The International Who's Who 2000

SIXTY-THIRD EDITION

EUROPA PUBLICATIONS LIMITED

First published 1935

Sixty-third Edition 1999

18 Bedford Square, London, WC1B 3JN
Tel: +44 171 580 8236
Fax: +44 171 580 3919
E-mail: europa@europapublications.co.uk
http://www.europapublications.co.uk

ISBN 1 85743 050 6

Library of Congress Catalog Card Number 35–10257

Also available on CD-ROM (ISBN 1 85743 072 7)
Book and CD-ROM combined (ISBN 1 85743 073 5)

PUBLISHER'S NOTE

The International Who's Who has been published annually by Europa Publications Limited since 1935 and provides biographical information on the most famous and talented men and women in the world today. We select the entries entirely on merit and our book is recognised by librarians in every country as a standard reference source in its field. It is compiled in our editorial offices at 18 Bedford Square, London, WC1B 3JN, England. We wish to make it clear that Europa Publications Limited has no connection with any other business purporting to produce a publication with the same title or a similar title to ours.

Cover photographs: GATES, William H. (Bill) III; CLINTON, Bill (William) J. and GORE, Albert, Jr.; HINGIS, Martina; PAVAROTTI, Luciano and SUTHERLAND, Dame Joan; HAWKING, Stephen W.; CASTRO RUZ, Fidel; AUNG SAN SUU KYI; CRUISE, Tom and KIDMAN, Nicole; ALBRIGHT, Madeleine Korbel; ANNAN, Kofi A.; MURDOCH, (Keith) Rupert; SOLZHENITSYN, Alexsandr Isayevich.

Typeset by UBL International and printed by Unwin Brothers Limited, The Gresham Press, Old Woking, Surrey

Bound by MPG Books Limited
Bodmin, Cornwall

(All members of the Martins Printing Group)

FOREWORD TO THE 63rd EDITION

This is the 63rd edition of THE INTERNATIONAL WHO'S WHO, which since its first publication in 1935 has become the standard reference work on the world's most famous and influential men and women. The present edition contains nearly 20,000 entries, of which nearly 1,000 appear for the first time.

In compiling THE INTERNATIONAL WHO'S WHO our aim is to create a reference book that answers the needs of readers seeking information on the lives of our most gifted contemporaries. We choose the entries entirely on merit and for their continuing interest and importance. Some are household names in every continent. Others are noted for their contributions in specialized fields or for their role in the political, economic, social or cultural life of their particular countries. The scope and diversity of the book is reflected in the range of activities represented, which includes architecture, art, business, cinema, diplomacy, engineering, fashion, journalism, law, literature, medicine, music, photography, politics, science, technology and theatre.

Each year new entrants are sent questionnaires with a request to supply biographical details. All existing entrants are also mailed, so that they may have an opportunity to make necessary additions and amendments. Supplementary research is done by the Editor and the Europa editorial department in order to ensure that the book is as up to date as possible on publication. Valuable assistance is also given by consultants and experts in particular fields or with specialized knowledge of certain countries.

This year we have included a special section to commemorate the millennium. It consists of 100 biographies of people, all having appeared in previous editions of the volume, whom we at Europa regard as having made a very significant contribution to shaping the Twentieth Century. All of these have been famous or notorious for a good deal longer than Andy Warhol's proverbial 15 minutes. This special section is to be found starting on page vii.

THE INTERNATIONAL WHO'S WHO 2000 edition is the first to be available on CD-ROM. Users will be able to search for biographees according to their nationality, professional activity, date of birth, place of education or leisure interest, or for any word occurring anywhere in THE INTERNATIONAL WHO'S WHO. This CD-ROM will make the unique store of knowledge contained in the book even more easily available.

Not many countries have their own who's who, and not all national who's whos are published annually. THE INTERNATIONAL WHO'S WHO represents in one volume a library of information from all countries that is not available elsewhere and is unrivalled in its balance and coverage.

May 1999.

ALPHABETIZATION KEY

The list of names is alphabetical, with the entrants listed under surnames. If part of an entrant's first given name is in parentheses, this will not affect his or her alphabetical listing.

All names beginning Mc and Mac are treated as though they began Mac, e.g. McDowell before MacEachen, MacFarlane after McFall, Macovescu after McNulty.

Names with Arabic prefixes are normally listed after the prefix except when requested by the entrant. In the case of surnames beginning De, Des, Du, van or von the entries are normally found under the prefix. Names beginning St. are listed as if they began Saint, e.g. St. Aubin after Sainsbury. As a general rule Chinese names are alphabetized under the first name.

Hyphenated surnames are listed under the first part, e.g. Twisleton-Wykeham-Fiennes, Sir Maurice Alberic. In the case of an entrant whose name is spelt in a variety of ways, who is known by a pseudonym or best known by another name, a cross reference is provided, e.g.

Kadhafi, Col. Mu'ammar Muhammed al- (see Gaddafi, Col. Mu'ammar Muhammed al-).

Le Carré, John (see Cornwell, David John Moore).

Lloyd, Chris(tine) Marie Evert (see Evert, Chris(tine) Marie).

100 ENTRIES FROM PREVIOUS EDITIONS OF THE INTERNATIONAL WHO'S WHO

1935–1999

ADENAUER, Konrad; German politician; b. 5 Jan. 1876; ed. Univs. of Freiburg, Munich and Bonn; practised law in Cologne; Deputy Mayor 1906, Senior Deputy Mayor 1911, Lord Mayor 1917; mem. Centre Party; mem. Provincial Diet of Rhine Province 1917–33; mem. Prussian Herrenhaus 1971, 1920; mem. Prussian State Council 1918–20, Pres. 1920–33; mem. Exec. Cttee. Centre Party until 1933; suspended from official duties as Lord Mayor March 1933, dismissed July 1933; imprisoned 1934 and 1944; again Lord Mayor of Cologne June-Oct. 1945; foundation mem. Christian Dem. Party of Rhineland Sept. 1945; Pres. CDU in British Zone March 1946; mem. British Zone Advisory Council March 1946–49; CDU mem. Provincial Diet of North Rhine; Leader CDU in Diet of North Rhine-Westphalia April 1947; represented North Rhine-Westphalia in Parl. Council of the three Western Zones Aug. 1948–49; Pres. Parl. Council Sept. 1948–49; Federal Chancellor 1949–63; Chair. CDU until 1966; Minister for Foreign Affairs 1951–55; mem. Académie des Sciences Morales et Politiques, Paris; 20 hon. degrees from Univs. of Cologne, Berlin-Charlottenburg, Yale, Harvard, Maryland, Georgetown, Marquette (Milwaukee), Ottawa, Teheran, Freiburg, Louvain, etc. *Publications:* Konrad Adenauer—Erinnerungen 1945–1953 1965. *Address:* Dr. Konrad Adenauerstrasse 8a, Rhöndorf/Rhein, German Federal Republic.
[*Died 19 April 1967.*]

ALI, Muhammad; American boxer; b. (as Cassius Marcellus Clay) 17 Jan. 1942, Louisville, Ky.; s. of Cassius Marcellus Clay Sr. and Odessa L. Grady; m. 1st Sonji Roi (dissolved 1966); m. 2nd Belinda Boyd (Khalilah Toloria) 1967 (divorced 1977); m. 3rd Veronica Porche 1977 (divorced 1986); m. 4th Yolanda Williams 1986; seven d. two s.; ed. Louisville; amateur boxer 1954–60, Olympic Games light-heavyweight champion 1960; professional boxer 1960–, won world heavyweight title Feb. 1964, defeating Sonny Liston; adopted name Muhammad Ali 1964; stripped of title after refusing to be drafted into U.S. Army 1967, won case in U.S. Supreme Court and returned to professional boxing 1970; regained world heavyweight title Oct. 1974, defeating George Foreman in Zaire; lost title to Leon Spinks 1978, regained title from Spinks 1978; 56 victories in 61 fights up to Dec. 1981; lost to Larry Holmes Oct. 1980; mem. of U.S. Black Muslim movement; Special Envoy of President Carter to Africa 1980 (to urge boycott of Olympic Games), of Pres. Bush to Iraq 1990 (prior to Operation Desert Storm); lit Olympic Flame, Atlanta, 1996; fmr. mem. Peace Corps Advisory Council; acted in films The Greatest 1976, Freedom Road 1980 and in Freedom Road (television) 1978; Hon. Consul-Gen. for Bangladesh in Chicago Feb. 1978. *Publications:* The Greatest: My Own Story (autobiography) 1975, Healing (with Thomas Hauser) 1996. *Address:* P.O. Box 187, Berrien Springs, MI 49103, U.S.A.

ARIAS, Dame Margot Fonteyn de, D.B.E.; British ballerina; b. (as Margaret Hookham) 18 May 1919; m. Roberto E. Arias 1955 (died 1989); ed. U.S.A. and China; as prima ballerina of the Royal Ballet Company, London, has danced all principal classical roles as well as leading roles in many modern ballets, and has appeared in many countries all over the world; *films include* I am a Dancer 1972; introduced and narrated B.B.C. TV series The Magic of Dance 1979; Pres. Royal Acad. of Dancing 1954–; Chancellor, Durham Univ. 1982–; Benjamin Franklin Medal 1973, Anglo-German Shakespeare Prize 1977; several hon. degrees, including Hon. Dr. (Durham) 1982, Order of Finnish Lion, Order of Estacio de Sá (Brazil) 1973, Chevalier Ordre of Merit of Duarte, Sanchez and Mella (Dominican Repub.) 1975. *Publications:* Margot Fonteyn (autobiog.) 1975, A Dancer's World 1978, The Magic of Dance 1980, Pavlova Impressions 1984, Swan Lake: as told by Margot Fonteyn (USA) 1989.
[*Died 21 February 1991.*]

ARMSTRONG, Louis; American musician; b. 4 July 1900, New Orleans; s. of Willie Armstrong and Mary Ann Armstrong; m. 1st Daisy Parker 1917 (dissolved); m. 2nd Lillian Hardin 1924 (dissolved); m. 3rd Alpha Smith (dissolved); m. 4th Lucille Wilson; joined Kid Ory's Band 1917, King Oliver's 1922; own band in Chicago 1925; tour of U.S. and Great Britain; tour of Holland and Scandinavia 1933–34, Australia and Europe 1954–55, Ghana 1956, Europe 1958 and 1959; has appeared in the films Every Day's a Holiday, Going Places, Cabin in the Sky, Jam Session, Doctor Rhythm, Glory Alley, The Strip, The Glen Miller Story, High Society, The Five Pennies; numerous recordings; composer of a large number of songs. *Address:* c/o Associated Booking Corporation, 50 West 57th Street, New York City, N.Y., U.S.A.
[*Died 6 July 1971.*]

AUNG SAN SUU KYI; Burmese politician; b. 19 June 1945, Rangoon; d. of the late Gen. Aung San; m. Michael Aris 1972 (died 1999); two s.; ed. St. Francis Convent, Methodist English High School, Lady Shri Ram Coll., Delhi Univ., St. Hugh's Coll., Oxford; Asst. Sec. Advisory Cttee. on Admin. and Budgetary Questions UN Secretariat, NY 1969–71; Resident Officer Ministry of Foreign Affairs, Bhutan 1972; Visiting Scholar Centre for S.E. Asian Studies, Kyoto Univ. 1985–86; Fellow Indian Inst. of Advanced Studies 1987; co-founder, Gen. Sec. Nat. League for Democracy 1988 (expelled from party), reinstated as Gen. Sec. Oct. 1995; returned from U.K. 1988; under house arrest 1988–95, house arrest lifted July 1995; Human Rights Prize 1991, Nobel Peace Prize 1991, Sakharov Prize 1990, Simón Bolívar Prize 1992, numerous hon. degrees. *Publications:* Aung San 1984, Burma and India: some aspects of colonial life under colonialism 1990, Freedom from Fear 1991, Towards a True Refuge 1993, Freedom from Fear and Other Writings 1995. *Address:* c/o National League for Democracy, 97B West Shwegondine Road, Bahan Township, Yangon, Myanmar.

BAIRD, John Logie; British television expert; b. 1888; m. Margaret Albu 1931; one s. one d.; ed. Larchfield School and Glasgow Univ.; gave world's first public demonstration of the television of the outlines of objects 1925, first of real images of living persons (to Royal Instn.) 1926; invention adopted by B.B.C. 1929; demonstrated noctovision (vision in total darkness by invisible rays) 1926, television in colour 1928; stereoscopic colour television 1942, telechrome 1944; Pres. Baird Television Ltd. 1927–39; Consulting Technical Adviser to Cable and Wireless Ltd. 1941–; Hon. Fellow Royal Society of Edinburgh; Fellow Physical Society; Associate Royal Technical Coll. *Address:* 3 Crescent Wood Road, Sydenham, London, S.E. 26.
[*Died 14 June 1946.*]

BECKETT, Samuel, M.A.; Irish author in French and English languages; b. 13 April 1906, Dublin; ed. Portora Royal School and Trinity Coll., Dublin; lecturer Ecole Normale Supérieure, Paris, 1928–30, Trinity Coll., Dublin 1930–32; now lives in Paris; Foreign Hon. mem. American Acad. of Arts and Sciences 1968; Prix Formentor 1961, Nobel Prize for Literature 1969, C.Lit. 1984; Croix de Guerre. *Publications:* Verse: Whoroscope 1930, Echo's Bones 1935; Novels: Murphy 1938, Watt 1944, Mercier et Camier 1946, Molloy 1951, Malone meurt 1952, L'Innommable 1953, Comment c'est, Imagination Dead Imagine 1966, Ill Seen, Ill Said 1982, Collected Poems in English and French 1977; Short Stories: More Pricks than Kicks 1934, Nouvelles et textes pour rien 1955, Le Dépeupleur 1971 (English Version The Lost Ones 1972), Four Novellas 1977, Company 1980; Stage Plays: En attendant Godot 1952 (English version Waiting for Godot), Fin de partie 1957 (English version Endgame), Krapp's Last Tape 1959, Happy Days 1960, Play 1963, Not I 1973, Rockaby 1981; Radio Plays: All that Fall 1957, Embers 1959, Words and Music 1961, Cascando 1964, Ends and Odds 1977, Stirrings Still 1989, Nohow On (novellas). TV Plays: Ghost Trio and ... But the Clouds 1977, Essay: Proust 1965; No's Knife; Collected Shorter Prose 1945–66 1967, Collected Poems in English and French 1977, Collected Poems (1930–78) 1984, Collected Shorter Plays 1984, Complete Dramatic Works 1986. *Address:* c/o Faber & Faber Ltd., 3 Queen Square, London, WC1, England.
[*Died 22 December 1989.*]

BEN GURION, David; Israeli politician; b. 16 Oct. 1886, Plonsk, Russian Poland; s. of Victor and Sheindel Grün; m. Paula Munweis 1917; one s. two d.; ed. privately and Istanbul Univ.; settled in Palestine 1906; exiled by Turks as Zionist 1915; went to U.S., where one of organizers of Jewish Legion, in which he himself served under Gen. Allenby; mem. Gen. Council Zionist Organization 1920; one of organizers of Jewish Labour Party (Mapai) and Gen. Fed. of Jewish Labour (Histadruth), and Sec.-Gen. of Fed. 1921–35; Chair. Jewish Agency for Palestine 1935–48; proclaimed Independence of Israel May 14th, 1948; Head of Provisional Govt. and Minister of Defence from then until March 1949; Prime Minister and Minister of Defence 1949–53, 1955–63; Leader of Mapai (Labour) Party; retired from Knesset 1970; Hon. Degrees Jewish Theological Seminary of America and Hebrew Univ. of Jerusalem; Bialik Literary Prize for Judaica 1952, Hadassah Henrietta Szold Award 1958; Hon. LL.D. (Brandeis Univ.) 1960, (Rangoon Univ.). *Publications:* Self-Government of Villayets 1914, Eretz Israel 1918, We and Our Neighbours 1920, The Labour Movement and Revisionism 1935, From

Class to Nation 1933, 1955, Mishmarot (essays on Labour Zionism) 1935, The Struggle (5 vols.) 1947–50, Israel at War 1951, Vision and Implementation (5 vols.) 1951–57, Mima-amad Leam 1955, Rebirth and Destiny of Israel 1954, Nezach Israel (Yiddish) 1953, En la Patria Libre 1954, The Sinai Campaign 1959, Israel: Years of Challenge (English) 1963, Ben Gurion looks back 1965, Dvarim Kehavayatam, Talks with Arabs, Michtavim Le Paula 1969, The Restored State of Israel (2 vols.) 1969, Iyunim Batanach 1969, Israel: A Personal History 1971, Igrot David Ben-Gurion 1971, Yehud Veye'ud 1971, Letters to Paula 1971, and many essays and articles. *Address:* Sdeh Boker, Negev, Israel.
[*Died 1 December 1973.*]

BERGMAN, Ingmar; Swedish film director and theatre producer; b. 14 July 1918, Uppsala; m. Ingrid Karlebovon Rosen 1971 (died 1995); eight c. by previous marriages; ed. Stockholm Univ.; producer Royal Theatre, Stockholm 1940–42; scriptwriter and producer Svensk Filmindustri 1940–44; theatre-dir. Helsingborg 1944–46, Gothenburg 1946–49, Malmo 1954–63; leading Dir. Royal Dramatic Theatre, Stockholm 1963; Dir. Mme de Sade Theatre 1989; Chair. European Cinema Soc. 1989–; has written the scripts of most of his films; mem. Swedish Acad. of Letters; Erasmus Prize 1965, Award for Best Dir. Nat. Soc. of Film Critics 1970, Order of the Yugoslav Flag 1971, Luigi Pirandello Int. Theatre Prize 1971, Goethe Award (Frankfurt) 1976, Gold Medal of Swedish Acad. 1977, European Film Award 1988, Le Prix Sonning 1989, Praemium Imperiale Prize (Japan) 1991, Dorothy and Lilian Gish Prize 1995; Dr. h.c. (Univ. of Rome) 1988; Commdr. Légion d'honneur 1985; author of plays A Painting on Wood, The City, The Rite (TV play), The Lie (TV play), Scenes from a Marriage (TV play); Dir. To Damascus 1974, The Merry Widow, Twelfth Night 1975, 1980, Tartuffe 1980, King Lear 1985, John Gabriel Borkman 1985, Miss Julie 1986, Hamlet 1986. *Films include:* Crisis 1945, It Rains on our Love 1946, A Ship Bound for India 1947, Music in Darkness 1947, Port of Call 1948, Prison 1948, Thirst 1949, To Joy 1949, Summer Interlude 1950, This Can't Happen Here 1950, Waiting Women 1952, Summer with Monika 1952, Sawdust and Tinsel 1953, A Lesson in Love 1954, Journey into Autumn 1955, Smiles of a Summer Night 1955, The Seventh Seal 1956, Wild Strawberries 1957, So Close to Life 1957, The Face 1958, The Virgin Spring 1959, The Devil's Eye 1960, Through a Glass Darkly 1961, Winter Light 1962, The Silence 1962, Now About these Women 1963, Episode in Stimulantia 1965, Persona 1966, The Hour of the Wolf 1967, Shame 1968, The Rite 1970, A Passion 1970, The Touch 1971, Cries and Whispers 1972, Scenes from a Marriage 1974 (film and TV), The Magic Flute (film and TV) 1975, Face to Face (film and TV) 1975, The Serpent's Egg 1977, Sonate d'automne 1978, Aus dem Leben der Marionetten 1980, Fåro Document 1980, Fanny and Alexander 1981, After the Rehearsal 1984; TV: Making Noise and Acting Up 1996; scriptwriter, Good Intentions 1989. *Publications:* Four Stories 1977, The Magic Lantern (autobiog.) 1988, Fanny and Alexander 1989, Images: My Life in Film 1993, Sunday's Child 1994, Private Confessions 1997.

BRADMAN, Sir Donald George, Kt., A.C.; Australian cricketer and company director; b. 27 Aug. 1908, Cootamundra, N.S.W.; s. of George and Emily Bradman; m. Jessie Menzies 1932 (died 1997); two s. (one deceased) one d.; ed. Bowral Intermediate High School; right-hand batsman; teams: N.S.W. 1927–34, South Australia 1935–49 (Capt. 1935–48); 52 Tests for Australia 1928–48, 24 as Capt., scoring 6,996 runs (average 99.9) including 29 hundreds; scored 28,067 first-class runs (average 95.1) with 117 hundreds—only Australian to score 100 hundreds; unequalled Test match and first-class averages; toured England 1930, 1934, 1938, 1948, scoring more than 2,000 first-class runs on each occasion; fmr. mem. Australian Bd. of Control for Int. Cricket, Chair. 1960–63, 1969–72; Vice-Pres. S. Australia Cricket Asscn. 1951–65, Pres. 1965–73; fmr. Australian Test Selector; fmr. mem. Stock Exchange of Adelaide; Champion Mt. Osmond Country Club (Golf) 1936, 1949; fmr. S. Australia Amateur Squash Champion; Life Vice-Pres. of M.C.C. 1988–. *Publications:* Don Bradman's Book 1930, How to Play Cricket 1935, My Cricketing Life 1938, Farewell to Cricket 1950, The Art of Cricket 1958, The Bradman Albums 1988. *Leisure interests:* cricket, tennis, golf, squash. *Address:* 2 Holden Street, Kensington Park, South Australia 5068, Australia.

BRECHT, Bertolt; German dramatist; b. 10 Feb. 1898, Augsburg; playwright and lyric poet; expressionist; deprived of German citizenship 1935; Stalin Peace Prize 1954. *Publications:* Baal 1922, Trommeln in der Nacht 1923 (awarded Kleist Prize), Dickicht 1924, Eduard II (an adaptation of Marlowe's play), Dreigroschenoper (founded on Beggar's Opera), Mahogany (with Kurt Weill), A Penny for the Poor, Mother, Der Gute Mann von Seuzan 1942, Films and Music (with Hanns Eisler), Fear and Misery in the Third Reich, Gesang an die Nachgeborenen, Mutter Courage und ihre Kinder 1940.
[*Died 14 August 1956.*]

CALLAS, Maria; Greek opera singer; b. 2 Dec. 1923, New York, U.S.A.; m. Giovanni Battista Meneghini 1947 (divorced 1971); ed. Athens Conservatoire; in Greece during 1939–45 war; studied under Elvira de Hidalgo; sang with Athens Opera; sang in Gioconda, Verona 1947; major rôles include, Madam Butterfly, Aida, Norma, Rigoletto, Medea, Tosca, etc.; has sung in Rome, Florence, Naples, Milan, New York, San Francisco, London, Mexico, Vienna, etc.; title role in film Medea 1970; numerous recordings. *Address:* 36 avenue George Mandel, Paris 16e, France; Monte Carlo, Monaco.
[*Died 16 September 1977.*]

CASTRO RUZ, Fidel, D.IUR.; Cuban politician; b. 13 Aug. 1928, m. Mirta Diaz-Bilart 1948 (dissolved 1955); one s.; ed. Jesuit schools in Santiago and Havana, Univ. de la Habana; law practice in Havana; began active opposition to Batista regime by attack on Moncada barracks at Santiago 26th July 1953; sentenced to 15 years' imprisonment 1953; amnestied 1956; went into exile in Mexico and began to organize armed rebellion; landed in Oriente Province with small force Dec. 1956; carried on armed struggle against Batista regime until flight of Batista Jan. 1959; Prime Minister of Cuba 1959–76; Head of State and Pres. of Council of State 1976–, Pres. of Council of Ministers 1976–; Chair. Agrarian Reform Inst. 1965–; First Sec. Partido Unido de la Revolución Socialista (PURS) 1963–65, Partido Comunista 1965– (mem. Political Bureau 1976–), Head Nat. Defence Council 1992—; Lenin Peace Prize 1961; Dimitrov Prize (Bulgaria) 1980; Hero of the Soviet Union 1963; Order of Lenin 1972, 1986, Order of the October Revolution 1976, Somali Order (1st Class) 1977, Order of Jamaica 1977, Gold Star (Vietnam) 1982. *Publications:* Ten Years of Revolution 1964, History Will Absolve Me 1968, Fidel (with Frei Betto) 1987, How Far We Slaves Have Come: South Africa and Cuba in Today's World (with Nelson Mandela) 1991. *Address:* Palacio del Gobierno, Havana, Cuba.

CHAPLIN, Sir Charles Spencer, Kt.; British film actor and producer; b. 16 April 1889, London; s. of Charles and Hannah Chaplin; m. 1st Mildred Harris 1918 (dissolved); m. 2nd Lita Grey 1924 (dissolved); two s. (one deceased); m. 3rd Paulette Goddard 1936 (dissolved); m. 4th Oona O'Neill, d. of late Eugene O'Neill, 1943; three s. five d.; formed own producing organization and built Chaplin Studios, Hollywood 1918; joint founder United Artists' Corpn. (with British affiliation Allied Artists); Officier de l'Instruction Publique (France); Commdr. Légion d'Honneur; Hon. D.Litt. (Oxford, Durham); Erasmus Prize 1965; mem. American Acad. of Arts and Sciences 1970; Life mem. Dirs. Guild of America 1975; Order of the Yugoslav Flag with Sash 1971; Acad. Award (Oscar) for services to cinema 1972. *Films include:* Shoulder Arms 1918, The Kid 1920, The Gold Rush 1925, The Circus 1928, City Lights 1931, Modern Times 1936, The Great Dictator 1940, Monsieur Verdoux 1947, Limelight 1952, A King in New York 1957, La Revue de Charlot, The Countess from Hong Kong 1966. *Publications:* My Autobiography 1964, My Life in Pictures 1974. *Address:* c/o United Artists Ltd., 142 Wardour Street, London, W1, England; Vevey, Vaud, Switzerland.
[*Died 25 December 1977.*]

CHURCHILL, Rt. Hon. Sir Winston Spencer, K.G., P.C., O.M., C.H., C.LIT., M.P., F.R.S., F.R.C.S., F.R.I.B.A., F.R.AE.S.; British politician and writer; b. 30 Nov. 1874; s. of Rt. Hon. Lord Randolph Churchill and Jennie Jerome; m. Clementine Hozier 1908; one s. four d. (two deceased); ed. Harrow and Sandhurst; entered Army 1895; served in Cuba with Spanish forces, with the Malakand Field Force at operations in Bajaui (India), with the Tirah Expeditionary Force (India), with the Nile Expeditionary Force, in South African War and in the First World War; Conservative M.P. for Oldham 1900–06; Liberal M.P. for North West Manchester 1906–08 and for Dundee 1908–22; Conservative M.P. for Epping Div. of Essex 1924–45; for Woodford 1945–; in Campbell-Bannerman and Asquith Mins. was successively Under-Sec. for Colonies 1906–08, Pres. Board of Trade 1908–10, Home Sec. 1910–11, First Lord of the Admiralty 1911–15, and Chancellor of the Duchy of Lancaster; in Lloyd George Min. was Min. of Munitions 1917–19, Sec. of State for War and Air 1918–21, and Sec. for the Colonies 1921–22; in Mr. Baldwin's second Min. was Chancellor of the Exchequer 1924–29; one of organisers of the India Defence League; First Lord of the Admiralty 1939–40; Chair. Cttee. of Service Mins. 1940; Prime Min., First Lord of the Treasury, and Min. of Nat Defence 1940–45, and 1951–55; resigned. Ministry of Defence 1952; Leader Conservative Party 1945–55; Pres. Constitutional Club 1940–; Lord Warden of the Cinque Ports 1941; Hon. Fellow Merton Coll. Oxford; Chancellor of Bristol Univ. 1930–; Col. 4th Queen's Royal Irish Hussars; Hon. Col. Royal Artillery, Royal Scots Fusiliers, Royal Sussex Regt., Heavy A.A. Regt. Royal Artillery; awarded Albert Gold Medal by Royal Society of Arts 1945; Hon. Freeman of Edinburgh, London, Wanstead and Woodford, Brussels, Antwerp, Aberdeen, Westminster, and numerous other towns and cities; Gold Medal of New York, Amsterdam, and Rotterdam; Hon. D.C.L. (Oxford); Hon. LL.D. of several British and foreign univs.; Hon. F.B.A. 1952; Hon. Citizen of the U.S.A. 1960. *Publications:* The Story of the Malakand Field Forces 1898, The River War 1899, London to Ladysmith 1900, Savrola 1900, Ian Hamilton's March 1900, Lord Randolph Churchill 1906, 1907, My African Journey 1908, Liberalism and the Social Problem 1909, The World Crisis 4 vols. 1923–29, My Early Life 1930, The Eastern Front 1931, Thoughts and Adventures 1922, Marlborough Vol. I 1933, Vol. II 1934, Vol. III 1936, Vol. IV 1938, Great Contemporaries 1937, Arms and the Covenant 1938, Step by Step 1939, Into Battle 1941, The Unrelenting Struggle 1942, The End of the Beginning 1943, The Dawn of Liberation 1945, Onwards to Victory, Victory, Secret Session Speeches 1946; War Memoirs: The Gathering Storm 1948, Their Finest Hour 1949, Grand Alliance 1950, The Hinge of Fate 1951, Closing the Ring 1952, Triumph and Tragedy 1954; A History of the English-Speaking Peoples, Vol. I: The Birth of Britain 1956, Vol. II: The New World 1956, Vol. III: The Age of Revolution 1957, Vol. IV: The Great Democracies 1958. *Address:* Chartwell, Westerham, Kent, England.
[*Died 24 January 1965.*]

DE GAULLE, Charles André Joseph Marie, Gen.; French army officer and politician; b. 22 Nov. 1890; ed. Saint-Cyr Acad.; served as Captain 1914–18 war; Gen. of Brigade and Commdr. 4th Armoured Div. 1940; Under-

Sec. Nat. Defence June 1940; Chief of Free French and later Pres. of French Nat. Cttee., London and Brazzaville 1940–42; Pres. of French Cttee. of Nat. Liberation, Algiers 1943; Pres. of Provisional French Govt. of French Republic, C.-in-C. French Armies 1944–46; founder Rassemblement du Peuple Française 1947; retired 1947–58; Prime Minister June 1958–Jan. 1959; Pres. of France Jan. 1959–April 1969. *Publications:* La Discorde chez l'Ennemi, Le Fil de l'Epée, Vers l'Armée de Métier, La France et son Armée, Discours et Messages, Mémoires de Guerre 1954, 1956, 1959. *Address:* "La Boisserie", Colombey-les-Deux-Eglises (Haute Marne), France.
[*Died 9 November 1970.*]

DIETRICH, Marlene; German-born American actress and singer; b. (as Maria Magdalena Dietrich) 27 Dec. 1901, Berlin; d. of Louis Erich Otto Dietrich and Josephine Felsing; step-d. of Edward von Losch; m. Rudolf Sieber 1924; one d.; ed. Augusta Victoria School, Berlin; début in Berlin: worked with Max Reinhardt 1922–29; emigrated to U.S. 1930; naturalized U.S. citizen 1937; numerous stage and cabaret appearances; Commdr. Légion d'honneur 1972, U.S. Medal of Freedom. *Films include:* The Blue Angel 1930, Morocco 1930, Dishonoured 1931, Shanghai Express 1932, Blonde Venus 1932. Song of Songs 1933, The Scarlet Empress 1934, The Devil is a Woman 1935, Desire 1936, The Garden of Allah 1936, Knight without Armour 1937, Angel 1937, Destry Rides Again 1939, Seven Sinners 1940, The Flame of New Orleans 1941, Manpower 1941, The Spoilers 1942, Kismet 1944, A Foreign Affair 1948, Stage Fright 1950, Rancho Notorious 1952, Around the World in Eighty Days 1956, Witness for the Prosecution 1957, Touch of Evil 1958, Judgement of Nuremburg 1961, Paris When It Sizzles, Just a Gigolo 1978. *Publication:* My Life (autobiog.) 1988. *Address:* c/o Regency Artists Ltd., 9200 Sunset Boulevard, Suite 823, Los Angeles, CA 90069, U.S.A.
[*Died 6 May 1992.*]

DISNEY, Walt (Walter Elias); American artist and film producer; b. 5 Dec. 1901, Chicago, Ill.; ed. Kansas City and Chicago schools; drove Red Cross Ambulance in France 1918–19; produced Alice comedies 1923–26, Oswald cartoons 1927, Mickey Mouse cartoons in sound 1928, Silly Symphonies, the first cartoon films in colour 1930, Snow White and the Seven Dwarfs in colour 1937, Pinocchio, Fantasia 1940, The Reluctant Dragon, Dumbo 1941, Bambi, Saludos Amigos 1942, Victory Through Air Power 1943, The Three Caballeros 1945, Make Mine Music, Song of the South 1946, Fun and Fancy Free 1947, Melody Time 1948, So Dear to my Heart, Ichabod and Mr. Toad, Seal Island 1949, Cinderella, Treasure Island, Beaver Valley 1950, Alice in Wonderland, Nature's Half-Acre 1951, Robin Hood 1952, The Sword and the Rose, Peter Pan, Bear Country, Prowlers of the Everglades 1953, The Living Desert, The Vanishing Prairie, 20,000 Leagues under the Sea, Lady and the Tramp, Davy Crockett, King of the Wild Frontier 1953–54, The Littlest Outlaw, The Great Locomotive Chase, Davy Crockett and the River Pirates, The African Lion 1955–56, Secrets of Life, Westward Ho the Wagons 1956–57, Old Yeller, Johnny Tremain 1957–58, Tonka, White Wilderness 1958, The Shaggy Dog, Sleeping Beauty, Darby O'Gill and the Little People, Third Man on the Mountain 1959, Swiss Family Robinson, Toby Tyler, Kidnapped 1960, Pollyanna, One Hundred and One Dalmatians, The Absent-minded Professor 1961, Moon Pilot, The Prince and the Pauper, Bon Voyage, In Search of the Castaways 1962, Son of Flubber 1963, Summer Magic 1963, Sword in the Stone 1963, Dr. Syn alias the Scarecrow 1963, The Horse without a Head 1963, Escapade in Florence 1963, The Magnificent Rebel 1963, The Misadventures of Merlin Jones 1964, The Three Lives of Thomasina 1964, The Waltz King 1964, The Incredible Journey 1964, A Tiger Walks 1964, Born to Sing 1964, The Moon-Spinners 1964, Mary Poppins 1964, That Darn Cat 1965, The Monkey's Uncle 1965. *Address:* 500 South Buena Vista Street, Burbank, Calif., U.S.A.
[*Died 15 December 1966.*]

EINSTEIN, Albert, PH.D.h.c., M.D.h.c., DR.h.c. (Oxford, Cambridge, Glasgow, Zürich, Madrid, Paris, Buenos Aires, Rostock, Brussels, Geneva, Manchester, Princeton, Harvard, London Univs.); American physicist; b. 14 March 1879, Ulm, Württemberg, Germany; ed. Zürich Univ.; Engineer Patent Office, Berne 1902; Lecturer in Mathematics and Physics, Zürich Univ. 1909; Prof. German, Univ. Prague 1911–12, Zürich Technical Univ. 1912; invited to Berlin by Prussian Acad. of Science 1914 and adopted German citizenship, renounced German citizenship 1933, now American citizen; Prof. of Physics Berlin Univ. and Dir. Kaiser Wilhelm Institute for Physics 1914–33; Prof. Coll. de France 1934; mem. Amsterdam, Copenhagen and Paris Acads. of Science; Nobel Prizeman for photo-electric effect; has lectured in London, Oxford, Cambridge and many American Univs.; permanent mem. with title of Prof. Emeritus Inst. for Advanced Study Princeton 1933–45; awarded Franklin Gold Medal 1935; staff mem. extra., U.S. Navy Ordnance Bureau (research work on explosives) 1943. *Publications:* Relativity 1920, Zur Einheitlichen Feldtheorie 1929, About Zionism 1930, Why War? (with Prof. Sigmund Freud) 1933, My Philosophy 1934, The World as I See It 1935, The Evolution of Physics (with Leopold Infeld) 1938, Out of My Later Years 1950. *Address:* 112 Mercer Street, Princeton, N.J., U.S.A.
[*Died 18 April 1955.*]

EISENHOWER, Dwight David; American army officer and politician; b. 14 Oct. 1890; (brother of Dr. Milton Eisenhower); ed. Abilene High School and U.S. Mil. Acad.; commissioned 2nd-Lieut. infantry, United States Army 1915, and advanced through grades to Gen. of Army Dec. 1944; graduated from Army War Coll. June 1928; Asst. Exec., Office of Asst. Sec. of War 1929–33; served in office of Chief of Staff 1933–35; Asst. to the Mil. Adviser in the Philippines 1935–40; Chief of Staff of 3rd Div. 1940; Chief of Staff IX Army Corps March 1941; Chief of Staff Third Army June 1941; Chief of War Plans Div., War Dept. Gen. Staff Feb. 1942; Asst. Chief of Staff in charge of Operations Div., Office of Chief of Staff April 1942; Commanding Gen., European Theatre June 1942; C.-in-C. Allied Forces, N. Africa Nov. 1942; Supreme Commander, Allied Expeditionary Forces Dec. 1943–45; Mil. Gov. of U.S. Occupied Zone in Germany May–Nov. 1945; Chief of Staff U.S. Army Nov. 1945–48; Pres. of Columbia Univ. 1948–53; Supreme Allied Commdr. Europe 1950–52; resigned from Army July 1952; President of the U.S.A. 1953–61; Chair. Editorial Board *Encyclopedia Americana* 1961–; holds over forty decorations including D.S.M. with four Oak Leaf Clusters, U.S. Navy D.S.M., Legion of Merit (all U.S.A.), Hon. G.C.B. and O.M. (both British), Grand Cordon, Légion d'Honneur and Médaille Militaire (France), and Order of Suvorov, First Degree (U.S.S.R.), numerous Hon. Degrees and City Freedoms. *Publications:* Crusade in Europe 1948, Mandate for Change, the White House Years 1963, Waging Peace, the White House Years 1956–61 1965, At Ease 1968. *Address:* Gettysburg, Penn., U.S.A.
[*Died 28 March 1969.*]

ELIOT, Thomas Stearns, O.M., A.M., D.LITT., LITT.D., LL.D., D. ès L., D.PHIL.; British (born American) poet, playwright and literary critic; b. 26 Sept. 1888; s. of Henry Ware Eliot and Charlotte Chauncy Eliot; m. 1st Vivienne Haigh (died 1947); m. 2nd Esmé Valerie Fletcher; ed. Harvard and Oxford Univs., and Univ. of Paris, Dir. Faber & Faber Ltd.; Charles Eliot Norton Prof. of Poetry at Harvard Univ. 1932–33; Pres. London Library 1952–; Hon. Fellow Magdalene Coll. Cambridge and Merton Coll. Oxford; Hon. Litt.D. Cambridge, Columbia, Bristol, Leeds, Harvard, Yale, Princeton, Washington, Rome, Sheffield; LL.D. Edinburgh and St. Andrews; D.Litt. Oxford and London; D. ès L. Paris, Aix-Marseille, Rennes; D.Phil. Munich; Officier de la Legion d'Honneur; Commandeur Ordre des Arts et des Lettres; mem. Ordre Pour le Mérite; foreign mem. Accademia dei Lincei Rome; Nobel Prize for Literature 1948, Hanseatic Goethe Prize 1954, Florentine Gold Medal 1959, Emerson-Thoreau Medal (American Acad. of Arts and Sciences) 1959. *Publications:* Knowledge and Experience in the Philosophy of F. H. Bradley 1916, 1964, The Waste Land 1922, The Sacred Wood 1920, Selected Essays 1932, The Use of Poetry and the Use of Criticism 1933, Elizabethan Essays 1934, Murder in the Cathedral (play) 1935, Collected Poems 1936, 1963, The Family Reunion (play) 1939, Practical Cats 1939, The Idea of a Christian Society 1939, A Choice of Kipling's Verse 1942, The Classics and the Man of Letters 1942, What is a Classic? 1944, Four Quartets 1944, Notes Towards the Definition of Culture 1948, Cocktail Party (play) 1949, Poetry and Drama 1951, The Confidential Clerk (play) 1954, On Poetry and Poets 1957, The Elder Statesman (play) 1959. *Address:* 24 Russell Square, London, W.C.1, England.
[*Died 4 January 1965.*]

ELIZABETH II (Elizabeth Alexandra Mary); Queen of Great Britain and Northern Ireland and of Her other Realms and Territories (see under Reigning Royal Families at front of book for full titles); b. 21 April 1926, London; d. of H.R.H. Prince Albert, Duke of York (later H.M. King George VI), and Duchess of York (now H.M. Queen Elizabeth The Queen Mother); succeeded to The Throne following Her father's death, 6 Feb. 1952; married, 20 Nov. 1947, H.R.H. The Prince Philip, Duke of Edinburgh, b. 10 June 1921; children: Prince Charles Philip Arthur George, Prince of Wales (heir apparent), b. 14 Nov. 1948; Princess Anne Elizabeth Alice Louise, The Princess Royal, b. 15 Aug. 1950; Prince Andrew Albert Christian Edward, Duke of York, b. 19 Feb. 1960; Prince Edward Antony Richard Louis, b. 10 March 1964. *Address:* Buckingham Palace, London, SW1A 1AA; Windsor Castle, Berkshire, SL4 1NJ, England; Palace of Holyroodhouse, Edinburgh, Scotland; Balmoral Castle, Aberdeenshire, AB35 5TB, Scotland; Sandringham House, Norfolk, PE35 6EN, England.

FAULKNER, William; American novelist; b. 25 Sept. 1897, New Albany, Miss., ed. Mississippi Univ.; served First World War with British Royal Flying Corps; Nobel Prize for Literature 1949; Pulitzer Novel Prize 1954. *Publications:* The Marble Faun 1925, Soldier's Pay 1926, Mosquitoes 1927, Sartoris 1929, The Sound and the Fury 1929, As I Lay Dying 1930, Sanctuary 1931, These Thirteen 1931, Green Boughs (poems) 1933, Pylon 1935, Absalom, Absalom! 1936, The Unvanished 1938, The Wild Palms 1939, The Hamlet 1940, Go Down Moses 1942, Intruder in the Dust 1948, Knight's Gambit (short stories) 1951, Collected Short Stories 1951, Requiem for a Nun 1951, The White Rose of Memphis 1953, A Fable 1954, Big Woods 1955, Uncle Willie and Other Stories, The Town 1958, The Mansion 1961. *Address:* Oxford, Miss., U.S.A.
[*Died 6 July 1962.*]

FELLINI, Federico; Italian film director; b. 20 Jan. 1920; m. Giulietta Masina 1943; screen writer: Quarta pagina 1942, Roma città aperta 1944–45, Paisa 1946, Il delitto di Giovanni Episcopo 1947, In nome della legge 1948–49, La città si difende 1951, Il brigante di Tacca di Lupo 1953, etc.; Dir. Lo sceicco bianco 1952, I vitelloni 1953, La strada (Oscar) 1954, Il bidone 1955, Le notti di Cabiria (Oscar) 1957, Fortunella 1958, La Dolce Vita (Cannes 1st Prize) 1960, The Temptation of Dr. Antonio (from Boccaccio 70) 1962, 8½ (Oscar) 1963, Giulietta degli spiriti (Golden Globe, Hollywood) 1964, Satyricon 1969, Never Bet the Devil Your Head (from Spirits of the Dead) 1969, I Clowns (television film) 1971, Roma 1972, Amarcord (New York Film Critics' Circle Award 1974) 1973, Casanova 1976, La Cité des

Femmes 1979, Orchestra Rehearsal 1979, And the Ship Sails On 1984, Ginger and Fred 1985, Intervista 1987, La Voce della Luna 1990, Trip to Tullum (with Milo Manara) 1990; has always written scripts for his own films. *Publications:* Amarcord 1974, Quattro film 1975. *Address:* 141a Via Margutta 110, Rome, Italy.
[*Died 31 October 1993.*]

FLEMING, Sir Alexander, Kt., F.R.S., M.B., B.S., F.R.C.S., F.R.C.P.; British bacteriologist; b. 6 Aug. 1881, Darvel; m. 1st Sarah Marion McElroy (died 1949); one s.; m. 2nd Amalia Coutsouris; ed. Kilmarnock Acad. and St. Mary's Hospital Medical School; Hunterian Prof. and Arris and Gale Lecturer, Royal Coll. of Surgeons; Capt. R.A.M.C. in First World War; Prof. of Bacteriology, St. Mary's Hospital Medical School 1928–48; discovered Lysozyme 1922, Penicillin 1929; Pres. Society for General Microbiology 1945; William Julius Mickle Fellowship, London Univ. 1941; Charles Mickle Fellowship, Toronto Univ. 1943; Culter Lecturer, Harvard Univ. 1945; Award of Merit, American Pharmaceutical Manfs. Asscn. 1943; Humanitarian Award, Variety-Clubs of America 1944; Cameron Prize, Univ. of Edinburgh 1944; John Scott Medal 1944; share in Nobel Prize for Medicine 1945; Moxon Medal, Royal Coll. of Physicians 1945; Harben Gold Medal, Royal Inst. of Public Health and Hygiene 1946; Albert Gold Medal, Royal Society of Arts 1946; Commdr. of Legion of Honour and Order of Public Health, France; Foreign Assoc. Acad. de Médécine, Paris; Corresp. of Acad. of Sciences, Inst. of France; mem. Pontifical Acad. of Sciences; foreign hon. mem. Palace of Royal Acads., Brussels; hon. mem. Academia de Medicina de Buenos Aires; Fellow Royal Society of Denmark; mem. Acad. of Athens; Rector Edinburgh Univ. 1952–; Hon. D.Sc. Pennsylvania, Harvard, Princeton, Durham, Dublin, Belfast; Hon. M.D. (Athens), Dr. h.c. (Paris, Brussels, Louvain, Liège and Rome). *Address:* 20 Danwers Street, London, S.W.3.
[*Died 11 March 1955.*]

FORD, Henry; American manufacturer; b. 30 July 1863, Dearborn, Mich.; ed. elementary schools; fmr. engineer Edison Illuminating Co.; founder 1903, Pres. 1903–18 and 1943–45; Ford Motor Co.; introduced profit-sharing system 1914; organised "peace ship", conf. of peace advocates which visited Europe 1915 to influence belligerent govts. to end war; mem. Wage Umpire Board 1918; mem. Society of Automotive Engineers and Detroit Board of Commerce; founder Henry Ford Hospital. *Publications:* My Life and Work 1925, To-day and To-morrow 1926, Moving Forward 1931. *Address:* Dearborn, Mich.
[*Died 7 April 1947.*]

FREUD, Sigmund, M.D., LL.D.; Austrian psychologist; b. 6 May 1856, Freiberg, Moravia; ed. Vienna Univ.; pioneer of psychoanalysis; Lecturer in Neuropathology Vienna 1885, Extra. Prof. 1902 and Prof. 1920; Editor *Jahrbuch der Psychoanalyse, Imago, International Journal of Psychoanalysis* and *Internationale Zeitschrift für ärztliche Psychoanalyse*; Goethe Prizewinner Frankfurt 1930. *Publications include:* Traumdeutung 1900, Psychopathologie des Alltagslebens 1904, Drei Abhandlungen zur Sexualtheorie 1905, Der Witz und seine Beziehungen zum Unbewussten 1905, Wahn und Träume in Jensens Gradiva 1907, Eine Kindheitserinnerung des Leonardo da Vinci 1910, Totem und Tabu 1913, Vorlesungen zur Einführung in die Psychoanalyse 1917, Jenseits des Luftprinzips 1920, Massenpsychologie und Ich-Analyse 1921, Das Ich und das Es 1923, Beiträge zur Psychologie des Liebeslebens 1924, Aus der Geschichte einer infantilen Neurose 1924, Psychoanalytische Studien an Werken der Dichtung und Kunst 1924, Die Frage der Laienanalyse 1926, Hemmung, Symptom und Angst 1926, Die Zukunft einer Illusion 1927, Dostojevksi und die Vatertötung 1928, Das Unbehagen in der Kultur, Neue Vorlesungen 1929, Gesammelte Schriften I-XII. *Address:* Ellesworthy Road, St. John's Wood, London, N.W.8.
[*Died 23 September 1939.*]

GANDHI, Mohandas Karamchand (Mahatma); Indian nationalist leader; b. 2 Oct. 1869; ed. Bhavnagar and London; led Satyagraha movement S. Africa 20 years; started and led Satyagraha movement 1918–19 and non-co-operation campaign 1920–21; associated with Khilafat agitation 1920–21; Pres. Indian Nat. Congress 1924–34 and 1940–41, resgnd.; inaugurated campaign for breach of Salt Laws 1930; Del. to Round Table Conf. 1931; imprisoned 1932–33 and 1942–44. *Publications:* Indian Home Rule, Universal-Dawn, Young India, Nava Jivan, Story of my Experiments with Truth, Self-restraint versus Self-indulgence, A Guide to Health, Satyagraha in South Africa. *Address:* Sevagram, Wardha (C.P.), India.
[*Died 30 January 1948.*]

GARCÍA MÁRQUEZ, Gabriel (Gabo); Colombian writer; b. 1928, Aracataca; m. Mercedes García Márquez; two s.; ed. secondary school and Univ. of Bogotá, Univ. of Cartagena; began writing books 1946; lived in Baranquilla; Corresp. Espectador in Rome, Paris; first novel published while living in Caracas, Venezuela 1957; est. bureau of Prensa Latina (Cuban press agency) in Bogotá; worked for Prensa Latina in Havana, Cuba, then as Deputy Head of New York Office 1961; lived in Spain, contributing to magazines, Mundo Nuevo, Casa de las Américas; went to Mexico; invited back to Colombia by Pres. July 1982; Rómulo Gallegos Prize 1972; Nobel Prize for Literature 1982. *Publications include:* La hojarasca (Leaf Storm) 1955, El coronel no tiene quien le escriba (No One Writes to the Colonel) 1961, La mala hora (In Evil Hour) 1962, Los funerales de la Mamá Grande (Big Mama's Funeral) 1962, Cien años de soledad (One Hundred Years of Solitude) 1967, La increíble y triste historia de la cándida Eréndira (Innocent Erendira and other stories) 1972, El otoño del patriarca (The Autumn of the Patriarch) 1975, Crónica de una muerte anunciada (Chronicle of a Death Foretold) 1981, El Olor de la Guayaba (Fragrance of Guava) 1982, El amor en los tiempos del cólera (Love in the Time of Cholera) 1984, Relato de un náufrago (The Story of a Shipwrecked Sailor) 1986, Miguel Littín's Adventure: undercover in Chile 1986, The General in His Labyrinth (translated from Spanish edn. of 1989) 1991, Amores Difíciles 1989, I Rent Myself Out to Dream 1989, Collected Stories 1991, Strange Pilgrims: Twelve Stories 1993, Of Love and Other Demons 1995, News of a Kidnapping 1997. *Address:* c/o Agencia Literaria Carmen Balcelos, Diagonal 580, Barcelona, Spain.

GATES, William Henry (Bill) III; American computer software executive b. 28 Oct. 1955, Seattle; s. of William Gates and Mary Maxwell; m. Melinda French 1994; one d.; ed. Lakeside School, Harvard Univ.; joined MITS 1975; Programmer for Honeywell 1975; Founder, Chair. Bd. Microsoft Corpn. (disk operating system, windows system) 1976–, now C.E.O.; Howard Vollum Award, Reed Coll. Portland, Ore. 1984; named CEO of Year Chief Executive Magazine. *Publications:* The Future 1994, The Road Ahead 1996. *Leisure interest:* tennis. *Address:* Microsoft Corporation, 1 Microsoft Way, Redmond, WA 98052, U.S.A.

GORBACHEV, Mikhail Sergeyevich; Russian politician; b. 2 March 1931, Privolnoye, Krasnogvardeisky Dist., Stavropol Territory; s. of Sergei Andreevich Gorbachev and Maria Panteleimonovna Gorbachev (née Gopcalo); m. Raisa Titarenko (now Gorbachev) 1953; one d.; ed. Faculty of Law, Moscow State Univ. and Stavropol Agricultural Inst.; began work as machine operator 1946; joined CPSU 1952; Deputy Head, Dept. of Propaganda, Stavropol Komsomol Territorial Cttee. 1955–56, Second, then First Sec. 1958–62; First Sec. Stavropol Komsomol City Cttee. 1956–58; Del. to CPSU Congress 1961, 1971, 1976, 1981, 1986, 1990; Party Organizer, Stavropol Territorial Production Bd. of Collective and State farms 1962; Head, Dept. of party bodies of CPSU Territorial Cttee. 1963–66; First Sec. Stavropol City Party Cttee. 1966–68; Second Sec. Stavropol Territorial CPSU Cttee. 1968–70, First Sec. 1970–78; mem. CPSU Cen. Cttee. 1971–91, Sec. for Agric. 1978–85, alt. mem. Political Bureau CPSU, Cen. Cttee. 1979–80, mem. 1980–91, Gen. Sec. CPSU Cen. Cttee. 1985–91; Deputy Supreme Soviet of U.S.S.R. 1970–89 (Chair. Foreign Affairs Comm., Soviet of the Union 1984–85), mem. Presidium 1985–88, Chair. 1988–89, Supreme Soviet of R.S.F.S.R. 1980–90, elected to Congress of People's Deputies of U.S.S.R. 1989, Chair. 1989–90; Pres. of U.S.S.R. 1990–91; Head Int. Foundation for Socio-Economic and Political Studies (Gorbachev Fund) 1992–; Head Int. Green Cross/Green Crescent 1993–; syndicated columnist for numerous leading newspapers worldwide 1992–; Nobel Peace Prize 1990; Jt. recipient Albert Schweitzer Leadership Award, Ronald Reagan Freedom Award 1992, Hon. Citizen of Berlin 1992; Freeman of Aberdeen 1993; Urania-Medaille (Berlin) 1996; Order of Lenin (three times), Orders of Red Banner of Labour, Badge of Honour and other medals. *Publications:* A Time for Peace 1985, The Coming Century of Peace 1986, Speeches and Writings 1986–90, Peace has no Alternative 1986, Moratorium 1986, Perestroika: New Thinking for Our Country and the World 1987, The August Coup (Its Cause and Results) 1991, December 1991: My Stand 1992, The Years of Hard Decisions 1993, Life and Reforms 1995. *Leisure interests:* literature, theatre, music, walking. *Address:* International Foundation for Socio-Economic and Political Studies, Leningradsky prosp. 49, 125468 Moscow, Russia. *Telephone:* (095) 943-99-90. *Fax:* (095) 943-95-94.

HAILE, Sellassie I, His Imperial Majesty; Emperor of Ethiopia, K.G. (original name Lij Tafari Makonnen); b. 23 July 1892; s. of late Ras Makonnen, cousin of Emperor Menelik II, and Woizero Yeshimebet; m. Woizero Menen 1911 (died 1962); six c.; proclaimed Regent and Heir to Imperial Throne 1916; invested with Grand Cordon of the Order of Solomon; took Ethiopia to League of Nations 1923; proclaimed abolition of slavery 1924; proclaimed King 1928; proclaimed Emperor after death of Empress Zauditu 1930; established Constitution 1931; following invasion by Italy 1935 forced to quit Addis Ababa 1936; appeared personally before League of Nations 1936; lived in England till 1940; rallied refugee patriots in Kenya and Sudan and crossed the frontier 1941; reinstated in capital 1941; reorganized Government, reopened Parliament, reinstituted State Bank of Ethiopia 1942; proclaimed new currency, established airlines, opened roads, reorganized army, navy and air force, built numerous schools, expanded industry and agriculture, founded the University Coll. of Addis Ababa and other colleges, organized a judiciary system, codified law and revised the Constitution 1955, entered into diplomatic relations with most of the important nations of the world; secured reintegration of Eritrea 1952, Grand Cross of the Order of the Legion of Honour; of the Annunsiata; of Leopold, Belgium; of the Lion d'Or de la Maison de Nassau, Luxembourg; Netherlands Order of Orange-Nassau; Danish Order of the Elephant; Brazilian Order of San Sebastian Guillaume; Mexican Order of the Aztec Eagle, Order of Military Merit of the Federal Republic of Germany; Order of the Star of Yugoslavia; Order of Military Merit of France; Order of Mohammed Ali of Egypt; Swedish Order of the Seraphim; Norwegian Order of St. Olaf; Greek Order of the Saviour; Order of Merit of the Italian Republic; Order of Suvorov U.S.S.R.; 1st Class Military Order of the White Lion Czechoslovakia; Ribbon of the Grand Cross of the Three Orders Portugal; Sudan Order of the Republic 1st Class; K.G., G.C.B. (Hon.); G.C.M.G. (Hon.); G.C.V.O. (Hon.); LL.D. (Hon.) Cantab., Columbia, Howard, McGill, Montreal, Michigan, Athens, Laval, Banaras, Moscow, Charles; D.C.L. (Hon.) Oxford; Hon. LL.D. (Ag.) Bonn. *Publication:* My Life and Ethiopia's Progress (autobiog.) 1972. *Address:* The

Imperial Palace, Addis Ababa, Ethiopia.
[*Died 27 August 1975.*]

HEMINGWAY, Ernest Miller; American novelist and war correspondent; b. 21 July 1899, Oak Park, Ill.; s. of Clarence Edmonds Hemingway and of Grace Hall; ed. Oak Park High School; American Acad. of Arts and Letters Award of Merit, Nobel Prize for Literature 1954. *Publications:* Three Stories and Ten Poems 1923, In Our Time 1924, The Torrents of Spring 1926, The Sun Also Rises 1926 (English edn. Fiesta 1927), Men Without Women 1927, A Farewell to Arms 1929, Death in the Afternoon 1932, Winner Takes Nothing 1933, Green Hills of Africa 1935, To Have and Have Not 1937, The Fifth Column and the First Forty-nine Stories 1938, For Whom the Bell Tolls 1940, Across the River and into the Trees 1950, The Old Man and the Sea 1952 (Pulitzer Prize 1953). *Address:* Finca Vigia, San Francisco de Paula, Cuba; c/o Guaranty Trust Co. of New York, 4 Place de la Concorde, Paris, France.
[*Died 2 July 1961.*]

HITCHCOCK, Sir Alfred Joseph, K.B.E.; American (b. British) film director; b. 13 Aug. 1899, London; m. Alma Reville 1926; one d.; ed. Univ. of London; joined Lasky Famous Players Corpn. 1920; Sr. Dir. British Int. Pictures; Hon. D.F.A. (Univ. of Calif., Santa Cruz) 1968; Hon. D.H.L. (Columbia) 1972; Life Achievement Award (American Film Inst.) 1978; Croix, Officier des Arts et des Lettres 1969, Commdr., Nat. Orders of Arts and Letters 1976. *Films produced under his direction include:* Blackmail, Juno and the Paycock, The Farmer's Wife, Hindle Wakes, Thirty-nine Steps, The Man Who Knew Too Much, Secret Agent, Sabotage, Young and Innocent, The Lady Vanishes, Jamaica Inn, Rebecca, Foreign Correspondent, Mr. and Mrs. Smith, Suspicion, Saboteur, Shadow of a Doubt, Lifeboat, Spellbound, Notorious, The Paradine Case, Rope, Under Capricorn, Stage Fright, Strangers on a Train, I Confess, Dial M for Murder, Rear Window, To Catch a Thief, The Trouble with Harry, The Wrong Man, Vertigo, North by Northwest, Psycho, The Birds, Marnie, Torn Curtain, Topaz, Frenzy, Family Plot; television series: Alfred Hitchcock Presents 1955–61, Alfred Hitchcock Hour 1963–65. *Publications:* Stories Not for the Nervous 1966, Stories that Scared Even Me 1968, Stories to Stay Awake By 1971, Supernatural Tales of Terror and Suspense 1974, Stories to be Read with the Door Locked; children's books: Monster Museum 1971, Haunted Houseful 1971.
[*Died 29 April 1980.*]

HITLER, Adolf; German politician; b. 20 April 1889, Braunau; ed. Elementary School and Lower Secondary School; fmr. house-painter; came to Munich 1912; served in German Army in First World War; wounded twice; founder and leader National Socialist German Labour Party 1919–45; sentenced to year's imprisonment for participation in abortive rising Nov. 1923; re-founded party after release Dec. 1924; defeated by Hindenburg in Presidential elections 1932; Chancellor of the Reich Jan. 1933; proclaimed Leader of Reich and Chancellor for life after death of Pres. Hindenburg Aug. 1933; Commander-in-Chief armed Forces 1938–45; assumed supreme command and responsibility armed forces Dec. 1941; Supreme Law Maker 1942; reptd. dead 1st May 1945, suicide on 29th April presumed. *Publications:* Mein Kampf I-II.
[*Died 30 April 1945.*]

HO Chi-Minh; Viet-Namese political leader; b. (as Nguyen Van Thanh) 19 May 1890, Kimlien; lived in France for some years; mem. French Socialist Party; organised Colonial Fed. and publ. *Pariah Weekly*; went to U.S.S.R. 1924; took part in Great Chinese Revolution 1925–27; went to Siam 1927 and imprisoned for political activities in Hong Kong 1931; led struggle for independence in Indo-China during Second World War; declared Pres. Democratic Republic of Viet-Nam 1945; refused to recognise Bay of Along Treaty with France 1948 and continued guerrilla warfare as leader of Vietminh; Hon. Chair. Nat. Cttee. of Lien-Viet Front (merger of Vietminh and Lien-Viet Leagues) and Chair. Laodong (newly formed Revolutionary Workers' Party) Mar. 1951; Pres. and Prime Minister of North Viet-Nam following July 1954 Armistice Agreement; relinquished Premiership Sept. 1955 but remained Pres., re-elected 1960; Order of Lenin 1967. *Publications:* Prison Diary, Selected Writings 1920–1966 1966. *Address:* Hanoi, Democratic Republic of Viet-Nam.
[*Died 3 September 1969.*]

JOYCE, James; Irish writer; b. 2 Feb. 1882, Dublin; ed. Clongowes Wood Coll., Belvedere Coll., and Royal Univ. of Ireland, Dublin; novelist, playwright and poet; has worked in Rome, Trieste, Zürich and Paris. *Publications:* Poems under the title of Chamber music, Pomes Penyeach, Collected Poems; short stories: Dubliners; novels: A Portrait of the Artist as a Young Man, Ulysses, Finnegans Wake; play: Exiles. *Address:* Paris XVI, 34 rue des Vignes.
[*Died 14 January 1941.*]

KARAJAN, Herbert von; Austrian conductor; b. 5 April 1908; ed. Salzburg Gymnasium and Mozarteum, Vienna Univ. and Conservatoire; successively Musical Dir. Ulm, Opera and Gen. Musical Dir. Aachen, Kapellmeister, Berlin State Opera, Conductor, Berlin Philharmonic Orch., Lifetime Dir. 1954–; Dir. Berlin Staatskapelle 1941–45; concert tours in Europe, U.S.A. and Far East 1945–; Artistic Dir. Berlin Philharmonic Orchestra 1955–56, Vienna State Opera 1956–64 (Dir. 1976–); mem. Bd. of Dirs., Salzburg Festival 1965–; Life Dir. Gesellschaft der Musikfreunde, Vienna; conducted at Salzburg and Lucerne Festivals; Mozart Ring 1957; Hon. D. Mus. (Oxford) 1978; Prix France-Allemagne 1970, UNESCO Music Prize 1983; Hon. Citizen of Berlin 1973. *Leisure interests;* skiing, mountaineering, flying, yachting, motoring, theatre, acoustical research. *Address:* c/o Festspielhaus, Salzburg, Austria.
[*Died 16 July 1989.*]

KARSH, Yousuf, C.C.; Canadian photographer; b. 23 Dec. 1908, Mardin, Armenia-in-Turkey; s. of Bahia and Amsih Karsh; m. 1st Solange Gauthier 1939 (died 1961); m. 2nd Estrellita Nachbar 1962; ed. Sherbrooke, Quebec and School of Art and Design, Boston, Mass.; Photo apprenticeship to John Garo of Boston; arrived in Canada from Armenia-in-Turkey 1925; specialized in portrait photography; Canadian citizen 1947; Visiting Prof. of Photography, Ohio Univ. 1967–69; Photographic Adviser to Expo 1970, Osaka, Japan 1969; Visiting Prof. of Fine arts, Emerson Coll., Boston 1972–73; numerous one-man exhbns., North America 1967–; touring exhbn. Men Who Make Our World Japan 1970, U.S.A. 1968–71, France, Germany, Netherlands 1971–73, Belgium, Arles 1974–75, Athens 1978 (now in perm. collection Museum of Contemporary Art, Tokyo, Nat. Gallery of Australia and Province of Alberta, Canada), Bradford, England 1983, Int. Center of Photography, New York 1983, 1992–93, Nat. Portrait Gallery, London 1984, Nat. Gallery Edin., Scotland 1984, Nat. Portrait Gallery, Helsinki 1985, Beijing, China 1985, Muscarelle Museum of Art, Coll. of William and Mary 1986, 80th Birthday Celebration, Barbican Centre, London 1988, retrospective exhbn. Nat. Gallery of Canada 1989, subsequently on tour; other exhbns. include Washington, D.C. 1993, Lausanne 1993, 85th Birthday Tribute exhbn., Bradford, England 1993, "American Legends", Int. Center of Photography 1993, Corcoran Gallery 1993, Mint Museum, Charlotte, N.C., "Karsh: Selected Portraits", Canadian Embassy, Washington, D.C. 1994, retrospective, Museum of Fine Arts, Boston, U.S.A. 1996, Detroit Inst. of Arts 1996–97, Tower Gallery, Yokohama, Japan 1997–98, 90th Birthday Tribute, Nat. Gallery, Ottawa 1998, "Karsh in London", Canada House, London 1998; film: Karsh: The Searching Eye 1986; eponymous annual lecture inaugurated at Museum of Fine Arts, Boston, 1998; fmr. Nat. Vice-Pres. now corp. mem. Muscular Dystrophy Asscns. of America 1970–; mem. Royal Acad. Arts and Sciences, Canada 1975; Trustee, Photographic Arts and Sciences Foundation 1970–; Hon. LL.D. (Queen's Univ., Kingston, Ont., Carleton Univ. and Savannah Coll. of Art and Design), Hon. D.H.L. (Dartmouth Coll. at Hanover, New Hampshire, Emerson Coll., Boston, Mass., Mount Allison Univs.), Hon. D.C.L. (Bishop's Univ., Quebec), LL.D. h.c. (Brooke Inst.) 1973, (Univ. of Mass.) 1978, (Hartford Univ.) 1980, (Tufts Univ.) 1982, D.F.A. (Syracuse Univ.) 1986, (Yeshiva Univ. N.Y.) 1989, (Columbia Coll.) 1990, (Univ. of British Columbia) 1990; Jerusalem Prize for Arts and Letters, Bezalel Acad., Israel 1997; Canada Council Medal 1965, Centennial Medal 1967, Gold Medal Americas Soc. 1989, Lotos Medal of Merit 1989; Univ. of Detroit President's Cabinet Annual Award 1979, Encyclopaedia Britannica Achievement in Life Award 1979, Silver Shingle Award, Boston Univ. Law School 1982, Creative Edge Award 1989, Master Photographer Award 1990, Medal of Canadian Confed. (125th anniversary) 1992. *Publications:* Faces of Destiny 1946, This is the Mass (English and French editions), This is Rome 1959, Portraits of Greatness 1959, This is the Holy Land 1961, In Search of Greatness (autobiog.) 1962, These are the Sacraments (co-author) 1963, The Warren Court 1964 (co-author), Karsh Portfolio 1967, Faces of our Time 1971, Karsh Portraits 1976, Karsh Canadians 1978, Karsh: A Fifty-Year Retrospective 1983, revised and augmented edn. 1996, American Legends 1992. *Leisure interests:* tennis, reading, archaeology, music. *Address:* 2 Commonwealth Avenue, Boston, MA 02116, U.S.A.

KENNEDY, John Fitzgerald, B.SC.; American politician; b. 29 May 1917, Boston, Mass.; s. of Joseph Kennedy and Rose (Fitzgerald) Kennedy; m. Jacqueline Bouvier; one s. one d. (and one s. deceased); ed. Harvard Univ.; served in U.S. Navy 1941–45; Corresp. Int. News Service 1945; mem. House of Reps. 1947–53; Senator from Massachusetts 1953–61; President of the United States 1961–63; Democrat. *Publications:* Why England Slept 1940, Profiles in Courage 1956, The Strategy of Peace 1960, To Turn the Tide 1962. *Address:* The White House, Washington, D.C., U.S.A.
[*Died 22 November 1963.*]

KEYNES, Baron, John Maynard Keynes, DR.h.c. (Oslo); British economist; b. 5 June 1883, Cambridge; s. of John Neville Keynes and Florence Ada Brown; m. Lydia Lopokova 1925; ed. Eton and King's Coll., Cambridge Univ.; Principal Treasury Rep. at the Paris Peace Conf., and Deputy for the Chancellor of the Exchequer on the Supreme Economic Council 1919; Fellow and Bursar King's Coll., Cambridge; Pres. Royal Economic Society; Editor *Economic Journal* 1912–; mem. Consultative Council to Treasury July 1940–; Dir. Bank of England; Chair. Arts Council of Gt. Britain. *Publications:* Economic Consequences of the Peace, A Treatise on Probability, A Revision of the Treaty, Essays in Persuasion, Essays in Biography, A Treatise on Money, General Theory of Employment, Interest and Money, How to Pay for the War. *Address:* 46 Gordon Square, London, W.C.1.
[*Died 21 April 1946.*]

KHOMEINI, Ayatollah Ruhollah; Iranian religious leader; b. 17 May 1900, Khomein; ed. in Khomein and at theological school, Qom; religious teacher in theological school, Qom; arrested in Qom after riots over Shah's land reforms June–Aug. 1963; in exile, Turkey 1964–65, Najaf, Iraq 1965–78, Neauphlé-le-Château, France Oct. 1978–Feb. 1979; while in exile aimed to create an Islamic Republic and from France was the most powerful influence on the revolution which toppled Shah Mohammad Reza Pahlavi; returned to Iran Feb. 1979; appointed Government of Mehdi Bazargan after collapse

of the Bakhtiar Government; returned to theological seminary, Qom, but continued as leader of Islamic movement March 1979–; under new constitution, became Velayat Faghih (religious leader) 1980–. *Publications:* The Goverment of Theologians (lectures whilst in exile) and numerous religious and political books and tracts. *Address:* Madresseh Faizieh, Qom; 61 Kuche Yakhchal Ghazi.
[*Died 4 June 1989.*]

KING, Martin Luther, Jr., A.B., B.D., PH.D.; American clergyman, b. 15 Jan. 1929, Atlanta, Ga.; s. of Martin Luther King and Alberta (Williams) King; m. Coretta Scott 1953; one s. one d.; ed. Morehouse Coll., Crozier Theol. Seminary, Boston Univ.; Pastor Dexter Avenue Baptist Church, Montgomery, Ala.; Pres. Montgomery Improvement Asscn.; Founder and leader, Southern Christian Leadership Council; mem. Nat. Asscn. for the Advancement of Colored Peoples; numerous awards for leadership Montgomery Movement; Hon. LL.D. (Jewish Theological Seminary); Hon. D.C.L. (Newcastle); Nobel Peace Prize 1964. *Publications:* Stride Towards Freedom 1958, Strength to Love 1964, Why We Can't Wait 1964. *Address:* 454 Dexter Avenue, Montgomery, Alabama, U.S.A.
[*Died 4 April 1968.*]

KISSINGER, Henry Alfred, M.A., PH.D.; American government official, university professor and consultant; b. 27 May 1923, Fuerth, Germany; m. 1st Anne Fleisher 1949 (divorced 1964); one s. one d.; m. 2nd Nancy Maginnes 1974; ed. George Washington High School, Harvard Coll., Harvard Univ.; went to U.S.A. 1938; naturalized U.S. Citizen 1943; U.S. Army 1943–46; Dir. Study Group on Nuclear Weapons and Foreign Policy, Council of Foreign Relations 1955–56; Dir. Special Studies Project, Rockefeller Brothers Fund 1956–58; Consultant, Weapons System Evaluation Group, Joint Chiefs of Staff 1956–60, Nat. Security Council 1961–63, U.S. Arms Control and Disarmament Agency 1961–68, Dept. of State 1965–68, and to various other bodies; Faculty mem. Harvard Univ. 1954–71; Dept. of Govt. and Center for Int. Affairs (on leave of absence 1969–71); Assoc. Dir. Harvard Univ. Center for Int. Affairs 1957–60; Dir. Harvard Int. Seminar 1951–71, Harvard Defense Studies Program 1958–71, Asst. to Pres. of U.S.A. for Nat. Security Affairs 1969–75; Sec. of State 1973–77; prominent in American negotiations for the Viet Nam settlement of Jan. 1973, and in the negotiations for a Middle East ceasefire 1973, 1974; Counsellor, Center for Strategic and Int. Studies 1977–, Trustee 1987–; Chair. Kissinger Associates, Inc. 1982–; mem. Pres.'s Foreign Intelligence Advisory Bd. 1984–90; Chair. Nat. Bipartisan Comm. on Cen. America 1983–84; Counsellor to Chase Manhattan Bank and mem. of its Int. Advisory Cttee.; Hon. Gov. Foreign Policy Asscn.; Sr. Fellow, Aspen Inst., syndicated columnist L.A. Times 1984–; Adviser to Bd. of Dirs. American Express, Revlon Group Inc., Continental Grain Co., Freeport McMoRan Inc., Hollinger Int.; Guggenheim Fellowship 1965–66, Woodrow Wilson Book Prize 1958, American Inst. for Public Service Award 1973, Nobel Peace Prize 1973, American Legion Distinguished Service Medal 1974, Wateler Peace Prize 1974, Presidential Medal of Freedom 1977, Medal of Liberty 1986, Hon. K.C.M.G. 1995 and many other awards and prizes. *Publications:* Nuclear Weapons and Foreign Policy 1956, A World Restored: Castlereagh, Metternich and the Restoration of Peace 1812–22 1957, The Necessity for Choice: Prospects of American Foreign Policy 1961, The Troubled Partnership: A Reappraisal of the Atlantic Alliance 1965, American Foreign Policy (3 essays) 1969, White House Years 1979, For the Record 1981, Years of Upheaval 1982, Observations: Selected Speeches and Essays 1982–84 1985, Diplomacy 1994 and numerous articles on U.S. foreign policy, international affairs and diplomatic history. *Address:* 350 Park Avenue, New York, NY 10022; Suite 400, 1800 K Street, N.W., Washington, DC 20006, U.S.A.

KOHL, Helmut, DR.PHIL.; German politician; b. 3 April 1930, Ludwigshafen; s. of Hans and Cäcilie (née Schnur) Kohl; m. Hannelore Renner 1960; two s.; ed. Univs. of Frankfurt and Heidelberg; Mem. of man. of an industrial union 1959; Chair. Christian Democrat Party (CDU), Rhineland-Palatinate 1966–73, Deputy Chair. CDU Deutschlands 1969–73, Chair. 1973–98; Minister-Pres. Rhineland-Palatinate 1969–76; Leader of the Opposition in the Bundestag 1976–82; Fed. Chancellor, Fed. Repub. of Germany 1982–98; Prof. h.c. (Tongji Univ., China) 1993; numerous hon. degrees; Karlspreis (Aachen) 1988, 1991; Jawarhal Nehru Award 1990; Konrad Adenauer Prize 1994, Leo Baeck Prize 1966; Grosses Bundesverdienstkreuz 1979. *Leisure interests:* reading, music, walking and swimming. *Address:* Marbacher Strasse 11, 67071 Ludwigshafen/Rhein-Oggersheim, Germany (Home).

LE CORBUSIER (Jeanneret), Charles-Edouard; French architect; b. 6 Oct. 1887, La Chaux-de-Fonds; s. of Georges-Edouard Jeanneret and Marie-Charlotte Amélie Perret; m. Yvonne Jeanne Victorine Gallis 1930; constructed first building at age of seventeen; planned new town of Bogotá, Chandigarh (capital of Punjab 1951–58), etc.; constructed pavilion l'Esprit Nouveau Int. Exhibition of Decorative Arts, Paris 1925, Centrosoyus (Min. of Light Industry, Moscow), Swiss Pavilion, Univ. City of Paris 1929–32; invited by Russian Govt. to make report on urbanisation of City of Moscow 1931; plan for construction of Soviet Palace 1932 (rejected); planned Univ. City of Brazil, Rio de Janeiro 1935, and Palace of Ministry of Education and Public Health, Rio de Janeiro 1935, and Palace of Ministry of Education and Public Health, Rio de Janeiro, with team of Brazilian architects; Pavillon des Temps Nouveaux, Paris 1937; "Unité d'Habitation" of Marseilles 1945–50; chief of architectural mission to U.S.A. 1945; construction Chapelle de Ronchamp 1952–55, "Unité d'Habitation", Nantes-Rezé 1953–54, Museum of Western Art, Tokyo, Museum of Knowledge, Ahmedabad, Convent at La Tourette; architect for Hosp. of St. John and St. Paul, Venice 1965; consultant for town and country planning to numerous govts.; Founder and Dir. *L'Esprit Nouveau* (review) 1919–25; first prize in contest for L.N. Palace, Geneva 1927, in int. contest for Palais du Centrosoyus, Moscow 1928; mem. Superior Comm. of Urbanism, Ministry of Colonies 1945; Ministry of Reconstruction 1945; Superior Council on Architecture; Direction-Gen. des Beaux Arts, Conseil Supérieur des Bâtiments Civils et Palais Nationaux 1945; Dir. l'Atelier de Bâtisseurs Le Corbusier, Paris; Pres. and Founder ASCORAL Asscn. of Constructors for Architectural Renovation, Paris; mem. French del. to U.N., N.Y. (headquarters construction); mem. Nat. Inst. of Arts and Letters, U.S.A.; Royal Gold Medal for Architecture for 1953; Grand Officier de la Légion d'Honneur; Dr. h.c. (Univ. of Zürich, Ecole Polytechnique Zürich and Univ. of Florence), Dr. Jur. h.c. (Cambridge), Dr. (h.c.) of Letters (Columbia, N.Y.). *Publications:* Vers une Architecture 1922, Urbanisme 1924, Quand les Cathédrales étaient blanches 1937, Destin de Paris 1941, Sur les quatres routes 1941, La Maison des Hommes 1942, Entretien avec les Etudiants des Ecoles d'Architecture 1943, La Charte d'Athènes 1943, Les 3 Etablissements Humains 1945, Manière de Penser l'Urbanisme 1947, Propos d'Urbanisme 1948, United Nations Headquarters 1947, L'Espace Indicible 1947, Le Modulor 1952, La Petite Maison 1954, Modulor 2 1955, Le Poème de l'Angle Droit 1955, My Work, 1961. *Address:* 35 rue de Sèvres, Paris 6e, France.
[*Died 27 August 1965.*]

LENNON, John Ono (formerly John Winston), M.B.E.; British songwriter and performer; b. 9 Oct. 1940, Liverpool; s. of Alfred Lennon and Julia Stanley; m. 1st Cynthia Powell 1962; one s.; m. 2nd Yoko Ono 1969; one s. one step-d.; ed. Dovedale Primary School, Quarrybank High School, Allerton and Liverpool Art College; plays guitar, organ, piano and harmonica; has written numerous songs with Paul McCartney; formed pop group The Quarrymen, while at Quarrybank High School 1955; appeared under various titles until formation of The Beatles 1960; appeared with The Beatles in the following activities: performances in Hamburg 1960, 1961, 1962, The Cavern, Liverpool 1960, 1961; toured Scotland, Sweden, U.K. 1963, Paris, Denmark, Hong Kong, Australia, New Zealand, U.S.A., Canada 1964, France, Italy, Spain, U.S.A. 1965, Germany, Spain, Philippines, U.S.A. 1966; attended Transcendental Meditation Course at Maharishi's Acad., Rishikesh, India Feb.–April 1968; formed Apple Corps Ltd., parent org. of The Beatles Group of Companies 1968; appeared in film How I Won the War 1967. *Publications:* In His Own Write 1964 (adapted as one-act play, Nat. Theatre 1968), A Spaniard in the Works 1965, You Are Here, Lennon Remembers 1972. *Recordings by the Beatles include:* Please, Please Me 1963, With the Beatles 1963, A Hard Day's Night 1964, Beatles for Sale 1965, Help! 1965, Rubber Soul 1966, Revolver 1966, Sergeant Pepper's Lonely Hearts Club Band 1967, The Beatles (White Album) 1968, Yellow Submarine 1969, Abbey Road 1969, Let It Be 1970. *Other recordings include:* Wedding Album 1969, John Lennon/Plastic Ono Band 1970, Imagine 1971, Mind Games 1973, Double Fantasy 1980. *Films:* (by the Beatles): A Hard Day's Night 1964, Help! 1965, Yellow Submarine (animated colour cartoon film) 1968; Let it Be 1970; T.V. film Magical Mystery Tour 1967. *Leisure interest:* working for peace. *Address:* c/o Apple Corps Ltd., 3 Savile Row, London, W.1, England; resident in U.S.A.
[*Died 8 December 1980.*]

LLOYD GEORGE OF DWYFOR, 1st Earl, cr. 1945; **Rt. Hon. David Lloyd George;** O.M., M.P., P.C.; British politician; b. 17 Jan. 1863, Manchester; s. of William George; m. 1st Margaret Owen 1888 (died 1941); two s. two d.; m. 2nd Frances Louise Stevenson 1943; solicitor 1884; Liberal M.P. for Carnarvon district since 1890; first came into prominence as vigorous opponent of Boer War and advocate of Welsh disestablishment; Pres. Board of Trade 1905–08; Chancellor of the Exchequer 1908–15; Min. of Munitions 1915–16; Sec. of State for War 1916; Prime Min. and First Lord of Treasury 1916–22; Hon. LL.D. Edin. Univ. 1918, Sheffield Univ. 1919; Jt.-Pres. Royal Inst. of Int. Affairs; leader Council of Action for Peace and Reconstruction 1935–. *Publications:* War Debts and Reparations 1932, War Memoirs I-VI, The Truth About the Peace Treaties. *Address:* House of Lords, London, S.W.1.
[*Died 26 March 1945.*]

MANDELA, Nelson Rolihlahla; South African politician and lawyer; b. 1918, Umtata, Transkei; s. of Chief of Tembu tribe; m. 1st Evelyn Mandela 1944 (divorced 1957); four c. (two deceased); m. 2nd Winnie Mandela 1958 (divorced 1996); two d.; m. 3rd Graca Machel (widow of fmr. Pres. Machel of Mozambique) 1998; ed. Univ. Coll. of Fort Hare, Univ. of the Witwatersrand; legal practice, Johannesburg 1952; Nat. organizer African Nat. Congress (ANC); on trial for treason 1956–61 (acquitted 1961); arrested 1962, sentenced to five years' imprisonment Nov. 1962; on trial for further charges 1963–64, sentenced to life imprisonment June 1964; released Feb. 1990; Deputy Pres. ANC 1990–91, Pres. 1991–97, mem. Nat. Exec. Cttee. 1991–; elected Pres. of South Africa May 1994–(99); Chancellor Univ. of the North 1992–; Jt. Pres. United World Colls. 1995–; Hon. LL.D. (Nat. Univ. of Lesotho) 1979, (City Coll. of City Univ. of New York) 1983, (Lancaster) 1984, (Strathclyde) 1985, (Calcutta) 1986, (Harare) 1987, (Kent) 1992, Hon. D.Litt. (Texas Southern Univ.) 1991; Dr. h.c. (Complutense) 1991; Hon. D.C.L. (Oxford) 1996, Cambridge (1996), Hon. LL.D. (London) 1996, Bristol (1996), (Nottingham) 1996, (Warwick) 1996, (De Montfort) 1996, (Glasgow Caledonian) 1996; Hon. Freeman of London; Jawaharlal Nehru Award (India) 1979, Bruno Kreisky Prize for Human Rights 1981, Freedom of City of Glasgow 1981, Hon. Citizen of Rome 1983, Simon Bolivar Int. Prize (UNESCO) 1983; Third World Prize 1985, Sakharov Prize 1988, Gaddafi Human Rights Prize 1989, Freeman of Dublin 1988, Bharat Ratna (India) 1990, Order of the Niger 1990, jt. winner Houphouët Prize (UNESCO) 1991, Nishan-e-Pakistan 1992, Asturias Prize 1992, Liberty Medal (U.S.A.) 1993; shared Nobel Prize for Peace 1993; Mandela-Fulbright Prize 1993; Hon. Bencher Lincoln's Inn 1994; Tun Abdul Razak Award 1994; Anne Frank Medal 1994. *Publications:* No Easy Walk to Freedom 1965, How Far We Slaves Have Come: South Africa and Cuba in Today's World (with Fidel Castro) 1991, Nelson Mandela Speaks: Forging a non-racial democratic South Africa 1993, Long Walk to Freedom 1994. *Address:* Office of the President, Private Bag X1000, Pretoria 0001, South Africa.

MANN, Thomas; German writer; b. 6 June 1875; Lübeck; m. Katja Pringsheim 1905; three s. three d.; novelist; fmr. mem. Comm. on Art and Literature of the L.N.; mem. American Acad. Arts; Fellow in Germanic Literature, U.S. Library of Congress; Nobel Prize for Literature 1929; Dr. h.c., Hon. Litt.D. (Yale, Columbia, Harvard, Princeton, Rutgers, Hobart, Cambridge). *Publications:* Buddenbrooks, Königliche Hoheit, Der Zauberberg, Der Tod in Venedig, Bemühungen, Joseph und seine Brüder, Leiden und Grösse der Meister, Lotte in Weimar, This War 1940, The Beloved Returns 1941, The Transposed Heads 1941, Order of the Day 1943, The Ten Commandments 1945, Joseph the Provider 1945, Doktor Faustus 1947, The Holy Sinner 1951. *Address:* Erlenbach, nr. Zürich, Switzerland.
[*Died 12 August 1955.*]

MAO Tse-tung; Chinese party leader; b. 26 Dec. 1893, Shaoshan, Hunan; m. 1st Yang K'asi-hui 1920; m. 2nd Chiang Ch'ing 1939; ed. Hunan Prov. No. 1 Middle School, Hunan Prov. No. 1 Normal School; Leader of Chinese Communist Revolution; organized New People's Soc. 1917; Library Asst. Peking Univ. Library 1918; edited, published *The Hsiang River Review* 1919; Principal, Elementary School, Hunan 1920–22; CCP activist in Hunan 1922–23; mem. Politburo, 3rd Cen. Cttee. of CCP 1923; Dir. Kuomintang Propaganda Dept. 1925; organized Autumn Harvest Uprising, Hunan 1927; Political Commissar Red Army 1928; mem. 6th Cen. Cttee. of CCP 1928; Chair. Cen. Chinese Soviet Repub. 1931–34; led Long March to Yenan 1934–36; Political Commissar, Chinese Worker-Peasant Red Army Coll. 1936; Principal, Yenan Party School 1942; Chair. Politburo, 7th Cen. Cttee. of CCP 1945; attended Chungking Conf. between CCP and Kuomintang 1945; assumed name of Li Te-sheng while heading CCP org., North Shensi 1947; directed mil. operations with Chou En-Lai from Hsiaoho 1947; led forces to Shensi-Chalae-Hopei Border Region 1948; Chair. Standing Cttee., Preparatory Cttee. for 1st Chinese People's Political Consultative Conf. 1949; Chair. Cen. People's Govt. 1949–54; Chair. People's Repub. of China 1954–59; Chair. 8th Cen. Cttee. of CCP 1956, mem. Standing Cttee. of Politburo 1956; Chair. 9th Cen. Cttee. of CCP 1969, mem. Standing Cttee. of Politburo 1969; Chair. 10th Cen. Cttee. of CCP 1973, mem. Standing Cttee. of Politburo 1973. *Publications:* articles and pamphlets collected in 4 vols. of Selected Works. *Address:* Central Committee of the Communist Party of China, Peking, People's Republic of China.
[*Died 9 September 1976.*]

MARCONI, Guglielmo, Marchese, Hon. G.C.V.O.; Italian physicist; b. 25 April 1874, Bologna; m. 1st Beatrice O'Brien 1905 (dissolved 1924); one s. two d.; m. 2nd Contessa Maria Cristina Bezzi-Scali; one d.; ed. Bologna and Florence; conducted wireless telegraphy experiments at Bologna; demonstrated his experiments to British Govt. 1896 and to Italian Govt. 1897; established first wireless communications between England and France 1899; effected transmission between Europe and America 1902; Nobel Prize winner for Physics 1909; invented new wireless system 1912; sent first message to Australia from England 1918; during War worked on short wave transmission experiments; Plenipotentiary Delegate to Peace Conf. 1919; lectured on short wave transmission New York Inst. of Radio Engineers; carried out experiments on yacht *Elettra* 1923–24; system adopted by British and Dominion Govts. 1924; Pres. Italian Royal Acad. 1930; Senator since 1918; Pres. Marconi Sounding Device Co. Ltd.; Joint Pres. Marconi Int. Marine Communication Co. Ltd.; Chair. Società Anonima Fiumana per le Radio Communicazione, Società Italiana Marconi, Rome; Dir. Cable and Wireless (Holding) Ltd., Cable and Wireless Ltd., Electric and Musical Industries Ltd., Gramophone Co. Ltd., Nederlandsche Seintoestellen Fabriek, Hilversum. *Address:* Via Condotti 11, Rome, Italy.
[*Died 20 July 1937.*]

MATISSE, Henri; French artist; b. 31 Dec. 1869, Cateau; ed. Ecole des Beaux Arts and with Gustave Moreau; mem. Société Nat. des Beaux-Arts, Salon d'Automne and Salon des Indépendants; winner Leningrad and Pennsylvania awards; Commdr. de la Légion d'Honneur Jan 1947. *Paintings include:* Desserts 1898, Italienne, Le Jeune Marin 1907, La Joie de Vivre 1907, Odalisque 1910, Femme au turban, La Musique 1911, Fenêtre à Tanger, Les trois soeurs 1917, Torse de jeune fille 1918, in Luxembourg Museum, Moscow State Museum of Western Art, and various European and American Galleries, designed chapel at Vence. *Address:* 132 boulevard Montparnasse, Paris 14, France.
[*Died 3 November 1954.*]

MITTERRAND, François Maurice Marie; French politician; b. 26 Oct. 1916, Jarnac, Charente; s. of Joseph and Yvonne (née Lorrain) Mitterrand; brother of Gen. Jacques Mitterrand; m. Danielle Gouze 1944; two s.; one d. by Anne Pingeot; ed. Collège Saint-Paul, Angoulême, Univ. of Paris; served 1939–40; taken prisoner, escaped back to France where active in P.O.W. and resistance movements; missions to London and Algiers 1943; Sec.-Gen. Org. for P.O.W.s, War Victims and Refugees 1944–46; journalist and mem. Paris Bar 1954; Deputy for Nièvre, Nat. Ass. 1946–58, 1962–81; Conseiller Général, Montsauche Dist. 1949; Minister for Ex-Servicemen, Sec. of State to Presidency of the Council, then Minister of State 1947–54; Nat. Pres. Union Démocratique et Socialiste de la Résistance 1951–52; Del. to Council of Europe July–Sept. 1953; Minister of the Interior 1954–55; Minister of State for Justice 1956–57; Political Ed. Le Courrier de la Nièvre; Councillor-Gen. for canton of Montsauche 1949–85; Pres. Gen. Council, Nièvre Dept. 1964–81; Mayor of Château-Chinon 1959–81; Senator for Nièvre 1959–62; Pres. of Fed. of Democratic and Socialist Left 1965–68; First Sec. Socialist Party 1971–81; Vice-Pres. The Socialist Int. 1972–81; Cand. for Pres. of France 1965, 1974; Pres. of France 1981–95; Grand Maître, Légion d'honneur, Croix de guerre, Rosette de la Résistance, Grand Cross Order of St. Charles (Monaco) 1984, Simon Wiesenthal Centre Prize 1984; Dr. h.c. (New York Univ.) 1988, (Univ. of Venice) 1992, (Gdansk) 1993. *Publications:* Aux frontières de l'union française, La Chine au défi 1961, Le coup d'état permanent 1964, Ma part de vérité 1969, Un socialisme du possible 1971, La rose au poing 1973, La paille et le grain 1975, Politique I 1977, L'abeille et l'architecte 1978, Ici et maintenant 1980, The Wheat and the Chaff: The Personal Diaries of the President of France 1971–81, Politique II 1982, Réflexions sur la politique extérieure de la France 1986, Mitterrand par lui-même 1992, Memoire à Deux Voix 1995 and many articles. *Leisure interest:* golf. *Address:* 22 rue de Bièvre, 75005 Paris, France (Home).
[*Died 8 January 1996.*]

MONROE, Marilyn; American actress; b. (as Norma Jean Baker) 1 June 1926; d. of Edward Mortensen and Gladys Baker (née Monroe); m. 1st Jim Dougherty (divorced); m. 2nd Joe DiMaggio 1954 (divorced); m. 3rd Arthur Miller 1956 (divorced 1961); Star of Tomorrow 1952, Best Actress of the Year, French Acad. of Motion Pictures 1958. *Films include:* Niagara, Asphalt Jungle, All About Eve, The Fireball, As Young as You Feel, Let's Make It Legal, Monkey Business, Gentlemen Prefer Blondes, How to Marry a Millionaire, The Seven Year Itch, Bus Stop, The Prince and the Showgirl, Some Like it Hot, The Misfits. *Address:* c/o M.C.A., 598 Madison Avenue, New York City, N.Y., U.S.A.
[*Died 31 August 1962.*]

MOORE, Henry, O.M., C.H., F.B.A.; British sculptor; b. 30 July 1898, Castleford, Yorks.; s. of Raymond Spencer Moore and Mary Baker; m. Irene Radetzky 1929; one d.; ed. Castleford Grammar School, Leeds School of Art and Royal Coll. of Art; Official War Artist 1940–42; Trustee, Tate Gallery 1941–48, 1949–56, Nat. Gallery 1955–63, 1964–74; mem. Royal Fine Art Comm. 1947–71, Arts Council 1963–67; formed Henry Moore Foundation 1977; 22 major exhbns. of work, London 1928–78, Leeds 1941, New York 1946, Chicago 1947, San Francisco 1947, Venice Biennale 1948 (First Prize for Sculpture), Cape Town 1951, Rotterdam 1953, Antwerp 1953, Sao Paulo 1953 (First Prize in Foreign Sculpture), Basel 1955, Paris 1957, Arnhem 1957, Edinburgh 1961, New York 1970, Munich 1971, Paris 1971, Florence 1972, Luxembourg 1973, Los Angeles 1973, Toronto 1974, Zürich 1976, Paris 1977, Madrid 1981; also tours in Australia 1947, Europe 1949–51, Scandinavia 1952–53, Germany 1953–54, U.S.A. 1955, Yugoslavia 1955, Canada, N.Z., Australia and South Africa 1955–58, Japan 1959, Spain and Portugal 1959, Poland 1959, Europe 1960–61, U.S.A. 1963, Latin America 1964–65, U.S.A. 1966–68, Eastern Europe 1966, Israel 1966, Canada 1967–68, Netherlands and Germany 1968, Japan 1969–70, Iran 1971, Scandinavia 1975–76; examples of work in Tate Gallery, London, British Museum, Nat. Gallery, Washington, Museum of Modern Art, New York, Albright Knox Art Gallery, Buffalo, and other public galleries in the U.K., U.S.A., Germany, Italy, Switzerland, Netherlands, Sweden, Denmark, Norway, France, Australia, Brazil, Israel, South Africa, Japan, etc.; Foreign mem. Swedish Royal Acad. of Fine Arts; Foreign Corresp. mem. Acad. Flamande des Sciences, Acad. des Lettres et Beaux Arts, Belgium; Foreign hon. mem. American Acad. of Arts and Sciences; Hon. Fellow Churchill Coll., Cambridge; Hon. D. Lit. (Leeds, London, Reading, Oxford, Hull, York, Durham), Hon. Dr. of Arts (Yale, Harvard), Hon. Dr. of Law (Cambridge, St. Andrews, Sheffield, Toronto, Manchester), Hon. Dr. of Eng. (Berlin), Hon. Dr. of Letters (Sussex, Warwick, Leicester, York, Columbia, Lancaster), Hon. Dr., R.C.A. 1967; Hon. Prof. Emer. of Sculpture, Carrara Acad. of Fine Arts; Feltrinelli Foundation Int. Sculpture Prize 1963, Erasmus Prize 1968, Einstein Prize 1968, Biancamano Prize 1973, Goslar Prize 1975; Order of Merit, (Fed. Repub. of Germany) 1968, (Italy) 1972, Commdr., Ordre des Arts et des Lettres (France) 1973, Decoration of Honour for Science and Art (Austria) 1978, Grand Cross of the Order of Merit (Fed. Repub. of Germany) 1980. *Works include:* Mother and Child, Reclining Figure, Madonna and Child, Three Standing Figures, Family Group, King and Queen, Reclining Figure (for Lincoln Center, New York), Sundial for *The Times* building, London. *Publications:* Heads, Figures and Ideas 1958, Henry Moore on Sculpture (with Philip James) 1966, Henry Moore at the British Museum 1981, Henry Moore (with John Hedgecombe) 1986. *Address:* Hoglands, Perry Green, Much Hadham, Herts., England. *Telephone:* Much Hadham 2566.
[*Died 31 August 1986.*]

MOUNTBATTEN OF BURMA, 1st Earl, cr. 1947; **Admiral of the Fleet Louis (Francis Albert Victor Nicholas) Mountbatten,** K.G., P.C., O.M., G.C.B., G.C.S.I., G.C.I.E., G.C.V.O., D.S.O., F.R.S.; b. 25 June 1900, British naval officer and public servant; ed. Locker's Park, Osborne, Dartmouth, Christ's

Coll., Cambridge; Naval Cadet 1913, Midshipman 1916, Sub-Lieut. 1918, Lieut. 1920, Lieut.-Commdr. 1928, Commdr. 1932, Capt. 1937, Cdre. 1941, Acting Vice-Adm. 1941, Acting Adm. 1943, substantive Rear-Adm. 1946, Vice-Adm. 1949, Adm. 1953, Adm. of the Fleet 1956; Col. of the Life Guards 1965, Col.-Commdt. Royal Marines 1965; served H.M.S. Lion 1916, Queen Elizabeth 1917, H.M. Submarine K6 1918, H.M.S. P31 1918, Renown 1920, 1921 (Prince of Wales tour to Australia and New Zealand 1920, and India, Japan and the Far East 1921), Repulse 1921, Revenge 1923; Signal School, Portsmouth 1924, R.N. Coll. Greenwich 1925; Asst. Fleet Wireless Signal Officer, Mediterranean Fleet 1927–28, Sr. Wireless Instr. 1929–31; Fleet Wireless Officer 1931–33; 2nd Destroyer Flotilla Signal and Wireless Officer 1928–29; commanded H.M.S. Daring 1934, Wishart 1935; Personal Naval A.D.C. to King Edward VIII 1936, to King George VI 1937–52; Capt. of Kelly and 5th Destroyer Flotilla 1939–41; in command aircraft carrier Illustrious to Oct. 1941; Adviser on Combined Operations 1941–42, Chief of Combined Operations and mem. of Chiefs of Staff Cttee. 1942–43; Supreme Allied Commdr. S.E. Asia 1943–46; Viceroy of India March–Aug. 1947; Gov.-Gen. of Dominion of India Aug. 1947–June 1948; Flag Officer Commanding First Cruiser Squadron, Mediterranean Fleet Oct. 1948–50; 4th Sea Lord, and Chief of Supplies and Transport June 1950–52; C.-in-C. Mediterranean 1952–54; C.-in-C. Allied Forces, Mediterranean 1953–54; First Sea Lord and Chief of Naval Staff 1955–59; Chief of Defence Staff and Chair. Chiefs of Staff Cttee. 1959–65; Gov. of Isle of Wight 1965, Lord Lieut. 1974–; Chair. of Nat. Electronics Council; Personal A.D.C. to H.M. the Queen 1953–; Legion of Merit and D.S.M. (U.S.A.); Grand Croix, Légion d'honneur and Croix de guerre; Grand Cross of the Lion (Netherlands), Grand Cross of Order of George I (Greece), Special Grand Cordon of the Cloud and Banner (China), Agga Maha Thiri Thudhamma (Burma), etc.; Hon. LL.D. (Cambridge, Leeds, Edin., Southampton, London, Sussex), Hon. D.C.L. (Oxford), Hon. D.Sc. (Delhi and Patna); Hon. Lieut.-Gen., Hon. Air Marshal.
[*Died 27 August 1979.*]

MURDOCH, (Keith) Rupert, A.C.; American (b. Australian) publisher; b. 11 March 1931, Melbourne, Victoria; s. of the late Sir Keith Murdoch and of Dame Elisabeth Murdoch; m. 1st Patricia Booker (divorced 1966); one d.; m. 2nd Anna Maria Torv 1967; two s. one d.; ed. Geelong Grammar School, Victoria, and Worcester Coll., Oxford; inherited Adelaide News 1952; has since built up Cruden Investments, a Murdoch family co. which owns 43 per cent of News Corpn. (Group C.E.O. 1979–, Chair. 1991–); has acquired newspapers, magazines and other interests in Australia, U.K., U.S.A. and Hong Kong, including: Australia—newspapers: The Australian (national), Daily Telegraph, Sunday Telegraph, Daily Mirror (Sydney), Sunday Sun (Brisbane), The News and Sunday Mail (Adelaide), The Sunday Times (Perth); U.S.A.—The Chicago Sun-Times, New York Post, Boston Herald, Mirror Newspapers Ltd., Nationwide News Pty. Ltd., Southdown Press Ltd., Cumberland Newspapers Ltd., (C.E.O. and fmr. Man. Dir. News Ltd. Group and associated cos. as above); magazines: TV Week, New Idea; television: Channel 10 (Sydney), Channel 10 (Melbourne, 50 per cent interest through Ansett Transport); other interests: Bay Books, Santos (energy), fmr. C.E.O. and Jt. Chair. Ansett Transport Industries. U.K.—newspapers: Sun, News of the World (national, acquired 1969), Berrows Org. (regional newspapers), C.E.O., Man. Dir. News Int. PLC (U.K.), Dir. 1969–, Chair. 1969–87, 1994–95, Chair., Pres. News America Publishing Inc.; acquired Times Newspapers Ltd. Feb. 1981, group includes The Times, The Sunday Times, The Times Literary Supplement, The Times Educational Supplement, The Times Higher Education Supplement; Dir. Times Newspapers Holdings 1981–, Chair. 1982–90, 1994–; magazines: City Magazines (Antique Collector's Guide, The Trader, Licensed Bookmaker); television: News Group Productions (U.S.A.), Skyband (U.S.A.), Satellite Television PLC (U.K.), 11.8 per cent stake in London Weekend Television; C.E.O. Sky Television Jan. 1989–, controlling stake in Star TV Asia 1993–; other interests: Townsend Hook (paper), Bemrose (printing), Convoys (transport), U.S.A.—newspapers: New York Post, others in San Antonio and Houston, Chair. News America Publishing Inc., City Post Publishing Corpn.; acquired Triangle Push Inc. 1988, Premiere 1988, William Collins PLC, Glasgow 1989–, acquired 20th Century Fox 1985–, Chair., C.E.O. Fox Inc. USA 1992–; magazines: Star, New York Magazine (including Cue and Village Voice); Today newspaper acquired 1987; Dir. United Technologies (U.S.) 1984; Dir. (non-exec.) Reuters Holdings PLC 1984–90; other interests: New York State Lotto; Commdr. of the White Rose (First Class) 1985; Kt. Order of St. Gregory the Great 1998. *Address:* 1 Virginia Street, London, E1 9XY, England; 2 Holt Street, Surry Hills, Sydney, N.S.W. 2000, Australia; News America Publishing Inc., 1211 Ave. of the Americas, 3rd Floor, New York, NY 10036, U.S.A.

NASSER, Col. Gamal Abdel; United Arab Republic (Egyptian) army officer and political leader; b. 15 Jan. 1918, Ben Mor, Egypt; m. 1944; three s. two d.; ed. El Masria Secondary School, Cairo, and Military Acad., Cairo; serving army officer until 1952; posted to Mil. Acad. 1942, graduated with distinction; fought in the Palestine war; led the coup d'état of July 23rd, 1952; Deputy Prime Minister and Minister of the Interior 1952–54; Prime Minister and Military Governor of Egypt 1954–56; Pres. of Egypt 1956–58; Pres. of United Arab Republic 1958–, also Prime Minister and Head of Arab Socialist Union June 1967–; Hero of the Soviet Union. *Address:* The Presidency, Cairo, U.A.R.
[*Died 28 September 1970.*]

NIXON, Richard Milhous, A.B., LL.B.; American politician (retd.); b. 9 Jan. 1913, Yorba Linda, Calif.; s. of Francis A. and Hannah (Milhous) Nixon; m. Thelma Catherine ("Pat") Ryan 1940; two d.; ed. Whittier Coll. and Duke Univ. Law School; practised law in Whittier 1937–42; Attorney with Office of Emergency Man., Washington, D.C. 1942; served with U.S. Navy 1942–46; attained rank of Lieut.-Commdr.; mem. Congress for 12th Calif. District 1947–50; Senator from Calif. 1950–53; Vice-Pres. of U.S.A. 1953–61; Republican candidate for Presidency (ran against John F. Kennedy) 1960; affiliated with law firm Adams, Duque and Hazeltine 1961–63; Republican Candidate for Gov., Calif. 1962; mem. Mudge, Stern, Baldwin and Todd 1963–64; partner, Nixon, Mudge, Rose, Guthrie, Alexander & Mitchell 1964–68; 37th Pres. of U.S.A. 1969–74, resigned 10 Aug. 1974; granted Presidential Pardon by Pres. Ford, Sept. 1974, after Watergate investigations; responsible for Viet-Nam Peace Settlement Jan. 1973; first U.S. Pres. to make official visit to People's Repub. of China Feb. 1972, U.S.S.R. May 1972; revisited China Feb. 1976, Sept. 1982; Foreign Assoc. Acad. des Beaux-Arts. *Publications:* Six Crises 1962, RN: Memoirs 1978, The Real War 1980, Leaders 1982, Real Peace: a Strategy for the West 1984, No More Vietnams 1986, 1999: Victory Without War 1988, In the Arena: A Memoir of Victory, Defeat and Renewal 1990, Seize the Moment: America's Challenge in a One Superpower World 1991. *Address:* Park Ridge, NJ; 142 East 65th Street, New York, NY 10021, U.S.A.
[*Died 22 April 1994.*]

NUREYEV, Rudolf (Hametovich); ballet dancer (b. U.S.S.R.); b. 17 March 1938, Razdolnaia; ed. Ufa and Leningrad Choreographic School; Winner Moscow Nat. Students Competition; joined Kirov Ballet, Leningrad as soloist 1958; sought political asylum in the West during tour in Paris 1961; joined Grand Ballet du Marquis de Cuevas 1961; London début Charity Gala 1961; appeared with Dame Margot Fonteyn and the Royal Ballet, London 1962, and became her principal partner; has since danced all over the world in over 80 ballets, including all the nineteenth century classics as well as contemporary roles in both classical and modern style; took Austrian citizenship 1982; Guest artist in 25 companies; Artistic Dir. Paris Opera Ballet 1983–89, Prin. Choreographer Nov. 1989–; Palais Garnier Dec. 1988–; appeared as King in The King and I 1989; Chevalier, Légion d'honneur; Choreographer Tancredi 1966, The Nutcracker 1967, Romeo and Juliet 1977, Manfred 1979, The Tempest 1982, Washington Square 1985, Cinderella 1986; revised and directed La Bayadère, Act III 1963, Raymonda 1964, Swan Lake 1964, The Sleeping Beauty 1966, Don Quixote 1970; Nutcracker; Raymonda (Dir.) 1983. *Films include:* An Evening with the Royal Ballet 1963, Romeo and Juliet 1966 and 1982, Swan Lake 1966, Le Jeune Homme et la Mort 1966, I am a Dancer 1972, Don Quixote 1972, Valentino 1977, Exposed 1982, Cinderella 1986. *Publication:* Nureyev, an autobiography. *Address:* c/o S. A. Gorlinsky Ltd., 33 Dover Street, London, W1X 4NJ, England.
[*Died 6 January 1993.*]

OLIVIER, Baron (Life Peer), cr. 1970, of Brighton; **Laurence Kerr Olivier,** Kt., O.M.; British actor and director; b. 22 May 1907; s. of the late Rev. G. K. Olivier and Agnes Louise Crookenden; m. 1st Jill Esmond 1930 (divorced 1940), one s.; m. 2nd Vivien Leigh 1940 (divorced 1961); m. 3rd Joan Plowright 1961, one s. two d.; ed. St. Edward's School, Oxford; First appearance, The Taming of the Shrew, Stratford 1922; Birmingham Repertory Co. 1925–28; subsequent appearances in London, New York, Paris and Denmark; Old Vic Theatre Co. 1944–45, 1949, toured Australia and New Zealand 1948; Actor-Manager, St. James's Theatre, London 1950–51; Shakespeare Memorial Theatre, Stratford-on-Avon 1955; Dir. Chichester Festival Theatre 1962–65, The National Theatre 1962–73; mem. South Bank Theatre Bd. 1967–; Hon. D.Litt. (Oxon., Manchester, London, Sussex), Hon. LL.D. (Edin.), Hon. M.A. (Tuft's); Chevalier, Légion d'honneur; Commdr., Order of Dannebrog (Denmark) and Grand Officer, Ordine al Merito della Repubblica (Italy); Acad. Award 1948; Sonning Prize (Denmark) 1966; Gold Medallion, Swedish Acad. of Literature 1968; Order of Yugoslav Flag with Gold Wreath 1971, Albert Medal, R.S.A. 1976; Hon. Acad. Award 1979. *Stage appearances include:* many Shakespearian, classical and modern plays; produced and appeared in Venus Observed, Caesar and Cleopatra, The Broken Heart, Uncle Vanya, etc.; National Theatre appearances include Uncle Vanya, Othello, Master Builder, Love for Love, The Dance of Death, A Flea in Her Ear, The Merchant of Venice, Long Day's Journey into Night, Saturday Sunday Monday, The Party; Dir. Eden End 1974. *Films include:* Wuthering Heights, Rebecca, Pride and Prejudice, 49th Parallel, Carrie, Beggar's Opera, The Devil's Disciple, Spartacus, The Entertainer, Term of Trial, Khartoum, Othello, The Shoes of the Fisherman, The Dance of Death 1968, Battle of Britain, Oh! What a Lovely War, Three Sisters 1969, David Copperfield, Nicholas and Alexandra, Lady Caroline Lamb, Sleuth, Seven Per Cent Solution 1975, Marathon Man 1975, A Bridge Too Far 1976, Jesus of Nazareth 1976, The Betsy 1977, The Boys from Brazil 1978, A Little Romance 1978, Dracula 1978, Clash of the Titans 1979, Inchon 1979, The Jazz Singer 1980, Richard Wagner 1982, The Bounty 1984, Wild Geese II 1984, Peter the Great; produced, directed and played in Henry V, Hamlet, Richard III and The Prince and the Showgirl. *Television appearances include:* John Gabriel Borkman, The Moon and Sixpence, The Power and the Glory, Long Day's Journey into Night, The Merchant of Venice, World at War (narrator) 1973, Love among the Ruins 1974, Jesus of Nazareth 1976, Brideshead Revisited (Emmy Award) 1978/80, A Voyage Round My Father 1982, King Lear 1982, Mr. Halpern and Mr. Johnson; television productions include The Best Play of the Year 19– (a series of plays) 1976, 1977, The Ebony Tower 1984. *Publication:* Confessions of an Actor 1982, On Acting 1986.

Leisure interests: tennis, flying, gardening. *Address:* c/o Wheelshare Ltd., 33/34 Chancery Lane, London, WC2A 1EW, England. *Telephone:* 01-405 8799.
[*Died 11 July 1989.*]

O'NEILL, Eugene Gladstone; American playwright; b. 16 Oct. 1888, New York; s. of James O'Neill and Ella Quinlan; m. 1st Kathleen Jenkins 1909; m. 2nd Agnes Boulton; m. 3rd Carlotta Monterey 1929; one s. one d. (one s. deceased) by previous marriages; ed. Princeton and Harvard Univs.; awarded Nobel Prize for Literature 1936. *Plays include:* The Moon of the Caribbees 1919, Beyond the Horizon 1920, The Emperor Jones 1921, The Hairy Ape 1922, Marco Millions 1924, Desire Under the Elms 1924, Strange Interlude 1927, Mourning Becomes Electra 1931, Ah, Wilderness! 1933, Days Without End 1933, The Iceman Cometh 1939, Long Day's Journey Into Night 1940, A Touch of the Poet 1942, A Moon for the Misbegotten 1943. *Address:* Random House, 20 East 57th Street, New York 22, N.Y., U.S.A.
[*Died 27 November 1953.*]

OPPENHEIMER, Robert; American physicist; b. 22 April 1904, New York; s. of Julius Oppenheimer and Ella (née Freedman) Oppenheimer; m. Katherine Harrison 1940; one s. one d.; ed. Univs. of Harvard, Cambridge and Göttingen; National Research Fellow 1927–28; Int. Educ. Board Fellow 1928–29; Prof. of Physics, Univ. of Calif. and Calif. Inst. of Technology 1929–47; Dir. Los Alamos Laboratory New Mexico 1943–45; Prof. of Physics, Inst. for Advanced Study, Princeton Oct. 1947–, Dir. 1947–66; Chair. Gen. Advisory Comm., Atomic Energy Comm. 1946–52. *Address:* Institute for Advanced Study, Princeton, N.J., U.S.A.
[*Died 18 February 1967.*]

ORWELL, George; British writer; b. 23 Jan. 1903; m. 1st Eileen O'Shaughnessy 1933 (died 1945); m. 2nd Sonia Mary Brownell 1949; ed. Eton; Indian Imperial Police (Burma) 1922–27; lived in Paris 1928–29; school teacher 1931–34; worked in bookseller's shop 1934–35; fought in Spanish Civil War (P.O.U.M. militia) 1936–37; mem. staff B.B.C. (Eastern Service) 1941–43; engaged in Freelance journalism 1930–; now Literary Editor of *Tribune*. *Publications:* Down and Out in Paris and London 1933, Burmese Days 1934, The Road to Wigan Pier 1937, Homage to Catalonia 1938, The Lion and the Unicorn 1941, Animal Farm 1945, Nineteen Eighty-Four 1949. *Address:* 10A Mortimer Crescent, London, N.W.6.
[*Died 21 January 1950.*]

PAULING, Linus Carl, PH.D., SC.D, L.H.D., U.J.D., D.H.C.; American university professor; b. 28 Feb. 1901; m. Ava Pauling (died 1981); ed. Oregon State Coll., Calif. Inst. of Tech. and Univs. of Munich, Copenhagen and Zürich: full-time Asst. in Quantitative Analysis, Oregon State Coll. 1919–20; part-time Asst. Chem., Mechanics and Materials, Oregon State Coll. 1920–22; Graduate Asst., Calif. Inst. of Tech. 1922–23, Teaching Fellow 1923–25, Research Assoc. 1925–26, Nat. Research Fellow, Chem. 1925–26; Fellow, John Simon Guggenheim Memorial Foundation 1926–27; Asst. Prof. of Chem., Calif. Inst. of Tech. 1927–29, Assoc. Prof. 1929–31, Prof. 1931–64; Prof. of Chem., Univ. of Calif., at San Diego 1967–69, Stanford Univ. 1969–74, Prof. Emer. 1974–; Pres. Linus Pauling Inst. of Science and Medicine 1973–75, Research Prof. 1973–; Chair. Div. of Chem. and Chemical Eng., Calif. Inst. of Tech., Dir. of the Gates and Crellin Laboratories 1936–58; George Fisher Baker Lecturer in Chem., Cornell Univ. 1937–38; Eastman Prof. Oxford Univ. 1948; Research Prof. Center for Study of Dem. Insts. 1963–67; mem. N.A.S., American Acad. of Arts and Sciences, Deutsche Akad. der Naturforscher Leopoldina; Hon. mem. or Fellow Chemical Soc. of London, Acad. of Sciences of Liège, Royal Inst., Swiss Chemical Soc., Chemical Soc. of Japan, Nat. Inst. Sciences India, Royal Norwegian Scientific Soc., Trondheim; foreign mem. Royal Soc., Norwegian Acad. Science and Letters, Acad. of Sciences U.S.S.R.; corresp. foreign mem. Accad. delle Scienze, Lisbon Acad. Science; Foreign Assoc. Acad. des Sciences (France); Hon. Fellow, Indian Acad. Sciences, Austrian Acad. of Science, European Soc. of Haematology, etc.; hon. degrees from numerous univs., awards include: Langmuir Prize 1931, William H. Nichols Medal 1941, Willard Gibbs Medal 1946, Theodore William Richards Medal 1947, Davy Medal 1947, Medal for Merit 1948, Gilbert Newton Lewis Medal 1951, Nobel Prize for Chem. 1954, for Peace 1962, Thomas Addis Medal 1955, John Phillips Memorial Award, Avogadro Medal 1956, Pierre Fermat Medal, Paul Sabatier Medal 1957, Lenin Prize 1970, Martin Luther King, Jr. Medical Award 1972, U.S. Nat. Medal of Science 1974, Lomonosov Gold Medal 1978, N.A.S. Award in Chemical Sciences 1979, Gold Medal of the Nat. Inst. of Social Sciences 1979, Priestley Medal 1984, American Chemical Soc. Award in Chemical Educ. 1987. *Publications:* The Structure of Line Spectra (with S. Goudsmit) 1930, Introduction to Quantum Mechanics, with Applications to Chemistry (with E. Bright Wilson, Jr.) 1935, The Nature of the Chemical Bond 1939, General Chemistry 1947, College Chemistry 1950, No More War! 1958, 1962, The Architecture of Molecules (with R. Hayward) 1965, The Chemical Bond 1967, Vitamin C and the Common Cold 1971, Vitamin C, the Common Cold and the Flu, Cancer and Vitamin C (with Ewan Cameron) 1979, How to Live Longer and Feel Better 1986. *Address:* Linus Pauling Institute of Science and Medicine, 440 Page Mill Road, Palo Alto, CA 94306; Salmon Creek 15, Big Sur, CA 93920, U.S.A.
[*Died 19 August 1994.*]

PAVAROTTI, Luciano, D.MUS.; Italian opera singer; b. 12 Oct. 1935, Modena; s. of Fernando Pavarotti and Adele (Venturi) Pavarotti; m. Adua Veroni 1961; three d.; ed. Istituto Magistrale; tenor range; début as Rodolfo in La Bohème at Reggio nell'Emilia 1961, Staatsoper Vienna, Royal Opera House, London 1963, La Scala 1965, Metropolitan Opera House, New York 1968, Paris Opera and Lyric Opera of Chicago 1973; début as Edgardo in Lucia di Lammermoor in U.S.A. (Miami) 1965; La Scala tour of Europe 1963–64; recitals and concerts abroad including the U.S.A. and Europe 1973–, tour of U.S.S.R. 1990; Pavarotti in the Park (London) 1991; about 30 albums 1964–79; appeared in MGM film Yes, Giorgio 1981; hon. degree (Pa.) 1979; Noce d'Oro Nat. Prize, Luigi Illica int. prize, first prize Gold Orfeo (Acad. du Disque Lyrique de France), Grammy Award for best classical vocal soloist 1981 and many other prizes; Grand Officer, Italian Repub., Légion d'honneur. *Publications:* Pavarotti: My Own Story (with William Wright), Grandissimo Pavarotti 1986, Pavarotti: My World (with William Wright) 1995. *Leisure interests:* tennis, painting, equitation. *Address:* c/o Herbert Breslin, 119 West 57th Street, New York, NY 10019, U.S.A. (Office); Via Giardini 941, 41040 Saliceta, Modena, Italy (Home).

PELÉ (Edson Arantes do Nascimento); Brazilian football player and author; b. 23 Oct. 1940, Três Corações; Minas Gerais State; s. of João Ramos do Nascimento and Celeste Arantes; m. Rosemeri Cholbi 1966 (divorced 1978); one s. two d.; m. Assiria Lemos 1994; ed. Santos Univ.; first played football at Baurú, São Paulo; Baurú Atlético Clube; joined Santos F.C. 1955; first int. game v. Argentina; played in World Cup 1958, 1962, 1966, 1970; finished career with New York Cosmos; Chair. Pelé Soccer Camps 1978–; Dir. Santos F.C. 1993–; Special Minister for Sports, Govt. of Brazil 1994–98; Dir. Soccer Clinics; three World Cup winners' medals; two World Club Championship medals; 110 int. caps, 97 goals for Brazil; 1,114 appearances for Santos, 1,088 goals; career total 1,282 goals in 1,364 games, 9 league championship medals, 4 Brazil cup medals; most goals in season 53 (1958); has appeared in several films, including Escape to Victory 1981, A Minor Miracle 1983, Hot Shot 1986; has composed numerous songs in Samba style; Goodwill Amb. for 1992, UN Conf. on Environment and Devt., Rio de Janeiro; Int. Peace Award 1978, WHO Medal 1989; Hon. K.B.E. 1997. *Publications:* Eu Sou Pelé 1962, Jogando com Pelé 1974, My Life and the Beautiful Game 1977, Pelé Soccer Training Program 1982, The World Cup Murders (novel) 1988. *Address:* 75 Rockefeller Plaza, New York, NY 10019, U.S.A.

PICASSO, Pablo Ruiz; Spanish painter; b. 25 Oct. 1881, Malaga; m. 1st Olga Koklova (died 1955); m. 2nd Jacqueline Roque 1961; ed. Barcelona; worked in Paris since 1901; founder and leader of the cubist school; designer for Diaghilev Ballet 1917–27; Dir. Prado Gallery Madrid 1936–39; painted murals for Spanish Pavilion, Paris Exhibition 1937, for UNESCO Building, Paris 1958; many hundreds of his works are in museums, galleries and pvt. collections throughout the world; although his most important work is in the field of painting, he has also executed a large number of drawings, sculptures, lithographs, ceramics and theatrical décors; he has also appeared in two films illustrating his work and techniques; Major Exhbn. Paris 1966; Sculpture Exhbn., London 1967; Lenin Peace Prize 1962. *Publications include:* engravings: The Dream and Life of General Franco 1937; plays: Le Désir attrapé par la Queue 1945, Les Quatres Petites Filles 1965. *Address:* Villa Californie, Cannes (A.-M.); and Mas Notre-Dame-de-Vic, par Mougins (A.-M.), France.
[*Died 8 April 1973.*]

PLANCK, Max, PH.D., M.D., D.SC.; German physicist; b. 23 April 1858; s. of Johann Julius Wilhelm Planck and Emma Patzig; ed. Munich and Berlin Univs.; originator of Quantum theory; Prof. of Physics Kiel Univ. 1885 and Berlin Univ. since 1889; mem. 1894 and Permanent Sec. since 1912 Prussian Acad. of Science. *Publications:* Prinzip der Erhaltung der Energie 1887, Vorlesungen über Thermodynamik 1897, Vorlesungen über die Theorie der Wärmestrahlung 1906, Einleitung in die theoretische Physik 1930, Where is Science Going? *Address:* Berlin-Grunewald, Wangenheimstr. 21.
[*Died 4 October 1947.*]

POL POT (also known as Saloth Sar, Tol Saut or Pol Porth), Cambodian politician; b. 19 May 1928, Memot; m. Khieu Ponnary 1956; worked on rubber plantation; joined anti-French resistance under Ho Chi Minh in 1940s; mem. Indo-Chinese CP until 1946, Pracheachon (Cambodian CP) 1946–89, leader 1962; mem. People's Representative Ass. representing rubber plantation workers 1976–79; Prime Minister 1976–79; overthrown after Vietnamese invasion of Kampuchea; charged with crimes of genocide; sentenced to death in absentia Aug. 1970; Commdr. of guerrilla army after invasion 1979–85 ("retd."); Dir. "Higher Inst. for Nat. Defence" 1985–89, returned to Cambodia Nov. 1991; reported dead 1996.
[*Died 14 April 1998.*]

PRESLEY, Elvis Aron; American entertainer; b. 8 Jan. 1935, Tupelo, Miss.; s. of Vernon Elvis Presley and Gladys Smith; m. Priscilla Beaulieu 1967 (dissolved); one d.; ed. East Tupelo School, L.C. Humes High School, Memphis, Tenn.; began singing career on contract to Memphis Sun Recording Studio; transferred to RCA Corpn., first RCA record *Heartbreak Hotel* 1956, also first Gold Record; has won more Gold Records than any other singer. *Recordings include:* singles Blue Suede Shoes, Love Me Tender, All Shook Up, Teddy Bear, Jailhouse Rock, I Got Stung, One Night, Stuck On You, The Girl of my Best Friend, Can't Help Falling in Love, Return to Sender, Crying in the Chapel, If I Can Dream, In the Ghetto, The Wonder of You, My Boy. *Film appearances include:* Love Me Tender 1956, Loving You 1957, King Creole 1958, G.I. Blues 1960, Flaming Star 1961, Wild in the Country 1961, Blue Hawaii 1961, Girls, Girls, Girls 1963, That's the Way it is 1971, Change of Habit 1971. Frequent cabaret performer; on programme televised

world-wide by satellite from Hawaii. *Leisure interests:* horse riding, karate, cinema. *Address:* Graceland, Elvis Presley Boulevard, Highway 51 South, Memphis, Tennessee, U.S.A.
[*Died 16 August 1977.*]

ROCKEFELLER, John Davison; American industrialist; b. 8 July 1839, Richford, N.Y.; s. of William Avery Rockefeller and Eliza Davison; m. Laura C. Spelman 1864 (died 1915); one s. one d.; Pres. Standard Oil Co. until 1911, when he retired from active business; created four great charitable corporations: the Rockefeller Foundation, Gen. Education Board, The Laura Spelman Rockefeller Memorial and the Rockefeller Inst. for Medical Research; his total philanthropic and charitable donations up to 1921 exceeded 500 million dollars. *Address:* 4 West 54th Street, New York City, U.S.A.
[*Died 23 May 1937.*]

ROOSEVELT, Franklin Delano, B.A., LL.D.; American politician; b. 30 Jan. 1882, Hyde Park, N.Y.; s. of James Roosevelt and Sara Delano Roosevelt; m. Anna Eleanor Roosevelt 1905; four s. one d.; ed. Harvard and Columbia Univ. Law School; admitted to New York Bar 1907; mem. firm of Carter Kedyard and Milburn 1907–10, and Roosevelt and O'Connor 1924–; mem. New York Senate 1910–13 (resigned); Asst. Sec. of the Navy 1913–20; Democrat nominee for Vice-Pres. of U.S. 1920; mem. Hudson-Fulton Celebration Comm. 1909, Plattsburg Centennial 1913; mem. Nat. Comm. Panama and Philippine Islands Exposition 1915; Overseer Harvard Univ. 1918–24; Governor New York 1929–33; President of U.S. March 1933–, re-elected Nov. 1936, for 3rd term Nov. 1940, for 4th term Nov. 1944. *Publications:* Whither Bound? 1926, The Happy Warrior 1928, Government—Not Politics 1932, Looking Forward 1933, On Our Way 1934, The Public Papers and Addresses of Franklin D. Roosevelt 1928–1940. *Address:* The White House, Washington, D.C.; and Hyde Park, Dutchess Co., N.Y., U.S.A.
[*Died 12 April 1945.*]

RUSSELL, 3rd Earl, cr. 1861; **Bertrand Arthur William Russell,** O.M., M.A., F.R.S.; British philosopher, mathematician and educationist; b. 18 May 1872, Trelleck; s. of Viscount John Amberley and Katherine Stanley; m. 1st Alys Whittall Pearsall Smith 1894 (divorced 1921); m. 2nd Dora Winifred Black 1921 (divorced 1935); one s. one d.; m. 3rd Patricia Helen Spence 1936 (divorced 1952); one s.; m. 4th Edith Finch 1952; ed. Trinity Coll., Cambridge; Fellow Trinity Coll., Cambridge 1895 and 1944–, Lecturer 1910–16; Chair. No Conscription Fellowship 1916; imprisoned for pacifist propaganda; fmr. Lecturer Univ. of California; appointed Lecturer in Mathematics, New York City Coll. 1940, appt. revoked; Prof. of Philosophy, Barnes Foundation 1940–43; Nobel Prize for Literature 1950, UNESCO Kalinga Prize 1957, Sonning Prize 1960. *Publications:* German Social Democracy 1896, Essay on the Foundations of Geometry 1897, Philosophy of Leibniz 1900, Principles of Mathematics 1903, Principia Mathematica (with Prof. A. N. Whitehead) 1910–13, Philosophical Essays 1910, Problems of Philosophy 1911, Our Knowledge of the External World as a Field for Scientific Method in Philosophy 1914, Principles of Social Reconstruction 1917, Mysticism and Logic 1918, Roads to Freedom 1918, Introduction to Mathematical Philosophy 1919, The Practice and Theory of Bolshevism 1920, The Analysis of Mind 1921, The Problem of China 1922, The ABC of Atoms 1923, (with Dora Russell) The Prospects of Industrial Civilization 1923, Icarus 1924, The ABC of Relativity 1925, What I Believe 1925, On Education 1926, Analysis of Matter 1927, An Outline of Philosophy 1927, Sceptical Essays 1928, Marriage and Morals 1929, The Conquest of Happiness 1930, The Scientific Outlook 1931, Education and the Social Order 1932, Freedom and Organisation 1814–1914 1934, In Praise of Idleness 1935, Which Way to Peace? 1936, The Amberley Papers (with Patricia Russell) 1937, Power: A New Social Analysis 1938, Let the People Think 1940, An Inquiry into Meaning and Truth 1941, A History of Western Philosophy 1946, Human Knowledge 1948, Authority and the Individual 1949, Unpopular Essays 1950, New Hopes for a Changing World 1951, The Impact of Science upon Society 1952, Satan in the Suburbs (fiction) 1953, Nightmares of Eminent Persons 1954, Human Society in Ethics and Politics 1954, Portraits from Memory 1956, Why I am not a Christian 1957, My Philosophical Development 1959, Wisdom of the West 1959, Has Man a Future? 1961, Fact and Fiction 1961, Unarmed Victory 1962, The Autobiography of Bertrand Russell 1872–1914 (Vol. I) 1967, War Crimes in Vietnam 1967, The Autobiography of Bertrand Russell 1914–1944 (Vol. II) 1968, The Autobiography of Bertrand Russell 1944–1967 (Vol. III) 1969. *Address:* Plas Penrhyn, Penrhyndeudraeth, Merionethshire, Wales.
[*Died 2 February 1970.*]

SAINT LAURENT, Yves (Henri Donat); French couturier; b. 1 Aug. 1936, Oran, Algeria; s. of Charles Mathieu Saint Laurent and Lucienne-Andrée Wilbaux; ed. Lycée d'Oran; worked with Christian Dior 1954–57, successor to Christian Dior 1957–60; Shareholder Société Yves Saint Laurent 1962–; consultant to Chinese govt. 1987–; designed costumes for: (ballets) Cyrano de Bergerac 1959, Adage et Variations, Notre-Dame de Paris 1965, Sheherezade 1973, Delicate Balance 1967; (films) The Pink Panther 1962, Belle de Jour 1967, La Chamade 1968, La Sirène du Mississippi 1969, L'Affaire Stavisky 1974; designed stage sets and costumes for: Les Chants de Maldoror 1962, Spectacle Zizi Jeanmaire 1961, 1963, 1968; exhbns.: Metropolitan Museum of Art, New York 1983, Beijing Museum of Fine Arts 1985, Musée des Arts de la Mode, Paris 1986; House of Painters of U.S.S.R. 1986, Hermitage Museum Leningrad (now St. Petersburg) 1987, Art Gallery of N.S.W. Sydney 1987, Sezon Museum, Tokyo 1990, Espace Mode Méditerrannée, Marseille 1993; Neiman-Marcus Award for fashions 1958, Oscar, Harper's Bazaar 1966, Int. Award of Council of Fashion Designers of America 1982, Best Fashion Designer Oscar 1985, Chevalier Légion d'honneur. *Address:* 5 avenue Marceau, 75116 Paris, France.

SARTRE, Jean-Paul; French writer; b. 21 June 1905, Paris; ed. Lycée Henri IV and Ecole Normale Supérieure, Paris; taught at Lycée du Havre, and later travelled in Egypt, Greece and Italy 1929–34; at Inst. Français, Berlin 1934; taught philosophy at Lycée Pasteur de Neuilly-sur-Seine 1935–39 and Lycée Condorcet; army 1939–41 (prisoner of war 1940–41); active in resistance movement 1941–44; resgnd. from teaching 1944; Founder Dir. Les Temps Modernes; was offered, but declined, Nobel Prize for Literature 1964; Dir. Tout 1970–74, Révolution 1971–74, Libération 1973–74, La France Sauvage 1973–. *Publications:* Philosophy: L'imagination 1936, Esquisse d'une théorie des émotions 1939, L'imaginaire, psychologie phénoménologique de l'imagination 1940, L'être et le néant 1943, Critique de la raison dialectique 1960, La transcendence de l'égo 1965; Novels: La nausée 1938, Le mur 1939, Les chemins de la liberté 1945; Plays: Les mouches 1943, Huis-clos 1944, Morts sans sépulture 1946, La putain respectueuse 1946, Les mains sales 1948, Le diable et le bon Dieu 1951, Nekrassov 1955, Les séquestrés d'Altona 1960; Essays: L'existentialisme est un humanisme 1946, Situations I-X 1947–, Qu'est-ce que la littérature? 1947, Baudelaire 1947, Saint Genet, comédien et martyr 1952, Merleau-Ponty vivant 1961, Le peintre sans privilège 1962, Marxisme et existentialisme (with Roger Garaudy) 1963, Les communistes et la paix 1969, Le spectre de Staline 1969, L'idiot de la famille (vol. III of biography of Flaubert) 1972; Screenplays: Les feux sont faits 1947, L'engrenage 1949; Les mots (memoirs) 1964. *Address:* Editions Gallimard, rue Sébastien-Bottin, 75007 Paris; 220 boulevard Raspail, 75014 Paris, France.
[*Died 15 April 1980.*]

SHAW, George Bernard; Irish playwright and philosopher, creative evolutionist, co-founder of Fabian socialism; b. 26th July 1856, Dublin; m. Charlotte Frances Payne-Townshend 1898 (died 1943); ed. domestic (mainly artistic); contributed weekly articles on music to *The Star* 1888–90 and on music and pictures to *The World* 1890–94; theatre critic to *The Saturday Review* 1895–98; Nobel Prizeman for Literature 1925. *Publications include:* more than fifty plays, incl. Mrs. Warren's Profession, Arms and the Man, Candida 1898, Man and Superman 1903, Major Barbara 1905, Androcles and the Lion 1913, Pygmalion 1914, Heartbreak House 1919, Back to Methuselah 1921, Saint Joan 1923, The Apple Cart 1929, and many novels, essays, treatises, etc. *Address:* Ayot Saint Lawrence, Welwyn, Herts.
[*Died 2 November 1950.*]

SHOSTAKOVICH, Dmitry Dmitryevich; Soviet pianist and composer; b. 25 Sept. 1906, Leningrad; m. 1st Nina Vasilievna Varzar (died 1954); one s. one d.; m. 2nd Irina Shostakovich; ed. Leningrad Conservatoire; studied under L. N. Nikolaev and M. O. Steinberg; Pianist in Leningrad Conservatoire 1927–37, Prof. 1937–71; Prof. Moscow Conservatoire 1943–48; artistic adviser, Bolshoi Theatre, Moscow 1954–; 1st Sec. Soviet Union of Composers 1960–68; mem. editorial board *Sovietskaya Muzyka*; State prizes for piano quintet 1941, 7th Symphony 1942, piano trio 1946; People's Artist of U.S.S.R. 1954; concert tour in Italy 1958; mem. U.S.S.R. Supreme Soviet 1959–; mem. Comm. for Public Education, Science and Culture of Soviet Union; Hon. mem. St. Cecilia Acad. of Music Jan. 1958; Diploma of Honour, St. Cecilia Acad. May 1958; Hon. D.Mus. (Oxon.) 1958, (Trinty Coll., Dublin) 1972; Lenin Prize for 11th Symphony 1958; Hero of Socialist Labour, Order of Lenin 1966; Hammer and Sickle Gold Medal, Royal Philharmonic Soc. (U.K.) 1966, State Prize 1968. *Works include:* fifteen symphonies, three ballets (Golden Age, Bolt, Clear Stream), three operas (Nose, Lady Macbeth of Mtsensk, Katerina Izamilova), symphonic suites, piano concertos, violin concertos, two cello concertos, three cantata-oratorios, six string quartets, music for films and theatrical productions, oratorio Song of the Forest 1949, oratorio Execution of Stepan Razin 66, operetta Cheryomushki 1958, symphonic poem October 1967, Sonata for Violin and Piano 1969. Address: U.S.S.R. Union of Composers, 8–10 Ulitsa Nezhdanovoy, Moscow, U.S.S.R.
[*Died 9 August 1975.*]

SIBELIUS, Jean Julius Christian, HON. R.A.M.; Finnish musician; b. 8 December 1865, Tavastehus; s. of D. Christian Sibelius and Maria (née Borg) Sibelius; m. Aino Järnefelt 1892; five d.; ed. Helsinki Univ., Berlin and Vienna Conservatoires; Composer; Hon. Prof.; Hon. Dr. Helsinki, Oxford, Yale and Heidelberg Univs.; hon. mem. Royal Acad. of Music London, Royal Philharmonic Soc. London, New York Nat. Society of Music, New York, Santa Cecilia Acad. Rome, Franz Liszt-Gesellschaft, Weimar etc.; corresp. mem. Acad. des Beaux-Arts, Paris, Akademie der Freien Künste, Berlin, Comitato del Congresso internazionale di Musica, Rome, Royal Swedish Acad. of Music, etc. *Works include:* seven symphonies, violin concerto, Saga, Karelia, Lemminkäinen, Finlandia, Valse Triste, Pelleas and Melisande, Luonnotar, Oceanides, Tapiola, Voces Intimae, Malinconia; about 200 pianoforte compositions and songs, etc. *Address:* Järvenpää, Finland.
[*Died 20 September 1957.*]

SINATRA, Frank; American singer, actor and composer; b. (as Francis Albert Sinatra) 12 Dec. 1915, Hoboken, N.J.; s. of Anthony Sinatra and Natalie Garaventi; m. 1st Nancy Barbato 1939 (divorced); one s. two d.; m. 2nd Ava Gardner 1951 (divorced); m. 3rd Mia Farrow 1966 (divorced 1968); m. 4th Barbara Marx 1976; ed. Drake Inst.; sang with Harry James and

Tommy Dorsey Bands; film début as singer 1941, as actor 1943; mem. Pres.'s Cttee. on Arts and Humanities 1982; Jean Hersholt Humanitarian Award, Motion Picture Acad. 1971; Hon. Citizen of Chicago 1975; Hon. Chief, Bophuthatswana 1981; Hon. D.Hum.Litt. (Nebraska) 1976; Cultural Award (Israel) 1977, Pied Piper Award (U.S.A. Soc. of Composers, Authors and Publrs.) 1980; Cross of Honour of Science and the Arts (Austria) 1984, Pres. Medal of Freedom 1985, Life Achievement Award, Nat. Asscn. for Advancement of Colored People 1987, Grammy Lifetime Achievement Award 1994. *Films include:* Higher and Higher 1943, Step Lively 1944, Anchors Aweigh 1945, Take Me Out to the Ball Game 1948, On the Town 1949, Double Dynamite 1950, From Here to Eternity (Acad. Award for Best Supporting Actor) 1953, Young at Heart 1954, The Tender Trap 1955, Not as a Stranger 1955, The Man with the Golden Arm 1956, Johnny Concho 1956, The Pride and the Passion 1956, Around the World in Eighty Days 1956, Guys and Dolls 1956, High Society 1956, Pal Joey 1957, The Joker is Wild 1957, Kings Go Forth 1958, Some Came Running 1958, A Hole in the Head 1959, Can Can 1959, Never So Few 1959, Ocean's Eleven 1960, The Devil at Four O'Clock 1961, Sergeants Three 1962, The Manchurian Candidate 1962, Four for Texas 1963, The List of Adrian Messenger 1963, Come Blow Your Horn 1963, Robin and the Seven Hoods 1964, None But the Brave (also dir.) 1964, Von Ryan's Express 1965, Marriage on the Rocks 1965, Cast a Giant Shadow 1966, Assault on a Queen 1966, The Naked Runner 1967, Tony Rome 1967, The Detective 1968, Lady in Cement 1968, Dirty Dingus Magee 1970, The First Deadly Sin 1981, Cannonball Run II (cameo), Who Framed Roger Rabbit (voice), Listen Up. *Publication:* A Man and His Art 1990. *Address:* Sinatra Enterprises, 9100 Wilshire Boulevard, # 455, Beverly Hills, CA 90212, U.S.A.
[*Died 15 May 1998.*]

SMUTS, Field Marshal Rt. Hon. Jan Christiaan, P.C., O.M., C.H., K.C., F.R.S., M.P.; South African politician; b. 24 May 1870; s. of J. A. Smuts; m. Sybella Margaretha Krige 1897; one s. four d. (one s. deceased); ed. Victoria Coll., Stellenbosch, and Christ's Coll., Cambridge; State Attorney South African Republic 1898; supreme Commander of Republican forces in Cape Colony 1901; Colonial Sec., Transvaal 1907; Commander of British forces, British East Africa 1916–17; mem. Imperial War Cabinet 1917–18; Min. of Interior and Mines 1910–12, of Finance 1912–13, and of Defence 1910–20; Prime Min. and Min. of Native Affairs 1919–24; Min. of Justice 1933–39; Prime Min., Min. of External Affairs and Defence Sept. 1939–48; Rector of St. Andrew's Univ. 1931–34; M.P. for Pretoria East; Leader United Party; Chancellor Cape Town Univ. 1936–; Officer Commanding Union Defence Forces 1940–48; awarded Albert Medal of Royal Society of Arts 1942; Chancellor Univ. of Cambridge 1948–; numerous decorations, city freedoms, and hon. degrees. *Publications:* Holism and Evolution 1926, Africa and Some World Problems 1930, Plans for a Better World 1942. *Address:* Doornkloof, Irene, near Pretoria.
[*Died 11 September 1950.*]

SOLZHENITSYN, Aleksandr Isayevich; Russian writer; b. 11 Dec. 1918, Kislovodsk; m. 1st Natalya Reshetovskaya (separated 1970); m. 2nd Natalya Svetlova; three s.; ed. Rostov Univ. and Correspondence Course in Literature, Moscow History and Literature Inst.; joined Army 1941, attended artillery school, commissioned 1942, served at front as Commdr. of Artillery Battery, and twice decorated for bravery; sentenced to eight years in a forced labour camp 1945–53; contracted, later cured of cancer; in exile in Siberia 1953–57; officially rehabilitated 1957; taught mathematics at secondary school, Ryazan; expelled from Writers' Union of U.S.S.R. Nov. 1969; expelled from U.S.S.R. Feb. 1974, lived in Vt., U.S.A.; ended exile as treason charges dropped 1991; returned to Russia, citizenship restored 1994; hosted A Meeting with Solzhenitsyn 1995; mem. American Acad. of Arts and Sciences 1969–, Russian Acad. of Sciences 1997–; Hon. Fellow, Hoover Inst. on War, Revolution and Peace 1975; Prix du Meilleur Livre Etranger (France) for The First Circle and Cancer Ward 1969, Nobel Prize for Literature 1970, Templeton Prize 1983; Hon. U.S. Citizen 1974. *Publications:* One Day in the Life of Ivan Denisovich 1962 (film 1971), Matryona's Home and An Incident at Krechetovka Station 1963 (short stories), For the Good of the Cause 1964 (short story), The First Circle (publ. U.S.A. and U.K. 1968), Cancer Ward (U.S.A. and U.K. 1968), The Easter Procession (short story), The Love Girl and the Innocent (play, U.K.) 1969, Collected Works (6 vols.) 1969, 1970, Stories and Prose Poems 1971, August 1914 1971, The Gulag Archipelago Vol. I 1973, Vol. II 1974, Vol. III 1976, Letter to Soviet Leaders 1974, Peace and Aggression 1974, Quiet Flows the Don: The Enigma of a Novel 1974, Candle in the Wind (play), The Oak and the Calf: Sketches of Literary Life in the Soviet Union 1975, The Nobel Prize Lecture 1975, Lenin in Zürich 1975, Détente (with others) 1976, Prussian Nights (poem trans. by Robert Conquest) 1977, Collected Works 1978–, Victory Celebrations, Prisoners (play) 1983, October 1916 1985, The Red Wheel, Live Not by Lies (essay) 1988, August 1914 (second version) 1989, Rebuilding Russia 1990, The Russian Question at the End of the 20th Century 1994, Invisible Allies (addendum to The Oak and the Calf) 1995, November 1916, Russia is Falling 1998. *Address:* P.O. Box 121, Cavendish, VT 05142, U.S.A.

SPIELBERG, Steven, B.A.; American film director; b. 18 Dec. 1947, Cincinnati, Ohio; s. of Arnold and Leah (née Posner) Spielberg; m. 1st Amy Irving 1985 (divorced 1989); two s.; m. 2nd Kate Capshaw; two d. (one adopted); ed. Calif. State Coll., Long Beach; won film contest with war film Escape to Nowhere 1961; dir. episodes of TV series, including Night Gallery, Marcus Welby, M.D., Columbo; directed 20-minute short Amblin'; Dir. TV films Duel 1971, Something Evil 1972; Dirs. Guild of America Award Fellowship 1986; Co-f. Dreamworks SKG 1995–; f. Starbright Foundation; Irving G. Thalberg Award 1987, Golden Lion Award (Venice Film Festival) 1993, B.A.F.T.A. Award 1994, Acad. Award for Schindler's List 1994, David Lean (B.A.F.T.A.); John Huston Award for Artists Rights 1995, Grosses Bundesverdienstkreuz 1998; Dr. h.c. (Univ. of S. Calif.) 1994; Hon. D.Litt. (Sussex) 1997; John Huston Award 1995. *Films directed:* The Sugarland Express 1974, Jaws 1975, Close Encounters of the Third Kind 1977, 1941 1979, Raiders of the Lost Ark 1981, E.T. (The Extra Terrestrial) 1982, Indiana Jones and the Temple of Doom 1984, The Color Purple (also produced) 1985, Empire of the Sun 1988; I Wanna Hold Your Hand (produced) 1978, Poltergeist (co-wrote and produced) 1982, Gremlins (produced) 1984, Young Sherlock Holmes 1985 (exec. producer), Back to the Future (co-exec. producer), The Goonies (writer and exec. producer) 1986, Batteries Not Included (exec. producer) 1986, The Money Pit (co-produced) 1986, An American Tail (co-exec. producer) 1986, Always 1989, Gremlins II (exec. producer), Dad (exec. producer), Joe versus the Volcano (exec. producer), Hook 1991, Cape Fear (co-exec. producer) 1992, Jurassic Park 1992, Schindler's List 1993, Casper (producer) 1995, Some Mother's Son 1996, Twister 1996 (exec. producer), The Lost World: Jurassic Park 1997, Amistad 1997, Deep Impact 1998, Saving Private Ryan 1998 (Acad. Award for Best Dir.). *Publication:* Close Encounters of the Third Kind (with Patrick Mann). *Address:* CAA, 9830 Wilshire Boulevard, Beverly Hills, CA 90212, U.S.A.

STALIN, Generalissimo Iosif Vissarionovich (Djugashvili), Marshal of the Soviet Union; Soviet statesman; b. 21 Dec. 1879; s. of Vissarion Djugashvili; m. 1st Yekaterina 1903 (died 1907); one s.; m. 2nd Nadejda Sergeyevna Alleuya 1918 (died 1932); one s. one d.; m. 3rd Rosa Kaganovich; ed. Seminary for Priests; Leader Marxist group in Tiflis 1897 and Party Cttee. 1900; arrested 1901; went into hiding and worked under various names (David, Nijeradze, Chizhikov, Ivanovich); deported to North Siberia for three years 1903, but escaped; Delegate to Bolshevik Conf. in Finland, First Congress at Stockholm 1906 and London Congress 1907; deported to Vologda Province 1908 but escaped; after Prague Conf. co-opted mem. Central Cttee. of Party 1912; worked on *Pravda* and *Zviezda*; deported but again escaped to Petersburg; led Bolshevik group in Duma; Dir. *Pravda*; arrested again and deported to Turukhan; returned to Petersburg after February Revolution as mem. Central Cttee. of Party; mem. of "The Five" during October Revolution and afterwards of "The Seven"; Commissar for Nationalisation 1917–23; Gen. Sec. of Central Cttee. of Communist Party since 1922; mem. Presidium Supreme Soviet of U.S.S.R. since 1925; mem. Council for Labour and Defence, Politbureau; Chair. Cttee. for drafting Constitution 1935; Chair. Council of People's Commissars 1941–46; Pres. Soviet Council of Mins. 1946–, State Cttee. of Defence 1941–46; Commissar of Defence and Commdr.-in-Chief 1941–46; Generalissimo of the Soviet Union 1945; awarded Order of Suvorov 1943, Order of Victory and Order of Red Banner 1944, Order of Victory and Title Hero of Soviet Union, June 1945. *Publications include:* Problems of Leninism, On the Opposition, Collected Articles, On Nationalities, On Lenin and Leninism. *Address:* Moscow, The Kremlin, U.S.S.R.
[*Died 5 March 1953.*]

STANISLAVSKY, Konstantin Sergeyevich; Soviet theatrical producer and actor; b. 1863; founded, with Komisarjevsky and Fedotov, the Society of Art and Literature 1888; worked as actor and producer; founder and Dir. the Moscow Art Theatre 1898–. *Publication:* Moja Zhisn i Iskustvo (My Life and Art). *Address:* Moscow, First Art Theatre, U.S.S.R.
[*Died 1938.*]

STEINBECK, John Ernst; American writer; b. 27 Feb. 1902, Salinas, Calif.; s. of John Ernst Steinbeck and Olive Hamilton; m. 1st Carol Henning 1930 (divorced 1943); m. 2nd Gwyn Conger 1943; m. 3rd Elaine Anderson 1950; ed. Stanford Univ.; Pulitzer Prize 1940, Nobel Prize for Literature 1962. *Publications:* Cup of Gold 1929, To a God Unknown 1933, Tortilla Flat 1935, In Dubious Battle 1936, Of Mice and Men, Red Pony 1937, The Grapes of Wrath 1939, Forgotten Village 1941, Sea of Cortez 1941, The Moon is Down 1942, Cannery Row 1945, The Wayward Bus 1947, The Pearl 1947, The Russian Journal 1948, Burning Bright 1950, East of Eden 1952, Sweet Thursday 1954, Pipe Dream 1954, Short Reign of Pippin IV 1957, Once there was a War, The Log from the Sea of Cortez 1958, The Winter of Our Discontent 1961, Travels with Charley 1962, America and the Americans 1966. *Address:* c/o McIntosh and Otis Inc., 18 East 41st Street, New York 17, N.Y., U.S.A.
[*Died 20 December 1968.*]

STRAVINSKY, Igor; American (born Russian) composer; b. St. Petersburg, Russia, 5 June 1882; m. Vera de Bosset 1940; naturalized French subject 1934; naturalized American subject 1945; Pres. English Bach Festival; Royal Philharmonic Soc. Gold Medal 1954; Sibelius Gold Medal 1955; mem. American Acad. of Arts and Letters. *Compositions include:* L'Oiseau de Feu 1910, Petrouchka 1911, Le sacre du Printemps 1913, Rossignol 1914, Renard 1916, Les Noces 1917–23, L'Histoire du Soldat 1918, Pulcinella 1919, Symphonies d'Instruments à vent 1920, Mavra 1922, Octour 1923, Concerto for Piano and Orchestra 1924, Oedipus-Rex 1926, Apollon Musagète 1927, Le Baiser de la Fée 1928, Capriccio for Piano and Orchestra 1929, Symphonie de Psaumes 1930, Concerto for Violin and Orchestra 1931, Persèphone 1933–34, Concerto for Two Pianos 1935, Jeu de Cartes 1936–37, Concerto for Chamber Ensemble 1937–38, Symphony in C 1940, Danses Concertantes 1942, Scènes de Ballet 1944, Symphony in 3 movements 1945, Orpheus

1947, Mass 1948, The Rake's Progress 1951, Cantata 1952, Septet 1953, Three Songs from William Shakespeare 1954, In Memoriam Dylan Thomas 1954, Canticum Sacrum 1956, Agon 1957, Threni 1958, Movements for Piano and Orchestra 1959, Gesualdo Monumentum 1960, The Flood (opera) 1962, Abraham and Isaac 1964, Elegy for J.F.K. 1964, Variation in Memory of Aldous Huxley 1965, Requiem Canticles 1966, The Song of the Nightingale 1967. *Address:* 1260 N. Wetherly Drive, Hollywood, Calif., U.S.A.
[*Died 6 April 1971.*]

TAYLOR, Elizabeth Rosemond; British film actress; b. 27 Feb. 1932, London; d. of Francis Taylor and Sara Sothern; m. 1st Conrad Nicholas Hilton, Jr. 1950 (divorced); m. 2nd Michael Wilding 1952 (divorced); two s.; m. 3rd Mike Todd 1957 (died 1958); one d.; m. 4th Eddie Fisher 1959 (divorced); m. 5th Richard Burton 1964 (divorced 1974, remarried 1975, divorced 1976); one adopted d.; m. 7th Senator John Warner 1976 (divorced 1982); m. 8th Larry Fortensky 1991 (divorced 1996); ed. Byron House, Hawthorne School, and Metro-Goldwyn-Mayer School; active in philanthropic and relief charitable causes internationally including Israeli War Victims Fund for the Chaim Sheba Hosp. 1976, UNICEF, Variety Children's Hosps., medical clinics in Botswana; initiated Ben Gurion Univ.-Elizabeth Taylor Fund for Children of the Negev 1982; supporter AIDS Project L.A. 1985; founder, Nat. Chair. Council for AIDS Research (AmFAR) 1985–, int. fund 1985–; founder Elizabeth Taylor AIDS Foundation 1991–; Commdr. Ordre des Arts et des Lettres 1985; Légion d'honneur (for work with AmFAR) 1987; Aristotle S. Onassis Foundation Award 1988, Jean Hersholt Humanitarian Acad. Award (for work as AIDS advocate), Life Achievement Award, American Film Inst. 1993, Lifetime Achievement Award, Screen Actors Guild 1998, BAFTA Fellowship 1999; honoured with dedication of Elizabeth Taylor Clinic, Washington 1993; licensed fragrances: Elizabeth Taylor's Passion, Passion for Men, White Diamonds/Elizabeth Taylor, Elizabeth Taylor's Diamonds and Emeralds, Diamonds and Rubies, Diamonds and Sapphires, jewelry: The Elizabeth Taylor Fashion Jewelry Collection for Avon. *Films include:* Lassie Come Home 1942, There's One Born Every Minute 1943, The White Cliffs of Dover 1943, Jane Eyre 1943, National Velvet 1944, Courage of Lassie 1946, Life with Father 1946, Cynthia 1947, A Date With Judy 1948, Julia Misbehaves 1948, Little Women 1948, Conspirator 1949, The Big Hangover 1949, Father's Little Dividend 1950, Father of the Bride 1950, A Place in the Sun 1950, Love is Better Than Ever 1951, Ivanhoe 1951, Rhapsody 1954, Elephant Walk 1954, Beau Brummel 1954, The Last Time I Saw Paris 1955, Giant 1956, Raintree Country 1957, Cat on a Hot Tin Roof 1958, Suddenly Last Summer 1959, Butterfield 8 1960, Cleopatra 1962, The VIPs 1963, The Sandpiper 1965, Who's Afraid of Virginia Woolf? 1966, The Taming of the Shrew 1967, The Comedians 1967, Reflections in a Golden Eye 1967, Doctor Faustus 1968, Boom 1968, Secret Ceremony 1968, The Only Game in Town 1969, Under Milk Wood 1971, X, Y and Zee 1972, Hammersmith is Out 1972, Night Watch 1973, Ash Wednesday 1974, The Driver's Seat 1975, Blue Bird 1976, A Little Night Music 1977, The Mirror Crack'd 1980, Between Friends 1983, The Young Toscanini 1988, The Flintstones 1994. *Television appearances include:* Divorce His, Divorce Hers 1973, Victory at Entebbe 1977, Return Engagement 1979, Between Friends 1982, Hotel (series) 1984, Malice in Wonderland 1986, North and South (mini-series) 1986, There Must be a Pony 1986, Poker Alice 1987, Sweet Bird of Youth 1989. *Plays include:* The Little Foxes (New York) 1981, (Los Angeles) 1981, (London) 1982, Private Lives (New York) 1983. *Publications:* World Enough and Time (with Richard Burton) 1964, Elizabeth Taylor 1965, Elizabeth Taylor Takes Off—On Weight Gain, Weight Loss, Self-Esteem and Self Image 1988. *Address:* c/o Nat Rubin, 245 Fifth Avenue, New York, NY 10016, U.S.A.

TERESA, Mother (Agnes Gonxha Bojaxhiu); Albanian-born Roman Catholic missionary; b. 27 Aug. 1910, Skopje, now fmr. Yugoslav repub. of Macedonia; joined Sisters of Loretto 1928; worked at Loretto insts. in Ireland and India; Principal St. Mary's High School, Calcutta; founded the Missionaries of Charity 1950, resgnd. as Head 1990, re-elected Sept. 1990; through the Missionaries of Charity has set up over fifty schools, orphanages and houses for the poor in India and other countries; opened Nirmal Hriday (Pure Heart) Home for Dying Destitutes 1952; started a leper colony in West Bengal 1964; Padma Shri 1962, Pope John XXIII Peace Prize 1971, Templeton Foundation Prize 1973, Nobel Peace Prize 1979, Bharat Ratna (Star of India) 1980; Hon. D.D. (Cambridge) 1977, Hon. O.B.E. 1978, Star of India 1980, Hon. Dr.Med. (Catholic Univ. of Sacred Heart, Rome) 1981, (Catholic Univ. of Louvain) 1982, Hon. Citizen of Assissi 1982, Hon. O.M. 1983, Presidential Medal of Freedom 1985, Woman of the Year Award 1989, Notre Dame Univ. Award 1992, Hon. Fellow Royal Coll. of Surgeons of Ireland 1992, Freedom of Dublin 1993. *Publications:* Gift for God 1975, Heart of Joy 1988, Living the Word 1990, Loving Jesus 1991, A Simple Path 1995. *Address:* 54A Acharya Jagadish Chandra Bose Road, Calcutta 700016, India. *Telephone:* (33) 297115.
[*Died 5 September 1997.*]

THATCHER, Baroness; (Life Peer) cr. 1992, of Kesteven in the County of Lincolnshire, **Rt. Hon. Margaret Hilda Thatcher,** L.G., O.M., P.C., M.A., B.SC., F.R.S.; British politician and barrister; b. 13 Oct. 1925; d. of the late Alfred Roberts and of Beatrice Ethel Stephenson; m. Denis Thatcher (now Sir Denis Thatcher, Bt.) 1951; one s. one d. (twins); ed. Grantham High School and Somerville Coll., Oxford; Research chemist 1947–51; called to the Bar, Lincoln's Inn 1953; M.P. for Finchley 1959–92; Parl. Sec. Ministry of Pensions and Nat. Insurance 1961–64; Chief Opposition Spokesman on Educ. 1969–70; Sec. of State for Educ. and Science 1970–74; Leader of Conservative Party 1975–90; Leader of H.M. Opposition 1975–79; Prime Minister 1979–90; First Lord of the Treasury and Minister for the Civil Service 1979–90; Pres. No Turning Back Group 1990–; Dir. Tiger Man. 1998–; Vice-Pres. Royal Soc. of St. George 1999–; Hon. Pres. Bruges Group 1991–; Chair. Advisory Bd. Univ. of London's Inst. of U.S. Studies 1994–; Hon. Bencher, Lincoln's Inn 1975; Hon. Master of the Bench of Gray's Inn 1983; Hon. Fellow Royal Inst. of Chem. 1979; Freedom of Royal Borough of Kensington and Chelsea 1979, of London Borough of Barnet 1980, of Falkland Is. 1983, of City of London 1989, of the City of Westminister 1990; Chancellor Univ. of Buckingham 1992–98, William and Mary Coll., Va. 1994–; mem. Worshipful Co. of Glovers 1983–, Int. Advisory Bd. British-American Chamber of Commerce 1993–; Hon. LL.D. (Univ. of Buckingham) 1986, Dr. h.c. (Rand Afrikaans Univ. S.A.) 1991, (Weizmann Inst. of Science) 1992, (Mendeleyev Univ.) 1993, (Brunel) 1996; MacArthur Foundation Fellowship 1992; Presidential Medal of Freedom (U.S.A.) 1991, Order of Good Hope (SA) 1991; Hilal-i-Imitaz 1996; Hon. Citizen of Gorasde 1993; Conservative. *Publications:* In Defence of Freedom 1986, The Downing Street Years 1979–1990 1993, The Path to Power 1995, The Collected Speeches of Margaret Thatcher 1997. *Address:* House of Lords, Westminster, London, SW1A 0PW; P.O. Box 1466, London SW1X 9HY, England.

TITO, Marshal (Josip Brož); Yugoslav politician; b. 7 May 1892; s. of Franjo and Marija Brož; m. 3rd Jovanka Budisavljevik 1952; two s.; two s. by previous marriages; mechanic; served in Austro-Hungarian Army 1914–15; imprisoned in Russian concentration camps 1915–17; participated in the Russian revolution; returned to Yugoslavia and worked as machinist and mechanic until 1927; Dist. Sec. of trade union of metal workers 1927–28; took active part in illegal Yugoslav Communist Party; sentenced to six years' imprisonment for conspiracy 1928; after release left the country, helped recruit Yugoslavs for the Int. Brigade in Spanish Civil War 1936–38; returned to Yugoslavia before World War II; after the German invasion organized Partisan Forces; elected Marshal of Yugoslavia and Pres. Nat. Liberation Cttee. 1943; Prime Minister and Minister of Nat. Defence 1945–53; Pres. of the Republic 1953–, Life Pres. 1974; Gen Sec. CP Secr. 1953–66, Chair. League of Communists 1966–, and Supreme Commdr. of the Armed Forces 1953–; Nat. Hero decoration (three times), Order of Lenin (U.S.S.R.), Hon. G.C.B. 1972, Jawaharlal Nehru Award for Int. Understanding 1974. *Address:* Office of the President of the Republic, Belgrade, Yugoslavia.
[*Died 4 May 1980.*]

WALES, Diana, Princess of; b. (as Diana Frances Spencer) 1 July 1961, Sandringham, Norfolk; d. of the late 8th Earl Spencer and of Countess Spencer (née Frances Roche, now Hon. Mrs. Peter Shand Kydd); m. H.R.H. The Prince of Wales 29 July 1981 (divorced 28 August 1996); two s., H.R.H. Prince William Arthur Philip Louis, b. 21 June 1982, H.R.H. Prince Henry Charles Albert David, b. 15 Sept. 1984; ed. Riddlesworth Hall Preparatory School, Diss, West Heath School, Sevenoaks; teacher Young England Kindergarten School, Pimlico, London 1979–81; Patron, Centrepoint, English Nat. Ballet, Great Ormond Street Hospital for Sick Children, The Leprosy Mission, The Royal Marsden Hospital, Nat. AIDS Trust; was fmrly. Patron of Welsh Nat. Opera, Royal School for the Blind, Leatherhead, The Malcolm Sargent Cancer Fund for Children, Pre-school Playgroups Asscn., Swansea Festival of Music and the Arts, Royal Coll. of Physicians and Surgeons of Glasgow, British Deaf Asscn., Nat. Children's Orchestra, The British Red Cross Youth Div., London City Ballet, Nat. Council for Child Health, Birthright, Help The Aged, The Commonwealth Soc. for the Deaf, Turning Point, Parkinson's Disease Soc., British Lung Foundation, British Sports Asscn. for the Disabled, Nat. Hosps. for Nervous Diseases, Relate; fmr. Pres. The Albany (community centre in the East End of London), Wales Craft Council, Barnardo's, Royal Acad. of Music, R.A.D.A., Nat. Meningitis Trust; fmr. Col.-in-Chief Royal Hampshire Regt., Light Dragoons; fmr. Sponsor H.M.S. Cornwall; Hon. Air Cdre. R.A.F. Wittering 1985–; Humanitarian Service Award 1995. *Address:* Kensington Palace, London W8, England.
[*Died 31 August 1997.*]

WAŁĘSA, Lech; Polish politician and trade union activist; b. 29 Sept. 1943, Popowo; s. of the late Bolesław and of Feliksa Wałęsa; m. Danuta Wałęsa 1969; four s. four d.; ed. primary and tech. schools; electrician, Lenin Shipyard, Gdańsk 1966–76, 1983–; Chair. Strike Cttee. in Lenin Shipyard 1970; employed Zremb and Elektromontaż 1976–80; Chair. Inter-institutional Strike Cttee., Gdańsk Aug.–Sept. 1980; co-founder and Chair. Solidarity independent trade union 1980–90, Chair. Nat. Exec. Comm. of Solidarity 1987–90; interned 1981–82; founder of Civic Cttee. attached to Chair. of Solidarity 1988–90; participant and co-Chair. Round Table Plenary debates 1989; Chair. Country Defence Cttee. 1990–95; Supreme Commdr. of Armed Forces of Polish Republic for Wartime 1990–95; Pres. of Polish Republic 1990–95; 60 hon. doctorates; Hon. citizen of Buffalo, N.Y. 1981, Osaka 1981; Man of the Year, Financial Times 1980, The Observer 1980, Die Welt 1980, Die Zeit 1981. L'Express 1981, Le Soir 1981, Time 1981, Le Point 1981; Awarded "Let us Live" peace prize of Swedish journal Arbetet 1981; Love International Award (Athens) 1981, Freedom Medal (Philadelphia) 1981, Medal of Merit, (Congress of Polish Community in U.S.A.) 1981, Free World Prize (Norway) 1982, Social Justice Award 1983, Nobel Peace Prize 1983, Human Rights Prize, Council of Europe 1989, White Eagle Order 1989, Meeting-90 Award (Rimini) 1990, and other awards and prizes.

Publication: Le Chemin d'espoir (autobiog.) 1987. *Leisure interests:* crossword puzzles, fishing. *Address:* ul. Polanki 54, 80-308 Gdańsk-Oliwa, Poland.

WATSON, James Dewey, B.S., PH.D.; American biologist; b. 6 April 1928, Chicago, Ill.; s. of James D. Watson and Jean Mitchell Watson; m. Elizabeth Lewis 1968; two s.; ed. Univ. of Chicago, and Univ. of Indiana; Research Fellow, U.S. Nat. Research Council, Univ. of Copenhagen 1950–51; Fellow U.S. Nat. Foundation, Cavendish Lab., Univ. of Cambridge, England 1951–53, 1955–56; Sr. Research Fellow in Biology, Calif. Inst. of Tech. 1953–55; Asst. Prof. of Biology, Harvard Univ. 1956–58, Assoc. Prof. 1958–61, Prof. 1961–76; Dir. Cold Spring Harbor Lab. 1968–93, Pres. 1994–; Assoc. Dir. NIH (USA) 1988–89, Dir. Nat. Center for Human Genome Research, NIH 1989–92; Newton-Abraham Visiting Prof., Oxford Univ., U.K. 1994; discovered structure of DNA (with F. W. Crick) 1953; mem. N.A.S., Danish Acad. of Arts and Sciences, American Acad. of Arts and Sciences, American Soc. of Biological Chemists; Sr. Fellow, Soc. of Fellows, Harvard Univ. 1964–70; Hon. Fellow of Clare Coll., Univ. of Cambridge 1967; mem. American Philosophical Soc. 1978; Foreign mem. Royal Soc. 1981, U.S.S.R. (now Russian) Acad. of Sciences 1989; Hon. D.Sc. (Chicago, Indiana, Long Island, Adelphi, Brandeis, Hofstra, Harvard, Rockefeller, State Univ. of New York, Albert Einstein Coll. of Medicine, Clarkson Coll., Stellenbosch, Fairfield, Cambridge, Oxford); Hon. LL.D. (Notre Dame) 1965; Hon. M.D. (Buenos Aires) 1986; Hon. D.Sc. (Rutgers Univ.) 1988, (Bard Coll.) 1991, (Melbourne) 1997; Eli Lilly Award in Biochem. 1959, Lasker Prize (American Public Health Asscn.) 1960, Nobel Prize for Medicine (with F.H.C. Crick and M.F.H. Wilkins) 1962, John J. Carty Gold Medal (Nat. Acad. of Sciences) 1971, Medal of Freedom 1977, Gold Medal Award, Nat. Inst. of Social Sciences 1984, Kaul Foundation Award for Excellence 1992, Capley Medal of Royal Soc. 1993, Nat. Biotech. Venture Award 1993; Lomosonov Medal 1994, Nat. Medal of Science 1997. *Publications:* Molecular Biology of the Gene 1965 (2nd edn. 1970, 3rd edn. 1976), The Double Helix 1968, The DNA Story 1981 (with John Tooze), Recombinant DNA: A Short Course 1983 (with others), The Molecular Biology of the Cell (with others) 1986, Recombinant DNA, 2nd edn. 1992 (with others); papers on structure of deoxyribonucleic acid (DNA), on protein synthesis and on the induction of cancer by viruses. *Address:* Cold Spring Harbor Laboratory, P.O. Box 100, Cold Spring Harbor, Long Island, New York, NY 11724 (Office); Bungtown Road, Cold Spring Harbor, New York, NY 11724, U.S.A. (Home). *Telephone:* (516) 367-8310.

WELLES, (George) Orson; American actor and producer; b. 6 May 1915, Kenosha, Wis.; s. of Richard Head Welles and Beatrice Ives; m. 1st Virginia Nicholson 1934 (divorced 1940); one s.; m. 2nd Rita Hayworth 1943 (divorced 1947); one d.; m. 3rd Paola Mori 1955; one d.; ed. Todd School, Woodstock, Ill.; fmr. actor Gate Theatre, Dublin; founded Mercury Theatre 1937, now Vice-Pres. and Dir. Mercury Productions; Producer, Writer and Dir. R.K.O. Radio Pictures 1939–40; mem. Actors Equity Asscn., American Fed. Radio Artists; Claire Senie Award for foremost achievement in American Theatre 1938; Commdr., Légion d'honneur 1982; Assoc. Ed. Free World Magazine; mem. American Acad. of Arts and Sciences 1970–; mem. Bd. Trustees, Simon Wiesenthal Cen. for Holocaust Studies 1981–; Special Acad. Award 1971; Life Achievement Award, American Film Inst. 1974, Fellow British Film Inst. 1983. *Directed plays:* Horse Eats Hat 1936, Dr. Faustus, Cradle Will Rock 1937, Julius Caesar 1937, Shoemaker's Holiday, Heartbreak House, Danton's Death 1938; produced and acted in Othello (London) 1951, Moby Dick (London) 1955, King Lear (New York) 1956; wrote and acted in Chimes at Midnight 1960. *Films:* Citizen Kane (wrote, produced, directed, acted) 1940, The Magnificent Ambersons (wrote, dir., prod.) 1942, Journey into Fear (wrote, prod., acted) 1942, Jane Eyre 1943, Tomorrow is Forever 1945, The Lady from Shanghai (wrote, prod., dir., acted) 1946, Macbeth (adapted, dir., acted) 1947, Black Magic 1947, The Third Man 1949, The Black Rose 1950, Versailles 1955, Confidential Report (wrote, dir., acted) 1955, Moby Dick 1955, Othello (adapted, dir., acted) 1956, The Long Hot Summer 1958, Compulsion 1959, Ferry to Hong Kong 1959, Crack in the Mirror 1960, David and Goliath 1961, The Trial, The V.I.P.s 1963, I'll Never Forget What's 'Is Name 1967, A Man for All Seasons 1967, The Kremlin Letter 1969, The Immortal Story (dir.) 1969, Waterloo 1970, Catch 22 1970, Ten Days' Wonder 1972, F for Fake (wrote, dir., acted) 1974, The Other Side of the Wind (dir.) 1974, Voyage of the Damned 1976, The Other Side of the Mountain 1977, Crossed Swords 1978, The Late Great Planet Earth 1978, Never Trust An Honest Thief. *Publications:* Mr. Arkadin 1957; Ed. with Roger Hill: Everybody's Shakespeare 1933, Mercury Shakespeare 1939; Play: Chimes at Midnight (film 1964). *Leisure interests:* prestidigitating, cartooning, swimming, reading. *Address:* c/o L. Arnold Weissberger, 120 East 56th Street, New York, N.Y. 10022; 10464 Bellago Road, Bel Air, Calif., U.S.A. (Home).
[*Died 10 October 1985.*]

WELLS, Herbert George, D.SC., HON. D.LIT. (Lond.); British writer; b. 21 September 1866, Bromley, Kent; s. of Joseph Wells; m. Amy Catherine Robbins (died 1927); two s.; ed. private school at Bromley, Kent, Midhurst Grammar School and Royal Coll. of Science; novelist, short story writer, sociological publicist and historian; sometime draper's apprentice and teacher; an early member of the Fabian Society, which published several of his pamphlets; Fellow Imperial Coll. Science and Technology. *Films produced:* Things to Come and The Man Who Could Work Miracles. *Publications include:* The Time Machine 1895, The War of the Worlds, The First Man in the Moon, Love and Mr. Lewisham, Kipps, The History of Mr. Polly, Tono Bungay 1909, The New Machiavelli 1911, The Dream 1924, The World of William Clissold 1926, The Shape of Things to Come 1933, The Outline of History 1920, The Science of Life (with Julian Huxley and G. P. Wells) 1929, The Work, Wealth and Happiness of Mankind 1932, Experiment in Autobiography 1934, The Anatomy of Frustration 1936, The Croquet Player 1936, Star Begotten 1937, Brynhild 1937, The Camford Visitation 1937, World Brain 1938, Apropos of Dolores 1938, The Holy Terror 1939, The Fate of Homo sapiens 1939, New World Order 1940 (amalgamated as The Outlook for Homo sapiens), Babes in the Darkling Wood 1940, You Can't be too Careful 1941, Phoenix 1942, The Conquest of Time 1942, Crux Ansata 1943, 1942–1944 (memoirs), The Happy Turning 1944, Mind at the end of its Tether 1945. *Address:* 13 Hanover Terrace, Regent's Park, London, N.W.1, England.
[*Died 13 August 1946.*]

WILHELM II, Friedrich Wilhelm Victor Albert Hohenzollern; ex-King of Prussia and ex-Emperor of Germany; b. 27 Jan. 1859, Potsdam, Berlin; eldest s. of Prince Friedrich Wilhelm of Prussia and Princess Victoria of Great Britain; m. 1st Princess Auguste Victoria, daughter of Friedrich, Duke of Augustenburg, 1881 (died 1921); six s. one d.; m. 2nd Princess Hermine of Schönaich-Carolath, b. Princess Reuss ä. L.; succeeded to the throne as King of Prussia and Emperor of Germany 1888; Adviser Good Neighbour Forum; Editor *The Caravan,* abdicated Nov. 9, 1918, and went into exile; lived at Doorn in Holland until German invasion 1940; now in Potsdam.
[*Died 5 June 1941.*]

WILLIAMS, Tennessee (Thomas Lanier), A.B.; American writer; b. 26 March 1911; s. of Cornelius Coffin Williams and Edwina (Dakin) Williams; ed. Univs. of Missouri and Iowa, and Washington Univ., St. Louis; awarded Pulitzer Prize 1948 and 1955, New York Drama Critics' Circle Award 1944, 1947, 1955, 1961. *Publications:* plays: Battle of Angels 1940, The Glass Menagerie 1944, You Touched Me (with Donald Windham) 1946, A Streetcar Named Desire 1947, Summer and Smoke 1948, The Rose Tattoo 1951, Camino Real 1953, Cat on a Hot Tin Roof 1955, Orpheus Descending 1957, Garden District (two plays: Suddenly Last Summer and Something Unspoken) 1958, Sweet Bird of Youth 1959, Period of Adjustment 1960, The Night of the Iguana 1961, The Milk Train Doesn't Stop Here Any More 1962 (Revised version 1963), Slapstick Tragedy 1966, The Two Character Play (U.S. title Outcry) 1967, The Seven Descents of Myrtle 1968, Will Mr. Merriweather Return from Memphis 1969, In the Bar of a Tokyo Hotel 1969, Small Craft Warnings 1972, The Red Devil Battery Sign 1974, The Eccentricities of a Nightingale 1976, Crève-coeur 1978, Vieux carré 1978, Clothes for a Summer Hotel 1980; screenplays: The Glass Menagerie 1950, A Streetcar Named Desire 1951, The Rose Tattoo (with Gore Vidal) 1955, Baby Doll 1956, Suddenly Last Summer 1959, The Fugitive King (based on Orpheus Descending) 1960, Boom (based on The Milk Train Doesn't Stop Here Any More) 1968; books: 27 Wagons Full of Cotton (one-act plays) 1946, One Arm and Other Stories 1948, The Roman Spring of Mrs. Stone (novel) 1950, Hard Candy: A Book of Stories 1954, In the Winter of Cities (poems) 1956, Three Players of a Summer Game (stories) 1960, The Knightly Quest (stories) 1967, Dragon Country (plays) 1970, Eight Mortal Ladies Possessed (stories) 1974, Moise and the World of Reason (novel) 1975, Memoirs (autobiography) 1975. *Address:* c/o Mitch Douglas, International Creative Management, 40 West 57th Street, New York, N.Y. 10019, U.S.A.
[*Died 25 February 1983.*]

YEATS, William Butler, Hon. D.LITT.; Irish poet; b. 13 June 1865, Dublin; s. of J. B. Yeats; m. Georgie Hyde Lees 1917; one s. one d.; ed. Godolphin School, London, and High School, Dublin; poet, dramatist and essayist; Nobel Prize for Literature 1923; joint-founder and Dir. Abbey Theatre, Dublin; Senator 1922–28. *Publications include:* The Wanderings of Oisin 1889, A Book of Irish Verse 1895, The Secret Rose 1897, The Wind among the Reeds 1899, Deirdre 1907, Plays for an Irish Theatre 1912, Michael Robartes and the Dancer 1921, Later Poems 1923, Plays and Controversies 1923, The Cat and the Moon 1931, Words for Music, Perhaps 1932, Wheels and Butterflies 1934, Collected Plays 1934, Full Moon in March 1935, Dramatis Personæ 1936. *Address:* The Abbey Theatre, Dublin, Ireland.
[*Died 28 January 1939.*]

ABBREVIATIONS

A.A.A.	Agricultural Adjustment Administration
A.A.A.S.	American Association for the Advancement of Science
A.A.F.	Army Air Force
A.A.S.A.	Associate of the Australian Society of Accountants
A.B.	Bachelor of Arts
AB	Aktiebolag
A.B.A.	American Bar Association
A.C.	Companion of the Order of Australia
A.C.A.	Associate of the Institute of Chartered Accountants
A.C.C.A.	Associate of the Association of Certified Accountants
Acad.	Academy, Académie
Accad.	Accademia
Accred.	Accredited
A.C.I.S.	Associate of the Chartered Institute of Secretaries
A.C.P.	American College of Physicians
A.C.S.	American Chemical Society
A.C.T.	Australian Capital Territory
ADC	Aide-de-camp
Adm.	Admiral
Admin.	Administrative, Administration, Administrator
A.E.	Air Efficiency Award
A.E.R.E.	Atomic Energy Research Establishment
A.F.	Air Force
A.F.C.	Air Force Cross
AfDB	African Development Bank
affil.	affiliated
AFL	American Federation of Labor
A.F.M.	Air Force Medal
AG	Aktiengesellschaft (Joint Stock Company)
Agric.	Agriculture
a.i.	ad interim
A.I.A.	Associate of Institute of Actuaries; American Institute of Architects
A.I.A.A.	American Institute of Aeronautics and Astronautics
A.I.B.	Associate of the Institute of Bankers
AICC	All-India Congress Committee
A.I.C.E.	Associate of the Institute of Civil Engineers
A.I.Ch.E.	American Institute of Chemical Engineers
AIDS	Acquired Immune Deficiency Syndrome
A.I.E.E.	American Institute of Electrical Engineers
A.I.M.E.	American Institute of Mining Engineers; Associate of the Institution of Mining Engineers
A.I.Mech.E.	Associate of the Institution of Mechanical Engineers
A.I.R.	All-India Radio
A.K.	Knight of the Order of Australia
Akad.	Akademie
AL	Alabama
Ala.	Alabama
A.L.S.	Associate of the Linnaean Society
Alt.	Alternate
A.M.	Master of Arts; Alpes Maritimes; Albert Medal; Member of the Order of Australia
Amb.	Ambassador
A.M.I.C.E.	Associate Member of the Institution of Civil Engineers
A.M.I.E.E.	Associate Member of the Institution of Electrical Engineers
A.M.I.Mech.E.	Associate Member of the Institution of Mechanical Engineers
A.N.U.	Australian National University
A.O.	Officer of the Order of Australia
A.P.	Andhra Pradesh
Apdo	Apartado
approx.	approximately
Apptd.	Appointed
AR	Arkansas
A.R.A.	Associate of the Royal Academy
A.R.A.M.	Associate of the Royal Academy of Music
A.R.A.S.	Associate of the Royal Astronomical Society
ARC	Agriculture Research Council
A.R.C.A.	Associate of the Royal College of Art
A.R.C.M.	Associate of the Royal College of Music
A.R.C.O.	Associate Royal College of Organists
A.R.C.S.	Associate of the Royal College of Science
A.R.I.B.A.	Associate of the Royal Institute of British Architects
Ariz.	Arizona
Ark.	Arkansas
A.R.S.A.	Associate of the Royal Scottish Academy; Associate of the Royal Society of Arts
A.S.L.I.B.	Association of Special Libraries and Information Bureaux
A.S.M.E.	American Society of Mechanical Engineers
Asoc.	Asociación
Ass.	Assembly
Asscn.	Association
Assoc.	Associate
A.S.S.R.	Autonomous Soviet Socialist Republic
Asst.	Assistant
ATV	Associated Television
Aug.	August
AZ	Arizona
b.	born
B.A.	Bachelor of Arts; British Airways
B.A.A.S.	British Association for the Advancement of Science
B.A.F.T.A.	British Academy of Film and Television Arts
B.Agr.	Bachelor of Agriculture
B.Agr.Sc.	Bachelor of Agricultural Science
B.A.O.	Bachelor of Obstetrics
B.A.O.R.	British Army of the Rhine
B.Arch.	Bachelor of Architecture
Bart.	Baronet
B.A.S.	Bachelor in Agricultural Science
B.A.Sc.	Bachelor of Applied Science
BBC	British Broadcasting Corporation
B.C.	British Columbia
B.C.C.	British Council of Churches
B.C.E.	Bachelor of Civil Engineering
B.Ch., B.Chir.	Bachelor of Surgery
B.C.L.	Bachelor of Civil Law; Bachelor of Canon Law
B.Com(m).	Bachelor of Commerce
B.C.S.	Bachelor of Commercial Sciences
B.D.	Bachelor of Divinity
Bd.	Board
B.D.S.	Bachelor of Dental Surgery
B.E.	Bachelor of Engineering; Bachelor of Education
BEA	British European Airways
B.Econs.	Bachelor of Economics
B.Ed.	Bachelor of Education
Beds.	Bedfordshire
B.E.E.	Bachelor of Electrical Engineering
B.E.M.	British Empire Medal
B.Eng.	Bachelor of Engineering
Berks.	Berkshire
B.F.A.	Bachelor of Fine Arts
B.F.I.	British Film Institute
B.I.M.	British Institute of Management
biog.	biography
BIS	Bank for International Settlements
B.L.	Bachelor of Laws
B.L.A.	Bachelor of Landscape Architecture
Bldg.	Building
B.Lit(t).	Bachelor of Letters
B.LL.	Bachelor of Laws
B.L.S.	Bachelor in Library Science
blvd.	boulevard
B.M.	Bachelor of Medicine
B.M.A.	British Medical Association
B.Mus.	Bachelor of Music
Bn.	Battalion
BNOC	British National Oil Corporation
BOAC	British Overseas Airways Corporation
B.P.A.	Bachelor of Public Administration
B.Phil.	Bachelor of Philosophy
Br.	Branch
Brig.	Brigadier
B.S.	Bachelor of Science; Bachelor of Surgery
B.S.A.	Bachelor of Scientific Agriculture
B.Sc.	Bachelor of Science
Bt.	Baronet
Bucks.	Buckinghamshire
c.	child, children

c.	circa
CA	California
C.A.	Chartered Accountant
Calif.	California
Cambs.	Cambridgeshire
Cand.	Candidate, Candidature
Cantab.	Of Cambridge University
Capt.	Captain
Cards.	Cardiganshire
C.B.	Companion of the (Order of the) Bath
CBC	Canadian Broadcasting Corporation
C.B.E.	Commander of (the Order of) the British Empire
CBI	Confederation of British Industry
C.Biol.	Chartered Biologist
C.B.I.M.	Companion of British Institute of Management
CBS	Columbia Broadcasting System
C.C.	Companion of Order of Canada
C.Chem.	Chartered Chemist
CCP	Chinese Communist Party
C.D.	Canadian Forces Decoration
Cdre.	Commodore
CDU	Christlich-Demokratische Union
C.E.	Civil Engineer, Chartered Engineer
CEAO	Communauté Economique de l'Afrique de l'Ouest
Cen.	Central
C.Eng.	Chartered Engineer
CENTO	Central Treaty Organization
C.E.O.	Chief Executive Officer
C.E.R.N.	Conseil (*now* Organisation) Européen(ne) pour la Recherche Nucléaire
C.F.R.	Commander of the Federal Republic of Nigeria
C.G.M.	Conspicuous Gallantry Medal
CGT	Confédération Général du Travail
C.H.	Companion of Honour
Chair.	Chairman, Chairwoman, Chairperson
Ch.B.	Bachelor of Surgery
Chem.	Chemistry
Ch.M	Master of Surgery
C.I.	Channel Islands
CIA	Central Intelligence Agency
Cia.	Compagnia (Company)
Cía.	Compañía (Company)
CID	Criminal Investigation Department
C.I.E.	Companion of (the Order of) the Indian Empire
Cie.	Compagnie (Company)
C.I.E.E.	Companion of the Institution of Electrical Engineers
C.I.MgT.	Companion Institute of Management
C.-in-C.	Commander-in-Chief
CIO	Congress of Industrial Organizations
C.I.S.	Commonwealth of Independent States
C.L.D.	Doctor of Civil Law (U.S.A.)
C.Lit.	Companion of Literature
C.M.	Canada Medal; Master in Surgery
CMEA	Council for Mutual Economic Assistance
C.M.G.	Companion of (the Order of) St. Michael and St. George
C.N.A.A.	Council for National Academic Awards
C.N.R.S.	Centre National de la Recherche Scientifique
CO	Colorado
Co.	Company; County
C.O.	Commanding Officer
COI	Central Office of Information
Col.	Colonel
Coll.	College
Colo.	Colorado
COMECON	Council for Mutual Economic Assistance
Comm.	Commission
Commdg.	Commanding
Commdr.	Commander, Commandeur
Commdt.	Commandant
Commr.	Commissioner
C.O.N.	Commander of Order of Nigeria
Conf.	Conference
Confed.	Confederation
Conn.	Connecticut
Contrib.	Contributor; contribution
C.O.O.	Chief Operating Officer
Corp.	Corporate
Corpn.	Corporation
Corresp.	Correspondent; Corresponding
CP	Communist Party; Caixa Postal (Post Office Box)
CPA	Commonwealth Parliamentary Association
C.P.A.	Certified Public Accountant
C.Phys.	Chartered Physicist
CPP	Convention People's Party (Ghana)
CPPCC	Chinese People's Political Consultative Conference
CPSU	Communist Party of the Soviet Union
cr.	created
C.Sc.	Candidate of Sciences
CSCE	Conference on Security and Co-operation in Europe
C.S.I.	Companion of (the Order of) the Star of India
CSIRO	Commonwealth Scientific and Industrial Research Organization
C.S.S.R.	Czechoslovak Socialist Republic
C.St.J.	Commander of (the Order of) St. John of Jerusalem
CT	Connecticut
Cttee.	Committee
C.V.	Commanditaire Vennootschap
C.V.O.	Commander of the Royal Victorian Order
d.	daughter(s)
D.Arch	Doctor of Architecture
D.B.	Bachelor of Divinity
D.B.A.	Doctor of Business Administration
D.B.E.	Dame Commander of (the Order of) the British Empire
DC	District of Columbia
D.C.	District of Columbia
D.C.E.	Doctor of Civil Engineering
D.C.L.	Doctor of Civil Law, Doctor of Canon Law
D.C.M.	Distinguished Conduct Medal
D.C.M.G.	Dame Commander of (the Order of) St. Michael and St. George
D.Cn.L.	Doctor of Canon Law
D.Comm.	Doctor of Commerce
D.C.S.	Doctor of Commercial Sciences
D.C.T.	Doctor of Christian Theology
D.C.V.O.	Dame Commander of the Royal Victorian Order
D.D.	Doctor of Divinity
D.D.R.	Deutsche Demokratische Republik (German Democratic Republic)
D.D.S.	Doctor of Dental Surgery
DE	Delaware
Dec.	December
D.Econ.	Doctor of Economics
Del.	Delegate, delegation, Delaware
Denbighs.	Denbighshire
D. en D.	Docteur en Droit
D. en Med.	Docteur en Medicine
D.Eng.	Doctor of Engineering
Dept.	Department
D.E.S.	Department of Education and Science
Desig.	Designate
D. ès L.	Docteur ès Lettres
D. ès Sc.	Docteur ès Sciences
Devt.	Development
D.F.	Distrito Federal
D.F.A.	Doctor of Fine Arts
D.F.C.	Distinguished Flying Cross
D.F.M.	Distinguished Flying Medal
D.H.	Doctor of Humanities
D.Hist.	Doctor of History
D.H.L.	Doctor of Hebrew Literature
D.H.S.S.	Department of Health and Social Security
D.Hum.Litt.	Doctor of Humane Letters
D.I.C.	Diploma of Imperial College
Dip.A.D.	Diploma in Art and Design
Dip.Agr.	Diploma in Agriculture
Dip.Ed.	Diploma in Education
Dip(l).Eng.	Diploma in Engineering
Dir.	Director
Dist.	District
D.Iur.	Doctor of Law
D. Iur. Utr.	Doctor of both Civil and Canon Law
Div.	Division; Divisional
D.Jur.	Doctor of Law
D.K.	Most Esteemed Family (Malaysia)
D.L.	Deputy Lieutenant
D.Lit(t).	Doctor of Letters; Doctor of Literature
D.L.S.	Doctor of Library Science
D.M.	Doctor of Medicine (Oxford)
D.M.D.	Doctor of Dental Medicine
D. Min. Sci.	Doctor of Municipal Science
D.M.S.	Director of Medical Services
D.Mus.	Doctor of Music
D.M.V.	Doctor of Veterinary Medicine
D.O.	Doctor of Ophthalmology
D.P.H.	Diploma in Public Health
D.P.M.	Diploma in Psychological Medicine
D.Phil.	Doctor of Philosophy
Dr. Agr.	Doctor of Agriculture
Dr.Ing.	Doctor of Engineering

Dr.Iur. Doctor of Laws
D(r).Med. Doctor of Medicine
Dr.Oec.(Publ.) Doctor of (Public) Economy
Dr.rer.nat. Doctor of Natural Sciences
Dr.rer.Pol. Doctor of Political Science
Dr.SC. Doctor of Sciences
Dr.Sc.Nat. Doctor of Natural Sciences
D.S. Doctor of Science
D.S.C. Distinguished Service Cross
D.Sc. Doctor of Science
D.Sc.S. Doctor of Social Science
D.S.M. Distinguished Service Medal
D.S.O. Companion of the Distinguished Service Order
D.S.T. Doctor of Sacred Theology
D.Tech. Doctor of Technology
D.Theol. Doctor of Theology
D.T.M.(& H.) Diploma in Tropical Medicine (and Hygiene)
D.U.P. Diploma of the University of Paris
D.Univ. Doctor of the University

E. East
EBRD European Bank for Reconstruction and Development
EC European Community, European Commission
ECA Economic Co-operation Administration; Economic Commission for Africa
ECAFE Economic Commission for Asia and the Far East
ECE Economic Commission for Europe
ECLA Economic Commission for Latin America
Econ(s). Economic(s)
ECOSOC Economic and Social Council
ECSC European Coal and Steel Community
ECWA Economic Commission for Western Asia
ed. educated; editor; edited
Ed. Editor
E.D. Efficiency Decoration; Doctor of Engineering (U.S.A.)
Ed.D. Doctor of Education
Edin. Edinburgh
Ed.M. Master of Education
Edn. Edition
Educ. Education
EEC European Economic Community
EFTA European Free Trade Association
e.h. Ehrenhalben (Honorary)
EIB European Investment Bank
E.M. Edward Medal; Master of Engineering (U.S.A.)
Emer. Emeritus
Eng. Engineering
Eng.D. Doctor of Engineering
E.N.O. English National Opera
ESCAP Economic and Social Commission for Asia and the Pacific
est. established
ETH Eidgenössische Technische Hochschule (Swiss Federal Institute of Technology)
Ets. Etablissements
EU European Union
EURATOM European Atomic Energy Community
Exec. Executive
Exhbn. Exhibition
Ext. Extension

f. founded
F.A.A. Fellow of Australian Academy of Science
F.A.A.S. Fellow of the American Association for the Advancement of Science
F.A.A.T.S. Fellow Australian Academy of Technological Sciences
F.A.C.C. Fellow of the American College of Cardiology
F.A.C.C.A. Fellow of the Association of Certified and Corporate Accountants
F.A.C.E. Fellow of the Australian College of Education
F.A.C.P. Fellow of American College of Physicians
F.A.C.S. Fellow of the American College of Surgeons
F.A.H.A. Fellow Australian Academy of the Humanities
F.A.I.A. Fellow of the American Institute of Architects
F.A.I.A.S. Fellow of the Australian Institute of Agricultural Science
F.A.I.M. Fellow of the Australian Institute of Management
FAO Food and Agriculture Organization
F.A.S. Fellow of the Antiquarian Socieity
F.A.S.E. Fellow of Antiquarian Society, Edinburgh
F.A.S.S.A. Fellow Academy of Social Sciences of Australia
F.B.A. Fellow of the British Academy
FBI Federal Bureau of Investigation
F.B.I.M. Fellow of the British Institute of Management
F.B.I.P. Fellow of the British Institute of Physics

F.C.A. Fellow of the Institute of Chartered Accountants
F.C.A.E. Fellow Canadian Academy of Engineering
F.C.G.I. Fellow of the City and Guilds of London Institute
F.C.I.A. Fellow Chartered Institute of Arbitrators
F.C.I.B. Fellow Chartered Institute of Bankers
F.C.I.C. Fellow of the Chemical Institute of Canada
F.C.I.S. Fellow of the Chartered Institute of Secretaries
F.C.M.A. Fellow Chartered Institute of Management Accountants

FCO Foreign and Commonwealth Office
F.C.S.D. Fellow Chartered Society of Designers
F.C.T. Federal Capital Territory
F.C.W.A. Fellow of the Institute of Cost and Works Accountants (now F.C.M.A.)

FDGB Freier Deutscher Gewerkschaftsbund
FDP Freier Demokratische Partei
Feb. February
Fed. Federation; Federal
F.Eng. Fellow, Fellowship of Engineering
F.F.C.M. Fellow of Faculty of Community Medicine
F.F.P.H.M. Fellow of the Faculty of Public Health Medicine
F.G.S. Fellow of the Geological Society
F.G.S.M. Fellow of the Guildhall School of Music
F.I.A. Fellow of the Institute of Actuaries
F.I.A.L. Fellow of the International Institute of Arts and Letters
F.I.A.M. Fellow of the International Academy of Management
F.I.A.M.S. Fellow of the Indian Academy of Medical Sciences
F.I.A.P. Fellow Institution of Analysts and Programmers
F.I.Arb. Fellow of the Institute of Arbitrators
F.I.B. Fellow of the Institute of Bankers
F.I.B.A. Fellow of the Institute of Banking Associations
F.I.Biol. Fellow of the Institute of Biologists
F.I.C.E. Fellow of the Institution of Civil Engineers
F.I.Chem.E. Fellow of the Institute of Chemical Engineers
F.I.D. Fellow of the Institute of Directors
F.I.E. Fellow of the Institute of Engineers
F.I.E.E. Fellow of the Institution of Electrical Engineers
F.I.E.E.E. Fellow of the Institute of Electrical and Electronics Engineers
F.I.J. Fellow of the Institute of Journalists
Fil.Lic. Licentiate in Philosophy
F.I.M. Fellow of the Institute of Metallurgists
F.I.M.E. Fellow of the Institute of Mining Engineers
F.I.Mech.E. Fellow of the Institute of Mechanical Engineers
F.I.M.I. Fellow of the Institute of the Motor Industry
F.Inst.F. Fellow of the Institute of Fuel
F.Inst.M. Fellow of the Institute of Marketing
F.Inst.P. Fellow of the Institute of Physics
F.Inst.Pet. Fellow of the Institute of Petroleum
F.I.P.M. Fellow of the Institute of Personnel Management
F.I.R.E. Fellow of the Institution of Radio Engineers
F.I.T.D. Fellow of the Institute of Training and Development
FL Florida
Fla. Florida
F.L.A. Fellow of the Library Association
FLN Front de Libération Nationale
F.L.S. Fellow of the Linnaean Society
F.MED.SCI. Fellow of Medical Science
fmr. former
fmrly. formerly
F.N.I. Fellow of the National Institute of Sciences of India
F.N.Z.I.A. Fellow of the New Zealand Institute of Architects
F.R.A.C.P. Fellow of the Royal Australasian College of Physicians
F.R.A.C.S. Fellow of the Royal Australasian College of Surgeons
F.R.Ae.S. Fellow of the Royal Aeronautical Society
F.R.A.I. Fellow of the Royal Anthropological Institute
F.R.A.I.A. Fellow of the Royal Australian Institute of Architects
F.R.A.I.C. Fellow of the Royal Architectural Institute of Canada
F.R.A.M. Fellow of the Royal Academy of Music
F.R.A.S. Fellow of the Royal Astronomical Society; Fellow of the Royal Asiatic Society
F.R.B.S. Fellow of the Royal Society of British Sculptors
F.R.C.A. Fellow of the Royal College of Anaesthetists
F.R.C.M. Fellow of the Royal College of Music
F.R.C.O. Fellow of the Royal College of Organists
F.R.C.O.G. Fellow of the Royal College of Obstetricians and Gynaecologists
F.R.C.P.(E.) Fellow of the Royal College of Physicians (Edinburgh)
F.R.C.P.I. Fellow of the Royal College of Physicians of Ireland
F.R.C.P. Fellow of the Royal College of Physicians (United Kingdom)
F.R.C.R. Fellow Royal College of Radiology
F.R.C.S.(E.) Fellow of the Royal College of Surgeons (Edinburgh)

F.R.Econ.S.	Fellow of the Royal Economic Society
F.R.E.S.	Fellow of the Royal Entomological Society
F.R.F.P.S.	Fellow of the Royal Faculty of Physicians and Surgeons
F.R.G.	Federal Republic of Germany
F.R.G.S.	Fellow of the Royal Geographical Society
F.R.Hist.S.	Fellow of the Royal Historical Society
F.R.Hort.S.	Fellow of the Royal Horticultural Society
F.R.I.B.A.	Fellow of the Royal Institute of British Architects
F.R.I.C.	Fellow of the Royal Institute of Chemists
F.R.I.C.S.	Fellow of the Royal Institute of Chartered Surveyors
F.R.Met.Soc.	Fellow of the Royal Meteorological Society
F.R.N.C.M.	Fellow of the Royal Northern College of Music
F.R.P.S.	Fellow of the Royal Photographic Society
F.R.S.	Fellow of the Royal Society
F.R.S.A.	Fellow of the Royal Society of Arts
F.R.S.A.M.D.	Fellow of the Royal Scottish Academy of Music and Drama
F.R.S.C.	Fellow of the Royal Society of Canada; Fellow of the Royal Society of Chemistry
F.R.S.E.	Fellow of the Royal Society of Edinburgh
F.R.S.L.	Fellow of the Royal Society of Literature
F.R.S.M.	Fellow of the Royal Society of Medicine
F.R.S.N.Z.	Fellow of the Royal Society of New Zealand
F.R.S.S.	Fellow of the Royal Statistical Society
F.R.S.S.A.	Fellow of the Royal Society of South Africa
F.R.T.S.	Fellow of the Royal Television Society
F.S.A.	Fellow of the Society of Antiquaries
F.S.I.A.D.	Fellow of the Society of Industrial Artists and Designers
F.T.I.	Fellow of the Textile Institute
F.T.S.	Fellow of Technological Sciences
F.W.A.A.S.	Fellow of the World Academy of Arts and Sciences
F.Z.S.	Fellow of the Zoological Society
GA	Georgia
Ga.	Georgia
GATT	General Agreement on Tariffs and Trade
G.B.	Great Britain
G.B.E.	Knight (or Dame) Grand Cross of (the Order of) the British Empire
G.C.	George Cross
G.C.B.	Knight Grand Cross of (the Order of) the Bath
G.C.I.E.	Knight Grand Commander of (the Order of) the Indian Empire
G.C.M.G.	Knight (or Dame) Grand Cross of (the Order of) St. Michael and St. George
G.C.S.I.	Knight Grand Commander of (the Order of) the Star of India
G.C.V.O.	Knight (or Dame) Grand Cross of the Royal Victorian Order
G.D.R.	German Democratic Republic
Gen.	General
GHQ	General Headquarters
Glam.	Glamorganshire
GLC	Greater London Council
Glos.	Gloucestershire
G.M.	George Medal
GmbH	Gesellschaft mit beschränkter Haftung (Limited Liability Company)
G.O.C. (in C)	General Officer Commanding (in Chief)
Gov.	Governor
Govt.	Government
GPO	General Post Office
Grad.	Graduate
G.R.S.M.	Graduate of the Royal School of Music
G.S.O.	General Staff Officer
Hants.	Hampshire
h.c.	honoris causa
H.E.	His Eminence; His (or Her) Excellency
Herefords.	Herefordshire
Herts.	Hertfordshire
H.H.	His (or Her) Highness
HI	Hawaii
H.L.D.	Doctor of Humane Letters
H.M.	His (or Her) Majesty
H.M.S.	His (or Her) Majesty's Ship
Hon.	Honourable; Honorary
Hons.	Honours
Hosp.	Hospital
HQ	Headquarters
H.R.H.	His (or Her) Royal Highness
HSP	Hungarian Socialist Party
HSWP	Hungarian Socialist Workers' Party
Hunts.	Huntingdonshire

IA	Iowa
Ia.	Iowa
IAEA	International Atomic Energy Agency
IATA	International Air Transport Association
IBA	Independent Broadcasting Authority
IBRD	International Bank for Reconstruction and Development (World Bank)
ICAO	International Civil Aviation Organization
ICC	International Chamber of Commerce
ICE	Institution of Civil Engineers
ICEM	Intergovernmental Committee for European Migration
ICFTU	International Confederation of Free Trade Unions
ICI	Imperial Chemical Industries
ICOM	International Council of Museums
ICS	Indian Civil Service
ICSID	International Centre for Settlement of Investment Disputes
ICSU	International Council of Scientific Unions
ID	Idaho
Ida.	Idaho
IDA	International Development Association
IDB	Inter-American Development Bank
I.E.E.	Institution of Electrical Engineers
I.E.E.E.	Institution of Electrical and Electronic Engineers
IFAD	International Fund for Agricultural Development
IFC	International Finance Corporation
IL	Illinois
Ill.	Illinois
ILO	International Labour Organization
IMCO	Inter-Governmental Maritime Consultative Organization
I.Mech.E.	Institution of Mechanical Engineers
IMF	International Monetary Fund
IN	Indiana
Inc.	Incorporated
Ind.	Indiana; Independent
Insp.	Inspector
Inst.	Institute; Institution
Int.	International
INTUC	Indian National Trades Union Congress
IOC	International Olympic Committee
IPU	Inter-Parliamentary Union
I.S.O.	Companion of the Imperial Service Order
ITA	Independent Television Authority
ITU	International Telecommunications Union
ITV	Independent Television
IUPAC	International Union of Pure and Applied Chemistry
IUPAP	International Union of Pure and Applied Physics
Jan.	January
J.C.B.	Bachelor of Canon Law
J.C.D.	Doctor of Canon Law
J.D.	Doctor of Jurisprudence
J.M.K.	Johan Mangku Negara (Malaysia)
J.P.	Justice of the Peace
Jr.	Junior
J.S.D.	Doctor of Juristic Science
Jt.	Joint
J.U.D.	Juris utriusque Doctor (Doctor of both Civil and Canon Law)
Ju.D.	Doctor of Law
J.U.Dr.	Juris utriusque Doctor (Doctor of both Civil and Canon Law), Doctor of Law
Kan.	Kansas
K.B.E.	Knight Commander of (the Order of) the British Empire
K.C.	King's Counsel
K.C.B.	Knight Commander of (the Order of) the Bath
K.C.I.E.	Knight Commander of (the Order of) the Indian Empire
K.C.M.G.	Knight Commander of (the Order of) St. Michael and St. George
K.C.S.I.	Knight Commander of (the Order of) the Star of India
K.C.V.O.	Knight Commander of the Royal Victorian Order
K.G.	Knight of (the Order of) the Garter
KGB	Committee of State Security (U.S.S.R.)
K.K.	Kaien Kaisha
KLM	Koninklijke Luchtvaart Maatschappij (Royal Dutch Airlines)
K.N.Z.M.	Knight of the New Zealand Order of Merit
K.P.	Knight of (the Order of) St. Patrick
KS	Kansas
K.St.J.	Knight of (the Order of) St. John of Jerusalem
K.T.	Knight of (the Order of) the Thistle

Kt.	Knight
Ky.	Kentucky
LA	Louisiana
La.	Louisiana
L.A.	Los Angeles
Lab.	Laboratory
Lancs.	Lancashire
LDP	Liberal Democratic Party
L.D.S.	Licentiate in Dental Surgery
Legis.	Legislative
Leics.	Leicestershire
L. en D.	Licencié en Droit
L. ès L.	Licencié ès Lettres
L. ès Sc.	Licencié ès Sciences
L.G.	Lady of (the Order of) the Garter
L.H.D.	Doctor of Humane Letters
L.I.	Long Island
Lic. en Der.	Licenciado en Derecho
Lic. en Fil.	Licenciado en Filosofía
Lic.Med.	Licentiate in Medicine
Lieut.	Lieutenant
Lincs.	Lincolnshire
Litt.D.	Doctor of Letters
LL.B.	Bachelor of Laws
LL.D.	Doctor of Laws
LL.L.	Licentiate of Laws
LL.M.	Master of Laws
L.M.	Licentiate of Medicine; or Midwifery
L.N.	League of Nations
L.Ph.	Licentiate of Philosophy
L.R.A.M.	Licentiate of the Royal Academy of Music
L.R.C.P.	Licentiate of the Royal College of Physicians
L.S.E.	London School of Economics
Ltd(a).	Limited; Limitada
L.Th.	Licentiate in Theology
L.V.O.	Lieutenant, Royal Victorian Order
m.	married; marriage; metre(s)
MA	Massachusetts
M.A.	Master of Arts
M.Agr.	Master of Agriculture (U.S.A.)
Maj.	Major
M.A.L.D.	Master of Arts in Law and Diplomacy
Man.	Manager, Managing, Management; Manitoba
M.Arch.	Master of Architecture
Mass.	Massachusetts
Math.	Mathematics, Mathematical
M.B.	Bachelor of Medicine
M.B.A.	Master of Business Administration
M.B.E.	Member of (the Order of) the British Empire
M.C.	Military Cross
MCC	Marylebone Cricket Club
M.C.E.	Master of Civil Engineering
M.Ch.	Master of Surgery
M.Ch.D.	Master of Dental Surgery
M.C.L.	Master of Civil Law
M.Com(m).	Master of Commerce
M.C.P.	Master of City Planning
MD	Maryland
Md.	Maryland
M.D.	Doctor of Medicine
M.Div.	Master of Divinity
M.D.S.	Master of Dental Surgery
ME	Maine
Me.	Maine
M.E.	Myalgic Encephalitis
mem.	member
M.Eng.	Master of Engineering (Dublin)
M.E.P.	Member European Parliament
M.F.A.	Master of Fine Arts
Mfg.	Manufacturing
Mfrs.	Manufacturers
Mgr.	Monseigneur; Monsignor
MI	Michigan
M.I.	Marshall Islands
M.I.A.	Master of International Affairs
M.I.C.E.	Member of the Institution of Civil Engineers
M.I.Chem.E.	Member of the Institution of Chemical Engineers
Mich.	Michigan
Middx.	Middlesex
M.I.E.E.	Member of the Institution of Electrical Engineers
Mil.	Military
M.I.Mar.E.	Member of the Institute of Marine Engineers
M.I.Mech.E.	Member of the Institution of Mechanical Engineers
M.I.Min.E.	Member of the Institution of Mining Engineers
Minn.	Minnesota
M.Inst.T.	Member of the Institute of Transport
Miss.	Mississippi
M.I.Struct.E.	Member of the Institution of Structural Engineers
M.I.T.	Massachusetts Institute of Technology
M.J.	Master of Jurisprudence
M.L.A.	Member of the Legislative Assembly, Master of Landscape Architecture
M.L.C.	Member of the Legislative Council
M.M.	Military Medal
MN	Minnesota
MO	Missouri
Mo.	Missouri
M.O.H.	Medical Officer of Health
Mon.	Monmouthshire
Mont.	Montana
Movt.	Movement
M.P.	Member of Parliament; Madhya Pradesh (India)
M.P.A.	Master of Public Administration (Harvard)
M.Ph.	Master of Philosophy (U.S.A.)
M.P.P.	Member of Provincial Parliament (Canada)
M.R.A.S.	Member of the Royal Asiatic Society
MRC	Medical Research Council
M.R.C.P.(E.)	Member of the Royal College of Physicians (Edinburgh)
M.R.C.P. (U.K.)	Member of the Royal College of Physicians (United Kingdom)
M.R.C.S.(E.)	Member of the Royal College of Surgeons (Edinburgh)
M.R.C.V.S.	Member of the Royal College of Veterinary Surgeons
M.R.I.	Member of the Royal Institution
M.R.I.A.	Member of the Royal Irish Academy
M.R.I.C.	Member of the Royal Institute of Chemistry
MRP	Mouvement Républicain Populaire
MS	Mississippi
M.S.	Master of Science; Master of Surgery
M.Sc.	Master of Science
M. Sc. S.	Master of Social Science
MT	Montana
M.T.S.	Master of Theological Studies
MU.Dr.	Doctor of Medicine
Mus.Bac. or B.	Bachelor of Music
Mus.Doc. or D.	Doctor of Music
Mus.M.	Master of Music (Cambridge)
M.V.D.	Master of Veterinary Medicine
M.V.O.	Member of the Royal Victorian Order
M.W.	Master of Wine
N.	North
N.A.S.	National Academy of Sciences (U.S.A.)
NASA	National Aeronautics and Space Administration
Nat.	National
NATO	North Atlantic Treaty Organization
Naz.	Nazionale
N.B.	New Brunswick
NBC	National Broadcasting Corporation
NC	North Carolina
N.C.	North Carolina
ND	North Dakota
N.D.	North Dakota
NE	Nebraska
N.E.	North East, Near East
Neb.	Nebraska
NEDC	National Economic Development Council
NERC	Natural Environment Research Council
Nev.	Nevada
NH	New Hampshire
N.H.	New Hampshire
N.I.H.	National Institute of Health
NJ	New Jersey
N.J.	New Jersey
NM	New Mexico
N.M.	New Mexico
Northants.	Northamptonshire
Notts.	Nottinghamshire
Nov.	November
NPC	National People's Congress
nr.	near
NRC	Nuclear Research Council
N.S.	Nova Scotia
N.S.F.	National Science Foundation
N.S.W.	New South Wales
N.T.	Northern Territory
NV	Nevada, Naamloze Vennootschap
N.W.	North West
N.W.T.	North West Territories

NY	New York
N.Y.	New York
N.Z.	New Zealand
N.Z.I.C.	New Zealand Institute of Chemistry
O.	Ohio
OAS	Organization of American States
OAU	Organization of African Unity
O.B.E.	Officer of (the Order of) the British Empire
O.C.	Officer of the Order of Canada
Oct.	October
OE	Order of Excellence (Guyana)
OECD	Organization for Economic Co-operation and Development
OEEC	Organization for European Economic Co-operation
O.F.S.	Orange Free State
OH	Ohio
O.J.	Order of Jamaica
OK	Oklahoma
Okla.	Oklahoma
O.M.	Member of the Order of Merit
O.N.	Order of Nigeria
Ont.	Ontario
O.N.Z.	Order of New Zealand
O.P.	Ordo Praedicatorum (Dominicans)
OPEC	Organization of the Petroleum Exporting Countries
O.P.M.	Office of Production Management
O.Q.	Officer National Order of Quebec
OR	Oregon
Ore.	Oregon
Org.	Organization
O.S.B.	Order of St. Benedict
Oxon.	Of Oxford University; Oxfordshire
PA	Pennsylvania
Pa.	Pennsylvania
Parl.	Parliament; Parliamentary
P.C.	Privy Councillor
PCC	Provincial Congress Committee
Pd.B	Bachelor of Pedagogy
Pd.D.	Doctor of Pedagogy
Pd.M.	Master of Pedagogy
PDS	Partei des Demokratischen Sozialismus
P.E.I.	Prince Edward Island
Pembs.	Pembrokeshire
PEN	Poets, Playwright, Essayists, Editors and Novelists (Club)
Perm.	Permanent
Ph.B.	Bachelor of Philosophy
Ph.D.	Doctor of Philosophy
Ph.Dr.	Doctor of Philosophy
Pharm.D.	Docteur en Pharmacie
Phila.	Philadelphia
Ph.L.	Licentiate of Philosophy
PLA	People's Liberation Army; Port of London Authority
PLC	Public Limited Company
P.O.(B.)	Post Office (Box)
P.O.W.	Prisoner of War
PPR	Polish Workers' Party
P.P.R.A.	Past President of the Royal Academy
P.Q.	Province of Quebec
PR	Puerto Rico
P.R.A.	President of the Royal Academy
Pref.	Prefecture
Prep.	Preparatory
Pres.	President
P.R.I.	President of the Royal Institute (of Painters in Water Colours)
P.R.I.B.A.	President of the Royal Institute of British Architects
Prin.	Principal
Priv. Doz.	Privat Dozent (recognized teacher not on the regular staff)
P.R.O.	Public Relations Officer
Proc.	Proceedings
Prof.	Professor
Propr.	Proprietor
Prov.	Province, Provincial
P.R.S.	President of the Royal Society
P.R.S.A.	President of the Royal Scottish Academy
P.S.M.	Panglima Setia Mahota
Pty.	Proprietary
Publ(s).	Publication(s)
Publr.	Publisher
Pvt.	Private
PZPR	Polish United Workers' Party
Q.C.	Queen's Counsel
Q.G.M.	Queen's Gallantry Medal
q.v.	quod vide (which see)
Q.P.M.	Queen's Police Medal
Q.S.O.	Queen's Service Order
R.A.	Royal Academy; Royal Academician; Royal Artillery
R.A.A.F.	Royal Australian Air Force
R.A.C.	Royal Armoured Corps
R.A.C.P.	Royal Australasian College of Physicians
R.A.F.	Royal Air Force
R.A.F.V.R.	Royal Air Force Volunteer Reserve
R.A.M.	Royal Academy of Music
R.A.M.C.	Royal Army Medical Corps
R.A.O.C.	Royal Army Ordnance Corps
R.C.	Roman Catholic
R.C.A.	Royal College of Art; Royal Canadian Academy; Radio Corporation of America
R.C.A.F.	Royal Canadian Air Force
RCP	Romanian Communist Party
R.C.P.I.	Royal College of Physicians of Ireland
Regt.	Regiment
R.E.M.E.	Royal Electric and Mechanical Engineers
Rep.	Representative; Represented
Repub.	Republic
resgnd.	resigned
retd.	retired
Rev.	Reverend
RI	Rhode Island
R.I.	Rhode Island
R.I.B.A.	Royal Institute of British Architects
R.M.A.	Royal Military Academy
R.N.	Royal Navy
R.N.R.	Royal Naval Reserve
R.N.V.R.	Royal Naval Volunteer Reserve
R.N.Z.A.F.	Royal New Zealand Air Force
R.P.	Member Royal Society of Portrait Painters
R.P.R.	Rassemblement pour la République
R.S.A.	Royal Scottish Academy; Royal Society of Arts
R.S.C.	Royal Shakespeare Company, Royal Society of Canada
RS.Dr.	Doctor of Social Sciences
R.S.F.S.R.	Russian Soviet Federative Socialist Republic
R.S.L.	Royal Society of Literature
Rt. Hon.	Right Honourable
Rt. Rev.	Right Reverend
R.V.O.	Royal Victorian Order
R.W.S.	Royal Society of Painters in Water Colours
s.	son(s)
S.	South
S.A.	South Africa; Société Anonyme, Sociedad Anónima
S.A.E.	Society of Aeronautical Engineers
Salop	Shropshire
S.A.L.T.	Strategic Arms Limitation Treaty
Sask.	Saskatchewan
S.B.	Bachelor of Science (U.S.A.)
SC	South Carolina
S.C.	South Carolina; Senior Counsel
SCAP	Supreme Command Allied Powers
Sc.B.	Bachelor of Science
Sc.D.	Doctor of Science
SD	South Dakota
S.Dak.	South Dakota
SDLP	Social and Democratic Liberal Party
SDP	Social Democratic Party
S.E.	South East
SEATO	South East Asia Treaty Organization
Sec.	Secretary
SEC	Securities and Exchange Commission
Secr.	Secretariat
SED	Sozialistische Einheitspartei Deutschlands (Socialist Unity Party of the German Democratic Republic)
Sept.	September
S.-et-O.	Seine-et-Oise
SHAEF	Supreme Headquarters Allied Expeditionary Force
SHAPE	Supreme Headquarters Allied Powers in Europe
S.J.	Society of Jesus (Jesuits)
S.J.D.	Doctor of Juristic Science
S.L.D.	Social and Liberal Democrats
S.M.	Master of Science
S.O.A.S.	School of Oriental and African Studies
Soc.	Society, Société
S.p.A.	Società per Azioni
SPD	Sozialdemokratische Partei Deutschlands

Sr.	Senior
S.R.C.	Science Research Council
S.S.M.	Seria Seta Mahkota (Malaysia)
S.S.R.	Soviet Socialist Republic
St.	Saint
Staffs.	Staffordshire
S.T.B.	Bachelor of Sacred Theology
S.T.D.	Doctor of Sacred Theology
S.T.L.	Licentiate of Sacred Theology
S.T.M.	Master of Sacred Theology
str.	strasse
Supt.	Superintendent
S.W.	South West
T.A.	Territorial Army
T.D.	Territorial Decoration; Teachta Dála (mem. of the Dáil)
Tech.	Technical, Technology
Temp.	Temporary
Tenn.	Tennessee
Tex.	Texas
Th.B.	Bachelor of Theology
Th.D.	Doctor of Theology
TH.Dr.	Doctor of Theology
Th.M.	Master of Theology
TN	Tennessee
Trans.	Translation; translator
Treas.	Treasurer
TU(C)	Trades Union (Congress)
TV	Television
TX	Texas
U.A.E.	United Arab Emirates
U.A.R.	United Arab Republic
UDEAC	L'Union Douanière et Economique de l'Afrique Centrale
UDR	Union des Démocrates pour la République
U.E.D.	University Education Diploma
U.K.	United Kingdom (of Great Britain and Northern Ireland)
UKAEA	United Kingdom Atomic Energy Authority
UMIST	University of Manchester Institute of Science and Technology
UMNO	United Malays National Organization
UN(O)	United Nations (Organization)
UNA	United Nations Association
UNCED	United Nations Council for Education and Development
UNCTAD	United Nations Conference on Trade and Development
UNDP	United Nations Development Programme
UNDRO	United Nations Disaster Relief Office
UNEF	United Nations Emergency Force
UNEP	United Nations Environment Programme
UNESCO	United Nations Educational, Scientific and Cultural Organisation
UNHCR	United Nations High Commissioner for Refugees
UNICEF	United Nations International Children's Emergency Fund
UNIDO	United Nations Industrial Development Organization
UNITAR	United Nations Institute for Training and Research
Univ.	University
UNKRA	United Nations Korean Relief Administration
UNRRA	United Nations Relief and Rehabilitation Administration
UNRWA	United Nations Relief and Works Agency
U.P.	United Provinces, Uttar Pradesh (India)
UPU	Universal Postal Union
U.S.A.	United States of America
U.S.A.A.F.	United States Army Air Force
U.S.A.F.	United States Air Force
U.S.N.	United States Navy
U.S.N.R.	United States Navy Reserve
U.S.S.	United States Ship
U.S.S.R.	Union of Soviet Socialist Republics
UT	Utah
VA	Virginia
Va.	Virginia
V.C.	Victoria Cross
VI	Virgin Islands
Vic.	Victoria
Vol(s).	Volume(s)
VT	Vermont
Vt.	Vermont
W.	West
WA	Washington (State)
W.A.	Western Australia
Warwicks.	Warwickshire
Wash.	Washington (State)
WCC	World Council of Churches
WCT	World Championship Tennis
WEU	Western European Union
WFTU	World Federation of Trade Unions
WHO	World Health Organization
WI	Wisconsin
Wilts.	Wiltshire
WIPO	World Intellectual Property Organization
Wis.	Wisconsin
WMO	World Meteorological Organization
Worcs.	Worcestershire
W.R.A.C.	Women's Royal Army Corps
W.R.N.S.	Women's Royal Naval Service
WV	West Virginia
W.Va.	West Virginia
WY	Wyoming
Wyo.	Wyoming
YMCA	Young Men's Christian Association
Yorks.	Yorkshire
YWCA	Young Women's Christian Association

REIGNING ROYAL FAMILIES

Biographical entries of most of the reigning monarchs and of certain other members of the reigning royal families will be found in their appropriate alphabetical order in the biographical section of this book. The name under which they can be found in the text of the book will be listed in this section in bold type.

BAHRAIN

Reigning Amir

SHEIKH HAMAD BIN ISA AL-**KHALIFA**; b. 28 January 1950; succeeded as Ruler of Bahrain on the death of his father, Sheikh Isa bin Sulman al-Khalifa; married 1968, Shaikha Saheeka bint Ebrahim al-Khalifa; three sons; assumed the title of Amir, March 1999.

BELGIUM

Reigning King

KING **ALBERT** FELIX HUMBERT THEODORE CHRISTIAN EUGENE MARIE; b. 6 June 1934; succeeded to the throne 9 August 1993, after the death of his brother, King Baudouin I; married 2 July 1959, Donna Paola Ruffo di Calabria (b. 11 September 1937).

Children of the King

Crown Prince Philippe, Duke of Brabant, b. 15 April 1960.

Prince Laurent, b. 19 October 1963.

Princess Astrid, b. 5 June 1962; m. Archduke Lorenz, September 1984; son Prince Amedeo, b. February 1986; daughter Princess Maria Laura, b. August 1988; son Prince Joachim, b. December 1991; daughter Louisa-Maria b. October 1995.

Father of the King

King Léopold III; b. 3 November 1901, died 25 September 1983; married (1) 4 November 1926, Princess Astrid of Sweden (b. 17 November 1905, died 29 August 1935); (2) 11 September 1941, Mlle Mary Lilian Baels (three children).

Sister of the King

Joséphine Charlotte, Princess of Belgium; b. 11 October 1927; married 9 April 1953, Prince Jean of Luxembourg (b. 5 January 1921) (five children).

BHUTAN

Reigning King

H.M. THE DRUK GYALPO JIGME SINGYE **WANGCHUCK**; b. 11 November 1955; succeeded to the throne 24 July 1972, on the death of his father, the Druk Gyalpo Jigme Dorji Wangchuk; crowned on 2 June 1974.

Queens

H.M. Queen Ashi Dorji Wangmo Wangchuck, b. 29 December 1955.

H.M. Queen Ashi Tshering Pem Wangchuck, b. 29 December 1957.

H.M. Queen Ashi Tshering Yandon Wangchuck, b. 21 June 1959.

H.M. Queen Ashi Sangay Choden Wangchuck, b. 11 May 1963.

Children

H.R.H. Dasho Jigme Khesar Namgyal Wangchuck, Crown Prince, b. 21 February 1980.

H.R.H. Prince Jigyel Ugyen Wangchuck, b. 16 July 1984.

H.R.H. Prince Khamsum Singye Wangchuck, b. 6 October 1985.

H.R.H. Prince Jigme Dorji Wangchuck, b. 14 April 1986.

H.R.H. Princess Chimi Yangzom Wangchuck, b. 10 January 1980.

H.R.H. Princess Sonam Dechen Wangchuck, b. 5 August 1981.

H.R.H. Princess Dechen Yangzom Wangchuck, b. 2 December 1981.

H.R.H. Princess Kesang Choden Wangchuck, b. 23 January 1982.

Parents of the King

The Druk Gyalpo Jigme Dorji Wangchuck, b. 1928; married 1953 Queen Ashi Kesang Wangchuck; succeeded to the throne 28 October 1952; died 21 July 1972.

Sisters of the King

H.R.H. Ashi Sonam Choden Wangchuck, b. 26 July 1953.

H.R.H. Ashi Dechen Wangmo Wangchuck, b. 8 September 1954.

H.R.H. Ashi Pem Pem Wangchuck, b. 12 March 1959.

H.R.H. Ashi Kesang Wangmo Wangchuck, b. 11 May 1961.

BRUNEI

Reigning Sultan and Yang di-Pertuan

H.M. Sultan Haji HASSANAL **BOLKIAH**; b. 15 July 1946; succeeded his father Sultan Haji Omar Ali Saifuddien II as 29th Sultan 5 October 1967, crowned 1 August 1968; married RAJA ISTERI PENGIRAN ANAK HAJJAH SALEHA, two sons, four daughters; also married PENGIRAN ISTERI HAJJAH MARIAM 1981, two sons, two daughters.

Brothers of the Sultan

H.R.H. Prince Mohamed Bolkiah.

H.R.H. Prince Haji Sufri Bolkiah.

H.R.H. Prince Haji Jefri Bolkiah.

CAMBODIA

Reigning King

KING **NORODOM SIHANOUK**; b. 31 October 1922; elected King April 1941; abdicated March 1955; took oath of fidelity to vacant throne 1960; elected Head of State on the death of his father 1960; deposed March 1970; elected as King 24 September 1993.

Children of the King

Princess Buppha Devi; b. 8 January 1943.

Prince Yuvaneath; b. 13 October 1943.

Prince Ranariddh; b. 2 January 1944.

Prince Ravivong; b. 1944; died 1973.

Prince Chakrapong; b. 21 October 1945.

Prince Naradipo; b. 10 February 1946; died 1977.

Princess Soriya Roeungsey; b. 1947; died 1977.

Princess Kantha Bopha; b. 1948; died 14 December 1952.

Prince Khemanourak; b. 1949; died 1977.

Princess Botum Bopha; b. 1951; died 1977.

Princess Socheata; b. 1953; died 1975.

Prince Sihamoni; b. 14 May 1953.

Prince Narindrapong; b. 18 Sept. 1954.

Princess Arun Rasmy; b. 2 Oct. 1955.

DENMARK

Reigning Queen

QUEEN **MARGRETHE II**; b. 16 April 1940; succeeded to the throne 14 January 1972, on the death of her father, King Frederik IX; married 10 June 1967, Count Henri de Laborde de Monpezat (Prince Henrik) (b. 11 June 1934).

Children of the Queen

Prince Frederik André Henrik Christian (heir-apparent); b. 26 May 1968.

Prince Joachim Holger Waldemar Christian; b. 7 June 1969; married 18 November 1995, Alexandra Christina Manley.

Parents of the Queen

King Frederik IX; b. 11 March 1899; died 14 January 1972; son of King Christian X and Queen Alexandrine; married 24 May 1935, Princess Ingrid of Sweden (b. 28 March 1910).

Sisters of the Queen

Princess Benedikte; b. 29 April 1944; married 3 February 1968, Prince Richard zu Sayn-Wittgenstein-Berleburg; son Prince Gustav, b. 12 January 1969; daughter Princess Alexandra, b. 20 November 1970; daughter Princess Nathalie, b. 2 May 1975.

Queen Anne-Marie of the Hellenes; b. 30 August 1946; married 18 September 1964, King Constantine II of the Hellenes; sons Prince Paul, b. 20 May 1967, Prince Nicholaos, b. 1 October 1969, Prince Filippos, b. 26 April 1986; daughters Princess Alexia, b. 10 July 1965, Princess Theodora, b. 9 June 1983.

JAPAN

Reigning Emperor

EMPEROR **AKIHITO**; b. 23 December 1933; succeeded his father 7th January 1989; enthroned 10 November 1990; married 10 April 1959, PRINCESS MICHIKO SHODA (b. 20 October 1934).

Children of the Emperor

Crown Prince Naruhito (Hironomiya), b. 23 February 1960, married 9 June 1993 Masako Owada.

Prince Fumihito (Ayanomiya), b. 30 November 1965; m. Kiko Kawashima 1990; two d.

Princess Sayako (Norinomiya), b. 18 April 1969.

Parents of the Emperor

Emperor Hirohito; b. 29 April 1901; married 26 January 1924, died 7 January 1989; Princess Nagako Kuni (b. 6 March 1903), daughter of Prince Kuni.

JORDAN

Reigning King

KING **ABDULLAH**; b. 30 January 1962; succeeded to the throne on the death of his father Hussein Ibn Talal, 7 February 1999; married 10 June 1993, Rania Yassin.

Children of the King

Prince Al Hussein; b. 28 June 1994.

Princess Iman; b. 7 September 1996.

Parents of the King

King Hussein Ibn Talal; b. 14 November 1935; died 7 February 1999; married 2nd Miss Antoinette Gardner, Princess Muna al-Hussein (divorced 1972).

Brothers and Sisters of the King

Crown Prince Hamzah bin Al Hussein; b. 29 March 1980.

Princess Alia; b. 13 February 1956; married 1st 11 July 1977 Nasser Wasfi Mirza (divorced 1983); son Prince Hussein Mirza; b. 12 February 1981; married 2nd 30 July 1988 Mohammad Farid Al Saleh; son Talal Al Saleh, b. 12 September 1989; son Abdul Hameed Al Saleh, b. 15 November 1991.

Prince Feisal; b. 11 October 1963; married 10 August 1987 Alia al-Tabba; daughter Princess Aya, b. 11 February 1990.

Princess Zein; b. 23 April 1968; married 3 August 1989 Majdi Farid Al Saleh; son Jafar Al Saleh, b. 9 November 1990.

Princess Aisha; b. 23 April 1968; married 26 July 1990 Zeid Juma'a; son Aoun Juma'a, b. 27 May 1992.

Princess Haya; b. 3 May 1974.

Prince Ali; b. 23 December 1975.

Prince Hashim; b. 10 June 1981.

Princess Iman; b. 24 April 1983.

Princess Raiyah; b. 9 February 1986.

KUWAIT

Reigning Amir

SHEIKH JABER AL-AHMAD AL-JABER AL-**SABAH**; b. 29 June 1926; succeeded his uncle, Sheikh Sabah al-Salim al-Sabah, 31 December 1977.

Crown Prince

SHEIKH SAAD AL-ABDULLAH AL-SALEM AL-**SABAH**; proclaimed Crown Prince 31 January 1978.

LESOTHO

Reigning King

KING **LETSIE III**; b. 17 July 1963; installed as King November 1990; abdicated January 1995; reinstalled 7th February 1996.

LIECHTENSTEIN

Reigning Prince

HANS-ADAM II; b. 14 February 1945; succeeded Franz Josef II, 13 November 1989; married 30 July 1967, COUNTESS MARIE KINSKY (PRINCESS MARIE).

Children of the Prince

Hereditary Prince Alois, b. 11 June 1968; married 3 July 1993, Duchess Sophie in Bavaria; son Prince Joseph Wenzel, b. 24 May 1995; daughter Princess Marie Caroline, b. 17 October 1996.
Prince Maximilian, b. 16 May 1969.
Prince Constantin, b. 15 March 1972.
Princess Tatjana, b. 10 April 1973.

Brothers and Sisters of the Prince

Prince Philipp; b. 19 August 1946; married 11 September 1971, Mademoiselle Isabelle de l'Arbre de Malander; sons, Prince Alexander, b. 19 May 1972; Prince Wenzeslaus, b. 12 May 1974; Prince Rudolf, b. 7 September 1975.

Prince Nicolas; b. 24 October 1947; married 20 March 1982, Princess Margaretha of Luxembourg; daughters, Princess Maria-Anunciata, b. 12 May 1985, Princess Marie-Astrid, b. 26 June 1987; son Prince Josef Emanuel, b. 7 May 1989.

Princess Nora; b. 31 October 1950; married 11 June 1988, Vicente Marques de Mariño; daughter Theresa Maria, b. 21 November 1992.

Prince Wenzel; b. 19 November 1962; died 28 February 1991.

LUXEMBOURG

Reigning Monarch

GRAND DUKE **JEAN**; b. 5 January 1921; succeeded 12 November 1964, on the abdication of his mother, Grand Duchess Charlotte; married 9 April 1953, JOSEPHINE CHARLOTTE, PRINCESS OF BELGIUM (b. 11 October 1927).

Children of the Grand Duke

Princess Marie-Astrid; b. 17 February 1954; married 6 February 1982, Charles Christian of Habsburg Lorraine, Archduke of Austria; daughter Marie-Christine Anne Astrid Zita Charlotte of Habsburg Lorraine, b. 31 July 1983, son Prince Imre, b. 8 December 1985, son Prince Christophe, b. 2 February 1988, son Prince Alexander, b. 26 September 1990, daughter Princess Gabriella, b. 26 March 1994.

Prince Henri; b. 16 April 1955; married 14 February 1981, Maria-Teresa Mestre; sons, Guillaume Jean Joseph Marie, b. 11 November 1981, Félix Léopold Marie Guillaume, b. 3 June 1984, Louis Xavier Marie Guillaume, b. 3 August 1986, daughter Alexandra Josephine Teresa Charlotte Marie Wilhelmina, b. 16 February 1991, son Sebastien Henri Marie Guillaume, b. 16 April 1992.

Prince Jean; b. 15 May 1957; married 27 May 1987, Hélène Suzanne Vestur; daughter Marie-Gabrielle, b. 8 December 1986, son Constantin Jean Philippe, b. 22 July 1988, son Wenceslas, b. 17 November 1990, son Carl-Johann, b. 15 August 1992.

Princess Margaretha; b. 15 May 1957; married 20 March 1982, Prince Nicolas of Liechtenstein; daughter, Princess Maria Annunciata, b. 12 May 1985, daughter Princess Marie-Astrid, b. 26 June 1987, son Prince Joseph-Emmanuel, b. 7 May 1989.

Prince Guillaume; b. 1 May 1963, married Sibilla Weiller, 24 September 1994; son Paul-Louis, b. 4 March 1998.

Parents of the Grand Duke

Grand Duchess Charlotte, Duchess of Nassau; b. 23 January 1896, died 9 July 1985; succeeded 15 January 1919; abdicated in favour of her son, Grand Duke Jean, 12 November 1964; married 6 November 1919, Prince Félix of Bourbon Parma (b. 28 September 1893, died 8 April 1970).

Brother and Sisters of the Grand Duke

Princess Elisabeth; b. 22 December 1922; married 9 May 1956, Duke François Ferdinand of Hohenberg (b. 13 September 1927, died 15 August 1977); two d.

Princess Marie-Adelaide; b. 21 May 1924; married 10 April 1958, Count Charles Joseph Henckel de Donnersmarck (b. 7 November 1928); three s. one d.

Princess Marie-Gabrielle; b. 2 August 1925; married 6 November 1951, Count Knud de Holstein-Ledreborg (b. 2 October 1919); seven d.

Prince Charles; b. 7 August 1927; married 1 March 1967, Joan Douglas Dillon; one s. one d.; died 26 July 1977.

Princess Alix; b. 24 August 1929; married 17 August 1950, H.H. Prince Antoine de Ligne (b. 8 March 1925); three s. three d.

MALAYSIA

*Supreme Head of State (Yang di-Pertuan Agong)**

SALAHUDDIN ABDUL AZIZ SHAH IBNI AL-MARHUM SULTAN HISAMUDDIN ALAM SHAH HAJI; Sultan of **Selangor**; b. 8 March 1926; installed as eleventh Yang-di Pertuan Agong 26 April 1999.

* Reign ends in 2004.

MONACO

PRINCE **RAINIER III**; b. 31 May 1923; succeeded his grandfather, Prince Louis II, 9 May 1949; married 18 April 1956, Miss GRACE PATRICIA KELLY, daughter of the late Mr. John Brendan Kelly and Mrs. Margaret Majer, of Philadelphia, U.S.A. (b. 12 November 1929, died 14 September 1982).

Children of the Prince

Princess Caroline Louise Marguerite; b. 23 January 1957; married 1st Philippe Junot, 28 June 1978 (divorced 1980, marriage annulled 1992); married 2nd Stefano Casiraghi, 29 December 1983 (died 3 October 1990); son, Andrea Albert Pierre, b. 8 June 1984; daughter, Charlotte Marie Pomeline, b. 3 August 1986; son, Pierre Rainier Stefano, b. 5 September 1987; married 3rd Prince Ernst August of Hanover, 23 January 1999.

Prince Albert Alexandre Louis Pierre; b. 14 March 1958.

Princess Stéphanie Marie Elisabeth; b. 1 February 1965; married 1st July 1995, Daniel Ducruet (divorced 5 October 1996); son Louis, b. 26 November 1992; daughter Pauline, b. 4 May 1994; daughter Camille Marie Kelly, b. 15 July 1998.

Parents of the Prince

Princess Charlotte, Duchess of Valentinois (b. 30 September 1898; died 16 November 1977); married 19 March 1920, Comte Pierre de Polignac (b. 24 October 1895), who thus became Prince Pierre of Monaco; he died 10 November 1964.

MOROCCO

Reigning King

KING **HASSAN II** (formerly Crown Prince Moulay Hassan); b. 9 July 1929; son of King Mohammed V (died 26 February 1961); became King of Morocco when he succeeded his father, 3 March 1961.

Children of the King

Princess Lalla Myriam; b. 26 August 1962; m. Fouad Fillali September 1984.

Prince Sidi Mohamed (Crown Prince); b. 21 August 1963.

Princess Lalla Asma; b. 1965; m. Khalid Bouchentouf 7 June 1987.

Princess Lalla Hasna; b. 1967; m. Khalid Benharbit 13 December 1991.

Prince Moulay Rachid; b. July 1970.

Brother and Sisters of the King

Prince Moulay Abdullah (deceased); married Lamia Solh.

Princess Lalla Aicha.

Princess Lalla Malika.

Princess Lalla Nezha (deceased).

Princess Lalla Amina.

Princess Lalla Fatima Zohra.

NEPAL

Reigning King

KING **BIRENDRA BIR BIKRAM SHAH DEV**; b. 28 December 1945; succeeded to the throne, 31 January 1972, on the death of his father King Mahendra; crowned 24 February 1975; married 1970, PRINCESS AISHWARYA RAJYA LAXMI DEVI RANA.

Children of the King

Crown Prince Dipendra Bir Bikram Shah Dev; b. 27 June 1971.

Princess Shruti Rajya Laxmi Devi Shah; b. 16 October 1976.

Prince Nirajan Bir Bikram Shah; b. 6 November 1978.

NETHERLANDS

Reigning Queen

QUEEN **BEATRIX** WILHELMINA ARMGARD; b. 31 January 1938; succeeded to the throne on the abdication of her mother, 30 April 1980; married 10 March 1966, PRINCE CLAUS GEORGE WILLEM OTTO FREDERIK GEERT OF THE NETHERLANDS, Jonkheer van Amsberg (b. 6 September 1926).

Children of the Queen

Prince Willem-Alexander Claus George Ferdinand, Prince of Orange-Nassau; b. 27 April 1967.

Prince Johan Friso Bernhard Christiaan David; b. 25 September 1968.

Prince Constantijn Christof Frederik Aschwin; b. 11 October 1969.

Sisters of the Queen

Princess Irene Emma Elisabeth; b. 5 August 1939; married 29 April 1964, Prince Carlos Hugo of Bourbon Parma (divorced 1981); sons Prince Carlos Javier Bernardo, b. 27 January 1970, Prince Jaime Bernardo, b. 13 October 1972; daughters Princess Margarita Maria Beatriz, b. 13 October 1972, Princess Maria Carolina Christina, b. 23 June 1974.

Princess Margriet Francisca; b. 19 January 1943; married 10 January 1967, Pieter van Vollenhoven; sons, Prince Maurits Willem Pieter Hendrik van Orange-Nassau van Vollenhoven, b. 17 April 1968, Prince Bernhard Lucas Emmanuel, b. 25 December 1969, Prince Pieter-Christiaan Michiel, b. 22 March 1972, Prince Floris Frederik Martÿn, b. 10 April 1975.

Princess Maria Christina; b. 18 February 1947; married 28 June 1975, Jorge Guillermo (divorced 1996); sons Bernardo Federico Tomás, b. 17 June 1977, Nicolas Daniel Mauricio, b. 6 July 1979; daughter, Princess Juliana Edenia Antonia, b. 8 October 1981.

Parents of the Queen

Princess **Juliana** (Louise Emma Marie Wilhelmina) of the Netherlands, Princess of Orange Nassau, Duchess of Mecklenburg; Princess of Lippe-Biesterfeld, etc.; b. 30 April 1909; succeeded to the throne on the abdication of her mother, 4 September 1948; inaugurated 6 September 1948; abdicated 30 April 1980; married 7 January 1937, Prince Bernhard Leopold Frederik Everhard Julius Coert Karel Godfried Pieter of the **Netherlands**, Prince of Lippe-Biesterfeld (b. 29 June 1911).

NORWAY

Reigning King

KING **HARALD** V; b. 21 February 1937; succeeded to the throne on the death of his father, King Olav V, 17 January 1991; married 29 August 1968, Miss Sonja Haraldsen (Queen Sonja).

Children of the King

Crown Prince Haakon Magnus; b. 20 July 1973.

Princess Märtha Louise; b. 22 September 1971.

Sisters of the King

Princess Ragnhild Alexandra; b. 9 June 1930; married 15 May 1953, Erling Lorentzen; three children.

Princess Astrid Maud Ingeborg; b. 12 February 1932; married 12 January 1961, Johan Martin Ferner; five children.

OMAN

Reigning Sultan

SULTAN **QABOOS BIN SAID**; b. 18 November 1940; succeeded to the throne on the abdication of his father, Sultan Said bin Taimur (1910–72), 23 July 1970.

QATAR

Reigning Amir

SHEIKH HAMAD BIN KHALIFA AL-**THANI**; b. 1950; succeeded his father, 27 June 1995.

SAUDI ARABIA

Reigning King

KING **FAHD IBN ABDUL AZIZ**; b. 1920; succeeded to the throne on the death of his brother, King Khalid, 13 June 1982.

Brothers of the King include

King Saud ibn Abdul Aziz; b. 15 January 1902; proclaimed King 12 November 1953, following the death of his father, King Abdul Aziz (Ibn Saud); relinquished the throne 1 November 1964; died 23 February 1969.

King Faisal ibn Abdul Aziz; b. 9 April 1906; acceded 1 November 1964; died 24 March 1975.

Amir Mohammed; b. 1912; died 1988.

King Khalid ibn Abdul Aziz; b. 1913; acceded 25 March 1975; died 13 June 1982.

Crown Prince Abdullah ibn Abdul Aziz; b. August 1921.

Amir Sultan; b. 1922.

SPAIN

Reigning King

KING **JUAN CARLOS I**; b. 5 January 1938; succeeded to the throne 22 November 1975; married 14 May 1962, Princess Sofía of Greece (b. 2 November 1938), daughter of the late King Paul of the Hellenes and Queen Frederica.

Children of the King

Princess Elena; b. 20 December 1963.

Princess Cristina; b. 13 June 1965.

Prince Felipe; b. 30 January 1968.

Parents of the King

Don Juan de Borbón y Battenberg, Count of Barcelona; b. 20 June 1913; married 1935, Doña María de las Mercedes de Borbón y Orleans; died 1 April 1993.

SWAZILAND

Reigning Monarch

KING MSWATI III; b. 19 April 1968; installed as Head of State 25 April 1986.

Father of the King

King Sobhuza II; b. 22 July 1899, died 21 August 1982.

SWEDEN

Reigning King

KING **CARL XVI GUSTAF**; b. 30 April 1946; succeeded to the throne 15 September 1973, on the death of his grandfather King Gustaf VI Adolf; married 19 June 1976, Silvia Renate Sommerlath (b. 23 December 1943); daughter, Victoria Ingrid Alice Désirée, b. 14 July 1977; son, Carl Philip Edmund Bertil, b. 13 May 1979; daughter, Madeleine Thérèse Amelie Josephine, b. 10 June 1982.

Parents of the King

Prince Gustaf Adolf, Duke of Västerbotten; b. 22 April 1906, died 26 January 1947; married 20 October 1932, Sibylla, Princess of Saxe-Coburg and Gotha (b. 18 January 1908, died 28 November 1972).

Sisters of the King

Princess Margaretha; b. 31 October 1934; married 30 June 1964, Mr. John Ambler; daughter, Sibylla Louise, b. 14 April 1965; sons, Charles Edward, b. 14 July 1966; James Patrick, b. 10 June 1969.

Princess Birgitta; b. 19 January 1937; married 25 May 1961, Prince of Hohenzollern Johann Georg; sons, Carl Christian, b. 5 April 1962; Hubertus, b. 9 June 1966; daughter, Desirée, b. 27 November 1963.

Princess Désirée; b. 2 June 1938; married 5 June 1964, Baron Niclas Silfverschiöld; son, Carl Otto Edmund, b. 22 March 1965; daughters, Christina Louise Madeleine, b. 29 September 1966, Hélène, b. 20 September 1968.

Princess Christina; b. 3 August 1943; married 15 June 1974, Tord Magnuson; sons, Carl Gustaf Victor, b. 8 August 1975, Tord Oscar Fredrik, b. 20 June 1977, Victor Edmund Lennart, b. 10 September 1980.

THAILAND

Reigning King

KING **BHUMIBOL ADULYADEJ**: b. 5 December 1927; succeeded to the throne on the death of his brother, King Ananda Mahidol, 9 June 1946; married 28 April 1950, MOM RAJAWONG SIRIKIT KITIYAKARA (b. 12 August 1932), daughter of H.H. Prince Nakkhatra Mongkol Kitiyakara, Krommuen Chandaburi Suranat.

Children of the King

Princess Ubol Ratana; b. 5 April 1951; married August 1972, Peter Ladd Jensen (relinquished Royal claims); daughter, Khun Ploy Pailin, b. May 1981, son, Khun Bhumi, b. August 1983, Khun Sirikitiya, b. 1985.

Crown Prince Vajiralongkorn; b. 28 July 1952; proclaimed Crown Prince December 1972; married 3 January 1977, Mom Luang Somsawalee Kitiyakara; daughter, Princess Bhajara Kitiyabha, b. 7 December 1978.

Princess Maha Chakri Sirindhorn; b. 2 April 1955.

Princess Chulabhorn; b. 4 July 1957; married 7 January 1982, Squadron Leader Virayuth Didyasarin; daughter, Princess Siribha Chutabhorn, b. 8 October 1982, daughter, Princess Aphithayadhorn Kittikhun, b. 6 May 1984.

Parents of the King

Prince Mahidol of Songkhla and Princess Sri Sangwalya.

Sister of the King

Princess Kalyani Vadhana.

TONGA

Reigning King

KING **TAUFA'AHAU TUPOU IV**; b. 4 July 1918; succeeded to the throne 15 December 1965, on the death of his mother, Queen Salote Tupou III; married 1947, Princess Halaevalu Mata'aho 'Ahome'e (b. 1926), (now Queen Halaevalu Mata'aho).

Mother of the King

Queen Salote Tupou III; b. 13 March 1900; married 1917, Prince Viliami Tungi (Prince Consort); died 15 December 1965.

Children of the King

Prince Tupouto'a (Crown Prince); b. 4 May 1948.

Princess Salote Mafile'o Pilolevu Tuku'aho Tuita; b. 17 November 1951; married 21 July 1976, Captain Ma'ulupekotofa Tuita.

Prince Fatafehi Alaivahamama'o Tuku'aho (known as Honorable Maátu); b. 17 December 1954.

Prince Lavaka Ata' Ulukalala (fmrly. known as 'Aho'eitu' Unuaki'otonga Tuku'aho); b. 12 July 1959; married 11 December 1982, Nanasipau'u Vaea (now Princess Nanasipau'u).

UNITED ARAB EMIRATES

Reigning Rulers

Ruler of Sharjah: Sheikh SULTAN BIN MUHAMMAD AL-**QASIMI**; succeeded to the throne 1972.

Ruler of Ras al-Khaimah: Sheikh SAQR BIN MUHAMMAD AL-**QASIMI**; succeeded to the throne 1948.

Ruler of Umm al-Qaiwan: Sheikh RASHID BIN AHMED AL-**MU'ALLA**; succeeded to the throne 1981.

Ruler of Ajman: Sheikh HUMAID BIN RASHID AL-**NUAMI**; succeeded to the throne 1981.

Ruler of Dubai: Sheikh MAKTOUM BIN RASHID AL-**MAKTOUM**; succeeded to the throne 1990.

Ruler of Abu Dhabi: Sheikh ZAYED BIN SULTAN AL-**NAHYAN**; succeeded to the throne 1966.

Ruler of Fujairah: Sheikh HAMAD BIN MUHAMMAD ASH-**SHARQI**; succeeded to the throne 1974.

UNITED KINGDOM

Reigning Queen

QUEEN **ELIZABETH II**; b. 21 April 1926; succeeded to the throne 6 February 1952, on the death of her father, King George VI; crowned 2 June 1953; married 20 November 1947, H.R.H. The Prince Philip, DUKE OF **EDINBURGH**, K.G., K.T., O.M., G.B.E., A.C., Q.S.O. (b. 10 June 1921), son of Prince Andrew of Greece and Princess Alice of Battenberg (Mountbatten).

Children of The Queen

The Prince Charles Philip Arthur George, Prince of **Wales**, Duke of Cornwall and Rothesay, Earl of Chester and Carrick, Baron of Renfrew, Lord of the Isles and Great Steward of Scotland, K.G., K.T., G.C.B., A.K., Q.S.O., A.D.C. (heir-apparent); b. 14 November 1948; married 29 July 1981, Lady Diana Frances Spencer (divorced 1996, died 1997); sons, Prince William Arthur Philip Louis, b. 21 June 1982; Prince Henry Charles Albert David, b. 15 September 1984.

The Princess Anne Elizabeth Alice Louise, The Princess **Royal,** G.C.V.O., Q.S.O.; b. 15 August 1950; married 1st 14 November 1973, Captain Mark Phillips (divorced 1992); son, Peter Mark Andrew, b. 15 November 1977; daughter, Zara Anne Elizabeth, b. 15 May 1981; married 2nd 12 December 1992, Commodore Timothy Laurence, M.V.O., R.N.

The Prince Andrew Albert Christian Edward, Duke of York, Earl of Inverness, Baron Killyleagh, C.V.O., A.D.C.; b. 19 February 1960; married Miss Sarah Ferguson 23 July 1986 (divorced 1996); daughter, Princess Beatrice Elizabeth Mary, b. 8 August 1988; daughter Princess Eugenie Victoria Helena, b. 23 March 1990.

The Prince Edward Antony Richard Louis, C.V.O.; b. 10 March 1964.

Parents of The Queen

King George VI; b. 14 December 1895; son of King George V and Queen Mary; married 26 April 1923, Lady **Elizabeth Angela Marguerite** Bowes-Lyon (b. 4 August 1900); succeeded to the throne 11 December 1936; died 6 February 1952.

Sister of The Queen

The Princess **Margaret Rose**, Countess of Snowdon, C.I., G.C.V.O.; b. 21 August 1930; married 6 May 1960, Antony Armstrong-Jones, later the Earl of Snowdon, G.C.V.O. (divorced 1978); son, David Albert Charles, Viscount Linley, b. 3 November 1961; daughter, Lady Sarah Frances Elizabeth Chatto, b. 1 May 1964.

The full titles of Queen Elizabeth II are as follows:

United Kingdom

"Elizabeth the Second, by the Grace of God, of the United Kingdom of Great Britain and Northern Ireland and of Her other Realms and Territories Queen, Head of the Commonwealth, Defender of the Faith."

Canada

"Elizabeth the Second, by the Grace of God, of the United Kingdom, Canada and Her other Realms and Territories Queen, Head of the Commonwealth, Defender of the Faith."

Australia

"Elizabeth the Second, by the Grace of God Queen of Australia and Her other Realms and Territories, Head of the Commonwealth."

New Zealand

"Elizabeth the Second, by the Grace of God, Queen of New Zealand and Her Other Realms and Territories, Head of the Commonwealth, Defender of the Faith."

Jamaica

"Elizabeth the Second, by the Grace of God, of Jamaica and of Her other Realms and Territories Queen, Head of the Commonwealth."

Barbados

"Elizabeth the Second, by the Grace of God, Queen of Barbados and of Her other Realms and Territories, Head of the Commonwealth."

The Bahamas

"Elizabeth the Second, by the Grace of God, Queen of the Commonwealth of The Bahamas and of Her other Realms and Territories, Head of the Commonwealth."

Grenada

"Elizabeth the Second, by the Grace of God, Queen of the United Kingdom of Great Britain and Northern Ireland and of Grenada and Her other Realms and Territories, Head of the Commonwealth."

Papua New Guinea

"Elizabeth the Second, Queen of Papua New Guinea and of Her other Realms and Territories, Head of the Commonwealth."

Solomon Islands

"Elizabeth the Second, by the Grace of God Queen of the Solomon Islands and of Her other Realms and Territories, Head of the Commonwealth."

Tuvalu

"Elizabeth the Second, by the Grace of God Queen of Tuvalu and of Her other Realms and Territories, Head of the Commonwealth."

Saint Lucia

"Elizabeth the Second, by the Grace of God, Queen of Saint Lucia and of Her other Realms and Territories, Head of the Commonwealth."

Saint Vincent and the Grenadines

"Elizabeth the Second, by the Grace of God, Queen of Saint Vincent and the Grenadines and of Her other Realms and Territories, Head of the Commonwealth."

Belize

"Elizabeth The Second, by the Grace of God, Queen of Belize and of Her Other Realms and Territories, Head of the Commonwealth."

Antigua and Barbuda

"Elizabeth the Second, by the Grace of God, Queen of Antigua and Barbuda and of Her other Realms and Territories, Head of the Commonwealth."

Saint Christopher and Nevis

"Elizabeth the Second, by the Grace of God, Queen of Saint Christopher and Nevis and of Her other Realms and Territories, Head of the Commonwealth."

The Republics of India, Ghana, Cyprus, Tanzania, Uganda, Kenya, Zambia, Malawi, Singapore, Botswana, Guyana, Nauru, The Gambia, Sierra Leone, Bangladesh, Sri Lanka, Malta, Trinidad and Tobago, Seychelles, Dominica, Kiribati, Zimbabwe, Vanuatu, Maldives, Namibia, Mauritius, South Africa, Fiji, Pakistan, Cameroon and Mozambique, together with the Federation of Malaysia, the Kingdom of Lesotho, the Kingdom of Swaziland, the Kingdom of Tonga, the Independent State of Samoa and the Sultanate of Brunei, recognize the Queen as "Head of the Commonwealth".

OBITUARY

** The biographies of some of those whose deaths were noted after the preparation of copy for this edition (completed in May 1999) still appear in the text. Their names are marked with an asterisk in the following list.*

Abacha, Gen. Sani	8 June 1998
Abiola, Chief Moshood Kashimawo Olawale	7 July 1998
*Abraham, Sir Edward Penley	8 May 1999
Adams, Charles Francis	5 Jan. 1999
Addison, John	7 Dec. 1998
*Adhikari, Man Mohan	26 April 1999
Ahrens, Joseph	—
Alby, Pierre	22 July 1998
Alport, 1st Baron; Cuthbert James McCall Alport	28 Oct. 1998
Ambler, Eric	22 Oct. 1998
Ambriere, Francis	July 1998
Ametistov, Ernest Mikhailovich	6 Sept. 1998
Anderson, David	—
Argaña, Luis María	23 March 1999
*Atwood, John Leland	5 March 1999
Aubert, Maurice	24 Oct. 1998
Baba, Corneliu	28 Dec. 1997
Balland, H.E. Cardinal Jean	1 May 1998
Ballestrero, H.E. Cardinal Anastasio Alberto	21 June 1998
Barraud, Henry	28 Oct. 1998
Bart, Lionel	3 April 1999
Beckingham, Charles Fraser	30 Sept. 1998
Beeby, Clarence Edward	10 March 1998
Beier, Friedrich-Karl	—
Bell, John Milton	—
Bender, Arnold Eric	21 March 1999
Bentley, Sir William	10 June 1998
Beriozova, Svetlana	10 Nov. 1998
Bertola, Giuseppe M.	—
*Bioy Casares, Adolfo	8 March 1999
*Bishop, Sir George Sidney	9 April 1999
Blackmun, Harry A.	4 March 1999
*Blech, Harry	9 May 1999
Boateng, Ernest Amano	11 July 1997
*Bogarde, Sir Dirk (Van den Bogaerde, Derek Niven)	8 May 1999
Box, Betty Evelyn	15 Jan. 1999
*Boyd, Arthur Merric Bloomfield	24 April 1999
Boyd-Carpenter, Baron; Rt. Hon. John Archibald Boyd-Carpenter	11 July 1998
Bradley, Thomas (Tom)	29 Sept. 1998
Brandon of Oakbrook, Baron; Henry Vivian Brandon	24 March 1999
Brinnin, John Malcolm	26 June 1998
Brook, Sir Robin (Ralph Ellis)	25 Oct. 1998
Brugmans, Hendrik	—
Brunner, Guido	2 Dec. 1997
Büchi, George H.	28 Aug. 1998
Bykov, Roland (Rolan) Anatolyevich	6 Oct. 1998
Caine, Sir Michael Harris	20 March 1999
Cairncross, Sir Alexander Kirkland	21 Oct. 1998
Callahan, Harry M.	15 March 1999
Callard, Sir Jack (Eric John)	2 Sept. 1998
Campen, Philippus Canisius Maria van	—
Candela (Outeriño), Félix	7 Dec. 1997
Cardwell, Donald Stephen Lowell	8 May 1998
Carmoy, Guy de	1 Oct. 1997
Casaroli, H.E. Cardinal Agostino	8 June 1998
Castaing, Raimond Bernard René	10 April 1998
*Cayzer, Baron; William Nicholas Cayzer	16 April 1999
Chadwick, John	24 Nov. 1998
Chiles, Lawton Mainor	12 Dec. 1998
Choonhavan, Maj. Gen. Chatichai	6 May 1998
Chornovil, Vyacheslav Maksimovich	25 March 1999
Christie, Ian Ralph	25 Nov. 1998
Ciszewski, Bohdan	14 April 1998
Clifford, Clark McAdams	10 Oct. 1998
Connell, Philip Henry	26 July 1998
Cookson, Dame Catherine	11 June 1998
Copp, (Douglas) Harold	7 March 1998
Cormack, Allan MacLeod	7 May 1998
Costa, Lucio	13 June 1998
Cudlipp, Baron; Hugh Cudlipp	17 May 1998
*Daube, David	24 Feb. 1999
Delamuraz, Jean-Pascal	4 Oct. 1998
Denning, Baron; Alfred Thompson Denning	5 March 1999
De Saeger, Jozef	—
Dixey, Paul Arthur Groser	19 Aug. 1998
Doroszkiewicz, Bazyl Włodzimierz	11 Feb. 1998
Douglas, William Wilton	2 July 1998
Dow, (John) Christopher (Roderick)	1 Dec. 1998
Drees, Willem	5 Sept. 1998
Drury, Allen Stuart	2 Sept. 1998
Dubinin, Nikolay Petrovich	26 March 1998
Dudintsev, Vladimir Dmitriyevich	23 July 1998
Dunn, Richard Johann	4 Aug. 1998
Dunnett, Alastair MacTavish	2 Sept. 1998
Dziewanowski, Kazimierz	19 Aug. 1998
*Ebtehaj, Abol-Hassan	24 Feb. 1999
Eccles, 1st Viscount, 1st Baron; David McAdam Eccles	24 Feb. 1999
Ehrlichmann, John Daniel	15 Feb. 1999
Einaudi, Giulio	5 April 1999
*Elion, Gertrude Belle	21 Feb. 1999
Emin, Gevorg	11 July 1998
English, Sir David	10 June 1998
Erben, Heinrich Karl	—
Everding, August	26 Jan. 1999
*Fabiani, Dante Carl	20 March 1999
Farlow, Tal(mage) Holt	25 July 1998
Fascell, Dante B.	28 Nov. 1998
Feuillère, Edwige	13 Nov. 1998
Flamand, Paul Henri	4 Aug. 1998
Françaix, Jean René Désiré	25 Sept. 1997
Frank, Sir (Frederick) Charles	5 April 1998
Frankel, Sir Otto Herzberg	21 Nov. 1998
Freeman, Sir Ralph	24 Aug. 1998
*Freund-Rosenthal, Miriam Kottler (Mrs. Harry Rosenthal)	16 Jan. 1999
Gable, Christopher	23 Oct. 1998
Gaddis, William	16 Dec. 1998
Gardelli, Lamberto	17 July 1998
*Gélinas, Gratien	16 March 1999
Gillmore of Thamesfield, Baron; David Howe Gillmore	20 March 1999
Godden, Rumer	8 Nov. 1998
Goldhaber, Gertrude Scharff	2 Feb. 1998
Goldwater, Barry Morris	29 May 1998
Goring, Marius	30 Sept. 1998
Gowing, Margaret Mary	7 Nov. 1998
Grade, Baron; Lew Grade	13 Dec. 1998
Grayson, Cecil	29 April 1998
Green, Julian	13 Aug. 1998
Greenborough, Sir John Hedley	3 July 1998
Griffith Joyner, Florence	21 Sept. 1998
Grotowski, Jerzy	14 Jan. 1999
*Guitton, Jean Marie Pierre	21 March 1999
Gurevich, Georgí Josifovich	18 Dec. 1998
Guth, Paul	29 Oct. 1997
Habeck, Fritz	—
*Hadjiolov, Asen. A.	—
Hallgrímsson, Geir	1 Sept. 1998
Halstead, John G. H.	—
Ham, James Milton	16 Sept. 1997
Hammond Innes, Ralph	10 June 1998
Häring, Bernhard	3 July 1998
Harsch, Joseph Close	3 June 1998
Hawkes, John	15 May 1998
Haxel, Otto Philipp Leonhard	—
Herbert, Zbigniew	28 July 1998
Heron, Patrick	20 March 1999
Herzberg, Gerhard	3 March 1999
Heslop-Harrison, John	July 1998
Hitchings, George Herbert	27 Feb. 1998
Hodgkin, Sir Alan Lloyd	20 Dec. 1998
Hodson, Henry Vincent	27 March 1999
Holub, Miroslav	14 July 1998
Hoover, Herbert William Jr.	19 May 1998
Hughes, Ted	29 Oct. 1998
Hunt, Baron; John Hunt	8 Nov. 1998
Hunt of Tanworth, Baron; John Joseph Benedict Hunt	8 Nov. 1998
Hussein Ibn Talal, King of Jordan	7 Feb. 1999
Ianni, Ronald William	—
Jackson, Gen. Sir William Godfrey Fothergill	12 March 1997
Jaeger, Richard	—

Jones, Geraint Iwan	3 May 1998
Jung, Nawab Mir Nawaz (M. Mir Khan)	—
Kadomtsev, Boris Borisovich	19 Aug. 1998
Kalmykov, Yury Khamzatovich	17 Dec. 1996
Kanin, Garson	13 March 1999
Kaske, Karlheinz	27 Sept. 1998
Kazin, Alfred	5 June 1998
*Keller, Andrew	7 Feb. 1999
Kemball, Charles	4 Sept. 1998
Kendall, Henry W.	15 Feb. 1999
Khalifa, H.H. Sheikh Isa bin Salman al-	6 March 1999
Killanin, 3rd Baron; Rt. Hon. Michael Morris	25 April 1999
Kinoshita, Keisuke	30 Dec. 1998
Knudsen, Semon Emil	6 July 1998
Koiter, Warner Tjardus	—
Kubrick, Stanley	7 March 1999
Kudsi, Nazem el	6 Feb. 1998
Kurosawa, Akira	6 Sept. 1998
Kurti, Nicholas	24 Nov. 1998
Ladgham, Bahi	13 April 1998
Latarjet, Raymond	3 June 1998
Laxness, Halldor	8 Feb. 1998
Leontief, Wassily	5 Feb. 1999
Lewin, Baron; Adm. of the Fleet Terence Thornton Lewin	23 Jan. 1999
Lhermitte, François Augustin	24 July 1998
Lighthill, Sir James	17 July 1998
Lilly, Malcolm Douglas	18 May 1998
Lindhard, Jens	—
Lini, Father Walter Hadye	21 Feb. 1999
Lloyd, George Walter Selwyn	3 July 1998
Long, Gerald	8 Nov. 1998
Lopes-Graça, Fernando	—
Lourié, Sylvain	27 June 1998
Lowry, Baron; Robert Lynd Erskine Lowry	15 Jan. 1999
Luhmann, Niklas	6 Nov. 1998
*McCrea, Sir William Hunter	25 April 1999
McDowall, Roddy	3 Oct. 1998
*McElroy, William David	17 Feb. 1999
MacGuigan, Hon. Mark Rudolph	—
McLennan, Sir Ian Munro	25 Oct. 1998
Mainsarra, Brig.-Gen. Ibrahim Barre	8 April 1999
Maltby, John Newcombe	13 Sept. 1998
Marais, Jean	8 Nov. 1998
Marples, Brian John	4 Oct. 1997
*Marston, Robert Quarles	14 March 1999
Masani, Minoo	27 May 1998
Mason, Philip	25 Jan. 1999
Massey, Daniel Raymond	25 March 1998
Medearis, Donald Norman, Jr.	—
Melchers, (Johann) Georg (Friedrich)	—
Mellish, Baron; Robert Joseph Mellish	10 May 1998
Mellon, Paul	Feb. 1999
Mende, Erich	6 May 1998
Menuhin, Yehudi	12 March 1999
Mercure, Jean	24 June 1998
Mezhelaitis, Eduardas Beniamino	6 June 1997
Mitchell, George Francis	25 Nov. 1997
Mitchison, Naomi	11 Jan. 1999
Modai, Itzhak	14 May 1998
Mokhehle, Ntsu	6 Jan. 1999
Moore, Brian	11 Jan. 1999
Moro, Peter	10 Oct. 1998
Motesiczky, Marie-Louise von	10 June 1996
Murdoch, Dame (Jean) Iris	9 Feb. 1999
Mutt, Viktor	9 Sept. 1998
Newton, Sir (Leslie) Gordon	31 Aug. 1998
Nguyen Co Thach	10 April 1998
Nicholas, Herbert George	3 July 1998
Nutting, Rt. Hon. Sir (Harold) Anthony	23 Feb. 1999
O'Neil, Thomas Francis	14 March 1998
Otumfuo Nana Opoku Ware II	25 Feb. 1999
Pacheco Areco, Jorge	29 July 1998
Pakula, Alan J.	19 Nov. 1998
Parker, Maynard Michael	16 Oct. 1998
Paton, Sir (Thomas) Angus (Lyall)	7 April 1999
Patterson, Gardner	26 June 1998
Pedersen, Olaf	3 Dec. 1997
Perkins, James Alfred	20 Aug. 1998
Phillips of Ellesmere, Baron; David Chilton Phillips	23 Feb. 1999
Pitzer, Kenneth Sanborn	26 Dec. 1997
Playfair, Sir Edward Wilder	21 March 1999
*Pliatzky, Sir Leo	4 May 1999
Pospelov, Germogen Sergeyevich	4 Nov. 1998
Prate, Alain	11 Sept. 1997
Prey, Hermann	23 July 1998
Prokhorov, Yevgeny Maratovich	1998
Prokoshkin, Yuriy Dmitriyevich	1 March 1997
Qian Zhongshu	19 Dec. 1998
Quilliot, Roger	17 July 1998
Radford, Courtenay Arthur Ralegh	27 Dec. 1998
Rafael, Gideon	10 Feb. 1999
Rayner, Baron; Derek George Rayner	26 June 1998
Reed, Oliver	2 May 1999
*Reedy, George Edward	21 March 1999
Reines, Frederick	26 Aug. 1998
Relly, Gavin Walter Hamilton	10 Jan. 1999
Reshtia, Sayed Qassem	26 March 1998
Robbins, Jerome	29 July 1998
Robotham, Hon. Sir Lascelles (Lister)	19 Feb. 1996
Rodbell, Martin	7 Dec. 1998
Rokhlin, Lieut.-Gen. Lev Yakovlevich	3 July 1998
*Rota, Gian-Carlo	19 April 1999
Rothermere, 3rd Viscount; Vere Harold Esmond Harmsworth	1 Sept. 1998
Rothschild, Baron Robert	—
Roux, Ambroise Marie Casimir	4 April 1999
Rouxel, Jean	19 March 1998
Rowland, Roland W. ("Tiny")	24 July 1998
Ru Zhijuan	1998
Rybakov, Anatoliy Naumovich	23 Dec. 1998
Sachs, Robert Green	14 April 1999
Sainsbury, Baron; Alan John Sainsbury	21 Oct. 1998
Sanford, Terry	18 April 1998
*Schawlow, Arthur Leonard	28 April 1999
Schnittke, Alfred	3 Aug. 1998
Schwarzschild, Martin	—
Seaborg, Glenn T(heodore)	25 Feb. 1999
Seefehlner, Egon Hugo	—
Segal, Irving Ezra	30 Aug. 1998
Sekhonyana, Evaristus Rets'elisitsoe	18 Nov. 1998
Seraphim, His Beatitude Archbishop	10 April 1998
Sertoli, Giandomenico	Jan. 1998
Seymour-Smith, Martin	1 July 1998
Sharif-Emami, Jafar	16 June 1998
Shepard, Alan B., Jr.	21 July 1998
Shevelyova, Yekaterina Vasilyevna	8 March 1998
Shu Tong	1998
Sijpesteijn, Pieter Johannes	May 1996
Sokolov, Vladimir Yevgenyevich	19 April 1998
Solovyev, Nikolay Nikolayevich	25 Sept. 1998
Soper, Baron; Rev. Donald Oliver Soper	22 Dec. 1998
Spilhaus, Athelstan Frederick	30 March 1998
Spivakovsky, Tossy	Aug. 1998
Stafleu, Frans Antonie	16 Dec. 1997
Stahr, Elvis J., Jr.	11 Nov. 1998
Starovoytova, Galiana Vasilyevna	20 Nov. 1998
*Steinberg, Saul	12 May 1999
Stoph, Willi	13 April 1999
Streibl, Max	11 Dec. 1998
Swaythling, 4th Baron; David Charles Samuel Montagu	1 July 1998
Tabarly, Eric Marcel Guy	13 June 1998
Thibau, Jacques Henri	28 Oct. 1998
Thode, Henry George	22 March 1997
Tilberis, Elizabeth	21 April 1999
Tillinghast, Charles C., Jr.	25 July 1998
Tuzo, Gen. Sir Harry Craufurd	7 Aug. 1998
Udall, Morris	12 Dec. 1998
Valentini Terrani, Lucia	11 June 1998
Varey, John Earl	28 March 1999
Vennamo, Veikko Emil Alexander	—
Vick, Sir (Francis) Arthur	2 Sept. 1998
Vieru, Anatol	9 Oct. 1998
Vonsovskiy, Sergey Vasiliyevich	28 Oct. 1996
Vu Van Mau	20 Aug. 1998
Wallace, George Corley	13 Sept. 1998
Way, Sir Richard	2 Oct. 1998
White, Raymond Walter Ralph	14 April 1998
Wichterle, Otto	18 Aug. 1998

Wilkie, Douglas Robert 21 May 1998
Wilkinson, John Frederick 13 Aug. 1998
Wu Yixia 1998

Xiao Yang 1998
Xin Fengxia 1998

Yang Shangkun 14 Sept. 1998
Ye Junjian (Chun-Chan Yeh) 1999
Yin Shoushi 1998
Yoshimura, Junzo 11 April 1997
Young, Freddie 1 Dec. 1998
Yu Qiuli, Lieut.-Gen. 1999
Zeidler, Sir David Ronald 16 March 1998
Zhivkov, Todor 5 Aug. 1998
Zorig, Sanjaasurengiin Oct. 1998

THE INTERNATIONAL WHO'S WHO

2000

A

AAKVAAG, Torvild; Norwegian business executive; b. 18 Jan. 1927, Baerum; s. of Torvild Aakvaag and Dagny Rivertz; m. Dagen Dahl 1952 (deceased); m. Ruth Kleppe 1990; trained as lawyer; attached to Norwegian Ministry of Foreign Affairs 1951–56; joined legal dept., Norsk Hydro 1956, Head of legal dept. 1967–70; Gen. Man. Petroleum Div. Norsk Hydro 1970–75, Exec. Vice-Pres. 1975, Deputy Pres. 1977, Pres. 1984–91, Chair. 1992–97. *Address:* c/o Norsk Hydro, Bygdoy alle 2 Oslo, Norway.

AARAAS, Hans Tandberg, DR.PHIL.; Norwegian professor of French literature; b. 21 July 1919, Skien; s. of the late Hans Aaraas and Hariet Aaraas; m. Kari Holter 1946; three s. two d.; ed. Univ. of Oslo; lecturer in Norwegian Language and Literature Univ. of Paris, Sorbonne 1949–53; Prof. of French Literature Univ. of Bergen 1961–86, Dean of Faculty 1968–70, Sr. Scholarship 1986–89; Bastian Prize for translation. *Publications:* Georges Bernanos 1959, Essai sur l'écrivain et le prêtre dans l'oeuvre de Bernanos 1967, Littérature et sacerdoce 1984, Peer Gynt A Dream of a Dreamer and his Dream 1995, translations, smaller studies and articles. *Address:* Paradisleitet 7, 5040 Paradis, Norway. *Telephone:* 55 91 01 09.

AARNES, Asbjørn Sigurd, D.PHIL.; Norwegian professor of European literature; b. 20 Dec. 1923, Vågbø; s. of Halvor Aarnes and Alida Olsen; m. Berit Alten 1950; one s. one d.; ed. Univ. of Oslo and Ecole Normale Supérieure, Paris; Prof. of European Literature, Univ. of Oslo 1964, Dir. Inst. d'études romanes 1966–70; Pres. Norwegian Acad. of Language and Literature 1966–84; mem. Norwegian Acad. of Science, various ed. bds. and cttees.; Chevalier, Ordre Nat. du Mérite; Chevalier, Légion d'honneur; Officier des palmes académiques. *Publications:* J. S. Welhaven 1955, Gérard de Nerval 1957, Nicolas Boileau 1961, The poetical phenomenon 1963, Dictionary of literary terms 1964, Pierre Le Moyne 1965, Ved Veiskille 1974, Maine de Biran 1976, Descartes Meditations 1980, French Thought and Philosophical Tradition 1981, Henri Bergson 1989, Perspektiver og profiler 1989, Cartesianische Perspektiven von Montaigne bis Paul Ricoeur 1991, Ed. Emmanuel Levinas, Den annens Humanisme 1993. *Leisure interests:* fishing. *Address:* Ostadalsveien 9, 0753 Oslo 7, Norway. *Telephone:* 22500789 (Home). *Fax:* 22500789.

AARON, David L., M.A.; American diplomatist; b. 21 Aug. 1938, Chicago; m. Chloe Aaron; one c.; ed. Occidental Coll. Calif. and Princeton Univ.; entered Foreign Service 1962; Political and Econ. Officer, Guayaquil, Ecuador; Int. Relations Officer, Dept. of State 1964–66; Political Officer, NATO, Paris 1966; Arms Control and Disarmament Agency; Sr. staff mem. Nat. Security Council 1972–74; Legis. Asst. to Sen. Walter Mondale 1974–75; Task Force Leader, Senate Select Cttee. on Intelligence 1975–76; mem. staff, Carter-Mondale presidential campaign; Transition Dir. with Nat. Security Council and CIA 1976–77; Deputy Asst. to Pres. for Nat. Security Affairs 1977–81; Vice-Pres. Oppenheimer & Co. Inc. 1981–85, Dir. Oppenheimer Int. 1984; Sr. adviser, Mondale presidential campaign; writer and lecturer, Lantz-Harris Agency 1985–93; consultant, 20th Century Fund 1990–92, Sr. Fellow 1992–93; U.S. Rep. to OECD 1993; U.S. Special Envoy for Cryptography 1996; Under-Sec. of Commerce for Int. Trade Nov. 1997–; Dr. h.c. (Occidental Coll.); Nat. Defense Medal. *Publications:* State Scarlet, Agent of Influence, Crossing by Night; articles in newspapers and journals. *Address:* Department of Commerce, International Trade Administration, 14th and Constitution Avenue, N.W., Washington, DC 20230, U.S.A. *Telephone:* (202) 482-2867. *Fax:* (202) 482-4821.

ABAKANOWICZ, Magdalena; Polish artist, weaver and sculptor; b. 20 June 1930, Falenty, nr. Warsaw; d. of Konstanty and Helena Abakanowicz; m. Jan Kosmowski 1956; ed. Warsaw Acad. of Fine Arts, mem. of ZAIKS Asscn. of authors; work includes monumental space forms of woven fibres, cycles of figurative sculptures of burlap, wood and clay, cast metal, stone, drawings, paintings with collage and gouache; Prof. 1979–90, Acad. of Fine Arts, Poznań; mem. Presidential Council for Culture 1992–; hon. mem. American Acad. of Arts and Letters 1996; Dr. h.c. (R.C.A.), London 1974, Rhode Island School of Design, Providence 1992; Minister of Culture and Art Prize (1st Class) 1965; Gold Medal VIII Int. Biennale of Arts, São Paulo 1965; State Prize 1972; Gottfried von Herder Prize 1979; Alfred Jurzykowski Foundation Prize 1982, Chevalier, Ordre des Arts et des Lettres, Paris 1985; Commdr.'s Cross, Order of Polonia Restituta, New York Sculpture Centre Award 1993, Leonardo da Vinci World Award of Arts 1997 and others. *Works:* Sculpture for Elbląg, relief woven composition for North Brabant Provincial Building, Netherlands; three-dimensional woven forms: Abakans Figurative sculptures, seated figures, Backs, Incarnations, War Games, Crowd; large outdoor installations: Katarsis (Italy), Negev (Israel), Space of Dragon (S. Korea), Space of Nine Figures (Germany), Becalmed Beings, Hiroshima, Sarcophagi in Glass Houses (U.S.A.), Manus (U.S.A.), Magnus (Italy); one-woman exhbns.: Zachęta State Gallery, Warsaw 1965, 1975, Kunsthaus Zürich 1968, Nat. Museum Stockholm 1970, Pasadena Art Museum 1970, Düsseldorf Kunsthalle 1972, Whitechapel Art Gallery, London 1975, Art Gallery of New South Wales, Sydney, Nat. Gallery of Victoria, Melbourne 1976, Henie-Onstad Foundation, Oslo, Sztuki, Łodz 1978, Musée d'Art Moderne de la Ville de Paris 1982, Museum of Contemporary Art, Chicago 1982, Musée d'Art Moderne, Montreal 1983, Xavier Fourcade Gallery, New York 1985, Virginia Museum of Fine Art, Richmond, Muku Gallery, Hiroshima 1987, Mücsarnok Palace of Exhbns., Budapest 1988, Turske a. Turske Gallery, Zürich 1988, Städel Kunstinstitut, Frankfurt 1989, Marlborough Gallery, New York 1989, 1993, Sezon Museum of Art, Tokyo 1991, Museum of Modern Art, Shiga 1991, Art Tower, Mito 1991, Hiroshima City Art Museum 1991, Walker Art Center, Minn. 1992, Inst. of Contemporary Art, New York, BWH, Kraków, Hiroshima City Museum 1993, Muzeum Sztuki, Łódź, Marlborough Gallery, Madrid, Fundació Miró, Mallorca 1994, Els Jardins de Can Altamira, Barcelona, Centre of Polish Sculpture, Orońsko, Centre for Contemporary Art, Warsaw, Yorks. Sculpture Park, Museum Royal Festival Hall, London, Museum Ludwig, Cologne, Hiroshima City Museum of Contemporary Art 1995; Oriel Mostyn, N. Wales, Centre for the Visual Arts, Charlottenborg, Exhbn. Hall, Copenhagen 1996, Marlborough Gallery, N.Y. 1997, Miami Art Museum 1997, Galeria Starmacha, Cracow 1998; group exhbns.: Biennale: Biennale de Lausanne 1962–79; Biennale of Art, São Paulo 1965, 1979, Venice Biennale 1968, 1980, ROSC, Dublin 1980, Nat. Gallery, Berlin 1982, Museum of Ateneum, Helsinki 1983, Biennale of Sculpture, Middelheim, Antwerp 1983, Biennale of Art, Sydney 1986, Storm Kings Art Center, New York 1987, Hirshhorn Museum, Washington, DC 1988, Fuji Sankei Biennale, Japan 1993, Royal Festival Hall, London, Museum Ludwig, Cologne, Hiroshima City Museum of Contemporary Art 1995, Marwan Hoss Gallery, Paris 1997, Guggenheim Museum, Bilbao 1997–98. *Leisure interests:* swimming, walking in the countryside and forests. *Address:* ul. Bzowa 1, 02-708 Warsaw, Poland. *Telephone:* (22) 486379.

ABALAKIN, Victor Kuzmich; Russian astronomer; b. 27 Aug. 1930; m.; three c.; ed. Odessa State Univ.; jr. researcher, Inst. of Geophysics, U.S.S.R. Acad. of Sciences 1953–55, Inst. of Theoretical Astronomy, U.S.S.R. Acad. of Sciences 1955–57, Head of Div. 1965–83; researcher, Odessa Astronomy Observatory 1960–63; docent, Odessa State Univ. 1963–65; Dir. Main Astronomy Observatory, Russian Acad. of Sciences 1983–; corresp. mem. U.S.S.R. (now Russian) Acad. of Sciences 1987–; main research in theoretical astronomy; U.S.S.R. State Prize. *Publications:* 5 books including Optical Localisation of the Moon 1981, numerous papers. *Address:* Main Astronomy Observatory, Pulkovskoye shosse 65, korp. 1, 196140 St. Petersburg, Russia. *Telephone:* (812) 298 2242 (Office); (812) 277 2881 (Home).

ABALKHAIL, Sheikh Mohamed Ali, B.A.; Saudi Arabian government official and financial executive; b. 1935, Buraida; s. of Ali Abdullah Abalkhail and Fatima Abdulaziz Othaim; m. 1966; two s. two d.; ed. Cairo Univ.; began career as Asst. Dir. of Office of Minister of Communications, later Dir.; Dir.-Gen. of Inst. of Public Admin.; Deputy Minister of Finance and Nat. Econ., then Vice-Minister, Minister of State, Minister for Finance and Nat. Econ. 1975–95; Chair. of Bd., Saudi Int. Bank, London; Chair. Center for Econ. and Man. Studies, mem. JP Morgan Int. Council; decorations from Belgium, Egypt, France, Niger, Pakistan, Saudi Arabia, Sudan, Germany, Morocco, Spain. *Leisure interests:* reading, some sports. *Address:* P.O. Box 287, Riyadh 11411, Saudi Arabia; Saudi International Bank, 1 Knightsbridge, London, SW1X 7XS, England. *Telephone:* (01) 478-1722, (01) 476-6965 (Riyadh). *Fax:* (01) 478-1904 (Riyadh).

ABALKIN, Leonid Ivanovich; Russian economist; b. 5 May 1930, Moscow; m. Abalkina (Satarova) Anna Vartanovna 1953; one s. one d.; ed. Inst. of Nat. Econ.; mem. CPSU 1956–91, mem. Cen. Cttee 1990–91; Deputy Head Acad. of Social Sciences of the Central Cttee. 1976–89, Head Faculty of Political Econ. 1978–86; Dir. Inst. of the Econ., Acad. of Sciences 1986–; mem. U.S.S.R. (now Russian) Acad. of Sciences 1987–, mem. of Presidium 1988–; Columnist, Trud; mem. ed. bds. of EKO and Voprosy ekonomiki;

U.S.S.R. People's Deputy 1989–91; Deputy Prime Minister, Chair. Comm. for Econ. Reforms 1989–91; adviser to Pres. Gorbachev 1991; mem. Govt.'s Econ Crisis Group 1998–; Ed.-in-Chief Voprosy Ekonomiki 1992–. *Publications:* Political Economy and Economic Policy 1970, Final Economic Results 1978, Direction—Acceleration 1986, New Type of Economic Thinking 1987, Perestroika—Ways and Problems 1989, Missed Chance 1991, To the Goal through Crisis: Destiny of Economic Reform 1992, At the Crossroads 1993, The Crisis Grip 1994, To Self-Perception of Russia 1995, Zigzags of Fate: Disappointments and Hopes 1996, Postponed Changes: The Lost Year 1997, Russia: The Choice 1998 and numerous articles in Soviet press on theoretical problems of political economy under socialism. *Leisure interests:* chess, gardening. *Address:* Institute of the Econ., Academy of Sciences of Russia, 117218 Moscow, Nakhimovsky Prospekt 32, Russia. *Telephone:* 129 02 54 (Office); 135 1085 (Home). *Fax:* 310-70 01.

ABASHIDZE, Aslan; Georgian politician and economist; b. 20 July 1938, Batumi; m. Maguli Gogitidze; one s. one d.; ed. Batumi State Inst., Tbilisi State Univ.; with Komsomol; Dir. Tech. Colls. No. 44, No. 105; Deputy Chair. Exec. Cttee., Public Deputies Council of Batumi; Minister of Civil Service, Autonomous Repub. of Ajaria, Georgia 1984–86; Deputy Minister of Civil Service, Repub. of Georgia; mem. Georgian Parl., Deputy Chair. 1990–95; Chair. Supreme Council of Autonomous Repub. of Ajaria, Georgia 1991–; est. Georgian Union of Revival Party 1991; Hon. Pres. Georgian Orientalist Assen.; mem. Int. Ind. Bureau's Council of European Parl.'s Humanitarian Subjects, Geneva; Hon. mem. Georgian Acad. of Political Science and Information; Order of Friendship; rank of Maj.-Gen. *Leisure interests:* drawing, model-making. *Address:* Gogebashvili Street 4, Apt. 24, Batumi 384503, Autonomous Republic of Ajaria, Georgia.

ABAZA, Mohamed Mahir, B.SC.; Egyptian politician and engineer; b. 12 March 1930, Sharkia; s. of Muhamed Osman Abaza; m. Ezdehar Abo El-Ela 1955; one s. one d.; ed. Cairo Univ.; engineer Ministry of Public Works 1951–64; Man. Egyptian Gen. Electricity Authority 1964–66; Dir.-Gen. Egyptian Electricity Authority 1966–72, Man. Dir. for Studies and Projects 1973–74; Insp. Gen. Rural Electrification Authority 1972–73; First Under-Sec. of State Ministry of Electricity and Energy 1975–80, Minister 1980–; mem. numerous comms., Inst. of Electric and Electronic Engineers, Thomas Alva Edison Foundation; Order of the Repub. (First Class, Egypt, France), Royal Order of the Poiar Star (Grand Cross, Sweden), Grand Cross of the Order of Merit (Germany, Italy). *Leisure interests:* philately, photography, reading, swimming. *Address:* Ministry of Electricity and Energy, Sharia Ramses, Cairo (Nasr City), Egypt. *Telephone:* (2) 2616317. *Fax:* (2) 2616302.

ABBADO, Claudio; Italian conductor; b. 26 June 1933, Milan; Music Dir. Teatro alla Scala Milano 1968–86, London Symphony Orchestra 1979–88, Vienna State Opera 1986–91; founder European Community Youth Orchestra 1978; Gen. Music Dir. of Vienna 1987–; founder and Music Dir. Gustav Mahler Jugend Orchestra 1988; founder and Artistic Dir. Modern Vienna (festival of contemporary art) 1988, Vienna Int. Competition for Composers 1991, Encounters in Berlin (Chamber Music Festival) 1992; Competitions of the Salzburg Easter Festival 1994; Artistic Dir. Berlin Philharmonic Orchestra 1989–; Artistic Dir. Easter Festival Salzberg 1994; Gran Croce d'Italia 1984, Cross of the Légion d'honneur, Bundesverdienstkreuz (Germany) 1992, Ehrenring of the City of Vienna 1994, etc.; Dr. h.c. (Aberdeen) 1986, (Ferrara) 1990, (Cambridge) 1994; recipient of major int. prizes for recordings. *Address:* Berliner Philharmonisches Orchester, Matthäikirchstrasse 1, 10785 Berlin, Germany.

ABBAS, Mahmoud, (alias Abu Mazen); Palestinian politician and civil servant; b. 1935, Safad, Galilea; ed. Damascus Univ., Moscow Univ.; civil servant U.A.E. –1967; mem. Fatah Cen. Cttee. 1967; elected to PLO Exec. Cttee. 1980, Head Pan-Arab and Int. Affairs Dept. 1984; participated in Middle East Peace Conf. Washington and in Norwegian-mediated peace talks with Israel. *Address:* c/o Palestinian National Authority, Jericho Area, West Bank.

ABBOUD, A. Robert, M.B.A., LL.B.; American banker; b. 29 May 1929, Boston, Mass.; s. of Alfred Abboud and Victoria Abboud; m. Joan Grover Abboud 1955; one s. two d.; ed. Harvard Coll., Harvard Law School, Harvard Business School; Asst. Cashier, Int. Dept., First Nat. Bank of Chicago 1960, Asst. Vice-Pres. Int. 1962, Vice-Pres. 1964, Sr. Vice-Pres. 1969, Exec. Vice-Pres. 1972, Vice-Chair. 1973, Deputy Chair. of Bd. 1974–75, Chair. of Bd. 1975–80; Pres., C.O.O. and Dir. Occidental Petroleum Corpn. 1980–84; Pres. A. Robert Abboud and Co., Fox Grove, Ill., 1984–; Chair. Braeburn Capital Inc. 1984–92; Chair. and C.E.O. First City Bancorp of Tex. Inc., Houston 1988–91, First City Nat. Bank of Houston 1988–91; fmr. Dir. of numerous cos.; Dir. Cities Service 1982–; Hart, Schaffner and Marx, AAR Corpn., ICN Biomedicals and ICN Pharmaceuticals, Inland Steel Co. *Publications:* Introduction of U.S. Commercial Paper in Foreign Markets—Premature and Perilous? 1970, A Proposed Course for U.S. Trade and Investment Policies 1971, A Proposal to Help Reverse the Narrowing Balance in the U.S. Balance of Trade 1971, The Outlook for a New Monetary System 1971, Opportunities for Foreign Banks in Singapore 1971, The International Competitiveness of U.S. Banks and the U.S. Economy 1972, Money in the Bank: How Safe is it? 1988. *Address:* A. Robert Abboud & Co., 212 Stone Hill Center, Fox River Grove, IL 60021 (Office); 209 Braeburn Road, Barrington Hills, IL 60010, U.S.A. (Home).

ABDALLAH, Ibrahim Saad El Din, PH.D.; Egyptian professor of business administration; b. 25 May 1925, Sharkia; m. Alia Hassan Hosny 1951; two s. one d.; ed. Cairo Univ., Univ. of Illinois; demonstrator Business Admin., Cairo Univ. 1946; Marketing Lecturer, Cairo Univ. 1955; with Cen. Ministry of Educ., Cairo 1959–60; with Ministry of Planning 1960–61; Sr. Expert, Sec. Gen., N.I.P. 1961–62; Prof. Man.; mem. Bd. Dirs. N.I.M.D. 1962–64; Under-Sec. Cen. Auditing Authority 1964–71; UNDP Project Man., Arab Inst. of Planning 1972–80; Dir. Third World Forum, Cairo 1981–. *Publications:* Principles of Marketing 1958, Managerial Policies and Socio-Economic Changes 1970, Movement of Arab Workers (co-author) 1980, The Crisis of the Socialist System 1989. *Leisure interests:* reading, walking. *Address:* 39 Dokki Street, P.O. Box 43, Orman, Cairo, Egypt.

ABDEL HALIM ABU-GHAZALA, Marshal Mohamed, M.SC.(ECON).; Egyptian politician and army officer; b. 1 Jan. 1930, El Behaira; m. 1953; two s. three d.; ed. War Coll., Egypt, U.S. Army War Coll.; fought in Palestine War 1948, Suez War 1956, Wars of June 1967 and Oct. 1973; rank of Major 1958, Col. 1966, Major-Gen. 1974, Lieut.-Gen. 1980, Marshal 1982; Commdr. of an Artillery Brigade 1968, an Artillery Div. 1969–71; Commdr. 2nd Field Army Artillery 1971 and 1973; Chief of Staff, Artillery Corps 1972 and 1973; Dir. Mil. Intelligence and Reconnaissance Dept. 1974–76; Defence Attaché, Embassy, U.S.A. 1976–80; Chief of Staff, Armed Forces 1980–81, C.-in-C. March 1981; also Minister of Defence and Mil. Production 1980–89; Deputy Prime Minister 1982–89; Asst. to Pres. of Egypt April 1989–; numerous awards and medals. *Publications include:* Soviet Military Strategy, History of Art of War (five vols.), The Guns Opened Fire at Noon (October War), Mathematics and Warfare, and 17 books on military affairs. *Leisure interests:* reading, chess, tennis, basketball, soccer. *Address:* c/o Presidential Palace, Abdeen, Cairo, Egypt.

ABDEL-LATIF, Ahmed; Saudi Arabian banker; fmr. Deputy Gov. Saudi Arabian Monetary Agency (SAMA); Man. Dir. Riyad Bank; Pres., C.E.O. Arab Banking Corpn. BSC 1995–. *Address:* Arab Banking Corporation, P.O. Box 5698, ABC Tower, Diplomatic Area, Manama, Bahrain. *Telephone:* 532235. *Fax:* 533163.

ABDEL-MALEK, Anouar I., D.LIT., PH.D.; Egyptian academic and writer; b. 23 Oct. 1924, Cairo; s. of Iskandar Abdel-Malek and Alice Zaki Ibrahim; m. Karin Konigseider 1961 (divorced 1965); one d.; ed. Coll. de la Sainte Famille, British Inst., Ain Shams Univ., Cairo and Univ. de Paris-Sorbonne; leading mem. Egyptian Nat. and Progressive Movt. 1941–; official, Nat. Bank of Egypt, Cairo 1941–42, Crédit Foncier Egyptien, Cairo 1943–46; Jt. Ed. Actualité, Cairo 1950–59; journalist, Le Journal d'Egypte, Cairo 1950–59; contrib. to Rose el-Yusef, Al-Magallah, Al Masa, Cairo 1950–59; teacher of philosophy, Lycée Al-Hurriya, Cairo 1958–59; Research Asst., Ecole Pratique des Hautes Etudes, Paris 1959–60; Research lecturer, later Research Reader, Research Prof., C.N.R.S., Paris 1960–, Dir. of Research 1970–90, Hon. Dir. 1991–; Project Co-ordinator, The UN Univ., Tokyo 1976–86; Prof. of Sociology and Politics, Faculty of Int. Relations, Ristumeikan Univ., Kyoto 1989–92; Adviser Nat. Centre for Middle East Studies, Cairo 1990–; mem. Bd. and Adviser, Centre for Asian Studies, Cairo Univ. 1994–; mem. Exec. Cttee., EEC Int. Sociological Assen. 1970–74, Vice-Pres. 1974–78; Visiting Prof., Univ. of Santiago, Chile 1969, Ain Shams 1975, Quebec 1986, Cairo 1992; Visiting Fellow, Clare Coll., Cambridge 1985, Life Assoc. 1986–; Ed. Library of the Contemporary Orient 1989, Ideas of the New World 1991; Prix du Jury de l'Amitié Franco-Arabe, Paris 1970, Gold Medal, Nasser Higher Mil. Acad. 1976. *Publications include:* Egypte, société militaire 1962, Idéologie et Renaissance Nationale: l'Egypte moderne 1969, La Pensée Politique Arabe Contemporaine 1970, Sociologie de l'Impérialisme 1970, La Dialectique Sociale 1972, Intellectual Creativity in Endogenous Culture 1983, The Transformation of the World 1985, The Egyptian Street and Thought 1989, Creativity and the Civilization Project 1991. *Leisure interests:* music, opera, ballet, theatre, cooking, swimming, walking, table-tennis, travelling, meditation. *Address:* 48 Nehru Street, 11351 Heliopolis (Cairo), Egypt (Home). *Telephone:* 33-1-44 23 78 01 (OFfice); 33-1-46 40 62 52 (Home). *Fax:* 20-2-244 3977.

ABDEL MEGUID, Ahmed Esmat, PH.D.; Egyptian diplomatist; b. 22 March 1923, Alexandria; s. of Mohamed Fahmy Abdel Meguid; m. Eglal Abou-Hamda 1950; three s.; ed. Faculty of Law, Alexandria Univ. and Univ. of Paris; Attaché and Sec., Embassy, London 1950–54; Head British Desk, Ministry of Foreign Affairs 1954–56, Asst. Dir. Legal Dept. 1961–63, Head Cultural and Tech. Assistance Dept. 1967–68; Counsellor, Perm. Mission to European Office of UN, Geneva 1957–61; Minister Counsellor, Embassy, Paris 1963–67; Official Spokesman of Govt. and Head Information Dept. 1968–69; Amb. to France 1969–70; Minister of State for Cabinet Affairs 1970–72; Head, Perm. Del. to UN 1972–82; Minister of Foreign Affairs 1984–91; Deputy Prime Minister 1985–91; Sec.-Gen. League of Arab States May 1991–; Chair. Cairo Preparatory Conf. for Geneva Peace Conf. 1977; Dir. Cairo Int. Arbitration Centre; mem. Politbureau, Nat. Democratic Party, Int. Law Assen., Advisory Council of the Inst. for Int. Studies, took part in UN confs. on the Law of the Sea 1959, on Consular Relations 1963 and on the Law of Treaties 1969; ordre nat. du Mérite 1967, Grand Croix 1971, 1st Class Decoration, Arab Repub. of Egypt 1970, and numerous foreign decorations. *Publications:* several articles in Revue égyptienne de droit international. *Address:* League of Arab States, Arab League Building, Tahrir Square, Cairo; 78 El Nile Street, Apt. 23, Giza, Cairo, Egypt (Home). *Telephone:* (2) 5750511.

ABDEL-RAHMAN, Aisha, PH.D. (pen name **Bint el-Shati**); Egyptian writer and university professor; ed. Cairo Univ.; Asst. Lecturer, Cairo Univ. 1939; Literary Critic Al Ahram 1942; Inspector in Arabic Languages and Literature, Ministry of Educ. 1942; Lecturer in Arabic, Ain Shams Univ. 1950–57, Asst. Prof. 1957–62, Prof. of Arabic Literature and Chair., Univ. Coll. for Women 1962–; mem. Higher Council of Arts and Letters 1960–; State Prize 1936, Acad. of Arabic Language Award for Textual Studies 1950, for Short Story 1954. *Publications:* Rissalet el Ghofram by Abul Ala'a 1950, New Values in Arabic Literature 1961, The Koran: Literary Interpretation 1962, Ibn Seeda's Arabic Dictionary 1962, Contemporary Arab Women Poets 1963; six books on illustrious women of Islam; two novels; four vols. of short stories. *Address:* 13 Agam Street, Heliopolis, Cairo, Egypt.

ABDELLAH, Faye Glenn, B.S., M.A., ED.D.; American nurse and psychologist; ed. Teachers' Coll., Columbia Univ.; first woman to be apptd. Deputy Surgeon General, U.S. Public Health Service 1981–89; Dean (a.i.) Univ. of Health Sciences 1993–96; Dean, Prof. Grad. School of Nursing, Uniformed Services Univ. of Health Sciences 1993–; numerous academic and professional awards including six hon. degrees. *Publications include:* Better Patient Care through Nursing Research (with E. Levine) 1986; more than 135 publs. (books, monographs and articles). *Leisure interests:* piano and swimming. *Address:* 3713 Chanel Road, Annandale, VA 22003, U.S.A. *Telephone:* (301) 443-4000.

ABDELLAH, Slaheddine, B.A.; Tunisian diplomatist; b. 25 March 1932, Kairouan; m. Nayla Ben Milad 1964; three c.; ed. Coll. Sadiki and Univ. of Lyon; joined Tunisian diplomatic service; Sec. Cairo 1957; Chargé d'Affaires, Tripoli 1958; Counsellor, Rabat 1959–60; Ministry of Foreign Affairs 1960–65; Minister Plenipotentiary, Washington, D.C. 1965–68; Amb. to Ethiopia (also accred, to Kenya, Tanzania, Malawi) and Perm. Rep. to OAU 1968–70; Amb. to Lebanon (also accred. to Jordan, Syria and Iraq) 1970–73; Sec. of State for Information 1974; Amb. to Egypt and Perm. Rep. to Arab League 1975–78; Amb. to Morocco 1978–84; Amb. Diplomatic Adviser 1985–86; Amb. Rep. to Arab League 1986–89; Amb. to Russia 1990–92, to Egypt 1993; Perm. Rep. to UN 1994–97; decorations from Tunisia, Egypt, Morocco, Lebanon. *Leisure interests:* swimming, golf, Arabic poetry and literature, history. *Address:* c/o Ministry of Foreign Affairs, place du Gouvernement, la Kasbah, Tunis, Tunisia.

ABDÉRÉMANE HALIDI, Ibrahim; Comoran politician; b. Anjouan Is.; fmr. teacher of philosophy; mem. Chuma Party; Minister of Interior 1990; leader Union des démocrates pour le développement (UDD); Prime Minister of the Comoros Jan.–May 1993; Minister of Transport, Tourism, Posts and Telecommunications 1996–97. *Address:* c/o Ministry of Transport, Tourism, Posts and Telecommunications, Moroni, The Comoros.

ABDESSALAM, Belaid, B.A.; Algerian politician; b. July 1928, Dehemcha; m.; four s. two d.; ed. Grenoble Univ.; fmr. Hon. Pres. Union Générale des Etudiants Musulmans Algériens (UGEMA); Instructor Front de Libération Nationale (FLN) School, Oujda; Political Adviser in Cabinet of M. Ben Khedda 1961; in charge of Econ. Affairs, FLN Provisional Exec. 1962; Pres., Dir.-Gen. Soc. Nat. pour la Recherche, la Production, le Transport, la Transformation et la Commercialisation des Hydrocarbures (SONATRACH) 1964–66; Minister of Industry and Energy 1966–77 (retaining SONATRACH post 1965–66), of Light Industry 1977–84; Prime Minister of Algeria and Minister of Economy 1992–93; Pres. of Special Econ. Comm. of Cen. Cttee. of FLN 1979–81; Chair. Council Org. of Arab Petroleum Exporting Countries 1974. *Address:* c/o Office of the Prime Minister, Palais du Gouvernement, Algiers, Algeria.

ABDNOR, James, B.A.; American politician; b. 13 Feb. 1923, Kennebec, S.D.; s. of Samuel J. and Mary (Wehby) Abdnor; ed. Univ. of Nebraska; teacher, coach, Presho, S.D. 1950–51; farmer, rancher, Kennebec 1945–; mem. 93rd–96th Congresses from S.D.; Chair. S.D. Young Republicans 1953–55; mem. S.D. Senate 1956–69, Pres. a.i. 1967–68; Lieut.-Gov. S.D. 1969–70; Senator from S. Dakota 1981–87; Admin. Small Business Administration, Washington 1987–89. *Address:* Kennebec, SD 57544, U.S.A.

ABDOU, Ahmed; Comoran politician; fmr. special adviser to Pres. Ahmed Abdallah Abderrahman; Prime Minister of the Comoros 1996–97.

ABDOULAYE, Souley; Niger politician and business executive; fmr. banker; Minister of Commerce, Transport and Tourism 1993–94; Prime Minister of Niger 1994–95; Minister of Transport 1996; mem. Convention démocratique et social-Rahana (CDS-Rahana). *Address:* c/o Ministry of Transport, Niamey, Niger.

ABDOU MADI, Mohamed; Comoran politician and tax inspector; m.; four c.; ed. Algeria, Poland; tax insp. Moroni 1988; convicted of fraud, served sentence as a domestic servant; Perm. Sec. CTRAP (org. funded by UN Devt. Programme to implement reforms in civil service) –1994; Sec.-Gen. Rassemblement pour la Démocratie et le Renouveau (RDR); Prime Minister of the Comoros 1994, also responsible for Public Works; Minister of Justice, Public Affairs, Employment, Professional Training, Administrative Decentralization and Institutional Reform 1998–. *Address:* Ministry of Justice, Public Affairs, Employment, Professional Training, Administrative Decentralization and Institutional Reform, B.P. 520, Moroni, The Comoros. *Telephone:* (73) 2411.

ABDRASHITOV, Vadim Yusupovich; Russian film director; b. 19 Jan. 1945, Kharkov, Ukraine; s. of Yusup Sh. Abdrashitov and Galina Abdrashitov; m. Natella G. Toidze; one s. one d.; graduated VGIK, Moscow, pupil of Romm; R.S.F.S.R. State Prize 1984, People's Artist of Russia. *Films include:* Witness for the Defence (U.S.S.R. Riga Prize) 1977, The Turning 1978, Foxhunting 1980, The Train has Stopped 1982, The Parade of the Planets 1984, Plumbum, or a Dangerous Game 1986 (Gold Medal at Venice Festival 1987), The Servant (Alfred Bauer Prize 1989) 1988, Armavir 1991, The Play for a Passenger 1995 (Silver Bear Award, Berlin Festival 1995), Time for a Dancer 1997. *Address:* 3d. Frunzenskaya 9, Apt. 211, 119270 Moscow, Russia. *Telephone:* (095) 242-35-54.

ABDUL, Paula; American pop singer and choreographer; b. 19 June 1962, Calif.; d. of Harry Abdul and Lorraine Abdul; m. 1st Emilio Estevez 1992 (divorced 1994); m. 2nd Brad Beckerman 1996; ed. Van Nuys High School, California State Univ.; choreographed works include: Janet Jackson's videos Torture, Control, When I Think of You, Nasty, and work for Duran Duran, Toto, The Pointer Sisters, ZZ Top, City of Crime video from Dragnet, Dolly Parton Christmas Special (TV), Tracey Ullman Show (TV), and films Coming to America, Bull Durham, The Doors; recordings include: Forever Your Girl 1988, Spellbound 1991.

ABDUL AL AZIZ BASHIR, Munir; Iraqi composer and performer; b. 28 Sept. 1930, Mosul; s. of Bashir Abdul Aziz; m. Gecsy Iren 1961; two s.; ed. high school and Fine Arts Inst. Baghdad; Instr. Fine Arts Acad. 1946–60; Dir. Community Arts Acad. 1950–56; Head, Music Dept. Baghdad Radio and TV 1949–60; Art Adviser and Gen. Dir. Music Dept. Iraqi Ministry of Culture and Information 1973–93; Gen. Dir. Babylon Int. Festival 1986–91; Vice-Pres. Int. Music Council (UNESCO) 1986–91; Sec.-Gen. Arab Acad. of Music 1974–; has performed solo Ud in more than 50 countries since 1954 and made many recordings; recipient of numerous honours and awards including Tchaikovsky Medal (U.S.S.R.), Chopin Medal (Poland), UNESCO Int. Prize and decorations from France, Spain, Poland, Italy, Jordan, Cuba etc. *Leisure interest:* reading. *Address:* Arab Academy of Music, Al-Mansour, P.O. Box 1650, Baghdad; The National Music Conservatory, P.O. Box 926687, Baghdad, Iraq. *Telephone:* 962-2-687620. *Fax:* 962-2-687621.

ABDUL LATIF, Haji Ibrahim, M.PHIL, M.LITT.; Brunei university lecturer and government official; b. 8 Jan. 1944, Brunei; m. Hajah Habibah binti Abdullah 1972; four s. one d.; ed. SMJA Malay School, Brunei, SOAS English School, Brunei, East West Centre, Univ. of Hawaii, British Museum Dept. of Ethnography, London and Univs. of N. Queensland and Cambridge; Research Asst. Brunei Museum 1965–70, Research Officer 1971–79, Curator of Ethnography 1980–83; Head of Research Unit, History Centre, Brunei 1983–86, Deputy Head 1986–88; Sr. lecturer, Univ. of Brunei Darussalam 1989–, Dir. Acad. of Brunei Studies 1993; Sec. Nat. Supreme Council, Malay Islam Monarchy, Brunei (ex officio); Pekerma Setia Brunei; Brunei Long Service Medal. *Publications:* A Short History of Brunei State Crest 1970, Bandar Seri Begawan (pictorial essay) 1976. *Address:* Academy of Brunei Studies, University of Brunei Darussalam, Bandar Seri Begawan 2028 (Office); 2, Simpang 254-23, Ban 3, Jan Mulaut, Sengkurong 2780, Brunei (Home). *Telephone:* 02-421518, 02-427001 Ext. 459 (Office); 02-672068 (Home). *Fax:* 02-427003 (Office).

ABDUL LATIF, Haji Jaya bin; Brunei diplomatist; b. 1939; m.; six c.; ed. Manchester Univ.; Govt. Deputy Agent, London 1981–82; Commr. to Malaysia 1982–84, High Commr. 1984–86; Amb. to the Philippines Oct. 1986–87; Perm Rep. of Brunei Darussalam to the UN 1987–93; Pres. Brunei State Youth Council 1977–80; fmr. mem. World Assembly of Youth, World Assembly of Muslim Youth and Asian Youth Council. *Address:* c/o Ministry of Foreign Affairs, Jalan Subok, Bandar Seri Begawan 1120, Brunei.

ABDUL MAJID, Mimi Kamariah, PH.D.; Malaysian professor of law; b. 5 Dec. 1952, Kuantan; m. Abdul Hadi Zakaria 1977; three d.; ed. Bukit Bintang Girls' Secondary School, Kuala Lumpur, Univ. of Malaya, Monash Univ., Australia; tutor, Faculty of Law, Univ. of Malaya 1976–79, lecturer 1979–87, Assoc. Prof. 1987–92, Prof. 1992, Dean, Faculty of Law 1992–94; *Publications:* Malaysian Law on Bail (co-author) 1986, Pentadbiran Keadilan Jenayah Di Malaysia (admin. of criminal justice) 1991, Undang-Undang Keluarga Di Malaysia (family law) 1992, Criminal Procedure in Malaysia 1995, Dangerous Drugs Laws 1995. *Address:* c/o Faculty of Law, University of Malaya, 50603 Kuala Lumpur, Malaysia. *Telephone:* 03-759 3903. *Fax:* 03-757 3239.

ABDUL-GHANI, Abdulaziz, M.A. (ECON); Yemeni politician and economist; b. 4 July 1939, Haifan, Taiz; s. of Abdulghani Saleh and Tohfa Moqbel; m. Aseya Hamza 1966; four s. one d.; ed. Teacher's High School, Aden Coll., Colorado Coll. and Colorado Univ.; teacher, Balquis Coll., Aden 1964–67; Minister of Health, Sana'a 1967–68, of Economy 1968–69; Prime Minister 1975–80, 1983–90, 1994–97; mem. Presidential Council 1990–94; mem. Gen. People's Congress (GPC); mem. Command Council 1975–78; Vice-Pres. 1980–83; Dir. Yemen Bank for Reconstruction and Devt. 1968; Gov. Cen. Bank of Yemen 1971–75; lecturer, Univ. of Sana'a 1972–74; Chair. Tech. Office Bd. of Planning 1969–71, Yemen Oil Co. 1971, Supreme Council for Reconstruction of Earthquake Affected Areas 1983; mem. Perm. Cttee 1983, of Presidential Advisory Council, Yemeni Econ. Soc.; Hon. Ph.D.; Mareb Sash (First Class) 1987. *Leisure interests:* swimming, hiking. *Address:* c/o Office of the Prime Minister, Sana'a; The Presidential Council, Sana'a, Yemen.

ABDULAH, Frank, M.A.; Trinidad and Tobago diplomatist (retd.); b. 8 Nov. 1928, Trinidad; s. of late Walter and Mildred Abdulah; m. 1st Norma Miller

1954 (divorced); four d.; m. 2nd Marie-Germaine Musso 1988; ed. Queen's Royal, Port of Spain, and Magdalen Coll., Oxford; Asst. Sec. Ministry of External Affairs 1962–63; First Sec., Kingston, Jamaica 1963–64; First Sec., Counsellor, London 1964-68; Counsellor, Ottawa 1968–70; Deputy Perm. Rep. to UN 1970–73, Amb. and Perm. Rep. 1975–82; Perm. Sec., Ministry of External Affairs 1973–75; High Commr. in U.K. 1983–85; Perm. Sec., Ministry of External Affairs 1985–88; Deputy Sec.-Gen. Caribbean Community Secr. 1989–93; Special Adviser to Pres. UN Gen. Ass. 1993–94, Pres. UN Asscn. of Trinidad and Tobago 1997–98. *Leisure interests:* music, sport. *Address:* 8 Nock Road, Maraval, Trinidad and Tobago.

ABDULAI, Yesufu Seyyid Momoh; Nigerian economist; b. 19 June 1940, Auchi; s. of Momoh Abdulai and Haijia Fatimah Abdulai; m. Zene Makonnen Abdulai 1982; three s. one d.; ed. Mount Allison Univ. and McGill Univ.; Tech. Asst. to Exec. Dir. for African Group 1, World Bank Group, Washington 1971–73, Adviser to Exec. Dir. 1973–78, Alternate Exec. Dir. for Africa Group 1 1978–80, Exec. Dir. 1980–82, Vice-Chair. Jt. Audit Cttee. Exec. Bd. 1980–82; Chair. Jt. Secr. African Exec. Dirs. of the World Bank Group and the IMF 1975–77; Man. Dir. and C.E.O. Fed. Mortgage Bank of Nigeria Jan. 1982–83; Dir.-Gen. OPEC Fund for Int. Devt. 1983–. *Leisure interests:* sport, reading, photography, listening to music. *Address:* OPEC Fund for International Development, Parkring 8, P.O. Box 995, 1011 Vienna, Austria. *Telephone:* 51-56-40. *Fax:* 513-92-38.

ABDULATIPOV, Ramazan Gadzhimuradovich, D.PHIL.SC.; Russian/Dagestan politician; b. 4 Aug. 1946, Guerguta, Dagestan; m.; two s. one d.; ed. Dagestan State Univ.; mem. CPSU 1973–91; CP work 1974–76; sr. teacher Dagestan Pedagogical Inst. 1975–76; Head of Murmansk Higher School of Marine Eng. 1978–87; Head of sector Div. of Int. Relations of CPSU Cen. Cttee. 1988–90; R.S.F.S.R. People's Deputy 1990–93, Chair. Council of Nationalities 1990–93; elected to Council of Fed. 1993, Deputy Chair. 1994–96; mem. State Duma 1995–97; Deputy Prime Minister 1997–98, Minister of Nat. Policy 1998–; participant of numerous peacemaking missions on N. Caucasus, Pres. Fed. of UNESCO Clubs in Russia; mem. Russian Acad. of Natural Sciences. *Publications:* Lenin's Policy of Internationalism in U.S.S.R., Internationalism and the Spiritual and Moral Development of the Peoples of Dagestan, What is the Essence of Your Being?, Power and Conscience, Nature and Paradoxes of National Consciousness. *Address:* Ministry of National Policy, Trubnikovsky per. 19, 191819 Moscow, Russia. *Telephone:* (095) 278-86-71; (095) 203-10-88.

ABDULLA OSMAN DAAR, Aden; Somali politician and businessman; b. 1908, Beledwin; ed. Govt. School, Somalia; served in Italian Admin. 1929–41; joined Somali Youth League 1944, Leader 1953, Pres. 1954–56, 1958–59; Pres. Nat. Ass. 1956–60, Constituent Ass. 1960; Pres. Somali Repub. 1961–67; Deputy to Nat. Ass. 1967–69; detained following coup 1969, released 1973. *Address:* c/o Government Offices, Mogadishu, Somalia.

ABDULLAH BIN AL HUSSEIN, H.M. King; Jordanian head of state and army officer; b. 30 Jan. 1962, Amman; s. of the late King Hussein Ibn Talal and of Princess Muna al-Hussein; m. Rania Yassin 1993 (now Queen Rania); one s. one d.; ed. Islamic Educ. Coll., St. Edmund's School, Surrey, Deerfield Acad., U.S.A., Sandhurst Mil. Acad., Oxford Univ.; commissioned Second Lieut. 1981, Reconnaissance Troop Leader 13th/18th bn. Royal Hussars (British Army), Fed. Repub. of Germany and England; rank of First Lieut. 1984; Platoon Commdr. and Co. second-in-command 40th Armoured Brigade, Jordan, Commdr. Tank Co. 91st Armoured Brigade 1985–86 (rank of Capt.); Tactics Instructor Helicopter Anti-Tank Wing, 1986–87; undertook advanced studies in int. affairs School of Foreign Service, Georgetown Univ., Washington 1987–88; Commdr. of a co. 17th Tank Bn., 2nd Guards Brigade then bn. second-in-command (rank of Major) 1989; attended Command and Staff Coll., Camberley, England 1990; Armour Rep. Office of the Insp. Gen. 1991, Commdr. 2nd Armoured Car Regt., 40th Brigade (rank of Lieut. Col.) 1992; promoted to rank of Col. 1993; Deputy Commdr. Jordanian Special Forces Jan.–June 1994; promoted to the rank of Brig. 1994 and assumed command of Royal Jordanian Special Forces; Commdr. of Special Operations Command Oct. 1997–; Pres. Jordan Nat. Football Fed.; Hon. Pres. Int. Tourism Golden Rudder Soc.; Head Nat. Cttee. for Tourism and Archaeological Film Production 1997–. *Leisure interests:* car racing, (fmr. Jordanian Nat. Rally Racing Champion), water sports, scuba diving, collecting ancient weapons and armaments. *Address:* Royal Hashemite Court, Amman, Jordan.

ABDULLAH, Farooq, M.B.; Indian politician; b. 21 Oct. 1937, Srinagar, Kashmir; s. of Sheikh Mohammad Abdullah and Begum Abdullah; m. Mollie Abdullah 1968; one s. three d.; Chief Minister, Jammu and Kashmir 1982–84, 1986–90; Pres. State Centre Labour Union, Jammu and Kashmir Nat. Conf.; Chair. Jammu & Kashmir Muslim Auquaf Trust, Sher-i-Kashmir Nat. Medical Inst. Trust; mem. of Parl. 1979–82, Nat. Integration Council. *Leisure interests:* golf, photography, walking. *Address:* Gupkar Road, Srinagar, Kashmir; 9 Safdarjung Lane, New Delhi 11001, India. *Telephone:* 74020 (Srinagar, Kashmir); 3011608 (New Delhi).

ABDULLAH BIN MOHD SALLEH, Tan Sri, B.A.; Malaysian petroleum executive and fmr. civil servant; b. 24 June 1926, Malacca; s. of Mohd. Salleh; m. Mahani Abdul Razak; two s. one d.; ed. High School, Malacca, Malay Coll., Kuala Kangsar, Univ. of Malaya in Singapore; posts in Admin. and Diplomatic Service 1955–71; Sec.-Gen. Ministry of Agric. and Fisheries 1972; Dir.-Gen. Public Service Dept. 1974; Chief Sec. to Govt. of Malaysia, Sec. to the Cabinet, Head of the Civil Service 1976–78; Chair. and Chief Exec. PETRONAS (Nat. Petroleum Co. of Malaysia) 1979–83, Pres. 1984–87. *Leisure interest:* golf. *Address:* 21 Jalan Setiajaya, Damansara Heights, Kuala Lumpur, Malaysia (Home). *Telephone:* 03-2550915.

ABDULLAH IBN ABDUL AZIZ AL-SAUD, H.R.H. Crown Prince; Saudi Arabian prince, army officer and politician; b. Aug. 1921; s. of the late King Abdul Aziz ibn Saud; brother of H.M. King Fahd (q.v.); Commdr. Nat. Guard 1962–; Second Deputy Prime Minister 1975–82, First Deputy Prime Minister and Commdr. of the Nat. Guard June 1982–; became Crown Prince June 1982. *Leisure interests:* hunting, horse racing. *Address:* Council of Ministers, Murabba, Riyadh 11121, Saudi Arabia. *Telephone:* (1) 488-2444.

ABDULLOJANOV, Abdumalik; Tajikistan politician; b. 6 Jan. 1949, Khodzent; ed. Odessa Inst. of Tech.; Deputy Chief Engineer, Deputy Dir. Kaizakum Mill 1971–73; Deputy Dir., Dir. Nauss Mill 1973–80; First Deputy Minister of Purchases Tajik S.S.R. 1980–86, of Bread Production 1986–87, Minister 1987–92; Chair. NON Corpn. Sept.–Nov. 1992; Prime Minister of Tajikistan 1992–93; Amb. to Russia 1993–95; unsuccessful Presidential Cand. Nov. 1994; mem. Acad. of Industry, fmr. U.S.S.R. Council of Ministers; leader Party of Popular Unity and Accord; lives in Russia.

ABDULOV, Aleksandr Gavrilovich; Russian actor; b. 29 May 1953, Fergana (Uzbekistan); one d.; ed. Lunacharsky State Inst. of Theatre; with Theatre of Leninsky Komsomol (now Lenkom) 1975–; debut as Lieut. Pluzhnikov in Missing from the Lists. *Plays include:* The Star and Death of Joaquin Murietta, Merciless Games, Yunona and Avos', Optimistic Tragedy, Enough Simplicity for Every Wise Man, Hamlet, Mourning Pray and others. *Films include:* Golden River 1977, Never Part with the Beloved 1980, A Woman in White 1982, Carnival 1982, Recipe of Her Youthfulness 1984, To Kill the Dragon 1988, The Barbarian and the Heretic 1997; numerous TV roles; Sec. Russian Union of Cinematographers 1992; People's Artist of Russia 1991. *Address:* Peschanaya str. 4, Apt. 3, 125252 Moscow, Russia (Home).

ABEL, Edward William, C.B.E., PH.D.; British professor of chemistry; b. 3 Dec. 1931, Mid Glamorgan; s. of Sydney J. Abel and the late Donna Maria Grabham; m. Margaret R. Edwards 1960; one s. one d.; ed. Bridgend Grammar School, Glamorgan, Univ. Coll. Cardiff and Northern Polytechnic, London; Research Fellow, Imperial Coll. London 1957–59; lecturer and Reader, Univ. of Bristol 1959–71; Prof. of Inorganic Chem. Univ. of Exeter 1972–97, Deputy Vice-Chancellor 1991–94; Visiting Prof. Univ. of B.C. 1970, Univ. of Japan 1971, Tech. Univ. of Brunswick 1973, A.N.U., Canberra 1990; mem. Council, Royal Soc. of Chem. 1978–82, 1983–98, Chair. Scientific Affairs Bd., Univ. Grants Cttee. 1986–89; Pres. Royal Soc. of Chem. 1996–98; other professional appts.; Tilden Medal, Royal Soc. of Chem. 1981. *Leisure interests:* gardening. *Address:* Department of Chemistry, University of Exeter, Exeter, Devon, EX4 4QD (Office); 1A Rosebarn Avenue, Exeter, Devon, EX4 6DY, England (Home). *Telephone:* (01392) 263489 (Office); (01392) 270272 (Home). *Fax:* (01392) 263434.

ABELEV, Garry Israyelevich; Russian immunologist; b. 10 Jan. 1928, Moscow; s. of Israel Abelev and Eugenia Abelev; m. Elfrida Cicart 1949; two s.; ed. Moscow State Univ.; sr. lab., researcher, Head of Lab., Head of Dept. N. Gamaleya Inst. of Epidemiology and Microbiology 1950–77; Head of Lab. Inst. of Carcinogenesis, Research Oncological Centre 1977–; Prof. Moscow State Univ.; Corresp. mem. U.S.S.R. (now Russian) Acad. of Sciences 1987–; research on immunology of tumours, immunochemistry, cell biochemistry; Abbot Prize, Gold Medal Cancer Research Inst. (U.S.A.), U.S.S.R. State Prize, Hon. mem. American Asscn. of Immunologists, European Soc. of Cancer Researchers, New York Acad. of Sciences. *Publications:* Virusology and Immunology of Cancer 1962, Alpha-Feto-Protein: 25 Years of Study, Tumour Biology 1989; articles in scientific journals of Russia and U.S.A. *Leisure interests:* music, history of science. *Address:* Cancer Research Center, 115478 Moscow, Kashirskoye Shosse 24, Russia. *Telephone:* (095) 323-59-10. *Fax:* (095) 324-12-05.

ABELSON, Philip Hauge, PH.D.; American physicist and editor; b. 27 April 1913, Tacoma, Wash.; s. of Ole Andrew and Ellen Hauge Abelson; m. Neva Martin 1936; one d.; ed. Washington State Coll. and Univ. of California at Berkeley; Asst. Physicist, Dept. of Terrestrial Magnetism, Carnegie Inst. of Washington 1939–41, Staff mem. (of Dept.) 1946–53, Dir. Geophysical Lab. 1953–71; Pres. Carnegie Inst. of Washington 1971–78, Trustee 1978–; Principal Physicist and Civilian-in-Charge, Naval Research Lab. Branch, Navy Yard, Philadelphia 1941–46; Co-Ed., Journal of Geophysical Research 1959–65; Ed., Science 1962–85; Resident Fellow Resources for the Future Inc. 1985–88; mem. Nat. Insts. of Health Biophysics and Biophysical Chemistry Study Section 1956–59, Gen. Advisory Cttee., to Atomic Energy Comm. 1960–63, Cttee. on Science and Public Policy of Nat. Acad. of Sciences 1962–63 and numerous other bodies; Consultant to Nat. Aeronautics and Space Admin. 1960–63; mem. N.A.S., A.A.A.S. (scientific advisor 1985–, Exec. Dir. (acting) 1989), American Philosophical Soc. and many other learned socs.; Pres. American Geophysical Union 1972–74, Int. Union of Geological Sciences 1972–76; Hon. D.Sc. (Yale) 1964, (Southern Methodist Univ.) 1969, (Tufts Univ.) 1976; D.H.L. (Univ. of Puget Sound) 1968; U.S. Navy Distinguished Civilian Service Medal 1945, Physical Sciences Award, Washington Acad. of Sciences 1950, Distinguished Alumnus Award, Washington State Univ. 1962, Hillebrand Award, Chemical Soc. of Washington 1962, Modern Medicine Award 1967, Joseph Priestley Award 1973, Kalinga Prize for Popularization of Science 1973, American Medical Asscn. Scientific

Achievement Award 1974; work includes identification of uranium fission products 1939–40, co-discovery of Neptunium 1940, separation of uranium isotopes 1943, biosynthesis in micro-organisms 1953, amino acids in fossils 1955, fatty acids in rocks 1956. *Publications:* author: Energy for Tomorrow 1975, Enough of Pessimism 1985; co-author: Studies in Biochemistry in Escherichia coli 1955; editor: Research in Geochemistry vols. 1 and 2 1959, 1967, Energy: Use, Conservation and Supply 1974, Food: Politics, Economics, Nutrition, and Research 1975, Materials: Renewable and Nonrenewable 1976, Electronics: The Continuing Revolution 1977. *Address:* A.A.A.S., 1200 New York Avenue, N.W., Washington, DC 20005, U.S.A.

ABERBACH, David, B.A., M.LITT., D.PHIL.; British professor; b. 17 Oct. 1953, London; s. of Prof. Moshe Aberbach and Rose (née Firsht) Aberbach; m. Mimi Skelker 1980; three d.; ed. Talmudical Acad. of Baltimore, Univ. Coll., London, Oxford Univ., Tavistock Clinic; lecturer Oxford and Cambridge Univs., Leo Baeck Coll. and Cornell Univ. 1982–86; Visiting Asst. Prof., McGill Univ. 1986–87, Assoc. Prof. Dept. of Jewish Studies 1987–; Visiting Prof. Univ. Coll. London 1992–93, 1998; Academic Visitor Sociology Dept. L.S.E. 1992–93, 1994–98. *Publications:* At the Handles of the Lock: Themes in the Fiction of S. J. Agnon 1984, Bialik 1988, Surviving Trauma: Loss, Literature and Psychoanalysis 1989, Realism, Caricature and Bias: The Fiction of Mendele Mocher Sefarim 1993, Imperialism and Biblical Prophecy 750–500 BCE 1993, Charisma in Politics, Religion and the Media: Private Trauma, Public Ideals 1996, Revolutionary Hebrew, Empire and Crisis 1998. *Leisure interests:* cinema, painting. *Address:* 32 Ravenshurst Avenue, London, NW4 4EG, England; Department of History, McGill University, 855 Sherbrooke Street West, Montreal, Quebec, H3A 2T7, Canada.

ABERCONWAY, 3rd Baron, of Bodnant; **Charles Melville McLaren;** British business executive; b. 16 April 1913; s. of 2nd Baron Aberconway, C.B.E. and of the late Christabel Aberconway; m. 1st Deirdre Knewstub 1941 (dissolved 1949); one s. two d.; m. 2nd Ann Lindsay Bullard 1949; one s.; ed. Eton Coll., and New Coll., Oxford; Barrister, Middle Temple 1937; Army service 1939–45; Chair. John Brown & Co. Ltd. 1953–78, Pres. 1978–84; Dir. English China Clays Ltd. 1935–87, Chair. 1963–84, Pres. 1984–; fmr Deputy Chair. Westland Aircraft Ltd. and Sun Alliance; Pres. Royal Horticultural Soc. 1961–84, Pres. Emer. 1984–; Commr. Gen. Int. Garden Festival, Liverpool 1984. *Leisure interests:* gardening, travel. *Address:* 25 Egerton Terrace, London, SW3 2DP, England; Bodnant, Tal-y-cafn, Colwyn Bay, Clwyd, North Wales.

ABIRACHED, Robert, D. ÈS L.; French writer and professor; b. 25 Aug. 1930, Beirut, Lebanon; m. Marie-France de Bailliencourt 1974; one s. one d.; ed. Lycée Louis-le-Grand and Ecole Normale Supérieure, Paris; Attaché C.N.R.S. 1960–64; Drama Critic Nouvel Observateur 1964–66; Literary and Drama Critic La Nouvelle Revue Française 1956–72; Lecturer, later Prof. Univ. of Caen 1969–81, Prof. and Dir. Dept. of Drama, Univ. of Paris X Oct. 1988–; Prof. Conservatoire nat. supérieure d'art dramatique 1993–97; Dir. Theatre and Exhibitions, Ministry of Culture 1981–88; Officier, Légion d'honneur, Officier du Mérite, Commandeur des Arts et Lettres, Officier des Palmes académiques; Prix Sainte-Beuve. *Publications:* Casanova ou la dissipation (essay) 1961, l'Emerveillée (novel) 1963, Tu connais la musique? (play) 1971, La crise du personnage dans le théâtre moderne (essay) 1978, Le théâtre et le Prince 1992. *Address:* Université de Paris X, 200 avenue de la République, 92000 Nanterre; 4 rue Robert-Turquan, 75016 Paris, France (Home).

ABLAITI ABDUREXITI; Chinese politician, b. March 1942, Yining, Xinjiang; ed. Xinjiang Eng. Coll.; joined CCP 1960; engineer then Vice-Pres. Xinjiang Uygur Autonomous Region Construction Survey and Design Acad., Vice-Dir. Xinjiang Uygur Autonomous Region Planning Comm.; Vice-Chair. Xinjiang Uygur Autonomous Region 1965–93; Chair. Xinjiang Uygur Autonomous Region, Vice-Sec. CCP Xinjiang Uygur Autonomous Region Cttee. 1993–; mem. CCP 15th Cen. Cttee. 1997–. *Address:* People's Government of Xinjiang Uygur Autonomous Region, Urumqi, Xinjiang, People's Republic of China.

ABLON, Ralph E.; American business executive; b. 1916, Tupelo, Miss.; m.; four c.; ed. Ohio State Univ.; Teacher, Ohio State Univ. 1938–39; worked for Luria Brothers and Co. 1939–62, Dir. 1962–; served in U.S. Navy during Second World War; Exec. Vice-Pres. Luria Brothers 1948–55, Pres. 1955–62; Chair. and C.E.O. Ogden Corpn. 1962–, Pres. 1972–86, Chair. 1992–. *Address:* Ogden Corporation, 2 Pennsylvania Plaza, New York, NY 10021, U.S.A.

ABOIMOV, Ivan Pavlovich; Russian diplomatist; b. 6 Nov. 1936, Zarechnoye, Orenburg Dist.; m.; two c.; ed. Liepaya Pedagogical Inst. Higher Diplomatic School; mem. CPSU –1991; Komsomol work 1959–69; sec., deputy head of dept. of Cen. Cttee. of Latvian CP 1963–69; Ministry of Foreign Affairs 1972–; counsellor in U.S.S.R. Embassy, Hungary 1972–79; First Sec. of European Dept., Ministry of Foreign Affairs 1979–83, Asst. to Minister 1983–84; minister counsellor, Embassy, Budapest 1984–86; chief of Personnel Admin., Ministry of Foreign Affairs 1986–88, Deputy Minister of Foreign Affairs 1988–90; Russian Amb. to Hungary 1990–96, to Finland 1996–97. *Address:* c/o Ministry of Foreign Affairs, 121200 Moscow, Smolenskaya-Sennaya pl. 32/34, Russia.

ABRAGAM, Anatole, D.PHIL.; French physicist; b. 15 Dec. 1914, Griva-Semgallen, Russia; s. of Simon Abragam and Anna Maimin; m. 1st Suzanne Lequesme 1944 (died 1992); m. 2nd Nina Gordon 1996; ed. Lycée Janson, Sorbonne, Oxford Univ.; Research Assoc., Centre Nat. de la Recherche Scientifique 1946; joined French Atomic Energy Comm. 1947, Physicist, later Sr. Physicist 1947–55, Head of Magnetic Resonance Lab. 1955–58, Head of Solid State Physics and Nuclear Physics Dept. 1959–65, Dir. of Physics 1965–70, Dir. of Research 1971–80; Prof. of Nuclear Magnetism, Coll. de France 1960–85; Pres. French Physical Soc. 1967; mem. Acad. of Sciences 1973–; Hon. Fellow, American Acad. of Arts and Sciences, Merton and Jesus Colleges, Oxford 1976; Foreign mem. U.S. N.A.S., Royal Soc.; Dr. h.c. (Kent) 1968, (Oxford) 1976, and others; Holweck Prize, London Physical Soc. 1958, Grand Prix Cognacq-Jay, Acad. of Sciences 1970, and others, Grand Croix, ordre nat. du Mérite, Commandeur, Légion d'honneur, Lorentz Medal 1982, Mateucci Medal 1992, Lomonosov Medal 1995. *Publications:* Discovery of Anomalous Hyperfine Structure in Solids 1950, Dynamic Polarization in Solids 1957, The Principles of Nuclear Magnetism 1961, Nuclear Anti-ferromagnetism 1969, Electron Paramagnetic Resonance of Transition Elements (with B. Bleaney) 1970, Nuclear Pseudomagnetism 1971, Nuclear Ferromagnetism 1973, Nuclear Magnetism: Order and Disorder (with M. Goldman) 1982, Reflexions of a Physicist 1985, La physique avant toute chose 1987, Time Reversal 1989. *Leisure interest:* English and Russian literature. *Address:* Collège de France, 3 rue d'Ulm, 75005 Paris (Office); 33 rue Croulebarbe, 75013 Paris, France (Home). *Telephone:* 4707 62 57 (Home).

ABRAHAM, Sir Edward Penley, Kt., C.B.E., D.PHIL., F.R.S.; British biochemist; b. 10 June 1913, Southampton; s. of Albert Penley Abraham and Mary Hearn; m. Asbjörg Harung 1939; one s.; ed. King Edward VI School, Southampton, Queen's Coll., Oxford; Fellow of Lincoln Coll., Oxford 1948–80; Reader in Chemical Pathology, Oxford Univ. 1960–64, Prof. of Chemical Pathology 1964–80, now Emer.; Hon. Fellow 1980–; Rockefeller Foundation Travelling Fellow at Univ. of Stockholm 1939, Univ. of Calif. 1948; CIBA Lecturer at Rutgers Univ., N.J. 1957; Guest Lecturer, Univ. of Sydney 1960; Rennebohm Lecturer, Univ. of Wis. 1967; L. P. Garrod Lecturer, London 1986; founder Funds for Research on Educ. in the Biological and Chemical Sciences; Hon. mem. American Acad. of Pharmaceutical Sciences 1967; Squibb Lecturer, Rutgers Univ., N.J. 1972; Hon. Fellow Queen's Coll. 1973, Linacre Coll. 1976, Lady Margaret Hall, Oxford 1978, Green Coll. 1981, Lincoln Coll. 1981, Wolfson Coll. 1982 and St. Peter's Coll. 1983; Foreign Hon. mem. American Acad. Arts and of Sciences 1983; Hon. D.Sc. (Exeter) 1980, (Oxford) 1984, (Strathclyde) 1989, (Harvard) 1997; Royal Soc. Royal Medal 1973, Scheele Medal (Sweden) 1975, Chem. Soc. Award in Medicinal Chemistry 1976, Royal Soc. Mullard Medal 1980, Int. Soc. of Chemotherapy Award 1983, Sarton Chair and Medal 1989. *Publications:* Biochemistry of Some Peptide and Steroid Antibiotics; part-author: Antibiotics, The Chemistry of Penicillin, General Pathology, Biosynthesis and Enzymic Hydrolysis of Penicillins and Cephalosporins; scientific papers on the penicillins and cephalosporins and other antibiotics. *Leisure interests:* walking, gardening. *Address:* Badger's Wood, Bedwells Heath, Boars Hill, Oxford, OX1 5JE, England. *Telephone:* (01865) 275571; (01865) 735395.

ABRAHAM, E. Spencer, J.D.; American politician; b. 12 June 1952, Lansing, Mich.; s. of Eddie Abraham and Juliette Sear Abraham; m. Jane Abraham; twin d.; ed. Michigan State Univ. E. Lansing and Harvard Law School; attorney, Lansing 1980–; Prof. Thomas M. Cooley Law School 1981–; Chair. Mich. Republican Party 1983–90; Chair. Mich. Del. Republican Nat. Convention 1984; Chair. Presidential Inaugural Cttee. Michigan 1985; Deputy Chief of Staff to Vice-Pres. Dan Quayle (q.v.) 1991–93; Co-Chair. Nat. Republican Congressional Cttee. 1991–93; Senator from Michigan 1994–; mem. Mich., American and D.C. Bar Asscns. *Address:* United States Senate, 239 Dirksen Senate Bldg., Washington, DC 20510, U.S.A.

ABRAHAM, F. Murray; American actor; b. 24 Oct. 1939, Pittsburgh; m. Kate Hannan 1962; two c.; ed. Texas Univ.; Prof. Brooklyn Coll. 1985–; Dir. No Smoking Please; numerous Broadway plays, musicals, TV appearances and films: *Films include:* Amadeus 1985, The Name of the Rose 1987; Russicum 1987, Slipstream, Hard Rain, Personal Choice, Eye of the Widow 1989, An Innocent Man 1990, Mobsters 1991, Bonfire of the Vanities 1991, By The Sword 1992, Last Action Hero 1993, Surviving the Game 1994, Nostradamus 1994, Mighty Aphrodite 1995, Children of the Revolution 1996, Mimic 1997, Star Trek IX 1998; narrator Herman Melville, Damned in Paradise 1985; Obie Award (for Uncle Vanya) 1984; Golden Globe Award 1985; Los Angeles Film Critics Award 1985; Acad. Award (for Amadeus) 1985. *Address:* William Morris Agency, 1325 Avenue of the Americas, New York, NY 10019, U.S.A.

ABRAHAMS, Ivor, R.A.; British sculptor and painter; b. 10 Jan. 1935, Lancs.; s. of Harry Abrahams and Rachel Kalisky; m. 1st Victoria Taylor 1966 (divorced 1974); one s. (deceased); m. 2nd Evelyne Horvais 1974; one s.; ed. Wigan Grammar School, Lancs., St. Martin's School of Art and Camberwell School of Art, London; visiting Lecturer in Sculpture and Drawing, Birmingham Coll. of Art 1960–64, Coventry Coll. of Art 1964–68; Visiting Lecturer, R.C.A., Slade School of Fine Art and Goldsmith's Coll. of Art 1970–80; many one-man and group exhbns. in Europe and U.S.A. since 1962; works in numerous public collections including Victoria and Albert Museum and Tate Gallery, London, Wedgwood Museum, Stoke-on-Trent, Walker Art Gallery, Liverpool, Arnolfini Gallery, Bristol, Nat. Gallery of Australia, Canberra, Bibliothèque Nationale, Paris, Museum of Modern Art and Metropolitan Museum of Modern Art, New York, Denver Museum, Colo., Fort Lauderdale Museum, Fla. Buymans Museum, Rotterdam, British

Council and Arts Council of G.B., Winston Churchill Fellow 1990. *Leisure interests:* books, postcards and golf. *Address:* c/o Royal Academy of Arts, Burlington House, Piccadilly, London, W1V 0DS, England.

ABRAHAMSEN, Egil, M.SC., DR.TECH.; Norwegian scientist; b. 7 Feb. 1923, Hvaler; s. of Anker Christian Abrahamsen and Aagot Abrahamsen (née Kjoelberg); m. Randi B. Wiborg 1951; one s. two d.; ed. Polytechnical Univ. of Norway, Univ. of Calif., Berkeley, U.S.A., Univs. of Durham, Newcastle upon Tyne, U.K.; surveyor Det Norske Veritas 1952–54, sr. surveyor 1954–57, prin. surveyor 1957–67, Deputy Pres. 1966–67, Vice-Pres. 1967, Pres. 1967–85; Ed. European Shipbldg. 1955–60; Chair. and mem. numerous Cttees.; Chair. Bd. of A/S Veda 1967–70, Bd. of Dirs. A.S. Computas 1967–83, Norsk Hydro 1985–92, The Abrahamsen Cttee. 1984–; Chair. Norwegian Telecom 1980–95, Royal Caribbean Cruise Line A/S (RCCL) 1985–89, OPAK 1985–, I.M. Skaugen 1990–, Eikland 1990–, Kosmos 1988–, IKO Group 1988–; Innovation 1990–; mem. Supervisory Bd. Den Norske Creditbank 1983–88. *Leisure interests:* skiing, tennis. *Address:* Maaltrostveien 35, 0390 Oslo, Norway. *Telephone:* 22 46 90 05. *Fax:* 22 14 71 04.

ABRAHAMSON, Gen. James A.; American defence official and air force officer; b. 19 May 1933, Williston, N.D.; s. of Norval S. Abrahamson and Thelma B. Helle; m. Barbara Jean Northcott 1959 (died 1985); one s. one d.; ed. M.I.T. and Univ. of Oklahoma; commissioned U.S.A.F. 1955, Lieut. Gen. 1982, Gen. 1987; Flight Instructor Bryan A.F. Base, Tex. 1957–59; Spacecraft Project Officer Vela Nuclear Detection Satellite Programme, L.A.A.F. Station 1961–64; Fighter Pilot Tactical Air Command 1964; Astronaut U.S.A.F. Manned Orbiting Lab. 1967–69; mem. staff Nat. Aeronautics and Space Council, White House 1969–71; Commdr. 4950th Test Wing U.S.A.F. 1973–74; Insp. Gen. A.F. Systems Command 1974–76; Dir. F-16 Fighter Programme 1976–80; Deputy Chief of Staff for Systems Andrews A.F. Base, Md. 1980–81; Assoc. Admin. for Space Transportation System, NASA HQ 1981–84; Dir. Strategic Defence Initiative Org. 1984–89; Pres. Transportation Sector, Exec. Vice-Pres. for Devt. Hughes Aircraft Co. 1989–92; Chair. Bd. Oracle Corp. 1992–95; investment banker Int. Air Safety, LLC, Washington 1995–; Lecturer of Astronautics A.I.A.A. 1993; numerous awards and medals. *Leisure interests:* sports, music and poetry. *Address:* International Air Safety, LLC, Washington Center E., 1001 G Street, N.W., Suite 200, Washington, DC 20001, U.S.A.

ABRAHAMSSON, Bo Axel; Swedish company executive; b. 20 July 1931, Stockholm; s. of Axel and Viola (née Ek) Abrahamsson; m. 1st Lili-Christine Engdahl 1959; m. 2nd Helène Westerlundh 1985; two s. three d.; ed. Royal Inst. of Tech., Stockholm; mem. of Bd. of Dirs. Gränges AB, Lamco, LIO, Platzer Bygg AB, Cominvest AB, Industri-Matematik AB, Fredells Trävaru AB, PIAB, Stena AB, Concordia Maritime AB, AB Forssjö Bruk; Pres. Motivation Bo, Abrahamsson AB, Stockholm 1982–87; mem. Industrial Cttee., Royal Swedish Acad. of Eng. Sciences. *Leisure interests:* golf, tennis, hunting, skiing.

ABRAMOVITZ, Max, M.S.; American architect; b. 23 May 1908, Chicago; s. of Benjamin Abramovitz and Sophia Maimon; m. 1st Anne Marie Causey 1937 (divorced); one s. one d.; m. 2nd Anita Brooks 1964; ed. Illinois and Columbia Univs., Ecole des Beaux Arts, Paris; mem. of Harrison, Fouilhoux & Abramovitz 1941–45, Harrison & Abramovitz 1945–76; Abramovitz-Harris-Kingsland 1976–85, Abramovitz, Kingsland, Schiff, New York 1985–; U.S. Army (Corps of Engineers) 1942–45; Deputy Dir. of Planning, UN, New York 1947–52; U.S. Air Force (Colonel) 1950–52; Fellow, American Inst. of Architects; mem. Architectural League of New York, American Soc. of Civil Engineers, Century Asscn.; fmr. Chair. and Dir. Regional Plan Asscn. Inc.; Trustee, Mount Sinai Hospital; Legion of Merit 1945; Hon. Dr. of Fine Arts, (Pittsburgh and Ill.); Award of Achievement, Univ. of Ill. Alumni Asscn. 1963; Fellow, Brandeis Univ. 1963. *Works include:* Jewish Chapel, U.S. Mil. Acad. (New York), Corning Glass Center (Corning, N.Y.) 1951, U.S. Steel Building, Alcoa Building (Pittsburgh), U.S. Embassy (Rio de Janeiro) 1952, U.S. Embassy (Havana) 1953, Three Chapels at Brandeis Univ. 1955, Corning Glass Building (New York) 1959, Philharmonic Hall, Lincoln Center for the Performing Arts (New York), Columbia Univ. Law School and Library (New York) 1962, Univ. of Illinois Assembly Hall (Champaign, Ill.) 1963, Phoenix Mutual Life Insurance Bldg. (Hartford, Conn.) 1964, Hilles Library, Radcliffe Coll., Cambridge, Mass. 1966, Beth Zion Temple, Buffalo, N.Y. 1967, Krannert Center for the Performing Arts, Urbana, Ill., Nationwide Insurance Co., Columbus, Ohio 1977, Tour GAN, La Défense, Paris 1977, La Banque Rothschild, Paris, Owens-Ill. World HQ, Toledo 1984. *Address:* 176 Honey Hollow Road, Pound Ridge, NY 10576, U.S.A. (Home).

ABRAMOVITZ, Moses, PH.D.; American economist; b. 1 Jan. 1912, New York; s. of Nathan Abramovitz and Betty Goldenberg Abramovitz; m. Carrie Glassev 1937; one s.; ed. Harvard Coll. and Columbia Univ.; Instructor and tutor in Econs. Harvard 1936–38; mem. research staff and Dir. of Business and Cycle Studies, Nat. Bureau of Econ. Research 1938–48; lecturer in Econs. Columbia Univ. 1940–42, 1946–48; Prin. Economist, Office of Strategic Services 1943–46; Prof. of Econs. and Coe Prof. of American Econ. History, Stanford Univ. 1948–77, Prof. Emer. 1977–; Pres. American Econ. Asscn. 1980, Western Econ. Asscn. 1988, Econ. History Asscn. 1990; Fellow Accad. Nazionale dei Lincei 1992; Hon. Ph.D. (Uppsala) 1985, (Ancona Univ.) 1992; Nitti Prize 1990. *Publications:* Inventories and Business Cycles 1950, Public Employment in Great Britain (with V. Eliasberg) 1957, Thinking About Growth 1989. *Address:* Department of Economics, Stanford University, Stanford, CA 94305; 762 Dolores Street, Stanford, CA 94305, U.S.A. (Home). *Telephone:* (415) 725-8437 (Office); (415) 328-1027 (Home). *Fax:* (415) 725-5702.

ABRAMS, Herbert Leroy, M.D.; American professor of radiology; b. 16 Aug. 1920, New York; s. of Morris Abrams and Freda (née Sugarman) Abrams; m. Marilyn Spitz 1943; one s. one d.; ed. Cornell Univ., State Univ. of New York; began medical practice Stanford Univ., faculty mem. School of Medicine 1951–67, Dir. Div. Diagnostic Roentgenology 1961–67, Prof. of Radiology 1962–67; Philip H. Cook Prof. of Radiology, Harvard Univ. 1967–85, now Prof. Emer., Chair. Dept. of Radiology 1967–80; Radiologist-in-Chief, Peter Bent Brigham Hosp., Boston 1967–80; Chair. Dept. of Radiology, Brigham & Women's Hosp., Boston 1981–85; Radiologist-in-Chief, Sidney Farber Cancer Inst., Boston 1974–85; Prof. of Radiology, Stanford Univ. Medical School 1985–90, Prof. Emer. 1990–; Clinical Prof. Univ. of California Medical School 1986–; Ed.-in-Chief Postgraduate Radiology 1980–, Cardiovascular and Interventional Radiology 1976–85; R.H. Nimmo Visiting Prof., Univ. of Adelaide 1976; numerous lectureships; mem.-in-residence Stanford Center for Int. Security and Arms Control 1985–; mem. Int. Blue Ribbon Panel on the Radiation Effects Research Foundation, Hiroshima and Nagasaki; mem. numerous medical asscns.; Fellow Nat. Cancer Inst.; Hon. Fellow Royal Coll. of Radiology, Royal Coll. of Surgeons (Ireland), Gold Medal (Asscn. Univ. Radiologists) 1984, Gold Medal (Radiological Soc., U.S.A.) 1995. *Publications include:* Congenital Heart Disease 1965, Coronary Arteriography: A Practical Approach 1983, Ed. Abrams Angiography 1983, The President has been Shot: Confusion, Disability and the 25th Amendment in the Aftermath of the Assassination Attempt on Ronald Reagan 1992, The History of Cardiac Radiology 1996, numerous articles for professional periodicals. *Leisure interests:* English and American Literature, tennis, music. *Address:* Stanford University School of Medicine, Stanford, CA 94305 (Office); 714 Alvarado, Stanford, CA 94305, U.S.A. (Home). *Telephone:* 415-723 6258 (Office); 415-424 8552 (Home). *Fax:* 415-725 7296.

ABRAMSKY, Jennifer, B.A.; British radio producer and editor; b. 7 Oct. 1946; d. of Chimen Abramsky and Miriam Nirenstein; m. Alasdair Liddell 1976; one s. one d.; ed. Holland Park School and Univ. of East Anglia; joined BBC Radio as Programme Operations Asst. 1969, Producer The World at One 1973, Ed. 1981, Jt. Producer special programme on Nixon 1974, Ed. PM 1978, Producer Radio Four Budget Programmes 1979–86, Ed. Today programme 1986–87, News and Current Affairs Radio 1987–93, est. Radio Four News FM 1991, Controller Radio Five Live and Ceefax 1993–, Dir. BBC Radio 1998–; mem. Econ. and Social Research Council 1992–, Editorial Bd. British Journalism Review 1993–; Hon. Prof. Thames Valley Univ. 1994; Woman of Distinction, Jewish Care 1990. *Leisure interests:* theatre, music. *Address:* BBC, Broadcasting House, Portland Place, London, W1A 1AA, England. *Telephone:* 0171-580 4468.

ABRASZEWSKI, Andrzej, M.A., LL.D.; Polish diplomatist; b. 4 Jan. 1938, Paradyz; s. of Antoni Abraszewski and Maria Zaleska; one s.; ed. Cen. School for Foreign Service, Warsaw, and Copernicus Univ., Toruń; researcher, Polish Inst. for Int. Affairs, Warsaw 1962–71; Sec. Polish Nat. Cttee. on the 25th anniversary of the UN 1970; Counsellor to the Minister for Foreign Affairs, Dept. of Int. Orgs., Ministry of Foreign Affairs, Warsaw 1971–83; mem. Polish del. to Gen. Ass. of the UN 1971–90, mem. Ad Hoc Working Group on UN's programme and budget machinery 1975, mem. Advisory Cttee. on Admin. and Budgetary Questions 1977–82, Vice-Chair. Fifth Cttee. (Admin. and Budgetary) of Gen. Ass. 1979, Chair. 1982, Cttee. on Contribs. 1983–88 (Vice-Chair. 1987–88); mem. Cttee. for Programmes and Co-ordination (Vice-Chair. 1989, Chair. 1990); Asst. to Deputy Minister for Foreign Affairs 1984–90; mem. UN Jt. Inspection Unit 1991–, Vice-Chair. 1993, 1998, Chair. 1994; awarded Prize of the Minister for Foreign Affairs. *Leisure interests:* boating, skiing, swimming. *Publications:* various papers on UN affairs. *Address:* Joint Inspection Unit, Office 501, GEC, United Nations, Palais des Nations, 1211 Geneva 10 (Office); 12D Chemin de Maisonneuve, 1219 Chatelaine, Geneva, Switzerland. *Telephone:* (22) 917-8425 (Office); (22) 797-1423 (Home). *Fax:* (22) 917-3033.

ABRIKOSOV, Aleksey Alekseyevich; Russian physicist; b. 25 June 1928, Moscow; s. of Aleksey Ivanovich Abrikosov and Fanny Davidovna Vulf; m. Svetlana Yuriyevna Bun'kova 1977; two s. one d.; ed. Moscow Univ.; Postgraduate Research Assoc., Research Worker, Inst. of Physical Problems, U.S.S.R. Acad. of Sciences 1948–65; Head of Dept., Landau Inst. of Theoretical Physics, U.S.S.R. Acad. of Sciences 1965–88, Dir. Inst. of High Pressure Physics 1988–91; Distinguished scientist Argonne Nat. Lab., Ill. 1991–; Research Assoc., Asst. Prof., Prof. Moscow Univ. 1951–68, Prof. Gorky Univ. 1971–72, Prof. Moscow Physical Eng. Inst. 1974–75, Head Chair. Theoretical Physics, Moscow Inst. of Steel and Alloys 1976–91; mem. U.S.S.R. (now Russian) Acad. of Sciences 1964; mem. American Acad. of Arts and Sciences 1991; Fellow American Physics Soc. 1992; Hon. Sc.D. (Moscow) 1955; D.S. h.c. (Lausanne) 1975; Lenin Prize 1966, Fritz London Award 1972, U.S.S.R. State Prize 1982, Landau Prize 1989, John Bardeen Prize 1991. *Publications:* Quantum Field Theory Methods in Statistical Physics 1962, Introduction to the Theory of Normal Metals 1972, Fundamentals of Metal Theory 1987, and works on plasma physics, quantum electro-dynamics, theory of superconductors, magnetism, astro-physics, quantum liquids and semimetals. *Leisure interests:* skiing, mountaineering. *Address:* Argonne National Laboratory, 9700 South Cass Avenue, Argonne, IL 60439, U.S.A. *Telephone:* (630) 252-5482.

ABRIL, Victoria; Spanish actress; stage appearances in Obras de Mihura, Company Tirso de Molina 1977, Viernes, día de libertad, Company L. Prendes 1977, Nuit d'Ivresse, Paris 1986; TV appearances. *Films:* Obsesión 1975, Robin and Marian 1975, Robin Hood 1975, Caperucita Roja 1975, Cambio de sexo 1975, La bien plantada 1976, Doña Perfecta 1976, Esposa y Amante 1977, La muchacha de las bragas de oro 1979, Asesinato en el Comité Central 1981, La Guerrillera 1981, La Colmena 1982, La batalla del porro 1982, Le Bastard 1982, La Lune dans le Caniveau 1982, Sem Sombra de pecado 1982, J'ai Epousé un ombre 1982, Rio Abajo 1982, Bajo el signo de Piscis 1983, Le Voyage 1983, Las bicicletas son para el verano 1983, L'Addition 1983, Rouge George 1983, La noche más hermosa 1984, Padre Nuestro 1984, After Dark 1984, L'Addition 1984, La hora bruja 1985, Tiempo de Silencio 1985, Max mon Amour 1985, Vado e torno 1985, El Lute 1987, El placer de matar 1987, Barrios altos 1987, El juego más divertido 1987, Ada dans la jungle 1988, Baton Rouge 1988, Sandino 1989, Atame 1989, A solas contigo 1990, Amantes 1990, Tie Me Up! Tie Me Down! 1991, High Heels 1992, Lovers 1992 (Silver Bead for Best Actress, Berlin Film Festival), Kika 1993, Gazon Maudit 1996.

ABSE, Dannie, D.LITT., M.R.C.S., L.R.C.P., F.R.S.L.; British author and physician; b. 22 Sept. 1923, Cardiff, Wales; s. of Rudolph Abse and Kate Shepherd; m. Joan Mercer 1951; one s. two d.; ed. St. Illtyd's Coll. Cardiff, Univ. Coll. Cardiff, King's Coll. London and Westminster Hosp., London; first book of poems published while still a medical student 1948; qualified as doctor 1950; Squadron-Leader R.A.F. 1951–55; doctor in charge of chest clinic at Cen. Medical Establishment, Cleveland St., London 1954–89; Writer in Residence, Princeton Univ., N.J., U.S.A. 1973–74; Pres. Poetry Soc. 1979–92, Welsh Acad. 1996; Hon. D. Litt. (Univ. of Wales) 1989; Fellow Welsh Acad. 1993; Welsh Arts Council Literature Prize; Jewish Chronicle Award; Cholmondeley Award 1983. *Publications:* Collected Poems 1948–1977, Pythagoras (a play), Ash on a Young Man's Sleeve 1954, Way Out in the Centre 1981, Ask the Bloody Horse 1986, Journals from the Ant Heap 1986, White Coat, Purple Coat 1989, The Music Lovers Literary Companion (with Joan Abse) 1989, Remembrance of Crimes Past 1990, The Hutchinson Book of Post-War British Poets (ed.) 1989, There was a Young Man of Cardiff 1991, On the Evening Road 1994, Intermittent Journals 1994, Twentieth-Century Anglo-Welsh Poetry 1997, A Welsh Retrospective 1997, Arcadia, One Mile 1998 and many others. *Address:* 85 Hodford Road, London, NW11 8NH; Green Hollows, Craig-yr-Eos Road, Ogmore-by-Sea, Glamorgan, South Wales.

ABSHIRE, David Manker, PH.D.; American diplomatist and administrator; b. 11 April 1926, Chattanooga, Tenn.; s. of James Ernest and Phyllis Patten Abshire; m. Carolyn Sample Abshire 1957; one s. four d.; ed. Baylor School, Chattanooga, U.S. Mil. Acad., West Point, N.Y., Georgetown Univ., Washington, D.C.; Exec. Dir. Center for Strategic and Int. Studies, Georgetown Univ. 1962–70, Chair. 1973–82, Pres. 1982–83; Asst. Sec. of State for Congressional Relations 1970–73; Perm. Rep. to NATO 1983–87; Special Counsellor to Pres. Jan.-April 1987; Chancellor Center for Strategic and Int. Studies (CSIS) April–Dec. 1987, Pres. 1988–; Co-ed. Washington Quarterly 1977–83; Chair. U.S. Bd. for Int. Broadcasting 1974–77; Dir. Nat. Security Group, Transition Office of Pres.-elect Reagan 1980–81; mem. Congressional Cttee. on the Org. of Govt. for the Conduct of Foreign Policy 1973–75; mem. Bd. Procter and Gamble 1987–96, Ogden Corpn., BP American Advisory Bd.; mem. Advisory Bd. Pres.'s Task Force on U.S. Govt. Int. Broadcasting 1991; Order of Crown (Belgium), Commdr. Ordre de Leopold (Belgium); Pres. Civilian Service Award 1989; Medal of Diplomatic Merit (Rep. of Korea) 1993; Order of the Lion of Finland (1st Class) 1994. *Publications include:* International Broadcasting: A New Dimension of Western Diplomacy 1976, Foreign Policy Makers: President vs. Congress 1979, The Growing Power of Congress 1981, Preventing World War III: A Realistic Grand Strategy 1988, The Global Economy 1990, Putting America's House in Order: The Nation as a Family 1996. *Leisure interest:* historical literature. *Address:* CSIS, Suite 1014, 1800 K Street, N.W., Washington, DC 20006; 311 South St Asaph Street, Alexandria, VA 22314, U.S.A. *Telephone:* 202-775-3212.

ABUBAKAR, Gen. Abdulsalami; Nigerian head of state and army officer; b. 13 June 1942, Minna; ed. Minna, Bida, Kaduna; joined Nigerian Army 1963, with UN peacekeeping force Lebanon 1978–79, Chief of Defence Staff and Chair. Jt. Chiefs of Staff of the Armed Forces 1993–98, fmrly. active in Cttee. of W. African Chiefs of Staff; Commdr. in Chief 1998–; Head of Govt. of Nigeria 1998–(99). *Address:* Office of the Head of State, Abuja, Nigeria.

ABU-GHAZALA, Marshal Mohamed Abdel Halim (see Abdel Halim Abu-Ghazala, Marshal Mohamed).

ABU-GHAZALEH, Talal; Palestinian/Jordanian management consultant and intellectual property expert; b. 22 April 1938, Jaffa; m. Nuha Salameh; two s. two d.; ed. American Univ. of Beirut; founder and Chair. Bd. of Dirs. Talal Abu-Ghazaleh Int. (TAGI) (mem. firm of Grant Thornton Int.), leading regional holding group of professional firms operating through 34 offices in Arab World and comprising, among others: Talal Abu-Ghazaleh & Co. (TAGCO), Abu-Ghazaleh Consultancy & Co. (AGCOC), Al-Dar Consulting Co. (ADCO), Talal Abu-Ghazaleh Assocs. Ltd. (TAGA), Arab Int. Projects Co. (AIPC), The First Projects Man. Co. (FBMC), Talal Abu-Ghazaleh Int. Man. Inc. (TAGIMI), TMP Agents, Arab Bureau for Legal Services (ABLE), Al-Dar Gen. Trading Co. (ADTCO); Chair. Arab Man. Soc. 1989–; numerous public and professional appts., etc.; Chevalier, Légion d'Honneur and decorations from Tunisia, Kuwait, Bahrain and Jordan; Hon. D.Hum.Litt. (Canisius Coll. Buffalo, N.Y.) 1988. *Publications:* Taxation in the Arab Countries, The Abu-Ghazaleh English-Arabic Dictionary of Accounting, Trade Mark Laws in the Arab Countries. *Address:* Talal Abu-Ghazaleh International, 23 Wadi El-Nil Street, Mohandessen City; P.O. Box 96, Imbaba 12411, Cairo, Egypt. *Telephone:* 3462951; 3479952. *Fax:* 3445729.

ABULFAZ ELCHIBEI (ALIYEV, Abulfaz Elchibei Kadyrgula ogly); Azerbaijani politician; b. 7 June 1938, Keleki, Nakhichevan Autonomous Repub.; ed. Azerbaijan State Univ.; lecturer Azerbaijan State Univ. 1969–74; as dissident arrested by KGB and imprisoned 1975–77; researcher Inst. of Manuscripts, Azerbaijan Acad. of Sciences 1977–92; Chair. People's Front of Azerbaijan 1989–; elected Pres. of Azerbaijan Repub. 1992–93, overthrown by Parl. June 1993; lived in exile in Keleki 1993–97; returned to Baku 1997. *Publications:* more than 50 works on oriental philosophy, history, literature, religion.

ABU MAZEN (see Abbas, Mahmoud).

ABUSHADI, Mohamed Mahmoud, PH.D., A.C.I.P.; Egyptian banker; b. 15 Aug. 1913, Fayoum; s. of Mahmoud and Seddika (Hashad) Abu Shadi; m. Colleen Althea Bennet 1947; two s. two d.; ed. Cairo Univ., Chartered Inst. of Patent Agents, and American Univ., Washington; Controller-Gen., Insurance Dept., Ministry of Finance 1949–52; Dir.-Gen. Govt. Insurance and Provident Funds 1953; Chair. and Man. Dir. Devt. and Popular Housing Co. 1954–55; Sub-Gov. Nat. Bank of Egypt 1955–60, Man. Dir. 1960–67, Chair. and Man. Dir. 1967–70; Chair. Union de Banques Arabes et Françaises (UBAF), Paris 1970–87, UBAF Bank Ltd., London 1971; Chair. Social Insurance Org. 1956–57; Chair. and Man. Dir. Cairo Insurance Co. 1956–57; Man. Dir. Cairo Bank 1956–57; Pres. Int. Bankers' Asscn. 1976–; Order of the Repub. (2nd Class), Order of Merit (1st Class), Commdr., Officier, Légion d'honneur. *Publications:* The Art of Central Banking and its Application in Egypt 1962, Central Banking in Egypt 1952, Will New York Attract Arab Capital? 1974, The Experience of the Arab-French Banks 1974, Oil Funds: The Search for Supplementary Recycling Mechanisms 1975, The Role of Finance in Promoting Arab European Business Co-operation 1976. *Leisure interests:* swimming, tennis, art. *Address:* 52 avenue Foch, 75016 Paris, France (Home).

ABYKAYEV, Nurtai Abykayevich; Kazakhstan politician and diplomatist; b. 15 May 1947, Dzhambul, Almaty Region; m.; three c.; ed. Ural Polytech. Inst., Almaty Higher CP School; has rank of Amb.; engineer Almaty factory of heavy machine construction 1972–76; CP functionary 1976–88; asst. to Chair. Council of Ministers of Kazakh S.S.R. 1988–89; asst. to First Sec. Cen. Cttee. CP of Kazakhstan 1989–90; Head Adm. of Pres. and Prime Minister Repub. of Kazakhstan, mem. Security Council 1990–95; Amb. to UK (also accred. to Denmark, Norway and Sweden) 1995–96; First Asst. to Pres. of Kazakhstan Sept. 1996–. *Address:* Residence of the President, Square of the Republic, 480091 Almaty, Republic of Kazakhstan. *Telephone:* (3272) 54 35 67, (3172) 15 11 53.

ACAR, Özgen; Turkish journalist; b. 29 Sept. 1938, Bor, Turkey; s. of Mihilmi Acar and Naciye (née Eren) Acar; m. Inci Güven 1980; one s.; ed. Ankara Univ.; Parl. Corresp. Cumhuriyet Daily Newspaper 1960–61, Econ. Corresp. 1961–63, Diplomatic Corresp. 1963–65, 1967–72, Investigative Corresp. 1990–92, 1994–, Ed.-in-Chief Istanbul 1992–94; Corresp. Reuters, Ankara 1972–74; Bureau Chief Milliyet Daily Newspaper Athens 1980–84, Ankara 1984–86, New York 1986–88; TV and Radio reporter; mem. Exec. Cttee. of Int. Fed of Journalists (IFJ) 1971, Adviser 1972–78; several journalism awards. *Publications:* numerous investigative reports. *Address:* Cumhuriyet Newspaper, Türkocaği 39 Cağaloğlu, Istanbul 34334, Turkey. *Telephone:* 5120505; 6611566. *Fax:* 5139095; 6611567.

ACCARDO, Salvatore; Italian violinist; b. 26 Sept. 1941, Turin; s. of Vincenzo and Ines Nea Accardo; m. Resy Corsi 1973; ed. Conservatorio S. Pietro a Majella, Naples and Accademia Musicale Chigiana, Siena; first professional recital 1954; won 1st prize Geneva Competition at age 15 and 1st prize Paganini Competition at age 17; repertoire includes concertos by Bartók, Beethoven, Berg, Brahms, Bruch, Paganini, Penderecki, Prokofiev, Saint-Saëns, Sibelius, Stravinsky and Tchaikovsky; plays with world's leading conductors and orchestras including Amsterdam Concertgebouw, Berlin Philharmonic, Boston Symphony, Chicago Symphony, Cleveland, La Scala, Milan, Santa Cecilia, Rome, BBC Symphony, London Symphony and Philharmonia; also appears as soloist/dir. with the English, Scottish and Netherlands Chamber Orchestras; Artistic Dir. Naples Festival. *Recordings include:* the Paganini Concertos and Caprices (Deutsche Grammophon), concerts by Beethoven and Brahms, complete works for violin and orchestra by Bruch, concertos by Mendelssohn, Dvořák, Sibelius and Tchaikovsky (Philips/Phonogram); Cavaliere di gran Croce 1982; numerous music prizes include Caecilia Prize (Brussels) and Italian Critics' Prize for recording of the Six Paganini Concertos and Diapuson d'Or for recording of the Sibelius Concerto. *Publications:* edn. Paganini Sixth Concerto, Paganini: Variations on "Carmagnola". *Leisure interests:* hi fi, electronics, sport and cooking.

ACCONCI, Vito, M.F.A.; American sculptor; b. 24 Jan. 1940, Bronx, New York; s. of Amilcar Acconci and Catherine Colombo; ed. Holy Cross Coll., Worcester, Mass., Univ. of Iowa; solo exhbns. at San Francisco Museum of Modern Art, Stedelijk Museum, Amsterdam, Museum of Contemporary Art, Chicago, Kunstverein, Cologne, Padiglione d'Arte Contemporanea, Milan,

Museum of Modern Art, New York, Museum für Angewandte Kunst, Vienna 1993, Museum d'Art Modern, Saint-Etienne 1994; exhbns. at Le Centre Nat. d'Art Contemporain de Grenoble 1991, Centro per l'Arte Contemporanea Luigi Pecci, Prato 1992; public comms.: The Palladium, New York 1986, Coca Cola Co., Atlanta 1987, St. Aubin Park, Detroit 1990, Autry Park, Houston 1990, Embarcadero Promenade, San Francisco 1992, Arvada Art Center, Arvada, Colo. 1992, La Fontaine Avenue School, Bronx, New York 1992; several awards from New York State Council of the Arts 1976, Nat. Endowment for the Arts; Guggenheim Foundation Fellowship 1979; Skowhegan Award 1980. *Leisure interests:* architecture, movies, music. *Address:* 39 Pearl Street, Brooklyn, New York, NY 11201, U.S.A. (Home). *Telephone:* (718) 852-6591. *Fax:* (718) 852-6591.

ACHARYA, Jayaraj, PH.D.; Nepalese diplomatist; b. 12 Nov. 1951, Tanahun; s. of late Nara Nath Acharya and of Ganga D. Acharya; m. Usha Acharya 1981; two s.; ed. Tribhuvan and Georgetown Univs.; lecturer in English, Tribhuvan Univ. 1978–84; Perm. Rep. of Nepal to UN 1991–95; Fulbright Scholar; five gold medals. *Publications:* Traditional Grammars: English & Nepali. A Study 1980, A Descriptive Grammar of Nepali and An Analyzed Corpus 1991, The Nepala-Mahatmya (Legends on the Sacred Places and Deities) 1992. *Leisure interest:* reading. *Address:* c/o Ministry of Foreign Affairs, Shital Niwas, Maharajganj, Kathmandu, Nepal.

ACHEBE, Chinua, B.A., F.R.S.L.; Nigerian writer; b. 16 Nov. 1930, Ogidi, Anambra State; s. of late Isaiah O. and Janet N. Achebe; m. Christie C. Okoli 1961; two s. two d.; ed. Government Coll., Umuahia, and Univ. Coll., Ibadan; Producer, Nigerian Broadcasting Corpn., Lagos 1954–58, Regional Controller, Enugu 1958–61, Dir. Voice of Nigeria, Lagos 1961–66; Sr. Research Fellow, Univ. of Nigeria, Nsukka 1967–72; Rockefeller Fellowship 1960–61; UNESCO Fellowship 1963; Foundation mem. Asscn. of Nigerian Authors 1982–; mem. Gov. Council, Lagos Univ. 1966, mem. E. Cen. State Library Bd. 1971–72; Founding Ed., Okike 1971–; Prof. of English, Univ. of Mass. 1972–75, Univ. of Conn. 1975–76, Univ. of Nigeria, Nsukka 1976–81, Prof. Emer. 1985–; Pro-Chancellor and Chair. of Council, Anambra State Univ. of Tech., Enugu, Nigeria 1986–88; Regents Lecturer, Univ. of Calif., Los Angeles 1984; Founding Ed. African Writers' Series (Heinemann) 1962–72; Dir. Heinemann Educational Books (Nigeria) Ltd., Nwamife (Publishers), Enugu; Pres. Asscn. of Nigerian Authors 1981–86; mem. Tokyo Colloquium 1981; Visiting Distinguished Prof. of English, City Coll., N.Y. 1989; Montgomery Fellow and Visiting Prof., Dartmouth Coll., Hanover 1990; Visiting Fellow, Ashby Lecturer Clare Hall, Cambridge 1993; Hon. mem. American Acad. of Arts and Letters 1982; Gov. Newsconcern Int. Foundation 1983; Hon. Fellow, Modern Language Asscn. of America 1974; Neil Gunn Int. Fellow 1975; Fellow, Ghana Asscn. of Writers 1975; Hon. D.Univ.; Hon. D.Litt. sixteen times; Hon. D.H.L. (Mass.), (Georgetown) 1990; Hon. LL.D. (P.E.I.); Dr. h.c. (Open Univ.) 1989; Margaret Wrong Memorial Prize 1959, Nigerian Nat. Trophy 1960, Jock Campbell New Statesman Award 1965, Commonwealth Poetry Prize 1972, The Lotus Prize (Afro-Asian writers) 1975, Order of the Federal Republic (Nigeria) 1979, Nigerian Nat. Merit Award 1979. *Publications:* Things Fall Apart 1958, No Longer at Ease 1960, Arrow of God 1964, A Man of the People 1966, Chike and the River 1966, Poems 1971, Girls at War 1972, Beware Soul Brother 1972, How the Leopard Got His Claws 1973, Morning Yet on Creation Day 1975, The Flute 1978, The Drum 1978, Anthills of the Savannah 1987, Hopes and Impediments—Selected Essays 1965–87 1988, Another Africa (jtly.) 1998. *Leisure interest:* music. *Address:* Bard College, P.O. Box 41, Annandale-on-Hudson, NY 12504, U.S.A.

ACHIDI ACHU, Simon; Cameroonian politician; b. 1934, Santa Mbu; ed. Cameroon Protestant Coll., Bali, Yaoundé Univ., Univ. of Besançon, France, Nat. School of Magistracy, Yaoundé; worked as agricultural asst., Cameroon Devt. Corpn. before entering univ.; fmr. interpreter, Presidency, Yaoundé, Chief Accountant, Widikum Council, Pres. North-West Provincial Co-operative Union Ltd.; Minister-del. in charge of State Reforms 1971; Minister of Justice and Keeper of the Seals 1972–75; in pvt. business 1975–88; elected Cameroon People's Democratic Movt. (CPDM) M.P. 1988; Prime Minister of Cameroon 1992–96. *Leisure interests:* farming, football. *Address:* c/o Prime Minister's Office, Yaoundé, Cameroon.

ACHILLE, Jean-Claude; French public administrator; b. 6 June 1926, Agen; m. 2nd Lise-Rose Rame 1961; one s.; ed. Ecole Polytechnique and Ecole des Mines, Paris; Engineer, coal mines, Bassin de Blanzy 1950–51; Engineer of Mines, Valenciennes, then Asst. to Chief Engineer, Douai Mines 1951–56; Tech. Councillor and Dir. of Offices at Ministry of Industry and Commerce 1956–59; Asst. Dir.-Gen. Gaz de France 1959–63; Dir.-Gen. Charbonnages de France 1963–68; Dir. Houillères du bassin du Nord et du Pas-de-Calais, Houillères du bassin de Lorraine 1963–68; Vice-Pres. Acadi 1967–; mem. Econ. and Social Cttee. European Community 1963–68; mem. Bd. of Dirs. Rhône-Poulenc, S.A. 1968, Dir.-Gen. 1968–76, Vice-Pres. 1975–77; mem. Advisory Council Banque de France 1975–; Pres. Union des Industries Chimiques 1977–91, Hon. Pres. 1991–; Pres. Fed. of Fertilizer 1978–; Vice-Pres. Soc. des Ingénieurs et Scientifiques de France 1987–; Dir. numerous other companies; Officier, Légion d'honneur, Chevalier des Palmes académiques, Officier du Mérite. *Address:* 14 rue de la République, 92800 Puteaux; 74 boulevard Maurice Barrès, 92200 Neuilly-sur-Seine, France.

ACHOUR, Habib; Tunisian trade union leader and politician; b. 1913; joined Néo-Destour party 1934; f. Union Générale Tunisienne de Travail (UGTT) with Farhat Hached 1946; arrested for inciting strikes 1947, 1952; elected Sec.-Gen. UGTT 1963–66; mem. Political Bureau, Parti Socialiste Destourien (PSD) 1947–66; imprisoned March–Sept. 1966; elected mem. Nat. Ass. 1969; readmitted to Political Bureau 1970 (–Jan. 1978) and re-elected Sec.-Gen. UGTT 1970 (–March 1978); sentenced to 10 years' hard labour following severe anti-govt. rioting Jan. 1978, later pardoned but remained under house arrest 1979; pardoned and released Nov. 1981; appointed Pres. UGTT 1981. *Address:* c/o Union Générale Tunisienne du Travail, 29 Place M'Hamed Ali, Tunis, Tunisia.

ACKEREN, Robert Van; German film maker, screenplay writer and producer; b. 22 Dec. 1946, Berlin; s. of Max and Hildegard Van Ackeren; ed. in film studies, Berlin; Prof. of Film, School of Arts, Cologne; German Film Prize, Ernst Lubitsch Prize, Federal Film Prize (Fed. Repub. of Germany), Prix Celuloide, Premio Incontri Int., Prix L'âge d'or and other awards. *Films:* Sticky Fingers 1966, Nou Nou 1967, Ja und Nein 1968, Für immer und ewig 1969, Blondie's No. 1 1971, Küss mich, Fremder 1972, Harlis 1973, Der letzte Schrei 1975, Belcanto 1977, Das andere Lächeln 1978, Die Reinheit des Herzens 1980, Deutschland Privat 1981, Die flambierte Frau 1983, Die Tigerin 1985, Die Venusfalle 1987, Die Wahre Geschichte von Männern und Frauen 1992. *Address:* Kurfürstendamm 132a, 10711 Berlin, Germany. *Telephone:* (30) 312 53 37. *Fax:* (30) 312 86 69.

ACKLAND, Joss (Sidney Edmond Jocelyn); British actor; b. 29 Feb. 1928, London; s. of Norman Ackland and Ruth Izod; m. Rosemary Jean Kirkcaldy 1951; two s. (one deceased) five d.; ed. Dame Alice Owens School, Cen. School of Speech Training and Dramatic Art; has worked in theatre since 1945; repertory includes Stratford-upon-Avon, Arts Theatre, Buxton, Croydon, The Embassy, Coventry, Oxford, Pitlochry; tea planter in Cent. Africa 1954–57; disc jockey in Cape Town 1955–57; mem. Old Vic Theatre Co. 1958–61; Artistic Dir Mermaid Theatre 1961–63; Dir The Plough and the Stars. *Theatre roles include:* Falstaff in Henry IV, Parts I and II, Hook and Darling in Peter Pan, Clarence Darrow in Never the Sinner, Mitch in A Streetcar Named Desire, Brassbound in Captain Brassbound's Conversion, Sir in the Dresser, Petruchio in Taming of the Shrew (Nat. tour), Gaev in The Cherry Orchard, Sam in Collaborators, Ill in The Visit, Eustace Perrin State in The Madras House, John Tarleton in Misalliance, Weller Martin in The Gin Game. *West End musical roles include:* Squeezum in Lock up Your Daughters, Romain Gary in Jean Seburg, Jorrocks in Jorrocks, Frederic in A Little Night Music, Perón in Evita. *Films include:* Seven Days to Noon 1949, Crescendo 1969, Lady Jane 1984, A Zed and Two Noughts 1985, The Sicilian 1986, To Kill a Priest 1987, White Mischief 1988, Lethal Weapon II, The Hunt for Red October, To Forget Palermo, Tre Colonne in Cronaca 1989, The Object of Beauty, The Sheltering Desert, The Bridge, A Murder of Quality 1990, Voices in the Garden 1992, Georgino, Occhio Pinocchio 1993, Nowhere to Run 1993, The Bible, Miracle on 34th Street, Mad Dogs and Englishmen, A Kid at the Court of King Arthur, Citizen X 1994, Daisies in December, Till the End of Time, Surviving Picasso, Deadly Voyage 1995, Swept from the Sea 1996, Firelight, My Giant 1997, Game of Mirrors, Son of Sandokan, Milk, Passion of Mind 1998. *TV appearances include:* Kipling, The Man who lived at the Ritz, When we are Married, The Barretts of Wimpole Street, Shadowlands, First and Last, They do it with Mirrors, Under the Sun. mem. Drug Helpline, Amnesty Int., Covent Garden Community Asscn. *Publications:* I Must Be in There Somewhere (autobiog.) 1989. *Leisure interests:* writing, painting, reading, 24 grandchildren. *Address:* c/o Jonathan Altaras, 13 Shorts Gardens, London, W.C.2, England.

ACKNER, Baron (Life Peer), cr. 1986, of Sutton in the County of West Sussex; **Desmond James Conrad Ackner,** P.C., M.A.; British judge; b. 18 Sept. 1920; s. of Conrad and Rhoda Ackner; m. Joan Evans 1946; one s. two d.; ed. Highgate School, Clare Coll., Cambridge; served in R.A. 1941–42, Admiralty Naval Branch 1942–45; called to Bar, Middle Temple 1945; Q.C. 1961; Recorder of Swindon 1962–71; Judge of Courts of Appeal of Jersey and Guernsey 1967–71; a Judge of the High Court of Justice, Queen's Bench Div. 1971–80; Judge of the Commercial Court 1973–80; presiding Judge, Western Circuit 1976–79; mem. Gen Council of Bar 1957–61, 1963–70, Hon Treas. 1964–66, Vice-Chair. 1966–68, Chair. 1968–70; Bencher, Middle Temple 1965, Deputy Treas. 1983, Treas. 1984; mem. Senate of the Four Inns of Court 1966–70, Vice-Pres. 1968–70; Pres. Senate of the Inns of Court and the Bar 1980–82; Lord Justice of Appeal 1980–86; Lord of Appeal in Ordinary 1986–92; Chair. Law Advisory Cttee., British Council 1980–90, mem. British Council 1991–, Lloyd's Arbitration Panel 1992–; Pres. Arbitration Appeal Panel, Securities and Futures Authority 1994–; Appeal Commr., Personal Investment Authority 1994–; Dir. City Disputes Panel 1994–98; Hon. mem. Canadian Bar Asscn. 1973–; Hon. Fellow Clare Coll., Cambridge 1983. *Leisure interests:* swimming, gardening, theatre. *Address:* House of Lords, Westminster, London SW1A 0PW; 4 Pump Court, Temple, London, EC4Y 7AN; Browns House, Sutton, nr. Pulborough, West Sussex, RH20 1PU, England. *Telephone:* 0171-219 3295, 0171-353 2656 (Temple); (01798) 869206 (Sussex).

ACKROYD, Norman, R.A., A.R.C.A.; British artist; b. 26 March 1938, Leeds; s. of Albert Ackroyd and Clara Briggs; m. 1st Sylvia Buckland 1963 (dissolved 1975); two d.; m. 2nd Penelope Hughes-Stanton 1978; one s. one d.; ed. Cockburn High School, Leeds, Leeds Coll. of Art, Royal Coll. of Art; Tutor in Etching, Central School of Art and Design 1965–; Prof. of Etching, Univ. of Indiana 1970; exhbns. at Mickelson Gallery, Wash. 1973, 1977, 1979, 1982, 1984, 1988, Anderson Oday Gallery, London 1979, 1988, Dolan

Maxwell Gallery, Phila. 1981, 1983, 1985, 1987, 1989; TV works include: Artists in Print (Etching) 1981, A Prospect of Rivers 1988; comms. include: Haringey Cultural Centre 1985, Lloyds Bank Tech. Centre, London 1990, British Airways 1991, Freshfields, London 1992, Tetrapak, London 1993; British Int. Print Biennale Prize 1974, 1982, Royal Soc. of Etchers and Engravers 1984, 85, Bronze Medal, Frechen, Germany 1986. *Publications include:* Landscapes and Figures, Etchings (with William McIllvannry) 1973, The Pictish Coast (with Douglas Dunn) 1988, St. Kilda: the furthest island 1989, Windrush 1990. *Leisure interests:* British history, archaeology, cricket. *Address:* c/o Royal Academy of Arts, Piccadilly, London, W1V 0DS, England. *Telephone:* 0171-378 6001.

ACKROYD, Peter, M.A., F.R.S.L.; British writer; b. 5 Oct. 1949, London; s. of Graham Ackroyd and Audrey Whiteside; ed. St. Benedict's School, Ealing, Clare Coll., Cambridge and Yale Univ.; Literary Ed. The Spectator 1973–77, Jt. Man. Ed. 1978–82; Chief Book Reviewer The Times 1986–; Mellon Fellow Yale Univ; Hon. D. Litt. (Exeter Univ.). *Publications: poetry:* London Lickpenny 1973, Country Life 1978, The Diversions of Purley 1987; *novels:* The Great Fire of London 1982, The Last Testament of Oscar Wilde 1983 (Somerset Maugham Prize 1984), Hawksmoor 1985 (Whitbread Award; Guardian Fiction Prize), Chatterton 1987, First Light 1989, English Music 1992, The House of Doctor Dee 1993, Dan Leno and the Limehouse Golem 1994, Milton in America 1996; *non-fiction:* Notes for a New Culture 1976, Dressing Up 1979, Ezra Pound and his World 1980, T.S. Eliot 1984 (Whitbread Award; Heinemann Awards), Dickens 1990, Introduction to Dickens 1991, Blake 1995, The Life of Thomas More 1998. *Address:* Anthony Sheil Associates Ltd., 43 Doughty Street, London, WC1N 2LF, England. *Telephone:* 0171-405 9351.

ACLAND, Sir Antony (Arthur), G.C.M.G., G.C.V.O.; British diplomatist; b. 12 March 1930, London; s. of late Brig. P. B. E. Acland; m. 1st Clare Anne Verdon 1956 (died 1984); two s. one d.; m. 2nd Jennifer McGougan (née Dyke) 1987; ed. Eton Coll., Christ Church, Oxford; joined diplomatic service 1953; at Middle East Centre for Arab Studies 1954; served in Dubai 1955, Kuwait 1956; Foreign Office 1958–62; Asst. Pvt. Sec. to Sec. of State 1959–62; mem. U.K. Mission to UN 1962–66; Head of Chancery, U.K. Mission, Geneva 1966–68; F.C.O. 1968–, Head of Arabian Dept. 1970–72; Prin. Pvt. Sec. to Foreign and Commonwealth Sec. 1972–75; Amb. to Luxembourg 1975–77, to Spain 1977–79; Deputy Under-Sec. of State, FCO 1980–82, Perm. Under-Sec. of State and Head of Diplomatic Service 1982–86; Amb. to U.S.A. 1986–91; Provost of Eton Nov. 1991–; Chancellor Order of St Michael and St George 1994–; Dir. Shell Transport and Trading 1991–, Booker PLC 1992–; Chair. of the Council of the Ditchley Foundation 1991–96, Chair. Tidy Britain Group 1991–96, Pres. 1996–; Trustee Nat. Portrait Gallery 1991–, Esmée Fairbairn Trust 1991–; Hon. D.C.L. (Exeter) 1988, (William and Mary Coll., U.S.A.) 1990, (Reading) 1991. *Address:* The Provost's Lodge, Eton College, Windsor, Berks., SL4 6DH, England.

ACOGNY, Germaine; Senegalese dancer and choreographer; b. Benin State, Nigeria; m. Helmut Vogt; f. pvt. professional dance school, Dakar; Dir. Mudra Africa Int. Dance School, Dakar –1983; dancer, choreographer with Peter Gabriel (q.v.) 1984; first solo performance Sahel 1984; collaborated with drummer Arona N'Diaye to stage Ye'ou, the Awakening 1985; performance at World of Music and Dance Festival 1993; London Dance and Performance Award for Ye'ou, the Awakening 1991.

ACZÉL, János D., F.R.S.C., PH.D.; Canadian (b. Hungarian) mathematician; b. 26 Dec. 1924, Budapest; s. of Dezsö Aczél and Irén Aczél; m. Susan Kende 1946; two d.; ed. D. Berzsenyi High School, Univ. of Budapest; Teaching Asst., Univ. of Budapest 1946–48; Statistician, Metal Workers' Trade Union, Budapest 1948; Asst. Prof., Univ. of Szeged 1948–50; Assoc. Prof. and Dept. Head, Tech. Univ., Miskolc 1950–52; Dept. Head, Assoc. Prof. then Prof., L. Kossuth Univ., Debrecen 1952–65; Prof., Univ. of Waterloo, Ont., Canada 1965, Distinguished Prof. Emer. 1993; many visiting professorships and fellowships, N. America, Europe, Africa, Asia and Australia 1963–; Chair. Int. Symposia on Functional Equations 1962–96, Hon. Chair. 1997–; mem. Canadian Math. Soc., American Math. Soc., Austrian Math. Soc., New York Acad. of Science; Foreign Fellow Hungarian Acad. of Sciences 1990; Fellow Royal Soc. of Canada 1971 (Convener Math. Div. 1974–75, Chair. Acad. of Science Editorial Cttee. 1977–78); donor L. Fejer-J. Aczél Scholarship, Univ. of Waterloo; M. Beke Award (J. Bolyai Math. Soc.) 1961, Award of Hungarian Acad. of Sciences 1962, Distinguished Prof., Univ. of Waterloo 1969, F.R.S.C. 1971, Cajal Medal (Nat. Research Council of Spain) 1988; Dr. h.c. (Karlsruhe) 1990, (Graz) 1995, (Katowice) 1996. *Publications:* over 250 articles and ten books, including A Short Course on Functional Equations Based upon Recent Applications to the Social and Behavioral Sciences 1987, Functional Equations in Several Variables (with J. Dhombres) 1989; Hon. Ed.-in-Chief Aequationes Math; Ed. Theory and Decision, Series B and six int. mathematical journals. *Leisure interests:* reading swimming, walking. *Address:* Department of Pure Mathematics, University of Waterloo, Waterloo, Ont., N2L 3G1 (Office); 97 McCarron Crescent, Waterloo, Ont., N2L 5M9, Canada (Home). *Fax:* (519) 725-0160.

ADA, Prof. Gordon Leslie, A.O., D.SC.; Australian research scientist; b. 6 Dec. 1922, Sydney; s. of W. L. Ada and Erica Flower; m. Jean MacPherson 1946; three s. one d.; ed. Fort Street Boy's High School, Sydney and Univ. of Sydney; Research Scientist Nat. Inst. for Medical Research, London 1946–48, Walter and Eliza Hall Inst., Melbourne 1948–68; Prof. Emer. Australian Nat. Univ.; mem. and Chair. Scientific Council, Int. Agency for Research on Cancer, Lyon; mem. Scientific and Tech. Advisory Cttee. WHO, UNDP and World Bank Special Programme on Tropical Diseases; mem. Global Advisory Council for Medical Research, WHO 1981–84; Chair. WHO Programme on Vaccine Devt. 1984–; Consultant WHO 1988–; Visiting Prof. Johns Hopkins School of Hygiene and Public Health, Baltimore 1988–; Fellow, Australian Acad. of Science. *Publications:* Antigens, Lymphoid Cells and the Immune Response (with G. J. V. Nossal) 1971; about 180 scientific papers on virology and immunology. *Leisure interests:* sailing, music, walking. *Address:* 71 Parkhill Street, Pearce, A.C.T. 2605, Australia. *Telephone:* (062) 86-2044.

ADAIR, Red (Paul Neal); American oil-well firefighter; b. 1915; m.; two c.; fmr. bomb disposal expert World War II; fmr. racing driver; worked in oil-well fire and gusher control with Myron McKinley 1939–59; with Red Adair Oil Well Fires and Blowouts Control Co., Houston 1959–94; handled Piper Alpha disaster 1988; capped oil well fires after 1991 Gulf War; has dealt with over 2,000 blowouts. *Address:* c/o Adair Enterprises, P.O. Box 747, Bellville, TX 77418, U.S.A.

ADAM, Ken, O.B.E.; British film designer; b. 1921, Berlin, Germany; ed. London Univ.; served in R.A.F. in W.W.II; started career as jr. draughtsman on a film set; Designer of about 60 films, including Around the World in Eighty Days, seven James Bond films, Dr Strangelove, Sleuth, Barry Lyndon (Acad. Award), The Deceivers, The Freshman, Patriots, Chitty Chitty Bang Bang, The Madness of King George (Acad. Award 1994), Boys on the Side, Bogus; designed sets for La Fanciulla del West, Royal Opera House, London.

ADAM, Robert; British architect; b. 10 April 1948, Hants.; s. of Robert W. Adam and Jessie M. Adam; m. Sarah J. Chalcraft 1970; one s. one d.; ed. Canford School and Regent Street Polytechnic; Dir. Winchester Design (Architects) Ltd. 1978–; Chair. Faculty of Architecture, British School at Rome 1992–; mem. R.I.B.A. Nat. Awards Cttee. 1988–; Bannister Fletcher Prize 1973; Rome Scholarship 1973–74. *Publications:* In Defence of Historicism 1981, Tin Gods 1989, Classical Architecture: A Complete Handbook 1990, Classical Design in the Late 20th Century 1990. *Address:* Winchester Design (Architects) Ltd., 9 Upper High Street, Winchester, Hants., SO23 8UT (Office); Crooked Pightle, Crawley, Winchester, Hants., SO21 2PN, England (Home). *Telephone:* (01962) 843843 (Office); (01962) 776480 (Home).

ADAM, Robert (Robin) Wilson: British petroleum executive; b. 21 May 1923, Aberdeen; s. of Robert Ross Adam and Agnes Wilson Adam; m. Marion Nancy Scott 1957; ed. Fettes Coll., Edinburgh; war service in India and Burma; joined Anglo-Iranian Oil Co. (later The British Petroleum Co.) as chartered accountant 1950, Asst. Chief Accountant 1959–64, with Cen. Planning Dept. 1964–67, Gen. Man. 1966–67; Dir. BP Chemicals 1966–68, Gen. Man. Finance and Planning Dept. 1967–69; Pres. BP North America Inc. 1969–72; Dir. BP Trading Ltd. 1973–75; Dir. Standard Oil Co. Inc. (SOHIO) 1972–76 and 1978–83; Man. Dir. The British Petroleum Co. PLC 1975–83, Deputy Chair. 1981–83; Dir. BP Canada (Inc.) 1972–84, Chair. 1981–82, BP (Southern Africa) Pty. Ltd. 1984; Dir. Gen. Accident PLC 1980–, Deputy Chair. 1987–; Dir. MEPC PLC 1982–88, Chair. 1984–88; Dir. London and Scottish Marine Oil Co. 1984–88, Chair. 1985–88; Dir. Dunlop PLC 1985–; Dir. TRW Inc. 1986–; mem. Council, Stock Exchange 1983–85. *Leisure interest:* watching cricket. *Address:* 25 Onslow Square, London, S.W.7., England.

ADAM, Theo; German concert singer; b. 1 Aug. 1926, Dresden; s. of Johannes Adam and Lisbeth (née Dernstorf); m. Eleonore Matthes 1949; one s. one d.; ed. Gymnasium and Conservatory; engagements with Dresden State Opera 1949, Bayreuth Festival 1952–80, Salzburg Festival 1969, 1970, 1980–89, 1992, 1995; mem. Deutsche Staatsoper, Berlin 1953–; has appeared with Vienna and Munich State Operas since 1967; Pres. of Curatorium Oper, Dresden 1985–; numerous recordings; Österreichischer Kammersänger, Bayerischer Kammersänger; Nat. Prize (First Class) of G.D.R. *Publications:* Seht, hier ist Tinte, Feder, Papier 1980, Die 100 Rolle, Wie schön ist doch der Musik 1996. *Leisure interest:* swimming. *Address:* Schillerstrasse 14, 01326 Dresden, Germany. *Telephone:* 0351/268 3997.

ADAMI, Franco; Italian sculptor; b. 19 Nov. 1933, Pisa; s. of Toscano Adami and Giuseppina Bertoncini; m. Jacqueline Sylvius; one s. two d.; ed. Istituto Leonardo da Vinci, Pisa, Scuola d'Arte, Cascina and School of Fine Arts, Florence; one-man shows include: Centroartemoderna, Pisa 1977, Galerie Matignon, Paris 1978, Galerie Mitkal, Abidjan 1979; other exhbns. include: Salon des Réalités Nouvelles 1976, Crédit Lyonnais, Paris 1980, Int. Exhbn. of Sculpture, Strasbourg 1981, European Biennale of Sculpture at Jouy-sur-Eure to mark anniversary of Treaty of Rome 1982, Musée Antoine Lecuyer, Saint Quentin 1983, Pisan Sculpture from XIV century to present day, Villa Medicis de San Giuliano 1983, UNICEF, Rouen 1986, Castello Malaspina, Carrara 1986, Galerie Triade, Barbizon 1987, Theodor Zink Museum, Kaiserlauten (Germany) 1987, Gallery K, Paris 1988, Salon 'Comparaisons', Paris 1988, Galerie Reymondin, Geneva 1989, FIAC 1989 and FIAC 1990, Galerie K, Paris, Art Jonction, Galerie Capazza, Nice 1990; Sculpture Prize of Cascina 1957; Prix Fernand Dupré for sculpture (France) 1981, Prix Charles Oulmont, Fondation de France 1987. *Leisure interests:* antiques, sculpture. *Address:* Via del Vicinato, Pontestrada, 55045 Pietrasanta, Italy (Studio); 250 rue du Faubourg Saint-Antoine, 75012 Paris, France. *Telephone:* (0) 584.73.37.17.

ADAMISHIN, Anatoly Leonidovich; Russian diplomatist and politician (retd.); b. 11 Oct. 1934, Kiev; m. Olga Adamishina; one d.; ed. Moscow State Univ.; diplomatic service 1957–; Third, then Second Sec. Embassy, Rome 1959–65; counsellor in First European Countries Dept., Ministry of Foreign Affairs 1965–71, counsellor in Dept. of Gen. Int. Problems 1973–78, head of First European Dept. 1978–86; mem. of Collegium, Ministry of Foreign Affairs 1979; Deputy Minister of Foreign Affairs 1986–90, First Deputy Minister 1992–94; Pres. U.S.S.R. Comm. for UNESCO 1987–90; U.S.S.R. (now Russian) Amb. to Italy 1990–92, to U.K. 1994–97; Minister for Co-operation with C.I.S. Countries 1997–98; mem. State Duma (Parl.) 1993–95. *Publication:* The Decline and Revival of the Great Power 1993. *Leisure interests:* classical music, opera, tennis. *Address:* c/o Minsotrudnichestru, Varvarka str. 7, 103012 Moscow, Russia.

ADAMKUS, Valdas; Lithuanian politician; b. 3 Nov. 1926, Kaunas, Lithuania; m. Alma Adamkiene; ed. Munich Univ., Univ. of Ill.; resistance movt. World War II; left Lithuania; on staff World YMCA, Sec.-Gen. and Chair. Chief Physical Training and Sports Cttee.; emigrated to U.S.A. 1949; worked in Chicago sports cars factory, draftsman Eng. Co.; f. Academic Sports Club of American Lithuanians 1951; Chair. Bd. of Santara Cen. of Lithuanian students in U.S.A. 1957–58; Vice-Chair., Chair. Santara-Sviesa Fed. of Lithuanian émigrés 1958–67; mem. of Bd. Lithuanian Community in U.S.A. 1961–64; Deputy Chair. Cen. Bd., mem., Chair. American Lithuanian Community; Chair. Org. Cttee. World Lithuanian Games 1983; fmr. Head Scientific Research Cen. Environment Protection Agency, Deputy Admin. for Mid-W., U.S.A., active participation in political life of Lithuania 1993–; Pres. of Lithuania Feb. 1998–; Dr. h.c. (Vilnius) 1989, (Indiana), (Ill.); Gold Medal of US Environment Protection Agency. *Address:* Office of the President, Gedimino prosp. 53, 2002 Vilnius, Lithuania (Office). *Telephone:* (2) 61 28 11, (2) 22 70 35.

ADAMOV, Yevgeny Olegovich, DR. TECH. SC.; Russian politician and engineer; b. 28 April 1939, Moscow; m.; two d.; ed. Moscow Aviation Inst.; engineer, Deputy Dir. I. Kurchatov Inst. of Nuclear Energy 1962–86; took part in Chernobyl Nuclear Power Station recovery work May–Aug. 1986; Dir., Constructor-Gen. Research Inst. of Energy Tech. 1986–88; Minister for Nuclear Energy March 1998–; mem. Russian Acad. of Eng., New York Acad. of Sciences. *Publications:* over 100 books, papers and articles on man., econs. of energy resources, nuclear energy, informatics. *Leisure interests:* reading books. *Address:* Ministry of Nuclear Energy, B. Ordynka str. 24/26, 101000 Moscow, Russia. *Telephone:* (095) 239 4908 (Office).

ADAMS, Brock(man), LL.B; American politician and lawyer; b. 13 Jan. 1927, Atlanta, Ga.; s. of Charles Leslie Adams and Vera Eleanor (née Beemer); m. Mary Elizabeth Scott 1952; two s. two d.; ed. Univ. of Washington and Harvard Law School; served U.S. Navy 1944–46; law practice 1952–61; U.S. Attorney for W. District of Wash. 1961–64; mem. House of Reps. 1965–76, mem. Interstate and Foreign Commerce Cttee. and Transportation sub-cttee., Chair. Budget Cttee. 1975–76; U.S. Sec. for Transportation 1977–79; U.S. Senator from Wash. 1987–93; partner Garvey, Schubert, Adams and Barer 1979–86; Instructor, American Inst. of Banking 1955–60; Chair. Presidential Campaign of J. F. Kennedy in W. Wash, 1960; mem. Dist. of Columbia, Wash. State and American Bar Asscns.

ADAMS, Bryan; Canadian rock singer; b. 5 Nov. 1959; Vancouver; signed contract with A&M Records 1979; albums include Cuts Like a Knife 1983, Reckless 1984, Into the Fire 1987, Waking up the Neighbours 1991, So Far So Good 1992, 18 'Til I Die 1996; 45 million albums sold worldwide (1995); awards, Diamond Sales Award (for Reckless), 12 Juno Awards, Recording Artist of the Decade, Canada; performed in Vietnam Jan. 1994. *Address:* c/o Press Department, A&M Records, 136–144 New King's Road, London, SW6 4LZ, England. *Telephone:* 0171-705 4343. *Fax:* 0171-731 4606.

ADAMS, Douglas (Noel), M.A.; British author; b. 11 March 1952, Cambridge; s. of Christopher Adams and Janet Dora (née Donovan) Adams (now Thrift); m. Jane Elizabeth Belson 1991; one d.; ed. Brentwood School, Essex, St. John's Coll., Cambridge Univ.; Radio and TV writer 1974–78; BBC Producer 1978, TV Script Ed. 1978–80; novelist 1979–. *Publications:* The Hitchhiker's Guide to the Galaxy 1979, The Restaurant at the End of the Universe 1980, Life, the Universe and Everything 1982, So Long, and Thanks for all the Fish 1984, The Meaning of Liff (with John Lloyd) 1984, The Original Hitch Hiker Radio Scripts 1985, Dirk Gently's Holistic Detective Agency 1987, The Long Dark Tea-time of the Soul 1988, Last Chance to See . . . (with Mark Carwardine) 1990, The Deeper Meaning of Liff (with J. Lloyd) 1990, Mostly Harmless 1992. *Leisure interest:* purchasing equipment for recreations he would like to take up. *Address:* c/o The Digital Village, 11 Maiden Lane, London, WC2E 7NA, England. *Telephone:* 0171-543 1700.

ADAMS, Gerard "Gerry"; Irish politician; b. 6 Oct. 1948, Falls Road, Belfast; s. of Gerard Adams and Annie Hannaway; m. Colette McCardle 1971; one s.; ed. St. Mary's Christian Bros. School, Belfast; worked as a barman; founder mem. Northern Ireland Civil Rights Asscn.; mem. Belfast Housing Action Cttee.; interned in Long Kesh under suspicion of being a terrorist March 1972; released to take part in secret London talks between Sec. of State for Northern Ireland and Irish Republican Army (IRA) July 1972; rearrested 1973, attempted to escape from Maze Prison, sentenced to 18 months' imprisonment, released Feb. 1977; charged with membership of Provisional IRA Feb. 1978, freed after 7 months because of insufficient evidence for conviction; Pres. of Sinn Féin Nov. 1983– (Vice-Pres. 1978–83); M.P. for Belfast West 1983–92, May 1997–; mem. N.I. Ass. for Belfast West 1998–; involved in peace negotiations with British Government; Thorr Award, Switzerland 1995. *Publications:* Falls Memory, Politics of Irish Freedom, Pathway to Peace 1988, Cage 11 (autobiog.) 1990, The Street and Other Stories 1992, Selected Writings 1994, Our Day Will Come (autobiog.) 1996, Before the Dawn (autobiog.) 1996, An Irish Voice 1997. *Address:* Sinn Féin, 55 Falls Road, Belfast, BT12 4PD, Northern Ireland.

ADAMS, Prof. Norman, R.A., A.R.C.A., F.R.S.A.; British painter and professor of fine art; b. 9 Feb. 1927, London; s. of Albert Henry Adams and Winifred Elizabeth Rose; m. Anna Teresa Butt 1947; two s.; ed. Harrow School of Art, Royal Coll. of Art, London; first exhbn. Young Contemporaries 1950; numerous solo exhbns. in London, N. England, Scotland and U.S.A.; exhbns. with British Council 1954–55; retrospective exhbn., R.A. 1988; fmr. teacher at St. Albans, Maidstone, Hammersmith Art Schools and Royal Acad. Schools; Head of Painting, Manchester Coll. of Art and Design 1962–71; elected Assoc. of Royal Acad. 1967; Visiting Tutor, Leeds Univ. 1973–76; Prof. of Fine Art and Dir. of King Edward VII Coll. Univ. of Newcastle upon Tyne 1981–86; Prof. of Painting, Royal Acad. of Arts, London 1986–, Keeper 1986–95; commissions: murals for St. Anselm's, Kennington, London 1971–72, Stations of the Cross for Our Lady of Lourdes, Milton Keynes 1974–75, Stations of the Cross St. Mary's (The Hidden Gem) Mulberry Street, Manchester (permanently installed in St. Mary's) 1995; Hon. mem. Royal Soc. of British Watercolourists 1990. *Public collections include:* Tate Gallery, London, Scottish Nat. Gallery of Modern Art, Edinburgh, Ulster Museum, Belfast, Nat. Gallery of New Zealand, Wellington. *Publications:* Alibis and Convictions 1978, A Decade of Painting 1971–81 1981, Angels of Soho 1988, Island Chapters 1991, Life on Limestone 1994. *Leisure interests:* art, music, literature. *Address:* 6 Gainsborough Road, London, W4 1NJ; Butts, Horton-in-Ribblesdale, Settle, N. Yorks, BD24 0HD, England (Homes). *Telephone:* 0181-747 3073; (01729) 860284.

ADAMS, Sir Philip George Doyne, K.C.M.G.; British diplomatist (retd.); b. 17 Dec. 1915, Wellington, New Zealand; s. of the late George Basil Doyne Adams and Arline Maud (née Dodgson) Adams; m. Hon. Mary Elizabeth Lawrence 1954; two s. two d.; ed. Lancing and Christ Church, Oxford; Vice-Consul, Beirut 1939–41; war service 1941; Third Sec., Cairo 1941–45; Amb. to Jordan 1966–70; Asst. Under-Sec. FCO 1970; Deputy Sec. Cabinet Office 1971–72; Amb. to Egypt 1973–75; Dir. Ditchley Foundation 1977–82; mem. Bd. British Council 1977–82, Marshall Aid Commemoration Comm. 1979–88. *Address:* 54 Sussex Square, London, W2 2SR, England.

ADAMS, Richard George, M.A., F.R.S.A., F.R.S.L.; British novelist; b. 9 May 1920, Newbury, Berks.; s. of Dr. E. G. B. Adams, F.R.C.S., and Lilian Rosa (Button) Adams; m. Barbara Elizabeth Acland 1949; two d.; ed. Bradfield Coll., Berks., and Worcester Coll., Oxford; army service 1940–46; Home Civil Service 1948–74; Pres. Royal Society for the Prevention of Cruelty to Animals 1980–82; Writer-in-Residence, Univ. of Florida, 1975, Hollins Coll., Va. 1976; Carnegie Medal 1972, Guardian Award for Children's Literature 1972, Medal of California Young Readers' Asscn. 1977. *Publications:* Watership Down 1972, Shardik 1974, Nature Through the Seasons, The Tyger Voyage 1976, The Plague Dogs 1977 (filmed 1982), The Ship's Cat 1977, Nature Day and Night 1978, The Girl in a Swing 1980 (filmed 1988), The Unbroken Web (The Iron Wolf) 1980, Voyage through the Antarctic 1982, Maia 1984, The Bureaucats 1985, A Nature Diary 1985, Occasional Poets: anthology (ed. and contributor) 1986, The Legend of Te Tuna 1986, Traveller 1988, The Day Gone By (autobiog.) 1990, Tales From Watership Down 1996. *Leisure interests:* chess, ornithology, folk-song, country pursuits, fly-fishing, travel. *Address:* 26 Church Street, Whitchurch, Hants., RG28 7AR, England.

ADAMS, Robert McCormick, Jr., PH.D.; American anthropologist; b. 23 July 1926, Chicago, Ill.; s. of Robert McCormick and Janet (Lawrence) Adams; m. Ruth S. Skinner 1953; one d.; ed. Univ. of Chicago; Instructor, Univ. of Chicago 1955–57, Asst. Prof. 1957–61, Assoc. Prof. 1961–62, Prof. 1962–84, Dir. Oriental Inst. 1962–68, 1981–83, Prof. of Anthropology 1963–, Dean of Social Sciences 1970–74, 1979–80, Univ. Provost 1982–84; Sec. Smithsonian Inst. 1984–93; Homewood Prof. Johns Hopkins Univ. 1984; Adjunct Prof. Univ. of Calif., San Diego 1993–; Chair. Ass. of Behavioral and Social Sciences, Nat. Research Council 1973–76; Visiting Prof., Harvard 1962, 1977, Univ. of Calif. (Berkeley) 1963; Annual Prof., Baghdad School, American Schools of Oriental Research 1966–67; Fellow Inst. for Advanced Study, Berlin 1995–96; field research in Iraq, Iran, Mexico, Saudi Arabia and Syria; Lewis Henry Morgan Prof., Univ. of Rochester 1965; Councillor, N.A.S. 1981 (mem.); mem. American Acad. of Arts and Sciences, American Anthropological Asscn., American Asscn. for the Advancement of Science, Middle East Studies Asscn., American Philosophical Soc., German Archaeological Inst.; Trustee, National Opinion Research Center 1970–94, Nat. Humanities Center 1976–83, Russell Sage Foundation 1978–91; U.C.L.A. Medal 1989; numerous hon. degrees. *Publications:* Land behind Baghdad: a History of Settlement on the Diyala Plains 1965, The Evolution of Urban Society: Early Mesopotamia and Prehispanic Mexico 1966, (with H. J. Nissen) The Uruk Countryside 1972, Heartland of Cities 1981, (with N. J. Smelser and D. J. Treiman) Behavioral and Social Science Research: A National Resource (2 Vols.) 1982, Paths of Fire 1996. *Leisure interests:* skiing, mountaineering. *Address:* 2810 31st Street, N.W., Washington, DC; P.O. Box ZZ, Basalt, CO 81621, U.S.A. *Telephone:* 202-965-0456; 303-927-3380 (Homes).

ADAMSON, Sir (William Owen) Campbell, Kt.; British business executive; b. 26 June 1922, Glasgow, Scotland; s. of John and Elsie (née Glendinning) Adamson; m. 1st Gilvray Allan 1945 (dissolved); two s. two d.; m. 2nd Josephine Lloyd Chandler; ed. Rugby School and Corpus Christi Coll., Cambridge; joined Baldwins Ltd. 1945; various posts in Steel Co. of Wales and Richard Thomas & Baldwins after mergers 1951–67, Dir. 1959; mem. Iron and Steel Fed. team visiting U.S.S.R. 1956; Industrial Adviser, Dept. of Econ. Affairs 1967, Senior Industrial Adviser 1967, Deputy Under Sec. of State 1968; Dir.-Gen. Confed. of British Industry 1969–76; Dir. Imperial Group 1976–86; Chair. Revertex Chemicals Jan. 1978–80; Chair. Barclays Tozer Ltd. (B.T.L.) 1977–81; Chair. Abbey National PLC 1978–91; Dir. Lazard Bros. and Co. 1977–87, Tarmac PLC. 1980–90; Chair. Renold PLC 1982–86; Chair. Re-Action Trust 1991–; founder mem. Social Science Research Council; mem. BBC Gen. Advisory Cttee.; mem. Council of Iron and Steel Inst. 1960–72; mem. Council, Industrial Soc.; Visiting Fellow, Lancaster Univ. 1970; Visiting Fellow Nuffield Coll., Oxford 1971–79; Gov. Rugby School 1980–93; Vice-Pres. Inst. of Employment Studies 1982–97; Pres. Nat. Council for Voluntary Orgs 1992–98; Hon. Fellow Corpus Christi Coll., Cambridge 1996; Hon. D.Soc.Sc. (Birmingham Univ.) 1993. *Leisure interests:* music, swimming, tennis. *Address:* 138 King's Road, London, SW3 4XB, England. *Telephone:* 0171-581 8669.

ADCOCK, Fleur, O.B.E., M.A., F.R.S.L.; British writer; b. 10 Feb. 1934, New Zealand; d. of Cyril John Adcock and Irene Robinson; m. 1st Alistair Teariki Campbell 1952 (divorced 1958); two s.; m. 2nd Barry Crump 1962 (divorced 1966); asst. lecturer Univ. of Otago 1958, Asst. Librarian 1959–61; with Alexander Turnbull Library 1962; with FCO 1963–79; freelance writer 1979–; Northern Arts Fellowship in Literature Univs. of Newcastle-upon-Tyne and Durham 1979–81; Eastern Arts Fellowship Univ. of E. Anglia 1984; writer-in-residence Univ. of Adelaide 1986; Buckland Award 1967, 1979; Jessie MacKay Award 1968, 1972; Cholmondeley Award 1976; N.Z. Book Award 1984. *Publications:* The Eye of the Hurricane 1964, Tigers 1967, High Tide in the Garden 1971, The Scenic Route 1974, The Inner Harbour 1979, Below Loughrigg 1979, The Oxford Book of Contemporary New Zealand Poetry 1982, Selected Poems 1983, The Virgin and the Nightingale: Medieval Latin Poems 1983, Hotspur: A Ballad for Music 1986, The Incident Book 1986, The Faber Book of 20th Century Women's Poetry 1987, Orient Express: Poems by Grete Tartler (translator) 1989, Time Zones 1991, Letters from Darkness: Poems by Daniela Crasnaru (translator) 1991, High Primas and the Archpoet (ed. and translator) 1994, The Oxford Book of Creatures (ed. with Jacqueline Simms) 1995, Looking Back 1997. *Address:* 14 Lincoln Road, London, N2 9DL, England. *Telephone:* 0181-444 7881.

ADDIS, Richard James, M.A.; British journalist; b. 23 Aug. 1956; s. of Richard Thomas Addis and Jane Addis; m. Eunice Minogue 1983; one s. two d.; ed. W. Downs Prep. School, Rugby, Downing Coll., Cambridge; with Evening Standard 1985–89; Deputy Ed. Sunday Telegraph 1989–91; Exec. Ed. Daily Mail 1991–95; Ed. Daily Express 1995–98, The Express on Sunday 1996–98. *Leisure interests:* dancing, tennis, elementary music-making.

ADDISON, Mark Eric, M.A., M.SC., PH.D.; British civil servant; b. 22 Jan. 1951; s. of Sydney Robert James Addison and Prudence Margaret Russell; m. Lucinda Clare Booth 1987; ed. Marlborough Coll., St. John's Coll., Cambridge, City Univ., Imperial Coll.; with Dept. of Employment 1978–95, Pvt. Sec. to Parl. Under-Sec. of State 1982, Pvt. Sec. to Prime Minister 1985–88; Regional Dir. London Training Agency 1988–91, Dir. Finance and Resource Man. 1991–94; Dir. Safety Policy Health and Safety Exec. 1994–98; Chief Exec. Crown Prosecution Service 1998–. *Leisure interests:* British motorbikes, windsurfing, photography. *Address:* Crown Prosecution Service, 50 Ludgate Hill, London, EC4, England.

ADEDEJI, Adebayo, B.SC. (ECON.), M.P.A., PH.D., the Asiwaju of Ijebu and Olotu'fore of Ijebu-Ode; Nigerian economist; b. 21 Dec 1930, Ijebu-Ode; s. of Mr. and Mrs. L. S. Adedeji; m. Susan Aderinola Ogun 1957; eight s. three d.; ed. Ijebu-Ode Grammar School, Univ. Coll., Ibadan, Univ. Coll., Leicester and Harvard Univ.; Asst. Sec., Ministry of Econ. Planning, W. Nigeria 1958–61, Principal Asst. Sec. (Finance) 1962–63; Deputy Dir. Inst. of Admin., Univ. of Ife 1963–66, Dir. 1967– (on leave of absence 1971); Prof. of Public Admin., Univ. of Ife 1968– (leave of absence 1971); Nat. Manpower Bd. 1967–71; Fed. Commr. for Econ. Devt. and Reconstruction 1971–75; Chair. Directorate, Nigerian Youth Services Corps 1973–75; UN Under-Sec.-Gen and Exec. Sec. UN Econ. Comm. for Africa 1975–91, Founder, Exec. Dir. African Centre for Devt. and Strategic Study (ACDESS) 1992–; Chair. Senate of UN Inst. for Namibia 1975; founder and editor, Quarterly Journal of Administration 1967–75; Fellow, Nigerian Inst. of Management, Nigerian Econ. Soc., African Acad. of Sciences, African Asscn. for Public Admin. and Man.; Pres. Nigerian Econ. Soc. 1971–72; Pres. African Asscn. for Public Admin. and Management 1974–83; Vice-Chair. Asscn. of Schools and Inst. of Admin. of Int. Inst. of Admin. Sciences 1970–; numerous awards, including Hon. D.Litt. (Ahmadu Bello Univ.), Hon. LL.D. (Dalhousie Univ., Univ. of Calabar, Univ. of Zambia), Hon. D.Sc. (Obafemi Awolowo Univ.) and numerous foreign decorations. *Publications:* A Survey of Highway Development in Western Nigeria 1960, Nigerian Administration and its Political Setting (Ed.) 1969, Nigerian Federal Finance: Its Development, Problems and Prospects 1969, Local Government Finance in Nigeria: Problems and Prospects (Co-ed.) 1972, Management Problems and Rapid Urbanisation in Nigeria (Co-ed.) 1973, The Tanzania Civil Service, a Decade after Independence 1974, Developing Research on African Administration: Some Methodological Issues (co-editor) 1974, Africa, The Third World and the Search for a New Economic Order 1977, Africa and the New International Economic Order: A Reassessment 1979, The Indigenization of the African Economy 1981, Economic Crisis in Africa: African Perspectives on Development Problems and Potentials (Co.-Ed.) 1985, Towards the Dawn of the Third Millennium and the Beginning of the Twenty-First Century 1986, Towards a Dynamic African Economy: Selected Speeches and Lectures 1975–1986 1989, African Within the World 1993, South Africa & Africa: Within or Apart? 1996, Nigeria: Renewal from the Roots? 1997, Comprehending and Mastering African Conflicts 1999. *Leisure interests:* photography, lawn tennis, golf, walking. *Address:* Asiwaju Court, Gra, Ijebu Ode, Nigeria. *Telephone:* 37-432208 (Office); 37-433000 (Home). *Fax:* 7-269-1746.

ADELI, Muhammad Hossein, PH.D.; Iranian banker; b. 1952, Ahwaz; m. Khadijeh Aryan; two s. one d.; fmr. Gov. Cen. Bank of Iran. *Leisure interest:* reading. *Address:* c/o Bank Markazi Jomhouri Islami Iran, P.O. Box 11365/8551, Ferdowsi Avenue, Tehran, Iran.

ADELMAN, Irma Glicman, PH.D.; American (b. Romanian) professor of economics; b. 14 March 1930, Romania; d. of the late Jacob Max Glicman and Raissa Etinger; m. Frank Louis Adelman 1950 (divorced 1979); one s.; ed. Univ. of Calif. at Berkeley; Asst. Prof., Stanford Univ. 1960–62; Assoc. Prof. Johns Hopkins Univ. 1962–66; Prof. of Econs. Northwestern Univ. 1967–72; Sr. Economist Devt. Research Centre, IBRD 1971–72; Prof. of Econs. Univ. of Md. 1972–79; Consultant U.S. Dept. of State 1963–72, IBRD 1968–, ILO, Geneva 1973–; Fellow Netherlands Inst. of Advanced Study, Cleveringa Chair Leiden Univ. 1977–78; Prof. of Econs. and Agric. and Resource Econs. Univ. of Calif. at Berkeley 1979–94, Emer. Prof. 1994–; Vice-Pres. American Econ. Asscn.; Fellow American Acad. of Arts and Sciences, Econometric Soc., Royal Soc. for the Encouragement of Arts 1990; Order of the Bronze Tower (South Korea). *Publications:* Theories of Economic Growth and Development 1964, Society, Politics and Economic Development (with C. T. Morris) 1967, Economic Growth and Social Equity in Developing Countries (with C. T. Morris) 1973, Income Distribution Planning (with Sherman Robinson) 1978, Comparative Patterns of Economic Development: 1850–1914 (with C.T. Morris) 1988, Village Economics (with J. Edward Taylor) 1996, Social Effects, The South Korean Miracle: How Replicable Is It? 1999. *Leisure interests:* art, theatre, music. *Address:* Agriculture and Natural Resources Department, 207 Gianninni Hall, University of California at Berkeley, Berkeley, CA 94720 (Office); 10 Rosemont Avenue, Berkeley, CA 94708, U.S.A. (Home). *Telephone:* 510 642-6417 (Office); 510 527-5280 (Home). *Fax:* 510 643-8911.

ADELMAN, Kenneth Lee, PH.D.; American government official; b. 9 June 1946, Chicago, Ill.; s. of Harry Adelman and Corinne Unger; m. Carol Craigle 1971; two d.; ed. Grinnell Coll., Georgetown Univ.; with U.S Dept. of Commerce 1968–70; Special Asst. VISTA, Washington, D.C. 1970–72; Liaison Officer, AID 1975–76; Asst. to Sec. of Defense 1976–77; Sr. Political Scientist, Stanford Research Inst. Arlington, Va. 1977–81; Amb. and Deputy Perm. Rep. to UN 1981–83; Dir. Arms Control and Disarmament Agency (ACDA) 1983–88; Vice-Pres. Inst. of Contemporary Studies 1988–; Instructor in Shakespeare, Georgetown Univ. 1977–79. *Publications:* The Defense Revolution (with N. Augustine) 1991 and articles in newspapers, magazines and professional journals. *Address:* Institute of Contemporary Studies, 4018 27th Street, North Arlington, VA 22207-5207, U.S.A.

ADELSOHN, Ulf, LL.B.; Swedish politician; b. 4 Oct. 1941, Stockholm; s. of Oskar and Margareta Adelsohn; m. Lena Liljeroth 1981; one s. one d.; legal adviser, Real Estate Co., Stockholm City 1968–70; Man.'s Asst., Swedish Confederation of Professional Asscns. 1970–73; Commr., Street and Traffic Dept., Stockholm City Admin. 1973–76; Mayor and Finance Commr. 1976–79; Minister for Transport and Communications 1979–81; mem. Riksdagen (Parl.) 1982–88; Leader Moderata Samlingspartiet (Conservative Party) 1981–86; County Gov. of Stockholm 1992–; Chair. Luftfartsverket (Civil Aviation Authority), Skansen (open air museum). *Publications:* Torsten Kreuger, Sanningen på väg (Torsten Kreuger, Truth on its Way) 1972, Kommunalmän: Hur skulle ni göra om det vore era egna pengar? (Local Politicians: What would you do if it was your money?) 1978, Ulf Adelsohn Partiledare 1981–86 (Leader of the Party 1981–86) 1987, Priset för ett liv (The Price for a Life) 1991. *Leisure interests:* ice hockey, tennis. *Address:* Slottsbacken 4, 11130 Stockholm, Sweden.

ÁDER, János, DR.IUR.; Hungarian politician; b. 1959, Csorna; s. of Terézia Szabó; m.; one s. two d.; ed. Révai Miklós Grammar School, Györ, Loránd Eötvös Univ., Budapest; council exec. Dist. VI, Budapest City Council 1983–85; researcher Sociology Research Inst., Hungarian Acad. of Sciences 1986–90; joined Fed. of Young Democrats (FIDESz) 1988, Vice-Chair. 1993–, Exec. Vice-Pres. 1997–; M.P. 1990–98, M.P. as rep. of FIDESz-Hungarian Civic Party coalition 1998–; Vice-Chair. of Parl. 1990–98; Pres. Nat. Ass. 1998–. *Leisure interests:* angling, soccer. *Address:* 1357 Budapest, Kossuth Lajos tér 1-3, Hungary. *Telephone:* (1) 268-4402. *Fax:* (1) 268-4806.

ADESINA, Segun, D.ED.; Nigerian professor of education; b. 5 Jan. 1941, Abeokuta, Ogun State; s. of Samuel Adesina and Georgiette Adesina; m. 1968; five c.; ed. Loyola Coll., Nigerian Coll. of Arts, Science & Tech., Univ. of Ife, and N. Ill. and Columbia Univs.; history tutor, Loyola Coll. 1965–66; Asst. lecturer in Educ. Univ. of Lagos Coll. of Educ. 1967–69, lecturer 1969–75; Sr. lecturer Univ. of Lagos Faculty of Educ. 1975–77, Assoc. Prof. 1977–78, Prof. of Educ. 1988, now Dir. Inst. of Educ.; Prof. of Educ. Ilorin

Univ.; Visiting Prof. and Provost, Univ. of Ife, Adeyemi Coll. of Educ. Ondo 1984–85; Exec. Sec. Nigerian Educational Research Council 1987; Adviser on Educ. UN Office, Geneva 1975–76; consultant, Unesco, Senegal 1984; numerous other academic and professional appts. etc.; Fellow, Nigerian Inst. of Admin. Man. Assoc. Inst. of Personnel Man., mem. Nigerian Inst. of Man., Presidential Cttee. on Brain Drain. *Publications:* Primary Education in Nigeria: A Book of Readings, co-Ed. Planning and Educational Development in Nigeria 1978. *Address:* Nigerian Educational Research Council, 3 Jibowu Street, P.O. Box 8058, Yaba, Lagos (Office); P.O. Box 41, Abeokuta, Nigeria (Home). *Telephone:* 01-822988 (Office); 039-232226 (Home).

ADESOLA, Akin Oludele, M.D., M.CH., F.R.C.S. (ENG.), F.A.C.S.; Nigerian university professor; b. 6 Nov. 1930, Aba, Nigeria; s. of Bamgboye F. Adesola and Felicia A. Adesola (née Dedeke); m. Oyebola Sodeinde 1959; two d.; ed. Abeokuta Grammar School, Univ. of Ibadan, Queen's Univ. of Belfast, Royal Coll. of Surgeons of England, Univ. of Rochester, U.S.A.; surgical tutor Queen's Univ. Belfast 1959–61; Sr. Buswell Fellow Univ. of Rochester, New York, U.S.A. 1963–64; Prof. of Surgery Univ. of Lagos 1967–88; Pres. W. Africa Soc. of Gastroenterology 1967–72, Nigerian Surgical Research Soc. 1975–79, W. Africa Coll. of Surgeons 1975–77; Chair. Nat. Orthopaedic Hospitals Man. Bd. 1977–78, Health Educ. Research and Man. Services 1989–, Bd. of Trustees W. African Coll. of Surgeons 1991–, Nat. Cttee. on Medical Care and Training 1991–; Vice-Chancellor Univ. of Ilorin 1978–81, Univ. of Lagos 1981–88; Chair. Asscn. of Commonwealth Univs. 1984–85; mem. Albert Schweitzer Int. Nomination Council 1984–, Commonwealth Expert Group on Distance Educ. 1986–88; Fellow Nigerian Acad. of Science 1986–; Consultant on Higher Educ. to IBRD 1988–, to Canadian Int. Devt. Agency 1988–; Ed. Nigerian Medical Journal 1970–80; mem. editorial Bd. British Journal of Surgery 1968–80; mem. Expert Panel Comm. on Commonwealth Studies, Commonwealth Secr. 1995–, Int. Steering Cttee. Leadership for Environment and Devt. (LEAD) Int., Rockefeller Foundation, N.Y. 1996–; Symons Medal for Distinguished Service to Commonwealth Univs. 1987, Distinguished Visitor Award, Carnegie Corpn. of New York 1988, Adesuyi Prize for Outstanding Contributions to Health in West Africa (West African Health Community) 1993; Hon. LL.D. (Queen's Univ. of Belfast) 1989. *Publications:* Coronary Thrombosis: The Influence of Meterological Changes 1960, Hyperparathyroidism and the Alimentary Tract 1960, Adult Intussusception In Western Nigeria 1964, Influence of Vasoactive Agents on Ascites 1965, Chronic Gastritis and Duodenal Ulcer in Nigerians 1974, Endoscopy in Upper Gastrointestinal Disease in Nigerians 1978, Technology in a Developing Economy 1983, The Nigerian University System: Meeting the Challenges of Growth in a Depressed Economy 1991, Anatomy of Service 1997. *Leisure interests:* golf, swimming, music. *Address:* 1 Ajani Olujare Street, Surulere, P.O. Box 51218, Falomo-Ikoyi, Lagos, Nigeria. *Telephone:* (1) 583-4470. *Fax:* (1) 583-4470.

ADEWOYE, Omoniyi; Nigerian university lecturer and fmr. politician; b. 27 Oct. 1939, Inisa, Osun State; s. of late Chief James Woye and Victoria Fadunke Woye; m. Margaret Titilayo 1967; five d.; ed. Kiriji Memorial Coll., Igbajo, Univ. of Ibadan and Columbia Univ., New York; Lecturer in History, Univ. of Ibadan 1968–75, Sr. Lecturer 1975, Prof. 1984–; Commr. for Econ. Devt., Western State 1975–76; Commr. for Finance and Econ. Devt., Oyo State 1976–77; Fed. Commr. for Econ. Devt. 1977–79; First Chair. Council of Ministers, Econ. Community of West African States 1977–78; Chair. Council of Ministers, Nigerian-Niger Jt. Comm. 1977–78; Consultant to Econ. Comm. for Africa on Econ. Integration in W. Africa 1982–83; Hon. Treas. Historical Soc. of Nigeria 1972–77; Woodrow Wilson Dissertation Scholarship (Columbia Univ.) 1967, Afgrad Fellowship (U.S.A.) 1964–68. *Publications:* The Legal Profession in Nigeria 1865–1962, 1977, The Judicial System in Southern Nigeria 1854–1954, 1977. *Leisure interests:* gardening, reading, writing, music. *Address:* P.O. Box 7321, Secretariat, Ibadan, Nigeria.

ADEY, Christopher, F.R.C.M.; British conductor; b. 19 Feb. 1943, London; m. Catherine Cave 1965 (divorced 1985); one s.; ed. Royal Acad. of Music, London; violinist with Hallé Orchestra 1963–65, London Philharmonic Orchestra 1967–71; Assoc. Conductor, BBC Scottish Symphony Orchestra 1973–76, Ulster Orchestra 1981–83; Conductor and Prof. Royal Coll. of Music 1979–; Dir. of Orchestral Studies, RCM Jr. Dept. 1973–84; now freelance conductor appearing as guest conductor with major orchestras in U.K., Europe, U.S.A. and Canada and with nat. and int. youth and student orchestras; Czechoslovakian Commemorative Medal 1986. *Address:* 137 Anson Road, Willesden Green, London, NW2 4AH, England.

ADHIKARI, Man Mohan, B.SC.; Nepalese politician; b. June 1920, Kathmandu; ed. Banares Hindu Univ., India; joined Quit India Movt. 1942; imprisoned in India for political activities for 18 months; returned to Nepal 1947; imprisoned in Nepal for political activities for three years; Gen. Sec. Nepal Communist Party (NCP) 1953; imprisoned for involvement in attempt to overthrow monarchy 1960–69; Pres. Communist Party of Nepal (Unified Marxist-Leninist—UML) 1991–; Prime Minister of Nepal 1994–95. *Address:* Communist Party of Nepal, Madan Nagar Balkhu, P.O. Box 5471, Kathmandu, Nepal.

ADIE, Kathryn (Kate), O.B.E., B.A.; British correspondent; b. 19 Sept. 1945; d. of John Wilfrid Adie and Maud (née Fambely) Adie; ed. Sunderland Church High School and Newcastle Univ.; technician and producer B.B.C. Radio 1969–76; Reporter B.B.C. T.V. South 1977–78, B.B.C. T.V. News 1979–81, Corresp. 1982–, Chief Corresp. 1989–; Hon. Prof. Sunderland Univ. 1995; Hon. M.A. (Bath) 1987, Hon. M.A. (Newcastle) 1990, Hon. D.Litt. (City) 1989, (Loughborough) 1991, (Sunderland) 1993, (Robert Gordon) 1996; Hon. M. Univ. (Open) 1996; RTS News Award 1981, 1987, Monte Carlo Int. News Award 1981, 1990, B.A.F.T.A. Richard Dimbleby Award 1989; Freeman of Sunderland 1990. *Address:* c/o BBC TV, Wood Lane, London, W12 7RJ, England. *Telephone:* 0181-576 8830.

ADIREKSARN, Pol. Gen. Pramara; Thai politician; b. 6 Jan. 1914; ed. Chulachomklao Royal Mil. Acad.; mil. career until 1951; Deputy Communications Minister 1951; MP for Saraburi 1956–; Industry Minister 1956; Deputy Premier 1975–76; Minister of Defence 1975; Minister of Agric. 1976; founded Chat Thai Party 1976, party leader 1976–86; fmr. Interior Minister, fmr. Industry Minister; Minister of Industry Sept.–Dec. 1990, of the Interior 1990–91. *Address:* c/o Ministry of the Interior, Bangkok 10200, Thailand.

ADJANI, Isabelle; French actress; b. 27 June 1955; two s., ed. Lycée de Courbevoie; Pres. Comm. d'avances sur recettes 1986–88. *Films:* Faustine et le bel été 1972, la Gifle 1974, l'Histoire d' Adèle H. 1975 (Best Actress, New York Critics 1976), le Locataire 1976, Barocco 1977, Violette et François 1977, Driver 1977, Nosferatu 1978, les Soeurs Brontë 1978, Possession 1980 (Best Actress, Cannes 1981), Clara et les chics types 1980, Quartet 1981 (Best Actress, Cannes 1982), l'Année prochaine si tout va bien 1981, Antonieta 1982, l'Eté meurtrier 1983 (Best Actress César 1984), Mortelle randonnée 1983, Subway 1985, Ishtar 1987, Camille Claudel 1988 (Best Actress César 1989, Best Actress Award, Berlin Film Festival 1989), La Reine Margot 1994 (Best Actress César 1995), Diabolique 1996. *Theatre:* la Maison de Bernarda Alba 1970, l'Avare 1972–73, l'Ecole des femmes 1973, Port-Royal 1973, Ondine 1974, Mademoiselle Julie 1983. *TV appearances include:* le Petit bougnat 1969, le Secret des flamands 1972, l'Ecole des femmes 1973, Top à Sacha Distel 1974, Princesse aux petits pois 1986. *Address:* c/o Phonogram, 89 blvd. Auguste Blanqui, 75013 Paris, France.

ADJI, Boukary; Niger politician and economist; Minister of Finance 1983–87; Deputy Gov. Cen. Bank of West African States (BCEAO) –1996; Prime Minister of Niger Jan.–Dec. 1996. *Address:* c/o Office of the Prime Minister, Niamey, Niger.

ADKISSON, Perry Lee, PH.D.; American entomologist; b. 11 March 1929, Hickman, Arkansas; s. of Robert L. Adkisson and Imogene (née Perry) Adkisson; m. Frances Rozelle 1956; one d.; ed. Univ. of Arkansas, Kansas State Univ. and Harvard Univ.; Asst. Prof. of Entomology Univ. of Missouri 1956–58; Assoc. Prof. of Entomology Texas A&M Univ. 1958–63, Prof. of Entomology 1963–67, Head, Dept. of Entomology 1967–78, Distinguished Prof. of Entomology 1967–, Vice-Pres. for Agric. and Renewable Resources 1978–80, Deputy Chancellor for Agric. 1980–83, Deputy Chancellor 1983–86, Chancellor 1986–91, Regent's Prof. 1991–95; Consultant Int. AEC, Vienna 1969–74; Chair. Texas Pesticide Advisory Comm. 1972; mem. panel on integrated pest control FAO, Rome 1971–78; mem. N.A.S., mem. Governing Bd. Int. Crop Research Inst. for Semi-Arid Tropics 1982–88, Standing Cttee. for Int. Plant Protection Congresses 1984–, Texas Science and Tech. Council 1986–, Advisory Cttee., Export-Import Bank of the U.S. 1987; Alexander Von Humboldt Award 1980, Distinguished Service Award, American Inst. of Biological Sciences 1987, Distinguished Alumni Award (Ark. Univ.) 1990, Wolfe Prize in Agric. 1994–95, World Food Prize 1997 and numerous others. *Publications:* Controlling Cotton's Insect Pests: A New System 1982; several papers on insect diapause and other entomological topics. *Leisure interests:* gardening, fishing. *Address:* The Texas A&M University, Entomology Department, College Station, TX 77843; The Reed House, 1 Reed Dr., College Station, TX 77843, U.S.A.

ADLER, Julius, PH.D.; American biologist and biochemist; b. 30 April 1930, Edelfingen, Germany; s. of Adolf Adler and Irma Stern; m. Hildegard Wohl 1963; one s. one d.; ed. Harvard Univ. and Univ. of Wisconsin; emigrated to U.S.A. 1938, naturalized U.S. citizen 1943; Postdoctoral Fellow, Wash. Univ., St. Louis 1957–59, Stanford Univ. 1959–60; Asst Prof., Depts. of Biochemistry and Genetics, Univ. of Wis. 1960–63, Assoc. Prof. 1963–66, Prof. 1966–92, Emer Prof. 1996–, Edwin Bret Hart Prof. 1972; Steenbock Prof. of Microbiological Sciences 1982–92; Dr. h.c. (Tübingen) 1987, (Regensburg) 1995; mem. American Acad. of Arts and Sciences, American Philosophical Soc., N.A.S., Wisc. Acad. of Sciences, Arts and Letters; Fellow American Asscn. for the Advancement of Science, American Acad. of Microbiology; Behring Lecturer, Philips Univ. of Marburg 1989, Hartman-Müller Memorial Lecturer, Univ. of Zürich 1984; Selman A. Waksman Microbiology Award, N.A.S. 1980, Otto-Warburg medal, German Soc. of Biological Chemistry 1986, Hilldale Award, Univ. of Wisconsin 1988, R.H. Wright Award, Simon Fraser Univ. 1988, Abbott-American Soc. for Microbiology Lifetime Achievement Award 1995, William C. Rose Award (American Soc. for Biochem. and Molecular Biology) 1996. *Publications:* research papers on the behaviour of simple organisms, especially bacteria. *Address:* Department of Biochemistry, University of Wisconsin-Madison, Madison, WI 53706; 1234 Wellesley Rd., Madison,WI 53705, U.S.A.

ADLER, Larry (Lawrence Cecil); American mouth organist; b. 10 Feb. 1914; s. of Louis Adler and Sadie Hack; m. 1st Eileen Walser 1938 (dissolved 1961); one s. two d.; m. 2nd Sally Cline 1969 (dissolved 1977); one d.; ed. Baltimore City Coll.; won Maryland Harmonica Championship 1927; first stage appearance, New York 1928; first British appearance in C. B. Cochran's Streamline revue 1934; first appearance as soloist with symphony orchestra,

Sydney, Australia 1939; jt. recital tours with dancer Paul Draper, U.S. 1941–49; soloist with New York Philharmonic and other major U.S. orchestras and orchestras in England, Japan and Europe; war tours for Allied Troops 1943, 1944, 1945, Germany 1947, 1949, Korea (British Commonwealth Div.) 1951, Israel (Six-Day War) 1967, (Yom Kippur War) 1973; numerous one-man TV shows; soloist, first performance of unpublished George Gershwin quartet (MS gift to Adler from Ira Gershwin) Edinburgh Festival 1963; works composed for him by Ralph Vaughan Williams, Malcolm Arnold, Darius Milhaud, Arthur Benjamin, Gordon Jacob and others. *Compositions include:* film scores for Genevieve, King and Country, High Wind in Jamaica, The Great Chase etc.; TV scores for BBC serial Midnight Men, various TV plays and documentaries; music for TV commercials, children's records, stage plays etc.; concert music, Theme and Variations, Camera III; one-man show, From Hand to Mouth, Edinburgh Festival 1965, other festivals 1965–; Duke Ellington Fellow, Yale Univ. 1988. *Publications:* How I Play 1937, Larry Adler's Own Arrangements 1960, Jokes and How to Tell Them 1963, It Ain't Necessarily So (autobiog.) 1985, Me and My Big Mouth 1994. *Leisure interests:* tennis, journalism, cycling, conversation. *Address:* c/o MBA Literary Agents, 45 Fitzroy Street, London, W1P 5HR, England.

ADLERCREUTZ, (Carl) Herman (Thomas), M.D., PH.D.; Finnish professor of clinical chemistry; b. 10 April 1932, Helsinki; s. of Erik and Elisabeth Adlercreutz; m. 1st Marie-Louise Gräsbeck 1956 (divorced 1974); m. 2nd Sirkka T. Neva 1976; one s. two d.; ed. Univ. of Helsinki; Research Fellow, Hormone Lab. Dept. of Obstetrics & Gynaecology, Karolinska Hosp. Stockholm 1958–61; Resident in Internal Medicine, Univ. of Helsinki 1961–64, Acting Asst. Prof. of Internal Medicine 1964–65, Assoc. Prof. of Clinical Chem. 1965–69, Acting Prof. of Clinical Chem. 1967–69, Prof. of Clinical Chem. 1969; Chief Physician, Central Lab. Helsinki Univ. Central Hosp. 1965; Research Prof. Acad. of Finland 1983–88; mem. thirteen foreign socs.; mem. numerous ed. bds. of journals, Comm. on Health and Science Asscn. of European Olympic Cttees. 1985–93; Finnish White Rose Order of Knighthood, The Tenth Dr R. Edwards Medal 1987, and other awards and distinctions. *Publications:* about 400 original publications mainly in the fields of steroid hormones, endocrinology, nutrition and cancer. *Leisure interests:* gardening, fishing, sport. *Address:* Riskutie 13, 00950 Helsinki, Finland (Home). *Telephone:* 358-0-320258 (Home).

ADNI, Daniel; Israeli concert pianist; b. 6 Dec. 1951, Haifa; ed. High Schools in Haifa and Tel-Aviv, Conservatoire of Music in Paris; first Recital in Haifa 1963; professional début, London 1970; New York début 1976; has played at most musical centres in the world incl. U.K., Germany, Israel, U.S.A., Japan, South Africa, Switzerland, Norway, Netherlands, Romania, Australia, New Zealand, Finland, Austria; made over 20 records for EMI-His Master's Voice; First Prize, Paris Conservatoire; First Prize, Young Concert Artists' Auditions, New York. *Leisure interests:* cinema, theatre, bridge, walks, sightseeing. *Address:* c/o 64 A Menelik Road, London, NW2 3RH, England. *Telephone:* 0171-794 4076. *Fax:* 0171-794 4076.

ADOLFO (Adolfo F. Sardiña); American fashion designer; b. 15 Feb. 1933, Cardenas, Matanzas, Cuba; ed. St. Ignacio de Loyola Jesuit School, Havana; served Cuban Army; apprentice, Cristóbal Balenciaga millinery salon, Paris 1950–52; apprentice millinery designer, Bergdorf Goodman, New York 1953–54; designer Emme (milliners), New York 1954–62; worked as unpaid apprentice, Chanel, New York summers of 1957, 1966; owner and head designer, Adolfo Inc., New York 1962–; designer, Adolfo Menswear Inc. and Adolfo Scarves Inc., New York 1978–; created perfume line for Frances Denny, New York 1979; mem. Council, Fashion Designers of America 1982.

ADOOR, Gopalakrishnan; Indian film maker; b. 3 July 1941, Adoor, Kerala; s. of late Madhavan Unnithan and Gouri Kunjamma; m. R. Sunanda 1972; one d.; mem. Working Group on Nat. Film Policy 1979–80; Dir. Nat. Film Devt. Corpn. 1980–83; mem. Faculties of Fine Arts, Univ. of Kerala, Calicut and Mahatma Gandhi Univs. 1985–89; Chair. Film & Television Inst. of India 1987–89, 1993–96; Chair. 7th Int. Children's Film Festival of India 1991; mem. Advisory Cttee. Nat. Film Archive of India 1988–90; Chair. Jury Singapore Int. Film Festival; mem. Jury, Int. Film Festival of India 1983, Venice Int. Film Festival 1988, Bombay Int. Festival 1990, Hawaii Int. Film Festival, Sochi Int. Film Festival, Alexandria Int. Film Festival; numerous int. film awards; awarded title of Padmashri 1984. *Films include:* Swayamvaran 1972, Kodiyettam 1977, Elippathayam 1981 (British Film Inst. Award), Mukhamukham 1984 (Int. Film Critics' Prize, New Delhi), Anantaram 1987, Mathilukal 1989 Vidheyan 1993, Kathapurushan 1995 and more than 24 short and documentary films. *Publications include:* plays: Vaiki vanna velicham 1961, Ninte rajyam varunnu 1963; The World of Cinema 1983; collections of essays. *Address:* Darsanam, Trivandrum, 695 017, Kerala, India. *Telephone:* (471) 551144. *Fax:* (471) 446567.

ADOUKI, Martin, D.JUR.; Republic of Congo diplomatist; b. 8 April 1942, Makoua; ed. Bordeaux and Paris Univs. and the Int. Inst. of Public Admin., Paris; Information Officer for the Group of African, Caribbean and Pacific Countries (ACP) in Brussels and attended negotiations between the ACP and the EEC; fmrly. Lecturer in Law at the Marien Ngouabi Univ., Brazzaville and later Special Adviser to the Prime Minister of the Congo; Perm. Rep. of the Congo to the UN 1985–94, to UN Security Council 1986–87, Pres. UN Security Council 1986–87, Chair. UN African Group Sept. 1986, Rep. of Chair. of OAU to UN 1986–87, Head Congo Del. to 43rd Session of Gen. Ass. 1988; mem. of the Zone of Peace and Co-operation in the South Atlantic 1988–90, mem. Del. of UN Special Cttee. on the Verification of Elections in Namibia 1989, Vice-Pres. UN Gen. Ass. (44th Session) 1989; Congolese Observer on the Gen. Elections in Nicaragua Feb. 1990, Head Congolese Del. to World Summit for Children Sept. 1990; Chair. 4th Cttee. of 45th Session of Gen. Ass. 1990–91; Amb. and Diplomatic Adviser to Pres. of the Congo 1998–. *Address:* c/o Ministry of Foreign Affairs and Co-operation, BP 2070, Brazzaville, Republic of Congo. *Telephone:* 81-47-14. *Fax:* 81-47-14.

ADOUM, Mahamat Ali; Chadian diplomatist; b. 14 Nov. 1947, Michimeré; m.; six c.; ed. Brazzaville Univ. (Congo), Laval Univ. Quebec and Johns Hopkins School of Advanced Int. Studies, Washington, D.C.; fmr. school teacher, headmaster and educ. inspector; First Counsellor, Embassy of Chad, Washington, D.C. 1977–79, Chargé d'Affaires 1979–81, 1982–83; Amb. to U.S.A. (also accred. to Canada 1983); Perm. Rep. to UN 1985–92; mem. Chad del. to UN Gen. Assembly 1978, 1979, 1982, to meetings of IBRD and IMF 1977–84. *Address:* c/o Ministry of Foreign Affairs, N'Djamena, Chad.

ADRIANO, Dino, F.C.C.A.; British business executive; b. 24 April 1943; s. of Dante Adriano and Yole Adriano; m. Susan Rivett 1996; two d.; ed. Strand Grammar School and Highgate Coll.; articled clerk, George W. Spencer & Co. 1959–64; Accounting Dept. trainee J. Sainsbury PLC 1964–65, Financial Accounts Dept. 1965–73, Br. Financial Control Man. 1973–80, Area Dir. Sainsbury's Cen. and Western Area 1986–89, Asst. Man. Dir. 1995–96, Deputy Chief Exec. 1996–97, Jt. Group Chief Exec. 1997–; Gen. Man. Homebase 1981–86, Man. Dir. 1989–95, Deputy Chief Exec. 1996–97; Dir. Laura Ashley PLC 1996–; Trustee Oxfam 1990–96, Adviser on Retail Matters 1996–. *Leisure interests:* opera, music, soccer, cookery. *Address:* Stamford House, Stamford Street, London, SE1 9LL, England. *Telephone:* 0171-921 7945.

ADVADZE, Valerian Sergeyevich, D.ECON.; Georgian economist and politician; b. 1930; fmr. Dir. Scientific Research Inst. for the Econs., Planning and Man. of the Econ. (attached to the Ministry of Econs. and Finance); fmr. Leader Union for Nat. Accord and Rebirth (Presidential Cand. 1991); U.S.S.R. People's Deputy 1989–91; Amb. to Russia 1992–95; Georgian Rep. Interstate Econ. Cttee. of CIS 1995–. *Address:* Georgian Embassy, Paliashvili Str. 6, Moscow, Russia. *Telephone:* (095) 291-2136.

ADVANI, Lal K.; Indian politician, fmr. journalist and social worker; b. 8 Nov. 1927, Karachi (now in Pakistan); s. of Kishinchand Advani and Gyani Advani; m. Kamala Jagtiani 1965; one s. one d.; ed. St. Patrick's High School, Karachi, D.G. Nat. Coll., Hyderabad, Sind, Govt. Law Coll., Bombay; joined Rashtriya Swayam Sevak Sangh (RSS, social work org.) 1942, Sec. of Karachi branch 1947; joined Bharatiya Jana Sangh (BJS) 1951; party work in Rajasthan until 1958, Sec. of Delhi State Jana Sangh 1958–63, Vice-Pres. 1965–67; mem. Cen. Exec. of BJS 1966; Joint Ed. of BJS paper Organizer 1960–67; mem. interim Metropolitan Council, Delhi 1966, leader of Jana Sangh Gp. 1966; Chair. of Metropolitan Council 1967; mem. Rajya Sabha 1970, head of Jana Sangh parl. gp. 1970; Pres. Bharatiya Jana Sangh 1973–77 (incorp. in Janata); detained during emergency 1975–77; Gen. Sec. Janata Party Jan.-May 1977; Minister of Information and Broadcasting 1977–79, of Home Affairs 1998–; Gen. Sec. Bharatiya Janata Party 1980–86, Pres. 1986–90, June 1993–; Leader of Opposition, Lok Sabha Dec. 1990–March 1991, 1991–96. *Publications:* A Prisoner's Scrap-Book, The People Betrayed. *Leisure interests:* theatre, cinema, books. *Address:* c/o Bharatiya Janata Party, 11 Ashok Road, New Delhi 110 001; C-1/6, Pandara Park, New Delhi, India. *Telephone:* 3782397 (Home). *Telephone:* (11) 3382234. *Fax:* (11) 3782163.

ADYEBO COSMAS, George; Ugandan politician and economist; fmr. Prin. Uganda Coll. of Commerce; mem. Nat. Resistance Council; Prime Minister of Uganda 1991–94. *Address:* c/o Office of the Prime Minister, P.O. Box 7006, Kampala, Uganda.

ADYRKHAYEVA, Svetlana Dzantemirovna; Russian/Ossetian ballerina; b. 12 May 1938, Ordzonikidze (now Vladikavkaz); d. of Taissya Gougkayeva and Dzantemir Adyrkhayev; m. Alexey Zakalinsky 1966; one d.; ed. Leningrad Choreographic School, Theatre Acad. of Russia; danced with Glinka Theatre of Opera and Ballet, Chelyabinsk 1955–58; with Odessa Opera and Ballet 1958–60; dancer at Bolshoi Theatre 1960–88; U.S.S.R. People's Artist 1984; Dir. Sveltlana Adyrkhayeva Ballet Theatre, Moscow. *Main roles include:* Odette-Odile, Princess Florine, Woman of the Bronze Mountain (Prokofiev's Stone Flower), Zarema (Asafiev's Fountain of Bakhchisaray), Mehmene Banu (Melikov's Legend of Love), Aegina (Khatchaturyan's Spartacus), Kitri (Minkus's Don Quixote). *Leisure interests:* reading, travelling. *Address:* 1 Smolensky per. 9, Apt. 74, 121099 Moscow, Russia. *Telephone:* (095) 241-13-62.

AFANASIYEV, Yuri Nikolaevich, D.HIS.SC.; Russian politician and historian; b. 5 Sept. 1934, Maina, Ulyanovsk region; m.; two c.; ed. Moscow State Univ., Acad. of Social Sciences; mem. CPSU 1956–90; instructor, then sec. Comsomol org. in Krasnoyarsk Region 1957–64, mem. of Comsomol Cen. Cttee. 1964–71; Deputy Head of Div. 1971, lecturer Higher Comsomol School 1971, Pro-rector 1972–83; sr. researcher Inst. of World History U.S.S.R. Acad. of Sciences 1983–87; Rector Moscow Inst. of History and Archives (now Russian Humanitarian Univ.) 1987–; U.S.S.R. People's Deputy 1989–91, mem. of Interregional Deputies' Group, People's Deputy of Russia 1991–92; Co-Chair. Democratic Russia Movt. 1991–92. *Publications:* works on problems of Russian history and contemporary politics. *Address:* Russian

Humanitarian University, ul. Chayanova 15, 125267 Moscow, Russia. *Telephone:* (095) 250 63 36 (Office); (095) 921 41 69 (Home).

AFANASIYEVSKY, Nikolai Nikolayevich; Russian diplomatist; b. 1 Oct. 1940, Moscow; m.; one s.; ed. Moscow Inst. of Int. Relations; mem. CPSU -1991; attaché, Embassy, Cameroon, 1964–66; with Ministry of Foreign Affairs 1966–76; del. to UN Gen. Ass. 1969; del. to CSCE, Geneva, Helsinki; 1973–75; counsellor, ministry counsellor, Embassy, Paris 1976–83; Deputy Chief of First European Dept., Ministry of Foreign Affairs 1983–86, Chief 1986–90; Amb. to Belgium and liaison to NATO 1990–94; Deputy Minister of Foreign Affairs 1994–98; Amb. to France 1998–. *Address:* Russian Embassy, boulevard Lannes 40-50, 75016 Paris, France. *Telephone:* (1) 45.04.05.50.

AFEWERKI, Issaias; Eritrean politician; b. 1945, Asmara; trained as engineer; joined Eritrean Liberation Front (ELF) 1966, mil. training in China 1966, Leader fourth regional area ELF 1968, Gen. Commdr. ELF 1969; founding mem. Eritrean People's Liberation Front (EPLF) now People's Front for Democracy and Justice (PFDJ) 1977, fmr. Asst. Sec. Gen., Sec. Gen. 1987; Chair. State Council, Nat. Ass.; Sec. Gen. Provisional Govt. of Eritrea 1991; assumed power May 1991; elected Pres. by Nat. Ass. June 1993–. *Address:* State Council, Asmara, Eritrea.

AFFANDI, Achmad; Indonesian politician; b. 27 Oct. 1927, Kuningan, W. Java; ed. Univ. of Indonesia, Bogor, Army Staff and Command Coll., Bandung and Univ. of Kentucky; teacher, Sr. High School and Teachers' Coll., Bogor 1953–57; Asst. Faculty of Agric., Bogor 1957–58, Asst. Lecturer 1959–60; Jr. Lecturer, Inst. of Agric., Bogor 1960–62, Lecturer 1962–64; Head, Bureau for Equipment and Campus Devt., Dept. of Higher Educ. and Science 1962–64; sr. official, Dept. of Defence and Security 1965–67; Dir. of Animal Husbandry, Bimas (Mass Guidance) poultry farming 1968–69; Agric. Attaché, The Hague 1969–71; Sec. Bimas Supervisory Body, Dept. of Agric. 1971–73; Insp.-Gen. Dept. of Agric. 1973–74; Dir.-Gen. of Food Crops, Dept. of Agric. 1974; Jr. Minister for Food Production 1978–83; Minister of Agric. 1983–88.

AFFLECK, James G., PH.D. American business executive; b. 1923; m.; ed. Princeton Univ.; joined American Cyanamid Co. 1947; successively research chemist, chemist, tech. rep., Man. New York New Products Office 1947–57; Man. Rubber Chem. Dept. 1957–61; Asst. Gen. Man. Commercial Devt. Div. 1961–64; Consumer Products 1964–65, Int. Divs. 1965–67; Gen. Man. Agricultural Div. 1967–71; Corporate Vice-Pres. 1971–72, Pres. 1972–76; Chair., Pres. and C.E.O. American Cyanamid 1976–82, Chair. 1982–; Dir. Potlatch Corpn., N.J. Bell, Prudential Insurance Co.; Trustee, Foundation of Coll. of Medicine and Dentistry, N.J., American Enterprise Inst., Jt. Council on Econ. Educ., Fairleigh Dickinson Univ.; mem. Bd. of Dirs. Pharmaceutical Mfrs. Asscn., Nat. Asscn. of Mfrs.

AFRAH, Maj.-Gen. Hussein Kulmia; Somali politician and army officer; b. 1920, Margeh; ed. Italian Secondary School, Mogadishu, and Italian Officers' Acad., Rome; shopkeeper until 1943; joined Police Force 1945; criminal investigation training in Kenya 1945; then instructor and translator, Police Training School Mogadishu; at Italian Secondary School Mogadishu 1950–54, Italian Officers' Acad. 1954–55; ADC to fmr. Pres. Osman 1960; mem. Supreme Revolutionary Council 1970–76, Vice-Pres. 1973–76; Chair. Econ. Cttee. 1973; Sec. of State for the Interior 1970–74; Deputy Head of State 1976–80, mem. Political Bureau, Somali Revolutionary Socialist Party 1976–; Pres. Adviser on Govt. Affairs 1980–84. *Address:* Somali Socialist Revolutionary Party Headquarters, Mogadishu, Somalia.

AFXENTIOU, Afxentis, M.A. (ECON.); Cypriot banker and government official; b. 11 Dec. 1932, Larnaca; s. of Costas Afxentiou and Terpsichore Panayi; m. 1st Stella Vanezis 1957 (deceased); one s. one d.; m. 2nd Egli Markides 1981; ed. Pancyprian Commercial Lyceum, Larnaca, Athens School of Econs. and Business and Univ. of Georgia; Hellenic Mining Co. Group 1955–62; Ministry of Finance 1962–79, Perm. Sec. 1973–79; Minister of Finance 1979–82; Gov. Cen. Bank of Cyprus 1982–; Gov. IMF 1982; fmr. Gov. for Cyprus, IBRD; fmr. Vice-Chair. Bd. Dirs. Cyprus Devt. Bank Ltd. *Leisure interests:* reading, walking, swimming. *Address:* 80 Kennedy Avenue, P.O. Box 5529, 1395 Nicosia, Cyprus. *Telephone:* 02-379800. *Fax:* 02-378153.

AGA KHAN IV, H.H. Prince Karim, B.A.; Spiritual leader and Imam of Ismaili Muslims; b. 13 Dec. 1936, Creux-de-Genthod, Geneva; s. of late Prince Aly Salomon Khan and of Princess Joan Aly Khan (now Viscountess Camrose, née Joan Barbara Yarde-Buller); m. Sarah Frances Croker-Poole 1969 (divorced 1995); two s. one d.; ed. Le Rosey, Switzerland, Harvard Univ., U.S.A.; became Aga Khan on the death of his grandfather Sir Sultan Mohamed Shah, Aga Khan III, G.C.S.I., G.C.I.E., G.C.V.O., 1957; granted title of His Highness by Queen Elizabeth II 1957, of His Royal Highness by the Shah of Iran 1959; founder Pres. Aga Khan Foundation 1967, Aga Khan Award for Architecture 1976–, Inst. of Ismaili Studies 1977–, Aga Khan Trust for Culture 1988; f. and Chancellor Aga Khan Univ., Pakistan 1983; Commdr. ordre du Mérite Mauritanien 1960; Grand Croix, ordre du Prince Henry du Gouvernement Portugais 1960, ordre Nat. de la Côte d'Ivoire 1965, de la Haute-Volta 1965, ordre Malgache 1966, ordre du Croissant Vert des Comores 1966; Grand Cordon ordre du Tadj de l'Empire d'Iran 1967, Nishan-i-Imtiaz, Pakistan 1970; Cavaliere di Gran Croce dell'Ordine al Merito della Repubblica (Italy) 1977; Grand Officier de l'ordre Nat. du Lion (Sénégal) 1982, Nishan-e-Pakistan, Pakistan 1983, Grand Cordon of Ouissam-al Arch (Morocco) 1986; Cavaliere del Lavoro (Italy) 1988; Commdr., Légion d'honneur (France) 1990, Gran Cruz Mérito Civil, Spain 1991; Hon. LL.D. (Peshawar Univ.) 1967, (Univ. of Sind) 1970, (McGill Univ., Montreal) 1983, (McMaster Univ.) 1987, (Wales Univ.) 1993; Hon. D.Litt. (London Univ.) 1989; recipient Thomas Jefferson Award in Architecture, Univ. of Virginia 1984, Honor Award AIA 1984, La Medalla de Oro del Consejo Superior de Colegios de Arquitectos, Spain 1987, Hon. Fellow R.I.B.A. 1991, Médaille d'Argent Académie d'Architecture, Paris 1991, Huésped de Honor de Granada, Spain 1991; Founder Pres. Yacht Club Costa Smerelda, Sardinia; mem. Royal Yacht Squadron 1982–. *Leisure interests:* breeding race-horses, yachting, golf, skiing. *Address:* Aiglemont, 60270 Gouvieux, France.

AGA KHAN, Prince Sadruddin; Iranian UN official; b. 1933, Paris; s. of Sultan Mohammed Shah, Aga Khan III and Andrée Josephine Carron; m. 1st Nina Sheila Dyer 1957 (divorced 1962); m. 2nd Catherine Sursock 1972; ed. Harvard Univ. and Harvard Univ. Graduate School for Arts and Sciences; UNESCO Consultant for Afro-Asian Projects 1958; Head of Mission and Adviser to UN High Commr. for Refugees 1959–60; UNESCO Special Consultant to Dir.-Gen. 1961; Exec. Sec. Int. Action Cttee. for Preservation of Nubian Monuments 1961; UN Deputy High Commr. for Refugees 1962–65, High Commr. 1965–77; Chargé de Mission, Consultant to Sec.-Gen. of UN 1978–; Chair. and founding mem. Independent Comm. on Internal Humanitarian Issues 1983–; UN Co-ordinator for Econ. and Humanitarian Programmes in Afghanistan 1988–91; Chief U.N. Operations in Iraq March–Dec. 1991; Publr. the Paris Review; Founder and Sec. Harvard Islamic Asscn.; Pres. Alp Action 1992, Council on Islamic Affairs, New York City; mem. Inst. of Differing Civilizations, Brussels; founder mem. and Pres. Groupe de Bellerive; Trustee World Wildlife Fund Int. (Vice-Pres. 1986–); Dr h.c. (Tufts Univ.) 1986, (Nice) 1988; Hon. LL.D. (Leeds) 1992; Commdr.'s Cross with Star of Order of Merit (Poland); Order of St. Sylvester The Pope; Order of Star of the Nile (Sudan); Order of Homayoun First Class (Iran); UN Human Rights Award 1978; Officier, Légion d'honneur (France) 1979; German UN Asscn. Dag-Hammarskjöld hon. medal 1990; Co-winner Olympia Prize, Alexander Onassis Foundation 1982; Commdr. of the Golden Ark (Netherlands) 1985, Man for Peace Award (Together for Peace Foundation) 1989. *Publications:* Lectures on Refugee Problems. *Leisure interests:* Islamic art, primitive art, photography, sailing. *Address:* Château de Bellerive, 1215 Collonge-Bellerive, Geneva, Switzerland. *Telephone:* (022) 468866.

AGAFANGEL (SAVVIN Alexey Mikhailovich); Metropolitan of Vinnitsa and Bratslav; Ukrainian ecclesiastic; b. 2 Sept. 1938, Burdino, Lipetsk Region; ed. Lipetsk Seminary, Moscow Theological Acad.; took monastic vows 1965; ordained as archimandrite 1967; Rector Odessa Seminary 1967–75; Bishop of Vinnitsa and Bratslav 1975–81; ordained as Archbishop 1981, Archbishop of Vinnitsa and Bratslav 1981–89; ordained as Metropolitan 1989, Metropolitan of Vinnitsa and Bratslav 1989–; People's Deputy of Ukraine; rep. of Russian Orthodox Church in Ukraine. *Address:* Ukrainian Orthodox Church, Pechersr hovasbery Lichnevolv Povstannia 21, Kiev, Ukraine. *Telephone:* 290-08-66.

AGAM, Yaacov; Israeli artist; b. 1928, Rishon Le-zion; m. Clila Agam 1954; two s. one d.; ed. Bezalel School of Art, Jerusalem, Atelier d'art abstrait, Paris; one-man exhbns. in Galerie Craven, Paris 1953, Galerie Denise René, Paris 1956, 1958, Palais des Beaux-Arts, Brussels 1958, Tel-Aviv Museum 1958, Suzanne Bollag Gallery, Zürich 1959, 1962, Drian Gallery, London 1959, Marlborough Gerson Gallery, New York 1966, Galerie Denise René, New York 1971, Guggenheim Museum, New York 1980, Tokyo, Osaka, Kawasaki 1989; travelling retrospective exhbn. Paris (Nat. Museum of Modern Art), Amsterdam, Düsseldorf, Tel-Aviv 1972–73. *Works include:* Transformes Musicales 1961, Double Metamorphosis, Shalom Liner 1964, Sculptures in the City, Reims 1970, sculpture and mural, President's mansion, Israel 1971, Water-Fire fountain, St. Louis 1971, Pompidou room, Elysée Palace 1972, environment, Elysée Palace, Paris 1972, mobile wall, School of Science, Montpellier 1972, design and realization of a square in La Défense, Paris, incl. water fountain and monumental sculpture 1973, Villa Regina, Miami (biggest painting in the world, at 300,000 sq. ft.) 1984, Homage to Mondrian (a whole building), L.A. 1984, Fire-Water Fountain, Tel-Aviv 1986, Visual Educ. System 1986, M.S. Celebration cruise ship 1987, Grand Prix Artec 1989, Nagoya, M.S. Fantasy cruise ship 1990; films produced incl. Recherches et inventions 1956, Le désert chante, 1957. *Publications:* 36 books covering his non-verbal visual learning method (visual alphabet). *Address:* 26 rue Boulard, Paris 75014, France. *Telephone:* 43-22-00-88.

AGANBEGYAN, Abel Gezevich; Russian/Armenian economist; b. 8 Oct. 1932, Tbilisi, Georgia; s. of Galina A. Aganbegyan; m. Zoya V. Kupriyanova 1953; one s. one d.; ed. Moscow State Econ. Inst.; mem. C.P.S.U. 1956–91; Economist, Gen. Econ. Dept., State Cttee. for Labour and Wages 1955–61; Head of Lab., Inst. of Econs. and Industrial Eng., Siberian Branch of U.S.S.R. Acad. of Sciences 1961–67, Dir. Inst. of Econs. and Industrial Eng. 1967–85; Prof. of Econs., Novosibirsk State Univ.; Prof. Acad. of Nat. Econ.; Chair. Cttee. for Study of Productive Forces and Natural Resources 1965–; Rector Acad. of Nat. Economy 1989–; mem. Presidium; Chair. All-Union Club of Managers; corresp. mem. U.S.S.R. (now Russian) Acad. of Sciences 1964, mem. 1974, Acad.-Sec. Dept. of Econ. 1986–89; Foreign mem. Bulgarian and Hungarian Acads. of Sciences; Corresp. F.B.A.; Dr. h.c. (Alicante and Łódź); two Orders of Lenin. *Publications:* Wages and Salaries in the U.S.S.R. 1959,

On the Application of Mathematics and Electronic Machinery in Planning 1961, Some Questions of Monopoly Price Theory with Reference to the U.S.A. 1961, Economical-Mathematical Analysis of Input-Output Tables in U.S.S.R. 1968, System of Models of National Economy Planning 1972, Management of the Socialist Enterprises 1979, Management and Efficiency: U.S.S.R. Economy in 1981–85 1981, Siberia—not by Hearsay (with Z. Ibragimova) 1981, Economic methods in planned management (with D. Kazakevich) 1985, Enterprise: managing scientific and technological progress (with V. Rechin) 1986; The Challenge: Economics of Perestroika 1987, Moving the Mountain: Inside Perestroika 1989, Measures and Stages of Improving U.S.S.R. Economy 1991. *Address:* Academy of National Economy, Prospect Vernadskogo 82, 117571 Moscow, Russia. *Telephone:* 434-83-89 (Office).

AGAPOV, Lieut-Gen. Boris Nikolayevich; Russian politician; b. 1946, Turkmenistan, m; one s. two d.; ed. Alma-Ata Higher Commanding School, Far E. Univ., Frunze Mil. Acad.; served in border forces in Middle Asia and Afghanistan; Deputy C.-in-C. border forces of Russia, Head Chief Operation Dept. 1991–93; Vice-Pres. Repub. of Ingushetia 1993–97; Deputy Sec. Security Council of Russian Fed. responsible for Inter-ethnic Problems and Emergency Situations June 1997–, several decorations. *Address:* Security Council, Ipatyevsky per. 4/10 entr. 6, Moscow, Russia (Office). *Telephone:* (095) 206 4396 (Office).

AGASSI, Andre; American tennis player; b. 29 April 1970, Las Vegas; m. Brooke Shields 1997; coached from age 13 by Nick Bollettieri, strength coach Gil Reyes; semi-finalist, French Open 1988, U.S. Open 1988, 1989; mem. U.S. team which defeated Australia in Davis Cup Final 1990; defeated Stefan Edberg to win inaugural ATP World Championship, Frankfurt 1991, finalist French Open 1990, 1991, U.S. Open 1990, 1995, Australian Open 1994; Men's Singles Wimbledon Champion 1992; won U.S. Open 1994, Canadian Open 1995; Australian Open 1995; winner Olympic Games tennis tournaments 1996; Asscn. of Tennis Professionals World Champion 1990. *Address:* International Management Group, 1 Brieview Plaza, Suite 1300, Cleveland, OH 44114, U.S.A.

AGEE, William J., M.B.A.; American business executive; b. 5 Jan. 1938, Boise, Ida.; s. of Harold J. and Suzanne (McReynolds) Agee; m. 1st Diane Weaver 1957; one s. two d.; m. 2nd Mary Cunningham 1982; one d.; ed. Stanford Univ., Boise Junior Coll., Univ. of Idaho, Harvard Univ.; with Boise Cascade Corpn. 1963–72; Sr. Vice-Pres. and Chief Financial Officer, Bendix Corpn. 1972–76, Pres. and C.O.O. 1976–77, Chair. and C.E.O. 1977–83, Pres. 1977–79; C.E.O. Semper Enterprises, Inc., Mass. 1983–; Chair., Pres. C.E.O. Morrison Knudsen Corpn. 1988–95; Dir. ASARCO, Equitable Life Assurance Soc. of U.S., Dow Jones & Co. Inc., Econ. Club of Detroit, Detroit Renaissance Inc., Nat. Council for U.S.-China Trade, Gen. Foods Corpn., Detroit Econ. Growth Corpn. 1978–, United Foundation, Nat. Council for U.S.-China Trade; mem. Conf. Bd., Council on Foreign Relations, Business Roundtable, American and other insts. of CPAs, Board of Dirs., Assocs. of Harvard Business School Feb. 1977–, United Negroes Coll. Fund Feb. 1977; Chair. Gov's. Higher Educ. Capital Investment Advisory Cttee., Pres's. Industrial Advisory Sub-cttee. on Econ. and Trade Policy 1978–79, Advisory Council Cranbrook Educational Community Aug. 1978, Trustee 1978; Trustee Urban Inst., Cttee. for Econ. Devt. May 1977, Citizen Research Council, Mich. March 1977; numerous hon. degrees. *Leisure interests:* tennis, golf, swimming.

AGLIETTA, Maria Adelaide; Italian politician; b. 4 June 1940, Turin; two d.; Nat. Sec. Radical Party, Italy 1976–77, Nat. Treas. 1979, Pres. Parl. Group 1979, Deputy 1983–86, 1987–89; Co-Pres. Green Group in European Parl. 1991–; mem. Chamber of Deputies, Italy, Foreign Affairs and Security Cttee. *Address:* European Parliament, rue Belliard 97-113, 1040 Brussels, Belgium; Via Algardi 8, 00157 Rome, Italy. *Telephone:* (2) 2845196 (Belgium); (6) 5811120 (Italy). *Fax:* 2847837 (Belgium).

AGNELLI, Giovanni, DR.JUR.; Italian industrialist; b. 12 March 1921, Turin; s. of Edoardo Agnelli and Princess Virginia Bourbon del Monte; brother of Umberto Agnelli (q.v.); m. Princess Marella Caracciolo di Castagneto 1953; one s. one d.; grandson of Giovanni Agnelli, founder of F.I.A.T. (mfrs of land, sea and air engines and vehicles); Vice-Chair. Fiat 1945–63, Man. Dir. 1963–66, Chair. 1966–96, Hon. Chair. 1996; Chair. Istituto Finanziario Industriale (IFI), Fondazione Giovanni Agnelli, La Stampa (newspaper); appointed Senator for Life 1991; Hon. Vice-Pres. Assoc. for the Monetary Union of Europe; mem. Exec. Bd. Confederation of Italian Industry, mem. Bd. Turin Industrial Asscn., Italian Stock Companies Asscn., Eurafrance (Paris); mem. Int. Advisory Council. Chase Manhattan Bank, Advisory Bd. Petrofina; mem. Advisory Bd. Bilderberg Meetings, The Hague; Cross for Military Valour. *Address:* Fiat S.p.A., 250 Via Nizza, Turin, Italy (Office). *Telephone:* 6861111.

AGNELLI, Susanna; Italian politician; b. 1922; sister of Giovanni Agnelli, (q.v.) and Umberto Agnelli (q.v.); mem. Parl. 1976; mem. European Parl. 1981; Senator 1983; mem. Nat. Council, Republican Party until 1992; Jr. Minister, Ministry of Foreign Affairs 1986–91; Minister of Foreign Affairs 1992–96. *Publications include:* memoirs. *Address:* c/o Ministry of Foreign Affairs, Piazzale della Farnesina 1, 00194 Rome, Italy.

AGNELLI, Umberto; Italian industrialist; b. 1 Nov. 1934, Lausanne, Switzerland; m. Allegra Caracciolo di Castagneto; two s. (one deceased) one d.; ed. Turin Univ.; mem. bd. IFI 1959–80, Vice-Chair., C.E.O. 1981–; Chair. SAI (insurance co.) 1960–76; mem. bd. FIAT S.p.A., Head Int. Operation Group 1964–73, Chair. FIAT France 1965–80, C.E.O. FIAT S.p.A. 1970–76, Vice-Pres. 1976–93, Chair. FIAT Auto 1980–90, mem. FIAT Int. Advisory Bd. 1993–; Chair. PIAGGIO S.p.A. (motorcycles) 1965–88 (mem. bd. 1988–), IVECO (heavy vehicle sector of FIAT Group) 1975–80, Teksid (metallurgical sector of FIAT Group) 1975–80, CRF (FIAT Research Centre) 1978–80, ISVOR (Inst. for Organizational Devt. of FIAT Group) 1978–80, IFIL 1983–, TORO (insurance co.) 1983–93; senator 1976–79; Chair. JUVENTUS 1956–61, Hon. Chair. 1970–; Chair. Italian Football Asscn. 1959–62; Vice-Pres. G. Agnelli Foundation 1966–; Chair. Cttee. of Common Market Automobile Constructors (ACEA, fmrly. CCMC) 1980–90, Int. Vienna Council (IVC) 1988–93 (Vice-Chair. 1993–); Pres. Italy-Japan Asscn. 1982–, LUISS (Univ. of Econ. Studies) Man. School 1986- (mem. bd. LUISS 1978–); Co-Chair. Italy-Japan Business Group 1989–; mem. ALLIANZ Advisory Cttee. 1980–, Steering Cttee. of European Roundtable Industrialists (ERT) 1983–94, European Advisory Cttee. of New York Stock Exchange 1985–96, TRILATERAL Comm. 1991–, Steering Cttee. of the Bilderberg Meetings 1994–, Int. Adviser Praemium Imperiale organised by Japanese Art Asscn., Fuji TV 1996–; Grand Ufficiale al Merito 1972, Grand Officier Légion d'Honneur 1992, Trade Award (Japan) 1995, Imperial Award Grand Cordon of the Sacred Treasure (Japan) 1996. *Leisure interests:* golf, modern art, skiing. *Address:* Corso Matteotti 26, 10121 Turin, Italy (Office). *Telephone:* (011) 6620444.

AGNEW, Harold Melvin, PH.D.; American physicist; b. 28 March 1921, Denver, Colo.; s. of Sam E. and Agusta (Jacobs) Agnew; m. Beverly Jackson 1942; one s. one d.; ed. Univs. of Denver and Chicago; Los Alamos Scientific Lab. 1943–46, Alt. Div. Leader 1949–61, Leader Weapons Div. 1964–70, Dir. Los Alamos Scientific Lab. 1970–79; Pres. GA Technologies Inc. 1979–85, Dir. 1985–; New Mexico State Senator 1955–61; Scientific Adviser, Supreme Allied Commdr. in Europe, Paris 1961–64; Chair. Army Scientific Advisory Panel 1965–70, mem. 1970–74; Chair. Gen. Advisory Cttee. U.S. Arms Control and Disarmament Agency 1972–76, mem. 1976–80; mem. Aircraft Panel, President's Scientific Advisory Cttee. 1965–73, U.S.A.F. Scientific Advisory Bd. 1957–69, Defense Scientific Bd. 1965–70, Govt. of N.M. Radiation Advisory Council 1959–61; Sec. N.M. Health and Social Services 1971–73; mem. Aerospace Safety Advisory Panel, NASA 1968–74, 1986; White House Science Council 1982–89; Adjunct Prof. Univ. Calif., San Diego 1988–; Woodrow Wilson Nat. Fellowship Foundation 1973–80; Dir. Charles Lee Powell Foundation 1993–; Fellow, American Physical Soc.; mem. N.A.S., Nat. Acad. of Eng.; Ernest Orlando Lawrence Award 1966; Enrico Fermi Award, Dept. of Energy 1978. *Leisure interests:* crafts, gardening, skiing, golf, tennis, fishing. *Address:* 322 Punta Baja Drive, Solana Beach, CA 92075, U.S.A. *Telephone:* (619) 481-8908. *Fax:* (619) 481-8908.

AGNEW, Jonathan Geoffrey William, M.A.; British investment banker; b. 30 July 1941; s. of late Sir Geoffrey Agnew and Hon. Doreen Maud Jessel; m. 1st Hon. Joanna Campbell 1966 (divorced 1985); one s. two d.; m. 2nd Marie-Claire Dreesmann 1990; one d.; ed. Eton Coll. and Trinity Coll. Cambridge; with The Economist 1964–65, IBRD 1965–67; with Hill Samuel & Co. 1967–73, Dir. 1971; Morgan Stanley & Co. 1973–82, Man. Dir. 1977; with J.G.W. Agnew & Co. 1983–86; Chief Exec. ISRO 1986; with Kleinwort Benson Group PLC 1987–93, Chief Exec. 1989–93; Chair. LIMIT PLC 1993–, Henderson Geared Income and Growth Trust PLC 1995–, Gerrard Group PLC 1998–; Dir. (non-exec.) Thos. Agnew & Sons Ltd. 1969–; Dir. (non-exec.) Nationwide Bldg. Soc. 1997, Deputy Chair. 1999–; mem. Council Lloyd's 1995–98. *Address:* Flat E, 51 Eaton Square, London, SW1W 9BE, England (Home). *Telephone:* 0171-390-6100 (Office); 0171-235 7589 (Home). *Fax:* 0171-390-6110 (Office).

AGNEW, Morland Herbert Julian, M.A.; British art dealer; b. 20 Sept. 1943, London; s. of late Sir Geoffrey Agnew and Hon. Doreen Maud Jessel; m. 1st Elizabeth Margaret Moncrieff Mitchell 1973 (divorced 1992); one s. two d.; m. 2nd Victoria Burn Callander 1993; one s.; ed. Eton Coll. and Trinity Coll. Cambridge; joined Thos. Agnew & Sons Ltd. 1965, Dir. 1968, Man. Dir. 1987–92, Chair. 1992–; Pres. British Antique Dealers Asscn. 1979–81; Chair. Soc. of London Art Dealers 1986–90. *Leisure interests:* opera, tennis, golf. *Address:* Thos. Agnew & Sons Ltd, 43 Old Bond Street, London, W1X 4BA; Egmere Farm House, Egmere, Nr. Walsingham, Norfolk, England.

AGNEW, Rudolph Ion Joseph, F.R.S.A.; British business executive; b. 12 March 1934; s. of Rudolph John and Pamela Geraldine (née Campbell) Agnew; m. Whitney Warren 1980; ed. Downside School; Commissioned Officer 8th King's Royal Irish Hussars 1953–57; joined Consolidated Gold Fields 1957; worked in South Africa, U.S.A., Canada and Australia; Chief Exec. Amey Roadstone Corpn. 1974–78, Chair. 1974–77; Exec. Dir. Consolidated Gold Fields PLC 1973, Deputy Chair. 1978–82, Group Chief Exec. 1978–89, Chair. 1983–89, mem. Cttee. of Man. Dirs. 1986–89; Chair., CEO TVS Entertainment 1990–93; Chair. Stena Sealink Ltd (fmrly. Sealink Stena Line) 1990–, Federated Aggregates PLC 1991–95, Bona Shipholding Ltd., Bermuda 1993–, LASMO PLC 1994–, Redland PLC 1995–97, Star Mining Corpn. 1995–; Jt. Chair. Global Stone Corpn. (Canada) 1993–94; Dir. (non-exec.) New London PLC 1985–96, Standard Chartered PLC 1988–97, Newmount Mining Corpn., U.S.A. 1989–, Hanson PLC 1989–91; Vice-Pres. Nat. Asscn. of Boys Clubs; mem. Council WWF (U.K.) 1989– (Trustee 1983–89); Fellow, Game Conservancy. *Leisure interest:* shooting. *Address:* 7 Eccleston Street, London, SW1X 9LX, England.

AGRAWAL, K.D., M. COMM.; Indian banker; b. 15 July 1938; ed. Allahabad Univ.; joined State Bank of India 1960; Chair. Gorakhpur Kshetriya Grameen Bank 1975–77; Chief Officer, Merchant Banking Div. State Bank of India 1981–84; Pres. and C.E.O. State Bank of India (Calif.) and State Bank of India (L.A. Agency) 1984–88; Gen. Man. (Operations), State Bank of India, Ahmedabad Circle 1988–91; Dir. (Finance), ACC Babcock Ltd. 1991–92; Chief Gen. Man. (Inspection and Audit), State Bank of India 1992–93; Chair. and C.E.O. Bank of Rajasthan Ltd. 1993–94; fmr. Chair. and Man. Dir. Industrial Finance Corpn. of India Ltd. (IFCI); Chair. Risk Capital & Tech. Finance Corpn. Ltd. (RCTC), Tourism Finance Corpn. of India Ltd. (TFCI), Tourism Advisory and Financial Services Corpn. of India Ltd. (TAFSIL), Inst. of Labour Devt. (ILD) Jaipur, IFCI Financial Services Ltd., IFCI Custodial Services Ltd., IFCI Investors' Services Ltd.; numerous other appts. *Address:* c/o Industrial Finance Corporation of India Ltd., IFCI Tower, 61 Nehru Place, New Delhi 110 019, India. *Telephone:* (11) 6487444. *Fax:* (11) 6488471.

AGRAWAL, Prabhu Lal; Indian business executive and engineer; b. 22 Oct. 1926, Udaipur, Rajasthan; s. of Trilok Chand Agrawal and Narayan Devi Agrawal; m. Pushpa Devi 1948; one s. one d.; ed. Banaras Hindu Univ. and Univ. of Sheffield; Lecturer, College of Mining and Metallurgy, Banaras Hindu Univ., then Asst. Prof. 1947–54, Reader 1954–56; Tech. Officer Rourkela Steel Plant, then Sr. Fuel Engineer, then Asst. Chief Fuel Engineer, then Supt. Energy & Economy Dept., then Chief Supt. 1965–66, Asst. Gen. Supt. 1966–69, Gen. Man. 1971–76, Man. Dir. 1976–78; Gen. Supt. Alloy Steels Plant 1969–70; Gen. Supt. Bokaro Steel Ltd. 1970–71; Chair. Steel Authority of India 1978–80; Tech. Adviser PT Krakatan Steel, Jakarta 1980–86; mem. judging panel for Prime Minister's Trophy for Best Operating Integrated Steel Plant 1992–97; Hon. mem. Indian Inst. of Metals 1980; Holker Fellow, Banaras Hindu Univ.; Uttar Pradesh Govt. Book Prize for Audyogik Indhan; Nat. Metallurgists Day Award; Bundesverdienstkreuz (1st Class); FIE Foundation Award, India 1980; Tata Gold Medal, Indian Inst. of Metals 1981, Platinum Medal, Indian Inst. of Metals 1993. *Publications:* Audyogik Indhan (Hindi); several technical papers and reports. *Leisure interests:* reading, social work, walking. *Address:* Narayan Villa, 56A New Fatehpura, Sukhadia Circle, Udaipur-313001, India. *Telephone:* (0294) 560380, (0294) 561722. *Fax:* (0294) 560380.

AGRAWALA, Surendra Kumar, M.A., LL.M., LL.D.; Indian university administrator and professor of law; b. 18 Jan. 1929, Bilgram; s. of late Radha Krishna and Tara Devi; m. Prof. Dr. Raj Kumari Agrawala 1959; one s.; ed. Allahabad and Lucknow Univs. and Harvard Law School; lecturer in Law, Lucknow Univ. 1953–62; Reader in Law, Aligarh Muslim Univ. 1962–65; Prof. and Head of Dept. Poona Univ. 1965–85, Prof. Emer.; Vice-Chancellor, Agra Univ. 1985–88; Sec.-Gen. Asscn. of Indian Univs. 1988–93; fmr. mem. Acad. Council, J. Nehru Univ.; mem. Court, Aligarh Muslim Univ.; Convener, U.G.C. Advisory Panel on Law; numerous professional appts., cttee. memberships etc.; K.M. Munshi Memorial Lecturer, Indian Law Inst. 1983. *Publications:* International Law: Indian Courts and Legislature 1965, Essays on the Law of Treaties (ed.) 1972, Legal Education in India: Problems and Perspectives (ed.) 1973, Proposed Indian Ombudsman 1971, Aircraft Hijacking and International Law 1975, New Horizons of International Law (ed.) 1983, Public Interest Litigation in India 1985; about 50 articles in anthologies and legal journals. *Leisure interests:* reading, writing, travel and sightseeing. *Address:* 3/454 Vishwas Khand, Gomtinagar, Lucknow, U.P., India. *Telephone:* (522) 309515.

AGRAWALA, Vasudeva Sharan, PH.D., D.LITT.; Indian writer and university professor; b. Aug. 1904; ed. Banaras Hindu Univ. and Lucknow Univ.; Curator, Mathura Museum 1931–39, Lucknow Museum 1940–45; Supt. Nat. Museum and Nat. Museum Branch of Archaeological Survey of India, New Delhi 1946–51; Prof. and Head of Dept. of Art and Architecture, Coll. of Indology, Banaras Hindu Univ. 1951; fmr. Pres. Museums Asscn. of India and other historical asscns.; Pres. All-India Prakrit Text Soc. 1964–. *Publications:* A Revised Catalogue of Mathura Museum 1950, India as Known to Panini 1953, Paninikalina Bharatavarsha 1955, Jayasi's Padamavata 1955, Kadambari: A Cultural Study 1958, Prithiviputra, or Essays on Indian Culture 1960, Sparks from the Vedic Fire 1962, The Thousand-Syllabled Speech of Vedic Symbolism, Vol. I 1963, Vidyapati's Kirtilata 1962, Matsya Purana: A Study 1963, Devi Mahatmya: Glorification of the Great Goddess 1963, Solar Symbolism of the Boar 1963, Vedic Lectures 1963, Harshacharita: A Cultural Commentary 1964, Vamana Purana: A Study 1964, Bharata Savitri, Vol. I 1957, Vol. II 1964, Chakradhvaja: The Wheel Flag of India 1964, Ancient Indian Folk-Cults 1964, Divyavadana 1965, Indian Art 1965, Heritage of Indian Art 1971. *Address:* c/o Department of Art and Architecture, College of Indology, Banaras Hindu University, Banaras 5, India.

AGT, Andries A. M. van; Netherlands politician; b. 2 Feb. 1931, Geldrop; s. of Frans van Agt and Anna Frencken; m. Eugenie Krekelberg 1958; one s. two d.; ed. Catholic Univ., Nijmegen. Worked at Ministry of Agric. and Fisheries, then Ministry of Justice 1958–68; Prof. of Penal Law, Univ. of Nijmegen 1968–; Minister of Justice 1971–77; Deputy Prime Minister 1973–77; Prime Minister and Minister of Gen. Affairs 1977–82; Minister of Foreign Affairs 1982; M.P. 1983; Gov. Prov. of Noord-Brabant 1983–87; Amb., Head Del. of European Communities, Tokyo 1987, later Washington –1995.

ÁGÚSTSSON, Helgi; Icelandic diplomatist; b. 16 Oct. 1941, Reykjavik; s. of Ágúst H. Pétursson and Helga Jóhannesdóttir; m. Hervör Jónasdóttir 1963; three s. one d.; ed. Commercial Coll. of Iceland and Univ. of Iceland; joined Ministry for Foreign Affairs 1970; First Sec. and Vice-Consul, London 1973–77; Dir. Defence Div. Ministry for Foreign Affairs and Icelandic Chair. U.S.-Icelandic Defence Council 1979; Minister-Counsellor, Washington, D.C. 1983–87; Deputy Perm. Under-Sec. Ministry for Foreign Affairs 1987; Amb. to U.K. (also accred. to Ireland, Netherlands and Nigeria) 1989–94; Perm. Under-Sec. Ministry for Foreign Affairs 1995–; fmr. Pres. Icelandic Basketball Fed.; Kt. Order of Dannebrog, Kt. Commdr. of White Rose, Grand Cross of Mérito Civil, Kt. Commdr. of Pole Star, Kt. Commdr. Order of the Falcon, Grand Cross Oranje-Nassau Order; Hon. G.C.V.O. *Leisure interest:* salmon fishing. *Address:* c/o Ministry for Foreign Affairs, Randararstigur 25, 150 Reykjavik, Iceland.

AGUTTER, Jenny; British actress and dancer; b. 20 Dec. 1952, Taunton; d. of Derek Brodie Agutter and Catherine (née Lynam); m. Johan Tham 1990; one s.; ed. Elmhurst Ballet School; film debut in East of Sudan 1964; has appeared in numerous TV films, dramas and series and on stage with RSC and Nat. Theatre; *Plays include:* Tempest, Spring Awakening, Hedda Gabler, Betrayal, The Unified Field, Breaking the Code, Love's Labour's Lost, Peter Pan. *Films include:* Ballerina 1964, I Start Counting, The Railway Children 1969, Walkabout, Logan's Run 1975, The Eagle Has Landed, Equus, Man in the Iron Mask, Riddle of the Sands, Sweet William, The Survivor 1980, An American Werewolf in London 1981, Secret Places 1983, Dark Tower 1987, King of the Wind 1989, Child's Play 2 1991, Freddie as Fro 7 1993, Blue Juice 1995, English Places, English Faces 1996. *TV includes:* Amy 1980, Not a Penny More, Not a Penny Less 1990, The Good Guys, Puss in Boots 1991, Love Hurts 1994, Heartbeat 1994, September 1995, 1996, The Buccaneers 1995, And The Beat Goes On 1996, A Respectable Trade 1997, Bramwell 1998. *Publication:* Snap 1983. *Leisure interest:* photography. *Address:* c/o JY Publicity, 54A Ebury Street, London, SW1W 9QD, England. *Telephone:* 0171-730 2112. *Fax:* 0171-730 5118.

AHDE, Matti Allan; Finnish politician; b. 23 Dec. 1945, Oulu; s. of Risto Ahde and Laila Ahde; m. Hilkka Riikonen; two s. one d.; worked as electrician and civil servant; M.P. 1970–90; Chair. State Youth Council 1971–75; mem. Exec. Finnish S.D.P. 1972–90, Oulu City Council 1972–84; Chair. State Sports Council 1975–77 (mem. 1978–83), Pres. Workers' Sports Fed. 1977–; Vice-Pres. Finnish Olympic Cttee. 1978–93, Finnish Nat. Opera 1980–, Finnish Sports Fed. 1994–; Chair. Bd. Trustees Finnish National Opera Foundation 1980–, Vice-Pres. 1981–; First Minister of the Interior 1982–83, Minister of the Environment 1983–87; Second Vice-Pres. of Finnish S.D.P. 1984–87, First Vice-Pres. 1987–90; Speaker of Parl. 1987–89; mem. Admin. Bd., Finnair 1988–91, Exec. Cttee. Int. Asscn. of State Lotteries 1990–; Man. Dir., Pres. Oy Veikkaus Ab 1990–. *Leisure interests:* sports, music. *Address:* Oy Veikkaus Ab, 01009 Vantaa, Finland. *Telephone:* (0) 85261.

AHERN, Bertie; Irish politician; b. 12 Sept. 1951, Dublin; m. Miriam P. Kelly 1975; two d.; ed. Rathmines Coll. of Commerce, Dublin and Univ. Coll., Dublin; formerly accountant, Mater Hosp., Dublin; mem. Dáil 1977–; mem. Dublin City Council 1979–, Lord Mayor 1986–87; Minister of State, Dept. of Taoiseach and of Defence March–Nov. 1982; Minister for Labour 1987–91, for Finance 1991–94; Pres. EC Council of Ministers for Social Affairs Jan.–June 1990; mem. Fianna Fáil, Pres. Nov. 1994–; Prime Minister of Ireland 1997–; fmr. mem. Bd. of Govs. IMF, World Bank, European Investment Bank (Chair. 1991–92), European Bank for Reconstruction and Devt., EU Council of Ministers for Econs. and Finance (ECOFIN); Grand Cross of O.M. (Germany). *Address:* Department of the Taoiseach, Government Buildings, Upper Merrion Street, Dublin 2; St Luke's, 161 Lower Drumcondra Road, Dublin 9, Republic of Ireland.

AHERN, Dermot, B.C.L.; Irish politician; b. Feb. 1955, Drogheda, Co. Louth; ed. Marist Coll., Dundalk, Univ. Coll., Dublin, Inc. Law Soc. of Ireland; fmrly. solicitor; mem. Louth Co. Council 1979–91; mem. Dáil Éireann Feb. 1987–; mem. various Parl. Cttees.; Asst. Govt. Whip 1988–91; Minister of State at Depts. of the Taoiseach and Defence, Govt. Chief Whip 1991–92; Minister for Social, Community and Family Affairs June 1997–; mem. British-Irish Parl. Body 1991– (Co-Chair. 1993–). *Address:* Department of Social, Community and Family Affairs, Aras Mhic Dhiarmada, Store Street, Dublin 1, Ireland (Office). *Telephone:* (1) 8748444. *Fax:* (1) 7043868.

AHLMARK, Per, B.A.; Swedish fmr. politician, journalist, novelist and poet; b. 15 Jan. 1939, Stockholm; s. of Prof. Axel Ahlmark; m. 1st (divorced); one s. one d.; m. 2nd Bibi Andersson (q.v.) 1978 (divorced); m. 3rd Lilian Edström; one s.; Leader of Young Liberals 1960–62; columnist for Expressen 1961–95, for Dagens Nyheter 1997–; mem. Parl. 1967–78; Deputy Chair. Swedish-Israeli Friendship Org. 1970–97; mem. Council of Europe 1971–76; mem. Royal Comms. on Literature, Human Rights, etc. in the 70s; Leader, Folkpartiet (Liberal Party) 1975–78; Deputy Prime Minister and Minister of Labour 1976–78; Deputy Chair. Martin Luther King Fund 1968–73; Chair. Swedish Film Inst. 1978–81; Founder and Deputy Chair. Swedish Comm. Against Antisemitism 1983–95; Adviser to Elie Wiesel Foundation for Humanity, New York 1987–; mem. UN Watch, Geneva 1993–; mem. Acad. Universelle des Cultures, Paris; Fellow Wissenschaftskolleg zu Berlin 1998–99; Hon. Fellow (Hebrew Univ., Jerusalem) 1992; Defender of Jerusalem Award 1986 (New York). *Publications:* An Open Sore, Tyranny and the Left, many political books, essays and numerous articles, three books of poetry, one novel. *Leisure interests:* books. *Address:* Folkungag 61, 11622 Stockholm, Sweden.

AHLSEN, Leopold; German author; b. 12 Jan. 1927, Munich; m. Ruth Gehwald 1964; one s. one d.; Gerhart Hauptmann Prize; Schiller-Förderungspreis; Goldener Bildschirm; Hörspielpreis der Kriegsblinden; Silver Nymph of Monte Carlo, Bundesverdienstkreuz and other awards. *Publications:* 13 plays, 23 radio plays, 56 television plays, 5 novels. *Leisure interest:* joinery. *Address:* Waldschulstrasse 58, 81827 Munich, Germany. *Telephone:* 089/ 4301466.

AHLSTRÖM, Krister Harry, M.SC.; Finnish business executive; b. 29 Aug. 1940, Helsinki; s. of Harry F. and Asta A. (née Seege) Ahlström; m. Anja I. Artto 1974; one s. four d.; ed. Helsinki Univ. of Technology; Product Eng., Gen. Man. and mem. Bd. of Man. Oy Wärtsilä Ab 1966–81; Dir. and mem. Exec. Bd. A. Ahlström Corpn. 1981–82, Pres. and C.E.O. 1982–98, Chair. 1998–. *Leisure interest:* sailing. *Address:* A. Ahlström Corporation, P.O. Box 329, Eteläesplanadi 14, 00101 Helsinki (Office); Itäinen Puistotie 2, 00140 Helsinki, Finland (Home). *Telephone:* 358 0 5039700 (Office). *Fax:* 358 0 5039729.

AHMAD, Datuk Abdul Ajib bin; Malaysian politician; b. 13 Sept. 1947, Segamat, Johore; ed. Malay Coll. Kuala Kangsar, Perak, Mara Inst. of Tech. and Univ. of Malaya; formerly served with Ministry of Foreign Affairs; later Exec., Shell Oil Co., Kuala Lumpur; Press Sec. to Dato Musa Hitam (Minister of Primary Industries, later Deputy Prime Minister) 1975–82; mem. State Ass. for Endau 1982–86; apptd. Menteri Besar Johor 1982; mem. Parl. 1986–; Minister, Prime Minister's Dept. 1986–87; mem. UMNO Supreme Council 1984–. *Leisure interests:* sport, reading. *Address:* c/o UMNO Baru, Menara Dato' Onn, 38th Floor, Jalan Tun Dr. Ismail, 50480 Kuala Lumpur, Malaysia.

AHMAD, Awang Mohammed Yussof, B.A.; Brunei diplomatist; b. 1944, Brunei; m.; two c.; ed. Western Australia and Manchester Univs.; Admin. Officer, Brunei Educ. Dept. 1972–75; Acting Dist. Officer of Belait Dist. and Chair. Belait and Seria Municipal Bd. 1975–76; Acting Sec. Public Service Comm. and Deputy Controller, Customs and Excise 1976; Sr. Admin. Officer, Office of the Gen. Adviser to the Sultan of Brunei Darussalam 1980–81; Deputy Dir. of the Establishment Dept. 1981; Dist. Officer, Tutong Dist. 1983–84; Amb. to the Philippines 1984–86; Perm. Rep. to the UN 1986–87. *Address:* c/o Ministry of Foreign Affairs, Bandar Seri Begawan, Brunei.

AHMED, Fakhruddin, M.A.; Bangladeshi diplomatist; b. 1 April 1931, Gopalgonj; s. of late A. A. F. Mohi; m. 1st Helen Ahmed 1963 (died 1984); m. 2nd Masuda Khan 1989; one s. one d.; ed. Dhaka Univ., Fletcher School of Law and Diplomacy, Boston, U.S.A.; with Foreign Service of Pakistan 1954–71, Junior Diplomatist, Saudi Arabia 1957–59, Vice-Consul, U.S.A. 1959–63, Second Sec., Iran 1963–65, First Sec., then Acting High Commr., Ghana 1967–68, served Ministry of Foreign Affairs 1968–71, Dir. 1968–70, Dir.-Gen. 1971; with Foreign Service of Bangladesh 1972, Additional Sec., then Foreign Sec., Ministry of Foreign Affairs 1972–76, Amb. to Italy (also to accred. to Switzerland), Perm. Rep. to FAO 1976–78, Amb. to Yugoslavia (also accred. to Greece, Albania) 1978–82, High Commr. in U.K. 1982–86 (also Amb. to Portugal 1983–86); Foreign Sec., Ministry of Foreign Affairs June 1986–May 1987; retd. from govt. service; mem. Observer Group for Sri Lanka Presidential Election 1988, Int. Observer Group Feb. 1989, SAARC Non-Governmental Observer Mission to Parl. Elections in Pakistan Oct. 1990; Adviser for Foreign Affairs with Cabinet rank 1990–91. *Leisure interests:* reading, writing, photography. *Address:* c/o Ministry of Foreign Affairs, 23/6 Mirpur Road, Topkhana Road, Dhaka (Office); 23/6, Mirpur Road, Shamoly, Dhaka, Bangladesh (Home). *Telephone:* 865290 (Office); 326533 (Home).

AHMED, Kazi Zafar, B.A.; Bangladeshi politician; b. 1 July 1940, Cheora; s. of Kazi Ahmed Ali; m.; three d.; ed. Dhaka Univ.; Office Sec. East Pakistan Students Union Cen. Cttee. 1957, Office Sec. 1957–62, Gen. Sec. 1962–63; imprisoned several times for political activities between 1963 and 1965; Pres. Bangla Sramik Fed. 1967; actively participated in struggle for independence 1971; Sec.-Gen. Cen. Cttee. Nat. Awami Party 1972–74; f. United People's Party 1974, Sec. Gen. 1974, Chair. Cen. Cttee. 1979; mem. Nationalist Front 1978 (later became part of Nat. Party); Ed. Nayajug; Minister of Educ. 1978, Deputy Prime Minister, also in charge of Ports, Shipping and River Transport 1986–87, Political Adviser to the Pres. and Minister of Information 1988–91; Prime Minister 1989–91; formed rival faction to Nat. Party with Shah Moazzen Hossein (q.v.) 1997. *Address:* c/o Jatiya Sangsad, Dhaka, Bangladesh.

AHMED, Moudud, M.A.; Bangladeshi politician; b. 1940, Noakhali; s. of the late Bara Moulana; m. Hasna Jasimuddin; two s.; ed. Dhaka Univ.; fmr. Gen. Sec. East Pakistan House, England; took an active part in struggle for independence, organising External Publicity Div. of Bangladesh Govt. in exile; Ed. Bangladesh (weekly); Lawyer, Bangladesh Supreme Court 1972–74; Gen. Sec. Cttee. for Civil Liberties Legal Aid 1974; imprisoned during State of Emergency 1974; Head, Bangladesh delegation to 32nd Session UN Gen. Ass. 1977; Adviser to Pres. 1977; Minister of Communications 1985–86, Deputy Prime Minister in charge of Ministry of Industries July 1986–88, Prime Minister and Minister of Industry 1988–89, Vice-Pres. 1989–90; under house arrest 1990–91, imprisoned Dec. 1991–; Fellow South Asian Inst. of Heidelberg Univ., Harvard Univ. Centre for Int. Affairs. *Publications:* Bangladesh Contemporary Events and Documents, Bangladesh Constitutional Quest for Autonomy 1974.

AHMED, Shahabuddin, B.A., M.A.; Bangladeshi head of state and judge; b. 1930, Pemal of Kendua, Greater Mymensingh Dist.; s. of Talukder Risat A. Bhuiyan; two s. three d.; ed. Dhaka Univ., Lahore Civil Service Acad., Univ. of Oxford; joined Civil Service of Pakistan 1954 as Sub-Divisional Officer, later Additional Deputy Commr.; transferred to Judicial Br. 1960; fmr. Additional Dist. and Sessions Judge, Dhaka, fmr. Dist. and Sessions Judge, Comilla and Chittagong; fmr. Registrar High Court of East Pakistan; elevated to High Court Bench 1972; mem. Labour Appellate Tribunal 1973–74; appointed Judge of Appellate Div. Supreme Court of Bangladesh 1980; Chief Justice 1990, 1991–95; Chair. Comm. of Enquiry into police shootings of students 1983, Nat. Pay Comm. 1984, Bangladesh Red Cross Soc. 1978–82; Acting Pres. of Bangladesh 1990–91, Pres. of Bangladesh Oct. 1996–. *Address:* Office of the President, Dhaka, Bangladesh.

AHMETI, Vilson; Albanian politician; b. 5 Sept. 1951; ed. Univ. of Tirana; engineer Vehicles Workshop, Tirana 1973–78; mem. Foreign Trade Dept. Makina-Import 1978–87; Deputy Minister of Food 1987; Minister of Industry March–June 1991, of Food June–Dec. 1991; Prime Minister of Albania 1991–92; convicted of abusing power Sept. 1993; sentenced to two years' imprisonment.

AHO, Esko Tapani, M.A.; Finnish politician; b. 20 May 1954, Veteli; s. of Kauko Kaleva Aho and Laura Kyllikki (née Harjupatana) Aho; m. Kirsti Hannele Söderkultalahti 1980; two s. one d.; Chair. Youth Org. of the Center Party 1974–80, Chair. Finnish Center Party (KESK) 1990–; Political Sec. to Minister of Foreign Affairs 1979–80; Trade Agent, Kannus 1980; Prime Minister of Finland 1991–95; mem. Parl. 1983–. *Leisure interests:* literature, tennis, theatre. *Address:* Centre Party of Finland, Pursimiehenkatu 15, 00150 Helsinki, Finland. *Telephone:* (9) 172721. *Fax:* (9) 653589.

AHOMADEGBÉ, Justin Tometin; Benin politician; b. 1917; ed. William Ponty School, Dakar, and School of Medicine, Dakar; medical work, Cotonou, Porto-Novo 1944–47; mem. Gen. Council, Dahomey 1947, Sec.-Gen. Bloc Populaire Africain; Sec.-Gen. Union Démocratique Dahoméenne (UDD) 1956; mem. Grand Council, A.O.F. 1957; mem. Dahomey Legis. Ass. 1959, Pres. 1959–60; medical work 1960–61; imprisoned 1961–62; Minister of Health, Public Works and Nat. Education 1963; Vice-Pres. of Dahomey, Pres. of Council of Ministers and Minister in Charge of Interior, Defence, Security and Information 1964–65, also in charge of the Plan 1965; mem. Presidential Council 1970–72; Head of State May-Oct. 1972; imprisoned 1972 released April 1981; f. Rally of Democratic Forces 1990. *Address:* c/o Ministry of Justice, Cotonou, Benin.

AHRENDS, Peter, A.A.DIPL. (HONS.), A.R.I.B.A.; British architect; b. 30 April 1933, Berlin, Germany; s. of Steffen Bruno Ahrends and Margarete Marie Sophie (née Visino) Ahrends; m. Elizabeth Robertson 1954; two d.; ed. King Edward VII School, Johannesburg, Architectural Assen., London; research into decoration in Islamic Architecture 1956; Visiting Critic and/or External Examiner Kumasi Univ., A.A. School of Architecture, Nova Scotia Tech. Univ., Strathclyde Univ.; with Steffen Ahrends & Partners, Johannesburg 1957–58; with Denys Lasdun & Partners 1959–60; with Julian Keable & Partners; teacher A.A. School of Architecture 1960–61; f. architectural practice Ahrends, Burton and Koralek 1961, Partner, Dir. 1961–; Visiting Prof. Kingston Polytechnic 1983–84; teacher conducted workshops A.A. School of Architecture, Canterbury Art School, Edin. Univ., Winter School, Edin., Plymouth Polytechnic, Plymouth Art School; Prof. Bartlett School of Architecture and Planning, Univ. Coll. London 1986–89; comms. include Trinity Coll. Library, Dublin 1961 and Arts Faculty Bldg. 1979, Templeton Coll., Oxford 1969, Nebenzahl House, Jerusalem 1972, Habitat Warehouse & Showroom, Wallingford 1974, Residential Bldg., Keble Coll., Oxford 1976, Nat. Gallery Extension 1982–85, Cummins Engines Factory, Shotts 1983, J. Sainsbury Supermarket, Canterbury 1984, W.H. Smith Retail HQ, Swindon 1985, Extension of Docklands Light Railway Station 1987, New British Embassy, Moscow 1988–99, Office Devt. for Stanhope Trafalgar 1990–, St. Mary's Hosp., Newport, Isle of Wight 1990, John Lewis Dept. Store, Kingston 1990, White Cliffs Heritage Centre, Dover 1991, Poplar Footbridge, London Docklands 1992, Quest Science Centre 1992–, Docklands Light Railway, Beckton Extension Stations 1993; exhbns. at R.I.B.A. Heinz Gallery 1980, Royal Architects Inst., Ireland 1981, Douglas Hyde Gallery, Dublin 1981, Braunschweig Tech. Univ., Hanover Tech. Univ., Finnish Architecture Museum, Helsinki 1982, Alvar Aalto Museum, Jyvaskyla 1982, Architectural Assen., Oslo 1983; mem. Design Council, Chair. U.K. Architects Against Apartheid 1988–; R.I.B.A. Good Design in Housing Award 1977, R.I.B.A. Architecture Award 1978, 1993, Structural Steel Design Award 1980, Structural Steel Design Commendation 1993. *Publications:* Ahrends, Burton & Koralek, Architects (monograph) 1991, numerous articles in professional journals. *Leisure interests:* architecture and architecture-related interests. *Address:* 7 Chalcot Road, London, NW1 8LH (Office); 16 Rochester Road, London, NW1 9JH, England (Home). *Telephone:* 0171-586 3311 (Office).

AHRLAND, Karin Margareta, LL.B.; Swedish politician; b. 20 July 1931, Torshälla; d. of Valfrid and Greta (née Myhlén) Andersson; m. 1st Hans F. Petersson 1958 (dissolved 1962); m. 2nd Nils Ahrland 1964; one s.; ed. Univ. of Lund; chief lawyer, County of Malmöhus 1971–76; mem. Riksdag (Parl.) 1976–; Minister for Public Health and Medical Services 1981–82; Del. UN Comm. of Status of Women 1976–79; Chair. Nat. Cttee. for Equality between Men and Women 1979–81; Chair. Nat. Arts Council 1980; Amb. 1989–90; with Consul, Montreal 1990–; Liberal. *Address:* c/o Ministry for Foreign Affairs, Gustav Adolfstorg 1, P.O. Box 16121, 103 39 Stockholm, Sweden.

AHRONOVITCH, Yuri (George); Israeli (Russian-born) conductor; b. 13 May 1932, Leningrad; s. of Michael Ahronovitch and Anna Eskina; m. Tamar Sakson 1973; ed. Leningrad Conservatorium, studied conducting with Kurt Sanderling and Nathan Rachlin; Conductor Saratov Philharmonic Orchestra 1956–57, Yaroslav Symphony Orchestra 1957–64; Chief Conductor Moscow Radio Symphony Orchestra 1964–72; left U.S.S.R. to settle in Israel 1972; opera début in Europe, Cologne 1973; début Royal Opera House Covent Garden (Boris Godunov) 1974; Chief Conductor Gürzenich Orchestra, Cologne 1975–, Stockholm Philharmonic Orchestra 1982.

AHRWEILER, Hélène, D. ÈS L.; French professor; b. 28 Aug. 1926, Athens, Greece; d. of Nicolas Glykatzi and Calliroe Psaltides; m. Jacques Ahrweiler 1958; one d.; ed. Univ. of Athens; Research Worker C.N.R.S. 1955–67, Head of Research 1964–67; Prof. Sorbonne 1967–; Pres. Univ. de Paris I 1976–81; Rector Acad., Chancellor Univs. of Paris 1982–89; Chair. and Pres. Terra Foundation for the Arts (Chicago); Sec.-Gen. Int. Cttee. of Historical Sciences 1980–90; Vice-Pres. conseil d'orientation du Centre Georges Pompidou 1975–89, conseil supérieur de l'Education Nationale 1983–89; Pres. Centre Georges Pompidou 1989–91; Pres. Univ. of Europe, Paris; Pres. Comité d'Ethique des Sciences (C.N.R.S.) 1994, European Cultural Center of Delphi (Greece); mem. Greek, British, Belgian, German and Bulgarian Acads; Dr. h.c. (Univs. of London, New York, Belgrade, Harvard (U.S.A.), Lima, New Brunswick (Canada), Athens Social Science Univ., American Univ. of Paris, Haifa); Officier, Légion d'honneur, Officier des Palmes académiques, Commdr. des Arts et des Lettres, numerous foreign decorations. *Publications:* Byzance et la Mer 1966, Etudes sur les structures administratives et sociales de Byzance 1971, l'idéologie politique de l'empire byzantin 1975, Byzance: les pays et les territoires 1976, Geographica 1981, contribs. to numerous books. *Leisure interests:* tennis, swimming. *Address:* Sorbonne, 47 rue des Ecoles, 75005 Paris (Office); 28 rue Guynemer, 75006 Paris, France (Home).

AHTISAARI, Martti; Finnish politician and diplomatist; b. 23 June 1937, Viipuri; s. of Oiva Ahtisaari and Tyyne Ahtisaari; m. Eeva Irmeli Hyvärinen 1968; one s.; UN Envoy, Head of operation monitoring Namibia's transition to independence 1989–90, Sr. envoy participated in peace-making efforts in fmr. Yugoslavia –1993; Pres. of Finland March 1994–. *Leisure interests:* golf, music, reading. *Address:* Office of the President, 00170 Helsinki, Finland. *Telephone:* 358-0-661133. *Fax:* 358-0-630292.

AI ZHONGXIN; Chinese painter; b. 13 Oct. 1915, Shanghai; m. Qian Lily, 1977; ed. Nanjing Central Univ. and in U.S.S.R.; Prof. Cen. Inst. of Fine Arts 1954–, Deputy Dir. 1980–; mem. Chinese Artists Asscn. Works include: Yellow River, Road to Ulumci, Seashore. *Publications:* Study of Xu Beihong, On Style of Painting, etc. *Address:* Central Institute of Fine Arts, Beijing, People's Republic of China.

AIBEL, Howard James, B.A., D.JUR.; American lawyer and business executive; b. 24 March 1929, New York; s. of David Aibel and Anne Aibel; m. Katherine W. Webster 1952; three s.; ed. Harvard Coll., Harvard Law School; admitted New York Bar 1952, served as Vice-Pres. of Asscn. of the Bar of New York City, Chair. Cttee. on Fed. Legislation, Assoc. White & Case, New York 1952–57; with Gen. Electric Co. 1957–64, Anti-Trust Litigation Counsel 1960–64; Trade Regulation Counsel ITT Corpn., New York 1964–66, Vice-Pres., Assoc. Gen. Counsel 1966–68, Gen. Counsel 1968–92, Sr. Vice-Pres. 1969–87, Exec. Vice-Pres. 1987–94, Chief Legal Officer 1992–94; Pres. Harvard Law School Asscn. of New York City 1992–93; partner Le Boeuf Lamb Greene & McRae 1994–; fmr. Trustee, Chair. Advisory Bd. School of Law, Bridgeport Univ. 1989–91, Chair. Exec. Cttee. Bd. of Dirs. American Arbitration Asscn. 1986–, Chair. Bd. of Dirs. 1995–98; Chair. Alliance of Resident Theaters, New York; Vice-Chair., Trustee The Fund for Modern Courts 1985–95, Vice-Pres. Harvard Law School Asscn. 1994–; mem. American Law Inst., New York County, New York State, American Bar Asscns.; mem. Bd. of Dirs. Sheraton Corpn. 1982–94, Farrel Corp. 1994–; Life Fellow American Bar Foundation; Trustee Int. Bar Asscn. Foundation, Lawyers' Cttee. for Civil Rights under Law 1991–95; consulting Trustee Nature Centre for Environmental Activities of Westport. *Address:* Le Boeuf Lamb Greene & McRae, 125 West 55th Street, New York, NY 10019 (Office); 183 Steep Hill Road, Weston, CT 06883, U.S.A. (Home). *Telephone:* (212) 424-8527 (Office); (203) 227-0738 (Home). *Fax:* (212) 424-8500 (Office); (203) 454-2072 (Home).

AICHINGER, Ilse; Austrian writer; b. 1 Nov. 1921, Vienna; m. Günter Eich (died 1972); ed. high school and Universität Wien; formerly worked with Inge Scholl at Hochschule für Gestaltung, Ulm; later worked as a reader for S. Fischer (publishers), Frankfurt and Vienna; Förderungspreis des Österreichischen Staatspreises 1952, Preis der Gruppe 47 1952, Literaturpreis der Freien und Hansestadt Bremen 1954, Immermannpreis der Stadt Düsseldorf 1955, Literaturpreis der Bayerischen Akademie 1961, Nyell Sachs-Preis, Dortmund 1971, City of Vienna Literature Prize 1974, Georg Tracke Prize 1979, Petrarca Prize 1982. *Publications:* Die Grössere Hoffnung (novel) 1948, Knöpfe (radio play) 1952, Der Gefesselte (short stories) 1953, Zu keiner Stunde (dialogues) 1957, Besuch im Pfarrhaus (radio play) 1961, Wo ich wohne (stories, dialogues, poems) 1963, Eliza, Eliza (stories) 1965, Nachricht von Tag (stories) 1970.

AIDA, Takefumi, PH.D.; Japanese architect and university professor; b. 5 June 1937, Tokyo; s. of Takeshi Aida and Chiyo Aida; m. Kazuko Aida 1966; one s. one d.; ed. School of Architecture, Waseda Univ., Tokyo; qualified architect 1967; Prof. Shibaura Inst. of Tech., Tokyo 1976, Prof. and Dean Dept. of Architecture and Eng. 1991–94; maj. works include: Memorial at Iwo-Jima Island, Tokyo 1983, Toy Block House X, Shibuya, Tokyo 1984, Tokyo War Dead Memorial Park, Bunkyo, Tokyo 1988, Saito Memorial Hall, Shibaura Inst. of Tech., Tokyo 1990, Community Centre, Kawasato 1993, Funeral Hall, Mizuho 1998; Japan Architects' Asscn. Annual Prize for Newcomers 1982; 2nd Prize Int. Doll's Houses Competition, England 1983. *Publications:* Architecture Note, Toy Block Houses III 1984, Toy Block House X 1986, Takefumi Aida Buildings and Projects 1990. *Leisure interest:* Shogi. *Address:* 1-3-2 Okubo, Shinjuku-ku, Tokyo 169, Japan. *Telephone:* 03-3205 1585. *Fax:* 3209-7960.

AIDA, Yukio; Japanese banker; b. 1 Feb. 1924, Tokyo; ed. Waseda Univ.; joined Nomura Securities Co. Ltd. 1947, Chief Man. Int. Dept. 1961–63, Dir. 1963–67, Man. Dir. 1967–71, Exec. Man. Dir. Int. Operation 1971–76, Exec. Vice-Pres. 1976–83, Sr. Adviser 1991, Hon. Chair. 1991–92, Chair. 1992–; Pres., CEO Nomura Investment Man. Co. Ltd. 1983–86, Chair. 1986–87, Sr. Adviser 1987–91. *Address:* Nomura Securities Co. Ltd., 6-40-8, Shimo-Shakujii, Nerima-ku, Tokyo 103, Japan. *Telephone:* (03) 3996-0886.

AIDOO, Ama Ata; Ghanaian writer; one d.; lecturer Cape Coast Univ. 1970–73; consultant at Univs. Acads. and Research Insts. in Africa, Europe and U.S.A.; Minister of Educ. 1982–83; Chair. African Regional Panel of the Commonwealth Writers' Prize 1990, 1991. *Publications include:* Novels: Our Sister Killjoy or Reflections from a Black-Eyed Squint 1977, Changes: A Love Story 1991, Poetry: Someone Talking to Sometime 1985, Birds and Other Poems, Plays: The Dilemma of a Ghost 1965, Anowa 1970, Short stories: No Sweetness Here 1970, The Eagle and The Chicken and Other Stories 1987, numerous contribs. to magazines and journals. *Address:* P.O. Box 4930, Harare, Zimbabwe. *Telephone:* (4) 731901.

AIGRAIN, Pierre Raoul Roger, D. ÈS SC.; French physicist; b. 28 Sept. 1924, Poitiers; s. of Marius and Germaine (née Ligault) Aigrain; m. Francine Bogard 1947; three s.; ed. secondary schools in Metz, Poitiers, Nancy, Annecy, Lycée Saint Louis, Paris, Naval School, Carnegie Inst. of Tech., Pittsburgh and Faculté des Sciences, Paris; Attaché, Research and Study Centre, French Navy 1948–50; Asst. Collège de France 1950–51; Engineer Atomic Energy Comm. 1951–52; Head of physics lectures, Faculté des Sciences, Lille 1952; mem. council and Nat. Sec. French Physics Soc. 1953, Sec.-Gen. 1959; Head of lectures Faculté des Sciences, Paris 1954, Titular Prof. gen. electrotechnology 1958–63, energy 1963–65; Vice-Pres. consultative cttee. for scientific and tech. research 1958–61; Scientific Dir. in charge of research and experimentation, Army ministry 1961–65; Dir. Higher Ed. Ministry of Nat. Ed. 1965–67, Gen. Del. for scientific and tech. research 1968–73; Prof. M.I.T. 1973–74; Gen. Tech. Dir. Thomson Group 1974–78; Admin. Fondation pour l'Innovation 1973; Pres. Admin. Council Institut des hautes études scientifiques 1977–78; Sec. of State in Charge of Research, Prime Minister's Office 1978–81; Dir.-Gen. (scientific and tech.) Thomson Brandt and Thomson C.S.F. 1981–83, Scientific Adviser to Pres. Thomson group 1983–92; Pres. Cttee. of Econ. and Industrial Co-operation between French and Chinese Business, Conseil nat. du Patronat Français 1984–93; Vice-Pres. de la Soc. française de physique 1987, then Pres.; Vice-Pres. Soc. des Ingénieurs et Scientifiques de France 1987–; mem. Atomic Energy Cttee. 1968–73, Conseil Supérieur de la langue française 1989–92; mem. Acad. des Sciences 1988; Pres. Conseil Scientifique de l'Inst. Nat. de Recherche en Informatique et en Automatique 1992–96; Foreign mem. Royal Swedish Acad. of Science; Assoc. mem. American Acad. of Sciences 1974–; Fellow Inst. of Electrical and Electronic Engineers; Foreign Assoc. Nat. Acad. of Eng. 1976–; Commdr., Légion d'honneur, Commdr. Ordre nat. du Mérite and Palmes académiques, Chevalier du Mérite agricole; Commdr. Nat. Order of Senegal, Order of Merit (Fed. Rep. Germany); Médaille de l'aéronautique; prix Robin (Soc. Française de Physique) 1974. *Publications:* Simples propos d'un homme de sciences 1984, numerous research papers on electronic circuits and semiconductors. *Address:* 56 rue de Boulainvilliers, 75016 Paris, France (Home).

AIKEN, Linda H., PH.D.; American nurse sociologist; b. 29 July 1943, Roanoke; d. of William Jordan and Betty Philips (Warner) Harman; one s. one d.; ed. Univ. of Florida, Gainesville, Univ. of Texas, Austin, Univ. of Wisconsin, Madison; nurse, Univ. of Fla. Medical Center 1964–65; Instructor, Coll. of Nursing, Univ. of Fla. 1966–67; Instructor, School of Nursing, Univ. of Mo. 1967–70, Clinical Nurse Specialist 1967–70; lecturer, School of Nursing, Univ. of Wis. 1973–74; Program Officer, Robert Wood Johnson Foundation 1974–76, Dir. of Research 1976–79, Asst. Vice-Pres. 1979–81, Vice-Pres. 1981–87; Prof. of Nursing and Sociology, Dir. Center for Health Services and Policy Research, Univ. of Pennsylvania 1988–; mem. Pres. Clinton's Nat. Health Care Reform Task Force 1993; Commr. Physician Payment Review Comm. Nat. Advisory Council, U.S. Agency for Health Care Policy and Research; Assoc. Ed. Journal of Health and Social Behaviour 1979–81; Jessie M. Scott Award, American Nurses Asscn. 1984, Nurse Scientist of the Year Award 1991. *Publications:* Nursing in the 1980s: Crises, Challenges, Opportunities (Ed.) 1982, Evaluation Studies Review Annual 1985 (co-Ed. with B. Kehrer) 1985, Applications of Social Science to Clinical Medicine and Health Policy (co-Ed. with D. Mechanic) 1986, Charting Nursing's Future (co-Ed. with C. Fagin) 1991, Hospital Restructuring in North America and Europe 1997. *Address:* University of Pennsylvania, 420 Service Drive, Philadelphia, PA 19104; 2209 Lombard Street, Philadelphia, PA 19146, U.S.A.

AILLAGON, Jean Jacques; French cultural official; b. 2 Oct. 1946, Metz; s. of Charles Aillagon and Anne-Marie Louis; two c.; ed. Univs. of Toulouse and Nanterre; Prof. of History and Geography, Lycée de Tulle 1973–76; Deputy Dir. Ecole Nat. Supérieure des Beaux-Arts 1978–82; Admin. Musée Nat. d'Art Moderne (Centre Pompidou) 1982–85; Asst. to Dir. of Cultural Affairs of City of Paris 1985–88; Del.-Gen. for Cultural Programmes of City of Paris 1988–93; Dir.-Gen. Vidéothèque de Paris 1992–93; Dir. of Cultural Affairs of City of Paris 1993–96; Pres. Centre Georges Pompidou 1996–; Pres. commission organizing year 2000 celebrations; Artistic Dir. Commissariat for France-Egypt Year 1996–98; Chevalier, Ordre nat. du Mérite, des Palmes Académiques. *Address:* Centre National d'Art et de Culture Georges Pompidou, 19 rue Beaubourg, 75004 Paris, France. *Telephone:* 01 44 78 49 60. *Fax:* 01 44 78 15 50.

AILLERET, François; French government official; b. 7 June 1937; s. of Pierre Ailleret; m.; four c.; served in Algeria and Côte d'Ivoire in early 1960s; various appts. at Paris Airport 1967–80; joined Electricité de France (EDF) 1980, Deputy Dir.-Gen. 1987, Dir.-Gen. 1994–96, Vice-Pres. 1996, Pres. EDF Int. 1996–; Pres. Int. Union of Electricity Producers and Distributors (UNIPEDE) 1997–; Admin. Pechiney 1996–; Officier, Légion d'honneur, Ordre nat. du Mérite, Croix de la Valeur militaire. *Address:* Electricité de France, 32 rue de Monceau, 75384 Paris; 33 rue Desnouettes, 75015 Paris, France.

AIMÉ, Jean-Claude C., M.B.A.; Haitian international civil servant; b. 10 Sept. 1935, Port-au-Prince; s. of Christian F. Aimé and Carmen Amelia Gautier; m. 1st Elizabeth B. Bettison 1963 (divorced 1991); m. 2nd Lisa M. Buttenheim 1992; ed. Harvard Coll., Univ. of Pennsylvania; joined UN 1962, Programme Officer Tunis 1963–64, Asst. Resident Rep. UNDP Algiers 1964–67, ILO Geneva 1967–69, Deputy Perm. Rep. UNDP Amman 1969–71, UN Relief Operation Dacca 1971–72, Rep. East African Community Arusha UNDP 1972–73, Resident Rep. UNDP Amman 1973–77, Senior Adviser UNIFIL Naqoura 1978, UN Sr. Adviser in the Middle East 1979–82, Dir. Office of Under-Secs.-Gen. for Special Political Affairs 1982–88, Exec. Asst. to Sec.-Gen. 1989–92, Asst. Sec.-Gen., Chief of Staff 1992–96, Exec. Sec. UN Compensation Comm., Geneva 1997–. *Leisure interests:* music, reading, squash, hunting. *Address:* United Nations Compensation Commission, Villa "La Pelouse", Palais des Nations, 1211 Geneva 10, Switzerland. *Telephone:* (22) 907-3800. *Fax:* (22) 907-0069.

AIMÉE, Anouk; French actress; b. (Françoise Dreyfus) 27 April 1932, Paris; d. of Henry Dreyfus and Geneviève Durand; m. 2nd Nico Papatakis 1951; one d.; m. 3rd Pierre Barouh 1966, 4th Albert Finney (q.v.) 1970 (divorced 1978); ed. Ecole de la rue Milton, Paris, Ecole de Barbezieux, Pensionnat de Bandd, Inst. de Megève and Cours Bauer-Therond. *Theatre includes:* Sud 1954, Love Letters 1990, 1994. *Films include:* Les mauvaises rencontres 1955, Tous peuvent me tuer, Pot bouille and Montparnasse 19 1957, La tête contre les murs 1958, Les drageurs 1959, La dolce vita, Le farceur, Lola, Les amours de Paris, L'imprévu 1960, Quai Notre Dame 1960, Le jugement dernier 1961, Sodome et Gomorrhe 1961, Les grands Chemins 1962, Education sentimentale 1962, Huit et demi 1962, Un homme et une femme 1966, Un soir un train 1967, The Appointment 1968, Model Shop 1968, Justine 1968, Si c'était à refaire 1976, Mon premier amour 1978, Salto nel vuoto 1979, La tragédie d'un homme ridicule 1981, Qu'est-ce qui fait courir David? 1982, Le Général de l'armée morte 1983, Vive la vie and Le succès à tout prix 1984, Un homme et une femme: vingt ans déjà 1986, Docteur Norman Bethune 1992, les Marmottes 1993, Les Cent et une Nuits 1995, Prêt-à-porter 1995. *Television:* Une page d'amour 1979. Commdr. des Arts et des Lettres. *Address:* Bureau Georges Beaume, 3 Quai Malaquais, 75006 Paris, France.

AIPIN, Yeremey Danilovich; Russian author; b. 27 June 1948; ed. Gorky Inst. of Literature; m.; two d.; People's Deputy 1990–91; Pres. Asscn. of Aboriginal Peoples of the N., Siberia and Far E. of Russia 1993–; mem. State Duma, Chair. Cttee. on Nat. Affairs 1993–96. *Publications include:* I am Listening to the Earth, Khanty or Star of Morning Dawn, In Wait for the First Snow and other works about peoples of N. Russia. *Address:* Pionerskaya str. 27 Apt. 72, 626200 Khanty-Mansiysk, Russia.

AIREY, Sir Lawrence, K.C.B., M.A.; British government administrator; b. 10 March 1926, Co. Durham; s. of Lawrence Clark Airey and Isabella Marshall Airey (née Pearson); m. Patricia Anne Williams 1953; two s. one d.; ed. Newcastle Royal Grammar School, Peterhouse, Cambridge, Nuffield Coll., Oxford; entered Civil Service 1949; Gen. Register Office 1949–56; Cabinet Office 1956–58; with H.M. Treasury 1958–80; Under-Sec. 1969–73, Deputy Sec. 1973–77; Second Perm. Sec. (Domestic Econ.) H.M. Treasury 1977; Chair. Bd. of Inland Revenue 1980–86; non-exec. Dir. Standard Life Assurance Co. 1987–94, Deputy Chair. 1988–94; Consultant Drivers Jonas Partners 1986–92; Research Fellow, Nuffield Coll., Oxford, 1961–62; mem. Bd. British Nat. Oil Corpn. 1976–77; mem. Govt. Contracts Review Bd. 1987–. *Leisure interest:* book collecting. *Address:* Lions House, Berwick-upon-Tweed, Northumberland, England.

AIRLIE, 13th Earl of, **David George Patrick Coke Ogilvy,** K.T., G.C.V.O., P.C.; British business executive; b. 17 May 1926, London; s. of 12th Earl of Airlie, K.T., G.C.V.O., M.C., and Lady Alexandra Marie Bridget Coke; m. Virginia Fortune Ryan 1952; three s. three d.; ed. Eton Coll.; Chair. Schroders PLC. 1977–84, Ashdown Investment Trust Ltd. 1968–84, J. Henry Schroder Bank AG (Switzerland) 1977–84, Baring Stratton Investment Trust PLC 1986–; Chair. Gen. Accident Fire and Life Assurance Corpn. PLC 1987–97; Dir. J. Henry Schroder Wagg & Co. Ltd. 1961–84, Schroder, Darling and Co. Holdings Ltd. (Australia) 1977–84, Schroders Inc. (U.S.A.) 1977–84, Schroder Int. Ltd. 1973–84, Scottish & Newcastle Breweries PLC 1969–83; Dir. Royal Bank of Scotland Group PLC 1983–93; Lord Chamberlain of the Queen's Household 1984–97; Lord Lieut. of Angus 1989–; Chancellor Univ. of Abertay Dundee 1994–; Gov. Nuffield Hosps.; Hon. Pres. Scout Asscn. in Scotland 1988–, J.P. Angus 1990; Hon. LL.D. (Univ. of Dundee) 1990. *Address:* Cortachy Castle, Kirriemuir, Angus, Scotland; 5 Swan Walk, Chelsea, London, SW3 4JJ, England. *Telephone:* (015754) 231.

AITCHISON, Craigie; British artist; b. 13 Jan. 1926, Scotland; s. of the late Rt. Hon. Lord Aitchison and of Lady Aitchison; ed. Slade School of Fine Art, London; British Council/Italian Govt. Scholarship for Painting 1955; Edwin Austin Abbey Premier Scholarship 1970; Lorne Scholarship 1974–75; Arts Council Bursary 1976; one-man exhbns. at Beaux Arts Gallery, Marlborough Fine Art, Rutland Gallery, Serpentine Gallery, 12 Duke Street Gallery and others, London, Compass Gallery, Glasgow, Scottish Arts Council, Edin., Kettle's Yard, Cambridge, Artis, Monte Carlo and others; Retrospectives, Harewood House, Leeds 1954–94, Gallery of Modern Art, Glasgow 1956–96; many mixed exhbns. in U.K., Italy, Japan, France and India; works in public collections including Tate Gallery, Arts Council of G.B., Contemporary Art Soc., London, Scottish Nat. Gallery of Modern Art, Scottish Arts Council, Walker Art Gallery, Liverpool and Newcastle Region Art Gallery, N.S.W., Australia, British Council exhbn., Israel Museum, Jerusalem 1992; fmr. R.A., resgnd. 1997, rejoined 1998; Prizewinner John Moores Liverpool Exhbn. 1974–75; Johnson's Wax Award for Best Painting at R.A. Summer Exhbn. 1982; Korn Ferry Int. Award, Royal Academy Summer Exhibition 1989, 1991; Jerwood Foundation Prize 1994. *Address:* c/o Royal Academy of Arts, Burlington House, Piccadilly, London, W1V 0DS, England.

AITKEN, Martin Jim, D.PHIL., F.R.S., F.R.A.S., F.S.A.; British physicist; b. 11 March 1922, Stamford, Lincs.; s. of Percy Aitken and Ethel Brittain; m. Joan Killick; one s. four d.; ed. Stamford School, Lincs., Wadham Coll., Oxford; war service as Radar Officer, R.A.F., Far East 1942–46; Research in Nuclear Physics, Clarendon Lab., Oxford 1949–56; Deputy Dir., Research Lab. for Archaeology and the History of Art, Oxford Univ. 1957–89; Prof. of Archaeometry, Oxford Univ. 1985–89; Fellow of Linacre Coll., Oxford 1965–89. *Publications:* Physics and Archaeology 1961, Archaeological Involvements of Physics (in Physics Reports, Vol. 40C) 1978, Thermoluminescence Dating 1985, Science-based Dating in Archaeology 1990, Introduction to Optical Dating 1998. *Leisure interest:* sailing-dinghy racing. *Address:* Ofslang House, Islip, Oxford, OX5 2SZ, England.

AITMATOV, Chingiz Torekulovich; Kyrgyzstan writer and diplomatist; b. 12 Dec. 1928, Sheker Village, Kirghizia; s. of late Torekul Aitmatov and of Nagima Aitmatova; m. Maria Urmatova 1974; three s. one d.; ed. Kirghiz Agricultural Inst.; writer 1952–; fmrly. Corresp. for Pravda; mem. CPSU 1959–91; First Sec. of Cinema Union of Kirghiz S.S.R. 1964–69, Chair. 1969–86; Chair. of Union of Writers of Kyrgyzstan 1986–; Cand. mem. Cen. Cttee. of CP of Kirghiz S.S.R. 1969–71, mem. 1971–90; People's Writer of Kirghiz S.S.R. 1968; Vice-Chair. Cttee. of Solidarity with Peoples of Asian and African Countries 1974–89; Deputy to U.S.S.R. Supreme Soviet 1966–89; People's Deputy of the U.S.S.R. 1989–91; mem. Presidential Council 1990–91; U.S.S.R. (now Russian) Amb. to Luxembourg 1990–92, to Belgium and Luxembourg 1992–96; mem. Kirghiz Academy of Science 1974, European Academy of Arts, Science and Humanity 1983, World Academy of Art and Science 1987; Chair. Issyk-Kul Forum 1986–; Chief Ed. Innostrannaya Literatura 1988–90; Lenin Prize for Tales of the Hills and the Steppes 1963; Austrian State Prize for European Literature 1994; Hero of Socialist Labour 1978, State Prize in Literature 1968, 1977, 1983 and other decorations and prizes from Germany, India, Turkey and U.S.A. *Publications include:* stories: Face to Face, Short Stories, Melody 1961, Tales of the Hills and the Steppes 1963; Stories 1967; Mother Earth and Other Stories 1989; novels: Djamilya 1959, My Poplar in a Red Kerchief 1960, Camel's Eye, The First Teacher, Farewell Gulsary, Mother Earth 1963, The White Steamship (English trans. 1972), The Lament of the Migrating Bird (English trans. 1972), The Ascent of Mount Fuji (with Muhamegjanov) 1973, co-author of Earth and Water 1978, Works (3 vols.) 1978, Early Storks 1979, Stories 1979, Piebald Dog, Running Along the Sea Shore, The Day Lasts More Than a Hundred Years 1980, Executioner's Block (English trans. 1987) 1986, The Place of the Skull, The White Cloud of Chingiz Khan 1991, A Conversation at the Foothill of Fudjiyama Mountain (with Daisaku Ikeda) 1992, The Brand of Cassandra (novel) 1994. *Leisure interest:* skiing. *Address:* Embassy of the Kyrgyz Republic, rue Tenbosch, 1050 Brussels, Belgium (Office); Toktogulstz 98, Apt. 9, 720000 Bishkek, Kyrgyzstan (Home).

AITMATOV, Ilgiz Torekulovich, PH.D., D.TECH.SC.; Kyrgyzstan scientist; b. 8 Feb. 1931, Frunze (now Bishkek); s. of Torokul Aitmatov and Naghima (née Abdulvaliyeva) Aitmatova; m. Rozalia Djamankulovna Djenchurayeva 1961; one s. two d.; ed. Moscow Inst. of Geological Survey; foreman, eng., Head anti-avalanche surveillance service, Kyrgyz Geological Man. 1954–57; jr. researcher, Head of Lab., Deputy Dir. Inst. of Physics and Mechs. of Rocks, Kyrgyz Acad. of Sciences 1960–64, Head of Lab. 1965–68, Deputy Dir. 1968–70, Dir. 1970–90, 1994–; mem. Kyrgyz Acad. of Sciences 1989–, Academician-Sec. Dept. of Physical, Math. and Geological Sciences 1989–90; mem. Political Council People's Republican Party of Kyrgyzstan 1992–; People's Deputy XII convocation 1990–94; mem. Pres. Council 1990–91;

Chair. Constant Comm. Soviet for Science, Tech., Industry, Power Industry and Communications 1984; Pres. Kyrgyz Acad. of Sciences 1990–93; U.S.S.R. State Prize 1989, Merited Worker of Science of Kyrgyzstan, People's Deputy of Kyrgyzstan, other medals and awards. *Publications:* 180 papers on geomechanics. *Address:* Institute of Rock Physics and Mechanics, O. Mederov Str. 98, 720035 Bishek (Office); 98 Toktoghul Str., Apartment 9, 720000 Bishkek, Kyrgyzstan (Home). *Telephone:* (31) 44-38-01 (Office); (31) 22-79-70 (Home).

AIZAWA, Hideyuki; Japanese politician; ed. Univ. of Tokyo; mem. House of Reps., Tottori Pref.; Vice-Minister of Finance; Vice-Chair. Policy Affairs Research Council Liberal Democratic Party (LDP); Dir.-Gen. Research Bureau, Treasury Bureau, (LDP); Chair. Cttee. on Judicial Affairs, Cttee. on Foreign Affairs; Dir.-Gen. Econ. Planning Agency, Minister of State 1990. *Address:* c/o Liberal Democratic Party, 1-11-23 Nagata-cho, Chiyoda-ku, Tokyo 100, Japan.

AJAYI, Jacob Festus Ade, PH.D.; Nigerian professor of history; b. 26 May 1929, Ikole-Ekiti; s. of late Chief E. Ade Ajayi and late Comfort F. Bolajoko Ajayi; m. Christie Akinleye-Martins 1956; one s. four d.; ed. Igbobi Coll. Lagos, Higher Coll. Yaba, Univ. Coll. Ibadan, Univ. Coll. Leicester and King's Coll. London; tutor, Ibadan Boys' High School 1948–49, 1951–52; Fellow, Inst. of Historical Research 1957–58; Lecturer, Sr. Lecturer, Univ. of Ibadan 1958–63, Prof. of History 1963–89; Fellow, Center for Advanced Study in the Behavioural Sciences, Stanford 1970–71; Vice-Chancellor, Univ. of Lagos 1972–78; Pro-Chancellor, Ondo State Univ., Ado-Ekiti 1984–88; mem. UN Univ. Council 1974–80, Chair. 1976–77; Chair. Int. African Inst. 1975–87; mem. Bureau, Asscn. of African Univs. 1973–80, Vice-Pres. 1976–80; mem. Bureau, Int. Asscn of Univs. 1980–90; Pres. Historical Soc. of Nigeria 1972–81; mem. UNESCO scientific cttee. for drafting The General History of Africa (ed. Vol. VI) 1970–93, Council, Nat. Univ. of Lesotho 1976–82, OAU Group of Eminent Persons for Reparation 1992–, editorial Bd. Encyclopaedia of Sub-Saharan Africa 1995–, Bd. of Trustees Nigerian Merit Award 1996–; mem. Bd. of Dirs. of SOWSCO 1994–; corresp. Fellow Royal Historical Soc., U.K.; Hon. Fellow School of Oriental and African Studies, Univ. of London 1994; Hon. LL.D. (Leicester) 1975, D. Litt. (Birmingham) 1984, D.Litt. (Ondo State Univ.) 1992; Bobapitan of Ikole-Ekiti and Onikoyi of Ife 1983; Nigerian Order of Nat. Merit 1986; Univ. of Lagos Anniversary Gold Medal 1987, Distinguished Africanist Award (African Studies Asscn. of U.S.A.) 1993. *Publications include:* Milestones in Nigerian History 1962, Yoruba Warfare 1964, Christian Missions in Nigeria, 1841–91: the Making of a New Elite 1965; Cementing Partnership: the Story of WAPCO 1960–90, History and the Nation and other Addresses, A Patriot to the Core: Samuel Ajayi Crowther 1993, History of the Nigerian Society of Engineers 1995, The African Experience with Higher Education 1996; ed. or jt. ed. of various vols. on African history. *Leisure interests:* table tennis, dancing. *Address:* P.O. Box 14617, University of Ibadan; 1, Ojobadan Avenue, Bodija Ibadan, Nigeria. *Telephone:* (02) 8101588 (Ibadan). *Fax:* (02) 8100064.

AJIBOLA, Hon. Prince Bola; Nigerian judge; b. 22 March 1934, Lagos; s. of Oba A. S. Ajibola and Adikatu Ashakun Ajibola; m. Olu Ajibola 1961; three s. two d.; ed. Holborn Coll. of Law, London Univ.; called to the English Bar (Lincoln's Inn) 1962; Prin. Partner, Bola Ajibola & Co., Lagos, Ikeja, Abeokuta and Kaduna, specializing in commercial law and int. arbitration; fmr. Attorney-Gen. and Fed. Minister of Justice; mem. Int. Court of Justice, The Hague 1991–94; mem. Nigerian del. to UN Gen. Ass. 1986; Temporary Pres. UN Gen. Ass., 17th Special Session on Narcotic Drugs 1990; Chair. Task Force for Revision of the Laws of the Fed. 1990; initiated first African Law Ministers Conf., Abuja 1989; Chair. Gen. Council of the Bar, Disciplinary Cttee. of the Bar, Advisory Cttee. on the Prerogative of Mercy; Pres. African Concern 1996–; mem. Nigeria Police Council, Int. Law Comm., Perm. Court of Arbitration, The Hague, ICC Court of Arbitration, Int. Maritime Arbitration Comm., Paris, Panel of Int. Arbitrators, London Inst. of Arbitrators, Int. Advisory Cttee. of World Arbitration Inst., U.S.A.; Judge IBRD Tribunal, Washington 1995–; Vice-Pres. Inst. of Int. Business Law and Practice, Paris; Nat. Chair. World Peace Through Law Centre; Ed. Nigeria's Treaties in Force 1970–1990, All Nigeria Law Reports 1961–1990; Ed.-in-Chief Justice; Gen. Ed. Fed. Ministry of Justice Law Review Series (7 vols.); Fellow Chartered Inst. of Arbitrators, Nigerian Inst. of Advanced Legal Studies; mem. Nigerian Bar Asscn. (Pres. 1984–85), African Bar Asscn., Int. Bar Asscn., Asscn. of World Lawyers, ICC, Commonwealth Law Asscn., World Arbitration Inst., Soc. for the Reform of Criminal Law, Hon. LL.D. (Buckingham) 1996. *Publications:* Principles of Arbitration 1980, The Law and Settlement of Commercial Disputes 1984, Law Development and Administration in Nigeria 1987, Integration of the African Continent Through Law 1988, Banking Frauds and Other Financial Malpractices in Nigeria 1989, Women and Children under Nigerian Law 1990, Scheme Relating to Mutual Assistance in Criminal Matters and the Control of Criminal Activities within Africa, and numerous other books on other legal topics. *Address:* c/o IBRD, 1818 H Street, N.W., Washington, DC 20433, U.S.A.; 141 Igbosere Road, Lagos, Nigeria.

AJMANI, Jagdish Chand, B.A.; Indian diplomatist; b. 4 April 1930, Shimla; s. of the late Dip Chand and Radha Ajmani; m. Asha Ajmani 1955; two s. two d.; ed. Modern School and MB Higher Secondary School, Delhi, St. Stephen's Coll., Delhi Univ. and Brasenose Coll., Oxford; joined Foreign service 1952; Third Sec. and Second Sec., Cairo 1955–57; Official Sec., Canberra 1957–60; First Sec., Baghdad 1960–63; Dir., Ministry of External Affairs 1963–67; Counsellor Tokyo 1967–69; attended Nat. Defence Coll., New Delhi 1970; Consul-Gen., Berlin and later Amb. to German Democratic Repub. 1974–77, to Fed. Repub. of Germany 1986–88; High Commr. in Australia 1977–80; Amb. to Italy 1980–84; Perm. Rep. to FAO 1980–84.

AJODHIA, Jules; Suriname politician; Vice-Pres. and Prime Minister of Suriname 1991–96; mem. Verenigde Hervormings Partij (VHP). *Address:* c/o Verenigde Hervormings Partij, Paramaribo, Suriname.

AKABUSI, Kriss, M.B.E.; British athlete; b. 28 Nov. 1958, London; s. of Daniel Akabusi and Clara Akabusi; m. Monika Udhöfer 1982; two d.; army sergeant and physical training instructor; mem. 4 × 400m relay team, Olympic Games 1984, 1988; European 4 × 400m relay records 1984, 1987; winner, U.K. 400m 1984, 400m hurdles (tie) 1987, AAA 400m 1988; winner 400m hurdles (British record), Commonwealth Games 1990.

AKAGAWA, Jiro; Japanese author; b. 29 Feb. 1948, Fukuoka; m. Fumiko Serita 1973; one d.; ed. Toho-gakuen High School; fmr. proof-reader for Japan Machinery Soc.; mem. Japanese Mystery Writers' Asscn. 1977–; All Yomimono Debut Writers' Award 1976; Kadokawa Publishing Book Award 1980. *Publications:* more than 350 works including novels: The School Festival for the Dead 1977, Ghost Train 1978, The Deduction of Tortoise-shell Holmes 1978, High School Girl with a Machine Gun 1978, The Requiem Dedicated to the Bad Wife 1980, Virgin Road 1983, Chizuko's Younger Sister 1989, The Ghost Story of the Hitokoizaka-Slope 1995. *Leisure interests:* classical music, watching movies. *Address:* 40-16-201 Ohyama-cho, Sibuya-ku, Tokyo 151, Japan.

AKAKA, Daniel Kahikina; American politician; b. 1 Sept. 1924, Honolulu; s. of Kahikina Akaka and Annie Kahoa; m. Mary M. Chong 1948; four s. one d.; ed. Univ. of Hawaii; schoolteacher, Hawaii 1953–60; Vice-Prin., Prin. Ewa Beach Elementary School, Honolulu 1960–64; Prin. Pohakea Elementary School 1964–65, Kaneohe Elementary School 1965–68; Dir. Hawaii Office of Econ. Opportunity 1971–74; special asst. human resources office of Gov. of Hawaii 1975–76; program specialist, Hawaii Compensatory Educ. 1978–79, 1985–91; mem. 95th–100th Congresses from 2nd Dist. of Hawaii 1977–91; Senator from Hawaii 1990–; Democrat. *Address:* United States Senate, 720 Senate Hart Bldg., Washington, DC 20510, U.S.A.

AKALAITIS, Joanne; American artistic director (retd.); b. 29 June 1932, Chicago; d. of Clement Akalaitis and Estelle Mattis; m. Philip Glass 1965 (divorced 1974); one s. one d.; ed. Univ. of Chicago and Stanford Univ. Grad. School; Artistic Dir. New York Shakespeare Festival 1991–92; works directed include Beckett's Cascando 1976, Dressed Like an Egg 1977, Dead End Kids 1980, A History of Nuclear Power (writer and dir. of play and film), Request Concert (Drama Desk Award) 1981, The Photographer 1983, Beckett's Endgame 1984, Genet's The Balcony 1985, Green Card (writer and dir.) 1986, Greg Buchner's Leon & Lena (and Lenz) 1987, Genet's The Screens 1987, Cymbeline 1989, 'Tis Pity She's a Whore 1992, Henry IV (Pts. I & II) 1991, Woyzeck 1992, In the Summer House 1993; Rockefeller Playwright Fellow; Rosamund Gilder Fellow; Guggenheim Fellow 1978; recipient of four Obies for distinguished direction. *Publication:* Green Card. *Leisure interest:* cooking. *Address:* Mabon Mines, 150 1st Avenue, New York, NY 10009, U.S.A.

AKAMATSU, Ryoko; Japanese politician; b. 24 Aug. 1929, Osaka; d. of Rinsaku Akamatsu and Asaka Akamatsu; m. Tadashi Hanami 1953; one s.; ed. Tsuda Coll. and Univ. of Tokyo; Ministry of Labour 1953, Dir. Women Workers' Div. 1970–72; Dir.-Gen. Yamanashi Labour Standard Bureau 1975–78; Counsellor in charge of Women's Affairs, Prime Minister's Office 1978–79; Minister, Perm. Mission to UN 1979–82; Dir.-Gen. Women's Bureau, Ministry of Labour 1982–85; Amb. to Uruguay 1986–89; Pres. Japan Inst. of Workers' Evolution 1989–93; Prof. Bunkyo Women's Coll. 1992–93; Minister of Educ., Science, Culture and Sports 1993–94. *Publications:* Girls Be Ambitious (autobiog.) 1990, Beautiful Uruguay 1990. *Leisure interests:* reading, swimming, listening to classical music. *Address:* 5-11-22-309, Roppongi, Minato-ku, Tokyo 106, Japan. *Telephone:* 03-3423-3534. *Fax:* 03-3423-3534.

AKASHI, Yasushi; Japanese diplomatist; b. 19 Jan. 1931, Akita; m.; two c.; ed. Univ. of Tokyo, Univ. of Virginia, Fletcher School of Law and Diplomacy and Columbia Univ.; Political Affairs Officer UN Secr. 1957–74; Chair. Univ. Seminar on Modern East Asia 1963–64; Amb. at Perm. Mission to UN, New York 1974–79; UN Under-Sec.-Gen. for Public Information 1979–87, for Disarmament Affairs 1987; UN Rep. in Cambodia 1992; Special Envoy to Fmr. Yugoslavia 1994–95; UN Under-Sec. for Humanitarian Affairs 1996–97, UN Emergency Relief Co-ordinator 1997–98; has represented Japan in Gen. Ass. and numerous UN confs. and orgs.; Chair. Budget and Finance Cttee. Governing Council UNDP 1978; mem. Advisory Cttee. on Admin. and Budgetary Questions 1974, 1977; Assoc. Columbia Univ. Seminars, Chair. Conf. of Mid-Career Asian Leaders on Devt. 1967; Dir. Int. Peace Acad., Better World Soc.; Sec. Founding Cttee. UN Univ.; fmr. Visiting Lecturer Univ. of Tokyo, Int. Christian Univ., Tokyo and Sophia Univ. *Publications:* The United Nations 1965, From the Windows of the United Nations 1984, The Lights and Shadows of the United Nations 1985, and numerous articles. *Address:* c/o United Nations, United Nations Plaza, New York, NY 10017, U.S.A.

AKAYEV, Askar Akayevich, D.TECH.; Kyrgyzstan politician; b. 10 Nov. 1944, Kyzyl-Baizak Keminsky dist.; s. of Akai Tokoyev and Aselj Tokoyeva; m. Mairam Akayeva 1970; two s. two d.; ed. Leningrad Inst. of Precise

Mechanics and Optics; lecturer; Prof. Frunze Politech. Inst. 1972–73, Chair. 1976–86; Prof. Inst. of Precise Mechanics and Optics 1973–76; Head of Science Dept. Cen. Cttee. Kyrgyz CP 1986–87; mem. CPSU 1981–91; fmr. mem. Cen. Cttee. Kyrgyz CP, Vice-Pres., Pres. Kirghiz S.S.R. (now Kyrgyzstan) Acad. of Sciences 1987–90; fmr. mem. CPSU Constitutional Compliance Cttee.; fmr. mem. U.S.S.R. Supreme Soviet Cttee. on Econ. Reform 1991; Exec. Pres. Kirghiz S.S.R. 1990, Pres. Kyrgyzstan 1991–; Hon. academician Int. Eng. Acad. and of Int. Acad. of Creation 1996. *Publications:* more than 80 articles on radiophysics problems and political problems. *Leisure interests:* travelling with the family, mountain skiing, mountaineering. *Address:* Government House, Bishkek 720003, Kyrgyzstan. *Telephone:* (31) 21 24 66. *Fax:* (31) 21 86 27.

AKBULUT, Yildirim; Turkish politician; b. 1935, Erzincan; m.; three c.; ed. Univ. of Istanbul; fmr. practising lawyer; Deputy for Erzincan 1983–; Prime Minister of Turkey 1989–91; mem. Motherland Party; fmr. Deputy Speaker of Parl., Speaker 1987–89; Minister of Interior 1986–87. *Address:* c/o Anavatan Partisi, 13 Cad. 3, Balgat, Ankara, Turkey.

AKCHURIN, Renat Suleimanovich, DR. MED.; Russian cardiosurgeon; b. 2 April 1946, Andijan, Uzbekistan; m. Natalya Pavlovna Akchurina; two s.; ed. Inst. of Medicine (now Seehenov Acad. of Medicine); general practitioner polyclinics 1970–73; ordinator, jr., sr. researcher Inst. of Clinical and Experimental Medicine 1973–84; in Baylor Univ., Texas, U.S.A. 1984; surgeon, Head Dept. of Cardiovascular Surgery Russian Cardiological Cen. 1984–; corresp. mem. Russian Acad. of Medical Sciences 1997; performed first heart and lung transplantation operations in U.S.S.R.; performs about 100 bypass operations a year, performed a bypass operation on Pres. Yeltsin 1996; patented several inventions of medical instruments; U.S.S.R. State Prize 1982. *Publications include:* over 180 scientific papers and articles. *Leisure interests:* music, hunting, cooking. *Address:* Cardiology Scientific Centre, Cherepkovskaya str. 15a, 121552 Moscow, Russia (Office). *Telephone:* (095) 415 0025 (Office).

AKE, Siméon; Côte d'Ivoirian lawyer, diplomatist and politician; b. 4 Jan. 1932, Bingerville; m. Anne Maud Bonful 1958; five c.; ed. Univs. of Dakar and Grenoble; Chef de Cabinet to Minister of Public Service, Ivory Coast 1959–61; First Counsellor, Ivory Coast Mission to UN 1961–63; Dir. of Protocol, Ministry of Foreign Affairs 1963–64; Amb. to U.K., Sweden, Denmark and Norway 1964–66; Perm. Rep. of Ivory Coast to UN 1966–77; Minister of Foreign Affairs 1977–90; Amb. accred. to Germany and Austria 1991; mem. Guiding Cttee., Parti démocratique de la Côte d'Ivoire (PDCI-RDA) Oct. 1975–; Commdr. ordre Nat. de la République de la Côte d'Ivoire, de l'ordre de St. Grégoire; Grand Officer, Légion d'honneur; distinctions from Belgium, Brazil, Spain, Cameroun. *Address:* 08 Boîte Postale 2102, Abidjan, Côte d'Ivoire.

AKENSON, Donald Harman, PH.D., D.LITT., F.R.S.A., F.R.S.C., F.R.HIST.S.; Canadian professor of history; b. 22 May 1941, Minneapolis, Minn.; s. of Donald Nels Akenson and Fern L. Harman Akenson; ed. Yale Coll. and Harvard Univ.; Allston Burr Sr. Tutor, Dunster House, Harvard Coll. 1966–67; Assoc. Prof. of History, Queen's Univ., Kingston, Ont. 1970–74, Prof. 1974–; Beamish Research Prof., Inst. of Irish Studies, Univ. of Liverpool 1998–; Guggenheim Fellow 1984–85; Chalmers Prize 1985, Landon Prize 1987, Grawemeyer World Peace Prize 1993; Molson Laureate 1996, D. Litt. (h.c.) McMaster Univ. 1995, D. Hum. Litt. (h.c.) Lethbridge Univ. 1995 and many other awards and distinctions. *Publications:* The Irish Education Experiment 1970, The Church of Ireland: Ecclesiastical Reform and Revolution 1800–1885 1971, Education and Enmity: The Control of Schooling in Northern Ireland 1920–50 1973, The United States and Ireland 1973, A Mirror to Kathleen's Face: Education in Independent Ireland 1922–60 1975, Local Poets and Social History: James Orr, Bard of Ballycarry 1977, Between Two Revolutions: Islandmagee, Co. Antrim 1798–1920 1979, A Protestant in Purgatory: Richard Whately: Archbishop of Dublin 1981, The Irish in Ontario: A Study of Rural History 1984, Being Had: Historians, Evidence and the Irish in North America 1985, The Life and Times of Ogle Gowan 1986, Small Differences: Irish Catholics and Irish Protestants, 1815–1921 1988, Half the World from Home: Perspectives on the Irish in New Zealand 1990, Occasional Papers on the Irish in South Africa 1991, God's Peoples: Covenant and Land in South Africa, Israel and Ulster 1992, The Irish Diaspora, A Primer 1993, Conor: A Biography of Conor Cruise O'Brien 1994, If the Irish ran the World: Montserrat 1630–1730, Surpassing Wonder: The Invention of the Bible and the Talmuds 1998; *novels:* The Lazar House Notebooks 1981, Brotherhood Week in Belfast 1984, The Orangeman: The Edgerston Audit 1987, At Face Value: The Life and Times of Eliza McCormack 1990; occasional papers and reviews. *Address:* Department of History, Queen's University, Kingston, Ont., K7L 3N6, Canada.

ÅKERMAN, Alf Knut Lennart, M.S.; Swedish business executive; b. 24 Feb. 1923, Lund; s. of Ernst Åke Åkerman and Hildur Åkerman (née Sonesson); m. Gun Widding 1953; three s. one d.; ed. Royal Univ. of Tech., Stockholm, Stockholm School of Econs., Massachusetts Inst. of Tech., U.S.A.; joined Reymersholms Gamla Ind. AB 1949, Head Research and Devt. Dept. 1956–58; Head Tech. and Devt. Dept. AB Marabou 1959–61, Deputy Man. Dir. 1961–67; Pres. and CEO Skandinaviska Banken, Stockholm 1968–71; Pres. and CEO Skandinaviska Enskilda Banken, Gothenburg 1972–84; Chair. Svenska Nestlé AB 1974–82, 1987–98, Erna and Victor Hasselblad Foundation 1983–98, Westpartner AB 1991–98, Trygg-Hansa Ins. 1985–94, Boliden AB 1974–86, Perstorp AB 1974–91, V. Hasselblad AB 1979–90, Sv. BP AB 1984–91, BASF Sv. AB 1981–94, SSPA Mar. Consult. AB 1984–91, Eng. Research Council of STU 1984–90; Mem. Bd. of Dirs. AB Färdig Betong 1987–, AB SKF 1973–93 (Deputy Chair. 1992–93), KABI-Pharmacia AB 1986–93, Mölnlycke AB 1975–93, NCC AB 1985–94, Forbo SA Zürich 1981–94; Ind. Bd. of Royal Swedish Acad. of Eng. Sciences 1963–85; mem. Royal Swedish Acad. of Eng. Sciences (Vice-Pres. 1985–87); Kt. Commdr. Royal Order of Wasa, Kings Medal (with Ribbon of Order of Seraphim) 1988, Govt Medal Illis Quorum 1988; Hon. D.Eng. (Chalmers Univ. of Tech., Gothenburg) 1985; Hon. D. Med. (Univ. of Gothenburg) 1991. *Leisure interests:* biochemistry, wildlife, archaeology, music. *Address:* Skandinaviska Enskilda Banken, S 405 04 Göteborg (Office); Box 76, S 429 22 Kullavik, Sweden (Home). *Telephone:* 031-62 22 05 (Office).

AKERS, John Fellows, B.S.; American business executive; b. 28 Dec 1934, Boston, Mass.; s. of Kenneth Fellows and Mary Joan (Reed) Akers; m. Susan Davis 1960; one s. two d.; ed. Yale Univ.; served U.S.N.R. 1956–60; joined IBM Corpn. as a Sales Trainee 1960, Vice-Pres. 1976, Asst. Group Exec. DP Product Group 1976–78, Vice-Pres., Group Exec. 1978–82, Sr. Vice-Pres., Group Exec. 1982–83; Pres. 1983–89, C.E.O. 1984–93, Chair. 1986–93; mem. Bd. New York Times Co., Pepsi Co.; mem. Bd. of Trustees Calif. Inst. of Tech., Metropolitan Museum of Art; mem. Pres. Bush's Educ. Policy Advisory Cttee., Pres.'s Advisory Cttee.; Chair. Bd. of Govs. United Way of America. *Address:* 1 Sturges Highway, Westport, CT 06880, U.S.A.

AKERS-JONES, Sir David, K.B.E., C.M.G., M.A.; British civil servant; b. 14 April 1927; s. of Walter George Jones and Dorothy Jones; m. Jane Spickernell 1951; one s. (deceased) one d.; ed. Worthing High School and Brasenose Coll. Oxford; with British India Steam Navigation Co. 1945–49; Malayan Civil Service 1954–57; Hong Kong Civil Service 1957–86, Sec. for New Territories and for District Admin., Hong Kong Govt. 1973–85, Chief Sec. 1985–86; Acting Gov. Hong Kong 1986–87; Hong Kong Affairs Advisor to China 1993–97; Chair. Nat. Mutual Asia Hong Kong 1987–, Hong Kong Housing Authority 1988–93, Global Asset Man. Hong Kong; Pres. Outward Bound Trust (Hong Kong) 1986–; Vice-Pres. WWF Hong Kong 1995–; Dir. Sime Darby Hong Kong, Hysan Devt. Co. Ltd., The China Investment Co.; mem. Council, Australian Nat. Gallery; Hon. Mem. R.I.C.S.; Hon. D.C.L. (Kent Univ.) 1987, Hon. LL.D. (Chinese Univ. of Hong Kong) 1988, Hon. D.Sc.S. (City Univ., Hong Kong) 1993. *Leisure interests:* painting, gardening, walking and music. *Address:* Dragon View, 128 Castle Peak Road, Tsing Lung Tau, New Territories, Hong Kong Special Administrative Region, People's Republic of China.

AKERT, Konrad, M.D.; Swiss professor of physiology; b. 21 May 1919, Zürich; m. Ruth Giger, 1947; three s. one d.; ed. Literarygymnasium Zürich, Medical School of the Univ. of Zürich; Instructor of Physiology at Johns Hopkins Univ., Baltimore, U.S.A. 1952; Asst. Prof. of Physiology, Univ. of Wisconsin, Madison 1953, Assoc. Prof. of Physiology 1955, Prof. of Anatomy and Physiology 1960; Prof. of Neurophysiology and Dir. of Brain Research Inst., Univ. of Zürich 1961–83, Dean of Faculty of Medicine 1974–76, Dir. of Physiology and Brain Research Insts. 1979–83, Rector 1984–88; Prof. of Physiology, Univ. of Zimbabwe 1988–89; Founder and Ed.-in-Chief of journal Brain Research 1966–76; Robert Bing Prize 1960, Otto Naegeli Prize 1969; Dr. h.c. (Geneva) 1976, (Freiburg) 1983; Hon. Research prof. (Academia Sinica Peking) 1980. *Publications:* about 340 scientific publications. *Leisure interests:* history, politics, mountaineering. *Address:* Bächtoldstrasse 1, CH-8044, Zürich, Switzerland. *Telephone:* (1) 382-1583.

AKHEDJAKOVA, Liya Medjidovna; Russian actress; b. 9 June 1938, Dniepropetrovsk; d. of Medjid Salekhovich Akhedjakov and Yulia Aleksandrovna Akhedjakova; m. Vladimir Nikolayevich Persyanov; ed. State Inst. of Theatre Art; actress Moscow Theatre of Young Spectator 1953–71; Sovremennik Theatre 1971–; People's Artist of Russia; leading roles in classical and contemporary plays including Shakespeare, Tennessee Williams; in cinema 1969–. *Films include:* Garage, Office Romance, Blessed Heavens, Twenty Days Without War, Lost Bus; State Prize, Nice Prize, People's Artist of Russia. *Address:* Udaltsova str. 12, Apt. 153, 117415 Moscow, Russia (Home). *Telephone:* (095) 131 60 41 (Home).

AKHMADULINA, Bella (Isabella Akhatovna); Russian poet; b. 10 April 1937, Moscow; d. of Ahat and Nadya (née Lazareva) Akhmadulin; m. 1st Yevgeniy Yevtushenko (q.v.) 1960; m. 2nd Yuriy Nagibin; m. 3rd Boris Messerer 1974; ed. Gorky Inst. of Literature; Hon. mem. American Acad. of Arts and Letters 1977; Sec. U.S.S.R. (now Russian) Writers' Union 1986–91, State Prize U.S.S.R. 1989; mem. bd. Russian PEN-Centre 1989–92. *Poems include:* The String 1962, The Rain 1963, My Ancestry 1964, Summer Leaves 1968, The Lessons of Music 1969, Fever and Other New Poems (trans. into English) 1970, Tenerezza 1971, The Rain 1974, Poems 1975, The Dreams about Georgia 1977, The Candle 1978, The Snowstorm 1978, The Mystery 1983, The Garden 1987, The Seaboard 1991, Selected Works (vols. 1–3) and translations from Georgian. *Address:* Chernyachovskogo str. 4, Apt. 37, 125319 Moscow, Russia. *Telephone:* 151-22-00.

AKHMEDOV, Khan A.; Turkmenistan politician (retd.); b. 16 June 1936, Pazau, Krasnovodsr Dist.; m.; four c.; ed. Tashkent Inst. of Railway; Transport Eng., Man. Railways of Middle Asia 1962–80; Head Dept. of Transport and Communications, Turkmenistan CP Cen. Cttee. 1980–85; First Sec. Ashkhabad City, CP Cttee. 1985–88; First Deputy Chair. Turkmen S.S.R. Council of Ministers 1988–89, Chair. 1989–90; Prime Minister of Turkmenistan 1990–91; Deputy Prime Minister 1991–92; Amb. to Turkey 1992–95; mem. Pres. Council.

AKHTAR, Muhammad, M.SC., PH.D., F.R.S.; British/Pakistani professor of biochemistry; b. 23 Feb. 1933, Punjab, India; s. of Muhammad Azeem Chaudhry; m. Monika E. Schürmann 1963; two s.; ed. Govt. Coll. Sargodha, Govt. Coll. Lahore, Univ. of Punjab and Imperial Coll., London; research scientist, Research Inst. for Medicine and Chem., Cambridge, Mass. 1959–63; Lecturer in Biochem. Univ. of Southampton 1963–66, Sr. Lecturer 1966–68, Reader 1968–73, Prof. 1973–98, Head Dept. of Biochem. 1978–93, Chair. School of Biochemical and Physiological Sciences 1983–87, Emer. Prof. of Biochemistry 1998–; Founding Fellow Third World Acad. of Sciences, Treasurer, mem. Council 1993; mem. Council Royal Soc. 1983–85; Biochemical Soc. Cttee. 1983–86; Sitara-I-Imtiaz (Pakistan); Flintoff Medal (Royal Soc. of Chemistry) 1993, TWAS Medal 1996. *Publications:* numerous articles in biochemical and chemical journals. *Address:* Department of Biochemistry, University of Southampton, Southampton, SO9 3TU, England (Office). *Telephone:* (01703) 594338.

AKI, Keiiti, PH.D.; American academic; b. 3 March 1930, Yokohama, Japan; s. of Koichi Aki and Fumiko Kojima; m. Haruko Uyeda 1956; three c.; ed. Univ. of Tokyo, Geophysical Inst.; Research Fellow, Calif. Inst. of Tech., U.S.A. 1958–60; Research Fellow and Assoc. Prof., Univ. of Tokyo 1960–66; Prof. of Geophysics, M.I.T. 1966–84, R. R. Schrock Prof. of Earth and Planetary Sciences 1982–84; W. M. Keck Foundation Prof. of Geological Sciences, Univ. of Southern Calif., U.S.A. 1984–; Science Dir., Chair. Bd. Dirs. Southern Calif. Earthquake Centre 1991–96; Distinguished Visiting Prof., Univ. of Alaska 1981–88; mem. Nat. Council for Earthquake Prediction Evaluation 1980–, Calif. Council for Earthquake Prediction Evaluation 1984–; Fellow A.A.A.S.; mem. N.A.S.; medal of the Seismological Society of America 1987; Hon. Foreign Fellow European Union of Geosciences 1987. *Publications:* (Co-author) Quantitative Seismology (Vol. I and II) 1980, Orogeny 1983. *Leisure interests:* swimming, skiing, sailing, surfing. *Address:* Department of Geological Sciences, University of Southern California, Los Angeles, CA 90089-0740 (Office); 3 Bis Impasse Jacarandas, La Reunion, CA 90277, U.S.A. (Home). *Telephone:* (213) 743-3510.

AKIHITO, Emperor of Japan; b. 23 Dec. 1933, Tokyo; s. of late Emperor Hirohito and of Empress Nagako; m. Michiko Shoda 1959; two s. one d.; ed. Gakushuin schools and Faculty of Politics and Econs. Gakushuin Univ.; official investiture as Crown Prince 1952; succeeded 7 Jan. 1989; crowned 12 Nov. 1990; has undertaken visits to some 37 countries and travelled widely throughout Japan; Hon. Pres. or Patron, Asian Games 1958, Int. Sports Games for the Disabled 1964, Eleventh Pacific Science Congress 1966, Japan World Exposition 1970, Int. Skill Contest for the Disabled 1981; Hon. Sec. Int. Conf. on Indo-Pacific Fish 1985; mem. Ichthyological Soc. of Japan; Hon. mem. Linnean Soc. (London). *Publications:* 25 papers in journal of Ichthyological Soc. of Japan. *Leisure interests:* taxonomic study of gobiid fish, natural history and conservation, history, tennis. *Address:* The Imperial Palace, 1-1 Chiyoda, Chiyoda-ku, Tokyo 100, Japan. *Telephone:* (3) 32131111.

AKILANDAM, Perungalur Vaithialingam (pseudonym Akilon); Indian Tamil writer; b. 27 June 1922, Perungular; s. of M. Vaithialingam and V. Amirdhammal; m.; three s. four d.; ed. Maharaja's Coll., Pudukkottai; writer 1940–; in Indian Post & Telegraph Dept. 1945–58; freelance writer 1958–; Sec. Tamil Writers' Asscn., Tiruchy 1953–57; Sec.-Gen. Fed. of All-India Tamil Writers 1962– (Vice-Pres. 1977–); Dir. Tamil Writers' Co-op. Soc. 1963; mem. Tamil Advisory Bd., Sahitya Akademi 1964–; Producer, Spoken Word in Tamil, All-India Radio, Madras 1965–; Pres. Tamil Writers' Asscn. 1967 (Vice-Pres. 1977–); Kalai Majai Prize for Penn 1946, Tamil Akademi Award for Nenjin Alaigai 1953, Sahitya Akademi Award for Vengaiyin Maindan 1963, Tamilnadu Govt. Award for Kayalvizhi 1968, for Erimalai 1973, Nehru Award for Soviet Land 1978. *Publications include:* novels: Penn 1946, Snehithi 1950, Nenjin Alaigai 1953, Pavai Vilakku 1958, Vengaiyin Maindan 1961, Ponmalar 1964, Kayalvizhi 1964, Chittirap Paavai 1967; short stories: Sakthival 1947, Nilavinilay 1950, Vazhi Pirandhadu 1952, Sahodarar Andro? 1963, Nellore Arisi 1967, Erimalai 1971. *Leisure interests:* reading and short travels. *Address:* 13 Kustian Beach Street, Santhome, Madras 600004, India. *Telephone:* 71020 (Office); 751173 (Home).

AKINKUGBE, Oladipo Olujimi, Atobase of Ife, Babalofin of Ijebu-Igbo, Adingbuwa of Ondo, Ikolaba Balogun Basegun of Ibadan, M.D., D.PHIL., D.T.M. & H., F.R.C.P.; Nigerian professor of medicine; b. 17 July 1933, Ondo; s. of Chief Odofin David Akinkugbe and Chief (Mrs.) Grace Akinkugbe; m. Dr. Folasade Dina 1965; two s.; ed. Govt. Coll., Ibadan, Univ. Coll., Ibadan, Univs. of London, Liverpool and Oxford; Lecturer in Medicine, Univ. of Ibadan 1964–66, Sr. Lecturer 1966–68, Prof. 1968–95, Emer. Prof. 1996, Dean of Medicine 1970–74, Chair. of Cttee. of Deans 1972–74, mem. Council 1971–74; Visiting Prof. Medicine, Harvard Univ. 1974–75; Principal, Univ. Coll., Ilorin 1975–77; Vice-Chancellor Univ. of Ilorin 1977–78, Ahmadu Bello Univ. 1978–79; Pro-Chancellor and Chair. Council, Port Harcourt Univ. 1986–; Pres. Nigerian Asscn. of Nephrology 1987–89, Nigerian Hypertension Soc. 1992–95; mem. Scientific Advisory Panel CIBA Foundation, Council of Int Soc. of Hypertension, WHO Expert Cttees. on Cardiovascular Diseases, Smoking Control, Professional and Tech. Educ. of Medical and Auxiliary Personnel, Sr. Consultant 1983–84, WHO Advisory Cttee. on Health Research 1990; Visiting Fellow, Balliol Coll., Oxford 1981–82; mem. Bd. of Trustees, Obafemi Awolowo Foundation, Nigerian Heartcare Foundation 1994– (also mem. Governing Council), Nigerian Educare Trust 1995, The Social Sciences and Reproductive Health Research Network 1996, Ajumogobia Science Foundation; Patron Sickle Cell Asscn. of Nigeria; mem. several editorial bds.; Commdr. Noble Order of the Niger 1979, Officier, ordre Nat. de la République de Côte d'Ivoire; Hon. D.Sc. (Ilorin) 1982, (Fed. Univ. Tech. Akure) 1994, (Port-Harcourt) 1997; Fellow Nigerian Acad. of Science; Searle Distinguished Research Award 1989; Nigerian Nat. Order of Merit 1997. *Publications include:* High Blood Pressure in the African 1972, Priorities in National Health Planning 1974 (Ed.), Hypertension in Africa (Ed.) 1975, Cardiovascular Diseases in Africa (Ed.) 1976, Clinical Medicine in the Tropics—Cardiovascular Disease 1986, many papers on hypertension and renal disease. *Leisure interests:* bird-watching, music, gardening. *Address:* Department of Medicine, University of Ibadan, Ibadan, Oyo State (Office); Summit, Olubadan Aleshinloye Way, Iyaganku, Ibadan, Nigeria (Home). *Telephone:* (0234) 22317717.

AKIYA, Einosuke: Japanese religious leader; b. 15 July 1930, Tokyo; s. of late Jubei Akiya and of Yuki Akiya; m. Akiko Ishida 1957; two s.; ed. Waseda Univ.; with Soka Gakkai 1951–, Young Men's Div. Chief 1956–59, Youth Div. Chief 1959–66, Dir. 1961–62, Vice-Gen. Dir. 1962–67, Gen. Admin. 1967–70, Vice-Pres. 1970–81, Pres. 1981–; Ed.-in-Chief Seikyo Shimbun 1968, Rep. Dir. 1975–81, Pres. 1987–90, Exec. Advisor 1990–; Gen. Dir. Soka Gakkai Int. 1981–92, Exec. Counsellor 1992–95, Deputy Pres. 1995–. *Leisure interests:* reading, music, theatre. *Address:* Soka Gakkai Headquarters, 32 Shinano-machi, Shinjuku-ku, Tokyo 160 (Office). *Telephone:* 03-3353-7111.

AKRAM, Wasim (see Wasim Akram).

AKSARANAN, Chokchai, M.SC.E., PH.D.; Thai senator and business executive; b. 8 July 1942, Ratchaburi; s. of Uthong Aksaranan and Linda Aksaranan; m. Saowaros Aksaranan; two s.; ed. Chulalongkorn Univ., Univ. of New Brunswick, Canada and Nat. Defence Coll.; Chair. Fed. of Thai Industries. *Address:* Federation of Thai Industries, Queen Sirikit National Convention Center, Zone C, 4th Floor, 60 New Ratchadapisek Road, Klongtoey, Bangkok 10110, Thailand.

AKSENENKO, Nikolai Yemelyanovich; Russian politician and administrator; b. 15 March 1949, Novoaleksandrovka, Novosibirsk Region; m.; two c.; ed. Novosibirsk Inst. of Railway Eng., Acad. of Nat. Econs.; metalworker, Novosibirsk Aviation Factory; worker on duty, Head of railway station, Head of sectors of E. Siberian and S.-E. Railways 1966–84; Deputy Dir. Murmansk Div., Oktyabrskaya Railway 1984–85; Dir. Leningrad–Finland Div., Oktyabrskaya Railway 1985–86; Deputy Dir., Chief Econ., First Deputy Dir., Oktyabrskaya Railway 1986–92; Deputy, First Deputy Minister of Railways of Russian Fed. 1994–97; Minister 1997–; mem. Govt. Comm. on Operational Problems 1997–. *Address:* MPS, Novobasmannaya str. 2, Moscow, Russia. *Telephone:* (095) 262 1002 (Office).

AKSU, Abdülkadir; Turkish politician; b. 1944, Diyarbakır; m., two c.; ed. Ankara Univ.; fmrly. Security Dir., Malatya, Acting Gov. of Kahramanmaraş, Deputy Security Dir., Gov. and Mayor of Rize, Gov. of Gaziantep; Deputy for Motherland Party 1987; Minister of the Interior 1989–91. *Address:* c/o Icisleri Bakanlığı, Bakanlıklar, Ankara, Turkey. *Telephone:* (4) 1285298.

AKSYONOV, Vasiliy Pavlovich; Russian writer; b. 20 Aug. 1932, Kazan; s. of Pavel V. Aksyonov and Yevgeniya Ginzburg; m. 1st Kira L. Mendeleva 1957; m. 2nd Maya A. Karmen; one s.; ed. Leningrad Medical Inst.; Physician 1956–60, Moscow Tubercular Dispensary 1960–; professional writer 1960–; emigrated to U.S.A. 1980; mem. Union of Russian Writers, Editorial Board Yunost; citizenship restored 1990. *Publications:* novels: Colleagues 1960, Starry Ticket 1961, 1970, Oranges from Morocco 1963, Time, My Friend, Time 1964, The Empty Barrels 1968, Love of Electricity 1971, My Grandpa is a Monument 1972, The Box Inside Which Something Knocks (children's book) 1976, Our Golden Ironware 1980, The Burn 1980, The Island of Crimea 1981, An Aristopheana 1981, Paper Landscape 1983, The Right to the Island 1983, Say 'Cheese' 1985, In Search of a Genre 1986, In Search of Melancholy Baby 1987, Our Garden Fronburg 1989, The Moscow Saga 1993, The Negative of a Positive Hero 1996, New Sweet Style 1998; collected stories: Catapult 1964, Half-Way to the Moon 1966, Wish You Were Here 1969; screenplay for films: Colleagues, My Young Friend, When They Raise the Bridges, Travelling 1967, The Murmar House 1972; play: On Sale 1965; travel: An Unusual Journey 1963, Twenty-Four Hours Non-Stop 1976, The Steel Bird and Other Stories 1978; joint ed. Metropol 1979, Four Temperaments (comedy) 1979. *Leisure interests:* music, travelling, running. *Address:* c/o Random House Inc., 201 East 50th Street, New York, NY 10022, U.S.A. *Telephone:* 915-45-63 (Moscow).

AKSYUCHITS, Viktor Vladimirovich; Russian politician; b. 27 Aug. 1949, Vardantsy, Minsk region; m. 2nd; four c.; ed. Riga Navigation School and Moscow State Univ.; mem. CPSU 1971–72; served in Navy, seasonal worker in Siberia and Far East; founder Orthodox Unity Church; edited Vybor; Chair. Duma of Russian Christian-Democratic Movt. 1990–92, Chair. of Political Council 1990–92; mem. Duma (Russian People's Congress) 1992–96; People's Deputy of Russia 1990–93; adviser to Deputy Prime Minister Boris Nemtsov 1997–98. *Address:* RNS, Bolshoi Karetni per. 20, Apt 2, 103051 Moscow, Russia. *Telephone:* 205-68-08 (Office); 438-66-79 (Home).

AKURGAL, Ekrem, PH.D.; Turkish archaeologist; b. 30 March 1911, Istanbul; ed. Germany; Prof. Univ. of Ankara 1941–81; has conducted excavations at Sinope, Phokaia, Daskyleion, Pitane and Erythrai 1953–, at Izmir 1967–; Visiting Prof., Princeton Univ. 1961–62, W. Berlin 1971–72, Vienna 1980–81; mem. Turkish Historical Soc. (Sec.-Gen. 1951–61), Turkish High Comm. for Ancient Monuments; mem. British, Austrian, Danish, French and Swedish Acads.; Hon. mem. Soc. for Promotion of Hellenic Studies, London, German, Austrian, American Inst. of Archaeology; Dr. h.c. (Bordeaux) 1961, (Athens) 1989, (Lecce) 1990; Goethe Medal (Fed. Repub. of Germany) 1979; Grand Prize, Turkish Ministry of Culture 1981. *Publications:* Griechische Reliefs aus Lykien 1942, Remarques stylistiques sur les reliefs de Malatya 1946, Späthethitische Bildkunst 1949, Phrygische Kunst 1955, Die Kunst Anatoliens von Homer bis Alexander 1961, Die Kunst der Hethiter 1961, Orient und Okzident 1966, Treasures of Turkey (with Mango and Ettinghausen) 1966, Urartäische und Altiranische Kunstzentren 1968, The Art and Architecture of Turkey 1981, Alt-Smyrna 1983, Ancient Civilizations and Ruins of Turkey (5th edn.) 1983, (8th edn. 1993), Griechische und Römische Kunst in der Turkey 1987, Turquie Akurgal-Mantran-Roux 1990. *Address:* Yalı Cadı 360/7, 35530 Karşiyaka, Izmir, Turkey (Home).

ALAGNA, Roberto; French opera singer; b. 7 June 1963, Clichy-sous-Bois; ed. Paris; m. (wife deceased); m. 2nd Angela Gheorghiu; debut as Alfredo in La Traviata, Glyndebourne Touring Opera; repertoire includes: Rodolfo in La Bohème, Lucia di Lammermoor, Rigoletto, L'elisir d'amore; recordings include: Duets and Arias (with Angela Gheorghiu), La Bohème 1996, Don Carlos 1996, La Rondine 1997; Personalité Musicale de l'Année 1994, Laurence Olivier Award for Outstanding Achievement in Opera 1995, Victor Award for Best Singer 1997. *Address:* c/o 76–78 avenue des Champs-Elysées, 75008 Paris, France.

ALAÏA, Azzeddine; French fashion designer; b. Tunis; ed. Ecole des Beaux Arts, Tunis; studied sculpture; worked with dressmakers specializing in copies of Parisian haute couture in Tunis and then began making his own designs for pvt. clients in Tunis; moved to Paris 1957; worked briefly at Christian Dior before moving to Guy Laroche workrooms for two seasons; also worked in Paris as cook and housekeeper; began made-to-order dressmaking business in 1960s; set up first atelier in Faubourg Saint Germain 1965–84; first ready-to-wear show, Bergdorf Goodman store, New York 1982; first Azzedine Alaïa boutique opened in Beverly Hills 1983; moved to Marais district of Paris 1984; retrospective exhbn. Museum of Modern Art, Bordeaux 1985; named Best Designer of Year by French Ministry of Culture 1985. *Address:* 18 rue de la Verrérie, Paris, France.

ALAIN, Marie-Claire; French organist; b. 10 Aug. 1926, Saint-Germain-en-Laye; d. of Albert and Magdeleine (Alberty) Alain; m. Jacques Gommier 1950; one s. one d.; ed. Institut Notre Dame, Saint-Germain-en-Laye, Conservatoire Nat. Supérieur de Musique, Paris; organ teacher, Conservatoire de Musique de Rueil-Malmaison; Lecturer, Summer Acad. for organists, Haarlem, Netherlands 1956–72; numerous concerts throughout world 1955–; lecturer at numerous univs. throughout world; expert on organology to Minister of Culture; Hon. D.Hum.Litt. (Colorado State Univ.); Hon. D.Mus. (Southern Methodist Univ., Dallas); numerous prizes for recordings and performances including Buxtehudepreis (Lübeck, Fed. Repub. of Germany); D.Hum.Litt. (Colorado State), Dr. h.c. (Acad. Sibelius, Helsinki); Prix Léonie Sonning, Copenhagen, Prix Franz Liszt, Budapest 1987, numerous other prizes; Officier, Légion d'honneur, Ordre du Mérite, Arts et Lettres. *Recordings:* over 250 records, including complete works of J. Alain, C. P. E. Bach, J. S. Bach, C. Balbastre, G. Böhm, N. Bruhns, D. Buxtehude, L. N. Clérambault, F. Couperin, L. C. Daquin, C. Franck, N. de Grigny, J. A. Guilain, G. F. Handel, J. Haydn, F. Mendelssohn, A. Vivaldi, etc. *Address:* 4 rue Victor Hugo, 78230 Le Pecq, France.

ALAINI, Mohsen Ahmed al-; Yemeni politician and diplomatist; b. 20 Oct. 1932, Bani Bahloul, N. Yemen; m. Aziza Abulahom 1962; two s. two d.; ed. Faculty of Law, Cairo Univ. and the Sorbonne, Paris; school-teacher, Aden 1958–60; Int. Confederation of Arab Trade Unions 1960–62; Minister of Foreign Affairs, Yemeni Repub. Sept.–Dec. 1962, 1974–80; Perm. Rep. to UN 1962–65, 1965–66, 1967–69; Minister of Foreign Affairs May–July 1965; Prime Minister Nov.–Dec. 1967, 1974–80; Amb. to U.S.S.R. 1968–70; Prime Minister, Minister of Foreign Affairs Feb. 1971 Sept. 1971–Dec. 1972, June 1974–Jan. 1975; Amb. to France Aug.–Sept. 1974, 1965–76, to U.K. 1973–74, to Fed. Repub. of Germany 1981–84, to U.S.A. 1984; Perm. Rep. to UN 1980–81. *Address:* c/o Ministry of Foreign Affairs, San'a, Yemen.

ALARCON, Fabián; Ecuadorian politician; fmrly. Speaker of Congress; Acting Pres. of Ecuador 6–10 Feb. 1997, Pres. of Ecuador 1997–98. *Address:* c/o Office of the President, Palacio Nacional, García Moreno 1043, Quito, Ecuador.

ALARCÓN DE QUESADA, Ricardo; Cuban diplomatist; b. 21 May 1937; s. of Roberto Alarcón de Quesada; m. Margarita Maza; one d.; ed. Univ. de Habana; Head of Student Section, Provincial Office of 26 July Revolutionary Movement 1957–59; Pres. Univ. Students' Fed., Sec. Union of Young Communists; Dir. for Regional Policies (Latin America), Ministry of Foreign Affairs 1962–66; mem. Governing Council of Inst. for Int. Politics, Ministry of Foreign Affairs, Deputy Minister of Foreign Affairs 1978, mem. Tech. Advisory Council 1980; Perm. Rep. of Cuba to the UN 1966–78; Pres. UNDP 1976–77; Alt. mem. Cen. Cttee. of CP of Cuba 1980–; mem. Politburo of CP 1992–; Perm Rep. to UN 1990; Minister of Foreign Affairs 1992–94; Pres. Nat. Ass. of People's Power 1993–. *Address:* Asamblea Nacional del Poder Popular, Havana; 42 Street No 2308 e/23 and 25 Streets, Municipio Playa, Cuba.

ALARCÓN MANTILLA, Luis Fernando, M.SC.; Colombian politician and engineer; b. Aug. 1951 Bucaramanga; m.; ed. Univ. of the Andes and M.I.T.; engineer with Mejía Millan y Perry Ltd and Prof. of Civil Eng. Univ. of the Andes 1980–83; Head of Public Investment Unit, Nat. Dept. of Planning 1983–84; Dir.-Gen. of Budget, Ministry of Finance and Public Credit 1984–86; economist at Banco Internacional de Desarrollo, Washington D.C. 1986; Vice-Minister at Ministry of Finance and Public Credit 1986–87, Minister 1987–91; mem. of Governing Council for Foreign Trade, Bd. of Banco de la República, Nat. Council for Econ. and Social Policy 1987–. *Address:* c/o Ministry of Finance and Public Credit, 7a, No 6-4J, Of. 308, Santa Fe de Bogotá, Colombia.

ALATAS, Ali; Indonesian diplomat; b. 4 Nov. 1932, Jakarta; s. of Abdullah Alatas; m. Yunisa Alatas 1956; three d.; ed. Acad. for Foreign Affairs and School of Law, Univ. of Indonesia; Financial and Econ. Ed. P.I.A. Nat. news agency, Jakarta; joined Ministry of Foreign Affairs 1954; Second Sec. (later First Sec.), Bangkok, Thailand 1956–69; Dir. Information and Cultural Affairs, Jakarta 1960–65, Dir. 1965–66, 1970–72; Counsellor (later Minister Counsellor), Washington, D.C. 1966–70; Sec. Directorate Gen. for Political Affairs, Jakarta, Chef de Cabinet to Minister of Foreign Affairs 1972–75; Minister of Foreign Affairs May 1988–; Perm. Rep. to UN 1976–78, 1982–84, 1985–87; Sec. to the Vice-Pres. of Indonesia 1978–82; Chair. First Cttee., 40th U.N. Gen. Ass. 1985; Indonesian Order of Merit. *Leisure interests:* golf, reading, music, swimming. *Address:* Ministry of Foreign Affairs, Jalan Taman Pejambon No. 6, Jakarta 10110, Indonesia.

ALATAS, Syed Hussein, PH.D.; Malaysian university vice-chancellor and sociologist; b. 17 Sept. 1928, Bogor, Indonesia; m.; one s. two d.; ed. Univ. of Amsterdam; Fullbright Visiting Prof. to USA 1965; Visiting Asian Fellow, A.N.U. Canberra 1973; corresp. Int. Social Science Journal, Paris 1973–; mem. Int. Sociological Asscn. 1976–; mem. Comm. on Challenges of Devt. Int. Union of Anthropological and Ethnological Studies 1979; founder mem. Int. Asscn. for Study of Peace and Prejudice, Nuremberg 1980; Research Fellow, Woodrow Wilson Int. Center for Scholars, Smithsonian Inst. Bldg. Washington, D.C. 1982–83; mem. Nat. Consultative Council, Fed. of Malaysia 1969–71; Nat. Unity Council 1971; mem. Senate, Parl. of Malaysia 1971; formerly Prof. and Head, Dept. of Malay Studies, Nat. Univ. of Singapore; Vice-Chancellor, Univ. of Malaya 1988–91; numerous professional affiliations, overseas lectureships etc. *Publications include:* The Sociology of Corruption 1968, Thomas Stamford Raffles: Reformer or Intriguer 1972, Modernization and Social Change in Southeast Asia 1972, The Intellectuals in Developing Societies 1977, The Myth of the Lazy Native 1977, The Problem of Corruption 1986. *Leisure interests:* reading, gardening.

ALBA, H.R.H., the Duke of; Jesús, D.PHIL.; Spanish philosopher; b. 9 June 1934, Madrid; m. the Duchess of Alba; five s. one d.; author of seven books; mem. Royal Spanish Academy. *Publications:* essays, poems, short stories, memoirs, art and poetry criticisms. *Address:* Palacio de Liria, 28008 Madrid, Spain.

ALBACETE CARREIRA, Alfonso; Spanish painter; b. 14 March 1950, Málaga; s. of Alfonso Albacete Carreira and María Albacete Carreira; m. Luisa Gómez 1986; one s. one d.; studied painting, with Juan Bonafé, and architecture; Asst. Juan Bonafé's studio 1967–69; studied painting Valencia 1969, then in Paris; first one-man exhbn., Madrid 1972; first exhbn. U.S.A., Center for Contemporary Art, Chicago 1989; works included in numerous collections of contemporary art. *Leisure interests:* botany, architecture. *Address:* Biasco de Garay 86, 6°A, Madrid 28015, Spain. *Telephone:* 5545640.

ALBARN, Damon; British singer, musician and songwriter; b. 23 March 1968, London; s. of Hazel Albarn and Keith Albarn; singer, keyboard player and songwriter with Blur (fmrly. named Seymour) 1989–; has toured worldwide; gold and platinum discs in U.K. *Singles include:* She's So High 1990, There's No Other Way 1991, Bang 1991, Popscene 1992, For Tomorrow 1993, Chemical World 1993, Sunday Sunday 1993, Girls and Boys 1994, To The End 1994, Parklife 1994, End Of A Century 1994, Country House 1995, Universal 1995, Charmless Man 1995, Beetlebum 1997, Song 2 1997, On Your Own 1997, MOR 1997. *Albums:* Leisure 1991, Modern Life is Rubbish 1993, Parklife 1994, The Great Escape 1995, Blur 1997, 13 1999. *Leisure interests:* football, Tae Kwon Do. *Address:* CMO, Unit 32, Ransomes Dock, 35–37 Parkgate Road, London, SW11 4NP, England.

ALBEE, Edward Franklin; American playwright; b. 12 March 1928; ed. Lawrenceville and Choate Schools, Washington, and Columbia Univ.; Comm. Chair. Brandeis Univ. Creative Arts Awards 1983, 1984; Pres. The Edward F. Albee Foundation Inc.; mem. Dramatists Guild Council, PEN America, The American Acad., Nat. Inst. of Arts and Letters; Gold Medal, American Acad. and Inst. of Arts and Letters 1980; inducted, Theater Hall of Fame 1985, Kennedy Center Award 1996. *Plays include:* The Zoo Story (Vernon Rice Award 1960) 1958, The Death of Bessie Smith 1959, The Sandbox 1959, Fam and Yam 1959, The American Dream (Foreign Press Asscn. Award 1961) 1960, Who's Afraid of Virginia Woolf? (Drama Critics' Circle Award for Best Play) 1961–62, stage adaptation of The Ballad of the Sad Café (Carson McCullers) 1963, Tiny Alice 1964, Malcolm (from novel by James Purdy) 1965, A Delicate Balance (Pulitzer Prize 1966) 1966, Everything in the Garden (after a play by Giles Cooper) 1967, Box 1968, Quotations from

Chairman Mao Tse-tung 1968, All Over 1971, Seascape (Pulitzer Prize 1975) 1974, Listening 1975, Counting the Ways 1976, The Lady from Dubuque 1977–79, Lolita (adapted from Vladimir Nabokov) 1979, The Man Who Had Three Arms 1981, Finding the Sun 1982, Marriage Play 1986–87, Three Tall Women (Pulitzer Prize 1994) 1990–91, Fragments 1993, The Play about the Baby 1996. *Leisure interest:* collecting art. *Address:* 14 Harrison Street, New York, NY 10013; Old Montauk Highway, Montauk, NY 11954, U.S.A.

ALBERS, Hans, DR. RER. NAT.; German business executive; b. 4 March 1925, Lingen; joined BASF, 1953, Deputy Chair. Man. Bd. until 1982, Chair. 1983–93; Chair. Verband der Chemischen Industrie eV 1986–. *Address:* BASF AG, 67056 Ludwigshafen, Germany.

ALBERT II; King of the Belgians; b. 6 June 1934; s. of King Léopold III and Queen Astrid; m. Donna Paola Ruffo Di Calabria 1959; two s. one d.; fmrly. Prince of Liège; fmr. Vice-Adm. of Navy; Pres. Caisse d'Epargne et de Retraite 1954–92; Pres. Belgian Red Cross 1958–93; Pres. Belgian Office of Foreign Trade 1962; apptd. by Council of Europe as Pres. of Conf. of European Ministers responsible for protection of cultural and architectural heritage 1969; participant in numerous int. confs. on environment including UN Conf. in Stockholm 1972; Chair. Belgian Cttee. of European Year of Renaissance of the City 1981; Hon. Pres. Belgian Olympic and Interfed. Cttee.; succeeded to the throne 9 Aug. 1993, following death of his brother King Baudouin I. *Address:* The Royal Palace, Brussels, Belgium.

ALBERT, Calvin; American sculptor; b. 19 Nov. 1918, Grand Rapids, Mich.; s. of Philip and Ethel Albert; m. Martha Neff 1941; one d.; ed. Inst. of Design, Chicago, Art Inst. of Chicago and Archipenko School of Sculpture; Teacher, New York Univ. 1949–52, Brooklyn Coll. 1947–49, Inst. of Design 1942–46; Prof. of Art, Pratt Inst. 1949–85, Prof. Emer. 1985–; 31 one-man exhbns. including Landmark, Stable and Borgenicht Galleries, New York, Palace of Legion of Honor, San Francisco, Art. Inst. of Chicago; retrospective exhbn. at Guildhall Museum, East Hampton, N.Y. 1979; other exhbns. in the U.S.A. and Galleria George Lester, Rome; sculpture and drawings in collections of Whitney Museum, Metropolitan Museum, Jewish Museum, Art Inst. of Chicago, Detroit Inst. of Arts, Univ. of Nebraska, Chrysler Museum of Art and Nelson-Atkins Museum of Art; Fulbright Advanced Research Grant to Italy 1961; Tiffany Grants 1963, 1965; Guggenheim Fellowship 1966; Nat. Inst. of Arts and Letters Award 1975. *Publication:* Figure Drawing Comes to Life (with Dorothy Seckler) 1987. *Leisure interest:* boating.

ALBERT, Carl Bert, B.C.L., LL.D.; American politician and lawyer; b. 10 May 1908; s. of Ernest H. Albert and Leona Scott; m. Mary Harmon 1942; one s. one d.; ed. Univ. of Oklahoma and Oxford Univ.; admitted to Oklahoma Bar 1936; Legal Clerk, Federal Housing Admin. 1935–37; practised law, Oklahoma City 1937; attorney and accountant Sayre Oil Co. 1937–38; law practice, Mattoon, Ill. 1938–39; legal dept., Ohio Oil Co. 1939–40; served army 1941–46; practised law, McAlester, Oklahoma 1946–47; mem. House of Reps. 1947–77, Democratic Whip 1955; Majority Leader 1962–71; Speaker of House of Reps. 1971–77; Bronze Star. *Publication:* Little Giant: The Life and Times of Speaker Carl Albert 1990. *Address:* 1831 Word Road, McAlaster, OK 74501, U.S.A.

ALBERTSSON, Per-Åke, PH.D.; Swedish professor of biochemistry; b. 19 March 1930, Skurup; s. of Albert Olsson and Frideborg Olsson; m. 1st Elisabet Godberg 1955 (divorced 1978); five s. one d.; m. 2nd Charlotte Erlanson 1978; three d.; ed. Swedish High School, Ystad and Univs. of Lund and Uppsala; lecturer in Biochem. Univ. of Uppsala 1960–65; Prof. of Biochem. Univ. of Umeä 1965–75, Univ. of Lund 1975–; research zoologist, Univ. of Calif. at Los Angeles 1961–62; Visiting Prof. Stanford Univ. 1971–72, Univ. of Calif. Berkeley 1984–85; mem. Swedish Acad. of Sciences, Swedish Acad. of Eng. Sciences, Röda Kapellet (symphonic band), City Council of Lund 1991–94; mem. Bd. Lunds Energi AB; Gold Medal, Swedish Acad. of Eng. Sciences; Gold Medal, Swedish Chem. Soc., Bror Holmberg Medal. *Publications:* Partition of Cell Particles and Macromolecules; over 140 scientific publs. in journals. *Leisure interests:* playing music with flute, recorder, trombone and euphonium, tennis. *Address:* Department of Biochemistry, Box 124, S-22100 Lund, Sweden (Office). *Telephone:* 46-46-222-8190 (Office). *Fax:* 46-46-222-4534.

ALBERTY, Robert Arnold, PH.D.; American professor of chemistry; b. 21 June 1921, Winfield, Kan.; s. of Luman H. and Mattie Arnold Alberty; m. Lillian Jane Wind 1944; one s. two d.; ed. Lincoln High School, Lincoln, Neb., Univ. of Nebraska and Univ. of Wisconsin; Instructor, Chemistry Dept., Univ. of Wis. 1947–48, Asst. Prof. 1948–50, Assoc. Prof. 1950–56, Prof. 1956–57, Assoc. Dean of Letters and Science 1962–63, Dean of Graduate School 1963–67; Prof. of Chemistry M.I.T. 1967–91, 1996–; Prof. Emer. 1991–96; Dean, School of Science 1967–82; mem. N.A.S. 1965–, American Acad. of Arts and Sciences 1968–, Inst. of Medicine 1973–; Chair. Comm. on Human Resources, Nat. Research Council 1971–77; Fellow, AAAS 1976–; Dir. Colt Industries 1978–88; Dir. Inst. for Defense Analysis 1980–86; Chair. Cttee. on Chemistry and Public Affairs, American Chemical Soc. 1980; Pres. Physical Chem. Div. IUPAC 1991–93; Eli Lilly Award for research in enzyme kinetics 1956; Hon. Dr. (Nebraska) 1967, (Lawrence) 1967. *Publications:* Physical Chemistry (co-author) 5th edn. 1979, Experimental Physical Chemistry (with others) 1962, co-author Physical Chemistry 1992. *Leisure interest:* designing and building a summer cabin. *Address:* Massachusetts Institute of Technology, Room 6-215, 77 Massachusetts Avenue, Cambridge, MA 02139 (Office); 7 Old Dee Road, Cambridge, MA 02138, U.S.A. (Home).

ALBERY, Tim; British theatre and opera director; b. 20 May 1952. *Plays directed include:* War Crimes 1981, Secret Gardens 1983, Venice Preserv'd 1983, Hedda Gabler 1984, The Princess of Cleves 1985, Mary Stuart 1988, As You Like It 1989, Berenice 1990, Wallenstein 1993, Macbeth 1996. *Operas directed include:* (for English Nat. Opera) Billy Budd 1988, Beatrice and Benedict 1990, Peter Grimes 1991, Lohengrin 1993; (for Opera North) The Midsummer Marriage 1985, The Trojans 1986, La Finta Giardiniera 1989, Don Giovanni 1991, Don Carlos 1992, Luisa Miller 1995; (for Welsh Nat. Opera) The Trojans 1987, Nabucco 1995; (for Scottish Opera) The Midsummer Marriage 1988, The Trojans 1990, Fidelio 1994; (for Australian Opera) The Marriage of Figaro 1992; (for Netherlands Opera) Benvenuto Cellini 1991, La Wally 1993; (for Bayerische Staatsoper) Peter Grimes 1993, Simon Boccanegra 1995, Ariadne Auf Naxos 1996; (for Batignano Festival, Italy) The Turn of the Screw 1983; (for Bregenz Festival, Austria) La Wally 1990; (for Royal Opera House) Cherubin 1994; (for Metropolitan Opera, New York) Midsummer Night's Dream 1996. *Address:* c/o Harriet Cruickshank, Cruickshank Cazenove, 97 Old South Lambeth Road, London, SW8 1XU, England.

ALBERY, Prof. Wyndham John, M.A., D.PHIL., F.R.S., F.R.S.C.; British professor of physical chemistry; b. 5 April 1936, London; s. of Michael James Albery and Mary Lawton Albery; ed. Winchester Coll., Balliol Coll., Oxford; Nat. Service 1955–56; Weir Jr. Research Fellow 1962, Fellow in Physical Chem., University Coll., Oxford 1964–78; Lecturer, Physical Chem., Univ. of Oxford 1964–78; Prof. of Physical Chem., Imperial Coll., London 1978–89, Visiting Prof. 1989; Master of University Coll., Oxford 1989–97; Visiting Prof., Harvard Univ. 1989; Chair. Burton-Taylor Theatre Man. Cttee. 1990–93; Gov. Rugby School 1987–; Tilden Lecturer Royal Soc. of Chemistry 1978; Hon. D.Sc. (Oxford) 1990; Electrochemistry Medal Royal Soc. of Chemistry 1989. *Publications:* Ring-Disc Electrodes 1971, Electrode Kinetics 1975; (two musicals with John Gould) Who Was That Lady? 1970, On the Boil 1972. *Leisure interests:* theatre, skiing. *Address:* 35 Falmouth House, Hyde Park Place, London W2 2NT, England. *Telephone:* 0171-262 3909.

ALBICOCCO, Gabriel Jean Fernand Joseph; French film director; b. 15 Feb. 1936, Cannes; s. of Quint Albicocco and Elisabeth Picchi; m. Hélène Tessier 1972; Sec.-Gen. Soc. des réalisateurs de films; Chevalier des Arts et des Lettres. *Films include:* La Fille aux yeux d'or 1962, Le Rat d'Amérique 1966, Le Grand Meaulnes 1968, L'Amour au féminin 1969, Le Coeur fou, de la Pilule à l'ordinateur 1970, Le Petit matin, Quint Jean-Baptiste, dit Quinto 1982.

ALBORCH BATALLER, Maria del Carmen, LL.D.; Spanish politician; b. 1948, Castellón del Rugat, Valencia; ed. Univ. of Valencia; lecturer in Commercial Law, Univ. of Valencia, Dean of Law 1985–86; Dir.-Gen. of Culture, Culture, Educ. and Science, Office of Autonomous Community of Valencia 1987; Dir.-Gen. of Scenic Arts, Cinema and Music Inst. Valencia; Dir.-Gen. of Cultural Insts. of Cultural, Educ. and Science Office, Dir., Man. Modern Art Inst. Valencia 1988–93; Minister of Culture 1993–96. *Address:* c/o Ministry of Culture, Plaza del Rey, Madrid, Spain.

ALBRECHT, Ernst Carl Julius, DR.RER.POL.; German politician and economist; b. 29 June 1930, Heidelberg; s. of Carl Albrecht, M.D., and Dr. Adda Albrecht (née Berg); m. Dr. Heidi Adele Stromeyer 1953; five s. two d.; ed. Univs. of Tübingen, Cornell, Basle, Bonn; Attaché to Council of Ministers, ECSC 1954; Head of Common Market section of Brussels conf. for preparation of Treaties of Rome 1956; C.E.O. to EEC Commr. Hans von der Groeben 1958; Deputy Head of Comm. del. at negotiations with Denmark, Ireland, Norway and U.K. for accession to EEC 1961–63; Dir.-Gen. for Competition, EEC Comm. 1967–70; Financial Dir. Bahlsens Keksfabrik, biscuit mfrs. 1971–76; mem. Landtag (Parl.) for Lower Saxony 1970–90, Minister-Pres. of Lower Saxony 1976–90; personal consultant to Prime Minister of Kyrgyzstan; Grosskreuz der Bundesrepublik Deutschland; Christlich-Demokratische Union (CDU). *Publication:* Der Staat—Idee und Wirklichkeit (The State—Ideal and Reality) 1976–90. *Address:* Am Brink 2B, 3167 Burgdorf, Germany. *Telephone:* (05136) 82141.

ALBRIGHT, Madeleine Korbel, PH.D.; American politician and professor of international affairs; b. Maria Jana Korbel 1938, Czechoslovakia; d. of Joseph Korbel; m. Joseph Albright (divorced); three d.; ed. Wellesley Coll. and Columbia Univ.; Prof. of Int. Affairs, Georgetown Univ.; Head, Center for Nat. Policy; fmr. legis. aide to Democratic Senator Edmund Muskie (q.v.); fmr. mem. Nat. Security Council staff in Carter Admin.; adviser to Democrat cands. Geraldine Ferraro 1984 and Michael Dukakis 1988; Perm. Rep. to UN 1993–97 (first foreign-born holder of this post); Sec. of State Jan. 1997–; Democrat. *Address:* Office of the Secretary of State, 2201 C Street, N.W., Washington DC 20520, U.S.A.

ALCHOURON, Guillermo E.; Argentine farmer; b. 4 Nov. 1933; m.; five c.; ed. Univ. of Buenos Aires; farmer specializing in breeding of Dutch Argentine and Jersey dairy cattle and milk production at Coronel Brandsen Estate; mem. Bd. of Dirs. Argentine Rural Soc. 1969–, Pres. 1984–; Pres. Argentine Soc. of Jersey Dairy Cattle; Counsellor, Foundation for Latin American Econ. Research 1969–, Argentine Council for Int. Relations 1987–; mem. Exec. Council, Int. Fed. of Agric. Producers; Gov. World Econ. Forum for Food and Farming Production; Pres. Agric. Soc.; del. to numerous int.

confs.; decorations from Spain, France, U.S.A., Germany and Italy. *Address:* La Juanita, Coronel Brandsen, Argentina.

ALCONADA ARAMBURU, Carlos Román Santiago, DR.; Argentine lawyer; b. 25 July 1920, La Plata; m. Balbina Maria Mogliano; nine s.; ed. Nat. Univ. La Plata; Law Prof.; Minister of Interior 1957–58, of Educ. and Justice 1963–66, 1983–86. *Address:* c/o Ministerio de Educación y Justicia, Marcelo T. de Alvear 1650, C.P. 1060, Buenos Aires, Argentina.

ALDA, Alan, B.S.; American actor; b. 28 Jan. 1936, New York; s. of Robert Alda and Joan Browne; m. Arlene Weiss; three d.; ed. Fordham Univ.; performed with Second City 1963; Broadway roles in The Owl and the Pussycat, Purlie Victorious, Fair Game for Lovers, The Apple Tree, Our Town (London) 1991, Jake's Women 1992, etc. *Films include:* Gone are the Days 1963, Paper Lion 1968, The Extraordinary Seaman 1968, The Moonshine War 1970, Jenny 1970, The Mephisto Waltz 1971, To Kill a Clown 1972, California Suite 1978, Same Time Next Year 1978, The Seduction of Joe Tynan (also wrote screenplay) 1979, Crimes and Misdemeanours (D.W. Griffith Award, NY Film Critics' Award) 1989, Whispers in the Dark 1992, And the Band Played On 1993, Manhattan Murder Mystery 1993, White Mile 1994, Canadian Bacon 1995, Everybody Says I Love You 1996, Murder at 1600 1997, Mad City 1997, The Object of My Affection 1998; actor, dir., writer of films: The Four Seasons 1981, Sweet Liberty 1986, A New Life 1987, Betsy's Wedding 1990. *TV includes:* The Glass House 1972, M*A*S*H 1972–83, Tune in America 1975, Kill Me If You Can (film) 1977; devised series We'll Get By 1975; Theatre World Award for Fair Game for Lovers; five Emmy Awards (Best Actor, Best Director and Best Writer), two Directors' Guild Awards, Writers' Guild Award, seven People's Choice Awards, Humanitas Award for Writing, five Golden Globe Awards for M*A*S*H; Trustee Museum of TV and Radio, Rockefeller Foundation; Pres. Appointee Nat. Comm. for Observance of Int. Women's Year 1976; Co-Chair. Nat. ERA Countdown Campaign 1982. *Address:* c/o Martin Bregman Productions, 641 Lexington Avenue, New York, NY 10022, U.S.A.

ALDER, Berni Julian, PH.D.; American theoretical physicist; b. 9 Sept. 1925, Duisburg, Germany; s. of Ludwig Alder and Ottilie Gottschalk; m. Esther Romella Berger 1956; two s. one d.; ed. Univ. of California (Berkeley), and California Inst. of Technology; Instructor, Univ. of Calif. (Berkeley) 1951–54; Theoretical Physicist, Univ. of Calif. Lawrence Livermore Nat. Lab. 1955–93; Prof. of Applied Science, Univ. of California at Davis 1987–93, Prof. Emer. 1993–; Nat. Science Foundation Sr. Post Doctoral Fellow, Weizman Inst. (Israel) and Univ. of Rome 1963–64; Van der Waals Prof., Univ. of Amsterdam 1971; Guggenheim Fellow, Cambridge (U.K.) and Leiden (Netherlands) 1954–55; Assoc. Prof., Univ. of Paris 1972; Hinshelwood Prof., Oxford Univ. 1986; Lorentz Prof., Univ. of Leiden 1990; Royal Soc. Lecturer 1991; Ed. Journal of Computational Physics; mem. N.A.S.; Hildebrand Award, American Chem. Soc. 1985; Fellow Japanese Promotion of Science 1989. *Publications:* many chapters in books and articles in journals. *Leisure interests:* hiking, skiing. *Address:* Lawrence Livermore National Laboratory, P.O. Box 808, Livermore, CA 94550, U.S.A. *Fax:* (510) 423-4371.

ALDERS, Hans; Netherlands politician; b. 17 Dec. 1942; ed. vocational school; fmr. junior man. in an employment agency; mem. Gelderland Prov. Ass. 1978, Leader Partij van de Arbeid (PvdA) Group 1979; mem. Parl. 1982–, Sec. PvdA Parl. Group 1987–89; Minister of Housing, Physical Planning and the Environment 1989–94. *Address:* Partij van Arbeid, Nicolaas Witsenkade 30, 1017 ZT Amsterdam, The Netherlands.

ALDINGTON, 1st Baron (cr. 1962); **Toby (Austin Richard William) Low,** P.C., K.C.M.G., C.B.E., F.R.S.A., D.S.O., T.D.; British industrialist and banker; b. 25 May 1914, London; s. of Col. Stuart Low, D.S.O. and Hon. Lucy Gwen, d. of Lord Atkin; m. Araminta, d. of Sir Harold MacMichael, G.C.M.G., D.S.O., 1947; one s. two d.; called to Bar 1939; Army Service 1939–45; Conservative M.P. 1945–62; Parl. Sec. to Ministry of Supply 1951–54; Minister of State, Bd. of Trade 1954–57; Deputy Chair. Conservative Party Org. 1959–63; Chair. Grindlays Bank Ltd. (fmrly. Nat. and Grindlays) 1963–76, Port of London Authority 1971–77, Gen. Advisory Council of BBC 1971–77; Chair. Sun Alliance and London Insurance Group 1971–85, Westland PLC 1977–85 (Pres. 1985), Man. Cttee. Inst. of Neurology (1961–79), Independent Schools Jt. Council 1986–89; Deputy Chair. Gen. Electric PLC 1968–84; Dir. Lloyds Bank PLC 1967–85, Citicorp N.A. (U.S.A.) 1969–84; Pres. British Standards Inst. 1986–89, Brain Research Trust 1987– (Chair. 1974–87); Hon. Fellow New Coll., Oxford; Warden of Winchester Coll. 1979–87; Chair. Leeds Castle Foundation 1984–94. *Leisure interests:* golf, gardening. *Address:* Knoll Farm, Aldington, Ashford, Kent, TN25 7BY, England. *Telephone:* (01233) 720292.

ALDISS, Brian Wilson, F.R.S.L.; British writer; b. 18 Aug. 1925, Norfolk; m. 2nd Margaret Manson 1965; two s. two d.; ed. Framlingham Coll. and West Buckland School; fmrly. soldier, draughtsman, bookseller and film critic; Literary Ed. Oxford Mail 1957–69; Pres. British Science Fiction Asscn. 1960–65; Joint-Pres. European Science Fiction Cttees. 1976–80; Chair. John W. Campbell Memorial Award 1976–77; Chair. Cttee. of Man. Soc. of Authors 1977–78; mem. Literature Advisory Panel, Arts Council 1978–80; Chair. Cultural Exchanges Cttee. of Authors 1978; Judge, Booker McConnell Prize 1981; Pres. World SF 1982–84; Ed. S.F. Horizons 1964–; Vice-Pres. H. G. Wells Soc., W. Buckland School 1997–; Hugo Award for Hothouse 1962, Nebula Award for The Saliva Tree 1965, Ditmar Award for World's Best Contemporary Science Fiction Writer 1969, British Science Fiction Asscn. Award for The Moment of Eclipse 1972, Eurocon III Merit Award for Billion Year Spree 1976, Jules Verne Award for Non-Stop 1977, 1st James Blish Award for Excellence in Criticism 1977, Pilgrim Award 1978, John W. Campbell Award 1983, Kurt Lasswitz Award 1984, I.A.F.A. Distinguished Scholarship Award 1986, J. Lloyd Eaton Award 1988. *Publications:* The Brightfount Diaries 1955, Space, Time & Nathaniel 1957, Non-Stop 1958, The Male Response 1959, Hothouse 1962, The Airs of Earth 1963, The Dark Light Years 1964, Greybeard 1964, Earthworks 1965, Best Science Fiction Stories of Brian W. Aldiss 1965, Cities and Stones: A Traveller's Jugoslavia 1966, Report on Probability A 1968, Barefoot in the Head 1969, Intangibles Inc., 1969, A Brian Aldiss Omnibus 1969, The Hand-Reared Boy 1970, The Shape of Further Things 1970, A Soldier Erect 1971, The Moment of Eclipse 1971, Brian Aldiss Omnibus 2 1971, Penguin Science Fiction Omnibus (ed.) 1973, Comic Inferno 1973, Billion Year Spree 1973, Frankenstein Unbound 1973, The Eighty-Minute Hour 1974, Hell's Cartographers (editor) 1975, Space Odysseys, Evil Earths, Science Fiction Art 1975, The Malacia Tapestry, Galactic Empires (2 vols.) 1976, Last Orders, Brothers of the Head 1977, Perilous Planets, A Rude Awakening 1978, Enemies of the System 1978, This World and Nearer Ones 1979, Pile 1979, New Arrivals, Old Encounters 1979, Moreau's Other Island 1980, Life in the West 1980, An Island called Moreau 1981, Foreign Bodies 1981, Helliconia Spring 1982, Science Fiction Quiz 1983, Helliconia Summer 1983, Seasons in Flight 1984, Helliconia Winter 1985, The Pale Shadow of Science 1985, ... And the Lurid Glare of the Comet 1986, Trillion Year Spree 1986 (Hugo Award 1987), Ruins 1987, Forgotten Life 1988, Science Fiction Blues 1988, Best SF Stories of Brian W. Aldiss 1988, Cracken at Critical 1989, A Romance of the Equator 1990, Bury my Heart at W.H. Smith's 1990, Dracula Unbound 1991, Remembrance Day 1993, A Tupolev Too Far 1993, Somewhere East of Life 1994, The Detached Retina 1995, At the Caligula Hotel (poems) 1995, The Secret of this Book 1995, Songs from the Steppes of Central Asia 1996, The Twinkling of an Eye 1998, When the Feast is Finished 1999. *Leisure interests:* the past, the future, obscurity. *Address:* Hambleden, 39 St. Andrews Road, Old Headington, Oxford, OX3 9DL, England. *Telephone:* (01865) 62464. *Fax:* (01865) 744435.

ALDRIDGE, (Harold Edward) James; British author and journalist; b. 10 July 1918; s. of William Thomas Aldridge and Edith Quayle Aldridge; m. Dina Mitchnik 1942; two s.; with Herald and Sun, Melbourne, Australia 1937–38, Daily Sketch and Sunday Dispatch, London 1939; with Australian Newspaper Service and North American Newspaper Alliance (as war correspondent), Finland, Norway, Middle East, Greece, U.S.S.R. 1939–45; correspondent for Time and Life, Teheran 1944; Rhys Memorial Award 1945; Lenin Peace Prize 1972. *Plays:* 49th State 1947, One Last Glimpse 1981. *Publications:* Signed With Their Honour 1942, The Sea Eagle 1944, Of Many Men 1946, The Diplomat 1950, The Hunter 1951, Heroes of the Empty View 1954, Underwater Hunting for Inexperienced Englishmen 1955, I Wish He Would Not Die 1958, Gold and Sand (short stories) 1960, The Last Exile 1961, A Captive in the Land 1962, The Statesman's Game 1966, My Brother Tom 1966, The Flying 19 1966, Living Egypt (with Paul Strand) 1969, Cairo: Biography of a City 1970, A Sporting Proposition 1973, The Marvellous Mongolian 1974, Mockery in Arms 1974, The Untouchable Juli 1975, One Last Glimpse 1977, Goodbye Un-America 1979, The Broken Saddle 1982, The True Story of Lilli Stubek 1984 (Australian Children's Book of the Year 1985), The True Story of Spit Mac Phee 1985 (Guardian Children's Fiction Prize), The True Story of Lola MacKellar 1993. *Leisure interests:* trout and salmon fishing. *Address:* c/o Curtis Brown, 28/29 Haymarket, London, SW1Y 4SP, England.

ALDRIN, Buzz, D.SC.; American astronaut; b. 20 Jan. 1930, Montclair, N.J.; s. of late Col. Edwin E. Aldrin and late Marion M. Aldrin; m. 1st (divorced 1978); two s. one d.; m. 2nd Lois Driggs-Cannon 1988; ed. U.S. Military Acad. and Massachusetts Inst. of Technology.; fmr. mem. U.S. Air Force; completed pilot training 1952; flew combat missions during Korean War; later became aerial gunnery instructor, Nellis Air Force Base, Nev.; attended Squadron Officers' School at Air Univ., Maxwell Air Force Base, Ala.; later Flight Commdr. 36th Tactical Fighter Wing, Bitburg, Germany; completed astronautics studies at M.I.T. 1963; selected by NASA as astronaut 1963; Gemini Target Office, Air Force Space Systems Div., L.A., Calif. 1963; later assigned to Manned Spacecraft Center, Houston, Tex.; pilot of backup crew for Gemini IX mission 1966; pilot for Gemini XII 1966; backup command module pilot for Apollo VIII; lunar module pilot for Apollo XI, landed on the moon 20 July 1969; Commdt. Aerospace Research Pilot School 1971–72; Scientific Consultant, Beverly Hills Oil Co., L.A.; Chair. Starcraft Enterprises; Fellow, American Inst. of Aeronautics and Astronautics; Hon. mem. Royal Aeronautical Soc.; several honorary degrees and numerous decorations and awards; retd. from U.S.A.F. 1972; Pres. Research & Eng. Consultants Inc. 1972–; consultant to JRW, Jet Propulsion Lab. *Publications:* First on the Moon: A Voyage with Neil Armstrong (with Michael Collins) 1970, Return to Earth 1973, Men From Earth 1989, The Tides of Tiber (with John Barnes) 1996. *Leisure interests:* scuba diving, snow skiing, Starcraft Enterprises. *Address:* 233 Emerald Bay, Laguna Beach, CA 92651, U.S.A.

ALEBUA, Rt. Hon. Ezekiel, P.C.; Solomon Islands politician; fmr. Deputy Prime Minister; Prime Minister of the Solomon Is. 1986–89; mem. Solomon Is. United Party (SIUPA). *Address:* c/o Office of the Prime Minister, Honiara, Solomon Islands.

ALEGRE, Norberto José d'Alva Costa; São Tomé e Príncipe politician; fmr. Minister of Econ. and Finance; Prime Minister of São Tomé and Príncipe 1992–94; mem. Partido de Convergência Democrática Grupo de Reflexão. *Address:* c/o Partido de Convergência Democrático Grupo de Reflexão, São Tomé, São Tomé and Príncipe.

ALEKPEROV, Vagit Yusufovich; Russian-Azerbaijani businessman; b. 1 Sept. 1950, Baku; m.; one s.; ed. Azerbaijan Inst. of Oil and Gas; Dir. oil-extraction Co. Kogalymneftegas 1984–90; Deputy, then First Deputy Minister of Oil and Gas Industry of U.S.S.R. 1990–91; Chair. Bd. Imperial Bank, Petrocommercial Bank; f. and Pres. Oil Co. LUKoil 1992–. *Publication:* Vertical Integrated Oil Companies in Russia. *Address:* LUKoil, Szetensky blvd. 11, 101000 Moscow, Russia. *Telephone:* (095) 927-4444.

ALEKSANDR, (Timofeyev, Nikolai Anatolyevich Archbishop of Saratov and Volsk; Russian ecclesiastic; b. 8 Aug. 1941, Teykovo; mil. service 1963–66; ed. Moscow Theological Acad.; became a monk 1971; lecturer, Moscow Theological Acad. 1973, Prof. 1981; Dean of Moscow Theological Acad. and Seminary 1982; Archbishop 1986–; Chair. of Educ. Cttee. of Holy Synod 1986. *Address:* Moscow Theological Academy and Seminary, Moscow, Russia.

ALEKSANDROV, Aleksandr Danilovich; Russian mathematician; b. 4 Aug. 1912, Volyn, Ryazan Region; s. of Daniel Aleksandrov and Elisabeth Bartoshevich; m. 1st Marianna Georg 1937 (divorced 1978); m. 2nd Svetlana Bogacheva 1980; one s., one d.; ed. Leningrad Univ.; Lecturer Leningrad Univ. 1933–, Rector 1952–64; mem. CPSU 1951–91; specialized in subject of convex bodies and general surfaces in geometry; corresp. mem. Acad. of Sciences of U.S.S.R. (now Russia) 1946–64, mem. 1964–; Head of Dept., Inst. of Math., Siberian Br. U.S.S.R. Acad. of Sciences 1964–86; Head of Dept. St. Petersburg Br. of Inst. of Math., Acad. of Sciences 1986–92, now Councillor; U.S.S.R. Master of Sport in Mountaineering 1949; mem. National Acad. (Italy) 1975; State prizewinner 1942, Lobachevsky Int. Prize 1951, Euler Medal 1992. *Publications:* The Internal Geometry of Convex Surfaces 1948, Convex Polyhedrons 1950, Two Dimensional Manifolds of Banded Curvature 1962, Foundations of Geometry 1988, Selected Works Part I. *Address:* Mathematical Institute, Fontanka 27, St. Petersburg 191011, Russia. *Telephone:* (812) 312-40-58 (Office); 272-58-52 (Home).

ALEKSANDROV, Aleksandr Pavlovich, PH.D.; Russian cosmonaut and pilot; b. 20 Feb. 1943, Moscow; m. Natalia Valentinovna Aleksandrova; one s. one d.; ed. Baumann Tech. Inst., Moscow; mem. CPSU 1970; after service in Soviet Army started work with Space Programme 1964–; took part in elaboration of control system of space-craft, Cosmonaut since 1978, participated in Soyuz-T and Salyut programmes; successfully completed 149-day flight to Salyut-7 orbital station with V. A. Lyakhov (q.v.) 1983 and effected space-walk, July 1987, with A. Victorenko and M. Fares; joined Yurii Romanenko in space, returned to earth Dec. 1987; completed 160-day flight on Mir Space Station; Chief, Dept. of Crew Training and Extra Vehicular Activity at Energya design and production firm; mem. Extra Vehicular Activity Cttee., IAF 1994–; Academician Int. Informatization Acad. 1997; Hero of Soviet Union 1983, 1987. *Address:* Khovanskaya Str. 3, 27, 129515, Moscow, Russia. *Telephone:* 5136788 (Office); 2155619 (Home). *Fax:* (095) 5136138.

ALEKSANDROV, Kiryll Sergeyevich, D.PHYSICAL-MATH.SC.; Russian physicist; b. 9 Jan. 1931; s. of Sergey Aleksandrov and Ljubov' Aleksandrov; m. Inga Chernjavskaja 1959; one d.; ed. Leningrad Electrotech. Inst.; worked as researcher Inst. of Crystallography; researcher, Vice-Dir. Kirensky Inst. of Physics, Siberian br. of U.S.S.R. Acad. of Sciences, Krasnoyarsk 1958–83, Dir. 1983–; Corresp. mem. U.S.S.R. Acad. of Sciences 1971, mem. 1984; Chair. Scientific Council on physics of segnetoelectrics and dielectrics, Dept. of Gen. Physics and Astronomy, Russian Acad. of Sciences; Vice-Chair. Krasnoyarsk Scientific Centre of Russian Acad. of Sciences. *Publications:* works in the field of crystal physics, structural phase transitions, physics of materials. *Leisure interests:* numismatics, mushroom hunting. *Address:* L. Kirensky Institute of Physics, 600036 Akademgorodok, Krasnoyarsk, Russia. *Telephone:* (3912) 43-26-35 (Office); 44-41-75 (Home). Fax: (3912) 43-89-23.

ALEKSEEVA, Tatyana Ivanovna; Russian anthropologist and biologist; b. 7 Dec. 1928; d. of Ivan Shacabrin and Varvara Majorova; m. Valery Alekseev; ed. Moscow State Univ.; jr., sr., leading, main researcher Research Inst. and Museum of Anthropology 1955–; corresp. mem. U.S.S.R. (now Russian) Acad. of Sciences 1991; research in study of influence of geographical and social medium on aboriginal population; mem. World Org. of Biologists. *Publications include:* Origin and Ethnic History of Russian People 1965, Ethnogenesis of East Slavs 1973, Geographical Medium and Biology of Man 1977, Adaptive Processes in Populations of Man 1986. *Leisure interests:* riding, pets. *Address:* Research Institute and Museum of Anthropology, Mokhovaya str. 11, 103009 Moscow, Russia. *Telephone:* (095) 203 3598 (Office); 331-3273 (Home).

ALEKSEYEV, Sergey Sergeyevich, D.JUR.; Russian lawyer; b. 28 July 1924, m.; two d.; ed. Sverdlovsk Inst. of Law; teacher, Prof., Head of Chair Sverdlovsk (now Yekaterinburg) Inst. of Law 1949–; Dir. Inst. of Philosophy and Law Ural Div. of U.S.S.R. Acad. of Sciences; Corresp. mem. U.S.S.R. Acad. of Sciences 1987; U.S.S.R. People's Deputy 1990–91; Chair. U.S.S.R. Cttee. of Constitutional Inspection 1990–91; Chair. Council of Research, Centre of Pvt. Law 1992–; author (with A. Sobchak) of one of projects of Constitution of Russia 1991–92; mem. Presidential Council of Russia 1993–95; U.S.S.R. State Prize; Merited Worker of Science of Russia. *Publications include:* General Theory of Law (Vol. 1-2, 1981–82), Theory of Law: Constitutional Concept 1991, Legal Civil Soc. 1991. *Leisure interests:* tourism, mountain skiing, reading. *Address:* Research Centre of Private Law, Yekaterinburg Branch, 620146 Yekaterinburg, Russia (Office). *Telephone:* (3432) 28-89-81 (Office).

ALEKSIY II, D.C.T. (b. A. M. Ridiguer); Russian Orthodox clergyman; b. 23 Feb. 1929, Tallinn, Estonia; ed. Leningrad (now St. Petersburg) Theological Acad.; ordained Priest 1950; Bishop of Tallinn and Estonia 1961–64; mem. Cen. Cttee. of World Council of Churches 1961–68; Vice-Chair. Dept. of External Church Relations, Moscow Patriarchate 1961–64; Archbishop 1961–, Admin. Manager of Moscow Patriarchy 1964–86, perm. mem. of Holy Synod 1964–, Chair. Teaching Cttee. of Moscow Patriarchate 1965–86; Metropolitan of Tallinn and Estonia 1968–86; Metropolitan of Leningrad and Novgorod 1986–90; Patriarch of Moscow and All Russia 1990–; Chair. of Presidium Conf. of European Churches 1987–92; U.S.S.R. People's Deputy 1989–91. *Address:* Moscow Patriarchate, Chisty per. 5, Moscow 119034, Russia. *Telephone:* 201-28-40. *Fax:* 201-25-04.

ALEMÁN LACAYO, Arnoldo; Nicaraguan politician; fmr. leader pro-Somoza Liberal Student Youth Org. in 1960s; imprisoned for alleged counter-revolutionary activity 1980; placed under house arrest 1989; Mayor of Managua 1990; Leader, Liberal Party Alliance 1996; Pres. of Nicaragua Jan. 1997–. *Address:* Oficina del Presidente, Managua, Nicaragua.

ALENTOVA, Vera Valentinovna; Russian actress; b. 21 Feb. 1942; m. Vladimir Menshov; one d.; ed. Studio School of Moscow Art Theatre; actress Moscow Pushkin Drama Theatre 1965. *Theatre roles include:* Three days Only, Children of the Sun, Scum, Lighting but not Heating, Chocolate Soldier; in cinema 1966–; numerous roles including Katerina in Moscow does not Trust Tears 1980, Time of Desires 1982; State Prize of Russia, Grand Prix Saint Michel; People's Artist of Russia 1992. *Address:* 3d Tverskaya-Yamskaya str. 52, Apt. 29, 125047 Moscow, Russia (Home). *Telephone:* (095) 250 8543 (Home).

ALESKEROV, Murtuz Nadzhaf ogly, DR.JUR.SC.; Azerbaijani politician; b. 20 Sept. 1928, Gyandzha; m.; two s. one d.; ed. Azerbaijan State Univ., Moscow Inst. of State and Law; sr. lecturer Azerbaijan State Univ. 1954–, Head of Chair of State Law 1965–, Prof. 1969, Rector 1993–96; after proclamation of independence of Azerbaijan took part in working out draft Constitution of new Repub.; participant in political activities since 1990; mem. Bd. of People's Front 1991–92, expelled for org. of rally in support of Heydar Alijev; Deputy Chair. Party Yeni Azerbaijan (New Azerbaijan) and mem. Political Council; elected Deputy to Milli Majlis (Nat. Ass.) 1995, Chair. 1996–; mem. Int. Juridical Asscn.; Merited Lawyer of Azerbaijan. *Publications:* author of numerous monographs, textbooks and of over 200 articles on problems of state and int. law. *Address:* Milli Majlis, Azizbekov prosp. 1, 370001 Baku, Azerbaijan. *Telephone:* (8922) 98-09-00.

ALEXANDER, Andrew Lamar, J.D.; American politician; b. 3 July 1940, Knoxville, Tenn.; s. of Andrew Lamar Alexander and Genevra F. Rankin; m. Leslee K. Buhler 1969; two s. two d.; ed. Vanderbilt and New York Univs.; mem. Bar of La. and Tenn.; law clerk to presiding justice, U.S. Court of Appeals (5th circuit), New Orleans; Assoc. Fowler, Rountree, Fowler & Robertson, Knoxville 1965; Legislative Asst. to Senator Howard Baker 1967–68; Exec. Asst. to Bryce Harlow, White House Congressional Liaison Office 1969–70; partner, Dearborn & Ewing, Nashville 1971–78; Gov. of Tenn. 1979–87; Chair. Leadership Inst. Belmont Coll. Nashville 1987–88; Pres. Univ. of Tenn. 1988–90; mem. Pres.'s Task Force on Federalism; Chair. Nat. Govs. Asscn. 1985–86, President's Comm. on Americans Outdoors 1985–87; mem. Bd. of Dirs. Corporate Child Care Inc., Nashville, Martin Marietta Corpn. Bethesda, Md.; U.S. Sec. of Educ. 1990–93; Counsel Baker, Donelson, Bearman and Caldwell 1993–; Chair. Republican Neighbourhood Meeting 1993–; recipient of various awards and distinctions; Republican. *Address:* Baker, Donelson, Bearman and Caldwell, 511 Union Street, Nashville, TN 37219, U.S.A.

ALEXANDER, Bill; British theatre director; b. 23 Feb. 1948, Hunstanton, Norfolk; s. of Bill Paterson and Rosemary Paterson; m. Juliet Harmer 1978; two d.; ed. St. Lawrence Coll. Ramsgate and Keele Univ.; began career at Bristol Old Vic directing Shakespeare and the classics and contemporary drama; joined R.S.C. 1977, Assoc. Dir. R.S.C. 1984–91, Artistic Dir. 1991–; productions for R.S.C. include: Tartuffe, Richard III 1984, Volpone, The Accrington Pals, Clay, Captain Swing, School of Night, A Midsummer Night's Dream (Olivier Award for Best Dir. 1986); other theatre work at Nottingham Playhouse, Royal Court Theatre, Victory Theatre, New York and Shakespeare Theatre, Washington, D.C.; Artistic Dir. Birmingham Repertory Co. 1993–, productions include: Othello, The Snowman, Macbeth, Dr. Jekyll and Mr. Hyde, The Alchemist, Awake and Sing, The Way of the World, Divine Right, The Merchant of Venice, Old Times, Frozen, Hamlet, The Tempest. *Leisure interest:* tennis. *Address:* Birmingham Repertory Theatre, Broad Street, Birmingham, B1 2EP; Rose Cottage, Tunley, Glos. GL7 6LP, England.

ALEXANDER, Brooke, B.A.; American art dealer and publisher; b. 26 April 1937, Los Angeles; s. of Richard H. Alexander and Marion C. Alexander; m. Carolyn Rankin 1967; two d.; ed. Yale Univ.; f. Brooke Alexander Inc. to publish and distribute graphic art 1968, expanded co. 1975; f. Brooke

Alexander Edns., opened separate gallery for graphics 1989; partner in Madrid gallery, Galería Weber, Alexander y Cobo 1991–; mem. Governing Bd. Yale Univ. Art Gallery 1988–. *Address:* 59 Wooster Street, New York, NY, U.S.A. *Telephone:* (212) 925-4338.

ALEXANDER, Christopher, PH.D.; American architect, professor and consultant; b. 4 Oct. 1936, Vienna, Austria; m. Pamela Patrick 1978; two d.; ed. Oundle, Trinity Coll., Cambridge, Harvard Univ.; fmrly. with Center for Cognitive Studies, Harvard, with Jt. Center for Urban Studies, Harvard Univ. and M.I.T. 1959–63; Prof. of Architecture Univ. of Calif., Berkeley 1963–98, Prof. in Grad. School 1998, Research Prof. in the Humanities 1965; Visiting Fellow Rockefeller Foundation Villa Serbelloni 1965; f., Pres., Dir. Center for Environmental Structure 1967–; Trustee Prince of Wales's Inst. for Architecture 1991–97; maj. works include: 35 bldgs. of New Eishin Univ., Tokyo, Linz Café, Linz, village school, Gujarat, low-cost housing in Mexico and Peru, Shelter for the Homeless, San José, numerous pvt. houses and public bldgs., Center for Environmental Structure has undertaken around 200 projects, including town and community planning worldwide; Fellow Harvard Univ. 1961–64, American Acad. of Arts and Sciences 1996; mem. Swedish Royal Acad. 1980–; Best Bldg. in Japan Award 1985; Seaside Prize 1994; numerous other awards and prizes. *Publications include:* Notes on the Synthesis of Form 1964, The Oregon Experiment 1975, The Linz Café 1981, A New Theory of Urban Design 1984, The Phenomenon of Life 1998, The Process of Creating Life 1998, The Luminous Ground 1998, over 200 articles in design journals. *Address:* 2701 Shasta Road, Berkeley, CA 94708, U.S.A.; Meadow Lodge, Binsted, near Arundel, W. Sussex, BN18 0LQ, England.

ALEXANDER, Clifford L., LL.D.; American government official and lawyer; b. 21 Sept. 1933, Harlem, New York; s. of Clifford and Edith (née McAllister) Alexander; m. Adele Logan 1959; one s. one d.; ed. Harvard Univ., Yale Univ.; practised as lawyer in New York, partner in Verner, Liipfert, Bernhard, McPherson and Alexander, law firm; Foreign Affairs Officer, Nat. Security Council Staff 1963–64; Deputy Special Asst., later Deputy Special Counsel to Pres. Lyndon Johnson 1964–67; Chair. Equal Employment Opportunity Comm. 1967–69, resigned; mem. Comm. for the Observance of Human Rights 1968; Special Amb. to Swaziland 1968; Partner in Arnold & Porter, law firm; news commentator and host, Cliff Alexander—Black on White TV programme 1971–74; Prof. of Law, Howard Univ. 1973–74; U.S. Sec. of the Army 1977–80; Pres. Alexander & Assocs. Inc. 1981–; mem. Bd. of Dirs. Pennsylvania Power & Light Co.; Adjunct Prof., Georgetown Univ.; Prof. Howard Univ., Washington; mem. Bd. of Dirs. Mexican-American Legal Defense and Educ. Fund, Dreyfus Third Century Fund Inc., MCI Corpn., Dreyfus Common Stock Fund, Dreyfus Tax Exempt Fund; mem. American and D.C. Bar Asscns.; fmr. mem. Bd. Overseers Harvard Univ.; Trustee, Atlanta Univ.; Hon. LL.D. (Univ. of Maryland, Atlanta Univ.); Frederick Douglass Award and other decorations. *Address:* Alexander & Assocs. Inc., 400 C Street, N.E., Washington, DC 20002; 512 A Street, S.E., Washington, DC 20003, U.S.A. (Home). *Telephone:* (202) 546 0111 (Office).

ALEXANDER, Jane; American actress and government official; b. 28 Oct. 1939, Boston; d. of Thomas Bartlett and Ruth Quigley (née Pearson); m. 1st Robert Alexander 1962 (divorced 1969); one s.; m. 2nd Edwin Sherin 1975; ed. Sarah Lawrence Coll., Edin. Univ.; Chair. Nat. Endowment for Arts 1993–97; mem. Bd. Dirs. Women's Action for Nuclear Disarmament 1981–88, Film Forum 1985–90, Nat. Stroke Asscn. 1984–91. *Broadway appearances include:* The Great White Hope 1968–69, Find Your Way Home 1974, Hamlet 1975, The Heiress 1976, Goodbye Fidel 1980, Night of the Iguana 1988, Shadowlands 1990–91, The Visit 1992. *Other stage appearances include:* Anthony and Cleopatra 1981, Hedda Gabler 1981, Approaching Zanzibar 1989. *Film appearances include:* The Great White Hope 1970, All the President's Men 1976, Kramer vs. Kramer 1979, Brubaker 1980, Sweet Country 1986, Glory 1989. *TV appearances include:* Eleanor and Franklin 1976, Playing for Time 1980, Kennedy's Children 1981, A Marriage: Georgia O'Keeffe and Alfred Stieglitz 1991, Stay the Night 1992; Tony Award for the Great White Hope 1969, Emmy Award for Playing for Time 1980, numerous other awards. *Publications:* The Bluefish Cookbook (with Greta Jacobs) 1979, (co-translator) The Master Builder (Henrik Ibsen). *Address:* c/o Mark Schwartz, William Morris Agency, 151 El Camino Drive, Beverly Hills, CA 90212, U.S.A.

ALEXANDER, Sir (John) Lindsay, Kt., M.A.; British banker; b. 12 Sept. 1920, Gloucester; s. of Ernest Daniel Alexander and Florence Mary Mainsmith; m. Maud Lilian Collard 1944; two s. one d.; ed. Alleyn's School and Brasenose Coll., Oxford; Man. Dir. Ocean Transport and Trading Ltd. 1955–71, Chair. 1971–80; Chair. Liverpool Port Employers' Asscn. 1964–67; Vice-Chair. Nat. Asscn. of Port Employers 1965–69; Chair. Cttee. of European Nat. Shipowners' Asscns. 1971–73; Vice-Pres. Chamber of Shipping of U.K. 1973–74, Pres. 1974–75; Dir. Lloyds Bank 1970–91 (Deputy Chair. 1980–88), Lloyds Bank Int. 1975–85 (Deputy Chair. 1979–80, Chair. 1980–85, Vice-Chair. Lloyds Bank U.K. Man. 1981–85), British Petroleum Co. Ltd. 1975–91; Dir. Hawker Siddeley Group 1981–91, Jebsen's Drilling PLC 1981–86; Dir. Wellington Underwriting Holdings Ltd. 1987–96; Dir. Britoil plc 1988–90; Dir. Lloyd's Abbey Life Group 1988–91; former Deputy Chair. Lloyds Merchant Bank Holdings Ltd., Lloyds Bank Canada; Fellow, Chartered Inst. of T.P.T. 1971; Hon. Fellow Brasenose Coll.; Companion, Inst. of Man. 1972; Commdr. Royal Order of St. Olav (Norway); Hon. mem. Master Mariners Co. 1974–. *Leisure interests:* gardening, music, photography. *Address:* c/o Lloyds Bank PLC, 71 Lombard Street, London, EC3P 3BS, England. *Telephone:* 0171-626 1500.

ALEXANDER, Jonathan James Graham, D.PHIL., F.B.A., F.S.A.; British professor of history of art; b. 20 Aug. 1935, London; s. of Arthur Ronald Brown and Frederica Emma Graham (who m. 2nd Boyd Alexander); m. 1st Mary Davey 1974 (dissolved 1994); one s.; m. 2nd Serita Winthrop 1996; ed. Magdalen Coll. Oxford; Asst., Dept. of Western Manuscripts, Bodleian Library, Oxford 1963–71; Lecturer, History of Art Dept., Univ. of Manchester 1971–73, Reader 1973–87; Prof. of Fine Arts Inst. of Fine Arts, New York Univ. 1988–; Lyell Reader in Bibliography, Oxford Univ. 1982–83; Sandars Lecturer, Cambridge Univ. 1984–85; Visiting Prof. Univ. Coll. London 1991–92; Hon. Fellow Pierpont Morgan Library 1995, John Simon Guggenheim Memorial Foundation Fellowship 1995–96, Distinguished Visiting Fellowship, La Trobe Univ. 1997, Visiting Fellow All Souls Coll., Oxford 1998. *Publications:* Illuminated Manuscripts in the Bodleian Library, Oxford (with Otto Pächt) (3 vols.) 1966, 1970, 1973, Italian Illuminated Manuscripts in the library of Major J. R. Abbey (with A. C. de la Mare) 1969, Norman Illumination at Mont St. Michel *c.* 966–1100 1970, The Master of Mary of Burgundy, A Book of Hours 1970, Italian Renaissance Illuminations 1977, Insular Manuscripts 6th–9th Century 1978, The Decorated Letter 1978, Illuminated Manuscripts in Oxford College Libraries, The University Archives and the Taylor Institution (with E. Temple) 1986, Age of Chivalry (Jt. Ed.), Art in Plantagenet England 1200–1400 1987, Medieval Illuminators and their Methods of Work 1993, The Painted Page: Italian Renaissance Book Illumination 1450–1550 (Ed.) 1994, The Townley Lectionary (introduction) 1997; articles in Burlington Magazine, Arte Veneta, Pantheon, Art Bulletin etc. *Address:* Institute of Fine Arts, 1 East 78th Street, New York, NY 10021, U.S.A. *Telephone:* (212) 772-5800. *Fax:* (212) 772-5807.

ALEXANDER KARADJORDJEVIC, H.R.H. Crown Prince of Yugoslavia; b. 17 July 1945, London; s. of H.M. King Peter II of Yugoslavia and H.R.H. Princess Alexandra of the Hellenes; m. 1st H.R.H. Princess Maria da Gloria of Orléans and Bragança 1972 (divorced 1983); m. 2nd Katherine Batis 1985; three s.; ed. Le Rosey, Switzerland, Gordonstoun, Scotland, Culver Mil. Acad., U.S.A., Royal Mil. Acad., U.K.; commissioned in British Army, 16th/5th The Queen's Royal Lancers, rank of Acting Capt. 1971; businessman working in Rio de Janeiro, New York, Chicago and London; in exile from birth, chose not to take the title of King on his father's death in 1970, whilst forced to live in exile; visited Belgrade for the first time Oct. 1991, returned on visits June 1992, 1995; British Army Ski Champion 1972. *Leisure interests:* skiing, scuba diving, underwater photography, family. *Address:* 36 Park Lane, London, W1Y 3LE, England. *Telephone:* 0171-493 3715 (Office). *Fax:* 0171-495 2889.

ALEXANDER, Sir Michael O'Donel Bjarne, G.C.M.G.; British diplomatist (retd.); b. 19 June 1936; s. of Conel Hugh O'Donel Alexander and Enid Constance Alexander (née Neate); m. Traute Anna Krohn 1960; two s. one d.; ed. St. Paul's School, King's Coll. Cambridge and Yale Univ., U.S.A. (Harkness Fellow); served R.N. 1956–57; joined H.M. Foreign (later Diplomatic) Service 1962; served Moscow 1963–65, Singapore 1965–68, London 1968–74 (Asst. Private Sec. to Sir Alec Douglas-Home and James Callaghan 1972–74), Geneva 1974–77; Deputy Head, later Head, of Personnel Operations Dept., F.C.O. 1977–79; Private Sec. (Overseas Affairs) to Prime Minister Margaret Thatcher 1979–81; Amb. to Austria 1982–86; Leader of U.K. Del. to Negotiations on Mutual Force Reductions in Cen. Europe 1985–86, Perm. Rep. on the N. Atlantic Council, Brussels 1986–92; Vice-Pres. British Atlantic Cttee. 1992–; Deputy Chair. Wasserstein Perella Eastern Europe 1992–97; Chair. RUSI 1993–, Capital SA (Bucharest), KINTO (Kiev) Sr. Adviser Bain & Co.; mem. Council, RUSI, Exec. Cttee. Anglo-Austrian Soc. *Publications:* articles on East-West relations and int. security. *Leisure interests:* reading and sport. *Address:* Washington Equity Partners, 1 Angel Court, London, EC2R 7HJ, England.

ALEXANDER, (Padinjarethalakal) Cherian, M.LITT., D.LITT.; Indian government official; b. 20 March 1921, Kerala; s. of Jacob and Mariama Alexander; m. Ackama Alexander 1942; two s. two d.; ed. India and U.K.; Indian Admin. Service, Kerala Cadre 1948; Devt. Commr. Small Scale Industries 1960–63; Sr. Adviser, Centre for Industrial Devt., UN, New York 1963–66; Chief UN Project on Small Industries and Chief Adviser to Govt. of Iran 1970–73; Devt. Commr. Small Scale Industries 1973–75; Sec. Foreign Trade, later Commerce Sec. 1975–78; Sr. Adviser, later Exec. Dir. and Asst. Sec.-Gen. Int. Trade Centre, UNCTAD-GATT, Geneva 1978–81; Prin. Sec. to Prime Minister of India 1981–85; High Commr. in U.K. 1985–88; Gov., Tamil Nadu 1988–89, Maharashtra 1993, Goa 1996. *Publications:* The Dutch in Malabar, Buddhism in Kerala, Industrial Estates in India. *Leisure interest:* reading. *Address:* c/o Raj Bhavan, Mumbai, Maharashtra, India.

ALEXANDER, Robert McNeill, M.A., PH.D., D.SC., F.R.S.; British professor of zoology; b. 7 July 1934, Lisburn, N. Ireland; s. of Robert Priestley Alexander and Janet (née McNeill) Alexander; m. Ann Elizabeth Coulton 1961; one s. one d.; ed. Tonbridge School and Cambridge Univ.; lecturer Univ. Coll. of N.Wales, Bangor 1958–69; Prof. of Zoology Univ. of Leeds 1969–; Sec. Zoological Soc. of London 1992–; Vice-Pres. Soc. for Experimental Biology 1993–95, Pres. 1995–97; Pres. Int. Soc. for Vertebrate Morphology 1997–; mem. Academia Europaea 1996; Hon. mem. American Soc. of Zoologists 1986; Scientific Medal (Zoological Soc. of London) 1969, Linnean Medal for Zoology (Linnean Soc. of London) 1979, Muybridge Medal (Int. Soc. for

Biomechanics) 1991. *Publications:* Functional Design in Fishes 1967, Animal Mechanics 1968, Size and Shape 1971, The Chordates 1975, The Invertebrates 1979, Locomotion of Animals 1982, Optima for Animals 1982, Elastic Mechanisms in Animal Movement 1988, Dynamics of dinosaurs and other extinct giants 1989, Animals 1990, Exploring Biomechanics 1992, The Human Machine 1992, Bones 1994, and many scientific papers. *Leisure interests:* local history and history of natural history. *Address:* Department of Biology, University of Leeds, Leeds, LS2 9JT, England (Office); 14 Moor Park Mount, Leeds, LS6 4BU, England (Home). *Telephone:* (0113) 2332911 (Office); (0113) 2759218 (Home). *Fax:* (0113) 275-9218.

ALEXANDER OF WEEDON, Baron (Life Peer) cr. 1988, **Robert Scott Alexander,** Q.C.; British banker and barrister; b. 5 Sept. 1936, Newcastle; s. of Samuel James Alexander and Hannah May Alexander; m. Marie Anderson; two s. one d.; ed. Brighton Coll. and King's Coll., Cambridge; called to the Bar (Middle Temple) 1961, Q.C. 1973, Bencher, 1979; Q.C. (N.S.W., Australia) 1983, Chair. of the Bar of England and Wales 1985–86; Chair. Panel of Takeovers and Mergers 1987–89; Deputy Chair. Nat. Westminster Bank PLC May–Oct. 1989, Chair. 1989–99; Trustee of Nat. Gallery 1986–93, The Economist 1990–; Gov. of Wycombe Abbey School 1986–92; non-exec. Dir. The RTZ Corpn. PLC 1991–96, The London Stock Exchange 1991–93 (Deputy Chair. Securities and Investments Bd. 1994–96); Chair. Deregulated Powers and Scrutiny Cttee., House of Lords 1995–; Hon. L.L.D. (Sheffield) 1991, (Buckingham Univ.) 1992, (Keele Univ.) 1993, (Exeter) 1994. *Leisure interests:* tennis, gardening. *Address:* c/o National Westminster Bank, 41 Lothbury, London, EC2P 2BP, England.

ALEXANDRA, H.R.H. Princess (see Ogilvy, the Hon. Mrs. Angus).

ALEXANDROV (see Aleksandrov).

ALEXEEV (see Alekseyev).

ALEXEEV, Dmitri Konstantinovich; Russian pianist; b. 10 Aug. 1947, Moscow; s. of Konstantin Alekseyev and Gertrude Bolotina; m. Tatiana Sarkisova 1970; one d.; ed. Moscow Conservatoire: studied under Dmitri Bashkirov; prizewinner Int. Tchaikovsky Competition, Moscow 1974, 5th Leeds Int. Piano Competition 1975 and other int. competitions; received Edison Award, Netherlands; performs regularly in the U.S.S.R., in U.K. and throughout Europe and U.S.A. and has toured Japan, Australia etc.; has performed with London Philharmonic Orchestra, London Symphony Orchestra, City of Birmingham Symphony Orchestra, the Royal Philharmonic Orchestra, St Petersburg Philharmonic Orchestra, Berlin Philharmonic, Chicago Symphony Orchestra, Philadelphia Orchestra, Royal Concertgebouw of Amsterdam, Israel Philharmonic and the Munich Bavarian Radio Orchestra; worked with Ashkenazy (q.v.), Boulez (q.v.), Dorati, Giulini (q.v.), Muti (q.v.), Kent Nagano, Klaus Tennstedt (q.v.), Michael Tilson Thomas (q.v.), Sian Edwards (q.v.), Valery Gergiev (q.v.), Andrew Litton (q.v.) and Yuri Temirkanov (q.v.); recordings include works by Bach, Brahms, Chopin, Grieg, Liszt, Prokofiev, Rachmaninov, Schumann, Shostakovich and Scriabin. *Address:* c/o IMG Artists, Media House, 3 Burlington Lane, Chiswick, London, W4 2TH, England. *Telephone:* 0181-233 5800.

ALEXIS, Francis, PH.D., LL.M.; Grenadian politician, author and lawyer; b. 3 Oct. 1947, Grenada; s. of John Everest Alexis and Anastasia Omega Alexis; m. Margaret de Bique 1973; three d.; ed. Grenada Boys' Secondary School, Univ. of West Indies, Hugh Wooding Law School and Univ. of Cambridge; fmr. clerk, Jonas Brown & Hubbards Ltd., Grenada; later civil servant, Grenada; Sr. Lecturer in Law, and Deputy Dean, Faculty of Law, Univ. of West Indies; Barrister-at-Law, Grenada; mem. Parl. 1984–; Minister of Labour, Co-operatives, Social Security and Local Govt. 1984–87; Attorney-Gen. and Minister of Legal Affairs and Labour 1987; Opposition M.P. 1987–90; founder mem. and Deputy Leader New Nat. Party 1986, Nat. Democratic Congress 1987–95; Attorney-Gen. and Minister of Legal Affairs and Local Govt. 1990–95; Acting Prime Minister on various occasions 1990–95; Leader Govt. Business, House of Reps. in Parl. 1990–95, Grenada Nat. Del. to the Windward Islands Political Union Talks 1991–92, to UN Gen. Ass. 1993, to Commonwealth Parl. Asscn. UK 1986, Canada 1994; Father of House of Reps. in Parl. 1995–; founder mem., Leader Democratic Labour Party 1995–; Vice-Pres. Grenada Bar Asscn. 1997–98. *Publications:* Commonwealth Caribbean Legal Essays 1981, Changing Caribbean Constitutions 1983, H. Aubrey Fraser: Eminent Caribbean Jurist 1985, The Constitution and You 1991; articles in law journals. *Leisure interests:* reading, writing, music. *Address:* Church Street, St. George's (Office); St. Paul's, St. George's, Grenada (Home). *Telephone:* (473) 440-6743 (Office); (473) 440-2378 (Home). *Fax:* (473) 440 6591.

ALFARO, Andreu; Spanish sculptor; b. 5 Aug. 1929, Valencia; s. of Andrés Alfaro and Teresa Hernández; m. Dorothy Hofmann 1954; three c.; began work as sculptor in Valencia 1958; joined Grupo Parpalló and participated in various collective exhbns. 1959–62; major one-man exhbn. Sala de la Dirección Gen. de Bellas Artes de Madrid 1967; first one-man exhbn. in Germany at Galerie Dreiseitel, Cologne 1974; one-man exhbn. org. by Ministry of Culture, Palacio Velázquez, Parque del Retiro de Madrid 1979; other one-man shows at Universidad Complutense de Madrid 1981, Antic Mercat del Born de Barcelona 1983; exhibited in Paris and Madrid 1989; retrospective exhbn. in Instituto Valenciano de Arte Moderno 1991; monumental open-air sculptures in Valencia, Barcelona, Madrid, Nüremberg, Cologne, Frankfurt, Munich; Gold Medal Salón Internacional de Marzo Valencia 1964, Creu de Sant Jordi 1982, Premi Alfons Roig 1991, Premio de Urbanismo, Arquitectura y Obra Pública del Ayto. de Madrid 1991; Premio Nacional de Artes Plásticas 1981. *Publications:* El Arte visto por los artistas 1987, Doce artistas de vanguardia en el Museo del Prado 1991; articles in reviews. *Address:* Urbanización Sta. Bárbara 138R, 46111 Rocafort, Valencia, Spain. *Telephone:* (96) 131 09 56.

ALFEROV, Zhores Ivanovich, D.PHYSICAL-MATH.SC.; Russian physicist; b. 15 March 1930; m.; two c.; ed. Leningrad Electrotech. Inst.;. researcher, Head of Lab. Ioffe Inst. of Physics and Tech. U.S.S.R. Acad. of Sciences 1972–87; Dir. 1987–; Corresp. mem. U.S.S.R. (now Russian) Acad. of Sciences 1972, mem. 1979; Vice-Pres. 1991–; Chair. Leningrad (now St. Petersburg) Scientific Centre 1990–; mem. State Duma 1995–; Ed.-in-Chief Physics and Tech. of Semiconductors; U.S.S.R. Lenin and State Prizes, Int. Arsenid Gallia Prize, Karpinsky Prize, Stuart Ballantine Gold Medal, mem. Acad. of Sciences of Germany, Poland, U.S.A., European Physical. Soc. *Publications:* scientific works on physics and tech. of semiconductors, quantum electronics. *Leisure interest:* history of Second World War. *Address:* Russian Academy of Sciences, Leninsky Prospekt 14, 117901 Moscow, Russia.

ALFONSÍN FOULKES, Dr. Raúl: Argentine politician and lawyer; b. 13 March 1926, Chascomus; m. María Barreneche; three s. three d.; ed. Liceo Militar General San Martín, Nat. Univ. of La Plata; journalist, Chascomus; f. El Imparcial newspaper; joined Movimiento de Intransigencia y Renovación 1944; mem. Unión Cívica Radical (Pres. 1983–91); Municipal Councillor, Chascomus 1950; mem. Buenos Aires Prov. Legislature 1952; imprisoned 1953; mem. Chamber of Deputies 1963–66, 1973–76; f. Movimiento de Renovación y Cambio 1966; Pres. of Argentina 1983–89; Dr. h.c. (Univ. of New Mexico) 1985, (Santiago de Compostela) 1988; Príncipe de Asturias Prize 1985, Shared Human Rights Prize of Council of Europe 1986.

ALGABID, Hamid; Niger politician; b. 1941, Tamont; m.; five c.; ed. Abidjan Univ.; fmr. Minister of State for Planning, Commerce and Transportation; fmr. Minister del. for Finance; Prime Minister of Niger 1983–88; fmr. Sec.-Gen. Org. of Islamic Conf. *Address:* c/o Organisation of the Islamic Conference, Kilo 6, P.O. Box 178, Jeddah 2411, Saudi Arabia.

ALGOSAIBI, Ghazi, PH.D.; Saudi Arabian diplomatist; b. 2 March 1940, Al-Hasa; s. of Abdul Rahman Algosaibi and Fatma Algosaibi; m. Sigrid Presser 1968; three s. one d.; ed. Univs. of Cairo, S. Calif. and London; Asst. Prof. King Saud Univ. Riyadh 1965, then Prof. and Head of Political Science and Dean, Faculty of Commerce; Dir. Saudi Railways 1974; Minister of Industry and Electricity 1975, of Health 1982; Amb. to Bahrain 1984, to U.K. and Ireland 1992–; numerous decorations. *Publications:* The Gulf Crisis: An Attempt to Understand; 10 collections of essays, 10 collections of poems, An Apartment Called Freedom 1996. *Leisure interests:* swimming, fishing, table tennis. *Address:* Royal Embassy of Saudi Arabia, 30 Charles Street, London, W1X 7PM, England. *Telephone:* 0171-917 3000. *Fax:* 0171-917 3330.

ALHAJI, Alhaji Abubakar; Nigerian politician; b. 22 Nov. 1938, Sokoto; m. Amina Abubakar 1965; three s. three d.; ed. Univ. of Reading and The Hague Inst. of Social Sciences; Deputy Perm. Sec. Ministry of Trade 1974; later Dir. of External Finance, Ministry of Finance; Minister of State for Budget and Planning and Special Advisor to the Pres. 1989–90; Minister of Finance and Econ. Devt. 1990; Sardauna of Sokoto 1990–; High Commr. in U.K. 1992–97; Hon. K.B.E. *Address:* c/o Ministry of Foreign Affairs, Maputo Street, PMB 130, Abuja, Nigeria.

ALHEGELAN, Sheikh Faisal Abdul Aziz al-; Saudi Arabian diplomatist; b. 7 Oct. 1929, Jeddah; s. of Sheikh Abdul Aziz Al-Hegelan and Fatima Al-Eissa; m. Nouha Tarazi 1961; three s.; ed. Faculty of Law, Fouad Univ., Cairo; Ministry of Foreign Affairs 1952–54; served Embassy in Washington, D.C. 1954–58; Chief of Protocol in Ministry 1958–60; Political Adviser to H.M. King Sa'ud 1960–61; Amb. to Spain 1961–68, to Venezuela and Argentina 1968–75, to Denmark 1975–76, to U.K. 1976–79, to U.S.A. 1979–83, to France 1996–; Minister of State and mem. Council of Ministers (Saudi Arabia) April–Sept. 1984, of Health 1984–96, Amb. to Paris 1996–; Chair. Bd. of Dirs., Saudi Red Crescent Soc. 1984–, Saudi Anti-Smoking Soc. 1985–; Chair. Bd. of Trustees, Saudi Council for Health Specialties 1992–; Order of King Abdulaziz, Gran Cruz Cordon of King Abdul Aziz, Order of Isabela la Católica (Spain), Gran Cordón, Orden del Libertador (Venezuela), Grande Oficial, Orden Riobranco (Brazil), May Grand Decoration (Argentina); Hon. K.B.E. *Leisure interests:* bridge, golf. *Address:* Embassy of Saudi Arabia, 5 av. Hoche, 75008 Paris, France; P.O. Box 25557, Riyadh 11576, Saudi Arabia. *Telephone:* 01.47.66.02.06. *Fax:* 01.44.40.25.76.

ALI, Ahmad Mohamed, LL.B., D.P.A.; Saudi Arabian development banker; b. 13 April 1932, Medina; s. of Mohamed Ali and Amina Ali; m. Ghada Mahmood Masri 1968; one s. three d.; ed. Cairo Univ., Univ. of Michigan, New York State Univ.; Dir. Scientific and Islamic Inst., Aden 1958–59; Deputy Rector King Abdul Aziz Univ., Jeddah 1967–72; Deputy Minister of Educ. for Tech. Affairs 1972–75; Pres. Islamic Devt. Bank 1975–94; Sec.-Gen. Muslim World League 1994–95; mem. King Abdul Aziz Univ. Council, King Saud Univ., Oil and Minerals Univ., Islamic Univ., Imam Mohammed Ben Saud Univ.; mem. Admin. Bd. Saudi Credit Bank, Saudi Fund for Devt. *Publications:* numerous articles and working papers on Islamic econs., banking and educ. *Leisure interests:* cycling, walking. *Address:* c/o Muslim World League, P.O. Box 537-538, Makkah, Saudi Arabia.

ALI, Sardar Asif Ahmad, M.A.; Pakistani politician; b. 21 Oct. 1940; s. of late Sardar Ahmad Ali; m.; three c.; ed. Lawrence Coll. Murree, Govt. Coll. Lahore, St. John's Coll. Oxford and Middle Temple, London; lecturer, F.C. Coll. Lahore 1966–68; adviser on agricultural and political affairs to Gov. of W. Pakistan 1969–70; Pres. Punjab Kissan Tanzeem (org. of peasants and small farmers) 1976–79; Sr. Vice-Pres. Majlis-i-Quaid-e-Azam 1978–81; Dir. Punjab Cooperative Union, Lahore 1982–84; Vice-Pres. Punjab Provincial Cooperative Bank Ltd. Lahore 1984–87; mem. Fed. Advisory Council 1981–83; mem. (independent) Nat. Ass. 1985–88, 1990–; mem. Taxation Reform Comm. 1985–87; Chair. Parl. Budget Cttee. 1991–92; mem. Public Accounts Cttee. 1991–93; fmr. Minister of State for Econ. Affairs; Minister of Foreign Affairs 1993. *Publications:* articles in newspapers and journals. *Leisure interests:* mountain-trekking. *Address:* c/o Ministry of Foreign Affairs, Constitution Avenue, Islamabad, Pakistan.

ALI, Muhammad; American boxer; b. (as Cassius Marcellus Clay) 17 Jan. 1942, Louisville, Ky.; s. of Cassius Marcellus Clay Sr. and Odessa L. Grady; m. 1st Sonji Roi (dissolved 1966); m. 2nd Belinda Boyd (Khalilah Toloria) 1967 (divorced 1977); m. 3rd Veronica Porche 1977 (divorced 1986); m. 4th Yolanda Williams 1986; seven d. two s.; ed. Louisville; amateur boxer 1954–60, Olympic Games light-heavyweight champion 1960; professional boxer 1960–, won world heavyweight title Feb. 1964, defeating Sonny Liston; adopted name Muhammad Ali 1964; stripped of title after refusing to be drafted into U.S. Army 1967, won case in U.S. Supreme Court and returned to professional boxing 1970; regained world heavyweight title Oct. 1974, defeating George Foreman in Zaire; lost title to Leon Spinks 1978, regained title from Spinks 1978; 56 victories in 61 fights up to Dec. 1981; lost to Larry Holmes Oct. 1980; mem. of U.S. Black Muslim movement; Special Envoy of Pres. Carter to Africa 1980 (to urge boycott of Olympic Games), of Pres. Bush to Iraq 1990 (prior to Operation Desert Storm); lit Olympic flame, Atlanta 1996; fmr. mem. Peace Corps Advisory Council; named Messenger of Peace, UN; Athlete of the Century, GQ Magazine; Lifetime Achievement Award, Amnesty Int.; acted in films The Greatest 1976, Freedom Road 1980 and in Freedom Road (television) 1978; Hon. Consul-Gen. for Bangladesh in Chicago Feb. 1978. *Publications:* The Greatest: My Own Story (autobiography) 1975, Healing (with Thomas Hauser) 1996. *Address:* P.O. Box 160, Berrien Springs, MI 49103, U.S.A.

ALI, Sadiq, B.A.; Indian politician; b. 1910, Udaipur, Rajasthan; s. of Shri Tahir Ali; m. Shrimati Shanti Sadiq Ali 1951; ed. Allahabad Univ; associated with Indian freedom movement 1930; Perm. Sec. All-India Congress Cttee. 1938–47; mem. Lok Sabha 1951–52, Rajya Sabha 1958–70; Gen. Sec. Indian Nat. Congress 1958–64, 1966–69; Pres. Opposition Congress Party 1971–73; Chief Ed. AICC Econ. Review 1960–69; Chair. Gandhi Nat. Museum and Library, New Delhi 1965–, Cen. Gandhi Smarak Nidhi 1991–; Gov. of Maharashtra 1977–80, of Tamil Nadu 1980–82; Chair. Gandhi Nat. Museum and Library, New Delhi 1965. *Publications:* Know Your Country, Congress Ideology and Programme, Culture of India, General Election 1957, Towards Socialist Thinking in Congress, Campaign Against Nuclear Arms. *Address:* A-23/139 Lodhi Colony, New Delhi 110003, India.

ALI, Saleh Ahmad al-; D.PHIL.; Iraqi professor of history; b. 1918, Mosul; m. Aida al-Ali 1954; two s. five d.; ed. High Teachers' Coll., Baghdad, Univs. of Cairo and Oxford; lecturer, then Asst. Prof., then Prof. 1949–; Head, Dept. of History, Coll. of Arts, Baghdad 1956–58; Dean, Inst. of Higher Islamic Studies, Baghdad 1964–68; Chief, Centre of Arabic Heritage Studies, Baghdad 1979–82; Pres. Iraqi Acad. 1978; Fuad Jalal Prize (Cairo). *Publications:* Social and Economic Organization in Basrah, Lectures on Arabic History, Extension of the Arabs, Studies in the Development of Arabic Thought and numerous articles. *Address:* c/o Iraqi Academy, Waziriyah, Baghdad, Iraq. *Telephone:* 25026 (Baghdad); 5511385.

ALI, Zine El Abidene ben; Tunisian politician; b. 3 Sept. 1936, Hammam Sousse; m.; three c.; ed. as graduate in electronics, Saint-Cyr Military Acad. (France), Chalons-sur-Marne School of Artillery (France), Special School of Intelligence and Security (U.S.A.); Head of Mil. Security 1958–74; Mil. and Naval Attaché, Rabat, Morocco 1974–77; mem. of Cabinet for Minister of Nat. Defence, Dir.-Gen. Nat. Security 1977–80; Amb. to Poland 1980–84; Sec. of State for Nat. Security 1984–85, Minister of the Interior 1986–87, Minister of State for the Interior May-Nov. 1987, Pres. of Tunisia Nov. 1987–; mem. politbureau of Parti Socialiste Destourien (PSD) 1986, Sec.-Gen. PSD 1986; Order of Merit of Bourguiba, Order of Independence, Order of the Repub., several foreign orders. *Address:* Présidence de la République, Tunis, Tunisia.

ALI SAMATER, Gen. Mohammed; Somali politician and army officer; b. 1931, Chisimaio; ed. Intermediate School, Mogadishu, Mil. Acad., Rome, Mil. Acad., Moscow; Commdt. Somali Police 1956, Maj.-Adjutant 1958–65; Brig.-Gen. Nat. Army 1967, Maj.-Gen. 1973; Sec. of State for Defence 1971–76, C.-in-C. Armed Forces 1971–78; fmr. Vice-Pres. Political Bureau, Somali Socialist Revolutionary Party; Minister of Defence 1976–81, 1982–89; First Vice-Pres. Supreme Revolutionary Council (now Council of Ministers) 1982–90; Prime Minister of Somalia 1987–90; Chair. Defence and Security Cttee., Supreme Council of the Revolution 1980–82, Vice-Pres. of Council 1981–82.

ALIA, Ramiz; Albanian politician; b. 1925, Shkodër; m. Semiram Alia; active in 1939–45 war; mem. of political shock 7th brigade; political leader 2nd Div.; fought in Yugoslavia at Kosova, Metohia, Sandjak, Political Commissar of the 5th Div.; First Sec. Cen. Cttee. Communist Youth –1955; Minister of Educ.; mem. of the Cen. Cttee. CP since the 1st Congress; since 4th Congress mem. of the Politburo, Sec. Cen. Cttee. CP, First Sec. April 1985–92; Vice-Chair. of the Gen. Council of the Democratic Front of Albania; Deputy to People's Ass. from 2nd Legislature; Pres. Presidium of People's Ass. (Head of State) 1982–92; under house arrest, imprisoned Aug. 1993; sentenced to nine years' imprisonment for abuse of power and violation of citizens' rights July 1994, released July 1995; acquitted of charges of genocide and crimes against humanity Oct. 1997.

ALIER, Abel, LL.B., LL.M.; Sudanese politician; b. 1933, Bor District, Upper Nile Province; s. of Kwai and Anaai Alier; m. Siama Fatma Bilal 1970; one d.; ed. Univs. of Khartoum and Yale; former advocate; District Judge in El Obeid, Wad Medani and Khartoum until 1965; participant in Round Table Conf. and mem. Twelve Man Cttee. to Study the Southern problem 1965; mem. Constitution Comms. 1966–67, 1968; fmr. mem. Law Reform Comm. and Southern Front; Minister of Supply and Internal Trade 1969–70; Minister of Works 1970–71; Minister of Southern Affairs 1971–72, of Construction and Public Works 1983–85; Vice-Pres. 1971–82; Pres. Supreme Exec. Council for the South 1972–78, 1980–81; mem. Political Bureau, Sudanese Socialist Union, Bd. of Dirs., Industrial Planning Corpn.; mem. Nat. Scholarship Bd.; Hon. LL.D. (Khartoum) 1978. *Leisure interests:* tennis, athletics, reading, history and literature. *Address:* c/o Ministry of Construction and Public Works, Sudan.

ALIMOV, Rashid; Tajikistan politician; b. 1953; m.; two c.; ed. Tajik Univ.; chair. trade union cttee. Tajik Univ. 1975–77; head of group of lecturers Cen. Comsomol Cttee. of Tajik S.S.R., instructor regional and city CP Cttees. Dushanbe; mem. div. of propaganda, First Sec. Frunze regional cttee. of Tajikistan CP 1988–89, Second Sec. Dushanbe City CP Cttee. 1989; Chair. Comm. on Problems of Youth, Supreme Soviet of Tajikistan 1989–91; State Counsellor to fmr. Pres. Nabiyev 1990–92; Minister of Foreign Affairs of Tajikistan 1992–94; Perm Rep. to UN 1994–. *Address:* Permanent Mission of Tajikistan to the United Nations, 136 East 67th Street, New York, NY 10021, U.S.A.; c/o Ministry of Foreign Affairs, Dushanbe, Tajikistan.

ALIMOV, Timur; Uzbekistan politician; b. 1936; ed. Tashkent Inst. of Irrigation Engineering and Agric. Mechanisation; engineer on construction of channel in Afghanistan 1960–62; senior engineer, Uzgiprovodkhoz 1962–65; senior engineer, Dir. of Tashkent reservoir div. 1965–67; mem. of CPSU 1967–91; Head of section of water supply and irrigation with Uzbek S.S.R. Council of Mins. 1967–75; Man., Uzbek S.S.R. Council of Ministers 1975–78; Pres. of Tashkent Exec. Cttee. of Uzbek CP. 1978–85; First Sec. of Tashkent Exec. Cttee. of Uzbek CP. 1985–91; Cand. mem. of CPSU Cen. Cttee. 1986–90; Adviser to the Pres. of Uzbekistan 1991–. *Address:* Office of the President, Uzbekistansky Prosp. 43, 700163, Tashkent, Uzbekistan. *Telephone:* (9932) 995746.

ALIMPIY (Alexander Kapitonovich Gusev); Russian ecclesiastic; b. 31 July 1929, Nizhny Novgorod; worked as fireman, served in army, was house-painter, stoker; ordained as deacon of Russian Old Belief Church 1967; deacon Old Belief Church in Gorky (now Nizhny Novgorod) 1967–86; elected Archbishop of Moscow and of All Russia on Ecumenical Council of Old Belief Church 1987; elected the First Old Belief Metropolitan of All Russia 1988. *Address:* Russian Old Belief Church Society, Pokrovsky Cathedral Church, Rogozksky pos. 29, Moscow, Russia. *Telephone:* (095) 361-5190.

ALINGTON, William Hildebrand, M.ARCH.; New Zealand architect; b. 18 Nov. 1929, Wellington; s. of Edward Hugh Alington and Beatrice McCrie Alington; m. Margaret Hilda Broadhead 1955; one s. two d.; ed. Hutt Valley High School, School of Architecture, Auckland Univ. Coll., School of Architecture Univ. of Illinois; architectural cadet and architect Head Office Ministry of Works, Wellington 1950–65; architect London Office Robert Matthew & Johnson-Marshall 1956–57; partner Gabites & Beard 1965–71, Gabites Toomath Beard Wilson & Partners 1971–72, Gabites Alington & Edmondson 1972–79, Gabites Porter & Partners 1978–83; Sr. Partner Alington Group Architects 1984–; Asst. Ed. NZIA Journal 1964–69; Pres. Architectural Centre 1970–72; Hon. lecturer Victoria Univ. of Wellington School of Architecture 1975–85, Tutor 1986–92; Vice-Pres. and Branch Chair. N.Z.I.A. 1977–79, mem. Council 1965–79; mem. Wellington Anglican Diocesan Synod 1972–90; major works include: Meteorological Office, Gisborne Courthouse, Upper Hutt Civic Centre, Massey Univ. Halls of Residence, VUW School of Music, Karori Baptist Church, St. Mary's Church Extension, New Plymouth. *Publications:* numerous articles in specialist journals. *Leisure interests:* gardening, painting, church government. *Address:* 60 Homewood Crescent, Wellington, New Zealand. *Telephone:* (04) 476 8495.

ALIYEV, Maj.-Gen. Heydar Alirza oglu; Azerbaijan politician; b. 10 May 1923, Nakhichevan; s. of Alirza Aliyev and Izzat Aliyeva; m. Zarifa Aziz gizi Aliyeva (died 1985); one s. one d.; ed. Inst. of Industry, Baku, Azerbaijan State Univ.; mem. CPSU 1945–91; official of security forces and mem. Council of Ministers of Nakhichevan Autonomous Republic 1941–49; on staff of Ministry of Foreign Affairs and Cttee. of State Security (KGB) of Azerbaijan S.S.R. 1949; Deputy Chair. KGB Azerbaijan S.S.R. 1964–67; rank of Maj.-Gen.; Cand. mem. Cen. Cttee. of CP of Azerbaijan (CPA) S.S.R. 1966–69, mem. Cen. Cttee. CPA 1969, mem. Bureau 1969, First Sec. Cen. Cttee. 1969–82; mem. Cen. Cttee. CPSU 1971–89, mem. Politburo of Cen. Cttee. CPSU 1976–87; Deputy to U.S.S.R. Supreme Soviet 1970–89, Vice Chair. Council of Union 1974–79; First Deputy Chair. U.S.S.R Council of Ministers

1982–87, retd. 1987; resumed political activities 1992, Chair. New Azerbaijan Party 1992–93, elected to Supreme Medjlis of Nakhichevan Autonomous Republic 1992; mem. and Vice Chair. Supreme Soviet of Azerbaijan Repub. 1992, Chair. Aug. 1993; Pres. of Azerbaijan Repub. Oct. 1993–; Hero of Socialist Labour (twice); Hon. mem. Int. Acad. of Architecture of Eastern Countries 1994; Dr. h.c. (Baku State Univ.) 1994, (Hojjat-Tapa Univ., Ankara) 1994. *Publications:* over 300 speeches, articles and books published on social, cultural, economic and political subjects. *Leisure interests:* paintings, poetry, sport. *Address:* Office of the President of the Republic of Azerbaijan, 19 Istiglaliyyat Str., 370001 Baku, Azerbaijan. *Telephone:* (8922) 92-88-54. *Fax:* 98 33 28; 98 08 02.

ALLADAYE, Lieut.-Col. Michel; Benin army officer; b. 1940, Abomey; m.; five c.; ed. Lycée Victor Ballot, Ecole Mil. de Saint-Cyr, Ecole Supérieure Technique du Génie, Versailles; Commdr. 1st Eng. Corps, Dahomey Armed Forces, Kandi 1963–67; promoted to rank of Capt. 1967; worked successively in Eng. Unit, Army Gen. Staff Command, Services Battalion Command; Commdr., Dir. Mil. Engs.; Minister of Foreign Affairs 1972–80, of Co-operation 1976–80, of Legislation and Social Affairs 1980–82, of Justice 1980–83; Vice-Pres. Parti de la Révolution Populaire du Bénin Defense and Security Comm. 1985; Chevalier, Légion d'honneur. *Address:* c/o Ministère de Justice, Cotonou, Benin.

ALLAIS, Maurice; French economist and engineer; b. 31 May 1911, Paris; s. of Maurice and Louise (Caubet) Allais; m. Jacqueline Bouteloup 1960; one d.; ed. Ecole Polytechnique and Ecole Nat. Supérieure des Mines de Paris; Dept. of Mines and Quarries 1937–43; Dir. Bureau de Documentation Minière 1943–48; econ. research 1948–70; Prof. of Economic Analysis, Ecole Nat. Supérieure des Mines de Paris 1944–88; Prof. of Econ. Theory, Inst. of Statistics, Univ. of Paris 1947–68; Dir. of Research, Centre Nat. de la Recherche Scientifique 1954–80; Dir. Centre for Econ. Analysis 1946–; Prof. Graduate Inst. of Int. Studies, Geneva 1967–70; Dir. Séminaire Clément Juglar d'Analyse Monétaire, Univ. of Paris-X (Nanterre) 1970–85; Foreign Assoc. mem. U.S. Nat. Acad. of Sciences; mem. Acad. des Sciences Morales et Politiques; Dr. h.c. (Groningen), Mons, American Univ. of Paris, Lisbon, Hautes Etudes Commerciales, Paris; numerous honorary doctorates from European and American Univs.; Lanchester Prize, American Soc. for Operations Research, Gold Medal, Société d'Encouragement pour l'Industrie Nationale, Gold Medal, Centre National de la Recherche Scientifique 1978, Prix Robert Blanché, Grand Prix Zerilli Marimó, Académie des Sciences Morales et Politiques, Nobel Prize for Econ. Sciences 1988 and other awards; Hon. Ingénieur Général au Corps des Mines; Commdr. Légion d'honneur, Officier Palmes académiques, Chevalier Ordre de l'Economie Nationale, Grand Officier, Ordre Nat. du Mérite. *Publications include:* A la Recherche d'un Discipline Economique 1943, Abondance ou misère 1946, Economie et intérêt 1947, Traité d'économie pure 1952, La gestion des houillères nationalisées et la théorie économique 1953, Les fondements comptables de la macroéconomique 1954, Le pendule paraconique 1957–59, Manifeste pour une société libre 1958, L'Europe unie, route de la prospérité 1960, Le Tiers-Monde au carrefour—Centralisation autoritaire ou planification concurrentielle 1962, L'Algérie d'Evian 1962, The Role of Capital in Economic Development 1963, Reformulation de la théorie quantitative de la monnaie 1965, L'Impôt sur le capital 1966, The Conditions of the Efficiency in the Economy 1967, Growth without Inflation 1968, Growth and Inflation 1969, La libéralisation des relations économiques internationales 1970, Les théories de l'équilibre économique général et de l'efficacité maximale 1971, Forgetfulness and Interest 1972, The General Theory of Surplus and Pareto's Fundamental Contribution 1973, Inequality and Civilization 1973, La création de monnaie et de pouvoir d'achat par le mécanisme du crédit 1974, The Psychological Rate of Interest 1974, L'inflation française et la croissance 1974, Classes sociales et civilisations 1974, Taux d'expansion de la dépense globale et vitesse de circulation de la monnaie 1975, Inflation répartition des revenus et indexation 1976, L'impôt sur le capital et la réforme monétaire 1977, Expected Utility Hypotheses and the Allais Paradox 1979, La théorie générale des surplus 1980, Frequency, Probability and Chance 1982, The Foundations of the Theory of Utility and Risk 1984, Determination of Cardinal Utility 1985, The Concepts of Surplus and Loss and the Reformulation of the Theories of Stable General Economic Equilibrium and Maximum Efficiency 1985, The Empirical Approaches of the Hereditary and Relativistic Theory of the Demand for Money 1985, Les conditions monétaires d'une économie de marchés 1987, Pour l'Indexation; Pour la Réforme de la Fiscalité 1990, L'Europe Face à son Avenir 1991, Erreurs et Impasse de la Construction Européenne 1992, Cardinalism 1994, Combats pour l'Europe 1994, l'Anisotropie de l'espace 1997. *Leisure interests:* history, physics, swimming, skiing. *Address:* 60 boulevard Saint Michel, 75006 Paris (Office); 15 rue des Gâtes-Ceps, 92210 Saint-Cloud, France (Home).

ALLAN, Alexander Claud Stuart, M.A., M.SC.; British civil servant and diplomatist; b. 9 Feb. 1951; s. of late Lord Allan of Kilmahew and of Maureen Catherine Flower Stuart-Clark; m. Katie Christine Clemson 1978; ed. Harrow School, Clare Coll., Cambridge, Univ. Coll., London; with H.M. Customs and Excise 1973–76, H.M. Treasury 1976–92, Prin. Pvt. Sec. to Chancellor of the Exchequer 1986–89; secondments in Australia 1983–84; Under Sec. for Int. Finance 1989–90, for Public Expenditure Policy, 1990–92; Prin. Pvt. Sec. to the Prime Minister 1992–97; High Commr. in Australia 1997–. *Leisure interests:* sailing, Grateful Dead music, computers, bridge. *Address:* British High Commission, Commonwealth Avenue, Yarralumla, A.C.T. 2600, Australia. *Telephone:* 6270-6666.

ALLAN, Andrew Norman, B.A., F.R.T.S.; British television executive; b. 26 Sept. 1943, Newcastle upon Tyne; s. of Andrew Allan and Elizabeth Allan (née Davidson); m. Joanna Forrest 1978; two s. one d. and two d. from previous m.; ed. Birmingham Univ.; presenter, ABC Television 1965–66; producer, Thames TV 1966–69, 1971–75; Head of News 1976–78; producer, ITN 1970; Dir. of Programmes, Tyne Tees TV 1978–83, Deputy Man. Dir. 1982–83, Man. Dir. 1983–84; Dir. of Programes, Cen. Ind. TV 1984–90, Man. Dir. 1993–94; Man. Dir. Cen. Broadcasting 1990–93; Chief Exec. Carlton TV 1994–95, Dir. of Programmes 1996–98. *Leisure interests:* reading, dining. *Address:* Wardington Lodge, Wardington, Banbury, Oxon., OX17 1SE, England.

ALLARDT, Erik Anders, M.A., PH.D.; Finnish university chancellor and professor of sociology; b. 9 Aug. 1925, Helsinki; s. of Arvid Allardt and Marita (née Heikel) Allardt; m. Sagi Nylander 1947; one s. two d.; ed. Univ. of Helsinki; Prof. of Sociology, Univ. of Helsinki 1958–85, Dean of the Faculty of Social Sciences 1969–70; Pres. Acad. of Finland 1986–91; Chancellor of the Åbo Acad. Univ. 1992–94; mem. European Science Foundation Exec. Council 1987–92, Vice-Pres. 1990–92; mem. bd. Scandinavia—Japan Sasakawa Foundation 1987–96; Founder mem. Academia Europaea 1988–; Fellow, Woodrow Int. Center for Scholars 1978–79; Visiting Prof. numerous countries and univs.; Hon. Dr. (Stockholm) 1978, (Åbo Akademi) 1978, (Uppsala) 1984, (Bergen) 1996. *Publications:* (with Rokkan) Mass Politics: Studies in Political Sociology 1970, Implications of the Ethnic Revival in Modern, Industrialized Society 1979, (with Lysgaard and Sørensen) Sociologin i Sverige, vetenskap, miljö och organisation 1988, The History of the Social Sciences in Finland 1997. *Address:* Unionsgatan 45B 40, HFIN00170 Helsinki, Finland. *Telephone:* 358-9-135-45-50. *Fax:* 358-9-135-29-26.

ALLCHIN, Frank Raymond, PH.D., F.B.A., F.S.A.; British university lecturer; b. 9 July 1923, Harrow; s. of Frank MacDonald Allchin and Louise Maude Wright; m. Bridget Gordon 1951; one s. one d.; ed. Regent Street Polytechnic School of Architecture and S.O.A.S., London; Lecturer in Indian Archaeology, S.O.A.S. 1954–59; Lecturer in Indian Studies, Cambridge 1959–72, Reader 1972–90, Emer. Reader 1990–; Fellow of Churchill Coll., Cambridge 1963–; Jt. Dir. British Archaeological Mission to Pakistan 1975–92; Dir. British Anuradhapura Project, Sri Lanka 1989–93; Jt. Founding Trustee, Ancient India and Iran Trust 1978–, Chair. 1996–. *Publications:* Co-author: The Birth of Indian Civilization 1968, The Rise of Civilization in India and Pakistan 1982, The Archaeology of Early Historic South Asia 1995, Origins of a Civilization. *Leisure interests:* walking, gardening. *Address:* 2 Shepreth Road, Barrington, Cambridge, CB2 5SB; 23 Brooklands Avenue, Cambridge, CB2 2BG, England. *Telephone:* (01223) 870494 (Shepreth Road); (01223) 356841 (Brooklands Avenue). *Fax:* (01223) 361125 (Brooklands Avenue).

ALLÈGRE, Claude Jean; French politician; b. 31 March 1937, Paris, France; s. of Prof. Roger Allègre and Lucette (née Hugoueneq) Allègre; m. Claude Blanche Simon 1967; three s. one d.; ed. Lycées Saint-Maur and Saint-Louis, Faculté des sciences, Paris; Asst. Univ. de Paris 1962–68; Dir. of Lab. of Geochemistry and Cosmochemistry Univ. de Paris VI and VII 1967–; Asst. Physician Inst. de physique du globe 1968–70, Dir. 1976–86; Prof. of Earth Sciences Univ. de Paris VII 1970–; Prof. of Earth Sciences Inst. of Tech., Mass. 1975–76; Special Adviser to Lionel Jospin 1988–92; M.E.P. 1989; Minister of Nat. Educ., Research and Tech. 1997–; Pres. admin council of Bureau de recherches géologiques et minières 1992–97; mem. of numerous socs.; Hon. mem. Union européenne de géosciences, European Biophysical Soc., Acad. of Arts and Sciences, Boston Philosophical Soc.; Foreign mem. Nat. Acad. of Sciences, U.S.A.; Crafoord Prize (Sweden) 1986; Officier, Légion d'honneur, Chevalier des Palmes académiques; numerous medals. *Publications include:* L'Ecume de la Terre 1983, De la Pierre à l'Etoile 1985, Les Fureurs de la Terre 1987, Economiser la Planète 1990, Introduction à une Histoire Naturelle 1992, L'Age des Savoires 1993, Ecologie des Villes, Ecologie des Champs 1993, L'Etat de la Planète 1994, La Défaite de Platon 1995, Questions de France 1996. *Address:* Ministère de l'Education nationale, de la Recherche et de la Technologie, 110 rue de Grenelle, 75700 Paris; Institut de physique du globe, 4 place Jussieu, 75005 Paris, France.

ALLÈGRE, Maurice Marie, L. EN D.; French research co-ordinator; b. 16 Feb. 1933, Antibes; s. of Guy Allègre and Renée-Lise Bermond; m. Catherine Pierre 1962; one s. one d.; ed. Ecole Polytechnique, Ecole nat. supérieure des Mines and Ecole nat. supérieure du pétrole et des moteurs; Researcher Direction des Carburants, Ministry of Industry 1957–62; Dir. Mines de l'Organisme Saharien 1962–64; Tech. Adviser to Ministry of Finance and Econ. Affairs 1965–67; Pres. Inst. de Recherche d'informatique et d'automatique 1968–74; Chief of Mission to New Caledonia 1975; Asst. Dir.-Gen. Inst. Français du Pétrole 1976–81; Pres. and Dir.-Gen. ISIS 1976–81; Pres. FRANLAB, COFLEXIP 1976–81, ANDRA (Nat. Radioactive Waste Man. Agency) 1993–98; Pres. Agence nat. de valorisation et de la Recherche (ANVAR) 1982–84; Dir. Scientific and Tech. Devt., Ministry of Research and Tech. 1982–84; Dir.-Gen. Bureau de Recherches Géologiques et Minières 1984–88, Pres. 1988–92. *Leisure interests:* photography, skiing, sailing. *Address:* 85 rue de Sèvres, 75006 Paris; 50 boulevard d'Aiguillon, 06600 Antibes, France.

ALLEN, Sir Douglas Albert Vivian, G.C.B. (see Croham, Baron).

ALLEN, Gary James, C.B.E., D.L., B.COM., F.C.M.A., C.B.I.M., F.R.S.A.; British business executive; b. 30 Sept. 1944, Birmingham; s. of Alfred Allen; m. Judith A. Nattrass 1966; three s.; ed. King Edward VI Grammar School, Aston, Birmingham and Liverpool Univ.; Man. Dir. IMI Range Ltd. 1973–77; Dir. IMI plc 1978–, Man. Dir. 1986–, also C.E.O.; Dir. (non-exec.) N. V. Bekaert SA, Belgium 1987–, Marley plc 1989–97 (Deputy Chair. 1993–97), Birmingham European Airways Ltd. 1989–91, The London Stock Exchange Ltd. 1994–; Chair. Optilon Ltd. 1979–84, Eley Ltd. 1981–85; mem. Nat. Council CBI 1986–; mem. Council, Birmingham Chamber of Industry and Commerce 1983–, Pres. 1991–92, mem. Bd. 1994–96; mem. Council Univ. of Birmingham 1985–90 and Hon. Life mem. Court 1984–; mem. Bd. Birmingham Royal Ballet 1993–; Pres. Midlands Club Cricket Conf. 1995–96; mem. Council Lord's Taverners 1995–. *Leisure interests:* sport, reading. *Address:* IMI plc, P.O. Box 216, Birmingham, B6 7BA, England (Office). *Telephone:* 0121-356 4848 (Office). *Fax:* 0121-356 7916 (Office).

ALLEN, Sir Geoffrey, Kt., PH.D., F.R.S., F.INST.P., F.P.R.I.; British polymer scientist and administrator; b. 29 Oct. 1928, Clay Cross, Derbyshire; s. of John James and Marjorie Allen; m. Valerie Frances Duckworth 1972; one d.; ed. Clay Cross Tupton Hall Grammar School, Univ. of Leeds; Postdoctoral Fellow, Nat. Research Council, Canada 1952–54; Lecturer, Univ. of Manchester 1955–65, Prof. of Chemical Physics 1965–75; Prof. of Polymer Science, Imperial Coll. of Science and Tech., Univ. of London 1975–76, of Chemical Tech. 1976–81, Fellow Imperial Coll. 1986; Exec. Adviser Kobe Steel Ltd. 1990–; Chair. Science Research Council 1977–81; Head of Research, Unilever PLC 1981–90, Dir. of Unilever responsible for Research and Eng. 1982–90, Non-Exec. Dir. Courtaulds 1987–93; Pres. PRI 1990–92; mem. Nat. Consumer Council 1993–; Vice-Pres. Royal Soc. 1991–93; Chancellor Univ. of E. Anglia 1994–; a Visiting Fellow, Robinson Coll., Cambridge 1980–; Hon. M.Sc. (Manchester); Dr h.c. (Open Univ.); Hon. D.Sc. (Durham) 1984, (Bath, Bradford, Keele, Loughborough) 1985, (Essex, Leeds) 1986, (Cranfield) 1988, (Surrey) 1989. *Leisure interests:* opera, walking, talking. *Address:* Kobe Steel Ltd., Alton House, 174 High Holborn, London, WC1V 7AA, England. *Telephone:* 0171-836 1225. *Fax:* 0171-240 7460.

ALLEN, John Frank, M.SC., M.A., PH.D., F.R.S., F.R.S.E; British professor of physics; b. 6 May 1908, Winnipeg, Canada; s. of Prof. Frank Allen and Sarah (née Harper) Allen; m. Elfriede Hiebert 1933 (divorced 1947); one adopted s.; ed. Univ. of Manitoba, Univ. of Toronto, Calif. Inst. of Tech. Univ. of Cambridge; with Ministry of Supply 1939–44; Lecturer and Fellow, St. John's Coll., Cambridge 1944–47; Prof. of Natural Philosophy, Univ. of St. Andrews 1947–78, Prof. Emer. 1978–. *Films:* Superfluid Helium 1983, The Meissner Effect 1985, The Standing Soliton 1986. *Publications:* numerous articles on low temperature research. *Address:* 2 Shorehead, St. Andrews, Fife, KY16 9RG, Scotland. *Telephone:* (01334) 472717.

ALLEN, John Robert Lawrence, D.SC., F.R.S., F.G.S., F.S.A.; British professor of sedimentology; b. 25 Oct. 1932; s. of George Eustace Allen and Alice Josephine (née Formby); m. Jean Mary Wood 1960; four s. one d.; ed. St. Philip's Grammar School, Birmingham, Univ. of Sheffield; mem. staff, Univ. of Reading 1959–, Prof. of Geology 1972–89, of Sedimentology 1989–93, Research Prof. Postgrad. Research Inst. for Sedimentology 1993–, Hon. Research Fellow in Archaeology; assoc. mem. Royal Belgian Acad. of Sciences; Hon. LL.D.; Lyell Medal, Geological Soc. 1980, David Linton Award, British Geomorphological Research Group 1983, Twenhofel Medal, Soc. of Econ. Paleontologists and Minerologists 1987, G.K. Warren Prize, N.A.S., U.S.A. 1990, Sorby Medal, Int. Asscn. of Sedimentologists 1994, Penrose Medal, Geological Soc. of America 1996. *Publications:* Current Ripples 1968, Physical Processes of Sedimentation 1970, Sedimentary Structures 1982, Principles of Physical Sedimentology 1985; numerous contribs. to professional journals. *Leisure interests:* music, opera, pottery, walking. *Address:* 17c Whiteknights Road, Reading, Berks., RG6 7BY, England. *Telephone:* (01189) 264621.

ALLEN, John Walter, M.A., F.R.S.E.; British physicist; b. 7 March 1928, Birmingham; s. of Walter Allen and Beryl Parsons; m. 1st Mavis Williamson 1956 (died 1972); m. 2nd Hania Szawelska 1981; one s.; ed. King Edward's School, Birmingham and Sidney Sussex Coll., Cambridge; R.A.F. Educ. Br. 1949–51; staff scientist, Ericsson Telephones, Nottingham 1951–56; Royal Naval Scientific Service, Services Electronics Research Lab. 1956–68; Visiting Prof. Stanford Univ. 1964–66; Tullis Russell Fellow, Univ. of St. Andrews 1968–72, Reader in Physics, Dir. of Wolfson Inst. of Luminescence 1972–81, Prof. of Solid State Physics 1981–. *Publications:* some 100 papers in scientific journals including the first account of a practical light-emitting diode. *Leisure interests:* archaeology, traditional dance. *Address:* Department of Physics and Astronomy, University of St. Andrews, North Haugh, St. Andrews, Fife, Scotland. *Telephone:* (01334) 463331.

ALLEN, Gen. Lew, Jr., M.S., PH.D.; American air force officer; b. 30 Sept. 1925, Miami; s. of the late Lew Allen and Zella Holman; m. Barbara McKelden Frink 1949; two s. three d.; ed. Gainesville Junior Coll., U.S. Mil. Acad. West Point, Air Tactical School Tyndall, Univ. of Illinois; Pilot, Carswell Air Force Base, Tex. 1946–50; Physicist, Los Alamos Scientific Laboratory, N.M. 1954–57; various posts Kirkland Air Force Base, N.M. 1957–61; Space Tech. Office and OSD, Washington, D.C. 1961–65; OSAF, Los Angeles, Calif. 1965–68; OSAF Washington, D.C. 1968–70; OSAF, Los Angeles, Calif. 1970–71; SAMSO, Los Angeles, Calif. 1971–73; c/s, HQ AFSC, Andrews Air Force Base, Md. 1973; Deputy to Dir. of Cen. Intelligence for the Intelligence Community 1973; Dir. NSA and Chief of Cen. Security Service, Fort Meade, Md. 1973–77; Commdr., AFSC, Andrews Air Force Base 1977–78; Vice-Chief of Staff USAF April-June 1978, Chief of Staff USAF 1978–82; Dir. Jet Propulsion Lab., Pasadena, Calif. 1982–90; Chair. Draper Lab., Boston 1991–95; mem. Nat. Acad. of Eng. 1977–; Defense Distinguished Service Medal, Distinguished Service Medal of the Air Force, Legion of Merit with 2 Oak Leaf Clusters, Joint Service Commendation and various other U.S. awards and medals, Order of Nat. Security (Repub. of Korea). *Leisure interests:* racquet ball, scuba diving, jogging. *Address:* c/o Draper Charles Stark Laboratory Inc., 555 Technology Square, Cambridge, MA 02139, U.S.A. *Telephone:* (818) 354-3405.

ALLEN, Mary; British arts administrator and fmr. actress; b. 22 Aug. 1951, London; d. of Fergus Allen and Joan Allen; m. 1st Robin Woodhead 1980 (dissolved 1990); m. 2nd Nigel Pantling 1991; appearances include The Rocky Horror Show; Man. Watermans Arts Centre, London; Deputy Sec. Gen. Arts Council of England 1992–94, Sec. Gen. 1994–97; Chief Exec. Royal Opera House, London 1997–98. *Publication:* A House Divided 1998. *Leisure interests:* gardening, cooking, theatre, collecting contemporary art. *Address:* 79 Aberdeen Road, London, N5 2XA, England. *Telephone:* 0171-226 5120.

ALLEN, Paul; American computer executive; ed. Washington State Univ.; co-f. Microsoft Corpn. 1975, Exec. Vice-Pres. 1975–83, also Dir.; f. Asymetrix Corpn. 1985–; f., Chair. Intervas Research; owner and Chair. Bd. Portland Trail Blazers (Ore.) 1988–; Dir. Egghead Discount Software, Darwin Molecular Inc.; fmrly. owner, Chair., Dir. Ticketmaster Holdings Group; currently Chair. Vulcan Northwest Inc. *Address:* The Paul Allen Group, Suite 530, 110 110th Avenue North East, Bellevue, WA 98004, U.S.A.

ALLEN, Percival, PH.D., F.R.S.; British geologist; b. 15 March 1917, Brede, Sussex; s. of the late Norman Williams Allen and Mildred Kathleen Allen (née Hoad); m. Frances Margaret Hepworth 1941; three s. one d.; ed. Rye Grammar School, Univ. of Reading; served in R.A.F. 1941–42; Asst. Lecturer Univ. of Reading 1945–46; Univ. Demonstrator, Univ. of Cambridge 1946–47, Lecturer 1947–52; Prof. of Geology, Univ. of Reading 1952–82, Emer. Prof. of Geology 1982–; Sec. Philpots Quarry Ltd.; Dean of Science Faculty, Univ. of Reading 1963–66; Visiting Prof., Univ. of Kuwait 1970; a Vice-Pres. Royal Soc. 1977–79; Pres. Geological Soc. 1978–80; Adviser UNDP Nile Delta Project 1972–75; Geology Consultant, India, for UNESCO/UNDP 1976–77; Algerian Sahara Glacials Expedition 1970; Tibet Geotraverse Follow-up 1986; Chair. Int. Confs. Organizing Cttees. of Seventh Int. Sedimentology Congress 1967, First European Earth and Planetary Physics Colloquium 1971, First Meeting European Geological Socs. 1975; Sec.-Gen. Int. Assoc. of Sedimentologists 1967–71; Chair. Royal Soc. Expeditions Cttee. 1974–; Royal Soc. Assessor to NERC 1977–80; Chair. Royal Soc., British Nat. Cttee. for Geology 1982–90, British Inst. for Geological Conservation 1987–90; U.K. Corresp. IGCP Project 245, 1986–91; U.K. Del. to Int. Union of Geological Sciences, Moscow 1984; Hon. mem. of Bulgarian Geological Soc., of Geological Asscn., Soc. Econ. Palaeontologists and Mineralogists and of Int. Asscn. of Sedimentologists; Council mem. Natural Environment Research Council 1971–74; Foreign Fellow, Indian Natural Sciences Acad.; Lyell Medal, Geological Soc. of London 1971. *Publications:* Papers on Purbeck-Wealden (Lower Cretaceous) and Torridonian (Proterozoic) sedimentology in various scientific journals from 1938 onwards. *Leisure interests:* chess, natural history, gardening, bicycling. *Address:* Postgraduate Research Institute for Sedimentology, University of Reading, Reading, RG6 6AB; Orchard End, Hazeley Bottom, Hartley Wintney, Hook, Hampshire, RG27 8LU, England. *Telephone:* (0118) 931 6713, ext. 7969 (Office); (01252) 842229 (Home). *Fax:* (01734) 310279.

ALLEN, Richard V.; American international business consultant; b. 1 Jan. 1936, Collingswood, N.J.; s. of C. Carroll Allen Sr. and Magdalen Buchman; m. Patricia Ann Mason 1957; three s. four d.; ed. Notre Dame Univ. and Univ. of Munich; helped found Cen. for Strategic and Int. Studies, Georgetown Univ. 1962; Consultant and fmr. Prof. Hoover Inst., Stanford Univ.; with Nat. Security Council 1968–69; int. business consultant; mem. Ronald Reagan's staff, campaigns 1976, Bd. Govs. Ronald Reagan Presidential Foundation 1985; Pres. Richard V. Allen Co., Washington 1982–90, Chair. 1991–; Head Nat. Security Council and Nat. Security Adviser 1981–82; Chair. Fed. Capital Bank 1987; Sr. Council for Foreign Policy and Nat. Security Affairs, Repub. Nat. Cttee. 1982–88; Bd. Dirs. Xsirius Inc. 1991–92; Distinguished Fellow and Chair. Asian Studies Center, The Heritage Foundation 1982; Chair. German-American Tricentenial Foundation 1983; Founding mem. U.S. Nat. Cttee. for Pacific Basin 1984; Sr. Fellow, Hoover Inst. 1983–; Hon. degrees (Hanover Coll.) 1981, (Korea Univ.) 1982; Order of Diplomatic Merit Ganghwa (Repub. of Korea) 1982, Kt. Commdr.'s Cross (Fed. Repub. of Germany) 1983, Order of Brilliant Star (Repub. of China) 1986, Sovereign Mil. Order of Kts. of Malta 1987. *Publications:* numerous books on political and economic affairs. *Address:* 905 16th Street, N.W., Washington, DC 20006, U.S.A. (Office).

ALLEN, Robert Eugene, B.A., LLD; American communications executive; b. 25 Jan. 1935, Joplin, Mo.; s. of Walter Allen and Frances Patton; m. Elizabeth Pfeffer 1956; two s. three d.; ed. Wabash Coll. and Harvard Business School; Indiana Bell Telephone Co. Inc. Indianapolis 1957–74; Vice-Pres., Gen. Man. Bell Telephone Co. of Pa. 1974–76; Vice-Pres., C.O.O., Dir. Ill. Bell Telephone Co., Philadelphia 1976–78; Vice-Pres. AT&T, Basking

Ridge, N.J. 1978–81; Pres., Chair. Bd. C&P Telephone Cos. Washington, D.C. 1981–83, Exec. Vice-Pres. Corporate Admin. and Finance 1983–84; Chair., C.E.O. AT&T Information Systems, Morristown, N.J. 1985; Pres., C.O.O. AT&T, New York 1986–88, Chair. and C.E.O. 1988–98; mem. Bd. Dirs. Bristol Myers Squibb Co., PepsiCo Inc., Fed. Reserve Bank of New York, etc.; five hon. degrees. *Address:* c/o AT&T International Inc., 32 Avenue of the Americas, New York, NY 10013, U.S.A.

ALLÉN, Sture, D.PHIL; Swedish professor of linguistics; b. 1928, Göteborg; s. of Bror G. Allén and Hanna Johansson; m. Solveig Janson 1954; three c.; ed. Univ. of Göteborg; Asst. Prof. of Scandinavian Philology, Univ. of Göteborg 1965–70, Prof. of Computational Linguistics 1979–93, Pro-Rector 1980–86; Assoc. Prof. of Computational Linguistics, Swedish Humanistic Research Council 1970–72, Prof. 1972–79; Perm. Sec. Swedish Acad. 1986–98; mem. Royal Soc. of Arts and Sciences of Göteborg, Royal Swedish Acad. of Letters, History and Antiquities, Acad. Europae, Royal Swedish Acad. of Eng. Sciences, Norwegian Acad. of Sciences and Letters; mem. Bd. of Dirs., Nobel Foundation 1987–; Hon. mem. Soc. of Swedish Literature in Finland; Coresp. mem. Icelandic Soc. of Sciences; mem. various comms. etc.; Dr. h.c. (Swedish Univ. of Åbo) 1988; several awards and distinctions, including Medal of King of Sweden in the Ribbon of the Order of Seraphim for Eminent Scientific and Cultural Achievements, Gothenburg City Medal (Gold) 1994, Knight Commdr. Order of the White Rose (Finland) 1994; Chester Carlson Research Prize 1988. *Publications:* author and co-author of numerous textbooks, dictionaries, glossaries, etc. *Address:* c/o Språkdata Group, Department of Swedish, University of Göteborg, P.O. Box 200, S-40530 Göteborg, Sweden.

ALLEN, Thomas, C.B.E., F.R.C.M., A.R.C.M.; British opera singer; b. 10 Sept. 1944, Seaham, Co. Durham; s. of Thomas Boaz and Florence Allen; m. 1st Margaret Holley 1968 (divorced 1986); one s.; m. 2nd Jeannie Gordon Lascelles 1988; ed. Robert Richardson Grammar School, Ryhope, Royal Coll. of Music, London; prin. baritone, Welsh Nat. Opera 1969–72, Royal Opera House, Covent Garden 1972–78, Glyndebourne Opera 1973, singing in Die Zauberflöte 1973, Le Nozze di Figaro 1974, Così fan Tutte 1975, Don Giovanni 1977, The Cunning Little Vixen 1977 and Simon Boccanegra, Billy Budd, La Bohème, L'Elisir d'Amore, Faust, Albert Herring, Die Fledermaus, La Traviata, A Midsummer Night's Dream, Beckmesser etc.; Queen's Prize 1967, Gulbenkian Fellow 1968; R.A.M. (Hon.) 1988; Hon. M.A. (Newcastle) 1984, Hon. D.Mus. (Durham) 1988. *Publication:* Foreign Parts: A Singer's Journal 1993. *Leisure interests:* painting, drawing, ornithology, golf, fishing. *Address:* c/o Askonas Holt Limited, Lonsdale Chambers, 27 Chancery Lane, London, WC2A 1PF, England.

ALLEN, Woody (Allen Stewart Konigsberg); American actor, writer, producer and director; b. 1 Dec. 1935, Brooklyn, New York; s. of Martin and Nettie (née Cherry) Konigsberg; m. 1st Harlene Rosen (divorced); m. 2nd Louise Lasser 1966 (divorced 1969); m. 3rd Soon-Yi Previn 1997; one s. by Mia Farrow (q.v.); ed. City Coll. of New York and New York Univ.; made his debut as a performer in 1961 at the Duplex in Greenwich Village; has performed in a variety of nightclubs across the U.S.; produced the play Don't Drink the Water at the Morosco Theater 1966, and at the Broadhurst Theatre 1969; made his Broadway début as Allan Felix in Play it Again, Sam, which he also wrote; play: The Floating Light Bulb 1981. *Films include:* What's New Pussycat? 1965, Casino Royale 1967, What's Up, Tiger Lily? 1967, Take the Money and Run 1969, Bananas 1971, Everything You Always Wanted to Know About Sex 1972, Play it Again, Sam 1972, Sleeper 1973, Love and Death 1976, The Front 1976, Annie Hall 1977, Interiors 1978, Manhattan 1979, Stardust Memories 1980, A Midsummer Night's Sex Comedy 1982, Zelig 1983, Broadway Danny Rose 1984, The Purple Rose of Cairo 1985, Hannah and her Sisters 1985, Radio Days 1987, September 1987, Another Woman 1988, Oedipus Wrecks 1989, Crimes and Misdemeanors 1989, Alice 1990, Scenes from a Mall, Shadows and Fog 1991, Husbands and Wives 1992, Manhattan Murder Mystery 1993, Bullets Over Broadway 1995, Mighty Aphrodite 1995, Everybody Says I Love You, Deconstructing Harry 1997, Celebrity; during the 1950s wrote for television performers Herb Shriner 1953, Sid Caesar 1957, Art Carney 1958–59, Jack Parr and Carol Channing, also wrote for the Tonight Show and the Gary Moore Show; Academy Award for Best Director, and Best Writer for Annie Hall, D.W. Griffith Award 1996. *Publications:* Getting Even 1971, Without Feathers 1975, Side Effects 1980, The Complete Prose 1994, has also contributed to Playboy and New Yorker. *Leisure interests:* chocolate milk shakes, poker, chess and baseball; also a noted clarinettist. *Address:* 930 Fifth Avenue, New York, NY 10021, U.S.A.

ALLENDE, Isabel; Chilean (Peruvian-born) writer; b. 8 Aug. 1942, Lima; d. of Francisca Llona Barros and Tomás Allende; m. 1st Miguel Frias 1962; one s. one d.; m. 2nd William Gordon 1988; journalist for Paula Magazine 1967–74, Mampato Magazine 1969–74; Channel 13 World Hunger Campaign 1964; Channel 7, various humorous programmes 1970–74; Maga-Cine-Ellas 1973; Admin. Marroco School, Caracas 1978–82; freelance journalist El Nacional newspaper, Caracas 1976–83; Visiting Teacher Montclair State Coll., N.J. 1985, Univ. of Virginia, Charlottesville 1988, Univ. of Calif., Berkeley 1989; Writer 1981–; Novel of the Year, Panorama Literario (Chile) 1983; Point de Mire (Belgium) 1985; Author of the Year and Book of the Year (Germany) 1984; Grand Prix d'Evasion (France) 1984; Colima for Best Novel (Mexico) 1985; Author of the Year (Germany) 1986; Mulheres Best Novel (Portugal) 1987; Dorothy and Jillian Gish Prize 1998. *Publications:* (novels) The House of the Spirits 1982, Of Love and Shadows 1984, Eva Luna 1989, Aphrodite 1998. (short stories) Tales of Eva Luna 1990, The Infinite Plan 1992, Paula (memoir) 1995; (children's story) La Gorda de Porcelana 1984. *Address:* 116 Caledonia Street, Sausalito, CA 94965, U.S.A.

ALLENDE, Jorge Eduardo, PH.D.; Chilean biochemist and molecular biologist; b. 11 Nov. 1934, Cartago, Costa Rica; s. of Octavio Allende and Amparo Rivera; m. Catherine C. Connelly 1961; three s. one d.; ed. Louisiana State and Yale Univs., U.S.A.; Research Assoc. Lab. of Prof. Fritz Lipmann at Rockefeller Univ. 1961–62; Asst. Prof. Dept. of Biochemistry, Univ. of Chile 1963–68, Assoc. Prof. 1968–71, Prof. of Biochemistry and Molecular Biology 1972–; Pres. Pan American Asscn. of Biochemical Socs. 1976; mem. Exec. Cttee. Int. Union of Biochemistry 1982–91, Int. Cell Research Org. 1976–; mem. Exec. Bd. Int. Council of Scientific Unions 1986–90; regional co-ordinator Latin American Network of Biological Sciences 1975–; mem. UNESCO Int. Scientific Advisory Bd. 1996–; Foreign Assoc. Inst. of Medicine, N.A.S.; Fogarty Scholar-in-Residence N.I.H., U.S.A.; Fellow Third World Acad. of Sciences; f. mem. Latin American Acad. of Sciences; mem. Chilean Acad. of Sciences, Pres. 1991–94; Hon. mem. Chilean Acad. of Medicine; Dr. h.c. (Buenos Aires) 1993; Chilean Nat. Prize in Natural Sciences 1992. *Publications:* 116 research articles in learned journals. *Leisure interests:* music, reading, swimming. *Address:* Departamento de Bioquímica, Facultad de Medicina, Universidad de Chile, Casilla 70086, Santiago 7, Chile. *Telephone:* (2) 737-6320. *Fax:* (2) 737-6320.

ALLER, Lawrence Hugh, M.A., PH.D.; American astronomer; b. 24 Sept 1913, Tacoma, Wash.; s. of late Leslie E. Aller and late Lena B. Aller; m. Rosalind Duncan Hall 1941; two s. one d.; ed. Univ. of California, Berkeley, and Harvard Univ. Soc. of Fellows, Harvard Univ. 1939–42; Asst. Prof. Indiana Univ. 1945–48; Assoc. Prof. Univ. of Michigan 1948–54, Prof. 1954–62; Prof. of Astronomy, Univ. of Calif., Los Angeles 1962–84, Prof. Emer. 1984–; Visiting Prof. Australian Nat. Univ. 1960–61, Univ. of Toronto 1961–62, Univ. of Sydney 1968, Univ. of Tasmania 1969, Univ. of Queensland 1977–78, Raman Inst., Bangalore 1978, Int. School of Advanced Studies, Trieste 1981, Univ. of S. Calif. 1983–84; Guest Investigator, Mount Wilson Observatory 1946–82; mem. N.A.S.; Fellow, American Acad. of Arts and Sciences; Russell Prize (American Astronomical Soc.) 1992. *Publications:* Atoms, Stars and Nebulae (with Leo Goldberg) 1942, Atmospheres of Sun and Stars 1953, 1963, Nuclear Transformations, Stellar Interiors and Nebulae 1954, Gaseous Nebulae 1956, Abundance of Elements 1961, Physics of Thermal Gaseous Nebulae 1984. *Leisure interests:* photography, travel. *Address:* Physics and Astronomy Department, University of California, Los Angeles, CA 90095 (Office); 18118 W. Kingsport Drive, Malibu, CA 90265, U.S.A. (Home). *Telephone:* (310) 825-3515 (Office); (310) 454-7498. *Fax:* (310) 206-2096.

ALLEST, Frédéric Jean Pierre d'; French engineer; b. 1 Sept. 1940, Marseilles; s. of Pierre and Luce d'Allest; m. Anne-Marie Morel 1963; three s.; ed. Ecole Saint Joseph and Lycée Thiers, Marseilles, Ecole Polytechnique and Ecole Nat. supérieure d'aéronautique; with Centre National d'Etudes Spatiales (CNES) 1966–70, Head of Ariane Project 1973–76, Dir. Ariane Programme 1976–82, Dir.-Gen. CNES 1982–89; with Europa III project, European Launcher Devt. Org. 1970–72; Pres. Soc. Arianespace 1980–90, Matra Transport 1992–, Matra Hachette 1993–; Dir.-Gen. Groupe Matra 1990–93, Groupe Lagardère 1996–; f. Marseille Provence 1988; Officier, Légion d'honneur, Officier ordre national du Mérite; Prix de l'aéronautique, James Watt Prize (Inst. of Mechanical Engineers) 1993. *Leisure interests:* sport, alpinism; *Address:* Groupe Lagardère, 121 ave de Malakoff, 75216 Paris Cedex 16 (Office); 6 rue Marcel Allegot, 92190 Meudon, France (Home).

ALLEY, Col. Alphonse; Benin politician and army officer; b. 9 April 1930, Bassila; s. of Amadou Alley and Amina Akim; m.; six c.; ed. primary schools at Lomé, Togo, secondary school in Senegal, and military colls. in France and Ivory Coast; joined 5th Senegalese Rifle Regt., Dakar; served in Indo-China 1950–53, Morocco 1955–56, Algeria 1959–61; returned to Dahomey 1961; Second-Lieut. Dahomeyan Army 1961, Capt. 1962, Major 1964, Lieut.-Col. 1967, Chief of Staff 1967; Pres. of Dahomey Dec. 1967–68; Sec.-Gen. for Nat. Defence 1970–72; arrested Feb. 1973, sentenced to twenty years' detention, in exile since 1974, granted amnesty 1984. *Leisure interests:* all forms of sport. *Address:* Carré 181–182, B.P. 48, Cotonou, Benin.

ALLEY, Kirstie; American actress; b. Wichita, Kan.; m. Parker Stevenson; one s. one d.; ed. Univ. of Kan.; stage appearances include: Cat on a Hot Tin Roof, Answers; regular TV show Cheers 1987–93, and other appearances in TV films and series. *Films:* Star Trek II, The Wrath of Khan 1982, One More Chance, Blind Date, Champions 1983, Runaway 1984, Summer School 1987, Look Who's Talking Too 1990, Madhouse 1990, Look Who's Talking Now 1993, David's Mother (TV film) 1994, Village of the Damned 1995, It Takes Two 1995, Sticks and Stones 1996, Nevada 1996, For Richer or Poorer 1997, Deconstructing Harry 1997, Toothless 1997. *Address:* Jason Weinberg and Associates, 122 East 25th Street, 2nd Floor, New York, NY 10010, U.S.A.

ALLEYNE, Sir George, Kt., M.D., F.R.C.P.; Barbadian physician; b. 7 Oct. 1932, Barbados; s. of Clinton Alleyne and Eileen (née Gaskin) Alleyne; m. Sylvan I. Chen 1958; two s. one d.; ed. Harrison Coll., Univ. of West Indies; Sr. Resident Univ. Hosp. of W. Indies 1963; Research Fellow Tropical Metabolism Research Unit, Jamaica 1964–72. Prof. of Medicine W. Indies Univ. 1972–81, Chair. Dept. of Medicine 1976–81; Head Research Unit Pan American Health Org. 1981–83, Dir. Health Programmes 1982–90, Asst.

Dir. 1990–95, Dir. 1995–; Hon. D.Sc. (W. Indies Univ.) 1988. *Leisure interests:* gardening, reading. *Publications include:* The Importance of Health: A Caribbean Perspective 1989, Public Health for All 1991, Health and Tourism 1992; over 100 articles in major scientific research journals. *Address:* Pan American Health Organization, 525 23rd Street, N.W., Washington, DC 20037, U.S.A. *Telephone:* (202) 974-3000. *Fax:* 974-3663.

ALLIALI, Camille Zahakro; Côte d'Ivoirian politician, lawyer and diplomatist; b. 23 Nov. 1926; m.; five c.; ed. Dakar Lycée and Lycée Champollion, Grenoble; fmr. Advocate, Court of Appeal, Abidjan; Press Sec. Parti Démocratique de la Côte d'Ivoire 1959, Deputy 1958–60; Vice-Pres. Nat. Ass., Ivory Coast 1957–60; Senator of French Community 1959–61; Amb. to France 1961–63; Perm. Del. UNESCO 1961–63; Minister of Foreign Affairs 1963–66; Minister of Justice 1966–83, Minister of State 1983–89; mem. Cen. Cttee. of Parti démocratique de la Côte d'Ivoire (PDCI); Commdr., Légion d'honneur and many other decorations. *Address:* c/o Parti Démocratique de la Côte d'Ivoire, Maison du Parti, Abidjan, Côte d'Ivoire.

ALLIANCE, Sir David, Kt., C.B.E., C.B.I.M., F.R.S.A.; British business executive; b. June 1932; ed. Iran; first acquisition, Thomas Hoghton (Oswaldtwistle) 1956; acquired Spirella 1968, then Vantona Ltd., 1975 to form Vantona Group 1975; acquired Carrington Viyella to form Vantona Viyella 1983, Nottingham Mfg. 1985, Coats Patons to form Coats Viyella 1986; Group Chief Exec. Coats Viyella 1975–90, Chair. 1989–; Chair. N. Brown Group 1968–, Tootal Group PLC 1991–; Hon. Fellow, UMIST; Hon. F.C.G.I. 1991; Hon. LL.D. (Manchester) 1989, (Liverpool) 1996; Hon. D.Sc. (Heriot-Watt) 1991. *Address:* Coats Viyella PLC, 28 Savile Row, London, W1X 2DD, England. *Telephone:* 0171-292 9200.

ALLIBONE, Thomas Edward, C.B.E., PH.D., D.SC., D.ENG., F.R.S., F.ENG.; British scientist; b. 11 Nov. 1903, Sheffield; s. of Henry James and Eliza Allibone; m. Dorothy Margery Boulden, L.R.A.M., A.R.C.M. 1931; two d.; ed. Sheffield and Cambridge Univs; High Voltage Lab. Metropolitan Vickers Co. 1930–44; Univ. of Calif. (British team, Atomic Bomb) 1944–45; Dir. Research Lab., Assoc. Electrical Industries, Aldermaston 1946–63; Scientific Adviser to A.E.I. Ltd. 1963; Dir. Assoc. Electrical Industries (Woolwich) Ltd. 1950–63; Chief Scientist, Central Electricity Generating Bd. 1963–70; External Prof. of Electrical Eng., Leeds Univ. 1967–79, Emer. Prof. 1979–; Visiting Prof. of Physics City Univ. 1971–, Robert Kitchin (Sadlers') Research Prof. 1983–, First Frank Poynton Visiting Prof. 1984–; Vice-Pres. Inst. Physics 1948–52; Chair. Research Cttee., Electrical Research Asscn. 1955–62; Vice-Pres. Royal Inst. 1955–57, 1969–72; mem. Council, Physical Soc. 1953–57, Council of Inst. of Electrical Engineers 1937–53, Advisory Council, Royal Mil. Coll., Shrivenham; Pres. Section A British Asscn. 1958, Inst. of Information Scientists 1967–69; Trustee, British Museum 1968–75; Hon. F.I.E.E., Hon. D.Sc., Hon. D.Eng.; Röntgen Medal, British Inst. of Radiology; Thornton and Cooper Hill Medals, Inst. of Electrical Engineers; Melchett Medal, Inst. of Fuel. *Publications:* High Voltage Electrical Phenomena and Thermonuclear Reactions, Release and Use of Atomic Energy, Rutherford, the Father of Nuclear Energy, The Royal Society and its Dining Clubs; contribution to Lightning and Lightning Protection, Cockcroft and the Atom 1984, Cambridge Physics in the Thirties 1984, The Making of Physicists 1987, Philately and the Royal Society 1990, research papers for Royal Soc. *Leisure interests:* history, archaeology, gardening, handicrafts. *Address:* York Cottage, Lovel Road, Winkfield, Windsor, Berks. SL4 2ES, England. *Telephone:* (01344) 88 4501.

ALLIMADI, E. Otema; Ugandan politician and diplomatist; b. 11 Feb. 1929, Kitgum; s. of the late Saulo Allimadi and of Susan (née Layado) Allimadi; m. Alice Lamunu 1954; six s. three d.; ed. in Uganda; N.C.O. in E. African Army Medical Corps. 1947–53; mem. Uganda Nat. Congress 1953, Nat. Admin. and Organizing Sec. 1956–59, Sec.-Gen. 1959, later Vice-Chair. Uganda People's Congress; Deputy Perm. Rep. to UN 1964–66; Amb. to U.S.A. 1966–71, concurrently Perm. Rep. to UN 1967–71; Minister of Foreign Affairs 1979–80; Prime Minister 1980–85; founder mem. Uganda People's Congress (UPC), fmr. Vice-Chair. *Address:* P.O. Box Gulu, Gulu District, Uganda.

ALLINSON, Sir Walter Leonard, K.C.V.O., C.M.G., M.A.; British diplomatist (retd.); b. 1 May 1926, London; s. of Walter and Alice Frances (Cassidy) Allinson; m. Margaret Patricia Watts 1951; three d.; ed. Friern Barnet Grammar School, Merton Coll., Oxford, Royal Coll. of Defence Studies; Asst. Prin., Petroleum Div., Ministry of Fuel and Power 1947–48; Asst. Prin., later Prin., Ministry of Educ. 1948–58 (Asst. Private Sec. to Minister 1953–54); First Sec., Commonwealth Relations Office 1958–60; served in Lahore and Karachi, Pakistan 1960–62, Madras and Delhi, India 1963–66; Deputy, later Head of Perm. Under-Sec.'s Dept., FCO 1968–70; Counsellor and Head of Chancery, later Deputy High Commr., Nairobi, Kenya 1970–73; Deputy High Commr. and Minister, Delhi, India 1975–78; British High Commr., Lusaka, Zambia 1978–80; Asst. Under-Sec. of State (Africa) 1980–82; High Commr. in Kenya and Amb. to UN Environment Programme 1982–86; Non-service mem. Home Office Consultancy Unit 1986–96; Vice-Pres. Royal Africa Soc. 1982–; mem. Governing Council, British Inst. in Eastern Africa 1986–92; Hon. Vice-Chair. Kenya Soc. 1990–; Chair. Finance Cttee. British Red Cross, Cornwall Branch 1996–98; Kenya Scouts Medal of Merit 1973. *Leisure interests:* rough gardening, walking, reading. *Address:* Tregarthen, Wendron, Helston, Cornwall, TR13 0NA, England.

ALLISON, Jr., Graham T., M.A., PH.D.; American professor of government and government official; b. 23 March 1940, Charlotte, N.C.; s. of Graham T. Allison, Sr. and Virginia Wright; m. Elisabeth K. Smith 1968; ed. Davison Coll. and Harvard and Oxford Univs.; Instr. of Govt., Harvard Univ. 1967–68, Asst. Prof. of Govt. 1968–70, Assoc. Prof. of Politics 1970–72, Prof. of Politics 1972–93, Assoc. Dean and Chair. Public Policy Program, John F. Kennedy School of Govt. 1975–77, Dean and Don K. Price Prof. of Politics, John F. Kennedy School of Govt. 1977–89, Douglas Dillon Prof. of Govt. John F. Kennedy School of Govt. 1989–93; Asst. Sec. of Defense for Policy and Plans, Dept. of Defense, Washington, D.C. 1993–94; Dir. Belfer Center for Science and Int. Affairs 1994–; numerous professional appts. *Publications include:* Essence of Decision: Explaining the Cuban Missile Crisis 1971, Sharing International Responsibilities: A Report to the Trilateral Commission 1983; co-author: Hawks, Doves and Owls: An Agenda for Avoiding Nuclear War 1985, Fateful Visions: Avoiding Nuclear Catastrophe 1988, Windows of Opportunity: From Cold War to Peaceful Competition 1989, Window of Opportunity: The Grand Bargain for Democracy in the Soviet Union 1991, Beyond Cold War to Trilateral Cooperation in the Asia-Pacific Region (with others) 1992, Avoiding Nuclear Anarchy 1996. *Leisure interests:* fishing, tennis. *Address:* Harvard University, 79 JFK Street, Cambridge, MA 02178 (Office); 69 Pinehurst Road, Belmont, MA 02178, U.S.A. (Home). *Telephone:* (617) 496-6099 (Office). *Fax:* (617) 495-1905 (Office).

ALLISON, Richard Clark, B.A., LL.B.; American judge; b. 10 July 1924, New York; s. of Albert F. and Anice (née Clark) Allison; m. Anne Elizabeth Johnston 1950; two s. one d.; ed. Univ. of Virginia; called to New York Bar 1948; practised in New York City 1948–52, 1954–55, 1955–; partner law firm Reid & Priest 1961–87; mem. Iran-U.S. Claims Tribunal, The Hague 1988–; mem. A.B.A. (Chair. Cttee. Latin American Law 1964–68, Int. Law Section 1976–77, Nat. Inst. on Doing Business in Far East 1972, Int. Legal Exchange Program 1981–85), Int. Bar Asscn. (Chair. Conf. 1986, Ethics Cttee. 1986–88); mem. Société Int. des Avocats, Inter-American Bar Asscn., American Foreign Law Asscn., American Arbitration Asscn. (Nat. Panel), Southwestern Legal Foundation, American Soc. of Int. Law, Council on Foreign Relations, American Bar Foundation, Asscn. of Bar of City of New York, Inst. for Transnat. Arbitration (Advisory Bd.), Raven Soc., SAR, St. Andrew's Soc., New York. *Publications:* Protecting Against the Expropriation Risk in Investing Abroad 1988; legal articles. *Address:* Iran-U.S. Claims Tribunal, Parkweg 13, 2585 JH The Hague (Office); 224 Circle Drive, Manhasset, New York, NY 11030, U.S.A. (Home). *Telephone:* (70) 352-00-64 (Office). *Fax:* (70) 350-24-56.

ALLOUACHE, Merzak; Algerian film director; b. 6 Oct. 1944, Algiers; s. of Omar and Fatma Allouache; m. Lazib Anissa 1962; one d.; worked in Nat. Inst. of Cinema, Algiers, later in Inst. of Film, Paris; after return to Algeria worked as Adviser, Ministry of Culture; Silver Prize, Moscow Festival; Tanit D'Or Prize, Carthage 1979. *Films include:* Our Agrarian Revolution (documentary) 1973, Omar Gatlato, Les aventures d'un héros, L'homme qui regardait les Fenêtres 1982. *Address:* Cité des Asphodèles, Bt D15, 183 Ben Aknoun, Algiers, Algeria. *Telephone:* 79 33 60.

ALMEIDA SERRA, José, M.ECON.; Portuguese civil servant and politician; b. 19 Dec. 1942, Pampilhosa da Serra; s. of José Augusto Serra and Maria da Encarnação Almeida; m. Maria de Lurdes Martins 1966; three d.; ed. Univ. of Lisbon and Massachusetts Inst. of Tech.; Sec. of State for Finance, IVth Provisional Govt. 1975; Dir. Banco de Fomento Nacional 1976–82; Sec. of State for Merchant Marine and Minister of the Sea, IX Constitutional Govt. 1983–85; Chair. Bd. Dirs. Siderurgia Nacional E.P. 1986–89; Exec. Dir. I.P. Financeira-Sociedade de Investimentos, Estudos e Participações Financeiras S.A. 1989; Dir. Gen. for Fisheries, European Comm. 1990–97. *Publications:* articles in professional journals.

ALMODÓVAR, Pedro; Spanish film director; b. 25 Sept. 1951, La Mancha; fronted a rock band; worked at Telefónica for ten years; started career with full-length super-8 films; made 16mm. short films, including Salome 1978–83; *Films include:* Pepe, Luci, Bom y otras montón, Laberinto de pasiones 1980, Dark Habits 1983, What Have I Done to Deserve This? 1985, Matador 1986, Law of Desire 1987, Women on the Verge of a Nervous Breakdown 1988 (Felix Award 1988), Tie Me Up, Tie Me Down 1990, Tacones Lejanos 1991, Kika 1993, The Flower of My Secret 1996, Live Flesh 1997. *Publications:* Fuego en las entrañas 1982, The Patty Diphusa Stories and Other Writings 1992. *Address:* c/o El Deseo SA, Ruiz Perelló 15, Madrid 28028, Spain; Miramax Films, 18 E. 48th Street, New York, NY 10017, U.S.A.

ALMOND, Gabriel Abraham, PH.D.; American educator; b. 12 Jan. 1911, Rock Island, Ill.; s. of the late David and Lisa Almond; m. Dorothea Kaufmann 1937; two s. one d.; ed. Univ. of Chicago; Fellow, Social Science Research Council 1935–36, 1946; Instructor, Political Science, Brooklyn Coll. 1939–42; Office of War Information, Washington 1942–45, War Dept., European Theatre of Operations 1945; Research Assoc. Inst. of Int. Studies, Yale Univ. 1947–49, Assoc. Prof. of Political Science 1949–51; Assoc. Prof. of Int. Affairs, Princeton Univ. 1951–54, Prof. 1954–57, Prof. of Politics 1957–59; Prof. of Political Science, Yale 1959–63; Prof. of Political Science, Stanford Univ. 1963, Exec. Head, Dept of Political Science, Stanford Univ. 1964–69; Visiting Prof. Univ. of Calif., Irvine 1987; Fulbright Lecturer Kiev State Univ. 1989; Consultant, Air Univ. 1948, Dept. of State 1950, Office of Naval Research 1951, Science Advisory Bd., U.S. Air Force 1960–61; Fellow, American Acad. of Arts and Sciences; Pres. American Political Science

Asscn. 1965–66; mem. Social Science Research Council 1956, American Philosophical Soc.; Fellow, Nat. Endowment for Humanities; N.A.S.; Overseas Fellowship, Churchill Coll., Cambridge 1972–73; Visiting Fellow A.N.U. 1983. *Publications:* The American People and Foreign Policy 1950, The Appeals of Communism 1954; editor The Struggle for Democracy in Germany 1949, The Politics of the Developing Areas 1960; co-author The Civic Culture 1963; Comparative Politics: A Developmental Approach 1966, Political Development 1970, Crisis, Choice and Change 1973, Comparative Politics; System, Process, Policy 1978, The Civic Culture Revisited 1980, Progress and its Discontents 1981, A Discipline Divided; Schools and Sects in Political Science 1990, Comparative Politics: A Theoretical Approach 1993. *Leisure interests:* carpentry, swimming, bird-watching. *Address:* 4135 Old Trace Road, Palo Alto, CA 94306, U.S.A.

ALMOND, Lincoln Carter, LL.B.; American lawyer and politician; b. 1936, Central Falls, R.I.; ed. Boston Univ.; called to R.I. Bar 1962; Admin. Town of Lincoln, R.I. 1963–67; U.S. Attorney, R.I. Dept of Justice, Providence 1967–78, 1981–93; pvt. law practice 1967–69, 1978–81; Pres. Blackstone Valley Devt. Foundation 1993–95; Gov. of Rhode Island 1995–. *Address:* Office of the Governor, State House, Providence, RI 02903, U.S.A.

ALMUNIA AMANN, Joaquín; Spanish politician; b. 1948, Bilbao; m.; two c.; ed. Univ. of Deusto; economist, various Spanish chambers of commerce in mem. countries of EEC; econ. adviser to Exec. Cttee., Unión General de Trabajo; Sec. for trade union relations, then head of Dept. of Research and Planning, then head of Perm. Cttee. for Political Man., Partido Socialista Obrero Español 1981, Sec.-Gen. 1997–; Minister of Labour and Social Security 1982–86; Minister of Public Admin. 1987–91; Pres. Socialist Parl. Group. *Address:* Plaza de las Cortes, 9, 4ª planta, 28014 Madrid, Spain.

ALOMAR, Raphael; French business executive; b. 28 July 1941, Tourcoing; s. of Raphaël Alomar and Jeanne Alomar (née Broutin); m. Nicole Labrunie 1964; three s.; ed. Sorbonne, Paris, Ecole des Hautes Etudes Commerciales and Ecole Nationale d'Admin. (E.N.A.); Sec. Gen. Etablissements Broutin 1966–69; Adviser to Gen. Man. Société Générale 1969–86; Prof. of Corp. Financial Man., E.N.A. 1974–82, Pres. Alumni Asscn. 1984–86, mem. Bd. Dirs. 1987–; Assoc. Gen. Man. Cie. de Navigation Mixte and of Via Banque 1986–93; Gov. Council of Europe Social Devt. Fund 1993–; Chevalier, Légion d'honneur, Commdr. Order of Isabella the Catholic. *Publication:* Financing Business Development 1981. *Address:* Council of Europe Social Development Fund, 55 avenue Kléber, 75116 Paris, France.

ALONEFTIS, Andreas P., M.B.A., F.A.I.A.; Cypriot business executive and government official; b. 24 Aug. 1945, Nicosia; s. of Polycarpos Aloneftis and Charitini Aloneftis; m. Nedi Georghiades 1967; one s. one d.; ed. New York Inst. of Finance Coll. of New York Stock Exchange, Southern Methodist Univ., Dallas, Tex., U.S.A.; served Nat. Guard 1964–66; studied finance and accountancy in U.K.; served 16 years in Cyprus Devt. Bank; Gen. Man. and Chief Exec. Officer, Cyprus Investment and Securities Corpn. Ltd. (CISCO) 1982–88; Minister of Defence 1988–93; Gen. Man. ALICO (Cyprus) 1993–95; Man. Dir. CYPRIALIFE Ltd. 1995–; Fellow Asscn. of Int. Accountants. *Address:* CYPRIALIFE Ltd., 2 Amphipoleos Str., Strovolos, P.O. Box 2535, 1522 Nicosia, Cyprus. *Telephone:* (2) 811562. *Fax:* (2) 428569.

ALONI, Shulamit; Israeli politician and lawyer; b. 1929, Tel Aviv; three s.; participated in the defence of Jerusalem during the War of Independence; worked as a teacher; columnist for several newspapers; producer of radio programmes dealing with legislation and legal procedures; f. Israel Consumers' Council, Chair. for four years; joined Mapai 1959; mem. Knesset (Labour) 1965–69; f. Civil Rights Movt. (CRM) 1973, CRM Minister without Portfolio June–Oct. 1974, CRM leader and MK 1974–, served on numerous cttees.; Minister of Educ. (representing the Meretz coalition) 1992, of Communications, Science and Tech. 1993–96; mem. Meretz (coalition party). *Publications include:* books on legal and political subjects. *Address:* c/o Ministry of Communications, 23 Yaffo Street, Jerusalem 91999, Israel. *Telephone:* (2) 706301. *Fax:* (2) 240029.

ALONSO, Alicia; Cuban ballet dancer, choreographer and ballet director; b. 21 Dec. 1920, Havana; d. of Antonio Martínez and Ernestina del Hoyo; m. 1st Fernando Alonso 1937; m. 2nd Pedro Simón 1975; one s. one d.; ed. Ballet School of Sociedad Pro-Arte Musical, Havana, School of American Ballet, U.S.A.; mem. American Ballet Caravan 1938–39, American Ballet Theater 1940–41, 1943–48, 1950–55, 1958–60, Ballet Russe, Monte Carlo 1955–59; danced with Greek Theatre, L.A., Calif. 1957–59, Washington Ballet 1958; Guest Artist, Teatro Colón, Buenos Aires 1958, Kirov and Bolshoi Ballets 1958, Royal Danish Ballet 1969, Paris Opera 1972, Rome Opera 1987; founder, prima ballerina assoluta, choreographer and Gen. Dir. Nat. Ballet of Cuba 1948–(99); has staged her versions of the maj. romantic and classical ballets in Paris, Rome, Milan, Naples, Vienna, Mexico, Sofia and Prague; mem. jury several int. ballet competitions, Advisory Council, Ministry of Culture and Nat. Cttee. of Writers, Artists' Union of Cuba, Kennedy Center Artistic Cttee., Washington, D.C.; many awards including Dance Magazine Annual Award 1958, Grand Prix of Paris 1966, 1970, Anna Pavlova Award, Univ. of Dance, Paris 1966, Gold Medal of Barcelona Liceo 1971, Annual Award of Gran Teatro de La Habana 1985; several honours including Hero of Work, Cuba, Order Félix Varela, Cuba, Order Aguila Azteca, Mexico, Order Isabel la Católica, Spain, Commdr. des Arts et Lettres. *Publication:* Dialogues with the Dance 1988. *Leisure interests:* films, music, scientific discoveries. *Address:* Calzada No. 510 entre D y E, C.P. 10400, El Vedado, Havana, Cuba. *Telephone:* (7) 55-2948. *Fax:* (7) 33-3317.

ALPER, Howard, PH.D., O.C., F.R.S.C.; Canadian professor of chemistry; b. 17 Oct. 1941, Montreal; s. of Max Alper and Frema Alper; m. Anne Fairhurst 1966; two d.; ed. Sir George Williams Univ., and McGill Univ.; NATO Postdoctoral Fellow, Princeton Univ. 1967–68; Asst. Prof. State Univ. of New York at Binghamton 1968–71, Assoc. Prof. 1971–74; Assoc. Prof. Univ. of Ottawa 1975–77, Prof. 1978–, Chair. Dept. of Chem. 1982–85, 1988–91, 1991–94, Asst. Vice-Pres. (Research) 1995–96, Vice-Pres. (Research) 1997–(2002); titular mem. European Acad. of Arts, Sciences and Humanities; Guggenheim Fellowship 1985–86; Killam Research Fellow 1986–88; Chemical Inst. of Canada Inorganic Chem. Award 1980, Catalysis Award 1984, Alfred Bader Award in Organic Chemistry 1990, Commemorative Medal (125th Anniversary of Canada) 1992, E. W. R. Steacie Award 1993, Urgel-Achambault Prize in Physical Sciences, Math. and Eng. (ACFAS) 1996, Chemical Inst. of Canada Medal 1997, Bell Canada Forum Award 1998. *Publications:* more than 400 papers and 25 patents in the area of organometallic chemistry and catalysis. *Address:* Department of Chemistry, University of Ottawa, Ottawa, Ont. K1N 6N5, Canada. *Telephone:* (613) 562-5189. *Fax:* (613) 562-5871.

ALPERT, Herb; American musician; b. 31 March 1935, Los Angeles; s. of Louis Alpert and Tillie Goldberg; m. 1st Sharon Mae Lubin 1956 (divorced); two c.; m. 2nd Lani Hall; one d.; ed. Univ. of S. Calif.; Co-owner and fmr. Pres. A&M Record Co., Co-Chair. 1962–, Almo Sounds 1994–; Leader, trumpeter, arranger, music group, Tijuana Brass 1962–; concert appearances include Atlanta Symphony 1988, Philharmonic Orch. of Florida, Miami 1988; recordings include: Fandango, Magic Man, Beat of the Brass, Lonely Bull, Solid Brass, South of the Border, What Now My Love, Whipped Cream, Wild Romance, Keep Your Eye on Me, Under a Spanish Moon, Second Wind 1996. *Address:* c/o Herb Alpert Foundation, 1414 Sixth Street, Santa Monica, CA 90401, U.S.A.

ALPERT, Joseph Stephen, M.D.; American professor of medicine; b. 1 Feb. 1942, New Haven, Conn.; s. of Zelly C. Alpert and Beatrice A. Kopsofsky; m. Helle Mathiasen 1965; one s. one d.; ed. Yale and Harvard Univs.; Instructor in Medicine, Peter Bent Brigham Hosp., Harvard Univ. 1973–74; Lieut-Commdr. U.S. Navy, Dir Coronary Care Unit, San Diego Naval Hospital and Asst. Prof. of Medicine, Univ. of Calif., San Diego 1974–76; Dir. Levine Cardiac Unit and Asst. Prof. of Medicine, Peter Bent Brigham Hospital and Harvard Univ. 1976–78; Dir. Div. of Cardiovascular Medicine and Prof. of Medicine, Univ. of Mass. Medical School 1978–92, Vice-Chair. Medicine Dept. 1990–; Budnitz Prof. of Cardiovascular Medicine 1988–92; Prof., Chair. of Medicine Dept. Ariz. Univ. 1992–; Fulbright Fellow, Copenhagen 1963–64; U.S. Public Health Service Fellow, Harvard and Copenhagen 1966–67; Nat. Inst. of Health Special Fellow, Harvard 1972–74; Fellow, American Coll. of Physicians, American Coll. of Cardiology (Trustee 1996–(2001)), American Heart Asscn. Clinical Council (Vice-Chair. 1991–92, Chair. 1993–95), American Coll. of Chest Physicians; Gold Medal of Univ. of Copenhagen and other awards. *Publications include:* The Heart Attack Handbook 1978, Physiopathology of the Cardiovascular System 1984, Modern Coronary Care 1990, Diagnostic Atlas of the Heart 1994; co-author of other books and author of more than 400 articles in scientific journals. *Leisure interests:* poetry, music, swimming, running, cooking, travel. *Address:* 1501 North Campbell Avenue, Tucson, AZ 85724 (Office); 3440 E. Cathedral Rock Circle, Tucson, AZ 85718, U.S.A. (Home). *Telephone:* (520) 626-6102 (Home). *Fax:* (520) 626-2919.

ALSOP, Will, F.R.S.A.; British architect; b. 12 Dec. 1947; s. of Francis Alsop and Brenda Hight; m. Sheila Bean 1972; two s. one d.; ed. Architectural Asscn.; teacher of Sculpture St. Martin's Coll.; worked with Cedric Price; fmrly. in practice with John Lyall; designed a ferry terminal in Hamburg; undertook design work on the Cardiff barrage; conducted feasibility studies to recycle the fmr. De Lorean car factory in Belfast; designed a govt. bldg. for Marseilles; est. own practice, collaborates with Bruce Maclean in producing architectural drawings; prin. Alsop & Störmer Architects 1979–; Hon. LL.D. (Leicester) 1996. *Publications:* City of Objects 1992, William Alsop Buildings and Projects 1992, William Alsop Architect: Four Projects 1993, Will Alsop and Jan Störmer, Architects 1993, Le Grand Bleu-Marseille 1994. *Address:* Bishop's Wharf, 39–49 Parkgate Road, London, SW11 4NP, England. *Telephone:* 0171-978 7878.

ALSTON, Richard Kenneth Robert, LL.M., B.COM., M.B.A.; Australian politician; ed. Xavier Coll., Melbourne, Melbourne and Monash Univs.; Senator for Vic. 1986–; Shadow Minister for Communications 1989–90, for Social Security, Child Care and Retirement Incomes 1990–92, for Social Security, Child Care and Superannuation 1992, for Superannuation and Child Care and Shadow Minister Assisting Leader on Social Policy 1992–93, for Communications and the Arts 1994–96; Minister for Communications and the Arts March 1996–, for Information Tech. Oct. 1998–; Deputy Leader of Opposition in Senate 1993–96, of Govt. in Senate March 1996–; Deputy Chair. Senate Standing Cttee. on Legal and Constitutional Affairs 1986, Jt. Parl. Cttee. on Nat. Crime Authority 1987; mem. Senate Standing Cttee. on Finance and Public Admin. 1987; State Pres. Liberal Party Vic. Div. 1979–82; mem. Amnesty Int. Parl. Group; Nat. Chair. Australian Council for Overseas Aid 1978–83; Chair. Afghan-Australia Council 1987–; Fed. Pres. UNA of Australia 1977–79; Gov. Nat. Gallery of Australia Foundation; Fellow Inst. of

Dirs. 1983–88. *Leisure interests:* Aboriginal art, modern literature, Oriental rugs, jogging, reading, pumping iron. *Address:* Parliament House, Canberra, A.C.T. 2600, Australia.

ALSTON, Robert John, B.A., C.M.G.; British diplomatist (retd.); b. 10 Feb. 1938; s. of Arthur William Alston and Rita Alston; m. Patricia Claire Essex 1969; one s. one d.; ed. Ardingly Coll., New Coll., Oxford; joined H.M. Diplomatic Service 1961, Third Sec. Kabul 1963, Eastern Dept. Foreign Office 1966, Head of Computer Study Team FCO 1969, First Sec., Econ., Paris 1971, First Sec. and Head of Chancery, Tehran 1974, Asst. Head, Energy, Science and Space Dept., FCO 1977, Head, Jt. Nuclear Unit, FCO 1978, Political Counsellor, U.K. Del. to NATO 1981, Head of Defence Dept., FCO 1984; Amb. to Oman 1986–90; seconded to Home Civil Service 1990–92; Asst. Under Sec. (Public Depts.), FCO 1992–94; High Commr. to New Zealand, to Western Samoa (non-res.) 1994–98; Gov. of Pitcairn 1994–98. *Leisure interests:* gardening, reading, listening to music. *Address:* 16 Carlisle Mansions, Carlisle Place, London, SW1P 1UX, England.

ALTBACH, Philip, G., PH.D.; American professor of education; b. 3 May 1941; m. Edith Hoshino 1962; two s.; ed. Univ. of Chicago; Lecturer on Educ., Harvard Univ. 1965–67; Asst. Prof., Assoc. Prof. Dept. of Educational Policy Studies, Univ. of Wisconsin-Madison 1967–75; Prof. Dept. of Educational Org., Admin. & Policy, State Univ. of New York, Buffalo 1975, Chair. 1985–88, Dir. Comparative Educ. Center 1978–94, Chair. Dept. of Social Foundations 1978–82, Adjunct Prof. School of Information and Library Studies 1982, Adjunct Prof. Dept. of Sociology 1991; Project Dir. Nat. Science Foundation study of higher educ. in newly industrialising countries 1988–90; Prof. School of Educ., Boston Coll. 1994–, J. Donald Monan S.J. Prof. of Higher Educ. 1996–; Dir. Centre for Int. Higher Educ. 1995–; Fulbright Research Prof. Univ. of Bombay 1968; Visiting Prof. Moscow State Univ. 1982, Univ. of Malaya 1983, School of Educ. Stanford Univ. 1988–89; Visiting Fellow, Hoover Inst., Stanford Univ. 1988–89; mem. numerous professional socs.; Consultant, Rockefeller Foundation; Senior Assoc. Carnegie Foundation for the Advancement of Teaching 1992–96; lecturer at many int. confs. and seminars. *Publications:* N. American Ed. of Higher Education; author or co-author of 14 books, book chapters, articles in professional journals etc. *Address:* Boston College, 207 Campion Hall, Chestnut Hill, MA 02167, U.S.A.

ALTES, Frederik Korthals; Netherlands politician and lawyer; b. 15 May 1931, Amsterdam; ed. Leiden Univ.; practised as solicitor; mem. First Chamber, States-Gen. 1981–82, 1991–; Minister of Justice 1982–89; Chair. Volkspartij voor Vrijheid en Democratie (VVD) 1975–81, Floor Leader in First Chamber, States-Gen. 1995–97, Pres. 1997; partner, Nauta Dutilh law firm 1990–96. *Address:* Oudorpweg 9, 3062 RB Rotterdam, Netherlands (Home). *Telephone:* 10-452 6163. *Fax:* 10-452 9491.

ALTHER, Lisa, M.A.; American writer and reviewer; b. 23 July 1944, Kingsport, Tenn.; d. of John Shelton Reed and Alice Greene Reed; m. Richard Alther 1966 (divorced); one d.; ed. Wellesley Coll., Radcliffe Coll.; editorial asst. Atheneum Publrs., New York 1967–68; freelance writer 1968–; lecturer, St. Michael's Coll., Winooski, Vt. 1980–81. *Publications:* Kinflicks 1975, Original Sins 1980, Other Women 1984, Bedrock 1990, Birdman and the Dancer 1993, Five Minutes in Heaven 1995. *Address:* 1086 Silver Street, Hinesburg, VT 05461, U.S.A. *Fax:* (802) 482-3141.

ALTMAN, Robert; American director, writer and producer; b. 20 Feb. 1925, Kansas City; m. 3rd Kathryn Reed; two s.; (also two s. one d. from two previous marriages); ed. Univ. of Missouri; Television work includes Bonanza, Kraft Theatre, Bus Stop, Combat, Cannes Film Festival Grand Prize for M*A*S*H; mem. Dirs. Guild of America. *Films include:* The Delinquents 1955, The James Dean Story 1957, Nightmare in Chicago 1964, Countdown 1968, That Cold Day in the Park 1969, M*A*S*H 1970, Brewster McCloud 1971, McCabe and Mrs. Miller 1972, Images 1972, The Long Goodbye 1973, Thieves Like us 1973, California Split 1974, Nashville 1975, Buffalo Bill and the Indians 1976, Welcome to LA 1977, The Late Show 1977, Three Women 1977, A Wedding 1979, Remember My Name 1979, Quintet 1979, A Perfect Couple 1979, Rich Kids 1979, Popeye 1980, Health 1980, The Easter Egg Hunt 1981, Come Back to the Five and Dime, Jimmy Dean, Jimmy Dean 1982, Secret Honor 1984, Fool for Love 1986, Aria (Segment) 1987, Beyond Therapy 1987, Vincent and Theo 1990 (cinema & TV), The Player 1991, Short Cuts 1992, Prêt à Porter 1994; producer: Mrs Parker and the Vicious Circle 1995, Kansas City, The Gingerbread Man 1998, The Cookie Fortune 1998; TV: The Laundromat 1984, The Dumb Waiter 1987, The Room 1987, The Caine Mutiny Court Martial 1987, Tanner '88 (co-dir.). *Address:* Sandcastle 5 Productions, 502 Park Avenue, Suite 15G, New York, NY 10022, U.S.A.

ALTMAN, Stuart Harold, PH.D.; American professor of health; b 8 Aug. 1937, Bronx, New York; s. of Sidney Altman and Florence Altman; m. Diane Kleinberg 1959; three d.; ed. City Coll. of New York and Univ. of California, Los Angeles; Labor Market Economist, Fed. Reserve Bd. 1962–64; Econ. Consultant and Manpower Economist, Office of Asst. Sec. of Defense, Washington, D.C. 1964–66; Asst Prof. of Econs., Brown Univ. 1966–68, Assoc. Prof. 1968–70; Univ. Fellow and Dir. of Health Studies, Urban Inst. 1970–71; Deputy Admin., Office of Health, Cost of Living Council, Dept. of Health, Educ. and Welfare 1973–74, Deputy Asst. Sec. for Planning and Evaluation (Health) 1971–76; Visiting Lecturer, Graduate School of Public Policy, Univ. of Calif., Berkeley 1976–77; Sol C. Chaikin Prof. of Nat. Health Policy, Heller School, Brandeis Univ. 1977–, Dean 1977; Chair. Prospective Payment Assessment Comm., U.S. Congress 1983–86, 1986–89; mem. N.A.S. Inst. of Medicine (mem. Governing Council 1982–83), Bd., Robert Wood Johnson Clinical Scholars, Bd. Beth Israel Hosp., Brookline, Mass. 1979–. *Publications:* The Growing Physician Surplus: Will it Benefit or Bankrupt the U.S. Health System 1982, Ambulatory Care: Problems of Cost and Access (with others) 1985, Will the Medicare Prospective Payment System Succeed? Technical Adjustments Can Make the Difference 1986 and other publs. *Leisure interests;* sailing, cross-country skiing, boating and tennis. *Address:* Institute for Health Policy, Heller Graduate School, POB 9110, Brandeis University, Waltham, MA 02254; 11 Bakers Hill Road, Weston, MA 02193, U.S.A. (Home). *Telephone:* (617) 736-3803 (Office); (617) 988-9144 (Home).

ALVA, Dinker Shanker, B.SC., B.SC. (TECH.); Indian industrialist; b. 2 July 1933, Mangalore, Karnataka; s. of the late Shanker Alva and Kamala Alva; m. Shashikala Alva 1960; one s. one d.; ed. Madras Univ.; Asst. Weaving Master, Delhi Cloth and Gen. Mills Ltd. 1954–58; Industrial Consultant IBCON Pvt. Ltd. 1958–60; Sales Exec. Bombay Dyeing and Mfg. Co. Ltd. 1960–66, Gen. Man. (Sales) 1969–74, Sales Dir. 1974–75, Dir. 1976–79, Pres. 1979–88, Man. Dir. 1988–; Gen. Man. Anglo-French Textiles Ltd. 1966–69; Dir. Archway Investment Co. Ltd., Sanghi Polyesters Ltd., Nat. Peroxide Ltd., Britannia Industries Ltd., Wadia BSN India Ltd., Indian Cotton Mills Fed.; mem. Governing Cttee. Bombay Textile Research Asscn.; Deputy Chair. Cttee. of Admin. Cotton Textiles Export Promotion Council; mem., Man. Cttee. All India Exporters' Chamber, The Bombay Millowners' Asscn. *Leisure interests:* music, reading, tennis. *Address:* Neville House, Ballard Estate, Bombay 400038 (Office); 426 Samudra Mahal, Dr. Annie Besant Road, Worli, Bombay 400 018, India. *Telephone:* 2618071/2615631 (Office); 4973535/4973536 (Home).

ALVA CASTRO, Luis; Peruvian politician and economist; b. Trujillo; ed. Universidad Nacional de Trujillo; fmr. Dir. Corporación de Desarrollo Económico y Social de la Libertad; Deputy for Libertad; has held various posts in Partido Aprista Peruano (now Alianza Popular Revolucionaria Americana) including Sec.-Gen. of Northern Regional Org., mem. Political Comm. and Nat. Sec. for Electoral Matters; Chair. Nat Planning Comm. of Partido Aprista Peruano; Second Vice-Pres. of Repub., Pres. Council of Ministers (Prime Minister) and Minister of Economy and Finance 1985–87. *Publications:* La Necesidad del Cambio, Manejo Presupuestal del Perú, En Defensa del Pueblo, Endeudamiento Externo del Perú, Deuda Externa: Un reto para los Latinoamericanos and other books and essays. *Address:* c/o Alianza Popular Revolucionaria Americana, Avenida Alfonso Ugarte 1012, Lima 5, Peru.

ALVAREZ, Aida, B.A.; American politician; b. Aguadilla, Puerto Rico; ed. Harvard Univ., former news reporter, presenter Metromedia TV, NY; fmr. reporter NY Post; fmr. mem. NY City Charter revision Comm.; fmr. Vice-Pres. NY City Health and Hospitals Corp.; investment banker First Boston Corp. NY, San Francisco 1986–93; Dir. Office Fed. Housing Enterprise Oversight 1993–; Dir. Small Business Admin. Jan. 1997–; fmr. mem. Bd. Dirs. Nat. Hispanic Leadership Agenda, NY Community Trust, Nat. Civic League; fmr. Chair. Bd. Municipal Assistance Corp./Victim Services Agency, NY; NY State Chair. Gore Presidential Campaign 1988; Nat. Co-Chair. Women's Cttee. Clinton Presidential Campaign 1992; mem. Pres. Econ. Transition Team 1992; Front Page Award 1982, Associated Press Award for Excellence 1982. LL.D. h.c. Iona Coll. 1985. *Address:* Small Business Administration, 409 3rd Street, Washington, DC 20024, U.S.A.

ALVAREZ, Mario Roberto; Argentine architect; b. 14 Nov. 1913, Buenos Aires; m. Jorgelina Ortiz de Rosas 1953; one s. one d.; ed. Colegio Nacional, Buenos Aires, and Univ. of Buenos Aires; in private practice, Buenos Aires 1937–, as Mario Roberto Alvarez and Assocs. 1947–; architect, Ministry of Public Works 1937–42; municipal architect, Avellaneda 1942–47; adviser, Secr. of Public Works, City of Buenos Aires 1958–62; Sec. to World Football Cup Stadium Comm., Buenos Aires 1972–78; Vice-Pres. Cen. Soc. of Architects 1953–55; exhibited, São Paulo Bienal 1957 and several other exhbns. of Argentine architecture in Buenos Aires and abroad; prizewinner in numerous int. architectural competitions; Hon. Fellow, American Inst. of Architects; Dr. h.c. (La Plata) 1982; Great Prize of the Nat. Fund of Arts 1976; Hon. mem. Inst. of City Planning, Peru 1979. *Address:* Mario Roberto Alvarez y Asociados, Solis 370, Buenos Aires, Argentina.

ALVAREZ ARMELLINO, Gen. Gregorio Conrado; Uruguayan politician and army officer; b. 26 Nov. 1925, Montevideo; s. of Gen. Gregorio Alvarez Lezama and Bianca Armellino de Alvarez Lezama; m. María del Rosario Flores 1978; one d.; ed. José Pedro Varela High School and Uruguay Mil. Coll.; Officer, Cavalry Regt. 1946–59; Head of Cavalry Operations Training, Mil. Coll. 1960–62; Chief of Republican Guard 1962–79; promoted to Gen. 1971; Joint Chief of Staff 1971–79; First Sec. Council of Nat. Security 1973–74; 4th Div. Army Commander 1974–78; C.-in-C. of the Army 1978–79; retd. from armed forces 1979; Pres. of Uruguay 1981–84; various military decorations. *Leisure interests:* horse-riding, fishing, hunting.

ALVAREZ RENDUELES, José Ramón, PH.D., LL.M.; Spanish central banker and university professor; b. 17 June 1940, Gijón; s. of Ramón Alvarez Medina; m. Eugenia Villar 1964; four s. one d; State Economist 1964; rank of Full Prof. in Public Finance 1973; Head of Econ. Studies in Planning Comm. 1969; Dir. Inst. of Econ. Devt. 1973; Tech. Sec.-Gen. Ministry of Finance 1973–75, Under-Sec. for Econ. 1975–76; Sec. of State for Econ. Affairs 1977–78; Gov. Bank of Spain 1978–84; Chair. COFIR 1988–93,

Productos Pirelli 1986–, Peugeot España 1996, Aceralia 1997; Pres. Prince of Asturias Foundation 1996–. *Publications:* Valoración actual de la imposición sobre consumo 1971, La Hacienda pública y el medio ambiente 1973. *Leisure interests:* golf, music, literature, lawn tennis. *Address:* La Masó 21, Madrid 28034 (Mirasierra), Spain (Home).

ALVEY, John, C.B., F.ENG., B.SC. (ENG.), F.I.E.E., F.R.S.A.; British engineer; b. 19 June 1925; s. of G.C.V. Alvey and H.E. Pellat; m. Celia E. Marson 1955; three s.; ed. Reeds School and Northampton Eng. Coll. (now City Univ.); Stock Exchange, London 1941–43; Service with R.N. 1943–46; Defence Science 1950–80; Dir. Admiralty Surface Weapons Establishment 1976–77; Chief Scientist, R.A.F. 1977–80; Sr. Dir. of Tech., British Telecom 1980–83, Man. Dir. for Procurement and Eng.-in-Chief 1983–86; Dir. (non-exec.) LSI Logic Ltd. 1986–91; Chair. SIRA 1987–94; Fellow, Queen Mary and Westfield Coll. 1988; Hon. D.Sc. (City Univ.), Hon. D.Tech. (CNAA) 1991; mem. Worshipful Co. of Engineers. *Publication:* The Alvey Committee Report 1982. *Leisure interests:* skiing, watching rugby, walking, reading, music, theatre. *Address:* 9 Western Parade, Emsworth, Hants., PO10 7HS, England.

AMAD, Hani Subhi al-, M.A., PH.D.; Jordanian librarian; b. 1938, Salt; s. of Subhi al-Amad and Suhaila al-Amad; m. Intesar Bashiti 1968; two s. two d.; ed. Salt Secondary School, Cairo Univ. and in U.S.A.; Librarian, Univ. of Jordan Library 1963–73, Dir. 1983; Librarian, Faculty of Arts & Human Sciences, Univ. of Moh. V, Rabat 1974–76; Dir.-Gen. Culture and Arts Dept., Amman 1977–78; Asst. Prof. Faculty of Arts, Univ. of Jordan 1979–, Asst. Dean 1981–83; Pres. Jordan Library Asscn. 1984–85; Jordanian Writers' Union 1987–. *Publications:* Jordan Folk Songs 1969, Jordan Folk Proverbs 1978, Cultural Policy in Jordan 1980, Studies in Biographical Sources 1981, Jordan Folk Elegies: Lamentation 1984, Directory of Notables in the Southern Region of Bilad Ash-Sham 1985, Literature of Writing and Authorship among Arabs: A General View 1986, Principles of Methodology in Arabic authorship extracted from Introductions 1987, Arab Character in the Biography of Princess That al-Himmah 1988. *Leisure interest:* reading and doing research. *Address:* c/o The Library, University of Jordan, Amman, Jordan.

AMADI, Elechi, B.SC.; Nigerian writer and fmr. teacher, army officer and administrative officer; b. 12 May 1934, Aluu, Rivers State; s. of Chief Wonuchukwu Amadi and Enwere Amadi; m. 1st Dorah Nwonne Ohale 1957, 2nd Priye Iyalla 1991; four s. eight d.; ed. Govt. Coll. Umuaphia, Univ. Coll. Ibadan, Brookings Inst., U.S.A.; worked as land surveyor 1959–60, teacher 1960–63; army officer (Capt.) 1963–66, with 3rd Marine Commandos during civil war 1968–69; Prin. Asa Grammar School 1967; Perm. Sec. Rivers State Govt. 1973–83, Commr. of Educ. 1987–89, of Lands and Housing 1989–90; Writer-in-residence and lecturer Rivers State Coll. of Educ. 1984–85, Dean of Arts 1985–86, Head Dept. of Literature 1991–93; Founder and Dir. Elechi Amadi School of Creative Writing 1997–; Rivers State Silver Jubilee Merit Award 1992, Ikwerre Ethnic Nationality Merit Award for Literature 1995. *Publications:* (novels) The Concubine 1966, The Great Ponds 1969, The Slave 1978, Estrangement 1986; (plays) Isiburu 1973, The Road to Ibadan 1977, Dancer of Johannesburg 1978; Sunset in Biafra (war diary) 1973; Ethics in Nigerian Culture (philosophy) 1982. *Leisure interests:* reading, music, playing the piano, billiards. *Address:* 7 Mbodo Road, Aluu, P.O. Box 331, Port Harcourt, Nigeria. *Fax:* (084) 230 238.

AMADO, Jorge; Brazilian novelist; b. 10 Aug. 1912, Itabuna, Bahia; s. of João Amado de Faria and Eulalia Leal Amado; m. Zelia Gattai 1945; one s. two d.; Calouste Gulbenkian Prize, Acad. du Monde Latin 1971; Nat. Literary Prize (Brazil); Nonnino Literary Prize (Italy); Commdr., Légion d'honneur, France. *Publications include:* Mar Morto, Jubiabá, The Violent Land, São Jorge dos Ilheus, Cacau, Suor, Capitães da Areia, ABC de Castro Alves, Bahia de Todos os Santos, O Amor do Soldado, Seara Vermelha, O Cavaleiro da Esperança, O Mundo da Paz, Os subterrâneos da Liberdade, Gabriela Cravo e Canela, Os velhos marinheiros, Os pastores da noite, Dona Flor e seus dois maridos! Tenda dos Milagres, Teresa Batista Cansada de Guerra, Tieta do Agreste e Farda, Fardão, Camisola de Dormir, O Menino Grapiúna, Tocaia Grande, Navegacio de Cabotagun, A Descoberta da América pelos Turcos. *Leisure interests:* reading, gardening, cats, poker. *Address:* Rua Alagoinhas 33, Rio Vermelho-Salvador, Bahia, Brazil. *Telephone:* 247-2165.

AMAMOU, Mohamed; Tunisian diplomatist; b. 7 Oct. 1933, Kairouan; s. of Mohamed Amamou and Zohra Saadi; m. Beya Boujdaria; one s. one d.; ed. Collège Sadiki and Inst. des Hautes Etudes; Chargé d'affaires, Jordan 1969–71; Amb. to Zaire 1972–73; Gen. Consul in Paris 1973–74; Amb. to Lebanon and Jordan 1974–78; Dir. of Political Affairs for the Arab World, Ministry of Foreign Affairs 1978–81; Chargé de mission, Ministry of Foreign Affairs 1981–85; Amb. to Morocco and Portugal (resident in Rabat) 1985–87, to Syria 1987–89; Sec. of State for Maghreb Affairs 1989–90; Prin. Adviser to Pres. of Tunisia 1990–91, Minister Adviser 1991; Sec.-Gen. of Arab Maghreb Union 1991–; Grand Officier Ordre de la République Tunisienne, Chevalier, Ordre Indépendance and several foreign decorations. *Address:* Arab Maghreb Union, 27 rue Okba, Agdal, Rabat, Morocco. *Telephone:* (7) 77 26 72. *Fax:* 77 26 93.

AMANDRY, Pierre, D. ES L.; French academic; b. 31 Dec. 1912, Troyes; s. of Albert Amandry and Marguerite Philippon; m. Angélique Pavlidi 1944; one s. one d.; ed. Ecole Normale Supérieure and Univ. of Paris/Sorbonne; Sec.-Gen. French Archaeological School, Athens 1942–49, Dir. 1969–81; Asst. Prof. Univ. of Paris 1949–50; Prof. Univ. of Strasbourg 1951–69; mem. Inst. de France (Acad. des Inscriptions et Belles Lettres); Assoc. mem. Acad. Royale de Belgique; foreign mem. Athens Acad.; Corresp. Fellow British Acad.; Hon. mem. British Soc. for Promotion of Hellenic Studies, Archaeological Inst. of America; Hon. Vice-Pres. Archaeological Soc. of Athens 1987; Officier, Légion d'honneur, decorations from Greece and Belgium. *Publications:* La mantique apollinienne à Delphes 1950, La colonne du Sphinx des Naxiens et le Portique des Athéniens à Delphes 1953, Collection Hélène Stathatos I. les bijoux antiques 1953, Collection Hélène Stathatos III. Objets antiques et byzantins 1963, and 150 articles in various periodicals. *Address:* 54 boulevard Saint Jacques, 75014 Paris, France. *Telephone:* (01) 45.87.17.07.

AMANN, Ronald, M.SOC.SC., PH.D.; British research administrator; b. 21 Aug. 1943, North Shields; s. of George Amann and Elizabeth Towell; m. Susan Peters 1965; two s. one d.; ed. Heaton Grammar School, Newcastle-upon-Tyne and Univ. of Birmingham; Consultant, OECD and Research Assoc. 1965–69; lecturer, Sr. lecturer in Soviet Science Policy, Univ. of Birmingham 1969–83, Dir. Centre for Russian and East European Studies (CREES) 1983–89, Prof. of Comparative Politics 1986 (on leave of absence), Dean Faculty of Commerce and Social Science 1989–91, Pro-Vice-Chancellor 1991–94; Chief Exec. and Deputy Chair. Econ. and Social Science Research Council (ESRC) 1994–; Visiting Fellow, Osteuropa Inst. Munich 1975; Specialist Adviser, House of Commons Select Cttee. on Science and Tech. 1976, mem. UK Tech. Foresight Steering Cttee., Cttee. on Public Understanding of Science (COPUS). *Publications:* co-author: Science Policy in the U.S.S.R. 1969, The Technological Level of Soviet Industry 1977, Industrial Innovation in the Soviet Union 1982, Technical Progress and Soviet Economic Development 1986. *Leisure interests:* walking, modern jazz, cricket. *Address:* Economic and Social Science Research Council, Polaris House, North Star Avenue, Swindon, SN2 1UJ; 26 Spring Road, Edgbaston, Birmingham, B15 2HA, England. *Telephone:* (01793) 413004. *Fax:* (01793) 413002.

AMANPOUR, Christiane; British broadcasting correspondent; b. 12 Jan. 1958, London; d. of Mohammad Amanpour and Patricia Amanpour; m. James Rubin (q.v.) 1998; ed. primary school in Tehran, Holy Cross Convent, U.K., New Hall School, U.K. and Univ. of Rhode Island; radio producer/research asst. BBC Radio, London 1980–82; radio reporter, WBRU Brown Univ. U.S.A. 1981–83; electronic graphics designer, WJAR, Providence, R.I. 1983; asst. CNN int. assignment desk, Atlanta, Ga. 1983; news writer, CNN, Atlanta 1984–86; reporter/producer, CNN, New York 1987–90; int. corresp. CNN 1990, Sr. int. corresp. 1994, Chief Int. Corresp. 1996–; assignments have included coverage of Gulf War 1990–91, break-up of U.S.S.R. and subsequent war in Tbilisi 1991, extensive reports on conflict in fmr. Yugoslavia and coverage of civil unrest and political crises in Haiti, Algeria, Somalia and Rwanda; Fellow, Soc. of Professional Journalists; Dr. h.c. (Rhode Is.); recipient of several awards including News and Documentary Emmy, George Foster Peabody Award, George Polk Award. *Leisure interests:* reading, riding, tennis, swimming, sky-diving. *Address:* c/o CNN International, CNN House, 19-22 Rathbone Place, London, W1P 1DF, England. *Telephone:* 0171-637 6800.

AMARI, Akira; Japanese politician; worked for Sony Corpn.; mem. House of Reps. of New Liberal Club for Ninami-Kanto; subsequently joined LDP, Deputy Sec.-Gen. LDP, Chief LDP Commerce and Industry Panel; Minister of Labour 1998–. *Leisure interests:* collecting antiques. *Address:* Ministry of Labour, 1-2-2, Kasumigaseki, Chiyoda-ku, Tokyo 100, Japan. *Telephone:* (03) 3593-1211. *Fax:* (03) 3502-6711.

AMATO, Giuliano; Italian politician; b. 13 May 1938, Turin; joined Italian Socialist Party (PSI) 1958, mem. Cen. Cttee. 1978–; Asst. Sec.; elected Deputy for Turin-Novara-Vercelli 1983, 1987; fmr. Under-Sec. of State, Presidency of Council of Ministers; Vice-Pres. Council of Ministers and Minister of the Treasury 1987–89; Prof. of Italian and Comparative Constitutional Law, Univ. of Rome; Nat. Deputy Sec. Italian Socialist Party 1988–92; Foreign debt negotiator for Albanian Govt. 1991–92; Prime Minister of Italy 1992–93. *Address:* Camera dei Deputati, Rome, Italy.

AMBANI, Dhirubhai; Indian business executive; b. 28 Dec. 1932, Gujarat; s. of Hirachand Ambani and Jamnaben Ambani; m. Kokilaben Ambani; worked as labourer, Aden; moved to Bombay 1985, traded in spices and yarn; f. Reliance textile and fibres co. 1966; Chair. Reliance Industries, Reliance Petrochemicals, Reliance Europe Ltd., Mudra Communications, Reliance Capital and Finance Trust. *Address:* Usha Kiran, 22 Carmichael Road, Bombay 400026, India.

AMBARTSUMOV, Yevgeniy Arshakovich; Russian politician, social scientist, political analyst and journalist; b. 19 Aug. 1929, Moscow; s. of Arshak Ambartsumov and Alexandra Vassilevskaia; m. Nina Ignatovskaia 1978; one s.; ed. Moscow Inst. of Int. Relations; with Novoye Vremya 1954–59, Problems of Peace and Socialism 1959–63; Sr. Scientific Researcher, Inst. of World Econs. and Int. Relations 1956–59, Head of Dept. Inst. of World Int. Labour Movt. 1966–69; Head of Dept., Inst. of Sociology 1969–73; Head of Dept. of Politics, Inst. of Economics of World Socialist System (now Inst. of Int. Economic and Political Studies) 1973–90; Russian People's Deputy 1990–93; Chair. Foreign Affairs Cttee. of Russian Supreme Soviet 1992–93; mem. State Duma (Parl.) 1993–94; mem. Presidential Council 1993–95, Amb. to Mexico, also accred. to Belize 1994–. *Publications include:* How Socialism Began: Russia under Lenin 1978, NEP: A Modern View 1988, Socialism: Past and Present (Ed.). *Leisure interest:* books. *Address:* Russian

Embassy, José Vasconcelos 204 (Hipódromo Condesa), Delegación Cuauhtemoc, 06140 México D.F., Mexico. *Telephone:* (5) 516-7633; (5) 273-1305. *Fax:* (5) 273-1545.

AMBARTSUMYAN, Sergey Aleksandrovich, D.TECH.; Armenian state official and scientist; b. 17 March 1922, Alexandropol (now Gumry); s. of Alexander G. Ambartsumyan and Anna V. Ambartsumyan; m. Seda A. Ambartsumyan 1949; one s. one d.; Rector Yerevan State Univ. 1977–92; Hon. Dir. Inst. of Mechanics 1993–; Academician Armenian Acad. of Sciences 1964– (Vice-Pres. 1975–77), Armenian Eng. Acad. 1992–, Armenian Philosophy Acad. 1993–; U.S.S.R. People's Deputy 1989–91, mem. Supreme Soviet 1979–91; Academician Int. Acad. of Astronautics; Hon. Pres. Armenian Acad. of Eng. 1997–; mem. Int. Acad. of Sciences, Educ., Industry and Arts 1997–; Hon. mem. Slovak. Acad. of Sciences, Int. Eng. Acad. 1991; Dr. h.c. (Bratislava) 1984; Hon. Prof. Peninsula Inst. of Information, Tech. and Business 1998; many awards and prizes. *Publications:* Theory of Anisotropic Shells 1961, Theory of Anisotropic Plates 1967, General Theory of Anisotropic Shells 1974, Magnetoelasticity of Thin Shells and Plates 1977, Different Modulus Theory of Elasticity 1982, Fragments of the Theory of Anisotropic Shells 1990, Some Problems of Electro-magneto-elasticity of Plates 1991, Vibrations and Stability of Current-carrying Elastic Plates 1991, Conductive Plates and Shells in Magnetic Field 1998; over 200 articles on mechanics of solids. *Leisure interests:* painting, literature, history. *Address:* Institute of Mechanics, 24 Marshal Bagramian Avenue, Yerevan 19, Armenia. *Telephone:* (2) 520644, 521503.

AMBRASEYS, Nicholas, PH.D., F.I.C.E., F.ENG.; British professor of engineering seismology; b. 19 Jan. 1929, Athens, Greece; s. of Neocles Ambraseys and Cleopatra Ambraseys; m. Xeni Stavrou 1955; ed. Univ. of Athens and Imperial Coll. of Science and Tech., Univ. of London; Prof. of Hydrodynamics, Nat. Tech. Univ. of Athens 1963–64; Lecturer in Soil Mechanics, Imperial Coll., London 1965–68, Reader in Eng. Seismology 1968–73, Prof. 1973–, Head of Eng. Seismology Section 1969–, Sr. Research Fellow 1995–, Sr. Research Investigator 1996–; led UN/UNESCO earthquake reconnaissance missions to Yugoslavia, Iran, Turkey, Pakistan, Romania, Algeria, Italy, E. Africa, Nicaragua and Cen. Africa 1963–81; mem. UN Advisory Bd. for reconstruction of Skopje 1964–69; Chair. British Nat. Cttee. for Earthquake Eng., ICE 1966–76; Vice-Pres. European Asscn. of Earthquake Eng. 1967–75; mem. and Chair. UNESCO Advisory Cttee. on Earthquake Risk 1971–81; mem. European Acad. 1996; Hon. Fellow, Int. Asscn. for Earthquake Eng. 1992; Dr. h.c. (Nat. Tech. Univ. Athens) 1993; Busk Medal for Scientific Discovery (Royal Geographical Soc.) 1975. *Publications;* A History of Persian Earthquakes (with G. Melville) 1982, The Seismicity of Egypt, Arabia and the Red Sea 1994, The Seismicity of Turkey 1995 and over 200 papers in scientific and eng. journals. *Leisure interests;* historical geography, archaeology, travel. *Address:* Department of Civil Engineering, Imperial College of Science and Technology, London, SW7 2BU; 19 Bede House, Manor Fields, London, SW15 3LT, England (Home). *Telephone:* 0171-589 5111 (College); 0181-788 4219 (Home).

AMELIO, Gilbert Frank, PH.D.; American business executive; b. 1 March 1943, New York; s. of Anthony Amelio and Elizabeth DeAngelis; m. Glenda Amelio; two s. one d. and one step-s. one step-d.; ed. Georgia Inst. of Tech.; Tech. Dir. and co-founder, Info Science, Atlanta 1962–65; mem. tech. staff, Bell Telephone Labs. Murray Hill, N.J. 1968–71; Div. Vice-Pres., Gen. Man. Fairchild, Mountain View, Calif. 1971–83; Pres. Semiconductor Products Div., Rockwell Int. Newport Beach, Calif. 1983–88; Pres. Communications Systems, Rockwell Int. Dallas 1988–91; Pres., C.E.O. Nat. Semiconductor Corpn. Santa Clara, Calif. 1991–96; C.E.O. Apple Computer Inc., Calif. 1996–97.

AMELING, Elly; Netherlands opera singer; b. (as Elisabeth Sara Ameling) 1938, Rotterdam; m. Arnold W. Beider 1964; studied singing with Jo Bollekamp, with Jacoba and Sam Dresden, and with Bodi Rapp; studied French art song with Pierre Bernac; has given recitals in Europe, S. Africa, Japan; début in U.S.A. 1968, annual tours of U.S.A. and Canada 1968–; has sung with Concertgebouw, New Philharmonic Orchestra, BBC Symphony Orchestra, Berlin Philharmonic, Cincinnati Symphony, San Francisco Symphony, Toronto Symphony, Chicago Symphony; has appeared in Mozart Festival, Washington, D.C. 1974, Caramoor Festival 1974, Art Song Festival, Princeton, N.J. 1974; major recordings, Mozart Concert, Handel Concert, Cantatas (Bach), Mörike Lieder (Wolf), Aimez-vous Handel?, Aimez-vous Mozart?, Christmas Oratorio (Bach), Symphony No. 2 (Mahler), Te Deum (Bruckner), Italienisches Liederbuch (Wolf); First Prize, Concours Int. de Musique, Geneva; Grand Prix du Disque, Edison Prize, Preis der Deutschen Schallplattenkritik, Stereo Review Record of the Year Award; Knight Order of Orange-Nassau.

AMERASINGHE, Chittharanjan Felix, B.A., LL.B., PH.D., LL.D.; Sri Lankan international lawyer; b. 2 March 1933, Colombo; s. of Samson Felix Amerasinghe, O.B.E. and Mary Victorine Abeyesundere; m. Wimala Nalini Pieris 1964; one s. two d.; ed. Royal Coll., Colombo, Trinity Hall, Cambridge Univ., Harvard Univ. Law School; supervisor in Law, Trinity Hall, Cambridge Univ. 1955–57; jr. exec., Caltex Oil Co., Colombo 1959–61; lecturer in Law, Univ. of Ceylon 1962–65, Sr. Lecturer 1965–68, Reader 1968–69, Prof. of Law 1969–71; Counsel, World Bank 1970–75, Sr. Counsel 1975–81, Exec. Sec. and Dir. of Secr., World Bank Admin. Tribunal 1981–96; Judge UN Tribunal, N.Y. 1997–; Consultant in Int. Law, Govt. of Ceylon 1963–70; mem. Ceylon Govt. Comm. on Local Govt. 1969; Hon. Prof. of Int. Law, Univ. of Colombo 1991–94; Adjunct Prof. of Int. Law, School of Law, American Univ. 1991–93; mem. Panel of Arbitrators, Commonwealth Secr. Arbitral Tribunal, Law of Sea Convention, Panel of UN Compensation Comm. for Kuwait; Exec. Council mem. American Soc. of Int. Law 1980–83; Assoc. mem. Inst. de Droit Int. 1981–87, mem. 1987–; mem. Int. Law Asscn. 1986–; mem. British Inst. of Int. and Comparative Law; mem. Sr. Editorial Bd., Project on Governing Rules of Int. Law, American Soc. of Int. Law; mem. Advisory Bd. and Hon. Cttee. Int. Inst. of Human Rights 1968–, Int. Inst. of Environmental Law 1987–, Sri Lanka Journal of Int. Law 1989–; Henry Arthur Thomas Classical Award, Cambridge Univ. 1953, Angus Classical Prize 1953, Clement Davies Prize for Law 1955, Major Scholar and Prize, Trinity Hall, Cambridge 1953–56, Trinity Hall Law Studentship 1956–59, Yorke Prize 1964, Research Fellowship, Harvard Univ. Law School 1957, Certificate of Merit, American Soc. of Int. Law 1988–89. *Publications:* Some Aspects of the Actio Iniuriarum in Roman-Dutch Law 1966, Defamation and Other Injuries in Roman-Dutch Law 1968, State Responsibility for Injuries to Aliens 1967, Studies in International Law 1969, The Doctrines of Sovereignty and Separation of Powers in the Law of Ceylon 1970, The Law of the International Civil Service (2 vols) 1988, Documents on International Administrative Tribunals 1989, Case Law of the World Bank Administrative Tribunal 1989, Local Remedies in International Law 1990, Principles of the Institutional Law of International Organizations 1996; articles in leading law and int. law journals. *Leisure interests:* religious reflection, classical and jazz music, art, artifacts, philately, photography, walking. *Address:* 6100 Robinwood Road, Bethesda, MD 20817, U.S.A. (Home). *Telephone:* (301) 229-2766 (Home).

AMERY, Carl (see Mayer, Christian).

AMES, Bruce Nathan, PH.D.; American professor of biochemistry; b. 16 Dec. 1928, New York; s. of Dr. M. U. and Dorothy Andres Ames; m. Dr. Giovanna Ferro-Luzzi 1960; one s. one d.; ed. Cornell Univ. and California Inst. of Tech.; Postdoctoral Fellow, Nat. Insts. of Health 1953–54, Biochemist 1954–60; Nat. Science Foundation Fellow, Labs. of F. C. Crick, Cambridge and F. Jacob, Paris 1961; Chief Section of Microbial Genetics, Lab. of Molecular Biology, Nat. Insts. of Health 1962–67; Prof. of Biochemistry, Univ. of Calif., Berkeley 1968–, Chair. Dept. of Biochemistry 1983–89; mem. Nat. Cancer Advisory Bd. 1976–82, N.A.S., American Acad. of Arts and Sciences; Fellow, American Asscn. for the Advancement of Science; Foreign mem. Royal Swedish Acad. of Sciences 1989; Eli Lilly Award, American Chem. Soc. 1964; Arthur Flemming Award 1966, Rosenstiel Award 1976, Fed. of American Socs. for Experimental Biology Award 1976, Wankel Award 1978, John Scott Medal 1979, Bolton L. Corson Medal 1980, New Brunswick Lectureship Award of American Soc. for Microbiology 1980, Gen. Motors Cancer Research Fund Charles S. Mott Prize 1983, Gairdner Foundation Award 1983, Tyler Prize for Environmental Achievement 1985, Spencer Award (American Chem. Soc.) 1986, Roger G. Williams Award in Preventive Nutrition 1989, Gold Medal American Inst. of Chemists 1991, Glenn Foundation Prize 1992, shared Japan Prize 1997, numerous other awards. *Publications:* scientific papers in areas of operons, biochemical genetics, histidine biosynthesis, mutagenesis, detection of environmental carcinogens and mutagens, oxygen radicals as a cause of aging and degenerative diseases, anticarcinogens, micronutrient deficiency. *Address:* University of California, Department of Molecular and Cell Biology, 401 Barker Hall, Berkeley, CA 94720 (Office); 1324 Spruce Street, Berkeley, CA 94709, U.S.A. (Home). *Telephone:* (510) 642-5165 (Office).

AMES, Michael McClean, PH.D., F.R.S.C.; Canadian professor of anthropology; b. 19 June 1933, Vancouver; s. of Ernest O. F. Ames and Elsie McClean; m. (separated); one s. one d.; ed. Univ of British Columbia and Harvard Univ.; Asst. Prof. of Sociology, McMaster Univ. 1962–64; Asst. Prof. Univ. of B.C. 1964, now Prof. of Anthropology; Dir. Museum of Anthropology, Univ. of B.C. 1974–; co-ed. of Manlike Monsters; consultant to various museums and projects since 1976; Guggenheim Fellowship 1970–71. *Publications:* Manlike Monsters on Trial 1980, Museums, The Public and Anthropology 1986, Cannibal Tours and Glass Boxes 1992; articles in academic and museum journals. *Leisure interests:* hiking, photography, running. *Address:* Museum of Anthropology, The University of British Columbia, 6393 N.W. Marine Drive, Vancouver, B.C. V6T 1Z2, Canada (Office). *Telephone:* 604-822-5887.

AMEY, Julian Nigel Robert, M.A.; British civil servant; b. 19 June 1949; s. of Robert Amey and Diana Amey (née Coles); m. Ann Victoria Brenchley 1972; three d.; ed. Wellingborough School, Magdalene Coll., Cambridge; Dir. Int. Sales and Marketing Longman Group Ltd. 1985–89; Exec. Dir. BBC English World Service 1989–94; seconded to Dept. of Trade and Industry 1994–96; Dir.-Gen. Canning House 1996–. *Publications:* Spanish Business Directory 1979, Portuguese Business Dictionary 1981. *Leisure interests:* cricket, tennis, travel. *Address:* Canning House, 2 Belgrave Square, London, SW1X 8PJ, England. *Telephone:* 0171-235 2303. *Fax:* 0171-235 3587.

AMIES, Sir (Edwin) Hardy, K.C.V.O., F.R.S.A.; British couturier; b. 17 July 1909; s. of late Herbert William Amies and of Mary Hardy; ed. Brentwood School; Trainee, W. & T. Avery, Birmingham 1930–34; Man. Designer Lachasse, Farm Street, London, W.1 1934–39; Intelligence Corps 1939–45; Dir. Hardy Amies Ltd. 1946–; opened Hardy Amies Boutique Ltd. 1950; Dressmaker to the Queen 1955–; Design Consultant to Alexandra Workwear

PLC (U.K.), Simon House Ltd. (New Zealand), Coppley Noyes and Randall, T. Lipson and Sons, Watson Bros., Carnaby Canada Leather MFG, Daito Woollen Spinning and Weaving Co. Ltd. (Japan), Michelsons Ltd. (U.K.), Australian Tie Co., Sovereign Industries (U.S.A.), Segye Corp. (Korea), Hsinger Garments (Taiwan), and numerous other companies; Chair. Inc. Soc. of London Fashion Designers 1959–60; Officier de l'Ordre de la Couronne (Belgium) 1946; Royal Designer for Industry 1964, British Knitting and Clothing Export Council Award 1989, Lifetime Contribution to Fashion Award 1989; numerous design awards. *Publications:* Just So Far 1954, ABC of Men's Fashion 1964, Still Here 1984, The Englishman's Suit 1994. *Leisure interests:* lawn tennis, gardening and opera. *Address:* Hardy Amies Ltd., 14 Savile Row, London, W1X 2JN (Office); The Old School, Langford, near Lechlade, Glos. GL7 3LF, England. *Telephone:* 0171-734 2436 (Office).

AMIN, Mahmoud, PH.D.; Egyptian petroleum geologist; b. 30 April 1920, Cairo; m. 1945; two s. one d.; ed. Cairo and London Univs. Deputy Gen. Man. of Exploration and Production, Egyptian Petroleum Corpn. 1958–68; Chair. Western Desert Petroleum Corpn. 1968–75; Asst. Sec.-Gen. OAPEC 1975–79, Petroleum Consultant 1979–. *Publications:* Economics of Petroleum Resources, about 25 scientific papers on geology and petroleum, about 100 articles on petroleum. *Address:* 20 Mohamed Hassan Street, Heliopolis, Cairo (Office); 391 Horyia Street, Apart. 802, Alexandria, Egypt (Home). *Telephone:* 836212/828266 (Office); 44958 (Home).

AMIN, Samir, D.ECON.; Egyptian economist; b. 4 Sept. 1931, Cairo; s. of Farid and Odette Amin; m. Isabelle Eynard 1957; ed. Univ. of Paris; Sr. Economist, Econ. Devt. Org., Cairo 1957–60; Tech. Adviser for Planning to Govt. of Mali 1960–63; Prof. of Econs., Univs. of Poiters, Paris and Dakar; Dir. UN African Inst. for Econ. Devt. and Planning 1970. *Publications:* Trois expériences africaines de développement, Mali, Guinée, Ghana 1965, L'économie du Maghreb (2 vols.) 1967, Le développement du capitalisme en Côte d'Ivoire 1968, Le monde des affaires sénégalaises 1968, Maghreb in the Modern World 1970, L'accumulation à l'échelle mondiale 1970, L'Afrique de l'ouest bloquée 1971, Le développement inégal 1973, The Arab Nation 1978, Class and Nation 1980. *Leisure interest:* history. *Address:* UN African Institute for Economic Development and Planning, B.P. 3186, Dakar; 64 rue Carnat, Dakar, Senegal. *Telephone:* 22577; 21133.

AMIN DADA, Field-Marshal Idi; Ugandan fmr. Head of State and army officer; b. 1925, Kakwa Region, West Nile; s. of late Amin Dada; joined King's African Rifles 1946; rank of Corporal 1949, Major 1963, Col. 1964; Deputy Commdr. of the Army 1964; Commdr. of the Army and Air Force 1966–70; rank of Brig.-Gen. 1967, Maj.-Gen. 1968, promoted Field-Marshal July 1975; leader of mil. coup d'état which deposed Pres. Milton Obote Jan. 1971; Pres. and Chief of Armed Forces 1971–79 (Life Pres. 1976–79 overthrown in Tanzanian invasion, fled Uganda); Minister of Defence 1971–75; Chair. Defence Council 1972–79; Minister of Internal Affairs 1973, of Information and Broadcasting 1973, of Foreign Affairs Nov. 1974–Jan. 1975, of Health 1977–79, of Foreign Affairs 1978, of Information, Broadcasting and Tourism, Game and Wildlife 1978–79, of Internal Affairs 1978–79; Chief of Staff of the Army 1974–79; Chair. OAU Ass. of Heads of State 1975–76, presided over Kampala Summit 1975, Addis Ababa Summit 1976; Heavyweight Boxing Champion of Uganda 1951–60; awarded eight highest mil. decorations of Uganda; Hon. LL.D. (Kampala) 1976; resident in Libya 1979–80; in exile in Jeddah, Saudi Arabia 1980–. *Telephone:* 966-2-693-3178.

AMIREDZHIBI, Chabua; Georgian writer and politician; b. 18 Nov. 1921, Tbilisi; s. of Erekle Amiredzhibi and Mariam Nakashidze; m. Tamar Djavakhishvili 1966; four s. two d.; as student of Tbilisi State Univ. was arrested for political activities 1944, sentenced to 15 years' imprisonment in Gulag, released 1959; ed. Tbilisi State Univ., A. Pushkin Tbilisi Pedagogical Inst.; Dir. Advertising-Information Bureau Goskinoprokat 1964–71; M.P. 1970–; Head Mematiane documentary film studio 1983–90; first published collection of short stories Road 1964, Tales for Children 1966, novel Data Tutashkhia 1974, Gora Mborgali 1995; author of numerous essays on literature, cinematography and culture; U.S.S.R. State Prize 1979, Sh. Rustaveli Prize 1995. *Leisure interests:* sports, football, basketball. *Address:* 8/45 Tamarashvili Street, 380062 Tbilisi, Georgia. *Telephone:* 23 06 75 (Home).

AMIS, Martin Louis, B.A.; British author; b. 25 Aug. 1949; s. of late Kingsley Amis and of Hilary Bardwell; m. 1st Antonia Phillips 1984 (dissolved 1996); two s. two d.; m. 2nd Isabel Fonseca 1998; ed. Exeter Coll. Oxford; Asst. Ed. 1971, Fiction and poetry Ed. Times Literary Supplement 1974; Literary Ed. New Statesman 1977–79; special writer for The Observer newspaper 1980–; Somerset Maugham Award (for The Rachel Papers) 1974. *Publications:* The Rachel Papers 1973, Dead Babies 1975, Success 1978, Other People: a mystery story 1981, Money 1984, The Moronic Inferno: and other visits to America 1986, Einstein's Monsters (five stories) 1987, London Fields 1989, Time's Arrow 1991, Visiting Mrs Nabokov and Other Excursions 1993, The Information 1994, God's Dice 1996, Night Train 1997, Heavy Water and Other Stories 1998. *Leisure interests:* tennis, chess, snooker. *Address:* c/o Wylie Agency (UK), 36 Parkside, 52 Knightsbridge, London, SW1X 7JP, England.

AMIT, Maj.-Gen. Meir, M.B.A.; Israeli politician and business executive; b. 17 March 1921, Tiberias; s. of Shimon and Haya Slutsky; m. Yona Kelman 1942; three d.; ed. Columbia Univ., New York; mem. Kibbutz Alonim 1939; served in Israeli Defence Forces 1948–68, fmr. Head of Mil. Intelligence and Head of Israeli Security Service; Pres. Koor Industries 1968–77; Minister of Transport and Communication 1977; mem. of Knesset 1977–81; man. consultant 1982; Chair. MA'OF 1982–85; Dir. Zim Lines, Israel Corpn. 1985, Yachin, DSI Teva Pharmaceutical, Lapidot Oil Drilling; Chair. Gen. Satellite Corpn., Spacecom, Satellite Communications, etc. *Leisure interests:* photography, collecting dolls and educational games. *Address:* 11 Hibat Zion Street, Ramat-Gan 52391, Israel. *Telephone:* 5708867. *Fax:* 5795712.

AMITAL, Yehuda; Israeli politician and rabbi; b. 1925, Transylvania; m.; five c.; in Nazi labour camp 1943–44; migrated to Israel 1944; yeshiva studies in Jerusalem; ordained in Jerusalem; joined Haganah during war of independence; Head, Yeshivat Har Etzion 1968–; f. Meimad, the Movt. for Religious Zionist Renewal 1993; Minister without Portfolio 1995–96; rank of capt. in army reserve. *Address:* The Knesset, Jerusalem, Israel.

AMITSUR, Shimshon Avraham, M.A., PH.D.; Israeli mathematician; b. 26 Aug. 1921, Jerusalem; s. of Jacob Amitsur and Rashke Amitsur; m. Sarah Frenkiel 1948; one s. two d.; ed. Hebrew Univ.; served British Army and Jewish Brigade 1942–46, Israel Army 1948–49; mem. Inst. for Advanced Studies, Princeton, N.J. 1952–54; Lecturer, Hebrew Univ. 1954–56, Assoc. Prof. 1956–60, Prof. 1960; Man. Project on High School Math. 1960–; mem. Israel Acad. of Sciences and Humanities (Chair. Science Section 1980–86); Hon. mem. London Math. Soc. 1989; D.Phil. h.c. (Univ. Ben Gurion, Israel) 1990; Israel Prize for Exact Science (with J. Levitzky 1953); Rothschild Prize for Math. 1969. *Publications:* about 115 scientific papers. *Address:* 43 Harlap Street, Jerusalem, Israel 92341. *Telephone:* (02)-63 69 65.

AMMAR, Mohamed Ali; Algerian politician; b. 1937; m.; six c.; ed. Univ. of Algiers; militant Nat. Liberation Front 1954; Head Algerian Gen. Worker's Union 1962–63; Divisional Inspector of Labour; Head Dept. Etudes et Conception du Parti; Pres. Comm. Volontariat, Comm. for Educ. and Training; Amb. to Libya; mem. Cen. Cttee. Nat. Liberation Front 1979–; Minister of Information and Culture 1988–89.

AMORIM, Celso Luiz Nunes; Brazilian diplomatist; ed. Rio-Branco Inst., Diplomatic Acad. Vienna and London School of Econs.; Minister-Counsellor, Embassy, The Hague; Chair. EMBRAFILME; Special Asst. to Ministry of Science and Tech.; Asst. Prof. Dept. of Political Science and Int. Relations, Univ. of Brasília; Perm. mem. Dept. of Int. Affairs, Inst. of Advanced Studies, Univ. of São Paulo; Amb. to UN, Geneva 1991–93; Minister of Foreign Affairs 1993–94. *Publications:* several works on political theory, int. relations, cultural policies and subjects connected with science and tech. *Address:* c/o Ministry of Foreign Affairs, Palácio do Itamaraty, Esplanada dos Ministérios, 70170 Brasília, DF, Brazil.

AMOSOV, Nikolai Mikhailovich; D.MED.; Russian/Ukrainian surgeon and biocybernetician; b. 6 Dec. 1913, Olkhovo, Vologda Region; s. of Michail Ivanovich Amosov and Elisaveta Kiryllovna Amosova; m. Lidia Denisenko 1944; one d.; ed. Arkhangelsk Medical Inst., Moscow Industrial Inst.; surgeon Cherepovets inter-regional hosp. 1939–41; chief surgery div., field hosp. 1941–46; Head Surgery Dept. Sklifovosky Inst. of Emergency Medicine in Moscow, Surgery Div. Bryansk regional hosp. 1946–52; work in Kiev 1952–; Scientific Sec. Clinics of Chest Surgery, Research Inst. of Tuberculosis and Chest Surgery 1952–68, Deputy Dir. responsible for research 1968–83; Head Div. of Biocybernetics, Inst. of Cybernetics, Ukrainian Acad. of Sciences 1960–, Head of Chair of Chest Surgery Inst. of Doctor's Training 1955–70; Prof., Dir. Kiev Research Inst. of Cardiovascular Surgery 1983–89, Hon. Dir. 1989–; first in U.S.S.R. to make prosthetic appliance of the mitral valve 1962, first in the world to use artificial valve with layer preventing thrombosis formation 1965, modified artificial blood circulation device, performed more than 600 operations on heart; advisor to Dir. Inst. of Cybernetics Ukrainian Acad. of Sciences; mem. Ukrainian Acad. of Sciences; Corresp. mem. Russian Acad. of Medical Sciences; Deputy of U.S.S.R. Supreme Soviet, U.S.S.R. People's Deputy 1989–91; Hero of Socialist Labour, Lenin Prize and other decorations. *Publications:* about 250 scientific works including 10 monographs on problems of surgery and biocybernetics, novels, short stories, memoirs. *Leisure interests:* sports, working out. *Address:* Institute of Cardiovascular Surgery, 11 Protasiv Yar, 252110 Kiev, Ukraine. *Telephone:* (44) 277-4322 (Office); (44) 225-6308 (Home). *Fax:* (44) 277-6422.

AMOUR, Salmin; Tanzanian politician; Pres. and Chair. Supreme Revolutionary Council of Zanzibar Oct. 1990–; Vice-Pres. C.C.M. (Revolutionary Party of Tanzania). *Address:* Office of the President, Supreme Revolutionary Council of Zanzibar, Zanzibar, Tanzania.

AMOUZEGAR, Jamshid, B.C.E., M.S., PH.D.; Iranian politician; b. 25 June 1923; s. of Turan and Habibollah Amouzegar; m. Ulrike Amouzegar 1951; ed. Univs. of Teheran, Cornell, Washington; UN Expert, Mission to Iran 1951; Chief, Eng. Dept 1952–55; Deputy Minister of Health 1955–58; Minister of Labour 1958–59, of Agriculture 1959–60; Consulting Eng. 1960–64; Chair. Int. Civil Service Advisory Bd. of UN 1962–67; Minister of Health 1964–65, of Finance 1965–74, of Interior and Employment 1974–76; Minister of State 1976–77; Sec.-Gen. Rastakhiz Party 1976–77, Jan.-Aug. 1978; Prime Minister of Iran 1977–78; Pres. OPEC 1974; fmr. Chief Oil Negotiator to Shah; First Order of the Taj. *Leisure interests:* listening to music, reading poetry.

AMOYAL, Pierre Alain Wilfred; French violinist; b. 22 June 1949, Paris; s. of Dr. Wilfred and Vera (Popravka) Amoyal; m. 2nd Leslie Chabot 1988; ed. Cours d'Etat, Vanves, Conservatoire Nat. Supérieur de Musique, Paris,

Univ. of Southern California, U.S.A. (studied with Jascha Heifetz, q.v.); invited by Sir Georg Solti to perform Berg's violin concerto with Orchestre de Paris 1971; invited by Pierre Boulez to perform Schoenberg's Concerto with Orchestre de Paris 1977; Prof. of Violin, Conservatoire Nat. Supérieur de Musique, Paris 1977–88; Lausanne Conservatory 1987–; numerous performances throughout world with orchestras including Royal Philharmonic, New Philarmonia, l'Orchestre Nat. de France, Residentie-Orkest, The Hague; First Prize, Conservatoire de Versailles 1960, Conservatoire Nat. Supérieur de Musique, Paris 1962, for chamber music, Conservatoire Nat. Supérieur de Musique; Prix Ginette Neveu; Prix Paganini; Prix Enesco 1970; Grand Prix du Disque 1974, 1977. *Numerous recordings including:* Symphonie espagnole (Lalo); Violin Concerto (Mendelssohn); Concertos Nos. 1 and 2 and 2 Sonatas (Prokofiev); Tartini's concertos; Third Concerto, Havanaise, and Rondo capriccioso (Saint-Saëns); Concerto No. 1 (Bruch); Concerto (Glazunov); Sonatas (Fauré); Horn Trio (Brahms); Concertos (Mozart); Concerto (Sibelius); Concerto (Tchaikovsky); Sonatas (Brahms); Concerto (Schoenberg); Chevalier, Ordre des Arts et des Lettres. *Leisure interests:* photography, literature, sport. *Address:* c/o Jacques Thelen, 252 rue du Faubourg Saint-Honoré, 75008 Paris, France.

AMRI SUED, Ismail; Rwandan government official; b. 1942, Kigombe, Ruhengeri; m. Nadia Musabeyezu 1975; one s. two d.; ed. Nat. Univ. of Rwanda, Univ. of Montreal and Catholic Univ., Louvain, Belgium; Research Asst. N.V. Philips (Eindhoven) 1969–70; Chief of Div. Ministry of Foreign Affairs 1973; Dir. Nat. Broadcasting Corpn. 1973–74; Adviser to Pres. on Foreign Policy 1974–79; Sec.-Gen. Organisation Commune Africaine et Mauricienne (OCAM) 1979–85; Amb. to Kenya 1985–89, to Côte d'Ivoire 1989–91; Chief of State Protocol 1992; Amb. to Egypt 1995, also accredited to Tunisia, Saudi Arabia, Kuwait, U.A.E., Oman; Commdr., Ordre Léopold II (Belgium), Ordre nat. de Mauritanie, Ordre nat. du Zaire, Ordre nat. du Mérite (France), Chevalier de la Reconnaissance Centrafricaine, Officier de l'Ordre Nat. de la Paix (Rwanda). *Publication:* L'adaption du travailleur africain à l'entreprise industrielle: cas de la Tanzanie 1971. *Leisure interests:* music, reading, ping-pong. *Address:* c/o Ministry of Foreign Affairs and Co-operation, BP 179, Kigali, Rwanda.

AMTE, Baba; B.A., LL.B.; Indian lawyer; b. 26 Dec. 1914, Hinganghat; s. of Devidai Amte and Laxmibai Amte; m. Sadhana Amte; two s.; ed. Christian Coll. Nagpur, Nagpur Univ., School of Tropical Medicines, Calcutta; joined Quit India movt., imprisoned 1942; Vice-Pres. Warora Municipality 1948; originator and developer of Maharogi Sewa Samiti leper complex near Nagpur which accommodates 1,400 lepers and includes a cottage hosp., out-patient clinic, shops, workshops, bank, schools, rehabilitation centre for the physically disabled and a technical coll.; UN Human Rights Award 1989; Templeton Prize for Progress in Religion (jointly with L. C. Birch, q.v.) 1990; numerous awards and prizes. *Publications:* numerous books of poems. *Address:* Maharogi Sewa Samiti, Warora, Anandwan, Dist. Chandrapur 442914, India. *Telephone:* 34 (Warora).

AMUDUN NIYAZ; Chinese party and government official; b. 1932; joined CCP 1953; First Sec. Urumqi Municipality CCP 1977–79; Vice-Chair. Govt. of Xinjiang Uygur Autonomous Region 1979–83; Chair. Standing Cttee. of Xinjiang Uygur Autonomous Region People's Congress 1985; Deputy Sec., Xinjiang Uygur Autonomous Region Cttee. CCP 1985; Chair. Xinjiang Uygur Autonomous Regional 8th People's Congress 1985, Standing Cttee. of 7th Xinjiang PC 1989–93, of 8th Xinjiang PC 1993–. *Address:* Standing Committee of Xinjiang Uygur Autonomous Region People's Congress, Urumqi, People's Republic of China.

AMUSATEGUI DE LA CIERVA, José María; Spanish banker; b. 12 March 1932, San Roque; s. of Antonio Amusategui de la Cierva and Dolores Amusategui de la Cierva; m. Amalia de León 1988 (divorced); six c.; ed. Colegio de Huérfanos de la Armada and Univ. of Madrid; state lawyer, Minister of Finance, Gerona 1959–70; Deputy Chair. Instituto Nacional de Industria 1970; Deputy Chair. Prodinsa 1974; Chair. Intelsa 1975, Astilleros Españoles 1980; Deputy Chair. Instituto Nacional de Hidrocarburos 1981; Chair. Campsa 1982; Man. Dir., Deputy Chair. Banco Hispano Americano 1985, Chair. 1991–99, also Pres.; Chair. Banco Cen. Hispano 1992–99; Co.-Chair. Banco Santander Cen. Hispanoamericano (BSCH) 1999–; Grand Cross of Civil Merit. *Leisure interests:* motorcycling, astronomy, botany. *Address:* Banco Santander Central Hispanoamericano, Alcalá 49, 28014 Madrid, Spain. *Telephone:* 532-8810. *Fax:* 531-6461.

AN MIN (Wang, An Min); Chinese university professor; b. 15 March 1922, Shandong; s. of Wang Jingxuan and Zhou Ailian; m. Wu Pei (Wu Guangrui) 1951; one s. one d.; ed. Ming Hsien High School and Nat. Cen. Univ.; mem. Friends Ambulance Unit 1941–49; mem. Faculty China Agric. Univ. 1949–, Head Dept. Animal Science 1979–82, Pres. Univ. 1982–87; Vice-Chair. Scientific and Tech. Cttee. Ministry of Agric. 1983–87, Consultant 1987–; Head Animal Science Section Nat. Academic Degree Cttee. 1984–92; Section Head Nat. Foundation for Natural Science 1986–; Pres. Domestic Animal and Poultry Information Centre 1984–87; Dir. Int. Goat Asscn. 1982, China Int. Conf. Centre for Science and Tech. 1984–; Vice-Chair. Chinese Asscn. of Agricultural Sciences 1983–87; Chief Ed. Chinese Journal of Animal Science 1980–84; mem. Standing Cttee. China Asscn. of Animal Science and Veterinary Medicine 1986–, China Asscn. for Science and Tech. 1987–91, Nat. Awarding Cttee. of Natural Science 1987–91; Deputy Chief Ed. China Agricultural Encyclopedia, Vol. Animal Science 1988–; Chief Ed. Biography of Chinese Scientists, Vol. Agricultural Animal Science 1989–; Dir. Dept. of Taiwan, Hong Kong and Macau Affairs, Ministry of Foreign Trade and Econ. Co-operation 1991–; Assoc. Chief Ed. China Animal Science 1993–; mem. Steering Cttee. Small Ruminant Production System Network of Asia 1990–; mem. Agricultural Consultant Group, Beijing Municipality 1990–. *Leisure interests:* music, theatre and travel. *Address:* 303 Building 15, China Agricultural University, Beijing 100094, People's Republic of China. *Telephone:* 62892955. *Fax:* (86-1) 2582332.

AN QIYUAN; Chinese government official and fmr. geologist; b. 1933, Lingtong Co., Shaanxi Prov.; ed. Dept. of Geology, Northwest China Univ.; joined CCP 1953; leader geological team of Songliao Petroleum Prospecting Bureau 1958–59; Dir. of Oil Mine and Chief, Underground Operation Section of 1st HQ Oil Extracting in Daqing 1964–65; Dir. Petroleum Geophysics Prospecting Bureau, Ministry of Petroleum 1973–77; Deputy Dir. State Seismological Bureau 1977–80, Dir. 1982–88; mem. Standing Cttee. CCP Shaanxi Prov. Cttee., Sec. CCP Xi'an Municipal Cttee. 1988; mem. Standing Cttee. CCPCC Comm. for Inspecting Discipline 1992–; Sec. CCP Shaanxi Prov. Cttee. 1994–. *Address:* Shaanxi Provincial Committee, Xi'an, Shaanxi Province, People's Republic of China.

AN SHIWEI (Imam al-Haj Salah); Chinese politician; b. 1919, Baoding, Heibei; s. of An Juzheng and An Lishi; m. An Xueqin 1948; four s. four d.; Imam, Mosque Shoupa Hutong, Beijing 1948; Vice-Pres. Islamic Asscn. of China 1978–; mem. Standing Cttee. 5th CPPCC, 8th CPPCC 1993–; mem. Presidium 6th CPPCC 1983–87; Vice-Chair. of Religious Affairs Comm. of 7th CPPCC 1988–; Pres. China Islamic Asscn. 1993–; Vice-Chair. Chinese Peace Cttee. for Religious Circles 1994–. *Leisure interest:* reading. *Address:* China Islamic Association, 103 Nan Hengxi Street, Xuanwu District, Beijing 100053, People's Republic of China. *Telephone:* 6723-4445.

AN ZHENDONG; Chinese government official and engineer; b. 5 Sept. 1930, Tangshan, Hebei; ed. Hebei Industry Coll. 1951; engineer, Qiqihar Admin. Railroad 1952–58; engineer Heilongjiang Sillicon Rectifier Factory 1963–67; Engineer, deputy factory dir. Harbin Rectifier Equipment Factory 1967–81; chief engineer 2nd Light Industry Bureau 1981–82; Vice-Gov. Heilongjiang 1983–90; Vice-Chair. Standing Cttee. Heilongjiang PPC 1990–93; Vice-Chair. 6th, 7th, 8th, 9th and 10th Cen. Cttee. Jiusan Soc., 6th, 7th deputy to the Nat. People's Congress; Vice-Pres. Chinese Package Soc.; Dir. Chinese Industry Econ. Soc.; named Model Worker of special grade of Harbin, the Model Worker of Heilongjiang Prov.; main inventions include: Signal and Radio Telephone in Railroad Cars 1958, Fire-fighting Automatic System in Cities 1963, Explosion proof Rectifier Equipment in Coal Mines 1973, Power Factor Electricity Regulator 1976. *Address:* c/o People's Congress Standing Committee of Heilonjiang, Nangang District, Harbin 150001, People's Republic of China. *Telephone:* (0451) 345314 (Office).

AN ZIJIE (T. K. Ann); Chinese politician; b. 1912, Dinghai Co., Zhejiang Prov.; Vice-Chair. Comm. for Drafting Basic Law of Projected Hong Kong Special Admin. Region 1985–91; perm. mem. 7th Nat. Cttee. CPPCC 1988–92, Vice-Chair. 8th Nat. Cttee. 1993–98, 9th Nat. Cttee. 1998–; fmr. Chair. Preparatory Cttee. Hong Kong Special Admin. Region. *Address:* National Committee of Chinese People's Political Consultative Conference, 23 Taiping Qiao Street, Beijing, People's Republic of China.

ANAND, Bal Krishan, M.B., B.S., M.D.; Indian physiologist; b. 19 Sept. 1917, Lahore; s. of V. D. Anand and Saraswati Anand; m. Kamla Puri 1942; one s. two d.; ed. Government Coll. and K.E. Medical Coll., Lahore; Prof. of Physiology, Lady Hardinge Medical Coll., New Delhi 1949–57, All India Inst. of Medical Sciences, New Delhi 1957–74 (Dean 1964–74), Prof. Emer. 1977–; Pres. XXVI Int. Congress of Physiological Sciences, New Delhi 1974; Asst. Dir. WHO. (S.E. Asia) 1974–77; Dir. Inst. of Medical Sciences, Srinagar 1982–85; Vice-Chancellor, Banaras Hindu Univ., Varanasi 1978; Pres. Indian Nat. Acad. of Medical Sciences; Pres. Nat. Bd. of Examinations 1979–82; Pres. Asscn. for Advancement of Medical Educ. 1984–86; Chair. Post-graduate Cttee. of Medical Council of India 1985–91; Chair. Physiology Cttee. of Indian Nat. Science Acad. 1988–91, Governing Council Vallahbhai Patel Chest Inst., Univ. of Delhi 1997–; Visiting Prof. Pa. Univ. School of Medicine 1968; Commonwealth Visiting Prof., Univ. of London 1966; Hon. Mem. Fed. of Asia Oceanic Physiological Soc. 1994; Hon. D.Sc. (Banaras) 1983; Rockefeller Foundation Fellow at Yale Univ. School of Medicine 1950–51; Fellow Nat. Acad. of Medical Sciences, Nat. Science Acad., Indian Acad. of Sciences; Indian Council of Medical Research Sr. Research Award 1962; Watumull Foundation Award in Medicine 1961; Sir Shanti Swaroof Bhatnagar Memorial Award for Scientific Research in Medicine 1963; Padma Shri 1966; Medical Council of India Silver Jubilee Research Award 1969; Dr. B. C. Roy Award for Eminent Medical Man 1984. *Leisure interests:* literature, photography, tennis, hiking. *Address:* B9/21, Vasant Vihar, New Delhi, India. *Telephone:* 6142627.

ANAND, Dev; Indian actor and film-maker; b. 1924, Gurdaspur; m. Kalpana Kartik; one s. one d.; est. Navketan Studios. *Films include:* Hum Ek Khain, The Guide 1965, Des Pardes 1978.

ANAND, Mulk Raj, PH.D.; Indian writer and critic; b. 12 Dec. 1905, Peshawar; s. of Lalchand Anand and Ishwar Kaur; m. 1st Kathleen van Gelder 1939 (divorced 1948); m. 2nd Shirin Vajifdar 1950; one d.; ed. Punjab and London Univs.; active in Nationalist and Gandhi movements; lecturer, London County Council; BBC broadcaster, film script writer, British Ministry of Information; edited (1956) various magazines; Leverhulme Fellow for Research in Hindustani literature; fmr. Editor Marg magazine, India; mem. Indian Nat. Acad. of Letters, Indian Nat. Acad. of Arts, Indian Nat. Book Trust; fmr. Tagore Prof. of Art and Literature, Punjab Univ., Chandigarh; Fellow, Nat. Acad. of Art, New Delhi; Padma Bhushan 1967; D.Litt. h.c. (Delhi, Benares, Andhra, Patiala, Shantiniketan); Laureate of Int. Peace Prize. *Publications:* Novels: The Bubble, Morning Face, Private Life of an Indian Prince, The Big Heart, The Sword and the Sickle, Across the Black Waters, Untouchable, Coolie, The Barbers' Trade Union, Seven Summers, etc.; Essays: Apology for Heroism, Seven Little Known Birds of the Inner Eye, Death of a Hero, etc. *Leisure interests:* environment, world peace. *Address:* Jassim House, 25 Cuffe Parade, Colaba, Bombay 400005, India. *Telephone:* Bombay 2181371.

ANAND PANYARACHUN; Thai politician and business executive; ed. Univ. of Cambridge; fmr. Amb. to Canada, U.S.A., U.N. and Fed. Repub. of Germany in 1970s; later Head, Ministry of Foreign Affairs; fmr. Exec. Chair. Saha Union (industrial conglomerate); fmr. Chair. Fed. of Industries; Prime Minister of Thailand 1991–92. *Address:* c/o Office of the Prime Minister, Government House, Thanon Nakhon Pathom Road, Bangkok 10300, Thailand.

ANANIASHVILI, Nina Gedevanovna; Georgian ballet dancer; b. 28 March 1963, Tbilisi, Georgia; d. of Gedevan Ananiashvili and Lia Gogolashvili; m. Gregory Vashadze 1988; ed. State Choreographic Schools of Georgia and Bolshoi Theatre, Moscow; joined Bolshoi Ballet 1981, now prima ballerina; has performed on tour worldwide with New York City Ballet, Royal Ballet, Royal Danish Ballet, Kirov Ballet, American Ballet Theatre, Royal Swedish Ballet, Ballet de Monte Carlo, The Munich Ballet and others; roles include: Giselle, Odette/Odile (Swan Lake) Aurora (Sleeping Beauty), Raimonda, Juliet (Romeo and Juliet), Nikya (La Bayadere); numerous awards include Grand Prix Int. Ballet Competition, Jackson 1986, People's Artist Repub. of Georgia and of Russia; State Prize 1992, (Russia) 1993. *Leisure interests:* antique books, modern painting. *Address:* 119270 Frunzenskaya nab. 46, Apt. 79, Moscow, Russia. *Telephone:* 242-5864. *Fax:* 476-3470.

ANANICH, Boris Vasilyevich; Russian historian; b. 4 March 1931; m.; one d.; ed. Leningrad State Univ.; chief researcher St. Petersburg br. Inst. of History, U.S.S.R. Acad. of Sciences; corresp. mem. U.S.S.R. (now Russian) Acad. of Sciences 1990, mem. 1994; research in history of Russia 19th–20th centuries, econ. history, internal policy. *Publications include:* Russia and International Capital 1897–1914, Essays on history of Financial Relations 1976, Banking Houses in Russia 1860–1914, Essays on history of Private Businesses 1991, numerous articles. *Address:* Institute of History, Russian Academy of Sciences, Petrozavodskaya str. 7, 197110 St. Petersburg, Russia. *Telephone:* (812) 235 4198 (Office).

ANANYEV, Anatoliy Andreyevich; Russian writer; b. 18 July 1925, Dzhambul, Kazakhstan; m. Tatyana Kharchenko 1957; one d.; ed. Kazakh State Univ.; mem. CPSU 1950–91; Deputy Ed. Znamya 1967–70; Ed.-in-Chief Oktyabr 1973–; Sec. U.S.S.R. Writers' Union 1976–91; Chair. Council of Independent Popular Pension Funds 1993–; People's Deputy of U.S.S.R. 1989–91; Hero of Socialist Labour 1984. *Publications:* Tales of Vernensk 1958, Small Cover 1959, The Shadow of Jesus 1961, The Trump Cards of the Monk Grigorii 1964, Tanks are Moving in Rhombus 1964, Miles of Love 1973, Years Without War, Vols 1–4 1975–84, Tables and Bells 1989, Faces of Immortal Power 1992, The Call for Ryurikovichi, or The Millennial Mystery of Russia (vols. 1–2) 1993–98, Collection of Works: (vols. 1–8) 1995–97. *Address:* Astrakhanski per. 5, Apt. 12, 129010 Moscow, Russia. *Telephone:* (095) 280-15-20.

ANAYA, Rudolfo, M.A.; American author; b. 30 Oct. 1937, Pastura, N.M.; s. of Martin Anaya and Rafaelita Mares; m. Patricia Lawless 1966; ed. Albuquerque High School, Browning Business School, Univ. of New Mexico; teacher Albuquerque public schools 1963–70; Dir. Counseling Center, Univ. of Albuquerque 1971–73; lecturer Univ. Anahuac, Mexico City 1974; Prof. Dept. of Language and Literature Univ. of N.M. 1974–93, Emer. Prof. 1993–; f., Ed. Blue Mesa Review 1989–93; Martin Luther King, Jr./César Chávez, Rosa Parks Visiting Prof. Univ. of Mich., Ann Arbor 1996; now Assoc. Ed. The American Book Review, Bd. Contributing Ed. The Americas Review, Advisory Ed. Great Plains Quarterly; Hon.D.Hum.Litt. (Albuquerque) 1981, (Marycrest Coll.) 1984, (New England) 1992, (Calif. Lutheran Univ.) 1994, (N.H.) 1997; Hon.Ph.D. (Santa Fe) 1991; Hon.D.Litt. (N.M.) 1996; f. PEN-N.M., Teachers of English and Chicano Language Arts 1991; f., Pres. N.M. Rio Grande Writers Asscn.; mem. Bd. Before Columbus Foundation; mem. Nat. Asscn. of Chicano Studies; recipient numerous awards. *Publications include:* Bless Me, Ultima 1972 (Premio Quinto Sol Award 1971), Heart of Aztlan 1976, Tortuga 1979 (American Book Award, Before Columbus Foundation 1979), Cuentos: Tales from the Hispanic Southwest (trans.) 1980, The Silence of the Llano (short stories) 1982, The Legend of La Llorona 1984, The Adventures of Juan Chicaspatas (poem) 1985, A Chicano in China 1986, Lord of the Dawn, The Legend of Quetzalcoatl 1987, Albuquerque 1992 (PEN-WEST Fiction Award 1993), The Anaya Reader (anthology) 1994, Zia Summer 1995, The Farolitos of Christmas 1995, Jalamanta, A Message from the Desert 1996, Rio Grande Fall 1996, Maya's Children 1997, Descansos: An Interrupted Journey (with Estevan Arellano and Denise Chávez) 1997; short stories in literary magazines in U.S.A. and internationally; has also ed. various collections of short stories. *Leisure interests:* reading, travel, apple orchards. *Address:* Department of Language and Literature, University of New Mexico, Albuquerque, NM 87131 (Office); 5324 Cañada Vista N.W., Albuquerque, NM 87120, U.S.A. (Home). *Fax:* (505) 899-0014 (Home).

ANBARI, Abdul-Amir al-, S.J.D.; Iraqi diplomatist; b. 10 Oct. 1934; m.; one s. two d.; ed. Univ. of Baghdad and Harvard Univ.; fmrly. held posts in Iraq Nat. Oil Co., OPEC and Iraqi Ministry of Oil; fmr. mem. Bd. State Org. for Oil Refineries, High Comm. for Marketing, Arab Petroleum Investment Corpn., Exec. Bd. of Org. of Arab Petroleum Exporting Countries (OAPEC); founding mem. Bd. of Trustees of Inst. of Int. Devt. Law, Rome; fmr. Judge, Judicial Tribunal of Arab Petroleum Exporting Countries; Exec. Chair. and Pres. Iraqi Fund for External Devt.; Gov. Islamic Devt. Bank; mem. Bd. of Govs. OAPEC Fund for Int. Devt.; Dir.-Gen. Multilateral Econ. Relations Dept. Ministry of Foreign Affairs 1984–85; Amb. to U.K. 1984–86; Amb. to U.S.A. 1986–88; Perm. Rep. to UN, New York 1988–92; Amb. to UNESCO, Paris 1992. *Address:* c/o Ministry of Foreign Affairs, Karradat Mariam, Baghdad, Iraq.

ANCRAM, Earl of; **Michael Andrew Foster Jude Kerr,** M.A., LL.D., P.C., Q.C.; British politician; b. 7 July 1945; s. of 12th Marquess of Lothian and Antonella, Marchioness of Lothian; m. Lady Jane Fitzalan-Howard 1975; two d.; ed. Ampleforth, Christ Church Coll., Oxford, Edinburgh Univ.; fmrly. in business, columnist Daily Telegraph (Manchester edn.), partner in tenanted arable farm; called to Scottish Bar 1970, practised law 1970–79; M.P. for Berwickshire and East Lothian Feb.-Oct. 1974, Edin. S. 1979–87, for Devizes 1992–; mem. House of Commons Energy Select Cttee. 1979–83; Parl. Under-Sec. of State Scottish Office 1983–87; Parl. Under-Sec. N.I. Office 1993–94, Minister of State 1994–96; Shadow Cabinet Spokesman for Constitutional Affairs 1997–; Chair. Conservative Party 1998–; Vice-Chair. Conservative Party in Scotland 1975–80, Chair. 1980–83; Chair. Northern Corp. Communications 1989–91; Dir. C.S.M. Parl. Consultants 1988–92; mem. Bd. Scottish Homes 1988–90; D.L. Roxburgh, Ettrick and Lauderdale 1990. *Leisure interests:* skiing, fishing, photography, folk singing. *Address:* House of Commons, London, SW1A 0AA, England. *Telephone:* 0171-219 4435. *Fax:* 0171-215 2528.

ANDENAES, Johannes, DR.JUR.; Norwegian professor of law; b. 7 Sept. 1912, Innvik; s. of Mads and Signe (née Mydland) Andenaes; m. Ida Rören 1939; two s. two d.; ed. Univ. of Oslo; Asst. judge 1936–37; Asst. Prof., Univ. of Oslo 1939, Prof. 1945–82, Dean, School of Law 1959–60, 1968–69, Rector 1970–72; Pres. Norwegian Acad. of Science and Letters 1977–81; Visiting Prof., Univ. of Pa. 1963, Chicago 1968, Minn. 1974; Visiting Fellow, All Souls Coll., Oxford 1971; Dr. jur. h.c. (Copenhagen, Uppsala, Bergen); Sellin-Glueck Award, American Soc. of Criminology 1979; Nordic Prize for legal scholarship 1981. *Publications:* Alminnelig Strafferett, Norsk straffeprosess, Statsforfatningen i Norge, Punishment and Deterrence, Norway and the Second World War, Det vanskelige oppgjöret, Spesiell Strafferett, Et liv blant paragrafer, Straffen som problem. *Address:* University of Oslo, Karl Johansgate 47, Oslo 1; Generallunden 23, 0381 Oslo 3, Norway (Home). *Telephone:* 22-859444 (Office); 22-524127 (Home).

ANDERS, Edward, PH.D., M.A.; American professor of chemistry; b. 21 June 1926, Liepaja, Latvia; s. of Adolph Alperovitch and Erica Leventals; m. Joan Elizabeth Fleming 1955; one s. one d.; ed. Univ. of Munich, Columbia Univ.; Instructor in Chem., Univ. of Ill. at Urbana 1954–55; Asst. Prof. of Chem. Univ. of Chicago 1955–60, Assoc. Prof. 1960–62, Prof. 1960–73, Horace B. Horton Prof. of Physical Sciences 1973–91; Visiting Prof. Calif. Inst. of Tech. 1960, Univ. of Berne 1963–64, 1970, 1978, 1980–81, 1983, 1987–88, 1989–90; Research Assoc. Field Museum of Natural History 1968–91; Fellow American Acad. of Arts and Sciences 1973–; mem. N.A.S. 1974–; Assoc. Royal Astronomical Soc., U.K. 1974–; Fairchild Distinguished Scholar, Calif. Inst. of Tech. 1992–93; Cleveland Prize, A.A.A.S. 1959; Smith Medal, N.A.S. 1971, Leonard Medal, Meteoritical Soc. 1974, Goldschmidt Medal, Geochemical Soc. 1990, Kuiper Prize, American Astronomical Soc. 1991, Hess Medal (American Geophysical Union) 1995. *Publications:* about 260 articles in scientific journals. *Leisure interests:* classical music, hiking, photography. *Address:* Hintere Engehaldenstrasse 12, 3004 Berne, Switzerland. *Telephone:* (31) 302-44-56. *Fax:* (31) 302-44-56.

ANDERSEN, Bodil Nyboe, M.SC.; Danish central banker; b. 9 Oct. 1940; ed. Univ. of Copenhagen; Asst. Prin. Ministry of Econ. Affairs 1966–68; Assoc. Prof. (Money and Banking), Univ. of Copenhagen 1968–80; Man. Dir. and mem. Man. Bd. Andelsbanken 1981–90; Group Man. Dir. Unibank and Unidanmark 1990; mem. Bd. Govs. Danmarks Nationalbank 1990–, Chair. Bd. of Govs. 1995–; Gov. for Denmark, IMF 1995–; with Gen. Council European Cen. Bank 1998–; mem. Bd. Dirs. Danish Foreign Policy Inst. 1972–78; mem. Senate, Univ. of Copenhagen 1977–80; Dir. Privatinvest 1978–80, CERD 1978–81, Great Belt Ltd. 1987–91, Danish Payment Systems Ltd. 1988–90, Industrial Mortgage Credit Fund 1991–92, etc.; mem. Council, European Monetary Inst. 1995–98. *Address:* Danmarks Nationalbank, Havnegade 5, 1093 Copenhagen K, Denmark. *Telephone:* 33 63 63 63. *Fax:* 33 63 71 01.

ANDERSEN, Ib; Danish ballet dancer; b. 14 Dec. 1954, Copenhagen; s. of Ingolf and Anna Andersen; ed. with Royal Danish Ballet; ballet dancer, Royal Danish Ballet 1973–80, Prin. Dancer 1975–80; Prin. Dancer, New York City Ballet 1980–94; Ballet Master Pittsburgh Ballet Theater 1994–; Nijinsky Prize. *Address:* Pittsburgh Ballet Theater, Pittsburgh, Pa., U.S.A.

ANDERSEN, Mogens; Danish painter; b. 8 Aug. 1916, Copenhagen; s. of late Einar F. T. Andersen and late Erna Ingeborg, née Andersen; m. Inger Therkildsen 1947; one s. one d.; ed. in Copenhagen under art master P. Rostrup Boyesen; art teacher Copenhagen 1952–59, Académie de la Grande Chaumière, Paris 1963; mem. cttee. Danish Art Exhbn. Arrangement 1956–58; Pres. Danish State Art Foundation 1977–80; mem. Royal Acad. of Fine Arts 1956, Prof. 1970–72; mem. PEN Club; Eckersberg Medal 1949, Thorvaldsen Medal 1984, Chevalier, Légion d'honneur, Kt. of Dannebrog, and other awards. *Exhibitions:* Copenhagen 1935–40, 1942–50, 1953–66, 1967; Paris 1950–74, 1981. *Private Exhbns.:* Copenhagen 1953, 1963, 1966, 1968, 1969, 1976 (retrospective), Alborg (Denmark) 1954, 1972, Lund (Sweden) 1959, Paris 1954, 1959, 1963, 1966, 1967, 1973, 1975, 1981, Warsaw 1973, Belgrade 1973, Zagreb, Randers 1981, Aarhus 1982, 1988, Budapest 1983, 1984, Pittsburgh 1987; group exhbns. in Europe and the U.S.A.; Venice Biennale 1968, retrospective Copenhagen 1988, Aarhus Kunstmuseum 1990, Glyptoteket, Copenhagen 1991, Mikael Andersen Gallery, Copenhagen 1991, 1993, 1996, Galerie Artcurial, Paris 1995, Århus Kunstmuseum 1995; paintings hung in Modern Museum, Skopje 1965, Bridgestone Museum, Tokyo, Kunstmuseum, Malmø, Kongelige Bibliotek, Copenhagen, and many other museums in Denmark, Sweden, Norway, Poland and U.S.A. *Major works:* Composition in Niels Bohr Inst., Copenhagen 1955, Mural, Central Library, Copenhagen 1958–59, Composition in Central Library, Århus 1964, October, State Art Museum 1964, Mural, Gentofte Town Hall 1971, Restaurante Copenhagen, Paris 1973, Handelsbanken, Copenhagen 1975, Northern Feather Inst., Danmarks Tekniske Højskole 1979, Panum-institutet, Copenhagen 1981, Kunstmuseum, Bochum 1981, Musikhuset, Aarhus 1982, Metalskolen, Holstebro, Skäfogaard, Mörke Konstmuseum, Lund, Mural in Sejs Church, Denmark 1989. *Publications:* Moderne fransk malerkunst 1948, Omkring Kilderne 1967, Nødigt, Men Dog Gerne 1976, Ungdomsrejsen 1979, Om Kunst og Samfund 1980, Huset 1986, Punktum, Punktum, Komma, Streg 1994. *Address:* Strandagervej 28, 2900 Hellerup, Copenhagen, Denmark. *Telephone:* (39) 62 02 66.

ANDERSEN, Ronald Max, M.S., PH.D.; American sociologist; b. 15 Feb. 1939, Omaha, Neb.; s. of Max Adolph Andersen and Evangeline Dorothy Andersen (née Wobbe); m. Diane Borella 1965; one d.; ed. Univ. of Santa Clara and Purdue Univ.; Research Assoc. Purdue Farm Cardiac Project, Dept. of Sociology, Purdue Univ. 1962–63; Assoc. Study Dir. Nat. Opinion Research Center, Univ. of Chicago 1963–66, Research Assoc. Center for Health Admin. Studies 1963–77; Instructor Grad. School of Business, Univ of Chicago 1966–68, Asst. Prof. 1968–72, Asst. Prof. Dept. of Sociology 1970–72, Assoc. Prof. Grad. School of Business, then Prof. 1974–90; Assoc. Dir. Center for Health Admin. Studies 1977–80, Dir. and Dir. Grad. Program in Health Admin. 1980–90; Chair. Ed. Bd. Health Admin. Press, Chicago, Ill. 1980–83, 1988–; Wasserman Prof. Health Services and Sociology Dept., Calif. Univ. at L.A. 1991–, Chair. Dept. of Health Services 1993–96; mem. numerous cttees., advisory panels etc.; mem. American Sociological Asscn., American Statistical Asscn., American Public Health Asscn. *Publications:* author and co-author of numerous books, monographs, book chapters and articles in professional journals. *Address:* UCLA School of Public Health, Los Angeles, CA 90024 (Office); 10724 Wilshire Boulevard, Apartment 312, Los Angeles, CA 90024, U.S.A. (Home).

ANDERSEN, Torkild, M.SC., DR.PHIL.; Danish professor of physics; b. 19 June 1934, Randers; m. Inger Bloch-Petersen 1957; one s. one d.; ed. Tech. Univ. Copenhagen; industrial chemist 1958–59; Asst. and Assoc. Prof. of Chem., Univ. of Aarhus 1958–71, Prof. of Physics (Atomic Physics) 1971–; Postdoctoral Fellow, Univ. of Cambridge 1961–63; Visiting Prof. Univ. of Colo. 1984–85, Flinders Univ. S. Australia 1988, 1994; Bd. mem. Carlsberg Foundation 1996–; mem. Royal Danish Acad. of Science; N. Bjerrum Prize 1972. *Publications:* 170 scientific contribs. to chemistry of physics journals. *Address:* Institute of Physics and Astronomy, University of Aarhus, Nordre. Ringgade, 8000 Aarhus C (Office); 37 Klokkerbakken, 8210 Aarhus V, Denmark (Home). *Telephone:* 8942-3740. *Fax:* 8612-0740.

ANDERSON, Campbell McCheyne, B.ECON.; Australian business executive; b. 17 Sept. 1941, Sydney; s. of Allen Taylor Anderson and Ethel Catherine Rundle; m. Sandra Maclean Harper 1965; two s. one d.; ed. Armidale School, N.S.W., Univ. of Sydney; audit clerk, Priestley and Morris 1958–59; with Boral Ltd. 1962–69; Gen. Man. then Man. Dir. Reef Oil Ltd. and Basin Oil Ltd. 1969–72; with Burmah Oil Australia Ltd. 1972–73, New York 1973–74, Div. Dir., then Chief Financial Officer, Burmah Oil Trading Ltd., U.K. 1974–75, Dir. 1975–76, Exec. Dir. Burmah Oil Co. Ltd. 1976–82, Man. Dir. Burmah Oil PLC 1982–85; Man. Dir. Renison Goldfields Consolidated Ltd. 1985, Man. Dir. and C.E.O. 1986–93, Dir. Consolidated Gold Fields PLC 1985–89; Man. Dir. North Ltd. 1994–; Chair. Energy Resources Australia Ltd. 1994–; Chair. Ampolex Ltd. 1991–96, Dir. 1996–97; Man. Dir. and Dir. of numerous cos. in U.K. and overseas; Pres. Australia/Japan Soc. of Vic. 1995–; Assoc. Australian Soc. of Certified Practising Accountants. *Leisure interests:* golf, shooting, horse-racing, swimming. *Address:* 193 Domain Road, South Yarra, Vic. 3041, Australia.

ANDERSON, Christopher (Chris), B. ECONS.; Australian journalist; b. 9 Dec. 1944; s. of C. F. and L. A. Anderson; m. Gabriella Douglas 1969; one s. one d.; ed. Picton High School, N.S.W., Univ. of Sydney, Columbia Univ., New York; journalist and political commentator 1962–76; Deputy Ed., later Ed., The Sun-Herald 1976–79; Deputy Ed., later Ed., The Sydney Morning Herald 1980–83, Ed.-in-Chief 1983–88; Man. Dir. and Group Ed. Dir. John Fairfax Ltd. 1987–90, Chief Exec. 1990–91; Man. Ed. Australian Broadcasting Corpn. 1993–95; Chief Exec. TV New Zealand Limited 1995–97, Optus Comm. *Address:* Optus Communications, 101 Miller Street, North Sydney, N.S.W. 2060, Australia. *Telephone:* (02) 9342-7001. *Fax:* (02) 9342-8001.

ANDERSON, David, M.A.; American diplomatist (retd.); b. 3 Jan. 1937, Scotland; s. of Alexander P. Anderson and Janet B. Anderson (née Brown); m. Doris Helen Heitmann 1979; one s. two d.; ed. Union Coll., Fletcher School of Law and Diplomacy; political officer Dept. of State, Yugoslavia 1962–65, Mali 1965–67, Berlin 1967–70, Brussels 1970–71, Bonn 1971–75; Dir Cen. European Affairs Dept. of State, Washington 1975–77; U.S. Minister Berlin 1978–81; Amb. to Yugoslavia 1981–85; Warburg Prof. internal relations Simmons Coll. Boston 1985–87; Dir. Aspen Inst., Berlin 1988–; mem. Council on Foreign Relations, Int. Inst. of Strategic Studies. *Leisure interests:* golf, reading. *Address:* Inselstrasse 10, 14129 Berlin, Germany. *Telephone:* 803-9041.

ANDERSON, Don L., PH.D.; American geophysicist; b. 5 March 1933, Frederick, Md.; m. Nancy Lois Ruth 1956; one s. one d.; ed. Rensselaer Polytechnic Inst. and California Inst. of Tech.; Geophysicist, Chevron Oil Co. 1955–56; Geophysicist, Geophysics Research Directorate, Air Force Cambridge Research Center 1956–58; Research Fellow, Calif. Inst. of Tech. 1962–63, Asst. Prof. 1963–64, Assoc. Prof. 1964–68, Prof. 1968–, Dir. Seismological Lab. 1967–89; Eleanor and John R. McMillan Chair. in Geophysics, Caltech. 1990–; Ed. Physics of the Earth and Planetary Interiors 1977; Assoc. Ed. Tectonophysics, Physics and Chemistry of the Earth, Journal of Geodynamics etc.; Pres. American Geophysical Union 1988–90, Past Pres. 1990–92; mem. Space Science Bd., Geophysics Research Forum (Chair. 1983–), Bd. on Earth Sciences of N.A.S., Arthur L. Day Award Cttee. N.A.S. (Chair. 1989–90) and several other cttees. and bds.; Fellow American Geophysical Union (Pres. 1986–88), A.A.A.S., Geological Soc. of America, N.A.S., Royal Astronomical Soc., American Philosophical Soc.; Hon. Foreign Fellow, European Union of Geosciences; mem. Seismological Soc. of America; Sloan Foundation Fellow 1964–67; H. Burr Steinbach Visiting Scholar, Woods Hole Oceanographic Inst. 1995; Distinguished Scientists Lecture Series, Trinity Univ. 1995; J.B. Macelwane Award, American Geophysical Union 1966, Sr. Fulbright-Hays Award (Australia) 1975, Newcomb Cleveland Prize (A.A.A.S.) 1976–77, NASA Distinguished Scientific Achievement Award 1977, Emil Wiechert Medal, German Geophysical Soc. 1986, Arthur L. Day Medal, Geological Soc. of America 1987, Gold Medal, Royal Astronomical Soc. 1988, Cloos Memorial Scholar, Johns Hopkins Univ. 1989, Bowie Medal, American Geophysical Union 1991. *Address:* Seismological Laboratory 252-21, California Institute of Technology, Pasadena, CA 91125 (Office); 669 Alameda Street, Altadena, CA 91001, U.S.A. (Home). *Telephone:* (818) 395-6901 (Office); (818) 797-7426 (Home). *Fax:* (818) 564-0715.

ANDERSON, Donald Thomas, A.O., D.SC., F.R.S.; Australian professor of biology; b. 29 Dec. 1931, Eton, England; s. of Thomas and Flora Anderson; m. Joanne T. Claridge 1960; one s.; ed. King's Coll., London; Lecturer in Zoology, Univ. of Sydney, Australia 1958, Sr. Lecturer 1963, Reader 1968, Prof. 1972, Challis Prof. of Biology 1984–91, Prof. Emer. 1992–; Visiting Prof., King's Coll., London 1970. *Publications:* Embryology and Phylogeny in Annelids and Arthropods 1973, Barnacles 1994, Atlas of Invertebrate Anatomy 1996, Invertebrate Zoology 1998. *Leisure interests:* photography, gardening. *Address:* 5 Angophora Close, Wamberal, N.S.W. 2260, Australia. *Telephone:* (02) 4384-6670.

ANDERSON, George Wishart, M.A., D.D., D. THEOL., F.B.A., F.R.S.E.; British academic; b. 25 Jan. 1913, Arbroath, Scotland; s. of George Anderson and Margaret Gordon Wishart; m. 1st Edith Joyce Marjorie Walter 1941 (deceased); one s. one d.; m. 2nd Anne Phyllis Walter 1959; ed. Arbroath High School, St. Andrews, Cambridge and Lund Univs.; Asst. Tutor Richmond Coll., Surrey 1939–41; R.A.F. Chaplain 1941–46; Lecturer in Old Testament Languages and Literature, Handsworth Coll. Birmingham 1946–56; Lecturer in Old Testament Literature and Theology, Univ. of St. Andrews 1956–58; Prof. of Old Testament Studies, Univ. of Durham 1958–62; Prof. of Old Testament Literature and Theology, Univ. of Edin. 1962–68, of Hebrew and Old Testament Studies 1968–82; Speaker's Lecturer in Biblical Studies, Univ. of Oxford 1976–80; Prof. Emer. 1982; Burkitt Medal for Biblical Studies (British Acad.). *Publications:* A Critical Introduction to the Old Testament 1958, The History and Religion of Israel 1966; translated He That Cometh (S. Mowinckel) 1956, The Ras Shamra Discoveries and Old Testament (A.S. Kapelrud) 1963, 1965; Ed. A Decade of Bible Bibliography 1967, Tradition and Interpretation 1979. *Leisure interests:* reading, music. *Address:* 51 Fountainhall Road, Edinburgh, EH9 2LH, Scotland. *Telephone:* 0131-667-2945.

ANDERSON, Gerry; British film maker; b. 14 April 1929; m. 1st Betty Wrightman 1952; two d.; m. 2nd Sylvia Thamm 1961 (divorced); one s.; m. 3rd Mary Robins 1981; one s.; Hon. Fellow British Kinematograph Sound and TV Soc.; *Television series include:* Adventures of Twizzle (52 shows) 1956, Torchy the Battery Boy (26 shows) 1957, Four Feather Falls (52 shows) 1958, Supercar (39 shows) 1959, Fireball XL5 (39 shows) 1961, Stingray (39 shows) 1962–63, Thunderbirds (32 shows screened in 20 countries) 1964–66 (Royal Television Soc. Silver Medal), Captain Scarlet (32 shows) 1967, Joe 90 (30 shows) 1968, The Secret Service (13 shows) 1968, UFO (26 shows) 1969–70, The Protectors (52 shows) 1971–72, Space 1999

(48 shows) 1973–76, Terrahawks (39 shows) 1982–83, Dick Spanner (26 shows) 1987, Space Precinct 1993–95, Lavender Castle 1997; numerous television commercials; Silver Arrow Award. *Films:* Thunderbirds are Go 1966, Thunderbird 6 1968, Doppelganger 1969.

ANDERSON, Gillian; British actress; b. 9 Aug. 1968, Chicago; m. Errol Clyde Klotz; one d.; ed. DePaul Univ., Chicago, Goodman Theater School, Chicago; worked at Nat. Theatre, London; appeared in two off-Broadway productions; best known for role as Special Agent Dana Scully in TV series The X Files (feature film 1998); TV films include Home Fire Burning 1992, When Planes Go Down 1996; presenter, Future Fantastic, BBC TV; Golden Globe Awards 1995, 1997. *Address:* c/o X-Files Production Office, Bldg. 10, 110–555 Brooks Avenue, Vancouver, B.C., V7J 3S5, Canada.

ANDERSON, Sir John Anthony, K.B.E., F.C.A.; New Zealand banker; b. 2 Aug. 1945, Wellington; m. Carol M. Anderson 1970; two s. one d.; ed. Christ's Coll. and Victoria Univ. of Wellington; Deloitte Haskins & Sells (chartered accountants), Wellington 1962–69; Guest & Bell (sharebrokers), Melbourne 1969–72; joined South Pacific Merchant Finance Ltd., Wellington 1972, Chief Exec. and Dir. 1979; Deputy Chief Exec. Nat. Bank of N.Z. (following merger of Southpac and Nat. Bank) 1988, Chief Exec. and Dir. 1990–; Chair. N.Z. Merchant Banks Asscn. 1982–89, Petroleum Corpn. of N.Z. Ltd. 1986–88, N.Z. Bankers Asscn. 1992–; Dir. N.Z. Steel Ltd. 1986–87, Lloyds Merchant Bank (London) 1986–92, Lloyds Bank NZA (Australia) 1989–97; Chair N.Z. Cricket Bd. 1995–; Pres. N.Z. Bankers Inst. 1990–; other professional and public appointments, affiliations etc.; recipient, 1990 Commemoration Medal. *Leisure interests:* rugby, cricket, golf, bridge. *Address:* The National Bank of New Zealand Ltd., 170–186 Featherston Street, P.O. Box 1791, Wellington 6000 (Office); 5 Fancourt Street, Karori, Wellington 5, New Zealand (Home). *Telephone:* (04) 4729459 (Office); (04) 4768949 (Home).

ANDERSON, John Bayard, J.D., LL.M.; American politician; b. 15 Feb. 1922, Rockford, Ill.; s. of E. Albin Anderson and the late Mabel Ring; m. Keke Machakos 1953; one s. four d.; ed. Univ. of Illinois, Harvard Law School; admitted to Ill. Bar 1946; practiced law, Rockford, Ill. 1946–48, 1950–52, 1955–56; Instructor, Northeastern Univ. Law School 1948–49; State Dept. Career Diplomatic Service 1952–55; Winnebago County, Ill., State's Attorney 1956–60; Congressman, 16th Dist., Ill. 1960–80; mem. U.S. House of Reps. 1960–79; Chair. House Republican Conf. 1969–79; Ind. cand. for U.S. Pres. 1980; Chair. Nat. Unity Party; Political Commentator WLS-TV, Chicago 1981; Visiting Prof. of Political Science Brandeis Univ. 1985, Univ. of Massachusetts 1985, Oregon State Univ. 1986, Nova Univ. Center for Study of Law 1987–96; Lecturer in Political Science, Bryn Mawr Coll. 1985; Visiting Prof. of Law, Washington Coll. of Law of American Univ., Washington, D.C. 1997–; Pres. World Federalist Asscn. 1992–; fmr. Trustee, Trinity Coll., Deerfield, Ill.; Hon. LL.D. (Ill., Wheaton Coll., Shimer Coll., Biola Coll., Geneva Coll., North Park Coll., Houghton Coll., Trinity Coll.). *Publications:* Between Two Worlds: A Congressman's Choice 1970, Vision and Betrayal in America 1975, Congress and Conscience (Ed.) 1970, The American Economy We Need But Won't Get 1984, A Proper Institution: Guaranteeing Televised Presidential Debates 1988. *Leisure interest:* writing occasional commentary or opinion piece on political affairs. *Address:* 3917 Massachusetts Avenue, N.W. Washington, DC 20016; 3300 36th Street, N.E., Fort Lauderdale, Florida, U.S.A.

ANDERSON, John Duncan, M.A.; Australian politician; b. 14 Nov. 1956; s. of D. A. Anderson; m. Julia Gillian Robertson 1987; one s. two d.; ed. Kings School, Parramatta, St. Paul's Coll., Univ. of Sydney; fmr. farmer and grazier; M.P. for Gwydir, N.S.W.; Deputy Leader NPA; Shadow Minister for Primary Industry 1993–96; Minister for Primary Industries and Energy 1996–98, for Transport and Regional Devt. 1998–; Nat. Party of Australia. *Leisure interests:* farming, shooting, reading, photography. *Address:* Department of Transport and Regional Development, GPOB 594, Canberra, A.C.T. 2601 (Office); 342–344 Conadilly Street, Gunnedah, N.S.W. 2380, Australia (Home).

ANDERSON, June; American soprano and concert and oratorio vocalist; b. Boston; *Roles include:* Queen of the Night in The Magic Flute, NY City Opera 1978, title role in Lucia di Lammermoor, Milwaukee Florentine Opera 1982 and Chicago 1990, Gulnara in Il Corsaro, San Diego Opera Verdi Festival 1982, I Puritani, Edmonton Opera 1982–83, title role in Semiramide, Rome Opera 1982–83 and Metropolitan Opera 1990, Rosina in The Barber of Seville, Seattle Opera and Teatro Massimo 1982–83, Cunigande in Candide 1989, Metropolitan Opera debut as Gilda in Rigoletto 1989; concert and oratorio vocalist: Chicago Pops Orchestra, Handel Festival Kennedy Centre, Denver Symphony, St. Louis Symphony, Cincinnati Symphony, Maracaibo (Venezuela) Symphony.

ANDERSON, Laurie, M.F.A.; American performance artist; b. 1947, Wayne, Ill.; d. of Arthur T. Anderson and Mary Louise (née Rowland) Anderson; ed. Columbia Univ.; Instructor in Art History, City Coll. of New York 1973–75; freelance critic Art News, Art Forum; composer and performer multi-media exhbns.; several recordings; wrote, directed and performed in film Home of the Brave 1986; one-woman shows include Barnard Coll. 1970, Harold Rivkin Gallery, Washington 1973, Artists' Space, New York 1974, Holly Solomon Gallery, New York 1977, 1980–81, Museum of Modern Art 1978, Queen's (N.Y.) Museum 1984; numerous group exhbns. 1972–; Artist-in-Residence, ZBS Media 1974; Guggenheim Fellow 1983. *Publications:* The Package 1971, October 1972, Transportation, Transportation 1973, The Rose and the Stone 1974, Notebook 1976, Artifacts at The End of a Decade 1981, Typisch Frac 1981, United States 1984, Laurie Anderson's Postcard Book 1990, Empty Places: A Performance 1991, Stories from the Nerve Bible 1993.

ANDERSON, Matthew Smith, PH.D.; British historian and fmr. university professor; b. 23 May 1922, Perth, Scotland; s. of Matthew Smith Anderson and Elizabeth Dobbie Redpath; m. Olive Ruth Gee (q.v.) 1954; two d.; ed. Perth Acad., Edinburgh Univ.; lecturer in Political History, London School of Econs. and Political Science 1953–61, Reader in Int. History 1961–72, Prof. 1972–85, Prof. Emer., London Univ. 1985–. *Publications:* Britain's Discovery of Russia 1958, Europe in the Eighteenth Century 1961, The Eastern Question, 1774–1923 1966, The Ascendancy of Europe, 1815–1914 1972, Peter the Great 1978, Historians and Eighteenth-Century Europe 1979, War and Society in Europe of the Old Regime 1618–1789 1988, The Rise of Modern Diplomacy, 1450–1919 1993, The War of the Austrian Succession, 1740–1748 1995, The Origins of the Modern European State System 1494–1618 1998. *Leisure interests:* golf, walking, photography. *Address:* 45 Cholmeley Crescent, Highgate, London, N6 5EX, England. *Telephone:* 0181-340 0272.

ANDERSON, Michael; British film director; b. 30 Jan. 1920, London; one s.; ed. in France; Co-Dir. Private Angelo (with Peter Ustinov) 1949; Dir. Waterfront 1950, Hell is Sold Out 1952, Night Was Our Friend, Dial 17, Will Any Gentleman?, The House of The Arrow 1952, The Dam Busters 1954, Around the World in Eighty Days 1956, Yangtse Incident 1957, Chase a Crooked Shadow 1957, Shake Hands with the Devil 1958, Wreck of the Mary Deare 1959–60, All the Fine Young Cannibals 1960, The Naked Edge 1961, Flight from Ashiya (in Japan) 1962, Operation Crossbow 1964, The Quiller Memorandum 1966, Shoes of The Fisherman 1969, Pope Joan 1970–71, Doc Savage (in Hollywood) 1973, Conduct Unbecoming 1974, Logan's Run (M.G.M. Hollywood) 1975, Orca—Killer Whale 1976, Dominique 1977, The Martian Chronicles 1978, Bells 1979–80, Millennium, Murder by Phone, Second Time Lucky, Separate Vacations, Sword of Gideon, Jeweller's Shop, Young Catherine, Millennium. *Address:* c/o Film Rights Ltd., 113–117 Wardour Street, London, W.1, England.

ANDERSON, Olive Ruth, M.A., B.LITT.; British professor of history; b. 27 March 1926, Edinburgh; d. of Donald H. F. Gee and Ruth (Clackson) Gee; m. Matthew Smith Anderson (q.v.) 1954; two d.; ed. King Edward VI Grammar School, Louth, Lincs., St. Hugh's Coll., Oxford; Asst. Lecturer in History, Westfield Coll., Univ. of London 1949–56, lecturer 1958–69, Reader 1969–86, Prof. and Head of Dept. 1986–89, Prof. and Deputy Head of Dept., Queen Mary & Westfield Coll. 1989–91, Emer. Prof. and Hon. Research Fellow 1991–, Fellow 1995–; James Ford Special Lecturer, Oxford Univ. 1992; mem. Acad. Council Univ. of London 1989–91 (Exec. Cttee. 1990–91); Councillor Royal Historical Soc. 1986–90, Vice-Pres. 1991–95; Trustee Theodora Bosanquet Trust 1995–98; mem. Finance Cttee. British Fed. of Women Grads. Charitable Foundation 1996–, Grants Cttee. 1998–. *Publications:* A Liberal State at War 1967, Suicide in Victorian and Edwardian England 1987. *Address:* Queen Mary & Westfield College University of London, History Dept., London, E1 4NS (Office); 45 Cholmeley Crescent, Highgate, London, N6 5EX, England (Home). *Telephone:* 0171-975 5016 (College).

ANDERSON, Reid Bryce; Canadian ballet director; b. 1 April 1949, New Westminster, B.C.; Prin. Dancer, Stuttgart Ballet 1969–83, Ballet Master, 1983–85; Artistic Dir. Ballet B.C. 1987–89, Nat. Ballet of Canada 1989–; Stuttgart Ballet 1996–; Bundesverdienstkreuz; John Cranko Prize 1989, 1996. *Address:* Stuttgarter Ballett, Oberer Schlossgarten 6, D-70173 Stuttgart, Germany. *Telephone:* (711) 20 32 235. *Fax:* (711) 20 32 491.

ANDERSON, Robert Geoffrey William, M.A., D.PHIL., F.R.S.E.; British museum director; b. 2 May 1944, London; s. of Herbert Patrick Anderson and Kathleen Diana Burns; m. Margaret Elizabeth Callis Lea 1973; two s.; ed. Woodhouse School, Finchley, St. John's Coll., Oxford; Keeper Science Museum, London 1980–84; Dir. Royal Scottish Museum 1984–85, Nat. Museums of Scotland 1985–92, British Museum 1992–; Curator School of Advanced Study, Univ. of London 1994–; Pres. British Soc. for the History of Science 1988–90, Scientific Instrument Comm. of the Int. Union of the History and Philosophy of Science 1982–97; mem. Bd. Boerhaave Museum, Leiden 1995–; Hon. D.Sc. (Edin.) 1995, (Durham) 1998; Dexter Award (American Chemical Soc.) 1986. *Publications:* The Playfair Collection 1978, Science in India 1982, Science, Medicine and Dissent (ed.) 1987, A New Museum for Scotland (ed.) 1990, Joseph Black: a Bibliography (with G. Fyffe) 1992, Making Instruments Count (jt. ed.) 1993. *Address:* The British Museum, London, WC1B 3DG, England.

ANDERSON, Robert Orville, B.A.; American business executive and cattle rancher; b. 13 April 1917, Chicago, Ill.; s. of Hugo Anderson and Hilda Nelson Anderson; m. Barbara Herrick Phelps 1939; two s. five d.; ed. Univ. of Chicago; founder and Pres. Hondo Oil and Gas Co. (fmrly. Malco Refineries Inc.) 1941–63; Founder and Owner, Lincoln County Livestock Co., New Mexico; Chair. Federal Reserve Bank of Dallas 1959–65; Dir. Northern Natural Gas Co. 1960–63; Chair. of Exec. Cttee. and Dir. The Atlantic Refining Co. 1963–65 (now ARCO), Chair. of Board 1965–85, C.E.O. 1965–82; Chair. The Observer Ltd. 1981–83, Deputy Chair. July 1983; Chair. of Bd., Diamond A. Cattle Co., Roswell, New Mexico; fmr. Chair. Hondo Oil and Gas Co.; mem. Nat. Petroleum Council 1954–; Hon. Chair. Aspen Inst.; Chair. Emer. Lovelace Foundation; Trustee Univ. of Chicago, Calif. Inst. of Technology; mem. Washington Inst. for Foreign Affairs 1963; official of numerous civic and business orgs. *Address:* c/o Hondo Oil and Gas Co., 10375 Richmond Avenue, Suite 900, Houston, TX 77042, U.S.A.

ANDERSON, Roy Arnold, M.B.A.; American financial executive; b. 15 Dec. 1920, Ripon, Calif.; s. of Carl Gustav Anderson and Esther Marie Johnson; m. Betty Leona Boehme 1948; two s. two d.; ed. Ripon Union High School, Humphrey's School of Business, Stanford Univ.; Man., Factory Accounting, Westinghouse Electric Corpn. 1952–56; Man., Accounting and Finance, also Dir., Management Controls, Lockheed Missiles and Space Co. 1956–65; Dir. of Finance, Lockheed Georgia Co. 1965–68; Asst. Treas. Lockheed Aircraft Corpn. (now Lockheed Corpn.) 1968–69, Vice-Pres. and Controller 1969–71, Senior Vice-Pres., Finance 1971–75, Vice-Chair. of Bd., Chief Financial and Admin. Officer 1975–77, Chair. and C.E.O. 1977–85, Dir., Chair. Exec. Cttee. and Consultant 1985–88, Chair. Emer. 1991–; Chair. Weingart Foundation 1993–. *Leisure interests:* gardening, golf, tennis. *Address:* c/o Lockheed Corporation, 606 S. Olive Street, 23rd Floor, Los Angeles, CA 90014, U.S.A. *Telephone:* (213) 689-8701.

ANDERSON, Roy Malcolm, PH.D., A.R.C.S., D.I.C., F.R.S.; British university professor of biology; b. 12 April 1947, Herts.; s. of James Anderson and Betty Watson-Weatherborn; m. 1st Dr. Mary Joan Mitchell 1975 (divorced 1989); m. 2nd Claire Baron 1990; ed. Duncombe School, Bengeo, Richard Hale School, Hertford, Imperial Coll., Univ. of London; IBM Research Fellow, Oxford Univ. 1971–73; Lecturer, King's Coll., Univ. of London 1973–77; Lecturer, Imperial Coll. 1977–80, Reader 1980–82, Prof. of Parasite Ecology 1982–93, Head of Dept. of Biology 1984–93; Linacre Prof. Oxford Univ. 1993–, Head Dept. of Zoology 1993–98, Dir. The Wellcome Trust Centre for the Epidemiology of Infectious Disease 1993–; Chair. Terrestrial Life Sciences Cttee., Nat. Environment Research Council; Patron Virgin Health Care Foundation; Chair. Infection and Immunity Panel for Wellcome Trust 1990–92; Council mem. Nat. Environment Research Council 1988–91, Advisory Council on Science and Tech. (ACOST) 1989–91, Royal Soc. 1989–92, Zoological Soc. 1988–90; mem. Bd. of Dirs., AIDS Policy Unit 1988–89, Spongiform Encephalopathy Advisory Cttee. 1997–; mem. Acad. of Medical Sciences 1998, Acad. Europaea 1998; Trustee, The Wellcome Trust 1991–92, Gov. 1992–; Fellow Inst. of Biology, Royal Soc. of Tropical Medicine and Hygiene, Royal Statistical Soc., Merton Coll., Oxford 1993–; Hon. M.R.C.P.; Hon. Sc.D. (East Anglia) 1997, (Stirling) 1998; Joseph Smadel Lecture (Infectious Diseases Soc. of America) 1994; Zoological Soc. Scientific Medal 1982, Huxley Memorial Medal 1983, C.A. Wright Memorial Medal 1986, David Starr Jordan Prize 1986, Chalmers Medal 1988, Weldon Medal 1989, John Grundy Lecture Medal 1990, Frink Medal 1993. *Publications:* Population Dynamics of Infectious Disease Agents: Theory and Applications (Ed.) 1982, Population Biology of Infectious Diseases (Jt. Ed. with R. M. May) 1982, Infectious Diseases of Humans: Dynamics and Control (with R. M. May) 1991. *Leisure interests:* hill walking, croquet, natural history, photography. *Address:* Merton College, Oxford, OX1 4JD, England.

ANDERSON, Theodore Wilbur, PH.D.; American professor of statistics and economics; b. 5 June 1918, Minneapolis, Minn.; s. of Theodore Wilbur Anderson and Evelynn Johnson Anderson; m. Dorothy Fisher 1950; one s. two d.; ed. North Park Coll., Northwestern Univ., Princeton Univ.; Research Assoc. Cowles Comm. for Research in Econs., Univ. of Chicago 1945–46; Instructor in Math. Statistics, Columbia Univ. 1946–47, Asst. Prof. to Prof. 1947–67, Chair. of Dept. 1956–60, 1964–65, Dir. Office of Naval Research, Dept. of Math. Statistics 1950–68; Prof. of Statistics and Econs., Stanford Univ. 1967–88, Prin. Investigator Nat. Science Foundation Project Dept. of Econs. 1969–83, Dept. of Statistics 1983–92; Prin. Investigator Army Research Office Project Dept. of Statistics 1982–92; Guggenheim Fellow, Univs. of Stockholm and Cambridge 1947–48; Academic Visitor, Imperial Coll. of Science and Tech., U.K., Univ. of London, Visiting Prof. of Math., Univ. of Moscow, Visiting Prof. of Statistics, Univ. of Paris 1967–68; Academic Visitor, L.S.E. 1974–75, Univ. of Southern Calif. 1989; Research Consultant, Cowles Foundation for Research in Econs. 1946–60; Consultant, Rand Corpn. 1949–66; Fellow, Center for Advanced Study in the Behavioral Sciences 1957–58, Visiting Scholar 1972–73, 1980; Distinguished Scholar, Calif. Inst. of Tech. 1980; Visiting Prof. of Econs., Columbia Univ. 1983–84, New York Univ. 1983–84; Sabbaticant, IBM Systems Research Inst. 1984; Research Assoc. Naval Postgraduate School 1986–87; Visiting Distinguished Prof. of Norwegian Council for Scientific and Industrial Research, Univ. of Oslo 1989; Fellow Acad. of Arts and Sciences 1974–; mem. N.A.S. 1976–; Pres. Inst. of Mathematical Statistics 1963, mem. Council; Vice-Pres. American Statistical Soc. 1971–73; Chair. Section U, Statistics, American Asscn. for the Advancement of Science 1990–91; mem. Econometric Soc., Inst. of Math. Statistics (mem. Council); Royal Statistical Soc., U.K.; American Math. Soc., Bernoulli Soc. for Math. Statistics and Probability, Indian Statistical Inst., Int. Statistical Inst., Statistical Soc. of Canada; Foreign mem. Norwegian Acad. of Science and Letters 1994; Hon. D.Lit. (North Park Coll.) 1988; Hon. D.Sc. (Northwestern Univ.) 1989; Hon. Ph.D. (Oslo) 1997; R. A. Fisher Award (Cttee. of Pres. of Statistical Socs.) 1985, Distinguished Alumnus Award, North Park Coll. 1987, Samuel S. Wilks Memorial Medal, American Statistical Asscn. 1988, Award of Merit, Northwestern Univ. Alumni Asscn. 1989. *Publications:* An Introduction to Multivariate Statistical Analysis 1958, 1984, The Statistical Analysis of Time Series 1971, A Bibliography of Multivariate Statistical Analysis (with S. D. Gupta and G. Styan) 1972, Introductory Statistical Analysis (with S. Sclove) 1974, An Introduction to the Statistical Analysis of Data (with S. Sclove) 1978, 1986, A Guide to MINITAB for the Statistical Analysis of Data (with B. Eynon) 1986, Collected Papers of T. W. Anderson 1943–85 1990, The New Statistical Analysis of Data (with J. D. Finn) 1996 and some 150 articles in statistical journals; Ed. and fmr. Ed. of numerous specialist journals. *Leisure interests:* tennis, swimming, travelling. *Address:* Department of Statistics, Sequoia Hall, Stanford University, Stanford, CA 94305-4065; 746 Santa Ynez Street, Stanford, CA 94305, U.S.A. (Home). *Telephone:* (650) 723-4732; (650) 327-5204 (Home). *Fax:* (650) 725-8977.

ANDERSON, Warren M., LL.B.; American business executive; b. 29 Nov. 1921, Brooklyn, New York; s. of John M. and Ida Peterson Anderson; m. Lillian Christensen 1947; ed. Colgate Univ., Western Reserve Univ.; joined Union Carbide Corpn. 1945; engaged in chemicals, plastics, gases, metals and carbons industries; responsible for operations in U.S.A., Europe, Latin America, Africa, Middle East; Vice-Pres. of Corpn. 1969, Exec. Vice-Pres. 1973–77, mem. Bd. of Dirs. 1974–, now of Exec. Cttee. of Bds.; Pres. and C.O.O., Union Carbide Corpn. 1977–82, Chair. and C.E.O. 1982–86. *Address:* 270 Park Avenue, New York, NY 10017, U.S.A. *Telephone:* (212) 551-4158.

ANDERSON, (William) Eric (Kinloch), D.LITT., F.R.S.E.; British college principal; b. 27 May 1936, Edinburgh; s. of W. J. Kinloch Anderson and Margaret Harper; m. Anne Elizabeth (Poppy) Mason 1960; one s. one d.; ed. George Watson's Coll., Univ. of St. Andrews and Balliol Coll. Oxford; asst. master, Fettes Coll. Edin. 1960–64, 1966–70, Gordonstoun School 1964–66; Headmaster, Abingdon School 1970–75, Shrewsbury School 1975–80, Eton College 1980–94; Rector, Lincoln Coll. Oxford 1994–; Chair. King George VI and Queen Elizabeth Foundation of St. Catherine's 1997–; Trustee Nat. Heritage Memorial Fund 1996–98, Chair. 1998–. *Publications:* The Journal of Walter Scott (ed.) 1972, The Percy Letters (Vol. IX) 1988; articles and reviews. *Leisure interests:* theatre, golf, fishing, walking. *Address:* Lincoln College, Oxford, OX1 3DR, England. *Telephone:* (01865) 279803. *Fax:* (01865) 279802.

ANDERSON, Capt. William R.; American naval officer; b. 17 June 1921, Bakerville, Tenn.; s. of Mr. and Mrs. D. H. Anderson; m. 1st Yvonne Etzel 1943 (divorced 1979); two s.; m. 2nd Patricia Walters 1980; one s. one d.; ed. Columbia Military Acad. and U.S. Naval Acad.; commissioned 1942; service in submarines 1942–59; Idaho Univ. Inst. of Naval Tactics 1951; Naval Reactors Branch, Atomic Energy Comm. 1956–57, 1959; Commdr. Nautilus, the world's first atomic submarine 1957–59 (Nautilus achieved the first Pacific-to-Atlantic under-ice transit and was the first ship to reach the North Pole 1958); Freedoms Foundation 1962–64; mem. U.S. House of Reps. 1964–72; Computer Corporate Exec. 1972–; Bronze Star Combat "V", Legion of Merit 1958, Christopher Columbus Int. Medal (Italy) 1958, Patron's Medal, Royal Geographical Soc. 1959, Freedom Leadership Award 1960, various war and campaign medals; Democrat. *Publications:* Nautilus 90 North 1959, First under the North Pole 1959, The Useful Atom 1966. *Address:* 10505 Miller Road, Oakton, VA 22124, U.S.A.

ANDERSON, William Summers; American business executive; b. 29 March 1919, Hankow, China; s. of William G. and Mabel Anderson; m. Janice Elizabeth Robb 1947; three d.; ed. Public and Thomas Hanbury School, Shanghai; Internal Auditor Hongkong and Shanghai Hotels Ltd. 1938–39; auditor Linstead and Davis 1940–41; war service 1941–45; Nat. Cash Register Corpn. (NCR) (U.K.) 1945, Man. NCR Hong Kong 1946–59, Vice-Pres. Far East and Chair. NCR Japan 1959–72, Corp. Pres. and Dir. 1972–, Chief Exec. Officer 1973–83, Chair. and Pres. 1974–76, Chair. 1976–84. *Publication:* Corporate Crisis—NCR and the Computer Revolution 1991. *Leisure interests:* sailing, golf. *Address:* P.O. Box 259, Pebble Beach, CA 93953, U.S.A.

ANDERSON-IMBERT, Enrique, PH.D.; American (b. Argentinian) university professor; b. 12 Feb. 1910, Argentina; s. of José Enrique Anderson and Honorina Imbert; m. Margot Di Clerico 1934; one s. one d.; ed. Univ. Nacional de Buenos Aires; Prof., Univ. Nacional de Cuyo, Argentina 1940–41, Univ. Tucumán, Argentina 1941–46, Univ. of Michigan 1947–65; First Victor S. Thomas Prof. of Hispanic American Literature, Harvard Univ. 1965; mem. American Acad. of Arts and Sciences 1967, Academia Argentina de Letras, 1978; City of Buenos Aires prize for novel Vigilia 1934. *Publications:* Vigilia 1934, El arte de la prosa en Juan Montalvo 1948, Historia de la literatura hispanoamericana 1954, El grimorio 1961, Vigilia-Fuga 1963, El gato de Cheshire 1965, Genio y figura de Sarmiento 1967, La originalidad de Rubén Darío 1967, La sandía y otros cuentos 1969, Una aventura de Sarmiento en Chicago 1969, La locura juega al ajedrez 1971, La flecha en el aire 1972, Los domingos del profesor 1972, Estudios sobre letras hispánicas 1974, La Botella de Klein 1975, Los primeros cuentos del mundo 1977, El realismo mágico 1978, Teoría y técnica del cuento 1979, Dos mujeres y un Julián 1982, La prosa 1984, La crítica literaria 1984, El tamaño de las brujas 1986, Nuevos estudios sobre letras hispanas 1986, Evocación de sombras en la ciudad geométrica 1989, El anillo de Mozart (included in Narraciones Completas) 1990, Mentiras y mentirosos en el mundo de las letras 1992, Y pensar que hace diez años 1994, Reloj de arena 1996, Amorios 1997, Modernidad y Postmodernidad 1997, La buena forma de un crimen 1998. *Address:* 4859 Golden Road, Pleasanton, CA 94566, U.S.A.

ANDERSSON, Bibi; Swedish actress; b. 11 Nov. 1935; d. of Josef and Karin Andersson; m. 1st Kjell Grede 1960; one d.; m. 2nd Per Ahlmark (q.v.) 1978 (divorced); ed. Terserus Drama School and Royal Dramatic Theatre School, Stockholm; Malmö Theatre 1956–59, Royal Dramatic Theatre, Stockholm

1959–62, 1968–; appearances at Uppsala Theatre 1962–; *Plays acted in include:* Erik XIV 1956, Tre systrar 1961, King John 1961, Le balcon 1961, La grotte 1962, Uncle Vanya 1962, Who's Afraid of Virginia Woolf? 1963, As You Like It 1964, After the Fall 1964–65, The Full Circle 1973, Twelfth Night 1975, The Night of the Tribades 1977, Twelfth Night 1980, Antigone 1981, A Streetcar Named Desire 1981, 1983, L'oiseau bleu 1981, Prisoners of Altona 1982, The Creditors 1984–85, Ett gästabud i Pestens tid 1986; *Films acted in include:* Sjunde inseglet (Seventh Seal) 1956, Smultronstället (Wild Strawberries) 1957, Nära livet (The Brink of Life) 1958, Sommarnöje Sökes (Summer House Wanted) 1958, Djävulens öga (Eye of the Devil) 1961, Älskarinnen (The Mistress) 1962, För att inte tala om alla dessa kvinnor (All Those Women) 1964, Juninatt (June Night) 1965, Ön (The Island) 1965, Syskonbädd (My Sister, My Love) 1966, Persona 1966, Duel at Diablo 1966, Story of a Woman 1968, The Girls 1969, The Kremlin Letter 1970, A Passion, The Touch 1971, Scenes from a Marriage 1974, I Never Promised you a Rose Garden, La rivale 1976, An Enemy of the People 1976, Babette's Feast, Quintet 1979, Svarte Fugler 1982, Berget på månens baksida 1982, Litt et Art 1989, The Hill on the Other Side of the Moon, Manika, Fordringsagare.

ANDERSSON, Claes, D.MED.; Finnish politician; b. 30 May 1937, Helsinki; s. of Oscar Andersson and Ethel Hjelt; m. Katriina Kuusi 1970; six c.; novelist and poet 1974; M.P. 1987–; fmrly. mem. Finnish People's Democratic League 1970–90, mem. Left-Wing Alliance 1990, Chair. 1990–; Chair. Finland's Swedish Union of Writers; Vice-Pres. Information Centre of Finnish Literature 1985–; Eino-Leino Prize 1985, five times recipient of State Prize of Literature. *Publications:* 14 collections of poems, three novels, 20 stage plays and several radio plays and an opera libretto. *Leisure interest:* amateur jazz piano. *Address:* Vasemmistoliitto, Siltasaarenkatu 6, 7th Floor, 00530 Helsinki, Finland. *Telephone:* (09) 774741. *Fax:* (09) 7747-4200.

ANDERSSON, Harriet; Swedish actress; b. 1932, Stockholm; theatre career commenced in chorus at Oscars Theatre; subsequently appeared in reviews and then started serious dramatic career at Malmö City Theatre 1953; now appears regularly at Kunigliga Dramatiska Teatern, Stockholm; best-known stage appearances include performances of Anne Frank in The Diary of Anne Frank, Ophelia in Hamlet, in The Beggar's Opera and in plays by Chekhov; numerous film appearances including several by Ingmar Bergman (q.v.): Summer with Monica 1953, Sawdust and Tinsel 1953, Women's Dreams 1955, Dreams of a Summer Night 1955, Through a Glass Darkly 1961, All Those Women 1964, Cries and Whispers 1973; films directed by Jörn Donner (q.v.): One Sunday in September 1963, To Love 1964, Adventure Starts Here 1965, Stimulantia 1965–66, Rooftree 1966, Anna 1970; other films include: Siska 1962, Dream of Happiness 1963, Loving Couples 1964, For the Sake of Friendship 1965, Vine Bridge 1965, The Serpent 1966, The Deadly Affair 1967, The Girls 1968, The Stake; German Film Critics' Grand Prize for Through a Glass Darkly; Swedish Film Asscn. plaque; Best Actress Award, Venice Film Festival 1964 (for To Love). *Address:* c/o Sandrew Film & Theater AB, Box 5612, 114 86 Stockholm, Sweden.

ANDERSSON, Leif Christer Leander, M.D., PH.D.; Finnish professor of pathology; b. 24 March 1944, Esse; s. of Herman Alfons Andersson and Elvi Alina Häll; m. Nea Margareta Gustavson 1971; one s. two d.; ed. Univ. of Helsinki; Visiting Investigator, Univ. of Uppsala 1975–76, Research Inst. of Scripps Clinic, La Jolla, Calif. 1989–90; Prof. of Pathology, Univ. of Helsinki 1981–; Research Prof. Finnish Acad. of Science 1988–92; Prof. of Pathology, Karolinska Inst., Stockholm, Sweden 1996–97, Head of Pathology, Karolinska Hosp. 1997–; Anders Jahres Medical Prize, Univ. of Oslo 1981. *Publications:* about 270 original publs. on cell biology, immunology, haematology, oncology and pathology. *Leisure interest:* Dixieland jazz. *Address:* University of Helsinki, Haartman Institute, Department of Pathology, P.O. Box 21 (Haartmaninkatu 3), 00014 Helsinki, Finland. *Telephone:* (09) 1911. *Fax:* (09) 1912-6675.

ANDERSSON, Sten; Swedish politician; b. 20 April 1923, Stockholm; m. Britta Andersson; three s. two d.; ed. Univ. of Stockholm; teacher and guide, Workers' Educ. Asscn.; mem. Social Democratic Youth League, later Branch Chair.; elected to Stockholm County Council 1950, mem. City Exec., Finance Cttee. and Real Estate Cttee.; Dist. Organizing Sec. Stockholm branch, Socialdemokratiska Arbetarepartiet (Social Democratic Labour Party—SAP) 1953, Branch Sec. 1958, Branch Chair. 1975, mem. Exec. Cttee. 1964; Sec. SAP 1962–82; mem. Parl. 1966; Minister of Health and Social Affairs 1982–85, of Foreign Affairs 1985–91. *Address:* c/o Swedish Social Democratic Labour Party, Sveavägen 68, 105 60 Stockholm, Sweden.

ANDERTON, James Patrick (Jim); New Zealand politician; b. 21 Jan. 1938, Auckland; m. twice; three s. one d.; ed. Seddon Memorial Tech. Coll., Auckland Teachers' Training Coll; teacher for two years; Child Welfare Officer Educ. Dept., Wanganui; Catholic Youth Movt. Organiser 1960–65; Sec. Catholic Diocesan Office, Auckland 1967–69; Export Man. UEB Textiles 1969–70; Man. Dir. Anderton Holdings 1971–; City Councillor Manukau 1965–68, Auckland 1974–77, Councillor Auckland Regional Authority 1977–80; joined Labour Party 1963, held posts at Electorate, Regional and Exec. levels, Pres. N.Z. Labour Party 1979–84, mem. Policy Council 1979–89; M.P. for Sydenham 1984; resigned from Labour Party 1989 and formed the New Labour Party; re-elected M.P. for Sydenham (now Wigram) 1990 as N.L.P. cand.; elected first leader of Alliance Party (formed 1991). *Leisure interests:* chess, cricket and classical guitar. *Address:* Parliament Buildings, Wellington, New Zealand (Office); 286a Selwyn Avenue, Spreydon, Christchurch, New Zealand (Home). *Telephone:* (04) 471 9590 (Office); (03) 365 5459 (Home).

ANDÒ, Salvatore; Italian politician and university lecturer in law; b. 13 Feb. 1945, Jonia, Catania; m.; two c.; lecturer in Public Law, Univ. of Catania; Chair. Consiglio Nazionale delle Opere Universitarie; Prov. Exec. Fed. of Young Socialists 1963–69; mem. Prov. Exec. Cttee. Catania Fed. of Italian Socialist Party (PSI) 1974–, mem. Exec. of Fed. 1975–, Deputy Sec. 1978–, mem. Regional Cttee. PSI; Parl. Deputy 1979–; Minister of Defence 1992–93. *Address:* c/o Italian Socialist Party, Via del Corso 476, 00186 Rome, Italy.

ANDO, Tadao; Japanese architect; b. 13 Sept. 1941, Osaka; m. Yumiko Kato 1970; one c.; began as professional boxer; taught himself architecture by observing bldgs. in Africa, America, Europe; founder, Dir. Tadao Ando Architect and Assocs. 1969–; Visiting Prof. Columbia, Harvard, Yale Univs.; designed art school for Benetton, Northern Italy, the Church of Light, Osaka, Japan, Children's Museum, Hyogo, Japan, Water Temple, Osaka, Rokko Housing Nr. Osaka; exhbn. at Royal Inst. of British Architects 1993; Gold Medal of Architecture (French Acad.), Carlsberg Architecture Prize, Pritzker Prize 1995, Imperial Praemium Prize 1996, Royal Gold Medal R.I.B.A. 1997. *Publications include:* Tadao Ando 1981, Tadao Ando: Buildings, Project, Writings 1984. *Address:* Tadao Ando Architect and Associates, 5-23 Toyosaki, 2-chome, Kita-ku, Osaka 531, Japan.

ANDOV, Stojan; Macedonian politician and economist; b. 1935, ed. Skopje Univ., Belgrade Univ.; worked as economist; political activities since late 1980s; one of fs. and mem. Exec. Bd. Liberal Party of Macedonia 1990; Deputy Chair. Repub. Exec. Cttee.; mem. Union Veche (Parl.) of Yugoslavia; took part in negotiations between Yugoslavia and European Econ. Community: Amb. of Yugoslavia to Iraq; del. to Nat. Ass. Repub. of Macedonia 1990–, Chair. 1990–96; Acting Pres. of Macedonia Oct. 1995–Jan. 1996; Head faction Reform Forces of Macedonia - Liberal Party, Co-Chair. 1996. *Address:* Sobranje, 11 Oktombri blvd., 91000 Skopje, Macedonia. *Telephone:* (91) 227 111 (Office).

ANDRÁSFALVY, Bertalan, PH.D.; Hungarian politician and ethnographer; b. 17 Nov. 1931, Sopron; s. of Károly Andrásfalvy and Judit Mezey; m. Mária Gere; three s.; ed. Budapest Univ.; with Museum of Szekszárd 1955, Transdanubian Research Inst. of the Hungarian Acad. of Sciences 1960–76, Archives of Baranya County and Museum of Pécs –1985; Exec., later dept. head ethnographic research group Hungarian Acad. of Sciences; Assoc. Prof. Janus Pannonius Univ. of Pécs 1989–93, Prof. 1993–; lecturer Eötvös Loránd Univ. of Budapest; mem. Cttee. Hungarian Democratic Forum; mem. of Parl. 1990–; Minister of Culture and Public Educ. 1990–93; Eriksson Prize of the Swedish Royal Acad., István Győrffy Memorial Medal of Hungarian Ethnographic Society; Hon. mem. Finnish Literature Soc.; Grand Silver Medal with Ribbon (Austria); Order of Merit Medium Cross with Star (Hungary), Grosse Verdienstkreutz (Germany), Grand Cross of Lion's Order of Knighthood (Finland). *Leisure interests:* gardening. *Address:* 7694 Hosszúhetény, Fő útca 26, Hungary (Home).

ANDRE, Carl; American sculptor; b. 16 Sept. 1935, Quincy, Mass.; s. of George H. Andre and Margaret M. (Johnson) Andre; ed. Phillips Acad., Andover, Mass., served U.S. Army 1955–56; went to New York 1957; worked as freight brakeman and conductor of Pa. Railroad 1960–64; first public exhbn. 1964, numerous public collections in U.S.A. and Europe. *Address:* c/o Paula Cooper, 534 West 21st Street, New York, NY 10011, U.S.A.; Konrad Fischer, Platanestrasse 7, 40233 Düsseldorf, Germany; Cooper Station, P.O. Box 1001, New York, NY 10276, U.S.A. (Home). *Telephone:* (212) 255-1105 (New York); (211) 68-59-08 (Düsseldorf).

ANDRÉ, Harvie, P.C., PH.D.; Canadian politician and engineer; b. 27 July 1940, Edmonton, Alberta; m. Joan Smith 1965; one s. two d.; ed. Univ. of Alberta, Calif. Inst. of Tech.; fmrly. Prof. of Eng., Univ. of Alberta and Consultant Engineer; elected M.P. 1972–93, fmrly. Caucus spokesperson on Nat. Defence, fmr. spokesperson on Energy, on Econ. Devt., on Treasury Bd., on Science and Tech., on Youth; fmr. mem. Standing Cttee. on External Affairs, on Nat. Defence, on Natural Resources and Public Works, on Finance, Trade and Econ. Affairs, fmr. mem. Special Jt. Cttee. on Senate Reform; Minister of Supply and Services 1984–85, Minister for Consumer and Corporate Affairs 1986–89, of Regional Industrial Expansion, Science and Tech. Jan. 1989–90, of State, and Govt. House Leader 1990–93; Pres. Cresvard Corpn. 1994–. *Address:* 819 Crescent Blvd., S.W., Calgary, Alta., T2S 1L3, Canada.

ANDRÉ, Maurice; French trumpeter; b. 21 May 1933, Alès, Gard; s. of Marcel André and Fabienne Volpélière; m. Lilianne Arnoult 1956; four c.; ed. Conservatoire national supérieur de musique, Paris; apprenticed as coal miner before formal music studies; won Prix d'honneur for trumpet; joined Paris Radio Orchestra; subsequently First Trumpet, Lamoureux Orchestra and other orchestras; played in jazz groups and chamber orchestras; now soloist with world's leading orchestras; specialises in baroque and contemporary music; Prof. of Trumpet, Paris Conservatoire 1967–; has made about 260 recordings, including 30 trumpet concertos; Chevalier de la Légion d'honneur; commdr. des Arts et des Lettres; First Prize, Geneva Int. Competition 1955, Munich Int. Competition 1963, Schallplattenpreis, Berlin 1970, Victoire de la musique 1987. *Leisure interests:* pen and ink drawing, gardening, swimming. *Address:* c/o de Valmalete Concerts, 7 rue Hoche, 92300 Levallois-Perret; Presles-en-Brie, 77220 Tournan-en-Brie, France.

ANDREA, Pat; Netherlands artist; b. 25 June 1942, The Hague; s. of Kees Andrea and Metty Naezer; m. 1st Cecile Hessels 1966 (divorced 1983); m. 2nd Cristina Ruiz Guiñazu 1993; three s. one d.; ed. Royal Acad. of Fine Arts, The Hague; paints in figurative style, focusing on personal deformaties, people in dramatic situations, sex and violence; has participated in numerous solo and collective exhbns. 1966–, including first museum show Haags Gemeentemuseum 1968, retrospective Museum of Modern Art, Arnheim 1975, Galerie Nina Dausset, Paris 1979, Paolo Baldacci Gallery, New York 1992, retrospective of works in Argentinian collections 1992, retrospectives Stedelijk Museum, Schiedam and Inst. Néerlandais, Paris 1994; represented in MOMA, New York, Centre Pompidou, Paris and Frisiras, Athens collections; Prof. Ecole Nat. Supérieur des Beaux Arts, Paris 1998–; Jacob Maris Prize 1968. *Publications:* (with H.P. de Boer) Nederlands gebarenboekje 1979, (with J. Cortazar) La Puñalada 1982, Pat Andrea: conversations avec Pierre Sterckx 1993. *Address:* 18 rue Henri Regnault, 75014 Paris, France. *Telephone:* (1) 45.45.44.23. *Fax:* (1) 40.44.75.75.

ANDREANI, Jacques; French diplomatist; b. 22 Nov. 1929, Paris; m. 1st Huguette de Fonclare; one s. one d.; m. 2nd Donatella Monterisi 1981; one s. one d.; ed. Inst. d'Etudes Politiques, Univ. of Paris and Ecole Nat. d'Admin.; Sec. French Embassy, Washington, D.C. 1955–60, Moscow 1961–64; Ministry of Foreign Affairs 1964–70; Deputy Rep. of France, NATO, Brussels 1970–72; Head, French Del. to CSCE, Helsinki and Geneva 1972–75; Asst. Sec. for European Affairs, Ministry of Foreign Affairs 1975–79; Amb. to Egypt 1979–81; Dir. of Political Affairs, Ministry of Foreign Affairs 1981–84; Amb. to Italy 1984–88; Chief of Staff, Ministry of Foreign Affairs 1988–89; Amb. to U.S.A. 1989–95; Special Asst. to Minister of Foreign Affairs 1995–; Officier, Légion d'honneur, Commdr. Ordre nat. du Mérite. *Leisure interests:* arts, music, golf. *Address:* Ministry of Foreign Affairs, 37 quai d'Orsay, 75007 Paris (Office); 40 rue Bonaparte, 75006 Paris, France (Home). *Telephone:* (33) 1.43 17 61 52 (Office); (33) 1.43 26 14 92 (Home). *Fax:* (33) 1.43 17 77 73 (Office).

ANDREEV, Aleksandr Fyodorovich, DR.PHYS.SC.; Russian physicist; b. 10 Dec. 1939, Leningrad; s. of Fyodor Andreev and Nina Andreeva; m. Tamara Turok 1960; one d.; ed. Moscow Physico-Tech. Inst.; jr. then sr. researcher 1964–79, Prof. 1979–; Deputy Dir. U.S.S.R. Acad. of Sciences, Kapitza Inst. for Physical Problems 1984–91, Dir. 1991–; Lorentz Prof. Univ. of Leiden 1992; Ed.-in-Chief Priroda 1993–, JETP 1997–; Corresp. mem. U.S.S.R. Acad. of Sciences 1981–87, mem. 1987; Vice-Pres. Russian Acad. of Sciences 1991–; Lomonosov Prize, U.S.S.R. Acad. of Sciences 1984, Lenin Prize 1986, Carus-Medaille de Deutschen Academie der Naturforscher Leopoldina, Carus-Preis der Stadt Schweinfurt 1987, Simon Memorial Prize (U.K.) 1995. *Address:* Academy of Sciences, Kapitza Institute for Physical Problems, Kosygin Street 2, 117334 Moscow, Russia. *Telephone:* (095) 9382029. *Fax:* (095) 938-20-30.

ANDREI, Ştefan; Romanian politician; b. 29 March 1931, Podari-Livezi, Dolj County; ed. Inst. of Civil Eng., Bucharest; Asst. Prof. Inst. of Civil Eng. and Inst. of Oil, Gas and Geology, Bucharest 1956–63; mem. Union of Communist Youth (UCY) 1949–54; joined student movement 1951; mem. Exec. Cttee. Union of Student Asscns. 1958–62; mem. Bureau Cen. Cttee. UCY 1962–65; mem. Romanian Communist Party (RCP) 1954–89; alt. mem. Cen. Cttee. RCP 1969–72, mem. 1972–89; First Deputy Head of Int. Section Cen. Cttee. 1966–72; Sec. Cen. Cttee. 1972–78; alt. mem. Exec. Political Cttee. 1974–89; mem. Perm. Bureau, Exec. Political Cttee. 1974–84; Minister for Foreign Affairs 1978–85; Secr. Cen. Cttee. 1985–87; Deputy Prime Minister 1987–89; mem. Grand Nat. Assembly 1975–89; mem. Nat. Council Front of Socialist Democracy and Unity 1980–89; several Romanian orders and medals.

ANDREJEVS, Georgs, D.MED.; Latvian politician and diplomatist; b. 30 Oct. 1932, Tukums; m. Anita Andrejeva; one s. one d.; ed. Latvian Medical Inst.; on staff Stradine Repub. Clinical Hosp. 1959–62; Asst. Prof., Head Dept. of Surgery, Chief Anaesthesiologist and Reanimatologist of Ministry of Health 1962–92; Deputy to Latvian Repub. Supreme Council; mem. Latvian People's Front; Sec. Comm. for Foreign Affairs of Supreme Council; Minister of Foreign Affairs 1992–93; mem. Saima (Parl.) 1993–95; Amb. to Canada 1995–98, to Council of Europe 1998–. *Address:* Latvian Mission to Council of Europe, 67075 Strasbourg Cédex, France.

ANDREN, Anders, L. ÈS L., M.B.A.; Swedish business executive; b. 30 July 1939, Gothenburg; s. of Erik Andren and Birgit Flodin; m. Monika Grohmann 1967; one s.; ed. Univ. of Stockholm and Institut européen de l'administration des affaires; Dir.-Gen. Electrolux Canarias S.A. 1968–70, Electrolux Belgique 1971–74; Pres.-Dir.-Gen. Electrolux S.A. France 1974–93, fmr. Chair., Man. Dir.; fmr. Pres. Supervisory Bd., Arthur Martin, Pres.-Dir. Gen. Groupe Esab S.A. France 1992–, Direct Ménager France 1993–; Hon. Pres. Swedish Chamber of Comerce in France. *Address:* Direct Ménager France S.A., 5 av. du Général de Gaulle, B.P. 171, 60305 Senlis cedex (Office); 13 Boucle d'en bas, 60270 Gouvieux, France (Home).

ANDRÉN, Carl-Gustaf, D.D.; Swedish university administrator; b. 7 July 1922, Slättåkra; s. of Rev. Victor and Andréa (née Johanson) Andrén; m. Karin E. Tengwall 1949; three s.; Asst. Prof. of Practical Theology, Lund Univ. 1957-64, Head of Admin. of Educ. 1964–67, Prof. of Practical Theology and Church Law 1967–80, Rector 1977–80; Chancellor of univs. and colls. in Sweden 1980–89; mem. several scientific socs. in Sweden. *Publication:* De septem sacramentis 1963.

ANDREOLI, Kathleen Gainor; American university administrator; b. 22 Sept. 1935, Albany, New York; d. of John Edward Gainor and Edmunda Ringelmann Gainor; m. Thomas Eugene Andreoli 1960; one s. two d.; ed. Georgetown Univ. and Vanderbilt Schools of Nursing and Univ. of Ala. School of Nursing, Birmingham; Staff Nurse, Albany Hosp. Medical Center, New York 1957; Instructor, various schools of nursing 1957–70; Educational Dir., Physician Asst. Program, Dept. of Medicine, School of Medicine, Univ. of Ala. 1970–75, subsequently Asst. then Assoc. of Nursing 1970–79, Prof. of Nursing 1979; Prof. of Nursing, Special Asst. to Pres. for Educational Affairs, Univ. of Texas Health Science Center, Houston 1979–82, Vice-Pres. for Educational Services, Interprofessional Educ. and Int. Programs 1983–87; Vice-Pres. Nursing Affairs and John L. and Helen Kellogg Dean of Coll. of Nursing Rush Univ., Chicago 1987–. mem. Nat. Advisory Nursing Council V.H.A. 1992, Advisory Bd. Robert Wood Johnson Clinic Nursing School Program, Visiting Cttee. Vanderbilt Univ. School of Nursing, numerous other bodies; Founders Award, N.C. Heart Asscn. 1970; numerous other awards. *Publications:* (jt.) Comprehensive Cardiac Care 1983, ed. Heart and Lung, Journal of Total Care 1971, contrib. articles in professional journals. *Leisure interests:* music, art, reading, bicycling, travelling. *Address:* Rush Presbyterian—St Luke's Medical Center, 600 South Paulina Street, Suite 1080, Chicago, IL 60612 (Office); 1212 South Lake Shore Drive, Chicago, IL 60605, U.S.A. (Home).

ANDREOTTI, Giulio; Italian politician and journalist; b. 14 Jan. 1919, Rome; s. of Philip Andreotti; m. Livia Danese 1945; two s. two d.; ed. Univ. of Rome; Pres., Fed. of Catholic Univs. in Italy 1942–45; Deputy to the Constituent Assembly 1945 and to Parl. 1946– (Life Senator 1992–); Under-Sec. in the Govts. of De Gasperi and Pella 1947–53; Minister for the Interior in Fanfani Govt. 1954; Minister of Finance 1955–58, of Treasury 1958–59, of Defence 1959–60, 1960–66, March-Oct. 1974, of Industry and Commerce 1966–68, for the Budget, and Econ. Planning and in charge of Southern Devt. Fund 1974–76, Chair. Christian Democratic Parl. Party in Chamber of Deputies 1948–72; Prime Minister 1972–73, 1976–79, 1989–92; Chair. Foreign Affairs Cttee., Chamber of Deputies; Minister of Foreign Affairs 1983–89; immunity lifted May 1993, charged with consorting with the Mafia March 1995; charged with murder Nov. 1995; Hon. L.L.D. (Beijing Univ.) 1991. *Publications:* Editor of Concretezza 1954–76, A Ogni morte di Papa 1980, Gli U.S.A. Visti da Vicino 1983, Diari 1976–79, Lives: Encounters with History Makers 1989, The U.S.A. Up Close 1992, Cosa Loro 1995, De Prima Republica 1996.

ANDRETTI, Mario Gabriele; American racing driver; b. 28 Feb. 1940, Montona, Italy; m. Dee Ann Hoch 1961; two s. one d.; began midget car racing in United States, graduating to United States Auto Club Nat. Formula; Indy Car Nat. Champion 1965, 1966, 1969, 1984; USAC Champion 1965, 1966, 1969, 1974; winner of Indianapolis 500 Miles 1969; winner of Daytona 500 Miles NASCAR stock car race 1967; began Formula 1 racing in 1968; World Champion 1978, third 1977; winner of Int. Race of Champions 1979; Pres. MA 500 Inc. 1968–, Newman/Haas Racing 1983–; Driver of the Year 1967, 1978, 1984, Driver of the Quarter Century 1992; all-time Indy Car lap leader (7,587). *Grand Prix wins:* 1971 South African (Ferrari), 1976 Japanese (Lotus-Ford), 1977 United States (Lotus-Ford), 1977 Spanish (Lotus-Ford), 1977 French (Lotus-Ford), 1977 Italian (Lotus-Ford), 1978 Argentine (Lotus-Ford), 1978 Belgian (Lotus-Ford), 1978 Spanish (Lotus-Ford), 1978 French (Lotus-Ford), 1978 German (Lotus-Ford), 1978 Dutch (Lotus-Ford). *Leisure interests:* snowmobiling, tennis, opera. *Address:* 457 Rose Inn Avenue, Nazareth, PA 18064, U.S.A.

ANDREW, Christopher Robert, M.B.E.; British rugby football player; b. 18 Feb. 1963, Richmond, Yorks.; m. Sara Andrew 1989; two d.; ed. Cambridge Univ.; chartered surveyor; fly-half; fmr. mem. Middlesbrough, Cambridge Univ., Nottingham, Gordon (Sydney, Australia) clubs; mem. Wasps Club 1987–91, 1992–96, Capt. until 1989–90; with Toulouse 1991–92, Barbarians, Newcastle Jan. 1996–; int. debut England versus Romania 1985; Five Nations debut England versus France 1985; Capt. England team, England versus Romania, Bucharest 1989; mem. Grand Slam winning team 1991, 1992; record holder for drop goals in ints.; retd. from int. rugby Oct. 1995; Devt. Dir. Newcastle Rugby Football Club Sept. 1995–. *Publication:* A Game and a Half 1995. *Leisure interests:* gardening, pushing a pram, golf. *Address:* c/o Newcastle RFC, Newcastle-upon-Tyne, NE3 2DT, England. *Telephone:* 0191-214 0422.

ANDREW, Edward Raymond, PH.D., SC.D., F.R.S., F.R.S.E.; British university professor; b. 27 June 1921, Boston, Lincs.; s. of late Edward R. Andrew and Anne Henderson; m. 1st Mary Farnham 1948 (died 1965); m. 2nd Eunice Tinning 1972; two d.; ed. Wellingborough School, Christ's and Pembroke Colls. Cambridge and Harvard Univ.; Scientific Officer, Royal Radar Establishment, Malvern 1942–45; Cavendish Lab. and Stokes Student, Cambridge Univ. 1945–48; Commonwealth Fund Fellow, Harvard Univ. 1948–49; lecturer in Natural Philosophy, St. Andrews Univ. 1949–54; Prof. of Physics, Univ. of Wales, Bangor 1954–64; Lancashire-Spencer Prof. of Physics, Nottingham Univ. 1964–83, Dean, Faculty of Science 1975–78; Grad. Research Prof. Univ. of Fla. 1983–; Fellow, Christ's Coll. Cambridge 1989, Clare Hall Cambridge 1996; Selby Fellow, Australian Acad. of Science 1989; Hon. mem.

British Biophysical Soc. 1992; Pres. Int. Soc. of Magnetic Resonance 1984–87; other professional appts.; Wellcome Medal, Royal Soc. 1984; Distinguished Service Medal, S.M.R.M.; Dr. h.c. (Turku) 1980, (Poznań) 1989, (Leipzig) 1990, (Wales) 1998. *Publications:* Nuclear Magnetic Resonance 1955, Clinical Magnetic Resonance (jtly.) 1990, Nuclear Magnetic Resonance at High Magnetic Fields 1992; articles in learned journals. *Leisure interest:* travel. *Address:* Department of Physics, University of Florida, Gainesville, FL 32611, U.S.A. *Telephone:* (352) 392-6691. *Fax:* (352) 392-3591.

ANDREW, Ludmilla; Canadian soprano opera singer; b. Canada, of Russian parentage; operatic début in Vancouver as Donna Elvira; British début as Madam Butterfly with Sadler's Wells Opera; noted for Russian song repertoire; has given many broadcasts of French, German and Russian song repertoire with Geoffrey Parsons; many recital tours; now appears regularly at world's leading opera houses and at maj. int. music festivals; roles include Aida, Anna Bolena, Leonore, Norma, Senta, Sieglinde and Turandot.

ANDREW, Sydney Percy Smith, M.A., F.R.S., F.ENG., F.I.CHEM.E., M.I.MECH.E; British chemical engineer; b. 16 May 1926; s. of Harold C. Andrew and Kathleen M. Andrew (née Smith); m. Ruth Harrison Kenyon 1986; ed. Barnard Castle School, King's Coll., Durham Univ., Trinity Hall, Cambridge; joined ICI, Billingham Div. 1950, Chemical Eng. Research 1951, Plant Engineer 1953, Section Man. Reactor Research 1955, Process Design 1959, Sr. Research Assoc., Group Man. Catalysts and Chemicals Research 1963–76; Consulting Chemical Engineer; Visiting Prof. Univ. of Bath 1988–; Chair. Resources Cttee. Inst. of Chem. Engineers; Hon. D.Sc. (Leeds) 1979. *Publications:* Catalyst Handbook 1970; papers on chemical eng., applied chem. and crop growth. *Leisure interests:* archaeology, ancient and medieval history. *Address:* 1 The Wynd, Stainton in Cleveland, Middlesbrough, TS8 9BP, England. *Telephone:* (01642) 596348.

ANDREWS, Anthony; British actor; b. 1 Dec. 1948, Hampstead, London; m. Georgina Simpson; one s. two d.; ed. Royal Masonic Public School; started acting 1967. *TV appearances include:* Doomwatch, Woodstock 1972, A Day Out, Follyfoot, Fortunes of Nigel 1973, The Pallisers, David Copperfield 1974, Upstairs, Downstairs 1975, French Without Tears, The Country Wife, Much Ado About Nothing 1977, Danger UXB 1978, Romeo and Juliet 1979, Brideshead Revisited 1980, Ivanhoe 1982, The Scarlet Pimpernel 1983, Columbo 1988, The Strange Case of Dr. Jekyll and Mr. Hyde 1989, Hands of a Murderer 1990, Lost in Siberia 1990, The Law Lord 1991, Jewels 1992, Ruth Rendell's Heartstones, Mothertime. *Films Include:* The Scarlet Pimpernel, Under the Volcano, A War of the Children, Take Me High 1973, Operation Daybreak 1975, Les Adolescents 1976, The Holcroft Covenant 1986, Second Victory 1987, Woman He Loved 1988, The Lighthorsemen 1988, Hannah's War 1988, Lost in Siberia (also producer) 1990, Haunted (also producer) 1995. *Plays:* 40 Years On, A Midsummer Night's Dream, Romeo and Juliet, One of Us 1986, Coming into Land 1986, Dragon Variation, Tima and the Conways. *Address:* c/o Peters Fraser & Dunlop Ltd, 503 The Chambers, Chelsea Harbour, London, SW10 0XF, England.

ANDREWS, David, B.C.L., S.C.; Irish politician; b. 15 March 1935, Dublin; m. Annette Cusack; two s. three d.; ed. Mount St. Joseph's Cistercian Coll., Co. Tipperary, Univ. Coll. Dublin and King's Inns, Dublin; mem. Dáil 1965–; Parl. Sec. to Taoiseach 1970–73; Govt. Chief Whip 1970–73; Minister of State, Dept. of Foreign Affairs 1977–79, Dept. of Justice 1978–79; Minister for Foreign Affairs 1992–93, for Defence and the Marine 1993–94, for Defence July–Oct. 1997, for Foreign Affairs Oct. 1997–; Opposition Spokesman on Tourism and Trade 1995–97; mem. New Ireland Forum, Consultative Assembly of Council of Europe, British-Irish Interparl. Body 1990–92; Fianna Fáil. *Leisure interests:* cinema, sport, walking. *Address:* Dáil Éireann, Leinster House, Dublin 2 (Office); 102 Avoca Park, Blackrock, Dublin, Ireland (Home). *Telephone:* (01) 6789911 (Office); (01) 6623851 (Home).

ANDREWS, David Roger Griffith, C.B.E., M.A., C.B.I.M., F.C.M.A.; British company executive; b. 27 March 1933, Hamilton, Ont., Canada; s. of C. and G.M. Andrews; m. Dorothy Ann Campbell 1963; two s. one d.; ed. Abingdon School and Pembroke Coll., Oxford; Assistant Controller, Ford of Europe 1968; Controller, British Leyland Motor Corpn. Ltd. 1969; Finance Dir., Austin Morris Ltd. 1970; Man. Dir. Power and Transmission Div. BLMC Ltd. 1973; Man. Dir. Leyland Int. 1975; Exec. Vice-Chair. B.L. Ltd. 1977–82, Dir. 1982–86; Chair. Leyland Group 1981–82, Landrover Group 1981–82, Chair. and C.E.O. Landrover-Leyland Group 1982–86; Chair. Gwion Ltd. 1986–96; Dir. Glaxo Trustees Ltd. 1983–91, Clarges Pharmaceutical Trustees Ltd. 1983–91, Foundation for Science and Tech. 1990–96; Foundation Medal 1996. *Address:* Gainford, Mill Lane, Gerrards Cross, Bucks., SL9 8BA, England. *Telephone:* (01753) 884310.

ANDREWS, John Hamilton, A.O., F.T.S., M.ARCH.; Australian architect; b. 29 Oct. 1933; s. of the late K. Andrews; m. Rosemary Randall 1958; four s.; ed. N. Sydney Boys' High School, Univ. of Sydney, Harvard Univ.; private practice, Toronto, Canada 1962, Sydney 1970–; mem. Staff, Univ. of Toronto School of Architecture 1962–67, Chair. and Prof. of Architecture 1967–69; mem. Visual Arts Bd., Australia Council 1977–80, Bd. mem. 1988–90; Chair. Architecture and Design Comm., Australia Council 1980–83, Founding Chair. Design Arts Bd., 1983–88; Architectural Juror, Australian Archives Nat. Headquarters Building 1979, Parl. House Competition 1979–80, The Peak, Hong Kong 1983, Hawaii Loa Coll. 1986, Governor Gen.'s Medals, Canada 1986; mem. R.I.B.A., Bd., Australia Council 1988–; Assoc. N.Z. Inst. of Architects; Foundation Mem. Australian Acad. of Design 1990; Fellow, Royal Architectural Inst. of Canada, Australian Acad. of Technological Science; Life Fellow, Royal Australian Inst. of Architects; Hon. Fellow, American Inst. of Architects; Hon. D. Arch. (Sydney) 1988; Centennial Medal (Canada) 1967; Massey Medal (Canada) 1967; Arnold Brunner Award, U.S. Acad. of Arts and Letters 1971; American Inst. of Architects Honour Award 1973; Gold Medal, Royal Australian Inst. of Architects 1980, Advance Australia Award 1982, Sulman Medal (Australia) 1983; Design Excellence 25 Year Award, Ontario Asscn. of Architecture, Scarborough Coll. 1989. *Principal works:* Scarborough Coll., Toronto, Harvard Graduate School of Design, Harvard Univ., Cameron Offices, Canberra, American Express Tower, Sydney, Intelsat Headquarters Building, Washington, D.C., Hyatt Hotel, Perth, Convention Centre Darling Harbour, Sydney, Convention Centre and Hyatt Hotel, Adelaide, World Congress Centre and Eden on the Yarra Hotel, Melbourne, The Octagon (office bldg.) Parramatta, Sydney, N.S.W., Veterinary Conf. Centre, Univ. of Sydney, N.S.W. *Publication:* Architecture: A Performing Art 1982. *Leisure interests:* fishing, surfing. *Address:* John Andrews International, P.O. Box 7087, McMahon's Point, N.S.W. 2060 (Office); Kiembah, Eugowra, N.S.W. 2806, Australia (Home). *Telephone:* (02) 9955 8808 (Office). *Fax:* (02) 9955 8188.

ANDREWS, Julie; British actress and singer; b. 1 Oct. 1935, Walton-on-Thames, Surrey, m. 1st Tony Walton 1959 (dissolved 1968); one d.; m. 2nd Blake Edwards 1969; one step-s. one step-d. and two adopted d.; first stage appearance at the age of twelve as singer, London Hippodrome; played in revues and concert tours; appeared in pantomime Cinderella, London Palladium; played leading parts in The Boy Friend, New York 1954, My Fair Lady 1959–60, Camelot, New York 1960–62, Victor, Victoria 1995/96; television play High Tor; several television shows including The Julie Andrews Hour 1972–73; Academy Award (Oscar) Best Actress 1964; three Golden Globe Awards, Emmy Award 1987, BAFTA Award 1989; work for UN Devt. Fund for Women. *Films:* Mary Poppins 1963, The Americanization of Emily 1964, The Sound of Music 1964, Hawaii 1965, Torn Curtain 1966, Thoroughly Modern Millie 1966, Star! 1967, Darling Lili 1970, The Tamarind Seed 1973, 10 1979, Little Miss Marker 1980, S.O.B. 1980, Victor/Victoria 1981, The Man Who Loved Women 1983, That's Life 1986, Duet For One 1986, The Sound of Christmas (TV) 1987. *TV appearances include:* Great Performances Live in Concert 1990, Our Sons 1991, The Julie Show 1992. *Publications:* Mandy 1972, Last of the Really Great Wangdoogles 1973.

ANDREWS, Kenneth Raymond, PH.D., F.B.A.; British professor of history; b. 26 Aug. 1921, London; s. of Arthur Andrews and Marion Andrews; m. Ottilie Kalman 1969; two step-s.; ed. Henry Thornton School, Clapham, London and King's Coll., London; Southend Polytechnic 1954–56; Chiswick Polytechnic 1956–63; Univ. of Liverpool 1963–64; Univ. of Hull 1964–86; Prof. of History 1979–88, part time 1986–88, Emer. 1988–; Vice-Pres. Hakluyt Soc. 1983–90. *Publications:* Elizabethan Privateering 1964, Drake's Voyages 1967, The Spanish Caribbean 1978, Trade, Plunder and Settlement 1984, Ships, Money and Politics 1991. *Address:* 8 Grange Drive, Cottingham, North Humberside, HU16 5RE, England.

ANDREYEV, Vladimir Alekseyevich; Russian actor and stage director; b. 1930; m. Natalia Selezheva; one s. one d.; ed. State Inst. of Theatre Arts Cinema (GITIS); actor with Yermolova Theatre Moscow 1952–70, chief dir. 1970–85, 1990–; mem. CPSU 1962–91; Chief. Dir. of Maly Theatre, Moscow 1985–88; teaches concurrently at GITIS, Prof. 1978–; mem. Int. Acad. for Life Preservation Problems 1993; U.S.S.R. People's Artist 1985; Stanislavsky State Prize 1980, 1993; *Roles include:* Aleksey in V. Rozov's It's High Time!, Vasilkov in Ostrovsky's Crazy Money, Golubkov in Bulgakov's Flight, Sattarov in Valeyev's I Give You Life, Dorogin in Zorin's Lost Story, Writer in Bunin's Grammar of Love. *Productions include:* Vampilov's plays: Last Summer in Chulimsk, and The Duck Hunt; Money for Mary (based on a work by V. Rasputin), The Shore (based on Yuriy Bondarev's novel), Uncle Vanya, Three Sisters (Chekhov). *Address:* Yermolova Theatre, Tverskaya 5, 103009 Moscow, Russia. *Telephone:* (095) 2038703.

ANDRIANOV, Nikolai Yefimovich; Russian gymnast; b. 14 Oct. 1952; m. Lubov Viktorovna Andrianova; ed. Moscow Inst. of Physical Culture; champion of Olympic Games, 15 Olympic medals (1972, 1976, 1980) including golden medals in free-style exercises 1972, in all-round competitions, on the rings, in jumps 1976, team championships and in jumps 1980; world champion 1974, 1978, 1979; numerous champion titles of Europe and U.S.S.R.; coach 1978–; chief coach U.S.S.R. (now Russian) team 1983–; Merited Master of Sports 1972. *Address:* Russian Federation of Gymnastics, Luzhnetskaya nab. 8, 119871 Moscow, Russia. *Telephone:* (095) 201 13 42 (Office); (9222) 23924 (Home).

ANDRIEȘ Andrei, D.PHYSICAL-MATH.SC.; Moldovan physicist; b. 24 Oct. 1933, Chișinău (Kishinev); s. of Mihail Andrieș and Maria Andrieș; m. Lidia Vasilievna Klimanova 1959; one s.; ed. Kishinev Univ., Ioffe Inst. of Physics and Tech., Leningrad; researcher Inst. of Applied Physics, Acad. of Sciences Moldavian S.S.R. 1962–64, Learning Sec. 1964–71, Head of Lab. Inst. of Applied Physics 1971–, Gen. Learning Sec. 1984–89, Dir. Centre of Optoelectronics 1993–; Corresp. mem. Acad. of Sciences Moldavian S.S.R. (now Acad. of Sciences of Moldova) 1978, mem. 1984, Pres. 1989–; State Prize of Moldova 1983; Merited Scientific Researcher 1984; mem. Eng. Acad. of Russian Fed. 1992, N.Y. Acad. of Sciences 1995, Int. Scientific Acad. of Life, the Universe and Nature, Toulouse 1997; numerous decorations and awards. *Publications:* over 300 works on new materials for photographic processes. *Leisure interests:* reading, travel. *Address:* Academy of Sciences of Moldova, Bd. Stefan cel Mare 1, 2001 Chişinău, Moldova. *Telephone:* (2) 26 14 78. *Fax:* (2) 23-35-87.

ANDRIESSEN, Franciscus H. J. J.; Netherlands politician and economist; b. 2 April 1929, Utrecht; ed. Univ. of Utrecht; Dir. Catholic Inst. for Housing 1954–72; mem. of Second Chamber, States-Gen. (Parl.) 1967–77, First Chamber 1980–; Minister of Finance 1977–80; Commr. for Competition Policy and Relations with the European Parl., Comm. of European Communities 1981–84; for Agric. and Fisheries 1984–85, for Agric. and Forestry 1986–89, for External Relations and Trade Policy 1989–93; special adviser KPMG 1993–; Pres. Inst. of the Euro 1993–; Prof. Univ. of Utrecht 1990–; mem. Catholic People's Party, Christian Democratic Appeal; Kt., Order of the Lion, Grand Cross of Order of Orange-Nassau, of Order of Leopold II, Commdr. du Mérite agricole. *Address:* Institut de L'Euro, 1 quai Jules Courmont, 69002 Lyon, France; KPMG European Headquarters, avenue Louise 54, 1050 Brussels, Belgium; clôs Henri Vaes 1, 1950 Kraainem, Netherlands (Home).

ANDRIESSEN, Jacobus Eije, M.A., PH.D.; Netherlands politician, economist and business executive; b. 25 July 1928, Rotterdam; m. Josephina Hoogeweij 1952; ed. Erasmus Univ., Rotterdam and Amsterdam Free Univ.; Dir. Dept. of Gen. Econ. Policy, Ministry of Econ. Affairs 1955–59; Prof., Law Faculty, Univ. of Amsterdam 1959–63; mem. Econ. and Social Cttee. EEC 1959–63; Minister of Econ. Affairs 1963–65, 1989–94; mem. and Chair. of Exec. Bd. Royal Packaging Industries Van Leer B. V. 1965–87; Prof. Free Univ., Amsterdam 1988–89, 1994–; Chair. Dutch Christian Employers Asscn. 1987–89, Rotterdam Philharmonic Orchestra Bd., Kröller Müller Museum Bd., Leiden Univ. Hosp.; dir. and adviser to several cos. and orgs. *Publications:* Development of Modern Price Theory 1955, Economics in Theory and Practice 1964, Riding the Wave 1987, Met Distantie 1998. *Leisure interests:* modern literature, classical music, films, golf. *Address:* Waldeck Pyrmantloch 16, 2243 Hm Wassenaar, Netherlands. *Telephone:* (70) 517-79-45. *Fax:* (70) 514-14-45.

ANDRIKIENE, Laima Liucija, DR.ECON.; Lithuanian politician; b. 1 Jan. 1958, Druskininkai, Lithuania; m. (husband deceased); one s.; ed. Vilnius State Univ., Manchester Univ., engineer, researcher Computation Cen. Lithuanian Research Inst. of Agric. Econ. 1980–88; Asst. to Deputy Chair. Council of Ministers Lithuanian S.S.R. 1989–90; deputy Supreme Soviet 1990; signatory to Act on Re-establishment of Independent State of Lithuania 1900; mem. Independence Party 1990–92; mem. Seimas (Parl.) 1992–; mem. Homeland Union Party (Lithuanian Conservatives) 1993–; Minister of Trade and Industry 1996–98, of European Affairs 1998–. *Address:* R. Seimas, Gedimino pr. 53, 2002 Vilnius, Lithuania (Office).

ANDRIYASHEV, Anatoliy Petrovich; Russian zoologist; b. 19 Aug. 1910, Montpellier, France; s. of P. E. Waitashevsky and N. Y. Andriasheva; m. Nina N. Savelyeva 1934; two d.; ed. Leningrad Univ.; Postgraduate, Research Assoc., Asst. Prof. Leningrad Univ. 1933–39; Sevastopol Biological Scientific Station 1939–44; Chief, Antarctic Research Div., Inst. of Zoology, U.S.S.R. (now Russian) Acad. of Sciences 1944–, Prof. 1970–; Vice-Pres. European Ichthyological Union 1979–82, Hon. mem. 1982–; Arctic and Bering Sea expeditions 1932, 1936, 1937, 1946, 1951; Antarctic expeditions 1955–58, 1971–72, 1975–76; Mediterranean and N. Atlantic expedition 1979; Corresp. mem. U.S.S.R. (now Russian) Acad. of Sciences 1966; Fellow Russian Acad. Natural Sciences 1994; Hon. Arctic explorer of the U.S.S.R. (now Russia) 1947–; Hon. Foreign mem. of American Soc. of Ichthyologists and Herpetologists; State prizewinner 1971; Leo S. Berg Academic Prize 1992, Soros Hon. Prof. 1996; Ed.-in-Chief Journal of Ichthyology 1977–88. *Publications:* works on ichthyology, marine zoogeography and Antarctic biology. *Leisure interest:* skiing. *Address:* Zoological Institute, Universitetskaya Nab. 1, Academy of Sciences, St. Petersburg 199034, Russia. *Telephone:* (812) 218-06-12. *Fax:* (812) 218-29-41.

ANDRONIKOF, Constantin, D.THEOL.; French interpreter, translator, author and professor; b. 16 July 1916, Petrograd, Russia; s. of Prince Yassé Andronikof and Helen von Wachter; m. 1st Nathaly de Couriss 1946 (deceased); m. 2nd Janet Wood 1989; two s. one d.; ed. Ecole Gerson, Lycée Janson-de-Sailly, Paris, Sorbonne and Inst. de Théologie Orthodoxe Saint-Serge, Paris; traffic officer, British Airways, Le Bourget 1936–38; official interpreter (Russian-English), French Ministry of Foreign Affairs 1946–76, of French Presidency (Elysée) 1962; Minister-Plenipotentiary (retd.); Acting Dean, Saint-Sergius Inst. until 1993, now Hon. Dean; Prof. Emer.; dir. Sophia collection, L'Age d'Homme, Lausanne, Paris; Officier, Légion d'honneur, Ordre nat. du Mérite. *Publications.* Le Sens des Fêtes I 1970, Le Cycle pascal (Sens des Fêtes II) 1985, Le Sens de la Liturgie 1988, Des Mystères sacramentals 1995; some 20 translations from English and Russian since 1939. *Leisure interests:* family (9 grandchildren), classical music, detective stories. *Address:* 26 rue Rosenwald, 75015 Paris, France. *Telephone:* 45-30-00-94.

ANDROUTSOPOULOS, Adamantios, LL.B., LL.M., J.D.; Greek politician; b. 1919, Psari, Greece, ed. Athens Univ., John Marshall Law School, Chicago, U.S.A., Chicago Univ.; Lawyer 1947; Prof. of Law, Chicago Industrial School; Scientific collaborator at Roosevelt Univ., Mundelein Coll., John Marshall Law School, Fengen Coll.; returned to Greece 1967; Minister of Finance 1967–71, of Interior 1971–73; Prime Minister 1973–74; mem. Athens Bar Asscn., American Judicature Soc., American Business Law Asscn. *Publications:* State Distributions and National Economy, The Problem of Causation in Maritime Law, Legal Terminology of the Greek-American Dictionary, The Spirit and Development of The American Law, The Testimony of a Prime Minister. *Address:* 63 Academias Street, 106 78 Athens, Greece.

ANDRUS, Cecil D.; American politician; b. 25 Aug. 1931, Hood River, Ore.; s. of Hal S. and Dorothy (Johnson) Andrus; m. Carol M. May 1949; three d.; ed. Oregon State Univ.; served U.S. Navy 1951–55; mem. Idaho Senate 1961–66; State Gen. Man. Paul Revere Life Insurance Co. 1967–70; Gov. of Idaho 1971–77, 1987–95; Chair. Nat. Govs. Conf. 1976; Sec. of Interior 1977–81; Dir. Beker Industries Corpn. 1981, Albertson's Inc. 1985–87, 1995–, Coeur d'Alene Mines 1995–, Albertson's, Inc. 1995–, Key Corp. 1996–; Hon. LL.D. (Gonzaga Univ., Spokane, Wash. 1975, Whitman Coll., Albertson Coll. of Idaho, Oregon State Univ., Univ. of Idaho, Idaho State Univ., Univ. of New Mexico); Democrat. *Leisure interests:* hunting, fishing, golf. *Address:* Andrus Center for Public Policy, Boise State University, 1910 University Drive, Boise, ID 83725, U.S.A. *Telephone:* (208) 385-4218. *Fax:* (208) 385-4208.

ANDSNES, Leif Ove; Norwegian pianist; b. 7 April 1970, Stavanger; ed. Bergen Music Conservatory; debut, Oslo 1987; British debut with Oslo Philharmonic, Edin. Festival 1989; U.S. debut with Cleveland Orchestra under Neeme Järvi 1990; recitals in London, Berlin, Vienna, Amsterdam, Glasgow; performs with Orchestre Nat. de France, Berlin Philharmonic, London Philharmonic, Chicago Symphony, City of Birmingham Symphony, BBC Philharmonic Orchestra, Bergen Philharmonic, L.A. Philharmonic, Japan Philharmonic, New York Philharmonic, Philadelphia Orchestra; recorded works of Brahms, Chopin, Grieg, Janacek, Liszt, Schumann; First Prize, Hindemith Competition, Frankfurt-am-Main and prizewinner at other int. competitions, Levin Prize (Bergen) 1988, Norwegian Music Critics Prize 1988, Grieg Prize (Bergen) 1990, Dorothy B. Chandler Performing Arts Award, Los Angeles 1992, Gilmore Prize 1997. *Address:* c/o Kathryn Enticott, IMG Artists, Media House, 3 Burlington Lane, London, W4 2TH, England. *Telephone:* 0181-233 5800. *Fax:* 0181-233 5801.

ANELL, Lars Evert Roland, M.B.A., M.A.; Swedish diplomatist; b. 23 Oct. 1941, Katrineholm, Sweden; s. of Evert Andersson and Margit Andersson; m. Kerstin Friis 1966; one s. three d.; ed. Stockholm School of Econs., Univ. of Stockholm; served Ministry of Finance 1966–70, Dir. for Planning and Research, Ministry for Foreign Affairs 1970–80, Dir. Gen. Swedish Agency for Research Co-operation with Developing Countries 1980–83, Sr. Advisor Prime Minister's Office 1983–86; Amb., Perm. Rep. of Sweden to UN orgs. in Geneva 1986 and EU; Chair. GATT Council 1990–91. *Publications:* The Other Society 1969, Should Sweden be Asphalted? 1971, Recession, The Western Economies and the Changing World Order 1981, Economic Crises in Theory and Practice 1986. *Address:* Permanent Mission of Sweden, C.P. 190, CH-1211 Geneva 20, Switzerland.

ANG LEE; Taiwanese film director; b. 1954, Taipei; m. Jane Lin; ed. New York Univ.; moved to U.S.A. 1978; winner of nat. script-writing contest (Taiwanese Govt.) 1990. *Films:* Pushing Hands 1992, The Wedding Banquet 1993, Eat Drink Man Woman 1995, Sense and Sensibility 1996, The Ice Storm 1998.

ANGEL, Heather Hazel, M.SC.; British wildlife photographer, author and lecturer; b. 21 July 1941, Fulmer, Bucks.; d. of Stanley Paul Le Rougetel and Hazel Marie Le Rougetel (née Sherwood); m. Martin Vivian Angel 1964; one s.; ed. 14 schools in U.K. and N.Z., Bristol Univ.; Special Prof., Dept. of Life Science, Nottingham Univ. 1994–; exhbns. include The Natural History of Britain and Ireland, Science Museum, London 1981, Nature in Focus, Natural History Museum, London 1987, The Art of Wildlife Photography, Nature in Art, Gloucester 1989; Kodak Calendar on The Thames 1987; TV programmes: Me and My Camera 1981, 1983, Gardener's World 1983, Nature 1984, Nocon on Photography 1988; featured in Japanese TV documentary, filmed in U.K. and Sri Lanka 1983; led British Photographic Del. to China 1985; Fellow, British Inst. of Prof. Photography; Hon. Fellow Royal Photographic Soc. (R.P.S.) (Pres. 1984–86); Hon. D.Sc. (Bath) 1986; Hood Medal (R.P.S.) for contrib. to advancement of nature photography through books, teaching, exhbns. etc. 1975; Médaille de Salverte, Société française de photographie 1984; Louis Schmidt Laureate, Biocommunications Asscn. 1998. *Publications:* Nature Photography: Its Art and Techniques 1972, Natural History of Britain and Ireland (co-author) 1982, The Family Water Naturalist 1982, The Book of Nature Photography 1982, The Book of Close-up Photography 1983, Heather Angel's Countryside 1983, A Camera in the Garden 1984, A View from a Window 1988, Nature in Focus 1988, Landscape Photography 1989, Animal Photography 1991, Kew: A World of Plants 1993, Photographing the Natural World 1994, Outdoor Photography: 101 Tips and Hints 1997, How to Photograph Flowers 1998, Pandas 1998. *Leisure interest:* travelling to remote parts of the world to photograph wilderness areas and unusual aspects of animal behaviour. *Address:* Highways, 6 Vicarage Hill, Farnham, Surrey, GU9 8HJ, England. *Telephone:* (01252) 716700. *Fax:* (01252) 727464.

ANGELINI, Arnaldo M.; Italian electrical and nuclear engineer; b. 2 Feb. 1909, Force, Ascoli Piceno Prov.; s. of Licinio and Anita Lucangeli Angelini; m. Livia Rossi 1937; two s. one d.; Man. Dir., Gen. Man. Terni Co.; Gen. Man. ENEL 1963–73, Chair. 1973–79, Hon. Pres. and Consultant 1979–; Pres. SIR Finanziaria S.p.A. and SIR Consorzio Industriale S.p.A. 1979–80; Prof. Electrical Eng., Univ. of Rome, Dir. Electric Eng. Inst.; Hon. Prof.,

Polytechnic Inst. of New York 1975–; fmrly. Vice-Pres. Comitato Nazionale per le Ricerche Nucleari; mem. Council Italian Forum for Nuclear Energy (FIEN), Pres. 1959–60; mem. Steering Cttee. Comitato Nazionale per l'Energia Nucleare 1960–73; mem. Scientific and Technical Cttee. EURATOM, Pres. 1961, Vice-Pres. 1964; mem. del. to Conf. on Peaceful Uses of Nuclear Energy, Geneva 1955, 1958, 1964, 1971; Hon. Exec. Vice-Pres. World Energy Conf.; Chair. Gen. Assembly, Org. of Nuclear Energy Producers (OPEN) 1976–79; New Acad. of Sciences 1981–; Pres. Associazione Elettrotecnica ed Elettronica Italiana (AEI) 1959–61, now Emer. mem. Gen. Presidency; Pres. Int. Union of Electric Energy Producers and Distributors (UNIPEDE) 1979–81; Fellow and Life mem. Inst. of Electrical and Electronic Eng.; National mem. Accad. Nazionale dei Lincei; Foreign Assoc., Nat. Acad. of Eng. of the U.S.A.; Fellow American Nuclear Soc.; mem. Soc. Française des Electriciens, and other socs.; Pugno Vanoni, Jona and Castellani Prizes (Italian Asscn. of Electrical Engs.), Simon Ramo Prize (I.E.E.E.). Eng. Leadership Recognition 1989. *Leisure interest:* amateur telescopes. *Address:* Enel S.p.A., Via G.B. Martini 3, Rome (Office); Via Francesco Coletti 5, 00191 Rome, Italy (Home). *Telephone:* (6) 85092207 (Office). *Fax:* (6) 85092082.

ANGELINI, H.E. Cardinal Fiorenzo; Italian ecclesiastic; b. 1 Aug. 1916, Rome; ordained priest 1940; elected Titular Bishop of Messene 1956, consecrated 1956; Archbishop 1985; cr. Cardinal 1991; Deacon of Santo Spirito in Sassia; Pres. Papal Council on Pastoral Work among Health Workers 1989; mem. Congregation for Evangelization of the Peoples, Papal Council on the Family, Papal Comm. on Latin America. *Address:* Via Anneo Lucano 47, 00136 Rome, Italy.

ANGELL, Wayne D., PH.D.; American economist; b. 28 June 1930, Liberal, Kansas; s. of Charlie Francis Angell and Adele Thelma Angell (née Edwards) m.; four c.; ed. Univ. of Kansas; Prof. Ottawa Univ. 1956, Dean 1969–72; mem. Kansas House of Reps 1961–67; Dir. Fed. Reserve Bank, Kansas City 1979–86; mem. of Fed. Reserve Bd. 1986–94; Chief Economist, Sr. Man. Dir. Bear Sterns & Co. Inc. 1994–. *Leisure interest:* tennis. *Address:* Bear Sterns & Co. Inc., 245 Park Avenue, New York, NY 10167 (Office); 1600 North Oak Street, Arlington, VA 22209, U.S.A. (Home).

ANGELOPOULOS, Theo; Greek film director; b. 27 April 1936, Athens; s. of Spyridon Angelopoulos and Katerina Krassaki; m. Phoebe Economopoulou 1980; three d.; ed. Univ. of Athens and the Inst. des Hautes Etudes Commerciales, Paris; film critic for the Athens daily Allaghi 1965; *directed:* Formix Story 1965, Broadcast 1968, Reconstruction 1970, Days of '36 1972, The Travelling Players 1974–75, The Hunters 1976–77, Megalexandros 1980, Athens 1984, Voyage to Cythera 1984, The Bee Keeper 1986, Landscape in the Mist 1988, The Hesitant Step of the Stork 1991, Ulysses Gaze 1995, Causes for Eternity; Best Foreign Film at Hyères Film Festival, George Sadoul Award, and five awards at the Thessaloniki Film Festival for Reconstruction; FIPRESCI Award, Berlin 1973 for Days of '36; FIPRESCI Grand Prix, Cannes, Golden Age Award, Brussels, Best Film of the Decade 1970–80, Italy, Grand Prix of the Arts and Best Film of the Year, Japan, Best Film of the Year, B.F.I., Interfilm Award, Berlin, Best Film, Figueira da Foz Film Festival, nine awards at the Thessaloniki Film Festival for The Travelling Players; Golden Hugo Award at the Chicago Film Festival 1978 for The Hunters; three awards at the Venice Film Festival for Megalexandros; Best screenplay and FIPRESCI Awards at the Cannes Film Festival for Voyage to Cythera; four awards at the Venice Film Festival, two awards at the Chicago Film Festival, Best European Film of the Year 1989 for Landscape in the Mist; Palme d'Or, Cannes Film Festival for Causes for Eternity; Chevalier des Arts et des Lettres (France). *Publications:* numerous screenplays. *Leisure interests:* cultivating tomatoes. *Address:* Solmou 18, 106 82 Athens (Office); Charitos 7, 106 75 Athens, Greece (Home). *Telephone:* 363-9120 (Office); 724-1406 (Home).

ANGELOU, Maya; American author; b. 4 April 1928, St. Louis; d. of Bailey Johnson and Vivian Baxter; one s.; Assoc. Ed. Arab Observer 1961–62; Asst. Admin., teacher School of Music and Drama, Univ. of Ghana 1963–66; feature Ed. African Review, Accra 1964–66; Reynolds Prof. Wake Forest Univ. 1981–; teacher of modern dance Rome Opera House, Hambina Theatre, Tel Aviv; has written several screenplays and films scores; theatre appearances include: Porgy and Bess 1954–55, Calypso 1957, The Blacks 1960, Mother Courage 1964, Look Away 1973; contrib. to Black Scholar, Essence, California Living, Ghanaian Times, Redbook, Ebony, Mademoiselle, Chicago Daily News, Harper's Bazaar, Cosmopolitan, Life, Sunday New York Times; Woman of Year in Communications 1976; TV appearances include: The Richard Pryor Special and Roots; producer Moon on a Rainbow Shawl 1988; Hon. Amb. to UNICEF 1996–; Dir. Down in the Delta (film) 1998; distinguished visiting prof. at several univs.; mem. various arts orgs.; Horatio Alger Award 1992, Grammy Award Best Spoken Word or Non-Traditional Album 1994, numerous other awards. *Publications include:* I Know Why the Caged Bird Sings 1970, Just Give Me A Cool Drink of Water 'Fore I Die 1971, Georgia, Georgia 1972, Gather Together In My Name 1974, Oh Pray My Wings Are Gonna Fit Me Well 1975, Singin' and Swingin' and Gettin' Merry Like Christmas 1976, And Still I Rise 1976, The Heart of a Woman 1986, All God's Children Need Travelling Shoes 1987, Now Sheba Sings the Song 1987, I Shall Not Be Moved 1990, Gathered Together in My Name 1991, Wouldn't Take Nothing for my Journey Now 1993, Collected Poems 1994, My Painted House, My Friendly Chicken and Me 1994, Phenomenal Woman 1995, Even the Stars Look Lonesome 1998. *Address:* c/o Dave La Camera, Lordly and Dame Inc., 51 Church Street, Boston, MA 02116, U.S.A. *Telephone:* (617) 482-3593. *Fax:* (617) 426-8019.

ANGELOZ, Eduardo César; Argentinian politician; b. 18 Oct. 1931, Río Tercero, Córdoba; m. Marta Marín; three c.; ed. Universidad Nacional de Córdoba; active mem. Unión Cívica Radical 1953–; Sec. Ministry of Public Works, Prov. of Córdoba 1955; Sec. Gen. Prov. Energy Corp., Córdoba 1956; Prov. Senator 1963; Nat. Senator, Sec. Comm. on Energy and Fuels, Nat. Senate 1973; mem. staff, OAS 1976; Gov. Prov. of Córdoba 1983–87, 1987–95; candidate in presidential elections 1989. *Publications:* El Tiempo de los Argentinos, Tiempo de la Transición; numerous essays and articles. *Address:* c/o Union Civica Radical, Buenos Aires, Argentina.

ANGENOT, Marc, D.PHIL., F.R.S.C.; Canadian professor of French and comparative literature; b. 21 Dec. 1941, Brussels; s. of Marcel Angenot and Zoé-Martha DeClercq; m. 1st Joséphine Brock 1966 (divorced 1976); one s. one d.; m. 2nd Nadia Khouri 1981; one d.; ed. Univ. Libre de Bruxelles; Prof. of French and Comparative Literature, McGill Univ. 1967–; Assoc. Dir Ecole des Hautes Etudes en Sciences Sociales, France 1985; Killam Fellowship 1987; Prix Biguet (Acad. Française) 1983; Prix des sciences humaines (Canada) 1996. *Publications:* Le Roman populaire 1975, Les Champions des femmes 1977, Glossaire pratique de la critique contemporaine 1979, La Parole pamphlétaire 1982, Critique de la raison sémiotique 1985, Le Cru et le faisandé 1986, Le Centenaire de la Révolution 1989, Ce que l'on dit des Juifs en 1889 1989, Mille huit cent quatre-vingt neuf 1989, L'Utopie collectiviste 1993, La Propagande socialiste 1996, Idéologies du ressentiment 1996; numerous articles and contributions in literary theory and discourse analysis. *Address:* 3460 McTavish Street, Montreal, Quebec H3A 1X9 (Office); 4572 Harvard Avenue, Montreal, Quebec, H4A 2X2, Canada. *Telephone:* (514) 488-1388. *Fax:* (514) 483-4428.

ANGERER, Paul; Austrian conductor, composer and instrumentalist; b. 16 May 1927, Vienna; s. of Otto and Elisabeth Angerer; m. Anita Rosser 1952; two s. two d.; ed. Hochschule für Musik und darstellende Kunst, Vienna; viola player, Vienna Symphony 1947, leading solo viola player 1953–57; viola player, Tonhalle Zürich 1948, Suisse Romande Orch., Geneva 1949; Dir. and Chief Conductor, Chamber Orch. of Wiener Konzerthausgesellschaft 1956–63; composer and conductor, Burgtheater, Vienna and Salzburg and Bregenz festivals 1960–; perm. guest conductor, Orchestra sinfonica di Bolzano e Trento "Haydn" 1964–90; first conductor, Bonn city theatre 1964–66; music dir. Ulm theatre 1966–68; Chief of opera, Salzburger Landestheater 1967–72; Dir. S.W. German Chamber Orch., Pforzheim 1971–82; Prof. Hochschule, Vienna 1983–92; leader of Concilium Musicum; several prizes including Austrian State Prize 1956, Theodor Körner Prize 1958, Vienna Cultural Prize 1983, Cultural Prize of Lower Austria 1987. *Works include:* orchestral pieces, chamber works, viola and piano concertos, a dramatic cantata, television opera, works for organ, harp, viola, harpsichord, etc.; numerous recordings both as soloist and conductor. *Address:* Esteplatz 3/26, A-1030 Vienna, Austria. *Telephone:* (1) 714 12 71. *Fax:* (1) 714 12 71.

ANGREMY, Jean-Pierre (Pierre-Jean Rémy); French diplomatist and writer; b. 21 March 1937, Angoulême; m. 1st Odile Cail (divorced); one s. one d.; m. 2nd Sophie Schmit 1986; one s.; ed. Institut d'études politiques, Paris; served Hong Kong 1963–64, Beijing 1964–66, London 1966–71, 1975–79; Cultural, Scientific and Tech. Relations, Paris 1971–72; seconded to ORTF 1972–75; seconded to Ministry of Culture and Communication 1979–84; Consul, Florence 1984–87; Dir.-Gen. Cultural, Scientific and Tech. Relations 1987–90; Amb. to UNESCO 1990–94; Dir. Académie de France, Rome 1994–97; Pres. Bibliothèque Nationale de France Jan. 1997–, mem. Acad. Française 1988. *Publications:* numerous novels and other publs. *Leisure interest:* collecting books. *Address:* Bibliothèque Nationale de France, 58 rue de Richelieu, 75084 Paris, France; 134 rue de Grenelle, 75007 Paris, France.

ANGUS, Sir Michael Richardson, Kt., B.SC., C.I.MGT.; British company director; b. 5 May 1930, Ashford, Kent; s. of William Richardson Angus and Doris Margaret Breach; m. Eileen Isabel May Elliott 1952; two s. one d.; ed. Marling School, Stroud, Bristol Univ.; served in R.A.F. 1951–54; joined Unilever PLC 1954, Marketing Dir. Thibaud Gibbs, Paris 1962–65, Man. Dir. Research Bureau 1965–67, Sales Dir. Lever Brothers, U.K. 1967–70, Dir. Unilever PLC and Unilever N.V. 1970–92, Toilet Preparations Co-ordinator 1970–76, Chemicals Co-ordinator 1976–80, Regional Dir. N. America 1979–84, Chair. and C.E.O. Unilever United States Inc., New York 1980–84, Chair. and C.E.O. Lever Brothers Co., New York 1980–84, Vice-Chair. Unilever PLC 1984–86, Chair. 1986–92, also Vice-Chair. Unilever NV; Vice-Pres. Netherlands-British Chamber of Commerce 1990–94; Deputy Pres. CBI 1991–92, 1994–95, Pres. 1992–94; Gov. Ashridge Man. Coll. 1974–, Chair. of Govs. 1991–; Jt. Chair. Netherlands-British Chamber of Commerce 1984–89; Chair. of Govs. Royal Agricultural Coll., Cirencester 1992–; Non-Exec. Dir. Whitbread PLC 1986– (Deputy Chair. Jan.–Aug. 1992, Chair. Aug. 1992–), Thorn EMI PLC 1988–93, British Airways PLC 1988– (Deputy Chair. 1989–); Dir. Nat. Westminster Bank PLC 1991– (Deputy Chair. 1991–94), The Boots Co. PLC 1994– (Chair. 1994–98, Deputy Chair. 1998–); Leverhulme Trust 1984–; mem. Council, British Exec. Service Overseas 1986– (Pres. 1998); mem. Council of Man., Ditchley Foundation 1994–; Hon. D.Sc. (Bristol) 1990, (Buckingham) 1994; Hon. LL.D. (Nottingham) 1996; Holland Trade Award 1990, Commdr. of Order of Oranje Nassau 1992.

Leisure interests: countryside, wine and mathematical puzzles. *Address:* Whitbread PLC, Chiswell Street, London, EC1Y 4SD, England. *Telephone:* 0171-606 4455. *Fax:* 0171-615 1012.

ANGYAL, Stephen John, O.B.E., PH.D., D.SC., F.A.A.; Australian (b. Hungarian) professor of organic chemistry; b. 21 Nov. 1914, Budapest; s. of Charles Engel and Maria Szanto; m. Helga Ellen Steininger 1941; one s. one d.; ed. Pazmany Peter Univ., Budapest; Research Chemist, Chinoin Pharmaceutical Works, Budapest 1937–40; Research Chemist, Nicholas Pty. Ltd., Melbourne, Australia 1941–46; Lecturer, Univ. of Sydney 1946–52; Nuffield Dominion Travelling Fellow 1952; Assoc. Prof. of Organic Chem., Univ. of N.S.W. 1953–60, Prof. 1960–80, Prof. Emer. 1980–, Dean of Science 1970–79; Fellow Royal Australian Chem. Inst.; Foreign mem. Hungarian Acad. of Science 1990; H.G. Smith Memorial Medal, Royal Australian Chem. Inst. 1958, Haworth Medal and Lectureship, Royal Soc. of Chem. 1980, Hudson Award, American Chemical Soc. 1987. *Publications:* Conformational Analysis (with others) 1965; about 200 research publs. in chemical journals. *Leisure interests:* swimming, skiing, bushwalking, music. *Address:* 304 Sailors Bay Road, Northbridge, N.S.W. 2063, Australia. *Telephone:* (02) 9958-7209. *Fax:* (02) 9385-6141.

ANIN, Patrick Dankwa, M.A., LL.B.; Ghanaian judge; b. 27 July 1928, Bekwai, Ashanti; m. Doris Marian Dadzie 1958; two s. two d.; ed. Achimota Coll., Selwyn Coll., Cambridge, and London School of Economics.; called to Bar, Middle Temple 1956, Called to Gold Coast Bar 1956; fmr. Dir. Bank of Ghana; mem. Electoral Comm. 1966–67; Commr. for Communications 1967–68, Commr. for External Affairs 1968–69; Justice of Appeal, Ghana Court of Appeal 1969; Chair. Bribery and Corruption Comm. 1971–74; Chair. Council of Univ. of Ghana, Legon 1976–78; Justice of Appeal, Court of Appeal of The Gambia, Nov. 1978–, Pres. 1993–. *Leisure interests:* reading, tennis. *Address:* Justice of Appeal's Chambers, Court of Appeal, Banjul, Gambia.

ANISTON, Jennifer; American actress; b. 11 Feb. 1969, Sherman Oaks, Calif.; d. of John Aniston; ed. New York High School of the Performing Arts. *Theatre includes:* For Dear Life, Dancing on Checker's Grave. *Films include:* Leprechaun 1993, She's the One 1996, Dream for an Insomniac 1996, 'Til There Was You 1996, Picture Perfect 1997, The Object of My Affection 1998. *TV includes:* Molloy (series) 1989, The Edge, Ferris Bueller, Herman's Head, Friends. *Address:* c/o CAA, 9830 Wilshire Blvd., Beverly Hills, CA 90212, U.S.A.

ANJARIA, Shailendra J.; Indian international finance official; b. 17 July 1946, Bombay; s. of Jashwantrai J. Anjaria and Harvidya Anjaria; m. Nishigandha Pandit 1972; two d.; ed. Univ. of Pennsylvania, Yale Univ. and London School of Econs.; economist, Exchange and Trade Relations Dept., IMF 1968; IMF office, Geneva 1973; Div. Chief 1980; Asst. Dir. and Adviser, Exchange and Trade Relations Dept. 1986; Asst. Dir. N. African Div. of African Dept. 1988; Dir. External Relations Dept. IMF 1991–. *Address:* International Monetary Fund, 700 19th Street, N.W., Washington, DC 20431, U.S.A.

ANKUM, Hans (Johan Albert), D.JUR.; Netherlands professor of Roman Law; b. 23 July 1930, Amsterdam; s. of Leendert and Johanna (née Van Kuykhof) Ankum; m. 1st Joke Houwink 1957 (divorced 1970); m. 2nd Pelline van Es 1971; one s. three d.; ed. Zaanlands Lyceum, Zaandam, Univ. of Amsterdam, Univ. of Paris; Asst. Roman Law and Juridical Papyrology, Univ. of Amsterdam 1956–60; Lecturer in Roman Law and Legal History, Univ. of Leyden 1960–63, Prof. 1963–69; Prof. of Roman Law, Legal History and Juridical Papyrology, Univ. of Amsterdam 1965–95; mem. Royal Dutch Acad. of Sciences 1986–; Winkler Prins award; Dr. h.c. (Aix-Marseille, Vrije Univs. Brussels and Ruhr Universität Bochum). *Publications:* De geschiedenis der 'Actio Pauliana'; numerous books and articles on Roman law and legal history. *Leisure interests:* classical music, history of art, travel. *Address:* Faculty of Law, University of Amsterdam, P.O. Box 1030, 1000 BA, Amsterdam Oudermanhuis poort 4–6 (Office); Zonnebloemlaan 8, NL-2111 ZG Aerdenhout, The Netherlands (Home). *Telephone:* (20)-5253408 (Office); (23)-5243036 (Home). *Fax:* (20)-5253495.

ANLYAN, William George, B.S., M.D.; American professor of surgery and medical consultant; b. 14 Oct. 1925, Alexandria, Egypt; s. of Armand Anlyan and Emmy Anlyan; two s. one d.; ed. Yale Univ. and Duke Univ. Hosp.; Instructor in Surgery Duke Univ. School of Medicine 1950–51, Assoc. 1951–53, Asst. Prof. of Surgery 1953–58, Assoc. Prof. 1958–61, Prof. 1961–89, Assoc. Dean 1963–64, Dean 1964–69; Assoc. Provost Duke Univ. 1969, Vice-Pres. for Health Affairs 1969–83, Chancellor for Health Affairs 1983–88, Exec. Vice-Pres. 1987–88, Chancellor 1988–90, Chancellor Emer. 1990–; numerous exec. posts Asscn. of American Medical Colls. 1965–, Distinguished Service Mem. 1974–, American Medical Asscn. 1971–74, American Surgical Asscn. 1964–; mem. Bd. of Dirs. Asscn. for Acad. Health Centers 1971–, Pres. 1974–75; mem. Research Strengthening Group for Special Programme for Research and Training in Tropical Diseases, WHO 1981–85, Chair. Univ. Council's Cttee. on Medical Affairs (WHO), Yale Univ. 1987–; mem. Council Govt.-Univ.-Industry Research Roundtable 1984–86; mem. several advisory and research cttees., N.C. 1965–; Consultant Gen. Surgery, Durham Veterans' Hosp. 1955–73; mem. U.S. dels. consulting on health and medical educ., China, Poland, Israel, Egypt, Saudi Arabia, Japan etc.; mem. Bd. of Regents Nat. Library of Medicine 1968–71, Chair. 1971–72, Consultant 1972–; mem. Bd. of Dirs. Wachovia Bank 1970–90, G.D. Searle and Co. 1974–90, Pearle Health Services Inc. 1983–85, N.C. Inst. of Medicine 1983–, Durham Chamber of Commerce Jan. 1988–; mem. Bds. of Visitors and Trustees numerous univs.; mem. numerous professional socs.; mem. Editorial Bd. The Pharos 1968–93; Trustee The Duke Endowment 1990–; Hon. D.S. (Rush Medical Coll.) 1973; Modern Medicine Award for Distinguished Achievement 1974, Gov.'s Award for Distinguished Meritorious Service 1978, Distinguished Surgeon Alumnus 1979, Yale Univ. School of Medicine, The Abraham Flexner Award, Asscn. of American Medical Colls. 1980, Civic Honor Award, Durham Chamber of Commerce 1981, Award of Merit, Duke Univ. Hosp. and Health Admin. Alumni Asscn. 1987, Lifetime Achievement Award 1995. *Publications:* contrib. and ed. several books; over 100 articles in professional journals on health and surgical topics. *Leisure interests:* piano, tennis. *Address:* Duke Medical Center, P.O. Box 3626, 109 Seeley G. Mudd Building, Durham, NC 27710, U.S.A. *Telephone:* (919) 684-3438. *Fax:* (919) 684-3518.

ANN-MARGRET; American actress, singer and dancer; b. 1941, Stockholm, Sweden; m. Roger Smith 1967; film début in Pocketful of Miracles 1961. *Films include:* State Fair, Bye Bye Birdie, Once A Thief, The Cincinnati Kid, Stagecoach, Murderer's Row, C.C. & Co., Carnal Knowledge, RPM, The Train Robbers, Tommy, The Twist, Joseph Andrews, Last Remake of Beau Geste, Magic, Middle Age Crazy, Return of the Soldier, I Ought to Be in Pictures, Looking to Get Out, Twice in a Lifetime, 52 Pick-Up 1987, New Life 1988, Something More, Newsies 1992, Grumpy Old Men 1993, Grumpier Old Men 1995. TV includes: Who Will Love My Children? 1983, A Streetcar Named Desire 1984, The Two Mrs Grenvilles 1987, Our Sons 1991, Nobody's Children, 1994, Following her Heart, Seduced by Madness: The Diane Borchardt Story 1996, Blue Rodeo 1996; also appears in cabaret. *Publication:* (with Todd Gold) Ann-Margret: My Story 1994. *Address:* William Morris Agency, 151 S. El Camino Drive, Beverly Hills, CA 90212, U.S.A.

ANNAKIN, Kenneth; British film director and writer; b. 10 Aug. 1914, Beverley, Yorks; s. of Edward Annakin and Jane Annakin; m. 1959; two d. (one deceased). *Films include:* Across the Bridge, Swiss Family Robinson, Very Important Person, The Longest Day, The Fast Lady, The Informers, Those Magnificent Men in Their Flying Machines, Battle of the Bulge, The Long Duel, Monte Carlo or Bust, Call of the Wild, Paper Tiger, The Fifth Musketeer, The Pirate, Cheaper to Keep Her, The Pirate Movie, Pippi Longstocking, Genghis Khan. *Screenplays:* The Crystals of Lemuria, Coco Chanel, Chiffon, Redwing. *Leisure interests:* travel, cinema, bridge. *Address:* c/o Denise Denny, 9233 Swallow Drive, Los Angeles, CA 90069, U.S.A.

ANNAN, Kofi A., M.SC., B.A.(ECONS); Ghanaian international civil servant; b. 1938; m.; one s. two d.; ed. Univ. of Science and Tech., Kumasi, Macalester Coll., St. Paul, Minn., U.S.A., Institut des Hautes Etudes Internationales, Geneva, Switzerland, Massachusetts Inst. of Tech., U.S.A.; held posts in UN ECA, Addis Ababa, UN, New York, WHO, Geneva 1962–71, Admin. Man. Officer, UN, Geneva 1972–74; Chief Civilian Personnel Officer, UNEF, Cairo 1974; Man. Dir. Ghana Tourist Devt. Co. 1974–76; Deputy Chief of Staff Services, Office of Personnel Services, Office of UNHCR, Geneva 1976–80, Deputy Dir. Div. of Admin., and Head Personnel Service 1980–83; Dir. of Admin. Man. Service, then Dir. of Budget, Office of Financial Services, UN, New York 1984–87, Asst. Sec.-Gen., Office of Human Resources Man. 1987–90; Controller Office of Programme Planning, Budget and Finance 1990–92; Asst. Sec.-Gen. Dept. of Peace-Keeping Operations 1992–93; Under-Sec.-Gen. 1993–96; UN Special Envoy (a.i.) to fmr. Yugoslavia 1995–96; Sec. Gen. of UN Jan. 1997–; Alfred P. Sloan Fellow, M.I.T. 1971–72. *Address:* United Nations, United Nations Plaza, New York, NY 10017, U.S.A.

ANNAN, Baron (Life Peer) cr. 1965, of Royal Burgh of Annan; **Noel Gilroy Annan,** O.B.E., M.A.; British university official; b. 25 Dec. 1916, London; s. of late James Gilroy Annan and Fannie Quinn; m. Gabriele Ullstein 1950; two d.; ed. Stowe School, King's Coll., Cambridge.; served in War Office, War Cabinet Offices and Mil. Intelligence 1940–44, France and Germany 1944–46; Gen. Staff Officer, Political Division, British Control Comm. 1945–46; Fellow, King's Coll., Cambridge 1944–56, 1966, Asst. Tutor 1947, Lecturer in Politics 1948–66, Provost 1956–66; Provost of Univ. Coll., London 1966–78; Vice-Chancellor, Univ. of London 1978–81; Gov. of Stowe School 1945–66, Queen Mary Coll. 1956–60; Senior Fellow, Eton Coll. 1956–66; mem. Gulbenkian Cttee. for Art in U.K. 1957–64, Chair. Educ. Cttee. 1971–76; mem. Academic Planning Board, Univ. of East Anglia 1960; Chair. Academic Planning Board, Univ. of Essex 1962; mem. Academic Advisory Board Brunel Univ. 1964; mem. Public Schools Comm. 1966–70; Chair. Cttee. on Future of Broadcasting 1974–77; Trustee, British Museum 1963–80, Nat. Gallery 1978–85 (Chair. 1980–85); Dir. Royal Opera House, Covent Garden 1967–78; F.R.Hist.S.; Fellow, Berkeley Coll., Yale 1963; Hon. Fellow, Univ. Coll., London 1968; Emer. Fellow, Leverhulme Trust 1984; Hon. D.Litt. (York, Ontario, New York Univ., London); D.Univ. (Essex); Hon. D.Laws (Univ. of Pennsylvania); Foreign Hon. mem. American Acad. of Arts and Sciences; Le Bas Prize 1948, James Tait Black Memorial Prize 1951, Clark Kerr Medal (Univ. of Calif., Berkeley) 1985. *Publications:* Leslie Stephen: His Thought and Character in Relation to His Time 1951, The Intellectual Aristocracy (in Studies in Social History, edited by J. H. Plumb) 1956, The Curious Strength of Positivism in English Political Thought 1959, Kipling's Place in the History of Ideas (in Kipling's Mind and Art) 1964, Roxburgh of Stowe 1965, Annan Report on the Future of Broadcasting 1977, Our Age 1990, Changing Enemies 1995, and articles in New York Review of Books and other periodicals. *Leisure interest:* writing English prose. *Address:* 45 Ranelagh Grove, London, SW1W 8PB, England. *Telephone:* 0171-730 4930.

ANNAUD, Jean-Jacques, L. ÈS L.; French film director and screenwriter; b. 1 Oct. 1943, Juvisy/Orge; s. of Pierre Annaud and Madeleine Tripoz; m. 1st Monique Rossignol 1970 (divorced 1980); one d.; m. 2nd Laurence Duval 1982; one d.; ed. Inst. des Hautes Etudes Cinématographiques, Paris and Univ. of Paris, Sorbonne; freelance commercial film dir. (500 films) 1966–75; feature film dir. 1975–. *Films include:* Black and White in Colour 1976 (Acad. Award for best Foreign Film), Hot Head 1979, Quest for Fire (César Award) 1981, Name of the Rose (César Award), The Bear 1988 (César Award), The Lover 1992, Wings of Courage 1994, Seven Years in Tibet 1997; Chevalier des Palmes académiques et du Mérite social, Officer des Arts et des Lettres. *Leisure interests:* books, old cameras. *Address:* c/o Repérage, 16 rue Saint-Vincent, 75018 Paris; 9 rue Guénégard, 75006 Paris, France (Home).

ANNE, H.R.H. The Princess (see Royal, H.R.H. The Princess.)

ANNENBERG, Walter H.; American diplomatist and publisher; b. 13 March 1908, Milwaukee, Wis.; s. of M. L. Annenberg; m. 1st Veronica Dunkelman (divorced); one d.; m. 2nd Leonore Cohn 1951; Pres. Triangle Publications Inc., Pa.; publishes TV Guide; Pres. M. L. Annenberg Foundation, Annenberg Fund; Amb. to U.K. 1969–75; Founder of Annenberg School for Communications at Univ. of Pa. and Univ. of S. Calif.; Trustee Nat. Trust for Historic Preservation, Univ. of Pa.; Emer. Trustee, Eisenhower Medical Center, Philadelphia Museum of Art; retd. Commdr., U.S.N.; several hon. degrees; Officier, Légion d'honneur; Commdr., Orders of Lion of Finland, Crown of Italy; Commdr. Order of Merit (Italy); Hon. K.B.E.; Presidential Medal of Freedom 1986, Hon. Old Etonian 1990, Churchill Bell Award 1993, Benjamin Franklin Award 1993, Nat. Medal of Arts 1993, American Legion Distinguished Service Medal 1994, Service to Democracy Award 1994, Univ. of Pa Medal for Distinguished Achievement 1994, Architect of Peace Award 1995, George Peabody Educ. Award 1995, Jefferson Award 1995, Steven J. Ross/Time Warner Technology Award 1996. *Address:* St. Davids Center, Suite A-200, 150 Radnor-Chester Road, St. Davids, PA 19087 (Office); Llanfair Road, Wynnewood, PA 19096, U.S.A. (Home). *Telephone:* (610) 342-9396. *Fax:* (610) 964-8688.

ANNESLEY, Sir Hugh, Kt.; British police officer; b. 22 June 1939, Dublin; m. Elizabeth Ann MacPherson 1970; one s. one d.; ed. St Andrew's Prep. School, Dublin and Avoca School for Boys, Blackrock; joined Metropolitan Police 1958; Asst. Chief Constable of Sussex with special responsibility for personnel and training 1976; Deputy Asst. Commr., Metropolitan Police 1981, Asst. Commr. 1985; Head Operations Dept., Scotland Yard 1987–89; Chief Constable of the Royal Ulster Constabulary 1989–96; mem. Nat. Exec. Inst., FBI 1986; Exec. Cttee. Interpol (British Rep. 1987–90, 1993–94); Queen's Police Medal 1986. *Address:* c/o Brooklyn, Knock Road, Belfast, BT5 6LE, Northern Ireland.

ANNIS, Francesca; British actress; d. of Anthony Annis and Mariquita Annis; one s. two d. by Patrick Wiseman; with R.S.C. 1975–78. *Plays include:* The Tempest, The Passion Flower Hotel, Hamlet, Troilus and Cressida, Comedy of Errors, The Heretic, Mrs Klein, Rosmersholm, Lady Windermere's Fan, Hamlet. *Films include:* Cleopatra, Saturday Night Out, Murder Most Foul, The Pleasure Girls, Run With the Wind, The Sky Pirates, The Walking Stick, Penny Gold, Macbeth, Krull, Dune, Under the Cherry Moon, Golden River, El Rio de Oro. *Television includes:* Great Expectations, Children in Uniform, Love Story, Danger Man, The Human Jungle, Lily Langtry (role of Lily), Madame Bovary, Partners in Crime, Coming Out of Ice, Why Didn't They Ask Evans?, Magnum P.I., Inside Story, Onassis—The Richest Man in the World 1990, Parnell and the Englishwoman 1991, Absolute Hell 1991, The Gravy Train 1991, Weep No More My Lady 1991, Between the Lines 1993, Reckless 1997, Deadly Summer 1997. *Address:* c/o ICM, 76 Oxford Street, London, W1N 0AX, England.

ANNORKWEI II, Nene, Q.M.C.; Ghanaian chief; b. 1900; ed. Wesleyan School, Accra; entered Nigerian civil service as Treasury Clerk 1919; transferred to Gold Coast 1930; promoted to Accountant 1944; elected Manche of Prampram 1948; appointed Treas. of Provincial Council, Eastern Province, and mem. Council's Standing Cttee. 1948; later Pres. Joint Provincial Council of Chiefs (representing Eastern and Western Regions); Chair. Ghana Museum and Monuments Board 1957–; Queen's Medal for Chiefs 1956. *Address:* Manche of Prampram, Prampram, Ghana.

ANSARI, Gholamreza, B.SC.; Iranian diplomatist; b. 22 Nov. 1955, Shahrood; m. Shahih Shirazi; four d.; ed. Allameh Tabatabaee Univ. Tehran; Gov.-Gen. Piranshahr City, Deputy Gov.-Gen. Azarbayejan Prov., Supt. of Gov.-Gen. of Azarbayejan Prov., Deputy Gen. Dir. of Foreign Nationals and Refugees Dept. 1980–88; Chargé d'Affaires Embassy, London 1992–. *Leisure interests:* reading, jogging, swimming. *Address:* Embassy of Iran, 16 Prince's Gate, London, SW7 1PT, England. *Telephone:* 0171-584 4153; 0171-225 3000. *Fax:* 0171-589 4440.

ANSELL, Barbara Mary, C.B.E., M.D., F.R.C.S., F.R.C.P.; British doctor; b. 30 Aug. 1923, Warwick; d. of Herbert Joseph Ansell and Annie Olivia Ansell; m. Angus Harold Weston; ed. King's High School for Girls, Warwick, Birmingham Medical School; Research Fellow, Research and Educ. Hosp., Chicago, U.S.A. 1953–54; Consultant Physician (Rheumatology), Canadian Red Cross Memorial Hosp., Taplow, Bucks. 1962, Wexham Park Hosp., Slough 1985–88; Head, Div. of Rheumatology, Clinical Research Centre, Northwick Park Hosp., Harrow, Middx. 1976–88; Chair. or mem. of several medical cttees. and orgs.; Hon. F.R.S.M. 1989, Queen's Prize, Birmingham Univ. 1944. *Publications:* Surgical Management of Juvenile Chronic Polyarthritis (with G.P. Arden) 1978, Rheumatic Disorders in Childhood 1980, Inflammatory Disorders in Muscle: in Clinics in Rheumatic Diseases 1984, Paediatric Rheumatology Update (co-ed.) 1991, Colour Atlas of Rheumatology (co-ed.) 1992. *Leisure interests:* opera, travel, cooking. *Address:* 9 Beaumont Road, Windsor, Berks. (Office); Dumgoyne, Templewood Lane, Stoke Poges, Bucks., SL2 4BG, England. *Telephone:* (01753) 662321 (Office).

ANSELL, Graham Keith, C.M.G., B.A.; New Zealand fmr. diplomatist and business executive; b. 2 March 1931, Lower Hutt, New Zealand; m. Mary Diana Wilson 1953; three s. one d.; ed. Horowhenua Coll., Palmerston North Boys' School and Victoria Univ., Wellington. Dept. of Industries and Commerce 1948–51, of External Affairs 1951–56; Second Sec., High Comm. to Ottawa 1956–59; Asst., then Acting Head, Econ. and Social Affairs Div., Dept. of External Affairs 1959–62; Deputy High Commr., Apia 1962–64, Canberra 1964–68; Head, Econ. Div., Ministry of Foreign Affairs 1968–71; Minister, N.Z. Embassy, Tokyo 1971–73; High Commr. in Fiji 1973–76, in Nauru 1974–76; Amb. to Belgium, Luxembourg and the European Communities (also accred. to Denmark) 1977–81; Dir. N.Z. Planning Council 1981–82; Amb. to Japan 1983–84; Deputy Sec. Ministry of Foreign Affairs 1984–85; High Commr. in Australia 1985–89; Chief Exec. Ministry of Foreign Affairs and Trade 1989–91; mem. N.Z. Meat Producers Bd. 1990–96; Dir. Nat. Bank of N.Z. 1991–, Asian N.Z. Meat Co. 1991–, N.Z. Bd., Colonial Mutual Insurance 1992–94; mem. Bd. Asia 2000 Foundation 1994–97; Chair. Advisory Bd., N.Z. Centre for Japanese Studies 1998–. *Leisure interests:* music, walking, gardening. *Address:* 13 Tainui Street, Raumati Beach, New Zealand.

ANSI, Saud bin Salim al-, B.A.; Omani diplomatist; b. 23 Dec. 1949, Salalah; s. of Salim Ansi and Sultana Ansi: m. 1976; two s. two d.; ed. Beirut Univ.; Ministry of Information and Culture and of Diwan Affairs 1974–75; Dir. Dept. of Research and Studies 1976–78; First Sec. Embassy, Tunis 1975–76, Consul-Gen., Karachi 1978–80, Amb. to Djibouti 1980–82, to Kuwait 1982–84; Perm. Rep. to the UN 1984–88; Under Sec. and Dir.-Gen. Council of Environment and Water Resources 1988–89; Sec.-Gen. Council of Educ. and Vocational Training 1990–92; Adviser to Ministry of Nat. Heritage and Culture 1993–94; Chief Information Dept., Ministry of Foreign Affairs 1995–. *Leisure interests:* reading, writing, sports, travelling. *Address:* P.O. Box 1128, Ruwi 112, Oman. *Telephone:* 701 207. *Fax:* 704 785.

ANSIMOV, Georgiy Pavlovich; Russian musical theatre director; b. 3 June 1922, Ladozhskaya; s. of Pavel Ansimov and Marija Sollertinskaja; m. 1st Irina Mikluho-Maklaj 1944 (died 1991); m. 2nd Lindmila Ansimova; ed. Lunarcharsky State Inst. of Theatre (under B.A. Pokrovsky); Producer at Bolshoi Theatre 1955–64, 1980–; Artistic Dir. and main producer, Moscow Operetta Theatre 1964–76; main productions: Story of a Real Man (Prokofiev); Carmen, The Tale of Tsar Sultan (Rimsky Korsakov), West Side Story, Orpheus in the Underworld, War and Peace (Prokofiev), Bethrothal in the Monastery (Prokofiev), The Golden Cock, Eugene Onegin, The Fiery Angel, Maddalena, The Taming of the Shrew, The Magic Flute, Sunset, Love for Three Oranges, The Tsar-Carpenter; Teaches at Lunarcharsky Inst., Prof. 1977–; Czechoslovakia State Prize 1960, U.S.S.R. People's Artist 1986. *Publications:* The Director in the Music Theatre 1980, Everything Begins Over Again Always 1983. *Leisure interest:* photography. *Address:* Theatralnaja pl. 1, 103009, Moscow (Office); Karetny Ryad 5/10-340, 103006 Moscow, Russia (Home). *Telephone:* (095) 2993953. *Fax:* (095) 2900597.

ANSON, Sir John, K.C.B., M.A.; British civil servant; b. 3 Aug. 1930, Yeovil; s. of late Sir Edward R. Anson and Frances Alison Anson (née Pollock); m. Myrica Fergie-Woods 1957; two s. two d.; ed. Winchester Coll., and Magdalene Coll., Cambridge; served H.M. Treasury 1954–68; Financial Counsellor, British Embassy, Paris 1968–70; Asst. Sec. Cabinet Office 1971–72, Under-Sec. 1972–74; Under-Sec. H.M. Treasury 1974–77, Deputy Sec. 1977–87; Head, Treasury Del. and Econ. Minister, British Embassy, Washington, D.C., and U.K. Exec. Dir. IMF and IBRD (World Bank) 1980–83; Second Perm. Sec. (Public Expenditure), H.M. Treasury 1987–90; Chair. Public Finance Foundation 1991–94, Retirement Income Inquiry 1994–96, House of Laity Southwark Diocesan Synod 1996–97; Treas. Council of Churches for Britain and Ireland 1990–92; Smith's Prize, Cambridge Univ. 1954. *Address:* 18 Church Road, Barnes, London, SW13 9HN, England. *Telephone:* 0181-748 6557.

ANSTEE, Dame Margaret Joan, D.C.M.G., M.A., B.SC. (ECON.); British United Nations official, lecturer and consultant; b. 25 June 1926, Writtle, Essex; d. of Edward C. Anstee and Anne A. Mills; ed. Chelmsford Co. High School for Girls, Newnham Coll. Cambridge and Univ. of London; Lecturer in Spanish, Queen's Univ. Belfast 1947–48; Third Sec. Foreign Office 1948–52; UN Tech. Assistance Bd. Manila 1952–54; Spanish Supervisor, Univ. of Cambridge 1955–56; UN Tech. Assistance Bd. Bogotá 1956–57, Uruguay 1957–59, Bolivia 1960–65; Resident Rep. UNDP Ethiopia and UNDP Liaison Officer with ECA 1965–67; Sr. Econ. Adviser, Office of Prime Minister, London 1967–68; Sr. Asst. to Commr. in charge of study of Capacity of UN Devt. System 1968–69; Resident Rep. UNDP, Morocco 1969–72, Chile (also UNDP Liaison Officer with ECLA) 1972–74; Deputy to UN Under Sec.-Gen. in charge of UN Relief Operation to Bangladesh and Deputy Co-ordinator of UN Emergency Assistance to Zambia 1973; with UNDP, New York 1974–78; Asst. Sec.-Gen. of UN (Dept. of Tech. Co-operation for Devt.) 1978–87; Under Sec.-Gen. UN 1987–93, Dir-Gen. of UN office at Vienna, Head of Centre for Social Devt. and Humanitarian Affairs 1987–92, Special Rep. of Sec.-Gen. for Angola and Head of Angolan Verification Mission 1992–93; Special Rep. of Sec.-Gen. to Bolivia 1982–92, for co-ordination of earthquake relief assistance to Mexico 1985–87; Co-ordinator of UN Drug Control Related Activities 1987–90, of Int. Co-operation for Chernobyl 1991–92; Sec.-Gen. 8th UN Congress on Prevention of Crime and Treatment of Offenders Aug. 1990; writer, lecturer, consultant and Adviser (ad honorem) to Bolivian Govt. 1993–; Hon. Fellow Newnham Coll. Cambridge 1991; Dr. h.c. (Essex) 1994; Hon. LL.D. (Westminster) 1996; decorations from Morocco, Bolivia and Austria; Reves Peace Prize. *Publications:* The Administration of International Development Aid 1969, Gate of the Sun: A Prospect of Bolivia 1970, Africa and the World (ed. with R. K. A. Gardiner and C. Patterson) 1970, Orphan of the Cold War: The Inside Story of the Collapse of the Angolan Peace Process 1992–93 1996. *Leisure interests:* writing, gardening, hill-walking (preferably in the Andes), bird-watching, swimming. *Address:* c/o PNUD, Casilla 9072, La Paz, Bolivia; c/o The Walled Garden, Knill, nr. Presteigne, Powys, LD8 2PR, Wales. *Telephone:* (01544) 267411 (Wales).

ANTES, Horst; German painter and sculptor; b. 28 Oct. 1936, Heppenheim; s. of Valentin Antes and Erika Antes; m. Dorothea Grossmann 1961; one s. one d.; ed. Heppenheim Coll.; worked in Florence, then Rome; Prof. at State Acad. of Fine Arts, Karlsruhe 1957–59, Berlin 1984–; mem. Acad. der Künste, Berlin, now living in Berlin, Karlsruhe and Tuscany, Italy; Villa Romana Prize, Florence 1962; Villa Massimo Prize, Rome 1963; UNESCO Prize, Venice Biennale 1966; Kulturpreis (Hesse) 1991; *One-man shows include:* Troisième Biennale de Paris, Museum Ulm, Städtische Galerie Munich, Gallery Stangl Munich, Galerie Defet, Nuremberg, Galerie Krohn, Badenweiler, Gimpel and Hanover Gallery, Zürich and London, Lefèbre Gallery, New York, 10th Biennale São Paulo, Staatliche Kunsthalle Baden-Baden, Kunsthalle Bern, Kunsthalle Bremen, Frankfurter Kunstverein, Badischer Kunstverein Karlsruhe, Galerie Gunzenhauser, Munich, Galerie Brusberg, Hanover and Berlin, Brühl, Schloss Augustenburg, Galerie Valentien, Stuttgart, Nishimura Gallery, Tokyo, Galerie Der Spiegel, Cologne, Kunsthalle, Bremen, Sprengel Museum, Hanover, Wilhelm-Hack Museum, Ludwigshafen, Guggenheim Museum, New York, Galerie Neumann, Düsseldorf, Städt. Galerie, Villingen-Schwerringen u. Kunstverein Hochrhein, Bad Säckingen, Galerie Levy, Hamburg, Freie Akad. der Künste, Hamburg, Galerie Bernd Lutze, Friedrichshafen, Palais Preysing, Munich, Haus der Kunst, Munich, Schloss Mosigkau, Dessau, Berlinische Galerie Pels-Lensden, Berlin, Galerie Organerie-Reinz, Cologne, Prinz Max Palais, Karlsruhe, Galerie Holbein, Lindau, Galerie Meyer-Ellinger, Frankfurt/Maine, Galleria d'Arte Narcisco, Turin, Keramik Museum, Stanfen, Galerie Werkstatt, Reinach, Galerie Uwe Sacksofsky, Heidelberg; numerous groups exhbns. Europe, U.S.A., Japan etc. *Catalogues:* Catalog of Etchings 1962–66 (G. Gerken) 1968, Catalog of Books (W. Euler) 1968, Catalog of Steel Sculptures (H.G. Sperlich) 1976, Catalog of Lithographs (B. Lutze) 1976, 25 Votive (1983/84). *Address:* Hohenbergstrasse 11, 76228 Karlsruhe (Wolfartsweier), Germany. *Telephone:* (0721) 491621.

ANTHONY, Rt. Hon. (John) Douglas, P.C., C.H.; Australian politician, farmer and business executive; b. 31 Dec. 1929, Murwillumbah; s. of Hubert Lawrence and Jessie (née Stirling) Anthony; m. Margot Macdonald Budd 1957; two s. one d.; ed. Murwillumbah High School, The King's School, Paramatta, and Queensland Agricultural Coll.; mem. House of Reps. 1957–84, Exec. Council 1963–72, 1975–83, Minister for the Interior 1964–67, of Primary Industry 1967–71, for Trade and Industry 1971–72, for Overseas Trade 1975–77, for Minerals and Energy Nov.-Dec. 1975, for Nat. Resources 1975–77, for Trade and Resources 1977–83; Deputy Prime Minister 1971–72, 1975–83; Deputy Leader Nat. Country Party of Australia (now Nat. Party of Australia) 1966–71, Leader 1971–84; Chair. Resource Finance Corp. Pty Ltd. 1987–; fmr. Chair. Mount Leyshon Gold Mines, Baskin-Robbins 31 Flavours; fmr. Dir. Poseidon Gold Ltd.; Dir. John Swire and Sons Pty Ltd. 1988–, Clyde Agric. Ltd. 1988–, Normandy Mining Ltd. 1996–; fmr. Chair. J.D. Crawford Fund 1986–; Chair. J.D. Steward Foundation (Univ. of Sydney) 1986–, Commonwealth Regional Telecommunications Infrastructure Fund 1997; Hon. Fellow Australian Acad. of Technological Sciences and Eng. 1990; Hon. LL.D. Victoria Univ. of Wellington 1983; Hon. D.Univ. (Sydney) 1997; Gold Medal Queensland Agric. Coll. 1985; Canberra Medal 1989; N.Z. Commemorative Medal 1990. *Leisure interests:* golf, tennis, swimming. *Address:* Sunnymeadows, Murwillumbah, N.S.W. 2484, Australia.

ANTHONY, Kenny; Saint Lucia politician; leader Saint Lucia Labour Party; Prime Minister of Saint Lucia May 1997–. *Address:* Office of the Prime Minister, New Government Bldgs., Castries, Saint Lucia. *Telephone:* 452-3980. *Fax:* 453-1648.

ANTICO, Sir Tristan, Kt., A.C.; Australian business executive; b. 25 March 1923; m. Dorothy Bridget Shields 1950; three s. four d.; ed. Sydney Boys' High School; Pres. Pioneer Int. Ltd.; fmr. Chair. Ampol Ltd, Ampol Exploration Ltd.; fmr. Dir. Qantas Airways Ltd.; Trustee Art Gallery N.S.W. Foundation, Randwick Racecourse; fmr. Chair. St. Vincent's Hosp.; fmr. Pres. Italian Chamber of Commerce; Pres. Pioneer Int. (fmrly. Concrete Services Ltd.) 1993–; fmr. mem. Export Devt. Advisory Council, numerous advisory Bds.; Commdr. Order of Star of Solidarity (Italy), Sovereign Mil. Hospitaller Order of St. John of Jerusalem of Rhodes and Malta, Kt. Commdr. Order of St. Gregory the Great. *Leisure interests:* horse-racing, horse-breeding, swimming, boating. *Address:* 161 Raglan Street, Mosman, Sydney, N.S.W. 2088, Australia (Home). *Telephone:* 969-4070 (Home).

ANTOINE, Frédéric, M.S.G.; Belgian journalist and academic; b. 27 Sept. 1955, Uccle; s. of Paul Antoine and Suzanne Degavre; m. Chantal Berque 1982; two s. one d.; ed. Catholic Univ. of Louvain; journalist L'Appel 1977, La Libre Belgique 1978; Research Asst. Communication Dept. Catholic Univ. of Louvain 1979; News Ed. Radio 1180, Brussels 1979; Prof. Media School I.A.D., Louvain-la-Neuve 1981; Prof. Communication Dept. Univ. of Louvain 1989, Dir. Research Unit on Mediatic Narrative (R.E.C.I.) 1991–; Ed. L'Appel 1992–. *Publications:* On Nous a Changé la Télé 1987, La Télévision à Travers ses Programmes 1988, Télévision In: Le Guide des Médias 1989–97, ed. La Médiamorphose d'Alain Vanderbiest 1994, ed. Coupures de Presse 1996. *Address:* Ruelle de la Lanterne, Magique 14, 1348 Louvain-la-Neuve; L'Appel, Rue du Hautmur 45, 4030 Liège (Offices); Montagne Street, JOB 12, 1180 Brussels, Belgium (Home). *Telephone:* 10-47-2814; 4-341-1004 (Offices); 2-374-1081 (Home). *Fax:* 10-47-3044; 4-341-1004 (Offices); 2-374-1081 (Home).

ANTON, Ioan, DR.ENG.; Romanian professor of fluid flow machinery; b. 18 July 1924, Vintere; s. of Mihai Anton; m. Viorica Flueraş 1949; one s. one d.; ed. Polytech. Inst. of Timişoara; Assoc. Prof. 1951, Prof. 1962; Dean, Faculty of Mech. Eng., Polytech. Inst. of Timişoara 1961–63, Head, Fluid Flow Machine Dept. 1962–73, 1982–90, Rector 1971–81; Corresp. mem. Romanian Acad. 1963–74, mem 1974–; Dir. Tech. Research Centre, Timişoara, Romanian Acad. 1969–70; Dir. Research Lab. for Hydraulic Machines, Timişoara 1970–74; Vice-Pres. Nat. Council for Science and Tech. 1973–79; Vice-Pres. Romanian Acad. 1974–90; Dir. of Research Centre for Hydrodynamics, Cavitation and Magnetic Fluids, Tech. Univ., Timişoara 1990–; Dir. Centre for Fundamental and Advanced Tech. Research, Romanian Acad. 1997–; mem. European Acad. of Sciences and Arts, N.Y. Acad. of Sciences 1997–; Dr. h.c. (Tech. Univ., Bucharest) 1998; State Prize 1953, Aurel Vlaicu Prize, Romanian Acad. 1958. *Publications:* Experimental Testing of Fluid Flow Machines (with A. Bărglăzan) 1952, Hydraulic Turbines 1979, Cavitation, Vol. 1 1984, Vol. 2 1985, Hydrodynamics of Bulb Type Turbines and Bulb Type Pump-Turbines (with V. Cîmpeanu and I. Carte) 1988 and over 238 papers on hydraulic machines, cavitation and boiling, and magnetic fluids; Ed.-in-Chief Revue Roumaine des Sciences Techniques. *Address:* 1900 Timişoara, Bd. Mihai Viteazul nr. 1, Romania. *Telephone:* (56) 191804.

ANTONAKAKIS, Dimitris; Greek architect; b. 22 Dec. 1933, Chania, Crete; m. Suzana Maria (née Kolokytha) Antonakakis (q.v.) 1961; one s. one d.; ed. School of Architecture, Nat. Tech. Univ. Athens; partnership with Suzana Antonakakis (q.v.), Athens 1959–; Asst. Instructor in Architecture, Nat. Tech. Univ. of Athens 1959–64, Instructor 1964–78, mem. teaching staff 1978–92; Founder and Co-Prin. (with S. Antonakakis) Atelier 66 1965; mem. and Treas. Admin. Cttee., Greek Architectural Asscn. 1962–63; Pres. Asscn. of Assts. and Instructors, Nat. Tech. Univ. 1975–77; Vice-Pres. Cen. Admin. Cttee., Asscn. of Assts. and Instructors of Greek Univs. 1976–77; mem. Int. Design Seminar, Tech. Univ. Delft 1987, Split 1988; Visiting Prof. M.I.T., U.S.A. 1994–, Nat. Tech. Univ. Athens 1997–; corresp. mem. Acad. d'Architecture, Paris; numerous awards and prizes. *Works include:* Archaeological Museum, Chios 1965–66, Hydra Beach Hotel, Hermionis 1965, vertical addition, house in Port Phaliron 1967–72, miners' housing complex, Distomo 1969, apartment bldg., Emm. Benaki 118, Athens 1973–74, Hotel Lyttos, Heraklion, Crete 1973–82, Zannas House, Philopappos Hill, Athens 1980–82, Gen. Hosp., Sitia, Crete 1982, Ionian Bank branch, Rhodes 1983, Heraklion, Crete 1987, Faculty of Humanities, Rethymnon, Crete 1982, Tech. Univ. of Crete, Chania 1982, Summer Theatre, Komotini 1989, Traditional Crafts Centre, Ioannina 1990, Museum of Acropolis, Athens 1990, Art Studio, Aegina 1990, office bldg., 342 Syngrou Ave., Athens 1990, Open Theatre, Thessaloniki 1995-96; several pvt. houses. *Publications:* numerous architectural articles. *Address:* Atelier 66, Emm. Benaki 118, Athens 114-73, Greece. *Telephone:* (01) 330 0323. *Fax:* (01) 330 0322.

ANTONAKAKIS, Suzana Maria; Greek architect; b. 25 June 1935, Athens; m. Dimitris Antonakakis (q.v.) 1961; one s. one d.; ed. School of Architecture, Nat. Tech. Univ., Athens; partnership with Dimitris Antonakakis, Athens 1959–; Founder and Co-Prin. (with Dimitris Antonakakis) Atelier 66 1965–88; mem. Admin. Cttee. Greek Architects Asscn. 1971–72; Pres. Dept. of Architecture, Tech. Chamber of Greece 1982–83; mem. Int. Design Seminar, Tech. Univ. Delft 1987, Split 1988; mem. Greek Secr. of U.I.A. 1985–; numerous awards and prizes. *Works include:* Archaeological Museum, Chios 1965–66, Hydra Beach Hotel, Hermionis 1965, vertical additions, House in Port Phaliron 1967–72, miners' housing complex, Distomo 1969, apartment bldg., Emm. Benaki 118, Athens 1973–74, Hotel Lyttos, Heraklion, Crete 1973–82, Zannas House, Philopappos Hill, Athens 1980–82, Gen. Hosp. Sitia, Crete 1982, Ionian Bank branch, Rhodes 1983, Heraklion, Crete 1987, Summer Theatre, Komotini 1989, Art Studio, Aegina 1990, office bldg., 342 Syngrou Ave., Athens 1990, Traditional Crafts Centre, Ioannina 1990, Museum of Acropolis, Athens 1990; several pvt. and holiday houses. *Publications:* numerous architectural articles; trans. Entretien (Le Corbusier) 1971. *Address:* Atelier 66, Emm. Benaki 118, Athens 114-73, Greece. *Telephone:* (01) 330 0323. *Fax:* (01) 330 0322.

ANTOÑANZAS PEREZ-EGEA, Juan Miguel, D.ENG.; Spanish business executive and engineer; b. 4 Oct. 1932, San Sebastián; s. of Adolfo Antoñanzas and Ana Pérez Egea; m. Pilar Toledo 1957; eight s. two d.; ed. Colegio del Pilar, Madrid, Madrid Univ.; Commercial Gen. Man., Barreiros 1959–62; Operations Gen. Man., Barreiros-Chrysler 1962–69; Gen. Man. Marconi Española (ITT) 1969–74; Asst. to Pres. Instituto Nacional de Industria 1974–75, Chair. and Exec. Pres. 1975–77; Chair. and Exec. Pres., SEAT, S.A. 1977–84; Vice-Chair. Técnicas Reunidas 1984–87; Exec. Dir. Russell Reynolds Assocs. 1988; dir. of numerous corpns.; Victor de Plata; Gran Cruz del Mérito Militar; Gran Cruz de Mauritania. *Leisure interests:* reading, art, theatre, outdoor living.

ANTONETTI, H. E. Cardinal Lorenzo; Italian ecclesiastic; b. 31 July 1922, Romagnano Sesia; ordained priest 1945; Archbishop, See of Roselle and Pro-Pres. of the Admin. of the Patrimony of the Apostolic See 1968–; cr. Cardinal Feb. 1998. *Address:* Administration of the Patrimony of the Holy See, Palazzo Apostolico, 00120 Città del Vaticano, Italy. *Telephone:* (6) 69884306. *Fax:* (6) 69883141.

ANTONIONI, Michelangelo, L. ECON. AND COMM.; Italian film director; b. 29 Sept. 1913, Ferrara; s. of Carlo Antonioni and Elisabetta Antonioni; m. 1st Letizia Balboni 1942; m. 2nd Enrica Fico 1986; ed. Univ. of Bologna; Film critic Corriere Padano and L'Italia Libera; City of Munich Prize 1968; Hon. Acad. Award 1995. *Films include:* Gente del Po 1943–47, Amorosa Menzogna 1949, N.U. 1948, Sette Canne un Vestito, La Villa dei Mostri, Superstizione 1949 (documentaries); Cronaca di un Amore 1950, La Signora Senza Camelie 1951–52, I Vinti 1952, Amore in Città 1953, Le Amiche 1955, Il Grido 1957, L'Avventura 1959 (Critics' Award, Cannes 1960), La Notte 1961 (Silver Bear, Berlin Film Festival 1961), L'Eclisse 1962, Il Deserto Rosso 1964 (Golden Lion, XXV Venice Film Festival 1964), Blow Up 1966 (Golden Palm, Cannes Film Festival 1967; Best Dir., Annual Awards of the Nat. Soc. of Film Critics), Zabriskie Point 1970, Chung Kuo-China 1972, The Passenger 1974, Il Mistero di Oberwald 1979, Identificazione di una Donna 1982 (Grand Prix, Cannes Film Festival 1982), Fumbha Mela 1989, Roma '90 1989, Beyond the Clouds 1995; Kt. Grand Cross, Order of Merit, Commdr. Ordre des Arts et des Lettres 1992, Légion d'honneur 1996. *Leisure interests:* tennis, ping-pong. *Address:* Via Flemming III, 00191, Rome (Office); Via Vincenzo Tiberio 18, 00191 Rome, Italy (Home).

ANTONOVA, Irina Aleksandrovna; Russian museum researcher; b. 20 March 1922, Moscow; ed. Moscow State Univ.; worked in Moscow Pushkin Museum of Fine Arts 1945–, sr. researcher 1945–61, Dir. 1961–; organizer of numerous exhbns. and regular exchange with museums of Europe and America; f. together with Sviatoslav Richter Festival of Arts December Nights accompanied by art shows 1981–; Vice-Pres. Int. Council of Museums 1980–92, Hon. mem. 1992–; mem. Russian Acad. of Educ. 1989; Corresp. mem. San-Fernando Acad., Madrid; State Prize 1995; Commdr. des Arts et des Lettres. *Publications:* more than 60 articles on problems of museum man., art of Italian Renaissance, contemporary painting. *Leisure interests:* swimming, cars, music, ballet. *Address:* Museum of Fine Arts, Volkhonka str. 12, Moscow, Russia. *Telephone:* 203 46 76 (Office).

ANTONOVICH, Ivan Ivanovich, DR. PHIL.; Belarus diplomatist; b. 1937, Brest Region; m.; two d.; ed. Minsk State Inst. of Foreign Languages, Inst. of Philosophy and Law; on staff UN Secr. New York 1969–74; Perm. Rep. of Belarus at UNESCO, rep. of Belarus in UN Comm. on Human Rights 1976–77; CP service 1977–87; Pro-rector, Prof. Acad. of Social Sciences at Cen. Cttee. CPSU 1987–90; mem. Politbureau, Sec. Cen. Cttee. of Russian CP; advisor to Pres. of Russian-American Univ., Dir. programmes of social-political analysis 1991–92; Dir. Centre of System Social-Econ. Studies, Acting Pro-rector Acad. of Man., Council of Ministers, Belarus Repub. 1992–93; Dir. Belarus Inst. of Scientific Information and Prognosis 1993–95; Deputy Minister of Foreign Affairs Belarus Repub. 1995–97, Minister 1997–98; mem. Russian Acad. of Social-Political Sciences, Acad of Geopolitics Belarus Repub.; Merited Worker of Science Belarus Repub. *Publications:* 15 books, numerous articles on problems of philosophy and int. relations. *Address:* Ministry of Foreign Affairs, Lenina str. 19, 220050 Minsk, Belarus (Office). *Telephone:* (3752) 27 29 41 (Office).

ANUSZKIEWICZ, Richard Joseph, M.F.A., B.S.; American artist; b. 23 May 1930, Erie, Pa.; s. of Adam Jacob Anuszkiewicz and Victoria Jankowski; m. Sarah Feeney 1960; one s. one d.; ed. Cleveland Inst. of Art, Yale Univ., Kent State Univ.; one-man exhbns. at Butler Art Inst., Youngstown, Ohio 1955, The Contemporaries, New York 1960, 1961, 1963, Sidney Janis Gallery, New York 1965–67, Dartmouth Coll. 1967, Cleveland Museum of Art 1967, Kent State Univ. 1968, Andrew Crispo Gallery, New York 1975, 1977, La Jolla Museum of Contemporary Art, Calif. 1976, Univ. Art Museum, Berkeley, Calif. 1977, Columbus Gallery of Fine Arts, Ohio 1977; represented in numerous group exhbns. including Museum of Modern Art 1960–61, 1963, 1965, Washington Gallery of Modern Art 1963, Tate Gallery, London 1964, Art Fair, Cologne 1967, etc.; represented in perm. collections at Museum of Modern Art, Whitney Museum of American Art, Albright-Knox Art Gallery, Butler Art Inst., Yale Art Gallery, Chicago Art Inst., Fogg Art Museum, Harvard Univ., etc.; artist-in-residence Dartmouth 1967, Univ. of Wis. 1968, Cornell Univ. 1968, Kent State Univ. 1968. *Publications:* articles in learned journals. *Address:* 76 Chestnut St., Englewood, NJ 07631, U.S.A.

ANWAR, Sheikh Muhammad, M.A.; Pakistani television executive; b. 25 March 1943, Amritsar, India; m.; four d.; ed. Fairfield Univ., Conn. and Pakistan Admin. Staff Coll.; contract producer/Dir. and scriptwriter, Pakistan Television (PTV), Lahore 1964–66, programme producer 1966–72, Exec. Producer, News and Current Affairs 1972–79, Deputy Controller, Overseas Div. PTV HQ, Islamabad 1979–80, Programme Manager, PTV, Rawalpindi/Islamabad 1980–81; Communications Consultant to the Ministry of Information and Broadcasting, Islamabad 1981–83; Deputy Controller of Programmes PTV HQ, Islamabad 1983–85, Producer Group-8, PTV, Lahore 1985–86, Gen. Man. PTV, Peshawar 1986–87, Controller Programme Planning PTV HQ, Islamabad 1988, Educational TV 1988, Programmes Training Acad. 1989–90, Programmes Admin. 1990–92, Int. Relations 1990–93, Controller Programmes Admin., Sport, Archives 1994–96; Gen., Man. PTV Centre, Lahore 1992–94; Controller PTV Acad., PTV HQ, Islamabad, Exec. Producer, Local Area Transmission, PTV, Lahore 1996–97; Visiting Prof. of Communications Quaid-e-Azam Univ. of Pakistan Information Services Acad. 1983–90; Examiner Fed. Public Services Comm. (Information Group); Visiting Prof. Fine Arts Dept., Punjab Univ. 1993; mem. Int. Inst. of Communication, London 1981, Royal TV Soc., London 1983–. *Address:* c/o PTV-Centre, Lahore (Office); 154-A, Model Town, Lahore, Pakistan (Home). *Telephone:* 9200611/9200651-9 (Office); 851169/856778 (Home).

ANYAOKU, Eleazar Chukwuemeka (Emeka), Ndichie Chief Adazie of Obosi, Ugwumba of Idemili, C.O.N., B.A.; Nigerian diplomatist; b. 18 Jan. 1933, Obosi; s. of the late Emmanuel Chukwuemeka Anyaoku, Ononukpo of Okpuno Ire and Cecilia Adiba (née Ogbogu); m. Ebunola Olubunmi Solanke 1962; three s. one d.; ed. Merchants of Light School, Oba, Univ. of Ibadan; Commonwealth Devt. Corpn., London and Lagos 1959–62; joined Nigerian Diplomatic Service 1962, mem. Nigerian Perm. Mission to UN, New York 1963–66; seconded to Commonwealth Secr., Asst. Dir. Int. Affairs Div. 1966–71, Dir. 1971–75, Asst. Sec.-Gen. of the Commonwealth 1975–77, elected Deputy Sec.-Gen. (Political) Dec. 1977, re-elected, 1984, Sec.-Gen. July 1990–; Minister of External Affairs, Nigeria Nov.–Dec. 1983; Sec. Review Cttee. on Commonwealth Intergovernmental Orgs. June–Aug. 1966; Commonwealth Observer Team for Gibraltar Referendum Aug.–Sept. 1967; mem. Anguilla Comm., West Indies Jan.–Sept. 1970; Deputy Conf. Sec., meeting of Commonwealth Heads of Govt., London 1969, Singapore 1971, Conf. Sec., Ottawa 1973, Kingston, Jamaica 1975; Leader, Commonwealth Mission to Mozambique 1975; Commonwealth Observer, Zimbabwe Talks, Geneva Oct.–Dec. 1976; accompanied Commonwealth Eminent Persons Group (EPG) S.A. 1986; Vice-Pres. Royal Commonwealth Soc. 1975–; mem. Council of Overseas Devt. Inst. 1979–90, Council of the Selly Oak Colls., Birmingham 1980–86, Council, Save the Children Fund 1984–90, Council of Int. Inst. for Strategic Studies, London 1987–, Int. Bd. of United World Colls. 1994–, World Comm. on Forests and Sustainable Devt. 1995–; Fellow R.S.A. 1989–; Hon. Fellow Inst. of Educ., London 1994, Coll. of Preceptors 1998; Hon. mem. Club of Rome 1992; Hon. D.Litt. (Ibadan) 1990, Hon. D.Phil. (Ahmadu Bello) 1991, Hon. LL.D. (Nigeria) 1991, (Aberdeen) 1992, (Reading) 1992, (Bristol) 1993, (Oxford Brookes) 1993, (Birmingham) 1993, (Liverpool) 1997, (London) 1997, (Nottingham) 1998; Dr. h.c. (Bradford) 1995; Livingston Medal, Royal Scottish Geographical Soc. 1996; Commdr. of the Order of the Niger (Nigeria) 1982; Freedom of City of London 1998. *Publications:* The Missing Headlines (vol. of speeches) 1997, essays in various publications. *Leisure interests:* tennis, athletics, swimming, reading. *Address:* Commonwealth Secretariat, Marlborough House, Pall Mall, London, S.W.1, England; Orimili, Okpuno Ire, Obosi, Anambra State, Nigeria. *Telephone:* 0171-839 3411. (London).

AOUN, Gen. Michel; Lebanese army officer; b. 1935, Beirut; attended Christian school, Beirut; enrolled in mil. school 1955; trained as artilleryman; training courses Châlons-sur-Marne, France 1958–59, Fort Seale, U.S.A. 1966, Ecole Supérieure de Guerre, France 1978–80; became Brigade Gen. 1984; C.-in-C. of Army 1984; following the abandoned presidential elections of Sept. 1988, outgoing Pres. Gemayel agreed to name him prime minister of an interim mil. admin.; following assassination of Pres. Mouawad in Nov. 1989, he refused to accept authority of successor, Pres. Elias Hrawi (q.v.); evicted from Baabda Presidential Palace by Syrian forces, refuge in French Embassy 1990–91, in exile in Marseilles, France 1991.

APEL, Hans Eberhard, DR.RER.POL.; German politician and economist; b. 25 Feb. 1932, Hamburg; m. Ingrid Schwingel 1956; two d.; ed. Hamburg Univ.; Apprentice, Hamburg export and import business 1951–54; Sec. Socialist Group in European Parl. 1958–61, Head, Econ., Finance and Transport Dept. 1962–65; mem. Bundestag 1965–90, Chair. Transport Cttee. 1969–72; Deputy Chair. Social Democratic Group in Bundestag 1969–72; mem. Nat. Exec., then Deputy Chair. Social-Democratic Party (SPD) 1970–88; Parl. Sec. of State, Fed. Ministry of Foreign Affairs 1972–74; Fed. Minister of Finance 1974–78, of Defence 1978–82; Dir. World Bank 1974. *Publications:* Edwin Cannan und seine Schüler 1961, Raumordnung in der Bundesrepublik 1964, Europas neue Grenzen 1964, Der deutsche Parlamentarismus 1968, Bonn, das Tagebuch eines Bundestagsabgeordneten 1972, 100 Antworten auf 100 Anfragen 1975, Der Abstieg 1990, Die deformierte Demokratie 1991, Der kranke Koloss 1994. *Leisure interests:* music, gardening, sport. *Address:* Rögenfeld 42c, 22359 Hamburg, Germany.

APEL, Karl-Otto, DR.PHIL.; German professor of philosophy; b. 15 March 1922, Düsseldorf; s. of Otto Apel and Elisabeth Gerritzen; m. Judith Jahn 1953; three d.; ed. Univs. of Bonn and Mainz; Prof. of Philosophy, Univ. of Kiel 1962–69, Univ. of Saarbrücken 1969–72, Univ. of Frankfurt-am-Main 1972–90, Prof. Emer. 1990–; many hon. degrees; Galileo Galilei Int. Prize 1988, F. Nietzsche Int. Prize 1989. *Publications include:* Idee der Sprache in der Tradition des Humanismus 1963, Transformation der Philosophie

1973, Der Denkweg von C. Peirce 1975, Die Erklären: Verstehen-Kontroverse in transzendentalpragmatischer Sicht 1979, Diskurs und Verantwortung (Vol. 1) 1988, (Vol. 2) 1999, Towards a Transcendental Semiotics (selected essays) 1994, Ethics and the Theory of Rationality (selected essays) 1997, Auseinandersekungen 1998, From a Transcendental-Semiotic Point of View 1998. *Leisure interest:* history of art. *Address:* Am Schillertempel 6, 65527 Niedernhausen, Germany. *Telephone:* 06127-2170. *Fax:* 06127-2058.

APONTE MARTÍNEZ, H.E. Cardinal Luis; American (Puerto Rican) ecclesiastic; b. 4 Aug. 1922, Lajas; s. of Santiago Evangelista Aponte and Rosa Martinez; ed. St. Ildefonso Seminary, San Juan and St. John's Seminary, Boston, Mass., U.S.A.; ordained priest 1950; Curate, Patillas, then Pastor of Santa Isabel; Sec. to Bishop McManus, Vice-Chancellor of Diocese of Ponce 1955–57; Pastor of Aibonito 1957–60; Chaplain to Nat. Guard 1957–60; Auxiliary Bishop of Ponce and Titular Bishop of Lares 1960–63; Bishop of Ponce 1963–64; Archbishop of San Juan 1964–; created Cardinal by Pope Paul VI 1973; Dir. of Devt. for Catholic Univ. of Puerto Rico 1960–63, fmr. Chancellor; Pres. Puerto Rican Episcopal Conf. 1966; Hon. LL.D. (Fordham) 1966; Hon. S.T.D. (Inter-American Univ. of Puerto Rico) 1969. *Address:* Arzobispado, Apartado S-1967, Calle San Jorge 201, Santurce, Puerto Rico 00902. *Telephone:* 725-4975.

APPEL, André, D.D., L.H.D., LL.D.; French ecclesiastic; b. 20 Dec. 1921, Strasbourg; s. of Georges Appel and Erna Meyer; m. Marjorie Pedersen 1950; three s. one d.; ed. Collège de Saverne, Univs. of Strasbourg, Paris and Tübingen; fmr. Chaplain Univ. of Paris; Sec.-Gen. French Protestant Fed. 1956–64; Pastor Temple Neuf, Strasbourg 1964–65; Sec.-Gen. Lutheran World Fed. 1966–74; Pres. Lutheran Church, Alsace and Lorraine 1974–87; Pres. Conf. des Eglises européennes 1974–86, also Pres. Nat. Alliance of French Lutheran Churches 1983–87.

APPEL, Karel Christian; Netherlands painter; b. 25 April 1921, Amsterdam; ed. Rijksakademie van Beeldende Kunsten, Amsterdam; began career as artist 1938; exhibitions in Europe, America and Japan 1950–; has executed murals in Amsterdam, The Hague, Rotterdam, Brussels and Paris; UNESCO Prize, Venice Biennale 1953; Lissone Prize, Italy 1958; Acquisition Prize, São Paulo Bienal 1959; Graphique Int. Prize, Ljubljana, Yugoslavia 1959; Guggenheim Nat. Prize, Netherlands 1951; Guggenheim Int. Prize 1961. *Publications:* Works on Paper 1980, Street Art 1985, Dupe of Being 1989, Complete Sculptures 1936–1990 1990, Karel Appel Sculpture: catalogue raisonné 1994. *Address:* c/o Galerie Statler, 51 rue de Seine, Paris, France (Office).

APPLEBY, Malcolm Arthur; British artist; b. 6 Jan. 1946, Beckenham, Kent; s. of James William Appleby and Marjory Stokes; m. Philippa Swann; one d.; ed. Hansdown Co. Secondary Modern School, Beckenham School of Art, Ravensbourne Coll. of Art, Cen. School of Arts and Crafts, Sir John Cass School of Art, R.C.A.; career artist, designer and engraver. *Leisure interests:* garden, life, work, family. *Address:* Aultbeag, Grandtully, by Aberfeldy, Perthshire, PH15 2QU, Scotland. *Telephone:* (01887) 840484.

APPLEYARD, Sir Raymond K., K.B.E., PH.D.; British scientist; b. 5 Oct. 1922, Birtley; m. Joan Greenwood 1947; one s. two d.; ed. Rugby School, Trinity Coll., Cambridge; Instructor in Physics and Biophysics, Yale Univ. 1949–51; Fellow in Natural Sciences, Rockefeller Foundation 1951–53; Assoc. Research Officer, Atomic Energy of Canada Ltd. 1953–56; Sec. UN Scientific Cttee. on the Effects of Atomic Radiation 1957–61; Dir. Biology Services, European Atomic Energy Community (EURATOM) 1961–73; Exec. Sec. European Molecular Biology Org. 1965–73; Sec. European Molecular Biology Conf. 1969–73; Dir.-Gen. Scientific and Tech. Information and Information Management, Comm. of European Communities 1973–81, for Information Market and Innovation 1981–86; Pres. Inst. of Information Scientists 1981–82, Inst. of Translation and Interpreting 1989–94; Hon. Dr. Med. (Ulm) 1977.

APRAHAMIAN, Felix; British music critic, writer and broadcaster; b. 5 June 1914, London; ed. Tollington School; contributor to musical press 1931–, nat. press 1937–; broadcaster 1942–; Asst. Sec. and Concert Dir. London Philharmonic Orchestra 1940–46; Consultant, United Music Publishers Ltd. 1946–64; Deputy Music critic Sunday Times 1948–89; Music Ed. The Listener 1966–67; Lecturer Richmond Adult Coll. 1969–88, Stanford Univ. in U.K. 1969–83, City Literary Inst. 1973–88, Morley Coll. 1975–82, Surrey Univ. 1986–; Visiting Prof. Univ. of E. London 1989–; Regents Lecturer, Univ. of Calif., Riverside 1991; Hon. Sec. The Organ Music Soc. 1935–70; Hon. R.C.O. 1973, BBC Cen. Music Advisory Cttee. 1958–61; Co-founder and organizer, Concerts de Musique Française 1942–64; Adviser, Delius Trust 1961–; mem. and Pres. Int. Music Juries, Geneva, Montreux and Biarritz 1963–; Hon. mem. Royal Philharmonic Soc. 1994; Hon. F.R.C.O. 1994; Hon. D.Mus. (City Univ.) 1995; Officier, Ordre des arts et des lettres. *Publications:* (Ed.) Ernest Newman's Essays from the World of Music 1956; More Essays from the World of Music 1958; Essays on Music from The Listener 1967–; co-ed. The Heritage of Music (Vol. 4) The Twentieth Century 1989. *Leisure interests:* horticulture, bibliophily. *Address:* 8 Methuen Park, London, N10 2JS, England. *Telephone:* 0181-883 3783. *Fax:* 0181-883 3783.

APTED, Michael; British film director; b. 10 Feb. 1941, Aylesbury; ed. Cambridge Univ.; started career as researcher, Granada TV 1963, then worked as investigative reporter for World in Action; dir. episodes of Coronation Street, comedy series The Lovers, children's series Folly Foot, Another Sunday and Sweet F.A., Kisses at Fifty, Poor Girl, Jack Point, UP documentary series including 28 UP and 35 UP; debut as feature film dir. with The Triple Echo 1972; *other films include:* Stardust 1975, The Squeeze 1977, Agatha 1979, Coal Miner's Daughter 1980, Continental Divide 1981, P'TangYang Kipperbang, Gorky Park 1983, Firstborn 1984, Critical Condition, Gorillas in the Mist 1988, Class Action 1990, Incident at Oglala, Thunderheart 1992, Blink 1993, Moving the Mountain 1993, Nell 1994, Extreme Measures 1996. *Address:* Michael Apted Film Co., 1901 Avenue of the Stars, Suite 1245, Los Angeles, CA 90067, U.S.A.

AQUINO, (Maria) Corazon (Cory), B.A.; Philippine politician; b. 25 Jan. 1933, Tarlac Prov.; d. of José Cojuangco, Sr.; m. Benigno S. Aquino, Jr. 1954 (assassinated 1983); one s. four d.; ed. Raven Hill Acad., Philadelphia, Notre Dame School, New York, Mount St. Vincent Coll., New York; in exile in U.S.A. with her husband 1980–83; mem. United Nationalist Democratic Org. (UNIDO) 1985–; President of the Philippines (after overthrow of régime of Ferdinand Marcos) 1986–92; William Fulbright Prize for Int. Peace 1996; Ramon Magsaysay Award for Int. Understanding 1998. *Address:* 25 Times Street., Quezon City, Philippines.

ARAFAT, Yasser (pseudonym of Mohammed Abed Ar'ouf Arafat); Palestinian resistance leader; b. 24 Aug. 1929, Jerusalem; m. Sulia Tawil 1991; ed. Cairo Univ.; joined League of Palestinian Students 1944, mem. Exec. Cttee. 1950, Pres. 1952–56; formed, with others, Al Fatah movt. 1956; engineer in Egypt 1956, Kuwait 1957–65; Pres. Exec. Cttee. of Palestine Nat. Liberation Movement (Al Fatah) June 1968–; Chair. Exec. Cttee. Palestine Liberation Org. 1968–, Pres. Cen. Cttee., Head, Political Dept. 1973–; Chair. Palestine Nat. Authority (PNA), also Minister of the Interior 1994–96; Pres. Palestine Legis. Council 1996–; Gen. Commdr. Palestinian Revolutionary Forces; shared Nobel Peace Prize 1994; addressed UN Gen. Assembly Nov. 1974; Joliot-Curie Gold Medal, World Peace Council Sept. 1975. *Address:* c/o Palestine National Authority, Jericho Area, West Bank.

ARAGALL GARRIGA, Giacomo (Jaime); Spanish opera singer (tenor); b. 6 June 1939, Barcelona; s. of Ramon Aragall and Paola Garriga; m. Luisa Aragall 1964; three s.; ed. with Jaume Francisco Puig, Barcelona and Vladimiro Badiali, Milan; winner int. competition, Busseto; debut at Teatro La Fenice de Venecia, Palermo, Metropolitan, New York 1968; opera appearances include: El Amico Fritz, La Bohème (La Scala, Milan), Madame Butterfly, La Favorita, La Traviata, Faust, Tosca, etc.; has sang in more than 100 opera productions at Gran Teatre del Liceu; numerous prizes include Peseta de Oro and Medalla de Plata for appearing at 1992 Olympics, Barcelona, Medalla de Oro de Bellas Artes 1992, etc. *Address:* c/o Stafford Law Associates, 6 Barham Close, Weybridge, Surrey, KT1 9PR, England.

ARAIZA, Francisco; Mexican opera singer; b. 4 Oct. 1950, Mexico City; s. of José Araiza and Guadalupe Andrade; m. Vivian Jaffray; one s. one d.; ed. Univ. of Mexico City, Mexico City and Munich Acads of Music; first engagement as lyric tenor in Karlsruhe, Fed. Repub. of Germany 1974; debut as Ferrando in Così fan Tutte 1975; debut at Zurich Opera House with Almaviva 1976, Perm. mem. 1977–; has become one of the leading tenors worldwide, performing at all the most important opera houses, as well as recitals accompanied by piano or orchestra; Kammersänger, Vienna State Opera 1988; has participated in festivals of Salzburg (debut under von Karajan 1980), Hohenems, Bayreuth, Edin., Pesaro, Verona, Aix-en-Provence; *Recordings include:* The Magic Flute, Faust, Das Lied von der Erde, Die schöne Müllerin; awarded Deutscher Schallplattenpreis, Orphée d'Or.

ARAÑA OSORIO, Gen. Carlos Manuel; Guatemalan army officer and politician; b. 17 July 1918; fmr. Commdr. Zacapa Brigade, Guatemala Army; fmr. Amb. to Nicaragua; mem. Movimiento de Liberación Nacional (MLN); Pres. of Guatemala 1970–74. *Address:* c/o Movimiento de Liberación Nacional, 5A Calle 1-20, Zona 1, Guatemala City, Guatemala.

ARANGIO-RUIZ, Gaetano; Italian professor of law; b. 10 July 1919, Milan; s. of Vincenzo and Ester Mauri Arangio-Ruiz; ed. Univ. of Naples; Prof. Int. Law, Univ. of Padua 1955–67, Univ. of Bologna 1968–74, Univ. of Rome 1974–; Visiting Prof. European Cen., Johns Hopkins School of Advanced Int. Studies 1967–75; Lecturer, Hague Acad. of Int. Law 1962, 1972, 1977, 1984; mem. UN Int. Law Comm. 1985–96; Special Rapporteur on State Responsibility 1987–96; mem. Int. Law Inst. *Publications:* Rapporti contrattuali fra Stati e organizzazione internaz. 1950, Gli enti soggetti 1951, Su la dinamica della base sociale 1954, The Normative Role of the UN General Assembly (Vol. III) 1972, L'Etat dans le sens du droit des gens et la notion du droit international, 'Oesterreichische Zeitschrift für Oeffentliches Recht' 1975–76, Human Rights and Non-Intervention in the Helsinki Final Act (Hague Acad. Recueil) Vol. IV 1977, The UN Declaration on Friendly Relations and the System of the Sources of International Law (Sijthoff) 1979, Le Domaine réservé 1984, Gen. Course in Int. Law, Hague Acad. 1984–95, Non-Appearance before the International Court of Justice (report to the Int. Law Inst.) 1991, Int. Law Inst. Yearbook. *Address:* Corso Trieste 51, 00198 Rome, Italy (Home). *Telephone:* (06) 49910219 (Office); (06) 8559720 and (0564) 819200 (Home).

ARANZADI MARTINEZ, José Claudio, B.A.; Spanish politician; b. 9 Oct. 1946, Bilbao; m.; ed. Bilbao Industrial Eng. School and Univ. of Paris; fmr. official, Banco de Vizcaya, Econ. Consultancy, Bancaya Group; worked for Study Services, Ministry of Industry, Dir. Tech. Bureau; fmr. Vice-Pres. Nat. Inst. of Industry and Energy, Vice-Pres. and Pres. Nat. Inst. of Industry;

Minister of Industry and Energy 1989–91, of Industry, Trade and Tourism 1991–93; del. to OECD. *Address:* c/o OECD, 2 rue André Pascal, 75775 Paris, France; c/o PSOE, Ferraz 68 y 70, 28008 Madrid, Spain. *Telephone:* 1-582-0444 (Madrid). *Fax:* 1-582-0422 (Madrid).

ARARKTSYAN, Babken Gurgenovich; Armenian politician; b. 1944, Yerevan; m.; three c.; ed. Yerevan State Univ., Moscow State Univ., Steklov Inst. of Math. U.S.S.R. Acad. of Sciences; researcher Computation Cen. and Inst. of Math. Armenian Acad. of Sciences 1968–75; researcher Inst. of Scientific and Tech. Information 1975–77; concurrently teacher, docent, Head of Chair. Yerevan State Univ. 1977–; published over 30 scientific articles and textbooks; mem. Cttee. Karabakh, mem. Exec. Bd. of Armenian Nat. Movt. 1988; mem., First Deputy Chair., Chair. Supreme Council of Armenia 1990–91, Armenian Parl. 1992–95; elected mem. Nat. Ass. Repub. of Armenia 1995–, Chair. 1995–98. *Address:* National Assembly, Marshal Bagzamyan Prosp. 26, 375019 Yerevan, Armenia. *Telephone:* (2) 52-46-14.

ARASHI, Qadi Abdul Karim al–; Yemeni politician; fmr. Minister for Local Govt. and the Treasury; Speaker of the Constituent People's Ass. 1978; Chair. Provisional Presidential Council June–July 1978; Vice-Pres. Yemen Arab Republic 1978–90; mem. Presidential Council of Yemen May 1990–. *Address:* Constituent People's Assembly, Sana'a, Yemen.

ARASKOG, Rand Vincent: American business executive; b. 30 Oct. 1931, Fergus Falls, Minn.; s. of Randolph Victor and Hilfred Mathilda Araskog; m. Jessie Marie Gustafson 1956; one s. two d.; ed. U.S. Mil. Acad. and Harvard Univ.; special asst. to Dir., Dept. of Defense, Washington, D.C. 1954–59; Dir. Marketing, aeronautical div., Honeywell Inc., Minneapolis 1960–66; Vice-Pres. ITT, Group Exec. ITT Aerospace Electronics, Components and Energy Group, Nutley, N.J. 1971–76; Pres. 1979–85, C.E.O. ITT Corpn., New York 1979–, Chair. Bd. and Exec. and Policy Comms. 1980–, also Dir., Chair., Pres., C.E.O. ITT Holdings Inc., New York; Chair. Nat. Security Telecommunications Advisory Cttee. 1983–; mem. Bd. of Govs., Aerospace Industries Asscn., Exec. Council, Air Force Asscn. *Publication:* ITT Wars 1989, numerous articles. *Address:* ITT Corporation, 1330 Sixth Avenue, New York, NY 10019, U.S.A.

ARAÚJO, H.E. Cardinal Serafim Fernandes de; Brazilian ecclesiastic; b. 13 Aug. 1924, Minas Novas; ordained priest 1949; Bishop 1959; Coadjutor, See of Belo Horizonte 1982, Archbishop 1986; cr. Cardinal Feb. 1998. *Address:* Cúria Metropolitana, Av. Brasil 2079, C.P. 494, 30140-002 Belo Horizonte, MG, Brazil. *Telephone:* (031) 261 3400. *Fax:* (031) 261 5713.

ARAÚJO SALES, H.E. Cardinal Eugénio de; Brazilian ecclesiastic; b. 8 Nov. 1920, Acari, Rio Grande do Norte; s. of Celso Dantas and D. Josefa de Araujo Sales; ordained 1943; Bishop 1954; Apostolic Administrator, See of São Salvador da Bahia until 1968; Archbishop of São Sebastião do Rio de Janeiro 1971–; cr. Cardinal 1969. *Leisure interest:* reading. *Address:* Palácio São Joaquim, Rua da Glória 446, 20241-150 Rio de Janeiro, RJ, Brazil. *Telephone:* 292-3132; 253-8148. *Fax:* 221-8093.

ARBATOV, Georgiy Arkadyevich; DR. HIST. SC.; Russian administrator and academician; b. 19 May 1923, Kherson; s. of Arkady Michailovich Arbatov and Anna Vasilievna Arbatova; m. Svetlana Pavlovna Goriacheva 1948; one s.; ed. Moscow Inst. for Int. Relations; Soviet Army 1941–44; mem. CPSU 1943–91; Ed. of publishing house for foreign literature and periodicals (Voprosy filosofii, Novoe vremya, Kommunist) 1949–60; Columnist Problems of Peace and Socialism 1960–62; Section Chief at Inst. of World Econ. and Int. Relations of U.S.S.R. Acad. of Sciences 1962–64; Worked for CPSU Cen. Cttee. 1964–67; Dir. Inst. of U.S. and Canadian Studies, U.S.S.R. (now Russian) Acad. of Sciences 1967–95, Hon. Dir. 1995–; Deputy U.S.S.R. Supreme Soviet 1974–89; People's Deputy of the U.S.S.R. 1989–91; personal adviser to Mikhail Gorbachev (q.v.) and other Soviet leaders including Brezhnev and Andropov, and to Boris Yeltsin (q.v.) until 1993; mem. Cen. Auditing Comm. of CPSU 1971–76; cand. mem. and mem. CPSU Cen. Cttee. 1976–89; mem. Palme Comm. 1980–91; mem. U.S.S.R. (now Russian) Acad. of Sciences 1974; Order of the Red Star 1943, Order of the Great Patriotic War, 1st Rank 1985. *Publications:* The System (published in U.S.A.) 1993, and other books and articles on history of Russian-American relations, disarmament, world economics, including A Delayed Recovery 1991. *Address:* U.S.A. and Canada Institute, 2/3 Khlebny per., Moscow G-69, 121814, Russia. *Telephone:* 2905875 (Office).

ARBEID, Murray; British fashion designer; b. 30 May 1935, London; s. of Jack Arbeid and Ida Davis; ed. Quintin School, London; apprenticed to Michael Sherard 1952; opened own business 1954–; designer and design consultant, Norman Hartnell 1988–89. *Leisure interests:* music, literature, art. *Address:* 202 Ebury Street, London, SW1W 8UN, England. *Telephone:* 0171-259 9292.

ARBER, Werner, PH.D.; Swiss microbiologist; b. 1929, Gränichen, Aargau; m.; two c; ed. Aargau Gymnasium, Eidgenössische Technische Hochschule, Zürich; Asst. at Laboratory of Biophysics, Univ. of Geneva 1953–58, Dozent then Extraordinary Prof. Molecular Genetics 1962–70; Research Assoc., Dept. of Microbiology, Univ. of Southern Calif. 1958–59; Visiting Investigator, Dept. of Molecular Biology Univ. of Calif., Berkeley 1970–71; Prof. of Microbiology, Univ. of Basel 1971–96, Rector 1986–88; Pres. Int. Council of Scientific Unions (ICSU) 1996–99; Joint Winner Nobel Prize for Physiology or Medicine 1978. *Address:* c/o Department of Microbiology, Biozentrum der Universität, Basel, 70 Klingelbergstrasse, CH-4056 Basel, Switzerland (Office). *Telephone:* (061) 2672130. *Fax:* (061) 2672118.

ARBHABHIRAMA, Anat, PH.D.; Thai scientist; b. 13 Jan. 1938; Bangkok; s. of Arun Arbhabhirama and Pathumporn Arbhabhirama; m. Mrs Benjarata 1966; three s.; ed. Chulalongkorn Univ., Bangkok, Asian Inst. of Tech., Bangkok, Colorado State Univ.; Vice-Pres. for Acad. Affairs and Provost, Asian Inst. of Tech. 1979–80; Deputy Minister of Agric. and Co-operatives 1980, Minister 1980–81; Head, Regional Research and Devt. Center, Asian Inst. of Tech. 1981–84; Pres. Thailand Devt. Research Inst. 1984–87; Chair. Intergovernmental Council of the Int. Hydrological Programme, UNESCO 1984–88; Gov. Petroleum Authority of Thailand 1987; Chair. PTT Exploration and Production Co. Ltd. 1988–, The Aromatics Co. Ltd. (Thailand) 1990–; Outstanding Researcher of the Year 1987. *Publications:* numerous articles and papers on water resources and hydraulics. *Leisure interests:* golf, jogging, chess. *Address:* c/o The Petroleum Authority of Thailand, 555 Vibhavadirangsit Road, Bangkok 10900, Thailand.

ARBOR, Patrick H.; American business executive; m.; two c.; ed. Loyola Univ. and Univ. of Chicago; fmr. teacher of math.; now Prin. Shatkin, Arbor, Karlov & Co. (independent futures trading co.); mem. Chicago Bd. of Trade 1965–, Chair. 1992–94; Chair. MidAmerican Commodity Exchange; mem. Bd. Dirs. Western New Independent States Enterprise Fund 1994–; fmr. mem. Bd. Dirs. First State Bank & Trust Co. of Park Ridge; numerous activities in banking, community affairs and charitable orgs. *Publications:* numerous articles on finance in professional and academic journals. *Leisure interest:* mountaineering. *Address:* c/o Chicago Board of Trade, La Salle at Jackson, Chicago, IL 60604, U.S.A. *Telephone:* (312) 435-3500.

ARBOUR, Louise, B.A., LL.L.; Canadian judge; b. 10 Feb. 1947, Montreal; ed. Univ. de Montréal; fmrly. clerk Supreme Court of Canada, teacher Osgoode Hall Law School, Toronto; called to bar Ont. 1977; Judge, Supreme Court of Ont. (High Court of Justice) 1987–90; Judge, Court of Appeal for Ont. 1990–96; Chief Prosecutor, Int. War Crimes Tribunals on fmr. Yugoslavia and Rwanda, The Hague 1996–. *Address:* 130 Queen Street W., Toronto, Ont., M5H 2N5, Canada (Home).

ARBULÚ GALLIANI, Gen. Guillermo; Peruvian government official and army officer; b. Trujillo; m. Bertha Tanaka de Azcárate; one s. two d.; ed. Chorillos Mil. Acad.; Sub-Lieut., Eng. Corps 1943, Lieut. 1946, Capt. 1949, Major 1955, Lieut.-Col.1959, Col. 1964, Brig.-Gen. 1971, Div. Gen. 1975–; fmr. Chief of Staff, 1st Light Div.; fmr. Dir. of Logistics; fmr. Chief of Operations, Armed Forces Gen. Staff; fmr. Dir. of Mil. Eng. Coll.; fmr. Instructor, Higher War Coll.; fmr. Adviser to Ministries of Mining and Fisheries; fmr. Pres. Empresa Pública de Servicios Pesqueros (State Fishing Corpn.); Pres. Joint Armed Forces Command; Prime Minister and Minister of Defence 1976–78, Amb. to Chile 1978–79, to Spain 1979–80; del. to Latin American Conf. of Ministers of Labour; rep. of Ministry of Foreign Affairs to negotiations for Andean Pact; rep. to 11th American Mil. Congress; Commdr. Mil. Order of Ayacucho; Jorge Chávez Award; Grand Officer of Peruvian Crosses of Aeronautical Merit, Naval Merit; Grand Cross, Peruvian Order of Mil. Merit; Grand Officer, Mayo Cross of Mil. Merit (Argentina). *Address:* c/o Ministry of Foreign Affairs, Lima, Peru.

ARCAND, Denys; Canadian film director; b. 25 June 1941, Deschambault, Québec; ed. Univ. of Montreal; worked at Office Nat. du Film, Canada 1962–65; Vice-Pres. Asscn. des Réalisateurs et Réalisatrices de films du Québec. *directed:* Seul ou avec d'autres (co-dir.) 1962, Champlain (short) 1963, Les Montréalistes (short) 1964, La Route de l'Ouest (short) 1965, Montréal, un jour d'été and Parcs Atlantiques (shorts) 1966, Volleyball 1967, On est au coton 1969, Québec: Dupléssis et après 1970, La maudite galette 1971, Réjeanne Padovani 1972, Gina 1974, La lutte des travailleurs d'hôpitaux (short) 1975, Le confort et l'indifférence 1980, Empire Inc. (TV) 1982, Le crime d'Ovide Plouffe 1984, Le déclin de l'empire Américain 1986, Jésus de Montréal 1989 (Cannes Jury Prize 1989), Love and Human Remains 1993.

ARCHER, Mary Doreen, PH.D., F.R.S.C.; British scientist; b. 22 Dec. 1944; d. of late Harold Norman Weeden and of Doreen Weeden (née Cox); m. Jeffrey Howard Archer (now Baron Archer of Weston-super-Mare, q.v.) 1966; two s.; ed. Cheltenham Ladies' Coll., St. Anne's Coll. Oxford, Imperial Coll. London; Jr. Research Fellow, St. Hilda's Coll. Oxford 1968–71; temporary Lecturer in Chem., Somerville Coll. Oxford 1971–72; Research Fellow, Royal Inst. of G.B. 1972–76; Lector in Chem., Trinity Coll. Cambridge 1976–86; Fellow and Coll. Lecturer in Chem., Newnham Coll. Cambridge 1976–86; Sr. Academic Fellow, De Montfort Univ. (fmrly. Leicester Polytechnic) 1990–; Visiting Prof., Dept. of Biochem., Imperial Coll. London 1991–; Visitor, Univ. of Herts. 1993–; Trustee Science Museum 1990–; mem. Council, Royal Inst. 1984–85, Cheltenham Ladies' Coll. 1991–; Chair. Nat. Energy Foundation 1990–; Dir. Anglia TV Group 1987–95, Mid Anglia Radio 1988–94, Cambridge & Newmarket FM Radio (now Q103) 1988–97, Addenbrookes Hosp. NHS Trust 1992–; mem. Council of Lloyd's 1989–92; Pres. Guild of Church Musicians 1989–. *Publications:* Rupert Brooke and the Old Vicarage, Grantchester 1989; contribs. to chemical journals. *Leisure interests:* conducting village choir, cats, squash, picking up litter. *Address:* The Old Vicarage, Grantchester, Cambridge, CB3 9ND, England. *Telephone:* (01223) 840213.

ARCHER OF WESTON-SUPER-MARE, Baron (Life Peer) cr. 1992, of Mark in the County of Somerset, **Jeffrey Howard Archer,** F.R.S.A.; British author and politician; b. 15 April 1940; s. of William and Lola (née Cook) Archer; m. Mary Weeden (q.v.) 1966; two s.; ed. Wellington School and Brasenose Coll., Oxford; mem. GLC for Havering 1966–70; mem. Parl. for Louth (Conservative) 1969–74; Deputy Chair. Conservative Party 1985–86. *Publications:* Not a Penny More, Not a Penny Less 1975, Shall we tell the President? 1977, Kane and Abel 1979, A Quiver Full of Arrows 1980, The Prodigal Daughter 1982, First Among Equals 1984, A Matter of Honour 1985, Beyond Reasonable Doubt (play) 1987, A Twist in the Tale 1988, Exclusive (play) 1989, As the Crow Flies 1991, Honour Among Thieves 1993, Twelve Red Herrings (short stories) 1994, The First Miracle (with Craigie Aitchison) 1994, The Fourth Estate 1996, The Collected Short Stories 1997, The Eleventh Commandment 1998. *Leisure interests:* theatre, cinema, cricket, auctioneering. *Address:* 93 Albert Embankment, London, SE1 7TY; The Old Vicarage, Grantchester, Cambridge, CB3 9ND, England.

ARCINIEGAS, Germán, D.L.; Colombian writer and diplomatist; b. 6 Dec. 1900, Bogotá; s. of Rafael Arciniegas and Aurora Angueyra; m. Gabriela Vieira 1926; two d.; ed. Univ. Nacional, Bogotá; Vice-Consul, London 1929; Chargé d'affaires, Buenos Aires 1940; Minister of Education, Republic of Colombia 1942–46; Visiting Prof. Univ. of Chicago 1944, Univ. of Calif. 1945, Columbia Univ. 1947; Prof. Columbia Univ. 1954–59; Amb. to Italy 1959–62, to Venezuela 1967–70, to Vatican City 1976–78; Dean, Faculty of Philosophy and Letters, Universidad de los Andes, Bogotá 1979–81; Pres. Acad. Colombiana de Historia 1980–; Ed. Cuadernos, Paris 1962–65, Amérique Latine, a monthly section of Revue des deux Mondes 1974–; Ed. Correo de los Andes 1979; mem. Acad. of History and Letters of Colombia; corresp. mem. acads. in Spain, Argentina, Mexico, Cuba, etc.; Hammarsjköld Prize 1967. *Publications:* El Estudiante de la Mesa Redonda 1932, América Tierra Firme 1937, Los Comuneros 1938, The Knight of El Dorado 1942, Germans in the Conquest of America 1943, The Green Continent 1944, Este Pueblo de América 1945, Caribbean, Sea of the New World 1946, The State of Latin America 1952, Amerigo and the New World 1955, Italia, Guía para Vagabundos 1959, América Mágica 1959, América Mágica II 1961, Cosas del Pueblo 1962, El Mundo de la Bella Simoneta 1962, Entre el Mar Rojo y el Mar Muerto 1964, Latin America: A Cultural History 1966, Genio y Figura de Jorge Isaacs 1967, Medio Mundo Entre un Zapato 1969, Nuevo Diario de Noé 1969, Colombia Itinerario y Espíritu de la Independencia 1969, Roma Secretísima 1972, América en Europa 1975, Fernando Botero 1978, El revés de la Historia 1979, Los Pinos Nuevos 1982, Bolívar y la Revolución 1984, OEA La Suerte de una Institución Regional 1985, De Pío XII a Juan Pablo II 1986, Bolívar, de San Jacinto a Santa Marta 1988, El Libertador y la guerrillera 1990, Germán Arciniegas: Su vida contada por él mismo 1990, En América nace la nueva historia 1990, Una Visión de América 1990, El Embajador 1990, América es otra cosa 1992, Cuadernos de un Estudiante Americano 1993, El Mundo cambió en América 1993, América Ladina 1994, Bolívar y Santander: Vidas Paralelas 1995, América nació entre libros 1996. *Leisure interest:* reading. *Address:* Academia Colombiana de Historia, Calle 10 No. 8-95, Apdo. Aéreo 14428, Bogotá, Colombia.

ARCULUS, Sir Ronald, K.C.M.G., K.C.V.O., M.A., F.B.I.M.; British diplomatist (retd.); b. 11 Feb. 1923, Birmingham; s. of the late Cecil Arculus, M.C., and Ethel Lilian Arculus; m. Sheila Mary Faux 1953; one s. one d.; ed. Solihull School, Exeter Coll., Oxford and Imperial Defence Coll.; served in Fourth Queen's Own Hussars 1942–45 (attained rank of Capt.); Foreign Office 1947; San Francisco 1948–50; La Paz 1950; Ankara 1953–56; Foreign Office 1957–60; First Sec. (Commercial), Washington 1961–65; Dir. of Trade Devt., New York 1965–68; Imperial Defence Coll. 1969; Head of Science and Technology Dept., FCO 1970–73; Minister (Economic), Paris 1973–77; Amb. to Law of Sea Conference 1977–79; Amb. to Italy 1979–83; Special Adviser to Government on Channel Tunnel trains 1987–88; Dir. Glaxo PLC 1983–91, Consultant 1992–95; Dir. of Appeals King's Medical Research Trust 1984–88; Freeman of the City of London; Gov. British Inst., Florence 1984–93; Consultant London and Continental Bankers Ltd. 1985–90, Trusthouse Forte 1983–86; Hon. Fellow Exeter Coll., Oxford 1989; Trustee, Glaxo Trustees Ltd. 1988–93. *Leisure interests:* travel, fine arts, music. *Address:* 20 Kensington Court Gardens, London, W8 5QF, England.

ARDALAN, Nader, M.ARCH.; architect and planner; b. 9 March 1938, Tehran, Iran; s. of Abbas Gholi Ardalan and Faranguis Davar Ardalan; m. 1st Laleh Bakhtiar 1962 (divorced 1976); one s. two d.; m. 2nd Shahla Ganji 1977; one s.; ed. New Rochelle High School, Carnegie-Mellon Univ. and Harvard Univ. Grad. School of Design; designer, S.O.M. 1962–64; Chief Architect, Nat. Iranian Oil Co. 1964–66; Design Parnter, Aziz Farmanfarmaian & Assocs. 1966–72; Man. Dir. Mandala Collaborative Tehran/Boston 1972–79; Prof. of Design, Tehran Univ. Faculty of Fine Arts 1972–77; Pres. Nader Ardalan Assocs. 1979–92; Prin. Jung/Brannen Assocs. Inc., Boston 1983–; Man. Prin. Jung/Brannen Assocs. Inc., Abu Dhabi 1992; Senior Vice-Pres. KEO Int. Consultants 1994–; Visiting Prof. Harvard Univ. Grad. School of Design 1977–78, 1981–83, Yale Univ. 1977, M.I.T. 1980; various other professional appts.; Aga Khan Award Steering Cttee. 1976–80; King Fahd Award 1987; design awards. *Publications.* Sense of Unity 1972, Habitat Bill of Rights 1976, Pardisan, Environmental Park 1976, Blessed Jerusalem 1985; articles in leading professional journals. *Leisure interests:* the study of sacred architecture, photography, swimming, hunting. *Address:* KEO International Consultants, P.O. Box 3679, Safat 13037, Kuwait. *Telephone:* (965) 243-8011. *Fax:* (965) 244-3969.

ARDANT, Fanny; French actress; b. 22 March 1949, Monte Carlo; theatre in France includes: Polyeucte, Esther, The Mayor of Santiago, Electra, Tête d'Or. *Films include:* Les Chiens 1979, Les uns et les autres, The Woman Next Door, The Ins and Outs, Life is a Novel, Confidentially Yours, Benevenuta, Desire, Swann in Love, Love Unto Death, Les Enragés, L'Eté prochain, Family Business, Affabulazione, Melo, The Family, La Paltoquet, Three Sisters, Australia, Pleure pas my love, Adventure of Catherine C., Afraid of the Dark, Rien que des mensonges, La Femme du déserteur, Amok, Colonel Chabert, Beyond the Clouds, Ridicule.

ARDEBERG, Arne Lennart, PH.D.; Swedish professor of astronomy; b. 10 Nov. 1940, Malmö; s. of Kurt Ardeberg and Elly Ardeberg; m. Margareta Vinberg 1969; one s. two d.; ed. Lund Univ.; staff astronomer, Lund Observatory 1965–69; staff astronomer, European Southern Observatory, La Silla, Chile 1969–73; Assoc. Prof. Lund Observatory 1973–79; Astronomical Dir. European Southern Observatory, La Silla 1979–81, Dir. 1981–83; Dir. Lund Observatory 1983–, Nordic Optical Telescope Scientific Asscn. 1984–; Dean, Faculty of Science, Lund Univ. 1987–; mem. Royal Swedish Acad. of Sciences, Royal Physiographical Soc. (Sweden), Royal Soc. of Sciences (Sweden); Wallmark Prize (Royal Swedish Acad. of Sciences) 1977. *Publications:* 160 publs. in int. journals and books on astronomy and physics. *Leisure interests:* mountaineering, forestry. *Address:* Lund Observatory, Box 43, S-221 00 Lund, Sweden. *Telephone:* 46 10 72 90; 46 10 73 00.

ARDEN, John; British playwright; b. 26 Oct. 1930, Barnsley; s. of Charles Alwyn Arden and Annie Elizabeth Layland; m. Margaretta Ruth D'Arcy (q.v.) 1957; five s. (one deceased); ed. Sedbergh School, King's Coll., Cambridge, and Edin. Coll. of Art; Fellow in Playwriting, Bristol Univ. 1959–60; Visiting Lecturer (Politics and Drama), New York Univ. 1967; Regent's Lecturer, Univ. of California, Davis 1973; Writer in Residence, Univ. of New England, Australia 1975; mem. Corrandulla Arts and Entertainment Club 1973, Galway Theatre Workshop 1975. *Plays:* All Fall Down 1955, The Life of Man 1956, The Waters of Babylon 1957, Live Like Pigs 1958, Serjeant Musgrave's Dance 1959, Soldier, Soldier 1960, The Happy Haven (with Margaretta D'Arcy) 1960, The Business of Good Government (with Margaretta D'Arcy) 1960, Wet Fish 1962, The Workhouse Donkey 1963, Ironhand 1963, Ars Longa Vita Brevis (with Margaretta D'Arcy) 1964, Armstrong's Last Goodnight 1964, Left Handed Liberty 1965, Friday's Hiding (with Margaretta D'Arcy) 1966, The Royal Pardon (with Margaretta D'Arcy) 1966, Muggins is a Martyr (with Margaretta D'Arcy and C.A.S.T.) 1968, The Hero Rises Up (musical with Margaretta D'Arcy) 1968, Two Autobiographical Plays 1972, The Ballygombeen Bequest (with Margaretta D'Arcy) 1972, The Island of the Mighty (with Margaretta D'Arcy) 1972, Keep Those People Moving (with Margaretta D'Arcy) 1972, The Non-Stop Connolly Show (with Margaretta D'Arcy) 1975, Pearl 1977, Vandaleur's Folly (with Margaretta D'Arcy) 1978, The Little Gray Home in the West (with Margaretta D'Arcy) 1978, The Making of Muswell Hill (with Margaretta D'Arcy) 1979, The Ingenious Gentleman, Don Quixote de la Mancha (adapted from Cervantes) 1980, Garland for a Hoar Head 1982, The Old Man Sleeps Alone 1982, The Manchester Enthusiasts (with Margaretta D'Arcy) 1984, Whose Is The Kingdom? (with Margaretta D'Arcy) 1988, A Suburban Suicide (with Margaretta D'Arcy) 1994, Six Little Novels by Wilkie Collins (adaptation for radio) 1997. Television documentary: Profile of Sean O'Casey (with Margaretta D'Arcy) 1973. Essays: To Present the Pretence 1977, Awkward Corners (with Margaretta D'Arcy) 1988; Novels: Silence Among the Weapons 1982, Books of Bale 1988, Cogs Tyrannic 1991, Jack Juggler and the Emperor's Whore 1995. *Address:* c/o Casarotto Ramsay Ltd, National House, 60–66 Wardour Street, London, W1V 3HP, England. *Telephone:* 0171-287 4450. *Fax:* 0171-287 9128.

ARDEN, Hon. Dame Mary (Howarth), M.A., LL.M, D.B.E.; British judge; b. 23 Jan. 1947; d. of the late Lieut.-Col. E. C. Arden and of M. M. (née Smith) Arden; m. Hon. Sir Jonathan Hugh Mance 1973; one s. two d.; ed. Huyton Coll., Girton Coll., Cambridge, Harvard Law School; called to the bar Gray's Inn 1971; admitted to Lincoln's Inn 1973, Bencher 1993; Q.C. 1986; D.T.I. Inspector Rotaprint PLC 1988–91; Attorney Gen. Duchy of Lancaster 1991–93; Judge of High Court of Justice, Chancery Div. 1993–; Chair. Law Comm. 1996–; bar mem. Law Soc.'s Standing Cttee. on Co. Law 1976–. *Leisure interests:* family activities, reading, swimming. *Address:* Royal Courts of Justice, Strand, London, WC2A 2LL, England.

ARDITO BARLETTA, Nicolás, PH.D., M.S.; Panamanian politician and economist; b. 21 Aug. 1938, Aguadulce, Coclé; s. of Nicolás Ardito Barletta and Leticia de Ardito Barletta; m. María Consuelo de Barletta; two s. one d.; ed. Univ. of Chicago and N. Carolina State Univ.; Cabinet mem. and Dir. Planning 1968–70; Dir. Econ. Affairs Org. of American States 1970–73; Minister of Planning 1973–78; Negotiator of econ. aspects of Panama Canal Treaties 1976–77; Vice-Pres. World Bank for Latin America and Caribbean 1978–84; founder and first Pres. Latin American Export Bank 1978; Pres. Latin American Econ. System (SELA) Constituent Ass.; Pres. of Panama 1984–85; Gen. Dir. of Int. Centre for Econ. Growth; Dir. Autoridad de la Región Interoceanía (ARI); mem. Bd. of Dirs. of several corpns., banks and policy insts.; decorated by several Latin American nations. *Publications:* numerous Latin American and Panamanian devt. studies. *Leisure interests:* tennis and music. *Address:* P.O. Box 7737, Panamá 9, Republic of Panama. *Telephone:* 228-7213. *Fax:* 228-8939.

ARDZINBA, Vladislav Grigoriyvich, D.HIS.SC.; Abkhaz politician and historian; b. 14 May 1945, Eshera, Abkhazia; m. Svetlana Ardzinba; one d.;

ed. Sukhumi Pedagogical Inst.; mem. CPSU 1967–91; researcher Inst. of Oriental Sciences, Moscow 1969–87; Dir. D. Gulia Abkhaz Inst. of Language, Literature and History, Georgian Acad. of Sciences 1987–90; U.S.S.R. People's Deputy 1989–91; Chair. Supreme Soviet of Abkhazia 1990–94; leader of independence movt., self-proclaimed Repub. of Abkhazia, Pres. 1994–. *Publications:* Rituals and Myths of Ancient Anatolia 1985, numerous papers. *Address:* Supreme Soviet of Abkhazia, Sukhumi, Georgia.

AREF, Maj.-Gen. Abdul Rahman Mohammed (brother of late President Abdul Salam Aref); Iraqi politician and army officer; b. 1916; ed. Baghdad Military Acad.; Head of Armoured Corps until 1962; Commdr. 5th Div. Feb. 1963–Nov. 1963; assisted in overthrow of Gen. Kassem 1963; mem. Regency Council 1965; Asst. Chief of Staff Iraqi Armed Forces Dec. 1963–64; Acting Chief of Staff 1964, Chief of Staff 1964–68; Pres. of Iraq 1966–68, also Prime Minister May-July 1967.

ARENDARSKI, Andrzej, PH.D.; Polish politician; b. 15 Nov. 1949, Warsaw; m. Agnieszka Łypacewicz; two s. one d.; ed. Warsaw Univ.; teacher, E. Dembowski Secondary School, Warsaw 1972–73, Inst. of Philosophy and Sociology of Polish Acad. of Sciences, Warsaw 1973–75; mem. Solidarity Trade Union 1980–; Ed.-in-Chief, underground journal Zeszyty Edukacji Narodowej 1981–82; co-f. Agric.-Industrial Soc., Konin 1988; mem. Soc. for Econ. and Econ. Action, Warsaw 1988–; co-f. Social Movt. for Econ. Initiatives SPRING 1988; Deputy to Sejm (Parl.) 1989–93; mem. Liberal Democratic Congress (KLD) 1989–94, Deputy Chair. KLD 1989–94, mem. KLD Political Council 1991–94; Pres., Nat. Chamber of Commerce 1990–; Minister of Foreign Econ. Co-operation 1992–93; Chair. Polish-Ukrainian Chamber of Commerce 1996–; Sec.-Gen. Polish Asscn. Industry, Commerce and Finance 1997–. *Publications:* contribs. to underground journals 1981–89; co-author: Polska lat 80-tych: Analiza stanu obecnego i perspektywy rozwoju sytuacji politycznej w Polsce 1984, Stan środowiska przyrodniczego 1984. *Leisure interests:* travel, sailing, art of cooking. *Address:* Krajowa Irba Gospodowna, ul. Tribacka 4, 00 074 Warsaw, Poland. *Telephone:* (22) 826 01 43.

ARENS, Moshe, M.K.; Israeli politician, professor and diplomatist; b. 7 Dec. 1925, Lithuania; ed. Massachusetts and California Insts. of Technology, U.S.A.; Assoc. Prof. of Aeronautical Eng. Technion (Israel Inst. of Tech.), Haifa; Deputy Dir. Israel Aircraft Industries, Lod; Amb. to U.S.A. 1982–83; Minister of Defence 1983–84, 1999– without Portfolio –1987, of Foreign Affairs 1988–90, of Defence 1990–92; elected to Knesset, mem. Knesset Finance Cttee. 1973; Israel Defence Prize 1971; Assoc. Fellow, A.I.A.A. *Publications:* Broken Covenant 1994, several books on propulsion and flight mechanics. *Address:* Ministry of Defence, Rehov Kaplan, Hakirya, Tel-Aviv 67659, Israel.

ARESPACOCHAGA Y FELIPE, Juan de; Spanish civil engineer and economist; b. 1920, Madrid; s. of Nicolás de Arespacochaga; m. Marta Llopiz 1949; one s. eight d.; ed. Univ. of Madrid; Pres. of Popular Group in the Senate; fmr. Lord Mayor of Madrid; Senator by royal nomination; fmr. Dir.-Gen. for Tourist Promotion; Chair. Acad. Internationale de Tourisme, Empresa Nacional de Turismo, Nat. Asscn. of Spanish Roads; Chair. Civil Eng. Asscn., mem. Nat. Coll. of Economists, Nat. Coll. of Civil Engineers, etc.; Grand Cross of Civil Merit and Orders from Italy, Portugal, Mexico, Tunisia and Lebanon. *Publications:* Las Obras Hidráulicas y la decadencia económica de España 1948, El aceite de Oliva, moneda mediterránea 1949, El multiplicador económico en las obras de riego 1956, Los transportes españoles y la integración europea 1959, Las inversiones de O.P. en la Plan Nacional 1979, Alcalde solo. *Leisure interests:* yacht, golf, winter sports. *Address:* c/o Senado, Las Cortes Generales, Madrid, Spain.

ARGERICH, Martha; Argentinian pianist; b. 5 June 1941, Buenos Aires; studied with V. Scaramuzzo, Friedrich Gulda, Nikita Magaloff, Madeleine Lipatti and Arturo Benedetto Michaelangeli; début Buenos Aires 1949; London début 1964; soloist with world's leading orchestras; First Prize Busoni Contest and Geneva Int. Music Competition 1957, Int. Chopin Competition, Warsaw 1965. *Address:* c/o Jacques Thelen Agence Artistique, 252 rue du Faubourg St. Honoré, 75008 Paris, France.

ARGUETA, Manlio; Salvadorean writer; has lived in exile in Costa Rica since 1973; won the Univ. of Central America prize for his novel One Day of Life 1980. *Publications:* One Day of Life 1980 (trans. into English 1984), Cuscatlán (novel) 1987. *Address:* c/o Chatto and Windus, 20 Vauxhall Bridge Road, London, SW1N 2SA, England.

ARGUETA ANTILLÓN, José Luis; Salvadorean university administrator; b. 16 July 1932, El Salvador; s. of Tomás Antillón and Andrea Argueta; m. María Luz Márquez 1969; four s. two d.; ed. Univs. of El Salvador and Chile; Prof., Univ. of El Salvador 1964–67, Sec. Faculty of Econ. Sciences 1967–69, Prof. Faculty of Investigative Econs. 1974–78, Asst. Dir. to the Dir. 1973–74, Dir. 1985–86, Asst. to Acting Rector 1979–80, Rector 1986–; Prof. and Researcher, Cen. American Univ. 1980–85; Dr. h.c. (Univ. of Simón Bolívar, Col.); Economist of the Year 1985. *Publications include:* Manual de Contabilidad Nacional 1967, La Economía Salvadoreana—Algunos Elementos de Análisis 1984, La Reedición de Reforma Universitaria de Córdoba—Una Necesidad Histórica 1989. *Leisure interest:* sport. *Address:* Universidad de El Salvador, Apdo 1703, San Salvador; Calle del Marmara no 18-A, Col Sardinas de Guadalupe, San Salvador, Ap. Post. 3210, El Salvador. *Telephone:* 23 1885.

ARGYRIS, John, D.SC.ENG., F.ENG., F.R.S., F.R.AE.S.; British professor of aeronautical structures; b. 19 Aug. 1916, Volos, Greece; s. of Nicolas Argyris and Lucie Argyris (née Caratheodory); m. Inga-Lisa Johansson 1953; one s.; ed. Technical Univs. in Athens, Munich and Zürich; research, J. Gollnow u. Sohn, Stettin; Research and Tech. Officer, Royal Aeronautical Soc. 1943–49; Sr. Lecturer, Dept. of Aeronautics, Imperial Coll. London 1949, Reader in Theory of Aeronautical Structures 1950, Prof. 1955–75, Visiting Prof. 1975–78, now Prof. Emer.; Dir. Inst. for Statics and Dynamics, Stuttgart 1959–84, Inst. of Computer Applications, Stuttgart 1984–; Prin. Ed. Journal of Computer Methods in Applied Mechanics and Eng. 1972–; Hon. Prof., Northwestern Polytech. Univ., Xian, China, Tech. Univ. of Beijing, Qinghua Univ.; Fellow A.A.A.S., A.I.A.A.; Life mem. A.S.M.E.; Hon. Life mem. New York Acad. of Sciences; Foreign Assoc. U.S. Nat. Acad. of Eng.; Hon. F.C.G.I.; Hon. F.R.Ae.S.; 16 hon. degrees; Silver Medal, R.Ae.S. 1971, Von Kármán Medal, A.S.C.E. 1975, Copernicus Medal, Polish Acad. of Sciences 1979, Timoshenko Medal, A.S.M.E. 1981, I. B. Laskowitz Award with Gold Medal in Aerospace Eng., New York Acad. of Sciences 1982, Royal Medal, Royal Soc. 1985, Daedalus Gold Medal, Sir George Cayley Inst. 1988, and other prizes and awards; Grosses Bundesverdienstkreuz (Fed. Germany) 1985, mit Stern 1990, Grand Cross of the Saviour (Greece) 1996, Golden Cross of the Order of Phoenix (Greece), Gold Medal of Volos 1996; Prince Philip Gold Medal of Royal Acad. of Eng. 1997; numerous other honours and awards. *Publications:* Handbook of Aeronautics (Vol. I) 1952, Energy Theorems and Structural Analysis 1960, Modern Fuselage Analysis and the Elastic Aircraft 1963, Recent Advances in Matrix Methods of Structural Analysis 1964, Introduction into the Finite Element Method (Vols. I, II and III) 1986–88, Dynamics of Structures 1991, An overview of aerolasticity 1992, The Dynamics of Chaos 1994; more than 545 articles in professional journals etc. *Leisure interests:* archaeology, nature, music, literature. *Address:* Institute of Computer Applications, 27 Pfaffenwaldring, D-70569 Stuttgart, Germany. *Telephone:* (711) 6853594. *Fax:* (711) 6853669.

ARIARAJAH, Wesley, TH.M., M.PHIL., PH.D.; Sri Lankan ecclesiastic; b. 2 Dec. 1941, Jaffna; s. of Ponniah David Seevaratnam and Grace Annalukshmi (née Sinnapu); m. Christine Shyamala Chinniah 1974; three d.; ed. Madras Christian Coll., United Theological Coll., Bangalore, Princeton (N.Y.) Seminary, Univ. of London; ordained in Methodist Church; Minister Methodist Church of Sri Lanka, Jaffna 1966–68; Lecturer Theological Coll. Lanka, Pilimatalawa 1969–71; Chair. North and East Dist., Methodist Church, Jaffna 1974–81; staff WCC programme on Dialogue with People of Living Faiths, Geneva 1981–83, Dir. 1983–93, Deputy Sec.-Gen. WCC 1993–97; Prof. of Ecumenical Theology, Drew Univ., N.J.; delivered Sixth Lambeth Interfaith Lecture 1987. *Publications:* Dialogue 1980, The Bible and People of Other Faiths 1986, Hindus and Christians: A Century of Protestant Ecumenical Thought, Did I Betray the Gospel?: The Letters of Paul and the Place of Women 1996, Not Without My Neighbour: Issues in Interfaith Dialogue 1998; Contrib. articles to specialist journals. *Leisure interest:* reading. *Address:* Seminary Hall, School of Theology, Drew University, Madison, NJ 07940 (Office); 34A Loantaka Way, Madison, NJ 07940, U.S.A. (Home). *Telephone:* (973) 408 3979 (Office); (973) 360 9296 (Home).

ARIAS-SALGADO Y MONTALVO, Fernando; Spanish diplomatist; b. 3 May 1938, Valladolid; s. of Gabriel Arias-Salgado y Cubas and Maria Montalvo; m. María Isabel Garrigues López-Chicheri 1969; one s. one d.; ed. Univ. of Madrid, Coll. of Lawyers, Madrid; entered Diplomatic School 1963; Sec. Perm. Del. of Spain to UN 1966–68; Adviser, UN Security Council 1968–69; Asst. Dir.-Gen. Promotion of Research, Ministry of Educ. and Science 1971, Asst. Dir.-Gen. of Int. Co-operation, Ministry of Educ. and Science 1972; Legal Adviser, Legal Dept. (Int. Affairs), Ministry of Foreign Affairs 1973–75, Dir. 1983–85; Counsellor, Spanish Del. to Int. Court of Justice 1975; Tech. Sec.-Gen. Ministry of Foreign Affairs 1976; Dir.-Gen. Radiotelevisión Española 1977–81; Amb. to U.K. Jan. 1981–83, to Tunisia 1993–96; Consul-Gen. for Spain, Zürich 1985–90; Perm. Rep. to Int. Orgs. in Vienna 1990–93. *Address:* c/o Ministry of Foreign Affairs, Plaza de la Provincial, 28071 Madrid, Spain.

ARIAS SÁNCHEZ, Oscar, PH.D.; Costa Rican politician and academic; b. 13 Sept. 1940; s. of Juan Arias Sánchez and Líllyan Arias Sánchez; m. Margarita Penõn; one s. one d.; m.; ed. Univ. of Costa Rica, Univ. of Essex, U.K.; Prof. School of Political Sciences Univ. of Costa Rica 1969–72; Financial Adviser to Pres. of Repub. 1970–72; Minister of Nat. Planning and Econs. Policy 1972–77; Int. Sec. Liberación Nacional Party 1975, Gen. Sec. 1979–83, 1983; Congressman in Legis. Ass. 1978–82; Pres. of Costa Rica 1986–90; mem. Bd. Cen. Bank 1972–77, Vice-Pres. 1970–72; ad hoc Comm. mem. Heredia's Nat. Univ. 1972–75; mem. Bd. Tech. Inst. 1974–77; mem. Rector's Nat. Council 1974–77; mem. Bd. Int. Univ. Exchange Fund, Geneva 1976; mem. N.-S. Roundtable 1977; has participated in numerous int. meetings and socialist conventions; instrumental in formulating the Cen. American Peace Agreement 1986–87; Dr. h.c. (Oviedo) 1988; Nobel Peace Prize 1987, Martin Luther King Award 1987, Príncipe de Asturias Award 1988, shared Philadelphia Liberty Medal 1991. *Publications:* Pressure Groups in Costa Rica 1970 (Essay's Nat. Award 1971), Who Governs in Costa Rica? 1976, Latin American Democracy, Independence and Society 1977, Roads for Costa Rica's Development 1977, New Ways for Costa Rican Development 1980, and several articles in newspapers and in nat. and foreign magazines. *Address:* Arias Foundation for Peace and Human Progress, Apdo 8-6410-1000, San José, Costa Rica. *Telephone:* (506) 55 29 55. *Fax:* (506) 55 22 44.

ARIAS STELLA, Javier; Peruvian politician and pathologist; b. 2 Aug. 1924, Lima; m. Nancy Castillo; four c.; ed. San Luis School, Universidad

Nacional Mayor de San Marcos and San Fernando Medical School; lectured in univs. in England, U.S.A., Argentina, Mexico and Brazil; work on pathology now known as the "Arias Stella Reaction or Phenomenon" published 1954; Nat. Sec.-Gen. Acción Popular (political party) 1959; Minister of Public Health 1963–65, 1967–68; in exile, Argentina 1973, Venezuela 1974; Minister for Foreign Affairs 1980–83; Perm. Rep. to the UN 1984–86; Hipolito Unanue (Peru), Premio Roussel Perú and numerous decorations. *Publications:* nearly 100 works on pathology.

ARIDOR, Yoram, M.JUR.; Israeli politician and lawyer; b. 24 Oct. 1933, Tel-Aviv; m.; three c.; ed. Hebrew Univ. of Jerusalem; mem. Knesset 1969–88, Chair. Cttee. for Interior and Environmental Affairs 1975–77, Chair. Sub-Cttee. for Constitutional Law 1975–77, mem. Cttee. for Legislation and Justice 1969–81, Deputy Minister in Prime Minister's office 1977–81; Minister of Finance 1981–83, also of Communications Jan.–July 1981; Chair. Herut (Freedom) Movt. in Histradrut (Gen. Fed. of Labour) 1972–77, mem. Cen. Cttee. Herut Movt. 1961–90, Chair. Secr. 1979–87; Amb. to UN 1990–92; fmr. Gov. IMF. *Address:* 38 Haoranim Street, Ramat-Efal, Israel (Home).

ARIE, Thomas Harry David, C.B.E., M.A., B.M., D.P.M., F.R.C.P., F.R.C.PSYCH., F.F.P.H.M.; British psychiatrist; b. 9 Aug. 1933, Prague, Czechoslovakia; s. of late Dr. O. M. Arie and H. Arie; m. Eleanor Aitken 1963; one s. two d.; ed. Balliol Coll., Oxford; Sr. Lecturer in Social Medicine, London Hosp. Medical Coll. 1962–74; Consultant Psychiatrist for Old People, Goodmayes Hosp. 1969–77; Foundation Prof. and Head, Dept. of Health Care of the Elderly, Nottingham Univ. 1977–95, Prof. Emer. 1995–; Visiting Prof. N.Z. Geriatrics Soc. 1980, Univ. of the Negev 1988, Univ. of Calif., L.A. 1991, Keele Univ. 1997; Consultant Psychiatrist to the Nottingham Hosps. 1977–95; Vice-Pres. Royal Coll. of Psychiatrists 1984–86, Chair. Specialist Section on Old Age 1981–86; Sec., Geriatric Psychiatry Section, World Psychiatric Asscn. 1983–89, Chair. 1989–93; Gov. Centre for Policy on Ageing 1992–; Council mem., Vice-Chair. Royal Surgical Aid Soc. (RSAS-AGE CARE); patron Abbeyfield Soc. *Publications:* Ed. Health Care of the Elderly 1981, Recent Advances in Psychogeriatrics (Vol. 1) 1985, (Vol. 2) 1992; papers on the care of the aged, old age psychiatry, epidemiology and educ. *Address:* Cromwell House, West Church Street, Kenninghall, Norfolk, NR16 2EN, England. *Telephone:* (01953) 887375. *Fax:* (01953) 887375.

ARIGONI, Duilio, DR.SC.TECHN.; Swiss professor of organic chemistry; b. 6 Dec. 1928, Lugano; s. of Bernardino Arigoni and Emma Arigoni (née Bernasconi); m. Carla Diener 1958 (died 1998); two s. one d.; ed. Swiss Fed. Inst. of Tech. (ETH), Zürich; Lecturer in Organic Chem., ETH Zürich 1961–62, Assoc. Prof. 1962–67, Full Prof. 1967–96; mem. Swiss Nat. Foundation for Scientific Research 1967–71, Bd. of Govs., Weizmann Inst. of Science, Rehovot, Israel 1979–, Bd. of Trustees, Sandoz Ltd. 1984–96, Novartis Ltd. 1996–; mem. Deutsche Akademie der Naturforscher Leopoldina, Accademia Nazionale delle Scienze, Rome; Foreign mem. Royal Soc., London; Hon. F.R.S.C.; Foreign Assoc. Nat. Acad. of Sciences, Washington; Davy Medal, Royal Soc. London 1983, R. A. Welch Award, Welch Foundation, U.S.A. 1985, Arthur C. Cope Award, American Chemical Soc. 1986, Wolf Prize, Israel 1989, Marcel Benoist Prize, Switzerland 1992, and other prizes and awards. *Publications:* over 170 publs. in scientific journals. *Leisure interest:* music, especially Bach, Mozart. *Address:* Laboratorium für org. Chemie, ETH-Zentrum, Universitätsstr. 16, 8092 Zürich (Office); Im Glockenacker 42, 8053 Zürich, Switzerland (Home). *Telephone:* 01/632 2891 (Office); 01/381 1383 (Home). *Fax:* 01/632 1154.

ARIKHA, Avigdor; Israeli artist and author; b. 28 April 1929, Bukovina; m. Anne Atik 1961; two d.; ed. Fine-Art, Bezalel, Jerusalem, Ecole des Beaux Arts, Paris and Sorbonne, Paris; since 1973 has painted exclusively from life; 23 one-man public insts. and 37 pvt. gallery exhbns. 1952–98; works in public collections including Musée du Louvre, Centre Pompidou, Paris, Tate Gallery, London, Hirshhorn Museum, Washington, D.C., Israel Museum, Jerusalem; painted portrait of H.M. Queen Elizabeth, The Queen Mother for Scottish Nat. Portrait Gallery 1983; curator Poussin exhbn., Louvre, Paris 1979, Ingres exhbn., Frick Collection, New York 1986, Israel Museum, Jerusalem, Musée des Beaux-Arts, Dijon, Museum of Fine Arts, Houston, U.S.A.; fmr. lecturer at univs. in U.S.A. and U.K.; has made several films for TV; Hon. Prof. Nat. Acad. of Fine Arts, China; D.Phil. h.c. (Hebrew Univ., Jerusalem) 1997; Grand Prix des Arts (City of Paris) 1987, Prix des Arts, des Lettres et des Sciences, Fondation du Judaïsme Français; Chevalier, Ordre des Arts et des Lettres. *Publications:* Peinture et Regard 1991, On Depiction—Writings on Art 1995; scholarly catalogues for exhbns. etc.; numerous essays and articles. *Address:* c/o Marlborough Fine Art, 6 Albemarle Street, London W1X 4BY, England.

ARIMA, Akito, D.SC.; Japanese university professor; b. 13 Sept. 1930; s. of Johji Arima and Kazuko Arima; m. Hiroko Aota 1957; one s. one d.; ed. Musashi Koto Gakko Coll., Univ. of Tokyo; Visiting Prof. Rutgers and Princeton Univs. 1967–68, State Univ. of New York, Stony Brook 1968, 1971–73; Prof. of Physics, Faculty of Science, Univ. of Tokyo 1975–, Dir. Computer Centre 1981–87, Dean of the Faculty of Science 1985–87, Vice-Pres. Univ. of Tokyo 1987–89, Pres. 1989–93; Pres. Inst. of Physical and Chemical Research (RIKEN) 1994–; mem. Science Council of Japan 1985–94; Nishina Memorial Prize 1978, Humboldt Prize 1987, John Price Wetherill Medal 1990, Bonner Prize 1993, Japan Acad. Prize 1993; Das Grosse Verdienstkreuz (Germany) 1990, Order of Orange Nassau (Netherlands) 1991; Hon. D.Sc. (Univ. of Glasgow). *Publication:* Interacting Boson Model 1987. *Leisure interests:* Haiku, calligraphy, reading. *Address:* Institute of Physical and Chemical Research, Hirosawa 2-1, Wako-shi, Saitama 351-01, Japan. *Telephone:* (048) 462-1111.

ARINZE, H.E. Cardinal Francis A.; Nigerian ecclesiastic; b. 1 Nov. 1932, Eziowelle, Onitsha; s. of Joseph Arinze Nwankwu and Bernadette M. Arinze; ordained 1958; consecrated Bishop (Titular Church of Fissiana) 1965; Archbishop of Onitsha 1967; elevated to Cardinal 1985; Pres. Pontifical Council for Inter-religious Dialogue. *Publications:* Partnership in Education 1965, Sacrifice in Ibo Religion 1970, Answering God's Call 1983, Alone With God 1986, Church in Dialogue 1990, Meeting Other Believers 1997. *Leisure interests:* tennis, reading. *Address:* Pontifical Council for Inter-Religious Dialogue, 00120 Vatican City, Italy. *Telephone:* (698) 83648, (698) 84321. *Fax:* (698) 84494.

ARISMUNANDAR, Lieut.-Gen. Wismoyo; Indonesian army officer; brother-in-law of fmr. Pres. Suharto (q.v.); fmrly. special forces commdr.; fmr. Army Deputy Chief, Army Chief 1993–. *Address:* c/o Ministry of Defence and Security, Jalan Merdeka Barat 13, Jakarta 10110, Indonesia.

ARISTIDE, Jean Bertrand; Haitian politician and fmr. ecclesiastic; b. Salut; m. Mildred Trouillot 1996; one d.; Roman Catholic priest; expelled from Salesian Order 1988; resgnd. from priesthood Nov. 1994; Pres. of Haiti Feb.–Oct. 1991, 1993–96; in exile in Caracas, Venezuela Oct. 1991; returned Oct. 1993 after resignation of junta. *Publications:* Haiti and the New World Order 1995, Dignity 1996. *Address:* c/o Office of the President, Port au Prince, Haiti.

ARJONA PÉREZ, Marta María; Cuban ceramic artist and sculptor; b. 3 May 1923, Havana; d. of Ernesto and Norak Arjona Pérez; ed. San Alejandro Nat. School of Beaux Arts and Paris; various exhbns. in Cuba and overseas 1945–52; Dir. Nuestro Tiempo Soc. Gallery 1953–59; Nat. Dir. of Plastic Arts, then Museums and Monuments 1959–77, Dir. of Cultural Heritage 1977–; Pres. Cuban Cttee., Int. Council of Museums; Medal, then Order of Raúl Gómez García 1975, 1982. *Works on view* include ceramic murals at the Palacio de la Revolución (with René Portocarrero) and Escuela V. I. Lenin (with Mariano Rodríguez). *Publications:* various articles in specialist periodicals. *Address:* Quinta B, no. 8605 entre 86 y 88, Miramar, Playa (Home); Calle A, no. 608 entre 25 y 27, Vedado, Havana, Cuba (Office). *Telephone:* 2-8155 (Home).

ARKAAH, Kow Nkensen, M.B.A.; Ghanaian politician; b. 14 July 1927; m. Marian Ribeiro Ayeh 1963; two s. three d.; ed. Mfantsipim Secondary School, Cape Coast, Achimota Coll., Lincoln Univ. Pa., U.S.A., Tufts Univ. Mass. and Harvard Univ.; asst. sales man. Socony Oil Corpn. New York 1954; retail sales man. Mobil Oil Ghana Ltd. 1955–57; Ministry of Trade 1958–65, Prin. Sec. 1965–66; Chief Exec. Ghana Industrial Holding Corpn. 1966–68; Supervising Prin. Sec. (with rank of Amb.), Ministry of Foreign Affairs 1968–69; Gen. Man. Ghana Nat. Trading Corpn. 1969–72; Man. Dir. Ghana Airways 1973; Man. Dir. Nat. Trading Corpn. of Gambia 1973–76; Man. Dir. Nat. Trading Co. of Sierra Leone 1976–78; Chief Exec. Ghana Nat. Procurement Agency 1978–79; Man. Dir. Ghana Oil Co. 1988–92; mem. Parl. 1979–81; consultant to numerous orgs.; leader of many govt. dels. 1958–81; Vice-Pres. of Ghana 1993; mem. Nat. Convention Party. *Address:* c/o National Convention Party, Accra, Ghana.

ARKHIPOVA, Irina Konstantinovna; Russian mezzo-soprano; b. 2 Jan. 1925, Moscow; d. of Wetoschkin Konstantin and Galda Evdokija; m. Piavkò Wladislav; one s.; attended vocal classes with Nadezda Malisheva at Inst. of Architecture, Moscow, from which graduated, 1948; entered Moscow Conservatoire 1959 (pupil of L. Savransky); stage début as soloist (Lubasha) of Tsar's Bridge with Sverdlovsk Opera and (Carmen) with Bolshoi Theatre, 1956, leading soloist –1988; mem. CPSU 1963–91; mem. U.S.S.R. Supreme Soviet 1962–66; People's Deputy 1989–91; Prof. at Moscow Conservatoire 1982–; Pres. Int. Union of Musicians, Irina Arkhipova Foundation; opera performances and song recitals since 1956 at Milan, Vienna, Paris, London and in U.S.A.; performs Russian, French and Italian repertoire, roles include Carmen, Amneris in Aida, Hélène in War and Peace, Eboli in Don Carlos; mem. Acad. of Creative Endeavours 1991, Int. Acad. of Sciences 1994; People's Artist of U.S.S.R. 1966; Lenin Prize 1978; Hero of Socialist Labour 1984, People's Artist of Kyrgyzstan 1993, State Prize 1997. *Publications:* My Muses 1992, Music of Life 1997. *Address:* Bryusov per. 2/14, Apt. 27, 103009 Moscow, Russia. *Telephone:* 229-60-29 (Office); 229-43-07 (Home).

ARKIN, Alan Wolf; American actor and director; b. 26 March 1934; s. of David and Beatrice Arkin; m. 2nd Barbara Dana; one s; two s. from first marriage; ed. Los Angeles City Coll., Los Angeles State Coll., Bennington Coll.; made professional theatre début with the Compass Players, St. Louis 1959; later joined Second City group, Chicago 1960; made New York début at Royal, in revue From the Second City 1961; played David Kolvitz in Enter Laughing 1963–64 (Tony Award 1963), appeared in revue A View Under The Bridge, 1964; Harry Berline in Luv; dir. Eh? at the Circle in the Square, 1966; Hail Scrawdyke 1966, Little Murders, 1969, White House Murder Case 1970; dir. The Sunshine Boys, Eh? 1972; dir. Molly 1973, Joan Lorraine 1974. *Films include:* The Russians Are Coming, the Russians Are Coming (Golden Globe Award) 1966, Women Times Seven 1967, Wait Until Dark 1967, Inspector Clouseau 1968, The Heart is a Lonely Hunter 1968, Popi 1969, Catch 22 1970, Little Murders (also dir.) 1971, Last of the Red Hot Lovers 1972, Freebie and the Bean 1974, Rafferty and the Gold Dust Twins

1975, Hearts of the West 1975, The In-Laws 1979, The Magician of Lublin 1979, Simon 1980, Chu Chu and the Philly Flash 1981, Improper Channels (Canadian Acad. Award) 1981, The Last Unicorn 1982, Joshua Then and Now (also dir., Canadian Acad. Award) 1985, Coupe de Ville 1989, Havana 1990, Edward Scissorhands 1990, The Rocketeer 1990, Glengarry Glen Ross 1992, Indian Summer 1993, So I Married an Axe Murderer 1993, Steal Big, Steal Little 1995, Mother Night 1995, Grosse Point Blank 1997, Gattaca 1998. *TV appearances include:* The Love Song of Barney Kempinski 1966, The Other Side of Hell 1978, The Defection of Simas Kudirka 1978, Captain Kangaroo, A Deadly Business 1986, Escape from Sobibor, Necessary Parties, Cooperstown, Taking the Heat, Doomsday Gun; Theatre World Award 1964 for Enter Laughing. New York Film Critics; Award Best Supporting Actor for Hearts of the West and for Heart is a Lonely Hunter. *Publications:* Tony's Hard Work Day, The Lemming Condition, Halfway Through the Door, The Clearing 1986, Some Fine Grampha 1995. *Address:* c/o William Morris Agency, 151 El Camino Drive, Beverly Hills, CA 90212, U.S.A.

ARLMAN, Paul, M.A.; Netherlands international civil servant and banker; b. 11 July 1946, Bussum; s. of Evert Arlman and Corrie Jacobs; m. Kieke Wijs 1971; one s. one d.; ed. Hilversum Grammar School, Rotterdam Econ. Univ., Peace Research Inst., Groningen and Nice European Inst., France; served in the Treasury, The Hague 1970–74, as Treasury Rep. to the Netherlands Embassy, Washington D.C. 1974–78; Div. Chief Treasury, The Hague 1978–81, Dir. and Deputy Asst. Sec. Int. Affairs 1981–86; Exec. Dir. IBRD, IDA, IFC, MIGA 1986–90; mem. Bd. of Dirs., EIB 1981–86, Chair. Bd. Policy Cttee. 1983–84; Sec.-Gen. Amsterdam Stock Exchange 1991–96; Dir. Int. Affairs Amsterdam Exchanges 1997–. *Leisure interests:* literature, tennis, skiing, outdoor sports. *Address:* Beursplein 5, 1012 JW Amsterdam (Office); Jan van Nassaustraat 33, 2596 BM The Hague, Netherlands (Home). *Telephone:* (20) 550-4004 (Office); (70) 3244938 (Home).

ARMACOST, Michael Hayden, M.A., PH.D. (brother of Samuel Henry Armacost, q.v.); American government official, politician and administrator; b. 15 April 1937, Cleveland, Ohio; s. of George H. and Verda Gay (Hayden) Armacost; m. Roberta June Bray 1959; three s.; ed. Carleton Coll., Friedrich Wilhelms Univ., Columbia Univ.; Assoc. Prof. Govt., Pomona Coll., Claremont, Calif. 1962–70; Wig Distinguished Prof. 1966; Special Asst. to Amb., American Embassy, Tokyo 1972–74, Amb. to Philippines 1982–84, to Japan 1989–93; mem. Policy Planning, Staff Dept., Washington 1974–77; Sr. Staff mem., Nat. Security Council, Washington 1977–78; Dep. Asst. Sec. Defence, Int. Security Affairs Defence Dept., Washington 1978–79; Principal Deputy Asst. Sec. E. Asian and Pacific Affairs 1980–81; Undersec. Political Affairs 1984–89; Amb. to Japan 1989; mem. Council on Foreign Relations; Visiting Prof. Int. Relations, Int. Christian Univ., Tokyo 1968–69; Pres. Brookings Inst., Washington, D.C. 1995–; Superior Honour Award, State Dept. 1976; Distinguished Civilian Service Award, Defence Dept. 1980; Presidential Distinguished Service Award; Sec. of State Distinguished Service Award; White House Fellow 1969–70. *Publications:* The Politics of Weapons Innovation 1969, The Foreign Relations of United States 1969. *Address:* Brookings Institution, 1775 Massachusetts Ave., N.W., Washington, DC 20036, U.S.A. *Telephone:* (262) 797-6200. *Fax:* (202) 797-6213.

ARMACOST, Samuel Henry, (brother of Michael Hayden Armacost, q.v.); American banker; b. 1939, Newport News, Va.; m. Mary Jane Armacost 1962; two d.; ed. Denison Univ., Granville, Ohio, Stanford Univ.; joined Bank of America as credit trainee 1961; London branch 1969–71; State Dept. Office of Monetary Affairs (executive exchange programme) 1971–72; Head Europe, Middle East and Africa Div., London 1977–79; Cashier Bank of America and Treasurer of its Holding Co. Bank-America Corpn. 1979–80; Pres. and C.E.O. Bank of America and Bank-America Corpn. 1981–86, Chair. and C.E.O. 1986 (resgnd); Investment Banker Merrill Lynch and Co. 1987; Man. Dir. Merrill Lynch Capital Markets 1988–. *Address:* c/o Merrill Lynch and Co. Inc., 100 Church Street, 12th Floor, New York, NY 10080, U.S.A.

ARMANI, Giorgio; Italian fashion designer; b. 11 July 1934, Piacenza; s. of late Ugo Armani and of Maria Raimondi; ed. Univ. of Milan; window dresser, then asst. buyer La Rinascente, Milan 1957–64; Designer and Product Developer Hitman (menswear co. of Cerruti group) 1964–70; freelance designer for several firms 1970; founded Giorgio Armani SpA with Sergio Galeotti 1975, achieved particular success with unconstructed jackets of mannish cut for women, trademarks also in babywear, underwear, accessories, perfume; appeared on cover of Time 1982; Dr. h.c. (Royal Coll. of Art, London) 1991; numerous awards including Cutty Sark 1980, 1981, 1984, 1986, 1987, (First Designer Laureate 1985), Ambrogino D'Oro, Milan 1982, Int. Designer Award, Council of Fashion Designers of America 1983, L'Occhio D'Oro 1984, 1986, 1987, 1988, L'Occhiolino D'Oro 1984, 1986, 1987, 1988, Time-Life Achievement Award 1987, Cristobal Balenciaga Award 1988, Woolmark Award, New York 1989, 1992, Senken Award, Japan 1989, Award from People for the Ethical Treatment of Animals, U.S.A. 1990, Fiorino d'Oro, Florence, for promoting Made in Italy image 1992, Hon. Nomination from Brera Acad., Milan 1993, Aguja de Oro Award, Spain, for Best Int. Designer 1993, Telva Triunfador Award, Madrid, for Best Designer of the Year 1993; Grand'Ufficiale dell'ordine al merito 1986, Gran Cavaliere 1987. *Leisure interests:* cinema, music, books. *Address:* Via Borgonuovo 21, 20121 Milan, Italy; Giorgio Armani Corpn, 114 Fifth Avenue, New York, NY 10011, U.S.A. *Telephone:* 02-801481 (Milan). *Fax:* 02-86461914 (Milan).

ARMATRADING, Joan; British singer and songwriter; b. 9 Dec. 1950, St. Kitts, West Indies; moved to Birmingham, U.K. 1958; began professional career in collaboration with lyric-writer Pam Nestor 1972; world tour 1995–96; Discs: 3 Silver, 28 Gold, 6 Platinum. *Recordings include:* Whatever's For Us 1973, Back To The Night 1975, Joan Armatrading 1976, Show Some Emotion 1977, My, Myself, I 1980, Walk Under Ladders 1981, The Key 1983, Secret Secrets 1985, The Shouting Stage 1988, Hearts and Flowers 1990, The Very Best of 1991, Square the Circle 1992, What's Inside (album) 1995.

ARMEY, Richard Keith, PH.D.; American politician; b. 7 July 1940, Cando, N.D.; s. of Glen Armey and Marion Gutschlog; m. Susan Byrd; three s. one d.; ed. Jamestown Coll., N.D. and Univs. of N. Dakota and Okla.; mem. Faculty of Econs. Univ. of Mon. 1964–65; Asst. Prof. West Tex. State Univ. 1967–68, Austin Coll. 1968–72; Assoc. Prof. North Tex. State Univ. 1972–77, Chair. Dept. of Econs. 1977–83; mem. U.S. House of Reps. from 26th Tex. Dist. 1985–; Majority Leader, House of Reps. Dec. 1995–; Republican. *Publications:* Price Theory 1977, The Freedom Revolution 1995, The Flat Tax 1996. *Address:* Suite 3050, 9901 Valley Ranch Parkway, Irving, TX 75063; U.S. House of Representatives, 301 Cannon Bldg., Washington, DC 20510, U.S.A.

ARMFIELD, Diana Maxwell, R.A., R.C.A.; British painter; b. 11 June 1920, Ringwood, Hants.; d. of Joseph Harold Armfield and Gertrude Mary Uttley; m. Bernard Dunstan 1949; three s.; ed. Bedales School, Slade School of Art, Cen. School of Arts & Crafts, London; teacher, Byam Shaw School of Art 1959–; Artist in Residence, Perth, Australia 1985, Jackson, Wyoming, U.S.A. 1989; numerous exhbns. U.K. including Browse & Darby, London 1979, 1981, 1984, 1987, 1990, 1993, 1996, also U.S.A., Australia and Netherlands; mem. New English Art Club, Royal W. of England Acad., Royal Cambrian Acad.; Hon. mem. Pastel Soc. *Leisure interests:* music, gardening. *Address:* 10 High Park Road, Kew, Richmond, Surrey, TW9 4BH, England; Llwynhir, Parc, Bala, Gwynedd, LL23 7YD, Wales.

ARMITAGE, Kenneth, C.B.E., R.A.; British sculptor; b. 18 July 1916, Leeds; m. 1940; ed. Leeds Coll. of Art and Slade School, London; teacher of Sculpture, Bath Acad. of Art 1947–56; Gregory Fellowship, Leeds Univ. 1953; British Council Visitor in Sculpture to Venezuela 1963–64; One-man exhbns. London 1952, 1957, 1962, 1965, New York 1954, 1956, 1958, 1962, Retrospective exhbn. Whitechapel Art Gallery, London 1959, Sala Mendoza, Caracas, Venezuela 1982; represented at Venice Biennale 1958; Guest Artist, City of Berlin 1967–69; Hakone Open-Air Sculpture, Japan 1969, one-man exhbn. touring Tokyo, Osaka, Nagoya 1978; retrospective exhbn., Paris 1985; Chelsea Harbour Sculpture Exhbn., London 1993, Yorkshire Sculpture Park 1996, Friend's Room 1996; sculpture Comm., new British Embassy, Brasília 1985–86; group exhbns. include Seoul Olympics Sculpture Exhibition 1988, World Expo, Brisbane 1988 and many in America and Europe; works in major public collections throughout the world; Hon. Dr. (R.C.A.) 1969, (R.A.) 1994; David Bright Prize Venice Biennale 1958. *Address:* 22A Avonmore Road, London, W14 8RR, England.

ARMSTRONG, Anne Legendre, B.A.; American politician, company director and diplomatist; b. 27 Dec. 1927, New Orleans, La.; d. of Armant and Olive Legendre; m. Tobin Armstrong 1950; three s. two d.; ed. Foxcroft School, Middleburg, Va., and Vassar Coll.; Republican Nat. Committee woman from Texas 1968–73; Republican Nat. Comm. Co-Chair. 1971–73; Counsellor to Pres. Nixon with cabinet rank 1973–74; Counsellor to Pres. Ford with cabinet rank 1974; resigned from govt. service 1974; Amb. to U.K. 1976–77; Dir. Halliburton, Boise Cascade, American Express Co.; Chair. English-Speaking Union of U.S. 1977–80, Pres.'s Foreign Intelligence Advisory Bd. 1981–90, Bd. of Trustees Center for Strategic and Int. Studies, Washington, D.C. 1987–, Public Policy Inst.; Co-Chair. Reagan-Bush Campaign 1980; Chair. Texas Women's Alliance 1985–89; mem. Visiting Cttee. JFK School of Govt., Harvard Univ. 1978–82, Comm. on Integrated Long-Term Strategy 1987, Gen. Motors Corpn. Advisory Council; mem. Bd. of Regents, Smithsonian Inst., 1978–94; Trustee American Assocs. of R.A., of Trust 1985–; Pres. Blair House Restoration Fund 1985–91, Nat. Thanksgiving Comm. 1986–94; Hon. LL.D. (Bristol, U.K.) 1976, (Washington and Lee) 1976, (Williams Coll., Mass.) 1977, (St. Mary's) 1978, (Tulane) 1978; Republican Woman of the Year Award 1979, Texan of the Year Award 1981, Texas Women's Hall of Fame 1986, Presidential Medal of Freedom 1987, Golden Plate Award, American Acad. of Achievement 1989. *Address:* Armstrong Ranch, Armstrong, TX 78338, U.S.A.

ARMSTRONG, C. Michael, B.S.; American business executive; b. 18 Oct. 1938, Detroit, Mich.; s. of Charles H. Armstrong and Zora Jean (née Brooks) Armstrong; m. Anne Gossett 1961; three d.; ed. Miami Univ., Dartmouth Inst.; joined IBM Corpn. 1961, Dir. systems man. marketing div. 1975–76, Vice-Pres. Market Operations East 1976–78, Pres. data processing div. 1978–80, Vice-Pres. plans and controls, data processing product group 1980–84, Asst. Group Exec. 1980–83, Group Exec. 1983–92, Sr. Vice-Pres. 1984–92, fmrly. Pres. IBM Corpn. Europe, Pres. and Dir. Gen. World Trade (Europe, Middle East, Africa) 1987–89; Chair. World Trade Corpn. 1989–92; Chair., C.E.O. Hughes Aircraft Co. 1992–93, Hughes Electronics Corpn. 1993–; Chair. Pres.'s Export Council 1994–; Chair., C.E.O. AT&T 1997–; Vice-Chair. World Affairs Council; Dir. Travelers Corpn., Times Mirror Co.; mem. Supervisory Bd. Thyssen-Bornemisza Group, Council on Foreign Relations, Nat. Security Telecommunications Advisory Cttee., Defence Policy

Advisory Cttee. on Trade (DPACT), numerous univ. advisory bds. *Address:* AT&T Corporation, Corporation Headquarters, 295 Maple Avenue, Basking Ridge, NJ 07920, U.S.A.

ARMSTRONG, David John, B.A.; Australian journalist; b. 25 Nov. 1947, Sydney; s. of Allan E. Armstrong and Mary P. Armstrong; m. Deborah Bailey 1980; two d.; ed. Marist Brothers High School Parramatta, Univ. of N.S.W.; Ed. The Bulletin 1985–86; Deputy Ed. The Daily Telegraph 1988–89; Ed. The Australian 1989–92; Ed. The Canberra Times 1992–93; Ed. South China Morning Post, Hong Kong 1993–94, Ed.-in-Chief 1994–. *Leisure interests:* reading, golf. *Address:* Morning Post Centre, 22 Dai Fat Street, Tai Po Industrial Estate, Tai Po, New Territory, Hong Kong Special Administrative Region, People's Republic of China.

ARMSTRONG, David Malet, A.O., B.PHIL., PH.D.; Australian professor of philosophy; b. 8 July 1926, Melbourne; s. of Capt. J. M. Armstrong and Philippa Suzanne Marett; m. Jennifer Mary de Bohun Clark 1982; ed. Dragon School, Oxford, England, Geelong Grammar School, Sydney and Oxford Univs.; Asst. Lecturer in Philosophy, Birkbeck Coll., London Univ. 1954–55; lecturer, Sr. Lecturer in Philosophy, Univ. of Melbourne 1956–63; Challis Prof. of Philosophy, Univ. of Sydney 1964–91, Emer. Prof. 1992–; Fellow Australian Acad. of Humanities; corresp. F.B.A. 1998. *Publications:* Berkeley's Theory of Vision 1961, Perception and the Physical World 1962, A Materialist Theory of the Mind 1968, Belief, Truth and Knowledge 1973, Universals and Scientific Realism 1978, The Nature of the Mind, and Other Essays 1983, What is a Law of Nature? 1983, Consciousness and Causality (with Norman Malcolm) 1984, A Combinatorial Theory of Possibility 1989, Universals, An Opinionated Instruction 1989, Dispositions: A Debate (with C. B. Martin and U. T. Place) 1996, A World of States of Affairs 1997, The Mind-Body Problem: An Opinionated Introduction 1999. *Address:* Department of Philosophy, Sydney University, Sydney, N.S.W. 2006; 206 Glebe Point Road, Glebe, N.S.W. 2037, Australia. *Telephone:* 9351-2466 (Office); 9660-1435 (Home). *Fax:* 9660-8846.

ARMSTRONG, Gillian; Australian film director; b. 18 Dec. 1950; ed. Swinburne Coll., Nat. Australian Film & TV School, Sydney; Dir. numerous short films and documentaries. *Feature films:* My Brilliant Career (Australian Film Inst. Award), Starstruck, Mrs. Soffel, Hard to Handle, High Tide, Fires Within, The Last Days of Chez Nous, Little Women.

ARMSTRONG, Neil A.; American astronaut and professor of engineering; b. 5 Aug. 1930, Wapakoneta, Ohio; m. Janet Shearon; two s.; ed. Purdue Univ. and Univ. of Southern California; naval aviator 1949–52, flew combat missions during Korean War; joined NASA Lewis Flight Propulsion Laboratory 1955, later transferred to NASA High Speed Flight Station, Edwards, Calif., as aeronautical research pilot, was X-15 project pilot flying to over 200,000 ft. and at approx. 4,000 m.p.h.; other flight test work included X-1 rocket research plane, F-100, F-101, F-104, F5D, B-47 and the paraglider; selected as astronaut by NASA Sept. 1962; command pilot for Gemini VIII 1966; backup pilot for Gemini V 1965, Gemini XI 1966; flew to the moon in Apollo XI July 1969, first man to set foot on the moon 20 July 1969; Chair. Peace Corps Nat. Advisory Council 1969; Deputy Assoc. Admin. for Aeronautics, NASA, Washington 1970–71; Prof. of Engineering, Univ. of Cincinnati 1971–79; Chair. Cardwell Int. Ltd. 1979–81; Chair. CTA Inc. 1982–92, AIL Systems Inc. 1989–; Dir. numerous cos.; mem. Pres's Comm. on Space Shuttle 1986, Nat. Comm. on Space 1985–86; mem. Nat. Acad. of Engineering; Fellow, Soc. of Experimental Test Pilots, American Inst. of Aeronautics and Astronautics, Royal Aeronautical Soc.; hon. mem. Int. Acad. of Astronautics; Hon. Fellow, Int. Astron. Fed.; numerous decorations and awards from 17 countries including Presidential Medal of Freedom, NASA Exceptional Service Award, Royal Geographical Soc. Gold Medal and Harmon Int. Aviation Trophy 1970.

ARMSTRONG, Robin Louis, B.A., PH.D., F.R.S.C.; Canadian professor of physics; b. 14 May 1935, Galt, Ont.; s. of Robert Dockstader Armstrong and Beatrice Jenny (née Grill) Armstrong; m. Karen Elisabeth Hansen 1960; two s.; ed. Univs. of Toronto and Oxford; Asst. Prof. of Physics Univ. of Toronto 1962–68, Assoc. Prof. 1968–71, Prof. 1971–90, Adjunct Prof. 1990–; Assoc. Chair. Physics Univ. of Toronto 1969–74, Chair. 1974–82, Dean Faculty of Arts and Science 1982–90; Visitante Distinguido, Univ. of Córdoba, Argentina 1989; Pres. and Prof. of Physics, Univ. of New Brunswick 1990–96; Acting Vice-Pres. Finance and Admin. Wilfrid Laurier Univ. 1997–; Pres. Canadian Inst. for Neutron Scattering 1986–89, Canadian Asscn. of Physicists 1990–91; Dir. Canadian Inst. for Advanced Research 1981–82, Huntsman Marine Lab. 1983–87; mem. Research Council of Canadian Inst. for Advanced Research 1982–, Natural Science and Eng. Research Council of Canada (NSERC) 1991–97 (mem. Exec. 1992–97, Vice-Pres. 1994–97); Rutherford Memorial Fellowship (Royal Soc. Canada) 1961; Herzberg Medal 1973; Medal of Achievement (Canadian Asscn. of Physicists) 1990, Commemorative Medal for 125th Anniversary of Canadian Confed. 1992. *Publications:* over 160 research articles on condensed matter physics in numerous journals. *Leisure interests:* golf, gardening. *Address:* University of Toronto, Department of Physics, 60 St. George Street, Toronto, Ont., M5S 1A7, Canada.

ARMSTRONG, Sheila Ann, F.R.A.M.; British opera and concert singer; b. 13 Aug. 1942, England; d. of William R. and Janet Armstrong; m. David E. Cooper 1980; ed. Hirst Park Girls' School, Ashington, Northumberland and Royal Acad. of Music; has appeared in opera at Glyndebourne, Scottish National Opera, Sadlers Wells, English Nat. Opera North and Royal Opera House, Covent Garden as well as giving recitals around the world with most of the maj. orchestras; has made extensive recordings; Pres. Kathleen Ferrier Soc.; Hon. M.A. (Newcastle); Hon. D.Mus. (Durham); Mozart Prize 1965, Kathleen Ferrier Memorial Award 1965. *Leisure interests:* collecting keys, interior decoration and design, flower-arranging, sewing, gardening and design. *Address:* Harvesters, Tilford Road, Hindhead, Surrey, GU26 6SQ, England.

ARMSTRONG OF ILMINSTER, Baron (Life Peer) cr. 1988, of Ashill in the County of Somerset; **Robert Temple Armstrong,** G.C.B., C.V.O., M.A.; British civil servant (retd.); b. 30 March 1927, Oxford; s. of Sir Thomas Armstrong and of Lady Armstrong (née Draper); m. 1st Serena Mary Benedicta Chance 1953 (divorced 1985) (died 1994); two d.; m. 2nd (Mary) Patricia Carlow 1985; ed. Eton Coll. and Christ Church, Oxford; Asst. Prin. Treasury 1950–55, Private Sec. to Economic Sec. 1953–54; Private Sec. to Chancellor of the Exchequer (Rt. Hon. R. A. Butler) 1954–55; Prin. Treasury 1955–64; Asst. Sec. Cabinet Office 1964–66; Asst. Sec. Treasury 1966–68; Prin. Private Sec. to Chancellor of the Exchequer (Rt. Hon. Roy Jenkins, q.v.) 1968; Under-Sec. Treasury 1968–70; Prin. Private Sec. to the Prime Minister 1970–75; Deputy Under-Sec. of State, Home Office 1975–77, Perm. Under-Sec. of State 1977–79; Sec. of the Cabinet 1979–87; Perm. Sec. Man. and Personnel Office 1981–87; Head, Home Civil Service 1981–87; Sec. Radcliffe Cttee. on Monetary System 1957–59; Sec. to the Dirs., Royal Opera House, Covent Garden 1968–87, Dir. 1988–93; Dir. Bristol and West Bldg. Soc. 1988–97 (Chair. 1993–97), Bank of Ireland and other cos.; Chair. Bd. of Trustees, Victoria and Albert Museum 1988–98; mem. Rhodes Trust 1975–97; Fellow, Eton Coll. 1979–94; Chancellor, Univ. of Hull Oct. 1994–; Hon. Student, Christ Church 1985; Hon. Bencher, Inner Temple. *Leisure interest:* music. *Address:* House of Lords, London, SW1A 0PW, England.

ÁRNASON, Tómas; Icelandic politician; b. 21 July 1923, Seydisfjörður; s. of Árni Vilhjálmsson and Gudrun (née Thorvardardóttir) Árnason; m. Thora Kristín Eiríksdóttir 1949; four s.; ed. Univ. of Iceland, Harvard Law School. Advocate at Akureyri 1949–51 and 1952–53; Advocate, Supreme Court 1964–72; Chief, Div. of Defence Affairs, Ministry of Foreign Affairs 1953–60; mem. of Parl. 1956, 1958, 1959, 1968–73, 1974–85; Minister of Finance 1978–79, of Trade and Commerce 1980–83; a Gov. Cen. Bank of Iceland 1985–; Man. Dir. of newspaper Tíminn 1960–64; Man. Dir. Econ. Devt. Inst. 1972–78; mem. del. to UN; mem. del. to North Atlantic Ass. 1974–78, 1983–84; mem. Central Cttee. of Progressive Party, Cashier 1968, Sec. 1978–83; mem. Bd. Nordic Investment Bank; Chair. Ministerial Council of EFTA 1982, mem. Steering Cttee. EFTA Industrial Devt. Fund for Portugal 1993. *Leisure interests:* golf, fishing. *Address:* Sedlabanki Íslands, Kalkofnsvegur 1, 150 Reykjavík; Efstaleiti 12, 103 Reykjavík, Iceland (Home). *Telephone:* (1) 686373 (Home).

ARNAUD, Jean-Loup, L.EN.D.; French government official; b. 25 Sept. 1942, Paris; s. of Raoul Arnaud and Emilienne Lapeyre; m. Lucienne Lavallée 1966; one d.; ed. Faculté de Droit, Paris and Ecole Nat. d'Admin.; Auditor, Cour des Comptes 1969, Advisory Counsellor 1976; assigned to Datar 1971–72; Tech. Counsellor, Cabinet of Sec. of State, André Rossi; assigned to financial aspects of reform of ORTF 1974–75; Advisory Counsellor, Cour des Comptes 1976; Tech. Counsellor, Cabinet of Minister of Culture and Environment 1977; Chief of Centre, Centre Nat. de la Cinématographie 1978; official in charge of relations with cinema, Soc. Nat. de Programme de France-Régions 3 (FR3) 1979–82; Admin. Soc. Française de Production Cinématographique 1983–; Head, Dept. of Cinema, Ministry of Culture and Communication 1986; Dir.-Gen. Soc. d'Edition de Programmes de Télévision 1987–; Admin. Fondation Européenne des métiers de l'image et du son (Femis) 1987; Dir.-Gen. Télé-Hachette 1989–; Vice-Pres. Union syndicale de la production audiovisuelle 1990–; Magistrate Cour des comptes; mem. Admin. Council of France 3 1993–. *Address:* Cour des comptes, 13 rue Cambon, 75001 Paris (Office); 55 rue de Seine, 75006 Paris, France (Home).

ARNAULT, Bernard; French business executive; b. 5 March 1949, Roubaix; s. of Jean Arnault and Marie-Jo Arnault (née Savinel) m. 1st Anne Dewavrin 1973 (divorced); two c.; m. 2nd Hélène Mercier 1991; two s.; ed. Ecole Polytechnique; joined Ferret-Savinel (family construction co.) 1971, Pres. 1978–84; lived in U.S.A. 1981–84; took over Boussac Saint-Frères (parent co. of Dior) 1985; Pres. LVMH (luxury goods group which includes Louis Vuitton bags, Moët Chandon champagne, Parfums Christian Dior, Hennessy and Hine cognac) 1989–, Chair. 1992–; Pres. Bd. of Dirs. Montaigne 1997–; fmr. Dir. Diageo; through holding co. Financière Agache owns fashion houses Dior, Lacroix and Céline and dept. store Bon Marché; Chevalier Légion d'honneur, Ordre nat. du Mérite. *Address:* 11 rue François 1er, 75008 Paris; 30 ave Hoche, 75008 Paris, France (Office).

ARNDT, Heinz Wolfgang, B.LITT., M.A.; Australian professor of economics; b. 26 Feb. 1915, Breslau (Wrocław); s. of F. G. Arndt; m. Ruth Strohsahl 1941; two s. one d.; ed. Oxford Univ., London School of Econs. (Leverhulme Research Fellow), U.K.; Research Asst. Royal Inst. of Int. Affairs 1941–43; Asst. Lecturer in Econs., Univ. of Manchester 1943–46; Sr. Lecturer in Econs., Univ. of Sydney, Australia 1946–50; Prof. of Econs., School of Gen. Studies, Australian Nat. Univ. (ANU) 1951–63, Dean Faculty of Econs. 1959–60, Prof. of Econs., Research School of Pacific Studies 1963–80, Deputy Chair. Bd. of Inst. of Advanced Studies 1976–78, 1978–80, Prof. Emer. and Visiting Fellow Nat. Centre for Devt. Studies 1981–; field work, Indonesia 1964–; Consultant, UNCTAD 1966, 1967; mem. Governing Council UN

Asian Inst. for Econ. Devt. and Planning, Bangkok 1969–75; Deputy Dir. Country Studies Div., OECD, Paris 1972; mem. Research Cttee., Australia-Japan Research Centre, ANU 1972–95; Chair. Expert Group on Structural Change and Econ. Growth, Commonwealth Secretariat, London 1980, Australian Steering Cttee., ASEAN-Australia Econ. Relations Research Project, ANU 1980–86; Consultant, UNIDO 1983–85, Asian Devt. Bank 1987, 1989–92; Pres. Econ. Soc. of Australia and N.Z. 1957–59, Australian Asscn. for Cultural Freedom 1977–85; Hon. Sec. Social Science Research Council of Australia 1957–59; Distinguished Fellow Australian Econ. Soc.; Ed. Bulletin of Indonesian Economic Studies 1965–82, Asian-Pacific Economic Literature 1986–; Jt. Ed. Quadrant 1981–83. *Publications:* The Economic Lessons of the Nineteen-Thirties 1944, The Australian Trading Banks 1957 and subsequent edns., The Rise and Fall of Economic Growth: A Study in Contemporary Thought 1978, The Indonesian Economy: Collected Papers 1984, A Course through Life: Memoirs of an Australian Economist 1985, Asian Diaries 1986, Economic Development: The History of an Idea 1987, The Indonesian Economy: As Seen by a Neighbour 1991, 50 Years of Development Studies 1993, Essays in International Economics 1944–1994, 1996, and several other books; articles in learned journals. *Leisure interests:* chess, music. *Address:* 14 Hopetoun Circuit, Deakin, A.C.T. 2600, Australia. *Telephone:* (06) 2492637 (Office); (06) 2733625 (Home). *Fax:* (06) 2798869.

ARNEDO ORBAÑANOS, Miguel Angel, B.L., B.ECONS.; Spanish banker; b. 15 May 1944, Haro; s. of Dionisio Arnedo and Vitorina Orbañanos; m. Ana Isabel Gómez Arbaiza 1971; one s.; Economist, Research Dept., Banco de España 1969; specialist in int. econ. 1973–; Deputy Dir. Monetary and Statistical Research 1981, Deputy Dir. for Foreign Relations 1984; mem. Cttee. on Capital Movts. and Invisible Transactions, OECD 1981–86; Vice-Pres. EIB 1986–92; mem. Court of Auditors. *Leisure interests:* literature, cinema, photography, jazz.

ARNELL, Richard Anthony Sayer; British composer and conductor; b. 15 Sept. 1917, London; s. of late Richard Sayer Arnell and Helène Marie Scherf; m. Joan Heycock 1992; three d. from previous marriages; ed. Mall School, University Coll. School and Royal Coll. of Music; Music consultant, BBC North American Service 1943–46; Lecturer, Trinity Coll. of Music, London 1948–87; Lecturer, Royal Ballet School 1958–59; Ed. "The Composer"1961–64; Visiting lecturer (Fulbright exchange), Bowdoin Coll., Maine, U.S.A. 1967–68; Visiting Prof., Hofstra Univ., N.Y. 1968–70; Music Dir. and mem. Bd. London Int. Film School 1975–89; Chair. Composers' Guild of G.B. 1974–75, 1977–79 (Vice-Pres. 1992–), Young Musicians' Symphony Orch. Soc. 1973–75, 1977–79, Saxmundham Music and Arts 1993–96 (Pres. 1996–); Music Dir. Ram Filming Ltd. 1980–91; Dir. A plus A Ltd. 1984–89; Chair. London Int. Film School Trust 1981–87; f., Chair. Friends of London Int. Film School 1982–87, Vice-Pres. 1987–; f., Chair. Friends of Trinity Coll. of Music Jr. Dept. 1986–87, Vice-Pres. 1987–; f., Chair. Tadcaster Civic Soc. Music and Arts 1988–91; Composer of the Year 1966 (Music Teachers' Asscn. Award); Tadcaster Town Council Merit Award 1991. *Compositions include:* Opera: Love in Transit 1953, Moonflowers 1958; Ballet scores: Punch and the Child 1947, Harlequin in April 1951, the Great Detective 1953, The Angels 1957, Giselle (re-orchestrated) 1965; Film scores: The Land 1941, The Third Secret 1963, The Visit 1964, The Man Outside 1966, Topsail Schooner 1966, Bequest for a Village 1969, Second Best 1972, Stained Glass 1973, Wires Over the Border 1974, Black Panther 1977, Antagonist 1980, Dilemma 1981, Toulouse Lautrec 1984, Light of the World 1988; other works: Symphonic Portrait, Lord Byron, for Sir Thomas Beecham 1953, Landscapes and Figures 1956, Petrified Princess, puppet operetta for BBC 1959; Robert Flaherty, Impression for Radio Eireann 1960, Musica Pacifica for Edward Benjamin 1963, Festival Flourish, for Salvation Army 1965, Piano Concerto for RPO 1967, Overture, Food of Love, for Portland Symphony Orch. 1968, My Ladye Greene Sleeves, for Hofstra Univ. 1968, Nocturne 1968, I Think of all Soft Limbs 1971, Astronaut One 1973, Life Boat Voluntary, for Royal Nat. Lifeboat Inst. 1974, Call, for LPO 1980, RVW's Almanac 1984, Six Lawrence Poems 1985, Ode to Beecham, for RPO 1986, Con Amore for Cantamus Girls Choir 1988, Xanadu for Harlow Choral Soc. 1993, Symphonic Statement for Pres. Mandela 1997; also six symphonies, two violin concertos, harpsichord concerto, two piano concertos, six string quartets, two quintets, organ works, music for string orch., wind ensembles, brass ensembles, song cycles and electronic music. *Leisure interests:* cooking, travel. *Address:* Benhall Lodge, Benhall, Suffolk, IP17 1JD, England. *Telephone:* (01728) 602014.

ARNETT, Emerson James, B.A., LL.M.; Canadian business executive; b. 29 Sept. 1938; s. of Emerson Lloyd Arnett and Elsie Audrey Rhind; m. Edith Alexandra Palk 1964; four c.; ed. Univ. of Man., Harvard Univ.; civil litigation section, Dept. of Justice, Ottawa 1964–65; Assoc. Pitblado and Hoskin (law firm), Winnipeg 1965–66; Asst. to Exec. Vice-Pres. Vickers and Benson Advertising, Toronto 1966–67; Assoc./Partner Davies, Ward and Beck (law firm), Toronto 1968–73; partner Stikeman, Elliott (law firm), Toronto 1973–97, Resident partner, Washington, D.C., 1993–96; Pres. and C.E.O. The Molson Cos. Ltd. 1997–. *Publications:* Doing Business (co-ed.); numerous law review and newspaper articles and conf. papers. *Leisure interests:* shooting, skiing, hiking, reading. *Address:* The Molson Companies Ltd., Scotia Plaza, 40 King Street West, Suite 3600, Toronto, Ont., M5H 3Z5, Canada.

ARNETT, Peter; American journalist and television reporter; b. 1934, New Zealand; m. (divorced); two c.; ed. Waitaki Coll., Oamaru, New Zealand; with Associated Press (AP) 1960–; war corresp. in Vietnam, Middle East, Nicaragua, El Salvador and Afghanistan; special writer for AP, New York; joined Cable News Network (CNN) 1981–; served as corresp. in Moscow for two years; later nat. security reporter, Washington, D.C.; CNN corresp. Baghdad 1991; Pulitzer prizewinner. *Publication:* Live from the Battlefield 1994. *Leisure interests:* collector of books and oriental statuary. *Address:* c/o CNN Building, 820 1st Street, NE, 9th Floor, Washington, DC 20002, U.S.A.

ARNOLD, Armin, PH.D., F.R.S.C.; Swiss/Canadian professor, writer and critic; b. 1 Sept. 1931, Zug, Switzerland; s. of Franz Arnold and Ida Baumgartner; ed. Univs. of Fribourg, London and Zürich; Asst. Prof. of German, Univ. of Alberta 1959–61, McGill Univ. 1961–64, Assoc. Prof. 1964–68, Prof. 1968–84, Auxiliary Prof. 1984–89; Dozent, Höhere Wirtschafts- und Verwaltungsschule, Olten 1984–93, Baden 1994–. *Publications include:* D. H. Lawrence and America 1958, James Joyce 1963, Die Literatur des Expressionismus 1966, Friedrich Dürrenmatt 1969, Prosa des Expressionismus 1972, Kriminalromanführer 1978, Alfred Doeblin 1996, etc. *Address:* 9E Rang Ste-Anne de la Rochelle, Quebec J0E 2B0, Canada; Rauchlenweg 332, 4712 Laupersdorf, Switzerland.

ARNOLD, Eve; photographer; b. Philadelphia, U.S.A.; m. Arnold Arnold (divorced); one s.; ed. New School for Social Research; joined Magnum Photographic Agency 1954; moved to U.K. 1961; has worked for Sunday Times, Time, Life, etc.; worked in U.K., U.S.A., China, fmr. U.S.S.R.; subjects include Marilyn Monroe, Joan Crawford, John and Anjelica Huston, Francis Bacon, Yves Montand, Margot Fonteyn, Rudolph Nureyev, Malcolm X, photographs examining the status of women, and numerous other topics; numerous exhbns. including Eve Arnold: In Retrospect, premièred Int. Center for Photography, N.Y., retrospective at Nat. Museum of Photography, Bradford 1996. *Publications include:* The Unretouched Woman, In China, In America, The Great British, Eve Arnold: In Retrospect 1996. *Address:* c/o Magnum Photographic Agency, Moreland Buildings, 2nd Floor, 5 Old Street, London, EC1V 9HL, England. *Telephone:* 0171-490 1771.

ARNOLD, Hans Redlef, PH.D.; German diplomatist and writer; b. 14 Aug. 1923, Munich; s. of Karl Arnold and Anne-Dora Volquardsen; m. Karin Baroness von Egloffstein 1954; three d.; ed. Univ. of Munich; joined Foreign Service, Fed. Repub. of Germany; served Embassy, Paris 1952–55, Foreign Office, Bonn 1955–57, Embassy, Washington 1957–61, Foreign Office 1961–68, sometime head of Foreign Minister Willy Brandt's office; Amb. to Netherlands 1968–72; Head, Cultural Dept., Foreign Office 1972–77; Amb. to Italy 1977–81; Insp.-Gen. German Foreign Service 1981–82; Amb. and Perm. Rep. to UN and Int. Orgs., Geneva 1982–86; lecturer Acad. of Political Science, Munich; several nat. and foreign decorations. *Publications:* Cultural Export as Policy? 1976, Foreign Cultural Policy 1980, The March (co-author) 1990, Europe on the Decline? 1993, Germany's Power 1995; regular contributions to periodicals and newspapers. *Address:* D-83083 Riedering-Heft, Germany. *Telephone:* (08032) 5255. *Fax:* (08032) 5255.

ARNOLD, James R., M.A., PH.D.; American professor of chemistry and space scientist; b. 5 May 1923, Metuchen, N.J.; s. of Abraham S. and Julia J. Arnold; m. Louise C. Arnold 1952; three s.; ed. Princeton Univ.; Asst. Princeton 1943, Manhattan Project 1943–46; Fellow, Inst. of Nuclear Studies, Univ. of Chicago 1946; Nat. Research Fellow, Harvard 1947; Asst. Prof., Univ. of Chicago 1949–55; Assoc. Prof., Princeton Univ. 1956–58; Assoc. Prof., Dept. of Chem., Univ. of Calif., San Diego 1958–60, Prof. 1960–92, Harold C. Urey Prof. 1983–92; Assoc. Ed. Moon 1972–; Dir. Calif. Space Inst. (S.I.O.), Univ. of Calif., San Diego 1980–89, interim Dir. 1996–97; prin. investigator Calif. Space Grant Consortium 1989–; recipient of lunar samples from Apollo and Soviet missions; mem. of N.A.S., A.A.A.S., A.C.S., American Acad. of Arts and Sciences; Nat. Council of World Federalists 1970–72; Guggenheim Fellow, India 1972–73; specialized in field of cosmic-ray produced nuclides, meteorites, lunar samples and cosmochemistry. *Publications:* over 100 articles in scientific reviews and journals. *Address:* University of California at San Diego, Department of Chemistry, Code 0524, La Jolla, CA 92093, U.S.A. *Telephone:* (619) 822-1597. *Fax:* (619) 534-7840.

ARNOLD, Sir Malcolm Henry, Kt., C.B.E., F.R.C.M., F.R.N.C.M.; British composer; b. 21 Oct. 1921, Northampton; s. of William Arnold and Annie Arnold; m. 1st Sheila Nicholson 1942; one s. one d.; m. 2nd Isobel Gray 1963 (died 1992); one s.; ed. Royal Coll. of Music, London; Prin. Trumpet, London Philharmonic Orchestra 1942–44 and 1946–48; served army 1944–46; full-time composer and conductor 1948–; Ivor Novello Award for music for Inn of Sixth Happiness 1952, Oscar for music for film Bridge on the River Kwai 1957, Ivor Novello Award for Outstanding Services to British Music 1986, Wavendon All Music Composer of the Year 1987; Hon. mem. Royal Northern Coll. of Music 1997; Hon. D.Mus. (Exeter) 1969, (Durham) 1982, (Leicester) 1984, (Trinity Coll. London) 1991; Dr. h.c. (Miami, Ohio) 1990; Hon. R.A.M. 1983; Bard of the Cornish Gorsedd 1969; Freeman City of London 1950; Hon. Freeman Borough of Northampton 1989. *Works include:* symphonies: No. 1 1949, No. 2 1953, No. 3 1957, No. 4 1960, No. 5 1961, No. 6 1967, No. 7 1973, No. 8 1978, No. 9 1986, Symphony for Brass Instruments 1979; overtures: Beckus the Dandipratt 1943, Tam O'Shanter 1955, Peterloo 1967; other compositions: 18 concertos, 5 ballets, 2 one-act operas, 2 string quartets, 2 brass quintets, and vocal, choral and chamber music. *Leisure interests:* reading, foreign travel. *Address:* c/o Diana Hirst, 55 Mamora Road, London, SE22 0RY; 26 Springfields, Attleborough, Norfolk, NR17 2PA, England. *Telephone:* 0181-299 1914 (London); (01953) 455420 (Norfolk). *Fax:* 0181-299 1914 (London); 01953 455420 (Norfolk).

ARNOLD, Roseanne (see Roseanne).

ARNOLD, Vladimir Igorevich, D.SC.; Russian mathematician; b. 12 June 1937, Odessa; s. of Igor Vladimirovich Arnold and Nina Alexandrovna Isakovich; m. Voronina Elionora Aleksandrovna 1975; one s.; ed. Moscow State Univ.; Asst. Prof., then Prof., Moscow State Univ. 1961–86; Prof. and chief scientific researcher Steklov Math. Inst., Moscow 1986–, Université Paris-Dauphine 1993–; Corresp. mem. U.S.S.R. (now Russian) Acad. of Sciences 1984–90, mem. 1990–; Foreign mem. Académie des Sciences, Paris, N.A.S., U.S.A., Academia Lincei, Rome, Royal Soc., London, Acad. of Arts and Sciences, Boston, U.S.A., London Math. Soc., American Philosophical Soc., European Acad.; Dr. h.c. (Univ. P. et M. Curie, Paris) 1979, (Warwick, U.K.) 1988, (Utrecht) 1991, (Bologna) 1991, (Universidad Complutense de Madrid) 1994, (Toronto) 1997; Moscow Math. Soc. Prize 1958, Lenin Prize 1965, Crafoord Prize 1982, Lobachevsky Prize 1992, Harvey Prize 1994, ADION Medal 1995. *Publications:* Ergodic Problems in Classical Mechanics (with A. Avez) 1967, Mathematical Methods of Classical Mechanics 1974, Catastrophe Theory 1981, Singularity Theory and its Applications (Vols. 1, 2) 1982, 1984, Huygens and Barrow, Newton and Hooke 1990, Topological Methods in Hydrodynamics 1997 and other publs. *Leisure interests:* skiing, canoeing, hiking. *Address:* Steklov Mathematical Institute, 8 Gubkina Street, GSP-1 Moscow 117966, Russia; (Jan.–June) CEREMADE, Université de Paris-Dauphine, Place du Mal de Lattre de Tassigny, Paris 75775, Cedex 16e, France. *Telephone:* 135-14-90 (Office, Moscow); 132-48-02 (Home, Moscow); 44.05.46.81 (Office, Paris); 40.01.92.08 (Home, Paris). *Fax:* 135-05-55 (Moscow); 44.05.45.99 (Paris).

ARNOTT, Struther, C.B.E., F.R.S.E., F.R.S.; British university vice-chancellor and scientist; b. 25 Sept. 1934; s. of Charles McCann and Christina Struthers Arnott; m. Greta Edwards 1970; two s.; ed. Hamilton Acad., Lanarkshire and Glasgow Univ.; Scientist, MRC Biophysics Research Unit, King's Coll. London 1960–70, Demonstrator in Physics 1960–67, Dir. of Postgraduate Studies in Biophysics 1967–70; Prof. of Molecular Biology, Purdue Univ., West Lafayette, Ind. 1970–86, Head, Dept. of Biological Sciences 1975–80, Vice-Pres. for Research and Dean, Graduate School 1980–86; Sr. Visiting Research Fellow, Jesus Coll. Oxford 1980–81; Nuffield Research Fellow, Green Coll. 1985–86; Principal and Vice-Chancellor, St. Andrews Univ. 1986–; Guggenheim Memorial Foundation Fellow 1985; Hon. Sc.D. (St. Andrews, U.S.A.) 1994; Hon. D.Sc. (Purdue) 1998. *Publications:* papers in learned journals on structures of fibrous biopolymers, especially nucleic acids and polysaccharides and techniques for visualizing them. *Leisure interests:* birdwatching, botanizing. *Address:* College Gate, St. Andrews, Fife, KY16 9AJ; The Principal's House, 9 The Scores, St. Andrews, Fife, KY16 9AR, Scotland. *Telephone:* (01334) 462545. *Fax:* (01334) 462543.

ARNOUL, Françoise (Françoise Gautsch); French actress; b. 9 June 1931, Constantine, Algeria; d. of Gen. Arnoul Gautsch and Jeanne Gradwohl; m. Georges Cravenne (divorced); ed. Lycée de Rabat, Lycée Molière (Paris) and Paris Conservatoire; Officier des Arts et des Lettres; *films include:* Nous irons à Paris, La maison Bonnadieu, Le désir et l'amour, La plus belle fille du monde, Les compagnons de la nuit, Les amants du Tage, French-Cancan, Des gens sans importance, Thérèse Etienne, La chatte, Asphalte, La bête à l'affût, Le bal des espions, La chatte sort ses griffes, La morte-saison des amours, Le testament d'Orphée, Les Parisiennes, Dimanche de la vie, Le Congrès s'amuse, Españolas en Paris 1970, Van der Valk 1972, Dialogue d'exiles 1975, Dernière sortie avant Roissy 1977, Ronde de Nuit 1984, Nuit Docile 1987, Voir L'Éléphant 1990; numerous TV roles; theatre debut in Les Justes (Camus), Versailles 1966; Chevalier Légion d'honneur. *Leisure interest:* dancing. *Address:* 53 rue Censier, 75005 Paris, France (Home).

ARNS, H.E. Cardinal Paulo Evaristo; Brazilian ecclesiastic; b. 14 Sept. 1921, Forquilhinha, Criciúma, Santa Catarina; s. of Gabriel and Helena Steiner Arns; ed. Univ. de Paris and Ecole des Hautes Etudes, Paris; taught theology and french, Univ. Católica de Petrópolis; pastoral work in Petrópolis; Aux. Bishop of São Paulo 1966; Archbishop of São Paulo, 1970–; Grand Chancellor of Pontificia Univ. Católica de São Paulo; mem. Sacred Congregation for the Sacraments (Vatican); mem. UN Int. Independent Comm. on Humanitarian Issues; cr. Cardinal by Pope Paul VI 1973; Nansen Prize (UN) 1985; Hon. LL.D. (Notre Dame, Ind., U.S.A.). *Publications:* numerous works and translations on religious and racial topics, including A Quem iremos, Senhor? 1968, Comunidade: União e Ação 1972, Sê Fiel 1977, Em Defesa dos Direitos Humanos 1978, Convite para Rezar 1978, Presença e Força do Cristão 1978, Discutindo o Papel da Igreja 1980, Os Ministérios na Igreja 1980, O que é Igreja 1981, Meditações para o Dia-a-Dia (vols. 1–4) 1981–83, Pensamentos 1982, Olhando o Mundo com São Francisco 1982, A Violência em nossos Dias 1983, Para Ser Jovem Hoje 1983, Santos e Heróis do Povo 1984. *Address:* Avenida Higienopolis, 890, C.P. 6778, 01064 São Paulo, S.P., Brazil. *Telephone:* (011) 826-0133. *Fax:* (011) 825-6806.

AROSEMENA MONROY, Carlos Julio, D.IUR.; Ecuadorean politician; b. 1920; Counsellor, Ecuadorean Embassy, Washington 1946–52; Chair. Chamber of Deputies 1952; Minister of Defence 1952–53; Vice-Pres. 1960–61; Pres. of Ecuador 1961–63.

ARPAILLANGE, Pierre Raymond, L. EN D.; French judge; b. 13 March 1924, Carlux, Dordogne; s. of Edmond Arpaillange and Eliette Bourgès; m. Nicole Sésia 1947; one s. two d.; ed. Lycée de Périgueux and Facultés de Droit, Paris and Toulouse; acting judge, Orléans 1949, Paris 1950; prosecutor, Meaux 1953; Supreme Court 1954–59; prosecutor, Versailles 1959, Paris 1962; Sec.-Gen. to Public Prosecutor, Court of Appeal and Supreme Court 1962; Tech. Counsellor 1965; Dir. Office of Guardian of Seals 1967–68; Dir. Office of Criminal Affairs and Pardons, Ministry of Justice 1968–74; mem. Audiovisual Council 1973; Dir. Office of Minister of Justice 1973–74; Counsellor, Supreme Court 1974–81; Procurator-Gen. Court of Appeal, Paris 1981–84, Supreme Court 1984–88; Guardian of the Seals and Minister of Justice 1988–90; Pres. Revenue Court 1990–93, Hon. Pres. 1993–; Grand Officier Légion d'honneur, Officier Ordre Nat. du Mérite, Officier des palmes académiques; Croix du combattant volontaire de la Résistance. *Address:* Cour des Comptes, 13 rue Cambon, 75100 Paris (Office); 54 avenue Théophile Gautier, 75016 Paris, France (Home).

ARQUETTE, Patricia; American actress; b. 8 April 1968; d. of Lewis Arquette and Mardi Arquette; m. Nicolas Cage (q.v.) 1995. *Films:* A Nightmare on Elm Street 3: Dream Warriors 1987, Far North 1988, The Indian Runner 1991, Prayer of the Rollerboys 1991, Ethan Frome 1993, Trouble Bound 1993, Inside Monkey Zetterland 1993, True Romance 1993, Holy Matrimony 1994, Ed Wood 1994, Infinity 1995, The Secret Agent 1998. *Films for TV include:* Daddy 1987, Dillinger 1991, Wildflower 1991, Betrayed by Love 1994, Lost Highway 1996, The Secret Agent 1996, Toby's Story 1998, The Hilo Country 1998, Stigmata 1998. *Address:* c/o U.T.A., 9560 Wilshire Blvd., 5th Floor, Beverly Hills, CA 90212, U.S.A.

ARQUETTE, Rosanna; American actress; b. 10 Aug. 1959, N.Y.; d. of Lewis Arquette; m. 1st (divorced); m. 2nd James N. Howard (divorced); m. 3rd. John Sidel 1993; f. Flower Child Productions. *Films include:* Gorp, Off the Wall, S.O.B., Baby, It's You, The Aviator, Desperately Seeking Susan, 8 Million Ways to Die, After Hours, Nobody's Tool, The Big Blue, Life Lessons, Black Rainbow 1989; Wendy Cracked a Walnut 1989, Sweet Revenge 1990, Baby, It's You 1990, Flight of the Intruder 1990, The Linguini Incident 1992, Fathers and Sons 1992, Nowhere to Run 1993, Pulp Fiction 1994, Beyond Rangoon 1995, Search and Destroy 1995, Crash 1996, Liar 1997, Gone Fishin' 1997, Buffalo '66 1997, Palmer's Pick Up 1998, I'm Losing You 1998, Homeslice 1998, Floating Away 1998. *TV films include:* Harvest Home, The Wall, The Long Way Home, The Executioner's Song, One Cooks, the Other Doesn't, The Parade, Survival Guide, A Family Tree, Promised a Miracle, Sweet Revenge, Separation, The Wrong Man, Nowhere to Hide.

ARRABAL, Fernando; Spanish writer; b. 11 Aug. 1932, Melilla; s. of Fernando Arrabal and Carmen Terán González; m. Luce Moreau 1958; one s. one d; ed. Univ. of Madrid; political prisoner in Spain 1967; now lives in Paris; founder "Panique" movt. with Topor, Jodorowsky, etc.; "Superdotado" award 1942, Ford Foundation Award 1959, Grand Prix du Théâtre 1967, Grand Prix Humour Noir 1968, Obie Award 1976, Premio Nadal (Spain) 1983, World's Theater Prize 1984, Medalla de Oro de Bellas Artes (Spain) 1989, Prix du Théâtre (Acad. française) 1993, Prix Int. Vladimir Nabokov 1994, Premio de Ensayo Espasa 1994, Grand Prix Soc. des Gens de Lettres 1996, Grand Prix de la Méditerranée 1996, Prix de la Francophonie 1998, Premio Mariano de Cavia 1998; Medal of Centre for French Civilization and Culture, New York 1997; Officier, Ordre des Arts et des Lettres 1984. *Publications: plays:* numerous plays including Le cimetière des voitures, Guernica, Le grand cérémonial, L'architecte et l'Empereur d'Assyrie, Le jardin des délices, Et ils passèrent des menottes aux fleurs, Le ciel et la merde, Bella ciao, La Tour de Babel, L'extravagante réussite de Jésus-Christ, Karl Marx et William Shakespeare, Les délices de la chair, La traversée de l'empire, Luly, Cielito; *novels:* Baal Babylone 1959, L'enterrement de la sardine 1962, Fêtes et rites de la confusion 1965, La tour prends garde, La reverdie, La vierge rouge, Bréviaire d'amour d'un haltérophile, L'extravagante croisade d'un castrat amoureux 1991, La tueuse du jardin d'hiver 1994, El Mono 1994, Le Funambule de Dieu 1998, Melilla 17 de Julio 1998; *poetry:* La pierre de la folie 1963, 100 sonnets 1966, Humbles paradis 1983, Liberté couleur de femme 1993, Arrabalesques 1994; *essays:* numerous, including Le 'Panique', Le New York d'Arrabal, Lettre au Général Franco, Greco 1970, Lettre à Fidel Castro 1983, Carta a José María Aznar 1992, Goya-Dali 1992, La Dudosa Luz del Día 1994. *Films:* directed and written: Viva la Muerte, J'irai comme un cheval fou, L'arbre de Guernica, L'odyssée de la Pacific, Le cimetière des voitures, Adieu Babylone!, J.-L. Borges (Una Vida de Poesía) 1998. *Leisure interest:* chess. *Address:* 22 rue Jouffroy d'Abbans, Paris 75017, France. *Fax:* (1) 42.67.01.26.

ARREAZA ARREAZA, Julio César, PH.D.; Venezuelan oil executive; b. 28 Feb. 1923; s. of the late Julio Arreaza Matute and Carmen Arreaza de Arreaza; m. Beatriz Bustamante de Arreaza 1949; three s. two d.; ed. Cen. Univ. of Venezuela; Lawyer 1948–59; Legal Adviser to Ministry of Mines and Hydrocarbons 1959–63; Dir.-Gen. Ministry of Mines and Hydrocarbons (frequently acting Minister) 1963–69; mem. Presidential Comm. for Oil Reversion, Head Legal Sub-Comm.; mem. High Level Comm. on aspects of nationalization of Oil Industry; First Vice-Pres. Designate Petróleos de Venezuela, S.A. 1975, confirmed as Vice-Pres. 1979, 1981; Comendador, Orden del Libertador, Orden Francisco Miranda (First Class), Mérito al Trabajo (First Class). *Address:* Avenida El Paseo, Quinta Marisela, Urb. Prados del Este, Caracas 1080, Venezuela. *Telephone:* 771061.

ARRIAGA, Gen. Kaúlza de; Portuguese army officer (retd.); b. 18 Jan. 1915, Oporto; s. of Manuel de Arriaga Nunes and Felicidade Oliveira de Arriaga; m. Maria do Carmo Formigal 1955; three s. two d.; ed. Univ. of Oporto, Portuguese Mil. Acad. and Portuguese Inst. for Higher Mil. Studies;

Under-Sec. of State for Aviation, later Sec. 1955–62; High Command Course 1963–64; Brig. 1964; Prof. of Strategy and Tactics, Inst. for High Mil. Studies 1964–69; Chair. Nuclear Energy Bd. 1967–69, 1973–74; Gen. 1968; C.-in-C. Portuguese Armed Forces in Mozambique 1970–73; mem. Overseas Council 1965–69, 1973–74; mem. Bd. of Dirs. and Exec. Chair. Soc. Portuguesa de Exploração de Petróleos (ANGOL Oil Corpn.) 1966–69, 1973–74; Chair. Shareholders' Meeting, Finicisa Synthetic Fibres Corpn. 1968–69, 1973–74; retd. May 1974; arrested during coup d'état Sept. 1974, released Jan. 1976, later successfully sued Portuguese State; mem. Council, Order of Christ 1966–74; Pres. Equestrian Fed. 1968–71; Grande-Oficial Ordem Militar de Cristo, Grã Cruz, Mérito Aeronáutico, Gran Cruz (Spain), Grande Oficial Ordem do Mérito Militar (Brazil), Grand Officier, Légion d'honneur (France), Commdr. Legion of Merit (U.S.A), and other Portuguese and foreign decorations. *Publications include:* Energia Atómica 1949, Portuguese National Defence during the Last 40 Years and in the Future 1966, Guerra e Política 1987, Maastricht 1992; numerous articles. *Address:* Avenida João XXI No. 9, 6°, 1000 Lisbon, Portugal. *Telephone:* 848.29.65/849.67.85.

ARRIGHI DE CASANOVA, Emile, D.IUR.; French civil servant and financial executive; b. 21 Oct. 1920, Bastia, Corsica; s. of Pierre and Catherine (Paoli) Arrighi de Casanova; m. Geneviève Barthelemy 1946; four c.; ed. Lycée Mignet, Univ. of Aix-en-Provence; Dir. of Internal Trade, Ministry of Industry and Trade 1951–59; Dir. of Industrial Expansion, Ministry of Industry 1959–65; Dir.-Gen. Chamber of Commerce and Industry of Paris 1965–77, Hon. Dir.-Gen. 1985–; Chair. Econ. and Social Cttee. for Corsica 1974–83; Conseiller d'Etat en Service extraordinaire 1976–79; Chair. Soc. du Marché d'Interêt national de Rungis 1977–81; Hon. Pres. Assoc. Nat. des docteurs en droit 1971–; Pres. Palais des congrès, Paris 1977–84, Institut du développement 1984–94; Vice-Pres. Groupement Nat. des Hypermarchés 1989–91; Pres. Egée France 1992–95, Institut de la Méditerranée 1994–; mem. Econ. and Social Council 1979– (Pres. 1984–94); Commdr. de la Légion d'honneur; Commdr. Légion d'honneur, Ordre nat. du Mérite, Ordre nat. du Mérite artisanal, Ordre nat. du Mérite commercial. *Address:* 7 rue Molitor, 75016 Paris; 11 boulevard du roi René, 13100 Aix-en-Provence, France.

ARRILLAGA, Josu, PH.D., D.SC., F.R.S.(N.Z.), F.I.E.E., F.I.E.E.E.; Spanish professor of electrical engineering; b. 21 Jan. 1934; s. of José María and María Mercedes Arrillaga; m. Greta Robinson 1968; two s. two d.; ed. in Spain and Univ. of Manchester Inst. of Science and Tech.; Industrial Engineer, ISOLUX, Spain 1955–59; A.E.I. Engineer, Manchester 1959–61; Research student UMIST 1961–66; Lecturer Salford Univ. 1966–67; Lecturer and Sr. Lecturer, UMIST 1967–75, Head Power Systems and High Voltage 1970–75; Prof. of Electrical Eng., Univ. of Canterbury, N.Z. 1975–, Head Dept. of Electrical and Electronic Eng. 1986–; Johns Hopkins prize, I.E.E. 1975. *Publications:* Computer Modelling of Power Systems, Power System Harmonics, HVDC Transmission, Computer Analysis of Power Systems, Power System Harmonic Analysis; 230 technical articles. *Leisure interest:* gardening. *Address:* 2/77 Hinau Street, Christchurch 4, New Zealand. *Telephone:* Christchurch 3439893.

ARRINDELL, Sir Clement Athelston, G.C.M.G., G.C.V.O., Q.C.; St. Christopher and Nevis civil servant and lawyer; b. 16 April 1932, St. Kitts, West Indies; s. of George E. Arrindell and Hilda I. Arrindell; m. Evelyn Eugenia O'Loughlin 1967; ed. St. Kitts-Nevis Grammar School (Island Scholar 1948) and Lincoln's Inn, London; practising barrister-at-law 1959–66; Dist. Magistrate 1966–74; Chief Magistrate 1975–77; Puisne Judge 1978–81; Gov. of St. Kitts-Nevis 1981–83; Gov.-Gen. of St Christopher and Nevis 1983–95. *Leisure interests:* gardening, piano playing, classical music. *Address:* The Lark, Bird Rock, St. Christopher and Nevis, West Indies.

ARRON, Henck Alphonsus Eugène; Suriname politician; b. 25 April 1936, Paramaribo; s. of J. S. Arron and Mrs. J. Arron-Halfhide; m. Antoinette Emelie Francis Leeuwin 1963; worked at Bank of Amsterdam, Netherlands; joined staff of Vervuurts (now Hakrin) Bank, Surinam; mem. Parl. 1963–80; Chair. Nationale Partij Surinam 1970–80; Minister of Finance in pre-independence govt. 1973–77; Prime Minister and Minister of Gen. Affairs and Foreign Affairs 1973–80 (deposed in coup); mem. Supreme Council 1985–87; Vice-Pres. and Prime Minister 1988–90; arrested Aug. 1980, released 1981; Man. Dir. Surinaamse Volkscredietbank 1982. *Leisure interests:* fishing, reading, music, pottery. *Address:* c/o Office of the Vice-President, Paramaribo, Suriname.

ARROW, Kenneth J., PH.D.; American professor of economics; b. 23 Aug. 1921, New York; s. of Harry I. and Lillian Arrow; m. Selma Schweitzer 1947; two s.; ed. The City College, Columbia Univ.; Capt. U.S. A.A.F. 1942–46; Research Assoc. Cowles Comm. for Research in Econ., Univ. of Chicago 1947–49; Asst. Assoc. and Prof. of Econs., Statistics and Operations Research, Stanford Univ., 1949–68; Prof. of Econs. Harvard Univ., 1968–79; Prof. of Econs. and Operations Research, Stanford Univ., 1979–91, Prof. Emer. 1991–; mem. N.A.S., American Acad. of Arts and Sciences, American Phil. Soc., Finnish Acad. of Sciences, British Acad., Inst. of Medicine, Pontifical Acad. of Social Sciences; Pres. Int. Soc. for Inventory Research 1983–90, Int. Econ. Asscn., Econometric Soc., American Econ. Asscn., Soc. for Social Choice and Welfare; Dir. various cos.; Hon. LL.D. (City Univ., Univ. of Chicago, Washington Univ., Univ. of Pennsylvania); Hon. Dr. of Social and Econ. Sciences (Vienna); Hon. Sc.D. (Columbia Univ.) 1973; D.Soc.-Sci. (Yale) 1974; Hon. Dr. (Univ. René Descartes) 1974; Hon. LL.D. (Hebrew Univ. Jerusalem) 1975, Hon. D. Pol. Sci. (Helsinki) 1976, Dr. h.c. (Univ. Aix-Marseille III) 1985, D.Litt. (Cambridge) 1985, D. Univ. (Uppsala) 1995; Nobel Memorial Prize in Econ. Science 1972; Order of the Rising Sun (Japan); John Bates Clark Medal; Von Neumann Prize; Medal of Univ. of Paris 1998. *Publications:* Social Choice and Individual Values 1951, 1963, Studies in the Mathematical Theory of Inventory and Production (with S. Karlin and H. Scarf) 1958, Studies in Linear and Nonlinear Programming (with L. Hurwicz and H. Uzawa) 1958, A Time Series Analysis of Inter-industry Demands (with M. Hoffenberg) 1959, Public Investment, The Rate of Return and Optimal Fiscal Policy (with M. Kurz) 1970, Essays in the Theory of Risk-Bearing 1971, General Competitive Analysis (with F. H. Hahn) 1971, The Limits of Organization 1973, Studies in Resource Allocation Processes (with L. Hurwicz) 1977, Collected Papers 1983–85, Social Choice and Multicriterion Decision Making (with H. Raynaud) 1985; about 200 articles in learned journals. *Leisure interests:* walking, music. *Address:* Department of Economics, Stanford Univ., Stanford, CA 94305-6072 (Office); 580 Constanzo Street, Stanford, CA 94305, U.S.A. (Home). *Telephone:* (650) 723 9165 (Office). *Fax:* (650) 725-5702 (Office).

ARSENIS, Gerassimos; Greek politician and economist; b. 1931, Cephalonia; m. Louka Katseli; three s. one d.; ed. Univ. of Athens and Massachusetts Inst. of Tech.; worked for United Nations 1960; Dir. Dept. of Econ. Studies, OECD Research Centre 1964–66, Sr. Official, Prebisch Group, UN 1966–73; Dir. UNCTAD 1973; Gov. Bank of Greece 1981–84; Minister of Nat. Economy 1982–84, of Finance and Nat. Economy 1984–85, of Merchant Marine June–July 1985, of Defence 1993–96, of Education and Religious Affairs 1996–; expelled from PASOK 1986; f. Democratic Initiative Group 1987, Leader 1987–89; returned to PASOK 1989, mem. Exec. Bureau 1990–; M.P. for Athens Dist. 1990–. *Address:* Ministry of Education and Religious Affairs, Odos Metropoleos 15, 105 57 Athens; 15 Valaoritou Street, 106 71 Athens, Greece. *Telephone:* (01) 3230461.

ARTEH GHALIB, Omar; Somali politician; b. 1930, Hargeisa; s. of the late Arteh Ghalib and Sahra Sheikh Hassan; m. Shakri Jirdeh Hussein 1954; six s. six d.; ed. St. Paul's Coll., Cheltenham, U.K. and Univ. of Bristol; Teacher 1946–49; Headmaster, various elementary schools 1949–54; Vice-Principal, Intermediate School, Sheikh, Somalia 1954–56; Principal, Intermediate School, Gabileh 1958; Officer in charge of Adult Educ. 1959; District Commr. in Public Admin. 1960–61; First Sec. Somali Embassy, Moscow 1961–62; Rapporteur, Special Cttee. on South-West Africa, UN 1962–63; Counsellor, Perm. Mission of Somalia at UN 1964; Amb. to Ethiopia 1965–68; mem. Somali Nat. Assembly 1969; Sec. of State for Foreign Affairs 1969–76; Minister of Culture and Higher Education 1976–78, in the President's Office 1978–80; mem. Cttee. for Social and Political Thought 1976–; Speaker, People's Ass. 1982–91; Prime Minister of Somalia 1991; attended numerous OAU Summit and Ministerial Confs.; numerous awards and decorations. *Publications include:* Back from the Lion of Judah. *Leisure interests:* reciting the Koran, writing, poetry, horse-riding, social welfare activities. *Address:* c/o Office of the President, People's Palace, Mogadishu, Somalia.

ARTÉS-GÓMEZ, Mariano; Spanish professor of mechanics; b. 5 March 1947, Murcia; s. of Mariano Artés and Elisa Gómez; m. María José Caselles 1973; three s.; ed. Universidad Politécnica de Madrid, Int. Centre for Theoretical Physics, Trieste; Asst. Prof. of Mechanics, Universidad Politécnica de Madrid 1971–78, Assoc. Prof. 1979–80; Prof. Universidad de Oviedo 1980–81; Prof. and Head of Dept. of Applied Math., Universidad Nacional de Educación a Distancia 1981–, Vice-Rector for Research 1986, Dean of Faculty of Industrial Eng. 1987, Rector 1987–96; mem. Asoc. Española de Informática y Automática, Asoc. Española de Ingeniería Mecánica, Soc. for Research into Higher Educ. (U.K.); Premio Citema 1975, Premio Extraordinario de Doctorado 1977, Laurel de Murcia 1987. *Publications:* El Papel Instrumental de la Informática en el Proceso Educativo 1975, Dinámica de Sistemas 1979, Mecánica 1982, numerous articles on informatics in educ. and applied mechanics. *Leisure interests:* music, reading. *Address:* Universidad Nacional de Educación a Distancia, Ciudad Universitaria, 28040 Madrid, Spain. *Telephone:* (1) 398 6420. *Fax:* (1) 398 6536.

ARTHUIS, Jean Raymond Francis Marcel; French politician; b. 7 Oct. 1944, Saint-Martin du Bois, Maine-et-Loire; s. of Raymond Arthuis and Marthe Cotin; m. Brigitte Lafont 1971; one s. one d.; ed. Coll. Saint-Michel, Château-Gontier, Ecole Supérieure de Commerce, Nantes and Inst. d'Etudes Politiques, Paris; chartered accountant, Paris 1971–86; Mayor of Château-Gontier 1971–; mem. Conseil, Gen., Mayenne, Château-Gontier canton 1976–, Pres. 1992–; Senator from Mayenne (Centrist Group) 1983–86, 1988–95; Sec. of State, Ministry of Social Affairs and Employment 1986–87, Ministry of Econ., Finance and Privatization 1987–88; Spokesman on Budget in Senate 1992–95; Minister of Econ. Devt. and Planning May–Aug. 1995, of Econ. and Finance 1995–97; Vice-Pres. Force Démocrate (fmrly. Centre des démocrates sociaux) 1995–; Chevalier du Mérite Agricole. *Publications:* Justice sinistrée, Démocratie en danger (co-author) 1991, Les Délocalisations et l'emploi 1993, Dans les coulisses de Bercy. Le Cinquième pouvoir 1998. *Address:* Mairie, 53200 Château-Gontier (Office); Conseil général de la Mayenne, 39 rue Mazagran, BP 1429, 53014 Laval cédex (Office); 8 rue René Homo, 53200 Château-Gontier, France (Home).

ARTHUR, James Greig, PH.D., F.R.S.C., F.R.S.; Canadian professor of mathematics; b. 18 May 1944, Hamilton; s. of John G. Arthur and Katherine (née Scott) Arthur; m. Dorothy P. Helm 1972; two s.; ed. Univ. of Toronto, Yale Univ.; Instructor Princeton Univ. 1970–72; Asst. Prof. Yale Univ.

1972–76; Prof. Duke Univ. 1976–79, Univ. of Toronto 1979–; Sloan Fellow 1975–77, Stracie Memorial Fellowship 1982–84; Synge Award in Math. 1987. *Publications:* numerous scientific papers and articles. *Leisure interests:* tennis, squash, golf. *Address:* 23 Woodlawn Avenue West, Toronto, Ont., M4V 1G6, Canada.

ARTHUR, Owen; Barbadian politician and economist; b. 17 Oct. 1949; m. Beverley Jeanne Batchelor 1978; ed. Harrison Coll., Univ. of W. Indies, Cave Hill, Univ. of W. Indies, Mona; Research Asst., Univ. of W. Indies, Jamaica 1973; Asst. Econ. Planner, Chief Econ. Planner Nat. Planning Agency, Jamaica 1974–79; Dir. of Econs. Jamaica Bauxite Inst. 1979–81; Chief Project Analyst Ministry of Finance, Barbados 1981–83; lecturer Dept. of Man. Univ. of W. Indies, Cave Hill 1986, Resident Fellow 1993; Senator 1983–; Parl. Sec. Ministry of Finance 1985–86; Chair. Barbados Labour Party (BLP) July 1993–; Prime Minister of Barbados, Minister of Defence and Security, Finance and Econ. Affairs and for the Civil Service Sept. 1994–. *Publications:* The Commercialisation of Technology in Jamaica 1979, Energy and Mineral Resource Development in the Jamaican Bauxite Industry 1981, The IMF and Economic Stabilisation Policies in Barbados 1984. *Leisure interests:* gardening, cooking. *Address:* Office of the Prime Minister, Government Headquarters, Bay Street, St. Michael, Barbados. *Telephone:* 426-3179. *Fax:* 436-9280.

ARTHURS, Harry William, O.C., F.R.S.C., LL.M.; Canadian barrister, professor of law and academic; b. 9 May 1935, Toronto; s. of Leon Arthurs and Ellen H. (Dworkin) Arthurs; m. Penelope Geraldine Ann Milnes 1974; two s.; ed. Univ. of Toronto, Harvard Univ., U.S.A.; Asst., Assoc. then full Prof. of Law, Osgoode Hall Law School, York Univ., Ont. 1961–, Dean of Law School 1972–77, Pres. York Univ. 1985–92, Emer. Pres. 1992–, Univ. Prof. 1995–; Assoc. Canada Inst. of Advanced Research 1995–98; mediator and arbitrator in labour disputes 1962–85; author, lecturer 1961–; Bencher, Law Soc. of Upper Canada 1979–83; mem. Econ Council of Canada 1978–81; Chair. Consultative Group, Research and Educ. in Law 1980–84; Chair. Council of Ont. Univs. 1987–89; Hon. LL.D. (Sherbrooke, McGill and Brock Univs., Law Soc. of Upper Canada), Hon. D. Litt (Lethbridge). *Publications:* Industrial Relations and Labour Law in Canada (co-author) 1984, Law and Learning (Report on Legal Research and Education in Canada) 1984, Without the Law: Administrative Justice and Legal Pluralism in Nineteenth Century England 1985. *Address:* Osgoode Law School, York University, 4700 Keele Street, North York, Ont., M3J 1P3 (Office); 11 Hillcrest Park, Toronto, Ont., M4X 1E8, Canada (Home). *Telephone:* (416) 736 5407 (Office). *Fax:* (416) 736 5736.

ARTSCHWAGER, Richard Ernst; American artist; b. 26 Dec. 1923, Washington, D.C.; m. 1st Elfriede Wejmelka 1947 (divorced 1970); one d.; m. 2nd Catherine Kord 1972 (divorced 1989); m. 3rd. Molly O'Gorman (divorced 1993); one s. one d.; m. 4th Ann Sebring 1995; ed. Cornell Univ.; studied with Amedee Ozenfant, New York 1949–50; baby photographer 1950–53; cabinet-maker 1953–65; has exhibited with Richard Bellamy and Leo Castelli also many group and one-man shows in U.S.A. and Europe 1963–. *Publication:* The Hydraulic Door Check 1967. *Address:* P.O. Box 12, Hudson, NY 12534, U.S.A.

ARTZT, Alice Josephine, B.A.; American classical guitarist and writer; b. 16 March 1943, Philadelphia, Pa.; d. of Harriett Green Artzt and Maurice G. Artzt; ed. Columbia Univ. and studied composition with Darius Milhaud and guitar with Julian Bream, Ida Presti and Alexandre Lagoya; taught guitar at Mannes Coll. of Music, New York 1966–69, Trenton State Univ. 1977–80; worldwide tours as soloist 1969–; f. Alice Artzt Guitar Trio (with M. Rutscho and R. Burley) 1989; tours in duo with R. Burley; mem. Bd. of Dirs. Guitar Foundation of America (Chair. 1986–89); several Critics' Choice awards. *Recordings include:* The Glory of the Guitar, Virtuoso Romantic Guitar, Tributes, Variations, Passacaglias and Chaconnes, American Music of the Stage and Screen. *Publications:* The Art of Practicing, The International GFA Guitarists' Cookbook (Ed.), Rythmic Mastery 1997; numerous articles in guitar and music periodicals. *Leisure interests:* hi-fi, travel, Chaplin movies. *Address:* 180 Claremont Avenue, Apartment 31, New York, NY 10027; 51 Hawthorne Avenue, Princeton, NJ 08540, U.S.A. *Telephone:* (212) 749-2027 (New York); (609) 921-6629 (Princeton). *Fax:* (212) 666-8798 (New York); (609) 924-0091 (Princeton).

ARTZT, Edwin Lewis, B.J.; American business executive; b. 15 April 1930, New York; s. of William Artzt and Ida Artzt; m. Ruth N. Martin 1950; one s. four d.; ed. Univ. of Oregon; Account Exec. Glasser Gailey Advertising Agency, Los Angeles 1952–53; joined Proctor & Gamble Co., Cincinnati 1953, Brand Man. Advertising Dept. 1956–58, Assoc. Brand Promotion Man. 1958–60, Brand Promotion Man. 1960, 1962–65, Copy Man. 1960–62, Advertisement Man. Paper Products Div. 1965–68, Man. Products Food Div. 1968–69, Vice-Pres. 1969, Vice-Pres., Acting Man. Coffee Div. 1970, Vice-Pres., Group Exec. 1970–75, Dir. 1972–75, 1980–95; Group Vice-Pres. Procter & Gamble Co., Europe, Belgium 1975–80; Pres. Procter & Gamble Int. 1980–89, Chair., C.E.O. 1995–; Vice-Chair. Procter & Gamble Co. 1980–89, Chair. 1989–95, C.E.O. 1989; Exec. Dir. Barilla G.E.R. SpA 1995–. *Address:* Procter & Gamble Co., 1 Procter and Gamble Plaza, Cincinnati, OH 45202, U.S.A.

ARUTIUNIAN, Alexander Grigor; Armenian composer; b. 23 Sept. 1920, Yerevan; s. of Gregori and Eleanor Arutiunian; m. Irina Odenova Tamara 1950; one s. one d.; ed. Yerevan Conservatory and Workshop at House of Armenian Culture, Moscow; mem. CPSU 1952–91; Artistic Dir. Armenian Philharmonic 1954–; Prof., Yerevan Conservatory 1962–; U.S.S.R. State Prize 1949, People's Artist of the U.S.S.R. 1970, Armenian State Prizes 1970, 1986, Kentucky Coll. Orpheus Award 1983, Khachaturian Prize 1986. *Compositions include:* Cantata on the Motherland 1949, Trumpet concerto 1950, Concertino for piano and orchestra 1951, Symphony 1957, Legend of the Armenian People for soloists, choir and orchestra 1961, French Horn concerto 1962, Concertino for cello 1964, Sinfonietta 1966, Sayat-Nova (opera) 1969, vocal series Memorial to Mother 1970, Piano concertos 1971, 1983, Reverend Beggars (musical comedy) 1972, Theme and Variations for trumpet and orchestra, Rhapsody for piano, percussion and string orchestra 1974, Oboe concerto 1977, Symphony for choir and percussion 1982, Armenian Scenes (brass quintet) 1984, concertos for flute and string orchestra 1985, for violin and string orchestra 1988, for trombone and orchestra 1990, for tuba and orchestra 1991, Suite for clarinet, violin and piano 1992, Rhapsody for trumpet and wind orchestra 1992, Suite for oboe, clarinet and piano 1994; chamber and vocal music, music for theatre and cinema. *Leisure interest:* memoirs. *Address:* Demirchian Str. 25, Apt. 19, 375002 Yerevan, Armenia. *Telephone:* (3742) 524785. *Fax:* (3742) 151938.

ARUTYUNYAN, Gagik Garushevich; Armenian politician; b. 1948, Gekhashen; ed. Yerevan Univ.; lecturer, Yerevan Inst. of Industry 1975–77; in Yugoslavia 1977–78; on staff Cen. Cttee. Armenian CP 1982–88; Head of Dept. 1988–90; joined Nationalist opposition; Deputy Chair. Armenian Supreme Soviet 1990–91; Vice-Pres. of Armenia Oct. 1991–; Acting Chair. Council of Ministers (Prime Minister) 1991–92; Chair. Constitutional Court 1995–. *Address:* Constitutional Court, Yerevan, Armenia.

ARUTYUNYAN, Khosrov; Armenian politician; b. 30 May 1948, Yerevan; m.; two c.; ed. Yerevan Polytech. Inst.; Head of Lab., Head of Dept., Dir. Ashtarak branch, Byurokan Observatory 1977–82; lecturer, Yerevan Polytechnic Inst. 1978–82; Dir. knitted goods factory 1983–87, Chair. Municipal Cttee. Charentsavan dist. 1991; mem. Armenian Supreme Soviet 1990–92; Chair. Comm. on problems of local self-governing 1990–92; mem. Parl. 1993–; Prime Minister of Armenia 1992–93; Deputy Chair. State Legal Comm., Adviser to Prime Minster 1995–; Pres. Nat. Ass. *Address:* National Assembly, 19 Marshal Bughramyan Avenue, 375095 Yerevan, Armenia. *Telephone:* 524614. *Fax:* 529826.

ARYAL, Krishna Raj, M.ED., M.A.; Nepalese politician, educationist and diplomatist; b. Dec. 1928, Kathmandu; m. Shanta Laxmi 1956; one s.; ed. Durbar High School, Tri-Chandra Coll., Allahabad Univ., India, Univ. of Oregon, U.S.A. Lecturer, Nat. Teachers' Training Centre 1954–56; Prof. Coll. of Educ., Dir. Publs. Govt. Educ. Devt. Project 1956–59; Ed. Education Quarterly 1956–59, Nabin Shikshya 1956–59; Founder, Admin. and Prin. Shri Ratna Rajya Laxmi Girls' Coll. 1961–71; Asst. Minister for Educ. 1971–72, Minister of State 1972–73, Minister 1973–75, Minister of Foreign Affairs 1975–79; Amb. to France also accred to Spain, Italy, Portugal and Israel and Perm. Dec. to UNESCO 1980–84; Chair. Asian Group and mem. Bureau Group 77, UNESCO 1982–83; Hon. mem. Raj Sabha 1985–90, Rastriya Panchayat (unicameral legis.) 1986–90; fmr. Sec. Cricket Asscn. of Nepal; Chair. Brahmacharya Ashram; Exec. mem. World Hindu Fed.; Gorakha Dakhinbahu (1st Class) Grand Cordon of Yugoslav Star, Order of the Rising Sun, 1st Class (Japan), Grand Officier, Order Nat. du Mérite (France), Order of Civil Merit, 1st Class (Spain), and other decorations. *Publications include:* Monarchy in the Making of Nepal (in English), Education for the Development of Nepal (in English), The Science of Education (Nepali). *Address:* 17/93 Gaihiri Dhara, Kathmandu, Nepal (Home).

ARZU IRIGOYEN, Alvaro Enrique; Guatemalan politician; leader Partido de Avanzada Nacional (PAN); Pres. of Guatemala Jan. 1996–. *Address:* Office of the President, Palacio Nacional, Guatemala City, Guatemala.

ARZUMANYAN, Aleksander Robertovich; Armenian politician and diplomatist; b. 24 Dec. 1959, Yerevan; m.; two c.; ed. Yerevan State Univ.; engineer Yerevan Research Inst. of Automatic Systems of City Man. 1985–88; Dir. Information Cen. Armenian Nat. Movt. 1989–90; asst. Chair. of Supreme Council of Armenia 1990–91; Rep. of Armenia to N. America 1991–92; Chargé d'Affaires to U.S.A. 1992–93; Perm. Rep. to UN 1992–; rank of Amb. 1992; took part and headed dels. of Armenia to int. meetings; elected Deputy Chair. 49th Gen. UN Ass., concurrently mem. Gen. Cttee. of UN and mem. Appellation Cttee. on resolutions of Admin. Court of UN 1994; Chair. Regional Group for E. Europe 1992–96; Minister of Foreign Affairs of Armenia 1996–98. *Address:* c/o Mashal Bagramyan str. 10, 375019 Yerevan, Armenia.

ASADOV, Eduard Arkadevich; Russian poet; b. 7 Sept. 1923, Merv, Turkmen S.S.R.; s. of Arkady Asadov and Lidya Asadova; m. 2nd Galina Asadova 1961; one s.; ed. Gorky Literary Inst., Moscow; Red Army 1941, seriously wounded and lost sight 1944; started publishing 1948; mem. CPSU 1951–91; ed. Gorky Inst. of World Literature Moscow. *Publications:* Again into the Line (Verse) 1948, Bright Roads 1951, Snowy Evening 1956, The Soldiers Have Returned from the War 1957, Galina 1960, Lyrical Limits 1962, I Love Forever 1965, Be Happy, Dreamers 1966, Isle of Romance 1969, Goodness 1972, I Fight, I Believe, I Love 1983, The Dream of Centuries 1985, The Highest Duty 1986, Collected Works (3 vols.) 1987–88, Fates and Hearts 1989, Letter from the Battle Front 1993, Never Surrender, People 1997. *Leisure interests:* music, especially gypsy songs, books, collecting funny names of streets and people. *Address:* Astrakhansky per., 5, Apt. 78, Moscow 129010, Russia. *Telephone:* 2801458.

ASAMOAH, Obed Y., J.S.D.; Ghanaian politician and lawyer; b. 6 Feb. 1936, Likpe Bala, Volta Region; s. of William and Monica Asamoah; m. Yvonne Wood 1964; two s. one d.; ed. Achimota Secondary School, Woolwich Polytechnic, London, King's Coll. London and Columbia Univ. New York; called to the Bar, Middle Temple, London 1960; upon return to Ghana practised as solicitor and advocate of Supreme Court of Ghana; lecturer, Faculty of Law, Univ. of Ghana, Legon 1965–69; fmr. Chair. Bd. of Dirs. of Ghana Film Industry Corpn., Ghana Bauxite Co.; mem. Constituent Ass. which drafted Constitution for Second Repub. of Ghana 1969; elected to Parl. (Nat. Alliance of Liberals) 1969; mem. Constituent Ass. which drafted third Republican Constitution 1979; Gen. Sec. United Nat. Convention (UNC) 1979, All People's Party (APP) 1981; Sec. for Foreign Affairs 1982–93; Minister of Foreign Affairs 1993; Attorney-Gen. and Minister of Justice Nov. 1993–; mem. Ghana Bar Asscn.; has served on several int. and public. orgs. *Publications:* articles in legal journals. *Leisure interests:* reading, farming. *Address:* Ministry of Justice, Accra, Ghana.

ASANBAYEV, Erik Magzumovich, D.ECON.; Kazakhstan politician; b. 1936, Baygabul, Turgai Dist.; m.; two c.; ed. Kazak Univ.; economist, Ministry of Finance 1958–59; lecturer Kazak Univ. 1959–63; Head of Dept., Inst. of Econs. 1963–67; Head of Dept., Deputy Minister of Finance 1967–75; mem. CPSU 1967–91; sr. posts in CP and Govt. 1975–88; Deputy Chair. Council of Ministers 1988–89; Sec. Cen. Cttee. Kazakh CP 1989–90; Chair. Kazak S.S.R. Supreme Soviet 1991; joined Socialist Party of Kazakstan Aug. 1991; Vice-Pres. Kazakstan 1991–96; Amb. to Germany 1996–. *Address:* House of the Government, Square of the Republic 64, 480091 Almaty, Kazakstan.

ASANGONO, Alejandro Evuna Owono; Equatorial Guinean politician and diplomatist; b. 23 May 1944, Nkumekien-Yebecon; s. of Martin Owono and Isabel Asangono; m. Julia Andeme Evuna 1967; two s. three d.; ed. School of Admin., then School of Diplomacy, Santa Isabel (now Malabo); served as Admin. Officer in Ministry of Interior 1966, 1969–71, also Ministry of Education 1967–68; First Sec. Perm. Mission to UN. 1972–74; Amb. to Ethiopia 1975; Roving Amb. and Envoy 1976–77; Perm. Rep. to UN 1977–80; Amb. to Spain 1980–81; Sec.-Gen. Ministry of Foreign Affairs and Co-operation 1982–85; Minister-Sec.-Gen., Prime Minister's Office 1986–89; Minister of State for Missions 1990; mem. Cen. Cttee. Partido Democrático 1990–. *Leisure interests:* hunting, farming. *Address:* c/o Presidencia de la República, Malabo, Equatorial Guinea.

ASANO, Teiji; Japanese business executive; b. 1906; ed. Tohoku Imperial Univ.; joined shipbuilding dept., Mitsui & Co. 1930; entered Tamano Shipyard Ltd. (predecessor of Mitsui Shipbuilding & Eng. Co. Ltd.) 1948; Man. Dir. Mitsui Shipbuilding & Eng. Co. 1958, Man. Dir. 1965, Vice-Pres. 1968, fmr. Chair. of Bd., Dir. and Counsellor 1973–76, Counsellor 1976–; Pres. Showa Aircraft Industry Co. Ltd. 1973–79, Chair. 1979. *Address:* c/o Mitsui Shipbuilding & Engineering Co. Ltd., 6-4, Tsukiji 5-chome, Chuo-ku, Tokyo, Japan. *Telephone:* 544-3000.

ASANTE, Samuel Kwadwo Boaten, LL.B., LL.M., J.S.D.; Ghanaian lawyer and international official; b. 11 May 1933, Asokore; s. of Daniel Y. Asante and Mary Baafi; m. Philomena Margaret Aidoo 1961; two s. three d.; ed. Achimota School, Univs. of Nottingham and London, and Yale Univ. Law School; State Attorney in the Ministry of Justice of Ghana 1960–61; Lecturer in Law and Acting Head of Law Dept., Univ. of Ghana 1961–65; Lecturer, Leeds Univ., U.K. 1965–66; Attorney World Bank, Washington, D.C. 1966–69; Adjunct Prof. of Law, Howard Univ. Law School, Washington, D.C. 1967–69; Solicitor-Gen. of Ghana 1969–74; mem. Arbitration Panel, Int. Cen. for Settlement of Investment Disputes, Washington, D.C. 1971–; Chair. Public Agreements Review Cttee. of Ghana 1972–77; Deputy Attorney-Gen. of Ghana 1974–77; Chief Legal Adviser, UN Comm. on Transnational Corpns., New York 1977–83, Dir. 1983–92; Dir. UN Legal Advisory Services for Devt. 1992–; Chair. Cttee. of Experts on Ghana Constitution 1991; Dir. Int. Third World Legal Studies Asscn., New York; mem. Bd. Dirs. Int. Devt. Law Inst., Rome; Taylor Lecturer, Lagos Univ. 1978; Consultant, Commonwealth Secr., African Devt. Bank and UNITAR; Guest Lecturer numerous univs. and institutions world-wide; Guest Fellow, Berkeley Coll., Yale Univ. 1964–65; fmr. Sterling, Fulbright and Aggrey Fellow; Fellow of World Acad. of Arts and Sciences 1975, Ghana Acad. of Arts and Sciences 1976; Visiting Fellow, Clare Hall, Cambridge Univ. 1978–79, Life mem.; Visiting Prof., Temple Univ. Law School, Philadelphia 1976; patron Int. Centre for Public Law, Inst. of Advanced Legal Studies, London Univ.; also Hon. Friend; mem. Int. Bar Asscn.; mem. Exec. Council, American Soc. of Int. Law 1979, mem. Gen. Legal Council, Ghana; mem. Advisory Bd., Foreign Investment Law Journal-ICSID Review; Ghana Book Award. *Publications:* Property Law and Social Goals in Ghana 1976, Transnational Investment Law and National Development 1979, and various articles in law journals. *Leisure interests:* tennis, golf, reading biographies. *Address:* United Nations, Room DC2-1320, New York, NY 10017, U.S.A. (Office); 412 Pinebrook Boulevard, New Rochelle, NY 10804, U.S.A. (Home).

ÅSBRINK, Erik, B.SC., B.A.; Swedish fmr. politician and business executive; b. 1 Feb. 1947, Stockholm; m. Anne-Marie Lindgren; three c.; ed. Univ. of Stockholm, Stockholm School of Economics; worked at Inst. for Soviet and E. European Econ. Affairs 1972; Nat. Inst. of Econ. Research 1972–74; Ministry of Finance 1974–76; Ministry of the Budget 1976–78; Research Sec., parl. group of Social Democratic Party (SDP) 1978–82; Under-Sec. of State, Ministry of Finance 1982–90; Minister for Fiscal and Financial Affairs, Ministry of Finance 1990–91, Minister of Finance 1996–; Man. Dir. Vasakronan AB 1993–, Pres. –1996; mem. Bd. 1st Nat. Pension Insurance Fund 1982–85; Chair. Lantbrukskredit AB 1983–85; Chair. State Housing Finance Corpn. 1984–85; Chair. Governing Bd. Sveriges Riksbank 1985–90; mem. Bd. 4th Nat. Pension Insurance Fund 1985–90; Vice-Chair. Systembolaget AB 1986–90; mem. Bd. AB Vin & Sprit AB (Swedish Wine and Spirits Corpn.) 1986–90, 1993–, AB Trav & Galopp 1989–90, Sparbanken Sverige AB 1991–93; Chair. Sparbanken Första 1992, Confortia AB 1993–, Swedish Bond Promotion 1993–; mem. Bd. ABB Investment Man. 1993–, Skandia-Banken 1994–, Swedish Concert Hall Foundation 1995–, SNS, Centre for Business and Policy Studies 1995–. *Address:* Ministry of Finance, Drottninggt. 21, 103 33 Stockholm, Sweden.

ÁSGRÍMSSON, Halldór; Icelandic politician; b. 8 Sept. 1947, Vopnafjörður; s. of Ásgrímur Halldórsson and Guðrún Ingólfsdóttir; ; m. Sigurjóna Sigurdardóttir; three d.; ed. Co-operative's Commercial Coll. and commerce univs. in Bergen and Copenhagen; Certified Public Accountant 1970; Lecturer in Auditing and Accounting, Univ. of Iceland 1973–75; mem. Parl. 1974–78, 1979–; mem. Bd. Cen. Bank of Iceland 1976–83, Chair. 1981–83; mem. Nordic Council 1977–78, 1979–83, 1991–95, Chair. 1982–83, Chair. Icelandic Del. 1982–83, mem. Presidium 1991–94, Chair. Liberal Group 1992–94; Minister of Fisheries 1983–91, of Nordic Co-operation 1985–87, 1995–, of Justice and Ecclesiastical Affairs 1988–89, of Foreign Affairs 1995–; Vice-Chair. Progressive Party 1980–94, Chair. 1994–; Vice-Pres. Liberal Int. 1994–; Kt. of Order of Falcon of Iceland. *Address:* c/o Progressive Party, P.O. Box 453, IS-121 Reykjavík, Iceland. *Telephone:* 562 4480. *Fax:* 562 3325.

ASH, Sir Eric Albert, Kt., C.B.E., PH.D., F.R.S., F.C.G.I., F.I.E.E., F.I.E.E.E., F.INST.P., F.ENG.; British professor of physics; b. 31 Jan. 1928, Berlin, Germany; s. of Walter Ash and Dorothea Ash (née Schwarz); m. Clare Babb 1954; five d.; ed. Univ. Coll. School and Imperial Coll., London; Research Fellow, Stanford Univ. 1952–54; Research Asst., Queen Mary Coll., London 1954–55; Research Engineer, Standard Telecommunications Labs. Ltd. 1955–63; Sr. Lecturer, Univ. Coll, London 1963–65, Reader 1965–67, Prof. of Electrical Eng. 1967-80, Pender Prof., and Head, Dept. of Electronic and Electrical Eng. 1980–85, Prof. of Electrical Eng. 1993–97, now Emer.; Rector, Imperial Coll., London 1985–93; Non-Exec. Dir. British Telecom 1987–93; Chair. BBC Science Advisory Cttee. 1987–, Chair. of Council, Vice-Pres. Royal Inst. 1995– (fmr. Sec., Man.); Trustee Science Museum 1987–, Wolfson Foundation 1988–; hon. degrees from Aston, Leicester, Edin., N.Y. Polytech., INPG Grenoble, Westminster, Sussex, Glasgow Univs. and Chinese Univ. of Hong Kong; Royal Medal (Royal Soc.) 1986; Nat. Order of Merit (France) 1990. *Publications:* papers on topics of physical electronics in various eng. and physics journals. *Leisure interests:* music, skiing, writing. *Address:* c/o Royal Society, 6 Carlton House Terrace, London, SW1Y 5AG, England.

ASH, Roy Lawrence, M.B.A.; American industrialist; b. 20 Oct. 1918, Los Angeles, Calif.; s. of Charles K. and Fay (Dickinson) Ash; m. Lila M. Hornbek 1943; three s. two d.; ed. Harvard Univ. Bank of America 1936–42, 1947–49; Private to Capt., U.S. A.F. 1942–46; Chief Financial Officer, Hughes Aircraft Co. 1949–53; Co-founder and Dir., Litton Industries Inc. 1953–72; Pres. 1961–72; mem. Bd. of Dirs. Bankamerica Corpn. 1968–72, 1976–91, Bank of America N.T. and S.A. 1964–72, 1978–91, Global Marine Inc. 1965–72, 1975–81, Pacific Mutual Life Insurance Co. 1965–72, Sara Lee Corpn. 1979–90; Los Angeles World Affairs Council 1968–72, (Pres. 1970–72), 1978–91; Chair. President's Advisory Council on Exec. Org. 1969–71; Asst. to the Pres. of the U.S.A. for Exec. Man. 1972–75; Dir. U.S. Office of Man. and Budget 1973–75; Chair. and Chief Exec. Officer, AM Int. 1976–81; Co-Chair. Japan-California Asscn. 1965–72, 1980–81; Vice-Chair. Los Angeles Olympic Organizing Cttee. 1979–84; mem. Bd. and Chair. L.A. Music Center Opera 1988–93; mem. The Business Roundtable 1977–81, The Conference Bd. 1977–, Bd. of U.S. Chamber of Commerce 1979–85; mem. Bd. of Trustees, California Inst. of Tech. 1967–72; Trustee, Cttee. for Econ. Devt. 1970–72, 1975–; Hon. LL.D. (Pepperdine) 1976; Kt. of Malta; Horatio Alger Award 1966. *Address:* 655 Funchal Road, Los Angeles, CA 90077, U.S.A. (Home).

ASHBERY, John Lawrence, M.A.; American author and critic; b. 28 July 1927, Rochester, N.Y.; s. of Chester F. and Helen L. Ashbery; ed. Deerfield Acad., Mass., Harvard Coll., Columbia and New York Univs.; copywriter, Oxford Univ. Press, New York 1951–54, McGraw-Hill Book Co. 1954–55; lived in France 1955–57, 1958–65; art critic European edn. New York Herald Tribune 1960–65; Paris corresp. Art News, N.Y. 1964–65, Exec. Ed. 1965–72; art critic, Art International, Lugano 1961–64; ed. Locus Solus 1960–62, Art and Literature, Paris 1963–66; Prof. of English and co-dir. MFA program in Creative Writing, Brooklyn Coll., N.Y. 1974–90; Poetry ed. Partisan Review, New York 1976–80; art critic, New York (magazine) 1978–80, Newsweek 1980–85; Chancellor American Acad. of Poets 1988–; leader, Foundation d'Art de la Napoule 1989; Charles P. Stevenson Prof. Bard Coll. 1990–; recipient of numerous awards and honours, including Pulitzer Prize 1975, MacArthur Award 1985. *Publications include:* non-fiction: Fairfield Porter 1983, R. B. Kitaj (with others) 1983, Reported Sightings: Art Chronicles 1957–1987 1989; novel: A Nest of Ninnies (with J. Schuyler) 1969; plays: Three Plays 1978; *poems include:* April Galleons 1987, Flow Chart 1992, Hotel Lautréamont 1992, And the Stars were Shining 1994, Can You Hear, Bird 1995. *Address:* c/o George Borchardt Incorporated, 136 East 57th

Street, New York, NY 10022; Bard College, Department of Languages and Literature, Annandale On Hudson, NY 12504, U.S.A.

ASHBURTON, 7th Baron, cr. 1835, **Sir John Francis Harcourt Baring,** Kt., K.G., K.C.V.O., M.A., F.I.B.; British merchant banker; b. 2 Nov. 1928, London; s. of 6th Baron Ashburton and Hon. Doris Mary Therese Harcourt; m. 1st Susan Mary Renwick 1955 (dissolved 1984); two s. two d.; 2nd Sarah Crewe 1987; ed. Eton Coll. and Trinity Coll., Oxford; Chair. Barings PLC 1985–89 (Dir. (non-exec.) 1989–94), Baring Bros. & Co. Ltd. 1974–89 (a Man. Dir. 1955–74); Dir. Royal Insurance Co. Ltd. 1964–82, (Deputy Chair. 1975–82), Dir. Outwich Investment Trust Ltd. 1965–86 (Chair. 1968–86), British Petroleum Co. 1982–95 (Chair. 1992–95); Dir. Dunlop Holdings 1981–84, Bank of England 1983–91, Baring Stratton Investment Trust PLC 1986–98 (Chair. 1986–98), Jaguar PLC 1989–91; mem. British Transport Docks Bd. 1966–71; Vice-Pres. British Bankers Asscn. 1977–81; mem. Pres.'s Cttee. CBI 1976–79, Gen. Council CBI 1976–80; Chair. Accepting Houses Cttee. 1977–81, NEDC Cttee. on Finance for Industry 1980–87; Pres. Overseas Bankers Club 1977–78; Rhodes Trustee 1970–, Chair. 1987–, Trustee Nat. Gallery 1981–87; Trustee and Hon. Treas. Police Foundation 1989–; mem. Exec. Cttee. Nat. Art Collections Fund 1989–; mem. Council Baring Foundation 1971–98, Chair. 1987–98; mem. Southampton Univ. Devt. Trust 1986–96 (Chair. 1989–96); Winchester Cathedral Trustee 1989– (Chair. 1993–); Lord Warden of the Stannaries, Duchy of Cornwall 1990–94, Receiver-Gen. 1974–90; High Steward Winchester Cathedral 1991–; D.L. Hants. 1994–; Fellow, Eton Coll. 1982–97; Hon. Fellow, Hertford Coll., Oxford 1976, Trinity Coll., Oxford 1989. *Address:* 3 Stanley House, 13 Stanley Crescent, London, W11 2NA; Lake House, Northington, Alresford, Hants., SO24 9TG, England.

ASHBY, Michael Farries, C.B.E., PH.D., F.R.S.; British professor of engineering materials; b. 20 Nov. 1935; s. of Lord Ashby and Elizabeth Helen Farries; m. Maureen Stewart 1962; two s. one d.; ed. Campbell Coll., Belfast, Queens' Coll., Cambridge; Asst., Univ. of Göttingen, Fed. Repub. of Germany 1962–65; Asst. Prof., Harvard Univ., U.S.A. 1965–69, Prof. of Metallurgy 1969–73; Prof. of Eng. Materials, Univ. of Cambridge 1973–89, Royal Soc. Research Prof., Dept. of Eng. 1989–; Ed. Acta Metallurgica 1974–96, Progress in Materials Science 1995–; mem. Akad. der Wissenschaften zu Göttingen 1980; Hon. M.A. (Harvard) 1969. *Publications:* Deformation Mechanism Maps 1982, Engineering Materials (vol. 1) 1989, (vol. 2) 1996, Materials Selection in Design 1992, Cellular Solids 1997. *Leisure interests:* music, design. *Address:* 51 Maids Causeway, Cambridge, CB5 8DE, England. *Telephone:* (01223) 303015.

ASHCROFT, John, J.D.; American politician; b. 9 May 1942, Chicago; m. Janet Elise; two s. one d.; ed. Yale Univ. and Univ. of Chicago; admitted, Missouri State Bar, U.S. Supreme Court Bar; Assoc. Prof. S.W. Missouri State Univ. Springfield; legal practice, Springfield, Mo. until 1973; State Auditor, Missouri 1973–75, Asst. Attorney-Gen. 1975–77, Attorney-Gen. 1977–84; Gov. of Missouri 1985–93; Senator from Missouri 1995–; recordings as gospel singer; Republican. *Publications:* College Law for Business (with Janet Elise), It's the Law 1979. *Address:* 316 Hart Senate Office Building, Washington, DC 20510, U.S.A.

ASHDOWN, Jeremy John Durham (Paddy); British politician; b. 27 Feb. 1941; s. of John W. R. D. Ashdown and Lois A. Ashdown; m. Jane Courtenay 1961; one s. one d.; ed. Bedford School; served Royal Marines 1959–71, Captain R.M.; joined Diplomatic Service, First Sec. Mission to U.N., Geneva 1971–76; Commercial Man.'s Dept., Westland Group 1976–78; Senior Man., Morlands Ltd. 1978–81; employee Dorset Co. Council 1982–83; Parl. spokesman for Trade and Industry 1983–86; Liberal/SDP Alliance spokesman on Education and Science 1987; Liberal M.P. for Yeovil 1983–88, Liberal Democrat M.P. for Yeovil 1988–; Leader Liberal Democrats 1988–99. *Publications:* Citizen's Britain: a Radical Agenda for the 1990s 1989, Beyond Westminster 1994. *Leisure interests:* walking, gardening, wine making. *Address:* Vane Cottage, Norton sub Hamdon, Somerset, TA14 6SG, England. *Telephone:* (01935) 882000.

ASHE, Sir Derick Rosslyn, K.C.M.G., M.A.; British diplomatist (retd.); b. 20 Jan. 1919, Guildford, Surrey; s. of Frederick Allen and Rosalind Ashe (née Mitchell); m. Rissa Guinness (née Parker) 1957; one s. one d.; ed. Bradfield Coll., Trinity Coll., Oxford; served in H.M. Forces 1940–46, mentioned in despatches 1945; Second Sec. Control Comm. for Germany 1947–49; Private Sec. to Perm. Under-Sec. of State for German Section, Foreign Office 1950–53; First Sec. La Paz 1953–55; Foreign Office 1955–57; First Sec. Information, Madrid 1957–61; Foreign Office 1961–62; Counsellor, Head of Chancery, Addis Ababa 1962–64, Havana 1964–66; Head of Security Dept., Foreign and Commonwealth Office 1966–69; Minister, Tokyo 1969–71; Amb. to Romania 1972–75, to Argentina 1975–77 (withdrawn Jan. 1976); alternate leader of U.K. del. to Disarmament Conf., Geneva 1977–79, to UN Special Session on Disarmament, New York 1977–78; Kt. Order of Orange-Nassau. *Leisure interests:* gardening, antiques. *Address:* Dalton House, Hurstbourne Tarrant, Andover, Hampshire, England. *Telephone:* (01264) 736276.

ASHER, Jane; British actress, writer and businesswoman; b. 5 April 1946; m. Gerald Scarfe (q.v.); two s. one d.; has appeared in numerous films, on TV and the London stage, and has written several best-selling books; Proprietor Jane Asher Party Cakes Shop and Sugarcraft 1990–; designer, consultant for Sainsbury's cakes 1992–; Pres. Nat. Autistic Soc.; Spokesperson and Consultant to McVities 1993–. *Films include:* Greengage Summer, Masque of the Red Death, Alfie, Deep End, Henry the Eighth and his Six Wives, Success is the Best Revenge, Dreamchild, Paris By Night, Walter (TV), Murder Most Horrid 1991, Closing Numbers (TV) 1994, The Choir (TV) 1995. *Plays include:* Henceforward . . ., School for Scandal 1990, Making It Better 1992. *Publications include:* The Moppy Stories 1987, Keep Your Baby Safe 1988, Calendar of Cakes 1989, Eats for Treats 1990, Time to Play 1993, Jane Asher's Book of Cake Decorating Ideas 1993, The Longing (novel) 1996, The Question (novel) 1998, Things We Do For Love (play) 1998. *Leisure interests:* reading, Times crossword. *Address:* c/o ICM, Oxford House, 76 Oxford Street, London, W1R 1RB; 24 Cale Street, London, SW3 3QU, England.

ASHIDA, Jun; Japanese fashion designer; b. 21 Aug. 1930, Kyoto; s. of Sadao Ashida and Ritsuko Ashida; m. Tomoko Tomita 1960; two d.; ed. Tokyo High School; studied under Jun-ichi Nakahara 1948–52; consultant designer to Takashimaya Dept. Store 1960; est. Jun Ashida Co. Ltd. and Jun Ashida label 1963; exclusive designer to H.I.H. (now Empress) Crown Princess Michiko 1966–76, designs for several mems. Imperial family; presented first collection in Paris 1977; launched Miss Ashida and Jun Ashida for Men labels 1985–86; opened shop Paris 1989; designed uniforms for Japanese Pavilion, Expo World Fair, Seville 1992, All Nippon Airways, Fuji Xerox, Imperial Hotel, Nomura Securities, Idemitsu Kosan, Tokyo Kaijo, Japanese team at Olympic Games, Atlanta 1996; mem. Postal Service Council of Ministry of Posts and Telecommunications; FEC Award 1971; Purple Ribbon Medal, Cavaliere, Ordine al Merito (Italy). *Publications:* Young Man (essays) 1986, Jun Ashida, 30 Years of Design 1993; articles on fashion and lifestyle in daily newspapers. *Leisure interests:* tennis, golf. *Address:* 1-3-3 Aobadai, Meguro-ku, Tokyo 153, Japan. *Telephone:* (03) 3463-8631. *Fax:* (03) 3463-8588.

ASHIHARA, Yoshinobu, B.A., M.ARCH., D.ENG.; Japanese architect; b. 7 July 1918, Tokyo; s. of Dr. Nobuyuki Ashihara and Kikuko Fujita; m. Hatsuko Takahashi 1944; one s. one d.; ed. Univ. of Tokyo and Harvard Univ. Graduate School; worked in architectural firms, Tokyo 1946–52; in Marcel Breuer's firm, New York 1953; visited Europe on Rockefeller Travel Grant 1954; Head, Yoshinobu Ashihara and Assocs. 1955–; Lecturer in Architecture, Hosei Univ., Tokyo 1955–59, Prof. of Architecture 1959–65; Prof. of Architecture, Musashino Art Univ., Tokyo 1964–70; Visiting Prof., School of Architecture and Building, Univ. of New South Wales, Australia 1966, Dept. of Architecture, Univ. of Hawaii 1969; Prof. of Architecture, Univ. of Tokyo 1970–79; Prof. Emer. Univ. of Tokyo, Musashino Art Univ.; Pres. Japan Architects' Asscn. 1980–82; Architectural Inst. of Japan 1985–87; mem. Japan Art Acad.; Hon. Fellow Architectural Inst. of Japan; Award of Architectural Inst. of Japan for Chuo-Koron Building 1960; Special Award of Architectural Inst. of Japan for Komazawa Olympic Gymnasium 1965; Minister of Educ. Award for Japan Pavilion, Expo 1967, Montreal; NSID Golden Triangle Award (U.S.A.) 1970, Japan Art Acad. Award 1984; Hon. F.A.I.A. 1979; Hon. Fellow Royal Australian Inst. of Architects 1987, Person of Cultural Merit 1991; Commendatore, Ordine al Merito (Italy) 1970, Order of Commdr. of Lion (Finland) 1985, of Cultural Merit 1998. *Works include:* Chuo-Koron Building, Sony Building, Komazawa Olympic Gymnasium 1965, Japanese Pavilion, Expo 67, Montreal, Fuji Film Bldg. 1969, Tokyo Metropolitan Art Space 1990. *Publications:* Exterior Design in Architecture 1970, The Aesthetic Townscape 1983, The Hidden Order 1989. *Leisure interests:* sauna, travelling. *Address:* Y. Ashihara, Architect and Associates, Sumitomo Seimei Building, 31-15 Sakuragaoka-cho, Shibuya-ku, Tokyo 150-0031 (Office); 47-10 Nishihara-3, Shibuya-ku, Tokyo 151-0066, Japan (Home). *Telephone:* (3) 3463-7461 (Office). *Fax:* (3) 3496-2596.

ASHKENASI, Shmuel; American violinist; b. 11 Jan. 1941, Tel-Aviv; m. Mihaela Ionescu Ashkenasi; two s.; ed. Curtis Inst. of Music, Philadelphia; Concert violinist since 1962; First violinist, Vermeer String Quartet; Prof. of Music, Univ. of Northern Ill. 1969–; First Prize, Merryweather Post Contest, Washington, D.C. 1958; Finalist, Queen Elizabeth Competition, Brussels 1959; Second Prize, Tchaikovsky Competition, Moscow 1962. *Leisure interests:* tennis, chess. *Address:* 3800 North Lake Shore Drive, Chicago, IL 60613, U.S.A. *Telephone:* (312) 348-5087.

ASHKENAZY, Vladimir; Icelandic/Russian concert pianist and conductor; b. 6 July 1937, Gorky, U.S.S.R.; s. of David Ashkenazy and Evstolia Ashkenazy (née Plotnova); m. Thorunn Sofia Johannsdóttir 1961; two s. three d.; ed. Central Music School, Moscow, and Moscow Conservatoire; Second Prize, Int. Chopin Competition, Warsaw 1955; Gold Medal, Queen Elizabeth Int. Piano Competition, Brussels 1956; Joint winner (with John Ogdon) Int. Tchaikovsky Piano Competition, Moscow 1962; Prin. Guest Conductor, Philharmonia 1982–83; Music Dir. Royal Philharmonic Orchestra 1987–94, Deutsches Symphonie-Orchester Berlin (fmrly. Berlin Radio Symphony) 1989–; Chief Conductor Czech Philharmonic Orchestra 1998–; Hon. R.A.M.; Hon. D.Mus. (Nottingham) 1995; Icelandic Order of the Falcon; concerts world-wide; many recordings. *Publication:* Beyond Frontiers (with Jasper Parrott) 1985. *Address:* Savinka, Käppelistr. 15, 6045 Meggen, Switzerland.

ASHMAWY, Muhammad Saïd al-, B.A.; Egyptian lawyer and writer; b. 1 Dec. 1932; Asst. of Dist. Attorney, Alexandria 1954; Dist. Attorney 1956; Judge 1961; Chief Prosecutor, Cairo 1973; Counsellor of State for Legislation 1977; Chief Justice High Criminal Court, Cairo 1985. *Publications:* Roots of Islamic Law 1979, Political Islam 1987, Islamic Caliphate 1990, Religion for the Future 1992, Veil and Tradition in Islam 1995, The Conflict between

Arabs and Israel 1997. *Leisure interests:* music, driving, tennis. *Address:* 9 Gezira al-Wosta Street, Zamalek-Cairo, Egypt 11211. *Telephone:* 2-340-2060. *Fax:* 2-340-2060.

ASHMORE, Admiral of the Fleet Sir Edward (Beckwith), G.C.B., D.S.C.; British naval officer; b. 11 Dec. 1919, Queenstown, Eire; s. of Vice-Adm. L. H. Ashmore, C.B., D.S.O., and T. V. Schutt; m. Elizabeth Mary Doveton Sturdee 1942; one s. one d.; ed. Royal Naval Coll., Dartmouth; served H.M.S. Birmingham, Jupiter, Middleton 1938–42; qualified Communications 1943; Staff, C.-in-C. Home Fleet 1944; Cruiser Squadron British Pacific Fleet 1945–46; mentioned in despatches 1946; Russian interpreter and Asst. Naval Attaché, British Embassy, Moscow 1946–47; Squadron Communications Officer 3rd Aircraft Carrier Squadron 50; Commdr. 1950; H.M.S. Alert 1952–53; Capt. 1955; Capt. (F) 6th Frigate Squadron, Commdg. Officer H.M.S. Blackpool 1958; Dir. of Plans, Admiralty and Ministry of Defence 1960–62; Commdr. British Forces Caribbean Area 1963–64; Rear-Adm. 1965; Asst. Chief of Defence Staff, Signals 1965–67; Flag Officer, Second-in-Command, Far East Fleet 1967–68; Vice-Adm. 1968; Vice-Chief Naval Staff 1969–71; Adm. 1970; C.-in-C. Western Fleet Sept.-Oct. 1971; C.-in-C. Fleet 1971–73; Chief of Naval Staff and First Sea Lord 1974–77; Chief of Defence Staff Feb.-Aug. 1977; First and Principal Naval ADC to Her Majesty the Queen 1974–77; Adm. of the Fleet 1977; Dir. Racal Electronics Ltd. 1978–97; Gov. Sutton's Hospital in Charterhouse 1975, Royal Naval Museum 1997. *Publication:* The Battle and the Breeze 1997. *Address:* c/o Naval Secretary, Victory Building, H.M. Naval Base, Portsmouth, Hants., England.

ASHRAWI, Hanan; Palestinian politician and academic; b. 1946; m. Emile Ashrawi; two d.; ed. American Univ. of Beirut, Univ. of Virginia; joined mainstream PLO Fatah faction; Prof. of English Literature, Chair. English Dept., Dean of Arts, Birzeit Univ., West Bank 1973–90; official spokeswoman for Palestinian Del. 1991–93; mem. Advisory Cttee. Palestinian Del. at Madrid Peace Conf. on Middle East; mem. Palestinian Independent Comm. for Palestinian Repub. (fmr. Head); f., Commr. Gen. Palestinian Ind. Comm. for Citizens' Rights 1993–95; mem. Palestinian Legis. Council 1996–; Minister of Higher Educ. 1996–98. *Publications:* A Passion for Peace 1994, This Side of Peace 1995. *Address:* c/o Ministry of Higher Education, P.O. Box 17360, Jerusalem, West Bank, via Israel.

ASHTAL, Abdalla Saleh al-, M.A.; Yemeni diplomatist; b. 5 Oct. 1940, Addis Ababa, Ethiopia; m. Vivian Eshoo al-Ashtal; one s. one d.; ed. Menelik II Secondary School, American Univ. of Beirut and New York Univ.; Asst. Dir. Yemeni Bank for Reconstruction Devt., Sanaa 1966–67; mem. Supreme People's Council, Hadramout Province 1967–68, Gen. Command Yemeni Nat. Liberation Front 1968–70; Political Adviser, Perm. Mission to UN 1970–72, Sr. Counsellor 1972–73, Perm. Rep. 1973–; Non-Resident Amb. to Canada 1974, to Mexico 1975–79, to Brazil 1985–91 (Pres. Security Council 1991). *Address:* Permanent Mission of Republic of Yemen to the United Nations, 413 East 51st Street, New York, NY 10022, U.S.A. *Telephone:* (212) 355-1730. *Fax:* (212) 750-9613.

ASHTON, Norman Henry, C.B.E., D.SC., F.R.C.P., F.R.C.S., F.R.C.PATH., F.R.C. OPHTH., F.R.S.; British university professor; b. 11 Sept. 1913; s. of Henry James Ashton and Margaret Ann Ashton; ed. West Kensington School, King's Coll. and Westminster Hosp. Medical School, London Univ.; Asst. Pathologist, Princess Beatrice Hosp. 1939; House Surgeon, House Physician, Sr. Casualty Officer, Westminster Hosp. London 1939–41; Dir. Pathology, Kent and Canterbury Hosp. 1941; Lieut. Col. R.A.M.C. 1946; Pathologist Gordon Hosp. 1947; Dir., Dept. of Pathology, Inst. of Ophthalmology 1948–78; Reader in Pathology, London Univ. 1953, Prof. 1957–78, Prof. Emer. 1978–; Visiting Prof., Johns Hopkins Hosp. 1959; Consultant Pathologist, Moorfields Eye Hosp. 1948–78, mem. Bd. of Govs. 1963–66, 1975–78; Fellow Royal Coll. of Ophthalmologists; Chair. British Diabetes Asscn. Cttee. on Blindness in Diabetes 1967–70; mem. Bd. of Govs., Royal Nat. Coll. for the Blind 1977–93; Life Pres., European Ophthalmic Pathology Soc.; Hon. Fellow Royal Soc. of Medicine, American Acad. of Ophthalmology, Royal Coll. of Ophthalmologists, Royal Coll. of Pathologists, Coll. of Physicians of Phila. 1976; Hon. mem., British Div., Int. Acad. of Pathology, American Ophthalmic Soc., American Assoc. of Ophthalmic Pathologists; Pres. Ophthalmological Soc. of the United Kingdom 1979–81; Visiting Research Fellow, Merton Coll. Oxford; Master, Soc. of Apothecaries of London 1984–85; Hon. Steward Westminster Abbey 1969–83; Hon. D.Sc. (Chicago); Helen Keller Int. Award for Vision Research 1998; Proctor Medal for Research in Ophthalmology (U.S.A.) 1957, Doyne Medal (Oxford) 1960, Bowman Medal 1965, Gonin Gold Medal 1978, 1st Jules Stein Award (U.S.A.) 1981, Lord Crook Gold Medal, Spectacle Makers' Co. 1989, Pisart Vision Award (U.S.A.) 1991, Buchanan Medal (Royal Soc.) 1996; Freeman of City of London; K.St.J. *Publications:* numerous articles in scientific journals. *Leisure interests:* painting, gardening. *Address:* 4 Blomfield Road, Little Venice, London, W9 1AH, England. *Telephone:* 0171-286 5536.

ASHWORTH, John Michael, PH.D., D.SC.; British biologist; b. 27 Nov. 1938, Luton; s. of Jack Ashworth and Mary Ousman; m. 1st Ann Knight 1963 (died 1985); one s. three d.; m. 2nd Auriol Stevens 1988; ed. Exeter Coll., Oxford, Leicester Univ., Brandeis Univ., U.S.A., Univ. of California, San Diego; Harkness Fellow, Commonwealth Fund, New York, N.Y. 1965–67; Lecturer, Biochemistry Dept., Univ. of Leicester 1967–71, Reader 1971–73; Prof., Biology Dept., Univ. of Essex 1973–79; Chief Scientist, Cen. Policy Review Staff, Cabinet Office 1976–81; Under-Sec. Cabinet Office 1979–81; Vice-Chancellor, Univ. of Salford 1981–89; Dir. L.S.E. and Political Science 1990–96; Chair. Bd. Nat. Computer Centre 1983–91, Nat. Accreditation Council for Certification Bodies 1984–88, British Library 1996–; mem. Bd. of Granada TV 1987–89, Dir. Granada Gp. 1990–; Dir. J. Sainsbury 1993–96; Hon. Fellow L.S.E 1997; Colworth Medal of Biochemical Soc. 1972; Hon. D.Sc (Salford) 1991. *Publications:* editor: Outline Studies in Biology; author: Cell Differentiation 1973, The Slime Moulds (with J. Dee) 1976, over 50 papers on biological and biochemical topics in scientific journals. *Address:* Garden House, Wivenhoe, Essex, CO7 9DB, England.

ASKEW, Reubin O'Donovan, LL.B.; American politician and lawyer; b. 11 Sept. 1928, Muskogee, Okla.; s. of Leo G. Askew and Alberta N. O'Donovan; m. Donna L. Harper 1956; one s. one d.; ed. Escambia County Public School System, Florida State Univ., Univ. of Florida Coll. of Law and Denver Univ.; Partner in law firm, Pensacola, Florida 1958–70; Asst. County Solicitor, Escambia Co., Florida 1956–58; mem. State of Florida House of Reps. 1958–62; State Senate 1962–70; Gov. of Florida 1971–79; U.S. Trade Rep. 1979–81; dir in law firm, Miami 1981–88; dir. Akerman, Senterfitt and Eidson 1988–; Chair. Education Commission of U.S.A. 1973; Chair. Southern Govs. Conf. 1974–78, Chair. Nat. Dem. Govs. Conference 1976, Nat. Govs. Conference 1976–77; Chair. Presidential Advisory Bd. on Ambassadorial Appointments 1977–79, Select Comm. on Immigration and Refugee Policy 1979; Visiting Fellow, Inst. of Politics, Harvard Univ. 1979; Chubb Fellow, Yale Univ.; Distinguished Service Prof. Fla. Atlantic Univ. Fort Lauderdale 1991; Hon. degrees Univ. of Notre Dame, Stetson Univ., Rollins Coll., Eckerd Coll., Florida Southern Coll., Saint Leo Coll., Miami Univ., Bethune-Cookman Coll., Univ. of West Fla., Barry Univ., Univ. of Florida, Univ. of Tampa, Belmont Abbey Coll.; John F. Kennedy Award, Nat. Council of Jewish Women 1973, Hubert Harley Award (American Judicature Soc.) 1973, Nat. Wildlife Fed. Award 1972, Outstanding Conservationist of Year Award, Florida Audubon Soc. 1972, Herbert H. Lehman Ethics Award 1973, Salvation Army Gen. William Booth Award 1973, Distinguished Community Service Award, Brandeis Univ., Ethics and Govt. Award, Common Cause; Order of COIF (Hon.) Coll. of Law, Univ. of Fla., Albert Einstein Distinguished Achievement Award, Yeshiva Univ.; Democrat; Presbyterian. *Publications:* Trade Services and the World Econ. 1983, Opinion: Public Welfare 1984. *Address:* Akerman, Senterfitt and Edison, 255 South Orange Avenue, P.O. Box 321, Orlando, FL 32802; College of Urban and Public Affairs, 220 South East 2nd Avenue, Fort Lauderdale, FL 33301, U.S.A. *Telephone:* (407) 843-7860.

ASKONAS, Brigitte Alice, PH.D., F.R.S.; British immunologist; b. 1 April 1923; d. of the late Charles F. Askonas and Rose Askonas; ed. McGill Univ., Montreal, Canada and Univ. of Cambridge, England; Research Student, School of Biochemistry, Univ. of Cambridge 1949–52; Immunology Div., Nat. Inst. for Medical Research, London 1953–88, Head 1977–88; Dept. of Bacteriology and Immunology, Harvard Medical School, Boston, Mass., U.S.A. 1961–62; Basel Inst. for Immunology, Switzerland 1971–72; Visiting Prof., Dept. of Medicine, St. Mary's Hosp. Medical School, London 1988–95, attached to Dept. of Immunology 1992–; Attached to Molecular Immunology Group, Inst. of Molecular Medicine, John Radcliffe Hosp., Oxford 1989–; Visiting Prof. Dept. of Biology, Imperial Coll. London 1995–; Fellow Acad. of Medical Science; Hon. mem. American Soc. of Immunology, Société française d'Immunologie, British Soc. of Immunology, German Soc. of Immunology; Hon. D.Sc. (McGill Univ.) 1987. *Publications:* scientific papers in various biochemical and immunological journals and books. *Leisure interests:* art, travel. *Address:* Infection and Immunity Section, Department of Biology, Imperial College of Science, Technology and Medicine, Sir Alexander Fleming Building, London, SW7 2AZ; 23 Hillside Gardens, London, N6 5SU, England. *Telephone:* 0171-594 5404/5 (Office); 0181-348 6792 (Home). *Fax:* 0171-584 9075.

ÅSLING, Nils Gunnar, B.SC.; Swedish banker and fmr. politician; b. 15 Dec. 1927, Åse; m. Karin Asling; twin s. one d.; ed. Schools of Agriculture, Torsta and Sånga-Säby, Stockholm School of Social Studies and Stockholm Univ.; mem. Swedish Parl. for Centre Party 1969–88, Cttee. on Finance 1973–76; Minister of Industry 1976–78, 1979–82; Chair. Swedish Asscn. of Co-operative Banks; Chair. Foreningsbankernas Bank; mem. bd. Fed. of Swedish Farmers 1983–92, Inlandsbanan AB, Företagshuset AB, Camfore group of cos., Svenska Rymdaktriebolaget (Spacecorpn.). *Publications:* The New Era 1955, Per Olof Sundman, a Portrait 1970, Ideas and Realities 1970, The Crisis and Reformation of Swedish Industry: The Perspective of Industrial Policies for the 1980s 1979, Struggle for Power or Collaboration 1983, Reason to Remember 1996. *Leisure interests:* art, literature. *Address:* N. Mälarstrand 62, 112 35 Stockholm (Office); Åse, 83047 Trångsviken, Sweden (Home). *Telephone:* (640) 40025. *Fax:* (640) 40446.

ASMAL, Kader, LL.M., M.A.; South African politician; b. 1934, Stanger; m. Louise Asmal; two s.; ed. Springfield Teachers' Training Coll.; law teacher Trinity Coll., Dublin for 27 years (during 30-year exile), Dean Faculty of Arts Trinity Coll., Dublin 1980–86; barrister Lincoln's Inn, London and King's Inn Dublin; returned from exile 1990; Prof. of Human Rights Univ. of W. Cape 1990–94; Minister for Water Affairs and Forestry, Govt. of Nat. Unity 1994–; f. British Anti-Apartheid Movement 1963, Chair. –1991; mem. Constitutional Comm. of African Nat. Congress (ANC) 1985–, ANC Nat. Exec. Comm. 1991–, Nat. Comm. for Emancipation of Women 1992–, mem. Nat. Ass. 1994–; mem. ANC negotiating team at Multi-Party Negotiating Forum 1993; UNESCO Prize for Teaching and Devt. of Human Rights 1985.

Publications: two books and over 150 articles on legal and political aspects of apartheid, labour law on Ireland and decolonization. *Address:* Ministry of Water Affairs and Forestry, Private Bag 9052, Cape Town 8000, Pretoria 0001, South Africa.

ASMODI, Herbert; German playwright; b. 30 March 1923, Heilbronn; m. T. Katja; ed. Ruprecht-Karl Universität, Heidelberg; war service 1942–45; studied 1947–52; freelance writer, Munich 1952–; wrote opera libretto Die Geschichte von dem kleinen blauen Bergsee und dem alten Adler (music by Wilfried Hiller) 1996; mem. PEN; Gerhart Hauptmann-Preis der Freien Volksbühne Berlin 1954, Tukan Prize, Munich 1971, Bayerischer Verdienstorden, Bundesverdienstkreuz. *Publications include:* plays: Jenseits vom Paradies 1954, Pardon wird nicht gegeben 1956, Tierjagt 1957, Die Menschenfresser 1959, Nachsaison 1970, Mohrenwäsche, Dichtung und Wahrheit 1969, Stirb und Werde 1965, Nasrin oder Die Kunst zu Träumen 1970, Marie von Brinvilliers 1971, Geld 1973; prose: Das Lächeln der Harpyjen 1987, Eine unwürdige Existenz 1988, Landleben 1991, Das Grosse Rendezvous 1993; poems: Jokers Gala 1975, Jokers Farewell 1977. *Address:* Kufsteiner Platz 2, 81679 Munich, Germany.

ASPE ARMELLA, Pedro, PH.D.; Mexican politician; b. 7 July 1950, Mexico City; ed. Mexican Autonomous Inst. of Tech., Massachusetts Inst. of Tech., U.S.A.; Co-ordinator of Econ. Consultancy for Finance and Public Credit Minister 1978–82; Chair. INEGI 1982–85; Deputy Minister of Budget Planning and Control, SPP 1985–87; Secretary of Budget and Programming 1987–88, of Finance and Public Credit 1988–94. *Address:* c/o Secretariat of State for Finance and Public Credit, Palacio Nacional, Patio Central, Piso 3, Desp. 3025, Centro C.P. 06066, Mexico City, Mexico.

ASPER, Israel Harold, Q.C., LL.M.; Canadian business executive and lawyer; b. 11 Aug. 1932, Minnedosa, Manitoba; s. of Leon and Cecilia Asper; m. Ruth M. Bernstein 1956; two s. one d.; ed. Kelvin High School, Winnipeg, and Univ. of Manitoba; with Drache, Meltzer, Essers, Gold & Asper 1957–59; f. Asper & Co. (now Buchwald, Asper & Co.), law firm, Winnipeg 1959, Sr. Partner Asper & Co. 1959–70; Sr. Partner Buchwald, Asper, Henteleff 1970–77; fmr. mem. Legis Ass., Man. fmr. Leader Liberal Party; Chair. of Bd. Global Television Network, Canwest Broadcasting Ltd., Canwest Communications Corpn, The Canwest Capital Group Inc., CanWest Trust Co., SaskWest TV Ltd, CPTV Inc.; Chair. and C.E.O. Canwest Global Communications Corpn., Canwest Int. Inc., TV3 Network Holdings Ltd.; mem. Bd. numerous cos. and orgs.; Hon. Lieut.-Col. Canadian Militia; Hon. Fellow Hebrew Univ. of Jerusalem; Univ. of Manitoba Alumni Award. *Publications:* The Benson Iceberg: A Critical Analysis of The White Paper on Tax Reform in Canada 1970; weekly newspaper column in Toronto Globe & Mail 1966–77. *Address:* 1063 Wellington Crescent, Winnipeg, Man. R3N 0A1, Canada (Home). *Telephone:* (204) 488-0050 (Home).

ASSAD, Lieut.-Gen. Hafiz al-; Syrian politician and army officer; b. 1928; m.; four s. (one s. deceased) one d.; ed. Military Coll., Aviation Coll; mem. Baath Party 1946–; formed Baathist Mil. Cttee. when in Egypt; dismissed from the army, rejoined 1963, promoted Gen. of Air Force 1964; Minister of Defence and Commdr. of Air Force 1966–70; Prime Minister 1970–71; Sec. Gen., Pres. Baath Party Nov. 1970–; Pres. of Syria March 1971–; mem. Pres. Council, Fed. of Arab Repubs. 1971; Pres. Syrian Nat. Progressive Front 1972–; Dr. h.c. (Damascus) 1972. *Address:* Office of the President, Damascus, Syria.

ASSAD, Nassir El-Din El-, M.A., PH.D.; Jordanian scholar; b. 13 Dec. 1923, Aqaba; s. of Mohammad Ahmed Jamil and Amina El-Assad; m. Awatif Hafez 1946; three s. one d.; ed. Univ. of Cairo; Dean, Faculty of Arts and Educ., Univ. of Libya 1959–61; Dean, Faculty of Arts, also Pres. of Univ., Univ. of Jordan 1962–68, Pres. 1978–80; Asst. Dir.-Gen. ALECSO 1970–77; Amb. to Saudi Arabia 1977–78; Pres. Royal Acad. for Islamic Civilization Research (Al Albait Foundation) 1980–; Minister of Higher Educ. 1985–89; Prof. Emer. Univ. of Jordan 1985–; mem. Upper House of Parl. 1993–97; King Faisal Int. Prize (Arabic Literature) 1981. *Publications:* 16 books and 55 papers including: Modern Literary Trends in Palestine and Jordan 1957, Modern Poetry in Palestine and Jordan 1961, Singing and Singing Girls in Pre-Islamic Arabia 1960, The Sources of Pre-Islamic Poetry 1956, Us and Our Times 1998. *Leisure interests:* reading, listening to music, walking. *Address:* Royal Academy for Islamic Civilization Research (Al Albait Foundation), P.O. Box 950361, Amman, 11195, Jordan. *Telephone:* (6) 5539471. *Fax:* (6) 5526471.

ASSAD, Rifat Al-, PH.D.; Syrian politician, newspaper publisher and fmr. army officer; b. 22 Aug. 1937, Kerdaha; s. of Ali Al-Assad and Na'issa Ibad; m. Lyn Al-Khayer 1973; eight s. eight d.; officer in Syrian Army 1963–94, founder and Commdr. of Defence Regts. 1965–84, mem. Regional Command of Syria 1975; Prof., Coll. of Law, Damascus Univ. 1976; Vice-Pres. of Syria 1984; Founder and Publr. Al-Forsan magazine, Damascus 1966–84, Paris and London 1984–92, Al-Shah daily newspaper, Paris 1988, Shaza magazine, Paris 1986, and Memo magazine, Cyprus 1986; Founder and Pres. League of Higher Studies, Grads. and Research 1974; many Syrian decorations; Légion d'honneur, Hon. Decoration of Morocco. *Publications:* many econ. and political articles in Arabic newspapers and magazines. *Leisure interests:* reading, sports, music. *Address:* c/o Mezzeh, Jabal, Damascus, Syria. *Telephone:* 6621623. *Fax:* 682080393.

ASSENMACHER, Ivan, M.D., D.SC.; French professor of physiology; b. 17 May 1927, Erstein; s. of Ivan Assenmacher and Mary (née Wetzel) Assenmacher; m. Violette Rochedieu 1952; two s. (one s. deceased); ed. Univs. of Strasbourg and Paris; Asst. Faculty of Medicine Univ. of Strasbourg 1950–53, Asst. Prof. 1953–57; Sub-Dir. Histophysiology Lab., Coll. de France, Paris 1957–59; Assoc. Prof. Univ. of Montpellier 1959–62, Prof. Physiology 1962–95, Prof. Emer. 1995–; Head of Neuroendocrinology Lab., C.N.R.S., Montpellier 1967–92; Exchange Prof. Physiology, Univ. of Calif., Berkeley 1976, 1982; mem. Acad. des Sciences 1982, Acad. Europea 1990; mem. Consultative Cttee. for Univs., Paris 1967–80, 1986–91, Nat. Cttee. for Scientific Research, Paris 1967–75, 1980–86, Gutachtergruppe für Neuroendokrinologie 1975–85, and Neuropeptide 1985–92, Deutsche Forschungsgemeinschaft, Bonn, Nat. Consultative Cttee. for a code of ethics for Life and Health Sciences 1986–91, French Nat. Comm. for UNESCO 1997–, Higher Council for Scientific and Technological Research, Paris 1992–95; Chevalier, Légion d'honneur, Officier, Ordre Nat. du Mérite, Officier Ordre Palmes Académiques, Médaille des Réfractaires 1944–45. *Publications:* Photorégulation de la Reproduction (with J. Benoît) 1970, Environmental Endocrinology (with D. S. Farner) 1978, Endocrine Regulations as Adaptive Mechanisms to the Environment (with J. Boissin) 1987. *Address:* Laboratory of Neuroendocrinology, Department of Health Sciences, University of Montpellier II, 34095 Montpellier (Office); 419 avenue d'Occitanie, 34090 Montpellier, France (Home). *Telephone:* (04) 67.52.28.25 (Office); (04) 67.63.22.20 (Home). *Fax:* (04) 67.52.28.25.

ASTACIO, Julio Ernesto; Salvadorean politician, physician and surgeon; b. 1932, San Salvador; m. Marta de Astacio; two s. one d.; ed. Univ. de El Salvador; specialized at Lady of Lourdes Hosp., Univ. of Pennsylvania, Walter Reed Hosp., Washington, D.C., U.S.A.; postgraduate studies in radiology, Saint Christopher's Children's Hosp., Philadelphia, Univs. of Munich and Erlange, Germany; fmr. Prof. of Radiology, Radiological Anatomy, Physiology and Pediatric Radiology, Univ. de El Salvador; fmr. Head of Radiology Dept., Benjamin Bloom's Children's Hosp., San Salvador and physician at the Mil. Hosp.; Vascular Radiologist, Salvadorian Inst. of Social Security Hosp.; Vice-Pres. of El Salvador 1977–79. *Address:* San Salvador, El Salvador.

ASTAFIEV, Viktor Petrovich; Russian writer; b. 1 May 1924, Ovsyanka Village, Krasnoyarsk District; s. of Lidia Ilyinichna and Pjotr Pavlovich Astafiev; brought up in orphanage; m. Maria Semenovna Korjakina 1975; one s. two d. (one deceased); ed. Higher Literary courses, U.S.S.R. Union of Writers; served in World War II; writer 1951–; People's Deputy 1989–91; Vice-Pres. European Forum of Writers; Hero of Socialist Labour 1989, U.S.S.R. State Prizes 1978, 1991, State Prize of Russia 1996; Pushkin Prize 1997. *Publications include:* novels: Till Next Spring 1953, The Snows are Melting 1958, Shooting Star 1962, Vasyutkin Lake 1962, Stories: Theft. Somewhere the War is Droning 1968, Blue Dusk 1968; Tales 1969; The Horse With the Pink Mane and Other Siberian Stories (Eng. trans.) 1970, The Last Bow 1971; The King-Fish (State Prize) 1972, The Light Afternoon and Other Tales 1973; The Sad Detective 1986, Condemned and Killed, (Vol. 1) 1992, (Vol. 2) 1994; stories The Last Bow (1954–1992), Shepherd and Shepherdess 1963–1990, Collected Works (six vols.) 1993, The Wish to Live is So Strong 1995, The Bridgehead 1995. *Leisure interest:* fishing. *Address:* Academia str. 14, Apt. 55, Krasnoyarsk 660036, Russia. *Telephone:* (3912) 43-78-10.

ASTOR, Hon. (Francis) David Langhorne; British journalist; b. 5 March 1912, London; s. of 2nd Viscount Astor; m. 1st Melanie Hauser 1945; one d.; m. 2nd Bridget Aphra Wreford 1952; two s. three d.; ed. Eton and Balliol Coll., Oxford; staff, Yorkshire Post 1936; served Second World War 1939–45; Foreign Ed. The Observer 1946–48, Ed. 1948–75, Dir. 1976–81; mem. Council Royal Inst. of Int. Affairs 1977; Croix de guerre. *Publication:* Peace in the Middle East: Super Powers and Security Guarantees (with V. Yorke) 1978. *Address:* 24 St Ann's Terrace, London, NW8 6PJ; Manor House, Sutton Courtenay, Oxon., OX14 4AD, England. *Telephone:* 0171-586 8689 (London); (01235) 848221.

ASTRUC, Alexandre, L. ÈS L.; French film director and author; b. 13 July 1923, Paris; s. of Marcel Astruc and Huguette Haendel; m. Elyette Helies 1983; ed. Lycée de Saint-Germain-en-Laye, Lycée Henri IV and Faculté des Lettres, Paris; journalist and film critic since 1945; TV reporter for Radio Luxembourg 1969–72; film critic, Paris Match 1970–72; contributor to Figaro-Dimanche 1977–; Chevalier, Légion d'honneur, Officier de l'Ordre du Mérite, Commdr. des Arts et des Lettres; various film prizes and other awards. *Films directed include:* Le Rideau cramoisi 1952, Les Mauvaises Rencontres 1955, Une Vie 1958, La Proie pour l'ombre 1960, Education sentimentale 1961, Evariste Galois 1965, La Longue Marche 1966, Flammes sur l'Adriatique 1968, Sartre par lui-même 1976; also TV films and series. *Publications:* Les Vacances 1945, La Tête la première, Ciel de Cendres 1975, Le Serpent Jaune 1976, Quand la chouette s'envole 1978, Le Permissionnaire 1982, Le Roman de Descartes 1989, De la caméra au stylo 1992, L'Autre versant de la colline 1993, Evadiste Galois 1994, Le Montreur d'ombres 1996. *Leisure interests:* mathematics, literature. *Address:* 168 rue de Grenelle, 75007 Paris, France (Home). *Telephone:* (1) 47.05.20.86.

ASYLMURATOVA, Altynai; Kazakhstan ballerina; b. 1962, Alma-Ata; m. Konstantin Zaklinsky; one d.; ed. Vaganova Ballet School, Leningrad; dancer with Kirov (now Mariinsky) Ballet 1980; numerous foreign tours including Paris 1982; U.S.A., Canada 1987. *Roles include:* Odette/Odile, in Swan Lake, Shirin, in Legend of Love, Kitzi in Don Quixote, Aurora in Sleeping Beauty,

Nike in Boyaderka, Giselle. *Address:* Mariinsky Theatre, Teatralnaya pl. 1, St. Petersburg, Russia. *Telephone:* 116-41-64 (Office); 315-57-24 (Home).

ATAEVA, Aksoltan Toreevna; Turkmenistan diplomatist, politician and medical practitioner; b. 6 Nov. 1944, Ashgabat; m. Tchary Pirmoukhamedov 1969; one s. one d.; ed. Turkmen State Medical Inst., Ashgabat; doctor, Hosp. No. 1, Ashgabat 1968–79, Asst. to Chief Dr. 1979–80; Vice-Dir. Regional Health Dept., Ashgabat 1980–85; Vice Minister of Health 1985–90, Minister 1990–94; Minister of Social Security 1994–95; Amb. Extraordinary and Plenipotentiary, Perm. Rep. to UN 1995–; mem. Democratic Party 1992–, Khalk Maslakhaty (Supreme People's Council of Turkmenistan) 1993–; Pres. Trade Unions of Turkmenistan 1994–95; Cand. of Science, Soviet Union Scientific Research Inst. for Social Hygiene and Health Care Man., Moscow 1985–89; Hon. Assoc. of Int. Acad. of Computer Sciences and Systems (Kiev, Ukraine) 1993; Gairat Medal 1992. *Publications:* 108 publs. and 2 monographs on health and maternity care. *Leisure interests:* books, arts, sports. *Address:* Permanent Mission of Turkmenistan to UN, 866 UN Plaza, Suite 424, New York, NY 10017, U.S.A. *Telephone:* (212) 486-8908.

ATANASOV, Georgi Ivanov; Bulgarian politician; b. 23 June 1933, Pravoslaven, Plovdiv; ed. Faculty of History, Univ. of Sofia; mem. Bulgarian CP (BCP) 1956–; First Sec. Sofia Komsomol City Cttee. 1953–62; mem. Komsomol Political Bureau and Sec. of Cen. Cttee. 1962–65, First Sec. 1965–68; cand. mem. BCP Cen. Cttee. 1962–66, Head of Dept. of Science and Educ., 1968–76, mem. BCP Cen. Cttee. 1966; mem. Dept. of Admin., 1976–78, Sec. 1977–86; mem. Political Bureau 1986; Deputy Chair. State Planning Cttee. 1980–81; Chair. Cttee. on State Control 1981–84; Pres. Council of Ministers 1986–90; charged with embezzlement Oct. 1992, convicted Nov. 1992; granted Presidential Pardon Aug. 1994.

ATAYEV, Khalykberdy; Turkmenistan politician and lawyer; b. 1943, Kipchik, Ashkhabad Region; ed. Turkmen Univ.; insp. Dept. of Legis. bodies, sr. consultant Supreme Court of Turkmen S.S.R.; Nebit-Dag City Court 1968–70; sr. judge Turkmen Regional Court 1970–72; mem. Supreme Court of Turkmen S.S.R. 1972–74; Chair. Krasnovodsk City Court 1974–88; Vice-Minister of Justice of Turkmen S.S.R. 1988–89, Minister 1989–91; Chair. Supreme Court of Turkmenistan 1991–92; Minister of Foreign Affairs 1992–95, Minster of Social Welfare 1996–97. *Address:* c/o Ministry of Social Welfare, Ashgabat, Turkmenistan. *Telephone:* (3632) 25-30-03.

ATHERTON, Alfred Leroy Jr., B.SC., M.A.; American diplomatist; b. 22 Nov. 1921, Pittsburgh; s. of Alfred Leroy Atherton and Joan (née Reed) Atherton; m. Betty Wylie Kittredge 1946; two s. one d.; ed. Harvard Univ.; joined Foreign Service 1947; Vice-Consul, Stuttgart and Bonn 1947–52; Second Sec., U.S. Embassy, Syria 1953–56; Consul, Aleppo, Syria 1957–58, Calcutta, India 1962–65; Int. Relations Officer, Bureau of Near Eastern and S. Asian Affairs, State Dept. 1959–61, Country Dir. (Iraq, Jordan, Lebanon, Syria) 1966–67, (Israel and Arab-Israeli Affairs) 1967–70; Deputy Asst. Sec. of State 1970–74, Asst Sec. of State 1974–78; Amb. at Large with Special Responsibility for Middle East Peace Negotiations 1978–79; Amb. to Egypt 1979–83; Dir.-Gen., Foreign Service, State Dept. 1983–85; Dir. The Harkness Fellowships 1985–91; Visiting Prof. Hamilton Coll. 1988, 1992, 1994, Mount Holyoke Coll. 1991; Chair. New York-Cairo Sister City Cttee. 1986–; mem. Bd. Dirs., US N.Z. Council 1987–; mem. Advisory Comm. for Initiative for Peace and Co-operation in Middle East in Search for Common Ground 1991– (Chair. 1992–); Trustee, the Una Chapman Cox Foundation 1985–87, Exec. Dir. 1989–; Pres. Distinguished Service Award 1983. *Leisure interests:* photography, travel. *Address:* Una Chapman Cox Foundation, 1726 M Street, N.W., Suite 800, Washington D.C. 20036 (Office); Apartment 5003, 4301 Massachusetts Avenue, N.W., Washington, D.C. 20016, U.S.A. (Home). *Telephone:* (202) 223-0887 (Office); (202) 244 1060 (Home).

ATHERTON, David, M.A., L.R.A.M., L.T.C.L., L.G.S.M.; British conductor; b. 3 Jan. 1944, Blackpool; s. of Robert and Lavinia Atherton; m. Ann Gianetta Drake 1970 (separated 1983); one s. two d.; ed. Cambridge Univ.; Répétiteur, Royal Opera House, Covent Garden 1967–68; Resident Conductor, Royal Opera House 1968–79; Artistic Dir. and Conductor, London Stravinsky Festival 1979–82, Ravel/Varese Festival 1983–84; début La Scala, Milan 1976, San Francisco Opera 1978, Metropolitan Opera, New York 1984; youngest-ever conductor at Henry Wood Promenade Concerts, London 1968; début Royal Festival Hall, London 1969; has conducted performances in Europe, Middle East, Far East, Australasia, N. America 1970–; Music Dir. and Prin. Conductor San Diego Symphony Orchestra 1980–87; Prin. Conductor and Artistic Adviser Royal Liverpool Philharmonic Orchestra 1980–83, Prin. Guest Conductor 1983–86; Prin. Guest Conductor BBC Symphony Orchestra 1985–89; Music Dir. and Prin. Conductor Hong Kong Philharmonic Orchestra 1989–; Music Dir. Mainly Mozart Festival, S. Calif. 1989–, London Sinfonietta 1967–73, 1989–91 (founder 1967); Prin. Guest Conductor BBC Nat. Orchestra of Wales 1994–97; Conductor of the Year Award, Composers' Guild of G.B. 1971, Edison Award 1973, Grand Prix du Disque Award 1977, Koussevitzky Award 1981, Int. Record Critics Award 1982, Prix Caecilia 1982. *Publications:* The Complete Instrumental and Chamber Music of Arnold Schoenberg and Roberto Gerhard (Ed.) 1973, Pandora and Don Quixote Suites by Roberto Gerhard (Ed.) 1973; Contrib. to The Musical Companion 1978, The New Grove Dictionary 1981. *Leisure interests:* travel, squash, theatre, computers. *Address:* c/o Askonas Holt Ltd., Lonsdale Chambers, 27 Chancery Lane, London, WC2A 1PF, England. *Telephone:* 0171-400 1700.

ATHERTON, Michael Andrew, O.B.E.; British cricketer; b. 23 March 1968, Manchester; s. of Alan Atherton and Wendy Atherton; ed. Manchester Grammar School and Downing Coll. Cambridge; right-hand opening batsman; leg-spin bowler; has played for Cambridge Univ. 1987–89 (Capt. 1988–89), Lancs. 1987–; England début 1989, 88 tests to 1 June 1999, 52 as Capt. (England record), scoring 6,045 runs (average 38.5) including 12 centuries; has scored 18,349 first-class runs (47 centuries) to 1 April 1999, including 1,193 in début season; toured Australia 1990–91, 1994–95 (Capt.); 53 limited-overs internationals (43 as Capt.) to 31 Dec. 1997. *Leisure interests:* decent novels, good movies, food, wine, travel, most sports, music. *Publication:* A Test of Cricket 1995. *Address:* c/o Lancashire County Cricket Club, Old Trafford, Manchester, M16 0PX, England.

ATHFIELD, Ian Charles, DIP.ARCH.; New Zealand architect; b. 15 July 1940, Christchurch; s. of Charles Leonard Athfield and Ella Agnes Taylor; m. Nancy Clare Cookson 1962; two s.; ed. Christchurch Boys High School, Auckland Univ. School of Architecture; a Principal of Structon Group Architects, Wellington 1965–68; own practice 1968–; Professional Teaching Fellowship, Victoria Univ. of Wellington 1987–88; winner Int. Design Competition for Housing, Manila, Philippines 1976; numerous awards include N.Z.I.A. Silver Medal 1970, Bronze Medal 1975, Gold Medal 1982; AA Award 1968, 1972; N.Z. Tourist and Publicity Design Award 1975; winner of over 50 design awards including for Wellington Civic Centre and Public Library; joint winner Design Competition for Low Cost Housing, Fiji 1978; AAA Monier Design Award 1983, N.Z.I.A. Branch Award 1984, N.Z.I.A. Nat. Design Award 1984, 1985, 1986, 1987, 1988; Environmental Design Award 1986, N.Z. Wool Bd. Award 1987, N.Z. Commemoration Medal 1996, Companion N.Z. Order of Merit 1997. *Leisure interests:* building, gardening. *Address:* P.O. Box 3364, Wellington (Office); 105 Amritsar Street, Khandallah, Wellington, New Zealand (Home). *Telephone:* (4) 499-1727. *Fax:* (4) 499-1960.

ATİLLA, İsmet; Turkish politician; b. 1940, Afyon; m.; ed. Social Services Acad.; Dir.-Gen. Bağ-Kur; advisor with Ministry of Labour and Social Security; deputy Doğru Yol Partisi (DYP) 1991–; Minister of Finance and Customs 1993–96. *Address:* c/o Doğru Yol Partisi, Selanik Cad. 40, Kızılay, Ankara, Turkey.

ATIYAH, Sir Michael Francis, Kt., O.M., SC.D., F.R.S., F.R.S.E.; British mathematician; b. 22 April 1929, London; s. of Edward Selim Atiyah and Jean (Levens) Atiyah; m. Lily Brown 1955; three s.; ed. Victoria Coll., Egypt, Manchester Grammar School and Trinity Coll. Cambridge; Research Fellow, Trinity Coll., Cambridge 1954–58, Hon. Fellow 1976, Master 1990–97, Fellow 1997; Fellow, Pembroke Coll., Cambridge 1958–61 (Hon. Fellow 1983), Univ. Lecturer 1957–61; Reader, Oxford Univ., and Fellow, St. Catherine's Coll., Oxford 1961–63, Hon. Fellow 1991; Savilian Prof. of Geometry, Oxford Univ., and Fellow of New Coll., Oxford 1963–69; Prof. of Mathematics, Inst. for Advanced Study, Princeton, N.J. 1969–72; Royal Soc. Research Prof., Oxford Univ. 1973–90, Fellow, St. Catharine's Coll., Oxford 1973–90; Dir. Isaac Newton Inst. of Math. Sciences, Cambridge 1990–96; Chancellor Univ. of Leicester 1995–; Hon. Fellow Darwin Coll., Cambridge 1992; Pres. London Mathematical Soc. 1974–76, Pres. Mathematical Assсn. 1981; mem. Science and Eng. Research Council 1984–89; Pres. Pugwash Confs. 1997–, Council Royal Soc. 1984–85, Pres. 1990–95; Foreign mem. American Acad. of Arts and Sciences, Swedish Acad. of Sciences, Leopoldina Acad. (Germany), N.A.S., Acad. des Sciences (France), Royal Irish Acad., Indian Nat. Science Acad., Australian Acad. of Sciences, Chinese Acad. of Sciences, American Philosophical Soc., Ukrainian Acad. of Sciences, Russian Acad. of Sciences, Georgian Acad. of Sciences, Venezuelan Acad. of Sciences; Hon. Prof. Univ. of Edin. 1997–; Hon. Fellow Royal Acad. of Eng. (U.K.) 1993; Hon. D.Sc. (Bonn, Warwick, Durham, St. Andrews, Dublin, Chicago, Edinburgh, Cambridge, Essex, London, Sussex, Ghent, Reading, Helsinki, Leicester, Rutgers, Salamanca, Montreal, Waterloo, Wales, Queen's-Kingston, Keele, Birmingham, Lebanon, Open Univ., Brown Univ., Oxford, Prague, Chinese Univ. Hong Kong); Dr. h.c. (UMIST) 1996; Fields Medal, Int. Congress of Mathematicians, Moscow 1966, Royal Medal of Royal Soc. (U.K.) 1968, De Morgan Medal, London Mathematical Soc. 1980, Copley Medal of Royal Soc. (U.K.) 1988, Feltrinelli Prize, Accademia Nazionale dei Lincei 1981, King Faisal Int. Prize for Science 1987, Benjamin Franklin Medal (American Philosophical Soc.), Nehru Medal (Indian Nat. Science Acad.); Commdr. Order of the Cedars; Order of Andreas Bello (Venezuela). *Publications:* K-Theory 1966, Commutative Algebra 1969, Geometry and Dynamics of Magnetic Monopoles 1988, The Geometry and Physics of Knots 1990. *Leisure interests:* gardening, music. *Address:* 3/8 West Grange Gardens, Edin., EH9 2RA, Scotland.

ATIYAT, Talal Moh'd Ismail, B.B.A., M.A.; Jordanian civil servant; b. 28 Dec. 1951, Amman; Chief of Div., Revenue Dept.; Dir. of Admin., UNESCO office; Dir. of Finance, Co-operative Bank; Asst. Gen. Dir., Dir. of Devt. Admin., Jordan Co-operative Corpn. 1995–. *Leisure interest:* reading. *Address:* Jordan Co-operative Corporation, Amman (Office); P.O. Box 930008, Housing Bank Complex, Amman, Jordan. *Telephone:* 665171 (Office); 711530 (Home).

ATKINS, Eileen, C.B.E.; British actress; b. 16 June 1934; d. of Arthur Thomas Atkins and of the late Annie Ellen Elkins; m. Bill Shepherd; ed. Latymer Grammar School, Edmonton and Guildhall School of Music and Drama. *Stage appearances include:* Twelfth Night, Richard III, The Tempest 1962, The Killing of Sister George 1965 (Best Actress, Evening Standard

Awards), The Cocktail Party 1968, Vivat! Vivat Regina! 1970 (Variety Award), Suzanne Andler, As You Like It 1973, St. Joan 1977, Passion Play 1981, Medea 1986, The Winter's Tale, Cymbeline 1988 (Olivier Award), Mountain Language 1988, A Room of One's Own 1989, Exclusive 1989, The Night of the Iguana 1992, Vita and Virginia 1993, Indiscretions 1995, John Gabriel Borkman 1996. *Films include:* Equus 1974, The Dresser 1984, Let Him Have It 1990, Wolf 1994. *TV appearances include:* The Duchess of Malfi, Sons and Lovers, Smiley's People, Nelly's Version, The Burston Rebellion, Breaking Up, The Vision, Mrs Pankhurst in In My Defence (series) 1990, A Room of One's Own 1990, The Lost Language of Cranes 1993, The Maitlands 1993, Cold Comfort Farm 1995. *Co-creator:* Upstairs Downstairs, The House of Eliott television series; B.A.F.T.A. Award 1985. *Address:* c/o Jonathan Altaras Associates, 27 Floral Street, London, WC2E 9DP, England.

ATKINSON, Anthony Barnes, M.A., F.B.A.; British professor of economics; b. 4 Sept. 1944, Caerleon; m. Judith Mary Mandeville 1965; two s. one d.; ed. Cranbrook School, Kent and Churchill Coll., Cambridge; Prof. of Econs., Univ. of Essex 1970–76; Head Dept. of Political Economy, Univ. Coll. London 1976–79; Prof. of Econs. L.S.E. 1980–92; Prof. of Political Economy, Cambridge Univ., Fellow Churchill Coll. 1992–94; Warden Nuffield Coll. Oxford 1994–; Ed. Journal of Public Economics 1972–97; mem. Royal Comm. on Distribution of Income and Wealth 1978–79, Retail Prices Index Advisory Cttee. 1984–, Pension Law Review Cttee. 1992–93, Conseil d'Analyse Economique 1997–; Fellow, St. John's Coll., Cambridge 1967–70; Fellow, Econometric Soc. 1984, Pres. 1988; Vice-Pres. British Acad. 1988–90; Pres. of the European Econ. Asscn. 1989, Hon. mem. American Econ. Asscn. 1985; Pres. Int. Econ. Asscn. 1989–92, Royal Econ. Soc. 1995–(98); Hon. Dr.rer.Pol., D.Sc.; UAP Prix Scientifique 1986; Frank E. Seidman Distinguished Award in Political Economy 1995. *Publications:* Poverty in Britain and the Reform of Social Security 1969, Unequal Shares 1972, The Economics of Inequality 1975, Distribution of Personal Wealth in Britain (with A. Harrison) 1978, Lectures on Public Economics (with J. E. Stiglitz) 1980, Social Justice and Public Policy 1983, Parents and Children (with A. Maynard and C. Trinder), Poverty and Social Security 1989, Economic Transformation in Eastern Europe and the Distribution of Income (with J. M. Micklewright) 1992, Public Economics in Action 1995, Incomes and the Welfare State 1996, Three Lectures on Poverty in Europe 1998. *Address:* 39 Park Town, Oxford, OX2 6SL, England.

ATKINSON, Conrad; British artist; b. 15 June 1940, Cleator Moor, Cumbria; m. Margaret Harrison 1967; two d.; ed. Whitehaven Grammar School, Carlisle and Liverpool Colls. of Art and Royal Acad. Schools, London; Granada Fellow in Fine Art 1967–68; Churchill Fellow in Fine Art 1972; Fellow in Fine Art, Northern Arts 1974–76; Lecturer, Slade School of Fine Art 1976–79; Visual Art Adviser to GLC 1982–86; Power Lecturer, Univ. of Sydney 1983; Artist-in-Residence, London Borough of Lewisham 1984–86, Edin. Univ. 1986–87; Adviser Labour Party 1985–86 (Visual Arts Policy); exhbns. include Strike at Brannans, ICA 1972, Work, Wages and Prices, ICA 1974, A Shade of Green on Orange Edge, Arts Council of N.I. Gallery, Belfast, Material, Ronald Feldman Fine Arts, New York, At the Heart of the Matter, ICA 1982, Ronald Feldman Fine Arts "Goldfish", New York 1985. *Leisure interest:* rock and roll music. *Address:* 172 Erlanger Road, London, SE14 5TJ, England. *Telephone:* 0171-639 0308.

ATKINSON, Sir Frederick John, K.C.B., M.A.; British economist; b. 7 Dec. 1919, London; s. of George E. Atkinson and Elizabeth S. Cooper; m. Margaret Grace Gibson 1947; two d.; ed. Jesus Coll., Oxford Univ.; Lecturer, Jesus and Trinity Colls., Oxford 1947–49; Econ. Adviser, Cabinet Office 1949–51, at Embassy, Washington 1951–54 and at Treasury 1955–69; Chief Econ. Adviser, Dept. of Trade and Industry 1970–73; Asst. Sec.-Gen. OECD 1973–75; Deputy Sec. Chief Econ. Adviser, Dept. of Energy 1975–77; Chief Econ. Adviser, Treasury 1977–79; Hon. Fellow, Jesus Coll., Oxford 1979–. *Publication:* (jt. author) Oil and the British Economy 1983. *Leisure interest:* reading. *Address:* 26 Lee Terrace, Blackheath, London, SE3 9TZ; Tickner Cottage, Church Lane, Aldington, Kent, TN25 7EG, England. *Telephone:* 0181-852 1040; (01233) 720 514.

ATKINSON, Harry Hindmarsh, PH.D.; British physicist; b. 5 Aug. 1929, Wellington, New Zealand; s. of late Harry Temple Hindmarsh and Constance Hindmarsh Shields; m. Anne Judith Barrett 1958; two s. one d.; ed. Canterbury Univ. Coll., N.Z., Corpus Christi Coll. and Cavendish Lab., Univ. of Cambridge; Asst. Lecturer of Physics, Canterbury Univ. Coll., N.Z. 1952–53; Research Asst., Cornell Univ., U.S.A. 1954–55; Sr. Research Fellow, A.E.R.E., Harwell 1958–61; Head, General Physics Group, Rutherford Lab. 1961–69; Staff Chief Scientific Adviser to U.K. Govt., Cabinet Office 1969–72; Head, Astronomy, Space and Radio Div., Science Research Council 1972–78, Under Sec. and Dir., Astronomy, Space and Nuclear Physics 1983–86; Under Sec. and Dir. of Science, Science and Eng. Research Council 1983–88, Under Sec. and Dir. (Special Responsibilities) 1988–92, Consultant 1992–; Chief Scientist (part-time) U.K. Loss Prevention Council 1990–; Chair. Anglo-Dutch Astronomy Cttee. 1981–88, Steering Cttee., Inst. Laue Langevin (ILL), Grenoble 1984–88; Vice-Chair. Council, European Space Agency 1981–84, Chair. 1984–87; U.K. del. Intergovernmental Panel on High Energy Physics 1983–91, Council of European Synchrotron Radiation Facility 1985–88; Assessor Univ. Grants Cttee. 1985–89; U.K. mem. S. African Astronomical Observatory Cttee. 1979–85, Anglo-Australian Telescope Bd. 1979–88; mem. NI Cttee. of Univ. Funding Council 1989–93; Co-ordinator Australia, N.Z., U.K. Science Scheme 1989–94. *Address:* Ampney Lodge, Bampton, Oxon., OX18 2JN, England. *Telephone:* (01993) 850 120. *Fax:* (01993) 851 529.

ATKINSON, Sir Robert, Kt., D.S.C., R.D., B.SC.ENG., F.ENG., F.I.MECH.; British business executive; b. 7 March 1916, Tynemouth, Northumberland; s. of Nicholas and Margaret Atkinson; m. 1st Joyce Forster 1941 (died 1973); one s. one d.; m. 2nd Margaret Hazel Walker 1977; ed. Christ Church School, Tynemouth Grammar School, Univ. of London; served World War II (D.S.C. and two bars; mentioned in despatches); Man. Dir. William Doxford 1957–61; Tube Investments 1961–67; Unicorn Industries 1967–72; Chair. Aurora Holdings 1972–; Chair. and Chief Exec. British Shipbuilders 1980–84. *Publications:* The Design and Operating Experience of an Ore Carrier Built Abroad 1957, Some Crankshaft Failures: Investigations into Causes and Remedies 1960, The Manufacture of Crankshafts (North East Coast of Engineers and Shipbuilders Gold Medal) 1961, British Shipbuilders' Offshore Division 1962, Productivity Improvement in Ship Design and Construction 1983. *Leisure interests:* salmon and trout fishing, walking, gardening. *Address:* Southwood House, Itchen Abbas, Winchester, Hants., SO21 1AT, England. *Telephone:* (01962) 779610.

ATKINSON, Rowan Sebastian, M.SC.; British actor and author; b. 6 Jan. 1955; s. of late Eric Atkinson and of Ella Atkinson; m. Sunetra Sastry 1990; ed. Durham Cathedral Choristers' School, St. Bees School and Univs. of Newcastle and Oxford; stage appearances include: Beyond a Joke, Hampstead 1978, Oxford Univ. revues at Edinburgh Fringe, one-man show, London 1981, The Nerd 1985, The New Revue 1986, The Sneeze 1988. *TV appearances:* Not the Nine O'Clock News 1979–82, Blackadder 1983, Blackadder II 1985, Blackadder the Third 1987, Blackadder Goes Forth 1989, Mr Bean, The Return of Mr Bean, The Curse of Mr Bean 1990–91, Rowan Atkinson on Location in Boston 1993, Full Throttle 1994, The Thin Blue Line 1995. *Films:* Never Say Never Again, The Tall Guy 1989, The Appointments of Dennis Jennings 1989, The Witches 1990, Four Weddings and a Funeral 1994, Hot Shots – Part Deux 1994, Bean: The Ultimate Disaster Movie 1997. *Leisure interests:* motor cars, motor sport. *Address:* c/o PBJ Management Ltd., 5 Soho Square, London, W1V 5DE, England. *Telephone:* 0171-287 1112.

ATLANTOV, Vladimir Andreevich; Russian tenor; b. 19 Feb. 1933, Leningrad; ed. Leningrad Conservatory (pupil of Natalya Bolotina); mem. CPSU 1966–88; joined Leningrad Kirov 1963; further study, La Scala, Milan 1963–65; won Tchaikovsky Competition 1966, and Int. Contest for Young Singers, Sofia 1967; soloist with Moscow Bolshoi Theatre 1968–88, with Vienna State Opera 1987–, Kammersänger 1987; R.S.F.S.R. People's Artist 1972, U.S.S.R. People's Artist 1976; major roles include German in The Queen of Spades, José in Carmen, Otello, Cavaradossi in Tosca; many tours and recordings.

ATOPARE, Sir Sailas, G.C.M.G.; Papua New Guinea Governor-General and civil servant; b. 1951; m.; ed. Jones Missionary Coll., Rabaul, E. New Britain Prov.; fmrly. Agriculture Officer, Dept. of Agric., Stocks and Fisheries, Asst. Transport Man., Dept. of Works and Supply, Man. and Sec. Assro-Watabung Rural Devt. Corpn.; mem. Nat. Parl. for Goroka Open, Eastern Highlands Prov. 1977; Gov.-Gen. 1997–; Sec.-Gen. Papua New Guinea Coffee Growers' Asscn.; K.St.J. *Address:* Office of the Governor, Port Moresby, Papua New Guinea.

ATRASH, Muhammad al-, PH.D.; Syrian international official; b. 13 Nov. 1934, Tartous; s. of Hassan Sayed al-Atrash and Aziza Sayed al-Atrash; m. Felicia al-Atrash 1958; two s. one d.; ed. American Univ., Beirut, Lebanon, American Univ., Washington, D.C., U.S.A., London School of Econs.; joined Cen. Bank of Syria 1963, Research Dept. 1963, Head of Credit Dept. 1966–70; Alt. Exec. Dir. IMF 1970–73; Deputy Gov. Cen. Bank of Syria 1974; Exec. Dir. IBRD 1974–76, IMF 1976–78; del. to Second Cttee. of UN Gen. Assembly, to UNCTAD and other int. econ. confs. 1963–70; part-time Lecturer, Univ. of Damascus 1963–70; mem. Deputies of IMF Interim Cttee. of the Bd. of Govs. on Reform of Int. Monetary System 1972–74; Assoc. mem. IMF Interim Cttee. 1974–76, ex officio mem. 1976–78; Minister of Economy and Foreign Trade 1980–82. *Publications:* articles in Al-Abhath (Quarterly of the American Univ. of Beirut) 1963, 1964, 1966. *Leisure interests:* swimming, walking, reading books on history and literature. *Address:* c/o Ministry of Economy and Foreign Trade, Damascus, Syria.

ATTALI, Bernard; French business executive; b. 1 Nov. 1943, Algiers; s. of the late Simon Attali and Fernande Abecassis; twin brother of Jacques Attali (q.v.); m. Hélène Scebat 1974; one d.; ed. Lycée Gauthier, Algiers, Lycée Janson-de-Sailly, Paris, Faculté de Droit, Paris, Inst. d'Etudes Politiques, Paris and Ecole Nat. d'Admin.; auditeur, Cour des Comptes 1968, adviser 1974; on secondment to Commissariat Général du Plan d'Equipement et de la Productivité 1972–74; Délégation à l'Aménagement du Térritoire et à l'Action Regionale (Datar) 1974–80, 1981–84; Finance Dir. Soc. Club Meditérranée 1980–81; Pres. Regional Cttee. of EEC 1981–84; Pres. Groupe des Assurances Nationales (Gan) 1984–86; Pres. Banque pour l'Industrie Française 1984–86; Adviser on European Affairs, Commercial Union Assurance 1986–88, Chair. Air France 1988–93; Pres. Supervisory Council, Sociétés Epargne de France 1986–88, Commercial Union lard 1986–88; Pres. Euroberlin 1988, Union de transports aériens (UTA) 1990, Asscn. des Transporteurs Aériens Européens (AEA) 1991; Vice-Pres. Supervisory Bd. BIGT 1995; Admin. Aérospatiale 1989, Air Inter 1990; Chief Adviser Revenue Court 1991–93; Chair. Supervisory Bd. Banque Arjil (part of Lagadère)

1993–96; Chair. Bankers Trust Co. France 1996–; Officier Ordre Nat. du Mérite, Chevalier, Légion d'honneur. *Publication:* Les Guerres du Ciel 1994. *Address:* Bankers Trust Company France, 12 rond-point des Champs-Elysées, 75008 Paris (Office); 12 avenue Pierre 1er de Serbie, 75016 Paris, France (Home).

ATTALI, Jacques; French international bank official and writer; b. 1 Nov. 1943, Algiers; s. of the late Simon Attali and of Fernande Attali; twin brother of Bernard Attali (q.v.); m. Elisabeth Allain 1981; one s. one d.; ed. Ecole Polytechnique, Inst. d'Etudes Politiques de Paris, Ecoles des Mines de Paris, Ecole Nat. d'Admin; started career as mining engineer, then Lecturer in Econs., Ecole Polytechnique; Auditeur, Council of State; Adviser to the Pres. 1981–91; State Councillor 1989–91; Pres. European Bank for Reconstruction and Development (EBRD), London 1991–93; Pres. Attali et Associés 1994–; mem. Council of State 1981–90, 1993–. *Publications:* Analyse économique de la vie politique 1972, Modèles politiques 1973, Anti-économique (with Marc Guillaume) 1974, La parole et l'outil 1975, Bruits, Essai sur l'économie politique de la musique 1976, La nouvelle économie française 1977, L'ordre cannibale 1979, Les trois mondes 1981, Histoires du temps 1982, La figure de Fraser 1984, Un homme d'influence 1985, Au propre et au Figuré 1988, La vie éternelle (novel) 1989, Millennium: Winners and Losers in the Coming World Order 1991, 1492 1991, Verbatim (Tome I) 1993, Europe(s) 1994, Verbatim (Tome II) 1995, Economie de l'Apocalypse 1995, Tome III 1996, Chemins de Sagesse 1996, Au delà de nulle part 1997, Dictionnaire du XXIe siècle 1998. *Address:* A & A, 28 rue Bayard, 75008 Paris, France.

ATTALIDES, Michalis A., PH.D; Cypriot diplomatist; b. 1941; m.; two c.; ed. L.S.E. and Princeton Univ.; lecturer in Sociology, Univ. of Leicester 1966–68; sociologist, Cyprus Town and Country Planning Project 1968–70; counterpart of UNESCO expert, Social Research Centre, Cyprus 1971, 1973–74; mil. service 1972; Guest Lecturer Otto Suhr Inst., Free Univ. of Berlin 1974–75; journalist 1975–76; worked in Int. Relations Service, House of Reps. of Cyprus 1977–89, Dir. 1979–; Amb., Dir. of Political Affairs Division B (Cyprus question), Ministry of Foreign Affairs 1989–91, Amb. of Cyprus to France (also accred. to Morocco, Portugal and Spain) 1991–95, Amb. to Belgium (also accred. to Luxembourg) and Perm. Del. of Cyprus to EU 1995–98, High Commr. in U.K. 1998–; Grand Officier, Ordre nat. du Mérite. *Publications:* Cyprus: Nationalism and International Politics 1980, Social Change and Urbanization in Cyprus: A study of Nicosia 1971. *Address:* Cyprus High Commission, 93 Park Street, London, W1Y 4ET, England. *Telephone:* 0171-499 8272. *Fax:* 0171-491 0691.

ATTALLAH, Naim Ibrahim, F.R.S.A.; British publisher and financial adviser; b. 1 May 1931, Haifa, Palestine; s. of Ibrahim Attallah and Genevieve Attallah; m. Maria Nykolyn 1957; one s.; ed. Coll. des Frères, Haifa and Battersea Polytechnic, London; Propr. Quartet Books 1976–, Women's Press 1977–, Robin Clark 1980–, Pipeline Books 1978–, The Literary Review 1981–, The Wire 1984–, Acad. Club 1989–, The Oldie 1991–94; Group Chief Exec. Asprey PLC 1992–96, Deputy Chair. Asprey (Bond Street) 1992–98; Man. Dir. Mappin and Webb 1990–95; Exec. Dir. Garrard 1990–95; Chair. Namara Group of cos. 1973–, launched Parfums Namara 1985, Avant L'Amour and Après L'Amour 1985, Naïdor 1987, L'Amour de Namara 1990; Hon. M.A. (Surrey) 1993; Retail Personality of the Year, U.K. Jewellery Awards 1993. *Films produced:* The Slipper and the Rose (with David Frost q.v.) 1975, Brimstone and Treacle (Exec. Producer) 1982, and several TV documentaries. *Theatre:* Happy End (Co-Presenter) 1975, The Beastly Beatitudes of Balthazar B. (Presenter and Producer) 1981, Trafford Tanzi (Co-Producer) 1982. *Publications:* Women 1987, Singular Encounters 1990, Of a Certain Age 1992, More of a Certain Age 1993, Speaking for the Oldie 1994, A Timeless Passion 1995, Tara and Claire (novel) 1996, Asking Questions 1996, A Woman a Week 1998, In Conversation with Naim Attalah 1998. *Leisure interests:* classical music, opera, theatre, cinema, photography and fine arts. *Address:* 51 Beak Street, London, W1R 3LF, England. *Telephone:* 0171-434 1529.

ATTAR, Mohamed Saeed Al-, PH.D.; Yemeni politician; b. 26 Nov. 1927; m.; one s. five d.; ed. Sorbonne, Paris; Research Assoc. Sorbonne and Inst. de Développement, Paris 1959–62; Gen. Man. Yemen Bank for Reconstruction and Devt. 1962–65, Chair. 1965–68; mem. High Econ. Comm. 1962–68; Ministry of Econ. 1965–68; Perm. Rep. of Yemen Arab Repub. to UN 1968–71, 1973–74; Roving Amb. 1971–73; Under-Sec.-Gen. of UN and Exec. Sec. Econ. Comm. for Western Asia (ECWA) 1974–85; Deputy Prime Minister, Minister of Devt. and Chair. Cen. Planning Org. 1985; Deputy Prime Minister and Minister of Industry 1990–95; Pres. Gen. Investment Authority 1993; Deputy Prime Minister and Minister of Oil and Mineral Resources 1995; mem. Supreme Council for Oil; many other public appts.; MARIB Legion decoration (Yemen); Légion d'honneur. *Publications include:* La Révolution Yemenite 1964; articles in magazines and newspapers. *Address:* c/o Ministry of Oil and Mineral Resources, P.O. Box 81, San'a, Yemen.

ATTAS, Haydar Abu Bakr al-; Yemeni politician; fmr. Minister of Construction; Prime Minister of People's Democratic Repub. of Yemen 1985–86; President (following overthrow of govt. of Ali Nasser Mohammed q.v.) 1986–90; Prime Minister of Repub. of Yemen 1990–94. *Address:* c/o Office of the Prime Minister, Sana'a, Yemen.

ATTASSI, Lt.-Gen. Louai; Syrian politician and army officer; b. 1926; ed. Syrian Military Acad., and Staff Officers' Coll., Homs.; took part in Palestinian war 1948; opposed Syrian break with Egypt 1961; Garrison Commdr., Aleppo April 1962; Mil. Attaché, Syrian Embassy, Washington 1962–63; C.-in-C. of Syrian Armed Forces and Pres. of Revolutionary Council March-July 1963.

ATTENBOROUGH, Baron (Life Peer) cr. 1993, of Richmond upon Thames in the London Borough of Richmond upon Thames, **Richard (Samuel) Attenborough,** Kt., C.B.E.; British actor, producer and director; b. 29 Aug. 1923; s. of late Frederick Attenborough and Mary Attenborough; brother of Sir David Attenborough (q.v.); m. Sheila Beryl Grant Sim 1945; one s. two d.; ed. Wyggeston Grammar School, Leicester, Royal Acad. of Dramatic Art, London; first stage appearance as Richard Miller in Ah! Wilderness, Palmers Green 1941; West End debut in Awake and Sing 1942; first film appearance In Which We Serve 1942; joined R.A.F. 1943; seconded to R.A.F. Film Unit for Journey Together 1944, demobilised 1946; returned to stage 1949; formed Beaver Films with Bryan Forbes (q.v.) 1959, Allied Film Makers 1960; Goodwill Amb. for UNICEF 1987–; Dir. Chelsea Football Club 1969–82; mem. British Actors' Equity Asscn. Council 1949–73, Cinematograph Films Council 1967–73, Arts Council of G.B. 1970–73; Chair. Actors' Charitable Trust 1956–88 (Pres. 1988–), Combined Theatrical Charities Appeals Council 1964–88 (Pres. 1988–), B.A.F.T.A. 1969–70 (Vice-Pres. 1971–94), Royal Acad. of Dramatic Arts 1970 (mem. Council 1963–), Capital Radio 1972–92 (Life Pres. 1992–), Help a London Child 1975–, UK Trustees Waterford-Kamhlaba School, Swaziland 1976– (Gov. 1987–), Duke of York's Theatre 1979–92, B.F.I. 1981–92, Goldcrest Films and TV 1982–87, Cttee. of Inquiry into the Arts and Disabled People 1983–85, Channel Four TV 1987–92 (Deputy Chair. 1980–86), British Screen Advisory Council 1987–96, European Script Fund 1988–96 (Hon. Pres. 1996); Gov. Nat. Film School 1970–81, Motability 1977–; Pres. Muscular Dystrophy Group of G.B. 1971– (Vice-Pres. 1962–71), The Gandhi Foundation 1983–, Brighton Festival 1984–95, British Film Year 1984–86, Arts for Health 1989–, Gardner Centre for the Arts, Sussex Univ. 1990– (Patron 1969–82); Dir. Young Vic 1974–84, Chelsea Football Club 1969–82; Trustee Tate Gallery 1976–82, 1994–96, Tate Foundation 1986–, Foundation for Sport and the Arts 1991–; Patron Kingsley Hall Community Centre 1982–, R.A. Centre for Disability and the Arts, Leicester 1990–; Pro-Chancellor Sussex Univ. 1970–98, Chancellor 1998–; Freeman of Leicester 1990; Hon. D. Litt. (Leicester) 1970, (Kent) 1981, (Sussex) 1987; Hon. D.C.L. (Newcastle) 1974; Hon. LL.D. (Dickinson, Penn.) 1983; Fellow King's Coll. London 1993; Evening Standard Film Award for 40 Years' Service to British Cinema 1983, Martin Luther King Jr. Peace Prize 1983, Padma Bhushan, India 1983, European Film Awards Award of Merit 1988, Fellow B.A.F.T.A., Hon. Fellow B.F.I. 1992, Shakespeare Prize for Oustanding Contrib. to European Culture 1992; Commdr. des Arts et des Lettres, Chevalier, Légion d'honneur, Dilys Powell Award 1995. *Stage appearances include:* The Little Foxes 1942, Brighton Rock 1943, The Way Back Home (Home of the Brave) 1949, To Dorothy a Son 1965, Sweet Madness 1952, The Mousetrap 1952–54, Double Image 1956–57, The Rape of the Belt 1957–58. *Film appearances include:* School for Secrets, The Man Within, Dancing with Crime, Brighton Rock, London Belongs to Me, The Guinea Pig, The Lost People, Boys in Brown, Morning Departure, Hell is Sold Out, The Magic Box, Gift Horse, Father's Doing Fine, Eight O'Clock Walk, The Ship that Died of Shame, Private's Progress, The Baby and the Battleship, Brothers in Law, The Scamp, Dunkirk, The Man Upstairs, Sea of Sand, Danger Within, I'm All Right Jack, Jet Storm, S.O.S. Pacific, The Angry Silence (also co-prod.) 1959, The League of Gentlemen 1960, Only Two Can Play, All Night Long 1961, The Dock Brief, The Great Escape 1962, Seance on a Wet Afternoon (also prod., Best Actor, San Sebastian Film Festival and British Film Acad.), The Third Secret 1963, Guns at Batasi (Best Actor, British Film Acad.) 1964, The Flight of the Phoenix 1965, The Sand Pebbles (Hollywood Golden Globe) 1966, Dr. Doolittle (Hollywood Golden Globe), The Bliss of Mrs. Blossom 1967, Only When I Larf 1968, The Last Grenade, A Severed Head, David Copperfield, Loot 1969, 10 Rillington Place 1970, And Then There Were None, Rosebud, Brannigan, Conduct Unbecoming 1974, The Chess Players 1977, The Human Factor 1979, Jurassic Park 1992, Miracle on 34th Street 1994. *Produced:* Whistle Down the Wind 1961, The L-Shaped Room 1962. *Directed:* Young Winston (Hollywood Golden Globe) 1972, A Bridge Too Far (Evening News Best Drama Award) 1976, Magic 1978, A Chorus Line 1985. *Produced and directed:* Oh! What a Lovely War (16 int. Awards), Gandhi (8 Oscars, 5 B.A.F.T.A. Awards, 5 Hollywood Golden Globes, Dirs'. Guild of America Award for Outstanding Directorial Achievement) 1980–81, Cry Freedom (Berlinale Kamera, BFI Award for Tech. Achievement) 1987, Chaplin 1992, Shadowlands 1993 (Alexander Korda Award for Outstanding British Film of the Year, BAFTA), In Love and War 1997, Grey Owl 1998. *Publications:* In Search of Gandhi 1982, Richard Attenborough's Chorus Line (with Diana Carter) 1986, Cry Freedom, A Pictorial Record 1987. *Leisure interests:* collecting paintings and sculpture, listening to music, watching football. *Address:* Old Friars, Richmond Green, Surrey, TW9 1NQ, England.

ATTENBOROUGH, Sir David Frederick, Kt., C.H., C.V.O., C.B.E., M.A., F.R.S.; British broadcaster and writer; b. 8 May 1926, London; s. of Frederick and Mary Attenborough; brother of Lord Attenborough (q.v.); m. Jane Elizabeth Ebsworth Oriel 1950 (died 1997); one s. one d.; ed. Wyggeston Grammar School, Leicester, and Clare Coll., Cambridge; Royal Navy 1947–49; Ed. Asst. in publishing house 1949–52; with BBC Television 1952–73, Trainee Producer BBC TV 1952–54, Producer of zoological, archaeological, travel, political and other programmes 1954–64, Controller BBC 2 1964–68, Dir. of Programmes, TV 1969–73; writer, presenter BBC series:

Tribal Eye 1976, Wildlife on One, annually 1977–, Life on Earth 1979, The Living Planet 1984, The First Eden 1987, Lost World, Vanished Lives 1989, The Trials of Life 1990, Life in the Freezer 1993, The Private Life of Plants 1995, The Life of Birds 1998; Pres. B.A.A.S. 1990–91, Royal Soc. for Nature Conservation 1991–96; mem. Man. Bd., BBC 1969–73; freelance broadcaster and writer 1973–; mem. Nature Conservancy Council 1975–82; Fellow, Soc. of Film and Television Arts 1980; Hon. Fellow, Clare Coll., Cambridge 1980, U.M.I.S.T. 1980; Int. Trustee, World Wild Life Fund 1979–86; Trustee, British Museum 1980–, Science Museum 1984–87, Royal Botanical Gardens, Kew 1986–92; Hon. D.Litt. (Leicester, London, Birmingham and City Univs.), Hon. D.Sc. (Liverpool, Ulster, Sussex, Bath, Durham, Keele and Heriot-Watt), Hon. LL.D. (Bristol and Glasgow) 1977, Hon. D.Univ. (Open Univ.) 1980, (Essex) 1987, Antwerp 1993; Dr. h.c. (Edin.) 1994; Special Award, Guild of TV Producers 1961, Silver Medal, Royal TV Soc. 1966, Silver Medal, Zoological Soc. of London 1966, Desmond Davis Award, Soc. of Film and TV Arts 1970, Founders Gold Medal, Royal Geographical Soc. 1985, UNESCO Kalinga Prize 1982, Medallist, Acad. of Natural Sciences, Philadelphia 1982, Encyclopedia Britannica Award 1987. *Publications:* Zoo Quest to Guiana 1956, Zoo Quest for a Dragon 1957, Zoo Quest in Paraguay 1959, Quest in Paradise 1960, Zoo Quest to Madagascar 1961, Quest under Capricorn 1963, The Tribal Eye 1976, Life on Earth 1979, The Zoo Quest Expeditions 1982; The Living Planet 1984, The First Eden, The Mediterranean World and Man 1987, The Trials of Life 1990, The Private Life of Plants 1994, The Life of Birds 1998 (BP Natural World Book Prize). *Leisure interests:* music, tribal art, natural history. *Address:* 5 Park Road, Richmond, Surrey, TW10 6NS, England.

ATTENBOROUGH, Philip John, C.B.E.; British book publisher; b. 3 June 1936; s. of John Attenborough C.B.E. and Barbara Attenborough (née Sandle); m. Rosemary Littler 1963; one s. one d.; ed. Rugby School, Trinity Coll., Oxford; joined Hodder & Stoughton 1957, Dir. 1963, Sales Dir. 1969; Chair. Hodder & Stoughton Ltd. and Hodder & Stoughton Holdings Ltd. 1975–93, Deputy Chair. Hodder Headline PLC 1993–96; Chair. The Lancet Ltd. 1977–91; Dir. Book Tokens Ltd. 1985–96; mem. Council, Publishers' Asscn. 1976–92, Pres. 1983–85; U.K. Rep. Fédération des Editeurs Européens 1986–93; mem. Exec. Cttee., Int. Publishers' Asscn. 1988–96, Vice-Pres. 1992–96; Chair., British Council Publishers' Advisory Cttee. 1989–93; Adviser, UNESCO Publishing 1992–95. *Publication:* The Rebirth of European Publishing: An Anglo-European Perspective of '1992' (essay) 1991. *Leisure interests:* trout fishing, watching cricket. *Address:* Coldhanger, Seal Chart, Sevenoaks, Kent, TN15 0EJ, England. *Telephone:* (01732) 761516.

ATTERSEE; Austrian artist; b. (as Christian Ludwig) 28 Aug. 1940, Pressburg; s. of Christian and Susanne Ludwig; ed. Akademie für Angewandte Kunst, Vienna; has worked as an artist since 1963; more than 200 one-man exhbns. in Germany, France, Netherlands, Italy, Austria and Switzerland, including Venice Biennale. *Publications:* Attersee Werksquer 1962–82, Attersee, Biennale Venedig 1984. *Leisure interest:* sailing. *Address:* Seilerstätte 5/14, 1010 Vienna, Austria. *Telephone:* (0) 222/513-2177.

ATTOLICO, Count Giacomo; Italian diplomatist; b. 4 Oct. 1928, Rio de Janeiro, Brazil; s. of Count Bernardo Attolico di Adelfia and Countess Eleonora Pietromarchi; m. Serena Magliucci 1963; two s. one d.; ed. Univ. of Rome; joined Ministry of Foreign Affairs 1954, Consul Brussels 1963–67, Counsellor, Beirut 1967–69; Press Counsellor, Paris 1969–73, Econ. Dept., Ministry of Foreign Affairs 1973–79, Deputy Dir.-Gen. Econ. Dept. 1979–82, Diplomatic Adviser to Pres. of Italy 1982–85, Dir.-Gen. for Econ. Affairs 1985–88, Amb. to France 1988–91, to U.K. 1991–95. *Address:* c/o Ministry of Foreign Affairs, Piazzale della Farnesina 1, 00194 Rome, Italy.

ATUN, Hakki, M.PHIL.; Turkish Cypriot politician, architect, city planner; b. 1935, Ergazi; s. of Mustafa Atun and Emine Atun; m. Suna Atun 1960; one s. one d.; ed. Istanbul Tech. Univ., Manchester Univ., Nottingham Univ.; with Cyprus Govt. Planning and Housing Dept. 1961–63, Turkish Cypriot Admin. Planning and Housing Dept. 1963–68, Dir. Planning and Public Works Dept. 1968–75, Under-Sec. of State for Housing 1975, Minister of Rehabilitation and Housing 1976–78, of Economy and Finance 1978–81, of Culture, Educ. and Youth 1981–83, of Housing 1983–85; mem. Turkish Cypriot Parl. 1976–, Speaker 1985–93; Prime Minister of 'Turkish Repub. of Northern Cyprus' 1993–96; mem. Nat. Union Party (UBP) 1976–92; f. The Democratic Party, Leader 1992–96, Speaker of Legis. Ass. 1996–98. *Address:* Legislative Assembly of "Turkish Republic of Northern Cyprus", Lefkoşa (Nicosia), via Mersin 10, Turkey. *Telephone:* 2274656. *Fax:* 2282161.

ATWATER, Horace Brewster, Jr., M.B.A.; American business executive (retd.); b. 19 April 1931, Minneapolis; s. of Horace Atwater and Eleanor Cook; m. Martha Clark 1955; one s. three d.; ed. Princeton and Stanford Univs.; Divisional Vice-Pres. and Dir. of Marketing, Gen. Mills Inc. 1958–65, Marketing Vice-Pres. 1965–70, Exec. Vice-Pres. 1970–76, C.O.O. 1976–81, Pres. 1977–82, C.E.O. 1981–95, Chair. Bd. 1982–95; mem. Bd. of Dirs. Merck & Co. Inc., GE. *Address:* 4900 IDS Center, 80 South 8th Street, Minneapolis, MN 55402, U.S.A. (Office).

ATWOOD, John Leland, A.B., B.S.; American engineer; b. 26 Oct. 1904; ed. Hardin Simmons Univ. and Univ. of Texas; Junior Engineer, Army Air Corps, Wright Field, Ohio 1928; Design Engineer, Douglas Aircraft Co. 1930–34; Vice-Pres. and Chief Engineer, North American Aviation Inc. (became North American Rockwell, now Rockwell Int. Corpn.) 1934, Pres.1948–70, Chief Exec. Officer 1960, Chair. of the Bd. 1962, Senior Consultant and Dir. 1970–78; mem. Soc. Automotive Engineers; numerous awards and prizes, including Hon. Fellow, American Inst. of Aeronautics and Astronautics, Pres. 1954; Nat. Aeronautic Asscn. Wright Brothers Memorial Trophy 1983–. *Address:* P.O. Box 1587, Vista, CA 92085, U.S.A.

ATWOOD, Margaret, C.C., A.M., F.R.S.C.; Canadian author; b. 18 November 1939, Ottawa; m. Graeme Gibson; one d.; ed. Univ. of Toronto and Harvard Univ.; taught at Univ. of British Columbia 1964–65, Sir George Williams Univ. 1967–68, Univ. of Alberta 1969–70, York Univ. 1971; Writer-in-residence, Univ. of Toronto 1972–73, Tuscaloosa, Alabama 1985; Berg Prof New York Univ. 1986, Maquarie Univ; Australia 1987; Guggenheim Fellowship 1981; several awards for poetry and fiction, including Commonwealth Literary Prize 1987; Hon. D.Litt. (Trent) 1973, (Concordia) 1980, (Trent Univ.), (Smith Coll.) 1982, (Univ. of Toronto) 1983, (Mount Holyoke) 1985, (Univ. of Waterloo) 1985, (Univ. of Guelph) 1985, (Oxford) 1998, Hon. LL.D. (Queen's Univ.) 1974; Centennial Medal (Harvard Univ.) 1990; Order of Ont. 1990; City of Toronto Book Awards, Coles Book of the Year, Canadian Booksellers Author of the Year 1989. *Publications:* poetry: The Circle Game 1966, The Animals in that Country 1969, The Journals of Susanna Moodie 1970, Procedures for Underground 1970, Power Politics 1971, You Are Happy 1974, Selected Poems 1976, Two Headed Poems 1978, True Stories 1981, Snake Poems 1983, Interlunar 1984, Selected Poems II 1986, Selected Poems 1966–1984, 1990, Margaret Atwood Poems 1965–1975, 1991, Morning in the Burned House 1995; fiction: The Edible Woman 1969, Surfacing 1972, Lady Oracle 1976, Dancing Girls 1977, Life Before Man 1979, Bodily Harm 1981, Encounters With the Element Man 1982, Murder in the Dark 1983, Bluebeard's Egg (short stories) 1983, Unearthing Suite 1983, The Handmaid's Tale 1985, Cat's Eye 1988, Wilderness Tips (short stories) 1991, The Robber Bride 1993, Bones and Murder 1995, The Labrador Fiasco 1996, Alias Grace (novel) 1996; non-fiction: Survival: a Thematic Guide to Canadian Literature 1972, Second Words: Selected Critical Prose 1982, (ed.) The New Oxford Book of Canadian Verse in English 1982, The Oxford Book of Canadian Short Stories in English (ed.) 1986, Interlunar 1988, The New Oxford Book of Canadian Short Stories in English 1995; children's books: Up in the Tree 1978, Anna's Pet 1980, For the Birds 1990, Princess Prunella and the Purple Peanut 1996; reviews and critical articles. *Address:* c/o McClelland & Stewart, 481 University Avenue, 9th Floor, Toronto, Ont., M5G 2E9; Oxford University Press, 70 Wynford Drive, Don Mills, Ont., M3C 1J9, Canada.

ATZMON, Moshe; Israeli conductor; b. 30 July 1931, Budapest, Hungary; m. 1954; two d.; ed. Tel-Aviv Acad. of Music, Guildhall School of Music, London; left Hungary for Israel 1944; played the horn professionally in various orchestras for several years; second prize Dimitri Mitropoulos Competition for Conductors, New York 1963; Leonard Bernstein Prize 1963; First Prize, Int. Conductors Competition, Liverpool, England 1964; has conducted in Israel, England, Australia, Germany, Sweden, Norway, Switzerland, Spain, Finland, Italy, Austria, Turkey and U.S.A.; Chief Conductor, Sydney Symphony Orchestra 1969–71; Chief Conductor, North German Symphony Orchestra 1972; Musical Dir. Basel Symphony Orchestra 1972–86; Chief Conductor Tokyo Metropolitan Orchestra 1979–83, Nagoya Symphony Orchestra 1987–92; Musical Dir. Dortmund Opera House and Philharmonic Orchestra 1991–. *Leisure interests:* reading, travelling. *Address:* Marignanostr. 12, 4059 Basel, Switzerland. *Telephone:* 061-35 65 32.

AUBERGER, Bernard, ING. CIVIL, L. EN D., DIPL.; French banker; b. 5 Dec. 1937, Gennevilliers; s. of Paul Auberger and Jeanne (née Geny) Auberger; m. Christine Baraduc 1963; three s. one d.; ed. Ecole des Mines, Paris, Inst. d'Etudes Politiques, Paris, Ecole Nat. d'Admin., Paris; Investigating Officer French Ministry of Finance 1966–70; Adviser to Gen. Man. Crédit Nat., Paris 1970–72; Financial Attaché French Embassy, New York 1972–74; Dir. of Cabinet for Under Sec. for Finance 1974; attached to Industrial Relations Cttee. 1974–75; Dir. Production and Trade, French Ministry of Agric. 1975–80; Cen. Man. Société Générale 1983–86; Insp. Gen. of Finances 1988; Advisor to Pres. of Paluel-Marmont 1990; Pres. Cortal Bank 1991–98, Banque Directe 1994–; Vice-Pres., Dir.-Gen. Crédit du Nord 1993–94, Chair., C.E.O. 1994–95; Pres. Asscn. Opéra Comique-Salle Favart 1994–; Dir. Compagnie bancaire 1991–, Banque Paribas 1994–97; mem. Econ. and Social Council 1982–; Gen. Man. Caisse Nat. de Crédit Agricole 1986–88; Adviser to Chair. Palvel-Marmont Group 1990; Chevalier Ordre Nat. du Mérite, Chevalier du Mérite Agricole, Chevalier, Légion d'honneur. *Address:* Compagnie Bancaire, 5 Avenue Kléber, 75116 Paris; 13 rue du Bois-Joli, 92190 Meudon, France (Home). *Telephone:* 45.34.08.78 (Home).

AUBERT, Guy, D. ÈS SC.; French scientific director; b. 9 May 1938, Costes, Hautes-Alpes; m. 1962; two d.; Research Assoc. Lab. d'Electrostatique et de Physique du Metal, C.N.R.S., Grenoble; Titular Prof. Univ. Scientifique et Médicale de Grenoble 1970, Vice-Pres. in charge of research 1981–84; Scientific Del. of C.N.R.S. for Rhône-Alpes region 1981–83; Dir. Ecole Normale Supérieure de Lyon 1985–94; Dir.-Gen. C.N.R.S. 1994–97; extraordinary mem. Conseil d'Etat 1997–; mem. Universities' Higher Council, French Physics Soc.; Officier ordre nat. du Mérite; Chevalier Légion d'honneur, des Palmes académiques, du Mérite agricole. *Publications:* papers in scientific journals. *Leisure interests:* skiing, tennis. *Address:* Conseil d'Etat, Palais Royal, 75100 Paris RP (Office); 79 Bvd. Suchet, 75016 Paris, France.

AUBERT, Pierre; Swiss politician and lawyer; b. 3 March 1927, La Chaux-de-Fonds; s. of the late Alfred and Henriette Erni Aubert; m. Anne-Lise

Borel 1953; one s. one d.; ed. Univ. of Neuchatel; mem. of local Assembly, La Chaux-de-Fonds 1960–68, Pres. 1967–68; mem. Legis. Ass. of Canton of Neuchâtel 1961–75, Pres. 1969–70; Labour mem. Council of States (upper house of Fed. Assembly) 1971–77; mem. Fed. Council (Govt.) 1978–87, Vice-Pres. Jan.–Dec. 1982; Pres. of Switzerland Jan.–Dec. 1983, Jan.–Dec. 1987; Head of Fed. Foreign Affairs Dept. 1978–87. *Leisure interests:* camping, boxing, skiing, cycling, theatre, watches.

AUBOUIN, Jean Armand, D. ÈS SC.; French academic; b. 5 May 1928, Evreux; m. Françoise Delpouget 1953; two d.; ed. Lycées Buffon and St.-Louis, Ecole Normale Supérieure (Saint-Cloud) and Univ. of Paris; Asst. Univ. of Paris 1952–62, Prof. 1962–90; mem. Acad. of Sciences Inst. of France 1981–, Vice-Pres. 1986–88, Pres. 1989–90, Pres. Inst. of France 1989; Pres. Société Géologique de France 1976, Int. Geological Congress 1980, Scientific Advisory Bds. of Bureau de Recherches Géologiques et Minières 1984–90, and Inst. Français de Recherche pour l'Exploitation de la Mer 1985–90; mem. Scientific Advisory Bds. of Inst. français du Pétrole 1983–92, of Fondation de France 1984–89, Planning Cttee. Int. Programme of Ocean Drilling 1980–84; Pres. Cttee. Geological Map of the World 1984–92; mem. Scientific Advisory Bds. of various geology-related programmes; mem. Bd. of Dirs. Office de Recherche Scientifique d'Outre-mer 1984–88, Bureau de Recherche Géologique et Minières 1988–93, Inst. océanographique, Paris and Monaco 1994– (Pres. Comité Perfectionnement 1992–); mem. Conseil Supérieur Recherche et Technologie 1981–86; Pres. French Cttee. of Int. Decade for the Reduction of Natural Disasters 1990–93, Parc Naturel du Verdun 1994–; Foreign mem. Accademia dei Lincei, Italy 1974–, Acad. of Sciences, U.S.S.R. (now Russia) 1976–, Acad. of Athens, Greece 1980–, Acad. Europaea 1988–, Acad. of Zagreb, Croatia 1990–, Acad. Royale Sciences, Arts et Lettres de Belgique 1994–, Deutsche Akademie der Naturforscher Leopoldina 1995–; Hon. mem. Geological Soc. of London 1976–; Hon. Fellow Geological Soc. of America 1980–; Hon. mem. Société Physique Histoire Naturelle (Geneva) 1990–; Dr. (h.c.) Univ. of Athens 1992; C.N.R.S. Medal 1959, Museo de la Plata Medal 1977, Dumont Medal (Société Géologique de Belgique) 1977, Ville de Paris Medal 1980; Prize Viquesnel (Soc. Géologique de France) 1962, Prize Charles Jacob (Acad. des Sciences) 1976, Gaudry Prize (Société Géologique de France) 1990, Gold Medal Académie Royale des Sciences de Belgique 1990, Chevalier Ordre des Palmes académiques 1965, Chevalier Ordre Nat. du Mérite 1981, Chevalier Légion d'honneur 1989. *Publications:* Géologie de la Grèce septentrionale 1959, Geosynclines 1965, Manuel de Cartographie (Co.Ed.) 1970, Précis de Géologie (Co-Ed., 4 vols.) 1968–79, approx. 400 scientific articles. *Leisure interests:* reading, mountain walking and swimming at sea. *Address:* Institut de Géodynamique, avenue Albert Einstein, Sophia Antipolis, 06560 Valbonne (Office); 27 avenue des Baumettes, 06000 Nice, France (Home). *Telephone:* (04) 93.95.42.22 (Office); (04) 93.86.03.76 (Home). *Fax:* (04) 93.65.27.17 (Office); (04) 93.86.03.76 (Home).

AUBRY, Cécile (pseudonym of Anne-José Bernard); French author and scriptwriter; b. 3 Aug. 1928, Paris; d. of Lucien Bénard Aubry and Marguerite Candelier; m. Prince Brahim el Glaoui 1951 (divorced); one s.; ed. Lycée Victor Duruy, Paris; appeared in prin. role in Clouzot's film Manon 1948; subsequent roles in films The Black Rose 1950, Barbe Bleue 1951 and in Italian and French films 1951; author of numerous television scripts and series 1961–72, including Poly, Belle et Sébastien, Sébastien Parmi les Hommes, Sébastien et la Mary Morgane, Le Jeune Fabre, etc.; Officier des Arts et des Lettres. *Publications:* three novels 1974–85, several children's books. *Address:* Le Moulin Bleu, 6 Chemin du Moulin Bleu, 91410 Saint-Cyr-sous-Dourdan, France. *Telephone:* 64 59 01 06.

AUBRY, Martine Louise Marie; French politician; b. 8 Aug. 1950, Paris; d. of Jacques Delors (q.v.) and Marie Lephaille; m. Xavier Aubry; one d.; ed. Inst. Saint-Pierre-Fourier, Lycée Paul-Valéry, Faculté de Droit, Paris, Inst. des Sciences Sociales du Travail, Inst. d'Etudes Politiques, Paris and Ecole Nat. d'Admin.; Ministry of Labour 1975–79; Instructor Ecole Nat. d'Admin. 1978; Dir. of preparations for econ. competition for admin. of Univ. Paris-Dauphine 1978; civil admin. Conseil d'Etat 1980–81; Deputy Dir. Pvt. Office of Minister of Labour 1981; special assignment for Minister of Social Affairs and Nat. Solidarity 1983–84; Dir. of Labour Relations, Ministry of Labour 1984–87; Maître des requêtes, Conseil d'Etat 1987; Deputy Dir.-Gen. Pechiney 1989–91; Minister of Labour, Employment and Professional Training May 1991–93; Pres. FACE 1993–97; First Asst. Mayor of Lille 1995–; Vice-Pres. Lille Urban Council 1995; mem. Nat. Ass. for Nord region June 1997– (Socialist Party); Minister of Employment and Social Affairs 1997–. *Publications:* Le Choix d'Agir 1994, Petit dictionnaire pour lutter contre l'extrême droite (jtly.) 1995, Il est grand temps . . . 1997. *Address:* Ministry of Employment and Social Affairs, 127 rue de Grenelle, 75700 Paris; FACE, 91 bis rue du Cherche Midi, 75006 Paris; Mairie de Lille, 59001 Lille, France.

AUCHINCLOSS, Kenneth, M.A.; American editor; b. 3 July 1937, New York; s. of Douglas Auchincloss and Eleanor Grant Auchincloss; m. Eleanor Johnson 1971; one s. one d.; ed. Harvard Coll. and Balliol Coll. Oxford; Asst. to Deputy Sec. U.S. Dept. of Commerce 1961; Exec. Asst. to U.S. Special Trade Rep. 1963; mem. staff, Inst. for Advanced Study 1965; Assoc. Ed. Newsweek 1966–68, Gen. Ed. 1968–72, Sr. Ed. 1972, Exec. Ed. 1972–76, Man. Ed. 1976–95, Ed. int. edition 1986–95, Ed.-at-large 1996–. *Leisure interest:* collecting books (fine printing). *Address:* Newsweek, 251 West 57th Street, New York, NY 10019 (Office); 40 East 62nd Street, New York, NY 10021, U.S.A. (Home). *Telephone:* (212) 445-4468 (Office). *Fax:* (212) 445-4450 (Office).

AUCHINCLOSS, Louis Stanton, LL.B., D.LITT.; American author and lawyer; b. 27 Sept. 1917; s. of Joseph Howland and Priscilla (née Stanton) Auchincloss; m. Adele Lawrence 1957; three s.; ed. Groton School, Yale Univ. and Univ. of Virginia; admitted to New York Bar 1941, Assoc. Sullivan and Cromwell 1941–51, Hawkins, Delafield and Wood, New York 1954–58, partner 1958–86; Lieut. U.S. Navy 1941–45; Pres. Museum of the City of New York; mem. Nat. Inst. of Arts and Letters. *Publications:* The Indifferent Children 1947, The Injustice Collectors 1950, Sybil 1952, A Law for the Lion 1953, The Romantic Egoists 1954, The Great World and Timothy Colt 1956, Venus in Sparta 1958, Pursuit of the Prodigal 1959, House of Five Talents 1960, Reflections of a Jacobite 1961, Portrait in Brownstone 1962, Powers of Attorney 1963, The Rector of Justin 1964, Pioneers and Caretakers 1965, The Embezzler 1966, Tales of Manhattan 1967, A World of Profit 1969, Motiveless Malignity 1969, Edith Wharton: A Woman in Her Time 1971, I Come as a Thief 1972, Richelieu 1972, The Partners 1974, A Winter's Capital 1974, Reading Henry James 1975, The Winthrop Covenant 1976, The Dark Lady 1977, The Country Cousin 1978, Persons of Consequence 1979, Life, Law and Letters 1979, The House of the Prophet 1980, The Cat and the King 1981, Watchfires 1982, Exit Lady Masham 1983, The Book Class 1984, Honorable Men 1985, Diary of a Yuppie 1986, Skinny Island 1987, The Golden Calves 1988, Fellow Passengers 1989, The Vanderbilt Era 1989, The Lady of Situations 1991, False Gods 1992, Three Lives 1993, Tales of Yesteryear 1994, Collected Stories 1994, The Education of Oscar Fairfax 1995, The Man Behind the Book 1996, La Gloire 1996, The Atonement 1997. *Address:* 1111 Park Avenue, New York, NY 10028, U.S.A. (Home).

AUCOTT, George William, B.S.; American company executive; b. 24 Aug. 1934, Philadelphia; s. of George William and Clara Anna (Nagel) Aucott; m. Ruth Tonetta Heller 1956; one s. two d.; ed. Ursinus Coll., Collegeville, Pa. and Harvard Univ.; served U.S. army 1957–60; joined Firestone Tire & Rubber Co. 1956, Pres. Firestone Industrial Products Co. 1978, Firestone Canada Inc. 1978–80, Vice-Pres. Mfg. parent co., Akron, Ohio 1980; Pres. and C.O.O. Firestone Int. 1982–91, Pres., C.O.O. World Tire Group 1988–; mem. Bd. of Dirs. and Exec. Vice-Pres. of Corpn. 1986–; Bd. Dirs. Akron United Way, 1968–73; Pres. and Dir. Akron YMCA 1969–73; mem. Bd. of Dirs. Rubber Mfrs. Asscn., Rubber Asscn. *Address:* 1200 Firestone Parkway, Akron, OH 44317 (Office).

AUDRAIN, Paul André Marie; French business executive; b. 17 May 1945, Chambéry, Savoie; s. of Jean Audrain and Margueritte Gubian; m. Danièle Pons 1967; two s.; ed. Lycée d'Etat de Chambéry, Lycée du Parc Lyon, Ecole Supérieure des Sciences Economiques et Commerciales, Paris; Engineer, IBM France 1969–70; Financial and Admin. Dir. Aiglon, Angers 1970–74; Financial Dir. Christian Dior 1974–79, then Sec. Gen., Financial and Admin. Dir. 1979–84, Chair. and C.E.O. 1984–85, Pres. 1985–86; Int. Dir. Financière Agache 1986–87; Chair. and C.E.O. Christian Lacroix 1987–88, Pierre Balmain 1988–89; C.E.O. Société Crillon 1990–93, Int. Consulting & Licensing. *Address:* 27 rue du Phare, Port Navalo, 56 640 Arzon (Home); 149 rue Saint Dominique, 75007 Paris, France. *Telephone:* (02) 97.53.85.45 (Office). *Fax:* (02) 97-53-63-76.

AUDRAN, Stéphane (see Dacheville, Colette).

AUERBACH, Frank; British artist; b. 29 April 1931, Berlin; s. of Max and Charlotte Auerbach; m. Julia Wolstenholme 1958; one s.; ed. St. Martin's School of Art, London, Royal Coll. of Art; one-man exhbns. at Beaux-Arts Gallery, London 1956, 1959, 1961, 1962, 1963, Marlborough Fine Art, London 1965, 1967, 1971, 1974, 1983, 1987, 1990, Marlborough Gallery Inc., New York 1969, Villiers Art Gallery, Sydney 1972, Univ. of Essex, Colchester 1973, Galleria Bergamini, Milan 1973, Marlborough, Zurich 1976, Retrospective Exhbn., Arts Council, Hayward Gallery, London, Fruit Market Gallery, Edinburgh 1978, Bernard Jacobson, New York 1979, Marlborough Gallery, New York 1982, 1994, Anne Berthoud, London 1983, Kunstverein, Hamburg 1986, Museum Folkwang, Essen, Centro de Arte Reina Sofia, Madrid 1987, Rijksmuseum Vincent Van Gogh, Amsterdam 1989, Paul Mellon Centre for British Art, Yale 1991, New Haven 1991, Nat. Gallery 1995, Campbell-Thibaud, San Francisco 1995, Rex Irwin, Sydney 1996; numerous group exhbns. including Carnegie Int. Exhbn., Pittsburg 1958, 1961, Gulbenkian Exhbn., London 1964, Peter Stuyvesant Foundation Collection, London 1967, New Spirit in Painting, Royal Acad. of Arts, London 1981, Westkunst, Cologne 1981, Venice Biennale 1982, The Hard-Won Image, Tate Gallery, London 1984, Venice Biennale 1986 (Golden Lion Award), British Art in the Twentieth Century, R.A., London 1987, The Pursuit of the Real, Manchester City Art Gallery 1990, Israel Museum, Jerusalem 1992–93, "From London", Edin., Luxembourg, Lausanne, Barcelona 1995–96; works in public collections in U.K., Australia, Brazil, U.S.A., Mexico, Israel, S. Africa, Canada; Silver Medal for Painting, Royal Coll. of Art. *Address:* c/o Marlborough Fine Art, 6 Albemarle Street, London, W1X 4BY, England.

AUERBACH, Stanley Irving, M.S., PH.D.; American ecologist; b. 21 May 1921, Chicago, Ill.; s. of Abraham and Carrie Friedman Auerbach; m. Dawn Patricia Davey 1954; two s. two d.; ed. Univ. of Illinois and Northwestern Univ.; Second Lieut. U.S. Army 1942–44; instructor, then Asst. Prof., Roosevelt Univ., Chicago 1950–54; Assoc. scientist, then scientist, Health Physics Div., Oak Ridge Nat. Laboratory 1954–59, Senior Scientist, Section Leader 1959–70, Dir. Ecological Sciences Div. 1970–72, Environmental Sciences Div.

1972–86, Sr. Research Adviser 1986–90; Visiting Research Prof. Radiation Ecology, Univ. of Georgia, Athens, Ga. 1964–90; Adjunct Prof., Dept. Ecology, Univ. of Tenn., Knoxville 1965–90; mem. U.S. Cttee. Int. Biological Program; Dir. Eastern Deciduous Forest Biome Project 1968–76; mem. Special Comm. on Biological Water Quality of Ohio River Valley Sanitation Comm. 1971–81, Bd. Environmental Consultants for Tenn.-Tombigbee Waterway, U.S. Army Corps of Engineers 1975–82, Energy Research and Devt. Admin. (ERDA) Ad Hoc Cttee. on Shallow Land Burial of Transuranic Waste 1976–80, Pres.'s Cttee. on Health and Ecological Effects on Increased Coal Utilization 1977–78, Research Advisory Cttee., Resources for the future 1978–81, Environmental Advisory Bd.-Chief of Engineers 1989–93; mem. Bd. of Trustees, Inst. of Ecology 1971–74, N.A.S.—NRC Bd. on Energy Studies, Bd. of Govs. American Inst. of Biological Sciences 1965–66, Ecological Soc. of America, Scientific Research Soc. of America (Pres. Oak Ridge Br. 1972–73), Cttee. on Energy and the Environment, N.A.S. Comms. on Physical Sciences, Nat. Resources (Chair. Environmental Studies Bd. 1983–86), Exec. Cttee. Science Advisory Bd., U.S. Environmental Protection Agency 1986–92; mem. British Ecological Soc., Nature Conservancy, Health Physics Soc., Soc. of Systematic Zoology; Radiation Research (A.A.A.S.); Leader, Interdisciplinary Review Group, Corps of Engineers, Tennessee-Tombigbee, Waterway project 1982. *Publications:* miscellaneous publications in ecology and radioecology. *Address:* 103 Wildwood Drive, Oak Ridge, TN 37830, U.S.A. (Home).

AUGSTEIN, Rudolf; German magazine publisher; b. 5 Nov. 1923, Hannover; s. of Friedrich Augstein and Gertrude (née Staaden); m.; four c.; ed. High School; Lieut., Second World War; Publr. Der Spiegel (weekly) 1947–; under arrest (for alleged political offence) Oct. 1962–Feb. 1963, elected Bundestag Nov. 1972, resigned Jan. 1973; mem. German PEN 1965–; FDP; Dr. h.c. (Bath) 1983, (Wuppertal) 1987; Hon. Senator Hamburg Univ. 1988, Hon. Citizen Hamburg 1994. *Publications:* Spiegelungen 1964, Konrad Adenauer 1964, Preussens Friedrich und die Deutschen 1968, Jesus Menschensohn 1972, Überlebensgross Herr Strauss 1980. *Address:* Spiegel-Verlag Rudolf Augstein GmbH & Co. KG, Brandstwiete 19, Ost-West-Strasse, 20457 Hamburg, Germany. *Telephone:* 040-3-00-71.

AUGUST, Bille; Danish film director; b. 9 Nov. 1948; ed. Christer Stroholm school of photography, Stockholm, Danish Film School; worked as cameraman on Homewards at Night, Manrape, The Grass is Singing, Love, before making first feature film 1978. *Television includes:* The World is So Big, So Big, May, Three Days with Magnus, Buster's World (series). *Feature films:* In My Life 1978, Zappa 1983, Twist and Shout 1986, Pelle the Conqueror 1989 (Oscar for Best Foreign Film, Palme d'Or, Cannes Film Festival, Golden Ram, Stockholm, Golden Globe, L.A.), The Best Intentions 1991, episode of The Young Indiana Jones, The House of the Spirits, Smilla's Feeling for Snow.

AUGUSTE, Yves L.; Haitian diplomatist; practised Law, Port-au-Prince 1946–50, 1959–65; served as 1st Sec. Haitian Embassies, Madrid and Washington D.C. 1950–57; Adviser on Trade to the OAS 1957–58; Teacher of Literature and Languages, Zaire 1965–69, Headmaster Bukavu Secondary School 1967–68; Prof. of French and Int. Relations, Lincoln Univ., Pa. 1970–75; Prof. of Haitian Culture, New York Univ. 1975; Prof. Seton Hall Univ., N.J. 1976–85; Deputy Perm. Rep. to the UN 1986–87, Perm. Rep. 1987–89, 1990. *Publications include:* two books on Haiti and the United States from 1804–62 and 1862–1900. *Address:* c/o Ministry of Foreign Affairs and Worship, Harry Truman Boulevard, Cité de l'Exposition, Port-au-Prince, Haiti.

AUGUSTINE, Norman Ralph; American aerospace industry executive; b. 27 July 1935, Denver; s. of Ralph Harvey Augustine and Freda Irene (Immenga) Augustine; m. Margareta Engman 1962; two c.; ed. Princeton Univ.; Research Asst., Princeton Univ. 1957–58; Program Man., Chief Engineer Douglas Aircraft Co. Inc., Santa Monica, Calif. 1958–65; Asst. Dir. of Defense Research and Eng., Office of Sec. for Defense, Washington, D.C. 1965–70; Vice-Pres. Advanced Systems, Missiles and Space Co., LTV Aerospace Corpn., Dallas 1970–73; Asst. Sec. Army, The Pentagon, Washington 1965–70, Under-Sec. 1973–75; Vice-Pres. Operations, Martin Marietta Aerospace Corpn., Bethesda, Md. 1977–82, Pres. Martin Marietta Denver Aerospace Co. 1982–85, Sr. Vice-Pres. Information Systems 1985, Pres. C.O.O. 1986–87, Vice-Chair. and C.E.O. 1987–88, Chair. and C.E.O. 1988–95; C.E.O. Lockheed Martin 1994, Pres. 1995–96, now Chair.; mem. Bd. of Dirs. Phillips Petroleum Co., Procter & Gamble Co., Riggs Nat. Bank Corpn.; mem. NATO Group of Experts on Air Defence 1966–70, NASA Research and Tech. Advisory Council 1973–75; Chair. NASA Space Systems and Tech. Advisory Bd. 1985–89; Fellow I.E.E.E., A.I.A.A.; mem. American Acad. of Arts and Sciences, Int. Acad. of Astronautics and other bodies; numerous hon. degrees; Nat. Eng. Award, American Asscn. of Eng. Socs. 1991, Goddard Medal, A.I.A.A. 1988, and other prizes and awards. *Publications:* Augustine's Laws, The Defense Revolution (co-author) 1990. *Address:* Lockheed Martin, 6801 Rockledge Drive, Bethesda, MD 20817, U.S.A.

AUKIN, David, B.A., F.R.S.A.; British television and film executive; b. 12 Feb. 1942, Harrow; s. of Charles Aukin and Regina Aukin; m. Nancy Meckler 1969; two s.; ed. St. Paul's School, London and St. Edmund Hall, Oxford; founder of Foco Novo and Jt. Stock Theatre cos. and admin. producer for various fringe theatre groups 1970–75; Admin. Dir. Hampstead Theatre 1975–79, Dir. 1979–84; Dir. Leicester Haymarket Theatre 1984–86; Exec. Dir. Royal Nat. Theatre of Great Britain 1986–90; Pres. Soc. of West End Theatres 1988–90; Head of Drama, Channel 4 TV 1990–97, Head of Film 1997–98; Jt. Chief Exec. HAL Films 1998–. *Address:* c/o Miramax, 45A Brewer Street, London, W1R 3FD, England.

AULENTI, Gae; Italian architect and designer; b. 4 Dec. 1927, Palazzolo dello Stella, Udine; d. of Aldo Aulenti and Virginia Gioia; divorced; one d.; ed. Faculty of Architecture, Milan Polytechnic; mem. editorial staff of review Casabella-Continuità 1955–65; Asst., Venice Faculty of Architecture 1960–62, Milan Faculty of Architecture 1964–67; own architecture, exhbn. design, interior design, industrial design, stage design practice, Milan 1956–; solo exhbn., Padiglione d'Arte Contemporanea (PAC), Milan 1979; group exhbn. Museum of Modern Art, New York 1972; *major recent works:* conversion of Gare d'Orsay into museum, Paris 1980–86; new interior design of Musée Nat. d'Art Moderne, Centre Georges Pompidou, Paris 1982–85; restoration of Palazzo Grassi, Venice 1986; conversion of Palau Nacional into Museu Nacional d'Art de Catalunya, Barcelona 1987–97; new access ramp to S. Maria Novella railway station, Florence 1990; Italian Pavilion at EXPO '92, Seville 1992; new gallery for temporary exhbns. at Triennale, Milan 1994; conversion of fmr. Leopolda railway station into venue for temporary exhbns., Florence 1996–; conversion of San Francisco Old Main Library into Asian Art Museum 1996–; reconstruction of La Fenice Theatre, Venice 1997–; *exhbn. installations:* Futurism 1986, German Expressionism 1997, and other exhbns. at Palazzo Grassi, Venice, The Italian Metamorphosis 1943–1968, Guggenheim Museum, New York and Kunstmuseum, Wolfsburg, Germany 1994–95; *stage designs:* Elektra, La Scala, Milan 1994, King Lear, Teatro Lirico, Milan 1995; *industrial design:* furniture, lamps, objects for Kartell, Knoll, Fontana Arte, Louis Vuitton, Tecno, Venini, Zanotta etc.; Hon. mem. American Soc. Interior Designers; Hon. Fellow American Inst. of Architects; Int. Prize for Italian Pavilion, Milan Triennale 1964, Praemium Imperiale for Architecture, Japan Art Asscn., Tokyo 1991; Chevalier, Légion d'honneur, Cavaliere di Gran Croce, Rome. *Leisure interests:* collecting paintings and sculptures. *Address:* 4 piazza San Marco, 20121 Milan, Italy. *Telephone:* (02) 8692613. *Fax:* (02) 874125.

AUMALE, Christian d', L. EN D.; French diplomatist (Ambassadeur de France); b. 23 May 1918, Lausanne, Switzerland; s. of Jacques and Elisabeth (née Le Bon de la Pointe) Aumale; m. Claude Darasse 1940; one s. one d. (deceased); ed. Lycée Condorcet, Faculté de Droit, Paris, London School of Econs. and Consular Acad., Vienna; Ministry of Foreign Affairs 1943–45, 1948–53, 1956–62; Second Sec., Copenhagen 1945–48; Counsellor, Tokyo 1953–56; Counsellor, then Minister, Bonn 1964; Asst. Dir. Econ. and Financial Affairs, Ministry of Foreign Affairs 1968; Amb. and Head of French Del. to OECD 1978–82; Rank of Amb. France 1982; Pres. Near and Middle East Comm., Conseil nat. du patronat français; Adviser on foreign affairs to Chair. Compagnie Lyonnaise des Eaux; Commdr. Légion d'honneur, Croix de guerre, Commdr. Ordre national du Mérite, Officier du Mérite agricole. *Address:* Lyonnaise des Eaux, 72 Avenue de la Liberté, 92753 Nanterre Cedex (Office); 6 rue Yvon Villarceau, 75116 Paris, France (Home).

AUMONT, Jean-Pierre (pseudonym of Jean-Pierre Philippe Salomons); French actor and playwright; b. 5 Jan. 1911, Paris; m. 1st Maria Montez 1942 (deceased); m. 2nd (divorced); m. 3rd Marisa Pavan 1956; two s. one d.; ed. Lycées Rollin and Buffon, Paris and Conservatoire nat. d'art dramatique; Officier, Légion d'honneur, Ordre nat. du Mérite, Croix de guerre, Commdr. des Arts et Lettres. *Stage appearances include:* Britannicus, la Machine infernale, Jules César, Flora, Tovaritch, Coup de soleil 1982, Pense à l'Afrique 1984; *films include:* Maman Colibri, Les Anges meurtriers, la Vie commence demain, le Diable à quatre heures, les Sept Péchés capitaux, la Nuit américaine 1972, le Chat et la Souris, Mahogany 1976, Nana, le désir: la Java des ombres 1983, l'Age Vermeil (TV) 1984, A Tale of Two Cities 1989, The Fighting Frenchman 1989, A Star for Two 1990, The Last Word 1990, Becoming Colette 1991, Senso 1991, Indiana Jones 1991, Georgino 1994, Jefferson in Paris 1994, La Propriétaire 1996. *Publications include:* l'Empéreur de Chine, l'Ile heureuse, un Beau Dimanche, Gigi, On Golden Pond. *Leisure interest:* writing. *Address:* c/o Lorcaster, 27 rue de Richelieu, 75001 Paris, France.

AUNG SAN SUU KYI; Burmese politician; b. 19 June 1945, Rangoon; d. of the late Gen. Aung San; m. Michael Aris 1972 (died 1999); two s.; ed. St. Francis Convent, Methodist English High School, Lady Shri Ram Coll., Delhi Univ., St. Hugh's Coll., Oxford; Asst. Sec. Advisory Cttee. on Admin. and Budgetary Questions UN Secretariat, NY 1969–71; Resident Officer Ministry of Foreign Affairs, Bhutan 1972; Visiting Scholar Centre for S.E. Asian Studies, Kyoto Univ. 1985–86; Fellow Indian Inst. of Advanced Studies 1987; co-founder, Gen. Sec. Nat. League for Democracy 1988 (expelled from party), reinstated as Gen. Sec. Oct. 1995; returned from U.K. 1988; under house arrest 1988–95, house arrest lifted July 1995; Human Rights Prize 1991, Nobel Peace Prize 1991, Sakharov Prize 1990, Simón Bolívar Prize 1992, numerous hon. degrees. *Publications:* Aung San 1984, Burma and India: some aspects of colonial life under colonialism 1990, Freedom from Fear 1991, Towards a True Refuge 1993, Freedom from Fear and Other Writings 1995. *Address:* c/o National League for Democracy, 97B West Shwegondine Road, Bahan Township, Yangon, Myanmar.

AURA, Matti Ilmari, LL.M.; Finnish business executive; b. 18 June 1943, Helsinki; s. of Teuvo Ensio Aura and Kielo Kaino Kivekäs; m. Marja H. Hiippala 1967; two s.; ed. Munkkiniemi High School and Univ. of Helsinki; lawyer, Finnish Export Credit Ltd. 1968–69, Confed. of Finnish Industries

1970–71; Man. Dir. Cen. Bd. of Finnish Wholesale and Retail Assen. 1972–85; Gen. Man. Cen. Chamber of Commerce of Finland 1986; Minister of Transport and Communications 1997–. *Address:* Ministry of Transport and Communications, P.O. Box 235, 00131 Helsinki (Office); Louhentie 1 H 25, 02130 Espoo, Finland (Home). *Telephone:* (09) 160 23 20 (Office); (358) 465610 (Home). *Fax:* (09) 160 25 87 (Office).

AURBACH, Gerhard, D.RER.POL.; German administrative official; b. 19 July 1936, Neuburg/Donau; m. Jennifer Thompson; two d.; ed. Univ. of Munich; Asst. Univ. of Munich, consultant, IFO Inst. (Econ. Research Inst.) Munich, consultant Fed. Ministry of Transport 1960–63; Admin. European Conf. of Ministers of Transport (ECMT) 1963, Prin. Admin. 1970, Head, Transport Policy Div. 1975, Deputy Sec.-Gen. 1986, Sec.-Gen. ECMT 1992–. *Publications:* articles on transport econs. and policy. *Leisure interests:* history, classical music, skiing, tennis. *Address:* European Conference of Ministers of Transport, 2 rue André Pascal, 75116 Paris Cedex 16, France. *Telephone:* (1) 45.24.82.00. *Fax:* (1) 45.24.97.42.

AURE, Aud Inger, CAND. JUR.; Norwegian politician; b. 12 Nov. 1942, Avcrøy; m.; three c.; mem. Kristiansund Municipal Council 1979–83; mem. Møre og Romsdal Co. Council 1984–95; mem. Cen. Exec. Cttee. Women's Org. Christian Democratic Party 1982–, Deputy Chair. 1986–88, Chair. 1988–94; Deputy mem. Storting for Møre og Romsdal Co. 1985–93, mem. 1989–90; mem. Standing Cttee. on Justice; Regional Employment Officer 1992–95; Mayor of Kristiansund 1995–; mem. Cen. Exec. Cttee. Christian Democratic Party 1995–; Minister of Justice Oct. 1997–. *Address:* Ministry of Justice and Police, Akersgt. 42, P.O. Box 8005 Dep., Oslo, Norway. *Telephone:* 22-24-51-00.

AUROUX, Jean; French politician; b. 19 Sept. 1942, Thizy, Rhône; s. of Louis and Jeanne (née Masson) Auroux; m. Lucienne Sabadie 1967; one s. one d.; ed. Lycée Jean Puy, Roanne, Faculté de Lyon; City Councillor, Roanne 1976–88, Mayor 1977–; mem., then Vice-Pres. Regional Assembly of Rhône-Alpes 1977–81; Pres. District de l'Agglomération Roanaisse 1991–; Parti Socialiste Nat. Del. for Housing 1978; mem. Nat. Assembly 1978–81, 1986–88, mem. Finance Cttee.; mem. Production and Exchange Cttee.; Minister of Labour 1981–82, Minister Del. attached to Social Affairs Ministry, in charge of Labour Affairs 1982–83, Sec. of State at Ministry of Industry and Research in charge of Energy 1983–84, at Ministry of Urban Planning, Housing and Transport 1984–85, Minister 1985–86; Pres. Socialist group in Nat. Ass. 1990–93; Pres. Féd. des maires des villes moyennes 1988–; mem. Conseil Nat. des Villes, Comité de Décentralisation. *Publication:* Géographie économique à usage scolaire. *Address:* Mairie, 42300 Roanne, France (Office).

AUSHEV, Lieut.-Gen. Ruslan Sultanovich; Russian/Ingush politician; b. 29 Oct. 1954, Volodarskoye, Kokchetav Region, Kazakhstan; s. of Sultan Aushev and Tamara Aushev; m. Aza Aushev 1983; one s. two d.; ed. Ordzhonikidze Gen. Troops School, M. Frunze Mil. Acad.; commdr. motorized infantry co., then platoon 1975–80; Chief of HQ, then Commdr. motorized bn. in Afghanistan 1980–82; Chief of Regt. HQ in Afghanistan 1985–87; Commdr. Motorized infantry Regt., then Deputy Commdr. motorized infantry div. Far East Command 1987–91; at Council of Heads of Govts. of CIS countries 1991–92; U.S.S.R. People's Deputy 1989–91; Head of Admin. in newly formed Ingush Repub. Nov.–Dec. 1992; elected Pres. of Repub. Ingushetia 1993–; mem. Council of Fed. of Russia 1993–; Hero of Soviet Union. *Leisure interest:* football. *Address:* Office of the President, J. Bazorkina prosp. 15, 366720 Nazran, Ingushetia, Russia (Office). *Telephone:* (87134) 231-07 (Nazran); (095) 334-2039 (Moscow). *Fax:* (095) 334-2039 (Moscow).

AUSTEN, K(arl) Frank, M.D.; American professor of medicine; b. 14 March 1928, Akron, Ohio; s. of Karl and Bertle J. Arnstein; m. Jocelyn Chapman 1959; two s. two d.; ed. Amherst Coll. and Harvard Medical School; Intern in Medicine, Mass. Gen. Hosp. 1954–55, Asst. Resident 1955–56, Sr. Resident 1958–59, Chief Resident 1961–62, Asst. in Medicine 1962–63, Asst. Physician 1963–66; Capt., U.S. Army Medical Corps, Walter Reed Army Inst. of Research 1956–58; U.S.P.H.S. Postdoctoral Research Fellow, Nat. Inst. for Medical Research, Mill Hill, London, U.K. 1959–61; Physician-in-Chief, Robert B. Brigham Hosp. Boston 1966–80; Physician, Peter Bent Brigham Hosp. Boston 1966–80; Chair. Dept. Rheumatology and Immunology, Brigham and Women's Hosp., Boston 1980–95, Dir. Inflammation and Allergic Diseases Research Section, Div. of Rheumatology and Immunology 1995–; Asst. in Medicine, Harvard Medical School 1961, Instr. 1962, Assoc. 1962–64, Asst. Prof. 1965–66, Assoc. Prof. 1966–68, Prof. 1969–72, Theodore Bevier Bayles Prof. of Medicine 1972–; Pres. Int. Soc. of Immunopharmacology 1994; numerous cttee. assignments, guest lectureships, etc.; mem. numerous professional orgs. and recipient of numerous prizes and awards. *Publications:* numerous publications on immunology, etc. *Leisure interests:* skiing, jogging, gardening. *Address:* Smith Building, One Jimmy Fund Way, Room 368, Boston, MA 02115; Brigham and Women's Hospital, PBB-B-2, 75 Francis Street, Boston, MA 02115, U.S.A.

AUSTIN, Colin François Lloyd, D.PHIL., F.B.A.; British classical scholar; b. 26 July 1941, Melbourne, Australia; s. of late Lloyd James Austin; m. Mishtu Mazumdar 1967; one s. one d.; ed. Lycée Lakanal, Paris, Manchester Grammar School, Jesus Coll. Cambridge (Scholar), Christ Church Oxford (Sr. Scholar) and Freie Universität, West Berlin; Research Fellow, Trinity Hall, Cambridge Univ. 1965–69, Dir. of Studies in Classics 1965–; Asst. Lecturer in Classics, Cambridge Univ. 1969–72, Lecturer 1973–88, Reader in Greek Language and Literature 1988–98, Prof. of Greek 1998–; Hallam Prize 1961, Browne Medal 1961, Porson Prize 1962. *Publications:* Nova Fragmenta Euripidea 1968, Menandri Aspis et Samia 1969–70, Comicorum Graecorum Fragmenta in papyris reperta 1973, Poetae Comici Graeci (with R. Kassel): vol. II Agathenor—Aristonymus 1991, vol. III 2 Aristophanes, Testimonia et Fragmenta 1984, vol. IV Aristophon—Crobylus 1983, vol. V Damoxenus—Magnes 1986, vol. VII Menecrates-Xenophon 1989, vol. VIII Adespota 1995, vol. VI 2 Menander, Testimonia et Fragmenta apud Scriptores Servata 1998. *Leisure interests:* cycling, philately, wine tasting. *Address:* Trinity Hall, Cambridge, CB2 1TJ (Office); 7 Park Terrace, Cambridge, CB1 1JH, England (Home). *Telephone:* (01223) 332520 (Office); (01223) 362732 (Home).

AUSTRIAN, Robert, M.D.; American physician and professor of medicine; b. 12 April 1916, Baltimore, Md.; s. of Charles Robert Austrian and Florence Hochschild Austrian; m. Babette Friedmann Bernstein 1963; ed. Johns Hopkins Univ.; numerous hosp. appts. at Johns Hopkins and other hosps. 1941–86; Consultant in Medicine, Veterans Admin. Hosp., Pa. 1968–91; Visiting Physician, Hosp. of the Univ. of Pa. 1962–; teaching appts. at Johns Hopkins Univ. School of Medicine, New York Univ. Coll. of Medicine, State Univ. of New York Coll. of Medicine 1942–62; John Herr Musser Prof. of Research Medicine 1962– (Chair. of Dept. of Research Medicine, Univ. of Pa. School of Medicine 1962–86), Prof. Emer. 1986–, Prof. of Medicine 1962–; Visiting Scientist, Dept. of Microbial Genetics, Pasteur Inst., Paris, France 1960–61; Dir. WHO Collaborating Centre for Reference and Research on Pneumococci, Univ. of Pa. School of Medicine 1978–; mem. WHO Expert Advisory Panel on Acute Bacterial Disease 1979–; mem. Editorial Bd. Antimicrobial Agents and Chemotherapy, Review of Infectious Diseases 1979–89, Vaccine; mem. Scientific Advisory Cttee., The Wistar Inst. 1985–87, mem. American Philosophical Soc. 1987–; Fellow A.A.A.S., American Acad. of Microbiology; Master, American Coll. of Physicians; mem. N.A.S.; Sr. mem. Inst. of Medicine 1992 and numerous socs.; Hon. D.Sc. (Philadelphia Coll. of Pharmacy and Science) 1981, (Pennsylvania) 1987, (State Univ. of New York) 1996; numerous awards including Lifetime Science Award, Inst. for Advanced Studies in Immunology and Aging 1997. *Publications:* Life with the Pneumococcus: Notes from the Bedside, Laboratory and Library 1985; 165 scientific articles in medical journals. *Leisure interests:* ornithology, philately. *Address:* Department of Research Medicine, University of Pennsylvania, The School of Medicine, 36th Street and Hamilton Walk, Philadelphia, PA 19104-6088, U.S.A. *Telephone:* (215) 662-3186.

AUTANT-LARA, Claude; French film director and author; b. 5 Aug. 1901, Luzarches; s. of Edouard and Louise (née Larapidie de L'Isle) Autant-Lara; m. Ghislaine Auboin (deceased); ed. Lycée Janson de Sailly, Mill Hill School, London, Ecole des Arts Décoratifs, and Ecole des Beaux-Arts; entered French film industry 1919; directed first short picture Faits-Divers 1923; Pres. Syndicat des Techniciens du Cinéma Français 1948–55, then Hon. Pres.; Pres. Fédération Nationale du Spectacle 1957–63, then Hon. Pres.; mem. Acad. des Beaux-Arts (Vice-Pres. 1989); mem. European Parl., Nat. Front June–Sept. 1989; Grand Prix de la Critique internationale 1947, and many other prizes; Chevalier de la Légion d'honneur; Officer ordre nat. du Mérite; Commandeur des Arts et des Lettres. *Principal films:* Le mariage de chiffon, Sylvie et le fantôme, Occupe-toi d'Amélie, Le diable au corps, Douce, The Red Inn, Game of Love, Le rouge et le noir, Seven Sins, Marguerite de la nuit, La traversée de Paris, En cas de malheur, La jument verte, Le bois des amants, Tu ne tueras point, Vive Henri-IV, Vive l'amour, Le Comte de Monte-Cristo, Le meurtrier, Le magot de Joséfa, Le journal d'une femme en blanc, Le nouveau journal d'une femme en blanc, Le plus vieux métier du monde 1967, Le franciscain de Bourges 1968, Les patates, Lucien Leuwen (TV serial) 1973, Gloria. *Publications:* Télémafia, La rage dans la coeur, Hollywood Cake Walk, Les Fourgons du Malheur 1987, Le Coq et Le Rat 1988. *Address:* 66 rue Lepic, 75018 Paris; La Poterie, 7 Calade St.-Roch, 06410 Biot, France.

AUTEUIL, Daniel; French actor; b. 1950, Algeria; one d. by Emmanuelle Béart (q.v.); worked in musical comedies in Paris; screen debut in L'Agression 1974; stage appearances include Le Garçon d'Appartement 1980; César for Best Actor in Jean de Florette and Manon des Sources 1986 (Award for Best Actor, Cannes). *Films:* Attention les Yeux 1975, La Nuit Saint-Germain des Près 1976, L'Amour Violé 1976, Monsieur Papa 1977, Les Héros n'ont pas Froid aux Oreilles 1978, A Nous Deux 1979, Bête Mais Discipliné 1979, Les Sous-Doués 1980, La Banquière 1980, Clara et les Chics Types 1980, Les Hommes Préfèrent les Grosses 1981, Les Sous-Doués en Vacances 1981, T'empêches Tout le Monde de Dormir 1981, Pour Cent Briques t'as Plus Rien 1981, L'Indic 1982, Que les Gros Salaires Lèvent le Doigt 1982, P'tit Con 1983, Les Fauves 1983, Palace 1983, L'Arbalete 1984, L'Amour en Douce 1984, Jean de Florette 1985, Manon des Sources 1985, Le Paltoquet 1986, Quelques Jours Avec Moi 1988, Romuald and Juliette 1989, Lacenaire 1989, Ma Vie Est Un Enfer 1991, Un Coeur en Hiver 1992, Ma Saison Préférée 1992, Quelques Jours Avec Moi, L'Elegant Criminel, Tout Ça Pour Ça 1993, La Séparation 1994, La Reine Margot 1994, Ma Saison Préférée 1994, The Eighth Day 1996, Les Voleurs 1998.

AVDEYEV, Aleksander Alekseyevich; Russian politician and diplomatist; b. 8 Sept. 1946, Kremenchug, Ukraine; m.; one s.; ed. Moscow State Inst. of Int. Relations; diplomatic service with U.S.S.R. Ministry of Foreign Affairs 1968–77; Second, First Sec., U.S.S.R. Embassy, France 1977–85;

Counsellor; Head of sector, First European Dept., U.S.S.R. Ministry of Foreign Affairs 1985–87; U.S.S.R. Amb. to Luxembourg 1987–90; First Deputy Head, First European Dept., Ministry of Foreign Affairs 1990–91; U.S.S.R. Deputy Minister of Foreign Affairs 1991–92; Amb. at Large, Russian Ministry of Foreign Affairs 1992–; Amb. to Bulgaria 1992–96; Deputy Minister of Foreign Affairs 1996–98, First Deputy Minister Oct. 1998–. *Address:* Ministry of Foreign Affairs, Smolenskaya-Sennaya str. 32/34, Moscow, Russia. *Telephone:* (095) 244 9225 (Office).

AVEDON, Richard; American photographer; b. 15 May 1923, New York; s. of Jack Avedon and Anna Polonsky; m. 1st Dorcas Nowell 1944; m. 2nd Evelyn Franklin 1951; one s.; ed. Columbia; staff photographer Harper's Bazaar 1945–65, mem. editorial staff Theatre Arts Magazine 1952–53, Vogue magazine 1966–90; photographer for New Yorker 1992–; one man exhbns. Smithsonian Inst. 62, Minneapolis Inst. of Arts 70, Museum of Modern Art 74, Marlborough Gallery, New York 75, Metropolitan Museum of Art, New York 1978, Univ. Art Museum, Berkeley, Calif. 1980, Amon Carter Museum, Fort Worth, Texas 1985, and American tour; retrospective Richard Avedon Evidence 1944–94 Whitney Museum of American Art, N.Y. 1994; Visiting Artist Harvard Univ. 1986–87; his work is represented in collections of many major museums and in private collections; Fellow Timothy Dwight Coll. Yale Univ. 1975–; Pres.'s Fellow Rhode Island School of Design 1978; Highest Achievement Medal Awards, Art Dirs. Show 1950; Popular Photography World's 10 Greatest Photographers 1958; Nat. Magazine Award for Visual Excellence 1976; Citation of Dedication to Fashion Photography, Pratt Inst. 1976; Chancellor's Citation, Univ. of Calif., Berkeley 1980; Art Dirs. Club Hall of Fame 1982, American Soc. of Magazine Photographers Photographer of the Year 1985, Best Photographic Book of the Year Award, Maine Photographic Workshop 1985, Dir. of the Year, Adweek magazine 1985; Dr. h.c. (R.C.A.) 1989, (Kenyon Coll., OH); Lifetime Achievement Award, Council of Fashion Designers of America (CFDA) 1989, Harvard Univ. Certificate of Recognition, Prix Nadar 1994, Mental Health Asscn. of N.Y. City Humanitarian Award 1996. *Publications:* Observations 1959, Nothing Personal 1964, Ed. Diary of a Century (photographs by Jacques Henri Lartigue, q.v.) 1970, Alice in Wonderland 1973, Portraits 1976, Rolling Stone Magazine, "The Family" 1976, Avedon: Photographs 1947–77 1978, In the American West 1985, An Autobiography 1993, Evidence 1944–1994 1994. *Address:* 407 East 75th Street, New York, NY 10021, U.S.A. *Telephone:* (212) 879-6325.

AVEN, Piotr Olegovich; Russian economist; b. 16 March 1955, Moscow; s. of Oleg P. Aven; ed. Moscow State Univ.; researcher Research Inst. of System Studies U.S.S.R. Acad. of Sciences 1981–88; Int. Inst. of Applied System Analysis in Vienna 1989–91, First Deputy Minister of Foreign Affairs, Chair. Cttee. of Foreign Econ. Relations 1991–92; Russian Minister of Foreign Econ. Relations Feb.–Dec. 1992; Pres., Deputy Chair. of Bd. Alpha Bank; Dir.-Gen. Fin-Pa Corpn. 1994–; mem. Political Council, Russian Choice Bloc. *Address:* Alpha Bank, Mashi Poryvayevoy str. 11, 107078 Moscow, Russia. *Telephone:* 974-25-15.

AVERINTSEV, Sergey Sergeyevich, D.PHIL.; Russian philologist; b. 10 Dec. 1937; m.; one s. one d.; ed. Moscow Univ.; researcher, sr. researcher, Head of Div., leading researcher Inst. of World Literature, U.S.S.R. Acad. of Sciences 1965–88, Head of section 1982–92; Prof. Moscow Univ. 1991, Head Dept. of Christian Culture 1992–; Prof. Inst. für Slavistik, Vienna Univ. 1994–; Corresp. mem. U.S.S.R. (now Russian) Acad. of Sciences 1987; mem. Russian Acad. of Natural Sciences; mem. Acad. Universelle de Culture 1991, Acad. Europea 1992, Acad. dell Science Social, Rome 1994; Pres. Asscn. of Culturologists of Russia; Chair. Bible Soc. of Russia; U.S.S.R. People's Deputy 1989–91; U.S.S.R. State Prize 1991; Leopold Lucas Prize, Tübingen Univ. 1995; Russia State Prize 1996. *Publications:* works on history and theory of literature, studies of Ancient, Byzantine, Latin and Syrian Literature, on history of Russian and West European Poetry including Plato and Greek Literature 1973, Poetry of Early Byzantine Literature 1977, From the Banks of Bosphorus to the Banks of Efrat 1987, contribs. to the Encyclopedia of Myths and Tales of Peoples of the World. *Address:* Moscow University, Vorob'yevy Gory, Philological Faculty, 119899 Moscow, Russia. *Telephone:* (095) 939-20-08, 939-54-38 (Moscow); (01) 4277-42830 (Vienna).

AVERY, Mary Ellen, A.B., M.D.; American physician; b. 6 May 1927, New Jersey; d. of William Clarence Avery and Mary Catherine Miller; ed. Wheaton Coll., Mass., Johns Hopkins School of Medicine; Eudowood Assoc. Prof. of Pediatrics, Johns Hopkins Univ. 1966–69; Prof. and Chairman, Pediatrics, Faculty of Medicine, McGill Univ., Physician-in-Chief, Montreal Children's Hosp. 1969–74; Thomas Morgan Rotch Prof. of Pediatrics, Harvard Medical School 1974–96, Dist. Emer. Prof. 1996–; Physician-in-Chief, Children's Hosp., Boston 1974–85; John and Mary Markle Scholar 1961–66; Trudeau Medal, American Thoracic Soc.; Dir. A.A.A.S.; mem. Council Inst. of Medicine; mem. N.A.S. 1994–, mem. council 1997–; Pres. American Paediatric Soc. 1990; numerous honorary degrees; Nat. Medal of Science 1991. *Publications:* The Lung and its Disorders in the Newborn Infant 1981, Born Early 1983, Diseases of the Newborn 1971, Pediatric Medicine 1988. *Address:* Children's Hospital, 221 Longwood Avenue, Boston, MA 02115-5817, U.S.A. *Telephone:* (617) 355-8330. *Fax:* (617) 732-4151.

AVERY, William Hinckley, A.M., PH.D.; American physicist (retd.); b. 25 July 1912, Fort Collins, Colo.; s. of Edgar Delano Avery and Mabel A. Gordon; m. Helen W. Palmer 1938; one s. one d.; ed. Pomona Coll. and Harvard Univ.; Postdoctoral Research Asst. Infrared Spectroscopy, Harvard 1937–39; Research Chemist, Shell Oil Co., St. Louis, Houston 1939–43; Head, Propulsion Div. Allegany Ballistics Lab. Cumberland, Md. 1943–46; Consultant in Physics and Chem. Arthur D. Little Co., Cambridge, Mass. 1946–47; Professional staff mem. Applied Physics Lab. Johns Hopkins Univ. 1947–73, Asst. Dir. Exploratory Devt. 1973–78, Dir. Ocean Energy Programs 1978–89, William H. Avery Propulsion Research Lab. named in his honour 1989; mem. various Govt. Advisory panels etc.; mem. American Chem. Soc.; Fellow, American Inst. of Aeronautics and Astronautics; Presidential Certificate of Merit 1948, Sir Alfred Egerton Award 1972, IR 100 Award 1979 and other awards and distinctions. *Publication:* (book) Ocean Thermal Energy Conversion 1992. *Address:* 724 Guilford Court, Silver Spring, MD 20901, U.S.A. *Telephone:* (301) 589-6552.

AVICE, Edwige, L. ÈS L.; French politician; b. 13 April 1945, Nevers; d. of Edmond Bertrant and Hélène Guyot; m. Etienne Avice 1970; ed. Cours Fénelon, Nevers, Lycée Pothier, Orléans, Univ. of Paris; worked for Nat. Cttee. for Housing Improvement 1970; Int. Dept., Crédit Lyonnais 1970–73; on staff of Dir.-Gen. of Paris Hospitals 1973–78; Pres. Asscn. Démocratique des Français de l'Etranger 1991–93, Pres. Financière de Brienne 1993; mem. Parti Socialiste (P.S.) 1972, mem. Exec. Bureau 1977, Nat. Secr. 1987–94, P.S. Nat. Del. for Nat. Service; mem. Nat. Assembly 1978–81, 1986–88; Minister-Del. for Free Time, Youth and Sports 1981–84; Sec. of State attached to the Minister of Defence 1984–86; Minister-Del. attached to the Minister for Foreign Affairs May 1988–91; Minister of Co-operation and Devt. 1991–93; Conseillère de Paris 1983–88. *Leisure interests:* travelling, music, swimming, walking, fencing. *Publication:* Terre d'élection 1993.

AVILA, Rev. Fernando Bastos de; Brazilian ecclesiastic and sociologist; b. 17 March 1918; ed. Univ. do Nova Friburgo (Brazil), Univ. de Louvain and Gregorian Univ., Rome; Prof. of Sociology, Pontificia Univ. Católica do Rio de Janeiro 1957; Social Dir. Nat. Catholic Immigration Comm. 1954–; mem. Council, Nat. Fed. of Trade 1960–; Dir. Inst. Brasileiro de Desenvolvimento (IBRADES). *Publications:* Economic Impacts of Immigration 1956, L'immigration au Brésil 1957, Introdução a Sociologia 1962, Solidarismo 1965, Pequena Enciclopédia de Moral Ecivismo 1967. *Address:* 115 rua Bambina-Botatogo, Rio de Janeiro, RJ, Brazil.

AVILDSEN, John Guilbert; American film director, cinematographer and editor; b. 21 Dec. 1935, Ill.; s. of Clarence John Avildsen and Ivy (Guilbert) Avildsen; m. Tracy Brooks Swope 1987; two s. one d.; ed. New York Univ.; Advertising Man. Vespa Motor Scooters 1959; served U.S. Army 1959–61; Asst. Dir. Greenwich Village Story 1961; worked as asst. cameraman and production man.; with Muller, Jordan & Herrick Industrial Films 1965–67. *Films include:* Turn On to Love 1967, Sweet Dreams 1968, Guess What We Learned in School Today 1969, Joe 1970, Cry Uncle 1971, Save the Tiger 1972, Inaugural Ball 1973, W.W. and the Dixie Dancekings 1974, Rocky 1976 (Acad. Award for best Director), Slow Dancing in the Big City 1978, The Formula 1980, Neighbors 1981, Travelling Hopefully 1982, A Night in Heaven 1983, The Karate Kid 1984, Happy New Year 1985, The Karate Kid II 1986, For Keeps 1987, The Karate Kid III 1989, Lean on Me 1989 (Image Award, NAACP), Rocky V 1990, The Power of One 1992, 8 Seconds 1994, Save the Everglades (documentary). *Television:* From No House to Options House (Emmy award); mem. Dirs. Guild of America, Motion Picture Photographers' Union, Motion Picture Eds. Union, Writers' Guild of America. *Address:* c/o United Talent Agency Martin Bauer, 9560 Wilshire Blvd., Fl. 5, Beverly Hills, CA 90212, U.S.A.

AVINERI, Shlomo; Israeli professor of political science; b. 20 Aug. 1933, Bielsko, Poland; s. of Michael Avineri and Erna Groner; m. Dvora Nadler 1957; one d.; ed. Shalva Secondary School, Tel-Aviv, Hebrew Univ., Jerusalem, and London School of Econs.; has lived in Israel since 1939; Prof. of Political Science, Hebrew Univ. Jerusalem 1971–, Dir. Eshkol Research Inst. 1971–74, Dean of Faculty of Social Sciences 1974–76; Dir.-Gen. Ministry of Foreign Affairs 1976–77; Dir. Inst. for European Studies, Hebrew Univ. 1997–; visiting appointments at Yale Univ. 1966–67, Wesleyan Univ., Middletown, Conn. 1971–72, Research School of Social Sciences, Australian Nat. Univ. 1972, Cornell Univ. 1973, Univ. of Calif. 1979, Queen's Coll., New York 1989, Oxford 1989; mem. Int. Inst. of Philosophy 1980–; Fellow, Woodrow Wilson Centre, Washington, D.C. 1983–84; Carlyle Lecturer, Oxford 1989; Guest Scholar, Brookings Inst., Washington, D.C. 1991, Cen. European Univ., Budapest 1994, Cardozo School of Law, N.Y. 1996–97, Northwestern Univ., Evanston 1997; British Council Scholarship 1961, Rubin Prize in the Social Sciences 1968, Naphtali Prize for study of Hegel 1977, Present Tense Award for Study of Zionism 1982, Israel Prize 1996. *Publications:* The Social and Political Thought of Karl Marx 1968, Karl Marx on Colonialism and Modernization 1968, Israel and the Palestinians 1971, Marx' Socialism 1972, Hegel's Theory of the Modern State 1973, Varieties of Marxism 1977, The Making of Modern Zionism 1981, Moses Hess—Prophet of Communism and Zionism 1985, Arlosoroff—A Political Biography 1989, Communitarianism and Individualism (co-author) 1992, Herzl's Diaries 1998. *Address:* Faculty of Social Sciences, Hebrew University of Jerusalem, Mount Scopus, 91 905 Jerusalem (Office); 10 Hagedud Ha-ivri Street, Jerusalem, Israel (Home). *Telephone:* (02) 588-3060 (Office); (02) 566-0862 (Home). *Fax:* (02) 532-2545.

AVNER, Yehuda; Israeli diplomatist; b. 30 Dec. 1928, Manchester, England; s. of George Avner and Rebecca Avner; m. Miriam Avner 1952; one s. three d.; ed. Manchester High School, London School of Journalism; emigrated to

Israel; Ed. of Publs., The Jewish Agency, Jerusalem 1956–64; with Ministry of Foreign Affairs 1964–67, Ed. of Political Publs. 1964–67, Dir. of Foreign Press Bureau 1972–74, Asst. to Prime Minister 1964–67, 1972–74; First Sec., then Counsellor, Embassy, Washington, D.C. 1968–72; seconded to Prime Minister's bureau 1974–77, Adviser to Prime Minister 1974–77, 1977–83; Amb. to U.K. 1983–88, to Australia 1992–96; Dir.-Gen. Clore Foundation 1989–90; Insp.-Gen. Israel Foreign Service 1990–92. *Publication:* "The Young Inheritors": A Portrait of Israeli Youth. *Leisure interests:* music, writing. *Address:* c/o Ministry of Foreign Affairs, Hakirya, Romena, Jerusalem 91950, Israel.

AVNET, Jonathan Michael, B.A.; American film company executive and film director; b. 17 Nov. 1949, Brooklyn, New York; m. Barbara Brody; one s. two d.; ed. Sarah Lawrence Coll., Univ. of Pennsylvania, Conservatory for Advanced Film Studies; Reader United Artists, L.A. 1974; Dir. Creative Affairs, Sequoia Pictures, L.A. 1975–77; Pres. Tisch/Avnet Productions, L.A. 1977–85; Chair. Avnet/Kerner Co., L.A. 1985–; Pres. Allied Communications Inc.; dir. and producer (films): Fried Green Tomatoes at the Whistle Stop Cafe (3 Golden Globes), The War, Up Close and Personal, George of the Jungle; producer, writer, dir. (TV series): Call to Glory 1984–85 (Golden Reel award), Between Two Women (Emmy Award); producer, exec. producer (films): Risky Business, Men Don't Leave, Less than Zero, When a Man Loves a Woman, Mighty Ducks, Deal of the Century, Miami Rhapsody, Three Musketeers; exec. producer: The Burning Bed, Silence of the Heart, Heatwave (4 Cable Ace awards, including Best Picture), Do You Know the Muffin Man, No Other Loved; Trustee L.A. Co. Opera; Fellow American Film Inst.; mem. Dirs. Guild of America, Writers Guild of America, Acad. of Motion Pictures Arts and Sciences. *Leisure interests:* basketball, skiing, biking.

AVRAMOVIĆ, Dragoslav, DR.JUR.; Serbian economist and lawyer; b. 14 Oct. 1919, Skopje; m. Maria Avramović; one s., two d.; participant resistance movt. 1941–44; Sec. Comm. on money exchange 1944–46; Deputy Sec. People's Bank of Yugoslavia 1944–46, counsellor 1951–53; counsellor Ministry of Finance 1948–53; asst. Law Faculty Belgrade Univ. 1948–53; on staff World Bank (IBRD) 1953–77; adviser Gen. Sec. Sector UNCTAD Geneva 1974–84; mem. W. Brandt Comm. Geneva 1978–79; econ. adviser Bank for Trade and Devt. Washington 1988–94; Dir. Cen. of European Movt. for Peace and Devt. Belgrade 1989; mem. Econ. Council, Govt. of Serbia 1989–94; Man. People's Bank of Yugoslavia 1994–96; Chief Co-ordinator of preparation of econ., social and financial programme for Yugoslavia 1995–97; mem. Advisory Group of experts on econ. problems Movt. of Non-allied Countries Geneva and Int. Comm. on problems of peace and food 1994–; Hon. Mem. Serbian Acad. of Sciences and Arts (SANU) 1994. *Publications:* over 50 scientific works on problems of stabilization of prices and production, industrialization of S. Asian and Latin American countries, econ. co-operation of developing countries, including Theory of Transfer, International Debts and Yugoslavia: What to Do?; author Programme of fight against inflation in Yugoslavia 1994. *Address:* SANU, Knez Mihailova str. 35, P.O. Box 366, 11000 Belgrade, Yugoslavia. *Telephone:* 187 144.

AVRIL, Pierre; French professor; b. 18 Nov. 1930, Pau; s. of Stanislas Avril and Geneviève Camion; m. Marie-Louise Hillion 1959; one s.; Asst. Pierre Mendès-France 1955–62, Ed.-in-Chief Cahiers de la Répub. 1960–62; sub.-ed. Soc. Gen. de Presse 1962–69; Prof. Faculté de Droit de Poitiers 1972–79, Univ. de Paris X 1979–88, Inst. d'études politiques 1982–97, Univ. de Paris II 1988–; chief consultant to magistrature 1998–. *Publications:* Le Régime politique de la Ve République 1964, Droit parlementaire (with others) 1988; Un président pour quoi faire? 1965, Essais sur les partis politiques 1990, La Ve République—histoire politique et constitutionnelle 1994, Les conventions de la Constitution 1997. *Address:* 48 rue Gay-Lussac, 75005 Paris, France (Home). *Telephone:* (1) 43.26.36.43.

AVRIL, Brig.-Gen. Prosper; Haitian politician and army officer; ed. Mil. Acad. Haiti and Univ. of Haiti Law School; fmr. adviser to deposed Pres. Jean-Claude Duvalier; adviser to mil.-civilian junta headed by Gen. Namphy and mem. Nat. Governing Council 1986; Commdr. Presidential Guard 1988; maj. participant in June 1988 coup which overthrew civilian govt. of Leslie Manigat; leader of coup which deposed regime of Gen. Namphy (q.v.) Sept. 1988; Pres. of Haiti 1988–90; in U.S.A. March 1990.

AWAD, Muhammad Hadi; Yemeni diplomatist; b. 5 May 1934; m. Adelah Moh'd Hadi Awad 1956; one s. three d.; ed. Murray House Coll. of Educ.; teacher 1953–59; Educ. Officer 1960–62; Chief Insp. of Schools 1963–65; Vice-Principal As-Shaab Coll. 1965–67; Perm. Rep. to Arab League 1968–70, concurrently Amb. to U.A.R., also accred. to Sudan, Lebanon, Libya and Iraq; Perm. Sec. Ministry of Foreign Affairs 1970–73; Amb. to U.K. 1973–80, concurrently to Spain and Sweden 1974–80, to Denmark, Portugal, the Netherlands 1975–80; Amb. to Tunisia and Perm. Rep. to the Arab League 1980–91; Dir. Western Europe Dept., Ministry of Foreign Affairs 1990–. *Leisure interest:* photography. *Address:* c/o Ministry of Foreign Affairs, P.O. Box 19262, Sana'a, Yemen.

AWADALLAH, Babikir; Sudanese politician and jurist; b. 1917, El Citaina, Blue Nile Province; ed. School of Law, Gordon Coll., Khartoum; District Judge 1947–54; resigned to become Speaker of Sudanese House of Reps. 1954–57; Judge of the Supreme Court 1957, Chief Justice 1964–69; Prime Minister and Minister of Foreign Affairs May-Oct. 1969; Deputy Chair. Revolutionary Council, Minister of Foreign Affairs 1969–70, Minister of Justice 1969–71, Deputy Prime Minister 1970–71; First Vice-Pres. of Sudan 1971–72. *Address:* c/o Sudanese Socialist Union, Khartoum, Sudan.

AWOONOR, Kofi Nyidevu, PH.D.; Ghanaian writer, teacher and diplomatist; b. 13 March 1935, Wheta; s. of Kosiwo and Atsu Awoonor; m.; four s. one d.; ed. Univ. of Ghana, Univ. Coll., London, and State Univ. of N.Y.; Research Fellow, Inst. of African Studies; Man. Dir. Film Corpn., Accra; Longmans Fellow, Univ. of London; Asst. Prof. and later Chair. Comparative Literature Program, State Univ. of N.Y., Stony Brook; Visiting Prof., Univ. of Texas, Austin and New School of Social Research, N.Y.; detained in Ghana for allegedly harbouring leader of coup 1975; on trial 1976, sentenced to one year's imprisonment Oct. 1976, pardoned Oct. 1976; fmr. Chair. Dept. of English and Dean of Faculty of Arts, Univ. of Cape Coast; Sec.-Gen. Action Congress Party; Amb. to Brazil 1984–90 (also accred. to Cuba 1988–90); Perm. Rep. to UN 1990–94; Contributing Ed., Transition and Alcheringa; Gurrey Prize for Poetry, Nat. Book Council Award for Poetry 1979, Longmans and Fairfield fellowships, Dillons Commonwealth Prize for Poetry (Africa Div.) 1989. *Publications:* poetry: Rediscovery 1964, Messages 1970, Night of My Blood 1971, House by the Sea 1978; prose: This Earth My Brother 1971, Guardians of the Sacred Word 1973, Ride Me Memory 1973, Breast of the Earth 1974 (history of African literature), Traditional African Literature (Series, Ed.), Alien Corn (novel) 1974, Where is the Mississippi Panorama 1974, Fire in the Valley: Folktales of the Ewes 1980, Until the Morning After (collected poems), The Ghana Revolution, Ghana: A Political History 1990, Comes the Voyage at Last 1991, The Caribbean and Latin American Notebook 1992. *Leisure interests:* jazz, walking, tennis, hunting. *Address:* c/o Secretariat for Foreign Affairs, POB M212, Accra, Ghana.

AXELROD, Julius, PH.D.; American biochemical pharmacologist; b. 30 May 1912, New York; s. of Isadore and Molly (Leichtling) Axelrod; m. Sally Taub 1938; two s.; ed. Coll. of the City of New York, New York Univ. and George Washington Univ. Lab.; Asst., Dept. of Bacteriology, New York Univ. Medical School 1933–35; Chemist, Laboratory of Industrial Hygiene 1935–46; Research Assoc., Third New York Univ. Research Div., Goldwater Memorial Hosp. 1946–49; Assoc. Chemist, Nat. Heart Inst., Nat. Inst. of Health 1949–50, Chemist 1950–53, Sr. Chemist 1953–55; Chief, Section on Pharmacology, Lab. of Chemical Science, Nat. Inst. of Mental Health, Health Services and Mental Health Admin., Dept. of Health, Educ. and Welfare 1955–84; Professorial lecturer George Washington Univ. 1959; Guest Researcher, Nat. Inst. of Mental Health 1984–; mem. Scientific Advisory Bd., Nat. Foundation, Brookhaven Nat. Lab., Center for Biomedical Educ., and many others; mem. Int. Brain Research Organization; Senior mem. Inst. of Medicine; Foreign mem. Royal Society; Fellow, American Coll. of Neuropsychopharmacology (mem. Council 1966–69); mem. A.C.S., American Soc. of Pharmacology and Experimental Therapeutics, American Soc. of Biological Chemists, A.A.A.S.; Fellow, American Acad. of Arts and Sciences, N.A.S.; corresp. mem. German Pharmacological Soc.; Foreign mem. Acad. der Naturforcher DDR; Hon. Sc.D. (Univ. of Chicago, Medical Coll. of Wisconsin, New York Univ, Medical Coll. of Pa. Univ. of Pa.); Hon. LL.D. (George Washington Univ.); Dr. h.c. (Univ. of Panama); Hon. LL.D. (Coll. of the City of New York), etc.; Gairdner Foundation Award 1967; Distinguished Achievement Award, George Washington Univ. 1968, Dept. of Health, Educ. and Welfare 1970, Modern Medicine Magazine 1970; Claude Bernard Medal, Univ. of Montreal 1969, Nobel Prize for Medicine or Physiology 1970, Albert Einstein Achievement Award, Yeshiva Univ. 1971, Torald Sollmann Award in Pharmacology 1973, Paul Hoch Award, American Psychopathological Asscn. 1975, etc.; several research awards, memorial lectureships etc. *Publications:* The Pineal 1968 (with Richard J. Wurtman and Douglas E. Kelly), 450 articles in professional journals, also abstracts and press articles. *Leisure interests:* music, reading. *Address:* Department of Health Education and Welfare, National Institute of Health, 9000 Rockville Pike, Room 3A-15, Bethesda, MD 20892 (Office); 10401 Grosvenor Place, Rockville, MD 20852, U.S.A. (Home). *Telephone:* (301) 493-6376.

AXER, Erwin; Polish theatre producer and director; b. 1 Jan. 1917, Vienna, Austria; s. of Dr. Maurycy Axer and Fryderyka Schuster; m. Bronisława Kreczmar 1945 (died 1973); two s.; ed. Nat. Acad. of Theatrical Art, Warsaw; Asst. Producer, Nat. Theatre, Warsaw 1938–39; Actor Polish Drama Theatre, U.S.S.R. 1939–41; Artistic Dir., Teatr Kameralny, Łódź 1946–49; Dir. and producer Teatr Współczesny (Contemporary Theatre) Warsaw 1949–81; Dir. and Chief Producer, Nat. Theatre, Warsaw 1954–57; Asst. Prof. Producers' Dept., State Higher Theatrical School, Łódź 1946–49, Warsaw 1949–57, Extraordinary Prof. 1957–66, Prof. Ordinary 1966–81, Prof. Emer. 1981–; mem. Presidential Council for Culture 1992–95; State Prizes for Artistic Achievement 1951, 1953, 1955, 1962, Nagroda Krytyki im. Boya-Żeleńskiego (Critics Award) 1960; Commdr. Cross of Polonia Restituta, Great Cross of Polonia Restituta 1996; Order of Banner of Labour (1st Class); other awards and prizes. *Productions include:* Major Barbara (Shaw) 1947, Niemcy (Kruczkowski) 1955, Kordian (Słowacki) 1956, Pierwszy dzień wolności 1959, Iphigenia in Tauris 1961, Kariera Arturo Ui (Brecht) Warsaw 1962, Leningrad 1963, Three Sisters (Chekhov) 1963, Düsseldorf 1967, Androcles and the Lion (Shaw), Warsaw 1964, Tango (Mrożek), Warsaw 1965, Düsseldorf 1966, Die Ermittlung (Weiss), Warsaw 1966, Le Piéton de l'Air (Ionesco), Warsaw 1967, Maria Stuart (Schiller), Warsaw 1969, Dwa Teatry (Szaniawski), Leningrad 1969, Matka (Witkiewicz) Warsaw 1970, Porträt eines Planeten, Düsseldorf 1970, Old Times and Macbeth, Warsaw 1972, Uncle Vanya, Munich 1972, Ein Fest für Boris, Vienna (Kainz Award) 1973, King

Lear (Bond), Warsaw, 1974, Endgame (Beckett), Vienna 1976, Kordian Warsaw 1977, Seagull (Chekhov), Vienna 1977, Biedermann und die Brandstifter (Max Frisch), Zürich 1978, Krawiec (Tailor by Mrożek), Warsaw 1979, Wesele (Wyspiański) New York 1962, Our Town, Leningrad 1979, John Gabriel Borkman, Zürich 1979, Triptychon (Frisch), Warsaw 1980, Die Schwärmer (Musil), Vienna 1980, Amphitryon (Kleist), Vienna 1982, Till Damascus (Strindberg), Munich 1983, Reigen (Schnizler), Vienna 1983, Vinzenz (Musil), Vienna 1985, Am Ziel (Bernhard), Berlin 1987, Nachtasyl (Gorky), Berlin 1987, Theatermacher (Bernhard), Warsaw 1990, When we Dead Awaken (Ibsen), Hamburg 1990, Emigranci (Mrożek), Bregenz 1990, Mein Kampf (Tabori), Hamburg 1992, The Widows, Warsaw 1992, Love in Crimea (Mrożek), Warsaw 1994, Ambassador 1995, Warsaw Semiramida (Wojtyszko) 1996, Am Ziel (Bernhard), Warsaw 1997. *Publications include:* Listy ze sceny I (Letters from the Stage) 1955, Listy ze sceny II 1957, Sprawy Teatralne (Theatrical Things) 1966, Ćwiczenia Pamięci (Exercises of the Memory) 1984, Exercises of the Memory Series II 1991, Exercises of the Memory Series III 1998, essays, serial, articles on theatre. *Address:* ul. Odyńca 27 m. 11, 02-606 Warsaw, Poland. *Telephone:* (22) 44-01-16.

AXFORD, David Norman, M.A., M.SC.(ELEC.), PH.D., C.ENG., F.I.E.E.; British meteorologist; b. 14 June 1934, London; s. of Norman Axford and Joy A. (Williams) Axford; m. 1st Elizabeth A. Stiles 1962 (divorced 1980); one s. two d.; m. 2nd Diana Bufton 1980; three step-s. one step-d.; ed. Merchant Taylors School, Plymouth Coll., St. John's Coll. Cambridge and Southampton Univ.; Scientific Officer, Kew Observatory 1960–62; Sr. Scientific Officer, various R.A.F. stations 1962–68; Prin. Scientific Officer, Meteorological Research Flight, Royal Aircraft Establishment, Farnborough 1968–76; Asst. Dir. (SPSO) Operation Instrumentation Branch 1976–80; Asst. Dir. (SPSO), Telecommunications 1980–82; Deputy Dir. Observational Services 1982–84; Dir. of Services and Deputy to Dir.-Gen. Meteorological Office 1984–89; Pres. N. Atlantic Ocean Station Bd. 1982–85; Chair. Cttee. of Operational World Weather Watch System Evaluations—N. Atlantic (CONA) 1985–89; Deputy Sec.-Gen. World Meteorological Org., Geneva 1989–1995, Special Exec. Adviser to Sec.-Gen. Jan–May 1995; Consultant Meteorologist 1995–; Consultant to Earthwatch Europe, Oxford 1996–; Hon. Sec. Royal Meteorological Soc. 1983–88, Vice-Pres. 1989–91; Trustee Thames Valley Hospice, Windsor 1996–98; mem. Exec. Cttee. British Asscn. of Former UN Civil Servants (BAFUNCS) 1996–, Vice-Chair. 1998; Chartered Meteorologist of Royal Meteorological Soc. 1994–; Groves Award 1972. *Publications:* articles in professional journals. *Leisure interests:* home and garden, food and wine. *Address:* Honey End, 14 Ock Meadow, Stanford-in-the-Vale, Oxon., SN7 8LN, England. *Telephone:* (01367) 718480.

AXFORD, Sir William Ian, Kt., M.SC., M.E., PH.D., F.R.S.; British/New Zealand scientist; b. 2 Jan. 1933, Dannevirke, N.Z.; s. of John Edgar Axford and May Victoria (née Thoresen) Axford; m. Catherine Joy Lowry 1955; two s. two d.; ed. Canterbury Univ. Coll., N.Z., Manchester Univ. and Cambridge Univ.; mem. staff Defence Research Bd., Canada 1960–62; Assoc. Prof., then Prof. of Astronomy, Cornell Univ., U.S.A. 1963–67; Prof. of Physics and Applied Physics, Univ. of Calif., San Diego, U.S.A. 1967–74; Ed. Journal of Geophysical Research 1969–73; Scientific mem. and Dir. Max Planck Inst. für Aeronomie 1974–82, 1985–; Vice-Chancellor, Victoria Univ. of Wellington, N.Z. 1982–85; Pres. Cttee. on Space Research 1986–94; Vice-Pres. Scientific Cttee. on Solar Terrestrial Physics 1986–90; Chair. Foundation for Research, Science and Tech., N.Z. 1992–95; Pres. European Geophysical Soc. 1990–92; Chair. Marsden Fund, N.Z. 1994–98; Assoc. Royal Astronomical Soc.; Fellow American Geophysical Union; Foreign Assoc. N.A.S.; mem. Acad. Europaea; Hon. mem. European Geophysical Soc.; Hon. F.R.S.N.Z.; Hon. Prof. (Gottingen); Hon. D.Sc. (Canterbury, N.Z.) 1996; Appleton Award (Union Radio-Scientifique Int.), J. A. Fleming Award (American Geophysical Union), Space Award (A.I.A.A.), Tsiolkovski Medal, Chapman Medal (Royal Astronomical Soc.) 1994, N.Z. Science and Tech. Medal (Royal Soc. of N.Z.) 1994, Scientist of the Year and New Zealander of the Year 1995. *Publications:* c. 250 scientific articles on various aspects of astrophysics, cosmic ray physics and space physics. *Leisure interests:* reading, family history. *Address:* 2 Gladstone Road, Napier, New Zealand; Max Planck Institut für Aeronomie, Postfach 20, 37189 Katlenburg-Lindau, Germany. *Telephone:* (6) 8352188 (N.Z.); (5556) 979 439 (Germany). *Fax:* (6) 8352176 (N.Z.); (5556) 979 149 (Germany).

AXWORTHY, Lloyd, M.A., PH.D.; Canadian politician and academic; b. 21 Dec. 1939; s. of Norman Joseph Axworthy and Gwen Jane Axworthy; m. Denise Ommaney 1984; one s.; ed. Princeton Univ.; fmr. Prof. of Political Science, Univ. of Winnipeg; fmr. mem. Man. Legis.; mem. House of Commons 1979–; fmr. Minister of Employment and Immigration, Minister responsible for Status of Women and Minister of Transport; Minister of Human Resources Devt. and Minister of Western Econ. Diversification 1993–96, of Foreign Affairs Jan. 1996–; Liberal Party. *Address:* Ministry of Foreign Affairs and International Trade, Lester B. Pearson Building, 125 Sussex Drive, Ottawa, Ont., K1A 0G2, Canada.

AYALA, Francisco Jose, PH.D.; American (naturalized) professor of genetics; b. 12 March 1934, Madrid, Spain; s. of Francisco and Soledad (née Pereda) Ayala; m. Hana Lostakova 1985; two s. (by previous m.); ed. Univ. of Madrid and Columbia Univ.; Research Assoc. Rockefeller Univ., New York 1964–65, Asst. Prof. 1967–71; Asst. Prof. Providence Coll., R.I. 1965–67; Assoc. Prof., later Prof. of Genetics Univ. of Calif., Davis 1971–87, Dir. Inst. of Ecology 1977–81, Assoc. Dean of Environmental Studies 1977–81; Distinguished Prof. of Biology Univ. of Calif., Irvine 1987–89, Donald Bren Prof. of Biological Sciences 1989–; Pres. A.A.A.S. 1994–95; mem. N.A.S., American Acad. of Arts and Sciences, American Philosophical Soc., Pres. Cttee. of Advisers on Science and Tech. 1994–; Dr. h.c. (León) 1982, (Madrid) 1986, (Barcelona) 1986, (Athens) 1991, (Vigo) 1996, (Islas Baleares) 1998. *Publications:* Studies in the Philosophy of Biology 1974, Molecular Evolution 1976, Evolution 1977, Evolving: The Theory and Processes of Organic Evolution 1979, Population and Evolutionary Genetics 1982, Modern Genetics 1984 and more than 600 scientific articles. *Leisure interests:* skiing, tennis, travel. *Address:* Department of Ecology and Evolutionary Biology, University of California, Irvine, CA 92697, U.S.A. (Office); 2 Locke Court, Irvine, CA 92612, U.S.A. (Home). *Telephone:* (949) 824-8293 (Office). *Fax:* (949) 824-2474.

AYALA-CASTAÑERES, Agustín, M.S., D.BIOL.; Mexican professor of micropaleontology; b. 28 Aug. 1925, Mazatlán; s. of Agustín Ayala and María Luisa Castañares; m. Alma Irma López 1957; one s. two d.; ed. Universidad Nacional Autónoma de México (UNAM) and Stanford Univ.; micropaleontologist, Pemex 1950–54; Prof. of Paleontology, Inst. Politécnico Nacional (IPN) 1955–60; Head, Dept. of Micropaleontology and Marine Science Dept. Inst. of Geology, UNAM 1956–67; Prof. of Micropaleontology, Faculty of Sciences, UNAM 1961–, Head, Dept. of Biology 1965–67, Dir. Inst. Biología 1967–73; full-time researcher, Centro de Ciencias del Mar y Limnología, UNAM 1970–81; Coordinator of Scientific Investigation, UNAM 1973–80; Assoc. researcher, Scripps Inst. of Oceanography, Univ. of Calif. San Diego 1968–; Chair. Nat. Cttee. Scientific Cttee. on Oceanic Research (SCOR) 1971–; Dir. Plan para crear una Infraestructura en Ciencias y Tecnologías del Mar, México-UNESCO 1974–80; Pres. Acad. de la Investigación Científica (AIC) 1975–76; Chair. Intergovernmental Oceanographic Comm. UNESCO 1977–82; Exec. Dir. Programa Nacional de Ciencia y Tecnología para el Aprovechamiento de los Recursos Marinos (PROMAR-CONACyT) 1974–80; Chair. Org. Cttee. Jt. Oceanographic Ass., Mexico 1988; mem. Bd. Trustees, Int. Center for Living Aquatic Resources Man. (ICLARM) 1989–94; Gen. Coordinator, Interinst. Comms. for Evaluation of Higher Educ. 1991–; Fellow, Geological Soc. of America; mem. Int. Asscn. of Plant Taxonomy and Nomenclauture, American Soc. of Ecology, American Soc. of Petroleum Geologists, Soc. of Econ. Paleontologists and Mineralogists, etc.; Dr. h.c. (Bordeaux) 1988. *Publications:* 52 articles on fossil foraminifera, marine geology, coastal lagoons and science policy. *Address:* Apartado Postal 70-157, México 04510 DF (Office); 43 Cerro del Jabalí, México 04320 DF, Mexico (Home).

AYALA-LASSO, José; Ecuadorean diplomatist and international civil servant; b. 29 Jan. 1932, Quito; m.; four c.; ed. Pontificia Universidad Católica del Ecuador, Universidad Cen. del Ecuador, Université Catholique de Louvain, Belgium; several foreign affairs posts at embassies in Japan, Repub. of Korea, China, Italy; Minister of Foreign Affairs 1977; fmr. Amb. to Belgium, Luxembourg, Peru, EEC; lecturer Int. Law Inst., Universidad Cen. del Ecuador; Deputy Legal Sec. Perm Comm. for the South Pacific; Perm. Rep. to UN 1989–94, Chair. Security Council Cttee. concerning fmr. Yugoslavia 1991; UN High Commr. for Human Rights 1994–97, Minister of Foreign Affairs 1997–; (Chair. working group to establish post of High Commr. for Human Rights 1993); Grand Cross, Nat. Order of Merit (Ecuador), numerous decorations from Japan, Belgium, Brazil, etc. *Address:* Ministry of Foreign Affairs, Avenida 10 de Agosto y Carrioń, Quito, Ecuador.

AYALON, David, M.A., PH.D.; Israeli professor of the history of the Islamic peoples; b. 17 May 1914, Haifa; s. of Michael and Rela Ayalon; m. Myriam Ayalon 1965; ed. Reali High School, Haifa and Hebrew Univ. of Jerusalem; Political Dept. Jewish Agency 1938–48; Ministry of Foreign Affairs 1948–49; Founder and Dir. Dept. of Middle East in Modern Times, Hebrew Univ. of Jerusalem 1949–63, Dir. Inst. of Asian and African Studies 1963–67; Visiting Prof. Princeton Univ. and Univ. of Calif. Berkeley 1967–68; mem. Inst. for Advanced Study, Princeton 1976–77; mem. Israeli Acad. of Sciences and Humanities 1961, Emer. 1983–; Rockefeller Fellow 1952–59; Israel Prize for the Humanities 1972; Rothschild Prize for the Humanities 1975. *Publications:* Arabic-Hebrew Dictionary of Modern Arabic (with P. Shinar) 1947, Gunpowder and Firearms in the Mamluk Kingdom: A Challenge to a Medieval Society 1956, The Great Yasa of Chingiz Khan—A Reexamination 1971–73, Studies on the Mamluks of Egypt 1977, The Mamluk Military Society 1979, Outsiders in the Lands of Islam 1988. *Address:* Institute of Asian and African Studies, Hebrew University of Jerusalem, 7 Kikar Magnes, Jerusalem 92304, Israel (Home). *Telephone:* (02) 633306 (Home).

AYARI, Chedli, L. EN D., D. ÈS SC.(ECON.); Tunisian economist, diplomatist and politician; b. 24 Aug. 1933, Tunis; s. of Sadok and Fatouma Chedly; m. Elaine Vatteau 1959; three c.; ed. Collège Sadiki and Inst. de Hautes Etudes; with Société Tunisienne de Banque 1958; Asst. Faculté de Droit et des Sciences Economiques et Politiques, Tunis 1959; Econ. Counsellor, Perm. Mission of Tunis at UN 1960–64; Exec. Dir. IBRD 1964–65; Dean, Faculté de Droit, Tunis 1965–67; Dir. C.E.R.E.S. 1967–69; Sec. of State in charge of Plan 1969–70; Minister of Nat. Educ., Youth and Sport 1970–71; Amb. to Belgium Feb.-March 1972; Minister of Nat. Economy 1972–74, of Planning 1974–75; Chair. of Bd. and Gen. Man. Arab Bank for Econ. Devt. in Africa March 1975; Prof. of Economics, Agrégé de Sciences Economiques, Tunis; Assoc. Prof. Univ. of Aix-Marseilles, Feb. 1989–; mem. UN Cttee. of Planning for Devt.; Dr. h.c. (Aix-Marseilles) 1972; Grand Officier Légion d'honneur, Grand Cordon, Ordre de la République. *Publications:* Les Enjeux méditerranéens 1992, La Méditerranée Economique 1992; books and articles on economic and monetary problems. *Leisure interest:* music. *Address:* Rue Tanit, Gammarth, La Marsa, Tunis, Tunisia (Home). *Telephone:* 270-038.

AYATSKOV, Dmitry Fedorovich; Russian politician; b. 9 Nov. 1950, Stolypino, Saratov Region; s. of Fedor Kuzmich Ayatskov and Anna Petrovna Ayatskov; m.; one s. one d.; ed. Saratov Inst. of Agric., Moscow Cooperation Inst.; machine-operator, electrician in kolkhoz; army service 1969–71; chief agronomist in kolkhozes, leading posts on maj. enterprises of region (Tantal, Saratovskoye) 1977–80; Vice-Mayor of Saratov 1992–96; Head of Admin. Saratov Region April 1996–; Gov. Sept. 1996–; mem. Council of Fed. of Russia 1993–. *Leisure interest:* history. *Address:* Office of the Governor, Moscovskaya str. 72, 410042 Saratov, Russia (Office). *Telephone:* (8452) 72 20 86 (Office). *Fax:* (8452) 24 20 89 (Office).

AYCKBOURN, Sir Alan, Kt., C.B.E.; British playwright and theatre director; b. 12 April 1939, London; s. of Horace Ayckbourn and Irene Maud Ayckbourn (née Worley); m. 1st Christine Helen Roland 1959 (divorced 1997); m. 2nd Heather Elizabeth Stoney 1997; two s.; ed. Haileybury; on leaving school went straight into the theatre as stage manager and actor with various repertory cos. in England; founder mem. Victoria Theatre Co., Stoke-on-Trent 1962–64; Drama Producer, BBC Radio 1964–70; Artistic Dir., Stephen Joseph Theatre, Scarborough 1971–; Prof. of Contemporary Theatre, Oxford 1992; Assoc. Dir. Bedroom Farce (Nat. Theatre) 1977, Sisterly Feelings (Nat. Theatre) 1980; Dir. Ten Times Table (West End) 1978, Joking Apart (West End) 1979, Season's Greetings (West End) 1982, Way Upstream (Nat. Theatre) 1982, Intimate Exchanges 1984, A Chorus of Disapproval (Nat. Theatre) 1985, Women in Mind (West End) 1986, Tons of Money (Nat. Theatre) 1986, A View from the Bridge (Nat. Theatre) 1987, A Small Family Business (Nat. Theatre) 1987, 'Tis Pity She's a Whore (Nat. Theatre) 1988, Henceforward . . . (West End) 1988; Man of the Moment (West End) 1990, The Revengers' Comedies (West End) 1991, Mr. A.'s Amazing Maze Plays (Nat. Theatre) 1993, Wildest Dreams (Royal Shakespeare Theatre) 1993, Time of my Life (Vaudeville) 1993, Two Weeks with the Queen (Nat. Theatre) 1994, Communicating Doors (West End) 1995, By Jeeves (West End) 1996, Things We Do For Love 1998; *Plays:* Relatively Speaking 1965, The Sparrow 1967, How the Other Half Loves 1969, Family Circles 1970, Time and Time Again 1971, Absurd Person Singular 1972 (Dir. 1990), The Norman Conquests 1973, Jeeves (book and lyrics for Andrew Lloyd Webber musical) 1975 (rewritten as By Jeeves 1996), Absent Friends 1974, Confusions 1974, Bedroom Farce 1975, Just Between Ourselves 1976, Ten Times Table 1977, Men on Women on Men (revue with music by Paul Todd) 1978, Joking Apart 1978, Sisterly Feelings 1979, Taking Steps 1979, Suburban Strains (musical play with music by Paul Todd) 1980, Season's Greetings 1980, Making Tracks (with Paul Todd) 1981, Way Upstream 1981, Intimate Exchanges 1982, Incidental Music (with Paul Todd) 1983, A Chorus of Disapproval 1984 (film 1988), The Westwoods 1984, Woman in Mind 1985, Mere Soup Songs (with Paul Todd) 1986, A Small Family Business 1986, Henceforward 1987, Man of the Moment 1988, The Revengers' Comedies 1989, Body Language 1990, This is Where We came in 1990, Callisto 5 1990, Othello (dir.) 1990, Wildest Dreams 1991, My Very Own Story 1991, Time of My Life 1992, Dreams from a Summer House (with music by John Pattison) 1992, Communicating Doors 1994, Haunting Julia 1994, The Musical Jigsaw Play 1994, A Word from our Sponsor (with music by John Pattison) 1995, The Champion of Paribanou 1996, Things We Do For Love 1997, Comic Potential 1998, The Boy Who Fell Into a Book 1998, Gizmo 1998; Hon. D.Litt. (Hull) 1981, (Keele, Leeds) 1987; Hon. Dr. (York) 1992, (Bradford) 1994, (Open Univ.) 1998; Evening Standard Award for Best New Comedy for Absurd Person Singular 1973, for Best New Play for The Norman Conquests 1974, for Best New Play for Just Between Ourselves 1977, Plays and Players Award for Best New Play for The Norman Conquests 1974, Variety Club of Great Britain Playwright of the Year 1974, Plays and Players Award for Best New Comedy for Joking Apart 1979, London Evening Standard Award, Olivier Award and Drama Award for Best Comedy for A Chorus of Disapproval 1985, London Evening Standard Award for Best New Play for A Small Family Business 1987, Plays and Players Director of the Year Award for a View from the Bridge 1987, London Evening Standard Award for Best Comedy for Henceforward . . . 1989, for Man of the Moment 1990, Lifetime Achievement Award (Writers' Guild) 1993, Mont Blanc de la Culture Award for Europe 1994, Writers' Guild of G.B. Award for Best West End Play for Communicating Doors 1996, British Regional Theatre Awards for Best Musical for By Jeeves 1996, Lloyds Pvt. Banking Playwright of the Year Award for Things We Do For Love 1998. *Publications:* The Norman Conquests 1975, Three Plays 1977, Joking Apart and other plays 1979, Sisterly Feelings and Taking Steps 1981, A Chorus of Disapproval, Woman in Mind, A Small Family Business, Henceforward . . ., Mr. A.'s Amazing Maze Plays 1989, Man of the Moment 1990, The Revengers' Comedies 1991, Time of my Life 1993, Wildest Dreams 1993, Communicating Doors 1995. *Leisure interests:* music, cricket, astronomy. *Address:* c/o Casarotto Ramsay Ltd., National House, 60–66 Wardour Street, London W1V 4ND, England. *Telephone:* 0171-287 4450. *Fax:* 0171-287 9128.

AYGI, Gennadi Nikolaevich; Chuvash poet; b. 21 Aug. 1934, Shamursino, Chuvash S.S.R.; ed. Gorky Literary Inst., Moscow; started writing in Russian rather than Chuvash 1960–; worked in Mayakovsky Museum, Moscow 1961–71; trans. and writer 1971–; Prix Paul Desfeuilles 1968 (for trans. of French poetry into Chuvash), Petrarca Prize (Italy) 1993, Ordre des arts et des lettres 1997. *Publications include:* Poetry 1954–71, Munich 1975; A Celebrated Winter, Paris 1982, Selected Poems 1954–1988, 1991, The Field—Russia 1990, The Winter Carouses 1991, Poetry as Silence 1994, Veronica's Notebook 1997. *Address:* Union of Chuvash Writers, Lenin Prosp. 4, Cheboksary, Russia.

AYKROYD, Daniel Edward; American actor; b. 1 July 1952, Ottawa; s. of Peter Hugh Aykroyd and Lorraine Gougeon Aykroyd; m. 1st Maureen Lewis 1974 (divorced); three s.; m. 2nd Donna Dixon 1984; two d.; ed. Carleton Univ., Ottawa; started as a stand-up comedian and worked on Saturday Night Live 1975–79; created and performed as The Blues Brothers (with the late John Belushi); albums include Made in America; Emmy Award 1976–77. *Films include:* 1941 1979, Mr. Mike's Mondo Video 1979, The Blues Brothers (also screenwriter) 1980, Neighbors 1981, Doctor Detroit 1983, Trading Places 1983, Twilight Zone 1983, Ghostbusters 1984, Nothing Lasts for Ever 1984, Into the Night 1985, Spies Like Us (also screenwriter) 1985, Dragnet (co-screenwriter) 1987, Caddyshack II 1988, The Great Outdoors 1988, My Stepmother is an Alien 1988, Ghostbusters II 1989, Driving Miss Daisy 1990, My Girl, Loose Canons, Valkemania, Nothing But Trouble 1991, Coneheads 1993, My Girl II 1994, North, Casper 1995 (also co-screenwriter), Sergeant Bilko 1996 (also co-screenwriter), Grosse Point Blank 1997 (also co-screenwriter), Blues Brothers 2000 1997, The Arrow 1997, Susan's Plan 1998 (also dir. and screenwriter). *Address:* c/o C.A.A., 9830 Wilshire Boulevard, Beverly Hills, CA 90212, U.S.A.

AYKUT, Imren; Turkish politician; b. 1941, Adana; s. of Şevket Şadi and Rahime Aykut; ed. Istanbul Univ. and Oxford Univ.; fmr man. of trades unions; industrial relations expert in Turkish glass industries; fmr. Sec.-Gen. Paper Industry Employers' Union; mem. Constitutional Ass. 1981; Deputy, Nat. Ass. 1983–; Minister of Labour and Social Security Dec. 1987–91; Govt. Spokesperson 1991; Pres. Turkish Inter-Parl. Gp. 1991–; Motherland Party. *Publications:* over 40 articles and research papers. *Leisure interests:* hand-made carpets, antiquities. *Address:* Türkiye Büyük Millet Meclisi, Parlamentolararasi Birlik Türk Grubu, Baskanigi, Ankara, Turkey. *Telephone:* (904) 4205431.

AYLING, Robert John; British airline executive; b. 3 Aug. 1946; m. Julia Crallan 1972; two s. one d.; ed. King's Coll. School, Wimbledon; joined Elborne, Mitchell & Co. 1968; legal adviser on British accession to the EC 1973–75, Head of Dept. of Trade aviation law br. 1978 (responsible for parl. bill that led to privatization of British Airways), Under-Sec. for EC, int. trade, competition issues 1981; with British Shipbuilders 1975; joined British Airways (legal and govt. affairs) 1985, Co. Sec. 1987, organized legal arrangements concerning BA's privatization Feb. 1987 and BA's acquisition of British Caledonian 1988, Dir. Human Resources 1988, Dir. Marketing and Operations 1991, Group Man. Dir. 1993–95, C.E.O. 1996–; Gov. King's Coll. School 1996; Hon. LL.D. (Brunel) 1996. *Address:* British Airways PLC, Waterside, P.O. Box 365, Harmondsworth, UB7 0GB, England. *Telephone:* 0181-759 5511. *Fax:* 0181-759 9597.

AYLMER, Gerald Edward, D.PHIL., F.B.A.; British historian; b. 30 April 1926, near Ludlow, Shropshire; s. of E. A. Aylmer and G. P. Aylmer née Evans; m. Ursula Adelaide Nixon 1955; one s. one d.; ed. Winchester Coll. and Balliol Coll. Oxford; J. E. Procter Visiting Fellow, Princeton Univ., U.S.A. 1950–51; Jr. Research Fellow, Balliol Coll. 1951–54; Asst. Lecturer, Modern History Dept., Univ. of Manchester 1954–57, Lecturer 1957–62; Prof. of History and Head of Dept., Univ. of York 1963–78; Visiting mem. of Inst. for Advanced Study, Princeton 1975; Master of St. Peter's Coll. Oxford 1978–91; Pres. Royal Historical Soc. 1984–88, Hon. Vice-Pres. 1989–; Hon. Vice-Pres. Cromwell Asscn. 1991, Historical Asscn. 1992; Chair. Royal Comm. on Historical Manuscripts 1989–94, Ed. Bd., History of Parl. Trust 1989–98; Hon. D.Litt. (Exeter) 1991, (Manchester) 1991. *Publications:* The King's Servants 1961, The Struggle for the Constitution 1963 (U.S. edn.: A Short History of 17th Century England), The Interregnum (Ed.) 1972, The State's Servants 1973, A History of York Minster (Ed. with R. Cant) 1977, The Levellers in the English Revolution 1975, Rebellion or Revolution? England 1640–60 1986. *Address:* The Old Captain's, Hereford Road, Ledbury, Herefordshire, HR8 2PX; 18 Albert Street, Jericho, Oxford, OX2 6AZ, England. *Telephone:* (01531) 670817 (Ledbury); (01865) 512383 (Oxford).

AYLWIN AZÓCAR, Patricio; Chilean politician, lawyer, university professor and consultant; b. 26 Nov. 1918, Viña del Mar; s. of Miguel Aylwin G. and Laura Azócar; m. Leonor Oyarzun Ivanovic 1948; five c.; Pres. Christian Democrat party (PDC) 1973, 1987–91; Senator 1965–73; leader opposition coalition rejecting Gen. Augusto Pinochet (q.v.) in nat. plebiscite Oct. 1988; opposition coalition cand. 1989; PDC cand. for Pres. 1989; Pres. of Chile 1990–94; Pres. Corporación Justicia y Democracia. *Publications:* El Juicio Arbitral 1943, La Transición Chilena. Discursos escogidos Marzo 1990–92, Crecimiento con Equidad. Discursos escogidos 1992–94, Justicia, Democracia y Desarrollo. Conferencias y discursos 1994–95. *Address:* Teresa Salas No. 786, Providencia, Santiago, Chile. *Telephone:* (562) 3411574. *Fax:* (562) 2042135.

AYNSLEY-GREEN, Albert, M.A., M.B.B.S., D.PHIL., M.R.C.S., F.R.C.P., F.R.C.P. (EDIN.); British paediatrician; b. 30 May 1943; m. Rosemary Boucher 1967; two d.; ed. Glyn Grammar School, Epsom and Univs. of London and Oxford; House Officer, Guy's Hosp. London, St. Luke's Hosp. Guildford, Radcliffe Infirmary, Oxford and Royal Postgrad. Medical School, Hammersmith 1967–70; Wellcome Research Fellow, Radcliffe Infirmary 1970–72, Clinical lecturer in Internal Medicine 1972–73, Sr. House Officer and Registrar in Paediatrics (also John Radcliffe Hosp.) 1973–74; European Science Exchange Fellowship, Univ. Children's Hosp. Zürich 1974–75; Clinical lecturer in Paediatrics, Univ. of Oxford 1975–78, Univ. lecturer 1978–83; Fellow, Green Coll. Oxford 1980–83, Royal Coll. of Paediatrics and Child Health; Prof. of Child Health and Head of Dept. Univ. of Newcastle-upon-Tyne 1984–93; Nuffield Prof. of Child Health, Univ. of London 1993–; Dir. of Clinical Research and Devt. Great Ormond St. Hosp. and Inst. of Child Health, London 1993–; numerous awards and distinctions etc. *Publications:* papers on child health. *Leisure interests:* family, walking, music, photography. *Address:* Institute of Child Health, 30 Guilford Street, London, WC1N 1EH, England. *Telephone:* 0171-813 8391. *Fax:* 0171-813 0387.

AYRE, Richard James, B.A.; British journalist; b. 1 Aug. 1949, Newcastle-upon-Tyne; s. of Thomas Henry Ayre and Beth Carson; ed. Univ. Coll., Durham; Pres. Univ. of Durham Students' Union 1969–70; producer and reporter BBC Northern Ireland 1973–76, Home News Ed. TV News 1979–84, Head of BBC Westminster 1989–92, Controller of Editorial Policy 1993–96, Deputy Chief Exec. BBC News 1996–; Benton Fellow Univ. of Chicago 1984–85. *Address:* BBC, Television Centre, Wood Lane, London, W.12 (Office); 69 Drayton Gardens, London, W13 0UG, England. *Telephone:* 0181-743 8000 (Office).

AYRES, Gillian, O.B.E.; British artist; b. 3 Feb. 1930; d. of Stephen Ayres and Florence Ayres; m. Henry Mundy (divorced); two s.; ed. St. Paul's Girls' School and Camberwell School of Art; teacher of art 1959–81, Sr. Lecturer, St. Martin's School of Art and Head of Painting, Winchester School of Art 1978–81; Sr. Fellow Royal Coll. of Art 1996; fmr. R.A., London, resgnd. 1997; Hon. D.Litt. (London); one-woman exhbns. include: Gallery One 1956, Redfern Gallery 1958, Moulton Gallery 1960, 1962, Kasmin Gallery 1965, 1966, 1969, William Darby Gallery 1976, Women's Int. Centre, New York 1976, Knoedler Gallery 1979, 1982, 1987, Museum of Modern Art, Oxford 1981, Sackler Gallery at Royal Acad., London 1997; retrospective exhbn. at Serpentine Gallery 1983; works have also appeared in group exhbns. in London, New York and Paris; works in public collections at Tate Gallery, London, Museum of Modern Art, New York and Gulbenkian Foundation, Lisbon; prizewinner, Tokyo Biennale 1963, Major Arts Council Bursary 1979, Charles Wolaston R.A. Award for best painting in the R.A. 1989, Gold Medal, Indian Triennale 1991. *Address:* c/o Gimpel Fils Gallery, 30 Davies Street, London, W.1, England.

AYYOUBI, Mahmoud Ben Saleh al-; Syrian politician; b. 1932; fmr. Dir.-Gen. for Admin. Affairs, Euphrates Dept.; Minister of Educ. 1969–71; Deputy Premier 1970–71; Vice-Pres. 1971–75; Prime Minister 1972–76; mem. Baath Party Regional Command 1971–75, Jan. 1980–. *Address:* c/o Baath Party, National Command, BP 849, Damascus, Syria.

AZA, Alberto; Spanish diplomatist; b. 22 May 1937, Tetuán, Morocco; s. of Alberto Aza and Marcela Arias; m. María Eulalia Custodio Martí 1963; two s. four d.; ed. Univ. of Oviedo and Madrid; joined Diplomatic Service 1965; served Libreville, Algiers, Rome, Madrid; Dir. Cabt. of Prime Minister of Spain 1977–83; Chief Dir. OAS, Latin America Dept., Ministry of Foreign Affairs 1983; Minister Counsellor, Lisbon 1983–85; Amb. to OAS, Washington, D.C. 1985–89 (also accred. to Belize); Amb. to Mexico 1990–92, to U.K. 1992–99; Gran Cruz del Mérito Civil 1979, Gran Cruz de la Order del Mérito Naval 1996; Hon. D.Litt. (Portsmouth) 1997. *Leisure interests:* golf, fishing, walking. *Address:* 24 Belgrave Square, London, SW1X 8QA, England. *Telephone:* 0171-235 8363. *Fax:* 0171-235 2026.

AZARNOFF, Daniel L(ester), M.S., M.D.; American physician and business executive; b. 4 Aug. 1926, Brooklyn, New York; s. of Samuel J. and Kate (Asarnow) Azarnoff; m. Joanne Stokes 1951; two s. one d.; ed. Rutgers Univ. and Univ. of Kansas; Instructor in Anatomy, Univ. of Kansas 1949–50, Research Fellow 1950–52, Intern 1955–56, Nat. Heart Inst. Resident Research Fellow 1956–58, Asst. Prof. of Medicine 1962–64, Assoc. Prof. 1964–68, Dir. Clinical Pharmacology Study Unit 1964–68, Assoc. Prof. of Pharmacology 1965–68, Prof. of Medicine and Pharmacology 1968, Dir. Clinical Pharmacology-Toxicology Center 1967–68, Distinguished Prof. 1973–78, Clinical Prof. of Medicine 1982–; Asst. Prof. of Medicine St. Louis Univ. 1960–62; Visiting Scientist, Fulbright Scholar, Karolinska Inst., Stockholm, Sweden 1968; Clinical Prof. of Pathology and Prof. of Pharmacology, Northwestern Univ. 1978–85; Clinical Prof. of Medicine, Univ. of Kan. Coll. of Health Sciences 1984; Sr. Vice-Pres. Worldwide Research and Devt., G. D. Searle & Co., Chicago 1978, Pres. Searle Research and Devt., Skokie, Ill. 1979–85; Pres. D. L. Azarnoff Assocs., Inc. 1987–; mem. Bd. of Dirs. De Novo Inc. 1994–; editorial Bd. Drug Investigation 1989–; Chair. Cttee. on Problems of Drug Safety, N.A.S. 1972–76; Consultant to numerous govt. agencies; mem. Nat. Comm. on Orphan Diseases, Dept. of Health and Human Services; mem. Bd. of Dirs. Oread Labs. Inc. 1993; Ed. Review of Drug Interactions 1974–77, Yearbook of Drug Therapy 1977–79; Series Ed. Monographs in Clinical Pharmacology 1977–; Fellow, American Coll. of Physicians, New York Acad. of Scientists; mem. American Soc. of Clinical Nutrition, American Nutrition Inst., American Fed. of Clinical Research, British Pharmacological Soc., Royal Soc. for the Promotion of Health, Inst. of Medicine (N.A.S.) and others; Ciba Award for gerontological research 1958, Rector's Medal (Univ. of Helsinki) 1968, Burroughs Wellcome Scholar 1964. *Address:* 210 Robin Road, Hillsborough, CA 94010, U.S.A. *Telephone:* (415) 340-9048.

AZCONA DEL HOYO, José; Honduran politician and engineer; b. 26 Jan. 1927, La Ceiba; s. of José Simón Azcona Vélez and Carmen Hoyo Pérez de Azcona; m. Miriam Bocock Selva; two s. one d.; ed. Universidad Nacional Autónoma de Honduras and Instituto Tecnológico de Estudios Superiores de Monterrey, Mexico; civil engineer, with special interest in low-cost housing, planning and urban devt.; Gen. Man. Federación Hondureña de Cooperativas de Vivienda Limitada 1973–82; started political activities when a student; Liberal cand. in 1963 gen. elections (interrupted by coup d'état); apptd. Sec. for Org. and Propaganda, Movimiento Liberal Rodista 1975; mem. Cen. Exec. Council 1977, Sec. Gen. 1981; Deputy to Congreso Nacional 1982–86; Minister of Communications, Public Works and Transport 1982–83; fmr. Pres. Liberal Party Cen. Exec. Council; Pres. of Honduras 1985–90. *Address:* c/o Partido Liberal, Tegucigalpa, Honduras.

AZCUNA, Adolfo, A.B., LL.B.; Philippines lawyer; b. 16 Feb. 1939; s. of Felipe Azcuna and Carmen Sevilla; m. Asuncion Aunario 1968; one s. three d.; ed. Ateneo de Manila and Univ. of Salzburg; elected del. 1971 Constitutional Convention 1971–73; mem. Constitutional Comm. 1986–87; Press Sec. 1989; Presidential spokesman and legal counsel 1989; Pres. Manila Hotel May 1997–; partner Azcuna, Yorac, Sarmiento, Arroyo & Chua Law Offices 1992–; Corazon Aquino Fellowship, Harvard Univ. 1990 (deferred). *Publications:* Doing Business in the Philippines, Foreign Judgment Enforcement in the Philippines, Asean Conflict of Law. *Leisure interests:* reading, biking. *Address:* Azcuna, Yorac, Sarmiento, Arroyo and Chua Law Offices, G/F, Cedar Mansions II, Amber Avenue, Ortigas Center, Pasig City, Philippines (Office); 140 CRM Avenue, Las Pinas, Metro Manila, Philippines (Home). *Telephone:* (2) 633-5981 (Office); 801-1685 (Home). *Fax:* (2) 633-2820 (Office).

AZIMOV, Yakhye Nuriddinovich; Tajikistan politician; b. 4 Dec. 1947, Khodjend, Tajikistan; m.; one s. two d.; ed. Tashkent Inst. of Textile Industry; worked Ura-Tubin Tricot factory 1971–75; engineer, head of rug production, Dir. Kairak-Kum rug factory 1975–82; deputy chief engineer, chief engineer, Dir.-General of rug productions 1982–96; Pres. Jt. Stock Co. Kolinkho, Kairakum Jan. 1996–; Chair. Council of Ministers (Prime Minister) of Tajikistan Feb. 1996–. *Address:* Council of Ministers, Rudaki prosp. 42, 743051 Dushanbe, Tajikistan (Office). *Telephone:* (3772) 21 18 71; 23 19 47 (Office).

AZINGER, Paul William; American golfer; b. 6 Jan. 1960, Holyoke, Mass.; m. Toni Azinger; two d.; ed. Florida State Univ.; started playing golf aged 5; turned professional 1981; won Phoenix Open 1987, Herz Bay Hill Classic 1988, Canon Greater Hartford Open 1989, MONY Tournament of Champions 1990, AT&T Pebble Beach Nat. Pro-Am 1991, TOUR Championship 1992, BMW Int. Open 1990, 1992, Memorial Tournament, New England Classic, PGA Championship, Inverness 1993; GWAA Ben Hogan Trophy 1995; mem. U.S. Ryder Cup Team 1989, 1991, 1993; broadcasting debut as reporter for NBC, 1995 Ryder Cup; PGA Tour Player of the Year 1987. *Publication:* Zinger (about his fight against cancer). *Leisure interest:* fishing. *Address:* P.G.A. Tour, 112 Tpc Boulevard, Ponte Vedra Beach, FL 33082, U.S.A.

AZIZ, Dato' Seri Paduka Rafidah, M.ECONS.; Malaysian politician; b. 4 Nov. 1943, Selama Perak; m. Mohammed Basir bin Ahmad; three c.; ed. Univ. of Malaya; tutor, Asst. Lecturer, Lecturer and Chair. Rural Devt. Div. Faculty of Econs. Univ. of Malaya 1966–76; mem. Parl. 1978–; Deputy Minister of Finance 1977–80; Minister of Public Enterprise 1980–88, of Int. Trade and Industry March 1988–; mem. UMNO Supreme Council 1975–; holder of many other public appts. and del. to numerous int. confs.; Ahli Mangku Negara, Datuk Paduka Mahkota Selangor. *Leisure interests:* reading, decoration, music, squash. *Address:* Ministry of International Trade and Industry, Block 10, Kompleks Rejabat Kerajaan, Jalan Duta, 50622 Kuala Lumpur, Malaysia. *Telephone:* (3) 6510033. *Fax:* (3) 6512306.

AZIZ, Tariq; Iraqi politician; b. 1936, Mosul; ed. Baghdad Univ.; mem. staff, Al-Jumhuriyah 1958; Chief Ed. Al-Jamahiir 1963; worked for Baath press in Syria until change of govt. in Feb. 1966; Chief Ed. Al-Thawra publishing house; mem. Revolutionary Command Council Gen. Affairs Bureau 1972; reserve mem. Arab Baath Socialist Party Leadership 1974–77; elected mem. Baath Regional Leadership 1977; Deputy Prime Minister 1981, 1991–; Minister of Foreign Affairs 1983. *Address:* Offices of the Deputy Prime Ministers, Karradat Mariam, Baghdad, Iraq.

AZIZ, Ungku Abdul, D.ECONS.; Malaysian professor and university administrator; b. 28 Jan. 1922, London, U.K.; m. Sharifah Azah Aziz; one d.; ed. Raffles Coll. and Univ. of Malaya in Singapore, Waseda Univ., Tokyo, Johore State Civil Service; Lecturer in Econs., Univ. of Malaya in Singapore till 1952; Head, Dept. of Econs., Univ. of Malaya, Kuala Lumpur 1952–61, Dean of Faculty 1961–65, Vice-Chancellor 1968–88, Royal Prof. of Econs. 1978; Pres. Nat. Co-operative Movement (ANGKASA) 1971, Asscn. of S.E. Asian Institutions of Higher Learning (ASAIHL) 1973–75; Chair. Asscn. of Commonwealth Univs. 1974–75, Malaysian Nat. Council for ASAIHL, Malaysian Examinations Council 1980–; mem. United Nations Univ. Council; Corresp. mem. of Advisory Bd., Modern Asian Studies 1973–75; mem. Econ. Asscn. of Malaysia, Int. Asscn. of Agricultural Economists, Joint Advisory Cttee. of FAO, UNESCO and ILO; mem. Nat. Consultative Council and Nat. Unity Advisory Council, Govt. of Malaysia; mem. numerous cttees. and orgs.; Fellow, World Acad. of Arts and Sciences 1965–; Tun Abdul Razak Foundation Award 1978, Japan Foundation Award 1981; Ordre des Arts et des Lettres (France) 1965; Special Award, Muslim Pilgrim Savings Fund Bd.

1988; Grand Cordon of the Order of the Sacred Treasure, Emperor of Japan 1989; ASEAN Achievement Award (Educ) 1992, Int. Academic Prize (City of Fukoka) 1993; Hon. D.Hum.Litt. (Univ. of Pittsburgh); Hon. Ed. D. (Chulalongkorn Univ.) Thailand 1977; Hon. D.Jur. (Waseda Univ.) Japan 1982; Hon. D. Litt. (Univ. of Warwick) 1982; Hon. D. Iur. (Univ. of Strathclyde) 1986; Hon. D. Econ. (Kebangsaan Univ. Malaysia) 1986; Hon. LL.D. (Buckingham) 1987; Hon. D. Iur. (Utara Univ. Malaysia) 1988. *Leisure interests:* jogging, reading and photography.

AZIZ M. IBRAHIM, Farouk Abdel, M.D., F.R.C.O.G.; Sudanese professor of obstetrics and gynaecology; b. 12 April 1941, Elgolid; s. of Abdel Aziz Mohamed and Zeinab Ahmed Hassan; m. Amal Abu Bakr Arbab 1975; two s. two d.; ed. Univ. of Khartoum; consultant and lecturer in Obstetrics and Gynaecology, Univ. of Khartoum 1972, Head of Dept. 1974, Assoc. Prof. 1980, Dir. E.D.C. 1985, Man. Health Learning Materials Project 1986, Dir. Staff Devt. Centre 1990; Dean Ahfad School of Medicine for Girls 1993; Chief Tech. Adviser WHO 1995–. *Publications:* 5 books on obstetrics and educ., 3 books on educ., obstetrics and reproductive health and family planning, 16 scientific papers on reproductive health. *Leisure interests:* photography, reading. *Address:* P.O. Box 543, Sana'a, Republic of Yemen. *Telephone:* (1) 216 337. *Fax:* (1) 251 216.

AZKOUL, Karim, PH.D.; Lebanese diplomatist and writer; b. 15 July 1915, Raschaya; s. of Najib Azkoul and Latifah Assaly; m. Eva Corey 1947; one s. one d.; ed. Jesuit Univ. of St. Joseph, Beirut, and Univs. of Paris, Berlin, Bonn and Munich. Prof. of History, Arab and French Literature, and Philosophy in various colls. in Lebanon 1939–46; Dir. of an Arabic publishing house and monthly Arabic review The Arab World, Beirut 1943–45; mem. Lebanese Del. to UN, New York 1947–50, Acting Perm. Del. to UN 1950–53; Head of UN Affairs Dept., Ministry of Foreign Affairs 1953–57; Head, Perm. Del. to UN 1957–59, Rapporteur Cttee. on Genocide 1948, Humanitarian, Cultural and Social Cttee. of Gen. Ass. 1951, Cttee. on Freedom of Information 1951; First Vice-Chair. Human Rights Comm. 1958; Chair. Negotiating Cttee. for Extra Budgetary Funds 1952–54; Consul-Gen. in Australia and New Zealand 1959–61; Amb. to Ghana, Guinea and Mali 1961–64, to Iran and Afghanistan 1964–66; Journalist 1966–68; Prof. of Philosophy, Beirut Coll. for Women 1968–72, Lebanese Univ. 1970–72; Chief Ed. The Joy of Knowledge, Arabic Encyclopedia (10 vols.) 1978–; mem. PEN, Emergency World Council, Hague 1971–; Vice-Chair. Cttee. for Defence of Human Rights in Lebanon; mem. Bd. of Trustees, Bd. of Management of Theological School of Balamand, Lebanon; Order of Cedar (Lebanon), Order of Holy Sepulchre (Jerusalem), Order of St. Marc (Alexandria), Order of the Brilliant Star (Republic of China), Order of Southern Star (Brazil), Order of St. Peter and Paul (Damascus). *Publications:* Reason and Faith in Islam (in German) 1938, Reason in Islam (in Arabic) 1946, Freedom (co-author) 1956, Freedom of Association (UN) 1968; trans. into Arabic Consciencism (Nkrumah) 1964; Arab Thought in the Liberal Age (Albert Hourani) 1969. *Leisure interests:* reading and writing.

AZNAR LÓPEZ, José María; Spanish politician; b. 1953, Madrid; m. Ana Botella; two s. one d.; ed. Universidad Complutense, Madrid; fmr. tax inspector; fmr. Chief Exec. Castile-Leon region; joined Rioja br. Alianza Popular 1978, Deputy Sec.-Gen. and mem. Cortes (Parl.) 1982; Premier Castilla y León Autonomous Region 1987; Pres. Partido Popular (PP, fmrly. Alianza Popular) 1990–; Prime Minister of Spain Feb. 1996–. *Address:* Prime Minister's Chancellery, Complejo de la Moncloa, 28071 Madrid, Spain. *Telephone:* (1) 3353535. *Fax:* (1) 5492739.

AZNAVOURIAN, Varenagh (pseudonym Charles Aznavour); French film actor and singer; b. 22 May 1924; m. 1st Micheline Rugel 1946; m. 2nd Evelyne Plessis 1955; m. 3rd Ulla Thorsel 1967; five c.; ed. Ecole centrale de T.S.F., Centre de spectacle, Paris; with Jean Dasté Company 1941; Man. Dir. French-Music 1965–; Roving UNESCO Amb. to Armenia 1995–; numerous song recitals in Europe and U.S.A.; Chevalier Légion d'honneur, des Arts et des Lettres; several prizes. *Films include:* La tête contre les murs 1959, Tirez sur le pianiste 1960, Un taxi pour Tobrouk, Le testament d'Orphée, Le diable et les dix commandements, Haute-infidélité 1964, La métamorphose des cloportes 1965, Paris au mois d'août 1966, Le facteur s'en va-t-en guerre 1966, Candy 1969, Les intrus 1973, Sky Riders, Intervention Delta, Folies bourgeoises, Dix petits nègres 1976, The Twist 1976, The Tin Drum 1979, Qu'est-ce qui a fait courir David? 1982, Les fantômes du chapelier 1982, La montagne magique 1983, Vive la vie 1984, Mangeclous 1988, Il Maestro 1992, les Années Campagne 1992. Film music includes: Soupe au lait, L'île du bout du monde, Ces dames préfèrent le mambo, Le cercle vicieux, De quoi tu te mêles Daniela, Douce violence, Les Parisiennes; also author and singer of numerous songs; composer of operetta Monsieur Carnaval 1965, Douchka 1973; Chevalier Légion d'honneur, des Arts et des Lettres; Grand Prix national de la chanson 1986. *Leisure interests:* photography, do-it-yourself. *Address:* c/o Levon Sayan, 76–78 avenue des Champs-Elysées, bureau 322, 75008 Paris, France.

AZUELA, Arturo; Mexican writer; b. 1938; fmr. mathematician and violinist in various symphony orchestras; published first novel 1973; mem. Academia Mexicana de la Lengua 1986–. *Publications:* El tamaño del infierno, La casa de las 1,000 vírgenes, Manifestación de silencios. *Address:* c/o Academia Mexicana de la Lengua, Donceles 66, Centro, Delegación Cuauhtémoc, 06010 México, D.F. Mexico.

AZUMA, Takamitsu, J.I.A., D.ARCH.; Japanese architect; b. 20 Sept. 1933, Osaka; s. of Yoshimatsu Azuma and Yoshiko (née Ikeda); m. Setsuko Nakaoka 1957; one d.; ed. Osaka Univ.; designer Ministry of Postal Service, Osaka 1957–60; Chief Designer Junzo Sakakura Architect & Assocs., Osaka 1960–63, Tokyo 1963–67; Prin. Takamitsu Azuma Architect & Assocs., Tokyo 1968–85; Instructor Univ. of Art and Design 1976–78, Tokyo Denki Univ. 1980–82, Tokyo Univ. 1983–85; Instructor Osaka Univ. 1981–85, Prof. 1985–; Instructor Osaka Art Univ. 1985–87; Architect Azuma Architects and Assocs. 1985–97; Emer. Prof. Osaka Univ. 1997–; Prof. Chiba Inst. of Tech. 1997–; mem. Architectural Inst. of Japan; Visiting Prof. School of Architecture, Washington Univ., St. Louis, U.S.A. 1985; 1st Prize Kinki Br., Inst. of Architects Competition 1957; Architectural Inst. of Japan Architectural Design Prize 1995. *Publications:* Revaluation of the Residence 1971, On the Japanese Architectural Space 1981, Philosophy of living in the City 1983, Device from Architecture 1986, Space Analysis of the Urban Residence 1986, White Book about Tower House 1987, On Urban Housing 1997. *Leisure interests:* travelling, reading, computing. *Address:* Azuma Architects & Assocs., 3-6-1 Minami-Aoyama Minato-ku, Tokyo 107-0016 (Office); 3-39-4 Jingumae, Shibuya-ku, Tokyo 150-0001, Japan (Home). *Telephone:* 03 3403 5593 (Office); 03 3404 0805 (Home).

B

BA JIN (LI YAOTANG); Chinese writer and journalist; b. 25 Nov. 1904, Chengdu, Sichuan Prov.; m. Xiao Shan 1944 (died 1972); one s. one d.; ed. Foreign Language School, Chengdu; studied in France and adopted name Ba Jin (taken from first syllable of Bakunin and the last of Kropotkin) 1926; Ed. fortnightly provincial Ban Yue 1928; writer and translator, Shanghai 1929; visited Japan 1934; Chief Ed. Shanghai Cultural Life Publishing House 1935; joined Lu Xun's China Literary Work Soc. 1936; Co-Ed. (with Mao Dun) Shouting Weekly and Bonfire Weekly 1937; Vice-Chair. Union of Chinese Writers 1953 (now Chair.); Deputy to NPC 1954; Chief. Ed. People's Literature 1957–58; Vice-Chair. China Fed. of Literary and Art Circles 1960; Chief Ed. Shanghai Literature 1961; in disgrace 1968–77; Vice-Chair. 5th Municipal CPPCC Cttee., Shanghai 1977–83; mem. Presidium 6th Nat. CPPCC Cttee. 1983–88; Vice-Chair. 7th Nat. Cttee. CPPCC 1988–93, 8th Nat. Cttee. 1993–98, 9th Nat. Cttee. 1998–; Exec. Council, China Welfare Inst. 1978–; Vice-Chair. China Fed. of Literary and Art Circles 1978–; Pres. China PEN Centre 1980–, Chinese Writers' Asscn. 1981–, China Literature Foundation 1986–; Hon. Pres. Fiction Soc. 1984–; Hon. Chair. China Shakespeare Research Foundation 1984–; Hon. mem. A.A.A.S. 1985; Medal of Int. Friendship, U.S.S.R. 1990. *Publications include:* Extinction 1928, The Family 1931, Trilogy of Love 1932–33, The History of the Nihilist Movement 1936, Spring 1937, Autumn 1940, Festival Day of Warsaw 1950, Living Among Heroes 1953, Three Comrades 1962, Essays by the Sickbed 1984. *Address:* c/o China PEN, Shatan Beijie 2, Beijing, People's Republic of China.

BAALI, Abdallah; Algerian diplomatist; b. 17 Oct. 1952; m. Rafika Baali; one s. one d.; now Perm. Rep. to UN, New York. *Address:* Permanent Mission of Algeria to the United Nations, 326 East 48th Street, New York, NY 10017, U.S.A.

BAATAR, Choisurengiin; Mongolian diplomatist; b. 24 Dec. 1950, Tsakhir soum, Arkhangai Prov.; s. of Ts. Choisuren and N. Dorjgochoo; m. S. Tserenjargal 1975; two s. one d.; ed. State Inst. of Int. Relations, Moscow; officer, Policy & Planning Dept. Ministry of Foreign Affairs 1975–; Pvt. Sec. of Minister for Foreign Affairs 1977–; served Embassy, Tokyo 1979–82, Vientiane 1982–; officer, Policy Planning Dept. Ministry of Foreign Affairs 1985–; officer. Foreign Relations Dept. Cen. Cttee. Mongolian People's Revolutionary Party (MPRP) 1986; mem. Presidium of State Great Hural (Parl.) 1980–; Head, Asia & Africa Dept. 1990–; Amb. to U.K. 1991–95; Deputy Minister of External Relations 1995–96; Exec. Sec. Nat. Security Council 1996. *Leisure interests:* reading, chess, snooker, billiards, hunting. *Address:* c/o Government House, National Security Council, Ulan Bator, Mongolia. *Telephone:* 3200 12.

BABA, Encik Abdul Ghafar Bin; Malaysian politician; b. 18 Feb. 1925, Kuala Pilah, Negeri Sembilan; ed. Sultan Idris Teachers' Training Coll., Tanjong Malim; school teacher 1949–55; mem. Fed. Legis. Council 1955; Chief Minister of Malacca 1955–67; Chair. MARA 1967; Senator and Minister without Portfolio 1967; Minister of Nat. and Rural Devt. 1969–74; Minister of Agric. and Rural Devt. 1974; Chair. Kompleks Kewangan Bd., Pegi Malaysia Bhd., Dunlop Estates Bhd. 1976–86; Deputy Prime Minister and Minister of Nat. and Rural Devt. 1986–93, Acting Prime Minister Jan. 1989; Vice-Pres. UMNO 1974, left UMNO Nov. 1993, rejoined March 1995. *Leisure interest:* golf. *Address:* c/o Ministry of National and Rural Development, Kewangar Complex, 5th Floor, Jalan Raja Laut, 50606 Kuala Lumpur, Malaysia.

BABADJHAN, Ramz (b. Babadzhanov, Ramz Nasyrovich); Uzbekistan poet and playwright; b. 1921, Uzbekistan; s. of Nasriddin Babadjhan and Salomat Babadjhan; m. 1947; one s. two d.; ed. Pedagogical Inst., Tashkent; Deputy Chair. Uzbek Writers' Union; mem. CPSU 1951–91; Chair. Uzbek Republican Cttee. on Relations with African and Asian Writers; Pres. Soc. on Cultural Relations with Compatriots Living Abroad "Vatan" 1990–94; first works published 1935; U.S.S.R. State Prize 1972. *Publications include:* Dear Friends, Thank You, My Dear, The Heart Never Sleeps, Selected Poetry, A Poet Lives Twice, Living Water, Yusuf and Zuleyha, 1001 Crane, Sides, Uncle and Nephew, You Cannot Deceive a Gipsy. *Leisure interests:* photography, travelling. *Address:* Levanevsky Str. 34, 700070 Tashkent, Uzbekistan. *Telephone:* 55-61-06.

BABANGIDA, Maj.-Gen. Ibrahim; Nigerian army officer (retd.) and fmr. Head of State; b. 17 Aug. 1941, Minna; m. Maryam King 1969; two s. two d.; ed. Niger provincial secondary school, Bida, Kaduna Mil. Training Coll. and Indian Mil. Acad.; commissioned 1963, Lieut. 1966; training with R.A.C., U.K. 1966; C.O. during Biafran civil war; Co Commdr. and Instructor, Nigerian Defence Acad. 1970–72; rank of Maj. then Lieut.-Col Armoured Corps 1974; trained at U.S. Army Armoury School 1974; promoted to Maj.-Gen., Dir. of Army Duties and Plans 1983; took part in overthrow of Pres. Shehu Shagari 1983; mem. Supreme Mil. Council and Chief Army Staff 1983–85; Pres. of Nigeria following coup overthrowing Maj.-Gen. Muhammadu Buhari (q.v.) 1985–93; Pres. Police Council 1989; Minister of Defence Dec. 1989–90; Hon. G.C.B. 1989. *Publications:* Civil and Military Relationship, The Nigerian Experience 1979, Defence Policy within the Framework of National Planning 1985. *Address:* Minna, Niger State, Nigeria.

BABAYEV, Agadzhan Geldyevich, DR. GEOG. SC.; Turkmenistan geographer; b. 10 May 1929, Mary; s. of Geldy Babayev and Ogulbek Babayev; m. Dunyagozel Palvanova 1951; two s. six d.; ed. State Pedagogical Inst., Ashkhabad (now Ashgabat), Turkmen State Univ.; Head Geography Dept., Turkmen State Univ. 1952–59; Deputy Dir. Desert Research Inst., Turkmen Acad. of Sciences 1959–60, Dir. 1960–; Chair. Scientific Council for Desert Problems 1967–; Ed.-in-Chief Problems of Desert Devt. 1967–; Dir. Turkmen Research and Training Centre on Desertification Control for ESCAP; mem. CPSU 1954–91; Deputy to U.S.S.R. Supreme Soviet 1979–89; mem. Cen. Auditing Cttee. CPSU 1990–91; Chair. Turkmen Soc. for Chinese-Soviet Friendship; mem. Turkmen Acad. of Sciences, Pres. 1975–86, 1989–93; Corresp. mem. U.S.S.R. (now Russian) Acad. of Sciences 1976; Academician, Islamic Acad. of Sciences; mem. Turkmen Geographical Soc.; Vice-Pres. Turkmens of the World Humanitarian Asscn.; Deputy, Turkmen Parl.; Sec. Democratic Party of Turkmenistan 1991–; Sign of Honour Award 1976, Heroic Labour Medal 1970, U.S.S.R. State Prize 1982, Academician Vavilov Medal 1976, Academician Karpinskii Medal 1990, Jerald Piel Medal 1992. *Publications:* eight monographs, over 200 articles for professional journals. *Address:* National Institute of Deserts, Flora and Fauna, 15 Bitarap Turkmenistan Street, Ashgabat 744000 (Office); 8 Kurban Durdy Street, Ashgabat 744020, Turkmenistan (Home). *Telephone:* (3632) 395427 (Office); (3632) 242683 (Home).

BABBITT, Bruce, LL.B.; American politician and lawyer; b. 27 July 1938; m. Hattie Coons; two c.; ed. Univ. of Notre Dame, Univ. of Newcastle, U.K., Harvard Univ. Law School; Attorney-Gen. Ariz 1975–78; Gov. of Arizona 1978–87; partner Steptoe & Johnson, Phoenix; Sec. of Interior Jan. 1993–; Chair. Nat. Groundwater Policy Forum 1984–; Pres. League of Conservation Voters; Marshall Scholar 1960–62; Thomas Jefferson Award, Nat Wildlife Fed. 1981, Special Conservation Award 1983; Democrat. *Publications:* Color and Light: The Southwest Canvases of Louis Akin 1973, Grand Canyon: An Anthology 1978. *Address:* Department of the Interior, 1849 C Street, N.W., Washington, DC 20240, U.S.A. *Telephone:* (202) 343-3171. *Fax:* (202) 208-5048.

BABBITT, Milton Byron, D.MUS., M.F.A.; American composer; b. 10 May 1916, Philadelphia; s. of Albert E. Babbitt and Sarah Potamkin; m. Sylvia Miller 1939; one d.; ed. New York and Princeton Univs.; Music Faculty, Princeton Univ. 1938–, Math. Faculty 1943–45, Bicentennial Preceptor 1953–56, Prof. of Music 1966–84, Prof. Emer. 1984–; Dir. Columbia-Princeton Electronic Music Center; mem. Faculty, Juilliard School 1971–; Fromm Prof., Harvard Univ. 1988; American Acad. Arts and Letters Award 1959; Guggenheim Fellow 1960–61; MacArthur Fellow 1986–91; Hon. D. Mus. (Glasgow); Hon. D.F.A. (Northwestern Univ.); Gold Medal, Brandeis Univ. 1970; Pulitzer Prize 1982, Schoenberg Inst. Award 1988, William Schuman Award 1992; mem. American Acad. of Arts and Sciences, and American Acad. of Arts and Letters. *Works include:* Music for the Mass 1940, Composition for Four Instruments 1948, Woodwind Quartet 1953, All Set 1957, Vision and Prayer 1961, Philomel 1964, Tableaux 1972, Reflections 1975, Solo Requiem 1977, Paraphrases 1979, Ars Combinatoria 1981, Melismata 1982, The Head of the Bed 1982, Canonic Form 1983, Piano Concerto 1985, Transfigured Notes 1986, The Joy of More Sextets 1986, Whirled Series 1987, Consortini 1989, Emblems 1989, Soli e Duettini 1989–90, Play It Again Sam 1989, Envoi 1990, Preludes, Interludes and Postlude 1991. *Publication:* The Function of Set Structure in the Twelve Tone System 1946. *Leisure interest:* philosophy. *Address:* 222 Western Way, Princeton, NJ 08540-5306, U.S.A.

BABCOCK, Horace W., PH.D.; American astronomer; b. 13 Sept. 1912, Pasadena, Calif.; s. of Harold D. Babcock and Mary G. (Henderson); m. 1st M. B. Anderson 1940; one s. one d.; m. 2nd Elizabeth M. Aubrey 1958; one s.; ed. California Inst. of Tech. and Univ. of California; Instructor, Yerkes and McDonald Observatories 1939–41; Staff mem. Radiation Lab., Mass. Inst. of Tech. 1941–42; Staff mem. Rocket Project, Calif. Inst. of Tech. 1942–45; Staff mem. Mount Wilson and Palomar Observatories 1946–, Asst. Dir. 1957–64, Dir. 1964–78; mem. N.A.S. (Draper Medal 1957), Council mem. 1973–76; founding Dir. Las Campanas Observatory (Chile) of Carnegie Inst. of Washington; mem. American Philosophical Soc., American Acad. of Arts and Sciences; Assoc. Royal Astronomical Soc.; Hon. Sc.D. (Newcastle) 1965; Eddington Medal, Royal Astronomical Soc. 1957, Gold Medal 1970, Bruce Medal, Astronomical Soc. of Pacific, U.S. Navy Bureau of Ordnance Devt. Award, Rank Prize for Opto-electronics 1993. *Publications:* Articles in scientific and technical journals, mainly on magnetic fields of the sun and stars, theory of the sun's magnetic field, rotation and mass distribution of the spiral galaxy in Andromeda, ruling of diffraction gratings, adaptive optics, telescope design, observatory devt. in southern hemisphere. *Address:* Observatories of the Carnegie Institution of Washington, 813 Santa Barbara Street, Pasadena, CA 91101 (Office); 2189 North Altadena Drive, Altadena, CA 91101, U.S.A. (Home). *Telephone:* (818) 577-1122 (Office).

BABENKO, Hector; Argentinian film director; b. 7 Feb. 1946, Buenos Aires; eight years in Europe as writer, house painter, door to door salesman, film extra etc. *Films:* Rei Da Nolte 1976, Lucio Flavio—Passageiro da Agonia 1978, Pixote 1980, Kiss of the Spider Woman 1985, Ironweed 1987, Naked

Tango 1990, At Play in the Fields of the Lords 1991. Best Foreign Film Award for Pixote (New York Film Critics).

BABICHEV, Vladimir Stepanovich, CAND. HIST.; Russian politician, b. 11 Jan. 1939, Sadovoye, Kalmyk Autonomous Repub.; m.; two d.; ed. Volgograd Inst. of Municipal Econ., Higher CP School at Cen. Cttee. CPSU, Acad. of Social Sciences at Cen. Cttee. CPSU; on staff Ministry of Communal Econ. Kalmyk Autonomous Repub. 1962–65; Minister 1969–74; Deputy Chair. Council of Ministers 1974–77; Sec. Repub. Cttee. CP 1977–81; Deputy Minister of U.S.S.R. Oil and Gas Industry 1982–83; Head All-Union Industry Co. Glavtyumengazprom 1983–86, insp., head of sector, Deputy Head Cadre Dept. Cen. Cttee. CPSU 1986–91; Deputy Dir.-General Gazmash br. of Russian Jt. Stock Co. Gazprom 1991–94; Minister, Head Govt. Admin. Dept. of Russian Fed. 1994–98; Deputy Chair. Govt. of Russian Fed. 1996–97; People's Deputy 1990–93; Chair. Exec. Bd. Political Movt. Our Home Russia Feb. 1996–. *Address:* Our Home is Russia Movement, Akademie Sakharov prospekt 12, 107078 Moscow, Russia. *Telephone:* (095) 921 8815.

BABIKIAN, Khatchik Diran; Lebanese politician and lawyer; b. 1924, Cyprus; m. 1956; five d.; ed. Collège Italien, Beirut, Faculté Française de Droit, Beirut, Faculté de Paris, Univ. of London; Barrister; Deputy for Beirut 1957, 1960, 1964, 1968, 1972, 1992; mem. Parl. Comm. on Justice; Pres. Traffic Comm., Parl. Comm. on Planning, Lebanese Management Asscn. 1972, 1992, 1995; Minister for Admin. Reform 1960–61; Minister of Public Health 1968–69, of Tourism 1969–70, of Information 1972–73, of Planning 1973, 1990–95, of Justice 1980–82, 1990–92; mem. Higher Court for the trial of the Presidents and Ministers 1994–97; Pres. Armenian Nat. Assembly 1972, 1976; Pres. Exec. Council Armenian Church of Cilicia 1983–97, Asscn. Libanaise contre la Drogue, Asscn. Libanaise pour le Diabète, Asscn. Libanaise pour l'Habitat; Vice-Pres. World Asscn. of French-Speaking Parliamentarians 1982, 1997; Personal Rep. of Pres. of Repub. at Conseil Perm. de la Francophonie 1992–97; Officier Légion d'honneur; Ufficiale, Ordine del Merito (Italy). *Leisure interests:* violin, languages. *Address:* Place de l'Etoile, Beirut (Office); Rue Abrine, Achrafié, Beirut, Lebanon (Home). *Telephone:* 335773 (Office); 322013 (Home).

BABIUC, Victor, D.IUR.; Romanian politician and lawyer; b. 3 April 1938, Răchiţi Commune, Botoşani Co.; s. of Victor Babiuc and Olga Babiuc; m. 1978; one d.; ed. Law School of Bucharest, Romanian Acad. for Econ. Studies, Univ. of Bucharest; juridical counsellor, judge in Braşov; chief juridical counsel Ministry of Foreign Trade, Sr. researcher at the World Economy Inst. 1977–90; mem. House of Deputies 1990–92; Minister of Justice 1990–91, Minister of the Interior, 1991–92; Vice-Pres. Democratic Party; Minister of Nat. Defence 1996–; Prof. of Commercial Law, Acad. of Econ. Studies of Bucharest 1994–; Pres. Perm. Comm. for Investigation into Corruption and Cases of Abuse and for Petitions –1992, Parl. Anticorruption Comm.; Pres. Int. Commercial Arbitration Court of Chamber of Commerce and Industry of Romania; mem. Panel of Arbitrators of American Arbitration Asscn., Moscow, Sofia, Abu Dhabi 1991–. *Publications:* over 100 works on economic law and int. commercial law. *Leisure interests:* theatre, walking, reading books on politics, history, memoirs. *Address:* c/o Camera Deputatilor, Casa Republicii, Str. 13 Decembrie, Sector 5, Bucharest (Office); Bd. Libertatii nr. 20, Sector 5, Bucharest, Romania (Home). *Telephone:* 6134073 (Office); 3103278, 3103279, 6505677 (Law Office); 3363109, 3351262 (Home). *Fax:* 3103280 (Law Office).

BABURIN, Sergey Nikolaevich, LL.D.; Russian politician; b. 31 Jan. 1959, Semipalatinsk; s. of Nikolay Baburin and Valentina Baburina; m. Tatiana Nikolaevna Baburina; four s.; ed. Omsk State Univ., Leningrad State Univ.; mem. CPSU 1981–91; mil. service in Afghanistan 1982–83; worked as lawyer; lecturer, Dean of Law Faculty, Omsk Univ. 1988–90; People's Deputy of R.S.F.S.R. (now Russia); mem. Supreme Soviet 1990–93; mem. Constitutional Comm. 1991–; Co-Chair. Exec. Bd. of All Russian Peoples' Union 1991; Co-Chair. Nat. Salvation Front 1992–; mem. State Duma (Parl.) 1995–, Deputy Chair. 1996–; Chair. All Russian People's Union 1994; Deputy Chair. Parl Ass. Union of Russia and Belarus. *Publications:* Russian Way: Selected Speeches and Essays 1990–95 1995, Russian Way: Losses and Acquisitions 1997, Territory of State: Law and Geopolitical Problems 1997. *Address:* State Duma, Okhotny Ryad 1, 103009 Moscow, Russia. *Telephone:* (095) 292-85-00; (095) 292-98-34.

BACALL, Lauren; American actress; b. 16 Sept. 1924, New York; m. 1st Humphrey Bogart 1945 (died 1957); 2nd Jason Robards 1961 (divorced); two s. one d. *Films include:* Two Guys from Milwaukee 1946, To Have and Have Not, The Big Sleep, Confidential Agent, Dark Passage, Key Largo, Young Man with a Horn, Bright Leaf, How to Marry a Millionaire, Woman's World, The Cobweb, Blood Alley, Written on the Wind, Designing Woman, The Gift of Love, Flame over India, Sex and the Single Girl, Harper, Shock Treatment 1964, Murder on the Orient Express 1974, The Shootist 1976, Health 1980, The Fan 1981, Appointment with Death 1988, Mr North 1988, Tree of Hands 1989, A Star For Two 1990, Misery 1990, All I Want for Christmas 1991, A Foreign Field 1993, The Portrait 1993, Prêt à Porter 1995, Le Jour et la Nuit 1996. *Plays:* Goodbye Charlie 1960, Cactus Flower 1966, Applause 1970 (Tony Award, Best Actress in a Musical 1970) (London 1972), Wonderful Town 1977, Woman of the Year 1981 (Tony Award 1981), Sweet Bird of Youth (London) 1985, The Visit (Chichester, U.K.). *Publications:* Lauren Bacall By Myself 1978, Lauren Bacall Now 1994. *Address:* c/o Johnnie Planco William Morris Agency, 1325 Avenue of the Americas, New York, NY 10019, U.S.A.

BACCOUCHE, Hedi; Tunisian politician; b. 1930; active mem. Tunisian Independence Movt.; Pres. Fed. des étudiants destouriens; detained by French authorities 1952; Dir. PSD Political Bureau –1987; Minister of Social Affairs April–Nov. 1987; Prime Minister 1987–89. *Address:* c/o Office of the Prime Minister, Tunis, Tunisia.

BACHA, Edmar Lisboa, PH.D.; Brazilian economist; b. 14 Feb. 1942; m. Maria Laura Cavalcanti; ed. Fed. Univ. of Minas Gerais, Yale Univ., U.S.A.; Research Assoc., M.I.T., Cambridge, Mass., U.S.A. 1968–69; Prof. of Econs., Vargas Foundation, Rio de Janeiro 1970–71, Univ. of Brasília 1972–78, Catholic Univ. of Rio de Janeiro 1979–93, Fed. Univ. of Rio de Janeiro 1996–; Pres. Statistical Office of Brazil, Rio de Janeiro 1985–86; Econ. Adviser to Brazilian Govt. 1993; Pres. Nat. Devt. Bank, Rio de Janeiro 1995; Visiting Prof. Harvard Univ. 1975, Columbia Univ. 1983, Yale Univ. 1984, Univ. of Calif. at Berkeley 1988, Univ. of Stanford 1989; mem. Exec. Cttee., Int. Econ. Asscn., Paris 1987–92, Cttee. for Devt. Planning, UN, New York 1987–94. *Publications:* Mitos de una Decada 1976, Models of Growth and Distribution for Brazil 1980, El Milagro y la Crisis 1986, Social Change in Brazil 1986, Recessão ou Crescimento 1987, Requirements for Growth Resumption in Latin America 1993. *Address:* Rua Marques de São Vicente 225, 22453 Rio de Janeiro, Brazil. *Telephone:* 55-21-274.2797.

BACHELIER, Bernard; French agronomist; b. 27 July 1950, Levallois Perret; ed. Inst. Nat. Agronomique, Paris-Grignon; worked in Africa for several years; Del. for Africa and Indian Ocean, Centre de Coopération Internationale en Recherche Agronomique pour de Développement (Cirad), Paris 1988–90; Pres. Cirad Centre, Montpellier 1993; Head of Devt. Research, Ministry of Educ. and Research 1993–96; Dir.-Gen. Cirad 1996–. *Address:* Centre de Coopération Internationale en Recherche Agronomique pour le Développement, 42 rue Scheffer, 75116 Paris (Office); 6 rue Danton, 92300 Levallois-Perret, France (Home).

BACHER, Aron ('Ali'), M.B., B.CH.; South African cricketer and administrator; b. 24 May 1942, Johannesburg; s. of Kopel Bacher and Rose Bacher; m. Shira Ruth Teeger 1965; two d.; ed. King Edward VII High School and Univ. of Witwatersrand; intern, Baragwanath and Natalspruit Hosps.; pvt. practice, Rosebank, Johannesburg 1970–79; Man. Dir. Delta Distributors (Pty.) Ltd. 1979–81; Man. Dir. The Transvaal Cricket Council 1981–86; Man. Dir. The South African Cricket Union 1986–91, United Cricket Bd. of South Africa 1991–; South African Sports Award Admin. 1991; Pres. Sports Award Admin. (Cricket) 1997; played for Transvaal 1959–74 (Capt. 1963–74); 12 tests for S. Africa 1965–70, 4 (all won) as Capt.; scored 7,894 first-class runs (18 centuries); toured England 1965; South African Sports Merit Award 1972; Paul Harris Fellow Award 1989; Jack Cheetham Memorial Award 1990; mem. Int. Jewish Sports Hall of Fame 1991. *Leisure interest:* jogging. *Address:* United Cricket Board of South Africa, P.O. Box 55009, Northlands, 2116 (Office); P.O. Box 55041, Northlands, 2116, South Africa (Home). *Telephone:* (011) 880-2810 (Office); (011) 883-2597 (Home).

BACHER, Robert Fox, B.S., PH.D.; American physicist; b. 31 Aug. 1905, Loudonville, Ohio; s. of Harry and Byrl (née Fox) Bacher; m. Jean Dow 1930; one s. one d.; ed. Univ. of Michigan; Nat. Research Fellow Physics, Calif. Inst. of Technology 1930–31, M.I.T. 1931–32; Alfred Lloyd Fellow, Univ. of Michigan 1932–33; Instructor, Columbia Univ. 1934–35; Instructor to Prof., Cornell Univ. 1935–49; Radiation Laboratory, M.I.T. 1940–45 (on leave 1943–45); Los Alamos Laboratory, Atomic Bomb Project 1943–46; Dir. of Laboratory of Nuclear Studies, Cornell Univ. 1946; mem. U.S. Atomic Energy Comm. 1946–49; Prof. of Physics, Calif. Inst. of Technology 1949–76, Prof. Emer. 1976–, Chair. Div. of Physics, Mathematics and Astronomy 1949–62, Provost 1962–70; mem. President's Science Advisory Cttee. 1953–55, 1957–60; Trustee, Carnegie Corpn. 1959–76, Claremont Graduate School 1971–, Universities Research Asscn. 1965–75 (Chair. 1969–73, Pres. 1973–74), Rand Corpn. 1950–60; Pres. Int. Union of Pure and Applied Physics 1969–72; mem. N.A.S., American Philosophical Soc., American Acad. of Arts and Sciences, American Physical Soc. (Pres. 1964), A.A.A.S.; awarded Medal for Merit by Pres. Truman Jan. 1946. *Publications:* Atomic Energy States (with S. Goudsmit) 1932. *Address:* California Institute of Technology, Pasadena, CA 91125, U.S.A.

BACHIRI, Mohamed; Moroccan administrator and engineer; b. 14 July 1948, Berkane; s. of Mimour Bachiri and Aïcha Bachiri; m. Badia Khelfaoui 1972; three c.; qualified civil engineer; responsible for public works, Berkane and Nador Provs. 1969; Asst. Dir. Moroccan Ports 1978; Regional Dir. of Public Works, Marrakesh 1983; Insp. Gen. Gen. Council of Public Works, f. and Dir. Al-Handassa Lwatania eng. journal 1991; now Dir. Gen. Port Dredging Co.; f. mem. Public Works Foundation; trophée d'Ingénieur Créateur. *Publications:* articles and editorials in Al Handassa Lwatania, contrib. to other prof. journals. *Leisure interest:* golf. *Address:* 3 Avenue Ma Al Aynine, Agdal, Rabat, Morocco. *Telephone:* 02-234640. *Fax:* 02-232600.

BACH NUÑEZ, Jaume; Spanish architect; b. 4 April 1943, Sabadell; s. of Miquel Bach Nuñez and Josefa Bach Nuñez; m. Carmen Triadó Tur 1978; two s.; ed. Tech. Univ. of Architecture, Barcelona (ETSAB); Assoc. Dols-Millet-Páez 1971; tutor, ETSAB 1971, 1972; in partnership with Gabriel Mora Gramunt (q.v.), Bach/Mora Architects 1976–; work includes grass hockey Olympic stadium, Terrassa 1989, cen. telephone exchange, Olympic Village, Barcelona 1992, apt. bldg., agric. complex, health clinic, etc.; tutor, Int. Lab. of Architecture and Urban Design, Urbino, Italy 1978; Design tutor, ETSAB 1978–; Visiting Prof. Univ. of Dublin 1993, Univ. of Hanover

1994; Hon. D. Arch. (Polytechnic Univ. of Barcelona) 1991; various professional awards. *Publications include:* Junge Architekten in Europa (jtly.) 1983, Young Spanish Architecture (jtly.) 1985. *Address:* Avenida Diagonal 335, 08037 Barcelona, Spain.

BACHRACH, Howard L., PH.D.; American biochemist; b. 21 May 1920, Faribault, Minn.; m. Shirley F. Lichterman 1943; one s. one d.; ed. Univ. of Minnesota; Chemist, Jos. Seagram & Co., Lawrenceberg, Ind. 1942; Research Asst., Explosives Research Lab., Carnegie Inst. of Tech., Nat. Defense Research Cttee., OSRD 1942–45; Research Asst., Univ. of Minn. 1945–49; Biochemist, Foot-and-Mouth Disease Research Mission, U.S. Dept. of Agric., Denmark 1949–50; Research Biochemist, Biochemistry and Virus Lab., Univ. of Calif., Berkeley 1950–53; Chief Scientist and Head, Biochemical and Physical Investigations, Plum Island Animal Disease Center, U.S. Dept. of Agric. 1953–81, Research Chemist 1981–89, Consultant-Collaborator 1990–95; developed unified comparative molecular pathways of animal virus replication 1978; first purification and visualization of polio virus 1953, and of foot-and-mouth virus 1958; first immunization of livestock with protein isolated from foot-and-mouth disease virus 1975; first production through gene splicing of an effective vaccine against any disease of animals or humans 1981; mem. N.A.S. (Communicating Member-Ed. of Proc.); Fellow, New York Acad. of Sciences; Hon. mem. American Coll. of Veterinary Microbiologists; many awards, including U.S. Presidential Citation 1965, A.A.A.S.-Newcomb Cleveland Prize 1982, American Chem. Soc. Kenneth A. Spencer Medal 1983, Nat. Medal of Science 1983, Nat. Award for Agricultural Excellence 1983 and Alexander von Humboldt Award 1983, USDA Agricultural Research Service, Science Hall of Fame 1987. *Publications:* 150 publs.; patent on FMD protein vaccine. *Address:* 355 Dayton Road, P.O. Box 1054, Southold, NY 11971; 10220 Andover Coach Circle G2, Lake Worth, FL 33467, U.S.A.

BACHYNSKI, Morrel Paul, PH.D., F.R.S.C., F.I.E.E.E.; Canadian physicist; b. 19 July 1930, Bienfait, Sask.; m. Slava Krkovic 1959; two d.; ed. Univ. of Saskatchewan and McGill Univ.; Lab. Dir., Microwave and Plasma Physics, RCA Ltd. 1960–65, Dir. Research 1965–75, Vice-Pres. Research and Devt. 1975–76; Pres. MPB Technologies Inc. 1977–; mem. Canadian Asscn. of Physicists (Pres. 1968), Asscn. of Scientific, Eng. and Tech. Community of Canada (Pres. 1974–75), Nat. Research Council of Canada (Chair. on Fusion 1977–87), Science Council of Canada; Fellow Canadian Aeronautics and Space Inst., American Physical Soc., Canadian Acad. of Eng.; Hon. LL.D. (Waterloo) 1993, (Concordia) 1997; Hon.D.Sc. (McGill) 1994; Prix Scientifique de Québec 1973, Canada Enterprise Award 1977, Queen's Silver Jubilee Medal 1977, Canadian Asscn. of Physicists Medal of Achievement 1984, Canadian Research Man. Medal of Achievement 1988, Canada Award for Business Excellence-Entrepreneurship 1989, 1990, Prix ADRIQ 1991, Canadian Asscn. of Physicists Medal for Industrial and Applied Physics 1995. *Publications:* The Particle Kinetics of Plasma (Co-Author) 1968; more than 80 publs. in scientific and eng. journals. *Leisure interest:* tennis. *Address:* MPB Technologies Inc., 151 Hymus Boulevard, Pointe Claire, Quebec, H9R 1E9 (Office); 78 Thurlow Road, Montreal, Quebec, H3X 3G9, Canada (Home).

BACKE, John David, M.B.A.; American communications executive; b. 5 July 1932, Akron, Ohio; s. of John and Ella A. (née Enyedy) Backe; m. Katherine Elliott 1955; one s. one d.; ed. Miami Univ., Ohio, and Xavier Univ., Ohio; various engineering, financial and marketing positions in General Electric Co. 1957–66; Vice-Pres. and Dir. of Marketing, Silver Burdett Co. 1966–68, Pres. 1968–69; Exec. Vice-Pres. General Learning Corpn. 1969, Pres. and C.E.O. 1969–73; Pres. of Publishing Group, CBS Inc. 1973–76, of CBS Inc. (also C.E.O.) 1976–80, Dir. of Business Marketing, Corpn. of New York 1978; Pres. C.E.O. Tomorrow Entertainment 1981–84, Chair. 1984–; Chair. Cinema Products, Los Angeles 1992–; Chair., C.E.O., Backe Group Inc. 1984–; Station WDKY-TV, Lexington 1985–93; Gulfshore Publ. Co., Naples 1986–; Gulfstream Newspapers, Pompano 1987–; Andrews Communications, Westtown, Pa. 1987–; Atlantic Publs., Accomac, Va. 1989–; Special Del. to UNESCO Conf. on publishing for Arabic-speaking countries 1972; mem. Nat. Advisory Cttee. for Illinois Univ. Inst. for Aviation; Hon. LL.D. (Miami and Xavier). *Leisure interest:* multi-engine piloting. *Address:* Backe Group Inc., Suite 210, 150 Strafford Avenue, Wayne, PA 19087, U.S.A. (Office).

BACKLEY, Steve; British athlete; b. 12 Feb. 1969, Sidcup, Kent; specializes in javelin; coached by John Trower; Commonwealth record-holder 1992 (91.46m.); Gold Medal European Jr. Championships 1987; Silver Medal World Jr. Championships 1988; Gold Medal European Cup 1989, 1997, Bronze Medal 1995; Gold Medal World Student Games 1989, 1991; Gold Medal World Cup 1989, 1994, 1998; Gold Medal Commonwealth Games 1990, 1994, Silver Medal 1998; Gold Medal European Championships 1990, 1994, 1998; Bronze Medal Olympic Games 1992, Silver Medal 1996; Silver Medal World Championships 1995, 1997.

BÄCKSTRÖM, Urban, PH.D.; Swedish banker; b. 25 May 1954, Sollefteå; s. of Sven-Ake Bäckström and Maj-Britt Filipsson; m. Ewa Hintze 1978; one s. one d.; ed. Stockholm Univ. and Stockholm School of Econs.; Research Asst. Inst. for Int. Econ. Studies, Stockholm 1978–80; First Sec. Int. Dept. Ministry of Foreign Affairs 1980–82; Chief Economist, Moderate Party 1982–83, 1986–89; Under-Sec. of State, Ministry of Finance 1991–93; now Gov. Sveriges Riksbank; Bd. mem. Bank for Int. Settlements 1994–. *Address:* Sveriges Riksbank, 10337 Stockholm, Sweden.

BACKUS, George Edward, S.M., PH.D., F.R.S.A.; American theoretical geophysicist; b. 24 May 1930, Chicago, Ill.; s. of late Milo Morlan Backus and of Dora (née Dare) Backus; m. 1st Elizabeth E. Allen 1961; two s. one d.; m. 2nd Marianne McDonald 1971; m. 3rd Varda Peller 1977; ed. Thornton Township High School, Harvey, Ill. and Univ. of Chicago; Asst. Examiner, Univ. of Chicago 1949–50; Junior Mathematician, Inst. for Air Weapons Research, Univ. of Chicago 1950–54; Physicist, Project Matterhorn, Princeton Univ. 1957–58; Asst. Prof. of Mathematics, M.I.T. 1958–60; Assoc. Prof. of Geophysics, Univ. of Calif. (La Jolla) 1960–62, Prof. 1962–94, Research Prof. 1994–95, 1995–; mem. Scientific Advisory Cttee. to NASA on jt. NASA/CNES Magnetic Satellites; Co.-Chair. Int. Working Group on Magnetic Field Satellites 1983–92; mem. Visiting Cttee. Inst. de Physique du Globe de Paris 1987; Guggenheim Fellowship 1963, 1971; Fellow American Geophysical Union, American Acad. of Arts and Sciences, R.S.A., Royal Astronomical Soc.; mem. N.A.S.; Foreign mem. Académie des Sciences de l'Institut de France; Gold Medal, Royal Astronomical Soc. 1986, John Adam Fleming Medal, American Geophysical Union 1986; Dr. h.c. (Inst. de Physique de Globe, Paris) 1995. *Publications:* numerous scientific works 1958–. *Leisure interests:* hiking, swimming, history, reading, skiing. *Address:* Institute of Geophysics and Planetary Physics, University of California at San Diego, La Jolla, CA 92093 (Office); 9362 La Jolla Farms Road, La Jolla, CA 92037, U.S.A. (Home). *Telephone:* (619) 534-2468 (Office); (619) 455-8972 (Home). *Fax:* (619) 534-8090.

BACKUS, John, A.M.; American computer scientist; b. 3 Dec. 1924, Philadelphia; m. 2nd Una Stannard 1968; two d.; ed. Columbia Univ.; Research Staff mem., Thomas J. Watson Research Center 1959–63; IBM Fellow, IBM Almaden Research Center, San José, Calif. 1963–91; consultant 1991–; Man. Incest Info., Bay Area 1992–; Visiting Prof., Univ. of California, Berkeley 1980; Fellow American Acad. of Arts and Sciences; mem. N.A.S., Nat. Acad. Eng.; D.Univ. (York, England) 1985; D.Sc. (Arizona) 1988, (Indiana) 1992; Dr. h.c. (Nancy I, France) 1989; awards include National Medal of Science 1975, A. M. Turing Award, Asscn. for Computing Machinery 1977, Charles Stark Draper Prize, Nat. Acad. of Eng. 1994. *Publications:* Systems Design of the IBM 704 Computer (with G. M. Amdahl) 1954, The Fortran Automatic Coding System (with others) 1957, The Syntax and Semantics of the Proposed International Algebraic Language of the Zürich ACM-GAMM Conference 1959, Report on the Algorithmic Language ALGOL 60 (with others) 1960, Can Programming Be Liberated from the von Neumann Style? A Functional Style and Its Algebra of Programs, (Communications of the Asscn. for Computing Machinery) 1978, Is Computer Science Based on the Wrong Fundamental Concept of Program? An Extended Concept in Algorithmic Languages (Holland) 1981. *Address:* 91 St. Germain Avenue, San Francisco, CA 94114, U.S.A. *Telephone:* (415) 731-8155.

BACON, Edmund Norwood, B.ARCH.; American architect and planner; b. 2 May 1910, Philadelphia; s. of Ellis W. and Helen Comly Bacon; m. Ruth Holmes 1938 (died 1991); two s. four d.; ed. Cornell Univ. and Cranbrook Acad.; Architectural Designer, Shanghai, China 1934; housing projects for W. Pope Barney, Architect, Philadelphia 1935; Supervisor of City Planning, Flint (Michigan) Inst. of Research and Planning; Man. Dir. Philadelphia Housing Asscn. 1940–43; Co-Designer Better Philadelphia Exhibition and Senior Land Planner, Philadelphia City Planning Comm.; Exec. Dir. Philadelphia City Planning Comm. 1949–70; Adjunct Prof., Univ. of Pa. 1950–87; Professional Adviser, Franklin Delano Roosevelt Memorial Competition 1959; mem. President's Citizens' Advisory Cttee. on Environmental Quality 1970; numerous awards. *Publication:* Design of Cities 1967 (revised 1974). *Films:* has produced/directed five films on architecture. *Address:* 2117 Locust Street, Philadelphia, PA 19103, U.S.A. (Home). *Telephone:* (215) 567-0693. *Fax:* (215) 567-1658.

BACON, Kevin; American actor; b. July 8 1958, Philadelphia; m. Kyra Sedgwick; one s. one d.; ed. Manning Street Actor's Theatre. *Stage appearances include:* Getting On 1978, Glad Tidyings 1979–80, Mary Barnes 1980, Album 1980, Forty-Deuce 1981, Flux 1982, Poor Little Lambs 1982, Slab Boys 1983, Men Without Dates 1985, Loot 1986. *Television appearances include:* The Gift 1979, Enormous Changes at the Last Minute 1982, The Demon Murder Case 1983, The Tender Age, Lemon Sky. *Film appearances include:* National Lampoon's Animal House 1978, Starting Over 1979, Hero at Large 1980, Friday the 13th 1980, Only When I Laugh 1981, Diner 1982, Footloose 1984, Quicksilver 1985, White Water Summer 1987, Planes, Trains and Automobiles 1987, End of the Line 1988, She's Having a Baby 1988, Criminal Law 1989, The Big Picture 1989, Tremors 1990, Flatliners 1990, Queens Logic 1991, He Said/She Said 1991, Pyrates 1991, JFK 1992, A Few Good Men 1992, The Air Up There 1994, The River Wild 1994, Murder in the First 1995, Apollo 13 1995, Sleepers 1996, Telling Lies in America 1997, Picture Perfect 1997, Digging to China 1997, Wild Things 1998, My Dog Skip 1999. *Address:* c/o Kevin Huvane, Creative Artists Agency, 9830 Wilshire Boulevard, Beverly Hills, CA 90212, U.S.A.

BACOT, John Carter, A.B., LL.B.; American banker (retd.); b. 7 Feb. 1933, Utica, N.Y.; s. of John Bacot and Edna Gunn; m. Shirley Schou 1960; two d.; ed. Hamilton Coll. Clinton, N.Y. and Cornell Univ.; admitted New York Bar 1959; with firm in Utica 1959–60; with Bank of New York, New York City 1960–, Pres. 1974–84, Chair. 1982–98, fmr. C.E.O.; mem. Bd. of Dirs. Home Life Insurance Co., Atlantic Reins. Co., Centennial Insurance Co., Bank of N.Y. Int. Corpn. *Address:* Bank of New York Co. Inc., 48 Wall

Street, Floor 3, New York, NY 10005; 48 Porter Place, Montclair, NJ 07042, U.S.A. (Home).

BACQUIER, Gabriel; French (baritone) opera singer; b. 17 May 1924, Béziers; s. of Augustin Bacquier and Fernande Severac; m. 1st Simone Teisseire 1943; one s.; m. 2nd Mauricette Bénard 1958; one s.; ed. Paris Conservatoire; debut at Théâtre Royal de la Monnaie, Brussels 1953; joined Opéra de Paris 1956; debut at Carnegie Hall 1960, Metropolitan Opera, New York 1961; has appeared at the Vienna State Opera, Covent Garden, La Scala, Opéra de Paris and most leading opera houses. Repertoire includes Otello, Don Giovanni, Pelléas et Mélisande, Damnation de Faust, Tosca, Falstaff; several recordings; Prix national du disque français 1964, and other prizes; Chevalier, Légion d'honneur, Officier, ordre nationale du Mérite, Officier des Arts et des Lettres. *Leisure interests:* painting, drawing. *Address:* c/o OIA, 16 avenue Franklin Roosevelt, 75008 Paris, France. *Telephone:* 227-33-84.

BÁCS, Ludovic; Romanian conductor and composer; b. 19 Jan. 1930, Petrila; s. of Ludovic Bács and Iuliana Bács (Venczel); m. Ercse Gyöngyver, 1952; two s.; ed. Dima Gh. Conservatory, Cluj-Napoca Tchaikovski Conservatory, Moscow, Cluj-Napoca Coll. of Philosophy 1948–49; began career as conductor Symphonic Orchestra of Romanian Radio, also Artistic Dir. 1964–; Prof. Bucharest Conservatory 1960–66, 1990–; Conductor Romanian Radio Chamber Orchestra 1990–; f. Musica rediviva 1966, the first group of performers to render ancient Romanian music; he conducted concerts in U.S.S.R., Poland, Czechoslovakia, Hungary, Bulgaria, the G.D.R., West Berlin, Fed. Germany, Holland, Switzerland, Spain, France; mem. Romanian Composers' Union; Cultural Merit Award, the Medal of Labour, Prize of the Theatre and Music Asscn. *Works include:* orchestration of Bach's Art of the Fugue (on record), numerous adaptations from 15th-18th century music: Bach, Monteverdi, Backfarg, from Codex Caioni a.o.; Suitá de Musicá Veche 17th–18th century, Variations Sinfoniques e Double Fugue sur une Théme Populaire Hongroise, Trois Madrigales pour Choeur. *Address:* Berthelot 63-64, Bucharest (Office); 31 D. Golescu, Sc III, E7 V ap.87, Bucharest 1, Romania (Home). *Telephone:* 6.37.37.94.

BADAWI, Datuk Abdullah Bin Haj, B.A.; Malaysian politician; b. 26 Nov. 1939, Pulau Pinang; m. Datin Endon bint Datuk Mahmud; ed. Univ. of Malaya; Asst. Sec. Public Service Dept. 1964; Asst. Sec. MAGERAN 1969; Asst. Sec. Nat. Security Council 1971; Dir. (Youth), Ministry of Sport, Youth and Culture 1971–74, Deputy Sec.-Gen. 1974–78; Minister without Portfolio, Prime Minister's Dept. 1982; Minister of Educ. 1984–86, of Defence 1986–87; mem. UMNO Supreme Council 1982–, Vice-Pres. 1984; many other public appts.; recipient of four awards. *Address:* Dewan Rakyat, Parliament Building, 50680 Kuala Lumpur, Malaysia.

BADAWI, Zeinab Mohammed-Khair, M.A.; television presenter; b. 3 Oct. 1959; d. of Mohammed-Khair El Badawi and Asia Malik; m. David Antony Crook 1991; one s. two d.; ed. Hornsey School for Girls, St. Hilda's Coll. Oxford and Univ. of London; presenter and journalist, current affairs and documentaries, Yorkshire TV 1982–86; current affairs reporter, BBC TV 1987–88; newscaster and journalist ITN Channel Four News 1988–; mem. Panel 2000. *Leisure interests:* languages, opera, yoga, reading. *Address:* ITN, 200 Gray's Inn Road, London, WC1X 8XZ, England. *Telephone:* 0171-833 3000.

BADDILEY, Sir James, Kt., M.A., PH.D., D.SC., SC.D., F.R.S.E., F.R.S.; British professor of chemical microbiology; b. 15 May 1918, Manchester; s. of the late James Baddiley and Ivy (Logan-Cato) Baddiley; m. Hazel M. Townsend 1944; one s.; ed. Manchester Grammar School and Univ. of Manchester; Beyer Fellow 1983–84; ICI Fellow, Univ. of Cambridge 1944–49; Fellow, Swedish Medical Research Council, Stockholm 1947–49; mem. of staff Dept. of Biochemistry, Lister Inst., London 1949–54; Prof. of Organic Chem., Univ. of Durham, Kings Coll., Newcastle 1955–63; Prof. of Organic Chem., Univ. of Newcastle upon Tyne 1963–77, Head of the School of Chem. 1968–78, Prof. of Chem. Microbiology 1977–83, now Emer. Prof.; Science and Engineering Research Council (SERC) Sr. Fellow, Univ. of Cambridge 1981–83, now Emer.; Dir. Microbiological Chem. Research Lab. 1975–83; mem. Science Research Council 1979–81; mem. Council, Royal Soc. 1977–79, SERC 1979–81; editorial Bds., Biochemical Preparations 1960–70, Biochimica et Biophysica Acta 1970–77; Cambridge Studies in Biotech. 1985–; Trustee EPA Cephalosporin Fund; Vice-Pres. Alzheimer's Research Trust; Fellow, Pembroke Coll., Cambridge; Hon. mem. American Soc. for Biochemistry and Molecular Biology; Rockefeller Fellow, Harvard Medical School 1954; Tilden Lecturer, Chemical Soc. 1959, Karl Folkers Prof., Univ. of Illinois 1962, Leeuwenhoek Lecturer, Royal Soc. 1967, Pedler Lecturer, Chem. Soc. 1978, Bose Endowment Lecturer, Bose Inst., Calcutta 1980; Hon. D.Sc. (Heriot-Watt) 1978, (Bath) 1986; Meldola Medal, Royal Inst. of Chem. 1947, Corday-Morgan Medal and Prize, Chem. Soc. 1952, Davy Medal, Royal Soc. 1974. *Publications:* numerous publications in bio-chem. and microbiological chem. *Leisure interests:* gardening, music, photography, fine arts, mountaineering. *Address:* Hill Top Cottage, Hildersham, Cambridge, CB1 6DA, England. *Telephone:* (01223) 893055.

BADGER, Sir Geoffrey Malcolm, Kt., A.O., PH.D.; Australian scientist; b. 10 Oct. 1916, Port Augusta, South Australia; s. of John McDougall Badger and Laura Mary Badger (née Brooker); m. Edith Maud Chevis 1941; ed. Geelong Coll., Gordon Inst. of Tech., Univs. of Melbourne, London and Glasgow; Finney-Howell Research Fellow, London 1939, 1940; Research Chemist, ICI Dyestuffs Ltd., Manchester 1941–43; Instructor Lieut., R.N. 1943–46; ICI Research Fellow, Univ. of Glasgow 1946–49; Sr. Lecturer, then Reader, then Prof. of Organic Chem., Univ. of Adelaide 1949–64, Prof. Emer. 1964–, Deputy Vice-Chancellor 1966–67, Vice-Chancellor 1967–77; mem. Exec., CSIRO (Canberra) 1964–65; Research Prof. 1977–79; Pres. Royal Australian Chemical Inst. 1964, Australian Acad. of Science 1974–78, ANZAAS 1979–80; Chair. Australian Science and Tech. Council, Canberra 1979–82, Order of Australia Asscn. 1989–92; H.G. Smith Medal 1951, A.E. Leighton Medal 1971, ANZAAS Medal 1981. *Publications:* six books and more than 200 scientific papers. *Leisure interests:* reading, writing, walking. *Address:* 1 Anna Court, West Lakes, South Australia 5021, Australia. *Telephone:* (8) 8449-4594.

BADIAN, Ernst, M.A., D.PHIL., LIT.D., F.B.A.; professor of history; b. 8 Aug. 1925; s. of Joseph and Sally (née Horinger) Badian; m. Nathlie A. Wimsett 1950; one s. one d.; ed. Christchurch Boys' High School, Canterbury Univ. Coll., Christchurch, N.Z. and Univ. Coll., Oxford; Asst. Lecturer in Classics, Victoria Univ. Coll., Wellington 1947–48; Rome Scholar in Classics, British School at Rome 1950–52; Asst. Lecturer in Classics and Ancient History, Univ. of Sheffield 1952–54; Lecturer in Classics, Univ. of Durham 1954–65; Prof. of Ancient History, Univ. of Leeds 1965–69; Prof. of Classics and History, State Univ. of N.Y. at Buffalo 1969–71; Prof. of History, Harvard Univ. 1971–82, John Moors Cabot Prof. 1982–98, Prof. Emer. 1998–; Fellow, American Acad. of Arts and Sciences, American Numismatic Soc.; corresp. mem. Austrian Acad. of Sciences, German Archaeological Inst.; foreign mem. Finnish Acad. of Sciences; Visiting Prof. and lecturer at many univs. in U.S.A., Canada, Australia, S. Africa, Europe etc.; Hon. Fellow Univ. Coll., Oxford; Hon. mem. Soc. for Roman Studies; Hon. D.Litt. (Macquarie). *Publications:* Foreign Clientelae (264—70 BC) 1958, Studies in Greek and Roman History 1964, Polybius 1966, Roman Imperialism in the Late Republic 1967, Publicans and Sinners 1972, From Plataea to Potidaea 1993, Zöllner und Sünder 1997; articles in classical and historical journals. *Leisure interests:* travel, reading. *Address:* Department of History, Harvard University, Cambridge, MA 02138, U.S.A. *Telephone:* (617) 496-5581. *Fax:* (617) 496-3425.

BADINTER, Robert, LL.D., A.M.; French lawyer and professor of law; b. 30 March 1928, Paris; s. of Simon Badinter and Charlotte Rosenberg; m. 1st Anne Vernon 1957; m. 2nd Elisabeth Bleustein-Blanchet 1966; two s. one d.; ed. Univ. of Paris, Columbia Univ., New York; Lawyer, Paris Court of Appeal 1951; Prof. of Law, Paris I (Sorbonne) 1974–81; Minister of Justice and Keeper of the Seals June 1981–86; Pres. Constitutional Council 1986–95; Pres. Court of Conciliation and Arbitration of the OSCE; Senator (Hauts de Seine) 1995. *Publications:* L'exécution 1973, Liberté, libertés 1976, Condorcet (with Elisabeth Badinter) 1988, Libres et égaux: L'émancipation des juifs sous la révolution française 1989, La prison républicaine 1992, C.3.3. 1995, Un antisémitisme ordinaire: Vichy et les avocats juifs 1940–44 1997. *Address:* 38 rue Guynemer, 75006 Paris, France (Home).

BADRAN, Ibrahim, PH.D.; Jordanian government official and foundation director; b. 19 July 1939; m.; four c.; ed. Univs. of Cairo and London; lecturer in Electrical Eng. Univ. of Libya, Tripoli 1970–74; Chief. Eng. and Head, Electricity Section, Consultancy and Architecture, Ministry of Planning, Baghdad 1974–76; Dir. of Planning and Dir. of Standards and Specifications, Jordan Electricity Authority 1978–80; Dir. of Energy, Ministry of Trade and Industry 1980–84; Sec.-Gen. Ministry of Energy and Natural Resources 1985–90; Sec.-Gen. (Under-Sec.) Ministry of Industry and Trade 1984–85, 1990–91; Adviser to Prime Minister 1991–94; Co-ordinator-Gen. of Peace Process, Ministry of Foreign Affairs 1994–95; Exec. Dir. Noor Al-Hussein Foundation 1995–; Chair. Bd. Dirs. Jordan Glass Co. 1985–87, Commercial Centers Cooperation-Jordan 1984–85, 1990–91; fmr. Dir. Jordanian Petroleum Refinery, Jordanian Phosphate Co., Jordan Valley Authority, Jordan Water Authority, Jordan Electricity Authority, Jordan Natural Resources Authority, Industrial Bank of Jordan etc.; Gov. for Jordan, IAEA 1982–90; numerous other professional and academic appts. and affiliations. *Publications:* author or co-author of 13 books on aspects of science, tech., nuclear energy, natural resources and devt. in the Arab world; two theoretical plays. *Address:* Noor Al-Hussein Foundation, P.O. Box 926687, Amman 11110, Jordan. *Telephone:* (962-6) 607460/693901. *Fax:* (962-6) 606994.

BADRAN, Mudar, B.A.; Jordanian politician and civil servant; b. 1934, Jerash; ed. Univ. of Damascus, Syria; Lieutenant and Legal Consultant, Jordanian armed forces 1957, Maj. and Legal Adviser to the Armed Forces Treasury 1962; Asst. Chief, Jordanian Foreign Intelligence 1965; Deputy Chief of Gen. Intelligence 1966, Chief 1968; Retd. Maj.-Gen. 1970; Chief Chamberlain of the Royal Court 1970, Sec.-Gen.; Nat. Security Adviser to H.M. King Hussein (q.v.) 1970; Minister in the Royal Court 1972; Nat. Security Adviser to King Hussein 1973; Minister of Educ. 1973–74; Chief of the Royal Court 1974–76; Minister of Defence and of Foreign Affairs 1976–79; Prime Minister 1976–79, 1980–84, 1989–91; also Minister of Defence 1980–84, 1989; mem. Nat. Consultative Council 1979–; fmr. mem. Exec. Council of the Arab Nat. Union; Hon. LL.D. (Leicester) 1991.

BADURA-SKODA, Paul; Austrian pianist; b. 6 Oct. 1927; s. of Ludwig Badura and Margarete Badura (née Winter); m. Eva Badura-Skoda (née Halfar); two s. two d.; ed. Realgymnasium courses in conducting and piano, Konservatorium der Stadt Wien, and Edwin Fischer's Master Class in Lucerne; regular concerts since 1948; tours all over the world as soloist and with leading orchestras; conductor of chamber orchestra 1960–; yearly master classes fmrly. in Edinburgh, Salzburg and Vienna Festival 1958–63; artist in residence, Univ. of Wisconsin, master classes in Madison, Wisconsin 1966–71; recorded over 200 L.P. records and CDs including complete Beethoven and Schubert sonatas; First Prize Austrian Music Competition 1947; Austrian Cross of Honour for Science and Arts (1st Order) 1976, Bösendorfer-Ring 1978. *Compositions:* Mass in D, Cadenzas to Piano and Violin Concertos by Mozart and Haydn, completion of 5 unfinished Piano Sonatas by Schubert 1976, and of unfinished Larghetto and Allegro for 2 Pianos by Mozart, Elegy for Piano 1980, Sonatine Romantique for Violin and Piano 1980. *Publications:* Interpreting Mozart on the Keyboard (with Eva Badura-Skoda), Die Klaviersonaten von Beethoven (with Jörg Demus) 1970, Interpreting Bach at the Keyboard; Editions of Schubert, Mozart, Chopin; numerous articles. *Leisure interest:* chess. *Address:* Zuckerkandlgasse 14, Vienna 1190, Austria. *Fax:* 47.32.77 (Vienna); (608) 238-8910 (Madison, Wis., U.S.A.).

BAER, Olaf; German baritone; b. 19 Dec. 1957, Dresden; s. of Ernst Edwin Baer and Dora Anneliese Pfennig; m. Carola Tantz 1993; ed. Music School 'Carl Maria von Weber', Dresden; mem. of Dresden Kreuzchores 1967–76; British début at Wigmore Hall 1983, American début in Bach's St. Matthew Passion with Chicago Symphony Orchestra 1987; Prin. Baritone with Dresden State Opera 1983–91; recital and concert tours in all major cities Europe, Australia, U.S.A. and Japan; winner of inaugural Walther Gruner Lieder Competition 1983. *Leisure interests:* all aspects of music, poetry, literature, painting. *Address:* Olbersdorferstrasse 7, 01324 Dresden, Germany. *Telephone:* (0351) 376952.

BAEZ, Joan; American folk singer; b. 9 Jan. 1941, Staten Island, N.Y.; d. of Albert V. and Joan (Bridge) Baez; m. David Harris 1968 (divorced 1973); one s.; ed. School of Fine and Applied Arts, Boston Univ.; began career as singer in coffee houses, appeared at Ballad Room, Club 47 1958–68, Gate of Horn, Chicago 1958, Newport, R.I., Folk Festival 1959–69, Town Hall and Carnegie Hall, New York 1962, 1967, 1968; gave concerts in black colls. in southern U.S.A. 1963; toured Europe and U.S.A. 1960s–1990s, Democratic Repub. of Viet Nam 1972, Australia 1985; recordings with Vanguard Records 1960–72, A & M Record Co. 1972–76, Portrait Records 1977–80, Gold Castle Records 1987–89, Virgin Records 1990–93, Guardian Records 1995–, Grapevine Label Records 1995–; awarded eight gold albums, one gold single; many TV appearances; began refusing payment of war taxes 1964; detained for civil disobedience opposing conscription 1967; speaking tour of U.S.A. and Canada for draft resistance 1967–68; Founder, Vice-Pres. Inst. for Study of Non-Violence (now called Resource Center for Non-violence) 1965–; Founder, Humanitas Int. Human Rights Comm. 1979–92; Gandhi Memorial Int. Foundation Award 1988; Chevalier, Légion d'honneur. *Publications:* Joan Baez Songbook 1964, Daybreak 1968, Coming Out (with David Harris) 1971, And then I wrote . . . (songbook) 1979, And a Voice to Sing With 1987. *Address:* Diamonds and Rust Productions, P.O. Box 1026, Menlo Park, CA 94026, U.S.A. *Telephone:* (415) 328-0266.

BAFILE, H.E. Cardinal Corrado; Italian ecclesiastic; fmr. Prefect of the S.C. for the Causes of Saints; b. 4 July 1903; s. of Vincenzo and Maddalena Tedeschini; ed. State Univ., Rome, and Lateran Univ., Rome; ordained priest 1936; Vatican Secretariat of State 1939–58; Privy Chamberlain to Pope John XXIII 1958–60; Papal Nuncio to Germany 1960–75; Titular Archbishop of Antiochia in Pisidia 1960–76; cr. Cardinal 1976, now Cardinal Priest. *Address:* 10 Via P. Pancrazio Pfeiffer, 00193, Rome, Italy.

BAGABANDI, Natsagiyn, M.SC.; Mongolian politician; b. 22 April 1950, Zavkhan Prov.; ed. Food Tech. Inst. of U.S.S.R.; served in Ulaanbaatar Brewery and Distillery 1972–75; Chief of dept. Mongolian People's Revolutionary Party's (MPRP) Cttee. of Cen. Prov. 1980–84; Chief of Div. adviser of Cen. Cttee. of MPRP 1978–90; Sec., Deputy Chair. of Cen. Cttee. of MPRP 1990–92, Chair. Feb.–June 1997; mem. of State Great Hural, Chair. 1992–96; Pres. of Mongolia May 1997–. *Address:* State Palace, Ulan Bator 12, Mongolia.

BAGAYEV, Sergey Nikolayevich; Russian physicist; b. 9 Sept. 1941; m.; one s.; ed. Novosibirsk State Univ.; researcher, jr., sr. researcher, head of lab. Inst. of Physics of Semiconductors, Siberian br. U.S.S.R. Acad. of Sciences 1965–78; head of lab., head of div., Deputy Dir. Inst. of Thermal Physics, Siberian br. U.S.S.R. Acad. of Sciences 1978–91; Deputy Dir. Inst. of Laser Physics, Siberian br. Russian Acad. of Sciences 1991–92; Dir. 1992–; corresp. mem. U.S.S.R. (now Russian) Acad. of Sciences 1990, mem. 1994; research in nonlinear laser spectroscopy of superhigh rarity, laser frequency standards, physics and their applications in precision physical experiments. *Publications include:* Narrow Resonances in Gas Laser in the Regime of Two-Frequency Generation 1974, Laser Frequency Standards 1986 and numerous articles. *Address:* Institute of Laser Physics, Siberian Branch of Russian Academy of Sciences, Akademik Lavrentyev pr. 1, 630090 Novosibirsk, Russia. *Telephone:* (3832) 354 289 (Office).

BAGAZA, Col. Jean-Baptiste; Burundian army officer and politician; b. 29 Aug. 1946, Rutovu, Bururi Prov.; m. Fausta Bagaza; four c.; ed. Ecole des Cadets, Brussels, and the Belgian Mil. School, Arlon; fmr. Asst. to Gen. Ndabemeye; Chief of Staff of the Armed Forces, rank of Lt.-Col.; led coup to overthrow Pres. Micombero Nov. 1976; Pres. of the Repub. of Burundi 1976–87, also Minister of Defence; Pres. Union pour le progrès national (UPRONA) 1976–87; promoted to Col. 1977; in exile abroad.

BAGGE, Sverre Hakon, PH.D.; Norwegian historian; b. 7 Aug. 1942, Bergen; s. of Sverre Olsen and Gunvor Bagge; m. Guro Mette Skrove; two s. one d.; lecturer Univ. of Bergen 1973, Sr. lecturer 1974, Prof. 1991–; awarded Brage Prize, Clara Lachmann's Prize. *Publications:* The Political Thought of the King's Mirror 1987, Society and Politics in Snorri Sturluson's Heimskringla 1991, From Gang Leader to the Lord's Anointed 1996. *Address:* Department of History, Sydnesplass 7, N-5007 Bergen (Office); Granlia 27, 5080 Eidsvag i Asane, Norway (Home). *Telephone:* 55 58 23 25 (Office). *Fax:* 55 58 96 54 (Office).

BAGGIO, Roberto; Italian footballer; m.; two c.; with Vicenza –1985, Fiorentina 1985–90, Juventus 1990–95, Milan 1995–97, Bologna 1997–98; Internazionale, Milan 1998–; European Player of the Year 1994, World Player of the Year 1994. *Leisure interest:* shooting ducks. *Address:* Bologna F.C. Via Casteldebole 10, 40132 Bologna, Italy.

BAGLAY, Marat Viktorovich, DR. JUR.; Russian lawyer; b. 13 March 1931, Baku; m.; three d.; ed. Rostov State Univ., Inst. of State and Law; researcher Inst. of State and Law 1957–62; Prof. Moscow Inst. of Int. Relations 1962–95; Head of Dept. Inst. of Int. Workers' Movt. Acad. of Sciences 1967–77; Pro-rector Acad. of Labour and Social Relations 1977-95; judge Constitutional Court of Russian Fed. 1996–, Chair. 1997–; assoc. mem. Russian Acad. of Sciences. *Publications include:* Way to Freedom, Constitutional Law of Russian Federation, numerous books and articles. *Address:* Constitutional Court of Russian Federation, Ilyinka str. 21, 103132 Moscow, Russia (Office). *Telephone:* (095) 206 17 62 (Office).

BAGNALL, Field Marshal Sir Nigel (Thomas), G.C.B., C.V.O., M.C.; British army officer; b. 10 Feb. 1927, India; s. of Lieut.-Col. Harry S. and Marjory M. Bagnall; m. Anna C. Church 1959; two d.; ed. Wellington Coll.; joined army 1945; commissioned into Green Howards 1946; 6th Airborne Div., Palestine 1946–48; Green Howards, Malaya 1949–53; Canal tour and Cyprus 1954–56; Staff Coll. 1957; Dir. of Borneo Operations, Gen. Staff Officer (Intelligence) 1966–67; command, 4/7 Royal Dragoon Guards, N. Ireland and British Army of the Rhine (BAOR) 1967–69; Sr. Directing Staff (Army), Joint Services Staff Coll. 1970; command, Royal Armoured Corps HQ 1 (British) Corps 1970–72; Defence Fellow, Balliol Coll., Oxford 1972–73; Sec. Chief of Staff Cttee. 1973–75; Gen. Officer Commanding 4th Div. 1975–77; Asst. Chief of Defence Staff (Policy), Ministry of Defence 1978–80; Commdr. 1st British Corps 1981–83; Commdr.-in-Chief BAOR and Commdr. Northern Army Group 1983–85; Chief of Gen. Staff 1985–88; Aide-de-Camp Gen. to the Queen 1985–88; Hon. Col. Commdt. Army Physical Training Corps 1981–85; Hon. Fellow Balliol Coll., Oxford 1986; Commdr.'s Cross of Merit 1993. *Publication:* The Punic Wars 1991. *Leisure interests:* walking, gardening, writing, reading, breeding waterfowl. *Address:* c/o Royal Bank of Scotland, 49 Charing Cross Road, London, SW1A 2DX, England.

BAGRATYAN, Hrand Araratovich; Armenian politician; b. 18 Oct. 1958, Yerevan; m.; one s.; ed. Yerevan Inst. of Nat. Econ.; jr. researcher, sr. researcher Inst. of Econs., Armenian Acad. of Sciences 1982–90; First Deputy Chair. Council of Ministers of Armenian S.S.R., Chair. State Cttee. on Econs. 1990–; Vice-Prime Minister, Minister of Econs. Repub. of Armenia 1991–93; Prime Minister of Armenia Feb. 1993–Oct. 1996. *Address:* c/o Office of the Prime Minister, Parliament Square 1, 375010 Yerevan, Armenia.

BAGRI, Baron; (Life Peer) cr. 1997; of Regents Park in the City of Westminster; **Raj Kumar Bagri,** C.B.E.; Indian international metals trader; b. 24 Aug. 1930; m. 1954; one s. one d.; joined a metals business in Calcutta 1946; moved into int. metals trading 1949; set up U.K. br. office of an Indian co. 1959; f. own company in U.K., Metdist Ltd., which became London Metal Exchange (LME) ring dealing mem. 1970, currently Chair. Minmetco (U.K. holding co. of Metdist Group of Cos.); joined LME's Man. Cttee. 1973, apptd. Dir. of LME 1983, Vice-Chair. 1990, Chair. 1993–; Trustee various orgs.; mem. Advisory Council Prince's Youth Business Trust, Governing Body S.O.A.S. *Leisure interest:* cricket. *Address:* Metdist Ltd., 80 Cannon Street, London, EC4N 6EJ; The London Metal Exchange Ltd., 56 Leadenhall Street, London, EC3A 2BJ, England. *Telephone:* 0171-606 8321 (Metdist Ltd.). *Fax:* 0171-606 6650.

BAGSHAWE, Kenneth Dawson, C.B.E., M.D., F.R.C.P., F.R.C.O.G., F.R.S.; British physician and medical oncologist; b. 17 Aug. 1925, Marple, Cheshire; s. of Harry Bagshawe and Gladys Bagshawe; m. 1st Ann A. Kelly 1946; m. 2nd Sylvia D. Lawler (née Corben) 1977 (died 1996); one s. one d.; ed. Harrow Co. School, London School of Econs. and St. Mary's Hosp. Medical School, Univ. of London; served R.N. 1943–46; Research Fellow, Johns Hopkins Hosp. 1955–56; Sr. Registrar, St. Mary's Hosp. 1956–60; Sr. Lecturer in Medicine, Charing Cross Hosp. Medical School 1961–63; Consultant Physician and Dir. Dept. of Medical Oncology 1961–90, Prof. Emer.; Prof. of Medical Oncology, Charing Cross Hosp. Medical School 1974–90; Chair., Zenyx Scientific Co. Ltd. 1996–, Enzacta 1998–; Vice-Chair. Council Cancer Research Campaign 1988–; Pres. Asscn. of Cancer Physicians 1986–93, British Asscn. for Cancer Research 1990–94; mem. various cancer research cttees. etc.; Fellow. Royal Coll. of Radiologists; Hamilton Fairley Lectureship 1989; Hon. D.Sc. (Bradford) 1990; Krug Award for Excellence in Medicine 1980; Edgar Gentilli Prize (R.C.O.G.) 1980, Galen Medal (London Soc. of Apothecaries) 1993. *Publications:* Choriocarcinoma 1969, Medical Oncology 1976, Germ Cell Tumours 1983, Antibody Directed Prodrug Therapy 1987 and articles in professional journals. *Leisure interests:* travel, walking, demolition and conservation. *Address:* Department of Surgery, 4N, Charing

Cross Hospital, London, W6 8RF (Office); 115 George Street, London, W1H T5A, England (Home). *Telephone:* 0181-846 7516 (Office); 0171-262 6033 (Home). *Fax:* 0181-846 7516 (Office); 0171-258 1365 (Home).

BAHADUR, Raj, B.SC., M.A., LL.B.; Indian politician and lawyer; b. 21 Aug. 1912; s. of Sunder Lal; m. Vidyawati Srivastava 1936; four s. one d.; ed. Maharaja's Coll., Jaipur, Agra Coll. and St. John's Coll., Agra; mem. Cen. Advisory Cttee. Bharatpur State 1939–42, Municipal Comm. 1941–42; resigned from these posts in connection with "Quit India" Movement; mem. Rep. Assembly 1943; imprisoned for participation in freedom struggle 1945 and 1947; Sec. Assembly Praja Parishad Party 1943–48, Gen. Sec. Matsya Union Congress Cttee. 1948–49; Pres. Bharatpur Bar Asscn. 1948–51; elected to Constituent Assembly of India 1948–50; mem. Union Parl. 1950–67, 1971–77; Sec. Congress Party in Parl. 1950–52; Deputy Minister, later Minister of State for Communications 1951–56; led Indian Del. to 10th Session of Int. Civil Aviation Org., Caracas; Minister of Communications 1956–57; Minister of State for Transport and Communications 1957–62; Minister of State for Transport 1962–63, Minister of Transport 1963–65, and of Civil Aviation 1965; Minister of Information and Broadcasting 1966–67; Advocate, Supreme Court of India 1967; Amb. to Nepal 1968–71; Minister of Parl. Affairs, Shipping and Transport 1971–73, of Communications 1973–74, of Tourism and Civil Aviation 1973–76; mem. Rajasthan P.C.C. and All-India Congress Cttee. 1956–82; mem. Rajasthan State Legis. Ass. June 1980–, Leader Congress (S) group; mem. Upper House of Raj Sabhā; awarded Tamrapatra 1974. *Leisure interest:* collecting books. *Address:* 3 Hospital Road, Jaipur, Rajasthan; N-33 Panchshila Park, New Delhi 110017, India. *Telephone:* 72458; 651577.

BAHARNA, Husain Mohammad al-, PH.D.; Bahraini lawyer and government minister; b. 5 Dec. 1932, Manama; s. of Mohammad Makki Al-Baharna and Zahra Sayed Mahmood; m.; three s. two d.; ed. Baghdad Law Coll., Iraq, London Univ., and Cambridge Univ., U.K.; mem. English Bar (Lincoln's Inn) and Bahraini Bar; Legal Adviser, Ministry of Foreign Affairs, Kuwait 1962–64; Legal Adviser and Analyst Arab Gulf Affairs, Arabian-American Oil Co., Saudi Arabia 1965–68; Legal Adviser, Dept. of Foreign Affairs, Bahrain 1969–70; Legal Adviser to the State and mem. Council of State, Pres. Legal Cttee. 1970–71; Minister of State for Legal Affairs 1971; mem. Del. of Bahrain to Sixth (Legal) Cttee. UN Gen. Ass. 1986, UN Int. Law Comm., Geneva 1987, Del. of Bahrain to Summit of Heads of State of Gulf Co-operation Council 1991; fmr. legal adviser and del. numerous int. confs. and summit meetings; Chair. Del. of Bahrain to UN Preparatory Comm. for Int. Sea Bed Authority and Int. Tribunal for Law of the Sea 1983; mem. Cttee. of Experts on Control of Transnational and Int. Criminality and for the est. of the Int. Criminal Court, Siracusa, Italy June 1990; Council mem. Centre for Islamic and Middle East Law, S.O.A.S., London Univ., Editorial Bd. Arab Law Quarterly; Hon. mem. Euro-Arab Forum for Arbitration and Business Law, Paris; mem. British Inst. of Int. and Comparative Law, American Soc. of Int. Law, Int. Law Asscn., Egyptian Soc. of Int. Law; Assoc. mem. Int. Comm. of Jurists; Arab Historian Medal (Union of Arab Historians) 1986. *Publications:* The Legal Status of the Arab Gulf States 1968, Legal and Constitutional Systems of the Arabian Gulf States (in Arabic) 1975, The Arabian Gulf States—Their Legal and Political Status and their International Problems 1975; articles in learned journals. *Leisure interest:* reading. *Address:* P.O. Box 790, Manama, Bahrain. *Telephone:* 255633. *Fax:* 270303.

BAHL, Kamlesh, LL.B., C.B.E., F.R.S.A.; British solicitor and administrator; b. 28 May 1956; d. of Swinder Nath Bahl and Leela Wati Bahl; m. Nitin Lakhani 1986; ed. Univ. of Birmingham; solicitor GLC 1978–81, British Steel Corpn. 1981–84, Texaco Ltd. 1984–87; Legal and Commercial Man. Data Logic Ltd. 1987–89, Co. Sec. 1989–93, also Man. Legal Services, legal consultant 1993–; Chair. Equal Opportunities Comm. 1993–; Chair. Law Soc. Commerce and Industry Group 1988–89, mem. Law Soc. Council 1990–, Deputy Vice-Pres. 1998–; Dir. (non-exec.) Parkside Health Authority 1990–93; mem. Justice Sub-Cttee. on Judiciary 1991–92, Ethnic Minorities Advisory Cttee. and Tribunals Cttee. 1991–94, Council and Standing Cttee. on Health Authorities, Nat. Asscn. of Health Authorities and Trusts 1993–94, Council of Justice 1993–94; independent mem. Diplomatic Service Appeal Bd., FCO 1993–; EC Rep. EC Consultative Comm. on Racism and Xenophobia 1994–. *Publication:* Managing Legal Practice in Business (ed.) 1989. *Leisure interests:* travelling, swimming, theatre, fund-raising for charity. *Address:* Overseas House, Quay Street, Manchester, M3 3HN, England. *Telephone:* 0161-833 9244. *Fax:* 0161-838 8201.

BAHNASSI, Afif, M.A., PH.D.; Syrian professor of art and architecture; b. 17 April 1928, Damascus; m. 1st Hiba Wadi 1962 (died 1966); m. 2nd Maysoun Jazairi 1971; four s. one d.; ed. Univ. of Syria and Sorbonne, Paris; Dir. Fine Arts Dept. 1959–71; Dir. Gen. of Antiquities and Museums of Syria 1972–88; mem. Arab Writers' Union 1967–; Chair. Fine Arts Asscn. of Syria 1968–; Prof. of History of Art and Architecture, Damascus Univ. 1988–. *Publications:* General History of Arts and Architecture 1962, L'esthétique de l'art arabe 1979, Arabic Modern Art 1979, Damascus 1981, L'Art et l'Orientalisme 1983, En Syrie 1986, The Ancient Syria 1987, The Great Mosque of Damascus 1988, Arab Architecture 1994, Dictionnaire d'Architecture 1994, Dictionnaire des termes de calligraphie, Enciclopédie de l'architecture Islamique 1996, The Great Mosque of San'a 1996, Formation of Damascus 1997, Aesthetics of al Tawhidi 1997, Discussion on Identity 1997, Aesthetics of Arabesque 1997, Criticism of Art 1997, Modernism and Postmodernism 1997, Islamic Tiles 1997, Arab Calligraphy 1997. *Leisure interests:* painting, sculpture. *Address:* 38 Gazzi Street, Damascus, Syria. *Telephone:* 3334554 (Office); 3311827 (Home). *Fax:* 2240198.

BAHNINI, Hadj M'Hammed, L. EN D., L. ÈS L.; Moroccan politican; b. 1914, Fez; ed. Lycée Gouraud (now Lyceé Hassan II), Rabat; Sec., Royal Palace; Magistrate, Haut Tribunal Chérifien; Instructor, Collège Impérial and Private Tutor to H.R.H. Crown Prince Moulay El Hassan, Prince Moulay Abdallah, Princess Lalla Aïcha and Princess Lalla Malika; Dir. of the Imperial Cabinet 1950–51; Del. Judge, Meknès 1951; exiled Dec. 1952–July 1954; Sec.-Gen. of the Cabinet 1955–72; Minister of Justice 1958–65; Minister of Admin. Affairs 1965–70; Minister of Nat. Defence 1970–71; Minister of Justice, Sec.-Gen. of Govt. 1971–72, also Deputy Prime Minister April–Nov. 1972; Minister of State for Culture 1972–81; Minister of State Without Portfolio 1981. *Address:* c/o Ministry of State, Royal Palace, Rabat, Morocco.

BAHR, Egon; German government official and journalist; b. 18 March 1922, Treffurt; m. Dorothea Grob 1945; one s. one d.; journalist 1945–, Contributor Die Neue Zeitung 1948–59, Das Tagesspiegel 1950; Chief Commentator RIAS (Rundfunk im amerikanischen Sektor Berlins) 1950–60; Dir. Press and Information Office of Berlin 1960–66; promoted to rank of Amb. in diplomatic service 1967; Dir. of Planning Staff, Diplomatic Service 1967–68; Ministerial Dir. 1968–69; State Sec., Bundeskanzleramt and Plenipotentiary of the Fed. Govt. in Berlin 1969–72; mem. of Parl. (Bundestag) 1972–90; Fed. Minister without Portfolio attached to the Fed. Chancellor's Office 1972–74, for Overseas Devt. Aid (Econ. Co-operation) 1974–76; Dir. Institut für Friedensforschung und Sicherheitspolitik 1984–94; mem. PEN 1974–, Ind. Comm. on Disarmament and Security 1980–; Theodor-Heuss-Preis 1976; Gustav-Heinemann-Bürgerpreis 1982. *Publications:* Was wird aus den Deutschen? 1982, Zum Europäischen Frieden 1988, Zu meiner Zeit 1996, Deutsche Interessen 1998. *Address:* Ollenhauerstrasse 1, 53113 Bonn, Germany.

BAI CHUNLI; PH.D.; Chinese chemist; b. 26 Sept. 1953, Liaoning; s. of Bai Fuxin and Li Fengyun; m. Li Chunfang 1981; one s.; ed. Peking Univ.; Research Asst., Changchun Inst. of Applied Chem., Chinese Acad. of Sciences (CAS) 1978, Research Assoc., Inst. of Chem. 1981–85; Visiting Research Assoc., Calif. Inst. of Tech., U.S.A. 1985–87; Assoc. Prof. and Dir. Study Group on Scanning Tunnelling Microscopy (STM), Inst. of Chem., CAS 1987–89, Prof. 1989–, Deputy Dir. 1992–96, Chair. Div. of Fundamental Research and Vice-Chair. Acad. Cttee. 1993–96, Vice-Pres. CAS 1996–; Visiting Prof. Inst. for Materials Research, Tohoku Univ., Japan 1991–92; Chair. 1st, 2nd, 3rd and 4th Nat. Confs. on STM; mem. Advisory Bd. Int. Organizing Cttee. of STM Conf., Co-Ed. Proc. STM '93; mem. Steering and Organizing Cttee. 1st and 2nd Asian Conf. on STM 1994, 1996; mem. editorial bds. journals of physics, ultramicroscopy and nanotechnology, vacuum science and tech., and analytical sciences; Pres. B-Y Research and Devt. Centre for Microscopic Instruments 1988–92; Sec.-Gen. and mem. Exec. Council Chinese Chemical Soc. 1994–; mem. Exec. Council China Material Research Soc. 1995–, Council Chinese Crystallographic Soc. 1994–, Chinese Vacuum Soc. 1990–, Exec. Council Engineers' Asscn. of CAS 1990–; Vice-Pres. All-China Youth Fed. 1995–; Pres. China Young Scientists' Asscn. 1996–; mem. CPPCC 1993–, alt. mem. 15th Cen. Cttee. 1997–; Fellow Third World Acad. of Sciences 1997–; Academician Chinese Acad. of Sciences 1997–; Outstanding Young Scholar Hong Qiu Shi Science and Tech. Foundation 1995; numerous prizes and awards. *Publications:* seven books and more than 200 papers in scientific journals. *Address:* Chinese Academy of Sciences, 52 San Li He Road, Beijing 100864, People's Republic of China. *Telephone:* (10) 62568158. *Fax:* (10) 62557908.

BAI DONGLU; Chinese pharmaceutical chemist; b. Feb. 1936, Dinghai Co., Zhejiang Prov.; s. of Bai Daxi and Zhang Yunxiao; m. Ni Zhifang 1969; one d.; Prof. Shanghai Inst. of Materia Medica, Academia Sinica; Science and Tech. Progress Award. *Publications:* more than 90 papers. *Leisure interest:* stamp collecting. *Address:* Shanghai Institute of Materia Medica, 294 Taiyuan Road, Shanghai 200031, People's Republic of China. *Telephone:* 21-64311833. *Fax:* 21-64370269.

BAI ENPEI; Chinese politician; b. Sept. 1946, Qingjian Co., Shaanxi Prov.; ed. Northwest Tech. Univ. 1965; joined CCP 1973; Vice-Sec. CCP Ya'nan Prefectural Cttee. 1983; Sec. CCP Yan'an Prefectural Cttee. 1985; alt. mem. 13th CCP Cen. Cttee. 1987; Vice-Sec. CCP Inner Mongolia Autonomous Regional Cttee. 1990; alt. mem. 14th CCP Cen. Cttee. 1992; Vice-Sec. CCP Qinghai Provincial. Cttee., Acting Gov. Qinghai Prov. 1997–; mem. 15th CCP Cen. Cttee. 1997–. *Address:* Office of the Governor, Qinghai Provincial Government, Xining City, Qinghai Province, People's Republic of China.

BAI JIEFU; Chinese politician; b. 1929, Suide Co., Shaanxi Prov.; joined CCP 1948; Vice-Pres. China Asscn. for Int. Friendship 1985–; Chair. 6th Beijing CPPCC Municipal Cttee. 1986–; Chair. 7th 1991–94; Deputy to 5th NPC 1983–87, 6th 1988–92; del. to CCP 13th Congress 1991; Exec. Pres. Soc. for Study of Anti-Japanese Agression War 1991–. *Address:* Beijing Chinese People's Political Consultative Council, 279 Dongsi Beidajie Street, Dongcheng District, Beijing 100007, People's Republic of China.

BAI JINIAN; Chinese party official; b. 1926, Shaanxi Prov.; joined CCP 1942; Sec. CCP Cttee., Shaanxi 1984–; mem. 12th Cen. Cttee. CCP 1985–87; mem. Standing and Econ. Cttee. 7th CPPCC 1988–92, 8th 1993–. *Address:* Shaanxi Provincial Chinese Communist Party, Xian, Shaanxi, People's Republic of China.

BAI LICHEN; Chinese administrator; b. 1941, Lingyuan, Liaoning; joined CCP 1971; mem. Standing Cttee. CCP Prov. Cttee. Liaoning 1985–87; Vice-Gov. Liaoning 1985–86; mem. 13th Cen. Cttee. CCP 1987–92, 14th Cen. Cttee. CCP 1992–97, 15th Cen. Cttee. 1997–; Chair. Ningxia Hui Autonomous Regional People's Govt. 1987–97; Deputy Sec. CPC Regional Cttee 1988–97; Sec. CCP Group, Nat. Office of Supply and Marketing Co-operatives 1997–; Vice-Chair. 9th Nat. Cttee. of CPPCC 1998–. *Address:* National Committee of the Chinese People's Political Consultative Conference, 23 Taiping Qiao Street, Beijing, People's Republic of China.

BAI QINGCAI; Chinese party and government official; b. 1932, Wutai Co., Shanxi Prov.; joined CCP 1955; Vice-Gov. of Shanxi Prov. 1983–93; mem. of Shanxi Standing Comm. CCP 1985–93; mem. 14th CCP Cen. Cttee. 1992–97; Gov. Shaanxi Prov. 1993–94; now Vice Chair. All-China Fed. of Supply and Marketing Co-operation; Deputy Sec. CCP Shaanxi Prov. Cttee; Vice-Chair. Environment and Resource Protection Cttee. of 9th NPC 1998–. *Address:* c/o Standing Committee of the National People's Congress, Beijing, People's Republic of China.

BAI SHANGWU; Chinese party official; b. 1928, Xing Co., Shanxi Prov.; joined CCP 1945; mem. Standing Cttee. CCP Prov. Cttee. Sichuan 1983–; Chair. Sichuan Prov. Political Science and Law Cttee. 1983–; Political Commissar Sichuan Prov. People's Govt. 1983–88, Vice-Chair. Standing Comm., Sichuan Prov. People's Congress 1988–; mem. 8th NPC 1993–. *Address:* Sichuan Provincial People's Government, Chengdu, People's Republic of China.

BAI SHOUYI (Djamal al-Din); Chinese historian; b. 1909; Dir. History Dept. of Beijing Teachers Coll. 1963–66; in disgrace during Cultural Revolution 1966–76; mem. China's NPC del. to Iran and Kuwait 1976; Dir. History Dept. of Beijing Teachers Univ. 1978–; Vice-Chair. Nationalities Cttee. 5th NPC 1979–83; Vice-Chair. China's Islamic Asscn. 1980–; mem. 6th NPC 1983–88; mem. 7th NPC 1988–92. *Publications:* An Outline History of China 1983. *Address:* Beijing Teachers University, Xizhimenwai Street, Beijing, People's Republic of China.

BAI SHUXIANG; Chinese ballerina; b. 1939; ed. Beijing Coll. of Dancing; Prin. Dancer Cen. Ballet Co. 1958–, Dir 1984–90; mem. 5th Nat. Cttee CPPCC 1978–82, 6th 1983–87, 7th 1988–92, 8th 1993–; Perm. mem. China Dancers' Asscn., now Chair.; First Grade Dancer of the Nat. (award); *Performances include:* Swan Lake, Giselle, The Fountain of Bakhchisarai, The Emerald, Sylvia, Red Women Army, Song of Yimeng, Song of Jiaoyang. *Address:* Chinese Dancers' Association, Di An Men Dong Dajie, Beijing 100009, People's Republic of China.

BAI XUESHI; Chinese artist; b. 12 June 1915, Beijing; s. of Dong and Bai Huanzhang; m. Xie Lin; two s. three d.; studied under Liang Shunian; specializes in landscape paintings; fmr. teacher Beijing Teachers' Inst. of Arts, Beijing Inst. of Arts; Prof. Cen. Acad. of Arts and Design; Pres. Beijing Research Soc. of Landscape Paintings; mem. Cttee. of 7th CPPCC 1988–; exhbns. in U.S.A., Japan, Hong Kong. *Works include:* Myriad Peaks Contending, Riverside Village, Riverboats in Springtime, Aspects of Lushan, Lijiang, Cool Waters of Lijiang, Cormorant Fishing. *Leisure interests:* Beijing opera and weiqi. *Address:* Central Academy of Arts and Design, Beijing, People's Republic of China. *Telephone:* 341308.

BAILAR, Benjamin Franklin, B.A., M.B.A.; American government official, educator and business executive; b. 21 April 1934, Champaign, Ill.; s. of late Dr. John C. Bailar, Jr. and Florence (née Catherwood) Bailar; m. Anne Tveit 1958; one s. one d.; ed. Univ. of Colorado, Harvard Graduate School of Business Admin.; Continental Oil Co. 1959–62; American Can Co. 1962–72, Vice-Pres. 1967–72; Senior Asst. Postmaster-Gen. U.S. Postal Service 1972–74, Deputy Postmaster-Gen. 1974, Postmaster-Gen. 1975–78; Exec. Vice-Pres., Dir. U.S. Gypsum Co., Chicago 1978–82; Pres. and C.E.O. Scott Publishing Co. 1983–85; Pres. Franklin Finance Corp. 1985–87; Dir. Dana Corpn., Toledo, Ohio 1980–, U.S. Can, Oakbrook, Ill. 1985–; Transco Energy Co. 1988–, First Interstate Bank 1990–, Smith Int. Inc. 1993–; Dean, Prof. of Admin., Jesse H. Jones Graduate School of Admin., Rice Univ. 1987–97. *Address:* 2121 Kirby Drive, Box 141, Houston, TX 77019, U.S.A.

BAILEY, David, F.R.P.S., F.S.I.A.D.; British photographer and film director; b. 2 Jan. 1938, London; s. of Herbert William Bailey and Gladys Agnes Bailey; m. 1st Rosemary Bramble 1960; m. 2nd Catherine Deneuve (q.v.) 1965; m. 3rd Marie Helvin (divorced 1985); m. 4th Catherine Dyer 1986; two s. one d.; self-taught; Photographer for Vogue, U.K., U.S.A., France, Italy and advertising photography 1959–; Dir. Commercials 1966–, TV documentaries 1968–; Exhbn. Nat. Portrait Gallery 1971; Photographers' Gallery 1973, Olympus Gallery 1980, 1982, 1983, Victoria and Albert Museum 1983; Int. Centre of Photography, New York 1984, Hamilton Gallery 1990, 1992; directed and produced TV film Who Dealt? 1993; documentary: Models Close Up 1998; dir. feature film The Intruder 1999. *Publications:* Box of Pinups 1964, Goodbye Baby and Amen 1969, Warhol 1974, Beady Minces 1974, Mixed Moments 1976, Trouble and Strife 1980, N.W.1 1982, Black and White Memories 1983, Nudes 1981–84 1984, Imagine 1985, The Naked Eye: Great photographs of the nude (with Martin Harrison) 1988, If We Shadows 1992, The Lady is a Tramp 1995, Rock & Roll Heroes 1997, Archive 1999. *Leisure interests:* photography, aviculture, travel, painting. *Address:* c/o Robert Montgomery and Partners, 3 Junction Mews, Sale Place, London, W.2, England. *Telephone:* 0171-439 1877.

BAILEY, D(avid) R(oy) Shackleton, LITT.D., F.B.A.; British academic; b. 10 Dec. 1917, Lancaster; s. of John Henry Shackleton Bailey and Rosamund Maud Giles; m. Kristine Zvirbulis 1994; ed. Gonville and Caius Coll. Cambridge; Fellow, Gonville and Caius Coll. 1944–55, Praelector 1954–55, Deputy Bursar 1964, Sr. Bursar 1965–68, Univ. Lecturer in Tibetan 1948–68; Fellow, Dir. of Studies in Classics, Jesus Coll. Cambridge 1955–64; Visiting Lecturer in Classics, Harvard Univ., U.S.A. 1963, Prof. of Greek and Latin 1975–82, Pope Prof. of Latin Language and Literature 1982–88, Prof. Emer. 1988–; Prof. of Latin, Univ. of Mich., Ann Arbor 1968–75, Adjunct Prof. 1989–; Nat. Endowment for Humanities Fellow, Visiting Fellow, Peterhouse, Cambridge 1980–81; Fellow, British Acad., American Acad. of Arts and Sciences; mem. American Philosophical Soc.; Hon. D.Litt. (Dublin) 1984; Charles J. Goodwin Award of Merit 1978, Kenyon Medal, British Acad. 1985. *Publications:* The Satapancasatka of Matrceta 1951, Propertiana 1956, Cicero's Letters, 10 vols. 1965–81, Cicero 1971, Profile of Horace 1982, Anthologia Latina I 1982, Horatius 1985, Cicero's Philippics 1986, Lucanus 1988, Cicero's Letters (4 vols.) 1988, Quintilian 1989, Martialis 1990, Martial (3 vols.) 1993, Homeoteleuton in Latin Dactylic Poetry 1994, Selected Classical Papers 1997 and others; Harvard Studies in Classical Philology (Ed.) 1978–85; articles on oriental and classical subjects in professional journals. *Leisure interest:* cats. *Address:* 303 North Division, Ann Arbor, MI 48104, U.S.A. *Telephone:* (734) 6658062.

BAILEY, Donovan; Canadian athlete and marketing consultant; b. 16 Dec. 1967, Manchester, Jamaica; one d. by Michelle Mullin; grew up in Jamaica and emigrated to Canada 1981; mem. Canada's winning 4 × 100m team, Commonwealth Games 1994; world indoor record holder for 50m 1996; Canadian 100m record holder 1995, 1996; World, Commonwealth and Olympic 100m record holder 1996. *Address:* c/o Athletics Canada, 1600 James Naismith Drive, Gloucester, Ont., K1B 5N4, Canada.

BAILEY, Norman Stanley, C.B.E., B.MUS.; British operatic and concert singer; b. 23 March 1933, Birmingham; s. of Stanley Ernest and Agnes Train (Gale) Bailey; m. 1st Doreen Evelyn Simpson 1957 (divorced 1983); two s. one d.; m. 2nd Kristine Ciesinski 1985; ed. East Barnet Grammar School, England, Boksburg High School, South Africa, Prince Edward School, Rhodesia, Rhodes Univ., South Africa, Akad. für Musik und Darstellende Kunst, Vienna; engaged full time at Linz Landestheater, Austria 1960–63, Wuppertaler Bühnen 1963–64, Deutsche Oper am Rhein, Düsseldorf and Duisburg 1964–67; Prin. Baritone English Nat. Opera, Sadler's Wells 1967–71; freelance 1971–; debut at La Scala, Milan 1967, Royal Opera House, Covent Garden 1969, Bayreuth Festival 1969, Paris Opera 1973, Vienna State Opera 1976, Metropolitan Opera, New York 1976; appearances Paris Opera, Edin. Festival, Hamburg State Opera, Munich State Opera; Prof. of Voice, Royal Coll. of Music, London. *Major recordings and TV films include:* Der fliegende Holländer, Die Meistersinger von Nürnberg, King Priam, Der Ring des Nibelungen, Macbeth, La Traviata, Falstaff; D. Mus. h.c. (Rhodes) 1986; awarded Hon. R.A.M. 1981, Sir Charles Santley Memorial Prize 1977. *Leisure interests:* golf, chess, micro-computing, mem. Baha'i World Faith. *Address:* 38 Manor Lane Terrace, Lewisham, London, SE13 5QS, England.

BAILEY, Paul, F.R.S.L.; British freelance writer; b. 16 Feb. 1937; s. of Arthur Oswald Bailey and Helen Maud Burgess; ed. Sir Walter St. John's School, London; Actor 1956–64, appearing in The Sport of My Mad Mother 1958 and Epitaph for George Dillon 1958; Literary Fellow at Univs. of Newcastle and Durham 1972–74; Bicentennial Fellowship 1976; Visiting Lecturer in English Literature, North Dakota State Univ. 1977–79; Somerset Maugham Award 1968; E. M. Forster Award 1978; George Orwell Memorial Prize 1978. *Publications:* At the Jerusalem 1967, Trespasses 1970, A Distant Likeness 1973, Peter Smart's Confessions 1977, Old Soldiers 1980, An English Madam 1982, Gabriel's Lament 1986, An Immaculate Mistake 1989, Hearth and Home 1990, Sugar Cane 1993, Kitty and Virgil 1998; ed. The Oxford Book of London 1995, numerous newspaper articles. *Leisure interests:* visiting churches, opera, watching tennis. *Address:* 79 Davisville Road, London, W12 9SH, England. *Telephone:* 0181-749 2279.

BAILIE, Roy; British business executive; ed. Harvard Business School; Chair CBI 1992–94, W. & G. Baird Holdings, N.I. Tourist Board; Vice-Pres. British Printing Industries Fed.; Dir. (non-exec.) Bank of England 1998–. *Address:* c/o Bank of England, Threadneedle Street, London, EC2R 8AH, England.

BAILLIE, A. Charles, M.B.A.; Canadian banker; ed. Trinity Coll., Univ. of Toronto, Harvard Business School, U.S.A.; joined The Toronto Dominion Bank 1964, Vice-Pres. and Gen. Man., U.S.A. Div. 1979, Sr. Vice-Pres. 1981, Exec. Vice-Pres., Corp. and Investment Banking Group 1984, Vice-Chair. 1992, Pres. The Toronto Dominion Bank 1995–, C.E.O. 1997–, Chair. 1998–; Dir. The Toronto Dominion Bank, AEtna Life Insurance Co. of Canada, AEtna Casualty & Surety Co. of Canada; Chair. Toronto Dominion Securities; Fellow Inst. of Canadian Bankers; mem. Bd. of Govs. The Shaw Festival; mem. Finance Cttee. and Investment Sub-Cttee. Nat. Cancer Inst.; mem. Corpn. of Trinity Coll. *Address:* The Toronto Dominion Bank, P.O. Box 1, Toronto Dominion Centre, Toronto, M5K 1A2, Canada.

BAILLY, Jean Paul Marie Henri; French industrialist; b. 5 June 1921, Orléans; s. of Paul M. E. Bailly and Maria J. L. Julien; m. Hélène V. Vienot 1946; one s. one d.; ed. Prytanée Militaire de La Flèche (Sarthe) and Ecole Polytechnique; engineer at collieries in Bassin du Nord and Pas de Calais 1946–54; Asst. Dir.-Gen., then Dir.-Gen. Mines de Zellidja and Fonderie de

Penarroya 1954–61; Asst. Dir.-Gen. Société des Ciments Lafarge 1961–66, Dir.-Gen. 1966–74; Pres. Dir.-Gen. Lafarge Coppée 1983–84, Hon. Pres. 1984–; Pres. Conseil d'admin. de la Société de l'industrie minérale 1984–90; Officier, Légion d'honneur. *Address:* 13 rue des Pyramides, 75001 Paris, France (Home).

BAILYN, Bernard, PH.D.; American historian; b. 10 Sept. 1922, Hartford, Conn.; s. of Charles Manuel Bailyn and Esther Schloss; m. Lotte Lazarsfeld 1952; two s.; ed. Williams Coll. and Harvard Univ.; mem. Faculty, Harvard Univ. 1953–, Prof. of History 1961–66, Winthrop Prof. of History 1966–81, Adams Univ. Prof. 1981–93, Prof. Emer. 1993–, James Duncan Phillips Prof. in Early American History 1991–93, Prof. Emer. 1993–; Dir. Charles Warren Center for Studies in American History 1983–94; Dir. Int. Seminar on History of Atlantic World 1995–; Ed.-in-Chief John Harvard Library 1962–70; Trevelyan Lecturer, Cambridge Univ. 1971; mem. American Historical Asscn. (Pres. 1981), American Acad. of Arts and Sciences, Nat. Acad. of Educ., American Philosophical Soc., Royal Historical Soc., Mass. Historical Soc., Mexican Acad. of History and Geography; Corresp. Fellow, British Acad. 1989; Robert H. Lord Award, Emmanual Coll. 1967; 8 hon. degrees. *Publications:* New England Merchants in the 17th Century 1955, Massachusetts Shipping 1697–1714: A Statistical Study 1959, Education in the Forming of American Society 1960, Pamphlets of the American Revolution 1750–1776, Vol. I 1965, The Ideological Origins of the American Revolution (Pulitzer and Bancroft Prizes 1968) 1967, The Origins of American Politics 1968, The Ordeal of Thomas Hutchinson (Nat. Book Award 1975) 1974, The Great Republic (co-author) 1977, Voyagers to the West (Pulitzer Prize 1986) 1986; co-ed.: The Intellectual Migration 1930–1960 1969, Law in American History 1972, Perspectives in American History 1967–77, The Press and the American Revolution 1980, Strangers Within the Realm 1990, The Debate on the Constitution (2 vols.) (jtly) 1993, On the Teaching Writing of History 1994. *Address:* 170 Clifton Street, Belmont, MA 02178, U.S.A.

BAINBRIDGE, Beryl, F.R.S.L.; British writer and actress; b. 21 Nov. 1934, Liverpool; d. of Richard and Winifred (née Baines) Bainbridge; m. Austin Davies 1954 (dissolved); one s. two d.; ed. Merchant Taylors' School, Liverpool, Arts Educational Schools, Tring; columnist Evening Standard 1987–; Hon. D. Litt. (Liverpool Univ.) 1988; Guardian Fiction Award for The Bottle Factory Outing, Whitbread Award for Injury Time. *Plays:* Tiptoe Through the Tulips 1976, The Warriors Return 1977, It's a Lovely Day Tomorrow 1977, Journal of Bridget Hitler 1981, Somewhere More Central (TV) 1981, Evensong (TV) 1986. *Publications:* A Weekend with Claude 1967, Another Part of the Wood 1968, Harriet Said . . . 1972, The Dressmaker 1973, The Bottle Factory Outing 1974, Sweet William 1975 (film 1980), A Quiet Life 1976, Injury Time 1977, Young Adolf 1978, Winter Garden 1980, English Journey (TV series) 1984, Watson's Apology 1984, Mum and Mr. Armitage 1985, Forever England 1986 (TV series 1986), Filthy Lucre 1986, An Awfully Big Adventure (staged 1992) 1989, The Birthday Boys 1991, Something Happened Yesterday 1993, Collected Stories 1994, Northern Stories (Vol. 5.) (ed. with David Pownall), Kiss Me Hardy 1996, Every Man For Himself 1996, Master George 1998. *Leisure interests:* reading, smoking. *Address:* 42 Albert Street, London, NW1 7NU, England. *Telephone:* 0171-387 3113.

BAIRD, Dugald Euan, B.A.; American oil industry executive; b. 16 Sept. 1937, Aberdeen, Scotland; s. of Dugald Baird and Matilda Deans Tennant; m. Angelica Hartz 1961; two c.; ed. Univs. of Aberdeen and Cambridge; joined Schlumberger Ltd. 1960, various field assignments Europe, Asia, Middle East, Africa until 1974, Personnel Man., Vice-Pres. (Operations) Schlumberger Technical Services, Paris 1974–79; Exec. Vice-Pres. (worldwide wireline operations) Schlumberger Ltd., New York 1979–86, Chair. Bd., Pres. and C.E.O. 1986–; Hon. LL.D. (Aberdeen) 1995, (Dundee) 1998. *Address:* Schlumberger Ltd., 277 Park Avenue, New York, NY 10172, U.S.A. *Telephone:* (212) 350-9481. *Fax:* (212) 350-9457.

BAIS, Ramesh; Indian politician; b. 2 Aug. 1948, Raipur, Madhya Pradesh; s. of late Khom Pal Bais; m.; one s. two d.; elected Councillor, Raipur Mun. Corpn. 1978, mem. Madhya Pradesh Legis. Ass. 1980, Lok Sabha 1989, 1996–; Vice-Pres. Madhya Pradesh Bharatiya Janata Party (BJP) 1989–90, 1994–96, mem. BJP Nat. Exec. 1993–; Minister of State for Steel and Mines 1998–; Chair. Seed and Agricultural Devt. Corpn. of Madhya Pradesh 1992–93. *Leisure interests:* woodcrafting, painting, interior decoration, gardening. *Address:* c/o Bharatiya Janata Party, 11 Ashok Road, New Delhi 110 001, India. *Telephone:* (011) 382234. *Fax:* (011) 3782163.

BAJAJ, Rahul, LL.B., M.B.A.; Indian industrialist; b. 10 June 1938, Calcutta; m. Rupa Bajaj 1961; two s. one d.; ed. St. Stephen's Coll., Delhi, Govt. Law Coll., Bombay, Harvard Univ.; Dir. Bajaj Auto Ltd. 1956–60, Chair. and Man. Dir. 1972–; Chair. Maharashtra Scooters Ltd. 1975–; Pres. Asscn. of Indian Automobile Mfrs. 1976–78, Mahratta Chamber of Commerce and Industries 1983–85, Confed. of Eng. Industry 1979–80; Chair. Devt. Council for Automobiles and Allied Industries 1975–77; mem. Exec. Cttee. Confed. of Eng. Industry 1978–, Governing Council, Automotive Research Asscn of India 1972–, Devt. Council for Automobiles and Allied Industries 1987–, World Econ. Forum's Advisory Council 1984–; Man of the Year Award (Nat. Inst. of Quality Assurance) 1975, Business Man of the Year Award (Business India Magazine) 1985. *Address:* 51 Mahatma Gandhi Road, Bombay 400 001, India (Office). *Telephone:* 0212-86250/83399 (Office); 0212-82857 (Home).

BAJAMAL, Abdulkader Abdulrahman, B.A.; Yemeni politician and economist; b. 18 Feb. 1946, Seiyun-Hadhramout; m. 1976; two s. two d.; ed. Cairo Univ.; First Deputy Minister of Planning and Devt. People's Democratic Repub. of Yemen 1978; lecturer in Econs. Aden Univ. 1978–80; Minister of Industry, Chair. Bd. Oil, Mineral and Electricity Auth. 1980–85; Minister of Energy and Minerals 1985; M.P. Repub. of Yemen (following union of fmr. People's Democratic Repub. of Yemen and fmr. Yemen Arab Repub.) 1990–91; Chair. Bd. Public Free Zone Authority 1991–94; Deputy Prime Minister 1994–97; Minister of Planning and Devt. 1994–97, 1998–; awarded Medal of Yemeni Unity, Medal of Yemeni Revolution, Medal of Yemeni Independence. *Publications:* New Administration Accountancy 1978, The Patterns of Development in the Arab Countries 1981 (jtly.), Policies and Guidelines for Privatization in the Republic of Yemen 1994. *Leisure interests:* sports, table tennis. *Address:* c/o Ministry of Planning and Development, P.O. Box 175, Sana'a, Republic of Yemen. *Telephone:* (1) 250118. *Fax:* (1) 250665.

BAJT, Aleksander, D.ECONS.; Slovenian professor of economics; b. 27 Feb. 1921, Ljubljana; s. of Aleš Bajt and Franja Bajt-Lukač; m. Dragica Zupanič 1946; ed. Law School, Univ. of Ljubljana; Dir. Slovenian Textile Ind. 1946–50; Asst. Prof. of Econs., Law School, Univ. of Ljubljana 1951–65, Prof. 1965–91; Visiting Prof. Univ. of Va. 1968–69; f. Econs. Inst. of Law Faculty 1963, Dir. 1963–93; Ed. Gospodarska gibanja 1971–87; mem. Slovenian Acad. of Arts and Sciences 1981. *Publications:* Marxist Law of Value 1953, Political Economy 1958, Introduction to Political Economy 1965, Principles of Economics 1967, Principles of Economic Analysis and Policy 1979, Alternative Economic Policy 1986, The Self-management Form of Social Property (in Serbocroat) 1988, and over 300 papers on economic subjects. *Address:* Pleteršnikova 32, Ljubljana, Slovenia. *Telephone:* 221-688 (Office); 312-160 (Home).

BAKA, András B., LL.D., PH.D.; Hungarian judge and professor of law; b. 11 Dec. 1952, Budapest; ed. St. Stephen's High School, Budapest and Eötvös Loránd Univ. Budapest; Research Fellow, Comparative Law Dept. Inst. for Legal and Admin. Sciences of Hungarian Acad. of Sciences 1978–82, Sr. Research Fellow, Constitutional and Admin. Dept. 1982–90; Prof. of Constitutional Law, Budapest School of Public Admin. 1990–; Dir.-Gen. and Pres. Bd. Budapest School of Public Admin. 1990–; mem. Parl. and Sec. Human Rights Comm. of Hungarian Parl. 1990–91; Judge, European Court of Human Rights 1991–; Visiting Prof. Brown Univ., Providence, R.I. 1986, Univ. of Va. 1987, Univ. of Calif. Berkeley 1987, Columbia Univ. New York 1987; Prof. Santa Clara Univ. School of Law, Inst. of Int. and Comparative Law, Santa Clara, Calif. 1991; Scientist Award, Hungarian Acad. of Sciences 1988. *Publications:* several publs. on minority rights. *Address:* School of Public Administration, 5 Ménesi Street, 1118 Budapest, Hungary. *Telephone:* (361) 186-9054. *Fax:* (361) 186-9429.

BAKATIN, Vadim Viktorovich; Russian politician; b. 6 Nov. 1937, Kiselevsk, Kemerovo Dist.; s. of Victor Aleksandrovich Bakatin and Nina Afanasievna Bakatina; m. Ludmila Antonovna; two s.; ed. Novosibirsk Construction Eng. Inst., Acad. of Social Sciences; supervisor, chief engineer, dir. of construction works 1960–71; mem. CPSU 1964–91; chief engineer of housing construction combine, Kemerovo 1971–73; Second Sec., Kemerovo City Cttee. 1973–75; Sec., Kemerovo Dist. Cttee. 1977–83; inspector, CPSU Cen. Cttee. 1985; First Sec. Kirov Dist. Cttee. 1985–87; mem. CPSU Cen. Cttee. 1986–90; First Sec. Kemerovo Dist. Cttee. 1987–88; U.S.S.R. Minister of Internal Affairs 1988–90; mem. Presidential Council Jan.–Nov. 1990; Head KGB Aug.–Dec. 1991, Interrepublican Security Service 1991–92; Vice-Pres. and Dir. Dept. of Political and Int. Relations Reforma Fund 1992–. *Publication:* The Deliverance from the KGB 1992. *Leisure interests:* painting, reading, tennis. *Address:* Kotelnicheskaya nab. 17, 103240, Moscow, Russia (Office). *Telephone:* 915-96-13.

BAKER, Alan, PH.D., F.R.S.; British mathematician; b. 19 Aug. 1939, London; s. of Barnet and Bessie Baker; ed. Stratford Grammar School, University Coll., London, and Trinity Coll., Cambridge; Fellow, Trinity Coll., Cambridge 1964–, Research Fellow 1964–68, Dir. of Studies in Math. 1968–74; Prof. of Pure Math. Univ. of Cambridge 1974–; Visiting Prof. Stanford Univ. 1974 and other univs. in U.S.A.; Guest Prof. ETH Zürich 1989; Fields Medal 1970, Adams Prize 1972; Hon. Fellow, Indian Nat. Science Acad.; mem. European Acad. 1998; Dr. h.c. (Univ. Louis Pasteur, Strasbourg) 1998. *Publications:* Transcendental Number Theory 1975, A Concise Introduction to the Theory of Numbers 1984, New Advances in Transcendence Theory (ed.) 1988; papers in scientific journals. *Leisure interests:* travel, photography, theatre. *Address:* Department of Pure Mathematics and Mathematical Statistics, 16 Mill Lane, Cambridge, CB2 1SB; Trinity College, Cambridge, CB2 1TQ, England. *Telephone:* (01223) 337999; (01223) 338400.

BAKER, Anita, American singer; b. 26 Jan. 1958, Toledo; m. Walter Bridgeforth, Jr. 1988; one s.; mem. funk band, Chapter 8, Detroit, 1978–80; worked as receptionist, Detroit 1980–82; Ind. singer and songwriter 1982–. *Records:* (with Chapter 8) I Just Wanna Be Your Girl 1980; (solo albums) The Songstress 1983, Rapture 1986 (Grammy award for Best Rhythm and Blues Vocal Performance 1987), Giving You the Best That I Got 1988 (Grammy awards for Best Rhythm and Blues Song, Best Rhythm and Blues Performance by a Female Artist 1988, Best Album 1989), Compositions 1990 (Grammy for Best Rhythm and Blues Performance 1990), Rhythm of Love 1994. *Songs include:* No More Tears, Caught Up in the Rapture, Sweet Love, Been So Long; NAACP Image Award, Best Female Vocalist and Best Album of the Year. *Address:* All Baker's Music, 345 N. Maple Drive, Beverly Hills, CA 90210, U.S.A.

BAKER, Carroll; American actress; b. 28 May 1931, Johnstown, Pa.; d. of William W. Baker and Virginia Duffy; m. 1st Jack Garfein 1955 (divorced); one s. one d.; m. 2nd Donald Burton 1982; ed. St. Petersburg Jr. Coll., Florida; Broadway appearances include All Summer Long 1954, Come on Strong 1962; toured Vietnam with Bob Hope (q.v.) 1966; mem. Acad. of Motion Picture Arts and Sciences; several acting awards. *Films include:* Giant 1956, Baby Doll 1957, The Big Country 1958, But Not for Me 1959, The Miracle 1959, Bridge to the Sun 1960, Something Wild 1961, How the West Was Won 1962, Station Six Sahara 1962, Carpetbaggers 1963, Cheyenne Autumn 1963, Mr Moses 1964, Sylvia 1964, Harlow 1965, The Harem 1967, Honeymoon 1968, The Sweet Body of Deborah 1968, Captain Apache 1971, Bad 1977, Watcher in the Woods 1980, Red Monarch 1983, The Secret Diary of Sigmund Freud 1983, Star 80 1983, Ironweed 1987, Native Son, Red Monarch, Kindergarten Cop, Blonde Fist, Cybereden. *Publications:* Baby Doll (autobiog.), A Roman Tale.

BAKER, Howard Henry, Jr., LL.B.; American politician, government official and attorney; b. 15 Nov. 1925, Huntsville, Tenn.; s. of Howard H. Baker and Dora Ladd; m. 1st Joy Dirksen 1951 (died 1993); one s. one d.; m. 2nd Nancy Kassebaum 1996; ed. The McCallie School, Chattanooga, Univ. of the South, Sewanee, Tennessee, Tulane Univ. of New Orleans, and Univ. of Tennessee Coll. of Law; U.S. Naval Reserve 1943–46; partner in Baker, Worthington, Barnett & Crossley 1949–66; Senator from Tennessee 1967–85; Minority Leader in the Senate 1977–81, Majority Leader 1981–85; partner Baker, Worthington, Crossley, Stansberry & Woolf 1985–87, 1988–95, Baker, Donelson, Bearman & Caldwell, Washington 1995–; mem. law firm Vinson and Elkins 1985–87; White House Chief of Staff 1987–88; del. to UN 1976; mem. Council on Foreign Relations 1973–; Int. Councillor, Center for Strategic and Int. Studies 1991–; mem. Inst. of Foreign Affairs 1992–; mem. Bd. The Forum for Int. Policy 1993–, Pres.'s Foreign Intelligence Advisory Bd. 1985–87, 1988–90; Int. Advisory Bd. Barrick Gold Corp., Bd. of Regents Smithsonian Inst.; Chair. Cherokee Aviation, Newstar Inc.; mem. Bd. of Dirs. United Technologies Corpn., Pennzoil Co.; several Hon. degrees; American Soc. of Photographers Award 1993, Presidential Medal of Freedom 1984; Republican. *Publications:* No Margin for Error 1980, Howard Baker's Washington 1982, Big South Fork Country 1993. *Leisure interests:* photography, tennis. *Address:* c/o Baker, Donelson, Bearman & Caldwell, 801 Pennsylvania Avenue, N.W., Washington, DC 20004, U.S.A.

BAKER, James Addison, III, LL.B.; American government official and lawyer; b. 28 April 1930, Texas; s. of James A. Baker, Jr., and Bonner Means; m. Susan Garrett 1973; eight c.; ed. Princeton Univ. and Univ. of Texas Law School; served U.S. Marine Corps 1952–54; with law firm Andrews, Kurth, Campbell and Jones, Houston, Texas 1957–75; Under-Sec. of Commerce under Pres. Ford 1975; Nat. Chair. Ford's presidential campaign 1976; Campaign Dir. for George Bush in primary campaign 1980, later joined Reagan campaign; White House Chief of Staff and on Nat. Security Council 1981–85; Trustee, Woodrow Wilson Int. Center for Scholars, Smithsonian Inst. 1977–; Sec. of the Treasury 1985–88, Sec. of State 1989–92; White House Chief of Staff and Sr. Counsellor 1992–93; Gov. Rice Univ. 1993; Sr. Partner Baker & Botts 1993–; UN Special Envoy to resolve W. Sahara Dispute 1997–; Co-Chair. Campaign to elect Bush as Pres. *Publication:* The Politics of Diplomacy 1995. *Leisure interests:* jogging, tennis, hunting. *Address:* Baker & Botts, 1 Shell Plaza, 910 Louisiana, Houston, TX 77002, U.S.A.

BAKER, Dame Janet, C.H., D.B.E., F.R.S.A.; British mezzo-soprano; b. 21 Aug. 1933, Hatfield, Yorks.; d. of Robert Abbott and May (née Pollard) Baker; m. James Keith Shelley 1957; ed. York Coll. for Girls, Wintringham, Grimsby; Pres. London Sinfonia 1986–; Chancellor Univ. of York 1991–; Trustee Foundation for Sport and the Arts 1991–; Hon. Fellow, St. Anne's Coll., Oxford 1975, Downing Coll., Cambridge 1985; Hon. D.Mus. (Birmingham) 1968, (Leicester) 1974, (London) 1974, (Hull) 1975, (Oxford) 1975, (Leeds) 1980, (Lancaster) 1983, (York) 1984, (Cambridge) 1984; Hon. LL.D. (Aberdeen) 1980; Hon. D.Litt. (Bradford) 1983; Kathleen Ferrier Memorial Prize 1956, Queen's Prize 1959, Shakespeare Prize, F.v.S. Foundation of Hamburg, Grand Prix, French Nat. Acad. of Lyric Recordings 1975, Leonie Sonning Prize (Denmark) 1979; Gold Medal of Royal Philharmonic Soc. 1990; Commdr. Ordre des arts et des lettres. *Publication:* Full Circle (autobiog.) 1982. *Leisure interest:* reading. *Address:* c/o Transart (UK) Ltd., 8 Bristol Gardens, London, W9 2JG, England.

BAKER, Rt. Rev. John Austin, M.A., M. LITT., D.D.; British ecclesiastic; b. 11 Jan. 1928, Birmingham; s. of George Austin Baker and Grace Edna Baker; m. Gillian Mary Leach 1974; ed. Marlborough Coll., Oriel Coll., Oxford and Cuddesdon Theological Coll.; ordained 1954; Official Fellow, Chaplain and Lecturer in Divinity Corpus Christi Coll., Oxford 1959–73; Lecturer in Theology Brasenose and Lincoln Colls., Oxford; Dorrance Visiting Prof. Trinity Coll., Hartford, Conn. 1967; Canon of Westminster 1973–82; Visiting Prof., King's Coll., London 1974–76; Sub-Dean of Westminster and Lector Theologiae 1978–82; Rector of St. Margaret's, Westminster 1978–82; Chaplain to Speaker of House of Commons 1978–82; Bishop of Salisbury 1982–93; mem. Church of England Doctrine Comm. 1967–81, 1984–87, Chair. 1985–87; mem. Standing Comm., WCC Faith and Order Comm. 1984–87; Emer. Fellow, Corpus Christi Coll., Oxford 1977–. *Publications include:* The Foolishness of God 1970, Travels in Oudamovia 1976, The Whole Family of God 1981, The Faith of a Christian 1996; numerous theological articles and trans. *Leisure interests:* music, travel. *Address:* 4 Mede Villas, Kingsgate Road, Winchester, Hants., SO23 9QQ, England. *Telephone:* (01962) 861388.

BAKER, John Hamilton, Q.C., PH.D., LL.D., F.B.A., F.R.HIST.S.; British professor of English legal history; b. 10 April 1944, Sheffield; s. of Kenneth Lee Vincent Baker and Marjorie Bagshaw; m. Veronica Margaret Lloyd 1968 (divorced 1997); two d.; ed. King Edward VI Grammar School, Chelmsford and Univ. Coll. London; Asst. Lecturer in Law, Univ. Coll. London 1965–67, Lecturer 1967–70; Barrister Inner Temple, London 1966; Librarian, Squire Law Library, Cambridge 1971–73; Lecturer in Law, Cambridge Univ. 1973–83, Reader in English Legal History 1983–88, Prof. 1988–, Fellow of St. Catharine's Coll. 1971–; Visiting Prof. N.Y. Univ. School of Law 1988–; Visiting Fellow All Souls Coll. Oxford 1995; Jt. Literary Dir. Selden Soc. 1981–90, Literary Dir. 1991–; Fellow of Univ. Coll. London 1991; Hon. Bencher, Inner Temple, London 1988; Corresp. Fellow American Soc. for Legal History 1992; Hon. Fellow Soc. for Advanced Legal Studies 1998; Hon. LL.D. (Chicago) 1991; Yorke Prize (Cambridge) 1975; Ames Prize (Harvard Law School) 1985. *Publications:* An Introduction to English Legal History 1971, The Reports of Sir John Spelman 1977, Manual of Law French 1979, The Order of Serjeants at Law 1984, English Legal MSS in the U.S.A. (Part I) 1985, The Legal Profession and the Common Law 1986, Sources of English Legal History (with S. F. C. Milsom) 1986, The Notebook of Sir John Port 1987, Readings and Moots at the Inns of Court 1990, English Legal MSS in the U.S.A. (Part II) 1990, Cases from the Lost Notebooks of Sir James Dyer 1994, Spelman's Reading on Quo Warranto 1997, Monuments of Endless Labours 1998. *Address:* St. Catharine's College, Cambridge, CB2 1RL, England. *Telephone:* (01223) 338317.

BAKER, John William; British business executive; b. 5 Dec. 1937; s. of Reginald Baker and Wilhelmina Baker; m. 1st Pauline Moore 1962; one s.; m. 2nd Gillian Bullen; ed. Harrow Weald Co. Grammar School and Oriel Coll., Oxford; served army 1959–61, Ministry of Transport 1961–70, Dept. of Environment 1970–74; Deputy C.E.O. Housing Corpn. 1974–78; Sec. Cen. Electricity Generating Bd. 1979–80, Bd. mem. 1980–89, Jt. Man. Dir. 1986–89; C.E.O. Nat. Power PLC 1990–95, Chair. 1995–97; Dir. (non-exec.) Royal Insurance (now Royal and Sun Alliance Insurance Group) 1995–, Medeva PLC; European Advisory Bd. mem. Air Products Inc., Bankers Trust; Int. Business Council mem. A.P. Höller; Chair. Groundwork Foundation 1995–, World Energy Council Exec. Ass. 1995–, English Nat. Opera 1996–, Medeva PLC 1996–. *Leisure interests:* tennis, bridge, music, theatre. *Address:* Medeva PLC, 10 St. James's Street, London, SW1A 1EF, England. *Telephone:* 0171-839 3888.

BAKER, Baron (Life Peer) cr. 1997, of Dorking in the County of Surrey, **Kenneth (Wilfred) Baker,** P.C., C.H.; British politician; b. 3 Nov. 1934, Newport, Wales; s. of W. M. Baker; m. Mary Elizabeth Gray-Muir 1963; one s. two d.; ed. St. Paul's School and Magdalen Coll. Oxford; nat. service 1953–55; served Twickenham Borough Council 1960–62; as Conservative candidate contested Poplar 1964, Acton 1966; Conservative M.P. for Acton 1968–70, St. Marylebone 1970–83, Mole Valley 1983–97; Parl. Sec. Civil Service Dept. 1972–74, Parl. Pvt. Sec. to Leader of Opposition 1974–75; Minister of State and Minister for Information Tech., Dept. of Trade and Industry 1981–84; Sec. of State for the Environment 1985–86, for Educ. and Science 1986–89; Chancellor of the Duchy of Lancaster and Chair. Conservative Party 1989–90; Sec. of State for the Home Dept. 1990–92; mem. Public Accounts Cttee. 1969–70; mem. Exec. 1922 Cttee. 1978–81; Chair. Hansard Soc. 1978–81, MTT PLC 1996–97; Sec. Gen. UN Conf. of Parliamentarians on World Population and Devt. 1978; Dir. (non-exec.) Hanson 1992–, Millennium Chemicals Inc., Inter-Hopper Ltd.; Adviser to ICL, Cable and Wireless, The Blackstone Group. *Publications:* I Have No Gun But I Can Spit 1980, London Lines (Ed.) 1982, The Faber Book of English History in Verse 1988, Unauthorized Versions (Ed.) 1990, The Faber Book of Conservatism (Ed.) 1993, The Turbulent Years 1993, The Prime Ministers, An Irreverent Political History in Cartoons 1995, The Kings and Queens: An Irreverent Cartoon History of the British Monarchy, The Faber Book of War Poetry 1996. *Leisure interest:* collecting books, political cartoons. *Address:* House of Lords, Westminster, London, S.W.1, England.

BAKER, Paul T., PH.D.; American professor of anthropology; b. 28 Feb. 1927, Burlington, Ia.; s. of Palmer Ward Baker and Viola (née Thornell) Laughlin; m. Thelma M. Shoher 1949; one s. three d.; ed. Univ. of New Mexico and Harvard Univ.; Research Scientist, U.S. Army Climatic Research Lab. 1952–57; Asst. Prof. of Anthropology, Penn. State Univ. 1957–61, Assoc. Prof. 1961–64, Prof. 1965–81, Head Dept. of Anthropology 1980–85, Evan Pugh Prof. of Anthropology 1981–87, Evan Pugh Prof. Emer. 1987–; Vice-Pres. Int. Union of Anthropological and Ethnological Sciences 1988–93, Sr. Vice-Pres. 1993–98; Pres. Int. Asscn. of Human Biologists 1980–89, American Asscn. of Physical Anthropologists 1969–71, Human Biology Council 1974–77; Chair. U.S. Man and Biosphere Program 1983–85; mem. N.A.S.; Huxley Medal (Royal Anthropological Soc., London) 1982, Gorjanovic-Krambergeri Medal (Croatian Anthropological Soc.) 1985, Order of the Golden Star with Necklace (Yugoslavia) 1988. *Publications:* The Biology of Human Adaptability (Co-Ed.) 1966, Man in the Andes: A Multidisciplinary Study of High Altitude Quechua 1976, The Biology of High Altitude Peoples (Ed.) 1978, The Changing Samoans: Behavior and Health in Transition 1986, Human Biology (co-author) 1988. *Leisure interest:* sailing. *Address:* 47-450 Lulani Street, Kaneohe, HI 96744, U.S.A. *Telephone:* (808) 239 8228.

BAKER, Raymond, PH.D., F.R.S.; British research scientist; b. 1 Nov. 1936; s. of Alfred Baker and May Golds; m. Marian Slater 1960; one s. two d.; ed. Ilkeston Grammar School and Univ. of Leicester; Postdoctoral Fellow, Univ. of Calif. at Los Angeles 1962–64; lecturer in Organic Chem. Univ. of Southampton 1964–72, Sr. lecturer 1972–74, Reader 1974–77, Prof. 1977–84; Dir. Wolfson Unit of Chemical Entomology 1976–84; Dir. of Medicinal Chem. Merck Sharpe Dohme Research Labs. 1984–89, Exec. Dir. 1989–96; Chief Exec. Biotech. and Biological Sciences Research Council 1996–; Visiting Prof. Univ. of Edin. 1988; Hon. D.Sc. (Nottingham Trent) 1990, (Aston) 1997. *Publications:* Mechanism in Organic Chemistry 1971; articles in professional journals. *Leisure interests:* golf, gardening. *Address:* Biotechnology and Biological Research Council, Polaris House, North Star Avenue, Swindon, SN2 1UH, England.

BAKER, Richard Douglas James, O.B.E., M.A.; British broadcaster and author; b. 15 June 1925; s. of Albert Baker and Jane I. Baker; m. Margaret C. Martin 1961; two s.; ed. Kilburn Grammar School and Peterhouse, Cambridge; Royal Navy 1943–46; actor 1948; teacher 1949; BBC Third Programme announcer 1950–53; BBC TV newsreader 1954–82; commentator for State Occasion Outside Broadcasts 1967–70; TV introductions to Promenade concerts 1960–95; panellist, Face the Music (BBC 2) 1966–79; presenter, Omnibus (BBC TV) 1983; presenter of various shows on BBC radio including Start the Week 1970–77, These You Have Loved 1972–77, Baker's Dozen 1978–87, Mainly for Pleasure, 1986–92, Comparing Notes 1987–95; presenter Classic Countdown for Classic FM radio 1995–97, Sound Stories Radio 3 1998–; Dir. Youth and Music; Trustee D'Oyly Carte Opera Co., etc.; mem. Broadcasting Standards Council 1988–93; Hon. Fellow, London Coll. of Music; Hon. R.C.M.; Hon. LL.D. (Strathclyde) 1979, (Aberdeen) 1983; TV Newscaster of the Year (Radio Industries Club), 1972, 1974, 1979, BBC Radio Personality of the Year (Variety Club of G.B.) 1984, Sony Gold Award for Radio 1996. *Publications:* Here is the News (broadcasts) 1966, The Terror of Tobermory 1972, The Magic of Music 1975, Dry Ginger 1977, Richard Baker's Music Guide 1979, Mozart 1982, London, a theme with variations 1989, Richard Baker's Companion to Music 1993, Franz Schubert 1997. *Leisure interests:* gardening, the gramophone. *Address:* c/o API Personality Management Ltd., 141–143 Drury Lane, London, WC2B 5TB, England. *Telephone:* 0171-379 4625.

BAKER, Russell Wayne, D.LITT.; American journalist and author; b. 14 Aug. 1925, London Co., Va.; s. of Benjamin R. Baker and Lucy E. Robinson; m. Miriam E. Nash 1950; two s. one d.; ed. Johns Hopkins Univ.; served U.S.N.R. 1943–45; with Baltimore Sun 1947–64; mem. Washington Bureau, New York Times 1954–62, author-columnist, editorial page 1962–; mem. American Acad., Inst. of Arts and Letters; Pulitzer Prize for distinguished commentary 1979; Pulitzer Prize for Biography 1983 and other awards; Chair. Pulitzer Prize Bd. 1992–; several hon. degrees. *Publications:* American in Washington 1961, No Cause for Panic 1964, All Things Considered 1965, Our Next President 1968, Poor Russell's Almanac 1972, The Upside Down Man 1977, Home Again, Home Again 1979, So This is Depravity 1980, Growing Up 1982, The Rescue of Miss Yaskell and Other Pipe Dreams 1983, The Good Times (memories) 1989, There's a Country in My Cellar 1990, Russell Baker's Book of American Humor 1993. *Address:* New York Times, 229 West 43rd Street, New York, NY 10036, U.S.A. (Office).

BAKER, William Oliver, B.S., PH.D.; American research chemist; b. 15 July 1915, Chestertown, Md.; s. of Harold M. and Helen (Stokes) Baker; m. Frances Burrill 1941; one s. one d. (deceased); ed. Washington Coll., Maryland, and Princeton Univ.; with A T and T Bell Labs. 1939–80, in charge of polymer research and devt. 1948–51, Asst. Dir. of Chemical and Metallurgical Research 1951–54, Dir. of Research, Physical Sciences 1954–55, Vice-Pres. Research 1955–73, Pres. 1973–79, Chair. of the Bd. 1979–80; Chair. Rockefeller Univ. 1978–90, Chair. Emer. 1990–; Chair. Andrew W. Mellon Foundation 1975–90, Chair. Emer. 1990–; Dir. Health Effects Inst. 1980–95; mem. N.A.S., Nat. Acad. of Engineering, Inst. of Medicine, American Philosophical Soc., American Acad. of Arts and Sciences, Nat. Comm. on Jobs and Small Business 1985–87, Nat. Comm. on Role and Future of State Colls. and Univs. 1985–87, Comm. on Science and Tech. of New Jersey 1985–, Nat. Council on Science and Tech. Educ., A.A.A.S. 1985–; numerous awards include Perkin Medal 1963, Priestley Medal 1966, Edgar Marburg Award 1967, A.S.T.M. Award to Executives 1967, Industrial Research Institute Medal 1970, Frederik Philips Award (Inst. of Elec. and Electronics Engineers) 1972, Industrial Research Man of the Year Award 1973, James Madison Medal, Princeton Univ. 1975, Gold Medal, American Inst. of Chemists 1975, Mellon Inst. Award 1975, American Chemical Soc. Parsons Award 1976, Franklin Inst. Delmer S. Fahrney Medal 1977, J. Willard Gibbs Medal, American Chemical Soc. 1978, Madison Marshall Award 1980, von Hippel Award, Materials Research Soc. 1978; Bush Medal, Nat. Science Foundation 1982, Nat. Security Medal 1983, Nat. Medal of Tech. (co-recipient) 1985, Nat. Medal of Science 1988, N.J. Thomas Edison Award 1988; and numerous hon. degrees. *Publications include:* Rheology, Vol. III 1960, Listen to Leaders in Engineering 1965, Perspectives in Polymer Science 1966, Science: The Achievement and the Promise 1968, 1942–1967, Twenty-five Years at RCA Laboratories: Materials Science and Engineering in the United States 1970, The Technological Catch and Society 1975, Science and Technology in America—An Assessment 1977, Resources of Organic Matter for the Future—Perspectives and Recommendations 1978; contributions to many symposia and publs., about 95 research papers in journals and holder of 13 patents. *Leisure interest:* natural history. *Address:* AT & T Bell Laboratories, 600 Mountain Avenue, Providence, NJ 07974, U.S.A. (Office). *Telephone:* (908) 582-3423.

BAKER, Wilson, M.A., PH.D., D.SC., F.R.S., F.R.S.C; British professor of organic chemistry (retd.); b. 24 Jan. 1900, Runcorn; s. of Harry Baker and Mary Baker; m. Juliet Elizabeth Glaisyer 1927; one s. two d.; ed. Liverpool Coll. Upper School, Victoria Univ. of Manchester; Asst. Lecturer in Chem., Univ. of Manchester 1924–27; Tutor in Chem., Dalton Hall, Manchester 1926–27; Univ. Lecturer and Demonstrator in Chem., Univ. of Oxford 1937–44; Alfred Capper Pass Prof. of Organic Chem., Univ. of Bristol 1945–65, Dean of Faculty of Science 1948–51, Emer. Prof. 1965–; Vice-Pres. Chemical Soc. 1957–60. *Publications:* numerous papers on organic chem., dealing chiefly with synthesis of natural products, devt. of synthetical processes, compounds of abnormal aromatic type, organic inclusion compounds, and the preparation of large-ring compounds, and the chem. of penicillin, publ. mainly in Journal of the Chemical Soc.; 2nd edn. of Sidgwick's The Organic Chemistry of Nitrogen (with T.W.J. Taylor) 1937. *Leisure interests:* walking, gardening, music, mineralogy. *Address:* Lane's End, 54 Church Road, Winscombe, North Somerset, England. *Telephone:* (0193) 484 3112.

BAKEWELL, Joan Dawson, B.A.; British broadcaster and writer; b. 16 April; d. of John Rowlands and Rose Bland; m. 1st Michael Bakewell 1955 (dissolved 1972); one s. one d.; m. 2nd Jack Emery 1975; ed. Stockport High School for Girls and Newnham Coll., Cambridge; TV critic The Times 1978–81, columnist Sunday Times 1988–90; Assoc. Newnham Coll., Cambridge 1980–91, Assoc. Fellow 1984–87; Gov. B.F.I. 1994–. *TV includes:* Sunday Break 1962, Home at 4.30 (writer and producer) 1964, Meeting Point, The Second Sex 1964, Late Night Line Up 1965–72, the Youthful Eye 1968, Moviemakers at the National Film Theatre 1971, Film 72, Film 73, Holiday 74, 75, 76, 77, 78 (series), Reports Action (series) 1976–78, Arts UK: OK? 1980, Heart of the Matter 1988–. *Publications:* The New Priesthood: British Television Today (jtly.) 1970, A Fine and Private Place (jtly.) 1977, The Complete Traveller 1977, The Heart of the Heart of the Matter 1996; contribs. to journals. *Leisure interests:* theatre, talk, travel. *Address:* Knight Ayton Management, 10 Argyll Street, London, W1V 1AB, England.

BAKHMIN, Vyacheslav Ivanovich; Russian engineer; b. 25 Sept. 1947, Tver; m.; one s.; ed. Moscow Inst. of Econ. Statistics; researcher Inst. of Molecular Biology 1971–, Inst. of Electronic Man. Machines 1971–73; engineer Computation Cen. Inst. of Information and Electronics 1973–79; sr. engineer Inst. of Public Hygiene and Org. of Public Health 1979–80; mem. human rights movt., arrested and imprisoned 1980–84; engineer, head of group Research Centre at Inst. of Applied Math. 1990; Head Div. of Global Problems and Humanitarian Co-operation Russian Ministry of Foreign Affairs 1991–92; Dir. Dept of Int. Humanitarian and Cultural Co-operation 1992–95; Dir. Inst. Open Soc. (Soros Foundation) 1995–. *Address:* Open Society, B. Kozlovsky per. 13/7, Moscow, Russia (Office). *Telephone:* (095) 921 20 65 (Office).

BAKHT, Sikander; Indian politician; b. 24 Aug. 1918, Delhi; s. of Hafiz Mohd Yusuf and N. Yusuf; m. Raj Sharma 1952; two s.; ed. Delhi Univ.; mem. of Indian Nat. Congress until 1969; mem. All-India Congress Cttee. (Org.), also mem. Working Cttee. 1969–77; mem. Delhi Metropolitan Council for 10 years; detained for 18 months during emergency 1975–76; mem. for Chandni Chowk, Lok Sabha 1977; Minister of Works, Housing, Supply and Rehabilitation 1977–79, Urban Affairs, Employment and External Affairs May 1996, of Industry 1998–; mem. and Gen. Sec. Janata Party 1977; Gen. Sec. Bharatiya Janata Party (BJP) 1980–82, Vice-Pres. 1982–93; mem. for Madhya Pradesh, Rajya Sabha 1990–96, April 1996–; Leader of Opposition in Rajya Sabha 1992–96, 1996–98. *Leisure interests:* sports, music. *Address:* 25 Tughlak Road, New Delhi 110011, India (Home). *Telephone:* 3793485 (Home). *Fax:* 011-3012376 (Home).

BAKLANOV, Grigoriy Yakovlevich; Russian author; b. 11 Nov. 1923, Voronezh; s. of Jakov Friedman and Ida Kantor; m. Elga Sergeeva 1953; one s. one d.; ed. Gorky Inst. of Literature, Moscow; served as soldier and officer 1941–45; mem. CPSU 1942–91; Ed.-in-Chief Znamya 1986–93; first works published 1950; U.S.S.R. State Prize 1982. *Publications include:* In Snegiri 1954, Nine Days 1958, The Foothold 1959, The Dead Are Not Ashamed 1961, July 41 1964, Friends 1975, Forever Nineteen 1980, The Youngest of the Brothers 1981, Our Man 1990, Time to Gather Stones 1989, Once it was the Month of May (scenario) 1990, The Moment Between the Past and the Future 1990, Come through the Narrow Gates 1993, Short Stories 1994, Kondratiy 1995, Short Stories 1996, And then the Marauders Come (novel) 1996, Life Granted Twice (memoirs). *Leisure interest:* gardening. *Address:* Lomonosovsky Prospekt 19, Apt. 82, 117311 Moscow, Russia. *Telephone:* 930-12-90. *Telephone and Fax:* 334-61-36.

BAKLANOV, Oleg Dmitrievich, B.ENG.; Russian politician; b. 17 March 1932, Kharkov; ed. All-Union Inst. of Energetics; engineer, sr. engineer, then dir. Kharkov technical appliances plant 1950–55; mem. CPSU 1953–91; gen. dir. of production unit 1975–76; Deputy Minister of Gen. Machine Construction (with special responsibility for the defence industry) in U.S.S.R. 1981–83, First Deputy Minister 1981–83, Minister 1983–88; mem. CPSU Cen. Cttee. 1986–91; Sec. Political Bureau 1988–91; Deputy to Supreme Soviet 1987–89; U.S.S.R. People's Deputy 1989–91; Hero of Socialist Labour 1976, Lenin Prize 1982; arrested 22 Aug. 1991 for involvement in failed coup d'état, on trial 1993–94, released on amnesty 1994; active in Communist movt.; mem. Political Council, Russian Public Union 1996–. *Address:* ROS, Szedny Tishinski Pereulok 10, Apt. 9, 123557 Moscow, Russia (Office). *Telephone:* 253-18-98.

BAKR, Rashid El Tahir; Sudanese politician; b. 1930, Karkoj; ed. Univ. of Khartoum; fmr. advocate; imprisoned for opposition to the regime of Gen. Ibrahim Abboud 1958–64; Minister of Animal Resources and Justice 1965; Amb. to Libya 1972–74; apptd. mem. Political Bureau, Sudanese Socialist Union (SSU) and Sec. Farmers' Union in the SSU 1972; Asst. Sec.-Gen. Sectoral Orgs., SSU 1974; Speaker, People's Nat. Assembly 1974–76, 1980–81; Second Vice-Pres. of Sudan 1976–80; Prime Minister 1976–77; Minister of Foreign Affairs 1977–80; Chair. OAU Council of Ministers 1978–79; Attorney-Gen. 1983–84; mem. group of 41 set up to revitalize policy-making organs of SSU Jan. 1982.

BAKR AL-HAKIM, Hojatoleslam Mohammed; Iraqi cleric and politician; s. of Grand Ayatollah Mohsen al-Hakim; ed. theological studies in Najaf; imprisoned for political activities 1977; escaped to Syria and then to Iran 1980; built up opposition movt. during Iran–Iraq War 1980–88; subsequently set up Supreme Ass. of Islamic Revolution in Iraq (Sairi), currently allied with other Iraqi opposition groups.

BALAGUER RICARDO, Joaquín; Dominican diplomatist and politician; b. 1 Sept. 1907, Villa Bisonó; s. of Joaquín Balaguer Lespier and Carmen Celia Ricardo Vda. Balaguer; ed. Univ. de Santo Domingo and Univ. de Paris à la Sorbonne; served Madrid 1932–35; Under-Sec. of Foreign Affairs 1936–40; Minister to Colombia 1940–46; Alt. Rep. to UN 1947; Minister of Foreign Affairs 1954–55, of Educ. and Arts 1955–57; Vice-Pres. of Dominican Repub. 1957–60, Pres. of the Dominican Repub. 1960, 1966–78, 1986–96; voluntary exile in U.S.A. 1962–65; Founder-Leader Partido Reformista Social Cristiano 1964–. *Address:* c/o PRSC, Avenida San Cristóbal, Ensanche La Fe, Apdo 1332, Santo Domingo, D.N., Dominican Republic.

BĂLĂIŢĂ, George; Romanian writer; b. 17 April 1935, Bacău; s. of Gheorghe Bălăiţă and Constantina Popa Bălăiţă; m. Lucia Gavril 1959; one s.; ed. Coll. of Philology; Ed. of cultural review Ateneu (Bacău) 1964–78; Dir. Cartea Românească publishing house, Bucharest 1982–90, Ed.-in-Chief Arc 1991–97; Vice-Pres. of the Romanian Writers' Union; Prize of the Romanian Acad. 1978; Prize of the Romanian Writers' Union 1975; Fulbright stipendiate 1980. *Major works:* novels: Lumea în două zile (The World in Two Days) 1975, Ucenicul neascultător (The Disobedient Apprentice) 1978; essays: A Provincial's Nights 1984, Gulliver in No Man's Land (essays) 1994. *Address:* 24-26 Bd. Lascăr Catargiu, Bucharest, Romania. *Telephone:* 650.48.59.

BALASSA, Iván; Hungarian ethnographer; b. 5 Oct. 1917, Báránd; s. of József Balassa and Edit Szabó; m. Éva Márton 1942; one s. one d.; ed. Univ. of Arts and Sciences, Debrecen; Scientific Adviser Hungarian Agricultural Museum; Hon. Pres. István Györffy Ethnographical Soc., János Kriza Ethnographical Soc. (Cluj-Kolozsvár), Culture Soc. of Bodrogköz (Kráľovský Chlmec Slovakia-Sárospatak); Titular Univ. Prof; hon. mem. Royal Acad. of Sciences of Denmark 1975–; mem. Royal Gustavus Adolphus Acad. of Sweden 1983–; holder of Herder Prize 1980. *Publications:* A magyar kukorica (The maize of Hungary) 1960, Karcsai mondák (Folk Tales of Karcsa) 1963, Földmüvelés a Hegyközben (Farming in the Hegyköz) 1964, Az eke és a szántás története Magyarországon (The History of the Plough and Ploughing in Hungary) 1973, Jankó János 1975, Magyar néprajz—in co-authorship with Gyula Ortutay (Hungarian Ethnography) 1979, Az arató-munkások Magyarországon 1848–1944 (Hired harvesters in Hungary) 1985, Hungarian Ethnography and Folklore 1985, Báránd története és néprajza (History and Ethnography of the Village of Báránd) 1985, A magyar parasztemetők (Hungarian Peasant Cemeteries) 1989, A szomszédos országok magyarjainak néprajza (Ethnography of Hungarians in the Neighbouring Countries) 1989, Csűry Bálint 1988, A magyar gabonatermeles néprajza (Ethnography of Hungarian Corn Production) 1990, Tokaj-Hegyalja szőleje és bora (Grapes and Wines of Tokaj-Hegyalja) 1991, A Székelyföldi Erdővidék temetői (Cemeteries of Székelyföld Erdővidék in Eastern Transylvania) 1992, Sárospatak történeti helyrajza. 16-20. század (Topography of the Town Sárospatak, 16th–20th centuries) 1994, Szabó T. Attila (1906–1987). Erdély nagy nyelvtudósa (The Most Important Linguist of Transylvania) 1996, Sárospatak határának helynevei (Geographical Names of the Outskirts of Sárospatak, with Daniel Kováts) 1997; about 760 studies in Hungarian and foreign journals. *Leisure interest:* gardening. *Address:* H-1015 Budapest, Batthyány utca 3, Hungary. *Telephone:* 201-72-61.

BALASSA, Sándor; Hungarian composer; b. 20 Jan. 1935, Budapest; s. of János Balassa and Eszter Bora; m. Marianna Orosz 1994; one s. one d.; ed. Budapest Conservatory and Music Acad. of Budapest; began career as a mechanic; entered Budapest Conservatory at age 17; studied composition under Endre Szervánszky at Budapest Music Acad., obtained diploma 1965; music dir. Hungarian Radio 1964–80; Teacher of instrumentation, Music. Acad. Budapest 1981; Erkel Prize 1972, Critics' Prize (Hungarian Radio) 1972, 1974, Listeners' Prize (Hungarian Radio) 1976, Distinction for Best Work of the Year, Paris Int. Tribune of Composers 1972, Merited Artist of the Hungarian People's Repub. 1978, Kossuth Prize 1983, Bartók-Pásztory Prize 1988. *Compositions include:* vocal: Legenda 1967, Antinomia 1968, Requiem for Lajos Kassák 1969, Cantata Y 1970, Motetta 1973, Tresses 1979, Kyrie for female choir 1981, The Third Planet, opera-cantata 1986, Oldott kéve for mixed choir 1992, Kelet népe for children's choir 1992, Damjanich's prayer for mixed choir 1993, Chant of Orphans 1995, Capriccio for Female Choir 1996, Spring Song, Autumn Song (for female choir) 1997, Woodcutter (for male choir) 1998; opera: Az ajtón kivül (The Man Outside) 1976, Karl and Anna 1992; instrumental: Dimensioni 1966, Quartetto per percussioni 1969, Xenia 1970, Tabulae 1972, The Last Shepherd 1978, Quintet for Brass 1979, The Flowers of Hajta 1984, Sonatina for harp 1993, Divertimento for two cimbaloms 1992, Little Garland (trio for flute, viola and harp) 1994, Five Brothers (piano) 1994, Bells of Nyirbátor (for twelve brass instruments) 1996, Sonatina for Piano 1996, Preludes and Fantasia for Organ 1996, Duets (for flute and harp) 1998; orchestral: Lupercalia 1971, Iris 1972, Chant of Glarus 1978, The Island of Everlasting Youth 1979, Calls and Cries 1980, A Daydreamer's Diary 1983, Three Phantasias 1984, Little Grape and Little Fish 1987, Tündér Ilona 1992, Prince Csaba for string orchestra 1993, Bölcske Concerto for string orchestra 1993, Dances of Mucsa 1994, Jánosnapi muzsika (solo violin) 1994, Vonósnégyes (string quartet) 1995, Sons of the Sun 1995, Four Portraits 1996, Number 301 Parcel 1997, Pécs Concerto 1998, Hungarian Coronation Music 1998. *Leisure interest:* nature. *Address:* str. 18 Sümegvár, 1118 Budapest, Hungary. *Telephone:* (1) 319-7049.

BALASURIYA, Stanislaus Tissa, B.A., S.T.L.; Sri Lankan ecclesiastic; b. 29 Aug. 1924, Kahatagasdigiliya; s. of William Balasuriya and Victoria Balasuriya; ed. Univ. of Ceylon, Gregorian Univ., Rome, Oxford Univ., Maris Stella Coll., Negombo, St. Patrick's Coll., Jaffna and St. Joseph's Coll., Colombo; helped found Aquinas Univ. with Fr. Peter Pillai Jan. 1954, Rector 1964–71; f. Centre for Soc. and Religion, Colombo Aug. 1971, Dir. 1971–, Citizens Cttee. for Nat. Harmony in Sri Lanka 1977–91; Visiting Prof. of Faith and Social Justice, Faculty of Theology, Univ. of Ottawa 1993–94; Ed. Logos, Quest, Voices of the Third World, Social Justice, Sadharanaya; Khan Memorial Gold Medal for Econs. *Publications:* Jesus Christ and Human Liberation, Eucharist & Human Liberation, Catastrophe July '83, Planetary Theology, Mary and Human Liberation, Liberation of the Affluent, Humanization Europe, Indicators of Social Justice, Third World Theology of Religious Life, Right Relationships: Re-rooting of Christian Theology 1991, Doing Marian Theology in Sri Lanka. *Leisure interests:* writing, organic farming. *Address:* Centre for Society and Religion, 281 Deans Road, Colombo 10, Sri Lanka. *Telephone:* 695425.

BALAYAN, Roman Gurgenovich; Armenian film director; b. 15 April 1941, Nagorno-Karabak Autonomous Region; m. Natalia Balayan; two s.; ed. Kiev Theatre Inst., U.S.S.R.; State Prize 1987. *Films include:* The Romashkin Effect, 1973, Kashtanka 1976, Biryuk (Morose) 1978, The Kiss 1983, Dream and Waking Flights 1983, Keep Me Safe, My Talisman 1985, Police Spy 1988, Lady Macbeth of Mtcentk 1989; TV Who's Afraid of Virginia Woolf 1992, The Tale of the First Love 1995. *Address:* Leningradsky Prosp. 33, Apt. 70, 125212 Moscow, Russia. *Telephone:* 159-99-74.

BALAYÉ, Simone, D. ÈS L.; French librarian; b. 14 March 1925, Versailles; d. of Fernand Balayé and Denise Fromont; ed. Lycée Victor Duruy, Paris, Jeanne d'Arc, Orléans, Lycée Camille Sée, Paris and Univ. of Paris (Sorbonne); Curator, Bibliothèque Nat., Paris 1950–90; Visiting Prof. Univ. of Ottawa, Canada 1970, Hebrew Univ., Jerusalem, Israel 1971; Zaharoff lecture, Oxford Univ., U.K. 1995; Sec. then Pres. Soc. des études staëliennes 1984–; Vice-Pres. Soc. française d'études sur le 18ème siècle, Paris 1985–97; Bd. mem. Soc. des études romantiques, Paris; mem. Bd. of Dirs., Asscn. Benjamin Constant, Lausanne, numerous other literary cttees.; corresp. mem. Soc. d'histoire et d'archéologie de Genève; Chevalier des arts et des lettres, des palmes académiques. *Publications include:* Lettres de Madame de Staël à Ribbing 1960, Les Carnets de voyages de Madame de Staël, contribution à la genèse de ses oeuvres (Broquette-Gonin Prize, Acad. Française) 1971, Madame de Staël: Lumières et liberté (Alfred Née Prize, Acad. Française) 1979, La Bibliothèque nationale des origines à 1800, (Roland de Jouvenel Prize, Acad. Française 1990) 1988, Madame de Staël: écrire, lutter, vivre 1994, Dix années d'exil de Mme. de Staël 1996; numerous articles in literary journals and conf. papers. *Address:* 44 rue Vaneau, 75007 Paris, 7ème, France. *Telephone:* (1) 45.49.30.03.

BALAZS, Artur Krzysztof, M.ENG.; Polish politician, trade union leader and farmer; b. 3 Jan. 1952, Ełk; s. of Adam Balazs and Irena Balazs; m. Jolanta Balazs 1973; three d.; ed. Agricultural Acad., Szczecin; worked in agric. service of Communal Office, Kołczewo 1974–76; own farm in Łuskowo 1976–; mem. Polish United Workers' Party (PZPR) 1975–81; active in Agric. Solidarity Independent Self-governing Trade Union 1980–81, participant 1st Nat. Congress of Solidarity of Pvt. Farmers Trade Union, Warsaw Dec. 1980; participant agric. strikes and co-signatory agreements in Ustrzyki, Rzeszów and Bydgoszcz 1981; mem. All-Poland Founding Cttee. of Solidarity of Private Farmers Trade Union, mem. Comm. for Realization of Rzeszów-Ustrzyki Agreements; interned Dec. 1981–Dec. 1982; mem. Presidium of Solidarity Provisional Nat. Council of Farmers 1987; mem. Inter-factory Strike Cttee. Szczecin Aug. 1988; mem. Civic Cttee. attached to Lech Wałęsa, Chair. of Solidarity Trade Union 1988–91; participant Round Table debates, mem. group for union pluralism and team for agric. matters Feb.–April 1989; mem. Episcopate Comm. for the Pastoral Care of Farmers 1989–; Deputy to Sejm (Parl.) 1989–93, 1997–; mem. Solidarity Election Action Parl. Club 1997–; Chair. Sejm Cttee. for Admin. and Internal Affairs 1992–93; Vice-Chair. Christian Peasant Party 1990–94, 1995–97, Chair. 1994–95; Vice-Chair. Conservative Peasant Party (SKL) 1997–; Chair. European Fund for the Devt. of Polish Villages 1990–; Minister, mem. Council of Ministers 1989–90, Minister without Portfolio Dec. 1991–92; mem. Senate 1995–97; mem. Cttee. for Agric. *Leisure interests:* press, politics. *Address:* Sejm RP, ul. Wiejska 4/6/8, 00-902 Warsaw, Poland. *Telephone:* (22) 694 1934.

BALÁZS, Éva H., PH.D.; Hungarian professor of modern history; b. 20 Dec. 1915, Székelyudvarhely; d. of Sándor Balázs and Judit Beczássy; m. Lajos Hunyady 1942; one s.; ed. Univ. of Budapest; Asst. Inst. of Political Science, Ministry of Foreign Affairs 1939–41; lecturer, Dept. of Medieval History, Univ. of Budapest 1945–54; Head, Dept. of History, Coll. of Pedagogy 1947; responsible for historians' affairs, Office of Prime Minister 1947–49; Fellow, Inst. of History, Hungarian Acad. of Sciences, 1949–61; lecturer, Dept. of Medieval and Modern World History, Univ. of Budapest 1961–77, Prof. 1978–87, Prof. Emer. 1987–, Head of Dept. 1982–87; Pres. jt. cttee. of French and Hungarian historians; mem. History Cttee. Hungarian Acad. of Sciences and Comm. of Austrian-Hungarian Historians; First Prize of Renovanda Hungariae Cultura Foundation 1996; Officier des Palmes académiques françaises, Laureate of Hungarian Acad., Officer's Cross of the Repub. of Hungary. *Publications:* The Age of Enlightenment 1964, Gergely Berzeviczy, the Reform Politician 1967, Paysannerie française-paysannerie hongroise (ed. and contrib.) 1973, Beförderer der Aufklärung in Mittel-und Osteuropa 1979, Noblesse 1981, Intellectuels 1985, Absolutisme Eclairé 1985, Vienna and Pest-Buda 1765–1800 1988, Magyarország történet 1989, Hungary and the Habsburgs, 1765–1800, Freemasons' Documents from 18th-century Habsburg Monarchy. *Leisure interests:* music, swimming. *Address:* Eötvös Egyetem, BTK, Piarista köz, Budapest, H-1364 (Office); 11 Érmelléki u. 7, Budapest, H-1026, Hungary (Home). *Telephone:* (1) 1353-986.

BALCEROWICZ, Leszek, D.ECON.SC., M.B.A.; Polish politician and economist; b. 19 Jan. 1947, Lipno; s. of Wacław Balcerowicz and Barbara Balcerowicz; m. 1977; two s. one d.; ed. Main School of Planning and Statistics, Warsaw, St. John's Univ., New York; staff Main School of Planning and Statistics, Warsaw 1970–, Inst. of Int. Econ. Relations 1970–80; Head, Research Team attached to Econ. Devt. Inst. 1978–, Scientific Sec. Econ. Devt. Inst. 1980–; Prof. of Comparative Int. Studies, Warsaw School of Econs. 1992–; mem. Polish United Workers' Party (PZPR) 1969–81; consultant, Network of Solidarity Independent Self-governing Trade Union 1981; Deputy Chair. Council of Ministers and Minister of Finance 1989–91, 1997–; Chair. Freedom Union (UW) 1994; Deputy to Sejm (Parl.) 1997–; mem. Council of Econ. Advisers to Pres. Wałesa; Head Int. for Comparative Int. Studies, Warsaw School of Econs.; Chair. Centre for Social and Econ. Research, Warsaw, Programme Bd., Foundation for Econ. Educ.; mem. Polish Econ. Soc. 1970–, Vice-Chair. Gen. Bd. 1981–82; mem. Polish Sociological Soc. 1983–, European Econ. Assen.; mem. Warsaw Civic Cttee. Solidarity 1989; Awards of Minister of Science, Higher Educ. and Tech. 1978, 1980, 1981, Ludwig Erhard Prize 1992. *Publications:* numerous scientific works on int. econ. relations and problems of econ. systems. *Leisure interests:* history, sport. *Address:* Ministerswo Finansów, ul. Swiętokrzysta 12, 00-916 Warsaw, Poland. *Telephone:* (22) 694 5555.

BALDERSTONE, Sir James Schofield; Australian company director (retd.) and grazier; b. 2 May 1921, Melbourne; s. of late J. S. Balderstone; m. Mary Tyree 1946; two s. two d.; ed. Scotch Coll., Melbourne; Gen. Man. and Dir. for Australia, Thomas Borthwick and Sons (Australia) 1953–67; Dir. Victorian Branch Bd., Australian Mutual Provident Soc. 1979–93, Deputy Chair. 1977–84, Chair. 1990–93, mem., Prin. Bd. 1979–93; Dir. Victoria State Bd. of Advice, Australian Mutual Provident Soc. 1962–89, Deputy Chair. 1977–89, Chair. 1984–89; Man. Dir. Stanbroke Pastoral Co. Pty. Ltd. 1964–81, Chair. 1982–93; Chair. Squatting Investment Co. 1966–73; Dir. Commercial Bank of Australia (merged to become Westpac Banking Corpn.) 1970–82, Dir., Deputy Chair. 1992–93; Dir. The Broken Hill Proprietary Co. Ltd. 1971–89, Chair. 1984–89; Dir. Woodside Petroleum Ltd. 1976–83, N.W. Shelf Devt. 1976–83, ICI Australia Ltd. 1981–84, Chase-AMP Bank 1985–91, Chair. 1990–91; Chair. Commonwealth Govt. Policy Discussion Group on Agric. 1981–82; Pres. Inst. of Public Affairs (Vic.) 1981–84; Chair. Scotch Coll. 1991–95; mem. Council of the Australian War Memorial 1994–, Dir. Council Australian War Memorial Foundation 1996–; Commdr.'s Cross of Order of Merit (Germany) 1991. *Leisure interests:* farming, reading, watching sport. *Address:* 115 Mont Albert Road, Canterbury, Vic. 3126, Australia (Home). *Telephone:* 98363137 (Home).

BALDESCHWIELER, John Dickson, PH.D.; American professor of chemistry; b. 14 Nov. 1933, Elizabeth, N.J.; s. of Emile L. Baldeschwieler and Isobel M. Dickson; m. Marlene Konnar 1991; two s. one d. from previous m.; ed. Cornell Univ. and Univ. of Calif., Berkeley; Asst. Prof. Harvard Univ. 1962–65; Assoc. Prof. Stanford Univ. 1965–67, Prof. of Chem. 1967–73; Deputy Dir. Office of Science and Tech. Exec. Office of Pres. of U.S.A. 1971–73; Prof. of Chem. Calif. Inst. of Tech. 1973–, Chair. Div. of Chem. and Chem. Eng. 1973–78; Chair. Bd. of Dirs. Vestar Research Inc. 1981–; mem. numerous advisory cttees. and comms.; Alfred P. Sloan Foundation Fellow 1962–65; American Chem. Soc. Award in Pure Chem. 1967. *Publications:* numerous articles in professional journals. *Leisure interests:* hiking, skiing, photography, music, travel. *Address:* Division of Chemistry and Chemical Engineering, California Institute of Technology, 127-72 Pasadena, CA 91125 (Office); P.O. Box 50065, Pasadena, CA 91115-0065, U.S.A. (Home).

BALDIN, Aleksandr Mikhailovich, DR.SC.; Russian physicist; b. 26 Feb. 1926, Moscow; s. of Mikhail Aleksandrovich Baldin and Ol'ga Lukyanovna Baldina; m. 1st 1954 (died 1962); m. 2nd 1977; one s. one d.; ed. Moscow Engineering-Physical Inst.; on staff of U.S.S.R. Acad. of Sciences Lebedev Physics Inst. 1949–68; Asst. Prof. at Moscow Univ. 1955–60, Prof. 1965; mem. of staff of Jt. Inst. for Nuclear Research (JINR), Dubna, 1961–; Dir. of Lab. of High Energy Physics of JINR 1968–; Prof. Moscow Physical Eng. Inst. 1971–; Chair. of Editorial Bd. of JINR Rapid Communications; Chair. Scientific Council on Physics of Electromagnetic Interactions, Russian Acad. of Sciences; Ed.-in-Chief Physics of Elementary Particles and Atomic Nuclei; State Prize 1973; mem. of U.S.S.R. (now Russian) Acad. of Sciences 1981–, Lenin Prize 1988, Veksler Prize 1997. *Leisure interest:* mountaineering. *Address:* Joint Institute for Nuclear Research, 141980 Dubna, Moscow District, Russia. *Telephone:* (095) 923-10-28, 926-22-76 (Office); (095) 926-22-12 (Home). *Fax:* (095) 975-23-81.

BALDOCK, Brian Ford, C.B.E., F.R.S.A., C.INST.M.; British business executive; b. 10 June 1934; s. of Ernest A. Baldock and Florence F. Baldock; m. 1st Mary Bartolo 1956 (divorced 1966); two s.; m. 2nd Carole Mason 1968; one s.; ed. Clapham Coll. London; army officer 1952–55; Procter & Gamble 1956–61; Ted Bates Inc. 1961–63; Rank Org. 1963–66; Smith & Nephew 1966–75; Revlon Inc. 1975–78; Imperial Group 1978–86; Dir. Guinness PLC 1986–96, Group Man. Dir. 1989–96, Deputy Chair. 1992–96; Chair. Portman Group 1989–96; Dir. PIC Int. (fmrly. Dalgety) 1992–, Marks & Spencer 1996–, WMC Communications 1996–, Cornhill Insurance 1996–. *Leisure interests:* theatre, opera, cricket. *Address:* Michael House, Baker Street, London, W1A 1DN, England. *Telephone:* 0171-935 4422.

BALDWIN, Alec (Alexander Rae Baldwin III); American actor, b. 3 April 1958, Masapequa, N.Y.; s. of Alexander Rae Baldwin, Jr. and Carol (née Martineau) Baldwin; m. Kim Basinger (q.v.) 1993; one d.; ed. George Washington and New York Univs., Lee Strasberg Theater Inst.; also studied with Mira Rostova and Elaine Aiken; mem. Screen Actor's Guild, American Fed. of TV and Radio Artists, Actors Equity Assen.; Theatre World Award (for Loot) 1986. *Stage appearances include:* Loot 1986, Serious Money 1988, Prelude to a Kiss 1990, A Streetcar Named Desire 1992. *Television appearances include:* The Doctors 1980–82, Cutter to Houston 1982, Knot's Landing 1984–85, Love on the Run 1985, A Dress Gray 1986, The Alamo: 13 Days to Glory 1986, Sweet Revenge 1990. *Film appearances include:* Forever Lulu 1987, She's Having a Baby 1987, Beetlejuice 1988, Married to the Mob 1988, Talk Radio 1988, Working Girl 1988, Great Balls of Fire 1989, The Hunt for Red October 1990, Miami Blues 1990, Alice 1990, The Marrying Man 1991, Prelude to a Kiss 1992, Glengarry Glen Ross 1992, Malice 1993, The Getaway 1994, The Shadow 1994, Heaven's Prisoners 1995, Looking for Richard 1996, The Juror 1996, Ghosts of Mississippi 1996, Bookworm 1997, The Edge 1997, Thick as Thieves 1998, Outside Providence 1998, Mercury Rising 1998 (also producer), The Confession 1999.

BALDWIN, Sir Jack Edward, Kt., PH.D., F.R.S.; British professor of chemistry; b. 8 Aug. 1938, London; s. of Frederick C. Baldwin and Olive F. Headland; m. Christine L. Franchi 1977; ed. Lewes County Grammar School and Imperial Coll., London; Asst. Lecturer in Chem., Imperial Coll. 1963, Lecturer 1966; Asst. Prof. Penn. State Univ. 1967, Assoc. Prof. 1969; Assoc. Prof. M.I.T. 1970, Prof. 1972; Daniell Prof. of Chem. King's Coll., London 1972; Prof. of Chem. M.I.T. 1972–78; Waynflete Prof. of Chem., Univ. of Oxford 1978–, Fellow Magdalen Coll. 1978–; Dir. Oxford Centre for Molecular Studies; Davy Medal, Royal Soc. 1993; Hon. D.Sc. (Warwick) 1988, (Strathclyde); Corday Morgan Medal, Chem. Soc. 1975; Karrer Medal, Univ. of Zürich 1984; Dr. P. Janssen Prize (Belgium) 1988; Davy Medal (Royal Soc.) 1994. *Publications:* papers in organic and biorganic chem. in Journal of American Chem. Soc. and Journal of Chem. Soc. *Address:* Dyson Perrins Laboratory, University of Oxford, South Parks Road, Oxford, OX1 3QY, England. *Telephone:* (01865) 557809.

BALDWIN, Peter, B.E.E., B.A.; Australian politician; b. 12 April 1951, Aldershot, U.K.; ed. Univ. of Sydney, Macquarie Univ.; fmr. engineer and computer programmer; mem. N.S.W. State Parl. (Upper House) 1976–82; Australian Labor Party mem. for Sydney, House of Reps. 1983–; Minister for Higher Educ. and Employment Services and Minister Assisting Treasurer 1990–93; Minister for Social Security 1993–96; Shadow Minister for Finance 1997–; mem. Parl. Cttee. on Foreign Affairs, Defence and Trade 1987–90, House of Reps. Standing Cttee. on Industry, Science and Tech. 1987–90. *Address:* Level 3, 10 Mallet Street, Camperdown, NSW 2050, Australia.

BALDWIN, Robert Roy, PH.D.; British university professor (retd.); b. 9 Feb. 1920, Widnes; m. Valerie Aucutt 1947; two d.; ed. Wallasey Grammar School and Emmanuel Coll., Cambridge; Physical Chemist, Thornton Research Centre, Shell Research Ltd 1941–47; Lecturer in Physical Chem., Hull Univ. 1947–57, Sr. Lecturer 1957–63, Reader 1963–66, Prof. 1966–84, Head, Chem. Dept. 1982–84, Prof. Emer. 1984–; Royal Chemical Soc. 1985 Award for "Reaction Kinetics." *Publications:* over 100 scientific research papers on combustion. *Leisure interests:* fell walking, music, photography, sport. *Address:* Chemistry Department, University of Hull, Cottingham Road, Hull, North Humberside, HU6 7RX, England. *Telephone:* 01482-444559.

BALESTRE, Jean-Marie; French editor and press executive; b. 9 April 1921, Saint-Rémy-de-Provence (Bouches-du-Rhône); s. of Joseph Balestre and Joséphine Bayol; ed. Lycée Charlemagne and Faculté de Droit, Paris; sub-ed., Sport et Santé 1937, L'Auto and Droit de Vivre 1938–40; Dir. Int. Gen. Presse 1947; Co-founder and Assoc. L'Auto Journal 1950, Dir.-Gen. 1952–71; Dir. Semaine du Monde 1953; Asst. Dir.-Gen. Soc. Edn. Diffusion

Presse 1970–; Dir. Presses Modernes de France, La Liberté de Seine-et-Marne, Centre-Presse, Oise-Matin, Edns. Professionnelles de France, Brunel Edns., Edns. Sport Auto, France Antilles; Dir. Robert Hersant press group 1969–; Dir. Agence Générale de Presse et d'Information (Hersant group) 1976–77; Treas. Office de Justification de la Diffusion de la Presse 1964–; Hon. Pres. Féd. Nat. de la Presse Hebdomadaire et Périodique; Pres. Féd. Française du Sport Automobile 1973–96, World Fed. of Automobile Clubs 1985–, Int. Fed. of Motor Sport 1978–96 (Hon. Pres. 1996–), Int. Automobile Fed. 1985–; Chevalier, Légion d'honneur, Officier, Ordre Nat. du Mérite, Médaille de la déportation pour faits de Résistance; Licence d'Or, Féd. Française du Sport Automobile 1976, Personnalité de l'année 1988. *Address:* c/o Fédération Française du Sport Automobile, 17–21 avenue du Général Mangin, 75781 Paris cedex 16, France.

BALGIMBAYEV, Nurlan Utebovich; Kazakhstan politician; b. 20 Nov. 1947; ed. Kazakh Polytech. Inst., Massachusetts Univ. U.S.A.; worked in petroleum industry; Minister of Petroleum and Gas Industry 1994–97; Pres. Kazakhoil 1997; Prime Minister of Kazakhstan 1997–. *Address:* House of Government, Astana, Kazakhstan. *Telephone:* (3172) 32 31 04 (Office).

BALL, Sir Christopher John Elinger, Kt., M.A., F.R.S.A.; British academic; b. 22 April 1935, London; s. of the late Laurence Elinger Ball and Christine Florence Mary (née Howe) Ball; m. Wendy Ruth Colyer 1958; three s. three d.; ed. St. George's School, Harpenden, Merton Coll., Oxford; Second Lieut. Parachute Regt. 1955–56; Lecturer in English Language, Merton Coll., Oxford 1960–61; Lecturer in Comparative Linguistics, School of Oriental and African Studies (Univ. of London) 1961–64; Fellow and Tutor in English Language, Lincoln Coll., Oxford 1964–69, Senior Tutor and Tutor for Admissions 1971–72, Bursar 1972–79; Warden, Keble Coll., Oxford 1980–88; Chancellor Univ. of Derby 1995–; Jt. Founding Ed. Toronto Dictionary of Old English 1970; mem. General Bd. of the Faculties 1979–82, Hebdomadal Council 1985–89, Council and Exec., Templeton Coll., Oxford 1981–92, Editorial Bd., Oxford Review of Educ. 1984–96, CNAA 1982–88; Chair. Bd. of Nat. Advisory Body for Public Sector Higher Educ. in England 1982–88, Oxford Univ. English Bd. 1977–79, Jt. Standing Cttee. for Linguistics 1979–83, Conf. of Colls. Fees Cttee. 1979–85, Higher Educ. Information Services Trust 1987–90, Educ.-Industry Forum 1988–90; Sec. Linguistics Asscn. G.B. 1964–67; Publications Sec. Philological Soc. 1969–75; Gov. St. George's School, Harpenden 1985–89, Centre for Medieval Studies, Oxford 1987, Brathay Hall Trust 1988–91, Manchester Polytechnic 1989–91; Founding Fellow in Kellogg Forum for Continuing Education, Oxford Univ. 1988–89, R.S.A. Fellow in Continuing Educ. 1990–92, Dir. of Learning 1992–; Founding Chair. Nat. Advisory Council for Careers and Educational Guidance (NACCEG); Pres. Nat. Campaign for Learning 1996–; Chancellor Univ. of Derby 1995–; Hon. Fellow (Lincoln Coll., Oxford) 1981, (Merton College, Oxford) 1987, (Keble College, Oxford) 1989, (Manchester Polytechnic) 1988, (Polytechnic of Cen. London) 1991, (Auckland Inst. of Tech., N.Z.) 1992; Hon. D. Litt (CNAA) 1989; Hon. D.Univ. (Univ. of N. London) 1993; Hon. D. Ed. (Greenwich Univ.) 1994. *Publications:* Fitness For Purpose 1985, Aim Higher 1989, Higher Education into the 1990s (Jt. Ed.) 1989, Sharks and Splashes!: The Future of Education and Employment 1991, Profitable Learning 1992, Start Right 1994; various contribs. to philological, linguistic and educ. journals. *Address:* 45 Richmond Road, Oxford, OX1 2JJ. *Telephone:* (01865) 310800.

BALL, James (see Ball, Sir (Robert) James).

BALL, Michael Ashley; British singer; b. 27 June 1962, Bromsgrove; s. of Tony Ball and Ruth (née Davis) Ball; ed. Plymouth Coll., Guildford School of Acting. *Theatre appearances include:* Godspell (debut), Aberystwyth 1984, The Pirates of Penzance, Manchester 1984, Les Misérables, London 1985–86, The Phantom of the Opera, London 1987–88, Aspects of Love, London 1989–90, New York, Passion, London 1996; represented U.K. Eurovision Song Contest 1992; several tours; own TV series 'Michael Ball' 1993, 1994; *film:* England My England 1995; *recordings include:* Michael Ball 1992, Always 1993, One Careful Owner 1994, First Love 1996; Gold Discs for four of his albums. *Address:* c/o James Sharkey Associates, 21 Golden Square, London W1R 3PA, England. *Telephone:* 0171-434 3801. *Fax:* 0171-494 1547.

BALL, Sir (Robert) James, Kt., PH.D., C.B.I.M., F.I.A.M.; British professor of economics; b. 15 July 1933, Saffron Walden; s. of Arnold James Hector Ball; m. 1st Patricia Mary Hart Davies 1954 (marriage dissolved 1970); one s. three d. (one d. deceased); m. 2nd Lindsay Jackson (née Wonnacott) 1970; one step-s.; ed. St. Marylebone Grammar School, Queen's Coll., Oxford, Univ. of Pennsylvania; R.A.F. 1952–54; Research Officer, Oxford Univ. Inst. of Statistics 1957–58; IBM Fellow, Univ. of Pa. 1958–60; Lecturer Univ. of Manchester 1960–63, Sr. Lecturer 1963–65; Prof. of Econs., London Business School 1984–98, Prof. Emer. 1998–, Deputy Prin. 1971–72, Prin. 1972–84; Dir. Barclays Bank Trust Co. Ltd. 1973–86, Tube Investments 1974–84, IBM U.K. Holdings Ltd. 1979–95, IBM UK Pensions Trust 1994–; Chair. Legal and General Group PLC. 1980–94, Royal Bank of Canada Holdings (UK) Ltd. 1995–98; Dir. LASMO 1988–94, Royal Bank of Canada 1990–98; Vice-Pres. Chartered Inst. of Marketing 1991–94; mem. Council British-N. American Cttee. 1985–98, Research Asscn. 1985–, Marshall Aid Commemoration Comm. 1987–94; Econ. Adviser, Touche Ross & Co. 1984–95; Trustee Foulkes Foundation 1984–, Civic Trust 1986–91, The Economist 1987–, ReAction Trust 1991–93; mem. Advisory Bd. IBM UK Ltd. 1995–98; Hon. D.Sc. (Aston) 1987, Hon. D.Soc.Sc. (Manchester) 1988; Freeman of City of London 1987. *Publications:* An Economic Model of the United Kingdom 1961, Inflation and the Theory of Money 1964, Inflation (ed.) 1969, The International Linkage of National Economic Models (ed.) 1972, Money and Employment 1982, The Economics of Wealth Creation (ed.) 1992, The British Economy at the Crossroads 1998, articles in professional journals. *Leisure interests:* chess, fishing, gardening. *Address:* London Business School, Sussex Place, Regent's Park, London, NW1 4SA, England (Office). *Telephone:* 0171-262 5050.

BALLADUR, Edouard, L. EN D.; French politician; b. 2 May 1929, Smyrna, Turkey; s. of Pierre Balladur and Emilie Latour; m. Marie-Josèphe Delacour 1957; four s.; ed. Lycée Thiers, Marseilles, Faculté de Droit, Aix-en-Provence, Inst. d'Etudes Politiques, Paris and Ecole Nationale d'Admin.; auditor, Conseil d'Etat 1957, Maître des requêtes 1963; adviser to Dir.-Gen. of ORTF 1962–63; mem. Admin. Council of ORTF 1967–68; Tech. Adviser, Office of Prime Minister Georges Pompidou 1966–68; Pres. French soc. for bldg. and devt. of road tunnel under Mont Blanc 1968–81; mem. Admin. Council, Nat. Forestry Office 1968–73; Asst. Sec.-Gen. Presidency of Repub. 1969, Sec.-Gen. 1974; Pres. Dir.-Gen. Générale de Service Informatique 1977–86; Pres. Compagnie Européenne d'Accumulateurs 1980–86; mem. Conseil d'Etat 1984–88, 1988–; Minister of the Econ., of Finance and Privatization 1986–88; Prime Minister of France 1993–95; mem. Nat. Ass.; Chevalier, Légion d'honneur. *Publications:* l'Arbre de mai 1979, Je crois en l'homme plus qu'en l'Etat 1987, Passion et longueur de temps (with others) 1989, Douze Lettres aux Français Trop Tranquilles 1990, Des Modes et Des Convictions 1992, Dictionnaire de la Réforme 1992, L'Action pour la Réforme 1995. *Address:* Counseil d'Etat, 75100 Paris; Assemblée nationale, 126 rue de l'Université, 75355 Paris, France.

BALLARD, James Graham; British novelist and short story writer; b. 15 Nov. 1930; s. of James Ballard and Edna Ballard (née Johnstone); m. Helen Mary Mathews 1954 (died 1964); one s. two d.; ed. Leys School, Cambridge and King's Coll. Cambridge. *Publications:* The Drowned World 1963, The 4-Dimensional Nightmare 1963, The Terminal Beach 1964, The Drought 1965, The Crystal World 1966, The Disaster Area 1967, The Atrocity Exhibition 1970, Crash 1973, Vermilion Sands 1973, Concrete Island 1974, High Rise 1975, Low-Flying Aircraft 1976, The Unlimited Dream Company 1979, Myths of the Near Future 1982, Empire of the Sun 1984, The Venus Hunters 1986, The Day of Creation 1987, Running Wild 1988, Memories of the Space Age 1988, War Fever 1990, The Kindness of Women 1991, The Terminal Beach (short stories) 1992, Rushing to Paradise 1994, A Users' Guide to the Millennium 1996, Cocaine Nights 1996. *Address:* 36 Old Charlton Road, Shepperton, Middx., TW17 8AT, England. *Telephone:* (01932) 225692.

BALLARD, Robert; American oceanographer; ed. Univs. of California, Southern California, Hawaii and Rhode Island; fmrly. comm. in Army Intelligence, later transferred to U.S.N.; served with U.S.N. in Vietnam war, now Commdr. U.S.N.R.; fmrly. Sr. Scientist and Dir. Centre for Marine Exploration, Woods Hole Oceanographic Inst., Cape Cod, Mass.; f. JASON project 1989; f. and Pres. Inst. for Exploration, Mystic, Conn. 1998; has led or participated in over 100 deep-sea expeditions including discoveries of German battleship Bismarck, R.M.S. Titanic 1985, warships from lost fleet of Guadalcanal, the Lusitania, Roman ships off coast of Tunisia 1997, U.S.S. Yorktown 1998; expeditions included first manned exploration of Mid-ocean Ridge, discovery of warm water springs and their fauna in Galapagos Rift, first discovery of polymetallic sulphides; has participated in numerous educ. programmes with major TV networks in Europe, Japan and U.S.A., hosted Nat. Geographic Explorer show 1989–91. *Publications:* Exploring the "Titanic" (with Rick Archbold), Bright Shark (novel) 1992, Explorer (children's book) 1992, The Lost Ships of Guadalcanal (with Rick Archbold) 1993, Explorations (autobiography) 1995, Exploring the "Lusitania" (with Spencer Dunmore) 1995, Lost Liners (with Rick Archbold) 1997; has also published more than 50 articles in scientific journals, and numerous popular articles. *Address:* Institute for Exploration, Mystic Aquarium, Coogan Boulevard, Mystic, CT 06355, U.S.A.

BALLE, Francis, D. ÈS L.; French professor; b. 15 June 1939, Fourmies; s. of Marcel Balle and Madeleine (née Leprohon) Balle; m. Marie Derieux 1972; three d.; ed. Inst. d'Etudes Politiques; philosophy teacher Ecole Normale d'Oran 1963–65; Asst. Lecturer Faculté des Lettres, Ecole de Journalisme, Algiers 1965–67, Univ. de Paris-Sorbonne 1967–70, Univ. René Descartes, Univ. Paris VI 1970–72; Lecturer Univ. de Droit, d'Econ. et de Sciences Sociales 1972, Prof. 1978–; Pres. statistical cttee. for TV action outside France 1997–; Dir. Inst. Français de Presse 1976–86, Inst. de Recherche et d'Etudes sur la Communication 1986–; Vice-Chancellor Univs. de Paris 1986–89; Visiting Prof. Univ. of Stanford, Calif. 1981–83; Dir. Information and New Techs. at Ministry of Nat. Educ. 1993–95, of Scientific Information, Tech. and of Libraries 1995–; Officier Ordre National de la Légion d'honneur, Palmes Académiques. *Publications:* Médias et Sociétés 1980, 1997, The Media Revolution in America and Western Europe 1984, Les nouveaux médias (with Gerard Eymery) 1987, 1996, Et si la Presse n'existait pas 1987, la Télévision 1987, le Mandarin et le marchand 1995, Dictionnaire des medias 1998. *Leisure interests:* music, painting. *Address:* 83 bis rue Notre Dame des Champs, 75006 Paris (Office); 18 rue Greuze, 75116 Paris, France (Home). *Telephone:* (1) 44.41.59.28 (Office); 47.27.78.31 (Home). *Fax:* (1) 43.26.15.78.

BALLESTEROS SOTA, Severiano; Spanish golfer; b. 9 April 1957, Pedreña, Santander; s. of Baldomero Ballesteros Presmanes and Carmen Sota

Ocejo; m. Carmen Botin Sanz 1988; two s. one d.; professional 1974–; won Spanish Young Professional title 1974; 72 int. titles; won Dutch Open and two major European tournaments and, with Manuel Pinero, World Cup 1976; won Opens of France, Switzerland and Japan, four other major tournaments in Europe, Japan and New Zealand, and World Cup, with Antonio Garrido 1977; won Opens of Japan, Germany, Kenya, Scandinavia and Switzerland and tournament in U.S.A. 1978; British Open Champion (youngest this century) 1979, 1984, 1988; second European and youngest ever winner U.S. Masters 1980; World Matchplay Title 1981, 1982, 1984, 1985; tied Gary Player's record of five victories in World Matchplay with his fifth win 1991; winner U.S. Masters 1980, 1983, Henry Vardon Trophy 1976, 1977, 1978, 1986, Ryder Cup 1979, 1983, 1985, 1987, British/Volvo PGA Championship 1983, 1991, Mallorca Open 1988, 1990, 1991, British Masters 1991, Dubai Open 1992; acted in film Escape to Paradise 1987; Príncipe de Asturias Award 1989; resident of Monaco. *Publication:* Trouble Shooting 1996. *Leisure interests:* ping-pong, chess, fitness, shooting, reading, music. *Address:* Fairway, S.A., Pasaje de Peña 2-4°, 39008 Santander, Spain; Houston Palace, 7 Avenue Princess Grace, 39009 Monte Carlo, Monaco. *Telephone:* (42) 31.45.12 (Spain). *Fax:* (42) 31.45.59 (Spain).

BALLIN, Ernst Hirsch (see Hirsch Ballin, Ernst).

BALOGUN, Kolawole, Chief Jagun of Otan, LL.B., PH.D.; Nigerian politician, lawyer and diplomatist; b. 1926, Osun, Oyo State; s. of Moses and Marian Balogun; ed. Govt. Coll., Ibadan; on staff of Nigerian Advocate, later radio announcer, then Asst. Ed. West African Pilot; legal studies in London 1948–51, called to the Bar 1951; Sec. London branch National Council of Nigeria and the Cameroons (NCNC) 1951; Nat. Sec. NCNC 1951–57; mem. of Fed. Parl. 1954; Fed. Minister without Portfolio 1955, of Information 1955–58; resigned from Govt. 1958; Nigerian Commr. in Ghana 1959–60, High Commr. 1960–61; fmr. mem. of Ministry of Foreign Affairs; Chair, Nigerian Nat. Shipping Line 1962–65; Commr. for Econ. Planning and Social Devt., Mil. Govt. of W. Nigeria 1967; Commr. for Educ. 1968–70. *Publications:* Government in Old Oyo Empire 1985, Osun State: Story of Its Creation 1992, Nigeria: June 12 Election 1996. *Leisure interests:* reading and writing. *Address:* Maye Lodge, P.O. Box 50, Osogbo, Nigeria. *Telephone:* (035) 234703.

BALSAI, István, D.IUR.; Hungarian politician; b. 5 April 1947, Miskolc; s. of József Balsai and Mária Szalontai; m. Ilona Schmidt; two s.; chemical laboratory asst. 1966; Eötvös Loránd Univ. Budapest faculty of political and legal sciences 1967–72; worked as adviser to Lawyers Asscn., Budapest; mem. Hungarian Democratic Forum 1988; mem. of Parl. 1990–; Minister of Justice 1990–94; leader of splinter group in Hungarian Democratic Forum 1998–; founding mem. Asscn. of Christian Intellectuals 1989–. *Leisure interest:* folk architecture. *Address:* Széchenyi rkp. 19, 1054 Budapest, Hungary. *Telephone:* (1) 268-5139. *Fax:* (1) 268-5978.

BALSEMÃO, Francisco Pinto (see Pinto Balsemão).

BALTHUS (see Klossowski de Rola, Comte Balthasar).

BALTIMORE, David, PH.D.; American biologist; b. 7 March 1938, New York, N.Y.; s. of Richard Baltimore and Gertrude Lipschitz; m. Alice Huang 1968; one d.; ed. Swarthmore Coll. and Rockefeller Univ.; Postdoctoral Fellow, Mass. Inst. of Technology (M.I.T.) 1963–64, Albert Einstein Coll. of Medicine, New York 1964–65; Research Assoc., Salk Inst., La Jolla, Calif. 1965–68; Assoc. Prof., M.I.T. 1968–72, Prof. of Microbiology 1972–95; Ivan R. Cottrell Prof. of Molecular Biology and Immunology M.I.T. 1994–; Inst. Prof. M.I.T. Cambridgeshire 1995–97; American Cancer Soc. Prof. of Microbiology 1973–83, 1994–; Dir. Whitehead Inst. for Biomedical Research 1982–90; Pres. Rockefeller Univ. 1990–91, Prof. 1990–94; Pres. Calif. Inst. of Tech. 1997–; mem. Nat. Insts. of Health Advisory Council on AIDS research, Chair. vaccine cttee. 1997–; Eli Lilly Award in Microbiology and Immunology 1971; U.S. Steel Foundation Award in Molecular Biology 1974; Nobel Prize 1975. *Address:* Massachusetts Institute of Technology, Room 68-380, 77 Massachusetts Avenue, Cambridge, MA 02139, U.S.A. *Telephone:* (617) 253-2135. *Fax:* (617) 253-2153.

BALTSA, Agnes; Greek opera singer; b. Lefkas; ed. Acad. of Music, Athens and in Munich (Maria Callas Scholarship); opera debut as Cherubino, Frankfurt 1968;debut at Vienna State Opera (Octavian) 1970, Salzburg Festival 1970, La Scala, Milan (Dorabella) 1976, Paris Opera and Covent Garden, London (Cherubino) 1976, Metropolitan Opera, New York (Octavian) 1980; mem. Deutsche Oper Berlin 1973–; performs at all major opera houses in world and has given concerts in Europe, U.S.A. and Japan with Karajan, Böhm, Bernstein, Muti, etc.; Österreichische Kammersängerin 1980, Deutscher Schallplattenpreis 1983, Prix Prestige Lyrique (French Ministry of Culture) 1984; has made about 30 operatic recordings. *Leisure interests:* swimming, fashion.

BAMERT, Matthias; Swiss conductor; b. 5 July 1942, Ersigen; m. Susan Exline 1969; one s. one d.; asst. conductor to Leopold Stokowski 1970–71; Resident Conductor Cleveland Orchestra 1971–78; Music Dir. Swiss Radio Orchestra, Basel 1977–83; Prin. Guest Conductor Scottish Nat. Orchestra 1985–90; Dir. Musica Nova Festival, Glasgow 1985–90, Lucerne Festival 1992–98; Music Dir. London Mozart Players 1993–; has appeared with Orchestre de Paris, Rotterdam Philharmonic, Cleveland Orchestra, Pittsburgh Symphony, Montreal Symphony, Royal Philharmonic Orchestra, London, London Philharmonic Orchestra, BBC Philharmonic, City of Birmingham Symphony Orchestra, and at BBC Promenade Concerts, London; has toured worldwide. *Address:* c/o Intermusica Artists Management Ltd., 16 Duncan Terrace, London, N1 8BZ, England. *Telephone:* 0171-278 5455. *Fax:* 0171-278 8434.

BAMFORD, Sir Anthony (Paul), Kt.; British construction executive; b. 23 Oct. 1945; s. of Joseph Cyril Bamford and Marjorie Griffin; m. Carole Gray Whitt 1974; two s. one d.; ed. Ampleforth Coll., Grenoble Univ.; joined J.C.B. 1962, Chair. and Dir. 1975–; Dir. Tarmac 1987–94; Pres. Staffs. Agricultural Soc. 1987–88, Burton-upon-Trent Conservative Asscn. 1987–90; Pres.'s Cttee. C.B.I. 1986–88; mem. Design Council 1987–89; Hon. M.Eng. (Birmingham) 1987; D.Univ. (Keele) 1988; D.Sc (Cranfield) 1994; Young Exporter of the Year (U.K.) 1972, Young Businessman of the Year (U.K.) 1979, Top Exporter of the Year (U.K.) 1995; Chevalier Ordre Nat. du Mérite (France) 1989, Commendatore della Repubblica Italiana 1995; D.L. Staffs., High Sheriff Staffs. 1985–86. *Leisure interests:* farming, gardening. *Address:* c/o J. C. Bamford Excavators Ltd., Rocester, Uttoxeter, Staffs., ST14 5JP, England.

BAMFORD, Clement Henry, PH.D., SC.D., D.SC., F.R.S.C., F.R.S.; British academic; b. 10 Oct. 1912, Stafford; s. of Frederic Jesse and Catherine Mary (née Shelley) Bamford; m. Daphne Ailsa Stephan 1938; one s. one d.; ed. King Edward VI School, Stafford, Trinity Coll., Cambridge; Fellow Trinity Coll., Cambridge 1937–41; with Special Operations Exec. 1942–45; with Fundamental Research Lab., Courtaulds Ltd., Maidenhead 1945–62; Dir. 1947–62; Campbell Brown Prof. of Industrial Chem., Univ. of Liverpool 1962–80, Prof. Emer. 1980–, Hon. Sr. Research Fellow, Dept. of Clinical Eng. 1981–96, Dean, Faculty of Science 1965–68, Pro-Vice-Chancellor 1972–75, Head of Dept., Inorganic, Physical and Industrial Chem. 1973–78; European Ed. Journal of Biomaterials Science, Polymer edn. 1988–96; Pres., Macromolecular Div. of Int. Union of Pure and Applied Chem. 1981–85; Life mem. Soc. of Chemical Ind., Royal Soc. of Chem.; Hon. mem. Soc. of Polymer Science, Japan 1996; Hon. D.Sc. (Univ. of Bradford) 1980, (Univ. of Lancaster) 1988; Meldola Medal, Royal Inst. of Chemistry 1941, Award in Macromolecules and Polymers, Royal Soc. of Chemistry 1977, Award for Distinguished Service in Advancement of Polymer Science, Soc. of Polymer Science, Japan 1989, George Winter Award, European Soc. for Biomaterials 1992. *Publications:* Synthetic Polypeptides (with others) 1956, Kinetics of Vinyl Polymerization by Radical Mechanisms (with others) 1958, Jt. Editor of series: Comprehensive Chemical Kinetics 1969–85; many scientific papers. *Leisure interests:* violin playing, gardening. *Address:* Broom Bank, Tower Road, Prenton, Birkenhead, Merseyside, L42 8LH, England (Home). *Telephone:* (0151) 608 3979 (Home).

BANANA, Rev. Dr. Canaan Sodindo, B.A., M.T.S.; Zimbabwean nationalist leader and ecclesiastic; b. 5 March 1936, Esiphezini, Essexvale Dist.; s. of Aaron Banana and Zibiya Banana; m. Janet Mbuyazwe 1961; three s. one d.; ed. Tegwani Training Inst., Epworth Theological Coll., Kansai Industrial Centre, Japan, Wesley Theological Seminary, U.S.A., Univ. of S.A.; Chaplain, Tegwani High School 1965–66; ordained Methodist at Epworth 1966; Prin. Matjinke Boarding School 1966; Chair. Bulawayo Council of Churches 1969–70, Southern Africa Urban Industrial Mission 1970–73; founder mem. and Vice-Pres. African Nat. Council (ANC) 1971–73; ANC rep. in U.S.A. and UN 1973–75; Chaplain American Univ. 1974–75; detained 1975–76; Press Spokesman for ANC 1976; attended Geneva Conf. on Rhodesia 1976; founder mem. and publicity sec. People's Movt. 1976; in detention several times and publs. banned in Rhodesia; Pres. Repub. of Zimbabwe 1980–87; f. Mushandira Pamure Project 1980; f. Kushinga-Phikelela Agric. Inst. 1981; Chancellor of Univ. of Zimbabwe 1983–88; led World Council of Churches Eminent Church Persons sanctions against S.A. 1989; Co-Chair. U.N. Panel on the operations of transnat. corpns. in S.A. Sept. 1989; Prof. of Classics, Religious Studies and Philosophy, Univ. of Zimbabwe 1989–; convicted on 11 charges of homosexual abuse 1998; sentenced to ten years imprisonment, nine suspended conditionally; Hon. LL.D. (American Univ., Univ. of Zimbabwe). *Publications:* The Zimbabwe Exodus, The Gospel According to the Ghetto, Theology of Promise, The Woman of My Imagination, The Ethos of Socialism 1987. *Leisure interests:* soccer, table tennis, lawn tennis. *Address:* c/o State House, Box 368, Harare, Zimbabwe. *Telephone:* (4) 26666.

BANBI, Hamdi El, DR.ENG.; Egyptian politician and petroleum engineer; b. 4 Oct. 1935, Assiut; ed. Cairo Univ., Tulsa and Texas A & M Univs., U.S.A.; Sr. Field Production Engineer, Asst. Production Man., Compagnie Orientale des Pétroles d'Egypte 1963–66; Asst. Prof., Azhar Univ., Cairo 1966–68; various posts, to Chief Petroleum Engineer, Operations Man., Western Desert Petroleum Co. (WEPCO) 1968–77; Chair. and Man. Dir. Gulf of Suez Petroleum Co. (GUPCO) 1977–88; Chair. Egyptian Gen. Petroleum Corp. (EGPC) 1988–91; Minister of Petroleum 1991–; Soc. of Petroleum Engineers (SPE) Distinguished Membership 1988, SPE Service Award of Middle East and African Region 1989, U.S. Bureau of Mines Certificate of Achievement. *Publications:* numerous papers in tech. journals. *Address:* Ministry of Petroleum and Mineral Resources, El-Mokhaim El-Daim Street, Nasr City, Cairo, Egypt. *Telephone:* 2622237. *Fax:* 2636060.

BANBURY, (Frederick Harold) Frith; British theatrical director, actor and manager; b. 4 May 1912, Plymouth; s. of Rear Admiral Frederick Arthur Frith Banbury and Winifred Fink; ed. Stowe School, Oxford Univ. and Royal Acad. Dramatic Art; made first stage appearance 1933 and appeared on the London stage, in plays and on television until 1947; has since concentrated on direction. *Plays directed include*: Dark Summer 1947, The Holly and the

Ivy 1950, Waters of the Moon 1951, The Deep Blue Sea 1951, Morosco (New York) 1952, A Question Of Fact 1953, Marching Song 1954, Love's Labours Lost, (Old Vic) 1954, The Diary of Anne Frank 1956, A Dead Secret 1957, Flowering Cherry 1957, A Touch of the Sun 1958, The Ring of Truth 1959, The Tiger and the Horse 1960, The Wings of the Dove 1963, The Right Honourable Gentleman (New York) 1965, Howards End 1967, Dear Octopus 1967, Enter a Free Man 1968, My Darling Daisy 1970, The Winslow Boy 1970, Captain Brassbound's Conversion 1971, Reunion in Vienna 1972, The Day After the Fair 1972, In U.S.A. 1973, Glasstown 1973, Ardèle 1975, Family Matter 1976, On Approval 1977, Motherdear 1980, Dear Liar 1982, The Aspern Papers 1984, The Corn is Green 1985, The Admirable Crichton 1988, Screamers 1989, and others in New York, Paris, Tel Aviv, Toronto, Hong Kong, Johannesburg, Nairobi, Sydney, Melbourne. *Leisure interest:* playing the piano. *Address:* 18 Park Saint James, Prince Albert Road, London, NW8 7LE, England.

BANCROFT, Anne; American actress; b. 17 Sept. 1931, New York; d. of Michael and Mildred (née DiNapoli) Italiano; m. 2nd Mel Brooks (q.v.) 1964; one s.; ed. Christopher Columbus High School, New York. *Theatre:* Broadway debut in Two for the Seesaw 1958, played Anne Sullivan in The Miracle Worker 1959–60; A Cry of Prayers 1968, Golda 1977, The Devils 1977, Mystery of the Rose Bouquet 1989. *Films:* The Miracle Worker, Don't Bother to Knock, Tonight We Sing, Demetrius and the Gladiators, The Pumpkin Eater, Seven Women, The Graduate 1968, Young Winston 1971, The Prisoner of Second Avenue 1974, The Hindenburg 1975, Lipstick 1976, Silent Movie 1976, The Turning Point 1977, Silent Movie, The Elephant Man 1980, To Be or Not to Be 1984, Agnes of God 1985, 84 Charing Cross Road 1986, Torch Song Trilogy 1989, Bert Rigby You're a Fool 1989, Broadway Bound 1992, How to Make An American Quilt 1995, Home for the Holidays 1995, The Homecoming 1996, Sunchasers 1997, GI Jane 1997, Critical Care 1997; wrote, directed and acted in Fatso; numerous TV appearances; Academy Award for film The Miracle Worker 1962; Golden Globe Award 1968; Emmy Award for Annie, the Woman in the Life of a Man 1970; Lifetime Achievement in Comedy Award, American Comedy Awards 1996. *Address:* c/o The Culver Studios, 9336 W Washington Boulevard, Culver City, CA 90232, U.S.A.

BANDA, Aleke Kadonaphani; Malawi politician and journalist; b. 19 Sept. 1939, Livingstone, Zambia; s. of Eliazar G. Banda and Lilian Phiri; m. Mbumba M. Kahumbe 1961; two s. one d.; ed. United Missionary School, Que Que and Inyati School, Bulawayo; Sec. Nyasaland African Contress (N.A.C.), Que Que Branch 1954; Gen. Sec. S. Rhodesia African Students Asscn. 1957–59; arrested and detained in Rhodesia 1959, deported to Nyasaland; Founder-mem. Malawi Congress Party (MCP), Sec.-Gen. 1959–73, mem. 1974–; Ed. Nyasaland TUC newspaper Ntendere Pa Nchito and mem. TUC Council 1959–60; Personal Political Sec. to Dr. Hastings Banda 1960–73; Sec. MCP Del. to Lancaster House Conf. resulting in self-govt. for Malawi 1960; Sec. to subsequent confs. 1960, 1962; Man. Ed. Malawi News 1959–66; Dir. Malawi Press Ltd. 1960; Dir.-Gen. Malawi Broadcasting Corpn. 1964–66; Nat. Chair. League of Malawi Youth and Commdr. Malawi Young Pioneers 1963–73; Dir. Reserve Bank of Malawi 1965–66; Minister of Devt. and Planning 1966–67, of Econ. Affairs (incorporating Natural Resources, Trade and Industry, and Devt. and Planning), and Minister of Works and Supplies 1967–68, of Trade and Industry (incorporating Tourism, Information and Broadcasting) 1968–69, of Finance and of Information and Tourism 1969–72, of Trade, Industry and Tourism 1972–73; dismissed from Cabinet posts and party 1973, reinstated as mem. party 1974; detained without trial May 1992; Minister of Finance, Econ. Planning and Devt. 1994–97, of Agriculture and Irrigation July 1997–; Campaign Chair. United Democratic Party; fmr. Chair. Nat. Bank of Malawi. *Leisure interest:* tennis. *Address:* Ministry of Agriculture and Irrigation, P.O. Box 30134, Capital City, Lilongwe 3, Malawi.

BANDAR IBN SULTAN IBN ABDULAZIZ AL-SAUD, M.A.; Saudi Arabian diplomatist and army officer; b. 2 March 1949, Taif; s. of H.R.H. Prince Sultan ibn Abdulaziz al-Saud; m. H.R.H. Princess Haifa bint Faisal ibn Abdulaziz al-Saud; two s. three d.; ed. R.A.F. Coll., Cranwell, U.S.A.F. Advanced Program and Johns Hopkins Univ.; fighter pilot, Royal Saudi Air Force 1969–82; in charge of special Saudi Arabian liaison mission to U.S.A. for purchase of AWACS and other defence equipment 1981; Defence and Mil. Attaché, Saudi Arabian Mil. Mission to U.S.A. 1982–83; Amb. to U.S.A. 1983–. *Leisure interests:* flying, racquetball, reading. *Address:* Royal Embassy of Saudi Arabia, 601 New Hampshire Avenue, N.W., Washington, DC 20037, U.S.A. *Telephone:* (202) 342-3800.

BANDARANAIKE, Sirimavo Ratwatte Dias; Sri Lankan politician; b. 17 April 1916, Ratnapura, Sabaragamuwa Prov.; d. of Barnes Ratwatte and Rosemund Mahawalatenne Ratwatte; m. S. W. R. D. Bandaranaike (Prime Minister of Ceylon 1956–59, died 1959) 1940; one. s. two d.; ed. St. Bridget's Convent, Colombo; Pres. of Sri Lanka Freedom Party 1960–; Prime Minister, Minister of Defence and External Affairs 1960–65; mem. Senate until 1965; Leader of Opposition 1965–70, 1988–; Prime Minister, Minister of Defence and Foreign Affairs, Planning, Econ. Affairs and Plan Implementation 1970–77; Prime Minister of Sri Lanka Nov. 1994–; mem. Parl. 1977–. *Leisure interests:* gardening, reading, cooking. *Address:* Prime Minister's Office, 150 R. A. de Mel Mawatha, Colombo 3; 65 Rosmead Place, Colombo 7, Sri Lanka. *Telephone:* (1) 433215. *Fax:* (1) 437017.

BANDEEN, Robert Angus, O.C., PH.D.; Canadian company executive; b. 29 Oct. 1930, Rodney, Ont.; s. of John Robert and Jessie Marie (Thomson) Bandeen; m. Mona Helen Blair 1958; four s.; ed. Univ. of Western Ontario and Duke Univ., U.S.A.; joined Canadian Nat. Railways 1955, Research and Devt. Dept. 1955–66, Dir. of Corporate Planning 1966–68, Vice-Pres. Corporate Planning and Finance 1968–71, Vice-Pres. Great Lakes Region, Toronto 1971–72, Exec. Vice-Pres. Finance and Admin. 1972–74, Pres. 1974–82, C.E.O. 1974–82; Pres. and Chair., Crown Life Insurance Co. 1982–84, Chair. and C.E.O. 1984–85; Pres. Crownx Inc. 1984–85, Vice-Chair. 1985–86; Pres. and C.E.O. Cluny Corpn. 1986–; Dir. numerous cos.; fmr. Chair. Counsel Life Insurance Co., Cytex Inc.; fmr. Chancellor Bishop's Univ., Lennoxville, Quebec; Gov. Olympic Trust of Canada; Senator Stratford Shakespearian Festival Foundation; Hon. LL.D. (W. Ont.) 1975, (Dalhousie) 1978, (Bishops) 1978, (Queens) 1982; Kt. St. J. 1980; Salzberg Medal (Syracuse Univ.) 1982. *Leisure interests:* tennis, skiing. *Address:* Cluny Corpn., #305 1166 Bay Street, Toronto, Ont., M5S 2X8, Canada.

BANDEIRA DE MELLO, Lydio Machado, DR.JUR.; Brazilian university professor emeritus; b. 19 July 1901, Abaete, Minas Gerais; s. of Dr. Lydio Alerano and Adélia Machado Bandeira de Mello; m. Amália Introcaso Bandeira de Mello 1928; two s. two d.; ed. Univ. of Brazil; Prof. of Criminal Law, Univ. of Minas Gerais 1952–71, Comparative Criminal Law 1959–71, Prof. Emer. 1972–. *Publications:* O Problema do Mal 1935, A Procura de Deus 1938, Responsabilidade Penal 1941, Prova Matemática da Existência de Deus 1942, Teoria do Destino 1944, Metafísica do Número 1946, A Predestinação Para O Bem 1948, Tabu, Pecado e Crime 1949, Dezessete Aventuras no Reino de Deus 1952, O Real e o Possível 1953, Manual de Direito Penal (Vols. 1-4) 1953–58, A Origem dos Sexos 1955, Filosofia do Direito 1957, Ontologia e Lógica da Contradição 1959, Metafísica do Tempo 1961, O Direito Penal Hispano-Luso Medievo (2 vols.) 1961, Tratado de Direito Penal, Crime e Exclusão de Criminalidade 1962, Da Responsabilidade Penal e Da Isenção de Pena 1962, Da Capitulação dos Crimes e da Fixação das Penas 1963, Metafísica da Gravitação 1963, Memória Espaço e Tempo (2 vols.) 1963, Cosmologia do Movimento 1965, Teologia Matemática 1965, Metafísica do Espaço 1966, A Pluralidade de Consciências 1967, Crítica Cosmológica de Física Quântica 1968, Fórmulas Gerais da Distribuição de Probabilidades 1968, Evangelho para Bacharéis 1969, O Criminoso, O Crime e a Pena 1970, Trabalhos de Algoritmia (Aritmética e Algebra) Superior 1971, A Existência e a Imortalidade da Alma 1972, As Credenciais da Razão 1973, Teoria Algébrica das Permutações Condicionadas 1972, Critíca do Principio de Razão Suficiente 1974, A Falibilidade da Indução 1974, A Conquista do Reino de Deus (2 vols.) 1975, O Possível Puro 1975, Cosmologia Científica 1976, Metafísica da Sensação 1977, A Matemática do Universo e a Matemática Dos Homens 1978, Voluntariedade da Vinda dos Homens para a Terra (A Genética Experimental 1979) 1980, Deus e cada Homem 1980, Sem Angústia Diante de Deus 1982, O Universo Físico Feito 1982, Para Receber Homens Livres 1982, Universos Abstratos em Possível Expansão Ilimitável 1983, Jesus meu Mestre 1984. *Leisure interests:* walking, cinema-going, philately. *Address:* Rua Rodrigues Caldas, 703 Belo Horizonte, Minas Gerais, Brazil. *Telephone:* 3370198.

BANDERAS, Antonio; Spanish film actor; b. 1960, Málaga; m. 1st Anna Banderas; m. 2nd Melanie Griffith 1996; began acting aged 14; performed with Nat. Theatre, Madrid for six years. *Films include:* Labyrinth of Passion, El Señor Galíndez, El Caso Almería, The Stilts, 27 Hours, Law of Desire, Matador, Tie Me Up! Tie Me Down!, Women on the Verge of a Nervous Breakdown, The House of Spirits, Interview with the Vampire, Philadelphia, The Mambo Kings, Love and Shadow, Miami Rhapsody, Young Mussolini, Return of Mariaolu, Assassins, Desperado, Evita, Never Talk to Strangers; Crazy in Alabama (dir.), The 13th Warrior. *Address:* c/o CAA, 9830 Wilshire Boulevard, Beverly Hills, CA 90212, U.S.A.; Agents Associés, 201 rue du Faubourg Saint-Honoré, 75008 Paris, France.

BANDLER, John William, PH.D., F.I.E.E., F.R.S.C., F.I.E.E.E.; Canadian professor of electrical and computer engineering; b. 9 Nov. 1941, Jerusalem; m. 3rd Beth Budd 1990; two d.; ed. Imperial Coll. London; Mullard Research Labs., Redhill, Surrey 1966; Univ. of Man. 1967–69; McMaster Univ. 1969, Prof. 1974; Chair. Dept. of Electrical Eng., McMaster Univ. 1978–79, Dean of Faculty 1979–81, Dir. of Research, Simulation Optimization Systems Research Lab. 1983–; Pres. Optimization Systems Assocs. Inc. 1983–97, Bandler Corpn. 1997–; ARFTG Automated Measurements Career Award for Automated Microwave Techniques 1994. *Publications:* more than 300 papers in journals and books and book chapters. *Address:* Department of Electrical and Computer Engineering, McMaster University, Hamilton, Ont., L8S 4K1, Canada. *Telephone:* (905) 525-9140. *Fax:* (905) 523-4407.

BANDLER, Vivica Aina Fanny; Finnish theatre director; b. 5 Feb. 1917, Helsingfors; d. of Erik von Frenckell and Ester Margaret Lindberg; m. Kurt Bandler 1943; ed. Univ. of Helsinki; with Helsingfors Student Theatre 1939; war service 1939–40, 1941–43; asst. film dir. in France 1939, Sweden 1945–46; started as theatre dir. Swedish Theatre, Helsingfors 1948; Head, theatre section, Helsinki's 400th anniversary 1950; f. Peasants' Theatre Group, Kylänpojat 1951; Man., Prin. Dir. Lilla Teatern, Helsingfors 1955–67, mem. Bd. 1983–; Man., Dir. Oslo Nye Teater, Norway 1967–69; Head Stockholm City Theatre, Sweden 1969–80; theatre dir. Sweden and Finland 1980–; Artistic Dir. Tampere Int. Theatre Festival, Finland 1989–95; Pres. Bd. of Swedish Theatre Union/Swedish Int. Theatre Inst. (ITI) 1978–92, mem. Exec. Cttee. ITI 1981–86, mem. Drama Cttee. 1990–92; mem. Bd. Nordic Theatre Union 1986–88; Pres. Theatre Acad. of Sweden, Stockholm 1992–; Patron Hangö Festival (Finland) 1996–97; theatre dir. Eri dance theatre (Finland) 1989–; Hon. mem. Swedish Authors' Asscn. in Finland, Union of Theatre Dirs., Finland; has written several dramatisations of novels, film scripts, musicals etc.; Golden Boot, awarded by daily newspaper Dagens Nyheter, Sweden, Medal of City of Stockholm, Medal of Swedish Parl. in Finland, August Award, Swedish Dramatists' Asscn., Letterstedt Foundation Medal for Nordic Co-operation, Thalia Award, Swedish Actors' Asscn., Finland Prize; Memory Medal of War 1939–40, Commdr. of Finnish Lion, Pro Finlandis (Finland), Commdr. Northern Star of Sweden. *Publications:* Adressaten okänd (Addressee Unknown) (with Carita Backström) 1992; articles about theatre, translations of plays, etc. *Address:* Upplandsgatan 28, S-113 28 Stockholm, Sweden; Villagatan 1 B, SF-00150 Helsinki, Finland. *Telephone:* (8) 314332 (Sweden); (9) 635483 (Finland).

BANERJI, Asoka Nath, B.SC., LL.B.; Indian politician; b. 19 Dec. 1917, Banaras; ed. Patna and Calcutta Univs.; served in army 1941–46; joined Indian Admin. Service 1947; various posts 1947–56; Deputy Gen. Man. Durgapur Steel Project 1956–61; Iron and Steel Controller for India 1961–63; Gen. Man. Rourkela Steel Plant 1964–67; Deputy Chair. Hindustan Steel Ltd. 1967–69; Dir.-Gen. Bureau of Public Enterprises 1969–73; Special Sec., Ministry of Industrial Devt. 1973–74; Sec., Ministry of Works and Housing 1974–76; Adviser to Gov. of Gujarat, Chair. Public Enterprises Selection Bd., Chair. Banking Service Comm. 1976; started legal practice in Supreme Court and Delhi High Court 1977–81; Gov. Himachal Pradesh 1981–83; Gov. Karnataka 1983–88.

BANGEMANN, Martin, D.JUR.; German politician and lawyer; b. 15 Nov. 1934, Wanzleben; s. of Martin Bangemann and Lotte Telge; m. Renate Bauer 1962; three s. two d.; ed. secondary school, Emden and Univs. of Tübingen and Munich; mem. Freie Demokratische Partei (FDP) 1963–, Deputy 1969, mem. Regional Exec. Baden-Württemberg FDP 1973–78 (resgnd.), mem. Nat. Exec. 1969– (resgnd. as Gen. Sec. 1975), Chair. FDP 1985–88; mem. Bundestag 1972–80, 1987–88, European Parl. 1979–84; Minister of Finance 1984–88; EEC (now EU) Commr. for Internal Market, Industry, relations with European Parl. 1989–92, for Industrial Affairs and Tech. 1993–95, for Industrial Affairs, Information and Telecommunications Technologies Jan. 1995–, a Vice-Pres. 1993–95; Fed. Cross of Merit with Star. *Leisure interests:* philosophy, horticulture. *Address:* c/o European Commission, 200 rue de la Loi, 1049 Brussels, Belgium.

BANGERTER, Norman Howard; American politician; b. 4 Jan. 1933, Granger, Utah; s. of William H. and Isabelle (Bawden) Bangerter; m. Colleen Monson 1953; four s. two d. and one foster s.; ed. Univ. of Utah and Brigham Young Univ.; Vice-Pres. B and H Real Estate Co. 1970–; Sec. Dixie-Six Land Devt. 1980; Pres. Bangerter Hendrickson Co. 1970–, NHB Construction Co. 1983–; mem. Utah House of Reps. 1974–84, Speaker 1981–84; Gov. of Utah 1985–93; Vice-Chair., Western Govs. Asscn. 1985–86; Vice-Chair., School Facilities Sub-cttee. Educ. 1991 Project, Nat. Gov.'s Asscn.; Republican. *Leisure interests:* golf, basketball, waterskiing, reading. *Address:* NHB Construction Corpn., 2976 West 10000 S South Jordan, UT 84095, U.S.A.

BANHAM, Sir John Michael Middlecott, Kt., M.A., L.L.D.; British business executive; b. 22 Aug. 1940; s. of Terence Middlecott Banham and Belinda Joan Banham; m. Frances Favell 1965; one s. two d.; ed. Charterhouse, Queens' Coll., Cambridge; with H.M. Foreign Service 1962–64; Dir. of Marketing, Wallcoverings Div., Reed Int. 1965–69; with McKinsey & Co. Inc. 1969, Assoc. 1969–75, Prin. 1975–80, Dir. 1980–83; Controller Audit Comm. for Local Authorities in England and Wales 1983–87; Dir.-Gen. CBI March 1987–92; Chair. WestCountry TV Ltd. 1992–, John Labatt (Europe) (now Labatt Breweries of Europe) 1992–95, ECI Ventures 1992–, Local Govt. Comm. for England 1992–95, Kingfisher 1996–; Deputy Chair. Tarmac Sept. 1993, Chair., C.E.O. 1994– (Dir. 1992–); Dir. Nat. Westminster Bank 1992–98, Nat. Power 1992–98; Man. Trustee Nuffield Foundation 1988–; Hon. Treas. Cancer Research Campaign 1991–; Hon. LL.D. (Bath) 1987, Hon. D.Sc. (Loughborough) 1989, (Exeter) 1993, (Strathclyde) 1995. *Publications:* Future of the British Car Industry 1975, Realising the Promise of a National Health Service 1977, The Anatomy of Change 1994, and numerous reports for Audit Comm. on educ., social services, housing, etc. 1984–87, and on the economy, skill training, infrastructure and urban regeneration for the CBI 1987–. *Address:* c/o Westcountry Management, 64A Neal Street, Covent Garden, London, WC2H 9PA (Office); Penberth, St. Buryan, nr. Penzance, Cornwall, England. *Telephone:* 0171-379 1697 (Office). *Fax:* 0171-379 1659 (Office).

BANHARN SILPAARCHA, Nai; Thai politician; b. 20 July 1932, Suphan Buri; m. Nang Jamsai; one s. two d.; ed. Bangkok Business Coll.; mem. Municipal Ass. Suphan Buri 1974; subsequently mem. Nat. Legis. Ass.; mem. Senate 1975; Deputy Sec.-Gen. Chat Thai Party; M.P. for Suphan Buri 1976–; Deputy Minister of Industry 1976–86; Minister of Communications 1986–88, of the Interior 1988–90. *Address:* c/o Ministry of the Interior, Atsadang Road, Bangkok 10200, Thailand.

BANI-SADR, Abolhasan; Iranian politician; b. 1933, Hamadan, W. Iran; s. of the Ayatollah Sayed Nasrollah Bani-Sadr; ed. Sorbonne and Teheran Univs.; supporter of Mossadeq (Prime Minister of Iran 1951–53); joined underground anti-Shah movement 1953; imprisoned after riots over Shah's land reforms 1963; in exile in Paris 1963–79; taught at the Sorbonne; close associate of the Ayatollah Ruhollah Khomeini, and returned to Iran after overthrow of Shah; Minister of Econ. and Financial Affairs 1979–80; Acting Foreign Minister Nov. 1979 (dismissed); President of Iran 1980–81; mem. Supervisory Bd. of Cen. Bank of Iran 1979; mem. Revolutionary Council 1979–81 (Pres. 1980–81); fled to France 1981, subsequently formed Nat. Council of Resistance to oppose the Govt. (in alliance with Massoud Rajavi, Leader of Mujaheddin Kalq, and Abdel-Rahman Ghassemlov, Leader of Democratic Party of Kurdistan, Nat. Democratic Front and other resistance groups), Chair. 1981–84. *Publications:* The Economics of Divine Unity, Oil and Violence, L'espérance trahie 1982, and numerous articles and pamphlets on economics and politics.

BANJO, Ladipo Ayodeji, PH.D.; Nigerian university administrator and linguist; b. 2 May 1934, Ijebu-Igbo, Ogun State; s. of late Ven. and Mrs. S. A. Banjo; m. Alice Mbamali; two s. two d.; ed. Nigerian Coll. of Arts, Science and Tech. Univs. of Glasgow and Leeds, Univ. of Calif. (Los Angeles), Univ. of Ibadan; Educ. Officer W. Nigeria 1960–64 (Sr. Educ. Officer Jan–Oct. 1966); lecturer Dept. of English, Univ. of Ibadan 1966–71, Sr. Lecturer 1971–73, Reader and Acting Head 1973–75, Prof. 1975–97, Head 1981, Dean Faculty of Arts 1977–79, Chair. Cttee. of Deans 1978–79, Deputy Vice-Chancellor 1981–84, Vice-Chancellor 1984–91, Prof. Emer. 1997–; Dir. Reading Centre 1970–72 (Co-Dir. 1966–70); Chair. Int. Panel on English Language, West African Examination Council 1979–85, Advisory Cttee. Nat. Language Centre 1980–85; Pres. West African Modern Languages Asscn. 1981–; Vice-Pres. Int. Fed. of Languages and Literatures 1985–89, Yoruba Studies Asscn. 1985–; J.P. Oyo State 1986–. *Publications:* Oral English 1971, Letter Writing 1973, Effective Use of English 1976, Developmental English 1985, New Englishes: A West African Perspective (Ed. with A. Bamgbose and A. Thomas) 1995, Making a Virtue of Necessity: An Overview of the English Language in Nigeria 1996, In the Saddle: a Vice-Chancellor's Story 1997. *Leisure interests:* music, photography, reading. *Address:* University of Ibadan, P.O. Box 14341, Ibadan, Oyo State, Nigeria. *Fax:* (02) 8104863.

BANKS, Iain; British author; b. 1954, Fife, Scotland; ed. Stirling Univ.; worked as technician, British Steel 1976, IBM, Greenock 1978. *Publications:* The Wasp Factory 1984, Walking on Glass 1985, The Bridge 1986, Espedair Street 1987, Canal Dreams 1989, The Crow Road 1992 (adapted as Channel 4 TV series 1996), Complicity 1993, Whit 1995; science fiction (under name Iain M. Banks): Consider Phlebas 1987, The Player of Games 1988, Use of Weapons 1990, The State of the Art 1991, Against a Dark Background 1993, Feersum Endjinn 1994, Excession 1996, A Song of Stone 1998, Inversions 1998. *Address:* c/o Little, Brown, Brettenham House, Lancaster Place, London, WC2E 7EN, England. *Telephone:* 0171-911 8000. *Fax:* 0171-911 8100.

BANKS, Russell; American author; b. 28 March 1940, Barnstead, N.H.; s. of Earl Banks and Florence Banks; m. 1st Darlene Bennett (divorced 1962); one d.; m. 2nd Mary Gunst (divorced 1977); three d.; m. 3rd Kathy Walton (divorced 1988); m. 4th Chase Twichell; ed. Colgate Univ. and Univ. of N.C. at Chapel Hill; fmr. teacher of creative writing at Emerson Coll. Boston, Univ. of N.H. at Durham, Univ. of Ala., New England Coll.; teacher of creative writing, Princeton Univ. 1982–; Fels Award for Fiction 1974; John Dos Passos Award 1985; American Acad. of Arts and Letters Award 1985. *Publications include:* poetry: Waiting to Freeze 1967, 30/6 1969, Snow: Meditations of a Cautious Man in Winter 1974; novels: Family Life 1975, Hamilton Stark 1978, The Book of Jamaica 1980, The Relation of My Imprisonment 1984, Continental Drift 1985, Affliction 1989, The Sweet Hereafter 1991; collected short stories: Searching for Survivors 1975, The New World 1978, Trailerpark 1981, Success Stories 1986; short stories in literary magazines. *Address:* 1000 Park Avenue, New York, NY 10028, U.S.A.

BANKS, Tony, B.A.; British politician; ed. Archbishop Tenison's Grammar School, Kensington, York Univ. and London School of Econs.; fmr. trade union research worker; Head of Research Amalgamated Union of Eng. Workers 1969–75; an Asst. Sec. Gen. Asscn. of Broadcasting and Allied Staffs 1976–83; Political Advisor to Minister for Overseas Devt. 1975; joined Labour Party 1964; GLC mem. for Hammersmith 1970–77, for Tooting 1981–86; Chair. Gen. Purposes Cttee. GLC 1975–77, Arts and Recreation Cttee. 1981–83, GLC 1985–86; mem. Select Cttee. H.M. Treasury 1986–87, Select Cttee. on Procedure 1987–97, Jt. Lords/Commons Cttee. on Private Bill Procedure 1987–88; mem. Council of Europe Parl. Ass. and W.E.U. 1989–97; M.P. for Newham North West 1983–97, West Ham 1997–; Parl. Under Sec. of State Dept. of Culture, Media and Sport 1997–; Chair. London Group of Labour M.P.s 1987–91; mem. Bd. English Nat. Opera 1981–83, London Festival Ballet 1981–83, Nat. Theatre 1981–85. *Publication:* Out of Order (jtly.) 1993. *Address:* House of Commons, London, SW1A 0AA; 306 High Street, Stratford, London, E15 1AJ, England. *Telephone:* 0181-555 0036.

BANNEN, Ian; British actor; b. 29 June 1928, Airdrie, Scotland; s. of John James Bannen and Clare Galloway; m. Marilyn Salisbury 1978; film début in Carlton Browne of the F.O. 1958; with the R.S.C. 1961–62. *Films include:* Station Six Sahara 1963, The Hill 1964, Flight of the Phoenix 1965, Penelope 1966, Lock up Your Daughters 1968, The Deserter 1970, Doomwatch 1972, The Mackintosh Man 1973, The Offence 1973, Bite the Bullet 1975, The Sweeney 1977, Watcher in the Woods 1979, Eye of the Needle 1980, Night Crossing 1980, Gandhi 1982, Gorky Park 1983, Lamb 1985, Defence of the Realm 1985, Hope and Glory 1987, The Courier 1987, George's Island 1988, Ghostdad, The Big Man 1990, Damage 1991, A Pin for a Butterfly 1993, Braveheart 1994, Dead Sea Reels, Something to Believe In, Waking Ned

1997, To Walk with Lions. *TV appearances include:* Tinker, Tailor, Soldier, Spy 1979, Uncle Vanya, Common Pursuit, Murder in Eden 1990, Arise and Go Now, Ashenden, The Treaty, Dr. Finlay, Series 2 1993, Series 3 1994, Series 4 1995, Measure for Measure 1994, The Politician's Wife 1994, Original Sin (mini-series). *Theatre includes:* Hamlet, As You Like It, Sergeant Musgrave's Dance (all with R.S.C.); The Iceman Cometh, Long Day's Journey Into Night, Translations (Critics' Award), All My Sons. *Leisure interests:* reading, walking, swimming, photography, music. *Address:* c/o London Management, 2–4 Noel Street, London, W1V 3RB, England. *Telephone:* 0171-287 9000.

BANNISTER, (Richard) Matthew, LL.B.; British broadcasting executive; b. 16 March 1957; s. of Richard Neville Bannister and Olga Margaret Bannister; m. 1st Amanda Gerrard Walker 1984 (died 1988); one d.; m. 2nd Shelagh Margaret Macleod 1989; one s.; ed. King Edward VII School, Sheffield, Nottingham Univ.; Presenter, BBC Radio Nottingham 1978–81; Reporter/Presenter Capital Radio, London 1981–83, Deputy Head News and Talks 1985–87, Head 1987–88; with Newsbeat, BBC Radio 1 1983–85; Man. Ed. BBC Greater London Radio 1988–91, Project Co-ordinator, BBC Charter Renewal 1991–93, Controller BBC Radio 1 1993–96, Dir. BBC Radio June 1996–98, Head of Production BBC TV 1999–. *Leisure interests:* rock music, collecting P. G. Wodehouse first edns. *Address:* BBC Television Centre, Wood Lane, London, W12 7RJ, England.

BANNISTER, Sir Roger G., Kt., C.B.E., D.M., F.R.C.P.; British athlete, consultant physician, neurologist and university administrator; b. 23 March 1929, London; s. of the late Ralph and of Alice Bannister; m. Moyra Elver Jacobsson; two s. two d.; ed. City of Bath Boys' School, Univ. Coll. School, Exeter and Merton Colls., Oxford, St. Mary's Hosp. Medical School, London; winner, Oxford and Cambridge Mile 1947–50; Pres. Oxford Univ. Athletic Club 1948; British Mile Champion 1951, 1953, 1954; world record one mile 1954, first sub-four minute mile 1954; Master Pembroke College, Oxford 1985–93; Hon. Consultant Neurologist, St. Mary's Hosp. Medical School, Nat. Hosp. for Neurology and Neurosurgery, London (non-exec. Dir.), London and Oxford Dist. and Region; Chair. St. Mary's Hosp. Devt. Trust; Chair. Govt. Working Group on Sport in the Univs. 1995–97; Chair. Clinical Autonomic Research Soc. 1982–84; mem. Physiological Soc., Medical Research Soc. Asscn. of British Neurologists; Fellow Imperial College; Hon. Fellow Exeter Coll., Oxford 1980, Merton Coll., Oxford 1986; Trustee Leeds Castle Foundation 1988–, St. Mary's Hosp. Medical School Devt. Trust 1994–; Hon. Fellow UMIST 1974; Hon. LL.D. (Liverpool) 1972; Hon. D.Sc. (Sheffield) 1978, (Grinnell) 1984, (Bath) 1984, (Rochester) 1986, (Williams) 1987; Dr. h.c. (Jyvaskylä, Finland); Hon. M.D. (Pavia) 1986; Hon. D.L. (Univ. of Victoria, Canada) 1994, (Univ. of Wales, Cardiff) 1995, (Loughborough) 1996, (Univ. of East Anglia) 1997; Hans-Heinrich Siegbert Prize 1977. *Publications:* First Four Minutes 1955 (now republished as Four Minute Mile 1989), Ed. Brain and Bannister's Clinical Neurology 1992, various medical articles on physiology and neurology, jt. Ed. Autonomic Failure 1993. *Address:* 21 Bardwell Road, Oxford, OX2 6SV, England. *Telephone:* (01865) 511413.

BANNON, John Charles, B.A., LL.B.; Australian politician; b. 7 May 1943; s. of C. Bannon; m. 1st Robyn Layton 1968 (dissolved); one d.; m. 2nd. Angela Bannon 1982; ed. St. Peter's Coll., Univ. of Adelaide; Industrial Advocate AWU 1969–73; Adviser to Commonwealth Minister of Labour and Immigration 1973–75; Asst. Dir. S. Australian Dept. of Labour and Industry 1975–77; mem. House Ass. 1977–93; Minister for Community Devt., Minister for Local Govt., Minister for Recreation and Sport 1978–79; Leader of the Opposition 1979–82; Premier and Treasurer of S. Australia, Minister of State Devt., and Minister for the Arts 1982–85; Premier and Treasurer of S. Australia and Minister for the Arts 1985–89; Premier and Treasurer of S. Australia 1982–92; Nat. Pres. Australian Labor Party 1988–91; Dir. Australian Broadcasting Corpn. 1994–, Adelaide Symphony Orchestra Bd.; mem. Council Constitutional Centenary Foundation 1995–; Ed. The New Federalist (Nat. Journal of Australian Fed. History) 1998. *Publications:* The Crucial Colony 1994; articles, monographs on Fed./State relations. *Leisure interests:* running, gardening. *Address:* Australian Broadcasting Corpn., 700 Harris Street, Ultimo, N.S.W. 2007, Australia. *Telephone:* 618 82012581. *Fax:* 618 82240062.

BANVILLE, John; Irish author; b. Wexford; m. Janet Durham; two s.; fmrly. night copy ed. on The Irish Times, Literary Ed. 1988–; recipient of Guinness Peat Aviation Prize for The Book of Evidence 1989. *Publications:* eight novels including: Birchwood, Dr Copernicus, Kepler, The Newton Letter, Mefisto, The Book of Evidence 1989, Ghosts 1993, Athena 1995, The Untouchable 1996. *Address:* c/o Sheil Land Associates Ltd., 43 Doughty Street, London, WC1N 2LF, England.

BANZER SUÁREZ, Gen. Hugo; Bolivian politician and army officer; b. 10 May 1926, Santa Cruz; s. of César Banzer and Luisa Suárez; m. Yolanda G. Prada 1962; two s. three d.; ed. Colegio Militar, La Paz; Commdr. Bolivian 4th Cavalry Regiment; Minister of Educ. and Culture 1964–66; Mil. Attaché Washington, D.C. 1967–69; Dir. Colegio Militar 1969–71; in exile Jan.-Aug. 1971; Pres. of Bolivia 1971–78, Aug. 1997–; overthrown in coup July 1978; Leader Acción Democrática Nacionalista 1980–93; in exile, Argentina, then Pres. cand. 1985; Order of Mil. Merit (U.S.A.), and other national and foreign decorations. *Address:* Oficina del Presidente, Palacio de Gobierno, Plaza Murillo, La Paz, Bolivia.

BAO TONG; Chinese political prisoner and former official; fmr. aide to CCP leader Zhao Ziyang; imprisoned following Tiananmen Square massacre 1989–96; now on probation.

BAO WENKUI; Chinese agronomist; b. 8 May 1916; ed. in U.S.A.; Prof. Chinese Acad. of Agricultural Sciences; Deputy, 5th NPC 1978–83; Dir. Inst. of Crop Breeding and Cultivation, Beijing 1981–; Deputy, 6th NPC 1983–88; mem. Dept. of Biology, Academia Sinica 1982–. *Address:* Chinese Academy of Agricultural Sciences, Baishiqiao Road, Haidian, Beijing 100081, People's Republic of China.

BAO XUDING; Chinese politician; b. Feb. 1939, Wuxi City, Jiangsu Prov.; ed. Shenyang School of Machine Bldg. 1958, CCP Cen. Party School 1986; joined CCP 1961; Vice-Dir. then Dir. Dept. of Machinery of Sichuan Prov. 1986; Dir. Sichuan Provincial Planning Comm. 1988; Vice-Minister of Machine Bldg. and Electronics Industries 1990; Vice-Minister of Machine Bldg. Industry 1993, Minister 1996–98; Vice-Minister State Devt. and Planning Comm. 1998–; mem. 15th CCP Cen. Cttee. 1997–. *Address:* c/o State Development and Planning Commission, 38 Yuetan Nan Jie, Beijing 100823, People's Republic of China.

BAPPOO, Sheilabai; Mauritian politician; b. June 1947; m. Dayanan Bappoo; two d.; ed. Henry Boswell and Queen Elizabeth Coll.; worked as teacher 1966–83; joined Mouvement Militant Mauricien (MMM) 1970, Pres. 1973; Municipal Councillor for MMM 1977–80; joined Mouvement Socialiste Mauricien (MSM) 1983; mem. Nat. Ass. 1983–; Minister for Women's Rights and Family Welfare 1983–86, of Labour and Industrial Relations, Women's Rights and Family Welfare 1986–91, of Women's Rights, Child Devt. and Family Welfare 1991–95. *Leisure interests:* reading, cooking, music. *Address:* c/o Mouvement Socialiste Mauricien, Sun Trust Building, 31 Edith Cavell Street, Port Louis, Mauritius.

BARAK, Lieut.-Gen. Ehud; Israeli government minister and fmr. army officer; b. 2 Feb. 1942, Israel; s. of Israel Barak and Esther Barak; m. Nava Cohen; three d.; ed. Hebrew Univ. Jerusalem and Stanford Univ. Calif.; enlisted in Israeli Defence Force (IDF) 1959; grad. Infantry Officers' course 1962; commando course, France 1963; Armoured Corps Co. Commdrs. course 1968; various command roles; also served in operations br. of Gen. Staff; active service in Six Day War 1967 and Yom Kippur War 1973; Commdr. Tank Commdrs. course 1974; Head, Gen. Staff Planning Dept. 1982–83; Dir. IDF Mil. Intelligence 1983–86; Commdr. Cen. Command 1986–87; Deputy Chief of Gen. Staff Israeli Defence Force 1987–91, Chief of Gen. Staff 1991–94; Minister of Interior July–Nov. 1995, of Foreign Affairs Nov. 1995–June 1996; Chair. Labour Party 1997–; mem. Knesset (Parl.) and of Parl. Security and Foreign Affairs Cttee. June 1996. *Leisure interest:* playing the piano. *Address:* Israel Labour Party, 110 Ha'yarkon Street, Tel-Aviv 61032; Knesset, Jerusalem, Israel. *Telephone:* (3) 5209222 (Tel-Aviv). *Fax:* (3) 5271744 (Tel-Aviv).

BARAKAT, Nayel, PH.D., F.INST.P.; Egyptian professor of experimental physics; b. 22 Sept. 1922, Cairo; s. of M.H. Barakat Bey and N. el Safty; m. Afaf Ali Nada 1956; one s. two d.; ed. Univs. of Cairo and London; lecturer, Alexandria Univ. 1951–54; lecturer, Ain Shams Univ. 1954–58, Asst. Prof. 1958–64, Prof. of Experimental Physics 1964–88, Prof. Emer. 1988–, Dean, Faculty of Science 1971–76; Cultural Counsellor and Dir. of Educ. Mission in Fed. Repub. of Germany, Netherlands and Denmark 1976–81; Hon. D.Sc. (London) 1992; Egyptian Nat. Award in Physics 1958, 1963; Nat. Award in Basic Science 1990. *Publications:* 85 papers in specialized journals. *Leisure interests:* Arabic and classical music, photography. *Address:* 4 Ibn Marawan Street, Appt. 504, Dokki, Cairo, Egypt. *Telephone:* 3484568.

BARALLE, Francisco Ernesto, M.D., PH.D.: British medical research scientist; b. 26 Oct. 1943, Buenos Aires, Argentina; s. of Juan Pedro Baralle and Maria Teresa Rossi; m. Maria Chiara Bolis 1968; one s. three d.; ed. Univs. of Buenos Aires and Naples; mem. Faculty and Research Fellow, Univ. of Buenos Aires 1966–74; Head of Chem. Research, Nat. Inst. of Pharmacology, Univ. of Buenos Aires 1970–74; staff scientist, MRC Lab. of Molecular Biology Cambridge 1974–80; Univ. lecturer, Sir William Dunn School of Pathology, Univ. of Oxford 1980–87, Fellow Magdalen Coll. 1980–87; Scientific Dir. Istituto Sieroterapico Milanese, Milan 1987–90; Dir.-Gen. Int. Centre for Genetic Eng. and Biotech. (ICGEB), UN Industrial Devt. Org. (UNIDO) 1990; Visiting Prof. at several Italian univs.; mem. European Molecular Biology Org.; Konex Prize 1993. *Publications:* more than 90 scientific and clinical publs. *Leisure interests:* squash, archaeology. *Address:* International Centre for Genetic Engineering and Biotechnology (ICGEB), Padriciano 99, 34012 Trieste, Italy. *Telephone:* (40) 3757337. *Fax:* (40) 226555.

BARAM, Uzi; Israeli politician; b. 1937, Jerusalem; co-f. Labour Party's Young Guard, Sec. 1966–70; Chair. Young Leadership Dept., World Zionist Org. 1972–75; Chair. Labour Party (Jerusalem br.) 1975–81, Sec.-Gen. 1984–88; Chair. Immigration and Absorption Cttee. 1984–92; Minister of Tourism 1992–96, fmrly. of Religious Affairs; mem. Knesset 1977–, Foreign Affairs and Defence Cttee. 1984–92. *Address:* c/o Ministry of Tourism, P.O. Box 1018, 24 Rehov King George, Jerusalem 91000, Israel.

BARAŃCZAK, Stanisław; Polish poet and literary critic; b. 13 Nov. 1946, Poznań; m.; one s. one d.; ed. Adam Mickiewicz Univ., Poznań; Asst. Adam Mickiewicz Univ. 1969–80; in the USA 1981–; Prof. Harvard Univ., jt. ed. Literary Publs. 1983–, Ed. monthly The Polish Review. *Collections of poetry* *include:* Korekta twarzy (Face correction) 1968, Jednym tchem (In one breath) 1970, Dziennik poranny (Morning Diary) 1972, Sztuczne oddychanie (Breathing Underwater) 1974, Ja wiem, że to niesłuszne (I know that it's wrong) 1977, Atlantyda (Atlantis) 1986, Widokówka z tego świata (A postcard from this World) 1988, Podróż zimowa (Winter Journey) 1994. *Criticism includes:* Ironia i harmonia (Irony and Harmony) 1973, Etyka i poetyka (Ethics and Poetry) 1979; Przed i po (Before and After) 1988, Tablica z Macondo (Board from Macondo) 1990; numerous translations of English, American and Russian poetry, and of William Shakespeare. *Address:* 8 Broad Dale, Newton Wille, MA 02160, U.S.A.

BARBA, Eugenio, M.A.; Danish theatre director; b. 29 Oct. 1936, Brindisi, Italy; s. of Emanuele Barba and Vera Gaeta; m. Judith Patricia Howard Jones 1965; two s.; ed. Univ. of Oslo, Theatre School, Warsaw and Jerzy Grotowski's Theatre Lab. Opole; founder and Dir. Odin Teatret (Interscandinavian Theatre Lab.) 1964–; more than 20 productions 1965–; founder and Dir. Int. School of Theatre Anthropology 1979–; mem. Bd. of Advisers, Int. Cttee. Théâtre des Nations 1975–80; mem. Bd. of Advisers, Int. Asscn. of Performing Arts Semiotics 1981–85; adviser, Danish Ministry of Culture 1981–82; UNESCO adviser, Centro de Estudios Teatrales, Museo de Arte Moderno, Bogotá 1983; adviser, Centre of Theatre Exchanges, Rio de Janeiro 1987–; lectures regularly at univs., theatre schools, etc.; Dr. h.c. (Århus) 1988; Danish Acad. Award 1980, Mexican Theatre Critics' Prize 1984, Diego Fabbri Prize 1986, Pirandello Int. Prize 1996. *Publications include:* In Search of a Lost Theatre 1965, The Floating Islands (drama) 1978, Il Brecht dell' Odin 1981, La Corsa dei Contrari 1981, Beyond the Floating Islands 1985, The Dilated Body 1985, Anatomie de l'Acteur (with N. Savarese) 1988, Brechts Aske, Oxyrhincus Evangeliet (two plays) 1986, The Secret Art of the Performer 1990, The Paper Canoe 1992, Theatre—Solitude, craft, revolt 1996; articles, essays etc. *Address:* Nordisk Teaterlaboratorium, Odin Teatret, Box 1283, 7500 Holstebro, Denmark. *Telephone:* (45) 97 42 47 77. *Fax:* (45) 97 41 04 82.

BARBARA, Agatha; Maltese politician; b. 11 March 1923, Zabbar; d. of late Joseph and Antonia (née Agius) Barbara; ed. Govt. Grammar School, Valletta; school teacher; mem. Labour Party 1946–82; Malta's first female M.P.; M.P. 1947–82; Minister of Educ. 1955–58, 1971–74, of Labour, Culture and Welfare 1974–81; Pres. of Repub. of Malta 1982–87; fmr. mem. ARP, later supervisor Victory Kitchens and Army Munitions Depot (World War II); fmr. Man. Freedom Press; mem. St. John Alliance (UK), Int. Social Democratic Women; Pres. Malta Labour Party Women's Club; Founder and Chair. Exec. Cttee. Malta Labour Party Women's Movement; Chair. The Samaritans—Malta 1988–; Patron ad vitam St. Michael's Band Club, Maltese Settlers' Club (Australia); Hon. mem. of several int. acads. of Science and Literature; Hon. Ph.D. (Beijing); Companion of Honour of Nat. Order of Merit, 50th Anniversary George Cross Medal, 50th Anniversary of Responsible Govt. Medal 1996; Grand Dame (Grand Cordon) S.O. St. John of Jerusalem Kts. Hospitaller 1996; numerous foreign honours and decorations. *Leisure interests:* philately, classical and modern music. *Address:* 'Il-Kenn Taghna', Wied Il-Ghajn Street, Zabbar, Malta. *Telephone:* 825208.

BARBENEL, Joseph Cyril, PH.D., F.R.S.E.; British bioengineer; b. 2 Jan. 1937, London; m. Lesley Mary Hyde Jowett 1964; two s. one d.; ed. Hackney Downs Grammar School, London, London Hosp. Dental School, Univ. of London, Queen's Coll., Univ. of St. Andrews, Univ. of Strathclyde, Glasgow; Dental House Surgeon, London Hosp. 1960; Royal Army Dental Corps 1960–62; gen. dental practice, London 1963; Lecturer, Dental Prosthetics, Univ. of Dundee 1967–69, Univ. of Strathclyde 1970, Sr. Lecturer, Bioeng. Unit 1970–82, Reader 1982–85, Prof. 1985–, Head Dept. 1992–98, Vice Dean (Research) Faculty of Eng. 1997–; Consulting Prof., Chongqing Univ., China; Visiting Prof. Tech. Univ. of Vienna; Chancellor Int. Faculty for Artificial Organs; Nuffield Foundation Award 1963–66. *Publications:* Clinical Aspects of Blood Rheology (with Lowe and Forbes) 1981, Pressure Sores (with Lowe and Forbes) 1983, Blood flow in Artificial Organs and Cardiovascular Prostheses (with co-eds.) 1988, Blood flow in the Brain (with co-eds.) 1988, numerous scientific papers. *Leisure interests:* music, theatre, reading. *Address:* University of Strathclyde Bioengineering Unit, Wolfson Centre, 106 Rottenrow, Glasgow, G4 0NW; 151 Maxwell Drive, Glasgow, G41, Scotland (Home). *Telephone:* (0141) 552 4400 Ext. 3221 (Office).

BARBER, Baron (Life Peer), cr. 1974, of Wentbridge in West Yorkshire; **Anthony Perrinot Lysberg Barber,** P.C., T.D.; British politician and former banker; b. 4 July 1920, Hull; s. of John Barber, C.B.E., and Katy Lysberg; m. 1st Jean Patricia Asquith 1950 (died 1983); two d.; m. 2nd Rosemary Youens 1989; ed. Retford School and Oriel Coll., Oxford; army service 1939–40, Royal Air Force 1940–45; mem. Parl. 1951–64, 1965–74; Parl. Private Sec., Air Ministry 1952–54; Govt. Whip 1955–57; Lord Commissioner of the Treasury 1957–58; Parl. Private Sec. to Prime Minister 1958–59; Econ. Sec. to the Treasury 1959–62; Financial Sec. to the Treasury 1962–63; Minister of Health 1963–64; Chair. Conservative Party 1967–70; Chancellor of Duchy of Lancaster June-July 1970; Chancellor of Exchequer 1970–74; Dir. British Ropes (now Bridon) 1964–70, 1974–83, several banks incl. Chartered Bank 1966–70, British Petroleum 1979–88; Chair. Redfearn Nat. Glass 1967, Standard Chartered Bank 1974–87, R.A.F. Benevolent Fund 1991–95; Vice Chair. Charing Cross and Westminster Medical School 1984–95; Deputy Lieut., West Yorks. 1987; mem. Cttee. of Inquiry into events leading to Argentine invasion of the Falkland Islands 1982, Commonwealth Group on S. Africa 1985; Hon. Fellow, Oriel Coll., Oxford 1971. *Address:* House of Lords, London, SW1A 0PW, England.

BARBER, Clarence Lyle, O.C., PH.D., F.R.S.C.; Canadian professor of economics; b. 5 May 1917, Wolseley, Sask.; s. of Richard Edward Barber and Lulu Pearl Lyons; m. Barbara Anne Patchet 1947; four s.; ed. Wolseley High School, Univ. of Saskatchewan, Clark Univ., Univ. of Minnesota, U.S.A.; served R.C.A.F. 1943–45; Statistician, Statistics Canada 1945–48; Asst. Prof., McMaster Univ. 1948–49; Assoc. Prof., Univ. of Manitoba 1949–55, Prof. 1956–83, Distinguished Prof. 1982, Prof. Emer. 1985–; Dir. of Research, Royal Comm. on Flood Cost-Benefit, Man. 1957–59; Adviser on Nat. Income, Govt. of Philippines 1959–60; Commr. Royal Comm. on Farm Machinery 1966–70, on Welfare, Man. 1972, Nat. Comm. on Inflation 1979, Royal Comm. on the Econ. Union and Devt. Prospects for Canada 1982–85; Pres. Canadian Asscn. of Univ. Teachers 1958–59, Canadian Econ. Asscn. 1972–73; Hon. LL.D. (Univ. of Guelph) 1988. *Publications:* Inventories and the Business Cycle 1952, Theory of Fiscal Policy Applied to a Province 1966, Collected Economic Papers 1982, Unemployment and Inflation 1980 and Controlling Inflation 1982 (both with J. C. P. McCallum); On the Origins of the Great Depression 1978, Can We Avoid Another Great Depression (essay) 1990, False Promises: The Failure of Conservative Economics 1993. *Leisure interests:* curling, skiing, bowling, bridge. *Address:* 766 Richmond Avenue, Victoria, B.C., V8S 3Z1, Canada. *Telephone:* (250) 595-6891.

BARBER, Frances; British actress; b. 13 May 1957, Wolverhampton; ed. Bangor and Cardiff Univs.; fmrly. with Hull Truck Theatre Co., Glasgow Citizens Theatre, Tricycle Theatre, R.S.C. *Television appearances include:* Clem, Jackie's Story, Home Sweet Home, Flame to the Phoenix, Reilly, Ace of Spies, Those Glory Glory Days, Hard Feelings, Behaving Badly, The Nightmare Year. *Film appearances include:* The Missionary 1982, A Zed and Two Noughts, White City, Castaway, Prick Up Your Ears, Sammy and Rosie Get Laid, We Think the World of You, The Grasscutter, Separate Bedrooms, Young Soul Rebels, Secret Friends. *Stage appearances include:* Night of the Iguana, Pygmalion, Closer.

BARBER, John Norman Romney; British business executive; b. 22 April 1919, Leigh-on-Sea, Essex; s. of George Ernest and Gladys Eleanor Barber; m. Babette Chalu 1941; one s.; Principal, Cen. Finance Dept., Ministry of Supply 1946–55; with Ford Motor Co. Ltd. 1955–65, Dir. of Finance 1962–65, Founder, Chair. Ford Motor Credit Co. 1963; Dir. of Finance, AEI Ltd. 1966; Finance Dir. Leyland Motor Corpn. 1967, Dir. of Finance and Planning, British Leyland Motor Corpn. 1968, Deputy Man. Dir. 1971, Deputy Chair. 1973–74; Deputy Chair. John E. Wiltshier Gp. Ltd. 1979–88; Chair. Aberhurst Ltd. 1976–89, A. C. Edwards Eng. Ltd. 1976–81; Dir. Acrow PLC 1977–85, Good Relations Group PLC 1980–87, Cox & Kings Holdings Ltd. 1980–81, Spear and Jackson Int. PLC 1980–86, C & K Consulting Group 1982–86, Cox & Kings Financial Services Ltd 1980–85, C & K Exec. Search Ltd 1981–85, Economists Advisory Group Ltd. 1981–, U.K. Investments Ltd. 1985–99, The Communication Group Holdings PLC 1990–99; Past Chair. Bd. of Trade Investments Grants Advisory Cttee.; fmr. mem. Royal Comm. on Medical Educ.; fmr. mem. Advisory Cttee. on Energy Conservation to Ministry of Energy; fmr. Vice-Pres., Soc. of Motor Mfrs. and Traders; Companion Inst. of Management. *Leisure interests:* motor sport, photography, reading, forestry. *Address:* Woodpecker Lodge, Romsey Road, Ower, Hants., SO51 6AE, England. *Telephone:* (01703) 811060. *Fax:* (01703) 811070.

BARBER, Lloyd Ingram, C.C., PH.D., LL.D.; Canadian professor and administrator; b. 8 March 1932, Regina, Saskatchewan; s. of Lewis Muir Barber and Hildred (née Ingram) Barber; m. Muriel Pauline (née Duna) MacBean 1956; three s. three d.; ed. Luther Coll., Univs. of Saskatchewan, Calif. and Washington; instructor in Commerce, Univ. of Sask. 1955, Asst. Prof. of Commerce 1957–64, Assoc. Prof. 1964, Prof. 1974–76, Dean 1965, Vice-Pres. 1968–74; Prof. of Admin. and Pres., Univ. of Regina, Sask. 1976–90, Pres. Emer. 1993–; Commr. Sask. Royal Comm. on Govt. Admin. 1964; Indian Claims Commr. 1969–77; Special Enquirer for Elder Indian Testimony 1977–81; Hon. Prof. Shandong Univ. 1986; Hon. LL.D. (Univs. of Alberta, Concordia and Regina); Saskatchewan Order of Merit; Hon. Sask. Indian Chief; Centennial Medal 1967, Vanier Medal 1979. *Publications include:* Youth in our Time (co-author) 1966, Barber Commission on SaskEnergy Report 1989. *Leisure interests:* hunting, fishing, sailing, swimming, travel, reading, gardening. *Address:* P.O. Box 510, Regina Beach, Sask., S0G 4C0, Canada (Home). *Telephone:* (306) 729-2336. *Fax:* (306) 729-4908.

BARBERÁ GUILLEM, Emilio, DR. MED.; Spanish university rector; b. 14 Feb. 1946, Valencia; s. of Edelmiro Barberá and Emilia Guillem; two s.; ed. Univ. of Valencia; Dir. Lab. of Quantitative Biol. Instituto Investigaciones Citológicas, C.A.M.P., Valencia 1969–74; Section Head, Centro Investigaciones Ciudad Sanit. 'La Fe' 1974–76; Investigator, Dept. of Pathology, Faculty of Medicine, Valencia 1976–79; Asst. Prof. Univ. of Valencia 1976–78, Assoc. Prof. 1978–79; Prof. Univ. of Valladolid 1979–80; Prof. of Histology and Gen. Embryology, Univ. del País Vasco 1980–; Dir. Dept. of Histology and Cellular Biology 1980, Rector 1986–92; other professional appts.; mem. Real Acad. de Medicina de Valencia, Real Acad. de Medicina de Vizcaya and nine int. biological socs. *Publications:* numerous scientific articles in int. reviews; book chapters. *Leisure interests:* photography, travel. *Address:* Universidad del País Vasco/Euskal Herriko Unibertsitatea, Edificio Rectorado, Apartado de Correos 1397, 48080 Bilbao, Spain. *Telephone:* (34) (4) 463.76.53.

BARBIERI, Fedora; Italian singer; b. 4 June 1919; ed. Trieste High School and Conservatoire; scholarship to Teatro Lirico, Florence 1940; debut as Fidalma in Cimarosa's The Secret Marriage, Teatro Comunale, Florence 1940; has appeared in leading roles at La Scala, Milan 1942–, Teatro Colón, Buenos Aires 1947–, Metropolitan Opera House, New York and Royal Opera House, Covent Garden, London 1950–; has also appeared at numerous important festivals and opera seasons in Italy, Germany, U.S.A., France, Spain, Portugal, Brazil, Austria, etc.; has sung leading roles in recordings of Aida, Il Trovatore, Requiem, Falstaff, Un Ballo in Maschera (Verdi), La Gioconda (Ponchielli), La Favorita and Linda di Chamonix (Donizetti), Suor Angelica (Puccini). *Address:* Viale Belfiore 9, Florence, Italy.

BARBOSA, Rubens Antonio, M.A.; Brazilian diplomatist; b. 13 June 1938, São Paulo; m. Maria Ignez Correa da Costa 1969; one s. one d.; ed. Univ. of Brazil, São Paulo and London School of Econs.; Exec. Sec. Brazilian Trade Comm. with Socialist Countries of E. Europe 1976–84; Chief of Staff of Minister of Foreign Affairs 1985–86; Under-Sec.-Gen. for Multilateral and Special Political Affairs 1986–87; Sec. for Int. Affairs, Ministry of Economy 1987–88; Amb. and Perm. Rep. to Latin American Integration Asscn. (ALADI) 1988–91; Pres. Cttee. of Reps. ALADI 1991–92; Under-Sec.-Gen. for Regional Integration, Econ. Affairs and Foreign Trade, Ministry of Foreign Affairs 1991–93; coordinator Brazilian section of Mercosul (Southern Cone Common Market) 1991–93; Amb. to U.K. 1994–; Pres. Asscn. of Coffee Producing Countries 1993–; Grand Cross, Order of Rio Branco, Commdr. Légion d'Honneur, Hon. L.V.O., Hon. G.C.V.O.; decorations from Argentina, Mexico and Italy. *Publications:* América Latina em Perspectiva: Integração Regional da Retórica à Realidade 1991; Panorama: Visto de Londres 1998; essays and articles in newspapers and magazines. *Leisure interests:* classical music, tennis. *Address:* Embassy of Brazil, 32 Green Street, London, W1Y 4AT, England. *Telephone:* 0171-629 6044. *Fax:* 0171-493 5105.

BARBOT, Ivan, L. ÈS L.; French police commissioner; b. 5 Jan. 1937, Ploeuc; s. of Pierre Barbot and Anne (née Le Calvez) Barbot; m. Roselyne de Lestrange 1971; three c.; ed. Lycée de Saint-Brieuc, Univ. of Paris; Prin. Pvt. Sec. to Chief Commr., Tarn-et-Garonne 1961; Prin. Pvt. Sec., later Dir. of Staff to Chief Commr., Haute-Savoie 1962; Dir. of Staff, Paris Region Pref. 1967; Deputy Chief Commr., Etampes 1969; Deputy Chief Commr. without portfolio, Official Rep. to the Cabinet 1974; Tech. Adviser to Minister of the Interior 1974–77; Sec.-Gen. Seine-Saint-Denis 1977–82; Chief Commr. and Supt., Dept. de la Charente 1982–85, du Var 1985–87; Dir.-Gén. Police nat. 1987–89; Pres. Interpol 1988–92; Prefect Poitou-Charentes 1989, Vienne 1989–91; with Prime Minister's office, responsible for security 1991–92; Pres. Admin. Council of French concessionary co. for the construction and exploitation of the road tunnel under Mont-Blanc 1992–94; Chair., C.E.O. OFEMA 1993–, SOFMA 1996–; Pres., Dir.-Gen. SOFEMA 1997–; Officier, Légion d'honneur, Commdr., Ordre national du Mérite. *Address:* SOFEMA, 58 ave Marceau, 75008 Paris (Office); 4 rue Marguerite, 75017 Paris, France (Home).

BARBOUR, Haley Reeves, J.D.; American politician; b. 22 Oct. 1947, Yazoo City, Miss.; s. of late Jeptha F. Barbour Jr. and LeFlore Johnson; m. Marsha Dickson 1971; two s.; ed. Univ. of Mississippi; field rep. Miss. Republican Party 1968, Deputy Exec. Dir. 1972–73, Exec. Dir. 1973–76; Regional Technician, Bureau of Census 1969–70; Exec. Dir. Southern Asscn. of Republican State Chairmen 1973–76; Southeastern U.S. Campaign Dir. Pres. Ford Cttee. 1976; Chair. 3rd Congressional Dist. Cttee. Miss. 1976–84; Republican nominee, U.S. Senate 1982; Municipal Judge, Yazoo City 1980–81, City Attorney 1981–85; Chair. Republican Nat. Cttee. 1993–97; Dir. Deposit Guarranty Corpn.; mem. Bd. Deposit Guarranty Nat. Bank; mem. Bd. Dirs. Amtrak & Mobil Telecommunications Technologies Inc. *Publication:* Agenda for America 1996. *Address:* Republican National Committee, Dwight D. Eisenhower Republican Center, 310 First Street, S.E., Washington, DC 20003, U.S.A.

BARBOUR, Very Rev. Robert Alexander Stewart, K.C.V.O., M.C., M.A., B.D., S.T.M., D.D.; British university professor and ecclesiastic (retd.); b. 11 May 1921, Edinburgh; s. of George F. Barbour and Helen V. Hepburne-Scott; m. Margaret Pigot 1950; three s. one d.; ed. Rugby School, Balliol Coll. Oxford, Univ. of St. Andrews and Yale Univ.; mil. service 1940–45; Lecturer and Sr. Lecturer in New Testament, New Coll. Univ. of Edin. 1955–71; Prof. of New Testament Exegesis, Univ. of Aberdeen 1971–85; Master, Christ's Coll. Aberdeen 1977–82; Chaplain-in-Ordinary to H.M. The Queen 1976–91; Dean, Chapel Royal in Scotland 1981–91; Prelate of Priory of Scotland of Order of St. John 1977–93; Moderator, Gen. Ass. of Church of Scotland 1979–80; Chair. Scottish Churches Council 1982–86; Hon. D.D. *Publications:* The Scottish Horse 1939–45 1950, Traditio-Historical Criticism of the Gospels 1972, What is the Church For? 1973. *Leisure interests:* music, forestry, walking. *Address:* Old Fincastle, Pitlochry, Perthshire PH16 5RJ, Scotland. *Telephone:* 01796 473209.

BARCHUK, Vasily Vasilievich, C.ECON.SC.; Russian politician and economist; b. 11 March 1941, Komsomolsk-on-Amur; m.; one d.; ed. All-Union Inst. of Finance and Econ. U.S.S.R. Acad. of Nat. Econ.; worked in tax inspection bodies in Khabarovsk Region 1958–72; staff-mem. R.S.F.S.R. Ministry of Finance 1972–84, U.S.S.R. Ministry of Finance 1986–91, Deputy Minister of Finance April–Nov. 1991; First Deputy Minister of Finance of Russia 1991–92, Minister 1992–93; Chair. of Bd., Pensions Fund of Russian Fed. 1993–. *Address:* Pensions Fund, Shabolovka str. 4, 117934, Moscow, Russia. *Telephone:* 237-36-37; 230-92-45. *Fax:* 959-83-53.

BARD, Allen J., PH.D.; American professor of chemistry; b. 18 Dec. 1933, New York; m. Frances Segal 1957; one s. one d.; ed. City Coll. of New York and Harvard Univ.; Thayer Scholarship 1955–56; Nat. Science Foundation Postdoctoral Fellowship 1956–58; joined chem. staff of Univ. of Tex., Austin 1958, Prof. of Chem. 1967, Jack S. Josey Prof. 1980–82, Norman Hackerman Prof. 1982–85, Hackerman-Welch Prof. 1985–; consultant to several labs. including E.I. duPont, Texas Instruments and several govt. agencies; research interests in application of electrochemical methods to study of chemical problems; Vice-Chair. Nat. Research Council; Ed.-in-Chief Journal of American Chemical Soc. 1982–; Chair. Nat. Acad. of Sciences Chemical Section 1996–; Gov. Weizmann Inst. 1995–; Fellow A.A.A.S.; mem. American Chemical Soc., Electrochemical Soc.; Ward Medal in Chem. 1955, Harrison Howe Award, American Chemical Soc. 1980, Carl Wagner Memorial Award, Electrochemical Soc. 1981, Bruno Breyer Memorial Medal, Royal Australian Chem. Inst. 1984, Fisher Award in Analytical Chem., American Chemical Soc. 1984, Charles N. Reilley Award, Soc. of Electroanalytical Chem. 1984; Dr. h.c. (Paris) 1986, New York Acad. of Sciences Award in Math. and Physical Sciences 1986, Willard Gibbs Award, American Chem. Soc. 1987, Olin-Palladium Award, Electrochem. Soc. 1987, Oesper Award, Univ. of Cincinnati 1989. *Publications:* Chemical Equilibrium 1966, Electrochemical Methods (with L. R. Faulkner) 1980; approx. 400 papers and book chapters; Ed. Electroanalytical Chemistry (15 vols.) 1966–, The Encyclopedia of the Electrochemistry of the Elements, 16 vols. 1973–82. *Address:* Department of Chemistry, University of Texas, Austin, TX 78712, U.S.A. (Office).

BARDER, Sir Brian Leon, K.C.M.G., B.A.; British diplomatist (retd.); b. 20 June 1934, Bristol; s. of Harry Barder and Vivien Young; m. Jane M. Cornwell 1958; two d. one s.; ed. Sherborne School and St. Catharine's Coll., Cambridge; Colonial Office 1957–64; U.K. Mission to UN, New York 1964–68; FCO 1968–70; First Sec. Moscow 1971–73; Counsellor, Canberra 1973–77; Canadian Nat. Defence Coll. 1977–78; Head of Southern Africa Dept., FCO 1978–82; Amb. to Ethiopia 1982–86, to Poland 1986–88; High Commr. in Nigeria and Amb. (non-resident) to Benin 1988–91; High Commr. in Australia 1991–94; Know How Fund Diplomatic Training Consultant 1996; mem. Bd. of Man. Royal Hosp. for Neurodisability 1996–; mem. English-Speaking Union Cttee. for Int. Debate and Communication Training 1996–. *Leisure interests:* music, computer, cycling. *Address:* 10 Melrose Road, London, SW18 1NE, England. *Telephone:* 0181-874 5909.

BARDINI, Adolfo, DR.ING.; Italian industrial executive; b. 9 April 1915, Genoa; s. of the late Emilio Bardini and Eugenia Baltuzzi; m. 1st Ernestina Zampaglione 1939; two d.; m. 2nd Mirella Noli Parmeggiani 1972; ed. Naples Univ.; Gen. Man. Fabbrica Macchine Industriali, Naples 1952–55; Dir. and Gen. Man. Nuova San Giorgio, Genoa 1955–62; Dir. and Gen. Man. Alfa Romeo S.p.A. 1962–74; Chair. Autodelta S.p.A. 1962–74, ANFIA (Italian Asscn. of Motor Vehicle Mfrs.) 1975–78, Turin Int. Motor Show 1975–78; Dir. C.M.I. S.p.A., Genoa 1975–82; Pres. C.L.C.A. (Comité de Liaison de la Construction Automobile pour les Pays de la Communauté Economique Européenne) 1978–80, Elettronica San Giorgio S.p.A. ELSAG, Genoa 1979–84, Hon. Chair. 1984–94. *Address:* Corso Monforte 36, 20122 Milan, Italy (Home).

BARDONNET, Daniel, D.JUR., DR.RER.POL.; French international lawyer; b. 18 May 1931, Moulins; s. of Louis Bardonnet and Marguerite Dory; m. Geneviève Paintaud-Briand 1958; two s.; ed. Lycée Banville, Moulins and Faculty of Law, Univ. of Paris; Prof. Faculty of Law, Univ. of Tananarive, Madagascar 1960–66, Univ. of Rabat, Morocco 1966–72; Fellow, Woodrow Wilson Int. Center for Scholars, Washington, D.C. 1972–73; Prof. Faculty of Law, Univ. of Paris XII 1973–77; Prof. Inst. d'Etudes Politiques de Paris 1975–84; legal adviser, French del. to Law of Sea Conf. 1976–82; Dir. Annuaire Français de Droit International 1977–94; Prof. Faculty of Law, Paris Univ. of Law, Econ. and Social Sciences 1977–94, Prof. Emer. 1994–; Sec.-Gen. Hague Acad. of Int. Law 1985–; mem. Scientific Council of Inst. du Droit Econ. de la Mer, Monaco 1985–98; mem. of the Curatorium, Hague Acad. of Int. Law 1999–; Assoc., mem. of Inst. of Int. Law 1987–; Judge, Tribunal for Nuclear Energy OECD 1990–95; arbitrator nominated by the French govt. under the U.N. Convention on the Law of the Sea 1998–; Prix Léon Juillot de la Morandière (Inst. de France) 1972; Chevalier Légion d'honneur, Officier des Palmes académiques, Grand croix ordre de José Cecilio del Valle (Honduras), Grand croix ordre de Mayo (Argentina), Officier Order of Orange Nassau (Pays Bas). *Publications:* Le Tribunal des Conflits, juge du fond 1959, L'évolution de la structure du Parti radical 1960, La Succession d'Etats à Madagascar 1970, Les frontières terrestres et la relativité de leur tracé 1976; articles in legal journals. *Leisure interests:* sea, forest, literature, 18th-century art. *Address:* 5 rue des Eaux, 75016, Paris, France (Home). *Telephone:* (1) 45.20.95.80. *Fax:* (1) 40.50.19.97.

BARDOT, Brigitte; French actress; b. 28 Sept. 1934, Paris; d. of Louis and Anne-Marie (Mücel) Bardot; m. 1st Roger Vadim (q.v.); m. 2nd Jacques Charrier; one s.; m. 3rd Gunther Sachs 1966 (dissolved 1969); ed. Paris Conservatoire; stage and film career 1952–; f., Pres. Fondation Brigitte Bardot; Étoile de Cristal from Acad. of Cinema 1966; Chevalier Légion d'honneur 1985; films include Manina: la fille sans voile, Le fils de Caroline chérie, Futures vedettes, Les grandes manoeuvres, La lumière d'en face, Cette sacrée gamine, La mariée est trop belle, Et Dieu créa la femme, En effeuillant la marguerite, Une parisienne, Les bijoutiers du clair de lune, En cas de malheur, La femme et le pantin, Babette s'en va-t-en guerre, Voulez-vous danser avec moi?, La vérité, Please not now?, Le mépris, Le repos du guerrier, Une ravissante idiote, Viva Maria, A coeur joie 1967, Two weeks in September 1967, Shalako 1968, Les femmes 1969, Les novices 1970, Boulevard du rhum 1971, Les pétroleuses 1971, Don Juan 1973, L'Histoire très bonne et très joyeuse de Colinot trousse-chemise 1973. *Publication:* Initiales BB 1996 (received Prix Paul Léautaud 1996). *Leisure interest:* swimming. *Address:* Fondation Brigitte Bardot, 45 rue Vineuse, 75016 Paris, France. *Telephone:* (1) 45.05.14.60. *Fax:* (1) 45.05.14.80.

BARENBOIM, Daniel, F.R.C.M.; Israeli concert pianist and conductor; b. 15 Nov. 1942, Buenos Aires, Argentina; s. of Prof. Enrique and Aida (née Schuster) Barenboim; m. 1st Jacqueline du Pré 1967 (died 1987); m. 2nd Elena Bashkirova 1988; two s.; ed. Santa Cecilia Acad., Rome; studied piano with his father and other musical subjects with Nadia Boulanger, Edwin Fischer and Igor Markevitch; début in Buenos Aires at age of seven; played Bach D Minor Concerto with orchestra at Salzburg Mozarteum at age of nine; has played in Europe regularly 1954–; yearly tours of U.S.A. 1957–; has toured Japan, Australia and S. America; has played with or conducted London Philharmonic, Philharmonia Orchestra, London Symphony Orchestra, Royal Philharmonic, Chicago Symphony Orchestra, New York Philharmonic, Philadelphia Orchestra, Israel Philharmonic, Vienna Philharmonic, Berlin Philharmonic; frequently tours with English Chamber Orchestra and with them records for E.M.I. (projects include complete Mozart Piano Concertos and late Symphonies); other recording projects include complete Beethoven Sonatas and Beethoven Concertos (with New Philharmonia Orchestra conducted by Klemperer); has appeared in series of Master-classes on BBC television; presented Festival of Summer Music on South Bank, London 1968, 1969; leading role in Brighton Festival 1967–69; appears regularly at Edinburgh Festival; conductor, Edinburgh Festival Opera 1973; Musical Dir. Orchestre de Paris 1975–89, Chicago Symphony Orchestra 1991–; Musical and Artistic Dir. Deutsche Staatsoper, Berlin 1992–; Beethoven Medal 1958; Paderewski Medal 1963; Beethoven Soc. Medal 1982; Hon. D.Mus. (Manchester) 1997. *Publication:* A Life in Music (jtly.) 1991. *Address:* c/o Daniel Barenboim Secretariat, 29 rue de la Coulouvrenière, 1204 Genève, Switzerland.

BARFOOT, Joan, B.A.; Canadian novelist and journalist; b. 17 May 1946, Owen Sound, Ont.; ed. University of Western Ont.; reporter, religion ed. Windsor Star 1967–69; feature and news writer Mirror Publications, Toronto 1969–73, Toronto Sunday Sun 1973–75; with London Free Press 1976–79, 1980–94; has taught journalism and creative writing at School of Journalism, Univ. of Western Ont. 1987–; Canadian del. First Int. Feminist Book Fair and Festival, U.K. 1983; juror Books in Canada First Novel Award 1987, Gov.-Gen.'s Award for English Language Canadian Fiction 1995, Trillium Literary Award 1996; mem. Writers' Union of Canada, PEN Canada; Books in Canada First Novel Award 1978, Marian Engel Award 1992. *Publications:* Abra 1978, Dancing in the Dark 1982, Duet for Three 1985, Family News 1989, Plain Jane 1992, Charlotte and Claudia Keeping in Touch 1994, Some Things About Flying 1997. *Address:* 286 Cheapside Street, London, Ont. N6A 2A2, Canada. *Telephone:* (519) 438-2207.

BARIANI, Didier, D. ÈS L.; French politician; b. 16 Oct. 1943, Bellerive sur Allier; m. Chantal Maufroy (divorced); two c.; ed. Inst. d'Etudes Politiques de Paris; Chargé de Mission, then Dept. Head, Conseil Nat. du Patronat Français 1969–74; Dir., later Chair. Bd. of Dirs., Centre de Perfectionnement et de Recherche des Relations Publiques 1974–79; Prin. Pvt. Sec. to Sec. of State for Environment, Ministry of Quality of Life June–Oct. 1974, to Sec. of State in charge of Public Admin., Prime Minister's Office 1974–76; Lecturer, Inst. d'Etudes Politiques de Paris 1975–79; Pres. Paris Fed. of Parti Radical Socialiste (PRS) 1973–78; Sec.-Gen. of party 1977–79, UDF Deputy for Paris 20th Arrondissement 1978–81, Vice-Pres. UDF Group in Nat. Ass. 1978–81, Nat. Vice-Pres. UDF 1979–83; Pres. PRS 1979–83, mem. Steering Cttee., Exec. Cttee. PRS 1971; mem. UDF Nat. Council 1978–; Paris Councillor 1983; Mayor 20th Arrondissement, Paris 1983–95, Deputy Mayor of Paris 1983–; Sec. of State, Ministry of Foreign Affairs 1986–88; Pres. Parti Radical 1979–83; Nat. Del. of UDF (relations with int. orgs.) 1988–92; Man. Société INFORG (Information, Communication et Organisation) 1977–; Pres. Parti Radical Fédération régionale de l'Ile de France 1988–; Exec. Vice-Pres. (in Nat. Ass.) UDF 1994–97; Jt. Sec.-Gen. responsible for UDF's relations with int. insts. 1992–96; mem. Nat. Ass. 1993–97; Titular Judge High Court of Justice 1995–97; Vice-Pres. Nat. Ass. 1995–97; Pres. France-Israel Friendship Group 1993–97. *Publication:* Les immigrés: Pour ou contre la France? 1985. *Address:* Hôtel de Ville de Paris, 75196 Paris RP, France.

BARING, Arnulf Martin, LL.D.; German academic; b. 8 May 1932, Dresden; m.; three d. one s.; ed. Univs. of Hamburg, Berlin, Freiburg, Columbia Univ., N.Y., U.S.A., Freie Univ. Berlin, Inst. of Admin. Science, Speyer and Fondation Nat. des Sciences Politiques, Paris; lecturer, Inst. for Public and Admin. Law, Freie Univ. Berlin 1956–58, in Political Science and Int. Relations 1966–68, Univ. Lecturer, Faculty of Econ. and Social Sciences 1968, Prof. of Political Science, Otto-Suhr-Inst. and John F. Kennedy Inst. 1969–, of Contemporary History and Int. Relations, Dept. of History 1976–; Research Assoc., Center for Int. Affairs, Harvard Univ. 1968–69; Political Ed. Westdeutscher Rundfunk 1962–64; Guest Prof. Stiftung für Wissenschaft und Politik, Ebenhausen, Sr. Research Assoc., Inst. for East-West Security Studies, New York, Fellow, Wilson Int. Center for Scholars, Washington, D.C. 1986–88; mem. Inst. for Advanced Study, Princeton, NJ 1992–93; Fellow, St. Antony's Coll., Oxford 1993–94. *Publications include:* Charles de Gaulle: Grosse und Grenzen (with Christian Tautil) 1963, Aussenpolitik in Adenauers Kanzlerdemokratie 1969, Sehr verehrter Herr Bundeskanzler, Heinrich von Brentano im Briefwechsel mit Konrad Adenauer 1949–64, 1974, Zwei zaghafte Riesen? Deutschland und Japan nach 1945 (co-ed.) 1977, Machtwechsel, Die Ära Brandt-Scheel 1982, Unser neuer Grössenwahn, Deutschland zwischen Ost und West 1988, Deutschland, was nun? 1991; contrib. to Frankfurter Allgemeine Zeitung, Westdeutscher und Norddeutscher Rundfunk, Sender Freies Berlin. *Leisure interests:* travel, rambling. *Address:* Freie Universität Berlin, FB Geschichtswissenschaften, Habelschwerdter Allee 45, 14195 Berlin (Office); Ahrenshooper Zeile 64, 14129 Berlin, Germany.

BARING, Hon. Sir John Francis Harcourt, (see Ashburton, Baron).

BARKAUSKAS, Antanas Stase; Lithuanian government official (retd.); b. 20 Jan. 1917, Paparchiai, Lithuania; s. of Stasys Barkauskas and Aleksandra Barkauskas; m. Zoya Yarashunaite 1961; one s. one d.; ed. Higher Communist Party School, Moscow, and Acad. of Social Sciences; mem. of Lithuanian Young Komsomol League 1940; Soviet official in Kaunas 1940–41; served in 16th Lithuanian Div. 1942–44; mem. CPSU 1942–90, party official in Kaunas during post-war period; Sec. Vilnius (later Kaunas) Regional Cttee. of Lithuanian C.P. 1950–53; Teacher, Head of Dept., Kaunas Polytechnic Inst. 1953–55; Head of Dept., Cen. Cttee. of Lithuanian C.P. 1959–60, mem. Cen. Cttee. 1960–90, Sec. of Cen. Cttee. 1961–75, mem. Secr. 1961–91, mem. Politburo 1962–66; Deputy to Supreme Soviet of Lithuania 1959–90, Chair. Supreme Soviet of Lithuanian S.S.R. 1959–75, Pres. of Presidium 1975–85; Deputy to Supreme Soviet of U.S.S.R. 1974–89, Vice-Chair. of Presidium 1976–85; mem. Cen. Auditing Cttee. of CPSU 1976–81; Cand. mem. Cen. Cttee., CPSU 1981–86 (retd.); Honoured Cultural Worker of Lithuanian S.S.R. 1967, Order of October Revolution 1971, Order of Red Banner of Labour 1965, 1973, Order of Red Star 1947, six medals. *Publications:* Country, Culture, Rural Life 1967, Culture and Society 1975, Lithuanian Countryside: Past, Present and Future (in English, French, German, Hungarian and Arabic) 1976. *Leisure interests:* fiction, travelling, sport. *Address:* Akmenų 7/1, Vilnius, Lithuania. *Telephone:* (2) 62-44-45.

BARKER, David James Purslove, M.D., PH.D., F.R.C.P.(U.K.), F.F.P.H.M., F.R.S.; British medical research director; b. 29 June 1938, London; s. of late Hugh Barker and Joye Barker; m. 1st Angela Coddington 1960 (deceased); m. 2nd Janet Franklin 1983; three s. two d. and one step-s. two step-d.; ed. Oundle School and Guy's Hosp. Univ. of London; Research Fellow, Dept. of Medicine, Univ. of Birmingham 1963, lecturer 1966; lecturer in Preventive Medicine, Makerere Univ. Uganda 1969; Sr. lecturer in Clinical Epidemiology, Univ. of Southampton, Prof. 1979–; Hon. Consultant Physician, Royal S. Hants. Hosp.; Dir. MRC Environmental Epidemiology Unit, Southampton 1984–; Royal Soc. Wellcome Gold Medal 1994. *Publications:* The Fetal and Infant Origins of Adult Disease 1992, Mothers, Babies and Disease in Adult Life 1994. *Leisure interests:* writing, drawing, golf, fishing. *Address:* MRC Environmental Epidemiology Unit, Southampton General Hospital, Southampton, SO16 6YD (Office); Manor Farm, East Dean, nr. Salisbury, Wilts., SP5 1HB, England (Home). *Telephone:* (01703) 777624 (Office); (01794) 340016 (Home). *Fax:* (01703) 704021 (Office).

BARKER, Horace Albert, PH.D., D.SC.; American professor of biochemistry; b. 29 Nov. 1907, Oakland, Calif.; s. of A. C. Barker and Nettie Barker; m. Margaret D. McDowell 1933; one s. two d.; ed. Stanford Univ.; Nat. Research Council Fellow in Biological Sciences, Hopkins Marine Station 1933–35; Gen. Educ. Bd. Fellow, Technical Univ., Delft, Holland 1935–36; Instructor in Soil Microbiology, Div. of Plant Nutrition, and Junior Soil Microbiologist in Agric. Experiment Station, Univ. of Calif. 1936–40, Asst. Prof. and Asst. Soil Microbiologist 1940–45, Assoc. Prof. and Assoc. Soil Microbiologist 1945–46, Prof. and Soil Microbiologist 1946–50, Prof. of Plant Biochemistry and Microbiologist 1950–57, Prof. of Microbial Biochemistry and Microbiologist 1957–59, Prof. of Biochemistry and Microbiologist 1959–75, Emer. Prof. 1975–; Chair. Dept. of Plant Nutrition 1949–50, Dept. of Plant Biochemistry 1950–53, Vice-Chair. Dept. of Agric. Biochemistry 1958–59, Chair. Dept. of Biochemistry 1962–64; on editorial boards of various scientific journals; mem. N.A.S., American Acad. of Arts and Sciences and other socs.; numerous awards including Gowland Hopkins Medal, Biochemistry Soc., London 1967, Nat. Medal of Science 1968. *Publications:* Bacterial Fermentations 1956; over 230 papers; research into various aspects of bacterial metabolism, including the synthesis and oxidation of fatty acids, fermentation of amino acids and purines, carbohydrate transformation and methane formation; isolation, structure and function of cobamide coenzymes; bacterial enzymes. *Leisure interests:* fishing and mountaineering. *Address:* Department of Biochemistry, H.A. Barker Hall, University of California, Berkeley, CA 94720, U.S.A. (Office); 561 Santa Clara Avenue, Berkeley, CA 94707, U.S.A. (Home). *Telephone:* (510) 642-5688 (Office).

BARKER, Pat; British author; b. 8 May 1943, Thornaby-on-Tees; m.; two c.; ed. London School of Econs.; Fawcett Prize 1983, Guardian Prize for Fiction 1993, Booker Prize for Fiction for The Ghost Road 1995. *Publications:* novels: Union Street 1982, Blow Your House Down 1984, The Century's Daughter 1986, The Man Who Wasn't There 1989; trilogy of First World War novels: Regeneration 1991, The Eye in the Door 1993, The Ghost Road 1995, Another World 1998. *Address:* c/o Gillon Aitken Associates, 29 Fernshaw Road, London, SW10 0TG, England. *Telephone:* 0171-351 7561. *Fax:* 0171-376 3594.

BARKIN, Ellen; American actress; b. 16 April 1955, New York; m. Gabriel Byrne 1988; one s.; ed. City Univ. of New York and Hunter Coll. Ind.; stage appearances include: Shout Across the River 1980, Killings on the Last Line 1980, Extremities 1982; TV appearances include Search for Tomorrow, Kent State 1981, We're Fighting Back 1981, Terrible Joe Moran 1984. *Films:* Diner 1982, Daniel 1983, Tender Mercies 1983, Eddie and the Cruisers 1983, The Adventures of Buckaroo Banzai 1984, Harry and Son 1984, Enormous Changes at the Last Minute 1985, Down by Law 1986, The Big Easy 1987, Siesta 1987, Sea of Love 1989, Johnny Handsome, Switch, Man Trouble 1992, Mac 1993, This Boy's Life 1993, Into the West 1993, Bad Company 1995, Wild Bill 1995, Mad Dog Time 1996, The Fan 1996.

BARKLEY, Richard C.; American diplomatist; b. 12 Dec. 1932, Chicago; m. Nina Margrethe Schultz 1982; two d.; ed. Michigan State Univ., East Lansing, Wayne State Univ., Detroit, Univ. of Freiburg, Fed. Republic of Germany; joined Foreign Service 1962; served in Norway, Finland, Dominican Republic, S. Africa and Fed. Repub. of Germany; Amb. to G.D.R. 1989–91, to Turkey 1991–94; mem. Bd. of Dirs. Inst. for Turkish Studies; Chair. Palace Arts Foundation Inc.

BARKWORTH, Peter Wynn; British actor and author; b. 14 Jan. 1929, Margate, Kent; s. of Walter W. Barkworth and Irene M. Barkworth; unmarried; ed. Stockport School and Royal Acad. of Dramatic Art; stage appearances in London include: Roar Like a Dove (Phoenix) 1957–60, The School for Scandal (Haymarket and New York) 1962, Crown Matrimonial (Haymarket) 1972, Donkeys' Years (Globe) 1976, Can You Hear Me at the Back? (Piccadilly) 1979–80, A Coat of Varnish (Haymarket) 1982, Siegfried Sassoon (Apollo) 1987, Hidden Laughter (Vaudeville) 1990–91, The Winslow Boy (Globe) 1994; TV series include: The Power Game 1966, Manhunt 1969, Winston Churchill: The Wilderness Years 1975, Telford's Change 1978, Late Starter 1984, The Price 1984; BAFTA Best Actor Award 1974, 1977; Royal Television Soc. Best Actor 1977; Writers' Guild Best Actor 1977; Hon. M.A. (Manchester). *Films include:* Where Eagles Dare 1968, Mr Smith, Escape from the Dark, Champions 1983, Wilde 1997. *Publications:* About Acting 1980, First Houses 1983, More About Acting 1984, The Complete About Acting 1991, For All Occasions 1997. *Leisure interests:* walking, gardening, looking at paintings. *Address:* 47 Flask Walk, London, NW3 1HH; 26 Marlborough Court, Earls Avenue, Folkestone, Kent, CT20 2PN, England. *Telephone:* 0171-794 4591; (01303) 245728.

BARLOG, Boleslaw; German theatre director and producer; b. 28 March 1906, Breslau (now Wrocław); m. Herta Schüster 1939; ed. Oberrealschule, Berlin; Asst. Producer, Volksbühne, Berlin 1930–33; Asst. Dir. UFA and TERRA films 1935–39, Dir. 1939–45; Dir.-Gen. Berlin Municipal Theatres 1945–72 (Schlosspark Theatre 1945–72, Schiller Theatre 1951–72, Schiller-Theatre Workshop 1959–72); mem. Carl-Zuckmayer Gesellschaft 1972–75, now Hon. Pres.; Hon. Prof. h.c.; mem. Acad. of Arts, Berlin; Hon. mem. Berlin Philharmonic; Grand Order of Merit with Star (Fed. Germany) 1950; Ordre National de l'Art et des Lettres. *Address:* Spindelmühler Weg 7, 12205 Berlin, Germany. *Telephone:* 8117314.

BARLOW, Gary; British singer, songwriter and producer; b. 20 Jan. 1971; singer, songwriter and producer with Take That 1990–96, solo 1996–; tours of Britain, Europe, Asia, Pacific 1992–95; gold discs in Austria, Belgium, Denmark, Finland, platinum discs in Germany, Ireland, two Brit awards, Nordoff Robbins Silver Clef Award for best band, numerous Smash Hits awards, Golden Camera Award (Berlin), Golden Otto Award for best band, MTV Award for Best Group in Europe, Ivor Novello Award for Most Performed Work and Best Selling Song 1996. *Released singles:* Do What U Like 1991, Promises 1991, Once You've Tasted Love 1992, It Only Takes A Minute 1992, I Found Heaven 1992, A Million Love Songs 1992, Could It Be Magic? 1992, Why Can't I Wake Up With You? 1993, Pray 1993, Relight My Fire 1993, Babe 1993, Everything Changes 1994, Love Ain't Here Anymore 1994, Sure 1994, Back For Good 1995, Never Forget 1995, Forever Love 1996. *Albums:* Take That and Party 1992, Everything Changes 1993, Nobody Else 1995, Greatest Hits 1996 (all with Take That), Open Road 1996 (solo). *Address:* c/o RCA Records, Music Recording, Bedford House, 69 Fulham High Street, London, S.W.6, England. *Telephone:* 0171-384 7500. *Fax:* 0171-371 9298.

BARLOW, Sir William, Kt., D.SC., F.ENG., F.I.E.E., F.I.MECH.E.; British engineer; b. 8 June 1924, Oldham; s. of Albert Edward and Annice Barlow; m. Elaine Mary Atherton Adamson 1948; one s. one d.; ed. Manchester Grammar School and Manchester Univ.; English Electric Co. Ltd. 1947–68; Man. Dir. English Electric Computers 1967–68; Chief Exec. Ransome Hoffmann Pollard Ltd. 1969–77, Chair. 1971–77; Chair. Post Office Corpn. 1977–80; Dir. Thorn EMI PLC 1980–89, Chair. of Eng. Group 1980–84; Dir. BICC PLC 1980–91, Chair. 1984–91; Chair. Ericsson Ltd. 1981–94, Metal Industries Ltd. 1980–84, SKF (U.K.) Ltd. 1990–92, Barking Power 1992–93, Kennedy and Donkin Ltd. 1997–; Chair. Design Council 1980–86, Eng. Council 1988–90; Dir. Racal Telecommunications PLC 1988; Dir. Vodafone Group (fmrly. Racal Telecom) 1988–98, Waste Man. Int. PLC 1992–98, Chemring Group PLC 1994–97 (Chair. 1997–); Pres. Royal Acad. of Eng. 1991–96; Vice-Pres. City and Guilds of London Inst. 1982–93; Gov. London Business School 1979–92; Pres. British Electrotechnical and Allied Mfrs. Asscn (BEAMA) 1986–87, Asscn. of Lancastrians 1992; Hon. D.Sc. (Cranfield Inst. of Tech.) 1979, (Bath) 1986, (Aston) 1988, Hon. D.Tech. (Liverpool Polytechnic) 1988, (City Univ.) 1989, (Loughborough) 1993, Hon. D.Eng. (UMIST) 1996. *Leisure interest:* golf, range. *Address:* 4 Parkside, Henley-on-Thames, Oxon., RG9 1TX, England. *Telephone:* (01491) 411101. *Fax:* (01491) 410013.

BÄRLUND, Kaj-Ole Johannes, M.SC. (ECON.); Finnish politician; b. 9 Nov. 1945, Porvoo; s. of Elis Bärlund and Meri Bärlund; m. Eeva-Kaisa Oksama 1972; one s. one d.; journalist, Finnish Broadcasting Co. 1967–71; Public Relations Officer, Cen. Org. of Finnish Trade Unions 1971–72; Legis. Sec. Ministry of Justice 1972–79; mem. Parl. 1979–91; Chair. Porvoo City Bd. 1979–87, Nat. Cttee. on Natural Resources 1979–83; Chair. Swedish Labour Union of Finland 1983–90; mem. Nordic Council, Vice-Chair. Nordic Council Social and Environment Cttee. 1983–87; mem. Exec. Bd. Finnish Broadcasting Co. 1982–83, Neste Oy 1983–90; Chair. Bureau of the Montreal Protocol 1989–90; Chair. UN/ECE Cttee. on Environmental Policy 1991–95; Minister of the Environment 1987–91; Dir.-Gen. Nat. Bd. of Waters and the Environment 1990–95; Dir.-Gen. Finnish Environment Agency 1995–; Dir. Environment and Human Settlements Div. UN/ECE 1995–; Chair. Peoples of Finland and Russia Friendship Soc. 1991–95; mem. Party Exec., Finnish Social Democratic Party 1984–91, Chair. Environmental Working Group 1981–87. *Leisure interests:* tennis, cross-country skiing, literature. *Address:* Environment and Human Settlements Division, Economic Commission for Europe, Palais des Nations, CH-1211 Geneva 10, Switzerland. *Telephone:* (22) 917 2370. *Fax:* (22) 907 0107.

BARNABY, Charles Frank, PH.D.; British physicist; b. 27 Sept. 1927, Andover, Hants.; s. of Charles H. Barnaby and Lilian Sainsbury; m. Wendy Elizabeth Field 1972; one s. one d.; ed. Andover Grammar School and Univ. of London; Physicist, U.K. Atomic Energy Authority 1950–57; mem. Sr. Scientific Staff, Medical Research Council, Univ. Coll. Medical School 1957–68; Exec. Sec. Pugwash Confs. on Science and World Affairs 1968–70; Dir. Stockholm Int. Peace Research Inst. (SIPRI) 1971–81; Prof. of Peace Studies, Free Univ., Amsterdam 1981–85; Dir. World Disarmament Campaign (U.K.) 1982–; Chair. Just Defence 1982–; Ed. Int. Journal of Human Rights. *Publications:* Man and the Atom 1971, Ed. Preventing the Spread of Nuclear Weapons 1971, Co-editor Anti-ballistic Missile Systems 1971, Disarmament and Arms Control 1973, The Nuclear Age 1976, Prospects for Peace 1980, Future Warfare (ed. and co-author) 1983, Space Weapons 1984, The Automated Battlefield 1986, The Invisible Bomb 1989, The Gaia Peace Atlas 1989, The Role and Control of Weapons in the 1990s 1992, How Nuclear Weapons Spread 1993, Instruments of Terror 1997; articles in scientific journals. *Leisure interests:* natural history. *Address:* Brandreth, Chilbolton, Stockbridge, Hants., England. *Telephone:* (01264) 860423 (Home). *Fax:* (01264) 860868.

BARNALA, Surjit Singh, LL.B.; Indian politician and lawyer; b. 21 Oct. 1925, Ateli, Gurgaon Dist. (now in Haryana); s. of Nar Singh and Jasmer Kaur; m. Surjit Kaur 1954; three s. one d.; ed. Lucknow Univ.; Shiromani Akali Dal M.P. for Barnala 1967–77; Educ. Minister of Punjab 1969–71; M.P. from Sangrur 1977; Union Agric., Irrigation and Food Minister in Janata Govt. 1977–80; elected Pres. Shiromani Akali Dal 1985; Chief Minister of Punjab 1985–87; Gov. Tamil Nadu 1990. *Leisure interests:* painting, reading, ecology. *Address:* Barnala Sangrur Dist., Punjab, India.

BARNARD, Christiaan Neethling, M.MED., M.D., M.S., PH.D., F.A.C.C.; South African heart surgeon (retd.) and farmer; b. 8 Oct. 1922, Beaufort West, Cape Province; s. of Adam Hendrik Barnard and Maria Elisabeth de Swart; m. 1st Aletta Gertruida Louw 1948 (divorced 1970); one s. (deceased) one d.; m. 2nd Barbara M. Zoellner 1970 (divorced 1982); two s.; m. 3rd Karin Setzkorn 1987; one s.; ed. Univ. of Cape Town; graduated as doctor 1946; intern, Groote Schuur Hospital, Cape Town 1947; then spent two years in general practice in Ceres; then Senior Resident Medical Officer, City Fever Hospital, Cape Town; returned to Groote Schuur Hospital; then Charles Adams Memorial Scholar, Univ. of Minnesota, concentrating on cardiothoracic surgery; on return to Groote Schuur Hospital concentrated on open-heart operations and cardiac research; Surgery of Common Congenital Cardiac Malformations (with V. Sehrire) 1968; Head of Cardiac Research and Surgery, Univ. of Cape Town 1968–83, Prof. Emer. 1984–; Sr. Consultant and Scientist in Residence, Okla. Heart Centre at Baptist Medical Centre, Okla. City 1985–; developed the Barnard Valve, for use in open-heart surgery; performed first successful open-heart operation in South Africa; performed first successful heart transplant operation in world 1967, first successful double heart transplant operation 1974; Hon. D.Sc. (Univ. of Cape Town). *Publications:* One Life (autobiography, with C. B. Pepper) 1970, Heart Attack: All You Have To Know About It 1971, The Unwanted (with S. Stander) 1974, South Africa: Sharp Dissection 1977, In the Night Season (with S. Stander) 1977, Best Medicine 1979, Good Life—Good Death 1980, The Body Machine 1981, The Living Body (with Karl Sabbagh) 1984, The Arthritis Handbook (jtly) 1984, The Second Life (autobiography) 1993, The Donor (novel) 1996. *Leisure interests:* power-boats, water skiing, fishing, flying. *Address:* 18 Silwood Road, Rondebosch 7700, South Africa.

BARNARD, Eric Albert, PH.D., F.R.S.; British biochemist; b. 2 July 1927; m. Penelope J. Hennessy 1956; two s. two d.; ed. Davenant Foundation School, King's Coll., Univ. of London; Nuffield Foundation Fellow, King's Coll. 1956–59, Asst. Lecturer 1959–60, Lecturer 1960–64; Assoc. Prof. of Biochemical Pharmacology, State Univ. of New York 1964–65, Prof. of Biochemistry 1965–76, Head Biochemistry Dept. 1969–76; Rank Prof. of Physiological Biochemistry, Imperial Coll. of Science and Tech., London

1976–85, Chair. Div. of Life Sciences 1977–85, Head Dept. of Biochemistry 1979–85; Dir. MRC Molecular Neurobiology Unit, Cambridge 1985–92; Dir. Molecular Neurobiology Unit, Prof. of Neurobiology, Royal Free Hospital School of Medicine, London Univ. 1992–; Rockefeller Fellow, Univ. of Calif., Berkeley 1960–61; Guggenheim Fellow, MRC Lab. of Molecular Biology, Cambridge 1971; Visiting Prof., Univ. of Marburg, Fed. Rep. of Germany 1965, Tokyo Univ. 1993; Visiting Scientist, Inst. Pasteur, France 1973; Ed.-in-Chief Receptors and Channels 1993–; mem. American Soc. of Biological Chemists, Int. Soc. of Neurochemistry; Cttee. mem. MRC; Josiah Macy Faculty Scholar Award, U.S.A. 1975, Medal of Polish Acad. of Sciences 1980, Ciba Medal and Prize 1985, Eastman Kodak Award (U.S.A.) 1988, Erspamer Int. Award for Neuroscience 1991. *Publications:* Ed. of eight scientific books; mem. editorial bd. four scientific journals; numerous papers in learned journals. *Leisure interest:* the pursuit of good claret. *Address:* Molecular Neurobiology Unit, Division of Basic Medical Sciences, Royal Free Hospital Medical School, Rowland Hill Street, London, NW3 2PF, England.

BARNARD, Lukas Daniël, M.A., D.PHIL.; South African intelligence officer and university professor; b. 14 June 1949, Otjiwarongo; s. of Nicolaas Evehardus Barnard and Magdalena Catharina Beukes; m. Engela Brand 1971; three s.; ed. Otjiwarongo High School, Univ. of O.F.S.; Senior Lecturer Univ. of O.F.S. 1976, Prof. and Head, Dept. of Political Science 1978; Dir.-Gen. Nat. Intelligence Service (fmrly. Dept. of Nat. Security) 1980–91, Head, Constitutional Development Service 1992; mem. several cttees. and bds.; S. African Police Star for Outstanding Service 1985, Order of the Star of S. Africa (Class 1), Gold 1987, Nat. Intelligence Service Decoration for Outstanding Leadership, Gold Nat. Intelligence Service Medal for Distinguished Service, Senior Service Award, Gold (CDS) 1992. *Publications:* one book, 26 articles in popular and technical scientific journals. *Leisure interest:* tennis. *Address:* c/o Constitutional Development, Private Bag X804, Pretoria 0001, South Africa. *Telephone:* 3412400.

BARNDORFF-NIELSEN, Ole Eiler, SC.D.; Danish professor of mathematical statistics; b. 18 March 1935, Copenhagen; m. Bente Jensen-Storch 1956; two s. two d.; ed. Univ. of Copenhagen and Aarhus Univ.; Prof. of Math. Statistics, Inst. of Math., Aarhus Univ. 1973–, Scientific Dir. Math. Centre 1995–; Ed.-in-Chief Bernoulli 1994–; mem. Royal Danish Acad. of Sciences and Letters 1980–, Academia Europaea 1990–; Dr.h.c. (Univ. Paul Sabatier, Toulouse) 1993. *Publications:* Information and Exponential Families in Statistical Theory 1978, Parametric Statistical Models and Likelihood 1988, Asymptotic Techniques for use in Statistics (with D. R. Cox) 1989, Inference and Asymptotics (with D. R. Cox) 1994, numerous scientific papers. *Leisure interests:* biography, blown sands, opera, tennis. *Address:* Department of Mathematics, Aarhus University, 8000 Aarhus (Inst.); Dalvangen 48, 8270 Højbjerg, Denmark (Home). *Telephone:* 89423188 (Inst.); 86271442 (Home).

BARNES, Dame (Alice) Josephine (Mary Taylor), D.B.E., M.A., D.M., F.R.C.P., F.R.C.S., F.R.C.O.G.; British obstetrician and gynaecologist; b. 18 Aug. 1912, Sheringham; d. of Rev. Walter Wharton Barnes and Alice Mary Ibbetson; m. Sir Brian Warren (divorced 1964) (died 1996); one s. two d.; ed. Oxford High School, Lady Margaret Hall, Oxford and Univ. Coll. Hospital; Consulting Obstetrician and Gynaecologist Elizabeth Garrett Anderson Hospital 1947–, Charing Cross Hospital 1954–; Surgeon Marie Curie Hospital 1947–67; appointments at Univ. Coll. Hospital, Samaritan Hospital, Queen Charlotte's Hospital, Radcliffe Infirmary; Pres. Medical Women Fed. 1966–67; Vice-Pres. Royal Coll. of Obstetricians and Gynaecologists 1975–78; Pres. Union Professionelle Int. de Gynécologie et d'Obstetrique 1977–79; Pres. Women's Nat. Cancer Control Campaign 1974–, Nat. Asscn. of Family Planning Doctors 1976–93; Pres. Section of History of Medicine, Royal Soc. of Medicine 1995–96; mem. Asscn. of Chartered Physiotherapists in Obstetrics and Gynaecology, British Medical Asscn. 1979–80, Royal Medical Benevolent Fund 1982–97; Fellow, Kings Coll., London 1985, mem. Council 1985–93; Fellow, Royal Holloway Coll. Univ. of London 1986; Hon. F.R.C.P.I. 1977; Hon. Fellow, Lady Margaret Hall, Oxford 1980; Hon. Bencher Gray's Inn 1992; Hon. M.D. (Liverpool) 1979; Hon. D.Sc. (Leicester) 1980, (Oxford) 1990; Hon. D.M. (Southampton) 1981; Commdr. du Bontemps de Médoc et des Graves 1966; Suckling Prize, F. T. Roberts Prize; Tuke Medal, Fellowes Medal. *Publications:* Gynaecological Histology 1948, The Care of the Expectant Mother 1954, Lecture Notes on Gynaecology 1966, Scientific Foundations of Obstetrics and Gynaecology (Ed. jointly) 1970, Essentials of Family Planning 1976; numerous contributions to medical literature; Hon. F.C.S.P. 1991. *Leisure interests:* music, gastronomy, motoring, foreign travel. *Address:* 1 Chartwell House, 12 Ladbroke Terrace, London, W11 3PG, England. *Telephone:* 0171-727 9832.

BARNES, Christopher Richard, O.C., C.M., B.SC., PH.D., F.R.S.C., P.GEOL.; Canadian geologist; b. 20 April 1940, Nottingham, England; m. Susan M. Miller 1961; three d.; ed. Univs. of Birmingham and Ottawa; NATO Research Fellow Univ. of Wales, Swansea 1964–65; Asst. Prof. Univ. of Waterloo 1965–70, Assoc. Prof. 1970–76, Prof. and Chair. 1976–81, Biology Dept. 1973–81, Adjunct Prof. 1981–82; Sr. Research Fellow Univ. of Southampton, U.K. 1971–72; Univ. of Cambridge 1980–81; Prof. and Head Memorial Univ. of Newfoundland 1981–87; Acting Dir. Centre for Earth Resources Research 1984–87; Dir.-Gen. Sedimentary and Marine Geosciences, Geological Survey of Canada 1987–89; Dir. for Earth and Ocean Research Univ. of Vic. 1989–, Dir. School of Earth and Ocean Sciences 1991–; Pres. Canadian Geoscience Council 1979, Geological Asscn. of Canada 1983–84, Acad. of Sciences, Royal Soc. of Canada 1990–93, Science Council of B.C. 1991–95; mem. Atomic Energy Control Bd. 1996–; Bancroft Award 1982; Geological Asscn. of Canada Nat. Lecturer 1978, Past-Pres.'s Medal 1977, Willis Ambrose Medal 1991. *Publications:* over 80 scientific works in geological journals. *Address:* School of Earth and Ocean Sciences, Univ. of Victoria, P.O. Box 3055, Victoria, B.C., V8W 3P6, Canada. *Telephone:* (250) 721 8847. *Fax:* (250) 721 6200.

BARNES, Clive Alexander, C.B.E.; British journalist, dance and theatre critic; b. 13 May 1927, London; m. Patricia Winckley 1958; one s. one d.; ed. King's Coll., London and Oxford Univ.; served R.A.F. 1946–48; Admin. officer, Town Planning Dept., London County Council 1952–61; also active as freelance journalist contributing articles, reviews and criticisms on music, dance, theatre, films and television to the New Statesman, The Spectator, The Daily Express, The New York Times, etc.; Chief dance critic, The Times, London 1961–65; Exec. Ed., Dance and Dancers, Music and Musicians, Plays and Players 1961–65; Dance Critic. The New York Times 1965–78, also Drama Critic (weekdays only) 1967–77; Assoc. Ed., Chief Drama and Dance Critic, New York Post 1977–; a New York Corresp. of The Times 1970–; Kt. Order of the Dannebrog (Denmark). *Publications:* Ballet in Britain Since the War, Frederick Ashton and His Ballet, Ballet Here and Now, Dance As It Happened, Dance in the Twentieth Century, Dance Scene: U.S.A.; Ed. Nureyev 1983. *Address:* c/o New York Post, 210 South Street, New York, NY 10002, U.S.A.

BARNES, Edward Larrabee, M.ARCH.; American architect; b. 22 April 1915, Chicago Ill.; s. of Cecil and Margaret H. (Ayer) Barnes; m. Mary E. Coss 1944; one s.; ed. Milton Acad., Harvard Coll. and Graduate School of Design; Sheldon Travelling Fellowship 1942; architectural practice in New York 1949–; Critic of Architectural Design, Pratt Inst., Brooklyn 1954–59, Yale School of Architecture 1957–64, Eliot Noyes Critic, Harvard Graduate School of Design 1979; Jefferson Prof., Univ. of Virginia 1980; work exhibited at Museum of Modern Art (New York), Carnegie Inst. (Pittsburgh, Pa.), Whitney Museum, New York and published in architectural magazines; Dir. Municipal Art Soc. of New York 1960; Fellow, American Inst. of Architects; Trustee, American Acad. in Rome 1963–78, Vice-Pres. 1973, First Vice-Chair. 1975; Trustee, Museum of Modern Art, New York, 1975–93, Life Trustee 1993–; Assoc. Nat. Acad. of Design 1969, Academician 1974–; Fellow, American Acad. of Arts and Sciences 1978; mem. American Acad. of Arts and Letters 1991–; Yale Award for Distinction in the Arts 1959, Arnold Brunner Prize, Nat. Inst. of Arts and Letters 1959, Silver Medal, Architectural League, (New York) 1960, A.I.A. Medal of Hon. (New York chapter) 1971, A.I.A. Collaborative Achievement in Architecture 1972, Hon. Award 1972, 1977, 1986, Harleston Parker Award, Boston Soc. of Architects 1972, Louis Sullivan Award 1979, Honor Award, Connecticut Soc. of Architects 1980, A.I.A. Architectural Firm Award 1980 (25 Year Award 1994), Thomas Jefferson Award 1981 (Univ. of Virginia), Honor Award, New Mexico Soc. of Architects 1983, Excellence in Design award, N.Y. State Asscn. of Architects 1984, Harvard Univ. 350th Anniversary Medal 1986, Interfaith Forum on Religion, Art and Architecture, Honor Award 1989, A.I.A. 25-year Award 1994, and other awards; Hon. Dr. of Fine Arts (Rhode Island School of Design) 1983, Hon. D.Hum.Litt. (Amherst Coll.) 1984. *Works include:* prefabricated house, private houses, camps, academic buildings and master plans, office bldgs. and corporate head-quarters, museums and botanical gardens including Haystack Mountain School of Arts and Crafts, Maine; master plans for State Univ. of New York at Purchase and Potsdam; office bldgs. for New England Merchants Nat. Bank, Boston, IBM headquarters in New York City and Mt. Pleasant, New York; master plan and office/retail complex, Crown Center, Kansas City; Walker Art Gallery, Minneapolis, Minn.; Sarah Scaife Gallery, Pittsburgh, Pa.; Chicago Botanic Garden, Dallas Museum of Art, Minn. Sculpture Garden, etc. *Leisure interests:* music, piano, sailing, climbing. *Address:* 975 Memorial Drive, Cambridge, MA 02138, U.S.A.

BARNES, John Arundel, D.SC., M.A., D.PHIL., F.B.A.; British sociologist; b. 9 Sept. 1918, Reading, Berks.; s. of Thomas D. Barnes and M. Grace Barnes; m. Helen F. Bastable 1942; three s. one d.; ed. Christ's Hosp., St. John's Coll. Cambridge, Univ. of Cape Town and Balliol Coll. Oxford; served RN 1940–46; Research Officer, Rhodes-Livingstone Inst. N. Rhodesia 1946–49; Lecturer, Dept. of Anthropology, Univ. Coll. London 1949–51; Fellow, St. John's Coll. Cambridge 1950–53; Simon Research Fellow, Univ. of Manchester 1951–53; Reader in Anthropology, London School of Econs. 1954–56; Prof. of Anthropology, Univ. of Sydney 1956–58, Australian Nat. Univ. 1958–69; Fellow, Churchill Coll. Cambridge 1965–66, 1969–; Prof. of Sociology, Univ. of Cambridge 1969–82; Visiting Fellow, Australian Nat. Univ. 1978–79, 1984–92, Program Visitor 1993–; Fellow, Acad. of Social Sciences, Australia; Wellcome Medal 1950, Rivers Medal 1959, Royal Anthropological Inst. *Publications:* Marriage in a Changing Society 1951, Politics in a Changing Society 1954, Three Styles in the Study of Kinship 1971, The Ethics of Inquiry in Social Science 1977, Who Should Know What? 1979, Models and Interpretations 1990, A Pack of Lies 1994. *Address:* Sociology Program, Research School of Social Sciences, Australian National University, Canberra, A.C.T. 0200, Australia. *Telephone:* (02) 6249 4037. *Fax:* (02) 6249 2114.

BARNES, Jonathan, F.B.A.; British professor of philosophy; b. 1942; s. of late A. L. Barnes and of K. M. Barnes; m. Jennifer Postgate 1965; two d.; ed. City of London School and Balliol Coll. Oxford; Fellow, Oriel Coll. Oxford 1968–78, Balliol Coll. 1978–94; Prof. of Ancient Philosophy, Univ. of Oxford 1989–94, Univ. of Geneva 1994–; visiting posts at Inst. for Advanced Study,

Princeton 1972, Univ. of Texas 1981, Wissenschaftskolleg zu Berlin 1985, Univ. of Alberta 1986, Univ. of Zurich 1987. *Publications:* The Ontological Argument 1972, Aristotle's Posterior Analytics 1975, The Presocratic Philosophers 1979, Aristotle 1982, Early Greek Philosophy 1987, The Toils of Scepticism 1991, Companion to Aristotle 1995. *Address:* Les Charmilles, 36200 Ceaulmont, France; 1 place de la Taconnerie, 1204 Geneva, Switzerland.

BARNES, Julian (Patrick), (also writes as Dan Kavanagh); British author; b. 1946; m. Pat Kavanagh; ed. City of London School, Magdalen Coll. Oxford; Lexicographer, Oxford English Dictionary Supplement 1969–72; TV Critic New Statesman 1977–81, Asst. Literary Ed. 1977–79; Contributing Ed. New Review, London 1977–78; Deputy Literary Ed. Sunday Times, London 1979–81; TV Critic The Observer 1982–86; Officier, Ordre des Arts et des Lettres 1995; Hon. Fellow Magdalene Coll., Oxford 1996–. *Publications:* Metroland, Duffy (as Dan Kavanagh) 1980, Fiddle City (as Dan Kavanagh) 1981, Before She Met Me 1982, Flaubert's Parrot (Prix Medicis 1986) 1984, Putting the Boot In (as Dan Kavanagh) 1985, Staring at the Sun 1986, Going to the Dogs (as Dan Kavanagh) 1987, A History of the World in 10½ Chapters 1989, Talking it Over (Femina Etranger Prize) 1991, The Porcupine (novel) 1992, Letters from London 1990–95, (articles) 1995, Cross Channel (short stories) 1996, Evermore 1996, England, England 1998. *Address:* c/o Peters, Fraser & Dunlop, 503/4 The Chambers, Chelsea Harbour, Lots Road, London, SW10 0XF, England.

BARNES, Peter John, M.A., D.M., D.SC., F.R.C.P.; British professor of thoracic medicine; b. 29 Oct. 1946, Birmingham; s. of late John Barnes and Eileen Barnes; m. Olivia Harvard-Watts 1976; three s.; ed. Leamington Coll., Cambridge Univ., Oxford Univ. Clinical School; medical positions Oxford, Brompton Hosp., Nat. Hosp., Univ. Coll. Hosp. 1972–78; Sr. Registrar Hammersmith Hosp. 1979–82; Sr. Lecturer, Consultant Physician Royal Postgrad. Medical School 1982–85 (MRC Research Fellow 1978–79); Prof. of Clinical Pharmacology Cardiothoracic Inst. 1985–87, of Thoracic Medicine Nat. Heart and Lung Inst. 1987–; Hon. Consultant Physician Royal Brompton Hosp. 1985–; MRC Travelling Fellow Cardiovascular Research Inst., San Francisco 1981–82; numerous awards. *Publications:* Asthma: Basic Mechanics and Clinical Management, The Lung: Scientific Foundations 1991, Pharmacology of the Respiratory Tract 1993, Conquering Asthma 1994, Molecular Biology of Lung Disease 1994, Asthma (2 vols.) 1997. *Leisure interests:* ethnic art, foreign travel, gardening. *Address:* Department of Thoracic Medicine, National Heart and Lung Institute (Imperial College), Dovehouse Street, London, SW3 6LY; 44 Woodsome Road, London, NW5 1RZ, England. *Telephone:* 0171-351 8174; 0171-485 6582. *Fax:* 0171-351 5675.

BARNES, Robert Henry, B.S., M.D.; American psychiatrist; b. 4 Nov. 1921, Worcester, Mass.; s. of Harry Elmer Barnes and Grace Stone Barnes; m. Beverly R. Feingold 1967; one s. one d. and one stepson; ed. Union Coll. Schenectady, New York, Duke Univ. and Univ. of Colorado; Instructor, Psychosomatic Medicine, Univ. of Colorado 1952–53, Asst. Prof. of Psychiatry, Duke Univ. 1953–56; Assoc. Prof., Prof. and Chair., Dept. of Psychiatry, Univ. of Missouri in Kansas City 1956–68; Exec. Dir Greater Kansas City Mental Health Foundation 1956–68; Acting Dir. Epidemiological Field Station, Kansas City, Missouri 1967–68; Prof. of Psychiatry, Univ. of Texas School of Medicine, San Antonio 1968–72; Prof. and Chair. Dept. of Chemistry, Texas Technical Univ. School of Medicine 1972; Fellow, American Psychiatric Asscn.; Consultant Nat. Inst. of Mental Health in Community Mental Health Programs and Epidemiology 1962–. *Publications:* A Community Concern (with Epps and McPartland) 1965; and 30 articles on geriatrics, psychosomatic medicine, electroencephalography, cerebral circulation, psychiatric education, and group therapy. *Leisure interests:* private flying, hunting, fishing, cooking.

BARNETT, Baron (Life Peer), cr. 1983, of Heywood and Royton in Greater Manchester; **Joel Barnett,** P.C., J.P.; British politician; b. 14 Oct. 1923; s. of Louis and Ettie Barnett; m. Lilian Goldstone 1949; one d.; ed. Derby Street Jewish School, Manchester Central High School; Certified Accountant 1974; Sr. Partner accountancy practice, Manchester 1953–74, 1979–80; served Royal Army Service Corps and British Mil. Govt. in Germany; mem. Borough Council, Prestwich, Lancs. 1956–59; Hon. Treas. Manchester Fabian Soc. 1953–65; Labour Cand. for Runcorn Div. of Cheshire 1959; M.P. for Heywood and Royton Div. of Lancashire 1964–83, mem. House of Commons Public Accounts Cttee. 1965–71, Chair. 1979–83; mem. Public Expenditure Cttee. 1971–74, Select. Cttee. on Tax Credits 1973–74; Vice-Chair. Parl. Labour Party Econ. and Finance Group 1966–67, Chair. 1967–70, 1972–74; Opposition Spokesman on Treas. Matters 1970–74; Chief Sec. to the Treas. 1974–79, mem. Cabinet 1977–79; mem. Hallé Cttee. 1982–93; Vice-Chair. Bd. of Govs., BBC 1986–93; Chair., Dir., consultant to a number of cos.; Chair. British Screen Finance Ltd 1985–, Hansard Soc. for Parl. Govt. 1984–90; Pres. Royal Inst. of Public Admin. 1989–92; Children's Medical Charity Trust PLC; Trustee Victoria and Albert Museum 1984–, Open Univ. Foundation 1994–; Gov. Birkbeck Coll., London Univ; Hon. Visiting Fellow, Univ. of Strathclyde 1980–; Hon. LL.D. (Strathclyde) 1983. *Publication:* Inside the Treasury 1982. *Leisure interests:* walking, conversation, reading, good food. *Address:* Flat 92, 24 John Islip Street, London, SW1P 4LG; 7 Hillingdon Road, Whitefield, Manchester, M25 7QQ, Lancs., England (Homes). *Telephone:* (0161) 766 3634.

BARNETT, Correlli Douglas, C.B.E., M.A.; British military historian; b. 28 June 1927, Norbury, Surrey; s. of Douglas A. Barnett and Kathleen M. Barnett; m. Ruth Murby 1950; two d.; ed. Trinity School, Croydon and Exeter Coll. Oxford; Intelligence Corps 1945–48; North Thames Gas Bd. 1952–57; public relations 1957–63; Keeper of Archives, Churchill Coll. Cambridge 1977–95; Defence Lecturer, Univ. of Cambridge 1980–83; Fellow Churchill Coll., Cambridge 1977–; mem. Cttee. London Library 1977–79, 1982–84; Hon. D.Sc. (Cranfield Univ.) 1993; Screenwriters' Guild Award for Best British TV Documentary (The Great War) 1964; F.R.S.L. Award for Britain and Her Army 1971; Winston Churchill Memorial Lecturer, Switzerland 1982; Chesney Gold Medal Royal United Services Inst. for Defence Studies 1991. *Publications:* The Hump Organisation 1957, The Channel Tunnel (with Humphrey Slater) 1958, The Desert Generals 1960, The Swordbearers 1963, Britain and Her Army 1970, The Collapse of British Power 1972, Marlborough 1974, Bonaparte 1978, The Great War 1979, The Audit of War 1986, Hitler's Generals 1989, Engage the Enemy More Closely 1991 (Yorkshire Post Book of the Year Award 1991), The Lost Victory: British Dreams, British Realities 1945–1950 1995. *Leisure interests:* gardening, interior decorating, eating, idling, mole-hunting. *Address:* Churchill College, Cambridge (Office); Catbridge House, East Carleton, Norwich, Norfolk, NR14 8JX, England (Home). *Telephone:* (01223) 336083 (Office); (01508) 570410 (Home).

BARNETT, Peter Leonard, A.M.; Australian journalist, broadcaster and administrator; b. 21 July 1930, Albany, Western Australia; s. of Leonard Stewart and Ruby Barnett; m. Siti Nuraini Jatim 1970; one s.; ed. Guildford Grammar School, Western Australia, Univ. of Western Australia; Canberra Rep. and Columnist, The Western Australian 1953–57; South-East Asia Corresp., Australian Broadcasting Comm. 1961, 1963, 1964, Jakarta Rep. 1962, New York and UN Corresp. 1964–67, Washington Corresp. 1967–70; News Ed., Radio Australia, Melbourne 1971–72, Washington Corresp. 1972–80, Controller, Melbourne 1980–84, Dir. 1984–89; Exec. Dir. Australian Broadcasting Corpn. 1984–89; Vice-Chair. Operating Cttee. Council for Econ. Devt. of Australia; Vice-Pres. Australian Inst. of Int. Affairs; Australia Award 1988; mem. Islamic Council of Vic. *Leisure interests:* swimming, gardening, literature, musical composition. *Address:* CEDA House, 123 Lonsdale Street, Melbourne 3000 (Office); 66/46 Lansell Road, Toorak, Vic. 3142, Australia (Home). *Telephone:* (03) 9827-5979 (Home).

BARNEVIK, Percy Nils, M.B.A.; Swedish business executive; b. 13 Feb. 1941, Simrishamn; s. of Einar and Anna Barnevik; m. Aina Orvarsson 1963; two s. one d.; ed. Gothenburg School of Econs., Stanford Univ., U.S.A.; Man. Admin. Devt., Group Controller, Sandvik AB 1969–75, Pres. U.S. subsidiary 1975–79, Exec. Vice-Pres. parent co. 1979–80, Chair. Sandvik AB Oct. 1983–; Pres. and Chief Exec. ASEA, Västerås 1980–92; C.E.O. ASEA Brown Boveri Group 1988–96, Chair. 1996–; Dir. Du Pont Co. 1991–; Dir. Skanska 1986–, Vice-Chair. 1991–92, Chair. 1992; mem. Prime Minister's Special Industry Advisory Cttee. 1994–. *Address:* ABB ASEA Brown Boveri Ltd., P.O. Box 8131, 8050 Zürich, Switzerland.

BARON, Carolyn, B.A.; American publishing executive, editor and author; b. 25 Jan. 1940, Detroit; d. of Gabriel Cohn and Viola Cohn; m. Richard W. Baron 1975; ed. Univ. of Mich.; Ed., Editorial Production Dir. Holt, Rinehart & Winston, New York 1965–71; Man. Ed. E.P. Dutton Co. Inc., New York 1971–74, Exec. Ed. 1974–75; Admin. Ed. Pocket Books, Simon & Schuster, New York 1975–78, Vice-Pres., Ed.-in-Chief 1978–79; Vice-Pres., Ed.-in-Chief Crown Publs., New York 1979–81; Vice-Pres. Dell Publishing Co. New York 1981–86, Sr. Pres., Publr. 1986–; Sr. Vice-Pres. Bantam, Doubleday,, Dell 1989–. *Publications:* The History of Labor Unions in the U.S. 1971, Re-entry Game 1974, Board Sailboats: A Buying Guide 1977; articles in magazines. *Address:* Dell Publishing Co. Inc., 1540 Broadway, New York, NY 10036, U.S.A.

BARON, Franklin Andrew Merrifield; Dominican business executive, politician and diplomatist; b. 19 Jan. 1923, Dominica; s. of Alexander and O. M. Baron; m. Sybil Eva McIntyre 1973; ed. Dominica Grammar School, St. Mary's Acad.; Man. A. A. Baron & Co. 1939–45, partner 1945–78, sole owner 1987–; mem. Dominica Legis. and Exec. Councils 1954–60; rep. of Dominica to Fed. Talks 1956–60; Founder and Political Leader, Dominica United People's Party 1957–66; Minister of Trade and Production 1956–60; Chief Minister and Minister of Finance 1960–61; Man. Dir. Franklyn Hotels Ltd. 1970–75; Man. Sisserou Hotel 1975–76; Chair. Dominica Tourist Bd. 1970–72, Dominica Electricity Services 1983–91, Nat. Commercial Bank of Dominica 1986–90, Fort Young Hotel Co. Ltd. 1986–, New Chronicle Newspaper 1990–, Paramount Printing Ltd. 1992–; Adviser, Barclays Bank Int. 1976–84; non-resident Amb. to U.S.A. 1982–86; Perm. non-resident Rep. to UN and to OAS 1982–, Chair. OAS 1985, 1993; non-resident High Commr. in U.K. 1986–92; mem. Industrial Devt. corpn. 1984–88. *Leisure interests:* gardening, reading. *Address:* 14 Cork Street, P.O. Box 57, Roseau (Office); Syb Bar Aerie, Champs Fleurs, Eggleston, Dominica (Home). *Telephone:* 809-448 2445 (Home).

BARÓN CRESPO, Enrique; Spanish politician; b. 1944, Madrid; m.; one s.; ed. Calasancio de las Escuelas Pías Coll., Instituto Católico de Dirección de Empresas, Ecole Supérieure des Sciences Economiques et Commerciales, Paris; mem. Federación Universitaria Democrática Española; mem. Unión Sindical Obrero 1964; ran legal and econ. consultancy with Agapito Ramos; mem. Convergencia Socialista and Federación de Partidos Socialistas (FPS); negotiated electoral coalition of FPS with the Partido Socialista Obrero Español (PSOE); mem. Congress of Deputies 1977–, PSOE spokesman for econ. affairs, public finance and the budget 1977–82; Minister of Transport and Tourism 1982–85; mem. European Parl. 1986–, Pres. 1989–92. *Leisure interests:* jazz, painting, walking, skiing. *Address:* Parlement Européen, 97/113 rue Belliard, 1040 Brussels, Belgium.

BARR, Rev. James, M.A., D.D., D.THEOL., F.B.A.; British university professor; b. 20 March 1924, Glasgow, Scotland; s. of Prof. and Mrs. Allan Barr; m. Jane J. S. Hepburn 1950; two s. one d.; ed. Daniel Stewart's Coll., Edinburgh, Univ. of Edinburgh; Minister, Church of Scotland, Tiberias, Israel 1951–53; Prof. of New Testament, Presbyterian Coll., Montreal, Canada 1953–55; Prof. of Old Testament, Univ. of Edinburgh 1955–61, Princeton Theological Seminary (N.J.) 1961–65; Prof. of Semitic Languages and Literatures, Univ. of Manchester 1965–76; Oriel Prof. of Interpretation of Holy Scripture, Univ. of Oxford 1976–78; Regius Prof. of Hebrew, Oxford 1978–89; Prof. of Hebrew Bible, Vanderbilt Univ., U.S.A. 1989–98, Distinguished Prof. 1994–98; mem. governing body SOAS 1980–85; Visiting Prof., numerous univs.; Currie Lecturer, Austin Theological Seminary, Tex. 1964; Guggenheim Memorial Fellowship for study in biblical semantics 1965; Cadbury Lecturer, Univ. of Birmingham 1969; F.B.A. 1969; Croall Lecturer, Univ. of Edinburgh 1970; Grinfield Lecturer on the Septuagint, Univ. of Oxford 1974–78; Firth Lecturer, Univ. of Nottingham 1978; Sprunt Lecturer, Richmond, Va. 1982; Schweich Lecturer British Acad. 1986, Sarum Lecturer Univ. of Oxford 1989, Read-Tuckwell Lecturer Bristol Univ. 1990, Gifford Lecturer, Edin. Univ. 1991, Hensley Henson Lecturer, Oxford Univ. 1997, Robertson Lecturer, Glasgow Univ. 1999; mem. Inst. for Advanced Study, Princeton, N.J. 1985; Schweich Lectures, British Acad. 1986; Fellow American Acad. of Arts and Sciences 1993; mem. American Philosophical Soc. 1993; Corresp. mem. Göttingen Acad. of Sciences, Fed. Repub. of Germany 1976, Norwegian Acad. 1977, Royal Swedish Acad. of Science, Uppsala 1991; Hon. mem. Soc. of Biblical Literature, U.S.A. 1983; D.D. Oxford Univ. 1981; numerous hon. degrees; Hon. Fellow, School of Oriental and African Studies, London 1975, Oriel Coll., Oxford 1980. *Publications:* The Semantics of Biblical Language 1961, Biblical Words for Time 1962, Old and New in Interpretation 1966, Comparative Philology and the Text of the Old Testament 1968, The Bible in the Modern World 1973, Fundamentalism 1977, Explorations in Theology 1980; Holy Scripture: Canon, Authority, Criticism 1983, Escaping from Fundamentalism 1984, The Variable Spellings of the Hebrew Bible 1988, The Garden of Eden and the Hope of Immortality 1992, Biblical Faith and Natural Theology 1993, The Concept of Biblical Theology 1999; editor: Oxford Hebrew Dictionary 1974–80. *Address:* 1432 Sitka Court, Claremont, CA 91711, U.S.A. *Telephone:* (909) 621-4189.

BARR, Roseanne, (see Roseanne).

BARR, William Pelham, M.A., J.D.; American lawyer; b. 23 May 1950, New York; s. of Donald Barr and Mary Ahern; m. Christine Moynihan 1973; three d.; ed. Columbia Univ., George Washington Univ.; staff officer CIA Washington 1973–77; barrister 1977–78; law clerk to U.S. Circuit Judge 1977–78, assoc. Shaw, Pittman, Potts & Trowbridge 1978–82, 1983–84, partner 1985–89, 1993–; deputy asst. dir. domestic staff policy The White House, Washington 1982–83; Asst. Attorney Gen. Office of Legal Counsel U.S. Dept. of Justice, Washington 1989–91; Attorney Gen. of U.S.A. 1991–93; mem. Virginia State Bar Asscn. DC Bar Asscn. *Address:* Shaw, Pittman, Potts and Trowbridge, 2300 N Street, N.W., Washington, DC 20037, U.S.A.

BARRAN, Sir David Haven, Kt.; British oil executive (retd.); b. 23 May 1912, London; s. of John N. Barran, Bt., and Alice M. Parks; m. Jane Lechmere Macaskie 1944; four s. (one deceased) three d.; ed. Winchester Coll. and Trinity Coll., Cambridge; Asiatic Petroleum Co. 1934–61, served Egypt, Sudan, Red Sea, India, London 1934–58, Pres. Asiatic Petroleum Corpn., New York 1958–61; Man. Dir. The Shell Petroleum Co., Shell Int. Petroleum Co. 1961–72; Principal Dir. Bataafse Petroleum Mij. N.V. 1961–72; Dir. Shell Transport and Trading Co. Ltd. 1961–83, Deputy Chair. 1964–67; Man. Dir. 1967–72, Chair 1967–72; Dir. Shell Oil Co. 1964–72, Chair. 1970–72; Dir. Midland Bank 1972–82, Deputy Chair. 1976–80, Chair. 1980–82; Dir. City Investment Co. of N.Y. 1972–84, Glaxo 1972–82, Gen. Accident Insurance 1972–83, Canadian Imperial Bank 1972–80, B.I.C.C. 1972–83, Standard Chartered Bank 1977–79. *Leisure interests:* gardening, golf, embroidery, (Pres. Embroiderers' Guild 1982–87). *Address:* 36 Kensington Square, London, W8 5HP; Brent Eleigh Hall, Sudbury, Suffolk, CO10 9NP, England (Home). *Telephone:* (01787) 247202.

BARRATT-BOYES, Sir Brian Gerald, K.B.E., M.B., CH.M., F.R.A.C.S., F.R.S.N.Z.; New Zealand cardiothoracic and vascular surgeon; b. 13 Jan. 1924, Wellington; s. of Gerald Boyes and Edna (Boyes) Barratt; m. 1st Norma Thompson (divorced 1986); five s.; m. 2nd Sara Monester 1986; ed. Wellington Coll. and Univ. of Otago; Fellowship, Cardiothoracic Surgery, Mayo Clinic 1953–55; N.Z. Nuffield Travelling Fellow, Univ. of Bristol, U.K. 1956; Sr. Thoracic Surgeon, Green Lane Hosp. Auckland 1957–65, Surgeon in Charge, Cardiothoracic Surgical Unit 1965–88; pvt. practice, Mater Misericordiae Hosp. (now Mercy Hosp.), Epsom, Auckland 1966–90; Hon. F.A.C.S.; Hon. F.R.C.S. 1985, Hon. F.R.C.S.T. 1987, Hon. F.A.C.C. 1989; Hon. F.R.A.C.P. 1995; Hon. D.Sc. 1985; R.T. Hall Prize Cardiology Soc. of Australia and N.Z. 1966, Réné Leriche Prize, Soc. Int. de Chirurgie 1987, Award for Excellence in Surgery, Royal Australasian Coll. of Surgeons 1994; featured on Famous New Zealanders postage stamp 1995. *Publications:* Heart Disease in Infancy: Diagnosis and Surgical Treatment 1973, Cardiac Surgery (with J. W. Kirklin) 1986. *Leisure interests:* farming, fishing, golf. *Address:* Greenhills, 982 Hibiscus Coast Highway, Waiwera, Auckland, New Zealand (Home).

BARRE, Raymond; French politician and international civil servant; b. 12 April 1924, Saint-Denis, Réunion; s. of René and Charlotte (née Déramond) Barre; m. Eve Hegedüs 1954; two s.; ed. Faculté de Droit, Paris, and Inst. d'Etudes Politiques, Paris; Prof. at Inst. des Hautes Etudes, Tunis 1951–54; Prof. at Faculté de Droit et de Sciences économiques, Caen 1954–63; Prof. Inst. d'Etudes politiques, Paris 1961, 1982–, Univ. de Paris I (Panthéon-Sorbonne) 1982, Faculté de Droit et Sciences économiques, Paris 1962; Dir. du Cabinet to Minister of Industry 1959–62; mem. Cttee. of Experts (Comité Lorain) studying financing of investments in France 1963–64; mem. Comm. of Gen. Econ. and Financing of Fifth Plan and other govt. cttees.; Vice-Pres. of Comm. of European Communities responsible for Econ. and Financial Affairs 1967–72; mem. Gen. Council, Banque de France 1973; Minister of Foreign Trade Jan.-Aug. 1976; Prime Minister 1976–78, 1978–81, also Minister of Economy and Finance 1976–78; mem. for Rhône, Nat. Assembly 1978–; Pres. Inst. d'études des relations internationales (IERI) 1988–, Convention libérale européenne et sociale (CLES) 1988–, Inst. int. du droit d'expression française 1989–, Pres. Supervisory Council of Aspen, France 1994–; Mayor of Lyon 1995–; numerous decorations. *Publications:* Economie politique 1956, Une politique pour l'avenir 1982, Réflexions pour demain 1982, Au Tournant du Siècle 1987, Questions de Confiance 1988. *Address:* Assemblée Nationale, 75355 Paris; Hôtel de Ville, place de la Comédie, 69001 Lyon (Office); 4–6 avenue Emile-Acollas, 75007 Paris, France (Home).

BARRÉ MAÏNASSARA, Ibrahim; Niger head of state and army officer; Chief of Staff of Gen. Armed Forces; mem. Nat. Salvation Council; Head of State of Niger Jan. 1996–. *Address:* Office of the President, Niamey, Niger.

BARRÉ-SINOUSSI, Françoise Claire, D. ÈS SC.; French scientist; b. 30 July 1947, Paris; d. of Roger Sinoussi and Jeanine Fau; m. Jean-Claude Barré 1978; ed. Lycée Bergson, Faculty of Science Paris VII and Paris VI; Research Asst. Inst. nat. de la Santé et de la recherche médicale (Inserm) 1975–80, Researcher 1980–86, Dir. of Research 1986–; Head of Lab., Biology of Retroviruses Unit, Inst. Pasteur 1988–92, Head of Unit 1993–; Prize of Fondation Körber pour la promotion de la Science européenne 1986, Prize of Acad. de médecine 1988, Faisal Prize for Medicine (Saudi Arabia) 1993; Chevalier Ordre nat. du Mérite, Chevalier Légion d'honneur. *Leisure interests:* theatre, reading. *Address:* Institut Pasteur, Unité de biologie des rétrovirus, 25 rue du Docteur Roux, 75724 Paris cedex 15, France.

BARREAS ARRECHEA, Ricardo Alfredo, DR. MED.; Argentinian politician and physician; b. 3 July 1934, Posadas; m. María Marta Preuciano; four c.; ed. Univ. de la Ciudad de Buenos Aires; Head, Dept. of Surgery, Hosp. Cen. de Posadas; Prin. Surgeon Sanatorio Nosiglia; fmr. mem. Juventud Radical Metropolitana; Vice-Pres. Dist. Misiones de la Unión Cívica Radical; Del. to Nat. Cttee., now Second Vice-Pres. Conducción Nacional U.C.R.; cand. for Gov., Prov. de Misiones 1973, 1975, Gov. 1983–87; Minister of Health and Social Affairs 1987–89; mem. Soc. Argentina de Gastroenterología, Soc. de Proctología, Soc. Argentina de Cirugía.

BARRETT, Charles Kingsley, D.D., F.B.A.; British professor of divinity (retd.); b. 4 May 1917, Salford, Lancs.; s. of Rev. F. Barrett and Clara Barrett (née Seed); m. Margaret E. Heap 1944; one s. one d.; ed. Shebbear Coll., Pembroke Coll. Cambridge and Wesley House, Cambridge; Lecturer in Theology, Durham Univ. 1945–58, Prof. of Divinity 1958–82; Visiting Lecturer and Prof. in various European countries, U.S.A., Canada, Australia and N.Z.; Pres. Studiorum Novi Testamenti Societas 1973–74; Hon. Fellow Pembroke Coll. Cambridge; mem. Royal Norwegian Soc. of Sciences and Letters 1991–; Hon. mem. Soc. of Biblical Literature (U.S.A.); Dr. h.c. (Hull, Aberdeen, Hamburg); Burkitt Medal for Biblical Study 1966; von Humboldt Forschungspreis 1988. *Publications:* The Holy Spirit and the Gospel Tradition 1947, The Gospel according to St. John 1955, 1978, From First Adam to Last 1962, Jesus and the Gospel Tradition 1967, The Epistles to the Corinthians 1968, 1973, The Signs of an Apostle 1970, Essays on Paul 1982, Essays on John 1982; Freedom and Obligation 1985; Church, Ministry and Sacraments in the New Testament 1985, Paul: An Introduction to his Thought 1994, The Acts of the Apostles, Vol. I 1994, Jesus and the Word 1996, The Acts of the Apostles, Vol. II 1998; several other books and many articles in learned journals and symposia. *Address:* 22 Rosemount, Plawsworth Road, Durham, DH1 5GA, England. *Telephone:* (0191) 386 1340.

BARRETT, Matthew W., O.C; Canadian banker; b. 20 Sept. 1944, Co. Kerry, Ireland; ed. Harvard Business School; joined Bank of Montreal, London, England 1962; moved to Canada 1967; Vice-Pres. Man. Services, Bank of Montréal 1978; Vice-Pres. B.C. Div. 1979; Sr. Vice-Pres. Eastern and Northern Ont. 1980; Sr. Vice-Pres. and Deputy Gen. Man. Int. Banking Group 1981; Sr. Vice-Pres. and Deputy Group Exec. Treasury Group 1984; Exec. Vice-Pres. and Group Exec. Personal Banking 1985; Pres. and C.O.O. 1987; C.E.O. 1989–, Chair. Bd. of Dirs. 1990–; Trustee, First Canadian Mortgage Fund; Dir. Harris Bankcorp. Inc. and subsidiaries, Nesbitt Burns Inc., Molson Cos. Ltd., Seagrams Co. Ltd.; various public appts.; Hon. LL.D. (St. Mary's Univ., Halifax, N.S.), (York Univ., Ont., Concordia Univ., Univ. of Waterloo); Hon. D.C.L. (Bishop's Univ.) 1993. *Leisure interests:* fly-fishing, tennis, reading. *Address:* Bank of Montréal, 129 rue St-Jacques ouest, Montréal, Québec, H2Y 1L6, Canada.

BARRIE, George Napier, B.A., LL.B., LL.D.; South African professor and advocate; b. 9 Oct. 1940, Pietersburg; m. Marie Howell 1970; two s. one d.; ed. Pretoria Univ., Univ. of S.A. and Univ. Coll. London; State advocate Supreme Court 1964–69; Sr. Law Adviser Dept. of Foreign Affairs 1970–80;

Prof. of Int. and Constitutional Law, Rand Afrikaans Univ. 1981–; Visiting Prof. Free Univ. of Brussels 1992; Leader of S.A. Del. to numerous int. confs.; mem. S.A. Del. to Int. Bar Assen. Conf. 1984, Nat. Advisory Council on Correctional Services. *Publications include:* Topical International Law 1979, Self-Determination in Modern International Law 1995 and numerous works and articles on int. and constitutional law; co-author: Nuclear Non-Proliferation: The Why and the Wherefore 1985, Constitutions of Southern Africa 1985, Law of South Africa 1986, Law of the Sea 1987, Bill of Rights Compendium 1996. *Leisure interest:* long distance running. *Address:* Faculty of Law, Rand Afrikaans University, P.O. Box 524, Auckland Park, Johannesburg 2006, South Africa. *Fax:* 011-4892049.

BARRINGTON, Edward John, B.A.; Irish civil servant and diplomatist; b. 26 July 1949, Dublin; m. Clare O'Brien 1972; one s.; ed. Univ. Coll. Dublin; Third Sec. Dept. of Foreign Affairs, EC Div. 1971–73, First Sec. 1973–75, First Sec. EC Perm. Rep. Office, Brussels 1975–80, First Sec. Press Section, HQ Aug.–Dec. 1980, Counsellor Political Div., HQ 1980–85, Asst. Sec.-Gen. Admin. Div., HQ 1985–89, Asst. Sec.-Gen. EC Div., HQ 1989–91, Asst. Sec.-Gen. Political Div. and Political Dir., HQ 1991–95, Deputy Sec. 1995; Amb. to U.K. Sept. 1995–. *Leisure interests:* cinema, hiking, jazz, theatre. *Address:* Embassy of Ireland, 17 Grosvenor Place, London, SW1X 7HR, England. *Telephone:* 0171-235 8483. *Fax:* 0171-235 2851.

BARRINGTON, Sir Nicholas John, K.C.M.G., C.V.O., F.R.S.A.; British diplomatist; b. 23 July 1934; s. of late Eric A. Barrington and Mildred Bill; ed. Repton School and Clare Coll. Cambridge; joined H.M. Diplomatic Service 1957; served Kabul 1959, U.K. Del. to European Communities, Brussels 1963, Rawalpindi 1965, Tokyo 1972–75, Cairo 1978–81; Minister and Head, British Interests Section, Teheran 1981–83; Asst. Under-Sec. of State, FCO 1984–87; Amb. to Pakistan 1987–89, High Commr. 1989–94; also Amb. (Non-Resident) to Afghanistan 1994; Chair. Man. Cttee. Southwold Summer Theatre 1995–; Co-Pres. Clare Coll. Devt. Programme, Cambridge 1995–; Trustee and Pres. of Friends of the Museum of Empire and Commonwealth, Bristol 1996–; mem. numerous bodies connected with Asia; Order of the Sacred Treasure, Japan 1975. *Leisure interests:* theatre, drawing, prosopography. *Address:* c/o Clare College, Cambridge, CB2 1TL, England.

BARRINGTON-WARD, Rt. Rev. Simon, M.A., D.D.; British ecclesiastic; b. 27 May 1930, London; s. of Robert McGowan Barrington-Ward and Margaret A. Radice; m. Dr. Jean Caverill Taylor 1963; two d.; ed. Eton Coll., Magdalene Coll. Cambridge and Westcott House, Cambridge; ordained, diocese of Ely 1956; Chaplain, Magdalene Coll. Cambridge 1956–60; Lecturer, Ibadan Univ. Nigeria 1960–63; Fellow and Dean of Chapel, Magdalene Coll. Cambridge 1963–69; Principal Church Missionary Soc. Coll. Selly Oak, Birmingham 1969–74; Gen. Sec. Church Missionary Soc. 1974–85; Canon, Derby Cathedral 1975–85; Chaplain to H.M. The Queen 1983–85; Bishop of Coventry 1985–97; Prelate to the Most Distinguished Order of St. Michael and St. George 1989; Asst. Bishop of Ely 1997—; Hon. Fellow Magdalene Coll. Cambridge 1997—; Hon. D.D. (Wycliffe Coll. Toronto) 1983; Hon. D.Litt. (Warwick Univ.) 1988. *Publications:* Love Will Out 1988, Christianity Today 1988, The Weight of Glory 1991, Why God? 1993, The Jesus Prayer 1996; articles and book chapters. *Leisure interests:* hill walking, music, cycling, calligraphy. *Address:* 4 Searle Street, Cambridge, CB4 3DB, England. *Telephone:* (01223) 740460.

BARRIONUEVO PEÑA, José; Spanish politician; b. 13 March 1942, Berja; m.; three c.; mem. Agrupación de Estudiantes Tradicionalistas; held posts in Sindicato Español Universitaria; became journalist; mem. Convergencia Socialista; town councillor, Madrid; Inspector de trabajo, Madrid 1971; Asst. Dir.-Gen. Ministry of Labour until 1979; socialist cand. in elections for Mayor of Madrid 1979; Minister of Interior 1982–88, of Transport, Tourism and Communications 1988–91; charged with kidnapping, misuse of public funds and assoc. with an outlaw band Jan. 1996; sentenced to ten years' imprisonment July 1998; partially pardoned and prison terms suspended Dec. 1998.

BARRIOS de CHAMORRO, Violeta; Nicaraguan politician; b. *c.* 1939; m. Pedro Joaquín Chamorro (died 1978); two s. two d.; ed. Our Lady of the Lake Catholic School, San Antonio and Blackstone Coll., U.S.A.; Pres. and Dir.-Gen. La Prensa (daily); Nat. Opposition Union cand. for Pres. 1989–90; Pres. of Nicaragua 1990–96, also Minister of Nat. Defence 1990. *Publication:* Dreams of the Heart (autobiography) 1996. *Address:* c/o Oficina del Presidente, Managua, Nicaragua.

BARRON, Derek Donald; British business executive (retd.); b. 7 June 1929; s. of Donald F.J. Barron and Hettie B. Barron; m. Rosemary I. Brian 1963; two s.; ed. Beckenham Grammar School and Univ. Coll. London; joined Ford Motor Co. Sales 1951; Tractor Group 1961; Tractor Man. Ford Italiana 1963; Marketing Assoc. Ford Motor Co., U.S.A. 1970; Gen. Sales Man. Overseas Markets 1971; Man. Dir. Ford Italiana 1973; Group Dir. Southern European Sales, Ford of Europe 1977; Sales and Marketing Dir. Ford Brazil 1979; Vice-Pres. Ford Motor de Venezuela 1982; Dir., Vice-Pres. Operations, Ford Brazil 1985; Chair., C.E.O. Ford Motor Co., Ltd. 1986–91; Chair. Ford Motor Credit Co. 1986–91.

BARRON, Sir Donald James, Kt., D.L., B.COM., C.A.; British businessman; b. 17 March 1921, Edinburgh; s. of Albert Gibson Barron and Elizabeth Macdonald; m. Gillian Mary Saville 1956; three s. two d.; ed. George Heriot's School, Edinburgh, Univ. of Edinburgh; joined Rowntree & Co. Ltd. 1952, Dir. 1961, Vice-Chair. 1965; Chair. Rowntree Mackintosh Ltd. 1966–81; Vice-Chair. Midland Bank PLC 1981–82 (Dir. 1972–87), Chair. 1982–87; mem. Bd. of Banking Supervision 1987–89; Vice-Chair. Canada Life Assurance Co. of Great Britain 1983–91, Chair. 1991–94 (Dir. 1980–96); Dir. Investors in Industry Group PLC 1980–91, Canada Life Unit Trust Mans. 1980–96 (Chair. 1982); mem. Council of C.B.I. 1966–81, Soc. Science Research Council 1971–72, Univ. Grants Cttee. 1972–81, Council Inst. of Chartered Accountants of Scotland 1980–81, Council of British Inst. of Management 1979–80; Trustee, Joseph Rowntree Foundation 1966–73, 1975–96, Chair. 1981–96; mem. NEDC 1983–85; Dir. Clydesdale Bank 1986–87; Gov. London Business School 1982–89; Treas. Univ. of York 1966–72, a Pro-Chancellor 1982–94; Hon. Dr. (Loughborough 1982, Heriot-Watt 1983, Council for Nat. Academic Awards 1983, Edinburgh 1984, Nottingham 1985, York 1986). *Leisure interests:* golf, tennis, travelling, gardening. *Address:* Greenfield, Sim Balk Lane, Bishopthorpe, York, YO2 1QH, England (Home). *Telephone:* (01904) 705675.

BARRON, John Penrose, M.A., D.PHIL., F.S.A.; British professor of Greek; b. 27 April 1934, Morley, Yorks.; s. of George Barron and Leslie Barron; m. Caroline M. Hogarth 1962; two d.; ed. Clifton Coll., Bristol and Balliol Coll. Oxford; Asst. lecturer, then lecturer in Latin, Bedford Coll. London 1958–64, in Archaeology, Univ. Coll. London 1964–67, Reader in Archaeology and Numismatics 1967–71; Prof. of Greek, Univ. of London (King's Coll.) 1971–91, Dean, Faculty of Arts 1976–80, Public Orator 1978–81, 1986–88, Dir. Inst. of Classical Studies 1984–91, Pro-Vice-Chancellor 1987–89; Dean, Univ. of London Insts. for Advanced Study 1989–91; mem. Univs. Funding Council 1989–93; Pres. Soc. for Promotion of Hellenic Studies 1990–93; Master St. Peter's Coll., Oxford 1991–; Chair. Conf. of Colls., Oxford 1993–95; Fellow, King's Coll; Gov. St. Paul's School, London 1991–, S.O.A.S., London 1989– (Vice-Chair. 1992–), Radley Coll. 1996–, Clifton Coll., Bristol 1996–; founder mem. Prince of Wales's Inst. of Architecture; Trustee Lambeth Palace Library 1998–. *Publications:* Greek Sculpture 1965, Silver Coins of Samos 1966. *Leisure interests:* travel, gardens. *Address:* Master's Lodgings, St Peter's College, Oxford, OX1 2DL, England. *Telephone:* (01865) 278862. *Fax:* (01865) 278862.

BARROT, Jacques, L. EN D.; French politician; b. 3 Feb. 1937, Yssingeaux, Haute-Loire; s. of Noël Barrot and Marthe Pivot; m. Florence Cattani 1982; one s. two d.; ed. Coll. d'Yssingeaux and Faculté de Droit, Paris and Inst. d'Etudes Politiques, Paris; Deputy to Nat. Ass. (Union Centriste) 1967–74, 1978, (Union pour la Démocratie Française) 1981–95; Sec. of State, Ministry of Equipment 1974–78; Minister of Commerce and Working Classes 1978–79, of Health and Social Security 1979–81; Pres. Conseil-Gen. Haute-Loire 1976–; Mayor of Yssingeaux 1989–; Minister of Labour, Social Dialogue and Participation 1995–97; Pres. Nat. Union for Environmental Improvement 1991–. *Publication:* Les Pierres de l'avenir 1978. *Leisure interest:* mountain sports. *Address:* Mairie, 43200 Yssingeaux; Conseil général de la Haute-Loire, 4 avenue du général de Gaulle, BP 310, 43011 Le-Puy-en-Veley cedex; Chemin de Lavée, 43200 Yssingeaux, France (Home).

BARROW, John David, B.SC., D.PHIL., F.R.A.S.; British professor of astronomy; b. 29 Nov. 1952, London; s. of late Walter Henry Barrow and Lois Miriam Barrow (née Tucker); m. Elizabeth Mary East 1975; two s. one d.; ed. Van Mildert Coll., Durham Univ., Magdalen Coll., Oxford; Lindemann Fellow, Astronomy Dept. Berkeley, Calif. Univ. 1977–78, Miller Fellow, Physics Dept. 1980–81; research lecturer Astrophysics Dept., Oxford Univ. 1978–80; lecturer Astronomy Centre, Sussex Univ. 1981, sr. lecturer, then Prof. 1989–, Dir. Astronomy Centre 1995–; Nuffield Fellow 1986–87, Leverhulme Royal Soc. Fellow 1992–93, PPARC Sr. Fellow 1994–; Gifford Lecturer (Glasgow Univ.) 1988, Samuel Locker Award 1989, Scott Memorial Lecture (Leuven) 1989, Collingwood Lecture (Durham) 1990, Spinoza Lecture (Amsterdam) 1993, George Darwin Lecture (Royal Astronomical Soc.) 1993, Elizabeth Spreadbury Lecture (UCL) 1993, BBV Lectures (Spain), Robert Boyle Memorial Lecture (Oxford) 1996. *Publications:* The Left Hand of Creation 1983, L'Homme et le Cosmos 1984, The Anthropic Cosmological Principle 1986, The World within the World 1988, Theories of Everything 1991, Perche il Mondo è Matematico? 1992, Pi in the Sky 1992, The Origin of the Universe 1994, The Artful Universe 1995, Impossibility 1998, Between Inner Space and Outer Space 1999. *Leisure interests:* athletics, books, theatre, writing. *Address:* Astronomy Centre, University of Sussex, Falmer, Brighton, Sussex BN1 9QJ, England. *Telephone:* (01273) 678574. *Fax:* (01273) 678097.

BARROW, Ursula Helen, M.A.; Belizean diplomatist; b. 31 Oct. 1955; ed. Newnham Coll., Cambridge Univ.; Econ. Devt. Planner, Planning Unit, Govt. of Belize 1978; consultant for small business affairs, urban planning and marketing, Frazier & Assocs. 1979–85; Counsellor and Deputy High Commr. in London 1988–89; Perm. Rep. to UN 1989–91; awarded Belize Open Scholarship 1974, Cambridge Commonwealth Trust Scholarship 1985. *Address:* c/o Ministry of Foreign Affairs, Economic Development and Education, P.O. Box 174, Belmopan, Belize.

BARROWCLOUGH, Sir Anthony Richard, Kt., Q.C.; British lawyer and civil servant; b. 24 June 1924; m. Mary Agnes Pery-Knox-Gore 1949; one s. one d.; ed. Stowe School and New Coll. Oxford; served war service as R.N.V.R. 1943–46; called to Bar, Inner Temple 1949, Bencher 1982; Recorder 1972–84; part-time mem. Monopolies Comm. 1966–69; mem. Council on Tribunals 1985–90; Parl. Commr. for Admin. and Health Service Commr.

for England, Wales and Scotland 1985–90; Chair. Dartmoor Steering Group 1990–. *Address:* The Old Vicarage, Winsford, near Minehead, Somerset, TA24 7JE, England.

BARRY, Brian Michael, M.A., D.PHIL., F.B.A.; British professor; b. 7 Aug. 1936, London; s. of James Frederick Barry and Doris Rose Barry; m. 1st Joanna Hill 1960 (dissolved 1989); one s.; m. 2nd Elizabeth Ann Parker 1991; ed. Taunton's School, Southampton and Queen's Coll., Oxford; Fellow Nuffield Coll., Oxford 1966–69, 1972–75; Prof. of Govt., Univ. of Essex 1969–72; Prof. of Political Science and Philosophy, Univ. of Chicago 1977–82; Prof. of Philosophy, Calif. Inst. of Tech. 1982–86; Prof. European Univ. Inst. 1986–87; Prof. of Political Science, L.S.E. 1987–; Fellow American Acad. of Arts and Sciences; Hon. D.Sc. (Southampton). *Publications:* Political Argument 1965, Sociologists, Economists and Democracy 1970, The Liberal Theory of Justice 1973, Theories of Justice 1989, Democracy, Power and Justice 1989, Democracy and Power 1991, Liberty and Justice 1991, Justice as Impartiality 1995. *Leisure interests:* cooking, playing the piano, London. *Address:* Department of Government, London School of Economics, Houghton Street, London, WC2A 2AE, England. *Telephone:* 0171-955 7175 (Office). *Fax:* 0171-831 1707.

BARRY, Edward William, B.A.; American publishing executive; b. 24 Nov. 1937, Stamford, Conn.; s. of Edward Barry and Elizabeth Cosgrove; m. Barbara H. Walker 1963; one s. one d.; ed. Univ. of Conn.; Pres. The Free Press, New York 1972–82, Oxford Univ. Press Inc., New York 1982–; Sr. Vice-Pres. Macmillan Publishing Co., New York 1973–82; mem. Exec. Council Professional and Scholarly Publications 1993, advisory Bd. Pace Univ. Grad. Program in Publishing 1990–, Bd. Dirs. Asscn. of American Publrs. 1995, mem. of other bodies. *Address:* Oxford University Press Inc., 198 Madison Avenue, New York, NY 10016 (Office); 62 High Rock Road, Stamford, CT 06903, U.S.A. (Home). *Telephone:* (212) 251-0416 (Office).

BARRY, John; b. John Barry Prendergast 1933, York; British soundtrack composer; formed group, The John Barry Seven 1957 left group 1962; stage musical, Billy 1974; first film score composed for Beat Girl; other film scores include music for Monte Walsh, The Lion in Winter, Midnight Cowboy (Acad. Award), Out of Africa (Acad. Award), The Ipcress File, Body Heat, Dances with Wolves (Acad. Award), From Russia with Love, Goldfinger, You Only Live Twice, Octopussy, The Cotton Club, A View to a Kill, Out of Africa (Acad. Award 1985), Dances with Wolves (Acad. Award 1990), Indecent Proposal, The Specialist.

BARRY, Marion Shepilov, Jr.; American politician; b. 6 March 1936, Itta Bena, Miss.; s. of Marion S. Barry and Mattie Barry; m. 1st Effi Barry 1978; one s.; m. 2nd Cara Masters Barry 1994; ed. LeMoyne Coll., Fisk Univ., Univs. of Kansas and Tennessee; Dir. of Operations, Pride Inc., Washington, D.C. 1967; co-founder, Chair. and Dir. Pride Econ. Enterprises, Inc., Washington, D.C. 1968; mem. Washington D.C. School Bd. 1971–74; mem. Washington City Council 1974–78; Mayor of Washington 1979–91; arrested and charged with possessing cocaine Jan. 1990; convicted, imprisoned for 6 months for possessing cocaine; re-elected Mayor 1995–98. *Address:* c/o Office of the Mayor, 1 Judiciary Square, 441 4th Street, NW, Washington, D.C. 20001, U.S.A.

BARRY, Peter; Irish politician; b. 1928, Cork; s. of Anthony and Rita Barry; m. Margaret O'Mullane 1957; four s. two d.; Man. Dir. of a tea firm; mem. of the Dáil 1969–; fmr. Chair. Oireachtas Cttee., Fine Gael Party; fmr. Lord Mayor of Cork and Chair. Cork and Kerry Regional Devt. Bd.; Fine Gael Spokesman on Labour and the Public Service 1972–73; Minister for Transport and Power 1973–76, for Educ. 1976–77; Fine Gael Spokesman on Finance and Econ. Affairs 1977–81; Minister for the Environment 1981–82; Fine Gael Spokesman on the Environment 1982; Minister for Foreign Affairs 1982–87; Opposition Spokesman on Foreign Affairs 1987–94, on industry and commerce 1991–94; Co-Chair. Anglo-Irish Conf. 1985–87; Deputy Leader Fine Gael Party 1979–87, 1991. *Address:* "Sherwood", Blackrock, Cork, Ireland.

BARRYMORE, Drew; American film actress; b. 22 Feb. 1975, Los Angeles; d. of John Barrymore Jr. and Jaid Barrymore; m. Jeremy Thomas 1994 (divorced); appeared in dog food commercial 1976; film debut in TV movie Suddenly Love 1978. *Films include:* Altered States 1980, E.T.: The Extra-Terrestrial 1982, Irreconcilable Differences 1984, Firestarter 1984, Cat's Eye 1985, See You In The Morning 1988, Guncrazy 1992, Poison Ivy 1992, Beyond Control: The Amy Fisher Story 1992, Wayne's World 2 1993, Bad Girls 1994, Boys On The Side 1995, Batman Forever 1995, Mad Love 1995, Scream 1996, Everyone Says I Love You 1996, All She Wanted 1997, Best Men 1997, Never Been Kissed (also producer) 1998, Home Fries 1998, The Wedding Singer 1998, Ever After 1998. *Address:* 1122 South Robertson Boulevard, #15, Los Angeles, CA 90035, U.S.A.

BARSALOU, Yves; French banking executive; b. 18 Sept. 1932, Bizanet; s. of Marcell Barsalou and Marie-Louise Salvan; m. Claire-Marie Vié 1955; two s.; ed. Ecoles de Carcassonne et Narbonne; mem. Dept. Centre of Young Farmers 1957–67; Pres. Caisse Locale de Crédit Agricole de Narbonne 1974–; mem. Cen. Cttee., then Vice-Pres. Caisse nat. du Crédit agricole (CNCA) 1981–88, Pres. 1988–, Chair. CNCA 1989; Vice-Pres. Fed. Nationale du Crédit Agricole (FNCA) 1992–; mem. Plenary Comm., Fed. nat. du Crédit agricole 1975–77, Dir. 1977–81, Pres. 1982–92; Vice-Pres., Pres. Fed. Int. du Crédit Agricole (CiCa) 1993–; Vice-Pres. Bd. Crédit Agricole Indosuez 1996; mem. Conseil econ. et social, numerous cttees.; Chevalier, Légion d'honneur, Cmmdr., Mérite agricole. *Address:* CNCA, 91–93 blvd Pasteur, 75015 Paris; 11200 Bizanet, France (Home).

BARSHAI, Rudolf Borisovich; Russian conductor; b. 28 Sept. 1924, Labinskaya, Krasnodar Territory; s. of Boris and Maria Barshai; ed. Moscow Conservatoire; performed in chamber ensembles with Shostakovich, Richter, Oistrakh, Rostropovich; founder and Artistic Dir. Moscow Chamber Orchestra 1956–77; Prin. Conductor and Artistic Adviser, Bournemouth Symphony Orchestra 1982–; Guest Conductor Orchestre Nat. de France; numerous tours abroad; author of orchestrations and arrangements for chamber orchestra of old and contemporary music; Hon. D.Mus. (Southampton). *Address:* Homberg Str. 6, 4433 Ramlinsburg, Switzerland. *Telephone:* (061) 931-1284. *Fax:* (061) 931-3564.

BARSHEFSKY, Charlene; American government official and lawyer; partner, Steptoe & Johnson (law firm), Washington, D.C.; formerly Deputy U.S. Trade Rep.; Acting U.S. Trade Rep. April–Nov. 1996; U.S. Trade Rep. March 1997–. *Address:* Office of the United States Trade Representative, Executive Office of the President, 600 17th Street, N.W., Washington, DC 20508, U.S.A.

BARSTOW, Dame Josephine Clare, D.B.E., B.A.; British opera singer; b. 27 Sept. 1940, Sheffield; d. of Harold Barstow and Clara Barstow; m. 1st Terry Hands 1964 (divorced 1968); m. 2nd Ande Anderson 1969 (died 1996); ed. Birmingham Univ.; taught English in London area for two years; début in operatic profession with Opera for All 1964; for short time co. mem. Welsh Nat. Opera, then English Nat. Opera; now freelance singer in all nat. opera houses in G.B. and in Paris, Vienna, Salzburg, Zürich, Geneva, Turin, Florence, Cologne, Munich, Berlin, U.S.S.R., Chicago, San Francisco, New York, Houston and many other American opera houses; *chief roles:* Violetta (Traviata), Leonora (Forza del Destino), Elisabeth (Don Carlos), Lady Macbeth, Leonore (Fidelio), Sieglinde, Arabella, Salome, Chrysothemis, Amelia, The Marshallin, Tosca, Mimi, Minnie, Manon Lescaut, Emilia Marty, Jenůfa, Katya Kabanova, Medea, Renata (The Fiery Angel), Katerina Ismailova, Kostelnicka (Jenůfa), Marie (Wozzeck); world premières of Tippet, Henze and Penderecki; *recordings include:* Verdi Recital Record with English National Opera Orchestra and Mark Elder, Amelia with Herbert von Karajan, Anna Maurant in Street Scene, Kate in Kiss Me Kate, Four Finales, Gloriana, Albert Herring; Hon. D.Mus. (Birmingham). *Leisure interests:* farming (cattle) and breeding Arabian horses. *Address:* c/o Askonas Holt, Lonsdale Chambers, 27 Chancery Lane, London, WC2A 1PF, England. *Telephone:* 0171-379 7700.

BARTELSKI, Lesław, LL.M.; Polish writer; b. 8 Sept. 1920, Warsaw; s. of Zygmunt and Zofia Ulanowska; m. Maria Zembrzuska 1947; one s. one d.; ed. Univ. of Warsaw; mem. of resistance movement 1939–44; mem. Sztuka i Naród (Art and Nation) 1942–44; Co-Ed. Nowiny Literackie 1947–48, Nowa Kultura 1953–63, Kultura 1963–72; mem. Presidium of Gen. Council, Union of Fighters for Freedom and Democracy 1969–79, Deputy Pres. 1979–90; mem. PEN; Chair. Warsaw Branch, Polish Writers' Asscn. 1972–78, mem. Polish Writers' Asscn. 1984–, Deputy Pres. 1989–; mem. Bd., Janusz Korczak Int. Asscn.; Visiting Prof., Univ. of Warsaw 1970–71, 1977–78; Vice-Pres. Warsaw City Council 1973–80; Lecturer on Cultural Research, Pvt. Higher School of Commerce 1993–96; State Prize (3rd class) 1951, Prize of Minister of Defence (2nd class) 1969, Pietrzak Prize 1969 and 1985, Warsaw Prize 1969, Prize of Minister of Culture and Art 1977 (1st class), Award of Pres. of Warsaw 1990; Commdr.'s Cross, Order of Polonia Restituta, Order of Banner of Labour (2nd class), Order of Cyril and Methodius (1st class) Bulgaria, Cross of Valour, Warsaw Insurgent Cross, Partisan's Cross. *Publications:* poems: Przeciw zagładrie 1948; novels include Ludzie zza rzeki 1951, Pejzaż dwukrotny 1958, Wodorosty 1964, Mickiewicz na wschodzie 1966, Dialog z cieniem 1968, Niedziela bez dzwonów 1973, Krwawe skrzydła 1975, Rajski ogród 1978; essays: Genealogia ocalonych 1963, Jeździec z Madary 1963, Cień wojny 1963, Walcząca Warszawa 1968, Z głową na karabinie 1974, Pamięć żywa 1977, Polscy pisarze współcześni 1944–74 (biographical dictionary) 1977, Kusociński 1979, Pieśń niepodległa 1988, Czas bitew 1993, Polscy pisarze współcześni 1939–91 (biographical dictionary) 1995; monograph: Powstanie Warszawskie 1965, Mokotów 1944, 1971, Pułk AK Baszta 1990, Krzyi AK 1993. *Leisure interests:* history of the Second World War, sport. *Address:* ul. F. Joliot Curie 17 m. 1, 02-646 Warsaw, Poland. *Telephone:* (22) 844-31-10.

BARTH, Else M.; Norwegian/Netherlands professor of logic and analytical philosophy; b. 3 Aug. 1928, Strinda, Norway; m. Hendrik A. J. F. Misset 1953; ed. Univs. of Oslo, Trondheim, Amsterdam and Leyden; Reader in Logic, Utrecht Univ. 1971–77; Prof. of Analytical Philosophy, Groningen Univ. 1977–87, of Logic and Analytical Philosophy 1987–; Pres. Evert Willem Beth Foundation 1976–; mem. Royal Netherlands Acad. of Arts and Sciences, Sciences, Norwegian Soc. of Sciences. *Publications:* The Logic of the Articles in Traditional Philosophy. A Contribution to the Study of Conceptual Structures 1974, Perspectives on Analytic Philosophy, in Mededelingen der Koninklijke Nederlandse Akademie van Wetenschappen, afd. Letterkunde, Nieuwe Reeks 1979, From Axiom to Dialogue—A philosophical study of logics and argumentation (with E. C. W. Krabbe) 1982, Argumentation: Approaches to Theory Formation. Containing the Contributions to the Groningen Conference on the Theory of Argumentation, October 1978 (Ed., with J. L. Martens) 1982, Problems, Functions, and Semantic Roles—A Pragmatist's Analysis of Montague's Theory of Sentence Meaning (with R. T. P. Wiche) 1986; numerous contribs. to learned journals and published lectures. *Leisure interests:* music, cultural and political philosophy, literature, skiing. *Address:* Filosofisch Instituut, University of Groningen, Westersingel 19, 9718 CA Groningen (Office); Kamperfoelieweg 16, 9765 HK Paterswolde; Nachtegaallaan 26, 2224 JH Katwijk aan Zee, The Netherlands (Home). *Telephone:* (050) 636146, 636148 (Office); (05907) 4315 (Paterswolde); (01718) 13353 (Katwijk aan Zee).

BARTH, John, M.A.; American novelist and professor of English; b. 27 May 1930, Cambridge, Md.; s. of John J. Barth and Georgia Simmons; m. 1st Harriette Anne Strickland 1950; two s. one d.; m. 2nd Shelly Rosenberg 1970; ed. Johns Hopkins Univ.; Instructor Pennsylvania State Univ. 1953, Assoc. Prof. until 1965; Prof. of English, State Univ. of New York at Buffalo 1965–73, Johns Hopkins Univ. 1973–91, Prof. Emer. 1991–; Nat. Acad. of Arts and Letters Award; Nat. Book Award 1973; Lannan Foundation Prize 1998; Rockefeller Foundation Grant; Brandeis Univ. Citation in Literature; Hon. Litt.D. (Univ. of Maryland). *Publications:* The Floating Opera 1956, The End of the Road 1958, The Sot-Weed Factor 1960, Giles Goat-Boy 1966; Lost in the Funhouse (stories) 1968, Chimera 1972, Letters 1979, Sabbatical 1982, The Friday Book (essays) 1984, The Tidewater Tales: A Novel 1987, The Last Voyage of Somebody the Sailor 1991, Once Upon a Time 1994, On With the Story (stories) 1996. *Address:* Writing Seminars, Johns Hopkins University, Baltimore, MD 21218, U.S.A.

BARTH, (Thomas) Fredrik (Weybye), M.A., PH.D.; Norwegian social anthropologist; b. 22 Dec. 1928, Leipzig; s. of Prof. Tom Barth and Randi Barth; m. Unni Wikan 1972; one s.; ed. Berg School, Oslo and Univs. of Chicago, U.S.A. and Cambridge, England; Research Fellow in Social Anthropology, Univ. of Oslo 1953–61; Prof. of Social Anthropology, Univ. of Bergen 1961–72, Univ. of Oslo 1973–86; Research Fellow, Ministry of Educ. and Science 1987–; Prof. of Anthropology, Boston Univ., U.S.A.; Visiting Prof. Columbia Univ. 1960, Univ. of Khartoum 1963–64, Yale Univ. 1972, Johns Hopkins Univ. 1977, Univ. of Calif. Berkeley 1980, City Univ. N.Y. 1987, Emory Univ. 1989–96, Harvard Univ. 1996–97; Retzius Medal, Stockholm; Huxley Medal, Royal Anthropological Inst., London; Dr. h.c. (Memorial Univ.) Newfoundland, (Edin.) 1996. *Publications:* Political Leadership Among Swat Pathans 1959, Nomads of South Persia 1961, Models of Social Organization 1964, Ethnic Groups and Boundaries 1969, Ritual and Knowledge among the Baktaman of New Guinea 1975, Selected Essays 1981, Sohar 1983, The Last Wali of Swat 1985, Cosmologies in the Making 1987, Balinese Worlds 1993. *Leisure interests:* travel, art. *Address:* Rödkleivfaret 16, 0393 Oslo 3, Norway. *Telephone:* (47) 22-147483. *Fax:* (47) 22-859960.

BARTHELMEH, Hans Adolf, DIPL. KFM; German business executive (retd.); b. 19 Sept. 1923, Cologne; s. of Johann and Gertrud (née Weiler) Barthelmeh; m. Helene Fries 1950; one s.; ed. Univ. of Cologne; Internal Auditor (taxes), Fed. Financial Admin., Cologne 1950–52; with Ford-Werke AG, Cologne 1952–; first, Head, Tax Dept., then Head depts., Finance Div. 1955–63; Chief Controller, Operations 1963–66; mem. Bd. of Man. (Finance) 1966–68, (Sales) 1968–71; Pres. and Chair. Man. Bd., Ford-Werke AG, Cologne, 1966–73; Gen. Man. Ford Motor GmbH, Salzburg, Austria 1957–59; Chair. Rank Xerox GmbH, Düsseldorf 1980–83; Chair. Bd. of Dirs. Ford-Credit AG, Cologne; mem. Man. Bd., Verband der Deutschen Automobilindustrie e.V., Frankfurt; fmr. mem. Bd. of Dirs. American Chamber of Commerce, Fed. Repub. of Germany; mem. Industry Cttee. Chamber of Industry and Commerce, Cologne; mem. Regional Council Deutsche Bank AG, Bd. of Dirs., Deutsche Automobil-Treuhand GmbH until 1973; Pres. and Chair. Man. Bd. Gildemeister AG, Bielefeld 1974–78; mem. Advisory Bd., Deutsche Bank AG, Düsseldorf, Supervisory Bd., Rank Xerox Austria; fmr. mem. Bd. of Dirs. Gildemeister Italiana S.p.A., Ponte S. Pietro, Gildemeister Maquinas Operatrizes S.A., Brazil. *Publications:* articles in business magazines. *Leisure interests:* swimming, walking, books on futurology, philosophy, psychology and history, playing the piano. *Address:* Herrenstrunder Strasse 2a, 51067 Cologne, Germany.

BARTHOLOMEOS I, Patriarch, D.CN.L.; Turkish Greek Orthodox ecclesiastic; b. 29 Feb. 1940, Hagioi Theodoroi, Island of Imvros; s. of Christos Archondonis and Merope Archondonis; ed. Theological School of Halki, Pontifical Oriental Inst., Rome, Ecumenical Inst. Bossey, Switzerland and Univ. of Munich; ordained deacon 1961, priest 1969; mil. service 1961–63; Asst. Dean, Theological School of Halki 1968; elevated to rank of Archimandrite 1970; Admin. Pvt. Patriarchal Office of Ecumenical Patriarch Dimitrios 1972–90; Metropolitan, See of Philadelphia, Asia Minor 1973; mem. Holy and Sacred Synod 1974; Metropolitan of Chalcedon 1990–91; Archbishop of Constantinople, New Rome and Ecumenical Patriarch 1991–; mem. Exec. and Cen. Cttees., WCC 1991–; mem. numerous dels. etc.; Dr. h.c. (Athens); Dr. h.c. (Holy Cross Orthodox School of Theology, Brookline, Mass.). *Address:* Chief Secretariat of the Holy and Sacred Synod of the Ecumenical Patriarchate, Greek Orthodox Church, Rum Ortodoks Patrikhanesi, 34220 Fener-Haliç, Istanbul, Turkey.

BARTHOLOMEW, Reginald; American diplomatist; b. 17 Feb. 1936, Portland, Maine; m. Rose-Anne Dognin; three s. one d.; ed. Dartmouth Coll., Chicago Univ.; instructor Chicago Univ. 1961–64; Wesleyan Univ., Conn. 1964–68; Deputy Dir. Policy Planning Staff, Dept. of State 1974; Deputy Dir. Politico-Mil. Affairs Bureau 1977, Dir. 1979–81; with Nat. Security Council 1977–79; Special Cyprus Co-ordinator 1981–82; Special Negotiator for U.S.-Greek defence and econ. co-operation negotiations 1982–83; Amb. to Lebanon 1983–86, to Spain 1987–89, to NATO 1992–93; Special Envoy of Pres. Clinton to Bosnia 1993; Amb. to Italy 1993; mem. Council on Foreign Relations. *Address:* c/o Department of State, International Security Affairs, 2201 C Street, N.W., Washington, DC, 20520, U.S.A.

BARTLETT, Boyd C., B.S.; American business executive; b. 21 Oct. 1925, Cameron, Wis.; s. of Roy M. Bartlett and Verna E. Boortz; m. Joyce M. Samborn 1946; two s. one d.; ed. Univ. of Wisconsin; joined Deere & Co. 1952, Vice-Pres. Farm Equipment and Consumer Products Marketing 1972–79, Sr. Vice-Pres. 1979–83, Exec. Vice-Pres. Operations 1983–85, Pres. and C.O.O. 1985–87; Dir. Quad City Devt. Group, Rock Island, Ill. 1979–85; mem. Farm and Industrial Equipment Inst., Farm Foundation. *Address:* c/o Deere & Co., John Deere Road, Moline, IL 61265, U.S.A.

BARTLETT, Jennifer, M.F.A.; American artist; b. 14 March 1941, Long Beach, Calif.; m. 1st Edward Bartlett 1964 (divorced 1972); m. 2nd Mathieu Carrière 1983; ed. Mills Coll., Oakland, Calif., Yale Univ. School of Art and Architecture; taught art at Univ. of Conn., Storrs 1964–72, School of Visual Arts, New York 1972; first New York exhbn., Alan Saret's SoHo gallery 1970; numerous one-woman and group exhbns. including: 1977 Documenta, Kassel, Fed. Repub. of Germany and 1980 Venice Biennale; works in numerous collections, including: Museum of Modern Art, Metropolitan Museum of Art, Whitney Museum of American Art, New York; Art Gallery of S. Australia, Adelaide, Rhode Island School of Design, Yale Univ. Art Gallery and Walker Art Cente, Minneapolis; large-scale murals and other works include: Rhapsody 1976, Swimmers Atlanta (Richard B. Russel Fed. Bldg., Atlanta, Ga.) 1979; 270 steel plates for Inst. for Scientific Information, Phila.; murals for AT&T Bldg., New York; sculpture and other objects for Volvo Corpn.'s HQ, Göteborg, Sweden; Harris Prize, Art Inst. of Chicago 1976, Award of American Acad. and Inst. of Arts and Letters 1983. *Address:* c/o Paula Cooper Gallery, 155 Wooster Street, New York, NY 10012, U.S.A.

BARTLETT, John Vernon, C.B.E., M.A., F.ENG., F.I.C.E., F.I.E.AUST., F.A.S.C.E.; British consulting engineer; b. 18 June 1927, London; s. of late Vernon F. Bartlett and of Olga (née Testrup) Bartlett; m. Gillian Hoffman 1951; four s.; ed. Stowe School and Trinity Coll., Cambridge; Engineer, John Mowlem & Co., Ltd. 1951–57; joined Mott Hay & Anderson (now Mott MacDonald Group) 1957, Partner 1966, Chair. 1973–88, Consultant 1988–95; Chair. British Tunnelling Soc, 1977–79; Pres. Inst. of Civil Engs. 1982–83; mem. Governing Body Imperial Coll. London 1991–95; Master Worshipful Co. of Engineers 1992–93; Telford Gold Medals 1971, 1973; S. G. Brown Medal, Royal Soc. 1973. *Publications:* Tunnels: Planning, Design and Construction (with T. M. Megaw) 1981, Ships of North Cornwall 1996; various professional papers. *Leisure interests:* sailing, maritime history. *Address:* 6 Cottenham Park Road, Wimbledon, London, SW20 0RZ, England (Home). *Telephone:* 0181-946 9576 (Home).

BARTLETT, Neil, B.SC., PH.D., F.R.S.; British chemist; b. 15 Sept. 1932, Newcastle upon Tyne; s. of Norman and Ann Willins (née Vock) Bartlett; m. Christina Isabel Cross 1957; three s. one d.; ed. Heaton Grammar School, Newcastle upon Tyne, King's Coll., Durham Univ.; Sr. Chemistry Master, The Duke's School, Alnwick, Northumberland 1957–58; Faculty mem. Dept. of Chem., Univ. of B.C., Canada 1958–66; Prof. of Chem. Princeton Univ., N.J., U.S.A. 1966–69; Scientist, Bell Telephone Labs., Murray Hill, N.J. 1966–69; Prof. of Chem. Univ. of Calif., Berkeley 1969–94; Prof. Emer. 1994, Prin. Investigator Lawrence Berkeley Lab. 1969–; Brotherton Visiting Prof., Chemistry Dept., Leeds Univ. 1981; Erskine, Visiting Fellow, Univ. of Canterbury, N.Z. 1983; Visiting Fellow, All Souls Coll., Oxford Univ. 1984; Assoc. of Inst. Jozef Stefan, Slovenia; mem. Leopoldina Acad., Halle 1969; Corresp. mem. Göttingen Acad. 1977, American Acad. of Arts and Sciences 1977, Nat. Acad. of Sciences 1979; Associé Etranger Acad. des Sciences, France 1989; Pierre Duhem Lecturer, Bordeaux Univ. 1998; D.Sc. h.c. (Waterloo) 1968, (Colby Coll.) 1971, Dr. h.c. (Bordeaux) 1976, (Newcastle upon Tyne) 1981, (Ljubljana) 1989, (Nantes) 1990, (McMaster) 1992; Hon. L.L.D. (Simon Fraser) 1993, Dr.rer.nat. h.c. (Freie Univ. Berlin) 1998; Research Corpn. Award 1965; Dannie Heineman Prize 1971; Robert A. Welch Award 1976, W. H. Nichols Medal, U.S.A. 1983, Moissan Fluorine Centennial Medal, Paris 1986, Prix Moissan 1988, American Chem. Soc. Award for Distinguished Service to Inorganic Chem. 1989, Pauling Medal (American Chem. Soc.) 1989, Award for Creative Work in Fluorine Chemistry (American Chem. Soc.) 1992, Bonner Chemiepreis 1992. *Publications:* The Chemistry of the Monatomic Gases (with F. O. Sladky, A. H. Cockett and K. C. Smith) 1973, Noble-Gas Compounds (with D. T. Hawkins and W. E. Falconer) 1978; more than 100 scientific papers including reports on the first preparation of the oxidised oxygen cation O_2^+ and the first true compound of a noble gas. *Leisure interests:* water-colour painting, antique silver. *Address:* Department of Chemistry, University of California, Berkeley, CA 94720; 6 Oak Drive, Orinda, CA 94563, U.S.A. (Home). *Telephone:* (510) 642-7259 (Office). *Fax:* (510) 642-8369.

BARTLETT DÍAZ, Manuel; Mexican politician; b. Feb. 1936, Puebla; ed. Nat. Univ. of Mexico, Univs. of Paris and Manchester; Adviser, Cen. Office of Credit, Ministry of Finance 1962–64; Asst. to Sec.-Gen., Nat. Fed. of Rural Workers 1963–64; Asst. Sec. PRI (Institutional Revolutionary Party) 1964–68; Prof. of Gen. Theory of the State, Nat. Univ. of Mexico 1968; various posts at Ministry of Interior 1969–76; Sec. Fed. Electoral Comm. 1970–76; Sec. Admin. Bd. Nat. Bank of Co-operative Devt. and Dir. of

Political Affairs, Ministry of Foreign Affairs 1976–79; Adviser to Minister of Programming and Budget 1979; Sec.-Gen. Nat. Exec. Cttee. of PRI 1981; Minister of the Interior 1982–88, of Public Educ. 1988–92. *Address:* c/o Secretariat of State for Public Education, República de Argentina y González Obregón 28, 06029, México, D.F., Mexico.

BARTLEY, Robert LeRoy, M.S.; American journalist; b. 12 Oct. 1937, Marshall, Minn.; s. of Theodore Bartley and Iva Radach; m. Edith Lillie 1960; three d.; ed. Iowa State Univ. and Univ. of Wisconsin; reporter, Grinnell (Ia.) Herald-Register 1959–60; staff reporter, Wall Street Journal, Chicago 1962–63, Philadelphia 1963–64; editorial writer, Wall Street Journal, New York 1964–70, Washington, D.C. 1970–71; Ed. editorial page, Wall Street Journal, New York 1972–78; Ed. Wall Street Journal 1979–, Vice-Pres. 1983–; mem. American Soc. of Newspaper Eds., American Political Science Asscn., Council on Foreign Relations; Pulitzer Prize for editorial writing 1980; Hon. LL.D. (Macalester Coll.) 1982, (Babson Coll.) 1987; Hon. H.H.D. (Adelphi) 1992. *Publication:* The Seven Fat Years 1992. *Address:* The Wall Street Journal, 200 Liberty Street, New York, NY 10281, U.S.A. *Telephone:* (212) 416-2000.

BARTOLI, Cecilia; Italian mezzo-soprano opera singer and recitalist; b. 4 June 1966, Rome; d. of Silvana Bazzoni; ed. Acad. of Santa Cecilia, Rome; professional career began with TV appearance aged 19; U.S. debut in recital at Mostly Mozart Festival, New York 1990; Paris debut as Cherubino in The Marriage of Figaro, Opéra de Paris Bastille 1990–91 season; debut, La Scala, Milan in Rossini's Le Comte Ory 1990–91 season; appeared as Dorabella in Così fan tutte, Maggio Musicale, Florence 1991; debut with Montreal Symphony Orch. and Philadelphia Orch. 1990–91 season; recitals in collaboration with pianist András Schiff (q.v.) since 1990; appeared in Marriage of Figaro and Così fan tutte conducted by Daniel Barenboim (q.v.) in Chicago Feb. 1992; debut at Salzburg Festival 1992; appeared in recital at Rossini bicentenary celebration at Lincoln Center, New York 1992; Grammy Award for Best Classical Vocal 1994. *Address:* J. F. Mastroianni Associates Inc., 80 Central Park West, Apartment 5E, New York, NY 10023, U.S.A.

BARTON, Anne, PH.D., F.B.A.; British professor of English; b. 9 May 1933; d. of Oscar Charles Roesen and Blanche Godfrey Williams; m. 1st William Harvey Righter 1957; m. 2nd John Bernard Adie Barton 1969; ed. Bryn Mawr Coll. and Cambridge Univ.; Lecturer History of Art, Ithaca Coll., N.Y. 1958–59; Rosalind Carlisle Research Fellow, Girton Coll. Cambridge 1960–62, Official Fellow in English 1962–72; Asst. Lecturer, Cambridge Univ. 1962–64, lecturer 1964–72; Hildred Carlile Prof. of English and Head Dept. of English, Bedford Coll., London 1972–74; Fellow and Tutor in English, New Coll., Oxford and Common Univ. Fund Lecturer 1974–84; Prof. of English, Cambridge Univ. 1984–; Fellow of Trinity Coll., Cambridge 1986–; mem. editorial Bds. Shakespeare Survey 1972–, Shakespeare Quarterly 1981–, Studies in English Literature 1976–, Romanticism 1995–; Hon. Fellow, Shakespeare Inst., Univ. of Birmingham, New Coll., Oxford; mem. Academia Europaea. *Publications:* Shakespeare and the Idea of the Play 1962; Ben Jonson, Dramatist 1984, The Names of Comedy 1990, Byron: Don Juan 1992, Essays, Mainly Shakespearean 1994; numerous essays in journals. *Leisure interests:* opera, travel, fine-arts. *Address:* Trinity College, Cambridge, CB2 1TQ; Leverington Hall, Wisbech, Cambridgeshire, PE13 5DE, England (Homes). *Telephone:* (01223) 338466 (Office).

BARTON, Glenys, M.A., R.C.A.; British artist; b. 24 Jan. 1944, Stoke-on-Trent; d. of Alexander James Barton and Gertrude Elizabeth Barton (née Farmer); m. Martin Hunt; one s.; ed. Royal Coll. of Art; part-time lecturer Portsmouth Polytechnic 1971–74, Camberwell School of Arts & Crafts 1971–87; *solo exhbns.:* Museum of Decorative Art, Copenhagen 1973, Oxford Gallery, Oxford 1973, Angela Flowers Gallery, London 1974, 1981, 1983, 1986, 1994, Gallery Het Kapelhuis, Amersfoort, Netherlands 1976, Germeentelijkmuseum, Leeuwarden, Netherlands 1976, Crafts Council Gallery, London 1977, Wedgwood New York 1978, Flowers East, London 1990, 1993, 1996, 1997, Nat. Portrait Gallery, London 1997, Manchester City Art Gallery 1997, City Museum and Art Gallery, Stoke-on-Trent 1998; numerous group exhbns., U.K. and abroad 1980–; works in numerous public collections including: Nat. Portrait Gallery, London, Royal Scottish Museum, Edin., Scottish Nat. Portrait Gallery, Edin., Victoria and Albert Museum, London, Potteries Museum, Stoke-on-Trent, Wedgwood Museum, Barlaston, and in Birmingham, Leeds, Leicester, Manchester, Norwich, Portsmouth, Reading, Southampton, Rotterdam, Melbourne, Pennsylvania, Leeuwarden and Stockholm. *Leisure interest:* gardening. *Address:* c/o Angela Flowers Gallery, 199–205 Richmond Road, London, E8 3NJ, England.

BARTON, Rev. John, M.A., D.PHIL., D.LITT.; British university professor; b. 17 June 1948, London; s. of Bernard A. Barton and Gwendolyn H. Barton; m. Mary Burn 1973; one d.; ed. Latymer Upper School, London and Keble Coll. Oxford; Jr. Research Fellow, Merton Coll. Oxford 1973–74; Univ. lecturer in Theology, Univ. of Oxford 1974–89, Reader in Biblical Studies 1989–91; Fellow, St. Cross Coll. Oxford 1974–91; Oriel and Laing Prof. of the Interpretation of Holy Scripture and Fellow, Oriel Coll. Oxford 1991–; Canon Theologian of Winchester Cathedral 1991–; Hon. D.Theol. (Bonn) 1998. *Publications:* Amos's Oracles Against the Nations 1980, Reading the Old Testament 1984, Oracles of God 1986, People of the Book? 1988, Love Unknown 1990, What is the Bible? 1991, Isaiah 1-39 1995, The Spirit and the Letter 1997, Making the Christian Bible 1997, Ethics and the Old Testament 1998, The Cambridge Companion to Biblical Interpretation 1998. *Address:* Oriel College, Oxford, OX1 4EW, England. *Telephone:* (01865) 276537.

BARTON, John Bernard Adie, C.B.E., M.A.; British drama director and adaptor; b. 26 Nov. 1928, London; s. of Sir Harold Montagu Barton and Lady Joyce Barton (née Wale); m. Anne Righter 1968; ed. Eton Coll. and King's Coll., Cambridge; Drama Lecturer, Univ. of Berkeley, Calif. 1953–54; Fellow, King's Coll. Cambridge 1954–59; Asst. Dir. (to Peter Hall) Royal Shakespeare Co. 1959, Assoc. Dir. 1964–91, Advisory Dir. 1991–. *Productions for R.S.C. include:* The Wars of the Roses (adapted, edited, co-directed) 1963, Love's Labour's Lost 1965, 1978, All's Well That Ends Well, Julius Caesar, Troilus and Cressida 1968–69, Twelfth Night, When Thou Art King 1969–70, Othello, Richard II, Henry V 1971, Richard II 1973, Dr. Faustus, King John (co-dir.), Cymbeline (co-dir.) 1974–75, Much Ado About Nothing, Troilus and Cressida, The Winter's Tale, King Lear, A Midsummer Night's Dream, Pillars of the Community 1976, The Way of the World 1978, The Merchant of Venice, Love's Labour's Lost 1978, The Greeks 1980, Hamlet 1980, Merchant of Venice, Two Gentlemen of Verona 1981, Titus Andronicus 1981, La Ronde 1982, Life's a Dream 1984, The Devils 1984, Waste 1985, Dream Play 1985, The Rover 1986, The Three Sisters 1988, Coriolanus 1989, Peer Gynt 1994, 1995, Cain 1995; also School for Scandal, Norway 1983, For Triumph Apollo 1983, The Vikings 1983; for Nat. Theatre, Oslo: Peer Gynt 1990, Measure for Measure, As You Like It 1991–92; The War That Still Goes On 1991. *Television productions:* Playing Shakespeare 1982, Mallory's Morte d'Arthur 1983, The War That Never Ends (scriptwriter) 1990. *Publications:* The Hollow Crown, The Wars of the Roses, The Greeks, La Ronde, The Rover. *Address:* 14 De Walden Court, 85 New Cavendish Street, London, W1M 7RA, England. *Telephone:* 0171-580 6196.

BARTOŠEK, Karel, DR.PHIL.; Czech historian and writer; b. 30 June 1930, Skutec; s. of Karel Bartošek and Frantiska Stepanková; m. Suzanne Bartošek (née Chastaing) 1959; one s. two d.; ed. Charles Univ., Prague; research asst., Inst. of History, Czechoslovak Acad. of Sciences 1960–68; resgnd. 1969; stoker 1972–82; researcher Inst. d'Histoire du Temps Présent, CNRS 1983–; Ed. Nouvelle Alternative 1986–. *Publications:* Les Aveux des Archives 1996, Le Livre noir du Communisme, crimes, terreurs, répressions (co-author) 1997. *Leisure interests:* swimming, skiing. *Address:* IHTP-CNRS, Bâtiment Laplace, ENS Cachan, 61 avenue du Président Wilson, 94235 Cachan Cédex; 6 rue du Moulin de la Pointe, 75013 Paris, France. *Telephone:* (1) 47.40.68.37; (1) 45.81.44.69. *Fax:* (1) 47.40.68.03.

BARTOSZCZE, Roman Bolesław; Polish politician and farmer; b. 9 Dec. 1946, Jaroszewice; m. Alicja Bartoszcze; three s. one d.; worked on family farm at Jaroszewice, then Sławęcin until 1966; nat. service 1966–68; runs own farm at Sławęcin 1968–; leader of nat. peasant strike, signatory Bydgoszcz Agreement 1981; interned Sept.–Dec. 1982; leader Solidarity Trade Union 1980– (jt. founder and Deputy Chair. Founding Cttee. of Farmers' Solidarity in Bydgoszcz province); mem. Presidium Nat. Founding Cttee. of Farmers' Solidarity 1981, Char. Bd. Bydgoszcz Region 1981, April 1989–; mem. Presidium Provisional Nat. Council of Farmers' Solidarity 1987; mem. Citizens' Cttee. attached to Chair. of Solidarity 1988–90; deputy to Sejm (Parl.) 1989–93; mem. United Peasant Party (ZSL) 1966–81, Polish Peasant Party (PSL) Wilanów group 1989–90, Peasant Party (PSL) 1990–91 (Pres. Chief Exec. Cttee. 1990–91). *Leisure interests:* reading, history of peasantry, mushroom picking. *Address:* Sławęcin 15, 88-100 Inowrocław, Poland.

BARTUREN DUEÑAS; Peruvian politician and civil servant; b. 5 Nov. 1936, Lima; ed. Universidad Nacional Mayor de San Marcos; taught at Graduate Business Admin. School 1965–66, subsequently at Public Admin. School; specialist in preparation and evaluation of investment projects, Interamerican Devt. Bank 1972–73; Head, Planning Office, Nat. Fisheries Co. 1970–73; Deputy Finance Dir. Centromin Perú 1979–84; Minister of Agric. 1985–86. *Address:* Avenida Salaverry s/n, Edificio M. de Trabajo, Lima, Peru. *Telephone:* 324040.

BARUCCI, Piero; Italian politician and banker; b. 1933; fmrly. sports reporter, then lecturer, Univs. of Siena and Florence; Chair. Monte dei Paschi di Siena 1983–87, Asscn. of Italian Banks (ABI) 1987–90; Man. Dir. Credito Italiano 1990–92; Minister of the Treasury 1992–94. *Address:* c/o Ministry of the Treasury, Via XX Settembre 97, 00187 Rome, Italy.

BARYSHNIKOV, Mikhail (Misha); Russian/American ballet dancer; b. 28 Jan. 1948, Riga, Latvia; s. of Nikolay and Aleksandra (née Kisselov) Baryshnikov; one d.; ed. Riga Ballet School and Kirov Ballet School, Leningrad; mem. Kirov Ballet Co. 1969–74; guest artist with many leading ballet cos. including American Ballet Theatre, Nat. Ballet of Canada, Royal Ballet, Hamburg Ballet, Fed. Repub. of Germany, Ballet Victoria, Australia, Stuttgart Ballet, Fed. Repub. of Germany, Alvin Ailey Co., U.S.A. 1974–; joined New York City Ballet Co. 1978, resigned 1979; Artistic Dir., American Ballet Theatre 1980–90; founder White Oak Dance Project 1990–; Stage début in Metamorphosis 1989; launched perfume Misha 1989; Gold Medal, Varna Competition, Bulgaria 1966, First Int. Ballet Competition, Moscow, U.S.S.R. 1968; Nijinsky Prize, First Int. Ballet Competition, Paris Acad. de Danse 1968. *Ballets (world premières):* Vestris 1969, Medea 1975, Push Comes to Shove 1976, Hamlet Connotations 1976, Other Dances 1976, Pas de Duke 1976, La Dame De Pique 1978, L'Après-midi d'un Faune 1978, Santa Fe Saga 1978, Opus 19 1979, Rhapsody 1980. *Films:* The Turning Point 1977, White Nights 1985, Giselle 1987, Dancers 1987, Dinosaurs

1991. *Choreography:* Nutcracker 1976, Don Quixote 1978, Cinderella 1984. *Publication:* Baryshnikov at Work 1977. *Address:* c/o Vincent & Farrell Associates, 157 West 57th Street, 502, New York, NY 10019, U.S.A.

BARZEL, Amnon, M.SC.; Israeli art writer, critic, consultant and museum director; b. 5 July 1935, Tel Aviv; m. Shafrira Glikson 1956; one s. one d.; ed. Hebrew Univ., Jerusalem, Sorbonne, Paris; Art Consultant for City of Tel Aviv 1975–76; Curator Biennale of Venice, Italy 1976–78, 1980, 'Two Environments', Forte Belvedere, Florence and Castle of Prato, Italy 1978, São Paulo Biennale, Brazil 1985; Founding Curator 'Contemporary Art Meetings', Tel Hai, Israel 1980–83, Villa Celle Art Spaces Collection, Giuliano Gori, Prato, Italy 1981–82; Founding Dir. Centre of Contemporary Art Luigi Pecci, Prato, Italy 1986–, Dir. School for Curators 1991–; Consultant for creation of Museum of Contemporary Art, Florence, Italy 1989; mem. Curatorial Cttee. for Int. Sculpture Centre (ISC), Washington, DC, U.S.A. 1990. *Publications:* Isaac Frenel 1973, Dani Karavan 1978, Art in Israel 1986, Europe Now 1988, Julian Schnable 1989, Enzo Cucchi 1989, Contemporary Russian Artists (jt. Ed.) 1990. *Leisure interests:* poetry, Holy contemporary philosophy. *Address:* Centro per l'Arte Contemporanea Luigi Pecci, Viale della Repubblica 277, 50047 Prato (Office); Via Giovanni Prati, 26, 50124 Florence, Italy (Home). *Telephone:* 0574-570620 (Office); 055-220098 (Home).

BARZEL, Rainer, DR. IUR.; German politician and civil servant; b. 20 June 1924, Braunsberg, East Prussia; s. of Dr. Candidus Barzel and Maria née Skibowski; m. 1st Kriemhild Schumacher 1948 (died 1980); one d. (deceased); m. 2nd Helga Henselder 1982 (died 1995); ed. Gymnasium, Braunsberg (East Prussia), Berlin, and Univ. of Cologne; Air Force, Second World War; Civil Service, North Rhine-Westphalia, Ministry for Fed. Affairs 1949–56, resigned 1956; mem. Bundestag 1957–87, Pres. 1983–84; Fed. Minister for All-German Affairs 1962–63; mem. Christian Democrat Party (CDU), Deputy and Acting Chair. CDU/CSU Parl. Group in Bundestag 1963–64, Chair. 1964–73; Chair. CDU 1971–73, Chair. Econ. Affairs Cttee. of Bundestag 1977–79, resigned 1979, Chair. Foreign Affairs Cttee. 1980–82; Co-ordinator for French-German Affairs 1980, 1986–90; Fed. Minister for Inter-German Affairs 1982–83; Pres. German-French Inst., Ludwigsburg 1980–83. *Publications:* Die geistigen Grundlagen der politischen Parteien 1947, Souveränität und Freiheit 1950, Die deutschen Parteien 1951, Karl Arnold—Grundlegung christlich-demokratischer Politik in Deutschland 1961, Gesichtspunkte eines Deutschen 1968, Es ist noch nicht zu spät 1976, Auf dem Drahtseil 1978, Das Formular 1979, Unterwegs—Woher und Wohin? 1982, Im Streit und umstritten 1986, Geschichten aus der Politik 1987, Ermland und Masuren—zu Besuch aber nicht als ein Fremder 1988, Plädoyer für Deutschland 1989, Sternstunden des Parlaments (Ed.) 1989. *Leisure interests:* skating, mountaineering, curling, archaeology. *Address:* c/o Görrestr. 15, Bundeshaus, 53179 Bonn, Germany.

BARZUN, Jacques, PH.D.; American writer and university professor; b. 30 Nov. 1907, Créteil, France; s. of Henri Martin and Anna-Rose Barzun; m. 1st Mariana Lowell 1936 (died 1979); two s. one d.; m. 2nd Marguerite Lee Davenport 1980; ed. Lycée Janson de Sailly and Columbia Univ.; Instructor in History, Columbia Univ. 1929, Asst. Prof. 1938, Assoc. Prof. 1942, Prof. 1945, Dean of Graduate Faculties 1955–58, Dean of Faculties and Provost 1958–67, Seth Low Prof. 1960, Univ. Prof. 1967–75; Prof. Emer. 1975; Literary Adviser, Scribner's 1975–93; fmr. Dir. Council for Basic Educ., New York Soc. Library, Open Court Publications Inc., Peabody Inst.; mem. Advisory Council, Univ. Coll. at Buckingham, Editorial Bd. Encyclopedia Britannica 1979–; mem. Acad. Delphinale (Grenoble), American Acad. and Inst. of Arts and Letters (Pres. 1972–75, 1977–78), American Historical Asscn., Royal Soc. of Arts, American Arbitration Asscn., American Philosophical Soc., Royal Soc. of Literature, American Acad. of Arts and Sciences; Extraordinary Fellow, Churchill Coll., Cambridge 1961; Chevalier Légion d'honneur. *Publications:* The French Race 1932, Race: A Study in Modern Superstition 1937, Of Human Freedom 1939, Darwin, Marx, Wagner 1941, Teacher in America 1945, Berlioz and the Romantic Century 1950, God's Country and Mine 1954, The Energies of Art 1956, Music in American Life 1956, The Modern Researcher 1957 (with H. Graff), The House of Intellect 1959, Classic, Romantic and Modern 1961, Science, the Glorious Entertainment 1964, The American University 1968, A Catalogue of Crime (with W. Taylor) 1971, On Writing, Editing and Publishing 1971, The Use and Abuse of Art 1974, Clio and the Doctors 1974, Simple and Direct 1975, Critical Questions 1982, A Stroll with William James 1983, A Word or Two Before You Go 1986, The Culture We Deserve 1989, Begin Here: On Teaching and Learning 1990; An Essay on French Verse for Readers of English Poetry 1991; Ed. Pleasures of Music 1951, The Selected Letters of Lord Byron 1953, New Letters of Berlioz (and trans.) 1954, The Selected Writings of John Jay Chapman 1957, Modern American Usage (with others) and numerous other books; Trans.: Diderot: Rameau's Nephew 1952, Flaubert's Dictionary of Accepted Ideas 1954, Evenings with the Orchestra 1956, Courteline: A Rule is a Rule 1960, Beaumarchais: The Marriage of Figaro 1961.

BASANG; Chinese party official; b. 1937, Lang, Tibet; ed. Tibetan Minorities Inst. 1956; served as a slave to the Landlord of Chika 1947–56; joined the CCP 1959; Vice-Chair. Tibet Autonomous Region Revolutionary Cttee. 1968–79; Sec. Secr. CCP Cttee. Tibet 1971–77; Chair. Women's Fed. of Tibet 1973; mem. 10th CCP Cen. Cttee. 1973; Chair. Langxian Co. Revolutionary Cttee. 1974; mem. Standing Cttee. 4th NPC 1975; 5th NPC 1978; Deputy Head Leading Group for Party Consolidation CCP Cttee. Tibet 1977; Sec. CPC 4th Tibet Autonomous Regional Cttee. 1977; Deputy Sec. 5th Autonomous Regional Cttee. 1977–; mem. CCP 11th Cen. Cttee. 1977; Deputy for Tibet to 5th NPC 1978; mem. Pres. 1979; Vice-Chair. People's Govt. of Tibet 1979–83; mem. 12th CCP Cen. Cttee. 1982–86; mem. Cen. Discipline Inspection Comm., CCPCC; Vice-Chair. CPPCC 6th Tibet Regional Cttee. Jan. 1993–. *Address:* Chinese Communist Party Tibet Autonomous Region, Lhasa, People's Republic of China.

BASAYEV, Col. Shamil; Russian Chechen army officer and politician; b. 14 Jan. 1965, Vedeno; m.; one s. one d.; ed. Moscow Inst. of Land Eng.; served in the Soviet army as fireman; cand. in Pres. elections Chechen Repub. Oct. 1991; participant of highjacking TU-134 from Mineralnye Vody to Turkey in protest against introduction of martial law to Chechnya Nov. 1991; returned to Chechnya as commdr. special task force of D. Dudayev, participant of armed units Confed. of Peoples of Caucasus 1991, Commdr.-in-Chief 1994; participant of mil. actions in Nagorny Karabakh (with Azerbaijan), Abkhazia (with separatists); Deputy Minister of Defence Self-Proclaimed Repub. of Abkhazia 1992; during civil war in Chechnya supported D. Dudayev 1994; after introduction of Russian troops one of leading field commdrs. of resistance; commdr. of group that attacked town of Budennovsk and took hostages June 1995; after removal of Russian troops cand. for Presidency of Chechen Repub. Ichkeria Jan. 1997; Deputy Prime Minister 1997–; Acting Prime Minister Jan.–Sept. 1998.

BASELITZ, Georg; German artist; b. 23 Jan. 1938, Deutschbaselitz, Saxony; m. Elke Kretzschmar 1962; two s.; ed. Gymnasium, Kamenz, Kunstakad. E. Berlin and Akad. der Künste, W. Berlin; Instructor Staatliche Akad. der bildenden Kunste, Karlsruhe 1977–78, Prof. 1978–83; Prof. Hochschule der Kunste, Berlin 1983–; exhbn. with Eugen Schönebeck, Pandemomnium, W. Berlin 1961; numerous one-man shows throughout Germany, Europe, U.K. and U.S.A. since 1963; contrib. to numerous group shows including Documenta 5, Kassel 1972, São Paulo Bienal 1975, Venice Biennale 1980, The New Spirit in Painting, Royal Acad. London 1981, Berlinart 1961–87, Museum of Modern Art, New York 1987; works in public collections including Kunsthalle, Hamburg, Hessisches Landesmuseum, Darmstadt, Sammlung Ludwig, Cologne, Stedelijk Museum, Amsterdam and Centre Pompidou, Paris. *Publications:* books, pamphlets, manifestos and articles. *Address:* Schloss Derneburg, 31188 Holle, Germany.

BASHARMAL, Khodaidad, M.SC., B.M.; Afghanistan public servant and physician; b. 15 July 1945, Laghman; m.; four c.; ed. Univ. of Nangrahar Medical School, Univ. of Texas, U.S.A.; fmrly. Physician, Good Samaritan Hosp., Ohio, lecturer, then Chief Physiology Dept., Jalalabad Medical School; Chief Admin. Eastern Zone 1980–83; Deputy Foreign Minister 1983–84; Pres. Dept. of Sciences and Public Health, Watan Party of Afghanistan 1984–87; Minister of Educ. 1987–90; Amb. to Poland 1990–91; Perm. Rep. of Afghanistan to UN 1991–92. *Address:* c/o Ministry of Foreign Affairs, Shah Mahmud Ghazi Street, Shar-i-Nau, Kabul, Afghanistan. *Telephone:* (93) 25441.

BASHIR, Lieut.-Gen. Omar Hassan Ahmad al-; Sudanese army officer; fmr. Brig.; overthrew govt. of Sadiq al-Mahdi (q.v.) in coup 30 June 1989; Chair. Revolutionary Command Council for Nat. Salvation, Pres. and Prime Minister of Sudan 1989–, Minister of Defence 1989–93. *Address:* Revolutionary Command Council, Khartoum, Sudan.

BASHKIROV, Dmitri Aleksandrovich; Russian pianist; b. 1 Nov. 1931, Tbilisi; s. of Alexandr Bashkirov and Ester Ramendik; m. 1st Vera Bashkirova 1954; one d.; m. 2nd Natalya Chumakova 1988; one s.; ed. Tbilisi State Conservatory; studied under A. Virsaladze, Moscow State Conservatory under A. Goldenweiser; winner Grand Prix M. Long Int. Competition Paris 1955; concerts since 1955; participated in Wiener Festwochen, Helsinki, Dubrovnik, Granada, Berlin and other festivals; repertoire includes works by Mozart, Schumann, Brahms, Debussy, Prokofiev; teacher Moscow State Conservatory 1957, Prof. 1976–90; Head of piano, Chair. Queen Sofia Higher School of Music, Madrid 1991–; mem. jury numerous int. competitions; master classes Acad. Mozarteum Salzburg, Sibelius Acad. Helsinki, Acad. of Music Jerusalem, Paris Conservatory and others. *Address:* 25 Martirez Oblatos, Pozuelo, Madrid, Spain. *Telephone:* 351 1175. *Fax:* 351 0788.

BASHMACHNIKOV, Vladimir Fedorovich; DR. ECON.; Russian politician; b. 27 March 1937; m.; three d.; ed. Urals State Univ.; worker, deputy chair. kolkhoz, Sverdlovsk Region 1959–62; teacher, docent, Prof. Urals State Univ. 1962–65; f. All-Russian Inst. of Labour (now All-Russian Inst. of Econ. and Man. in Agric.) 1964–72, Deputy Dir. 1972–84; consultant Econ. Dept. Cen. Cttee. CPSU 1984–89; mem. Cttee. on Land Reform Cen. Cttee. CPSU 1989–91; active participant movt. for privatization of land, mem. State Duma; mem. faction Our Home Russia; mem. Cttee. on Agrarian Problems 1995–; Pres. Asscn. of Farmers' and Agric. Co-operatives of Russia 1991–; Chair. Union of Land-Owners of Russia 1994; mem. Co-ordination Council, Round Table Business of Russia. *Publications:* over 150 books and articles on org. of labour in agric. *Address:* Association of Farmers' and Agricultural Co-operatives of Russia, Orlikov per 3, Suite 405, 107139 Moscow, Russia (Office). *Telephone:* (095) 204 4027 (Office).

BASHMET, Yuri Abramovich; Russian viola player; b. 24 Jan. 1953, Rostov-on-Don; m. Natalia Bashmet; one d.; ed. Moscow State Conservatory; concerts since 1975; gave recitals and played with maj. orchestras of Europe, America and Asia; played in chamber ensembles with Sviatoslav Richter, Vladimir Spivakov, Victor Tretyakov and others; restored chamber repertoire for viola and was first performer of music by contemporary composers, including concertos by Alfred Schnittke, Giya Kancheli, Aleksander Tchaikovsky; f. and dir. Chamber Orchestra Soloists of Moscow 1989–; prize winner of int. competitions in Budapest 1975, Munich 1976; f. Yuri Bashmet Int. Competition for Young viola players 1994–; People's Artist of Russia 1986, State Prize of Russia 1993, Sonning Prize (Denmark) 1995. *Address:* c/o ICM Artists Ltd., 40 West 57th Street, New York, NY 10019, U.S.A. (Agent); Briyusov per. 7, Apt. 16, 103009 Moscow, Russia (Home). *Telephone:* 229-73-25 (Home).

BASILASHVILI, Oleg Valeriyanovich; Russian actor and politician; b. 26 Sept. 1934, Moscow; m. Galina Mshanskaya; two d.; ed. Moscow Art Theatre; debut Leningrad Theatre of Lenin's Komsomol 1956–59; leading actor Leningrad (now St. Petersburg) Bolshoi Drama Theatre of Tovstonogov 1959–; several leading roles, including Gayev (The Cherry Orchard), Voynitsky (Uncle Vanya), Khlestakov (The Government Inspector); active participant of democratic movt. since end of 1980s, People's Deputy of Russia 1990–93; People's Actor of Russia 1977, U.S.S.R. People's Actor 1984, State Prize of Russia 1978, Order of Friendship 1994. *Films include:* Alive Corpse 1969, Business Love Affair 1977, Autumn Marathon 1979, Railway Station for Two 1983, The Promised Heaven 1991, The Prophecy 1992, The Ticket in the Red Theatre 1994; also TV. *Address:* Borodinskaya str. 13, Apt. 58, 196180 St. Petersburg, Russia (Home). *Telephone:* 113-55-56 (Home).

BASIN, Yefim Vladimirovich; Russian politician and engineer; b. 3 Jan. 1940, Khislovichi, Tambov Region; m.; one s. one d.; ed. Belarus Inst. of Transport Eng., Acad. of Nat. Econs.; master, chief engineer, Head, Yaroslavl Construction Dept. 1962–69; Deputy Man., chief eng., Gortransstroi, Gorky (now Nizhny Novgorod) 1969–72; Head Construction Dept., Pechorstroi 1972–78; First Deputy Head Glavbamstroi 1980–86; U.S.S.R. Deputy Minister of Transport Construction; Head, Glavbamstroi and Bamtransstroi production cos. 1986–90; Deputy, State Duma of R.S.F.S.R.; mem. Supreme Soviet; Chair. Cttee. on Construction, Architecture and Housing 1990–92; Chair. State Cttee. on Problems of Architecture and Construction 1992–94; Minister of Construction 1994–97; Chair. State Cttee. on Construction Policy 1997–98; First Deputy Head, Complex of Perspective Construction, then Head, Dept. of Construction Devt., Moscow Govt. May–Oct. 1998; Chair. State Cttee. of Russian Fed. on Construction, Architecture and Housing Policy Oct. 1998–; Hero of Socialist Labour, Merited Constructor of Russian Fed. *Address:* State Committee on Construction, Stroiteley str. 8, korp. 2, 117987 Moscow, Russia. *Telephone:* (095) 930 1755 (Office).

BASINGER, Kim; American actress; b. 8 Dec. 1953, Athens, Ga.; d. of Don Basinger; m. 1st Ron Britton 1980 (divorced 1990); m. 2nd Alec Baldwin 1993; model 1971–76; first TV role 1976. *Films include:* Hard Country 1981, Mother Lode 1982, Never Say Never Again 1982, The Man Who Loved Women 1983, The Natural 1984, 9½ weeks 1985, Fool for Love 1985, No Mercy 1986, Batman 1989, The Marrying Man 1990, Too Hot to Handle 1991, Final Analysis 1992, Cool World 1992, The Real McCoy 1993, Getaway 1994, Wayne's World II 1994., Pret-à-Porter 1994, L.A. Confidential 1997 (Acad. Award and Golden Globe for Best Supporting Actress). *Address:* c/o Rick Nicita, CAA, 9830 Wilshire Boulevard, Beverly Hills, CA 90212; c/o Judy Hofflund, Hofflund Polone, 9465 Wilshire Boulevard, Suite 820, Beverly Hills, CA 90212, U.S.A.

BASINSKI, Zbigniew Stanislaw, O.C., D.PHIL., D.SC., F.R.S.C., F.R.S.; Canadian scientist; b. 28 April 1928, Wolkowysk, Poland; s. of Antoni and Maria Zofia Anna (née Hilferding) Basinski; m. Sylvia Joy Pugh 1952; two s.; ed. Lyceum of Krzemieniec, Poland, Univ. of Oxford; Research Asst., Univ. of Oxford 1951–54; staff mem. Dept. of Mechanical Eng. (Cryogenic Lab.), Massachusetts Inst. of Tech. 1954–56; Prin. Research Officer, Head of Materials Physics, Div. of Physics, Nat. Research Council of Canada 1956–87; Research Prof. Inst. for Materials Research, Dept. of Materials Science and Eng., McMaster Univ., Hamilton 1987–92, Prof. Emer. 1992–; Ford Distinguished Visiting Prof., Carnegie Inst. of Tech., Pittsburgh, Penn. 1964–65; Commonwealth Visiting Prof., Univ. of Oxford (Fellow of Wolfson Coll.) 1969–70; Overseas Fellow, Churchill Coll., Cambridge 1980–81; Dr. h.c. (Stanisław Staszic Univ. Acad. of Mining and Metallurgy, Kraków 1991). *Publications:* numerous research papers, mainly on crystal defects and mechanical properties of metals. *Address:* The Brockhouse, Institute for Materials Research, McMaster University, 1280 Main Street West, Hamilton, Ont., L8S 4M1, Canada (Office); 98 Bluebell Crescent, Ancaster, Ont., L9K 1G1, Canada (Home). *Telephone:* (905) 525-9140 Ext. 3498 (Office); (905) 648-5435 (Home).

BASIR, Ismail; Malaysian banker; b. 1927, Taiping, Perak State; ed. Serdang Agricultural Coll. and Durham Univ.; Lecturer, Universiti Pertanian Malaysia; Asst. Agricultural Officer Serdang Agricultural Coll.; Dir. Agric. Dept., Dir.-Gen. Agric., later Exec. Dir. Johore State Devt. Corpn.; Chair. Nat. Padi and Rice Authority 1981–, Food Industries Malaysia 1981–; Exec. Chair. Bank Bumiputra Malaysia Bhd. 1985; Head BMF, Kewangan Bumiputra, Bumiputra Merchant Bankers 1985; Dir. Bank Negara 1981, and of several other cos.

BASOLO, Fred, PH.D.; American professor of chemistry; b. 11 Feb. 1920, Coello, Ill.; s. of John and Catherine Basolo; m. Mary P. Basolo 1947; one s. three d.; ed. Southern Illinois Normal Univ. and Univ. of Illinois; Research Chemist, Rohm & Haas Chemical Co. 1943–46; Instructor, subsequently Asst. Prof., Assoc. Prof. and Prof. of Chem., Northwestern Univ. 1946–, Chair. of Chem. Dept. 1969–72, Morrison Prof. of Chem. 1980–90, Charles E. and Emma H. Morrison Prof. Emer. 1990–; NATO Distinguished Prof., Tech. Univ. of Munich 1969; NATO Sr. Scientist Fellow, Italy 1981; numerous visiting lectureships U.S.A., Australia, Europe and Asia; Ed.-in-Chief Chemtracts 1988–; Assoc. Ed. Inorganic Chemica Acta Letters 1977–; mem. Editorial Bd. Inorganica Chemica Acta 1967–, and other publs.; Hon. D.Sc. (Southern Ill.) 1984; Hon. Prof. Lanzhou Univ., China 1985; Fellow A.A.A.S. (Chair. Chem. Section 1979); mem. American Chemical Soc. (mem. Bd. of Dirs. 1982–84, Pres. 1983), N.A.S., Chemical Soc. (London); Hon. mem. Italian Chemical Soc.; Foreign mem. Accademia Naz. dei Lincei, Italy; corresp. mem., Chemical Soc. of Peru 1983; Fellow, American Acad. of Arts and Sciences 1983, Japanese Soc. for the Promotion of Science 1979; Guggenheim Fellow, Copenhagen 1954–55; Sr. Nat. Research Foundation Fellow, Rome 1962–63; American Chemical Soc. Award for Research in Inorganic Chem. 1964, Award for Distinguished Service in Inorganic Chem. 1975, Dwyer Medal Award 1976, Oesper Memorial Award 1983, IX Century Medal of Bologna Univ. 1988, Harry and Carol Mosher Award 1990, Padua Univ. Medal 1991, Chinese Chemical Soc. Medal 1991, Chemical Pioneer Award (American Inst. of Chemists) 1992, Humboldt Sr. U.S. Scientist Award 1992, Gold Medal Award (American Inst. of Chemists) 1993, Joseph Chatt Medal (Royal Soc. of Chem.) 1996, Josiah Willard Gibbs Medal (American Chemical Soc.) 1996; numerous other awards and honours. *Publications:* Mechanisms of Inorganic Reactions (with R. G. Pearson), Coordination Chemistry (with R. C. Johnson—several edns. in trans.); more than 350 scientific publs. *Address:* Department of Chemistry, Northwestern University, 2145 Sheridan Road, Evanston, IL 60208, U.S.A.

BASOV, Nikolai Gennadievich; Russian physicist; b. 14 Dec. 1922, Usman; s. of Prof. Gennadiy Fedorovich Basov and Zinaida Andreyevna Molchanova; m. Kseniya Tikhonovna Nazarova 1950; two s.; ed. Moscow Inst. of Physical Engineers; P. N. Lebedev Physical Inst. 1950–, Vice-Dir. 1958–73, Dir. 1973–89, Dir. Quantum Radiophysics Div. 1989–; founded Laboratory of Quantum Radiophysics 1963–; Prof. Moscow Inst. of Physical Engs. 1963–; Deputy of U.S.S.R. Supreme Soviet 1974–89, mem. Presidium 1982–89; mem. CPSU 1951–91; Corresp. mem. U.S.S.R. (now Russian) Acad. of Sciences 1962–66, mem. 1966–, mem. Presidium 1967–; fellow Optical Soc. of America, Indian Nat. Science Acad., Hon. mem. Int. Acad. of Sciences, European Acad. of Sciences and Arts (Salzburg), mem. Akad. der Wissenschaften der DDR, Berlin, Deutsche Akad. der Naturforscher Leopoldina, Bulgarian Acad. of Sciences, Polish Acad. of Sciences, Czechoslovak Acad. of Sciences, Royal Swedish Acad. of Eng. Sciences, European Acad. of Arts, Sciences and Humanities (Paris); Hon. Dr. Prague Polytechnic Inst., Polish Military-Tech. Acad., Jena Univ., Pavia Univ., Italy, Madrid Polytechnic Univ., Karl Marx Stadt Tech. Univ.; Vice-Chair. Exec. Council of World Fed. of Scientific Workers 1976–83, Vice-Pres. of World Fed. of Scientific Workers 1983–90, Hon. mem. 1990–, Chair. of Bd., All-Union Soc. Znanie, U.S.S.R. 1978–90; Hon. Chair. 1990–; Chief Ed. Priroda (Nature) popular science magazine 1967–90, Adviser 1990–, Soviet Journal of Quantum Electronics 1971–, Journal of Soviet Laser Research 1980–; jtly. created first quantum generator-maser, Madrid Polytechnic Univ. 1984; Lenin Prize 1959, Nobel Prize for Physics 1964, Order of Lenin (five times), Hero of Socialist Labour 1969, 1982, Gold Medal of Czechoslovak Acad. of Sciences 1975, A. Volta Gold Medal 1977; E. Henkel Gold Medal (G.D.R.) 1986, Order of Kirill and Methodii (Bulgaria) 1981, Order of the Patriotic War 1985, Commdr.'s Cross Order of Merit (Poland) 1986, Kalinga Prize, UNESCO 1986, Gold Medal Slovak Acad. of Sciences 1988, U.S.S.R. State Prize 1989, Lomonosov Gold Medal 1990, Edward Teller Medal (U.S.A.) 1991. *Publications:* various works on semiconducting laser, quantum frequency standards, theory of powerful impulses of hard-bodied lasers. *Leisure interests:* photography, skiing. *Address:* P. N. Lebedev Physical Institute, 53 Leninsky Prospect, Moscow, Russia (Office). *Telephone:* 135-21-57.

BASSANI, Giorgio; Italian writer; b. 1916; ed. Univ. of Bologna; Chief Ed. Botteghe Oscure 1948–60, Dir. of Literary Series with Feltrinelli including Il Gattopardo, G. di Lampedusa 1957–63; Teacher History of Theatre, Accademia d'Arte Drammatica 1957–68; Vice-Pres. Radio Televisione Italiana 1964–65; mem. Italia Nostra 1955– (Pres. 1966); Strega Prize 1956, Viareggio Prize 1962, Campiello Prize 1969, Nelly Sachs Prize 1969. *Publications:* Cinque storie ferraresi 1956, Gli occhiali d'oro (novel) 1958, Il giardino dei Finzi-Contini (novel) 1962, L'alba ai vetri (poems) 1963, Dietro la porta (novel) 1964, Le parole preparate (essays) 1966, L'airone (novel) 1968, Heron 1970, Epitaffio (poems) 1974.

BASSANI, Giuseppe Franco, DR.SC.; Italian professor of physics; b. 29 Oct. 1929, Milan; s. of Luigi Bassani and Claretta Riccadonna; m. Serenella Figini 1959; one s. one d.; ed. Univs. of Pavia and Illinois; research physicist, Argonne Nat. Lab. 1960–65; Prof. of Physics, Univ. of Pisa 1965–70, Univ. of Rome 1970–80, Scuola Normale Superiore, Pisa 1980–; Nat. mem. Accademia dei Lincei; Dr.h.c. (Toulouse) 1979, (Lausanne) 1986, (Purdue Univ., W. Lafayette, U.S.A.) 1994. *Publications:* Electronic States and Optical Transitions in Solids (co-author) 1975 and articles in professional journals. *Leisure interest:* history. *Address:* Scuola Normale Superiore, Pisa 56100, Italy. *Telephone:* 050-509111 (Office); 050-580524 (Home).

BASSEY, Shirley, C.B.E.; British popular singer; b. 8 Jan. 1937, Tiger Bay, Cardiff, Wales; d. of late Eliza Mendi; m. 1st Kenneth Hume; m. 2nd Sergio Novak; four c. (one deceased); sang at Astor Club, London; signed up for Such is Life by impresario Jack Hylton 1955; started making records 1956;

appeared in cabaret New York 1961; records include Banana Boat Song, As I Love You, Kiss Me Honey Honey Kiss Me, As Long As He Needs Me, theme song for film Goldfinger 1964; album I Am What I Am 1984; many awards including 20 gold discs and 14 silver discs for sales in U.K., Netherlands, France, Sweden and other countries; Best Female Singer (TV Times) 1972, 1973, (Music Week) 1974, Britannia Award 1977, Best Female Entertainer (American Guild of Variety Artists) 1976.

BASSIOUNY, Mohamed Abdel Aziz; Egyptian diplomatist; b. 31 July 1937, Cairo; s. of Abdel Aziz Bassiouny; m. Nagwa Elsabouny; one s. one d.; ed. Egyptian Mil. Acad.; served Egyptian Army 1956–80; mem. teaching staff, Mil. Acad. 1959–66; Mil. Attaché to Syria 1968–76, Liaison Officer between Egyptian and Syrian Commands, War of Oct. 1973; Brig.-Gen. in Egyptian Army 1978; Mil. Attaché to Iran 1978–80; joined Foreign Service 1980; Counsellor, then Minister Plenipotentiary, Embassy, Tel Aviv 1980, Amb. to Israel 1986–; participated all Egyptian-Israeli talks on normalization of relations and on Taba dispute; Hon. Dr. (Ben Gurion Univ., Israel) 1995; twelve mil. decorations from Egyptian Army; High Medal of Honour for Bravery with rank of Kt., Syria. *Publications:* several articles on Egyptian-Israeli relations, the peace process and the Taba talks. *Leisure interests:* sport, reading. *Address:* Egyptian Embassy, 54 Basel Street, Tel Aviv 62744, Israel. *Telephone:* 03-546 4151. *Fax:* 03-544 1615.

BASSOLE, Bazomboué Léandre, M.A.; Burkinabè diplomatist; b. 21 Sept. 1946, Koudougou; s. of late Bassole Baourla and of Kanki Eyombie; m. Louise Ouedraogo 1975; four s. one d.; ed. Higher Educ. Centre, Ouagadougou, Univ. of Bordeaux and Int. Inst. for Public Admin., Paris; Counsellor State Protocol Dept., Legal Affairs and Claims Dept. and Int. Co-operation Dept. of Ministry of Foreign Affairs 1975–76, Dir. for Admin. and Consular Affairs 1976–77; Second Counsellor, later First Counsellor, Upper Volta Embassy, Paris 1977–81; First Counsellor, Perm. Mission of Upper Volta to the UN 1981–82, Chargé d'affaires 1982–83, Perm. Rep. of Upper Volta (now Burkina Faso) to the UN 1983–86; Amb. to U.S.A. March–Aug. 1986; Minister of External Affairs and Co-operation 1986–87; Amb. to Canada 1988–91, to Côte d'Ivoire 1991–; Chair. UN Security Council Aug. 1984, Oct. 1984, Dec. 1985. *Leisure interests:* classical music, soccer, cycling, swimming, movies. *Address:* Embassy of Burkina Faso, 2 ave. Terrasoun de Fougères, 01 BP 908, Abidjan, Côte d'Ivoire. *Telephone:* 32 13 55.

BÁSTI, Juli; Hungarian actress; b. 10 Aug. 1957, Budapest; d. of Lajos Básti and Zsuzsa Zolnay; one s.; ed. Acad. of Dramatic Arts, Budapest; mem. Csiky Gergely Theatre co., Kaposvár 1980–85, Katona József Theatre co. 1985–; stage roles include Beatrice (The Changeling), Ophelia (Hamlet), Helena (Midsummer Night's Dream), Lady Anne (Richard III), Mother Ubu (King Ubu), Masha (Three Sisters), Anna Andrejevna (The Government Inspector), Anna Petrovna (Platonov); musicals: Velma Kelly in Chicago, Sally in Cabaret 1993; films: Wasted Lives 1980, The Red Countess 1983, The Followers 1983, Laura 1986, The Horoscope of Jesus Christ 1988, The Bride of Stalin 1990, The Holidaymaker 1990; Best Actress Award, San Remo 1982, Moscow 1985, Award for Best Acting in Theatre in Budapest 1985, Jászay Marit Prize 1985, Kossuth Prize 1993. *Leisure interest:* forests. *Address:* Krecsányi utca 6, 1025 Budapest, Hungary. *Telephone:* 2742219 (Home).

BASU, Jyoti, B.A.; Indian politician and lawyer; b. 1914; ed. Loreto Day School, St. Xavier's School, St. Xavier's Coll.; went to England, called to Middle Temple Bar; during stay in England actively associated with India League and Fed. of Indian Students in England, Sec. of London Majlis, and came in contact with CP of Great Britain; returned to Calcutta 1940; a leader of fmr. Eastern Bengal Railroad Workers' Union; elected to Bengal Legis. Council 1946; after Partition remained a mem. of W. Bengal Legis. Ass.; arrested for membership of CP after party was banned 1948, but released on orders of High Court; became Chair. Editorial Bd. Swadhinata; mem. W. Bengal Legis. Ass. 1952–72; fmr. Sec. Prov. Cttee. of CP, mem. Nat. Council, Cen. Exec. Cttee. and Nat. Secr. until CP split 1963; subsequently mem. Politbureau, CP of India (Marxist); imprisoned 1948, 1949, 1953, 1955, 1963, 1965; Deputy Chief Minister and Minister in charge of Finance in first United Front Govt. 1967, Deputy Chief Minister in second United Front Govt.; M.P. for Satgachia 1977; subsequently Leader of Left Front Legislature Party; Chief Minister of W. Bengal 1977–. *Address:* Chief Minister's Secretariat, Writers' Bldg., Calcutta, India.

BATA, Thomas John, C.C.; Canadian (b. Czech) shoe industry executive; b. 17 Sept. 1914, Prague; s. of the late Tomas Bata and Marie Bata; m. Sonja Ingrid Wettstein 1946; one s. three d.; ed. pvt. schools England and Switzerland and Acad. of Commerce, Uherske, Hradiste; emigrated to Canada 1939, became Canadian citizen 1942; served as Capt. in Canadian Reserve Army; Hon. Chair. Bata Ltd.; Chair. Bata Shoe Foundation, Cttee. on Devt. of Business and Industry Advisory Cttee., OECD, Bohemiae Foundation, Czech Repub., Canada Czech Repub. Chamber of Commerce, Toronto etc.; mem. Bd. of Dirs. Canadian Council for Int. Business; mem. Comm. on Int. Trade and Investment Policy of ICC, Business Council on Nat. Issues, Operation Enterprise Advisory Cttee. of American Man. Asscn., Advisory Council, Canadian Exec. Service Org., Advisory Cttee. East/West Enterprise Exchange, York Univ., Toronto, Chief Exec. Org., Young Presidents' Org. (Founding mem. and Past Pres.), World Bank's Advisory group on Pvt. Sector Devt. Research, Exec. Bd. Canadian Cttee. of Council for Security Co-operation in Asia Pacific, Bd. of Govs. Canadian Export Asscn., Bd. of Govs. Nat. Ballet Guild of Canada; Fellow Int. Acad. of Man.; Paul Harris Fellow (Rotary); Hon. D.Sc. (Univ. of Econs., Prague); Hon. Dr. (Tech. Univ., Brno). *Leisure interests:* tennis, skiing, scuba diving, riding, aviation. *Address:* 44 Park Lane Circle, Don Mills, Ont., M3C 2N2, Canada.

BATALOV, Aleksey Vladimirovich; Russian film actor and director; b. 20 Nov. 1928, Moscow; m. Gitana Azkad'yevna Leonchenko; ed. Moscow Arts Theatre Studio; actor with Cen. Theatre of Soviet Army 1950–53; with Moscow Art Academic Theatre 1953–60; film début 1954; Order of Lenin, People's Artist of U.S.S.R. 1976; teacher VGIK 1976–, Prof. 1979–. *Roles include:* Aleksei Zhurbin in A Large Family 1954, Sasha in The Rumyantsev Case 1956, Boris in The Cranes Are Flying 1957, Gusev in Nine Days in One Year 1962, Pavel Vlasov in Mother 1964, Gurov in The Lady with the Lap-dog 1965, Golubkin in The Flight 1971, Georgi Ivanovich in Moscow Does Not Believe in Tears 1980. *Films directed:* The Overcoat 1960, The Three Fat Men 1966, The Living Corpse 1969, The Flight 1971, The Gambler 1973. *Publication:* Fate and Craftsmanship 1984. *Address:* VGIK, Wilgelm Piek str. 3, 129226 Moscow (Office); Serafimovicha 2, Apt. 91, 109072 Moscow, Russia (Home). *Telephone:* 181-13-14 (Office); 238-16-29 (Home).

BATBAYAR, Bat-Erdeniin, B.SC.; Mongolian politician and scientist; b. 1955, Arkhangai Prov.; ed. Mongolian State Univ., Imperial Coll. Univ. of London; teacher at secondary school, Hentii Prov. 1982–84; scientist, Inst. of Microbiology 1984–; Founding mem. Democratic Socialist Movt.; Founding mem. Mongolian Social Democratic Party, Chair. 1990–94; mem. State Great Hural 1996–; Minister of Finance 1998–99 (resgnd.). *Address:* Mongolian Social Democratic Party, P.O. Box 578, Ulan Bator 11, Mongolia. *Telephone:* 322055; 328425. *Fax:* 322055.

BATBEDAT, Jean, LL.B.; French diplomatist; b. 15 Feb. 1926, Paris; s. of Gérard Batbedat and Jeanne (née Laborde) Batbedat; m. Suzanne Magnier 1956; one s. one d.; ed. Paris Univ., Nat. School of Oriental Languages, Paris; Vice-Consul, French Consulate Gen., Calcutta 1953–55; First Sec. French Embassy, New Delhi 1959–61; Inst. des Hautes Etudes de Défense Nat., Paris 1962; Counsellor, French Embassy, Tunis 1962–66, Moscow 1966–69; Jt. Dir., Direction du Personnel 1974; Jt. Dir.-Gen., Dir.-Gen. des Relations Culturelles 1981; French Amb. to Ireland, Dublin 1982–85, Dir. Diplomatic Archives and Documentation, Ministry of Foreign Affairs, Paris 1985–90; Officier Légion d'honneur; Commdr. Ordre Nat. du Mérite. *Publications:* La Petite Marche du Telengana 1968, Le Dieu Assassiné 1974, Roman de la Begum Sombre 1980, Si l'Adour avait voulu 1987, Le mercenaire du Gange 1995, etc. *Address:* 8 rue de Jarente, 75004 Paris, France. *Telephone:* 42.74.08.55.

BATCHELOR, George Keith, PH.D., F.R.S.; British professor of applied mathematics; b. 8 March 1920, Melbourne, Australia; s. of George C. Batchelor and Ivy C. Berneye; m. Wilma M. Rätz 1944 (died 1997); three d.; ed. Essendon High School, Melbourne Boys' High School, Univs. of Melbourne and Cambridge; Research Officer, Div. of Aeronautics, Commonwealth Council for Scientific and Industrial Research, Melbourne 1941–44; Fellow, Trinity Coll., Cambridge 1947–; ed. Journal of Fluid Mechanics 1956–; Lecturer, Univ. of Cambridge 1948–59, Reader in Fluid Dynamics 1959–64, Head, Dept. of Applied Mathematics and Theoretical Physics 1959–83, Prof. of Applied Math. 1964–83, Prof. Emer. 1983–; Chair. European Mechanics Cttee. 1964–87, U.K. Nat. Cttee. for Theoretical and Applied Mechanics 1967–73; mem. Royal Soc. of Sciences of Uppsala, Sweden; Foreign mem. Polish Acad. of Sciences, American Acad. of Arts and Sciences, Foreign assoc. French Acad. of Sciences, N.A.S.; Corresp. mem. Australian Acad. of Sciences; Hon. D.Sc. (Grenoble) 1959, (Tech. Univ. of Denmark) 1974, (McGill Univ., Montreal) 1986, (Univ. Mich.) 1990, (Univ. of Melbourne) 1994, (KTH, Stockholm) 1995; Adams Prize, Cambridge Univ. 1951, Agostinelli Prize, Accademia dei Lincei 1986, Royal Medal, Royal Soc. 1988, Timoshenko Medal, A.S.M.E. 1988, Taylor Medal, Soc. of Eng. Science 1997. *Publications:* The Theory of Homogenous Turbulence 1953, An Introduction to Fluid Dynamics 1967, The Life and Legacy of G. I. Taylor 1996. *Address:* Department of Applied Mathematics and Theoretical Physics, University of Cambridge, Cambridge CB3 9EW, (Office); Cobbers, Conduit Head Road, Cambridge, CB3 0EY, England (Home). *Telephone:* 01223-337915 (Office); 01223-356387 (Home).

BATE, Jennifer Lucy, B.A., F.R.C.O., L.R.A.M., A.R.C.M.; British organist; b. 11 Nov. 1944, London; d. of Horace Alfred Bate and Dorothy Marjorie Bate; ed. Bristol Univ.; Shaw Librarian, L.S.E. 1966–69; full-time concert career 1969–; has performed worldwide; has organized several teaching programmes; collaboration with Olivier Messiaen 1975–92; designed portable pipe organ with N.P. Mander Ltd. 1984 and a prototype computer organ 1987; F. J. Read Prize (Royal Coll. of Organists), Young Musician 1972, voted Personnalité de l'Année, France 1989, one of the Women of the Year, U.K. 1990–97; hon. Italian citizenship for services to Music 1996. *Compositions:* Toccata on a Theme of Martin Shaw, Introduction and Variations on an Old French Carol, Four Reflections, Homage to 1685, The Spinning Wheel, Lament, An English Canon, Variations on a Gregorian Theme. *Recordings:* concertos and solo works of all periods; prizes include Grand Prix du Disque (Messiaen), Diapason d'Or, Prix de Répertoire (France), Preis der deutschen Schallplatten Kritik (Germany) and M.R.A. Award for 18th century series From Stanley to Wesley. *Leisure interests:* cooking, theatre, philately, gardening. *Address:* 35 Collingwood Avenue, Muswell Hill, London, N10 3EH, England. *Telephone:* 0181-883 3811. *Fax:* 0181-444 3695.

BATEMAN, Barry Richard James, B.A.; British investment executive; b. 21 June 1945; m. Christine Bateman; one s.; ed. Univ. of Exeter; investment analyst Hoare Govett 1967–72, Research Dir. 1972–75; Marketing Dir. Datastream 1975–81; Sr. Marketing Dir. Fidelity Int. Man. Ltd. 1981–86, Man. Dir. Fidelity Investment Ltd. 1986–97, Pres. Fidelity Int. Ltd. 1991–; Chair. Unit Trust Asscn. 1991–93. *Address:* Fidelity Investment Management Limited, Oakhill House, 130 Tonbridge Road, Hildenborough, Tonbridge, Kent, TN11 9DZ, England. *Telephone:* (01732) 361144. *Fax:* (01732) 777441.

BATEMAN, Leslie Clifford, C.M.G., D.SC., PH.D., F.R.S.; British scientist; b. 21 March 1915, Yiewsley; s. of Charles Samuel Bateman and Florence Skinner; m. 1st Marie Pakes 1945 (died 1967); two s.; m. 2nd Eileen Jones 1973; one step-s. one step-d.; ed. Univ. Coll., London, and Oriel Coll., Oxford; Chemist, Natural Rubber Producers' Research Asscn., England 1941–53, Dir. of Research 1953–62; Controller of Rubber Research, Malaysia 1962–74; Special Adviser, Malaysian Rubber Research and Devt. Bd. 1974–75; Sec.-Gen. Int. Rubber Study Group 1976–83; Jubilee Foundation Lecturer 1971, Inst. of the Rubber Industry; Hon. D.Sc. (Malaya) 1968, (Aston) 1972; Fellow, Univ. Coll., London 1974; Colwyn Medal 1962, Panglima Setia Makhota, Malaysia 1974. *Publications:* Ed. and contributor to The Chemistry and Physics of Rubber-like Substances 1963; numerous publs. in Journal of Chemical Society, etc. and on the techno-economic position of the natural rubber industry. *Leisure interests:* outdoor activities, particularly cricket and golf. *Address:* 3 Palmerston Close, Welwyn Garden City, Herts, AL8 7DL, England. *Telephone:* (01707) 322391.

BATEMAN, Robert McLellan, B.A., LL.D., O.C.; Canadian artist; b. 24 May 1930, Toronto; s. of Joseph W. and Anne McLellan Bateman; m. 1st Suzanne Bowermann 1960; two s. one d.; m. 2nd Birgit Freybe 1975; two s.; ed. Univ. of Toronto; high school art teacher for 20 years; began full-time painting 1976, numerous museum exhbns. since 1959, including the Smithsonian Inst. 1987; mem. Niagara Escarpment Comm. 1970–85; Master Artist, Leigh Yawkey Woodson Museum 1982; Hon. life mem. Fed. of Canadian Artists, Canadian Wildlife Fed., Audubon Soc., World Wildlife Fund Int. etc.; nine hon. degrees; Queen Elizabeth II Jubilee Medal 1977, Officer Order of Canada 1983, Medal of Honour, World Wildlife Fund 1985, Rachel Carson Award 1996, Golden Plate Award 1998. *Address:* Gulf Islands, British Columbia, Canada.

BATENIN, Vyacheslav Mikhailovich; DR. PHYS.-MATH. SC.; Russian physicist; b. 12 March 1939; m.; one s.; ed. Moscow Energy Inst.; engineer, sr. engineer, Deputy Dir. Inst. of High Temperatures U.S.S.R. (now Russian) Acad. of Sciences 1962–, Dir. 1987–; corresp. mem. U.S.S.R. Acad. of Sciences 1987. *Publications include:* works on physics of gas explosion and low-temperature plasma, problems of applied superconductivity and magnetic hydrodynamics, unconventional energy sources. *Leisure interests:* tennis, travelling. *Address:* Institute of High Temperatures (IVTAN), Izhorskaya str. 13/19, 127112 Moscow, Russia (Office). *Telephone:* (095) 484 23 11 (Office); (095) 331 32 52 (Home).

BATES, Alan, C.B.E.; British actor; b. 17 Feb. 1934, Allestree, Derbys.; s. of Harold A. Bates and Florence M. Wheatcroft; m. Victoria Ward 1970 (died 1992); twin s. (one s. died 1990); ed. Belper Grammar School and Royal Acad. of Dramatic Art (RADA); spent one year with Midland Repertory Co., Coventry; Hon. D.Litt. (Derby) 1997; *subsequent stage appearances in London include roles in* The Mulberry Bush, Look Back in Anger (also in Moscow and New York), The Country Wife, In Celebration, Long Day's Journey into Night (also at Edinburgh Festival), The Caretaker (also in New York), The Four Seasons, Hamlet (also in Nottingham), Butley (also in New York, Los Angeles and San Francisco), Life Class, Otherwise Engaged 1975–76, The Seagull 1976, Stage Struck; has also appeared at Canadian Shakespeare Festival, Stratford, Ont. in title role of Richard III and as Ford in The Merry Wives of Windsor; also in Poor Richard (New York), Venice Preserved (Bristol), The Taming of the Shrew (Stratford-upon-Avon), A Patriot for Me (London and Chichester) 1983, Dance of Death 1985, Yonadab 1985, Melon 1987, Ivanov 1989, Much Ado About Nothing 1989, Muse of Fire 1989, Stages (Nat. Theatre) 1992, The Showman 1993, Rat in the Skull 1995, The Master Builder 1995, Simply Disconnected 1996, Fortune's Fool 1996, Life Support 1997. *Films:* The Entertainer 1960, Whistle Down the Wind 1961, A Kind of Loving 1962, The Running Man 1962, The Caretaker 1963, Nothing but the Best 1964, Zorba the Greek 1965, Georgy Girl 1965, King of Hearts 1966, Far from the Madding Crowd 1966, The Fixer 1967, Women in Love 1968, The Three Sisters 1969, The Go-Between 1971, A Day in the Death of Joe Egg 1972, Butley 1973, The Impossible Object 1973, In Celebration 1974, Royal Flash 1974, An Unmarried Woman 1977, The Shout 1977, The Rose 1978, Nijinsky 1979, The Trespasser 1980, Quartet 1981, The Return of the Soldier 1982, The Wicked Lady 1982, Duet for One 1987, Prayer for the Dying 1987, The Lair of the White Worm 1989, Dr M. 1989, Force Majeure, Hamlet 1990, 102 Boulevard Haussmann 1990, Mister Frost 1990, Secret Friends 1991, Shuttlecock 1991, Losing Track 1991, Silent Tongue 1992, The Grotesque 1996. *Television:* Two Sundays, Plaintiff and Dependant, The Collection, The Mayor of Casterbridge, Very Like a Whale, A Voyage Round my Father 1982, An Englishman Abroad 1983, Dr. Fischer of Geneva or the Bomb Party 1984, Pack of Lies 1988, 102 Boulevard Haussmann 1991, Two Lumps of Ice 1992, Silent Tongue 1995; received Tony Award for Butley, Broadway, New York 1973, Variety Club Award for Otherwise Engaged 1975, An Englishman Abroad, Separate Tables 1983, Unnatural Pursuits 1992, Hard Times 1993, Oliver's Travels 1995. *Leisure interests:* squash, swimming, tennis, driving, travelling, reading. *Address:* c/o Chatto & Linnit Ltd., Prince of Wales Theatre, Coventry Street, London, W1V 7FE, England.

BATES, Kathy; American actress; b. 28 June 1948, Memphis, Tenn.; d. of Langdon Doyle Bates and Bertye Kathleen (née Talbot); m. Tony Campisi 1991; ed. White Station High School, Southern Methodist Univ.; singing waitress Catskill mountains, cashier Museum of Modern Art, Manhattan. *Theatre work includes:* Varieties 1976, Crimes of the Heart 1979 (won Pulitzer Prize 1981), The Art of Dining 1979, Goodbye Fidel 1980, Chocolate Cake 1980, Extremities 1980, The Fifth of July 1981, Come Back to the 5 & Dime Jimmy Dean, Jimmy Dean 1982, 'night, Mother 1983 (Outer Critics Circle Award), Days and Nights Within 1985, Rain of Terror 1985, Deadfall 1985, Curse of the Starving Class 1985, Frankie and Johnny in the Clair de Lune 1987 (Obie Award), The Road to Mecca 1988. *Films include:* Taking Off 1971, Straight Time 1978, Summer Heat 1987, Arthur 2 on the Rocks 1988, High Stakes 1989, Dick Tracy 1990, White Palace 1990, Men Don't Leave 1990, Misery 1990 (Acad. Award for Best Actress 1991, Golden Globe Award from Hollywood Foreign Press Asscn.), Prelude to a Kiss 1991, At Play in the Fields of the Lord 1991, The Road to Mecca 1991, Fried Green Tomatoes at the Whistle Stop Café 1991, Used People 1992, A Home of our Own 1993, North 1994, Curse of the Starving Class 1994, Diabolique 1996, The War at Home 1996, Primary Colors 1998, Swept from the Sea 1998, Titanic 1998, A Civil Action 1999. *TV work includes guest roles in:* The Love Boat, St. Elsewhere, Cagney & Lacey, L.A. Law, China Beach, All my Children; *TV films include:* Johnny Bull, Uncommon Knowledge, No Place like Home, One for Sorrow—Two for Joy, Signs of Life, Murder Ordained, Straight Time, Hostages, The West Side Waltz 1995, The Late Shift 1996. *Address:* c/o Susan Smith and Associates, 121 N. San Vicente Blvd., Beverly Hills, CA 90211, U.S.A.

BATESON, Paul Patrick Gordon, PH.D., F.R.S.; British university professor; b. 31 March 1938, Chinnor Hill, Oxon.; s. of Richard Gordon Bateson and Solvi Helene Berg; m. Dusha Matthews 1963; two d.; ed. Westminster School, Univ. of Cambridge; Stanford Medical Centre, Univ. of Calif.; Sr. Asst. in Research Sub-Dept. of Animal Behaviour, Univ. of Cambridge 1965–69, Dir. 1976–80, Lecturer in Zoology 1969–78, Reader in Sub-Dept. of Animal Behaviour 1978–84, Prof. of Ethology 1984–; Provost of King's Coll. Cambridge 1988–; Pres. Council Zoological Soc. of London 1989–; mem. Council Museums and Galleries Comm. 1995–; Trustee Inst. for Public Policy Research 1988–; Scientific Medal (Zoological Soc. of London) 1976. *Publications:* (with others) Defended to Death 1983, Ed. Perspectives in Ethology 1973, Growing Points in Ethology 1976, Mate Choice 1983, The Domestic Cat: the biology of its behaviour 1988, Ed. The Development and Integration of Behaviour 1991. *Address:* Sub-Department of Animal Behaviour, University of Cambridge, Madingley, Cambridge, CB3 8AA (Office); Provost's Lodge, King's College, Cambridge, CB2 1ST, England (Home). *Telephone:* 01954-210301 (Office); 01223-355949 (Home).

BATHURST, Adm. of the Fleet Sir (David) Benjamin, G.C.B., D.L.; British naval officer; b. 27 May 1936; s. of late Group Capt. Peter Bathurst and Lady Ann Bathurst; m. Sarah Peto 1959; one s. three d.; ed. Eton Coll. and Britannia Royal Naval Coll. Dartmouth; joined Royal Navy 1953; qualified as pilot 1960, as helicopter instr. 1964; Fleet Air Arm appts.; Sr. Pilot, 820 Naval Air Squadron; C.O. 819 Naval Air Squadron; H.M.S. Norfolk 1971; naval staff 1973; C.O. H.M.S. Ariadne 1975; Naval Asst. to First Sea Lord 1976; Capt. 5th Frigate Squadron, H.M.S. Minerva 1978; Royal Coll. of Defence Studies 1978; Dir. of Naval Air Warfare 1982; Flag Officer, Second Flotilla 1983–85; Dir.-Gen. Naval Manpower and Training 1985–86; Chief of Fleet Support 1986–89; C.-in-C. Fleet, Allied C.-in-C. Channel and C.-in-C. Eastern Atlantic Area 1989–91; Vice-Chief of Defence Staff 1991–93; First Sea Lord and Chief of Naval Staff 1993–95. *Leisure interests:* gardening, shooting, fishing. *Address:* c/o Coutts & Co., 440 Strand, London, WC2R 0QS, England.

BATIZ CAMPBELL, Enrique; Mexican conductor; b. 4 May 1942, Mexico City, D.F.; s. of José Luis Bátiz and María Elena Campbell; m. 1st Eva María Zuk 1965 (divorced 1983); one s. one d.; m. 2nd Elena Campbell Lombardo; ed. Centro Universitario México, Southern Methodist Univ., Dallas, Tex., U.S.A., Juilliard School, New York, Warsaw Conservatoire, Poland; Founder-conductor Orquesta Sinfónica del Estado de México 1971–83, 1990–; Artistic Dir. Orquesta Filarmónica de la Ciudad de México 1983–90; Prin. Guest Conductor Royal Philharmonic Orchestra, London 1984–; Guest Conductor with 130 orchestras; decorated Officer, Order of Rio Branco (Brazil) 1986. *Leisure interest:* swimming. *Address:* International Artists' Management, 340 West 57th Street, New York, NY 10019, U.S.A. (Agent); Cerrada Rancho de los Colorines No. 11, Col Huipulco Tabla del Llano, Código Postal 14380, Zona Postal 22, México, D.F., 7, 34, Mexico. *Telephone:* (525) 671-4216 (Agent); (72) 14 46 84 (Office). *Fax:* (72) 15 62 16.

BATLINER, Gerard, DR.IUR.; Liechtenstein lawyer; b. 9 Dec. 1928, Eschen; s. of Andreas and Karolina Batliner; m. Christina Negele 1965; two s.; ed. Grammar School, Schwyz, Switzerland, and Univs. of Zürich, Fribourg, Paris, and Freiburg im Breisgau; practice at County Court of Principality of Liechtenstein 1954–55; Lawyer, Vaduz 1956–62, 1970–; Vice-Pres. Progressive Burgher Party 1958–62; Deputy Mayor of Eschen 1960–62; Head of Govt. of Principality of Liechtenstein 1962–70; Pres. Liechtenstein Parl.

1974–77, Vice-Pres. 1978–81; Head of Liechtenstein Parl. Del. to the Council of Europe 1978–81; a Vice-Pres Parl. Assembly, Council of Europe, session 1981–82; mem. European Comm. on Human Rights 1983–90, European Comm. for Democracy through Law 1991–; Arbitrator at Court of O.S.C.E. 1995–; Chair. Scientific Council of Liechtenstein-Inst. 1987–97; mem. Scientific Council of Liechtenstein Inst. 1998–; Ed.-in-Chief Liechtenstein Politische Schriften (Liechtenstein Political Publications); Dr. h.c. (Basel) 1988; Fürstlicher Justizrat 1970; Grand Cross of the Liechtenstein Order of Merit, Grand Silver Cross of Honour (Austria). *Publications:* various publs. in field of political science. *Address:* Am Schrägen Weg 2, FL-9490 Vaduz, Liechtenstein.

BATT, Neil Leonard Charles, A.O., B.A.; Australian politician; b. 14 June 1937, Hobart; s. of Clyde Wilfred Luke and Miriam (née Wilkie) Batt; m. 1st Anne Cameron Teniswood 1962 (divorced 1986); three d.; m. 2nd Dr. Karen Green 1986; one s., two d.; ed. Hobart High School, Univ. of Tasmania; Secondary School teacher 1960–61 and 1964–66; mem., House of Ass., Tasmanian Parl. 1969–80, 1986–89; Minister of Transport and Chief Sec. 1972–74, Minister for Educ. 1974–77, Deputy Premier and Treasurer 1977–80, Minister for Forests 1978–80, Minister for Finance 1979–82; Nat. Pres. Australian Labor Party 1978–80; Dir. TNT Group of Cos. for Vic. and Tasmania 1982–86, Resident Dir. TNT Man. Pty. Ltd. 1982–86; Leader of Opposition 1987–89; Exec. Dir. Health Benefits Council of Vic.; Chair. Heine Man. Ltd.; Dir. Eurolynx Ltd 1994–; Ombudsman for Tasmania 1989–91; mem. Jackson Cttee.; Trustee, Nat. Gallery of Vic. 1983–86, Treas. 1984–86; Commr. of Commonwealth Serum Labs. 1983–86, Chair. 1984–86; mem. Bd. of Australian Opera 1983–96. *Leisure interests:* swimming, yachting. *Publications:* The Great Depression in Australia 1970, The Role of the University Today 1977, Information Power 1977. *Address:* 38 Burnett Street, St Kilda, Vic. 3182, Australia.

BATT, Philip E.; American politician and farmer; b. 4 March 1927, Wilder, Idaho; m. Jacque Fallis 1948; one s. two d.; Chair. Idaho State Republican party; fmr. mem. Idaho State Senate; fmr. Lieut.-Gov. of Idaho; Gov. of Idaho 1995–99. *Address:* c/o Office of the Governor, P.O. Box 83720, Boise, ID 83720, U.S.A.

BATTAGLIA, Adolfo; Italian politician; b. 10 Feb. 1930, Viterbo; graduated in law; worked as journalist with Annuario Politico Italiano, La Stampa, Il Mondo, Panorama and Voce Repubblicana; Republican Deputy 1972; fmrly. Under-Sec. for Foreign Affairs, and for Defence, Chair. Radical Party (PRI) Parl. Group, mem. Constitutional Affairs Comm., Comm. of Inquiry into P2; Minister of Industry 1989–91. *Address:* c/o Ministry of Industry, Via Vittorio Veneto 33, 00187, Rome, Italy.

BATTEN, Alan Henry, PH.D., D.SC., F.R.S.C.; Canadian astronomer; b. 21 Jan. 1933, Whitstable, England; s. of George Cuthbert Batten and Gladys (Greenwood) Batten; m. Lois Eleanor Dewis 1960; one s. one d.; ed. Wolverhampton Grammar School, Univs. of St. Andrews and Manchester; Research Asst., Univ. of Manchester and Jr. Tutor, St. Anselm Hall of Residence 1958–59; Post-doctoral Fellow, Dominion Astrophysical Observatory, Victoria, B.C., Canada 1959–61, staff mem. 1961–91, Sr. Research Officer 1976–91, Guest Worker 1991–; Visiting Erskine Fellow, Univ. of Canterbury, N.Z. 1995; Vice-Pres. Astronomical Soc. of Pacific 1974–76; Pres. Canadian Astronomical Soc. 1974–76, Royal Astronomical Soc. of Canada 1976–78 (Hon. Pres. 1994–98), Comm. 30 of Int. Astronomical Union 1976–79, Comm. 42 1982–85; Vice-Pres. Int. Astronomical Union 1985–91; mem. Advisory Council, Centre for Studies in Religion and Society, Univ. of Vic. 1993– (Chair. 1997–); mem. Editorial Bd., Journal of Astronomical History and Heritage; Queen's Silver Jubilee Medal 1977. *Publications:* The Determination of Radial Velocities and their Applications (Co-Ed.) 1967, Extended Atmospheres and Circumstellar Matter in Close Binary Systems (Ed.) 1973, Binary and Multiple Systems of Stars 1973, Resolute and Undertaking Characters: The Lives of Wilhelm and Otto Struve 1988, Algols (Ed.) 1989; over 150 scientific papers. *Leisure interest:* campanology. *Address:* Dominion Astrophysical Observatory, 5071 West Saanich Road, Victoria, B.C., V8X 4M6 (Office); 2987 Westdowne Road, Victoria, B.C., V8R 5G1, Canada (Home). *Telephone:* (250) 363 0001 (Office); (250) 592-1720 (Home). *Fax:* (250) 363-0045.

BATTEN, Sir John Charles, K.C.V.O., M.D., F.R.C.P.; British physician; b. 11 March 1924; s. of the late Raymond Wallis Batten and of Gladys Charles; m. Anne Margaret Oriel 1950; one s. two d. (and one d. deceased); ed. Mill Hill School, St. Bartholomew's Medical School; jr. appointments, St. George's Hospital and Brompton Hospital 1946–58; Surgeon Capt., Royal Horse Guards 1947–49; Physician, St. George's Hospital 1958–79, Brompton Hospital 1959–86, King Edward VII Hospital for Officers 1968–89, King Edward VII Hospital, Midhurst 1969–89; Physician to H.M. Royal Household 1970–74, Physician to H.M. the Queen 1974–89, Head H.M. Medical Household 1982–89; Dorothy Temple Cross Research Fellow, Cornell Univ. Medical Coll., New York 1954–55; Deputy Chief Medical Referee, Confederation Life Insurance Co. 1958–74, Chief Medical Officer 1974–95; Examiner in Medicine, London Univ. 1968; Marc Daniels Lecturer, Royal Coll. of Physicians 1969; Croonian Lecturer, Royal Coll. of Physicians 1983; mem. Bd. of Govs., Brompton Hospital 1966–69, Medical School Council, St. George's Hospital 1969, Man. Cttee., King Edward VII Hospital Fund, Council, Royal Soc. of Medicine 1970, Chair. Medical and Survival Cttee. RNLI 1992–94; Censor, Royal Coll. of Physicians 1977–78, Sr. Censor 1980–81, Vice-Pres. 1980–81; Hon. Physician to St. George's Hospital 1980–, Royal Brompton Hosp. 1986–; Consultant to King Edward VII Convalescent Home, Isle of Wight 1975–85; Pres. Cystic Fibrosis Trust 1984–, Medical Protection Soc. 1987–95. *Publications:* articles in medical books and journals. *Address:* 7 Lion Gate Gardens, Richmond, Surrey, TW9 2DF, England. *Telephone:* 0181-940 3282.

BATTERSBY, Sir Alan Rushton, Kt., PH.D., D.SC., SC.D., F.R.S.; British chemist; b. 4 March 1925, Leigh; s. of William and Hilda Battersby; m. Margaret Ruth Hart 1949 (died 1997); two s.; ed. Leigh Grammar School, Manchester Univ., St. Andrews Univ.; Lecturer in Chem., St. Andrews Univ. 1948–53, Bristol Univ. 1954–62; Prof. of Organic Chem., Liverpool Univ. 1962–69, Cambridge Univ. 1969–92, Emer. Prof. 1992–; Hon. D.Sc. (Rockefeller) 1977, Hon. LL.D. (St. Andrew's) 1977; Hon. D.Sc. (Bristol) 1994, (Liverpool) 1996; Corday-Morgan Medal and Prize 1961, Tilden Lectureship and Medal 1963, Hugo Müller Lectureship and Medal 1972, Flintoff Medal 1975, Paul Karrer Medal 1977, Davy Medal 1977, Max Tishler Award and Lectureship (Harvard) 1978, W. von Hofmann Award and Lectureship 1979, Medal for Chemistry of Natural Products 1979, Pedlar Lectureship and Medal 1980, Roger Adams Award and Medal, American Chemical Soc. 1983, Davy Medal, Royal Soc. 1984, Baker Lectureship, Cornell Univ. 1984, Havinga Medal 1984, Longstaff Medal 1984, Royal Medal 1984, Robert Robinson Lectureship 1985, Antonio Feltrinelli Int. Prize for Chemistry, Accademia Nazionale dei Lincei, Italy 1986, Varro Tyler Award, Purdue, U.S.A. 1987, Medal of Société Royale de Chimie, Belgium 1987, Adolf Windaus Medal and Lectureship German Chem. Soc. 1987, Marvel Lectureship, Illinois, U.S.A. 1989, Gilman Lectureship, Iowa, U.S.A. 1989, Wolf Foundation Chemistry Prize 1989, Kurt Alder Lectureship, Univ. of Cologne, Germany 1991, Arun Guthikonda Award and Lectureship, Columbia Univ., U.S.A. 1991, W. von Hofmann Memorial Medal 1992, Romanes Lectureship, Edin. Univ. 1993, Univ. Lectureship, Ottawa 1993, William Dauben Lectureship, Univ. of Calif., Berkeley, U.S.A. 1994, Alexander Cruickshank Lectureship, Gordon Confs., U.S.A. 1994, Tetrahedron Prize 1995, Linus Pauling Distinguished Lectureship, Oregon State Univ., U.S.A. 1996, Hans-Herloff Inhoffen Medal and Prize, Germany 1997. *Publications:* original papers in the major chemical journals. *Leisure interests:* trout fishing, camping, hiking, gardening, classical music. *Address:* University Chemical Laboratory, Lensfield Road, Cambridge, CB2 1EW (Office); 20 Barrow Road, Cambridge, CB2 2AS, England (Home). *Telephone:* (01223) 336400 (Office); (01223) 63799 (Home). *Fax:* (01223) 336362.

BATTLE, Kathleen, M.MUS.; American opera singer; b. Portsmouth, Ohio; d. of Ollie Layne Battle and Grady Battle; ed. Coll.-Conservatory of Music, Univ. of Cincinnati; professional début in Brahms Requiem, Cincinnati May Festival, then Spoleto Festival, Italy 1972; début Metropolitan Opera, New York as shepherd in Wagner's Tannhäuser 1977; regular guest with orchestras of New York, Chicago, Boston, Philadelphia, Cleveland, L.A., San Francisco, Vienna, Paris and Berlin, at Salzburg, Tanglewood and other festivals, and at the major opera houses including Metropolitan, New York, Covent Garden, London, Paris and Vienna; appearances in 1985/86 season include Sophie in Der Rosenkavalier and Susanna in Figaro, Metropolitan New York, U.S. première parts of Messiaen's St. Francis of Assisi with Boston Symphony Orchestra and recitals U.S.A. and in Toronto, Paris, Vienna and Florence; appearances in 1986/87 season include Zerbinetta in Ariadne auf Naxos and Adina in L'Elisir d'amore, Metropolitan New York and recitals in Japan, London, Salzburg and Vienna; recordings include Brahms Requiem and Songs, Mozart Requiem, Don Giovanni, Seraglio and concert arias, Verdi's Un Ballo in Maschera and Berg's Lulu Suite; New Year's Eve Gala, Vienna; planned recordings include Fauré Requiem; Dr. h.c. (Cincinnati and Westminster Choir Coll., Princeton), Grammy Award 1987, 1988. *Leisure interests:* gardening, cooking, sewing, piano, dance. *Address:* c/o Columbia Artist Management Inc., 165 West 57th Street, New York, NY 10019, U.S.A.

BATTLE, Lucius Durham, A.B., LL.B.; American educationist; b. 1 June 1918, Dawson, Ga.; s. of Warren L. Battle and Jewel B. Durham; m. Betty Davis 1949; two s. two d.; ed. Univ. of Florida; Man. of student staff, Univ. of Florida Library 1940–42; Assoc. Admin. Analyst, War Dept. 1942–43; U.S. Naval Reserve 1943–46; Foreign Affairs Specialist, Dept. of State, Washington 1946–49; Special Asst. to Sec. of State 1949–53, 1961–64, also Exec. Sec. Dept. of State 1961–62; First Sec., Copenhagen 1953–55; Deputy Exec. Sec. NATO, Paris 1955–56; Asst. Sec. of State for Educational and Cultural Affairs 1962–64; Amb. to United Arab Repub. 1964–67; Asst. Sec. of State for Near Eastern and S. Asian Affairs, Washington 1967–68; Vice-Pres. for Corporate Affairs, Communications Satellite Corpn., Washington, D.C. 1968–73, Senior Vice-Pres. for Corporate Affairs 1974–80; Pres. Middle East Inst., Washington, D.C., 1973–74, 1986–90; Lucius D. Battle Associates 1984–85; mem. Advisory Council, Center for U.S.-European Middle East Co-operation 1981–; Chair. UNESCO Gen. Conf., Paris 1962; Adviser, Foundation for Middle East Peace 1981, Pres. 1994–; mem. Bd. of Dirs. World Council of Washington, D.C. 1980; mem. Nat. Bd. Smithsonian Assocs. 1981–85; Vice-Pres. Colonial Williamsburg Inc., Williamsburg Restoration Inc. 1956–61; Pres. Bacon House Foundation; Trustee, Meridan House Int., American Univ. Cairo, The Jordan Soc. 1982; mem. Bd. of Dirs. Foreign Policy Asscn., School of Advanced Int. Studies, Middle East Inst., George C. Marshall Research Foundation, First American Bank, N.A. 1982; mem. Bd. Nat. Defense Univ. Foundation 1982–; mem. Founders' Council, Inst. for

Study of Diplomacy, Georgetown Univ. 1978–87; mem. Advisory Bd. Faith and Hope, WAFA WAL AMAL, Center for Contemporary Arab Studies, Georgetown Univ., Inst. for Psychiatry and Foreign Affairs; mem. American Foreign Service Asscn. (Pres. 1962–63), Nat. Study Comm. on Records and Documents of Federal Officials, Dept. of State Fine Arts Cttee.; Communications exec. Dir. COMSAT Gen. Corpn.; Chair. Nat. Cttee. to honour the 14th Centennial of Islam 1979–; Chair. The Johns Hopkins Foreign Policy Inst., School for Advanced Int. Studies, The Johns Hopkins Univ., Washington, D.C. 1980–84; Order of Republic (1st class), Egypt 1978. *Address:* Middle East Institute, 1761 North Street, N.W., Washington, DC 20036-3882 (Office); 4856 Rockwood Parkway, N.W., Washington, DC 20016, U.S.A. (Home). *Telephone:* (202) 244-9109 (Home).

BATTS, Warren Leighton; American business executive; b. 4 Sept. 1932, Norfolk, Va.; s. of John Leighton and Allie Belle (née Johnson) Batts; m. Eloise Pitts 1957; one d.; Georgia Inst. of Tech., Harvard; with Kendall Co. 1963–64; Exec. Vice-Pres. Fashion Devt. Co. 1964–66; Vice-Pres., Douglas Williams Assocs. 1966–67; Founder, Triangle Corpn. 1967, Pres. and Chief Exec. Officer 1967–71; Vice-Pres., Mead Corpn. 1971–73, Pres. 1973–80, Chief Exec. Officer 1978–80; Pres. Dart Industries 1980–81, Pres. Dart & Kraft 1981–86; Chair. Premark Int. Inc. 1986–97, C.E.O. 1986–96; Chair., C.E.O. Tupperware Corpn. 1996–97; Trustee Northwestern Univ. 1989, Children's Memorial Hospital, Chicago 1984–. *Address:* c/o Premark International Inc., 1717 Deerfield Road, IL 60015, U.S.A. *Telephone:* (312) 405-6300.

BATTY, Sir William (Bradshaw), Kt.; British motor executive (retd.); b. 15 May 1913, Manchester; s. of Rowland and Nellie Batty; m. Jean Ella Brice 1946; one s. one d. (one s. deceased); ed. Hulme Grammar School, Manchester; apprentice toolmaker, Ford Motor Co. Ltd. 1930, company trainee 1933; Man. Tractor Div. 1955; Gen. Man. Tractor Group 1961; Dir. of Car and Truck Group 1964; Exec. Dir. Ford Motor Co. Ltd. 1963, Man. Dir. 1967–73, Chair. 1972–76; Dir. Henry Ford and Son Ltd., Cork 1965–76; Chair. Ford Motor Credit Co. Ltd. 1968–76, Automotive Finance Ltd. 1970–76; Dir. Ford Lusitana SARL, Portugal 1973–76; Pres. Soc. of Motor Mfrs. and Traders 1975–76, Vice-Pres. 1976–. *Leisure interests:* golf, sailing, gardening. *Address:* Glenhaven Cottage, Riverside Road West, Newton Ferrers, Plymouth, Devon, England. *Telephone:* (01752) 872415.

BATU BAGEN; Chinese party and government official; b. 1924, Zhenlai Co., Jilin Prov.; s. of Chen and Ne Garibu; m. 1950; three d.; joined CCP 1946; Deputy 1st, 2nd, 4th, 5th, 6th and 7th Inner Mongolia Autonomous Regional People's Congress, Chair. 1983–93; mem. Presidium 4th, 5th, 6th and 7th Autonomous Regional People's Congress; Deputy for Inner Mongolia 4th, 5th, 6th and 7th NPC; mem. Presidium 6th, 7th NPC; Vice-Chair. Autonomous Regional Govt. Inner Mongolia 1979–83; alt. mem. Cen. Cttee. CCP 1982–92; mem. Standing Cttee. 8th CPPCC and Vice-Chair. Ethnic Affairs Cttee. CPPCC 1993–; Leader 8th Prov. Spoken and Written Mongolian Language Co-ordination Group 1983–; Vice Chair. China Sports Asscn. for the Elderly 1992; Vice-Pres. China Yellow River Culture, Econs. and Devt. Research Inst. 1993; Pres. Inner Mongolia Yellow River Culture, Econs. and Devt. Research Inst. 1995. *Leisure interests:* tennis, calligraphy. *Address:* Bldg. 4, Inner Yard, 1 Qingcheng Lane, Huhhot 010015, People's Republic of China. *Telephone:* (0471) 4951419.

BAT-ÜÜL, Erdeniin; Mongolian politician; b. 1 July 1957, Ulan Bator; m. B. Delgertuja 1977; two s. one d.; teacher, First Constructing Tech. Training School, Ulan Bator 1981–82, secondary school Höbsögöl Prov. 1982–85; scientist, Observatory of Acad. of Sciences 1985–89; Founder-mem. Mongolian Democratic Union, mem. Gen. Co-ordinating Council 1989–, Gen. Coordinator Political Consultative Centre 1990–; Deputy to Great People's Hural 1990–92, 1996–; mem. Political Consultative Centre of Mongolian Democratic Party 1992–; mem. Gen. Council and Dir. Political Policy Inst. of Mongolian Nat. Democratic Party 1992–, Regional Sec. 1993–, Gen. Sec. and Presidium of Co-ordinating Council of Mongolian Democratic Union 1993–. *Address:* Mongolian National Democratic Party, Ulan Bator, Mongolia (Office); Suchbaatar District 1-40,000, 62-1-4 Ulan Bator, Mongolia (Home). *Telephone:* 372810 (Office); 321105 (Home). *Fax:* 976-1-372810.

BATURIN, Yuri Mikhailovich, D.JUR.; Russian politician; b. 12 June 1949, Moscow; ed. Moscow Inst. of Physics and Tech., All-Union Inst. of Law, Moscow State Univ.; worked in research production union Energia 1973–80; Inst. of State and Law U.S.S.R. (now Russian) Acad. of Sciences; on staff of Pres. Mikhail Gorbachev admin. 1991; mem. Pres.'s Council 1993–; asst. to Pres. on legal problems 1993–94, on Nat. Security Problems 1994–97; mem. Council on Personnel Policy of Pres. 1994–97; Sec. Defence Council of Russian Fed. 1996–97; Asst. to Pres., Chair. Cttee. for Mil. Ranks and Posts 1996–98; took part in space flight to Mir Station Sept. 1998.

BAUCHARD, Denis Michel Bertrand; French diplomatist; b. 20 Sept. 1936; s. of Charles Bauchard and Marguerite Duhamel; m. Geneviève Lanoë 1961; two s. two d.; ed. Inst. of Political Studies, Ecole national d'administration; Civil Admin., Ministry of Finance 1964–66, 1968–74; Financial Attaché Nr. and Middle East, French Embassy Beirut 1966–68; Asst. to Minister 1974–76; Financial Counsellor, French Mission to UN 1977–81; Deputy Asst. Sec., Ministry of Foreign Affairs 1981–85; Asst. Sec. 1986–89; Ambassador to Jordan 1989–93; Asst. Sec. Ministry of Foreign Affairs (N. Africa and Middle East) 1993–96; Chief of Staff to Minister of Foreign Affairs 1996–97; Amb. to Canada 1998–; Chevalier, Légion d'honneur; Officier, Ordre national du mérite. *Publications:* Le Jeu Mondial des pétroliers 1970, Economie financière des collectivités locales 1972. *Address:* French Embassy, 42 Sussex Drive, Ottawa, Ont., K1M 2C9, Canada; Ministry of Foreign Affairs, Service de la valise (Ottawa), 37 Quai d'Orsay, 75007 Paris; 91 rue de Rennes, 75006 Paris, France (Home).

BAUCUS, Max, LL.B.; American senator; b. 11 Dec. 1941, Helena, Mont.; m. Wanda Minge 1983; one s.; ed. Helena High School, Stanford Univ. and Stanford Law School; staff attorney, Civil Aeronautics Bd., Washington, D.C. 1967–69; legal staff, Securities and Exchange Comm. 1969–71; legal asst. to Chair. S.E.C. 1970–71; private law practice, Missoula, Mont. 1971; Acting Exec. Dir. and Cttee. Coordinator, Mont. Constitutional Convention; elected to Montana State Legislature 1972; two terms in U.S. House of Reps. for Mont. Western Dist., mem. House Appropriations Cttee. and Deputy Whip; Senator from Montana 1979–; Chair. Senate Int. Trade Sub-Cttee. of Finance, Senate Environment and Public Works Cttee., Senate Agric. and Intelligence Cttee.; mem. several other sub-cttees.; Democrat. *Address:* 511 Hart, Senate Building, Washington, DC 20510, U.S.A.

BAUDO, Serge; French conductor; b. 16 July 1927, Marseille; s. of Etienne Baudo and Geneviève Tortelier; m. Madeleine Reties 1947; one s. one d.; ed. Conservatoire national supérieur de musique, Paris; Music Dir. Radio Nice 1957–59; Conductor Paris Opera Orchestra 1962–66; titular Conductor and Orchestral Dir. a.i. Orchestre de Paris 1968–70; Music Dir. Opéra de Lyon 1969–71, Orchestre Nat. de Lyon 1971–87; has conducted many of world's leading orchestras; Founder Berlioz Festival, Lyon 1979–89; Chevalier, ordre national du mérite; Officier des Arts et des Lettres; de la Légion d'honneur; numerous prix du disque. *Address:* Musicaglotz, 11 rue Le Verrier, 75006 Paris; Jas du Ferra, Chemin Charré, 13600 Ceyreste, France (Home).

BAUDOUIN, Jean-Louis, B.A., B.C.L., PH.D.; Canadian lawyer and professor of law; b. 8 Aug. 1938, Boulogne, France; s. of Louis Baudouin and Marguerite Guerin; m.; four d.; ed. Univ. of Paris, McGill Univ., Montreal, Canada; admitted to Bar of Quebec 1959; Prof. of Law, Univ. of Montreal 1963–; Commr., Law Reform Comm. of Canada 1976–78, Vice-Chair. 1978–80, Judge, Court of Appeal, Quebec 1989–; mem. Royal Soc. of Canada. *Publications:* Les Obligations 1970, La Responsabilité Civile 1973, Le Secret Professionnel 1964, Produire l'Homme: de quel Droit? 1987, Ethique de la Mort 1992, Droit à la Mort 1992. *Leisure interests:* windsurfing, fishing, winetasting. *Address:* Court House, 1 Notre Dame East, Montreal, H2Y 1B6 (Office); 875 Antonine Maillet, Montreal, Quebec, H2V 2Y6, Canada (Home).

BAUDRIER, Jaqueline; French journalist and diplomatist; b. 16 March 1922, Beaufai; m. 1st Maurice Baudrier (divorced); m. 2nd Roger Perriard 1957; ed. Univ. of Paris; political reporter, Actualités de Paris news programme, and foreign news reporter and presenter on various news programmes, Radiodiffusion-Télévision Française 1950–60; Sec.-Gen. Soutien fraternel des journalistes 1955; Ed.-in-Chief of news programmes, Office de Radiodiffusion-Télévision Française (ORTF) 1963–66, in charge of main news programme 1966–68; Asst. Dir. of radio broadcasting, in charge of information 1968–69; Dir. of Information, 2nd TV channel (A2) 1969–72; Dir. 1st TV channel network (TF1) 1972–74; Chair. Radio-France (nat. radio broadcasting co.) 1975–81; mem. Bd. of Dirs. Télédiffusion de France (nat. TV broadcasting co.) 1975–81; Pres. Communauté radiophonique des programmes de langue française 1977–79; Vice-Chair. Programming Comm. Union européenne de radiodiffusion 1978, re-elected 1980; Perm. Rep. of France to UNESCO 1981–85; mem. Exec. Cttee., UNESCO 1984–85, Comm. nat. de la Communication et des Libertés 1986–89; columnist Quotidien de Paris 1989; Pres. Cosmo Communications 1989–95; columnist, mem. ed. bd. L'Observatoire de la Télévision 1993–; Pres. Channel 5 TV Programming Comm. 1995; Vice-Pres. Nat. Comm. for UNESCO 1996; prix Maurice Bourdet 1960, prix Ondes 1969; Chevalier Légion d'honneur, Officier, Ordre nationale du Mérit; numerous other awards. *Address:* 60 quai Louis Blériot, 75016 Paris, France (Home).

BAUDYŠ, Antonín, DIP.TECH.; Czech politician and academic; b. 9 Sept. 1946, Prague; m.; two s.; ed. Czech Univ. of Tech., Prague; teacher Dept. of Precision Mechanics and Optics, Czech Univ. of Tech., Prague 1969–89; Reader 1988; mem. Christian and Democratic Union-Czechoslovak People's Party (CDU-CPP) 1970–; mem. of Presidium, Cen. Cttee. of CDU-CPP Nov. 1989–; Vice-Premier, Govt. of Czech Repub. 1989–92; Minister of Defence of Czech Repub. 1992–94; pvt. consultant 1994–; Cross of the Order of Merit, Kts. of Malta. *Publications:* 15 lecture notes, author and co-author of many patents and inventions in optics and precision mechanics, author of various improvements of mechanical and optical equipments. *Address:* Christian Democratic Party-Czech People's Party, Malostranské nám. č. 28, 110 00 Prague 1, Czech Republic. *Telephone:* 53 17 19.

BAUER, Baron (Life Peer), cr. 1983, of Market Ward in the City of Cambridge, **Peter Thomas Bauer,** M.A., F.B.A.; British economist; b. 6 Nov. 1915, Budapest, Hungary; ed. Scholae Piae (Budapest) and Gonville and Caius Coll., Cambridge; Fellow Gonville and Caius Coll. Cambridge 1946–60, 1968–; Reader, Agricultural Econ, Univ. of London 1947–48; Univ. Lecturer in Econ., Cambridge Univ. 1948–56, Smuts Reader in Commonwealth Studies 1956–60; Prof. of Econ. (with special reference to econ. devt. and underdeveloped countries), Univ. of London 1960–83, Prof. Emer. 1983–; Hon. Fellow L.S.E. 1997. *Publications:* The Rubber Industry 1948, West African Trade 1954, The Economics of Under-developed Countries (with B. S. Yamey) 1957, Economic Analysis and Policy in Under-developed Countries 1958, Indian Economic Policy and Development 1961, Markets, Market

Control and Marketing Reform (Selected Papers, with B. S. Yamey) 1969, Dissent on Development: Studies and Debates in Development Economics 1972, Equality, The Third World and Economic Delusion 1981, Reality and Rhetoric: Studies in the Economics of Development 1984, The Development Frontier 1991; numerous articles on economic subjects. *Address:* House of Lords, Westminster, London, S.W.1, England (Office).

BAULIEU, Etienne-Emile, D. EN MED., D. ÈS SC.; French biochemist; b. 12 Dec. 1926, Strasbourg; s. of Léon Blum and Thérèse Lion; m. Yolande Compagnon 1947; two s. one d.; ed. Lycée Pasteur, Neuilly-sur-Seine, Faculté de Médecine and Faculté des Sciences, Paris; Intern, Paris Hosps. 1951–55; Chef de Clinique, Faculté de Médecine, Paris 1955–57, Assoc. Prof. of Biochemistry 1958; Visiting Scientist, Dept. of Obstetrics, Gynaecology and Biochemistry, Columbia Univ. New York 1961–62; Dir. Research Inst. 33, Hormones Lab., Inst. Nat. de la Santé et de la Recherche Médicale (INSERM) 1963–; Prof. of Biochemistry, Faculté de Médecine de Bicêtre, Univ. Paris-Sud 1970; Prof. at Collège de France 1993, a chair. 1994–; Consultant, Roussel Uclaf; mem. Editorial Bds. several French and int. journals; mem. and Past Pres. INSERM, Fondation pour la Recherche Médicale Française; Pres. Société Française d'Endocrinologie 1978; mem. Organizing Cttee. Karolinska Symposia on Reproductive Endocrinology, NCI-INSERM Cancer and Hormones programme (Past French Scientific Chair.), fmr. mem. Scientific Advisory Bd. WHO Special Programme in Human Reproduction; inventor of RU486 abortion pill; mem. Inst. de France (Acad. des Sciences); Foreign Assoc. mem. N.A.S. (U.S.A.) 1990; Hon. mem. American Physiological Soc. 1993; Dr. h.c. (Ghent) 1991, (Karolinska Inst.) 1994; Hon. Dr. (Tufts) 1991, (Worcs. Foundation, Shrewsbury) 1994; Reichstein Award, Int. Soc. of Endocrinology 1972, Grand Prix Scientifique 1989, de la Ville de Paris 1974, First European Medallist of Soc. of Endocrinology (G.B.) 1985, Albert & Mary Lasker Clinical Research Award 1989, Premio Minerva, Rome 1990, Christopher Columbus Discovery Award in Biomedical Research (Genoa and N.I.H.) 1992, Nat. Award, American Asscn. for Clinical Chem. 1992, Grand Prix Scientifique, Fondation pour la Recherche Médicale, Paris 1995, and numerous other prizes and awards; Commdr. Légion d'honneur; Chevalier Ordre Nat. du Mérite. *Publications:* Génération pilule 1992, numerous specialist papers. *Address:* Laboratoire des hormones, Hôpital de Bicêtre, 94270 Le Kremlin-Bicêtre, France.

BAUM, Bernard René, PH.D., F.R.S.C.; Canadian scientist; b. 14 Feb. 1937, Paris, France; s. of Kurt Baum and Marta Berl; m. Danielle Habib 1961; one d.; ed. Hebrew Univ., Jerusalem; Research Scientist, Plant Research Inst., Dept. of Agric., Ottawa, Canada 1966–74; Sr. Research Scientist, Biosystematics Research Inst., Agric. Canada, Ottawa 1974–80, Prin. Research Scientist, Biosystematics Research Centre 1980–90, Prin. Research Scientist, Centre for Land and Biological Resources Research 1990–95, Eastern Cereal and Oilseed Research Centre 1996–; Section Chief, Cultivated Crops Section 1973–77, Section Head, Vascular Plants Section 1982–87, Acting Dir., Geostrategy Div., Devt. Policy Directorate 1981–82; mem. Acad. of Sciences (Royal Soc. of Canada), Botanical Soc. of America, Societé Botanique de France, Int. Asscn. for Plant Taxonomy and other socs.; Founder mem. Hennig Soc.; Fellow Linnean Soc., London; George Lawson Medal, Canadian Botanical Asscn. 1979. *Publications:* Material of an International Oat Register 1973, Oats: wild and cultivated. A monograph of the genus Avena 1977, The Genus Tamarix 1978, Barley Register 1985, Triticale Register; 200 scientific publs. *Leisure interests:* swimming long distance, classical music. *Address:* Eastern Cereal and Oilseed Research Centre, Agriculture Canada, Central Experimental Farm, Ottawa, Ont., K1A 0C6 (Office); 15 Murray Street, Suite 408, Ottawa, Ont., K1N 9M5, Canada (Home). *Telephone:* (613) 759 1821 (Office); (613) 241 5871 (Home).

BAUM, Warren C., PH.D.; American international finance official; b. 2 Sept. 1922, New York; s. of William and Elsie Baum; m. Jessie Scullen 1946; two d.; ed. Columbia Coll. and Harvard Univ.; with Office of Strategic Services 1942–46; Economic Co-operation Admin. 1949–51; Mutual Security Agency 1952–53; Economist, RAND Corpn. 1953–56; Chief, Office of Network Study, Fed. Communications Comm. 1956–59; Economist, European Dept. World Bank 1959–62; Div. Chief, European Dept. 1962–64; Asst. Dir. in charge of Transportation, Projects Dept. 1964–68; Deputy Dir., Projects Dept. July 1968; Assoc. Dir., Projects Nov. 1968–72; Vice-Pres. Projects Staff 1972–83, Vice-Pres. 1983–; Chair. Consultative Group on Int. Agricultural Research 1974–83, Chair. Emer. 1984–. *Publications:* The Marshall Plan and French Foreign Trade 1951, The French Economy and the State 1956, Investing in Development 1985. *Address:* 1818 H. Street, N.W., Washington, DC 20433, U.S.A.

BAUM, H.E. Cardinal William Wakefield, S.T.D., S.T.L.; American ecclesiastic; b. 21 Nov. 1926, Dallas, Tex.; s. of Harold E. and Mary Leona (Hayes) White, step-father Jerome C. Baum; ed. Kenrick Seminary, St. Louis and Univ. of St. Thomas Aquinas, Rome; ordained to priesthood 1951; Assoc. Pastor, St. Aloysius, St. Therese's and St. Peter's parishes, Kan. City, Mo. 1951–56; Instructor and Prof., Avila Coll., Kan. City 1954–56; 1958–63; Admin. St. Cyril's Parish, Sugar Creek, Mo. 1960–61; Hon. Chaplain of His Holiness the Pope 1961; Peritus (Expert Adviser), Second Vatican Council 1962–65; First Exec. Dir. Bishops' Comm. for Ecumenical and Interreligious Affairs, Washington 1964–67, Chair. 1972; mem. Jt. Working Group of reps. of Catholic Church and World Council of Churches 1965–69; mem. Mixed Comm. of reps. of Catholic Church and Lutheran World Fed. 1965–66; Chancellor, Diocese of Kan. City, St. Joseph 1967–70; Hon. Prelate of His Holiness the Pope 1968; Pastor, St. James Parish, Kan. City 1968–70; Bishop, Diocese of Springfield-Cape Girardeau 1970; mem. Synod of Bishops 1971; Archbishop of Washington 1973–80; Chancellor of the Catholic Univ. 1973–80; Cardinal 1976; Prefect, Sacred Congregation for Catholic Educ. 1980–91; Grand Penitentiary Cardinal 1990–; Permanent Observer-Consultant for Vatican Secretariat for Promoting Christian Unity; Chair. USCC-NCCB Doctrine Cttee., Cttee. for Pastoral Research and Practices; mem. Secretariat for Non-Christians; Hon. D.D., Muhlenberg Coll., Allentown, Pa. 1967, Georgetown Univ., Wash., St. John's Univ., Brooklyn, N.Y. *Leisure interests:* reading, music. *Publications:* The Teaching of Cardinal Cajetan on the Sacrifice of the Mass 1958, Considerations Toward the Theology on the Presbyterate 1961. *Address:* Via Rusticucci 13, 00193, Rome, Italy.

BAUMAN, Robert Patten, B.A., M.B.A.; American business executive; b. 27 March 1931; s. of John Nevan Bauman, Jr. and Lucille Miller Patten; m. Patricia Hughes Jones 1961; one s. one d.; ed. Ohio Wesleyan Univ., Harvard School of Business; joined Gen. Foods Corpn. 1958, Corp. Vice-Pres. 1968, Group Vice-Pres. 1970, Exec. Vice-Pres. and Corp. Dir. 1972–81; Dir. Avco Corpn. 1980, Chair. and C.E.O. 1981–85; Vice-Chair. and Dir. Textron Inc. 1985–86; Chair. and Chief Exec. Beecham Group 1986–89, C.E.O. SmithKline Beecham 1989–94; Chair. British Aerospace PLC 1994–98, BTR PLC, London 1998–; Dir. Cap Cities/ABC Inc., Union Pacific Corpn., Trustee, Ohio Wesleyan Univ. *Publication:* Plants as Pets 1982. *Leisure interests:* growing orchids, paddle tennis, jogging, tennis, photography, golf, sailing.

BAUMAN, Zygmunt, PH.D.; British professor of sociology; b. 19 Nov. 1925, Poznań, Poland; s. of Moritz Bauman and Sophia Bauman (née Cohn); m. Janina Lewinson 1948; three d.; ed. Univ. of Warsaw; held Chair. of Gen. Sociology, Univ. of Warsaw 1964–68, now Prof. Emer.; Prof. of Sociology, Univ. of Tel-Aviv 1968–71, Univ. of Leeds 1971–91, now Prof. Emer.; Dr. h.c. (Oslo Univ.) 1997; Amalfi Prize for sociology and social sciences 1989, Theodor W. Adorno Prize 1998. *Publications:* Culture as Praxis 1972, Hermeneutics and Social Science 1977, Memories of Class 1982, Legislators and Interpreters 1987, Modernity and the Holocaust 1989, Modernity and Ambivalence 1990, Intimations of Postmodernity 1991, Thinking Sociologically 1991, Mortality, Immortality and other life strategies 1992, Postmodern Ethics 1993, Life in Fragments 1995, Postmodernity and its Discontents 1996, Globalization: the human consequences 1998, Work, Consumerism and the New Poor 1998, In Search of Politics 1999. *Leisure interest:* photography. *Address:* 1 Lawnswood Gardens, Leeds, LS16 6HF, England. *Telephone:* (0113) 267 8173. *Fax:* (0113) 267 8173.

BAUMANIS, Aivars; Latvian diplomatist and journalist; b. 23 Dec. 1937, Riga; s. of Arturs Baumanis and Elza Finks; m. Anita Baumanis 1979; three s. one d.; ed. Latvian Univ.; investigator, City Police Dept. of Riga 1961–64; corresp. foreign news desk of Latvian Radio 1964–71; ed. Liesma (magazine) 1971–74; corresp. Padomfu Faunatne (newspaper) 1974–80; Exec. Sec. Furmala (newspaper) 1980–88, Ed.-in-Chief 1986–88; Dir. Latvian br. Novosti News Agency 1988–90; Dir. Latvian news agency Leta 1990–91; Amb. and Perm. Rep. of Latvia to UN Dec. 1991–. *Publications:* articles in various Latvian newspapers and magazines 1966–91. *Leisure interests:* jazz, movies, literature. *Address:* 333 East 50th Street, New York, NY 10022, U.S.A. *Telephone:* (212) 935-3005. *Fax:* (212) 888-3607.

BAUMANN, Herbert Karl Wilhelm; German composer and conductor; b. 31 July 1925, Berlin; s. of Wilhelm and Elfriede (née Bade) Baumann; m. Marianne Brose 1951; two s.; ed. Berlin Classical High School, Schillergymnasium and Int. Music Inst.; conductor, Tchaikovsky Symphony Orch. 1947; composer and conductor, Deutsches Theater, Berlin 1947–53, Staatliche Berliner Bühnen: Schillertheater and Schlossparktheater 1953–70, Bayerisches Staatsschauspiel: Residenztheater, Munich 1971–79; freelance composer 1979–; several recordings. *Works include:* stage music (ballets: Alice in Wonderland, Rumpelstilzchen), music for radio, cinema and television, orchestral, chamber and choral works, several suites for plucked instruments and works for organ. *Leisure interests:* travelling and wandering, reading, especially books on fine arts. *Address:* Franziskanerstrasse 16, Apt. 1419, 81669 Munich, Germany. *Telephone:* 089-480 77 45. *Fax:* 089-480 77 45.

BAUMEL, Jacques; French politician; b. 6 March 1918, Marseille; m. Louise-Jacqueline Bachelot 1959; two d.; Deputy for Hauts-de-Seine (R.P.R.); Mayor of Rueil-Malmaison; fmr. govt. minister and senator; Vice-Pres. Comm. on Nat. Defence and the Armed Forces; Vice-Chair. Parl. Ass., Council of Europe; Pres. Defence Cttee. W.E.U., Forum du Futur; Chair Ass. Nationale de Téléspectateurs français; mem. French del. to U.N. 1984–; Pres. Conseil nat. des collectivités territoriales pour l'audiovisuel (CNCTA) 1989–; Chevalier, Légion d'honneur; Compagnon de la Libération; Croix de guerre; Médaille de la Résistance. *Publication:* Une Certaine Idée de la France 1985. *Address:* Assemblée nationale, 75355 Paris (Office); 13 boulevard Foch, 92500 Rueil-Malmaison, France (Home). *Telephone:* 1.47.08.41.18 (Office). *Fax:* 1.47.08.64.16 (Office).

BAUMOL, William Jack, PH.D.; American professor of economics; b. 26 Feb. 1922, New York; s. of Solomon and Lillian Baumol; m. Hilda Missel 1941; one s. one d.; ed. Coll. of City of New York and Univ. of London; jr. economist, U.S. Dept. of Agriculture 1942–43, 1946; Asst. Lecturer, London School of Econs. 1947–49; Asst. Prof. Dept. of Econs., Princeton Univ. 1949–52, Prof. of Econs. 1952–92, Prof. Emer. and Sr. Research Economist 1992–; Dir. C.V. Starr Center for Applied Econs., New York Univ. 1971–;

Prof. of Econs. New York Univ. 1971–; Pres. Eastern Econ. Asscn. 1978–79, Asscn. of Environmental and Resource Economists 1979, American Econ. Asscn. 1981, Atlantic Econ. Soc. 1985; mem. N.A.S.; Hon. Fellow, L.S.E.; Hon. doctorates, Stockholm School of Econs., Univ. of Basle, etc.; Frank E. Seidman Award, Political Econ. 1987. *Publications:* 30 books including: Economic Dynamics 1951, Business Behavior, Value and Growth 1959, Economic Theory and Operations Analysis 1961, Performing Arts: The Economic Dilemma (with W. G. Bowen) 1966, Theory of Environmental Policy (with W. E. Oates) 1975, Economics, Environmental Policy, and the Quality of Life (with W. E. Oates and S. A. Batey Blackman) 1979, Economics: Principles and Policy (with A. S. Blinder) 1979, Contestable Markets and the Theory of Industry Structure (with J. C. Panzar and R. D. Willig) 1982, Productivity Growth and U.S. Competitiveness (ed. with K. McLennan) 1985, Superfairness: Applications and Theory 1986 (Best Book in Business, Man. and Econs., Asscn. American Publishers), Microtheory: Applications and Origins 1986, Productivity and American Leadership: The Long View (with S. A. Batey Blackman and E. N. Wolff) 1989, The Information Economy and the Implications of Unbalanced Growth (with L. Osberg and E. N. Wolff) 1989, The Economics of Mutual Fund Markets: Competition versus Regulation (jtly.) 1990, (co-author) Perfect Markets and Easy Virtue: Business Ethics and the Invisible Hand 1991, Entrepreneurship, Management and the Structure of Payoffs 1993, Toward Competition in Local Telephony (with G. Sidak) 1994. *Leisure interests:* woodcarving, painting. *Address:* Department of Economics, New York University, 269 Mercer Street, New York, NY 10003 (Office); 100 Bleecker Street, Apt. 29A, New York, NY 10012, U.S.A. (Home). *Telephone:* (212) 998-8943 (New York Univ.). *Fax:* (212) 995 3932.

BAUSCH, Pina; German dancer and choreographer; b. 27 July 1940, Solingen; one s.; ed. Folkwang School, Essen, Juilliard School, New York; mem. Dance Company Paul Sanasardo and Donya Feuer, danced at Metropolitan Opera New York, New American Ballet 1960–62; became soloist, Folkwang-Ballett 1962, choreographer, 1968–73, Dir. 1968–73; f. Tanztheater Wuppertal 1973; Head Dance Dept., Folkwang Hochschule Essen 1983–89; Artistic Dir. Folkwang-Tanzstudio 1983–. *Choreographed works include:* Fritz, Iphigenie auf Tauris, Adagio — Fünf Lieder von Gustaf Mahler 1974, Orpheus und Eurydike, Frühlingsopfer 1975, Die Sieben Todsünden 1976, Blaubart, Komm Tanz mit Mir, Renate Wandert aus 1977, Café Müller, Kontakthof 1978, Arien, Keuschheitslegende 1979, Bandoneon 1980, Walzer, Nelken 1982, Auf dem Gebirge hat Man ein Geschrei gehört 1984, Two Cigarettes in the Dark 1985, Viktor 1986, Ahnen 1987, Die Klage der Kaiserin, Palermo, Palermo 1989, Tanzabend II 1991, Das Stück mit dem Schiff 1993, Ein Trauerspiel 1994, Danzón 1995, Nur Du 1996, Der Fensterputzer 1997; numerous prizes and awards; Commdr. Ordre des Arts et des Lettres (France), Cruz da Ordem Militar de Santiago de Espada (Portugal), Pour le Mérite Orden, Bundesverdienstkreuz mit Stern. *Address:* Tanztheater Wuppertal, Spinnstr. 4, 42283 Wuppertal, Germany. *Telephone:* 202-5634253. *Fax:* 202-5638171.

BAUTIER, Robert-Henri; French archivist and museum curator; b. 19 April 1922, Paris; s. of the late Edgar Bautier and Suzanne Voyer; m. Anne-Marie Regnier 1948; one d.; ed. Ecole des Chartes, Sorbonne and Ecole des Hautes Etudes; archivist, Nat. Archives 1943; Head Archivist, Archives départementales de la Creuse 1944; mem. Ecole Française de Rome 1945; Keeper, Archives de France 1948; Prof. Ecole Nat. des Chartes 1961–90; Curator Musée Jacquemart-André, Chaalis Abbey 1990–; Pres. Comm. Int. de Diplomatique 1980 (then Hon. Pres.), Cttee. Historic and Scientific Works, Ministry of Nat. Educ. 1989–, Société française d'Héraldique et Sigillographie; mem. Inst. de France (Acad. des Inscriptions et Belles Lettres); Assoc. Fellow, British Acad.; Fellow, Medieval Acad. of America; Assoc. mem. Belgian Acad.; mem. Académie internationale d'Héraldique etc.; Chevalier Légion d'honneur, Officier Ordre nat. du Mérite, Commdr. des Palmes Académiques, des Arts et Lettres and other distinctions; fellow of numerous French provincial acads. and learned socs. *Publications:* numerous books and more than 300 articles in learned journals. *Address:* 13 rue de Sévigné, 75004 Paris; Les Rabuteloires, 45360 Chatillon-sur-Loire, France. *Telephone:* (01) 48.87.23.38.

BAVADRA, Adi Kuini Teimumu Vuikaba, B.A.; Fiji politician; b. 23 Dec. 1949, Ba; d. of late Senator Ratu Qoro Latianara and of Lanieta Vuni Latianara; m. 1st Dr. Timoci Bavadra, fmr. Prime Minister of Fiji (died 1989); m. 2nd Clive Speed 1991; two s. two d. and eight step-c.; ed. Suva Grammar School, Univ. of the South Pacific, Australian Nat. Univ.; rep. Fiji Public Service Asscn. women at world conf. org. by Public Service Int. 1984; Pres. Fiji Labour Party (FLP) 1989–91; lived in Australia 1991–94; stood as All Nationals Congress (ANC) cand. in gen. elections 1994, Pres. ANC (now merged with Fijian Asscn.-FA) 1994; head, official Fiji del. to World Conf. on UN End of Decade for Women, Nairobi; past Pres. Fiji Public Servants Asscn. (women's wing), Univ. of S. Pacific Alumni Asscn. *Leisure interests:* reading, Bible study, political debates, biographical documentaries of world leaders and literary figures. *Address:* General Post Office 633, Suva, Fiji. *Telephone:* 320 533. *Fax:* 320 533.

BAVARIA, Duke of, Albrecht Luitpold Ferdinand Michael; b. 3 May 1905, Munich, Germany; s. of the late Rupprecht Kronprinz von Bayern and Marie Gabriele Herzogin in Bayern; m. 1st Marie Gräfin Draskovich von Trakostjan 1930 (died 1969); m. 2nd Marie-Jenke Gräfin Keglevich von Buzin (died 1983); two s. two d.; ed. Wittelsbacher Gymnasium, Munich, Ettal monastery and Univ. of Munich; succeeded his father as head of Royal House of Bavaria (House of Wittelsbach) 1955; Hon. Senator and Dr. med. vet. h.c., Univ. of Munich. *Publications:* Über Rehe in einem Steirischen Gebirgsrevier 1975. *Address:* Schloss Nymphenburg 11, 80638 Munich, Germany. *Telephone:* 089-17 22 25.

BAVIN, Rt. Rev. Timothy John, M.A.; British ecclesiastic; b. 17 Sept. 1935, Northwood, England; s. of Edward and Marjorie Bavin; ed. St. George School, Windsor, Brighton Coll., Worcester Coll., Oxford Univ., Cuddesdon Coll.; Asst. Priest, St. Alban's Cathedral, Pretoria 1961–64; Chaplain, St. Alban's Coll., Pretoria 1964–69; Asst. Priest, Uckfield, Sussex, England 1969–71; Vicar, Church of the Good Shepherd, Brighton 1971–73; Dean of Johannesburg 1973–74, Bishop Nov. 1974–84; Bishop of Portsmouth, England 1985–95; Monk, Order of St. Benedict, Alton Abbey 1996–; mem. Oratory of the Good Shepherd 1987–95; Hon. Fellow Royal School of Church Music 1991–. *Leisure interests:* music, walking, gardening. *Address:* Alton Abbey, Alton, Hants., GU34 4AP, England.

BAWDEN, Nina Mary, C.B.E., M.A., J.P., F.R.S.L.; English novelist; b. 19 Jan. 1925, London; d. of Charles Mabey and Ellalaine Ursula May Mabey; m. 1st H. W. Bawden 1947; two s. (one deceased) one d.; m. 2nd Austen S. Kark (q.v.) 1954; two step-d.; ed. Ilford County High School, Somerville Coll., Oxford; Asst., Town and Country Planning Asscn. 1946–47; J.P., Surrey 1968; Pres. Soc. of Women Writers and Journalists 1981–; Guardian Prize for Children's Literature 1975; Yorkshire Post Novel of the Year Award 1976. *Publications:* The Birds on the Trees 1970, Anna Apparent 1972, George Beneath a Paper Moon 1974, Afternoon of a Good Woman 1976, Familiar Passions 1979, Walking Naked 1981, The Ice House 1983, Circles of Deceit 1987, Family Money 1991, In My Own Time (autobiog.) 1994; for children: Carrie's War, The Peppermint Pig, The Runaway Summer, The Finding 1985, Princess Alice 1985, Keeping Henry 1988, The Outside Child, Humbug 1992, The Real Plato Jones 1993, Granny the Pag 1995, A Nice Change 1997, Devil By The Sea 1997, Off the Road 1998. *Leisure interests:* theatre, cinema, travel, croquet. *Address:* 22 Noel Road, London, N1 8HA, England; 19 Kapodistriou, Nauplion 21100, Greece.

BAWOYEU, Jean Alingue; Chadian politician; b. 18 Aug. 1937, N'djamena; s. of Marc Alingue Bawoyeu and Tabita Poureng; m. Esther Azina 1960; three s. four d.; fmr. Pres. of Nat. Ass.; Prime Minister of Chad 1991–92; Chair. Union pour la Démocratie et la République. *Address:* B.P. 1122, N'Djamena, Chad.

BAXANDALL, Michael David Kighley, M.A., F.B.A.; British historian; b. 18 Aug. 1933, Cardiff; s. of David K. Baxandall and Sarah I.M. Thomas; m. Katharina D. Simon 1963; one s. one d.; ed. Manchester Grammar School, Downing Coll. Cambridge, and Univs. of Pavia and Munich; Asst. Keeper, Dept. of Sculpture, Victoria & Albert Museum, London 1961–65; Lecturer in Renaissance Studies, Warburg Inst. Univ. of London 1965–72, Reader in History of the Classical Tradition 1973–80, Prof. of History of the Classical Tradition 1980–81; Slade Prof. of Fine Art, Univ. of Oxford 1974–75; A.D. White Prof.-at-Large, Cornell Univ. 1982–88; Prof. of Art History, Univ. of Calif. Berkeley 1987–96, Prof. Emer. 1996–; Mitchell Prize for History of Art 1980; Prix Vasari de l'Essai Etranger 1986. *Publications:* Giotto and the Orators 1971, Painting and Experience in 15th Century Italy 1972, The Limewood Sculptors of Renaissance Germany 1980, Patterns of Intention 1985, jtly. Tiepolo and the Pictorial Intelligence 1994, Shadows and Enlightenment 1995. *Address:* 405 Doe Library, University of California, Berkeley, CA 94720, U.S.A.

BAXENDELL, Sir Peter Brian, Kt., C.B.E., B.SC., A.R.S.M., F.ENG.; British petroleum engineer; b. 28 Feb. 1925, Runcorn; s. of Lesley Wilfred Baxendell and Evelyn Gaskin; m. Rosemary Lacey 1949; two s. two d.; ed. St. Francis Xavier's Coll., Liverpool, Royal School of Mines, Imperial Coll., London; with Royal Dutch/Shell Group 1946–95; Anglo-Egyptian Oilfields 1947–50; Compañía Shell de Venezuela 1950–63; Tech. Dir. Shell-BP Nigeria 1963–66, Man. Dir. 1969–72; Shell Int. London, Eastern Region 1966–69; Chair. Shell U.K. 1973–79; Man. Dir. Royal Dutch/Shell Group 1973–85; Vice-Chair. Cttee. of Man. Dirs. 1979–82, Chair. 1982–85; Chair. Shell Transport and Trading 1979–85, Dir. 1973–95; Dir. Hawker Siddeley Group 1984–91, Chair. 1986–91; Dir. Inchcape PLC 1986–93; Dir. Sun Life Assurance Co. of Canada 1986–97; mem. Univ. Grants Cttee. 1983–89; Fellow, Imperial Coll. Science and Tech., London 1983, mem. Governing Body 1983– (Deputy Chair. 1992–); Hon. D.Sc. (Heriot-Watt) 1982, (Queen's, Belfast) 1986, (London) 1986, (Loughborough) 1987; Commdr. Order of Orange-Nassau. *Leisure interests:* fishing, tennis. *Address:* c/o Royal Dutch/Shell Group, Shell Centre, London, S.E.1, England (Office). *Telephone:* 0171-934 2772.

BAXTER, Glen; British artist; b. 4 March 1944, Leeds; s. of late Charles and of Florence Baxter; m. Carole Agis; one s. one d.; ed. Cockburn Grammar School, Leeds and Leeds Coll. of Art; has exhibited his drawings in New York, San Francisco, Venice, Amsterdam, Tokyo and Paris and represented U.K. at the Sydney Biennale 1986, Adelaide Festival 1992, Hôtel Furkablick (Switzerland) 1993; major retrospective at Musée de l'Abbaye Sainte-Croix, Les Sables d'Olonne, France 1987; illustrated Charlie Malarkey and the Belly Button Machine 1986. *Publications:* The Impending Gleam 1981, Atlas 1982 and Glen Baxter: His Life: The Years of Struggle 1983, Jodhpurs in the Quantocks 1986, Welcome to the Weird World of Glen Baxter 1989, The Billiard Table Murders, A Gladys Babbington Morton Mystery 1990, Glen Baxter Returns to Normal 1992, The Collected Blurtings of Baxter 1993,

The Further Blurtings of Baxter 1994, The Wonder Book of Sex 1995, Glen Baxter's Gourmet Guide 1997. *Leisure interests:* croquet, dozing. *Address:* c/o Aitken and Stone, 29 Fernshaw Road, London, SW10 0TG.

BAXTER, Rodney James, SC.D., F.A.A., F.R.S.; Australian professor of mathematical physics; b. 8 Feb. 1940, London, England; s. of Thomas J. Baxter and Florence Baxter; m. Elizabeth A. Phillips 1968; one s. one d.; ed. Bancroft's School, Essex, Trinity Coll., Cambridge and Australian Nat. Univ.; Reservoir Engineer, Iraq Petroleum Co. 1964–65; Research Fellow, Australian Nat. Univ. 1965–68; Asst. Prof. Mass. Inst. of Tech. 1968–70; Fellow, Australian Nat. Univ. 1971–81; Prof. Dept. of Theoretical Physics, Research School of Physical Sciences, Australian Nat. Univ. 1981–, jtly. with School of Mathematical Sciences 1989–; Royal Soc. Research Prof. Univ. of Cambridge 1992, Sr. Fellow 1992–; Pawsey Medal, Australian Acad. of Science 1975, Boltzmann Medal, Int. Union of Pure and Applied Physics 1980, Dannie Heineman Prize, American Inst. of Physics 1987, Massey Medal, Inst. of Physics 1994. *Publication:* Exactly Solved Models in Statistical Mechanics 1982, contribr. to professional journals. *Leisure interest:* theatre. *Address:* Theoretical Physics I.A.S., Australian National University, Canberra, ACT 0200, Australia.

BAYE, Nathalie; French actress; b. 6 July 1948, Mainneville; one d. by Johnny Hallyday; ed. Conservatoire nat. d'art dramatique de Paris; *stage appearances include:* Galapages 1972, Liola 1973, les Trois Soeurs 1978, Adriana Monti 1986, les Fausses Confidences 1993, la Parisienne 1995. *Films include:* Two People 1972, La nuit américaine 1973, La gueule ouverte 1974, La Gifle 1974, Un jour la fête 1974, Le Voyage de noces 1975, Le plein de super 1976, Mado 1976, L'homme qui aimait les femmes 1977, Monsieur Papa 1977, la Communion solennelle 1977, la Chambre verte 1978, Mon premier amour 1978, La Mémoire courte 1978, Sauve qui peut 1979, Je vais craquer 1979, Une semaine de vacances 1980, Provinciale 1980, Beau-père, Une étrange affaire, L'Ombre rouge and Le retour de Martin Guerre 1981, La Balance (César for Best Actress 1983) 1982, J'ai épousé une ombre 1982, Notre histoire 1983, Rive droite, rive gauche 1984, Détective 1984, Le neveu de Beethoven 1985, Lune de Miel 1985, De guerre lasse 1987, En toute innocence 1988, la Baule-les-Pins 1990, un Week-end sur deux 1990, The Man Inside 1990, L'Affaire Wallraff 1991, La Voix 1992, Mensonges 1993, La Machine 1994, Les Soldats de L'Espérance 1994. *Address:* c/o Artmédia, avenue Georges V, 75008 Paris, France.

BAYER, Oswald; German ecclesiastic and professor of theology; b. 30 Sept. 1939, Nagold; s. of Emil and Hermine Bayer; m. Eva Bayer 1966; ed. Tübingen, Bonn and Rome; Vicar, Evangelische Landeskirche, Württemberg 1964; Asst. Univ. of Tübingen 1965–68; Evangelical Stift, Tübingen 1968–71; Priest, Taebingen 1972–74; Prof. of Systematic Theology, Univ. of Bochum 1974–79, Univ. of Tübingen 1979–, Dir. Inst. of Christian Ethics 1979–95. *Publications:* several books on theological and philosophical topics. *Address:* Evangelisch-theologische Fakultät der Universität Tübingen, Liebermeisterstr. 18, 72076 Tübingen (Office); Herrlesberg 36, 72074 Tübingen, Germany (Home). *Telephone:* 07071-2972882 (Office); 07071-81897 (Home).

BAYERO, Alhaji Ado; Nigerian administrator; b. 1930, Kano; s. of Alhaji Abdullahi Bayer, Emir of Kano; m. Halimatu Sadiya; ed. Kano Middle School; clerk, Bank of W. Africa; M.P., N. House of Ass. 1955–57; Chief of Kano Native Authority Police 1957–62; Amb. to Senegal 1962–63; Emir of Kano 1963–; Chancellor, Univ. of Nigeria, Nsukka, E. Nigeria 1966–75, Chancellor Univ. of Ibadan 1975–85. *Leisure interests:* photography, riding, reading. *Address:* c/o University of Ibadan, Ibadan, Nigeria.

BAYH, Evan, B.S., J.D.; American politician; b. 26 Dec. 1955, Terre Haute, Ind.; s. of Birch Evans Bayh Jr. and Marvella Hern; m.; ed. Indiana Univ. and Univ. of Virginia; Sec. of State of Indiana 1987–89; Gov. of Indiana 1989–97; partner Baker & Daniel Assocs. Indianapolis 1997–; Senator from Indiana 1998–; Democrat. *Address:* U.S. Senate, 306 Hart Senate Office Building, Washington, DC 20510; Baker & Daniel Associates, 300 N Meridian, Suite 2700, Indianapolis, IN 46204, U.S.A.

BAYI, Filbert; Tanzanian athlete; b. 22 June 1953, Karatu, Arusha Region; s. of late Sanka Bayi and of Magdalena Qwaray; m. Anna Lyimo 1977; two s. two d.; joined Air Transport Battalion (TPDF), Dar es Salaam; beat Tanzanian Nat. Champion over 1,500 m., Dar es Salaam 1972; 1,500 m. Gold Medal Nat. Championships, Dar es Salaam 1972, All African Games, Lagos, Nigeria (record time) 1973; first competed Europe June 1973; 1,500 m. Gold Medal (world record), Commonwealth Games, Christchurch, New Zealand 1974; has competed on all five continents; Athletic Nat. Coach; Army Chief Coach ATHL; Sec. TAAA Tech. Cttee.; mem. TAAA Exec. Cttee.; IAAF Athletic Coaching Lecturer; Nat. Chief Instructor and Athletic Coach. *Leisure interests:* reading, sports, watching TV. *Address:* P.O. Box 60240, Dar es Salaam, Tanzania. *Telephone:* (051) 43961. *Fax:* (051) 43961.

BAYKAM, Bedri; Turkish painter, writer and politician; b. 26 April 1957, Ankara; s. of Suphi and Mutahhar Baykam; m. Sibel Yağci; one c.; ed. French Lycée, Istanbul, Univ. of Paris I (Panthéon-Sorbonne), France, California Coll. of Arts and Crafts, Oakland, Calif., U.S.A.; 67 solo exhbns. Paris, Brussels, Rome, New York, Istanbul, Munich, Stockholm, Helsinki, London 1963–67; mem. Cen. Bd. CHP (Republican Party of the People) 1995–98; Painter of the Year, Nokta magazine 1987, 1989, 1990, 1996–97. *Publications include:* The Brain of Paint (Boyanin Beyni) 1990, Monkey's Right to Paint 1994, Mustafa Kemal's on Duty Now 1994, Secular Turkey Without Concession 1995, Fleeting Moments, Enduring Delights 1996, His Eyes Always Rest on Us 1997, The Color of the Era 1997, The Years of 68 1998. *Leisure interests:* tennis, football, music. *Address:* Palanga Cad 33/23, Ortaköy, Istanbul 80840, Turkey. *Telephone:* 212-2584464. *Fax:* 212-2273465.

BAYLEY, John Oliver, F.B.A., M.A.; British professor of English literature; b. 27 March 1925; s. of F. J. Bayley; m. (Jean) Iris Murdoch 1956 (died 1999); ed. Eton and New Coll. Oxford; served in army 1943–47; mem. St. Antony's and Magdalen Colls. Oxford 1951–55; Fellow and Tutor in English, New Coll. Oxford 1955–74; Warton Prof. of English Literature and Fellow, St. Catherine's Coll. Oxford 1974–92. *Publications:* In Another Country (novel) 1954, The Romantic Survival: A Study in Poetic Evolution 1956, The Characters of Love 1961, Tolstoy and the Novel 1966, Pushkin: A Comparative Commentary 1971, The Uses of Division: unity and disharmony in literature 1976, An Essay on Hardy 1978, Shakespeare and Tragedy 1981, The Order of Battle at Trafalgar 1987, The Short Story: Henry James to Elizabeth Bowen 1988, Housman's Poems 1992, Alice (novel) 1994, The Queer Captain (novel) 1995, George's Lair (novel) 1996, The Red Hat 1997. *Address:* c/o St. Catherine's College, Oxford, England.

BAYLEY, Stephen, M.A.; British design consultant, writer, exhibition organiser and museum administrator; b. 13 Oct. 1951, Cardiff; s. of Donald Bayley and Anne Bayley; m. Flo Fothergill 1981; one s. one d.; ed. Quarry Bank School, Liverpool, Manchester Univ., Liverpool School of Architecture; Lecturer in History of Art, The Open Univ. 1974–76, Univ. of Kent 1976–80; Dir. Conran Foundation and subsequently The Boilerhouse Project and The Design Museum 1980–90; Prin. Eye-Q Ltd. (design consultancy) 1991–; Creative Dir. New Millennium Experience Co. 1997–98 (resgnd.); lectured throughout the U.K. and abroad; Periodical Publrs. Asscn. Magazine, Columnist of the Year 1995; Chevalier des Arts et des Lettres (France). *Publications include:* In Good Shape 1979, The Albert Memorial 1981, Harley Earl and the Dream Machine 1983, Conran Directory of Design 1985, Sex, Drink and Fast Cars 1986, Commerce and Culture 1989, Taste 1991, General Knowledge 1996; contribs. to newspapers and magazines; numerous exhbn. catalogues. *Leisure interests:* travel-related services, solitary sports, books. *Address:* 74 Fentiman Road, London, SW8 1LA, England. *Telephone:* 0171-820 8899.

BAYM, Gordon Alan, A.M., PH.D.; American physicist and educator; b. 1 July 1935, New York; s. of Louis and Lillian Baym; two s. two d.; ed. Cornell Univ., Harvard Univ.; Fellow, Universitetets Institut for Teoretisk Fysik, Copenhagen 1960–62; Lecturer, Univ. of Calif., Berkeley 1962–63; Prof. of Physics, Univ. of Ill., Urbana 1963–; Visiting Prof., Univs. of Tokyo and Kyoto 1968, Nordita, Copenhagen 1970, 1976, Niels Bohr Inst. 1976, Univ. of Nagoya 1979; Visiting Scientist, Academia Sinica, Beijing 1979; mem. Advisory Bd. Inst. of Theoretical Physics, Santa Barbara, Calif. 1978–83; mem. sub-cttee. on theoretical physics, physics advisory cttee., Nat. Scientific Foundation (NSF) 1980–81, mem. Physics Advisory Cttee. 1982–85; mem. Nuclear Science Advisory Cttee., Dept. of Energy/NSF 1982–86; mem. Ed. bd. Procs. N.A.S. 1986–92; Trustee Assoc. Univ. Inc. 1986–90; Fellow, A.A.A.S., American Acad. of Arts and Sciences, American Physical Soc.; Research Fellow, Alfred P. Sloan Foundation 1965–68; NSF postdoctoral fellow 1960–62; Trustee, Assoc. Univs. Inc. 1986–90; Assoc. Ed. Nuclear Physics; mem. American Astronomical Soc., Int. Astronomical Union, N.A.S.; Sr. U.S. Scientist Award, Alexander von Humboldt Foundation 1983. *Publications:* Quantum Statistical Mechanics (jt. author) 1962, Lectures on Quantum Mechanics 1969, Neutron Stars 1970, Neutron Stars and the Properties of Matter at High Density 1977, Landau Fermi-Liquid Theory (jtly.) 1991. *Leisure interests:* photography and mountains. *Address:* Loomis Laboratory of Physics, University of Illinois, 1110 West Green Street, Urbana, IL 61801, U.S.A. *Telephone:* (217) 333-4363. *Fax:* (217) 333-9819.

BAYNE, Sir Nicholas Peter, K.C.M.G., M.A., D.PHIL.; British diplomatist (retd.); b. 15 Feb. 1937, London; s. of the late Capt. Ronald Bayne, R.N. and of Elizabeth (née Ashcroft) Bayne; m. Diana Wilde 1961; three s. (one deceased); ed. Eton Coll. and Christ Church, Oxford; joined H.M. Diplomatic Service 1961; served Manila 1963–66, Bonn 1969–72; seconded to H.M. Treasury 1974–75; Financial Counsellor, Paris 1975–79; Head of Econ. Relations Dept., FCO 1979–82; Royal Inst. of Int. Affairs 1982–83; Amb. to Zaire, also accred. to Congo, Rwanda, Burundi 1983–84; Amb. and Perm. Rep. to OECD 1985–88; Deputy Under-Sec. of State, FCO 1988–92; High Commr. in Canada 1992–96; Visiting Fellow, L.S.E. 1997–. *Publication:* Hanging Together: the Seven-Power Summits (with R. Putnam) 1984. *Leisure interests:* reading, sightseeing. *Address:* 2 Chetwynd House, Hampton Court, Surrey, KT8 9BS, England.

BAYROU, François; French politician; b. 25 May 1951, Bordères, Basses-Pyrénées; s. of Calixte Bayrou and Emma Sarthou; m. Elisabeth Perlant; three s. three d.; ed. Lycée de Nay-Bourdettes, Lycée Montaigne, Bordeaux and Univ. of Bordeaux III; Prof. Pau 1974–79; special attachment to Office of Minister of Agric. 1979; Ed.-in-Chief, Démocratie Moderne (weekly) 1980–; Nat. Sec. Centre des Démocrates Sociaux (now Force démocrate) 1980–86, Deputy Sec.-Gen. 1986–94, Pres. 1994–; Conseiller Gen. Pau 1982; Pres. Conseil Gen. des Pyrénées-Atlantiques 1992–; Conseiller Régional, Aquitaine 1982–86; Town Councillor, Pau 1983–; Adviser to Pierre Pflimlin (Pres. of Ass. of EC) 1984–86; Deputy to Nat. Ass. 1986–93; Gen. Del. Union pour la Démocratie Française (UDF) 1989–91, Sec. Gen. 1991–94; Minister of Nat. Educ. 1993–95, also of Higher Educ., Research and Professional Training

1995–97; Pres. Parti Populaire Européenne 1996–. *Publication:* 1990–2000, la Décennie des mal-appris 1990, Henri IV, le roi libre 1994, le Droit au sens 1996. *Address:* Assemblée nationale, 75355 Paris; Force démocrate, 133 bis rue de l'Université, 75007 Paris; Conseil général des Pyrénées-Atlantiques, 2 rue du Maréchal Joffre, BP 1615, 64016 Pau cedex; 27 rue Duboué, 64000 Pau, France (Home).

BAYÜLKEN, Ümit Halûk; Turkish diplomatist; b. 7 July 1921, Istanbul; s. of Staff Officer H. Hüsnü Bayülken and Melek Bayülken; m. Valihe Salci 1952; one s. one d.; ed. Lycée of Haydarpasa, Istanbul, and Univ. of Ankara (Political Sciences); Ministry of Foreign Affairs 1944–; Reserve Officer in Army 1945–47; Vice-Consul, Frankfurt (Main) 1947–49; First Sec., Bonn 1950–51; Ministry of Foreign Affairs 1951–53; First Sec. Turkish Perm. Mission to UN 1953–57, Counsellor 1957–59; Turkish Rep. to London Joint Cttee. on Cyprus 1959–60; Dir.-Gen., Policy Planning Group, Ankara 1960–63, Deputy Sec.-Gen. for Political Affairs 1963–64, Sec.-Gen. 1964–66; Amb. to U.K. 1966–69, concurrently accred. to Malta May 1968–July 1969; Perm. Rep. of Turkey to UN 1969–71; Minister of Foreign Affairs 1971–74; Sec.-Gen. CENTO 1975–77; Sec.-Gen. of the Presidency 1977–80; Minister of Defence 1980–83; M.P. from Antalya 1983–87; Pres. Atlantic Treaty Asscn. (Turkey) 1987–90; Pres. of Turkish Parl. Union 1992–; Hon. G.C.V.O. (U.K.), Order of Isabel la Católica (Spain), Grosses Bundesverdienstkreuz (Fed. Repub. of Germany), numerous other int. awards; Hon. mem. Mexican Acad. Int. Law, etc. *Publications:* lectures, articles, studies and essays on minorities, Cyprus, principles of foreign policy, int. relations and disputes, including the Cyprus Question in the UN 1975, Collective Security and Defence Organizations in Changing World Conditions 1976, Turkey and the Regional Security Interests 1991. *Leisure interests:* music, painting, reading. *Address:* Nergiz Sokak no. 15/20, Cankaya, Ankara, Turkey. *Telephone:* 127-0858.

BAZ, Farouk El-, PH.D; Egyptian/American scientist; b. 1 Jan. 1938, Zagazig; s. of late El-Sayed El-Baz and of Zahia Hammouda; m. Catherine Patricia O'Leary 1963; four d.; ed. Ain Shams Univ., Cairo, Assiut Univ., Missouri School of Mines and Metallurgy, Univ. of Missouri, Massachusetts Inst. of Tech., Heidelberg Univ., Germany; demonstrator, Geology Dept., Assiut Univ. 1958–60; lecturer, Mineralogy-Petrography Inst., Univ. of Heidelberg 1964–65; exploration geologist, Pan-American UAR Oil Co., Cairo 1966; Supervisor, Lunar Science Planning and Operations, BellComm, Bell Telephone Labs., Washington, D.C. for Apollo Program Dir., NASA 1967–72; Research Dir., Center for Earth and Planetary Studies, Nat. Air and Space Museum, Smithsonian Inst., Washington, D.C. 1973–82; Science Adviser to Pres. Anwar Sadat of Egypt 1978–81; Vice-Pres. for Science and Tech. and for Int. Devt., Itek Optical Systems, Lexington, Mass. 1982–86; Dir. Center for Remote Sensing, Boston Univ. 1986–; pioneering work in applications of space photography to understanding of arid terrain; Pres. Arab Soc. of Desert Research; numerous honours and awards, including NASA Apollo Achievement Award, Exceptional Scientific Achievement Medal and Special Recognition Award, Award for Public Understanding of Science and Tech., A.A.A.S. 1992; Order of Merit (First Class), Egypt. *Publications:* Say it in Arabic 1968, Astronaut Observations from the Apollo-Soyuz Mission 1977, Egypt as seen by Landsat 1979, Desert Landforms of Southwest Egypt 1982, Deserts and Arid Lands 1984, The Geology of Egypt 1984, Physics of Desertification 1986, The Gulf War and the Environment 1994. *Leisure interests:* reading history, travel, swimming. *Address:* Center for Remote Sensing, Boston University, Boston, MA 02215, U.S.A. *Telephone:* (617) 353-5081. *Fax:* (617) 353-3200.

BAZAINE, Jean, L. ÈS L.; French painter; b. 21 Dec. 1904, Paris; s. of Léon Bazaine and Clémence Temblaire; executed stained glass windows for church at Assy 1946, at Saint Séverin, Paris 1966, Villeparisis 1958, Ste Roseline (Les Arcs) 1970, Berlens (Switzerland) 1979, La Madeleine (Brittany) 1981, cathedral of St Dié (Vosges) 1986; ceramic mural and windows at Audincourt 1951–54, ceramic mural at UNESCO 1960, and Maison de la Radio, Paris 1963, Sénat (Palais de Luxembourg, Paris) 1988, Cluny metro 1988, church at Concarneau (Brittany) 1996; exhibited Galerie Carré, Galerie Maeght, Paris; retrospective exhbns., Berne 1958, Eindhoven 1959, Hanover 1963, Zürich 1963, Oslo 1963, Paris 1965, Grand Palais, Paris 1990, Halmstad, Sweden 1992, Charlottenborg, Denmark 1992; rep. at Biennali of Venice, São Paulo, Carnegie, Grand Palais, Paris; Grand Prix Nat. des Arts 1964; Commdr. Ordre des Arts et des Lettres 1979; paintings in most of the leading museums in U.S.A. and Europe. *Publications:* Notes sur la peinture d'aujourd'hui 1948, Exercice de la peinture 1973, Le Temps de la Peinture 1990. *Address:* Galerie Louis Carré et Cie, 10 avenue de Messine, 75008 Paris (Office); 36 rue Pierre Brossolette, 92140 Clamart, France (Home).

BAZIN, Marc Louis, L. EN D.; Haitian politician; b. 6 March 1932, Saint-Marc; s. of Louis Bazin and Simone St. Vil; m. Marie Yolène Sam 1981; ed. Lycée Petion, Port-au-Prince, Univ. of Paris, Solvay Inst. Brussels and American Univ. Washington, D.C.; Admin. Asst. Ministry of Foreign Affairs 1950; Prof. of Civic Educ. Lycée Petion, Haiti 1951; Legal Adviser, Cabinet Rivière (real estate agency), Paris 1958; Lecturer in Commercial Law, Paris 1960; Tech. Adviser, Treasury Dept., Rabat, Morocco 1962, Deputy Gen. Counsel 1964; Technical Adviser, Ministry of Finance, Rabat 1965; Sr. Loan Officer, IBRD, Washington, D.C. 1968; Deputy Chief IBRD Mission in West Africa, Ivory Coast 1970; Div. Chief, IBRD, Washington, D.C. 1972; Dir. Riverblindness Program, WHO, Upper Volta 1976; Man. Dir. Industrial Devt. Fund, Port-au-Prince 1980; Minister of Finance and Econ. Affairs 1982; Special rep. of IBRD at UN 1982; Div. Chief for int. orgs. IBRD 1986; Pres. Mouvement pour l'Instauration de la Démocratie en Haiti (MIDH) allied with ANDP 1986–; Prime Minister of Haiti 1992–93; Officer, Order of the Ouissam Alaouite (Morocco); Knight of Nat. Order of Merit (Burkina Faso). *Address:* 114 ave Jean Paul II, Port-au-Prince, Haiti.

BEALE, Geoffrey Herbert, M.B.E., PH.D., F.R.S., F.R.S.E.; British research scientist; b. 11 June 1913, London; s. of Herbert Walter and Elsie Beale; m. Betty Brydon McCallum 1949 (dissolved 1969); three s.; ed. Imperial Coll., Univ. of London; mem. Research Staff, John Innes Horticultural Inst. 1935–40; Intelligence Corps (war service) 1940–45; with Carnegie Inst., Cold Spring Harbor, New York 1946–47; Rockefeller Fellow, Indiana Univ. 1947–48; Lecturer in Genetics, Edinburgh Univ. 1948–63, Royal Soc. Research Prof. 1963–78, Hon. Research Prof. 1978–; Visiting Research Worker, Chulalongkorn Univ., Bangkok. *Publications:* Genetics of Paramecium aurelia 1954, Extranuclear Genetics (with Jonathan Knowles) 1978, Malaria Parasites (with Sodsri Thaithong) 1992. *Leisure interests:* music, languages. *Address:* 23 Royal Terrace, Edinburgh, EH7 5AH, Scotland. *Telephone:* (0131) 557-1329.

BEALES, Derek Edward Dawson, LITT.D., F.B.A.; British professor of history; b. 12 June 1931, Felixstowe; s. of the late Edward Beales and Dorothy K. Dawson; m. Sara J. Ledbury 1964; one s. one d.; ed. Bishop's Stortford Coll. and Sidney Sussex Coll. Cambridge; Research Fellow, Sidney Sussex Coll. Cambridge 1955–58, Fellow 1958–; Asst. Lecturer in History, Univ. of Cambridge 1962–65, Lecturer 1965–80, Prof. of Modern History 1980–97; Prof. Emer. 1997–; Stenton Lecturer, Univ. of Reading 1992, Birkbeck Lecturer, Trinity Coll., Cambridge 1993; Recurring Visiting Prof., Cen. European Univ., Budapest 1995–; Ed. Historical Journal 1971–75; mem. Standing Cttee. for Humanities, European Science Foundation. *Publications:* England and Italy 1859–60 1961, From Castlereagh to Gladstone 1969, The Risorgimento and the Unification of Italy 1971, History and Biography 1981, History, Society and the Churches (with G. Best) 1985, Joseph II, Vol. I: In the Shadow of Maria Theresa 1987, Mozart and the Habsburgs 1993, Sidney Sussex Quatercentenary Essays (with H. B. Nisbet) 1996; numerous articles. *Leisure interests:* music, walking, bridge. *Address:* Sidney Sussex College, Cambridge, England. *Telephone:* (01223) 338800.

BEALL, Donald Ray, B.S., M.B.A.; American business executive; b. 29 Nov. 1938, Beaumont, Calif.; s. of Ray C. Beall and Margaret (née Murray) Beall; m. Joan Frances Lange 1961; two s.; ed. San Jose State Coll. and Univ. of Pittsburgh; various financial and management positions, Ford Motor Co., Newport Beach, Calif., Philadelphia and Palo Alto, Calif. 1961–68; Exec. Dir. Corporate Financial Planning, Rockwell Int., El Segundo, Calif. 1968–69, Exec. Vice-Pres. Electronics Group 1969–71; Exec. Vice-Pres. Collins Radio Co., Dallas 1971–74; Pres. Collins Radio Group, Dallas, Rockwell Int. 1974–76, Pres. Electronics Operations 1976–77, Exec. Vice-Pres. 1977–79; Pres. Rockwell Int. 1979–88, C.O.O. 1979–88, Chair., C.E.O. Feb. 1988–98, C.E.O. 1988–97, now Chair. Exec. Cttee.; mem. Pres.'s Export Council 1981–85; mem. bd. overseers Univ. of Calif. Irvine 1988–. *Leisure interests:* tennis and boating. *Address:* Rockwell International Corporation, Suite 700, 600 Anton Boulevard, Costa Mesa, CA 92628, U.S.A.

BEAN, Sean; British actor; b. 17 April 1958, Sheffield, Yorks.; m. 2nd Melanie Hill; ed. Royal Acad. of Dramatic Art; professional debut as Tybalt in Romeo and Juliet, Watermill Theatre, Newbury; other stage appearances include: The Last Days of Mankind and Der Rosenkavalier at Citizens' Theatre, Glasgow, Who Knew Mackenzie? and Gone, Theatre Upstairs, Royal Court, Romeo in Romeo and Juliet, RSC, Stratford-upon-Avon 1986, Captain Spencer in The Fair Maid of the West, RSC, London; TV appearances include Clarissa, Fool's Gold and role of Mellors in BBC dramatization of Lady Chatterley's Lover, role of Sharpe in TV series. *Films:* Caravaggio, Stormy Monday, War Requiem, The Field, Patriot Games, Gone With The Wind, Goldeneye, When Saturday Comes, Anna Karenina, Ronin. *Address:* c/o ICM Ltd., Oxford House, London, W1R 1RB, England.

BEARN, Alexander Gordon, M.D., F.A.C.P.; American (b. British) pharmaceutical executive and professor of medicine; b. 29 March 1923, Cheam, England; s. of Edward Gordon Bearn; m. Margaret Slocum 1952; one s. one d.; ed. Epsom Coll. and Guy's Hospital, Univ. of London; Postgraduate Medical School, London 1949–51; Asst. to Prof., Rockefeller Univ., New York, U.S.A. 1951–64, Prof. 1964–66, Adjunct Prof., Visiting Physician 1966–; Prof. and Chair. Dept. of Medicine, Cornell Univ. Medical Coll. 1966–77; Physician-in-Chief New York Hosp. 1966–77; Stanton Griffis Distinguished Medical Prof. 1976–80; Prof. of Medicine, Cornell Univ. Medical Coll. 1966–89, Prof. Emer. 1989–; Sr. Vice-Pres., Medical and Scientific Affairs, Merck Sharp & Dohme Int. 1979–88; mem. Council Fogarty Centre, Nat. Insts. Health 1990–; mem. N.A.S., American Philosophical Soc.; Pres. American Soc. of Human Genetics 1971; Lowell Lecture, Harvard Univ. 1958; Alfred Benzon Prize (Denmark); Hon. M.D. (Catholic Univ., Korea), Dr. h.c. (René Descartes, Paris). *Publications:* Progress in Medical Genetics (Ed.) 1962–87, Cecil Loeb Textbook of Medicine (Assoc. Ed.) 1963, 1967, 1971, 1975, numerous articles in medical and scientific journals. *Leisure interest:* aristology. *Address:* The Rockefeller University, 1230 York Avenue, New York, NY 10021 (Office); 241 South 6th Street, #2111, Philadelphia, PA 19106, U.S.A. (Home). *Telephone:* (212) 570-7920 (Office).

BÉART, Emmanuelle; French actress; b. 14 Aug. 1965, Gassin; d. of Guy Béart (q.v.); one d. by Daniel Auteuil (q.v.); ed. drama school; began acting career with appearance as a child in Demain les Momes 1978. *Films:* Un Amour Interdit, L'Enfant Trouvé 1983, L'Amour en Douce 1984, Manon des Sources 1985, Date with Angel 1987, A Gauche en Sortant de l'Ascenseur 1988, Les Enfants du Désordre 1989, Capitaine Fracasse 1990, La Belle Noiseuse 1991, J'embrasse Pas 1991, Un Coeur en Hiver 1991, Ruptures 1992, L'Enfer 1993, Mission Impossible 1995, Nelly and M. Arnaud 1995.

BÉART, Guy; French singer, composer, engineer and author; b. 16 July 1930, Cairo, Egypt; s. of David Behart-Hasson and Amélia Taral; one s. one d.; ed. Lycée Henri IV, Paris and Ecole Nat. des Ponts et des Chaussées; music transcriber, Prof. of Math., then Eng. 1952–57; subsequently made début in cabaret in Paris; composed songs for Zizi Jeanmaire, Juliette Greco, Patachou, Maurice Chevalier, etc.; recitalist in various Paris theatres and music-halls; composer of more than 200 songs, also film music (including L'Eau vive, Pierrot la tendresse and La Gamberge); author and producer of TV series Bienvenue 1966–72; Chevalier, Légion d'honneur, Officier, Ordre Nat. du Mérite, Commdr. des Arts et des Lettres; Grand Prix, Acad. du Disque 1957, Grand Prix du Disque, Acad. Charles Cros 1965, Grand prix de la chanson Sacem 1987; Prix Balzac 1987; Grand Médaille de la Chanson française (Académie Française) 1994. *Leisure interest:* chess. *Address:* Editions Temporel, 2 rue du Marquis de Morès, 92380 Garches, France (Office).

BEASLEY, David Muldrow, J.D.; American politician; b. 26 Feb. 1957, Lamar, S.C.; s. of Richard L. Beasley and Jacqueline A. Blackwell; m. Mary Wood Payne; ed. Clemson Univ. and Univ. of S. Carolina; practising attorney; Rep. for S.C. State, Dist. 56 1979–92; Majority Leader, S.C. House of Reps. 1987; Gov. of S. Carolina 1995–98; Republican. *Address:* c/o Office of the Governor, State House, POB 11369, Columbia, SC 29211, U.S.A.

BEATRIX, Queen of the Netherlands; **Beatrix Wilhelmina Armgard;** b. 31 Jan. 1938, Baarn; d. of Queen Juliana (q.v.) and Bernhard, Prince of the Netherlands (q.v.); succeeded to the throne on abdication of her mother 30 April 1980; m. Claus George Willem Otto Frederik Geert von Amsberg 10 March 1966; children: Prince Willem-Alexander Claus George Ferdinand, Prince of Orange, b. 27 April 1967; Prince Johan Friso Bernhard Christiaan David, b. 25 Sept. 1968; Prince Constantijn Christof Frederik Aschwin, b. 11 Oct. 1969; ed. Baarn Grammar School, Leiden State Univ.; Hon. K.G. *Address:* c/o Government Information Service, Press and Publicity Department, Binnenhof 19, 2513 AA The Hague, Netherlands. *Telephone:* 070-3564136.

BEATSON, Jack; British professor of law and barrister; b. 3 Nov. 1948, Haifa, Israel; s. of late John James Beatson and Miriam White; m. Charlotte H. Christie-Miller 1973; one s. one d.; ed. Whittingehame Coll. Brighton and Brasenose Coll. Oxford; lecturer in Law, Univ. of Bristol 1972–73; Fellow and Tutor in Law, Merton Coll. Oxford 1973–93, Hon. Fellow 1994–; Rouse Ball Prof. of Law, Univ. of Cambridge 1993–; Fellow, St. John's Coll. Cambridge 1994–; Dir. Centre for Public Law, Cambridge 1997–; Visiting Prof. Osgoode Hall Law School, Toronto 1979, Univ. of Va. Law School 1980, 1983; Sr. Visiting Fellow, Nat. Univ. of Singapore 1987; Law Commr. for England and Wales 1989–94; Recorder of Crown Court 1994–; mem. Monopolies and Mergers Comm. 1995–; Hon. Bencher, Inner Temple. *Publications:* Administrative Law: Cases and Materials (with M. Matthews), The Use and Abuse of Restitution 1991; Jt. Ed. Chitty on Contracts (27th edn. 1994), Good Faith and Fault in Contract Law 1995, Jt. Ed. European Public Law 1998. *Leisure interests:* gardening, travelling. *Address:* St. John's College, Cambridge, CB2 1TP, England.

BEATTIE, Ann, M.A.; American author; b. 8 Sept. 1947, Washington; d. of James Beattie and Charlotte Crosby; m. Lincoln Perry; ed. American Univ. and Univ. of Connecticut; Visiting Asst. Prof. Univ. of Va., Charlottesville 1976–77, Visiting Writer 1980; Briggs Copeland lecturer in English, Harvard Univ. 1977; Guggenheim Fellow 1977; mem. American Acad. and Inst. of Arts and Letters (Award in literature 1980), PEN, Authors' Guild; Hon. L.H.D. (American Univ.). *Publications:* Chilly Scenes of Winter 1976, Distortions 1976, Secrets and Surprises 1979, Falling in Place 1990, Jacklighting 1981, The Burning House 1982, Love Always 1985, Where You'll Find Me 1986, Alex Katz (art criticism) 1987, Picturing Will 1990, What Was Mine (story collection) 1991, My Life Starring Dara Falcon 1997. *Address:* c/o Janklow & Nesbit, 598 Madison Avenue, New York, NY 10022, U.S.A.

BEATTIE, Hon. Sir David Stuart, G.C.M.G., G.C.V.O., Q.C., Q.S.O., LL.D.; New Zealand administrator and lawyer; b. 29 Feb. 1924, Sydney, Australia; s. of Joseph Nesbitt Beattie and Una Mary Beattie; m. Norma Macdonald 1950; three s. four d.; ed. Dilworth School and Univ.; Naval Officer, Second World War; barrister and solicitor; Judge of Supreme Court 1969–80; Gov.-Gen. of New Zealand 1980–85; Chair. N.Z. Int. Festival of the Arts 1987–; Chair. N.Z. Meat Industry Asscn. Inc. 1988–; Commr. to examine Fijian courts and judicial system 1993–94; Pres. Auckland District Law Soc. 1964; N.Z. Services rugby 1944–45; Chair. Royal Comm. on Courts 1977–79, Winston Churchill Trust 1976–80, Admiralty Reform Cttee. 1973; Patron N.Z. Rugby Football Union 1982–96; Pres. N.Z. Olympic and Commonwealth Games Asscn. 1989; Chair. N.Z. Selection Cttee., Harkness Fellowships of New York; several directorships 1986; Olympic Order 1994. *Leisure interests:* golf, tennis, fly-fishing, music. *Address:* 18 Golf Road, Heretaunga, Upper Hutt, Wellington, New Zealand (Home).

BEATTY, Perrin, B.A.; Canadian politician; b. 1 June 1950, Toronto; s. of Martha Beatty; m. Julia Kenny 1974; two s.; ed. Upper Canada Coll., Univ. of Western Ont.; Special Asst. to Minister of Health, Ont.; mem. House of Commons 1972–; Minister of State for Treasury Bd. 1979; Minister of Nat. Revenue 1984–85; Solicitor-Gen. for Canada 1985–86, Acting Solicitor-Gen. 1989; Minister of Defence 1986–89, of Nat. Health and Welfare 1989–91, of Communications 1991–93, of External Affairs 1993; Pres. and C.E.O. Canadian Broadcasting Corpn. 1995–; mem. Special Jt. Cttee. on Constitution 1978, Chair. Progressive Conservative Caucus Cttee. on Supply and Services, Spokesperson on Communications; Co-chair. of Standing Jt. Cttee. on Regulations and other Statutory Instruments; Caucus spokesperson on Revenue Canada; Chair. of Caucus Cttee. on Fed. Prov. Relations and of Progressive Conservative Task Force on Revenue Canada 1983. *Leisure interests:* music, woodwork and reading. *Address:* CBC, 1500 Bronson, P.O. Box 8478, Ottawa, Ont., K1G 3J5, Canada.

BEATTY, Warren, American actor; b. 30 March 1937, Richmond, Virginia; s. of Ira Beatty and Kathlyn Maclean; m. Annette Bening 1992; one s. two d.; ed. Stella Adler Theatre School. *Film appearances include:* Splendor in the Grass 1961, Roman Spring of Mrs. Stone 1961, All Fall Down 1962, Lilith, 1965, Mickey One 1965, Promise Her Anything 1966, Kaleidoscope 1966, Bonnie and Clyde 1967, The Only Game in Town 1969, McCabe and Mrs. Miller 1971, Dollars 1972, The Parallax View 1974, Shampoo (producer and co-screenwriter) 1975, The Fortune 1976, Heaven Can Wait (producer, co-dir. and co-screenwriter) 1978, Reds (producer, dir., Acad. Award for Best Dir. 1981) 1981, Ishtar 1987, Dick Tracy 1989, Bugsy 1991, Love Affair, Bulworth (also dir.) 1998. *TV appearances include:* Studio One and Playhouse 90; theatre roles include: A Loss of Roses 1960, Commdr. Ordre des Arts et des Lettres. *Address:* C.A.A., 9830 Wilshire Boulevard, Beverly Hills, CA 90212, U.S.A.

BEAUCE, Thierry M. de; French government official; b. 14 Feb. 1943, Lyon; s. of Bertrand Martin de Beauce and Simone de la Verpillere; m. Diane Segard; two d.; ed. Univ. of Paris and Ecole Nat. d'Admin.; civil admin., Ministry of Cultural Affairs 1968–69; seconded to office of Prime Minister 1969–73; Tech. Adviser, Pvt. Office of Pres. of Nat. Ass. 1974; seconded to Econ. Affairs Directorate, Ministry of Foreign Affairs 1974–76; Cultural Counsellor, Japan 1976–78; Second Counsellor, Morocco 1978–80; Vice-Pres. for Int. Affairs Société Elf Aquitaine 1981–86; Dir.-Gen. of Cultural, Scientific and Tech. Relations, Ministry of Foreign Affairs 1986–87; State Sec. attached to Minister of Foreign Affairs 1988–91; Adviser to the Pres. for African Affairs 1991–94; Vice-Pres. of Conf. for Yugoslavia 1992; Amb. to Indonesia 1995–97; Dir. of Int. Affairs Vivendi (fmrly. Compagnie générale des eaux) 1997–; Deputy Pres. Asscn. of Democrats 1989–; Chevalier, Légion d'honneur. *Publications:* Les raisons dangéreuses (essay) 1975, Un homme ordinaire (novel) 1978, L'Ile absolue (essay) 1979, Le désir de guerre 1980, La chute de Tanger (novel) 1984, Nouveau discours sur l'universalité de la langue française 1988, Le livre d'Esther 1989, la République de France 1991, La Nonchalence de Dieu 1995. *Address:* Vivendi, 52 rue d'Anjou, 75008 Paris; 73 avenue Franklin Delano Roosevelt, Paris 8, France (Home).

BEAUDOIN, Gérald-A., O.C., Q.C., M.A., LL.D.; Canadian politician, lawyer and university professor; b. 15 April 1929, Montreal; s. of Armand Beaudoin and Aldéa St.-Arnaud; m. Renée Desmarais 1954; four d.; ed. Univs. of Montreal, Toronto, Ottawa; pvt. practice with Paul Gérin-Lajoie Q.C. in Montreal 1955–56; mem. Advisory Counsel, Dept. of Justice, Ottawa 1956–65; Asst. Parl. Counsel, House of Commons 1965–69; Prof. of Constitutional Law, Univ. of Ottawa 1969–89, Visiting Prof. 1989–94, Emer. Prof. 1994–, Dean of Law 1969–79, Assoc. Dir., Human Rights Center 1981–86, Dir. 1986–88; Vice-Pres. Institut de droit d'expression française 1973–; Pres. Int. Comm. of Jurists (Canadian section) 1990–92; Chair. Senate Standing Cttee. on Legal and Constitutional Affairs 1993–96; mem. Canadian Senate Sept. 1988–; mem. Pepin-Robarts Royal Comm. (Task Force on Canadian Unity) 1977–79; Co-Chair. Senate and House of Commons Jr. Cttee. on Formula of Amendment (Beaudoin-Edwards) 1991, on the Renewal of Canada (Beaudoin-Dobbie) 1991–92; mem. Académie des lettres du Québec, Royal Soc. of Canada; Titular mem. Int. Acad. of Comparative Law; Prix du doyen 1953; Medal of ACFAS 1987, Ramon John Hnatyshyn Award for Law 1997. *Publications:* Essais sur la Constitution 1979, Le partage des pouvoirs, 3rd edn. 1983, La Constitution du Canada 1990; Ed. The Supreme Court of Canada 1986, Charter Cases 1987, Your Client and the Charter 1989, As the Charter Evolves 1990, The Charter: Ten Years Later 1992; Co-Ed. Canadian Charter of Rights and Freedoms 1982, Perspectives canadiennes et européennes des droits de la personne 1986, 1989; over 100 articles on the Canadian Constitution. *Leisure interests:* reading, travels. *Address:* Senate Bldg., Centre Block, Room 474-F, Ottawa, Ont., K1A 0A4 (Office); Faculty of Law, Civil Law Section, 57 Louis Pasteur, University of Ottawa, Ottawa, Ont., K1N 6N5 (Office); 4 St.-Thomas, Hull, Quebec, J8Y 1L4, Canada (Home). *Telephone:* (613) 995-6128 (Office); (819) 771-4742 (Home). *Fax:* (613) 943-0685.

BEAUMONT, (John) Michael; Seigneur of Sark and engineer (retd.); b. 20 Dec. 1927, Egypt; s. of the late Lionel Beaumont and Enid Beaumont (née Ripley); m. Diana La Trobe-Bateman 1956; two s.; ed. Loughborough Coll.; chief stress engineer Beagle Aircraft 1965–69, chief tech. engineer 1969–70; sr. engineer guided weapons, Filton 1970–74; inherited Fief of Sark 1974. *Leisure interests:* theatre, music, gardening. *Address:* La Seigneurie de Sark, Channel Islands, GY9 0SF. *Telephone:* (01481) 832017. *Fax:* (01481) 832628.

BEAUMONT, Lady Mary Rose, B.A.; British art historian; b. 6 June 1932, Petersfield; d. of Charles Edward Wauchope and Elaine Margaret

Armstrong-Jones; m. Lord Beaumont of Whitley, The Rev. Timothy Wentworth Beaumont 1955; one s. two d.; ed. Prior's Field School, Godalming, Surrey, Courtauld Inst. of Fine Art, Univ. of London; art critic for Art Review 1978–96; lecturer in Modern Art for Christies' Educ. 1978–; exhbn. curator for British Council in E. Europe and Far East 1983–87; exhbn. curator The Human Touch, Fischer Fine Art Gallery 1986, The Dark Side of the Moon, Rhodes Gallery 1990, Three Scottish Artists, Pamela Auchincloss Gallery, New York 1990; Picker Fellow Kingston Polytechnic 1986–87; lecturer in Humanities Dept. City & Guilds School of Art 1996–; mem. Exec. Cttee. of Contemporary Art Soc. 1979–89. *Publications include:* An American Passion: The Susan Kasen Summer and Robert D. Summer Collection of Contemporary British Painting (contrib. artists' profiles) 1995, Open Studio: Derek Healey 1997, Jean MacAlpine: Intervals in Light 1998. *Leisure interests:* reading novels, listening to opera. *Address:* 40 Elms Road, London, SW4 9EX, England. *Telephone:* 0171-498 8664. *Fax:* 0171-498 8664.

BEAVEN, Peter Jamieson, DIP.ARCH., A.R.I.B.A., F.N.Z.I.A.; New Zealand architect; b. 13 Aug. 1925, Christchurch; s. of Eric Tamate Beaven and Maria Joan Jamieson; m. Anne Mary Beaglehole 1952; one s. two d.; ed. Christ's Coll., Christchurch, Univ. Coll., Auckland; Sub-Lieut. Royal Naval Volunteer Reserve, Far East; practised in Christchurch for twenty years; founded first N.Z. Civic Trust; Chair. Environment Advisory Cttee., Christchurch City Council; Principal, Beaven Hunt Assocs.; Gold Medal, N.Z. Inst. of Architects 1966, various merit awards in N.Z. architecture. *Leisure interests:* yachting, sketching, painting, walking, reading. *Publications:* Urban Renewal Report (N.Z. Govt.), co-author New Zealand Architecture 1840-1970 1973. *Address:* Beaven Hunt Associates, P.O. Box 1766, Christchurch (Office); 22 Salisbury Street, Christchurch 1, New Zealand (Home).

BEAZLEY, Kim Christian, M.A., M.PHIL.; Australian politician; b. 14 Dec. 1948, Perth; s. of Kim Edward Beazley; m. 1st Mary Beazley 1974 (divorced 1989); two d.; m. 2nd Susannah Beazley 1990; one d.; ed. Univ. of Western Australia, Oxford Univ.; fmr. Lecturer in Social and Political Theory, Murdoch Univ. Perth; M.P. for Swan 1980–96, for Brand 1996–; Minister for Aviation 1983–84, for Defence Dec. 1984–90; for Transport and Communications 1990–91, of Finance 1991, of Employment, Education and Training 1991–93, of Finance 1993–96; Deputy Prime Minister 1995–96; Special Minister of State 1983–84; Leader of the House 1988–96; Leader of Labor Party March 1996–. *Address:* c/o ALP, Centenary House, 19 National Circuit, Barton, ACT 2600, Australia.

BEBEAR, Claude; French businessman; b. 29 July 1935, Issac; s. of André Bebear and Simone (née Veyssière); m. Catherine Dessagne 1957; one s. two d.; ed. Lycées of Périgueux and St. Louis, Paris; joined Ancienne Mutuelle 1958, Dir. Gen. 1975; Dir.-Gen., Pres. AXA 1982–, AXA-UAP 1997–, Chair. 1996–; Dir.-Gen. Finaxa; numerous directorships; Hon. Pres. Inst. des Actuaires Français 1989–; Chevalier, Légion d'honneur, Officier, Ordre Nat. du Mérite. *Address:* AXA, 21–23 avenue Matignon, 75008 Paris, France. *Telephone:* 40 75 5700.

BECERRA BARNEY, Manuel Francisco; Colombian politician and lawyer; b. 22 Nov. 1951; m.; two s. one d.; ed. Instituto La Salle, Bogotá and Externado de Colombia, Bogotá; Prof. at Univ. Javeriana, Bogotá; Pres. of Colombian Del. to Ibero-American Parl., Madrid; Gov. of Valle Prov. 1986–88; Minister of Educ. 1988–90; mem. of Peace Verification Comm.; Pres. of Educative Cttee. for Nat. Peace Dialogue. *Publications include:* The Exorbitant Clause in Administrative Contracts. *Address:* c/o Ministry of Education, Centro Administrativo Nacional, Of. 501, Avda Eldorado, Santa Fe de Bogotá, Colombia.

BECHERER, Hans Walter, M.B.A.; American business executive; b. 19 April 1935, Detroit, Mich.; s. of Max Becherer and Mariele Specht; m. Michele Beigbeder 1959; one s. (deceased) one d.; ed. Trinity Coll., Hartford, Conn. and Munich and Harvard Univs.; Exec. Asst. Office of Chair. Deere & Co., Moline, Ill. 1966–69; Gen. Man. John Deere Export, Mannheim, Germany 1969–73; Dir. Export Marketing, Deere & Co., Moline, Ill. 1973–77, Vice-Pres. 1977–83, Sr. Vice-Pres. 1983–86, Exec. Vice-Pres. 1986–87, Pres. 1987–90, C.O.O. 1987–89, C.E.O. 1989–, Chair. 1990–; Dir. Schering-Plough Corpn. 1989–, Allied Signal Inc. 1991–, Chase Manhattan Corpn. and Chase Manhattan Bank 1998; mem. The Business Roundtable, Chase Manhattan Bank Int. Advisory Cttee. 1990–98, The Business Council 1992–; Trustee Cttee. for Econ. Devt. 1990. *Address:* Deere & Company, One John Deere Place, Moline, IL 61265 (Office). *Telephone:* 309-765-4116 (Office).

BECHERT, Heinz, D.PHIL.; German professor of Indology; b. 26 June 1932, Munich; s. of Rudolf Bechert and Herta Bechert; m. Marianne Würzburger 1963; ed. Univs. of Munich and Hamburg; Research Asst. Univ. of Saarbrücken 1956–61; Univ. of Mainz 1961–64; Prof. of Indology Univ. of Göttingen 1965–; Visiting Prof. Yale Univ. 1969–70, 1974–75; Research Fellow Japan Soc. for the Promotion of Science 1990; mem. Akademie der Wissenschaften in Göttingen 1968, Académie Royale de Belgique 1973, Royal Swedish Acad. of Literature, History and Antiquities 1988, Acad. Europaea 1989. *Publications:* author and editor of 30 books and 210 contribs. in academic journals. *Address:* Hermann-Föge-Weg 1a, 37073 Göttingen, Germany. *Telephone:* (551) 485765.

BECK, Béatrix Marie; Swiss writer; b. 30 July 1914; ed. Lycée de St. Germain-en-Laye and Université de Grenoble; fmr. Sec. to André Gide; journalist; mem. Jury, Prix Fémina; Prix Goncourt for Léon Morin, prêtre; Prix Félix Fénéon; Prix Fondation Delmas 1979. *Publications:* Barny, Une mort irrégulière, Léon Morin, prêtre, Des accommodements avec le ciel, Le premier mai, Abram Krol, Le muet, Cou coupé court toujours.

BECK, Brian Edgar, M.A., D.D.; British ecclesiastic; b. 27 Sept. 1933, London; s. of late A. G. Beck and C. A. Beck; m. Margaret Ludlow 1958; three d.; ed. City of London School, Corpus Christi Coll., Cambridge and Wesley House, Cambridge; Asst. Tutor Handsworth Coll. 1957–59; ordained Methodist Minister 1960; Circuit Minister, Suffolk 1959–62; St. Paul's United Theological Coll., Limuru, Kenya 1962–68; Tutor Wesley House, Cambridge 1968–80, Prin. 1980–84; Sec. Methodist Conf. of G.B. 1984–98, Pres. 1993–94; Co.-Chair. Oxford Inst. of Methodist Theological Studies 1976–; Sec. E. African Church Union Consultation Worship and Liturgy Cttee. 1963–68; mem. World Methodist Council 1966–71, 1981–98. *Publications:* Reading the New Testament Today 1977, Christian Character in the Gospel of Luke 1989, Community-Unity-Communion 1998, Rethinking Wesley's Theology 1998, (contrib. to) Christian Belief, A Catholic-Methodist Statement 1970, Unity the Next Step? 1972, Suffering and Martyrdom in the New Testament 1981, and articles in theological journals. *Leisure interests:* walking and DIY. *Address:* 26 Hurrell Road, Cambridge, CB4 3RH, England. *Telephone:* (01223) 312260. *Fax:* (01223) 312260.

BECK, Conrad; Swiss composer; b. 16 June 1901, Lohn, Schaffhausen; m. Friedel Ehrsam 1941; two s.; ed. Konservatorium, Zürich; further musical studies in Paris with Ibert, Honegger and Roussel 1923–32; Ludwig Spohr Prize, City of Brunswick, Composers Prize of Asscn. of Swiss composers, Kunstpreis, City of Basel; Commdr. Order of Cultural Merit, Monaco 1973. *Principal works:* seven symphonies, many other symphonic works, concertos, two oratorios, cantatas, chamber music, etc., including Der Tod zu Basel (Miserère), Die Sonnenfinsternis, Elegie. *Leisure interest:* mountaineering. *Address:* St. Johann Vorstadt 82, Basel, Switzerland.

BECK, Sir Edgar (Charles), Kt., C.B.E., F.ENG., F.I.C.E.; British engineer; b. 11 May 1911; s. of Edgar Bee and Nellie Stollard (née Osborne) Beck; m. Mary Agnes Sorapure 1933 (divorced 1972); three s. two d.; m. 2nd Anne Teresa Corbould 1972; ed. Lancing Coll., Jesus Coll., Cambridge; joined John Mowlem & Co. Ltd. as engineer 1933, Dir. 1940, Man. Dir. 1958, Chair. 1961–79, Pres. 1981–; Dir. Scaffolding G.B. Ltd. 1942 (Chair. 1958–78), Builders' Insurance Ltd. 1959 (Deputy Chair. 1969); mem. Export Credits Guarantee Dept. Advisory Council 1964–69; Pres. Fed. of Civil Eng. Contractors 1971–75; Chair. Export Group for the Constructional Industries 1959–63; British Hospitals Export Council 1964–75; Underwriting mem. Lloyd's 1955–. *Leisure interests:* golf, salmon fishing. *Address:* Mill Cottage, Wilsford-cum-Lake, Wilts., SP4 7BP, England.

BECK, James (Henry); American art historian; b. 14 May 1930; s. of Samuel Beck and Margaret Weisz; m. Darma Tercinod 1956; one s. one d.; ed. Oberlin Coll., New York and Columbia Univs.; Asst. Prof. Univ. of Ala. 1958–59, Ariz. State Univ. 1959–61; joined Columbia Univ. 1961, Prof. of Art History 1972–, Chair. Dept. of Art History 1984–90, Visiting Assoc. Prof. Princeton Univ. 1970; f. ArtWatch Int., Pres. 1992–; Herodotus Fellow Inst. for Advanced Study, Princeton Univ. 1967; Fellow Harvard Univ. Centre for Italian Renaissance Studies 1967–68, 1972, Visiting Scholar 1983; Guggenheim Fellow 1973–74. *Publications include:* Marioano di Jacopo detto il Taccola, 'Liber Tertius' 1969, Jacopo della Quercia e San Petronio 1970, Michelangelo: A Lesson in Anatomy 1975, Raphael 1976, Masaccio: The Documents 1978, Leonardo's Rules of Painting: An Unconventional Approach to Modern Art 1979, Italian Renaissance Painting 1981, The Doors of the Florentine Baptistry 1985, The Sepulchral Monument for Ilaria del Caretto by Jacopo della Quercia 1988, Jacopo della Quercia 1991, The Tyranny of the Detail 1992, The Culture, the Business and the Scandal 1993, Raphael, the Camera della Segnatura 1993. *Address:* Columbia University, 826 Schermerhorn Hall, New York, NY 10027 (Office); 435 Riverside Drive, New York, NY 10025, U.S.A. (Home).

BECK, John C., M.D.; American professor of medicine; b. 4 Jan. 1924, Audubon, Ia.; s. of Wilhelm and Marie Beck; one s.; ed. McGill Univ.; Physician-in-Chief, Royal Victoria Hospital 1964–74, Sr. Physician, Dept. of Medicine 1974–81; Prof. of Medicine, Univ. of Calif., San Francisco 1974–79; Visiting Prof. U.C.L.A. 1978–79, Dir. Multicampus Div. of Geriatric Medicine, School of Medicine, U.C.L.A. 1979–93, Prof. of Medicine, U.C.L.A. 1979–; Dir. Calif. Geriatric Educ. Center 1987–93, Dir. Emer. 1993–; numerous other professional appts. *Publications:* articles in professional journals. *Address:* U.C.L.A. School of Medicine, Division of Geriatric Medicine and Gerontology, 10833 La Conte, 32-144 CHS, Los Angeles, CA 90024; 1562 Casale Road, Pacific Palisades, CA 90272, U.S.A.

BECKENBAUER, Franz; German footballer; b. 11 Sept. 1945; s. of the late Franz Beckenbauer Sr. and of Antonia Beckenbauer; m. Brigitte Wittmann; three s.; ed. Northern Coll. of Insurance Studies; played for Bayern Munich and New York Cosmos football clubs; won West German Cup (with Bayern Munich) 1966, 1967, 1969, 1971, West German Championship 1972, 1974, European Cup Winners 1967, European Cup 1974–76, World Club Championship 1976; won European Nations Cup (with West German Nat. Team) 1972, World Cup 1974; won North American Championship (with New York Cosmos) 1977, 1978–80; European Footballer of the Year 1972, 1976, West German Footballer of the Year 1980; Professional Football Man. 1977–, Man. West German Nat. Team 1984–90; Tech. Dir. Marseilles

1990–; Consultant Olympique Marseilles; U.S. Soccer Fed. 1990–; fmr. coach; f. Franz Beckenbauer Foundation 1982; Adviser Mitsubishi Mrawa Football Club 1992–; Bayern Verdienstorden 1982; Order of FIFA (Int. Football Fed.) 1984. *Publication:* Einer wie ich (Someone like Me). *Address:* DFB, Otto-Fleck-Schneise 6, 6000 Frankfurt/Main 71, Germany. *Telephone:* (0611) 71 04 05.

BECKER, Boris; German tennis player; b. 22 Nov. 1967, Leimen, near Heidelberg; s. of Karl-Heinz and Elvira Becker; m. Barbara Feltus; one s.; started playing tennis at Blau-Weiss Club, Leimen; won West German Jr. Championship 1983; subsequently runner-up U.S. Jr. Championship; coached by Ion Tiriac since 1984; quarter-finalist Australian Championship, winner Young Masters Tournament, Birmingham, England 1985, Grand Prix Tournament, Queen's 1985; won Men's Singles Championship, Wimbledon 1985 (youngest ever winner and finalist; beat Kevin Curren), also won 1986, 1989, finalist 1988, 1990, 1991, 1995; finalist Benson and Hedges Championship, Wembley, London 1985; Masters Champion 1988, finalist 1989; U.S. Open Champion 1989; Semi-finalist French Open 1989; winner Davis Cup 1989, Australian Open Championships 1991, 1996, IBM/ATP Tour Championship 1992, 1995, Grand Slam Cup 1996; Sportsman of the Year 1985, Hon Citizen Leimen 1986, named World Champion 1991, 36 titles (Nov. 1992). *Leisure interests:* football, basketball, chess, backgammon. *Address:* Nusslocher Strasse 51, 69181 Leimen, Baden, Germany.

BECKER, Carl Johan; Danish archaeologist; b. 3 Sept. 1915, Copenhagen; s. of Carl and Henny Becker (née Döcker); m. Birgit Hilbert 1949; three d.; ed. Metropolitanskolen, Univ. of Copenhagen; Asst., Nat. Museum 1934–41, Asst.-Keeper 1941–52; Prof. of Prehistoric Archaeology, Univ. of Copenhagen 1952–85, Dean Faculty of Arts 1963–64, mem. Konsistorium 1964–70; Chief Ed. Acta Archaeologica 1948–84; mem. Royal Danish Acad. of Sciences and Letters, Danish Research Council for the Humanities 1968–75; Corresp. Fellow, British Acad.; mem. Cttee. of Thai-Danish Archaeological Expedition and numerous European Prehistoric and Archaeological socs; Knight First Class Order of Dannebrog. *Publications:* Enkeltgravkulturen på de danske Øer 1936, Mosefundne Lerkar fra Yngre Stenalder 1948, Die Mittel-Neolithischen Kulturen in Südskandinavien 1955, 1971, Förromersk Jernalder i Syd-og Midtjylland 1961, Studies in Northern Coinages of the Eleventh Century 1981, Nörre Sandegård, Arkaeologiske undersøgelser på Bornholm 1990, Stendygegrve og Kulthuse (jtly.) 1997. *Leisure interest:* numismatics. *Address:* Chr. Wintersvej 4C, 1., DK-1860 Frederiksberg C, Denmark. *Telephone:* 33.26.29.11.

BECKER, Gary Stanley, PH.D.; American economics educator; b. 2 Dec. 1930, Pottsville, Pa.; s. of Louis William and Anna Siskind Becker; m. 1st Doria Slote 1954 (deceased); m. 2nd Guity Nashat 1979; two s. two d.; ed. Princeton Univ., Univ. of Chicago; Asst. Prof., Univ. of Chicago 1954–57; Asst. and Assoc. Prof. of Econs. Columbia Univ. 1957–60, Prof. of Econs. 1960, Arthur Lehman Prof. of Econs. 1968–69; Ford Foundation Visiting Prof. of Econs., Univ. of Chicago 1969–70, Univ. Prof., Dept. of Econs, 1970–83, Depts. of Econs. and Sociology 1983–, Chair. Dept. of Econs. 1984–85; Research Assoc., Econs. Research Center, N.O.R.C. 1980–; mem. N.A.S., Int. Union for the Scientific Study of Population, American Philosophical Soc. and American Econ. Asscn. (Pres. 1987), Mont Pelerin Soc. (Dir. 1985–, Pres. 1990–92); Fellow, American Statistical Asscn., Econometric Soc., Nat. Acad. of Educ., American Acad. of Arts and Sciences; Hon. degrees Hebrew Univ. of Jerusalem 1985, Knox Coll., Galesburg, Ill. 1985, Univ. of Ill., Chicago 1988, State Univ. of New York 1990, Princeton Univ. 1991; W. S. Woytinsky Award (Univ. of Mich.) 1964, John Bates Clark Medal (American Econ. Asscn.) 1967, Frank E. Seidman Distinguished Award in Political Econ. 1985, Merit Award (Nat. Insts. of Health) 1986, John R. Commons Award, Nobel Prize for Economic Sciences 1992. *Publications:* The Economics of Discrimination 1957, Human Capital 1964, Human Capital and the Personal Distribution of Income: Analytical Approach 1967, Economic Theory 1971, Essays in the Economics of Crime and Punishment (ed., with William M. Landes) 1974, The Allocation of Time and Goods over the Life Cycle (with Gilbert Ghez) 1975, The Economic Approach to Human Behavior 1976, A Treatise on the Family 1991, Accounting for Tastes 1996, The Economics of Life 1996; columnist Business Week 1985–, numerous articles in professional journals. *Address:* Department of Economics, 1126 East 59th Street, Chicago, IL 60637; 1308 E. 58th Street, Chicago, IL 60637, U.S.A. (Home). *Telephone:* (312) 702-8168 (Office). *Fax:* (312) 702-8490.

BECKER, Gert O.; German company executive; b. 21 Aug. 1933, Kronberg; s. of Otto Becker and Henriette (née Syring); m. Margrit Bruns 1960; one s. one d.; ed. Akademie für Welthandel, Frankfurt; Sales Dept., Degussa, Frankfurt 1956; with rep. office in Teheran, Iran 1960, with subsidiary in São Paolo, Brazil 1963, Div. Man., Frankfurt 1966, Dir. 1971, Man. Dir. Degussa, Frankfurt 1977–96, fmr. Pres. and C.E.O.; Pres. Asscn. of Chemical Industries 1994–95. *Leisure interests:* literature, book collecting, golf. *Address:* Friedrichstrasse 100, 61476 Kronberg, Germany.

BECKER, Jürgen; German writer and editor; b. 10 July 1932, Cologne; s. of Robert and Else (née Schuchardt) Becker; m. 1st Mare Becker 1954 (dissolved 1965); one s.; m. 2nd Rango Bohne 1965; one step-s. one step-d.; ed. Univ. of Cologne; various jobs until 1959; freelance writer and contributor to W. German Radio 1959–64; Reader at Rowohlt Verlag 1964–65; freelance writer; living in Cologne, Berlin, Hamburg and Rome; Dir. Suhrkamp-Theaterverlag 1974; Head of Drama Dept., Deutschlandfunk Köln; Writer in Residence, Warwick Univ. 1988; mem. Akademie der Künste Berlin, Deutsche Akademie für Sprache und Dichtung Darmstadt, PEN Club; Förderpreis des Landes Niedersachsen 1964, Stipendium Deutsche Akad. Villa Massimo, Rome 1965, 1966, Group 47 Prize 1967, Literaturpreis der Stadt Köln 1968, Literaturpreis, Bavarian Acad. of Arts 1980, Kritikerpreis 1981, Bremer Literaturpreis 1986, Heinrich-Böll Prize 1995. *Publications:* Phasen (Text and Typogramme with Wolf Vostell) 1960, Felder (short stories) 1964; Ränder (short stories) 1968, Bilder, Häuser (Radio Play) 1969, Umgebungen (short stories) 1970, Schnee (poems) 1971, Das Ende der Landschaftsmalerei (poems) 1974, Erzähl mir nichts vom Kreig (poems) 1977, In der verbleibenden Zeit (Poetry) 1979, Erzählen bis Ostende (short stories) 1981, Gedichte 1965–1980 (collected poems) 1981, Fenster und Stimmen (Poems) 1982, Odenthals Künste (Poems) 1986, Das Gedicht von der wieder-vereinigten Landschaft (Poem) 1988, Das Englische Fenster (Poems) 1990, Frauen mit dem Rücken zum Betrachter (short stories) 1989, Foxtrott im Erfurter Stadion 1993, Das fehlende Rest 1997; Ed. Happenings (documentary with Wolf Vostell) 1965. *Address:* Am Klausenberg 84, 51109 Cologne, Germany. *Telephone:* 84-11-39.

BECKETT, Rt. Hon. Margaret Mary; British politician; b. 15 Jan. 1943, Ashton-under-Lyne, Lancs.; d. of Cyril and Winifred Jackson; m. Leo Beckett 1979; two step-s.; ed. Notre Dame High School, Manchester and Norwich, Manchester Coll. of Science and Tech., John Dalton Polytechnic; eng. apprentice (metallurgy), Associated Electrical Industries, Manchester, subsequently Experimental Officer, Univ. of Manchester; researcher (Industrial Policy), Labour Party HQ; Labour M.P. for Lincoln 1974–79, for Derby South 1983–; Parl. Pvt. Sec., Minister for Overseas Devt. 1974–75; Asst. Govt. Whip 1975–76; Minister, Dept. of Educ. 1976–79; Prin. Researcher, Granada TV 1979–83; Opposition Spokeswoman with responsibility for Social Security 1984–89, for Health Oct. 1994–97; Shadow Chief Sec. 1989–92; Shadow Leader of House, Campaigns Co-ordinator, Deputy Leader of Opposition 1992–94, Leader of Opposition May–July 1994; Shadow Sec. of State for Health 1994–95; Shadow Pres. of Bd. of Trade 1995–97; Pres. of Bd. of Trade and Sec. of State for Trade and Industry 1997–98; Pres. of Council and Leader of the House of Commons 1998–; mem. Labour Party Nat. Exec. Cttee. 1980–81, 1985–86, 1988–98, Transport & General Workers Union Parl. Labour Party Group; apptd. to Privy Council 1993. *Leisure interests:* cooking, reading, caravanning. *Address:* House of Commons, London, SW1A 0AA, England.

BECKETT, Sir Terence (Norman), K.B.E., D.L., B.SC.(ECON.), F.ENG., F.I.MECH.E.; British business executive; b. 13 Dec. 1923, Walsall, Staffs.; s. of Horace Norman and Clarice Lillian (née Allsop) Beckett; m. Sylvia Gladys Asprey 1950; one d.; ed. Wolverhampton and S. Staffs. Tech. Coll., London School of Econs.; Capt. Royal Electrical and Mechnical Eng., served in Britain, India and Malaya 1945–48; joined Ford Motor Co. as Man. Trainee 1950, Styling Man., Briggs Motor Bodies Ltd. (Ford subsidiary) 1954, Admin. Man., Engineer, then Man. Product Staff 1955, Gen. Planning Man., Product Planning Staff 1961, Man. Marketing Staff 1963, Dir., Car Div., Ford Motor Co. Ltd. 1964, Exec. Dir. 1966, Dir. of Sales 1968, Vice-Pres. European and Overseas Sales Operations, Ford of Europe 1969–73; Man. Dir., Chief Exec., Ford Motor Co. Ltd. 1974–80, Chair. 1976–80; fmr. Chair. Ford Motor Credit Co. Ltd.; Dir. (non-exec.) CEGB 1987–90, Deputy Chair. 1990; Pro-Chancellor Univ. of Essex 1989–98 (Chair. 1989–95); fmr. Dir. ICI, Ford Nederland N.V., Ford Lusitana S.A.R.L., Portugal, Henry Ford & Son Ltd., Ireland, Ford Motor Co. A/S, Denmark, Ford Motor Co. AB, Sweden, Automotive Finance Ltd.; fmr. mem. of Council CBI, Dir.-Gen. 1980–87, mem. Council and Exec. Cttee. Soc. of Motor Mfrs. and Traders; mem. NEDC 1980–87; mem. Court and Council Essex Univ. 1985–98, Top Salaries Review Body 1987–92; Chair. Governing Body of London Business School, London Business School Trust Co. Ltd. 1979–86, Council of Motor Cycle Trades Benevolent Fund; Gov., Cranfield Inst. of Tech., Nat. Inst. of Econ. and Social Research, London School of Econs.; Patron, Manpower Services Comm. Award Scheme for Disabled People; Hon. mem. R.E.M.E. Inst. 1990; Hon. Fellow (Sidney Sussex Coll., Cambridge) 1981–, (London Business School) 1987–, (L.S.E.) 1995–; Hon. D.Sc. (Cranfield Inst. of Tech.) 1977, (Heriot-Watt) 1981; Hon. D.Sc.Econ. (London) 1982; Hon. D.Tech. (Brunel) 1991, (Wolverhampton) 1995; Hon. D.Univ. (Essex) 1995; Hon. D.Litt. (Anglia) 1998; Hambro Businessman of the Year Award 1978; BIM Gold Medal 1980. *Leisure interests:* ornithology, music. *Address:* c/o Barclays Bank PLC, 74 High Street, Ingatestone, Essex, England.

BECKWITH, Athelstan Laurence Johnson, D.PHIL., F.A.A., F.R.S.; Australian professor of organic chemistry; b. 20 Feb. 1930, Perth, W.A.; s. of Laurence A. and Doris G. Beckwith; m. Phyllis Kaye Marshall 1953; one s. two d.; ed. Univ. of Western Australia and Balliol Coll., Oxford Univ.; Research Scientist, CSIRO, Melbourne 1957–58; Lecturer in Chem., Univ. of Adelaide 1958–62, Prof. of Organic Chem, 1965–81; Lecturer, Imperial Coll., Univ. of London 1962–63; Visiting Prof., Univ. of York 1968; Prof. of Organic Chem., A.N.U. 1981–96, Emer. Prof. 1997–, Dean 1989–91; Pres. Royal Australian Chemical Inst. 1984–85; Vice-Pres. Australian Acad. of Science 1985–86; Chair. Ed. Bd. Australian Journals of Science 1988–94; Syntex Pacific Coast Lecturer 1986, Rayson Huang Lecturer 1989, Kharasch Lecturer 1990, Centenary Lecturer 1991; Rennie Memorial Medal 1960, Centenary Medal 1991, Organic Chemistry Medal 1992; Carnegie Fellow 1968; H. G. Smith Memorial Medal 1980, Leighton Medal 1997. *Publications:* numerous scientific papers and reviews in chemistry journals, etc. *Leisure* *interests:* reading, performing music, model-making, golf. *Address:* Research School of Chemistry, Australian National University, Canberra, A.C.T. 0200 (Office); 3/9 Crisp Circuit, Bruce, A.C.T. 2617, Australia (Home). *Telephone:* (02) 6253-0696. *Fax:* (02) 6253-0737.

BEDDALL, David; Australian politician; b. 27 Nov. 1948, Manchester, U.K.; m. Helen Beddall; one d.; two s. from previous marriage; mem. staff Commonwealth Banking Corpn. 1967–78; Loans Officer, Australian Guarantee Corpn. Ltd. 1978–83; commercial finance consultant 1979–83; mem. House of Reps. for Fadden, Queensland 1983, for Rankin 1984–; Minister for Small Business and Customs 1990–93, for Communications 1993, for Resources 1993–96; Chair. Jt. Standing Cttee. on Foreign Affairs and Defence 1984–87, House of Reps. Standing Cttee. on Industry, Science and Tech. 1987–93. *Address:* Inala Plaza, Corsair Avenue, Inala, Queensland 4077; House of Representatives, Canberra, A.C.T. 2600, Australia.

BEDDOME, John MacDonald; Canadian oil executive; b. 20 Sept. 1930, Vernon, B.C.; m. Barbara McCarthy; one s. one d.; ed. Univ. of British Columbia; with Gulf Oil Canada 1952–71; with Dome Petroleum Ltd. 1971–88, Pres. and C.O.O. 1983–88; Pres. and C.E.O. Polar Gas Ltd 1989–91, Polar Delta Project 1989–91, Alberta Natural Gas Ltd 1991–; Chair. & Dir. TransCanada Pipelines 1979–83; Dir. PanArctic Oils Ltd. 1981–88, Encor Energy Corpn. Ltd., Ipsco Inc. 1986–, Morgan Hydrocarbons Inc. 1989–, Western Gas Marketing 1989–, Canadian Petroleum Asscn. 1986–88, Pan Canadian Petroleum 1992–.

BEDFORD, David, A.R.A.M.; British composer; b. 4 Aug. 1937, London; s. of L. H. Bedford and L. F. K. Duff; m. 1st M. Parsonage 1958 (divorced); two d.; m. 2nd S. Pilgrim 1969 (divorced); two d.; m. 3rd Allison Powell 1994; one s. one d.; ed. Lancing Coll. and R.A.M.; teacher of Music, Whitefield School, Hendon, London 1966–69, Queen's Coll., Harley Street, London 1969–80; Assoc. Visiting Composer, Gordonstoun School 1980–81; Youth Music Dir. English Sinfonia 1986–93, Composer in Asscn. English Sinfonia 1993–, Imogen Holst Fellow in Composition, Dartington Coll. of Arts 1996–; Patron Barnet Schools Music Asscn. 1987; since 1980 freelance composer and arranger; compositions: Music for Albion Moonlight 1965, Star Clusters 1971, The Golden Wine 1974, Star's End 1974, The Rime of the Ancient Mariner 1978, The Death of Baldur 1979, Sun Paints Rainbows 1982, Symphony No. 1 1983, Symphony No. 2 1985, some music for film The Killing Fields 1984, Absolute Beginners 1985, The Mission 1986, Into Thy Wondrous House 1986, Ma non Sempere 1987, Gere Curam Mei Nobis (for Katherine) 1987; Licentiate of Trinity Coll. of Music. *Leisure interests:* squash, film and cricket. *Address:* 39 Shakespeare Road, Mill Hill, London, NW7 4BA, England. *Telephone:* 0181-959 3165.

BEDFORD, Steuart John Rudolf, B.A., F.R.C.O., F.R.A.M.; British conductor; b. 31 July 1939, London; s. of L. H. and Lesley (Duff) Bedford; m. 1st Norma Burrowes (q.v.) 1969 (divorced 1980); m. 2nd Celia Harding 1980; two d.; ed. Lancing Coll., Sussex, Oxford Univ., Royal Acad. of Music.; operatic training as repetiteur, asst. conductor, Glyndebourne Festival 1965–67; English Opera Group (later English Music Theatre), Aldeburgh and London 1967–73; Co-Artistic Dir., English Musical Theatre 1976–, Artistic Dir. English Sinfonia 1981–, Artistic Dir. (also Exec. Artistic Dir.) Aldeburgh Festival 1987–98; freelance conductor, numerous performances with English Opera Group, Welsh Nat. Opera, Metropolitan Opera, New York (operas include Death in Venice, The Marriage of Figaro), Royal Danish Opera; also at Royal Opera House, Covent Garden (operas include Owen Wingrave, Death in Venice, Così fan tutte) Santa Fe Opera, Teatro Colón, Buenos Aires, Brussels, Lyon etc.; conductor for BBC, Netherlands Radio, Belgian Radio; recordings include works by Britten, Shostakovich, Saxton; Medal of the Worshipful Co. of Musicians. *Leisure interests:* golf, skiing. *Address:* c/o Harrison-Parrott Ltd., 12 Penzance Place, London, W11 4PA, England.

BEDFORD, Sybille, O.B.E., C.LIT.; British author; b. 16 March 1911, Berlin; d. of Maximilian von Schoenebeck and Elizabeth Bernhard; m. Walter Bedford 1935; ed. pvt. schools in France and England; literary journalist 1930s–. *Leisure interests:* wine, food, reading, travel. *Publications:* A Visit to Don Otavio 1953, A Legacy 1956, The Best We Can Do 1958, The Faces of Justice 1961, A Favourite of the Gods 1968, A Compass Error 1968, Aldous Huxley: A Biography (Vol. I) 1973, (Vol. II) 1974, Jigsaw 1989, As It Was 1990. *Address:* c/o Lutyens & Rubinstein, 231 Westbourne Park Road, London, W11 1EB, England. *Telephone:* 0171-792 4853.

BEDI, Bishan Singh, B.A.; Indian cricketer; b. 25 Sept. 1946, Amritsar; s. of late Gyan Singh Bedi and Rajinder Kaur Bedi; m. 1st Glenith Jill Bedi 1969; one s. one d.; m. 2nd Inderjit Bedi 1980; ed. Punjab Univ.; employed by Steel Authority of India, New Delhi; slow left-arm bowler; played for Northern Punjab 1961–62 to 1966–67, Delhi 1968–69 to 1980–81, Northamptonshire 1972–77; played in 67 Tests for India (1967–68 to 1979), 22 as captain, taking 266 wickets (average 28.7); took 1,560 first-class wickets; toured England 1971, 1974, 1976 and 1975 (World Cup); Hon. Life mem. M.C.C. 1981, nat. selector; Padma Shri 1969; Arjuna Award 1971. *Leisure interests:* reading, photography, swimming and letter-writing. *Address:* Ispat Bhawan, Lodhi Rd, New Delhi 3, India. *Telephone:* 43133.

BEDIE, Henri Konan, L. EN D.; Côte d'Ivoire politician; b. 1934, Dadiekro; m. Henriette Koinzan Bomo 1958; two s. two d.; ed. Univ. of Poitiers; Asst. Dir. Caisse de Sécurité de la Côte d'Ivoire 1959–60; Counsellor, French Embassy, Washington, D.C. March–Aug. 1960; mem. Perm. Mission to UN 1960; Chargé d'Affaires, Embassy of Côte d'Ivoire, Washington, D.C. Aug.–Dec. 1960; Amb. to U.S.A. 1960–66; Minister-Del. for Econ. and Financial Affairs 1966–68; Minister of Economy and Finance 1968–75; Special Adviser, IFC 1976–80; re-elected Deputy, Nat. Ass. 1980; Pres. Nat. Ass. 1980, re-elected 1985, 1986; mem. Political Bureau, Parti Démocratique de la Côte d'Ivoire (PDCI); Pres. Office Africain et Malgache de la Propriété Industrielle; President of Côte d'Ivoire Dec. 1993–. *Address:* Présidence de la République, Abidjan, Côte d'Ivoire.

BEDJAOUI, Mohammed; Algerian lawyer; b. 21 Sept. 1929, Sidi-Bel-Abbès; s. of Benali Bedjaoui and Fatima Oukili; m. Leila Francis 1962; two d.; ed. Univ. of Grenoble and Institut d'Etudes Politiques, Grenoble; Lawyer, Court of Appeal, Grenoble 1951; research worker at Centre Nat. de la Recherche Scientifique (CNRS) Paris 1955; Legal Counsellor of the Arab League in Geneva 1959–62; Legal Counsellor Provisional Republican Govt. of Algeria in Exile 1958–61; Dir. Office of the Pres. of Nat. Constituent Ass. 1962; mem. Del. to UN 1957, 1962, 1977, 1978–82; Sec.-Gen. Council of Ministers, Algiers 1962–63; Pres. Soc. Nat. des Chemins de Fer Algériens (SNCFA) 1964; Dean of the Faculty of Law, Algiers Univ. 1964; Minister of Justice and Keeper of the Seals 1964–70; mem., special reporter, Int. Law Comm. 1965–82; Amb. to France 1970–79; Perm. Rep. to UNESCO 1971–79, to UN 1979–82; Vice-Pres. UN Council on Namibia 1979–82; mem. UN Comm. of Inquiry (Iran) 1980; Pres. Group of 77 1981–82; Judge Int. Court of Justice 1982–97 (Pres. 1994–97); Pres. African Soc. of Int. and Comparative Law 1993–; Head Algerian del. to UN Conf. on Law of the Sea 1976–80; mem. Int. Inst. of Law; Carnegie Endowment for Int. Peace 1956; ordre du Mérite Alaouite, Morocco; Order of the Repub., Egypt; Commdr. Légion d'honneur (France), ordre de la Résistance (Algeria). *Publications:* International Civil Service 1956, Fonction publique internationale et influences nationales 1958, La révolution algérienne et le droit 1961, Succession d'états 1970, Terra nullius, droits historiques et autodétermination 1975, Non-alignment et droit international 1976, Pour un nouvel ordre économique international 1979, Droit international: bilan et perspectives 1992. *Address:* c/o International Court of Justice, Peace Palace, Carnegieplein 2, 2517 KJ, The Hague, Netherlands; 39 rue des Pins, Hydra, Algiers, Algeria. *Telephone:* (070) 392 44 41 (The Hague); (213-2) 60-30-89 (Algiers).

BEDNARSKI, Krzysztof; Polish sculptor; b. 25 July 1953, Cracow; m.; two s.; ed. Acad. of Fine Arts (ASP), Warsaw; worked for Laboratorium Theatre of J. Grotowski, Wrocław 1976–82. *Works include:* monument of Fellini now under construction in Rimini, and of Krzysztof Kieślowski's grave Warsaw; works in numerous collections. *Leisure interest:* beer drinking. *Address:* ul. Nowowiejska 28/55, 02-010 Warsaw, Poland; 00-186 Roma, Via Dei Banchi Vecchi 134, Italy. *Telephone:* (22) 628 95 48 (Warsaw); 06/6896068 (Rome). *Fax:* 06/6896068 (Rome).

BEDNORZ, George, PH.D.; German physicist; b. 16 May 1950; ed. Swiss Federal Inst. of Tech., Zürich; with IBM Research Lab., Rüschlikon, Zürich 1982–; shared Nobel Prize for Physics for discovery of new super-conducting materials 1987. *Address:* IBM Zürich Research Laboratory, Säumerstrasse 4, CH-8803 Rüschlikon, Zürich, Switzerland. *Telephone:* 41-1-72 48 111.

BEDSER, Sir Alec Victor, Kt., C.B.E.; British cricketer and company director; b. 4 July 1918, Reading; s. of the late Arthur and Florence Beatrice Bedser; ed. Monument Hill Secondary School, Woking; served R.A.F. 1939–46; right-arm fast-medium bowler and right-hand lower-order batsman; played for Surrey 1939–60; played in 51 Tests for England 1946–55, taking then record 236 wickets (average 24.8) including 104 against Australia; took 1,924 first-class wickets; toured Australia 1946–47, 1950–51 and 1954–55; mem. England Cricket Selection Cttee. of Test and County Cricket Bd. 1962–83, Chair. 1968–81; Asst. Man. (to the late Duke of Norfolk) MCC tour to Australia 1962–63, Man. MCC tour to Australia 1974–75, to Australia and India 1979–80; Pres. Surrey C.C.C. 1987–88, fmr. Vice-Pres. and cttee. mem.; started office equipment firm in partnership with twin brother, Eric A. Bedser 1955; now consultant, Initial Cleaning Services. *Publications:* Our Cricket Story (with Eric A. Bedser) 1951, Bowling 1952, Following On (with Eric A. Bedser) 1954, May's Men in Australia 1959, Cricket Choice 1981, Twin Ambitions (autobiog. with Alex Bannister) 1986. *Leisure interests:* cricket, golf, gardening, charities.

BEEBY, Thomas Hall; American architect; b. 12 Oct. 1941, Oak Park, Ill.; m. 1st Marcia D. Greenlease 1960 (divorced 1973); one s. one d.; m. 2nd Kirsten Peltzer 1975; two s.; ed. Lower Merion High School, Ardmore, Pa., Gresham's School, Holt (U.K.), Cornell and Yale Univs.; Assoc. C.F. Murphy Assocs. Chicago 1965–71; partner, Hammond Beeby & Assocs. Chicago 1971–76; partner, Hammond Beeby & Babka, Chicago 1976–; Assoc. Prof. Dept. of Architecture, Ill. Inst. of Tech., Chicago 1973–80; Dir. School of Arch. Univ. of Ill. at Chicago 1980–85; Dean, Prof. School of Arch. Yale Univ. 1985–91, Adjunct Prof. 1992–; work includes office bldgs., shopping centres, housing, libraries, hosps., public bldgs. etc.; contributor to numerous exhbns. of architecture and design in U.S.A. and Europe including Venice Biennale 1980; Distinguished Building Award, American Inst. of Architects, Chicago Chapter (several times); Nat. Design Award 1984, 1987, 1989, 1991, 1993. *Publications:* articles in professional journals. *Address:* Hammond Beeby and Babka Inc., 440 N. Wells Street, Chicago, IL 60610, U.S.A.

BEELEY, Sir Harold, K.C.M.G., C.B.E., M.A.; British diplomatist; b. 15 Feb. 1909, London; s. of Frank Arthur Beeley; m. Karen Brett-Smith (née Shields) 1958; one step-s. three d., two step-d.; ed. Highgate School and Queen's

Coll., Oxford; lecturer at Univs. of Sheffield, London, Oxford and Leicester 1930–39; entered Foreign Service 1946; Counsellor, Copenhagen 1949–50, Baghdad 1950–53, Washington 1953–55; Amb. to Saudi Arabia 1955; Asst. Under-Sec. Foreign Office 1956–58; Deputy Perm. Rep. to UN 1958–61; Amb. to United Arab Republic 1961–64, 1967–69; Perm. Rep. of U.K. to Disarmament Conf., Geneva 1964–67; retired from Diplomatic Service 1969; lecturer, Queen Mary Coll., London 1969–75; Pres. Egypt Exploration Soc. 1969–88; Chair. World of Islam Festival Trust 1973–96; Chair. Arab-British Centre 1977–81, Egyptian-British Chamber of Commerce 1981–92; mem. Bd. Arab-British Chamber of Commerce 1979–81. *Publication:* Disraeli 1936. *Address:* 38 Slaidburn Street, London, SW10 0JW, England.

BEENE, Geoffrey; American fashion designer; b. 30 Aug. 1927, Haynesville, La.; s. of Albert Beene and Lorene Waller; ed. Tulane Univ., Univ. of S. Calif., Traphagen School of Fashion and Acad. Julien, Paris; designer for Samuel Winston 1949–50, Harmay 1950–57, Teal Traina 1958–62; Pres. and Designer, Geoffrey Beene Inc. New York 1962–; work represented in Costume Inst., Metropolitan Museum of Art; recipient of numerous awards including Council of Fashion Designers of America Award 1981, 1985, 1987, Achievement in Creative Arts, Philadelphia Coll. of Art 1986. *Address:* Geoffrey Beene Inc., 250 W. 39th Street, 9th Floor, New York, NY 10018, U.S.A.

BEER, Otto F., DR. PHIL.; Austrian writer, journalist and professor; b. 8 Sept. 1910, Vienna; s. of Leopold J. and Emma (née Pabst) Beer; m. Gerty Mothwurf 1949 (died 1985); ed. Univ. of Vienna; Ed. Neues Wiener Journal and Neues Wiener Tagblatt until 1939; Chief Ed. Salzburger Nachrichten 1945; Drama Critic, Welt am Abend 1946–48, Der Standpunkt, Merano 1948–52, Neues Österreich, Vienna 1952–67, Österreichischer Rundfunk 1967, Süddeutsche Zeitung 1967. *Publications:* Zehnte Symphonie 1952, Wiedersehen in Meran 1952, Ich-Rodolfo-Magier 1965, Christin-Theres 1967; comedies: Man ist nur zweimal jung 1955, Bummel durch Wien 1971, Der Fenstergucker 1974, Einladung nach Wien 1977. *Leisure interest:* music. *Address:* Lederergasse 27, 1080 Vienna, Austria. *Telephone:* 405-04-84.

BEERING, Steven Claus, M.D.; American university president; b. 20 Aug. 1932, Berlin, Germany; s. of Steven and Alice Friedrichs Beering; m. Jane Pickering 1956; three s.; ed. Univ. of Pittsburgh; Prof. of Medicine 1969–; Asst. Dean, Indiana Univ. School of Medicine 1969–70, Assoc. Dean 1970–74, Dean 1974–83, Dir. Indiana Univ. Medical Center 1974–83; Pres. Purdue Univ. and Purdue Univ. Research Foundation 1983–; numerous awards and prizes. *Publications:* numerous articles in professional journals. *Leisure interests:* music, photography, reading, travel. *Address:* Purdue University, 1031 Hovde Hall, Room 200, West Lafayette, IN 47907-1031 (Office); 500 McCormick Road, West Lafayette, IN 47906-4911, U.S.A. (Home). *Telephone:* 317-494-9708 (Office); 317-743-9933 (Home).

BEERS, Charlotte Lenore; American business executive; b. 26 July 1935, Beaumont, Tex.; d. of Glen Rice and Frances Bolt; m. Donald C. Beers 1971; one d.; ed. Baylor Univ. Waco, Tex.; Group Product Man. Uncle Ben's Inc. 1959–69; Sr. Vice-Pres., Dir. Client Services, J. Walter Thompson 1969–79; C.O.O. Tatham-Laird & Kudner, Chicago, Man. Partner, Chair. and C.E.O. 1979–; Vice-Chair. RSCG Group Roux Seguela, Cayzac & Goudard, France; Chair. and C.E.O. Ogilvy & Mather Worldwide, New York, Ogilvy Group Inc., New York, Chair. Emer. 1997–. *Address:* Ogilvy Group Inc., Ogilvy & Mather Worldwide Inc., 309 West 49th Street, #12, New York, NY 10019, U.S.A.

BEEVERS, Harry, PH.D.; American biologist; b. 10 Jan. 1924, Shildon, England; s. of Norman and Olive Beevers; m. Jean Sykes 1949; one s.; ed. Univ. of Durham; post-doctoral research, Univ. of Oxford 1946–50; Asst. Prof. of Biology, Purdue Univ. 1950–53, Assoc. Prof. 1953–58, Prof. 1958–69; Prof. of Biology, Univ. of Calif., Santa Cruz 1969–90, Prof. Emer. 1990–; Pres. American Soc. of Plant Physiologists 1961; Sr. U.S. Scientist, Alexander von Humboldt Foundation 1986; Fellow Crown Coll., Univ. of Calif. Santa Cruz 1969; mem. N.A.S.; Fellow American Acad. of Arts and Sciences 1973; mem. Deutsche Botanische Gesellschaft 1982, Academia Nazionale dei Lincei 1991; Foreign mem. Academia Europaea; Sigma Xi Research Award, Purdue Univ. 1958; McCoy Research Award 1968, Stephen Hales Award, American Society of Plant Physiologists 1970; Hon. D.Sc. (Purdue Univ.) 1971, (Univ. of Newcastle upon Tyne) 1974, (Nagoya Univ.) 1986. *Publications:* Respiratory Metabolism in Plants 1961; 200 articles on plant metabolism in scientific journals. *Leisure interest:* gardening. *Address:* Biology Department, University of California, Santa Cruz, CA 95064 (Office); 46 South Circle Drive, Santa Cruz, CA 95060, U.S.A. (Home). *Telephone:* (408) 458-9295 (Home).

BEFFA, Jean-Louis Guy Henri; French business executive; b. 11 Aug. 1941, Nice; s. of Edmond Beffa and Marguerite Feursinger; m. Marie-Madeleine Brunel-Grasset 1967; two s. one d.; ed. Lycée Masséna, Nice, Ecole Nat. Supérieure des Mines and Inst. d'Etudes Politiques, Paris; Mining Engineer Clermont-Ferrand 1967; motor fuel man. 1967–74; head of refinery service 1970–73; Asst. to Dir. 1973–74; Chief Mining Eng. 1974; Dir. of Planning, Cie. de Saint-Gobain-Pont-à-Mousson 1975–77; Dir.-Gen. Société Pont-à-Mousson 1978, Pres. Dir.-Gen. 1979–82; Deputy Dir. (Pipelines) Saint-Gobain-Pont-à-Mousson 1978, Dir 1979–82; Dir.-Gen. Cie. de Saint-Gobain 1982–86, Pres., Dir.-Gen. 1986–; Pres. Inst. de L'Histoire de L'Industrie (Idni) 1992–; Pres. Supervisory Bd. Poliet 1996–; Vice-Pres. Companie Générale des Eaux 1992–; mem. int. consultative cttee. Chase Manhattan Bank (fmrly. Chemical Bank) 1986–, American Telephone & Telegraph 1987; mem. Admin. Council Ecole Polytechnique 1993–; Admin. Banque Nat. de Paris, Cie. Gen. des eaux, Cie. de Suez et de Petrofina; Chevalier de la Légion d'honneur, Officier de l'Ordre Nat. du Mérite. *Leisure interests:* swimming, golf. *Address:* Les Miroirs, 92096 la Défense cedex, France (Office).

BEG, Gen. Mirza Aslam; Pakistani army officer; b. 2 Aug. 1931, Azamgarh, Uttar Pradesh, India; m.; one s. two d.; ed. Shibli Coll. Azamgarh, Command and Staff Coll. Quetta and Nat. Defence Coll. Rawalpindi; commissioned 1952; served in Baluch (Infantry) Regt.; joined Special Service Group (Commandos) 1961; Brig. Maj. of an Infantry Brigade during India-Pakistan war 1965; Lieut.-Col. 1969; in command, Infantry Bn., India-Pakistan war 1971; staff appts.; Chief Instr. Armed Forces War Course, Nat. Defence Coll.; Brig. in command of Infantry Brigade 1974; Maj.-Gen. in command Infantry Div. 1978; Chief of Gen. Staff 1980–85; Lieut.-Gen. 1984; Corps Commdr. 1985; Gen. and Vice-Chief of Army Staff 1987; Chief of Army Staff 1988–91; Nishan-e-Imtiaz (Mil.), Hilal-e-Imtiaz (Mil.), Sitara-e-Basalat, Tongil (First Class) Medal (S. Korea), U.S. Legion of Merit. *Address:* c/o Office of the Chief of Army Staff, General Headquarters, Rawalpindi, Pakistan.

BEGGS, James Montgomery, M.B.A.; American business executive; b. 9 Jan. 1926, Pittsburgh, Pa.; s. of the late James A. Beggs and Elizabeth M. Beggs; m. Mary Elizabeth Harrison 1953; two s. three d.; ed. U.S. Naval Acad., Harvard Grad. School of Business Admin.; with U.S. Navy 1947–54; Gen. Man. Underseas Div., Westinghouse Electric Corpn. 1955–60, Gen. Man. Systems Operating Div. 1960–63, Vice-Pres. Defense and Space Cen. and Gen. Man. Surface Div. 1963–67, Corpn. Dir. Purchases and Traffic 1967–68; Assoc. Admin. Office of Advanced Research and Tech., NASA 1968–69, Admin. 1981–85; Under-Sec. U.S. Dept. of Transport 1969–73; Man. Dir. Operations, Summa Corpn. 1973–74; Exec. Vice-Pres. Aerospace, Gen. Dynamics Corpn. 1974–81; Pres. DGI 1987–89; Chair. MAKAT, Inc. 1988–; Chair. Spacehab. 1988–; numerous honorary degrees; Goddard Memorial Trophy 1988. *Leisure interests:* golf, hunting. *Address:* 1925 North Lynn Street, Suite 1101, Arlington, VA 22209 (Office); 5408 Falmouth Road, Bethesda, MD 20814, U.S.A. (Home). *Telephone:* (301) 229-9372 (Home). *Fax:* (301) 229-2415 (Home).

BÉGUIN, Bernard, L. ÈS L.; Swiss journalist; b. 14 Feb. 1923, Sion, Valais; s. of Bernard Béguin and Clemence Welten; m. Antoinette Waelbroeck 1948; two s. two d.; ed. Geneva High School, Geneva Univ. and Graduate Inst. of Int. Studies; Swiss Sec. World Student Relief 1945–46; corresp. at U.N. European Headquarters; Journal de Genève 1946–70, Foreign Ed. 1947, Ed.-in-Chief 1959–70; Diplomatic Commentator, Swiss Broadcasting System 1954–59, Swiss T.V. 1959–70; Head of Programmes, Swiss French-speaking TV 1970–73; Deputy Dir. Radio and T.V. 1973–86; Cen. Pres. Swiss Press Asscn. 1958–60, Hon. mem. 1974–; Visiting Prof. in Professional Ethics, Univ. of Neuchâtel 1984–88; Pres. Swiss Press Council 1985–90; Pres. Swiss Ind. Authority on Complaints concerning Broadcasting Programmes 1991–92; consultant with UNESCO (assessment of the media environment), Belarus 1994; mem. Fed. Comm. on Cartels 1964–80; mem. Bd., Swiss Telegraphic Agency 1968–71. *Publication:* Journaliste, qui t'a fait roi? Les médias entre droit et liberté, 1988. *Leisure interests:* sailing, camping. *Address:* 41 avenue de Budé, 1202 Geneva 1, Switzerland. *Telephone:* 733-75-30.

BEHREND, Hilde, PH.D., B.SC.(ECON.); British economist; b. 13 Aug. 1917, Berlin, Germany; d. of Dr. F. W. Behrend and Marie Behrend (née Zöllner); ed. Grammar School, Berlin and London School of Economics; came to Britain 1936; teaching and secretarial posts 1938–42; Grammar School teacher of German and French 1944–49; Asst. Lecturer and Research Fellow, Faculty of Commerce and Social Science, Univ. of Birmingham 1949–54; lecturer, Edinburgh Univ. 1954–64, Sr. lecturer 1964–72, Reader 1972–73, Personal Chair. in Industrial Relations 1973–82, Prof. Emer., Hon. Fellow; mem. of various research bodies on incomes, etc.; mem. Manpower Services Comm., Lothian (Dist.) Manpower Cttee. 1976–79. *Publications:* Absence Under Full Employment 1951, A National Survey of Attitudes to Inflation and Incomes Policy 1966 (with Harriet Lynch and Jean Davies), Incomes Policy and the Individual (with Harriet Lynch, Howard Thomas and Jean Davies) 1967, Views on Pay Increases, Fringe Benefits and Low Pay 1970, Views on Income Differentials and the Economic Situation 1970, Incomes Policy, Equity and Pay Increase Differentials 1973, Attitudes to Price Increases and Pay Claims 1974, How to Monitor Absence from Work: from Head-Count to Computer 1978, Problems of Labour and Inflation 1984, Information and Government (Ed. Davidson and White) (contrib.) 1988, and numerous articles in academic journals. *Leisure interests:* walking, sketching, indoor plants.

BEHRENS, Hildegard; German opera singer; b. Oldenburg; m. Seth Schneidmann; ed. Freiburg Music Conservatory; opera debut, Freiburg 1971; resident mem. Deutsche Oper am Rhein, Düsseldorf; has appeared with Frankfurt Opera, Teatro Nacional de San Carlo, Lisbon, Vienna State Opera, Metropolitan Opera, New York; soloist, Chicago Symphony Orchestra 1984. *Address:* c/o Herbert H. Breslin Inc., W 57th Street, New York, NY 10019, U.S.A.

BEHRMAN, Richard Elliot, M.D., J.D.; American professor of pediatrics; b. 13 Dec. 1931, Philadelphia, Pa.; s. of Robert Behrman and Vivian Keegan; m. Ann Nelson 1954; one s. three d.; ed. Amherst Coll., Harvard Univ., Univ.

of Rochester and Johns Hopkins Univ.; Oregon Regional Primate Research Center and Univ. of Oregon Medical School 1965–68; Prof. of Pediatrics and Dir. Neonatal Intensive Care Unit and Nurseries, Univ. of Ill. Coll. of Medicine 1968–71; Prof. and Chair. Dept. of Pediatrics and Dir. Babies Hospital, Columbia Univ. Coll. of Physicians and Surgeons 1971–76; Prof. and Chair. Dept. of Pediatrics and Dir. Dept. of Pediatrics, Rainbow Babies and Children's Hosp. Case Western Reserve Univ. School of Medicine 1976–82; Dean, School of Medicine, Case Western Reserve Univ. 1980–89, Vice-Pres. Medical Affairs 1987–89; Dir. Centre for Future of Children, Davis and Lucile Pakard FD 1989; Prof. Stanford Univ. and UCSF 1989; Chair. Bd. of Dirs., Lucile Pakard Foundation for Children 1997–; mem. Bd. of Dirs., UCSF Stanford Health Care 1997–; mem. several ed. bds.; Fellow American Acad. of Pediatrics; mem. Inst. Medicine, N.A.S. *Publications:* The Future of Children (Ed.) 1990, Essentials of Paediatrics (Ed.) 1993, Nelson Textbook of Paediatrics (Ed.) 1995. *Leisure interests:* running, hiking, reading. *Address:* Center for Future of Children, 300 Second Street, Los Altos, CA 94022 (Office); 15 Crest Road, Belvedere, CA 94920, U.S.A. (Home). *Telephone:* (415) 948-3696 (Office); (415) 435-9066 (Home). *Fax:* (415) 948-6798.

BEI SHIZHANG, DR. RER. NAT.; Chinese biologist, university professor and institute director; b. 10 Oct. 1903, Ningpo; s. of Bei Qingyang and Chen Ahua; m. Cheng Ihming 1931; two s. two d.; ed. Tongji Medical and Eng. School, Shanghai and Univ. of Freiburg i. Breisgau, Univ. of München, Univ. of Tübingen; Asst. Inst. of Zoology, Univ. Tübingen 1928–29; returned home 1929; Assoc. Prof., Prof. and Chair. of Dept. of Biology, Univ. of Zhejiang 1930–50, Dean of Science Faculty 1949–50; Dir. Inst. of Experimental Biology, Chinese Acad. of Sciences 1950–58; Chair. Dept. of Biophysics, Univ. of Science and Tech., China 1958–64; Dir. Inst. of Biophysics, Chinese Acad. of Sciences 1958–83, Hon. Dir. 1985–; Pres. Chinese Zoological Soc. 1978–83, Chinese Biophysical Soc. 1980–83, (Hon. Pres. 1983–86); Deputy Ed.-in-Chief Scientia Sinica 1958–83, Encyclopedia of China 1984–; Ed.-in-Chief Acta Biophysica Sinica 1985–91; mem. Div. of Biological Sciences, Chinese Acad. of Sciences; mem. 1st 1954, 2nd 1959, 3rd 1964, 4th 1975, 5th 1978 and 6th 1983 NPC. *Publications:* Cell Reformation, Series 1 (24 papers) 1988, Series 2 (18 papers), in preparation; other studies on cell reformation, chromatin, DNA and histones in yolk granules; several articles in Science Record and Scientia Sinica. *Address:* Institute of Biophysics, Chinese Academy of Sciences, Da Tun Road 15, Chao Yang District, 100101 Beijing, People's Republic of China. *Telephone:* 6202-2029; 6255-1064; 6255-4575. *Fax:* 6202-7837.

BEICKLER, Ferdinand; German automobile executive; b. 2 Nov. 1922, Mainz; m.; two s.; joined Adam Opel AG, Rüsselsheim, as apprentice tool-maker 1937, studied mechanical eng.; Tech. Dir. Bochum plant 1964, Chief of operations, Bochum 1966–70, Mfg. Dir. and mem. Bd. of Mans. 1970–82, Chair. Bd., Man. Dir. 1982–87; Chair. Supervisory Bd. Adam Opel 1987–95; Vice-Pres. Gen. Motors Corpn. 1986–87; Man. Dir. Vauxhall Motors Ltd., Luton, U.K. 1979; Bundesverdienstkreuz 1975. *Leisure interests:* classical music, golf. *Address:* c/o Adam Opel AG, Bahnhofsplatz 1, 65428 Rüsselsheim, Germany.

BEINEIX, Jean-Jacques; French film director; b. 8 October 1946, Paris; Asst. Dir. 1970–77; films directed: Le Chien de Monsieur Michel 1971, Diva 1980, La Lune dans le caniveau (The Moon in the Gutter) 1983, 37.2° le matin (Betty Blue) 1985, Roselyne and the Lions 1989.

BEIT-ARIÉ, Malachi, M.A., M.L.S., PH.D.; Israeli university professor and palaeographer; b. 20 May 1937, Petah-Tiqva; s. of Meir Beit-Arié and Esther (née Elpiner) Beit-Arié; m. Dalia Mamut 1958; one s. two d.; ed. Hebrew Univ., Jerusalem; Dir. The Hebrew Palaeography Project, Israel Acad. of Sciences and Humanities 1965–, Inst. of Microfilmed Hebrew Manuscripts 1970–78; Sr. Lecturer in Codicology and Palaeography, Hebrew Univ. 1975–78, Assoc. Prof. 1979–83, Prof. 1984–; Dir. Nat. and Univ. Library 1979–90; Chair. Int. Advisory Council Jewish Nat. Library 1991–; Visiting Fellow Wolfson Coll., Oxford 1984–85; Visiting Researcher IRHT (CNRS) Paris 1991; Visiting Scholar Harvard Univ. 1992; Anne Frank Awards for poetry 1961. *Publications:* These Streets, Those Mountains (lyrics) 1963, The Hills of Jerusalem and All the Pain (poems) 1967, Manuscrits médiévaux en caractères hébraiques (with C. Sirat), Parts I-III 1972–86, Hebrew Codicology 1977, The Only Dated Medieval MS Written in England 1985, Medieval Specimens of Hebrew Scripts 1987, The Makings of the Medieval Hebrew Book 1993, Hebrew Manuscripts of East and West: Towards Comparative Codicology 1993, Catalogue of the Hebrew MSS in the Bodleian Library (Supplement) 1994. *Leisure interest:* classical music. *Address:* P.O. Box 34165, Jerusalem 91341 (Office); 9 Bustanai Street, Jerusalem 93229, Israel (Home). *Telephone:* (02) 5619270 (Office); (02) 5633940 (Home). *Fax:* (02) 6511771.

BEITZ, Berthold; German industrialist; b. 26 Sept. 1913; m. Else Hochheim 1939; three d.; ed. secondary school; bank apprentice; employment in Shell, Hamburg; in charge of the Galician oilfields, Poland 1939–44; Deputy Chair. British Zonal Insurance Control Dept. 1946; Dir.-Gen. Iduna Germania Insurance Co. 1949–53; General-bevollmächtigter Dr. Alfried Krupp von Bohlen and Halbach 1953–67; Chair. Bd. of Curators, Alfried Krupp von Bohlen und Halbach-Stiftung; Chair. Cttee. of the Max-Grundig Foundation; Hon. mem. Int. Olympic Cttee; Chair. Bd., Ruhr Cultural Foundation (Kulturstiftung Ruhr); mem. 'pro ruhrgebiet' Cttee.; Direktorium der Univ. Witten-Herdecke; Hon. Chair. Supervisory Bd., Fried. Krupp AG Hoesch-Krupp, Essen, Inst. for East-West Security Studies, N.Y.; Hon. Gov. Ernst-Moritz-Arndt Univ. (Greifswald); Hon. mem. Nat. Olympic Cttee., Univ. of Essen; Dr. h.c. (Jagiellonian Univ., Poland); Hon. Dr. (Greifswald Univ.); Yad Vashem Medal (Israel), Grosses Bundesverdienstkreuz mit Stern und Schulterband, Grosskreuz des Verdienstordens der Bundesrepublik Deutschland, Commandorium with Star of Order of Merit (Poland), First Class Order of Madara Reiter (Bulgaria); Freeman of the City of Essen; Ehrenbürger der Hanestadt Greifswald; numerous other decorations including B'nai B'rith Medal. *Leisure interests:* yachting, hunting, jazz, modern painting. *Address:* Weg zur Platte 37, 45133 Essen, Germany. *Telephone:* 0201-188-1.

BÉJART, Maurice (Jean); French choreographer, dancer and stage director; b. 1 Jan. 1927; s. of Gaston Béjart and Germaine Berger; ed. Lycée de Marseilles; début as ballet dancer with Marseilles Opera 1945; with int. Ballet 1949–50, Royal Opera, Stockholm 1951–52; co-founded Les Ballets de l'Etoile, later Ballet-Théâtre de Paris, 1954 (Dir. 1954–59); Artistic Dir. Béjart Ballet Lausanne (fmrly. Twentieth Century Ballet Co.) 1960– (became Béjart Ballet Lausanne 1987); Dir. Mudra Sch 1972; mem. Inst. (Académie des Beaux-Arts) 1994; Grand Prix Nat. de la Musique 1970, Prix Erasme de la Danse 1974, Chevalier des Arts et Lettres, Commdr. Ordre de Léopold 1982, Ordre du Soleil Levant (Japan) 1986, Grand Officier Ordre de la Couronne (Belgium) 1988, Imperial Award (Japan) 1993. *Principal works include:* La Belle au Boa, Symphonie pour un homme seul 1955, Orphée 1958, le Sacre du Printemps 1959, Boléro 1961, The Tales of Hoffmann 1962, The Merry Widow, The Damnation of Faust, l'Oiseau de Feu 1964, Roméo and Juliet 1966, Messe pour le Temps Présent 1967, Firebird 1970, Song of a Wayfarer, Nijinsky: Clown de Dieu 1971, Le Marteau sans Maître, la Traviata 1973, Ce que l'amour me dit 1974, Notre Faust 1975, Heliogabale, Pli selon pli 1976, Petrouchka 1977, Gaîté Parisienne, Ce que la Mort me dit 1978, Mephisto Waltzer 1979, Casta Diva, Eros Thanatos 1980, The Magic Flute, les Chaises, Light, les Uns et les Autres (film) 1981, Wien Wien nur du Allein, Thalassa Mare Nostrum 1982, Salome, Messe pour le Temps Futur, Vie et mort d'une marionnette humaine 1983, Dionysos 1984, Le Concours, la Chauve Souris 1985, Arepo, Malraux ou la Métamorphose des Dieux 1986, Trois Etudes pour Alexandre, Souvenir de Léningrad, Après-midi d'un Faune, Fiche Signalétique, 1987, Patrice Chéreau . . ., Dibouk, Et Valse, Piaf, Paris-Tokyo, A force de partir . . . 1988, 1789 et nous, Elegie pour elle, L . . ., aile 1989, Ring um den Ring 1990, Nijinsky Clown de Dieu 1990, Pyramides 1990, M pour B 1990, Mort Subite 1991, Maurice Béjart (co-choreographer) 1991, Ballade de la rue Athina, Le Mandarin merveilleux, King Lear/Prospero, Sissi, Les Chaises 1994, le Presbytère 1997, Jérusalem, cité de la paix 1997. *Publications:* Mathilde, ou le temps perdu (novel) 1963, La Reine Verte (play) 1963, L'Autre chant de la danse 1974, Un instant dans la vie d'autrui 1979, La mort subite 1991, Maurice Béjart 1991 (jtly), la Vie de qui? 1997. *Address:* Rudra Béjart Lausanne, case postale 25, 1000 Lausanne 22, Switzerland.

BEKHTEREVA, Natalya Petrovna, DR. MED. SC.; Russian physiologist; b. 7 July 1924, Leningrad; d. of Pyotr Vladimirovich Bekhterev and Zinaida Vasilievna Bekhtereva; m. 1st Vsevolod Medvedev 1948 (divorced 1973); m. 2nd Ivan Kastelian 1973 (died 1990); one s.; ed. Leningrad Medical Inst., mem. CPSU 1959–91; junior research worker at U.S.S.R. Acad. of Medical Sciences Inst. of Experimental Medicine 1950–54; on staff of Neuro-surgical Inst. of Ministry of Health 1954–62; Head of Lab., Deputy Dir. Inst. of Experimental Medicine 1962–, Dir. 1970–90; Scientific Dir. Inst. of the Human Brain, Russian Acad. of Science 1990–; U.S.S.R. People's Deputy 1970–74, 1989–91; Corresp. mem. Austrian Acad. of Sciences; Foreign mem. Cuban Physiological Soc.; Hon. mem. Czechoslovakian Neurochirurgical Soc. J.E. Purkyne, Hungarian Electrophysiological Soc.; mem. Finnish Acad. of Sciences, U.S.S.R. (now Russian) Acad. of Sciences 1981–, U.S.S.R. (now Russian) Acad. of Medical Sciences 1975; Fellow Academia Medicina et Psychiatria (U.S.A.); U.S.S.R. State Prize Winner 1985; McCulloch Medal, U.S.A. Cybernetics Soc., Hans Berger Medal, G.D.R. Electrophysiological Soc., Medal of Bulgarian Union of Research Workers, Bechterev's Gold Medal, Russian Acad. of Sciences, Century Award of the Int. Org. of Psychophysiology 1998. *Publications:* over 300 publs. in Russian and English on physiology of mental activity, structural and functional org. of physiological activity of brain, incl. The Healthy and Diseased Human Brain 1985. *Leisure interests:* painting, music. *Address:* Institute of the Human Brain, Pavlova Street 9, St. Petersburg 197376, Russia. *Telephone:* 234-22-21 (Office). *Fax:* 234-32-47.

BEKSIŃSKI, Zdzislaw; Polish painter; b. 24 Feb. 1929, Sanok; m.; one s.; ed. Cracow Tech. Univ.; mem. of Asscn. of Polish Artists (ZPAP) 1962–83, 1989; collaborated with Piotr Dmochowslú, Paris 1980–94; numerous one-man exhbns. in Poland, France, Germany and Japan. *Leisure interests:* collecting records, computer graphic art. *Address:* ul. Sonaty 6. m. 314, 02-744 Warsaw, Poland. *Telephone:* 47 05 87.

BELAFONTE, Harry; American singer; b. 1 March 1927, New York; s. of Harold George Belafonte Sr. and Malvene Love Wright; m. 2nd Julie Robinson 1957; one s. three d.; ed. George Washington High School, New York.; in Jamaica 1935–39; service with U.S. Navy 1943–45; American Negro Theater; student at Manhattan New School for Social Research Dramatic Workshop 1946–48; first engagement at the Vanguard, Greenwich Village; European tours 1958, 1976, 1981, 1983, 1988; Pres. Belafonte Enterprises

Inc.; Goodwill Amb. for UNICEF 1987; Host Nelson Mandela Birthday Concert, Wembley 1988; Broadway appearances in Three For Tonight, Almanac, Belafonte At The Palace, and in films Bright Road, Carmen Jones 1952, Island in the Sun 1957, The World, the Flesh and the Devil 1958, Odds Against Tomorrow 1959, The Angel Levine (also producer) 1969, Grambling's White Tiger 1981, White Man's Burden; produced with Sidney Poitier Buck and the Preacher 1971 (also acted), Uptown Saturday Night 1974; Emmy Television Award for Tonight with Belafonte 1960; Producer Strolling 20's 1965, A Time for Laughter 1967, Harry and Lena 1970, Beat Street 1984; concerts in U.S.A., Europe 1989, Canada 1990, U.S.A. and Canada 1991, N. America, Europe and Far East 1996; mem. bd. N.Y. State Martin Luther King Jr. Inst. for Nonviolence 1989–; numerous awards including Golden Acord Award, Bronx Community Coll. 1989, Mandela Courage Award 1990; Hon. D.Hum. (Park Coll., Mo.) 1968, Hon. D.Arts, New School of Social Research, New York 1968, Hon. D.C.L. (Newcastle) 1997, numerous other hon. doctorates. *Leisure interests:* photography, water skiing, recording.

BÉLANGER, Gerard, M.A., M.SOC.SC.; Canadian professor of economics; b. 23 Oct. 1940, St. Hyacinthe; s. of Georges Bélanger and Cécile Girard; m. Michèle Potvin 1964; one d.; ed. Princeton and Laval Univs.; Prof. Dept. of Econs. Laval Univ. 1967–, Prof. of Econs. 1977–; Research Co-ordinator, Howe Inst. Montreal 1977–79; mem. Task Force on Urbanization, Govt. of Quebec 1974–76; Sec. Acad. of Letters and Social Sciences, Royal Soc. of Canada 1985–88; Woodrow Wilson Fellow. *Publications:* The Price of Health 1972, Le financement municipal au Québec 1976, Taxes and Expenditures in Québec and Ontario 1978, Le prix du transport au Québec 1978, L'économique du secteur public 1981, Croissance du Secteur Public et Fédéralisme 1988. *Address:* Department of Economics, Université Laval, Québec, G1K 7P4, Canada. *Telephone:* (418) 656-5363 (Office). *Fax:* (418) 656-2707.

BELAÚNDE TERRY, Fernando; Peruvian politician and architect; b. 7 Oct. 1913; ed. France and U.S.A.; mem. Chamber of Deputies 1945–48; Dean in School of Architecture, Lima 1948–56; Leader Acción Popular (AP) 1956–; Presidential Candidate 1956, 1962; Pres. of Peru 1963–68 (deposed by military coup); fled to New York Oct. 1968; lecturing at Harvard Univ. Nov. 1968; returned to Peru briefly Dec. 1970, deported at end of month, returned Jan. 1976; Pres. of Peru July 1980–85. *Publications:* Peru's Own Conquest (autobiog.). *Address:* Acción Popular, Paseo Colón 218, Lima 1, Peru.

BÉLAVAL, Philippe Marie; French library executive and civil servant; b. 21 Aug. 1955, Toulouse; s. of Jacques Bélaval and Marie-Thérèse (née Chazarenc) Bélaval; ed. Faculté des Sciences Sociales de Toulouse, Inst. d'études politiques de Toulouse; trainee at École nationale d'admin. 1977–79, auditor 1979; technical adviser Conseil d'Etat 1983–84, counsel 1984, rep. of Sec. of State for Budget and Consumption 1984–86; Asst. Dir. Office of Minister of Public Affairs and Admin. Reform 1988–89, Dir. 1989–90; Dir.-Gen. Théâtre nationale de l'Opéra de Paris 1990–92; Dir.-Gen. Bibliothèque nationale de France 1994–98; Dir.-Gen. Archives de France 1998-; Pres. Admin. Council Groupe vocal de France 1985–90; Council of State 1996; mem. Admin. Council of École des chartes; Sr. lecturer Inst. d'études politiques de Paris; Chevalier Ordre du Mérite, des Arts et des Lettres. *Address:* Archives de France, 60 rue des Francs-Bourgeois, 75141 Paris Cedex 03; Conseil d'État, place du Palais Royal, 75100 Paris, France.

BELCHIOR, Murillo, M.D.; Brazilian physician; b. 26 April 1913, Rio de Janeiro; s. of Carlos de Britto Bayma Belchior and Laura Bastos Belchior; m. Jean Shafer Belchior 1945; two d.; ed. Colégio Santo Inàcio, Univs. of Brazil and Michigan and Harvard Univ.; Chief, Clinical Dept., Santa Casa Hosp. 1942–; Dir. for int. health, Ministry of Health 1963–69; Pres. Fed. Council of Medicine 1968, Council of Int. Org. of Medical Sciences 1979–96, U.S.-Brazil Cultural Inst. 1974–; mem. New York Acad. of Sciences; Fellow, Royal Soc. of Medicine (U.K.); Eisenhower Fellow. *Leisure interests:* cultural matters. *Address:* Rua Bolívar, 7 apto. 6 (Copacabana), 20.061 Rio de Janeiro, Brazil. *Telephone:* 236.6429.

BELIGAN, Radu; Romanian actor; b. 14 Dec. 1918, Galbeni, Bacău County; m.; four c.; ed. Bucharest Conservatoire; started career at Muncă şi Lumină (Work and Light) Theatre in Bucharest, then played at Alhambra and Nat. Theatre; Prof. Inst. of Drama and Film Art Bucharest 1960–68; Merited Artist 1953, People's Artist 1962; Dir. Teatrul de Comedie 1960–68; Dir. Nat. Theatre 1969–89; Chair. Int. Theatre Inst.; mem. Cen. Cttee. Romanian CP 1969–89; mem. Exec. Bureau Nat. Council Front of Socialist Democracy and Unity 1980–89; performances in classic and modern Romanian plays and int. repertoire (Shakespeare, Gogol, Chekhov, Albee, Dürrenmatt and others). *Publications:* Pretexte şi subtexte (Pretexts and Understatements), essays, 1968; Luni, marţi, miercuri (Monday, Tuesday, Wednesday), Memoirs 1978. *Address:* Str. Spătarului 36, 70241 Bucharest, Romania.

BELIN, Roger, D.IUR.; French civil servant; b. 21 March 1916, Paris; m. Christiane Bressac 1961; ed. Univ. of Paris Law Faculty, Paris School of Political Sciences; Auditeur Conseil d'Etat 1943; Chargé de Mission, Présidence du Conseil 1944; Maître des Requêtes, Conseil d'Etat 1949; mem. Atomic Energy Cttee. 1951; Dir. Présidence du Conseil 1955; Sec.-Gen. of the Govt. 1958; Pres. Régie autonome des transports parisiens 1964–81; Hon. Conseiller d'Etat 1981; Pres. Union Int. des Transports Publics 1973–79; Man. Dir. of newspaper Le Parisien 1982–84; Chargé de Mission to Edouard Balladur (Minister of State, of Economy, of Finance, of Privatisation) 1986–88; Grand Officier Légion d'honneur. *Address:* 9 boulevard Flandrin, 75116 Paris, France (Home).

BELL, Baron (Life Peer) cr. 1998, of Belgravia in the City of Westminster, **Timothy John Leigh Bell,** Kt., F.I.P.A.; British public relations executive; b. 18 Oct. 1941; s. of Arthur Leigh Bell and Greta Mary Bell (née Findlay); m. Virginia Wallis Hornbrook 1988; one s. one d.; ed. Queen Elizabeth's Grammar School, Barnet, Herts.; with ABC Television 1959–61, Colman Prentis & Varley 1961–63, Hobson Bates 1963–66, Geers Gross 1966–70; Man. Dir. Saatchi & Saatchi 1970–75, Chair. and Man. Dir. Saatchi & Saatchi Compton 1975–85; Group Chief Exec. Lowe Howard-Spink Campbell Ewald 1985–87, Deputy Chair. Lowe Howard-Spink & Bell PLC 1987–89; Chair. Lowe-Bell Communications 1987–, Chime Communications 1994–; f. Lowe Bell Govt. Relations 1993–; arranged man. buy-out of Lowe Bell Communications 1989; Special Adviser to Chair. Nat. Coal Bd. 1984–86; mem. South Bank Bd. 1985–86; Chair. Charity Projects 1984–93, Pres. 1993–; Dir. Centre for Policy Studies; mem. Industry Cttee. SCF, Public Relations Cttee. Greater London Fund for the Blind 1979–86, Council Royal Opera House 1982–85, Public Affairs Cttee., Worldwide Fund for Nature 1985–88; Gov. B.F.I 1983–86. *Address:* 7 Hertford Street, London, W1Y 7DY, England (Office).

BELL, (Ernest) Arthur, C.B., PH.D., C.CHEM., F.R.S.C., C.BIOL., F.I.BIOL., F.L.S.; British scientist; b. 20 June 1926, Gosforth, Northumberland; s. of Albert and Rachel Enid (née Williams) Bell; m. Jean Swinton Ogilivie 1952; two s. one d.; ed. Dame Allan's School, Newcastle upon Tyne, King's Coll., Newcastle, Univ. of Durham, Trinity Coll., Univ. of Dublin; Research Chemist, ICI 1946–47, Demonstrator and holder of Sarah Purser Research Award, Trinity Coll., Dublin 1947–49, Asst. to Prof. of Biochemistry 1949–53; Lecturer in Biochemistry, King's Coll., London 1953–64, Reader 1964–68, Prof. of Biology and Head of Dept. of Plant Sciences 1972–81, Dean of Natural Science 1980–81; Prof. of Botany, Univ. of Texas at Austin 1968–72; Dir. Royal Botanic Gardens, Kew Nov. 1981–88; Consultant Dir. CAB Int. Mycological Inst. 1982–88; mem. Working Party on Naturally Occurring Toxicants in Foods 1983–95; Sr. Foreign Scientist Fellow of Natural Science Foundation of U.S.A.; Visiting Prof. Univ. of Kansas 1964, Univ. of Sierra Leone 1977, King's Coll., London 1982–, Univ. of Reading 1982–88; Sr. Commonwealth Visiting Fellow, Australia 1980; Cecil H. and Ida Green Visiting Prof. Univ. of British Columbia 1987; Visiting Prof. Univ. of Texas at Austin 1988–90, Adjunct Prof. 1991–; Scientific Dir., Texas Botanical Garden Soc. 1988–; mem. Royal Mint Advisory Cttee. 1992–98; Fellow, King's Coll., London 1982; Vice-Pres. Linnean Soc. of London 1982; Pres., Plant Biology Section, British Asscn. for the Advancement of Science 1985–86; Hon. mem. Phytochemical Soc. of Europe 1985–; Visiting Fellow, Japan Soc. for the Promotion of Science 1986; Pres. King's Coll. London Asscn. 1986–88; Hon. Fellow, Trinity Coll. Dublin Ireland 1990, Emer. Leverhulme Fellow 1991–93. *Publications:* numerous publs. on plant biochemistry, chemotaxonomy and chemical ecology. *Leisure interests:* walking, travel, watching rugby football. *Address:* 3 Hillview, Wimbledon, London SW20 0TA, England. *Telephone:* 0181-946 2626.

BELL, Geoffrey Lakin, B.SC.ECON.; British international banker; b. 8 Nov. 1939, Grimsby; s. of late Walter Lakin Bell and of Anne Bell; m. Joan Rosine Abel 1973; one d.; ed. Grimsby Tech. High School and London School of Econs.; H.M. Treasury 1961–63; Visiting Economist Federal Reserve System 1963–64; H.M. Treasury and Lecturer, L.S.E. 1964–66; Adviser British Embassy, Washington 1966–69; joined J. Henry Schroder Wagg and Co. Ltd. 1969, Asst. to Chair. 1969–72; Dir. and Exec. Vice-Pres. Schroder Int. Ltd.; Dir. Schroder Bermuda Ltd.; Exec. Sec. Group of Thirty 1978–; Pres. Geoffrey Bell and Co. Ltd. Aug. 1982–; Chair. Guinness Mahon Holdings 1987–93; mem. Court of Govs. L.S.E. 1994–. *Publication:* The Euro-Dollar Market and the International Financial System 1973, contrib. The Times and numerous academic and other publications. *Address:* Apt. 15A, 455 East 57th Street, New York, NY 10022, U.S.A.; 17 Abbotsbury House, Abbotsbury Road, London, W14 8EN, England. *Telephone:* (212) 838-1193 (U.S.A.); 0171-603 9408 (England).

BELL, John Anthony, O.B.E. A.M.; Australian theatre director and actor; b. 1 Nov. 1940, Newcastle; s. of Albert Bell and Joyce Feeney; m. Anna Volska 1965; two d.; ed. Maitland Marist Bros. High School, N.S.W. and Univ. of Sydney; actor with Old Tote Theatre Co. 1963–64, with RSC U.K. 1964–69; co-founder, Nimrod Theatre Co. 1970–85; founder and Artistic Dir. Bell Shakespeare Co. 1990–; roles include King Lear, Macbeth, Shylock, Malvolio and Richard III; Hon. D. Litt. *Leisure interests:* reading, music, painting. *Address:* The Bell Shakespeare Company, Level 1, 88 George Street, The Rocks, N.S.W. 2000, Australia.

BELL, Joshua; American violinist; b. 9 Dec. 1967, Indiana; youngest guest soloist at a Philadelphia Orchestra Subscription concert 1982; European tour with St. Louis Symphony 1985; German tour with Indianapolis Symphony 1987; guest soloist with numerous orchestras in U.S.A., Canada, U.K., Germany and Czech Repub.; has also appeared in U.S.A. and Europe as a recitalist; played première of violin concerto by Nicholas Maw, written for him, with Philharmonia Orchestra 1993; Visiting Prof. at Royal Acad. of Music. *Recordings:* Mendelssohn and Bruch concertos with the Academy of St. Martin-in-the-Fields and Sir Neville Marriner, Tchaikovsky and Wieniawski concertos with the Cleveland Orchestra and Vladimir Ashkenazy, recital album of Brahms, Paganini, Sarasate and Wieniawski with Samuel

Sanders, Lalo Symphonie Espagnole and Saint-Saens Concerto with Montreal Symphony Orchestra and Charles Dutoit, Franck, Fauré and Débussy, Chausson Concerto for violin, piano and string quartet with Thibaudet and Isserlis, Poème with Royal Philharmonic Orchestra and Andrew Litton, Mozart Concertos 3 and 5 with the English Chamber Orchestra and Peter Maag, Prokofiev violin concertos with Montreal Symphony Orchestra and Charles Dutoit, Barber and Walton concertos and Bloch Baal Shem with Baltimore Symphony Orchestra and David Zinman, recital disc with Olli Mustonen. *Leisure interests:* chess, computers, golf, tennis and baseball. *Address:* c/o IMG Artists, Media House, 3 Burlington Lane, Chiswick, London, W4 2TH, England.

BELL, Martin, M.A., O.B.E.; British broadcaster; b. 31 Aug. 1938; s. of late Adrian Bell and Marjorie Bell (née Gibson); m. 1st Nelly Gourdon 1971 (divorced); two d.; m. 2nd Rebecca Sobel 1985 (divorced 1993); m. 3rd Fiona Goddard 1998; ed. The Leys School, Cambridge, King's Coll., Cambridge; joined BBC 1962, news asst., Norwich 1962–64, gen. reporter, London and overseas 1964–76, Diplomatic Corresp. 1976–77, Chief N. American Corresp. 1977–89, Berlin Corresp. BBC TV News 1989–93, Vienna Corresp. 1993–94, Foreign Affairs Corresp. 1994–96, Special Corresp., Nine O'Clock News 1997; has reported from over 70 countries, and has covered wars in Vietnam, Middle East 1967, 1973, Angola, Rhodesia, Biafra, El Salvador, Gulf 1991, Nicaragua, Croatia, Bosnia; M.P. (Ind.) for Tatton 1997–; Royal TV Soc. Reporter of the Year 1976, 1992, TV and Radio Industries Club Newscaster of the Year 1995, Inst. of Public Relations Pres.'s Medal 1996; Dr. h.c. (Derby) 1996; Hon. M.A. (E. Anglia) 1997, (Aberdeen) 1998. *Publication:* In Harm's Way 1995. *Address:* House of Commons, Westminster, London, SW1A 0AA, England.

BELL, William Edwin, C.B.E., B.SC.; British oil industry executive; b. 4 Aug. 1926, Leicester; s. of Cuthbert Edwin Bell and Winifred Mary Simpson; m. Angela Josephine Vaughan 1952; two s. two d.; ed. Birmingham Univ. and Royal School of Mines, Imperial Coll. of Science and Tech., London; joined Royal Dutch Shell Group 1948; Dir. Shell U.K. Ltd. and Gen. Man. Shell U.K. Exploration and Production 1973; Man. Dir. Shell U.K. Ltd. 1976–79; Dir. Shell Int. Petroleum Co. Ltd. and Middle E. Regional Coordinator 1980–84; Chair. Enterprise Oil PLC 1984–91, Deputy Chair. (non-exec.) 1991–; Pres. U.K. Offshore Operators' Asscn. 1975–76; Dir. (non-exec.) Costain Group PLC 1982–92; mem. Advisory Bd., Brown and Root (U.K.) Ltd. 1983–92. *Leisure interests:* yachting and golf. *Address:* Fordcombe Manor, Fordcombe, nr. Tunbridge Wells, Kent, TN3 0SE, England. *Telephone:* (01892) 740214.

BELLAMY, Carol, J.D.; American agency administrator; b. 1942, Plainfield, N.J.; ed. Gettysburg Coll. and New York Univ.; Asst. Commr. Dept. of Mental Health and Mental Health Retardation Service, New York; with Peace Corps, Guatemala; Assoc. Cravath, Swaine & Moore, New York; mem. New York State Senate; Man. Dir Morgan Stanley & Co. New York; Dir. Peace Corps, Washington, D.C. 1993–95; Exec. Dir. UNICEF 1995–. *Address:* UNICEF, 3 United Nations Plaza, New York, N.Y. 10017, U.S.A.

BELLAMY, Christopher William, M.A., Q.C.; British judge; b. 25 April 1946, Waddesdon, Bucks.; s. of William Albert Bellamy and Vyvienne Hilda Bellamy (née Meyrick); m. Deirdre Patricia Turner 1989; one s. two d.; ed. Tonbridge School, Brasenose Coll., Oxford; called to the Bar, Middle Temple 1968 (Bencher 1994), in full-time practice 1970–92, Q.C. 1986, Asst. Recorder 1989–92; Judge of Court of First Instance of the EC 1992–; Gov. Ravensbourne Coll. of Design and Communication 1988–92. *Publication:* Common Market Law of Competition (jtly.) 1973. *Leisure interests:* family life, walking, history. *Address:* Court of First Instance of the European Communities, 2925GD Luxembourg. *Telephone:* (352) 4303 3494/3562.

BELLAMY, David James, O.B.E., PH.D., F.I.BIOL.; British botanist, writer and broadcaster; b. 18 Jan. 1933, London; s. of Thomas Bellamy and Winifred Green; m. Rosemary Froy 1959; two s. three d.; ed. Chelsea Coll. of Science and Tech. and Bedford Coll., London Univ.; Lecturer, then Sr. Lecturer, Dept. of Botany, Univ. of Durham 1960–80, Hon. Prof. of Adult and Continuing Educ. 1980–82; Visiting Prof. Massey Univ., N.Z. 1988–89; Special Prof. of Botany Nottingham Univ. 1987–; TV and radio presenter and scriptwriter; TV series include: Life in Our Sea 1970, Bellamy on Botany 1973, Bellamy's Britain 1975, Bellamy's Europe 1977, Botanic Man 1978, Up a Gum Tree 1980, Backyard Safari 1981, The Great Seasons 1982, Bellamy's New World 1983, End of the Rainbow Show 1986, S.W.A.L.L.O.W. 1986, Turning the Tide 1986, Bellamy's Bugle 1986, 1987, 1988, Bellamy on Top of the World 1987, Bellamy's Journey to the Centre of the World 1987, Bellamy's Bird's Eye View 1989, Wheat Today What Tomorrow? 1989, Moa's Ark 1990, Bellamy Rides Again 1992, Blooming Bellamy 1993, 1994, Routes of Wisdom 1993, The Peak 1994, Bellamy's Border Raids 1996, Westwatch 1997, A Welsh Herbal 1998, Salt Solutions 1999, Buzz of Biodiversity 1999; Founder Dir. Conservation Foundation; Pres. WATCH 1982; Pres. Youth Hostels Asscn. 1983; Pres. Population Concern 1988–, Nat. Asscn. of Environmental Educ. 1989–, Plantlife 1995–, Wildlife Trust's Partnership 1996–, British Inst. of Cleaning Science 1997–; Dir. David Bellamy Assocs. (environmental consultants) 1988–97; Pres. Council Zoological Soc. of London 1991–94; Hon. Fellow of the Linnaean Soc., of CIWEM; Dr. h.c. (C.N.A.A.) 1990; Dutch Order of the Golden Ark 1989, UNEP Global 500 Award 1990. *Publications include:* Peatlands 1974, Life Giving Sea 1977, Half of Paradise 1979, The Great Seasons 1981, Discovering the Countryside with David Bellamy (Vols. I, II) 1982, (Vols. III, IV) 1983, The Mouse Book 1983, The Queen's Hidden Garden 1984, Bellamy's Ireland 1986, Bellamy's Changing Countryside (4 vols.) 1988, England's Last Wilderness 1989, Wetlands 1990, Wilderness Britain 1990, Moa's Ark 1990, How Green Are You? 1991, Tomorrow's Earth 1992, World Medicine 1992, Poo, You and the Poteroo's Loo 1997, Bellamy's Changing Countryside 1998 and books connected with TV series. *Leisure interests:* children and ballet. *Address:* Mill House, Bedburn, Bishop Auckland, Co. Durham, DL13 3NN; c/o The Conservation Foundation, 1 Kensington Gore, London, SW7 2AR, England.

BELLANY, John, C.B.E., R.A.; British artist; b. 18 June 1942, Port Seton, Scotland; s. of Richard Weatherhead Bellany and Agnes Maltman Bellany; m. 1st Helen Margaret Percy 1965 (remarried 1986); two s. one d.; m. 2nd Juliet Gray (née Lister) 1979 (deceased 1985); ed. Cockenzie Public School, Preston Lodge, Prestonpans, Edin. Coll. of Art, R.C.A., London; lecturer in Fine Art, Winchester School of Art 1969–73; Head of Faculty of Painting, Croydon Coll. of Art 1973–78; Visiting Lecturer in Painting, R.C.A. 1975–85; lecturer in Fine Art, Goldsmiths' Coll., Univ. of London 1978–84; Fellow Commoner, Trinity Hall, Cambridge 1988; one-man exhbns. include: Arts Council Touring Show 1978, Rosa Esman Gallery, New York 1982, 1983, 1984, Ikon Gallery, Birmingham, Walker Art Gallery, Liverpool, Graves Art Gallery, Sheffield, Christine Abrahams Gallery, Melbourne, Nat. Portrait Gallery, London 1986, Galerie Kirkhaar, Amsterdam 1986, Fischer Fine Art, London 1989, Retrospective, Scottish Nat. Gallery of Modern Art, Kunsthalle, Hamburg, Serpentine Gallery, London, Ruth Siegel Gallery, New York 1990, Raab Gallery, Berlin, Ruth Siegel Gallery, U.S.A. 1990, Fitzwilliam Museum, Cambridge, Fischer Fine Art, London 1991, Kelvingrove Museum, Glasgow, Beaux Arts Gallery 1992, Berkeley Square Gallery, London 1993, Beaux Arts Gallery, London 1997; Hon. R.S.A.; Dr. h.c. (Edin.) 1996; Hon. D.Lit. (Edin.) 1998; Arts Council Award 1981, Jt. 1st Prize, Athena Int. Award 1985. *Publications:* Scottish National Galleries 1986, National Portrait Gallery, London 1986. *Leisure interests:* opera, motoring. *Address:* 2 Windmill Drive, London, SW4 9DE, England; 19 Great Stuart Street, Edinburgh, EH2 7TP, Scotland (Homes).

BELLEN, Heinz, DR. PHIL.; German professor of ancient history; b. 1 Aug. 1927, Neuss/Rhein; s. of Heinrich Bellen and Elisabeth Hussmann; m. Agnes Meuters 1958; two d.; secondary school teacher, Düsseldorf 1957–62; Asst. Prof. Cologne 1962–68, Lecturer, 1968–73; Prof. of Ancient History, Univ. of Mainz 1974–93; mem. Mainz Acad. 1975–. *Publications:* Studien zur Sklavenflucht im römischen Kaiserreich 1971, Die germanische Leibwache der römischen Kaiser 1981, Metus Gallicus-Metus Punicus 1985, Grundzüge der römischen Geschichte (Vol. I) 1994, (Vol. II) 1998, Ed.: Forschungen zur antiken Sklaverei 1978, Politik-Recht-Gesellschaft 1997. *Address:* Saarstrasse 21, 55099 Mainz (Office); Alfred-Nobel Strasse 23, 55124 Mainz, Germany (Home). *Telephone:* (06131) 472919.

BELLET, Pierre Rémy; French lawyer (retd.); b. 7 Sept. 1911, Maisons-Laffitte; s. of Daniel Bellet and Lilly Bourgeois; m. Annette Hirchberg 1946; three s.; ed. Lycée Janson-de-Sailly, Univ. of Paris, Ecole des Sciences Politiques; trainee lawyer, Paris Court of Appeal 1933–35, Pres. of Chamber 1964–65; 1st Vice-Pres. Seine Tribunal de Grande Instance 1965–68, Pres. 1968–72; Councillor, Court of Cassation 1968, Pres. of Chamber 1972–77, First Pres. 1977–80; Vice-Pres. Cttee. of Int. Private Law 1965–71, Pres. 1971–; Pres. Admin. Council, Ecole Nat. de la Magistrature; Pres. Comm. Nat. de l'informatique et des libertés 1978–79; Chair. 2nd Chamber, Iran-U.S.A. Arbitration Tribunal 1981–83; Pres. Council of Int. Arbitration Franco-Arab Chamber of Commerce 1983–; Vice-Pres. Juristes européens; Dr. h.c. (Glasgow, Geneva); Prize, Paris Faculty of Law; Grand Officier, Légion d'honneur, Commdr. ordre nat. du Mérite. *Leisure interests:* sailing, painting. *Address:* 15 avenue du Président Wilson, 75116 Paris, France. *Telephone:* 4723-50-61 (Home).

BELLINGHAM, Alastair John, C.B.E.; British professor of haematology; b. 27 March 1938, London; m. Valerie Jill Morford 1963 (died 1997); three s.; ed. Tiffin Boys' School, Univ. Coll. Hosp. Medical School, London; Sr. Lecturer, Hon. Consultant Haematology Dept., Univ. Coll. Hosp. Medical School 1971; Prof. of Haematology Univ. of Liverpool 1974, King's Coll., Univ. of London 1984–97; Pres. British Soc. for Haematology 1992–93, Royal Coll. of Pathologists 1993–96. *Leisure interests:* photography, wine and viticulture. *Publications:* numerous publs. on red cell physiology and biochemistry, inherited red cell abnormalities, sickle cell disease. *Address:* Broadstones, Teffont Magna, Salisbury, Wilts., SP3 5QP, England. *Telephone:* (01722) 716267.

BELLINI, Mario; Italian architect; fmrly. designer for Olivetti office machines; exhbns. include: The Renaissance from Brunelleschi to Michelangelo—The Representation of Architecture, Venice 1994, Paris 1995, Berlin 1995; commissions include: Tokyo design centre, Sakurada Dori Dist., Villa Erba int. congress and exhbn. centre, Cernobbio on Lake Como, exhbn. bldgs. for Milan Trade Fair. *Address:* c/o Architecture Centre, 66 Portland Place, London W.1, England.

BELLOCH JULBE, Juan Alberto; Spanish politician; b. 3 Feb. 1950, Mora de Rubielos (Teruel); m.; one s.; mem. Democratic Justice; founder, Asscn. Judges for Democracy, Asscn. Magistrats Européens pour la démocratie et les libertés; founder and Pres. Asscn. for the Human Rights of the Basque Country; Judge, La Gomera, Berga Vic y Alcoy from 1975; Magistrate and Pres. Court of Justice of Biscay 1981–90; mem. Gen. Council of Judiciary

1990–93; Minister of Justice 1993–96, of the Interior 1994–96. *Address:* c/o PSOE, Ferraz 68 y 70, 28008 Madrid, Spain. *Telephone:* 1-582-0444. *Fax:* 1-582-0422.

BELLOW, Saul, B.S.; American writer; b. 10 June 1915, Quebec, Canada; s. of Abraham and Liza (née Gordon) Bellow; m. 5th Janis Freedman 1989; three s. (from fmr. m.); ed. Northwestern Univ.; Professor, Univ. of Minn. 1946–48; Prof. Princeton Univ. 1952–53; Prof. Univ. of Chicago 1964–; mem. Faculty, Boston Univ.; mem. Comm. on Social Thought 1963–; Nat. Book Award, Inst. of Arts and Letters 1953, Ford Foundation Grant 1959, Prix Int. de Littérature 1965, U.S. Nat. Book Award for The Adventures of Augie March 1954, Herzog 1965, Mr. Sammler's Planet 1971, Pulitzer Prize for Humboldt's Gift 1976, Nobel Prize for Literature 1976; Fellow, American Acad. of Arts and Sciences, Commandeur, Légion d'honneur; Malaparte Literary Award 1984, Nat. Medal of Arts 1988, Nat. Book Foundation Medal 1990. *Publications:* include contributions to numerous magazines and journals; also Dangling Man 1944, The Victim 1947, The Adventures of Augie March 1953, Seize the Day 1956, Henderson the Rain King 1959, Herzog 1964, Mosby's Memoirs and Other Stories 1968, Mr. Sammler's Planet 1969, Humboldt's Gift 1975, To Jerusalem and Back: A Personal Account (non-fiction) 1976, The Dean's December 1981, Him with His Foot in His Mouth and Other Stories 1984, More Die of Heartbreak 1987, A Theft (novella) 1989, The Bellarosa Connection (novella) 1989, Something to Remember Me By 1991, Occasional Pieces 1993, It All Adds Up (essays) 1994, The Actual 1997. *Address:* c/o Committee on Social Thought, University of Chicago, 1126 East 59th Street, Chicago, IL 60637, U.S.A.

BELLUGI, Piero; Italian conductor; b. 14 July 1924, Florence; s. of Mario Bellugi and Giulia Favilli; m. Ursula Herzberger 1954 (divorced); five c.; ed. Conservatorio Cherubini, Florence, Accademia Chigiana, Siena, Akad. des Mozarteums, Salzburg, and Tanglewood, Mass., U.S.A.; Musical Dir. Oakland (Calif.) and Portland (Ore.) Symphony Orchs. 1955–61; Perm. conductor, Radio Symphony Orch., Turin 1967; Prof. courses for orchestral players and conductor, Italian Youth Orchestra 1981–; guest conductor, La Scala, Milan (début 1961), Vienna State Opera, Rome Opera, Aix-en-Provence Festival, Berlin Radio, Paris, Rome S. Cecilia, Chicago, San Francisco Operas, etc.; Hon. mem. Nat. Acad. Luigi Cherubini of Music, Letters and Arts. *Address:* 50027 Strada in Chianti, Florence, Italy. *Telephone:* (55) 858556. *Fax:* (55) 858116.

BELMONDO, Jean-Paul; French actor, b. 9 April 1933, Neuilly-sur-Seine; s. of Paul Belmondo; m. 1959 (divorced 1967); one s. two d. (one deceased); ed. Ecole Alsacienne, Paris, Cours Pascal and Conservatoire nat. d'art dramatique; started career on the stage; mainly film actor since 1957; Pres. French Union of Actors 1963–66; Pres. Annabel Productions 1981–; Dir. Théâtre des Variétés 1991–; Prix Citron 1972; Légion d'honneur; Chevalier, ordre nat. du Mérite, Arts et des Lettres. *Plays acted in include:* L'hôtel du libre-échange, Oscar, Trésor-Party, Médée, La mégère apprivoisée, Kean 1987, Cyrano de Bergerac 1990, Tailleur pour Dames 1993, La Puce à l'oreille 1996. *Films acted in include:* Sois belle et tais-toi, A pied, à cheval et en voiture, les Tricheurs, Charlotte et son Jules, Drôle de dimanche 1958, Les Copains du dimanche, Mademoiselle Ange, A double tour, Classe tous risques, Au bout de souffle, L'Amour, La Novice, La Ciociara, Moderato Cantabile, Léon Morin Prêtre, Le Doulos 1962, Dragées au poivre, L'Aîné des Ferchaux, Peau de banane, 100,000 dollars au soleil 1963, Two Women, The Man From Rio, Echappement libre 1964, Les tribulations d'un Chinois en Chine, Pierrot le Fou 1965, Paris, brûle-t-il? 1966, Le Voleur 1966, Casino Royale 1967, The Brain 1969, La Sirène du Mississippi 1969, Un Homme qui me plaît 1970, Borsalino 1970, The Burglars 1972, La Scoumoune 1972, L'Héritier 1972, Le Magnifique 1973, Stavisky 1974, Peur sur la ville 1975, L'Incorrigible 1975, L'Alpageur, Le corps de mon ennemi 1976, L'Animal 1977, Flic ou Voyou 1979, L'As de as (also produced) 1982, Le Marginal 1983, Joyeuses Pâques, Les Morfalous 1984, Hold-up 1985, Le Solitaire 1987, Itinéraire d'un enfant gâté (César for Best Actor 1988), L'Inconnu dans la Maison 1992, Les Cent et une Nuits 1995, Les Misérables 1995, Désiré 1996, Une chance sur deux 1998. *Publication:* 30 Ans et 25 Films (autobiog.) 1963. *Address:* Annabel Productions, 5 rue Clément Marot, 75008 Paris; Théâtre des Variétés, 7 blvd. Montmartre, 75002 Paris, France.

BELNAP, Nuel, PH.D.; American professor of philosophy; b. 1 May 1930, Evanston, Ill.; s. of Nuel Dinsmore and Elizabeth (Dafter) Belnap; m. 1st Joan Gohde 1953; m. 2nd Gillian Hirth 1982; four c.; m. 3rd Birgit Herbeck 1997; ed. Univ. of Illinois, Yale Univ.; instructor in Philosophy, then Asst. Prof., Yale Univ. 1958–63; Assoc. Prof. of Philosophy, Univ. of Pittsburgh 1963–66, Prof. 1966–, Alan Ross Anderson Distinguished Prof. of Philosophy 1984–, Prof. of Sociology 1967–, of History and Philosophy of Science 1971, of Intelligent Systems 1988–93; Visiting Fellow, Australian Nat. Univ., Canberra 1976; mem. several editorial bds.; Sterling Jr. Fellow 1955–56, Fulbright Fellow 1957–58, Morse Research Fellow 1962–63, Guggenheim Fellow 1975–76. *Publications:* Bindex 1974, Computer Programs Tester 1976; (Co-author) The Logic of Questions and Answers 1976, Entailment: The Logic of Relevance and Necessity (Vol. I) 1975, (Vol. II) 1992, The Revision Theory of Truth 1993 (with Anil Gupta). *Address:* Department of Philosophy, University of Pittsburgh, Fifth Avenue, Pittsburgh, PA 15260 (Office); 5803 Ferree Street, Pittsburgh, PA 15217, U.S.A. (Home). *Telephone:* (412) 624-5777 (Office); (412) 521-3897 (Home). *Fax:* (412) 624-5377 (Office).

BĚLOHLÁVEK, Jiří; Czech musician and conductor; b. 24 Feb. 1946, Prague; m. Anna Fejérová 1971; two d.; ed. Acad. of Performing Arts, Prague; Conductor, Orchestra Puellarum Pragensis (a chamber orchestra), Prague 1967–72; lectureship with Czech Philharmonic Orchestra 1970–71; Conductor, State Philharmonic Orchestra, Brno 1972–77; Chief Conductor, Prague Symphony Orchestra 1977–89; Conductor, Int. Philharmonic Youth Orchestra, Prague 1987–; Conductor, Czech Philharmonic 1981–90, Prin. Conductor and Music Dir. 1990–92; freelance conductor 1993–; Musical Dir. Prague Chamber Philharmonic Orchestra (PCPO) 1994–; chief Guest Conductor BBC Symphony Orchestra 1995–, Guest Conductor Nat. Theatre Prague 1998–; Prof. Acad. of Music, Prague 1995–; concert performances in many countries; many recordings for Czechoslovak Radio, TV; Supraphon Prize 1977, Artist of Merit 1986, Supraphon Golden Disc 1986, 1987, 1994, Diapason d'Or 1992. *Leisure interests:* gardening, hiking. *Address:* Prague Chambre Philharmony, 110 00 Prague 1, Czech Republic. *Telephone:* 5796 0172. *Fax:* 5796 0173.

BELONOGOV, Aleksandr Mikhailovich; Russian diplomatist; b. 15 May 1931; s. of Mikhail N. Belonogov and Lidya A. Elizazova; m. Natalia Zimina 1962 (deceased); two d.; ed. Moscow Inst. of Int. Relations; entered Ministry of Foreign Affairs 1954, staff mem. Legal Dept. and Dept. of Int. Econ. Orgs. 1954–62, Sr. Counsellor, then Head of Unit, then Deputy Head Dept. of Int. Policy Planning 1967–84; Second, then First Sec. at Soviet Embassy, London 1962–67; Amb. to Egypt 1984–86; Perm. Rep. of U.S.S.R. to UN 1986–90; Deputy Minister of Foreign Affairs 1990–92; Amb. to Canada 1992–98; holds various govt. orders and medals. *Publication:* White House and Capitol Hill—Partners and Rivals 1984. *Address:* Ministry of Foreign Affairs, Smolenskaya-Sennaya 32/34, 121200 Moscow, Russia.

BELOTSERKOVSKY, Oleg Mikhailovich; Russian mathematician; b. 29 Aug. 1925; m.; two c.; ed. Moscow State Univ.; sr. researcher Computer Cen. U.S.S.R. (now Russian) Acad. of Sciences; Rector Moscow Inst. of Physics and Eng.; corresp. mem. U.S.S.R. Acad. of Sciences 1972, mem. 1979; Dir. Inst. of Design Automatization; Lenin Prize, N. Zhukovsky Golden Medal; mem. Int. Acad. of Astronautic Fed. *Publications:* Numerical Methods in Dynamics of Liquids 1981, Numerical Modelling in Mechanics of Solid Media 1984, Computational Mechanics: Contemporary Problems and Results 1991 and numerous others. *Leisure interests:* tennis, swimming. *Address:* Institute of Design Automatization, Russian Academy of Sciences, 2 Brestskaya str. 19/18, 123056 Moscow, Russia. *Telephone:* (095) 250 0262 (Office).

BELOUS, Oleg Nikolayevich; Russian diplomatist; b. 1951; ed. Moscow Inst. of Int. Relations; on staff U.S.S.R. (later Russian) Ministry of Foreign Affairs 1973–; Counsellor, Russian Embassy to Belgium 1991–94; Deputy Dir. First European Dept. 1994–96; Dir.; Dept. of All-European Co-operation 1996–98; Perm. Rep. of Russia to Org. of Security and Co-operation in Europe (OSCE), Vienna. *Address:* Permanent Mission of Russian Federation to Organization of Security and Co-operation, Erzherzog Karl-strasse 182, 1220 Vienna, Austria. *Telephone:* (431) 22 53 91 (Office).

BELOV, Marshal Andrei Ivanovich; Russian army officer (retd.); b. 19 Aug. 1917, Pskov; joined CPSU 1941; served in Soviet army 1938–; Mil. Electro-Technical Acad.; fought in Finno-Soviet War of 1939–40; tank signals engineer 1940; Chief of signals of mechanized corps on Southern, 1st Ukranian, 3rd Byelorussian, 2nd Baltic Fronts 1942–45; Chief of signals of mechanized corps of 1st Far Eastern Front Aug.–Sept. 1945; Sr. lecturer, head of faculty, Mil. Signals Acad. 1945–57; Chief of army signals of Turkestan Mil. Dist. 1957–60, of Strategic Rocket Forces 1960–68; First Deputy Chief, Army Signals, Ministry of Defence 1968–70, Chief. 1970–87; rank of Marshal (Signals) 1973; Deputy Chief of Staff of Soviet Forces 1977–87; Insp.-Adviser Ministry of Defence 1987–92; U.S.S.R. State Prize 1977, Lenin Prize 1981, Order of Lenin, Order of Red Banner, Order of Red Star (three times) and other decorations. *Address:* c/o Ministry of Defence, Myasnitskaya 37, 103175 Moscow, Russia. *Telephone:* 296-89-00.

BELOV, Vasiliy Ivanovich: Russian writer; b. 23 Oct. 1932, Timonikha, Vologda; fmr. mem. CPSU and U.S.S.R. Union of Writers; worked on kolkhoz, received industrial training at a FZO school, then as a joiner and mechanic; served in Soviet Army; staff writer on regional newspaper 'Kommunar' in Gryazovets (Vologda) 1950s; secondary ed. (evening classes) 1956–59; Ed. Literary Inst. of Union of Writers 1959–64; People's Deputy of U.S.S.R. 1989–91, mem. U.S.S.R. Supreme Soviet 1989–91; U.S.S.R. State Prize 1981. *Publications include:* My Village in the Forest 1961, Hot Summer 1963, Tisha and Grisha 1966, Carpenter Stories 1968 (English trans. 1969), An Ordinary Affair 1969, Village Tales 1971, Day after Day 1972, The Hills 1973, Looks can Kiss 1975, On the Eve 1972–87, All is Ahead 1986. *Address:* Maltseva ul. 19, Apt. 26, 160001 Vologda, Russia. *Telephone:* (81722) 2-94-65.

BELSHAW, Cyril Shirley, PH.D., F.R.S.C.; Canadian anthropologist and writer; b. 3 Dec. 1921, Waddington, N.Z.; s. of Horace Belshaw and Marion L. S. (née McHardie) Belshaw; m. Betty J. Sweetman 1943 (deceased); one s. one d.; ed. Auckland Univ. Coll. and Victoria Coll., Wellington (Univ. of New Zealand), London School of Econs.; Dist. Officer and Deputy Commr. for Western Pacific, British Solomon Islands 1943–46; Sr. Research Fellow, Australian Nat. Univ. 1950–53; Prof. Univ. of British Columbia 1953–86, Prof. Emer. 1986–; Dir. Regional Training Centre for UN Fellows, Van. 1961–62; Ed. Current Anthropology 1974–84; mem. numerous UNESCO comms., working parties and consultancy groups; Pres. Int. Union of Anthropological and Ethnological Sciences 1978–83, XIth Int. Congress of Anthropological and Ethnological Sciences 1983; Exec. American Anthropological Assoc. 1969–70; Chair. Standing Cttee. Social Sciences and Humanities

Pacific Science Assn. 1968–76; Hon. Life mem. Royal Anthropological Inst. 1978, Pacific Science Assn. 1981; Ed. The Anthroglobe Journal 1998–; Propr. Webzines of Vancouver; Man. Ed. EVE-Enjoy Vancouver Electronically 1997–. *Publications:* Island Administration in the South West Pacific 1950, Changing Melanesia 1954, In Search of Wealth 1955, The Great Village 1957, The Indians of British Columbia (with others) 1958, Under the Ivi Tree 1964, Anatomy of a University 1964, Traditional Exchange and Modern Markets (eds. in 5 languages) 1965, The Conditions of Social Performance 1970, Towers Besieged 1974, The Sorcerer's Apprentice 1976, The Complete Good Dining Guide to Restaurants in Greater Vancouver 1984, Where is Utopia - Controlling Social Evolution 1998, On Disappearance, Accusation and the Unknown. *Leisure interests:* gardening, photography, travel, restaurants. *Address:* Suite 28, 1201 Lamey's Mill Road, Vancouver, B.C. V6H 3S8, Canada. *Telephone:* (604) 739-8190. *Fax:* (604) 739-8190.

BELSKY, Igor Dmitriyevich; Russian choreographer; b. 28 March 1925, Leningrad; m. Lyudmila Alekseyeva; one s.; ed. Leningrad Choreography School (now Acad. of Russian Ballet); dancer with Leningrad Kirov Theatre of Opera and Ballet 1943–63; teacher of folk character dance at Leningrad Choreography School 1946–73; Producer and Choreographer, Leningrad Kirov Theatre of Opera and Ballet 1959–62, Chief Choreographer 1962–66, teacher of Choreography Leningrad Conservatory 1966–; Choreographer with Kirov Ballet 1973–77, Prof. 1982–; with Cairo Ballet, Egypt 1977; Art Dir. St. Petersburg Ballet 1979–92; Pres. Vaganova Ballet Acad., St. Petersburg 1992–; People's Artist of the R.S.F.S.R. 1966. *Principal roles:* Rotbart (Swan Lake), Nurali (Fountain of Bakhchiserai), Tybalt (Romeo and Juliet), Shurale (Yarushllin's Shurale), Severyan (Prokofiev's Stone Flower), Mako (Karayev's Thunder Road). *Chief productions:* Shores of Hope (Petrov) 1959, Leningrad Symphony (Shostakovich) 1961, Humpbacked Horse (Shchedrin) 1963, Eleventh Symphony (Shostakovich) 1966, The Nutcracker (Tchaikovsky) 1969, Icarus (Slonimsky) 1974. *Address:* Academy of Russian Ballet, Rossi str. 2, St. Petersburg, Russia. *Telephone:* (812) 311-1431. *Fax:* 315-5390.

BELSTEAD, 2nd Baron (cr. 1938); **John Julian Ganzoni,** Bt., P.C., J.P., M.A.; British politician; b. 30 Sept. 1932; s. of 1st Baron Belstead and of the late Gwendolen Gertrude Turner; ed. Eton Coll. and Christ Church, Oxford; Parl. Under-Sec. of State Dept. of Educ. and Science 1970–73, N. Ireland Office 1973–74, Home Office 1979–82, Minister of State FCO 1982–83, Ministry of Agric., Fisheries and Food 1983–87, Dept. of Environment 1987–88; Lord Privy Seal and Leader of the House of Lords 1988–90; Paymaster Gen. N. Ireland Office 1990–92; Chair. The Parole Bd. 1992–97; Chair. Assn. Governing Bodies of Public Schools 1974–79; J.P., Borough of Ipswich 1962; D.L., Suffolk 1979, Lord-Lieut. of Suffolk 1994–. *Leisure interests:* lawn tennis, sailing, skiing. *Address:* House of Lords, London, SW1A 0PW, England.

BELTRÁN, Washington; Uruguayan newspaper executive and former politician; b. 6 April 1914, Montevideo; s. of Washington Beltrán and Elena Mullin de Beltrán; m. Esther Storace Arrosa de Beltrán 1943; three s. three d.; ed. Univ. de la República; joined El País 1939, Sub-Dir. 1949–61, Co-Dir. 1961–; mem. House of Reps. 1946, 1955; founded Reconstrucción Blanca and Unión Blanca Democrática groups, both within Partido Nacional; elected Senator 1959, 1967, 1971; mem. Consejo Nacional de Gobierno 1962–67, Pres. of Uruguay 1965–66; proscribed by mil. govt. 1973–80; since 1980 has dedicated most of time to journalism, especially editorials (collected in a book 1985); attended UNICEF World Conf. 1982; Amb. Plenipotentiary to Vatican and companion to Pope on his visit to Uruguay 1987; Pres. Sino-Uruguayan Foundation; Círculo de Tenis de Montevideo; numerous decorations from many countries. *Publication:* Pamperada Blanca 1990. *Address:* El País, Plaza Cagancha 1162, 11100 Montevideo, Uruguay. *Telephone:* (2) 9011929. *Fax:* (2) 9020632.

BELTRÃO, Alexandre Fontana; Brazilian coffee executive; b. 28 April 1924, Curitiba, Paraná; s. of late Alexandre Beltrão and of Zilda Fontana Beltrão; m. Anna Emilia Beltrão 1964; two c.; ed. Instituto Santa Maria, Curitiba, Univ. de São Paulo, Escola Nacional de Engenharia, Rio de Janeiro; asst. engineer 1944; army officer 1945–46; asst. engineer, Dept. of Soil Mechanics, Inst. de Pesquisas Tecnológicas, São Paulo 1948; trained in regional planning at Inst. Nat. d'Aerophotogrametrie, Ministère de la Reconstruction, Paris and at Ministry of Works, London 1950–51; founder and Dir. of SPL (Planning Services Ltd.) 1954–; observer, Govt. of State of Paraná to UN Int. Coffee Conf. 1962; special adviser to Pres. Brazilian Coffee Inst. 1964; Chief Brazilian Coffee Inst. Bureau, N.Y. 1965–67; Pres. World Coffee Promotion Cttee. of Int. Coffee Org. 1965–67; Exec. Dir. Int. Coffee Org. 1968–94; Sec. of Science and Tech., Paraná 1994–; Commdr. Order of Rio Branco. *Publications:* Paraná and the Coffee Economy 1963, essay on Economy of States of Paraná, Pará and Ceará (Brazil) 1958.

BELYAKOV, Rostislav Apollosovich, DR.TECH.SCI.; Russian mechanical scientist; b. 4 March 1919; m. Lyudmila Nikolayevna Shvernik; one s.; ed. Ordzhonikidze Aviation Inst., Moscow; mem. CPSU 1944–91; leading positions as engineer and designer 1941–57; deputy gen. designer ANPK "MIG" 1957–71, gen. designer 1972–98, gen. design adviser 1998–; corresp. mem. of U.S.S.R. (now Russian) Acad. of Sciences 1974, mem. 1981–; Hero of Socialist Labour 1971, 1982, U.S.S.R. State Prize 1952, Lenin Prize 1972; Deputy to U.S.S.R. Supreme Soviet 1974–89; A. N. Tupolev Gold Medal. *Publications:* papers on aircraft construction. *Address:* ANPK "MIG", Leningradskoye Sh. 6, 125299 Moscow, Russia. *Telephone:* 158-18-72. *Fax:* 158-78-26.

BELYAYEV, Sergey Georgiyevich; DR.TECH.SC.; Russian politician; b. 6 April 1954, Gatchina, Leningrad Region; m.; two c.; ed. Leningrad Polytech. Inst.; worked on energy plants construction sites of Caucasus, Baltic Repub., Karelia 1977–80; pedagogue, docent, Deputy Dean, head of lab. Leningrad Polytech. Inst. 1980–90; started political career in 1990; Chair. Soviet of People's Deputies Krasnogvardeysky Dist. of Leningrad, deputy Leningrad City Soviet 1990–93; Deputy Chair. City Construction Comm., Deputy Mayor on Public Relations Problems 1991–93; Deputy Chair then First Deputy Chair. State Cttee. on Property of Russia 1993–95; Dir.-Gen. Fed. Dept. on problems of bankruptcy 1993–95; Chair. State Cttee. on Property of Russia 1995–96; one of organizers political union Our Home - Russia 1995; mem. State Duma (Parl.) 1995–, leader faction Our Home - Russia 1995–97, independent mem. 1997–. *Leisure interest:* tennis. *Address:* State Duma, Okhotny Ryad 1, 103265 Moscow, Russia. *Telephone:* (095) 292 6429 (Office).

BELYAYEV, Spartak Timofeyevich, DR.SC.; Russian physicist; b. 27 Oct. 1923, Moscow; m.; two c.; ed. Moscow State Univ.; junior research worker, senior research worker, Head of Laboratory, I. Kurchatov Inst. of Nuclear Energy 1952–62; Inst. of Nuclear Physics, Siberian Dept., Acad. of Sciences 1962–78; Head of Dept., Kurchatov Inst. 1980–; Prof., Rector, Novosibirsk State Univ. 1965; Corresp. mem. U.S.S.R. (now Russian) Acad. of Sciences 1964–68, mem. 1968–; mem. CPSU 1943–91. *Publications:* scientific works in field of theory of atomic nucleus, particle movement in cyclotron, physics of relativistic plasma, statistic physics of quantum, many body systems. *Address:* Russian Scientific Centre Kurchatov Institute, Kurchatova 46, D-182 Moscow, Russia. *Telephone:* 196-92-06.

BELZA, Svyatoslav Igorevich; Russian literary and music critic; b. 26 April 1942, Chelyabinsk; s. of Igor Belza and Zoya Gulinskaya; m. Nina Kulagina 1969 (divorced 1982); two s.; ed. Moscow State Univ.; researcher Inst. of World Literature U.S.S.R. (now Russian) Acad. of Sciences 1965–; f. and reviewer TV programme Music on TV 1988–97; Man. and Artistic Dir. TV programme Music on TV 1995–97; actively works as literary critic and TV broadcaster; mem. Russian Union of Writers; mem. Acad. of Russian Art, Acad. of Russian TV; Merited Worker of Art; Officer Cross of Merit (Poland) 1998, Order of St. Nicholas (Ukraine) 1998. *Publications include:* Homo legens 1983, 1990, and over 300 literary works and reviews. *Leisure interests:* reading, travel. *Address:* Stroiteley str. 4, korp. 7, Apt. 9, Moscow, Russia (Home). *Telephone:* (095) 930 3661 (Home). *Fax:* (095) 930 3661 (Home).

BEN ALI, Mohamed; Tunisian actor, writer and producer; b. 17 Feb. 1932, Tunis; m. 1957; one s. four d.; ed. secondary educ.; journalist, actor, writer and producer 1952–; f. Groupe Théâtral Radio Tunisienne 1952–, Groupe Théâtre Populaire 1954–; Deputy Mayor of Ezzahra 1980–82; Municipal Councillor 1985–90; Dir. Festival of Ezzahra 1987–90; mem. Assn. Tunisienne Droit d'Auteur et Compositeur, Union des Acteurs Professionels; various awards from Ministry of Culture and Assn. Audio-Visuelle. *Leisure interests:* reading, travel. *Address:* 10 rue Gabes, 2034 Ezzahra, Tunisia. *Telephone:* 451888, 388941.

BEN BELLA, Mohammed; Algerian politician; b. 1916; Warrant Officer in Moroccan regiment during Second World War (decorated); Chief O.A.S. rebel military group in Algeria 1947; imprisoned 1949–52 (escaped); directed Algerian nat. movement from exile in Libya 1952–56; arrested Oct. 1956; held in France 1959–62; Vice-Premier, Algerian Nationalist Provisional Govt., Tunis 1962, Leader, Algerian Political Bureau, Algeria 1962, Premier of Algeria Sept. 1962–65, Pres. of Algeria Sept. 1963–65; detained 1965–80; restricted residence, Msila 1979–80; freed 1981; returned from exile Sept. 1990; Chair. Int. Islamic Comm. for Human Rights, London 1982–; Lenin Peace Prize 1964.

BEN-DAVID, Zadok; Israeli sculptor; b. 1949, Bayhan, Yemen; s. of Moshe and Hana Ben-David; m. Dana Pugach 1991; ed. Acad. of Art and Design, Jerusalem, Reading Univ. 1974–75 and St. Martin's School of Art, London 1975–76; Sculpture teacher at St. Martin's School of Art 1977–82, Ravensbourne Coll. of Art and Design, Bromley 1982–85; first one man show at Air Gallery, London 1980; Exhbns. (solo and group) in Antwerp, London, New York, Jerusalem, Melbourne, Munich, Glasgow, Tel Aviv 1984–; represented Israel in the Biennale di Venezia, Italy 1988. *Publications:* (catalogues) Zadok Ben-David 1987, The Israeli Pavilion—The Venice Biennale 1988. *Address:* 65 Warwick Avenue, London, W9 2PP, England (Home). *Telephone:* 0171-266 0536 (Home). *Fax:* 0171-266 3892.

BEN-ELIEZER, Benjamin; Israeli politician and army officer; b. 1936, Iraq; emigrated to Israel 1949; career officer Israel Defence Forces (IDF), Commdr. Six Day War 1967, served on IDF Mil. Mission to Singapore 1970–73, Commdr. Yom Kippur War 1973, First C.O. Southern Lebanon 1977–78, Commdr. Judea and Samaria 1978–81; Govt. Co-ordinator of Activities in the Administered Areas 1983–84; Minister of Housing and Construction 1992–96; mem. Knesset 1984–, served on Foreign Affairs Cttee. 1988–92; Labour. *Address:* c/o Ministry of Construction and Housing, P.O. Box 18110, Kiryat Hamemshala (East), Jerusalem 91180, Israel. *Telephone:* (02) 847211. *Fax:* 02-822114.

BEN ELISSAR, Eliahu, PH.D.; Israeli politician and diplomatist; b. 2 Aug. 1932, Radom, Poland; s. of Eliezer Israel Gottlieb and Haja Dobrzynski; m.

Nitza Efrony 1979; one s.; ed. Sorbonne, Paris, and Univ. of Geneva; escaped from Poland to Palestine 1942; returned to Europe as student 1950; Govt. service Israel and abroad until 1965; Corresp. for L'Aurore and Le Journal de Genève in Israel; active mem. of Herut Movement; elected to Cen. Cttee. of Herut 1970, Party Spokesman 1971, Herut Exec. Cttee. 1972, Herut Directorate 1978; in charge of Information Dept. during Likud nat. election campaigns 1973, 1977; Chair. Herut World Exec. 1988–91; mem. Bd. of Govs. Jewish Agency 1989–92; Del. to World Zionist Congress 1972, 1987, 1992; Dir.-Gen. Prime Minister's Office 1977–80; Head of Israel's first del. to Cairo, Mena House talks 1977; Israel's First Amb. to Egypt 1980–81; mem., Knesset 1981–98; Amb. to U.S.A. 1996–98, to France 1998–; mem. Foreign Affairs and Defence Cttee. 1981–82, 1984–89, 1993– (Chair. 1982–84, 1989–92); mem. Knesset Faction Exec. 1984–92; mem. del. to Madrid Conf. 1991; mem. del. to UN Gen. Ass. 1992; mem. Advisory Cttee. Israeli Council on Foreign Relations; mem. Public Council Eibshitz Inst. of Holocaust Studies; founding mem. Cttee. Menachem Begin Heritage Foundation; Grand Officier, Ordre de l'Ethiopie 1964, Grand Cruz Extraordinaria, Orden de la Democracia (Colombia) 1980. *Publications:* La Politique Etrangère du IIIème Reich et les Juifs, La Guerre israélo-arabe. *Address:* Israeli Embassy, 3 rue Rabelais, 75008 Paris, France.

BEN-NATAN, Asher; Israeli diplomatist; b. 15 Feb. 1921, Vienna; s. of Nahum Ben-Natan and Berta Ben-Natan; m. Erika (Rut) Frudt 1940; one s. one d.; ed. Z. P. Hayut Hebrew Coll., Vienna and Institut des Hautes Etudes Internationales, Geneva; co-founder and mem. Kibbutz Mederot-Zeraim 1938–44, latterly Sec. and Treas.; Political Dept., Jewish Agency 1944–45; on mission to Europe to organize rescue of Jews and illegal immigration to Palestine: attached to office of Head of Jewish Agency 1945–47; Ministry of Foreign Affairs 1948–51; studies in Geneva 1951–53; Govt. Rep. on Bd. of Red Sea Inkodeh Co. 1953–56, Gen. Man. 1955–56; Rep. of Ministry of Defence in Europe 1956–58; Dir.-Gen. Ministry of Defence 1959–65; Amb. to Fed. Repub. of Germany 1965–70, to France 1970–75; Political Adviser to Minister of Defence 1975–78; Adviser to Prime Minister on Special Affairs 1985–; Amb. on Special Mission 1993; Chair. Ben-Gurion Foundation 1983–; Pres. Israel-German Asscn. 1973–; Dr. h.c. (Ben Gurion Univ.) 1990; D.Phil. h.c. (Ben Gurion Univ.) 1997; Officier Légion d'honneur; Commdr. ordre nat. (Ivory Coast); Commdr. ordre de l'Etoile équatoriale (Gabon); Louis Waiss Peace Prize 1974. *Publications:* Briefe an den Botschafter 1970, Dialogue avec des Allemands 1973. *Address:* 89 Haim Levanon Street, Tel-Aviv 69345, Israel. *Telephone:* 6413398.

BENACERRAF, Baruj; American (b. Venezuelan) professor of pathology; b. 29 Oct. 1920, Caracas, Venezuela; m. Annette Dreyfus 1943; one d.; ed. Lycée Janson, Paris, Columbia Univ., New York, Medical Coll. of Virginia; Internship, Queens General Hospital, New York 1945–46; army service 1946–48; Research Fellow Dept. of Microbiology, Coll. of Physicians and Surgeons, Columbia Univ., N.Y. 1948–50; Chargé de Recherches, CNRS, Hôpital Broussais, Paris 1950–56; Asst. Prof. of Pathology, New York Univ. School of Medicine 1956–58, Assoc. Prof. of Pathology 1958–60, Prof. of Pathology 1960–68; Chief, Lab. of Immunology, Nat. Inst. of Allergy and Infectious Diseases, Nat. Insts. of Health, Bethesda, Md. 1968–70; Fabyan Prof. of Comparative Pathology and Chair. Dept. of Pathology, Harvard Medical School, Boston, Mass. 1970–91; mem. Immunology "A" Study Section, Nat. Insts. of Health 1965–69; Scientific Advisor World Health Org. for Immunology; Trustee and mem. Scientific Advisory Bd., Trudeau Foundation 1970–77; mem. Scientific Advisory Bd. Mass. General Hospital 1971–74; mem. Bd. of Govs. Weizmann Inst. of Science; Chair. Scientific Advisory Cttee., Centre d'Immunologie de Marseille, CNRS-INSERM; Pres. American Asscn. of Immunologists 1973–74; Pres. Fed. of American Socs. for Experimental Biology 1974–75; Pres. Dana-Farber Cancer Inst., Boston, Mass. 1980–92; Pres. Int. Union of Immunological Socs.; Fellow, American Acad. of Arts and Sciences; mem. American Asscn. of Immunologists, American Asscn. of Pathologists and Bacteriologists, American Soc. for Experimental Pathology, Soc. for Experimental Biology and Medicine, British Asscn. for Immunology, French Soc. of Biological Chemistry, Harvey Soc., New York Acad. of Sciences, American Acad. of Sciences, Inst. of Medicine; Rabbi Shai Shacknai Prize in Immunology and Cancer Research (Hebrew Univ. of Jerusalem) 1974, T. Duckett Jones Memorial Award, Helen Hay Whitney Foundation 1976, Nobel Prize for Physiology or Medicine 1980, Nat. Medal of Science 1990. *Address:* 111 Perkins Street, Jamaica Plain, MA 02130, U.S.A.

BENACHENHOU, Mourad, M.ECON., D.SOC.; Algerian economist and government minister; b. 30 July 1938, Tlemcen; s. of late Mohammed Benachenhou and Rostane Hiba; m. Norya Berbar 1962; two s. one d.; ed. Univ. D'Alger, Univ. de Bordeaux, Univ. of Maryland; Officer Nat. Liberation Army 1956–62; Adviser, Ministry of Agric. 1965–66; Dir. Nat. Agronomic Inst., Algiers 1966–78; Dir. Higher Ed. 1971–78; Dir. Centre of Research on Agronomy 1978–82; Perm. Sec. Ministry of Finance 1982–90; int. consultant 1990–93; Minister of Econ. Affairs 1993–94, of Industrial Restructuring and Participation 1994–96, of Industry 1996; Exec. Dir. World Bank 1982; Médaille de la Résistance. *Publications:* Higher Education in Algeria 1976, The Future of the University 1979, Debt and Democracy 1992, Inflation and Devaluation 1993. *Leisure interests:* tennis, chess, computers, reading, writing. *Address:* c/o Ministry of Industry, Le Colisée, Rue Roccas, Algiers, Algeria.

BENAKIS, Anna, DR. JUR.; Greek politician and professor of criminal law; b. 12 Dec. 1934, Athens; m. Linos Benakis 1957; ed. Pierce Coll. of Athens and Univs. of Athens and Bonn; Asst., Asst. Prof., Univ. of Athens, Univ. of Bonn, Max-Planck Inst. for Int. Criminal Law, Freiburg 1962–78; Consultant on Higher Educ. to Ministry of Educ. 1975–77, 1980–81; mem. Legal Comms. of Ministry of Justice 1977–81; mem. foreign teaching staff, Temple Univ. Philadelphia 1981–85; now Prof. of Criminal Law, Univ. of Athens; mem. Parl. 1981–; Speaker on legal and educ. matters, Nea Democratia Party 1981–89; Alt. Minister of Educ. 1989; Alt. Minister of Culture 1991; Minister of Culture 1991; Minister of Justice 1992–93; Vice-Pres. Greek Soc. for Criminal Law 1988–. *Publications:* four books and several articles on criminal matters; political articles. *Leisure interests:* water skiing, swimming, classical music, literature. *Address:* Skoufa 75, 10680 Athens (Office); Sina 58, 10672 Athens, Greece (Home). *Telephone:* 3602634, 3602863 (Office); 3636818 (Home). *Fax:* 3602633 (Office); 3645179 (Home).

BÉNARD, André Pierre Jacques; French business executive; b. 19 Aug. 1922, Draveil, Essone; s. of Marcel Bénard and Lucie Thalmann; m. Jacqueline Preiss 1946; one s.; ed. Lycée Janson-de-Sailly, Lycée Georges Clémenceau, Nantes, Lycée Thiers, Marseilles, Ecole Polytechnique, Paris; joined Royal Dutch/Shell Group 1946; with Société Anonyme des Pétroles Jupiter 1946–49; Shell Petroleum Co. Ltd., London 1949–50; Head of Bitumen services, Société des Pétroles Shell Berre 1950–58, Head Nat. Activities Dept. 1958–59; Asst. Dir.-Gen. Société pour l'Utilisation Rationnelle des Gaz 1960–61, Pres. Dir.-Gen. 1962–64; Marketing Man. Shell Française 1964–67, Pres. Man. Dir. 1967–70; Regional Co-ordinator Europe 1970; Dir. Shell Petroleum N.V. 1970; Dir. The Shell Petroleum Co. Ltd. 1970, Barclays Bank SA, Paris 1989–; Man. Dir. Royal Dutch Petroleum Co. 1971–83, mem. Supervisory Bd. 1983–; Admin. Royal Dutch 1983–, INSEAD 1983–, La Radiotechnique 1983–; Hon. Pres., French Chamber of Commerce and Industry, in the Netherlands 1980–; Jt. Chair. Eurotunnel 1986–90, Pres. Admin. Council 1990–94; Prix Descartes 1982; Médaille des Evadés; Médaille de la Résistance; Chevalier de l'ordre nat. du Mérite, Commdr. Légion d'honneur, Commdr. Order of Orange Nassau, Chevalier du Mérite agricole; Hon. K.B.E. *Leisure interest:* golf.

BÉNASSY, Jean-Pascal, PH.D.; French economist and researcher; b. 30 Dec. 1948, Paris; s. of Jean Bénassy and Jeannine Bénassy; ed. Ecole Normale Supérieure, Paris, Univ. of Berkeley, California, U.S.A.; research assoc. CEPREMAP 1973–; Dir. of Research C.N.R.S. 1981–; Dir. Laboratoire d'Economie Politique, Ecole Normale Supérieure 1984–88; Dept. of Econs. Ecole Polytechnique 1987–; Fellow Econometric Soc. 1981, mem. Council 1990–92; Guido Zerilli Marimo Prize, Acad. des Sciences Morales et Politiques 1990. *Publications:* The Economics of Market Disequilibrium 1982, Macroéconomie et théorie du Déséquilibre 1984, Macroeconomics: An Introduction to the Non-Walrasian Approach 1986, Macroeconomics and Imperfect Competition 1995, numerous articles in specialized journals. *Address:* CEPREMAP, 142 rue du Chevaleret, 75013 Paris, France. *Telephone:* 01 40 77 84 62. *Fax:* 01 44 24 38 57.

BENAUD, Richard ('Richie'), O.B.E.; Australian cricketer; b. 6 Oct. 1930; s. of Louis Richard and Irene Benaud; m. Daphne Elizabeth Surfleet 1967; two s. by previous marriage; ed. Parramatta High School; right-hand middle-order batsman and right-arm leg-break and googly bowler; played for New South Wales 1948–49 to 1963–64 (captain 1958–59 to 1962–63); played in 63 Tests for Australia 1951–52 to 1963–64, 28 as captain, scoring 2,201 runs (average 24.4) including 3 hundreds, taking 248 wickets (average 27.0); first to score 2,000 runs and take 200 wickets in Tests; scored 11,719 runs (23 hundreds) and took 945 wickets in first-class cricket; toured England 1953, 1956 and 1961; int. sports consultant; TV Commentator, BBC 1960–99, Channel Nine 1977–, Channel 4 1999–. *Publications:* Way of Cricket 1960, Tale of Two Tests 1962, Spin Me a Spinner 1963, The New Champions 1965, Willow Patterns 1972, Benaud on Reflection 1984, The Appeal of Cricket 1995, Anything But . . . An Autobiography 1998. *Leisure interest:* golf. *Address:* 19/178 Beach Street, Coogee, New South Wales 2034, Australia. *Telephone:* Sydney 9664-1124.

BENAWA, Abdul Raouf; Afghanistan writer and administrator; b. 1913; ed. Ganj Public School, Kandahar; mem. Language Dept. Afghan Acad. 1939; mem. Words Dept. Afghan Acad. and Asst. Information Dept. 1940; Dir. Publication Dept. Afghan Acad. 1941; Gen. Dir. Pushtu Tolana; Sec. Afghan Acad. and Dir. Kabul magazine; proprietor of weekly magazine Hewad; mem. History Dept. 1950, Dir. Internal Publ. Dept. 1951, Gen. Dir. 1952; Press Attaché India 1953–56; Pres. Radio Kabul 1956–63; Press and Cultural Counsellor, Cairo 1963. *Publications:* Women in Afghanistan, Mir Wiess Neeka, Literary Sciences, Pushtu Songs, De Ghanamo Wazhai, Pushtoonistan, A Survey of Pushtoonistan, Rahman Baba, Pir mohammad-Kakar, Khosh-hal Khan se Wai, Pushtoo Killi, Vol. 4, Kazim Khan-e-Shaida; translations: Mosa-fir Iqbal, Geetan-Jali Tagoor, Da Darmistatar Pushtoo Seerane, Leaders of Pashtoonistan, History of Hootaki, Preshana afkar (poem), Da zra khwala, Pashto writers today (2 vols.), Pashto reader for schools, Pachakhan (A leader of Pashtoni), Landei (public poems); plays: I-Zoor gonahgar (Old criminal), Ishtebah (confusion), Kari bar asal, Aashyanae aqab, Zarang Chaoki der khater, Hakoomat baidar.

BENDA, Ernst; German politician and lawyer; b. 15 Jan. 1925, Berlin; s. of Rudolf and Lilly (Krasting) Benda; m. Waltraut Vorbau 1956; one s. one d.; ed. Kant-Gymnasium, Berlin-Spandau, Humboldt Univ., Freie Univ. Berlin, Univ. of Wisconsin; war service; prisoner-of-war; Humboldt Univ. 1946–48; Freie Univ., Berlin 1948–51; Univ. of Wis. 1949–55; Dist. appointment, Spandau 1951–54; mem. Berlin House of Reps. 1955–57, Bundestag 1957–71; in practice as lawyer 1956–71; Chair. Berlin Christian Democratic Union Youth Dept. 1952–54; mem. Fed. Govt. 1966; Under-Sec. in Interior Ministry; Minister of the Interior 1968–69; Pres. Fed. Constitutional Court, Karlsruhe 1971–83; Prof. Constitutional Law Univ. of Freiburg 1983–93; Chair. Media Council Berlin-Brandenburg 1993–; Hon. Prof., Law Faculty, Trier Univ. 1977; Hon. D.Jur. (Würzburg Univ.) 1974. *Publications:* Notstandsverfassung und Arbeitskampf 1963, Rechtsstaat und Verjährung 1965, Industrielle Herrschaft und sozialer Staat 1966, Die Notstandsverfassung 1966, Der Rechtsstaat in der Krise 1971, Verfassungsprozessrecht 1992. *Leisure interest:* sailing. *Address:* Käthe-Kollwitz Strasse 46, 76227 Karlsruhe, Germany. *Telephone:* (0721) 404661. *Fax:* (0721) 496634.

BENDA, Václav, PH.D.; Czech politician, mathematician and computer expert; b. 8 Aug. 1946, Prague; m.; six c.; ed. Charles Univ., Prague; lecturer, Faculty of Mathematics and Physics, Charles Univ., Prague 1970–77; signed Charter 77, 1977; stoker 1977–79; founding mem., Cttee. for Protection of the Unjustly Prosecuted 1978–; spokesman for Charter 77, 1979; refused to leave Czechoslovakia 1979; imprisoned on charges of subversion of the state 1979–83; labourer 1983–89; co-founder of the Movt. for Civic Freedom; Chair. Exec. Cttee. of Christian Democratic Party Dec. 1989–, Chair. Christian Democratic Party 1990–93, First Deputy Chair. 1994–1995; mem. of ODS/Civic Democratic Party (Civic Democratic Party and CHDP merged 1996); mem. Exec. Cttee. Civic Democratic Party/ODS 1995 as mem. of CHDS, as mem. of ODS 1996–; Deputy to House of People, Fed. Ass. of Czechoslovakia 1989–92, Chair. House June–Dec. 1992, mem. Presidium, Fed. Ass. Czechoslovakia 1990–1992, Vice-Chair. June–Dec. 1992; Dir. Inst. for Documenting and Investigating Crimes under Communism 1994–98; mem. Senate 1996–; Medal for Merit 1998. *Publications:* publisher of journal Paraph (in samizdat) 1985–89, The Black Girl (prose), About the Terrible Fight with the Monster (children's fairytales), 4 vols. of letters from prison. *Address:* Karlovo nám. 18, Prague 2–120 00; Senate of the Czech Republic, Valdštejnský palác, Prague 1–118–01, Czech Republic. *Telephone:* (02) 298676 (Home); (02) 5707 1111 (Office).

BENDITT, Earl Philip, M.D.; American pathologist; b. 15 April 1916, Philadelphia, Pa.; s. of Milton Benditt and Sarah (Schoenfeld) Benditt; m. Marcella Wexler 1945; four s.; ed. Swarthmore Coll., Harvard Medical School and Univ. of Chicago; Instructor in Pathology, Univ. of Chicago 1944–47, Asst. Prof. 1947–52, Assoc. Prof. 1952–57; Prof. and Chair. Dept. of Pathology, Univ. of Wash., Seattle 1957–81, Prof. of Pathology 1981–86, Prof. Emer. 1986–; Distinguished Physician, Seattle Veterans' Admin. Hosp. 1988–; Visiting Scholar, Sir William Dunn School of Pathology, Univ. of Oxford 1979–80; Welcome Foundation Visiting Prof. Cornell Univ. Medical School 1987; Fellow, N.A.S., A.A.A.S. *Publications:* 230 papers on pathology and related subjects. *Leisure interests:* sailing, art. *Address:* 3717 East Prospect Street, Seattle, WA 98112, U.S.A. *Telephone:* (206) 322-5731.

BENDJEDID, Col. Chadli (see Chadli, Col. Bendjedid).

BENDUKIDZE, Kakha Avtandilovich; Russian business executive; b. 20 April 1956, Tbilisi, Georgia; ed. Tbilisi State Univ., Moscow State Univ.; researcher, Inst. of Biochem. and Physiology of Micro-organisms, U.S.S.R. (now Russian) Acad. of Sciences 1981–; Head, Lab. of Molecular Genetics, Inst. of Biotech., U.S.S.R. Ministry of Medical Industry 1985–89; f., mem. Bd. Dirs., Bioprocess 1988–90; Gen. Man. People's Oil Investment-Industrial European-Asian Corpn. NIPEK 1993–; Dir.-Gen. Urals machine-construction factory 1997–; mem. Presidium, All-Union Movt. Businessmen for New Russia 1993–94; mem. Council on Industrial Policy and Enterprise, Govt. of Russian Fed. 1994–98; mem. State Cttee. on Econ. Policy and Supporting Econ. Structures 1995–98; mem. Reform-Club Interaction. *Address:* M. Yermolayevsky per. 27, 103379 Moscow, Russia. *Telephone:* (095) 974 6024 (Office).

BENEDETTI, Mario; Uruguayan writer; b. 14 Sept. 1920, Paso de los Toros, Tacuarembo; s. of Brenno Benedetti and Matilde Farrugia; m. Luz López; ed. Colegio Alemán; Journalist on Marcha (weekly) and Literary, Film and Theatre Critic on El Diario, Tribuna Popular and La Mañana; visited Europe 1957, 1966–67. *Publications:* Fiction: Esta mañana 1949, El último viaje y otros cuentos 1951, Quién de nosotros 1953, Montevideanos 1959, La Tregua 1963, Gracias por el Fuego 1965, La muerte y otras sorpresas 1968; Plays: Ustedes por ejemplo 1953, El Reportaje 1958, Ida y Vuelta 1958; Poetry: La víspera indeleble 1945, Sólo mientras tanto 1950, Poemas de la Oficina 1956, Poemas del Hoyporhoy 1965, Inventario 1965, Contra los puentes levadizos 1966, A ras de sueño 1967; Essays: Peripecia y novela 1948, Marcel Proust y otros ensayos 1951, Literatura uruguaya siglo XX 1963, Letras del continente mestizo 1967, Sobre artes y oficios 1968.

BENEDICTO, Roberto S., A.A., LL.B., LL.M.; Philippine lawyer, banker and diplomatist; b. 17 April 1917, La Carlota, Negros Occidental; m. Julita Campos; one d.; ed. Univ. of the Philippines, George Washington Univ., U.S.A.; Major in the Philippines Armed Forces 1941–45; Acting Provincial Fiscal, Negros Occidental 1945; Prof. Commercial Law, Far Eastern Univ. 1948–55; Gov. Devt. Bank of the Philippines 1957–59; Exec. Vice-Pres. Treas. Philippine Commercial and Industrial Bank 1962–65; fmr. Pres., Vice-Chair. Philippine Nat. Bank; mem. Monetary Bd., Cen. Bank of the Philippines; alt. Gov. IMF, IBRD 1966–70; Amb. to Japan 1972–78; mem. Cabinet Exec. Cttee. Aug. 1982; Pres. Nat. Sugar Trading Corpn.; Chair., Philippine Sugar Comm.; Pres. Nat. Sugar Trading Corpn.; Chair. Republic Planters Bank 1978–80; Vice-Chair., Kilusan ng Bagong Lipunan, Region VI 1978–81; mem. Bd. of Regents, Univ. of Philippines 1982; Pres. Boy Scouts of Philippines 1982; Philippine Legion of Merit, Philippine Defense Medal, Philippine American Defense Medal, Asiatic Pacific Theatre Medal, Philippine Liberation Medal (First Class), Order of the Rising Sun, Outstanding Citizen of Manila. *Address:* Kanlaon Towers, Roxas Boulevard, Metro Manila, Philippines (Home).

BENEDIKTSSON, Einar, M.A.; Icelandic diplomatist; b. 30 April 1931, Reykjavík; s. of Stefan M. Benediktsson and Sigridur Oddsdóttir; m. Elsa Petursdóttir 1956; three s. two d.; ed. Colgate Univ., N.Y., Fletcher School of Law and Diplomacy, Mass., London School of Econs., Inst. des Etudes Européennes, Turin, Italy; with Org. for European Econ. Co-operation, Paris 1956–60; Head of Section, Ministries of Econ. Affairs and Commerce 1960–64, Ministry of Foreign Affairs 1964, 1968–70; Counsellor, Icelandic Embassy, Paris 1964–68; Perm. Rep. to Int. Orgs., Geneva 1970–76; Chair. EFTA Council 1975; Amb. to France 1976–82 (also accred. to Spain, Portugal and Cape Verde, Perm. Rep. to OECD and UNESCO), to U.K. 1982–86 (also accred. to Netherlands, Ireland and Nigeria), to Belgium and E.C. (also accred. to Luxembourg) 1986–91 (and Perm. Rep. to NATO 1986–90), to Norway 1991–93 (also accred. to Poland and the Czech and Slovak Federal Repub.); Amb. to U.S.A. 1993; Commdr. Order of Falcon (Iceland), various foreign decorations. *Address:* c/o Ministry of Foreign Affairs, Raudarárstíg 25, 150 Reykjavík, Iceland.

BENEŠOVÁ, Libuše, D.PHIL.; Czech politician; b. 5 July 1948, Benešov; m. Jiří Beneš; one d.; ed. Charles Univ., Prague; Mayor of Lešany 1990–93; Chief Dist. Officer Civic Democratic Party, Prague-West 1993–95; Vice-Minister of Finance 1995–97; Senator 1997–, Chair of Senate 1998–. *Leisure interests:* cooking, gardening, knitting, reading, sewing. *Address:* The Senate, Valdštejnské nám. 4, 118 11 Prague 1, Czech Republic. *Telephone:* (2) 27-93-51.

BENETTON, Luciano; Italian business executive; s. of Rosa Benetton; m. Maria-Teresa Benetton (separated); f. Benetton 1963, now Pres. Benetton Group; mem. Italian Senate 1992–94; facing fraud charges 1997; awarded Civiltà Veneta 1986; Premio Creatività 1992. *Address:* Benetton Group SpA, Via Minelli, 31050 Ponzano (Treviso), Italy. *Telephone:* 422-4491. *Fax:* 422-449586.

BENFLIS, Ali; Algerian politician; b. 8 Sept. 1944, Batna; m.; four c.; ed. Univ. of Algiers; juge au tribunal Blida 1968; Deputy Dir. Cttee. on Infant Delinquancy, Ministry of Justice 1969; Public Prosecutor, Batna 1970; Procurator Gen., Constantine 1971–74; Pres. of the Bar, East Algeria 1983, mem. 1974–88; Founding mem. of Algerian League for Human Rights 1987; Pres. of the Bar, Batna 1987; Pres. Eastern Region, Algerian League for Human Rights 1987; Minister of Justice 1988–91; head of legal firm 1993–. *Address:* Boite postale 57, Hydra, Algiers, Algeria. *Telephone:* 02.59.18.63; 02.60.29.98.

BENFREHA, Ahmed; Algerian politician; b. 1940, Mascara; m.; three c.; ed. Inst. Abdelhamid Ben Badis, Constantine, Univ. de la Zitouna and Univ. of Algiers; research worker Agronomie-Inst. de recherches; chargé de mission, Ministry of Agric.; Cen. Dir. Ministry of Agric.; Head of Student Cell, Nat. Liberation Front, Tunis; Deputy Nat. Popular Assembly; Sec. of State for Fishing 1980–82, Fishing and Maritime Transport 1982–84; Minister of Public Works 1984–88, Hydraulics and Forests 1988–89; mem. Central Cttee. Nat. Liberation Front 1979–. *Address:* le Grand Séminaire, Kouba, Algiers, Algeria. *Telephone:* (2) 58-95-00.

BENGSTON, Billy Al; American artist; b. 7 June 1934, Dodge City, Kan.; one d.; ed. Los Angeles City Coll., Calif. Coll. of Arts & Crafts, Oakland and Otis Art Inst.; instructor Chouinard Art Inst. Los Angeles 1961; lecturer, Univ. of Calif. at Los Angeles 1962–63; Guest Artist, Univ. of Okla. 1967; Guest Prof. Univ. of Colo. 1969; Guest lecturer, Univ. of Calif. at Irvine 1973; Exec. Dir. Westfall Arts 1995–98; numerous one-man exhbns.; works in numerous public collections including Museum of Modern Art, New York, Whitney Museum of American Art, New York, Solomon R. Guggenheim Museum, New York, San Francisco Museum of Art, The Beaubourg, Paris; Nat. Foundation for the Arts Grant 1967; Tamarind Fellow 1968, 1982, 1987; Guggenheim Fellowship 1975; various commissions and other awards. *Leisure interests:* running, swimming, films. *Address:* 805 Hampton Drive, Venice, CA 90291, U.S.A. *Telephone:* (310) 450-2131.

BENGU, Sibusiso Mandlenkosi Emmanuel, PH.D.; South African politician; b. 8 May 1934, Kranskop; s. of Rev. Jackonia Bengu and Augusta Bengu; m. Ethel Funeka 1961; one s. four d.; Prin. Dlangezwa High School 1968–76; Publicity Sec. Natal African Teachers' Asscn. 1969–71; Dir Students' Advisory Services, Univ. of Zululand 1977–78; Exec. Sec. for Research and Social Action, Lutheran World Fed., Geneva 1978–91; Rector, Vice-Chancellor Univ. of Fort Hare 1991–94; Minister of Educ. Govt. of Nat. Unity 1994–99; First Gen. Sec. Inkatha Freedom Party, now mem. A.N.C. *Publications:* African Cultural Identity and International Relations 1975, Chasing Gods Not our Own 1975, Mirror or Model. *Address:* c/o Ministry of Education, Private Bag X603, Pretoria 0001, South Africa.

BENGZON, Cesar, B.A., LL.B.; Philippine judge; b. 29 May 1896; ed. Ateneo de Manila and Univ. of the Philippines; Law Clerk, Bureau of Justice 1919, Special Attorney, then Asst. Attorney 1920, Solicitor-Gen. 1931; Dean and Prof. of Law, Univ. of Manila 1928–32; Under-Sec. of Justice and Chair. Bd.

of Pardons 1933; Assoc. Justice, Court of Appeals 1936; Assoc. Justice, Supreme Court 1945; Prof. of Law, Univ. of Santo Tomás and Philippine Law School 1948–54; Chair. Senate Electoral Tribunal 1950–57; Chief Justice Supreme Court 1961; Judge, Int. Court of Justice, The Hague 1966–76; mem. Philippine Acad. of Sciences and Humanities 1964–; Pres. Philippine Section, Int. Comm. of Jurists 1964, 1966; mem. Nat. Research Council 1964–, American Judicature Soc. 1965, Philippine Soc. of Int. Law 1965–; LL.D. h.c. Univ. of Manila 1957, Ateneo de Manila Univ. 1964, Univ. of the Philippines 1964. *Address:* c/o National Council of the Philippines, Gen. Santos, Bicutan, Taguig, Philippines.

BENHAMOUDA, Boualem D.IUR.; Algerian politician and lexicographer; b. 8 March 1933, Cherchell; m.; two s. one d.; Minister of Ex-Combatants 1965–70, of Justice 1970–77, of Public Works 1977–80, of the Interior 1980–82, of Finance 1982–86; mem. Political Bureau of Nat. Liberation Front (FLN) 1979–, Chair. FLN Cttee. on Educ. Training and Culture 1979–80, Gen. Sec. FLN 1996–; responsible for the Inst. of Global Studies of Strategy (political and econ. matters) 1986–90. *Publications:* The Keys of Arabic Language 1991, The Arabic Origin of some Spanish Words 1991, The Democratic Practice of Power (Between Theory and Reality) 1992, Spanish-Arabic Pocket Dictionary 1993, The Arabic Origin of About 1000 French Words, General French-Arabic Dictionary 1996, General Arabic-French Dictionary 1999. *Leisure interests:* reading, studying, cultural travel. *Address:* 5 rue des Frères Zennouche, El-Biar, Algiers, Algeria.

BENHIMA, Mohamed, M.D.; Moroccan politician and physician; b. 25 June 1924, Safi; s. of Tayeb Benhima and Ben Hida; m.; four c.; ed. Faculté de Médecine de Nancy, France; Chief Medical Officer, Had Court District 1954–56; Chief of Cen. Service for Urban and Rural Hygiene 1956–57; Head of Personal Office of Minister of Public Health 1957–58; Asst. Dir. Admin., Ministry of Public Health 1958–60; Sec.-Gen. Ministry of Public Health Jan.–April 1960; Gov. of Provinces of Agadir and Tarfaya 1960–61; Minister of Public Works 1961–62, 1963–65, 1967, of Commerce, Industry, Mines, Handicrafts and Merchant Marine 1962–63, of Nat. Educ., Arts, Youth and Sport 1965–67; Prime Minister 1967–69; Minister of State for Agric. and Agrarian Reform 1969–70; Minister of Internal Affairs 1972–73; Minister of State for Co-operation and Training 1973–77, for the Interior 1977–79; decorations from Govts. of Belgium, Morocco, Sweden, Ethiopia, Tunisia, Liberia, France, Italy, Niger, Libya, Ivory Coast, Guinea, Cameroon and United Arab Republic. *Address:* Km. 5.5, Route des Zaërs, Rabat, Morocco.

BENIGNI, Roberto; Italian actor, director and writer; b. 27 Oct. 1952, Misericordia, Tuscany. *Films include:* Belingua ti voglio bene (actor, writer) 1977, Down By Law (actor) 1986, Tutto Benigni (actor, writer) 1986, Johnny Stecchino (dir., actor, writer), Night on Earth (actor) 1992, Son of the Pink Panther (acted) 1993, Mostro (dir., actor, writer), Life is Beautiful (dir., actor, writer, Acad. Award for Best Actor and Best Foreign Film) 1998, Asterisk and Obelisk (actor) 1998.

BENING, Annette; American actress; b. 1958, Topeka, Kan.; m. 1st Steven White (divorced); m. 2nd Warren Beatty (q.v.) 1992; three c.; stage appearances in works by Ibsen, Chekhov and Shakespeare in San Diego and San Francisco; other stage roles in Coastal Disturbances, The Great Outdoors. *Films:* Valmont, The Grifters, Regarding Henry, Guilty by Suspicion, Bugsy, Love Affair, The American President, Richard III, Blue Vision, Mars Attacks!, Against All Enemies, The Siege, In Dreams. *Address:* c/o Kevin Huvane, C.A.A., 9830 Wilshire Boulevard, Beverly Hills, CA 90212, U.S.A.

BENJAMIN, Edouard E., M.A.; Guinean international civil servant; b. 11 August 1941, Conakry; s. of Rev. Martin Luther Benjamin and Emilie Wright Benjamin; m. Danielle Fignolé 1968; two s. two d.; ed. Univ. of Bucknell, Pa., Yale Univ. and American Univ., Washington D.C.; Ministry of Foreign Affairs 1968–69; Head of Cabt. of Sec.-Gen. of OAU, Addis Ababa 1969–73; IBRD, Washington, D.C. 1974–86; Minister of Planning and Int. Co-operation 1986–89, of Economy and Finance 1989–92; Exec. Sec. Econ. Community of W. African States (ECOWAS) 1993–97. *Address:* c/o Economic Community of West African States, Secretariat Building, Asokoro, Abuja, Nigeria. *Telephone:* (9) 5231858. *Fax:* (9) 2637052.

BENJAMIN, George William John, F.R.C.M.; British composer, conductor and pianist; b. 31 Jan. 1960, London; s. of William Benjamin and Susan (née Bendon) Benjamin; ed. Westminster School, Paris Conservatoire, King's Coll., Cambridge, IRCAM, Paris; first London orchestral performance, BBC Proms Aug. 1980; Prince Consort Prof. of Composition, Royal Coll. of Music 1994–; has performed and lectured on own and other contemporary music in G.B., Europe, U.S.A., Australia and Far East; Prin. Guest Artist, Hallé Orchestra 1993–; Carte Blanche at Opéra Bastille, Paris March 1992; founding Artistic Dir. Wet Ink Festival, San Francisco Symphony Orchestra 1992, Meltdown Festival, South Bank 1993; Featured Composer, 75th Salzburg Festival 1995, Artistic Consultant BBC Sounding the Century 1996–99; Lili Boulanger Award, U.S.A. 1985, Koussevitzky Int. Record Award 1987, Grand Prix du disque de l'Académie Charles Cros 1987, Gramophone Contemporary Award 1990, Chevalier Ordre des arts et lettres 1996, Edison Award 1998. *Publications:* orchestral works: Ringed by the Flat Horizon 1980, A Mind of Winter 1981, At First Light 1982, Jubilation 1985, Antara 1987, Sudden Time 1993, Three Inventions for Chamber Orchestra 1995, Sometime Voices 1996; chamber music: Piano Sonata 1978, Octet 1978, Flight 1979, Sortilèges 1981, Three Studies for Piano 1985, Upon Silence 1990, Viola, Viola 1997. *Address:* c/o Faber Music, 3 Queen Square, London, WC1N 3AU, England.

BENJELLOUN, Tahar; Moroccan writer; b. 1944, Fes; m. 1986; two s. two d.; ed. Lycée Regnault de Tanger, Faculté de Lettres de Rabat and Univ. of Paris; columnist Le Monde 1973–; mem. haut conseil de la francophonie, conseil supérieur de la langue française; Chevalier des Arts et des Lettres, Légion d'honneur; Médaille du Mérite national (Morocco); Prix Goncourt 1987; Global Tolerance Award (UN) 1998. *Publications:* Harrouda 1973, la Reclusion solitaire 1976, les Amandiers sont morts de leurs blessures (poems) 1976, La plus haute des Solitudes 1977, Moha le fou, Moha le sage 1978, la Prière de l'absent 1980, L'Écrivain public 1983, l'Enfant de sable 1985, la Nuit sacrée 1987, Jour de Silence à Tanger 1990, Les Yeux baissés 1991, Giacometti 1991, l'Ange aveugle 1992, l'Homme rompu 1994, le premier Amour est toujours le dernier 1995, les Raisins de la galère 1995, Poésie complète 1995, la Nuit de l'erreur 1997, le Racisme expliqué à ma fille 1998. *Address:* Editions du Seuil, BP 80, 27 rue Jacob, 75261 Paris cedex 06, France (Office).

BENMAATI, Nadir; Algerian politician; b. 1944; m.; two c.; civil servant for construction and housing 1970–, business devt. 1970–77; Cen. Dir., Dir.-Gen., Sec. Gen. Union of Algerian Sociologists and Economists 1983–88; Minister of Construction, Housing and Regional Development 1988–89. *Address:* Route des 4 Canons, Tagarins, Algiers, Algeria.

BENMAKHLOUF, Alexandre; French lawyer; b. 9 Sept. 1939, Oran, Algeria; s. of Tahar Benmakhlouf and Sylviane Jan; m. Gabrielle Steinmann 1965; one s. one d.; Deputy Public Prosecutor, Meaux 1970, Versailles 1972; seconded to Chancellery 1974–84; Pres. Nanterre Magistrates' Court 1984–86; Deputy Sec.-Gen. Professional Asscn. of Magistrates 1984–86; Adviser to Prime Minister Jacques Chirac 1986–89; Legal Adviser to Jacques Chirac, Mayor of Paris 1989–91; Pres. Court of Appeal, Versailles 1991–93; Dir. of Civil Affairs and Dir. of Cabinet of Guardian of the Seal, Ministry of Justice 1993–96; Attorney-General, Court of Appeal 1996–97, Solicitor-General 1997–. *Address:* Cour d'Appel, Palais de Justice, blvd. du Palais, 75001 Paris, France.

BENN, Rt. Hon. Tony, P.C., M.A., M.P.; British politician; b. 3 April 1925, London; s. of William Wedgwood Benn (1st Viscount Stansgate), P.C. and Margaret Eadie (Holmes); m. Caroline de Camp 1949; three s. one d.; ed. Westminster School and New Coll., Oxford; R.A.F. Pilot 1943–45; Oxford Univ. 1946–49; Producer, BBC 1949–50; Labour M.P. for Bristol S.E. 1950–60, compelled to leave House of Commons on inheriting peerage 1960, re-elected and unseated 1961, renounced peerage and re-elected 1963, contested and lost Bristol East seat in 1983, re-elected as mem. for Chesterfield March 1984–; Nat. Exec. Labour Party 1959–94; Chair. Fabian Soc. 1964; Postmaster-Gen. 1964–66; Minister of Technology 1966–70, of Power 1969–70; Shadow Minister of Trade and Industry 1970–74; Sec. of State for Industry and Minister of Posts and Telecommunications 1974–75; Sec. of State for Energy 1975–79; Vice-Chair. Labour Party 1970, Chair. 1971–72; Chair. Labour Party Home Policy Cttee. 1974–82; Cand. for Leadership of Labour Party 1976, 1988, for Deputy Leadership 1971, 1981; Pres. EEC Energy Council 1977; Pres. Socialist Campaign Group of Labour M.P.s 1987–; fmr. mem. Bureau Confed. of Socialist Parties of the European Community; Hon. LL.D. (Strathclyde Univ.), Hon. LL.D. (Williams Coll., U.S.A.), (Brunel), Hon. D.Tech. (Bradford), Hon. D.Sc. (Aston). *Publications:* The Privy Council as a Second Chamber 1957, The Regeneration of Britain 1964, The New Politics 1970, Speeches by Tony Benn 1974, Arguments for Socialism 1979, Arguments for Democracy 1981, Parliament, People and Power 1982, The Sizewell Syndrome 1984, Writings on the Wall 1984, Out of the Wilderness: Diaries 1963–67, 1987, Office without Power: Diaries 1968–72, 1988, Fighting Back 1988, Against the Tide: Diaries 1973–76, 1989, Conflicts of Interest: Diaries 1977–80, 1990, A Future for Socialism 1991, End of an Era: Diaries 1980–90 1992, Common Sense: A new Constitution for Britain (with Andrew Hood) 1993, Years of Hope—Diaries 1940–1962 1994, The Benn Diaries 1940–1990 1995; The BBC Benn Tapes (audio tapes) 1994, 1995, Writings on the Wall (with Roy Bailey) (audio tape) 1996; Speaking Up in Parliament (video) 1993. *Address:* House of Commons, Westminster, London, S.W.1, England.

BENNACK, Frank Anthony, Jr.; American publishing executive; b. 12 Feb. 1933, San Antonio; s. of Frank Bennack and Lula Connally; m. Luella Smith 1951; five d.; ed. Univ. of Maryland and St. Mary's Univ.; advertising account exec. San Antonio Light 1950–53, 1956–58, advertising man. 1961–65, asst. publr. 1965–67, Publr. 1967–74; Gen. Man. (newspapers), Hearst Corpn. New York 1974–76, Exec. Vice-Pres. and C.O.O. 1975–78, Pres. and C.E.O. 1978–; Chair. Museum of TV and Radio, N.Y. City 1991–; mem. Bd. of Dirs. Mfrs. Hanover Trust Co., New York; Pres. Tex. Daily Newspaper Asscn. 1973–; Dir. American Newspaper Publrs. Asscn. *Address:* Hearst Corporation, 959 8th Avenue, New York, NY 10019; The Museum of TV and Radio, 25 W 52nd Street, New York, NY 10019, U.S.A.

BENNET, Douglas J., Jr., PH.D.; American public administrator; b. 23 June 1938, Orange, N.J.; s. of Douglas and Phoebe Bennet; m. 1st Susanne Klejman 1959 (divorced 1995); m. 2nd Midge Bowen Ramsey 1996; two s. one d.; ed. Wesleyan Univ., Middletown, Conn., Univ. of Calif. (Berkeley) and Harvard Univ.; Asst. to Econ. Adviser (Dr. C. E. Lindblom), Agency for Int. Devt., New Delhi 1963–64; Special Asst. to Amb. Chester Bowles, U.S. Embassy, New Delhi 1964–66; Asst. to Vice-Pres. Hubert Humphrey

1967–69; Admin. Asst. to Senator T. F. Eagleton 1969–73, to Senator A. Ribicoff 1973–74; Staff Dir. Senate Budget Cttee. 1974–77; Asst. Sec. of State, Congressional Relations 1977–79; Admin. U.S. Agency for Int. Devt. 1979–81; Pres. Roosevelt Center for American Policy Studies 1981–83; Pres., C.E.O. Nat. Public Radio (NPR) 1983–93; Asst. Sec. of State, Int. Organizational Affairs, Dept. of State 1993–95; Pres. Wesleyan Univ. 1995–; mem. Council of Foreign Relations, North South Round Table, Soc. for Int. Devt., Carnegie Endowment Study on Organizing Int. Financial Co-operation in 1980s; Dir. Overseas Educ. Fund, KTI Corpn. *Publications:* articles in newspapers and journals. *Leisure interests:* sailing, skiing. *Address:* Office of the President, Wesleyan University, 229 High Street, Middletown, CT 06457 (Office); 269 High Street, Middletown, CT 06457, U.S.A. (Home). *Telephone:* (202) 822-2010 (Office).

BENNETT, Alan; British playwright and actor; b. 9 May 1934; s. of Walter Bennett and Lilian Mary Peel; ed. Leeds Modern School, Exeter Coll., Oxford; Jr. Lecturer, Modern History, Magdalen Coll., Oxford 1960–62; co-author and actor Beyond the Fringe, Edin. 1960, London 1961, New York 1962; author and actor On the Margin (television series) 1966, Forty Years On (play) 1968; Evening Standard Film Award 1996; *Plays:* Getting On 1971, Habeas Corpus 1973, The Old Country 1977, Enjoy 1980, Kafka's Dick 1986, Single Spies 1988, The Wind in the Willows (adapted for Nat. Theatre) 1990, The Madness of George III 1991 (film 1995). *Television scripts:* A Day Out (film) 1972, Sunset Across the Bay (TV film) 1975, A Little Outing, A Visit from Miss Prothero (plays) 1977, Doris and Doreen, The Old Crowd, Me! I'm Afraid of Virginia Woolf, All Day on the Sands, Afternoon Off, One Fine Day 1978–79, Intensive Care, Our Winnie, A Woman of No Importance, Rolling Home, Marks, Say Something Happened, An Englishman Abroad 1982, The Insurance Man 1986, Talking Heads (Olivier Award) 1992, 102 Boulevard Haussmann 1991, A Question of Attribution 1991, Talking Heads 2 1998. *Films:* A Private Function 1984, Prick Up Your Ears 1987, The Madness of King George 1994. *Television Documentaries:* Dinner at Noon 1988, Poetry in Motion 1990, Portrait or Bust 1994, The Abbey 1995. *Publications:* Beyond the Fringe (with Peter Cook, Jonathan Miller (q.v.) and Dudley Moore (q.v.)) 1962, Forty Years On 1969, Getting On 1972, Habeas Corpus 1973, The Old Country 1978, Enjoy 1980, Office Suite 1981, Objects of Affection 1982, The Writer in Disguise 1985, Two Kafka Plays 1987, Talking Heads 1988, Single Spies 1989, The Lady in the Van 1991, The Wind in the Willows (adaptation) 1991, The Madness of George III 1992, Writing Home 1994, The Madness of King George (screenplay) 1995, The Clothes They Stood Up In 1998, Talking Heads 2 1998, The Complete Talking Heads 1998; regular contrib. to London Review of Books. *Address:* c/o Peters; Fraser & Dunlop, The Chambers, Chelsea Harbour, Lots Road, London SW10 0XF, England. *Telephone:* 0171-344 1000.

BENNETT, Bob, B.A.; American politician and businessman; b. 18 Sept. 1933, Salt Lake City, Utah; s. of Wallace Bennett; m. Joyce McKay; six c.; ed. Univ. of Utah; served in U.S.A.F. 1951–57; propr. Bennett Paint & Glass Co.; Congressional liaison official for Transportation Dept., Washington, DC 1968–70; became lobbyist after acquiring Robert Mullen's public relations firm 1970; C.E.O. Franklin Quest 1984–92; Campaign Adviser to fmr. U.S. Senator Wallace Bennett 1962; Republican U.S. Senator from Utah 1993–. *Address:* U.S. Senate, Washington, DC 20510, U.S.A.

BENNETT, Emmett Leslie, PH.D.; American classical scholar; b. 12 July 1918, Minneapolis, Minn.; s. of Emmett L. Bennett and Mary C. Buzzelle; m. Marja Adams 1942; five c.; ed. Univ. of Cincinnati; Research analyst, U.S. War Dept. 1942–45; taught in Dept. of Classics, Yale Univ. 1947–58; Fulbright Research Scholar, Athens 1953–54, Cambridge 1965; mem. Inst. for Advanced Study, Guggenheim Fellow, Visiting Lecturer in Greek, Bryn Mawr Coll. 1955–56; Dept. of Classical Languages, Univ. of Texas 1958–59; Univ. of Wis. Inst. for Research Humanities 1959–, Acting Dir. 1968–69, 1972–75, Dept. of Classics 1960–, Moses S. Slaughter Prof. of Classical Studies 1978–88, Emer. 1988–; Visiting Scholar, Univ. of Texas 1989–; Visiting Prof., Univ. of Colorado 1967, of Cincinnati 1972; Elizabeth A. Whitehead Prof., American School of Classical Studies 1986–87; Adjunct Prof., Dept. of Classics, Univ. of Texas-Austin 1992–93, 1995; corresp. mem. German Archaeological Inst.; Hon. Councillor Archaeological Soc. of Athens; mem. Comité Int. Permanent des Etudes Mycéniennes, Archaeological Inst. of America, American Philological Asscn.; Gold Cross (Greece) 1991. *Publications:* The Pylos Tablets 1951 and 1956, The Mycenae Tablets 1953 and 1958, Mycenaean Studies 1964, Ed., Nestor 1957–77, etc. *Address:* 746 West Main Street, Suite 309, Madison, WI 53715, U.S.A. *Telephone:* (608) 257-2279. *Fax:* (608) 257-4173.

BENNETT, Hywel; British actor and director; b. 8 April 1944, Garnant, South Wales; s. of Gorden Bennett and Sarah Gwen Lewis; m. 1st Cathy McGowan 1967 (divorced 1988); one d.; m. 2nd Sandra Layne Fulford 1998; one d.; ed. Henry Thornton Grammar School, Clapham, London, and Royal Acad. of Dramatic Art; London stage debut as Ophelia in Youth Theatre's Hamlet, Queen's Theatre 1959; played in repertory, Salisbury and Leatherhead 1965. *Stage roles include:* Puck in A Midsummer Night's Dream, Edin. Festival 1967; Prince Hal in Henry IV (Parts I and II), Mermaid 1970; Antony in Julius Caesar, Young Vic 1972; Stanley in The Birthday Party, Gardner Cen., Brighton 1973; Hamlet (touring S. Africa) 1974; Danny in Night Must Fall, Sherman, Cardiff 1974 and Shaw, 1975; Jimmy Porter in Look Back in Anger, Belgrade, Coventry 1974; Konstantin in the Seagull (on tour), Birmingham Repertory Co. 1974, Otherwise Engaged, Comedy Theatre 1978, Terra Nova, Chichester 1979, The Case of the Oily Levantine, Her Majesty's 1980, She Stoops to Conquer, Nat. Theatre 1984–85; Andrey in Elijah Moshinksy's production of The Three Sisters, Albery Theatre 1987, Treasure Island 1990; has directed several plays including Rosencrantz and Guildenstern are Dead, Leatherhead 1975, A Man for All Seasons, Birmingham 1976, I Have Been Here Before, Sherman Theatre, Cardiff 1976, Otherwise Engaged, Library Theatre, Manchester 1978, What the Butler Saw, Theatre of Wales, Cardiff 1980, Fly Away Home (also producer), Hammersmith 1983. *Films include:* The Family Way 1966, Twisted Nerve 1968, The Virgin Soldiers 1969, Loot 1970, Percy 1971, Alice in Wonderland 1972, Endless Night 1972, Murder Elite, War Zone, Frankie and Johnnie 1985, The Twilight Zone, Checkpoint Chiswick, Age Unknown, Married to Malcolm 1997, Misery Harbour 1998. *TV appearances include:* Romeo and Juliet, The Idiot, Unman, Wittering and Zigo, A Month in the Country, Malice Aforethought (serial), Shelley (two series), Tinker, Tailor, Soldier, Spy (serial) 1979, Coming Out, Pennies From Heaven, Artemis '81, The Critic, The Consultant, Absent Friends, Checkpoint Chiswick, The Secret Agent, A Mind to Kill, Casualty, Virtual Murder, Shelley, The Other Side of Paradise, Trust Me, Frontiers, Karaoke, Harpur and Isles, Hospital, many voice-overs and narrations; radio plays; Hon. Fellow Univ. of Wales, Cardiff 1997. *Leisure interests:* fishing, cooking, golf, painting, walking, swimming, reading and solitude. *Address:* c/o James Sharkey Associates, Third Floor, 21 Golden Square, London, W1R 3AG; 116 Lots Road, Chelsea Creek, London S.W.10, England (Home). *Telephone:* 0171-434 3801.

BENNETT, Jack Franklin, PH.D.; American economist; b. 17 Jan. 1924, Macon, Ga.; s. of Andrew Jackson Bennett and Mary Eloise Franklin Bennett; m. Shirley Elizabeth Goodwin 1949; three s. one d.; ed. Woodrow Wilson High School, Washington, D.C., Yale and Harvard Univs.; Communications Officer, U.S. Navy 1944–46; Joint U.S./U.K. Export-Import Agency, Berlin 1946; Econ. Co-operation Admin. 1950; Special Asst. to Admin., Tech. Co-operation Admin. 1951–53; Sr. Economist, Presidential Comm. on Foreign Econ. Policy 1953–54; Foreign Exchange Analyst, Standard Oil Co. (N.J.) 1955; Presidential Citizens' Cttee. on Mutual Security 1956–57: European Financial Rep., Standard Oil (N.J.) 1958–60, Asst. Treas., Exec. Asst. to Chair. 1961–64, Chief Economist, Man. Co-ordination and Planning 1965–66, Gen. Man. Supply Dept. Humble Oil 1967–69, Dir. and Vice-Pres. Esso Int. 1969–71, Sr. Vice-Pres. and Dir. Exxon 1975–88; Deputy Under-Sec. for Monetary Affairs U.S. Treasury Dept. 1971–74, Under-Sec. March-July 1974, Under-Sec. for Monetary Affairs 1974–75; Alexander Hamilton Award 1974. *Publications:* articles in Foreign Affairs, Journal of Finance, Economia Internazionale. *Leisure interests:* swimming, tennis, inventing. *Address:* 141 Taconic Road, Greenwich, CT 06831, U.S.A. (Office).

BENNETT, Jana Eve, B.A., M.SC.; British broadcasting executive; b. 6 Nov. 1957, Cooperstown, U.S.A.; m.; one s. one d.; ed. Bognor Comprehensive, St. Anne's Coll., Oxford, L.S.E.; News trainee BBC 1979, fmrly. Asst. Producer The Money Programme, Producer Newsnight, Producer/Dir. Panorama, Series Producer Antenna, Ed. Horizon, Head of BBC Science; now BBC Dir. of Production; Golden Nymph Award (Panorama), B.A.F.T.A., Emmy, Prix Italia (Horizon). *Leisure interests:* mountaineering, music, children. *Address:* Room 6004, BBC Television Centre, Wood Lane, London, W12 7RJ, England.

BENNETT, Martin Arthur, PH.D., D.SC., F.R.S., F.A.A., F.R.S.C.; British/Australian professor of chemistry; b. 11 Aug. 1935, Harrow; s. of Arthur Edward Charles Bennett and Dorothy Ivy Bennett; m. Rae Elizabeth Matthews 1964; two s.; ed. Haberdashers' Aske's Hampstead School, Imperial Coll. of Science and Tech., London; Postdoctoral Fellow Univ. of S. Calif. 1960–61; Turner and Newall Fellow Univ. Coll. London 1961–63, lecturer 1963–67; Fellow Research School of Chemistry, Australian Nat. Univ. 1967–70, Sr. Fellow 1970–79, Professorial Fellow 1979–91, Prof. 1991–; various professorial and visiting fellowships in Canada, Germany, U.S.A. and Japan; Max Planck Soc. Research Award 1994; Nyholm Medal, Royal Soc. of Chemistry 1991. *Leisure interests:* golf, reading, foreign languages. *Publications:* chapters on ruthenium in Comprehensive Organometallic Chemistry; over 200 papers in journals. *Address:* Research School of Chemistry, Australian National University, Canberra, ACT 0200 (Office); 21 Black Street, Yarralumla, ACT 2600, Australia (Home). *Telephone:* (26) 249-3639 (Office); (26) 282-4154 (Home). *Fax:* (26) 249-3216.

BENNETT, Maxwell Richard, B.ENG., D.SC., F.A.A.; Australian professor of physiology; b. 19 Feb. 1939, Melbourne; s. of Herman Adler Bennett (Bercovici) and Ivy G. Arthur; m. Gillian R. Bennett 1965; one s. one d.; ed. Christian Brothers Coll., St Kilda, Melbourne and Univ. of Melbourne; John & Alan Gilmour Research Fellow, Univ. of Melbourne 1965; Lecturer in Physiology, Univ. of Sydney 1969, Reader 1973, Prof. of Physiology 1991–, Dir. Neurobiology Research Centre 1982–90; Scientific Adviser Nat. Research School of Biological Sciences, Australian Medical Research and Devt. Corpn.; Convener Sydney Inst. of Biomedical Research 1995; Opening Plenary Lecture, World Congress of Neuroscience 1995; Founder Fed. Australian Scientific and Tech. Socs. 1985, Fed. Australian Socs. for Experimental Biology 1988; Chair. Programme Cttee. Inaugural Congress Int. Soc. for Autonomic Neuroscience; Convener Sydney Inst. of Biomedical Research 1995; Deputy Chair. Australian Neural Networks Soc.; Pres. Australian Neuroscience Soc. 1989–92; Vice-Pres. Int. Soc. for Autonomic Neuroscience 1995; Scientific Adviser Australian Medical Research and Devt. Corp. 1992–; mem. Australia Prize Cttee. 1992; Goddard Medal Nat. Heart Foundation 1996, Ramaciotti Medal for Biomedical Research 1996, Perpetual Trustees

Prize in Biomedical Research 1996, Australian Heart Foundation Goddard Prize 1996, Renenessin Research Prize Nat. Heart Foundation 1998, Burnet Medal and Lecture Australian Acad. of Science 1999. *Publications:* Autonomic Neuromuscular Transmission 1972, Development of Neuromuscular Synapses 1983, Optimising Research and Development 1985, The Idea of Consciousness 1997, History of the Synapse 1999. *Leisure interests:* history and philosophy of science, science policy. *Address:* Department of Physiology, University of Sydney, N.S.W. 2006, Australia. *Telephone:* (2) 9351 2034.

BENNETT, Michael Vander Laan, B.S., D.PHIL.; American professor of neuroscience; b. 7 Jan. 1931, Madison, Wis.; s. of Martin Toscan Bennett and Cornelia Vander Laan Bennett; m. 1st Ruth Berman 1963 (divorced 1993); one s. one d.; m. 2nd Ruth Suzanne Zukin 1998; ed. Yale Univ. and Oxford Univ., England; research worker, Dept. of Neurology, Coll. of Physicians and Surgeons, Columbia Univ. 1957–58, Research Assoc. 1958–59; Asst. Prof. of Neurology, Columbia Univ. 1959–61, Assoc. Prof. 1961–66; Prof. of Anatomy, Albert Einstein Coll. of Medicine 1967–74; Co-Dir. Neurobiology Course, Marine Biological Lab. 1970–74; Prof. of Neuroscience, Albert Einstein Coll. of Medicine 1974–, Dir. Div. of Cellular Neurobiology 1974–, Chair. Dept. of Neuroscience 1982–96, Sylvia and Robert S. Olnick Prof. 1986–; Rhodes Scholar 1952; Sr. Research Fellowship, Nat. Inst. of Health 1960–62; Fellow, Nat. Neurological Research Foundation 1958–60, A.A.A.S., New York Acad. of Sciences; mem. N.A.S., American Assen. of Anatomists, American Physiological Soc., American Soc. for Cell Biology, American Soc. of Zoologists, Biophysical Soc., Soc. for Neuroscience, Soc. of Gen. Physiologists; mem. Editorial Bds. Brain Research 1975–, Journal of Cell Biology 1983–85, Journal of Neurobiology 1969– (Assoc. Ed. 1979–93), Journal of Neurocytology 1980–82, Journal of Neuroscience. *Publications:* over 250 papers in scholarly journals and books. *Leisure interests:* running, hiking, skiing and scuba. *Address:* Albert Einstein College of Medicine, Department of Neuroscience, Bronx, NY 10461, U.S.A. (Office). *Telephone:* (718) 430-2536 (Office). *Fax:* (718) 430-8944.

BENNETT, Sir Richard Rodney, Kt., C.B.E., A.R.A.M., F.R.A.M.; British composer; b. 29 March 1936, Broadstairs, Kent; s. of H. Rodney Bennett and Joan Esther Bennett; ed. Leighton Park School, Reading, Royal Acad. of Music, London and under Pierre Boulez, Paris; commissioned to write two operas by Sadler's Wells 1962; Prof. of Composition, Royal Acad. of Music 1963–65, Visiting Prof. 1995–; Vice-Pres. Royal Coll. of Music 1983; mem. Gen. Council, Performing Right Soc. 1975–; Arnold Bax Soc. Prize for Commonwealth Composers 1964; Anthony Asquith Memorial Award for Murder on the Orient Express film music, Soc. of Film and TV Awards 1974. *Compositions:* The Approaches of Sleep 1959, Journal, Calendar, Winter Music 1960, The Ledge, Suite Française, Oboe Sonata 1961, Nocturnes, London Pastoral, Fantasy 1962, Aubade, Jazz Calendar, String Quartet No. Four, Five Studies 1964, Symphony No. 1 1965, Epithalamion 1966, Symphony No. 2 1967, Wind Quintet, Piano Concerto 1968, Jazz Pastoral 1969, Oboe Concerto 1970, Guitar Concerto 1971, Viola Concerto 1973, Commedia I-IV 1972–73, Spells (choral) 1975, Serenade for Youth Orchestra 1977; Opera: The Mines of Sulphur 1964, A Penny for a Song 1966, Victory 1969, All the King's Men (children's opera) 1969; Isadora (ballet) 1981; Film Music: Indiscreet, Devil's Disciple, Blind Date, The Mark, Only Two Can Play, Wrong Arm of the Law, Heavens Above, Billy Liar, One Way Pendulum, The Nanny, The Witches, Far from the Madding Crowd, Billion Dollar Brain, The Buttercup Chain, Secret Ceremony, Figures in a Landscape, Nicholas and Alexandra, Lady Caroline Lamb, Voices, Murder on the Orient Express, Equus, Sherlock Holmes in New York, L'Imprecateur, The Brinks Job, Yanks, Return of the Soldier, Four Weddings and a Funeral; TV music for series include: Hereward the Wake, The Christians, The Ebony Tower, Poor Little Rich Girl. *Leisure interests:* cinema, modern jazz. *Address:* c/o Novello & Co., 8–9 Frith Street, London, W1V 5TZ, England.

BENNETT, Roy Frederick, F.C.A.; Canadian business executive; b. 18 March 1928, Winnipeg, Man.; s. of late Charles William Bennett and Gladys Mabel Matthews; m. Gail Cook Bennett 1978; two s. two d.; ed. Collegiate Inst., N. Toronto and Inst. of Chartered Accountants; with Ford Motor Co. of Canada Ltd., Asst. Controller 1960–62, Dir. Vehicle Marketing 1962–63, Dir. Corporate Planning 1963–64, Gen. Marketing Man. 1964–65, Vice-Pres. Finance 1965–70, Dir. 1966–, Pres. and C.E.O. 1970–81, Chair. and C.E.O. 1981–82; Chair. Bennecon Ltd. 1982–; Chair. Bd. Jannock Ltd.; Dir. Bell Canada Inc.; Chair. Bd. Midland Walwyn Inc., Talisman Energy Inc., Zalev Metals Ltd.; Hon. LL.D. *Leisure interests:* golf, tennis, skiing. *Address:* Suite 1416, Commercial Union Tower, P.O. Box 59, Toronto Dominion Bank Tower, Toronto, Ont. M5K 1E7, Canada. *Telephone:* (416) 365-1418. *Fax:* (416) 365-1419.

BENNETT, Tony (Anthony Dominick Benedetto), MUS.D; American singer and entertainer; b. 3 Aug. 1926, Astoria; s. of John Benedetto and Anna Suraci; m. 1st Patricia Beech 1952 (divorced 1971); two c.; m. 2nd Sandra Grant 1971 (divorced 1984); two d.; ed. American Theatre Wing, NY and Univ. of Berkeley; frequent appearances on TV and in concert. *Records include:* The Art of Excellence 1986, Bennett/Berlin 1988, Astoria: Portrait of the Artist 1990, Perfectly Frank 1992 (Grammy award for Best Traditional Vocal Performance), Steppin' Out 1993 (Grammy award for Best Traditional Pop Vocal), The Essence of Tony Bennett 1993, MTV Unplugged 1994 (Grammy award Album of the Year, Best Traditional Pop Vocal), Here's to the Ladies 1995; owner and recording artist with Improv Records; paintings exhibited at Butler Inst. of American Art, Youngstown, Ohio 1994; Gold records for recordings of Because of You, I Left My Heart in San Francisco; Grammy Award for Best Traditional Pop Vocal Performer 1998.

BENNETT, William John, PH.D., J.D.; American administrator and politician; b. 31 July 1943, Brooklyn; m. Mary Glover 1982; Asst. to Pres., Boston Univ. 1972–76; Exec. Dir. Nat. Humanities Center, N.C. 1976–79, Pres. 1979–81; Assoc. Prof. N.C. State Univ., Raleigh 1979–81, Univ. of N.C. 1979–81; Pres. Nat. Endowment for Humanities 1981; Sec. for Educ. 1985–88; Dir. Nat. Drug Policy 1989–90; fmr. Democrat, joined Republican Party 1986.

BENNETT, William Richards; Canadian politician and businessman; b. 14 April 1932, Kelowna, B.C.; s. of the late William Andrew Cecil Bennett (Premier of B.C. 1952–72) and of Annie Elizabeth May (Richards) Bennett; m. Audrey Lyne James 1955; four s.; ed. Kelowna High School; established business including 17 companies, starting with retail furniture and appliance stores in B.C.; mem. B.C. Legis. Ass. for Okanagan S. 1973; Leader Social Credit Party in B.C. Nov. 1973; Premier of B.C. Dec. 1975–86 (resgnd.). *Leisure interests:* tennis, skiing, jogging. *Address:* 1475 Pritchard Drive, Westbank, B.C. V4T 1X4, Canada.

BENNEY, Adrian Gerald Sallis, C.B.E.; British gold- and silversmith; b. 21 April 1930, Hull; s. of Ernest Alfred Sallis Benney and Aileen Mary Benney; m. Janet Edwards 1957; three s. one d.; ed. Brighton Grammar School, Brighton Coll. of Art, Royal Coll. of Art; est. first workshop in London 1955, Consultant Designer, Viners Ltd. 1957–67; commenced designing and making Reading civic plate 1963; Prof. of Silversmithing and Jewellery, R.C.A. 1974–83; Export Adviser and Designer, Selangor Pewter, Kuala Lumpur 1986–; Adviser to U.K. Atomic Energy Ceramics Centre 1979–83; Chair. Govt. India Hallmarking Survey 1981; British Hallmarking Council 1983–88; has staged several major exhbns.; Liveryman, Worshipful Co. of Goldsmiths 1964; Freeman, City of London 1964; Freeman, Borough of Reading 1984; Hon M.A. (Leicester) 1963; Royal Designer to Industry 1971; royal warrants of appt. to the Queen, the Duke of Edinburgh, Queen Elizabeth the Queen Mother and the Prince of Wales. *Leisure interests:* landscape gardening, painting. *Address:* 73 Walton Street, London, SW3 2HT (Office); The Old Rectory, Cholderton, Nr. Salisbury, Wilts., SP4 0DW, England (Home). *Telephone:* (0171) 589 7002 (Office); (01890) 629614 (Home). *Fax:* (0171) 581 2573 (Office); (01980) 629461 (Home).

BENOIT DE COIGNAC, Henri Elie Marie; French diplomatist; b. 3 Oct. 1935, Rodez (Aveyron); s. of Emile Benoit de Coignac and Madeleine Bonnefous; m. Nadine Vimont 1966; two s. one d.; ed. Collège Saint-Joseph, Sarlat, Lycée Henry IV, Lycée Louis-le-Grand, Faculté de Droit, Univ. of Paris; Asst., Staff Dept., Ministry of Foreign Affairs, Paris 1963–65, Second Sec., Mexico 1965–67, Second Sec. then First Sec., Washington, D.C. 1967–71, First Sec. Tunis and Chief of Press and Information Service 1971–74, Counsellor in charge of Political Affairs 1974, Cultural Counsellor and Counsellor for Tech. and Scientific Co-operation in India 1975–77, Diplomatic Adviser to Nat. Defence Gen. Sec. and Auditeur, Nat. Defence Inst. for Higher Studies (IHEDN) 1978–79, First Counsellor, Buenos Aires 1979–82, Rep. of Pres. of France (Viguier) in Andorra 1982–84, Chief of Protocol in Paris 1984–88, Minister Plenipotentiary 1986, Amb. to Spain 1988–93, to Morocco 1993–95; Diplomatic Advisor to French Govt. 1996–97; Amb. to Ireland Nov. 1997–; Ordre nat. du Mérite, Chevalier Légion d'honneur. *Leisure interests:* tennis, golf. *Address:* French Embassy, 36 Ailesbury Road, Ballsbridge, Dublin 4, Ireland (Office); 26 rue des Boulangers, 75005 Paris; Domaine de Farinières, Saint-Germain des Prés, 81700 Puylaurens, France (Homes). *Telephone:* (353-1) 260 1666 (Office). *Fax:* (353-1) 283 0178 (Office).

BENSLIMANE, Abdelkader; Moroccan politician; b. 1932; ed. Toulouse Univ., France; joined Ministry of Finance 1957; Amb. to France 1961–63; attached to Maghreb Consultative Comm., Ministry of Finance; Amb. to Belgium 1972; Minister of Trade, Industry, Mines and Merchant Marine 1972–74, of Finance 1974–77; fmr. Chair. and Gen. Man. Banque Nationale pour le Développement Economique, Rabat 1978–84; Amb. to Fed. Rep. of Germany 1984–86. *Address:* Place des Alaouites, B.P. 407, Rabat, Morocco.

BENSON, Andrew Alm, PH.D.; American biochemist and plant physiologist; b. 24 Sept. 1917, Modesto, Calif.; s. of Carl B. Benson and Emma C. Alm; m. 1st Ruth Carkeek 1942 (divorced 1969); m. 2nd Dorothy Dorgan Neri 1971; one s. three d. (two deceased); ed. Modesto High School, Univ. of Calif., Berkeley and Calif. Inst. of Tech.; Instructor, Univ. of Calif., Berkeley 1942–43; Research Assoc. Stanford Univ. 1944–45; Asst. Dir. Bioorganic Group, Radiation Lab., Univ. of Calif., Berkeley 1946–54; Assoc. Prof. of Agricultural Biological Chemistry Pennsylvania State Univ. 1955–60, Prof. 1960–61; Prof.-in-Residence, Physiological Chem. and Biophysics, U.C.L.A. 1961–62; Prof. Scripps Inst. of Oceanography, Univ. of Calif., San Diego 1962–88, Prof. Emer. 1988–, Asst. Dir. 1966–70, Dir. Physiology Research Lab. 1970–77; mem. advisory Bd. Marine Biotech. Inst. Co. Ltd., Tokyo 1990–, N.A.S., A.A.A.S., American Acad. of Arts and Sciences; Dr. h.c. (Oslo, Paris) and other awards and distinctions. *Publications:* Path of Carbon in Photosynthesis 1947–55, Wax in Oceanic Food Chains 1975, Arsenic Metabolism, a Way of Life in the Sea 1984, Methanol Metabolism and Plant Growth; 280 articles in scientific journals. *Address:* Scripps Institution of Oceanography, La Jolla, CA 92093-0202 (Office); 6044 Folsom Drive, La Jolla, CA 92037, U.S.A. (Home). *Telephone:* 619-534-4300 (Office). *Fax:* 619-534-7313 (Office).

BENSON, Sir Christopher John, Kt., F.R.I.C.S.; British business executive and chartered surveyor; b. 20 July 1933, Wheaton Aston; m. Margaret Josephine Bundy 1960; two s.; ed. Worcester Cathedral King's School, Inc. Thames Nautical Training Coll. H.M.S. Worcester; Midshipman R.N.R. 1949–52; Sub-Lieut. R.N.V.R. 1952–53; worked as chartered surveyor and agricultural auctioneer 1953–64; Dir. Arndale Devts. Ltd. 1965–69; Chair. Dolphin Devts. Ltd. 1969–71, Dolphin Farms Ltd. 1969–, Dolphin Property (Man.) Ltd. 1969–; Asst. Man. Dir. The Law Land Co. Ltd. 1972–74; Dir. Sun Alliance and London Insurance Group 1978–84, Chair. Sun Alliance Insurance Group PLC 1993–96 (Dir. 1988, Vice-Chair. 1991, Deputy Chair. 1992), Deputy Chair. Royal and Sun Alliance Insurance Group PLC 1996– (Chair. 1996–97); Advisor to British Petroleum Pension Fund 1979–84; Underwriting Mem. of Lloyd's 1979–; mem. Council CBI 1979–; Pres. British Property Fed. 1981–83; Dir. House of Fraser PLC 1982–86; Chair. London Docklands Devt. Corpn. 1984–88; Chair. Reedpack Ltd. 1989–90; Man. Dir. MEPC PLC 1976–88, Chair. 1988–93; Chair. Housing Corpn. 1990–94; Chair. Boots Co. PLC 1990–94 (Dir. 1989); Chair. Games For Good Causes PLC 1993–94; Chair. Costain Group PLC 1993–96; Chair. Funding Agency For Schools 1994–97; Deputy Chair. Thorn Lighting Group PLC 1994–; Chair. Albright and Wilson PLC 1995–; Chair. Devt. Bd. Macmillan Cancer Relief 1995–; Pres. Nat. Deaf Children's Soc. 1995–; Vice-Pres. R.S.A. 1992–97; Hon. Vice-Pres. Nat. Fed. of Housing Asscns. 1994–; Hon. Fellow Wolfson Coll. Cambridge 1990–, Chartered Inst. of Bldg. 1992–, Royal Coll. of Pathologists 1992–; Hon. Bencher, Hon. Soc. of Middle Temple 1984–; mem. Court of Worshipful Co. of Watermen and Lightermen of the River Thames; Liveryman of Guild of Air Pilots and Air Navigators; numerous other public and charitable interests. *Leisure interests:* opera, ballet, farming in Wiltshire, flying, swimming. *Address:* 43 New Bond Street, London, W1X 9HB, England. *Telephone:* 0171-399 2300. *Fax:* 0171-399 2309.

BENSON, Hon. Edgar John, P.C., B.COM.(M.), LL.D., F.C.A.; Canadian politician and chartered accountant; b. 28 May 1923, Cobourg, Ont.; m. Barbara L. Scrymgeour; ed. Queen's Univ., Kingston, Ontario; joined firm England, Leonard and Macpherson (chartered accountants), Kingston, Ont. 1952; Asst. Prof. of Commerce, Queen's Univ., Kingston 1952–62; M.P. 1962–72; Parl. Sec. to Minister of Finance 1963–64; Minister of Nat. Revenue 1964–68; Pres. of Treasury Bd. 1965–68; Minister of Finance 1968–72, also Receiver-Gen. 1968–72; Minister responsible for Cen. Mortgage and Housing Corpn. 1968–72; Minister of Nat. Defence Jan.-Oct. 1972; Pres. Canadian Transport Comm. 1972–82; Amb. to Ireland 1982–86; Liberal.

BENSON, Sidney William, PH.D.; American professor of chemistry; b. 26 Sept. 1918, New York; s. of Julius Benson and Dora Cohen; m. Anna Bruni 1986; one s. one d.; ed. Stuyvesant High School, Columbia Coll. and Harvard Univ.; Postdoctoral Research Fellow, Harvard Univ. 1941–42; Instructor in Chem., Coll. of City of New York 1942–43, Group Leader, Manhattan Project 1943; Asst. Prof., Univ. of Southern Calif. 1943–48, Assoc. Prof. 1948–51, Prof. of Chemistry 1951–64, 1976–91, Distinguished Prof. Emer. 1989; Scientific Co-Director, Loker Hydrocarbon Research Inst. 1977–90, Emer. 1991–; Chair. Dept. of Kinetics and Thermochemistry, Stanford Research Inst. 1963–76; mem. Int. Editorial Bd., Elsevier Publishing Co., Amsterdam, Netherlands 1965–; Founder and Ed.-in-Chief Int. Journal of Chemical Kinetics 1967–83, Ed. Emer. 1983–; G.N. Lewis Lecturer, Univ. of Calif., Berkeley 1989; mem. Editorial Bd. Journal of Physical Chem. 1981–84; Fellow, A.A.A.S., American Physical Soc.; Foreign mem. Indian Acad. Science 1989; mem. American Chemical Soc., N.A.S.; Guggenheim Fellow, Chemical Kinetics and Fulbright Fellow to France 1950–51; N.S.F. Sr. Research Fellow 1957–58, in France 1971–72; Dr. h.c. (Univ. of Nancy) 1989; American Chemical Soc. Award in Petroleum Chem. 1977, Tolman Medal 1978; Fellowship Award of the Japanese Soc. for Promotion of Science 1980; Irving Langmuir Award in Chemical Physics, American Chemical Soc. 1986; Polanyi Medal for Work in Chemical Kinetics (Royal Soc.) 1986, American Chemical Soc. Award, Orange Co. 1986, U.S.C. Award, Presidential Medallion 1986, Emer. Faculty Award, Univ. of S.C. 1990, Kapitsa Gold Medal Award, Russian Acad. of Nat. Science 1977. *Leisure interests:* skiing, swimming and tennis. *Address:* University of Southern California, University Park, MC-1661 Los Angeles, CA 90089-1661; 1110 North Bundy Drive, Los Angeles, CA 90049, U.S.A. (Home). *Telephone:* (213) 740-5964 (Office); (310) 471-5841 (Home). *Fax:* (213) 740-6679.

BENTELE, Raymond F., B.S.; American business executive (retd.); b. 1936; m.; ed. N.E. Missouri State Coll.; accountant, S.D. Leidesdorf & Co. 1960–65; Treasurer, Controller, Germania Savings and Loan Asscn. 1965–67; joined Mallinckrodt, Inc. 1967, Asst. Controller 1969–71, Controller 1971–74, Vice-Pres. 1974–76, Vice-Pres. Finance and Admin. 1976–77, Vice-Pres. Int. Group 1977–78, Sr. Vice-Pres., Group Exec. 1978–79, Pres. and C.E.O. 1979–86; Sr. Vice-Pres. Int. Minerals & Chemical Corpn. 1986–89, Exec. Vice-Pres. 1989–92, Vice-Chair. (bd. of dirs.) 1991–92. *Address:* c/o Mallinckrodt, Inc., 675 McDonnell Boulevard, P.O. Box 5840, St. Louis, MO 63134, U.S.A.

BENTHAM, Richard Walker, B.A., LL.B., F.R.S.A.; British professor of law; b. 26 June 1930; s. of Richard H. Bentham and Ellen W. Fisher; m. Stella W. Matthews 1957; one d.; ed. Trinity Coll. Dublin and Middle Temple, London; called to Bar 1955; Lecturer in Law, Univ. of Tasmania 1955–57, Univ. of Sydney 1957–61; Legal Dept. British Petroleum Co. PLC 1961–83, Deputy Legal Adviser 1979–83; Prof. of Petroleum and Mineral Law and Dir. Centre for Petroleum and Mineral Law Studies, Univ. of Dundee 1983–90, Prof. Emer. 1991–; Russian Petroleum Legislation Project (Univ. of Houston, World Bank, ODA) 1991–96; mem. Council ICC Inst. of Int. Business Law and Practice 1988–95; British nominated mem. panel arbitrators I.E.A. Dispute Settlement Centre; mem. Bd. Scottish Council for Int. Arbitration 1988–98; mem. Int. Law Asscn., Int. Bar Asscn. *Publications:* publications in learned journals in the U.K. and overseas. *Leisure interests:* cricket, military history. *Address:* Earlham, 41 Trumlands Road, St. Marychurch, Torquay, Devon, TQ1 4RN, England. *Telephone:* (01803) 314315.

BENTLEY, (Charles) Fred, O.C., M.SC., PH.D., F.R.S.C.; Canadian professor of soil science; b. 14 March 1914, Mass., U.S.A.; s. of Charles F. Bentley and Lavina A. (née MacKenzie) Bentley; m. Helen S. Petersen 1943; one s. one d.; ed. Univ. of Alberta and Minnesota; Instructor in Soil Science Univ. of Minn. 1942–43; Instructor and Asst. Prof. Soil Science Univ. of Sask. 1943–46; Faculty mem. Soil Science Univ. of Alberta 1946–79, Dean Faculty of Agric. 1959–68, Prof. Emer. 1979–; Special Adviser, Agric., Canadian Int. Devt. Agency 1968–69; mem. Bd. of Govs. Int. Devt. Research Centre 1970–74; Chair. of Bd. Int. Crops Research Inst. for Semi-Arid Tropics, Hyderabad, India 1972–82, Int. Bd. for Soil Research and Man., Bangkok, Thailand 1983–87; Consulting Agrologist, Int. Devt. Volunteer 1979; Hon. D.Sc. (Guelph) 1984, Alberta 1990; Fellow American Asscn. for Advancement of Science 1962, Agric. Inst. of Canada, Canadian Soc. of Soil Science, American Soc. of Soil Science, American Soc. of Agronomy, Royal Soc. of Canada; Pres. Int. Soc. of Soil Science 1975; Queen's Silver Jubilee Medal; Alberta Order of Excellence 1987, M. H. Bennett Award, Soil and Water Conservation Soc. 1989; numerous other awards and distinctions. *Publications:* over 100 scientific reports and papers. *Leisure interests:* world development, international affairs, agriculture and human welfare. *Address:* 13103-66 Avenue, Edmonton, Alberta, T6H 1Y6, Canada. *Telephone:* (403) 435-6523.

BENTLEY, Gerald Eades, Jr., D.PHIL., D.LITT., F.R.S.C.; American/Canadian scholar and professor of English; b. 23 Aug. 1930, Chicago, Ill.; s. of Gerald Eades Bentley and Esther Felt Bentley; m. Elizabeth Budd 1952; two d.; ed. Princeton Univ. and Oxford Univ., U.K.; Instructor, Univ. of Chicago Dept. of English 1956–60; Asst., later full Prof. of English, Univ. of Toronto, Canada 1960–96; Fulbright Lecturer, Univ. of Algiers 1967–68, Univ. of Poona, India 1975–76, Fudan Univ., Shanghai, People's Repub. of China 1982–83; Visiting Fellow, Univ. Coll., Swansea 1985, Univ. of Hyderabad (India) 1988, Fudan Univ. (China) 1988; Guggenheim Fellow, London 1958–59; Fellow of Canada Council and successor Social Science and Humanities Research Council of Canada 1963–64, 1970–71, 1977–78, 1984–85, 1991–94, 1995–(98); Harold White Fellow, Nat. Library of Australia 1989, Connaught Fellow 1991–92; Rockefeller Research Fellow Bellaggio, Italy 1991; Prof./Visiting Research Fellow Princeton Univ. 1992, Merton Coll. Oxford 1993, Hatfield Coll., Durham 1996; Visiting Lecturer Australian Defence Force Acad. 1997; Co-founder Conf. on Editorial Problems 1964–, Chair. 1991–96; Jenkins Award for Bibliography. *Publications include:* Ed. William Blake, Vala, or The Four Zoas 1963, Ed. William Blake's Writings, 2 vols. 1978, Blake Records 1969, Blake Books 1977, Blake Records Supplement 1988, Blake Studies in Japan 1994, Blake Books Supplement 1995; The Early Engravings of Flaxman's Classical Designs 1964, A Bibliography of George Cumberland 1975, Editing Eighteenth Century Novels (Ed.) 1975, George Cumberland, the Captive of the Castle of Sennaar (Ed.) 1991. *Leisure interests:* book collecting, travel. *Address:* 246 MacPherson Avenue, Toronto, Ont., M4V 1A2, Canada. *Telephone:* (416) 922-5613.

BENTON, Peter Faulkner, M.A.; British industrial consultant; b. 6 Oct. 1934, London; s. of S. Faulkner Benton and Hilda Benton; m. Ruth S. Cobb 1959; two s. three d.; ed. Oundle School and Queens' Coll. Cambridge; jr. man. positions in Unilever, Shell Chemicals and Berger, Jenson and Nicholson 1959–64; consultant, McKinsey & Co., London and Chicago 1964–71; Dir. Gallaher Ltd. 1971–77; Man. Dir. Post Office Telecommunications 1978–81; Deputy Chair. British Telecom 1981–83; Chair. European Practice, Nolan, Norton & Co. 1984–87, Enfield Dist. Health Authority 1986–92; Vice-Pres. European Council of Man. 1989–92; Dir. Singer & Friedlander Ltd. 1983–89, Tandata Holdings PLC. 1983–89, Turing Inst. 1985–95, Woodside Communications Ltd. 1995–96; Dir. Gen. British Inst. of Man. 1987–92; Chair. Enterprise Support Group 1993–96; Chair. Visiting Group Inst. for Systems and Eng. Informatics, Italy 1993–94, Visiting Group Inst. for Systems, Informatics and Safety, Italy 1996–; Adviser to Arthur Andersen 1992–98; mem. Int. Advisory Bd. for Science and Tech. to Govt. of Portugal 1996–, Industrial Devt. Advisory Bd. (DTI) 1988–94; Adviser to Stern Stewart Inc. 1996–; mem. Exec. Cttee. Atheneum 1997–; Chair. Delhi Conf. on Indian Infrastructure 1998; Adam Smith Lecturer 1991; I.E.E. Award 1994. *Publication:* Riding the Whirlwind 1990. *Leisure interests:* reading, golf, sailing. *Address:* Northgate House, Highgate Hill, London, N6 5HD, England. *Telephone:* 0181-341 1122. *Fax:* 0181-341 1133.

BENTON, Philip Eglin, Jr., M.B.A.; American business executive; b. 31 Dec. 1928, Charlottesville, Va.; s. of Philip Eglin and Orient Nichols; m. Mary Ann Zadosko 1974; one s. four d.; ed. Dartmouth Coll. and Amos Tuck School; Ford Motor Co. 1953–, Vice-Pres. Truck Operations, Ford of Europe 1977–79, Ford Div. Detroit 1979–81, Sales Operations, N. American Auto Operations Detroit 1981–85, Exec. Vice-Pres. Diversified Products, Dearborn, Mich. 1985–86, Ford Int. Automotive Operations, Dearborn 1986–87, Pres. Ford Automotive Group, Dearborn 1987–90, Pres. and C.O.O. Ford Motor Co. 1990–93.

BENTSEN, Lloyd Millard, Jr., LL.B.; American politician; b. 11 Feb. 1921, Mission, Tex.; s. of the late Lloyd M. Bentsen and of Edna Ruth (Colbath) Bentsen; m. Beryl A. Longino 1943; two s. one d.; ed. Univ. of Texas, Austin; served U.S. Army 1942–45; County Judge, Hidalgo County, Tex. 1946–48; mem. House of Reps. 1948–54; Pres. Lincoln Consolidated, Houston, until 1970; U.S. Senator from Tex. 1971–93; Sec. of Treasury 1993–94; cand. for U.S. Vice-Pres. (with Michael Dukakis, q.v.) in 1988 presidential election; mem. Senate Finance Cttee., Chair. 1988–93, Senate Environment and Public Works Cttee., Jt. Econ. Cttee., Senate Commerce Cttee. 1987–93; Chair. New Holland NV 1996–; Distinguished Flying Cross; Air Medal with Three Oak Leaf Clusters; Democrat. *Address:* c/o Treasury Department, 15th Street and Pennsylvania Avenue, Washington, DC 20220, U.S.A.

BENTZON, Niels Viggo; Danish composer; b. 24 Aug. 1919; s. of the late Viggo and Karen Emma (née Hartmann) Bentzon; ed. Danish Royal Conservatory; musical works: thirteen symphonies, six piano concertos, opera: Faust, choral works, five ballets, concertos for flute and harmonica, pieces for chamber orchestra, string quartet and piano. *Address:* Egernvej 39, 2000 Copenhagen, Denmark.

BENZER, Seymour, PH.D.; American biologist; b. 15 Oct. 1921, New York; s. of Mayer Benzer and Eva Naidorf; m. 1st Dorothy Vlosky 1942 (died 1978); two c.; m. 2nd Carol Miller 1980; one c.; ed. Brooklyn Coll. and Purdue Univ.; Asst. Prof. of Physics Purdue Univ. 1947–53, Assoc. Prof. of Biophysics 1953–58, Prof. 1958–61, Stuart Distinguished Prof. 1961–67; Biophysicist Oak Ridge Nat. Laboratory 1948–49; Research Fellow Calif. Inst. of Technology 1949–51, Visiting Assoc. 1965–67, Prof. of Biology 1967–75, Boswell Prof. of Neuroscience 1975; Fulbright Research Scholar, Pasteur Inst., Paris 1951–52; Senior Nat. Science Foundation Research Fellow Cambridge 1957–58; Fellow, American Asscn. for the Advancement of Science; mem. N.A.S., Harvey Soc., Biophysical Soc., American Acad. of Arts and Sciences, American Philosophical Soc., Foreign mem. Royal Soc. London; Dr. h.c. (Purdue) 1968, (Columbia) 1974, (Yale) 1977, (Brandeis) 1978, (City Univ. of New York) 1978, (Univ. of Paris) 1983; awards include Sigma Xi Research Award 1957, Ricketts Award, Univ. of Chicago, Lasker Award 1971, Prix Charles-Leopold Mayer, French Acad. of Sciences 1975, Harvey Prize, Technion, Israel 1977, Warren Triennial Prize, Mass. General Hosp. 1977, Dickson Prize, Carnegie-Mellon Univ. 1978, Nat. Medal of Science (U.S.A.) 1983, Rosenstiel Award, Brandeis Univ. 1986, T. H. Morgan Medal, Genetics Soc. of America 1986, Lashley Award, American Philosophical Soc. 1988, Gerard Medal, Soc. for Neuroscience 1989, Helmerich Award for Retina Research 1990, Wolf Foundation Award for Medicine 1991, Bristol-Myers Squibb Award for Neuroscience 1992, Crafoord Prize (Royal Swedish Acad. of Sciences) 1993, Feltrinelli Prize (Accademia dei Lincei) 1994, Mendel Medal (Genetical Soc. of G.B.) 1994. *Publications:* The Elementary Units of Heredity 1957, Induction of Specific Mutations with 5-bromouracil 1958, Topology of the Genetic Fine Structure 1959, Topography of the Genetic Fine Structure 1961, A Change from Nonsense to Sense in the Genetic Code 1962, On the Role of Soluble Ribonucleic Acid in Coding for Amino Acids 1962, A Physical Basis for Degeneracy in the Genetic Code 1962, Adventures in the rII Region 1966, Isolation of Behavioral Mutants of Drosophila by countercurrent Distribution 1967, Genetic Dissection of the Drosophila Nervous System by means of Mosaics 1970, Mapping of Behavior in Drosophila Mosaics 1972, Genetic Dissection of Behavior 1973, Dunce, a Mutant of Drosophila Deficient in Learning 1976, Monoclonal Antibodies against the Drosophila Nervous System 1982, Antigenic Cross-Reaction between Drosophila and Human Brain 1983, Neuronal Development in the Drosophila Retina, Monoclonal Antibodies as Molecular Probes 1984, from Monoclonal Antibody to Gene for a Neuron-Specific Glycoprotein in Drosophila 1985, Molecular Characterization and Expression of Sevenless, a Gene involved in Neuronal Pattern Formation in the Drosophila Eye 1987, The Fly and Eye 1990, numerous other publs. on neurogenetics. *Address:* 2075 Robin Road, San Marino, CA 91108, U.S.A. (Home).

BENZI, Roberto; Italian/French conductor; b. 12 Dec. 1937, Marseille; s. of Giuseppe Benzi and Maria Pastorino; m. Jane Rhodes 1966; studied conducting with Andre Cluytens; début as conductor, France 1948; tours in Europe and S. America 1949–52; opera conducting début 1954; conducted Carmen, Paris Opera 1959; guest conductor Europe, Japan, Israel, Mexico, Canada, U.S.A., South Africa and main music festivals; Music Dir. Bordeaux-Aquitaine Orchestra 1973–87, Arnhem Philharmonic 1989–98, Dutch Nat. Youth Orchestra 1991–96; Chevalier, Légion d'honneur, Ordre National du Mérite and des Palmes Académiques, Order of Orange-Nassau. *Publications:* orchestrations of Brahms op. 23 Schumann Variations 1970, Brahms op. 24 Variations and Fugue on a theme by Handel 1973, Rossini Thème et Variations 1978, Erik Satie Je te veux, valse 1987. *Leisure interests:* wildlife, astronomy, cycling. *Address:* 12 Villa Sainte Foy, 92200 Neuilly-sur-Seine, France. *Telephone:* (1) 46.24.27.85. *Fax:* (1) 46.24.55.73.

BERDENNIKOV, Grigory Vitalievich; Russian diplomatist; b. 24 Dec. 1950, Moscow; m.; one d.; ed. Moscow Inst. of Int. Relations; diplomatic service 1973–, sec., atttaché Mission in UN, New York 1973–78, sec. of div. U.S.S.R. Ministry of Foreign Affairs 1978–81, Second then First Sec. Mission to UN, Geneva 1981–86, Counsellor, Chief of Div., Deputy Chief Dept. of Armament Reduction and Disarmament, U.S.S.R. (now Russian) Ministry of Foreign Affairs 1986–92, Deputy Minister of Foreign Affairs of Russia 1992–94; Perm. Rep. to Disarmament Conf. Geneva 1994–97; Dir. Dept. of Security and Disarmament, Ministry of Foreign Affairs 1997–. *Address:* Ministry of Foreign Affairs, Smolenskaya Sennaya 32/34, Moscow, Russia.

BEREND, T. Iván; Hungarian economic historian; b. 11 Dec. 1930, Budapest; s. of Mihály Berend and Elvira Gellei; two d.; ed. Univ. of Economics and Univ. of Sciences, Faculty of Philosophy, Budapest; Asst. lecturer, Karl Marx Univ. of Economics 1953, sr. lecturer 1960, Prof. of Econ. History 1964–, Head of Dept. 1967–85, Rector 1973–79; Prof. of History Univ. of Calif. at L.A. 1990–, Dir. Center for European and Russian Studies 1993–; Gen. Sec. Hungarian Historical Soc. 1966–72, Pres. 1975–79; Corresp. mem. Hungarian Acad. of Sciences 1973–79, mem. 1979–, Pres. 1985–90; Fellowship, Ford Foundation, New York 1966–67; Visiting Fellow, St. Antony's Coll., Oxford 1972–73; Visiting Prof. Univ. of Calif., Berkeley 1978; Visiting Fellow, All Souls Coll., Oxford 1980; Fellow, Woodrow Wilson Int. Center for Scholars, Washington 1982–83; Co-Chair. Bd. of Dirs. Inst. for E.-W. Security Studies 1986; mem. Exec. Cttee. of Int. Econ. Soc. 1982–86, Vice-Pres. 1986–; First Vice-Pres. Int. History Asscn. 1990–95, Pres. 1995–; Corresp. mem. Royal Historical Soc. 1981, British Acad. 1989, Austrian Acad. of Sciences 1989, Czechoslovak Acad. of Sciences 1988; Hon. D. Litt. (St. John's Univ., New York) 1986, (Glasgow) 1990, (Janus Pannonius Univ., Pécs) 1994; Kossuth Prize 1961, State Prize 1985. *Publications:* (with György Ránki): Magyarország gyáripara 1900–1914 1955, Magyarország gyáripara a II. világháboru elött és a háboru idöszakában 1933–1944 1958, Magyarország a fasiszta Németország "életterében" 1960, Magyarország gazdasága az I. világháboru után 1919–1929 1966, Economic Development in East-Central Europe in the 19th and 20th Centuries 1974, Hungary—A Century of Economic Development, Underdevelopment and Economic Growth, The European Periphery and Industrialization 1780–1914 1982, The Hungarian Economy in the Twentieth Century 1985, The European Economy in the Nineteenth Century 1987; (as sole author): Ujjáépités és a nagytöke elleni harc Magyarországon 1945–1948 1962, Gazdaságpolitika az elsö ötéves terv meginditásakor 1948–1950 1964, Öt elöadás gazdaságról és oktatásról 1978, Napjaink a történelemben 1980, Válságos évtizedek 1982, Gazdasági utkeresés 1983, The Crisis Zone of Europe 1986, Szocializmus és reform 1986, The Hungarian Economic Reforms 1990, Central and Eastern Europe 1944–93 — Detour from the Periphery to the Periphery 1997. *Leisure interest:* tennis. *Address:* Department of History, University of California, Los Angeles, 405 Hildgard Avenue, Los Angeles, CA 90096, U.S.A. *Telephone:* (310) 825-1178.

BERENDT, John; American writer; b. 5 Dec. 1939, Syracuse, N.Y.; s. of Ralph Berendt and Carol (Deschere) Berendt; ed. Nottingham High School, Syracuse, Harvard Univ.; Assoc. Ed. Esquire 1961–79, columnist 1982–94; Ed. New York magazine 1979–82. *Publication:* Midnight in the Garden of Good and Evil 1994. *Address:* c/o Random House, 201 East 50th Street, New York, NY 10022, U.S.A.

BÉRENGER, Paul Raymond, B.A.; Mauritian politician; b. 26 March 1945, Quatre Bornes; m. Arline Perrier 1971; one s. one d.; ed. Collège du Saint Esprit, Univ. of Wales and Sorbonne, Paris; Gen. Sec. Mouvement Militant Mauricien 1969–82; Minister of Finance 1982–83, of Foreign Affairs 1991, M.P. 1982–83; Deputy Prime Minister and Minister of Foreign Affairs and Int. and Regional Co-operation 1995; Gov. IMF, African Devt. Bank/African Devt. Fund. *Leisure interests:* reading, swimming. *Address:* Wellington Street, Quatre Bornes, Mauritius (Home). *Telephone:* 54-1998 (Home).

BERENGER, Tom; American actor; b. 31 May 1950, Chicago; ed. Univ. of Missouri; stage appearances in regional theatre and off-Broadway including The Rose Tattoo, Electra, Streetcar Named Desire, End as a Man; TV appearances include: One Life to Live (series), Johnny We Hardly Knew Ye, Flesh and Blood, If Tomorrow Comes. *Films:* Beyond the Door 1975, Sentinel, Looking for Mr Goodbar, In Praise of Older Women, Butch and Sundance: The Early Days, The Dogs of War, The Big Chill, Eddie and the Cruisers, Fear City, Firstborn, Rustler's Rhapsody, Platoon, Someone to Watch Over Me, Shoot to Kill, Betrayed, Last Rites, Major League, Love at Large, The Field, Shattered, Chasers, Sniper 1993, Sliver 1993, Major League 2 1994, Last of the Dogmen 1994, Gettysburg 1994, The Substitute. *Address:* c/o C.A.A., 9830 Wilshire Boulevard, Beverly Hills, CA 90212, U.S.A.

BERENGO GARDIN, Gianni; Italian photographer; b. 10 Oct. 1930, Santa Margherita Ligure; s. of Alberto Berengo Gardin and Carmen Maffei Berengo Gardin; m. Caterina Stiffoni 1957; one s. one d.; began working as photographer 1954; has lived and worked in Switzerland, Rome, Venice; living in Milan 1965–; photographs originally published by Il Mondo magazine, now published by maj. magazines in Italy and worldwide; over 70 personal exhibns. including Cologne Photokina, Montreal Expo, Venice Biennale, Milan, Rome, Venice, Arles, London, Lausanne, Paris, Vienna, New York; photographs in perm. collections of Museum of Modern Art, New York, Bibliothèque Nationale Paris, Eastman House, Rochester, N.Y., Musée de l'Elysée, Lausanne, Museum of Aesthetic Art, Beijing; Mois de la Photo Brassaï Award, Paris 1990; Leica Oskar Barnack Award, Arles 1995. *Publications:* over 150 photographic books. *Leisure interests:* photography, farming, his little dog Olivia. *Address:* Via S. Michele del Carso 21, 20144 Milan, Italy. *Telephone:* (2) 4692877. *Fax:* (2) 4692877.

BERESFORD, Bruce; Australian film director; b. 16 Aug 1940, Sydney; s. of Leslie Beresford and Lona Beresford; m. 1st Rhoisin Beresford 1965; two s. one d.; m. 2nd Virginia Duigan 1989; one d.; ed. Univ. of Sydney; worked in advertising; worked for Australian Broadcasting Comm.; went to England

1961; odd jobs including teaching; film ed. Nigeria 1964–66; Sec. to British Film Inst.'s Production Bd. 1966; feature film dir. 1971–; directed many short films 1960–75. *Directed feature films:* The Adventures of Barry Mackenzie 1972, Barry Mackenzie Holds His Own 1974, Side by Side 1975, Don's Party 1976, The Getting of Wisdom 1977, Money Movers 1979, Breaker Morant 1980, Puberty Blues 1981, The Club 1981, Tender Mercies 1983, King David 1984, Crimes of the Heart 1986, Fringe Dwellers 1986, Aria (segment) 1987, Her Alibi 1988, Driving Miss Daisy 1989 (Acad. Award Best Film 1990), Mr. Johnson 1990, Black Robe 1990, Rich in Love 1993, A Good Man in Africa 1993, Silent Fall 1994, The Last Dance 1995, Paradise Road 1996, Double Jeopardy 1998. *Address:* c/o Anthony A. Williams, 50 Oxford Street, Paddington, N.S.W. 2021, Australia.

BERESFORD, Meg, B.A.; British peace campaign organizer; b. 5 Sept. 1937, Birmingham; d. of John Tristram Beresford and Anne Isobel Northcroft (née Stuart Wortley); m. William Tanner 1959; two s.; ed. Sherborne School for Girls, Dorset and Univ. of Warwick; Founder mem. and Co-ordinator, Campaign Atom, Oxford 1980–81; elected to Nat. Council Campaign for Nuclear Disarmament (CND) 1980; Organizing Sec. European Nuclear Disarmament 1981–83; Vice-Chair. CND 1983–85, Gen. Sec. 1985–90; Staff Coordinator, The Iona Community 1991–94; Asst. Dir. Wiston Lodge, YMCA 1994–97, Man. 1997–. *Publication:* Into the Twenty First Century 1989. *Leisure interests:* walking, the environment, reading and art. *Address:* Wiston Lodge, Wiston, Biggar, ML12 6HT, Scotland. *Telephone:* (018995) 228.

BEREZOVSKY, Boris Abramovich; DR.MATH.SC.; Russian businessman, mathematician and politician; b. 23 Jan. 1946, Moscow; m.; four c.; ed. Moscow Inst. of Wood Tech., Moscow State Univ.; engineer Research Inst. of Testing Machines, Equipment and Measurement Devices 1968–69; engineer Hydrometeorological Research Cen. 1969; engineer, researcher, head of div. Inst. of Problems of Man. 1969–87; author of over 100 scientific articles on applied math., theory of man.; Corresp. mem. Russian Acad. of Sciences 1991; supervisor of introduction of automatization on Togliatti Car Works (VAZ) 1973–91; one of founders and Dir.-Gen. LOGOVAZ Co. 1991–96, 1997–; Dir.-Gen. All-Union Automobile Alliance (AVVA) 1993–96; Deputy Chair. Bd. of Dirs. Public Russian TV 1995–96; Deputy Sec. Security Council of Russian Fed. 1996–97; Exec. Sec. C.I.S. 1998–; f. Charity Foundation Triumph 1994. *Address:* Secretariat of C.I.S., Kirova Street 17, 220050, Minsk, Belarus. *Telephone:* (172) 293517. *Fax:* (172) 272339.

BEREZOVSKY, Boris Vadimovich; Russian pianist; b. 4 Jan. 1969, Moscow; ed. Moscow Conservatoire; m. 1989; winner, Prize of Hope competition, city of Ufa 1985; fourth prize, Leeds Int. Piano Competition 1987; London début, Wigmore Hall 1988; Gold Medal, Int. Tchaikovsky Piano Competition, Moscow 1990; appeared with Soviet Festival Orchestra, London 1990; recitals in New York, Washington, London, Amsterdam, Salzburg, Moscow, Leningrad, Tokyo, Osaka, etc.; appearances with Leningrad (now St. Petersburg) Philharmonic Orchestra, Bayerische Rundfunk Orchestra, Munich and Royal Philharmonic Orchestra, London. *Address:* IMG Artists, 3 Burlington Lane, London, W4 2TH, England. *Telephone:* 0181-233 5800.

BERG, Adrian, M.A., A.R.C.A.; British artist; b. 12 March 1929, London; s. of Charles Berg and Sarah (née Sorby) Berg; ed. Charterhouse, Gonville and Caius Coll. Cambridge, Trinity Coll. Dublin, St. Martin's and Chelsea Schools of Art and Royal Coll. of Art; one-man exhbns. in London, Florence, Düsseldorf, Montreal, Toronto and Chicago; Arts Council Serpentine Gallery, Paintings 1977–86; touring exhbn., "A Sense of Place", Barbican Centre, London, Bath, Plymouth, Gwent, Sheffield, Newcastle-upon-Tyne, Edin., 1993–94; R.A. Elect 1992; Hon. Fellow R.C.A. 1994; several prizes including Gold Medal, Florence Biennale 1973, Maj. Prize, Tolly Cobbold Eastern Arts Asscn. Exhbn. 1981 and Third Prize, John Moores Liverpool Exhbn. 1982–83, First Nat. Trust Foundation for Art Award 1987. *Leisure interests:* music, reading, travel, walking. *Address:* The Piccadilly Gallery, 16 Cork Street, London, W1X 1PF, England. *Telephone:* 0171-629 2875.

BERG, Bernard; Luxembourg politician; b. 14 Sept. 1931, Dudelange; m. Christine Schaffner 1957; one s.; ed. State Industrial School, Labour High School; Sec. of Labour Del. of Arbed steel works at Dudelange; then Vice-Chair. Cen. Labour Del. of Arbed Steel Corpn; then Chair. of Cen. Labour Del. of Arbed Corpn. and Chair. of Labour Del. of Arbed works at Dudelange; mem. Cen. Cttee. of Luxembourg Workers' Trade Union, later Vice-Chair., then Chair.; mem. Council of Gen. Confed. of Labour; mem. Chamber of Deputies 1968–74; Minister of Labour and Social Security, also of Family, Housing and Social Welfare 1974–79, Vice-Pres. of Govt. (Deputy Prime Minister) 1976–79; Deputy Chair. Parl. Group 1979–84; Minister of Social Security 1984–89; Socialist. *Address:* c/o Ministry of Social Security, 26, rue Zithe, 2763 Luxembourg.

BERG, Christian, D.PHIL.; Danish professor of mathematics; b. 2 June 1944, Haarslev; m. Margrete Vergmann 1967; one s. one d.; ed. Univ. of Copenhagen; Assoc. Prof., Univ. of Copenhagen 1972, Prof. of Math. 1978–, Chair. Math. Dept. 1996–; Pres. Danish Mathematical Soc. 1994–98; mem. Danish Natural Sciences Research Council 1985–92, Royal Danish Acad. of Sciences and Letters 1982–; Gold Medal Univ. of Copenhagen 1970. *Publications:* Research monographs: Potential theory on locally compact abelian groups (with Forst) 1975, Harmonic Analysis on Semigroups (with Christensen and Ressel) 1984, papers on potential theory and analysis. *Address:* Department of Mathematics, Universitetsparken 5, 2100 Copenhagen Ø, Denmark. *Telephone:* 35320728. *Fax:* 35320704.

BERG, Eivinn; Norwegian diplomatist; b. 31 July 1931, Sandefjord; s. of Morten Berg and Ester Christoffersen; m. Unni Berg 1957; one s. two d.; ed. Norwegian Coll. of Econs. and Business Admin., Bergen, Norway; entered Foreign Service 1957; Attaché and Vice-Consul, Chicago 1957–60; Ministry of Foreign Affairs 1960–63, 1968–70; First Sec. Norwegian Perm. Del. to EFTA/GATT, UN Office, Geneva 1963–66, Head of Dept., EFTA 1966–68; Counsellor of Embassy, Brussels, and Norway's Mission to EEC 1970–73; Dir. Int. Affairs Norwegian Shipowners Asscn., Oslo 1973–78; Deputy Dir.-Gen. Ministry of Foreign Affairs (Dept. of External Econ. Affairs) 1978–80, Dir.-Gen. 1980–81, State Sec., Ministry of Foreign Affairs 1984–88; Amb. and Perm. Rep. of Norway to NATO 1984–88, to European Union 1989–96; Chief Negotiator European Economic Area 1990–92, for possible accession of Norway to EU 1993–94, for Schengen Agreement 1995–96; Sr. Adviser on int. and European affairs to Statoil, Norske Skog, Statkraft; Commdr., Order of the Crown, Belgium 1974, Commdr., Henrique Infante, Portugal 1980, Caballero Gran Cruz al Mérito Civil, Spain 1982, Grand Lion Order of the Lion, Finland 1983, Grand Officier, Order Nat. du Mérite, France 1984, Commdr., Royal Order of St. Olav, Norway 1987. *Leisure interests:* golf, sailing, mountain hiking. *Address:* Aasstubben 64, 0381 Oslo, Norway. *Telephone:* 22 52 50 08. *Fax:* 22 52 51 88.

BERG, Jeffrey Spencer, B.A.; American theatrical agent; b. 26 May 1947, L.A.; ed. Univ. of California, Berkeley; fmrly. head literature div. Creative Man. Assocs., fmrly. Vice-Pres.; Vice-Pres. Motion Picture Dept. Int. Creative Man. 1975–80, Pres. 1980–85, Chair. and C.E.O. 1985–; Dir. Josephson Int. Inc., Marshall McLuhan Center of Global Communication; Pres. Letters and Science Exec. Bd. Univ. of Calif., Berkeley; Co-Chair. Calif. Information Tech. Council; Trustee Univ. of Berkeley Foundation. *Address:* International Creative Management, 8942 Wilshire Boulevard, Beverly Hills, CA 90211, U.S.A.

BERG, Knut, M.A., D.PHIL.; Norwegian art historian; b. 4 Aug. 1925, Oslo; s. of Arno and Signe (née Mowinckel-Larsen) Berg; m. Marcia W. Robinson 1953; two s. one d.; ed. Univ. of Oslo; research scholar, Univ. of Oslo 1953–65; curator, Dept. of Prints and Drawings, Nasjonalgalleriet 1965–73, Dir. Nasjonalgalleriet 1973–96; mem. Norwegian Acad. of Science and the Humanities, Norwegian Cultural Council; Chair. State Cttee. for Cultural Exchanges with Foreign Countries 1981, Soc. for Benefit of City of Oslo 1980; mem. numerous other bds. and cttees.; Hon. mem. Norwegian Soc. of Art Historians. *Publications:* Studies in Tuscan Twelfth Century Illumination 1968, King Magnus Haakonson's Laws of Norway 1983; ed. History of Norwegian Art (Vol. 1–7) 1981–83, Dictionary of Norwegian Artists 1981–86. *Address:* c/o Nasjonalgalleriet, Universitetsgaten 13, Oslo 1; Haakon den Godes vei 18, Oslo, Norway. *Telephone:* 14 28 04.

BERG, Paul, PH.D., F.A.A.A.S.; American biochemist; b. 30 June 1926, New York; s. of Harry Berg and Sarah Brodsky; m. Mildred Levy 1947; one s.; ed. Pennsylvania State Univ. and Western Reserve Univ.; Postdoctoral Fellow, Copenhagen Univ., Denmark 1952–53; Postdoctoral Fellow, Wash. Univ., St. Louis, Mo. 1953–54, Scholar in Cancer Research 1954–57, Asst. to Assoc. Prof. of Microbiology 1955–59; Prof. of Biochemistry, Stanford Univ. School of Medicine, Stanford, Calif. 1959–, Willson Prof. of Biochem. 1970–94, Chair Dept. 1969–74, Dir. Beckman Center for Molecular and Genetic Medicine 1985–, Robert W. Cahill Prof. of Cancer Research 1994–; Dir. Nat. Foundation for Biomedical Research 1994–; Chair. Nat. Advisory Cttee. Human Genome Project 1990–92; dir. several cos.; Sr. Post-Doctoral Fellow of Nat. Science Foundation 1961–68; Non-resident Fellow Salk Inst. 1973–83; Foreign mem. Académie des Sciences, France 1981; mem. Inst. Medicine, N.A.S. and several other professional bodies; Pres. American Soc. of Biological Chemists 1974–75; Eli Lilly Prize in Biochemistry 1959, Calif. Scientist of the Year 1963, V. D. Mattia Award 1972, shared Nobel Prize for Chem. 1980, Nat. Medal of Science and other awards and prizes. *Leisure interests:* travel, art, and sports. *Address:* Stanford University School of Medicine, Beckman Center, B-062, Stanford, CA 94305, U.S.A. (Office). *Telephone:* (415) 723-6170 (Office).

BERGANT, Boris; Slovenian journalist and broadcasting executive; b. 19 April 1948, Maribor; s. of Evgen Bergant and Marija Bergant; m. Verena Bergant 1969; one s.; fmrly. Ed. foreign affairs, Ed.-in-Chief of News TV Slovenia; fmr. radio journalist; now Deputy Dir.-Gen. Int. Relations and Programme Cooperation RTV Slovenija; Pres. Slovenian Journalist Asscn. 1986–90; mem. Admin. Council European Broadcasting Union 1990–92, 1996–, Vice-Chair. TV programme cttee. 1993, mem. radio cttee. 1993; Pres. Circom-Regional 1989–92, 1995–; awarded Tomšičeva nagrada prize for best journalistic achievement in Slovenia; awards at Monte Carlo, New York and Leipzig TV festivals. *Leisure interests:* tennis, golf. *Address:* Radio-televizija Slovenija, 1550 Ljubljana, Kolodvorska 2–4, Slovenia. *Telephone:* (61) 175 2151. *Fax:* (61) 175 2150.

BERGANZA, Teresa; Spanish mezzo-soprano; b. 16 March 1935, Madrid; d. of Guillermo and Ascensión Berganza; m. 1st Felix Lavilla 1957; one s. two d; m. 2nd José Rifa 1986; début in Aix-en-Provence 1957, in England, Glyndebourne 1958; has sung at La Scala, Milan, Opera Roma, Metropolitan, New York, Chicago Opera House, San Francisco Opera, Covent Garden, etc.; has appeared at festivals in Edinburgh, Holland, Glyndebourne; concerts in France, Belgium, Holland, Italy, Germany, Spain, Austria, Portugal,

Scandinavia, Israel, Mexico, Buenos Aires, U.S.A., Canada, etc.; appeared as Rosina in Il Barbiere di Siviglia, Covent Garden 1967; sung Carmen, at opening ceremony of Expo 92, Seville, also at opening ceremonies Barcelona Olympics 1992, mem. Real Academia de Bellas Artes de San Fernando, Spanish Royal Acad. of Arts 1994; Premio Lucrezia Arana; Premio extraordinario del Conservatorio de Madrid; Grande Cruz, Isabel la Católica; Harriet Cohen Award, Int. Critic Award 1988; Commdr., Ordre des Arts et des Lettres. *Film:* Don Giovanni. *Publication:* Flor de Soledad y Silencio 1984. *Leisure interests:* art, music, reading. *Address:* La Rossiniana, Archanda 5, P.O. Box 137, 28200 San Lorenzo del Escorial, Madrid, Spain. *Telephone:* (1) 8960941 (Madrid). *Fax:* (1) 8960816 (Madrid).

BERGE, Gunnar; Norwegian politician; b. 29 Aug. 1940, Etne; m.; sheet metal worker; mem. Stavanger City Council 1963–67; Chair. Rogaland Co. AUF (Norwegian Labour Youth League) 1965–66; mem. Storting 1969, Chair. Standing Cttee. on Finance 1978–81, Vice-Chair. 1981; Minister of Finance 1986–89, of Local Govt. and Labour 1993; fmr. Vice-Pres. of Lagting. *Address:* c/o Ministry of Local Government, Møllergt. 43, P.O. Box Box 8004 Dep., 0030 Oslo 1, Norway.

BERGÉ, Pierre Vital Georges; French business executive; b. 14 Nov. 1930, l'Ile d'Oléron; s. of Pierre Bergé and Christiane (née Sicard) Bergé; ed. Lycée Eugène-Fromentin, La Rochelle; Dir. and Ed.-in-Chief la Patrie mondiale 1949–61; f. and Dir.-Gen. Yves Saint Laurent 1961, Pres. 1971–; Pres. Yves Saint Laurent of America Inc., New York 1971–; Chair. Asscn. of Theatres of the Paris Opera 1988–94, Hon. Pres. 1994–; Pres. Chambre syndicale du prêt-à-porter des couturiers et des créateurs de mode 1988–93; Goodwill Amb. for UNESCO 1993; Dir. Lundis musicaux de l'Athénée 1977; Admin. Cttee. for the Devt. and Promotion of Textile and Design, Fondation Cartier Parsons School of Design 1985–, Pres. 1991–; Pres. Inst. français de la mode 1985–; Pres., Dir.-Gen. Yves Saint Laurent Parfums (merged with Elf-Sanofi) 1987–93; Chevalier Légion d'honneur, Ordre nat. du Mérite, Commdr. des Arts et des Lettres, Officer Order of Orange-Nassau (Netherlands). *Publications:* Bernard Buffet 1957, Liberté, j'écris ton nom 1991, l'affaire Clovis 1996, studies on Pierre Mac-Orlan, Henry de Montherlant, Jean Anouilh, Francis Carco and Jean Giono. *Leisure interest:* modern art. *Address:* Yves Saint Laurent, 5 avenue Marceau, 75116 Paris (Office); 5 rue Bonaparte, 75006 Paris, France (Home).

BERGEN, Candice Patricia; American actress and photo-journalist; b. 9 May 1946, Beverly Hills; d. of Edgar and Frances (née Westerman) Bergen; m. Louis Malle 1980 (died 1995); one d.; ed. Westlake School for Girls, Univ. of Pa.; *Films include:* The Group 1966, The Sand Pebbles 1966, The Day the Fish Came Out 1967, Vivre Pour Vivre 1967, The Magus 1968, Getting Straight 1970, Soldier Blue 1970, The Adventurers 1970, Carnal Knowledge 1971, The Hunting Party 1971, T. R. Baskin 1972, 11 Harrowhouse 1974, Bite the Bullet 1975, The Wind and the Lion 1976, The Domino Principle 1977, A Night Full of Rain 1977, Oliver's Story, 1978, Starting Over 1979, Rich and Famous 1981, Gandhi 1982, Stick 1985, Au Revoir les Enfants (co-Dir.) 1987, Murphy Brown (TV series Emmy Award 1989, 1990) 1989, 1990, Tim (TV movie) 1996; photojournalist work has appeared in Vogue, Cosmopolitan, Life and Esquire. *Publications:* The Freezer, (in Best Short Plays of 1968), Knock Wood (autobiog.) 1984. *Address:* c/o William Morris Agency, 151 El Camino, Beverly Hills, CA 90212, U.S.A.

BERGER, Helmut; Austrian actor; b. 1942, Salzburg; ed. Feldkirk Coll., Univ. of Perugia, Italy; first film role in Luchino Visconti's Le Streghe 1966; other film roles: The Young Tigers, The Damned, Do You Know What Stalin Did To Women?, The Garden of the Finzi-Continis, The Picture of Dorian Gray, A Butterfly with Bloody Wings, The Greedy Ones, The Strange Love Affair, Ludwig, Ash Wednesday, Conversation Piece, The Romantic Englishwoman, Orders to Kill, Madame Kitty, Merry-Go-Round, Code Name: Emerald, The Glass Heaven, Faceless, The Betrothed, The Godfather Part III.

BERGER, John; British author and art critic; b. 5 Nov. 1926, London; s. of late S.J.D. Berger and Miriam Berger (née Branson); ed. Cen. School of Art and Chelsea School of Art, London; began career as painter and teacher of drawing; exhbns. at Wildenstein, Redfern and Leicester Galleries, London; Art Critic Tribune, New Statesman; Visiting Fellow B.F.I. 1990–; numerous TV appearances including Monitor, two series for Granada; Scenario: La Salamandre (with Alain Tanner), Le Milieu du Monde, Jonas (New York Critics Prize for Best Scenario of Year 1976); George Orwell Memorial Prize 1977. *Publications:* fiction: A Painter of Our Time 1958, The Foot of Clive 1962, Corker's Freedom 1964, G (Booker Prize, James Tait Black Memorial Prize) 1972, Pig Earth 1979, Once in Europa 1989, Lilac and Flag 1991, To The Wedding 1995, Photocopies 1996; theatre: Question of Geography (with Nella Bielski) 1984 (staged in Marseille, Paris and by R.S.C., Stratford), Francisco Goya's Last Portrait (with Nella Bielski) 1989; non-fiction: Marcel Frishman 1958, Permanent Red 1960, The Success and Failure of Picasso 1965, A Fortunate Man: the story of a country doctor (with J. Mohr) 1967, Art and Revolution, Moments of Cubism and Other Essays 1969, The Look of Things, Ways of Seeing 1972, The Seventh Man 1975 (Prize for Best Reportage, Union of Journalists and Writers, Paris 1977), About Looking 1980, Another Way of Telling (with J. Mohr) 1982, And Our Faces, My Heart, Brief as Photos 1984, The White Bird 1985 (U.S.A. as The Sense of Sight 1985), Keeping a Rendezvous (essays and poems) 1992; translations: (with A. Bostock): Poems on the Theatre by B. Brecht 1960, Return to My Native Land by Aime Cesaire 1969; Oranges for the Son of Alexander Levy by Nella Bielski (with Lisa Appignanesi) 1982. *Address:* Quincy, Mieussy, 74440 Taninges, France.

BERGER, Samuel; American government official; b. 28 Oct. 1945, Sharon, Conn.; ed. Cornell Univ., Harvard Univ., mem. Bar, D.C. 1971; Legis. Asst. to Senator Harold E. Hughes 1971–72; Special Asst. to Mayor John V. Lindsay, N.Y. 1972; Deputy Dir. Policy Planning Staff Dept. of State 1977–80; partner Hogan & Hartson; Asst. Dir. Nat. Security Presidential Transitional Team 1992; Deputy Asst. to Pres. for Nat. Security Affairs 1993–96; Nat. Security Adviser Jan. 1997–. *Address:* c/o National Security Council, Old Executive Office Building, 17th Street and Pennsylvania Avenue, N.W., Washington, D.C. 20504, U.S.A. (Office). *Telephone:* 202-456-9392.

BERGER, Thomas Louis, B.A.; American author; b. 20 July 1924, Cincinnati, Ohio; s. of Thomas C. Berger and Mildred Berger; m. Jeanne Redpath 1950; ed. Univ. of Cincinnati and Columbia Univ. Grad. School; mil. service 1943–46; Distinguished Visiting Prof. Southampton Univ. 1975–76; Visiting lecturer, Yale Univ. 1981, 1982; Regents lecturer, Univ. of Calif. (Davis) 1982; Dial Fellow 1962; Rosenthal Award, Nat. Inst. of Arts and Letters 1965; Western Heritage Award 1965; Hon. Litt.D. (Long Island) 1986. *Publications:* Crazy in Berlin 1958, Reinhart in Love 1962, Little Big Man 1964, Killing Time 1967, Vital Parts 1970, Other People (play) 1970, Regiment of Women 1973, Sneaky People 1975, Who Is Teddy Villanova? 1977, Arthur Rex 1978, Neighbors 1980, Reinhart's Women 1981, The Feud 1983, Nowhere 1985, Being Invisible 1987, The Houseguest 1988, Changing the Past 1989, Orrie's Story 1990, Meeting Evil 1992, Robert Crews 1994, Suspects 1996, The Return of Little Big Man 1999. *Leisure interest:* cooking. *Address:* P.O. Box 11, Palisades, NY 10964, U.S.A.

BERGERON, André Louis; French trade unionist and printer; b. 1 Jan. 1922, Suarce; s. of Louis and Marie (née Voëlin) Bergeron; m. Georgette Monnier 1954; ed. Tech. Coll., Belfort; printer 1936–48; Sec.-Gen. of Typographical Union, Belfort 1946–47; Force-Ouvrière 1947–48, Perm. Sec. Belfort Area 1948; Sec.-Gen. Fédération Force Ouvrière du Livre 1948–50; Regional Del. Force Ouvrière and mem. Exec. Cttee. 1950–56, mem. Bureau de la Confédération 1956–63, Sec.-Gen. Force Ouvrière 1963–89; mem. exec. cttee. Féd. graphique internationale 1957, Pres. 1958–86, 1988–; Pres. Org. commune de consommateurs, agriculteurs-consommateurs 1985–; Vice-Pres. Union national pour l'emploi dans l'industrie et le commerce (UNEDIC) 1986, Pres. 1989–90. *Publications:* Lettre ouverte à un syndiqué 1975, Ma route et mes combats 1976, Quinze cents jours 1984, Tant qu'il y aura du grain à moudre 1988, Je revendique le bon sens 1996. *Address:* 14 rue du Stade-Buffalo, 92120 Montrouge, France (Home).

BERGERSEN, Fraser John, D.SC., F.A.A., F.R.S.; Australian research scientist; b. 26 May 1929, New Zealand; s. of Victor E. and Arabel H. (Young) Bergersen; m. Gladys I. Heather 1952; two s. one d.; ed. Hamilton High School, New Zealand, Univs. of Otago and New Zealand; Assoc., Bacteriology Dept., Univ. of Otago 1952–54; joined Div. of Plant Industry, CSIRO 1954, Chief Research Scientist 1972–94, Hon. Research Fellow 1994–96; Visiting Fellow A.N.U. 1994–95, 1999–, Univ. Fellow 1996–98; Australian Acad. of Science Council 1987–93, Foreign Sec. 1989–93; Research Assoc. Univ. of Wisconsin 1958–59; Royal Soc. Commonwealth Fund Fellow, Univ. of Sussex 1973; David Rivett Medal, CSIRO 1968. *Publications:* Methods for Evaluating Biological Nitrogen Fixation 1980, Root Nodules of Legumes: Structure and Functions 1982; more than 160 papers on microbiology and biological nitrogen fixation. *Leisure interests:* music, gardening. *Address:* Division of Biochemistry and Molecular Biology, School of Life Sciences, Australian National University, Canberra, A.C.T. 0200 (Office); 13 Ferdinand Street, Campbell, Canberra, A.C.T. 2612, Australia (Home). *Telephone:* (02) 6249 2840 (Office); (02) 6247 7413 (Home). *Fax:* (02) 6249 0313 (Office).

BERGET, Grete Anni; Norwegian politician and journalist; b. 25 March 1954, Vinstra; d. of Bjarne Berget and Gudrun Berget; m. Per Ritzler 1989; one d.; ed. Oppland District Coll., Norwegian School of Journalism and Crafts School; journalist, local radio and newspapers, Lillehammer 1978–82; Ed. Labour Youth org. newspaper 1982–84; journalist, Arbeiderbladet, Oslo 1984–88; Dir. of Information, Office of Prime Minister 1988–89; Political Counsellor to Prime Minister Brundtland 1989–91; Minister of Children and Family Affairs 1991. *Leisure interests:* being with husband and child; mountain tours, winter and summer skiing, soccer, music. *Address:* c/o Ministry of Children and Family Affairs, Akersgt. 59, Postboks 8036 Dep, 0030 Oslo, Norway. *Telephone:* 22-34-90-90. *Fax:* 22-34-95-15.

BERGGREN, Bo Erik Gunnar; Swedish company executive; b. 11 Aug. 1936, Falun; s. of Tage Berggren and Elsa Höglund; m. Gunbritt Haglund 1962; two s. two d.; ed. Royal Inst. of Tech.; metallurgical research and devt., STORA Kopparbergs Bergslags AB (now STORA), Domnarvet 1962–68, Mill Man., Söderfors 1968–74, Exec. Vice-Pres., Falun 1975–78, Pres. 1984–92, C.E.O. 1984–94, Chair. Bd. 1992–, Chair. Bd. STORA Stockholm 1995–98; Pres. Incentive AB, Stockholm 1978–84; mem. Prime Minister's Special Industry Advisory Cttee. 1994–; Chair. Astra, SAS (Sweden), SAS (Sverige) AB; Vice-Chair. Investor, Fed. of Swedish Industries, Skandinaviska Enskilda Banken; mem. Bd. Telefonaktiebolaget L M Ericsson, Danisco A/S, Royal Inst. of Tech.; mem. Int. Council J. P. Morgan & Co. Inc., Robert Bosch Internationale Beteiligungen Advisory Cttee., Royal Swedish Acad. of Eng. Sciences, of Forestry and Agric.; King's Medal 12th dimension with Ribbon of Order of the Seraphim 1987; Dr. h.c. (Royal Inst. of Tech.,

Stockholm) (Dalhousie Univ.) 1996. *Leisure interests:* the arts, family, music. *Address:* c/o STORA, P.O. Box 16 100, S-103 22 Stockholm, Sweden. *Telephone:* (8) 6136600. *Fax:* (8) 1062821.

BERGGREN, Thommy; Swedish actor; b. 1937; ed. The Pickwick Club (private dramatic school), Atelierteatern, Stockholm, and Gothenburg Theatre; Gothenburg Theatre 1959–63; Royal Dramatic Theatre, Stockholm 1963; *plays acted in include:* Gengangaren (Ibsen) 1962, Romeo and Juliet 1962, Chembalo 1962, Who's Afraid of Virginia Woolf 1964. *Films acted in include:* Pärlemor 1961, Barnvagnen (The Pram) 1962, Kvarteret Korpen (Ravens End) 1963, En söndag i september (A Sunday in September) 1963, Karlek 65 (Love 65) 1965, Elvira Madigan 1967, The Black Palm Trees 1969, The Ballad of Joe Hill 1971.

BERGH, Birger, D.PHIL.; Swedish professor of Latin; b. 25 June 1935, Luleå; s. of Elsa Bergh and Ragnar Bergh; m. Gunilla Åselius 1958 (divorced 1987); two s. one d.; ed. Uppsala Univ.; Asst. Prof. of Latin, Uppsala Univ. 1968–75; Prof. of Latin, Lund Univ. 1975–. *Publications:* Critical Editions of St. Bridget's Revelations, (Books V, VI and VII) 1967, 1971, 1991 of Mathias Lincopensis' Testa Nucis and Poetria 1996; works on Latin linguistics, studies in Swedish neo-Latin. *Leisure interest:* music. *Address:* Sandgatan 12, 22350 Lund, Sweden. *Telephone:* (46) 222-83-76.

BERGIN, Patrick; Irish actor; b. 1954, Dublin; m. Paula Bergin; teacher of juvenile delinquents and children with learning disabilities in London until 1980; full-time actor in repertory theatre, TV and film 1980–; TV appearances include: Boon, Hard Cases, The Real Charlotte (series) 1990, Robin Hood 1991, The Hummingbird Tree (BBC film) 1992, Act of Betrayal, They, Frankenstein. *Films include:* Those Glory, Glory Days, Sleeping With The Enemy 1991, Patriot Games 1992, Map of the Human Heart 1992, Love Crimes 1992, Double Cross.

BERGKAMP, Dennis; Netherlands footballer; b. 20 May 1969, Amsterdam; striker; played for Ajax Amsterdam 1986–92, Inter Milan 1992–95, Arsenal, London, U.K. 1995–, for Holland 1990–. *Address:* c/o Arsenal F.C., Arsenal Stadium, Avenell Road, London, N5 1BU, England.

BERGLUND, Paavo Allan Engelbert, Finnish conductor; b. 14 April 1929, Helsinki; s. of Hjalmar and Siiri (Loiri) Berglund; m. Kirsti Kivekäs 1958; one s. two d.; ed. Sibelius Acad. Helsinki; Violinist, Finnish Radio Symphony Orchestra 1949–56, Conductor 1956–62, Prin. Conductor 1962–71; Prin. Conductor Bournemouth Symphony Orch. 1972–79, Helsinki Philharmonic Orch. 1975–79; Prin. Conductor Royal Stockholm Philharmonic Orchestra 1987–91, Royal Danish Orchestra 1993–; State Award for Music 1972; Hon. O.B.E. *Recordings:* complete Sibelius symphonies incl. first recording of Kullervo Symphony 1971–77, Má Vlast (Smetana), Shostakovich symphonies 5, 6, 7, 10, 11, many other recordings. *Publication:* A Comparative Study of the Printed Score and the Manuscript of the Seventh Symphony of Sibelius 1970. *Address:* Munkkiniemenranta 41, 00330 Helsinki 33, Finland.

BERGMAN, Ingmar; Swedish film director and theatre producer; b. 14 July 1918, Uppsala; m. Ingrid Karlebovon Rosen 1971 (died 1995); eight c. by previous marriages; ed. Stockholm Univ.; producer Royal Theatre, Stockholm 1940–42; scriptwriter and producer Svensk Filmindustri 1940–44; theatre-dir. Helsingborg 1944–46, Gothenburg 1946–49, Malmo 1954–63; leading Dir. Royal Dramatic Theatre, Stockholm 1963; Dir. Mme de Sade Theatre 1989; Chair. European Cinema Soc. 1989–; has written the scripts of most of his films; mem. Swedish Acad. of Letters; Erasmus Prize 1965, Award for Best Dir. Nat. Soc. of Film Critics 1970, Order of the Yugoslav Flag 1971, Luigi Pirandello Int. Theatre Prize 1971, Goethe Award (Frankfurt) 1976, Gold Medal of Swedish Acad. 1977, European Film Award 1988, Le Prix Sonning 1989, Praemium Imperiale Prize (Japan) 1991, Dorothy and Lilian Gish Prize 1995; Dr. h.c. (Univ. of Rome) 1988; Commdr. Légion d'honneur 1985; author of plays A Painting on Wood, The City, The Rite (TV play), The Lie (TV play), Scenes from a Marriage (TV play); Dir. To Damascus 1974, The Merry Widow, Twelfth Night 1975, 1980, Tartuffe 1980, King Lear 1985, John Gabriel Borkman 1985, Miss Julie 1986, Hamlet 1986. *Films include:* Crisis 1945, It Rains on our Love 1946, A Ship Bound for India 1947, Music in Darkness 1947, Port of Call 1948, Prison 1948, Thirst 1949, To Joy 1949, Summer Interlude 1950, This Can't Happen Here 1950, Waiting Women 1952, Summer with Monika 1952, Sawdust and Tinsel 1953, A Lesson in Love 1954, Journey into Autumn 1955, Smiles of a Summer Night 1955, The Seventh Seal 1956, Wild Strawberries 1957, So Close to Life 1957, The Face 1958, The Virgin Spring 1959, The Devil's Eye 1960, Through a Glass Darkly 1961, Winter Light 1962, The Silence 1962, Now About these Women 1963, Episode in Stimulantia 1965, Persona 1966, The Hour of the Wolf 1967, Shame 1968, The Rite 1970, A Passion 1970, The Touch 1971, Cries and Whispers 1972, Scenes from a Marriage 1974 (film and TV), The Magic Flute (film and TV) 1975, Face to Face (film and TV) 1975, The Serpent's Egg 1977, Sonate d'automne 1978, Aus dem Leben der Marionetten 1980, Fårö Document 1980, Fanny and Alexander 1981, After the Rehearsal 1984, Private Confessions 1998; TV: Making Noise and Acting Up 1996; scriptwriter, Good Intentions 1989. *Publications:* Four Stories 1977, The Magic Lantern (autobiog.) 1988, Fanny and Alexander 1989, Images: My Life in Film 1993, Sunday's Child 1994, Private Confessions 1997.

BERGMAN, Stephenie Jane, DIP.A.D.; British artist; b. 18 April 1946, London; d. of Jack 'Kid' Berg and Morya Bergman; ed. St Paul's Girls' School and St. Martin's School of Art; one-woman exhbns. at Garage Art Ltd., London 1973, 1975, Nottingham 1976, Cambridge 1977, Chester 1978, Anthony Stokes, London, 1978, 1980, Riverside Studios, London 1980, Crafts Council Gallery 1984, Butler's House, Kilkenny 1984; has participated in group exhbns. in London, France, Belgium, Australia, Zimbabwe, including 25 Years of Painting, Royal Academy, London 1976; Gulbenkian Award 1975. *Leisure interest:* horse racing.

BERGMANN, Barbara Rose, M.A., PH.D.; American professor of economics; b. 20 July 1927, New York; d. of Martin Berman and Nellie Wallenstein; m. Fred H. Bergmann 1965; one s. one d.; ed. Cornell and Harvard Univs.; economist, U.S. Bureau of Statistics, New York 1949–53, New York Metropolitan Regional Study 1957–61; Instr. Harvard Univ. 1958–61; Sr. Research Assoc. Harvard Econ. Research Project 1960–61; sr. staff economist, Council of Econ. Advisers, Washington, D.C. 1961–62; Assoc. Prof. Brandeis Univ. 1962–64; mem. sr. staff, Brookings Inst. Washington, D.C. 1963–65; sr. econ. adviser, AID, Washington, D.C. 1966–67; Prof. of Econs. Univ. of Md. College Park 1971–88; Distinguished Prof. of Econs. American Univ. Washington, D.C. 1988–97, Prof. Emer. 1997–; Vice-Pres. American Econ. Asscn. 1976; Columnist on econ. affairs N.Y. Times 1981–82, L.A. Times 1983–; Pres. American Asscn. of Univ. Profs. 1990–92. *Publications:* Projection of a Metropolis (co-author) 1961, The Impact of Highway Investment on Development (co-author), A Microsimulated Transactions Model of the U.S. Economy (co-author) 1985, The Economic Emergence of Women 1986, Saving Children from Poverty: What the United States Can Learn From France 1995, In Defense of Affirmative Action 1996. *Address:* Department of Economics, American University, Washington, DC 20016 (Office); 5430 41st Place, N.W., Washington, DC 20015, U.S.A. (Home). *Telephone:* (202)-885-2725 (Office); (202)-537-3036 (Home). *Fax:* (202)-885-3790 (Office).

BERGMANN, Christine, DR. RER. NAT.; German politician; b. 7 Sept. 1939, Dresden; m. Volker Bergmann 1963; one s. one d.; ed. Leipzig Univ.; fmrly. worked as apothecary; freelance work then full-time employee in pharmaceutics propagation Berlin Pharmaceutical Inst. 1967–77, Head of Dept. 1977; mem. Social Democratic Party of Germany (SPD) 1989–, State Chair. Berlin 1989, mem. Party Exec. Cttee. and Presidium 1995–; Fed. Minister of Family Affairs, Sr. Citizens, Women and Youth 1998–; Pres. Berlin Ass. of City Councillors 1990–91, elected Mayoress of Berlin and Senator 1991. *Address:* Ministry of Family Affairs, Senior Citizens, Women and Youth, Rochusstrasse 8–10, 53123 Bonn, Germany. *Telephone:* (228) 9300. *Fax:* (228) 930-22-21.

BERGMANN, Felix, PH.D., M.D.; Israeli pharmacologist and academic; b. 17 Aug. 1908, Frankfurt/Oder; s. of Yehuda Bergmann and Hedwig Bergmann; m. Sarah Sulski 1938; one s. one d.; ed. Univ. of Berlin; Research Assoc. Weizman Inst. of Science, Rehovot, Israel 1934–46; Head Dept. of Pharmacology, Medical School, Jerusalem 1947–78, Emer. Prof. 1978–; Research Assoc., Coll. of Physicians and Surgeons, Columbia Univ., New York 1950–; Visiting Prof. Harvard Medical School 1946–47, Columbia Univ. 1947–48, 1958–59, Nat. Inst. for Medical Research, London 1977, Univ. of Cape Town 1987; mem. Israeli Acad. of Science, Hon. mem. Physiological Soc. of South America. *Publications:* over 350 publs. on organic chemistry, physiology, pharmacology and toxicology. *Leisure interest:* archaeology. *Address:* Department of Pharmacology, Medical School, Jerusalem 91010; Disraeli Street 3, Jerusalem 92222, Israel (Home). *Telephone:* (02) 428741 (Office); (02) 631138 (Home).

BERGNER, Christoph, DR. AGRAR; German politician; b. 24 Nov. 1948, Zwickau; m.; three c.; ed. Univs. of Jena and Halle; mem. Christian Democratic Union (CDU) without office in fmr. G.D.R. 1971; Research Asst. Inst. of Biochemistry of Plants, Univ. of Halle 1974; mem. Landtag (State Parl.) of Saxony-Anhalt 1990–; Vice-Chair. Saxony-Anhalt CDU Asscn. 1991–; Chair. CDU Parl. Party in Landtag 1991–93, 1994; Minister-Pres. of Saxony-Anhalt 1993–94. *Address:* Tannenweg 37, 06120 Halle, Germany.

BERGONZI, Carlo; Italian opera singer; b. 13 July 1924, Busseto, Parma; m. Adele; two c.; ed. Parma Conservatory; début (baritone) as Figaro (Il Barbiere di Siviglia) at Lecce 1948; début as tenor in title role of Andrea Chénier, Teatro Petruzzelli, Bari 1951; subsequently appeared at various Italian opera houses including La Scala, Milan; U.S. début in Il Tabarro and Cavalleria Rusticana, Lyric Opera, Chicago 1955; appeared at Metropolitan Opera, New York in Aïda (as Radames) and Il Trovatore (as Manrico) 1955–56; now appears at all the major opera houses in Europe, and also in U.S.A. and South America; repertoire includes many Verdi roles.

BERGQUIST, Dame Patricia Rose, D.B.E., PH.D., D.SC., F.R.S.N.Z.; New Zealand professor of zoology; b. 10 March 1933, Auckland; d. of William and Bertha E. Smyth; m. Peter L. Bergquist 1958; one d.; ed. Takapuna Grammar School and Univ. of Auckland; Lecturer in Zoology, Auckland Univ. 1958; Post-doctoral research, Yale Univ. 1961–64; subsequently career concentrated on sponge biology, chemistry, chemo-taxonomy; pioneered application of chem. and pharmacology of marine sponges to resolving maj. questions of sponge phylogeny and relationships; int. consultant in marine sponge taxonomy and marine ecology; Prof. of Zoology (Personal Chair.), Univ. of Auckland 1981–, Head of Dept. 1986–, Asst. Vice-Chancellor (Academic) 1989–96, Deputy Vice-Chancellor 1996, Special Asst. to Vice-Chancellor 1997–98. *Publications:* more than 120 articles in professional journals. *Leisure interests:* fishing, stamp collecting, classical music. *Address:* School of Biological Sciences, University of Auckland, Private Bag 92019, Auckland 1, New Zealand. *Telephone:* (9) 3737599.

BERGSAGEL, John Dagfinn, PH.D.; Danish (b. Canadian) musicologist; b. 19 April 1928, Outlook, Sask.; s. of Rev. Dr. Knut Bergsagel and Alma Josephine Bergsagel née Anderson; m. 1st Sondra Rubin 1953 (divorced); 2nd Ingrid Charlotte Sørensen 1965; three s. one d.; ed. Gordon Bell High School, Winnipeg, Man., Univ. of Manitoba, St. Olaf Coll., Minn., U.S.A., Cornell Univ., U.S.A., Oxford Univ., U.K., Royal Acad. of Music, London, U.K.; Lecturer, Concordia Coll., Minn. 1954–55; Assoc. Prof., Ohio Univ. 1955–59, Exec. Ed. Early English Church Music, Oxford, U.K. 1961–76; Tutor in History of Music, Oxford Univ. 1962–67, Lecturer, New Coll. 1966–67; Sr. Lecturer in Musicology, Manchester Univ. 1967–70; Lecturer in History and Theory of Music, Univ. of Copenhagen 1970–81, Prof. of Musicology 1981–98; Dir. Monumenta Musicae Byzantinae, Exec. Bd. Foundation for Publishing of Works of Niels W. Gade; Sr. Arts Fellow of Canada Council 1959; Gulbenkian Foundation Grant 1961; Fellow Royal Danish Acad. of Sciences and Letters, Norwegian Acad. of Science and Letters, Academia Europaea (Chair. Musicology Section, mem. Council); Order of Dannebrog. *Publications:* The Collected Works of Nicholas Ludford 1963, Early Tudor Masses I–II 1963, 1976, Engelske Anthems fra det 16. århundrede 1973, Musikk i Norge i Middelalder og Renessanse 1982, Music in Denmark at the Time of Christian IV: vol. 2, Music for Instrumental Ensemble 1988, vol. 6, Anonymous Mass and Occasional Motets (with H. Glahn) 1988; numerous articles, contribs. to encyclopaedias, transls. of many scholarly works. *Address:* Strandvejen 63, 2100 Copenhagen Ø, Denmark. *Telephone:* 39 20 02 02.

BERGSON, Abram, PH.D.; American professor of economics; b. 21 April 1914, Baltimore, Md.; m. Rita Macht 1939; three d.; ed. Johns Hopkins and Harvard Univs.; Asst. Prof. of Econs. Univ. of Texas 1940–42; mem. staff, Office of Strategic Services, Washington, D.C., then Chief, Russian Econ. Subdiv. 1944–45; various posts, finally Prof. of Econs. Columbia Univ. 1946–56; consultant, The Rand Corpn. 1948–88; Prof. of Econs. Harvard Univ. 1956–71, George F. Baker Prof. of Econs. 1971–84, Prof. Emer. 1984–; Dir. Regional Studies Program—Soviet Union 1961–64, Dir. Russian Research Center 1964–68, Acting Dir. 1969–70, Dir. 1977–80, Frank W. Taussig Research Prof. 1970–71; mem. American Reparations Del. Moscow 1945, Social Science Advisory Bd., U.S. Arms Control and Disarmament Agency 1966–73, Chair. 1971–73; consultant various Fed. agencies; Chair. Advisory Cttee. on Nat. Income Estimates, World Bank 1983; mem. Nat. Acad. of Sciences, American Philosophical Soc.; Fellow, American Acad. of Arts and Sciences, Econometric Soc.; mem. Council, Int. Econ. Assen. 1974–77; Pres. Comparative Econ. Assen. 1981; Trustee Nat. Council for Soviet and East European Research 1987–88; Award, Distinguished Contribution, American Assen. for the Advancement of Slavic Studies 1975; Distinguished Fellow, American Econ. Assen.; Hon. LL.D. (Windsor) 1979, Hon. D.H.L. (Brandeis) 1985. *Publications:* several books, including The Structure of Soviet Wages: A Study in Socialist Economics 1944, Real National Income of Soviet Russia since 1961, The Economics of Soviet Planning 1964, Essays in Normative Economics 1966, Planning and Productivity under Soviet Socialism 1968, Productivity and the Social System—The U.S.S.R. and the West 1978, Welfare, Planning and Employment: Selected Essays in Economic Theory 1982, The Soviet Economy: Towards the Year 2000 (co-ed. with Herbert Levine, and contrib.) 1983; Planning and Performance In Socialist Economies 1989; numerous articles and papers. *Address:* Department of Economics, Harvard University, Cambridge, MA 02138 (Office); 334 Marsh Street, Belmont, MA 02178, U.S.A. (Home). *Telephone:* 617-484 9171 (Home). *Fax:* (617) 495-8319.

BERGSTRÖM, Lars, PH.D.; Swedish professor of philosophy; b. 17 July 1935, Stockholm; m. Ulla von Heland 1960; one s.; ed. Stockholm Univ.; Assoc. Prof., lecturer in Philosophy Stockholm Univ. 1967–74, Prof. of Practical Philosophy 1987–; Prof. of Practical Philosophy, Uppsala Univ. 1974–87. *Publications:* The Alternatives and Consequences of Actions 1966, Objektivitet 1972, Grundbok i Värdeteori 1990. *Leisure interests:* music, tennis. *Address:* Department of Philosophy, Stockholm University, S-106 91 Stockholm; Reimersholmsgatan 39, S-117 40 Stockholm, Sweden. *Telephone:* (08) 669 8899.

BERIO, Luciano; Italian composer; b. 24 Oct. 1925; s. of Ernesto Berio and Ada dal Fiume; m. 1st Cathy Berberian 1950 (dissolved 1964, deceased 1983); one d.; m. 2nd Susan Oyama 1964 (dissolved 1971); one s. one d.; m. 3rd Talia Pecker 1977; two s.; ed. Liceo Classico and Conservatorio G. Verdi, Milan; founder of Studio de Fonologia Musicale, Italian Radio; Teacher of Composition and Lecturer at Mills Coll. (Calif.), Darmstadt, and Harvard Univ.; now Prof. of Composition, Juilliard School of Music, N.Y.; Wolf Prize 1990, Imperial Praemium Prize 1996. *Compositions include:* 5 Variazioni 1951, Nones for Orchestra 1954, Alleluyah I and II 1955–57, Thema (Omaggio a Joyce) 1958, Circles 1960, Visage 1961, Epifanie 63, Passagio 1962, Laborintus II 1965, O King 1968, Sinfonia 1969, This Means That ... 1970, Opera 1970, Sequenzas for solo instruments, A-Ronne for eight voices 1974–75, Coro for Chorus and Orchestra 1975–76, La Ritirata Notturna di Madrid 1975, Ritorno degli Snovidenia 1977, La Vera Storia 1978, Corale 1981, Un Re in Ascolto 1982, Requies 1983, Voci 1984, Requires 1985, Formazioni 1986, Ricorrenze 1987, Concerto II 1988, Ofanim 1988, Canticum Novissimi Testamenti 1989, Rendering (Schubert) 1990, Continuo 1991. *Address:* Il Colombaio, Radicondoli, Siena, Italy.

BERISHA, Sali, PH.D.; Albanian politician and cardiologist; b. 15 Oct. 1944, Tropoje; m.; two c.; ed. Tirana Univ.; worked as cardiologist in Tirana Cardiology Clinic; fmr. mem. Albanian Workers' Party; co-f. Democratic Party, leader 1991–97, elected Chair. Sept. 1991; Pres. of Albania 1992–97; mem. Nat. Medical Research Cttee.; mem. European Cttee. on Medical Scientific Research 1986–. *Publications:* political articles in newspapers.

BERKELEY, Michael Fitzhardinge, F.R.A.M.; British composer; b. 29 May 1948, London; s. of Sir Lennox Berkeley and Freda Elizabeth Berkeley; m. Deborah Jane Coltman-Rogers 1979; one d.; ed. Westminster Cathedral Choir School, The Oratory School, Royal Acad. of Music; writer on music and arts for the Observer, Vogue and The Listener 1970–75; presents music programmes (including Proms) for BBC TV 1975–; BBC Radio 3 announcer 1974–79; Dir. Britten-Pears Foundation 1996–; mem. Exec. Cttee. Assen. of Professional Composers 1982–84, Cen. Music Advisory Cttee., BBC 1986–90; Music Panel Adviser to Arts Council 1986–90; Visiting Prof. Huddersfield Univ. (fmrly. Polytechnic) 1991–94; Artistic Dir. Cheltenham Festival July 1995–; Co-Dir. Spitalfields Festival 1994–97; apart from concert works, has written music for film, TV and Radio; The Guinness Prize for composition 1977; Assoc. of R.A.M. 1984. *Major works include:* Meditations for Strings, Oboe Concerto, Fantasia Concertante, Gregorian Variations (orchestra), For The Savage Messiah (piano quintet), Or Shall We Die? (oratorio to text by Ian McEwan), 4 String quartets, Piano Trio, Songs of Awakening Love, Entertaining Master Punch, Clarinet Concerto, Speaking Silence, Baa Baa Black Sheep (opera), Viola Concerto, Catch Me If You Can (chamber), Dark Sleep (keyboard). *Leisure interests:* walking, farming, reading. *Address:* c/o Rogers, Coleridge and White Ltd., 20 Powis Mews, London, W11 1JN, England. *Telephone:* 071-221 3717.

BERKOFF, Steven; British actor, writer and director; b. 3 Aug. 1937, Stepney, London; s. of Alfred Berkoff and Pauline Berkoff; m. 1st Alison Minto 1970; m. 2nd Shelley Lee 1976 (divorced). *Films include:* Octopussy, First Blood 2, Beverly Hills Cop, Absolute Beginners, War and Remembrance (TV) 1988, The Krays 1990, Decadence 1994. *Plays/Productions include:* Agamemnon (London) 1973, The House of Usher 1974, The Trial 1976, East 1978, Hamlet 1980, Greek 1980, Decadence 1981, Agamemnon (USA) 1984, Harry's Xmas 1985, Kvetch 1986, 1991, Sink the Belgrano 1987, Coriolanus 1988, Metamorphosis 1988, Salome 1989, The Trial 1991, Brighton Beach Scumbags? 1994; Dir. West (London) 1983, Acapulco (L.A.) 1990, One Man (London) 1993, Coriolanus 1996, Mermaid 1996, Massage (L.A. and Edin.) 1997. *Publications:* America 1988, I am Hamlet 1989, A Prisoner in Rio 1989, The Theatre of Steven Berkoff (photographic) 1992, Coriolanus in Deutschland 1992, The Murder of Jesus Christ (play) 1993, Overview-Collected Essays Free Association (autobiog.) 1996, Graft: Tales of an Actor 1998. *Leisure interest:* paddle tennis, roller blades, wind surfing. *Address:* c/o Joanna Marston, 1 Clairville Grove Mews, London, SW7 5AH, England.

BERLIET, Paul; French industrialist; b. 5 Oct. 1918, Lyon; s. of Marius and Louise (née Saunière) Berliet; m. Colette Vignon-Carret 1942; two s. two d.; ed. Lycée Ampère, Lyon; Deputy Dir.-Gen. Société Automobiles M. Berliet 1954–58, Admin. Dir.-Gen. 1958–62, Pres., Dir.-Gen. 1962–74, Vice-Pres. and Dir.-Gen. 1975–78; Admin. Citröen S.A. 1968–75; Pres. Bd. Saviem 1975–76; Vice-Pres. Renault Véhicules Industriels (RVI) 1978–; Pres. Fondation de l'Automobile Marius Berliet 1982, Comité Rhône-Alpes de la Chambre de Commerce Franco-Arabe 1980–89, Comm. du commerce extérieur de la Chambre de commerce de Lyon 1983–88; Officier, Légion d'honneur, Commdr. Ordre Nat. des Arts et Lettres. *Address:* Fondation de l'Automobile Marius Berliet, 39 avenue Esquirol, 69003 Lyon; 9 rue du Docteur Mouisset, Lyon, France.

BERLINER, Robert W., B.S., M.D.; American physician; b. 10 March 1915, New York; s. of William M. Berliner and Anna Weiner; m. Lea Silver 1941; two s. two d.; ed. Yale Univ. and Columbia Univ.; Intern, Presbyterian Hosp., New York 1939–41; Resident Physician, Goldwater Hosp., New York 1942–43; Research Fellow, Goldwater Memorial Hosp., and Asst. in Medicine, New York Univ. Coll. of Medicine 1943–44; Research Asst., Goldwater Memorial Hosp., and Instructor in Medicine, New York Univ. Coll. of Medicine 1944–47; Asst. Prof. of Medicine, Columbia Univ. 1947–50; Research Assoc., Dept. of Hosps., City of New York 1947–50; Chief, Lab. of Kidney and Electrolyte Metabolism, Nat. Insts. of Health, Bethesda, Md. 1950–62; Special Lecturer, George Washington School of Medicine, Wash., D.C. 1951–; Dir. of Intramural Research, Nat. Heart Inst., Nat. Insts. of Health 1954–68; Dir. of Labs. and Clinics, Nat. Insts. of Health 1968–69, Deputy Dir. for Science 1969–73; Prof. Lecturer, Georgetown Univ. Schools of Medicine and Dentistry 1964–73; Prof. of Physiology and Medicine, Dean, Yale Univ. School of Medicine 1973–85, Dean Emer. 1985–; Dir. Pew Scholars Programme in Biomedical Sciences 1984–91; mem. N.A.S. (Council 1978–81), American Acad. of Arts and Sciences, American Heart Assen.; Pres. American Soc. of Nephrology 1968, Soc. for Experimental Biology and Medicine 1978–81; mem. numerous other medical socs.; Distinguished Service Award, Dept. of Health, Educ. and Welfare 1962, Homer W. Smith Award in Renal Physiology 1965, Alumni Award for Distinguished Achievement, Coll. of Physicians and Surgeons, Columbia Univ. 1966, Bicentennial Medal, Coll. of Physicians and Surgeons, Columbia Univ. 1967, Distinguished Achievement Award by Modern Medicine 1969, American Heart Assen. Research Achievement Award 1970, A. Ross McIntyre Award (Univ. of Neb.) 1974, Joseph Mather Smith Prize 1978, Ray G. Daggs Award, American Physiological Soc. 1982, David M. Hume Memorial Award 1983, George M. Kober Medal

1984, A. N. Richards Award, ISN 1987. *Publications:* approx. 100 publs. in medical literature. *Leisure interests:* hiking, birdwatching, music. *Address:* Yale University School of Medicine, Sterling Hall of Medicine, 333 Cedar Street, New Haven, CT 06510 (Office); 36 Edgehill Terrace, Hamden, CT 06517, U.S.A. (Home). *Telephone:* (203) 785-4490 (Office); (203) 777-1379 (Home).

BERLUSCONI, Silvio; Italian politician and businessman; b. 1936, Milan; ed. Univ. of Milan; started building and property devt. business aged 26; built up Fininvest, major conglomerate with interests in commercial TV, printed media, publishing, advertising, insurance and financial services, retailing and football; worked on Milan 2 Housing project 1969; Canale 5 network began broadcasting 1980; bought Italia 1 TV network 1983, Rete 4 TV network 1984; took stake in La Cinq commercial TV network 1985, Chain, Cinema 5 (largest in Italy); bought Estudios Roma 1986; Milan AC Football Club 1986; La Standa (Italy's largest dept. store chain) 1988; Chair. Arnoldo Mondadori Editore S.p.A. Jan.–July 1990, (half-share) 1991; f., Pres. Forza Italia political movt. 1993–, began full-time political career Jan. 1994, declaring he had stepped down from exec. posts in Fininvest; led Forza Italia to win general elections in alliance with Lega Nord and Alleanza Nazionale parties March 1994; Prime Minister April–Dec. 1994; indicted, ordered to stand trial on fraud and illegal party financing charges July 1996 together with Bettino Craxi (q.v.), also charged with authorizing bribery of tax officials, on trial Nov. 1996; sentenced to two years and 4 months' imprisonment for breaking political party funding laws July 1998; sentenced to two years and 9 months for bribing tax officials July 1998. *Address:* c/o Forza Italia, Via dell'Umiltà 48, 00187 Rome, Italy.

BERMAN, Harold Joseph, M.A., LL.B.; American professor of law; s. of Saul Berman and Emma Kaplan Berman; b. 13 Feb. 1918, Hartford, Conn.; m. Ruth Harlow Berman 1941; two s. two d.; ed. Dartmouth Coll., London School of Econs., Yale Univ. and Yale Law School; James Barr Ames Prof. of Law, Harvard Univ. 1948–85, Prof. Emer. 1984–; mem. Exec. Cttee. of Russian Research Center, Harvard Univ. 1952–84; Robert W. Woodruff Prof. of Law, Emory Univ. 1985–; Fellow, Carter Center, Dir. of U.S.-Russian Affairs 1985–; Founder and Co-Dir. American Law Center in Moscow 1991–; Co-founder, Vice-Chair. World Law Inst. 1997; other professional appts.; Dr. h.c. (Catholic Univ. of America) 1991, (Va. Theological Seminary) 1995, (Univ. of Ghent) 1997; Scribes Book Award, American Bar Asscn. 1984; Bronze Star Medal. *Publications:* Justice in the U.S.S.R.: An Interpretation of Soviet Law 1950 (revised edn. 1963), The Nature and Functions of Law: An Introduction for Students of the Arts and Sciences 1958, Law and Revolution: The Formation of the Western Legal Tradition 1983, Faith and Order: The Reconciliation of Law and Religion 1993. *Leisure interests:* tennis, bridge, music. *Address:* Emory University School of Law, Gambrell Hall G534, Atlanta, GA 30322, U.S.A. *Telephone:* (404) 727-6503. *Fax:* (404) 727-0299.

BERMAN, Yitzhak; Israeli lawyer and politician; b. 1913, Russia; s. of Jacob Berman and Miriam Berman; ed. Teacher Training Coll., Jerusalem, Univ. Coll., London and Inner Temple, London; settled in Palestine 1921; served in British Army 1942–45; mem. Irgun Zevayi Leumi, later Major, Israeli Defence Force 1948–50; Gen. Man. Willis Overland & Kaizer Assembly Plant, Haifa 1950–54; private law practice, Tel-Aviv 1954–; fmr. mem. Liberal Party; mem. Knesset 1977–84, Speaker March 1980–81; Minister of Energy 1981–82. *Leisure interests:* reading, theatre, hiking. *Address:* 9 Bavli St., P.O. Box 32351, Tel-Aviv 61322, Israel. *Telephone:* (03) 6052392.

BERN, Howard Alan, PH.D.; American professor of biology and research endocrinologist; b. 30 Jan. 1920, Montreal, Canada; s. of Simeon Bern and Ethel Bern; m. Estelle Bruck 1946; one s. one d.; ed. Univ. of California, Los Angeles; mil. service 1942–46; Nat. Research Council Predoctoral Fellow in Biology, U.C.L.A. 1946–48; Instructor in Zoology, Univ. of Calif., Berkeley, Asst. Prof. 1950–56, Assoc. Prof. 1956–60, Prof. of Zoology 1960–89, Prof. of Integrative Biology 1989–90, Prof. Emer. 1990–, research Endocrinologist, Cancer Research Lab. 1960–; research interests: comparative endocrinology of prolactin, control of prolactin secretion, mammary gland biology, long-term effect of perinatal exposure to hormones; hormones and genital epithelial cell growth, developmental endocrinology and growth of fishes; neurosecretion; Fellow, A.A.A.S., American Acad. of Arts and Sciences; Foreign Fellow, Indian Nat. Science Acad., Accad. Nazionale dei Lincei (Italy), Acad. of Sciences of Naples; Assoc. Nat. Museum of Natural History, Paris; mem. N.A.S., American Soc. of Zoologists (Pres. 1967), Int. Soc. of Neuroendocrinology, Soc. for Experimental Biology and Medicine, Endocrine Soc., American Physiological Soc.; Hon. mem. Japan Soc. of Comparative Endocrinology, Japan Soc. of Zootechnical Science; Visiting Prof. at numerous univs.; Dr. h.c. (Rouen); Hon. LL.D. (Hokkaido); Hon. Ph.D. (Yokohama). *Publications:* A Textbook of Comparative Endocrinology (with A. Gorbman) 1962; co-ed. of six books and author of numerous other publs. *Leisure interests:* collection of art and antiquities. *Address:* Department of Integrative Biology, University of California, Berkeley, CA 94720-3140, U.S.A. *Telephone:* (510) 642-2940. *Fax:* (510) 643-6264.

BERN, Lars A. V., PH.D.; Swedish business executive; b. 21 Oct. 1942, Sundsvall; s. of John-Eric Bern and Helena Richter; m. Britt-Marie Bern 1966; Pres. and C.E.O. The ÅF-Group 1979–89, Incentive AB 1989–90; Pres. and Deputy Chair. Swedish Environmental Research Inst. (IVL) 1985–89; Pres. Fläkt AB 1991. *Leisure interest:* yachting.

BERNABE, Franco; Italian business executive; b. 18 Sept. 1948, Vipiteno; s. of Bruno Bernabe and Clara Frigerio; m. Maria Grazia Curtetto; one s. one d.; ed. Univ. of Turin; Fellow, Einaudi Foundation and Prof. of Econs. Univ. of Turin 1973; Sr. Economist, OECD, Paris 1976; Chief Economist, FIAT, Turin 1978; Asst. to Chair. ENI S.p.A. 1983, Dir. Corp. Devt., Planning and Control 1986, now Man. Dir. and C.E.O. *Publications include:* Financial Structure and Economic Policy in Italy 1975, Labour Market and Unemployment (with A. Boltho) 1982, Industrial Policies and Industrialization: The Case of the Automobile Industry 1982. *Address:* ENI S.p.A., Piazzale E. Mattei 1, 00144 Rome, Italy. *Telephone:* (06) 59825445; (06) 59822706. *Fax:* (06) 59822492.

BERNABEI, Ettore; Italian journalist and broadcasting executive; b. 1921; ed. Univ. of Florence; Director Il Giornale del Mattino (Florence) 1951–56, Il Popolo (Rome) 1956–60; Ed. La Nazione del Popolo (Florence); Dir.-Gen. Radiotelevisione Italiana 1961–74; Pres. Italstat 1974.

BERNABÒ-BREA, Luigi; Italian archaeologist; b. 27 Sept. 1910, Genoa; ed. Univs. of Genoa and Rome and Italian School of Archaeology, Athens; Insp., Archaeological Museum, Taranto 38; Supt. of Antiquities for Liguria 1939–41, for Eastern Sicily 1941–73; Dir. Archaeological Museum, Syracuse 1941; founder and Dir. Aeolian museum, Lipari; Dir. Italian archaeological mission to Poliochni, Lemnos; mem. Acad. Naz. dei Lincei. *Publications:* Gli scavi nella Caverna delle Arene Candide di Finale Ligure, Vol. I 1946, Vol. II 1956, La scultura funeraria tarantina 1952, Akrai 1956, Sicily before the Greeks 1958, Poliochni, Vol. I 1964, Vol. II 1976; (in collaboration with Madeleine Cavalier) Mylai 1960, Meligunis Lipara, Vol. I 1960, Vol. II 1965, Vol. III 1968, Vol. IV 1978, Vol. V 1990, Vol. VI 1992, Vols. VII and VIII 1995, Vol. IX 1998, Menandro e il teatro greco nelle terracotte Liparesi 1981, Gli Eoli e l'inizio dell'età del bronzo nelle Eolie e nell'Italia meridionale 1985, La ceramica policroma Liparese di età ellenistica 1986, Isole Eolie: Vulcanologia, Archeologia 1992, Ceramica figuratà del IV sec. a.c. rinvenuta a Lipari 1997, Maschere ellenistiche della tragedia greca 1998, Maschere e personaggi del teatro greco nelle terracotte liparesi 1998. *Leisure interest:* Japanese art. *Address:* c/o Museo Eoliano, I 98055 Lipari, Aeolian Islands, Italy. *Telephone:* (090) 9812348.

BERNADOTTE, Graf (Gustaf) Lennart (Nicolaus Paul); Swedish administrator; b. 8 May 1909, Stockholm; s. of Prinz Wilhelm of Sweden and Princess Marie Pavlovna; m. 1st Karin Nissvandt 1932–72; 2nd Sonja Haunz 1972; four s. five d.; ed. studies in forestry and land economy; owner, Insel Mainau, Lake Constance 1932–74 (now belongs to Lennart Bernadotte Foundation); Hon. Pres. Deutsche Gartenbaugesellschaft, Nobelpreisträgertagungen, Lindau; Hon. Senator, Technische Hochschule, Hannover; Hon. mem. Royal Horticultural Soc.; Dr. sc.agr. h.c. (Univ. of Hohenheim) numerous decorations and awards including Grosses Bundesverdienstkreuz mit Stern und Schulterband, Albert Schweitzer Gold Medal. *Address:* Schloss Mainau, D-7750 Insel Mainau, Germany. *Telephone:* 07531/303-0.

BERNADOTTE, Count Sigvard Oscar Fredrik, B.A.; Swedish industrial designer; b. 7 June 1907; s. of late King Gustav VI of Sweden; m. Marianne Lindberg 1961; ed. Uppsala Univ., Royal Acad. of Arts, Stockholm and Munich; designed silverware, textiles, bookbindings, glass, porcelain 1930–; Partner, Bernadotte & Bjørn (Industrial Design) 1949–63, own firm Bernadotte Design AB 1964–; Pres. Int. Council of Socs. of Industrial Design (ICSID) 1961–63, foreign mem. 1961–63, 1967–; Speaker German Advisory Service for Land Husbandry 1962–; Hon. Dr. Univ. of Stuttgart-Hohenheim; awarded Gold Medal, Silver Medal and Diploma at the Milan Triennale. *Address:* Villagatan 10, Stockholm, Sweden. *Telephone:* 10-20-20.

BERNARD, Claire Marie Anne; French violinist; b. 31 March 1947, Rouen; d. of Yvan Bernard and Marie Chouquet; ed. Conservatoire Régional de Musique, Rouen and Conservatoire Nat. Supérieur de Musique (C.N.S.M.), Paris; began professional career as solo violinist 1965; mem. jury, Tchaikovsky Int. Competition, Moscow 1974; Prof. of Violin at state-run conservatoires and music schools in France; Asst. Conservatoire national supérieur de musique, Lyon 1990–; Prof. C.N.R., C.N.S.M.; recordings include works by Khatchatourian, Prokofiev, Barber, Milhaud, Mozart, Haydn and Sarasate; Chevalier, Ordre Nat. du Mérite; other awards and prizes. *Leisure interests:* painting, gymnastics, swimming. *Address:* 53 rue Rabelais, 69003 Lyon, France (Home).

BERNARD, Daniel Louis; French diplomatist; b. 13 Sept. 1941, Lyon; s. of Célestin Bernard and Marie Corsat; m. Monique Beaumet 1964; two s. one d.; ed. Lycée du Parc, Lyon, Faculté des Lettres de Lyon, Ecole nationale d'admin.; Vice-Consul Dublin 1967–71, UN Affairs Dept., Ministry of Foreign Affairs 1975–77, First Sec., Perm. Mission to EC, Brussels 1977–81, Tech. Adviser to Office of Minister of External Relations 1981–83, in charge of int. affairs, Ministry of Industry and Research 1984, Tech. Adviser to Office of Prime Minister 1984–86, Insp., Gen. Inspectorate of Foreign Affairs 1986, seconded to Comm. of EC 1987–88, Official Rep., Pres. of Nat. Ass. 1988–90, Head of Press, Information and Communication, and Spokesman, Ministry of Foreign Affairs 1990–92, Minister Plenipotentiary 1991, Head, Office of Minister of State, Ministry of Foreign Affairs 1992–93; Amb. to Netherlands 1993–95, to U.K. 1997–, Perm. Rep. to UN in Geneva 1995–97. *Address:* French Embassy, 58 Knightsbridge, London, SW1X 7JT, England.

BERNARD, Lucien, M.D.; French public health official; b. 30 Nov. 1913, Paris; s. of Noel Bernard and Paule Delage; m. Marguerite Hamelin 1939;

one s. two d.; ed. Faculté de Paris and Inst. Pasteur, Paris; Dir. of Health Services and Prof. of Microbiology, School of Medicine, Rheims 1941–44; Chief of Communicable Diseases branch and Int. Health at Ministry of Public Health 1946–56; Asst. to Dir.-Gen. of Public Health 1956–58; Dir. of Health Services, Regional Office for S.E. Asia, World Health Org. (WHO) 1958–63, Dir. in the office of the Dir.-Gen., Geneva, and Personal Rep. of the Dir.-Gen. at Regional Office for Africa 1963–64; Asst. Dir.-Gen. WHO Feb. 1964–77; Corresp. Nat. Acad. of Medicine, Paris; Officier, Légion d'honneur, Croix de guerre 1939–45, etc. *Publications:* on microbiology, epidemiology and public health administration. *Leisure interests:* music, oriental art. *Address:* 29 route de Malagnou, 1208 Geneva, Switzerland. *Telephone:* 735-33-71.

BERNE, Robert Matthew, A.B., M.D.; American professor of physiology; b. 22 April 1918, Yonkers, New York; s. of Nelson Berne and Julia Stahl; m. Beth Goldberg 1944; two s. two d.; ed. Univ. of North Carolina, Chapel Hill and Harvard Medical School; Intern, Asst. Resident, Mount Sinai Hosp. of New York 1943–44; U.S. Army Medical Corps 1944–46; Resident in Medicine, Mount Sinai Hosp. 1947–48; Research Fellow in Physiology, Western Reserve Univ. 1948–49, Instructor 1949–50, Sr. Instructor 1950–52, Asst. Prof. 1952–55, Assoc. Prof. 1955–61, Prof. 1961–66; Chair. and Charles Slaughter Prof. of Physiology, Univ. of Va. 1966–88, Alumni Prof. of Physiology 1988–94, Prof. (Emer.) 1995–; mem. Bd. Science Counsel Nat. Heart, Lung and Blood Inst. 1986–; mem. N.A.S., Inst. of Medicine, Nat. Acad. of Sciences 1988, American Acad. of Arts and Sciences 1995; Fellow A.A.A.S., American Coll. Cardiology; Carl J. Wiggers Award for significant contrib. towards understanding of circulation in health and diseases 1975; Research Achievement Award, American Heart Asscn. 1979; Gold Heart Award, American Heart Asscn. 1985, Jacobi Medallion 1987, Virginia Lifetime Science Achievement Award 1989, Daggs Award 1990, Inventor of the Year Award (Va.) 1992, and numerous other awards. *Publications:* The Heart, in Handbook of Physiology 1979, Cardiovascular Physiology (with M. N. Levy) 1981, The Regulatory Function of Adenosine (with others) 1983, Physiology (Ed., with M. N. Levy) 1983, Principles of Physiology (Ed. with M. N. Levy) 1990; 243 scientific papers. *Leisure interests:* tennis and fishing. *Address:* University of Virginia School of Medicine, Dept. of Molecular Physiology, Box 10011, Charlottesville, VA 22906 (Office); 1851 Wayside Place, Charlottesville VA 22903, U.S.A. (Home). *Telephone:* 804 924-0173 (Office); 804 295-9745 (Home). *Fax:* 804 982-1631.

BERNEA, Horia Mihai; Romanian painter; b. 14 September 1938; s. of Ernest Bernea and Maria Bernea; m. Margareta Cucu 1963; ed. Coll. of Physics, Coll. of Architecture Bucharest and Coll. of Fine Arts Bucharest; one-man exhbns. in England, Scotland, France, Poland, Venice Bienniale 1978, 1980, Netherlands, Romania, U.S.A., France, Budapest 1992; Gen. Man. Romanian Peasants' Museum 1990–; mem. Fine Arts Union in Romania (Chair. 1990); leader Young Artists' Union, Romania 1976–81; numerous prizes. *Address:* Muzeul Ţăranlui Român, Şos. Kiseleff 3, 71268 Bucharest; 29, E. Pangratti Street, Sector 1, Bucharest (Studio), 7 Ferme 'L' Street, jud. Ilfov, Otopeni, Romania (Home). *Telephone:* 231 1141 (Studio); 791 1155 (Home). *Fax:* 312 9875.

BERNER, Peter, DR.MED.; Austrian psychiatrist and neurologist; b. 15 Nov. 1924, Karlsbad; s. of Emil Berner and Grete Berner; m. Claire Leenhardt 1955; one s. two d.; ed. Vienna Univ., Psychiatric Neurological Clinic, Vienna Univ.; Mental Health Adviser to UNHCR, Geneva 1960–62; Visiting Prof., Lausanne 1966–67; Asst. Dir. Psychiatric Clinic, Vienna Univ. 1969–71, Head 1971–1991; Visiting Prof., Paris 1986–87; Sec.-Gen. World Psychiatric Asscn. 1977–83; mem. Royal Coll. of Psychiatrists; Foreign Assoc. mem. Société médico-psychologique, Paris; Corresp. mem. German Asscn. of Psychiatrists and Neurologists, American Psychiatrists Asscn., Académie Nationale de Médicine. *Publications:* 4 scientific books, 365 scientific papers. *Leisure interests:* literature, painting. *Address:* 14 rue Mayet, 75006 Paris, France. *Telephone:* (01) 40.65.97.88. *Fax:* (01) 40.65.97.92.

BERNERD, Elliott; British property developer; b. 23 May 1945; s. of the late Geoffrey Bernerd and of Trudie Malawar (née Melzack); m. 1st Susan Elizabeth Lynton 1968 (divorced 1989); two d.; m. 2nd Sonia Ramsey (née Ramalho) 1992; Chair. Chelsfield PLC 1987–, London Philharmonic Trust 1987–94, Wentworth Group Holdings Ltd. 1990–, South Bank Foundation 1996–. *Leisure interests:* tennis, skiing. *Address:* Chelsfield PLC, 67 Brook Street, London, W1Y 2NJ, England. *Telephone:* 0171-493 3977.

BERNES, Thomas Anthony, B.A.; Canadian government official; b. 21 March 1946, Winnipeg; m. Ann Boyd 1974 (divorced 1997); one s. one d.; ed. Univ. of Manitoba; Dir. Gen. Trade Policy, Dept. of Industry, Trade and Commerce 1981–82, Economic Policy Planning Secr. 1982–83; Head Gen. Trade Policy Div., OECD 1983–85; Dir. GATT Affairs, Dept. of Foreign Affairs and Int. Trade, Govt. of Canada 1985–87; Dir. Internal Econ. Relations, Dept. of Finance 1987–88, Gen. Dir. Int. Trade and Finance Br. 1988–91, Exec. Dir. Coordinating Secr. on Canadian Unity, Office of the Deputy Minister 1991–92, Asst. Deputy Minister, Int. Trade and Finance Br. 1992–95; G7 Finance Deputy 1995–96; Alt. Gov. for Canada, IMF, Asia Devt. Bank, African Devt. Bank and Inter-American Devt. Bank 1996; Dir. Canadian Export Devt. Corpn. 1996; Exec. Dir. IMF 1996–. *Address:* 700 19th Street, N.W., Washington, DC 20431, U.S.A. *Telephone:* (202) 623-7783. *Fax:* (202) 623-4712.

BERNHARD LEOPOLD FREDERIK EVERHARD JULIUS COERT KAREL GODFRIED PIETER, H.R.H. Prince (see under Netherlands).

BERNHARD, Sandra; American actress, comedienne and singer; b. 6 June 1955, Flint, Mich.; d. of Jerome Bernhard and Jeanette Bernhard; stand-up comedienne in nightclubs in Beverly Hills 1974–78. *Films include:* Cheech and Chong's Nice Dreams 1981, The King of Comedy 1983 (Nat. Soc. Film Critics Award), Sesame Street Presents: Follow That Bird 1985, Track 29 1988, Without You I'm Nothing 1990, Hudson Hawk 1991, Truth or Dare 1991, Inside Monkey Zetterland 1993, Dallas Doll 1994, Unzipped 1995, Catwalk 1995, Somewhere in the City 1997, Lover Girl 1997, The Apocalypse 1997, Exposé 1998. *Stage appearances (solo):* Without You I'm Nothing 1988, Giving Till It Hurts 1992. *TV appearances:* Living in America (host) 1990, Roseanne (series). *Albums:* I'm Your Woman (co-author 8 songs) 1985, Without You I'm Nothing 1989. *Publications include:* Confessions of a Pretty Lady 1988, Love Love and Love 1993. *Address:* Gold, Marshak, Liedtke and Associates, 3500 West Olive Avenue, Burbank, CA 91505; c/o Susan DuBow, 9171 Wilshire Boulevard, Beverly Hills, CA 90210, U.S.A.

BERNHEIM, Antoine, D.E.S. EN D., L. ÈS SC.; French business executive; b. 4 Sept. 1924, Paris; s. of Léonce Bernheim and Renée-Marcelle Schwob d'Héricourt; m. Francine Bernard 1947; one s. one d.; ed. Lycée Janson-de-Sailly, Univs. of Paris and Grenoble; partner 1954, later Prés. Dir. Gen. Soc. française gén. immobilière (fmrly. Bernheim Frères et Fils) 1967–72; Man. Partner Lazard Frères et Cie. 1967–, Gen. Partner and mem. Exec. Bd. Lazard Partners 1984–; mem. Bd. of dirs. 1967, Prés. Dir. Gén. La France IARD et Vie 1972; Prés. Dir. Gén. La France SA 1974–; Prés. Dir. Gén. Euromarché 1981–91; Vice-Prés. Dir. Gén. Eurafrance 1984–; partner 1973–, mem. Supervisory Cttee. 1976, Vice-Prés. 1982–95, Prés. Generali France Holding 1995–; partner, Vice-Pres. then Pres. Generali SpA, Trieste; Prés. Euralux 1973–; mem. Supervisory Bd. then Vice-Prés. Printemps SA 1972; dir. and Vice-Pres. Mediobanca 1988–; mem. Supervisory Bd. 1988–, dir. then Vice-Pres. Bd. of dirs. LVMH Moët Hennessy Louis Vuitton 1992–; mem. Supervisory Bd. 1981, Vice-Pres. Pinault-Printemps 1992–93; Dir. Eridania Béghin-Say Group and numerous other partnerships and directorships; Commdr. Légion d'honneur. *Address:* Société Lazard Frères, 121 blvd. Haussmann, 75008 Paris; la France Assurances, 7–9 blvd. Haussmann, 75009 Paris; 64 ave. Henri-Martin, 75116 Paris, France (Home).

BERNIK, France, PH.D.; Slovenian academic.; b. 13 May 1927, Ljubljana; s. of Franc Bernik and Cecilija Bernik (née Smole); m. Marija Kanc 1956; one d.; ed. Univ. of Ljubljana; teaching asst. Slovene Literature Univ. of Ljubljana 1951–57; Ed., Sec. Slovenska Matica, Ljubljana 1961–71; affiliated with Slovenian Acad. of Sciences and Arts Research Centre 1972–; Scientific Adviser Inst. for Slovene Literature and Literary Sciences 1977–, assoc. mem. 1983, mem. 1987, Pres. Slovenian Acad. of Sciences and Arts 1992–; lecturer, Visiting Prof. various univs.; Soc. for Slovene Studies, Bloomington, U.S.A. 1992, mem., Senator Academia Scientiarum et Artium Europaea, Salzburg 1993; mem. Croatian Acad. of Sciences and Arts 1994, numerous editorial bds.; Commdr. Ordre de Saint Fortunat 1996; Int. Cultural Diploma of Honour 1996; Eques commendator Ordinis sancti Gregorii Magni 1997; Golden Honorary Decoration of Freedom of Repub. of Slovenia 1997. *Publications:* The Lyrics of Simon Jenko 1962, Cankar's Early Prose 1976, Simon Jenko 1979, Problems of Slovene Literature 1980, Typology of Cankar's Prose 1983, Ivan Cankar: A Monograph 1987, Slovene War Prose 1941–80 1988, Studies on Slovene Poetry 1993, Slowenische Literatur im Europäischen Kontext 1993, Ivan Cankar: Ein slowenischer Schriftsteller des europäischen Symbolismus 1997, Ed.-in-chief Collected Works of Slovene Poets and Writers 1981–. *Address:* Slovenian Academy of Sciences and Arts, Novi trg 3, 1000 Ljubljana (Office); Zidovska 1, 1000 Ljubljana, Slovenia (Home). *Telephone:* 61–1256 068. *Fax:* 61–1253-423.

BERNINI, Carlo; Italian politician; Prof. of Transport Man., Univ. of Padua; Pres. Province of Treviso 1970–80; elected Pres. of Veneto Region 1980; Minister of Transport 1990–92. *Address:* c/o Ministry of Transport, Piazza della Croce Rossa 1, 00161 Rome, Italy.

BERNINI, Giorgio; Italian politician, lawyer and university lecturer; b. 9 Nov. 1928, Bologna; ed. Univ. of Bologna; lecturer in Commercial Law, Univ. of Bologna; fmr. adviser to EC (now EU) and Italian Govt. on questions of int. commercial law, customs tariffs, and technology transfer; entered politics Jan. 1994, Forza Italia Senator March 1994–; Minister for Foreign Trade 1994–95; Chair. Int. Council for Arbitration. *Publications:* articles in specialized journals and in daily newspapers. *Address:* c/o Forza Italia, Via dell'Umiltà 48, 00187, Rome, Italy.

BERNSTEIN, Alexander; British business executive; b. 15 March 1936; s. of late Cecil Bernstein and of Myra Ella Lesser; m. 1st Vanessa Anne Mills 1962 (divorced 1993); one s. one d.; m. 2nd Angela Mary Serota 1995; ed. Stowe School, St. John's Coll. Cambridge; Man. Dir. Granada TV Rental Ltd. 1964–68, Chair. 1977–86; Jt. Man. Dir. Granada TV Ltd. 1971–75; Chair. Granada Group PLC 1979–96 (Dir. 1964–96); acquired Forte PLC 1996; Dir. Waddington Galleries 1966–; Trustee Civic Trust for the North-West 1964–86, Granada Foundation 1968–; Chair. Royal Exchange Theatre 1983–94; mem. of Court, Univ. of Salford 1976–87, Univ. of Manchester 1983–; Hon. D.Litt. (Salford) 1981, Hon. D. Univ. (Manchester) 1996. *Leisure interests:* modern art, skiing, gardening. *Address:* c/o Waddington Galleries, 11 Cork Street, London, W1X 1PD, England.

BERNSTEIN, Carl, LL.D.; American journalist and author; b. 14 Feb. 1944, Washington; s. of Alfred Bernstein and Sylvia Walker; m. Nora Ephron 1976 (divorced); two s.; ed. Univ. of Maryland and Boston Univ.; copyboy, reporter, Washington Star 1960–65; reporter Elizabeth (N.J.) Journal 1965–66, Washington Post 1966–76; Washington bureau chief, ABC 1979–81; corresp. ABC News, New York 1981–84; Corresp., contrib. Time Magazine 1990–91; Visiting Prof. New York Univ. 1992–93; Drew Pearson Prize for investigative reporting of Watergate 1972; George Polk memorial award and other awards for journalism. *Publications:* All the President's Men (with Bob Woodward) 1974, The Final Days (with Bob Woodward) 1976, Loyalties: A Son's Memoir 1989. *Address:* c/o Janklow & Nesbit Assocs., 598 Madison Avenue, New York, NY 10022, U.S.A.

BERNSTEIN, Robert Louis; American publisher; b. 5 Jan. 1923, New York City; s. of Alfred and Sylvia Bernstein; m. Helen Walter 1950; three s.; ed. Harvard Univ.; U.S. Army Air Force 1943–46; with Simon & Schuster (book publrs.) 1946–57, Gen. Sales Man. 1950–57; Random House Inc. 1958–, Vice-Pres. (Sales) 1961–63, First Vice-Pres. 1963–65, Pres. and C.E.O. 1966–89, Chair. 1975–89; Publr. at large, Adviser John Wiley & Sons Inc. 1991–98; Vice-Chair. Asscn. of American Publrs. 1970–72, Chair. 1972–73; Chair. Asscn. of American Publrs. Cttee. on Soviet-American Publishing Relations 1973–74, on Int. Freedom to Publish 1975; Chair. U.S. Helsinki Watch Cttee., New York, 1979–92, Founding Chair. 1992; Chair. Fund for Free Expression 1975–90, Founding Chair. 1990; Chair. Human Rights Watch; fmr. mem. Council on Foreign Relations, Nat. Advisory Cttee. Amnesty Int.; mem. Americas Watch, Asia Watch, M.E. Watch, Africa Watch, Advisory Cttee. Carter-Menil Human Rights Foundation, Advisory Bd. Robert F. Kennedy Foundation Human Rights Award; Vice-Pres. Bd. of Dirs. Aaron Diamond Foundation, The Century Asscn.; Dr. of Laws New School for Social Research 1991; Human Rights Award (Lawyers' Cttee. for Human Rights) 1987, Spirit of Liberty Award for the American Way 1989, Barnard Medal of Distinction, Barnard Coll. 1990, Liberty Award, Brandeis Univ. 1994; other awards. *Leisure interests:* skiing, tennis, swimming. *Address:* 10 East 53rd Street, 20th Floor, New York, NY 10022, U.S.A. (Office).

BERNSTEN, Thorbjørn; Norwegian politician and trade union official; b. 15 April 1935, Oslo; m. Adda Bernsten; ed. Tech. Coll., Officers' Training School; with Nylands Shipyard 1951–66; Information Sec. Norwegian Union of Iron and Metalworkers, Leader 1965–66; Leader Akers mek. Verksted A.S. 1962–64; Chair., later Deputy Chair. Oslo Municipal Consultative Cttee. for Trade and Industry 1969–83; Deputy Chair. Labour Party 1989–; Minister of the Environment 1990–97; mem. Cttee. of Reps. Oslo Labour Party 1962– (Chair. 1976–82), Standing Cttee. on Local Govt. and the Environment 1973– (Chair. 1989–90), Storting (Parl.) 1977–. *Address:* c/o Det Norske Arbeiderpartei, Youngstorget 2, P.O. Box 8743, 0028 Oslo, Norway.

BEROV, Lyuben; Bulgarian politician and economist; fmr. econ. advisor to Pres. Zhelev (q.v.); Prime Minister of Bulgaria 1992–94; mem. Movt. for Rights and Freedoms (MRF). *Address:* c/o Movement for Rights and Freedoms, Ivan Vazov, Tzarigradsko Shosse 47/1, 1408 Sofia, Bulgaria.

BERRI, (Claude) (pseudonym of Langmann, Claude Beri); French film director; b. 1 July 1934, Paris; s. of Hirsh Langmann and Beila Bercu; m. Anne-Marie Rassam 1967; two c.; ed. Lycée Turgot, Paris; theatre and film actor 1951–63; writer and dir. of films 1963–; Grand Prix de l'Acad. du Cinéma 1986. *Films include:* Le Poulet 1963 (Acad. Award for best short film 1966), Le Vieil Homme et l'Enfant 1966, Mazel Tov ou le Mariage 1968, Le Pistonné 1970, Le Cinéma de Papa 1971, Sex-Shop 1972, Le Mâle du Siècle 1975, La Première Fois 1976, Un Moment d'égarement 1977, Je vous aime 1980, Le Maître d'Ecole 1981, Tchao Pantin 1983, Jean de Florette 1986, Manon des Sources 1986, Uranus 1990, My Dog Stupid 1990, Germinal 1993, La Reine Margot 1994, Lucie Albrac 1996; producer The Bear 1989. *Address:* Renn Espace d'Art Contemporain, 7 rue de Lille, 75007 Paris; Production, 10 rue Lincoln, 75008 Paris, France.

BERRIDGE, Sir Michael John, Kt., PH.D., F.R.S.; British biologist; b. 22 Oct. 1938, Gatooma, Rhodesia (now Zimbabwe); s. of George Kirton Berridge and Stella Elaine Hards; m. Susan Graham Winter 1965; one s. one d.; ed. Univ. Coll. of Rhodesia and Nyasaland, Univ. of Cambridge; Post-doctoral Fellow, Univ. of Va. 1965–66; Post-doctoral Fellow, Case Western Reserve Univ. 1966–67, Research Assoc. 1967–69; Sr. Scientific Officer, Unit of Invertebrate Chemistry and Physiology, Univ. of Cambridge 1969–72, Prin. Scientific Officer 1972–78, Sr. Prin. Scientific Officer, Unit of Insect Neurophysiology and Pharmacology 1978–90, Hon. Prof. of Cell Signalling 1994–; Deputy Chief Scientific Officer, Lab. of Molecular Signalling, Babraham Inst., Cambridge 1990–, Head of Signalling 1993–; mem. Soc. of Gen. Physiologists, Acad. Europaea 1989–, European Molecular Biology Org. 1991–; Hon. mem. Japanese Biochemical Soc.; Hon. life mem. Soc. for Experimental Biology; mem. numerous editorial bds. including Biochemical Journal 1987–, Journal of Endocrinology 1989–, Molecular Biology of the Cell 1989–, Advances in Second Messenger and Phosphoprotein Research 1990–, Journal of Basic and Clinical Physiology and Pharmacology 1990–, Journal of Experimental Biology 1993–; Advisory Ed. BioEssays 1994–; Foreign Corresp., Acad. Royale de Médecine de Belgique 1994–; Fellow Trinity Coll. Cambridge 1972–; Trustee, Isaac Newton Trust 1991–; has given numerous memorial lectures; Gov. Strangeways Research Lab. 1987–; main area of research concerns the mode of action of hormones and neurotransmitters at the cellular level; Dr. h.c. (Limburgs Universitair Centrum, Belgium) 1993; Feldberg Prize 1984, King Faisal Int. Prize in Science 1986, Louis Jeantet Prize in Medicine 1986, William Bate Hardy Prize, Cambridge Philosophical Soc. 1987, Dr. H. P. Heineken Prize for Biochemistry and Biophysics 1994, Wolf Foundation Prize in Medicine, Israel 1995, Massry Prize, U.S.A. 1996; numerous awards and medals including Gairdner Foundation Int. Award 1988, Baly Medal, Royal Coll. of Physicians 1989, Royal Medal, Royal Soc. 1991. *Publications:* more than 100 scientific papers. *Leisure interests:* gardening, golf. *Address:* 13 Home Close, Histon, Cambridge, CB4 4JL, England. *Telephone:* (01223) 232416.

BERRILL, Sir Kenneth, G.B.E., K.C.B., B.SC.(ECON.), M.A.; British economist; b. 28 Aug. 1920, London; s. of Stanley Berrill and Lilian Blakeley; m. 1st Brenda West 1941 (divorced); one s.; m. 2nd June Phillips 1950 (divorced 1976); one s. one d.; m. 3rd Jane Marris 1977; ed. London School of Econs. and Trinity Coll., Cambridge; H.M. Treasury (Cen. Econ. Planning Staff) 1947–49; lecturer in Econs., Cambridge Univ. 1949–69; Prof. M.I.T. 1962; Special Adviser, H.M. Treasury 1967–69; Brit. Nat. Comm. for UNESCO 1967–70; Gov. Admin. Staff Coll. Henley 1969–85; mem. Council for Scientific Policy 1969–72; Chair. Univ. Grants Cttee. of G.B. 1969–73, Moneda Chile Fund 1995–; mem. Advisory Bd. for Research Councils 1972–73, 1976–78; mem. Advisory Council for Applied Research and Devt. 1977–80; apptd. Head of Govt. Econ. Service and Chief Econ. Adviser to H.M. Treasury 1973–74; Head Cen. Policy Review Staff, Cabinet Office 1974–80; Chair. Vickers Da Costa and Co. 1981–85, Securities and Investment Bd. 1985–88; Deputy Chair. Universities Superannuation Scheme 1980–85; Vice-Pres. Council, Royal Econ. Soc. 1986–; Dir. Nippon Credit Gartmore Investment Man. Ltd. 1990–98; Chair. Commonwealth Equities Fund 1990–95; mem. Advisory Bd., Royal Coll. of Defence Studies 1974–80; mem. Stock Exchange (London) 1980–85; mem. Review Bd. for Govt. Contracts 1981–85; Deputy Chair. Gen. Funds Investment Trust 1981–85; Chair. Robert Horne Group 1987–90; mem. Council Lloyds of London 1983–88; Pro-Chancellor and Chair. of Council of Open Univ. 1983–96; sometime Econ. Adviser to OECD, IBRD, Guyana, Cameroon, Turkey; City Councillor, Cambridge 1964–69; Fellow Open Univ. 1997; Hon. Fellow (L.S.E., King's Coll. and St. Catharine's Coll., Cambridge, King's Coll. London, Open Univ.; James S. McDonnell Fellow (WIDER) 1988, 1990, Trustee, London Philharmonic Orchestra 1987–; Hon. LL.D. (Bath, Cambridge, East Anglia, Leicester), Hon. D.Univ. (Open Univ.), Hon. D.Tech. (Loughborough), Hon. Sc.D. (Aston). *Leisure interests:* sailing, music, gardening. *Address:* Salt Hill, Bridle Way, Grantchester, Cambs., CB3 9NY, England (Home). *Telephone:* (01223) 840335. *Fax:* (01223) 845939.

BERRY, Brian Joe Lobley, M.A., PH.D., F.B.A.; American geographer, policy analyst and planner; b. 16 Feb. 1934, Sedgley, Staffs., U.K.; s. of Joe and Gwendoline (Lobley) Berry; m. Janet E. Shapley 1958; one s. two d.; ed. Univ. Coll., London and Univ. of Washington; Asst. Prof., then Prof. Univ. of Chicago 1958–76; Faculty mem. Brookings Inst. 1966–76; Prof. Harvard Univ. 1976–81; Prof. and Dean, School of Urban and Public Affairs, Carnegie Mellon Univ. 1981–86; Prof. Univ. of Tex. at Dallas 1986–; Fellow, Univ. Coll. London 1983; mem. N.A.S., American Acad. of Arts and Sciences, Asscn. of American Geographers, American Inst. of Certified Planners, Weimar School of Land Econs., Inst. of British Geographers; numerous awards and prizes; Victoria Medal, Royal Geographical Soc. 1988; Hon. A.M. (Harvard) 1976. *Publications:* numerous books and articles. *Leisure interests:* family history, genealogy, travel. *Address:* School of Social Sciences, University of Texas-Dallas, 2404 Forest Ct., McKinney, TX 75070, U.S.A. (Home). *Telephone:* (972) 883-2041 (Office); (972) 562-1058 (Home).

BERRY, Chuck (Charles Edward Anderson Berry); American singer and composer; b. 18 Oct. 1926, St. Louis; m. Thermetta Suggs 1948; four c.; popular artiste in rock and roll, plays guitar, saxophone, piano; concert and TV appearances 1955–; Grammy Award for Life Achievement 1984. *Albums:* After School Sessions 1958, One Dozen Berry's 1958, New Juke Box Hits 1960, Chuck Berry 1960, More Chuck Berry 1960, On Stage 1960, You Can Never Tell 1964, Greatest Hits 1964, Two Great Guitars 1964, Chuck Berry in London 1965, Fresh Berrys 1965, St. Louis to Liverpool 1966, Golden Hits 1967, At the Fillmore 1967, Medley 1967, In Memphis 1967, Concerto in B Goods 1969, Home Again 1971, The London Sessions 1972, Golden Decade 1972, St. Louis to Frisco to Memphis 1972, Let the Good Times Roll 1973, Golden Decade (Vol. II) 1973, (Vol. V) 1974, Bio 1973, Back in the U.S.A. 1973, I'm a Rocker 1975, Chuck Berry 75 1975, Motorvatin' 1976, Rockit 1979, Chess Masters 1983. The Chess Box 1989, Missing Berries 1990, Rarities 1990, On the Blues Side 1993. *Films:* Go, Johnny Go, Rock, Rock, Rock 1956, Jazz on a Summer's Day 1960, Let the Good Times Roll 1973, Hail! Hail! Rock 'n' Roll 1987. *Publication:* Chuck Berry: The Autobiography 1987. *Address:* Berry Park, 691 Buckner Road, Wentzville, MO 63385, U.S.A.

BERRY, L. Michael; Canadian diplomatist; b. 28 Sept. 1937, Bolton, U.K.; s. of Leonard Berry and Margaret (née Wynne) Berry; m. Linda Kathleen Randal 1963; one s. two d.; ed. McGill Univ.; entered Canadian Dept. of External Affairs 1964, served in Berlin 1966–68 and London 1971–75; High Commr. in Singapore 1979–82; Amb. to OECD 1988–91; High Commr. in Australia 1991–95; Canadian Special Co-ordinator for the Reconstruction of Former Yugoslavia 1995–97; Diplomat-in-Residence Malaspina Univ., B.C. 1997–. *Leisure interests:* skiing, golf, cricket, music, investment. *Address:*

541 St. Andrews Road, Qualicum Beach, B.C. V9K 1L5, Canada. *Telephone:* (250) 752-9360. *Fax:* (250) 752-9372.

BERRY, Nabih; Lebanese politician and lawyer; b. 1938, Sierra Leone; s. of Mustapha Berri; m. 1st; six c.; m. 2nd; ed. Makassed, Ecole de la Sagesse, Beirut, Univ. Libanaise, Univ. of Paris; lawyer 1963–; led student movement, Unions of Lebanese Univs.; Pres. Shi'ite Amal Movement 1980–; fmr. State Minister of Reconstruction and the South, of Justice, of Hydraulic and Electrical Resources; led Liberation Bloc 1992 parl. elections, Liberation and Devt. Bloc 1996; Pres. Nat. Ass. 1992–. *Address:* Assemblée Nationale, Beirut, Lebanon.

BERRY, Richard Stephen, PH.D., A.M.; American professor of chemistry; b. 9 April 1931, Denver, Colo.; s. of Morris Berry and Ethel (Alpert) Berry; m. Carla Lamport Friedman 1955; one s. two d.; ed. Harvard Univ.; Instructor, Univ. of Mich. 1957–60; Asst. Prof. Yale Univ. 1960–64; Assoc. Prof. Univ. of Chicago 1964–67, Prof. Dept. of Chem., James Franck Inst. 1967–89, James Franck Distinguished Service Prof. 1989–; Gaest Prof. Univ. of Copenhagen 1967, 1979; Consultant Argonne Nat. Lab. 1976–, Los Alamos Science Lab. 1975–; Visiting Prof., Univ. de Paris-Sud 1979–80; Hinshelwood Lecturer, Oxford 1980; Chair., Numerical Data Advisory Bd., National Research Council 1978–84; Newton Abraham Prof., Oxford Univ., England 1986–87; mem. Visiting Comm. of Applied Physics, Harvard Univ. 1977–81; mem. N.A.S.; mem. numerous cttees. and orgs.; Foreign mem. Royal Danish Acad. of Sciences; Fellow, A.A.A.S., American Acad. of Arts and Sciences (Vice-Pres. 1995–(98)); MacArthur Prize Fellow, Alexander von Humboldt Preistraeger 1993. *Publications:* (with L. Gaines and T. V. Long II) TOSCA: The Social Costs of Coal and Nuclear Power 1979, (with S. A. Rice and J. Ross) Physical Chemistry 1980; approximately 200 scientific papers in specialist journals. *Leisure interests:* music, skiing, hiking and climbing, photography, fly fishing. *Address:* Department of Chemistry, University of Chicago, 5735 S. Ellis Avenue, Chicago, IL 60637 (Office); 5317 S. University Ave., Chicago, IL 60615, U.S.A. (Home). *Telephone:* (312) 702-7021 (Office). *Fax:* (312) 702-7052.

BERRY, Walter; Austrian baritone singer; b. 8 April 1929, Vienna; s. of Franz Berry and Hilde Jelinek; m. 1st Christa Ludwig (q.v.) 1957 (divorced 1970); one s.; m. 2nd Brigitte Hohenecker 1973; ed. Vienna School of Eng. and Vienna Music Acad.; student mem. Vienna State Opera 1950–53, ordinary mem. 1953–; awarded title Kammersaenger by Austrian Govt. 1963; Guest singer at openings of opera houses in Vienna, Munich, Berlin, Tokyo, New York (Metropolitan Opera), at festivals in Salzburg, Munich, Aix-en-Provence, Lucerne, Netherlands, Stockholm, Saratoga; appearances in New York, Chicago, Buenos Aires, Tokyo, London, Paris, Berlin, Munich, etc.; Prizes from Music Concourses in Vienna, Verviers and Geneva. Roles include: Wozzeck, Ochs von Lerchenau, Barak, Olivier, Escamillo, Pizarro, Telramund, Klingsor, Wotan, Amonasro, Scarpia, Figaro, Guglielmo, Leporello; Mozart Prize. *Leisure interests:* listening to and taping music, yachting, swimming, archaeology, photography.

BERRY, Wendell, M.A.; American author; b. 5 Aug. 1934, Henry County, Ky.; m. Tanya Amyx 1957; one s. one d.; ed. Univ. of Ky.; mem. Faculty, Univ. of Ky. 1964–77, 1987–, Distinguished Prof. of English 1971–72. *Publications:* novels: Nathan Coulter 1962, A Place on Earth 1967, The Memory of Old Jack 1974; short stories: The Wild Birds 1986; poetry: The Broken Ground 1964, Openings 1968, Findings 1969, Farming: A Handbook 1970, The Country of Marriage 1973, Clearing 1977, A Part 1980, The Wheel 1982, Collected Poems 1985, Sabbaths 1987; essays: The Long-Legged House 1969, The Hidden Wound 1970, The Unforseen Wilderness 1971, A Continuous Harmony 1972, The Unsettling of America 1977, Recollected Essays 1965–80 1981, The Gift of Good Land 1981, Standing by Words 1985; co-ed. Meeting the Expectations of the Land 1985, Home Economics 1987, What Are People For? 1990, Harland Hubbard: Life and Work 1990, Standing on Earth 1991, Another Turn of the Crank. *Address:* Port Royal, KY 40058, U.S.A.

BERSON, Jerome Abraham, M.A., PH.D.; American professor of chemistry; b. 10 May 1924, Sanford, Fla.; s. of Joseph and Rebecca Bernicker Berson; m. Bella Zevitovsky 1946; two s. one d.; ed. City Coll. of New York, Columbia and Harvard Univs.; Asst. Prof., Univ. of Southern Calif. 1950–53, Assoc. Prof. 1953–58, Prof. 1958–63; Prof., Univ. of Wis. 1963–69, Yale Univ. 1969–79, Irénée duPont Prof. 1979–92, Sterling Prof. 1992–94, Sterling Prof. (Emer.) 1994–; Chair. Dept. of Chem., Yale Univ. 1971–74; Dir. Div. of Physical Sciences and Eng. 1983–90; Sherman Fairchild Distinguished Scholar, Calif. Inst. of Tech. 1974–75; mem. N.A.S.; Fellow, American Acad. of Arts and Sciences; Nat. Research Council Post-doctoral Fellow; American Chem. Soc. (Calif. Section) Award 1963, James Flack Norris Award in Physical Organic Chemistry 1978, Sr. U.S. Scientist Award, Alexander von Humboldt Foundation 1980; Townsend Harris Medal 1984; William H. Nichols Medal 1985, Roger Adams Award 1987, Nat. Insts. of Health Merit Award 1989, Arthur C. Cope Scholar Award 1992, Oesper Award 1998. *Publications:* scientific papers on organic chem. published mostly in Journal of the American Chemical Society. *Leisure interests:* hiking, squash. *Address:* Department of Chemistry, Yale University, Box 208107, New Haven, CT 06520-8107, U.S.A. *Telephone:* (203) 432-3970. *Fax:* (203) 432-6144.

BERTHELOT, Yves M.; French statistician and economist; b. 15 Sept. 1937, Paris; m. Dosithée Yeatman 1961; three s. one d.; ed. Ecole Polytechnique and Ecole Nationale de la Statistique et de l'Administration Economique; Dir. of Studies in the Ministry of Planning, Ivory Coast 1965–68; Chief of the Study of Enterprises Div., then Chief of Service of Programmes of INSEE (Institut national de la Statistique et des Etudes Economiques) 1971–75; Chief, Service des Etudes et Questions Int., French Ministry of Co-operation 1976–78; Dir of Research, Devt. Centre of OECD, Paris 1978–81; Dir. CEPII (Prospective Studies and Int. Information Centre) 1981–85; Deputy Sec.-Gen. of UNCTAD 1985–93; Exec. Sec. UN Econ. Comm. for Europe 1993–. *Publications:* numerous articles on economics. *Leisure interests:* sailing, skiing. *Address:* United Nations Economic Commission for Europe, Palais des Nations, CH-1211 Geneva 10 (Office); 54 quai Gustav-Ador, 1207 Geneva, Switzerland; 3 rue Auguste Comte, 75006 Paris, France.

BERTHELSEN, Asger, DR.PHIL.; Danish geologist; b. 30 April 1928, Aarhus; s. of O.V. Berthelsen and Charlotte Berthelsen (neé Jensen); m. 1st Suoma I. Påhlman-Carlsson 1954 (died 1971); one d.; m. 2nd Mona D. Hansen (died 1979); m. 3rd Inge Halberg 1985; ed. Copenhagen and Neuchatel Univ.; State Geologist 1959; Prof. of Geology, Aarhus Univ. 1961, Copenhagen Univ. 1966–92; mem. Royal Danish Acad. of Science, Academia Europaea; Denmark Geology Prize 1993; Order of Dannebrog (1st Class). *Publications:* On the geology of the Rupshu District 1953, Geology of Tovqussap Nuna 1960, Precambrian of Greenland 1965, Geological Map of Ivigtut 1975, Geologi pa Rösnäs 1975, Den lille Tektoniker 1976, The EUGENO-S Project 1988, A Continent Revealed: The European Geotraverse Project (Co-author) 1992, Rejsen til den blaa Sø 1998. *Leisure interest:* oil painting. *Address:* Geological Institute, Øster Voldgade 10, 1350 Copenhagen K (Office); Jägersborg Alle 199 St. tv. 2820, Gentofte, Denmark (Home). *Telephone:* 35 32 24 24 58 (Office); 39 76 26 22 (Home). Fax: 33 14 83 22.

BERTHOIN, Georges Paul, L. EN D., L. ÈS SC.; French civil servant; b. 17 May 1925, Nérac; s. of Jean Berthoin and Germaine Mourgnot; m. 1st Anne W. Whittlesey (deceased); m. 2nd Pamela Jenkins 1965; two s. four d.; ed. Univ. of Grenoble, Ecole des Sciences Politiques, Paris and Harvard and McGill Univs.; Private Sec. to Minister of Finance 1948–50; Head of Staff, Prefecture of Alsace-Lorraine-Champagne 1950–52; Prin. Pvt. Sec. M. Jean Monnet, Pres. of ECSC 1952–55; Counsellor for Information, ECSC 1955–56; Deputy Chief Rep. of ECSC in U.K. 1956; Acting Chief Rep. of Comm. of EEC 1967–68, Deputy Chief Rep. 1968–71, Chief Rep. 1971–73; Exec. mem. Trilateral Comm. 1973–75, European Chair. 1975–92, Hon. Chair. 1993–; Int. Chair of European Movement 1978–81; Dir. Int. Peace Acad., New York; Bd. mem. Aspen-Berlin Inst.; mem. Int. Advisory Bd. Johns Hopkins Univ., Bologna, Nine Wise Men Group on Africa; Aspen Inst. Distinguished Fellow; Chevalier, Légion d'honneur, Médaille militaire, Croix de guerre, Médaille de la Résistance. *Leisure interests:* art, theatre, walking, collecting objects. *Address:* 67 avenue Niel, 75017 Paris, France.

BERTI, Luciano; Italian art historian; b. 28 Jan. 1922, Florence; s. of Ferdinando and Ines Berti; m. Anna Maria Tinacci 1959; ed. Univ. of Florence; attached to Superintendency of Florence 1949; arranged new museums of Casa Vasari, Arezzo 1950, Palazzo Davanzati 1955, Il Museo di Arezzo 1958, Il Museo di S. Giovanni Valdarno 1959, Museum of Verna 1961, Museum of S. Croce, Florence 1962; Dir. Museums of Arezzo, San Marco and Acad., Florence; Dir. Museo Nazionale del Bargello; Dir. Uffizi Gallery, Florence 1969–87; Dir. Monuments, Pisa Gallery 1973–74; Dir. of Galleries, Florence 1974–87; mem. Consiglio Superiore 1976–80; Pres. Casa Buonarroti 1990–; Gold Medal, Ministry of Cultural Heritage; Dott. Laurea in Lettere; Libera docenza in Storia dell'Arte. *Publications:* Filippino Lippi 1957, Masaccio 1964, Pontormo 1964, Pontormo disegni 1965, Il Principe dello Studiolo 1967, Il Museo tra Thanatos ed Eros 1973–74, Catalogue to the Uffizi Gallery 1979, I Disegni di Michelangelo in Casa Buonarroti 1985; various articles and catalogues. *Leisure interests:* history of art, museology. *Address:* Casa Buonarroti, Via Ghibellina 70, 50122, Florence (Office); Via Giusti 6, Florence, Italy (Home). *Telephone:* 244938 (Home).

BERTINI, Catherine, B.A.; American international public servant; b. 30 March 1950, Syracuse, New York; d. of Fulvio Bertini and Ann Vino Bertini; m. Thomas Haskell 1988; ed. Cortland High School, N.Y., State Univ. of New York at Albany; Youth Dir., New York Republican State Cttee. 1971–74, Republican Nat. Cttee. 1975–76; Man., Public Policy, Container Corpn. of America 1977–87; Dir. Office of Family Assistance, U.S. Dept. of Health and Human Services 1987–89; Acting Asst. Sec., U.S. Dept. of Health and Human Services 1989, Asst. Sec. U.S. Dept. of Agriculture 1989–92; Exec. Dir. World Food Programme of UN, Rome 1992–; mem. UN Sec.-Gen.'s Panel of High-Level Personalities on African Devt. 1992–; Fellow Inst. of Politics, Harvard Univ. 1986; Commr. Ill. State Scholarship Comm. 1979–84, Ill. Human Rights Comm. 1985–87; Leadership in Human Services Award, American Public Welfare Asscn. 1990; Excellence in Public Service Award, American Acad. of Pediatrics 1991; Leadership Award, Nat. Asscn. of WIC Dirs. 1992, Quality of Life Award, Auburn School of Human Sciences 1996. *Address:* World Food Programme, Via Cristoforo Colombo 426, 00145 Rome, Italy. *Telephone:* (6) 5228-2000. *Fax:* (6) 5228-2834.

BERTOLI, H.E. Cardinal Paolo; Vatican diplomatist; b. 1 Feb. 1908, Poggio Garf (Lucca); s. of Carlo and Aride Poli; ordained priest 1930; Sec. Apostolic Nunciature, Belgrade 1933–38, France 1938–42; Chargé d'affaires a.i., Antilles Apostolic Nunciature, Port-au-Prince, Haiti 1942–46; Counsellor, Apostolic Nunciature, Berne 1946–52; Head of Mission of Emigration to S. America; Titular Archbishop of Nicomedia 1952; Apostolic Del. in Turkey 1952–53, Apostolic Nuncio in Colombia 1953–59, in Lebanon 1959–60; France 1960–69; Prefect of Congregation for the Causes of Saints

1969–73; cr. Cardinal 1969; Suburbicarian Bishop of Frascati 1979–; Camerlengo of the Roman Catholic Church 1979–85. *Address:* 8 Piazza della Città, Leonina 1, 00193 Rome, Italy.

BERTOLUCCI, Bernardo; Italian film director; b. 16 March 1940, Parma; s. of Attilio Bertolucci; m. Clare Peploe 1978; worked with Pier Paolo Pasolini on Accattone; directed: La Commare Secca 1962, Prima della Rivoluzione 1964, Il Fico Infruttuoso in Vangelo 70 1968, Partner 1970, La Strategia del Ragno 1970, Il Conformista 1970, Last Tango in Paris 1972, 1900 1975, La Luna 1979, Tragedy of a Ridiculous Man 1981, The Last Emperor 1986, The Sheltering Sky 1989, Little Buddha 1993, Stealing Beauty 1995, I Dance Alone 1996, Besieged 1998; European Film Award 1988. *Publications:* In cerca del mistero (poems) 1962 (Viareggio Prize 1962). *Address:* c/o Recorded Picture Company, 24 Hanway Street, London, W1P 9DD, England; c/o Jeff Berg, ICM, 8942 Wilshire Boulevard, Beverly Hills, CA 90211, U.S.A.

BERTOUILLE, André; Belgian politician; b. 29 Jan. 1932, Renaix; s. of Paul Bertouille and Virginia (née Delem) Bertouille; m. Marie-Louise Lison 1953; one d.; Sec. of State for Walloon Region 1980; Minister and mem. Walloon Regional Exec. 1981; Minister for Nat. Educ. 1983–85; Minister, mem. Exécutif de la Communauté française of Belgium 1985–88. *Leisure interests:* genealogy, public law. *Address:* Rue du Becquerelle 22, 7500 Tournai, Belgium. *Telephone:* (069) 21.40.74. *Fax:* (069) 21.40.74.

BERTRANOU, Armando Victorio; Argentinian professor of agricultural economics; b. 14 May 1942, Mendoza; s. of Pablo Luis Bertranou and Susana Angélica Saligari; m. Clara Alicia Jalif 1965; two s. two d.; ed. Universidad Nacional de Cuyo, Univ. of California, Davis; Titular Prof., Faculty of Agricultural Sciences, Universidad Nacional de Cuyo, Rector April 1988–. *Publications:* many articles and papers on irrigation and water man. *Leisure interests:* aerobics, rugby, rowing. *Address:* Universidad Nacional de Cuyo, Centro Universitario, Parque General San Martín, 5500 Mendoza; Paso de los Andes 966, 5500 Mendoza; Casilla de Correo 589, 5500 Mendoza, Argentina. *Telephone:* 2-52152; 2-53219; 2-31352.

BERTUCCELLI, Jean-Louis Augusto; French film producer; b. 3 June 1942, Paris; s.of Louis Bertuccelli and Charlotte Feral; one d.; ed. Conservatoire Régional de Musique de Nice and Faculté des Sciences, Marseille; musician, then sound engineer 1964–66; film producer 1966–; TV corresp. reporting on Japan, Thailand, Hong Kong, Bolivia, Mexico, South Africa, Senegal, U.S.A. and Spain 1968–73; Chevalier des Arts et des Lettres. *Films include:* Remparts d'argile (Prix Jean Vigo) 1970, Paulina 1980, Docteur Françoise Gailland 1975, L'Imprécateur 1977, Interdit aux moins de treize ans 1982, Aujourd'hui Peut-être 1991, Momo 1992, L'Institut 1993, Le Clandestin 1993, Le Serment d'Hypocrate 1996; also short films, TV films and series etc.; Chevalier des Arts et des Lettres. *Address:* 9 rue Bénard, 75014, Paris, France.

BESCH, Werner Walter, DR.PHIL.; German professor of German; b. 4 May 1928, Erdmannsweiler, Schwarzwald; s. of Matthias and Elisabeth (née Fuss) Besch; m. Katharina Müller 1957; one s. two d.; Prof. of German Language and Early German Literature, Ruhr Univ., Bochum 1965–70, Univ. of Bonn 1970–; Rector, Univ. of Bonn 1981–83, Pro-Rector 1983–85; mem. Wiss-Rat., Inst. für deutsche Sprache, Mannheim 1976–; Corresp. mem. Heidelberg Akad. der Wissenschaften; mem. Nordrhein-Westfälische Akad. der Wissenschaften. *Publications:* Lautgeographie u. Lautgeschichte im obersten Neckar-u. Donaugebiet 1961, Sprachlandschaften u. Sprachausgleich im 15. Jahrhundert 1967, Dialekt/Hochsprache-Kontrastiv 1977, Handbuch Dialektologie 1983, Handbuch Sprachgeschichte 1985, Duzen, Siezen, Titulieren. Zur Anrede im Deutschen heute und gestern 1996. *Leisure interests:* joinery, skiing, walking. *Address:* Hobsweg 64, 53125 Bonn, Germany (Home).

BESSIAH, Boulaem; Algerian politician; b. 1930, El-Bayadh; m.; two c.; mem. Secr. gén. du Conseil nat. de la revolution algérienne 1959–62; Amb. to Benelux, EEC, Egypt; Sec.-Gen. Ministry of Foreign Affairs; Special Envoy of the Pres. of Algeria to numerous Heads of State; Dir. Algerian Del., many sessions of the Arab League, OAU, Islamic Conf. and non-aligned States; Amb. to Kuwait; fmr. Minister of Information and Culture, Posts and Telecommunications, Culture and Tourism; Minister of Foreign Affairs 1988–89; mem. Central Cttee. of FLN 1979–. *Address:* c/o Front de Libération Nationale, 7 rue du Stade, Hydra, Algiers, Algeria.

BESSMERTNOVA, Natalya Igorevna; Russian ballet dancer; b. 19 July 1941, Moscow; d. of Igorj Borisovich Bessmertnov and Antonia Yakovlevna Bersmertnova; m. Yuriy N. Grigorovich (q.v.); ed. Bolshoi Theatre Ballet School (pupil of M. Kozhukhova and S. Golovkina); soloist with Bolshoi Theatre Ballet 1961–63; prima ballerina Bolshoi Theatre Ballet 1963–95; ballet mistress/tutor 1994–95; founder, Pres. European Dance Acad. 1996–; gives masterclasses abroad; Anna Pavlova Prize 1970, People's Artist, U.S.S.R. 1976, U.S.S.R. State Prize 1977, Lenin Prize 1986. *Important roles include:* Mazurka and 7th Valse (Chopiniana), Pas de trois (Swan Lake), variations (Class-concert), Giselle (Giselle), The Muse (Paganini, music by Rachmaninov), Florin (Sleeping Beauty), Leila (Leila and Medjnun, by Balasanyan), Shirin (Legend of Love), Odette-Odile (Swan Lake), Girl (Le Spectre de la Rose), Maria (The Fountain of Bakhtchisaray), Phrygia (Spartacus), Juliet (Romeo and Juliet), Masha (The Nutcracker), Nikia (The Kingdom of Shades), Rita (Golden Age), Valentina (The Angara), Aurora (Sleeping Beauty), Anasthasia (Ivan the Terrible), Raymonda. *Address:* Sretenskii blvd. 6/1, Apt. 9, Moscow 101000, Russia. *Telephone:* (095) 925-6431 (home). *Fax:* (095) 925-6557.

BESSMERTNYKH, Aleksandr Aleksandrovich, PH.D.; Russian politician and diplomatist; b. 10 Nov. 1933, Biisk; s. of Alexander and Maria Bessmertnykh; m.; one s. one d.; ed. Moscow State Inst. of Int. Relations; joined Diplomatic Service 1957, with Embassy, Washington 1970–83; fmr. arms control negotiator; First Deputy Foreign Minister (with special responsibility for North America and the Middle East) 1987–90, Deputy 1986; Amb. to U.S.A. 1990–91; Minister of Foreign Affairs Jan.–Aug. 1991; mem. CP Cen. Cttee. 1990–91; Head Policy Analysis Center Soviet (now Russian) Foreign Policy Asscn. 1991–92, Pres. March 1992–, Chair. World Council of fmr. Foreign Ministers May 1993–. *Leisure interests:* literature, classical music, tennis. *Address:* Yakovo-Apostolski per. 10, Moscow 103064, Russia. *Telephone:* 975-21-67. *Fax:* 975-21-90.

BESSON, Luc; French film director; b. 18 March 1959, Paris; one d. with Anne Parillaud; worked as an asst. on films in Paris and Hollywood; first asst. for several advertising films; two features (Homme libre and Les Bidasses aux grandes manoeuvres) and four shorts; f. Les Films du Loup 1982. *Films directed:* Le Dernier Combat 1982, Subway 1984, The Big Blue 1988, Nikita 1990, Atlantis 1991, The Professional 1994, Leon 1994, The Fifth Element 1996, Joan of Arc 1999. *Address:* c/o CBC, 11 rue de la Croix Boissée, 91540 Mennecy, France.

BEST, George; British footballer; b. 22 May 1946; s. of Richard Best and late Anne Best (née Withers); m. 1st Angela Macdonald Janes 1978 (divorced); one s.; m. 2nd Alexandra Jane Pursey 1995; joined Manchester United 1963, 361 League appearances (137 goals), 46 Football Asscn. Cup competition appearances (21 goals), 25 League Cup competition appearances (9 goals), 34 European competition appearances (11 goals); rep. N. Ireland 37 times; Irish Footballer of the Year 1967, European Footballer of the Year 1968, British Footballer of the Year 1968, Sportswriters' Footballer of the Year 1968, Sportsman of the Year 1969, 1971, Sky TV Greatest Sportsman Award 1995, Total Sport Magazine Greatest Sportsman of All Time; now sports commentator Sky TV. *Leisure interests:* reading, crosswords, travel, films, sports. *Address:* c/o British Sky Broadcasting Ltd., Grant Way, Middx., TW7 5QD, England.

BESTUZHEV-LADA, Igor Vassilyevich, DR. HIST.; Russian sociologist and historian; b. 12 Jan. 1927; m.; two d.; ed. Inst. of Int. Relations; researcher Inst. of History U.S.S.R. Acad of Sciences 1967–68; researcher Inst. of Social Studies; Head of sector Inst. of Sociology U.S.S.R. Acad of Sciences; Sec. Russian Acad of Educ.; teacher, Prof. Moscow State Univ.; Chair Lce. Bd. Russian Pedagogical Soc. *Leisure interests:* classic literature, book design. *Address:* Russian Academy of Education, Pogodinskaya str. 8, 119905 Moscow, Russia (Office). *Telephone:* (095) 245 1641 (Office).

BETANCUR CUARTAS, Belisario; Colombian politician; b. 1923, Amaga, Antioquia; m.; one s. two d.; mem. House of Reps., later Senator; Conservative Party Presidential Cand. 1962, 1970, 1978, Pres. of Colombia 1982–86; Minister of Labour 1963; Amb. to Spain 1974.

BETHE, Hans Albrecht, PH.D.; Alsatian-born American physicist; b. 2 July 1906; m. Rose Ewald 1939; one s. one d.; ed. Goethe Gymnasium (Frankfurt/Main), and Frankfurt/Main and Munich Univs.; Lecturer German Univs. 1928–33, Manchester and Bristol Univs. (England) 1933–35; Asst. Prof. Cornell Univ. 1935–37, Prof. 1937–75, Prof. Emer. 1975–; Dir. Theoretical Physics Div. Los Alamos Scientific Lab. 1943–46; mem., Pres.'s Science Advisory Cttee. 1956–59; mem. American Philosophical Soc., N.A.S., American Physical Soc. (Pres. 1954), American Astronomical Soc.; Foreign mem. Royal Soc. (London); Hon. D.Sc. (Birmingham) 1956, (Manchester) 1981; Presidential Medal of Merit 1946, Max Planck Medal 1955, Enrico Fermi Award 1961, Nobel Prize for Physics 1967, Vannevar Bush Award (N.A.S.) 1985. *Publications:* Elementary Nuclear Theory 1947, Mesons and Fields 1955, Intermediate Quantum Mechanics 1964, 1968; contributions to Handbuch der Physik 1933, 1957, Review of Modern Physics 1936–37, etc., and to scientific journals. *Address:* Newman Laboratory, Cornell University, Ithaca, NY 14853, U.S.A.

BETTELHEIM, Charles, D. EN D., L. ÈS L.; French economist; b. 20 Nov. 1913, Paris; s. of Henri Bettelheim and Lucienne Jacquemin; m. Lucette Beauvallet 1937; three s. two d.; ed. Paris Univ.; Dir. Centre for Social Studies and Int. Relations, Ministry of Labour, Paris 1944–48; French rep. Conf. on Trade and Employment 1947; Dir. at Ecole Pratique des Hautes Etudes 1948–; Head of UN Mission for Tech. Assistance to Indian Govt. 1955–56; Prof. at Ecole Nat. d'Administration; Prof. at Inst. d'Etudes du Développement Economique et Social 1958–; mem. French Sociological Inst.; Dir. of the review Problèmes de Planification 1948–, Centre d'Etudes des Modes d'Industrialisation (C.E.M.I.) at Ecole des Hautes Études en Sciences Sociales 1986–; Lauréat de l'Institut. *Publications:* La Planification soviétique 1939, Les problèmes théoriques et pratiques de la planification 1946, L'économie allemande sous le Nazisme 1946, Bilan de l'économie française de 1918 à 1946 1947, Esquisse d'un tableau économique de l'Europe 1948, Initiations aux recherches sur les idéologies économiques et les réalités sociales 1948, Emploi et chômage devant la théorie économique 1949, L'économie soviétique 1950, Auxerre en 1950 1950, Théories contemporaines de l'emploi 1951, Nouveaux aspects de la théorie de l'emploi 1952, Long-Term Planning Problems 1956, Foreign Trade and Planning for Economic

Development 1956, Studies in the Theory of Planning 1959, Some Basic Planning Problems 1960, Teoria de la Planificación 1961, Problemas Teóricos y Prácticos de la Planificación 1962, L'Inde indépendante 1962, Planification et croissance accélérée 1964, La construction du socialisme en Chine 1965, Los Marcos Socioeconómicos y la organización de la planificación Social 1966, Problèmes théoriques et pratiques de la planification 1966, La transition vers l'économie socialiste 1968, India Independent 1968, Calcul économique et formes de propriété 1970, Révolution culturelle et organisation industrielle en Chine 1973, Les luttes de classes en U.R.S.S.—1917–1923 1974, Les luttes de classes en U.R.S.S.—1923–1930 1977, 1930–1941 Part One, 1994, China since Mao 1978, Les luttes de classe en U.R.S.S.—1930–41, Vol. 1, Les dominés 1982, Vol. 2 Les dominants 1983, Moscou, Place du Manège 1984, Orwell et il 1984 del Socialismo reale (jtly.) 1984, Rethinking Marxism (Chapter 3) 1985, Parcours, Markets within Planning (Chapter 1) 1988, Il Socialismo Irrealizato (jtly.) 1992, essays in various publs. *Address:* EHESS, Cemi, 105 boulevard Raspail, 75006 Paris, France.

BETTENCOURT SANTOS, Humberto; Cape Verde diplomatist; b. 17 Feb. 1940, Santo Antao Island; s. of Severino Santos and Inacia Santos; m.; two c.; ed. Catholic Univ. of Louvain, Belgium; mem. del. in negotiations on colonial dispute with Portugal 1975; elected Deputy to Nat. Ass. 1975, re-elected 1980; Dir.-Gen. Fisheries 1975–82; Amb. to EC and to Nordic and Benelux countries 1982–87; Perm. Rep. of Cape Verde to UN 1987–91; mem. Nat. Comm. on Law of the Sea 1979–82; int. consultant; dir. of pvt. computer training centre; pvt. consultant in econ. and fisheries for FAO and UNDP 1991–. *Leisure interests:* music (guitar), tennis, golf.

BETTS, Donald Drysdale, M.SC., PH.D., F.R.S.C.; Canadian professor of physics; b. 16 May 1929, Montreal; s. of Wallace Havelock Betts and Mary Drysdale Betts; m. 1st Vilma Mapp 1954 (divorced 1981); m. 2nd Patricia Giles McWilliams 1986; three s. one d. two step-s.; Queen Elizabeth High School, Halifax, Dalhousie Univ., Halifax and McGill Univ.; Nat. Research Council Fellow Univ. of Alberta, Edmonton 1955–56, Asst. Prof. of Physics 1956–61, Assoc. Prof. 1961–66, Prof. 1966–80; Dean of Arts and Science Dalhousie Univ. 1980–88, of Science 1988–90, Prof. Emer. 1994–; Visiting Prof. of Physics King's Coll., London 1970–71, of Chemistry and Physics Cornell Univ., New York Jan.–June 1975, Univ. of N.S.W. 1991, 1993; Gordon Godfrey Visiting Research Prof. of Theoretical Physics, Univ. of N.S.W. 1995–(2000); Dir. Theoretical Physics Inst. Univ. of Alberta 1972–78; Ed. Canadian Journal of Physics 1992–; Pres. Canadian Asscn. of Physicists 1969–70; Fellow Japan Soc. for Promotion of Science 1982; NATO Science Fellowship 1963–64; Nuffield Fellowship 1970; Peter Kirkby Medal for Outstanding Service to Canadian Physics (Canadian Asscn. of Physicists) 1996. *Publications:* some 90 refereed articles in physics journals. *Leisure interests:* game of Go, hiking, gardening, badminton and swimming. *Address:* Department of Physics, Dalhousie University, Halifax, B3H 3JS, Canada (Office); 8 Simcoe Place, Halifax, Nova Scotia, B3M 1H3, Canada (Home). *Telephone:* (902) 494-2834 (Office); (902) 494-5124 (Office); (902) 443-3916 (Home). *Fax:* (902) 494-2835.

BEUTLER, Ernest, M.D.; American research scientist and professor of medicine; b. 30 Sept. 1928, Berlin, Germany; s. of Alfred David and Kaethe (Italiener) Beutler; m. Brondelle Fleisher 1950; three s. one d.; ed. Univ. of Chicago; Resident in Medicine, Univ. of Chicago Clinics 1951–53, Asst. Prof., Univ. of Chicago 1956–59; Chair. Div. of Medicine, City of Hope Medical Centre, Duarte, Calif. 1959–78; Chair. Dept. of Clinical Research, Scripps Clinic and Research Foundation, La Jolla, Calif. 1978–82, Chair. Dept. of Basic and Clinical Research 1982–89, Dept. Molecular and Experimental Medicine 1989–, Head, Div. of Haematology-Oncology 1982–87; Clinical Prof. of Medicine, Univ. of Southern Calif., Los Angeles 1964–79, Univ. of Calif., San Diego, La Jolla, Calif. 1979–; Spinoza Chair. Univ. of Amsterdam, Netherlands 1991; mem. N.A.S., American Acad. of Arts and Sciences, Asscn. of American Physicians; Hon. D.Ph. (Tel Aviv Univ.) 1993; Gairdner Award 1975, Blundell Prize 1985, Mayo Soley Award (Western Soc. for Clinical Investigation) 1992, Fifth Nat. Award for Excellence in Clinical Research (NIH Gen. Clinical Research Centers Program) 1993, City of Medicine Award 1994. *Publications:* author of eight books and numerous articles in medical periodicals. *Leisure interests:* music and computer programming. *Address:* Scripps Research Institute, 10550 North Torrey Pines Road, La Jolla, CA 92037; 2707 Costebelle Drive, La Jolla, CA 92037, U.S.A. (Home). *Telephone:* (619) 784-8040 (Office); (619) 457-5790 (Home). *Fax:* (619) 784-2083.

BEVAART, Jacob; Netherlands business executive; b. 15 Feb. 1942, Amsterdam; m. J. J. Griffioen 1965; three s.; ed. Univ. of Amsterdam; Dir. Concertgebouw Amsterdam 1975–82; Dir.-Gen. Chamber of Commerce and Industry for Amsterdam Feb. 1984–; Chair. Buvoha Soc. (Trade Information Bureau), Judicial Comm. European Chambers of Commerce, Brussels, Consumer Arbitration Bd. for Public Utilities, The Hague; mem. Bd. of Man. Buma/Sterma (Co-operative Copyright Orgs.) 1982–, Amsterdam Tourists Asscn.; mem. Bd. Amsterdam Ports Asscn., Univ. of Amsterdam Foundation for Econ. Research; Deputy Judge Utrecht Dist. Court. *Address:* Chamber of Commerce and Industry for Amsterdam, De Ruyterkade 5, 1013 AA Amsterdam, Netherlands. *Telephone:* (20) 531-4602. *Fax:* (20) 531-4699.

BEVAN, Sir Timothy Hugh, Kt.; British banker; b. 24 May 1927, London; s. of Hugh Bevan and Pleasance Scrutton; m. Pamela Murray (née Smith) 1952; two s. two d.; ed. Eton Coll.; called to the Bar, Middle Temple 1950; Dir. Barclays Bank Ltd. (now Barclays Bank PLC) 1966–93, Vice-Chair. 1968, Deputy Chair. 1973, Chair. 1981–87; Dir. Barclays Int. Ltd. 1971; Dir. BET Public Ltd. Co. 1987–92, Chair. 1988–91; Dir. Foreign and Colonial Investment 1988–98 (Deputy Chair 1993–98); fmr. Dir. Soc. Financière Européenne 1967, Commercial Union Assurance Co. Ltd., Union Discount Co. of London Ltd.; Chair. Cttee. London Clearing Bankers 1983–85; Chair. City Communications Centre 1982–83. *Leisure interests:* sailing, gardening. *Address:* c/o Barclays Bank PLC, 54 Lombard Street, London, EC3V 9EX, England.

BEVERIDGE, Sir Gordon Smith Grieve, Kt., PH.D., A.R.C.S.T., F.R.S.E., F.ENG., F.I.CHEM.E., M.R.I.A.; British academic; b. 28 Nov. 1933, St. Andrews, Scotland; s. of the late Victor B. Beveridge and Elizabeth F. (née Grieve) Beveridge; m. Geertruida H.J. Bruyn 1963; two s. one d.; ed. Inverness Royal Acad., Univ. of Glasgow, Royal Coll. of Science & Tech. Glasgow and Univ. of Edin.; Asst. Lecturer Univ. of Edin. 1956–60, Lecturer 1962–67; Post-doctoral Harkness Fellow of Commonwealth Fund, Univ. of Minn. 1960–62; Sr. Lecturer, Reader, Heriot-Watt Univ. 1967–71; Prof. of Chemical Eng. and Head, Dept. of Chemical and Process Eng. Univ. of Strathclyde 1971–86; Pres. and Vice-Chancellor, Queen's Univ. Belfast 1986–97; mem. of Court, Univ. of Stirling 1997–; industrial consultant; Chair. Cremer & Warner Group of cos. 1985–90; Chair. and Dir. of Navan at Armagh; many other professional appts.; mem. Eng. Council 1981–95; Chair. Radioactive Waste Man. Advisory Cttee. 1995–; Pres. Retirement Asscn. of Northern Ireland 1986–96; mem. of Bd., British Council 1997–; Hon. Fellow Royal Coll. of Surgeons in Ireland 1995; numerous hon. degrees; Companion Inst. of Man. *Publications:* Optimization: theory and practice (with R.S. Schechter) 1970; articles in learned journals. *Leisure interests:* walking, Marlburian war games, Irish, Dutch and Scottish history, family history. *Address:* 6 Brompton Road, Bangor, BT20 3RE, Northern Ireland. *Telephone:* 02147-451-381.

BEVERLOO, Cornelis Van; Netherlands painter; b. 1922; ed. Amsterdam Acad. of Fine Arts; co-founder, with Appel and Constant, of the experimental "Reflex" group; co-founder of "Cobra" group 1948; rep. at numerous exhibitions, including Brussels Int. Exhibition 1958, Dunn Int. Exhibition, London 1963; works under the name of "Corneille".

BEWKES, Jeff; American broadcasting executive; fmrly. Exec. Vice-Pres. Home Box Office Inc., Pres., C.O.O. 1991–, Chair., C.E.O. 1995–. *Address:* Home Box Office Inc., 1100 Avenue of the Americas, New York, NY 10036, U.S.A.

BEWLEY, Thomas Henry, M.A., M.D.; Irish consultant psychiatrist; b. 8 July 1926, Dublin; s. of Geoffrey Bewley and Victoria Jane Wilson; m. Beulah Knox 1955; one s. four d.; ed. St. Columba's Coll., Dublin, Trinity Coll., Dublin Univ.; trained at St. Patrick's Hosp., Dublin, Maudsley Hosp., London and Univ. of Cincinnati, U.S.A.; Consultant Psychiatrist, Tooting Bec and St. Thomas' Hosps., London 1961–88; Emer. Consultant St. Thomas' Hosp.; mem. Standing Advisory Cttee. on Drug Dependence 1966–71, Advisory Council on Misuse of Drugs 1972–84; Consultant Adviser on Drug Dependence to Dept. of Health and Social Security 1972–81; Consultant WHO 1969–78; Hon. Sr. Lecturer, St. George's Hosp. Medical School, Univ. of London 1974–96; Pres. Royal Coll. of Psychiatrists 1984–87 (Dean 1977–82); Jt. Founder and mem. Council, Inst. for the Study of Drug Dependence 1967–96; F.R.C.P. (London and Ireland); Hon. F.R.C. Psych.; Hon. C.B.E. *Publications:* Handbook for Inceptors and Trainees in Psychiatry 1976; papers on drug dependence, medical manpower and side effects of drugs. *Leisure interest:* Irish Georgian Society (London Chapter). *Address:* 4 Grosvenor Gardens Mews North, London, SW1W 0JP, England. *Telephone:* 0171-730 9592 (Home).

BEXON, Roger, C.B.E., M.A., M.S.; British business executive; b. 11 April 1926, London; s. of the late Macalister Bexon, and Nora Hope (née Jenner) Bexon; m. Lois Loughran Walling 1951; one s. one d.; ed. Denstone Coll., St. John's Coll., Oxford Univ., Tulsa Univ., U.S.A.; Geologist, Trinidad Petroleum Devt. Co. Ltd. 1946–57; managerial positions with British Petroleum Co. Ltd. (B.P.), E. Africa 1958–59, Libya 1959–60, Trinidad 1961–64, London 1964–66, Man. North Sea Operations 1966–68, Gen. Man., Libya 1968–70, Regional Co-ordinator for Middle East, London 1971–73, Gen. Man. Exploration and Prodn., London 1973–76, Man. Dir. B.P. Exploration Co. Ltd., London 1976–77, Man. Dir. B.P. 1981–86, Deputy Chair. Dec. 1983–86, Chair. B.P. Gas Ltd. 1981–86, Chair B.P. Exploration Co. Ltd. 1981–86; Dir. and Sr. Vice-Pres. Standard Oil Co., Cleveland, Ohio 1977–80, Dir. 1982–86; Dir. B.P. Canada Inc. 1981–87; Dir. BICC PLC 1985–92; Dir. Fenner PLC 1986–89; Dir. Lazard Bros. & Co. Ltd. 1986–91, Dir. Cameron Iron Works, Inc. 1986–89; Chair. Laporte PLC 1986–95, Goal Petroleum PLC 1990–96; Dir. Astec (BSR) PLC 1989–95. *Leisure interests:* reading, golf, Times crosswords, swimming. *Address:* c/o 22 Hill Street, London, W.1., England.

BEYER, Frank Michael; German composer and professor of composition; b. 8 March 1928, Berlin; s. of Oskar Beyer and Margarete (née Löwenfeld) Beyer; m. Sigrid Uhle 1950; one s. one d.; ed. Berliner Kirchenmusikschule, Staatliche Hochschule für Musik (HDK), piano training in Leipzig; began career in church music; Scholarship, Cité Internationale des Artes Paris 1968; Docent Berliner Kirchenmusikschule 1953–62; with Hochschule für Musik Berlin, Prof. of Composition 1968–; initiated range of 'musica nova sacra' 1970–85; promoter Inst. für Neue Musik 1990; Supervisory mem. of Gema 1973–83; Exec. mem. German Music Bds. 1978–82; mem. Akademie der Künste Berlin 1979–, Dir. of Music Div. 1986–; mem. Bayerischen Akademie der Schönen Künste 1981–; Kunstpreis Berlin for Young Generation 1957, Bernhard-Sprengel Prize 1962, Preis Jeunesse Musicale 1967. *Compositions:* Orchestral and chamber music, organ and solo piano works, music for TV films. *Leisure interest:* philosophy. *Address:* Söhtstrasse 6, 12203 Berlin, Germany. *Telephone:* 030/8338051.

BEYNON, John David Emrys, PH.D., F.ENG; British professor of electronics and college principal; b. 11 March 1939, Risca, Gwent; s. of John Emrys Beynon and Elvira Beynon; m. Hazel Janet Hurley 1964; two s. one d.; ed. Univ. of Wales and Univ. of Southampton; Scientific Officer, Radio Research Station, Slough 1962–64; lecturer, Sr. Lecturer, then Reader, Univ. of Southampton 1964–67; Prof. of Electronics, Univ. of Wales Inst. of Science and Tech., Cardiff 1977–79; Head, Dept. of Electronic and Electrical Eng., Univ. of Surrey 1979–83, Pro Vice-Chancellor 1983–87, Sr. Pro Vice-Chancellor 1987–90; Prin. King's Coll., Univ. of London 1990–92; Hon. Fellow Univ. Coll. of Swansea 1990; mem. British Library Advisory Council, Ind. TV Comm. *Publications:* Charge-coupled Devices and Their Applications (with D. R. Lamb) 1980, papers on plasma physics, semi-conductor devices and integrated circuits and eng. educ. *Leisure interests:* music, photography, travel. *Address:* 13 Great Quarry, Guildford, Surrey, GU1 3XN, England.

BEYNON, John Herbert, D.SC., C.CHEM., F.R.S.C., C.PHYS., F.INST.P., F.R.S.; British professor of chemistry; b. 29 Dec. 1923, Ystalyfera, Wales; s. of Leslie Ewart and Phyllis (née Gibbon) Beynon; m. Yvonne Lilian Fryer 1947; Scientific Officer, Tank Armament Research 1943–47; Man. and Sr. Research Assoc., Physical Chemistry Research, ICI Dyestuffs Div. 1952–74; Prof. of Chemistry and Dir. Mass Spectrometry Center, Purdue Univ., U.S.A. 1969–75; Assoc. Prof. of Molecular Sciences, Univ. of Warwick 1972–74; Visiting Prof. Univ. of Essex 1982–; Royal Soc. Research Prof. Univ. of Wales, Swansea 1974–86, Research Prof. 1987–, Prof. Emer. 1991–; Chair. Science Curriculum Devt. Cttee., Cttee. for Wales 1983–88; Ed.-in-Chief Rapid Communications in Mass Spectrometry 1987–97; mem. Editorial Bd. Organic Mass Spectrometry 1967–88, 1992–94, Int. Journal of Mass Spectrometry and Ion Processes 1967–97, Mass Spectrometry Reviews 1984–, Biological Mass Spectrometry 1992–94, J. Mass Spectrometry 1995–97; Chair. Swansea Sports Club 1988–92; Dir. Swansea Cricket and Football Club 1991–92; Founder Pres. European Mass Spectrometry Soc. 1993–; Assoc. Inst. Jožef Stefan, Yugoslavia, Hon. mem. mass spectrometry Socs. of Japan, China, Italy and Yugoslavia, Hon. Fellow Bosnian Chem. Soc. 1982; Fellow Univ. of Wales Swansea 1988–; Hon. D.Sc. (Purdue Univ., U.S.A.) 1995, (Babeş-Bolyai Univ., Romania) 1997; 3M-Boomer Award 1965, Hasler Award for Spectroscopy 1979, Jan. Marc Marci Medal 1984, Gold Medal of the Int. Mass Spectrometry Soc. 1985, Frank H. Field and Joe L. Franklin Award of the American Chemical Soc. 1987, Aston Medal of British Mass Spectrometry Soc. 1990, Gold Medal, Italian Chemical Soc. 1992. *Publications:* 10 books and over 400 scientific papers. *Leisure interests:* photography, golf, rugby. *Address:* 17 Coltshill Drive, Mumbles, Swansea, SA3 4SN, Wales. *Telephone:* 01792-368718 (Home). *Fax:* 01792-368718.

BEZOS, Jeff; American media executive; b. 1963; ed. Princeton Univ.; with Bankers Trust Co. 1988–90; joined D. E. Shaw & Co. 1990, Sr. Vice-Pres. 1992–94; f., Chair., C.E.O. Amazon.com Inc. 1995–. *Address:* Amazon.com, 1516 2nd Avenue, Seattle, WA 98101, U.S.A.

BHABHA, J. J., B.A.; Indian industrialist; b. 21 Aug. 1914, Bombay; ed. Cathedral High School, Bombay, Gonville and Caius Coll., Cambridge, Lincoln's Inn, London; Chair. Tata Services Ltd., Tata McGraw-Hill Publishing Co. Ltd., Associated Bldg. Co. Ltd.; Dir. Tata & Sons Ltd., Indian Hotels Co. Ltd., Tata Ltd., London, RDI Print and Publishing Pvt. Ltd., Titan Industries Ltd., Stewarts and Lloyds of India Ltd., Tata Press Ltd.; Chair. and Trustee-in-Charge Nat. Centre for the Performing Arts; Vice-Chair. and Man. Trustee Sir Dorabji Tata Trust; Trustee Lady Tata Memorial Trust, J.H. Bhabha Memorial Trust, Prince of Wales Museum of Western India, etc.; Chair. Governing Bd. Tata Inst. of Social Sciences; mem. Council Nat. Inst. Advanced Studies, Tata Memorial Centre for Cancer Research and Treatment; mem. numerous public insts.; Pres. Nat. Soc. of the Friends of Trees; Vice-Pres. Nat. Soc. for Clean Cities; Kt. Commdr. of the Order of Merit (Italy) 1976, Commdr.'s Cross of the Order of Merit (Fed. Repub. of Germany) 1978, Commdr.'s Cross of the Order of the Crown, Belgium 1979, Austria Award of Honour 1984. *Address:* Tata Sons Ltd., Bombay House, 24 Homi Mody Street, Bombay 400 001 (Office); 12 Little Gibbs Road, Malabar Hill, Bombay 400 006, India (Home). *Telephone:* 204-9131 (Office).

BHADESHIA, Harshad Kumar Dharamshi Hansraj, PH.D., F.R.S., F.INST.P., F.I.M.; British metallurgist; b. 27 Nov. 1953, Nairobi, Kenya; s. of Dharamshi Hansraj Bhadeshia and Narmda Bhadeshia; m. (divorced); two d.; ed. Univ. of Canterbury; demonstrator Cambridge Univ. 1981–85, lecturer 1985–94, Reader in Physical Metallurgy 1994–; Royal Soc. Armourers and Brasiers' Medal, Rosenheim Medal. *Publications include:* Geometry of Crystals 1987, Bainite in Steels 1992, (jtly.) Steels 1995. *Leisure interest:* television. *Address:* University of Cambridge, Department of Materials Science and Metallurgy, Pembroke Street, Cambridge, CB2 3QZ, England. *Telephone:* (01223) 334301. *Fax:* (01223) 334567.

BHAGAT, Bali Ram; Indian politician; b. 1 Oct. 1922; ed. Patna Coll.; Secretary Bihar Provincial Congress Cttee. 1949; mem. Provisional Parl. 1950–52, Lok Sabha 1952–77, Speaker 1976–77; Parl. Sec. Ministry of Finance 1952–55; Deputy Minister for Finance 1955–63; Minister of State for Planning 1963–67, for Defence March-Nov. 1967, for External Affairs 1967–69, 1985–86; Minister in charge of Foreign Trade and Supply 1969–70; Minister for Steel and Heavy Industry 1970–71, of External Affairs 1985–86; Speaker, Lok Sabha 1976–77. *Address:* B-7, Maharani Bagh, New Delhi 110065, India.

BHAGWATI, Prafulla Chandra, B.A., LL.B.; Indian judge; b. 21 Dec. 1921; s. of Watvarlal Bhagwati; m. Prabhavati Bhagwati 1949; three d.; ed. Univ. of Bombay; practising lawyer specializing in constitutional and company cases, High Court, Bombay; Judge, Gujarat High Court 1960, Chief Justice of Gujarat 1967; Judge, Supreme Court of India 1973, Chief Justice of India 1985–86; Samuel Rubin Fellow, Columbia Univ. 1984; fmr. Pres. Indian Law Inst., Indian Chapter of Int. Law Asscn.; Int. Award, Int. Bar Asscn.; LL.D. h.c. (Andhra Univ.). *Leisure interests:* philosophy, literature, Sanskrit.

BHAJAN LAL, Chaudhri; Indian politician; b. 6 Oct. 1930; ed. Bahwal Nagar, W. Pakistan; mem. Haryana Legis. Ass. 1968–, Minister in Haryana Cabinet 1970–75, Minister for Co-operation, Dairy Devt., Animal Husbandry, Labour and Employment 1978–79; Chief Minister of Haryana 1979–86, 1991–96; mem. Rajya Sabha 1986–; Union Minister of Environment and Forests Oct. 1986–88, of Agric. and Rural Devt. 1988–89. *Leisure interests:* nature, wildlife. *Address:* Chief Ministers Secretariat, Chandigarh, India.

BHANDARI, Sunder Singh, M.A., LL.B.; Indian politician and lawyer; b. 12 April 1921, Udaipur, Rajasthan; s. of Sujan Singh Bhandari and Phool Kanwar; Advocate Mewar High Court 1942–43; headmaster, Shiksha Bhawan, Udaipur 1943–46; Gen. Sec. Bharatiya Jana Sangh, Rajasthan 1951–57, All India Gen. Sec. 1967–77, All India Vice-Pres. Bharatiya Janata Party 1981–98; mem. Rajya Sabha 1966–72, 1976–82, 1992–98; Deputy Leader Janata Parl. Party 1977–80; Chair. Petition Cttee. Rajya Sabha 1992–94, Parl. Standing Cttee. on Transport and Civil Aviation 1996–98; Gov. of Bihar 1998–; mem. Indian del. to Inter-Parl. Union, Lisbon 1978, Seoul 1997. *Leisure interests:* reading, social service. *Address:* Mograwadi, Udaipur; 3/16 Kalkaji Extn., New Delhi; Raj Bhavan, Patna, India. *Telephone:* 485520 (Udaipur); 641-9891 (New Delhi); 226626 (Patna).

BHARGAVA, Pushpa Mittra, PH.D.; Indian scientist; b. 22 Feb. 1928, Ajmer, Rajasthan; s. of Dr. Ram Chandra Bhargava and Gayatri Devi Bhargava; m. Edith Manorama Patrick 1958; one s. one d.; ed. Lucknow Univ.; lecturer, Dept. of Chemistry, Osmania Univ., Hyderabad, then mem. staff Cen. Labs. Hyderabad; Post-doctoral Fellow, Univ. of Madison 1953–56; at Nat. Inst. for Medical Research, U.K. 1957–58; joined Regional Research Lab. (now Indian Inst. of Chemical Tech.) 1958–77; Dir. Centre for Cellular and Molecular Biology, Hyderabad 1977–90, CSIR Distinguished Fellow 1990–93; Visiting Prof. Collège de France, Paris; Scientific adviser in several industries; has worked by invitation at McArdle Lab. for Cancer Research, U.S.A., Nat. Inst. for Medical Research, U.K., Institut du Radium, France, Max-Planck Institut für Biophysikalische Chemie, Germany; has given over 250 lectures to int. meetings worldwide; Founder Guha Research Conf.; Founder-mem. Soc. for Study of Reproduction (U.S.A.); Past-Pres. Soc. of Biological Chemists; mem. numerous other Indian and int. professional socs. and standing or ad hoc cttees. of Int. Cell Research Org. and other int. orgs.; fmr. or current mem. several editorial bds. of scientific journals; Fellow Indian Nat. Science Acad., Indian Acad. of Sciences, Nat. Acad. of Sciences (India), Nat. Acad. of Medical Sciences (India), World Acad. of Arts and Sciences; Corresp. mem. American Asscn. for Cancer Research and other bodies; Hon. D.Sc. (Univ. of Burdwan); Life Fellow, Clare Hall, Cambridge, U.K.; numerous prizes and awards, including Nat. Citizens Award 1988; Padma Bhushan conferred by Pres. of India 1986; Chevalier, Légion d'honneur 1998. *Publications:* several books, including Proteins of Seminal Plasma 1989; numerous articles. *Leisure interests:* fine arts, reading, current affairs, sports, music, films, photography. *Address:* Anveshna Consultancy Services, 12-13-414/4 Street No. 1, Tarnaka, Hyderabad 500 017, India. *Telephone:* 7017789, 7823517. *Fax:* 40-7017857; 40-7173387.

BHATTACHARYA, Basu; Indian film director, producer and writer; b. 31 Jan. 1936, Murshidabad, W. Bengal; m. Rinki Bhattacharya 1963; one s. two d.; Pres. Indian Film Dirs. Asscn. 1978–85; Dir. Nat. Film Devt. Corpn. 1980–87; mem. Nat. Film Policy Working Group; mem. Jury, Moscow Int. Film Festival 1981; recipient of numerous film awards. *Films include:* Teesri Kasam 1966, Anubhav 1972, Sparsh 1981, Griha Pravesh 1982, Panchvati 1986. *Leisure interests:* poetry, painting, gardening. *Address:* Gold Mist, 36 Carter Road, Bandra, Bombay 50, India. *Telephone:* 6424727.

BHATTACHARYYA, Birendra Kumar, B.SC., M.A., PH.D.; Indian journalist and writer; b. 16 March 1924, Suffry Sibsagar, Assam; s. of Sashidhar and Aideo Bhattacharyya; m. Binita Bhattacharyya 1958; two s. one d.; ed. Jorhat Government High School, Cotton Coll., Gauhati, Calcutta Univ. and Gauhati Univ.; fmr. Science Teacher, Ukrul High School, Manipur; Ed. Ramdhenu 1951–61, Sadiniya Navayung 1963–67; lecturer in Journalism, Gauhati Univ. 1974–; Exec. mem. Janata Party, Assam; Sec. Archaeological Soc. of Assam; Sahitya Akademi Award for Assamese Literature 1961, Jnanpitho Award 1979. *Publications:* novels: Iyaruingam (won Akademi Award), Rajpathe Ringiai (Call of the Main Street), Mother, Sataghai (Killer), Mrityunjay, Pratipad, Nastachandra, Ballart, Kabar Aru Phul, Ranga Megh, Daint; collections of short stories: Kolongajioboi (Still Flows the Kolong), Satsari (Necklace); Aurobindo (biography), A Survey of Assamese Modern Culture (in Assamese), Munichunir Pohar, Kalar Humuniyah, Naga Kakar

Sadhu, Chaturanga, Phul Konwarar Pathighora, Sandhya Swar. *Address:* Kharghuli Development Area, Guwahati 781004, India. *Telephone:* 25019.

BHATTARAI, Krishna Prasad; Nepalese politician; b. 24 Dec. 1924, Banaras, India; s. of late Sankata Prasad Bhattarai and Lalita Devi; unmarried; served 14 years' imprisonment for opposition to absolute monarchy in Nepal; Pres. Nepali Congress Party (banned for 29 years until 1990); Prime Minister of Nepal (presiding over interim multiparty govt.) 1990–91. *Address:* Nepali Congress Central Office, Baneshwar, Kathmandu, Nepal. *Telephone:* 977-01-534397.

BHAVSAR, Natvar, B.A., A.M., M.F.A.; artist; b. 7 April 1934, Gothava; s. of Prahladji Bhavsar and Babuben Bhavsar; m. Janet Brosious Bhavsar; three c.; ed. Gujarat Univ., Univ. of Pennyslvania, U.S.A.; art instructor Univ. of Rhode Island, Kingston, U.S.A.; numerous solo exhbns. including ART Cologne, ACP Viviane Ehrli Gallery 1998; recent group exhibitions include: Galleria Civica d'Arte, Italy (Il Sud del Mondo. L'Altra Arte Contemporanea) 1991; work in public collections including: Australian Nat. Gallery, Boston Museum of Fine Arts, Solomon R. Guggenheim Museum, Metropolitan Museum of Art, M.I.T., Philadelphia Museum of Art; work in numerous pvt. collections; John D. Rockefeller III Fund Fellowship 1965–66, John Simon Guggenheim Memorial Foundation Fellowship 1975–76, Vishva Gurjari 1988. *Publication:* Monogram 1998. *Address:* 131 Greene Street, New York, NY 10012, U.S.A. *Telephone:* (212) 674 1293.

BHICHAI RATTAKUL, Nai; Thai politician; b. 16 Sept. 1926, Bangkok; m. Nang Charoye; two s. one d.; ed. St. Peter's School, Bangkok, St. Stephen's Coll., Hong Kong; fmr. Man. Dir. Jawarad Co. Ltd., Pres. Thai Pharmaceutical Mfrs. Asscn., Vice-Pres. Druggists Asscn. of Thailand, Dir. Thai Chamber of Commerce, Bd. of Trade, and of Asscn. of Thai Industries, rep. of Thai Employers to Gen. Confs. of ILO, Geneva, Deputy mem. Asian Advisory Cttee. of ILO; joined Democrat Party 1958; M.P. for Bangkok Metropolis 1969–71, 1975–; mem. Nat. Convention, Nat. Legis. Ass., Constitution Scrutiny Cttee. 1973; Minister of Foreign Affairs 1975–86; Deputy Prime Minister 1986–90; Deputy Leader Democrat Party. *Address:* c/o Government House, Nakhan Pathan Road, Bangkok 10300, Thailand.

BHUMIBOL ADULYADEJ; King of Thailand; b. 5 Dec. 1927, Cambridge, Mass., U.S.A.; ed. Bangkok and Lausanne, Switzerland; youngest son of Their Royal Highnesses Prince and Princess Mahidol of Songkla; succeeded his brother, the late King Ananda Mahidol, June 1946; married Her Majesty the present Queen Sirikit, daughter of H.H. the late Prince Chandaburi Suranath, 28th April 1950; formal Coronation 5th May 1950; one son, H.R.H. Crown Prince Maha Vajiralongkorn, b. 1952; three daughters, H.R.H. Princess Ubol Ratana, b. 1951, H.R.H. Princess Maha Chakri Sirindhorn, b. 1955, H.R.H. Princess Chulabhorn, b. 1957. *Address:* Chitralada Villa, Bangkok, Thailand.

BHUTTO, Benazir; Pakistani politician; b. 21 June 1953; d. of the late Zulfikar Ali Bhutto (died 1979) and of Begum Nusrat Bhutto (q.v.); m. Asif Ali Zardari 1987; one s. two d.; ed. Harvard Univ. and Lady Margaret Hall, Oxford; under house arrest 1977–84; leader in exile of Pakistan People's Party with her mother Nusrat and involved in the Movt. for the Restoration of Democracy in Pakistan 1984–; Co-Chair. Pakistan People's Party (PPP), Chair. Dec. 1993–; returned to Pakistan 1986; Prime Minister of Pakistan 1988–90, 1993–96, also fmr. Minister of Finance and Econ. Affairs; removed from position by Presidential decree and charged with corruption and abuse of power Aug. 1990; dismissed by Presidential decree Nov. 1996, dismissal upheld by Supreme Court Jan. 1997; charged with corruption and money laundering July 1998; charged with taking bribes Oct. 1998; Opposition Leader 1990–93; Head. Parl. Foreign Affairs Cttee. 1993–96; Dr. h.c. (Harvard) 1989, (Lady Margaret Hall, Oxford) 1989. *Publication:* Daughter of The East (autobiog.) 1988. *Address:* Pakistan People's Party, 70 Clifton, Karachi 75600, Pakistan.

BHUTTO, Begum Nusrat; Pakistani politician; b. 1934; widow of Zulfikar Ali Bhutto (died 1979); two s. two d. (Benazir Bhutto q.v.); fmr. first lady of Pakistan; Co-Chair. Pakistan People's Party (PPP) –1993 and involved in the Movt. for the Restoration of Democracy in Pakistan 1984–. *Address:* c/o Pakistan People's Party, 70 Clifton, Karachi 75600, Pakistan.

BIANCHERI, Boris, B.L.; Italian diplomatist; b. 3 Nov. 1930, Rome; m.; one s. one d.; ed. Univ. of Rome; entered diplomatic service 1956, Office of the Sec. of State, Ministry of Foreign Affairs 1956–58; Italian Embassy, Athens 1959; Econ. Affairs Dept., Ministry of Foreign Affairs 1964–67, Counsellor 1967–71; Sec.-Gen. of Govt. Comm. for 1970 Universal Osaka Exhbn. 1968; Political Counsellor, Italian Embassy, London 1972–75; Head of Office of Sec.-Gen. Ministry of Foreign Affairs 1975–78, Chef de Cabinet Sec. of State for Foreign Affairs 1978, Minister Plenipotentiary 1979; Amb. to Japan 1980–84; Dir.-Gen. Personnel and Admin., Ministry of Foreign Affairs 1984, Dir.-Gen. Political Affairs 1985; Amb. to U.K. 1987–91, to U.S.A. 1991. *Leisure interests:* gardening, boating, swimming, horse-riding. *Address:* c/o Ministry of Foreign Affairs, Piazzale della Farnesinal, 00194 Rome, Italy.

BIANCHI, Tancredi; Italian professor of banking economics; ed. Bocconi Univ., Milan; Prof. of Banking Econs. Bocconi Univ., Milan 1979; Pres. Associazione Bancaria Italiana (ABI) 1991–. *Address:* Associazione Bancaria Italiana, Piazza del Gesú 49, 00186 Rome, Italy.

BIANCINI, Angelo; Italian sculptor; b. 1911; ed. Accademia di Santa Luca; Prof. and Artistic Dir. Istituto d'Arte, Faenza; Regular Exhibitor Venice Biennali and Rome Quadriennali 1934–58; international exhibitor throughout the world; Prize, Milan Triennale 1940, Venice Biennale 1958. Major works: three statues. Galleria d'Arte Moderna, Rome, Canadian Temple, Rome, Mosaic Marist Fathers' International Coll. etc. *Address:* Istituto d'Arte di Ceramica, Faenza, Italy.

BIANCO, Jean-Louis; French civil servant; b. 12 Jan. 1943, Neuilly-sur-Seine; s. of Louis Bianco and Gabrielle (née Vandries) Bianco; m. Martine Letoublon 1971; three s.; ed. Lycée Janson-de-Sailly and Inst. d'études politiques, Paris; Auditor Conseil d'Etat 1971; Official Rep. Group central des villes nouvelles 1973–74; attached to Ministry of Health 1976–79; Counsel Conseil d'Etat 1976; Official Rep. Syndicat intercommunal de devt. Durance-Bléone 1979–81; Official Rep. to the advisers of the Pres. 1981; Sec.-Gen. to the Pres. 1982–91; Minister of Social Affairs and Integration 1991–92, of Equipment, Transport and Housing April 1992–93; mem. Regional Council of Provence 1992–, Pres. 1998–; Mayor of Digne-les-Bains (Alpes de Haute Provence) 1995–; Deputy from Alpes de Haute-Provence (Socialist) June 1997–. *Address:* Conseil d'Etat, Palais Royal, 75100 Paris RP; Mairie, 1 boulevard Maître Bret, 04000 Digne-les-Bains; Conseil général des Alpes de Haute-Provence, 13 rue du Docteur Romieu, 04000 Digne-les-Bains, France.

BIČKAUSKAS, Egidijuš; Lithuanian politician and lawyer; b. 29 May 1955, Prienai; m. Jurate Bičkauskienė; ed. Vilnius Univ.; investigator, special cases investigator Procurator's Gen. Office 1978–89; joined People's Front Movt. Sajudis 1988; Deputy of U.S.S.R Supreme Soviet 1989–90; elected to Parl. Restoration Seimas of Repub. of Lithuania 1990–92, signatory of the Lithuanian Repub. Independence Restoration Act 1990; Head Lithuanian diplomatic mission to Moscow 1990–96; mem. Parl. (Seimas) of Repub. of Lithuania, Deputy Chair. 1992–; Deputy Chair., head of faction in Seimas of Centre Party of Lithuania 1996–. *Address:* L R Seimas, Gedimino p.2 53, LT-2600 Vilnius (Office); Laurų 35, LT 2046 Vilnius, Lithuania. *Telephone:* (3702) 225493 (Home).

BIDDISS, Michael Denis, PH.D., F.R.HIST.S.; British professor of history and author; b. 15 April 1942, Farnborough, Kent; s. of Daniel Biddiss and Eileen Biddiss (née Jones); m. Ruth Margaret Cartwright 1967; four d.; ed. Queens' Coll., Cambridge, Centre des Hautes Etudes Européennes, Univ. of Strasbourg; Fellow in History, Downing Coll., Cambridge and Dir. of Studies in History, Social and Political Sciences 1966–73; lecturer, then Reader in History, Univ. of Leicester 1973–79; Prof. of History, Univ. of Reading 1979–, Dean Faculty of Letters and Social Sciences 1982–85; Visiting Prof., Univ. of Victoria 1973, Univ. of Cape Town 1976, 1978, Univ. of Cairo 1985, Monash Univ., Australia 1989, Univ. of Nanjing, China 1997; Chair. History at the Univs. Defence Group 1984–87; mem. Council, The Historical Asscn. 1985– (Pres. 1991–94), Vice-Pres. Royal Historical Soc. 1995– (mem. Council 1988–92); Lister Lecturer, B.A.A.S. 1975; Hon. Fellow Faculty of the History of Medicine (Pres. 1994–98), Soc. of Apothecaries 1986–, Osler Medallist, Soc. of Apothecaries of London 1989, Locke Medallist, Soc. of Apothecaries of London 1996. *Publications:* Father of Racist Ideology 1970, Gobineau: Selected Political Writings (Ed.) 1970, Disease and History (co-author) 1972, The Age of the Masses 1977, Images of Race (Ed.) 1979, Thatcherism (co-ed.) 1987, The Nuremberg Trial and the Third Reich (co-author) 1992, The Uses and Abuses of Antiquity (co-ed.) 1999. *Leisure interests:* cricket, music, mountain walking, art, opera. *Address:* Department of History, University of Reading, Whiteknights, Reading, RG6 6AA, England. *Telephone:* (0118) 931 8146.

BIDDLE, Martin, O.B.E., M.A., F.B.A., F.S.A., F.R.HIST.S.; British archaeologist; b. 4 June 1937, North Harrow, Middx; s. of Reginald S. Biddle and Gwladys F. Baker; m. Birthe Kjølbye 1966; two d. and two d. by previous m.; ed. Merchant Taylors' School and Pembroke Coll. Cambridge; Asst. Insp. of Ancient Monuments, Ministry of Public Building and Works 1961–63; lecturer in Medieval Archaeology, Univ. of Exeter 1963–67; Visiting Fellow, All Souls Coll. Oxford 1967–68; Dir. Winchester Research Unit. 1968–; Dir. Univ. Museum and Prof. of Anthropology and History of Art, Univ. of Pa. 1977–81; lecturer of The House, Christ Church, Oxford 1983–86; Astor Sr. Research Fellow in Medieval Archaeology, Hertford Coll. Oxford 1989–; Prof. of Medieval Archaeology, Univ. of Oxford 1997–; dir. excavations and investigations at Nonsuch Palace 1959–60, Winchester 1961–71, Repton (with wife) 1974–88, 1993, St. Alban's Abbey (with wife) 1978, 1982–84, 1991, 1994–95, Holy Sepulchre, Jerusalem (with wife) 1989–90, 1992, 1993, 1998, Qasr Ibrim, Egypt (with wife) 1990, 1992, 1995; archaeological consultant to Canterbury Cathedral, St. Alban's Abbey, Eurotunnel etc.; mem. Royal Comm. on Historical Monuments for England 1984–95; Trevelyan Lecturer, Univ. of Cambridge 1991; Pres. Soc. for Medieval Archaeology 1995–; Frend Medal, Soc. of Antiquaries (with Birthe Biddle) 1986. *Publications:* The Future of London's Past (with C. Heighway) 1973, Winchester in the Early Middle Ages (with others) 1976, The History of the King's Works, Vol. IV, Pt. 2 (with others) 1982, King Arthur's Round Table 1990, Approaches in Urban Archaeology 1990, Object and Economy in Medieval Winchester 1990, Das Grab-Christi 1998, Nonsuch Palace 1997; papers in learned journals. *Leisure interests:* travel, especially Hellenic travel, architecture, Renaissance art. *Address:* 19 Hamilton Road, Oxford, OX2 7PY, England. *Telephone:* (01865) 513056. *Fax:* (01865) 559017.

BIDE, Sir Austin (Ernest), Kt., B.SC., F.R.S.C., C.B.I.M., C.CHEM.; British business executive; b. 11 Sept. 1915, London; s. of Ernest Arthur and Eliza (Young) Bide; m. Irene Ward 1941; three d.; ed. Univ. of London; mem. of staff, Dept. of Govt. Chemist until 1940; Research Dept. Glaxo Laboratories Ltd., Deputy Sec. 1954, Sec. 1959; Dir. Glaxo Group Ltd. 1963; Deputy Chair. Glaxo Holdings Ltd. 1971–73, Chief Exec. 1973–80, Chair. 1973–85, Hon. Pres. 1985–95; mem. Council CBI 1974–85, Chair, Research and Tech. Cttee. 1977–86, mem. Pres.'s Cttee. 1983–85; mem. Council British Inst. of Management 1976–88, Companions Cttee. 1976–84, Chair. Finance Cttee. 1976–79, Vice-Pres. 1992–, Dir. and Chair. B.I.M. Foundation 1977–79; Dir. British Leyland (now BL Ltd.) 1977–86 (non-exec. Deputy Chair. 1980–82, non-exec. Chair. 1982–86), J. Lyons and Co. 1977–78; mem. Working Party on Biotechnology, Council of the Imperial Soc. of Knights Bachelor 1980–; Chair. Visiting Cttee. of the Open Univ. 1982–88; Chair. CGEA (U.K.) Ltd. 1991–, Onyx (U.K.) Ltd 1991–, Comatech (U.K.) Ltd 1992–, Tyseley Waste Disposal 1994–; mem. Advisory Cttee. on Industry to Vice-Chancellors and Prins. of Univs. of U.K. 1984–87; mem. Review Body, Univ. Grants Cttee., mem. Council of Inst. of Manpower Studies 1985–91, Adam Smith Inst. 1985 (Chair. 1986–); Chair. Q-Ca Ltd 1985–88, Microtest Research Ltd. 1987–90; Chair. United Environmental Systems Ltd. 1988–90; Dir. Oxford Consultancy Ltd. 1988– (Chair. 1994–); Trustee, British Motor Industry Heritage Trust 1983–86; mem. Court of British Shippers' Council 1984–92 (Chair. 1989–92); Chair. Salisbury Cathedral Appeal Cttee. 1987–92; mem. MRC 1986; Hon. Fellow, Vice-Pres. Inst. of Industrial Mans. 1983, Hon. Fellow Inst. of Chemical Engineers; Hon. Fellow, Inst. of Biotechnological Studies, mem. Advisory Council 1985–89; Hon. D.Sc. (Queen's, Belfast), Hon. Dr. h.c. (C.N.A.A.) 1990; Fellow St. Catharine's Coll., Cambridge. *Leisure interests:* fishing, handicrafts.

BIDEN, Joseph Robinette, Jr., J.D.; American politician; b. 20 Nov. 1942, Scranton, Pa.; s. of Joseph R. Biden and Jean F. Biden; m. 1st Neilia Hunter (deceased); two s. one d. (deceased); m. 2nd Jill Tracy Jacobs 1977; one d.; ed. Univ. of Delaware, Newark and Syracuse Univ. Coll. of Law, N.Y.; Trial Attorney in the Public Defender's Office, Del. 1968; Founder of Biden & Walsh Law Firm, Wilmington; mem. New Castle Co., del. and American Bar Asscns., American Trial Lawyers' Asscn.; admitted to practise before the Del. Supreme Court; mem. New Castle Co. Council 1970–72; Senator from Delaware 1972–, serving as a mem. of the Cttee. on Foreign Relations, Judiciary Cttee. (Chair.); named to the Democratic Steering Cttee.; Democrat. *Leisure interests:* sports, history, public speaking, American architecture. *Address:* 221 Russell Building, Washington, DC 20510, U.S.A. (Office). *Telephone:* (202) 224-5045 (Office).

BIDWELL, Charles Edward, PH.D.; American professor of education and sociology; b. 24 Jan. 1932, Chicago; s. of Charles L. Bidwell and Eugenia Campbell Bidwell; m. Helen Claxton Lewis 1959; one s.; ed. Univ. of Chicago; Lecturer in Sociology, Harvard Univ. 1959–61, Assoc. Prof. 1965–70, Prof. of Educ. and Sociology 1970–85, Reavis Prof. Educ. and Sociology 1985–, Chair. Dept. of Educ. 1978–88; Chair. Dept. of Sociology 1988–94; Dir. Ogburn-Stouffer Center 1988–94; Guggenheim Fellow 1971–72; Fellow A.A.A.S.; mem. Nat. Acad. of Educ. *Publications:* The School as a Formal Organization, in Handbook of Organizations (Ed. J. March) 1965, The Organization and its Ecosystem (with J.D. Kasarda) 1985. *Leisure interests:* skiing and reading. *Address:* Department of Sociology, 5848 S. University Avenue, Chicago, IL 60637, U.S.A.

BIDWELL, Sir Hugh Charles Philip, G.B.E.; British business executive; b. 1 Nov. 1934; s. of Edward and late Elisabeth Bidwell; m. Jenifer C. Webb 1962; two s. one d.; ed. Stonyhurst Coll.; nat. service 1953–55 (commissioned E. Surrey Regt.); Viota Foods 1957–70, Dir. 1962–70; Dir. Robertson Foods 1968–70; Chair. Pearce Duff & Co. 1970–85, Gill & Duffus Foods 1984–85; non-exec. Dir. Argyll Group plc 1990–95, Rothschild Asset Man. Ltd. 1992–98, Alpha Airports Group PLC 1994–; Chair. British Invisibles 1991–94, Royal Tokaji Wine Co. (Hungary) Ltd. 1997–; Chair. (non-exec.) London Tourist Bd. Ltd. 1992–93, Julius Group PLC 1993–97, Applied Distribution (Group) Ltd. 1993–; Deputy Chair. ITE Group PLC 1996–; mem. Exec. Cttee. Food Mfrs'. Fed. 1973–86; mem. Council London Chamber of Commerce and Industry 1976–85, and numerous other trade orgs.; Pres. British Food Export Council 1980–87; Alderman, Billingsgate Ward, City of London 1979–96, Sheriff 1986–87, Lord Mayor of London 1989–90. *Leisure interests:* golf, fishing, tennis, cricket, shooting. *Address:* Byron House, 112A Shirland Road, London, W9 2EQ, England (Office). *Telephone:* 0171-286 9720.

BIEBER, Owen F.; American labour official; b. 28 Dec. 1929, North Dorr, Mich.; s. of Albert F. Bieber and Minnie Schwartz Bieber; m. Shirley M. Van Woerkom 1950; three s. two d.; ed. High School; elected Regional Dir., United Auto Workers (UAW, now United Automobile, Aerospace and Agricultural Implement Workers of America) Region 1D 1974–80, Vice-Pres. Int. Union 1980–83, Pres. 1983–; Hon. D.Hum. (Grand Valley Coll.), Hon. Dr. Sc. (Ferris State Coll.). *Address:* United Auto Workers (UAW), 8000 E. Jefferson Avenue, Detroit, MI 48214, U.S.A. (Office). *Telephone:* 313 926 5201 (Office).

BIEDENKOPF, Kurt Hans, DR.JUR.; German politician and lawyer; b. 28 Jan. 1930, Ludwigshafen; s. of Wilhelm and Agathe (Schmidt) Biedenkopf; m. 2nd Ingrid Ries 1979; Prof. of Law, Ruhr Univ., Bochum 1964–70, Rector 1967–69; Chair. Govt. Comm. on co-determination 1968–70; Gen. Sec. Christian Democratic Party (CDU) 1973–77, Vice-Pres. 1977–83; Pres. CDU Regional Asscn., North Rhine-Westphalia 1980–84; mem. Bundestag 1976–80, 1987–90; Prime Minister of Saxony 1990–; Chair. Kuratorium Trust of Devt. and Peace; mem. Exec. Bd. Henkel Corpn., Düsseldorf 1971–73; mem. Bd. Inst. for Econ. and Social Policy, Bonn 1977–; mem. Bd. German Nat. Trust; mem. Landtag of North Rhine-Westphalia 1980–88; mem. Senate Max Planck Gesellschaft; Dr.jur. h.c. (Davidson Coll.) 1974, (Georgetown) 1978, (New School for Social Research, New York) 1993, (Katholic Univ., Brussels) 1994. *Publications:* Vertragliche Wettbewerbsbeschränkung und Wirtschaftsverfassung 1958, Grenzen der Tarifautonomie 1964, Fortschritt in Freiheit 1974, Die programmierte Krise-Alternativen zur staatlichen Schuldenpolitik 1979, Die neue Sicht der Dinge 1985, Zeitsignale—Parteienlandschaft im Umbruch 1989, Einheit und Erneuerung 1994. *Leisure interests:* skiing, sailing. *Address:* Archivstrasse 1, 01095 Dresden, Germany.

BIEGMAN, Nicolaas H, PH.D.; Netherlands diplomatist; b. 23 Sept. 1936, Apeldoorn; s. of Nicolaas Biegman and Aukje de Boer; m. Mirjana Cibilic; two s.; ed. Univ. of Leiden; lecturer in Turkish and Persian, Univ. of Leiden 1960–62; various posts in Netherlands foreign service 1963–84; Amb. to Egypt 1984–88; Dir.-Gen. for Int. Cooperation, Ministry of Foreign Affairs 1988–92; Perm. Rep. to UN 1992–97; Perm. Rep. to NATO 1998–; Order of The Netherlands Lion, Order of Merit, United Arab Repub. *Publications:* The Turco-Ragusan Relationship 1967, Egypt-Moulids, Saints, Sufis 1990, Egypt's Sideshows 1992, An Island of Bliss 1993, Mainly Manhattan 1997. *Leisure interest:* photography. *Address:* c/o Ministry of Foreign Affairs, Bezuidenhouseweg 67, P.O. Box 20061, 2500 EB The Hague, The Netherlands.

BIELECKI, Jan Krzysztof, M.SC.; Polish politician and economist; b. 3 May 1951, Bydgoszcz; s. of Anastazy Bielecki and Janina Bielecka; m. Barbara Bielecka 1976; one s. one d.; ed. Gdańsk Univ.; Asst. Gdańsk Univ. 1973–77; head of research unit Centre for Training Managerial Staff, Ministry of Trade and Ministry of Machine Industry 1972–82; trade union and workers' rights activist, expert for econ. affairs Solidarity Trade Union 1980–81; continued union activity under martial law as assoc. of underground regional and nat. authorities; lorry driver 1982–85; man. Doradca consulting co-operative, Sopot 1985–91; deputy to Sejm (Parl.) 1989–93 (mem. Civic Parl. Club 1989–91, leader Parl. Liberal-Democratic Congress Club); Prime Minister of Poland Jan.–Dec. 1991; Minister for European Integration 1992–93; mem. Liberal-Democratic Congress (mem. Provisional Bd., the Presidium) 1989–94; Dir. EBRD. *Leisure interests:* horse riding, tennis, football. *Address:* European Bank for Reconstruction and Development, 1 Exchange Square, London EC2 2EA, England.

BIELER, Manfred, M.A.; German writer; b. 3 July 1934, Zerbst; s. of Richard and Elsbeth (née Tietz) Bieler; m. Marcella Matejovská 1966; one s. two d.; ed. Humboldt Univ., Berlin; mem. German Writers' Union 1956–57, freelance writer 1957–; fisherman on G.D.R. trawler 1960; resident in Prague, Czechoslovakia 1964–68; emigrated to Fed. Repub. of Germany 1968; mem. Bavarian Acad. of Fine Arts, PEN Club. *Publications:* Bonifaz 1963, Maria Morzek 1969, Der Passagier 1971, Der Mädchenkrieg 1975, Der Kanal 1978, Ewig und drei Tage 1980, Der Bär 1983 (novels), Walhalla, Lit. Parodien 1988, Still wie die Nächtlichen Memoiren eines Kindes 1989, numerous plays for radio and television. *Leisure interests:* playing cembalo, painting. *Address:* Gustav-Meyrink-Strasse 17, 81245 Munich, Germany. *Telephone:* 089 8342855.

BIERICH, Marcus, PH.D.; German business executive; b. 29 April 1926; ed. Univs. of Münster and Hamburg; Bankhaus Delbrück Schickler & Co. 1956–61; Dir. Mannesmann AG, Düsseldorf 1961–67, mem. Man. Bd. 1967–80; mem. Man. Bd. Allianz Versicherungs-AG, Munich 1980–84; Chair. Man. Bd. Robert Bosch GmbH, Stuttgart 1984–94, Chair. Supervisory Bd. 1993–; Hon. Dr. rer. oec. (Bochum). *Address:* c/o Robert Bosch GmbH, Postfach 106050, 70049 Stuttgart, Germany.

BIERRING, Ole, LL.M.; Danish diplomatist; b. 9 Nov. 1926, Copenhagen; s. of Knud and Ester M. (Lorck) Bierring; m. Bodil E. Kisbye 1960; one s. three d.; ed. Univ. of Copenhagen and Princeton Univ., U.S.A.; joined Ministry of Foreign Affairs 1951; served in Washington, D.C. 1956–58, Vienna 1960–63, Brussels (NATO) 1968–72; Under-Sec. for Political Affairs 1976–80, Deputy Perm. Under-Sec. 1980; Amb. to France 1980–84; Amb. and Perm. Rep. to UN 1984–88, Rep. on the Security Council 1985–86; Amb. to NATO 1988–95; Observer to WEU 1993–95; Amb.-at-Large 1995–96; Commdr. Order of Dannebrog (1st class) and other decorations. *Leisure interests:* music, sailing. *Address:* Rysensteensgade 6, 5 tv, 1564 Copenhagen V, Denmark. *Telephone:* 33.91.66.36.

BIESHEUVEL, Barend Willem; Netherlands politician and agriculturist; b. 5 April 1920, Haarlemmerliede; m. Wilhelmina Meuring 1945; one s. two d.; ed. Free Univ. of Amsterdam; Ministry of Agriculture 1945–47; Sec. for Foreign Relations, Fed. of Agriculture 1947–52; Gen. Sec. Nat. Protestant Farmers' Union 1952–59, Pres. 1959–63; mem. States-Gen. (Parl.) 1957–63, 1963–; mem. European Parl.; Deputy Prime Minister, Minister of Agriculture and Fisheries 1963–67; leader of Anti-Revolutionary Parliamentary Group 1967–71; Prime Minister 1971–73; Pres. Supervisory Bd. Nat. Investment Bank 1973–91; mem. Supervisory Bd. CSM NV 1975–92, Royal Dutch Airlines (KLM) 1986–92. *Address:* Ter Hoffsteedeweg 4-B, 2051 ER Overveen, Netherlands (Home). *Telephone:* (023) 526 5754. *Fax:* (023) 526 5831.

BIESHU, Mariya Lukyanovna; Moldovan singer (soprano); b. 3 Aug. 1935, Moldova; d. of Luca Bieshu and Tatiana Bieshu; m. Arcady Rodomsky 1965; ed. Kishinev Conservatoire; soloist with Moldovan Folk Orchestra 1958–60; with Moldovan Opera and Ballet 1961–; postgrad. studies at La Scala, Milan 1965–67; Prof. Kishinev Conservatoire 1980–; Roles include: Tosca 1962, Desdemona in Othello 1967, Leonora in Il Trovatore 1969, Zemphira in Aleko 1973, Mimi in La Bohème 1977, Turandot 1979, Iolanta 1979, Elizabeth of Valois in Don Carlos 1985, Amelia in A Masked Ball 1989, Abigail in Nabucco 1991; awards include: 1st Prize Int. Puccini Competition, Tokyo 1967, People's Artist of U.S.S.R. 1970, Lenin Prize 1982. *Leisure interests:* dogs, open country. *Address:* 24 Pushkin Str., Chişinău 2012, Moldova.

BIFFEN, Baron (Life Peer) cr. 1997, of Tanar in the County of Shropshire, **John Biffen,** P.C., B.A.; British politician; b. 3 Nov. 1930; s. of Victor W. Biffen; m. Sarah Wood (née Drew) 1979; one step-s. one step-d.; ed. Dr. Morgan's Grammar School, Bridgwater, Jesus Coll., Cambridge; M.P. for Oswestry 1961–83, for Shropshire North 1983–97; with Tube Investments Ltd. 1953–60; with Economist Intelligence Unit 1960–61; Chief Sec. to the Treasury 1979–81, Sec. of State for Trade 1981–82; Lord Privy Seal and Leader of the Commons 1983–87; Dir. Glynwed Int. 1987–, J. Bibby and Sons 1988–97, Rockware Group 1988–91, Barlow Int. PLC 1997–; Trustee The London Clinic 1994–; Deputy Lieut. of Shropshire 1993; Conservative. *Publication:* Inside the House of Commons 1989. *Address:* Tanat House, Llanyblodwel, Oswestry, Shropshire, SY10 8NQ, England.

BIFFI, H.E. Cardinal Giacomo; Italian ecclesiastic; b. 13 June 1928, Milan; ordained 1950; consecrated Bishop (Titular Church of Fidene) 1975; Archbishop of Bologna 1984; elevated to Cardinal 1985. *Address:* Arcivescovado, Via Altabella 6, 40126 Bologna, Italy. *Telephone:* (051) 238.202.

BIGELEISEN, Jacob, A.B., M.S., PH.D.; American chemist; b. 2 May 1919, Paterson, N. J.; s. of Harry and Ida (Slomowitz) Bigeleisen; m. Grace Alice Simon 1945; three s.; ed. New York Univ., Washington State Univ. and Univ. of California (Berkeley); S.A.M. Labs., Columbia Univ. (Manhattan District) 1943–45; Ohio State Univ. 1945–46; Univ. of Chicago 1946–48; Assoc. to Senior Chemist, Brookhaven Nat. Laboratory 1948–68; Prof. of Chemistry, Univ. of Rochester 1968–78, Chair. Dept. of Chemistry 1970–75, Tracy H. Harris Prof., Coll. of Arts and Sciences 1973–78, Leading Prof. of Chemistry, State Univ. of New York (Stony Brook) 1978–89, Vice-Pres. for Research 1978–80, Dean of Graduate Studies 1978–80, Distinguished Prof. and Emer. Prof. 1989–; Visiting Prof. Cornell Univ. 1953; Hon. Visiting Prof., Eidgenössische Technische Hochschule, Zürich 1962–63; Senior Postdoctoral Fellow, Nat. Science Foundation 1962–63; Gilbert N. Lewis Lecturer, Univ. of Calif. 1963; Visiting Distinguished Prof., State Univ. of New York (Buffalo) 1966; Guggenheim Fellow 1974–75; mem. N.A.S., Chair. Assembly of Math. and Physical Science 1976–80, Councilor 1982–85; Fellow, American Acad. of Arts and Sciences, American Physical Soc., A.A.A.S.; American Chem. Soc. Nuclear Applications to Chemistry Award 1958, E. O. Lawrence Memorial Award and Presidential Citation 1964, Distinguished Alumnus Award (Washington State Univ.) 1983. *Publications:* Calculation of Equilibrium Constants of Isotopic Exchange Reactions 1947, Relative Reaction Velocities of Isotopic Molecules 1949, The Significance of the Product and Sum Rules to Isotope Fractionation Studies 1957, Statistical Mechanics of Isotope Effects in Condensed Systems 1961, Quantum Mechanical Foundations of Isotope Chemistry 1974, and numerous publs. on ionization of strong electrolytes, organic photochemistry, semiquinones, acids and bases and particularly theoretical and experimental studies on the chemistry of isotopes. *Address:* 461 Graduate Chemistry Building, State University of New York, Stony Brook, Stony Brook, NY 11794; P.O. Box 217, Saint James, NY 11780, U.S.A. *Telephone:* (516) 632-7905. *Fax:* (516) 632-7960.

BIGGAM, Sir Robin Adair, Kt.; British business executive and chartered accountant; b. 8 July 1938, Carluke; s. of Thomas Biggam and Eileen Biggam; m. Elizabeth McArthur (née McDougall) Biggam 1962; one s. two d.; ed. Lanark Grammar School; C.A. Peat Marwick Mitchell 1960–63, ICI 1964–81; Finance Dir. 1981–84; Exec. Dir. Dunlop 1984–85; Chair. Cadcentre Ltd 1983–86; Non Exec. Dir. Chloride Group PLC 1985–87, Lloyds Abbey Life plc (fmrly. Abbey Life Group) 1985–90, Redland Group PLC 1991–, British Aerospace PLC 1994–; Man. Dir. BICC PLC 1986–87, C.E.O. 1987–91, Deputy Chair. 1991–, Chair. 1992–96; Dir. Fairey Group PLC 1995– (Chair. 1996–); Chair. Independent TV Comm. 1996–. *Leisure interests:* golf, gardening, swimming. *Address:* Independent Television Commission, 33 Foley Street, London, W1P 7LB, England.

BIGGS, Barton Michael, M.B.A.; American executive; b. 26 Nov. 1932, New York; s. of William Richardson and Georgene Biggs; m. Judith Anne Lund 1959; one s. two d.; ed. Yale and New York Univs.; First Lieut. U.S. Marine Corps 1955–59; research analyst E. M. Hutton & Co. 1961–65, asst. to Chair. 1962–, partner 1965; co-f. Fairfield Partners 1965, Man. Partner 1965–73; partner and Man. Dir. Morgan Stanley & Co. 1973–, Man. Research Dept. 1973–79, 1991–93; Chair. and C.E.O. Morgan Stanley Asset Man. Co. 1980–, mem. Man. Cttee. 1987–, mem. Exec. Cttee. Bd. Dirs. 1991–; Chair. Morgan Stanley Funds; Dir. Rand McNally & Co. *Address:* Morgan Stanley & Co., Room 311, 1221 Avenue of the Americas, 22nd Floor, New York, NY 10020, U.S.A.

BIGGS, Sir Norman Parris, Kt.; British banker; b. 23 Dec. 1907, Newry, Co. Down; s. of John G. Biggs and Mary Sharpe Dickson; m. Peggy Helena Stammwitz 1936 (died 1990); two s. one d.; ed. John Watson's School, Edinburgh; Bank of England 1927–46; Dir. Kleinwort, Sons & Co. Ltd. 1946–52; Dir. Esso Petroleum Co. 1952–57, Man. Dir. 1957–64, Vice-Chair. 1964–66; Vice-Pres. (Finance) Esso Europe Inc. 1966–67; Chair. Esso Petroleum Co. Ltd. 1968–71; Chair. United Int. Bank Ltd. 1970–79, Deputy Chair. Privatbanken Ltd. 1980–83; Chair. Williams and Glyn's Bank Ltd. 1972–76; Deputy Chair. Nat. and Commercial Banking Group Ltd. 1974–76; Dir. Gillett Bros. Discount Co. Ltd. 1963–77, Royal Bank of Scotland 1974–76, Banco de Bilbao 1981–87; mem. Bullock Cttee. on Industrial Democracy 1975–76. *Address:* Northbrook, Danworth Lane, Hurstpierpoint, Sussex, BN6 9LW, England. *Telephone:* (01273) 832022.

BIGGS, Peter Martin, C.B.E., D.SC., F.R.S., F.R.C.V.S., F.R.C.PATH., C.BIOL., F.I.BIOL., F.R.S.; British veterinary scientist; b. 13 Aug. 1926, Petersfield; s. of Ronald and Cecile (née Player) Biggs; m. Alison Janet Molteno 1950; two s. one d.; ed. Bedales School, Petersfield, Cambridge School, Mass.; with R.A.F. 1944–48; with Royal Veterinary Coll., London 1948–53; Research Asst., Dept. of Veterinary Anatomy, Univ. of Bristol 1953–55; Lecturer in Veterinary Clinical Pathology, Dept. of Veterinary Medicine 1955–59; Prin. Scientific Officer, Houghton Poultry Research Station 1959–66, Sr. Prin. Scientific Officer 1966–1971, Deputy Dir. 1971–74, Dir. 1974–86; Dir. Inst. for Animal Health 1986–88; Chief Scientific Officer 1981–88; Visiting Prof. of Veterinary Microbiology, Royal Veterinary Coll. London 1982–; Andrew D. White Prof.-at-Large, Cornell Univ., U.S.A. 1988–94; Vice Pres. British Veterinary Asscn. 1996–98; Fellow Inst. of Biology 1973, Pres. 1990–92; Fellow Royal Coll. of Pathologists 1978, Royal Coll. of Veterinary Surgeons 1979, Royal Veterinary Coll. 1983; Hon. Fellow Royal Agricultural Soc. of England 1986; Wolf Foundation Prize in Agric. 1989; Dalrymple—Champneys Cup and Medal of the British Veterinary Asscn.; Hon. Doc. of Veterinary Medicine (Ludwig-Maximilians Univ., Munich), Dr. h.c. (Univ. of Liège) and numerous others. *Publications:* more than 100 scientific papers. *Leisure interests:* music making, boating. *Address:* 'Willows', London Road, St. Ives, Huntingdon, Cambridgeshire, PE17 4ES, England. *Telephone:* (01480) 463471. *Fax:* 01480 463471.

BIGI, Federico; San Marino politician and judge; b. 21 March 1920, Reggio Emilia, Italy; m. Wanda Cherubini; two d.; ed. Univs. of Bologna and Urbino; fmr. journalist; lecturer, Liceo Classico Statale di San Marino; mem. Provisional Govt. 1943; mem. Congresso di Stato 1943; mem. Parl. 1943–93, mem. Consiglio Grande e Generale 1993–; Sec. of State for Internal Affairs 1951, for Foreign and Political Affairs 1957–72; Pres. Società Unione Soccorso di San Marino; Vice-Pres. Cassa de Risparmio; Judge, European Court of Human Rights, Strasbourg 1991–; mem. various Italian Acads.; recipient of numerous foreign decorations. *Address:* c/o European Court of Human Rights, Council of Europe, 67075 Strasbourg Cedex, France.

BIGNONE, Maj.-Gen. Reynaldo Benito; Argentinian politician and army officer; b. 21 Jan. 1928, Morón; m. Nilda Raquel Belen; three c.; ed. Nat. Mil. Acad., Superior War Coll.; Capt. 1954; Commdr. Cadet Corps, Nat. Mil. Acad. 1970; Sec. to Army High Command 1973; Deputy Commdr., later Commdr. Nat. Mil. Insts. 1980–81; fmr. Dir. Nat. Mil. Acad. and Sec.-Gen. of Army; retd. from active service Dec. 1981; Pres. of Argentina 1982–83; arrested Jan. 1984, released June 1984.

BIGOT, Charles André Marie; French aviation engineer; b. 29 July 1932, Angers; s. of Charles Bigot and Marcelle Pousset; m. Marie-Odile Lambert 1959; one s. three d.; ed. Ecole Sainte-Geneviève, Versailles, Ecole Nat. Supérieure de l'Aéronautique, Ecole Polytechnique and Cranfield Coll. of Aeronautics; aeronautical eng. 1957–61; Tech. Dir. of Aeronautical Services, CNRS 1961–63; Dir. of launch vehicle div., Centre Nat. des Etudes Spatiales (CNES) 1963–70; Deputy Dir. Centre Spatial de Brétigny 1970–71; Dir. of Devt. Air Inter 1971–75; Tech. Dir. Soc. d'Etudes et de Réalisations Industrielles (Seri-Renault Eng.) 1975–76, Dir.-Gen. 1975–80; Commercial Dir. Soc. Nat. Industrielle Aérospatiale (Snias) 1980; Dir.-Gen. Arianespace 1982–90, Pres.-Dir.-Gen. 1990–; mem. Int. Acad. of Astronautics, Acad. Nat. de l'Air et de l'Espace; Chevalier, Légion d'honneur, Commandeur, Ordre Nat. du Mérite, Médaille de Vermeil (CNES). *Address:* Arianespace, bd. de l'Europe, BP 117, 91006 Evry cedex; 3 rue Saint-Laurent, 91360 Villemoisson-sur-Orge, France. *Telephone:* (1) 69.04.62.59.

BÍLÁ, Lucie (Hana Zaňáková); Czech singer; b. 7 April 1966, Otvovice; d. of Josef Zanák; partner Petr Kratochvíl; one s.; co-owner Theatre Ta Fantastika, Prague; has toured throughout W. Europe; has performed in charity concerts in Czech Repub.; numerous awards including Czech Grammy Prize 1992–96, Most Popular Singer (Czech Repub.) 1994–97, Czech Musical Acad. Prize 1997. *Albums:* Missariel 1993, Lucie Bílá 1994, Binoculars 1995, Stars as Stars 1998. *Theatre includes:* Les Misérables 1992, Dracula 1995, Rat-Catcher 1996. *Film:* King Ubu. *Leisure interest:* family. *Address:* Theatre Ta Fantastika, Karlova ul. 8, 110 00 Prague 1, Czech Republic. *Telephone:* (2) 24-23-25-32; (2) 24-23-27-11.

BILALI, Mohamed Gharib; Tanzanian politician; fmr. govt. official; Chief Minister Supreme Revolutionary Council of Zanzibar Oct. 1995–; mem. C.C.M. (Party for Democracy and Progress). *Address:* Office of the Chief Minister, Supreme Revolutionary Council of Zanzibar, Zanzibar, Tanzania.

BILBY, Bruce Alexander, PH.D., F.R.S.; British professor of theory of materials and consultant; b. 3 Sept. 1922, London; s. of George A. Bilby and Dorothy J. (née Telfer) Bilby; m. 1st Hazel J. Casken 1946 (dissolved 1964);

two s. one d.; m. 2nd Lorette W. Thomas 1966; two s.; ed. Dover County Grammar School, Peterhouse, Cambridge, and Univ. of Birmingham; Royal Soc. Sorby Research Fellow, Univ. of Sheffield 1951–57, J. H. Andrew Research Fellow 1957–58, Reader in Theoretical Metallurgy 1958–62, Prof. of Theoretical Metallurgy 1962–66, Prof. of the Theory of Materials 1966–84, Prof. Emer. 1984–; Rosenhain Medal 1963, Griffith Medal 1994. *Publications:* scientific papers in learned journals. *Leisure interest:* sailing. *Address:* Department of Mechanical Engineering, University of Sheffield, Mappin Street, Sheffield, S1 3JD (Office); 32 Devonshire Road, Totley, Sheffield, S17 3NT, England (Home). *Telephone:* (0114) 222 2000 (Office); (0114) 236 1086 (Home).

BILDT, Carl; Swedish politician; b. 15 July 1949; m. Mia Bohman 1984; one s. one d.; ed. Univ. of Stockholm; Ed. Svensk Linje 1969–73; Chair. Confed. of Liberal and Conservative Students 1973–74, European Democrat Students 1974–76; mem. Stockholm County Council 1974–77; Political Advisor on Policy Co-ordination Ministry of Econ. Affairs 1976–78; Under-Sec. of State for Co-ordination and Planning at the Cabinet Office 1979–81; M.P. 1979–; mem. Exec. Cttee. Moderate Party 1981–; mem. Parl. Standing Cttee. on Foreign Affairs 1982–86; mem. Advisory Council on Foreign Affairs 1982–; mem. Submarine Defence Comm. 1982–83; mem. 1984 Defence Policy Comm. 1984–87; Chair. Moderate Party 1986–; Prime Minister of Sweden 1991–94; EU Peace Envoy in fmr. Yugoslavia 1995; High Rep. of the Int. Community in Bosnia and Herzegovina 1995–97; mem. Int. Inst. for Strategic Studies, London; Vice-Chair. Int. Democrat Union (IDU) 1989–92, Chair. 1992–. *Publications:* Landet som steg ut i kylan 1972, Framtid i frihet 1976, Hallanning, svensk, europe 1991, Peace Journey 1999. *Address:* Sveriges Riksdag, 10012 Stockholm, Sweden. *Telephone:* 786 4000.

BILGRAV-NIELSEN, Jens; Danish politician; b. 14 May 1936, Ølstrup; teacher 1963–65; mem. Folketing (Parl.) 1966–77, 1979–; Minister of Energy 1988; mem. Gen. Council, Radical Liberal Party 1973–, Deputy Chair. Parl. Group 1973–73, Nat. Council 1977–79; mem. N. Schleswig Cttee., Liaison Cttee. of Prime Minister's Dept., Defence Comm. 1969–73, Radio Council 1982–87, Finance Cttee. 1968–71, 1979–88; Minister of Energy 1988–90; Chair. Finance Cttee. 1990–. *Address:* Dyrehavegard, Engelsholm, 7182 Bredsten, Denmark.

BILHEIMER, Rev. Robert Sperry, B.A., B.D.; American ecclesiastic; b. 28 Sept. 1917, Denver, Colo.; s. of George Steven and Katherine Elizabeth Bilheimer; m. Dorothy Dodge 1942; three s.; ed. Phillips Exeter Acad., Yale Univ., Yale Divinity School; Minister, Westminster Presbyterian Church 1946–48; Sec. The Inter-Seminary Movement 1945–48; Programme Sec., World Council of Churches, New York 1948–54, Assoc. Gen. Sec., Dir. of the Division of Studies, Geneva 1954–63; Senior Minister, Central Presbyterian Church, Rochester, N.Y. 1963–66; Dir. Int. Affairs Programs, The Nat. Council of Churches of Christ in the U.S.A. 1966–74; Exec. Dir. Inst. for Ecumenical and Cultural Research, St. John's Univ. 1974–84; Hon. D.D. (Chicago Theological Seminary 1954, Butler Univ. 1954, Hamilton Coll. 1980). *Publications:* What Must the Church Do? 1947, The Quest for Christian Unity 1952, Faith and Ferment (Ed.) 1983, A Spirituality for the Long Haul 1984, Breakthrough, the Emergence of the Ecumenical Tradition 1989. *Leisure interests:* trout fishing, photography.

BILLAUD, Bernard; French civil servant; b. 3 Sept. 1942, Béziers; m. Claude Devitry 1967; two s. one d.; ed. Inst. d'etudes politiques de Paris and Ecole nat. d'admin.; Auditor 1968, Public Auditor Cour des Comptes 1976, Conseiller maître 1989; Adviser to French Embassy, Holy See 1974–76; Official Rep. to the Prime Minister 1976; Sr. Lecturer Institut d'études politiques de Paris 1977–92; Dir. of Staff, Mayor of Paris 1979–83; mem. comm. Vieux Paris 1983–; Pres. comm. on historical works of Ville de Paris 1983–; Dir.-Gen. Int. Relations, Paris 1983–84; Gen. Commr. of the French Language 1987–89; Prime Minister's Rep. of Admin. Council of AFP 1993–98, France 3 1995–98; Vice-Pres. organizing cttee. for 'de la Gaule à la France' 1996. *Publication:* l'Aide de l'Etat à l'enseignement privé 1966. *Leisure interest:* history. *Address:* 77 rue Claude Bernard, 75005 Paris, France (Home).

BILLESKOV-JANSEN, Frederik Julius, DR.PHIL.; Danish professor; b. 30 Sept. 1907, Hvidbjerg; s. of Hans Billeskov-Jansen and Bothilde Schack-Schou; m. Vibeke Collet Henrichsen 1938; one s. two d.; ed. Københavns Universitet; Asst. lecturer in Danish, Univ. of Copenhagen 1935–38, Prof. 1941–77; lecturer, Univ. de Paris à la Sorbonne 1938–41; Ed. Orbis Litterarum 1943–50; mem. Emer. Royal Danish Acad. of Sciences and Letters, mem. Int. Asscns. of Comparative Literature and of German Language and Literature, mem. Danish Acad.; Pres. Søren Kierkegaard Soc., Alliance Française, Copenhagen; Commdr. Order of Dannebrog, Ingenio & Arti, Officier, Légion d'honneur, Officier, Ordre des Palmes académiques. *Publications:* Danmarks Digtekunst I-III 1944–58, Holberg som Epigrammatiker og Essayist 1939, Editions of Holberg: Moralske Tanker 1943, Epistler 1954, Memoirer 1963, Vaerker i tolv Bind 1969–71, Ludvig Holberg 1974; Søren Kierkegaards Litteraere Kunst 1951, Søren Kierkegaards: Vaerker i Udvalg 1950, Poetik (Vols. I and II) 1941–48, Den Danske Lyrik 1961–66, Esthétique de l'œuvre d'art littéraire 1948, L'Age d'or 1953, Anthology of Danish Literature (French edn. 1964, English edn. 1971, Italian edn. 1973, Dutch edn. 1973, Japanese edn. 1976, German edn. 1978, Portuguese edn. 1981, Spanish edn. 1984), Verdens Litteraturhistorie I-XII (Chief Ed.) 1971–74, Verdenslitteratur 1982, Humanitas Christiana; also articles in Scandinavian and international reviews. *Address:* Frydendalsvej 20, 1809 Frederiksberg C., Denmark. *Telephone:* 31-316369.

BILLINGHAM, Rupert Everett, M.A., D.PHIL., D.SC., F.R.S.; British zoologist; b. 15 Oct. 1921, Warminster, Wilts.; s. of Albert Everett Billingham and Helen Louise Green; m. Jean Mary Morpeth 1951; two s. one d.; ed. Oxford Univ.; Lecturer, Dept. of Zoology, Birmingham Univ. 1947–51; Research Fellow of British Empire Cancer Campaign, and Hon. Research Assoc., Dept. of Zoology, Univ. Coll. London 1951–57; mem. Wistar Inst. of Anatomy and Biology, Philadelphia, U.S.A. 1957–65; Prof. of Zoology, Univ. of Pa. 1958–71; Prof. and Chair. Dept. of Medical Genetics, and Dir. Phipps Inst. of Medical Genetics, Univ. of Pa. School of Medicine 1965–71; Prof. and Chair. Dept. of Cell Biology and Anatomy, Univ. of Tex. Health Science Centre at Dallas, Tex. 1971–86, Prof. Emer. 1990–; Pres. The Transplantation Soc. 1974–76, Int. Soc. for Immunology of Reproduction 1983–86; Fellow, New York Acad. of Sciences, American Acad. Arts and Sciences; Fellow Royal Soc. 1961–; Hon. D.Sc., Trinity Coll. (Conn.); Alvarenga Prize, Coll. of Physicians of Philadelphia; Hon. Award Medal, American Asscn. of Plastic Surgeons; F. L. Adair Award, American Gynaecological Soc. 1971; Peter Medawar Prize for The Immunobiology of Mammalian Reproduction (jtly.) (The Transplantation Soc.) 1994. *Publications:* Transplantation of Tissues and Cells (ed. with W. K. Silvers) 1961, Wound Healing (ed. with W. Montagna) 1964, Epithelial-Mesenchymal Interactions (ed. with R. Fleischmajer) 1968, Immunology and the Skin (ed. with W. Montagna) 1971, The Immunobiology of Transplantation (with W. K. Silvers) 1971, The Immunobiology of Mammalian Reproduction (with A. E. Beer) 1976, numerous scientific publications on tissue transplantation immunology, immunological tolerance, immunological aspects of mammalian reproduction and the biology of skin, in Royal Soc. and other journals. *Leisure interests:* gardening, travel. *Address:* R.R.3–Box 86P, Vineyard Haven, MA 02568, U.S.A. *Telephone:* (508) 693-7939.

BILLINGTON, James Hadley, PH.D.; American historian and librarian; b. 1 June 1929, Bryn Mawr, Pa.; s. of Nelson Billington and Jane Coolbaugh; m. Marjorie A. Brennan 1957; two s. two d.; ed. Princeton Univ. and Univ. of Oxford; army service 1953–56; Instructor in History, Harvard Univ. 1957–58, Fellow, Russian Research Center 1958–59, Asst. Prof. of History 1958–61; Assoc. Prof. of History, Princeton Univ. 1962–64, Prof. 1964–73; Dir. Woodrow Wilson Int. Center for Scholars, Washington, D.C. 1973–87; Librarian of Congress, Library of Congress, Washington, D.C. 1987–; Visiting Research Prof. Inst. of History of U.S.S.R. Acad. of Sciences 1966–67, Univ. of Helsinki 1960–61, Ecole des Hautes Etudes en Sciences Sociales, Paris 1985, 1988; visiting lecturer to various univs. in Europe and Asia etc.; Guggenheim Fellow 1960–61; mem. American Acad. of Arts and Sciences, American Philosophical Soc.; Chair. Bd. of Foreign Scholarships (Fulbright Program) 1971–73; writer/host The Face of Russia (TV series) 1998; Chevalier Ordre des Arts et des Lettres, Gwangha Medal (Repub. of Korea), Woodrow Wilson Award 1992, Kt. Commdr.'s Cross of the Order of Merit (Germany) 1996; 22 hon. degrees. *Publications:* Mikhailovsky and Russian Populism 1958, The Icon and the Axe: An Interpretive History of Russian Culture 1966, Fire in the Minds of Men: Origins of the Revolutionary Faith 1980, Russia Transformed: Breakthrough to Hope 1992, The Face of Russia 1998; contribs. to books and journals. *Address:* Library of Congress, First and Independence Avenues, Washington, DC 20540-1000, U.S.A. *Telephone:* (202) 707-5205. *Fax:* (202) 707-1714.

BILLINGTON, Kevin, B.A.; British film, theatre and television director; b. 12 June 1934; s. of Richard and Margaret Billington; m. Lady Rachel Mary Pakenham 1967; two s. two d.; ed. Bryanston School and Queens' Coll. Cambridge; film dir. BBC programme Tonight 1960–63; documentary film dir., BBC 1963–67; Chair. BAFTA 1989–90, 1990–91; *feature films:* Interlude 1967, The Rise and Rise of Michael Rimmer 1969, The Light at the Edge of the World 1970, Voices 1974, Reflections 1984; *scripts:* Looking For Love 1997, Loving Attitudes 1997, Bodily Harm 1999; *television films:* And No One Can Save Her 1973, Once Upon a Time is Now (documentary) 1978, The Music Will Never Stop (documentary) 1979, Henry VIII 1979, The Jail Diary of Albie Sachs 1980, The Good Soldier 1981, Outside Edge 1982, The Sonnets of William Shakespeare 1984, The Deliberate Death of a Polish Priest 1986, Heartland 1989, A Time to Dance 1991; *plays directed:* Find Your Way Home 1970, Me 1973, The Birthday Party 1974, The Caretaker 1975, Bloody Neighbours 1974, Emigrés 1976, The Homecoming 1978, Quartermaine's Terms 1982, The Deliberate Death of a Polish Priest 1985, The Philanthropist 1986, The Lover, and A Slight Ache (double bill) 1987, The Breadwinner 1989, Veterans Day 1989, Quartermaine's Terms 1993, Old Times 1994, Six Characters in Search of an Author 1999; Screenwriters' Guild Award 1966, 1967, Guild of TV Producers and Directors Award 1966, 1967. *Leisure interests:* swimming, football (Queen's Park Rangers). *Address:* The Court House, Poyntington, Sherborne, Dorset, DT9 4LF; 33 Courtnell Street, London, W2 5BU, England. *Telephone:* 0171-727 4811.

BILLINGTON, Michael Keith, B.A.; British drama critic and author; b. 16 Nov. 1939, Leamington Spa; s. of Alfred R. Billington and Patricia Bradshaw; m. Jeanine Bradlaugh 1977; one d.; ed. Warwick School and St. Catherine's Coll. Oxford; Public Liaison Officer, Theatre Royal, Lincoln 1962–64; writer on theatre, film and cinema, The Times 1965–71; Drama Critic, The Guardian 1971–, Country Life 1988–; presenter of various BBC Radio arts programmes including Options, Kaleidoscope, Meridian, etc. 1971–91; writer on London arts scene for The New York Times 1984–94;

writer and presenter of TV profiles of Peter Hall, Alan Ayckbourn, Peggy Ashcroft 1988–90; IPC Critic of the Year 1974, Theatre Critic of the Year 1993, 1995. *Publications:* The Modern Actor 1973, Alan Ayckbourn 1983, Tom Stoppard 1987, Peggy Ashcroft 1988, One Night Stands 1993, The Life and Work of Harold Pinter 1996. *Leisure interests:* cricket, opera, travel. *Address:* 15 Hearne Road, London, W4 3NJ, England. *Telephone:* 0181-995 0455.

BILNEY, Gordon, B.D.S., B.A.; Australian politician and fmr. diplomatist; b. 21 June 1939, Renmark, S. Australia; s. of Neil Joseph Bilney and Elaine May (née Aitchison) Bilney; m. Elizabeth Gunton 1967 (divorced 1995); two d.; ed. Univ. of Adelaide; mem. personal staff successive Ministers for Foreign Affairs 1973–75; joined Diplomatic Service, Dept. of Foreign Affairs 1966, served in Jakarta, Manila, Geneva, Paris, then High Commr. in West Indies 1980–82, Head OECD, EC and Energy Br. Dept. of Foreign Affairs Econ. Div. 1982–83; mem. House of Reps. for Kingston 1983–96; Minister for Defence Science and Personnel 1990–93; Minister for Devt. Co-operation and for Pacific Island Affairs 1993–96; Chair. Parl. Jt. Cttee. on Foreign Affairs, Defence and Trade 1987; Labor Party. *Leisure interests:* gardening, reading, fishing, tennis, chess. *Address:* 2 Jervois Terrace, Marino, S.A. 5049, Australia.

BIN LADEN, Osama; Saudi Arabian guerrilla leader; b. Jeddah, Saudi Arabia; s. of late Mohammad bin Laden; joined troops fighting against Soviet Union in Afghanistan 1979; co-f. group to send aid to Afghan resistance and establish recruitment centres mid-1980s; f. org. to support Islamic opposition movements 1988; expelled from Saudi Arabia for anti-govt. activities 1991, from Sudan following pressure from U.S.A. and UN 1996; continues to support Islamic extremist activities from Afghanistan.

BINAISA, Godfrey Lukwongwa, LL.B.; Ugandan politician and lawyer; b. 30 May 1920, Kampala; ed. King's Coll., Budo, Makerere Univ., King's Coll., London, Lincoln's Inn, London; in private legal practice 1956–62, 1967–79; mem. of Uganda Nat. Congress, later of Uganda People's Congress; Attorney-Gen. 1962–67; Pres. Uganda Law Soc., Chair. Law Devt. Centre 1968; mem. Uganda Judicial Service Comm. 1970; Chair. Organizing Cttee. for Commonwealth Lawyers' Conf., 1972; went into exile; in legal practice in New York; returned to Uganda 1979 after fall of Govt. of Pres. Idi Amin Dada (q.v.); Pres. of Uganda 1979–80, also Minister of Foreign Affairs June–July 1979, Minister of Defence; Chancellor, Makerere Univ. 1979–80; under house arrest 1980–81; left Uganda Jan. 1981; went to Britain.

BINCHY, Maeve; Irish writer; b. 28 May 1940; d. of William Binchy and Maureen Blackmore; m. Gordon Snell 1977; teacher of History and French, Pembroke School, Dublin 1961–68; columnist, Irish Times 1968–; Hon. D.Lit. (Queen's Belfast) 1998. *Publications:* (short stories) Central Line 1978, Silver Wedding 1979, Victoria Line 1980, Dublin Four 1982, The Lilac Bus 1984; (novels) Light a Penny Candle 1982, London Transports 1983, Echoes 1985, Firefly Summer 1987, Circle of Friends 1990, Copper Beech 1992, The Glass Lake 1994, Evening Class 1996. *Address:* c/o The Irish Times, 11–15 D'Olier Street, Dublin 2; Dalkey, Co. Dublin, Ireland.

BINDER, Theodor, M.D.; Peruvian physician; b. 1919; ed. Hebel-Gymnasium Lörrach, Univs. of Freiburg, Strasbourg, and Basel, and Swiss Tropical Inst., Basel; Clinic Chief, Swiss Tropical Inst. 1947–48; Public Health Officer, Oxapampa, Peru 1948–50; Staff, Medical School, Nacional Mayor de San Marcos de Lima 1951–56; Founder of Clinic for the Poor, and constructor of Hospital, Pucallpa 1956–60, Inauguration Hospital Amazónico Albert Schweitzer, Yarinacocha, Pucallpa 1960, Dir. 1960–; Founder and Dir. Instituto Tropical Amazónico 1963–; Exec. Dir. Amazonian Indian Int. Devt., Toronto and New York 1971–. *Publications:* Philosophy: Friedrich Nietzsche 1950, Goethe's Iphigenia and the Ethics 1951, A. Schweitzer as a Philosopher 1954, Heroism as an Attitude towards Life 1956, Personal Ethics in a Depersonalizing Age 1963, Tristes Tropiques or Land of Hope 1968, The Right to an Independent Development in the Third World 1970, Sense and Nonsense of the Christian Mission among Jungle Indians 1970, Problems of Intercultural Relations 1971; Medicine: Congenital Malaria 1950, Treatment of Hypertension 1952, Latin-America: Nonanalytical Psychotherapy 1958, Histoplasmosis in Eastern Peru 1964, Dermatomycosis and Deep Mycosis in Eastern Peru 1965, etc.

BINDING, Günther, DR.ING., DR.PHIL.; German professor of art and architecture; b. 6 March 1936, Koblenz; s. of Kurt Binding and Margot (née Masur); m. Elisabeth Dietz 1969; one s. two d.; ed. gymnasium in Arnsberg and Cologne, Technische Hochschule, Aachen, and Univs. of Cologne and Bonn; Dir. Lower Rhine section, Rheinisches Landesmuseum, Bonn 1964–70; Prof., Univ. of Cologne 1970–, Rector 1981–83, Pro-rector 1983–85; Vice-Pres. W. German Rectors' Conf. 1982–84; Ruhrpreis für Kunst und Wissenschaft 1966, Josef-Humar-Preis 1986, Rheinland-Taler 1987. *Publications:* 30 books and 280 articles about European architecture and history of art. *Address:* Wingertsheide 65, 51427 Berg.-Gladbach, Germany. *Telephone:* 02204/64956.

BINGAMAN, Jeff, J.D.; American politician and lawyer; b. 3 Oct. 1943, Silver City, N.M.; s. of Jesse Bingaman and Beth Ball; m. Ann Kovacovich 1968; one s.; ed. Harvard and Stanford Univs.; admitted to N.M. Bar 1968; partner Campbell, Bingaman & Black, Santa Fe 1972–78; Attorney-Gen., N.M. 1979–82; Senator from New Mexico Jan. 1983–; Democrat. *Address:* U.S. Senate, 703 Hart Senate Building, Washington, DC 20510 (Office); P.O. Box 5775 Santa Fe, NM 87502, U.S.A. (Home).

BINGHAM, John, C.B.E., F.R.S.; British scientist; b. 19 June 1930; s. of Thomas Frederick Bingham and Emma Maud Lusher; m. Jadwiga Anna Siedlecka 1983; one s.; mem. staff Plant Breeding Inst., Cambridge 1954–86, Deputy Chief Scientific Officer Plant Breeding Int. Cambridge Ltd. 1981–91; research in plant breeding has culminated in production of improved winter wheat varieties for British Agric.; Pres. Royal Norfolk Agric. Asscn 1991; Hon. Fellow Royal Agric. Soc. of England 1983; Mullard Medal of Royal Soc. 1975, Royal Agric. Soc. of England Research Medal 1975; Massey Ferguson Nat. Award for Services to U.K. Agric. 1984. *Leisure interests:* farming and wildlife conservation. *Address:* Hereward Barn, Church Lane, Mattishall Burgh, Dereham, Norfolk, NR20 3QZ, England. *Telephone:* (01362) 858354.

BINGHAM OF CORNHILL, Baron (Life Peer) cr. 1996, of Boughrood in the County of Powys, **Thomas (Henry) Bingham,** Kt., P.C., M.A.; British judge; b. 13 Oct. 1933; s. of late Dr. T. H. Bingham and Dr. C. Bingham; m. Elizabeth Loxley 1963; two s. one d.; ed. Sedbergh School, Balliol Coll. Oxford; called to Bar, Gray's Inn 1959, Bencher 1979; Standing Jr. Counsel to Dept. of Employment 1968–72; Q.C. 1972; Recorder of Crown Court 1975–80; Judge, High Court of Justice, Queen's Bench Div. and Judge, Commercial Court 1980–86; a Lord Justice of Appeal 1986–92; Master of the Rolls 1992–96; Lord Chief Justice of England 1996–; Leader, Investigation into supply of petroleum and petroleum products to Rhodesia 1977–78; mem. Lord Chancellor's Law Reform Cttee.; Chair. Inquiry into the Supervision of BCCI 1991–92; Commr. Interception of Communications 1985, 1992–94; Chair. numerous other comms.; Special Trustee St. Mary's Hosp. 1985–92 (Chair. 1988–92). *Publication:* Chitty on Contracts (Asst. Ed.) (22nd edn. 1961). *Address:* Royal Courts of Justice, Strand, London, W.C.2, England.

BINKERT, Pius; Swiss businessman; b. 22 May 1923, Laufenburg; m. Yolanda Binkert-Gerster; four s. two d.; ed. Business Schools of Schwyz and Fribourg; Man. Dir. AG für Keramische Industrie Laufen and Tonwarenfabrik Laufen AG 1953–70; Del. of Bd. Keramik Holding AG Laufen 1971–88; mem. Cttee. Bd. of Dirs. Keramik Holding SA Laufen; mem. Cttee. Bd. of Dirs. Alusuisse-Lonza S.A., Zürich; mem. Bd. of Dirs. Swiss Bank Corpn., Basel; mem. Bd. Swiss Life Insurance Co., Zürich, mem. Bd. of cos. associated with Forbo Holding S.A., Keramik Holding S.A. *Leisure interests:* swimming, skiing, music, hunting. *Address:* Obere Hohe 10, CH-4242 Laufen, Switzerland. *Telephone:* 061 89 66 31.

BINMORE, Kenneth George, PH.D., F.B.A.; British professor of economics; b. 27 April 1940, London; s. of Ernest Binmore and Maud Binmore (née Holland); m. Josephine Ann Lee 1972; two s. two d.; ed. Imperial Coll., London Univ.; Prof. of Mathematics L.S.E. 1974–88; Prof. of Econs., Univ. of Mich. 1988–93, Univ. Coll. London 1993–; Dir. Centre for Econ. Learning and Social Evolution 1995–; Fellow Econometric Soc. *Publications include:* Mathematical Analysis 1977, Economics of Bargaining 1986, Playing Fair; Game Theory and the Social Contract I 1994, Just Playing: Game Theory and the Social Contract II 1998. *Leisure interest:* philosophy. *Address:* Department of Economics, University College London, Gower Street, London, WC1E 6BT, England (Office); Newmills, Whitebrook, Monmouth, Gwent, NP5 4TY, Wales (Home). *Telephone:* 0171-380 7864 (Office); (01600) 860 691 (Home).

BINNIG, Gerd; German physicist; b. 20 July 1947, Frankfurt-am-Main; m. Lore Wagler 1969; one s. one d.; mem. Physics group, IBM Zürich Research Lab. Rüschlikon 1978–, Group Leader 1984–; Assignment to IBM Almaden Research Centre, San José, collaboration with Stanford Univ., Calif. 1985–86, 1987; IBM Fellow 1986; Visiting Prof. Stanford Univ. 1986–; Hon. Prof. (Univ. of Munich) 1986–; Hon. Fellow (Royal Microscopical Soc.) 1988; Foreign Assoc. mem. Acad. of Sciences, Wash. 1987; mem. IBM Acad. 1989, Bd. Mercedes Automobil Holding AG 1989–93, Bd. Daimler Benz Holding 1990–; shared Nobel Prize for Physics (with E. Ruska and H. Rohrer) 1986; Physics Prize of German Physical Soc. 1982, Otto Klung Prize 1983, shared King Faisal Int. Prize for Physics and Hewlett Packard Europhysics Prize 1984, Eliot Cresson Medal (Franklin Inst., Phila.) 1987; D.S.M., O.M. (Fed. Repub. Germany) 1987; Minnie Rosen award (Ross Univ., N.Y.) 1988, Bayerischer Verdienstorden 1992. *Leisure interests:* music, sports. *Address:* Zurich IBM Research Laboratory, Säumer Strasse 4, CH-8803 Rüschlikon, Switzerland. *Telephone:* (1) 7248-111.

BINNS, Malcolm; British concert pianist; b. 29 Jan. 1936, Nottingham; s. of Douglas Priestley Binns and May Walker; ed. Bradford Grammar School, Royal Coll. of Music; soloist with maj. British orchestras 1960–; toured with Scottish Nat. Orchestra and Limbourg Orchestra 1987–88; has performed many times at the Promenade Concerts and broadcast regularly on the BBC; more than 30 recordings, including Balakirev Piano Concertos 1 and 2 and Rimsky-Korsakov Piano Concerto (English Northern Philharmonia) 1992; concerts at Aldeburgh, Leeds, Three Choirs and Canterbury Festivals; Chappell Medal 1956, Medal of Worshipful Co. of Musicians 1956. *Leisure interest:* gardening. *Address:* 233 Court Road, Orpington, Kent, BR6 9BY, England. *Telephone:* (01689) 31056.

BINOCHE, Juliette; French actress; b. Paris; d. of Jean-Marie Binoche and Monique Stalens; one s. by Andre Halle; ed. Nat. Conservatory of Drama and private theatrical studies. *Films include:* Les nanas, La vie de famille,

Rouge Baiser, Rendez-Vous, Mon beau-frère a tué ma soeur, Mauvais Sang, Un tour de manège, Les amants du Pont-Neuf, The Unbearable Lightness of Being, Wuthering Heights 1992, Damage 1992, Trois Couleurs: Bleu 1993, Le Hussard sur le Toit 1995, The English Patient (Acad. Award for Best Supporting Actress 1996, Berlin Film Festival Award 1996, B.A.F.T.A. Award 1997); play Naked (Almeida, London) 1998. *Address:* c/o UTA, 9560 Wilshire Boulevard, Floor 5, Beverly Hills, CA 90212, U.S.A.

BIO, Brig.-Gen. Julius Maada; Sierra Leonean army officer; fmr. Vice-Chair. Supreme Council of State; Chair. Sierra Leone Nat. Provisional Ruling Council Jan.–June 1996.

BIOBAKU, Saburi Oladeni, C.M.G. PH.D.; Nigerian historian and university official; b. 16 June 1918, Abeokuta; s. of Sanni Oloyede Biobaku and Saudatu Ayinke Biobaku; m. Muhabat Folasade Agusto 1949; four s.; ed. Government Coll., Ibadan, Higher Coll., Yaba, Univ. Coll. Exeter, Trinity Coll. Cambridge and Inst. of Historical Research, London; Master, Govt. Coll., Ibadan 1941–44; Educ. Officer Govt. Coll., Umuahia 1947–50; Asst. Liaison Officer for Nigerian Students in U.K., Colonial Office, London 1951–53; Registrar, Univ. Coll., Ibadan 1953–57; Sec. to Premier and Exec. Council, W. Nigeria 1957–61; Pro Vice-Chancellor, Dir. Institutes of African Studies and of Public Admin., Univ. of Ife 1961–65; Vice-Chancellor, Univ. of Zambia Feb.-March 1965; Vice-Chancellor, Dir. Inst. of African Studies, Univ. of Lagos 1965–72; Research Prof. and later Dir. Inst. of African Studies, Univ. of Ibadan 1976–83; Chair. Cttee. of Vice-Chancellors, Nigeria 1967–70, Standing Cttee., Encyclopaedia Africana 1968, Antiquities Comm. 1967–79; mem. Exec. Bd. Asscn. of African Univs. 1967–72; Pres. Historical Soc. of Nigeria 1968–71; Chair. Management Consultants Services Ltd. 1972–76, 1983–; Chair. Nigerian Textile Mills plc 1977; created Aare of Iddo 1958, Agbaakin of Igbore, Abeokuta 1972, Maye of Ife 1980, Baapitan of Egbaland 1980, Baloguen of Iddo 1981; Fellow, Nigerian Inst. of Man. 1980; Historical Soc. of Nigeria 1980; Hon. Fellow, W. African Asscn. of Surgeons 1968. *Publications:* The Origin of the Yoruba 1955, The Egba and their Neighbours 1957, African Studies in an African University 1963, Sources of Yoruba History 1972, Living Cultures of Nigeria (Ed.) 1977, When We Were Young 1992, A Window on Nigeria 1995. *Address:* 2 Alhaji B.A., Agusto Close, Ilupeju, Lagos; P.O. Box 7741, Lagos, Nigeria. *Telephone:* (1) 961430.

BIOKE MALABO, Capt. Cristino Seriche; Equatorial Guinean politician and army officer; Second Vice-Pres. and Minister of Health 1981–82; Prime Minister of Equatorial Guinea 1982–91; Minister of Govt. Co-ordination, Planning, Economic Devt. and Finance 1982–86, of Health 1986, now in Charge of Political and Admin. Co-ordination. *Address:* c/o Oficina del Primer Ministro, Malabo, Equatorial Guinea.

BIONDI, Alfredo; Italian politician and lawyer; 29 June 1928, Pisa; m. Giovanna Susak; two c.; fmr. mem. Liberal Party (PLI), Nat. Sec. 1985–86; PLI Deputy 1968–92; Unione di Centro (Liberta) Deputy 1992–94, Forza Italia Deputy March 1994–; Minister of Justice 1994–95. *Address:* c/o Ministero di Grazie e Giustizia, Via Arenula 71, 00186 Rome, Italy.

BIONDI, Frank J., Jr., M.B.A.; American business executive; b. 9 Jan. 1945, New York; s. of Frank Biondi and Virginia Willis; m. Carol Oughton 1974; two d.; ed. Princeton and Harvard Univs.; Assoc. corporate finance, Prudential Securities, New York 1969, Shearson-Lehman Inc. New York 1970–71; Prin. Frank Biondi & Assocs. New York 1972; Dir. business analysis, Teleprompter Corpn. New York 1972–73; Asst. Treas., Assoc. Dir. Business Affairs, Children's TV Workshop, New York 1974–78; Dir. Entertainment Planning, HBO, New York 1978, Vice-Pres. programming operations 1979–82, Exec. Vice-Pres. Planning and Admin. 1982–83, Pres. and C.E.O. 1983, Chair. and C.E.O. 1984; Exec. Vice-Pres. entertainment business sector, The Coca-Cola Co. 1985; Chair. and C.E.O. Coca-Cola TV 1986; Pres., C.E.O. and Dir. Viacom Int. Inc. New York 1987–; Pres., C.E.O. and Dir. Viacom Inc. 1987–96; Chair., C.E.O. Universal Studios Inc. 1996–98; Dir. Seagram 1996–. *Address:* c/o Seagram Co. Ltd., 1430 Peel Street, Montreal, Quebec H3A 1S9, Canada.

BIRCH, Bill; New Zealand politician; b. 1934, Hastings; m.; four c.; qualified as surveyor; served six years as Deputy Mayor of Pukekohe; Nat. Party M.P. 1972–; apptd. Jr. Opposition Whip 1974–75, Sr. Govt. Whip 1975; successively, Minister of Energy, of Regional Devt., of Nat. Devt., and of Science and Tech. 1978–84; Opposition Leader of House 1985–90; Minister of Labour and Immigration 1990–93, also of Employment 1991–93; Minister of Health 1993–94, of Finance 1994–, Treasurer 1998–, also fmrly. of Revenue. *Address:* Parliament Buildings, Wellington, New Zealand.

BIRCH, Bryan John, PH.D., F.R.S.; British mathematician; b. 25 Sept. 1931, Burton-on-Trent; s. of Arthur Birch and Mary Birch; m. Gina Margaret Christ 1961; two s. one d.; ed. Shrewsbury School and Trinity Coll., Cambridge; Research Fellow, Trinity Coll. 1956–60; Sr. Research Fellow, Churchill Coll., Cambridge Univ. 1960–62; Sr. Lecturer, later Reader, Univ. of Manchester 1962–65; Reader in Mathematics., Oxford Univ. 1966–85, Prof. of Arithmetic 1985–98, Fellow of Brasenose Coll. 1966–, Professorial Fellow 1985–98; Del. of Oxford Univ. Press 1988–98. *Publications:* scholarly articles, particularly on number theory. *Leisure interests:* theoretical gardening, listening to music, watching marmots. *Address:* Green Cottage, Boars Hill, Oxford, OX1 5DQ; Mathematical Institute, 25–29 St. Giles, Oxford, OX1 3LB, England. *Telephone:* (01865) 735367; (01865) 273525.

BIRCH, L. Charles, B.AGR.SC., D.SC.; Australian academic; b. 8 Feb. 1918, Melbourne; s. of Harry Milton Birch and Honoria Eleanor Hogan; ed. Scotch Coll., Melbourne, Univs. of Melbourne and Adelaide; Research Fellow, Waite Agricultural Research Inst., Adelaide 1939–46; Sr. Overseas Research Scholar, Zoology Dept., Univ. of Chicago, U.S.A. 1946, Oxford Univ., U.K. 1947; Sr. Lecturer in Zoology, Univ. of Sydney 1948–54, Reader in Zoology 1954–60, Challis Prof. of Biology 1960–83, Prof. Emer. 1984–; Fulbright Research Scholar, Zoology Dept., Columbia Univ., New York 1954; Visiting Prof. Univ. of Minn. 1958; Visiting Prof. of Genetics, Univ. of Calif., Berkeley 1967; Fellow Australian Acad. of Science; mem. Club of Rome; David Syme Prize, Univ. of Melbourne 1954, Eminent Ecologist Award, Ecological Soc. America 1988, Gold Medal, Ecological Soc. Australia 1988, Templeton Prize 1990. *Publications:* Nature and God 1965, Confronting the Future 1976; (Co-author) The Distribution and Abundance of Animals 1954, Genetics and the Quality of Life 1975, The Liberation of Life 1981, The Ecological Web 1984, On Purpose 1990, Liberating Life 1990, Regaining Compassion 1993, Feelings 1995, Living with the Animals 1997. *Leisure interests:* surfing, music (organ). *Address:* 5A/73 Yarranabbe Road, Darling Point, N.S.W. 2027, Australia. *Telephone:* (02) 362-3788.

BIRCH, Peter Gibbs, C.B.E.; British business executive; b. 4 Dec. 1937; m. Gillian Benge 1962; three s. one d.; ed. Allhallows School, Devon; served Royal West Kent Reg. 1957–58; with Nestlé Co. 1958–65; Sales Man. Gillette 1965, Gen. Sales Man. Gillette Australia 1969, Man. Dir. Gillette NZ 1971, Gen. Man. Gillette SE Asia 1973, Group Gen. Man. Gillette, Africa, Middle East, Eastern Europe 1975, Man. Dir. Gillette UK 1981; Dir. Abbey Nat. (fmrly. Abbey Nat. Bldg. Soc.) 1984–, Chief Exec. 1984–88, Chief Exec. Abbey Nat. PLC 1988–98; Dir. Hoskyns Group 1988–93, Argos 1990–, Scottish Mutual 1992–, Dalgety 1993–, N. M. Rothschild and Sons 1998–; mem. Bd. Land Securities PLC 1997– (Chair. 1998–), Dah Sing Financial Holdings 1997–; Chair. Trinity PLC 1998–; Chair. Council of Mortgage Lenders 1991–92; Pres. Middx. Asscn. of Boys' Clubs 1988–. *Leisure interests:* active holidays, swimming. *Address:* N. M. Rothschild and Sons, New Court, St. Swithins Lane, London, EC4P 4DU, England. *Telephone:* 0171-280 5000.

BIRD, Harold Dennis 'Dickie', M.B.E.; British international umpire and cricketer; b. 19 April 1933, Barnsley, Yorks.; s. of James Harold Bird and Ethel Bird; ed. Raley Secondary Modern School, Barnsley; right-hand batsman and right-arm medium-fast bowler; teams: Yorkshire 1956–59, Leicestershire 1960–64; scored 3,314 runs (average 20.71) with 2 hundreds; First-Class Umpire 1970–; umpired 67 Test matches (world record 1973–96) and 93 Limited-Overs Internationals (1973–97), including 1975, 1979, 1983 and 1987–88 World Cups (officiating in the first 3 finals) and seven Sharjah tournaments; served on Int. Umpires Panel 1994 to 1995–96; Hon. life mem. Yorks. Co. Cricket Club, Leics. Co. Cricket Club, Marylebone Cricket Club; Dr. h.c. (Sheffield Hallam) 1995, (Leeds) 1996; voted Yorks. Personality of the Year 1977, Yorkshireman of the Year 1996. *Publications:* Not Out 1978, That's Out 1985, From the Pavilion End, Dickie Bird, My Autobiography 1997. *Leisure interest:* watching football. *Address:* White Rose Cottage, 40 Paddock Road, Staincross, Barnsley, Yorks. S75 6LE.

BIRD, Lester Bryant, B.A.; Antiguan politician; b. 21 Feb. 1938; m.; one s. four d.; ed. Antigua Grammar School, Univ. of Michigan and Gray's Inn, London; lawyer in pvt. practice 1969–76; Chair. Antigua Labour Party (ALP) 1971–; Senator, Upper House of Parl. and Leader of Opposition in Senate 1971–76; mem. Parl. 1976–; Deputy Premier and Minister of Econ. Devt., Tourism and Energy 1976–81; Deputy Prime Minister and Minister of Foreign Affairs, Econ. Devt., Tourism and Energy 1981–91; Minister of External Affairs, Planning and Trade 1991–94; Prime Minister of Antigua & Barbuda 1994–, and Minister of External Affairs, Planning, Social Services and Information 1994, of Communications, Civil Aviation and Int. Transport 1996–98, of Foreign Affairs, Social Services, Civil Aviation and Int. Transport and Information 1998–; del. to numerous Caribbean and int. confs. *Address:* Office of the Prime Minister, Factory Road, St. John's, Antigua, West Indies.

BIRD, Vere Cornwall, Sr.; Antiguan politician; b. 9 Dec. 1909, St. John's; ed. St. John's Boys' School; joined Salvation Army as teenager; trained at Salvation Army Training School, Trinidad, then posted to Grenada; mem. Exec. Antigua Trades and Labour Union (AT&LU) on its foundation, 16 Jan. 1939; Pres. AT&LU 1943–67; elected mem. Legis. Council of Antigua 1945, re-elected 1946 (also mem. Exec. Council), 1951 (also a Chair. of Cttees., Exec. Council –1956); Minister of Trade and Production 1956–60; first Chief Minister of Antigua 1960–67; Premier of Antigua 1967–71, 1976–81; lost seat in Gen. Election 1971; re-elected to Parl. 1976, 1980, 1984, 1990; Prime Minister of Antigua and Barbuda 1981–93; Minister of Planning, External Affairs, Defence and Energy 1981–82, of Finance 1982–84; attended Caribbean Union Confs., Trinidad 1945, St. Kitts 1946, Jamaica 1947; West Indian Govt. Confs., Lancaster House, London 1953, 1956; with Errol Barrow (Barbados) and Forbes Burnham (Guyana), formed Caribbean Free Trade Asscn. 1965; Leader del. to U.K. which gained Assoc. Statehood for Antigua 1966; Leader del. to U.K. which gained full independence for Antigua from Britain Dec. 1980; Leader Antigua Labour Party; Chancellor Bryant House Schools and Univ.; Nat. Hero of Antigua and Barbuda 1996, Kt. Grand Cross, Order of Emperor Haile Selassie I 1996. *Leisure interest:* reading. *Address:* Tomlinsons, St. John's, Antigua, West Indies.

BIRENDRA BIR BIKRAM SHAH DEV, King of Nepal; b. 28 Dec. 1945, Kathmandu; s. of late King Mahendra and Princess Indra; m. Queen Aishwarya Rajya Laxmi Devi Shah 1970; two s. one d.; ed. St. Joseph's Coll.,

Darjeeling, Eton Coll., England, Univ. of Tokyo and Harvard Univ.; has travelled extensively throughout Europe, North and South America, U.S.S.R., Iran, Japan, China and several African countries; Grand Master of all medals and decorations of the Kingdom of Nepal; Supreme Commdr.-in-Chief, Royal Nepalese Army; Patron Royal Nepal Acad. of Science and Tech., King Mahendra Trust for Nature Conservation, Lumbini Devt. Trust, Pashupati Area Devt. Trust; Chancellor Tribhuvan Univ., Mahendra Sanskrit Univ.; Hon. Field-Marshal (U.K.) 1980 and numerous other decorations; came to the throne 31 Jan. 1972, crowned 24 Feb. 1975. *Leisure interests:* nature conservation, riding, painting. *Address:* Narayanhity Royal Palace, Kathmandu, Nepal.

BIRIDO, Omer Yousif, M.A.; Sudanese diplomatist; b. 1939; m. 1966; five c.; ed. Univ. of Khartoum and Delhi Univ., India; Third Sec., Sudan Embassy, New Delhi 1963–66, Second Sec., London 1966–69; Deputy Dir., Consular Dept., Ministry of Foreign Affairs 1969–71; Counsellor Sudan Embassy, Kampala 1971–73; Minister Plenipotentiary, Perm. Mission of Sudan to the UN, New York 1973–76; Dir. Dept. of Int. Orgs., Ministry of Foreign Affairs 1976–77, Dir. Dept. of African Affairs 1977–78; Perm. Rep. to UN, Geneva and Vienna, also mem. Sudan Del. and Rep. to Second Cttee. at UN Gen. Ass. 1979–83; Perm. Rep. to UN 1984–86; Amb. to Saudi Arabia 1989–96. *Address:* c/o Ministry of Foreign Affairs, Nasseriya Street, Riyadh 11124, Saudi Arabia.

BIRINDWA, Faustin; Democratic Republic of the Congo politician; b. Southern Kivu Region; m.; co-f. Union pour la démocratie et le progrès social (UDPS); Minister of Finance in Tshisekedi Govt. Oct. 1991; formed breakaway faction within UDPS Feb. 1993, expelled for "political truancy" March 1993; appointed Prime Minister by political "conclave" controlled by Pres. Mobutu March 1993; Tshisekedi appointed Prime Minister by Nat. Conclave Aug. 1992; replaced by Kengo Wa Dondo (q.v.) June 1994.

BIRK, Roger Emil; American business executive; b. 14 July 1930, St. Cloud, Minn.; s. of Emil Birk and Barbara E. (née Zimmer) Birk; m. Mary Louise Schrank 1955; one s. three d.; ed. St. John's Univ., Collegeville, Minn.; Div. Dir. of Operations, Merrill, Lynch, Pierce, Fenner & Smith 1970–74, mem. Bd. of Dirs. 1971, Pres. 1974–76; mem. Bd. of Dirs. Merrill, Lynch & Co. Inc. (parent co.) 1974, Pres. 1976–81, Chair. of Bd. 1980–85, Chair. Emer. 1985–, C.E.O. 1980–84, mem. Advisory Council; Vice-Chair. Bd., New York Stock Exchange 1983–85; Chair. Bd. Int. Securities Clearing Corpn. 1986–87; Pres. and C.O.O. Fed. Nat. Mortgage Asscn., Wash. 1987–; Trustee Notre Dame Univ. 1981–. *Leisure interest:* golf. *Address:* Federal National Mortgage Association, 3900 Wisconsin Avenue, NW, Washington, DC 20016, U.S.A. (Office).

BIRKAVS, Valdis; Latvian politician; b. 28 July 1942, Riga; s. of Voldemars Birkavs and Veronika Birkavs (née Zihelmane); m. Aina Zileva 1967; one s.; ed. Riga Industrial Polytech. School, Univ. of Latvia; expert, sr. researcher, Head of div. Latvian Research Lab. of Forensic Medicine and Criminology 1969–86; lecturer, Univ. of Latvia 1969–86, Deputy Dean Law Faculty 1986–89; Founder and Pres. Latvian Bar Asscn. 1988–; Deputy to Supreme Council of Latvian Repub. from Popular Front of Latvia 1990–93, Deputy Chair. Legis. Cttee., Deputy Chair. Supreme Council of Latvian Repub. 1992–93; Prime Minister of Latvian Repub. 1993–94; Minister of Foreign Affairs 1994–. *Leisure interests:* tennis, yachting, reading, downhill skiing. *Address:* Ministry of Foreign Affairs, Brīvības blvd. 36, Riga 1395, Latvia. *Telephone:* 7016101. *Fax:* 7828121.

BIRKE, Adolf Mathias, PH.D., F.R.HIST.S.; German professor of modern and contemporary history; b. 12 Oct. 1939, Wellingholzhausen; s. of Matthias Birke and Maria Birke (née Enewoldsen); m. 1st Linde D. Birn 1968, 2nd Sabine Volk 1988; one s. two d.; ed. Univ. of Berlin, Univ. of Cambridge, U.K.; Prof. of Modern History, Free Univ. of Berlin 1979; Visiting Prof. of German and European Studies, Trinity Coll., Univ. of Toronto, Canada 1980–81; Asst. St. Antony's Coll., Oxford; Prof. of Modern History, Univ. of Bayreuth 1982–85, Univ. of Munich 1995–; Dir. German Historical Inst., London 1985–94; Chair. Prince Albert Soc. 1983–95; Cusanuswerk Grant 1962; Heisenberg Fellow 1979; Fed. Cross of Merit 1996. *Publications:* Bischof Ketteler und der deutsche Liberalismus 1971, Pluralismus und Gewerkschaftsautonomie 1978, Britain and Germany 1987, Nation ohne Haus. Deutschland 1945–1961 1989, Prince Albert Studies (Ed.) Vols. I–XIII 1983–95, Die Herausforderung des europäischen Staatensystems 1989, Princes, Patronage and the Nobility (ed. with R. Asch) 1991, The Quest for Stability (ed. with R. Ahmann and M. Howard) 1992, Control Commission for Germany (British Element) (11 vols.) Inventory (ed. with H. Booms and O. Merker) 1993, Die Bundesrepublik Deutschland. Verfassung, Parlament und Parteien 1997; numerous articles on 19th- and 20th-century German and English history. *Leisure interests:* music, walking. *Address:* University of Munich, Wagmüllerstr. 23/II, 80538 München; Herzogstr. 60/II, 80803 München, Germany. *Telephone:* (089) 21106-52. *Fax:* (089) 21106-93.

BIRKERTS, Gunnar, F.A.I.A.; American architect; b. 17 Jan. 1925, Riga, Latvia; s. of the late Peter Birkerts and of Merija Shop Birkerts; m. Sylvia Zvirbulis 1950; two s. one d.; ed. Technische Hochschule, Stuttgart, Germany; went to U.S.A. 1949; est. own practice 1959, Pres. Gunnar Birkerts and Assocs. Inc. 1963–; Prof. of Architecture, Univ. of Mich. 1959–90; numerous guest lectureships U.S.A., Canada, Mexico and Europe; Architect in Residence, American Acad. in Rome 1976; Fellow Latvian Architects' Asscn.; mem. Latvian Acad. of Sciences; Hon. Dr. (Riga Tech. Univ., Latvia) 1990; over 50 awards for projects; work exhibited U.S.A., Italy, Brazil, Latvia, Estonia, Yugoslavia. *Major projects include:* Lincoln Elementary School, Columbus, Ind., Fed. Reserve Bank of Minneapolis, Contemporary Arts Museum, Houston, Tex., IBM Corp. Computer Center, Sterling Forest, New York, Corning Museum of Glass, New York, Law Library Addition, Univ. of Mich., Ann Arbor, Coll. of Law Bldg., Univ. of Iowa, St. Peter's Lutheran Church, Columbus, Ind., Domino's World HQ Bldg., Ann Arbor Mich., Law School, Ohio State Univ., Columbus, Cen. Library Addition, Univ. of Calif. at San Diego, Kemper Museum of Contemporary Art, Kan. City, Mo., U.S. Embassy, Caracas, School of Law Addition, Duke Univ., Durham, N.C.; Library, Univ. of Mich.-Flint. *in progress:* Sports Centre, Venice, Italy, Novoli Multi-Use Centre, Florence, Italy, Nat. Library, Riga, Latvia, Univ. of Turin, Italy, Performing Arts Center, Mich. Technological Univ., Houghton; Marriott Library Expansion, Univ. of Utah, Market Master Plan, Riga, Latvia. *Address:* Gunnar Birkerts Architects, Inc., 1830 E. Tahquamenon Street, Bloomfield Hills, MI 48302, U.S.A. *Telephone:* (248) 626-5661. *Fax:* (248) 626-5101.

BIRKIN, Sir Derek, Kt., T.D.; British business executive; b. 30 Sept. 1929, S. Elmsall, Yorks.; s. of Noah and Rebecca (née Stranks) Birkin; m. Sadie Smith 1952; one s. one d.; ed. Hemsworth Grammar School; Man. Dir. Velmar Ltd. 1966–67, Nairn Williamson Ltd. 1967–70; Man. Dir. Tunnel Holdings Ltd. 1971–75, Chair. and Man. Dir. 1975–83; Dir. Rio Tinto-Zinc Corpn. 1982–96, Deputy Chief Exec. 1983–85, Chief Exec. and Deputy Chair. 1985–91, Chair. 1991–96; Chair. Watmoughs (Holdings) PLC 1996–; Dir. Smiths Industries Ltd. 1977–84, British Gas Corpn. 1982–85, George Wimpey PLC 1984–92, CRA Ltd. (Australia) 1985–94, Rio Algom Ltd. (Canada) 1985–92, The Merchants Trust PLC 1986–, British Steel Corpn. 1986–92, Barclays Bank PLC and Barclays PLC 1990–94, Merck & Co. Inc. (USA) 1992–, Carlton Communications PLC 1992–; mem. Council, Industrial Soc. 1986–97, U.K. Top Salaries Review Body 1986–89, Bd. Unilever PLC 1993–, Royal Opera House Bd. 1993–97. *Leisure interests:* opera, rugby, cricket. *Address:* 21 Manchester Square, London, W1M 5AP, England.

BIRKIN, Jane; French (b. British) actress and singer; b. 14 Dec. 1946, London; d. of David Birkin and Judy Campbell; m. John Barry (divorced) (q.v.); one d.; one d. by Serge Gainsbourg, one s. with Jacques Doillon. *Theatre includes:* Carving a Statue 1964, Passion Flower Hotel 1965, la Fausse suivante 1985, l'Aide-Mémoire 1993. *Films include:* The Knack 1965, Blow Up 1966, les Chemins de Katmandou 1969, Je t'aime moi non plus 1976, Mort sur le nil 1978, Jane B par Agnès V 1988, Noir comme le souvenir 1995. *Recordings of songs by Serge Gainsbourg include:* C'est la vie qui veut ça, la Baigneuse de Brighton, Je t'aime moi non plus (Le Métier trophy 1970), Di doo dah, le Canari est sur le balcon, Baby Song, Si ça peut te consoler, Tu n'es pas le premier garçon, Lolita Go Home, Love for Sale, la Ballade, Ex-fan des sixties, Baby Alone in Babylone (Grand Prix du disque, Acad. Charles-Cros); Gold Leaf Award Canada 1968, Triomphe du cinéma 1969, 1973, Victoire de la musique (for best female singer) 1992; Chevalier des Arts et des Lettres. *Address:* VMA, 10 avenue George V, 75008 Paris, France.

BIRKS, Jack, C.B.E., PH.D., F.ENG., F.INST.PET.; British business executive; b. 1 Jan. 1920, Chapeltown, Sheffield; s. of the late Herbert Horace Birks and of Ann Birks; m. Vere Elizabeth Burrell-Davis 1948; two s. two d.; ed. Ecclesfield Grammar School, Univ. of Leeds; served with REME in Europe and India (despatches, rank of Captain) 1941–46; Exploration Research Div., Anglo-Iranian Oil Co. 1948–57; Man. of Petroleum Eng. Research, BP Research Centre, Sunbury 1957–59; Vice-Pres. Exploration, BP North America 1959–62; various posts then Dir. and Gen. Man. Iranian Oil Exploration and Production Co. 1962–70; Gen. Man. Exploration and Production Dept., British Petroleum Co. Ltd. 1970–72; Tech. Dir. BP Trading Ltd. and Deputy Chair. BP Trading Exec. Cttee. 1972–77; Man. Dir. British Petroleum Co. Ltd. 1978–82; Chair. BP Minerals Int. 1981–82 (Dir. 1982–85), BP Coal 1981–82, LAE Energy Inc. 1981–88, London American Energy NV 1981–88, Charterhouse Petroleum PLC 1982–86, NMI Ltd. (now British Maritime Tech. Ltd.) 1982–85, Midland and Scottish Resources 1994–; Dir. George Wimpey 1981–90, Jebsens Drilling UK 1982–89; Pres. Inst. of Petroleum 1984–86; Chair. British Maritime Tech. Ltd. 1985–95; Dir. Petrofina (U.K.) Ltd. 1986–89, Mountain Petroleum PLC 1986–91 (Chair. 1988–91); Chair. North American Gas Investment Trust PLC 1989–95; Dir. Bellwether Exploration Co. 1988–, Midland & Scottish Resources PLC 1989–97 (Chair. 1992–97), Gulf Indonesia Resources Ltd. 1997–; Fellow Inst. of Mining and Metallurgy. *Publications:* articles in journals, scientific papers about oilfields developments and North Sea oil. *Leisure interests:* tennis, golf. *Address:* High Silver, High Street, Holt, Norfolk, NR25 6BN, England. *Telephone:* (01263) 712847.

BIRLA, Ganga Prasad, B.SC.; Indian industrialist; b. 2 Aug. 1922, Calcutta; s. of the late B. M. Birla and Rukmani Devi Birla; m. Nimala Devi Birla 1952; one s. one d.; ed. Calcutta Univ.; Chair. Hindustan Motors Ltd., Orient Paper & Industries Ltd. 1957–; Man. Dir. Birla Brothers Pvt. Ltd. 1982–; Chair. Bd. of Govs. Birla Inst. of Tech., Ranchi, Birla Inst. of Scientific Research; Pres. Bd. of Govs. Calcutta Medical Research Inst., Man. Cttee. B.M. Birla Heart Research Centre, Calcutta; Pres. Indian Paper Mills Asscn., Calcutta 1947–48, 1954–55, 1955–56, Employers' Asscn., Calcutta 1962–63, 1964–65; mem. Red Cross Soc. *Leisure interests:* music, art, literature, archaeology, sport, travel. *Address:* 9/1 R.N. Mukherjee Road, Calcutta 700

001 (Office); Birla House, 8/9 Alipore Road, Calcutta 700 027, India (Home). *Telephone:* 248 0135 (Office); 479 1285 (Home).

BIRNSTIEL, Max Luciano, DR. SC. NAT.; Swiss scientist; b. 12 July 1933, Salvador, Brazil; s. of Max Birnstiel and Dalila Varella; m. Margaret I. H. Chipchase 1961; one s. one d.; ed. Eidgenössische Tech. Hochschule Zürich; Postdoctoral Fellow, Biology Div., Calif. Inst. of Tech., Pasadena 1960–63; lecturer, MRC, Epigenetics Research Group, Univ. of Edin. 1963–66, Sr. lecturer 1966–69, Reader 1969–71, Prof. 1971–72; Prof. and Head Inst. of Molecular Biology II, Univ. of Zürich 1972–86; Man. Dir. Research Inst. of Molecular Pathology 1987–96; Consultant to Helmut Horden Foundation 1989–; Dr. Sc. Nat. h.c. (Fribourg), Dr. Phil. h.c. (Lund and Guelph, Toronto); Otto Naegli Prize 1979; Foreign Assoc. N.A.S. *Publications:* Structure and Function of Major and Minor snRNAs (ed.) 1988, and publs. in various scientific journals. *Leisure interest:* gardening. *Address:* Research Institute of Molecular Pathology, Dr. Bohr-Gasse 7, 1030 Vienna, Austria. *Telephone:* (01) 797 30/500.

BIRRELL, Sir James Drake, Kt., F.C.A., F.C.B.S.I.; British building society executive; b. 18 Aug. 1933; s. of James R. Birrell and Edith M. Drake; m. Margaret A. Pattison 1958; two d.; ed. Belle Vue Grammar School, Bradford; articled clerk, Boyce Welch & Co. 1949–55; R.A.F. 1955–57; chartered accountant, Price Waterhouse 1957–60; accountant, ADA Halifax 1960–61; man. accountant, Empire Stores 1961–64; Dir. and Co. Sec. John Gladstone & Co., 1964–68; with Halifax Bldg. Soc. 1968–93, Chief Exec. 1988–93; Dir. (non-exec.) Securicor 1993–, Wesleyan Gen. Assurance Soc. 1993–; mem. Bldg. Soc.'s Comm. 1994–. *Leisure interests:* golf, gardening, archaeology, local history. *Address:* Kinnesswood, Greenroyd Avenue, Skircoat Green, Halifax, HX3 0JN, England. *Telephone:* (01422) 345278.

BIRT, Sir John, Kt., M.A., F.R.T.S.; British broadcasting executive; b. 10 Dec. 1944, Liverpool; s. of Leo Vincent and Ida Birt; m. Jane Frances Lake 1965; one s. one d.; ed. St. Mary's Coll., Liverpool, St. Catherine's Coll., Oxford; Television Producer of Nice Time 1968–69, Jt. Editor World in Action 1969–70, Producer of The Frost Programme 1971–72, Exec. Producer of Weekend World 1972–74, Head of Current Affairs, London Weekend Television (LWT) 1974–77, Co-Producer of The Nixon Interviews 1977, Controller of Features and Current Affairs, LWT 1977–81, Dir. of Programmes 1982–87; Deputy Dir. Gen. BBC 1987–92, Dir. Gen. Dec. 1992–; Vice-Pres. Royal TV Soc. 1994– (Fellow 1989); mem. Media Law Group 1983–94, Working Party on New Techs. 1981–83, Broadcasting Research Unit, Exec. Cttee. 1983–87, Int. Museum of TV and Radio, New York, Opportunity 2000 Target Team, Business in the Community 1991–; Visiting Fellow Nuffield Coll., Oxford 1991–; Hon. Fellow Univ. of Wales, Cardiff 1997. *Leisure interest:* walking. *Address:* c/o BBC, Broadcasting House, Portland Place, London, W1A 1AA, England.

BIRT, Lindsay Michael, A.O., C.B.E., PH.D., D.PHIL., F.A.I.M.; Australian professor of biochemistry and academic; b. 18 Jan. 1932, Melbourne; s. of the late Robert Birt and Florence Elizabeth Chapman; m. Jenny Tapfield 1959; two s.; ed. Univ. of Melbourne, and Oxford Univ.; lecturer in Biochemistry, Univ. of Melbourne 1960–63, Sr. Lecturer 1964; Sr. Lecturer, Univ. of Sheffield 1964–67; Foundation Prof. and Head, Dept. of Biochemistry, A.N.U. 1967–73, Emer. Prof. 1974; Vice-Chancellor (desig.), then Vice-Chancellor, Univ. of Wollongong 1973–81; Vice-Chancellor and Prin., Univ. of New South Wales 1981–92; Chair. Australian Science and Tech. Council 1992–93; Hon. D. Litt. (Wollongong), Hon. LL.D. (Sheffield). *Publication:* Biochemistry of the Tissues (with W. Bartley and P. Banks) 1968. *Leisure interests:* music, art, drama, cricket, golf, Australian Rules football. *Address:* 85 Florida Road, Palm Beach, N.S.W. 2108, Australia (Home).

BIRTWISTLE, Sir Harrison, Kt.; British composer; b. 1934, Accrington, Lancs.; m. Sheila Birtwistle 1958; three s.; ed. Royal Manchester Coll. of Music and Royal Acad. of Music, London; Dir. of Music, Cranborne Chase School 1962–65; Visiting Fellow Princeton Univ. (Harkness Int. Fellowship) 1966; Cornell visiting Prof. of Music, Swarthmore Coll., Pa. 1973–74; Slee Visiting Prof., New York State Univ., Buffalo, N.Y. 1975; Assoc. Dir. Nat. Theatre 1975–88; Composer-in-Residence London Philharmonic Orchestra 1993–; Henry Purcell Prof. of Composition King's Coll., London Univ. 1994–; Hon. Fellow Royal Northern Coll. of Music 1990; Grawemeyer Award (Univ. of Louisville, Ky.) 1987; works have been widely performed at the major festivals in Europe including the Venice Biennale, the Int. Soc. of Contemporary Music Festivals in Vienna and Copenhagen, the Warsaw Autumn Festival and at Aldeburgh, Cheltenham and Edinburgh; formed, with Peter Maxwell Davies (q.v.), The Pierrot Players. *Works: operatic and dramatic:* The Mark of the Goat (cantata) 1965–66, The Visions of Francesco Petrarca (sonnets for baritone and orchestra) 1966, Punch and Judy (one-act opera) 1966–67; *orchestral works:* Chorales for Orchestra 1962–63, Three Movements with Fanfares 1964, Nomos 1968, The Triumph of Time 1970; *for instrumental ensemble:* Refrains and Choruses 1957, Monody for Corpus Christi 1959, The World is Discovered 1960, Entr'actes and Sappho Fragments 1964, Ring a Dumb Carillon 1965, Tragoedia 1965, Three Lessons in a Frame 1967, Verses for Ensembles 1969, Grimethorpe Aria 1973; *choral works: Narration:* Description of the Passing of a Year 1964, Carmen Paschale 1965; *additional compositions:* The Mask of Orpheus (opera) 1974–81, Down By The Greenwood Side 1969, Nenia on the Death of Orpheus 1970, Melencolia I 1976, Silbury Air 1977, Meridian, For O For O the Hobby Horse is Forgot 1977, agm. 1979, On the Sheer Threshold of the Night 1980, Pulse Sampler 1980, Yan Tan Tethera 1983, Still Movement, Secret Theatre 1984, Earth Danses, Words Overhead 1985, Fanfare for Will 1987, Endless Parade 1987, Gawain (opera) 1990, Four Poems by Jaan Kaplinski 1991, The Second Mrs Kong 1992, Antiphonies 1992, Cry of Anubis 1995, Panic 1995, Pulse, Shadows 1997, Exody 1998; also several pieces of instrumental music. *Address:* c/o Allied Artists Agency, 42 Montpelier Square, London, SW7 1JZ, England.

BISCHOFF, Winfried Franz Wilhelm ('Win'), B.COM.; German merchant banker; b. 10 May 1941, Aachen; s. of late Paul Helmut and Hildegard (née Kühne) Bischoff; m. Rosemary Elizabeth Leathers 1972; two s.; ed. Marist Bros., Johannesburg and Univ. of the Witwatersrand; Man. Dir. Schroders Asia Ltd. (fmrly. Schroders & Chartered Ltd.), Hong Kong 1971–82; Dir. J. Henry Schroder & Co. Ltd., London 1978, Head of Int. Issues 1982, Head of Corp. Finance 1983, Chair. 1983–94; Dir. Schroders PLC 1983, Group Chief Exec. 1984–95, Chair. 1995–; Dir. (non.-exec.) Cable and Wireless plc., Deputy Chair 1995–. *Leisure interests:* opera, music, golf. *Address:* Schroders PLC, 120 Cheapside, London, EC2V 6DS, England (Office). *Telephone:* 0171-382 6000 (Office).

BISHER, Ilmar, DR.SC.IUR; Latvian politician and lawyer; b. 1 Nov. 1930, Riga, Latvia; m. 1st Benita Samuilova 1958 (divorced 1975), m. 2nd Aina Bullite 1975; two s.; ed. Latvia Univ.; professor of law, Latvia Univ.; mem. Latvian Popular Front 1989–92; U.S.S.R. People's Deputy (representing Latvian constituency) 1989–91; Deputy Chair. U.S.S.R. Supreme Soviet Council of Nationalities 1989–90; First Vice-Chair. Council of Ministers of Latvia 1990–91, Counsellor to Prime Minister 1991–93; barrister, Chair. Bisers & Partneri 1993–; Pres. Latvian Certificate Fund 1994–95, Asscn. of Securities Market Participants 1994–95; mem. Constitutional Comm., Democratic Party of Latvia 1992–, Parl. 1995–. *Address:* Sporta St. 1, Apt. 3, LV-1001 Riga, Latvia.

BISHOP, Sir George Sidney, Kt., C.B., O.B.E., B.SC.; British company executive; b. 15 Oct. 1913, Wigan, Lancs. (now Greater Manchester); s. of late J. and M. Bishop; m. 1st Marjorie Woodruff (divorced 1961); one d.; m. 2nd Una Padel 1961; ed. Ashton-in-Makerfield Grammar School, London School of Econs.; social service work in distressed areas 1935–38; South West Durham Survey 1939; Ministry of Food 1940; Private Sec. to Minister of Food 1945–49; Under-Sec. Ministry of Agric., Fisheries and Food 1949–59, Deputy Sec. 1959–61; Dir. Booker McConnell Ltd. 1961–82, Vice-Chair. 1970–71, Chair. 1972–79; Chair. Int. Sugar Council 1957; Vice-Chair. Int. Wheat Council 1959; Chair. Bookers Agricultural Holdings Ltd. 1964–70; Dir. Nigerian Sugar Co. Ltd. 1966–70; mem. Panel for Civil Service Manpower Review 1968–70, Royal Comm. on the Press 1974–77; Dir. Barclays Bank Int. 1972–83, Agricultural Mortgage Corpn. Ltd. 1973–79, Barclays Bank 1974–83, Rank Hovis McDougall 1976–84, Int. Basic Economy Corpn., U.S.A. 1981–83; Chair. Overseas Devt. Inst. 1977–84; Pres. West India Cttee. 1977–, Britain-Nepal Soc. 1979–89; Gov. Nat. Inst. of Econ. and Social Research 1968–; Vice-Pres. Royal Geographical Soc. 1981–84, Pres. 1984–87; mem. Council of CBI 1973–79. *Leisure interests:* mountaineering, photography. *Address:* Brenva, Egham's Wood Road, Beaconsfield, Bucks., HP9 1JX, England. *Telephone:* (01494) 673096.

BISHOP, James Drew, B.A.; British journalist; b. 18 June 1929, London; s. of late Sir Patrick Bishop and Vera Drew; m. Brenda Pearson 1959; two s.; ed. Haileybury Coll., Hertford and Corpus Christi Coll., Cambridge; reporter, Northampton Chronicle 1953; editorial staff of The Times (London) 1954–70, Foreign Corresp. 1957–64, Foreign News Ed. 1964–66, Features Ed. 1966–70; Ed. The Illustrated London News 1971–87, Newsweek Int. Diary 1977–88; Dir. Int. Thomson Publishing Co. 1980–85; Editorial Dir. Orient Express, Connections and Natural World Magazines 1981–94; Ed.-in-Chief Illustrated London News Publs. 1987–94; contrib. to The Annual Register 1960–88, mem. Advisory Bd. 1970–; Chair. Editorial Bd. Natural World 1981, Asscn. of British Eds. 1987–95; Trustee Nat. Heritage 1994–. *Publications:* A Social History of Edwardian Britain 1977, Social History of the First World War 1982, The Story of The Times (with O. Woods) 1983, Illustrated Counties of England (ed.) 1985, The Sedgwick Story 1998. *Address:* 11 Willow Road, London NW3 1TJ, England (Home). *Telephone:* 0171-435 4403 (Home).

BISHOP, John Michael, M.D.; American scientist; b. 22 Feb. 1936; m. 1959; two c.; ed. Gettysburg Coll. and Harvard Univ.; intern in internal medicine Mass. Gen. Hosp., Boston 1962–63, Resident 1963–64; Research Assoc. in Virology, N.I.H., Washington, D.C. 1964–66, Sr. Investigator 1966–68, Asst. Prof. to Assoc. Prof. 1968–72; Prof. of Microbiology and Immunology, Univ. of Calif. Medical Center, San Francisco 1972–, Prof. of Biochemistry and Biophysics 1982–; Dir. G. W. Hooper Research Foundation 1981–; Univ. Prof. Univ of Calif. Medical Center, San Francisco 1994–, Chancellor 1998–; Gairdner Foundation Int. Award 1984; Medal of Honor, American Cancer Soc. 1984; Nobel Prize for Physiology or Medicine 1989, and many other awards and distinctions. *Address:* University of California Medical Center, Box 0552, San Francisco, CA 94143-0552, U.S.A.

BISHOP, Sir Michael (David), Kt., C.B.E.; British business executive; b. 10 Feb. 1942; s. of Clive Bishop and Lilian Frost; ed. Mill Hill School; joined Mercury Airlines, Manchester 1963, British Midland Airways Ltd. 1964–; Chair. British Midland PLC (fmrly. Airlines of Britain Holdings PLC) 1978–, Manx Airlines 1982, Loganair 1978; Deputy Chair. Channel 4 TV Corpn. 1991–93, Chair. 1993–97; Chair. D'Oyly Carte Opera Trust Ltd. 1989–;

Deputy Chair. Airtours PLC 1996– (Dir. 1987–); Dir. Williams PLC 1993; Hon. D. Tech. (Loughborough Univ. of Tech.) 1989; Hon. D. Litt. (Salford) 1991, Hon. LL.D. (Nottingham) 1993, Hon. D.Univ. (Cent. England) 1993, Hon. D.Litt. (Coventry) 1994. *Address:* Donington Hall, Castle Donington, Derby, DE74 2SB, England. *Telephone:* (01332) 854000.

BISHOP, Peter Orlebar, A.O., M.B., B.S., D.SC., F.A.A., F.R.S.; Australian academic; b. 14 June 1917, Tamworth, N.S.W.; s. of the late Ernest John Hunter Bishop and Mildred Alice Havelock Vidal; m. Hilare Louise Holmes 1942; one s. two d.; ed. Barker Coll., Hornsby, N.S.W., Sydney Univ. Medical School; Resident Medical Officer and Neurological Registrar, Royal Prince Alfred Hosp., Sydney 1941–42; Surgeon Lieut., R.A.N.R. 1942–46; Fellow, Postgraduate Cttee. in Medicine, Univ. of Sydney 1946–50; at Nat. Hosp. for Nervous Diseases, London 1946–47 and Dept. of Anatomy, Univ. Coll., London 1947–50; Fellow, Dept. of Surgery, Univ. of Sydney 1950–51, Sr. lecturer 1951–54, Reader 1954–55, Prof. and Head 1955–67, Dept. of Physiology, Univ. of Sydney; Prof. and Head of Dept. of Physiology, Australian Nat. Univ., Canberra 1967–82, Prof. Emer. 1983–; Visiting Fellow, Dept. of Behavioural Biology, Australian Nat. Univ., 1983–84; Research Assoc. Univ. of Sydney 1987–; Visiting Prof. Osaka Univ. Medical School 1974, Keio Univ. Medical School Tokyo 1982, Katholieke Univ., Leuven 1984–85, Univ. of Zürich 1985; Visiting Fellow, St. John's Coll., Cambridge 1986; hon. mem. various socs.; Hon. M.D. (Univ. of Sydney) 1983; Australia Prize (jtly.) 1993. *Leisure interest:* bushwalking. *Address:* Department of Anatomy, University of Sydney, N.S.W. 2006 (Office); 139 Cape Three Points Road, Avoca Beach, N.S.W. 2251, Australia (Home).

BISHOP-KOVACEVICH, Stephen (see Kovacevich, Stephen.)

BISIGNANI, Giovanni, LL.M.; Italian airline executive; b. 1946, Rome; m.; one d.; ed. Univ. of Rome and Harvard Business School; Sr. Asst. Prof. in Public Law, Univ. of Rome 1969; with First Nat. City Bank, New York 1970; research and econ. planning, EFIM, Rome 1973; Asst. to Pres. ENI, Rome 1976; Corp. Vice-Pres. and Asst. to Pres. IRI, Rome 1979, Corp. Vice-Pres. (Foreign Affairs) 1981, Corp. Sr. Vice-Pres. and Head of Foreign Affairs 1983; Man. Dir. and C.E.O. Alitalia 1989; Chair. Galileo Int. (global computer reservation system group) 1993–; mem. Bd. Galileo Distribution System Ltd., ILVA (IRI steel co.), Italo-German Chamber of Commerce, Inst. for Int. Affairs. *Publications:* articles on law, economic and financial subjects in professional publs. *Address:* c/o Alitalia, Palazzo Alitalia, Piazzale Giulio Pastore, 00144, Rome, Italy.

BISSAT, Bahaeddine; Lebanese politician and engineer; b. 1923, Saida; s. of Sobhi Bissat and Mariam Mekkawi; m. Itaff Bissat 1950; two s. one d.; Pres. Order of Engineers and Architects 1970–72, 1974, 1975–; Chair. al-Makassed Soc., Saida, Lebanese Standards Inst. (LIBNOR); Minister of Hydraulic and Electric Resources, Housing and Co-operatives 1982–84; Pres. Bahaeddine Bissat UNIBUILD Contracting Co.; mem. Higher Council and Urban Planning. *Leisure interests:* reading, travelling. *Address:* P.O.B. 11-6460, 804 Corniche Mazraa, Beirut, Lebanon. *Telephone:* 300736; 301568.

BISSELL, Claude T(homas), C.C., PH.D.; Canadian university administrator; b. 10 Feb. 1916, Meaford, Ont.; s. of George Thomas Bissell and Maggie Editha (Bowen) Bissell; m. Christina Flora Gray 1945; one d.; ed. Runnymede Collegiate Inst., Toronto, Cornell and Toronto Univs; Reuben Wells Leonard Fellowship 1936, Cornell Fellowship 1937; Instructor in English, Cornell Univ. 1938–41; lecturer in English, Toronto Univ. 1941–42; served in Canadian Army in Europe 1942–45; on staff of Khaki Coll. England 1945–46; Asst. Prof. of English, Dean in Residence, Univ. Coll. Toronto Univ. 1947; Asst. to Pres. Toronto Univ. 1948, Assoc. Prof. 1951, Vice-Pres. of Univ. 1952–56, Pres. 1958–71, Univ. Prof. 1971–83, now Emer.; Pres. Carleton Univ., Ottawa 1956–58; Chair. Canada Council 1960–62; Pres. Nat. Conf. Canadian Univs. and Colls., World Univ. Service of Canada 1962–; Chair. Canadian Univs. Foundation 1962–; Pres. World Univ. Service of Canada 1962–63; Visiting Prof. of Canadian Studies on William Lyon Mackenzie King Endowment, Harvard Univ. 1967–68; Chair. Carnegie Foundation for Advancement of Teaching 1966; Hon. mem. American Acad. of Arts and Sciences 1968; Hon. D.Litt. (Manitoba, Laval, Western Ont., Lethbridge, Leeds, Toronto), Hon. LL.D. (McGill, Queen's, New Brunswick, Carleton, Montreal, St. Lawrence, British Columbia, Michigan, York, Windsor, St. Andrews and Columbia Univs.); Companion of the Order of Canada 1969. *Publications:* Great Canadian Writing 1966, The Strength of the University 1968, Halfway Up Parnassus, A Personal Account of the University of Toronto, 1932–1971, Ed. and Contrib. to University College: A Portrait 1853-1953, Canada's Crisis in Higher Education, Our Living Tradition, The Humanities in the University 1977, The Young Vincent Massey 1981, The Imperial Canadian 1982; many articles. *Leisure interests:* swimming, photography. *Address:* 229 Erskine Avenue, Toronto, Ont. M4P 1Z5, Canada (Home). *Telephone:* 483-9616 (Home).

BISSET, Jacqueline; British actress; b. 13 Sept. 1944, Weybridge; ed. French Lycée, London; film début in The Knack 1965. *Other films include:* Two for the Road 1967, Casino Royale 1967, The Sweet Ride 1968, The Detective 1968, Bullitt 1968, The First Time 1969, Airport 1970, The Grasshopper 1970, The Mephisto Waltz 1971, Believe in Me 1971, The Life and Times of Judge Roy Bean 1972, Stand Up and Be Counted 1972, The Thief Who Came to Dinner 1973, Day for Night 1973, Murder on the Orient Express 1974, The Spiral Staircase 1974, End of the Game 1974, St. Ives 1975, The Deep 1976, Le Magnifique 1977, Sunday Woman 1977, The Greek Tycoon 1978, Secrets 1978, Too Many Chefs 1978, I Love You, I Love You Not 1979, When Time Ran Out 1980, Rich and Famous 1981, Inchon 1981, Class 1982, Under the Volcano 1983, Forbidden 1986, Choices 1986, High Season 1988, Scenes from the Class Struggle in Beverly Hills 1989, Wild Orchid 1989, La Cérémonie 1995, The Maid, A Judgement in Stone, Once You Meet a Stranger 1996, The Honest Courtesan 1996, Let the Devil Wear Black 1998. *Address:* c/o William Morris Agency, 151 El Camino Drive, Beverly Hills, CA 90212, U.S.A.; VMA, 10 avenue George V, 75008 Paris, France.

BISSINGER, Frederick Lewis, M.E., M.S., J.D.; American chemical executive; b. 11 Jan. 1911, New York; s. of Jacob Frederick Bissinger and Rosel (Ensslin) Bissinger; m. 1st Julia E. Stork 1935 (deceased); one s. one d.; m. 2nd Barbara S. Simmonds 1993; ed. Stevens Inst. of Technology and Fordham Univ.; Chemistry Instructor, Stevens Inst. of Technology 1933–36; lawyer, Pennie, Davis, Marvin & Edmonds 1936–42; various exec. positions, including Pres., Industrial Rayon Corpn. 1942–61; Group Vice-Pres. Midland-Ross Corpn. 1961–62; Vice-Pres. and Dir. Stauffer Chem. Corpn. 1962–65; Vice-Pres. Allied Chemical Corpn. 1965–66, Dir. 1966–76, Exec. Vice-Pres. 1966–69, Pres. 1969–74, Vice-Chair. 1974–76; Counsel to Pennie & Edmonds 1976–; Chair. Bd. Trustees, Stevens Inst. of Tech. 1971–83, Chair. Emer. 1983–; Trustee Fordham Univ. 1970–75, Emer. 1985–; Dir. Selas Corpn.; Former Dir. Midlantic Nat. Bank, Nat. Starch and Chemical Corpn., Neptune Int. Corpn., Otis Elevator Corpn., Rheingold Corpn.; mem. Bar N.Y., Dist. of Colo., Ohio, Supreme Court. *Address:* 9 West Irving Street, Chevy Chase, MD 20815, U.S.A. *Telephone:* (301) 657-8373.

BISSON, Thomas Noel, PH.D.; American professor of medieval history; b. 30 March 1931, New York; s. of Thomas A. Bisson and Faith W. Bisson; m. Margaretta C. Webb 1962; two d.; ed. Port Washington (N.Y.) High School, Haverford Coll., Univ. of Calif. (Berkeley) and Princeton Univ.; Instructor in History, Amherst Coll. 1957–60; Asst. Prof. Brown Univ. 1960–65; Assoc. Prof. Swarthmore Coll. 1965–67; Assoc. Prof. Univ. of Calif. (Berkeley) 1967–69, Prof. 1969–87; Prof. Harvard Univ. 1986–, Henry Charles Lea Prof. of Medieval History 1988–, Chair. Dept. of History 1991–95; mem. American Philosophical Soc.; Fellow, Medieval Acad. of America (Pres. 1994–95), Royal Historical Soc., British Acad. etc.; Guggenheim Fellow 1964–65; Dr h.c. (Barcelona) 1991. *Publications:* Assemblies and Representation in Languedoc in the Thirteenth Century 1964, Medieval Representative Institutions: Their Origins and Nature 1973, Conservation of Coinage: Monetary Exploitation and its Restraint in France, Catalonia and Aragon (c. AD 1000–c. AD 1225) 1979, Fiscal Accounts of Catalonia under the Early Count-Kings 1151–1213 (2 vols.) 1985, The Medieval Crown of Aragon: a Short History 1986, Medieval France and her Pyrenean Neighbors 1989, Tormented Voices: Power, Crisis, and Humanity in Rural Catalonia 1140–1200 1998; articles in journals. *Leisure interests:* classical music, English literature. *Address:* Department of History, Robinson Hall, Harvard University, Cambridge, MA 02138 (Office); 21 Hammond Street, Cambridge, MA 02138, U.S.A. (Home). *Telephone;* (617) 495-5221 (2504) (Office).

BISTA, Kirti Nidhi, M.A.; Nepalese politician; b. 1927; ed. Tri-Chandra Coll., Kathmandu and Lucknow Univ.; Assistant Minister for Education 1961–62, Minister for Educ. 1962–64, for Foreign Affairs 1964; Vice-Chair. Council of Ministers and Minister for Foreign Affairs and Educ. 1964–66; Vice-Chair. Council of Ministers and Minister for Foreign Affairs and Econ. Planning 1966–67; Deputy Prime Minister and Minister for Foreign Affairs and Educ. 1967–68, Perm. Rep. to UN 1968–69; Prime Minister 1969–70, 1971–73, 1977–79, Minister of Finance, Gen. Admin. and Palace Affairs 1969–73, of Finance, Palace Affairs and Defence 1978–79; mem. Royal Advisory Cttee. 1969–70; Leader Nepalese dels. to UN Gen. Assemblies 1964, 1965, 1966, and to UNESCO Gen. Confs. 1962, 1964, 1966, and to various other confs; accompanied H.M. the King on many State Visits; Order of the Right Hand of Gurkhas (First Class), Fed. German Order of Merit, Légion d'honneur. *Address:* Gyaneshwor, Kathmandu, Nepal (Home).

BISWAS, Abdul Rahman; Bangladeshi politician; fmr. Speaker, House of Ass.; Pres. of Bangladesh 1991–96. *Address:* c/o Office of the President, Dhaka, Bangladesh.

BITARAF, Habibollah, M.S.; Iranian government official; b. 1956, Yazd; m. Zahra Mansurie 1981; three d.; ed. Tehran Univ., Gov.-Gen. 1987–90; Deputy Minister for Energy 1991–95, Exec. Man. of Karon 3 and 4 (dam and energy plant) project 1995–97, Minister for Energy 1997–. *Publication:* Fluid Mechanics. *Leisure interests:* studying, mountaineering, table tennis, pilgrimage, travelling. *Address:* Ministry of Energy, no. 81, Felestin Shoumali Ave., Tehran 14154, Iran. *Telephone:* (0098-21) 898541. *Fax:* (0098-21) 895344.

BITAT, Rabah; Algerian politician; b. 19 Dec. 1925, Constantine Region; two s. one d.; joined Parti du Peuple Algérien 1940, Mouvement pour le Triomphe des Libertés démocratiques 1947; participated in formation of Organisation spéciale 1948; detained, sentenced to 10 years; participated in foundation of Comité révolutionnaire d'Unité et d'Action 1954, later of Front de Libération National; arrested March 1955, held in France till 1962; hunger strike, granted political status after being appointed Minister of State in Provisional Revolutionary Govt. of Algerian Repub. 1958; mem. Political Bureau, in charge of Party Org. 1962–63; Deputy Premier 1962–63, Third Deputy Premier 1963; in exile in France 1963–65; Minister of State 1965–66; Minister of State in charge of Transport 1966–77; Pres. Nat.

People's Assembly 1977–90; acting Pres. of Algeria 1978–79; Pres. Arab Parl. Union 1981, African Parl. Union 1984; mem. Exec. Cttee. Int. Parl. Union 1984, Vice-Pres. 1986. *Address:* c/o National People's Assembly, 18 Boulevard Ziroulh Youcef, Algiers, Algeria.

BITOV, Andrei Georgevich; Russian writer; b. 27 May 1937, Leningrad; m. Inga Petkevich; one d.; evacuated 1939–44; ed. Leningrad Mining Inst. worked as stevedore and lathe-operator 1958–62; researcher, Leningrad Mining Inst. 1962; started publishing 1960; mem. of 'Young Prose' group in 1960s with Aksyonov (q.v.) and Gladilin (q.v.); contributor to Metropol 1979; Pres. Russian PEN Centre 1992–; Andrey Bely Prize (Russia), Best Foreign Book Prize (Paris), Pushkin Prize (Germany), State Prize (Russia). *Publications include:* The Big Balloon 1963, Such a Long Childhood 1965, A Summer Place 1967, Apothecary Island 1968, Way of Life 1972, Seven Journeys 1976, Days of Man 1976, Pushkin House 1978, Sunday (short stories) 1980, A Man in the Landscape 1987, The Flying Monakhov 1990, We Woke Up in a Strange Country 1991, Awaiting Monkeys 1993, Empire in Four Dimensions (collected works), (Vols.) 1–4 1996. *Address:* Krasnoprudnaya str. 30/34, Apt. 14, 107140 Moscow, Russia. *Telephone:* (095) 209-45-89 (Office); (095) 264-12-93 (Home).

BITSCH, Hans-Ullrich; German architect and industrial designer; b. 13 June 1946, Essen; s. of Prof. Heinz W. and Lore L. (née Falldorf) Bitsch; m. Evelyn R. Koch 1981; two s.; ed. High School, Saarbrücken, State Coll. of Art, Saarbrücken, and Illinois Inst. of Tech.; architect, Univ. of Saarbrücken 1968; Instructor Int. Inst. of Design, Washington, D.C. 1969; Visiting Lecturer, Harrington Inst., Chicago, Ill. 1970–71; Prof. Dept. of Architecture, Düsseldorf Univ. 1972–; Pres. German Inst. of Interior Architects 1977–82; Visiting Prof., Univ. of Texas 1981; Pres. Professor Bitsch & Assocs. (design and architectural office), Düsseldorf; work represented in Smithsonian Inst., Design Collection, Stuttgart, and Stiftung Preussischer Kulturbesitz; several awards for architecture and design. *Publications:* Menschengerechte Gestaltung des Kassenarbeitsplatzes 1978, Farbe und Industrie-Design 1982, Design und Formentwicklung von Stuhlen 1988, Visuelle Wahrnehmung in Architektur und Design 1989, Projekt Hotel 1992. *Leisure interests:* skiing, sailing, photography. *Address:* Kaiser-Wilhelm-Ring 23, RiveGauche, 4000 Düsseldorf-Oberkassel 11, Germany. *Telephone:* (0211) 553820.

BIYA, Paul, L. EN D.; Cameroonian politician; b. 13 Feb. 1933, Mvomeka'a; m. 1st Jeanne (née Atyam) (deceased); one c.; m. 2nd Chantal Biya 1994; ed. Ndem Mission School, Edea and Akono Seminaries, Lycée Leclerc, Yaoundé, Univ. of Paris, Inst. d'Etudes Politiques, Inst. des Hautes Etudes d'Outre-Mer, Paris; Head of Dept. of Foreign Devt. Aid 1962–63; Dir. of Cabinet in Ministry of Nat. Educ., Youth and Culture 1964–65; on goodwill mission to Ghana and Nigeria 1965; Sec.-Gen. in Ministry of Educ., Youth and Culture 1965–67; Dir. of Civil Cabinet of Head of State 1967–68; Minister of State, Sec.-Gen. to Pres. 1968–75; Prime Minister 1975–82; Pres. of Cameroon Nov. 1982–; Second Vice-Pres., Central Cttee., mem. Union Nationale Camerounaise (UNC), Pres. 1983–85; Pres. Rassemblement Démocratique du Peuple Camerounais (RDPC) 1985–; mem. Politbureau; Commdr. de l'Ordre de la Valeur Camerounaise, Commdr. of Nat. Order of Fed. Repub. of Germany and of Tunisia, Grand Cross of Nat. Order of Merit of Senegal, Grand Officier, Légion d'honneur. *Publication:* Communal Liberalism 1987. *Address:* Office of the President, Yaoundé, Cameroon. *Telephone:* 23-40-25.

BIZIMUNGU, Pasteur; Rwandan politician; mem. Front patriotique rwandais (FPR); Pres. of Rwanda July 1994–. *Address:* Office of the President, BP 15, Kigali, Rwanda. *Telephone:* 75432.

BJARNASON, Gudmundur; Icelandic politician; b. 9 Oct. 1944, Húsavík; s. of Bjarni Stéfánsson and Jakobina Jónsdóttir; m. Vigdís Gunnarsdottir; three d.; ed. Húsavík Secondary School and Co-operative Coll.; with Co-operative Soc., Húsavík 1963–67; Húsavík Br. Co-operative Bank of Iceland 1967–77, Br. Dir. 1977–80; elected mem. Húsavík Town Council 1970, Chair. 1974; mem. Althing 1979–; Minister of Health and Social Security 1987–91, of Environment and Agric. April 1995–; mem. Althing Appropriation Cttee. 1979–87 and 1991–, Vice-Chair 1983–87; Chair. Cttee. on Housing Affairs; mem. jt. cttee. on public projects; Bd. Research Council; mem. Icelandic del. to Parl. Ass. of Council of Europe. *Address:* Ministry of the Environment, Vornarstraeti 4, 150 Reykjavík; Varnasel 1, 109 Reykjavík, Iceland. *Telephone:* 5578953. *Fax:* 562 4604.

BJARNASON, Matthias; Icelandic politician and businessman; b. 15 Aug. 1921, Isafjordur; s. of Bjarni Bjarnason and Audur Johannesdóttir; m. Kristin Ingimundardóttir 1944; one d. one s.; ed. Commercial Coll. of Iceland; Man. ferry co., Isafjordur 1942–68, Isafjordur Fishing Vessels' Mutual Insurance Soc. 1960–74; Man. Kögur Fishing Co. 1959–66; mem. Bd. Isfirdingur Fishing Co. 1947–59, Chair. 1950–59; mem. Isafjordur Town Council 1946–70, Chair. 1950–52; Chair. Bd. Isafjordur Electric Power Works 1946–51; Ed. Vesturland 1953–59; mem. Bd. Union of Icelandic Fishing Vessel Owners 1962–74, also other owners' socs.; mem. Cttee. State Shipping Authority 1966–; Supplementary mem. Althing 1963–67, mem. for West Fjords 1967–; Chair. Icelandic Fishing Vessels Joint Insurance Inst. 1967–74; mem. Bd. Icelandic Fish Industries Fund 1969–74, Employment Equalization Fund 1970–71, Econ. Devt. Inst. 1972–; Chair. Exec. Cttee. Fish Industry Bd. 1968–74; mem. Independence Party, on Cen. Cttee. 1970–; Minister of Fisheries, Health and Social Security 1974–78, of Health, Social Security and Communications 1984–85, of Trade and Commerce 1985–87. *Leisure interests:* reading, travelling. *Address:* Tjaldanes 5, Gardabaer, Iceland. *Telephone:* (1) 25000.

BJELKE-PETERSEN, Hon. Sir Johannes, K.C.M.G.; Australian politician; b. 13 Jan. 1911, Dannevirke, New Zealand; s. of Carl G. and Maren (née Poulsen) Bjelke-Petersen; m. Florence Gilmour 1952; one s. three d.; ed. Taabinga Village Primary School, correspondence courses and private studies; Farmer; mem. Queensland Legislative Assembly 1947–; Minister for Works and Housing, Queensland 1963–68, later of Aboriginal and Island Affairs, and Police; Leader of Country (National) Party of Queensland 1968–87, (split 1987), Leader New Nat. Party of Australia (right wing of old party) 1987–88; Premier of Queensland 1968–87. *Leisure interests:* flying, reading, bush-walking. *Address:* P.O. Box 141, Kingaroy, Queensland 4610, Australia.

BJERREGAARD, Ritt; Danish politician; b. 19 May 1941, Copenhagen; d. of Rita Bjerregaard; m. Søren Mørch 1966; mem. Parl. 1971–95; Minister of Educ. 1973, 1975–78, for Social Affairs 1979–81; Chair. Parl. Group, Social Democratic Party (SDP) 1981–92, 1987–92, Deputy Chair. 1982–87; Chair. Parl. Cttee. on Public Accounts 1990–95; mem. Parl. Assembly of Council of Europe 1990–95; Pres. Danish European Movt. 1992–94; Vice-Pres. Parl. Ass. of CSCE 1992–95; Vice-Pres. Socialist Int. Women 1992–94; EU Commr. for Environment 1995–; mem. Trilateral Comm., Centre for European Policy Studies. *Publications:* several books on politics in general and the role of women in politics. *Leisure interests:* her apple farm, organic farming, the environment. *Address:* European Commission, 200 rue de la Loi, 1049 Brussels, Belgium.

BJERVE, Petter Jakob, CAND. OECON., D.PHIL.; Norwegian economist and fmr. politician; b. 27 Sept. 1913, Stjördal; s. of Petter Jakob Bjerve and Kristine Arnstad; m. Rannveig Bremer 1942; three s.; ed. Univ. of Oslo; Research Asst. Economics Inst., Oslo Univ. 1939–40; Research Fellow, Oslo Univ. 1945–49; Chief of Div. Ministry of Finance 1945–49; Dir.-Gen. Central Bureau of Statistics of Norway 1949–60, 1963–80; Visiting Prof., Stanford Univ. 1954–55; Minister of Finance 1960–63; mem. advisory missions to Zambia 1964, Sri Lanka 1971; Adviser to the Govt. of Pakistan 1968–69, Bangladesh 1973, Sri Lanka 1976, Bangladesh 1979, 1982; mem. tax inquiry comm. Zimbabwe 1983–85; UN Consultant on UN Handbook of Statistical Orgs. 1977; mem. Labour Party. *Publications:* Hva krigen kostet Norge (What the War Cost Norway) 1945, Government Economic Planning and Control 1950, Planning in Norway 1947–56, 1959, Trends in Norwegian Planning 1945–1975, 1976, 2 Addresses on Statistical Co-operation 1976, 3 Decades of the Conference of European Statisticians: Past Achievements and Perspectives for the Future 1982, International Trends in Official Statistics 1985, Economy, Population Issues and Statistics; Selected Works by Petter Jakob Bjerve; Ed. Cen. Bureau of Statistics 1985, Ragnar Frisch og Økosirksystemet 1987, Economic Planning and Policy 1989, International Cooperation on Statistics 1991, Technical Advice in Pakistan 1991, Why did we get the National Budget? 1991, Technical Advice on Official Statistics in Bangladesh 1992, Analysis and Evaluation of the Macroeconomic Policy in 1986–1992 1993, Development Assignment in Sri Lanka 1994, The Influence of Ragnar Frisch on Macroeconomic Planning and Policy in Norway 1995, Contributions of Ragnar Frisch to National Accounting 1996, Nasjonalbudsjettet 50 år 1997, Befolkningskommisjonen gjennom 50 år 1998. *Leisure interests:* fishing, gardening. *Address:* Breidablikkvn. 10D, 1167 Oslo, Norway (Home). *Telephone:* 22283759.

BJÖRCK, Anders; Swedish politician; b. 19 Sept. 1944; m. Py-Lotte Björck; one d.; Nat. Pres. Swedish Young Moderates 1966–71; M.P. 1968–; mem. Parl. Ass. Council of Europe 1976–91, Pres. (Speaker) 1989–91; Minister of Defence 1991–94; First Deputy Speaker of Swedish Parl. 1994–; mem. Bd. Swedish Broadcasting Co. 1978–91, Swedish TV Co. 1979–91; mem. numerous govt. comms. dealing with constitutional matters, the mass media, environmental protection. *Publications:* various articles on defence, foreign policy and constitutional issues. *Address:* Swedish Parliament, 10012 Stockholm, Sweden. *Telephone:* (8) 786-4000.

BJÖRK (b. Björk Gudmundsdóttir); Icelandic singer and songwriter; b. 21 Nov. 1965, Reykjavík; one c.; made first album "Bjork" 1977; formed several bands including Exodus, Tappi Tikarrass; mem. The Sugarcubes (fmrly. Kukl) 1986–92; singles with The Sugarcubes include: Birthday; albums with The Sugarcubes: Life's Too Good, Here Today, Tomorrow Next Week!, Stick Around For Joy; solo artist 1992–; singles include: Human Behaviour, Venus As A Boy, Big Time Sensuality, Violently Happy, Play Dead, Army Of Me, Blow A Fuse (It's Oh So Quiet), Hyperballad; albums: Debut 1993, Post (platinum disc in U.K.); Best Int. Female Award (MTV European Music awards). *Address:* One Little Indian Records, 250 York Road, London, SW11 3SJ, England. *Telephone:* 0171-924 1661. *Fax:* 0171-924 4274.

BJÖRK, Anita; Swedish actress; b. 25 April 1923, Tällberg Dalecarlia; m. Stig Dagerman (deceased); one s. two d.; ed. Royal Dramatic Theatre School, Stockholm; has toured around U.S.A., Canada, U.K. and France; numerous stage appearances at Royal Dramatic Theatre, Stockholm, including Miss Julie 1951, Agnes (Brand, Ibsen), Celia (The Cocktail Party, Eliot), Rosalind (As You Like It, Shakespeare), Juliet (Romeo and Juliet, Shakespeare), Eliza (Pygmalion, Shaw), Solange (Les Bonnes, Genet), The girl (Look Back in Anger, Osborne), Johanna (Les séquestrés d'Altona, Sartre), Siri von Essen (Night of The Tribades, P. O. Enquist), Madame Arkadina (The Seagull, Chekhov) 1982-83, Hanna Luise Heiberg (Life of the Rainsnakes,

Enquist), Christa Wolf (Kassandra, Wolf). *Films acted in include:* Himlaspelet 1942, Räkna de lyckliga stunderna blott (Count Your Blessings) 1944, Hundra dragspel och en flicka (One Hundred Concertinas and a Girl) 1946, Ingen väg tillbaka (No Return) 1947, Kvinna utan ansikte 1947, Det kom en gäst (There Came a Guest) 1947, Pa dessa skuldror (On these Shoulders) 1948, Människors rike (The Realm of Men and Women) 1949, Kvartetten som sprängdes (The Quartet that was Broken) 1950, Fröken Julie 1950–51 (First Prize, Cannes Film Festival), Han glömde henne aldrig 1952, Night People 1953, Die Hexe 1954, Giftas 1955, Der Cornet 1955, Moln över Hellesta (Dark Clouds over Hellesta) 1956, Sängen om den eldröda blommen 1956, Gäst i eget hus (Guest in One's Own House) 1957, Mannekäng i rött 1958, Tärningen är kastad 1960, Goda vänner trogna grannar 1960, Vita frun 1962, Älskande par 1964, Mme. de Monfreuil (The Marchioness of Sade), Mother and Daughter 1990; Swedish Critics' Award 1990. *Address:* AB Baggensgatan 9, 111 31 Stockholm, Sweden. *Telephone:* (8) 209747.

BJORK, Claes; Swedish business executive; joined Skanska AB 1967, moved to U.S.A. 1971, responsible for Skanska's construction operations in U.S.A. 1983, Pres. Skanska (USA) Inc. 1987, Sr. Vice-Pres. Skanska AB, Head Skanska USA Operations –1997, mem. Group Man. Skanska AB 1995–, Pres., Group Chief Exec. May 1997–; Chair. Swedish-American Chamber of Commerce 1992–95; mem. Bd. Banister Foundation 1990–. *Address:* Skanska AB, 182 25 Danderyd, 205 33 Malmö, Sweden. *Telephone:* (40) 144000. *Fax:* (40) 40144540.

BJÖRKMAN, Olle Erik, PH.D., D.SC.; American professor of plant biology; b. 29 July 1933, Jönköping, Sweden; s. of Erik Gustaf Björkman and Dagmar Kristina Björkman (Svensson); m. Monika Birgit Waldinger 1955; two s.; ed. Univs. of Stockholm and Uppsala; Research Fellow, Swedish Natural Science Research Council, Univ. of Uppsala 1961–63; Postdoctoral Fellow, Carnegie Inst. Washington, Stanford, Calif. 1964–65, Faculty mem. 1966–, Prof. of Biology by courtesy, Stanford Univ. 1977–; mem. Cttee. on Carbon Dioxide Effects, U.S. Dept. of Energy 1977–82, Cttee. on Bioscience Research in Agric. 1984–85; Scientific Adviser, Desert Research Inst., Nevada 1980–81; mem. Editorial Bd. Planta 1993–96; mem. N.A.S.; Fellow, American Acad. of Arts and Sciences, A.A.A.S.; Corresp. (Foreign) mem. Australian Acad. of Sciences, Foreign mem. Royal Swedish Acad. of Sciences; Linnaeus Prize, Royal Swedish Physiographic Soc. 1977, The Stephen Hale's Award, American Soc. of Plant Physiologists 1986, The Selby Award, Australian Acad. of Sciences 1987. *Publications:* Experimental Studies on the Nature of Species V (co-author) 1971, Physiological Processes in Plant Ecology 1980, more than 170 articles in scientific journals. *Leisure interest:* opera. *Address:* Carnegie Institution Department of Plant Biology, Stanford, CA 94305, U.S.A. (Office); 3040 Greer Road, Palo Alto, CA 94303, U.S.A. (Home). *Telephone:* (650) 325-1521 (Office); (650) 858-0880 (Home). *Fax:* (650) 325-6857.

BJÖRN, H. Lars Olof, PH.D.; Swedish professor of plant physiology; b. 8 March 1936, Visby, Gotland; s. of Hilding Björn and Anna-Lisa Björn; m. Gunvor S. Berg 1959; two d.; ed. Univs. of Lund and Calif. (Berkeley); Prof. of Plant Physiology, Agric. Univ. of Denmark 1971–72, Univ. of Lund 1972; mem. Royal Swedish Acad. of Sciences; Scandinavian Soc. for Plant Physiology Award for Popularization of Science 1982, 1987, Linnaeus Prize for Botany (Royal Physiological Soc.) 1983, N.G. Rosen's Prize for Popularization of Science 1985, UNEP Citation of Excellence in recognition of outstanding contribution to the protection of the Earth's ozone layer. *Publications include:* Optiska och Elektriska Analysmetoder 1965, The Effect of Light on the Development of Root Plastids 1967, Light and Life 1976, Vital and Vicious Atoms 1989. *Leisure interests:* photography, popular science (writing and reading). *Address:* c/o Department of Plant Physiology, Lund University, Box 117, S-221 00 Lund (Office); Småskolevägen 26, 22367 Lund, Sweden (Home). *Telephone:* 4646 10 77 97 (Office); 4646 13 37 13 (Home).

BJØRNHOLM, Sven, DR.PHIL.; Danish physicist; b. 8 Sept. 1927, Tønder; s. of Lieut.-Col. H. L. Bjørnholm and Inger Hillerup; m. Iran Park 1957; two s. one d.; ed. Tech. Univ. of Denmark, Sorbonne, Paris and Univ. of Copenhagen; Research Asst. Niels Bohr Inst. Copenhagen 1955–68; Assoc. Prof. Univ. of Copenhagen 1968–96; visiting scientist at research insts. in France, U.S.S.R., U.S.A., Germany and Brazil 1951–97; mem. Bd. Int. Fed. of Insts. of Advanced Study 1972–77, Danish Natural Science Research Council 1973–79, Danish Energy Policy Council 1976–86, Int. Union of Pure and Applied Physics (IUPAP) Comm. on Nuclear Physics 1978–84, European Community Comm. on Research and Devt. 1980–82; Pres. Danish Physical Soc. 1978–80; mem. Royal Danish Acad., Danish Acad. of Tech. Sciences, Royal Physiographical Soc. of Lund, Sweden, Danish Pugwash Cttee.; Ole Rømer Award 1965, Ulrich Brinch Award 1973, Officier, Ordre des Palmes Académiques. *Publications:* Energy in Denmark 1990–2005 1976, and articles on the structure and reactions of atomic nuclei and metal clusters, including fission, in professional journals. *Address:* The Niels Bohr Institute, Blegdamsvej 17, 2100 Copenhagen Ø (Office); Frederiksberg Alle 45, 1820 Frederiksberg C, Denmark (Home). *Telephone:* 35-32-52-94 (Office); 31-22-48-85 (Home).

BJØRNVIG, Thorkild Strange, DR. PHIL.; Danish poet and writer; b. 2 Feb. 1918; s. of Adda and Theodor Bjørnvig; m. 1st Grete Damgaard Pedersen 1946, 2nd Birgit Hornum 1970; two s. one d.; ed. Cathedral School, Aarhus, and Univ. of Aarhus; mem. Danish Acad. 1960; several prizes. *Publications:* poetry: Stjaernen bag gavlen 1947, Anubis 1955, Figur og Ild 1959, Vibrationer 1966, Ravnen 1968, Udvalgte digte 1970, Morgenmørke 1977, Den dobbelte Lykke 1982, Gennem Regnbuen 1987, Siv vand og måne 1993; essays: Rilke og tysk Tradition 1959, Begyndelsen 1960, Kains Alter 1964, Oprør mod neonguden 1970, Virkeligheden er til 1973, Pagten, mit venskab med Karen Blixen 1974, Delfinen 1975, Stoffets Krystalhav 1975, Det religiøse menneskes ansigter 1975, Også for naturens skyld 1978, Barnet og dyret i industrisamfundet 1979, Abeguder, Miljødigte 1975–80 1981, Den følende planet 1988, Epidemeteus Miljødigte 1980–90 1991, Digtere 1991. *Address:* Issehoved, 8305 Samsø, Denmark.

BJURSTRÖM, Per Gunnar, PH.D.; Swedish professor; b. 28 March 1928, Stockholm; s. of Gunnar and Claire (née Hellgård) Bjurström; m. 1st Eva Gunnars 1957 (dissolved 1983); two d.; m. 2nd Görel Cavalli-Björkman; Asst. curator, Nationalmuseum 1950–68, curator of prints and drawings 1968–79; Dir. Nat. Swedish Art Museums 1980–89; guest prof., Yale Univ. 1968; Prof. Nat. Gallery of Art, Washington 1990–91; mem. Bd. Gen. Art Asscn. of Sweden 1964–, Prince Eugen's Waldemarsudde 1980–89; Vice-Chair. Soc. of Art History 1965–91; Chair. Int. Cttee. of Museums of Fine Art 1983–88; mem. Royal Acad. of Letters, History and Antiquities and Royal Acad. of Fine Art, Ateneo Veneto, Venice. *Publications:* Giacomo Torelli and Baroque Stage Design 1961, Stage Design in Sweden 1964, Feast and Theatre in Queen Christina's Rome 1966, German Drawings in Swedish Public Collections 1972, French Drawings in Swedish Public Collections 1976, 1982, 1986, Italian Drawings in Swedish Public Collections 1979, Johan Tobias Sergel 1975, Three Decades of Swedish Graphic Art 1946–1976, Roman Baroque Scenery 1977, Philip von Schantz 1979, Claude Lorrain Sketchbook 1984, Nationalmuseum 1792–1991 1992, Karl Axel Pehrson 1992, I, Alexander Roslin 1993. *Address:* Folkungagatan 142, 116 30 Stockholm, Sweden. *Telephone:* (08) 641-7093. *Fax:* (08) 641-7093.

BLACK, Conrad M., P.C., O.C., LITT.D., LL.D.; Canadian publisher and business executive; b. 25 Aug. 1944, Montreal, Quebec; s. of George Montegu and Jean Elizabeth (Riley) Black; m. 1st Joanna Catherine Louise Black 1978 (divorced 1991); two s. one d.; m. 2nd Barbara Amiel 1992; ed. Carleton, Laval, McGill; Chair. and C.E.O. Ravelston Corpn. Ltd.; acquired Daily Telegraph newspaper group 1985; Chair. The Telegraph PLC 1987; Chair. Saturday Night Magazine Inc.; Chair. and C.E.O. Hollinger Int. Inc. 1985, Chair. Chairs. Exec. Cttee.; Chair. Bd. and Exec. Cttee Argus Corpn Ltd.; Deputy Chair. American Publishing Co. (now Hollinger Int.), John Fairfax (Australia); Dir. Canadian Imperial Bank of Commerce; Dir. Brascan Ltd., The Spectator (1828) Ltd., UniMédia Inc., Eaton's of Canada Ltd., Financial Post Co. Ltd., Key Publishers Co. Ltd., Southam Inc. (Chair., C.E.O. 1994–), Sotheby's 1997–; Patron The Malcolm Muggeridge Foundation; mem. Advisory Bd., The Nat. Interest, Washington, D.C., Steering Cttee. and Advisory Group, Bilderberg Meetings, Chair.'s Council, Americas Soc., Int. Inst. for Strategic Studies, Gulfstream Aerospace Corpn.; Hon. LL.D. (St. Francis Xavier) 1979, (McMaster) 1979, (Carleton) 1989, Hon. Litt.D. (Windsor) 1979. *Publications:* Duplessis 1977, A Life in Progress 1994. *Address:* c/o Hollinger Inc., 10 Toronto Street, Toronto, Ont. M5C 2B7, Canada; 1 Canada Square, Canary Wharf, London, E14 5DT, England. *Telephone:* (416) 363-8721 (Toronto). *Fax:* (416) 364-2088 (Toronto).

BLACK, Sir Douglas Andrew Kilgour, Kt., M.D., F.R.C.P.; British physician; b. 29 May 1913, Delting, Shetland; s. of Rev. Walter Kilgour Black and Mary Jane Crichton; m. Mollie Thorn 1948; one s. two d.; ed. St. Andrews Univ.; Lecturer, Reader and Prof., Dept. of Medicine, Manchester Univ. 1946–77, now Emer., Sir Arthur Sims Commonwealth Travelling Prof. 1971; on secondment as Chief Scientist, Dept. of Health and Social Security 1972–77; Pres. Royal Coll. of Physicians, London 1977–83; Pres. Inst. of Medical Ethics 1984–; Pres. British Medical Asscn. 1985–86; Lectureships (Royal Coll. of Physicians, London): Goulstonian 1953, Bradshaw 1965, Lumleian 1970, Harveian 1977; Hon. D.Sc. (St. Andrews) 1972, Hon. D.Sc. (Manchester) 1978, (Cambridge) 1994; Kt.St.J. 1989. *Publications:* Sodium Metabolism in Health and Disease 1952, The Logic of Medicine 1968, Essentials of Fluid Balance (4th edn.) 1967, An Anthology of False Antithesis 1984, Invitation to Medicine 1987, Recollections and Reflections 1987. *Leisure interests:* reading and writing. *Address:* The Old Forge, Duchess Close, Whitchurch-on-Thames, Reading, RG8 7EN, England. *Telephone:* (0118) 9844693.

BLACK, Sir James (Whyte), Kt., F.R.C.P., F.R.S.; British professor of analytical pharmacology; b. 14 June 1924; m. Rona McLeod Mackie 1994; ed. Beath High School, Cowdenbeath and Univ. of St. Andrews; Asst. Lecturer in Physiology, Univ. of St. Andrews 1946; lecturer in Physiology, Univ. of Malaya 1947–50; Sr. Lecturer Univ. of Glasgow Veterinary School 1950–58; with ICI Pharmaceuticals Ltd. 1958–64, Head of Biological Research and Deputy Research Dir. Smith, Kline & French, Welwyn Garden City 1964–73; Prof. and Head of Dept. of Pharmacology, Univ. College, London 1973–77; Prof. of Analytical Pharmacology, King's Coll. Hosp. Medical School, Univ. of London 1984–93, now Emer. Prof.; Chancellor Dundee Univ. 1992–; Dir. Therapeutic Research, Wellcome Research Labs. 1978–84; mem. British Pharmacological Soc. 1961–; Mullard Award, Royal Soc. 1978, Nobel Prize for Physiology or Medicine 1988; Hon. Fellow R.S.C. 1989; Hon. Assoc. mem. Royal Coll. of Veterinary Surgeons 1990; Hon. M.D. (Edin.) 1989; Hon. D.Sc. (Glasgow) 1989, (Oxford) 1996. *Address:* Analytical Pharmacology Unit, Rayne Institute, 123 Coldharbour Lane, London, SE5 9NU; 3 Ferrings, Dulwich, London, SE21 7LU, England; University of Dundee, Dundee, DD1 4HN, Scotland. *Telephone:* 0171-274 7437.

BLACK, Kent March; American business executive; b. 25 Oct. 1939, Carrollton, Ill.; s. of Kenneth Wilbur and Alta Jane (March) Black; m. Karen Anne Jones 1960; two d.; ed. Univ. of Illinois; joined Rockwell Int. 1962, various posts to Exec. Vice-Pres. and C.O.O. 1989; mem. Advisory Cttee. Nat. Security Telecom 1989–. *Address:* c/o Rockwell International Corporation, P.O. Box 5090, Costa Mesa, CA 92628, U.S.A.

BLACK, Robert Denis Collison, M.A., PH.D., F.B.A., M.R.I.A.; British economist; b. 11 June 1922, Dublin; s. of William R. and Rose M. (née Reid) Black; m. Frances M. Weatherup 1953; one s. one d.; ed. Sandford Park School, Dublin and Trinity Coll., Dublin; Deputy for Prof. of Political Econ., Trinity Coll. Dublin 1943–45; Asst. Lecturer in Econ. Queen's Univ. Belfast 1945–46, Lecturer 1946–58, Sr. Lecturer 1958–61, Reader 1961–62, Prof. 1962–85, Prof. Emer. 1985–, Pro-Vice-Chancellor 1971–75; Rockefeller Postdoctoral Fellow, Princeton Univ. 1950–51; Visiting Prof. Yale Univ. 1964–65; Research Fellow, Japan Soc. for Promotion of Science 1980; Hon. D.Sc. (Queen's Univ.) 1988; Hon. Fellow, Trinity Coll., Dublin 1982, Distinguished Fellow, History of Econs. Soc., U.S.A. 1987. *Publications:* Economic Thought and the Irish Question 1817–1870 1960, Catalogue of Pamphlets on Economic Subjects 1750–1900 1969, Readings in the Development of Economic Analysis 1971, Papers and Correspondence of W. S. Jevons (Vols. I-VII) 1972–81, Ideas in Economics (Ed.) 1986, Economic Theory and Policy in Context 1995. *Leisure interests:* travel, music, classic cars. *Address:* Queen's University, Belfast, BT7 1NN, Northern Ireland. *Telephone:* (01232) 245133.

BLACK, Robert Lincoln, M.D.; American pediatrician; b. 25 Aug. 1930, Los Angeles; s. of Harold Black and Kathryn Stone; m. Jean Wilmott McGuire 1953; two s. one d.; ed. Stanford Univ., Kings County Hosp., Brooklyn, Stanford Univ. Hosp., Palo Alto; Capt. U.S. Air Force Medical Corps 1956–58; Asst. Clinical Prof., Stanford Univ. 1962–68, Assoc. Prof. 1968–79, Prof. of Pediatrics 1980; mem. Bd. of Educ. Monterey Peninsula Unified School Dist. 1965–73; mem. Bd. Dirs. Lyceum of Monterey Peninsula 1973–; mem. Bd. Mid Coast Health System Agency 1975–81; mem. various cttees. of American Acad., of Pediatrics 1962–, Alt. Chapter Chair. 1984–87; Consultant, State of Calif. Dept. of Health Service 1962–, and of Office of Statewide Health Planning 1975–81; mem. State Maternal, Child, Adolescent Health Care Bd. 1984–93; currently Pediatrician with pvt. practice; mem. Inst. of Medicine, N.A.S., Calif. State Maternal, Child, Adolescent Health Bd. *Publications:* California Health Plan for Children, California's Use of Health Statistics in Child Health Planning. *Leisure interests:* music, hiking, travel, photography. *Address:* 920 Cass Street, Monterey, CA 93940 (Office); 976 Mesa Road, Monterey, CA 93940, U.S.A. (Home). *Telephone:* (408) 372-5841 (Office); (408) 372-2594 (Home).

BLACK, Shirley Temple; American actress and diplomatist; b. 23 April 1928, Santa Monica, Calif.; d. of George F. and Gertrude Temple; m. 1st John Agar, Jr. 1945 (dissolved 1949); one d.; m. 2nd Charles A. Black 1950; one s. one d.; ed. privately and Westlake School for Girls; career as film actress commenced at 3½ years; first full-length film was Stand Up and Cheer; narrator/actress in TV series Shirley Temple Storybook 1958; hostess/actress Shirley Temple Show 1960; Del. to UN, New York 1969–70; Amb. to Ghana 1974–76, to Czechoslovakia 1989–92; White House Chief of Protocol 1976–77; mem. U.S. Comm. for UNESCO 1973–; mem. U.S. Delegation on African Refugee Problems, Geneva 1981; Dir. Nat. Multiple Sclerosis Soc.; Dame, Order of Knights of Malta (Paris) 1968; American Exemplar Medal 1979, Gandhi Memorial Int. Foundation Award 1988; numerous state decorations. *Films include:* Little Miss Marker, Baby Take a Bow, Bright Eyes, Our Little Girl, The Little Colonel, Curly Top, The Littlest Rebel, Captain January, Poor Little Rich Girl, Dimples, Stowaway, Wee Willie Winkie, Heidi, Rebecca of Sunnybrook Farm, Little Miss Broadway, Just Around the Corner, The Little Princess, Susannah of the Mounties, The Blue Bird, Kathleen, Miss Annie Rooney, Since You Went Away, Kiss and Tell, That Hagen Girl, War Party, The Bachelor and the Bobby-Soxer, Honeymoon. *Publication:* Child Star 1988. *Address:* c/o Academy of Motion Picture Arts & Sciences, 8949 Wilshire Blvd., Beverly Hills, CA 90211, U.S.A.

BLACK, Stanley, O.B.E.; British conductor, composer and pianist; b. 14 June 1913, London; m. Edna Kaye 1947; one s. one d.; ed. schools in London; BBC Staff conductor 1944–52; Musical Dir. Assoc. British Film Studios, Elstree 1952–61; freelance 1962–; guest conductor, BBC Concert Orchestra 1965–; has composed and musically directed scores of some 95 British and Anglo-American productions since 1944; as conductor has appeared with most of the major British orchestras; conducting tours in Japan, Korea, Scandinavia, Belgium, Netherlands, New Zealand, Australia, Canada and U.S.A.; records for Decca; Life Fellow Inst. of Arts and Letters 1963–, and numerous others; Freedom of the City of London 1988; several gold awards. *Leisure interests:* theatre, literature, music, children, grandchildren. *Address:* 43 Viceroy Court, Prince Albert Road, London, NW8 7PR, England.

BLACKADDER, Elizabeth, O.B.E., R.A., R.S.A., M.A.; British artist; b. 24 Sept. 1931, Falkirk, Scotland; m. John Houston 1956; ed. Falkirk High School, Edinburgh Coll. of Art and Edinburgh Univ.; teacher of art, St. Thomas of Aquin's School, Edin. 1958–59; librarian, Fine Art Dept. Univ. of Edin. 1959–61; teacher, Edin. Coll of Art 1962–86; regular one-woman shows, Mercury Gallery, London 1965–; other individual shows include: 57 Gallery, Edin. 1959, The Scottish Gallery, Edin. 1961, 1966, Vaccarino Gallery, Florence 1970, Theo Waddington Gallery, Toronto 1981–82, Lillian Heidenberg Gallery, New York 1986; Scottish Arts Council retrospective exhbn. Edin., Sheffield, Aberdeen, Liverpool, Cardiff 1981–82; participant in numerous group shows in U.K., U.S.A., Canada etc. British Painting 1952–77; Royal Acad. London 1977; work includes drawings and watercolours (especially botanical), prints, lithographs, portraits, tapestries and stained glass (window commissioned by Nat. Library of Scotland 1987); Hon. Fellow Royal Soc. of Edin.; Hon. D.Litt. (Heriot-Watt Univ.) 1989, (Strathclyde) 1998; Dr. h.c. (Univ. of Edinburgh) 1990; Hon. LL.D (Aberdeen) 1997; jt. winner, Watercolour Foundation Award, R.A. Summer Exhbn. 1988. *Publication:* Favourite Flowers (with Deborah Kellaway) 1994. *Address:* 57 Fountainhall Road, Edin. EH9 2LH; c/o Royal Scottish Academy, The Mound, Edin. EH2 2EL, Scotland.

BLACKBOURN, David Gordon, PH.D., F.R.HIST.S.; British professor of history; b. 1 Nov. 1949, Spilsby, Lincs.; s. of Harry Blackbourn and Pamela Jean Blackbourn (née Youngman); m. Deborah Frances Langton 1985; one s. one d.; ed. Leeds Modern Grammar School, Christ's Coll., Cambridge; Research Fellow, Jesus Coll., Cambridge 1973–76; lecturer in History, Queen Mary Coll., London Univ. 1976–79, Birkbeck Coll. 1979–85, Reader in Modern History 1985–89, Prof. of Modern European History 1989–92; Prof. of History Harvard Univ. 1992–97, Coolidge Prof. of History 1997–; lectures and contribs. to confs. in U.K., Ireland, Germany, France, Italy, Yugoslavia, U.S.A. and Canada 1973–; Fellow Inst. for European History, Mainz, Fed. Republic of Germany 1974–75; Research Fellow, Alexander von Humboldt Foundation, Bonn-Bad Godesberg, Fed. Repub. of Germany 1984–85; Visiting Kratter Prof. of German History, Stanford Univ., Calif., U.S.A. 1989–90; Fellow Guggenheim Foundation, New York 1994–95; Sec. German History Soc. 1978–81, mem. Cttee. 1981–86; mem. Acad. Man. Cttee., German Historical Inst., London 1983–92; mem. Editorial Bd. Past and Present 1988–; mem. European Sub-cttee. of Labour Party Nat. Exec. Cttee. 1978–80, Academic Man. Cttee., Inst. for European History, Mainz, Germany 1995–. *Publications:* Class, Religion and Local Politics in Wilhelmine Germany 1980, The Peculiarities of German History (with Geoff Eley) 1984, Populists and Patricians: Essays in Modern German History 1987, Volksfrömmigkeit und Fortschrittsglaube im Kulturkampf 1988, The German Bourgeoisie (ed. with Richard J. Evans) 1991, Marpingen: Apparitions of the Virgin Mary in Bismarckian Germany 1993, The Fontana History of Germany: the Long Nineteenth Century, 1780–1918 1997; scholarly articles in English, German, French, Serbo-Croat, Japanese and Italian; contribs. to several magazines and the B.B.C. *Leisure interests:* family, reading, music, sport, politics. *Address:* Minda de Gunzburg Center for European Studies, Harvard University, 27 Kirkland Street, Cambridge, MA 02138, U.S.A. *Telephone:* (617) 495-4303, ext. 228 (Office). *Fax:* (617) 495-8509.

BLACKBURN, Jeffrey Michael, F.C.I.B., F.R.S.A.; British business executive; b. 16 Dec. 1941, Manchester; m. 2nd Louise Clair Jouny 1987; two s.; one s. one d. from previous marriage; Chief Man. Business Advisory Service with Lloyds Bank 1979–83; Dir., C.E.O. Jt. Credit Card Co. Ltd. (Access) 1983–87, Leeds Perm. Bldg. Soc. 1987–93; Dir. and C.E.O Halifax Bldg. Soc. 1993–97, Halifax PLC 1997–; mem. Chartered Inst. of Man. *Leisure interests:* the arts. *Address:* Halifax PLC, Trinity Road, Halifax, West Yorks., HX1 2RG, England.

BLACKBURN, Simon W., PH.D., D.PHIL.; British professor of philosophy; b. 12 July 1944, Bristol; s. of Cuthbert Blackburn and Edna Blackburn; m. Angela Bowles 1968; one s. one d.; ed. Clifton Coll. Bristol and Trinity Coll. Cambridge; Research Fellow, Churchill Coll. Cambridge 1967–69; Fellow and Tutor in Philosophy, Pembroke Coll. Oxford 1969–90; Ed. MIND 1984–90; Edna J. Koury Distinguished Prof. of Philosophy, Univ. of N.C. 1990–; Adjunct Prof. A.N.U. 1993–. *Publications:* Reason and Prediction 1970, Spreading the Word 1984, Essays in Quasi-Realism 1993, Oxford Dictionary of Philosophy 1994, Ruling Passions 1998. *Leisure interests:* mountaineering, photography, sailing. *Address:* Department of Philosophy, CB 3125, Caldwell Hall, University of North Carolina, Chapel Hill, NC 27599; 313 Woodhaven Road, Chapel Hill, NC 27514, U.S.A. *Telephone:* (919) 968-2498.

BLACKMAN, Honor; actress; film début in Fame is the Spur 1947. *Films include:* Green Grow the Rushes 1951, Come Die My Love 1952, The Rainbow Jacket 1953, The Glass Cage 1954, Dead Man's Evidence 1955, A Matter of Who 1961, Goldfinger 1964, Life at the Top 1965, Twist of Sand 1967, The Virgin and the Gipsy 1970, To the Devil a Daughter 1975, Summer Rain 1976, The Cat and the Canary 1977, Talos—The Mummy. *TV appearances include:* Four Just Men 1959, Man of Honour 1960, Ghost Squad 1961, Top Secret 1962, The Avengers 1962–64, The Explorer 1968, Visit from a Stranger 1970, Out Damned Spot 1972, Wind of Change 1977, Robin's Nest 1982, Never the Twain 1982, The Secret Adversary 1983, Lace 1985, The First Modern Olympics 1986, Minder on the Orient Express 1986, Dr Who 1986, William Tell 1986, The Upper Hand (TV series). *Address:* c/o Jean Diamond, London Management, 2–4 Noel Street, London, W1V 3RB, England.

BLACKSTAD, Theodor Wilhelm, M.D.; Norwegian professor of anatomy; b. 29 July 1925, Iveland; s. of Leif Blackstad and Alfhild (née Holmsen); m. Ebba Helene Dietrichson 1952; two d.; ed. Univ. of Oslo; anatomy teacher, Univ. of Oslo 1953, Prof. of Medicine 1977–91, Prof. Emer. 1991–; Prof. of Medicine, Univ. of Aarhus, Denmark 1967; Sr. Research Fellow Norwegian Research Council 1991–95; Monrad-Krohn and Nansen prizes. *Publications:* (recently) articles on computer-based analysis of brain morphology. *Address:*

Department of Anatomy, Inst. of Basic Medical Sciences, Sognsvannsveien 9, P.O. Box 1105 Blindern, 0317 Oslo (Office); Jernbaneveien 83, 1320 Stabekk, Norway (Home). *Telephone:* 22851271. *Fax:* 22851278.

BLACKSTONE, Baroness (Life Peer) cr. 1987, of Stoke Newington in Greater London, **Tessa Ann Vosper Blackstone,** PH.D.; British politician and fmr. college principal; b. 27 Sept. 1942, London; d. of Geoffrey Vaughan Blackstone, C.B.E., G.M., and Joanna Blackstone; m. Tom Evans 1963 (marriage dissolved); one s. one d.; ed. Ware Grammar School, London School of Economics, Univ. of London; Assoc. Lecturer, Enfield Coll. 1965–66; Asst. Lecturer, then Lecturer, Dept. of Social Admin., L.S.E. 1966–75; Fellow, Centre for Studies in Social Policy 1972–74; Adviser, Cen. Policy Review Staff, Cabinet Office 1975–78; Prof. of Educational Admin., Univ. of London Inst. of Educ. 1978–83; Deputy Educ. Officer (Resources), then Clerk and Dir. of Educ., Inner London Educ. Authority 1983–87; Master, Birkbeck Coll., Univ. of London 1987–97; Minister of State in Dept. of Educ. and Employment 1997–; Opposition Spokesperson on Educ. and Science, House of Lords 1990–92, on Foreign Affairs 1992–97; Dir. Royal Opera House 1987–97; Chair. General Advisory Council BBC 1987–91; Chair. Bd. of Trustees, Inst. for Public Policy Research 1988–97; Trustee British Museum (Natural History) 1992–97; Dir. Thames TV 1991–92; Fellow Birkbeck Coll., Univ. of London 1997–; Hon. D.Lit. (Bristol Polytechnic) 1991, Hon. D. Litt. (Bradford); Hon. D.Univ. (Middx.); Hon. LL.D. (Aberdeen) 1994, (St. Andrews) 1995; Dr. h.c. (Strathclyde) 1996; Hon. Dauphine (Sorbonne, Paris) 1998. *Publications:* A Fair Start 1971, Education and Day Care for Young Children in Need 1973, Social Policy and Administration in Britain 1975; co-author: Students in Conflict 1970, The Academic Labour Market 1974, Disadvantage and Education 1982, Education Policy and Educational Inequality 1982, Response to Adversity 1983, Testing Children 1983, Inside the Think Tank: Advising the Cabinet 1971–83, 1988, Prisons and Penal Reform 1990, Race Relations in Britain 1997. *Leisure interests:* tennis, walking, ballet, opera. *Address:* Department for Education and Employment, Sanctuary Buildings, Great Smith Street, London, SW1P 3BT, England. *Telephone:* 0171-925 6243.

BLACKWELL, Baron (Life Peer) cr. 1997, of Woodcote in the County of Surrey, **Norman Roy Blackwell,** PH.D., M.B.A.; British civil servant; b. 29 July 1952, London; m. Brenda Clucas 1974; three s. two d.; ed. Latymer Upper School, Trinity Coll., Cambridge, Wharton Business School, Univ. of Pa. (Thouron Scholar); Jr. Exhibitioner R.A.M. 1963–69; Chair. Cambridge Univ. Conservative Asscn. 1973; with Strategic Planning Unit, Plessey Co. 1976–78, McKinsey & Co. 1978–86, 1988–95 (partner 1984), Prime Minister's Policy Unit 1986–88 (Head 1995–97); Dir. of Group Devt. NatWest Group 1997–; Deputy Chair. British Urban Regeneration Asscn. 1991–92. *Leisure interests:* classical music, walking. *Address:* c/o NatWest Group, 41 Lothbury, London, EC2P 2BP, England.

BLACKWELL, Julian Toby; British bookseller; b. 10 Jan. 1929; s. of the late Sir Basil H. Blackwell and Marion C. Soans; m. Jennifer J.D. Wykeham 1953; two s. one d.; ed. Winchester Coll. and Trinity Coll., Oxford; served 5th Royal Tank Regt. 1947–49; 21st SAS (TA) 1950–59; Dir. and Chair. various Blackwell cos. since 1956; Chair. The Blackwell Group Ltd. 1980–94; Pres. Blackwell Ltd 1995–, Chair. 1996–; Chair. Council, ASLIB 1966–68; Pres. Booksellers' Asscn. 1980–82; Chair. Thames Business Advice Centre 1986–97, Heart of England TEC 1989–94, Fox FM 1989–, Cottontail Ltd. 1990–; Chair. Son White Memorial Trust 1991–; D.L. (Oxfordshire) 1988. *Leisure interests:* sawing firewood, sailing. *Address:* c/o 50 Broad Street, Oxford, OX1 3BQ, England. *Telephone:* (01865) 792111.

BLAGOVOLIN, Sergei Yevgenyevich, D.SC.ECON.; Russian political scientist; b. 22 Aug. 1939, Moscow; m. 1st Victoria Fedorova 1969; m. 2nd Elena Kondrashova 1976; one d.; ed. Moscow State Univ.; Inst. of World Economy and Int. Relations (IMEMO) 1962–, Deputy Dir. 1992–; Pres. Inst. for Nat. Security and Strategic Studies 1991–; mem. Coordinating Council, European-Atlantic Asscn. 1992–; mem. Council on Foreign Policy, Ministry of Foreign Affairs 1993–, Presidential Council of Russia 1994–96; mem. Political Council and Chair. Moscow City Org. of Democratic Choice of Russia Party 1994–; Dir.-Gen. Russian Public TV (ORT) 1995–97; Pres. Fin.-Prom. Corpn. 1997–; mem. Bd. Int. Inst. for Strategic Studies, London 1993–; Fellow, World Acad. of Art and Science; mem. Russian Acad. of Natural Sciences. *Publications:* Arms Race: Reasons, Consequences, Ways for Elimination 1987, Army and Society 1991, La Difesa Europea Proposte e Sfide 1991, Russia in the Far East and Pacific Region 1994. *Leisure interests:* poetry, driving, football. *Address:* Apt. 5, Bld. 1/15-A, Kotelnicheskaya Nab., 109240 Moscow, Russia. *Telephone:* 120-35-68 (Office); 915-49-30 (Home). *Fax:* 120-12-82.

BLAHNIK, Manolo; Spanish couturier; b. 28 Nov. 1943, Santa Cruz, The Canary Islands; ed. Univ. of Geneva; f. and Dir. Manolo Blahnik Int. Ltd.; opened shop in Chelsea, London 1973, U.S.A. 1981; Biannual collections in London and New York; Fashion Council of America Award 1988, 1991, 1997, American Leather New York Award 1991, British Fashion Award 1992, Nieman Marcus Award 1993, mem. F. N. Hall of Fame 1997. *Publications:* various int. publs. on fashion. *Leisure interests:* painting, reading. *Address:* 15 West 55th Street, New York, NY 10019, U.S.A.; 49–51 Old Church Street, London, S.W.3., England. *Telephone:* 0171-352 8622.

BLAINEY, Geoffrey Norman, A.O.; Australian historian and author; b. 11 March 1930, Melbourne; s. of Rev. Samuel C. Blainey and Hilda Blainey; m. Ann Heriot 1957; one d.; ed. Ballarat High School, Wesley Coll., Univ. of Melbourne; freelance historian 1951–61; Reader in Econ. History, Univ. of Melbourne 1963–68, Prof. 1968–76, Ernest Scott Prof. 1977–88, Dean of Faculty of Arts 1982–87; Prof. of Australian Studies, Harvard Univ. 1982–83; columnist in daily newspapers 1974–; Chair. Australia Council 1977–81, Fed. Govt.'s Australia-China Council 1979–84, Commonwealth Literary Fund 1971–73; Pres. Council, Queen's Coll., Univ. of Melbourne 1971–89; Chair. Australian Selection Cttee. Commonwealth Fund (Harkness) Fellowships 1983–90; Chancellor Univ. of Ballarat 1994–; Dir. Royal Humane Soc. 1996–; Gov. Ian Potter Foundation 1991–; Councillor Australian War Memorial 1997–; Gold Medal, Australian Literature Soc. 1963, Capt. Cook Bicentenary Literary Award 1970, Britannica Award for dissemination of learning, N.Y. 1988. *Publications include:* The Peaks of Lyell 1954, Centenary History of the University of Melbourne 1957, Gold and Paper: a History of the National Bank 1958, Mines in the Spinifex 1960, The Rush That Never Ended 1963, The Tyranny of Distance 1966, Across a Red World 1968, The Rise of Broken Hill 1968, The Steel Master 1971, The Causes of War 1973, Triumph of the Nomads: A History of Ancient Australia 1975, A Land Half Won 1980, Our Side of the Country 1984, All for Australia 1984, The Great Seesaw 1988, A Game of Our Own 1990, Eye on Australia 1991, Odd Fellows 1992, The Golden Mile 1993, Jumping over the Wheel 1993, A Shorter History of Australia 1994, White Gold 1997, A History of AMP 1999. *Leisure interests:* travel, wood-chopping, Australian football. *Address:* P.O. Box 257, East Melbourne, Vic. 3002, Australia. *Telephone:* 03-9417 7782.

BLAIR, Rt. Hon. Anthony Charles Lynton (Tony), P.C.; British politician; b. 6 May 1953, Edinburgh; s. of Leo Blair and late Hazel Blair; m. Cherie Booth (q.v.) 1980; two s. one d.; ed. Fettes Coll., Edin., St. John's Coll., Oxford; barrister, specializing in Trade Union and Employment law; M.P. for Sedgefield 1983–; Shadow Treasury Spokesman 1984–87, Trade and Industry Spokesman 1987–88, Energy Spokesman 1988–89, Employment Spokesman 1989–92, Home Affairs Spokesman 1992–94; Leader of the Labour Party July 1994–, Prime Minister, First Lord of the Treasury and Minister for the Civil Service May 1997–; Hon. Bencher Lincoln's Inn 1994; Hon. LL.D. (Northumbria) 1995. *Publication:* New Britain: My Vision of a Young Country 1996. *Address:* 10 Downing Street, London SW1A 2AA; Myrobella, Trimdon Station, County Durham, TS29 6DU, England. *Telephone:* 0171-270 3000.

BLAIR, Gordon Purves, C.B.E., PH.D., D.SC., F.ENG., F.I.MECH.E.; British professor of mechanical engineering; b. 29 April 1937, Larne, Northern Ireland; s. of Gordon Blair and Mary H.J. Blair; m. Norma Margaret Millar 1964; two d.; ed. Larne Grammar School and The Queen's Univ. of Belfast; Asst. Prof., Mechanical Eng., New Mexico State Univ. 1962–64; Lecturer in Mechanical Eng., Queen's Univ. Belfast 1964–71, Sr. Lecturer 1971–73, Reader 1973–76, Prof. 1976–96, Prof. Emer. 1997–, Prof. and Head of Dept. of Mechanical and Industrial Eng. 1982–88, Dean of Faculty 1985–88, Pro-Vice-Chancellor 1989–94; consultant to many industries world-wide on engine design; Fellow S.A.E.; Colwell Technical Merit Award (S.A.E.); Crompton Lanchester Medal (I.Mech.E.); Trident TV Award (IBA). *Publications:* The Basic Design of Two-Stroke Engines 1990, The Design and Simulation of Two-Stroke Engines 1996, 90 tech. papers in int. journals. *Leisure interests:* golf, fishing, motorcycling. *Address:* Ashby Building, The Queen's University of Belfast, Belfast, BT9 5AH, Northern Ireland. *Telephone:* (01232) 370368. *Fax:* (01232) 370372.

BLAIS, Marie-Claire, C.C.; Canadian writer; b. 5 Oct. 1939, Quebec City; d. of Fernando Blais and Veronique Nolin; ed. Quebec, Paris and United States; Guggenheim Foundation Fellowship, New York 1963, 1964; Hon. Prof. Calgary Univ. 1978; Dr. h.c. (York Univ., Toronto) 1975; Order of Canada; Prix de la langue française 1961, Prix France-Québec 1964, Prix Médicis 1966, Prix de l'Acad. Française 1983, Prix Athanase-David (Québec) 1983, Prix Nessim Habif (Acad. Royale de Belgique) 1991, and others. *Publications:* La belle bête 1959, Tête blanche 1960, Le jour est noir 1962, Existences (poems), Une saison dans la vie d'Emmanuel 1965, L'insoumise 1966, David Sterne 1967, Manuscrits de Pauline Archange 1968, Vivre, vivre 1969, Les voyageurs sacrés 1966, Les apparences 1970, Le loup 1972, Un Joualonais sa Joualonie 1973, Une liaison parisienne 1976, Les nuits de l'underground 1978, Le sourd dans la ville 1980, Visions d'Anna 1982, Pierre 1984 (novels); Pays voilés (poems) 1964; L'océan 1967, L'exécution 1968, Fièvre 1974, La nef des sorcières 1976, Sommeil d'hiver 1985, Fière 1985 (plays), L'île (play) 1988, L'ange de la solitude (novel) 1989, Un jardin dans la tempête (play) 1990, Parcours d'un Ecrivain: Notes Americaines (essay) 1993, L'Exile (short stories) 1993. *Leisure interests:* painting and drawing, biking, handwriting analysis. *Address:* 4411 Rue St. Denis, Apt. 401, Montréal, H2J 2LN, Quebec, Canada.

BLAIS, Pierre, B.A., LL.L.; Canadian politician; b. 30 Dec. 1948, Berthier-sur-Mer, Quebec; m. Chantal Fournier; two s. two d.; ed. Laval Univ.; partner, Montmagny law practice 1976–84; Prof. Univ. du Québec à Rimouski 1982; Prof. Laval Univ. 1982–84; Parl. Sec. to Minister of Agric. 1984–86, to Deputy Prime Minister 1987–87; Minister of State (Agric.) 1987–93, Minister of Consumer and Corp. Affairs 1990–93; Minister of Justice and Attorney-Gen. 1993; Privy Council Pres. 1993; Solicitor-Gen. of Canada 1989–90; Progressive Conservative. *Leisure interests:* skiing, reading, swimming. *Address:* Langlois, Gaudreau s.e.n.c., 801 chemin St-Louis, bur. 160, Quebec, G1S 1C1, Canada. *Telephone:* (418) 682-1212. *Fax:* (418) 682-2272.

BLAKE, Baron (Life Peer), cr. 1971, of Braydeston, Norfolk; **Robert Norman William Blake,** M.A., F.B.A., J.P.; British academic; b. 23 Dec. 1916, Blofield, Norfolk; s. of William J. Blake and Norah L. Daynes; m. Patricia M. Waters 1953 (died 1995); three d.; ed. King Edward VI School, Norwich, and Magdalen Coll., Oxford; mil. service during World War II (R.A.), P.O.W. in Italy 1942–44, escaped 1944; MI6 1944–46; Lecturer in Politics, Christ Church, Oxford 1946–47, Student and Tutor in Politics 1947–68, Hon. Student 1977; Censor 1950–55; Sr. Proctor 1959–60; Ford's Lecturer in English History 1967–68; mem. Hebdomadal Council 1959–81; Provost, The Queen's Coll., Oxford 1968–87; Pro-Vice-Chancellor, Univ. of Oxford 1971–87; Jt. Ed. Dictionary of Nat. Biog. 1980–90; Pres. Electoral Reform Soc. 1986–93; mem. Royal Comm. on Historical Manuscripts (Chair. 1982–89), Bd. of Trustees of British Museum; Rhodes Trustee 1971–87, Chair. 1983–87; mem. Bd. of Channel 4 TV 1983–87; Hon. D.Litt. (Glasgow) 1972, (East Anglia) 1983, (Buckingham) 1988. *Publications:* The Private Papers of Douglas Haig (ed.) 1952, The Unknown Prime Minister (Life of Andrew Bonar Law) 1955, Disraeli 1966, The Conservative Party from Peel to Churchill 1970, The Office of Prime Minister 1975, A History of Rhodesia 1977, Disraeli's Grand Tour 1982, The English World (ed.) 1982, The Conservative Party from Peel to Thatcher 1985, The Decline of Power 1985, Salisbury: the man and his policies (co-ed.) 1987, World History: From 1800 to the Present Day (ed.) 1988, Churchill (co-ed.) 1993, The Conservative Party from John Peel to Major 1997. *Address:* Riverview House, Brundall, Norfolk, NR13 5LA, England. *Telephone:* (0603) 712133.

BLAKE, John Clemens, M.A., R.C.A.; American artist; b. 11 Jan. 1945 Providence, R.I.; s. of John Holland Blake and Elizabeth Clemens (now Romäno); ed. Carnegie Inst. of Tech. (now Carnegie-Mellon Univ.), Yale Univ., Royal Coll. of Art, London; freelance visual artist in various media including drawing, installations, photographic constructions, audio constructions, film, etc.; approx. 40 solo exhbns. in Europe and U.S.A. 1972–, including Victoria and Albert Museum, London, Museum of Modern Art, Oxford, Project Studios One (PS1), New York, ICA, London, Krzysztofory, Krakow, Poland, Corps de Garde, Groningen, de Vleeshal, Middelburg and Bonnefantenmuseum, Maastricht, Netherlands, Orchard Gallery, Londonderry, Northern Ireland; teaching has included Hull Polytechnic 1975–76; London Coll. of Printing 1978–82; S. Glamorgan Inst. of Higher Educ., S. Wales 1983–84; Fulbright Fellow 1967–69; Nat. Endowment (U.S.A.) 1977; Arts Council Award (U.K.) 1979; Hokkaido Foundation Award (Japan) 1984. *Publications:* John Blake 1980, de Vleeshal 1983, Their Eyes 1983, Drawings and Constructions 1986. *Address:* Oz. Voorburgwal 131, 1012-ER Amsterdam, Netherlands. *Telephone:* (020) 277-740.

BLAKE, Sir Peter, K.B.E.; New Zealand yachtsman; b. 1 Oct. 1948, Auckland; m. Pippa Blake 1979; one s. one d.; ed. Takapuna Grammar School, Auckland Tech Inst.; began sailing at age eight; aged 18 built own 23 ft. keelboat in which he won N.Z. championships; moved to England 1971; winner Fastnet Race 1979, 1989; winner, Sydney-Hobart Race 1980, 1984; winner Round Australia Two-Handed Race 1988, Whitbread Round the World Race 1989–90; C.E.O. Team New Zealand Ltd., America's Cup Defence 2000 1994–; NZ Yachtsman of the Year 1982, 1989–90, NZ Sports Personality of the Year 1989, NZ Sportsman of the Year 1990; numerous other awards. *Address:* Longshore, 3 Western Parade, Emsworth, Hants., PO10 7HS, England. *Telephone:* (01243) 377027.

BLAKE, Peter, B.ARCH., F.A.I.A.; American architect; b. 20 Sept. 1920, Berlin, Germany; one s. one d; ed. Bootham School, York, Univ. of London, Regent Street Polytechnic, London, Univ. of Pa. and Pratt Inst. School of Architecture; apprentice architect, London 1938–39, Philadelphia 1940–42; Curator, Dept. of Architecture and Industrial Design, Museum of Modern Art, New York 1948–50; Assoc. Ed., later Ed.-in-Chief, The Architectural Forum, New York 1950–72; registered architect 1956–; architectural practice, New York, Boston, Washington, D.C. and Berlin 1956–; Ed.-in-Chief, Architecture Plus, New York 1972–75; Chair. School of Architecture, Boston Architectural Center 1975–79; Chair. Dept. of Architecture and Planning, Catholic Univ. of America, Washington, D.C. 1979–86, Prof. of Architecture 1979–91, Prof. Emer. 1991–; Visiting Prof. Washington Univ. St. Louis 1991–93; bldgs. and projects include: apt. bldg., Berlin; various experimental theatres in New York, Nashville, Tenn. and elsewhere; institutional and industrial bldgs. in U.S.A. and Europe; housing projects and several exhbns. *Publications:* The Master Builders 1960, God's Own Junkyard 1964, Form Follows Fiasco—Why Modern Architecture Hasn't Worked 1977, No Place Like Utopia 1993; contribs. to books and articles in newspapers, magazines and journals. *Leisure interests:* photography. *Address:* 140 Elm Street, Branford, CT 06405-3501, U.S.A. *Telephone:* (203) 488-7644. *Fax:* (203) 488-7644.

BLAKE, Peter Thomas, C.B.E., R.A.; British artist; b. 25 June 1932; s. of Kenneth William Blake; m. 1st Jann Haworth 1963 (dissolved 1982); two d.; m. 2nd Chrissy Wilson 1987; one d.; ed. Gravesend Tech. Coll., Gravesend School of Art, Royal Coll. of Art; third assoc. artist of Nat. Gallery, London 1994–96; works exhibited in Inst. of Contemporary Art 1958, 1960, Guggenheim Competition 1958, Cambridge 1959, Royal Acad. 1960, Musée d'Art Moderne, Paris 1963; retrospective exhbn. City Art Gallery, Bristol 1969, Tate Gallery, London 1983, Nat. Gallery, London 1996; works in perm. collections, Trinity Coll., Cambridge, Carlisle City Gallery, Tate Gallery, Arts Council of G.B., Museum of Modern Art, New York, Victoria and Albert Museum, and other maj. galleries; Dr. h.c. (R.C.A.). *Publications:* illustrations for Oxford Illustrated Old Testament 1968, several Arden Shakespeares and in various periodicals and magazines. *Address:* c/o Waddington Galleries Ltd., 11 Cork Street, London, W1X 2LT, England.

BLAKE, Quentin Saxby, O.B.E., M.A., F.C.S.D.; British artist, illustrator and teacher; b. 16 Dec. 1932, Sidcup, Kent; s. of William Blake and Evelyn Blake; ed. Downing Coll, Cambridge, London Inst. of Educ., Chelsea School of Art; freelance illustrator since 1957; Tutor, Royal Coll. of Art 1965–86, Head of Illustration Dept. 1978–86, Visiting Prof. 1989–; Senior Fellow Royal Coll. of Art 1988. *Publications:* illustrations for over 150 works for children and adults, including collaborations with Roald Dahl, Russell Hoban (q.v.), Joan Aiken, Michael Rosen, John Yeoman. *Address:* Flat 8, 30 Bramham Gardens, London, SW5 0HF, England. *Telephone:* 0171-373 7464.

BLAKEMORE, Colin (Brian), PH.D., SC.D., D.SC., F.I.BIOL., C.BIOL., F.MED.SCI., F.R.S.; British neuro-physiologist and professor of physiology; b. 1 June 1944, Stratford-on-Avon; s. of Cedric Norman and Beryl Ann Blakemore; m. Andrée Elizabeth Washbourne 1965; three d.; ed. King Henry VIII School, Coventry, Corpus Christi Coll., Cambridge, Univ. of Calif. Berkeley; Harkness Fellowship, Univ. of Calif. 1965–67; Univ. Demonstrator, Physiological Laboratory, Cambridge 1968–72; Lecturer in Physiology, Cambridge 1972–79; Fellow and Dir. of Medical Studies, Downing Coll. 1971–79; Visiting Prof. New York Univ. 1970, M.I.T. 1971; Locke Research Fellow, Royal Soc. 1976–79; Waynflete Prof. of Physiology, Oxford 1979–; Professorial Fellow of Magdalen Coll. Oxford 1979–; Chief Exec. European Dana Alliance for the Brain 1996–; Pres. British Asscn. for the Advancement of Science 1997–98, British Neuroscience Asscn. 1997–; Vice-Pres. B.A.A.S. 1990–; Visiting Scientist, The Salk Inst., San Diego 1982–83; Dir. McDonnell-Pew Centre for Cognitive Neuroscience, Oxford 1990–, MRC Interdisciplinary Research Centre for Cognitive Neuroscience, Oxford 1996–; Assoc. Dir. MRC Research Centre in Brain and Behaviour, Oxford 1990–; Visiting Prof. McMaster Univ. 1992; mem. Editorial Bd. Perception 1971, Behavioral and Brain Sciences 1977, Journal of Developmental Physiology 1978–86, Experimental Brain Research 1979–89, Language and Communication 1979, Reviews in the Neurosciences 1984–, News in Physiological Sciences 1985, Clinical Vision Sciences 1986, Chinese Journal of Physiological Sciences 1988, Advances in Neuroscience 1989–, Vision Research 1993–; Hon. mem. Physiological Soc. 1998; Assoc. Ed. NeuroReport 1989–; Hon. Assoc. Rationalist Press Asscn. 1986–; Ed.-in-Chief IBRO News 1986–; Leverhulme Fellowship 1974–75; BBC Reith Lecturer 1976; Lethaby Prof., R.C.A., London 1978; Storer Lecturer, Univ. of Calif. at Davis 1980, Regents' Prof. 1995–96; Macallum Lecturer, Univ. of Toronto 1984; Fellow World Econ. Forum 1994–98, Hon. Fellow Corpus Christi Coll., Cambridge 1994–, Founder Fellow Acad. of Medical Sciences 1998–; Foreign mem. Royal Netherlands Acad. of Arts and Sciences 1993; mem. Worshipful Co. of Spectacle Makers and Freeman of the City of London 1997, mem. Livery 1998; Patron and mem. Professional Advisory Panel Headway (Nat. Head Injuries Asscn.) 1997–; Patron Asscn. for Art, Science, Eng. and Tech. (ASCENT) 1997–; Hon D.Sc. (Aston) 1992, (Salford) 1994; Robert Bing Prize, Swiss Acad. of Medical Sciences 1975, Man of the Year (Royal Soc. for Disability and Rehabilitation) 1978; Christmas Lectures for Young People, Royal Inst. 1982; John Locke Medal, Worshipful Soc. of Apothecaries 1983, Netter Prize of Acad. Nat. de Médecine, Paris 1984, Bertram Louis Abrahams Lecture, Royal Coll. of Physicians 1986, Cairns Memorial Lecture and Medal, Soc. of British Neurological Surgeons 1986, Norman McAllister Gregg Lecture and Medal, Royal Australian Coll. of Ophthalmologists 1988, Royal Soc. Michael Faraday Medal 1989, Robert Doyne Medal, Oxford Ophthalmology Congress 1989, John P. McGovern Science and Society Lecture and Medal 1990, Montgomery Medal 1991, Sir Douglas Robb Lectures, Univ. of Auckland 1991, Osler Medal (Royal Coll. of Physicians) 1993, Ellison-Cliffe Medal (Royal Soc. of Medicine) 1993, Charles F. Prentice Award (American Acad. of Optometry) 1994, Annual Review Prize Lecture (Physiological Soc.) 1995, Centenary Lecture, Univ. of Salford 1996, Alcon Prize 1996, Newton Lecture 1997, Cockcroft Lecture, UMIST 1997, Memorial Medal (Charles Univ., Czech Repub.) 1998. *Publications:* Ed. Handbook of Psychobiology 1975, Mechanics of the Mind 1977, Ed. Mindwaves 1987, The Mind Machine 1988, Ed. Images and Understanding 1990, Vision: Coding and Efficiency 1990, Sex and Society 1999; contributions to Constraints on Learning 1973, Illusion in Art and Nature 1973, The Neurosciences Third Study Program 1974 and to professional journals. *Leisure interests:* running and the arts. *Address:* University Laboratory of Physiology, Parks Road, Oxford OX1 3PT, England (Office). *Telephone:* (01865) 272471.

BLAKEMORE, Michael Howell; Australian theatre and film director; b. 18 June 1928, Sydney; s. of Conrad Blakemore and Una Mary (née Litchfield) Blakemore; m. 1st Shirley Bush 1960; one s.; m. 2nd Tanya McCallin 1986; two d.; ed. The King's School, N.S.W., Sydney Univ., Royal Acad. of Dramatic Art, U.K.; actor with Birmingham Repertory Theatre, Shakespeare Memorial Theatre etc. 1952–66; Co-Dir. Glasgow Citizens' Theatre 1966–68 (first production The Investigation); Assoc. Artistic Dir. Nat. Theatre, London 1971–76; Dir. Players, New York, U.S.A. 1978; Resident Dir. Lyric Theatre, Hammersmith, London 1980; *Productions include:* A Day in the Death of Joe Egg 1967, Arturo Ui 1969, The National Health 1969, Long Day's Journey into Night 1971, The Front Page, Macbeth 1972, The Cherry Orchard 1973, Design for Living 1973, Separate Tables 1976, Plunder 1976, Privates on Parade 1977, Candida 1977, Make and Break 1980, Travelling North 1980, The Wild Duck 1980, All My Sons 1981, Noises Off 1982 (Drama Desk Award, New York 1983–84), Benefactors 1984, Lettice and Lovage

1987, Uncle Vanya 1988, City of Angels 1989, Lettice and Lovage 1990, After the Fall 1990, The Ride Down Mount Morgan 1991, Tosca (Welsh Nat. Opera) 1992, The Sisters Rosensweig 1994, Death Defying Acts 1995, Now You Know 1995, Sylvia 1996, The Life 1997, Copenhagen 1998; films: A Personal History of the Australian Surf 1981, Privates on Parade 1983, Country Life (writer and dir.) 1994; Best Dir., London Critics 1972. *Publication:* Next Season (novel) 1969. *Leisure interest:* surfing. *Address:* 18 Upper Park Road, London, NW3 2UP, England. *Telephone:* 0171-483 2575. *Fax:* 0171-483 2476.

BLAKENEY, Allan Emrys, P.C., O.C., Q.C., L.L.B., M.A.; Canadian politician (retd.); b. 7 Sept. 1925, Bridgewater, Nova Scotia; s. of John Cline Blakeney and Bertha May Davies; m. 1st Mary Elizabeth Schwartz 1950 (died 1957); one s. one d.; m. 2nd Anne Gorham; one s. one d.; ed. Dalhousie and Oxford Univs; Sec. and legal adviser to Crown Corpn., Govt. of Saskatchewan 1950–55; Chair. Sask. Securities Comm. 1955–58; partner law firm of Davidson, Davidson & Blakeney 1958–60; mem. Legis. Ass. 1960–88 (retd.); Govt. of Sask. Minister of Educ. 1960–61, Provincial Treas. 1961–62, Minister of Health 1962–64, Leader of the Opposition 1970–71, Premier 1971–82, Leader of the Opposition 1982–87; mem. Senate, Univ. of Sask. 1960–62; Chair. of Wascana Centre Authority 1962–64; partner Griffin, Blakeney, Beke (law firm) 1964–70; Pres. New Democratic Party of Canada 1969–71; Laskin Prof. of Constitutional Law, Osgoode Hall Law School, York Univ. 1988–90; Law Foundation Prof. of Public Law, Univ. of Saskatchewan 1990–91, Visiting Scholar 1991–; Dr. h.c. (Mount Allison Univ.) 1980, (Dalhousie) 1980, (York) 1991, (Univ. of W. Ont.) 1991, (Univ. of Regina) 1993, (Univ. of Saskatchewan) 1995. *Publications:* Political Management in Canada (with S. Borins) 1992, articles on public affairs. *Address:* 1752 Prince of Wales Avenue, Saskatoon, Saskatchewan, S7K 3E5, Canada.

BLAKENHAM, 2nd Viscount (cr. 1963), of Little Blakenham; **Michael John Hare,** P.C., O.B.E., D.L.; British business executive; b. 25 Jan. 1938, London; s. of the late 1st Viscount Blakenham and Hon. Beryl N. Pearson; m. Marcia P. Hare 1965; one s. two d.; ed. Eton Coll. and Harvard Univ.; mil. service 1956–57; with English Electric Co. 1958; Lazard Bros. 1961–63; Standard Industrial Group 1963–71; Doulton & Co. 1972–77; Chief Exec. Pearson PLC 1978–83, Chair. 1983–97, Chief Exec. 1983–93; Chair. Financial Times 1983–93; Partner Lazard Partners 1984– (Dir. Lazard Bros. 1975–97); Dir. Sotheby's Holdings Inc. 1987–, MEPC PLC 1990– (Chair. 1993–98); mem. Int. Advisory Bd. Lafarge 1979–97 (Dir. 1997–); mem. Int. Advisory Gp. Toshiba 1997–; Dir. UK-Japan 2000 Group 1990–; Chair. Royal Soc. for Protection of Birds 1981–86; Pres. Sussex Wildlife Trust 1983–; mem. House of Lords Select Cttee. on Science and Tech. 1984–88, Nature Conservancy Council 1986–90; Trustee The Royal Botanic Gardens, Kew 1991– (Chair. 1997–); Conservative. *Address:* House of Lords, London, SW1A 0PW, England.

BLAMEY, Norman Charles, O.B.E., R.A.; British painter; b. 16 Dec. 1914, London; s. of Charles H. Blamey and Ada Blamey (née Beacham); m. Margaret Kelly 1948; one s. ed. Holloway School and School of Art, The Polytechnic, Regent Street, London; Lecturer and Sr. Lecturer, School of Art, Regent St. Polytech. 1938–63; military service 1941–46; Sr. Lecturer, Chelsea School of Art, London 1963–79; Visitor at Ruskin School of Drawing and of Fine Art, Univ. of Oxford 1978–80; Visitor (since 1975) at Royal Acad. Schools, London; retrospective exhbn. Norwich, Bath, London 1992, Fine Art Soc., London 1996. *Works include:* mural decoration, St. Luke's, Leagrave, Beds. 1956, Lutheran Church of St. Andrew, Ruislip Manor, Middx. 1964, official portraits since 1975 and works in perm. collections including Tate Gallery, Chantry Bequest, King George V Gallery, Port Elizabeth, S.A., Pa. State Univ. Museum of Art, U.S.A., La Salle Coll. Art Gallery, Philadelphia., U.S.A., Victoria and Albert Museum, London, and Southampton Art Gallery; Roy Miles Award 1978, Rowney Bicentenary Award 1983, Charles Wollaston Award 1984, Korn/Ferry Carré/Orban Int. Award 1995. *Leisure interest:* walking. *Address:* 39 Lyncroft Gardens, London, NW6 1LB, England. *Telephone:* 0171-435 9250.

BLANC, Christian; French airline executive; b. 17 May 1942, Talence, Gironde; s. of Marcel Blanc and Emcarma Miranda; m. Asa Hagglund 1973; two d.; ed. Ecole Montgolfier, Bordeaux, Lycée Montesquieu, Bordeaux and Inst. d'Etudes Politiques, Bordeaux; Asst. Dir. Sopexa-Scandinavie 1969; Société centrale d'équipement du territoire 1970–74; Chef du bureau, State Secr. for Youth and Sport 1974–76; Asst. Del.-Gen. Agence technique interministérielle pour les loisirs et le plein air 1976–80; Dir. du Cabinet to Edgard Pisani, mem. of Comm. of EC, Brussels 1981–83; Prefect, Commr., République des Hautes-Pyrénées 1983–84; special govt. assignment, New Caledonia 1985; Prefect for Seine-et-Marne 1985–89; Special Prefect 1989; Pres.-Dir.-Gen. RATP 1989–93; Pres. Air France (Admin. Council) 1993–97; Chevalier, Légion d'honneur; Chevalier Ordre Nat. du Mérite. *Publication:* Le Lièvre et La Tortue (jtly.) 1994.

BLANC, Georges; French chef, author and business executive; b. 2 Jan. 1943, Bourg-en-Bresse; s. of Jean Blanc and Paule Blanc (née Tisserand); m. Jacqueline Masson 1966; two s.; ed. Ecole Hôtelière de Thonon-les-Bains; worked at Réserve de Beaulieu and Grand Hôtel de Divonne; mil. service as chef to Adm. Vedel on the Foch and the Clémenceau; returned to work in family business 1965, became head of firm 1968; Man. Dir. Georges Blanc S.A.; Maître Cuisinier de France 1975; finalist in Meilleur Ouvrier de France competition 1976; has organized numerous events abroad to promote French cuisine; Founder mem., Second Vice-Pres. Chambre Syndicale de la Haute Cuisine Française 1986; Muncipal Councillor, Vonnas 1989; Officier, Ordre nat. du Mérite, Commandeur du Mérite agricole, Officier des Arts et des Lettres, Chevalier, Légion d'honneur. *Publications:* Mes recettes 1981, La cuisine de Bourgogne (Co-author), La nature dans l'assiette 1987, Le livre blanc des quatre saisons 1988, Les Blanc (jtly.) 1989, Le Grand Livre de la Volaille (jtly.) 1991, De la vigne à l'assiette 1995. *Leisure interests:* skiing, tennis. *Address:* Le Mère Blanc, 01540 Vonnas (Ain), France. *Telephone:* (4) 74-50-90-90.

BLANC, Pierre-Louis, M. EN D., M. ÈS L.; French diplomatist; b. 18 Jan. 1926; s. of Lucien Blanc and Renée Blanc; m. 1st (wife deceased); one s. two d.; m. 2nd Jutta Freifrau von Cramm 1988; ed. Univ. of Paris, Paris Inst. of Political Studies and Ecole Nat. d'Admin.; served French embassies in Rabat 1956, Tokyo 1962, Madrid 1965; served Office of Pres. of Repub. 1967–69; pvt. staff of Gen. de Gaulle 1969–70; Acting Deputy Dir. for Asia/Oceania, Govt. of France 1969–71; Cultural Counsellor, London 1971–75; Deputy Dir. for Personnel and Gen. Admin. Ministry of Foreign Affairs 1975; Dir. Ecole Nat. d'Admin. 1975–82; Amb. to Sweden 1982–85, to Greece 1985–87; Perm. Rep. to UN 1987–91; Pres. Council of Francophone Affairs 1992–; Vice-Pres. Soc. des Amis des Archives de France 1994–. *Address:* Quartier de Gergouven, 84560 Ménerbes, France.

BLANC, Raymond René Alfred; French chef; b. 19 Nov. 1949, Besançon; s. of Maurice Blanc and Anne-Marie Blanc; m. Katalin Blanc 1991 (separated 1994); two s. (by previous marriage); ed. Besançon Tech. Coll.; various positions 1968–76, Mil. Service 1970–71; Man. and Chef de cuisine, Bleu, Blanc, Rouge, Oxford 1976–77; opening of Les Quat'Saisons, Oxford as Chef Proprietor 1977; opening of Maison Blanc, patisserie and boulangerie 1978, Dir. and Chair. 1978–88; opening of Le Manoir aux Quat'Saisons 1984; opening of Le Petit Blanc, Oxford 1996 and in Cheltenham 1998; weekly recipe column in the Observer 1988–90; mem. Acad. Culinaire de France, British Gastronomic Acad.; mem. Restaurateurs Asscn. of G.B.; European Chef of the Year 1989; Personalité de l'Année 1990; many awards for both the restaurant and hotel; Blanc Mange (TV series) 1994. *Publications:* Recipes from Le Manoir aux Quat'Saisons 1989, Cooking for Friends 1991, Blanc Mange 1994; contributor: Take Six Cooks 1986, Taste of Health 1987, Masterchefs of Europe 1988, Best Restaurants of Great Britain 1989, Gourmet Garden 1990, European Chefs 1990, A Blanc Christmas 1996, Blanc Vite 1998. *Leisure interests:* classical music, opera, swimming, tennis. *Address:* Le Manoir aux Quat'Saisons, Church Road, Great Milton, Oxford, OX44 7PD, England. *Telephone:* (01844) 278881 (Office). *Fax:* (01844) 278847.

BLANCHARD, Francis, L.L.B.; French international civil servant; b. 21 July 1916, Paris; s. of Antoine and Marie (née Séris) Blanchard; m. Marie Claire Boué 1940 (deceased); two s. (one deceased); ed. Univ. of Paris; French Ministry of the Interior 1942–47; Int. Org. for Refugees, Geneva 1947–51; Int. Labour Office, Geneva 1951; Asst. Dir.-Gen. 1956–68, Deputy Dir.-Gen. 1968–74, Dir.-Gen. 1974–89; Préfet 1956, Hon. Préfet 1977; mem. French Econ. and Social Council 1989–94; mem. council Centre d'étude des revenus et des coûts 1989–, de la population et de la famille 1990–, Econ. and Social Council 1989; Dr. h.c. (Brussels, Manila, Seoul and Cairo Univs.); Officier Légion d'honneur. *Leisure interests:* skiing, tennis. *Address:* Prébailly, 01170 Gex (Ain), France (Home). *Telephone:* 04-50-41-51-70 (Home).

BLANCHARD, James J., M.B.A., J.D.; American politician; b. 8 Aug. 1942, Detroit, Mich.; m. Paula Parker (divorced); m. 2nd Janet Eifert; one s.; ed. Michigan State Univ. and Univ. of Minnesota; admitted to Mich. Bar 1968; Legal Aid, elections bureau, Office of the Sec. of State, Mich. 1968–69; Asst. Attorney-Gen., Mich. 1969–74, Admin. Asst. to Attorney-Gen. 1970–71, Asst. Deputy Attorney-Gen. 1971–72; mem. House of Reps. 1975–83; Gov. of Mich. 1983–91; Partner Verner, Liipfert, Bernhard. McPherson and Hand 1991–93, 1996–; Amb. to Canada 1993–96; fmr. mem. Pres.'s Comm. on Holocaust; Democrat; numerous awards including Foreign Affairs Award for Public Service 1996. *Address:* 1901 15th Street, N.W., 700 Washington, D.C. 20005, U.S.A.

BLANCHARD, Olivier Jean, PH.D.; French professor of economics; b. 27 Dec. 1948, Amiens; m. Noelle Golinelli 1973; three d.; ed. Univ. of Paris and Massachusetts Inst. of Tech.; Asst. Prof. Harvard Univ. 1977–81, Assoc. Prof. 1981–83; Assoc. Prof. M.I.T. 1983–85, Prof. of Econs. 1985–, Class of 1941 Prof. 1994–, Chair. Econs. Dept. 1998–; Vice-Pres. American Econ. Asscn. 1995–96; Fellow, Econometric Soc.; mem. American Acad. of Arts and Sciences. *Publications:* Lectures on Macroeconomics (with S. Fischer) 1989, Reform in Eastern Europe 1991, Pour l'Emploi et Cohésion Sociale 1994, Spanish Unemployment: Is There a Solution? 1994, The Economics of Transition 1996, Macroeconomics 1997. *Leisure interest:* tennis. *Address:* Department of Economics, E52-252, Massachusetts Institute of Technology, Cambridge, MA 02139, U.S.A. *Fax:* (617) 253-1330.

BLANC-LAPIERRE, André Joseph Lucien, D. ÈS SC.; French scientist; b. 7 July 1915, Lavaur; s. of Victor Blanc-Lapierre and Jeanne Garrigues; m. Jacqueline Masson 1940 (deceased); two s. six d.; ed. Ecole Normale Supérieure de Paris; Staff mem., Ecole Normale Supérieure 1940–44; Head of electronic Dept., Centre National d'Etudes des Télécommunications 1945–48; Prof. Univ. of Algiers and Dir. Inst. d'Etudes Nucléaires 1948–61; Prof. Univ. of Paris XI 1961–83; Dir. Laboratoire de l'Accélérateur Linéaire, Paris 1961–69; Dir.-Gen. Ecole Supérieure d'Electricité 1969–78; Pres. Consultative Cttee. for Scientific and Tech. Research 1963–65; Pres. Comm. for Scientific Research of Plan 1964–66; Pres. Council Nuclear Safety and Information 1987–90; mem. Acad. des Sciences 1970–, Vice-Pres. 1983–84, Pres. 1985–86; mem. Acad. Pontificale des Sciences; Grand Officier Légion d'honneur, Ordre nat. du Mérite, Commdr. des Palmes académiques; several prizes. *Publications:* numerous books and articles in professional journals. *Leisure interests:* bridge, travel. *Address:* Résidence Voltaire, 92290 Châtenay-Malabry, France (Home).

BLANCO, Salvador Jorge; Dominican Republic politician; b. 1926; Attorney-Gen. 1965; mem. comm. negotiating withdrawal of U.S. troops from Dominican Repub. 1965; mem. Senate; presidential cand. Partido Revolucionario Dominicano (PRD) 1982; Pres. Dominican Repub. 1982–86; sentenced to 20 years' imprisonment for misappropriation of public funds Aug. 1991.

BLANCO, Serge; French rugby football player; b. 31 Aug. 1958, Caracas, Venezuela; m. Lilianne Blanco; two s.; fmr. fitter, Dassault aeronautical factory, now promotions rep., Pernod; plays for Biarritz Olympique; first B cap, France v. Wales 1978, first full cap, France v. S. Africa 1980; 66 caps (won 41, drawn 3, lost 22); 26 tries.

BLANCO-CERVANTES, Raúl; Costa Rican politician and chest specialist; b. 1903, San José, s. of Macedonio Blanco Alvarez and Dolores Cervantes Castro; m. Dora Martín Chavarría 1939; one s. four d.; ed. Liceo de Costa Rica and Ludwig-Maximilians-Univ. München; Medical Dir., Sanatorio Carlos Durán 1933–67; Dir. of Anti-Tuberculosis Dept., Ministry of Public Health 1937–67; Minister of Public Health 1948–49; Pres. Coll. of Physicians and Surgeons of Costa Rica 1946, 1947; Dir.-Gen. of Assistance, Ministry of Public Health 1950, 1951; First Vice-Pres. of Costa Rica 1953–58, 1962–66; Acting Pres. of Costa Rica 1955; Dir. Hospital Nacional para Tuberculosis 1958–; Pres. Colegio de Médicos y Cirujanos de Costa Rica 1946–47; Hon. mem. Sociedad Mexicana de Tisiología; mem. of WHO Expert Advisory Panel on tuberculosis 1954–71; Gov. American Thoracic Soc., American Coll. of Chest Physicians until 1966; First Pres. and Founder Sociedad Centroamericana de Tisiología; several decorations. *Leisure interests:* reading, gardening. *Address:* Apdo. 918, San José, Costa Rica. *Telephone:* 21-20-82.

BLANCO ESTRADE, Juan Carlos; Uruguayan politician; b. 9 June 1934, Montevideo; ed. Univ. de Montevideo; worked in Banco Hipotecario, Uruguay; Central Govt. office, later President's office, until 1965; Gen. offices of OAS, and simultaneously alternate Rep. of Latin-American Asscn. of Free Trade (LAFTA) 1965–68; Dir. LAFTA 1968–71; Under-Sec. for Foreign Affairs 1971–72; Minister for Foreign Affairs 1972–76; Perm. Rep. to UN 1982–85. *Address:* c/o Ministerio de Asuntos Exteriores, Montevideo, Uruguay.

BLANCO-ZAVALA, David, B.A.; Bolivian banker; b. 6 Jan. 1946; s. of Humberto Blanco and Gabriela Zavala; m. María Eugenia Sejas 1973; three d.; ed. Univ. of Chile, American Univ., Washington, D.C.; Prof., School of Econs., Univ. of Chile 1970–71; Prof. of Econ. Policy, Catholic Univ. of Bolivia 1971–72; Econ. Adviser, Cen. Bank of Bolivia 1971–72; Financial Adviser to Pres. of Bolivia 1972–73; Under-Sec. of Finance 1973–77, Minister of Finance 1977–78, 1989; Dir. Cen. Bank of Bolivia 1975–77; Corporación Minera de Bolivia 1976–77; Gov. Inter-American Devt. Bank 1977–78; Gov. World Bank 1977; Alt. Exec. Dir. (Argentina, Bolivia, Chile, Paraguay, Uruguay) World Bank 1978–80, Exec. Dir. (incl. Peru) 1980–82. *Leisure interests:* tennis, swimming, skiing. *Address:* c/o Ministry of Finance, Calle Bolívar, La Paz, Bolivia.

BLANCPAIN, Marc (pseudonym Marc Benoni); French writer; b. 29 Sept. 1909; m. Denise Mazedier 1948; three s.; ed. Collèges d'Hirson et de Laon, Univ. de Nancy, Univ. de Paris à la Sorbonne and Ecole Normale Supérieure, Saint-Cloud; teacher, Ecole Internationale de Genève 1931–35, Lycée Français, Cairo 1935–39; Sec.-Gen. of Alliance Française 1945–78, Pres. 1978–93, Hon. Pres. 1993; Pres. Carnegie Comm., France 1984–; mem. PEN Club, Soc. des Gens de Lettres, Acad. Stanislas, Acad. des Sciences d'Outre-Mer; Commdr. Légion d'honneur, Croix de guerre 1939–44, Commdr. Ordre des Palmes académiques, Grand Officier, Ordre national du Mérite, Commdr. Ordre des Arts et des Lettres, and orders from Peru, Chile, Senegal, Brazil and Belgium; Grand Prix du Roman, Acad. Française 1945, Prix Courteline 1946, Prix Scarron 1955, Prix Engelmann (Belgium) 1956, Grand Prix du Rayonnement Français (Acad. Française) 1961. *Publications include:* novels: Le solitaire 1945, Les contes de la lampe á graisse 1946, Le carrefour de la désolation 1951, Ulla des Antipodes 1967, La femme d'Arnaud vient de mourir 1958, La Folle Marquise 1990; essays: Voyages et verres d'eau 1952, Les lumières de la France 1967; for children: Contes de Vermeil 1958; short stories: Vincennes Neuilly 1963; also: Les peupliers de la Prétentaine 1961, Grandes heures d'un village de la frontière 1964, Les truffes du voyage 1965, Aujourd'hui, l'Amérique latine 1966, La saga des amants séparés, Vol. I 1969, Vol. II 1970, Vol. III 1972–, Le plus long amour 1971, En français malgré tout 1973, Nous l'appelions Bismarck 1974, Paul-Emile et Emily 1977, Quand Guillaume II gouvernait "de la Somme aux Vosges" 1980, Histoires du Périgord 1982, La vie quotidienne au temps des invasions 1814–1944 1983, Le sentier de la douane, La bachelière de Landouzy 1984, Le mardi de Rocroi 1985, Monsieur le Prince 1986, Anne de Montmorency 1988, Histoire tragique de la frontière du nord 1991, La Fontaine avant La Fontaine 1995. *Address:* 12 boulevard Jean Mermoz, 92200 Neuilly-sur-Seine, France (Home). *Telephone:* 47-47-92-10 (Home).

BLAND, Sir (Francis) Christopher (Buchan), Kt.; British business executive; b. 29 May 1938; s. of James Bland and Jess Brodie; m. Jennifer Mary, Viscountess Enfield 1981; one s. and two step-s. two step-d.; ed. Sedbergh and Queen's Coll. Oxford; 2nd Lieut. 5th Royal Inniskilling Dragoon Guards 1956–58; Lieut. N. Irish Horse (TA) 1958–69; Dir. N. Ireland Finance Corpn. 1972–76; Deputy Chair. IBA 1972–80; Chair. Sir Joseph Causton & Sons 1977–85, LWT (Holdings) 1984–94, Century Hutchinson Group 1984–89, Life Sciences Int. (fmrly. Philicom) PLC 1987–, NFC 1994–; Dir. Nat. Provident Inst. 1977–88, Storehouse PLC 1988–93; mem. for Lewisham, GLC 1967–70; mem. Burnham Cttee. 1970; Chair. Bow Group 1969–70; Ed. Crossbow 1971–72; mem. Prime Minister's Advisory Panel on Citizen's Charter 1991–94; Chair. NHS Review Group on Nat. Training Council and Nat. Staff Cttees. 1982, Hammersmith and Queen Charlotte's Hosps. (fmrly. Hammersmith) SHA 1982–94, Hammersmith Hosps. NHS Trust 1994–, BBC Bd. of Govs. 1996–; *Leisure interests:* fishing, skiing. *Address:* 10 Catherine Place, London, SW1E 6HF; Blissamore Hall, Clanville, Andover, Hants., SP11 9HL, England. *Telephone:* 0171-834 0021 (London); (01264) 772274 (Andover).

BLANDY, John Peter, C.B.E., M.A., D.M., M.CH., F.R.C.S., F.A.C.S.; British professor of urology and consultant surgeon; b. 11 Sept. 1927, Calcutta, India; s. of Sir E. Nicolas Blandy and Dorothy Kathleen, née Marshall; m. Anne Mathias 1953; four d.; ed. Clifton Coll., Balliol Coll., Oxford, London Hosp. Medical Coll.; House Physician and House Surgeon, London Hosp. 1952, Surgical Registrar and Lecturer in Surgery 1956–60, Sr. Lecturer 1961, Consultant Surgeon 1964–92, now Consulting Surgeon; served R.A.M.C. 1953–55; Exchange Fellow, Presbyterian St. Luke's Hosp., Chicago, U.S.A. 1960–61; Resident Surgical Officer, St. Paul's Hosp. 1963–64; Consultant Surgeon, St. Peter's Hosp. for the Stone 1969–92, now Consulting Surgeon; Prof. of Urology, Univ. of London 1969–92, Prof. Emer. 1992–; mem. B.M.A., Royal Soc. of Medicine (Hon. Fellow 1995), Council, Royal Coll. of Surgeons 1982–94 (Vice-Pres. 1992–94), Int. Soc. of Pediatric Urology Surgeons, Int. Soc. of Urological Surgeons, British Asscn. of Urological Surgeons (Pres. 1984), European Asscn. of Urology (Pres. 1986–88); Pres. European Bd. of Urology 1991–92; Fellow Asscn. of Surgeons; Hon. Fellow Balliol Coll. Oxford, Royal Coll. of Surgeons, Ireland 1992, Urological Soc. of Australasia, Mexican Coll. of Urology, American, Dutch, Canadian, Romanian and Danish Urological Asscns. etc.; St. Peter's Medal, Freyer Medal, Diaz Medal 1988. *Publications:* Tumours of the Testicle (with A.D. Dayan and H.F. Hope-Stone) 1970, Transurethral Resection 1971, Urology (Ed.) 1976, Lecture Notes on Urology 1976, Operative Urology 1978, The Prostate (Ed. with B. Lytton) 1986, Urology for Nurses (with J. Moors) 1989, Urological and Genital Cancer (ed. with R. T. D. Oliver and H. F. Hope-Stone) 1989, Urology (with C. G. Fowler) 1995; papers in scientific journals. *Leisure interests:* painting and sculpture. *Address:* 362 Shakespeare Tower, Barbican, London, EC2Y 8NJ, England. *Telephone:* 0171-638 4095. *Fax:* 0171-638 4095.

BLANNING, Timothy Charles William, LITT.D, F.B.A.; British professor of history; b. 21 April 1942, Wells, Somerset; s. of Thomas Walter Blanning and Gwendolen Marchant-Jones; m. Nicky Susan Jones 1988; ed. King's School, Bruton, Somerset, Sidney Sussex Coll., Cambridge; Research Fellow, Sidney Sussex Coll. 1965–68, Fellow 1968–, Asst. Lecturer in History, Cambridge Univ. 1972–76, lecturer 1976–87, Reader in Modern European History 1987–92, Prof. of Modern European History 1992–. *Publications:* Joseph II and Enlightened Despotism 1970, Reform and Revolution in Mainz 1743–1803 1974, The French Revolution in Germany 1983, The Origins of the French Revolutionary Wars 1986, The French Revolution: Aristocrats versus Bourgeois? 1987, Joseph II 1994, The French Revolutionary Wars 1787–1802 1996, The French Revolution: Class War or Culture Clash? 1998; Ed.: The Oxford Illustrated History of Modern Europe 1996, The Rise and Fall of the French Revolution 1996, History and Biography: Essays in Honour of Derek Beales. *Leisure interests:* music, gardening. *Address:* Sidney Sussex College, Cambridge, CB2 3HU, England. *Telephone:* (01223) 338800.

BLASHFORD-SNELL, Col. John Nicholas, O.B.E., F.R.S.G.S.; British explorer, author and broadcaster; b. 22 Oct. 1936, Hereford; s. of Rev. Prebendary Leland John Blashford Snell and Gwendolen Ives Sadler; m. Judith Frances Sherman 1960; two d.; ed. Victoria Coll., Jersey, R.M.A., Sandhurst; Commissioned Royal Engineers 1957; Commdr. Operation Aphrodite (Expedition), Cyprus 1959–61; Instructor Jr. Leaders Regt. Royal Engineers 1962–63; Instructor, R.M.A., Sandhurst 1963–66; Adjt. 3rd Div. Engineers 1966–67; Commdr. The Great Abbai Expedition (Blue Nile) 1968; attended Staff Coll., Camberley 1969; Chair. Scientific Exploration Soc. 1969–; Commdr. Dahlak Quest Expedition 1969–70, British Trans-Americas Expedition (Darien Gap) 1971–72; Officer Commdg. 48th Field Squadron Royal Engineers 1972–74; Commdr. Zaire River Expedition 1974–75; C.O. Jr. Leaders Regt. Royal Engineers 1976–78; Dir. of Operations Operation Drake 1978–81; Staff Officer Ministry of Defence 1978–91, Consultant 1992–; Commdr. Fort George Volunteers 1982; Operations Dir. Operation Raleigh 1982–88, Dir.-Gen. 1989–91; Dir. SES Tibet Expedition 1987; Leader Kalahari Quest Expedition 1990, Karnali Quest Expedition 1991, Karnali Gorges Expedition 1992, numerous exploration projects thereafter; Chair. Explorers' Club (British Chapter), Operation New World 1995–; Hon. D.Sc. (Durham Univ.); Hon. D.Eng. (Bournemouth Univ.) 1997; The Livingstone Medal, The Darien Medal, The Segrave Trophy, Freeman of the City of Hereford, Paul Harris Fellow (Rotary Int.), Royal Geographical Soc. Patrons' Medal 1993, Gold Medal (Inst. of Royal Engineers) 1994. *Publications:* Weapons and

Tactics (with T. Wintringham) 1972, Where the Trails Run Out 1974, In the Steps of Stanley 1975, Expeditions the Experts' Way (with A. Ballantine) 1977, A Taste for Adventure 1978, Operation Drake (with M. Cable) 1981, Mysteries, Encounters with the Unexplained 1983, Operation Raleigh, The Start of an Adventure 1987, Operation Raleigh, Adventure Challenge (with Ann Tweedy) 1988, Operation Raleigh, Adventure Unlimited (with Ann Tweedy) 1990, Something Lost Behind the Ranges 1994, Mammoth Hunt (with Rula Lenska) 1996. *Leisure interests:* shooting, photography, food and wine. *Address:* c/o Scientific Exploration Society, Expedition Base, Motcombe, nr. Shaftesbury, Dorset, SP7 9PB, England.

BLASS, Bill (William) Ralph; American fashion designer; b. 22 June 1922, Fort Wayne, Ind.; s. of Ralph Aldrich and Ethyl (Keyser) Blass; mil. service with 603rd Combat Engineers during World War II; Asst. Designer, David Crystal 1950–51, Anna Miller & Co. 1951–59; designer, Maurice Rentner Ltd. (now Bill Blass Ltd.) 1959–, Vice-Pres. 1963–70, Pres. Bill Blass Ltd. 1970–; Trustee, New York Public Library 1986–; mem. Council, Fashion Designers of America; Coty Award, American Fashion Critics 1961, 1963, 1970, Men's Coty Award 1968, 1971, 1982, 1983, Hall of Fame Award 1970; Cartier Santos Award 1965, Print Council Award 1971, Great American Designers Award 1974, American Fashion Awards 1975, Cutty Sark Hall of Fame Award 1979, American Lifetime Achievement Award, Council of Fashion Designers 1987 and many other awards. *Address:* Bill Blass Ltd., 550 7th Avenue, New York, NY 10018, U.S.A.

BLASSE, George, D.SC.; Netherlands professor of chemistry; b. 28 Aug. 1934, Amsterdam; m. S. Vel 1961; three s.; ed. Univ. of Amsterdam; employed at Nat. Defence Lab. 1958–60, Philips Research Labs. 1960–70; Prof. of Solid State Chem., Univ. of Utrecht 1970; mem. Royal Dutch Acad. of Sciences; Gold Medal Chem. Soc. *Publications:* articles in journals. *Leisure interest:* bird watching. *Address:* J. F. Kennedylaan 36, Bunnik, Netherlands.

BLATHERWICK, Sir David Elliott Spiby, K.C.M.G., O.B.E., M.A.; British diplomatist; b. 13 July 1941, Lincoln; s. of Edward S. Blatherwick; m. (Margaret) Clare Crompton 1964; one s. one d.; ed. Lincoln School and Wadham Coll. Oxford; Foreign Office 1964; Second Sec. Kuwait 1968–70; First Sec. Dublin 1970–73; FCO 1973–77; Head of Chancery, Cairo 1977–80; Northern Ireland Office, Belfast 1981–83; FCO 1983–85; sabbatical, Stanford Univ. 1985–86; Head of Chancery, Perm. Mission to UN, New York 1986–89; Prin. Finance Officer and Chief Insp. FCO 1989–91; Amb. to Ireland 1991–95, to Egypt 1995–99. *Publication:* The Politics of International Telecommunications 1987. *Leisure interests:* walking, sailing, music. *Address:* c/o Foreign and Commonwealth Office, King Charles Street, London, S.W.1, England.

BLATTY, William Peter, M.A., D.HUM.LITT.; American author; b. 7 Jan. 1928, New York; s. of Peter and Mary (née Mouakad) Blatty; m. Julie Alicia Witbrodt 1983; three s. three d.; ed. Georgetown Univ., George Washington Univ. and Seattle Univ.; served in U.S.A.F. 1951–54; ed. with U.S. Information Agency 1955–57, Publicity Dir. Univ. Southern Calif. 1957–58, Public Relations Dir. Loyola Univ., Los Angeles 1959–60. *Publications:* Which Way to Mecca, Jack? 1959, John Goldfarb, Please Come Home 1963, I, Billy Shakespeare 1965, Twinkle, Twinkle, 'Killer' Kane 1966, The Exorcist 1970, I'll Tell Them I Remember You 1973, The Exorcist: From Novel to Film 1974, The Ninth Configuration 1978, Legion 1983. *Author of screenplays:* The Man from the Diner's Club 1961, Promise Her Anything 1962, A Shot in the Dark 1964, The Great Bank Robbery 1967, What Did You Do in the War, Daddy? 1965, Gunn 1967, Darling Lili 1968, The Exorcist 1973, The Exorcist III 1990; *Film directed:* The Ninth Configuration 1981; awards include: Golden Globe award for best movie screenplay (Twinkle, Twinkle, 'Killer' Kane, The Exorcist) 1981, Academy Award of Acad. Motion Picture, Arts and Sciences 1973.

BLAU, Peter Michael, PH.D.; American professor of sociology; b. 7 Feb. 1918, Vienna, Austria; s. of Theodore Blau and Bertha Selka; m. 1st Zena Smith 1948; m. 2nd Judith Fritz 1968; two d.; ed. Elmhurst Coll., Ill., Columbia Univ.; Instructor, Wayne State Univ. 1949–51, Cornell Univ. 1951–53; Asst. Prof., Univ. of Chicago 1953–58, Assoc. Prof. 1958–63, Prof. 1963–70; Pitt Prof. of American History and Insts., Univ. of Cambridge 1966–67; Prof. Columbia Univ. 1970–88, Quetelet Prof. 1977–88, Chair Sociology Dept. 1982–85; Visiting Prof., State Univ. of New York at Albany 1978–79, Distinguished Prof. 1979–82; Robert Broughton Distinguished Research Prof., Univ. of N.C. Chapel Hill 1988–; Hon. D. Litt. (Elmhurst Coll.) 1974; ASA Sorokin Award 1968, ASA Distinguished Scholarship Award 1980. *Publications:* The Dynamics of Bureaucracy 1955, Bureaucracy in Modern Society 1956, Formal Organizations: A Comparative Approach (with W. Richard Scott) 1962, Exchange and Power in Social Life 1964, The American Occupational Structure (with Otis Dudley Duncan) 1967, The Structure of Organizations (with Richard A. Schoenherr) 1971, The Organization of Academic Work 1973, On the Nature of Organizations 1974, Approaches to the Study of Social Structure (Ed.) 1975, Inequality and Heterogeneity 1977, Crosscutting Social Circles (with Joseph E. Schwartz) 1984, Continuities in Structural Inquiry (ed. with R. K. Merton) 1984, Structural Contexts of Opportunities 1994. *Leisure interests:* theatre, reading, travel. *Address:* University of North Carolina, Chapel Hill, NC 27514 (Office): 12 Cobb Terrace, Chapel Hill, NC 27514, U.S.A. (Home). *Telephone:* (919) 929-7885. *Fax:* (919) 962-7568.

BLAUDIN De Thé, Guy (see de Thé, Guy Blaudin).

BLAYNEY, John; Irish judge; b. 13 March 1925, Dublin; s. of Alexander Blayney and Mary Stanton; m. Bernadette Boullier 1953; four s. two d.; ed. Belvedere Coll., Glenstal Abbey School, Univ. Coll. Dublin and Kings Inns, Dublin; called to Bar 1948; practised on North-Eastern Circuit 1948–74; Asst. lecturer in Law, Univ. Coll. Dublin 1958–68; called to Inner Bar 1974; Judge, High Court 1986; Judge, Supreme Court 1992–97. *Leisure interests:* reading, music, cinema, theatre, rugby (capped for Ireland 1950), tennis. *Address:* 67 Park Avenue, Dublin 4, Ireland. *Telephone:* (01) 269110.

BLEANEY, Brebis, C.B.E., F.R.S., D.PHIL.; British physicist and university professor; b. 6 June 1915, London; s. of Frederick Bleaney and Eva Johanne Petersen; m. Betty Isabelle Plumpton 1949; one s. one d.; ed. St. John's Coll., Oxford; lecturer in Physics, Oxford 1945–57; Fellow of St. John's Coll., Oxford 1947–57, Hon. Fellow 1968–; Dr. Lee's Prof. of Experimental Philosophy, Oxford 1957–77; Fellow of Wadham Coll. 1957–; Royal Soc. Warren Research Fellow 1977–80, Leverhulme Emer. Fellow 1980–82; many visiting Professorships; Corresp. mem. Acad. des Sciences de l'Institut de France 1974–78, Associé Etranger 1978–; Abigail and John Van Vleck lecturer, Minneapolis 1985; Foreign Hon. mem. American Acad. Arts and Sciences 1978–; D.Sc. h.c. (Porto) 1987; Hughes Medal, Royal Soc. 1962; C. V. Boys Prize, Physical Soc. of London 1952, ISMAR Prize 1983, Holweck Prize, British and French Physical Socs. 1984, Zavoisky Award (Kazan) 1992, Hon. Prof., Kazan Univ. 1994. *Publications:* Electricity and Magnetism (with B. I. Bleaney) 1957, Electron Paramagnetic Resonance (with A. Abragam) 1970. *Leisure interests:* music, tennis, travel. *Address:* Clarendon Laboratory, Parks Road, Oxford, OX1 3PU; Garford House, Garford Road, Oxford, England (Home). *Telephone:* 272324 (Laboratory); 559589 (Home).

BLEASDALE, Alan; British playwright and novelist; b. 23 March 1946; s. of George Bleasdale and Margaret Bleasdale; m. Julia Moses 1970; two s. one d.; ed. Wade Deacon Grammar School, Widnes, Padgate Teachers Training Coll.; schoolteacher 1967–75; Hon. D.Litt. (Liverpool Polytechnic) 1991; B.A.F.T.A. Writers Award 1982, Royal TV Soc. Writer of the Year 1982; Best Writer Monte Carlo Int. TV Festival 1996 (for Jake's Progress). *Publications:* Scully 1975, Who's Been Sleeping in My Bed 1977, No More Sitting on the Old School Bench 1979, Boys from the Blackstuff 1982, Are You Lonesome Tonight? (Best Musical, Evening Standard Drama Awards 1985) 1985, No Surrender (film script) 1986, Having a Ball 1986, It's a Madhouse 1986, The Monocled Mutineer (televised 1986) 1986, GBH (TV series) 1991, On the Ledge 1993, Jake's Progress (TV) 1995. *Leisure interest:* rowing. *Address:* c/o Harvey Unna & Stephen Durbridge Ltd., 24 Pottery Lane, Holland Park, London, W11 4LZ, England. *Telephone:* 0171-727 1346.

BLECH, Harry, C.B.E., F.R.S.A., F.R.A.M.; British conductor; b. 2 March 1910, London; s. of Polish parents; m. 1st Enid Lessing 1935; one s. two d.; m. 2nd Marion Manley 1957; one s. three d.; ed. Central London Foundation, Trinity Coll. of Music and Manchester Coll. of Music; with B.B.C. Symphony Orchestra 1930–36; Founder mem. Blech Quartet 1933–50, London Wind Players 1942, London Mozart Players 1949, Haydn-Mozart Soc. 1949, London Mozart Choir 1952; Conductor Royal Acad. of Music Chamber Orchestra 1961–65; Hon. mem. Royal Acad. of Music; Fellow, Royal Manchester Coll. of Music, Trinity Coll. of Music. *Leisure interest:* reading. *Address:* The Owls, 70 Leopold Road, Wimbledon, London, SW19 7JQ, England. *Telephone:* 0181-946 8135.

BLECHA, Karl; Austrian politician; b. 16 April 1933, Vienna; s. of Karl Matthias Blecha and Rosa Blecha; m. 1st Ilse Steinhauser 1965; m. 2nd Burgunde Teuber 1982; two d.; ed. Univ. of Vienna; became vocational adviser in Vienna Employment Exchange and later worked as reader in publishing firm; Founder, Dir. Inst. for Empiric Social Research 1963–75; mem. Lower Austrian SPÖ (Austrian Socialist Party) Exec. 1964–90; mem. Nationalrat 1970–89; Gen. Sec. SPÖ H.Q. 1976–81, Vice-Chair. SPÖ 1981–89; Federal Minister of the Interior 1983–89; Dir. Mitropa Inst. for Econ. and Social Research, Vienna 1989–; fmr. Chair. Socialist Student Movt., Socialist Young Generation, Austrian Asscn. for Cultural Affairs; Pres. Austrian Soc. for Promotion of Research 1994–; *Address:* Mitropa Institute, Reinergasse 38, A-1050 Vienna, Austria.

BLEEHEN, Norman Montague, C.B.E., M.A., F.R.C.P., F.R.C.R.; British professor of clinical oncology; b. 24 Feb. 1930, Manchester; s. of Solomon Bleehen and Lena Bleehen; m. Tirza Loeb 1959; ed. Haberdashers' Aske's Hampstead School and Univ. of Oxford; Registrar and Sr. Registrar, The Middx. Hosp. London and Mt. Vernon Hosp. Northwood 1961–67; Research Fellow, Dept. of Radiology, Stanford, Calif. 1966–67; Locum Consultant Radiotherapist, The Middx. Hosp. 1967–69; Prof. of Radiotherapy and Head, Academic Dept. of Radiotherapy, Middx. Hosp. Medical School 1969–75, Hon. Consultant Radiotherapist 1975; Cancer Research Campaign Prof. and Head of Dept. of Clinical Oncology and Radiotherapeutics, Univ. of Cambridge 1975–95; Hon. Consultant, Dir. MRC Unit, Clinical Oncology and Radiotherapeutics 1975–95; Dir. Radiotherapeutic Centre, Addenbrooke's Hosp. Cambridge 1984–92; Fellow St. John's Coll., Cambridge 1976–; Hon. F.A.C.R.; Dr. h.c. (Bologna). *Publications:* contributions to numerous books and scientific journals. *Leisure interests:* reading, music, television. *Address:* 21 Bentley Road, Cambridge, CB2 2AW, England (Home).

BLEGEN, Judith; American opera and concert singer; b. Lexington, Ky.; d. of Dr. Halward Martin and Dorothy Mae (Anderson) Blegen; m. 1st Peter Singher 1967 (divorced 1975); one s.; m. 2nd Raymond Gniewek 1977; ed. Curtis Inst. of Music, Philadelphia, Pa., Music Acad. of the West, Santa

Barbara, Calif.; leading soprano, Nuremberg Opera, Fed. Republic of Germany 1965–68, Staatsoper, Vienna, Austria 1968–70, Metropolitan Opera, New York 1970–; Vienna roles include Zerbinetta (Ariadne auf Naxos), Rosina (The Barber of Seville), Aennchen (Der Freischütz), Norina (Don Pasquale); numerous performances at Metropolitan include Marzelline (Fidelio), Sophie (Werther), Mélisande (Pelléas et Mélisande), Sophie (Der Rosenkavalier), Adina (L'Elisir d'amore), Juliette (Roméo et Juliette), Susanna (The Marriage of Figaro); other appearances include Susanna (The Marriage of Figaro), San Francisco, title-role in Manon, Tulsa Opera, Gilda (Rigoletto), Chicago, Despina (Così fan tutte), Covent Garden, Blondchen (The Abduction from the Seraglio), Salzburg Festival, Mélisande (Pélleas et Mélisande), Spoleto Festival, Susanna (The Marriage of Figaro), Edinburgh Festival, Sophie, Paris Opera; Fulbright Scholarship, Grammy Awards. *Numerous recordings, including:* La Bohème (Puccini), Carmina Burana (Orff), Symphony No. 4 (Mahler), Harmonienmesse (Haydn), The Marriage of Figaro (Mozart), A Midsummer Night's Dream (Mendelssohn), Lord Nelson Mass (Haydn), Gloria (Poulenc), Peer Gynt Suite (Grieg), Lieder recital (Richard Strauss and Hugo Wolf), baroque music recital. *Address:* c/o Thea Dispeker, 59 East 54th Street, New York, NY 10022, U.S.A.

BLEGVAD, Mogens, DR. PHIL.; Danish professor of philosophy; b. 25 June 1917, Copenhagen; s. of Dr Olaf Blegvad Overlaege and Gudrun Schrøder; m. 1st Marianne Holm 1942–56; m. 2nd Victoria Britt-Mari Persson 1961; two s. one d.; ed. Univ. of Copenhagen; Psychologist, Copenhagen Municipal Inst. of Vocational Psychology 1943–48; Librarian, Royal Library, Copenhagen 1949–58; Lecturer, Danish Library School 1960–64; Prof. of Philosophy, Univ. of Copenhagen 1964–87; Prof. Emer. 1987–; Chair. Danish Soc. for Legal and Social Philosophy 1989–96; Fellow, Royal Danish Acad. of Sciences and Letters. *Publications:* The Naturalistic Fallacy 1959, Morals and Conscience 1963, Social Thought through One Hundred Years—Themes and Figures 1984, On Morals and Ethics 1986, The Royal Danish Academy of Sciences and Letters 1942–92 1992. *Leisure interests:* music, theatre, films. *Address:* Soldalen 7, 2100 Copenhagen Ø, Denmark. *Telephone:* 39293778.

BLEICKEN, Jochen, DR.PHIL.; German professor of history; b. 3 Sept. 1926, Westerland/Sylt; s. of Max Bleicken and Marie (née Jensen) Bleicken; ed. Univs. of Kiel and Frankfurt a. M.; Asst. Althistorische Seminar, Göttingen 1955–62, Teacher in Early History 1961; Prof. in Ancient History, Hamburg 1962–67, Frankfurt a. M. 1967–77, Göttingen 1977–91; Prof. Emer. 1991–; mem. Wissenschaftlich Geschichte, Johann Wolfgang Goethe Univ., Frankfurt 1967–, Deutschen Archäologischen Instituts (DAI) 1976–, Akad. der Wissenschaften in Göttingen 1978. *Publications:* Das Volkstribunat der klassische Republik 1955, Staatliche Ordnung und Freiheit in der Römische Republik 1972, Lex Publica: Studien zu Gesetz und Recht in der Römische Republik 1975, Verfassung und Sozialgeschichte der Römische Kaiserzeit 1981, Geschichte der Römische Republik 1982, Die Athenische Demokratie 1985, Die Verfassung der Römische Republik 1985, Augustus: Eine Biographie 1998. *Leisure interest:* numismatics. *Address:* Obernjesaer Strasse 8, 37133 Friedland, Germany. *Telephone:* 05504-381.

BLENDON, Robert J., SC.D., M.P.H., M.B.A.; American professor of health policy and political analysis; b. 19 Dec. 1942, Philadelphia, Pa.; s. of Edward G. Blendon and Theresa M. Blendon; m. Marie C. McCormick 1977; ed. Marietta Coll., Univ. of Chicago and Johns Hopkins Univ.; Instructor Johns Hopkins Univ. School of Hygiene and Public Health, Baltimore 1969, Asst. to Assoc. Dean (Health Care Programs) 1969–70, Asst. Prof. 1970–71, Asst. Dir. for Planning and Devt., Office of Health Care Programs 1970–71; Special Asst. for Health Affairs to Deputy Under-Sec. for Policy Co-ordination, Dept. of Health Educ. and Welfare 1971–72, Special Asst. for Policy Devt. to Asst. Sec. for Health and Scientific Affairs 1971–72; Visiting Lecturer, Princeton Univ. 1972–80, Co-ordinator, Medicine in Modern America Course 1980–; Sr. Vice-Pres. The Robert Wood Johnson Foundation 1980–87; Prof. Dept. of Health Policy and Political Analysis, Harvard Univ. School of Public Health 1987–, Chair. 1987–96; Prof. Kennedy School of Govt. 1995– and numerous other professional appts. *Publications:* articles in professional journals. *Address:* Harvard University School of Public Health, 677 Huntington Avenue, Boston, MA 02115 (Office); 478 Quinobequin Road, Newton, MA 02468, U.S.A. *Telephone:* (617) 432-4502.

BLESSED, Brian; British actor; b. 9 Oct. 1936; s. of William Blessed and Hilda Wall; m. Hildegard Zimmermann 1978; one d.; ed. Bolton-on-Dearne Secondary Modern School; studied at Bristol Old Vic; subsequently worked in repertory cos., mainly Nottingham and later Birmingham Repertory Co.; appeared with RSC as Claudius in Hamlet, Hastings in Richard III, Exeter in Henry V; appearances with Nat. Theatre include State of Revolution, Metropolis, Cats, The Lion in Winter; one-man show An Evening with Brian Blessed; numerous TV appearances including role of Fancy Smith in Z Cars and roles in BBC serializations of The Three Musketeers, I, Claudius, My Family and Other Animals, Black Adder and Tom Jones. *Films:* Flash Gordon, Return to Treasure Island, Trojan Women, Man of La Mancha, Henry V, War and Remembrance, Robin Hood Prince of Thieves, Prisoners of Honour, Much Ado About Nothing, Hamlet, King Lear. *Publications:* The Turquoise Mountain, The Dynamite Kid, Nothing's Impossible, Blessed Everest. *Leisure interests:* mountaineering, judo (black belt), Koi Carp and animal welfare. *Address:* c/o Derek Webster, Associated International Management, 5 Denmark Street, London, WC2H 8LP, England. *Telephone:* 0171-836 2001. *Fax:* 0171-379 0848.

BLETHYN, Brenda Anne; British actress; b. 20 Feb. 1946; d. of William Charles Bottle and Louisa Kathleen Bottle; partner Michael Mayhew 1977; ed. St. Augustine's R.C. School, Ramsgate, Thanet Tech. Coll., Guildford School of Acting; with Nat. Theatre (now Royal Nat. Theatre) 1975–90. *Theatre appearances include:* Mysteries 1979, Steaming 1981, Double Dealer 1982, Benefactors 1984, Dalliance 1987, A Doll's House 1987, Born Yesterday 1988, The Beaux' Stratagem 1989, An Ideal Husband 1992, Wildest Dreams 1993, The Bed Before Yesterday 1994, Habeas Corpus 1996, Absent Friends (New York) 1996. *Films:* The Witches, A River Runs Through It 1992, Secrets and Lies 1996, Remember Me 1996, Music From Another Room 1997, Girls' Night 1997, Little Voice 1999. *Television includes:* Henry VI (Part I) 1981, King Lear 1983, Chance in a Million 1983–85, The Labours of Erica 1987, The Bullion Boys 1993, The Buddah of Suburbia 1993, Sleeping with Mickey 1993, Outside Edge 1994–96, First Signs of Madness 1996; mem. Poetry Soc. 1976–; numerous awards including Best Actress Award for Secrets and Lies, Cannes Film Festival 1996, Boston Film Critics 1997, L.A. Film Critics 1997, Golden Globe 1997, London Film Critics 1997, BAFTA 1997. *Leisure interests:* reading, swimming, cryptic crosswords. *Address:* c/o ICM, 76 Oxford Street, London, W1N 0AX, England. *Telephone:* 0171-636 6565.

BLEVIN, William Roderick, A.M., D.SC., F.T.S.E., F.A.A.; Australian research physicist; b. 31 Oct. 1929, Inverell, N.S.W.; s. of late W. R. Blevin and Elizabeth McRae; m. Doreen Graham 1952; one s. two d.; ed. Tamworth High School, N.S.W. and Univ. of Sydney; Research Scientist to Chief Research Scientist, Div. of Physics, CSIRO 1953–79; Chief Standards Scientist, Div. of Applied Physics, CSIRO 1980–88, Chief of Div. 1988–94, Hon. Research Fellow 1994–; Expert Consultant, U.S. Nat. Bureau of Standards 1973; mem. of Council, Univ. of New England 1976–84; mem. Nat. Standards Comm. 1980–94, Chair. 1981–85; Pres. Consultative Cttee. for Photometry and Radiometry 1980–96; mem. Int. Cttee. of Weights and Measures 1982–, Vice-Pres. 1992–96, Sec. 1996–. *Leisure interest:* gardening. *Address:* CSIRO Division of Telecommunications and Industrial Physics, P.O. Box 218, Lindfield, N.S.W. 2070 (Office); 61 Boronia Avenue, Cheltenham, N.S.W. 2119, Australia (Home). *Telephone:* (612) 9413 7320 (Office); (612) 9876 5835 (Home). *Fax:* (612) 9876 3043.

BLEWETT, Neal, A.C., M.A., PH.D., F.R.HIST.S.; Australian politician; b. 24 Oct. 1933, Sydney; s. of James Blewett and Phyllis Blewett (née Kerrison); m. Jill Myford 1962 (deceased 1988); one s. one d.; ed. Launceston High School, Tasmania, Univ. of Tasmania, Oxford Univ.; Lecturer, Oxford Univ. 1959–64; Prof., Dept. of Political Theory and Insts., Flinders Univ. 1974–77; M.P. for Bonython, S. Australia 1977–94; Minister for Health 1983–87, for Community Services and Health 1987–90, for Trade and Overseas Devt. 1990–91, Minister for Social Security 1991–93; High Commr. in U.K. 1994–98; Pres. Australian Inst. of Int. Affairs 1998–; mem. Exec. Bd. WHO 1995–98; fmr. mem. Jt. House Cttee. on Foreign Affairs and Defence; fmr. mem. parl. dels. visiting several overseas countries; Australian Labor Party. *Publications:* Playford to Dunstan: The Politics of Transition (with Dean Jaensch) 1971, The Peers, the Parties and the People 1972. *Leisure interests:* reading, walking, cinema. *Address:* 32 Fitzroy Street, Leura, New South Wales 2780, Australia.

BLEY, Carla Borg; American jazz composer; b. 11 May 1938, Oakland, Calif.; d. of Emil Carl Borg and Arlene Anderson; m. 1st Paul Bley 1959 (divorced 1967); m. 2nd Michael Mantler 1967 (divorced 1992); one d.; ed. public schools; freelance composer 1956–; pianist, Jazz Composers Orchestra, New York 1964–; European concert tours with Jazz Realities 1965–66; founder, WATT 1973–; toured Europe with Jack Bruce Band 1975; leader, Carla Bley Band, touring U.S.A. and Europe 1977–; composed and recorded: A Genuine Tong Funeral 1967, Escalator Over the Hill (opera) 1970–71 (Oscar du Disque de Jazz 1973), Tropic Appetites 1973; composed chamber orchestra 3/4 1974–75, Mortelle Rautonnée (film score) 1983; recordings include: Dinner Music 1976, The Carla Bley Band—European Tour 1977, Music Mecanique 1979, Fictitious Sports 1980, Social Studies 1980, Carla Bley Live! 1981, Heavy Heart 1984, I Hate to Sing 1984, Night Glo 1985, Sextet 1987, Live 1987, Duets 1988, Fleur Carnivore 1989, The Very Big Carla Bley Band 1991, Go Together 1993, Big Band Theory 1993, Songs with Legs 1995, Goes to Church 1996, Fancy Chamber Music 1998; Cultural Council Foundation grantee 1971, 1979; Guggenheim Fellow 1972; Nat. Endowment for Arts grantee 1973; Winner, int. jazz critics' poll, Down Beat magazine seven times (1966, 1971, 1972, 1978, 1979, 1980, 1983), Best Composer of Year, Down Beat readers' poll 1984 and Composer/Arranger of Year 1985–92, Best in Field Jazz Times critics' poll 1990, Prix Jazz Moderne for The Very Big Carla Bley Band (Acad. du Jazz) 1992, Best Arranger Down Beat critics' poll 1993, 1994. *Address:* c/o Watt Works, P.O. Box 67, Willow, NY 12495, U.S.A.

BLIER, Bertrand; French film director; b. 14 March 1939, Paris; s. of the late Bernard Blier and of Gisele Brunet; m. Catherine Florin 1973; one d.; also one s. by Anouk Grinberg; ed. Lycée Claude Bernard, Paris; worked as asst. to several film directors; Grand Prix Nat. du Cinema 1989. *Films include:* Hitler, connais pas 1963, Si j'étais un espion (Breakdown) 1967, Les valseuses (Making It) 1974, Calmos 1975, Préparez vos mouchoirs (Oscar for Best Foreign Film) 1977, Buffet froid (three Césars) 1979, Beau-père 1981, La femme de mon pote (My Best Friend's Girl) 1983, Notre histoire (Separate Rooms) 1984, Tenue de soirée 1986, Trop belle pour toi (Cannes Special Jury Prize 1989) 1988, Merci la Vie 1991, Tango 1992, Un Deux

Trois—Soleil 1993, Mon Homme 1996. *Publications:* several novels and film scripts. *Address:* Artmédia, 10 avenue George V, 75008 Paris (Office); 11 rue Marguerite, 75017 Paris, France (Home).

BLIKLE, Andrzej, PROF. MATH.; Polish mathematician and confectioner; b. 24 Sept. 1939, Warsaw; s. of Jerzy Blikle and Aniela Blikle; m.; one s.; ed. Warsaw Univ.; Prof. 1976; master of confectioner's trade 1975; scientific worker Inst. of Math. Polish Acad. of Sciences 1963–71; Computational Centre Polish Acad. of Sciences 1971–77; Inst. of Computer Science Polish Acad. of Sciences 1977–; Pres. A. Blikle Ltd. 1991–; mem. Polish Math. Society 1962–, Polish Information Processing Society 1981– (Pres. 1987), Asscn. for Theoretical Computer Science 1982–, Academiae Europaeae 1993. *Leisure interests:* skiing, wind surfing, films, history. *Address:* ul. Czarnieckiego 82, 01-541 Warsaw, Poland. *Telephone:* (22) 39 63 65. *Fax:* (22) 843 06 01.

BLIM, Richard Don, M.D.; American pediatrician; b. 8 Nov. 1927, Kansas City; s. of Miles Blim and Latha Daniels Blim; m. Myrle Tingstad 1952; two s. one d.; ed. Univ. of Kansas; Pres. Kansas City S.W. Pediatric Soc. 1963; Pres. Mo. Chapter American Acad. of Pediatrics 1964–67; Exec. Bd. American Acad. of Pediatrics 1973–79, Vice-Pres. 1979–80, Pres. 1980–81; Dir. Medical Affairs, St. Luke's Hosp. 1989–; Pres. Pediatrics Assocs. 1970–89; Pres. Univ. of Kansas Medical Alumni 1973; mem. Inst. of Medicine 1983–; Pres. of Health Plan Mid America 1984–88; Outstanding Medical Alumnus, Univ. of Kansas 1978; Grulee Award, American Acad. of Pediatrics 1984. *Publications:* several articles on paediatrics. *Leisure interest:* golf. *Address:* St. Luke's Hospital, 44 Wornall, Kansas City, MO 64111 (Office); 304 West 172nd Street, Belton, MO 64012, U.S.A. (Home). *Telephone:* (816) 932-3601 (Office). *Fax:* (816) 932-5990 (Office).

BLINDER, Alan Stuart, A.B., PH.D.; American professor of economics; b. 14 Oct. 1945, Brooklyn, New York; s. of Morris Blinder and Shirley Blinder; m. Madeleine Schwartz 1967; two s.; ed. Princeton Univ., London School of Econs., Mass. Inst. of Tech.; Deputy Asst. Dir. Congressional Budget Office 1975; Gordon S. Rentschler Memorial Prof. of Econs., Princeton Univ., N.J. 1982–, Dir. Center for Econ. Policy Studies 1989–93, Co.-Dir. 1996–; mem. Council of Econ. Advisers to Pres. Clinton 1993–94; Vice-Chair. Bd. of Govs. of Fed. Reserve System 1994–96; Vice-Chair. G7 Group 1997–; Fellow American Acad. of Arts and Sciences 1991–; mem. American Philosophical Soc. 1996–. *Publications include:* Growing Together: An Alternative Economic Strategy for the 1990s 1991, Economics, Principles and Policy (jtly.) 1997, Central Banking in Theory and Practice 1998, Asking About Prices: A New Approach to Understanding Price Stickiness (jtly.) 1998. *Leisure interests:* tennis, skiing. *Address:* Department of Economics, Princeton University, 105 Fisher Hall, Princeton, NJ 08544, U.S.A. *Telephone:* (609) 258-3358. *Fax:* (609) 258-5398.

BLIN-STOYLE, Roger John, D.PHIL., F.R.S.; British academic; b. 24 Dec. 1924, Leicester; s. of C. B. and A. M. (née Nash) Blin-Stoyle; m. Audrey Elizabeth Balmford 1949; one s. one d.; ed. Alderman Newton's Boys' School, Leicester, Wadham Coll., Oxford; Lecturer in Mathematical Physics Birmingham Univ. 1953–54; Sr. Research Officer in Theoretical Physics Oxford 1952–62, Fellow and Lecturer in Physics Wadham Coll. 1956–62, Hon. Fellow 1987; Visiting Assoc. Prof. of Physics M.I.T. 1959–60; Dean, School of Mathematical and Physical Sciences Sussex Univ. 1962–68, Prof. of Theoretical Physics 1962–90, Emer. Prof. 1990–, Pro-Vice-Chancellor 1965–67, Deputy Vice-Chancellor 1970–72, Pro-Vice-Chancellor (Science) 1977–79; Chair. School Curriculum Devt. Cttee. 1983–88; Pres. Inst. of Physics 1990–92, Asscn. for Science Educ. 1993–94; Rutherford Medal and Prize, Inst. of Physics 1976; Hon. D.Sc. (Sussex) 1990. *Publications:* Theories of Nuclear Moments 1957, Fundamental Interactions and the Nucleus 1973, Nuclear and Particle Physics 1991, Eureka! Physics of Particles, Matter and the Universe 1997; Ed. Students Physics Series and various articles in scientific and educational journals. *Leisure interest:* making music. *Address:* School of Chemistry, Physics and Environmental Sciences, University of Sussex, Brighton, Sussex, BN1 9QJ (Office); 14 Hill Road, Lewes, Sussex, BN7 1DB, England (Home). *Telephone:* 01273 606755 (Office); 01273 473640 (Home).

BLISS, John William Michael, PH.D., F.R.S.C.; Canadian historian and writer; b. 18 Jan. 1941, Kingsville, Ont.; s. of Quartus Bliss and Anne L. Crow; m. Elizabeth J. Haslam 1963; one s. two d.; ed. Kingsville Dist. High School and Univ. of Toronto; Teaching Asst. Harvard Univ. 1967–68; Dept. of History, Univ. of Toronto 1968–72, Prof. 1975–; numerous awards including Tyrrell Medal, Royal Soc. of Canada 1988. *Publications:* A Living Profit 1974, A Canadian Millionaire: The Life of Sir Joseph Flavelle 1978, The Discovery of Insulin 1982, Banting: A Biography 1984, Northern Enterprise: Five Centuries of Canadian Business 1987, Plague: A Story of Smallpox in Montreal 1991, Right Honourable Men: The Descent of Canadian Politics from Macdonald to Mulroney 1994. *Address:* Department of History/History of Medicine, University of Toronto, 88 College Street, Toronto, M5G 1L4, Canada. *Fax:* 416-971-2160.

BLISS, Timothy Vivian Pelham, PH.D., F.R.S.; British neuroscientist; b. 27 July 1940, Weymouth; s. of Pelham Marryat Bliss and Elizabeth Bliss (née Sproule); m. 1st Virginia Catherine Morton-Evans 1975; one step-s. one step-d.; m. 2nd Isabel Frances Vasseur; two step-s.; one d. by Katherine Clough; ed. McGill Univ., Montreal; mem. of scientific staff MRC at Nat. Inst. for Medical Research 1967–, Head Div. of Neurophysiology 1988–, Head Neurosciences Group 1996–; Visiting Prof. Dept. of Physiology, Univ. Coll. London 1993–; Fellow Acad. of Medical Sciences 1998; Bristol Myers Squibb Prize for Neuroscience 1991, Feldberg Prize 1994. *Publications:* over 80 papers in scientific journals relating to the neural basis of learning and memory. *Leisure interests:* architecture, food, wine. *Address:* National Institute for Medical Research, Mill Hill, London, NW7 1AA, England.

BLISSETT, William, PH.D. F.R.S.C.; Canadian professor of English; b. 11 Oct. 1921, Saskatchewan; s. of Ralph R. Blissett and Gladys Jones; ed. Univs. of British Columbia and Toronto; lecturer in English, Univ. of Toronto 1948–50; Assoc. Prof. Univ. of Sask. 1950–57, Prof. 1957–60; Prof. and Head, Dept. of English, Huron Coll. Univ. of W. Ont. 1960–65; Prof. of English, Univ. Coll. Univ. of Toronto 1965–87, Prof. Emer. 1987–; Hon. Fellow, Huron Coll. 1966; recipient of Festschrift, Craft and Tradition (ed. H. B. De Groot and A. M. Leggatt), with list of publs. 1990. *Publications:* The Long Conversation, A Memoir of David Jones 1981; numerous articles on Spenser, Shakespeare, Jonson, literary Wagnerism, T. S. Eliot, David Jones. *Leisure interests:* travel, opera, book collecting. *Address:* University College, University of Toronto, Toronto, M5S 1A1 (Office); 36 Castle Frank Road, Apt. 212, Toronto, M4W 2Z7, Canada (Home). *Telephone:* (416) 924-1297 (Home).

BLIX, Hans Martin, LL.D., PH.D.; Swedish international official and lawyer (retd.); b. 28 June 1928, Uppsala; s. of Gunnar and Hertha (née Wiberg) Blix; m. Eva Kettis 1962; two s.; ed. Uppsala Univ., Univ. of Cambridge, Columbia Univ., New York, Univ. of Stockholm; Asst. Prof. of Int. Law, Univ. of Stockholm 1960–63; Legal Consultant on Int. Law, Foreign Ministry 1963–76; Under-Sec. of State for Int. Devt. Co-operation, Foreign Ministry 1976–78, 1979–81; Minister for Foreign Affairs 1978–79; Dir.-Gen. Int. Atomic Energy Agency (IAEA), Vienna 1981–97; mem. Swedish del. to UN Gen. Assembly 1961–81; mem. del. to Conf. on Disarmament, Geneva 1962–78. *Publications:* Treaty-Making Power (dissertation), Statsmyndigheternas Internationella Förbindelser (monograph) 1964, Sovereignty, Aggression and Neutrality 1970, The Treaty-Maker's Handbook 1973, and articles in scientific journals. *Leisure interests:* skiing, hiking, art. *Address:* c/o International Atomic Energy Agency, Wagramerstrasse 5, P.O. Box 100, A-1400 Vienna, Austria.

BLOCH, Konrad, PH.D.; American (b. German) biochemist; b. 21 Jan. 1912; s. of Frederick Bloch and Hedwig Bloch (née Steiner); m. Lore Teutsch 1941; one s. one d.; ed. Technische Hochschule, Munich, and Columbia Univ.; emigrated to U.S.A. 1936, naturalized 1944; Instructor and Research Assoc., Columbia Univ. 1939–46; Asst. Prof. of Biochemistry, Univ. of Chicago 1946–50, Prof. 1950–54; Higgins Prof. of Biochemistry, Harvard Univ. 1954–82; Prof. Emer. 1982–; Fellow American Acad. of Sciences; mem. N.A.S., American Philosophical Soc. 1966; Foreign mem. Royal Soc 1985; Fritzsche Award, American Chemical Soc. 1964, Nobel Prize for Medicine with Prof. Theodor Lynen for discoveries concerning the mechanism and regulation of cholesterol and fatty acid metabolism 1964, U.S. Nat. Medal of Science 1987. *Publication:* Lipid Metabolism 1961. *Address:* c/o Department of Chemistry, Medical School, Harvard University, 12 Oxford Street, Cambridge, MA 02138, U.S.A. *Telephone:* (617) 495 4069.

BLOCK, Herbert Lawrence (Herblock); American cartoonist; b. 13 Oct. 1909, Chicago; s. of David Julian Block and Tessie Lupe; ed. Lake Forest Coll., Ill., Art Inst., Chicago; editorial cartoonist Chicago Daily News 1929–33; Nat. Educ. Asscn. Service 1933–43; served World War II; editorial cartoonist The Washington Post 1946–; Pulitzer Prize 1942, 1954, 1979, American Newspaper Guild Award 1948, Heywood Broun Award 1950, Sidney Hillman Award 1953, Reuben Award, Nat. Cartoonists Soc. 1957, Lauterbach Award for Civil Liberties 1959, Florina Lasker Award, New York Civil Liberties Union 1960, Distinguished Service Journalism Award 1963, Bill of Rights Award 1966, Nat. Headliners Award 1976, Power of Printing Award 1977, Nat. Press Club 4th Estate Award 1977, Nat. Educ. Asscn. Human Relations Award 1979, Hubert H. Humphrey Civil Rights Award 1987, Exceptional Merit Media Award 1990, Robert F. Kennedy Memorial Special Recognition Award 1994, etc.; Hon. LL.D. (Lake Forest Coll.) 1957; Hon. Litt.D. (Rutgers Univ.) 1963; Hon. L.H.D. (Williams Coll. 1969, Haverford Coll. 1977, Univ. of Md. 1977). *Publications:* The Herblock Book 1952, Herblock's Here and Now 1955, Herblock's Special for Today 1958, Straight Herblock 1964, The Herblock Gallery 1968, Herblock's State of the Union 1972, Herblock Special Report 1974, Herblock On All Fronts 1980, Herblock Through the Looking Glass 1984, Herblock At Large 1987, Herblock: A Cartoonist's Life 1993, Bella and Me: Life in the Service of a Cat 1995; designed U.S. postage stamp commemorating 175th anniversary of Bill of Rights 1966. *Address:* The Washington Post, 1150 15th Street N.W., Washington, DC 20071, U.S.A.

BLOCK, Ned Joel, PH.D.; American professor of philosophy; b. 22 Aug. 1942, Chicago; s. of Eli Block and Blanche Rabinowitz; m. Susan Carey 1970; one d.; ed. Mass. Inst. of Tech., St. John's Coll. Oxford and Harvard Univ.; Asst. Prof. MIT 1971–77, Assoc. Prof. 1977–83, Prof. of Philosophy, Dept. of Linguistics and Philosophy 1983–96, Chair. of Philosophy 1989–95; Prof. of Philosophy New York Univ. 1996– Pres. Soc. for Philosophy and Psychology 1978–79; Chair. MIT Press Cognitive Science Bd. 1992–95; NSF Fellow 1985–86, 1988–89; Fellow, American Council of Learned Socs., Center for Study of Language and Information; Guggenheim Fellow; Sloan Foundation Fellow. *Publications:* The IQ Controversy (with G. Dworkin) 1976, Readings in Philosophy of Psychology (Vol. 1) 1980, (Vol. 2) 1981, Imagery 1981, The Nature of Consciousness (with O. Flanagan and G. Güzeldere).

Address: Dept. of Philosophy, New York University, Main Bldg., 100 Washington Square E., New York, NY 10003 (Office); 29 Washington Square, New York, NY 10003, U.S.A. (Home). *Telephone:* (212) 998 8322. *Fax:* (212) 995 4179.

BLOEMBERGEN, Nicolaas, DR.PHIL.; American (naturalized 1958) professor of applied physics; b. 11 March 1920, Dordrecht, Netherlands; s. of Auke Bloembergen and Sophia M. Quint; m. Huberta D. Brink 1950; one s. two d.; ed. Univs. of Utrecht and Leiden; Research Fellow, Leiden Univ. 1947–49; Soc. of Fellows, Harvard Univ. 1949–51, Gordon McKay Assoc. Prof. 1951–57, Prof. of Applied Physics 1957, Rumford Prof. of Physics 1974–80, Gerhard Gade Univ. Prof. 1980; Guggenheim Fellow 1957; Lorentz Guest Prof., Leiden 1973; Raman Visiting Prof., Bangalore Univ. 1979; Visiting Prof., Coll. de France 1980; mem. N.A.S. (U.S.A.); Corresp. mem. Royal Dutch Acad. of Sciences; Foreign Assoc. mem. Acad. des Sciences, Inst. de France 1981–; Commdr., Order of Orange 1988; foreign mem., Indian Acad. of Sciences, Akad. Leopoldina (G.D.R.), Royal Norwegian Inst. of Science; Hon. D.Sc. (Laval Univ., Quebec, Univ. of Conn., Hartford Univ., Univ. of Mass., Univ. of Cen. Fla.); Hon. D.Sc. (Moscow State Univ.) 1997, (N. Carolina State Univ.) 1998; Buckley Prize, American Physical Soc., Liebmann Prize, Inst. of Radio Engineers, Ballantine Medal, Franklin Inst., Royal Dutch Acad. of Arts and Sciences, Half Moon Trophy, Netherland Club of New York, Nat. Medal of Science 1974, Lorentz Medal, Royal Dutch Acad. of Sciences 1978, Frederick Ives Medal, Optical Soc. of America 1979, Alexander von Humboldt Senior U.S. Scientist Award, Munich 1980, shared Nobel Prize in Physics 1981 for contribution to development of laser spectroscopy, Medal of Honor, Inst. of Electrical and Electronics Engineers 1983. *Publications:* Nuclear Magnetic Relaxation 1961, Nonlinear Optics 1965, Encounters in Magnetic Resonance 1996, Encounters in Nonlinear Optics 1996, over 300 papers in professional journals. *Leisure interests:* travel, skiing, tennis. *Address:* Pierce Hall, Harvard University, Cambridge, MA 02138, U.S.A.

BLOKHIN, Oleg Vladimirovich; Ukrainian footballer; b. 1953, Ukraine; m. Irina Deryugina; ed. Kiev Physical Culture Inst. and Kiev Univ.; played for Dinamo, Kiev 1974–86, scoring over 200 goals; concurrently mem. Soviet nat. team; seven times Champion U.S.S.R.; Coach Olympiacos (Greece) 1988–94; Golden Boot Award 1975. *Address:* c/o Ministry of Youth and Sport, Espladra 42, 252023 Kiev, Ukraine. *Telephone:* 220-02-00.

BLOM-COOPER, Sir Louis Jacques, Kt., Q.C., F.R.S.A.; British lawyer and author; b. 27 March 1926; s. of Alfred Blom-Cooper and Ella Flesseman; m. 1st 1952 (dissolved 1970); two s. one d.; m. 2nd Jane E. Smither 1970; one s. two d.; ed. Seaford Coll., King's Coll., London, Municipal Univ. of Amsterdam and Fitzwilliam Coll., Cambridge; army service 1944–47; called to Bar, Middle Temple 1952, Bencher 1978; mem. Home Sec.'s Advisory Council on the Penal System 1966–78; Chair. Howard League for Penal Reform 1973–84, Vice-Pres. 1984–; Chair. Panel of Inquiry into death of Jasmine Beckford 1985; on several comms. of inquiry 1986–87; Judge Court of Appeal, Jersey and Guernsey 1989–96; Ind. Commr. for the Holding Centres, Northern Ireland 1993–99; Chair. Mental Health Act Comm. 1987–94, Press Council 1989–90, Nat. Asscn. for Victim Support Schemes (NASS) 1994–; Dr. h.c. (Ulster) 1995; Hon. Litt.D. (E. Anglia) 1997. *Publications:* Bankruptcy in Private International Law 1954, The Law as Literature 1962, The A6 Murder (A Semblance of Truth) 1963, A Calendar of Murder (with T. P. Morris) 1964, Language of the Law 1965, Separated Spouses (with O. R. McGregor and C. Gibson) 1970, Final Appeal: A Study of the House of Lords in its Judicial Capacity (with G. Drewry) 1972, ed. Progress in Penal Reform 1975, Law and Morality (with G. Drewry) 1976, The Falling Shadow (jtly.) 1995, The Birmingham Six and Other Cases 1997; articles in legal journals, etc. *Leisure interests:* watching and reporting on Association football, reading, music, writing, broadcasting. *Address:* 2 Ripplevale Grove, London, N1 1HU, England; Glebe House, Montgomery, Powys, SY15 6QA, Wales. *Telephone:* 0171-607 8045 (London); (01686) 668458 (Montgomery).

BLOMSTEDT, Herbert Thorson; Swedish music director and conductor; b. 7 Nov. 1927, Springfield, Mass., U.S.A.; s. of Adolphe Blomstedt and Alida Armintha Thorson; m. Waltraud Regina Peterson 1955; four d.; ed. Royal Acad. of Music, Stockholm and Uppsala Univ.; Music Dir., Norrköping Symphony Orchestra 1954–61; Prof. of Conducting, Swedish Royal Acad. of Music 1961–70; Perm. Conductor, Oslo Philharmonic 1962–68; Music Dir. of Danish Radio Symphony Orchestra 1967–77, of Dresden Staatskapelle Orchestra 1975–85, of Swedish Radio Symphony Orchestra 1977–82; Music Dir. and Conductor, San Francisco Symphony Orchestra 1985–; Hon. Conductor NHK Symphony, Tokyo 1985; Hon. D.Mus. (Andrews); Jenny Lind Scholarship, Swedish Royal Acad. of Music; Kt. Royal Order of the North Star (Sweden); Kt. Royal Order of Dannebrog (Denmark); Litteris et Artibus, Gold Medal (Sweden). *Leisure interests:* hiking, reading, art. *Address:* San Francisco Symphony Orchestra, 201 Van Ness, San Francisco, CA 94102, U.S.A.; Interartists, Frans van Mierisstraat 43, 1071 RK, Amsterdam, Netherlands. *Telephone:* 415-552-8000.

BLOOM, Claire; British actress; b. 15 Feb. 1931, London; d. of Edward Bloom and Elizabeth Grew; m. 1st Rod Steiger (q.v.) 1959 (divorced 1969); one d.; m. 2nd 1969; m. 3rd Philip Roth 1990 (divorced 1995); ed. London, Bristol and New York; Oxford Repertory Theatre 1946, Stratford-on-Avon 1948; first major stage appearances in The Lady's Not For Burning 1949, Ring Around the Moon 1950; at Old Vic 1951–53, Duel of Angels 1956. *Other stage performances include:* Andromache in The Trojan Women 1964, Sascha in Ivanov, London 1966, Nora in A Doll's House, New York 1971, London 1973, Hedda Gabler in Hedda Gabler, New York 1971, Mary, Queen of Scots in Vivat, Vivat Regina!, New York 1972, A Streetcar Named Desire, London (Evening Standard Drama Award for Best Actress) 1974, The Innocents, U.S.A. 1976, Rosmersholm, London 1977, The Cherry Orchard, Chichester Festival 1981, When We Dead Awaken 1990, The Cherry Orchard, U.S.A. 1994, Long Day's Journey into Night, U.S.A. 1996, Electra, New York 1998; Fellow, Guildhall School of Music and Drama 1975. *Films include:* Limelight, Man Between, Richard III, Alexander the Great, Brothers Karamazov, Buccaneer, Look Back in Anger, Three Steps to Freedom 1960, The Brothers Grimm, The Chapman Report 1962, The Haunting 1963, 80,000 Suspects 1963, Alta Infedeltà 1963, Il Maestro di Vigevano 1963, The Outrage 1964, Spy Who Came in from the Cold 1965, Charly 1966, Three into Two Won't Go 1967, Illustrated Man 1968, Red Sky at Morning 1970, A Doll's House 1973, Islands in the Stream 1975, The Clash of the Titans 1979, Always 1984, Sammy and Rosie Get Laid 1987, Brothers 1988, Crimes and Misdemeanours 1989, Mighty Aphrodite 1994, Daylight 1995. *Television appearances:* A Legacy 1975, The Orestea 1978, Henry VIII 1979, Brideshead Revisited 1979, Hamlet 1980, Cymbeline 1982, Separate Tables 1982, The Ghost Writer 1982, King John 1983, Time and the Conways 1984, Shadowlands 1985, Promises to keep us 1985, Oedipus the King 1985, Lightning Always Strikes Twice 1985; mini series in U.S.A.: Ellis Island 1984, Florence Nightingale 1984, Liberty 1985, Anastasia 1986, Queenie 1986, The Belle of Amherst 1986, Intimate Contact 1987, A Shadow on the Sun 1988, The Camomile Lawn 1991, The Mirror Crack'd from Side to Side 1992, Remember 1993, A Village Affair 1994, Family Money 1996. Also performs her one woman show These are Women, A Portrait of Shakespeare's Heroines, throughout the U.S.A. *Publications:* Limelight and After 1982, Leaving a Doll's House 1996. *Leisure interests:* walking, music. *Address:* c/o Jeremy Conway, 18–21 Jermyn St, London SW1Y 6HB, England.

BLOOM, Harold, PH.D.; American professor of humanities; b. 11 July 1930, New York; s. of William Bloom and Paula Lev; m. Jeanne Gould 1958; two s.; ed. Cornell and Yale Univs.; mem. Faculty, Yale Univ. 1955–, Prof. of English 1965–77, DeVane Prof. of Humanities 1974–77, Prof. of Humanities 1977–, Sterling Prof. of Humanities 1983–; Visiting Prof. Hebrew Univ. Jerusalem 1959, Breadloaf Summer School 1965–66, Soc. for Humanities, Cornell Univ. 1968–69; Visiting Univ. Prof. New School of Social Research, New York 1982–84; Charles Eliot Norton Prof. of Poetry, Harvard Univ. 1987–88; Berg Visiting Prof. of English, New York Univ. 1988–; mem. American Acad. of Arts and Sciences, American Acad. and Inst. of Arts and Letters, American Philosophical Soc.; Guggenheim Fellow 1962; Fulbright Fellow 1955; Newton Arvin Award 1967; Melville Cane Award, Poetry Soc. of America 1970; Zabel Prize, American Inst. of Arts and Letters 1982; MacArthur Prize Fellowship 1985; Hon. Dr. Saint Michael's Coll. and other insts. *Publications:* Shelley's Mythmaking 1959, The Visionary Company 1961, Blake's Apocalypse 1963, Commentary to Blake 1965, Yeats 1970, The Ringers in the Tower 1971, The Anxiety of Influence 1973, Wallace Stevens: The Poems of Our Climate 1977, A Map of Misreading 1975, Kabbalah and Criticism 1975, Poetry and Repression 1976, Figures of Capable Imagination 1976, The Flight to Lucifer: A Gnostic Fantasy 1979, Agon: Towards a Theory of Revisionism 1981, The Breaking of the Vessels 1981, The Strong Light of the Canonical 1987, Freud: Transference and Authority 1988, Poetics of Influence: New and Selected Criticism 1988, Ruin the Sacred Truths 1989, The Book of J 1990, The American Religion 1991, The Book of Kabbalah 1991, The Western Canon 1994, Omens of Millennium 1996, Shakespeare: The Invention of the Human 1998. *Address:* 179 Linden Street, New Haven, CT 06511, U.S.A.

BLOOM, Myer, PH.D., F.R.S.C., F.A.P.S.; Canadian professor of physics; b. 7 Dec. 1928, Montreal; s. of Israel Bloom and Leah Ram; m. Margaret P. Holmes 1954; one s. one d.; ed. Baron Byng High School, McGill Univ. and Univ. of Illinois at Urbana; NRC Travelling Postdoctoral Fellow, Univ. of Leiden, Netherlands 1954–56; Research Assoc. Univ. of B.C. 1956–57, Asst. Prof. 1957–60, Assoc. Prof. 1960–63, Prof. of Physics 1963–94; Emer. Prof. 1995–; Visiting Prof. Harvard 1964–65, Kyoto Univ. 1965, Univ. de Paris Sud 1971–72, 1978–79, Univ. of Rome 1986, Danish Tech. Univ. 1986; mem. Canadian Asscn. of Physicists; Alfred P. Sloan Fellow 1961–65; Fellow Canadian Inst. for Advanced Research 1991–; Hon. D.Tech. (Tech. Univ. of Denmark) 1994; Hon. D.Iur. (Concordia Univ., Montreal) 1995; Steacie Prize 1967, Biely Prize 1969; Canadian Asscn. of Physicists Gold Medal 1973; Science Council of B.C. Chair.'s Award for Career Achievements 1992, Izaak Walton Killam Memorial Prize for Natural Sciences 1995. *Publications:* numerous research and review articles. *Leisure interests:* hiking, skiing, squash, wine-making. *Address:* Department of Physics, University of British Columbia, 6224 Agriculture Road, Vancouver, B.C., V6T 1Z1 (Office); 5669 Kings Road, Vancouver, B.C., V6T 1K9, Canada (Home). *Telephone:* (604) 822-2136 (Office). *Fax:* (604) 822-5324.

BLOOM, Stephen Robert, M.A., M.D., F.R.C.P.; British physician, educator and biomedical researcher; b. 24 Oct. 1942, Maidstone, Kent; s. of Arnold Bloom and Edith Nancy Bloom (née Fox); m. Margaret Janet Sturrock 1965; two s. two d.; ed. Univ. of Cambridge; Medical Unit Registrar, Middx. Hosp., London 1970–72; MRC Clinical Research Fellow 1972–74; Sr. Lecturer, Royal Postgrad. Medical School, Hammersmith Hosp. 1974–78, Reader in Medicine 1978–82, Prof. of Endocrinology 1982–, Head Dept. of Endocrinology and Metabolic Medicine. *Publications:* Gut Hormones (ed.) 1978, Endocrine Tumours 1985, Surgical Endocrinology 1992. *Leisure interests:* jogging, classical music, computing. *Address:* Division of Endocrinology and Metabolism, Royal Postgraduate Medical School, Hammersmith Hospital, Du Cane Road, London, W12 0NN, England.

BLOOMBERG, Michael; American business executive; b. 14 Feb. 1942; Boston; two c.; ed. Johns Hopkins Univ., Harvard Univ.; with Salomon Brothers (investment bank) –1981; founder, Chief Exec., Chair. Bloomberg Financial Markets 1981–; founder, Pres. Bloomberg L.P. 1982–; Chair. Bd. Trustees Johns Hopkins Univ.; Trustee Big Apple Circus, Lincoln Center for Performing Arts, Jewish Museum, NY, Metropolitan Museum of Art and numerous other bodies. *Publication:* Bloomberg by Bloomberg (autobiog.) 1998. *Address:* Bloomberg LP, 499 Park Avenue, FL. 15, New York, NY 10022, U.S.A.

BLOOMFIELD, Sir Kenneth Percy, K.C.B., M.A.; British civil servant; b. 15 April 1931, Belfast; s. of late Harry Percy Bloomfield and Doris Bloomfield; m. Mary E. Ramsey 1960; one s. one d.; ed. Royal Belfast Academic Inst. and St. Peter's Coll., Oxford; joined N. Ireland Civil Service 1952; Private Sec. to Ministers of Finance 1956–60; Deputy Dir. British Industrial Devt. Office, New York 1960–63; Asst. later Deputy Sec. to Cabinet, N. Ireland 1963–72; Under-Sec. N. Ireland Office 1972–74; Perm. Sec. Office of Exec. N. Ireland 1974–75; Perm. Sec. Dept. of Environment, N. Ireland 1975–81, Dept. of Econ. Devt. 1981–84; Head, N. Ireland Civil Service and Second Perm. Under-Sec. of State, N. Ireland Office 1984–91; Nat. Gov., Chair. Broadcasting Council for N. Ireland, BBC 1991–; Chair. Children in Need Trust 1992–; BBC Audit Cttee.; Chair. N. Ireland Chief Execs. Forum, Higher Educ. Council for N. Ireland; Pres. Ulster People's Coll. 1996–; mem. N. Ireland Advisory Bd. Bank of Ireland, Green Park Trust; numerous other appointments; Hon. Fellow St. Peter's Coll. Oxford; Hon. LL.D. (Belfast). *Leisure interests:* reading history and biographies, writing, swimming. *Publication:* Stormont in Crisis (a memoir) 1994. *Address:* BBC (NI), Broadcasting House, Ormeau Avenue, Belfast, BT2 8HQ, Northern Ireland. *Telephone:* (01232) 338000.

BLOUIN, Georges Henri, LL.B; Canadian diplomatist; b. 4 June 1921, Montreal; s. of Charles-Henri Blouin and Hermine Panneton; m. Denise Angers 1949 (deceased); one s. one d. ; ed. Coll. Ste.-Marie, Montreal and Univ. of Montreal; joined foreign service 1949; served New Delhi, San Francisco, Athens, Brussels 1951–65; Amb. to Cameroon (also accred. to Gabon, Chad, Cen. African Repub.) 1965–67; Minister, Washington, D.C. 1967–70; Dir.-Gen. of Personnel, Dept. of External Affairs 1970–73; Amb. to Spain (also accred. to Morocco) 1973–77; Asst. Deputy Minister for External Affairs 1977–79; Amb. to Netherlands 1979–83; Chief of Protocol of Canadian Govt. 1983–85. *Leisure interests:* golf, walking. *Address:* 130 Rideau Terrace, Ottawa, Ont., K1M 0Z2, Canada.

BLOUT, Elkan R(ogers), A.B., PH.D.; American biochemist; b. 2 July 1919, New York; s. of Eugene and Lillian Blout; m. 1st Joan Dreyfus Blout 1939; two s. one d.; m. 2nd Gail Ferris Blout 1985; one d.; ed. Phillips Exeter Acad. and Princeton and Columbia Univs.; Assoc. Dir. of Research, Polaroid Corpn. 1948–58, Vice-Pres. and Gen. Man. of Research 1958–62; Lecturer on Biophysics, Harvard Medical School 1960–62, Prof. of Biological Chem. 1962–89, Edward S. Harkness Prof. of Biological Chem. 1964–90, Emer. Prof. 1990–, Chair. Dept. of Biological Chem. 1965–69, Dean Academic Affairs, Harvard School of Public Health 1978–89, Chair. Dept. of Environmental Science and Physiology 1986–88, Dir. Div. of Biological Sciences 1987–91; Dir. Center for Blood Research 1972–92, CHON Corpn. 1974–83; Scientific adviser, Affymax Research Inst. 1988–; Gov. Weizmann Inst. of Science, Rehovot, Israel 1977–; mem. Finance Cttee., N.A.S. 1976–, Inst. of Medicine 1979–, Advisory Cttee. on the U.S.S.R. and Eastern Europe 1979–84; mem. Boston Biomedical Research Inst. 1972– (Vice-Pres. 1990–94), Finance Cttee. American Soc. of Biological Chemists 1973–82, Corpn. of the Museum of Science, Boston 1974–, Advisory Council of the Dept. of Biochemical Sciences, Princeton Univ. 1974–83 and of Programme in Molecular Biology 1983–95, Finance Cttee. American Acad. Arts and Sciences 1976–, Conseil de Surveillance, Compagnie Financière du Scribe 1975–81, Editorial Bd. International Journal of Peptide and Protein Research 1978–89, Editorial Bd. Journal of the American Chemical Society 1978–82, Assembly of Math. and Physical Sciences, Nat. Research Council 1979–82, Scientific Advisory Council, American Cttee. for the Weizmann Inst. of Science 1979–, Governing Bd., Nat. Research Council 1980–92, Council, N.A.S. 1980–92, Exec. Cttee. of Governing Bd., Nat. Research Council 1980–92, Investments Advisory Cttee., Fed. of American Socs. for Experimental Biology 1981–85, Council, Int. Org. for Chemical Sciences in Devt. 1981– (Vice-Pres. and Treas. 1985–), Comm. on Physical Sciences, Maths, and Resources, Nat. Research Council 1982–87; Treas. Nat. Acad. of Sciences 1980–92, Advisory Council of the Program in Molecular Biology, Princeton Univ. 1983–95; mem. Bd. of Dirs., ESA Inc. 1985–91, Auburn Investment Man. Corpn. (also Investment Manager) 1985–; mem. Bd. of Dirs., Nat. Health Research Foundation 1985–92, Organization for Chemical Sciences in Devt. 1985–, and Sec.-Treas., Nat. Acads. Corpn. 1986–92; Chair., Research Advisory Cttee., Children's Hosp. Medical Center 1986–90; Prof. and Dir. Emer. Harvard School of Public Health 1991–; Sr. Advisor for Science, Food and Drug Admin. 1991–; Gen. Partner, Gosnold Investment Fund Ltd. Partnership; Chair. Budget Comm., American Acad. of Arts and Sciences, Treas. 1992–98; Pres. Inst. for Int. Vaccine Devt.; mem. Sr. Advisory Bd. The Encyclopedia of Molecular Biology 1991, Council of Visitors Marine Biological Lab. 1992–, Kuratorium of the German–American Academic Council 1995–; Foreign mem. Russian Acad. of Sciences 1976; Nat. Research Fellow, Harvard Univ.; Fellow, American Acad. of Arts and Sciences, A.A.A.S., Optical Soc. of America, New York Acad. of Sciences; Trustee, Bay Biochemical Research 1973–82, Boston Biomedical Research Inst. 1972– (Vice-Pres. 1990–94); Hon. A.M. (Harvard Univ.) 1962, Hon. D.Sc. (Loyola Univ.) 1976; Class of 1939 Achievement Award, Princeton Univ. 1970, Nat. Medal of Science Award 1990, Ralph F. Hirschmann Award in Peptide Chemistry, American Chem. Soc. 1991. *Publications:* Various articles in specialized journals, including Journal of American Chemical Society, etc. *Leisure interests:* boating, deep-sea fishing. *Address:* Dept. of Biological Chemistry and Molecular Pharmacology, Harvard Medical School, 240 Longwood Avenue, Boston, MA 02115 (Office); 1010 Memorial Drive, Apt. 12A, Cambridge, MA 02138, U.S.A. (Home).

BLOW, David Mervyn, PH.D., F.R.S., F.INST.P.; British professor of biophysics; b. 27 June 1931; s. of Rev. Edward Mervyn Blow and Dorothy Laura Blow; m. Mavis Sears 1955; one s. one d.; ed. Kingswood School, Corpus Christi Coll., Cambridge; Fulbright Scholar, Nat. Inst. of Health, Bethesda, Md. and M.I.T., U.S.A. 1957–59; MRC Unit for Study of Molecular Biological Systems, Cambridge 1959–62; MRC Lab. of Molecular Biology, Cambridge 1962–77; Coll. Lecturer and Fellow, Trinity Coll., Cambridge 1968–77; Prof. of Biophysics, Imperial Coll., Univ. of London 1977–94, Head, Dept. of Physics 1991–94, Prof. (Emer.), Sr. Research Fellow 1994–; Dean of Royal Coll. of Science 1981–84; Pres. British Crystallographic Asscn. 1984–87; foreign assoc. mem. Acad. des Sciences, Paris 1992; Biochemistry Soc. CIBA Medal 1967, Charles Léopold Meyer Prize 1979, Wolf Foundation Prize for Chem. 1987. *Publications:* papers and reviews in scientific journals. *Leisure interests:* walking, sailing. *Address:* Blackett Laboratory, Imperial College of Science, Technology and Medicine, University of London, Prince Consort Road, SW7 2BZ; 1 Meeting Street, Appledore, Bideford, North Devon, EX39 1RH, England. *Telephone:* 0171-594 7683; (01237) 471106.

BLOW, Isabella; English stylist and fashion consultant; b. Nantwich, Cheshire; d. of Sir Evelyn Delves Broughton and Helen Mary Shore; m. Detmar Blow 1989; ed. Heathfield School, Ascot and Columbia Univ., New York; various jobs including domestic cleaner, shop asst., waitress, etc.; worked on American Vogue, The Tatler, British Vogue magazines; Fashion Dir. The Sunday Times 1997–; contrib. to The Face and other periodicals. *Leisure interests:* art, Gloucester Cathedral, rare breeds of agricultural animals and birds, reading, my husband. *Address:* 5 Theed Street, London, SE1 8ST, England.

BLOW, Sandra, R.A.; British artist; b. 14 Sept. 1925; d. of Jack Blow and Lily Blow; ed. St. Martin's School of Art, Royal Acad. Schools, Accademia di Belle Arti, Rome; tutor, Painting School, R.C.A. 1960–75; one-person exhbns.: Gimpel Fils 1952, 1954, 1960, 1962, Saidenbury Gallery, New York 1957, New Art Centre, London 1966, 1968, 1971, 1973, Francis Graham-Dixon Gallery 1991; group exhbns. in U.K., U.S.A., Italy, Denmark and France; works in collections of Peter Stuyvesant Foundation, Nuffield Foundation, Arts Council of G.B., Arts Council of Northern Ireland, Walker Art Gallery, Liverpool, Allbright Knox Art Gallery, Buffalo, New York, Museum of Modern Art, New York, Tate Gallery, Gulbenkian Foundation, Ministry of Public Bldg. and Works, Contemporary Art Soc.; silk screen prints in Victoria and Albert Museum, Fitzwilliam Museum, Cambridge, City of Leeds Art Gallery, Graves Art Gallery, Sheffield; painting purchased for liner Queen Elizabeth II; won British Section of Int. Guggenheim Award 1960; Second Prize, John Moore's Liverpool Exhbn. 1961; Arts Council Purchase Award 1965–66. *Address:* c/o Royal Academy of Arts, Piccadilly, London, W1V 0DS, England.

BLÜM, Norbert, DR.PHIL.; German politician; b. 21 July 1935, Rüsselsheim; s. of Christian and Margarete (née Beck) Blüm; m. Marita Binger 1964; one s. two d.; ed. Volksschule; apprentice, Opel AG, Rüsselsheim, 1949–53, toolmaker 1953–57; worked in building trade and as lorry driver while studying evenings 1957–61; univ. student in Cologne and Bonn 1961–67; Ed. Soziale Ordnung 1966–68; Chief Man. Social Comm. of Christian Democrat employees' asscn. 1968–75, Regional Chair. Rhineland-Palatinate 1974–77, Fed. Chair. 1977–87; mem. Fed. Exec. C.D.U. 1969–; mem. Bundestag 1969–; Deputy Chair. CDU 1981–; Senator for Fed. Affairs for Berlin 1981; Minister of Labour and Social Affairs 1982–98; Regional Chair. CDU North Rhine-Westphalia. *Publications:* Reaktion oder Reform—Wohin geht die CDU 1972, Gewerkschaften zwischen Allmacht und Ohnmacht 1979, Werkstücke 1980, Die Arbeit geht weiter—zur Krise der Erwerbsgesellschaft 1983, 40 Jahre Socialstaat Bundesrepublik Deutschland (Hrsg.) 1989, Politikals Balanceakt 1993, Dann Willichs mal probieren-Geschichten vom Lachen und Weimen 1994, Sommerfrische-Regentage inclusive 1995. *Leisure interests:* reading, walking. *Address:* c/o Bundesministerium für Arbeit und Sozialordnung, Rochusstrasse 1, 53123 Bonn, Germany.

BLUM, Yehuda Z., M.JUR., PH.D.; Israeli diplomatist and lawyer; b. 2 Oct. 1931, Bratislava; m. Moriah Rabinovitz-Teomim; two s. one d.; ed. Hebrew Univ., Jerusalem, Univ. of London; detained in Nazi concentration camp of Bergen-Belsen 1944; Asst. to Judge Advocate-Gen. of Israel Defence Forces 1956–59; Senior Asst. to Legal Adviser, Ministry for Foreign Affairs 1962–65; UNESCO Fellow, Univ. of Sydney July-Aug. 1968; Office of UN Legal Counsel Sept.-Dec. 1968; Senior Research Scholar, Univ. of Michigan Law

School 1969; Visiting Prof., School of Law, Univ. of Texas, Austin 1971, New York Univ. 1975–76, Univ. of Mich. Law School 1985, Univ. of Southern Calif., Los Angeles 1991–92; mem. Israeli del., Third UN Conference on Law of the Sea 1973, 31st Session of UN Gen. Assembly 1976; Perm. Rep. to UN 1978–84; Hersch Lauterpacht Prof. of Int. Law, Hebrew Univ., Jerusalem 1991; Law Ed. Encyclopedia Hebraica 1973–; Jabotinsky Prize 1984; Dr. Jur. h.c. (Yeshiva Univ.) 1981. *Publications:* Historic Titles in International Law 1965, Secure Boundaries and Middle East Peace 1971, For Zion's Sake 1987, Eroding the UN Charter 1993. *Address:* Faculty of Law, Hebrew University, Mount Scopus, Jerusalem, Israel. *Telephone:* (02) 588-2562.

BLUMBERG, Baruch Samuel, M.D., PH.D., F.R.C.P.; American research physician; b. 28 July 1925, New York; s. of late Meyer and of Ida (Simonoff) Blumberg; m. Jean Liebesman 1954; two s. two d.; ed. Union Coll., Schenectady, Columbia Univ. Coll. of Physicians and Surgeons, Balliol Coll., Oxford; served U.S. Navy 1943–46; Intern and resident, First (Columbia) Div., Bellevue Hosp., New York 1951–57; Ship's Surgeon 1952; Fellow in medicine, Presbyterian Hosp., New York 1953–55; Dept. of Biochem., Oxford Univ., U.K. 1955–57; Chief of Geographic Medicine and Genetics Section, Nat. Insts. of Health, Bethesda, Md. 1957–64; Assoc. Dir. for Clinical Research, Inst. for Cancer Research, Philadelphia 1964–86, Vice-Pres. for Population Oncology, Fox Chase Cancer Centre 1986–89; Univ. Prof. of Medicine and Anthropology, Univ. of Pennsylvania 1977–; George Eastman Visiting Prof., Univ. of Oxford 1983–84, Raman Visiting Prof., Indian Acad. of Sciences, Bangalore, India, Jan.–April 1986; Ashland Visiting Prof., Univ. of Ky. 1986–87; Master Balliol Coll., Oxford 1989–94; attending physician, Pa. Hosp., Hosp. of Univ. of Pennsylvania; Fox Chase Distinguished Scientist and Sr. Adviser to Pres., Fox Chase Cancer Centre 1989–; mem. Assen. of American Physicians, various other medical socs.; Fellow, N.A.S.; Hon. Fellow, Balliol Coll., Oxford 1976; numerous hon. degrees; Bernstein Award, Medical Soc. of New York, 1969, Passano Award 1974, Modern Medicine Distinguished Achievement Award 1975, Karl Landsteiner Award 1975, Showa Emperor Memorial Award, Japan, 1994, shared Nobel Prize in Physiology or Medicine for discoveries concerning new mechanisms for origin and dissemination of infectious diseases 1976, and numerous other awards. *Publications:* Australia Antigen and the Biology of Hepatitis B 1977; numerous papers to scientific journals. *Leisure interests:* canoeing, mountain walking, cycling. *Address:* Fox Chase Cancer Center, 7701 Burholme Avenue, Fox Chase, Philadelphia, PA 19111, U.S.A. (Office). *Telephone:* (215) 728-3164 (Office).

BLUMENTHAL W(erner) Michael, PH.D.; American business executive; b. 3 Jan. 1926, Germany; s. of Ewald Blumenthal and Rose Valerie (Markt) Blumenthal; ed. Univ. of California at Berkeley and Princeton Univ; went to U.S. 1947, naturalized 1952; Research Assoc., Princeton Univ. 1954–57; Vice-Pres., Dir. Crown Cork Int. Corpn. 1957–61; Deputy Asst. Sec. of State for Econ. Affairs, Dept. of State 1961–63; also served as U.S.A. Rep. to UN Comm. on Int. Commodity Trade; President's Deputy Special Rep. for Trade Negotiations (with rank of Amb.) 1963–67; Chair. U.S. Del. to Kennedy Round tariff talks in Geneva; Pres. Bendix Int. 1967–70; Dir. Bendix Corpn. 1967–77, Vice-Chair. June-Dec. 1970, Pres. and Chief Operating Officer 1971–72, Chair. and C.E.O. 1972–77; Sec. of the Treasury 1977–79; Dir. Burroughs Corpn. (now Unisys) 1979–90, Vice-Chair. 1980, C.E.O. 1981–90, Chair. 1990; Sr. Advisor Lazard Frères & Co 1990–96; mem. Bd. of Dirs. Daimler-Benz InterServices, Int. Advisory Bd. Chemical Bank, Tenneco Co., The Business Council, Charter Trustee Emer., Princeton Univ. *Leisure interests:* tennis, skiing. *Address:* 227 Ridgeview Road, Princeton, NJ 08540, U.S.A.

BLUMGART, Leslie Harold, B.D.S., M.D., F.A.C.S., F.R.C.S., F.R.C.S.E., F.R.C.P.S.; British professor of surgery; b. 7 Dec. 1931, South Africa; s. of Harold Herman Blumgart and Hilda Blumgart; m. 1st Pearl Navias 1955 (deceased), 2nd Sarah Raybould Bowen 1968; two s. two d.; ed. Jeppe High School, Johannesburg, Univ. of Witwatersrand, Johannesburg, Univ. of Sheffield, England; Sr. Lecturer and Deputy Dir., Dept. of Surgery, Welsh Nat. School of Medicine, Cardiff 1970–72; St. Mungo Prof. of Surgery, Univ. of Glasgow, Hon. Consultant Surgeon, Glasgow Royal Infirmary 1972–79; Prof. of Surgery and Dir. Dept. of Surgery, Royal Postgraduate Medical School, Univ. of London and Hon. Consultant, Hammersmith Hosp., London 1979–86; Prof. of Visceral and Transplantion Surgery, Univ. of Berne and Inselspital Bern, Switzerland 1986–91; Enid A. Haupt Prof. of Surgery, Memorial Sloan-Kettering Cancer Center 1991–, Chief of Section of Hepato-Biliary Surgery 1995–, Dir. Hepato-Biliary Program; Prof. of Surgery, Cornell Univ. Medical Coll. 1993, American Surgery Soc.; Moynihan Fellowship, Assen. of Surgeons of G.B. and Ireland 1972; Hon. mem. Soc. for Surgery of the Alimentary Tract, U.S.A., Danish Surgical Soc. 1988, Assen. Française Chirurgie; mem. Hong Kong Surgical Soc., Hellenic Surgical Soc., L.A. Surgical Soc.; Pres. Int. Biliary Assen. 1986; Hon. mem. Yugoslav Soc. of Surgery; Hon. D.Sc.; Order of Prasidda Prabala Gorkha-Dakshin Bahu (Nepal) 1984. *Publications include:* Essentials of Medicine and Surgery for Dental Students (with A. C. Kennedy), 4th edn. 1982, The Biliary Tract, in Clinical Surgery Int., vol. 5 1982, Liver Surgery, in Clinical Surgery Int., vol. 12 (with S. Bengmark) 1986, Surgery of the Liver and Biliary Tract, Vols. 1 and 2 1988, Difficult Problems in General Surgery 1989; numerous publs. concerned with medical educ., gastrointestinal surgery and aspects of oncology with particular interest in surgery of the liver, pancreas and biliary tract. *Leisure interests:* watercolour painting, wood carving. *Address:* Memorial Sloan-Kettering Cancer Center, 1275 York Avenue, New York, NY 10021 (Office); 447 East 57th Street, 3E, New York, NY 10022, U.S.A. (Home). *Telephone:* (212) 639-5526 (Office); (212) 755-0836 (Home). *Fax:* (212) 794-5852 (Office).

BLUNDELL, Pamela, DIP. FASHION; British fashion designer; ed. Southampton Univ., Epsom School of Art & Design; fmrly. worked on samples, design and marketing with late John Flett; numerous freelance clients including English Nat. Opera, Liberty of London; fmr. lecturer St. Martin's School of Art, London; formed Copperwheat Blundell with Lee Copperwheat (q.v.) 1993; Visiting Lecturer Cen. St. Martin's School of Art, Univ. of Nottingham, Brighton Polytechnic 1991–95; winner Courtaulds knitwear competition; Smirnoff Fashion Award for Best Young Designer 1987; Young Designer of the Year 1994 (with Lee Copperwheat). *Address:* Copperwheat Blundell, 14 Cheshire Street, London, E2 6EH, England. *Telephone:* 0171-613 0651. *Fax:* 0171-729 8600.

BLUNDELL, Sir Tom Leon, Kt., D.PHIL., F.R.S.; British professor of biochemistry; b. 7 July 1942, Brighton; s. of Horace Leon Blundell and Marjorie Blundell; m. Bancinyane Lynn Sibanda 1987; one s. two d.; ed. Steyning Grammar School and Brasenose Coll., Oxford; jr. research fellow in molecular physics, Linacre Coll. 1968–70; lecturer, Hertford Coll., Oxford 1970–72; lecturer in Biological Sciences, Sussex Univ. 1973–76; Prof. of Crystallography, Birkbeck Coll., London Univ. 1976–90; Sir William Dunn Prof. of Biochemistry, Univ. of Cambridge 1995–, Fellow Sidney Sussex Coll. 1995–, Head Dept. of Biochem., 1996–; Dir.-Gen. Agricultural and Food Research Council 1991–94; Dir. Int. School of Crystallography 1982–; Chair. Scientific Advisory Bd. Bioprocessing Ltd. 1996–; Chief Exec. Biotechnology and Biological Sciences Research Council 1994–96; Dir. (non-exec.) Celltech 1997–; Scientific Adviser Oxford Molecular Ltd. 1996–; mem. R. & D. Bd. SmithKline Beecham 1997–, Bd. Babraham Inst., Cambridge; Hon. Dir. of Imperial Cancer Research Fund Unit of Structural Molecular Biology 1989–96; Chair. Biological Sciences, Science and Eng. Research Council (SERC) 1983–87, SERC 1989–90, AFRC Council and Food Cttee. 1985–90, Advisory Council on Science and Tech. 1988–90; Consultant, Pfizer 1983–90; mem. Academia Europaea 1993, Council, Royal Soc. 1997–; Fellow, EMBO 1985–; Fellow Birkbeck Coll., Univ. of London 1997; Foreign Fellow, Indian Nat. Science Acad. 1994; Hon. Fellow Royal Agricultural Soc. of England 1993; Hon. Fellow, Brasenose Coll., Oxford 1989–, Linacre Coll., Oxford 1991–; Professional Fellow, Sidney Sussex Coll., Cambridge 1995–; numerous hon. degrees; Gold Medal, Inst. of Biotechnologies 1987, Sir Harry Krebs Medal 1987, CIBA Medal 1988, Feldberg Prize 1988, Medal of Soc. for Chemical Industry 1995, Nat. Equal Opportunities Award 1996. *Publications include:* Protein Crystallography 1976, Progress in Biophysics and Molecular Biology (Ed.) 1980–; various publs. in Nature, Journal of Molecular Biology. *Leisure interests:* opera, playing jazz, foreign travel, walking. *Address:* Department of Biochemistry, 80 Tennis Court Road, University of Cambridge, Cambridge, CB2 1GA, England. *Telephone:* (01223) 333628. *Fax:* (01223) 766082.

BLUNDEN, Sir George, Kt., M.A.; British central banker; b. 31 Dec. 1922, Sutton, Surrey; s. of George Blunden and Florence Holder; m. Anne Bulford 1949; two s. one d.; ed. City of London School, Univ. Coll., Oxford; war service, Royal Sussex Regt. 1941–45; Bank of England 1947–55; Economist, Balance of Payments Div., Int. Monetary Fund 1955–58; various posts, Bank of England 1958–65, Deputy Principal, Discount Office 1965–67, seconded to Monopolies Comm. 1968, Deputy Chief Cashier 1968–73, Chief of Man. Services 1973–74, responsible for banking supervision with rank of Head of Dept. 1974–76, Exec. Dir. 1976–84, Non-Exec. Dir. 1984–85, Deputy Gov. 1986–90; Chair. Group of Ten Cttees. on banking supervision 1975–77 and on payments systems 1981–83; Chair. London Pensions Fund Authority 1990–92; Jt. Deputy Chair. Leopold Joseph Holdings 1984–85, 1990–94; Pres. Inst. of Business Ethics 1994–96; Chair. Centre for Study of Financial Innovation 1995–; Adviser Union Bank of Switzerland (London br.) 1990–94. *Address:* Crossfield Farmhouse, Hindringham, Fakenham, Norfolk, NR21 0PS, England. *Telephone:* (01328) 878509.

BLUNKETT, David, B.A., M.P.; British politician; b. 6 June 1947; m. (divorced); three s.; ed. Sheffield Univ.; worked for E. Midlands Gas Bd. before entering univ.; subsequently taught industrial relations and politics at Barnsley Coll. of Tech.; joined Labour Party 1963; mem. Sheffield City Council 1970–87, Leader 1980–87; mem. S. Yorks. Co. Council 1973–77; M.P. for Sheffield Brightside 1987–; elected to Nat. Exec. Cttee. (NEC) of Labour Party 1983, Chair. NEC Local Govt. Cttee. 1984; Local Govt. Front Bench Spokesman in Opposition's Environment Team 1988–92; Shadow Sec. of State for Health 1992–94, for Educ. 1994–95, for Educ. and Employment 1995–97; Sec. of State for Educ. and Employment May 1997–; Vice-Chair. Labour Party 1992–93, Chair. 1993–94. *Publications:* On a Clear Day (autobiog.) 1995; co-author: Local Enterprise and Workers' Plans 1981, Building from the Bottom: the Sheffield Experience 1983, Democracy in Crisis: the Town Halls Respond 1987, On a Clear Day 1995. *Leisure interests:* walking, sailing, poetry. *Address:* House of Commons, London, SW1A 0AA, England. *Telephone:* 0171-219 4043. *Fax:* 0171-219 5903.

BLUNT, Charles William, B.ECON., C.P.A.; Australian politician and businessman; b. 19 Jan. 1951; s. of late R. S. G. Blunt; m. Gail Blunt; two s.; mem. House of Reps. (for Richmond, N.S.W.) 1984–90; Shadow Minister for Sport, Recreation and Tourism 1984, for Social Security 1985, for Community Service 1987; Exec. Dir. Nat. Party 1980–84, Leader 1989–90; C.E.O. American Chamber of Commerce in Australia 1990–. *Leisure interests:* tennis, squash, golf. *Address:* Suite 4, Gloucester Walk, 88 Cumberland Street, Sydney, N.S.W. 2000, Australia.

BLY, Robert, M.A.; American writer and poet; b. 23 Dec. 1926, Madison, Minn.; s. of Jacob Thomas Bly and Alice (Aws) Bly; m. 1st Carolyn McLean 1955 (divorced 1979); m. 2nd Ruth Counsell 1980; five c.; ed. Harvard Univ. and Univ. of Iowa; served U.S. Navy 1944–46; first book, Silence in the Snowy Fields, publ. 1962; f. The Fifties 1958, later The Sixties and Seventies Press; f. American Writers Against the Vietnam War 1966; Fulbright Award 1956–57; Amy Lowell Fellow 1964–65; Guggenheim Fellow 1965–66; Rockefeller Foundation Fellow 1967; Nat. Book Award in Poetry 1968. *Publications include:* (poems) Silence in the Snowy Fields 1962, The Light Around the Body 1967, This Tree Will Be Here for a Thousand Years 1979, Sleepers Joining Hands 1973, Jumping out of Bed 1973, Old Man Rubbing his Eyes 1975, The Man in the Black Coat 1982, Loving a Woman in Two Worlds 1985, Selected Poems (ed.) 1986, The Moon on a Fencepost 1988, Meditations on the Insatiable Soul 1994, Morning Poems 1997; (prose poems) The Morning Glory 1973, This Body is Made of Camphor and Gopherwood 1977; (criticism) Leaping Poetry 1975; Ed. Forty Poems Touching on Recent American History 1967, A Poetry Reading Against the Vietnam War 1966 and The Sea and the Honeycomb 1966; trans. of vols. of poetry from Swedish, Norwegian, German, Spanish and Hindi. *Address:* 1904 Girard Avenue South, Minneapolis, MN 55403, U.S.A.

BLYTH OF ROWINGTON, Baron (Life Peer) cr. 1995, of Rowington in the County of Warwickshire; **James Blyth,** Kt., F.R.S.A., M.A.; British business executive; b. 8 May 1940; s. of Daniel Blyth and Jane Power Carlton; m. Pamela Anne Campbell Dixon 1967; one d. (one s. deceased); ed. Spiers School, Glasgow Univ.; Mobil Oil Co. 1963–69; Gen. Foods Ltd. 1969–71; Mars Ltd. 1971–74; Dir. and Gen. Man. Lucas Batteries Ltd. 1974–77, Lucas Aerospace Ltd. 1977–81; Dir. Joseph Lucas Ltd. 1977–81; Head of Defence Sales, Ministry of Defence 1981–85; Man. Dir. Plessey Electronic Systems 1985–86; Man. Dir. Plessey Co. PLC 1986–87; C.E.O. Boots Co. PLC 1987–, Deputy Chair. 1994–98, Chair. 1998–; Non-Exec. Dir. Imperial Group PLC 1984–86, Cadbury-Schweppes PLC 1986–90, British Aerospace 1990–94, Deputy Chair. 1994; mem. Council, Soc. of British Aerospace Cos. 1977–81; Gov. London Business School 1987–96; Pres. Middle East Asscn. 1988–92; Chair. Advisory Panel on Citizen's Charter 1991–97; Patron Combined Services Winter Sports Asscn. 1997–; Hon. LL.D. (Nottingham) 1992. *Leisure interests:* skiing, tennis, paintings, theatre. *Address:* Boots Co. PLC, Nottingham, NG2 3AA, England.

BO, Jørgen; Danish architect; b. 8 April 1919, Copenhagen; s. of Alf and Anne Marie Bo; m. Gerda Bennike 1941 (divorced 1966); two s. two d.; ed. Royal Danish Acad. of Fine Arts; own firm since 1943; tech. consultant for Soc. for Preservation of Natural Amenities of Denmark 1944–52; mem. Danish Nature Conservancy Bd. 1952–61; mem. Charlottenborg Adjudicating Bd. 1958–61; mem. Slotsholm Cttee. 1961–63; mem. San Cataldo Council, Italy 1966; Fellow, Royal Danish Acad. in Rome 1968–70; consultant planner for Danish Nat. Museum; mem. of various int. juries; Fellow, Royal Danish Acad. of Fine Arts, Prof. 1960–89; Kt. of the Dannebrog. *Works include:* domestic housing 1945–58, the Louisiana Museum 1956–58, Educ. Centre, Monastir, Tunisia 1960, Museum of Music History 1965, IBM HQ in Denmark 1968–73, Danish Embassy in Brasília 1968–73, IBM Int. Educ. Centre, Belgium 1969–75, Ny Carlsberg Glyptotek 1971–78, restoration work for Carlsberg Foundation and Royal Danish Acad. 1973–76, Extension of Louisiana Museum, Art Museum, Bochum, and offices and housing in Baghdad 1978–83, Lübcke Museum, Hamm, Fed. Repub. of Germany 1984–, Weisbord Pavilion, Israel Museum, Jerusalem 1987–88, 20th Century Art Pavilion, Israel Museum 1988. *Address:* Lindevangsvej 22, 3460 Birkerød, Denmark.

BO YIBO; Chinese government official (retd.); b. 1908, Dinxian Co.; m. Hu Ming (died 1966); five s. two d.; ed. Taiyuan Elementary School and Beijing Univ.; joined Chinese CP 1925; arrested for subversive activities 1932; organized Sacrifice for Nat. Salvation League in Taiyuan 1937; during Sino-Japanese War was Chair. S.E. Admin. Office of Shanxi Govt., Commdr. Taiyuan Mil. Area and Special Commissar in 3rd Admin. Commissar's Office 1937–45; mem. Cen. Cttee. of CP 1945–67; Chair. Shanxi-Hebei-Shandong-Henan Border Region Govt. 1945–47, also reportedly Vice-Chair. Revolutionary Mil. and Political Acad. for Korean Cadres, Yenan; Deputy Political Commissar Cen. China PLA, Commdr. 8th Column 1947–48; Political Commissar N. China Mil. Area, First Vice-Pres. N. China People's Govt., Chair. N.E. Finance and Econ. Cttee. and mem. CPN China Bureau 1948; mem. Preparatory Cttee. for CPPCC 1949; mem. Govt. Admin. Council, Vice-Chair. Cttee. of Finance and Econs., and Minister of Finance 1949–53; Political Commissar Suiyuan Mil. Area 1949; mem. Bd. All-China Fed. of Co-operatives 1950; Chair. Govt. Econ. Investigation Cttee. (led anti-corruption drive) 1951; mem. State Planning Comm. 1952–67, Deputy Chair. 1962–67; mem. Constitution Drafting Cttee. 1953; mem. NPC 1954–67, May 1979–; Chair. State Construction Comm. 1954–56; Head of Third Office, State Council 1955–59; Vice-Chair. Planning Comm. for Scientific Devt. 1956–67; Chair. State Econ. Comm. 1958–67; Alt. Mem. Politburo of CP 1958–69; Vice-Premier 1958–67; Deputy Dir. State Office of Industry and Communications 1959–61, Dir. 1961–67; criticized during Cultural Revolution 1966; arrested 1967; rehabilitated 1979; Vice-Premier, State Council 1979–82; Minister in Charge of State Machine Building Comm. 1979–82; mem. 11th Cen. Cttee. CCP 1979–82; Vice-Chair. Cen. Advisory Comm., CCP 1982–92; State Councillor, State Council 1982–83; Vice-Minister, State Comm. for Restructuring Econ. System 1982–83; mem. Party Cttee. of Special Orgs. 1983–92; Vice-Chair. Cen. Party Consolidation Comm. 1983–; mem. Presidium 14th CCP Nat. Congress 1992; Hon. Pres., Finance Soc., Acad. of Social Sciences 1980–; Hon. Chair. China Council for Promotion of Int. Trade 1984–; Hon. Chair. Bd. of Dirs. China Nat. Tech. Import Corpn. 1984–; Hon. Pres. Beijing Garment Asscn. 1984–; Hon. Chair. All-China Fed. of Handicraft Cooperatives 1986–, China Council for Promotion of Int. Trade (China Chamber of Int. Commerce); Hon. Pres. Industrial Economy Soc. May 1988–, Township Enterprises Asscn. Jan. 1990–, Nat. Self-Employed Workers Asscn., Political Restructuring Research Soc., numerous other appointments. *Address:* c/o The State Council, Beijing, People's Republic of China.

BOARDMAN, Baron (Life Peer), cr. 1980, of Welford in the county of Northamptonshire; **Thomas Gray Boardman,** M.C., T.D., D.L.; British company director and lawyer; b. 12 Jan. 1919, Staverton Hall, Northants; s. of John Clayton and Janet Boardman; m. Norah Mary Deirdre Chaworth-Musters (née Gough) 1948; two s. one d.; ed. Bromsgrove School; served Northamptonshire Yeomanry 1939–45, later Commdr.; qualified solicitor 1947; Conservative M.P. for Leicester South West, later for Leicester South 1967–74; Minister for Industry 1972–74; Chief Sec. to the Treasury Jan.-March 1974; Pres. Asscn. of British Chambers of Commerce 1977–80; Chair. Steetley PLC 1978–83, Heron Int. N.V. 1993–95; Dir. Nat. Westminster Bank (Chair. 1983–89), MEPC PLC 1980–89, Pritchard Services Group 1982–83; mem. Advisory Bd. LEK, Council of Aims of Industry; Trustee Prince's Youth Business Trust 1986–93; High Sheriff of Northants. 1979–80; one of H.M. Lieuts. City of London 1990–; Hon. Treas. Conservative Party 1980–82. *Leisure interests:* riding, foxhunting. *Address:* 29 Tufton Court, Tufton Street, London, SW1P 3QH; The Manor House, Welford, Northamptonshire, NN6 6HX, England (Home). *Telephone:* 0171-222 6793 (London); (0185 8575) 235 (Home).

BOARDMAN, Christopher (Chris) Miles, M.B.E., M.SC.; British cyclist; b. 26 Aug. 1968; m. Sally-Anne Edwards 1988; three s. one d; ed. Hilbre Secondary School, and Withens Coll.; has competed in nine World Championships; holder of various nat. records and 20 nat. titles; Bronze medal, Commonwealth Games, Edinburgh 1986; two Bronze Medals, Commonwealth Games, Auckland 1990; Gold Medal, 4,000m. individual pursuit, Olympic Games, Barcelona 1992, Double World Champion (pursuit and time trial) 1994; winner Tour de France Prologue and holder Yellow Jersey 1994, 1997, 1998; World Record for distance cycled in one hour 1993 and 1996; won World 4,000m. cycling championships, broke his own world record Sept. 1996; Hon. D.Sc. (Brighton) 1997. *Leisure interests:* carpentry, swimming, family. *Address:* c/o Beyond Level Four Ltd., Lindfield House, Station Approach, Meols, Wirral, L47 8XA, England. *Telephone:* (0151) 632 3383 (Office).

BOARDMAN, Sir John, Kt., M.A., F.S.A., F.B.A.; British archaeologist; b. 20 Aug. 1927; s. of late Frederick Boardman and Clare Wells; m. Sheila Stanford 1952; one s. one d.; ed. Chigwell School and Magdalene Coll. Cambridge; Asst. Dir. British School, Athens 1952–55; Asst. Keeper, Ashmolean Museum, Oxford 1955–59; Reader in Classical Archaeology, Univ. of Oxford 1959–78, Lincoln Prof. of Classical Archaeology and Art 1978–94, Hon. Fellow 1995; Fellow, Merton Coll. Oxford 1973–78, Hon. Fellow 1978–, Sub-warden 1975–78; Prof. of Ancient History, Royal Acad. of Arts 1989–; conducted excavations on Chios 1953–55, Crete 1964–65, Tocra, Libya 1964–65; Visiting Prof. Columbia Univ. 1965; Geddes-Harrower Prof. Univ. of Aberdeen 1974; Fellow, Inst. of Etruscan Studies, Florence 1983, Austrian and German Archaeological Insts.; Foreign mem. Royal Danish Acad.; Assoc. mem. Acad. des Inscriptions et des Belles Lettres, Inst. de France; corresp. mem. Bavarian Acad. of Sciences; Hon. M.R.I.A.; Hon. R.A.; Dr. h.c. (Athens) 1991, (Sorbonne) 1994; Kenyon Medal (British Acad.) 1995. *Publications include:* Cretan Collection in Oxford 1961, Island Gems 1963, Archaic Greek Gems 1968, Athenian Black Figure Vases 1974, Escarabeos de Piedra de Ibiza 1984, The Oxford History of the Classical World (with others) 1986, Athenian Red Figure Vases: Classical period 1989, Oxford History of Classical Art 1993, The Diffusion of Classical Art in Antiquity 1994, Greek Sculpture, Later Classical 1995, Early Greek Vase Painting 1997, articles in learned journals. *Address:* 11 Park Street, Woodstock, Oxford, OX20 1SJ, England. *Telephone:* (01993) 811259. *Fax:* 01865 278082.

BOARDMAN, Norman Keith, A.O., PH.D., SC.D., F.T.S.E., F.A.A., F.R.S.; Australian biochemist; b. 16 Aug. 1926, Geelong, Vic.; s. of William R. and Margaret Boardman; m. Mary C. Shepherd 1952; two s. five d.; ed. Melbourne Univ. and St. John's Coll., Cambridge; Research Officer, Wool Research Section, CSIRO 1949–51; Sr. Research Scientist, Div. of Plant Industry, CSIRO 1956–61, Prin. Research Scientist 1961–64; Fulbright Scholar, Univ. of Calif., Los Angeles 1964–65; Sr. Prin. Research Scientist, Div. of Plant Industry, CSIRO 1966–68, Chief Research Scientist 1968–77, mem. of Exec., CSIRO 1977–85, Chair. and Chief Exec. 1985–86, C.E.O. 1986–90, post-retirement Fellow 1990–97; Pres. Australian Biochem. Soc. 1976–78; Chair. Nat. Science and Industry Forum 1998–; Treas. Australian Acad. of Science 1978–81; Dir. Sirotech Ltd. 1986–90, Landcare Australia Ltd. 1990–98; Sec. for Science Policy, Australian Acad. of Science 1993–97; mem. Australian Research Grants Cttee. 1971–75, Australian Nat. Univ. Council 1979–89, 1990–91, Australian Centre for Int. Agric. Research (ACIAR) 1982–88, CRA

Scientific Advisory Bd. 1983–98, Prime Minister's Scientific Council 1989–90; Fellow Australian Acad. of Tech. Sciences and Eng.; David Syme Research Prize, Melbourne Univ. 1967; Lemberg Medal, Australian Biochem. Soc. 1969. *Publications:* scientific papers on plant biochemistry, particularly photosynthesis and structure, function and biogenesis of chloroplasts. *Leisure interests:* listening to music, fishing, reading, tennis. *Address:* 6 Somers Crescent, Forrest, A.C.T. 2603, Australia. *Telephone:* (02) 6295-1746 (Home). *Fax:* (02) 6295-1158.

BOASE, Martin, M.A.; British advertising and marketing executive; b. 14 July 1932, Sheffield; s. of Alan Boase and Elizabeth Grizelle Boase, née Forster; m. 1st Terry Ann Moir 1960 (divorced 1971); one s. one d.; m. 2nd Pauline Valerie Brownrigg 1974; one s. one d.; ed. Rendcomb Coll., New Coll., Oxford; with Pritchard Wood and Partners 1961–68; Partner, The Boase Massimi Pollitt Partnership (subsequently Boase Massimi Pollitt PLC, now part of Omnicom UK PLC), Chair. 1977–89; Chair. Omnicom UK PLC 1989–95, Predator Three PLC 1990–; Chair. Advertising Asscn. 1987–92, Kiss 100 FM 1993–, Maiden Outdoor 1993–, British TV Advertising Awards Ltd. 1993–, Herald Investment Trust 1994–, Investment Trust of Investment Trusts 1995–, Heal's 1997–; Dir. Omnicom Group Inc. 1989–93, EMAP PLC 1991–, Taunton Cider PLC 1993–, Matthew Clark PLC 1995–. *Leisure interest:* the Turf. *Address:* c/o Omnicom UK PLC, 12 Bishops Bridge Road, London, W2 6AA, England.

BOCHEŃSKI, Jacek; Polish writer; b. 29 July 1926, Lvov; m.; one d.; ed. State College of Theatrical Arts, Warsaw; ed. magazines Pokolenie, Przegląd Kulturalny, Zapis; Head Polish PEN Club 1996–. *Publications include:* prose: Fiołki przynoszą nieszczęście (Violets bring bad luck) 1949, Zgodnie z prawem (In Accordance with Law) 1952, Tabu (Taboo) 1965, Krwawe speciały włoskie (Bloody Italian Rarities) 1982, Stan po zapaści (After the Collapse) 1987, Retro 1990; essays: Boski Juliusz (Divine Julius) 1961, Nazo poeta 1969; several articles. *Address:* PEN Club Polski, ul. Krakowskie Przedmieście 87/89, 00-079 Warsaw, Poland. *Telephone:* (22) 826 57 84. *Fax:* (22) 826 57 84.

BOCK, Dieter; German business executive; b. Dessau, Germany; m. Olga Giro 1985; four s.; ed. Marburg and Munich Univs. attorney at law and tax adviser; apprentice for law firm Boesebeck and Barz, Frankfurt; then with accountancy firm; f. own consultancy firm, Frankfurt 1973; est. first partnership for real estate investment, Munich 1974; f. Advanta Man. AG 1985; owns Laerstate BV, Netherlands; Chair. of the Supervisory Bd. of Advanta AG 1986–; Chair. of the Supervisory Bd. of Kempinski Hotels; Jt. Chief Exec. of Lonrho 1993–94, C.E.O. 1994–96, Deputy Chair. 1996–97; Pres. TrizecHahn (Europe) 1997–; Vice-Chair. TrizecHahn Corpn. 1997–; sponsor of cultural and artistic activities. *Address:* 18A St. James's Place, London, SW1A 1NH, England.

BOCK, Edward John, M.S.; American chemicals executive; b. 1 Sept. 1916, Fort Dodge, Ia.; s. of Edward J. and Maude (Juday) Bock; m. Ruth Kunerth 1941; two s. two d.; ed. Iowa State Univ.; joined Monsanto Co. as an engineer 1941; Plant Man. Columbia, Tenn. 1948; Assoc. Dir. of Marketing, Inorganic Chemicals Div. 1956, Dir. of Marketing 1957, Asst. Gen. Man. 1958, Vice-Pres. 1960, Gen. Man. 1960, Vice-Pres. (Admin.), mem. Bd. of Dirs. and mem. Exec. Cttee. 1965; mem. Corporate Devt. Cttee. 1967; Pres. of Monsanto Co., Chair. Corporate Devt. Cttee. and Exec. Cttee. 1968–72; Dir. ENRON Corpn., Midcoast Aviation Inc., Harbour Group Ltd. 1976; Pres. and C.E.O. Cupples Co., St. Louis 1976–84; mem. Bd. of Govs., Iowa State Univ. Foundation; Anson Marston Eng. Award; Nat. College Football Hall of Fame 1970. *Leisure interests:* amateur radio, golf, hunting, boating. *Address:* 2232 Clifton Forge, St. Louis, MO 63131, U.S.A.

BOCK, Hans, PH.D.; German professor of inorganic chemistry; b. 5 Oct. 1928, Hamburg; s. of Paul Bock and Hedwig (née Lis) Bock; m. Dr. Luise (née Eisenreich) Bock 1954; two s. three d.; ed. Ludwigs Maximilians Univ., Munich; Visiting Scientist, Fed. Inst. of Tech., Zürich 1965–68; Prof. and Dir. Johann Wolfgang Goethe Univ., Frankfurt 1969–; Adjunct Prof. Univ. of Michigan, Ann Arbor, U.S.A. 1983–84; External Scientific mem. Max Planck Soc. 1977–; mem. Acad. of Science, Mainz 1984–; Corresp. mem. Acad. of Science, Göttingen 1986, Acad. of Natural Scientists Leopoldina, Halle 1991, Bavarian Acad. of Sciences 1994; Dr. h.c. (Hamburg) 1988, (Montpellier) 1993; Chemistry Award, Acad. of Science, Göttingen 1969, Frederic Stanley Kipping Award, A.C.S. 1974, Wilhelm Klemm Award of the German Chemical Soc. 1987, Hieber Award 1993; Heyrovsky Medal, Prague Acad. of Science 1996. *Publications:* 500 scientific publs. in int. journals, The HMO Model and its Application, (3 vols., with Edgar Heilbronner) 1965–68. *Leisure interests:* Norman art, oenology. *Address:* c/o Institut für Anorganische Chemie der J. W. Goethe-Universität, Marie-Curie-Str. 11, 60439 Frankfurt am Main (Office); Rombergweg 1A, 61462 Königstein, Germany (Home). *Telephone:* (069) 7982-9180 (Office); 06174-931016 (Home). *Fax:* (069) 7982-9188.

BOCK, Jerry (Jerrold Lewis); American composer; b. 23 Nov. 1928, New Haven; s. of George and Rebecca (Alpert) Bock; m. Patricia Faggen 1950; one s. one d.; ed. Univ. of Wisconsin; wrote scores for high school and coll. musicals; author of sketches for television 1951–54; mem. N.Y. Bd. Educiradio broadcasts 1961–; composed songs for film Wonders of Manhattan 1956; composed music for show Mr. Wonderful 1956, and with Sheldon Harnick (q.v.) The Body Beautiful 1958, Fiorello 1959 (Pulitzer Prize, Antoinette Perry (Tony) Awards), Tenderloin 1960, She Loves Me 1963, Fiddler on the Roof 1964, The Apple Tree 1966, The Rothschilds 1970, Jerome Robbins Broadway 1989, A Stranger Among Us 1992; mem. Wilderness Soc., Horticultural Soc., New York, Broadcast Music Inc., American Civil Liberties Union; Johnny Mercer Award, Songwriters Hall of Fame 1990, Theatre Hall of Fame 1990.

BOCUSE, Paul; French restaurateur; b. 11 Feb. 1926, Collonges-au-Mont-d'Or (Rhône); s. of Georges Bocuse and Irma Roulier; m. Raymonde Duvert 1946; one s. one d.; ed. Ecole primaire, Collonges-au-Mont-d'Or and Pensionnat Saint-Louis, Lyons; restaurateur (in business passing from father to son since 1765), Collonges-Mont-d'Or; restaurateur, French Pavilion, Disneyworld, Orlando, Fla., U.S.A.; Pres. Asscn. Eurotoques 1989–, L'Ecole des Arts Culinaires et de l'Hôtellerie Ecully 1991–95; Pres. Meilleur Ouvrier de France—Section Cuisine-Restauration; mem. Asscn. des maître-cuisiniers de France; Officier, Légion d'honneur, Officier Mérite nat., Chevalier des palmes académiques, Officier du Mérite agricole. *Publications:* La Cuisine du marché 1976, Bocuse dans votre cuisine 1982, La cuisine du gibier (in collaboration) 1984, Bon Appétit 1989, Cuisine de France 1990, La bonne chère 1995. *Leisure interest:* underwater fishing. *Address:* Restaurant Paul Bocuse, 40 rue de la Plage, 69660 Collonges-au-Mont d'Or, France. *Telephone:* 72.42.90.90. *Fax:* 72.27.85.87.

BOD, Péter Ákos, PH.D.; Hungarian economist and politician; b. 28 July 1951, Szigetvár; s. of Andor Bod and Rózsa Nagy; m. Katalin Monostori; one d.; ed. high-school, Miskolc, Univ. of Budapest; worked as researcher, later dept. head, Inst. for Econ. Planning; UNDP adviser in Ghana; mem. of Parl. (Hungarian Democratic Forum) 1990–91; Minister of Industry and Trade 1990–91; Pres. Nat. Bank of Hungary 1991–94; mem. bd. EBRD, London 1995–97; Chief Economic Adviser, Prime Minister's Office 1998–. *Publication:* The Entrepreneurial State in the Contemporary Market Economy 1987 and articles on economic policy. *Leisure interests:* tennis, soccer, music, reading. *Address:* Prime Minister's Office, 1051 Budapest, Kossuth tér. 4, Hungary. *Telephone:* (1) 268-3526. *Fax:* (1) 268-3527.

BODE, Thilo, PH.D.; German business executive and consultant; b. 1947, nr. Munich; ed. Munich and Regensberg Univs.; int. consultant Lahmeyer Int., Frankfurt; Project Man. German Bank for Reconstruction and Devt. 1978–81; ind. consultant for int. orgs., govts. and businesses 1981; Special Asst. to Chief Exec. of int. pvt. corpn. 1986; Exec. Dir. Greenpeace Germany 1989–95, Greenpeace Int. 1995–. *Address:* Greenpeace International, Keizergracht 176, Amsterdam 1016 DW, Netherlands.

BODELÓN, Rogelio, DR. ING.; Spanish business executive; b. 21 Sept. 1936, Ponferrada; s. of Carlos Bodelón and Adela Bodelón; ed. Escuela Técnica Superior Ingenieros Industriales, Madrid; mem. Bd. of Dirs. Sefanitro 1973–77; Commercial Dir. HIDRONITRU 1977–83; Gen. Dir. ENSIDESA 1983–88; Asst. Dir. Instituto Nacional de Industria (INI) Aug. 1988–; Pres. AGCISA Jan. 1989–; Vice-Pres. TARNOS, S.A. 1991–; mem. Bd. of Dirs. Ferroatlántica 1993–, Fertiberia 1995–, SEFANITRO 1997–. *Publications:* numerous articles in newspapers. *Leisure interests:* golf, dominoes. *Address:* Paseo Habana 26-6-12, 28036 Madrid, Spain. *Telephone:* 561 45 86. *Fax:* 563 68 40.

BODEN, Margaret Ann, M.A., PH.D., SC.D., F.B.A.; British professor of philosophy and psychology; b. 26 Nov. 1936, London; d. of Leonard F. Boden and Violet D. (Dawson) Boden; m. John R. Spiers 1967 (divorced 1981); one s. one d.; ed. Newnham Coll., Cambridge (Major Scholar) and Harvard Grad. School (Harkness Fellow); lecturer in Philosophy, Univ. of Birmingham 1959–65; lecturer, then Reader in Philosophy and Psychology, Univ. of Sussex 1965–80, Prof. 1980–, Founding Dean School of Cognitive and Computing Sciences 1987; Curator Univ. of London Inst. for Advanced Study 1995–; co-founder, Harvester Press Ltd. 1970, Dir. 1970–85; Vice-Pres. British Acad. 1989–91, Royal Inst. of G.B. 1993–95, Chair. of Council, Royal Inst. of G.B. 1993–95; mem. Advisory Bd. for the Research Councils 1989–90, Council, Royal Inst. of Great Britain 1992–95, Academia Europaea 1993–, Animal Procedures Cttee. 1995–; Fellow American Asscn. for Artificial Intelligence 1993–. *Publications:* Purposive Explanation in Psychology 1972, Artificial Intelligence and Natural Man 1977, Piaget 1979, Minds and Mechanisms 1981, Computer Models of Mind 1988, Artificial Intelligence in Psychology 1989, The Philosophy of Artificial Intelligence (ed.) 1990, The Creative Mind 1990, Dimensions of Creativity (ed.) 1994, Artificial Intelligence and the Mind (co-ed.) 1994, The Philosophy of Artificial Life (ed.) 1996, Artificial Intelligence (ed.) 1996. *Leisure interests:* dressmaking, travelling. *Address:* c/o School of Cognitive and Computing Sciences, University of Sussex, Brighton, BN1 9QH, England. *Telephone:* (01273) 678386. *Fax:* (01273) 671320.

BODEWITZ, Hendrik Wilhelm, PH.D.; Netherlands professor of Sanskrit; b. 13 Oct. 1939, Gramsbergen; s. of Johan Adriaan Bodewitz and Jennigjen Lenters; m. Janneke van Uchelen 1964; one s. one d.; ed. Lyceum Coevorden, Univ. of Utrecht; lecturer in Sanskrit, Utrecht Univ. 1966–68, Prof. 1976–92, Dean of Faculty 1980–82 and 1984–86; Sr. Lecturer, Leiden Univ. 1969–76, Prof. 1992–; mem. Netherlands Royal Acad.; founding mem. Academia Europaea; Ed. Indo-Iranian Journal, Gonda Indological Studies; Co-Ed. Groningen Oriental Studies; Sec. Gonda Foundation. *Publications:* Jaiminīya Brāhmaṇa I, 1-65, with a study of the Agnihotra and the Prāṇāgnihotra 1973, The daily evening and morning offering according to the Brāhmaṇas 1976, The Jyotiṣṭoma Ritual: Jaiminīya Brāhmaṇa I, 66-364 1990. *Address:* Stolberglaan 29, 3583 XL Utrecht, Netherlands. *Telephone:* (030) 2510047.

BODIN, Manfred; German banker; b. 14 Nov. 1939, Münster; m.; Stadtsparkasse, Münster 1960–64; Stadtsparkasse, Witten 1964–70; mem. Man. Bd. Kreissparkasse Recklinghausen 1970–75, Chair. Man. Bd. 1976–83; Chair. Man. Bd. Sparkasse Essen 1984–91; Chair. Man. Bd. NORD/LB 1991–; Dr. h.c. (Essen). *Address:* Norddeutsche Landesbank Girozentrale, Georgsplatz 1, 30159 Hannover, Germany. *Telephone:* 511-361-0. *Fax:* 49-511-361-4765.

BODMAN, Samuel Wright, III, SC.D.; American business executive; b. 26 Nov. 1938, Chicago, Ill.; s. of Samuel W. Bodman Jr. and Lina B. Bodman; m. 1st Lynda Schubert 1984; three c.; m. 2nd Diane Barber 1997; ed. Cornell Univ. and Massachusetts Inst. of Tech.; Instructor, M.I.T. 1964, Asst. Prof. 1964–68, Assoc. Prof. 1968–70, Dir. School of Chemical Eng. Practice, American Cyanamid Co. 1965–67; Tech. Dir. American Research and Devt. Corpn. 1964–70; Founding Partner Fidelity Ventures Ltd. 1970–86, Vice-Pres. Commercial Devt. 1971–75, Pres. Fidelity Man. and Research Co. 1976–86, Pres. and C.O.O. FMR Corpn. (parent holding co. of Fidelity Investments) 1982–86, Exec. Vice-Pres. and Dir. Fidelity Group of Mutual Funds 1980–86; Pres. and C.O.O. Cabot Corpn. 1987–88, Chair. 1988–, C.E.O. 1988; Dir. Cabot Corpn., Bank of Boston Corpn., Westvaco Inc., Continental Cablevision Inc., Index Tech. Corpn.; Trustee Mitre Corpn., Babson Coll., Isabella Stewart Gardner Museum, New England Aquarium; mem. Corpn., M.I.T., Chair. Chemical Eng. Visiting Cttee.; mem. American Acad. of Arts and Sciences. *Address:* Cabot Corporation, 75 State Street, Boston, MA 02109, U.S.A. *Telephone:* (617) 342-6103.

BODMER, Sir Walter Fred, Kt., PH.D., F.R.C.PATH., F.R.S.; British research scientist; b. 10 Jan. 1936, Frankfurt-am-Main, Germany; s. of Ernest J. and Sylvia E. Bodmer; m. Julia G. Pilkington 1956; two s. one d.; ed. Manchester Grammar School and Univ. of Cambridge; Research Fellow, Clare Coll., Cambridge 1958–60, Fellow 1961, Hon. Fellow 1989; Demonstrator, Dept. of Genetics, Univ. of Cambridge 1960–61; Fellow, Visiting Asst. Prof., Dept. of Genetics, Stanford Univ. 1961–62, Asst. Prof. 1962–66, Assoc. Prof. 1966–68, Prof. 1968–70; Prof. of Genetics, Univ. of Oxford 1970–79; Vice-Pres. Royal Inst. 1981–82; Pres. Royal Statistical Soc. 1984–85; Pres. British Asscn. for Advancement of Science 1987–88, Chair. of Council 1996–; mem. Advisory Bd. for the Research Councils 1983–88; Chair. BBC Science Consultative Group 1981–87; mem. BBC Gen. Advisory Council; Pres. Asscn. for Science Ed. 1989; Chair. Bd. of Trustees, British Museum (Natural History) 1989–93; Pres. Human Genome Org. 1990–92; Dir.-Gen. Imperial Cancer Research Fund 1991–96 (Dir. of Research 1979–91); Chancellor of Salford Univ. 1996–; Prin. Hertford Coll., Oxford Sept 1996–; Chair. Cttee. on the Public Understanding of Science (COPUS) 1990–94; Pres. Int. Fed. of Asscns. for the Advancement of Science and Tech. 1992–94; Hon. Vice-Pres. Research Defense Soc. 1990–; non-exec. Dir. Fisons PLC 1990–96; Foreign Hon. mem. American Acad. of Arts and Sciences, American Asscn. of Immunologists; Foreign Assoc. N.A.S.; Hon. Fellow, Green Coll., Oxford, Clare Coll., Cambridge, Royal Soc. of Medicine; Foreign mem. Acad. of Sciences 1988–; Hon. F.R.C.P.; Hon. F.R.C.S., Hon. F.R.S.E.; Hon. M.D. (Bologna, Birmingham); Hon. D.Sc. (Bath), (Oxford), (Hull), (Edinburgh) 1990, (Aberdeen) 1994, (Lancaster) 1994, (London), (Plymouth), (Salford) 1996, (UMIST) 1997; Hon. D.Univ. (Surrey) 1990; William Allan Memorial Award (American Soc. of Human Genetics) 1980, Conway Evans Prize (Royal Coll. of Physicians/Royal Soc.) 1982, Rabbi Shai Shacknai Memorial Prize Lectureship in Immunology and Cancer Research 1983, John Alexander Memorial Prize and Lectureship (Univ. of Pa. Medical School) 1984, Rose Payne Distinguished Scientist Lectureship 1985, Ellison Cliffe Lecture and Medal 1987. *Publications:* co-author, The Genetics of Human Populations 1971, Our Future Inheritance—Choice or Chance? 1974, Genetics, Evolution and Man 1976, The Book of Man 1993; papers in scientific and medical journals. *Leisure interests:* playing piano, riding, swimming. *Address:* Hertford College, Oxford, OX1 3BW, England.

BODSTRÖM, Lennart, PH.D.: Swedish politician; b. 1928, Gothenburg; ed. Gothenburg and Uppsala Univs.; lecturer Political Science Dept., Uppsala Univ. 1961–63; mem. Research staff Swedish Cen. Org. of Salaried Employees 1964, Deputy Gen. Man. 1966–70, Chair. 1970; mem. Econ. Planning Council 1970; Vice-Chair. Bd. Cen. Fed. of People and Defence 1970–82; mem. Consultative Cttee. EFTA 1970–82; mem. Bd. Council of Nordic Trade Unions 1973–82; mem. Trade Union Advisory Cttee. OECD 1970, Chair. 1980–82; mem. Bd. Int. Confed. of Free Trade Unions 1981–82; Minister of Foreign Affairs 1982–85, of Educ. and Cultural Affairs 1985–89; Amb. to Norway 1989–94; Chair. Nat. Union of Students 1959; mem. Directorate Nat. Bd. of Univs. and Colls. 1969–74; mem. Swedish Labour Market Bd. 1970–82. *Address:* Odengatan 71, 11322 Stockholm, Sweden.

BOEHM, Gottfried Karl, DR.PHIL.; German art historian; b. 19 Sept. 1942, Braunau, Bohemia; s. of Karl and Olga Boehm; m. Margaret Hunold 1980; one d.; ed.; Univs. of Cologne, Vienna and Heidelberg; lecturer, History of Art, Ruhr Univ. Bochum 1975–79, Prof. 1977; Prof. of History of Art, Justus Liebig Univ., Giessen 1979–86, Univ. of Basel 1986–; Vice-Pres. Inst. für die Wissenschaften vom Menschen, Vienna 1981–. *Publications:* Studien zur Perspektivität, Philosophie und Kunst in der frühen Neuzeit 1969, Zur Dialektik der ästhetischen Grenze 1973, Philosophische Hermeneutik 1976, Die Hermeneutik und die Wissenschaften 1978, Bildnis und Individuum, Über den Ursprung der Porträtmalerei in der italienischen Renaissance 1985, Paul Cézanne, Montagne Sainte-Victoire 1988, Konrad Fiedler, Schriften zur Kunst 1991, Was ist ein Bild? 1994, Beschreibungskunst-Kunstbeschreibung. Ekphrasis von der Antike bis zut Gegenwart 1995, articles and contributions, etc. *Address:* Kunstgeschichtliches Seminar, St. Alban-Graben-16, CH-4051 Basel (Office); Sevogelplatz 1, CH-4051 Basel, Switzerland (Home). *Telephone:* 061-2723595 (Office); 061-3116241 (Home). *Fax:* 061-2723073.

BOEKELHEIDE, Virgil Carl, PH.D.; American professor of chemistry; b. 28 July 1919, S. Dakota; s. of Charles F. Boekelheide and Eleanor Toennies; m. Caroline A. Barrett 1945; two s. one d.; ed. Univ. of Minnesota; Instructor, Univ of Illinois 1943–46; Asst. Prof. Univ. of Rochester 1946–60; Prof. of Chem., Univ. of Oregon 1960–; mem. N.A.S. 1962–; Guggenheim Fellow 1953–54; Swiss American Foundation Fellow 1960; Roche Anniversary Fellow 1963–64; Welch Lecturer 1968; Fulbright Distinguished Prof., Yugoslavia 1972; Distinguished Scholar Exchange Program, People's Repub. of China 1981; mem. Bd. of Eds. Organic Reactions 1956–, Organic Syntheses 1956–64, Journal of American Chemical Society 1964–74; mem. Council for Int. Exchange of Scholars (Sr. Fulbright-Hayes Awards); Centenary Lecturer, Royal Soc. of G.B. 1983–; Alexander v. Humboldt Prize (Fed. Repub. of Germany) 1974–75; Coover Award 1981. *Publications:* over 200 original research papers. *Leisure interests:* tennis and music. *Address:* 2017 Elk Drive, Eugene, OR 97403, U.S.A.

BOENISCH, Peter H.; German journalist; b. 4 May 1927, Berlin; s. of Konstantin Boenisch and Eva Boenisch (née Premysler); m. 1st Victoria von Schack 1959 (divorced); m. 2nd Julia Schramm 1998; one d.; ed. Dr. Hugo Eckner Coll., Berlin Univ.; Political Ed. Die Neue Zeitung 1945–49; Ed. Tagespost 1949–52; Special Asst. to Pres. Nordwest-Deutsche-Rundfunk 1952–55; Ed. Kindler Publishing Co. 1955–59, Springer Publishing Corpn. (Berliner Illustrierte, Bild-Zeitung, Bild am Sonntag) 1959–81; Chair. Ed. Bd. Die Welt 1978–81; fmr. Vice-Chair. Axel Springer Group, responsible for planning and development; Chief Govt. Spokesman and Leader, Fed. Press and Information Office 1983–85; Man. Dir of Burda Magazines 1986–92; Bundesverdienstkreuz, Bayerischer Verdienstorden 1976, Order of Leopold II (Belgium) 1985. *Leisure interests:* golf, antiques. *Address:* Kaltenbrunnerstr. 14, 83703 Gmund, Germany.

BOESAK, Rev. Allan; South African clergyman; b. 23 Feb. 1946, Kakamas; s. of Andreas Boesak and Sarah Helena Boesak; m. 1st Dorothy Rose Martin 1969; one s. three d.; m. 2nd Elna Botha 1991; prominent anti-apartheid campaigner; elected Pres. World Alliance of Reformed Churches, Geneva 1982; Pres. Asscn. of Christian Students in S.A. 1984–90; Pres. S.A. Council of Churches 1984–87; fmr. mem. Dutch Reformed Mission Church; Leader ANC in Western Cape 1991; Dir. Foundation for Peace and Justice 1991; faces 32 theft and corruption charges 1997; on trial for fraud Aug. 1998; sentenced to six years' imprisonment March 1999; Hon. D.D. (Victoria) 1983, (Yale) 1984, (Interdenominational Theological Centre Atlanta) 1985; Hon. D.Iur. (Warwick) 1989; Third World Prize 1989, numerous other awards and hon. degrees; co-f. United Democratic Front 1983. *Publication:* A Call for an End to Unjust Rule 1986, If This is Treason, I am Guilty (Speeches) 1988. *Address:* c/o African National Congress, P.O. Box 61884, Marshalltown 2107, South Africa.

BOETSCH, Wolfgang, DR. JUR.; German politician; b. 8 Sept. 1938, Bad Kreuznach; m.; two c.; ed. Univ. of Würzburg and Verwaltungshochschule, Speyer; municipal lawyer, Kitzingen 1968–74; legal adviser to Govt. of Lower Franconia 1974; mem. Christian Social Union (CSU) 1960–; mem. Würzburg City Council 1972–76; mem. Bavarian Parl. 1974–76; Chair. of CSU, Würzburg 1973–91, also mem. Presidium of CSU; mem. Bundestag 1976–; Minister for Posts and Telecommunications 1993–97. *Address:* Waltherstrasse 5a, 97074 Würzburg, Germany. *Telephone:* (0931) 83080. *Fax:* (0931) 14-8872.

BOEYNANTS, Paul Van Den; Belgian politician; b. 22 May 1919; ed. Collège Saint-Michel; fmr. butcher; mem. Chamber of Reps. 1949–; Minister of Middle Classes 1958; Dir. 1958 Exhbn., Brussels; Chair. Social Christian Party 1961–68, 1979–81; Minister of State 1969; Prime Minister 1966–68, (acting) 1978–79; Deputy Prime Minister 1979–81; Minister of Defence 1972–79, of Brussels Affairs 1974–77; kidnapped Jan. 1989, released Feb. 1989. *Address:* 5 Kalfhoek, 8300 Knokke-Le Zoute, Belgium.

BOFF, Leonardo Genezio Darci, D.PHIL., D.THEOL.; Brazilian professor of theology, writer and editor; b. 14 Dec. 1938, Concórdia, S.C.; s. of Mansueto Boff and Regina Fontana Boff; ed. Inst. Teológico Franciscano, Petrópolis and Nat. Univ. of Rio de Janeiro; Prof. of Systematic Theology and of Franciscan Spirituality, Inst. Teológico Franciscano, Petrópolis, Rio de Janeiro 1971–92, also Prof. of Theology of Liberation; Adviser to Latin American Conf. of Religions (CLAR) 1971–80, to Nat. Conf. of Brazilian Bishops (CNBB) 1971–80; mem. Editorial Bd. of Revista Eclesiástica Brasileira 1971–92; mem. Bd. of Dirs. Vozes publishing house 1971–92; Pres. Bd. of Eds., Theology and Liberation collection 1985–; mem. Editorial Bd. Concilium; ordered by Roman Curia to begin unspecified period of "obedient silence" 1985; Dr. h.c. (Turin, Lund); Paz y Justicia Award, Barcelona; Menschenrechte in der Kirche Award, Herbert Haag Foundation, Fed. Repub. of Germany and Switzerland. *Publications:* Jesus Christ Liberator 1971, Die Kirche als Sakrament im Horizont der Welterfahrung 1972, Theology of Captivity and Liberation 1972, Ecclesiogenesis 1977, The Maternal Face of God 1979, Church: Charism and Power 1980, Theology Listening to People 1981, St. Francis: A Model for Human Liberation 1984, Trinity and Society 1988, The Gospel of the Cosmic Christ 1989, The

New Evangelization: The Perspective of the Oppressed 1990, Ecology and Spirituality 1991, Mística e Espiritualidade 1994, Nova Era: a Consciência Planetária 1994. *Leisure interests:* gardening, social work at the "favelas", child minding. *Address:* Pr. Martins Leão 12/204, Alto Vale Encantado, 20531-350 Rio de Janeiro, Brazil. *Telephone:* (21) 326-5293. *Fax:* (21) 326-5293.

BOFILL, Ricardo; Spanish architect; b. 5 Dec. 1939, Barcelona; s. of Emilio Bofill and Maria Levi; two s.; ed. Ecole Française, Barcelona, architectural studies in Geneva; founder mem. and leader Taller de Arquitectura (design team), Paris, Barcelona; works incl. Les Espaces d'Abraxas, Marne-la-Vallée, Les Echelles du Baroque, Paris, Antigone, Montpellier, Le Lac and Le Viaduc, Versailles, airports (Barcelona), theatres (Metz and Barcelona), offices, wine cellars Congress Palace, Madrid, Christian Dior Corpn. HQ, Paris, Shepherd School of Music, Houston, Tex., U.S.A., 77 W. Wacker office tower, Chicago, Ill., U.S.A., Harajuku United Arrows shopping centre, Tokyo; exhbns. incl. Architectural Asscn., London Jan. 1981, Museum of Modern Art, New York June–Sept. 1985. *Address:* Taller de Arquitectura, 14 Avenue Industria, 08960 Saint Just Desvern, Barcelona, Spain; 154 rue de l'Université, 75007 Paris, France. *Telephone:* (3) 4999900 (Spain); (1) 45.56.03.03 (France).

BOFINGER, Helge; German architect and university professor; b. 30 March 1940, Stettin/Pommern; s. of Christa Bofinger and Hans Ullrich Bofinger; m. Margret Schreib Schmitz-Mathies 1965; ed. Ratsgymnasium Goslar, Tech. Univ. of Brunswick; Scientific Asst. T.U. Brunswick 1968–69; est. own office Bofinger and partner with Margret Bofinger, Brunswick 1969–81, Berlin 1974–, Wiesbaden 1978–; Asst. Prof., Univ. of Dortmund 1979–81, Prof. of Design and Bldg. Theory, Faculty of Architecture 1986–; Hon. Prof., Univ. of Buenos Aires, Argentina 1985; Visiting Prof. and Lecturer, Venice, Amsterdam, Rotterdam, Buenos Aires, São Paulo, Brasília, Curitiba, Shanghai 1984–91; projects and bldgs. include: Castle Park, Brunswick 1972–74, Unitèhabitation, Göttingen 1972–74, Piazza Ledenhof, Osnabrück 1976–77, school, Riedland 1977–79, Villa S. Kronberg 1980–82, German Cinema Museum 1979–84, Frankfurt Fair Bldg. 1984, IBA Berlin, Wilhemstr., Stresemannstr. 1981, 1988–89, Telecommunications bldg., German Post/Telecom 1987–90, Commerzbank bldg., Frankfurt 1991, SPD headquarters, Berlin 1992, town hall extension, Saarbrücken 1992; rep. in numerous exhbns. Germany, U.S.A., Canada, Israel, Italy, Argentina, U.K., France, U.S.S.R. 1979–90; Deubau Special Prize 1979, German Architectural Prize 1983, Hon. Prize, Transcaucasian Biennale, Tbilisi 1988. *Publications:* Architecture in Germany 1979, Young Architects in Europe 1983; numerous contribs. to German and int. architectural magazines. *Leisure interest:* architecture. *Address:* Biebricher Allee 49, 65187 Wiesbaden, Germany. *Telephone:* (0611) 87094. *Fax:* (0611) 87095.

BOGAERS, Petrus Clemens Wilhelmus Maria, DRS.ECON.; Netherlands politician and trade unionist; b. 2 July 1924, Cuyk a/d Maas; s. of Petrus P. M. J. Bogaers and Henrica Maria Hermans; m. 1st Femmigje Visscher 1950 (divorced 1980); m. 2nd Yvonne M. H. L. Bogaers 1981 (divorced 1986); m. 3rd Ida Heyne 1994; four s. three d.; ed. Episcopal Coll. Grammar School, Roermond, and Tilburg School of Economics; official Red Cross Army 1945; Asst. to Prof. v.d. Brink 1947; Econ. Adviser to Roman Catholic Workers' Union 1948, Head Scientific Advisory Section 1957–63; mem. Socio-Economic Council 1954; mem. EEC Econ. and Social Cttee. 1958; mem. Second Chamber, Netherlands Parl. 1959; Minister of Housing and Building 1963–65; Minister of Housing and Physical Planning 1965–66; Pres. Gooiland Region 1968–74, Netherlands Asthma Foundation 1976–89 (Hon. mem. 1989); mem. Supervisory Bds. various Dutch cos. 1976–95; Sec. Employee Participation Foundation BERGEYK 1986–96; mem. Supervisory Bd. Dutch Employee Participation Inst. 1994–96; Dutch Efficiency Prize 1963; Officer Order of Orange-Nassau 1963, Queens House Medal of Orange-Nassau 1965, Commdr. Order of Orange-Nassau 1966. *Leisure interests:* reading, tennis, open-air life. *Address:* Volta Street 53, Amersfoort, Netherlands. *Telephone:* (33) 4615093.

BOGARDE, Sir Dirk (Van den Bogaerde, Derek Niven), Kt.; British actor; b. 28 March 1921, Hampstead, London; ed. Allan Glen's School, Glasgow, Univ. Coll. School, London, and Chelsea Polytechnic; Army Service 1940–46; Chevalier de l'Ordre des Arts et des Lettres 1982, Commdr. 1990; Hon. D.Litt. (St. Andrews Univ.) 1985; BAFA Acad. Award 1988. *Roles in plays include:* Cliff in Power without Glory 1947, Orpheus in Point of Departure 1950, Nicky in The Vortex 1953, Alberto in Summertime 1955–56, Jezebel 1958. *Films include:* Hunted, Appointment in London, They Who Dare, The Sleeping Tiger, Doctor in the House, Doctor at Sea, Doctor at Large, The Spanish Gardener, Cast a Dark Shadow, Ill Met by Moonlight, A Tale of Two Cities, The Wind Cannot Read, The Doctor's Dilemma, Libel, Song Without End, The Angel Wore Red, The Singer Not the Song, Victim, H.M.S. Defiant, Password is Courage, The Mind Benders, I Could Go on Singing, The Servant, Doctor in Distress, Hot Enough for June, High Bright Sun, King and Country, Darling ..., Modesty Blaise, Accident, Our Mother's House, Sebastian, Justine, The Fixer, Upon This Rock, The Damned, Death in Venice, The Serpent, The Night Porter, Permission to Kill, Providence, A Bridge Too Far, Despair, Daddy Nostalgie (These Foolish Things) 1990; adapted for TV and starred in May We Borrow Your Husband 1986. *Publications:* A Postillion Struck by Lightning (autobiog.) 1977, Snakes and Ladders (autobiog.) 1978; A Gentle Occupation (novel) 1980, Voices in the Garden (novel) 1981, An Orderly Man (autobiog.) 1983, West of Sunset (novel) 1984, Backcloth (autobiog.) 1986, The Complete Autobiography 1988, A Particular Friendship 1989, Jericho (novel) 1992, Great Meadow (autobiog.) 1992, A Short Walk from Harrods 1993, A Period of Adjustment (novel) 1994, Cleared for Take Off 1995, Closing Ranks (novel) 1997, For the Time Being 1998. *Address:* c/o J.A.A., 27 Floral Street, London, WC2E 3DP, England.

BOGDANOR, Vernon, C.B.E., M.A., F.R.S.A., F.B.A.; British professor of government; b. 16 July 1943, London; s. of Harry Bogdanor and Rosa Weinger; m. Judith Beckett 1972; two s.; ed. Queen's Coll. and Nuffield Coll. Oxford; Fellow, Brasenose Coll. Oxford 1966–, Sr. Tutor 1979–85, 1996–97; mem. Council of Hansard Soc. for Parl. Govt. 1981–; Special Adviser, House of Lords Select Cttee. on European Communities 1982–83; adviser to Govts. of Czech Repub., Slovakia, Hungary and Israel on constitutional and electoral matters 1988–; Reader in Govt. Univ. of Oxford 1989–96, Prof. of Govt. 1996–; Special Adviser, House of Commons Public Service Cttee. 1996; mem. U.K. del. to CSCE Conf. Oslo 1991; Mishcon Lecturer 1994. *Publications:* Devolution 1979, The People and the Party System 1981, Multi-party Politics and the Constitution 1983, What is Proportional Representation? 1984, The Blackwell Encyclopaedia of Political Institutions (ed.) 1987, Comparing Constitutions (co-author) 1995, The Monarchy and the Constitution 1995, Politics and the Constitution 1996, Power and the People 1997. *Leisure interests:* music, walking, talking, journalism. *Address:* Brasenose College, Oxford, OX1 4AD, England. *Telephone:* (01865) 277830. *Fax:* (01865) 277822.

BOGDANOV, Aleksey Alekseyevich; Russian biochemist; b. 11 Oct. 1935; s. of Aleksey Bogdanov and Irina Bogdanova; m. Suzanna Bogdanova; two s.; ed. Moscow State Univ.; jr., sr. researcher, docent Moscow State Univ. 1958–69, Prof. 1973–; head of dept. 1969–; corresp. mem. U.S.S.R. (now Russian) Acad. of Sciences 1984, mem. 1994; research in bioorganic chem. and molecular biology; U.S.S.R. State Prize. *Publications include:* Chemistry of Nucleic Acids and their Components 1978, Advanced Organic Chemistry of Nucleic Acids (VCH) 1994; numerous articles in scientific journals. *Leisure interest:* classical music. *Address:* Moscow State University, Vorobyevy gory, 119899 Moscow, Russia. *Telephone:* (095) 939 3143 (Office).

BOGDANOV, Michael, M.A.; British theatre director; b. 15 Dec. 1938, London; s. of Francis Bogdin and Rhoda Rees; m. Patricia Ann Warwick 1966; two s. two d.; ed. Trinity Coll., Dublin, Munich Univ., Sorbonne; Producer/Dir. Radio Telefis Eireann 1966–68; Asst. Dir. R.S.C. 1969–71; Assoc. Dir. Tyneside Theatre Co. 1971–73; Dir. Phoenix Theatre, Leicester 1973–77; Dir. Young Vic Theatre 1978–80; Assoc. Dir. Nat. Theatre 1980–88, also Co. Dir.; founded (with Michael Pennington) English Shakespeare Co. 1986–, Artistic Dir. 1986–; Intendant Deutsches Schauspielhaus, Hamburg 1989–; Fellow Trinity Coll., Univ. of Dublin 1997; Hon. Fellow Univ. of Sunderland 1997; Hon. Prof. Univ. of Wales 1993; Sr. Fellow De Montfort Univ. 1992; Assoc. Peter Brook's (q.v.) production of A Midsummer Night's Dream, R.S.C. 1971; Two Gentlemen of Verona, Teatro Escobar, São Paulo, Brazil, Rabelais (Jean-Louis Barrault) 1971; Dir. Gawain and the Green Knight, Hunchback of Notre Dame, Nat. Theatre 1977, The Taming of the Shrew, R.S.C., Hamlet, Stuttgart, and Düsseldorf 1978–79, Shadow of a Gunman, Knight of the Burning Pestle, R.S.C., The Seagull, Tokyo 1980; Dir. The Romans in Britain, Mayor of Zalamea, The Hypochondriac, A Spanish Tragedy, Uncle Vanya, all for Nat. Theatre; Hiawatha (Nat. Theatre Christmas production) 1980, 1981, 1982; Lorenzaccio, You Can't Take it With You, National Theatre 1983; Hamlet, Dublin Abbey Theatre 1983, Romeo and Juliet, Tokyo Imperial Theatre 1983; The Story of a Horse, Ancient Mariner, both for Nat. Theatre 1984; The Mayor of Zalamea, Washington 1984, Measure for Measure, Stratford, Ont. 1985, Mutiny, London 1985, Donnerstag Aus Licht, Covent Garden 1985, Romeo and Juliet, Royal Shakespeare Co. 1986, Julius Caesar, Hamburg 1986, Henry IV (parts I and II), Henry V, U.K., Europe, Canada, U.S.A. 1986–87, Reineke Fuchs, Hamburg 1987, The Wars of the Roses (7 play history cycle) 1987–89 (Dir. of the Year, Laurence Olivier award 1989); Montag aus Licht, (Stockhausen) La Scala 1988; Coriolanus, The Winter's Tale, Macbeth, The Tempest, The Venetian Twins, R.S.C. 1993, 1998, Hair, Old Vic 1993, Peer Gynt 1995, Faust 1996, Macbeth 1997, Timon of Athens 1997; Dir. of Year, Soc. of West End Theatres, for the Taming of the Shrew 1979; Hon. Fellow Welsh Coll. of Music and Drama 1994. *Television includes:* Channel 4 series Shakespeare Lives, also for Channel 4, Hiawatha, Macbeth (Channel 4), The Tempest in Bute Town (BBC Wales) 1996, A Light in the Valley (BBC). *Film:* Shakespeare on the Estate 1995 (received B.A.F.T.A. Award). *Publications:* Hiawatha 1981, The Magic Drum 1983, Ancient Mariner, The English Shakespeare Company (jtly.) 1992. *Leisure interests:* cricket, reading, music, wine. *Address:* c/o The English Shakespeare Company, 21–33 Meard Street, London, W1V 3HQ, England.

BOGDANOV, Vsevolod Leonidovich; Russian journalist; b. 6 Feb. 1944, Arkhangelsk Region; m.; two d.; ed. Leningrad State Univ.; corresp., ed. in newspapers, radio and TV Magadan 1961–76; Head Chief Dept. of Periodicals State Cttee. of Publs. 1976–89; Dir.-Gen. TV programmes State Radio and TV Cttee. 1989–92; Chair. Russian Union of Journalists 1992–. *Leisure interests:* book rarities, fishing, hunting, Russian cuisine, music. *Address:* Union of Journalists, Zubovsky blvd. 4, 119021 Moscow, Russia (Office). *Telephone:* (095) 201 5101 (Office).

BOGDANOVICH, Peter; American film director, writer, producer and actor; b. 30 July 1939, Kingston, N.Y.; s. of Borislav and Herma (Robinson) Bogdanovich; m. 1st Polly Platt 1962 (divorced 1970); two d.; m. 2nd L. B.

Straten 1988; Actor, American Shakespeare Festival, Stratford, Conn. 1956, N.Y. Shakespeare Festival 1958; Dir., Producer off-Broadway plays, The Big Knife 1959, Camino Real, Ten Little Indians, Rocket to the Moon 1961, Once in a Lifetime 1964; film feature-writer for Esquire, New York Times, Village Voice, Cahiers du Cinéma, Los Angeles Times, New York Magazine, Vogue, Variety etc. 1961–; Owner The Holly Moon Co. Inc. 1992–; mem. Dirs. Guild of America, Writers' Guild of America, Acad. of Motion Picture Arts and Sciences; N.Y. Film Critics' Award (1971) and B.A.F.T.A. Award for Best Screenplay (The Last Picture Show) 1971, Writers' Guild of America Award for Best Screenplay (What's Up, Doc?) 1972, Pasinetti Award, Critics' Prize, Venice Festival (Saint Jack) 1979, and other awards and prizes. *Films include:* The Wild Angels (2nd Unit Dir., co-wrote, acted in) 1966, Targets (dir., co-wrote, produced, acted in) 1968, The Last Picture Show (dir., co-wrote) 1971, Directed by John Ford (dir., wrote) 1971, What's Up Doc? (dir., co-wrote, prod.) 1972, Paper Moon (dir., prod.) 1973, Daisy Miller (dir., prod.) 1974, At Long Last Love (dir., wrote, prod.) 1975, Nickelodeon (dir., co-wrote) 1976, Saint Jack (dir., co-wrote, acted in) 1979, They All Laughed (dir., wrote) 1981, Mask (dir.) 1985, Illegally Yours (dir., prod.) 1988, Texasville (dir., prod., wrote) 1990, Noises Off (dir., exec. producer) 1992, The Thing Called Love (dir.) 1993, Who The Devil Made It (dir.) 1997; *Television:* The Great Professional: Howard Hawks (co-dir., wrote), BBC 1967; regular commentator for CBS This Morning 1987–89, actor in Northern Exposure, CBS 1993, Fallen Angels 1995, Painted Word 1995, To Sir With Love II 1996. *Publications:* The Cinema of Orson Welles 1961, The Cinema of Howard Hawks 1962, The Cinema of Alfred Hitchcock 1963, John Ford 1968, Fritz Lang in America 1969, Allan Dwan, the Last Pioneer 1971, Pieces of Time, Peter Bogdanovich on the Movies 1961–85, The Killing of the Unicorn: Dorothy Stratten (1960–80) 1984, A Year and a Day Calendar (ed.) 1991, This is Orson Welles (with Orson Welles) 1992, Who the Devil Made It 1997. *Address:* c/o William Pfeiffer, 30 Lane of Acres, Haddonfield, NJ 08033, U.S.A.

BOGIANCKINO, Massimo, PH.D.; Italian opera director; b. 10 Nov. 1922, Rome; s. of Edoardo T. Bogianckino and Fiorangela Liberi; m. Judith Matthias 1950; ed. Conservatory of Music and Acad. Santa Cecilia, Rome and Univ. of Rome; fmr. musicologist and concert pianist; Dir. Enciclopedia dello Spettacolo 1957–62; Dir. Accademia Filarmonica, Rome 1960–63; Dir. Teatro dell' Opera, Rome 1963–68; Artistic Dir. Festival of Two Worlds, Spoleto 1968–71; Dir. of Concert Programs, Accad. Santa Cecilia, Rome 1970–71; Artistic Dir. La Scala, Milan 1971–74; Gen. Man. Teatro Comunale, Florence 1974–82; Admin. Gen. Paris Opera 1982–; Grosses Bundesverdienstkreuz (Fed. Repub. of Germany). *Publications:* L'arte clavicembalistica di D. Scarlatti 1956 (English version 1968), Aspetti del teatro musicale in Italia e in Francia nell' età Barocca 1968, Le canzonette e i madrigali di V. Cossa 1981.

BOGLE, Ellen Gray; Jamaican diplomatist and government official; b. 9 Oct. 1941, St. Andrew; d. of Victor Gray Williams and Eileen Averil Rampie; one s. one d.; ed. St. Andrew High School, Univ. of the West Indies; Dir. Foreign Trade Div., Ministry of Foreign Affairs, with responsibility for formulation of Jamaica's Foreign Trade policy 1978–81; Dir. Jamaica Nat. Export Corpn.; High Commr. in Trinidad & Tobago 1981–89; High Commr. in U.K. 1989–94; Amb., Ministry of Foreign Affairs and Foreign Trade 1996–; has represented Jamaica at numerous int. confs.; Order of Distinction (Commdr.). *Leisure interests:* gardening, reading, cooking, table tennis. *Address:* Ministry of Foreign Affairs and Foreign Trade, 21 Dominica Drive, Kingston 5, Jamaica.

BOGNER, Willy; German business executive, film director and producer; b. 23 Jan. 1942, Munich; s. of Willy and Maria Bogner; m. Sonia Ribeiro 1973; ed. Altes Realgymnasium, Munich, and business and technical studies in Munich and Hohenstein; Man. Willy Bogner GmbH & Co. KG (sportswear co.), Willy Bogner Film GmbH, Munich; mem. German Nat. Olympic Cttee.; dir. of documentary, advertising, sports (esp. skiing) films, etc. and special cameraman for James Bond films 1960–; several times German ski champion and participated in Winter Olympics 1960, Squaw Valley 1960, Innsbruck 1964, and World Ski Championships, Chamonix 1962, Portillo (Chile) 1966. *Films include:* Skivision 1974, 1975, 1979, Skifaszination, Ski Fantasie 1981, Crystal Dreams 1982, Feuer und Eis 1986, Feuer, Eis und Dynamit 1990, White Magic 1994. *Leisure interests:* sport (tennis, skiing, golf), sailing, flying, filming and photography. *Address:* Firma Willy Bogner GmbH & Co. KG, Sankt-Veit-Strasse 4, 81673 Munich, Germany. *Telephone:* (089) 41491.

BOGOLEPOV, Nikolai Nikolayevich, DR. MED.; Russian physiologist; b. 30 Nov. 1933, Moscow; m. Lidia Nikolayevna Rybina; two d.; ed. Moscow Inst. of Medicine; corresp. mem. Russian Acad. of Medical Sciences 1988–; researcher, head of lab., Dir. Research Inst. of Brain 1957–; mem. Scientific Soc. of Anatomy, Histology; mem. Int. Brain Research Org.; main research in morphology and structure of brain. *Publications include:* 8 books and over 200 scientfic papers and articles. *Address:* Obukha str. 5, 107120 Moscow, Russia (Office). *Telephone:* (095) 917 5007 (Office].

BOGOLYUBOV, Mikhail Nikolayevich; Russian philologist; b. 24 Jan. 1918, Kiev; m.; two c.; ed. Leningrad Univ.; service in the army 1941–45; lecturer and Researcher Leningrad Univ. 1944–60, Prof. 1959–, Dean Oriental Dept. 1960–95, Hon. Dean 1995–; Corresp. mem. U.S.S.R. (now Russian) Acad. of Sciences 1966–, mem. 1990; researcher into oriental philology and Iranian languages; ed. Russian translation of Mahabharata 1987. *Address:* St. Petersburg State Univ., Oriental Faculty, 11 Universitetskaya Naberezhnaya, St. Petersburg, Russia. *Telephone:* (812) 218-77-32 (Office); (812) 448-51-46 (Home).

BOGOMOLOV, Aleksey Fedorovich, DR.TECH.SC.; Russian physicist; b. 2 June 1913, Sitskoe Village, Smolensk Region; ed. Moscow Power Inst.; Postgraduate, Research Assoc. Moscow Power Inst. 1937–41; Army Service 1941–45; mem. CPSU 1944; Asst. Prof. Head of Chair, Moscow Power Inst. 1945–58, Prof., Dir. and Chief Constructor 1958–89, Hon. Dir. 1989–; worked on radio-telescope; Merited Scientist of R.S.F.S.R.; mem. U.S.S.R. Acad. of Sciences 1984; Hero of Socialist Labour 1957; Lenin Prize 1960, U.S.S.R. State Prizes 1978, 1986. *Publications:* Works on radiophysics and radio engineering. *Address:* Moscow Power Institute, 14 Krasnokazarmennaya ulitsa, Moscow, Russia. *Telephone:* (095) 362-56-52 (Office); (095) 132-00-26 (Home).

BOGOMOLOV, Oleg Timofeyevich; Russian economist; b. 20 Aug. 1927, Moscow; s. of T. I. Bogomolov and K. P. Zhelybaeva; m. 1st Larisa Sokolova, one s. (died 1962); m. 2nd Inna Yermakova 1966 (divorced 1977); m. 3rd Tatyana Yarikova 1978; ed. Moscow Inst. of Foreign Trade; Ministry of Foreign Trade 1949–50; with CMEA 1954–56; Scientific Inst. for Economical Researches of State Cttee. for Planning 1956–62; mem. CPSU 1950–90, Head of Advisors Group (Cen. Cttee.) 1962–69; Section Chief, Econ. Research Inst., State Planning Cttee. 1958–62; lecturer, then Prof. Moscow Univ. 1967–77; Dir. Inst. of Econs. of the World Socialist System of Acad. of Sciences (now Inst. of Int. Econ. and Political Studies) 1969–; Pres. Int. Econ. Asscn. 1992–, Council of Ministers Cttee. for Mutual Cooperation with Socialist Countries 1970–86; People's Deputy of U.S.S.R. 1989–91; Deputy, State Duma (Parl.) 1993–95; mem. U.S.S.R. (now Russian) Acad. of Sciences 1981, Exec. Cttee. of Int. Social Science Council, UNESCO 1996–; decorations include Order of October Revolution, Order of Red Banner (twice). *Publications:* Socialism between Past and Future 1990, Russia and the Commonwealth of Independent States; Trends and Risks of Post-Soviet Development; Europe in Global Change 1993; Market Transformation in Russia: Prospects Still Uncertain; Economics in a Changing World of the Tenth Congress of the IEA 1994, Reformy glazami amerikanskikh i rossijskikh ucheynykh 1996. *Leisure interests:* photography, music, tennis. *Address:* Institute of International Economic and Political Studies, 117418, Novo-Cheremushkinskaya 46, Moscow, Russia. *Telephone:* (095) 120-82-00 (Office). *Fax:* (095) 310-70-61.

BOGORAD, Lawrence, PH.D.; American biologist; b. 29 Aug. 1921, Tashkent, U.S.S.R.; s. of Boris and Florence (Bernard) Bogorad; m. Rosalyn G. Sagen 1943; one s. one d.; ed. Univ. of Chicago; Instructor, Dept. of Botany, Univ. of Chicago 1948–51, Asst. Prof. 1953–57, Assoc. Prof. 1957–61, Prof. 1961–67; Visiting Investigator, Rockefeller Inst. 1951–53; Prof. Dept. of Biology, Harvard Univ. 1967–92, Maria Moors Cabot Prof. of Biology 1980–92, Prof. Emer. 1992–; Chair. Dept. of Biology 1974–76; Dir. Maria Moors Cabot Foundation, Harvard Univ. 1976–87; mem. N.A.S., N.A.S. Council 1989–92, Chair. Botany Section 1974–77, Ed. and Chair. Editorial Bd. Proceedings of the N.A.S. 1991–; mem. American Philosophical Soc., Space Studies Bd. 1995–; Foreign mem. Royal Danish Acad. of Sciences and Letters; Fellow, American Acad. of Arts and Sciences; Pres. American Soc. of Plant Physiologists 1968; Pres. Soc. of Developmental Biology 1983–84; mem. Bd. of Dirs. A.A.A.S. 1982–86, Pres. 1986–87, Chair. Bd. of Dirs. 1987–88; Fulbright Fellowship 1960, Stephen Hales Award 1982 and other academic awards. *Publications:* various papers in scientific journals. *Address:* Harvard University, Department of Molecular and Cellular Biology, 16 Divinity Avenue, Cambridge, MA 02138, U.S.A.

BOGOSIAN, Eric, B.A.; American actor; b. 24 April 1953, Boston; s. of Henry Bogosian and Edwina Bogosian; m. Jo Anne Bonney 1990; ed. Univ. of Chicago and Oberlin Coll.; author, star, Off-Broadway productions, Men Inside, New York Shakespeare Festival 1982, Funhouse, New York Shakespeare Festival 1983, Actor's Playhouse, New York 1983, Drinking in America, American Place, New York 1986, Talk Radio, New York Shakespeare Festival 1987, Sex, Drugs, Rock & Roll, Orpheum Show Theatre, New York 1990; Pounding Nails in the Floor with my Forehead 1994, Surburbia 1994, Office Killer 1997, Deconstructing Harry 1997; appearances in several TV shows and films including Caine Mutiny Court Martial, Drinking in America, Talk Radio 1988, Sex, Drugs, Rock & Roll, Under Siege 2; Obie Award 1986, 1990, 1994; Drama Critics Circle Award; Berlin Film Festival Silver Bear Award 1988.

BOGSCH, Arpad, LL.D.; American international official and lawyer; b. 24 Feb. 1919, Budapest, Hungary; s. of Arpad Bogsch and Emilia Taborsky; one s. one d.; m. Adèle Frankhauser 1994; ed. Univs. of Budapest and Paris and George Washington Univ., Washington, D.C.; attorney-at-law, Budapest 1942–48; legal officer, UNESCO, Paris 1948–54; legal counsellor, U.S. Copyright Office, Washington, D.C. 1954–63; Deputy Dir.-Gen. World Intellectual Property Org. Geneva 1963–73, Dir.-Gen. 1973–97; Hon. Prof. of Law, Beijing Univ. 1991; Dr. h.c. (Jabalpur) 1978, (George Washington Univ.) 1985, (Colombo) 1987, (Kyung Hee Univ. Repub. of Korea) 1991, (Eötvös Lóránd Univ. Budapest) 1991, (Bucharest) 1991, (Delhi) 1992, (Prague) 1994, (Kiev) 1995, (Mathias Bel, Slovakia) 1996, (Tbilisi) 1996, (Riga) 1997, numerous awards and decorations. *Publications:* books and articles in the field of patents, trademarks and copyright. *Leisure interest:* music. *Address:* c/o World Intellectual Property Organization (WIPO), 34 chemin des Colombettes, 1211 Geneva 20, Switzerland. *Telephone:* (022) 730-9111. *Fax:* (022) 733-5428.

BOGUSLAVSKY, Mark Moiseyevich, D.JUR.; Russian professor of law; b. 8 June 1924, Moscow; m. 1st Iren Gorodetskaya 1960; m. 2nd Valentina Mazourova 1993; ed. Moscow Univ.; prof. and sr. researcher, U.S.S.R. (now Russian) Academy of Sciences Inst. of State and Law; Arbiter Int. Commercial Court of Arbitration at Moscow; specialist in pvt. and econ. int. law, intellectual property, and foreign investment legislation; mem. Bd. Russian Asscn. of Int. Law. *Publications:* numerous publications on pvt. international law. *Address:* Institute of State and Law, Russian Academy of Sciences, Znamenka str. 10, 119841 Moscow, Russia. *Telephone:* (095) 202-48-32. *Fax:* (095) 291-85-74.

BOHAN, Marc; French couturier; b. 22 Aug. 1926; s. of Alfred Bohan and Geneviève Baudoux; m. Huguette Rinjonneau (deceased); one d.; ed. Lycée Lakanal, Sceaux; Asst. with Piguet 1945, later with Molyneux and Patou; Dior organization, London 1958, later Paris; Artistic Dir. Soc. Christian Dior 1960–89; Artistic Dir. Hartnell, London 1990–92; Chevalier, Légion d'honneur, Ordre de Saint-Charles (Monaco). *Leisure interests:* classical music, theatre, reading, riding, antiques. *Address:* 35 rue du Bourg à Mont, 21400 Châtillon sur Seine, France.

BOHIGAS GUARDIOLA, Oriol; Spanish architect; b. 10 Dec. 1925, Barcelona; s. of Pere Bohigas and María Guardiola; m. Isabel Arnau 1957; five c.; founder-mem. of Grupo R 1951; partnership with Josep Martorell 1952; Special Technician in town-planning, Instituto de Estudios de Administración Local 1961; partnership with David Mackay 1963; lecturer, Escuela Técnica Superior de Arquitectura, Barcelona 1964–66, Prof. 1971–, Dir. 1977–80; Head of town-planning, Barcelona City Council 1980–84, Adviser to Mayor 1984–; mem. Accad. Nazionale di San Luca de Roma; prizes from Foment de les Arts Decoratives for best building in Barcelona 1959, 1962, 1966, 1976, 1979, Delta de Plata (industrial design) 1966; First Prize, Internationale Bauhausstellung Berlin 1980. *Publications include:* Barcelona entre el pla cerda i el barraquisme 1963, Arquitectura modernista 1968–1969, Les escoles tecniques superiors i l'estructura professional 1968, 1970, Contra una arquitectura adjetivada 1969, La arquitectura española de la Segunda República 1970, 1978, Polemica d'arquitectura catalana 1970, Reseña y catálogo de la arquitectura modernista 1972, Proceso y erótica del diseño 1972, 1979, Once arquitectos 1976, Catalunya. Arquitectura i urbanisme durant la republica 1978, Reconstrucció de Barcelona 1984. *Address:* calle Calvet, 71 Barcelona 21; calle Camp, 61 Barcelona 22, Spain.

BOHL, Heinrich Friedrich; German politician and lawyer; b. 5 March 1945, Rosdorf, Göttingen; s. of Heinrich Bohl and Gerda Heyden; m. Elisabeth Bocking; two s. two d.; ed. Univ. of Marburg; lawyer 1972–, notary 1976–; mem. CDU and Jungen Union (JU) 1963–; local Chair. JU Marburg-Biedenkopf 1964–70; Dist. Chair. JU Mittelhessen 1969–73; mem. Provincial Parl. Hessen 1970–80, Chair. Legal Cttee. 1974–78; Acting Chair. CDU Landtagsfraktion 1978–80; Chair. CDU Kreistagsfraktion Marburg-Biedenkopf 1974–90; mem. Fed. German. Parl. 1980–, Parl. Man. CDU/CSU Bundestagsfraktion 1984–91; Fed. Minister for Special Tasks and Head of Fed. Chancellery 1991–98; Head of Press and Information, Fed. Govt. 1998; Bundesverdienstkreuz (1st Class) 1987. *Address:* c/o Federal Chancellery, 53113 Bonn, Adenauerallee 139–141 (Office); Bundestag, 5300 Bonn, Germany (Office); Finkenstrasse 11, 35043 Marburg-Cappel, Germany (Home). *Telephone:* 41333 (Home).

BÖHME, Helmut, DR. PHIL.; German university president; b. 30 April 1936, Tübingen; s. of Helmut B. Böhme and Elisabeth Müller; m. Bertheide Mittinger 1982; one s. three d.; ed. Univs. of Tübingen and Hamburg; Prof. 1969; Pres. Darmstadt Univ. 1971–; Hon. Ph.D. *Publications include:* Deutschlands Weg zur Grossmacht 1966, Prolegomena 1968; essays and other publs. on history of banking. *Leisure interest:* painting. *Address:* Karolinenplatz 5, 64289 Darmstadt, Germany. *Telephone:* 161.

BOHR, Aage Niels, DR.PHIL., D.SC.; Danish physicist; b. 19 June 1922, Copenhagen; s. of Prof. Niels Bohr and Margrethe Nørlund; m. 1st Marietta Bettina (née Soffer) (died 1978); two s. one d.; m. 2nd Bente Scharff (née Meyer) 1981; ed. Univ. of Copenhagen; Assoc. D.S.I.R., London 1943–45; Research Asst., Inst. of Theoretical Physics, Copenhagen 1946; Prof. of Physics, Univ. of Copenhagen 1956; Dir. Niels Bohr Inst. 1963–70, Nordita 1975–81; mem. Danish, Norwegian, Pontifical, Swedish, Polish, Finnish, Yugoslav Acads. of Science, Nat. Acad. of Sciences, U.S.A., American Acad. of Arts and Sciences, American Philosophical Soc., Royal Physiograph Soc., Lund, Sweden, Acad. of Tech. Sciences, Copenhagen, Deutsche Acad. der Naturforscher Leopoldina; Hon. Ph.D. (Oslo, Heidelberg, Trondheim, Manchester, Uppsala); Dannie Heineman Prize 1960, Pius XI Medal 1963, Atoms for Peace Award 1969, Ørsted Medal 1970, Rutherford Medal 1972, John Price Wetherill Medal 1974, Nobel Prize for Physics 1975, Ole Rømer Medal 1976. *Publications:* Rotational States of Atomic Nuclei 1954, Nuclear Structure Vol. I 1969, Vol. II 1975 (with Ben R. Mottelson). *Address:* c/o Niels Bohr Institute, Blegdamsvej 15–17, 2100 Copenhagen, Denmark.

BOHRER, Karl Heinz, PH.D.; German academic; b. 26 Sept. 1932, Cologne; m. Undine Gruenter 1991; one s. one d.; Prof. of History of Modern Literature, Univ. of Bielefeld; Ed. Merkur; Joseph E. Drexel Prize 1968; J.H. Merck Prize 1978. *Publications:* Die gefährdete Phantasie oder Surrealismus und Terror 1970, Der Lauf des Freitag—Die lädierte Utopie und der Dichter 1973, Die Ästhetik des Schreckens 1978, Plötzlichkeit. Der Augenblick des ästhetischen Scheins 1981, Mythos und Moderne 1983, Der romantische Brief, Die Entstehung aesthetischer Subjektivität 1987, Nach der Natur, Über Politik und Ästhetik 1988, Die Kritik der Romantik 1989, Das absolute Präsens, Die Semantik ästhetischer Zeit 1994, Der Abschied. Theorie der Trauer 1996. *Address:* 11 rue Robert Planquette, 75018 Paris, France; Franziskastr. 9, Cologne, Germany.

BOIDEVAIX, Serge Marie-Germain, L. ÈS L., L. EN D.; French diplomatist; b. 15 Aug. 1928, Aurillac, Cantal; s. of Jean Boidevaix and Hélène Orcibal; m. Francine Savard 1966; two d.; ed. Lycée d'Aurillac, Lycée Louis-le-Grand, Faculté de Droit and Faculté des Lettres, Paris and Ecole Nat. d'Admin.; joined Ministry of Foreign Affairs 1954; served Vienna, Washington, D.C. and Bonn; Adviser, Pvt. Office of Minister of Defence 1969–73; Dir. Office of Minister of Foreign Affairs 1973–74; Adviser on int. affairs and cooperation, Office of Prime Minister 1974–76; Amb. to Poland 1977–80, to India 1982–85, to Germany 1986–92; Deputy Sec.-Gen. Ministry of Foreign Affairs 1985–86; Sec. Gen. 1992–93; Sr. mem. Council of State 1993–; Officier, Légion d'honneur, Commdr. Ordre Nat. du Mérite. *Leisure interests:* tennis, hunting. *Address:* Conseil d'Etat, 75100 Paris RP; 8 rue des Eaux, 75016 Paris, France.

BOISDEFFRE (Néraud le Mouton de), Pierre Jules Marie Raoul; French diplomatist, writer and broadcasting official; b. 11 July 1926, Paris; s. of Gen. de Boisdeffre; m. Béatrice Wiedemann-Goiran 1957; three s.; ed. Lycée Condorcet, Collège Stanislas, Ecole Libre des Sciences Politiques, Ecole Nationale d'Administration and Harvard Univ.; Civil Servant, Ministry of Nat. Educ. 1950–55; Deputy Dir. of Press Affairs, Ministry of Foreign Affairs 1958–63; Dir. of Sound Broadcasting, Office de Radiodiffusion et Télévision Française (O.R.T.F.) 1963–68; Cultural Counsellor, French Embassy, London 1968–71, Brussels 1972–77, Ministry of Foreign Affairs 1977–78; Minister Plenipotentiary 1979; Amb. to Uruguay 1981–84, to Colombia 1984–88; Perm. Rep. to the Council of Europe 1988–91; Officier de la Légion d'honneur, Commdr., Ordre national du Mérite, Commdr. des Arts et des Lettres, Officier des Palmes académiques, Grand-Croix l'Ordre de San Carlos (Colombia), Officier de l'Etoile Polaire, Commdr. de l'Ordre de la Couronne, Commdr. de l'Ordre national du Cèdre, Commdr. de l'Ordre du Christ; Grand Prix de la Critique (for Métamorphose de la littérature) 1950; Prix Alfred de Vigny 1994 (for Contre le Vent Majeur). *Publications include:* Métamorphose de la littérature (Vol. I de Barrès à Malraux, Vol. II de Proust à Sartre) 1950, Où va le roman? 1962, Les écrivains français d'aujourd'hui 1963, Histoire de la littérature de langue française (1930–85), 10 Edns., Une anthologie vivante de la littérature d'aujourd'hui I 1965, II 1966, La cafetière est sur la table 1967, Lettre ouverte aux hommes de gauche 1969, Les écrivains de la nuit, les poètes français d'aujourd'hui 1973, La foi des anciens jours 1977, Les nuits, L'île aux livres, Paroles de vie, la Belgique 1980, L'église au milieu du Gué 1981; critical portraits: Barrès parmi nous 1952, André Malraux 1952, Kafka (with R. M. Albéres) 1960, Barrès 1962, Giono 1965, Vie d'André Gide (Vol. I: Gide avant la fondation de la N.R.F.) 1970, De Gaulle malgré lui 1978, L'Ile aux Livres 1980, Les Nuits (short stories) 1980, André Malraux, la mort et l'histoire 1996, Pierre Loti 1996; Theatre: Goethe m'a dit 1981; Contre le vent majeur (memoirs) 1994, Le Lion et le Renard (de Gaulle-Mitterrand) 1998. *Address:* 5 cité Vaneau, 75007 Paris; 33 Place du Marche, 36400 La Chatre, France (Homes). *Telephone:* (1) 45-55-17-34.

BOISSET, Yves; French author and film director; b. 14 March 1939, Paris; s. of Raymond Boisset and Germaine Bonnet; m. Micheline Paintault 1964; two s.; ed. Lycée Louis-le-Grand, Faculté des Lettres, Paris and Inst. des Hautes Etudes Cinématographiques; journalist on Cinéma, Paris-Jour etc. 1958–63; Asst. dir. to Yves Ciampi 1959, to Jean-Pierre Melville 1962, Claude Sautet and Antoine Bourseiller 1964, Vittorio de Sica and René Clément 1965, Ricardo Freda 1966; dir. for television and films 1967–; Chevalier des Arts et des Lettres. *Films include:* Coplan sauve sa peau 1968, Cran d'arrêt 1969, Un condé 1970, Le Saut de l'ange 1971, L'Attentat 1972, R.A.S. 1973, Dupont Lajoie 1974, Folle à tuer 1975, Le Juge Fayard dit le Sheriff 1976 (Prix Louis Delluc 1977), Un taxi mauve 1977, La Clé sur la porte 1978, La Femme flic 1979, Allons z'enfants 1981, Espion lève-toi 1982, Le Prix du danger 1983, Canicule 1984, Bleu comme l'Enfer 1986, La Travestie 1988, Radio Corbeau 1989, La Tribu 1991. *Publication:* 20 ans de cinéma américain 1962. *Address:* 61 boulevard Inkerman, 92200 Neuilly-sur-Seine, France.

BOISSIEU DEAN DE LUIGNÉ, Gen. Alain Henri Paul Marie-Joseph de; French army officer; b. 5 July 1914, Chartres; s. of Henri de Boissieu Dean de Luigné and Marguérite Froger de Mauny; m. Elizabeth de Gaulle, d. of Gen. Charles de Gaulle, 1946; one d.; ed. Saint-Cyr Mil. Acad.; Cavalry Second Lieut. 1938, First Lieut, 1940; prisoner of war, escaped, later detained in U.S.S.R.; joined Free French Forces 1941; Capt. 1942; Staff, High Commr. in Indian Ocean 1944–45; Maj. 1945, Lieut.-Col. 1953; Commdg. Officer 4th Regiment of Chasseurs, Algeria 1956–58; Col. 1958; Chief Mil. Staff, High Commr. in Algeria 1958; Chief of Staff Armoured Directorate 1959; Commdg. Officer 2nd Armoured Brigade 1962; Brig.-Gen. 1964; Commdg. Gen. Saint-Cyr Mil. Acad. and Ecole Mil. Inter-Armes de Coëtquidan 1964–67; Commdg. Gen. 7th Div. 1967; Maj.-Gen. 1968; Inspector of Armour 1969; Lieut.-Gen. 1970; mem. Army Council 1971; Gen., Chief of Staff of French Army 1971–75; fmr. Grand Chancellor, Légion d'honneur, fmr. Chancellor, Ordre national du Mérite 1975–81; Grand Croix Légion d'honneur, Compagnon de la libération, Grand Croix de l'Ordre national du Mérite, Croix de guerre, Croix de la Valeur militaire, Knight of Malta; Hon. K.B.E., and other decorations. *Leisure interests:* riding, hunting. *Address:* 233 rue de Vaugirard, 75015 Paris, France.

BOISSON, Jacques-Louis, LL.D.; Monegasque diplomatist; b. 8 Jan. 1940, Monaco; m. Carmen Gómez Parejo; one s.; ed. Institut d'Etudes Politiques, Institut de Droit Int., Paris; int. civil servant (responsible for training, research and protection of human rights) UNESCO 1968–83; Amb. to France 1984–93; Perm. Rep. to UN Aug. 1993–; Ordre de St. Charles de Monaco. *Publications:* Le Particularisme Institutionnel de la Principalité de Monaco 1966, Le Droit de la Nationalité Monégasque 1968, numerous articles on the protection and promotion of int. human rights. *Leisure interests:* baroque music, opera, philosophy, poetry. *Address:* Permanent Mission of Monaco to United Nations, 866 United Nations Plaza, Suite 520, New York, NY 10017, U.S.A.; 48 blvd. du Jardin Exotique, 98000 Monaco. *Telephone:* 8320721 (U.S.A.); 93255964 (Monaco). *Fax:* 8325358 (U.S.A.).

BOJART ORTEGA, Rafael; Argentinian university professor; b. 12 April 1920, Buenos Aires; s. of Rafael Bojart Ceballos and Hemilce Ortega; m. Haydée Albistur Pando 1944; two s.; ed. Univs. de Buenos Aires, El Salvador, Barcelona and Columbia Univ., New York; Founder Academia de Estudios Históricos Bartolomé Mitre 1958, Univ. de Morón 1960, Instituto Enrique Larreta 1964, Academia Internacional de Historia 1965, Instituto Americano de Futurología 1975; Pres. Academia de Estudios Históricos Bartolomé Mitre, Academia Internacional de la Historia; Dir. Instituto Moderno de Arte; fmr. Rector, Univ. de Morón; mem. Real Academia Hispano-americana de Cádiz, Academia Argentina de Diplomacia, Academia de Estudios Parlamentarios y Legislativos Internacionales, Instituto de Cultura Americana de Madrid, Instituto Argentino Hispánico, Asociación Internacional de Derecho, Academia de Letras (Uruguay), Club des intellectuels français, Univ. Int. Moctezuma, World Constituent Assembly, U.S.A.; Médaille Etoile Civique, Paris, Gran Cruz del Inst. de Estudios Franciscanos, Médaille Grand Prix Humanitaire de France. *Publications:* Introducción a la filosofía, Filosofía de la Historia, La Poesía Epica Medieval, La Estética Contemporánea, La Esencia de la Poesía, El Motivo de la Angustia en el Existencialismo, La Poesía de Carlos Obligado, La Inteligencia en el Gobierno de los Pueblos, Ricardo Rojas y el Futuro de América, El Hispanismo en Larreta, La Poesía de César Rosales, Como Hacer un Best Seller, Qué es la Futurologia, Borges Escritor, La Fuerza del Occidente, Una Obra Inédita de Enrique Larreta, Que Piensa Arnold Toynbee del Futuro, El Universo y el Hombre, La Paz Internacional en el Pensamiento de Churchill y Kennedy; novels: La Música de la Montaña, El Hombre Nuevo, Una Aventura en el Año 2000, Hombres Celebres del Siglo XX; plays: Polichinela, Los Hijos que no Nacieron.

BØJER, Jørgen R. H.; Danish diplomatist; b. 5 March 1940, Hjørring; s. of Svend Rud Hansen Bøjer and Ingeborg Bøjer (née Frederiksen); m. Lone Heilskov 1964; two d.; ed. Univ. of Aarhus, Institut d'Etudes Politiques, Paris; Foreign Service Officer 1967; Sec. of Embassy, Prague 1971; Head of Section Ministry of Foreign Affairs, Copenhagen 1973, Dir. 1982, Deputy Undersec. 1992; Visiting Fellow Stanford Univ. 1978; Counselor Embassy, Washington, D.C. 1979; Amb. to Egypt (also accred. to Sudan and Somalia), then to Austria, Slovenia, Bosnia and Herzegovina; Perm. Rep. to Int. Orgs. in Vienna 1993; Perm. Rep. to UN 1997–. *Address:* Permanent Mission of Denmark to the United Nations, One Dag Hammarskjold Plaza, 885 Second Avenue, 18th Floor, New York, NY 10017, U.S.A.

BOK, Derek, M.A., J.D.; American university administrator; b. 22 March 1930, Bryn Mawr, Pa.; s. of late Curtis Bok and Margaret Plummer (now Mrs. W. S. Kiskadden); m. Sissela Ann Myrdal (d. of Karl Gunnar and Alva Myrdal q.v.) 1955; one s. two d.; ed. Univs. of Stanford, Harvard, George Washington and Inst. of Political Science, Paris Univ.; served U.S. Army 1956–58; Asst. Prof. of Law, Harvard Univ. 1958–61, Prof. 1961–, Dean 1968–71; Dean, 300th Anniversary Univ. Prof. 1991–; Harvard Law School 1968–71; Pres. Harvard Univ. 1971–91. *Publications include:* The First Three Years of the Schuman Plan, Cases and Materials on Labor Law (with Archibald Cox), Labor and the American Community (with John Dunlop), The Federal Government and the University, Beyond the Ivory Tower: Social Responsibilities of the Modern University 1982, Higher Learning 1986, Universities and the Future of America 1990, The Cost of Talent 1993, The State of the Nation 1997. *Leisure interests:* gardening, tennis, swimming. *Address:* Harvard University, J.F.K. School of Government, Cambridge, MA 02138, U.S.A. *Telephone:* 617-495-1502.

BOKERIA, Leonid Antonovich, DR. MED. SC.; Russian cardiologist; b. 21 Dec. 1939; m.; two c.; ed. I. M. Sechenov Medical Inst., Moscow; with A. Bakulev Scientific Centre of Cardio-Vascular Surgery (SCCVS) 1968–, Dir. 1991–; Dir., Prof. Burakovsky Research Inst. of Cardiosurgery at SCCVS; mem. Russian Acad. of Medicine; main research in cardio-vascular surgery, hyperbaric oxygenation, treatment of cardiopulse violation problems; Lenin Prize 1975, U.S.S.R. State Prize 1986. *Publications:* articles on cardiosurgery. *Leisure interests:* painting, collecting of encyclopaedias and dictionaries. *Address:* A. Bakulev Scientific Centre, Leninsky prosp. 8 korp. 7, 117931 Moscow, Russia. *Telephone:* (095) 414 7571 (Office).

BOKROS, Lajos, PH.D.; Hungarian banker; b. 26 June 1954, Budapest; s. of Lajos Bokros and Irén (née Szarka) Bokros; m. Edit Bártfai; one s. one d.; ed. Univ. of Econs. Budapest, Univ. of Panama; researcher Financial Research Inst., Budapest 1980–85, Chief Public Finance Div. 1986–87; Deputy Head Econ. Dept. Nat. Bank of Hungary 1988–89, Dir. Capital Market Dept. 1989–91; Chair. Budapest Stock Exchange 1990–95; Chair., C.E.O. Budapest Bank 1991–95; Minister of Finance 1995–96; mem. bd. of dirs. State Property Agency 1990–91, mem. Council of Dirs. World Bank 1996. *Publications:* Development Commodity Production, Market Economy 1984, Market and Money in the Modern Economy 1985. *Address:* c/o World Bank, 1818 H Street, N.W., Washington, D.C. 20433, U.S.A.

BOKSENBERG, Alexander, C.B.E., PH.D., F.R.S.; British astronomer; b. 18 March 1936; s. of Julius Boksenberg and Ernestina Steinberg; m. Adella Coren 1960; one s. one d.; ed. Stationers' Co.'s School, Univ. of London; S.R.C. Research Asst., Dept. of Physics and Astronomy, Univ. Coll. London 1960–65, Lecturer in Physics 1965–75, Head of Optical and Ultraviolet Astronomy Research Group 1969–81, Reader in Physics 1975–78, SRC Sr. Fellow 1976–81, Prof. of Physics and Astronomy 1978–81; Sherman Fairchild Distinguished Scholar Calif. Inst. of Tech. 1981–82; Dir. Royal Greenwich Observatory 1981–93, Royal Observatories (Royal Greenwich Observatory, Royal Observatory, Edin., Isaac Newton Group of Optical Telescopes, Canary Islands, Jt. Astronomy Centre, Hawaii) 1993–96; Research Prof. Univ. of Cambridge and PPARC Sr. Research Fellow Univs. of Cambridge and London 1996–; Extraordinary Fellow Churchill Coll., Cambridge 1996–; Visiting Prof., Dept. of Physics and Astronomy, Univ. Coll. London 1981–, Astronomy Centre, Univ. of Sussex 1981–89; Hon. Prof. of Experimental Astronomy, Univ. of Cambridge 1991–; Exec. Ed. Experimental Astronomy 1995–; Hon. Pres. Astronomical Soc. of Glasgow; Chair. New Industrial Concepts Ltd. 1969–81; Pres. West London Astronomical Soc. 1978–; Chair. SRC Astronomy Cttee. 1980–81 and numerous other cttees. on astronomy 1980–; mem. ESA Hubble Space Telescope Instrument Definition Team 1973–, S.A. Astronomical Observatory Advisory Cttee. 1978–85, British Council Science Advisory Cttee. 1987–91, Fachbeirat of Max Planck Institut für Astronomie 1991–95, past mem. of over 30 other councils, bds., cttees. etc. 1970–; Fellow Royal Astronomical Soc. 1965–, Royal Soc. 1978–, Univ. Coll. London 1991–; Dr. h.c. (l'Observatoire de Paris) 1982, Hon. D.Sc. (Sussex) 1991; Freeman 1984, Liveryman 1989; mem. of court 1994; Asteroid (3205) named Boksenberg 1988. *Publications:* Modern Technology and its Influence on Astronomy 1990 (ed.), 220 contribs. to learned journals. *Leisure interest:* skiing. *Address:* University of Cambridge, Institute of Astronomy, The Observatories, Madingley Road, Cambridge, CB3 0HA, England. *Telephone:* (01223) 339909.

BOLDON, Ato; Trinidadian athlete; b. 30 Dec. 1973, Port of Spain; ed. Univ. of Calif. at L.A.; resident in U.S.A. since 1988; coached by John Smith; Cen. American and Caribbean record-holder at 60m. indoors (6.49 seconds), 100m. (9.86 seconds) and 200m. (19.77 seconds); Gold Medal World Jr. Championships 100m. and 200m. 1992; fourth Commonwealth Games 100m. 1994; Bronze Medal World Championships 100m. 1995; Gold Medal NCAA Championships 100m. 1996; Bronze Medals Olympic Games 100m. and 200m. 1996; Gold Medal World Championships 200m. 1997; Gold Medal Goodwill Games, New York 200m. 1998; Gold Medal Commonwealth Games 100m. 1998.

BOLDUC, J.P., B.A.; American business executive; b. 17 July 1939; m.; four c.; ed. St. Cloud State Univ.; qualified as certified internal auditor; fmr. Asst. Sec., U.S. Dept. of Agric.; Vice-Pres.-Partner, Booz-Allen & Hamilton Inc. 1977–83; C.O.O. for Pres. Reagan's Pvt. Sector Survey on Cost Control in Fed. Govt. 1982–84; Sr. Vice-Pres. W.R. Grace & Co. 1983–86, Chief Financial Officer and Vice-Chair. 1986–90, Pres. and C.O.O. 1990–93, Pres., C.E.O. 1993–95; Dir. several pvt. corpns. *Address:* c/o W.R. Grace & Co., One Town Center Road, Boca Raton, FL 33486, U.S.A.

BOLDYREV, Yuri Yuryevich; Russian politician; b. 29 May 1960, Leningrad; m. 1990; one s.; ed. Leningrad Electrotech. Inst., Leningrad Inst. of Finance and Econs.; worked as engineer Cen. Research Inst. of Vessel Electronics and Tech. 1983–89; mem. CPSU 1987–90; U.S.S.R. People's Deputy 1989–91; del. of 28 CPSU Congress; left CPSU 1990; mem. Council of Reps., then of Co-ordination Council of Democratic Russia Movt. 1990–91; mem. Higher Advisory Council to Chair. of Russian Supreme Soviet (later to Pres. of Russian Fed.) 1990–92; consultant Russian Govt. Feb.–March 1992; Chief State Inspector of Russian Fed., Chief Control Man. of Admin. of Presidency 1992–93; mem. Centre of Econ. and Political Research (Epicentre) 1993–94; mem. Duma (Parl.) 1993–95, Deputy Chair Yabloko Movt. 1993–95, left Party Sept. 1995; Deputy Chair. Accountant Chamber of Russian Fed. 1995–. *Address:* Accountant Chamber, Gilyarovskogo str. 31, Suite 1, 129090 Moscow, Russia (Office). *Telephone:* (095) 284-8732 (Office). *Fax:* (095) 284-8666.

BOLGER, Dermot; Irish author; b. 1959, Finglas, Dublin; s. of Roger Bolger and late Bridie Flanagan; m. Bernadette Clifton 1988; two s.; ed. St. Canice's BNS, Finglas and Benevin Coll. Finglas; worked as factory hand, library asst. and professional author; Founder and Ed. Raven Arts Press 1979–82; Founder and Exec. Ed. New Island Books, Dublin 1992–; mem. Arts Council of Ireland 1989–93; elected mem. Aosdana 1991; Playwright in Association, The Abbey (Nat.) Theatre 1997; recipient of various awards. *Publications include:* novels: Night Shift 1985, The Woman's Daughter 1987, The Journey Home 1990, Emily's Shoes 1992, A Second Life 1994, Father's Music 1997, Finbar's Hotel (co-author) 1997; plays: The Lament for Arthur Cleary 1989, Blinded by the Light 1990, In High Germany 1990, The Holy Ground 1990, One Last White Horse 1991, A Dublin Bloom 1994, April Bright 1995; TV films: The Disappearance of Finbar 1996, Edward No Hands 1996; poetry: The Habit of Flesh 1979, Finglas Lilies 1980, No Waiting America 1981, Internal Exile 1986, Leinster Street Ghosts 1989. *Leisure interests:* soccer, golf. *Address:* c/o A.P. Watt, 20 John Street, London, WC1N 2DR, England.

BOLGER, James Brendan, P.C.; New Zealand politician and farmer; b. 31 May 1935, Taranaki; s. of Daniel Bolger and Cecilia (née Doyle) Bolger; m. Joan Maureen Riddell 1963; six s. three d.; ed. Opunake High School; farmer sheep and beef cattle; owner Hereford cattle stud, Te Kuiti; mem. Parl. 1972–; Minister of Fisheries and Assoc. Minister of Agric. 1977–78; Minister of Labour 1978–84, of Immigration 1978–81; Deputy Leader Nat. Party 1984–86, Leader 1986–90; Prime Minister 1990–97; Amb. to U.S.A. 1998–; Br. Chair. Federated Farmers 1967–72, Sub-Prov. Chair. 1970–72, Vice-Pres. Waikato Prov. 1971–72; del. to various ILO confs., Pres. 1983; Hon. D.Sc. (Khon Kaen Univ., Thailand) 1994; Queen's Silver Jubilee Medal 1977, N.Z. Commemoration Medal 1990, N.Z. Suffrage Centennial Medal 1993. *Address:* New Zealand Embassy, 37 Observatory Circle, NW, Washington DC 20008, U.S.A.

BOLIN, (Axel) Bertil; Swedish international official and lawyer; b. 8 Nov. 1923, Törnevalla; s. of A. G. and Gotty Bolin; one s. one d.; ed. Univ. of Uppsala; Legal Adviser to Swedish Confed. of Trade Unions 1954–62, Dir. for Int. Affairs 1962; mem. Swedish Del. to UN Gen. Assembly 1962–68; Chair. Industrial Devt. Bd. 1966–67; mem. ILO Gov. Body 1965–68, Asst. Dir.-Gen. 1968–74, Deputy Dir.-Gen. 1974–89; mem. Int. Comm. of Jurists, Int. Asscn. for Industrial Relations, Swedish Labour Law Asscn., several Swedish Royal Comms.; Onassis Foundation Prize 1995. *Publications:* Swedish Labour Law, Holidays with Pay (in Swedish), Labour Market and Trade Unions in Developing Countries (in Swedish), Consumer Rights. *Leisure interests:* skiing, tennis, gardening.

BOLING, Edward J., M.S., ED.D.; American academic; b. 19 Feb. 1922, Sevier County, Tenn.; s. of Sam R. and Nerissa (Clark) Boling; m. Carolyn Pierce 1950; three s.; ed. Univ. of Tennessee and George Peabody Coll.; with Union Carbide Corpn. of Oak Ridge, Tenn. 1951–54; State Budget Dir. 1954–58; Commr. of Finance and Admin. 1958–61; Vice-Pres. for Devt. and Admin., Univ. of Tenn. 1961–70, Pres. Univ. of Tenn. 1970–88, Pres. Emer. 1988–; Univ. Prof. 1988–92; mem. Educ. Comm. of States 1970–92, mem. Southern Regional Educ. Bd. 1957–61, 1970–81, 1983–90, 1992–; Chair. Tenn. Resource Valley 1991–92. *Publications:* Forecasting University Enrolment (with D. A. Gardiner) 1952, Methods of Objectifying the Allocation of Tax Funds to Tennessee State Colleges 1961. *Leisure interests:* boating, tennis, skiing. *Address:* Suite 731, Andy Holt Tower, University of Tennessee, Knoxville, TN 37996, U.S.A. *Telephone:* 615-974-3500 (Office); 615-523-6882 (Home).

BOLKHOVITINOV, Nikolai Nikolaevich, D.HIST.; Russian historian; b. 26 Oct. 1930, Moscow; s. of Nikolai Bolkhovitinov and Lidiia (née Komarova) Bolkhovitinova; m. Ludmila Povel'nenko 1965; ed. Moscow Inst. of Int. Relations; on staff Dept. of History of Diplomacy U.S.S.R. Ministry of Foreign Affairs 1957–58; jr., sr. researcher Inst. of History 1958–68; sr., leading researcher, head of Centre for North American Studies, Inst. of World History U.S.S.R. Acad. of Sciences 1968–; corresp. mem. U.S.S.R. (now Russian) Acad. of Sciences 1987, full mem. 1992; research in history of U.S.A. and history of int. relations in 18th–19th centuries, Russian-American relations and foreign policy of Russia, geographic discoveries on N. Pacific and in N. America; mem. Russian Geographical Soc., New York Acad. of Sciences; Koontz Memorial Award (American Historical Asscn.); State Prize of Russian Fed. *Publications include:* Monroe's Doctrine 1959, U.S.A.: Problems of History and Contemporary Historiography 1980, History of Russian America 1732–1867 1997, series of monographs on history of Russian-American relations and numerous articles. *Leisure interest:* tennis. *Address:* Institute of World History, Russian Academy of Sciences, Leninskii pr. 32A, 117334 Moscow, Russia. *Telephone:* (095) 938 0097 (Office); (095) 210 2741 (Home). *Fax:* (095) 938 2286.

BOLKIAH, H.R.H. Prince Jefri; Brunei politician; fmrly. Minister of Culture, Youth and Sports, Deputy Minister of Finance; Minister of Finance 1988–97; Chair. Royal Brunei Airlines. *Address:* c/o Ministry of Finance, Bandar Seri Begawan, Brunei. *Telephone:* (02) 242405.

BOLKIAH, H.R.H. Prince Mohamed; Brunei politician; ed. Royal Mil. Acad., Sandhurst, U.K.; Minister of Foreign Affairs 1988–. *Address:* Ministry of Foreign Affairs, Jalan Subok, Bandar Seri Begawan, Brunei. *Telephone:* (02) 261177.

BOLKIAH MU'IZUDDIN WADDAULAH, H.M. Sultan Sir Muda Hassanal, D.K., P.S.P.N.B., P.S.N.B., P.S.L.J., S.P.B.M. P.A.N.B.; Sultan of Brunei; b. 15 July 1946; s. of former Sultan Sir Muda Omar Ali Saifuddin, K.C.M.G.; m. 1st Rajah Isteri Anak Saleha 1965; one s. five d.; m. 2nd Pengiran Isteri Hajjah Mariam 1981; two s. two d.; ed. privately, and Victoria Inst., Kuala Lumpur, Malaysia, and Royal Mil. Acad., Sandhurst; Appointed Crown Prince and Heir Apparent 1961; Ruler of State of Brunei Oct. 1967–; Prime Minister of Brunei Jan. 1984–, Minister of Finance and Home Affairs 1984–86, of Defence Oct. 1986–, also of Finance and of Law; Hon. Capt. Coldstream Guards 1968, Hon. Marshal R.A.F. 1992; Sovereign and Chief of Royal Orders instituted by Sultans of Brunei. *Address:* Istana Darul Hana, Bandar Seri Begawan, Brunei; The Aviary, Osterley, England. *Telephone:* (02) 229988 (Brunei). *Fax:* (02) 241717.

BOLLARD, Edward George, C.B.E., PH.D.; New Zealand plant physiologist; b. 21 Jan. 1920, Athlone, Westmeath, Ireland; s. of Edward D. and Elizabeth (née Allen) Bollard; m. 1st Constance M. Esmond 1947 (died 1971); m. 2nd Joy E. Cook 1972; two s. one d.; ed. Mount Albert Grammar School, Auckland, and Univs. of Auckland and Cambridge; with N.Z. Dept. of Scientific and Industrial Research 1948–80, latterly Dir. Div. of Horticulture and Processing; Hon. Prof., Univ. of Auckland 1973, Pro-Chancellor 1989–90; Fellow, Royal Soc. of N.Z., Pres. 1981–85; Harkness Fellow, Cornell Univ. 1956–57; Hector Medal, Royal Soc. of N.Z. 1972; Jubilee Medal 1977; Hon. D.Sc. (Auckland). *Publications:* Science and Technology in New Zealand: Opportunity for the Future 1986; Further Prospects for Horticulture: The Continuing Importance of Research 1996; research papers in the field of plant nutrition and on the development of the horticultural industry in N.Z. *Leisure interest:* keel boat sailing. *Address:* 22 Dunkerron Avenue, Epsom, Auckland, Auckland 1003, New Zealand. *Telephone:* (09) 520-6894.

BOLLING, Claude; French jazz pianist, composer and band leader; b. 10 April 1930, Cannes; s. of Henri Bolling and Geneviève Brannens; m. Irène Dervize-Sadyker 1959; two s.; studied with private music teachers including Bob Colin, Earl Hines, Maurice Duruflé, Willie 'The Lion' Smith, André Hodeir; compositions and recordings: piano solos, duos, trios and all instrumental combinations including jazz, big band and symphony orchestra; collaborated with Roy Eldridge, Lionel Hampton, Duke Ellington's men and many other jazz musicians and vocalists; written and recorded with Jean-Pierre Rampal (Suite for Flute), Alexandre Lagoya (Guitar Concerto), Maurice Andre (Toot Suite), Pinchas Zukerman (Suite for Violin), Yo-Yo Ma (Suite for Cello); composed more than 100 film soundtrack scores including, The Awakening, Le Jour et l'Heure, Borsalino, Lucky Luke, Le Magnifique, Willie and Phil, California Suite, La Mandarine, L'Homme en Colère, Flic Story, le Mur de l'Atlantique, On ne meurt que deux fois, Netchaiev est de retour; for television: Jazz Memories, Les Brigades du Tigre, Chantecler; many jazz and variety shows; U.S. and Canada Gold Records, Médaille d'or Maurice Ravel, Officier Arts et Lettres, Chevalier Ordre Nat. du Mérite, Chevalier Légion d'honneur, Hon. Citizen of L.A. *Leisure interests:* ecology, model railroading. *Address:* 20 avenue de Lorraine, 92380 Garches, France. *Telephone:* (1) 47-41-41-84. *Fax:* (1) 47-01-03-63.

BOLSHAKOV, Aleksey Alekseyevich; Russian politician and radio engineer; b. 17 Dec. 1939, Dno, Pskov Dist.; m.; two s.; ed. M. Bonch-Bruyevich Electromechanical Inst. of Telecommunications, Leningrad; worked as engineer in factories of Leningrad, Dir.-Gen. production union Dalnaya Svyaz; First Deputy Chair. Leningrad City Exec. Cttee., Chair. Planning Comm. 1988–91; Dir.-Gen. Jt.-Stock Co. Vysokoskorostnye Linii 1991–94; one of initiators of construction of high-speed St. Petersburg-Moscow highway; Chair. Intergovernmental Cttee. of C.I.S. 1994–; Deputy Chair. Russian Council of Ministers 1994–96, First Deputy Chair. 1996–97. *Address:* c/o House of Government of the Russian Federation, Krasnopresnenskaya nab. 2, 103274 Moscow, Russia.

BOLTANSKI, Christian; French artist; b. 6 Sept. 1944, Paris; recent one-man shows include: Museum of Contemporary Art, Chicago, Museum of Contemporary Art, Los Angeles, New Museum of Contemporary Art, New York, Galerie Pablo and Pandora van Dijk, Rotterdam, Ydessa Hendeles Art Foundation, Toronto, El Caso, Centro de Arte Reina Sofia, Madrid, Maria Goodman Gallery, New York 1988; Galerie Ghislaine Hussenot, Paris, Vancouver Art Gallery, Museum of Contemporary Art, Basle, Jean Bernier Gallery, Athens, Marika Malacorda Gallery, Geneva, Univ. Art Museum, Berkeley, Calif., Israel Museum, Jerusalem, Foksal Museum, Warsaw 1989; Galerie des Beaux Arts, Brussels, Kaufmann Gallery, Basle, Whitechapel Gallery, London, Musée de Grenoble, Inst. of Contemporary Arts, Nagoya, Marion Goodman Gallery, New York 1990; Kunsthalle, Hamburg, Lisson Gallery, London 1991; Lost: New York Project 1995; participant in numerous group exhbns. in Europe, U.S.A., Canada and Australia; Prof. Ecole Nationale Supérieure des Beaux Arts 1986; Grand Prix nat. de la Sculpture 1990. *Publications:* L'Album de la Famille B. 1971, Les Compositions Photographiques 1976, Murales 1977. *Address:* 146 boulevard Carmélina, 92240 Malakoff, France.

BOMBASSEI FRASCANI DE VETTOR, Giorgio; Italian diplomatist; b. 29 June 1910, Florence; s. of Alfredo Bombassei Frascani de Vettor and Margherita Tidone Peri; m. Eli Tramontani 1940; one s.; ed. Università degli Studi, Florence and Inst. of Political and Social Sciences "Cesare Alfieri", Florence; Italian Diplomatic Service 1933–, served Egypt, U.S.A., France, Ceylon, U.S.S.R., Switzerland, Brazil 1933–50; Deputy Dir. of Int. Co-operation, Ministry of Foreign Affairs 1952, Deputy Dir.-Gen. of Political Affairs 1956; Perm. Rep. of Italy to Council of Europe 1957–61; Amb. to Luxembourg 1961–65; Perm. mem. Italian Del. to Special Council of Ministers of ECSC 1961–65; Amb. to Netherlands 1965–67; Perm. Rep. of Italy to the European Communities 1967–76; Vice-Pres. EIB and Vice-Chair. Bd. Dirs. 1976–82, Hon. Vice-Pres. June 1982–; Grand Cross Officer Order of Merit (Italy), Medal of Freedom (U.S.A.), Knight S.M. Order of Malta; and other decorations. *Leisure interests;* golf, bridge. *Address:* 8 rue de Crayer, 1000 Brussels, Belgium. *Telephone:* (02) 6480701.

BOMERS, Henricus J.A.; Netherlands ecclesiastic; b. 19 April 1936, Eibergen; Novitiate, Lazarist Fathers 1957; ordained 1964; Lecturer in Philosophy, Interdiocesan Seminary, Addis Ababa 1967–73; Regional Superior, Lazarist Fathers in Ethiopia 1973–78; Sec.-Gen. for Food Aid 1973–74; Apostolic Vicar of Gimma, Ethiopia 1977; Bishop of Haarlem 1983–.

BON JOVI, Jon; American rock singer; m. Dorothea Bon Jovi; two c.; f. rock band Bon Jovi, singer, songwriter 1984–; band's recordings include single Runaway, albums Slippery When Wet, New Jersey, Keep The Faith,

Cross Road 1994 (12m copies sold worldwide), These Days 1996; world tour 1995; films: Moonlight and Valentino, The Leading Man; band won Best Int. Group Brit Award 1995. *Address:* c/o Dawn Bartlett, Mercury Press Office, P.O. Box 1425, Chancellors House, Chancellors Road, London, W6 9QB, England. *Telephone:* 0181-910 5733. *Fax:* 0181-910 5893.

BÓNA, István, PH.D.; Hungarian archaeologist and historian; b. Feb. 1930, Heves; ed. Pázmány Péter Univ.; with Hungarian Nat. Museum 1952–53; museum dir. 1953–54; with Dept. of Archaeology Eötvos Loránd Univ. of Arts and Sciences 1954–57, asst. 1957–59, asst. lecturer 1959–64, Asst. Prof. 1964–75, Prof. 1975–, Head Ancient and Early History Dept. 1987–95, Head Postgrad. Course 1995–; has carried out archaeological excavations at Bronze Age cemeteries and settlements unearthing Longobard, Gepid, Avar and early Hungarian burial places and settlements 1951–; Pres. Archaeological Cttee. Hungarian Acad. of Sciences 1980–90, Sec. 1975–80; mem. editorial bd. Acta Archaeologica; corresp. mem. Hungarian Acad. of Sciences 1990–, mem. 1998–; awarded Kuzsinsky Bálint Medal 1963, Rómer Flóris Medal 1984, Acad. Prize 1987, Széchenyi Prize 1998. *Publications:* Die Langobarden in Ungarn 1956, VII századi avar települések és Árpád kori magyar falu Dunaújvárosban 1973, Mittelbronzezeitliche Tell-Siedlung bei Békés 1974 (jtly.), A középkor hajnala 1974, Die Mittlere Bronzezeit Ungarns 1975, Die Graebefelder von Intercisa (jtly.) 1976, Az Őskor története Magyarországon, A népvándorlás kora és a kora középkor története Magyarországon, Magyarország története (Vol. I) 1984, Dáciától Erdőelvéig, Erdély története I 1986, Völkerwanderung und Frühmittelalter (271–895), Zeit des ungarisch-slawischen Zusammenlebens (895–1172), Geschichte Siebenbürgens 1990, Dunapentele története 1991, Das Hunnenreich 1991, Bronzezeit in Ungarn (ed.) 1992, Az Árpádok korai várai 1998. *Address:* 2400 Dunaújváros, Görbe u. 4, Hungary.

BOND, Alan, A.O.; Australian business executive; b. 22 April 1938, London, England; s. of Frank Bond and Kathleen Bond; m. 1st Eileen Hughes 1956 (divorced); two s. two d.; m. 2nd Diana Bliss 1995; ed. Perivale School, London and Fremantle Boys' School, W.A.; f. and Exec. Chair. Bond Corpn. Holdings Ltd. 1969–90, now consultant; interests in brewing, property, oil and gas, electronic media, minerals, airships; arrested on fraud charges Dec. 1990; judged liable for debts Sept. 1991; declared bankrupt April 1992; sentenced to 2½ years for dishonesty; served three months in prison; released and retrial ordered Aug. 1992; found not guilty after retrial Nov. 1992; sentenced quashed; facing further charges of fraud 1994; found guilty of four charges Aug. 1996; sentenced to three years' imprisonment for fraud 1996; sentenced for four years' imprisonment for fraud Feb. 1997; sentence extended to seven years Aug. 1997; Syndicate Head America's Cup Challenge 1983 Ltd.; Australia Winners of 1983 America's Cup Challenge; named Australian of the Year 1977. *Leisure interest:* yachting.

BOND, Alan Maxwell, PH.D., D.SC., F.A.A., F.R.A.C.I., F.R.S.C.; Australian professor of chemistry; b. 17 Aug. 1946, Cobden, Vic.; s. of late Ian T. Bond and Joyce M. Bond; m. Tunde-Maria Bond 1969; two s.; ed. Univ. of Melbourne; Research Fellow, Dept. of Inorganic Chem. Univ. of Melbourne 1973–78; Foundation Prof. of Chem. Deakin Univ. 1978–90; Prof. of Chem. La Trobe Univ. 1990–95, Monash Univ. 1995–, also Deputy Head Dept. of Chemistry; 150th anniversary Royal Soc. of Chem. Robert Boyle Fellow in Analytical Chem. Univ. of Oxford 1991; Hinshelwood Lecturer Univ. of Oxford 1998; mem. Council Australian Acad. of Science 1993–96, Vice-Pres. 1995–96; Fulbright Fellow 1972; Fellow, Japan Soc. for Promotion of Science 1990; Erskine Fellowship 1993; Fed. of Asian Chemical Socs. Foundation Lectureship 1993; Rennie Medal 1975, David Syme Prize 1978, Australian Analytical Chem. Medal 1989, Stokes Medal 1992, Liversidge Award, Australian and N.Z. A.A.S. 1992, Australian Research Council Special Investigator Award 1997–99. *Publications:* Modern Polarographic Methods in Analytical Chemistry 1981; more than 450 publs. on different aspects of electrochemistry. *Leisure interest:* cricket. *Address:* Department of Chemistry, Monash University, Clayton, Vic. 3168 (Office); 7 Canterbury Road, Toorak, Vic. 3142, Australia (Home). *Telephone:* (03) 9905 1338 (Office); (03) 827 8466 (Home). *Fax:* (03) 9905 4597 (Office).

BOND, Christopher Samuel; American politician and lawyer; b. 6 March 1939, St. Louis; s. of Arthur Doerr and Elizabeth Green Bond; m. Carolyn Reid 1967; one s.; ed. Deerfield Acad., Mass., Woodrow Wilson School of Public and Int. Affairs, Princeton Univ., Univ. of Virginia; Clerk, Fifth Circuit, U.S. Court of Appeals 1963–64; with law firm, Covington and Burling, Washington, D.C. 1964–67; private practice 1968; Asst. Attorney-Gen., Chief Counsel of Consumer Protection Div. 1969–70; State Auditor, Missouri 1970–72; Gov. of Missouri 1973–77, 1981–84; Chair. Republican Govs.' Asscn. 1974–75, Midwestern Govs.' Conf. 1976; Exec. Cttee. Nat. Govs.' Conf. 1974–75; Chair. NGA Cttee. on Econ. Devt. 1981-82; Pres. Great Plains Legal Foundation, Kansas City, Mo. 1977–81; Partner, law firm Gage and Tucker, Kansas City and St. Louis 1981–87; Senator from Missouri Jan. 1987–; Hon. LL.D. (Westminster and William Jewell Colls., Mo.) 1973, Hon. D.Litt. (Drury Coll., Springfield, Mo.) 1976; Republican. *Address:* US Senate, Russell Senate Building, Room 293, Washington, DC 20510 (Office); 14 S. Jefferson Road, Mexico, MO 65265, U.S.A. (Home).

BOND, Edward; British playwright and director; b. 18 July 1934, London; m. Elisabeth Pablé 1971; Resident Theatre Writer, Univ. of Essex 1982–83; winner, George Devine Award, John Whiting Award 1968; Hon. D.Litt. (Yale) 1977. *Publications:* plays: Saved 1965, Narrow Road to the Deep North 1968, Early Morning 1968, The Pope's Wedding 1971, Passion 1971, Black Mass 1971, Lear 1972, The Sea 1973, Bingo 1974, The Fool 1976, A-A-America! (Grandma Faust and The Swing) 1976, Stone 1976, The Bundle 1978, The Woman 1979, The Worlds 1980, Restoration 1981, Summer: A Play for Europe 1982, Derek 1983, Human Cannon 1985, War Plays (Red Black and Ignorant, The Tin Can People, Great Peace) 1985, Jackets 1989, In the Company of Men 1989, September 1990, Olly's Prison (TV) 1992, Tuesday (TV) 1993, Coffee: A Tragedy 1994, At the Inland Sea (A Play for Young People) 1996, Eleven Vests (A Play for Young People) 1997, The Crime of the Twenty-First Century 1999; librettos: We Come to the River 1977, The English Cat 1983; translations: Chekhov's The Three Sisters 1967, Wedekind's Spring Awakening 1974, Wedekind's Lulu: A Monster Tragedy 1992; others: Theatre Poems and Songs 1978, Collected Poems 1978–1985, 1987, Notes on Post-Modernism 1990, Letters (5 vols.) 1994–98. *Address:* c/o Casarotto Ramsay, National House, 60–66 Wardour Street, London, W1V 3HP, England. *Telephone:* 0171-287 4450. *Fax:* 0171-287 9128.

BOND, John; banker; b. 24 July 1941; m. Elizabeth Parker; one s. two d.; joined The Hongkong and Shanghai Banking Corpn. 1961; worked in Hong Kong, Thailand, Singapore, Indonesia and U.S.A.; Chief Exec. Wardley (merchant banking subsidiary) 1983; Gen. Man. and C.E.O. Hongkong and Shanghai Banking Corpn. Americas 1988–89, Chair 1997–; Chair. Hongkong Bank of Canada 1987–97; Dir. (Exec. Dir. Americas) Hongkong and Shanghai Banking Corpn. 1988–, Exec. Dir. Banking 1990; Dir. (non-exec.) London Stock Exchange 1994–, British Steel 1994–98; Pres. and C.E.O. Marine Midland Banks, Inc., U.S.A. (subsidiary of HSBC Holdings PLC) 1991–93, now Chair.; Chair. Midland Bank PLC 1998–; Chair. British Bank of the Middle East 1998–; Group C.E.O. HSBC Holdings PLC 1993–98, Chair. 1998– (Dir. 1990–); Dir. (non-exec.) Visa Int. 1995–97, Orange PLC 1996–; Gov. The English-Speaking Union 1997–. *Address:* HSBC Holdings PLC, 10th Floor, 10 Lower Thames Street, London, EC3R 6AE, England. *Telephone:* 0171-260 9158.

BOND, Julian; American civil rights leader; b. 14 Jan. 1940; s. of Horace Mann Bond and Julia Agnes (née Washington); m. 1st Alice Louise Clopton 1961 (divorced 1989); three s. two d.; m. 2nd Pamela Sue Horowitz 1990; ed. Morehouse Coll.; co-founder, Cttee. on Appeal for Human Rights, Atlanta Univ. 1960, later Exec. Sec.; co-founder Student Non-violent Co-ordinating Cttee. 1960, Communications Dir. 1961–66; reporter, feature writer Atlanta Inquirer 1960–61, Man. Ed. 1963; mem. Ga. House of Reps. 1966–75, excluded 1966 by House for criticizing U.S. involvement in Viet Nam, exclusion overruled in Supreme Court; mem. Ga. Senate 1975–87; Prof. Drexel Univ. 1988–89; Pappas Fellow, Univ. of Pennsylvania 1989; Visiting Prof. Harvard Univ. 1989, 1991, Univ. of Va. 1990; Distinguished Prof. American Univ. 1990–; Prof. Univ. of Va. 1993–; Chair. Bd., Southern Elections Fund, Nat. Asscn. for the Advancement of Colored People 1998–; Pres. Emer. Southern Poverty Law Center; Pres. Inst. of Southern Studies; mem. Bd. of Dirs. Delta Ministry Project of Nat. Council of Churches, Robert F. Kennedy Memorial Fund, Martin Luther King Jr. Center for Social Change, Centre for Community Change, Southern Regional Council, New Democratic Coalition, and other bodies; mem. Nat. Advisory Council of American Civil Liberties Union, Southern Correspondents Reporting Racial Equality Wars, hon. degrees from 15 Colls. and Univs. *Publications:* A Time to Speak, A Time to Act, poems and articles in books and periodicals. *Address:* 5435 41st Place, N.W., Washington, DC 20015, U.S.A. *Telephone:* (202) 244-1213.

BONDAREV, Yuriy Vasiliyevich, Russian writer; b. 15 March 1924, Orsk; s. of Vasili Vasilevich Bondarev and Claudia Iosifovna Bondareva; m. Valentina Nikitichna Mosina 1950; two d.; ed. Gor'kiy Inst., Moscow 1951; writer 1949–; mem. CPSU 1944–91; First Deputy Chair. of R.S.F.S.R. Writers' Union, Chair. of Bd. 1990–93; Pres. Yedineniye (Unity) Asscn. 1995–; served Soviet Army 1941–45; Deputy to Supreme Soviet 1975–80 and Deputy Chair.; Co-Chair. Int. Community of Writers' Unions; Hero of Socialist Labour 1984, two State prizes, Lenin Prize, R.S.F.S.R. Prize, Tolstoy Prize 1993, Sholokhov Prize 1994. *Publications include:* novels: On the Big River 1953, Young Commanders 1956, Fire for the Battalions 1957, Last Salute 1959, Silence 1962, Relatives 1965, Hot Snow 1969, The Shore 1975, A Choice 1980, The Game 1984, Temptation 1991, Instants (essays) 1981–87 and 1987–94; Collected works (8 vols.) 1993–94, Non-Resistance to Evil 1994. *Leisure interest:* collecting painting albums. *Address:* Lomonosovsky Prospekt N19, Apt. 148, 117311 Moscow, Russia. *Telephone:* 930-26-51.

BONDEVIK, Kjell Magne; Norwegian politician; b. 3 Sept. 1947, Molde; s. of Margit Bondevik and Johs Bondevik; m. Björg Bondevik 1970; two s. one d.; ed. Free Faculty of Theology, Univ. of Oslo; ordained minister 1979; Deputy Chair. Christian Democratic youth asscn. 1968–70, Chair. 1970–73; Deputy mem. Storting 1969–73, mem. 1973–; Political Vice-Chair. Christian Democratic Party 1975–83, Chair. 1983–95; Minister of Church and Educ. 1983–86, of Foreign Affairs 1989–90, Deputy Prime Minister 1985–86; Prime Minister of Norway 1997–; Chair. Christian Democratic Party's Parl. Group 1981–83, 1986–89, 1990–; Hon. D.Tech. (Brunel) 1997. *Address:* c/o Stortingel, Karl Johansgt. 22, 0026 Oslo 1, Norway.

BONDI, Sir Hermann, K.C.B., M.A. F.R.S.; British mathematician; b. 1 Nov. 1919, Vienna, Austria; s. of late Samuel and Helene Bondi; m. Christine M. Stockman 1947; two s. three d.; ed. Real Gymnasium, Vienna, and Trinity

Coll., Cambridge; Fellow, Trinity Coll., Cambridge 1943–49, 1952–54; Lecturer in Math., Cambridge Univ. 1948–54; Research Assoc. Cornell Univ. 1951, Harvard Coll. Observatory 1953; Visiting Prof. Cornell Univ. 1960; Prof. of Math. King's Coll., Univ. of London 1954–71, Titular Prof. 1971–84, Prof. Emer. 1985–; Dir.-Gen. European Space Research Org. (ESRO), Paris 1967–71; Chief Scientific Adviser to Ministry of Defence 1971–77; Chief Scientist Dept. of Energy 1977–80; Chair. Offshore Energy Bd., Dept. of Energy 1977–80, Advisory Council on Research and Devt. for Fuel and Power 1977–80, Severn Barrage Cttee. 1978–81; Chair. and Chief Exec. Natural Environment Research Council 1980–84; Fellow, Royal Soc. 1959, Royal Astronomical Soc. (Sec. 1956–64), Cambridge Philosophical Soc.; Chair. Nat. Cttee. for Astronomy 1964–67; Pres. Inst. of Math. and its Applications 1974–75, Asscn. of British Science Writers 1981–83, British Humanist Asscn. 1982–, Pres. Hydrographical Soc. 1985–87; Master, Churchill Coll., Cambridge 1983–90, Fellow 1990–; Hon. Fellow Regent's Coll. 1988, Inst. of Physics 1992, Inst. of Math. and its Applications 1993, Indian Acad. of Sciences 1996; Hon D.Sc. (Sussex, Bath, Surrey) 1974, (York) 1980, (Southampton) 1981, (Salford) 1982, (Birmingham) 1984, (St. Andrews) 1985, (Vienna) 1993, (Plymouth) 1995; Gold Medal (Inst. of Math. and its Applications) 1988, G. D. Birla Int. Award for Humanism 1990, Planetary Award (Asscn. of Space Explorers) 1993, Pres.'s Decoration for Science and Arts (Austria) 1997. *Publications:* Cosmology 1960, The Universe at Large 1961, Relativity and Common Sense 1964, Assumption and Myth in Physical Theory 1967, Science, Churchill and Me (autobiog.) 1990, numerous papers. *Address:* Churchill College, Cambridge, CB3 0DS, England.

BONDURANT, Stuart, B.S., M.D.; American professor and university administrator; b. 9 Sept. 1929, Winston-Salem, N.C.; m. 1st Margaret Fortescue 1954 (divorced); one s. two d.; m. 2nd Susan Haughton Ehringhaus 1991; ed. Univ. of North Carolina at Chapel Hill, Duke Univ. School of Medicine, Durham, N.D.; Assoc. Dir. Indiana Univ. Cardiovascular Research Centre, Indiana Univ. Medical Center, Indianapolis, Ind. 1961–67; Chief, Medical Br. Artificial Heart-Myocardial Infarction Program, Nat. Health Inst., Nat. Insts. of Health 1966–67; Prof. and Chair., Dept. of Medicine, Albany Medical Coll., Physician-in-Chief, Albany Medical Center Hosp., New York 1967–74, Pres. and Dean 1974–79; Prof. of Medicine, Univ. of N.C. 1979–, Dean, Univ. of N.C. School of Medicine 1979–94; Dir. Center for Urban Epidemiology Studies, N.Y. Acad of Medicine 1994–96; Hon. F.R.C.P. (E.); Hon. D.Sc. (Indiana 1980). *Address:* University of North Carolina School of Medicine, Dept. of Medicine CB. 7005, Chapel Hill, NC 27599; 623 Greenwood Road, Chapel Hill, NC 27514, U.S.A. (Home.) *Telephone:* (919) 966-4161 (Office).

BONELL, Carlos Antonio; British musician, teacher, guitarist and composer; b. 23 July 1949, London; m. Pinuccia Rossetti 1971; two s.; ed. William Ellis School, London and Royal Coll. of Music, under John Williams (q.v.); solo début as guitarist, Wigmore Hall, London 1971; concerto début with Royal Philharmonic Orchestra 1975; American début, Avery Fisher Hall, New York 1978; concert appearances with all the prin. British orchestras; appearances with John Williams, Teresa Berganza (q.v.), Pinchas Zukerman (q.v.) 1975–; formed Carlos Bonell Ensemble 1983; Prof. Royal Coll. of Music 1972–, London Coll. of Music 1983–; Hon. A.R.C.M. *Recordings include:* Guitar Music of Spain 1975, Guitar Music of the Baroque 1976, Showpieces 1981, Rodrigo Concerto 1981, Paganini Trios and Quartets 1983, Twentieth Century Music for Guitar 1987, Once Upon a Time, with Xer-Wai (violin) 1992, Walton Bagatelles and Anon in Love 1993, Britten Folksongs (with Philip Langridge) 1994, The Sea in Spring 1997, The Private Collection 1998. *Publications:* 20 First Pieces 1982, Tarrega: Fantasia on "La Traviata", 3 Spanish Folk Songs, Purcell: Music from the Fairy Queen, Fantasy for 3 Guitars 1995, Technique Builder 1997, Complete Guide to Sight Reading 1999. *Leisure interests:* reading, walking, snooker. *Address:* c/o Upbeat Management, Sutton Business Centre, Restmor Way, Wallington, Surrey, SM6 7AH, England. *Telephone:* 0181-773 1223. *Fax:* 0181-669 6752.

BONET, Pep; Spanish architect and designer; b. 19 Nov. 1941, Barcelona; m. Marta Monné 1964; three s.; ed. High School of Architecture, Barcelona; f. Studio Per architectural practice, with Cristian Cirici, Lluis Clotet and Oscar Tusquets 1965; began producing furniture and bldg. components, co-f. B.D. Ediciones de Diseño 1972; taught at School of Architecture, Barcelona 1975–78, Washington School of Architecture, St. Louis, Mo., U.S.A. 1981; Deltas ADI-FAD award 1967, 1976, 1986, 1990, 1991, Azulejo de Oro award 1970, Nat. Restoration award 1980, FAD award for architecture 1965, 1970, 1972, 1987, Architecture and Town Planning award 1987 for Triángulo de Oro Sports Centre, Madrid. *Major works include:* (Feria de Barcelona) Plaza Universo 1983–85, Rius i Taulet pavilion 1987, Iberia pavilion 1987, Lleida-Parallel pavilion 1989; Triángulo de Oro Sports Centre 1985, Canillejas civic centre 1985 (Madrid); Granollers Olympic sports centre, COOB-92. *Leisure interest:* playing jazz (tenor saxophone). *Address:* C/Pujades 63, 08005 Barcelona, Spain. *Telephone:* (93) 4855494. *Fax:* (93) 3091472.

BONETTI, Mattia; Swiss designer, decorator and artist; b. 2 May 1952, Lugano; s. of Giorgio Bonetti and Stella Frossard; m. Isabelle Forestier 1990; two d.; ed. Centro Scolastico Industrie Artistiche, Lugano; Exhbns.: Musée des Arts Décoratifs, Bordeaux 1985, Galerie Neotu, Paris 1985–87, 1993, 1994, Furniture of the 20th Century, New York 1985, 1987, 1988, Mairie de Villeurbanne 1986, Vic. and Albert Museum, London 1988, 1994, Seibu, Tokyo, Japan, 1989, Galerie Wunderhaus, Munich 1990, Galerie Néotú, New York 1990, 1993, Galleria Ex-Ante, Rome 1990, Galleria Iannone, Milan 1992, Galerie Wohn Tendenz, Innsbruck 1993, Musée de Riom, France 1993, Galerie Naila de Monbrison, Paris 1993, Liberty, London 1993, Kulturring, Sundern 1994, Galerie Raab, Berlin 1994, Design Museum, Frankfurt 1994, La Monnaie de Paris 1995, "Premises" group show, Guggenheim Museum, New York 1998, David Gill Gallery, London 1999; decorated Bernard Picasso's Boisgeloop Castle 1987, Christian Lacroix Showroom and Graphics 1987–88; designs for cafeteria, Schloss Regensburg Museum, Germany 1990, Banque Bruxelles-Lambert, Geneva 1991, packaging for Nina Ricci Cosmetics 1992, 1994, Water Carafe design for Ricard 1995, designed tramway for city of Montpellier 1998; Hon. Citizen City of Villeurbanne; "Créateurs de l'Année 1991" (France), Chevalier, Ordre des Arts et des Lettres 1995. *Publication:* Mattia Bonetti & Elizabeth Garouste 1990. *Leisure interests:* swimming, photography. *Address:* 1 rue Oberkampf, 75011 Paris, France. *Telephone:* (1) 48-05-86-51.

BONFIELD, Sir Peter Leahy, Kt., C.B.I.M., C.B.E., F.ENG.; British business executive; b. 3 June 1944; m. Josephine Houghton 1968; ed. Loughborough Univ.; Div. Dir. Texas Instruments Inc. 1966–81; Group Exec. Dir. Worldwide Operations, Int. Computers Ltd. 1981–84; Man. Dir. Int. Computers Ltd. 1984; Chair. and Man. Dir. STC Int. Computers Ltd. 1986–90; Deputy Chief Exec. STC PLC 1987–90; Chair. ICL PLC 1990–97, Deputy Chair. 1997–, C.E.O. 1990–95; Chair. DESC Ltd. 1990–95; Dir. (non-exec.) BICC PLC 1992–96; C.E.O. British Telecommunications PLC 1996– (merged with MCI 1996 to form Concert); Dir. Zeneca Gp. 1995–; Fellow Chartered Inst. of Marketing, British Computer Soc., Royal Soc. of Arts 1992; Dr. h.c. (Open Univ.) 1997; Hon. Dr. Tech. (Loughborough) 1988, (Brunel) 1997. *Leisure interests:* music, sailing, jogging. *Address:* British Telecommunications PLC, BT Centre, 81 Newgate Street, London, EC1D 7AT, England. *Telephone:* 0171-356 5000. *Fax:* 0171-356 5221.

BONGARD-LEVIN, Grigory Maximovich; Russian historian; b. 26 Aug. 1933, Moscow; s. of Maxim Bongard-Levin and Lussy Bongard-Levin; m. Irina Bongard-Levin (deceased) 1956; one s.; ed. Moscow State Univ.; jr., sr. researcher. head of div. Inst. of Oriental Studies U.S.S.R. Acad. of Sciences 1956–87, chief researcher 1987–; Corresp. mem. U.S.S.R. (now Russian) Acad. of Sciences 1987, mem. 1990; Ed.-in-Chief Vestnik Drevnei Istorii; mem. Nat. Cttee. of History of Russia; head Comm. on Sanskrit Studies at Asscn. of Oriental Studies; Hon. Fellow Royal Asiatic Soc., London 1997; Dr. h.c. Sarnath Tibetan Inst. 1991; Nehru Prize 1975, Gold Medal, Asiatic Soc. of Bengal 1979; U.S.S.R. State Prize 1988, Int. Prize of St. Mark, Venice 1990. *Publications:* works on culture, and ethnogenesis of peoples of Asia, of old civilisations of Orient and W., including books Ancient India 1969, India of the Epoch of Mauryas 1974, Ancient Indian Civilisation 1980, From India to Scythia 1983, India in Ancient Times, Indian Texts from Central Asia (2 vols.) 1985–90, Scythian Novel 1997. *Leisure interests:* paintings, literature, antique furniture. *Address:* Institute of Oriental Studies, Rozhdestvenka 12, 103777 Moscow (Office); 117334, Leninsky Prospekt 2, R. 1503, VDI, Moscow, Russia (Home). *Telephone:* (095) 938 5228 (Office); (095) 245 4696 (Home). *Fax:* (095) 938 1912 (Office).

BONGO, Martin; Gabonese politician; b. 4 July 1940, Lekei; ed. Ecole Normale de Mitzic; fmrly. school dir. in Franceville, then Insp. for Primary Instruction for Upper-Ogooué Region; fmr. Dir. of Cabinet to the Vice-Pres.; Deputy Dir. of Cabinet to the Pres. 1968–69; Commr.-Gen. for Information April-Dec. 1969; Sec. of State to the Presidency, for Penitentiary Services 1969–70, for Nat. Educ. in charge of Special Missions 1970–72, Head of State's Personal Rep. 1972–73; Minister of Educ. and Scientific Research 1973–75, of Nat. Educ. 1975–76, of Foreign Affairs and Co-operation 1976–81, of State for Foreign Affairs and Co-operation 1981–89; Commdr. Order of the Equatorial Star, Grand Officer, Nat. Order of Merit (Mauritania), Grand Officer, Order of Merit (Italy), Commdr. Ordre national du Mérite. *Address:* c/o Ministère des Affaires Etrangères et de la Coopération, Libreville, Gabon.

BONGO, Omar (Albert-Bernard); Gabonese politician; b. 30 Dec. 1935, Lewai, Franceville; m.; three c.; ed. primary school at Bacongo (Congo—Brazzaville) and technical coll., Brazzaville; Civil Servant; served Air Force 1958–60; entered Ministry of Foreign Affairs 1960; Dir. of Private Office of Pres. Léon Mba 1962, in charge of Information 1963–64, Nat. Defence 1964–65; Minister-Del. to Presidency in charge of Nat. Defence and Co-ordination, Information and Tourism 1965–66; Vice-Pres. of Govt., in charge of Co-ordination, Nat. Defence Planning, Information and Tourism 1966–67; Vice-Pres. of Gabon March-Nov. 1967, Pres. 1967–, Minister of Defence 1967–81, of Information 1967–80, of Planning 1967–77, Prime Minister 1967–75, Minister of the Interior 1967–70, of Devt. 1970–77, of Women's Affairs 1976–77, and numerous other portfolios; Pres. UDEAC 1981; Founder and Sec.-Gen. Parti Démocratique Gabonais 1968; High Chancellor, Ordre Nat. de l'Etoile Equatoriale; decorations from the Ivory Coast, Niger, Chad, Cameroon, Central African Republic, Mauritius, Togo, Taiwan, Zaire, France, U.K. and Guinea. *Address:* Présidence de la République, Boîte Postale 546, Libreville, Gabon. *Telephone:* 26-90.

BONHAM CARTER, Helena; British actress; b. 26 May 1966; (great granddaughter of fmr. British Prime Minister Lord Asquith); d. of Hon. Raymond Bonham Carter and Elena Bonham Carter; TV appearances include A Pattern of Roses, Miami Vice, A Hazard of Hearts, The Vision, Arms and the Man, Beatrix Potter. *Films include:* Lady Jane, A Room with a View, Maurice, Francesco, The Mask, Getting it Right, Hamlet, Where Angels Fear to Tread, Howard's End 1991, A Dark Adapted Eye (TV) 1994,

Mary Shelley's Frankenstein 1994, The Glace Bay Miners' Museum 1994, A Little Loving 1995, Mighty Aphrodite 1995, Twelfth Night 1996; Margaret's Museum 1996, Parti Chinois 1996, The Theory of Flight 1997, Keep the Aspidistra Flying 1997, The Wings of the Dove 1998, The Revengers' Comedies 1998, Woman Talking Dirty 1999; face of Yardley Cosmetics Co.; play The Barber of Seville 1992, Trelawny of the "Wells" 1992. *Address:* c/o Conway van Gelder Limited, 18/21 Jermyn Street, London, SW1Y 6HP, England. *Telephone:* 0171-287 0077.

BONIN, Bernard, D. EN SC. (ECON.), F.R.S.C.; Canadian economist; b. 29 Sept. 1936, Joliette; s. of Georges Bonin and Thérèse Racette; m. Andrée Gregoire 1960; one s. one d.; ed. Ecole des Hautes Etudes Commerciales, Montréal and Univ. of Paris; Prof. of Econs. Ecole des Hautes Etudes Commerciales, Montréal 1962–74; Asst. Deputy Minister for Immigration, Govt. of Quebec 1974–77, for Intergovernmental Affairs 1977–81; Prof. of Econs., Ecole Nat. d'Admin. Publique, Montreal 1979–88; Deputy Gov. Bank of Canada 1988–94, Sr. Deputy Gov. 1994–. *Publications:* L'investissement étranger à long terme au Canada 1967, A propos de l'association économique Canada-Québec 1980, L'entreprise multinationale et l'état 1984, Innovation industrielle et analyse économique 1988. *Leisure interests:* music, reading, sport. *Address:* Bank of Canada, 234 Wellington Street, Ottawa, Ont. K1A 0G9, Canada (Office). *Telephone:* (613) 782-7713 (Office).

BONINGTON, Sir Christian John Storey, C.B.E.; British mountaineer, writer and photographer; b. 6 Aug. 1934; s. of Charles Bonington and Helen Anne (née Storey) Bonington; m. Muriel Wendy Marchant 1962; three s. (one s. deceased); ed. Univ. Coll. School and R.M.A.; Royal Tank Regt. 1956–59; Instructor Army Outward Bound School 1959–61; Man. Trainee Unilever 1961–62; writer and photographer 1962–; Vice-Pres. Army Mountaineering Asscn. 1980–; Pres. LEPRA 1985–, British Orienteering Fed. 1986–, British Mountaineering Council 1988–91 (Vice-Pres. 1976–79, 1985–88), Council for Nat. Parks 1992–, The Alpine Club 1995–; Hon. Fellow UMIST, Lancs. Poly.; Hon. M.A. (Salford); Hon. D.Sc. (Sheffield) 1976, (Lancaster) 1983; Hon. D.C.L. (Northumbria) 1996; Hon. D.Univ. (Sheffield Hallam) 1998; Founders Medal (Royal Geographical Soc.) 1971, Lawrence of Arabia Medal 1986, Livingstone Medal 1991; David Livingstone Medal Royal Scottish Geographical Soc. 1991, Fellow Lancs. Polytechnic. *Numerous climbs include:* Annapurna South Face Expedition 1970, British Everest Expedition 1972, Brammah, Himalayas 1973, Changabang, Himalayas 1974, British Everest Expedition (first ascent, S.W. Face) 1975, Mount Vinson, Antarctica 1983, Panch chuli II, Himalayas (first ascent, W. Ridge) 1992, Maslin, Greenland (first ascent) 1993, Rangrik Rang, India (first ascent) 1994, Drangnag-Ri, Nepal (first ascent) 1995; reached Everest summit 1985; *Publications include:* I Chose to Climb (autobiog.) 1966, The Next Horizon (autobiog.) 1973, Quest for Adventure 1981, The Everest Years 1986, Mountaineer 1989, The Climbers 1992, Sea, Ice and Rock (jtly.) 1992. *Leisure interests:* mountaineering, orienteering. *Address:* Badger Hill, Hesket Newmarket, Wigton, Cumbria, CA7 8LA, England. *Telephone:* (016974) 78286. *Fax:* (016974) 78238.

BONINO, Emma, PH.D; Italian politician; b. 9 March 1948, Bra, Turin; ed. Univ. of Milan; mem. Chamber of Deputies 1976–1983, re-elected 1986, 1992, 1994; Pres. Parl. Group, Radical Party 1981; mem. European Parl. 1979–; founder, Centro Informazione Sterilizzazione e Aborto 1975; Pres. Transnat. Radical Party 1991–93, Sec. 1993–95; EC Commr. for Consumer Policy, EC Humanitarian Office and Fisheries 1995–. *Address:* European Commission, Breydel 10/54, Avenue d'Auderghem 45, 1040 Brussels, Belgium. *Telephone:* (2) 956447.

BONNEFOY, Yves Jean, L. ÈS L.; French writer; b. 24 June 1923, Tours; s. of Elie Bonnefoy and Hélène Maury; m. Lucille Vines 1968; one d.; ed. Lycée Descartes, Tours, Faculté des Sciences, Poitiers, and Faculté des Lettres, Paris; Prof. Collège de France 1981; contributor to Mercure de France, Critique, Encounter, L'Ephémère, La Nouvelle Revue Française etc.; has travelled in Europe, Asia and N. America; lectures or seminars at Brandeis, Johns Hopkins, Princeton, Geneva, Nice, Yale and other univs.; Prix Montaigne 1980, Grand Prix de poésie (Acad. Française) 1981, Prix Florence Gould 1987, Grand Prix national 1993, Prix de la Fondation Cino-del-Duca 1995; Commdr. des Arts et des Lettres and numerous other prizes; Hon. D. Hum Litt. (American Coll., Paris, Univ. of Chicago, Univ. of Neuchâtel, Trinity Coll., Dublin). *Publications:* poems: Du mouvement et de l'immobilité de Douve 1953 (English 1968), Hier régnant désert 1958, Pierre écrite 1964 (English 1976), Selected Poems 1968, Dans le leurre du seuil 1975, Poèmes (1947–1975) 1978, Ce qui fut sans lumière 1987, Entretiens sur la Poesie 1990, Début et fin de la neige 1991; essays: L'Improbable 1959, Arthur Rimbaud 1961 (English translation 1973), Un rêve fait à Mantoue 1967, Le nuage rouge 1977, Rue traversière 1977; on art: Peintures murales de la France Gothique 1954, Miró 1963, Rome 1630 1969, L'Arrière-Pays 1972, Entretiens sur la poésie 1981, La Présence et l'Image 1983, Récits en rêve 1987, La Vérité de Parole 1988, Alberto Giacometti 1991, La vie errante 1993, Remarques sur le dessin 1993, Dessin, couleur et lumière 1995, Théâtre et poésie: Shakespeare et Yeats, l'Encore aveugle 1998; co-editor L'Ephémère, translations of Shakespeare, W.B. Yeats. *Address:* Collège de France, 11 place Marcelin Berthelot, 75005 Paris, France.

BONNEMAIN, François; French broadcasting executive and fmr. journalist; b. 9 Oct 1942; ed. Centre de formation des journalistes de Paris; with Associated Press (AP), Agence France-Presse (AFP), then France-Soir; joined TF 1 TV channel, in charge of political news 1972; Ed. in Chief TF 1 1977; apptd. Ed. FR 3 TV channel 1981; Dir. News and Current Affairs, France-Inter 1982; Political Ed. Hebdo (weekly magazine); Tech. Adviser to Prime Minister (Jacques Chirac, q.v.) on Audiovisual Information 1986–88, to Mayor of Paris (Chirac) 1988–94; Man. Dir. Radio-Télévision française d'outre-mer (RFO) 1994–95; mem. Conseil Supérieur de l'audiovisuel (CSA) 1996–. *Address:* Conseil Supérieur de l'Audiovisuel (CSA), Tour Mirabeau, 39–43 quai André Citröen, 75739 Paris cedex 15, France. *Telephone:* (1) 40-58-38-00. *Fax:* (1) 40-58-36-57.

BONNER, Elena Georgievna; Russian human rights activist and writer; b. 25 Feb. 1923, Moscow; m. Andrei Sakharov 1970 (deceased); one s. one d; ed. 1st Leningrad Medical Inst.; active as nurse 1941–45; partially blinded; lieut. 1945; doctor 1953–83; founder of Moscow group to monitor observation of 1975 Helsinki accords; regular visitor to Sakharov during latter's exile in Gorky 1980–84; sentenced to five years' exile 1984, released 1986; political activist after husband's death; Chair. Comm. for perpetuation of Andrei Sakharov's memory. *Publications:* Alone Together 1986 (memoirs), P.S. (post scriptum) 1991.

BONNER, Gerald, M.A., F.S.A.; British university professor; b. 18 June 1926, London; s. of Frederick J. Bonner and Constance E. Hatch; m. Priscilla J. Hodgson 1967; one s. one d.; ed. The Stationers' Co.'s School, London and Wadham Coll. Oxford; mil. service 1944–48; Asst. Keeper, Dept. of Manuscripts, British Museum 1953–64; lecturer in Theology, Univ. of Durham 1964, promoted to personal Readership 1969, Reader Emer. 1989–; Convener and Sec. Bedan Conf. Durham 1973; Distinguished Prof. of Early Christian Studies, Catholic Univ. of America 1991–94; delivered Cathedral Lecture, Durham 1970, Augustine Lecture, Villanova Univ. Pa., 1970, Otts Lectures, Davidson Coll. N.C. 1992; Johannes Quasten Medal 1994. *Publications:* The Warfare of Christ 1962, St. Augustine of Hippo: Life and Controversies 1963, Famulus Christi: Essays in Commemoration of the Thirteenth Centenary of the Venerable Bede (ed.) 1976, God's Decree and Man's Destiny 1987, St. Cuthbert, His Cult and His Community (ed. with D. Rollason and C. Stancliffe), Church and Faith in the Patristic Tradition: Augustine, Pelagianism and Early Christian Northumbria 1996; articles in the Augustinus-Lexikon (Basle) and other learned journals. *Leisure interests:* reading, antiquarianism, (moderate) wine-drinking and any sort of history. *Address:* 7 Victoria Terrace, Durham, DH1 4RW, England. *Telephone:* (0191) 386-3407.

BONNER, John Tyler, PH.D., D.SC.; American biologist; b. 12 May 1920, New York; s. of Paul Hyde Bonner and Lilly Marguerite Stehli; m. Ruth Ann Graham 1942; three s. one d.; ed. Harvard Univ.; U.S. Air Corps 1942–46; Asst. Prof., then Prof., Princeton Univ., N.J. 1947–, George M. Moffett Prof. 1966–, Chair. Dept. of Biology 1965–77, 1983–84, 1987–88, Prof. Emer. June 1990–; Bernard Visiting Prof., Williams Coll. 1989; Raman Visiting Prof., Indian Acad. of Sciences 1990; Sheldon Travelling Fellow, Panama, Cuba 1941; Rockefeller Travelling Fellow, Paris 1953; Guggenheim Fellow, Edin. 1958, 1971–72; Nat. Science Foundation Sr. Postdoctoral Fellow, Cambridge, England 1963; Commonwealth Foundation Book Fund Fellow, Edin. 1971 and 1984–85; Josiah Macy Jr. Foundation Book Fund Fellow, Edin. 1978; Fellow American Acad. of Arts and Sciences, A.A.A.S.; Hon. Fellow Indian Acad. of Sciences; mem. American Philosophical Soc., N.A.S.; mem. Oxford Surveys in Evolutionary Biology 1982–93; fmr. mem. Editorial Bd. American Naturalist, American Scientist and other publs. *Publications:* Morphogenesis: An Essay on Development 1952, Cells and Societies 1955, The Evolution of Development 1958, The Cellular Slime Molds 1959, The Ideas of Biology 1962 (several edns. in transl.), Size and Cycle 1965, The Scale of Nature 1969, On Development: The Biology of Form 1974, The Evolution of Culture in Animals 1980 (several edns. in trans.), On Size and Life 1983, The Evolution of Complexity 1988, Life Cycles 1993, Sixty Years of Biology: Essays on Evolution and Development 1996; Ed. abridged edn. of Growth and Form (D'Arcy Thompson) 1961. *Leisure interests:* fishing, walking. *Address:* Department of Ecology and Evolutionary Biology, Guyot Hall, Princeton University, Princeton, NJ 08544 (Office); 52A Patton Avenue, Princeton, NJ 08540, U.S.A. (Home). *Telephone:* (609) 258-3841 (Office); (609) 924-1255 (Home).

BONNER, Paul Max; British television executive; b. 30 Nov. 1934, Banstead, Surrey; s. of Frank and Jill Bonner; m. Jenifer Hubbard 1956; two s. one d.; ed. Felsted School; with Longmans Green & Co., Publrs. 1952; trainee reporter, Southend Standard 1953; Nat. Service 1953–55; Asst. Press Officer, E.K. Cole Ltd. 1955; freelance work for Evening Standard 1955; Trainee Studio Asst., BBC, Bristol 1955–56, Studio Man. 1956–58, Acting Asst. Producer, Talks Dept., West Region 1958–59, Production Asst., Talks Dept., TV 1961–65, Sr. Producer, Travel and Features Programmes 1965–74, Ed. BBC Community Programmes 1974–77, Special Asst. to Controller BBC2 1977, Chair. Small Integrated Multi-Role Production Unit Study Group 1977, Head of Science and Features Dept., TV 1978–81; Channel Controller, Channel Four TV Co. Ltd. 1981–83, Controller of Programmes and Exec. Dir. 1983–87; Dir. of Programme Planning Secr. ITV Asscn. 1987–92, Dir. ITV Network Centre Secr. 1993–94; Dir. House of Commons Broadcasting Unit Ltd. 1989–94; Chair. Edin. TV Festival 1979; a Man., Royal Inst. 1982–85; Gov. of Nat. Film and TV School 1981–88; Bd. mem., Broadcasting Support Services 1981–93; Chair. Media Group, Cttee. on Public Understanding of Science 1981–93; Fellow Royal TV Soc. *Publications:* The Third Age of Broadcasting 1983, Ind. TV in Britain (Vol. 5: ITV and IBA 1981–92) 1998. *Leisure interests:* photography, sailing, walking.

Address: North View, Wimbledon Common, London, SW19 4UJ, England. *Telephone:* 0171-843 8082.

BONNET, Christian, D. EN D.; French politician and industrialist; b. 14 June 1921, Paris; s. of Pierre Bonnet and Suzanne Delebecque; m. Christiane Mertian 1943; five c. (one s. deceased); ed. Univ. of Paris and Ecole des sciences politiques; Pres. Les Grandes Marques de la conserve 1952–61, Del. Conseil supérieure de la conserve; MRP Deputy for Morbihan 1956–58; Deputy for the second constituency of Morbihan 1956–83; Gen. Councillor, Belle-Ile 1958, 1964, 1970, 1976, 1982; Mayor of Carnac 1964–; fmr. Sec.-Gen. Républicains Indépendants; Chair. Cttee. on the Merchant Marine budget; Pres. Supervisory Council, Caisse des dépots et consignations; Sec. of State for Supply, Housing and Territorial Devt. 1972–74; Minister of Agric. 1974–77, of the Interior 1977–81; Senator for Morbihan 1983. *Address:* Palais du Luxembourg, 75291 Paris Cedex 06 (Office); 56340 Carnac, France (Home).

BONNEY, Barbara; American soprano opera singer; b. 14 April 1956, Montclair, NJ; d. of Alfred Bonney III and Janet Gates; m. 1st Håkan Hagegård 1989; m. 2nd Maurice Whittaker; ed. Univ. of New Hampshire and Mozarteum, Salzburg; maj. appearances include: Der Rosenkavalier, Covent Garden 1984, Metropolitan Opera, New York 1990, Die Zauberflöte, La Scala 1985, Falstaff, Metropolitan Opera 1990, The Marriage of Figaro, Covent Garden 1995; noted especially for Mozart and Strauss interpretations; appears regularly as recitalist accompanied by Geoffrey Parsons; recordings of works by Schönberg, Haydn, R. Strauss, Donizetti, Mozart, Mendelssohn, Wolf etc. *Leisure interests:* textiles, interior decorating, calligraphy. *Address:* c/o IMG, 3 Burlington Lane, Chiswick, London, W4 2TH, England. *Telephone:* 0181-233 5000. *Fax:* 0181-233 5801.

BONNEY, J. Dennis, B.S., LL.M.; American business executive (retd.); b. 22 Dec. 1930, Blackpool, England; s. of John P. Bonney and Isabel Evans; m. Elizabeth Shore-Wilson; four s. two d.; ed. Oxford Univ. and Univ. of California, Berkeley; lawyer (self-employed), Liverpool 1956–59; Exec. Iraq Petroleum Co., London and Baghdad 1959–60; Exec. Standard Oil Co. (now Chevron Corp), San Francisco 1960–, elected Vice-Pres. 1972, Dir. 1986, Vice-Chair. 1987–95. *Leisure interests:* music, tennis, sailing. *Address:* c/o Chevron Corporation, 225 Bush Street, San Francisco, CA 94104, U.S.A. *Telephone:* (415) 894-3232.

BONNICI, Carmelo Mifsud (see Mifsud Bonnici, Carmelo).

BONNICI, Josef, B.A.(HONS.), M.A., PH.D(ECON.); Maltese economist and politician; b. 15 April 1953; m. Rita Oliva; two c.; ed. Univ. of Malta and Simon Fraser Univ., Canada; Sr. Lecturer in Econs. Deakin Univ., Australia; Prof. of Econ. Univ. of Malta 1988; Econ. Advisor to Prime Minister 1988–92; appointed advisor to Council of Europe in Co-ordinated Social Research Programme 1992; mem. Parl. 1992–; Parl. Sec. Ministry of Finance 1993–95; Minister of Econ. Services 1995–96; Shadow Minister and Opposition Spokesman for Econ. Devt. 1996–98; Minister for Econ. Services 1998–; mem. Del. to Org. for Security and Co-operation in Europe, to Council of Europe, Jt. Malta EU Parl. Cttee.; Dr. h.c. (Rikkyo) 1996; Nationalist Party. *Publications:* books and articles on econs. in Malta and in professional econ. journals. *Address:* Ministry for Economic Services, Auberge d'Aragon, Valletta CMR 02, Malta. *Telephone:* 2262637. *Fax:* 226261.

BONNICI, Ugo Mifsud (See Mifsud Bonnici, Ugo).

BONO (b. Paul Hewson); Irish rock singer; b. 10 May 1960; s. of Bobby Hewson and Iris Hewson; m. Alison Stewart 1982; two d.; educ. Mount Temple School; formed band with friends, Dublin 1976, named U2 1978. *Recordings include:* Boy 1980, October 1981, War 1983, Under a Blood Red Sky 1983, The Unforgettable Fire, The Joshua Tree 1987, Desire 1988, Rattle and Hum 1988, When Love Comes to Town 1989, Achtung Baby 1991, The Fly 1991, Stay 1993, Discotheque 1997, The Sweetest Thing 1998; film Rattle and Hum 1988; numerous national and int. tours; Several prizes and awards for recordings and videos. *Address:* c/o Regine Moylett Publicity, First Floor, 145A Ladbroke Grove, London, W10 6HJ, England. *Telephone:* 0171-221 0554. *Fax:* 0171-221 8532.

BONYNGE, Richard, A.O., C.B.E.; Australian conductor; b. 29 Sept. 1930, Sydney; s. of C. A. Bonynge; m. Dame Joan Sutherland (q.v.) 1954; one s.; trained as a pianist; début as conductor with Santa Cecilia Orchestra, Rome 1962; conducted first opera Faust, Vancouver 1963; has conducted in most of leading opera houses; Artistic Dir., Principal Conductor Sutherland/Williamson Int. Grand Opera Co., Australia 1965; Artistic Dir. Vancouver Opera Assen. 1974–78; Musical Dir. Australian Opera 1975–86. Has conducted La Sonnambula, La Traviata, Faust, Eugene Onegin, L'Elisir d'amore, Orfeo 1967, Semiramide, Florence 1968, Giulio Cesare, Lucia di Lammermoor, Hamburg, New York 1969–71, Norma and Orfeo, N.Y. 1970, The Tales of Hoffmann, N.Y. 1973, Sydney Opera House 1974. *Major recordings include:* Alcina, La Sonnambula, Norma, Beatrice di Tenda, I Puritani, Faust, Semiramide, Lakmé, La Fille du Régiment, Messiah, Don Giovanni, Les Huguenots, L'Elisir d'amore, Lucia di Lammermoor, Rigoletto, The Tales of Hoffmann, Thérèse (Massenet), numerous orchestral works, ballet including Giselle, Coppélia, Sylvia, The Nutcracker, Sleeping Beauty, Swan Lake. *Publication:* The Joan Sutherland Album (with Dame Joan Sutherland) 1986. *Address:* c/o Ingpen and Williams, 14 Kensington Court, London W8 5DN, England.

BOOKOUT, John Frank, Jr., M.A.; American petroleum executive; b. 31 Dec. 1922, Shreveport, La.; s. of the late John Frank and Lena (Hagen) Bookout; m. Mary Carolyn Cook 1946; one s. two d.; ed. Centenary Coll., Shreveport, La., Univ. of Texas, Austin, Tex.; joined Shell Oil Co., Geologist, Tulsa, Okla. 1950–59, Man. Exploration Div. 1959–61, Area Exploration Man., Denver, Colo. 1961–63, the Hague, Netherlands 1963–64, Exploration Man., New Orleans 1964, Man. Exploration and Production Econs. Dept., New York 1965, Vice-Pres. Denver Area 1966, Vice-Pres. Southeastern Exploration and Production Region 1967–70; Pres. and Chief Exec. Officer, Shell Canada Ltd. 1970–74; Exec. Vice-Pres. Shell Oil Co. 1974–76, Pres., Dir. and Chief Exec. Officer 1976–87; Dir. Exec. Comm. Shell Petroleum Inc. 1988–; Dir. Royal Dutch Petroleum 1988–93; Dir. Irving Trust Co., Houston Chamber of Commerce, Methodist Hospital, Houston, Safeway Stores Inc., Royal Dutch Shell; mem. Bd. of Visitors Tulane Univ., Southern Regional Advisory Bd. of Inst. of Int. Educ., British-North America Cttee., Geology Foundation Advisory Council of Texas Univ., Man. Cttee. American Petrol Inst., Advisory Cttee. of Houston Reg. Minority Purchasing Council, American Assen. of Petrol Geologists, Business Roundtable, Nat. Petroleum Council, The Conf. Bd., Business Higher Educ. Forum of American Council on Educ.; Trustee U.S. Council of Int. Chambers of Commerce, Foundations for Business, Politics and Econs.; Hon. D.Sc. (Tulane). *Leisure interests:* hunting, fishing. *Address:* 1 Shell Plaza, 900 Louisiana Street, Suite 5050, Houston, TX 77002 (Office); P.O. Box 2463, Houston, TX 77252, U.S.A. (Home).

BOOLELL, Sir Satcam, Kt., Q.C., LL.B.; Mauritian politician; b. 11 Sept. 1920, New Grove; s. of Sahadewoo Boolell and Cossilah Choony; m. 1st Premila K. Inderjeet (died 1986); two s. one d.; m. 2nd Myrtha Poblete; ed. L.S.E., U.K.; called to Bar (Lincoln's Inn) 1952; mem. Legis. Council of Moks-Flacq (Ind.) 1953; joined Labour Party 1955; Minister of Agric. and Natural Resources 1959–67, 1968–82, of Educ. 1967–68, of Econ. Planning and Devt. 1984; Pres. Mauritius Labour Party 1983–92; Deputy Prime Minister, Attorney-Gen., Minister of Justice and of External Affairs and Emigration 1986–87, 1987–90; High Commr. in U.K. 1996– (also accred. to Sweden, Norway, Denmark, Finland and Holy See); Hon. D.C.L. (Univ. of Mauritius) 1985; Commdr. Légion d'honneur 1990. *Publications:* Untold Stories 1996, Reminiscences of Travels Abroad 1998. *Leisure interests:* reading travel literature, walking in the countryside, numismatics. *Address:* Mauritius High Commission, 32-33 Elvaston Place, London, SW7 5NW, England. *Telephone:* 0171-581 0294. *Fax:* 0171-823 8437.

BOOMS, Hans, DR.PHIL.; German historian and archivist; b. 22 June 1924, Haldern/Reis; s. of Theodor Booms and Agnes Kamps; m. 1st Renate Welter 1949; m. 2nd Brigitte Ludwig 1981; one s. two d.; ed. Gymnasium, Emmerich and Univ. of Cologne; Hon. Prof. Univ. of Cologne 1970; Pres. Fed. Archives of Fed. Republic of Germany 1972–; Pres. Int. Council on Archives 1984–88; Bundesverdienstkreuz 1982, Commdr. Ordre de la Couronne de Chêne. *Publications:* historical and archival books and articles. *Address:* Potsdamerstrasse 1, 56075 Koblenz (Office); Emser Landstrasse 9, 56112 Lahnstein, Germany (Home). *Telephone:* 0261-505-200 (Office); 02621-7845 (Home).

BOOMSTRA, Sjoerd, D.JUR.; Netherlands financial executive; b. 12 Sept. 1913, Rotterdam; m. Henny Brons 1954; two c.; ed. secondary school, Bandung, Indonesia, Univ. of Leiden; Netherlands Clearing Inst. and Deviezen Inst. 1938; joined Ministry of Finance 1945, Deputy Dir., then Dir. External Finance 1953; Vice-Pres. EIB 1970–76, Hon. Vice-Pres. 1976–. *Address:* Ridderlaan 23, The Hague, Netherlands. *Telephone:* 3244167.

BOON, David Clarence, M.B.E.; Australian cricketer; b. 29 Dec. 1960, Launceston, s. of Clarence Leonard Boon and Lesley Mary Boon; m. Philippa Louise Wright 1983; one s. two d.; ed. Launceston Church Grammar School; right-hand batsman; teams: Tasmania 1978–79 to 1998/99 (Capt. 1992–93 to 1998/99), Durham, England (Capt.) 1997–, for Australia played 107 test matches 1984–96, scoring 7,422 runs (average 43.6) including 21 hundreds and holding 99 catches; toured England 1985, 1989 and 1993; by Oct. 1998 had scored 22,314 first-class runs (67 hundreds); 181 limited-overs internationals; Marketing Man. Trust Bank Australia 1991–; Patron Road Trauma Support Group, World Vision, Int. Cricketer of the Year 1987. *Publications:* In the Firing Line (with A. Mark Thomas). Under the Southern Cross (autobiog.) 1996. *Leisure interests:* gardening, golf. *Address:* Trust Bank, Level 1A, 79 St. John Street, Launceston, Tasmania 7250; c/o Australian Cricket Board, 90 Jollimont Street, Vic. 3002, Australia; c/o Durham County Cricket Club, County Ground, Riverside, Chester-le-street, Co. Durham, DH3 3QR, England.

BOONZAIER, Hugh Murray; South African stockbroker; b. 31 July 1933, Cape Town; m. Helen Mary Liebenberg 1961; one s. one d.; ed. Observatory Boys' High School and Univ. of Cape Town; qualified as chartered accountant 1956; Accountant, Cape Portland Cement, various jobs, London, England, Man. Trainee, Alcan Aluminium, Pietermaritzburg, then Johannesburg; became mem. Johannesburg Stock Exchange (J.S.E.) 1963, mem. Cttee. 1974–86, Pres. 1985–86; Dir. J. D. Anderson & Co. Inc. 1963–93, Allied Bldg. Soc. 1986–90, African Cables Ltd. 1987–90, Allied Group Ltd. 1988–90, Allied Bank Ltd. 1988–90, Allied Insurance Ltd. 1988–90; Non-broking mem. Davis Borkum Hare 1993–; Hon. Life mem. J.S.E. 1986. *Address:* Box 2269, Cape Town 8001, South Africa.

BOORMAN, John, C.B.E.; British film director, producer and screenwriter; b. 18 Jan. 1933; s. of George and Ivy (Chapman) Boorman; m. Christel Kruse

1956; one s. three d.; ed. Salesian Coll., Chertsey; Broadcaster and critic, BBC Radio, also contributor to Manchester Guardian and magazines 1950–54; army service 1951–53; Film Editor, ITN London 1955–58; Dir. and Producer Southern TV 1958–60; Head of Documentaries, Bristol, BBC TV; left BBC to work as film director; Chair. Nat. Film Studios of Ireland 1975–85; Gov. British Film Inst. 1983–94; Best Director Prize, Cannes Festival 1970, 1998, many film awards; Chevalier de l'Ordre des Arts et Lettres 1985. *Television:* founded magazine Day by Day, Dir. The Citizen 1963, The Newcomers 1960–64. *Films:* Catch us if you Can 1965, Point Blank 1967, Hell in the Pacific 1968, Leo the Last 1969, Deliverance 1970, Zardoz 1973, The Heretic 1976, Excalibur 1981, The Emerald Forest 1985, Hope and Glory 1987 (Golden Globe Award 1988), Where the Heart Is 1989, I Dreamt I Woke Up 1991, Beyond Rangoon 1994, Two Nudes Bathing 1995, The General 1998. *Publications:* The Legend of Zardoz 1973 (novel), Money into Light 1985, Hope into Light 1987, Projections 1 1992, Projections 2 1993, Projections 3 1994, Projections 4½ (Co.-ed.) 1995, Projections 5 1996, Projections 6 1997, Projections 7 1997, Projections 8 1998; co-ed. A Year in Film 1993. *Leisure interests:* hacking the Wicklow Hills, losing gracefully at tennis, skiing in the wake of my kids. *Address:* Merlin Films, 16 Upper Pembroke Street, Dublin 2, Ireland. *Telephone:* (1) 6764376. *Fax:* (1) 6764368.

BOORSTIN, Daniel J., M.A., LL.D.; American historian, author and administrator; b. 1 Oct. 1914, Atlanta, Ga.; s. of late Samuel Boorstin and Dora Olsan; m. Ruth Carolyn Frankel 1941; three s.; ed. Harvard Coll., Balliol Coll., Oxford, Cambridge and Yale Univs.; Harvard Coll. and Harvard Law School 1938–42; Office of Lend-Lease Admin., Washington 1942; Asst. Prof., Swarthmore Coll. 1942–44; Prof. of American History and Preston and Sterling Morton Distinguished Service Prof. of History, Univ. of Chicago 1944–69; Prof. American History, Univ. of Paris 1961–62; Pitt Prof. American History and Institutions and Fellow, Trinity Coll. Cambridge 1964–65; Dir. Nat. Museum of History and Tech. 1969–73; mem. Comm. on Critical Choices for Americans 1973–; Shelby and Kathryn Cullom Davis Lecturer, Graduate Inst. of Int. Studies, Geneva 1973–74; Senior Historian Smithsonian Inst., Washington, D.C. 1973–75; The Librarian of Congress 1975–87, Librarian Emer. 1987–; mem. Bd. Trustees Colonial Williamsburg, Bd. Dirs. Thomas Gilcrease Museum, Comm. on Critical Choices for Americans, Bd. Editors Encyclopedia Britannica; mem. task force on exploration NASA 1989–91, NASA Task Force on Exploration 1989, Cafritz Foundation Bd. of Dirs. 1991; numerous hon. degrees; Pulitzer Prize for History 1974, and several other prizes; Chevalier Légion d'honneur 1984, Grand Officer of the Order of Prince Henry the Navigator (Portugal) 1985, Japanese Order of the Sacred Treasure, (First Class) 1986, Watson-Davis Prize of the History of Science (Soc. for Discoverers) 1986, Charles Frankel Prize of the Nat. Endowment for the Humanities 1989, Nat. Book Award Medal for Distinguished Contribution to American Letters 1989. *Publications include:* The Mysterious Science of the Law 1941, Delaware Cases 1792-1830 (3 vols.) 1943, The Lost World of Thomas Jefferson 1948, The Genius of American Politics 1953, The Americans: The Colonial Experience 1958, America and the Image of Europe 1960, The Image or What Happened to the American Dream 1962, The Americans: The National Experience 1965, The Landmark History of the American People (2 vols.) 1968, 1970, The Decline of Radicalism 1969, The Sociology of the Absurd 1970, The Americans: The Democratic Experience 1973, Democracy and its Discontents 1974, The Exploring Spirit 1976, The Republic of Technology 1978, A History of the United States (with Brooks Kelley) 1980, The Discoverers 1983, Hidden History 1987, The Creators 1992, Cleopatra's Nose 1994, The Daniel J. Boorstin Reader 1995; Ed.: An American Primer 1966, American Civilization 1972, The Seekers 1998. *Leisure interests:* gardening, bird watching, hiking. *Address:* Library of Congress, Washington, DC 20540 (Office); 3541 Ordway Street, N.W., Washington, DC 20016, U.S.A. (Home). *Telephone:* (202) 707-1500 (Office); (202) 966-1853 (Home).

BOOS, Georgy Valentinovich; Russian politician; b. 22 Jan. 1963, Moscow; m.; one d.; ed. Moscow Energy Inst.; sr. engineer, All-Union Research Inst. of Light Tech., also teacher of math., secondary school 1986–91; f., Dir.-Gen., then Pres., Svetoservis Co. 1991–96; mem. State Duma 1996–98; Head, State Taxation Service of Russian Fed. Sept.–Dec. 1998; Minister of Revenue Dec. 1998–; Pres., Nat. Soc. of Light Tech.; designer of architectural illumination of Moscow 1996; State Prize. *Address:* Ministry of Revenue, Neglinnaya str. 23, 103381 Moscow, Russia. *Telephone:* (095) 925 4847 (Office).

BOOTH, Cherie, Q.C., LL.D., F.R.S.A.; British barrister; b. 23 Sept. 1954, Bury, Lancs.; d. of Anthony Booth and Gale Booth (née Smith); m. Anthony Charles Lynton Blair (Tony Blair, q.v.); two s. one d.; ed. Seafield Grammar School, Crosby, Liverpool, L.S.E.; called to Bar (Lincoln's Inn) 1976; pupillage with Alexander Irvine (now Lord Irvine of Lairg, q.v.) 1976–77; Tenant New Court Chambers 1977–91, 4/5 Gray's Inn Square, London 1991–; appointed Q.C. April 1995; Asst. Recorder 1996–; Gov. London School of Econs. 1998–; Fellow John Moores Univ., Liverpool (Chancellor 1998–). *Leisure interests:* reading, working out, the arts. *Address:* 4/5 Gray's Inn Square, Gray's Inn, London, WC1R 5AY, England.

BOOTH, Chris; New Zealand sculptor; b. 30 Dec. 1948, Kerikeri, Bay of Islands; m.; one s.; ed. Ilam School of Fine Arts, Univ. of Canterbury, Christchurch; undertook specialist sculpture studies with Barbara Hepworth, Denis Mitchell, John Milne and Quinto Ghermandi 1968–70; numerous solo and collective exhbns.; represented in public and pvt. collections; mem. Artists Alliance, N.Z.; int. mem. Royal Soc. of British Sculptors 1990–; Christchurch/Seattle Sister City Comm. Award 1996, Nillumbik Art in Public Places Award 1997, Greenham Common Trust Award 1998; Winner 10th Millfield Int. Sculpture Comm., Somerset, England 1998, Artists in Industry Project, Victoria, Australia 1998. *Television documentaries include:* When a Warrior Dies 1991, documentary on bombing of Greenpeace ship Rainbow Warrior 1995, Sculpture in the Park 1996. *Publications include:* Chris Booth Sculpture 1993, Balanced Stone 1998. *Address:* 192 Stone Store Hill, Kerikeri, Bay of Islands, New Zealand. *Telephone:* (9) 407-9769. *Fax:* (9) 407-5359.

BOOTHROYD, Rt. Hon. Betty, P.C., M.P.; British politician; b. 8 Oct. 1929, Dewsbury, Yorks.; d. of Archibald Boothroyd and Mary Boothroyd; ed. Dewsbury Coll of Commerce and Art; sec. Labour Party H.Q. 1955–60; legis. asst. to U.S. congressman, Washington, D.C. 1960–62; sec. and personal asst. to various sr. Labour politicians 1962–73; mem. Hammersmith Borough Council 1965–68; contested various elections and by-elections 1957–70; mem. Parl. for W. Bromwich 1973, for W. Bromwich West 1974–92; Asst. Govt. Whip 1974–76; mem. Labour Party Nat. Exec. 1981–87; a Deputy Speaker 1987–92; Speaker of the House of Commons 1992–; Chancellor Open Univ. 1994–; several hon. degrees from British univs. including Hon. D.C.L. (Oxford) 1995. *Address:* Speaker's House, Westminster, London, SW1A 0AA, England.

BORCHERS, Elisabeth; German editor; b. 27 Feb. 1926, Homberg; d. of Rudolf Sarbin and Claire (née Beck) Sarbin; m. (divorced); two s.; Ed. Luchterhand 1960–71, Suhrkamp Verlag and Insel Verlag 1971–; mem. PEN, Acad. of Sciences and Literature, Mainz, Acad. of Language and Poetry, Darmstadt; Erzahlerpreis Suddeutscher Rundfunk, German Industry Culture Prize, Roswitha-Gedenk-Medaille 1976, Friedrich-Hölderlin-Preis 1986. *Publications:* poetry, prose, translations, children's books. *Address:* Arndtstrasse 17, 60325 Frankfurt, Germany. *Telephone:* (069) 74 63 91.

BORCHERT, Jochen; German politician; b. 25 April 1940, Nahrstedt, Kreis Stendal; m.; two c.; ed. studies in agric. and econs.; mem. Christian Democratic Union (CDU) 1965–; mem. Bochum City Council 1976–80; mem. Bundestag 1980–, Vice-Pres. Farmers' Assn., Westfalen-Lippe; Chair. Absatzforderungsfonds der Deutschen Land- und Ernährungswirtschaft; CDU/CSU Spokesman on Budgetary Policy in Bundestag; Minister of Agric. Food and Forestry 1993–98; Fed. Chair. Protestant Working Group CDU/CSU, mem. Fed. Bd. CDU. *Address:* c/o Bundesministerium für Ernährung, Landwirtschaft und Forsten, Rochusstrasse 1, 53123 Bonn, Germany.

BORD, André; French politician; b. 30 Nov. 1922, Strasbourg; s. of Alphonse Bord and Marie-Anne Sigrist; m. 1st Germaine Fend (deceased); two s.; m. 2nd Francine Heisserer 1981; ed. Saint-Etienne Coll., Strasbourg; mem. of Nat. Assembly 1958–66, 1967, 1968, 1973, 1978; mem. Municipal Council, Strasbourg 1959–89, Deputy Mayor 1959–81; mem. Conseil Général, Strasbourg-Est 1961-79, of Strasbourg 8 1973–79; Pres. Corbeil-Général du Bas-Rhin 1967–79; Pres. Groupe de l'Union démocratique européenne, European Parl. 1961–66, mem. European Parl. 1982–84; Sec. of State for Interior 1966–72, for Ex-Servicemen and War Victims 1972–77, for Relations with Parl. 1977–78; Sec.-Gen. UDR 1975–76; Founder, Pres. Asscn. for Industrial Devt., Alsace 1967; Pres. Regional Council of Alsace 1973–77, Commission Interministérielle de Coopération France–République Fédérale d'Allemagne 1986–; Médaille militaire, Médaille de la France libre, Médaille de la Résistance; Croix de guerre avec palme; Grand Officer, Order of Orange-Nassau (Netherlands), Order of Polonia Restituta (Poland), Officier Légion d'honneur, and others. *Address:* Ministry of Foreign Affairs, 23 rue Lapérouse, 75775 Paris, cedex 16; 27 route de Wolfisheim, 67810 Holtzheim, France.

BORDABERRY AROCENA, Juan María; Uruguayan politician; b. 17 June 1928, Montevideo; s. of Domingo Bordaberry and Elisa Arocena de Bordaberry; m. Josefina Herrán Puig; seven s. one d.; ed. Univ. Montevideo; Chair., Nat. Meat Bd. 1959; mem. Hon. Comm. for Agric. Devt. Plan 1960; mem. Nat. Wool Bd. 1960–62; Chair. Comm. Against Foot and Mouth Disease 1962; mem. Senate 1962–64; Chair. Liga Federal de Acción Ruralista 1964; Minister of Agric. 1969–72; Pres. of Uruguay 1972–76 (deposed). *Address:* Joaquín Suárez 2868, Montevideo, Uruguay. *Telephone:* 20-14-12.

BORDER, Allan Robert, A.O.; Australian cricketer; b. 27 July 1955, Cremorne, Sydney; s. of John and Sheila Border; m. Jane Hiscox 1980; two s.; ed. Mosman Primary School, N. Sydney Tech. School, N. Sydney Boys' High School; fmr. clerk; work in motor trade; left-hand middle-order batsman, left-arm slow bowler; teams: N.S.W. 1976–80, Glos., England 1977 (1 match), Queensland 1980–96 (Capt. 1983–89), Essex, England 1986–88; Capt. Australian Nat. Team 1984–94; 156 (record) Tests for Australia 1978–94, including record unbroken sequence of 153 matches, record 93 (unbroken sequence 1984–94) as Capt., scoring 11,174 runs (average 50.5) including 27 hundreds, and then holding record 156 catches; scored 27,131 first-class runs (70 hundreds); toured England 1979 (World Cup), 1980, 1981, 1983 (World Cup), 1985, 1989, 1993 (last three as Capt.); then record 273 limited-overs internationals, record 178 as Capt.; with Ronald McConnell Holdings 1980–84; with Castlemaine Perkins 1984–. *Publication:* A Peep at the Poms 1986. *Address:* c/o Australian Cricket Board, 90 Jolimont Street, Jolimont, Vic. 3002, Australia.

BORDIER, Roger; French writer; b. 5 March 1923; s. of Robert Bordier and Valentine Jeufraux; m. Jacqueline Bouchaud; ed. secondary school; journalist in the provinces, later in Paris; contributor to Nouvelles Littéraires and Aujourd'hui; radio and television writer; Prix Renaudot 1961. *Publications:* poems: Les épicentres 1951; novels: La cinquième saison 1959, Les blés 1961, Le mime 1963, L'Entracte 1965, Un âge d'or 1967, Le tour de ville 1969, Les éventails 1971, L'océan 1974, Meeting 1976, Demain l'été 1977; plays: Les somnambules 1963, Les visiteurs 1972; essays: L'objet contre l'art 1972, Le progrès: Pour qui? 1973, L'art moderne et l'objet 1978; novels: La grande vie 1981, Les temps heureux 1983, La longue file 1984, 36 La fête 1985, La belle de mai 1986, Les saltimvanques de la Révolution 1989, Vel d'hib 1989, Les fusils du 1er Mai 1991, Chroniques de la Cité Joyeuse 1995. *Address:* 8 rue Geoffroy St. Hilaire, 75005 Paris, France. *Telephone:* 535-22-56.

BORDYUZHA, Col.-Gen. Nikolai Nikolayevich; Russian politician; b. 22 Oct. 1949, Orel; m.; one s.; service in army and state security forces 1972–91; First Deputy Head, Personnel dept., Fed. Agency of Govt. Communications and Information of Russian Presidency 1991–92; Deputy Commdr., Frontier Forces 1992–95; Deputy Dir., Fed. Frontier Service, C.-in-C., Frontier Forces 1995–98; mem. Russian Security Council March 1998–, Sec. Sept. 1998–, Head Office of the Pres. Dec. 1998–. *Address:* Security Council of Russian Federation, Ipatyevsky per. 4/10, entr. 6, Moscow, Russia. *Telephone:* (095) 206 4396 (Office).

BOREL, Jacques; French writer, teacher and critic; b. 17 Dec. 1925, Paris; s. of Pierre Borel and Lucie Dubée; m. Christiane Idrac 1948; one s. four d.; ed. Lycée Henri IV, Paris and Univ. de Paris; teacher, Lycée de Clermont-Ferrand 1952–56, Lycée Rodin, Paris 1956–67; Visiting Prof. Middlebury Coll. 1966, Portland State Coll. 1967, Univ. of Hawaii 1968, Univ. of Calif. (Irvine) 1969, Univ. of Calif. (Riverside) 1980, Univ. of N.Y. 1983; Literary Adviser Gallimard 1969–75, Balland 1978–82; Cultural Attaché, French Embassy in Belgium 1984–86; contributes poems and essays to Nouvelle Revue Française, Critique, Cahiers du Chemin, Mercure de France, Botteghe Oscure, Cahiers du Sud, Figaro, etc.; Prix Goncourt 1965, Grand Prix Société des Gens de Lettres pour l'ensemble de l'oeuvre 1993; Chevalier Arts et Lettres 1971, Officier 1986. *Publications:* Ed.: Verlaine's Complete Works 1959–60, Poetical Works 1962, Complete Works in Prose 1972; novels: L'adoration 1965, Le retour 1970, Histoire de mes vieux habits 1979, Le déferlement 1993; play: Tata ou de l'éducation 1967; essays: Marcel Proust 1972, Commentaires 1974, Poésie et nostalgie 1979, Sur les poètes 1998, L'effacement 1998; diaries: La dépossession 1973, Un voyage ordinaire 1975; autobiography: Petite histoire de mes rêves 1981, L'Aven Différé 1997; Short stories: L'attente 1989, La clôture 1989, Commémorations 1990; Poems: Sur les murs du temps 1990; Translated: James Joyce's The Cat and the Devil 1966, Collected Poems 1967, Prefaces to Romanciers au travail 1967, Du Bellay's Poetical Works 1967, Guillevic's Terraqué 1968, Fargue's Vulturne and Epaisseurs 1971, Francis Jammes' De l'Angélus de l'aube à l'Angélus du soir 1971, Verlaine's Poèmes Saturniens, Fêtes galantes, Romances sans paroles 1973, Victor Hugo: Choix de poèmes 1983, Paroles écrites 1986, L'enfant voyeur 1987, Lettres d'Europe 1988. *Address:* 22 rue Charles de Gaulle, 91440 Bures-sur-Yvette, Essonne; 68 rue du Moulin, 91120 Palaiseau, Essonne, France. *Telephone:* 01 69 07 57 29; 01 60 10 33 57.

BOREL, Jacques Paul; French restaurant and hotel executive; b. 9 April 1927, Courbevoie; s. of William and Marie (née Le Monnier) Borel; m. Christiane Roubit 1949; two s. one d.; ed. Lycées Condorcet and Carnot, Paris, Ecole des Hautes Etudes Commerciales; mem. Sales Force IBM France 1950–57, Man. Saigon (Viet Nam) Branch Office IBM; Founder Restaurant Chain Jacques Borel 1957, became Compagnie des Restaurants Jacques Borel (CRJB) 1960, then Jacques Borel Int. (J.B. Int.) 1970, Pres., Dir.-Gen. –1977; Pres. J.B. Enterprises Soc. 1977; Dir. Sofitel Jacques Borel, Jacques Borel Belgie NV-Belgique SA, Jacques Borel Do Brasil, Jacques Borel Deutschland, Jacques Borel Italia, Jacques Borel Nederland, Jacques Borel Iran, Jacques Borel Misr (Egypt), Jacques Borel Venezuela, Hoteles Jacques Borel (Barcelona), Farah Maghreb (Casablanca); Founder Syndicat Nat. des Restaurants Economiques 1966, become Syndicat Nat. des Chaînes d'Hôtels et de Restaurants de Tourisme et d'Entreprise 1970, Pres. until 1972, then Founder-Pres.; Pres. Groupement HEC Tourisme-Hôtellerie. *Leisure interests:* music, painting, sailing. *Address:* 100 avenue du Président Kennedy, 75016 Paris, France.

BOREN, David L., M.A., J.D.; American politician and lawyer; b. 21 April 1941, Washington, D.C.; s. of Lyle H. and Christine (McKown) Boren; m. 1st; one s. one d.; m. 2nd Molly W. Shi 1977; ed. Yale, Oxford and Oklahoma Univs. Rhodes Scholar 1965; mem. Okla. House of Reps. 1966–74; Chair. Govt. Dept., Okla. Baptist Univ. 1969–74; Gov. of Okla. 1975–79; Senator from Okla. 1979–94; Pres. Univ. of Okla. 1994–. *Leisure interests:* family, reading, rowing, tennis. *Address:* University of Oklahoma, 660 Parrington Oval, Norman, OK 73019; 750 West Boyd, Norman, OK 73019, U.S.A. (Home).

BORG, Alan Charles Nelson, C.B.E., PH.D., F.S.A.; British museum director; b. 21 Jan. 1942; s. of late Charles J. N. Borg and Frances M. O. Hughes; m. 1st Anne Blackmore 1964 (divorced); one s. one d.; m. 2nd Lady Caroline Hill 1976; two d.; ed. Westminster School, Brasenose Coll. Oxford and Courtauld Inst. of Art; lecteur d'anglais, Univ. d'Aix-Marseille 1964–65; lecturer History of Art, Ind. Univ. 1967–69; Asst. Prof. of History of Art, Princeton Univ. 1969–70; Asst. Keeper of the Armouries, H.M. Tower of London 1970–78; Keeper, Sainsbury Centre for Visual Arts, Univ. of E. Anglia 1978–82; Dir.-Gen. Imperial War Museum 1982–95; Chair. Nat. Inventory of War Memorials 1988–95, Advisory Cttee. on Public Records 1993; Dir. Vic. and Albert Museum Oct. 1995–; Pres. Elizabethan Club 1994–. *Publications include:* Architectural Sculpture in Romanesque Provence 1972, European Swords and Daggers in the Tower of London 1974, Torture and Punishment 1975, Heads and Horses 1976, Arms and Armour in Britain 1979, The Vanishing Past 1981, War Memorials 1991; articles in learned journals. *Leisure interests:* fencing, music, travel. *Address:* Victoria and Albert Museum, Cromwell Road, London, SW7 2RL; Telegraph House, 36 West Square, London, SE11 4SP, England.

BORG, Björn Rune; Swedish tennis player and business executive; b. 6 June 1956, Södertälje; s. of Rune Borg; m. 1st Mariana Simionescu 1980 (divorced 1984); one s. by Jannike Bjorling; m. 2nd Loredana Berte 1989 (divorced 1992); ed. Blombacka School; professional player since 1972; Italian Champion 1974, 1978; French Champion 1974, 1975, 1978, 1979, 1980, 1981; Wimbledon Champion 1976, 1977, 1978, 1979, 1980 (runner-up 1981); WCT Champion 1976; Grand Prix Masters Champion 1980, 1981; World Champion 1979, 1980; played Davis Cup for Sweden 1972, 1973, 1974, 1975, 1976, 1977, 1978, 1979, 1980; Winner Stockholm Open 1980; announced retirement from tennis Jan. 1983; returned to competitive tennis Feb. 1992; f. Björn Borg Enterprises Ltd. *Publication:* Bjorn Borg—My Life and Game (with Eugene Scott) 1980. *Leisure interest:* fishing. *Address:* c/o International Management Group, The Pier House, Strand on the Green, Chiswick, London W4 3NN, England.

BORG, Kim, M.SC.; Finnish singer; b. 7 Aug. 1919, Helsinki; s. of Kaarlo Borg and Hilkka Stenius; m. Ebon Ringblom 1950; one s. one d.; ed. Helsinki Inst. of Technology and Sibelius-Acad., Helsinki. Début, Helsinki 1945; Royal Theatre, Copenhagen 1952–70; Finnish Nat. Opera 1952–70; Munich State Opera 1956–57; Glyndebourne Opera Co. 1956, 1959 and 1968; Metropolitan Opera Co., New York 1959–62; Royal Theatre, Stockholm 1963–75; Hamburg State Opera 1964–69; Prof. Royal Conservatory, Copenhagen 1972–89; guest appearances at State Opera, Vienna and Bolshoi Theatre, Moscow; tours in Europe, N. and S. America, Asia, Australia and Africa; numerous recordings; composed chamber music and orchestral music; Chair. Det danske Sangselskab 1972–82; mem. Bd. Dirs. Danish-Finnish Soc.; Dr. h.c.; Commdr. Finnish Lion; Cross of Liberty (Finland); Kt. of White Rose (Finland); Kt. of Dannebrog (Denmark); Pro-Finlandia Medal; Hon. Cross for Arts and Sciences (Austria), Commdr. of North Star (Sweden), Sibelius Medal, Finnish Mil. Medal. *Leisure interests:* Scandinavian co-operation, literature. *Publications:* Suomalainen laulajanaapinen (ABC for the Finnish singer) 1972, Muistelmia (memoirs) 1992. *Address:* Österbrogade 158, 2100 Copenhagen, Denmark. *Telephone:* 39290731; 42190027.

BORG, Per O.; Swedish businessman and civil servant; b. 27 Sept. 1943; m. Kerstin Borg Wallin; two c.; ed. Univ. of Gothenburg; served Ministry of Finance 1969–71, Ministry of Commerce 1971–78, of Defence 1978–81; Man. Dir. IMPOD 1981–82; Under-Sec. of Defence 1982–88; Dir. Gen. FMV 1988–. *Leisure interests:* opera, sailing, skiing. *Address:* FMV, 115 88 Stockholm, Sweden. *Telephone:* 46 8 782 6350.

BORG, Tonio, LL.D.; Maltese politician and lawyer; b. 12 May 1957; s. of Carmelo Borg and Maria Gemma Zarb; m. Adele Galea 1982; one s. two d.; ed. St. Aloysius Coll. and Univ. of Malta; lecturer in Public Law, Univ. of Malta; exec. mem. of European Union Young Christian Democrats 1983–85; Dir. Mid-Med Bank 1987–92; Pres. of Nationalist Party Gen. Council 1988; mem. of European Cttee. for Prevention of Torture and Inhuman or Degrading Punishment or Treatment 1990–95; M.P. 1992–; mem. Planning Authority 1992–95; mem. of Council of Europe Ass. 1992–96; mem. Jt. Parl. Cttee of the European Parl. and Maltese House of Reps. 1992–95, 1996–98; Minister for Home Affairs 1995–96, 1998; Nationalist Party. *Leisure interests:* reading, cycling. *Address:* Ministry for Home Affairs, Casa Leoni, 476 St. Joseph High Road, St. Venera, HMR 18, Malta. *Telephone:* 485100-5. *Fax:* 493744.

BORGE, Victor; American entertainer; b. 3 Jan. 1909, Copenhagen; s. of Bernhard and Frederikke (née Lichtinger) Borge; m. Sarabel Sgaper; two s. three d. (including one s. and one d. by previous marriage); ed. Borgerdydskolen and Copenhagen Conservatoire, and in Berlin and Vienna under Frederic Lamond and Egon Petri; concert pianist 1922–34; revue, theatre and film career as composer, actor and musical comedian 1934–; numerous stage, TV and radio appearances in U.S.A., Europe, Australia, N.Z., Far East; guest conductor numerous orchestras; Nat. Chair. CARE Pub. Service Cttee., Multiple Sclerosis Soc.; settled in U.S.A. 1940, U.S. citizen 1948; Hon. D. Mus. (Butler Univ., Dana Coll., Neb.); Order of Dannebrog, Order of Vasa (Sweden) 1972, Order of St. Olav (Norway) 1973, Order of the White Rose (Finland) 1981. *Publication:* My Favourite Intervals 1974. *Leisure interest:* boating. *Address:* Field Point Park, Greenwich, CT 06830; c/o Gurtman & Murtha Associates, 450 7th Avenue, 603, New York, NY 10123, U.S.A.

BORGE MARTÍNEZ, Tomás; Nicaraguan politician, writer and journalist; b. 13 Aug. 1930, Matagalpa; s. of Tomás Borge Delgado and Ana Martínez Rivera; m. 1st Yelba Mayorga (assassinated by Nat. Guard 1979); m. 2nd Josefina Cerda; eight d.; ed. Nat. Univ. León and Granada; first took part in activities against Somoza 1943, sentenced to eight years in prison 1956, escaped 1958, founder Frente Sandinista de Liberación Nacional (FSLN) 1961, guerrrilla leader in Río Coco-Bocay, Pancasán and in clandestine struggle in the cities, captured by Somoza's agents 1976 and sentenced to 180 years of imprisonment, suffered torture and thirty months isolation, liberated in 1978 after attack on Nat. Palace; mem. Nat. Directorate FSLN 1978–; Minister of the Interior 1979–90, Adjoint Commdr. Armed Forces, First Vice-Pres. Perm. Conference of Political Parties in Latin America (COPPPAL); founder Espartaco (magazine) 1946 and El Universitario (newspaper) 1950; Dr. h.c. Autonomous Univ. of Puebla, Mexico 1981; jury mem. Festival of New Latin Amercian Film 1990, House of Americas Award 1991. *Publications:* Carlos, el Amanecer ya no es una Tentación 1979, Los Primeros Pasos 1981, Estamos Creando una Nueva Sociedad 1981, La Mujer en la Revolución 1983, La Revolución Combate Contra la Teología de la Muerte 1983, El Axioma de la Esperanza 1984, Nicaragua: Justicia y Revolución 1986, Cristianismo y Revolución 1987, Una Relación Mágica 1989, La Paciente Impaciencia (House of America Award) 1989, La Ceremonia Esperada 1990. *Leisure interest:* film. *Address:* Apartado 1229, Managua, Nicaragua. *Telephone:* 43853-52.

BORGEAUD, Pierre, DIPL.ENG; Swiss business executive; b. 31 March 1934; m.; three c.; ed. Swiss Fed. Inst. of Tech.; Research Dept. of Sulzer Bros. Ltd 1959–73, Man. of Sulzer Eng. Works and of Swiss Locomotive and Machine Works, Winterthur 1973–75, Gen. Man., Sulzer Bros. Ltd. (now Sulzer Man. Ltd.) 1975–81, Pres., C.E.O. 1981–88 (Chair. 1988–); Chair. Presidential Bd. of Swiss Fed. of Commerce and Industry 1987–93; mem. Bd. of Dirs. Winterthur Insurance Co., Swiss Bank Corpn., Bühler Ltd., Pirelli Int. Ltd. *Address:* Sulzer Ltd., Zuercherstr. 12, CH-8401 Winterthur, Switzerland. *Telephone:* (052) 262 20 91. *Fax:* (052) 262 01 25.

BORGEN, Kjell; Norwegian politician; b. 21 Oct. 1939, Oslo; m.; Municipal Projects Leader and local Mayor 1968–77; mem. Storting 1977; Chair. Standing Cttee. on Communications 1981–85; Vice-Chair. Standing Cttee. on Local Govt. and the Environment, until 1986; Minister of Communications 1986–88, of Local Govt. 1988–89, 1990–92. *Address:* c/o Ministry of Local Government, Møllergt. 43, P.O. Box 8112, Dep., 0030 Oslo 1, Norway.

BORGES, Jacobo; Venezuelan painter; b. 28 Nov. 1931; ed. Escuela de Artes Plásticas Cristóbal Rojas, Caracas and Ecole des Beaux Arts, Paris; mem. of Young Painters' Group and Illustrator of magazines and record covers while in Paris 1951–56, also exhibited in French Nat. Exhbns.; Prof. of Scenography and Plastic Analysis, Escuela de Artes Plásticas Cristóbal Rojas, Caracas 1958–65; Prof. of Scenography, Theatre School of Valencia and Dir. Experimental Art Centre, Univ. Central de Venezuela 1966–; one-man exhbns. in Caracas at Galeria Lauro 1956, Museo de Bellas Artes 1956, Galeria G 1963 and Galeria Techo 1965; represented in numerous group exhbns. including São Paulo Bienal 1957, 1963, 1965, Venice Biennale 1958, Brussels World Fair 1958, and Int. Exhbns. at Guggenheim Museum, New York 1964, 1965; Nat. Painting Prize 1963, Armando Reverón Bienal Prize 1965. *Major works:* La Lámpara y la Silla 1951, La Pesca 1957, Sala de Espera 1960, Todos a la Fiesta 1962, Ha Comenzado el Espectáculo 1964, Altas Finanzas 1965; series of Las Jugadoras and Las Comedoras de Helados 1965–66. *Address:* c/o Museo de Bellas Artes, Avenida los Caobos, Caracas, Venezuela.

BORGNINE, Ernest; American actor; b. 24 Jan. 1917, Hamden, Conn.; s. of Charles B. and Anna (née Baselli) Borgnine; m. Tova Newman 1972; ed. New Haven public schools, Randall School of Dramatic Arts, Hartford; *Films include:* From Here to Eternity, Bad Day at Black Rock, Marty, Violent Saturday, Square Jungle, Three Brave Men, Hell Below, The Rabbit Trap, Man on String, Barabbas, Flight of the Phoenix 1966, The Oscar 1966, The Split, Ice Station Zebra, The Dirty Dozen 1968, Willard 1971, The Poseidon Adventure 1972, Emperor of the North 1972, Sunday in the Country 1974, Law and Disorder 1975, Convoy 1978, Goin' South 1979, The Black Hole 1980, All Quiet on the Western Front 1980, Last Days of Pompeii 1984, Dirty Dozen: The Next Mission 1985, Any Man's Death 1990, Mistress 1992; numerous TV appearances including Little House on the Prairie, Love Boat, Murder She Wrote; Acad. Award for Best Performance in Marty 1956.

BORGOMEO, Rev. Pasquale, S.J., D.LIT.; Italian ecclesiastic; b. 20 March 1933, Naples; s. of Vincenzo Borgomeo and Letizia De Meo; ed. Pontano Coll.; entered Soc. of Jesus 1948; ordained Priest 1963; Ed.-in-Chief Vatican Radio 1970–78, Programme Dir. 1978–83, Asst. Dir. Gen. 1983–85, Dir. Gen. 1985–; mem. Bureau Univ. Radiophonique et Télévisuelle Int., Paris 1976–98, Bd. of Dirs Centro Televisivo Vaticano 1983–97; Pres. Int. Broadcasting Working Party of European Broadcasting Union 1983–93; Consultant to Pontifical Council for Social Communications 1989–, Unione Cattolica Stampa Italiana 1997–. *Publication:* L'Eglise de ce temps dans la prédication de Saint Augustin 1972. *Address:* Vatican Radio, 00120 Vatican City (Office); Via dei Penitenzieri, 20, 00193 Rome, Italy (Home). *Telephone:* (6) 698-83945 (Office); (6) 689-77240 (Home).

BORISEVICH, Nikolai Aleksandrovich; Belarus physicist; b. 21 Sept. 1923; m. Irina Pavlovna Borisevich 1949; two s.; ed. Byelorussian Univ., Minsk; served in Soviet Army 1941–45; Deputy Dir. Inst. of Physics, Byelorussian Acad. of Sciences 1955–69 (Head of Lab. 1957–); Head of Lab. Lebedev Inst. of Physics, U.S.S.R. (now Russian) Acad. of Sciences 1987–; Deputy to U.S.S.R. Supreme Soviet 1969–89; mem. Byelorussian (Belarus) Acad. of Sciences 1969 (Pres. 1969–87, Hon. Pres. 1992); Corresp. mem. U.S.S.R. (now Russian) Acad. of Sciences 1972–81, mem. 1981; Foreign mem. Czechoslovakian Acad. 1977, Slovenian Acad. of Sciences and Arts 1981; titular mem. European Acad. of Arts, Sciences and Humanities 1991; Hon. Ph.D. (Iena) 1985; U.S.S.R. State Prize 1973; Hero of Socialist Labour 1978; Lenin Prize 1980, State Prize 1998. *Address:* P. N. Lebedev Institute of Physics, B-333, Leninski Prospekt 53, 117924 Moscow, Russia. *Telephone:* (095) 135-75-98 (Office); (095) 129-25-46 (Home).

BORJA CEVALLOS, Rodrigo, LL.D.; Ecuadorean politician and academic; b. 1937; m. Carmen Calisto de Borja; one s. three d.; ed. Cen. Univ. of Ecuador; Deputy in Nat. Congress 1962–82; Founder and Leader Partido Izquierda Democrática; Prof. of Political Sciences, Cen. Univ. of Ecuador 1963–88; Pres. of Ecuador 1988–92; Pres. Law School Asscn., Cen. Univ. of Ecuador 1958; mem. Special Comm. of Lawyers on Ecuador's Political Constitution 1966. *Publications:* Political Constitutional Law (2 vols.) 1964, 1971, Democratic Socialism 1983; numerous essays. *Address:* c/o Office of the President, Palacio Nacional, García Moreno 1043, Quito, Ecuador.

BORK, Robert Heron, J.D.; American judge, lawyer and educationalist; b. 1 March 1927, Pittsburgh; s. of Harry Philip Bork and Elizabeth Kunkle; m. 1st Claire Davidson 1952 (died 1980); two s. one d.; m. 2nd Mary Ellen Pohl 1982; ed. Univ. of Chicago; admitted to Illinois Bar 1953; Assoc., mem. Kirkland, Ellis, Hodson, Chaffetz & Masters 1955–62; Assoc. Prof. Yale Law School 1962–65, Prof. of Law 1965–73, Chancellor Kent Prof. of Law 1977–79, Alexander M. Bickel Prof. of Public Law 1979–81; Solicitor-Gen. 1973–77; Acting Attorney-Gen. 1973–74; mem. Kirkland & Ellis, Washington 1981–82; Circuit Judge for Dist. of Columbia Circuit 1982–88; nominated as Justice of U.S. Supreme Court and rejected by Senate 1987; John M. Olin Scholar in Legal Studies, American Enterprise Inst. 1988–; Resident Scholar, American Enterprise Inst., Washington, D.C. 1977, adjunct scholar 1977–82; Co-Chair. Bd. of Trustees Federalist Soc.; mem. perm. cttee. Oliver Wendell Holmes Devise 1989; Fellow, American Acad. of Arts and Sciences; Francis Boyer Award, American Enterprise Inst. 1984; Hon. LL.D. (Creighton Univ.) 1975, (Notre-Dame) 1982; Hon. D.Hum.Litt. (Wilkes-Barre Coll.) 1976, Juris Dr. h.c. (Brooklyn Law School) 1984; Shelby Cullom Davis Award 1989. *Publication:* The Antitrust Paradox: A Policy at War with Itself 1978, The Tempting of America: The Political Seduction of the Law 1990, Slouching Towards Gomorrah 1996. *Address:* 5171 Palisade Lane, N.W., Washington, DC 20016, U.S.A. (Home). *Telephone:* (202) 862-5851 (Office).

BORKH, Inge; Swiss soprano opera singer; b. 26 May 1921; ed. Drama School, Vienna, and Vienna Acad.; theatre performances (dancing, piano) in Vienna and Milan, then in Switzerland in German version of Konsul (Menotti); Int. career 1951–, Bayreuth, Paris, Vienna, Edinburgh Festival; first visit to U.S.A. 1953; World Première of Irische Legende (Egk) 1955; appeared as Salome and Elektra, Carnegie Hall, New York 1958; Metropolitan Opera, N.Y. 1958; Bavarian Court Singer 1963; appeared at opening of Nationaltheater, Munich, in Die Frau ohne Schatten 1963; Grand Prix du Disque for Elektra, Antigone (Orff), and Schönberg's Gurrelieder; Reinhard Ring Award 1973. *Address:* D 7000 Stuttgart 75, Florentinerstrasse 20, Apt. 2018, Germany. *Telephone:* 47022018.

BORKO, Yuri Antonovich, DR. ECON.; Russian economist; b. 6 Feb. 1929, Rostov on Don; m. Yelena Borisovna Borko; two s.; ed. Moscow State Univ.; researcher Inst. of World Econ. and Int. Relations U.S.S.R. Acad. of Sciences 1962–63; Ed. and mem. of bd. journal World Econ. and Int. Relations 1963–69; Head of Div. Inst. of Information on Social Sciences Acad of Sciences 1970–90; founder, Deputy Dir., Prof. Inst. of Europe, Russian Acad. of Sciences; Pres. Asscn. of European Studies 1992–. *Publications include:* works on problems of European integration, European Community policy and int. relations between Russia and European Community. *Address:* Institute of Europe, Mokhovaya str. 8, stroenye 3b, 103873 Moscow, Russia (Office). *Telephone:* (095) 201 6775, 201 6704 (Office). *Fax:* (095) 200 4298 (Office).

BORLAUG, Norman Ernest, PH.D.; American agricultural scientist; b. 25 March 1914, Cresco, Ia.; s. of Henry O. and Clara (Vaala) Borlaug; m. Margaret G. Gibson 1937; one s. one d.; ed. Univ. of Minnesota; with U.S. Forest Service 1938–39; Instructor, Univ. of Minn. 1941; Microbiologist, E. I. DuPont de Nemours Foundation 1942–44; Research Scientist, Wheat Rockefeller Foundation, Mexico 1944–60, Centro Internacional de Mejoramiento de Maíz y Trigo (Int. Maize and Wheat Improvement Center), Mexico 1964–79; Leonard L. Klinck Lecturer, Agric. Inst. of Canada 1966; mem. Citizens' Comm. on Science, Law and Food Supply 1973, Comm. on Critical Choices for America 1973, Council of Agric. Science and Tech. 1973–; Assoc. Dir. Rockefeller Found. 1960–63, Life Fellow 1983–, Consultant 1983; A. D. White Distinguished Prof. at Large, Cornell Univ. 1983–85; Distinguished Prof. of Int. Agriculture, Texas A+M Univ. Jan.–May 1984; mem. N.A.S.; Nobel Peace Prize 1970; Foreign mem. Royal Swedish Acad. of Agric. and Forestry 1971, Indian Nat. Science Acad. 1973; Hon. Foreign mem. Acad. Nacional de Agronomia y Veterinaria de Argentina, N. I. Vavilovi Acad. (U.S.S.R.); Hon. Fellow Indian Soc. of Genetics and Plant Breeding 1968; Life Fellow Rockefeller Foundation 1983–; Hon. D.Sc. (Punjab Agric. Univ.) 1969, (Royal Norwegian Agric. Coll.) 1970, (Mich. State Univ.) 1971, (Univ. of Florida) 1973, and others; Medal of Freedom 1977 and numerous Mexican awards. *Leisure interests:* hunting, fishing, baseball, wrestling, football, golf. *Address:* Texas A+M University System, Department of Soil and Crop Science, College Station, TX 77843 (Office); 15611 Ranchita Drive, Dallas, TX 75248, U.S.A. (Home).

BORMAN, Frank; American astronaut and business executive; b. 14 March 1928, Gary, Ind.; s. of Edwin Borman and late Marjorie Borman; m. Susan Bugbee 1950; two s.; ed. U.S. Military Acad., Calif. Inst. of Tech.; pilot training, Williams Air Force Base, Arizona; assigned to various fighter squadrons in U.S. and Philippines; Instructor in Thermodynamics and Fluid Mechanics, U.S. Mil. Acad. 1957; Master's degree from Calif. Inst. of Tech. 1957; graduated from U.S. Air Force Aerospace Research Pilots School 1960; Instructor 1960–62; selected by NASA as astronaut Sept. 1962; Command Pilot Gemini VII 1965; Commdr. Apollo VIII spacecraft which made flight round the moon Dec. 1968; Deputy Dir. for Flight Operations, NASA, until May 1969; Field Dir. of a NASA Space Station Task Group 1969–70; Vice-Pres. Eastern Airlines Inc. 1970–74, Vice-Pres. for Eastern Operations 1974–75, Pres. 1975–85, C.E.O. 1975–86, Chair. of Bd. 1976–86; Vice-Chair., mem. Bd. of Dirs. Texas Air Corp. 1986–92; now Chair. Bd. Autofinance Group Inc., Chair., C.E.O., Dir. Patlex Corp. 1992–, dir. other cos.; NASA Exceptional Service Medal, Harmon Int. Aviation Trophy 1966, Gold Space Medal, Int. Aeronautics 1969, Encyclopedia Britannica Achievement in Life Award 1980. *Leisure interests:* restoring aeroplanes, building model aeroplanes. *Address:* Patlex Corporation, 250 Cotorro Court, Suite A, Las Cruces, NM 88005; Autofinance Group Inc., Suite 350, Oakmont Circle 1, 601 Oakmont Lane, Westmont, IL 60559, U.S.A. *Telephone:* (505) 523-8081 (Las Cruces). *Fax:* (505) 524-4050 (Las Cruces).

BORN, Gustav Victor Rudolf, D.PHIL., M.B., CH.B., F.R.S, F.R.C.P.; British professor of pharmacology; b. 29 July 1921; s. of the late Prof. Max Born; m. 1st Wilfrida Ann Plowden-Wardlaw 1950 (divorced 1961); two s. one d.; m. 2nd Dr Faith Elizabeth Maurice-Williams 1962; one s. one d.; ed. Oberrealschule, Göttingen, Germany, Perse School, Cambridge, Edin. Acad. and Univs. of Edin. and Oxford; Medical Officer, R.A.M.C. 1943–47; Medical Officer, Graham Research Lab., Univ. Coll. Hosp. Medical School, London 1947–49; Studentship, training in research methods of MRC 1949–52; mem. scientific staff, Toxicology Research Unit, MRC 1952–53; Sr. Research Officer Nuffield Inst. for Medical Research and Medical Lecturer St. Peter's Coll., Oxford 1953–60; Vandervell Prof. of Pharmacology, Royal Coll. of Surgeons and London Univ. 1960–73; Sheild Prof. of Pharmacology, Cambridge Univ. and Fellow, Gonville and Caius Coll. Cambridge 1973–78; Prof of Pharmacology, King's Coll., London Univ. 1978–86, Prof. Emer. 1986–, Dir. William Harvey Research Inst., St. Bartholomew's Hospital Medical Coll. 1989–; Dir. Int. Inter-Univ. Research Centre, Perugia 1995–; Fellow; fmr. mem. Council of the Int. Soc. of Thrombosis and Haemostasis (Pres. 1977–79), Cttee. of British Pharmacological Soc., Working Party on Antihaemophilic Globulin of MRC, Official Cttee. of Enquiry into Relationship of Pharmaceutical Industry with Nat. Health Service, Medical Advisory Bd., British Council and numerous other cttees. and bds.; Hon. D.Sc. (Bordeaux, Paris, Brown Univ.), Hon. M.D. (Münster, Leuven, Edin., Munich, Loyola Univ., Chicago); Hon. Fellow St. Peter's Coll., Oxford; Chevalier de l'Ordre National du Mérite; mem. Akademie Leopoldina; Hon. Life mem. New York Acad. of Sciences; Royal Soc. Royal Medal, Paul Morawitz Prize, Robert Pfleger Prize, Alexander von Humboldt Award 1995, other prizes and awards. *Leisure interests:* music, history. *Address:* The William Harvey Research Institute, St. Bartholomew's and the Royal London School of Medicine and Dentistry, Charterhouse Square, London, EC1M 6BQ; 5 Walden Lodge, 48 Wood Lane, London, N6 5UU, England. *Telephone:* 0171-982 6070 (College). *Fax:* 0171-982 6071.

BORNER, Silvio, DR.OEC.; Swiss professor of economics; b. 24 April 1941; s. of Walter Borner and Meta Borner; m. Verena Barth 1966; two d.; ed. St. Gall Grad. School and Yale Univ.; Prof. of Econs. Univ. of St. Gallen 1974–78, of Political Econs. Univ. of Basle 1978–. *Publications:* Die 'sechste Schweiz'—überleben auf dem Weltmarkt, New Forms of Internationalization: An Assessment, Einführung in die Volkswirtschaftslehre, International Finance and Trade in a Polycentric World. *Leisure interests:* sports (active) and culture. *Address:* Institut für Volkswirtschaft, WWZ UniversitätBasel, Petersplatz 1, CH-4003 Basle, Switzerland. *Telephone:* 061/29-31-11.

BORODINA, Olga Vladimirovna; Russian mezzo-soprano; b. 29 July 1963, Leningrad; d. of Vladimir Nikolaevich and Galina Fedorovna Borodins; one s.; ed. Leningrad Conservatory (student of Irina Bogacheva); soloist of Kyrov (now Mariinsky) Theatre of Opera and Ballet 1987–; debut as Siebel (Faust); winner of First Prizes: All-Union Glinka Competition 1987, Int. Rosa Poncell Competition (New York) 1987, Int. Francisco Vignas Competition (Barcelona) 1989; leading parts in operas Eugene Onegin (Olga), Khovanshchina (Marfa), Prince Igor (Konchakovna), Queen of Spades (Poline), Sadko (Lubava), Boris Godunov (Marina Mnichek), Cin-derella (Cinderella); on tour with Mariinsky Theatre in most European countries; debut in U.S.A. with Mariinsky Theatre 1992, solo recitals 1993–; debut in U.K. as Delilah, Covent Garden. *Address:* c/o Askonas Holt, Lonsdale Chambers, 27 Chancery Lane, London, WC2A 1PF, England.

BOROSS, Péter, PH.D.; Hungarian politician; b. 27 Aug. 1928, Nagybajom; m.; two c.; ed. Eötvös Loránd Univ. of Budapest; with Budapest Metropolitan Council 1951–56; dismissed for revolutionary cttee. and revolutionary council membership of 1956; kept under police surveillance until 1959; employed as unskilled worker 1964; organized catering and tourist coll. training; Catering chain dir. 1971; mem. Council Coll. of Trade and Catering; mem. Hungarian League of Human Rights, Hungarian Chamber of Economy; Founder Nation Bldg. Foundation 1988; Minister of State for the Office of Information and the Office of Nat. Security 1990–94; Minister of the Interior 1990–93; Prime Minister of Hungary 1993–94; mem. Parl. 1994–98; Chair. Nat. Security Cttee. of Parl. 1994–96; Sr. Counsellor and Advisor to Prime Minister 1998–; mem. Hungarian Democratic Forum Nat. Presidium 1993–. *Address:* 1055 Budapest, Kossuth Lajos tér 1–3, Hungary. *Telephone:* (1) 268-3000. *Fax:* (1) 268-4888.

BOROVKOV, Aleksandr Alekseyevich; Russian mathematician; b. 6 March 1931, Moscow; s. of Aleksey and Klaudia Borovkov; m. Svetlana Borovkov 1975; two s.; ed. Moscow Univ.; Postgraduate, Research Assoc. Moscow Univ. 1954–60; Head of Dept. Inst. of Math., Siberian Branch U.S.S.R. (now Russian) Acad. of Sciences 1960–, Deputy Dir. 1981–; lecturer 1961–, Prof., Head of Chair Novosibirsk Univ. 1965–; Corresp. mem. U.S.S.R. (now Russian) Acad. of Sciences 1966–90, mem. 1990–; mem. Int. Statistical Inst. and Bernulli Soc.; State Prize 1979. *Publications:* Stochastic Processes in Queuing Theory 1976, Wahrscheinlichkeitstheorie 1976, Asymptotic Methods in Queuing Theory 1980, Statistique Mathématique 1987, works on contiguous problems of theory probabilities and mathematical statistics. *Address:* Institute of Mathematics, Universitetsky prospekt 4, Novosibirsk 90, Russia. *Telephone:* (3832) 35-40-80 (Office); (3832) 35-63-83 (Home).

BOROVOI, Konstantin Natanovich, C.TECH.SC.; Russian politician and businessman; b. 30 June 1948, Moscow; m.; two d.; ed. Moscow Inst. of Railway Eng., Moscow State Univ.; worked in field of applied math., taught in Moscow State Univ. and Inst. of Land Utilization 1975–87, business activities since 1987–; publishes journal We and Computer 1988–90; co-founder and Pres. Russian Stock and Raw Materials Exchange 1990–92; Pres. Agency of Econ. News 1990; Chair. Bd. of All-Russian Nat. Commercial Bank 1990–; Pres. Russian Investment Co. Rinako 1991–; mem. Council of Businessmen of Pres. of Russia 1991–; Co-chair. Foundation of External Policy of Russia 1992–; founder Commercial TV Co. 1992–; founder and Co-Chair. Party of Econ. Freedom 1992–; mem. State Duma Dec. 1995–; Pres. Borovoi Trust Co. 1995–. *Publications:* The Price of Freedom, numerous articles. *Leisure interest:* tennis. *Address:* Economic Freedom Party, Novoslobolskaya, str. 9, Korp. 3, 103030 Moscow, Russia. *Telephone:* (095) 973-12-18 (Office); (095) 250 95 02 (Home).

BOROWSKI, Marek Stefan; Polish politician; b. 4 Jan. 1946, Warsaw; m.; one s.; ed. fmr. Main School of Commerce (now Main School of Planning and Statistics), Warsaw; Sr. Economist Centrum supermarket, Warsaw 1968–82; Ministry of Nat. Economy 1982–91, Deputy Minister 1989–91; deputy to Sejm (Parl.) 1991–; Deputy Prime Minister, Minister of Finance and Head Econ. Cttee. of Council of Ministers 1993–94; Minister/Head Council of Ministers Office 1994–96; Vice-Marshal of Sejm 1996–; mem. Polish United Workers' Party (PZPR) 1967–68, 1975–90; mem. Social Democracy of Polish Repub. 1990–. *Leisure interests:* literature, film, theatre. *Address:* Sejm RP, ul. Wiejska 4/6/8, 00-902 Warsaw, Poland. *Telephone:* (22) 694 25 00.

BORRELL FONTELLES, José, D.ECON.SCI.; Spanish politician; b. 24 April 1947, Pobla Segur, Lerida; m.; two c.; ed. Polytechnic Univ. and Complutense Univ. Madrid, Stanford Univ., U.S.A.; mem. Socialist Workers' Party (PSOE) Madrid 1975–; fmr. Dir. Dept. of Systems CESPA (Compañía Española de Petróleos); Deputy, Treasury and Economic Planning for Provincial Del. Madrid 1979; Under-Sec. Budget and Public Spending 1982–84, Sec. of State for the Treasury 1984–86, Deputy for Barcelona in the Legis. Ass. 1986–91; Minister of Public Works and Transport 1991–96, of the Environment 1993–96. *Address:* c/o Ministerio de Obras Públicas y Transportes, Nuevos Ministerios, 28071 Madrid, Spain.

BORRELLI, Mario, M.SC.; Italian sociologist; b. 19 Sept. 1922, Naples; s. of Gennaro Borrelli and Lucia Morvillo; m. Jilyan West 1971; one d.; ed. Posillipo Theological Univ., School of States Archives, Naples, London School of Econs.; Founder of "Casa dello Scugnizzo", Naples 1950 (Pres. 1993–); Founder-Dir. Lo Scugnizzo (monthly magazine) 1950–; Founder Materdei Community Centre, Naples 1970. *Publications:* La Concezione Copernico Galileiana e la Filosofia di Tomaso D'Aquino 1961, La Relazione tra il Conservatorio dei Poveri di Gesù Cristo e l'Oratorio di Napoli 1961, Il Largo dei Girolamini 1962, A Streetlamp and the Stars 1963, Memorie Baroniane dell'Oratorio de Napoli 1963, Opere e Documenti sul Baronio Presso The British Museum Library 1964, I Documenti dell'Oratorio Napoletano 1964, Le Testimonianze Baroniane dell'Oratorio di Napoli, Documenti sul Baronio Presso The Bodleian Library, L'Epistolario del Giusto Calvino nei suoi Rapporti col Baronio 1965, L'Architetto Nencioni Dionisio Di Bartolomeo 1967, Le Costituzioni dell' Oratorio Napoletano 1968, Diario delle Baracche 1969, Unearthing the Roots of the Sub-Culture of the South Italian Sub-Proletariat 1969, Socio-political Analysis of the Sub-Proletarian Reality of Naples and Lines of Intervention for the Workers of the Centre 1973, Basic Concepts for Community Action in the Urban Sub-Proletariat 1974, Practical Directions for Intervention in a Community Action in Favour of the Urban Sub-Proletariat 1974, Hypothesis of the Existence of a "Peripheral" Europe with consequent different types of Social Policy Intervention 1975, Exclusion from the Productive Process, Social Deviance and Mental Illness 1975, Alimentation and Directions of Social Intervention among the Neapolitan Sub-Proletariat 1975, Communication and Consciousness-Raising 1975, Socio-political Analysis of the Neapolitan Reality and Programme of Intervention for the Social Operators of the Centre 1976, Integration between Peace Research, Peace Education and Peace Action 1977, New Trends in the International Division of Labour and their Effects on the Conditions of Workers in Industrialized and "Third World" Countries 1977, Tourism as an Expression of Economic Subordination: Relationships between Emigration and Tourism 1977, Italian Compulsory School and Mental Retardation 1978, Human Needs, Human Rights and Peace Education (An Analysis by Means of the Practical Experience of the Materdei Community Centre of Naples), Exploration of the Preliminary Conditions for a Defensive and Economic Strategy for Central Europe leading to its Balance Insertion in the Mediterranean and African Areas 1981, Human Rights and a Methodology for Peace 1983, The Development of the Concept of Peace Education in the IPRA Archipelago 1983, An Approach to the Political Dimension of Disarmament Education 1984, The Periphery of Europe and the Community Integration of 1992 (an Analysis from the Southern Italian Scene) 1990, 4 contributions to Council of Europe research on street children. *Address:* Via Vecchia, S. Gennaro, 100/A-Pozzuoli, Naples, Italy. *Telephone:* (081) 526-57-01 (Home).

BORRIE, Baron (Life Peer) cr. 1995, of Abbots Morton in the County of Hereford and Worcester; **Gordon Borrie,** Kt., Q.C., F.R.S.A.; British lawyer; b. 13 March 1931; s. of Stanley Borrie; m. Dorene Toland 1960; ed. John Bright Grammar School, Llandudno and Univ. of Manchester; called to Bar, Middle Temple 1952; Bencher 1980; Barrister, London 1954–57; Lecturer, later Sr. Lecturer in Law, Coll of Law 1957–64, Univ. of Birmingham 1965–68, Prof. of English Law and Dir. Inst. of Judicial Admin. 1969–76, Dean Faculty of Law 1974–76; Dir.-Gen Office of Fair Trading 1976–92; Dir. Woolwich Bldg. Soc. 1992–; Dir. (non-exec.) Three Valleys Water Services 1992–, Mirror Group Newspapers 1993–, Telewest Communications 1994–, General Utilities 1998–; mem. Parole Bd. for England and Wales 1971–74, Consumer Protection Advisory Cttee. 1973–76, Equal Opportunities Comm. 1975–76; Pres. Inst. of Trading Standards Admin. 1992–97; Chair. Comm. on Social Justice 1992–94, Money Advice Trust 1993–95; mem. Council of Ombudsman for Corp. Estate Agents 1992–98; Labour cand. Croydon 1955, Ilford 1959; Gov. Birmingham Coll. of Commerce 1966–70; Hon. LL.D. (City of London Polytechnic) 1989, (Manchester Univ.) 1990, (Hull Univ.) 1991, (Dundee Univ.) 1993, (Nottingham Trent Univ.) 1996, (Univ. of the West of England) 1997. *Publications:* Commercial Law 1962, The Consumer, Society and the Law (with Prof. A. L. Diamond) 1963, Law of Contempt (with N. V. Lowe) 1973, The Development of Consumer Law and Policy 1984. *Leisure interests:* gastronomy, piano playing, travel. *Address:* Manor Farm, Abbots Morton, Worcestershire, WR7 4NA; 1 Plowden Buildings, Temple, London EC4Y 9BU, England. *Telephone:* (01386) 792330; 0171-353 4434.

BORRIE, Wilfred David, C.B.E., M.A.; Australian demographer; b. 2 Sept. 1913, Waimate, New Zealand; s. of Peter and Isobella Borrie; m. Alice H. Miller 1941; one d.; ed. Waitaki Boys High School, Oamaru, New Zealand, Univ. of Otago, N.Z. and Cambridge Univ; Lecturer, Social History and Econs., Sydney Univ. 1944–46, Senior Lecturer 1946–48; Research Fellow, Research School of Social Sciences, Australian Nat. Univ. 1949–52, Reader 1952–57, Prof. and Head of Dept. of Demography 1957–68, Dir. Research School of Social Sciences 1968–73, Prof. of Demography 1973–78, Emer. Prof. 1979–; Visiting Prof., Office of Population Research, Princeton Univ. 1959–60; Vice-Pres. Int. Union for Scientific Study of Population 1961–63; Pres. Social Science Research Council of Australia 1962–64, Australian Council of Social Services 1963–64, Australian and New Zealand Asscn. for the Advancement of Science (ANZAAS) 1975; Chair. UN Population Comm. 1965–69; Chair. and Dir. Nat. Population Inquiry 1970–78; Dir. Acad. of Social Sciences in Australia 1979–85; mem. Immigration Planning Council of Australia 1965–74, Australian Population and Immigration Council 1972–81; Patron Australian Population Asscn. 1980–; Laureate Int. Union for the Scientific Study of Population 1996; Hon.D.Litt (Tasmania) 1975, Hon. D.Sc. (Sydney) 1979; Hon. LL.D. (Australian Nat. Univ.) 1982, Laureate IUSSP 1996. *Publications:* Immigration 1948, Population Trends and Policies 1949, Italians and Germans in Australia 1954, The Cultural Integration of Immigrants (Part I and General Ed.) 1959, Australia's Population Structure and Growth (with G. Spencer) 1965, The Growth and Control of World Population 1970, Population Environment and Society 1973, Population and Australia (First Report of the Nat. Population Inquiry, 2 vols.) 1975, Supplementary Report (Recent Trends and their Implications) 1978, Implications of Australian Population Trends (Ed.) 1981, Immigration to New Zealand 1854–1938, The European Peopling of Australasia: A Demographic History, 1788–1988 1994. *Leisure interests:* reading, walking, gardening. *Address:* 49 The Grange, 67 MacGregor Street, Deakin, A.C.T. 2600, Australia. *Telephone:* 02814114.

BORST, Piet, M.D., PH.D.; Netherlands biochemist; b. 5 July 1934, Amsterdam; s. of Prof. J. Borst and A. Borst-de Geus; m. Jinke C. S. Houwing 1957; two s. one d.; ed. Gymnasium, Amsterdam, Univ. of Amsterdam; research asst. Lab. of Biochemistry Univ. of Amsterdam 1958–61; post-doctoral research Fellow, Dept. of Biochemistry New York Univ. 1963–64; Prof. of Biochemistry and Molecular Biology Univ. of Amsterdam 1965–83, Head of Section for Medical Enzymology, Lab. of Biochemistry 1966–83, Dir. Inst. of Animal Physiology 1972–80, Extraordinary Prof. of Clinical Biochemistry 1983–; Dir. of Research Netherlands Cancer Inst., Amsterdam 1983–; mem. European Molecular Biology Org. 1974, Royal Netherlands Acad. of Arts and Sciences 1978, Hollandsche Maatschappij der Wetenschappen 1983, Academia Europaea 1989; Foreign mem. Royal Soc. 1986, Foreign Assoc. N.A.S. 1991; Foreign Hon. mem. American Acad. of Arts and Sciences 1995; Royal Dutch/Shell Prize for the Life Sciences 1981, Federatie van Medisch Wetenschappelijke Verenigingen Prize 1984, Paul-Ehrlich and Ludwig-Darmstaedter Prize (jtly.) 1984, Ricketts Award of Univ. of Chicago 1989, Dr. G. Wander Award of the Wander Foundation, Berne 1990, Gold Medal of the Genootschap voor Natuur-, Genees- en Heelkunde, Amsterdam 1990, Dr. H.P. Heineken Prize for Biochem. and Biophysics, Amsterdam 1992, Gold Medal of the Koch Foundation, Bonn 1992. *Publications:* over 300 scientific articles in biochemistry, molecular biology and cell biology. *Leisure interests:* tennis, windsurfing, skiing, cello. *Address:* Netherlands Cancer Institute, Plesmanlaan 121, 1066 CX Amsterdam (Office); Meentweg 87, 1406 KE Bussum, Netherlands (Home). *Telephone:* 20-512 2881 (Office); 35-691 4453 (Home).

BORTEN, Per; Norwegian politician and agronomist; b. 3 April 1913, Fla Gauldal; s. of Lars and Karen Borten; m. Magnhild Rathe 1948; three c.; ed. Norwegian Agricultural Univ; Asst. Head, Tech. Section, Provincial Agric. Admin., Sör-Tröndelag 1946–65; Chair. Fla Municipal Council 1945, Provincial Council, Sör-Tröndelag 1948; fmr. Head of Youth Movement of Agrarian Movement, Sör-Tröndelag; mem. Storting 1950–77, Pres. Odelsting 1961–65, 1973–77; Chair. Senterpartiet 1955–67, Chief Spokesman 1958–65; Prime Minister 1965–71; *Address:* c/o Storting, Oslo, Norway.

BORZOV, Valeriy Filippovich; Ukrainian athlete; b. 20 Oct. 1949, Sambor, Lvov Region, Ukraine; s. of Philipp Petrovich Borzov and Valentina Georgiyevna Borzova; m. Lyudmila Turishcheva 1978; one d.; competed Olympic Games Munich 1972, winning gold medals at 100 m. and 200 m.; bronze medal at 100 m., Montreal 1976; European Junior Champion 100 m. and 200 m. 1968; European Champion 100 m. 1969; 100 m. and 200 m. 1971, 100 m. 1974; European Indoor Champion 60 m. 1970, 1971, 1972, 50 m. 1974, 1975, 1976; held European record at 100 m. and 200 m. and World record at 60 m.; Merited Master of Sport; Minister of Sport and Youth Ukrainian Repub. 1990–96; Chair. State Cttee. for Physical Culture and Sport 1996–97; Pres. Nat. Olympic Cttee. of Ukraine 1990–; mem. Int. Olympic Cttee., Jt. Asscn. of Summer Olympic Sports 1994–. *Leisure interests:* fishing, hunting. *Address:* c/o National Olympic Committee of Ukraine, Esplanadna Street 42, 252023 Kiev, Ukraine. *Telephone:* (44) 220-05-50. *Fax:* (44) 220-05-09.

BOSCH GAVIÑO, Juan; Dominican Republic politician and writer; b. 1909; ed. La Vega and Santo Domingo; founded literary group Las Cuevas (The Caves); exile in Puerto Rico and Cuba, travelled extensively in Latin America 1937–61; founded Partido Revolucionario Dominicano 1939, Leader until 1973; founded Partido de la Liberación Dominicana 1973, Leader until 1994; fmr. Prof. of Inst. of Political Science of Costa Rica; Pres. of Dominican Repub. Feb.-Sept. 1963 (deposed by mil. coup); unsuccessful candidate for Presidency 1966, 1978, 1982, 1986, 1990 and 1994. *Publications:* Camino Real (Royal Path—short stories), Indios (Indians), La Mañosa (The Shrew—novel), Mujeres en la Vida de Hostos (Women in the life of Hostos), Hostos—El Sembrador (Hostos, the Sower), Dos Pesos de Agua (Two Pesos worth of Water), Ocho Cuentos (Eight Tales), La Muchacha de la Guaira (The Girl from La Guaira), Cuba, la Isla Fascinante (Cuba, the Fascinating Island), Cuentos de Navidad (Christmas Stories), Life of Bolívar, Cuentos escritos en el Exilio (Tales written in Exile), Trujillo: Causas de una tiranía sin Ejemplo (Trujillo: Causes of a Tyranny without Equal), The Unfinished Experiment: Democracy in the Dominican Republic 1965, David 1966, Pentagonism 1969.

BOSHER, John Francis, PH.D., F.R.S.C., F.R.HIST.S; Canadian professor of history; b. 28 May 1929, Sidney, B.C.; s. of John Ernest Bosher and Grace Simister; m. Kathryn Cecil Berry 1968; one s. three d.; ed. Univ. of British Columbia, Univ. of Paris and Univ. of London; Jr. Admin. Asst. and Personnel Selection Officer Civil Service Comm., Ottawa 1951–53; Asst. Lecturer King's Coll., London 1956–59; Asst. Prof. Univ. of British Columbia 1959–67; Prof. of History Cornell Univ. 1967–69, York Univ., Toronto 1969–96; Visiting Fellow All Souls Coll., Oxford 1991–92. *Publications:* The Single Duty Project: A Study of the Movement for a French Customs Union in the 18th Century 1964, French Finances 1775–1795: From Business to Bureaucracy 1970, French Society and Government: Essays in Honour of Alfred Cobban (Ed.) 1973, The Canada Merchants 1713–1763, 1987, The French Revolution 1988, Men and Ships in the Canada Trade 1660–1760: a Biographical Dictionary 1992, Business and Religion in the Age of New France 1600–1760 1994, The Gaullist Attack on Canada 1998; numerous articles on France. *Leisure interests:* gardening and music. *Address:* 280 Chapel Street, Ottawa, Ont. K1N 7Y9, Canada. *Telephone:* (613) 565-6724.

BOSHOFF, Carel Willem Hendrik, M.A., D.D.; South African theologian; b. 9 Nov. 1927, Nylstroom; s. of W. S. and A. M. Boshoff; m. Anna Verwoerd, d. of late Hendrik Verwoerd (Prime Minister of S.A. 1958–66) 1954; five s. two d.; ed. Nylstroom High School, Pretoria Univ.; Missionary Dutch Reformed Church 1953–63, Sec. of Missions 1963–66; Prof. and Head of Dept. of Theology, Missiology and Science of Religion, Univ. of Pretoria 1967–88, Dean, Theology Faculty 1978–80; Chair. S.A. Bureau of Racial Affairs (SABRA) 1972–; Chair. N. G. Kerkboekhandel 1976–88; Chair. Afrikaner Volkswag Cultural Org. 1984–, Council of Inst. for Missiological Research 1978–88; Exec. Chair. Afrikaner Vryheidstigting 1988–; Chair., Dir. Orania Bestuurdienste Ltd. 1990–; Leader, Die Voortrekkers 1981–89; mem. numerous theological and scholarly cttees.; Pres. Burger Council Afrikaner Vryheidstigting 1994–; Provincial Leader, Freedom Front of Northern Cape 1994–; mem. legislature, Province of Northern Cape 1994–. *Publications:* Die Begin van die Evangelie van Jesus Christus 1963, Uit God Gebore 1968,

Die Nuwe Sendingsituasie 1978, Swart Teologie van Amerika Tot in Suid-Afrika 1980. *Leisure interests:* small farming, breeding Nooitgedracht ponies, hiking. *Address:* P.O. Box 27, Orania 8752, South Africa. *Telephone:* (053) 207 0061 (Office); (053) 207 0008 (Home). *Fax:* (053) 207 0114.

BOSKIN, Michael Jay, PH.D.; American economist, government official, university educator and consultant; b. 23 Sept. 1945, N.Y.; s. of Irving Boskin and Jean Boskin; m. Chris Dornin 1981; ed. Univ. of California, Berkeley; Asst. Prof. Stanford Univ., Calif. 1970–75, Assoc. Prof. 1976–78, Prof. 1978–; Dir. Centre for Econ. Policy Research 1986–89; Wohlford Prof. Econs. 1987–89; Chair. of the Pres.'s Council of Econ. Advisers 1989–93; Chair. Congressional Comm. on the Consumer Price Index; Friedman Prof. of Econs. and Hoover Inst. Sr. Fellow, Stanford Univ., Calif. 1993–; Pres. Boskin & Co., Calif. 1993–; Research Assoc. Nat. Bureau of Econ. Research 1976–; Visiting Prof. Harvard Univ., Mass. 1977–78; Faculty Research Fellow Mellon Foundation 1973; Distinguished Faculty Fellow Yale Univ. 1993; Scholar American Enterprise Inst.; mem. Bd. of Dirs. Exxon Corp., Oracle Corp., Airtouch Communications, Healthcare Compace Corp.; several prizes and awards. *Publications:* Too Many Promises: The Uncertain Future of Social Security 1986, Reagan and the Economy: Successes, Failures, Unfinished Agenda 1987, Frontiers of Tax Reform 1996, Capital Technology and Growth 1996, Toward a More Accurate Measure of the Cost of Living 1996; contrib. articles in various professional journals. *Leisure interests:* tennis, skiing, reading, theatre. *Address:* Stanford University, 213 HHMB, Stanford, CA 94305, U.S.A.

BOSSANO, Hon. Joseph J., B.SC. (ECON.), B.A.; Gibraltarian politician; b. 10 June 1939; ed. Gibraltar Grammar School, Birmingham Univ., Univ. of London; m. 1st Judith Baker 1967 (dissolved 1988); three s. one d.; m. 2nd Rose Torilla 1988; factory worker 1958–60; merchant seaman 1960–64; Sec. Integration with Britain Movt. 1964; mem. Man. Cttee. Tottenham Constituency Labour Party 1965–68; fmr. mem. IWBP Exec. Cttee.; Leader Gibraltar Socialist Labour Party 1977–; Leader of the Opposition 1984–88, 1996–; Sec. Gibraltar Br. Commonwealth Parl. Asscn. 1980–88; Br. Officer TGWU (Gibraltar) 1974–88; Chief Minister of Gibraltar, with responsibility for Information 1988–96. *Leisure interests:* carpentry, fishing, thinking and linguistics. *Address:* c/o 6 Convent Place, Gibraltar.

BOSSARD, André, D.IUR.; French international police official (retd.); b. 18 June 1926, St. Ouen; s. of Charles and Aline (Sirugue) Bossard; m. Francine Agen 1956; two d.; ed. Lycée Louis le Grand, Paris Univ.; called to Bar 1949; joined police service with rank of Commissaire 1950, Commissaire Principal 1958, Commissaire Divisionnaire 1968; Tech. Adviser at Police Judiciaire HQ 1970; Head of a Div. Int. Criminal Police Org. (INTERPOL) 1971–77; Contrôleur Gén. de la Police Nat. 1977; Sec.-Gen. INTERPOL 1978–85; Visiting Adjunct Prof., Univ. of Illinois 1988–91, 1998; Hon. Research Fellow, Univ. of Exeter 1991; Chevalier Légion d'honneur. *Publications:* Transnational Crime and Criminal Law 1987, Law Enforcement in Europe 1993, Carrefours de la grande truanderie 1998. *Leisure interest:* painting. *Address:* 228 rue de la Convention, 75015 Paris, France. *Telephone:* 01-48-28-21-45.

BOSSI, Umberto; Italian politician; b. 1941, Cassano Magnago, Varese; m. (separated); two c. by Manuela Marrone; ed. Pavia Univ.; founded Lombard Autonomy League 1982; Leader, Lombard League 1984–; Senator 1987; Sec. Fed. of Northern League Movts. 1989–; sentenced to five months' imprisonment for libel and eight months for illegal financing of his party Nov. 1995. *Address:* Lega Nord, Milan, Italy. *Telephone:* (2) 6070379. *Fax:* (2) 66802766.

BOSSIDY, Lawrence Arthur, B.A.; American business executive; b. 5 March 1935, Pittsfield, Mass.; m. Nancy Bossidy 1956; three s. six d.; ed. Colgate Univ.; joined Gen. Electric Co. 1957, Vice-Chair. 1984–91; Chair., C.E.O. Allied Signal Inc. 1991–; sometime Chair. and Dir. Gen. Electric Credit Corpn. New York; dir. numerous cos. *Address:* Allied Signal Inc., P.O. Box 300, 101 Columbia Road, Morristown, NJ 07960, U.S.A.

BOSSON, Bernard; French politician; b. 25 Feb. 1948, Annecy; s. of Charles Bosson and Claire Bosson; m. Danielle Blaise 1976; one d.; ed. Coll. Saint-Michel and Faculté de droit de Lyon; barrister, Annecy 1976–; Mayor of Annecy 1983–; Deputy to Nat. Ass. 1986–93, 1995–; Sec. of State, Ministry of the Interior 1986, Del. Minister, Ministry of Foreign Affairs 1986–88; Minister of Public Works, Transport and Tourism 1993–95; Deputy Vice-Pres. Del. for EC 1988; Vice-Pres. Mouvement européen 1990–97; Sec.-Gen. Centre des Démocrates sociaux 1991; mem. Union pour la démocratie française. *Address:* Assemblée nationale, 75355 Paris; Mairie, 74000 Annecy, France.

BØSTERUD, Helen; Norwegian politician; b. 15 Feb. 1940, Oslo; mem. Akershus Co. Council 1975–79; mem. Storting 1977; State Sec. Ministry of Health and Social Affairs 1980–81; Chair. Storting's Standing Cttee. on Justice 1981–86, on Defence 1989–94; Minister of Justice 1986–89; Dir.-Gen. Directorate for Civil Defence and Emergency Planning 1993–. *Address:* Directorate for Civil Defence and Emergency Planning, Sandakervn 12, P.O. Box 8136, Dep. 0033, Oslo, Norway.

BOSTRÖM, Rolf Gustav, PH.D.; Swedish professor of space physics; b. 15 April 1936, Kalmar; s. of Gustav Boström and Greta Boström (née Bergström); m. Barbro Karlsson 1962; one s.; ed. Royal Inst. of Tech.; Research Assoc., Dept. of Plasma Physics, Royal Inst. of Tech. 1961–71, Sr. Physicist 1971–75, Assoc. Prof. 1975–76; Prof. Uppsala Div. of Swedish Inst. of Space Physics (fmrly. Uppsala Ionospheric Observatory) 1976–; Head Dept. of Space Physics, Uppsala Univ. 1988–96; mem. Royal Swedish Acad. of Sciences. *Publications:* scientific papers on space plasma physics. *Leisure interests:* hiking, angling. *Address:* Swedish Institute of Space Physics, Uppsala Division, 75591 Uppsala (Office); Klippvägen 22, 75652 Uppsala, Sweden (Home). *Telephone:* 46-18 303610 (Office); 46-18 320261 (Home).

BOT, Bernard Rudolf, D.JUR.; Netherlands diplomatist; b. 21 Nov. 1937, Djakarta, Indonesia; s. of Th. H. Bot and E.W. van Hal; m. Christine Bot-Pathy 1962; three c.; ed. St. Aloysius Coll. The Hague, Univ. of Leiden, Acad. of Int. Law, The Hague and Harvard Law School; Deputy Perm. Rep. of Netherlands to North Atlantic Council, Brussels 1982–86; Amb. to Turkey 1986–89; Sec.-Gen. Ministry of Foreign Affairs 1989–92; Perm. Rep. to European Union 1992–; Kt., Order of Netherlands Lion and other decorations. *Publication:* Non-recognition and Treaty Relations 1968. *Leisure interests:* cycling, painting, skiing. *Address:* Permanent Mission of the Netherlands to the European Union, avenue Hermann Debroux 48, 1160 Brussels, Belgium. *Telephone:* 679.15.11. *Fax:* 679.17.75.

BOTCHWEY, Kwesi, J.S.D.; Ghanaian politician and lawyer; b. 13 Sept. 1942; m.; three c.; ed. Univ. of Ghana, Legon and Yale and Mich. Univs.; lecturer, Univs. of Zambia and Dar es Salaam; Sr. lecturer, Faculty of Law, Univ. of Ghana 1974; consultant, UN Univ. Project on Socio-Cultural Alternatives in the Transformation of the World; Sec. for Finance 1982–92; Minister of Finance & Economic Planning 1993–95; mem. Asscn. of Third World Economists. *Address:* c/o Ministry of Finance and Economic Planning, P.O. Box M40, Accra, Ghana.

BOTELHO, João; Portuguese film director; b. 11 May 1949, Lamego; ed. Nat. Conservator Film School, Lisbon; involved in film socs. in Coimbra and Oporto; film critic for newspapers; f. film magazine M. *Films include:* Alexandre e Rosa (short, co-dir.) 1978, Conversa acabada (The Other One) 1980, Um adeus português (A Portuguese Goodbye) 1985, Tempos difíceis (Hard Times) 1987. *Address:* c/o Associação Portuguesa de Realizadores, Rua de Palmeira 7, r/c, 1200 Lisbon, Portugal.

BOTERO; Colombian artist; b. 19 April 1932, Medellín; s. of David and Flora Botero; m. Cecilia Botero 1964; four c.; first group exhbn., Medellín 1948; first one-man exhbn., Galería Leo Matiz, Bogotá 1951; studied at Acad. San Fernando and El Prado Museum, Madrid 1952; visited Paris and Italy and studied art history with Roberto Longhi, Univ. of Florence 1953–54; lived in Mexico 1956; one-man exhbn. Pan American Union, Washington, D.C. 1957, Colombia 1958–59; lived in New York 1960–; first one-man exhbn. in Europe, Baden-Baden and Munich 1966; visited Italy and Germany 1967, studied work of Dürer; travelling retrospective exhbn. of 80 paintings in five German museums 1970; one-man exhbn. Hanover Gallery, London 1970; moved to Paris 1973; concentrated on Sculpture 1976–77, first one-man exhbn. of sculpture, Foire Int. d'Art Contemporain, Paris 1977; retrospective exhbn., Hirshorn Museum and Sculpture Garden, Washington, D.C. 1979; first one-man exhbn. in Japan, Tokyo, Osaka 1981; paintings in public collections in Belgium, Finland, Germany, Israel, Italy, S. America, Spain and U.S.A.; Guggenheim Nat. Prize for Colombia 1960.

BOTERO RESTREPO, Oscar; Colombian politician and army officer; b. 11 May 1933, Armenia, Caldas; s. of Jaime Botero and Felisa Restrepo; m. Lucía Restrepo Mejía 1963 (died); three s.; ed. Univ. of Gran Colombia and José María Cordova Mil. School; commdr. Intelligence Bn. 1967–70; commdr. Charry Solano Bn. 1971–72; Chief of Mil. Household of the Palacio Nacional 1973–74; Mil. Attaché, Colombian Embassy, Madrid 1974–76; Chief of Dept. of E-1 Commando 1976; Commdr. 8th Brigade 1977–78; Chief of Dept. of D-2 of Jt. Staff 1979–81; Commdr. 5th Brigade 1981–82; Chief of Mil. Household of the Presidency 1982–83; Commdr. 5th Div. 1983–84; Army Inspector 1984–85; Second-in-Command and Army Chief of Staff 1985–86; Commdr. of Army 1986–88; Gen. Commdr. of Mil. Forces 1988–89; Minister of Nat. Defence 1989; rank of Gen. 1987; Commdr. of Order of the Liberator, Star of Carabobo; Cross of the Land Forces of Venezuela. *Address:* c/o Ministry of National Defence, Avda Eldorado, Bogotá, Colombia.

BOTHA, Matthys Izak, B.A., LL.B.; South African diplomatist (retd.); b. 31 Oct. 1913, Bloemfontein; s. of Johannes H. J. Botha and Anna M. J. Botha (née Joubert); m. Hester le Roux (née Bosman) 1940; two s.; ed. Selborne Coll., East London and Univ. of Pretoria; Dept. of Finance 1931–44; Dept. of Foreign Affairs 1944–85, Washington 1944–51, UN, New York 1951–54; Head of Political Div., Dept. of Foreign Affairs, Pretoria 1955–58; Minister to Switzerland 1959–60; Minister, London 1960–62; Perm. Rep. to UN 1962–70; Amb. to Canada 1970–73, to Italy and Panama 1973–76, also accred. to Costa Rica and El Salvador 1973–74, to U.K. 1977–78, to Ciskei 1983–85; mem. Transvaal Bar; mem. Probus Club Southern Africa, Huguenot Soc.; Kt. Grand Cross, Order of Merit (Italy). *Leisure interests:* swimming, golfing, cycling. *Address:* 7 de Jongh Street, Strand, Cape Province 7140, South Africa.

BOTHA, Pieter Willem, D.M.S., M.P.; South African politician; b. 12 Jan. 1916, Paul Roux district, O.F.S.; m. 1st Anna Elizabeth Rossouw 1943 (died 1997); two s. three d.; m. 2nd Barbara Robertson 1998; ed. Univ. of Orange Free State; mem. Parl. for George 1948–84; Chief Sec. Cape Nat. Party 1948–58, Deputy Minister of the Interior 1958–61; Minister of Community Devt., Public Works and Coloured Affairs 1961–66, of Defence 1966–80, of Nat. Security 1978–84; Prime Minister 1978–84; State Pres. of South Africa

1984–89; C.-in-C. of the Armed Forces 1984–89; Leader Nat. Party 1978–89; Leader Nat. Party in Cape Prov. 1966–86; Chancellor Univ. of Stellenbosch 1984–88; faces criminal charges in refusing to appear before the Truth and Reconciliation Comm. 1998; Dr. h.c. (Univ. of O.F.S.); Decoration for Meritorious Service (S.A.) 1976, Order of the Star of S.A. and various foreign awards. *Publication:* Voice from the Wilderness (autobiog.). *Leisure interests:* horse riding, hunting game, reading, walking. *Address:* Die Anker, Wilderness 6560, South Africa.

BOTHA, Roelof Frederik (Pik), B.A., LL.B.; South African politician; b. 27 April 1932, Rustenburg; m. 1st Helena Bosman 1953; two s. two d.; m. 2nd Ina Joubert 1998; ed. Volkskool, Potchefstroom, Univ. of Pretoria; joined Dept. of Foreign Affairs 1953; served with diplomatic missions in Europe 1956–66; mem. S. African legal team in S.W. Africa case, Int. Court of Justice, The Hague 1963–66, 1970–71; Agent of S. African Govt., Int. Court of Justice 1965–66; Legal Adviser Dept. of Foreign Affairs 1966–68, Under-Sec. and Head S.W. Africa and UN sections 1968–70; mem. Parl. for Wonderboom 1970–74, for Westdene 1977–94, re-elected 1994–96, served on various select Parl. cttees. 1970–74; Sec. Foreign Affairs Study Group of Nat. Party's mems. of Parl. 1974; Amb. and Perm. Rep. to UN 1974–77; Amb. to U.S.A. 1975–77; Minister of Foreign Affairs 1977–94, of Mineral and Energy Affairs 1994–96, for Information 1980–86; mem. S. African Del. to UN Gen. Assembly 1967–69, 1971, 1973–74; Leader Nat. Party in Transvaal 1992–96; Grand Cross, Order of Good Hope, Decoration for Meritorious Service (S.A.), Grand Cordon, Order of the Brilliant Star (Taiwan). *Leisure interests:* hunting and fishing. *Address:* P.O. Box 16176, Pretoria North 0116, South Africa.

BOTHAM, Ian Terence, O.B.E.; British cricketer (retd.); b. 24 Nov. 1955, Heswall, Cheshire; m. Kathryn Waller 1976; one s. two d.; ed. Buckler's Mead Secondary School, Yeovil; right-hand batsman, right-hand, fast-medium bowler; teams: Somerset 1974–86 (Capt. 1984–85), Worcs. 1987–91, Queensland 1987–88, Durham 1992–93; 102 Tests for England 1977–92, 12 as Capt., scoring 5,200 runs (average 33.5) including 14 hundreds, taking 383 wickets (average 28.4) and holding 120 catches; scored 1,673 runs and took 148 wickets v. Australia; became first player to score a century and take 8 wickets in an innings in a Test Match, v. Pakistan (Lord's) 1978; took 100th wicket in Test cricket in record time of 2 years 9 days 1979; achieved double of 1,000 runs and 100 wickets in Tests to create world record of fewest Tests (21), and English records of shortest time (2 years 33 days) and at youngest age (23 years 279 days) 1979; became first player to have scored 3,000 runs and taken 250 wickets in Tests (55) Nov. 1982; first player to score a century and take 10 wickets in a Test Match, v. India; scored 19,399 runs (38 hundreds) and took 1,172 wickets in first-class cricket; toured Australia 1978–79, 1979–80, 1982–83 and 1986–87; has also played soccer for Scunthorpe United and Yeovil; mem. Sky cricket commentary team; Tech. Dir. of bowling, England Cricket Team 1996–; mem. MCC Cricket Cttee. 1995, Sports Council 1995–. *Publications include:* It Sort of Clicks 1986, Cricket My Way 1989, Botham: My Autobiography 1994, The Botham Report (with Peter Hayter) 1997. *Leisure interests:* shooting, golf, flying, fishing. *Address:* c/o Ludorum Management Ltd., 33 Tooley Street, London, SE1 2QF, England. *Telephone:* 0171-403 8200. *Fax:* 0171-403 8210.

BOTHWELL, Thomas Hamilton, D.SC., M.D., F.R.C.P., F.R.S.S.A.; South African physician and professor of medicine; b. 27 Feb. 1926; s. of Robert Cooper Bothwell and Jessie Isobel (née Hamilton) Bothwell; m. Alexandrine Moorman Butterworth 1957; one s. two d.; ed. St. John's Coll., Johannesburg, Univ. of Witwatersrand and Univs. of Oxford and Washington; physician, later Sr. Physician Dept. of Medicine, Univ. of the Witwatersrand 1956–67, Prof. of Medicine and Head Dept. of Medicine 1967–91; Chief Physician Johannesburg Hosp. 1967–91; Dir. MRC Iron and Red Cell Metabolism Research Unit, Univ. of the Witwatersrand 1969–91, Dean of Medicine 1992–93, Hon. Professorial Research Fellow 1993–; Hon. F.A.C.P.; Dr. h.c. (Univs. of Cape Town, Natal, Witwatersrand); Gold Medal, S.A. Medical Research Council. *Publications:* 250 articles in the field of iron metabolism, 50 chapters and two books: Iron Metabolism 1962, Iron Metabolism in Man 1979. *Leisure interests:* reading, walking, dogs. *Address:* Faculty of Medicine, University of the Witwatersrand, Medical School, 7 York Road, Parktown 2193, Johannesburg, South Africa.

BOTT, Martin Harold Phillips, M.A., PH.D., F.R.S.; British professor of geophysics; b. 12 July 1926, Stoke-on-Trent; s. of Harold Bott and Dorothy Bott (née Phillips); m. Joyce Cynthia Hughes 1961; two s. one d.; ed. Clayesmore School, Dorset, Keble Coll. Oxford (army short course) and Magdalene Coll. Cambridge; Nat. Service in army (Royal Signals) 1945–48, rank of Lieut.; Turner & Newall Research Fellow, Univ. of Durham 1954–56, Lecturer in Geophysics 1956–63, Reader 1963–66, Prof. 1966–88, Research Prof. in Geophysics 1988–91, Emer. Prof. 1991–; Head of Dept. of Geological Sciences 1970–73, 1976–82; Chair. British Nat. Cttee. for Geodesy and Geophysics 1985–89; Murchison Medal, Geological Soc. of London 1977, Clough Medal, Geological Soc. of Edin. 1979, Sorby Medal, Yorks. Geological Soc. 1981, Wollaston Medal, Geological Soc. of London 1992. *Publications:* The Interior of the Earth 1971, Structure and Development of the Greenland-Scotland Ridge: new methods and concepts (Co-Ed.) 1983, Sedimentary Basins of Continental Margins and Cratons (Ed.) 1976, and many scientific papers in journals. *Leisure interests:* Reader (Anglican Church), mountain walking, garden slavery, etc. *Address:* 11 St Mary's Close, Shincliffe, Durham, DH1 2ND, England.

BOTT, Raoul, D.SC.; American (naturalized) mathematician; b. 24 Sept. 1923, Budapest, Hungary; s. of Rudolph and Margit (Kovacs) Bott; m. Phyllis H. Aikman 1947; one s. three d.; ed. McGill Univ. and Carnegie Inst. of Tech.; mem. Inst. for Advanced Study, Princeton 1949–51, 1955–57; Instructor in Math., Univ. of Mich. 1951–52, Asst. Prof. 1952–55, Prof. 1957–59; Prof. of Math., Harvard Univ. 1959–, Higgins Prof. of Math. 1967–79, Graustein Prof. of Math. 1969–; Ed. Topology, Annals of Mathematics 1958–59, American Journal of Mathematics 1969; mem. Nat. Acad. of Sciences, American Math. Soc., American Acad. of Arts and Sciences, French Acad. of Sciences; Master Dunster House 1978–84; Hon. Fellow London Math. Soc. 1983, St. Catherine's Coll., Oxford 1984; Nat. Medal of Science 1987; several hon. degrees and awards. *Leisure interests:* music, swimming, skiing. *Address:* Mathematics Department, Harvard University, Science Center, 1 Oxford Street, Cambridge, MA 02138 (Office); 1 Richdale Avenue No. 9, Cambridge, MA 02140, U.S.A. (Home). *Telephone:* (616) 864-2482 (Home).

BOTTAI, Bruno; Italian diplomatist; b. 10 July 1930, Rome; ed. Univ. of Rome; entered Ministry of Foreign Affairs 1955; served Tunis, Brussels, London, Vatican and Ministry of Foreign Affairs 1955–76; Amb. to the Holy See and the Sovereign Mil. Order of Malta 1979; Dir.-Gen. of Political Affairs, Ministry of Foreign Affairs 1981–85; Amb. to U.K. 1985–87; Sec.-Gen. Ministry of Foreign Affairs 1987–93; Amb. to the Holy See 1994–97; Pres. Società Dante Alighieri 1996–. *Leisure interest:* modern paintings. *Address:* Palazzo Firenze, Piazza Firenze 27, 00186 Rome, Italy.

BOTTO DE BARROS, Adwaldo Cardoso; Brazilian international official; b. 19 Jan. 1925, Aracajú, Sergipe; m. Neida de Moura Botto de Barros 1951; one s. two d.; ed. Mil. Coll. of Resende, Mil. Eng. Inst., Catholic Univ. of São Paulo and Getulio Vargas Foundation; Chief Eng. railway construction 1952–54; Dir. of industries in São Paulo and Curitiba 1955–64; Dir. Handling Sector, São Paulo Pref., Financial Adviser to São Paulo Eng. Faculty and Adviser on industrialization of Suzano Prefecture, São Paulo 1965–71; Regional Dir. Brazilian Telegraph and Post Office Enterprise, São Paulo 1972–74; Pres. Brazilian Telegraph and Post Office Enterprise, Brasilia 1974–84; Chair. Exec. Council, Universal Postal Union (UPU) 1979–84, Dir.-Gen. Int. Bureau 1985–94; numerous awards and honours. *Leisure interests:* philately, sport. *Address:* Rua Manuel Guedes, 522 aptº 71, Haim Bibi, 04536-070 São Paulo-SP, Brazil.

BOTTOMLEY, Rt. Hon. Virginia Hilda Brunette Maxwell, P.C., B.A., M.SC., J.P., M.P.; British politician; b. 12 March 1948; d. of W. John Garnett; m. Peter Bottomley, M.P.; one s. two d.; ed. Putney High School, Univ. of Essex, L.S.E.; researcher for Child Poverty Action Group and lecturer in a further educ. coll. 1971–73, Psychiatric Social Worker Brixton and Camberwell Child Guidance Units 1973–84; Vice-Chair. Nat. Council of Carers and their Elderly Dependants 1982–88; Dir. Mid Southern Water Co. 1987–88; mem. MRC 1987–88; M.P. Surrey South-West May 1984–; Parl. Pvt. Sec. to Minister of State for Educ. and Science 1985–86, to Minister for Overseas Devt. 1986–87, to Sec. of State for Foreign and Commonwealth Affairs 1987–88; Parl. Under-Sec. of State Dept. of Educ. and Science 1988–89; Sec. Conservative Backbench Employment Cttee. 1985; Fellow Industry Parl. Trust 1987; Minister of State (Minister for Health) 1982–92; Sec. of State for 1992–95, with responsibility for Family Policy 1994–95; Sec. of State for Nat. Heritage 1995–97; Co-Chair. Women's Nat. Comm. 1991–92; mem. Court of Govs. L.S.E. 1985–, British Council 1997–, House of Commons Select Cttee. on Foreign Affairs 1997–; J.P. Inner London 1975 (Chair. Lambeth Juvenile Court 1981–84); Conservative; Hon. LL.D. (Portsmouth) 1992. *Leisure interest:* family. *Address:* House of Commons, London, SW1A 0AA, England. *Telephone:* 0171-219 6499.

BOUBAKER, Sidi Mohamed Ould; Mauritanian politician; b. 19 May 1954; ed. Nat. School of Admin., Univ. of Nancy; fmr. civil servant; Sec.-Gen. Democratic and Social Republican Party (DSRP); fmr. Minister of Finance; Prime Minister of Mauritania 1992–96. *Address:* c/o Office of the Prime Minister, Nouakchott, Mauritania.

BOUBLIL, Alain Albert; French author and dramatist; b. 5 March 1941, Tunis; four s.; two Tony Awards, Two Grammy Awards, two Victoire de la Musique Awards, Molière Award (all for Les Misérables), Evening Standard Drama Award (for Miss Saigon), Laurence Olivier Award (for Martin Guerre). *Publications:* wrote libretto and lyrics for: La Révolution Française 1973, Les Misérables 1980, Abbacadabra 1984, Miss Saigon 1989, Martin Guerre 1996; Le Journal d'Adam et Eve (play) 1994. *Leisure interests:* theatre, opera, cinema, tennis. *Address:* c/o Cameron Mackintosh Limited, 1 Bedford Square, London, WC1B 3RA, England. *Telephone:* 0171-637 8866. *Fax:* 0171-436 2683.

BOUCETTA, M'Hamed, L. EN D.; Moroccan politician; b. 1925, Marrakesh; one s. four d.; ed. Ecole Sidi Mohamed, Lycée Moulay Idriss, Fez, Univ. of Paris, France, Inst. des Etudes Supérieures, Paris; worked as lawyer in Casablanca; joined Istiqlal Party 1944, Dir. Al-Istiqlal (party newspaper) 1955, mem. Political Bureau 1956, Exec. Cttee. 1963–, Sec.-Gen. 1974–98; Sec. of State for Foreign Affairs 1956; Minister of Justice 1961–63; M.P. 1977–; Minister of State without Portfolio March-Oct. 1977, 1984–85, for Foreign Affairs 1977–84, and for Co-operation 1977–81, Minister of State without Portfolio in Interim Govt. 1985. *Address:* Istiqlal, 4 Avenue Ibnou Toumert, Rabat, Morocco. *Telephone:* (7) 730951. *Fax:* (7) 725354.

BOUCHARD, Benoît, B.A.; Canadian politician; b. 16 April 1940, Roberval, Quebec; m. Jeannine Lavoie; three c.; ed. Laval Univ.; teacher Coll. Classique, Coll. Notre-Dame, then Prin. Coll. Notre-Dame and Villa étudiante, Roberval; Dir.-Gen. St. Felicien CEGEP 1979–; alderman, Roberval 1973–80; Minister of State (Transport) Sept. 1984–85, Minister of Communications 1985–86, of Employment and Immigration 1986–88, of Transport 1988–90, of Industry, Science and Tech. 1990–91, of Nat. Health and Welfare 1991–93; Amb. to France 1993–96. *Address:* Ménard Avenue, Roberval, Quebec, Canada.

BOUCHARD, Lucien, B.A., B.SC.; Canadian politician; b. 22 Dec. 1938, Saint-Coeur-de-Marie, Lac Saint-Jean, Quebec; m. Audrey Best; one s. one d.; ed. Laval Univ.; admitted Quebec Bar 1964; pvt. law practice in Chicoutimi until 1985; mem. numerous comms. and orgs. connected with labour relations, both in public and pvt. sectors; Pres. Saguenay Bar 1978; Amb. to France 1985–88; Sec. of State of Canada 1988; M.P. 1988–; Minister of the Environment 1989–90; resgnd. from Conservative Party 1990 to lead Bloc Québécois; Chair. and Leader, Bloc Québécois 1993–96; Leader Parti Québécois Jan. 1996–; Leader of Opposition, House of Commons 1993–95; Prime Minister of Quebec Jan. 1996–. *Publications:* À visage découvert 1992; articles in legal and labour relations journals. *Address:* Office of the Prime Minister, 885 Grande-Allée Est, 3e étage, Québec, PQ G1A 1A2, Canada.

BOUCHARDEAU, Huguette; French politician; b. 1 June 1935, Saint-Etienne; d. of Marius Briaut and Rose (née Noel) Briaut; m. Marc Bouchardeau 1955; one s. two d.; teacher of philosophy, Lycée Honoré d'Urfé 1961–70; lecturer in educ. sciences, Univ. of Lyon 1970; Sec.–Gen. Parti Socialiste unifié 1979–83; unsuccessful presidential cand. 1981; Sec. of State for Environment and Quality of Life 1983–84; Minister for the Environment 1984–86; f., Ed. H.B. Editions 1995–; Mayor Aigues-Vives June 1995–. *Publications:* Pas d'histoire, les femmes 1977, Hélène Brion: La voie feministe 1978, Un coin dans leur monde 1980, Le ministère du possible 1986, Choses dites de profil 1988, George Sand, La lune et les sabots 1990, Rose Noël 1990, La grande verrière 1991, Carnets de Prague 1992, Le Déjeuner 1993, La Famille Renoir 1994, Simone Weil 1995. *Address:* H.B. Editions, 3 Grand Rue, 30670 Aignes-Vives (Office); 41 rue de Calvisson, 30670 Aigues-Vives, France (Home).

BOUCHIER, Ian Arthur Dennis, C.B.E., M.B., CH.B., M.D., F.R.C.P., F.R.C.P.E., F.R.S.A., F.R.S.E., F.F.P.H.M., F.I.BIOL.; British professor of medicine; b. 7 Sept. 1932, Cape Town, S. Africa; s. of E. A. Bouchier and May Bouchier; m. Patricia N. Henshilwood 1959; two s.; ed. Rondebosch Boys' High School and Univ. of Cape Town; junior staff positions, Groote Schuur Hosp. Cape Town 1955–60; Registrar, Lecturer, Royal Free Hosp. London 1961–63; Research Fellow, Instr. Boston Univ. 1963–65; Sr. Lecturer, Univ. of London 1965–70, Reader in Medicine 1970–73; Prof. of Medicine, Univ. of Dundee 1973–86, Univ. of Edin. 1986–97; Sec.-Gen. World Org. of Gastroenterology 1982–90, Pres. 1990–98; Chief Scientist for Scotland 1992–97; mem. Chief Scientist Cttee.; Visiting Prof. Univ. of Michigan 1979, Madras Medical Coll. 1981, McGill Univ. 1983, Royal Postgrad. Medical School 1984, Univ. of Hong Kong 1988, China Medical Univ. 1988, Univ. of Dunedin 1989, Keio Univ. 1991; mem. Council British Soc. of Gastroenterology 1987–90 (Pres. 1994–95); mem. Council, Royal Soc. of Edin. 1986–89; mem. Council British Soc. of Gastroenterology 1992–; Fellow, Inst. of Biology; Hon. mem. South African Soc. of Gastroenterology, Japanese Soc. of Gastroenterology; Corresp. mem. Italian Soc. of Gastroenterology, Royal Catalonian Acad. of Medicine; mem. numerous editorial bds.; Hon. F.C.P. (South Africa). *Publications:* 28 textbooks and 550 articles mainly on gastroenterological topics. *Leisure interests:* music of Berlioz, history of whaling, cooking. *Address:* 8A Merchiston Park, Edin., EH10 4PN, Scotland.

BOUDART, Michel, M.A., PH.D.; American professor of chemical engineering; b. 18 June 1924, Brussels, Belgium; s. of François Boudart and Marguerite Swolfs; m. Marina M. D'Haese 1948; three s. one d.; ed. Princeton Univ.; Asst. then Assoc. Prof. Princeton Univ. 1954–61; Prof. Univ. of Calif. (Berkeley) 1961–64, adjunct Prof. of Chemical Eng. 1994–; Prof. of Chemical Eng. Stanford Univ. 1964–80, William M. Keck Prof. 1980–94, Prof. Emer. 1994–; mem. tech. advisory bd. British Petroleum 1992–98, Nova 1997–, numerous editorial bds.; co-founder and Dir. Catalytica Inc. 1973; mem. N.A.S., Nat. Acad. of Eng., American Acad. of Arts and Sciences, Calif. Acad. of Sciences. *Publications include:* Kinetics of Chemical Processes 1968, Kinetics of Heterogeneous Catalytic Reactions 1984 (with G. Djéga-Mariadassou), jt. ed. Catalysis: Science and Technology, 11 vols. 1981–96, (with Marina Boudart and René Bryssinck) Modern Belgium 1990. *Address:* Department of Chemical Engineering, Stanford University, CA 94305 (Office); 512 Gerona Road, Stanford, CA 94305, U.S.A. (Home). *Telephone:* (415) 4748 (Office).

BOUDOURIS, Georges; Greek university professor and engineer; b. 11 Sept. 1919, Kyparissia; s. of Odysseas Boudouris and Eustathia Rombola; m. Irma Terzakis 1952; two s.; ed. Nat. Tech. Univ. of Athens, École Supérieure d'Électricité, Paris and Univ. of Paris; Scientific Research C.N.R.S., Paris 1955–66; Asst. Prof. École Supérieure d'Électricité 1964–65; Consultant Univ. of Patras, Greece 1965–66; Assoc. Prof. Agricultural High School of Athens 1966–68; returned to France in 1968, became naturalised citizen but retained Greek nationality; Prof. Polytechnic Inst. and Univ. of Grenoble 1968–76; returned to Greece 1976; Prof. of Physics Nat. Tech. Univ. of Athens 1976–87, Rector 1983–86, re-elected 1986, resgnd. 1987, Prof. Emer. 1987–; fmr. Visiting Prof. Univs. of Pisa and Paris; Gov. Hellenic Telecommunication Org. 1981–82; Pres. Nat. Foundation of Scientific Research 1982–83; Vice-Pres. Greek Cttee. for UNESCO 1982–85, Pres. 1989–; mem. Perm. Cttee. Conf. of European Univ. Rectors 1983–87, Exec. Cttee. European Scientific Foundation 1982–84, Admin. Council Community of Mediterranean Univs. 1983–87, Council for Higher Educ., Greek Ministry of Nat. Educ. 1983–87, mem. numerous other scientific, cultural and social orgs. and insts.; hon. medal for participation in the Nat. resistance. *Publications:* about 60 research papers on electromagnetism, atomic and molecular physics, 15 textbooks, and numerous articles, reports and other publs. concerning univ. educ., energy problems and peace protection. *Leisure interests:* social and cultural activities, classical music. *Address:* Odos Xiroyanni 56, Zografou 157.71, Athens, Greece. *Telephone:* 7796 560.

BOUDRIA, Don; Canadian politician; b. 1949, Hull, Quebec; m. Mary Ann Morris 1971; one s. one d.; ed. Univ. of Waterloo; fmr. fed. govt. employee, holding various positions including Chief Purchasing Agent; fmr. Councillor, Cumberland Township; mem. Ontario Legis. 1981–84; founding Pres. Ont. Section, Int. Asscn. of French-speaking Parliamentarians; mem. Parl. 1984–; fmr. Chief Govt. Whip and Chair. Ont. Liberal Caucus; Minister for Int. Cooperation and Minister responsible for Francophonie 1996–97; Leader of Govt. in House of Commons 1997–. *Address:* House of Commons, Confederation Building Room 380, Ottawa, Ont., K1A 0A6, Canada.

BOUGIE, Jacques, O.C.; Canadian business executive; b. 1947, Montreal; ed. Univ. of Montreal; joined Alcan 1979, Man. Beauharnois Works, then various positions in Winnipeg, Toronto and Montreal in product devt., planning and gen. man., responsible for fabricating operations in N. America, Pres., C.O.O. Alcan Aluminium Ltd. 1989–93, Pres., C.E.O. 1993–; Canadian Chair. Canada-Japan Business Cttee.; Vice-Chair. Business Council on Nat. Issues; mem. Bd. Dirs. Royal Bank of Canada, Bell Canada, Asia Pacific Foundation of Canada. *Address:* Office of the President, Alcan Aluminium Limited, 1188 Sherbrooke Street W., Montreal, Québec, H3A 3G2, Canada.

BOUHAFS, Abdelhak; Algerian government official; b. 15 Aug. 1945; m.; one c.; ed. Algiers and Grenoble Univs.; with Sonatrach 1974, Asst. to Vice-Pres. and responsible for devt. and for valorization of hydrocarbons 1974–80, Co-ordinator of Energy Studies 1980–83; joined Ministry of Energy and Petrochemical Industries 1983; Dir.-Gen. of Energy Coordination and of Commercialization 1984–86; responsible for Studies and Synthesis in sphere of Int. Relations 1986–88; Chef de Cabinet to Minister of Energy and Petrochemical Industries 1988–89; Dir.-Gen. Sonatrach 1989. *Address:* c/o Sonatrach, 10 rue du Sahara, Hydra, Algiers, Algeria.

BOULANGER, Daniel; French writer; b. 24 Jan. 1922, Compiègne, Oise; s. of Michel Boulanger and Hélène Bayard; m. 2nd Clémence Dufour; four s. three d.; ed. Petit Séminaire Saint-Charles, Chauny; sub-editor, Affaires économiques 1946–48; writer 1948–; wrote scripts or screenplays for over 100 films, including L'Homme de Rio 1963, Le Roi de Coeur (Prix Louis-Delluc) 1969, L'Affaire Dominici 1973, Toute une vie 1974, Une femme fidèle 1976, Chouans 1988; numerous plays; mem. Académie Goncourt 1983; Prix Pierre de Monaco for his complete body of work 1979, Prix Kléber Haedens 1983; Officier Légion d'honneur, Officier Ordre nat. du Mérite, Commdr. des Arts et des Lettres. *Publications include:* (novels, novellas and short stories) Les Noces du Merle 1963 (Prix de la Nouvelle 1963), Retouches 1969 (Prix Max Jacob 1970), Vessies et Lanternes 1971 (Prix de l'Académie française 1971), Fouette Cocher 1974 (Prix Goncourt de la nouvelle 1974), La Confession d'Omer 1991, Un Eté à la diable 1992, Ursacq 1993, A la courte paille 1993, Le Retable Wasserfall et Etiquettes 1994, Caporal Supérieur 1994, Le Miroitier 1995, Taciturnes 1995, Tombeau d'Héraldine 1997, Talbard 1998; several collections of poetry. *Address:* 22 rue du Heaume, 60300 Senlis, France.

BOULARÈS, Mohamed Habib; Tunisian politician, writer and journalist; b. 29 July 1933, Tunis; s. of Sadok Ben Mohamed and Zoubeida Bent Abdelkader Aziz; m. Line Poinsignon 1966; one d.; ed. Collège Sadiki, Tunis; mem. staff exec. office, Parti Destourien 1955; Deputy Ed. daily Essabah 1956; in charge of publications, Ministry of Information 1957; Ed. Nat. Radio news service 1958; Ed. Al Amal (Parti Destourien daily newspaper) 1960; first Man. Dir. Tunis Afrique Presse news agency 1961; Dir. Radio Télévision Tunisienne, Dir. of Information, Ministry of Cultural Affairs and Information 1962; mem. Econ. and Social Council 1964–70; Minister of Cultural Affairs and Information 1970; Dir. Ecole Internationale de Bordeaux, France 1972–73; teacher, Institut de Langues Orientales, Paris for four years; mem. Parl. 1981–86, 1989–94, 1994–; Amb. to Egypt 1988; Minister of Culture 1988–89, of Culture and Information April 1989–90, of Foreign Affairs 1990–91, of Nat. Defence Feb.–Oct. 1991; Special Adviser to Pres. of Repub. March 1990; Pres. Nat. Ass. 1991–94; (Mediterranean Africa prize of Asscn. des Ecrivains en langue française ADELF) 1984; Grand Officier Ordre de l'Indépendence, Grand Cordon Ordre de la République, Commdr. Ordre du 7 Novembre, numerous foreign decorations. *Publications:* L'Islam, la peur et l'espérance (trans. in English); several other non-fiction works and plays. *Address:* c/o Assemblée Nationale, 2000 Le Bardo, Tunis, Tunisia. *Telephone:* 01 510-200. *Fax:* 01 514-608.

BOULEZ, Pierre, C.B.E.; French composer and conductor; b. 26 March 1925, Montbrison; s. of Léon Boulez and Marcelle Calabre; ed. Paris Conservatoire; studied with Messiaen, Vaurabourg-Honegger and Leibowitz; Dir. of Music to Jean-Louis Barrault theatre co. 1948; aided by Barrault and Madeleine Renaud Barrault he founded the Concert Marigny which later became the Domaine Musicale, Paris; Prin. Guest Conductor Cleveland Symphony

Orchestra 1968; Prin. Conductor BBC Symphony Orchestra 1971–75; Musical Dir. New York Philharmonic 1971–77; Dir. Inst. de Recherches et de Coordination Acoustique/Musique (IRCAM) 1975–91, Hon. Dir. 1992–; Prof. Collège de France 1976–95; Vice-Pres. Opéra Bastille 1985–91; Prin. Guest Conductor Chicago Symphony Orchestra 1995–; conducted the centenary production of Wagner's Ring, Bayreuth 1976–80; Dr. h.c. (Cambridge) 1980, (Bâle) 1980, (Los Angeles) 1984, (Oxford) 1987. (Brussels) 1988; Praemium Imperiale, Japan Art Asscn. 1989, Polar Music Prize Sweden 1996; *Works:* First Piano Sonata 1946, Sonatina for Flute and Piano 1946, Le Visage Nuptial (5 poems of René Char for 2 solo voices, female choir and orch.) 1946–50, Second Piano Sonata 1948, Le Soleil des Eaux (2 poems of René Char for voice and orch.) 1948, Livre pour Quattuor (string quartet) 1949, Le Marteau sans Maître (cantata for voice and instruments to texts by René Char, also ballet 1965) 1955, Structures (2 pianos) 1964, Third Piano Sonata 1957–58, Improvisations sur Mallarmé (soprano and chamber ensemble) 1958, Doubles (orch.) 1958, Poésie pour Pouvoir (orch.) 1958, Tombeau (soprano and orch.) 1959, Pli selon Pli 1958–62, Figures—doubles-prismes 1964/74, Eclats and Eclats Multiples 1965, Domaines 1968–69, Cummings ist der Dichter 1970, Explosante-fixe for 8 solo instruments 1973, Rituel 1974, Messagesquisse 1977, Notations 1979, Répons 1981–86, Dérive 1984, Dialogue de l'ombre double 1984, Mémoriale 1985, le Visage nuptial 1989, Dérive 2 1993, Explosante-fixe for 3 solo flutes and large ensemble 1993. *Publications:* Penser la musique aujourd'hui 1966, Relevés d'apprenti (essays) 1967, Par volonté et par hasard 1975, Points de repère 1981, Le pays fertile: Paul Klee 1989, Orientations: Collected Writings 1986. *Address:* IRCAM, 1 place Igor Stravinsky, 75004 Paris, France; Postfach 22, 76481 Baden-Baden, Germany.

BOULTING, Roy; British film producer and director; b. 21 Nov. 1913; s. of Arthur Boulting and Rose Bennet; twin brother of the late John Boulting; m. Hayley Mills (q.v.) 1971 (divorced 1977); m. (5th) Sandra Payne 1978; ed. Reading School; formed independent film production co. with John Boulting 1937; war service, RAC, finishing as Capt.; Dir. British Lion Films Ltd. 1958–72; Jt. Man. Dir. Charter Film Productions Ltd. 1973–. *Films produced include:* Brighton Rock 1947, Seven Days to Noon 1950, Privates Progress 1955, Lucky Jim 1957, I'm All Right Jack 1959, Heaven's Above! 1962. *Films directed include:* Pastor Hall 1939, Thunder Rock 1942, Fame is the Spur 1947, The Guinea Pig 1948, High Treason 1951, Singlehanded 1952, Seagulls over Sorrento, Crest of the Wave 1953, Josephine and Men 1955, Run for the Sun 1955, Brothers in Law 1956, Happy is the Bride 1958, Carlton-Browne of the FO 1958–59, I'm All Right Jack 1959, The Risk 1960, The French Mistress 1960, Suspect 1960, The Family Way 1966, Twisted Nerve 1968, There's a Girl in My Soup 1970, Soft Beds, Hard Battles 1974, Danny Travis 1978, The Last Word 1979, The Moving Finger (for BBC TV) 1984. *Play:* Favourites 1976; Dr. (h.c.) Royal Coll. of Arts 1990. *Address:* Charter Film Productions Ltd., Twickenham Film Studios, St. Margarets, Twickenham, Middlesex, TW1 2AW, England (Office).

BOUMA, Johannes, PH.D.; Netherlands soil scientist; b. 29 Oct. 1940, 't Bildt; s. of S. Bouma and J. Bouma (née Werff); m. Marianne Wiebols 1969; one s. one d.; ed. Agricultural Univ., Wageningen, Univ. of Wisconsin, Madison; Asst. Prof. Soils Dept., Univ. of Wis., Madison 1969–73, Assoc. Prof. 1973–75; Head of Soil Physics Dept., Netherlands Soil Survey Inst., Wageningen 1975–82, Deputy Dir. in charge of research 1982–86; Prof. of Soil Science, Agricultural Univ., Wageningen 1986–; mem. Netherlands Scientific Council for Govt. Policy 1998–; mem. Royal Dutch Acad. of Sciences 1989; corresp. mem. German Soil Science Asscn.; Fellow Soil Science Soc. of America. *Publications:* various articles in tech. journals. *Leisure interests:* jogging, cycling. *Address:* Laboratory of Soil Science, P.O. Box 37, Agricultural University, 6700 AA Wageningen, Netherlands (Office); Spoorbaanweg 35, 3911 CA Rhenen, Netherlands (Home).

BOUQUET, Carole; French actress; b. 1953; two s.; Face of Chanel No. 5. *Films include:* Cet Obscur Objet du Désir 1977, Buffet Froid 1979, Le Manteau d'Astrakan 1979, For Your Eyes Only 1981, Le Jour des Idiots 1981, Bingo Bango 1982, Dream One 1983, Mystère 1983, Dagobert 1984, Rive droite, Rive gauche 1984, Double Messieurs 1985, Special Police 1985, Le Mal d'Aimer 1986, Jenatsch 1986, On se dépêche d'en rire 1987, Bunker Palace Hotel 1988, Trop Belle pour toi 1988, Grosse Fatigue, A Business Affair.

BOURBON BUSSET, Comte Jacques Louis Robert Marie de; French diplomatist and writer; b. 27 April 1912, Paris; s. of François de Bourbon, Comte de Busset, and Guillemette de Colbert; m. 1st Laurence Ballande 1944; three s. one d.; m. 2nd 1997; ed. Ecole Normale Supérieure, Paris; embassy attaché 1939; Pres. French Red Cross 1944–45; Dir. de Cabinet, Ministry of Foreign Affairs 1948–52, Dir. of Cultural Affairs 1952–56, Minister 1954; mem. Acad. Française 1981; Grand Prix Roman de l'Académie Française 1957, Prix Marcel Proust 1980. *Publications:* 38 works including Le Livre de Laurence (10 vols.), Lettre à Laurence 1987, L'Audace d'aimer 1990, L'Instant perpétuel 1991, L'Esprit de la forêt 1993, L'Amour Confiance 1995, La Tendresse Inventive 1996. *Address:* 91610 Ballancourt, France. *Telephone:* (6) 4932902.

BOURDEAU, Philippe François, PH.D.; Belgian fmr. EC official and university professor; b. 25 Nov. 1926, Rabat, Morocco; s. of Michel Bourdeau and Lucienne Imbrecht; m. Flora Gorirossi 1954; three d.;. ed. Gembloux, Belgium and Duke Univ. U.S.A.; Asst. Prof. State Univ. of N.C. 1954–56, Yale Univ. 1956–58, 1960–62; Prof. Univ. of Belgian Congo 1958–60; Head, Radiobiology Dept. EURATOM, Jt. Research Centre, Ispra, Italy 1962–71; Head of Div. then Dir. research programmes in environment and in non-nuclear energy, Comm. of EC, Brussels 1971–91; Prof. Univ. Libre de Bruxelles 1972–; Head, European Environment Agency Task Force 1991; Chair. Scientific Cttee., European Environmental Agency (EEA); Fellow, A.A.A.S. *Publications:* scientific papers in the fields of environment policy, ecophysiology, ecotoxicology. *Leisure interests:* reading, sport. *Address:* EEA, Kongens Nytorv 6, 1050 Copenhagen K, Denmark; U.C.B., CP 130/02, 50 ave F. D. Roosevelt, 1050 Brussels, Belgium.

BOURDIEU, Pierre; French professor of social sciences; b. 1 Aug. 1930, Denguin; s. of Albert Bourdieu and Noémi Duhau; m. Marie-Claire Brizard 1962; three s.; ed. Ecole Normale Supérieure; Prof., Lycée de Moulins 1954–55; Asst., Faculty of Arts, Algiers 1958–60, Faculty of Arts, Paris 1958–60; Dir. of Educ., Faculty of Arts, Lille 1961–64; Dir. of Studies, Ecole pratique des hautes études 1964–; Ecole normale supérieure 1964–84; Dir. Collection "Le Sens Commun" (Editions de Minuit) 1964–92; Visiting mem. Inst. for Advanced Studies, Princeton 1972–73; mem. Scientific Council of Max Planck Inst. für Bildungsforschung 1974–76; Ed. review Actes de la recherche en Sciences Sociales 1975–, Liber 1989–; Consulting Ed. American Journal of Sociology 1975; mem. Ed. Bd. The Sociological Review 1976, Media, Culture and Society 1980; Dir. Centre de sociologie européenne (CSE) of Collège de France, and Ecole des hautes études en Sciences Sociales 1985–; Prof., Coll. de France 1981–; mem. American Acad. of Arts and Sciences. *Publications* (in English): The Algerians 1958, The Inheritors 1964, Reproduction in Education, Society and Culture 1970, Outline of a Theory of Practice 1972, Algeria 1960 1977, Distinction 1979, Homo Academicus 1984, Language and Symbolic Power 1991, An Invitation to Reflexive Sociology 1992 (jtly.), The Rules of Art 1996, The State Nobility 1996, Acts of Resistance. Against the New Myths of Our Time 1998, Practical Reason. On the Theory of Action 1998, On Television and Journalism 1998; contrib. The Field of Cultural Production: Essays on Art and Literature (ed. R. Johnson) 1993. *Address:* Collège de France, 52 rue du Cardinal Lemoine, 75005 Paris, France.

BOUREAU, Edouard; French academic; b. 31 Jan. 1913, Maine-et-Loire; s. of Edouard Boureau and Elise (née Decouard) Boureau; m. Jane Vallet 1943; two s.; Deputy Dir. Museum Nat. d'Histoire Naturelle 1946–59; Prof. of Paleobotany, Univ. Pierre-et-Marie-Curie, Paris 1959–81, Prof. Emer. 1981–; Sec.-Gen., Pres. Org. int. de la Paléobotanique 1954–80; mem. Acad des Sciences (Inst. de France) 1977–; Laureat Acad. des Sciences 1950–65, Officier des Palmes Académiques 1949, Chevalier, Légion d'honneur 1992. *Publications:* Anatomie végétale (3 vols) 1954–57, Traite de Paléobotanique (4 vols) 1964–75; World Report on Paleobotany (9 vols) 1954–73, Les Sphénophytes 1971, La Terre, Mère de la vie? 1986. *Leisure interest:* scientific history. *Address:* 64 rue de Paris, 94340 Joinville-Le-Pont, France. *Telephone:* (1) 48 83 83 61.

BOURGES, Hervé; French administrator and journalist; b. 2 May 1933, Rennes, Ile-et-Vilaine; s. of Joseph Bourges and Marie-Magdeleine Desjeux; m. Marie-Thérèse Lapouille 1966; ed. Lycée de Biarritz, Coll. Saint-Joseph, Reims, École supérieure de journalisme; Ed. then Ed.-in-Chief Témoignage Chrétien 1956–62; attached to the Keeper of the Seals 1959–62, Dir. Algerian Ministry of Youth and Popular Education, attached to Ministry of Information; Asst. Lecturer Univ. de Paris II 1967–; f. and Dir. École supérieure de journalisme de Yaoundé, Cameroun 1970–76; Dir. then Pres. Admin. Council École nat. supérieure de journalisme de Lille 1976–80; Dir. Information Service and Dir.-Gen.'s Messenger UNESCO 1980–81, Amb. to UNESCO 1994–95; Dir. then Dir.-Gen. Radio France Int. 1981–83; Chair. Dir.-Gen. TV Française 1 (T.F.1) 1983–87, Hon. Pres. 1987–93; Hon. Pres. Admin. Council, École Supérieure de Journalisme de Lille 1992–; Dir.-Gen. Radio Monte Carlo (RMC) 1988; Pres., Dir.-Gen. Société financière de radiodiffusion (Sofirad) 1989–91; Pres. Canal Horizon 1990–91, Conseil Supérieur de L'Audio-Visuel (CSA) 1995–; Docteur d'état en sciences politiques; Chevalier, Légion d'honneur; Croix de la Valeur Militaire. *Publications:* L'Algérie à l'épreuve du pouvoir 1967, La Révolte étudiante 1968, Décoloniser l'information 1978, Les cinquante Afriques (jtly.) 1979, Le village planétaire (jtly.) 1986, Une Chaîne sur les bras 1987, Un amour de télévision (jtly.) 1989, La Télévision du Public 1993. *Address:* Conseil Supérieur de l'Audiovisuel, tour Mirabeau, 39–43 quai André Citroën, 75739 Paris cedex 15; 12 rue Magellan, 75008 Paris, France. *Telephone:* (1) 45-68-10-00. *Fax:* (1) 45-67-16-90.

BOURGES, Yvon, L. EN D.; French politician and overseas administrator; b. 29 June 1921, Pau; s. of Jacques Bourges and Nancy Dardenne; m. Odile Fontaine 1943; two s. three d.; ed. Univ. de Rennes; Chef de Cabinet to Prefect of the Somme 1944–45, of Bas-Rhin 1945–47; Sub-Prefect of Erstein 1947–48; with Ministry of Overseas Territories 1948, Dir. de Cabinet, High Comm. in French Equatorial Africa 1948–51, in French West Africa 1951–56; Gov. Upper Volta 1956–58; High Commr. (French) Equatorial Africa 1958–61; Chef de Cabinet, Ministry of Interior 1961–62; Deputy for Ille-et-Vilaine 1962–80; Mayor of Dinard 1962–67, 1971–89; Sec. of State for Scientific Research 1965–66, for Information 1966–67, for Co-operation 1967–72; Minister of Commerce 1972–73, of Defence 1975–80; Chair. Regional Council of Brittany 1986–98; mem. Senate 1980–, EU Cttee. of the Regions; Chevalier Légion d'honneur and numerous foreign decorations. *Address:* Palais du Luxembourg, 75291 Paris Cedex 06, France.

BOURGUIBA, Habib Ben Ali; Tunisian politician; b. 3 Aug. 1903, Monastir; m. 1st Mathilde Lorrain 1927 (divorced 1961, deceased 1976); one s.; m. 2nd Wassila Ben Ammar 1962 (divorced 1986); ed. Univ. of Paris, Ecole Libre des Sciences Politiques; active in politics and journalism since 1928; mem. Destour Party 1921, broke away and formed Neo-Destour Party (outlawed by the French) 1934; imprisoned by the French 1934–36 and 1938–43; escaped to Middle East 1945, travelled to promote Tunisian independence 1945–49, world tour during Tunisian negotiations with French Govt. 1951; arrested 1952, placed under surveillance at Tabarka (Jan.), imprisoned at Remada (March), in solitary confinement, Ile de la Galite (May) until 1954; released 1954, under surveillance in France 1954–55, during negotiations; returned to Tunisia following Franco-Tunisian Agreements 1955; Pres. Tunisian Nat. Assembly, Prime Minister, Pres. of the Council, Minister of Foreign Affairs, of Defence 1956–57, Head of Cabinet 1957–87; Pres. of Tunisia 1957–87, Pres. for Life 1975–87; Pres. Neo-Destour Party (Pres. for Life 1974); under house arrest, Mornag, S. Tunisia 1987–; Ordre du Sang, Ordre de la confiance en diamants. *Publications:* Le Destour et la France 1937, La Tunisie et la France 1955.

BOURGUIBA, Habib, Jr., L ÈS D.; Tunisian diplomatist (retd.); b. 9 April 1927, Paris, France; s. of fmr. Pres. Habib Bourguiba (q.v.); m. Neila Zouiten 1954; two s. one d.; ed. Collège Sadiki, Law School, France; collaborated in nat. liberation movement, especially 1951–54; Counsellor, Tunisian Embassy, Washington 1956–57; Amb. to Italy 1957–58, to France 1958–61, to U.S.A. 1961–63, to Canada 1961–62, to Mexico 1962–63; Perm. Rep. to UN 1961–62; Sec.-Gen., Govt. of Repub. 1963–64; in charge of Dept. of Youth and Sports, Dept. of Tourism, Nat. office of Artisanship and Information Dept. 1963–64; elected mem. Nat. Assembly Nov. 1964; Sec. of State for Foreign Affairs 1964–70; Special Adviser to the Pres. 1977–86; Pres., Gen. Man. Banque de Développement de l'Economie de la Tunisie 1971–88; consultant 1988–; many Tunisian and foreign decorations. *Leisure interests:* staying home with family, computers, golf. *Address:* Le Colisée, 45 avenue Habib Bourguiba, B. 258, Tunis 1001 (Office); Dar Essalam, 14 rue Chedli Zouiten, La Marsa 2070, Tunisia (Home). *Telephone:* 340938 (Office); 271505 (Home). *Fax:* 342248 (Office); 742666 (Home).

BOURGUIGNON, Philippe Etienne, M.SC.ECON., M.B.A.; French business executive; b. 11 Jan. 1948, Salins les Bains; s. of Jacques Bourguignon and Paule Clément; m. Martine Lemardeley 1977; one s. one d.; ed. Univ. of Aix; analyst, Synthèse Documentaire, Paris 1971–72; Project Man. Systembau, Munich 1973; Vice-Pres. Devt. Accor, Novotel Asia, Middle East 1974–79; Exec. Vice-Pres. Accor North America, New York 1979–84; Pres. and C.E.O. Accor Asia Pacific, Los Angeles 1984–88; Sr. Vice-Pres. Real Estate Devt. Euro Disney, Paris 1989–92; Pres. Euro Disney SA, Paris 1992, Chair. and C.E.O. 1993–97; Exec. Vice-Pres. for Europe Walt Disney Co. 1996–97; Chair. Bd. of Dirs. Club Méditerranée 1997–; Pres. Young Pres. Org. 1990; mem. Bd. of Dirs. American Chamber of Commerce in France; Chevalier Légion d'honneur, mem. Econ. Council Confed. of French Industries and Services; Chair. YPO French Chapter 1990. *Leisure interests:* sailing, reading. *Address:* Club Méditerranée, 11 rue Cambrai, 75019 Paris, France (Office).

BOURHANE, Ali; Comoran international civil servant; b. 2 April 1946, Comoros; m. Beatrice Bourhane; one s. one d.; ed. Univ. of Bordeaux and Ecole Nationale d'Administrations, Paris; Research Fellow, Univ. of Toulouse 1971; Prof. of Math. Comoros 1972–75; civil servant 1980–85; Sr. Economist, IMF, Washington, D.C. 1985–90; Alt. Exec. Dir. IBRD 1990–94, Exec. Dir. 1994–. *Leisure interests:* reading (religion, African history and anthropology, devt. econs.), tennis, running. *Address:* International Bank for Reconstruction and Development, 1818 H Street, N.W., Washington, DC 20433 (Office); 3 Greenlance Court, Potomac, MD 20854, U.S.A. (Home). *Telephone:* (202) 458-1153 (Office); (301) 299-1933 (Home).

BOURHANE, Nourdine; Comoran politician; Prime Minister of Comoros 1997–98. *Address:* c/o Office of the Prime Minister, B.P. 421, Moroni, Comoros.

BOURJAILY, Vance, B.A., D.LIT.; American novelist; b. 17 Sept. 1922, Cleveland, Ohio; s. of Monte Ferris and Barbara Webb Bourjaily; m. 1st Bettina Yensen 1946; one s. two d.; m. 2nd Yasmin Mogul 1985; one s.; ed. Handley High School, Va. and Bowdoin Coll., Maine; American Field Service 1942–44; U.S. Army 1944–46; Publisher, Record, New Castle, Va. 1947–48; Staff Writer, San Francisco Chronicle 1949–50; Ed. Discovery 1951–53; Instructor, Mexico City Coll. 1953; Dramatic Critic, The Village Voice 1955–56; freelance TV writer 1956–57; Visiting lecturer, Univ. of Iowa 1957–59, Prof. 1961; Specialist, U.S. State Dept. 1960; Boyd Prof. of English, La. State Univ. 1985–. *Publications:* novels: The End of My Life 1947, The Hound of Earth 1953, The Violated 1957, Confessions of a Spent Youth 1960, The Man Who Knew Kennedy 1967, Brill Among the Ruins 1970, Now Playing at Canterbury 1976, The Great Fake Book 1986, Old Soldier 1990, Fishing by Mail: The Outdoor Life of a Father and Son 1993; non-fiction: The Unnatural Enemy 1963, Country Matters 1973; plays: Time is a Dancer 1950, The Quick Years 1956, Confessions 1971. *Leisure interests:* politics, mycology, conservation. *Address:* c/o Owen Laster, William Morris Agency, 151 El Camino Drive, Beverly Hills, CA 90212, U.S.A. *Telephone:* (504) 766-6231 (Home).

BOURJINI, Salah Amara, M.A.(ECONS.), PH.D.; Tunisian United Nations official; b. 17 Jan. 1938, Lekef; m. 1967; one s. two d.; eng. in planning and statistics, Tunis 1963–67; lecturer in Econs. Univ. of Kansas 1969–72; Prof. Univ. of Tunis 1972–80; Adviser to Minister of Economy 1972–76; Deputy Dir.-Gen. Ministry of Foreign Affairs 1976–80; Deputy UN Resident Rep. and UN Coordinator, Algeria 1980–82; Chief, Div. for Regional Programme, Arab States, UNDP, New York 1982–87; UN Resident Rep. and UN Coordinator, Iraq 1987–92; UN Resident Rep. and UN Coordinator, Libya 1992–; Chevalier de la République; various UN service awards. *Publications:* Human Capital Investment and Economic Growth 1974, New International Economic Order 1978; articles on devt., educ. and trade. *Leisure interests:* tennis, swimming, music. *Address:* United Nations Development Programme, P.O. Box 358, Tripoli, Libya. *Telephone:* 218-21 33 30 855. *Fax:* 218-21 33 30 856.

BOURKE, William Oliver; American business executive; b. 12 April 1927, Chicago, Ill.; s. of Robert E. and Mabel E. D'Arcy Bourke; m. 1st Mary C. Cassell 1948; m. 2nd Elizabeth M. Philbey 1970; three s. one d.; ed. DePaul Univ.; Asst. Gen. Sales Man., Studebaker Corpn., South Bend, Ind. 1952–56; Exec. Vice-Pres. Ford Motor Co., Dearborn, Mich. 1956–80; Pres. Reynolds Metal Co. (now Reynolds Aluminium) 1981–88, C.E.O. 1986–92, Chair. 1988–92; Dir. Dart & Kraft Inc., Abex Corpn., Robertshaw Controls Co. *Address:* c/o Reynolds Metals Company, 6601 West Broad Street, Richmond, VA 23230, U.S.A.

BOURNE, Charles Beresford, LL.D., S.J.D., F.R.S.C.; Canadian professor of law and barrister; b. 19 Feb. 1921, Barbados, W.I.; s. of Rev. Beresford Bourne and Lilian M. Ward; m. Barbara J. Farmer; one s. two d.; ed. The Lodge School, Barbados, Univ. of Toronto, St. John's Coll. Cambridge and Harvard Law School; Asst. Prof. of Law, Univ. of Saskatchewan 1947–50; Assoc. Prof. of Law, Univ. of B.C. 1950–57, Prof. 1957–86, Prof. Emer. 1986–; Ed.-in-Chief, Canadian Yearbook of Int. Law 1962–93; Read Medal (Canadian Council of Int. Law). *Publications:* articles in legal journals especially on the law of international water resources and constitutional law. *Leisure interests:* reading, walking, gardening, bridge, croquet. *Address:* 1822 East Mall, Vancouver, B.C., V6T 1Z1; 1576 Newton Crescent, Vancouver, B.C., V6T 1W7, Canada. *Telephone:* (604) 822-5624 (Office); (228) 0590 (Home). *Fax:* (604) 822-8108.

BOURNE, Larry Stuart, PH.D., F.R.S.C.; Canadian professor of geography and planning; b. 24 Dec. 1939, London, Ont.; s. of Stuart H. Bourne and Florence (Adams) Bourne; m. Paula T. O'Neill 1967; one s. one d.; ed. Univs. of Western Ontario, Alberta and Chicago; Asst. Prof. of Geography, Univ. of Toronto 1967–69, Assoc. Prof. and Assoc. Dir., Centre for Urban and Community Studies (CUCS) 1969–72, Prof. and Dir. 1973–78, 1979–84, Prof. of Geography and Planning, Co-ordinator of Grad. Studies 1985–89, 1991–94; Dir. Grad. Planning Program 1996–98; Visiting Scholar, Univ. of Monash, Australia and L.S.E., U.K. 1972–73, Centre for Environmental Studies, London, U.K. 1978–79; Visiting Prof., Univ. of Alberta, Univ. of Tex., U.S.A. 1984, Marburg (W. Germany) 1985, Melbourne 1988, Meiji Univ., Tokyo 1991; Chair. Comm. on Urban Systems and Devt., Int. Geographical Union 1988–92; consultant to local, nat. and int. agencies; Pres. Canadian Asscn. of Geographers 1993–94, North American Regional Science Council 1994–95; Award for Scholarly Distinction, Canadian Asscn. of Geographers 1985, Honors Award, Asscn. of American Geographers 1985, Award for Service to Geography (Ont. Div. Canadian Asscn. of Geographers) 1990. *Publications:* 18 books, including Internal Structure of the City 1971, Urban Systems: Strategies for Regulation 1975, The Geography of Housing 1981, Urbanization and Settlement Systems 1984, Urban Systems in Transition 1986, The Changing Geography of Urban Systems 1989, Urbanization and Urban Growth 1991, Changing Social Geography of Canadian Cities 1993; numerous articles in journals. *Address:* Department of Geography, University of Toronto, 100 St. George Street, Toronto, Ont., M5S 3G3 (Office); 26 Anderson Avenue, Toronto, Ont., M5P 1H4, Canada (Home). *Fax:* (416) 978-6729.

BOURSEILLER, Antoine; French theatre director and producer; b. 8 July 1930, Paris; s. of Marcel Edouard Bourseiller and Denise Fisteberg; m. Chantal Darget 1966 (deceased); one s. one d.; Dir. of Theatre, Studio des Champs-Elysées 1960–63, Poche 1964–66, Centre Dramatique National de Marseille 1966–75, Recamia 1975–78, Orléans 1980–82; Dir.-Gen. Opéra-Théâtre de Lorraine de Nancy 1982–96; Dir. (plays): Va donc chez Torpe 1961, Axel 1963, L'Amérique 1964, Metro Fantôme 1965, Striptease 1965, Silence, l'arbre. . . 1967, Les Brigands 1972, Jean Harlow 1972, Leuco 1974, Kennedy's Children 1975, La Tour 1976, S.T. 1979; (opera): La Clémence de Titus (Aix-en-Provence Festival) 1973, Le Barbier de Seville (Théâtre Lyrique du Sud) 1979, Mireille (Geneva) 1981, (London) 1983, Carmen (Nancy) 1981, Woyzeck (Angers) 1982; Boulevard Solitude 1984, Cantate d'Octobre, Erwartung 1986, Donna Abbandonata 1987, King Priam 1988 (all at Lorraine); Lulu (Nantes), Lady Macbeth de Mtsensk (Nancy) 1989; La Noche Triste (Opera) 1989, Lohengrin (Opera) 1994, L'Homme de Mancha 1998; Chevalier, Légion d'honneur; Commdr. des Arts et Lettres. *Address:* 20 Villa Seurat, 75014 Paris, France. *Telephone:* (1) 43.35.26.17.

BOUTALEB, Abdelhadi, B.A.; Moroccan politician and educationist; b. 28 Dec. 1923, Fez; m. Touria Chraïbi 1946; two s. one d.; ed. Al Qarawiyin Univ.; Prof. of Arabic History and Literature, and Tutor to Prince Moulay Hassan and Prince Moulay Abdallah; Founder-mem. Democratic Party of Independence 1944–51, Shura and Istiqlal Party 1948, mem. Politburo –1959; campaigned, through the Party, for Moroccan independence, and for this purpose attended UN Session, Paris 1951, and Negotiating Conf. at Aix-les-Bains 1955; Minister of Labour and Social Affairs 1956; Chief Ed. of journal Al-Rai-Alaam 1956–61; Amb. to Syria 1962; Sec. of State, Ministry of Information Nov. 1962, Ministry of Information, Youth and Sports Jan. 1963; Interim Minister in Charge of Mauritania and Sahara Nov. 1963; Minister of Justice 1964–67, of Nat. Educ. and Fine Arts 1967; Minister of State 1968; Minister of Foreign Affairs 1969–70; Pres. Chamber of Reps. 1970–71; lecturer in Constitutional Law and Political Insts., Rabat Law Univ. 1974, in Constitutional Law and Political Insts. 1979–; Amb. to U.S.A., 1974–76, to Mexico 1976; Adviser to H.M. Hassan II 1977–78, 1992–96, Tutor to Crown Prince Sidi Mohamed 1978; Minister of State in Charge of Information 1978; Dir.-Gen. Islamic Educ., Scientific and Cultural Org., Rabat May 1982; Vice-Pres. Int. Comm. for the Presentation of Int. Cultural Heritage 1983–; mem. Royal Acad. for Islamic Civilization Research, Royal Acad. of Morocco 1982, Hon. Cttee. of Pascual de Gayancos Arab-Spanish Foundation 1985; Commdr. of the Throne of Morocco, Grand Cordon of the Repub. of U.A.R., and other decorations. *Publications:* many cultural and literary works. *Leisure interests:* sports, music, reading. *Address:* 100 rue des Oudayas, 20300 Casablanca, Morocco. *Telephone:* (2) 61-82-85. *Fax:* (2) 62-11-95.

BOUTEFLIKA, Abdul Aziz; Algerian politician; b. 2 March 1937, Oujda; ed. Morocco; Major, Nat. Liberation Army and Sec. of Gen. Staff; mem. Parl. for Tlemcen 1962; Minister of Youth, Sports and Tourism 1962–63, of Foreign Affairs 1963–79; Counsellor to the Pres. March 1979–80; mem. F.L.N. Political Bureau 1964–81, mem. Cen. Cttee. 1989; mem. Revolutionary Council 1965–79; led negotiations with France 1963, 1966, for nationalization of hydrocarbons 1971; leader of dels. to many confs. of Arab League, OAU 1968, Group of 1977 1967, Non-aligned countries 1973, Pres. 7th Special Session of UN Gen. Assembly 1975, Int. Conf. on Econ. Co-operation, Paris 1975–76; Pres. 29th UN Gen. Ass. 1974; mem. Nat. Council Moujahidin (Nat. Liberation Army) 1990–. *Address:* 138 Chemin Bachir Brahimi, El Biar, Algiers, Algeria. *Telephone:* 60 34 59.

BOUTIN, Bernard Louis, PH.B.; American management consultant; b. 2 July 1923, Belmont, N.H.; s. of Joseph L. Boutin and Annie E. (Laflam) Boutin; m. Alice M. Boucher 1945; six s. five d.; ed. St. Michael's Coll., Winooski, Vt., and Catholic Univ. of America, Washington, D.C.; Pres. and Treas., Boutin Insurance Agency Inc., Laconia, N.H. 1948–63; Proprietor, Boutin Real Estate Co., Laconia 1955–63; Mayor of Laconia 1955–59; Deputy Admin. Gen. Services Admin. (G.S.A.), Washington D.C. Feb.-Nov. 1961; Admin. G.S.A. 1961–64; Exec. Vice-Pres. Nat. Asscn. Home Builders 1964–65; Admin. of Small Business Admin. 1966–67; Deputy Dir. Office of Econ. Opportunity 1965–66; Exec. Sanders Assoc. Inc. 1967–69; Chair. N.H. State Bd. of Educ. 1968–69; mem. Nat. Highway Safety Comm. 1969–70; Democratic Candidate for Gov. of N.H. 1958, 1960; Pres. St. Michael's Coll. 1969–75; Exec. Vice-Pres. Burlington Savings Bank (Vt.) 1975–76, Pres., Treas., Trustee 1976–80; Treas. and Trustee Medical Center Hospital of Vermont 1978–80; Dir. New England College Fund 1979–80; Dir. First Deposit Nat. Bank 1991–94; numerous awards including Kt. of the Equestrian Order of the Holy Sepulchre of Jerusalem; Hon. LL.D. (St. Michael's Coll.); Hon. L.H.D. (Plymouth Coll. of the Univ. of New Hampshire), Hon. H.H.D. (Franklyn Pierce Coll.). *Publication:* Echos of Me 1991. *Leisure interests:* golf, fishing. *Address:* P.O. Box 1547, Laconia, NH 03247; 26 Wildwood Village, Laconia, NH 03246, U.S.A. *Telephone:* (603) 528-1014.

BOUTROS, Fouad; Lebanese politician and lawyer; b. 1918, Beirut; m. Tania Shehade 1953; one s. two d.; ed. Coll. des Frères, Beirut; Judge, Civil and Mixed Commercial Court, Beirut 1944–47; Judge Mil. Tribunal and Court Lawyer 1947–50; Govt. Lawyer 1951–57; Minister of Nat. Educ. and of the Plan 1959–60; mem. Chamber of Deputies 1960–; Deputy Speaker, Chamber of Deputies 1960–61; Minister of Justice 1961–64; Vice-Pres. of the Council, Minister of Educ. and Defence 1966; Vice-Pres., Council of Ministers, Minister of Foreign Affairs and of Tourism Feb.-Oct. 1968; Deputy Prime Minister and Minister of Foreign Affairs 1976–82, of Defence 1976–80; numerous decorations. *Publications:* numerous lectures and political articles in the press, in Arabic and French. *Leisure interests:* reading, walking. *Address:* Sursock Street, Fouad Boutros Building, Beirut, Lebanon (Home). *Telephone:* 201500 (Home). *Fax:* 428933 (Office).

BOUTROS GHALI, Boutros, LL.B., PH.D.; Egyptian international civil servant and politician; b. 14 Nov. 1922, Cairo; m. Leia Nadler; ed. Cairo Univ. and Paris Univ.; fmr. Prof. of Int. Law and Int. Relations and Head Dept. of Political Sciences, Cairo Univ. 1949–77; fmr. mem. Cen. Cttee. Arab Socialist Union; Pres. Cen. of Political and Strategic Studies; f. Al Ahram Al Iktisadi, Ed. 1960–75, f. Al-Siyassa Ad-Dawlya, Ed.; Minister of State for Foreign Affairs 1977–91, Deputy Prime Minister for Foreign Affairs 1991–92; Sec. Gen. of UN 1992–96; Sec.-Gen. Francophonie 1997–; Vice-Pres. Egyptian Soc. of Int. Law; mem. Cttee. on Application of Conventions and Recommendations of Int. Labour Org.; mem. Int. Comm. of Jurists, Geneva, and Council and Exec. Cttee. of Int. Inst. of Human Rights, Strasbourg; mem. UN Comm. of Int. Law 1979–92, Secretariat Nat. Democratic Party 1980–92, Parl. 1987–92; Onassis Foundation Prize 1995. *Publications include:* Contribution à l'étude des ententes régionales 1949, Cours de diplomatie et de droit diplomatique et consulaire 1951, Le principe d'égalité des états et les organisations internationales 1961, Foreign Policies in World Change 1963, L'Organisation de l'unité africaine 1969, La ligue des états arabes 1972, Les Conflits des frontières en Afrique 1973; also numerous books in Arabic and contributions to periodicals. *Leisure interests:* the works of Matisse, collecting old pens from the Ottoman Empire. *Address:* 2 avenue Epnipgiza, Cairo, Egypt (Home).

BOUYGUES, Corinne Suzanne Marie Edmée; French broadcasting executive; b. 24 Aug. 1947, Laval; d. of Francis Bouygues and Monique Teze; m. Sergio Gobbi 1995; two s. one d.; Head of Public Relations Compagnie Européene de Publication (CEP) 1979–81; Press Attaché Bouygues Group 1981, Asst. Dir. Communication 1987–89, Dir.-Gen. Communication 1989–; Dir. of Communication TF1 1989, Asst. Dir. Gen. TF1 Publicity 1990–91, Dir. Gen. 1991, Admin. 1992, Admin. TF1 1993, Chair., Dir. Gen. TF1 Enterprises 1995, of Une Musique 1994–97, of Téléshopping S.A. 1994–97. *Address:* Villa Montmorency, 21 Avenue des Tilleuls, 75016 Paris, France (Home).

BOVIN, Aleksandr Yevgeniyevich; Russian journalist and diplomatist; b. 9 Aug. 1930, Leningrad; s. of Yevgeni Bovin and Agnessa Bovin; m. Lena Bovin 1962; one d.; ed. Rostov Univ.; mem. CPSU 1952–91; party and man. work in Krasnodar Dist. 1954–56; served on editorial staff of Kommunist 1959–63; adviser, Chief of advisers group, Cen. Cttee. CPSU 1963–72; political observer for Izvestiya 1972–91, 1997–; mem. Cen. Auditing Comm., CPSU 1981–86; Russian Amb. to Israel 1991–97. *Leisure interest:* business. *Address:* Tverskaya str. 18, 103791 Moscow (Office); B. Pirogovskaya str. 5, Apt. 79, 119021 Moscow, Russia (Home). *Telephone:* (095) 299 6136 (Office); (095) 245 19 94 (Home).

BOVONE, H.E. Cardinal Alberto; Italian ecclesiastic; b. 11 June 1922, Frugarolo; ordained priest 1945; Archbishop, See of Cesarea in Numidia and Pro-Prefect Congregation for the Causes of Saints 1984; cr. Cardinal Feb. 1998. *Address:* Congregation for the Causes of Saints, Piazza Pio XII 10, 00193 Rome, Italy. *Telephone:* (6) 69884247. *Fax:* (6) 69881935.

BOWE, Riddick Lamont; American professional boxer (retd.); b. 1967, Brooklyn; s. of Dorothy Bowe; m. Judy Bowe 1986; one s. two d.; amateur boxer 1982–89, professional boxer 1989–, won World Boxing Asscn., World Boxing Confed., Int. Boxing Fed. titles 1992, World Boxing Asscn., Int. Boxing Fed. titles 1993, World Boxing Org. title 1995, defeating two challengers in that year to retain title; Silver Medal Super Heavyweight Div., Olympic Games, Seoul, 1988; ranked Undisputed Heavyweight Champion 1992–93, 1995; retd. from boxing 1996; briefly with U.S. Marine Corps; pleaded guilty to fed. charge of abduction June 1998.

BOWEN, Lionel Frost, A.C.; Australian politician; b. 28 Dec. 1922, Sydney; m. Claire Bowen 1953; five s. three d.; ed. Univ. of Sydney; fmrly. in practice as solicitor; mem. N.S.W. Parl. 1962–69; mem. House of Reps. (Fed. Parl.) 1969–90; Postmaster-Gen., Special Minister of State and Minister for Mfg. Industry 1972–75; Deputy Leader of Opposition 1977–83; Deputy Prime Minister, Minister for Trade and Minister assisting Prime Minister in Commonwealth-State Affairs 1983–84, Deputy Prime Minister, Attorney-Gen. 1984–90; Minister assisting the Prime Minister 1984–88, Vice-Pres. of Exec. Council 1984–87; Deputy Chair. Advertising Standards Cttee. 1990; Chair. Nat. Gallery, Canberra 1991–94, Verus Investments Ltd., The Benwood Property Trust 1997–; Australian Labor Party. *Address:* 24 Mooramie Avenue, Kensington, N.S.W. 2033, Australia.

BOWEN, Most. Rev. Michael George, S.T.L., PH.L.; British ecclesiastic; b. 23 April 1930, Gibraltar; s. of late Maj. C. L. J. Bowen and late Mary J. Pedley; ed. Downside Abbey School, Trinity Coll., Cambridge, and Gregorian Univ., Rome; wine trade 1951–52; Venerable English Coll., Rome 1952–59; ordained R.C. priest 1958; curate, Earlsfield and Walworth, Diocese of Southwark 1959–63; teacher of Theology, Pontifical Beda Coll., Rome 1963–66; Chancellor, Diocese of Arundel and Brighton 1966–70, Coadjutor Bishop 1970–71, Bishop of Arundel and Brighton 1971–77; Archbishop and Metropolitan, Diocese of Southwark 1977–; Vice-Pres. Catholic Bishops' Conf. England and Wales 1996–; Freeman of City of London 1984. *Leisure interests:* golf, tennis. *Address:* Archbishop's House, 150 St. George's Road, London, SE1 6HX, England. *Telephone:* 0171-928 2495. *Fax:* 0171-928 7833.

BOWEN, Ray M.; PH.D.; American university administrator; b. 30 March 1936, Fort Worth, TX; s. of Winfred Herbert Bowen and Elizabeth Williams Bowen; m. Sara Elizabeth Gibbons Bowen 1958; one s. one d.; ed. Texas A&M Univ., California Inst. Tech.; Assoc. Prof. Mechanical Eng., Louisiana State Univ. 1965–67; Prof. Mechanical Eng., Rice Univ. 1967–83, Chair. Dept. Mechanical Eng. 1972–77; Div. Dir. Nat. Science Foundation 1982–83, Acting Asst. Dir. Eng. to Dep. Asst. Dir. 1990–91; Prof. and Dean of Eng. Univ. of Kentucky 1983–89; Vice-Pres. Academic Affairs, Okla. State Univ. 1991–93, Interim Pres. 1993–94; Pres. Texas A&M Univ. 1993–; Soc. of Scholars, Johns Hopkins Univ.; A.S.E.E. Fellows. *Publications:* Introduction to Continuum Mechanics for Engineers; Introduction to Vectors and Tensors (co-author); Rational Thermodynamics (contrib.); contrib. numerous articles in professional journals. *Leisure interests:* travelling, opera. *Address:* Office of the President, Texas A&M University, Room 805, Rudder Tower, College Station, TX 77843, U.S.A. *Telephone:* 409-845-2217. *Fax:* 409-845-5027.

BOWEN, William Gordon, PH.D.; American academic; b. 6 Oct. 1933, Cincinnati, Ohio; s. of Albert A. Bowen and Bernice Pomert; m. Mary Ellen Maxwell 1956; one s. one d.; ed. Denison and Princeton Univs.; Asst. Prof. of Econs., Princeton Univ. 1958–61, Assoc. Prof. 1961–65, Prof. 1965–87; Dir. of Graduate Studies, Woodrow Wilson School of Public and Int. Affairs, Princeton Univ. 1964–66; Provost, Princeton Univ. 1967–72, Pres. 1972–87;

Pres. Andrew W. Mellon Foundation, New York 1988–; Dir. NCR Corpn. 1975–; Regent Smithsonian Inst. 1980, now Regent Emer.; Trustee, Denison Univ. 1966–75, 1992–, Center for Advanced Study in the Behavioral Sciences 1973–84, 1986–. *Publications:* The Wage-Price Issue: A Theoretical Analysis 1960, Performing Arts: The Economic Dilemma (with W. J. Baumol) 1966, The Economics of Labor Force Participation (with T. A. Finegan) 1969, Ever the Teacher 1987, Prospects for Faculty in the Arts and Sciences 1989 (with J. A. Sosa), In Pursuit of the PhD 1992 (with Neil L. Rudenstine), Inside the Boardroom: Governance by Directors and Trustees 1994, (with T. Nygren, S. Turner and E. Duffy) The Charitable Nonprofts 1994. *Leisure interests:* swimming, tennis, reading. *Address:* Andrew W. Mellon Foundation, 140 East 62nd Street, New York, NY 10021, U.S.A. (Office).

BOWER, Gordon, M.S., PH.D.; American professor of psychology; b. 30 Dec. 1932, Scio, Ohio; s. of Clyde W. Bower and Mabelle Bosart Bower; m. Sharon Anthony 1957; one s. two d.; ed. Western Reserve (now Case Western Reserve) and Yale Univs.; Asst. Prof. Stanford Univ. 1959, Assoc. Prof. 1963, Prof. 1965, A. R. Lang Chair Prof. 1975–, Chair. Dept. of Psychology 1978, Assoc. Dean, Stanford Univ. 1983–85; Ed. The Psychology of Learning and Motivation 1964–; mem. N.A.S., American Acad. of Arts and Sciences, Soc. of Experimental Psychologists. *Publications:* co-author of five books. *Leisure interests:* reading, sport. *Address:* Department of Psychology, Stanford University, Stanford, CA 94305, U.S.A.

BOWERING, George Henry, M.A.; Canadian writer and lecturer; b. 1 Dec. 1936, Penticton, B.C.; s. of Ewart Bowering and Pearl Bowering (née Brinson); m. Angela Luoma 1962; one d.; ed. Univ. of British Columbia; served Royal Canadian Air Force 1955–58; lecturer Univ. of Calgary 1963–66; Writer-in-Residence Sir George Williams Univ., Montréal 1967–71; lecturer Simon Fraser Univ., Burnaby, B.C. 1972–; Gov.-Gen.'s Award (poetry) 1967, (fiction) 1980. *Publications:* Mirror on the Floor 1967, A Short Sad Book 1977, Burning Water 1980, Caprice 1987, Harry's Fragments 1990, Shoot! 1994, Parents from Space 1994, Piccolo Mondo 1998. *Leisure interests:* baseball, fastball. *Address:* 2499 W. 37 Avenue, Vancouver, BC V6M 1P4, Canada. *Fax:* (1-604) 266 9000.

BOWERS-BROADBENT, Christopher Joseph, F.R.A.M.; British organist and composer; b. 13 Jan. 1945, Hemel Hempstead; s. of Henry W. Bowers-Broadbent and Doris E. Mizen; m. Deirdre Cape 1970; one s. one d.; ed. Berkhamsted School and Royal Acad. of Music; chorister, King's Coll. Cambridge 1954–58; appointed organist and choirmaster of St. Pancras Parish Church 1965–88, West London Synagogue 1973– and Gray's Inn 1983–; debut organ recital, Camden Festival 1966; Prof. of Organ, Royal Acad. of Music 1976–92; Recordings include: Trivium, O Domina Nostra, Meditations Sur; operas include: The Pied Piper 1972, The Seacock Bane 1979, The Last Man 1983. *Leisure interest:* sketching. *Address:* 94 Colney Hatch Lane, Muswell Hill, London, N10 1EA, England. *Telephone:* 0181-883 1933. *Fax:* 0181-883 1933.

BOWIE, David (David Robert Jones); British musician and actor; b. 8 Jan. 1947, Brixton, London; s. of Hayward Jones and Margaret Mary (née Burns) Jones; m. 1st Angela Barnett 1970 (divorced 1980); one s.; m. 2nd Iman Abdul Majid (q.v.) 1992; singer/songwriter 1967–; first hit single Space Oddity 1969, numerous tours and TV appearances; *recordings include:* The Man Who Sold The World, Hunky Dory 1971, The Rise and Fall of Ziggy Stardust and the Spiders From Mars 1972, Aladdin Sane, Pin Ups 1973, David Live, Diamond Dogs 1974, Young Americans 1975, Station to Station 1976, Low, Heroes 1977, Lodger (with Brian Eno) 1979, Scary Monsters and Super Creeps 1980, Let's Dance 1983, Never Let me Down 1987, Tin Machine (with group) 1989; *appeared in films:* The Man Who Fell to Earth 1976, Just a Gigolo 1981, The Hunger 1983, Merry Christmas Mr Lawrence 1983, Ziggy Stardust and the Spiders from Mars 1983, Absolute Beginners 1986, Labyrinth 1986, The Last Temptation of Christ 1988, The Linguini Incident 1990, Basquiat 1996; appeared in play The Elephant Man, New York 1980; appeared in TV play Baal (Brecht) 1982; exec. producer and wrote musical score for The Delinquents 1989. *Leisure interests:* boxing, martial arts instruction, listening to Polish and Chinese Communist music. *Address:* c/o Isolar, Suite 220, 641 5th Avenue, New York, NY 10022, U.S.A.

BOWIE, Stanley Hay Umphray, D.SC., F.R.S., F.ENG., F.R.S.E., F.M.S.A., F.S.A.-(SCOT.); British economic geologist; b. 24 March 1917, Bixter; s. of James Cameron Bowie and Mary Nicolson; m. Helen Elizabeth Pocock 1948; two s.; ed. Aberdeen Grammar School, Univ. of Aberdeen; with Meteorological Office 1942; commissioned R.A.F. 1943–46; Geologist, Sr. Geologist, Prin. Geologist, Geological Survey of Great Britain (GSGB) 1946–55, Chief Geologist, Atomic Energy Div. 1955–68; Chief Geochemist, Asst. Dir. Inst. of Geological Sciences 1968–77; Chief Consultant Geologist to UKAEA 1955–77; Visiting Prof. of Applied Geology, Univ. of Strathclyde 1968–85; Prin. Investigator Apollo 11 and 12 Lunar samples 1969–71; Geological Consultant 1977–97; Dir. Liquid Crystals Ltd. 1977–; Visiting Prof., Royal School of Mines, Imperial Coll. 1985–92; Chair. Comm. on Ore Microscopy, Int. Mineralogical Asscn. 1970–78; Chair. Steering Cttee., Mineral Deposits of Europe 1970–89; Chair. DOE Research Advisory Group, Radioactive Waste Man. 1984–85; Chair. Shetland Sheep Breeders' Group 1989–91, Vice-Pres. 1992–; Hon. Fellow Inst. Mining and Metallurgy; Silver Medal R.S.A., Sr. Kilgour Research Scholarship, Mitchell Prize for Geology (Univ. of Aberdeen), Team mem. Queen's Award for Tech. Achievement 1990. *Publications:* contrib. to Nuclear Geology 1954, Physical Methods in Determinative Mineralogy 1967, Applied Environmental Geochemistry 1963, The Bowie Simpson System for the Microscopic Determination of Ore Minerals (with P. R. Simpson) 1980 and others, Ed. (Jt.) Uranium Prospecting Handbook 1972, Mineral Deposits of Europe 1978, Environmental Geochemistry and Health 1985, Radon and Health—The Facts (with C. Bowie) 1991, Shetland Sheep 1994, Shetland Wool 1994, Shetland Cattle 1995; numerous articles on rare breeds of domesticated animals. *Leisure interests:* photography, gardening, survival of endangered breeds of domesticated animals. *Address:* Tanyard Farm, Clapton, Crewkerne, Somerset, TA18 8PS, England.

BOWLES, Erskine; American government official; b. 1945; s. of Hargrove "Skipper" Bowles; m. Crandall Bowles; three c.; with Morgan Stanley & Co. New York; Bowles Hollowell Conner & Co. Charlotte, N.C. 1975–93; Admin. Small Business Admin. Washington, D.C. 1993–94; Deputy Chief of Staff, The White House, Washington, D.C. 1994–97, Chief of Staff to Pres. 1997–99. *Address:* c/o The White House, Washington, DC 20500, U.S.A.

BOWLES, Paul; American composer and writer; b. 30 Dec. 1910, New York; s. of Dr. Claude Dietz Bowles and Rena (Winnewisser) Bowles; m. Jane Auer 1938; ed. Univ. of Virginia and in Berlin and Paris; Music Critic for New York Herald Tribune 1942–45; recipient of Guggenheim Fellowship and Rockefeller Grant. *Compositions of music for films, for the theatre:* Doctor Faustus, Twelfth Night, The Glass Menagerie, Cyrano de Bergerac, Watch on the Rhine, Summer and Smoke, Sweet Bird of Youth, The Milk Train Doesn't Stop Here Any More, etc.; scores for ballets: Yankee Clipper, Pastorela (American Ballet Company), Colloque Sentimental (Marquis de Cuevas); operas: Denmark Vesey, The Wind Remains, Yerma; and a number of sonatas, concertos, etc.; also wrote novels, The Sheltering Sky, Let it come Down, The Spider's House, Up Above the World, Too Far From Home; short stories, collections, A Little Stone, The Hours after Noon, A Hundred Camels in the Courtyard, Pages from Cold Point, Things Gone and Things Still Here, Midnight Mass, Call at Corazón, Unwelcome Words 1989; non-fiction, Their Heads are Green, Yallah! Without Stopping, Points in Time; Poetry: Scenes, The Thicket of Spring, Next to Nothing; trans. No Exit (by Jean-Paul Sartre), A Life Full of Holes (by Driss ben Hamed Charhadi), Love with a Few Hairs, The Lemon (by Mohammed Mrabet), M'Hashish, the Boy Who Set the Fire (by Mohammed Mrabet), For Bread Alone (by Mohamed Choukri), Jean Genet in Tangier (by Mohamed Choukri), Tennessee Williams in Tangier (by Mohamed Choukri), The Oblivion Seekers (by Isabelle Eberhardt), Look and Move On (by Mohammed Mrabet), Harmless Poisons, Blameless Sins (by Mohammed Mrabet), The Big Mirror (by Mohammed Mrabet), The Beach Café (by Mohammed Mrabet), Five Eyes (by five Moroccans), The Chest (by Mohammed Mrabet), Marriage With Papers (by Mohammed Mrabet), A Distant Episode 1989, The Beggar's Knife, Dust on her Tongue, The Pelcari Project (three vols. by Rodrigo Rey Rosa), The Oblivion Seekers. *Address:* 2117 Tanger Socco, Tangier, Morocco; c/o William Morris Agency, Inc., 1350 Avenue of the Americas, New York, NY 10019, U.S.A.

BOWMAN, John, M.A., B.D., D.PHIL., F.A.H.A.; Australian university professor and ecclesiastic; b. 13 May 1916, Ayr, Scotland; s. of Matthew Bowman and Sarah (née Andrew) Bowman; m. Margaret Fanny Stanton 1944; two s. five d.; ed. Ayr Acad., Glasgow Univ., Christ Church, Oxford Univ.; lecturer in Hebrew, Faculties of Arts and Divinity, Glasgow Univ. 1945–46; Sr. Lecturer, Head of Dept. of Semitic Languages and Literature, Leeds Univ. 1946–59; Prof., Univ. of Melbourne, Dept. of Middle Eastern Studies 1959–78, Prof. Emer. 1978–; Sr. Acad. Assoc., Dept. of Fine Arts, Classics and Archaeology; ordained priest 1954; became Australian citizen 1961; founder and Ed. Abr Nahrain 1961–80; current research: Qur'an and the Gospel; UNESCO Fellow 1964. *Publications:* The Gospel of Mark: the New Christian Jewish Passover Haggadah 1964, Samaritanische Probleme. Studien zum Verhältnis von Samaritanertum, Judentum und Urchristentum 1966, The Fourth Gospel and the Jews 1979, Samaritan Documents 1979. *Leisure interests:* planting trees, walking. *Address:* 15 Haines Street, North Melbourne, Vic. 3051, Australia.

BOWN, Jane Hope, C.B.E.; British photographer; b. 13 March 1925, Ledbury; d. of Charles Wentworth Bell and Daisy Bown; m. Martin Grenville Moss 1954; two s. one d.; ed. William Gibbs School for Girls, Faversham, Kent; photographer for the Observer 1950–; Hon. D.Litt. (Bradford). *Publications:* The Gentle Eye 1980, Women of Consequence 1985, Men of Consequence 1986, The Singular Cat 1988, Pillars of the Church 1991, Jane Bown Observer 1996. *Leisure interests:* animals, the country, antiques. *Address:* Old Mill House, 50 Broad Street, Alresford, Hants., SO24 9AN, England. *Telephone:* (01962) 732419.

BOWNESS, Sir Alan, Kt., C.B.E.; British art historian; b. 11 Jan. 1928; s. of George and Kathleen (née Benton) Bowness; m. Sarah Hepworth-Nicholson; one s. one d.; ed. Univ. Coll. School, Downing Coll., Cambridge, Courtauld Inst. of Art, Univ. of London; with Friends' Ambulance Unit and Friends' Service Council 1946–50; Regional Art Officer, Arts Council of G.B. 1955–57; Courtauld Inst. 1957–79, Deputy Dir. 1978–79; Reader, Univ. of London 1967–78, Prof. of History of Art 1978–79; Visiting Prof. Humanities Seminar, Johns Hopkins Univ., Baltimore 1969; Dir. Tate Gallery 1980–88, Henry Moore Foundation 1988–94 (Trustee 1984–88, 1994–); mem. Arts Council 1973–75, 1978–80, Art Panel 1960–80 (Vice-Chair. 1973–75, Chair. 1978–80), Arts Film Cttee. 1968–77 (Chair. 1972–75); mem. Fine Arts Cttee., British Council 1960–69, 1970–93 (Chair. 1981–93); mem. Exec. Cttee.,

Contemporary Art Soc. 1961–69, 1970–86, Cultural Advisory Cttee., U.K. Nat. Comm. for UNESCO 1973–82; Gov. Chelsea School of Art 1965–88; Hon. Sec. Asscn. of Art Historians 1973–76; Dir. Barbara Hepworth Museum, St. Ives, Cornwall 1976–88; mem. Council Royal Coll. of Art 1978–99; Trustee Handel House Museum 1994– (Chair. 1997–); Hon. Fellow 1984; mem. int. juries for Premio Di Tella, Buenos Aires 1965, São Paulo Bienal 1967, Lehmbruck Prize, Duisburg 1970; Rembrandt Prize 1982, Venice Biennale 1986; Hon. Fellow, Downing Coll., Cambridge 1980, Bristol Polytechnic 1980, Royal Coll. of Art 1982; Hon. D.Lit. (Liverpool) 1988, (Leeds) 1995, (Exeter) 1996; Chevalier Ordre des Arts et des Lettres 1973. *Publications:* William Scott Paintings 1964, Impressionists and Post Impressionists 1965, Henry Moore: complete sculpture 1955–64 1965, Modern Sculpture 1965, Barbara Hepworth Drawings 1966, Alan Davie 1967, Recent British Painting 1968, Gauguin 1971, Barbara Hepworth: complete sculpture 1960–69 1971, Modern European Art 1972, Ivon Hitchens 1973, Picasso 1881–1973 (contrib.) 1973, The Genius of British Painting (contrib.) 1975, Henry Moore: complete sculpture 1964–73 1977, Henry Moore: Complete Sculpture 1974–80 1983, Henry Moore: Complete Sculpture 1981–86 1988, The Conditions of Success 1989, British Contemporary Art 1910–1990 (contrib.) 1991, Bernard Meadows 1995. *Address:* 91 Castelnau, London, SW13 9EL; 16 Piazza, St. Ives, Cornwall, England. *Telephone:* 0181-846 8520; (01736) 795444.

BOWRING, Edgar Rennie Harvey, M.C., M.A., C.B.I.M.; British company executive and lawyer; b. 5 Nov. 1915, Calif., U.S.A.; s. of Arthur and Margaret Bowring; m. Margaret Grace Brook 1940; two s. one d.; ed. Eastbourne Coll., Clare Coll., Cambridge, and Yale Univ.; served Kent Yeomanry and Royal Artillery 1939–46; admitted solicitor 1949; Partner, Cripps Harries Hall and Co. 1950–55; Solicitor, Dir. C. T. Bowring and Co. (Insurance) Ltd. 1960–73; mem. Lloyd's 1962–; Dir. C. T. Bowring and Co. Ltd. 1963–81; Chair. English and American Insurance Co. Ltd. 1966–77, Deputy Chair. and Chief Exec. C. T. Bowring (Insurance) Holdings Ltd. 1970–73; Chair. Crusader Insurance Co. Ltd. 1973–77; Chair. Bowmaker Ltd. 1973–77; Chair. The Bowring Group of Companies 1973–78; Dir. Singer and Friedlander 1971–77; Deputy Pres. Insurance Inst. of London 1970–71, Pres. 1971–72; Dir. Marsh and McLennan Cos. Inc. 1980–88, Advisory Dir. 1988–95; Fellow, Corpn. of Insurance Brokers. *Leisure interests:* golf, gardening. *Address:* Leopards Mill, Horam, Sussex, England. *Telephone:* (01435) 812687.

BOWRING, Peter, C.B.E., F.R.S.A., F.Z.S.; British company director; b. 22 April 1923, Bromborough; s. of Frederick Clive and Agnes Walker (née Cairns) Bowring; m. Barbara Ekaterina Brewis 1946 (divorced); one s. one d.; m. 2nd Carol Gillian Hutchings 1979 (divorced); m. 3rd Carole Mary Dear 1986; ed. Shrewsbury School; commissioned, Rifle Brigade 1942, served in Egypt, North Africa, Italy and Austria (mentioned in despatches); Dir. C. T. Bowring & Co. Ltd. 1956; Chair. C. T. Bowring Trading (Holdings) Ltd. 1967; Deputy Chair. C. T. Bowring and Co. Ltd. 1973; Chair. Bowmaker (Plant) Ltd. 1972–83, Bowmaker Ltd. 1978–82, C. T. Bowring & Co. Ltd. 1978–82; Dir. Marsh and McLennan Companies Inc. 1980–85, Vice-Chair. 1982–84; Dir. Aldeburgh Foundation 1975–90, Chair. 1982–89, Vice-Pres. 1991–; Chair. Help the Aged Ltd. 1977–87, Pres. 1987–; Chair. Inter-Action Social Enterprise Trust Ltd. 1989–91; Master Co. of World Traders 1989–90; Trustee Zoological Soc. Devt. Trust 1987–90, Ironbridge Gorge Museum Devt. Trust 1987–93 (Companion 1993), Upper Severn Navigation Trust 1987–; mem. Lloyds 1968–98; Worshipful Company of Insurers; Company of Watermen and Lightermen; Freeman of City of London; Bd. of Govs. St. Dunstan's Educational Foundation 1974–94, Chair. 1977–90 (Companion 1998); Bd. Govs. Shrewsbury School 1969–97; Dir. Independent Primary and Secondary Educ. Trust 1986–, Centre for Policy Studies 1983–88, City Arts Trust 1984–94 (Chair. 1987–94), Int. Human Assistance Programs Inc. 1985–89, Rhein Chemie Holding GmbH 1968–; Fellow Inst. of Dirs. *Leisure interests:* photography, sailing, motoring, music, walking, cooking. *Address:* 79 New Concordia Wharf, Mill Street, London, SE1 2BB, England. *Telephone:* 0171-237 0818.

BOWYER, William, R.A., R.P., R.W.S.; British artist; b. 25 May 1926; m. Vera Mary Small 1951; two s. one d.; ed. Burslem School of Art, Royal Coll. of Art; Head of Fine Art, Maidstone Coll. of Art 1971–82; Hon. Sec. New English Art Club. *Leisure interests:* cricket, snooker. *Address:* 12 Cleveland Avenue, Chiswick, London, W4 1SN, England. *Telephone:* 0181-994 0346.

BOX, John Allan Hyatt, O.B.E., A.R.I.B.A., F.R.S.A.; British set designer; b. 27 Jan. 1920; s. of late Allan Cyril Box and of Bertha Storey; m. 1st Barbara Courtenay Linton 1944; m. 2nd Doris Lee 1953 (deceased); two d.; ed. Ceylon, Highgate School, School of Architecture, London Polytechnic; served R.A.C., Royal Tank Regt. 1940–46 (despatches); has worked in films 1948–. *Films designed include:* The Million Pound Note 1954, The Inn of the Sixth Happiness 1958, Our Man in Havana 1959, The World of Suzie Wong 1960, Lawrence of Arabia 1962 (Acad. Award), Doctor Zhivago 1965 (Acad. Award), A Man For All Seasons 1967 (B.A.F.T.A. Award), Oliver! 1968 (Acad. Award), Nicholas and Alexandra 1971 (Acad. Award), Travels With My Aunt 1972, The Great Gatsby 1974 (B.A.F.T.A. Award), Rollerball 1975 (B.A.F.T.A. Award), A Passage to India 1984, Black Beauty 1994, First Knight 1995, producer The Looking Glass War 1969; B.A.F.T.A. Award for special contrib. to films 1991, Royal Designer for Industry R.S.A. 1992. *Leisure interests:* painting, art, cricket, rugby. *Address:* 5 Elm Bank Mansions, The Terrace, Barnes, London, SW13 0NS, England. *Telephone:* 0181-876 9125.

BOXER, Barbara, B.A.; American politician; b. 11 Nov. 1940, Brooklyn, New York; d. of Ira Boxer and Sophie (Silvershein) Levy; m. Stewart Boxer 1962; one s. one d.; ed. Brooklyn Coll.; stockbroker, New York 1962–65; journalist, Assoc. Ed. Pacific Sun 1972–74; Congressional Aide to Rep. 5th Congressional Dist. San Francisco 1974–76; mem. Marin Co. Bd. of Supervisors, San Rafael, Calif. 1976–82, Pres. 1980–81; Democrat mem. 98th–102nd Congresses from 6th Calif. Dist., Senator from California Jan. 1993–; mem. Bd. of Dirs. Golden Gate Bridge Highway and Transport Dist., San Francisco 1978–82; Pres. Democratic New Mems. Caucus 1983; numerous awards. *Address:* U.S. Senate, 112 Hart Senate Office Building, Washington, DC 20510, U.S.A.

BOYARCHUK, Aleksander Alekseyevich; Russian astrophysicist; b. 21 June 1931, Grozny; s. of Alexei Boyarchuk and Maria Boyarchuk; m. Margarita Yevgenyevna Boyarchuk (née Kropotova) 1955; one s.; ed. Leningrad State Univ.; researcher, Deputy Dir. Crimea Astrophysical Observatory U.S.S.R. Acad. of Sciences 1953–87; Dir. Inst. of Astronomy 1987–; mem. U.S.S.R. (now Russian) Acad. of Sciences 1987; Acad.-Sec. Dept. of Gen. Physics and Astronomy 1996–; published over 200 works on astrospectroscopy, physics of star atmospheres, construction of astronomic equipment, cosmic studies, Ed.-in-Chief Astronomical journal, Pres. Int. Astronomical Union 1991–94; mem. Int. Astronomical Acad., Royal Astronomical Soc. of U.K., American Astronomical Soc., American Physical Soc.; U.S.S.R. State Prize. *Address:* Institute of Astronomy, Pyatnitskaya str. 48, 109017 Moscow, Russia. *Telephone:* (095) 951 5461 (Office). *Fax:* (095) 230 2081 (Office).

BOYCE, Adm. Sir Michael (Cecil), K.C.B., O.B.E.; British naval officer; b. 2 April 1943, Cape Town, S.A.; s. of Commdr. Hugh Boyce and Madeleine Boyce (née Manley); m. Harriette Gail Fletcher 1971; one s. one d.; ed. Hurstpierpoint Coll., British Royal Naval Coll., Dartmouth; joined R.N. 1961; qualified Submariner 1965, TAS 1970, served in H.M. submarines Anchorite, Valiant and Conqueror 1965–72, commanded H.M. submarines Oberon 1973–74, Opossum 1974–75, Superb 1979–81, frigate H.M.S. Brilliant 1983–84, Capt. (SM) Submarine Sea Training 1984–86; Royal Coll. Defence Staff 1988; Sr. Naval Officer ME 1989; Dir. Naval Staff Duties 1989–91; Flag Officer, Sea Training 1991–92, Surface Flotilla 1992–95; Commdr. Anti-Submarine Warfare Striking Force 1992–94; Second Sea Lord and C.-in-C. Naval Home Command 1995–97; Flag ADC to the Queen 1995–97; C.-in-C. Fleet, C.-in-C. Eastern Atlantic Area and Commdr. Naval Forces N.W. Europe 1997–98; First Sea Lord Oct. 1998–; Gov. Alleyn's School 1995–. *Leisure interests:* squash, tennis, photography, windsurfing. *Address:* Ministry of Defence, Whitehall, London, S.W.1, England.

BOYCOTT, Brian Blundell, F.R.S.; British professor of biology; b. 10 Dec. 1924, Croydon, Surrey; s. of Percy Blundell Boycott and Doris Eyton Lewis; m. Marjorie Mabel Burchell 1950; two s. (one deceased); ed. Royal Masonic School, Birkbeck Coll., Univ. of London; Tech., Nat. Inst. Medical Research; Asst. Lecturer in Zoology, Univ. Coll., Univ. of London 1946–47, Hon. Research Asst. Anatomy 1947–52, Lecturer in Zoology 1952–62, Univ. Reader in Zoology 1962–68, Prof. of Zoology 1968–70; Prof. of Biology, MRC 1971–89, Dir. Cell Biophysics Unit 1980–89; Prof. Emer. Univ. of London 1990–; Visiting Prof. Univ. Coll., London Univ. 1997; Fellow King's Coll. London 1990–; Hon. Sr. Research Fellow, Guy's Hosp.; mem. Advisory Council, British Library Bd. 1976–80, Council Open Univ. 1975–87, Council Royal Soc. 1976–78, Academic Consultative Cttee. Open Univ., MRC Neurosciences and Mental Health Bd. 1989–91; Scientific Medal (Zoological Soc.), London 1965, Hon. Dr. (Open Univ.). *Publications:* articles on structure and function of nervous systems in scientific journals. *Address:* c/o Department of Visual Science, Institute of Ophthalmology, 11–43 Bath Street, London, EC1V 9EL, England. *Telephone:* 0171-608 6878. *Fax:* 0171-608 6850.

BOYCOTT, Geoffrey, O.B.E.; British cricketer; b. 21 Oct. 1940, Fitzwilliam, Yorks.; s. of late Thomas Wilfred Boycott and Jane Boycott; ed. Kinsley Modern School and Hemsworth Grammar School; fmrly. in civil service; right-hand opening batsman; teams: Yorkshire 1962–86 (Capt. 1971–78), Northern Transvaal 1971–72; 108 Tests for England 1964–82, 4 as Capt., scoring then record 8,114 runs (average 47.7) including 22 hundreds; scored 48,426 first-class runs (151 hundreds); completed 100 hundreds for Yorkshire 1985, 7th batsman to achieve this for a county; toured Australia 1965–66, 1970–71, 1978–79 and 1979–80; fined and given a suspended three month prison sentence for assault Jan. 1998, Grasse, sentence on appeal; conviction upheld Nov. 1998; only Englishman to achieve average of 100 in English County season 1971; repeated this achievement in 1979; scored 100th hundred, England v. Australia, Headingly, Leeds Aug. 1977; became 18th batsman in history of game to score 100 hundreds and the first to achieve this in a Test Match; mem. Gen. Cttee.; cricket commentator. *Publications:* Geoff Boycott's Book for Young Cricketers 1976, Put to the Test: Ashes Series in Australia 1978/79 1979, Geoff Boycott's Cricket Quiz 1979, Boycott on Batting 1980, Opening Up 1980, In the Fast Lane 1981, Master Class 1982, Boycott—The Autobiography 1987, Boycott on Cricket 1990. *Leisure interests:* golf, tennis. *Address:* c/o Yorkshire County Cricket Club, Headingley Cricket Ground, Leeds, Yorks., LS6 3BY, England.

BOYCOTT, Rosie; British journalist and author; b. 13 May 1951; d. of Charles Boycott and Betty Boycott; m. David Leitch (divorced); one d.; ed. Cheltenham Ladies Coll., Kent Univ.; f. Spare Rib 1972; est. Virago Books 1973; worked on Village Voice (magazine), New York; subsequently edited Arabic women's magazine in Kuwait; Features Ed. Honey; Deputy Ed. Daily

Mail's Male and Femail pages; Ed. Discount Traveller; commissioning Ed. The Sunday Telegraph; Deputy Ed. Harpers & Queen 1989; Deputy Ed. and Features Ed. (British) Esquire 1991, Ed. 1992–96, of Ind. on Sunday 1996–98, of the Ind. 1998, of the Express April 1998–, of the Express on Sunday April 1998–. *Address:* Express Newspapers PLC, Ludgate House, 245 Blackfriars Road, London, SE1 9UX, England. *Telephone:* 0171-928 8000.

BOYD, Alan Stephenson, LL.B.; American politician and transportation executive; b. 20 July 1922, Jacksonville, Fla.; s. of Clarence and Elizabeth (Stephenson) Boyd; m. Flavil Townsend 1943; one s.; ed. Univ. of Virginia; Chair. U.S. Civil Aeronautics Bd. 1961–65; U.S. Under-Sec. of Commerce 1965–66; first U.S. Sec. of Transportation 1966–69; Pres. Ill. Cen. Gulf Railroad 1969–76; U.S.-U.K. Bilateral Air Traffic Negotiation Leader 1977; Pres. and Chair. Amtrak 1978–82; Chair. and Pres. Airbus Industrie North America 1982–86, Pres. and C.E.O. 1986–; Trustee, Anser Inc. 1969–. *Leisure interests:* golf, historic preservation. *Address:* 2301 Connecticut Avenue, N.W., Washington, DC 20008, U.S.A. (Home).

BOYD, Arthur Merric Bloomfield, A.C., O.B.E.; Australian painter; b. 24 July 1920, Murrumbeena; s. of Merric Boyd and Doris Gough; m. Yvonne Lennie 1945; one s. two d.; taught painting and sculpture by parents and grandfather; painted and exhibited in Australia 1937–59, in England 1959–; first one-man exhbn. London 1960; retrospectives: Whitechapel Gallery, London 1962, Adelaide 1964, N.S.W. Art Gallery 1993–94; designed for Ballet at Edinburgh Festival and Sadler's Wells Theatre 1961, Covent Garden Opera House 1963; designed 160m² tapestry for Parl. House, Australia 1988; Britannica Award for Distinguished Service to Art 1979, Australian of the Year Award 1995. *Address:* Bundanon, Bundanon Road, Nowra, N.S.W. 2541, Australia.

BOYD, Sir John Dixon Iklé, K.C.M.G., M.A.; British diplomatist (retd.) and university administrator; b. 17 Jan. 1936, Cambridge; s. of late Prof. James Dixon Boyd and of Amélie Lowenthal; m. 1st Gunilla Ingregerd Rönngren 1968 (divorced 1977); one s. one d.; m. 2nd Julia Raynsford 1977; three d.; ed. Westminster School, Clare Coll., Cambridge, Yale Univ.; joined Foreign Service 1962; in Hong Kong 1962–64, Beijing 1965–67; at FCO 1967–69, Asst. Under-Sec. of State 1984, Deputy Under-Sec. of State 1987–89, Chief Clerk 1989–92; with Embassy, Washington 1969–73; First Sec. Embassy, Beijing 1973–75; on secondment to Treasury 1976; Econ. Counsellor Embassy, Bonn 1977–81; Counsellor (Econ. and Social Affairs) Perm. Mission to UN 1981–84; Political Adviser, Hong Kong 1985–87; Amb. to Japan 1992–96; Master Churchill Coll., Cambridge 1996–; Chair. Bd. of Govs. Bedales School 1966–, David Davies Memorial Inst. 1997–, Trustees of Cambridge Union 1997–; Vice-Chair. Menuhin Prize 1996–; Hon. Fellow Clare Coll. Cambridge 1994; Gov. R.S.C. 1996–; Trustee Sir Winston Churchill Archive Trust 1996–, British Museum 1996–, Margaret Thatcher Archive Trust 1997–, Cambridge Foundation 1997–, The Wordsworth Trust 1997–; Dir. (non-exec.) British Nuclear Fuels PLC 1997–; mem. ASEM 'Vision Group' 1998–; Syndic Fitzwilliam Museum 1997–. *Leisure interests:* music, fly-fishing. *Address:* Master's Lodge, Churchill College, Cambridge, CB3 0DS, England. *Telephone:* (01223) 336226. *Fax:* (01223) 336177.

BOYD, Joseph Aubrey, M.S., PH.D.; American business executive; b. 25 March 1921, Oscar, Ky.; s. of Joseph R. Boyd and Relda J. Myatt; m. Edith A. Atkins 1942; two s.; ed. Univs. of Ky. and Mich.; Instr., Asst. Prof. of Electrical Eng. Univ. of Ky. 1947–49; mem. Faculty, Univ. of Mich. 1949–62, Prof. of Electrical Eng. 1958–62, Dir. Willow Run Labs. 1958–62, Dir. Inst. of Science and Tech. 1960–62; Exec. Vice-Pres. Radiation Inc., Melbourne, Fla. 1962–63, Pres. 1963–72; Exec. Vice-Pres. Electronics, Harris Corpn. Cleveland (now in Melbourne, Fla.) 1967–71, Exec. Vice-Pres. Operations 1971–72, Dir. 1972–87, Chair. Exec. Cttee. 1987–, Pres. 1972–85; Chair., C.E.O. Fairchild Space and Defence Corpn. 1992–94, Fairchild Controls 1994–; consultant, Inst. for Defense Analyses 1956–, Nat. Security Agency 1957–62; special consultant to Army Combat Surveillance Agency 1958–62; Chair. Advisory Group, Electronic Warfare, Office of Dir. of Defense Research, Dept. of Defense 1959–61, consultant 1959–; Fellow, A.A.A.S., Inst. of Electrical and Electronic Engs. *Publications:* articles in professional journals. *Address:* Fairchild Controls, 540 Highland Street, Frederick, MD 21701 (Office); 4650 Hamilton Terrace, Vero Beach, FL 32967, U.S.A. (Home).

BOYD, Sir Robert Lewis Fullarton, Kt., C.B.E., PH.D., A.C.G.I., F.R.S.; British emeritus professor of physics and chartered engineer; b. 19 Oct 1922, Saltcoats, Ayrshire; s. of late Dr. and Mrs. W. J. Boyd; m. 1st Mary Higgins 1949 (died 1996); two s. one d.; m. 2nd Betty Robinson 1998; ed. Whitgift School, Croydon, Imperial and Univ. Colls., London; experimental officer, Admiralty Mining Establishment 1943–46; Research Asst., Dept. of Math., Univ. Coll., London 1946–49, ICI Research Fellow 1949–50, ICI Research Fellow, Dept. of Physics 1950–52, Lecturer in Physics 1952–58, Reader 1959–62, Prof. 1962–83, Hon. Research Fellow 1983–88; Dir. Mullard Space Science Lab., Univ. Coll., London 1965–83; Prof. of Astronomy (part-time), Royal Inst. 1961–67; Fellow, Inst. of Physics, Inst. of Elec. Engs., Royal Astron. Soc.; Hon. D.Sc. (Heriot Watt) 1979, Fellow, Univ. Coll. London 1988. *Publications:* over 100 scientific books and papers. *Leisure interests:* elderly Rolls-Royce motor cars and "live steam" model making. *Address:* Bethaven, 9 Cherwell Gardens, Chandlers Ford, Eastleigh, Hants., SO53 2NH, England. *Telephone:* (01703) 273717.

BOYD, William Andrew Murray, M.A., F.R.S.L.; British author; b. 7 March 1952; s. of Dr Alexander Murray Boyd and Evelyn Boyd; m. Susan Anne (née Wilson) Boyd 1975; ed. Gordonstoun School, Glasgow Univ., Jesus Coll., Oxford; lecturer in English, St. Hilda's Coll., Oxford 1980–83; TV critic, New Statesman 1981–83. *Publications include:* A Good Man in Africa (Whitbread Prize 1981, Somerset Maugham Award 1982) 1981, (screenplay) 1994, On the Yankee Station 1981, An Ice-Cream War (John Llewellyn Rhys Prize) 1982, Stars and Bars 1984 (screenplay 1988), School Ties 1985, The New Confessions 1987, Scoop (screenplay) 1987, Brazzaville Beach (McVities Prize and James Tait Memorial Prize) 1990, Aunt Julia and the Scriptwriter (screenplay) 1990, Mr. Johnson (screenplay) 1990, Chaplin (screenplay) 1992, The Blue Afternoon (novel) 1993, A Good Man in Africa (screenplay) 1994, The Destiny of Nathalie "X" 1995, Cork 1995, Armadillo 1997. *Leisure interests:* tennis, strolling. *Address:* c/o The Agency, 24 Pottery Lane, Holland Park, London, W11 4LZ, England.

BOYD DE LA GUARDIA, Aquilino Edgardo; Panamanian diplomatist and lawyer; b. 30 March 1921; m. Dora Brind; five s.; ed. La Salle, Panama City, Holy Cross Coll., U.S.A., Univs. de la Habana and Panamá; First Sec. Cuba 1946–47, Washington 1947–48; mem. Panama Nat. Assembly 1948–64; Pres. Nat. Assembly 1949; Minister Foreign Affairs 1956–58, 1976–77; Perm. Rep. to UN 1962–67, 1968–76, 1983–86; Amb. to U.S.A. 1983–86, to U.K. 1994–97. *Address:* c/o Ministry of Foreign Affairs Panamá 4, Panama.

BOYD OF MERTON, 2nd Viscount (cr. 1960); **Simon Donald Rupert Lennox-Boyd,** M.A.; British business executive; b. 7 Dec. 1939, London; s. of the late Alan Lennox-Boyd (Viscount Boyd of Merton) and of Lady Patricia Guinness; m. Alice Clive 1962; two s. two d.; ed. Eton, Christ Church Coll., Oxford; Dir. Iveagh Trustees Ltd. 1967; Deputy Chair. Arthur Guinness & Sons 1981–86; Trustee, Guinness Trust 1974–; Chair. Stonham Housing Asscn. 1992–. *Leisure interests:* forestry. *Address:* 9 Warwick Square, London, SW1V 2AA; Ince Castle, Saltash, Cornwall, PL12 4QZ, England. *Telephone:* 0171-821 1618 (Warwick Square); (01752) 842672 (Saltash).

BOYER, Paul Delos, PH.D.; American professor of biochemistry; b. 31 July 1918, Provo, Utah; s. of Dell Delos Boyer and Grace Guymon; m. Lyda Wicker 1939; one s. two d.; ed. Brigham Young Univ. and Univ. of Wisconsin; Research Asst., Univ. of Wis. 1939–43; Instructor, Stanford Univ. 1943–45; Assoc. Prof., Univ. of Minn. 1947–53, Prof. 1953–56, Hill Prof. of Biochem. 1956–63; Prof. of Biochemistry, Univ. of Calif. at Los Angeles 1963–, Dir. Molecular Biology Inst. 1965–83, Biotechnology Program 1985–89; mem. Nat. Acad. of Sciences; Fellow, American Acad. of Arts and Sciences, Vice-Pres. Biological Sciences 1985–87; Pres. American Soc. of Biol. Chemists 1969–70; Guggenheim Fellowship 1955; American Chem. Soc. Award 1955; Tolman Medal 1981; Rose Award (American Soc. of Biochemistry and Molecular Biology) 1989; shared Nobel Prize for Chem. 1997; Dr. h.c., Univ. of Stockholm 1974. *Publications:* Author or co-author of over 200 scientific papers in biochem. and molecular biology; Ed. Annual Biochemistry Review 1964–89, Ed. Biochemical and Biophysical Research Communications 1968–80, The Enzymes 1970–. *Leisure interest:* tennis. *Address:* University of California at Los Angeles, Molecular Biology Institute, 408 Hilgard Avenue, Los Angeles, CA 90024 (Office); 1033 Somera Road, Los Angeles, CA 90077, U.S.A. (Home). *Telephone:* (213) 825-1416 (Office).

BOYER, Yves, PH.D.; French defence research director; b. 9 Oct. 1950, Blois; m. Isabelle Kraft 1978; one s. one d.; ed. Inst. d'Etudes Politiques, Paris and Paris-Panthéon Univ.; Deputy Gen. Sec. SOFRESA, Paris 1978–80; Bureau des Etudes Stratégiques et des Négociations Internationales, Secr. Gén. de la Défense Nationale 1980–82; Defence Consultant and Research Assoc. Int. Inst. for Strategic Studies, London 1982–83; Sr. Researcher, Inst. Français des Relations Internationales 1983–88; Research Fellow, Woodrow Wilson Center 1986; now Deputy Dir. CREST, Ecole Polytechnique; Prof. Army Acad. 1986–, Staff Coll. 1992–; mem. Bd. Centre d'Analyse de la Sécurité Européenne (CASE); Ed. Les Cahiers du CREST.

BOYER SALVADOR, Miguel; Spanish politician; b. 5 Feb. 1939, San Juan de Luz, France; m. 1st Elena Arnedo; two s.; m. 2nd Isabel Preysler 1988; graduated in physics and econ. sciences; joined Spanish Socialist Workers' Party 1960, imprisoned for 6 months for political activities; fmr. economist, Studies Group of Banco de España; Dir. Studies, Nat. Industrial Inst., Strategic Planning Group, Explosivos Rio Tinto S.A., Strategic Planning, Nat. Hydrocarbons Inst.; Minister of Economy, Finance and Commerce 1982–85; Chair. Banco Exterior de España 1985–88, Cartera Central, Grueyersa 1989–93; Vice-Chair. FCC Construcción 1993–; Gov. IBRD; Rep. to IDB 1983–85. *Address:* Avda. General Perón 36, 28020 Madrid, Spain. *Telephone:* (34-1) 556-70-00. *Fax:* (34-1) 556-90-07.

BOYLE, Danny; British film director; b. 20 Oct. 1956, Bury, Lancs.; Artistic Dir. Royal Court Theatre 1982–87; received Golden Ephebe Award 1997; produced Elephant (TV Film) 1989; dir. The Greater Good (TV series) 1991, Mr. Wroe's Virgins (TV) 1993, Not Even God is Wise Enough (TV) 1993. *Films:* Shallow Grave 1994, Trainspotting 1996, A Life Less Ordinary 1996; exec. producer Twin Town 1996. *Address:* c/o ICM, 6th Floor, 76 Oxford Street, London, W1N, 0AT, England.

BOYNTON, Robert Merrill, PH.D.; American professor of psychology; b. 28 Oct. 1924, Evanston, Ill.; s. of Merrill Holmes Boynton and Eleanor Matthews Boynton; m. 1st Alice Neiley 1947 (died 1996); three s. one d.; m. 2nd Sheleah Maloney 1998; ed. Amherst Coll. and Brown Univ.; Asst. Prof., Univ. of Rochester 1952–57, Assoc. Prof. 1957–61, Prof. 1961–74, Dir. and Founder, Center for Visual Science 1963–71, Chair. Dept. of Psychology

1971–74; Prof., Dept. of Psychology, Univ. of Calif. at San Diego 1974–91, Emer. Prof. 1991–; Assoc. Dean, Graduate Studies and Research 1987–91; Chair. Visual Sciences B Study Section, Nat. Inst. of Health 1972–75; Chair. Bd. of Eds. Vision Research 1982–85; mem. N.A.S.; Fellow A.A.A.S.; Godlove Award, Inter-society Color Council 1982, Tillyer Medal, Optical Soc. of America 1972, Ives Medal and Quinn Prize, Optical Soc. of America 1995, Prentice Award, American Acad. of Optometry 1997. *Publications:* Human Color Vision 1979; 150 scientific articles and 12 articles on baseball. *Leisure interest:* baseball research. *Address:* Department of Psychology C-009, University of California at San Diego, La Jolla, CA 92093; 376 Bellaire Street, Del Mar, CA 92014, U.S.A. (Home). *Telephone:* (619) 534-3976 (Univ.); (619) 481-0263 (Home).

BOYSE, Edward Arthur, M.D., F.R.S.; British/American research physician; b. 11 Aug. 1923, Worthing, Sussex; s. of Arthur Boyse and Dorothy V. (née Mellersh) Boyse; m. 1st Jeanette Grimwood 1951; two s. one d.; m. 2nd Judith Bard 1987; ed. St. Bartholomew's Hosp. Medical School, Univ. of London; various hospital appts. 1952–57; Research Fellow in Pathology, Guy's Hospital, London 1957–60; Assoc. mem. Sloan-Kettering Inst., New York 1964–67, mem. 1967–89; Prof. of Biology, Cornell Univ. Grad. School of Medical Sciences 1969–89; Adjunct Prof. of Pathology New York Univ. School of Medicine 1964; Distinguished Prof. of Microbiology and Immunology, Univ. of Ariz. 1989–94, Prof. Emer. 1994–; Harvey Lecturer 1975; Fellow American Acad. of Arts and Sciences 1977, N.A.S. 1979; Cancer Research Inst. Award in Tumour Immunology 1975; Isaac Adler Award of Rockefeller and Harvard Univs. 1976. *Publications:* papers relating to genetics and immunology to devt. and cancer. *Address:* Department of Microbiology and Immunology, University of Arizona, Health Sciences Center, 1501 N. Campbell Ave, Tucson, AZ 85724, U.S.A.

BOZANGA, Simon-Narcisse; Central African Republic politician; b. 26 Dec. 1942, Bangassou; Dir. of Legal Studies, Ministry of Foreign Affairs 1972–74, Sec.-Gen. 1974–78; Amb. to Gabon 1978–79; Sec.-Gen. to Govt. 1979–80; Minister of Justice 1980–81; Prime Minister and Head of Govt. April–Sept. 1981 (deposed by mil. coup); Dir.-Gen. Société Centrafricaine des Hydrocarbures (CentraHydro) 1982.

BOZER, Prof. Dr. Ali Husrev; Turkish jurist; b. 28 July 1925, Ankara; s. of Mustafa Fevzi Bozer and Zehra Bozer; m.; three s.; ed. Ankara and Neuchâtel Univs. and Harvard Law School; Asst. judge, Ankara 1951; Asst., Faculty of Law, Ankara Univ. 1952–60, Agrégé 1955–60, Head of Dept. 1961, Prof. of Commercial Law 1965–; lawyer at bar, Ankara 1952–; Dir. Inst. de Recherche sur le Droit commercial et bancaire 1960–; Judge, European Court of Human Rights 1974–76; mem. Admin. Council, Turkish Radio-TV Corpn. 1968–71, Vice-Pres. 1971–73; Minister of Customs and Monopolies 1981–83, of State for Relations with EEC 1986–90; Deputy Prime Minister and Minister of State 1989–90; Minister of Foreign Affairs Feb.–Oct. 1990. *Publications:* Les droits d'administration et de jouissance des père et mère sur les biens de l'enfant, Nantissement commercial, Aperçu général sur le droit des assurances sociales en droit turc, Droit commercial pour les employés de banques, Papiers valeurs pour les employés de banques; monographs and articles in several reviews in Turkish and French. *Leisure interest:* tennis. *Address:* Ahmet Rasim sok. 35/5, Çankaya, Ankara, Turkey. *Telephone:* 271845, 191322.

BOŽOVIĆ, Radoman, PH.D.; Yugoslav politician and economist; b. 1953, Serbia; m.; two c.; ed. Belgrade Univ.; academic 1976–89; fmr. deputy to Vojvodina Ass., later head of provincial govt.; mem. Socialist Party of Serbia (SPS) (fmrly. League of Communists of Yugoslavia (LCY)); Deputy Serbian Ass. 1990–, Head SPS parl. group.; Prime Minister of Serbia 1991–92; Chair. Council of Citizens, Fed. Ass. 1992–97; f. Bancor Group Sept. 1997; Prof. Univ. Subotica. *Publications:* numerous books and articles including Political Economy (2 vols.), Accumulation and Economic Development, Types of Prosperity in Socialism, Problems of Economic System Reform in Yugoslavia. *Address:* Veće gzotana SRY Yugoslavijc, Belgrade, Serbia, Yugoslavia.

BRABHAM, Sir Jack (John Arthur), Kt., O.B.E.; Australian professional racing driver (retd.); b. 2 April 1926, Sydney, Australia; m. 1st Betty Evelyn (divorced); three s.; m. 2nd Margaret Brabham; ed. Hurstville Tech. Coll., Sydney; served in R.A.A.F. 1944–46; started own engineering business 1946; Midget Speedway racing 1946–52; numerous wins driving a Cooper-Bristol, Australia 1953–54; went to Europe 1955; Australian Grand Prix 1955, 1963; World Champion, Formula II 1958; Formula II Champion of France 1964; World Champion Driver 1959–60, 1960–61, 1966; First in Monaco and U.K. Grandes Epreuves 1959; won Grand Prix of Netherlands, Belgium, France, U.K., Portugal, Denmark 1960, Belgium 1961, France 1966, 1967, U.K. 1966; began building own cars 1961; Chair. Jack Brabham (Worcester Park) Ltd., Jack Brabham (Ewell) Ltd.; Dir. Engine Devts. Ltd.; Ferodo Trophy 1964, 1966; RAC Gold Medal 1966, BARC Gold Medal 1959, 1966, 1967; Formula I Mfrs. Championship 1966, 1967. *Publications:* Jack Brabham's Book of Motor Racing 1960, When the Flag Drops 1971. *Address:* 5 Ruxley Lane, Ewell, Surrey, KT19 0JB, England; P.O. Box 654, Miranda, N.S.W. 2228, Australia.

BRABOURNE, 7th Baron, cr. 1880; **John Ullick Knatchbull,** 16th Bt., cr. 1641, C.B.E.; British film and television producer; b. 9 Nov. 1924; s. of 5th Baron Brabourne and Lady Doreen Geraldine Browne; m. Lady Patricia Edwina Victoria Mountbatten (Countess Mountbatten of Burma) 1946; four s. (and one s. deceased) two d.; ed. Eton Coll. and Univ. of Oxford; Copyright Promotions Group 1974–; Dir. Thames TV 1978– (Chair. 1990–93); Dir. Thorn EMI 1981–86; Gov. BFI 1979–94 (Fellow 1985); Gov. Nat. Film School 1980–95; mem. British Screen Advisory Council 1985–; Trustee, British Acad. of Film and Television Arts (BAFTA), Science Museum, Nat. Museum of Photography, Film and TV; Gov. United World Colls.; Pro-Chancellor, Univ. of Kent; other public appts.; Dr. h.c. (Kent) 1991. *Films produced:* Harry Black 1958, Sink the Bismarck! 1959, H.M.S. Defiant 1961, Othello 1965, The Mikado 1966, Romeo and Juliet, Up the Junction 1967, Dance of Death 1968, Tales of Beatrix Potter 1971, Murder on the Orient Express 1974, Death on the Nile 1978, Stories from a Flying Trunk 1979, The Mirror Crack'd 1980, Evil Under the Sun 1982, A Passage to India 1984, Little Dorritt 1987; producer TV series: Nat. Gallery 1974, A Much-Maligned Monarch 1976, Leontyne 1987. *Address:* Mersham Productions Ltd., 41 Montpelier Walk, London, SW7 1JH (Office); Newhouse, Mersham, Ashford, Kent, TN25 6NQ, England (Home). *Telephone:* (01233) 503636. *Fax:* (01233) 502244.

BRACHER, Karl Dietrich, DR. PHIL.; German political scientist and historian; b. 13 March 1922, Stuttgart; s. of Theodor Bracher and Gertrud Zimmermann; m. Dorothee Schleicher 1951; one s. one d.; ed. Gymnasium, Stuttgart, Univ. of Tübingen and Harvard Univ.; Research Asst. and Head of Dept., Inst. of Political Science, Berlin 1950–58; lecturer, German Hochschule für Politik, Berlin; Privatdozent and Prof. Free Univ., Berlin 1955–58; Prof. of Political Science and Contemporary History, Univ. of Bonn 1959–; Pres. Comm. for History of Parl. and Political Parties, Bonn 1962–68; Fellow, Center for Advanced Study in the Behavioral Sciences, Stanford, U.S.A. 1963–64; Chair. German Asscn. of Political Science 1965–67; mem. Inst. for Advanced Study, Princeton, U.S.A. 1967–68, 1974–75; mem. Wilson Center, Wash. 1980–81; Chair. Bd., Inst. für Zeitgeschichte, Munich 1980–88, German Asscn. of Foreign Policy, German PEN Centre; Visiting Prof. Oxford Univ. 1971, Tel Aviv Univ. 1974, European Univ. Inst. (Florence) 1975–76; Hon. mem. American Acad. of Arts and Sciences; Corresp. Fellow, British Acad., American Philosophical Soc., Austrian Akad. der Wissenschaften; mem. Deutsche Akad. für Sprache und Dichtung, Rhenish-Westfalian Acad. of Sciences; Ed. Vierteljahrshefte für Zeitgeschichte; mem. Editorial Bd., Politische Vierteljahresschrift until 1970, Neue Politische Literatur, Bonner Historische Forschungen, Journal of Contemporary History, Government and Opposition, Societas, Zeitschrift für Politik, Tempo Presente, Risorgimento, European Journal of Int. Affairs, History of the Twentieth Century, Bonner Schriften zur Politik und Zeitgeschichte, Quellen zur Geschichte des Parliamentarismus, Modern Constitutionalism and Democracy (joint editor) 2 vols. 1966, Nach 25 Jahren (editor) 1970, Bibliographie zur Politik (joint editor) 1970, 1976, 1982, Dokumente zur Deutschlandpolitik 1972–, Nationalsozialistische Diktatur 1983, Das Gewissen steht auf 1984, Geschichte der BR Deutschland 1981–87; Hon. D. Hum. Litt., Dr. Jur., Dr. Rer. Pol.; Dr. h.c. (Paris); Ordre pour le Mérite. *Publications:* Conscience in Revolt (with others) 1954, Die Auflösung der Weimarer Republik 1955, Staat und Politik (with E. Fraenkel) 1957, Die Nationalsozialistische Machtergreifung (with others) 1960, Propyläen Weltgeschichte (Vol. 9) 1960, The Foreign Policy of the Federal Republic of Germany 1963, Problems of Parliamentary Democracy in Europe 1964, Adolf Hitler 1964, Deutschland zwischen Demokratie und Diktatur 1964, Theodor Heuss 1965, Internationale Beziehungen (with E. Fraenkel) 1969, The German Dictatorship (English, Italian, Spanish, French, Japanese, Hebrew trans.) 1970, Das deutsche Dilemma 1971 (English trans. 1974), Western Europe (in Times History of Our Times) 1971, Democracy (in Europe Tomorrow) 1972, Zeitgeschichtliche Kontroversen 1976, Die Krise Europas seit 1917 1976 and 1992 (Italian trans.), Schlüsselwörter in der Geschichte 1978, Geschichte und Gewalt 1981, Zeit der Ideologien 1982 (English, Spanish and Italian trans. 1985), Die totalitäre Erfahrung 1987, Die Weimarer Republik 1988, Deutschland zwischen Krieg und Frieden 1991, Deutschland 1933–1945 1992, Wendezeiten der Geschichte 1992, Verfall und Fortschritt im Denken der frühen römischen Kaiserzeit 1987, Hitler et la dictature allemande 1995, Turning Points in Modern Times 1995. *Leisure interest:* piano music. *Address:* Universität Bonn, Stationsweg 17, 53127 Bonn, Germany. *Telephone:* 284358.

BRACHES, Ernst; Netherlands professor (retd.); b. 8 Oct. 1930, Padang, Indonesia; s. of Gottfried Daniel Ernst Braches and Zeni Jansz; m. Maartje van Hoorn 1961; three s. and one foster s.; ed. Univ. of Amsterdam; Asst. Univ. of Amsterdam 1957–65; Keeper, Western Printed Books, Univ. Library, Leiden 1965–73; Asst. Dir. Rijksmuseum Meermanno-Westreenianum, The Hague 1973–77; Librarian, Univ. of Amsterdam 1977–88; Prof. History of the Printed Book, Univ. of Amsterdam; hon. mem. Soc. de la Reliure Originale, Paris. *Publications:* Het Boek als Nieuwe Kunst 1973, Engel en Afgrond 1983; publications on Goethe, Henry James, Thomas Mann, typography etc. *Leisure interest:* Borneo in World War II. *Address:* Vrijburglaan 53, 2051 LB Overveen, Netherlands (Home). *Telephone:* (023) 5253246 (Home). *Fax:* (023) 5253246 (Home).

BRADBEER, Sir (John) Derek (Richardson), Kt., M.A., O.B.E., T.D.; British lawyer; b. 29 Oct. 1931; s. of William Bertram Bradbeer and Winifred Richardson; m. Margaret Elizabeth Chantler 1962; one s. one d.; ed. Canford School, Sidney Sussex Coll. Cambridge; admitted Solicitor 1959; partner Wilkinson Maughan (fmrly. Wilkinson Marshall Clayton & Gibson) 1961–; mem. Criminal Injuries Compensation Bd. 1988–; mem. Council, Law Soc. 1973–, Vice-Pres. 1986–87, Pres. 1987–88; Pres. Newcastle upon Tyne Inc. Law Soc. 1982–83; Gov. Coll. of Law 1983– (Chair. 1990–); Chair. North

East Water 1992–; D.L. Tyne and Wear 1988; Vice-Chair. N. of England T.A. & V.R.A. 1988–90, Chair. 1990–. *Leisure interests:* reading, gardening, sport. *Address:* Forge Cottage, Shilvington, Ponteland, Newcastle upon Tyne, NE20 0AP, England. *Telephone:* (01670) 775214.

BRADBURY, Malcolm Stanley, C.B.E., M.A., PH.D., F.R.S.L.; British author and professor of American studies; b. 7 Sept. 1932, Sheffield, Yorks.; s. of Arthur and Doris Ethel (Marshall) Bradbury; m. Elizabeth Salt 1959; two s.; ed. Univ. Coll., Leicester, Queen Mary Coll., Univ. of London, Univ. of Manchester, Indiana Univ.; Staff Tutor in Literature and Drama, Dept. of Advanced Educ., Univ. of Hull 1959–61; lecturer in English Language and Literature, Univ. of Birmingham 1961–65; lecturer, later Senior lecturer and Reader, School of English and American Studies, Univ. of East Anglia 1965–70, Prof. of American Studies 1970–95, Prof. Emer. 1995–; Visiting Fellow, All Souls, Oxford 1969; Visiting Prof., Univ. of Zürich 1972, Visiting Fellow St. John's Coll., Oxford 1995; Royal Soc. of Literature Prize for The History Man 1975; mem. Man. Cttee. Booker Prize 1984–91; Hon. Fellow, Queen Mary Coll., London 1985; Hon. D.Litt. (Leicester) 1986, (Birmingham) 1989, (Hull) 1994, (Nottingham) 1996; Int. Emmy Award for Porterhouse Blue (TV Series) 1988, Monte Carlo Award for The Gravy Train 1991. *Publications:* Eating People is Wrong (novel) 1959, Evelyn Waugh 1962, E. M. Forster: a Collection of Critical Essays (editor) 1965, Stepping Westward (novel) 1965, What is a novel? 1969, A Passage to India: a Casebook 1970, A Penguin Companion to Literature: Vol. III, American Literature (with E. Mottram) 1971, The Social Context of Modern English Literature 1972; Possibilities: Essays on the State of the Novel 1973, The History Man (novel) 1975, Modernism (with J. W. MacFarlane) 1976, Who Do You Think You Are? (short stories) 1976, The Novel Today (editor) 1977, An Introduction to American Studies (with H. Temperley) 1981, Saul Bellow 1982, The After Dinner Game (plays) 1982, All Dressed Up and Nowhere To Go 1982, The Modern American Novel 1983, Rates of Exchange (novel) 1983, Why Come to Slaka 1986, No Not Bloomsbury 1986, Cuts: A Very Short Novel 1987, Structuralism's Hidden Hero: My Strange Quest for Henri Mensonge 1987, The Penguin Book of Modern Short Stories (ed.) 1987, No, Not Bloomsbury (essays) 1987, The Modern World: Ten Great Writers 1988, Unsent Letters 1988, Anything More Would be Greedy (TV drama series), The Green Man (adapted for TV) 1989, The Gravy Train (TV drama series) 1990, Cold Comfort Farm (adapted for TV and film) 1994; From Puritanism to Postmodernism: A History Of American Literature (with R. Ruland) 1991, The Gravy Train Goes East 1991, New Writing 1992, Doctor Criminale 1992, The Modern American Novel 1992, New Writing 2 1993, The Modern British Novel 1993, Dangerous Pilgrimages 1995, Class Work 1995, The Atlas of Literature 1996, Inside Trading (play) 1996, A Touch of Frost (TV) 1997, Dalziel and Pascoe (adapted for TV) 1996–97, Kavanagh QC (TV) 1997, Inspector Morse (adapted for TV) 1998, Diderot at the Hermitage (novel) 1998; numerous critical articles; many TV scripts. *Leisure interest:* reading other people's books. *Address:* c/o Curtis Brown Literary Agents, Haymarket House, 28/29 Haymarket, London, SW1Y 4SP, England.

BRADBURY, Ray (Douglas); American author; b. Aug. 1920, Ill.; s. of Leonard Bradbury and Esther Bradbury; m. Marguerite McClure 1947; four d.; Pres. Science-Fantasy Writers of America 1951–53; mem. Bd. of Dirs. Screen Workers Guild of America 1957–61. *Publications include:* Dark Carnival 1947, The Meadow (play) 1948, The Martian Chronicles 1950, The Illustrated Man 1951, It Came from Outer Space (screenplay) 1952, Fahrenheit 451 1953, The Golden Apples of the Sun 1953, Moby Dick (screenplay) 1954, The October Country 1955, Switch on the Night 1955, Dandelion Wine 1957, A Medicine for Melancholy (play as The Day it Rained Forever) 1966, Icarus Montgolfier Wright (screenplay) 1961, R is for Rocket 1962, Something Wicked This Way Comes 1962, The Anthem Sprinters and Other Antics (play) 1963, The World of Ray Bradbury (play) 1964, The Machineries of Joy (short stories) 1964, The Vintage Bradbury 1965, The Wonderful Ice-Cream Suit (play) 1965, The Autumn People 1965, Tomorrow Midnight 1966, The Pedestrian (play) 1966, S is for Space 1966, The Picasso Summer (screenplay) 1968, I Sing the Body Electric! 1969, Christus Apollo (play) 1969, Old Ahab's Friend and Friend to Nosh, Speaks His Piece: A Celebration 1971, The Halloween Tree 1972, The Wonderful Ice Cream Suit and Other Plays: For Today, Tomorrow and Beyond Tomorrow 1972, When Elephants Last in the Dooryard Bloomed (poetry) 1972, The Small Assassin 1973, Zen and the Art of Writing 1973, Mars and the Mind of Man 1973, The Son of Richard III 1974, Long After Midnight (stories) 1976, Pillar of Fire and Other Plays 1976, Where Robot Mice and Robot Men Run Round in Robot Towns, New Poems Both Light and Dark 1977, Beyond 1984 1979, The Stories of Ray Bradbury 1980, The Ghosts of Forever 1981, The Haunted Computer and the Android Pope 1981, The Last Circus 1981, The Complete Poems of Ray Bradbury 1982, The Love Affair 1983, The Dinosaur Tales 1983, A Memory for Murder 1984, Forever and the Earth 1984, Death is a Lonely Business (novel) 1985, The Toynbee Convector 1989, A Graveyard for Lunatics (novel) 1990, Yestermorrow, Obvious Answers to Impossible Futures, Green Shadows, White Whale 1992, Journey to Far Metaphor: Further Essays on Creativity, Writing, Literature and the Arts 1994, The First Book of Dichotomy, The Second Book of Symbiosis 1995, Driving Blind 1998. *Leisure interests:* oil painting, ceramics, collecting native masks. *Address:* 10265 Cheviot Drive, Los Angeles, CA 90064, U.S.A.

BRADEMAS, John, D.PHIL.; American politician and former university president; b. 2 March 1927, Mishawaka, Ind.; s. of Stephen Brademas and Beatrice Goble; m. Mary Briggs 1977; ed. Harvard Univ. and Univ. of Oxford; legis. asst. to Senator Pat McNamara; admin. asst. to Rep. Thomas L. Ashley 1955; exec. asst. to presidential nominee Stevenson 1955–56; Asst. Prof. of Political Science, St. Mary's Coll. Notre Dame, Ind. 1957–58; mem. 86th–96th Congresses from 3rd Ind. Dist.; Chief Deputy Majority Whip 93rd–94th Congresses; Majority Whip 95th–96th Congresses; Pres. New York Univ. 1981–92; fmr. Chair. Fed. Reserve Bank of New York; Dir. RCA/NBC, Scholastic Inc., New York Stock Exchange, Rockefeller Foundation, Co-Chair, American Asscn. for the Advancement of Science; mem. Cen. Comm. WCC, Trilateral Comm.; many other public appts.; Fellow, American Acad. of Arts and Sciences; George Peabody Award 1980; Hon. Fellow Brasenose Coll., Oxford; numerous hon. degrees and other awards and distinctions. *Publications:* Anarcosindicalismo y revolución en España, 1930–37 1974, Washington, D.C. to Washington Square 1986, The Politics of Education: Conflict and Consensus on Capitol Hill 1987. *Address:* c/o Office of the President, New York University, 53 Washington Square South, New York, NY 10012, U.S.A.

BRADFORD, Barbara Taylor; British author and journalist; b. 10 May 1933, Leeds, England; d. of Winston Taylor and Freda Walker; m. Robert Bradford 1963; ed. privately; reporter, Yorkshire Evening Post 1949–51, Women's Ed. 1951–53; Fashion Ed. Woman's Own 1953–54; columnist, London Evening News 1955–57; Exec. Ed. London American 1959–62; Ed. Nat. Design Center Magazine 1965–69; syndicated columnist, Newsday Specials, Long Island 1968–70; nat. syndicated columnist, Chicago Tribune-New York (News Syndicate), New York 1970–75, Los Angeles Times Syndicate 1975–81; Hon. D. Lit. (Leeds) 1990. *Publications:* Complete Encyclopaedia of Homemaking Ideas 1968, A Garland of Children's Verse 1968, How to be the Perfect Wife 1969, Easy Steps to Successful Decorating 1971, Decorating Ideas for Casual Living 1977, How to Solve your Decorating Problems 1976, Making Space Grow 1979, A Woman of Substance (novel) 1979, Luxury Designs for Apartment Living 1981, Voice of the Heart 1982, Hold the Dream 1984, Act of Will (novel) 1986, To Be The Best 1988, The Women in his Life (novel) 1990, Remember (novel) 1991, Angel (novel) 1993, Everything to Gain (novel) 1994, Dangerous to Know (novel) 1995, Love in Another Town (novel) 1995, Her Own Rules 1996, A Secret Affair 1996, Power of a Woman 1997, A Sudden Change of Heart 1998. *Address:* Bradford Enterprises, 450 Park Avenue, New York, NY 10022, U.S.A. *Telephone:* (212) 308 7390. *Fax:* (212) 935 1636.

BRADFORD, Max; New Zealand politician and economist; b. 1942; m. Rosemary Bradford; two step-c.; fmr. mem. staff of Treasury and of IMF, Washington, D.C., Chief Exec. N.Z. Bankers' Asscn.; econ. and financial consultant; Nat. Party M.P. for Tarawera (now for Rotorua) 1990–; Minister of Labour, Energy, Immigration and Business Devt. 1996–98, of Labour, Energy, Defence, Revenue, Enterprise and Commerce 1998–; fmr. Chief Exec. Nat. Party. *Address:* Ministry of Labour, P.O. Box 3705, Wellington, New Zealand. *Telephone:* (04) 915-4000. *Fax:* (04) 495-4015.

BRADFORD, William E.; Canadian insurance executive; b. 14 Oct. 1933, Montreal; s. of the late Elwood Joseph Bradford and Jessie (née Murray) Bradford; m. Dolores MacDonnell 1954; three s. four d.; ed. Concordia Univ., Montreal; with Northern Electric Co. Ltd. 1950–59, Canada Iron Foundries Ltd. 1959–62; Asst. Controller, Reynolds Extrusion Co. Ltd. 1962–66; Vice-Pres. and Controller, Churchill Falls (Labrador) Corpn. Ltd. 1967–70; Vice-Pres. and Sr. Financial Officer, Brinco 1970–74; Exec. Vice-Pres. for Finance, Bank of Montreal 1975, for Finance and Admin. 1976, Exec. Vice-Pres. and Deputy Gen. Man. Domestic Banking 1978, also Gen. Man. 1979, Exec. Vice-Pres., Chief Gen. Man. Bank of Montreal 1980, Pres. 1981–83, Deputy Chair. 1983–87; Pres. and C.E.O. N. American Life Assurance Co. (now Manulife Financial) 1987–93, Deputy Chair. and C.E.O. 1993–; Fellow, Certified Gen. Accountants' Asscn. of Ont., Financial Execs. Inst. *Leisure interests:* tennis, squash, golf, skiing, hunting, fishing. *Address:* Manulife Financial, 5650 Yonge Street, North York, Ont., M2M 4G4; 1333 Watersedge Road, Mississauga, Ont., L5J 1A3, Canada (Home). *Telephone:* (416) 229-3010 (Office).

BRADLEE, Benjamin Crowninshield; American newspaper editor; b. 26 Aug. 1921, Boston; s. of Frederick Bradlee and Josephine deGersdorff; m. 1st Jean Saltonstall 1942; one s.; m. 2nd Antoinette Pinchot 1956; one s. one d.; m. 3rd Sally Quinn 1978, one s.; ed. Harvard Univ.; reporter, N.H. Sunday News, Manchester 1946–48, Washington Post 1948–51; Press Attaché, U.S. Embassy, Paris 1951–53; European corresp. Newsweek, Paris 1953–57; reporter, Washington Bureau, Newsweek 1957–61, Sr. Ed. and Chief of Bureau 1961–65; Man. Ed. Washington Post 1965–68, Vice-Pres. and Exec. Ed. 1968–91, Vice-Pres. at Large 1991–; Chair. History of St. Mary's City Comm. 1992–; Burton Benjamin Award 1995. *Publications:* That Special Grace 1964, Conversations with Kennedy 1975, A Good Life: Newspapering and Other Adventures (autobiog.) 1995. *Address:* c/o Washington Post, 1150 15th Street, N.W., Washington, DC 20071 (Office); 3014 N. Street, N.W., Washington, DC 20007, U.S.A. (Home).

BRADLEY, Bill, M.A.; American politician; b. 28 July 1943, Crystal City, Mo.; s. of Warren W. Bradley and Susan Crowe; m. Ernestine Schlant 1974; one d.; ed. Princeton and Oxford Univs.; player, New York Knickerbockers Professional Basketball Team 1967–77; Senator from New Jersey 1979–96; Payne Dist. Prof., Inst. for Int. Studies, Stanford Univ., Calif. 1997–; Democrat. *Publications:* Life on the Run 1976, The Fair Tax 1984, Time Present, Time Past 1996. *Address:* 1661 Page Mill Road, Palo Alto, CA 94304, U.S.A. (Home).

BRADLEY, Clive, C.B.E., M.A.; British publishing and communications executive; b. 25 July 1934, London; s. of late Alfred Bradley and Annie K. Bradley; ed. Felsted School, Essex, Clare Coll. Cambridge and Yale Univ.; B.B.C. 1961–63; Broadcasting Officer, Labour Party 1963–65; Political Ed., The Statist 1965–67; Group Labour Adviser, Int. Publishing Corpn. and Deputy Gen. Man. Mirror Group Newspapers 1967–73; Dir. The Observer 1973–75; Chief Exec. The Publishers Asscn. 1976–98, adviser on digital information 1997–; Dir. Confed. of Information Communication Industries 1984–. *Publications:* many articles and broadcasts on politics, econs. and current affairs. *Leisure interests:* politics, reading, walking. *Address:* 1 Kingsway, London, WC2B 6XF (Office); 8 Northumberland Place, Richmond upon Thames, Surrey, TW10 6TS, England (Home). *Telephone:* 0171-565 7474 (Office); 0181-940 7172 (Home).

BRADLEY, Daniel Joseph, PH.D., F.R.S., F.I.E.E.E., F.INST.P.; Irish professor of optical electronics; b. 18 Jan. 1928; s. of John and Margaret Bradley; m. Winefriede M. T. O'Connor 1958; four s. one d.; ed. St. Columb's Coll., Derry, St. Mary's Training Coll., Belfast, Birkbeck and Royal Holloway Colls., London; primary school teacher, Londonderry 1947–53, secondary school teacher, London area 1953–57; Asst. Lecturer, Royal Holloway Coll. 1957–60; lecturer, Imperial Coll. of Science and Tech. 1960–64; Reader, Royal Holloway Coll. 1964–66; Prof. and Head of Dept. of Pure and Applied Physics, Queen's Univ., Belfast 1966–73; Prof. of Optics, Imperial Coll. 1973–80, Head, Dept. of Physics 1976–80, Emer. Prof. London Univ. 1980–; Prof. of Optical Electronics, Trinity Coll., Dublin 1980–; Visiting Scientist M.I.T. 1965; Consultant, Harvard Observatory 1966; Chair. Laser Facility Cttee. S.R.C. 1976–79, British Nat. Cttee. for Physics 1979–80, Quantum Electronics Comm. IUPAP 1982; mem. Rutherford Lab. Establishment Cttee. S.R.C. 1977–79, Science Bd., S.R.C. 1977–80; mem. Council, Royal Soc. 1979–80; Fellow, Optical Soc. of America; Fellow Trinity Coll., Dublin; mem. Royal Irish Acad.; D.Sc.h.c. (New Univ., Ulster) 1983, (Belfast) 1986; Thomas Young Medal, Inst. of Physics 1975; Royal Medal, Royal Soc. 1983, Charles Hard Townes Award of Optical Soc. of America 1989. *Publications:* papers on optics, lasers, spectroscopy, chronoscopy and astronomy in learned journals. *Leisure interests:* television, walking. *Address:* Trinity College, Dublin 2, Ireland.

BRADLEY, David John, M.A., D.M., F.R.C.P., F.R.C.PATH., F.F.P.H.M., F.I.BIOL.; British professor of tropical hygiene; b. 12 Jan. 1937; s. of Harold Bradley and Mona Bradley; m. Lorne M. Farquhar 1961 (divorced 1989); two s. two d.; ed. Wyggeston Grammar School, Leicester, Selwyn Coll. Cambridge and Univ. Coll. Hosp. Medical School, London; Univ. Coll. Hosp. 1960–61; Medical Research Officer, Ross Inst. Bilharzia Research Unit, Mwanza, Tanzania 1961–64; lecturer, Makerere Medical School, Univ. of E. Africa 1964–66, Sr. lecturer in Preventive Medicine 1966–69; Royal Soc. Tropical Research Fellow 1969–73; Sr. Research Fellow, Staines Medical Fellow, Exeter Coll. Oxford 1971–74; Clinical Reader in Pathology, Univ. of Oxford Clinical Medical School 1973–74; Prof. of Tropical Hygiene, Univ. of London, Dir. and Head of Dept. Ross Inst. of Tropical Hygiene, London School of Hygiene and Tropical Medicine 1974–, Chair. Div. of Communicable and Tropical Diseases 1982–88; Visiting Prof. Univ. of Wales Coll. of Medicine 1995–; numerous professional appointments, consultancies to int. orgs. etc.; corresp. mem. German Tropenmedizingesellschaft; foreign corresp. mem. Royal Belgian Acad. of Medicine; other awards and distinctions. *Publications:* five books and more than 150 papers on tropical medicine and related topics. *Leisure interests:* natural history, landscape gardens, travel. *Address:* Department of Infections and Tropical Diseases, London School of Hygiene and Tropical Medicine, Keppel Street, London, WC1E 7HT (Office); The Retreat, Woodperry Road, Beckley, Oxford, OX3 9UZ, England (Home). *Telephone:* 0171-927 2216 (Office); (01865) 358897 (Home). *Fax:* 0171-580 9075 (Office).

BRADLEY, Donald Charlton, PH.D., D.SC., F.R.S.C., F.R.S.A., F.R.S.; British inorganic chemist; b. 7 Nov. 1924; m. 1st Constance Joy Hazeldean 1948 (died 1985); one s.; m. 2nd Ann Levy (née MacDonald) 1990; ed. Hove Co. School for Boys, Birkbeck Coll., Univ. of London; Research Asst., British Electrical and Allied Industries Research Asscn. 1941–47; Asst. Lecturer in Chem., Birkbeck Coll. 1949–52, Lecturer 1952–59; Prof. of Chem., Univ. of Western Ont. 1959–64; Prof. of Inorganic Chem., Queen Mary Coll., Univ. of London 1965–87, Emer. Prof. 1988–, Head of Chem. Dept. 1978–82, Fellow 1988; Chair. Bd. of Studies in Chem. and Chemical Industries, Univ. of London 1977–79; mem. Senate, London Univ. 1981–87, Soc. of Chem. Industry; M.R.I. (mem. Council 1987–93, Hon. Sec. 1988–93); Exec. Ed. Polyhedron 1982–97; Ludwig Mond Medal and Lectureship, Royal Soc. of Chemistry 1987, Royal Medal, Royal Soc. 1998. *Publications:* (jt. author) Metal Alkoxides 1978, numerous scientific papers. *Leisure interests:* travelling, gardening, music, archaeology. *Address:* Department of Chemistry, Queen Mary and Westfield College, Mile End Road, London, E1 4NS, England.

BRADMAN, Sir Donald George, Kt., A.C.; Australian cricketer and company director; b. 27 Aug. 1908, Cootamundra, N.S.W.; s. of George and Emily Bradman; m. Jessie Menzies 1932 (died 1997); two s. (one deceased) one d.; ed. Bowral Intermediate High School; right-hand batsman; teams: N.S.W. 1927–34, South Australia 1935–49 (Capt. 1935–48); 52 Tests for Australia 1928–48, 24 as Capt., scoring 6,996 runs (average 99.9) including 29 hundreds; scored 28,067 first-class runs (average 95.1) with 117 hundreds—only Australian to score 100 hundreds; unequalled Test match and first-class averages; toured England 1930, 1934, 1938, 1948, scoring more than 2,000 first-class runs on each occasion; fmr. mem. Australian Bd. of Control for Int. Cricket, Chair. 1960–63, 1969–72; Vice-Pres. S. Australia Cricket Asscn. 1951–65, Pres. 1965–73; fmr. Australian Test Selector; fmr. mem. Stock Exchange of Adelaide; Champion Mt. Osmond Country Club (Golf) 1936, 1949; fmr. S. Australia Amateur Squash Champion; Life Vice-Pres. of M.C.C. 1988–. *Publications:* Don Bradman's Book 1930, How to Play Cricket 1935, My Cricketing Life 1938, Farewell to Cricket 1950, The Art of Cricket 1958, The Bradman Albums 1988. *Leisure interests:* cricket, tennis, golf, squash. *Address:* 2 Holden Street, Kensington Park, South Australia 5068, Australia.

BRADMAN, Godfrey Michael, F.C.A.; British business executive; b. 9 Sept. 1936; s. of William I. Bradman and Anne B. Goldsweig; m. Susan Bennett 1975; two s. three d.; Sr. Partner, Godfrey Bradman & Co. (chartered accountants) 1961; Chair. London Mercantile Corpn. 1969; Chair. Rosehaugh PLC 1979–91; Chair. European Land and Property Corpn. PLC 1992–, European Land and Property Investments Co. 1993–, Ashpest Finance Ltd. 1993–, Jt. Chair. Vic. Quay 1993–, Pondbridge Europe Ltd. 1994–; founder, mem. CLEAR (Campaign for Lead-Free Air) 1981–91; jt. founder and Pres. Campaign for Freedom of Information 1983–, Founder, Chair. Citizen Action, European Citizen Action 1983–91; Chair. Friends of the Earth Trust 1983–91; Dir. AIDS Policy Unit 1987–90; Pres. Soc. for the Protection of Unborn Children Educational Trust 1987–; mem. Council UN Int. Year of Shelter for the Homeless 1987; mem. governing body London School of Hygiene and Tropical Medicine 1988–91; founder and Jt. Chair. Parents Against Tobacco Campaign; Founder Opren Victims Campaign; Hon. Fellow King's Coll. London; Hon. D.Sc. (Salford). *Leisure interests:* his children, reading, horseriding. *Address:* 15 Hanover Terrace, London, NW1 4RJ, England.

BRADSHAW, Anthony David, M.A., PH.D., F.I.E.E.M., F.L.S., F.R.S.; British ecologist; b. 17 Jan. 1926; m. Betty Margaret Bradshaw; three d.; ed. St. Paul's School, London, Jesus Coll., Cambridge; Lecturer Univ. Coll. N. Wales, Bangor 1952–63, Sr. Lecturer 1963–64, Reader in Agricultural Botany 1964–68; Holbrook Gaskell Prof. of Botany, Univ. of Liverpool 1968–88, Prof. Emer. 1988–; mem. Nature Conservancy Council 1969–78, Natural Environment Research Council 1969–74; Bd. of Man. Sports Turf Research Inst. 1976–; Pres. British Ecological Soc. 1981–83, Inst. of Ecology and Environmental Man. 1991–94; Pres. Merseyside Environment Trust; mem. Bd. of Man. Groundwork Trust, St. Helens, Knowsley, Sefton 1982–; Hon. D.Sc. (Lancaster) 1998. *Publications:* (jt. ed.) Teaching Genetics 1963, (with M. J. Chadwick) The Restoration of Land 1980, (with others) Quarry Reclamation 1982, (with others) Mine Wastes Reclamation 1982, (with R. A. Dutton) Land Reclamation in Cities 1982, (jt. ed.) Ecology and Design in Landscape 1985, Transforming our Waste Land (with A. Burt) 1986, (jt. ed.) The Treatment and Handling of Wastes 1991, Trees in the Urban Landscape (with B. Hunt and T. J. Walmsley) 1995, numerous learned papers. *Leisure interests:* sailing, gardening, landscape appreciation. *Address:* 58 Knowsley Road, Liverpool, L19 0PG, England. *Telephone:* 0151-280 2292. *Fax:* 0151-291 4987.

BRADSHAW, Peter, B.A., F.R.S.; British professor of aerodynamics; b. 26 Dec. 1935, Torquay; s. of J. W. N. Bradshaw and F. W. G. Bradshaw (née Finch); m. Sheila Dorothy Brown 1969; ed. Torquay Grammar School, St. John's Coll., Cambridge; Scientific Officer, Aerodynamics Div., Nat. Physical Lab., Teddington 1957–69; Sr. Lecturer, Dept. of Aeronautics, Imperial Coll., Univ. of London 1969–71, Reader 1971–78, Prof. of Experimental Aerodynamics 1978–88; Thomas V. Jones Prof. of Eng., Dept. of Mechanical Eng., Stanford Univ. 1988–95, Emer. Prof. 1996–; Hon. D. Sc. (Exeter) 1990; Royal Aeronautical Soc. Bronze Medal 1971, Royal Aeronautical Soc. Busk Prize 1972, AIAA Fluid Dynamics Award 1994. *Publications:* Experimental Fluid Mechanics 1964, An Introduction to Turbulence 1971, Momentum Transfer in Boundary Layers (with T. Cebeci) 1977, Engineering Calculation Methods for Turbulent Flow (with T. Cebeci and J. H. Whitelaw) 1981, Convective Heat Transfer (with T. Cebeci) 1984. *Leisure interests:* ancient history, walking. *Address:* Thermosciences Division, Department of Mechanical Engineering, Stanford Univ., Stanford, CA 94305-3030, U.S.A. *Telephone:* (415) 725-0704.

BRADY, Conor, M.A.; Irish journalist; b. 24 April 1949, Dublin; s. of Conor Brady and Amy MacCarthy; m. Ann Byron 1971; two s.; ed. Mount St. Joseph Cistercian Abbey, Univ. Coll. Dublin; Asst. Ed. The Irish Times 1978–81; Ed. The Sunday Tribune 1981–82; Deputy Ed. The Irish Times 1984–86, Ed. 1986–, Dir. Irish Times Ltd. 1986–; Award for Outstanding Work in Irish Journalism 1979. *Publication:* Guardian of the Peace 1974. *Leisure interests:* travel, reading, swimming. *Address:* c/o The Irish Times, 10–16 d'Olier Street, Dublin 2, Ireland. *Telephone:* 6792022. *Fax:* (1) 6793910.

BRADY, James S., B.S., J.D.; American government official and lawyer; b. 17 Sept. 1944, Grand Rapids, Mich.; s. of George Joseph and Emily Mae (Sherman) Brady; m. Catherine Ann Yared 1966; two s., one d.; ed. Univs. of Western Michigan and Notre Dame; admitted to Mich. bar 1969; assoc. Roach, Twohey, Maggini and Brady law firm 1969–77, partner 1972–77; Adjunct Prof. Cooley Law School, Lansing, Mich. 1975–76; U.S. Attorney Western Dist., Mich. Grand Rapids 1977–81; mem. Miller, Johnson, Snell and Cummiskey 1981–, Chair. Litigation Section 1992–; Press Sec. to Pres.

Reagan 1981; mem. American, Fed., Mich. and Grand Rapids bar asscns., State Bar, Mich., American Trial Lawyers' Asscn.; Presidential Medal of Freedom 1996. *Address:* 800 Calder Plaza Building, Grand Rapids, MI 49503 (Office); 1700 Fisk S.E., Grand Rapids, MI 49506, U.S.A. (Home).

BRADY, Nicholas F.; American politician and financier; b. 11 April, 1930, New York; s. of James C. Brady and Eliot Brady; m. Katherine Douglas 1952; two s. one d.; ed. Yale and Harvard Univs.; with Dillon, Read and Co. Ltd. 1954–82, fmr. Chair., C.E.O. 1982–; Chair., Exec. Comm. Purolator Courier Corpn. Inc. Basking Ridge, N.J. 1983–; U.S. Treasury Sec. 1988–93; appointee to U.S. Senate from N.J. 1982; Chair. Templeton Latin American Investment Trust 1994–, Derby Overseas Investments 1996–; Dir. Bessemer Securities Corpn., Doubleday & Co., Wolverne World Wide Inc., ASA Ltd., Media Gen. Inc., NCR Corpn.; mem. MX Missile Options Panel, Cen. American Study Comm.; Chair. Jockey Club, New York. *Address:* Templeton Latin America Investment Trust PLC, Saltire Court, 20 Castle Terrace, Edin., EH1 2EH, Scotland. *Telephone:* 0131-469 4000. *Fax:* 0131-228 4506.

BRADY, Roscoe Owen, M.D.; American medical research scientist; b. 11 Oct. 1923, Philadelphia, Pa.; s. of Roscoe O. and Martha Roberts Brady; m. Bennett Carden Manning 1972; two s.; ed. Pennsylvania State Univ., Harvard Medical School and Univ. of Pennsylvania; Thyroid Clinic Assoc., Univ. of Pa. School of Medicine 1950–52; Officer-in-Charge, Dept. of Chemistry, U.S. Naval Medical School 1952–54; Section Chief. Nat. Inst. of Neurological Diseases and Blindness (now Nat. Inst. of Neurological Disorders and Stroke) 1954–67, Acting Chief, Laboratory of Neurochemistry 1967–68, Asst. Chief 1969–71, Chief, Developmental and Metabolic Neurology Branch 1972–; Professorial Lecturer, Dept. of Biochemistry, George Washington Univ. School of Medicine 1963–73; Adjunct Prof. of Biochemistry, Dept. of Biochemistry, Georgetown Univ. School of Medicine 1965–; mem. of medical staff Children's Hosp. Wash. 1992–; mem. N.A.S., Inst. of Medicine (N.A.S.); Gairdner Foundation Int. Award, Passano Foundation Award, Lasker Foundation Award, Cotzias Award, American Acad. of Neurology, Kovalonko Medal, N.A.S., Aldert Foundation Prize, Harvard Medical School, and other awards and prizes. *Publications:* Neurochemistry of Nucleotides and Amino Acids (ed. with D. B. Tower) 1960, The Basic Neurosciences (ed.) 1975, The Molecular Basis of Lysosomal Storage Disorders (ed. with J. A. Barranger) 1984 and 400 scientific publs. *Leisure interests:* piano, tennis, bridge. *Address:* Building 10, Room 3D04, National Institutes of Health, 9000 Rockville Pike, Bethesda, MD 20892 (Office); 6026 Valerian Lane, Rockville, MD 20852, U.S.A. (Home). *Telephone:* (301) 496-3285 (Office); (301) 881-3474 (Home).

BRADY, Mgr. Sean, D.CN.L.; Irish ecclesiastic; b. 16 Aug. 1939, Laragh, Co. Cavan; s. of late Andrew Brady and Teresa Smith; ed. Caulfield Nat. School, St. Patrick's Coll. Cavan, St. Patrick's Coll. Maynooth, Irish Coll. Rome and Lateran Univ.; ordained priest 1964; language teacher, St. Patrick's Coll. Cavan 1967–80; Diocesan Sec. Kilmore 1973–80; Vice-Rector, Irish Coll. Rome 1980, Rector 1987–94; Parish Priest, Ballyhaise 1994; Coadjutor Archbishop of Armagh 1995–96, Archbishop of Armagh and Primate of All Ireland 1996–. *Leisure interests:* Gaelic football. *Address:* Ara Coeli, Armagh, BT61 7QY, Northern Ireland. *Telephone:* 01861-522045. *Fax:* 01861-526182.

BRAGG, Baron (Life Peer), cr. 1998, of Lington in the County of Cumbria, **Melvyn Bragg,** M.A., F.R.S.L., F.R.T.S.; British author and television presenter; b. 6 Oct. 1939; s. of Stanley Bragg and Mary E. Park; m. 1st Marie-Elisabeth Roche 1961 (deceased); one d.; m. 2nd Catherine M. Haste 1973; one s. one d.; ed. Nelson-Thomlinson Grammar School, Wigton and Wadham Coll. Oxford; BBC Radio and TV Producer 1961–67; TV Presenter and Ed. The South Bank Show for ITV 1978–; Head of Arts, London Weekend TV 1982–90, Controller of Arts 1990–; Deputy Chair. Border TV 1985–90, Chair. 1990–96; novelist 1964–; writer and broadcaster 1967–; mem. Arts Council and Chair. Literature Panel of Arts Council 1977–80; Pres. Cumbrians for Peace 1982–, Northern Arts 1983–87, Nat. Campaign for the Arts 1986–; Gov. L.S.E. 1997–; mem. Bd. Really Useful Co. 1989–90; Hon. D.Litt. (Liverpool) 1986, (Council for Nat. Academic Awards) 1990, Lancaster) 1990, (South Bank) 1997; Dr. h.c. (Open Univ.) 1989; Domus Fellow, St. Catherine's Coll. Oxford 1990; Hon. Fellow Lancashire Polytechnic 1990; numerous awards. *Plays:* Mardi Gras 1976, Orion 1977, The Hired Man 1984, King Lear in New York 1992. *Screenplays:* Isadora, Jesus Christ Superstar, Clouds of Glory (with Ken Russell). *Publications:* Speak for England 1976, Land of the Lakes 1983, Laurence Olivier 1984, Rich, The Life of Richard Burton 1988, The Seventh Seal: a study on Ingmar Bergman 1993; *novels:* For Want of a Nail 1965, The Second Inheritance 1966, Without a City Wall 1968, The Hired Man 1969, A Place in England 1970, The Nerve 1971, Josh Lawton 1972, The Silken Net 1974, A Christmas Child 1976, Autumn Manoeuvres 1978, Kingdom Come 1980, Love and Glory 1983, The Maid of Buttermere 1987, A Time to Dance (televised 1992) 1990, Crystal Rooms 1992, Credo 1996, The Sword and the Miracle 1997, On Giant's Shoulders 1998. *Address:* 12 Hampstead Hill Gardens, London, NW3 2PL, England.

BRAHAM, Allan John Witney, PH.D.; British fmr. gallery curator and author; b. 19 Aug. 1937, Croydon; s. of Dudley Braham and Florence Mears; m. Helen Clare Butterworth 1963; two d.; ed. Dulwich Coll., London Univ. and the Courtauld Inst.; Asst. Keeper Nat. Gallery 1962, Deputy Keeper 1973, Keeper and Deputy Dir. 1978–88; Hitchcock Medal, Bannister Fletcher Prize for writings. *Publications include:* François Mansart (with Peter Smith) 1973, Carlo Fontana: The Drawings at Windsor (with Hellmut Hager) 1977, The Architecture of the French Enlightenment 1980, El Greco to Goya 1981, Italian Paintings of the Sixteenth Century 1985. *Address:* 15A Acol Road, London, NW6 3AA, England (Home).

BRAHIMI, Abdelhamid, D.ECON.; Algerian politician; b. 2 April 1936, Constantine; m.; one c.; officer, Nat. Liberation Army 1956–62; Wali of Annaba (govt. rep. in province of Annaba) 1963–65; Dir. O.C.I. (Algerian-French Bd. for promotion of industrial co-operation) 1968–70; Prof. of Econs., Univ. of Algiers 1970–75; Chair. SONATRACH Inc., U.S.A. 1976–78; Minister of Planning and Regional Devt. 1979–83; Prime Minister of Algeria 1984–88.

BRAHMANANDA Palahally Ramaiya, PH.D.; Indian professor of economics; b. 27 Sept. 1926, Bangalore; s. of Ramaiya and Jayalakshamma Ramaiya; ed. Mysore Univ. and Bombay Univ.; Research Asst., Bombay Univ. 1950–54, Lecturer in Econs. 1954–56, Reader in Monetary Econs. 1956–63, Prof. 1963–89, Dir. Dept. of Econs. 1976–86; Nat. Fellow I.C.S.S.R. 1977–79, R.B.I. Nat. Prof. 1990; Ed. Indian Economic Journal 1956; Nat. Lecturer in Econs., Univ. Grants Comm.; Pres. Indian Econs. Asscn. 1977; Nat. Fellow in Econs., Univ. Grants Comm. 1978–81; Best Teacher Award, Govt. of Maharashtra 1983; Visiting Prof. Delhi Univ. 1985. *Publications:* Planning for a Shortage Economy 1952, Economics of Electricity Planning 1952, Planning for an Expanding Economy 1956 (all with C. N. Vakil), Studies in Welfare Maximization 1959, The new Classical vs. the Neo-Classical Economics 1967, The Gold-Money Rift—A Classical Theory of International Liquidity 1969, Explorations in the New Classical Theory of Political Economy and a Connected Critique of Economic Theory 1974, Determinants of Real National Income and of Price Level 1976, The Falling Economy and How to Revive It 1977, Planning for a Futureless Economy—A Critique of the 6th Plan 1978, Growthless Inflation by Means of Stockless Money 1980, Essays in Honour of Professor V. L. D'Souza (ed. with D. M. Nanjundappa and B. K. Narayan) 1980, The I.M.F. Loan and India's Economic Future 1982, Productivity in the Indian Economy: Rising Inputs for Falling Outputs 1982, Employment Policy in a Developing Country: A Case Study of India, Vols. I–II (ed. with A. Robinson and L. K. Deshpande) 1983, New Models for the American Economy 1985; Keynes' 'General Theory': A New-Classical Critique 1986, Monetary Theory—A Real Angle 1986; over 300 articles on different aspects of economic theory and the Indian economy. *Address:* c/o Department of Economics, University of Bombay, Vidyanagari P.O., Vidyanagari Marg, Bombay 400098, India; No. 12, Kalappa Block, Basavanagudi, Bangalore 560004, India. *Telephone:* 602822.

BRAIBANT, Guy; French public servant; b. 5 Sept. 1927, Paris; s. of Charles Braibant and Evelyne Curiel; m. Françoise Fabiani 1989; one s. one d. by previous marriage; ed. Ecole Nat. d'Admin., Inst. d'Etudes Politiques de Paris; Auditeur, Conseil d'Etat 1953–60, Counsel 1960–78, Conseiller d'Etat 1978–85, Chair. Reports and Studies Section 1985–92, Vice-Pres. Comm. Supérieure de Codification 1989–; Dir.-Gen. Int. Inst. of Admin. Sciences 1979–81, Pres. 1992–95; Head of Mission, Minister of Transport 1981–84; Prof., Inst. d'Etudes Politiques de Paris 1971; Commdr., Légion d'honneur, Commdr. Ordre Nat. du Mérite. *Publications:* Les grands arrêts de la jurisprudence administrative 1956, Le contrôle de l'administration et la protection des citoyens 1973, Le droit administratif français 1985, Les archives en France 1996, Données personelles et société de l'information 1998. *Address:* Commission Supérieure de Codification, 72 rue de Varenne, 75007 Paris (Office); 208 rue de Rivoli, 75001 Paris, France (Home).

BRAININ, Norbert, O.B.E.; British (b. Austrian) violinist; b. 12 March 1923, Vienna; s. of Adolph Brainin and Sophie Brainin; m. Kathe Kottow 1948; one d.; ed. Vienna High School, started studies Vienna; emigrated to U.K. 1938; studied with Carl Flesch and Max Rostal; won Carl Flesch prize for solo violinists, Guildhall School of Music, London 1946; fmrly. leader of Amadeus String Quartet, which he founded 1947; founder Leader of Ensemble Amadeus 1988–; Prof. of Chamber Music, Hochschule für Musik, Cologne 1976–92; Prof. for Chamber Music R.A.M. 1986–93, Prof. annual Amadeus Quartet course; Prof. of violin Scuola di Musica di Fiesole 1980, of Quartet playing, Reichenau, Austria, of violin playing Hochschule für Musik "Franz Liszt", Weimar 1995; D. Univ. (York) 1968; Grand Cross of Merit, First Class (Fed. Repub. of Germany) 1972; Cross of Hon. for Arts and Science (Austria) 1972. *Address:* 19 Prowse Avenue, Bushey Heath, Herts., WD2 1JS, England. *Telephone:* 0181-950 7379.

BRAITHWAITE, Eustace, M.SC.; Guyanese author and diplomatist; b. 27 June 1922; ed. New York Univ. and Cambridge Univ.; R.A.F., Second World War; schoolteacher, London 1950–57; Welfare Officer, London County Council 1958–60; Human Rights Officer, World Veterans Foundation, Paris 1960–63; lecturer and Educ. Consultant, UNESCO, Paris 1963–66; Perm. Rep. of Guyana to UN 1967–68; Amb. to Venezuela 1968–69; Franklin Prize; Ainsfield Wolff Literary Award for To Sir, With Love. *Publications:* To Sir, With Love 1959 (film 1967), A Kind of Homecoming 1961, Paid Servant 1962, A Choice of Straws, 1965, Reluctant Neighbours 1972, Honorary White 1976.

BRAITHWAITE, Sir Rodric Quentin, G.C.M.G.; British fmr. diplomatist; b. 17 May 1932, London; s. of Henry Warwick Braithwaite and Lorna Constance Davies; m. Gillian Mary Robinson 1961; four s. (one deceased) one d.; ed. Bedales School, Christ's Coll., Cambridge; Mil. Service 1950–52; joined Foreign Service 1955; Third Sec. Jakarta 1957–58; Second Sec.

Warsaw 1959–61; Foreign Office 1961–63; First Sec. (Commercial) Moscow 1963–66; First Sec. Rome 1966–69; FCO 1969–72, Head of European Integration Dept. (External) 1973–75, Head of Planning Staff 1979–80, Asst. Under Sec. of State 1981, Deputy Under-Sec. of State 1984–88; Head of Chancery, Office of Perm Rep. to EEC, Brussels 1975–78; Minister, Commercial, Washington 1982–84; Amb. to Soviet Union 1988–92; Foreign Policy Adviser to Prime Minister 1992–93; Sr. Adviser, Deutsche Bank 1994–; Chair. Britain Russia Centre 1994–, Moscow School of Political Studies 1998–; mem. European Strategy Bd. ICL 1994–, Supervisory Bd. Deutsche Bank Moscow 1998–, Bd. UralMash Zavody (Moscow and Ekaterinburg) 1998–; mem. Royal Acad. of Music 1992– (Chair. of Govs. 1998–); Hon. Fellow Christ's Coll. Cambridge, Royal Acad. of Music; Visiting Fellow All Souls Coll. Oxford 1972–73; Dr. h.c. (Birmingham) 1998. *Publication:* Engaging Russia (with Blackwill and Tanaka) 1995. *Leisure interests:* chamber music (viola), sailing, Russia. *Address:* Deutsche Bank, 23 Great Winchester Street, London, EC2P 2AX, England.

BRAKKE, Myron Kendall, PH.D.; American research chemist (retd.); b. 23 Oct. 1921, Minn.; s. of John T. and Hulda C. Marburger Brakke; m. Betty-Jean Einbecker 1947; two s. two d.; ed. Rochester Jr. Coll., Minnesota and Univ. of Minnesota; Research Assoc., Brooklyn Botanic Garden, Brooklyn, New York 1947–52, Univ. of Illinois 1952–55; Research Chemist, U.S. Dept. of Agric. Lincoln, Neb. 1955–86; Prof. of Plant Pathology, Univ. of Nebraska 1955–86, Prof. Emer. 1986–; mem. N.A.S., A.A.A.S., American Chem. Soc. and numerous professional socs. etc.; Hon D.Sc. (Nebraska) 1946; several achievement awards. *Publications:* more than 100 research articles. *Leisure interests:* reading, gardening, forestry. *Address:* Route 1, Box 57, Crete, NE 68333, U.S.A.

BRAKS, Gerrit J. M., M.AGR.; Netherlands politician; b. 23 May 1933, Odiliapeel; s. of Theodorus H. Braks and Helena Johanna Kroef; m. Frens Bardoel 1965; two s. three d.; ed. Agricultural Univ., Wageningen; worked on parents' farm -1955; Asst. Govt. Agricultural Advisory Service, Eindhoven 1955–58; Directorate for Int. Econ. Co-operation, Ministry of Agric. and Fisheries 1965–66; Deputy Agricultural Attaché, Perm. Mission of Netherlands to EEC, Brussels 1966–67; Sec. North Brabant Christian Farmers' Union (NCB), Tilburg 1967–69; Agricultural Counsellor, Perm. Mission of Netherlands to EEC 1969–77; mem. Second Chamber of Parl. 1977–80, 1981–82; Chair. Standing Cttee. on Agric., Second Chamber 1979–80 parl. year; Minister of Agric. and Fisheries 1980–81, 1982–90; mem. First Chamber of Parl. 1991–; Pres. Catholic Broadcasting Org. 1991–96; Chair. and Pres. Céhavé Farmers Cooperative 1995–; mem. Interparl. Benelux Council 1996–; Commdr. Order of Netherlands Lion. *Leisure interests:* gardening and golf. *Address:* Rumenbergstraat 4, 5271 AG Sint–Michielsgertel, Netherlands. *Telephone:* 073-551-4759. *Fax:* 073-551-7353.

BRAMALL, Life Peer (cr. 1987), of Bushfield in the County of Hampshire; **Field Marshal Sir Edwin (Noel Westby) Bramall,** K.G., G.C.B., O.B.E., M.C.; British army officer; b. 18 Dec. 1923, Tunbridge Wells, England; s. of Maj. Edmund Haselden Bramall and Katherine Bridget (Westby) Bramall; m. Dorothy Avril Wentworth Vernon 1949; one s. one d.; ed. Eton Coll.; commissioned in Kings Royal Rifle Corps 1943, served in North-west Europe 1944–45; occupation of Japan 1946–47; Instructor, School of Infantry 1949–51; served Middle East 1953–58; Instructor, Army Staff Coll. 1958–61; on staff of Lord Mountbatten with special responsibility for reorg. of Ministry of Defence 1963–64; CO 2nd Green Jackets (Kings Royal Rifle Corps) 1965–66; Commdr. 5th Airportable Brigade 1967–69; G.O.C 1st Div. BAOR 1972–73; rank of Lieut. Gen. 1973; Commdr. British Forces Hong Kong 1973–76; Col. Commdt. 3rd Royal Green Jackets 1973–84; Col. 2nd Goorkhas 1976–86; rank of Gen. 1976; C.-in-C. U.K. Land Forces 1976–78; Vice-Chief of Defence Staff (Personnel and Logistics) 1978–79; Chief of Gen. Staff and ADC Gen. to H.M. The Queen 1979–82; rank of Field Marshal 1982; Chief of Defence Staff 1982–85; Lord Lieut. of Greater London 1986–98; Pres. of M.C.C. 1988–89; Trustee Imperial War Museum 1983–, Chair. 1989–98; J.P. London 1986; K.St.J. 1986. *Publication:* The Chiefs: The Story of the United Kingdom Chiefs of Staff (co-author). *Leisure interests:* cricket, painting, travel, tennis. *Address:* House of Lords, London, SW1A 0PW, England.

BRANAGH, Kenneth; British actor and director; b. 10 Dec. 1960, Belfast; s. of William Branagh and Frances Branagh; m. Emma Thompson 1989 (divorced 1998); ed. Meadway Comprehensive School, Reading, Royal Acad. of Dramatic Art; Bancroft Gold Medal RADA 1982; f. Renaissance Theatre Co. 1987 (resgnd. 1994), Renaissance Films PLC 1988 (resgnd. 1994), Shakespeare Film Co. 1999; mem. bd. BFI 1993–97; Officer Ordre des Arts et des Lettres. *Theatre:* Another Country 1982 (Soc. of W. End Theatres Award for Most Promising Newcomer), The Madness 1983, Francis, Henry V, Hamlet, Love's Labours Lost, Golden Girls, Tell Me Honestly (wrote and dir.) 1986, Romeo and Juliet (prod. and dir.) 1986, Napoleon (dir.) 1987, Twelfth Night 1987, Much Ado About Nothing, As You Like It, Hamlet (dir.), Look Back in Anger 1989, Napoleon: The American Story 1989, King Lear (actor, dir.) 1989, Midsummer Night's Dream (actor, dir.) 1989, Uncle Vanya (co-dir.) 1991, Coriolanus (actor), Hamlet (actor, RSC) 1992. *TV:* The Boy in the Bush, Billy (Trilogy), To the Lighthouse, Maybury, Derek, Coming Through, Ghosts, Fortunes of War, Strange Interlude, The Lady's Not for Burning, Shadow of a Gunman. *Radio:* Hamlet (actor, dir.) 1992, Romeo and Juliet (actor, dir.) 1993, King Lear (actor) 1994. *Films:* High Season, A Month in the Country, Henry V (actor, dir., writer) (Evening Standard Best Film, N.Y. Film Critics Circle Best Dir. Award) 1989, Dead Again (actor, dir.) 1991, Peter's Friends (actor, dir., prod.) 1992, Swing Kids (actor) 1992, Swan Song (dir.) 1992, Much Ado about Nothing (actor, dir.) 1993, Mary Shelley's Frankenstein, Othello (actor) 1995, In the Bleak Midwinter (dir., writer) 1995, Hamlet 1996, The Theory of Flight 1997, The Proposition 1997, The Gingerbread Man 1997, Celebrity 1998, Wild, Wild West 1998, Love's Labour's Lost (dir.); Hon. D. Litt. (Queen's Univ., Belfast) 1990; B.A.F.T.A. Award (best dir.) 1990. *Publications:* Public Enemy (play) 1988, Beginning (memoirs) 1989; The Making of Mary Shelley's Frankenstein 1994, In the Bleak Midwinter 1995. *Address:* Shepperton Studios, Studio Road, Shepperton, Middx, TW17 0QD, England.

BRANCA, Vittore (Felice Giovanni), D.LITT.; Italian educationist; b. 9 July 1913, Savona; s. of Antonio Branca and Lucia Branca; m. Olga Montagner 1938; one s. three d.; ed. Univ. of Pisa; Prof. Accad. della Crusca, Florence 1937–48; Prof. of Italian Literature, Maria Assunta Univ., Rome 1948–50; Prof. of Italian Literature, Univ. of Catania 1950–53, Univ. of Padua 1953–; Rector Univ. of Bergamo 1968–72; Head, Div. of Arts and Letters, UNESCO 1950–53; Hon. Pres. Int. Asscn. for Study of Italian Language and Literature; Gen. Sec. and Pres. Fondazione Giorgio Cini 1953–96; mem. Cttee. Int. Fed. of Modern Languages and Literatures; literary adviser to publishing houses; Ed. Lettere Italiane and Studi sul Boccaccio (magazines) and of numerous series of classical texts and essays; Pres. Istituto Veneto Scienze Lettere e Arti 1979–85; mem. Accad. dei Lincei, Accad. Arcadia, Accad. Polacca della Scienze, Acad. du Monde Latin (Inst. de France), Medieval Acad. of America, Hon. mem. Modern Language Asscn. of America, American Acad. of Arts and Sciences, Union of Writers, Moscow, British Acad.; Dr. h.c. (Univs. of Budapest, New York, Bergamo, Paris Sorbonne, McGill Univ.); Gold Medal of Italian Ministry of Educ. and of Polish Ministry of Culture. *Publications:* editions and critical studies of St. Francis, Petrarch, Boccaccio, Poliziano, Alfieri, Manzoni, other classical authors and Romanticism; methodological works including Boccaccio Medievale 1958, Filologia e critica 1977, Poliziano e l'umanesimo della parola 1983, Dizionario critico della letteratura italiana 1986, Mercanti scrittori 1987, Ponte Santa Trinità 1988, Esopo Toscano 1989, Tradizione delle opere di Giovanni Boccaccio 1991, Esopo Veneto 1992, Con Amore Volere 1996, La Sapienza civile 1998, Writers of the Italian Renaissance 1999. *Leisure interests:* swimming, climbing. *Address:* San Marco 2885, Venice, Italy. *Telephone:* 5289819.

BRANDAUER, Klaus Maria; Austrian actor; b. 1944; m. Karin Brandauer 1965; ed. Acad. of Music and Dramatic Arts, Stuttgart; mem. Burgtheater, Vienna; extensive stage repertoire; Cannes Film Festival Prize for film Mephisto 1981; Acad. Award (Oscar) for title role in film Mephisto 1982; appeared as Jedermann at Salzburg Festival 1983, as Speer, Almeida Theatre, London 1999. *Films include:* Mephisto 1980, Colonel Redl 1985, Out of Africa 1985, Burning Secret 1988, Hannussen 1988, Russia House, Angel in Hell 1989, Streets of Gold 1989, The French Revolution 1989, The Artisan (also dir.), Becoming Colette 1991, White Fang 1991, The Resurrected, Seven Minutes (also dir.), Felidae (voice); TV appearance in Quo Vadis? *Address:* Bartensteingasse 8/9, A-1010 Vienna, Austria.

BRANDO, Marlon; American actor; b. 3 April 1924, Omaha; s. of Marlon and Dorothy Penebaker (née Myers) Brando; m. 1st Anna Kashfi 1957 (divorced 1959); one s.; m. 2nd Movita Brando (divorced); one c.; ed. Shattuck Military Acad. *Stage appearances include:* I Remember Mama, Candida, A Flag is Born, The Eagle has Two Heads, A Streetcar Named Desire, etc. *Film appearances include:* The Men 1950, A Streetcar Named Desire 1951, Viva Zapata 1952, Julius Caesar 1953, The Wild Ones 1953, Desirée 1954, On the Waterfront 1954, Guys and Dolls 1955, Teahouse of the August Moon 1956, Sayonara 1957, The Young Lions 1958, The Fugitive Kind 1960, The One-Eyed Jacks (also Dir.) 1960, Mutiny on the Bounty 1962, The Ugly American 1963, Bedtime Story 1964, The Saboteur 1965, The Chase 1966, Appaloosa 1966, A Countess from Hong Kong 1967, Southwest to Sonora 1966, Reflections in a Golden Eye 1967, Candy 1968, The Night of the Following Day 1969, Queimada 1970, The Nightcomers 1971, The Godfather 1972, Last Tango in Paris 1972, The Missouri Breaks 1975, Apocalypse Now 1977, Superman 1978, The Formula 1980, Dry White Season 1989, Jericho (wrote and acted in) 1989, The Freshman 1989, Christopher Columbus 1992, Don Juan DeMarco 1994, The Island of Dr. Moreau 1996, The Brave 1997. *TV appearance:* Roots: The Next Generations 1979; Acad. Award for the best actor of the year 1954, Golden Globe Award for the most popular actor 1972; refused Oscar for The Godfather 1973. *Publication:* Brando: Songs My Mother Taught Me 1994. *Address:* Tetiarou Island, South Pacific.

BRANDT, Cornelis J.; Netherlands business executive and journalist; b. 14 Feb. 1913, Amsterdam; m. W. J. van den Bosch 1937; two s.; ed. Netherlands Inst. of Chartered Accountants; began career as accountant and Sec. to agricultural and banking organizations; Acting Ed.-in-Chief Amsterdamsche Effectenblad and Het Financieele Dagblad 1943–49; Financial Ed. De Telegraaf 1949–52, Ed.-in-Chief 1952–79; Man. Dir. 1964–79; Chair. of the Bd. of Dirs. N.V. Holdingmaatschappij De Telegraaf 1979–. *Publication:* Preference Shares 1946. *Leisure interest:* bridge.

BRANDT, Elmar, DR.PHIL.; German cultural institute director; b. 18 Nov. 1936, Berlin; s. of Arthur Brandt and Anna Maria Brandt (née Monscheuer); m. Holle Behncke 1983; one d. one step-s.; ed. Univs. of Frankfurt/Main, Berlin and Munich; Dir. Goethe-Institut, Yaoundé, Cameroon 1965–68,

Deputy Dir. Goethe-Institut, Tokyo 1968–70, Dir. Goethe-Institut Osaka, Japan 1970–77, Head, Media Dept., Goethe-Institut Head Office, Munich 1977–83, Dir. Goethe-Institut, São Paulo, Brazil 1983–89, London 1989–95; Rome 1995–. *Publications include:* Fundamentals of a Theory of Meaning 1963–64, Current Problems of Consumer Protection 1978, The Woman in the Twentieth Century 1988, New Strategies of Urban Planning 1992. *Leisure interests:* gardening, photography, painting. *Address:* 50 Prince's Gate, Exhibition Road, London, SW7 2PH, England. *Telephone:* 0171-411 3400. *Fax:* 0171-581 0974.

BRANITZKI, Heinz; German business executive; b. 23 April 1929, Zülz; s. of Ludwig Branitzki and Agnes Apostel; m. Else Quadt 1952; ed. Gymnasium zum Grauen Kloster, Berlin and Freie Univ. Berlin; Chair. Man. Bd. of Porsche AG, Stuttgart; Dr. h.c.

BRANSCOMB, Lewis McAdory, M.S., PH.D.; American physicist; b. 17 Aug. 1926, Asheville, N.C.; s. of Bennett Harvie Branscomb and Margaret Vaughn Branscomb; m. Anne Wells 1951; one s. one d.; ed. Duke and Harvard Univs.; Instructor in Physics, Harvard Univ. 1950; Lecturer in Physics, Univ. of Maryland 1950–51; Chief, Atomic Physics Section, Nat. Bureau of Standards, Washington, D.C. 1954–60, Chief Atomic Physics Div. 1960–62; Chair. Jt. Inst. for Laboratory Astrophysics 1962–65, 1968–70; Chief, Lab. Astrophysics Div., Nat. Bureau of Standards, Boulder, Colo. 1962–69; Dir. Nat. Bureau of Standards 1969–72; Chief Scientist, Vice-Pres. IBM Corpn. 1972–86; Prof., Dir. Public Policy Program Kennedy School of Govt., Harvard Univ. 1986–96, AETNA Prof. in Public Policy and Corp. Man. 1988–96, now Emer., Telluride Inst. 1996–; mem. tech. assessment advisory council, Office of Tech. Assessment, U.S. Congress 1990–95; mem. Bd., Mobil Corpn., MITRE Corpn.; mem. Nat. Acad. of Sciences, Inst. of Medicine, Nat. Acad. of Eng.; Fellow, American Acad. of Arts and Sciences, American Philosophical Soc.; mem. Nat. Acad of Public Admin., Harvard Univ. Bd. of Overseers, Comm. on Global Information/Infrastructure 1995–; Trustee, Carnegie Inst. of Washington 1973–90, Vanderbilt Univ., Nat. Geographic Soc., Woods Hole Oceanographic Inst.; several awards and hon. degrees. *Publications:* Empowering Technology 1993, Confessions of a Technophile 1994, Korea at the Turning Point 1996, numerous articles in professional journals. *Leisure interests:* skiing, sailing. *Address:* Kennedy School of Government, Harvard University, 79 J. F. Kennedy Street, Cambridge, MA 02138, U.S.A.

BRANSON, Richard; British business executive; b. 18 July 1950; s. of Edward James Branson; m. 1st 1969 (dissolved); m. 2nd Joan Templeman 1989; one s. one d.; ed. Stowe School; set up Student Advisory Centre (now Help) 1970; founded Virgin mail-order co. 1969, first Virgin record shop 1971, recording co. 1973, nightclub (The Venue) 1976, Virgin Atlantic Airlines 1984; f. and Chair. Virgin Retail Group, Virgin Communications, Virgin Travel Group, Voyager Group; took Virgin Music Group public 1986, bought back shares 1988 (rotating chairmanship 1991, Chair. 1991–92, now Life Pres. after sale of shares); Group also includes publishing, broadcasting, construction, heating systems, holidays; Chair. UK 2000 1986–88, Pres. 1988–; Dir. Intourist Moscow Ltd. 1988–; f. The Healthcare Foundation 1987, Virgin Radio 1993, Virgin Rail Group Ltd. 1996; launched Virgin Cola (drink) 1994; captured Blue Riband Title for Fastest Atlantic Crossing 1986, Segrave Trophy 1987; crossed Pacific in hot air balloon with Per Lindstrand 1991. *Publication:* Losing My Virginity 1998. *Leisure interest:* sailing. *Address:* c/o Virgin Group PLC, 120 Campden Hill Road, London, W8 7AR, England. *Telephone:* 0171-229 1282.

BRANSTAD, Terry Edward, B.A., J.D.; American state governor; b. 17 Nov. 1946, Leland, Iowa; s. of Edward Arnold Branstad and Rita Garland; m. Christine Ann Johnson 1972; two s. one d.; ed. Univ. of Iowa and Drake Univ.; admitted to Iowa Bar; sold interest in Branstad/Schwarm, Lake Mills, Iowa; farmer, Lake Mills; mem. Iowa House of Reps. 1972–78; Lieut.-Gov. of Iowa 1979–82, Gov. of Iowa Jan. 1983–98; Republican. *Address:* c/o State Capitol, Des Moines, IA 50319, U.S.A.

BRASH, Donald Thomas, M.A., PH.D.; New Zealand banker; b. 24 Sept. 1940; s. of Rev. Dr. Alan A. Brash and Mrs Brash; m. 1st Erica Beatty 1964, 2nd Je Lan Lee 1989; two s. one d.; ed. Christchurch Boys' High School, Canterbury Univ. and Australian Nat. Univ.; Gen. Man. Broadbank Corpn. Ltd. 1971–81; Gen. Man. Finance and Computer Sector, Fletcher Challenge Ltd. 1981–82; Man. Dir. N.Z. Kiwifruit Authority 1982–86; Man. Dir. Trust Bank Group 1986–88; Gov. Reserve Bank of New Zealand 1988–; mem. N.Z. Monetary and Econ. Council 1974–78, N.Z. Planning Council 1977–80; Chair. various cttees. etc. *Publications:* New Zealand's Debt Servicing Capacity 1964, American Investment in Australian Industry 1966. *Address:* Reserve Bank of New Zealand, 2 The Terrace, P.O. Box 2498, Wellington, New Zealand. *Telephone:* (4) 472-2029.

BRASSEUR, Claude; French actor; b. 15 June 1936, Paris (as Claude Espinasse); s. of late Pierre Espinasse (known as Pierre Brasseur) and of Odette Joyeux; m. 2nd Michèle Cambon 1970; one s.; ed. René Girard and René Simon drama schools, Paris. *Plays include:* Un ange passe, L'enfant du dimanche, Match 1964, La calèche 1966, Britannicus 1966, Du côté de chez l'autre 1971, Les jeux de la nuit 1974, Georges Dindin 1987, Le Souper 1989, Dîner de cons 1993, la Dernière salve 1995. *Films include:* Rue des prairies, Les yeux sans visage 1959, Le noeud de vipères, La verte moisson, Pierrot la tendresse 1960, Le caporal épinglé, La bride sur le cou 1961, Germinal 1962, Dragées au poivre, Peau de banane 1963, Bande à part, Lucky Joe 1964, L'enfer (unfinished), Le chien fou, Du rififi à Paname 1966, Un homme de trop, Caroline chérie 1967, La chasse royale, Catherine ou il suffit d'un amour 1968, Le viager, Le portrait de Marianne, Un cave 1971, Une belle fille comme moi 1972, Bel ordure 1973, Les seins de glace 1974, Il faut vivre dangereusement, L'agression 1975, Attention les yeux 1976, Barocco, Le grand Escogriffe, Un éléphant ça trompe énormément 1976, Monsieur papa, Nous irons au paradis, L'état sauvage 1977, L'argent des autres, Une histoire simple 1978, La guerre des polices 1979, La boume 1980, Une langouste au petit déjeuner, Une robe noire pour un tueur, L'ombre rouge, Une affaire d'hommes 1981, Josepha, Guy de Maupassant 1982, Légitime violence 1982, T'es heureuse? Moi toujours 1983, la Crime 1983, Signes extérieurs de richesse 1983, Souvenir, Le Léopard 1984, Palace 1985, Les loups entre eux 1985, La gitane 1986, Taxi Boy 1986, Descente aux enfers 1986, Georges Dindin 1988, Radio Corbeau 1989, l'Union sacrée 1989, l'Orchestre Rouge 1989, Dancing Machine 1990, Sale comme un Ange 1991, Le Bal des Casse-Pieds 1992, le Souper 1992, le Fil de L'Horizon 1993. *Television appearances include:* Le paysan parvenu, La misère et la gloire, Don Juan, Le mystère de la chambre jaune (as Rouletabille), Les eaux mêlées, Vidocq, Les nouvelles aventures de Vidocq, l'Équipe, l'Argent; Beatrix Dussane trophy 1974, Caesar awards for Best Supporting Actor in Un éléphant ça trompe énormément 1976, Best Actor in La guerre des polices 1980; Chevalier, Ordre Nat. du Mérite. *Leisure interests:* boxing, swimming, football, bobsleighing, skiing. *Address:* c/o Artmédia, 10 ave Georges V, 75008 Paris, France.

BRATHWAITE, Sir Nicholas, Kt., O.B.E., B.ED.; Grenadian politician; b. 8 July 1925, Carriacou; s. of Charles Brathwaite and Sophia Brathwaite; m.; three s. one d.; ed. Univ. of West Indies; fmr. teacher, Sr. Tutor, Prin. Teachers' Coll.; fmrly. Chief Educ. Officer; fmr. Minister of Social Affairs; fmr. Commonwealth official; Chair. Interim Council set up after U.S. invasion of Grenada and deposition of fmr. mil. govt. 1983–84; leader Nat. Democratic Congress (NDC) 1989–94; Prime Minister 1990–95, also fmr. Minister of Home Affairs, Nat. Security, Foreign Affairs, Personnel and Man. and Carriacou and Petit Martinique Affairs. *Address:* c/o House of Representatives, St. George's, Grenada.

BRATKOWSKI, Andrzej, D.ENG.; Polish politician and building engineer; b. 10 Nov. 1936, Warsaw; s. of Stefan Bratkowski and Julia Bratkowski; m. Yolanta Bratkowski 1962; two s.; ed. Tech. Univ., Cracow; for many years worked on bldg. sites, including Turoszów Electric Power Station; mem. Polish United Workers' Party (PZPR) 1956–90, subsequently Labour Solidarity Union 1991–92; co-organizer and Pres. Mutual Insurance Soc.; Deputy to Sejm (Parl.) 1989–91, Chair. Sejm Cttee. of Bldg. and Housing Policy 1989–91; Minister of Land Man. and Construction 1992–93; mem. Acad. of Eng. 1994–. *Leisure interest:* Economic History of Poland. *Address:* ul. Okrąg 8/10A m. 22, 00-407 Warsaw, Poland (Home). *Telephone:* (22) 629 98 01.

BRAUER, Arik; Austrian artist; b. 4 Jan. 1929, Vienna; s. of Simon Moses Brauer and Hermine Brauer; m. Naomi Dahabani 1957; three d.; ed. Wiener Kunstakademie; underground, Vienna 1942–45; after studies in Vienna travelled in Africa, France, Spain, Austria, Greece and Israel 1950–58, U.S.A., E. Africa, Ethiopia, Japan 1965–74; Prof. Acad. of Fine Arts Vienna 1986; one-man exhbns. 1956–, in Austria, Germany, Switzerland, France, Denmark, Liechtenstein, Italy, Canada, Sweden, Yugoslavia, Bulgaria, Norway, Japan, Israel and U.S.A.; world travelling exhbn. 1979–; group exhbns., incl. travelling exhbns. with Wiener Schule des Phantastischen Realismus 1962–, in W. Europe, U.S.A., S. America, Poland, Yugoslavia, Israel, Iran, Turkey, Japan; Scenery for The Seven Mortal Sins (Vienna 1972), Bomarzo (Zürich 1970); scenery and costumes for Medea (Vienna 1972), The Magic Flute (Paris 1977); book, design and costumes for Sieben auf einen Streich (Vienna 1978); mural design for Univ. of Haifa, Israel 1982–; designer Brauerhaus, Vienna 1983–95; Guest Lecturer, Int. Summer Acad. for Fine Arts, Salzburg 1982, 83; two gold records for Erich Brauer LP (poetry, music and songs) 1971. *Publications:* Zigeunerziege 1976, Runde Fliegt 1983. *Leisure interests:* alpinism, skiing, windsurfing. *Address:* Academy of Fine Arts, Schillerplatz 3, Vienna 1010, Austria. *Telephone:* 58 816 257.

BRAUER, Jerald Carl, A.B., B.D., PH.D.; American historian of Christianity and educator; b. 16 Sept. 1921, Fond du Lac, Wisconsin; s. of Carl L. and Anna M. Brauer; m. Muriel I. Nelson 1945; two s. one d.; ed. Carthage Coll., Northwestern Lutheran Theological Seminary and Univ. of Chicago; Instructor, Church History and History of Christian Thought, Union Theological Seminary, New York City 1948–50; Asst. Prof. of Church History, Federated Theological Faculty, Univ. of Chicago 1950–54, Assoc. Prof. 1954–59, Prof. 1959–; Dean, Federated Theological Faculty 1955–60; Visiting Prof. Univ. of Frankfurt 1961; Naomi Shenstone Donnelley Prof. History of Christianity 1969–91, Prof. Emer. 1991–, Dean, Divinity School 1960–70; Frederick W. Bateson Senior Prof. in Residence 1994–; Visiting Lecturer Univ. of Tokyo and Kokugakin Univ. 1966; mem. Bd. of Augustana Coll., Carthage Coll. 1958– (Trustee Emer. 1990); mem. Bd. of Theological Educ., Lutheran Church in America 1961–70, Pres. 1961–68; mem. Bd. of Govs., International House 1970–95 (Life Gov. 1995), Chair. 1973–91; Fellow, Center for Policy Studies, N.Y. Educ. Dept. 1969–78, Nat. Endowment of the Humanities 1977–78; Visiting Fellow, Center for the Study of Democratic Insts. 1972, 1974; Trustee, Council on Religion and Int. Affairs, Chair. of Bd. 1979–83; Del. of Lutheran Church in America to Lutheran World Fed. Assembly, Helsinki 1963; Observer to Vatican Council Sessions 1964, 1965;

mem. American Soc. of Church History, Pres. 1961; Hon. D.D. (Miami), Hon. L.L.D. (Carthage Coll.), Hon. S.T.D. (Ripon Coll.), Hon. L.H.D. (Gettysburg Coll.). *Publications:* Protestantism in America 1953, rev. edn. 1966, Luther and the Reformation (with Jaroslav Pelikan) 1953, Basic Questions for the Christian Scholar 1954, John Nuveen: A Life of Service 1896–1968, 1997; Ed.: The Future of Religions by Paul Tillich 1966, Essays in Divinity (8 vols.) 1967, My Travel Diary by Paul Tillich 1970, Westminster Dictionary of Church History 1971, Religion and the American Revolution 1976, The Lively Experiment Continued 1987, Chicago Studies in the History of American Religions, 21 vols. (Co-ed. with M. E. Marty) 1991, The Unrelieved Paradoxi Studies in the Theology of Franz Bibfeldt (co-ed. with M. E. Marty) 1994. *Leisure interests:* painting, music, drama. *Address:* Swift Hall 300C, Univ. of Chicago, Chicago, IL 60637 (Office); 5620 South Blackstone Avenue, Chicago, IL 60637, U.S.A. (Home). *Telephone:* (773) 702-8232 (Office); (773) 493-6886 (Home). *Fax:* (773) 702-8223.

BRAUMAN, John I., PH.D.; American professor of chemistry; b. 7 Sept. 1937, Pittsburgh, Pa.; s. of Milton and Freda S. Brauman; m. Sharon Lea Kruse 1964; one d.; ed. M.I.T. and Univ. of California (Berkeley and Los Angeles); Asst. Prof., Stanford Univ. 1963–69, Assoc. Prof. 1969–72, Prof. 1972–80, J. G. Jackson-C. J. Wood Prof. 1980–, Chair. 1979–83, 1995–96; Deputy Ed. Science 1985–; mem. Editorial Bds. several journals including Nouveau Journal de Chimie 1977–85, Chemical Physics Letters 1982–85, Chemical and Engineering News 1982–84, Journal of Physical Chemistry 1985–87; mem. Nat. Research Council Bd. on Chemical Sciences and Tech., advisory panels of NASA, Nat. Science Found., Atomic Energy Comm.; mem. N.A.S. and A.A.A.S.; Award in Pure Chemistry and Harrison-Howe Award, American Chemical Soc., James Flack Norris Award in Physical Organic Chemistry, Arthur C. Cope Scholar Award. *Publications:* over 270 publs. in scientific journals. *Address:* Department of Chemistry, Stanford University, Stanford, CA 94305 (Office); 849 Tolman Drive, Palo Alto, CA 94305, U.S.A. (Home). *Telephone:* (415) 723-3023 (Office); (415) 493-1378 (Home).

BRAUN, Carol Moseley (see Moseley-Braun, Carol)

BRAUN, Ewa; Polish interior decorator and art director; b. 2 Aug. 1944, Kraków; ed. Warsaw Univ.; costume designer Documentary Film Producers 1967–72, interior decorator, art dir. Film Production Agency 1972–; mem. History of Art Soc. 1971–; mem. Polish Film Asscn. 1994–; interior decorations and designs in over 60 films including: Illumination 1972, Nikodem Dyzma's Career 1979, Queen Bona 1980, C.K Dezerterzy 1985, Wonderful Child (Gdańsk Bronze Lion 1987) 1986, Europe, Europe 1989, Schindler's List (Acad. Award 1994) 1993, Les Milles 1994, Holy Week 1995, Bandit 1996, Last Chapter 1996, Brother of Our God 1997, Jacob the Liar 1997, Deserters' Gold 1998. *Leisure interests:* movies, travels, music, literature. *Address:* Agencja Produkcji Filmowej, ul. Puławska 61, 02-295 Warsaw, Poland. *Telephone:* (22) 845 40 41 (Office).

BRAUN, Pinkas; Swiss actor and director; b. 7 Jan. 1923, Zürich; s. of Chaja and Nathan Braun; m. (divorced); one s. one d.; ed. drama school, Zürich; mem. of co. of Schauspielhaus Zürich 1945–50, 1952–56; own co. 1950–51; freelance 1957–; has undertaken theatre work as actor and Dir. in Germany, Austria and Israel, and television and cinema work in Germany, Austria, France, Italy and U.K. *Roles include:* Woyzeck, Baron (in Nachtasyl), Pelegrin (in Santa Cruz), Salieri (in Amadeus), Shylock (in The Merchant of Venice), Iago (in Othello), Otto Frank (in The Diary of Anne Frank), George Bernard Shaw (in The Best of Friends). *Publications:* translation into German of Edward Albee's plays. *Address:* Unterdorf, CH 8261 Hemishofen /SH, Switzerland. *Telephone:* 052-741 3370.

BRAUNFELS, Michael; German composer, pianist and teacher; b. 3 April 1917, Munich; s. of Walter and Bertele (von Hildebrand) Braunfels; m. Mechthild Russel 1954; two s. three d.; studied piano in Basle under Paul Baumgartner and composition with Frank Martin; concert pianist in all West European music centres, Near East, Asia and Africa 1949–; Prof. of Piano, Cologne Music Coll. 1954–. *Compositions include:* 2 piano concertos, Cembaloconcerto 1956, Oboe concerto 1960, Symphony for 12 celli 1975, Concerto for cello and piano with orchestra 1976, Concerto for string trio and string orch. 1978, Das Parlament (variations for orchestra) 1982, Sinfonietta serena seria 1984, The King's Messenger (musical for children), chamber music, lieder and piano music. *Leisure interest:* history. *Address:* Dransdorferstrasse 40, 50968 Cologne, Germany. *Telephone:* (0221) 383660.

BRAUNWALD, Eugene, M.D.; American professor of medicine; b. 15 Aug. 1929, Vienna, Austria; m. 1st Nina Starr 1952; two d.; m. 2nd Elaine Smith 1994; ed. New York Univ.; successively Chief, Section of Cardiology, Clinic of Surgery, Cardiology Br. and Clinical Dir. Nat. Heart, Lung & Blood Inst. 1958–68; Prof. and Chair. Dept. of Medicine, Univ. of Calif. San Diego School of Medicine 1968–72; Hersey Prof. of Theory and Practice of Medicine, Harvard Medical School 1972–96, Distinguished Hersey Prof. of Theory and Practice of Medicine 1996–, Faculty Dean for Academic Programs 1996–; Sr. Consultant in Medicine Mass. Gen. Hosp. 1994–; Vice-Pres. Academic Programs Partners Healthcare System 1996–; Herrmann Blumgart Prof. of Medicine 1980–89; Chair. Dept. of Medicine, Peter Bent Brigham Hosp. (now Brigham & Women's Hosp.) 1972–96; J. Allyn Taylor Int. Prize in Medicine 1993; five hon. degrees and many other awards. *Publications:* over 900 articles, reviews and book chapters. *Address:* Partners Healthcare, 800 Boylston Street, Boston, MA 02199, U.S.A.

BRÄUTIGAM, Hans Otto, D.JUR., LL.M.; German diplomatist and politician; b. 6 Feb. 1931, Völklingen, Saar; s. of Maximilian Bräutigam and Margarethe Senewald; m. Dr. Hildegard Becker 1961; two s. one d.; ed. Bonn Univ. and Harvard Law School; research asst. in int. law, Heidelberg 1958–62; served in foreign service of Fed. Repub. of Germany 1962–74; Deputy Head, Perm. Representation of Fed. Repub. of Germany to German Democratic Repub. (G.D.R.) 1974–77, Dir. Fed. Chancellor's Office, Bonn 1977–80; Foreign Office, Bonn 1980–82, Head 1982–89; Perm. Rep. of Fed. Repub. of Germany to UN 1989–90; Brandenburg Minister of Justice 1990–. *Leisure interests:* arts, mountain climbing. *Address:* c/o Brandenburg Ministry of Justice, Heinrich-Mann-Allee 107, 14473 Potsdam; Schedestrasse 1–3, 53113 Bonn, Germany. *Telephone:* (0288) 915000.

BRAWNE, Michael, M.ARCH., M.A., F.R.I.B.A.; British architect; b. 5 May 1925, Vienna; m. 1st Rhoda Dupler 1954; m. 2nd Charlotte Baden-Powell 1983; two s. one d.; ed. Univ. of Edinburgh, Architectural Asscn., London and Mass. Inst. of Tech.; Prin. Michael Brawne & Assocs. 1964–; lecturer, Univ. of Cambridge 1964–78; Prof. of Architecture, Univ. of Bath 1978–90; designer of numerous exhbns. including Henry Moore, Tate Gallery, London 1968, Ceramic Art of China, Victoria & Albert Museum, London 1971, The Age of Neo-Classicism, Royal Acad. London 1972, Arts of Islam, Hayward Gallery, London 1976, The Architecture of Information, British Pavilion, Venice Biennale 1996; museums in Dorchester, Bath, Rochdale and Barnsley; also museums and library in Germany and projects for museums in Jordan and Oman; multi-screen audio-visual shows for museums in London, Paris and Berlin; UNESCO consultant on library design in Sri Lanka, Pakistan, Yemen, Mozambique, China and Yugoslavia; architect, Nat. Library of Sri Lanka. *Publications:* The New Museum 1965, University Planning and Design (ed.) 1967, Libraries, Architecture and Equipment 1970, Arup Associates 1983, The Museum Interior 1983, Museum für Kunsthandwerk 1992, From Idea to Building 1992, Kimbell Art Museum 1992, The University of Virginia: The Lawn 1994, The Getty Center 1998. *Leisure interests:* architecture, travel, gardening. *Address:* 28 College Road, Bath, BA1 5RR, England. *Telephone:* (01225) 319242. *Fax:* (01225) 442857.

BRAY, Kenneth Noel Corbett, PH.D., F.R.S., C.ENG., M.S.E., M.R.AE.S., M.A.I.A.A.; British professor of applied thermodynamics; b. 19 Nov. 1929; s. of Harold Bray and Effie Bray; m. Shirley Culver 1958; two s. one d.; ed. Univs. of Cambridge and Southampton and Princeton Univ.; research eng. Handley Page Aircraft 1955–56; Univ. of Southampton 1956–85, Dean, Faculty of Eng. and Applied Science 1975–78, Head, Dept. of Aeronautics and Astronautics 1982–85; Hopkinson and ICI Prof. of Applied Thermodynamics, Univ. of Cambridge 1985–96; Fellow Girton Coll., Univ. of Cambridge 1985–; Visiting Prof. M.I.T. 1966–67, Univ. of Calif. (San Diego) 1975, 1983. *Publications:* papers on topics in gas dynamics, chemically reacting flows, molecular energy transfer processes and combustion. *Leisure interests:* walking, wood-carving, gardening. *Address:* 23 De Freville Avenue, Cambridge, CB4 1HW, England.

BRAYBROOKE, David, PH.D.; Canadian philosopher, university professor and author; b. 18 Oct. 1924, Hackettstown, N.J.; s. of Walter Leonard Braybrooke and Netta Rose Foyle; m. 1st Alice Boyd Noble 1948 (divorced 1982); two s. one d.; m. 2nd Margaret Eva Odell 1984 (divorced 1994); m. 3rd Gomyo Michiko 1994; ed. Hobart Coll., New School for Social Research, Downing Coll., Cambridge, U.K., Harvard and Cornell Univs., U.S.A., New College, Oxford, U.K.; Instructor, History and Literature, Hobart and William Smith Colls. 1948–50; Teaching Fellow, Econ., Cornell Univ. 1950–52; Instructor, Philosophy, Univ. of Mich., U.S.A. 1953–54, Bowdoin Coll. 1954–56; Asst. Prof. of Philosophy, Yale Univ., U.S.A. 1956–63; Assoc. Prof. of Philosophy and Politics, Dalhousie Univ., Halifax 1963–65, Prof. 1965–88, McCulloch Prof. of Philosophy and Politics 1988–90, Prof. Emer. 1990–; The Centennial Comm. Prof. in the Liberal Arts Univ. of Texas at Austin 1990–; Fellowship American Council of Learned Socs. 1952–53; Rockefeller Foundation Grant 1959–60; Guggenheim Fellow 1962–63; Leave Fellowships, Canada Council etc.; Visiting Fellow, Wolfson Coll., Cambridge, U.K. 1985–86. *Publications:* A Strategy of Decision: Policy Evaluation as a Social Process (with C. E. Lindblom) 1963, Philosophical Problems of the Social Sciences 1965, Three Tests for Democracy 1968, Traffic Congestion Goes through the Issue-Machine 1974, Ethics in the World of Business 1983, Philosophy of Social Science 1987, Meeting Needs 1987, Logic on the Track of Social Change (with B. Bryson and P. K. Schotch) 1995, Social Rules 1996. *Leisure interests:* reading (poetry, fiction, history), listening to music, walking, swimming. *Address:* Department of Political Science, Dalhousie University, Halifax, N.S. B3H 4H6 (Office, Canada); 1 Prince Street 510, Dartmouth, N.S. B2Y 4L3, Canada (Home, Canada); Department of Government, University of Texas at Austin, Austin, TX 78712 (Office, U.S.A.); 1500 Scenic Drive, 300, Austin, TX 78703, U.S.A. (Home, U.S.A.). *Telephone:* (902) 494-3810 (Dept. of Philosophy, Dalhousie, Canada); (902) 466 3660 (Home, Canada); (512) 471 5121 (Dept. of Govt. Texas Univ.); (512) 479 8963 (Home, U.S.A.).

BRAYFIELD, Celia Frances; British journalist and writer; b. 21 Aug. 1945, Wembley Park; d. of late Felix Brayfield and Ellen (née Jakeman) Brayfield; one d.; ed. Grenoble Univ.; feature writer Daily Mail 1969–71, TV critic Evening Standard 1974–82, The Times 1983–88; columnist Sunday Telegraph 1989–90; contrib. to numerous other media. *Publicat*
The Truth About Fame 1985, Pearls 1987, The Prince 1990, Wh
Harvest 1995, Bestseller 1996, Leafy 1998, Getting Home 19

c/o Curtis Brown Ltd., Haymarket House, 28/29 Haymarket, London, SW1Y 4SP, England. *Telephone:* 0171-396 6600. *Fax:* 0171-396 0110.

BRAZAUSKAS, Algirdas Mikolas, D.ECON.; Lithuanian politician; b. 22 Sept. 1932, Rokishkis; s. of Zofija Brazauskienė and Kazimieras Brazauskas; m. Julija Styraitė-Brazauskienė 1958; two d.; ed. Kaunas Polytechnic Inst.; Sr. Engineer Kaunas Hydroelectric Power Station 1956–57; Chair. Energy Bldg. Trust Bd. 1958–65; Minister for the Construction Materials Industry of Lithuanian S.S.R. 1965–67; Deputy, Supreme Council of Lithuania 1967–90; First Deputy Chair. of State Planning Cttee., Lithuanian S.S.R. 1967–77; cand. mem. Cen. Cttee. of Lithuanian CP 1966–76, mem. 1976–92, sec. Cen. Cttee. of Lithuanian CP. 1977–88, first sec. 1988–90; Chair. Democratic Labour Party 1990–93; Chair. Presidium Lithuanian S.S.R. 1990; Deputy Chair. U.S.S.R. Supreme Soviet 1990; Deputy Premier of Lithuania 1990–91; acting Pres. of Lithuania 1992; elected Pres. of Lithuania 1993–97. *Publications:* Lithuanian Divorce 1998; numerous articles. *Leisure interest:* yachting. *Address:* Turniškių 30, 2016 Vilnius, Lithuania.

BREAM, Julian, C.B.E., F.R.C.M.; British guitarist and lutanist; b. 15 July 1933, London; m. 1st Margaret Williamson; one adopted s.; 2nd Isobel Sanchez 1980 (dissolved); ed. Royal Coll. of Music; began professional career Cheltenham 1947, London début, Wigmore Hall 1950; has made many transcriptions for guitar of Romantic and Baroque works; commissioned new works from Britten, Walton, Henze and Arnold; tours throughout the world, giving recitals as soloist and with the Julian Bream Consort (f. 1960); many recitals with Sir Peter Pears and Robert Tear and as guitar duo with John Williams (q.v.); 60th Birthday Concert, Wigmore Hall, London 1993; Fellow Royal Northern Coll. of Music 1983; Hon. D.Univ. (Surrey) 1968, Hon. D.Mus. (Leeds) 1984; Villa-Lobos Gold Medal 1976; numerous recording awards. *Leisure interests:* playing the guitar, cricket, table tennis, gardening, backgammon. *Address:* c/o Hazard Chase, 16–20 Regent Street, Cambridge, CB2 1DB, England.

BREARLEY, John Michael (Mike), O.B.E.; British cricketer and psychoanalyst; b. 28 April 1942, Harrow, Middlesex; s. of Horace and Midge Brearley; partner Mana Sarabhai; two c.; ed. City of London School and St. John's Coll., Cambridge; right-hand opening batsman, occasional wicket-keeper; played for Cambridge Univ. 1961–64, captained Cambridge Univ. 1963, 1964; awarded county cap (Middlesex) 1964; Capt. of Middlesex (winning County Championships four times and Gillette Cup twice) 1971–82; Test debut 1976; Capt. of England 1977–80, 1981 (four Tests); went on tours of South Africa 1964–65, Pakistan 1967, India, Sri Lanka and Australia 1976–77, Pakistan 1977–78, Australia 1978–79, Australia and India 1979–80; holds record for most runs scored at Cambridge Univ. (4,310 at an average of 38.48) 1964; scored 312 not out for M.C.C. under-25 v. North Zone, Peshawar 1966–67; Lecturer in Philosophy, University of Newcastle upon Tyne 1968–71. *Publications:* (with Dudley Doust) The Return of the Ashes 1978, (with Dudley Doust), The Ashes Retained 1979, Phoenix: the Series that Rose from the Ashes 1982, The Art of Captaincy 1985, Arlott in Conversation with Mike Brearley (with John Arlott) 1986. *Address:* c/o Middlesex County Cricket Club, Lord's Cricket Ground, St. John's Wood Road, London, NW8 8QN, England. *Telephone:* 0171-289 1300.

BREAUX, John B., J.D.; American politician; b. 1 March 1944, Crowley, La.; s. of Ezra Breaux and Katie Breaux; m. Lois Gail Daigle 1964; two s. two d.; ed. Southwestern Univ. and State Univ. of Louisiana; called to La. Bar 1967; Partner Brown, McKernan, Ingram and Breaux 1967–68; Legislative Asst. to U.S. Congressman 1968–69; Dist. Asst. 1969–72; mem. 92nd-99th Congresses from 7th Dist., La. 1971–87; Senator from Louisiana Jan. 1987–; mem. House of Democrats Policy and Steering Cttee., Finance Cttee. 1990–; mem. Senate Cttee. on Commerce, Science and Transportation, on Environment and Public Works, Special Cttee. on Aging, Democratic Leadership Council; Chair. Nuclear Regulation Subcttee, Democratic Senatorial Campaign Cttee., Nat. Water Alliance 1987–88; fmr. Chair House Subcttee. on Fisheries and Wildlife and the Environment; American Legion Award; Neptune Award, American Oceanic Org. 1980; Democrat. *Address:* 516, Hart Senate Office Building, U.S. Senate, Washington, DC 20510, U.S.A. *Telephone:* (202) 224-4623.

BRECHER, Michael, PH.D., F.R.S.C.; Canadian professor of political science; b. 14 March 1925; s. of Nathan Brecher and Gisela Hopmeyer; m. Eva Danon 1950; three d.; ed. McGill and Yale Univs.; mem. Faculty, McGill Univ. 1952–, Angus Prof. of Political Science 1993–; Pres. Int. Studies Asscn. 1999–(2000); Visiting Prof. Univ. of Chicago 1963, Hebrew Univ. Jerusalem 1970–75, Univ. of Calif. Berkeley 1979, Stanford Univ. 1980; Nuffield Fellow 1955–56; Rockefeller Fellow 1964–65; Guggenheim Fellow 1965–66; f. Shashtri Indo-Canadian Inst. 1968; Watumull Prize (American Hist. Asscn.) 1960; Killam Awards (Canada Council) 1970–74, 1976–79; Woodrow Wilson Award (American Political Science Asscn.) 1973, Fieldhouse Award for Distinguished Teaching (McGill Univ.) 1986, Distinguished Scholar Award (Int. Studies Asscn.) 1995; many other awards and distinctions. *Publications:* The Struggle for Kashmir 1953, Nehru: A Political Biography 1959, The New States of Asia 1963, Succession in India 1966, India and World Politics 1968, Political Leadership in India 1969, The Foreign Policy System of Israel 1972, Israel, the Korean War and China 1974, Decisions in Israel's Foreign Policy 1975, Studies in Crisis Behavior 1979, Decisions in Crisis 1980, Crisis and Change in World Politics 1986, Crises in the 20th Century (Vol I, II) 1988, Crisis, Conflict and Instability 1989, Crises in World Politics 1993, A Study of Crisis 1997; over 80 articles in journals. *Address:* McGill University, 855 Sherbrooke Street West, Montreal, P.Q., H3A 2T7, Canada; 5 Dubnov Street, Jerusalem, Israel (Home). *Telephone:* (514) 398-4816 (Office). *Fax:* (514) 398-1770.

BRECKENRIDGE, Alasdair Muir, C.B.E., M.D., M.SC., F.R.C.P., F.R.C.P.E., F.R.S.E.; British professor of clinical pharmacology; b. 7 May 1937, Arbroath, Scotland; s. of Thomas Breckenridge and Jane Breckenridge; m. Jean M. Boyle 1967; two s.; ed. Bell-Baxter School, Cupar, Fife and Univ. of St. Andrews; House Physician and Surgeon, Dundee Royal Infirmary 1961–62; House Physician, Registrar, Lecturer, Sr. Lecturer, Hammersmith Hosp. and Royal Postgrad. Medical School 1963–74; Prof. of Clinical Pharmacology, Univ. of Liverpool 1974–; mem. Cttee. on Safety of Medicines 1981–; Councillor Int. Union of Pharmacology 1981–87; Foreign Sec. British Pharmacological Soc. 1983–91, Dir. Research and Devt., Mersey Region 1992–; Chair. Mersey Regional Health Authority Jan.–July 1993; mem. Council Royal Coll. of Physicians 1983–86, Panel of Tropical Diseases, Wellcome Trust 1984–88, Council MRC 1992–; Vice-Chair. Advisory Cttee. on Drugs 1985–; mem. WHO Steering Cttee. on Chemotherapy of Malaria 1987–91, MRC Physiological Systems and Disorders Bd. 1987–91; Cen. Research and Devt. Cttee Nat. Health Service 1991–95; Dir. Research and Devt. Mersey Region 1992–94, N.W. Region 1994–96; Chair. N.W. Regional Office of the Nat. Health Service 1996–; Goulstonian Lecturer, Royal Coll. of Physicians 1975; Paul Martini Prize for Clinical Pharmacology 1974; Poulson Medal (Norwegian Pharmacological Soc.) 1988; Lilly Prize (British Pharmacological Soc.) 1993. *Publications:* articles in scientific and medical journals. *Leisure interests:* stock market, golf. *Address:* Department of Pharmacology and Therapeutics, University of Liverpool, Liverpool, L69 3BX (Office); Cree Cottage, Feather Lane, Wirral, L69 3BX, England (Home). *Telephone:* 0151-709 6022 (Office); 0151-342 1096 (Home).

BREDIN, Frédérique Marie Denise Colette; French politician; b. 2 Nov. 1956, Paris; d. of Jean-Denis Bredin and Danièle Hervier; m. Jean-Pascal Beaufret 1985; two c.; ed. Inst. d'Etudes Politiques, Paris and Ecole Nat. d'Admin.; Insp. Gen. of Finance 1980–84; special assignment to Minister of Culture 1984–86, to Pres. of Repub. 1986–88; Socialist Deputy to Nat. Ass. 1988–91, 1995–, to European Parl. 1994–96; Mayor of Fécamp 1989–95; Minister of Youth and Sport 1991–93; Nat. Sec. Socialist Party, with responsibility for Culture and Media 1996–. *Address:* Assemblée Nationale, 75355 Paris, France.

BREDIN, Jean-Denis, L. ÈS L.; French lawyer; b. 17 May 1929, Paris; m. Danièle Hervier; two s.; ed. Lycée Charlemagne and Facultés de Droit et des Lettres, Paris; advocate, Court of Appeal, Paris 1950–; Prof. Faculté de Droit, Rennes 1958, Lille 1967; Adviser to Council for Higher Educ. 1968–69; Prof. of Pvt. Law, Univ. of Paris-Dauphine 1969; Prof. Univ. of Paris I 1971–93, Prof. Emer. 1993–; Vice-Pres. Mouvement des radicaux de gauche 1976–80; Pres. Man. Bd. Bibliothèque Nationale 1983–88; Vice-Pres. Comm. Moinot 1981; Pres. Comm. for Reform of Cinema 1982; Adviser on Audiovisual Matters to Prime Minister 1985; mem. Acad. Française (Prix Gobert 1984). *Publications include:* Traité de droit commercial international 1967, La République de Monsieur Pompidou 1974, Les Français au pouvoir 1977, Eclats 1976, L'Affaire 1983, Un coupable 1985, L'Absence 1986, La Tâche 1988, Weisbuch 1989, Un enfant sage 1990, Mademoiselle et autres nouvelles 1991, Battements de coeur 1991, Bernard Lazare 1992, Comédie des Apparences 1994, Encore un peu de temps 1996, Convaincre, dialogues sur l'éloquence 1997, L'Affaire 1998. *Address:* 130 rue du Faubourg Saint-Honoré, 75008 Paris; Institut de France, 23 quai de Conti, 75006 Paris, France.

BREDSDORFF, Elias, DR. PHIL.; Danish author and retd. university reader; b. 15 Jan. 1912, Roskilde; s. of Thomas Bredsdorff and Margrete Lunn; m. 1st Marlie Brande 1935; m. 2nd Anne Lise Neckelmann 1954; one s. one d.; ed. Roskilde Grammar School, Copenhagen Univ. and Univ. Coll. London; lecturer, Vordingborg Teachers' Training Coll. 1939–43; underground activities in Danish Resistance Movt. 1943–45; Ed. Frit Danmark 1945–46; Queen Alexandra Lecturer in Danish, Univ. Coll. London 1946–49; lecturer in Danish, Univ. of Cambridge 1949–60, Reader and Head of Dept. of Scandinavian Studies 1960–79; Fellow, Peterhouse, Cambridge 1963–79, Fellow Emer. 1979–; Ed. Scandinavica 1962–75; Fellow, Royal Danish Soc.; Hans Christian Andersen Award 1975. *Publications:* D. H. Lawrence 1937, Hans Christian Andersen and Charles Dickens 1956, Hans Christian Andersen og England 1954, Henrik Pontoppidan og Georg Brandes 1–2 1964, Den store nordiske krig om seksualmoralen 1973, Hans Christian Andersen: The Story of his Life and Work 1975, Aerkedansk (12 essays) 1992, Kjeld Abell. Et brevportraet 1993, H. C. Andersen og Georg Brandes 1994, Medmennesker og Modmennesker 1994. *Leisure interest:* travel. *Address:* Kronprinsesse Sofiesvej 28, 2000 Copenhagen F, Denmark. *Telephone:* 31 199117.

BREEDEN, Richard, B.S., D.IUR.; American administrator; b. 1949, Long Island, NY; m.; three c.; ed. Stanford Univ., Harvard Law School; teacher Law School of Miami Univ.; Assoc. Cravath, Swain & Moore and Willkie, Farr & Gallagher 1976–81; Exec. Asst. to Under Sec. Dept. of Labor 1981–82; Deputy Counsel to Vice-Pres. Bush and Staff Dir. White House Regulatory Task Force 1982–85; partner Baker & Botts 1985–89; Asst. to Pres. Bush for Issues Analysis; Chair. US Securities and Exchange Comm. 1989–93. *Publications:* numerous articles for professional periodicals. *Address:* c/o Office of the Chairman, Securities and Exchange Commission, 450 50th Street, N.W., Washington, DC 20549-0001, U.S.A.

BREGGIN, Peter R., B.A., M.D.; American psychiatrist; b. 5 Nov. 1936, New York; m. 3rd Ginger Ross 1984; one c. (and three c. from two previous marriages); ed. Harvard Coll., Case Western Reserve School of Medicine, State Univ. of New York, Massachusetts Mental Health Centre; consultant Nat. Inst. of Mental Health 1966–68; psychiatrist in pvt. practice 1968–; f., Dir. Int. Center for Study of Psychiatry and Psychology 1972–; Adjunct Prof. of Conflict Resolution George Mason Univ. 1990–96; Faculty Assoc. Dept. of Counselling Johns Hopkins Univ. 1996–; Ed. numerous journals, including Journal of Mind and Behaviour, Int. Journal of Risk and Society in Medicine, The Humanistic Psychologist, Review of Existential Psychology and Psychiatry, The Psychotherapy Patient, Charges; Ludwig von Mises Award of Merit 1987, Minn. Mental Health Asscn. Advocacy Award 1990, honours from Harvard Coll. *Publications:* Toxic Psychiatry 1991, Talking Back to Prozac (with Ginger Breggin) 1994, Brain-Disabling Treatments in Psychiatry 1997, The Heart of Being Helpful 1997. *Address:* 4628 Chestnut Street, Bethesda, MD 20814, U.S.A. *Telephone:* (301) 652-5580. *Fax:* (301) 652-5924.

BRÉGOU, Christian Robert; French publisher; b. 19 Nov. 1941, Neuilly-sur-Seine, Hauts-de-Seine; ed. École Supérieure des Sciences Économiques et Commerciales; apptd. Financial Dir. Havas Group 1971; Dir.-Gen. C.E.P. Communication 1975, Pres. 1979–97; Pres. Dir.-Gen. Groupe de la Cité 1988, Groupe Expansion 1994, l'Express 1995–97; adviser Socpresse SA 1997. *Address:* 218 boulevard Saint-Germain, 75007 Paris, France.

BREGVADZE, Nani Georgievna; Georgian singer; b. 21 July 1938; ed. Tbilisi Conservatoire (pianoforte class under Machutadze); soloist with Georgian State Philharmonia 1959–, with Georgian popular orchestra 'Rero' 1959–64, with 'Orera' 1964–80; specializes in Georgian music and Russian romances; has toured abroad on numerous occasions; People's Artist of U.S.S.R. 1983; Hon. Citizen of Tbilisi 1995; Order of Honour 1995; People's Artist of Georgia 1996; State Prize of Georgia 1997. *Address:* Irakly Abashidze str. 18A, Apt. 10, 380079 Tbilisi, Georgia. *Telephone:* (32) 22-37-22.

BREIEN, Anja; Norwegian film director; ed. Inst. des hautes études cinématiques, France; dir. of short films and feature films 1967–. *Short films include:* 17. Mai—en film om ritualer 1969, Ansikter 1971, Murer rundt fengslet 1972, Herbergister 1973, Mine Søsken, goddag 1974, Gamle 1975, Solvorn 1997. *Feature films include:* Vokse opp (Part 1 of Dager fra 100 år) 1967, Voldtekt (Rape) 1971, Hustruer (Wives) 1975, Den Allvarsamme Leken (Games of Love and Loneliness) 1977 (Silver Hugo Award, Chicago 1977), Arven (Next of Kin/The Inheritance) 1979, Forfølgelsen (Witch Hunt) 1981, Papirfuglen (Paper Bird) 1984 (Silver Hugo Award, Chicago 1984), Hustruer—ti år etter (Wives—Ten Years After) 1985, Smykketyven (Twice upon a Time) 1990, Hustruer III (Wives III) 1996; has also written script for film Trollsyn (Second Sight), dir. Ola Solum 1994. *Address:* c/o Norsk Film, Filmparken-Wedel Jarlsbergs vei 36, 1342 Jar; Mellbyedalen 8, 0287 Oslo, Norway. *Telephone:* 67.52.53.00 (Jar). *Fax:* 67.12.51.08 (Jar).

BREITENSTEIN, (Fredrik) Wilhelm, LL.M.; Finnish diplomatist; b. 17 May 1933, Tampere; s. of B. Rafael Breitenstein and Ebba Huikarinen; m. 1st Dorrit I. Martin (divorced 1977); one s. three d.; m. 2nd Satu Marjatta Lefkowitz 1978; one d.; ed. Univ. of Helsinki; intern, UN Secr. New York 1957–58; Ministry of Foreign Affairs 1960–62, 1966–68, 1978–83; Attaché and Sec. of Embassy, Perm. Mission to UN, New York 1962–66; Deputy Perm. Rep. to EFTA and Int. Orgs. Geneva 1968–72, Perm. Mission to UN, New York 1972–78; Gov. Asian Devt. Bank 1978–83, African Devt. Bank 1978–83; Alt. Gov. Inter-American Devt. Bank 1978–83; Perm. Rep. to OECD and UNESCO 1983–91; Perm. Rep. to UN 1991–; del. to numerous UN and other int. confs. *Leisure interests:* art and antiques. *Address:* Permanent Mission of Finland to the United Nations, 866 United Nations Plaza, 2nd Floor, New York, NY 10017, U.S.A. *Telephone:* (212) 355-2100. *Fax:* (212) 759-6156.

BREITSCHWERDT, Werner, DR.ING.; German business executive and consultant; b. 23 Sept. 1927, Stuttgart; m. Nelly Breitschwerdt; two c.; joined Daimler-Benz AG 1953, mem. Admin. Bd. 1979, Chair. 1983–87; mem. Supervisory Bd. Continental AG, Dornier GmbH, Zahnradfabrik Friedrichshafen AG, Keiper KG, Mercedes-Benz subsidiaries, MTU GmbH; Ed. Züblin AG; Ehren-Senator Univ. of Heidelberg; Hon. Prof. Univ. of Karlsruhe; Hon. Dr. Ing. (Bochum) 1982; Bundesverdienstkreuz. *Address:* Daimler-Benz AG, c/o Mercedes-Benz AG, F506, 70322 Stuttgart, Germany.

BREKHOVSKIKH, Leonid Maksimovich, D.SC.; Russian physicist; b. 6 May 1917, Strunkino Village, Arkhangelsk Region; s. of Maxim Vasiljevich and Nadezda Alexandrovna Brekhovskikh; m. Lidia Andreevna Popova 1940; one s. two d.; ed. Perm. State Univ; jr. research worker, sr. research worker, Deputy Head of Dept., Inst. of Physics, U.S.S.R. Acad. of Sciences 1939–54; Dir. Inst. of Acoustics 1954–64, Head of Laboratory 1964–80; Head Ocean Acoustics Dept. Shirsov Inst. of Oceanology 1980–; discovered (with others) super-distant propagation of sound in the sea and existence of mesoscale eddies in the sea; Head of Dept. of Oceanography, Physics of Atmosphere and Geography, U.S.S.R. (now Russian) Acad. of Sciences 1969–91; Counsellor Presidium of Russian Acad. of Sciences 1991–; mem. CPSU 1959–91; Prof. Moscow Univ. 1953–75, Moscow Physics Tech. Inst. 1975–97; Corresp. mem. U.S.S.R. (now Russian) Acad. of Sciences 1953–68, mem. 1968–; mem. N.A.S. 1991–; State Prize 1950, 1976, Lenin Prize 1970, Rayleigh Gold Medal, British Inst. of Acoustics, Karpinsky Prize 1986, F.V.S. Foundation, Hamburg; Hero of Socialist Labour 1987; Munk Medal of Oceanographic Soc. 1996. *Publications:* numerous scientific works in fields of ocean acoustics, radiophysics and theoretical physics. *Leisure interest:* yoga exercises. *Address:* P. P. Shirshov Oceanology Institute, Russian Academy of Sciences, Krasikova 23, B-218 Moscow, Russia. *Telephone:* (095) 124 85 38; 938-14-63. *Fax:* (095) 124 59 83.

BREMAN, Jan; Netherlands professor of comparative sociology; b. 24 July 1936, Amsterdam; Dir. Centre of Asian Studies, Univ. of Amsterdam; Prof. Inst. of Social Studies, The Hague; extensive anthropological research in India and Indonesia 1962–; devt. consultant on social policies in Asia; mem. Nat. Advisory Council on Devt. Cooperation in the Netherlands; mem. Royal Netherlands Acad. of Sciences. *Publications:* Patronage and Exploitation 1974, Landless Labour in Colonial Java 1984, Of Peasants, Migrants and Paupers 1985, Taming the Coolie Beast 1989, Beyond Patronage and Exploitation 1993, Wage Hunters and Gatherers 1993. *Address:* Oude Hoogstraat 24, 1012 CE Amsterdam, Netherlands. *Telephone:* 20-5252745. *Fax:* 20-525 2446.

BREMER, Jon, D(R.)MED.; Norwegian professor of medical biochemistry; b. 5 Dec. 1928, Ås; s. of late Anders H. Bremer and Anna Bjorkum; m. Eli Sakshaug 1958; two s. one d.; ed. Oslo Univ.; Research Fellowship, Norwegian Cancer Soc. 1960–66; Assoc. Prof. of Clinical Biochem., Univ. of Oslo 1966–72, Prof. of Medical Biochem. 1972–95; Vice-Chair. Norwegian Medical Research Council 1975–78, Chair. 1978–81; mem. Norwegian Acad. of Science and the Humanities; Anders Jahres Sr. Prize for Medical Research 1985. *Publications:* numerous publs. on metabolism of fatty acids. *Leisure interests:* outdoor activities (skiing, hiking), art, travel, literature. *Address:* Institute of Medical Biochemistry, University of Oslo, P.O. Box 1112, Blindern, Oslo (Office); Damvegen 31, 0587 Oslo 5, Norway (Home). *Telephone:* 22 85 1066 (Office); 22 15 2016 (Home). *Fax:* (2) 285-10-58.

BREMI, Ulrich; Swiss business executive and politician; b. 6 Nov. 1929, Zürich; s. of Heinrich Bremi-Sennhauser and Johanna Bremi-Sennhauser; m. Anja Bremi-Forrer; two d.; ed. School of Mechanical Eng., Winterthur and Swiss Fed. Inst. of Tech. Zürich; C.E.O. Kaba Holding Ltd. Zürich 1962–90; Chair. Bd. Neue Zürcher Zeitung 1988–, Georg Fischer AG 1989–98, Swiss Reinsurance Co. 1992–, Flughafe-Immobilien-Gesellschaft 1992–; mem. Swiss Nat. Parl. 1975–91, Chair. 1990–91. *Address:* Swiss Reinsurance Company, Mythenquai 50/60, P.O. Box 8022, Zürich, Switzerland. *Telephone:* 41 1 285 35 53. *Fax:* 41 1 285 41 80.

BRENCHLEY, Thomas Frank, C.M.G., M.A.; British diplomatist (retd.); b. 9 April 1918, Stockton-on-Tees; s. of Robert B. and Alice (née Brough) Brenchley; m. Edith Helen Helfand 1946 (died 1980); three d.; ed. Merton Coll., Oxford and the Open Univ.; served in British Army 1939–46; entered Civil Service 1947, transferred to Foreign Office 1949; served in Singapore, Cairo, Foreign Office and Middle East Centre for Arabic Studies 1950–59; Khartoum, Jeddah and Foreign Office 1960–66; Asst. Under-Sec. for Middle East Affairs, Foreign and Commonwealth Office 1967–68; Amb. to Norway 1968–72, to Poland 1972–74; Deputy Sec., Cabinet Office 1975–76; Deputy Sec.-Gen., C.E.O. Arab-British Chamber of Commerce 1976–83; Chair. Inst. for the Study of Conflict 1983–89, Research Inst. for the Study of Conflict and Terrorism 1989–94; Dir. Center for Security Studies, Washington, D.C. 1988–90; Pres. Int. Inst. for the Study of Conflict, Geneva 1989–91; Chair. Travellers' Club London 1991–94. *Publications:* Britain and the Middle East: An Economic History 1945–1987, 1989, Aegean Conflict and the Law of the Sea 1990. *Leisure interests:* collecting books, chess. *Address:* 19 Ennismore Gardens, London, S.W.7, England. *Telephone:* 0171-584 7981.

BRENDEL, Alfred; Austrian pianist and writer; b. 5 Jan. 1931, Wiesenberg; s. of Ing. Albert and Ida (née Wieltschnig) Brendel; m. 1st Iris Heymann-Gonzala 1960 (divorced 1972); one d.; m. 2nd Irene Semler 1975; one s. two d.; studied piano under Sofija Deželić (Zagreb), Ludovika v. Kaan (Graz), Edwin Fischer (Lucerne), Paul Baumgartner (Basel), Edward Steuermann (Salzburg); studied composition under A. Michl (Graz) and harmony under Franjo Dugan (Zagreb); first piano recital 1948; concert tours through Europe, Latin America, North America 1963–; Australia 1963, 1966, 1969, 1976; has appeared at many music festivals, including Salzburg 1960–, Vienna, Edinburgh, Aldeburgh, Athens, Granada, Puerto Rico and has performed with most of the major orchestras of Europe and U.S.A., etc.; numerous recordings, including complete piano works of Beethoven, Schubert's piano works 1822–28; mem. Acad. of Arts and Sciences (U.S.A.); Hon. R.A.M.; Hon. D.Mus. (London) 1978, (Oxford) 1983, (Exeter) 1998; Hon. Fellow, Exeter Coll. Oxford 1987; Hon. D.Litt. (Sussex) 1981; Hon. D. (Warwick) 1991, (Yale) 1992, (Cologne) 1995; Premio Città de Bolzano, Concorso Busoni 1949, Grand Prix du Disque 1965, Edison Prize (five times 1973–87), Grand Prix des Disquaires de France 1975, Deutscher Schallplattenpreis (four times 1976–84, 1992), Wiener Flötenuhr (six times 1976–87), Gramophone Award (six times 1977–83), Japanese Record Acad. Award (five times 1977–84), Japanese Grand Prix 1978, Franz Liszt Prize (four times 1979–83), Frankfurt Music Prize 1984, Diapason D'Or Award 1992, Heidsieck Award for Writing on Music 1990; Commdr., Arts et Lettres 1985; Hon. K.B.E. 1989, Ordre pour le Mérite (Germany) 1991. *Publications:* essays on music and musicians in Phono, Fono Forum, Österreichische Musikzeitschrift, Music and Musicians, Hi-Fi Stereophonie, New York Review of Books, Die Zeit, Frankfurter Allgemeine Zeitung, Musical Thoughts and Afterthoughts 1976, Music Sounded Out (essays) 1990, Fingerzeig 1996, Störendes Lachen Während des Jaworts 1997, On Many 1998, etc. *Leisure interests:* books, theatre, the visua baroque and romanesque architecture, unintentional humour, kitsch. *Address:* c/o Ingpen and Williams, 26 Wadham Road, London, SW15 2LR, England. *Telephone:* 0181-874 3222.

BRENNAN, Edward A.; American business executive; b. 16 Jan. 1934, Chicago; s. of Edward Brennan and Margaret Bourget; m. Lois Lyon 1955; three s. three d.; ed. Marquette Univ.; joined Sears, Roebuck and Co., Madison, Wis. as salesman 1956, held several positions in co.'s nat. HQ and elsewhere, Exec. Vice-Pres. South 1977, Pres. of Sears 1980, Chair. and C.E.O. Sears Merchandise Group 1981, Pres. and C.O.O. Sears, Roebuck and Co. 1984–86, Chair., Pres. and C.E.O. 1986–95; Exec. Adviser Seiyu Ltd. 1995–; mem. Bd. of Trustees Atlanta, DePaul and Marquette Univs. and Chicago Museum of Science and Industry; mem. Bd. of Govs. United Way of America; mem. Chicago Urban League 1980–. *Address:* c/o Sears, Roebuck and Co., 3333 Beverly Road, Hoffman Estates, IL 60179, U.S.A.

BRENNAN, Hon. Sir (Francis) Gerard, A.C., K.B.E., LL.B.; Australian judge; b. 22 May 1928, Rockhampton, Queensland; s. of Hon. Mr. Justice F.T. Brennan; m. Patricia O'Hara 1953; three s. four d.; ed. Christian Brothers' Coll. Rockhampton, Downlands Coll. Toowoomba and Univ. of Queensland, Brisbane; admitted to Bar 1951, Q.C. 1965; Pres. Bar Assn. of Queensland 1974–76, Australian Bar Assn. 1975–76, Admin. Review Council 1976–79, Admin. Appeals Tribunal 1976–79; mem. Exec. Law Council of Australia 1975–76, Australian Law Reform Comm. 1975–77; Additional Judge, Supreme Court of A.C.T. 1976–81; Judge, Australian Industrial Court 1976–81, Fed. Court of Australia 1977–81; Justice, High Court of Australia 1981–95; Chief Justice of Australia 1995–98; Foundation Scientia Prof., Univ. of N.S.W. 1998–; Hon. LL.D. (Trinity Coll.). *Address:* c/o Suite 2604, Piccadilly Tower, 133 Castlereagh Street, Sydney, N.S.W. 2000, Australia.

BRENNAN, Séamus, B.A., M.COMM.; Irish politician; b. 16 Feb. 1948, Salthill, Galway; s. of late James Brennan and of Teresa Brennan; m. Ann O'Shaughnessy 1972; two s. four d.; ed. St. Joseph's Secondary School, Galway, Univ. Coll., Galway; has worked as an accountant and management consultant; Gen. Sec. Fianna Fáil party 1973–80; Govt. Deputy Whip Seanad Éireann 1977–81; Senator 1977–81; Dáil deputy for Dublin South 1981–; Minister of State, Dept. of Industry and Commerce with responsibility for Trade and Marketing 1987–89; Minister for Tourism and Transport 1989–92, for Educ. 1992–93, for Commerce and Technology 1993–94; Front Bench spokesperson on Transport, Energy and Communications 1994–97; Minister of State to the Taoiseach, Govt. Chief Whip and Minister of State at the Dept. of Defence 1997–; mem. Oireachtas Cttee. on Procedure and Privileges 1977–81; Vice-Chair. Oireachtas Cttee. on State Sponsored Bodies 1981; mem. Jt. Cttee. on commercial state sponsored bodies, and Small Business 1994–97; mem. Oireachtas Jt. Cttee. on the Secondary Legislation in the EEC 1982; mem. Dublin Co. Council 1985–87. *Leisure interests:* boating, golf, reading, tennis. *Address:* 31 Finsbury Park, Churchtown, Dublin 14, Ireland.

BRENNER, Sydney, C.H., M.B., D.PHIL., F.R.S., F.R.C.P.; British scientist; b. 13 Jan. 1927, Germiston, South Africa; s. of Morris Brenner and Lena Blacher; m. May Woolf Balkind; three s. (one step-s.) two d.; ed. Univ. of the Witwatersrand, Johannesburg, and Oxford Univ.; Lecturer in Physiology, Univ. of Witwatersrand 1955–57; mem. Scientific Staff, M.R.C. 1957–92, Dir. M.R.C. Lab. of Molecular Biology, Cambridge 1979–86, Dir. Molecular Genetics Unit, Cambridge 1986–92; mem. Scripps Inst., La Jolla, Calif. 1992–94; Dir. Molecular Sciences Inst., Berkeley, Calif. 1996–; mem. Medical Research Council 1978–82, 1986–90; Fellow of King's Coll., Cambridge 1959–; Hon. Prof. of Genetic Medicine, Univ. of Cambridge Clinical School 1989–; Foreign Hon. mem. American Acad. of Arts and Sciences 1965, Hon. mem. Deutsche Akademie der Natursforscher Leopoldina 1975, Soc. for Biological Chemists 1975; Foreign Assoc. N.A.S. 1977; Hon. F.R.S.E.; Foreign mem. of American Philosophical Soc. 1979; Foreign Assoc. Royal Soc. of S. Africa 1983, Hon. Fellow, Exeter Coll. 1985; Foreign mem. of Real Academia de Ciencias 1985; External Scientific mem. Max Planck Soc. 1988; mem. Acad Europaea 1989; Hon. Fellow Indian Acad. of Sciences 1989; Hon. mem. Chinese Soc. of Genetics 1989; Hon. Fellow Royal Coll. of Pathologists 1990; Hon. mem. Assoc. of Physicians of G.B. and Ireland 1991; Corresp. Scientifique Emérite de l'INSERM, Associé Etranger Académie des Sciences, France, Fellow American Acad. of Microbiology; Hon. D.Sc. (Dublin, Witwatersrand, Chicago, London, Leicester, Oxford); Hon. LL.D. (Glasgow); Hon. D.Litt (Singapore); Warren Triennial Prize 1968, William Bate Hardy Prize, Cambridge Philosophical Soc. 1969, Gregor Mendel Medal of German Acad. of Science Leopoldina 1970, Albert Lasker Medical Research Award 1971, Gairdner Foundation Annual Award (Canada) 1978; Royal Medal of Royal Soc. 1974, Prix Charles Leopold Mayer, French Acad. 1975, Krebs Medal, Fed. of European Biochemical Socs. 1980, Ciba Medal, Biochemical Soc. 1981, Feldberg Foundation Prize 1983, Neil Hamilton Fairley Medal, Royal Coll. of Physicians 1985, Croonian Lecturer Royal Soc. of London 1986, Rosenstiel Award, Brandeis Univ. 1986, Prix Louis Jeantet de Médecine (Switzerland) 1987, Genetics Soc. of America Medal 1987, Harvey Prize, Israel Inst. of Tech. 1987, Hughlings Jackson Medal, Royal Soc. of Medicine 1987, Waterford Bio-Medical Science Award (The Research Inst. of Scripps Clinic) 1988, Kyoto Prize (Inamori Foundation) 1990, Gairdner Foundation Award (Canada) 1991, Copley Medal (Royal Soc.) 1991, King Faisal Int. Prize for Science (King Faisal Foundation) 1992, Bristol-Myers Squibb Award for Distinguished Achievement in Neuroscience Research 1992. *Address:* Kings College, Cambridge, CB2 1ST (Office); 17b St. Edward's Passage, Cambridge, CB2 3PJ, England. (Home).

BRENT, Richard Peirce, PH.D., F.A.A., F.I.E.E.E.; Australian professor of computing science; b. 20 April 1946, Melbourne; s. of Oscar Brent and Nancy Brent; m. Erin O'Connor 1969; two s.; ed. Melbourne Grammar School, Monash Univ., Stanford Univ., U.S.A.; Research Scientist, IBM T. J. Watson Research Center, Yorktown Heights, New York, U.S.A. 1971–72; Research Fellow etc., A.N.U., Canberra 1972–78, Prof. of Computer Sciences 1978–98, now Adjunct Prof.; Prof. of Computing Science, Oxford Univ. 1998–; Fellow Assn. for Computing Machinery, U.S.A.; Australian Math. Soc. Medal 1984; Forsythe Memorial Lecturer 1990. *Publications:* Algorithms for Minimization without Derivatives 1973, Topics in Computational Complexity and the Analysis of Algorithms 1980. *Leisure interests:* music, chess, astronomy. *Address:* Oxford University Computing Laboratory, Wolfson Building, Parks Road, Oxford, OX1 3QD, England. *Telephone:* (01865) 283504.

BRENTON, Howard, B.A.; British playwright; b. 13 Dec. 1942, Portsmouth; s. of Donald and Rosalind Brenton; m. Jane Fry 1970; two s.; ed. Chichester High School for Boys and St. Catharine's Coll., Cambridge; resident writer, Royal Court Theatre, London 1972–73; writer-in-residence, Warwick Univ. 1978–79; Granada Artist in Residence, Univ. of Calif. at Davis 1997; John Whiting Award 1970, Standard Best Play of the Year Award 1976, Standard Best Play of the Year (jtly. with David Hare) 1985. *Publications:* Revenge 1969, Christie in Love 1969, Hitler Dances 1972, Magnificence 1973, Brassneck (with David Hare) 1973, The Churchill Play 1974, Government Property 1975, The Saliva Milkshake 1975, Weapons of Happiness 1976, Sore throats 1979, Plays for the Poor Theatre 1980, The Romans in Britain 1980, Thirteenth Night 1981, The Genius 1983, Sleeping Policemen (with Tunde Ikoli) 1983, Bloody Poetry 1984, Pravda (with David Hare) 1985, Dead Head 1986, Greenland 1988, Diving for Pearls (novel) 1989, Iranian Nights (with Tariq Ali) 1989, Hess is Dead 1990, Moscow Gold (with Tariq Ali) 1990, Berlin Bertie 1992, Hot Irons (Essays and Diaries) 1995, Playing Away (opera) 1994, Goethe's Faust, Parts I and II 1995, Plays I 1996, Plays II 1996, Ugly Rumours (with Tariq Ali) 1998. *Leisure interest:* painting. *Address:* c/o Cassarotto Ramsay Ltd., 60/66 National House, Wardour Street, London, WC1V 3HP, England. *Telephone:* 0171-287 4450.

BRESLOW, Lester, M.D., M.P.H.; American professor of public health; b. 17 March 1915; s. of Joseph Breslow and Mayme Danziger; m. Devra Miller 1967; three s.; ed. Univ. of Minnesota; Dist. Health Officer, Minn. 1941–43; U.S. Army 1943–46; Chief, Bureau of Chronic Diseases, Calif. Dept. of Public Health 1946–60, Div. of Preventative Medicine 1960–65; Dir. Calif. Dept. of Public Health 1965–68; Prof. School of Public Health, Univ. of Calif. (Los Angeles) 1968–, Dean 1972–80, Dir. for Cancer Control Research, Jonsson Comprehensive Cancer Center 1982–86, Dir. Health Promotion Center 1986–91; consultant Nat. Cancer Inst. 1981–; Sedwick Medal, American Public Health Assn.; Lasker Award; Dana Award. *Publication:* Health and Ways of Living: The Alameda County Study 1983; Health-Trac Award. *Leisure interest:* gardening. *Address:* 10926 Verano Road, Los Angeles, CA 90077, U.S.A. (Home).

BRESLOW, Ronald Charles, PH.D.; American professor of chemistry; b. 14 March 1931, Rahway, N.J.; s. of Alexander Breslow and Gladys Fellows; m. Esther Greenberg 1956; two d.; ed. Harvard Univ.; Instructor, Columbia Univ. 1956–59, Assoc. Prof. 1959–62, Prof. 1962–67, Mitchill Prof. of Chem. 1966–, Univ. Prof. 1992–; Ed. Benjamin Inc. 1962–; Sloan Fellowship 1961–63; Fellow A.A.A.S. 1986; mem. Nat. Acad. of Sciences, American Acad. of Arts and Sciences, American Philosophical Soc., Exec. Cttee. of Organic Div. of American Chemical Soc.; mem. Ed. Bd. Organic Syntheses 1965–, Bd. of Eds. Journal of Organic Chem. 1968, Tetrahedron, Tetrahedron Letters 1977, Chemical Eng. News 1980–83; Hon. mem. Korean Chemical Soc. 1996, Royal Soc. of Chem. (U.K.) 1996; Procurator, N.A.S. 1984; Trustee, American-Swiss Foundation for Scientific Exchange Inc. 1969–71; Chair. Div. of Organic Chem., American Chemical Soc. 1970–71, Pres. of Soc. 1996; Chair. Div. of Chem., N.A.S. 1974; Chair. Dept. of Chem., Columbia Univ. 1976–; mem. Advisory Bd., Chemical and Engineering News 1980; Chair. Bd. of Scientific Advisers, Sloan Foundation 1981–; mem. Bd. of Scientific Advisers, Gen. Motors 1982–; Centenary Lecturer, London Chemical Soc. 1972; Trustee, Rockefeller Univ. 1981–; A. R. Todd Visiting Prof., Univ. of Cambridge 1982; Foreign Fellow Indian Acad. of Science 1992; Annual Ciba Foundation Lecturer, London 1982; American Chemical Soc. Award in Pure Chem. 1966; Fresinius Award 1966, Mark van Doren Award 1969, Baekeland Medal 1969, Harrison Howe Award 1974, Remsen Medal 1977, Roussel Prize 1978, American Chemical Soc. James Flack Norris Award in Physical Organic Chemistry 1980, Richards Medal in Chemistry 1984, Arthur Cope Award 1987, George Kenner Award 1988, Nichols Medal 1989, Nat. Acad. of Sciences Chemistry Medal 1989, Paracelsus Medal, Swiss Chemical Soc. 1990, U.S. Nat. Medal of Science 1991, Priestley Medal, American Chemical Soc. 1999. *Publications:* Organic Reaction Mechanisms 1965; over 350 scientific papers. *Address:* 566 Chandler Laboratories, Department of Chemistry, Columbia University, New York, NY 10027, U.S.A. *Telephone:* (212) 854-2170.

BRESSANI, Ricardo, PH.D.; Guatemalan biochemist; b. 28 Sept. 1926, Guatemala; s. of César Bressani and Primina Castignoli de Bressani; m. Alicia Herman 1949; five s. two d.; ed. Univ. of Dayton, Iowa State Univ. and Purdue Univ.; Visiting Prof. M.I.T., Rutgers Univ.; Ed.-in-Chief, Archivos

Latino-americanos de Nutrición; Head and Research Dir., Div. of Agric. and Food Sciences, Inst. of Nutrition of Cen. America and Panama (INCAP) 1988–; mem. Directive Cttee. Agroindustrial Rural Devt. (PRODAR) Costa Rica 1991–; Corresp. Academic mem., Acad. of Medical, Physical and Natural Sciences of Guatemala 1990–; Foreign mem. N.A.S. (U.S.A.); mem. American Inst. of Food Technologists; Dr. h.c. (Purdue), (Universidad del Valle de Guatemala); Babcock Hart Award 1970, McCollum Award 1976, World Science Award "Albert Einstein" 1984, Abraham Horowitz Award 1990. *Publications:* over 450 scientific publications in related professional fields including books, monographs and articles in scientific journals. *Leisure interests:* swimming, horseback-riding. *Address:* Institute of Nutrition of Central America and Panama, Calzada Roosevelt zona 11, 01011 Guatemala City (Office); Instituto de Investigación Universidad del Valle de Guatemala, 18 avenida 11-95 zona 15, 01015, Vista Hermosa III, Guatemala City (Office); 6a calle "A" 7-74 zona 9, Guatemala City, 01009 Guatemala (Home). *Telephone:* 72 37 62-8 Ext. 221 (Inst. of Nutrition); 380 336/40 (University); 326125 (Home). *Fax:* 380 212.

BRESSON, Robert; French film writer and director; b. 25 Sept. 1901, Bromont-Lamothe (Puy-de-Dôme); s. of Léon Bresson and Marie-Elisabeth Clausels; m. 1st Leidia van der Zee; m. 2nd Marie-Madeleine van der Mersch; ed. Lycée Lakanal, Sceaux; started as painter; made first film 1934; Hon. Pres. Soc. des Réalisateurs de films 1968; Officier Légion d'honneur, Grand Croix Ordre nat. du Mérite, Commdr. Arts et Lettres; Grand Prix du Cinéma français 1943, 1951, Prix Louis-Delluc 1950, Grand Prix du Film d'avant garde 1950, Grand Prix des Arts et des Lettres 1978, Akira Kurosowa Award 1988 and numerous foreign awards. *Films directed include:* les Anges du péché 1943, Les dames du Bois de Boulogne 1945, Journal d'un curé de campagne 1951 (Venice Film Festival Grand Prize 1951), Un condamné à mort s'est échappé 1956 (Best Dir. Award, Cannes 1957), Pickpocket 1959 (prix du Meilleur Film de l'année 1960), Procès de Jeanne d'Arc 1962 (prix spécial, Cannes Festival 1962), Au hasard, Balthasar 1966, Mouchette 1966 (prix du Cinéma français 1967, Hommage unanime du jury Cannes 1967, grand prix, Panama Festival 1968), Une femme douce 1969 (Coquille d'argent, Festival de Saint Sébastien), Quatre nuits d'un rêveur 1971, Lancelot du lac 1974, Le diable probablement 1977 (Ours d'argent, Berlin 1977), l'Argent (Grand Prix, Cannes festival 1983); Golden Lion, Venice Film Festival 1989; Felix Award (European Film Acad.) 1994, prix René Clair 1995. *Publication:* Notes sur le cinématographe 1975. *Address:* 49 quai de Bourbon, 75004 Paris, France.

BRETH, Andrea; German theatre director; b. 31 Oct. 1952, Rieden, Allgau; d. of Prof. Herbert Breth and Maria Breth (née Noether); ed. Darmstadt, Heidelberg; dir. Bremen, Hamburg, Berlin 1976, Zürich, Bochum 1980, Freiburg (Bernarda Albas Haus, Lorca) 1984, Schauspielhaus Bochum (Le Sud, Green; The Last, Gorki) 1986–90, Burgtheater, Vienna (Zerbrochener Krug, Kleist) 1990, Schaubuhne Berlin (Einsamer Weg, Schnitzler) 1991 and (Nachtasyl, Gorki) 1992, Burgtheater Vienna (End of the Beginning, O'Casey) 1991, Tschulimsk, Wampilow (Letzten Sommer) 1992, Kaiser (Von morgens bis mitternachts) 1993, (Hedda Gabler) 1993, (Orestes) 1995, (Die Möwe) 1995; mem. Berlin Acad. of Arts; Deutscher Kritiker Preis, Nordrhein-Westfalen Forderpreis, Kortner Preis. *Leisure interests:* literature, music, paintings. *Address:* Kurfürstendamm 153, 10709 Berlin, Germany.

BRETSCHER, Mark Steven, M.A., PH.D., F.R.S.; British/Swiss research scientist; b. 8 Jan. 1940, Cambridge; s. of Hanni Bretscher (née Greminger) and Egon Bretscher; m. Barbara M. F. Pearse (q.v.) 1978; one s. one d.; ed. Abingdon School, Gonville and Caius Coll., Cambridge; Research student, Gonville and Caius Coll., Cambridge 1961–64; Scientific Staff mem. MRC, Lab. of Molecular Biology, Cambridge 1965–, Head, Div. of Cell Biology 1984–95; Visiting Prof. Harvard Coll., U.S.A. 1974–75, Stanford Univ., U.S.A. 1984–85; Friedrich-Miescher Prize 1979. *Publications:* scientific papers in professional journals. *Leisure interest:* silviculture. *Address:* Medical Research Council, Laboratory of Molecular Biology, Hills Road, Cambridge, CB2 2QH (Office); Ram Cottage, Commercial End, Swaffham Bulbeck, Cambridgeshire, CB5 0ND, England (Home). *Telephone:* (01223) 248011 (Office); (01223) 811276 (Home). *Fax:* (01223) 412142.

BREUEL, Birgit; German business executive and politician; b. 1937, Hamburg; m. Ernst Breuel 1959; three s.; ed. Univs. of Hamburg, Oxford and Geneva; mem. Hamburg State Parl. 1970; Minister of Econs. Lower Saxony 1978, of Finance 1986–90; mem. CDU Bundesvorstand, Bonn 1986; Chief Exec. Treuhandanstalt, Berlin (formed to manage and/or sell all fmrly. state-owned cos. in East Germany) 1990, Pres. 1991–95; Gen. Sec. Expo 2000, Hannover 1995–; mem. Bd. Volkswagen AG, Norddeutsche Landesbank AG, Deutsche Bundesbahn AG, Salzgitter AG, PREAG; Chair. Bd. Deutsche Messe AG, Hannover; adviser, Hamburg-Mannheimer Versicherung AG, Zweites Deutsches Fernsehen; coordinator and chief del. for EXPO 2000, Hannover; Senator, Max Planck Gesellschaft, Munich.

BREUER, Rolf E., DR. JUR.; German banker; deputy mem. of Bd. of Managing Dirs. Deutsche Bank AG, Frankfurt, C.E.O. 1997–; Chair. Supervisory Bd. Deutsche Grundbesitz Anlagegesellschaft mbH, Cologne, Deutsche Vermögensbildungsgesellschaft mbH, Frankfurt, Lombardkasse AG, Frankfurt; Vice-Chair. Supervisory Bd. Deutscher Auslandskassenverein AG, Frankfurt, Frankfurter Kassenverein AG, Frankfurt; mem. of Bd. Asia Fund Management Co. S.A., Luxembourg; Chair. Deutsche Bank Capital Markets (Asia), Euro-Clear Clearance System Ltd., London; Vice-Chair. Deutsche Bank Capital Corp., Frankfurt, Deutsche Bank Capital Markets Ltd., London. *Address:* Deutsche Bank, Taunusanlage 12, 60325, Frankfurt am Main, Germany.

BREWER, Derek Stanley, LITT.D., PH.D.; British professor of English; b. 13 July 1923, Cardiff; s. of Stanley Leonard Brewer and Winifred Helen Forbes; m. Lucie Elisabeth Hoole 1951; three s. two d.; ed. Crypt Grammar School, Gloucester, Magdalen Coll., Oxford; war service in infantry 1942–45; Asst. Lecturer then lecturer, Univ. of Birmingham 1949–56, Sr. Lecturer 1958–64; Prof. Int. Christian Univ., Tokyo 1956–58; lecturer, Univ. of Cambridge 1965–76, Reader 1976–83, Prof. 1983–90, Emer. Prof. 1990–; f. D. S. Brewer Ltd. (now part of Boydell and Brewer), publrs. of academic books; Fellow, Emmanuel Coll., Cambridge 1965–77, Master 1977–90, Life Fellow 1990–; Hon. degrees from Univs. of Keio (Tokyo), Harvard, York, Birmingham, Paris IV (Sorbonne), Liège, Williams Coll., U.S.A.; Seatonian Prize for Poetry nine times; Hon. mem. 1981 and Medal, Japan Acad. 1997; Corresp. Fellow Medieval Soc. of America 1987; Franqui Prof. des Sciences Humaines (Belgium) and Medal 1998. *Publications include:* Chaucer 1953, Proteus 1958, Chaucer's Parlement of Foulys (ed.) 1960, Malory's Morte d'Arthur Parts 7 and 8 (ed.) 1968, Chaucer and his World 1978, Symbolic Stories 1980, English Gothic Literature 1983, Introduction to Chaucer 1984, Medieval Comic Tales (ed.) 1996, A Critical Companion to the Gawain-poet (ed.) 1996, and numerous other publs. *Leisure interests:* reading, walking. *Address:* Emmanuel College, Cambridge, CB2 3AP, England. *Telephone:* (01223) 334200. *Fax:* (01223) 241104.

BREWER, Leo, PH.D.; American professor of chemistry; b. 13 June 1919, St. Louis, Mo.; s. of Abraham and Hannah (Resnik) Brewer; m. Rose Strugo 1945; one s. two d.; ed. Calif. Inst. of Tech. and Univ. of California (Berkeley); Research Assoc. Manhattan Dist. Project, Univ. of Calif. (Berkeley); Research Assoc. Lawrence Berkeley Lab. (Univ. of Calif.) 1943–61, Head Inorganic Materials Div. 1961–75, Prin. Investigator 1961–94; Assoc. Dir. Lawrence Berkeley Lab. 1967–75; Asst. Prof. Coll. of Chem., Univ. of Calif. 1946–50, Assoc. Prof. 1950–55, Prof. 1955–89, Prof. Emer. 1989–; mem. N.A.S. 1959–, American Acad. of Arts and Sciences 1979–; Great Western Dow Fellow 1942, Guggenheim Fellow 1950, Berkeley Fellow 1992; Leo H. Baekland Award 1953, E. O. Lawrence Award 1961, Palladium Medal and Award of Electrochemical Soc. 1971, Distinguished Alumni Award (Calif. Inst. of Tech.) 1974, William Hume-Rothery Award 1983, Henry B. Linford Award 1988, Berkeley Citation 1989, Extractive Metallurgy Science Award 1991; several hon. lectureships 1963–67, 1970–72, 1974, 1979, 1981, 1983, 1986, 1989. *Publications:* Thermodynamics (co-author) 1961 and numerous articles in professional journals. *Leisure interest:* gardening. *Address:* Department of Chemistry M.C. 1460, University of California, Berkeley, CA 94720 (Office); 15 Vista del Orinda Road, Orinda, CA 94563, U.S.A. (Home). *Telephone:* (510) 643-5555. *Fax:* (510) 642-4136.

BREWER, Richard George, PH.D.; American atomic physicist; b. 8 Dec. 1928, Los Angeles; s. of Louis Ludwig and Elise Brewer; m. Lillian Magidow 1954; one s. two d.; ed. California Inst. of Technology and Univ. of California, Berkeley; Instructor, Harvard Univ. 1958–60; Asst. Prof., Univ. of Calif., Los Angeles 1960–63; IBM Research Staff mem., San José, Calif. 1963–73; Consulting Prof., Applied Physics, Stanford Univ. 1977–; IBM Fellow, San José, Calif. 1973–94, Fellow Emer. 1994–; mem. N.A.S. 1980; Fellow American Physical Soc. and Optical Soc. of America; Albert A. Michelson Gold Medal, Franklin Inst. 1979; Distinguished Alumni Award, C.I.T. 1994. *Publications:* more than 145 papers in scientific journals. *Leisure interests:* growing magnolias, classical music, reading Italian literature. *Address:* 730 De Soto Drive, Palo Alto, CA 94303, U.S.A.

BREYER, Stephen, B.A., LL.B.; American judge; b. 15 Aug. 1938, San Francisco, Calif.; s. of Irving Breyer and Anne Breyer; m. Joanna Hare 1967; one s. two d.; ed. Stanford Univ., Magdalen Coll. Oxford and Harvard Law School; law clerk to Mr Justice Goldberg, U.S. Supreme Court 1964–65; Special Asst. to Asst. Attorney-Gen. Antitrust Div. U.S. Dept. of Justice 1965–67; Asst. Prof. of Law, Harvard Univ. 1967–70; Prof. of Law, Harvard Law School 1970–80; Prof. Kennedy School of Govt. Harvard Univ. 1977–80; lecturer, Harvard Law School 1981–; Asst. Special Prosecutor, Watergate Special Prosecution Force 1973; Special Counsel, Admin. Practices Subcttee. U.S. Senate Judiciary Cttee. 1974–75; Chief Counsel, Senate Judiciary Cttee. 1979–80; Circuit Judge, U.S. Court of Appeals for the First Circuit 1980–94, Chief Judge 1990–94; mem. U.S. Sentencing Comm. 1985–89; Assoc. Justice, Supreme Court of U.S.A. 1994–; Visiting lecturer, Coll. of Law, Sydney 1975; Visiting Prof. Univ. of Rome 1993; Fellow, American Acad. of Arts and Sciences. *Publications:* The Federal Power Commission and the Regulation of Energy (with P. MacAvoy) 1974, Administrative Law and Regulatory Policy (with R. Stewart) 1979, Regulation and Its Reform 1982, Breaking the Vicious Circle: Towards Effective Risk Regulation 1993; numerous articles and book chapters. *Address:* Supreme Court of the United States, 1 First Street, N.E., Washington, DC 20543, U.S.A. (Office). *Telephone:* (202) 479-3000 (Office).

BREZIS, Haim; French professor of mathematics; b. 1 June 1944, Riom-ès-Montagnes; s. of Jacob Brezis and Rebecca Brezis; m. Michal Govrin 1982; two d.; ed. Univ. of Paris; Prof. Pierre et Marie Curie Univ. 1974–; Visiting Prof. New York Univ., Univ. of Chicago, Princeton Univ., M.I.T., Hebrew Univ.; Visiting Distinguished Prof. Rutgers Univ.; mem. Acad. des Sciences, Academia Europaea; Foreign Hon. Mem. American Acad. of Arts and Sciences; Hon. mem. Romanian Acad. *Publications:* Analyse Fonctionnelle 1983, Ginzburg-Landau vortices 1994. *Leisure interest:* Hebraic studies. *Address:* Analyse Numérique, Université Pierre et Marie Curie, 4 place Jussieu, 75252 Paris Cedex 05 (Office); 18 rue de la Glacière, 75640 Paris Cedex 13, France (Home). *Telephone:* (33.1) 44 27 42 98 (Office); (33.1) 43 36 15 10 (Home). *Fax:* (33.1) 44 27 72 00.

BRIALY, Jean-Claude; French actor and director; b. 30 March 1933, Aumale, Algeria; s. of Roger Brialy and Suzanne Abraham; ed. Coll. Saint-Etienne and Conservatoire d'art dramatique, Strasbourg; Dir. Théâtre Hébertot 1977, Théâtre des Bouffes Parisiens 1986–, Anjou Festival; numerous stage, TV and film appearances; *dir. films:* Eglantine 1971 (Prix Jean Le Duc, Acad. Française), Les Volets clos 1973, L'Oiseau rare 1973, Un amour de pluie 1974, Quelques hommes de bonne volonté, Un Bon petit diable 1983; Chevalier, Légion d'honneur, Officier, Ordre Nat. du Mérite, Commdr. des Arts et des Lettres; recipient of César awards for roles in films Julie pot de colle 1976 and Les Innocents 1988. *Other recent films include:* La nuit de Varennes 1982, La Fille de Trieste, Sarah, Cap canaille, Mortelle randonnée, Le Démon dans l'île, Edith et Marcel, Stella, La Crime 1983, Pinot simple flic 1984, Le Mariage du siècle 1985, Inspecteur Lavardin, Suivez mon regard, Le Débutant 1986, Grand guignol, Levy et Goliath, Le Moustachu, Maladie d'amour 1987, Comédie d'Eté, Au bonheur des chiens 1990, S'en Fout la Mort 1990, Août 1992, Les Cents et Une Nuits 1995. *Television appearances include:* Quelques Hommes de Bonne Volonté 1983, Mariage Mortel 1991. *Theatre appearances include:* Le Negre 1986, La Jalousie 1992. *Publication:* Les Volets clos 1973. *Leisure interests:* collecting old watches and books; swimming and riding. *Address:* Théâtre des Bouffes Parisiens, 4 rue Monsigny, 75002 Paris (Office); 25 Quai Bourbon, 75004 Paris, France (Home).

BRIANÇON, Pierre, LL.M.; French journalist; b. 3 Aug. 1954, Tunis, Tunisia; s. of Claude Briançon and Geneviève Pochard; three c.; ed. Université Paris II, Institut d'Etudes Politiques, Paris; journalist, Forum International 1979; Econs. and Business Ed. Libération 1981–88, Moscow Corresp. 1988–91, U.S.A. Bureau Chief, Washington 1992–95, Ed.-in-Chief 1996–98; contrib. France Inter radio 1982–86. *Publications:* A Droite en sortant de la gauche? 1986, Héritiers du désastre 1992. *Address:* c/o Libération, 11 Rue Béranger, 75003 Paris, France. *Telephone:* 01-42-76-17-89. *Fax:* 01-42-76-16-37.

BRIDGEMAN, John Stuart; B.SC., T.D., F.R.S.A.; British business executive; b. 5 Oct. 1944; s. of late Alfred George Bridgeman and Edith Celia Bridgeman (née Watkins); m. Lindy Jane Fillmore 1967; three d.; ed. Whitchurch School, Cardiff, Univ. Coll., Swansea, McGill Univ., Montreal; with Alcan Industries 1966–69, Aluminium Co. of Canada 1969–70, Alcan Australia 1970, Commercial Dir. Alcan U.K. 1977–80, Vice-Pres. (Europe) Alcan Basic Raw Materials 1978–82, Man. Dir. Extrusion Div. British Alcan Aluminium P.L.C. 1983–87, British Alcan Enterprises 1987–91, Dir. Corp. Planning Alcan Aluminium Ltd., Montreal 1992–93, Man. Dir British Alcan Aluminium P.L.C. 1993–95; Dir.–Gen. of Fair Trading 1995–; Visiting Prof. of Man. Keele Univ. 1992–; Chair. N. Oxon. Business Group 1984–92, Enterprise Cherwell Ltd. 1985–91, N. Oxon Coll. 1989; Vice-Pres. Aluminium Fed. 1995, U.K.-Canada Chamber of Commerce 1995–96 (Pres. 1997–98); Gov. N. Oxon Coll. 1985–; Man. Dir. Heart of England Trading and Enterprise Council 1989–; Command T.A. and Reserve Forces 1978, Queen's Own Yeomanry 1981–84, Maj. R.E.M.E. (V) 1985–94, Staff Coll. 1986, mem. T.A.V.R.A. Oxon. and E. Wessex 1985–; mem. British Aiways N.E. Consumer Council 1978–81, Defence Science Advisory Council 1991–94, Nat. Employer Liaison Cttee. for Reserve Forces 1992–, U.K.-Canada Colloquium 1993–; numerous trusteeships; High Sheriff, Oxon. 1995–96; D.L. (Oxon.) 1989; U.S. Aluminium Asscn. Prize 1988; F.R.G.S.; Dr. h.c. (Sheffield Hallam) 1996. *Leisure interests:* education, gardening, public affairs, shooting, skiing. *Address:* Office of Fair Trading, Field House, Bream's Buildings, London, EC4A 1PR, England. *Telephone:* 0171-269 8919.

BRIDGEMAN, Viscountess Victoria Harriet, M.A., F.S.A.; British fine arts specialist and library executive; b. 30 March 1942, Co. Durham; d. of Ralph Meredyth Turton and Mary Blanche Turton (née Chetwynd-Stapylton); m. Viscount Bridgeman 1966; four s.; ed. St. Mary's School, Wantage, Trinity Coll., Dublin; Exec. Ed. The Masters 1965–69; Ed. Discovering Antiques 1970–72; est. own co. producing books and articles on fine and decorative arts; f., Man. Dir. The Bridgeman Art Library; European Woman of the Year (Arts Section) Award 1997. *Leisure interests:* reading, family, travel. *Publications:* Encyclopaedia of Victoriana, Needlework: An Illustrated History, The British Eccentric 1975, Society Scandals 1977, Beside the Seaside 1977, Guide to the Gardens of Europe 1980, The Last Word 1982 (all jtly. with Elizabeth Drury), eight titles in Connoisseur's Library series. *Address:* The Bridgeman Art Library, 17–19 Garway Road, London, W2 4PH (Office); 19 Chepstow Road, London, W2 5BP; Watley House, Sparsholt, Nr. Winchester, Hants., SO21 2LU, England. *Telephone:* 0171-727 4065 (Office); 0171-727 5400 (London); (01962) 776297 (Hants.). *Fax:* 0171-792 8509 (Office); (01962) 776297 (Hants.).

BRIDGES, 2nd Baron; **Thomas Edward Bridges,** G.C.M.G., M.A.; British diplomatist (retd.); b. 27 Nov. 1927, London; s. of Edward, 1st Baron Bridges, K.G., and Hon. Katharine D. Farrer; m. Rachel M. Bunbury 1953; two s. one d.; ed. Eton and New Coll., Oxford; joined diplomatic service 1951; served Bonn, Berlin, Rio de Janeiro, Athens and Moscow; Asst. Private Sec. to Foreign Sec. 1963–66; Private Sec. (Overseas Affairs) to Prime Minister 1972–74; Commercial Minister, Washington, D.C. 1976–79; Deputy Sec. (for int. econ. affairs), FCO 1979–83; Amb. to Italy Feb. 1983–87; Dir. Consolidated Gold Fields PLC 1988–89; mem. Select Cttee. on the European Communities, House of Lords 1988–92, 1994–; Chair. U.K. Nat. Cttee. of UNICEF 1989–97; Ind. Bd. mem. Securities and Futures Authority Ltd. 1989–97. *Address:* 56 Church Street, Orford, Woodbridge, Suffolk, IP12 2NT, England.

BRIDGES, Alan; British film director; b. 28 Sept. 1927; m. Eileen Middleton 1954; one s. one d.; dir. of numerous films and dramas for TV including The Intrigue, The Ballad of Peckham Rye, Alarm Call: Z Cars, The Brothers Karamazov, The Idiot, Days to Come, Great Expectations, Les Miserables, Dear Brutus etc. *Films include:* Act of Murder, Invasion, The Lie, The Wild Duck, Shelley, The Hireling (Golden Palm Award, Best Film, Cannes Festival 1973), Brief Encounter, Out of Season, Summer Rain, The Girl in Blue Velvet, Very Like a Whale, Rain on the Roof, The Return of the Soldier, The Shooting Party, Displaced Persons, Apt Pupil, Secret Places of the Heart, Fire Princess, Pig Robinson. *Address:* 2B High Street, Shepperton, Middx., TW7 9AW, England.

BRIDGES, Jeff; American actor; b. 4 Dec. 1949, Los Angeles; s. of the late Lloyd Bridges and of Dorothy Bridges; m. Susan Bridges; three d.; acting début at the age of 8. *Films include:* Halls of Anger 1970, The Last Picture Show 1971, Fat City 1971, Bad Company 1972, The Last American Hero 1973, The Iceman Cometh 1973, Thunderbolt and Lightfoot 1974, Hearts of the West 1975, Rancho Deluxe 1975, King Kong 1976, Stay Hungry 1976, Somebody Killed her Husband 1978, Winter Kills 1979, The American Success Company 1980, Heaven's Gate 1980, Cutter's Way 1981, Tron 1982, Kiss Me Goodbye 1982, The Last Unicorn 1982, Starman 1984, Against All Odds 1984, Jagged Edge 1985, 8 Million Ways to Die 1986, The Morning After 1986, Nadine 1987, Tucker, the Man and his Dream 1988, See You in the Morning 1990, Texasville 1990, The Fabulous Baker Boys 1990, The Fisher King 1991, American Heart, The Vanishing, Blown Away 1994, Fearless 1994, Wild Bill, White Squall 1995, The Mirror Has Two Faces 1996, The Big Lebowski 1997, Arlington Road 1998. *Address:* c/o Creative Artists Agency, 9830 Wilshire Boulevard, Beverly Hills, CA 90212, U.S.A.

BRIDGES, Sir Phillip Rodney, Kt., C.M.G., Q.C.; British lawyer; b. 9 July 1922; s. of Capt. Sir Ernest and Lady Bridges; m. 1st Rosemary Ann Streeten 1951 (dissolved 1961); two s. one d.; m. 2nd Angela Mary (née Dearden) Huyton; ed. Bedford School, England; army service 1941–47, Capt. Royal Artillery with Royal West African Frontier Force, W. Africa, India, Burma; admitted as solicitor England 1951; barrister and solicitor, The Gambia 1954; Solicitor-Gen. of The Gambia 1961, Attorney-Gen. 1964, Chief Justice 1968–82. *Address:* Weavers, Coney Weston, Bury St. Edmunds, Suffolk, England. *Telephone:* (01359) 221 316.

BRIERLEY, Sir Ronald Alfred, Kt.; New Zealand business executive; b. 2 Aug. 1937, Wellington; ed. Wellington Coll.; Chair. Brierley Investments Ltd. 1961–89 (Founder 1961, Founder Pres. 1990–); Deputy Chair. Bank of N.Z. 1987–89; Chair. Industrial Equity Pacific Ltd. 1966–90, Guinness Peat Gp. PLC 1990–, Tozer Kemsley & Millbourn Holdings PLC 1986, The Citizens & Graziers Life Assurance Co. Ltd. 1990–91; Dir. Ariadne Australia Ltd 1989–91, The Australian Gas Light Co. 1987–, Australian Oil & Gas Corpn. Ltd., Mid-East Minerals Ltd. 1992–, Metals Exploration Ltd. 1992–, Tyndall Australia Ltd. 1992–, Advance Bank Australia 1990–; mem. N.Z. Cricket Council, N.Z. Cricket Foundation; Dir. Sydney Cricket & Sports Ground Trust. *Leisure interests:* cricket, ballet, stamp collecting, chess. *Address:* Guinness Peat Group PLC, 2nd Floor, 21–26 Garlick Hill, London, EC4V 2AU, England.

BRIERS, Richard David, O.B.E.; British actor; b. 14 Jan. 1934, Merton; s. of Joseph Briers and Morna Richardson; m. Ann Davies 1957; two d.; ed. Rokeby Prep. School, Wimbledon, Ridgeway School, Wimbledon and Royal Acad. of Dramatic Art; London début in Gilt and Gingerbread, Duke of York's Theatre 1956; other stage roles include appearances in: Arsenic and Old Lace 1965, Relatively Speaking 1966, The Real Inspector Hound 1968, Cat Among the Pigeons 1969, The Two of Us 1970, Butley 1972, Absurd Person Singular 1973, Absent Friends 1975, Middle Age Spread 1979, The Wild Duck 1980, Arms and the Man 1981, Run for Your Wife 1983, Why Me? 1985, The Relapse 1986, Twelfth Night 1987, King Lear 1990, Midsummer Night's Dream 1990, Coriolanus 1991, Uncle Vanya 1991, Home 1994, A Christmas Carol 1996, The Chairs 1997; television series include: Brothers-in-Law, Marriage Lines, The Good Life, OneUpManShip, the Other One, Norman Conquests, Ever-Decreasing Circles, All in Good Faith, If You See God, Tell Him 1993. *Films:* Henry V 1988, Much Ado About Nothing 1992, Swan Song 1993, Mary Shelley's Frankenstein 1995, In the Bleak Midwinter 1995, Hamlet 1996. *Publications:* Natter Natter 1981, Coward and Company 1987, A Little Light Weeding 1993, A Taste of the Good Life 1995. *Leisure interests:* gardening, reading. *Address:* Hamilton Asper Management, Ground Floor, 24 Hanway Street, London, W1P 9DD, England. *Telephone:* 0171-636 1221.

BRIGGS, Baron (Life Peer), cr. 1976, of Lewes in the County of Sussex; **Asa Briggs,** M.A., B.SC., F.B.A.; British historian; b. 7 May 1921, Keighley, Yorks.; s. of William Walker Briggs and Jane Briggs; m. Susan Anne Banwell 1955; two s. two d.; ed. Keighley Grammar School and Sidney Sussex Coll., Cambridge; Fellow, Worcester Coll., Oxford 1945–55, Reader in Recent

Social and Econ. History, Univ. of Oxford 1950–55; Prof. of Modern History, Leeds Univ. 1955–61; Prof. of History, Univ. of Sussex 1961–76, Dean of Social Studies 1961–65, Pro-Vice-Chancellor 1961–67, Vice-Chancellor 1967–76; Provost Worcester Coll., Oxford 1976–91; Chancellor, Open Univ. 1979–94; Pres. Workers Educational Asscn. 1958–67; Chair. Appts. Comm. Press Council 1972–88; mem. Univ. Grants Cttee. 1959–67; Trustee, Int. Broadcast Inst. 1968–86; Gov. British Film Inst. 1970–76, Hon. Trustee 1990–; Chair. European Inst. of Educ. 1974–84; mem. Council of UN Univ. 1974–80; Chair. Cttee. on Nursing 1970–72, Heritage Educ. Group 1976–86, Commonwealth of Learning 1988–93; Pres. Social History Soc. 1976–, Ephemera Soc. 1984–, Victorian Soc. 1983–; Vice-Pres. Historical Asscn. 1986–; Vice-Chair. of Council, UN Univ. 1974–80; Hon. mem. American Acad. of Arts and Sciences 1970–; Hon. LL.D., Hon. D.Litt., Hon. D.Sc.; Marconi Medal for Services to Study of Broadcasting 1975; Medal of French Acad. for Architecture 1982. *Publications:* Patterns of Peacemaking (with D. Thomson and E. Meyer) 1945, History of Birmingham, 1865-1938 1952, Victorian People 1954, Friends of the People 1956, The Age of Improvement 1959, Ed. Chartist Studies 1959, History of Broadcasting, Vol. I 1961, Vol. II 1965, Vol. III 1970, Vol. IV 1979, Vol. V 1995, Victorian Cities 1963, The Nineteenth Century (editor) 1970, Cap and Bell (with Susan Briggs) 1972, Essays in the History of Publishing (editor) 1974, Essays in Labour History 1918–1939 1977, Governing the BBC 1979, From Coalbrookdale to the Crystal Palace 1980, The Power of Steam 1982, Marx in London 1982, A Social History of England 1983 (revised edn. 1994) (Haut-Brion: An Illustrious Lineage 1994), The BBC—The First Fifty Years 1985, The Collected Essays of Asa Briggs, (vol. 1, 2, 3), The Franchise Affair (with Joanna Spicer) 1986, Victorian Things 1988, The Longman Encyclopedia (ed.) 1989, The Channel Islands: Occupation and Liberation 1940–45 1995, Fins de Siècle (co-ed.) 1996; co-author Modern Europe 1789–1989 1996, The History of Bethlem 1997. *Leisure interest:* travel. *Address:* The Caprons, Keere Street, Lewes, Sussex, England (Home). *Telephone:* (01273) 474704 (Home). *Fax:* (01273) 814462.

BRIGGS, Raymond Redvers, N.D.D., D.F.A.; British writer, illustrator and cartoonist; b. 18 Jan. 1934, Wimbledon; s. of Ernest R. Briggs and Ethel Bowyer; m. Jean T. Clark 1963 (died 1973); ed. Rutlish School, Merton, Wimbledon School of Art and Slade School of Fine Art, London; free-lance illustrator 1957–; children's author 1961–; awards include Kate Greenaway Medal 1966, 1973, B.A.F.T.A. Award, Francis Williams Illustration Award (Victoria & Albert Museum) 1982, Broadcasting Press Guild Radio Award 1983, Children's Author of the Year 1992, Kurt Maschler Award 1992. *Publications*: The Strange House, 1961, Midnight Adventure 1961, Sledges to the Rescue 1963, Ring-a-Ring o' Roses 1962, The White Land 1963, Fee Fi Fo Fum 1964, The Mother Goose Treasury 1966, Jim and the Beanstalk 1970, The Fairy Tale Treasury 1972, Father Christmas 1973, Father Christmas Goes on Holiday 1975, Fungus the Bogeyman 1977, The Snowman 1978, Gentleman Jim 1980, When the Wind Blows 1982 (stage and radio version 1983, animated film version 1987), The Tinpot Foreign General and the Old Iron Woman 1984, The Snowman Pop-Up 1986, Unlucky Wally 1987, Unlucky Wally Twenty Years On 1989, The Man 1992, The Bear 1994, Ethel and Ernest 1998. *Leisure interests*: second-hand books, walking, gardening. *Address*: Weston, Underhill Lane, Westmeston, nr. Hassocks, Sussex, England.

BRIGGS, Winslow Russell, M.A., PH.D.; American biologist; b. 29 April 1928, St. Paul, Minn.; s. of John Briggs and Marjorie (Winslow) Briggs; m. Ann Morrill 1955; three d.; ed. Harvard Univ.; Instructor in Biological Sciences, Stanford Univ. 1955–57, Asst. Prof. 1957–62, Assoc. Prof. 1962–66, Prof. 1966–67; Prof. of Biology, Harvard Univ. 1967–73, Stanford Univ. 1973–93; Dir. Dept. of Plant Biology, Carnegie Inst. of Washington, Stanford 1973–93; Guggenheim Fellow 1973–74; mem. Nat. Acad. of Sciences; Stephen Hales Award American Society of Plant Physiologists 1994, Sterling Hendricks Award, American Chem. Soc. and U.S. Dept. of Agric. 1995. *Publications:* Life on Earth (with others) 1973; articles in professional journals. *Leisure interests:* hiking, Chinese cooking. *Address:* Department of Plant Biology, Carnegie Institution of Washington, 260 Panama St., Stanford, CA 94305; 480 Hale Street, Palo Alto, CA 94301, U.S.A.

BRIGHTMAN, Baron (Life Peer), cr. 1982, of Ibthorpe in the County of Hampshire; **John Anson Brightman,** Kt., P.C.; British lawyer; b. 20 June 1911, St. Albans, Herts.; s. of William Henry Brightman and Minnie Boston (née Way) Brightman; m. Roxane Ambatielo 1945; one s.; ed. Marlborough Coll., St John's Coll., Cambridge; called to the bar, Lincoln's Inn 1932; Able Seaman 1939–40; Lieut.-Commdr. R.N.V.R. 1940–46; Asst. Naval Attaché Ankara 1944; Q.C. 1961; Bencher 1966; Attorney-Gen., Duchy of Lancaster, and Attorney and Serjeant within the County Palatine of Lancaster 1969–70; a Lord Justice of Appeal 1979–82; a Lord of Appeal in Ordinary 1982–86; Judge, Nat. Industrial Relations Court 1971–74; mem. Gen. Council of the Bar 1956–60, 1966–70, Cttee. on Parl. Procedures for Tax Simplification 1996; Hon. Fellow, St. John's Coll., Cambridge 1982. *Leisure interests:* arctic travel, sailing, skiing, mountain walking. *Address:* House of Lords, London, SW1A 0PW, England. *Telephone:* 0171-219 2034.

BRIGHTMAN, Sarah; British actress and singer; d. of Grenville Brightman and Pauline Brightman (née Hall); m. Andrew Lloyd Webber (q.v.), 1984 (divorced 1990); partner Frank Peterson; fmr. mem. Pan's People and Hot Gossip groups. *Performances include:* Cats, Requiem, The Phantom of the Opera, Aspects of Love (music all by Andrew Lloyd Webber), I and Albert, The Nightingale, The Merry Widow, Trelawney of the Wells, Relative Values, Dangerous Obsession; concerts world-wide. *Address:* c/o Sunhand Limited, 63 Grosvenor Street, London, W1X 9DA, England. *Telephone:* 0171-493 7831.

BRIGHTY, (Anthony) David, C.M.G., C.V.O.; British diplomatist (retd.); b. 7 Feb. 1939; m. 1st Diana Porteous 1963 (divorced 1979, died 1993); two s. two d.; m. 2nd Jane Docherty 1982 (divorced 1996); m. 3rd Susan Olivier 1997; ed. Clare Coll. Cambridge; entered FCO 1961; Third Sec. Brussels 1962–64; Third Sec. Havana 1964–66, Second Sec. 1966–67; FCO 1967–69; Asst. Man. S.G. Warburg & Co. 1969–71; FCO 1971–73; Head of Chancery, Saigon 1973–75; First Sec. U.K. Mission, New York 1975–78; Royal Coll. of Defence Studies 1979; FCO 1979–83; Counsellor, Lisbon 1983–86; Dir. of Cabinet of Sec.-Gen. to NATO, FCO 1986–87; Amb. to Cuba 1989–91; Amb. to Czech Repub. and Slovakia (non-resident) 1991–94; Amb. to Spain and Andorra (non-resident) 1994–98. *Address:* 15 Provost Road, London, NW3 4ST, England.

BRILLINGER, David Ross, PH.D., F.R.S.C.; Canadian professor of statistics; b. 27 Oct. 1937, Toronto; s. of Austin C. Brillinger and Winnifred E. Simpson; m. Lorie Silber 1961; two s.; ed. Univ. of Toronto and Princeton Univ.; lecturer in Math. Princeton Univ., concurrently mem. tech. staff, Bell Telephone Labs. 1962–64; lecturer, then Reader, London School of Econs. 1964–69; Prof. of Statistics, Univ. of Calif. Berkeley 1969–; Guggenheim Fellow 1975–76, 1982–83; Fellow American Acad. of Arts and Sciences 1993; Wald Lecturer 1983; R. A. Fisher Award 1991, Gold Medal, Statistical Soc. of Canada 1992. *Publications:* Time Series: Data Analysis and Theory 1975, Directions in Time Series 1980; ed. International Statistical Review 1987–91. *Publications:* Time Series: Data Analysis and Theory 1975, Directions in Time Series 1980. *Address:* Department of Statistics, University of California, Berkeley, CA 94720, U.S.A. *Telephone:* (510) 642-0611.

BRIM, Orville Gilbert, PH.D.; American foundation administrator and author; b. 7 April 1923, Elmira, New York; s. of Orville Gilbert and Helen Whittier Brim; m. Kathleen J. Vigneron 1944; two s. two d.; ed. Yale Univ.; Instructor in Sociology, Univ. of Wis. 1952–53, Asst. Prof., Sociology 1953–55; Sociologist, Russell Sage Foundation, New York 1955–60, Asst. Sec. 1960–64, Pres. 1964–72; author and consultant 1972–74; Pres. Foundation for Child Devt. 1974–85; Chair., Bd. of Dirs., Automation Eng. Lab. 1959–67, Special Comm. on the Social Sciences, Nat. Science Foundation 1968–69; mem. Drug Research Bd., N.A.S. 1964–65; Vice-Chair., Bd. of Trustees, American Insts. for Research 1971–88, Chair. 1988–90; MacArthur Foundation Research Cttee. on Successful Aging 1985–90; Dir. McArthur Foundation Research Network on Successful Midlife Devt. 1990–; Pres. Life Trends Inc. 1991–; Interim Pres. Social Science Research Council 1998–99; Kurt Lewin Memorial Award 1979; Soc. Research in Child Devt. Award for Distinguished Scientific Contribs. to Child Devt. Research 1985. *Publications:* Sociology and the Field of Education 1958, Education for Child Rearing 1959, Personality and Decision Processes 1962, Intelligence: Perspectives 1964, Socialization after Childhood: Two Essays 1966, American Beliefs and Attitudes Toward Intelligence 1969, The Dying Patient 1979; Ed.: Lifespan Development and Behavior, Vols. 2–5 1979–83, Constancy and Change in Human Development 1980, Ambition: How we manage success and failure throughout our lives 1992. *Leisure interests:* sports and world ocean beaches. *Address:* Life Trends, Inc., P.O. Box 2846, Vero Beach, FL 32960 (Office); 503 River Drive, Vero Beach, FL 32963, U.S.A. (Home). *Telephone:* (561) 778-8899 (Office); (561) 231-3329 (Home).

BRINDLE, Ian, F.C.A., B.A.; British business executive; b. 17 Aug. 1943; s. of John Brindle and Mabel (née Walsh) Brindle; m. Frances Elisabeth Moseby 1967; two s. one d.; ed. Blundells School, Manchester Univ.; articled Price Waterhouse London 1965, Toronto 1975, admitted to partnership 1976, mem. Supervisory Cttee. 1988–, Dir. Auditing and Business Advisory Services 1990–91, Sr. Partner 1991–; mem. Auditing Practices Cttee. Consultancy Cttee. of Accounting Bodies 1986–90, Chair. 1990; mem. Accounting Standards Bd. 1993–; mem. Council Inst. of Chartered Accountants in England and Wales; mem. Financial Reporting Council 1995–; Auditor Duchy of Cornwall 1993–. *Leisure interests:* tennis, golf. *Address:* Price Waterhouse, Southwark Towers, 32 London Bridge Street, London, SE1 9SY (Office); Milestones, Packhorse Road, Bessels Green, Sevenoaks, Kent, TN13 2QP, England (Home).

BRINDLEY, Giles Skey, M.A., M.D., F.R.C.P., F.R.S.; British physiologist; b. 30 April 1926; s. of late Arthur James Benet and Dr. Margaret Beatrice Marion Skey; m. 1st Lucy Dunk Bennell 1959 (dissolved); m. 2nd Dr. Hilary Richards 1964; one s. one d.; ed. Leyton Co. High School, Downing Coll., Cambridge, London Hosp. Medical School; clinical and research posts 1950–54; Russian Language Abstractor, British Abstracts of Medical Sciences 1953–56; Demonstrator, then Lecturer and Reader in Physiology, Univ. of Cambridge 1954–68; Prof. of Physiology, Univ. of London Inst. of Psychiatry 1968–91, Prof. Emer. 1991–; Hon. Dir. MRC Neurological Prostheses Unit 1968–92; partner Brindley Surgical Implants 1991–; Hon. Consultant Physician Maudsley Hosp. 1971–92; Hon. F.R.C.S. 1988; Fellow King's Coll., Cambridge 1959–62, Trinity Coll., Cambridge 1963–68; Chair. Editorial Bd. Journal of Physiology 1964–66; Visiting Prof. Univ. of Calif., Berkeley 1968; Liebrecht-Franceschetti Prize, German Ophthalmological Soc. 1971, Feldberg Prize, Feldberg Foundation 1974, St. Peter's Medal, British Asscn. of Urological Surgeons 1987. *Publications:* Physiology of the Retina and Visual Pathway 1960, numerous scientific papers. *Leisure* *interests:* skiing, designing and playing musical instruments. *Address:* 102 Ferndene Road, London, SE24 0AA, England. *Telephone:* 0171-274 2598. *Fax:* 0171-738 6116.

BRINK, André Philippus; South African writer; b. 29 May 1935, Vrede; s. of Daniel and Aletta (née Wolmarans) Brink; m.; three s. one d.; ed. Potchefstroom Univ., Sorbonne, Paris; began writing at an early age; first novel (Afrikaans) published 1958; on return from Paris became mem. and spokesman of young Afrikaans writers' group Sestigers; returned to Paris 1968; went back to South Africa to resist apartheid through writing; novel Kennis van die Aand banned 1973 (first Afrikaans novel to be banned); began to write in English as well; dir. several plays, but abandoned theatre owing to censorship; resumed playwriting 1996; founder-mem. Afrikaans Writers' Guild; Prof. of Afrikaans and Dutch Literature, Rhodes Univ. (previously lecturer) 1980–89; Prof. of English, Univ. of Cape Town 1990–; C.N.A. Award for Literature, South Africa 1965, 1978 and 1982, Martin Luther King Memorial Prize 1979, Prix Médicis Etranger, France 1979; Légion d'honneur 1983; Commdr. Ordre des Arts et des Lettres 1992; Hon. D.Litt. (Witwatersrand Univ.) 1992, (Univ. of Free State) 1997; Biannual Freedom of Speech Prize by Monismanien Foundation, University of Uppsala 1991, Premio Mondello (Italy) 1997. *Publications include:* novels: Looking on Darkness 1974, An Instant in the Wind 1976, Rumours of Rain 1978, A Dry White Season 1979, A Chain of Voices 1982, Mapmakers (essays) 1983, The Wall of the Plague 1984, The Ambassador 1985, States of Emergency 1988, An Act of Terror 1991, The First Life of Adamastor 1993, On the Contrary 1993, Imaginings of Sand 1996, Reinventing a Continent (essays) 1996, Devil's Valley 1998; several plays 1965–75, The Jogger 1997. *Address:* Department of English, University of Cape Town, Rondebosch 7700, South Africa. *Fax:* (021) 685 3945.

BRINK, Andries Jacob, M.D., F.R.C.P., D.SC.; South African professor of medicine; b. 29 Aug. 1923, Potchefstroom; s. of Andries J. Brink and Petronella J. Havenga; m. Maria Ruskovich 1949; two s. two d.; ed. Jeppe High School, Univs. of Witwatersrand, Pretoria, and Stellenbosch; Post-Graduate Medical School, Hammersmith Hosp., London 1951; Fellow in Paediatrics, Johns Hopkins Hosp., U.S.A. 1952; Internist, Sr. Lecturer, Univ. of Pretoria 1953–56; Founder Prof. Dept. of Medicine, Univ. of Stellenbosch 1956, Chief Cardiologist and Founder, Dept. of Cardiology 1956–78, Dean, Faculty of Medicine 1971–83; Dir. Molecular and Cellular Cardiac Research Unit, MRC 1956–69; Pres. (part-time) S.A. Medical Research Council 1969–83, Full-time Pres. 1984–89; Man. Dir. Clinics Cardive Publishing Co. 1990–; Tygerberg Clinical Trial Centre 1991–; Nat. Dir. MC Research Pty. Ltd. 1998–; mem. Bd. Scientific Advisory Council 1972–83, 1990–94; S.A. Medical and Dental Council 1971–83; Founder Heart Foundation of S.A.; Founder-Ed. Cardiovascular Journal of S.A.; D.Sc. h.c. (Natal) 1976, (Potchefstroom); 35 major awards and prizes, including Recht Malan Award, (for Dictionary of Afrikaans Medical Terms), Merit Awards (Gold), S.A. Medical Research Council 1986; Decoration for Meritorious Service. *Publications:* 120 scientific and general medical publications, including 6 books and Medical Dictionary. *Leisure interests:* reading, music, cycling, painting, oenology, viticulture. *Address:* P.O. Box 62, Durbanville, 7550 (Office); 13 Lindenberg Avenue, Durbanville 7550, South Africa (Home). *Telephone:* (021) 96-8129 (Office); (021) 96-1786 (Home). *Fax:* (021) 96-8984.

BRINK, David Maurice, D.PHIL., F.R.S.; British physicist; b. 20 July 1930, Tasmania, Australia; s. of Maurice Ossian Brink and Victoria May (née Finlayson) Brink; m. Verena Wehrli 1958; one s. two d.; ed. Friends' School, Hobart, Univ. of Tasmania, Univ. of Oxford; Rhodes Scholar 1951–54, Rutherford Scholar 1954–58; Lecturer, Balliol Coll., Oxford 1954–58, Fellow and Tutor 1958–93; Instructor M.I.T. 1956–57; Moseley Reader in Theoretical Physics 1989–93; Prof. of History in Physics Trento Univ., Italy 1993–98; Rutherford Medal and Prize, Inst. of Physics 1982. *Publications:* Angular Momentum 1962, Nuclear Forces 1965, Semi-Classical Methods in Nucleus—Nucleus Scattering 1985. *Leisure interests:* bird-watching, mountaineering. *Address:* 34 Minster Road, Oxford, OX4 1LY, England (Home). *Telephone:* (01865) 246127 (Home).

BRINK, Frank, Jr., B.S., M.S., PH.D.; American biophysicist; b. 4 Nov. 1910, Easton, Pa.; s. of Frank Brink, Sr., and Lydia (Wilhelm) Brink; m. Marjory Gaylord 1939; one s. one d.; ed. Easton High School, Pennsylvania State Univ., Calif. Inst. of Tech. and Univ. of Pennsylvania; Research Asst. Johnson Research Foundation, Univ. of Pennsylvania 1937–38; Fellow 1938–40; Instructor in Physiology, Cornell Medical Coll., New York City 1940–41; Johnson Foundation Fellow and Lecturer in Biophysics, Univ. of Pa. 1941–47, Asst. Prof. 1947–48; Assoc. Prof. Johns Hopkins Univ. 1948–53; Prof. and mem. Rockefeller Inst. (now Univ.) 1953–81, acting Dean of Graduate Studies 1954–58, Dean of Graduate Studies 1958–72, Detlev W. Bronk Prof. 1974–81, Prof. Emer. July 1981–; White Fellowship, Pa. State Coll. (now Univ.); Lalor Fellowship, Univ. of Pa.; mem. Nat. Acad. of Sciences, American Acad. of Arts and Sciences; Hon. D.Sc. (Rockefeller Univ.) 1983. *Publications:* articles in scientific journals. *Leisure interest:* reading. *Address:* Pine Run, Apt. E-1, Ferry and Iron Hill Roads, Doylestown, PA 18901, U.S.A. (Home). *Telephone:* (215) 348-1792 (Home).

BRINKHUES, Josef; German ecclesiastic; b. 21 June 1913, Aachen; s. of Heinrich Brinkhues and Cläre (neé Führen); m. Dr. Ilse Volckmar 1946; one s. one d.; ed. Frankfurt and Bonn; ordained priest 1937; consecrated bishop 1966; mem. Int. Old Catholics Bishops' Conf. of Utrecht Union 1966–1986; Bishop Emer. of Old-Catholic Church in Germany. *Leisure interest:* music. *Address:* Oberdorf 18, 53347 Impekoven/Alfter, Germany. *Telephone:* (0228) 64 33 01.

BRINKLEY, David; American broadcaster (retd.); b. 10 July 1920, Wilmington, N.C.; s. of William G. Brinkley and Mary West; m. 1st Ann Fischer 1946; three s.; m. 2nd Susan Adolph 1972; one c.; reporter, Wilmington, N.C. Star-News 1938–41; reporter, bureau man. various cities, United Press Asscn. 1941–43; news writer, broadcaster, radio and TV, NBC, Washington 1943–, Washington Corresp. 1951–81; Anchorman, This Week (ABC) 1981–97; duPont Award, Peabody Award, and other awards for journalism; Presidential Medal of Freedom 1992. *Publications:* David Brinkley (autobiog.) 1996, David Brinkley's Homilies 1996, Everybody is Entitled to my Opinion 1996. *Address:* c/o ABC News, 1717 DeSales Street, N.W., Washington, DC 20036, U.S.A.

BRINKMAN, Leonard Cornelis (Eelco), DR. RER.POL.; Netherlands politician; b. 5 Feb. 1948, Dirksland; m. J. Salentijn; three c.; ed. Gymnasium, Dordrecht, Free Univ., Amsterdam; research post in the Public Admin. Dept., Free Univ. 1969–74; mem. Co-ordination Office for North of West Holland conurbation 1974–75; Head of Office of Sec.-Gen., Ministry of Home Affairs 1976–79, Dir.-Gen. Jan. 1980–82; Minister for Welfare, Health and Cultural Affairs 1982–89; Christian Democratic Alliance. *Publications:* articles on public admin. in specialist journals. *Address:* c/o Ministry of Welfare, Public Health and Culture, Sir Winston Churchilllaan 362-366, P.O.B. 5406, 2280 EH Rijswijk, Netherlands.

BRISVILLE, Jean-Claude Gabriel; French author; b. 28 May 1922, Bois-Colombes/Hauts-de-Seine; s. of Maurice Brisville and Geneviève Gineste; m. 2nd Irène Kalaschnikowa 1963; one s. one d. by first m.; ed. Lycée Jacques Decour, Paris; literary journalist 1946–; Reader, Hachette 1951–58; Sec. to Albert Camus 1957–59; Deputy Literary Dir. Juillard 1959–64, Literary Dir. 1964–70; Head of Drama Video Section, ORTF 1971–75; Literary Dir. Livre de poche 1976–81; Chevalier des Arts et des Lettres; Prix du Théâtre de la Société des Auteurs et Compositeurs Dramatiques (SACD). *Publications:* narrative works: Prologue 1948, D'un amour (Prix Sainte-Beuve) 1954, La Fuite au Danemark 1962, La Zone d'ombre 1976; plays: Le Fauteuil à bascule (Prix Ibsen, Prix de la meilleure création dramatique) 1982, Le Bonheur à Romorantin, L'entretien de M. Descartes avec M. Pascal le jeune, La Villa bleue, Les Liaisons dangereuses (adaptation), Le Souper (Prix du Théâtre, Acad. Française) 1990, L'Officier de la Garde 1990, L'Antichambre 1991, Contre-jour 1993, Dernière Salve 1995; essays; stories for children. *Address:* SACD, 12 rue Ballu, 75009 Paris, France.

BRITTAN, Rt. Hon. Sir Leon, Kt., P.C., Q.C.; British politician and barrister; b. 25 Sept. 1939, London; s. of the late Dr. Joseph Brittan and of Rebecca Brittan; brother of Sir Samuel Brittan (q.v.); m. Diana Peterson 1980; two step-d.; ed. Haberdashers' Aske's School, Trinity Coll., Cambridge, Yale Univ.; Chair. Cambridge Univ. Conservative Asscn. 1960; Pres. Cambridge Union 1960, debating tour of U.S.A. 1961; called to Bar, Inner Temple 1962 (Bencher 1983); Chair. Bow Group 1964–65; contested N. Kensington seat 1966, 1970; Ed. Crossbow 1966–68; mem. Political Cttee. Carlton Club, Cttee. of the British Atlantic Group of Young Politicians 1970–78; Vice-Chair. of Govs. of Isaac Newton School 1968–71; M.P. for Cleveland and Whitby 1974–83, for Richmond (N. Yorks.) 1983–89; Queen's Counsel 1978; apptd. mem. Privy Council 1981; U.K. Commr. with responsibility for Competition Policy and Financial Insts., Comm. of the European Communities (now European Comm.) 1989–92, for Econ. Relations 1993–94, for External Trade (with N. America and parts of Asia) Jan. 1995–, a Vice-Pres. 1989–; Vice-Chair. Parl. Conservative Party Employment Cttee. 1974–76; Opposition Spokesman on Devolution and House of Commons Affairs 1976–78, on Devolution and Employment 1978–79; Minister of State, Home Office 1979–81; Chief Sec. to the Treasury 1981–83, Home Sec. 1983–85; Sec. of State for Trade and Industry 1985–86; Dir. Phicom 1987–; Distinguished Visiting Fellow Inst. of Policy Studies 1988; Hersch Lauterpacht Memorial Lecturer, Univ. of Cambridge 1990; Chair. Soc. of Conservative Lawyers 1986–89; Vice-Chair. Nat. Asscn. of School Govs. and Mans. 1970–78; Chancellor Univ. of Teesside 1993–; Hon. D.C.L. (Newcastle) 1990, (Durham) 1992; Hon. LL.D. (Hull) 1990, (Bath) 1995; Dr. h.c. (Edinburgh) 1991; Hon. D.L. (Bradford) 1992; Hon. D.Econ. (Korea Univ.). *Publications:* contributed to The Conservative Opportunity, jt. author Milestones for the Sixties, Rough Justice, Infancy and the Law, How to Save your Schools, A New Deal for Health Care 1988, Defence and Arms Control in a Changing Era 1988, Discussions on Policy 1989, Monetary Union: the Issues and the Impact 1989, Europe: Our Sort of Community (Granada Guildhall Lecture) 1989, Hersch Lauterpacht Memorial Lectures (Cambridge Univ.) 1990, European Competition Policy 1992, Europe: The Europe We Need 1994. *Leisure interests:* walking, cricket, opera. *Address:* European Commission, 200 rue de la Loi, 1049 Brussels, Belgium.

BRITTAN, Sir Samuel, Kt., M.A.; British economist and journalist; b. 29 Dec. 1933, London; brother of Sir Leon Brittan (q.v.); ed. Kilburn Grammar School, Jesus Coll., Cambridge; journalist on The Financial Times 1955–61, prin. economic commentator 1966–, Asst. Ed. 1978–; Econs. Ed. The Observer 1961–64; Adviser, Dept. of Econ. Affairs 1965; Research Fellow, Nuffield Coll. 1973–74, Visiting Fellow 1974–82; Visiting Prof., Chicago Law School, U.S.A. 1978; Hon. Prof. of Politics Univ. of Warwick 1987–92; Hon. Fellow Jesus Coll., Cambridge 1988; mem. Peacock Cttee. on Finance of the BBC

1985–86; Hon. D. Litt. (Heriot-Watt Univ.) 1985; first winner Sr. Wincott Award for financial journalists 1971, Ludwig Erhard Prize 1987, George Orwell Prize for political journalism 1980. *Publications:* Steering the Economy, Left or Right: The Bogus Dilemma 1968, The Price of Economic Freedom: A Guide to Flexible Rates 1970, Is There an Economic Consensus? 1973, Capitalism and the Permissive Society 1973 (new edn. A Restatement of Economic Liberalism 1988), The Delusion of Incomes Policy (with Peter Lilley) 1977, The Economic Consequences of Democracy 1977, How to End the 'Monetarist' Controversy 1981, Role and Limits of Government: Essays in Political Economy 1983, There Is No Such Thing As Society 1993, Capitalism with a Human Face 1995. *Address:* The Financial Times, Number 1, Southwark Bridge, London, SE1 9HL, England. *Telephone:* 0171-873 3000.

BRITTEN, Roy John, PH.D.; American biophysicist and molecular biologist; b. 1 Oct. 1919, Washington, D.C.; s. of Rollo H. Britten and Marion (Hale) Britten; m. (divorced); two s.; m. 2nd Jacqueline Aymar Reid 1986; ed. Univ. of Virginia, Johns Hopkins and Princeton Univs.; staff mem. Biophysics Group, Dept. of Terrestrial Magnetism, Carnegie Inst. of Washington 1951–71; inventor, quadrupole focusing of energetic beams; discoverer, repeated DNA sequences in genomes of higher organisms; Visiting Assoc. Calif. Inst. of Tech. and staff mem. Dept. of Terrestrial Magnetism, Carnegie Inst. of Washington 1971–73; Sr. Research Assoc. Calif. Inst. of Tech. and staff mem. Carnegie Inst. of Washington 1973–81; Distinguished Carnegie Sr. Research Assoc. in Biology, Calif. Inst. of Tech. and staff mem. Carnegie Inst. of Washington 1981–; Adjunct Prof. Univ. of Calif., Irvine 1992–; mem. N.A.S., Acad. Arts and Sciences. *Publications:* articles in professional journals. *Leisure interests:* inventing, sailing. *Address:* Kerckhoff Marine Laboratory, California Institute of Technology, 101 Dahlia Avenue, Corona del Mar, CA 92625, U.S.A. *Telephone:* (949) 675 2159.

BRIZOLA, Leonel; Brazilian politician; b. 1922, Carazinho, Rio Grande do Sul; s. of the late José Brizola; m. Neusa Goulart 1950; ed. Tech. School, Porto Alegre; shoeshine boy; warehouse labourer; joined Brazilian Labour Party (PTB) 1945; State Deputy, Constituent Ass., Rio Grande do Sul; State Sec. for Public Works; elected Fed. Deputy 1954; Mayor of Porto Alegre 1955; Gov. Rio Grande do Sul 1958; Fed. Deputy, State of Guanabara, Rio de Janeiro 1962; exiled for attempt to org. armed resistance to mil. regime 1964; lived in Uruguay until 1977; expelled from Uruguay under pressure from Brazilian military 1977; lived in Lisbon 1977–79; returned to Brazil 1979; Leader, Democratic Labour Party (PDT); Vice-Pres. Socialist Int. 1979; Gov. Rio de Janeiro 1982–86. *Address:* Partido Democrático Trabalhista, Rua 7 de Septembro 141, 4°, 20050 Rio de Janeiro, R.J., Brazil.

BROACKES, Sir Nigel, Kt.; British businessman; b. 21 July, 1934, Wakefield; s. of the late Donald and Nan Broackes; m. Joyce Horne 1956 (died 1993); two s. one d.; ed. Stowe School; with Stewart & Hughman Ltd. 1952–55; Man. Dir. Trafalgar House Investments Ltd. 1958, Deputy Chair. and Jt. Man. Dir. 1968, Chair. 1968–92, Hon. Pres. 1992–; Chair. London Docklands Urban Devt. Corpn. 1981–84, Ship and Marine Tech. Requirements Bd. 1972–77; Deputy Chair. Offshore Energy Tech. Bd. 1975–77; non-exec. Dir. The Distillers Co. PLC 1985–86; British Chair. Euroroute 1984–86; mem. Advisory Council, Victoria and Albert Museum 1980–83; Chair. Crafts Council 1991–97; Trustee Nat. Maritime Museum 1987–96; fmr. Trustee Royal Opera House Trust. *Publication:* A Growing Concern 1979. *Address:* 41 Chelsea Square, London, SW3 6LH; Checkendon Court, Checkendon, Nr. Reading, Oxon., RG8 0SR, England.

BROADBENT, Edward Granville, M.A., SC.D., F.R.AE.S., F.I.M.A., F.R.S., F.ENG.; British scientist; b. 27 June 1923, Huddersfield, Yorks.; s. of Joseph C. F. and Lucetta (née Riley) Broadbent; m. Elizabeth B. Puttick 1949; ed. Huddersfield Coll. and St. Catharine's Coll., Cambridge; Govt. Scientist, Royal Aircraft Establishment, Farnborough 1943–83, Deputy Chief Scientific Officer (Aerodynamics Dept.) 1969–83, Consultant 1983–85; Visiting Prof. Dept. of Math., Imperial Coll., London 1983–; Consultant, Royal Armament Research and Defence Establishment, Fort Halstead 1983–85; fmr. F.R.S.A.; Simms, Wakefield and Gold Medals, Royal Aeronautical Soc. *Publications*: various scientific papers. *Leisure interests*: music, theatre, chess, duplicate bridge, garden. *Address*: Imperial College, Huxley Building, Queen's Gate, London, SW7 2BZ (Office); 11 Three Stiles Road, Farnham, Surrey, GU9 7DE, England (Home). *Telephone*: 0171-594 8501 (Office); (01252) 714621.

BROADBENT, Hon. John Edward, O.C., PH.D.; Canadian politician and professor; b. 21 March 1936, Oshawa, Ont.; s. of Percy E. Broadbent and Mary A. Welsh; m. Lucille Munroe 1971; one s. one d.; ed. High School in Oshawa, Univ. of Toronto, London School of Econs. and Political Science; Prof. of Political Science, York Univ., Ont. 1965–68; mem. House of Commons 1968–89; Co-Chair. Policy Review Cttee. for New Democratic Party Fed. Convention 1969; Chair. Fed. Caucus 1972–74, Parl. Leader of Fed. Caucus 1974–75; Nat. Leader of New Democratic Party 1975–89; Vice-Pres. Socialist Int. 1978–90, Hon. Pres. 1991–; Pres. Int. Centre for Human Rights and Democratic Devt. 1990–96; J. S. Woodsworth Chair. Inst. for the Humanities, Simon Fraser Univ. 1997–; LL.D. h.c. (Dalhousie Univ.) 1990, (York Univ.) 1991, D.Litt. (Trinity Coll., Oxford Univ.) 1990, (Toronto Univ.) 1990. *Publications:* The Liberal Rip-Off 1970. *Leisure interests:* reading contemporary fiction, listening to music, skiing. *Address:* 1386 Nicola, Apt. 30, Vancouver, B.C., V6G 2G2, Canada.

BROCK, William Emerson, B.S.; American politician; b. 23 Nov. 1930, Chattanooga; s. of William Emerson Jr. and Myra (Kruesi) Brock; m. 1st Laura Handly 1957 (deceased); three s. one d.; m. 2nd Sandra S. Mitchell 1986; ed. McCallie School and Washington and Lee Univ.; with Brock Candy Co., Chattanooga 1956–63; mem. House of Reps. 1963–71; U.S. Senator from Tenn. 1971–77; Chair. Republican Nat. Cttee. 1977–80; U.S. Trade Rep. (Cabinet status) 1981–85; U.S. Sec. of Labor 1985–87; Chair. Dole for Pres. Cttee. 1987–88; Chair. The Brock Group 1987–. *Address:* 1155 Connecticut Avenue, N.W., Washington, DC 20036, U.S.A.

BROCK, William Ranulf, M.A., PH.D., F.B.A., F.R.HIST.S.; British historian; b. 16 May 1916, Farnham, Surrey; s. of Stewart E. Brock and Katherine Temple Roberts; m. Constance H. Brown 1950; one s. one d.; ed. Christ's Hospital, Horsham and Trinity Coll. Cambridge; Fellow, Selwyn Coll. Cambridge 1947–, Life Fellow 1967; Prof. of Modern History, Univ. of Glasgow 1967–81, Prof. Emer. 1981–. *Publications:* Lord Liverpool and Liberal Toryism 1941, Character of American History 1960, An American Crisis 1865–67 1963, Conflict and Transformations, U.S.A. 1844–77 1973, Parties and Political Conscience 1979, Scotus Americanus 1981, Investigation and Responsibility 1984, Welfare, Democracy and the New Deal 1988, Selwyn College: a history (with P. H. M. Cooper) 1994. *Leisure interest:* antiques. *Address:* 49 Barton Road, Cambridge, CB3 9LG, England. *Telephone:* (01223) 313606.

BROCKES, Jeremy Patrick, PH.D., F.R.S.; British biologist; b. 29 Feb. 1948, Haslemere; s. of Bernard Brockes and Edna Heaney; ed. St. John's Coll., Cambridge, Edinburgh Univ.; asst., then Assoc. Prof. of Biology Caltech 1978–83; mem. MRC Biophysics Unit, King's Coll., London 1983–88; mem. Ludwig Inst. for Cancer Research 1988–97; Prof. of Cell Biology Univ. Coll. London 1992–97, MRC Research Prof. Dept. of Biochemistry 1997–; various scientific medals. *Publication:* Amphibian Limb Regeneration: Rebuilding a Complex Structure. *Leisure interest:* soprano saxophone. *Address:* Department of Biochemistry and Molecular Biology, University College London, Gower Street, London, WC1E 6BT, England.

BROCKHOUSE, Bertram Neville, C.C., PH.D., F.R.S.; Canadian physicist; b. 15 July 1918, Lethbridge, Alberta; s. of Israel Bertram Brockhouse and Mable Emily Neville Brockhouse; m. Doris Isobel Mary Miller 1948; four s. two d.; ed. Univ. of British Columbia, Univ. of Toronto; served with Royal Canadian Navy 1939–45; lecturer Univ. of Toronto 1949–50; Research Officer Atomic Energy of Canada Ltd. 1950–59, Head Neutron Physics Br. 1959–62; Prof. of Physics, McMaster Univ. 1962–84, Prof. Emer. 1984–; Foreign mem. Royal Swedish Acad. of Sciences, American Acad. of Arts and Sciences; shared Nobel Prize for Physics 1994 for pioneering neutron scattering techniques and elaboration on theory of phonons; Hon. D.Sc. (Waterloo) 1969, (McMaster) 1984, (Toronto) 1995, (Univ. of B.C.) 1996; Dr. h.c. (Dalhousie) 1996, (Lethbridge) 1997. *Publications:* numerous articles. *Leisure interests:* natural philosophy, social bridge. *Address:* P.O. Box 7338, Ancaster, Ont., L9G 3N6, Canada. *Telephone:* (905) 648-6329. *Fax:* (905) 648-7246.

BROCKINGTON, Ian Fraser, M.PHIL., M.D., F.R.C.P., F.R.C.PSYCH.; British professor of psychiatry; b. 12 Dec. 1935, Chillington, Devon; s. of Fraser Brockington and Joyce Brockington; m. Diana Hilary Pink 1969; two s. two d.; ed. Winchester Coll., Univ. of Cambridge, Univ. of Manchester Medical School; Wellcome Research Fellow, Royal Postgraduate Medical School and Univ. of Ibadan, Nigeria 1966–69; Visiting Prof. Univ. of Chicago, U.S.A. 1980–81, Washington Univ., St. Louis, U.S.A. 1981; Prof. of Psychiatry, Univ. of Birmingham 1983–; Pres. The Marcé Society 1982–84; founder and first Chair. Women's Mental Health section, World Psychiatric Asscn.; Cottman Fellow, Monash Univ. 1988. *Publications:* papers on African heart diseases 1966–80, on schizoaffective psychosis, methods of clinical psychiatric research, pregnancy related psychiatric disorders; Motherhood and Mental Illness (with R. Kumar) 1982, Motherhood and Mental Health 1996. *Leisure interests:* family activities, choral singing, French, Italian and German literature, restoring Tudor farmhouse. *Address:* Faculty of Medicine and Dentistry, University of Birmingham, Edgbaston, Birmingham, B15 2TT; Lower Brockington Farm, Bredenbury, Bromyard, Herefordshire, England (Home). *Telephone:* 0121-627 2858 (Office); (0188548) 3245 (Home).

BRÖDER, Ernst-Günther, D.ECON.; German banker and economist; b. 6 Jan. 1927, Cologne; ed. Univs. of Cologne, Mainz, Freiburg and Paris; mem. corpn. staff, Bayer AG, Leverkusen 1956–61; Projects Dept. World Bank (IBRD) 1961–64; joined Kreditanstalt für Wiederaufbau 1964, Deputy Man. 1968–69, Man. 1969–75, mem. Man. Bd. 1975–84, Man. Bd. Spokesman 1980–84; Dir. European Investment Bank (EIB) 1980–84, Pres. and Chair. Bd. of Dirs. 1984–93, Hon. Pres. 1993–; Chair. Inspection Panel, IBRD 1994–96, mem. 1997–; mem. Supervisory Bd. DEG Deutsche Finanzierungsgesellschaft für Beteiligungen in Entwicklungsländern GmbH 1980–84; mem. Panel of Conciliators, Int. Centre for Settlement of Investment Disputes 1976–, Special Advisory Group, Asian Devt. Bank 1981–82. *Address:* World Bank, 1818 H Street, N.W., Washington, DC 20433, U.S.A.

BRODER, Samuel, M.D.; American physician; b. 24 Feb. 1945, Łódź, Poland; m. Gail Broder; two d.; moved to U.S.A. 1949; ed. Univ. of Mich. Ann Arbor and Stanford Univ.; clinical assoc. Nat. Cancer Inst. (NCI), Bethesda, Md. 1972, investigator, medicine br. 1975, sr. investigator, metabolism br. 1976, in charge of lab. overseeing new drug trials 1981–89; Dir. NCI 1989–; has played prominent role in HIV research. *Publications:* AIDS: Modern Concepts and Therapeutic Challenges (ed.) 1987; more than 250 articles. *Leisure interests:* long walks, playing cards, cinema, dinner with friends.

Address: Office of the Director, National Cancer Institute, National Institutes of Health, 9000 Rockville Pike, Building 31, Bethesda, MD 20892, U.S.A.

BRODERICK, Matthew; American actor; b. 21 March 1962, New York; s. of James Broderick and Patricia Broderick; m. Sarah Jessica Parker 1997; stage appearances: Valentine's Day (workshop production), Torch Song Trilogy, Brighton Beach Memoirs (Tony Award), Biloxi Blues; film appearances: War Games, Ladyhawke, 1918, On Valentine's Day, Ferris Bueller's Day Off, Project X, Biloxi Blues, Torch Song Trilogy, Glory, Family Business, The Freshman, Lay This Laurel, Glory, Out on a Limb, The Night We Never Met, The Lion King (voice), Road to Welville, Mrs. Parker and the Vicious Circle, The Cable Guy, Addicted to Love, Godzilla, Election; TV appearances: Master Harold . . . and the Boys, Cinderella. *Address:* c/o C.A.A., 9830 Wilshire Boulevard, Beverly Hills, CA 90212, U.S.A.

BRODIE, Harlow Keith Hammond, M.D.; American academic; b. 24 Aug. 1939, Stamford; s. of Lawrence Sheldon and Elizabeth Hammond Brodie; m. Brenda Ann Barrowclough 1967; three s. one d.; ed. Princeton Univ. and Columbia Univ. College of Physicians and Surgeons; Asst. Resident in Psychiatry, Columbia-Presbyterian Medical Center, New York 1966–68; Clinical Assn., Sec. on Psychiatry, Lab. of Clinical Science, Nat. Inst. of Mental Health 1968–70; Asst. Prof., Dept. of Psychiatry, Stanford Univ. School of Medicine 1970–74; Program Dir., Gen. Clinical Research Center, Stanford Univ. School of Medicine 1973–74; Prof. and Chair., Dept. of Psychiatry, Duke Univ. School of Medicine 1974–82; Chief, Psychiatry Service, Duke Univ. Hosp. 1974–82; Chancellor Duke Univ. 1982–85, Acting Provost 1982–83, Pres. 1985–93, Pres. Emer. 1993–, James B. Duke Prof. of Psychiatry and Behavioral Sciences 1981–, Prof. Dept. of Psychology, Prof. Law 1980–; Chair. Cttee. on Substance Abuse and Mental Health Issues in AIDS Research 1992–; mem. Coll. of Physicians and Surgeons of Columbia Univ. Asscn. of Alumni Gold Medal 1985, Carnegie Council on Adolescent Devt. 1986–, Nat. Review and Advisory Panel for Improving Campus Race Relations, Ford Foundation 1990–; Hon. LL.D. (Richmond) 1987. *Publications:* co-author Modern Clinical Psychiatry 1982, co-ed. American Handbook of Psychiatry (Vol. 8) 1986, co-ed. Critical Problems in Psychiatry, Signs and Symptons in Psychiatry, Aids and Behavior: An Integrated Approach 1994, Keeping an Open Door: Passages in a University Presidency 1996; also numerous articles. *Leisure interests:* tennis, reading, hiking. *Address:* 205 East Duke Building, Duke Univ., Durham, NC 27708 (Office); 63 Beverly Drive, Durham, NC 27706, U.S.A. *Telephone:* (919) 493-2447 (Home).

BRODIE, James William, O.B.E., M.SC., F.R.S.N.Z.; New Zealand scientist; b. 7 Oct. 1920, Bebington, Cheshire, U.K.; s. of James Thomas Fielding Brodie and Isabella Garner; m. Audrey Jacobsen 1945; two s.; ed. Napier Boys' High School, Victoria Coll., Univ. of New Zealand; with N.Z. Lands and Survey Dept. 1937–45; staff of Head Office, N.Z. Dept. of Scientific and Industrial Research 1945–49, Geophysics Div. 1949–54, Dir. N.Z. Oceanographic Inst. 1954–1977; Dir. Fisheries Research Div., N.Z. Marine Dept. 1964–67; Consultant on Marine Sciences, UNESCO; S.E. Asia, Paris, Indonesia 1965–79, Marine Science Adviser for S.E. Asia, Jakarta, Indonesia 1978–79, Chair. West Pacific Oceanographic Workshop, Tokyo 1979; Chair. Tech. Advisory Group, S. Pacific Offshore Prospecting, ESCAP 1975, 1976, 1978, Chair. Marine Geoscience Symposium, Suva, Fiji 1976; Pres. Geological Soc. of N.Z. 1960–61, N.Z. Marine Sciences Soc. 1966–67; Hon. Librarian Royal Soc. of N.Z. 1965–78, Home Sec. 1983–87, Vice-Pres. 1986–87; Ed. N.Z. Stamp Collector 1980–85; mem. Bd. of Trustees, Nat. Art Gallery and Museum 1982–92, Project Devt. Bd., Museum of N.Z. 1988–92; Marsden Medal, N.Z. Asscn. of Scientists 1978; N.Z. Marine Sciences Soc. Award 1985, Fellow Royal Philatelic Soc. of N.Z. 1978, Rhodes Medal 1988. *Publications:* Bathymetry of the N.Z. Region 1964, Terawhiti and the Goldfields 1986, The First Seven Thousand: A Jubilee History of Scots College 1991; Ed. (with Audrey Brodie) Haddenham Quaker History 1988, N.Z. Journeys of Lucy Violet Hodgkin 1989, Seeking a New Land: Quakers in New Zealand 1993, Go Anywhere, Do Anything: New Zealanders in the Friends' Ambulance Unit in China 1945–1951 1996, Keeping Touch: the Quaker Population in Nineteenth Century New Zealand 1998, Remembrances of Friends Past: Lives of New Zealand Quakers 1843–1998 1998; papers on geological and marine science topics; philatelic monographs. *Leisure interests:* archaeology, historical research. *Address:* 1 Fettes Crescent, Wellington 3, New Zealand. *Telephone:* (4) 3886894.

BRODY, Alexander, B.A.; American advertising executive; b. 28 Jan. 1933, Budapest, Hungary; s. of John Brody and Lilly Pollatschek; ed. Princeton Univ.; with Young & Rubicam Inc. 1953–83; Vice-Pres., Man. Young & Rubicam Inc., Frankfurt, Germany 1965–70; Sr. Vice-Pres., Head, European Operations, Young & Rubicam Inc. 1967–70; Int. Pres. Young & Rubicam Inc., Brussels and New York 1970–82; Pres. and C.E.O. DYR Worldwide, New York 1984–87; Pres. Int. Ogilvy & Mather Worldwide 1987–93, consultant 1993–, now Pres. and C.E.O. Int. Operations. *Address:* Ogilvy & Mather Worldwide, Worldwide Plaza, 309 W. 49th Street, New York, NY 10019, U.S.A.

BRODY, Jane Ellen, M.S.; American journalist; b. 19 May 1941, Brooklyn; d. of Sidney Brody and Lillian Kellner; m. Richard Engquist 1966; twin s.; ed. New York State Coll. of Agric., Cornell Univ. and Univ. of Wis.; reporter, Minn. Tribune 1963–65; science writer, personal health columnist, New York Times 1965–; mem. Advisory Council, New York State Coll. of Agric. 1971–77; numerous awards including Howard Blakeslee Award, American Heart Asscn. 1971; Science Writers' Award, ADA 1978; J.C. Penney-Univ. of Mo. Journalism Award 1978; Lifeline Award, American Health Foundation 1978. *Publications:* Secrets of Good Health (with R. Engquist) 1970, You Can Fight Cancer and Win (with A. Holleb) 1977, Jane Brody's Nutrition Book 1981, Jane Brody's New York Times Guide to Personal Health 1982, Jane Brody's Good Food Book 1985, Jane Brody's Good Food Gourmet 1990, Jane Brody's Good Seafood Book (with Richard Flaste) 1994, Jane Brody's Cold and Flu Fighter 1995, Jane Brody's Allergy Fighter 1997. *Address:* c/o New York Times, 229 W. 43rd Street, New York, NY 10036, U.S.A.

BROERS, Sir Alec Nigel, Kt., SC.D., F.ENG., F.R.S.; British professor of electrical engineering; b. 17 Sept. 1938, Calcutta; s. of Alec W. Broers and Constance A. (Cox) Broers; m. Mary T. Phelan 1964; two s.; ed. Geelong Grammar School, Melbourne Univ. and Gonville & Caius Coll. Cambridge; mem. research staff and man. of photon and electron optics groups, IBM Thomas Watson Research Center 1965–80; Man. Semiconductor Lithography and Process Devt. and Advanced Devt. IBM East Fishkill Lab. 1981–84; mem. Corp. Tech. Cttee. IBM Corp. H.Q. 1984; Prof. of Electrical Eng., Univ. of Cambridge 1984–96, Emer. 1996–; Head Electrical Div. 1984–92, of Dept. of Eng. 1992–96; Fellow, Trinity Coll. Cambridge 1984–90; Master, Churchill Coll., Cambridge 1990–96; Vice-Chancellor, Univ. of Cambridge 1996–; Foreign Assoc., Nat. Acad. of Eng. (U.S.A.); IBM Fellow 1977; Hon. D.Eng. (Glasgow) 1996; Hon. D.Sc. (Warwick) 1997; Prize for Industrial Applications of Physics, American Inst. of Physics 1982; Cledo Brunetti Award, Inst. of Electrical and Electronic Engs. 1985. *Publications:* patents, papers and book chapters on electron microscopy, electron beam lithography and integrated circuit fabrication. *Leisure interests:* music, small-boat sailing, skiing, tennis. *Address:* The Old Schools, Trinity Lane, Cambridge CB2 1TN, England. *Telephone:* (01223) 332291.

BROKAW, Thomas John, B.A.; American journalist; b. 6 Feb. 1940, Webster, S. Dak.; s. of Anthony O. Brokaw and Eugenia Conley; m. Meredith Lynn Auld 1962; three d.; ed. Univ. of S. Dakota; morning news ed. KMTV, Omaha 1962–65; news ed., anchorman, WSB-TV, Atlanta 1965–66; reporter, corresp., anchorman KNBC-TV, Los Angeles 1966–73; White House corresp. NBC, Washington, D.C. 1973–76; anchorman, Saturday Night News, New York 1973–76; host, Today Show, New York 1976–82; anchorman, NBC Nightly News 1982–, Corresp. Exposé NBC 1991–; mem. advisory cttee. Reporters Cttee. for Freedom of Press, Gannett Journalism Center, Columbia Univ.; trustee, Norton Simon Museum of Art, Pasadena, Calif.; Dr. h.c. (Washington Univ. St. Louis, and Syracuse and Hofstra Univs.). *Publication:* The Greatest Generation 1999. *Address:* NBC News, 30 Rockefeller Plaza, New York, NY 10112, U.S.A.

BROMLEY, David Allan, PH.D., F.R.S.A.; American professor of physics; b. 4 May 1926, Westmeath, Ont., Canada; s. of Milton E. and Susan (Anderson) Bromley; m. Patricia J. Brassor 1949 (died 1990); one s. one d.; ed. Queen's Univ., Kingston, Ont., and Univ. of Rochester, N.Y.; operating engineer, Hydro Electric Power Comm., Ont. 1947–48; research officer, Nat. Research Council of Canada 1948; Instructor, then Asst. Prof. of Physics, Univ. of Rochester 1952–55; Sr. Resident Officer, Atomic Energy Canada Ltd. 1955–60; Assoc. Prof. of Physics, Yale Univ. 1960–61, Prof. 1961–89, Chair. Dept. of Physics 1970–77, Henry Ford II Prof. of Physics 1972–93, Sterling Prof. of Sciences 1994–, Dean of Eng., Yale Univ. 1994; mem. White House Science Council 1981–92; Science and Tech. Asst. to the Pres., Washington 1989–92, Chair. Pres.'s Council Advisers on Science and Tech. 1989–92, Fed. Coordinating Council, Science, Eng. and Tech. 1989–93, Dir. Office of Science and Tech. Policy 1989–93; discovered first nuclear molecules, created first completely integrated computer-based nuclear data acquisition system; Dir. and consultant of several cos. and mem. various scientific advisory bodies; Pres. A.A.A.S. 1981–85; Pres. Int. Union of Pure and Applied Physics 1984–87; Assoc. Ed. of several learned journals; Fellow, A.A.A.S., American Physical Soc., Brazilian Acad. of Sciences 1987–, Royal Soc. of S.A. 1988–; Benjamin Franklin Fellow, Royal Soc. of Arts. 1979; several hon. degrees and other distinctions. *Publications:* Large Electrostatic Accelerators 1976, Detectors in Nuclear Science 1978, Nuclear Science in China 1980, Heavy Ion Science, 8 vols. 1984, numerous scientific and tech. publs. *Address*: Yale University, A. W. Wright Nuclear Laboratory, 272 Whitney, Box 6666, New Haven, CT 06511; 35 Tokeneke Drive, North Haven, CT 06473, U.S.A. (Home).

BRON, Eleanor, B.A.; British actress and author; b. 14 March 1938, Stanmore; d. of Sydney Bron and Fagah Bron; ed. North London Collegiate School and Newnham Coll. Cambridge; started at Establishment Night Club, toured U.S.A. 1961; TV satire, Not So Much a Programme, More a Way of Life; wrote and appeared in TV series Where was Spring?, After That This; TV appearances in Rumpole, Dr Who, French & Saunders, Absolutely Fabulous, Vanity Fair; BBC TV Play for Today: Nina, A Month in the Country, The Hour of the Lynx, The Blue Boy; Dir. Actors' Centre 1982–93, Soho Theatre Co. 1994–; *stage appearances include:* Private Lives, Hedda Gabler, Antony & Cleopatra, Madwoman of Chaillot, Hamlet; appeared at Royal Exchange in Uncle Vanya, Heartbreak House, Oedipus, The Prime of Miss Jean Brodie, Present Laughter; appeared at Nat. Theatre in The Duchess of Malfi, The Cherry Orchard, the Real Inspector Hound, The Miser, The White Devils, Dona Rosita The Spinster, A Delicate Balance, Be My Baby, Making Noise Quietly. *Films:* Help!, Alfie, Two for the Road, Bedazzled, Women in Love, The National Health, Turtle Diary, Little Dorritt,

The Attic, Deadly Advice, Black Beauty, A Little Princess. *Publications include:* Song Cycle (with John Dankworth) 1973; verses for Saint-Saëns Carnival of the Animals 1975; Is Your Marriage Really Necessary? (with John Fortune) 1972, Life and Other Punctures 1978, The Pillow Book of Eleanor Bron 1985, Desdemona—If You Had Only Spoken! (translation) 1992, Double Take (novel) 1996. *Address:* c/o Rebecca Blond, 69A King's Road, London, SW3 4WX, England. *Telephone:* 0171-351 4100. *Fax:* 0171-351 4600.

BRØNDSTED, Mogens; Danish professor of Nordic literature; b. 12 Nov. 1918, Copenhagen; s. of Prof. Johannes Brøndsted; m. Else Baadsgaard 1947; two s. one d.; lecturer Oslo Univ. 1946–50, Uppsala Univ. 1950–57; librarian Kongelige Bibliotek, Copenhagen 1957–61; lecturer Univ. of Copenhagen 1961–63, Asst. Prof. 1963–66; Prof. of Nordic Literature, Odense Univ. 1966–88, Rector 1966–71; Dr. Phil.h.c. (Uppsala). *Publications:* Henrik Hertzes teater 1946, Henrik Ibsen antologi 1951, Danske i Norge 1953, Digtning og skaebne 1958, Meir Goldschmidt 1965, Goldschmidts fortaellekunst 1967, Danmarks litteratur (with S. M. Kristensen) 1963, Oehlenschlägers Fynsrejse 1970, H. C. Andersen og avisen 1972, Ed. Nordens litteratur I-II 1972. *Leisure interest:* music. *Address:* Åløkken 50, 5250 Odense SV, Denmark. *Telephone:* 65-961884.

BRONFMAN, Charles Rosner, O.C.; Canadian industrialist; b. 27 June 1931, Montreal, Quebec; s. of the late Samuel Bronfman and of Saidye (Rosner) Bronfman; m. 2nd Andrea Morrison 1982; one s. one d. from previous m.; ed. Selwyn House School, Montreal, P.Q., Trinity Coll., Port Hope, Ont., McGill Univ., Montreal; joined The Seagram Co. Ltd. 1951, Dir. and Vice-Pres. 1958–71, Exec. Vice-Pres. 1971–75, Chair. Exec. Cttee. 1975–94, Deputy Chair. 1979–86, Co.-Chair. 1986–; fmr. Chair. Cemp Investments Ltd.; Hon. Chair. Canada-Israel Securities Ltd.; Dir. E.I. du Pont de Nemours Co., Canadian Council of Christians and Jews, Power Corpn. of Canada; Hon. Chair. and Dir. Super-Sol Ltd., Israel; Chair. Montreal Expos Baseball Club. *Leisure interests:* tennis, golf. *Address:* The Seagram Company Ltd., 1430 Peel Street, Montreal, Quebec H3A 1S9, Canada. *Telephone:* (514) 849-5271.

BRONFMAN, Edgar M., B.A.; American business executive; b. 20 June 1929, Montreal, Quebec; s. of late Samuel Bronfman and of Saidye (Rosner) Bronfman; ed. Trinity Coll. School, Port Hope, Ont., Williams Coll., Williamstown, Mass., and McGill Univ., Montreal; exec. in charge of co.'s plants in Canada, Distillers Corpn.-Seagrams Ltd. 1953–55; Chair. Admin. Cttee., Joseph E. Seagram & Sons Inc., N.Y. 1955, Pres. and Dir. 1957–71; Pres. Distillers Corpn.-Seagrams (now The Seagrams Co. Ltd.), Montreal July 1971–75, Chair. and C.E.O., N.Y. May 1975– (Co.-Chair. Nov. 1986–); now Chair. and C.E.O. Joseph E. Seagram and Sons Inc.; Dir. Int. Exec. Service Corps., American Technion Soc.; Chair. Clevepak Corpn., Pres. World Jewish Congress; Dir. E.I. duPont de Nemours & Co., United Negro Coll. Fund, Weizmann Inst. of Science, American Cttee.; Trustee Salk Inst. for Biological Studies, Mt. Sinai Hosp. and School of Medicine; mem. Bd. of Dirs. Inter-racial Council for Business Opportunity; mem. Foreign Policy Asscn., Center for Inter-American Relations Inc., Cttee. for Econ. Devt., Dir. U.S.-U.S.S.R. Trade and Econ. Council, Inc., etc.; Chevalier Légion d'honneur. *Address:* Joseph E. Seagram and Sons Inc., 375 Park Avenue, New York, NY 10152, U.S.A. (Office); 1430 Peel Street, Montreal, PQ H3A 1S9, Canada.

BRONFMAN, Edgar M., Jr.; American business executive; b. 1955; m.; with J. Seagram Corpn. 1976–, Asst. to Pres. 1982, Man. Dir. Seagram Europe 1982–84, Pres. House of Seagram 1984–88, Exec. Vice-Pres. U.S. Operations 1988–89; Pres. and C.O.O. J.E. Seagram Corpn. New York 1989–; now Pres. and C.E.O. Seagram Co. Ltd.; Acting Pres. MCA Inc. 1995–. *Address:* Joseph E. Seagram & Sons Inc., 375 Park Avenue, New York, NY 10152, U.S.A.; The Seagram Co. Ltd., 1430 Peel Street, Montreal, PQ H3A 1S9, Canada.

BRONIAREK, Zygmunt; Polish journalist and broadcaster (retd.); b. 27 Aug. 1925, Warsaw; s. of Wacław Broniarek and Marianna Broniarek; m. Elżbieta Sarcewicz 1972; ed. Main School of Planning and Statistics, Warsaw; Radiotelegraphic operator and stenographer, Czytelnik publishers, Warsaw 1945–48; Corresp. Trybuna Ludu 1950–90, Perm. Corresp. in U.S.A. 1985; in U.S.A. 1955, 1958, 1974, Latin America 1956, Paris 1959–60, 1969–73, Washington 1960–67, East Africa 1975, West Africa 1976, Nordic Countries 1977–82; mem. Polish United Workers' Party (PZPR) 1956–90; Corresp., Polish Radio and TV, for Finland and Sweden; Chair. Polish Asscn. of Int. Journalists and Writers 1974–77; mem. Bd. of Foreign Press Asscn., Stockholm 1979–81; mem. Presidium of Journalists' Asscn. Polish People's Repub. 1983–85; Vice-Pres. Polish Club of Int. Journalism 1984–85, mem. of Bd. 1991–; Corresp. Trybuna Ludu, L.A. Olympic Games 1984; Special Corresp. in Australia 1984; Corresp. Trybuna Ludu, U.S.A. 1985–90; Presenter The Guests of Mr. Broniarek (TV), The Inner History of the Great Policy (TV) 1983, Behind the Scenes of Int. Politics (TV) 1983–85, retd. 1990; Int. Journalists Club of Polish Journalistic Asscn. Prize 1978, Golden Screen Award of Weekly Ekran 1984, Victor Prize (TV) 1985, Polish Club of Int. Journalism (1st Prize) 1990; Bolesław Prus Award, First Class (SD PRL) 1984; Gold Cross of Merit, Commdr's. Cross Order of Polonia Restituta, Order of Banner of Labour (Second Class) 1984, Commdr.'s Cross with star of Infante Dom Henrique the Navigator (Portugal), Hon. Silver Ace of Polish Promotion Corpn. 1995. *Publications:* Od Hustonu do Missisipi 1956, Gorące dni Manhattanu 1960, Walka o Pałac Elizejski 1974, Kto się boi rewolucji (co-author) 1975, Angola zrodzona w walce 1977, Jak się nauczyłem sześciu języków 1977, Od Kissingera do Brzezińskiego 1980, Szaleństwo zbrojeń (co-author) 1982, Źródła spirali zbrojeń (co-author) 1985, Szczeble do Białego Domu 1986, Tajemnice Nagrody Nobla 1987, Ronald Reagan w Białym Domu 1989, Jak nauczyłem się ośmiu języków 1991, Biały Dom i Jego Prezydenci 1992, Tygodnik Popularny, Wesoła spowiedź 1993, Książę Karol w Polsce 1994, Sekrety korespondenta zagranicznego 1995, Okiem światowca 1999. *Leisure interests:* good company, good food. *Address:* ul. Gałczyńskiego 12 m. 9, 00-362 Warsaw, Poland. *Telephone:* (22) 826 33 04; 12 06 15.

BRONSON, Charles (Charles Buchinsky); American actor; b. 3 Nov 1922, Ehrenfield, Pa.; m. 1st Harriet Tendler (divorced); two c.; m. 2nd Jill Ireland 1969 (deceased); one d. two step-c.; played small parts in Hollywood films in the 1950s before coming into prominence in The Magnificent Seven 1960; other films include: A Thunder of Drums, 1961, Lonely Are the Brave 1962, The Great Escape 1963, The Sandpiper 1965, Battle of the Bulge 1965, This Property is Condemned 1966, The Dirty Dozen 1967, Guns for San Sebastian 1969, Rider in the Rain 1969, Twinky 1969, You Can't Win Them All 1970, Cold Sweat 1971, The Family 1971, Chato's Land 1972, The Mechanic 1972, The Valachi Papers 1972, Wild Horses 1973, The Stone Killer 1973, Mr. Majestyck 1974, Death Wish 1974, Breakout 1975, Hard Times 1975, Breakheart Pass 1976, From Noon till Three 1976, St. Ives 1976, The White Buffalo 1976, Telefon 1977, Love and Bullets 1979, Cabo Blanco, Death Wish II 1981, Murphy's Law 1986, Assassination 1987, Messenger of Death 1988, Kinjite 1989, The Indian Runner 1991, Death Wish V 1993, Dead to Rights 1995; television includes Raid on Entebbe 1976, The Legend of Jesse James, Act of Vengeance 1986; also appeared on many American series during 1950s and 1960s. *Address:* c/o William Morris Agency, 1515 S. El Camino Drive, Beverly Hills, CA 90212, U.S.A.

BROOK, Adrian G., PH.D.; Canadian professor of chemistry; b. 21 May 1924, Toronto; s. of Frank A. Brook and Beatrice M. Wellington; m. Margaret E. Dunn 1954; two s. one d.; ed. Lawrence Park Collegiate and Univ. of Toronto; Lecturer in Chem. Univ. of Toronto 1953–56, Asst. Prof. 1956–60, Assoc. Prof. 1960–62, Prof. 1962–89, Acting Chair. Dept. of Chem. 1969–71, Chair. 1971–74, Chair. Univ. of Toronto Research Bd. 1976–81, Univ. Prof. 1987, Univ. Prof. Emer. 1989–; Nuffield Fellow 1950–51; Stanley Kipping Award (American Chem. Soc.) 1973; CIC Medal (Chem. Inst. of Canada) 1986, Killam Prize (Canada Council) 1994. *Publications:* over 140 papers on aspects of organic chemistry. *Leisure interests:* windsurfing, computer hacking. *Address:* Department of Chemistry, University of Toronto, Toronto, M5S 3H6 (Office); 7 Thornwood Road, Apt. 202, Toronto, M4W 2R8, Canada (Home). *Telephone:* (416) 978-3573 (Office); (416) 920-8383 (Home). *Fax:* (416) 978-8775.

BROOK, Peter Stephen Paul, C.H., C.B.E.; British theatre and film director; b. 21 March 1925; s. of Simon Brook; m. Natasha Parry 1951; one s. one d.; ed. Westminster and Gresham's Schools, and Magdalen Coll., Oxford; joined Royal Shakespeare Co. 1962; Producer, Co-Dir. Royal Shakespeare Theatre; founded Int. Theatre Research Centre, Paris 1970, has toured with group in Iran, W. Africa; Hon. D.Litt. (Birmingham), (Strathclyde) 1990; Freiherr von Stein Foundation, Shakespeare Award 1973, Wexner Prize (Ohio State Univ.) 1991, Onassis Int. Award 1993, Times Award 1994; Officier, Ordre des Arts et des Lettres, Légion d'honneur, Praemium Imperiale. *Productions include:* Dr. Faustus 1943, Pygmalion, King John, Lady from the Sea 1945, Romeo and Juliet (at Stratford) 1947, Dir. of Productions at Covent Garden Opera 1949–50, The Beggar's Opera (film) 1952, Faust (at Metropolitan Opera, N.Y.) 1953, The Dark is Light Enough (London) 1954, House of Flowers (N.Y.) 1954, Cat on a Hot Tin Roof (Paris) 1956, Eugene Onegin (N.Y.) 1958, View from the Bridge (Paris) 1958, The Fighting Cock (N.Y.) 1959, Moderato Cantabile (film) 1960, Irma la Douce 1960, Lord of the Flies (film) 1962, King Lear 1963, The Physicists (N.Y.) 1964, The Marat/Sade (N.Y.) 1965 (film) 1966, US 1966, Tell Me Lies (film) 1968, Oedipus (Seneca) 1968, A Midsummer Night's Dream 1970, King Lear (film) 1971, The Conference of the Birds 1973, Timon of Athens (Paris) 1974, The Ik (Paris) 1975, (London) 1976, (U.S.A.) 1976, Ubu (Paris) 1977, Meetings with Remarkable Men (film, also dir. screenplay) 1977, Antony and Cleopatra (Stratford and London) 1978, Measure for Measure (Paris) 1978, Conference of the Birds, L'os (Festival Avignon and Paris) 1979, (New York) 1980, The Cherry Orchard (Paris) 1981, (New York) 1988, (Moscow) 1989, La Tragédie de Carmen (opera) (Paris) 1981, Le Mahabharata (Avignon and Paris) 1985, (World tour) 1988, Woza Albert! (Paris) 1989, The Mahabharata (film) 1989, La Tempête (Paris) 1990, Impressions de Pelléas (opera) 1992, L'Homme Qui (Paris) 1993, 1997, The Man Who 1994, Oh! Les Beaux Jours (Lausanne) 1995, (Paris) 1996, Don Giovanni (opera) 1998, Je suis un phénomène (Paris) 1998. *Publications:* The Empty Space 1968, The Shifting Point: Forty years of theatrical exploration 1946–87, 1988, There Are No Secrets 1993, The Open Door: Thoughts on Acting and the Theatre 1993, Threads of Time (autobiog.) 1998, Avec Shakespeare 1998. *Address:* c/o C.I.C.T., 13 blvd. de Rochechouart, 75009 Paris, France.

BROOK, Robert H., M.D., SC.D., F.A.C.P.; American professor of medicine; b. 3 July 1943, New York; s. of Benjamin N. Brook and Elizabeth Berg; m. 1st Susan Weiss 1966; m. 2nd Jacqueline Kosecoff 1981; one s. three d.; ed. Univ. of Arizona, Johns Hopkins Medical School, Johns Hopkins School of Hygiene and Public Health; mil. service, U.S. Public Health Services 1972–74; Dir. Health Sciences Program, Rand Corpn. 1990–, Vice-Pres. 1998–; Prof. of Medicine and Public Health, Univ. of California Center for the Health Sciences 1974–; Dir. Robert Wood Johnson Clinical Scholar Program 1974–; mem. Inst. of Medicine, Nat. Acad. of Sciences, American Soc. of Clinical Investigation, American Assen. of Physicians; Commendation Medal; Richard and Hinda Rosenthal Foundation Award; Baxter Health Services Research Prize 1988; Sonneborn Distinguished Lecturer, Univ. of Pa., Distinguished Health Services Researcher, Assen. of Health Services Research; Robert J. Glaser Award of Soc. of Gen. Internal Medicine, Johns Hopkins Soc. of Scholars; Hollister Univ. Lecturer, Northwestern Univ. *Publications:* over 300 articles on medicine. *Leisure interests:* tennis, swimming, golf. *Address:* The Rand Corporation, P.O. Box 2138, 1700 Main Street, Santa Monica, CA 90406 (Office); 1474 Bienvenida Avenue, Pacific Palisades, CA 90272, U.S.A. (Home).

BROOKE, Christopher Nugent Lawrence, C.B.E., M.A., LITT.D., F.B.A., F.R.HIST.S., F.S.A.; British historian; b. 23 June 1927, Cambridge; s. of Zachary Nugent Brooke and Rosa Grace (Stanton) Brooke; m. Rosalind Beckford Clark 1951; three s. (one deceased); ed. Gonville and Caius Coll. Cambridge, Fellow 1949–56, 1977–; Asst. Lecturer, Univ. of Cambridge 1953–54, Lecturer 1954–56; Prof. of Medieval History, Univ. of Liverpool 1956–67; Prof. of History, Westfield Coll., Univ. of London 1967–77; Dixie Prof. of Ecclesiastical History, Univ. of Cambridge 1977–94; Hon. D. Univ. (York) 1984; Pres. Soc. of Antiquaries 1981–84; Corresp. Fellow, Medieval Acad. of America; Corresp. mem. Monumenta Germaniae Historica; Fellow Società Internazionale di Studi Francescani; mem. Royal Comm. on Historical Monuments 1977–83, Reviewing Comm. on Export of Works of Art 1979–82; corresp. mem. Bavarian Acad. of Sciences. *Publications:* The Dullness of the Past 1957, From Alfred to Henry III 1961, The Saxon and Norman Kings 1963, Europe in the Central Middle Ages 1964, Time the Archsatirist 1968, The Twelfth Century Renaissance 1969, Structure of Medieval Society 1971, Medieval Church and Society (selected papers) 1971, Marriage in Christian History 1977, A History of Gonville and Caius College 1985, The Church and the Welsh Border in the Central Middle Ages 1986, The Medieval Idea of Marriage 1989, A History of the University of Cambridge IV, 1870–1970 1993; co-author of numerous works, including Gilbert Foliot and his Letters (with A. Morey) 1965, London 800–1216 (with G. Keir) 1975, Popular Religion in the Middle Ages, 1000–1300 (with Rosalind Brooke) 1984, Oxford and Cambridge (with Roger Highfield and Wim Swaan) 1988, David Knowles Remembered (with R. Lovatt, D. Luscombe and A. Sillem) 1991; ed. of numerous works, including Oxford (fmrly. Nelson's) Medieval Texts, Nelson's History of England (Gen. Ed.); articles and reviews in professional journals. *Address:* Gonville and Caius College, Cambridge, CB2 1TA, England.

BROOKE, Edward William, LL.D.; American politician and lawyer; b. 26 Oct. 1919, Washington, D.C.; s. of Edward and Helen Brooke; m. 2nd Anne Fleming 1979; ed. Howard Univ. and Boston Univ; admitted to Mass. Bar 1948; Chair. Finance Comm., Boston 1961–62; Attorney-Gen. of Mass. 1963–67; U.S. Senator from Mass. 1967–79; Chair. Boston Opera Co.; fmr. Partner, O'Connor and Hannan, Washington, D.C.; Chair. Nat. Low-Income Housing Coalition 1979–; Counsel Csaplar and Bok, Boston 1979–; Ltd. Partner, Bear and Stearns, N.Y. 1979; Fellow, American Bar Assen., American Acad. of Arts and Sciences; numerous hon. degrees; Republican. *Address:* Oconnor and Hannah, 1919 Pennsylvania Avenue, N.W., Washington, DC 20006, U.S.A. (Office).

BROOKE, Rt. Hon. Peter Leonard, C.H., M.A., M.B.A.; British politician; b. 3 March 1934, London; s. of Lord Brooke of Cumnor, C.H., P.C. and Baroness Brooke of Ystradfellte, D.B.E.; m. 1st Joan Smith 1964 (died 1985); four s. (one deceased); m. 2nd Lindsay Allinson 1991; ed. Marlborough Coll., Balliol Coll., Oxford, Harvard Business School, U.S.A.; Research Assoc., IMEDE, Lausanne and Swiss Corresp. of Financial Times 1960–61; Spencer Stuart Man. Consultants 1961–79, Chair. of parent co. 1974–79; M.P. for City of London and Westminster S. 1977–97, of Cities of London and Westminster 1997–; Govt. Whips' Office 1979–83; Dept. of Educ. and Science Parl. Under-Sec. 1983–85; Minister of State, H.M. Treasury 1985–87, Paymaster Gen. 1987–89; Chair. Conservative Party 1987–89; Sec. of State for Northern Ireland 1989–92, for Nat. Heritage 1992–94; Trustee, Wordsworth Trust 1976–, Cusichaca Project 1978–; Lay Adviser, St. Paul's Cathedral 1980–; Chair. Churches Conservation Trust 1995–; lay mem. Univ. of London Council 1992–94; Trustee Conf. on Training in Architectural Conservation; Sr. Fellow, R.C.A. 1987; Presentation Fellow, King's Coll. London 1989. *Leisure interests:* churches, conservation, cricket, visual arts. *Address:* House of Commons, London, SW1A 0AA, England.

BROOKE-LITTLE, John Philip Brooke, M.A., C.V.O., F.S.A.; British heraldic official; b. 6 April 1927; s. of late Raymond Brooke-Little; m. Mary Lee 1960; three s. one d.; Clayesmore School, New Coll., Oxford; mem. Earl Marshal's Staff 1952–53; Gold Staff Officer at Coronation of Queen Elizabeth II 1953; Bluemantle Pursuivant of Arms 1956–67; Richmond Herald 1967–80; Registrar Coll. of Arms 1974–82, Librarian 1974–94, Treas. 1978–95; Norroy and Ulster King of Arms, King of Arms, Registrar and Kt. Attendant on the Most Illustrious Order of St. Patrick 1980–95; Clarenceux King of Arms 1995–97; f., Chair. Heraldry Soc. 1947–97, Pres. 1997–; Chair. Govs. Clayesmore School 1971–83; Chair. Harleian Soc. 1984–; Pres. English Language Literary Trust 1985–; Dir. Heralds' Museum 1991–; Fellow Soc. of Genealogists 1969; Adviser on heraldry to Nat. Trust, Shrievalty Assen. 1983–; Hon. Fellow Inst. of Heraldic and Genealogical Studies 1979, numerous other appointments; K.St.J. 1975; Kt. of Malta 1955, numerous decorations. *Publications:* Royal London 1953, Pictorial History of Oxford 1954, Boutell's Heraldry (several edns. 1963–83), Knights of the Middle Ages 1966, Prince of Wales 1969, Fox-Davies Complete Guide to Heraldry 1969, Kings and Queens of Great Britain 1970 (jtly.), An Heraldic Alphabet 1973, Beasts in Heraldry 1974 (jtly.), The British Monarchy in Colour 1976, Royal Arms, Beasts and Badges 1977, Royal Ceremonies of State 1979, articles on genealogy and heraldry. *Leisure interests:* cooking. *Address:* Heyford House, Lower Heyford, Bicester, Oxon., OX6 3NZ, England. *Telephone:* (01869) 340337.

BROOKES, Baron (Life Peer), cr. 1975, of West Bromwich, West Midlands; **Raymond Percival Brookes,** Kt.; British business executive; b. 10 April 1909, West Bromwich, Staffs.; s. of William Percival and Ursula Brookes; m. Florence E. Sharman 1937; one s.; ed. West Bromwich School, Kenrick Tech. Coll.; apprenticed as engineer 1923; joined GKN as joint Gen. Man. of Carringtons Ltd. 1941, subsequently Man. Dir. and Chair.; Chair. GKN Forgings and Castings Ltd. 1965–74; fmr. Chair. Joseph Sankey and Sons Ltd. (now GKN Sankey Ltd.); Dir. GKN PLC (fmrly. Guest Keen and Nettlefolds Ltd.) 1953, Deputy Group Man. Dir. 1962, Group Man. Dir. 1964, Group Chair. and Man. Dir. (subsequently relinquished Man. Directorship) 1964, Group Chair. and C.E.O. 1966–75, Life Pres. 1975–; part-time mem. British Steel Corpn. 1967–68; First Pres. British Mechanical Eng. Confederation 1968–70; Vice-Pres. Eng. Employers' Fed. 1967–75; mem. Council Soc. of Motor Mfrs. and Traders Ltd. 1969–, mem. Exec. Cttee. 1970–, Pres. 1974–75; mem. Council CBI 1968–75, BNEC 1969–71, Wilberforce Court of Inquiry into electricity supply industry dispute Jan. 1971, Industrial Development Advisory Bd. 1972–75, Man. Bd. UNI-Cardan Group Lohmar, Fed. Repub. of Germany 1975–78; former Chair. Rea Brothers (Isle of Man) Ltd.; Dir. AMF Inc. U.S.A. (retd. 1979), Mannin Industries Ltd., Mannin Trust Bank Ltd. (retd. 1980); non-Exec. Dir. Plessey Co.; Hon. Fellow, Inst. of Sales Engineers 1973; Pres. Motor Ind. Research Assen. 1973–75. *Leisure interests:* fly-fishing, golf. *Address:* GKN PLC, P.O. Box 55, Redditch, Worcs., B98 0TL, England; Mallards, Santon, Isle of Man.

BROOKNER, Anita, C.B.E.; British teacher and author; b. 16 July 1928; d. of Newson and Maude Brookner; ed. James Allen's Girls' School, King's Coll., London, Courtauld Inst. and Paris; Visiting Lecturer, Univ. of Reading 1959–64; Slade Prof., Univ. of Cambridge 1967–68; lecturer, Courtauld Inst. of Art 1964, Reader 1977–87; Fellow, New Hall, Cambridge, King's Coll. London; Hon. D. Litt. (Loughborough Univ. of Tech.) 1990, Dr. h.c. (Smith Coll., U.S.A.); Booker Prize for Fiction for Hôtel du Lac 1984. *Publications:* Watteau 1968, The Genius of the Future 1971, Greuze: the rise and fall of an Eighteenth Century Phenomenon 1972, Jacques-Louis David 1980, The Stories of Edith Wharton (ed.) 1988; novels: A Start in Life 1981, Providence 1982, Look at Me 1983, Hôtel du Lac 1984, Family and Friends 1985, A Misalliance 1986, A Friend from England 1987, Latecomers 1988, Lewis Percy 1989, Brief Lives 1990, A Closed Eye 1991, Fraud 1992, A Family Romance 1993, A Private View 1994, Incidents in the rue Laugier 1995, Altered States 1996, Visitors 1997, Soundings 1997, Falling Slowly 1998; articles in Burlington Magazine etc. *Address:* 68 Elm Park Gardens, London, SW10 9PB, England. *Telephone:* 0171-352 6894.

BROOKS, Diana B.; American business executive; b. 1950; m. Michael C. Brooks; two c.; ed. Yale Univ.; lending officer Nat. Banking Group, Citibank 1973–79; fmrly. Sr. Vice Pres., then Pres., C.E.O. Sotheby's N. America; Pres., C.E.O. Sotheby's N. and S. America 1990–; Pres., C.E.O. Sothby's Holdings Inc. 1994–; Pres. Council of Assocs. Frick Art Reference Library; Dir. New York City Partnership; Trustee Yale Univ., Deerfield Acad., Allen-Stevenson School. *Address:* Sotheby's, 1334 York Avenue, New York, NY 10021, U.S.A.

BROOKS, Garth (Troyal Garth Brooks), B.S.; American country music singer; b. 7 Feb. 1962, Tulsa, Okla.; s. of Troyal Raymond and Colleen Carroll Brooks; m. Sandy Mahl 1986; two c.; ed. Oklahoma State Univ. *Albums:* Garth Brooks, No Fences (Acad. Country Music Album of the Year 1991), Ropin' The Wind 1991, Beyond the Season 1992, The Chase 1992, In Pieces 1993, The Hits 1994. *Songs include:* The Dance (Acad. Country Music Song of Year 1991), Friends in Low Places (Acad. Country Music Single Record of Year 1991), If Tomorrow Never Comes (American Music Country Song of Year 1991), The Thunder Rolls, We Shall Be Free, Somewhere Other Than The Night, Learning to Live Again. *Television specials:* This is Garth Brooks 1992, This is Garth Brooks Too 1994, Garth Brooks: The Hits 1995; Acad. Country Music Entertainer of the Year award 1991, 1992, 1993, 1994, Male Vocalist of the Year award 1991, Horizon Award, Country Music Assen. Entertainer of the Year award 1991, 1992, Grammy award for Best Male Country Vocalist 1992, Best Male Country Music Performer 1992, 1993, Best Male Musical Performer, People's Choice Awards 1992–95; inducted into Grand Ole Opry. *Address:* 1111 17th Ave., S. Nashville, TN 37212, U.S.A.

BROOKS, Gwendolyn; American writer; b. 7 June 1917, Topeka, Kan.; d. of David Brooks and Keziah Wims; m. Henry Blakely 1939; one s. one d.; ed. Englewood High School and Wilson Junior Coll; Poet Laureate for State of Illinois 1968; Teacher of poetry at Northeastern Illinois State Coll., Columbia Coll., Chicago and Elmhurst Coll.; Jefferson Lecturer 1994; mem. Nat. Inst., American Acad. of Arts and Letters, Poetry Soc. of America, Nat. Assen. for Advancement of Colored People, Third World Press; cited for creative writing by American Acad. of Arts and Letters 1946; Guggenheim Fellow 1946, 1947; Pulitzer Prize for Poetry for Annie Allen 1950; Anisfield-Wolf Award 1969, Shelley Memorial Award, Nat. Endowment for the Arts

Award 1989, Nat. Book Award for Distinguished Contrib. to U.S. Letters 1994, Nat. Medal of Arts 1995. *Publications:* A Street in Bronzeville 1945, Annie Allen 1949, Maud Martha 1953, Bronzeville Boys and Girls 1956, The Bean Eaters 1960, Selected Poems 1963, In the Mecca 1968, Riot 1969, Family Pictures 1970, Aloneness 1971, Report From Part One (autobiog.) 1972, Tiger who wore White Gloves 1974, Beckonings 1975, Primer for Blacks 1980, Young Poet's Primer 1980, To Disembark 1981, The Near-Johannesburg Boy 1986, Blacks 1987, Gottschalk and the Grande Tarantelle 1988, Winnie 1988, Children Coming Home 1991, Report From Part Two 1995. *Address:* 5530 S South Shore Drive, Apartment 2A, Chicago, IL 60637, U.S.A.

BROOKS, Harvey, A.B., PH.D.; American physicist; b. 5 Aug. 1915, Cleveland, Ohio; s. of Chester Kingsley Brooks and Elizabeth Brown Brooks; m. Helen Gordon Lathrop 1945; one s. three d.; ed. Yale and Harvard Univs; Soc. of Fellows, Harvard Univ. 1940–41, Research Assoc. Harvard Underwater Sound Laboratory 1942–45; Gordon McKay Prof. of Applied Physics 1950–75, Benjamin Pierce Prof. of Tech. and Public Policy 1975–86, Prof. Emer. 1986–, Dean of Eng. and Applied Physics 1957–75; Asst. Dir. Ordnance Research Laboratory, Pa. State Univ. 1945–46; Assoc. Laboratory Head, Knolls Power Laboratory, Gen. Electric Schenectady 1946–50; Ed.-in-Chief Physics and Chemistry of Solids; Dir. Raytheon Co.; mem. Bd. of Trustees, German Marshall Fund, Case Western Reserve Univ., Tufts Univ., Woods Hole Oceanographic Inst., Environmental Law Inst.; fmr. Pres. American Acad. of Arts and Sciences; mem. UN Advisory Cttee. on Science and Technological Devt. 1987–91; mem. Council on Library Resources, Nat. Acad. of Eng., Nat. Acad. of Sciences, American Philosophical Soc.; Hon. D.Sc.; Ernest Orlando Lawrence Award 1960. *Publications:* The Government of Science 1968; numerous articles in Physical Review, Nuclear Science and Engineering, and other scientific journals. *Address:* Harvard University, J.F.K. School of Government, 79 J.F.K. Street, Cambridge, MA 02138, U.S.A.

BROOKS, Mel (Melvin Kaminsky); American actor, writer, producer and director; b. 1926, New York; m. 1st Florence Baum; two s. one d.; m. 2nd Anne Bancroft (q.v.) 1964; one s.; script writer for TV series Your Show of Shows 1950–54, Caesar's Hour 1954–57, Get Smart 1965; set up feature film production co. Brooksfilms; *films include:* The Critic (cartoon) 1963, The Producers 1968, The Twelve Chairs 1970, Blazing Saddles 1974, Young Frankenstein 1974, Silent Movie 1976, High Anxiety 1977, The Elephant Man (producer) 1980, History of the World Part I 1981, My Favourite Year 1982 (producer), To Be or Not to Be 1983 (actor, producer), Fly I 1986 (producer), Spaceballs 1987 (actor, producer), 84 Charing Cross Road 1987, Fly II 1989 (producer), Life Stinks (actor, dir., producer) 1991, Robin Hood: Men in Tights 1993, Dracula: Dead and Loving It 1995; Academy awards for The Critic 1964, The Producers (Best Screenplay) 1968. *Address:* c/o The Culver Studios, 9336 W. Washington Boulevard, Culver City, CA 90232, U.S.A.

BROOME, David McPherson, C.B.E.; British farmer and professional show jumper; b. 1 March 1940, Cardiff; s. of Fred and Amelia Broome; m. Elizabeth Fletcher 1976; three s.; ed. Monmouth Grammar School for Boys; European Show Jumping Champion, riding Sunsalve, Aachen 1961, riding Mr. Softee, Rotterdam 1967 and Hickstead 1969; World Champion, riding Beethoven, La Baule (France) 1970; Professional Champion of World, riding Sportsman and Philco, Cardiff 1974; mem. of six British Olympic teams (including Barcelona 1992); Master of Foxhounds. *Publications:* Jump-Off 1970, Horsemanship (with S. Hadley) 1983. *Leisure interests:* hunting, shooting, golf. *Address:* Mount Ballan Manor, Crick, Chepstow, Gwent, NP6 4XP, Wales. *Telephone:* (01291) 420778.

BROPHY, Theodore F., B.A., LL.B.; American business executive; b. 4 April 1923, New York; s. of Frederick H. and Muriel W. (née Osborne) Brophy; m. Sallie M. Showalter; one s. one d.; ed. Yale Univ. and Harvard Univ. Law School; Assoc. law firm of Root, Ballantine, Harlan, Bushby & Palmer 1950–55; Gen. Counsel, The Lummus Co. 1955–58; GTE Corpn., Counsel 1958–59, Vice-Pres. and Gen. Counsel 1959–68, Exec. Vice-Pres. 1968–69, Dir. 1969, Pres. 1972–76 and 1992–95, Chair. and C.E.O. 1976–88; Chair. U.S. Del., World Admin. Conf. on Space Services –1988; Dir. Procter and Gamble Co., Readers' Digest Asscn.; Trustee Dewitt and Lilla Wallace Readers' Digest Funds, Smith Coll., Kent School; mem. American Bar Asscn. and Past Chair. Public Utility Law Section; mem. Fed. Communications Bar Asscn.; Public mem. Admin. Conf. of the U.S. 1970–72. *Address:* 60 Arch Street, Greenwich, CT 06830, U.S.A. (Office).

BROSNAN, Pierce; Irish actor; b. 16 May 1953, Navan, Co. Meath; s. of Tom Brosnan and May Smith; m. Cassandra Harris (died 1991); one s.; one s. by Keely Shaye Smith; ed. Drama Center; London stage appearances include Wait Until Dark, The Red Devil Battery Sign (cast in role of McCabe in British premiere by Tennessee Williams), Filumenia; TV appearances include role of detective in Remington Steele (series), Noble House (NBC mini-series), Nancy Astor, Around the World in Eighty Days, The Heist, Murder 101, Victim of Love, Live Wire, Death Train, Robinson Crusoe 1994. *Films:* The Mirror Crack'd 1980, The Long Good Friday, Nomads, The Fourth Protocol, Taffin, The Deceivers, Mister Johnson, The Lawnmower Man, Mrs Doubtfire 1993, Love Affair 1994, Robinson Crusoe 1995, Mars Attacks! 1996, The Mirror Has Two Faces 1996, Dante's Peak 1997, The Nephew 1998; role of James Bond in Goldeneye 1994, Tomorrow Never Dies 1997, The World is Not Enough 1999.

BROUGHTON, Martin Faulkner, F.C.A.; British business executive; b. 15 April 1947, London; s. of Edward Broughton and Laura Faulkner; m. Jocelyn Mary Rodgers 1974; one s. one d.; ed. Westminster City Grammar School; joined British-American Tobacco Co. 1971; Souza Cruz, Brazil 1980–85, Finance Dir. 1984; Finance Dir. Eagle Star 1985–88; Finance Dir. BAT Industries 1988–90; Chair. Wiggins Teape (then part of BAT) 1989–90; Sr. Finance Dir. BAT Industries 1990–92; Group Man. Dir. Financial Services 1992–, Group Chief Exec. and Deputy Chair. 1993–; Chair. Eagle Star 1992–93, C.B.I. Cos. Cttee. 1995–, Urgent Issues Task Force, Accounting Standards Bd. 1991–95; Dir. (non-exec.) Whitbread 1993–; mem. Takeover Panel 1996–. *Leisure interest:* occasional golf. *Address:* BAT Industries PLC, Windsor House, 50 Victoria Street, London, SW1H 0NL, England. *Telephone:* 0171-222 7979. *Fax:* 0171-222 0122.

BROUWENSTYN, Gerarda; Netherlands opera singer; studied in Amsterdam; joined the Amsterdam opera and subsequently became First Soprano; has appeared in London, Berlin, Stuttgart, Brussels, Copenhagen, Paris, Vienna, Bayreuth, Barcelona, Buenos Aires, etc.; repertoire includes Forza del Destino, Tosca, Aida, Otello, Un Ballo in Maschera, Tannhäuser, Die Walküre, Die Meistersinger, Le Nozze di Figaro, Jenufa, Troubadour, Cavalleria Rusticana, Don Carlos, etc.; Order of Orange-Nassau.

BROWALDH, Tore, B.A., LL.M., DR.ENG., DR.ECON.; Swedish banker; b. 23 Aug. 1917, Västerås; s. of Ernfrid and Ingrid (née Gezelius) Browaldh; m. Gunnel Ericson 1942; three s. one d.; Financial Attaché Swedish Legation, Washington, D.C. 1943; Asst. Sec. Swedish Royal Cttee. of Post-War Econ. Planning 1944–45: Admin. Sec. Swedish Industrial Inst. for Econ. and Social Research 1944–45; Sec. Bd. of Man., Svenska Handelsbanken 1946–49, Chief Gen. Man. 1955–66, Chair. 1966–78, Vice-Chair. 1978–88, Hon. Chair. 1988–; Dir. Econ., Social, Cultural and Refugee Dept., Sec.-Gen. Council of Europe 1949–51; Exec. Vice-Pres. Confed. of Swedish Employers 1951–54; mem. Bd. Swedish Bankers Asscn., Chair. 1959–61; Chair. AB Industrivärden 1966–88, Svenska Cellulosa AB 1960–88, Swedish IBM, Swedish Unilever AB; Deputy Chair. Nobel Foundation 1966–88, AB Volvo; mem. Bd. IBM World Trade Corpn. 1976–88; mem. Advisory Bd. Unilever, Rotterdam 1976–88; mem. Bd. Dag Hammarskjöld Foundation 1961–63, Swedish Govt. Research Advisory Bd. 1966–70, Swedish Govt. Industrial Policy Comm. 1968–70, Swedish Govt. Econ. Planning Comm. 1962–; Special Adviser to Int. Fed. of Insts. for Advanced Studies; mem. UN Group to Study Multinational Corpns.; mem. Swedish Royal Acad. of Sciences 1980, Swedish Acad. of Eng. Sciences, Royal Acad. of Arts and Sciences, Uppsala; St. Erik Medal, Commdr. Order of Vasa, Commdr. Grand Cross Order of the Northern Star. *Publications:* Management and Society 1961, The Pilgrimage of a Journeyman 1976, The Road Ahead 1980, Ascent and Tailwind 1984. *Leisure interests:* playing jazz on piano, golf, computer technology. *Address:* Svenska Handelsbanken, Kungsträdgårdsgatan 2, S-106 70 Stockholm (Office); 14 Sturegatan, 114 36 Stockholm, Sweden (Home). *Telephone:* 08-229120 (Home).

BROWDER, Felix Earl, M.A., PH.D.; American professor of mathematics and university administrator; b. 31 July 1927, Moscow, Russia; s. of Earl Browder and Raissa Berkmann; m. Eva Tislowitz 1949; two s.; ed. Yonkers High School and Princeton Univ.; C.L.E. Moore Instr. in Math. M.I.T. 1948–51; Instr. in Math. Boston Univ. 1951–53; U.S. Army 1953–55; Asst. Prof. of Math. Brandeis Univ. 1955–56; from Asst. Prof. to Prof. Yale Univ. 1956–63; Prof. of Math. Univ. of Chicago 1963–72, Louis Block Prof. of Math. 1972–82, Max Mason Distinguished Service Prof. 1982–87, Chair. Math. Dept. 1971–76, 1979–85; Visiting Prof. M.I.T. 1961–62, 1977–78; Vice-Pres. for Research Rutgers Univ. 1986–91, Univ. Prof. 1986–; Pres. (elect) American Mathematical Soc. 1988; ed. numerous journals; Dr. h.c. (Paris) 1990; mem. N.A.S. (mem. Council 1992–95, Governing Bd. Nat. Research Council 1994–95); Fellow, American Acad. of Arts and Sciences. *Publications:* Problèmes non-linéaires 1966, Functional Analysis and Related Fields 1970, Nonlinear Functional Analysis (2 vols.) 1970, 1976, Mathematical Heritage of Henri Poincaré 1984, Nonlinear functional analysis and its applications (2 vols.) 1985, numerous papers in mathematical journals. *Leisure interests:* reading, especially in philosophy, history and classics. *Address:* Rutgers University, P.O. Box 201, New Brunswick, NJ 08903, U.S.A. *Telephone:* (732) 445-4878 (Office); (732) 297-6040 (Home).

BROWN, Alexander Claude, PH.D., D.SC., F.R.S.S.A.; South African professor of zoology and marine biology; b. 19 Aug. 1931, Cape Town; s. of Alexander John Brown and Doris Hilda (née Todd) Brown; m. Rosalind Jane Roberts 1957; three s.; ed. Rhodes Univ. and Univ. of Cape Town; lecturer in Zoology, Rhodes Univ. 1954; Research Officer Council for Scientific and Industrial Research 1954–57; lecturer and Sr. Lecturer Univ. of Cape Town 1957–74; Prof. and Head Dept. of Zoology 1975–96, Prof. Emer. 1997–; Dir. Univ. Centre for Marine Studies 1997–; Deputy Dean, Faculty of Music 1970–80; worked at the Univs. of London, Manchester, Cambridge and Plymouth Marine Lab.; expeditions to Chile and Antarctica; mem. Ed. Bd. Journal of Experimental Marine Biology and Ecology; Past Pres. Royal Soc. of South Africa; Life Fellow Univ. of Cape Town; Gold Medal, Zoological Soc. of Southern Africa, Gilchrist Medal for Outstanding Marine Research. *Publications:* Ed. A History of Scientific Endeavour in South Africa (Royal Soc. of South Africa), several textbooks; Ed. Transactions of the Royal Soc. of South Africa 1968–72; Ecology of Sandy Shores (with A. McLachlan) 1990; about 180 research papers on the ecophysiology of sandy beach animals and marine pollution. *Leisure interests:* music, musicological research. *Address:*

Department of Zoology, University of Cape Town, Rondebosch 7701 (Office); 10 Monroe Road, Rondebosch 7708, South Africa (Home). *Telephone:* 6503603 (Office); 613504 (Home). *Fax:* 6503301 (Office).

BROWN, Arthur Joseph, C.B.E., M.A., D.PHIL., F.B.A.; British professor of economics; b. 8 Aug. 1914, Great Warford, Cheshire; s. of Joseph and Adelene Brown; m. Joan Hannah Margaret Taylor 1938; three s. (one deceased); ed. Bradford Grammar School and Queen's Coll. Oxford; Fellow of All Souls Oxford 1937–46; Foreign Research and Press Service (Foreign Office) 1940–43; Foreign Office Research Dept. (Head of Econ. Section) 1943–45; Econ. Adviser, Econ. Section, Cabinet Office 1945–47; Prof. of Econs., Univ. of Leeds 1947–79, Pro-Vice-Chancellor 1975–77, Emer. Prof. 1979–; Pres. Royal Econ. Soc. 1976–78, Vice-Pres. 1978–; Hon.D.Litt. (Bradford, Sheffield, Kent); Hon. LL.D. (Aberdeen); Hon. Fellow Queen's Coll. *Publications:* Applied Economics: Aspects of the World Economy in War and Peace 1948, The Great Inflation 1939–51 1955, The Framework of Regional Economics in the United Kingdom 1972, World Inflation since 1950 1985. *Leisure interests:* gardening, walking. *Address:* 24 Moor Drive, Leeds, LS6 4BY, England. *Telephone:* (0113) 275 5799.

BROWN, Cedric Harold, F. ENG., F.I.GAS E., F.I.C.E.; British business executive; b. 7 March 1935; s. of late William H. Brown and Constance Frances; m. Joan Hendry 1956; one s. three d.; ed. Sheffield, Rotherham and Derby Colls. of Tech.; East Midlands Gas Bd. 1953–59; Eng. Asst. Tunbridge Wells Borough Council 1959–60; eng. posts, E. Midlands Gas Bd. 1960–75; Dir. of Eng. E. Midlands Gas 1975–78; joined British Gas Corpn. (now British Gas PLC) 1978; Dir. Morecambe Bay Project 1980–87; Regional Chair. British Gas W. Midlands 1987–89; Dir. and Man. Dir. Exploration and Production 1989; Man. Regional Services 1989–91; Sr. Man. Dir. 1991; Chief Exec. British Gas PLC 1992–96; Pres. IGasE 1996–97; Dir. Bow Valley Industries 1988–; mem. Advisory Council on Business and the Environment 1993–95. *Publications:* tech. papers. *Leisure interests:* sport, countryside, places of historic interest. *Address:* CB Consultants Limited, 1 Great Cumberland Place, London, W1H 7AL, England.

BROWN, David Arthur, PH.D., D.SC., M.R.I.A.; British emeritus professor of inorganic chemistry; b. 5 June 1929, High Wycombe; s. of Arthur Percy Brown and Fanny Catherine (née Withell) Brown; m. Rita Brown; two s. four d.; ed. Watford Grammar School, Queen Mary Coll., King's Coll., Cambridge; lecturer, Univ. Coll. Dublin 1959, Prof. of Inorganic Chem. 1964, Head of Dept. 1974–77, 1983–86, 1989–, Dean of Faculty of Science 1984–87, mem. of Governing Body 1979–81, 1985–87; Pres. Inst. of Chem. of Ireland 1976–77; Boyle-Higgins Medal 1996. *Publications:* over 180 publs. on organometallic chem., bioinorganic chem. and theoretical chem. *Leisure interests:* walking, travelling, reading, music. *Address:* Department of Chemistry, University College, Belfield, Dublin 4, Ireland. *Telephone:* Dublin 7062297.

BROWN, Denise Scott, R.I.B.A., M.ARCH., M.C.P.; American architect and urban planner; b. 3 Oct. 1931, Nkana, Zambia; d. of Simon Lakofski and Phyllis (Helpker) Lakofski; m. 1st Robert Scott Brown 1955 (died 1959); m. 2nd Robert Charles Venturi (q.v.) 1967; one s.; ed. Kingsmead Coll. and Univ. of Witwatersrand, S.A., Architectural Asscn., London, U.K., Univ. of Pennsylvania, U.S.A.; Asst. Prof., Univ. of Pa. 1960–65; Assoc. Prof., Head Urban Design Program, Univ. of Calif. at L.A. 1965–68; with Venturi, Rauch and Scott Brown, Phila. 1967–, partner 1969–89, Prin. Venturi, Scott Brown and Assocs. Inc. 1989–; Visiting Prof. of Architecture, Univ. of Calif. at Berkeley 1965, Yale Univ. 1967–70; Eliot Noyes Design Critic in Architecture, Harvard Univ. 1989–90; Policy Panellist Design Arts Program, Nat. Endowment for the Arts 1981–83; mem. Bd. of Dirs. Cen. Phila. Devt. Corpn. 1985–, Urban Affairs Partnership, Phila. 1987–91; mem. American Planning Asscn., Architectural Asscn., London, Soc. Architectural Historians and numerous others; Hon. D.F.A. (Oberlin Coll.) 1977, (Parsons School of Design) 1985, (Phila. Coll. of Art) 1985, (Univ. of Pa.) 1994, Hon. D.Eng. (Tech. Univ. of Nova Scotia) 1991, Hon. D. Hum. Litt. (N.J. Inst. of Tech.) 1984, (Pratt Inst.) 1992, (Phila. Coll. of Textiles and Science) 1992, Hon. D.Arch. (Miami) 1997; Chicago Architecture Award 1987, Order of Merit (Italy) 1987, Nat. Medal of Arts (U.S. Presidential Award) 1992, The Philadelphia Award, The Benjamin Franklin Award (Royal Soc. for the Arts) 1993, ACSA–AIA Jt. Award for Excellence in Architecture Educ., Topaz Medallion 1996. *Publications:* Learning from Las Vegas 1972 (co-author), A View from the Campidoglio: Selected Essays 1953–84 (co-author) 1985, Urban Concepts 1990; numerous contribs. to professional journals. *Address:* Venturi, Scott Brown and Associates Inc., 4236 Main Street, Philadelphia, PA 19127, U.S.A. *Telephone:* (215) 487-0400. *Fax:* (215) 487-2520.

BROWN, Donald David, M.S., M.D.; American biologist; b. 30 Dec. 1931, Cincinnati, Ohio; s. of Louise R. Brown and Albert L. Brown; m. Linda Weil 1957; one s. two d.; ed. Walnut Hills High School, Cinn. Dartmouth Coll and Univ. of Chicago; Intern, Charity Hosp., New Orleans 1956–57, Sr. Asst. Surgeon, U.S. Public Health Service, Bethesda 1957–59; Postdoctoral Fellow, Pasteur Inst. 1959–60, Dept. of Embryology, Carnegie Inst. of Washington, Baltimore 1960–62, staff mem. 1963–, Dir. 1976–94; Prof., Dept. of Biology, Johns Hopkins Univ. 1968–; Pres. Life Sciences Research Foundation 1981; Pres. American Soc. of Cell Biology 1992; U.S. Steel Award in Molecular Biology 1973, V. D. Mattia Award 1976, Boris Pregel Award, New York Acad. of Science 1977, Rose Harrison-ISDB Award 1981, Ernst W. Bertner Award, Texas Univ. Cancer Center 1982, Louisa Gross Horwitz Award, Columbia Univ. 1985, Rosensteil Award 1985, Feodor Lynen Medal, Miami Winter Symposium 1987. *Address:* Carnegie Institution Washington, 115 W. University Parkway, Baltimore, MD 21210 (Office); 5721 Oakshire Road, Baltimore, MD 21209, U.S.A. (Home).

BROWN, Donald S., B.A.; American administrator; b. 2 April 1928; m.; three s.; ed. Antioch Coll., Ohio; Asst. Program Officer, U.S. Agency for Int. Devt. (AID), mission to Iran 1956–58, to Libya 1958–60, Program Officer, mission to Somalia 1960–63, then to the Sudan; Exec. Sec., Washington, D.C. 1963–65, Deputy Dir. then Dir., mission to Zaire 1967–70, to Morocco 1970–72, Deputy Asst. Admin. of Africa Bureau 1972–76; Dir., mission to Egypt 1976–82, Special Asst. to Admin. of AID 1982–; Woodrow Wilson Fellow, Univ. of Princeton 1965–66; Vice-Pres. Int. Fund for Agricultural Devt. (IFAD) 1983–96. *Address:* c/o International Fund for Agricultural Development, Via del Serafico 107, 00142 Rome, Italy.

BROWN, Edmund Gerald, Jr., A.B., J.D.; American politician and lawyer; b. 7 April 1938, San Francisco; s. of Edmund G. Brown (q.v.) and Bernice Layne; ed. Univ. of California at Berkeley, Yale Law School; Research Attorney, Calif. Supreme Court 1964–65, Attorney, Los Angeles 1966–69; Sec. of State, Calif. 1971–74; Gov. of Calif. 1975–83; Chair. Calif. State Democratic Party 1989–90; unsuccessful Democratic Presidential Cand. 1992; partner Reavis and McGarth; Trustee, Los Angeles Community Colls. 1969.

BROWN, Fred, PH.D., F.R.S.; British chemist; b. 31 Jan. 1925, Clayton, Lancs.; s. of Fred Brown and Jane E. Fielding; m. Audrey Alice Doherty 1948; two s.; ed. Burnley Grammar School, Victoria Univ. of Manchester; Head, Biochem. Dept., Animal Virus Research Inst., Pirbright, Surrey 1955–83, Deputy Dir. 1980–83; Head, Virology Dept., Wellcome Biotechnology Ltd. 1983–90; Adjunct Prof. of Epidemiology, Yale Univ. 1990–97; Professorial Fellow Queen's Univ., Belfast 1986–; Scientific Sec. Int. Asscn. of Biological Standardisation; Visiting Scientist, U.S. Dept. of Agric., Plum Inst., Animal Disease Center, New York 1995–; Hon. D.Sc. (Queen's Univ., Belfast) 1992. *Publications*: numerous papers on virology. *Leisure interests*: fell walking, reading scientific biographies, watching cricket and association football. *Address*: Plum Island Animal Disease Center, Greenport, P.O. Box 848, NY 11944-0848, U.S.A. (Office); Syndal, Glaziers Lane, Normandy, Surrey GU3 2DF, England (Home); 14 Cromwell Place, Old Saybrook, CT 06475, U.S.A. (Home). *Telephone*: (516) 323-2500 (Office); (01483) 811107 (Home in England); (203) 388 1527 (CT Home).

BROWN, Gordon (see Brown, James Gordon).

BROWN, Hank, J.D., LL.M.; American politician; b. 12 Feb. 1940, Denver, Colo.; s. of Harry W. Brown and Anna M. Hanks; m. Nana Morrison 1967; one s. two d.; ed. Univ. of Colo. and George Washington Univ.; tax accountant, Arthur Andersen 1967–78; admitted, Colo. Bar 1969; asst. to Pres. Monfort of Colo. Inc., Greeley 1969–70, corporate counsel 1970–71, Vice-Pres. Monfort Food Distributing 1971–72, Vice-Pres. corporate devt. 1973–75, int. operations 1975–78, lamb div. 1978–80; mem. U.S. House of Reps. (97th–101st) Congresses from Colo. 4th Dist.; mem. Colo. State Senate 1972–76, Asst. Majority Leader 1974–76; Senator from Colorado (102nd Congress) 1991–97; mem. Senate Judiciary, Budget and Foreign Affairs Cttees. 1991–97; Co-Dir. Centre for Public Policy and Contemporary Policies Univ. of Denver 1997–98; Pres. Univ. of N. Colo. 1998–; Republican. *Address:* University of Northern Colorado, Center for Public Policy and Contemporary Studies, 1322 43rd Avenue, Greeley, CO 80634, U.S.A.

BROWN, Harold, PH.D.; American fmr. government official and physicist; b. 19 Sept. 1927, New York City; s. of A. H. Brown and Gertrude Cohen; m. Colene McDowell 1953; two d.; ed. New York City public schools and Columbia Univ.; Lecturer in Physics, Columbia Univ. 1947–48, Stevens Inst. of Tech. 1949–50; Univ. of Calif. Radiation Laboratory, Berkeley 1950–52; Livermore Radiation Laboratory, 1952–61, Dir. 1960–61; mem. Polaris Steering Cttee., Dept. of Defense 1956–58; Consultant to Air Force Scientific Advisory Bd. 1956–57; mem. Scientific Advisory Cttee. on Ballistic Missiles to Sec. of Defense 1958–61; mem. President's Science Advisory Cttee. 1961; Sec. of Air Force 1965–69; Pres. Calif. Inst. of Tech. 1969–77; U.S. Sec. of Defense 1977–81; Distinguished Visiting Prof. of Nat. Security Affairs, School of Advanced Int. Studies, Johns Hopkins Univ. 1981–84, Chair. Johns Hopkins Univ. Foreign Policy Inst. 1984–92; business consultant 1981–; Dir. Philip Morris, Cummins Engine Co., Evergreen Holdings Inc., Mattel; Partner E. M. Warburg, Pincus and Co. 1990–; Counselor Center for Strategic and Int. Studies 1992–; mem. Del. to Strategic Arms Limitation Talks 1969; mem. N.A.S.; Hon. D.Eng. (Stevens Inst. of Tech.), Hon. LL.D. (Long Island Univ., Gettysburg Coll., Occidental Coll., Univ. of Calif., Univ. of S.C., Franklin and Marshall Coll., Brown Univ.), Hon. D.Sc. (Univ. of Rochester). *Publications:* Thinking About National Security 1983, The Strategic Defense Initiative: Shield or Snare? (ed.) 1987. *Leisure interests:* tennis, swimming, reading. *Address:* 1800 K Street, Suite 400, N.W., Washington, DC 20006, U.S.A.

BROWN, Headley Adolphus, PH.D.; Jamaican central bank governor; b. 12 Nov. 1930, St. Thomas; s. of Victor Rose; m. Alice Brown; two c.; ed. Kingston Tech. High School, Univ. of West Indies; Research Economist, Ministry of Industry and Trade 1964–66, Chief Economist 1966–72; Dir. Sectoral and Social Planning, Nat. Planning Agency 1972–75; mem. tech. group which designed framework for EEC/ACP Agreement, Jamaica's rep., tech. group which designed common external tariff for Caricom 1972–75;

Dir. Econ. Stabilization Comm. 1976–77; Trade Admin. 1977–81; Chief Tech. Dir. Nat. Planning Agency 1981–84; Dir. Gen. Planning Inst. of Jamaica, Chair. Bd. of Dirs. 1984; Gov. Bank of Jamaica, Chair. Bd. of Dirs. 1985; Alt. Gov. IMF, World Bank, Caribbean Devt. Bank, Inter-American Devt. Bank 1985; Chair. Nat. Export-Import Bank of Jamaica 1985; Dir. Bd. of Nat. Investment Bank of Jamaica 1985, Bd. of Pegasus Hotels of Jamaica 1985; Commdr. of Order of Distinction, Order of Jamaica. *Leisure interests:* lawn tennis, cricket, reading. *Address:* 23 Dillsbury Avenue, Kingston 6, Barbican, Jamaica (Home).

BROWN, Helen Gurley (see Gurley Brown, Helen).

BROWN, James; American singer and broadcasting executive; b. 17 June 1928; m. Adrienne Brown; leader, Famous Flames (musical group) 1956–; now solo performer and recording artist with King, Smash Records; Pres. J.B. Broadcasting, Ltd. 1968–, James Brown Network 1968–; arrested Dec. 1988 for attempted assault, received six-year sentence; *films include:* Come to the Table 1974, The Blues Brothers 1980; recordings include Original Disco Man, Please, Please, Hot on the One, Poppa's Got a Brand New Bag, Gravity, The Big Payback, Living in America; more than 75 albums recorded including I'm Real 1988, Universal James 1992; Grammy award 1965; 44 Gold Record awards. *Address:* c/o Brothers Management Associates, 141 Dunbar Avenue, Fords, NJ 08863, U.S.A.

BROWN, Rt. Hon. (James) Gordon, P.C., M.A., PH.D.; British politician; b. 20 Feb. 1951, Glasgow; s. of the late Rev. Dr. J. Brown and of J. Elizabeth Brown; ed. Kirkcaldy High School and Edin. Univ.; Rector, Edin. Univ. 1972–75, Temporary Lecturer 1976; Lecturer, Glasgow Coll. of Tech. 1976–80; Journalist and Current Affairs Ed., Scottish TV 1980–83; M.P. (Labour) Dunfermline East 1983–; Chair. Labour Party Scottish Council 1983–84; Opposition Chief Sec. to the Treasury 1987–89; Shadow Sec. of State for Trade and Industry 1989–92; Shadow Chancellor of the Exchequer 1992–97; Chancellor of the Exchequer May 1997–; mem. Nat. Union of Journalists, Transport and Gen. Workers' Union. *Publications:* The Red Paper on Scotland (ed.) 1975, The Politics of Nationalism and Devolution (with H. M. Drucker) 1980, Scotland: the real divide (ed.) 1983, Maxton 1986, Where there is Greed 1989, John Smith: Life and Soul of the Party (with J. Naughtie) 1994, Values, Visions and Voices (with T. Wright) 1995. *Leisure interests:* reading, writing, football and tennis. *Address:* The House of Commons, London, SW1A 0AA, England. *Telephone:* 0171-219 6345.

BROWN, Jesse; American politician and government official; b. 27 March 1944, Detroit; m.; two c.; ed. Chicago City Coll., Roosevelt Univ., Chicago, Catholic Univ., Washington, D.C.; served in Marine Corps (wounded in Vietnam) 1963–65; joined staff Disabled American Veterans (DAV), Chicago 1967, Head, Nat. Service Office, Washington, D.C. 1973–76, Head, Nat. Appeals Staff 1976–81, Chief of Claims, Nat. Service and Legis. HQ 1981–83, Deputy Nat. Service Dir. 1983–89, Exec. Dir. 1989–93; Sec. of Veterans' Affairs Jan. 1993–. *Address:* Department of Veterans' Affairs, 810 Vermont Avenue, NW, Room 1000, Washington, DC 20420, U.S.A. *Telephone:* (202) 273-4800. *Fax:* (202) 273-4877.

BROWN, Sir John Gilbert Newton, Kt., C.B.E., F.R.S.A.; British publisher; b. 7 July 1916, London; s. of John Brown and Molly Purchas; m. Virginia Braddell 1946; one s. two d.; ed. Lancing Coll., Hertford Coll., Oxford; Man. Oxford Univ. Press, Bombay 1937–40, London 1946–49, Sales Man. 1949–55, Deputy Publr. 1955, Publr. 1956–74, Publr. Gen. Div. and Deputy Sec. 1974–80; served R.A. 1940–41, Japanese P.O.W. 1942–45; Chair. B. H. Blackwell Ltd. 1980–83, Basil Blackwell Ltd. (fmrly. Basil Blackwell Publrs. Ltd.), Univ. Bookshops (Oxford) Ltd.; Dir. Blackwell Group Ltd. 1980–87, Vice-Pres. 1987–; Dir. Willshaws Ltd., Manchester 1966–89, Book Tokens Ltd. 1973–89, Archival Facsimiles Ltd. 1986–89, John Brown Publishing Ltd. 1989–; mem. Publrs. Asscn., Pres. 1963–65; mem. Bd. British Library 1974–80; mem. Bd. British Council; Prof. Fellow of Hertford Coll., Oxford; Jt. Treas. Royal Literary Fund. *Leisure interest:* gardening. *Address:* B. H. Blackwell Ltd., 50 Broad Street, Oxford, OX1 3BQ (Office); Milton Lodge, Great Milton, Oxon., OX44 7NJ, England (Home). *Telephone:* (01844) 279217 (Home).

BROWN, John Joseph, A.O.; Australian politician; b. 19 Dec. 1931, Sydney; s. of Norman Leslie Brown and Eva May Spencer; m. Jan Murray 1963; four s. one d.; ed. Sydney Univ.; worked as distributor and co. dir. in wholesale meat business; Alderman, Parramatta City Council 1977–70; M.P. for Parramatta, N.S.W. 1977–90; Minister for Sport, Recreation and Tourism 1983–87 (also Minister assisting the Minister for Defence), for Admin. Services 1983–84; Chair. N.S.W. Wholesale Meat Traders' Asscn. 1974–76, Tourism Task Force Ltd. 1989–, Environmental Choice 1992–94; Dir. Tourism Assets Ltd. 1992–, Sea World Man. Ltd. 1993–, Duty Free Operators Accreditation Bd. 1998–; mem. Australasian Meat Industry Employees' Union; Labor Party. *Leisure interests:* golf, jogging, horse racing, theatre, opera, gardening. *Address:* Tourism Task Force Limited, Level 9, Westfield Towers, 100 William Street, Sydney, N.S.W. 2000, Australia.

BROWN, Lawrence Michael, D.SC., M.A., PH.D., F.R.S.; Anglo-Canadian physicist; b. 18 March 1936, Windsor, Ont.; s. of B. W. and Edith Brown; m. Susan Drucker 1965; one s. two d.; ed. Univ. of Toronto, Univ. of Birmingham, England; work in Cambridge 1960–, Fellow, Gonville and Caius Coll. 1963–77, Univ. Demonstrator in Physics 1966, Reader in Structure and Properties of Materials, Dept. of Physics 1983–90, Prof. of Physics 1990–; Fellow and Coll. Lecturer in Natural Science (Physical), Robinson Coll. 1977–; Rosenhain Medal, Metals Soc. 1980, Robert Franklin Mehl Award, T.M.S. 1991. *Publications:* many papers in Philosophical Magazine and Acta Metallurgica. *Leisure interests:* reading, gardening. *Address:* Cavendish Laboratory, Madingley Road, Cambridge, CB3 0HE; 74 Alpha Road, Cambridge, CB4 3DG, England (Home). *Telephone:* (01223) 337291 (Office); (01223) 62987 (Home).

BROWN, Michael Stuart, B.A., M.D.; American professor of genetics; b. 13 April 1941, New York; s. of Harvey Brown and Evelyn Katz; m. Alice Lapin 1964; two d.; ed. Univ. of Pennsylvania; Intern, then Resident, Mass. Gen. Hosp. Boston 1966–68; served with U.S. Public Health Service 1968–70; Clinical Assoc. Nat. Inst. of Health 1968–71; Asst. Prof. Univ. of Texas Southwestern Medical School, Dallas 1971–74, Paul J. Thomas, Prof. of Genetics and Dir. Center of Genetic Diseases 1977–; mem. N.A.S. and other scientific socs.; Pfizer Award (American Chemical Soc.) 1976; Lounsbery Award (N.A.S.) 1979, Lita Annenberg Hazen Award 1982, Albert Lasker Medical Research Award 1985, Nobel Prize in Medicine or Physiology 1985, Nat. Medal of Science U.S.A. 1988. *Address:* University of Texas Health Science Center, Department of Molecular Genetics, 5323 Harry Hines Boulevard, Dallas, TX 75235, U.S.A.

BROWN, Rt. Hon. Nicholas Hugh, P.C., B.A.; British politician; b. 13 June 1950; s. of late R. C. Brown and of G. K. Brown (née Tester); ed. Swatenden Secondary Modern School, Tunbridge Wells Tech. High School, Univ. of Manchester; trade union officer Gen. and Municipal Workers' Union, Northern Region 1978–83; mem. Newcastle-upon-Tyne City Council 1980–83; M.P. for Newcastle-upon-Tyne E. 1983–97, for Newcastle-upon-Tyne E. and Wallsend 1997–; Labour spokesman on Legal Affairs 1987–92, on Treasury Affairs 1988–94, on Health 1994–95; Deputy Chief Opposition Whip 1995–97; Chief Whip and Parl. Sec. to the Treasury 1997–98, Sec. of State for Agric., Fisheries and Food 1998–. *Address:* House of Commons, London, SW1A 0AA, England.

BROWN, Norman Wesley, M.B.A.; American advertising executive; b. 27 Jan. 1931, Columbus, Ohio; s. of Leonard Brown and Alvena Folker; m. 1st Blanche Brown; one s. one d.; m. 2nd Lynn Godfrey 1980; two s.; ed. Ohio State and Harvard Univs.; Account Exec. Foote, Cone & Belding, Los Angeles 1959–63, Account Supt. 1963–73, Gen. Man. 1973–79; Gen. Man. Foote, Cone & Belding, Chicago 1979–81, Pres. 1981–, C.E.O. 1982–, also Chair.; Chair. Bd. and C.E.O. Foote, Cone & Belding Communications Inc., Chicago. *Address:* Foote, Cone & Belding Communications Inc., 101 E. Erie Street, Chicago, IL 60611, U.S.A.

BROWN, Robert (Bob), B.ECONS., DIP.ED.; Australian politician; b. 2 Dec. 1933, Pelaw Main, Hunter Valley, N.S.W.; m. Joy Hirschausen 1960; one s. one d.; ed. Maitland Boys' High School, Univ. of Sydney; active in local govt. politics, Greater Cessnock 1969–80; mem. for Cessnock, N.S.W. Legis. Ass. 1978–80; mem. for Hunter, House of Reps. 1980–84, mem. for Charlton 1984–; Minister for Land Transport and Shipping Support 1988–90, Minister for Land Transport 1990–93. *Publications include:* Student Economics Parts 1 and 2 1982, The Australian Economy 1989. *Leisure interests:* collecting, photography, music, theatre. *Address:* Suite 4, Level 3, Harbour Park Centre, 251 Wharf Road, Newcastle, N.S.W. 2300, Australia. *Telephone:* (02) 4926 4277. *Fax:* (02) 4929 4654.

BROWN, Robert Hanbury, A.C., D.SC., M.I.E.E., A.R.A.S., F.A.A., F.R.S.; British professor of astronomy and consulting engineer; b. 31 August 1916, Aruvankadu, India; s. of Col. B. H. Brown and Joyce Brown (née Blaker); m. Heather Chesterman 1952; two s. one d.; ed. Tonbridge School, Kent, Brighton Tech. Coll., City and Guilds Coll., Univ. of London; Scientific Officer Air Ministry (radar) 1936–42; Hon. Comm. Flight Lieut. R.A.F. 1940–45; Asst. Head Combined Research Group, Naval Research Lab., Washington, D.C. 1942–45; Prin. Scientific Officer Telecommunications Research Establishment and Head Navigation Div., Ministry of Supply 1945–47; Partner Sir Robert Watson-Watt and Partners Ltd. 1947–49; Prof. Radio-Astronomy Univ. of Manchester 1949–64; Prof. Physics (Astronomy) Univ. of Sydney, Australia and Dir. Narrabri Observatory 1964–81, Foundation Research Fellow 1982–88, Emer. Prof.; Pres. Int. Astronomical Union 1982–85; Hon. mem. Royal Inst. of Navigation 1997; Hon. F.A.Sc. 1975, Hon. F.N.A. 1975; Hon. D.Sc. (Sydney, Monash); numerous awards including Hughes Medal of The Royal Soc. 1971, Britannica Australia Medal 1971, Michelson Medal of Franklin Inst. 1982, Eddington Medal (Royal Astronomical Soc.) 1994. *Publications:* The Exploration of Space by Radio (with A. C. B. Lovell) 1960, The Intensity Interferometer 1974, Man and the Stars 1978, Photons, Galaxies and Stars 1985, The Wisdom of Science 1986, Boffin, A Personal Story of the Early Days of Radar, Radioastronomy and Quantum Optics 1991. *Address:* White Cottage, Penton Mewsey, Andover, Hants, SP11 0RQ, England. *Telephone:* (01264) 772334.

BROWN, Robert McAfee, M.DIV., PH.D.; American professor and clergyman; b. 28 May 1920, Illinois; s. of George William Brown and Ruth McAfee Brown; m. Sydney Elise Thomson 1944; three s. one d.; ed. Amherst Coll., Union Theological Seminary, Columbia Univ.; U.S. Navy Chaplain, Pacific 1945–46; Asst. Chaplain, Instructor in Religion, Amherst Coll. 1946–48; Instructor, Union Theological Seminary 1950–51; Prof. and Head of Dept. of Religion, Macalester Coll. 1951–53; Auburn Prof. of Systematic Theology, Union Theological Seminary 1953–62; Prof. of Religious Studies, Stanford Univ. 1962–76; Prof. of Ecumenics, Union Theological Seminary 1976–79;

Prof. of Theology and Ethics, Pacific School of Religion 1979–86, Prof. Emer. 1986; Fulbright Scholar 1949–50; Montgomery Fellow, Dartmouth Coll. 1966; Hanley Distinguished Prof., Santa Clara, Calif. Univ. 1990; several hon. doctorates. *Publications:* numerous books, including The Spirit of Protestantism 1961, the Ecumenical Revolution 1967, Religion and Violence 1973, Is Faith Obsolete? 1974, Making Peace in the Global Village 1981, Elie Wiesel: Messenger to All Humanity 1982, Unexpected News: Reading the Bible with Third World Eyes 1984, Saying Yes and Saying No: On Rendering to God and Caesar 1986, Spirituality and Liberation: Overcoming the Great Fallacy, Gustavo Gutierrez: An Introduction to Liberation Theology 1990, Persuade Us to Rejoice: The Liberating Power of Fiction 1992, Liberation Theology: An Introductory Guide 1993, Reclaiming the Bible: Words for the Nineties 1994, Speaking of Christianity 1997; several trans. *Leisure interests:* cello, carpentry, grandchildren. *Address:* 2090 Columbia Street, Palo Alto, CA 94306, U.S.A. *Telephone:* (415) 857-0870.

BROWN, Ronald Drayton, PH.D.; Australian professor of chemistry; b. 14 Oct. 1927, Melbourne; s. of William Harrison Brown and Linda Grace Drayton; m. Florence Catherine Mary Stringer 1950; two s. one d.; ed. Wesley Coll., Melbourne, Univs. of Melbourne and London; lecturer, Univ. Coll., London, U.K., Melbourne Univ.; Prof. of Chem., Monash Univ. 1960–, Head Chem. Dept. 1959–92; current research interests cover theoretical chem., spectroscopy, galactochemistry and life in space; past Pres. Comm. 51 (Bioastronomy) of Int. Astronomical Union; mem. of Exec. Cttee and Bureau, Int. Union of Pure and Applied Chem.; Fellow Australian Acad. of Science (fmr. mem. Council and Vice-Pres. of Physical Sciences); Matthew Flinders Lecturer 1988; Masson Medal, Royal Chemical Inst. 1948, Rennie Medal 1951, Smith Medal 1959; David Syme Prize for Research, Univ. of Melbourne 1959; Edgeworth-David Medal, Royal Soc. of N.S.W. 1961; Royal Soc. Medal of Victoria 1977. *Publications:* Manual of Elementary Practical Chemistry (co-author), Atomic Structure and the Theory of Valency, The ABZ of Valency, Valency. *Leisure interests:* badminton, golf, skiing, squash, tennis. *Address:* Department of Chemistry, Monash University, Wellington Road, Clayton, Vic., 3168 (Office); 3 Moonya Rd, Glen Iris, 3146 Vic., Australia (Home). *Telephone:* (03) 9905 4550 (Office); (03) 9885 4069 (Home).

BROWN, Tina, M.A.; British writer and magazine editor; b. 21 Nov. 1953, Maidenhead; d. of George Hambley Brown and Bettina Iris Mary (née Kohr) Brown; m. Harold Evans (q.v.) 1981; one s. one d.; ed. Univ. of Oxford; columnist, Punch magazine 1978; Ed.-in-Chief Tatler Magazine 1979–83, of Vanity Fair Magazine, New York 1984–92, London 1991–92; Ed. The New Yorker 1992–98; Most Promising Female Journalist, Katherine Pakenham Prize Sunday Times 1973, Young Journalist of the Year 1978. *Publications:* Under the Bamboo Tree (play) 1973 (Sunday Times Drama Award), Happy Yellow (play) 1977, Loose Talk 1979, Life as A Party 1983. *Address:* c/o New Yorker Magazine Inc., 20 West 43rd Street, New York, NY 10036, U.S.A.

BROWN, Trisha; American choreographer; b. Aberdeen, Wash.; f. The Trisha Brown Dance Co., Pres. 1970–. *Works Include:* Walking on the Walls, Roof Piece 1973, Son of Gone Fishin' 1981, Bessie 1984, Lateral Pass 1985, Newark 1987, For M.G.: The Movie 1991, Astral Converted 1991, Another Story: As in Falling 1993, If You Couldn't See Me 1994, Foray Forêt 1995, You Can See Us 1995, Twelve Ton Rose 1996; numerous awards; Chevalier Ordre des Arts et des Lettres 1988. *Address:* 211 West 61st Street, Floor 4, New York, NY 10023, U.S.A. (Office).

BROWN, William Charles Langdon, C.B.E.; British banker; b. 9 Sept. 1931, London; s. of Charles Leonard Brown and Kathleen May Tizzard; m. Nachiko Sagawa 1959; one s. two d.; ed. John Ruskin School, Croydon, Ashbourne Grammar School, Derbyshire; with Chartered Bank of India, Australia and China, serving throughout Far East 1954–75, Area Gen. Man., Hong Kong 1975–87, Sr. Gen. Man. (London) for Asia Pacific Region 1987; Exec. Dir. Standard Chartered Bank PLC (SCB) 1987, Man. Dir. 1988, Deputy Group Chief Exec. 1988, Group Deputy Chair. 1989–91, non-exec. Dir. 1991–94; Dir. and Treasurer Royal Commonwealth Soc. 1991–95, Commonwealth Trust 1991–95; Dir. the HongKong Investment Trust PLC 1991–97; Dir. (non-exec.) Kexim Bank U.K. Ltd. 1992–, Arbuthnot Latham & Co. Ltd. 1993–; Chair. (non-exec.) Atlantis Japan Growth Fund Ltd. 1996–; Unofficial mem. Legis. Council of Hong Kong 1980–85; Hon. Dr. Soc. Sc. (Chinese Univ., Hong Kong) 1987. *Leisure interests:* mountain walking, yoga, skiing, philately, photography, classical music. *Address:* Penthouse B, 15 Portman Square, London, W1H 9HD; Appleshaw, 11 Central Avenue, Findon Valley, Worthing, Sussex, BN14 0DS, England. *Telephone:* 0171-487 5741; (01903) 873 175. *Fax:* 0171-486 3005; (01903) 873 175.

BROWNBACK, Sam, B.S., J.D.; American politician; b. Parker, Kan.; m. Mary Brownback; three c.; ed. Kansas State Univ. and Univ. of Kansas; partner, law firm in New York; Instr. in Law, Kansas State Univ.; City Attorney, Ogden and Leonardville, Kan.; mem. 104th Congress 1994–97; Senator from Kansas 1997–; Republican. *Address:* United States Senate, 303 Hart Senate Office Building, Washington, DC 20510, U.S.A.

BROWNE, Sir Edmund John Phillip, Kt., M.A., M.S., F.ENG., F.I.M.M.; British business executive; b. 20 Feb. 1948, Hamburg, Germany; s. of late Edmund J. Browne and of Paula Browne; ed. King's School, Ely, Univ. of Cambridge and Stanford Univ.; Group Treas. and Chief Exec. BP Finance Int. 1984–86; Exec. Vice-Pres. and Chief Financial Officer, Standard Oil Co., Ohio 1986–89, C.E.O. 1987–89; Chief Exec. BP Exploration Co., Ltd. 1989–95; Man. Dir. British Petroleum Co. PLC 1991–, Group Chief Exec. July 1995–, now Chair.; Chair. Advisory Council, Grad. School of Business 1991–; Dir. Redland PLC 1993, SmithKline Beecham 1995–, Intel Corpn. 1997–; Trustee British Museum 1995–. *Leisure interests:* ballet, opera. *Address:* British Petroleum Company PLC, Britannic House, 1 Finsbury Circus, London, EC2M 7BA, England. *Telephone:* 0171-496 4488.

BROWNE-WILKINSON, Baron (Life Peer) cr. 1991, of Camden, in the London Borough of Camden; **Nicolas Christopher Henry Browne-Wilkinson,** P.C., Q.C., B.A.; British judge; b. 30 March 1930, London; s. of Canon A. R. Browne-Wilkinson and Molly Browne-Wilkinson; m. Ursula de Lacy Bacon 1955 (died 1987); three s. two d.; m. Hilary Tuckwell 1990; ed. Lancing Coll., Magdalen Coll., Oxford; called to Bar, Lincoln's Inn 1953, Bencher 1977; Q.C. 1972; Jr. Counsel to Registrar of Restrictive Trading Agreements 1964–66, to Attorney-Gen. in Charity Matters 1966–72, in bankruptcy, to Dept. of Trade and Industry 1966–72; a Judge of the Courts of Appeal of Jersey and Guernsey 1976–77; a Judge of the High Court, Chancery Div. 1977–83; a Lord Justice of Appeal 1983–85; Vice-Chancellor of the Supreme Court 1985–91; a Lord of Appeal in Ordinary 1991–, Sr. Lord 1998–; Pres. Employment Appeal Tribunal 1981–83, Senate of the Inns of Court and the Bar 1984–86; Fellow St. Edmund Hall (Oxford) 1986, Magdalen Coll. 1993. *Leisure interests:* gardening, music. *Address:* House of Lords, London, SW1A 0PW, England. *Telephone:* 0171-219 3202.

BROWNER, Carol; American politician and lawyer; b. 1956; m. Michael Podhorzer; one s.; gen. counsel of a cttee. of Fla. Legis. 1979–83; Assoc. Dir. Citizen Action, Washington, D.C. 1983–86; mem. staff Senator Lawton Chiles (q.v.) 1986–89; mem. staff Senate Cttee. on Energy and Natural Resources 1989; Legis. Dir. on staff of Senator Al Gore (q.v.) 1989–90; Head Dept. of Environmental Regulation, State of Fla. 1990–93; Admin. Environmental Protection Agency (EPA) Jan. 1993–. *Address:* Environmental Protection Agency, 401 M Street, SW, Washington, DC 20460, U.S.A. *Telephone:* (202) 382-4700. *Fax:* (202) 382-7886.

BROWNING, Most Rev. Edmond L., B.D.; American ecclesiastic; b. 11 March 1929, Texas; s. of Edmond L. Browning and Cora M. Lee; m. Patricia Sparks 1953; four s. one d.; ed. Univ. of the South, Sewanee, Tenn., School of Theology, Sewanee and Japanese Language School, Okinawa; First missionary Bishop of Okinawa 1968–71; Bishop-in-Charge, Convocation of American Churches in Europe 1971–74; Exec. for Nat. and World Mission, Episcopal Church Center 1974–76; Bishop of Hawaii 1976–85; Presiding Bishop, Episcopal Church, U.S.A. 1986–98. *Address:* 5164 Imai Road, Hood River, OR 97031, U.S.A.

BROWNING, Keith Anthony, PH.D., A.R.C.S., D.I.C., F.R.S.; British meteorologist; b. 31 July 1938, Sunderland; s. of late James Anthony Browning and of Amy Hilda Greenwood; m. Ann Baish 1962; one s. two d.; ed. Imperial Coll. of Science and Tech., Univ. of London; Research Atmospheric Physicist, Air Force Cambridge Research Labs., Mass., U.S.A. 1962–66; Prin. then Chief Meteorological Officer, Meteorological Office Radar Research Lab., Royal Signals and Radar Establishment, Malvern, Worcs. 1966–74, 1975–85; Chief Scientist, Nat. Hail Research Experiment, Nat. Center for Atmospheric Research, Boulder, Colo., U.S.A. 1974–75; Deputy Dir. (Physical Research), Meteorological Office, Bracknell, Berks. 1985–89, Dir. of Research 1989–91; Visiting Scientist, Joint Centre for Mesoscale Meteorology, Univ. of Reading 1991–92, Dir. 1992–; Prof. in Dept. of Meteorology, Univ. of Reading 1995–; Chair. Meteorology & Atmospheric Physics Sub-Cttee. of British Cttee. for Geodesy and Geophysics 1985–89; mem. Natural Environment Research Council 1984–87; Visiting Prof., Dept. of Meteorology, Univ. of Reading 1988–94; Pres. Royal Meteorological Soc. 1988–90; mem. Academia Europaea, Jt. Scientific Cttee., World Climate Research Programme 1992–94; Foreign Assoc., Nat. Acad. of Eng. (U.S.A.) 1992–; awards from Royal Meteorological Soc., American Meteorological Soc. and Inst. of Physics; Fellow American Meteorological Soc.; Chartered Meteorologist, Royal Meteorological Soc. *Publications:* numerous articles on meteorology. *Leisure interests:* home and garden. *Address:* Joint Centre for Mesoscale Meteorology, University of Reading, P.O. Box 243, Reading, RG6 6BB, England. *Telephone:* (01189) 316521. *Fax:* (01189) 318791.

BROWNLEE, George, D.SC., PH.D., F.K.C.; British professor of pharmacology; b. 8 Sept. 1911, Edinburgh; s. of late George R. Brownlee and Mary C. C. Gow; m. 1st Margaret P. M. Cochrane 1940 (died 1970); three s.; m. 2nd Betty J. Gaydon 1977 (divorced 1981); ed. Tynecastle School and Heriot-Watt Coll., Edinburgh and Univ. of Glasgow; mem. scientific staff, Wellcome Research Labs. 1939–49, MRC Toxicology Unit, Carshalton 1949; Reader in Pharmacology, King's Coll. London 1949–55, Prof. of Pharmacology 1955–78, Prof. Emer. 1978–. *Publications:* Experimental Pharmacology (with J. P. Quilliam) 1952; contribs. to scientific journals. *Leisure interests:* herbals, history of medicine, making things. *Address:* 602 Gilbert House, Barbican, London, EC2Y 8BD, England. *Telephone:* 0171-638 9543.

BROWNLIE, Albert Dempster, M.COM.; New Zealand university vice-chancellor (retd.); b. 3 Sept. 1932, Fiji; m.; two d.; ed. Univ. of New Zealand; economist, N.Z. Treasury 1954–55; lecturer then Sr. Lecturer in Econs., Assoc. Prof. Univ. of Auckland 1956–64; Nuffield Foundation Dominion Travelling Fellow, Nuffield College, Oxford, U.K. 1963; Prof. and Head Dept. of Econs., Univ. of Canterbury 1965–77, Asst. Vice-Chancellor (Bldgs. and Site Devt.) 1974–77, Vice-Chancellor 1978–98; mem. Sixth and Seventh Groups of Experts on Programming Techniques, ECAFE 1968–69; Ed. N.Z. Econ. Papers 1970–73; Chair. N.Z. Monetary and Econ. Council 1972–78;

mem. Commonwealth Experts Group on a New Int. Econ. Order 1975–77, Commonwealth Experts Group on World Econ. Crisis 1980; Chair. Australia-N.Z. Foundation 1978–83; Chair. N.Z. Vice-Chancellors' Cttee. 1983–84, 1993; Queen Elizabeth II Silver Jubilee Medal 1977. *Address:* c/o University of Canterbury, Private Bag 4800, Christchurch 1, New Zealand.

BROWNLIE, Ian, C.B.E., Q.C., D.C.L., F.B.A.; British int. law practitioner and academic; b. 19 Sept. 1932, Liverpool; s. of Amy Isabella Atherton and John Nason Brownlie; m. 1st Jocelyn Gale 1957; one s. two d.; m. 2nd Christine Apperley, LL.M. 1978; ed. Alsop High School, Liverpool, Hertford Coll. Oxford and King's Coll. Cambridge; called to Bar (Gray's Inn) 1958; in practice 1967–; Q.C. 1979; Bencher of Gray's Inn 1988; Fellow Wadham Coll. Oxford 1963–76; Prof. of Int. Law, London Univ. (attached to L.S.E.) 1976–80; Chichele Prof. of Public Int. Law, Oxford and Fellow of All Souls 1980–(99); Dir. of Studies, Int. Law Assen. 1982–91; lecturer, Hague Acad. of Int. Law 1995; Judge, European Nuclear Energy Tribunal 1995–, Pres. 1996–; mem. Inst. of Int. Law 1983; Commdr., Order of Merit of the Norwegian Crown. *Publications:* International Law and the Use of Force by States 1963, Principles of Public International Law 1966, Encyclopaedia of African Boundaries 1979, State Responsibility, Part I 1983, Liber Amicorum for Lord Wilberforce 1987; British Year Book of International Law (Jt. Ed.) 1974–. *Leisure interests:* travel, book collecting, maps. *Address:* All Souls College, Oxford, OX1 4AL; 2 Hare Court, Temple, London, EC4Y 7BH (Chambers); 43 Fairfax Road, Chiswick, London, W4 1EN, England (Home). *Telephone:* (01865) 279342 (Coll.); 0171-583 1770 (Chambers); 0181-995 3647 (Home).

BROWNLOW, Kevin; British film historian and television director; b. 2 June 1938, Crowborough, Sussex; s. of Robert Thomas Brownlow and Niña Fortnum; m. Virginia Keane 1969; one d.; ed. University College School, Hampstead; joined World Wide Pictures 1955; became film Ed., then jt. Dir. 1964; with Thames TV 1975–90. *Films* include: It Happened Here 1964, Winstanley 1975 (both with Andrew Mollo). *Television* includes 13-part series Hollywood 1980, three-part Unknown Chaplin 1983, three-part British Cinema 1986, three-part Buster Keaton—A Hard Act to Follow 1987, two-part Harold Lloyd 1988, three-part D. W. Griffith 1993, six-part Cinema Europe: the other Hollywood 1995 (all with David Gill). *Publications:* Parade's Gone By . . . 1968, The War, the West and the Wilderness 1978, Napoleon (Abel Gance's Classic Film) 1983, Behind the Mask of Innocence 1990, David Lean: A Biography 1996, Mary Pickford Rediscovered 1999. *Address:* c/o Photoplay Productions, 21 Princess Road, London, N.W.1, England (Office). *Telephone:* 0171-722 2500.

BROWSE, Sir Norman Leslie, Kt., M.D., F.R.C.P., F.R.C.S.; British surgeon; b. 1 Dec. 1931, London; s. of Reginald Browse and Margaret Browse; m. Jeanne Menage 1957; one s. one d.; ed. St. Bartholomew's Hosp. Medical Coll. and Univ. of Bristol; Capt. R.A.M.C. 1957–59; Sr. House Officer and Registrar, Bristol 1959–62; lecturer in Surgery, Westminster Hosp. 1962–65; Harkness Fellow, Research Assoc. Mayo Clinic, Rochester, Minn. 1964–65; Reader in Surgery and consultant surgeon, St. Thomas' Hosp. 1965–72, Prof. of Vascular Surgery 1972–81, Prof. of Surgery 1981–96, consulting surgeon 1996–; Hon. consultant to Army and R.A.F. 1980–96; Prof. of Surgery, United Medical and Dental Schools 1981–96; Prof. Emer. Univ. of London 1996–; Pres. Royal Coll. of Surgeons of England 1992–95; Chair., Jt. Consultants Cttee. 1994–98, Lord Brock Memorial Trust 1994–; Vice-Chair. British Vascular Foundation 1997–; various fellowships and other professional distinctions. *Publications:* Physiology and Pathology of Bed Rest 1964, Symptoms and Signs of Surgical Disease 1978, Reducing Operation for Lymphoedema 1986, Diseases of the Veins 1989. *Leisure interests:* marine art, medieval history, sailing. *Address:* Corbet House, Butes Lane, Alderney, GY9 3UW, Channel Islands.

BROYLES, William Dodson, Jr., M.A.; American journalist; b. 8 Oct. 1944, Houston; s. of William Dodson and Elizabeth (née Bills) Broyles; m. Sybil Ann Newman 1973; one s. one d.; ed. Rice Univ., Houston, Oxford Univ.; U.S. Marine Corps Reserve 1969–71; teacher Philosophy U.S. Naval Acad. 1970–71; Asst. Supt. Houston Public Schools 1971–72; Ed.-in-Chief Texas Monthly 1972–82; Ed.-in-Chief California Magazine 1980–82; Ed.-in-Chief Newsweek Magazine 1982–84; Columnist, U.S. News and World Report 1986; Co-producer, exec. consultant China Beach (T.V. programme) 1988–; screenwriter Apollo 13 1995; Bronze Star.

BRUBAKER, Charles William, B.ARCH.; American architect; b. 28 Sept. 1926, South Bend, Ind.; s. of Ralph Brubaker and Mary Brubaker; m. Elizabeth Rogers 1955; two s. one d.; ed. Univ. of Tex. at Austin; architect Perkins & Will, architects, Chicago 1950–58, partner 1958–70, Vice-Pres. 1980–85, Pres. 1985–86, Vice-Chair. 1986–; architect for numerous school, coll. and univ. bldgs. and responsible for campus planning both in U.S.A. and worldwide; Fellow, American Inst. of Architects, Chancellor 1988–89. *Publication:* Planning Flexible Learning Places 1977. *Leisure interests:* sketching, history of architecture, music, sailing. *Address:* Perkins and Will Inc., 330 N. Wabash Avenue, Chicago, IL 60611 (Office); 82 Essex Road, Winnetka, IL 60093, U.S.A. (Home). *Telephone:* (708) 446-2624 (Home).

BRUBECK, David Warren, B.A.; American musician; b. 6 Dec. 1920, Concord, Calif.; s. of Howard P. Brubeck and Elizabeth Ivey; m. Iola Whitlock 1942; five s. one d.; ed. Pacific and Mills Colls.; Leader Dave Brubeck Octet, Trio and Quartet 1946–; formed Dave Brubeck Quartet 1951; numerous tours and recordings; many awards from trade magazines, Metronome, Downbeat, Billboard, Melodymaker; Hon. Ph.D. (Univ. of Pacific, Fairfield Univ., Univ. of Bridgeport, Mills Coll., Niagara Univ., Kalamazoo Coll.); Jazz Pioneer Award, BMI 1985; Compostela Humanitarian Award 1986; Connecticut Arts Award 1987; American Eagle Award, Nat. Music Council 1988; Gerard Manley Hopkins Award 1991; Nat. Medal of the Arts 1994; mem. American Jazz Hall of Fame 1995, Lifetime Achievement Award Nat. Acad. of Recording Arts and Sciences 1996; Duke Ellington Fellow, Yale Univ.; composer of 250 jazz pieces and songs. *Extended works:* ballets: Points on Jazz 1962, Glances 1976; orchestral: Elementals 1963, They All Sang Yankee Doodle 1976; flute and guitar: Tritonis 1979; piano: Reminiscences of the Cattle Country 1946, Four by Four 1946; Oratorios: The Light in the Wilderness 1968, Beloved Son 1978, Voice of the Holy Spirit 1985; cantatas: Gates of Justice 1969, Truth is Fallen 1971, La Fiesta de la Posada 1975, In Praise of Mary 1989; chorus and orchestra: Pange Lingua Variations 1983, Upon this Rock Chorale and Fugue 1987, Lenten Triptych 1988, Joy in the Morning 1991; Mass: To Hope! A Celebration 1980; SATB Chorus: I See, Satie 1987, Four New England Pieces 1988; Earth is our Mother 1992. *Address:* Derry Music Company, 601 Montgomery Street, Suite 800, San Francisco, CA 94111; c/o Sutton Artists Corporation, 20 West Park Avenue, Suite 305, Long Beach, NY 11561; Box 216, Wilton, CT 06897, U.S.A.

BRUCE, Christopher, C.B.E.; British artistic director and choreographer; b. 3 Oct. 1945, Leicester; s. of Alexander Bruce and Ethel Parker; m. Marian Meadowcroft 1967; two s. one d.; ed. Rambert School, London; dancer, Ballet Rambert, London 1963–80; Assoc. Dir. Ballet Rambert 1975–79, Assoc. Choreographer 1979–87; Assoc. Choreographer, English Nat. Ballet (fmrly. London Festival Ballet), London 1986–91; Resident Choreographer, Houston Ballet 1989–; Artistic Dir. Rambert Dance Co. 1994–; choreographer for Kent Opera, Nederlands Dans Theater, Ballet du Grand Théâtre de Genève, etc.; *ballets include*: George Frideric 1969, for those who die as cattle 1971, There Was a time 1972, Weekend 1974, Ancient Voices of Children 1975, Black Angels 1976, Cruel Carden 1977, Night with Waning Moon 1979, Dancing Day 1981, Ghost Dances 1981, Berlin Requiem 1982, Concertino 1983, Intimate Pages 1984, Ceremonies 1986, Swansong 1987, Symphony in Three Movements 1989, Waiting 1993, Crossing 1994, Meeting Point 1995 (for "United We Dance" Int. Festival celebrating 50 years of UN), Quicksilver (tribute to Marie Rambert to celebrate Rambert Dance Co.'s 70th anniversary) 1996, Stream 1996, Four Scenes 1998; Evening Standard Inaugural Dance Award 1974; Int. Theatre Inst. Award 1993; Evening Standard Ballet Award 1996. *Address:* Rambert Dance Company, 94 Chiswick High Road, London, W4 1SH, England. *Telephone:* 0181-995 4246. *Fax:* 0181–747 8323.

BRUCKMANN, Gerhart, PH.D., M.P.; Austrian politician and statistician; b. 9 Jan. 1932, Vienna; s. of Friedrich Bruckmann and Anny (née Pötzl) Bruckmann; m. Hilde Bartl 1961; two s.; ed. Univ. of Graz, Vienna and Rome, Antioch Coll., U.S.A.; with Austrian Fed. Chamber of Commerce 1957–67; Prof. of Statistics, Univ. of Linz 1967–68, Univ. of Vienna 1968–92; Dir. Inst. for Advanced Studies 1968–73; Consultant Int. Inst. for Applied Systems Analysis 1973–83, Council mem. 1983–86; M.P. 1986–94; Bd. mem. Austrian Sr. Citizens' Union 1998–; Exec. Officer European Sr. Citizens' Union 1998–; mem. Austrian Acad. of Sciences, Club of Rome. *Publications:* Auswege in die Zukunft 1974, Sonnenkraft statt Atomenergie 1978, Groping in the Dark (with D. Meadows and J. Richardson) 1982, Megatrends für Österreich 1988, Österreicher wer bist du? 1989. *Leisure interest:* collecting anchor building blocks. *Address:* Österr. Seniorenbund, Lichtenfelsgasse 7, A-1010 Vienna (Office); Zehenthofgasse 11, 1190 Vienna, Austria (Home). *Telephone:* (431) 40126-151 (Office).

BRUCKNER, Pascal, D. ÈS L.; French writer and lecturer; b. 15 Dec. 1948, Paris; s. of René Bruckner and Monique Bruckner; m. Violaine Barret 1970 (divorced 1973); one s.; also one d. by Caroline Thompson; ed. Lycée Henri IV, Univs. de Paris I (Sorbonne), Paris VII (Jussieu); annual travels in Asia 1977–90; lecturer Inst. d'Etudes Politiques, Paris 1990–; Visiting Prof. Univs. of San Diego and New York 1986–95; Prix Médicis 1995, Prix Renaudot 1995; Chevalier des Arts et des Lettres. *Publications:* Le Nouveau Désordre Amoureux 1977, Le Divin Enfant 1992, La Tentation de l'Innocence 1995, Les Voleurs de Beauté 1997. *Leisure interests:* piano, sports, fantasy films. *Address:* 8 rue Marie Stuart, 75002 Paris, France. *Telephone:* (1) 40.26.68.79. *Fax:* (1) 40.56.34.38.

BRUECKNER, Keith Allan, M.A., PH.D.; American professor of physics; b. 19 March 1924, Minneapolis, Minn.; s. of Leo John and Agnes Holland Brueckner; m. Bonnie Brueckner; two s. one d.; ed. Univs. of Minnesota and California (Berkeley), Inst. for Advanced Study, Princeton; Asst. Prof. Indiana Univ. 1951–54, Assoc. Prof. 1954–55; Physicist, Brookhaven Nat. Lab. (N.Y.) 1955–56; Prof. of Physics, Univ. of Pa. 1956–59; Prof. of Physics, Univ. of Calif. (San Diego) 1959–; Vice-Pres. and Dir. of Research, Inst. for Defense Analyses, Wash., D.C. 1961–62; Tech. Dir. KMS Tech. Center, San Diego 1968–71; Exec. Vice-Pres. and Tech. Dir. KMS Fusion Inc., Ann Arbor 1971–74; Consulting Ed., Pure and Applied Physics Series, Academic Press 1964–; mem. N.A.S.; Hon. D.Sc. (Indiana Univ.) 1976; Dannie Heinemann Prize for Mathematical Physics 1963. *Publications:* Numerous articles in scientific journals. *Leisure interests:* mountain climbing, skiing, sailing, surfing. *Address:* Department of Physics, University of California at San Diego, La Jolla, CA 92093, U.S.A. (Office). *Telephone:* (619) 452-2892 (Office).

BRUEL, Jean-Marc André; French business executive; b. 18 Feb. 1936, Akbou, Algeria; s. of René Bruel and Jeanine Poirson; m. Anne-Mary Barthod

1962; two s. two d.; ed. Ecole Centrale des arts et Manufactures; Head of tech. services, Rhodiaceta, Brazil 1964; Dir. nylon polyester factory, Rhône-Poulenc, Brazil 1968; Deputy Dir.-Gen. of textile production Rhône-Poulenc, Brazil 1971; Deputy Dir.-Gen. Div. of plant hygiene, groupe Rhône-Poulenc 1975, Dir.-Gen. 1976; Asst. to Pres. and mem. Exec. Cttee. Rhône-Poulenc 1979–80, Deputy Dir.-Gen. 1980, Dir.-Gen. 1982–84; mem. Exec. Cttee. Sandoz, Basle 1985–87; Dir.-Gen. Rhône Poulenc 1987–92, Vice-Pres. 1992–; Pres. Rhône Poulenc Chimie 1987–92; Vice-Pres. European Council of Fed. of Chemical Industry (Cefic) 1988; Pres. Soc. of Chemical Industry 1993–94, Villette Enterprises 1995–, Institut Curie 1998–. *Leisure interests:* tennis, sailing. *Address:* Rhône Poulenc, 25 quai Paul Doumer, 92408 Courbevoie Cedex (Office); 105 bis rue de Longchamp, 92200 Neuilly-sur-Seine, France (Home).

BRUGGER, Ernst; Swiss politician and banker; b. 10 March 1914, Bellinzona; s. of Alois Brugger and Ida Müller; m. Eleonora Ringer 1937; five s.; ed. Univs. of Zürich, London, Paris; Secondary school teacher, Gossau 1936; Deputy to Kantonsrat 1947–59; Mayor of Gossau 1949–59; mem. Zürich Canton Govt. 1959–69, Dir. of Interior and Justice Depts. 1959–67, Dir. of Public Economy Dept. 1967–69; mem. Fed. Council 1970–78, Vice-Pres. Jan.-Dec. 1973, Pres. Jan.-Dec. 1974; Head of Fed. Dept. of Public Economy 1970–78, retd. from Govt. Feb. 1978; Chair. Finland-EFTA Jt. Council at Ministerial level and of Consultative Cttee. 1974; Chair. of Bd. of Dirs. Swiss Volksbank -1986, Swiss charitable org. Pro-Infirmis; Radical Democrat. *Leisure interest:* mountaineering. *Address:* 'Berg', 8625 Gossau 2H, Switzerland. *Telephone:* (01) 935 16 73.

BRUGUERA, Sergi; Spanish tennis player; b. 16 Jan. 1971, Barcelona; s. of Luis Bruguera; coached by his father; Nat. Jr. Champion 1987; turned professional 1988; winner French Open 1993, 1994.

BRUMBACK, Charles Tiedtke, C.P.A.; American communications executive (retd.); b. 27 Sept. 1928, Toledo; s. of John Brumback and Frances Tiedtke; m. Mary Howe 1951; two s. two d.; ed. Princeton Univ. and Univ. of Toledo; with Arthur Young & Co. 1950–57; Business Man., Vice-Pres., Treas., Pres., C.E.O., Dir. Sentinel Star Co. (subsidiary of Tribune Co.), Orlando, Fla. 1957–81; Pres. and C.E.O. Chicago Tribune 1981–88, Pres. and C.O.O. 1988–90, C.E.O. 1990–95, Chair. 1993–95, Dir. 1981–96; mem. Bd. of Dirs. Tribune Co., Chicago, Chair. 1993–94; Chair Northwestern Healthcare Network 1994–98, Newspaper Asscn. of America 1994–95; Bronze Star. *Address:* Tribune Co., 435 N. Michigan Avenue, Chicago, IL 60611; 1500 N. Lake Shore Drive, Columbus, IL 60610, U.S.A.

BRUNDIN, Clark Lannerdahl, B.S., PH.D.; American university administrator and engineer; b. 21 March 1931, Los Angeles, Calif.; s. of late Ernest Brundin and late Elinor (née Clark) Brundin; m. Judith Anne Maloney 1959; two s. two d.; ed. Whittier High School, Calif. Inst. of Tech. and Univ. of Calif., Berkeley; electronics petty officer, US Navy 1951–55; Assoc. in Mech. Eng., Univ. of Calif., Berkeley 1956–57, Research Engineer, Inst. of Eng. Research 1959–63; Demonstrator Dept. of Eng. Science, Univ. of Oxford 1957–58, lecturer 1963–85; Vice-Chair. Gen. Bd. of Faculties, Univ. of Oxford 1984–85; Fellow and Tutor in Eng., Jesus Coll., Oxford 1964–85, Sr. Tutor 1974–77, Estates Bursar 1978–84, Hon. Fellow 1985–; Gov. Oxford Polytechnic 1978–83, Cokethorpe School 1983–96, Magdalen Coll. School 1987–, Coventry School Foundation; Vice-Chancellor Univ. of Warwick 1985–92; Visiting Prof. Univ. of Calif., Santa Barbara 1978; Visiting Scholar Center for Study of Higher Educ., Univ. of Calif. Berkeley 1997–; Chair. Anchor Housing Asscn. 1985–91; Dir. Blackwell Science Ltd. 1990–98; Dir. Heritage Projects (Oxford) 1986–97, Oxford Univ. School of Man. Studies 1992–96, Finsbury Growth Trust PLC 1995–, Charities Aid Foundation America 1997– (Pres. 1998–); Pres. Templeton Coll., Oxford 1992–96; mem. Eng. Bd., C.N.A.A. 1976–82. *Publications:* articles on rarefied gas dynamics and education. *Leisure interests:* sailing, mending old machinery, all types of music. *Address:* Jesus College, Oxford, OX1 3DW, England (Office).

BRUNDTLAND, Gro Harlem, M.D., M.P.H.; Norwegian politician and physician; b. 20 April 1939, Oslo; d. of Gudmund and Inga Harlem; m. Arne Olav Brundtland 1960; three s. (one deceased) one d.; ed. Oslo and Harvard Univs.; Consultant, Ministry of Health and Social Affairs 1965–67; Medical Officer, Oslo City Health Dept. 1968–69; Deputy Dir. School Health Services, Oslo 1969; Minister of Environment 1974–79; Deputy Leader Labour Party 1975–81, Leader Labour Parl. Group 1981–92; Prime Minister of Norway Feb.–Oct. 1981, 1986–89, 1990–96; mem. Parl. Standing Cttee. on Foreign Affairs, fmr. mem. Parl. Standing Cttee. on Finance; mem. of Storting (Parl.) 1977–97; Dir.-Gen. WHO July 1998–; Chair. UN World Comm. on Environment and Devt.; fmr. Vice-Chair. Sr. Secondary Schools' Socialist Asscn., Students' Asscn. of Labour Party; Third World Prize for Work on Environmental Issues 1989, Indira Gandhi Prize 1990, Onassis Foundation Award 1992. *Publications:* Articles on preventive medicine, school health and growth studies. *Leisure interest:* cross-country skiing. *Address:* World Health Organization Avenue Appia, 1211 Geneva 27, Switzerland; Th. Løvstads vei 19, N-0286 Oslo 2, Norway (Home).

BRUNEI, Sultan of (see Bolkiah).

BRUNER, Jerome Seymour, PH.D.; American professor of psychology; b. 1 Oct. 1915, New York; s. of Herman Bruner and Rose Bruner; m. 1st Katherine Frost 1940 (divorced 1956); one s. one d.; m. 2nd Blanche Marshall McLane 1960 (divorced 1984); m. 3rd Carol Fleisher Feldman; ed. Duke and Harvard Univs.; U.S. Intelligence 1941–42; Assoc. Dir. Office of Public Opinion Research, Princeton 1942–44; Political Intelligence, France 1943; Research, Harvard Univ. 1945–72, Prof. of Psychology 1952–72, Dir. Center for Cognitive Studies 1961–72; Ed. Public Opinion Quarterly 1943–44; Lecturer, Salzburg Seminar 1952; Bacon Prof., Univ. of Aix-en-Provence 1965; Watts Prof. of Psychology, Oxford Univ. 1972–80; Univ. Prof., New School for Social Research, New York 1981–88; Research Prof. of Psychology, New York Univ. 1988–, Sr. Researcher Fellow, Law School 1991–; Hon. D.Sc. (Northwestern) 1965, (Sheffield) 1970, (Bristol) 1965, (Columbia) 1991, Hon. M.A. (Oxford) 1972, Hon. LL.D. (Temple) 1965, (Cincinnati) 1966, (New Brunswick) 1969, (Yale) 1978, Hon. D.Litt. (North Mich.) 1969, (Duke) 1969, (York Univ.) 1993, Dr. h.c. (Sorbonne) 1974, (Leuven) 1976, (Ghent) 1977, (Madrid) 1986, (Free Univ. Berlin) 1988, (Rome) 1992; mem. American Acad. of Arts and Sciences; Fellow, New York Inst. for the Humanities; Int. Balzan Foundation Prize 1987. *Publications:* Mandate from the People 1944, The Process of Education 1960, On Knowing: Essays for the Left Hand 1962, Toward a Theory of Instruction 1966, Processes of Cognitive Growth: Infancy, (Vol. 111) 1968, The Relevance of Education 1971, Under Five in Britain 1980, Communication as a Language 1982, In Search of Mind 1983, Child's Talk 1983, Actual Minds, Possible Worlds 1986, Acts of Meaning 1990, The Culture of Education 1996; also co-author of several books. *Leisure interest:* sailing. *Address:* 200 Mercer Street, New York, NY 10012, U.S.A. *Telephone:* (212) 674 7816. *Fax:* (212) 673 6118.

BRUNETTA, Renato; Italian professor of labour economics; b. 26 May 1950, Venice; ed. Marco Foscarini Liceo Classico, Venice and Univs. of Padua, Cambridge and Rotterdam; researcher in political sciences, Univ. of Padua 1975–77, Prof. of Labour Econs. 1978–82; Gen/Sec. Fondazione G. Brodolini, Rome 1980–; Ed. Economia & Lavoro (quarterly review), Rome 1980–; chief consultant, econ. adviser to Italian Ministry of Labour 1983–88; Sec. Italian Asscn. of Labour Economists 1985–87; Vice-Pres., OECD Manpower and Social Affairs Cttee. 1986–88; founder and Ed. Labour (4-monthly journal) 1987–; Pres. Comm. on Information for CNEL (Nat. Council of Economy and Labour) 1989–94, European Asscn. of Labour Economists 1989–93, Scientific Cttee. on European Integration of Ministry of Foreign Affairs 1990–92; Prof. of Labour Econs. Rome Univ. II 'Tor Vergata' 1990–; Premio Saint Vincent (for econs.) 1988, mem. ASPEN-Italy 1989–, Taskforce for Programming and Econ. Policy, Ministry of the Budget 1990–; Councillor, CNEL 1995–; Premio Tarantelli (for econs.) 1993. *Publications:* Economia del Lavoro 1981, Multilocalizzazione produttiva come strategia d'impresa 1983, Squilibri, conflitto, piena occupazione 1983, Spesa pubblica e conflitto 1987, Microeconomia del lavoro: Teorie e analisi empiriche 1987, Labour Relations and Economic Performance (ed.) 1990, Il Modello Italia 1991, Economics for the New Europe 1991, Il conflitto e le relazioni di lavoro negli anni '90 1992, Disoccupazione, Isteresi, Irreversibilita 1992, Retribuzione, costo del lavoro. Regolazione e deregolazione; il capital umano; la destrutturazione del mercato (Ed.) 1992, La fine della società dei salariati 1994, Sud: Alcune idee perché il Mezzogiorno non resti com'è 1995; articles and essays on labour econs. and industrial relations. *Leisure interests:* photography, history of Venice, gastronomy. *Address:* Fondazione Cassa di Risparmio di Venezia, S. Marco 2847, 30124 Venice, Italy. *Telephone:* (41) 5226805. *Fax:* (41) 5225573.

BRUNHART, Hans; Liechtenstein politician; b. 28 March 1945, Balzers; s. of Andreas and Rosa Brunhart; m. Bernadette Biedermann 1972; one s.; ed. Lyceum Gutenberg in Balzers, Univs. of Freiburg and Basel, Switzerland; Dir. Liechtenstein Nat. Library and Liechtenstein State Archives, Vaduz 1972–74; Deputy to Head of Govt. 1974–78; Head of Govt. 1978–93; Head Depts. Foreign and External Affairs, Educ., Finance and Bldg. 1982–93; Grand Cross, Liechtenstein Princely Order of Merit, Grosses Goldenes Ehrenzeichen am Bande für Verdienste (Austria), Grand Cross of the Order of Pius IX, "Piano". *Publications:* contributions to Der Schriftsteller und sein Verhältnis zur Sprache 1971, 2 essays in Liechtenstein Politische Schriften 1972, 1973.

BRUNI-SAKRAISCHIK, Claudio Alberico; American (b. Italian) art consultant and critic; b. 5 May 1926, Udine, Italy; s. of Bruno Bruni and Caterina Ellero; ed. Univs. of Bologna and Rome; Pres. La Medusa Gallery Inc., New York; Art Expert by appt. of Tribunal of Rome; Curator Gen. Catalogue of Works of Giorgio de Chirico; Vice-Pres. Giorgio and Isa de Chirico Foundation, Rome; Hon. Pres. Italian Art Dealers' Asscn.; lectures on de Chirico. *Publications:* General Catalogue of the Works of Giorgio de Chirico (vols. 1–9), several books and articles on the artist. *Address:* 128 East 72nd Street, New York, NY 10021, U.S.A.; Via Margutta 60, 00187 Rome, Italy. *Telephone:* (212) 744-5593 (New York); 320 7749 (Rome).

BRUNO, Franklin Roy (Frank), M.B.E.; British boxer; b. 16 Nov. 1961, London; s. of late Robert Bruno and of Lynette Bruno (née Cambell); m. Laura Frances Mooney 1990; one s. two d.; ed. Oak Hall School, Sussex; began boxing with Wandsworth Boys' Club, London 1970; mem. Sir Philip Game Amateur Boxing Club 1977–80; won 20 out of 21 contests as amateur; professional career 1982–96; won 38 out of 42 contests as professional 1982–89; European heavyweight champion 1985–86 (relinquished title), World heavyweight title challenges against Tim Witherspoon 1986, Mike Tyson 1989; staged comeback, won first contest 1991; lost 4th World Title Challenge against Lennox Lewis Oct. 1993; World Heavyweight Boxing Champion 1995–96, lost title to Mike Tyson 1996; appearances in pantomimes 1990, 1991; fmr. presenter, BBC TV; SOS Sports Personality of the

Year 1990; TV Times Sports Personality of the Year 1990; announced retirement Aug. 1996. *Publication:* Personality: From Zero to Hero (with Norman Giller) 1996. *Leisure interests:* music, training. *Address:* c/o P.O. Box 2266, Brentwood, Essex, CM15 0AQ, England. *Fax:* (01277) 822209.

BRUNSCHWIG, Jacques, D. ÈS LETT.; French professor of history of ancient philosophy; b. 27 April 1929, Paris; s. of Robert Brunschwig and Isabelle Vidal-Naquet; m. Hélène Blancherie 1960; one s. one d.; ed. Lycée Carnot, Lycée Henri IV, Paris, Ecole Normale Supérieure, Univ. of Paris; instructor, Univ. of Paris 1953–57; researcher, C.N.R.S. 1957–66; Asst. Lecturer, Univ. of Paris 1966–69; Head of Courses, Univ. of Picardie, Amiens 1969–76; Prof., Univ. of Paris X (Nanterre) 1976–88; Prof. of History of Ancient Philosophy, Univ. of Paris I 1988–94, Prof. Emer. 1994–; Visiting Fellow Christ's Coll. Cambridge 1999; Corresp. Fellow British Acad. *Publications:* Aristote, Topiques (critical edn., French trans. and notes) 1967, Papers in Hellenistic Philosophy 1994, Etudes sur les philosophes hellénistiques 1995, Le Savoir grec (co-ed. with G.E.R. Lloyd) 1996; about 60 contribs. to books and learned journals. *Leisure interest:* music. *Address:* 10 rue des Jardinets, 92160 Antony, France. *Telephone:* (1) 42-37-62-61. *Fax:* 42-37-35-62.

BRUNT, Peter Astbury, M.A., F.B.A.; British professor of ancient history; b. 23 June 1917, Croydon; s. of Rev. Samuel Brunt and Gladys Eileen Brunt; ed. Ipswich School, Oriel Coll., Oxford; Temporary Civil Servant 1940–45; Craven Fellow, Oxford Univ. 1946–47; Lecturer in Ancient History, Univ. of St. Andrews 1947–51; Fellow and Tutor, Oriel Coll., Oxford 1951–67; Fellow and Sr. Bursar, Gonville and Caius Coll., Cambridge 1968–70; Camden Prof. of Ancient History, Oxford, and Fellow of Brasenose Coll. 1970–82, Prof. Emer. 1982–; Hon. Fellow of Oriel Coll., Oxford. *Publications:* Italian Manpower 225 B.C.–A.D. 14 1971, Social Conflicts of Roman Republic 1971, Arrian's Anabasis and Indica, 2 vols. (ed.) 1976, The Fall of the Roman Republic and related essays 1988, Roman Imperial Themes 1990, Studies in Greek History and Thought 1992, numerous articles and reviews in academic journals. *Address:* 37 Woodstock Close, Woodstock Road, Oxford, OX2 8DB, England. *Telephone:* (01865) 553024.

BRUNTON, Sir Gordon Charles, Kt.; British business executive; b. 27 Dec. 1921, London; s. of Charles A. Brunton and Hylda Pritchard; m. 1st Nadine Sohr 1946 (divorced 1965); one s. (one s. deceased) two d.; m. 2nd Gillian A. Kirk 1966; one s. one d.; ed. Cranleigh School and London School of Econs.; war service 1942–46; joined Tothill Press 1947, Exec. Dir. 1956; Man. Dir. Tower Press Group 1958; Exec. Dir. Odhams Press 1961; joined Thomson Org. 1961, Dir. 1963, Man. Dir. and C.E.O. Int. Thomson Org. PLC (fmrly. Thomson British Holdings), and Thomson Org. Ltd. 1968–84; Man. Dir. Thomson Publications 1961; Chair. Thomson Travel 1965–68; Pres. Int. Thomson Org. Ltd. 1978–84; Dir. Times Newspapers Ltd. 1967–81, Bemrose Corpn. 1974 (Chair. 1978–91), Sotheby Parke Bernet Group PLC 1978–85, Cable and Wireless PLC 1981–91, Yattendon Investment Trust PLC 1985–; fmr. non-exec. Dir. Cable and Wireless PLC, South Bank Bd. (Arts Council); Pres. Periodical Publishers' Asscn. 1972–74, 1981–82, Nat. Advertising Benevolent Soc. 1973–75; Chair. Econ. Devt. Council for Civil Eng. 1978–84, Appeals Cttee., Independent Adoption Soc., Communications and Gen. Consultants Ltd. 1985–, Mercury Communications Ltd. 1986–90, Cavendish Shops 1985–93, Community Industry Ltd. 1985–92, The Racing Post plc 1985–97, Ingersoll Publications 1988–91, Verity Group PLC (fmrly. Wharfedale PLC) 1991–97, Green Field Leisure Group Ltd 1992–, PhoneLink PLC 1993–, Euram Consulting Ltd., Focus Investments Ltd., Cavendish Retail, Racing Int. Ltd. and other limited cos.; Gov. and Fellow L.S.E., Henley Man. Coll. 1983–86; Pres. The History of Advertising Trust 1981–84; mem. Council, Templeton Coll. (fmrly. Oxford Cen. for Man. Studies); mem. South Bank Bd., Arts Council 1985–92. *Leisure interests:* books, breeding horses. *Address:* North Munstead, North Munstead Lane, Godalming, Surrey, GU8 4AX, England. *Telephone:* (01483) 416313.

BRUSKIN, Grisha (Brouskine Grigori); Russian artist; b. 21 Oct. 1945, Moscow; s. of David Brouskin and Bassia Strunina; m. 1st Ludmila Dmitrieva 1975 (divorced 1978); m. 2nd Alexandra Makarova 1982; one d. one adopted s.; ed. Art High School, Moscow, Moscow Textile Inst.; became mem. Soviet Artists' Union 1968; work includes paintings, gouaches, drawings, sculptures, performances; work included in first Sotheby's auction in Moscow, designed poster for Chicago Art Exhbn. 1988; now lives and works in New York, U.S.A.; solo exhbns. in Moscow 1976, 1984, Vilnius, Lithuania 1983, Marlborough Gallery, New York 1990; numerous group exhbns. including The Painter and Modernism, Moscow 1987, 100 Years of Russian Art, Barbican, London and in Chicago, Berne, Seoul, Cologne, Chicago, New York, Barcelona, Paris, Munich, Düsseldorf, Lisbon, Brussels, Berlin, Copenhagen 1988–; works in Art Inst. of Chicago, Jewish Museum, New York, Museum of Modern Art, New York, Nat. Museum of Israel, Jerusalem etc. *Leisure interests:* literature, music.

BRUSTAD, Tor; Norwegian biophysicist; b. 20 Dec. 1926; s. of Johan Ludvig and Aslaug Brustad; m. Berte-Marie Brustad 1953; one s. two d.; ed. Univs. of Oslo and California; Research Fellow, Univ. of Oslo 1953–54, Norwegian Cancer Soc. 1954–57, U.S. Nat. Acad. of Sciences 1957–59; Research Assoc. Univ. of California 1959–60; Chair. Dept. of Biophysics, Norsk Hydro's Inst. for Cancer Research (Chair. Exec. Council 1975–84), Oslo 1962–; Chair. Dept. of Medical Physics, The Norwegian Radium Hospital (Chair. Admin. Council 1978–81), Oslo 1968–; Prof. of Radiation Biophysics, Univ. of Trondheim 1970; mem. Norwegian Acad. of Science and Letters, Royal Norwegian Soc. of Science and Letters 1978; Kt. Royal Norwegian Order of St. Olav (1st Class) 1995. *Publications:* on radiation effects on various biological systems. *Address:* Institute for Cancer Research, Montebello 0310, Oslo 3 (Office); Nordveien 30, 1342 Jar, Norway (Home). *Telephone:* 22935635 (Office); 67149750 (Home). *Fax:* 22732944.

BRUSTEIN, Robert, M.A., PH.D.; American drama critic, actor and producer; b. 21 April 1927, New York, N.Y.; m. 1st Norma Cates 1962 (deceased 1979); one s. one step-s; m. 2nd Doreen Beinart 1996; two step-c.; ed. Amherst Coll. Yale Univ. Drama School, Columbia Univ.; played about 70 roles in theatre groups and TV plays 1950–; Instructor, Cornell Univ. 1955–56, Vassar Coll. 1956–57; lecturer, Columbia Univ. 1957–58, Asst. Prof. 1958–63, Assoc. Prof. 1963–65, Prof. 1965–66; Prof. of English, Yale Univ., Dean of Yale Drama School, Artistic Dir. and Founder, Yale Repertory Theatre 1966–79; Artistic Dir. and Founder American Repertory Theatre Ensemble, Loeb Drama Center, Cambridge, Mass. 1979–; Prof. of English, Harvard Univ. 1979–; Drama Critic, The New Republic 1959–67, 1978–, Contributing Ed. 1959–79; host and writer, The Opposition Theatre (Net TV) 1966–; regular contributor to New York Times 1972–; Founder, Artistic Dir. Yale Repertory Theatre 1966–79; Advisory Ed., Theatre Quarterly 1967–; Guest Critic, The Observer, U.K. 1972–73, 1978–, Contributing Ed. 1959–; Trustee, Sarah Lawrence Coll. 1973–77; Panel mem. Nat. Endowment for the Arts 1970–72, 1981–84; mem. Nat. Acad. Arts and Sciences; Fulbright Fellow 1953–55, Guggenheim Fellow 1961–62, Ford Fellow 1964–65; George G. Nathan Prize in Criticism 1962, George Polk Memorial Award in Criticism 1964, Jersey City Journal Award in Theatre Criticism 1967; Eliot Norton Award for Theatre; New England Theatre Conf. Award for Excellence in Theme, Award, Outstanding Achievement in American Theater, New England Theater Council 1985, Tiffany Award for Excellence in Theater, Soc. for Performing Arts Administrators 1987; American Acad. of Arts and Letters Distinguished Services to Arts Award 1995; Litt.D. (Lawrence Univ.) 1968, (Amherst Coll.) 1972, L.H.D. (Beloit Coll.) 1975; Hon. Dr. of Arts (Bard Coll.) 1981. *Publications:* Introduction to The Plays of Chekhov 1964; Ed. The Plays of Strindberg 1964; author: The Theatre of Revolt 1964, Seasons of Discontent 1965, The Third Theatre 1969, Revolution as Theatre 1971, The Culture Watch 1975, The Plays and Prose of Strindberg (editor), Critical Moments 1980, Making Scenes 1981, Who Needs Theatre 1987, Reimagining American Theatre 1991, Dumbocracy in America 1994, Demons 1995 (play), Nobody Dies on Friday 1996 (play); articles in well-known journals and newspapers. *Address:* Loeb Drama Center, Harvard University, Cambridge, MA 02138, U.S.A.

BRUTON, John Gerard, B.A., B.L.; Irish politician and farmer; b. 18 May 1947, Dublin; s. of Matthew Joseph Bruton and Doris Mary Delany; m. Finola Gill 1981; one s. three d.; ed. Clongowes Wood Coll., Univ. Coll., Dublin, King's Inn, Dublin; mem. Dáil Éireann (House of Reps.) 1969–; Fine Gael Spokesman on Agric. 1972–73; Parl. Sec. to Minister for Educ. 1973–77, to Minister for Industry and Commerce 1975–77; Fine Gael Spokesman on Agric. 1977–81, on Finance Jan.–June 1981; Minister of Finance 1981–82, of Industry, Trade, Commerce and Tourism 1982–86, of Finance 1986–87; Deputy Leader of Fine Gael 1987–90, Leader 1990–, Fine Gael Spokesman on Industry and Commerce 1987–89, on Educ. 1989–90; mem. Parl. Ass., Council of Europe 1989–91, British-Irish Parl. Body 1993–94; Prime Minister of Ireland 1994–97; Barrister; Hon. Citizen, Sioux City, Iowa, U.S.A. *Leisure interests:* history, folk music, tennis. *Address:* Dáil Éireann, Leinster House, Dublin 2; Cornelstown, Dunboyne, County Meath, Ireland (Home). *Telephone:* 6183117 (Office). *Fax:* 6184141 (Office).

BRUTUS, Dennis, B.A.; South African educationist and poet; b. 28 Nov. 1924, Salisbury, S. Rhodesia (now Harare, Zimbabwe); s. of Francis Henry Brutus and Margaret Winifred (née Bloemetjie); m. May Jaggers 1950; four s. four d.; ed. Paterson High School, Port Elizabeth, Fort Hare and Witwatersrand Univs.; language teacher, Paterson High School, Cen. Indian High School; office boy and law student, Witwatersrand Univ.; imprisoned for opposition to apartheid 1964–65, exiled 1966, political asylum in U.S.A. 1983; Dir. World Campaign for Release of S. African Political Prisoners; worked for Int. Defence and Aid Fund, fmrly. UN Rep.; Visiting Prof. Denver Univ.; Prof. of English, Northwestern Univ., Evanston, Ill.; Visiting Prof., English Dept., African and Afro-American Studies and Research Center, Univ. Tex., Austin, 1974–75; Visiting Prof., Dept. of English, Amherst Coll., Mass. 1982–83, Dartmouth Coll., N.H. 1983; Adjunct Prof. Northeastern Univ., Boston, Mass. 1984; Pres. S. African Non-Racial Olympic Cttee. (SAN-ROC); Chair. Int. Campaign Against Racism in Sport (ICARIS), Africa Network 1984–; Dir. Program on African and African-American Writing in Africa and the Diaspora 1989–; Interport lecturer Univ. of Pittsburg; Founding Chair., Exec. mem. African Literature Asscn., fmr. Chair. ARENA (Inst. for Study of Sport and Social Issues); mem. of Bd., Black Arts Celebration, Vice-Pres. Union of Writers of the African People; mem. Bd. of Dirs. UN Asscn. of Chicago and Ill., Editorial Bd. Africa Today; Dir. Troubadour Press; Fellow, Int. Poetry Soc.; mem. Modern Language Asscn. 1972, Int. Platform Asscn. 1979–, Int. Jury Books Abroad Award 1976; Hon. H.L.D. (Worcester State Coll.) 1982; Mbari Prize for Poetry in Africa, Chancellor's Prize for Bilingualism (Univ. of S. Africa); Freedom Writers' Award, Kenneth David Kaunda Humanism Award, Academic Excellence Award, Nat. Council for Black Studies 1982, UN Human Rights Day Award 1983. *Publications:* Sirens, Knuckles, Boots 1963, Letters to Martha 1968, Poems from Algiers 1970, Thoughts Abroad (John Bruin) 1971, A Simple Lust 1973, China

Poems 1975, Strains 1975, Stubborn Hope 1978, 1979, 1983, Salutes and Censures 1980. *Leisure interests:* sport, music, chess.

BRYAN, Sir Arthur, Kt.; British company director; b. 4 March 1923, Stoke-on-Trent; s. of William Woodall Bryan and Isobel Alan (née Tweedie); m. Betty Ratford 1947; one s. one d.; ed. Longton High School; served with R.A.F.V.R. 1941–45; joined Wedgwood Ltd. 1947, sales rep. 1949, Asst. London Man. 1950–53, London Man. and Gen. Man. of Wedgwood Rooms 1953–59, Gen. Sales Man. 1959–60; Dir. and Pres. Josiah Wedgwood & Sons Inc. of America 1960–62; Man. Dir. Wedgwood PLC 1963–85; Chair. 1968–86; Pres. Waterford Wedgwood Holdings PLC 1986–88; Dir. Waterford Glass Group PLC 1986–88; Dir. Friends' Provident Life Asscn. 1985–92, U.K. Fund Inc. 1987–, Dartington Crystal Group 1995–; Pres. British Ceramic Mfrs. Fed. 1970–71; mem. Court, Univ. of Keele; Chair. Consumer Market Advisory Cttee., Dept. of Trade and Industry 1988–; Companion, British Inst. of Man. 1968; Fellow, Inst. of Marketing, Royal Soc. of Arts 1964; Companion, Inst. Ceramics; K. St. J. 1972; Lord Lieut. of Staffordshire 1968–93. *Leisure interests:* walking, reading. *Address:* Parkfields Cottage, Tittensor, Stoke-on-Trent, Staffs, ST12 9HQ, England (Home).

BRYAN, John Henry, B.A.; American business executive; b. 5 Oct. 1936, West Point, Miss.; s. of John H. Bryan, Sr.; m. Neville Frierson Bryan 1958; two s. two d.; ed. Southwestern Univ. (now Rhodes Coll.), Memphis; joined Bryan Packing Co. 1960, Pres., C.E.O. 1968–74; Exec. Vice-Pres., Dir. Sara Lee Corpn. March–Oct. 1974, Pres. 1974–75, C.E.O. 1975–, Chair. 1976–; Dir. (non-exec.) Gen. Motors 1993–; mem. Bd. of Dirs. Amoco Corpn., First Chicago Corpn., The First Nat. Bank of Chicago; fmr. Chair. and mem. Bd. of Dirs. of Grocery Mfrs. of America, Inc.; mem. Business Roundtable, bds. Catalyst, Nat. Women's Econ. Alliance, Art Inst. of Chicago; Dir. Business Cttee. for Arts; Prin. of Chicago United; Trustee Rush-Presbyterian-St. Luke's Medical Center, Univ. of Chicago; Trustee Cttee. for Econ. Devt. *Address:* Sara Lee Corpn., 3 First National Plaza, Chicago, IL 60602-4260, U.S.A. (Office). *Telephone:* (312) 726-2600 (Office).

BRYAN, Richard H., LL.B.; American politician; b. 16 July 1937, Washington; m.; three c.; ed. Univ. of Nev. and Hastings Coll. of Law, Univ. of Calif.; admitted to Nev. Bar 1963, U.S. Supreme Court Bar 1967; Deputy Dist. Attorney, Clark Co., Nev. 1964–66; Public Defender, Clark Co. 1966–68; Counsel Clark Co. Juvenile Court 1968–69; mem. Nev. Assembly 1969–71; Nev. Senate 1973–77; Attorney-Gen., Nev. 1979–82; Gov. of Nevada Jan. 1983–89; Senator from Nevada Jan. 1989–; Democrat. *Address:* U.S. Senate, 269 Russell Senate Office Bldg., Washington, DC 20510, U.S.A.

BRYANT, John Martin, M.A., C.ENG., F.I.M.; British business executive; b. 28 Sept. 1943, Cardiff; s. of William George Bryant and Doris Bryant; m. Andrea Irene Emmons 1965; two s. one d.; ed. W. Monmouth School, Pontypool, St. Catharine's Coll., Cambridge; grad. trainee Steel Co. of Wales 1965–68; various tech., production, personnel positions British Steel 1968–78, Works Man. Hot Rolled Products 1978–87, Dir. Coated Products 1987–90, Dir. Tinplate 1990–92, Man. Dir. Strip Products 1992–96, Exec. Dir. 1996–98, Chief Exec. 1999–; Dir. Bank of Wales 1996–. *Leisure interests:* all sports, particularly squash and rugby, family. *Address:* British Steel PLC, 15 Marylebone Road, London, NW1 5JD, England.

BRYANT, Michael, C.B.E.; British actor; b. 5 April 1928; m. Judith Mary Coke 1990; has acted on stage in London and Broadway and in TV drama series; appearances with Nat. Theatre, London 1977–; Assoc. Dir. Royal Nat. Theatre 1996–; Council mem. Royal Acad. of Dramatic Art (RADA); Trustee Nat. Theatre Foundation. *Plays include:* Five Finger Exercise, Ross, and over 50 plays at the Royal Nat. Theatre. *Films include:* A Life for Ruth, The Mindbenders, Goodbye Mr Chips, The Happy Family, Nicholas and Alexandra, The Ruling Class, A Fortunate Man, Caravan to Vaccares, Gandhi, Sakharov. *Address:* 19 Deanhill Court, Upper Richmond Road, London, SW14 7DJ, England.

BRYANT, Thomas Edward, M.D., J.D.; American physician and attorney; b. 17 Jan. 1936, Ala.; s. of Howard Edward Bryant and Alibel Nettles Bryant; m. Lucie Elizabeth Thrasher 1961 (divorced); one s. one d.; ed. Emory Univ., Atlanta; Dir. of Health Affairs, U.S. Office of Econ. Opportunity 1969–70; Pres. Nat. Drug Abuse Council 1970–78; Chair. Pres. Comm. on Mental Health 1977–78; Dir. Children of Alcoholics Foundation 1983–; mem. Inst. of Medicine, N.A.S. 1972; Chair. The Public Cttee. on Mental Health 1977–79, Council for Understanding Mental Illnesses 1983–87, Aspirin Foundation of America 1987–, Non-Profit Man. Assocs. Inc. 1988–; Exec. Dir. Co. Behavioural Health Inst. 1997–; Practising Attorney specializing in Health Law with Webster and Sheffield 1980–; Pres. The Friends of the Nat. Library of Medicine 1985–. *Address:* Non Profit Management Associates Inc., 1555 Connecticut Ave., NW, Suite 200, Washington, D.C. 20036, U.S.A.

BRYANTSEV, Dmitri Aleksandrovich; Russian choreographer; b. 18 Feb. 1947, Leningrad; ed. Leningrad Higher School of Choreography, Moscow State Inst. of Theatre; soloist Moscow Choreographic Ensemble Classical Ballet 1966–77; works as ballet master and choreographer since 1975; staged a number of productions including Choreographic Miniatures (Kirov Theatre), Gussars' Ballad by T. Khrennikov (Kirov and Bolshoi Theatres 1979, 1980); chief ballet master K. Stanislavsky and V. Nemirovich-Danchenko Musical Theatre 1985–; staged numerous productions, including Othello, Corsar, Optimistic Tragedy, Hunchback Horse; author of TV ballet productions Galatea, Old Tango; staged dances in opera productions including Dead Souls by R. Shchedrin (Bolshoi Theatre) and drama productions (Turandot, Taganka Theatre); People's Artist of Russia 1989. *Address:* Musical Theatre, Bolshaya Dmitrovka 17, 103009 Moscow, Russia. *Telephone:* (095) 229 2835 (Office).

BRYARS, (Richard) Gavin, B.A.; British composer and professor of music; b. 16 Jan. 1943, Goole, Yorks.; s. of Walter Joseph Bryars and Miriam Eleanor Bryars; m. Angela Margaret Bigley 1971 (divorced 1993); two d.; ed. Goole Grammar School, Sheffield Univ. and private composition study with George Linstead; freelance Double Bassist 1963–66; freelance Composer/Performer 1968–70; Lecturer in Dept. of Fine Art, Portsmouth Polytechnic 1969–70; Sr. Lecturer, School of Fine Art, Leicester Polytechnic 1970–78, Sr. Lecturer and Head of Music, School of Performing Arts 1978–85, Prof. of Music 1985–96; mem. Collège de Pataphysique, France 1974–; Ed. Experimental Music Catalogue 1972–81; British Rep. Int. Soc. for Contemporary Music Festival 1977; Arts Council Comms. 1970, 1980, 1982, Bursary 1982. *Works include:* The Sinking of the Titanic 1969, Jesus' Blood Never Failed Me Yet 1971, Out of Zaleski's Gazebo 1977, The Vespertine Park 1980, Medea (opera with Robert Wilson) 1982, My First Homage 1978–82, Effarene 1984, String Quartet No.1 1985, Pico's Flight 1986, By the Vaar 1987, The Invention of Tradition 1988, Glorious Hill 1988, Cadman Requiem 1989, String Quartet No. 2 1990, The White Lodge 1991, Three Elegies for Nine Clarinets 1994, After Handel's Vesper 1995, The Adnan Songbook 1996, Doctor Ox's Experiment 1997 (opera); recordings on Editions EG, Crépuscule and ECM (Munich). *Leisure interests:* cricket (mem. Yorks. County Cricket Club) and detective fiction. *Address:* c/o Erica Bolton and Jane Quinn Ltd., 8 Pottery Lane, London, W11 4LZ; c/o Schott and Co. Ltd., 48 Great Marlborough Street, London, W1V 2BN, England. *Telephone:* 0171-221 5000 (Bolton and Quinn); 0171-494 1487 (Schott).

BRYDON, Donald Hood, O.B.E.; British investment executive; b. 25 May 1945; s. of James Hood Brydon and Mary Duncanson (née Young); m. 1st Joan Victoria Brydon 1971 (divorced 1995), one s. one d.; m. 2nd Corinne Susan Jane Brydon 1996; ed. George Watson's Coll., Edin., Univ. of Edinburgh; with Econs. Dept. Univ. of Edin. 1967–70; with British Airways Pensions Fund 1970–77; Barclays Investment Man.'s Office 1977–81, Deputy Man. Dir. Barclays Investment Man. Ltd. 1981–86; Dir. BZW Investment Man. 1986–88, Man. Dir. 1988–91, Chair., C.E.O. BZW Asset Man. Ltd. 1991–94, Chair. (non-exec.) 1994–95, Deputy Chief Exec. Barclays de Zoete Wedd 1994–96, Acting C.E.O. 1996; Chair., C.E.O. AXA Asset Man. Europe 1997–; Dir. Stock Exchange 1991–; Dir. Edin. Inca Investment Trust 1996–. *Publications:* Economics of Technical Information Services (jtly) 1972. *Address:* Stock Exchange, London, E.C.2, England.

BRYMER, Charles; American business executive; fmrly. with BBDO Inc. Houston and New York; joined Interbrand Group (int. consultancy specializing in brands and branding) 1985, now C.E.O. *Address:* Interbrand Schechter Inc., 437 Madison Avenue, New York, NY 100022, U.S.A. *Telephone:* (212) 752-4400. *Fax:* (212) 752-4503.

BRYMER, Jack, O.B.E., F.G.S.M., F.G.C.L.; British clarinettist; b. 27 Jan. 1915, South Shields, Co. Durham; s. of John Brymer and Mary Dixon; m. Joan Richardson 1939; one s.; ed. Goldsmith's Coll., London Univ.; Prin. Clarinet, Royal Philharmonic Orchestra 1947–63, BBC Symphony Orchestra 1963–72, London Symphony Orchestra 1972–87; Prof., Royal Acad. of Music 1950–56; Prof. of Clarinet, Royal Mil. School of Music, Kneller Hall 1970–73; Prof. of Clarinet Guildhall School of Music and Drama 1981–; mem. Wigmore Ensemble, Prometheus Ensemble, London Baroque Ensemble, Delme Ensemble, Robles Ensemble and Dir./Founder London Wind Soloists; worldwide soloist recitals and numerous recordings; lecturer on musical topics on radio and television; two demonstration films on history, development and use of the clarinet as a solo and orchestral instrument; Fellow Northern Coll. of Music; Hon. F.R.A.M.; Hon. M.A. (Newcastle) 1973; Hon. D.Mus. (Kingston) 1992, (De Montfort, Leicester) 1995; Cobbett Medal of Worshipful Co. of Musicians 1989. *Publications:* The Clarinet 1976, From Where I Sit (autobiog.) 1978, In the Orchestra 1987, Learn the Clarinet (video) 1990. *Leisure interests:* golf, tennis, swimming, gardening, carpentry, photography. *Address:* 31 Sycamore Court, Hoskins Road, Oxted, Surrey, RH8 9JQ, England. *Telephone:* (01883) 712843.

BRYNGDAHL, Olof, DR.; Swedish university professor; b. 26 Sept. 1933, Stockholm; s. of Carl Olof Bryngdahl and Ingeborg M. Pihlgren; m. Margaretha Schraut 1959; ed. Royal Inst. of Tech. Stockholm; Research Assoc. Inst. for Optical Research, Stockholm 1956–64; staff mem. Xerox Research Lab. Rochester, NY 1964–65; Man. IBM Research Lab. San José, Calif. 1966–69; Sr. scientist, IBM Research Lab. Yorktown Heights N.Y. 1970; Prin. scientist, Xerox Research Lab. Palo Alto, Calif. 1970–77; Prof. Inst. d'Optique, Univ. of Paris 1975–76; Prof. Univ. of Essen 1977–; Fellow, Optical Soc. of America. *Publications:* more than 200 scientific articles; 14 patents in optics. *Address:* University of Essen, 45117 Essen, Universitätsstrasse 2, Germany. *Telephone:* 49-201-1832562.

BRYNIELSSON, Harry Anders Bertil; Swedish executive; b. 20 March 1914, Stockholm; s. of Georg and Gurli Brynielsson; m. Wera Wahrenby 1940; two s. one d.; ed. Royal Inst. of Tech., Stockholm; with Kema-Bolagen, Stockholm 1936–43; Man. Dir. LKB-Produkter Fabriks Aktiebolag, Stockholm 1943–51; Man. Dir. Aktiebolaget Atomenergi (Swedish Atomic Energy Co.) 1951–69; mem. Bd. Boliden AB 1955–84; Pres. European Atomic Energy Soc. 1958–61; Chair. Swedish Corrosion Inst. 1972–90, Swedish Plant

Inspection 1975–85; Svenska B.P. 1979–84; Delegation for Scientific and Tech. Information 1979–85; mem. Swedish Acad. of Eng. Sciences.

BRYNTSALOV, Vladimir Alekseyevich; Russian businessman; b. 23 Nov. 1946, Cherkessk; m. 1st; one d.; m. 2nd Natalya Bryntsalova; one s. one d.; ed. Inst. of Construction and Eng.; engineer, then Head Construction Dept. in Stavropol 1970–80; expelled from CPSU for construction of a house of his own; pvt. enterprising activities started late 1980s; f. co-operative Pchelka (Bee) 1987, set up candles factory 1988; in Moscow since 1989; bought stock shares of pharmaceutical factories, f. Co. Ferein 1992– (produces over one third of all medicaments in Russia); mem. State Duma (Parl.) 1995–, joined Our Home—Russia faction 1997; Cand. for Presidency of Russia 1996. *Address:* Ferein, Nagatinskaya str. 1, 113105 Moscow, Russia. *Telephone:* (095) 111 0079 (Office).

BRYSON, Adm. Sir Lindsay Sutherland, K.C.B., D.SC., D.ENG., F.ENG., F.R.S.E., F.R.AE.S.; British naval officer (retd.) and engineer; b. 22 Jan. 1925, Glasgow; s. of James McAuslan Bryson and Margaret Whyte; m. Averil Curtis-Willson 1951; one s. two d.; ed. Allan Glen's School, Glasgow; entered Royal Navy as Electrical Mechanic 1945, rank of Lieut. 1948, Commdr. 1960, Capt. 1967; Commdg. Officer, R.N. Air Station, Lee-on-Solent 1970–71; Dir. Naval Guided Weapons 1973–75; Dir. Surface Weapon Projects as Commodore 1975–76; rank of Rear-Adm. 1977; Dir. Gen. Weapons (Navy) 1977–80; rank of Vice-Adm. 1979; Chief Naval Engineer Officer 1979–80; Controller of the Navy 1981–84; rank of Admiral 1983; retd. from Navy 1985; Pres. I.E.E.. 1985–86; Dir. (non-exec.) ERA Tech. Ltd. 1985 (Chair. 1990–97), Molins PLC 1988; Chair. Marine Technology Directorate Ltd. 1986–92; Lord Lieut. of E. Sussex 1989–; Pres. Soc. of Underwater Tech. 1989–91; Chair. of Council, Sussex Univ. 1989–95; Chair. New Sussex Opera 1990–, Brighton Festival Trust 1990–, Brighton Coll. Council 1990–98; Pres. Asscn. of Project Mans. 1991–95; Chair. Brighton West Pier Trust 1995–; Chair. Old Market Trust 1996–; Hon. Fellow, Paisley Coll. of Tech. 1986; Hon. F.I.E.E. 1991; Hon. F.I. Mech. E. 1991; Hon. Fellow Asscn. of Project Mans. 1996; Trustee Hanover Band 1997–; Hon. D.Sc. (Strathclyde) 1987; Hon. D.Eng. (Bristol) 1988; Hon. LL.D. (Sussex) 1995. *Leisure interests:* opera, sailing. *Address:* 74 Dyke Road Avenue, Brighton, Sussex, BN1 5LE, England. *Telephone:* (0273) 553638. *Fax:* (0273) 562478.

BRZEZINSKI, Zbigniew K., PH.D.; American (naturalized 1958) professor of government; b. 28 March 1928, Warsaw, Poland; m. Emilie Anna (Muska) Benes 1955; two s. one d.; ed. McGill and Harvard Univs.; settled in N. America 1938; Instructor in Govt. and Research Fellow, Russian Research Center, Harvard Univ. 1953–56; Asst. Prof. of Govt., Research Assoc. of Russian Research Center and of Center for Int. Affairs, Harvard Univ. 1956–60; Assoc. Prof. of Public Law and Govt., Columbia Univ. 1960–62, Prof. 1962–89 (on leave 1966–68, 1977–81) and Dir. Research Inst. on Communist Affairs 1961–77 (on leave 1966–68); mem. Policy Planning Council, Dept. of State 1966–68; mem. Hon. Steering Cttee., Young Citizens for Johnson 1964; Dir. Foreign Policy Task Force for Vice-Pres. Humphrey 1968; Asst. to the Pres. for Nat. Security Affairs 1977–81; Counsellor, Center for Strategic and Int. Studies, Washington, D.C. Jan. 1981–; now Robert Osgood Prof. of American Foreign Policy, Paul Nitze School of Advanced Int. Studies, Johns Hopkins Univ. 1989–; Fellow, American Acad. of Arts and Sciences 1969–; mem. Nat. Security Council 1977–81, Council on Foreign Relations, New York, Bd. of Trustees, Freedom House; Guggenheim Fellowship 1960, Ford Fellowship 1970; Presidential Medal of Freedom 1981; Hon. Dr. (Alliance Coll.) 1966, (Coll. of the Holy Cross) 1971, (Fordham Univ.) 1979, (Williams Coll.) 1986, (Georgetown Univ.) 1987, (Catholic Univ. of Lublin) 1990, (Warsaw Univ.) 1991. *Publications include:* Political Controls in the Soviet Army 1954, The Permanent Purge—Politics in Soviet Totalitarianism 1956, Totalitarian Dictatorship and Autocracy (co-author) 1957, The Soviet Bloc—Unity and Conflict 1960, Ideology and Power in Soviet Politics 1962, Africa and the Communist World (Ed. and contrib.) 1963, Political Power: U.S.A./U.S.S.R. (co-author) 1964, Alternative to Partition: For a Broader Conception of America's Role in Europe 1965, Dilemmas of Change in Soviet Politics (Ed. and contrib.) 1969, Between Two Ages: America's Role in the Technetronic Era 1970, The Fragile Blossom: Crisis and Change in Japan 1972, Power and Principle 1983, Game Plan 1986, The Grand Failure: The Birth and Death of Communism in the 20th Century, 1989, Out of Control 1993, The Grand Chessboard: American Primacy and its Geostrategic Imperatives 1997. *Address:* Centre for Strategic and International Studies, Suite 400, 1800 K Street, N.W., Washington, DC 20006, U.S.A. (Office).

BU HE (YUN SHUGUANG); Chinese party and government official; b. 24 March 1926, Inner Mongolia; s. of late Ulanfu and Yun Ting; m. Zhulanqiqige 1947; one s. two d.; ed. Yan'an Inst. for Nationalities and Nationalities Coll. of Yan'an Univ.; joined CCP 1942; Lecturer and Deputy Dir. Political Dept. of Nei Mongol Autonomous Coll. in Chifeng 1946; CCP Br. Sec. and Dir. of Nei Mongol Art Troupe 1947–53; Leading Party Group Sec. and Deputy Dir. Nei Mongol Cultural Bureau 1954–64; Acting mem. Standing Cttee. of CCP Cttee., Nei Mongol and Sec. and Dir. of CCP Cttee. of Cultural and Educ. Comm., Nei Mongol 1966; Sec. Municipal Party Cttee. of Baotou 1974–77; Dir. Propaganda Dept. of CCP Cttee., Nei Mongol 1978; Deputy Dir. State Nationalities Affairs Comm. 1978–81; Sec. CCP Cttee. and Mayor of Huhhot City 1978–81; Deputy Sec. CCP Cttee., Nei Mongol 1981–82; mem. of 12th CCP Central Cttee. 1982–87; Deputy Sec. CCP Cttee. and Chair. Provincial Govt., Nei Mongol 1983–; mem. 13th CCP Cen. Cttee. 1987–92; Vice-Chair. 8th NPC Standing Cttee. 1993–98, 9th NPC 1998–; Chair. Regional Fed. of Literary and Art Circles 1954–65; mem. 2nd, 3rd, 4th Council of Chinese Fed. of Literary and Art Circles. *Publications:* The Basic Knowledge of Autonomy in the Nationalities Region, the Nationalities Theory of Marxism and the Party's Nationalities Policies, The Animal Husbandry in Inner Mongolia Today, In the Sea of Poems (poetry collection), Bu He's Collection of Theses in Literature and Art. *Leisure interests:* calligraphy, literature and art-writing. *Address:* Office of the Regional Governor, Hohhot, Nei Mongol, People's Republic of China.

BUALLAY, Kassim Muhammad, B.B.A.; Bahraini diplomatist; b. 15 March 1942, Muharraq; s. of Muhammad Buallay and Balkees Buallay; m. Satia Buallay 1969; two s. two d.; ed. American Univ. of Beirut; supervisor, Bursaries Section, Ministry of Educ. 1963–69; int. civil servant, UNESCO, Paris 1970–74; Amb. to France 1974–79, to Tunisia 1987–94; Dir. of Econ. Affairs, Ministry of Foreign Affairs, Bahrain 1979–87; Perm. Rep. to UN, New York 1994–; Ordre nat. du Mérite, France, decorations of Morocco (Alawite) and Tunisia. *Leisure interests:* reading, theatre, music, tennis, gastronomy. *Address:* 2 UN Plaza, 25th Floor, New York, NY 10017, U.S.A. *Telephone:* (212) 223-6205. *Fax:* (212) 319-0687.

BUBKA, Sergey Nazarovich; Ukrainian athlete; b. 4 Dec. 1963, Voroshilovgrad (now Lugansk); s. of Nazar Bubka and Valentina Bubka; m. Lilya Tioutiounik 1983; two s.; world champion pole vaulter 1983; 16 world records, from 5.85m 1984 to 6.13m 1992, including world's first 6m jump, Paris 1985; 18 world indoor records, from 5.81m in 1984 to 6.15m in 1993; Olympic gold medal 1988; now represents OSC Berlin; lives Paris and Donetsk. *Address:* c/o State Committee of Physical Culture and Sport, 42 Esplanadnaya, 252023 Kiev, Ukraine. *Telephone:* (44) 220 02 43. *Fax:* (44) 220 02 94.

BUCARAM ORTIZ, Abdala Jaime, LL.M., ED.M.; Ecuadorean politician; b. 20 Feb. 1952, Guayaquil; s. of Jacobo Bucaram Elmalhin and Rina Ortiz Caicedo de Bucaram; m. María Rosa Pulley Vergara; three s. one d.; ed. Colegio Salesiano "Cristóbal Colón", Univ. Estatal de Guayaquil; rep. Ecuador Olympic Games, Munich 1972; holder of nat. Jr. 100m. record (10.5 seconds); a founder of Ecuador's Naval Sports Foundation, has been responsible for codes of conduct for sporting orgs., etc.; taught at Colegio San José La Salle, training colls. for marines, navy, etc.; Gov.-Gen. of Police, Guayas 1979–80, Advisor to nat. Superintendency; Prov. Councillor for Guayas 1980; f. Partido Roldosista Ecuatoriano 1982, Chief Exec. 1983–85, 1991–93; Mayor of Guayaquil 1984; Presidential cand. (Partido Roldosista) 1988, 1992; Pres. of Ecuador 1996–97; granted political asylum in Panama 1997; sentenced in absentia to two years' imprisonment on charges of slandering two political rivals; Dir. various agricultural, commercial and media cos.; Pres. Fondo de Desarrollo Urbano de Guayaquil (FODUR) 1984–85; numerous sporting awards at nat. and regional level including Vicecampeón Sudamericano de Atletismo. *Publications:* Ideario Político del Partido Roldosista Ecuatoriano con sus antecedentes históricos: Principios y Estatutos, Principios de Liberación Nacional, Principios de Justicia Social, Principios de Democracia, Principios de Política Humanística, Principios de Libertad, Desarrollo Económico, Principios de Política Internacional, Las verdades de Abdalá, Roldos y Abdalá: Epopeya del pensamiento ecuatoriano. *Leisure interests:* football, athletics and basketball.

BUCCI, Maurizio, B.L.; Italian diplomatist; b. 29 Aug. 1923, Sant'Angelo del Pesco (Isernia); s. of Onorato Bucci and Tina Marracino; m. Anna Maria Costa 1956; one d.; ed. Terenzio Mamiani High School, Rome, and Univ. of Rome; entered diplomatic service 1949; Second Sec. Italian Mission to NATO 1952; Deputy Consul-Gen. Paris 1955; First Sec. Luxembourg 1958; Chief of Cabinet of Vice-Pres. of EEC Exec. Cttee. 1961; Counsellor, Italian Mission to European Communities, Brussels 1963; Head, Research and Planning Div., Econ. Dept., Ministry of Foreign Affairs 1968; Amb. to Syria 1973–76, to Brazil 1976–79; Dir. Gen. of Econ. Affairs, Ministry of Foreign Affairs 1979–84; Perm. Rep. to UN 1984–89; Gran Croce, Merito Repubblica Italiana. *Address:* Via Monte Zebio 25, 00195 Rome, Italy.

BUCCLEUCH, 9th Duke of, cr. 1663, **AND QUEENSBERRY,** 11th Duke of, cr. 1684; **Walter Francis John Montagu Douglas Scott,** K.T., V.R.D., J.P.; Baron Scott of Buccleuch, Earl of Buccleuch, Baron Scott of Whitchester and Eskdaill, Earl of Doncaster and Baron Tynedale (England), Earl of Dalkeith, Marquis of Dumfriesshire, Earl of Drumlanrig and Sanquhar, Viscount of Nith, Torthorwold, and Ros, Baron Douglas; b. 28 Sept. 1923, London; s. of 8th Duke of Buccleuch, K.T., P.C., G.C.V.O. and Vreda Esther Mary Lascelles; m. Jane McNeill 1953; three s. one d.; ed. Eton, Christ Church, Oxford; served R.N.V.R. World War II: M.P. (C) Edin. North 1960–73; Parl. Pvt. Sec. to Sec. of State for Scotland 1962–64; Chair. Asscn. of Lord Lieuts. 1990–; Pres. Royal Asscn. for Disability and Rehabilitation, Buccleuch Heritage Trust 1985–, Living Landscape Trust 1986–; Pres. Royal Highland and Agric. Soc. of Scotland 1969, Malcolm Sargent Cancer Fund for Children, Scotland 1974–, St. Andrew's Ambulance Asscn., Royal Scottish Agric. Benevolent Inst., Scottish Nat. Inst. for War Blinded, Royal Blind Asylum and School, Galloway Cattle Soc., E. of England Agric. Soc. 1976, Commonwealth Forestry Asscn., Royal Scottish Forestry Soc. 1994–96; Chair. Asscn. of Lord Lieuts. 1990–; Vice-Pres. Royal Scottish Soc. for Prevention of Cruelty to Children; Hon. Pres. Movedun Foundation for Animal Welfare, Scottish Agric. Org. Soc.; DL Selkirk 1955, Midlothian 1960, Roxburgh 1962, Dumfries 1974; JP Roxburgh 1975; Chancellor of the Order of the Thistle 1992; Hon. Capt. R.N.R.; Capt. the Queen's Body Guard for Scotland, Royal Co. of Archers; Lord-Lieut. of Roxburgh 1974–98, of Ettrick and Lauderdale 1975–98; Countryside Award, Countryside Comm. and Country Landowners Asscn. 1983, Bledisloe Agric. Award 1992. *Leisure interests:* works of art, historic buildings, country sports, painting, classical music, travel. *Address:* Bowhill, Selkirk, TD7 5ET, Scotland. *Telephone:* (01750) 20732.

BUCHACHENKO, Anatoly Leonidovich, DR. CHEM. SC.; Russian chemical physicist; b. 7 Sept. 1935, Arkhangelsk region; s. of L. P. Buchachenko and A. S. Buchachenko; m. M. S. Buchachenko 1960; one s. one d.; ed. Gorky Univ.; post-grad., jr. then sr. scientific asst. 1958–68; Head of Lab. of U.S.S.R. (now Russian) Acad. of Sciences Inst. of Chemical Physics 1970–, Vice-Dir. 1989–94, Dir. 1994–96; Head of Dept. 1996; Head of Dept. of Chemical Kinetics, Moscow State Univ. 1988–; Prof. 1975–; mem. U.S.S.R. (now Russian) Acad. of Sciences 1987; State Prize 1977, Lenin Prize 1986. *Publications:* works on the physical chemistry of free radicals, chemical reactions, spin chemistry, molecular ferromagnets. *Leisure interests:* wood architecture modelling. *Address:* N. N. Semenov, Institute of Chemical Physics of the Russian Academy of Sciences, Kosygin Street 4, 117977 Moscow, Russia. *Telephone:* (095) 137-32-32 (Office); (095) 331 31 70 (Home). *Fax:* (095) 938-2484.

BUCHANAN, Sir Colin Douglas, Kt., C.B.E.; British town planner; b. 22 Aug. 1907, Simla, India; s. of William Ernest and Laura Kate Buchanan; m. Elsie Alice Mitchell 1933 (died 1984); two s. one d.; ed. Berkhamsted School and Imperial Coll. of Science and Technology, London; with Public Works Dept., Sudan 1930–32; Regional Planning Studies with F. Longstreth-Thompson, London 1932–35; at Ministry of Transport 1935–39; served with Royal Engineers 1939–46; at Ministry of Town and Country Planning (later Ministry of Housing and Local Govt.) 1946–61; Urban Planning Adviser, Ministry of Transport 1961–63; Prof. of Transport, Imperial Coll., London 1963–72; Dir. School of Advanced Urban Studies, Univ. of Bristol 1973–75; Visiting Prof., Imperial Coll. 1975–78; Consultant with Colin Buchanan and Partners and to various public authorities; mem. Comm. on Third London Airport 1968–70, Royal Fine Art Comm. 1972–73; Pres. Council for the Protection of Rural England 1980–85, Friends of the Vale of Aylesbury 1985–; Gold Medal, Town Planning Inst. 1968; Int. Road Fed. "Man of the Year" 1971, Fritz Schumacher Prize 1971, Inst. of Highways and Transportation Award 1992, Automobile Asscn. Nat. Motoring Award 1994. *Publications:* Mixed Blessing, the Motor in Britain 1958, Traffic in Towns 1963, Bath: A Study in Conservation 1969, No Way To the Airport: The Stansted Controversy 1981, and numerous papers on town planning and related subjects. *Leisure interests:* painting in pastels, photography, caravanning. *Address:* Appletree House, Lincombe Lane, Boars Hill, Oxford OX1 5DU, England. *Telephone:* (01865) 739458.

BUCHANAN, Isobel; British opera singer; b. 15 March 1954, Glasgow; d. of Mr and Mrs S. Buchanan; m. Jonathan King (actor Jonathan Hyde) 1980; two d.; ed. Cumbernauld Comprehensive High School and Royal Scottish Acad. of Music and Drama; professional début in Sydney, Australia with Richard Bonynge and Joan Sutherland 1976–78; British début, Glyndebourne 1978; U.S. and German débuts 1979; Vienna Staatsoper début 1979; ENO début 1985, Paris Opera début 1986; now freelance artist working with all major opera cos. and orchestras; has made several recordings. *Leisure interests:* cooking, reading, gardening, yoga, knitting.

BUCHANAN, James McGill, M.A., PH.D.; American academic; b. 3 Oct. 1919, Murfreesboro, Tenn.; s. of James Buchanan and Lila Scott; m. Anne Bakke 1945; ed. Middle Tenn. State Coll. and Univs. of Tenn. and Chicago; Prof. of Econs. Univ. of Tenn. 1950–51, Fla. State Univ. 1951–56, Univ. of Va. 1956–62; Paul. G. McIntyre Prof. of Econs. Univ. of Va. 1962–68; Prof. of Econs. Univ. of Calif. Los Angeles 1968–69; Univ. Distinguished Prof. of Econs. Va. Polytechnic Inst. 1969–83, Dir. Center for Study of Public Choice 1969–88, Advisory Gen. Dir. 1988–; Univ. Distinguished Prof. of Econs. George Mason Univ. 1983–; Fulbright Research Scholar, Italy 1955–56; Ford Faculty Research Fellow 1959–60; Fulbright Visiting Prof. Univ. of Cambridge 1961–62; Nobel Prize for Econs. 1986; Seidman Award 1984; Fellow, American Acad. of Arts and Sciences; Distinguished Fellow, American Econ. Asscn.; Dr. h.c. (Giessen) 1982, (Zürich) 1984, (Valencia) 1987, (Lisbon) 1987, (Fairfax) 1987, (London) 1988, (Rome) 1993, (Bucharest) 1994, (Catania) 1994, (Valladolid) 1996. *Publications:* author and co-author of numerous books on financial policy and other econ. matters; articles in professional journals. *Address:* Center for the Study of Public Choice, George Mason University, Buchanan House Mail Stop 1 E6, Fairfax, VA 22030 (Office); P.O. Box G, Blacksburg, VA 24063, U.S.A. (Home).

BUCHANAN, John Machlin, D.SC., PH.D.; American professor of biochemistry; b. 29 Sept. 1917, Winamac Ind.; s. of Harry J. and Eunice B. (Miller) Buchanan; m. Elsa Nilsby 1948; two s. two d.; ed. De Pauw Univ., Univ. of Michigan and Harvard Univ.; Instructor, Dept. of Physiological Chem., School of Medicine, Univ. of Pa. 1943–46, Asst. Prof. 1946–49, Assoc. Prof. 1949–50, Prof. 1950–53; Nat. Research Council Fellow in Medicine, Nobel Inst., Stockholm 1946–48; Prof., Head, Div. of Biochem., Dept. of Biology, M.I.T. 1953–67, Wilson Prof. of Biochem. 1967–88, Prof. Emer. 1988–; mem. Medical Fellowship Bd. 1954–; Fellow, Guggenheim Memorial Foundation; mem. N.A.S., American Soc. of Biological Chemists, American Chem. Soc., Int. Union of Biochemists, American Acad. of Arts and Sciences; Eli Lilly Award in Biological Chem., A.C.S. 1951. *Address:* Room 68-333B, Department of Biology, Massachusetts Institute of Technology, Cambridge, MA 02139 (Office); 56 Meriam St., Lexington, MA 02420, U.S.A. (Home).

BUCHANAN, J. Robert, M.D.; American professor of medicine; b. 8 March 1928, Newark, N.J.; m. Susan Carver; one s. one d.; ed. Amherst Coll. and Cornell Univ. Medical School; Intern, then Asst. Resident Physician, New York Hosp. 1954–58, Research Fellow in Medicine 1956–57; Research Fellow in Endocrinology, Cornell Univ. Medical Coll., New York 1960–61; WHO Travelling Fellow 1963; Instructor in Medicine, Cornell Univ. Medical Coll. 1961–63, Asst. Prof. 1963–67, Asst. to Chair. Dept. of Medicine 1964–65, Assoc. Dean 1965–69, Clinical Assoc. Prof. 1967–69, Assoc. Prof. 1969–71, Prof. 1971–76, Acting Dean, then Dean 1969–76; Prof. of Medicine, Univ. of Chicago, Ill. 1977–82; Assoc. Dean, Pritzker School of Medicine, Chicago 1978–82; Prof. of Medicine, Harvard Medical School, Boston, Mass. 1982; Gen. Dir., Mass. Gen. Hosp. 1982–94; Gen. Dir. Emer. 1994–; physician at hosps. in New York, Chicago and Boston 1956–; mem. Admin. Bd., Council of Teaching Hosps. 1984–89, mem. Exec. Council 1985–; Dir. Mass. Div., American Cancer Soc. 1984–; Bd. of Dirs. Bank of New England 1986–91, AMI Holdings 1991–, Exec. Cttee. Mass. Hosp. Asscn. 1987– (Chair. 1990–91), Charles River Labs.; Chair. Council of Teaching Hosps., Asscn. of American Medical Colls. 1988–89; mem. N.A.S. Cttee. to review Inst. of Medicine, American Cancer Soc., Mass. Div., Soc. of Medical Admins.; Chair. Educ. Comm. for Foreign Medical Grads. 1994–; Fellow American Coll. of Physicians. *Publications:* numerous papers and articles in journals. *Address:* RSTAR/ATI, One Cambridge Center, Cambridge, MA 02142 (Office); 19 Shipway Place, Charlestown, MA 02129, U.S.A. (Home).

BUCHANAN, Patrick Joseph, M.S.; American government official and journalist; b. 2 Nov. 1938; s. of William Buchanan and Catherine Crum; m. Shelley A. Scarney 1971; ed. Georgetown and Columbia Univs.; editorial writer, St. Louis Globe Democrat 1962–64, asst. editorial writer 1964–66; Exec. Asst. to Richard Nixon 1966–69; Special Asst. to Pres. Nixon 1969–73; consultant to Pres. Nixon and Ford 1973–74; Asst. to Pres., Dir. of Communications, White House, Washington, D.C. 1985–87; syndicated columnist, political commentator, New York Times special features 1975–78, Chicago Tribune-New York News Syndicate 1978–85, Tribune Media Services 1987–91, 1993–; commentator, NBC Radio Network 1978–82; TV Show Cable News Network 1982–85, 1987–91, 1993–95, 1997–; appeared as host and panellist in TV shows 1978–; Ed.-in-Chief PJB—From the Right (newsletter) 1990–91; moderator Capital Gang TV show CNN 1988–92; Chair. The American Cause 1993–95, 1997–, Pat Buchanan & Co., Mutual Broadcasting System 1993–95; Candidate for Republican Presidential nomination 1992, 1996; Republican. *Publications:* The New Majority 1973, Conservative Votes, Liberal Victories 1975, Right from the Beginning 1988; Barry Goldwater, The Conscience of A Conservative 1990. *Address:* 1017 Savile Lane, McLean, VA 22101, U.S.A.

BUCHHEIM, Lothar-Günther; German author and publisher; b. 6 Feb. 1918, Weimar, Thüringen; m. Diethild Wickboldt 1955; one s. one d.; ed. Dresden Acad., Art Acad., Munich; served in German navy; f. Kunstbuchverlag, Feldafing, and started collection, "the most important private collection", of the work of German Expressionists; owner and publr. Buchheim Verlag, Feldafing; Dr. h.c. (Duisburg) 1985; Ernst-Hoferichter Prize, Munich 1993; Bundesverdienstkreuz, Grosses Verdienstkreuz des Verdienstordens, Bayerischer Verdienstorden, Ehrenbürger von Chemnitz, Grosses Verdienstkreuz mit Stern des Verdienstordens, Bayerischer Maximiliansorden 1998. *Publications:* Tage und Nächte steigen aus dem Strom 1941, Die Künstlergemeinschaft "Brücke" 1956, Der Blaue Reiter und die Neue Künstlervereinigung München 1958, Graphik des deutschen Expressionismus 1959, Max Beckmann 1959, Otto Mueller 1963, Das Boot 1973, U-Boot-Krieg 1976, Staatsgala 1977, Mein Paris 1977, Die Tropen von Feldafing 1978, Staatszirkus 1978, Der Luxusliner 1980, U 96 1981, Der Film-Das Boot 1981, Das Segelschiff 1982, Die U-Boot-Fahrer 1985, Das Museum in den Wolken 1986, Zu Tode gesiegt-Der Untergang der U-Boote 1988, Malerbuch 1988, Die Festung 1995, Jäger im Weltmeer 1996. *Address:* Biersackstr. 23, D-82340 Feldafing, Germany. *Telephone:* 08157 1221. *Fax:* 08157-3143.

BUCHTHAL, Fritz, M.D.; Danish neurophysiologist; b. 19 Aug. 1907, Witten, Germany; s. of Sally Buchthal and Hedvig Weyl; m. Margaret A. Lennox, M.D.; ed. Albert-Ludwig-Universität, Freiburg im Breisgau, Germany, Stanford Univ., Calif., U.S.A., and Humboldt-Universität zu Berlin; Asst. in Physiology, Univ. of Berlin 1930–32; Inst. for Theory of Gymnastics, Copenhagen Univ. 1933–43; Physiological Inst., Lund Univ. 1943–45; Dir. Inst. of Neurophysiology, Copenhagen Univ. 1946–77, Prof. of Neurophysiology 1955–77; Chief, Dept. of Neurophysiology, Univ. Hospital 1945–77; Consultant, Nat. Inst. of Health, U.S.A. 1959; Visiting Scientist, Nat. Inst. of Neurological and Communicative Disorders and Stroke, Nat. Inst. of Health, Bethesda 1982–84, Consultant 1984–; Consultant Dept. of Neurology, San Francisco Calif., Calif.-Pacific Medical Centre 1985–; Visiting Prof. Univ. of California 1962, Academia Sinica 1964, N.Y. Univ. 1965; mem. Royal Danish Acad. Sciences 1946, Danish Acad. of Technical Sciences, Royal Swedish Acad. of Sciences 1968, Royal Soc. of Sciences (Sweden) 1972, Polish Acad. of Sciences 1988; Hon. Fellow Royal Soc. Medicine 1991; Hon. mem. French Neurological Soc., British Asscn. of Neurologists, Polish Neurological Soc., Danish Neurological Soc., American Neurological Asscn., American Acad. of Neurophysiology, San Francisco Neurological Soc., German EEG Soc., English EEG Soc., Italian and Danish EEG and Clinical Neurophysiological Soc., American Soc. for Electrodiagnosis and Electromyography, Polish Soc. for EEG and Clinical Neurophysiology; Corresp. mem. German Physiological and Neurological Socs., Italian Neurological Soc., Acad. de Ciencias Médicas, Cordoba; Hon. M.D. (Münster, Zürich, Lund, Munich); Hon. D.Sc. (Medical Coll., Wisconsin); numerous awards. *Publications:* Mechanical Properties of Muscle Fibre 1942, Rheology of Muscle 1951, An Introduction to Electromyography 1957, Electrophysiological Aspects of Myopathy 1963, Evoked Action Potential and Conduction Velocity in Human Sensory Nerve 1966, Electrical and Mechanical Responses of Normal and Myasthenic Muscle 1968, Human Nerve Potentials Evoked by Tactile Stimuli 1982. *Leisure interest:* gardening. *Address:* 289 El Cielito Road, Santa Barbara, CA 93105, U.S.A. *Telephone:* (805) 966-5304.

BUCHWALD, Art; American journalist, author and playwright; b. 20 Oct. 1925, New York; s. of Helen Kleinberger and Joseph Buchwald; m. Ann McGarry 1952; one s. two d.; ed. Univ. of Southern Calif., Los Angeles; columnist, Herald Tribune, Paris 1948–62, Wash. 1962–; syndicated columnist to 550 newspapers throughout the world 1952–; Prix de la Bonne Humeur; Pulitzer Prize for Outstanding Commentary 1982; Horatio Alger Award 1989; mem. American Acad. and Inst. of Arts and Letters 1986. *Publications:* Paris After Dark, Art Buchwald's Paris, I Chose Caviar, More Caviar, A Gift from the Boys, Don't Forget to Write, How Much Is That in Dollars? 1961, Is It Safe to Drink the Water? 1962, I Chose Capitol Punishment 1963, And Then I Told the President 1965, Son of the Great Society 1967, Have I Ever Lied to You? 1968, Oh, to Be a Swinger 1970, Getting High in Government Circles 1971, I Never Danced at the White House 1973, I Am Not a Crook 1974, Washington Is Leaking 1976, Down the Seine and Up the Potomac 1977, The Buchwald Stops Here 1978, Laid Back in Washington with Art Buchwald 1981, While Reagan Slept 1983, You *Can* Fool All of the People All of the Time 1985, I Think I Don't Remember 1987, Whose Rose Garden Is It Anyway? 1989, Lighten Up, George 1991, Leaving Home: A Memoir 1994, I'll Always Have Paris (memoir) 1996. *Address:* 2000 Pennsylvania Avenue, N.W., Washington, DC 20006, U.S.A. *Telephone:* Washington 393-6680.

BUCHWALD, Christoph; German publishing executive; fmrly. Ed. Hanser, Munich; fmrly. Publr. Luchterhand Literaturverlag; now with Suhrkamp Verlag K.G., Frankfurt 1998–. *Address:* Suhrkamp Verlag KG, 60019 Frankfurt a.M., Postfach 101945, Germany. *Telephone:* (69) 756010. *Fax:* (69) 75601522.

BUCKINGHAM, Prof. Amyand David, C.B.E., F.R.S.; Australian professor of chemistry; b. 28 Jan. 1930, Sydney; s. of the late Reginald Joslin Buckingham and Florence Grace Buckingham; m. Jillian Bowles 1965; one. s. two d.; ed. Barker Coll., Hornsby, N.S.W., Univ. of Sydney, Corpus Christi Coll., Cambridge; Lecturer, then Student and Tutor, Christ Church, Univ. of Oxford 1955–65, Univ. Lecturer in Inorganic Chem. 1958–65; Prof. of Theoretical Chem., Univ. of Bristol 1965–69; Prof. of Chem., Univ. of Cambridge 1969–97, Fellow, Pembroke Coll., Cambridge 1970–97, Emer. 1997–; Pres. Faraday Div. of Royal Soc. of Chem. 1987–89, Cambridge Univ. Cricket Club 1990–; foreign mem. American Acad. of Arts and Sciences; mem. NY Acad. of Sciences, American Chemical Soc. *Publications:* over 250 papers in scientific journals, The Laws and Applications of Thermodynamics 1964, Organic Liquids: Structure, Dynamics and Chemical Properties 1978, The Principles of Molecular Recognition 1993. *Leisure interests:* cricket, tennis, woodwork, travel, walking.

BUCKLAND, David John; British artist and theatre director; b. 15 June 1949, London; s. of Denis Buckland and Valarie Buckland; partner, Siobhan Davies 1978; one s. one d.; ed. Dorchester Secondary Modern School, Dorset, Hardye's Grammar School, Dorchester, Deep River High School, Ottawa and London Coll. of Printing; principal one-man exhbns. Photographers Gallery London, 1977, 1987, Air Gallery, London 1978, Sander Gallery New York 1979, 1984, Moria Kelly Gallery, London 1981, Pompidou Centre, Paris 1982, Tom Peek Gallery, Amsterdam 1985, Espace Photo, Paris 1988, Nat. Portrait Gallery 1999; has participated in group exhbns. and work appears in public collections in London, New York, Chicago, Los Angeles, Paris etc.; Artistic Dir. Siobhan Davies Dance Co.; lecturer, Royal Coll. of Art, London Coll. of Printing, Chicago Art Inst.; 21 set and costume designs for dance including Rambert Dance Co., Siobhan Davies Dance Co., English Nat. Ballet and work for TV; Northern Arts Fellow 1972–73; Kodak Bursary 1978; Minn. First Bank Award 1988–90. *Leisure interests:* multi-hull sailor, arts/theatre, travel, hill-walking. *Address:* 239 Royal College Street, London, NW1 9LT, England. *Telephone and Fax:* 071-485 3228.

BUCKLAND, Sir Ross, Kt., F.C.I.S.; Australian business executive; b. 19 Dec. 1942, Sydney; s. of William Buckland and Elizabeth Buckland; m. Patricia Bubb 1966; two s.; ed. Sydney Boys' High School; various positions in banking, eng. and food industries 1958–66; Dir. Finance and Admin. Elizabeth Arden Pty. Ltd. 1966–73; Kellogg (Australia) Pty. Ltd. 1973–77, 1978; Man. Dir. Kellogg Salada Canada Inc., Pres. and Chief Exec. 1979–80; Chair. Kellogg Co. of G.B. Ltd., Dir. European Operations and Vice-Pres. Kellogg Co. U.S.A. 1981–90; Chief Exec. Unigate PLC 1990–; Fellow Inst. of Grocery Distribution, Chartered Inst. of Secs. and Admins., Australian Soc. of Certified Practising Accountants. *Leisure interest:* walking. *Address:* Unigate PLC, Unigate House, Wood Lane, London W12 7RP, England. *Telephone:* 0181-749 8888. *Fax:* 0181-576 6003.

BUCKLE, (Christopher) Richard (Sandford), C.B.E.; British writer, critic and exhibition designer; b. 6 Aug. 1916; ed. Marlborough Coll. and Balliol Coll., Oxford; founded "Ballet" 1939; army service 1940–46; Ballet Critic, The Observer 1948–55, Sunday Times 1959–75; Dir. Theatre Museum Asscn. 1978–; organizer The Diaghilev Exhibition, Edinburgh Festival and London 1954, The Observer Film Exhibition, London 1956, Telford Bicentenary Exhibition 1957, Epstein Memorial Exhibition, Edinburgh 1961, The Shakespeare Exhibition (for Quatercentenary), Stratford-on-Avon and Edinburgh 1964; designer, Exhibition Rooms, Harewood House, Yorks. and area in "Man in the Community" Pavilion, Expo 1967 exhbn. Montreal, Gala of Ballet, London 1971, Happy and Glorious exhbn. London 1977; Plays: Gossip Column, Q Theatre 1953 and Family Tree, Worthing 1956. *Publications:* John Innocent at Oxford (novel) 1939, The Adventures of a Ballet Critic 1953, In Search of Diaghilev 1955, Modern Ballet Design 1955, The Prettiest Girl in England 1958, Harewood (a guide book) 1959, Dancing for Diaghilev (the Memoirs of Lydia Sokolova) 1960, introductions to Epstein Drawings 1962, and Epstein: An Autobiography 1963, Jacob Epstein: Sculptor 1963, Monsters at Midnight (ltd. edn.) 1966, The Message, a Gothick Tale of the A1 (ltd. edn.) 1969, Nijinsky 1971, Diaghilev 1978, U and Non-U revisited (Ed.) 1978, Self Portrait with Friends: Selected Diaries of Cecil Beaton 1926–74 (Ed.) 1979, Buckle at the Ballet (selected criticism) 1980, Designing for the Dancer (with others) 1981, The Most Upsetting Woman (autobiog.) 1981, In the Wake of Diaghilev (autobiog.) 1982, The Englishman's Room (contrib.) 1986, Sir Iain Moncrieffe of that Ilk (contrib.) 1986, George Balanchine, Ballet Master (with John Taras) 1988. *Address:* Roman Road, Gutch Common, Semley, Shaftesbury, Dorset, SP7 9BE, England.

BUCKLEY, James Lane, LL.B.; American judge; b. 9 March 1923, New York, N.Y.; s. of William F. Buckley and Aloise Steiner Buckley; m. Ann F. Cooley 1953; five s. one d.; ed. Yale Univ.; served U.S. Navy 1943–46; Senator from New York 1971–77; Under-Sec. of State for Security Assistance 1981–82; Pres. Radio Free Europe—Radio Liberty 1982–85; Circuit Judge, U.S. Court of Appeals, D.C. Circuit 1985–; Co-Chair. U.S. Del. to UN Conf. on Environment, Nairobi 1982; Chair. U.S. Del. to UN Conf. on Population, Mexico City 1984; Republican. *Publication:* If Men Were Angels 1975. *Leisure interest:* natural history. *Address:* United States Court of Appeals, 333 Constitution Avenue, N.W., Washington, DC 20001, U.S.A.

BUCKLEY, Stephen, M.F.A.; British artist and university professor; b. 5 April 1944, Leicester; s. of Nancy Throsby and Leslie Buckley; m. Stephanie James 1973; one s. one d.; ed. Univs. of Newcastle upon Tyne and Reading; taught at Canterbury Coll. of Art 1969, Leeds Coll. of Art 1970, Chelsea School of Art 1971–80; Artist in Residence, King's Coll., Cambridge 1972–74; Prof., Head Dept. of Fine Art, Univ. of Reading 1994–; one-man exhbns. throughout world including Museum of Modern Art, Oxford 1985, Yale Center for British Art, New Haven, Conn., U.S.A. 1986; worked with Rambert Dance Co., London 1987–88; works in public collections in Chile, Sweden, U.K., Venezuela, U.S.A., N.Z., Australia; comms. include Neal St. Restaurant 1972, mural painting for Penguin Books 1972, Leith's Restaurant 1973; prizewinner, John Moores Exhbn. 1974, 1985, Chichester National Art Exhbn. 1975, Tolly-Cobbold Exhbn. 1977. *Address:* Department of Fine Art, University of Reading, 1 Earley Gate, Whiteknights Road, Reading, RG6 6AT, England. *Telephone:* (0118) 931 8050. *Fax:* (0118) 926 2667.

BUCKLEY, William Frank, Jr.; American editor and author; b. 24 Nov. 1925, New York; s. of William Frank and Aloise (Steiner) Buckley; m. Patricia Taylor 1950; one s.; ed. Univ. of Mexico and Yale Univ.; formerly on staff American Mercury; Ed. National Review 1955–88, Ed.-in-Chief 1988–90, Ed.-at-Large 1991–; syndicated columnist 1962–; host of weekly television series Firing Line 1966–; lecturer New School for Social Research 1967; mem. U.S.I.A. Advisory Comm. 1969–72; mem. U.S. del. to UN 1973; contrib. to Harper's, Esquire, Foreign Affairs, Atlantic, etc.; Presidential Medal of Freedom 1991; numerous hon. degrees. *Publications:* God and Man at Yale 1951, Up from Liberalism 1959, Rumbles Left and Right 1963, The Unmaking of a Mayor 1966, The Jeweler's Eye 1968, The Governor Listeth 1970, Cruising Speed 1971, Inveighing We Will Go 1972, Four Reforms 1973, United Nations Journal 1974, Execution Eve 1975, Saving the Queen 1976, Airborne, Stained Glass 1978, A Hymnal 1978, Who's on First 1980, Marco Polo, If You Can 1982, Atlantic High 1982, Overdrive 1983, The Story of Henri Tod 1984, See You Later, Alligator 1985, Right Reason (articles and essays) 1985, The Temptation of Wilfred Malachey 1986, High Jinx 1986, Racing through Paradise 1987, Mongoose R.I.P. 1988, On the Firing Line 1989, Gratitude 1990, Tucker's Last Stand 1990, Wind Fall: The End of the Affair 1992, Happy Days Were Here Again 1993, A Very Private Plot 1994, Buckley! The Right Word 1996, Nearer My God—An Autobiography of Faith 1998; co-author McCarthy and His Enemies 1954; Ed. The Committee and Its Critics 1962, Odyssey of a Friend 1970, Did You Ever See a Dream Walking 1970. *Leisure interests:* skiing, sailing, music. *Address:* National Review, 215 Lexington Avenue, New York, NY 10016, U.S.A. *Telephone:* (212) 679-7330.

BUCKSTEIN, Mark, J.D., B.S.; American lawyer; b. 1 July 1939, New York; s. of Henry Buckstein and Minnie Buckstein; m. Rochelle J. Buchman 1960; one s. one d.; ed. New York Univ. Law School and City Coll. of New York; Sr. Partner, Baer, Marks & Upham (law firm), New York 1968–86; Special Prof. of Law, Hofstra Univ. School of Law 1981–93; Adjunct Prof. of Law, Rutgers Univ. Law School 1993–96; Sr. Vice-Pres. and Gen. Counsel, Trans World Airlines Inc. 1986; Exec. Vice-Pres., Gen. Counsel GAF and Int. Speciality Products, N.J. 1993–96; Counsel, Greenberg, Traurig, Fort Lauderdale, Fla. 1996–. *Leisure interests:* tennis, puzzles, reading, music. *Address:*

Greenberg Traurig, 515 East Las Olas Boulevard, Fort Lauderdale, FL 33301 (Office); 5038 Windsor Parke Drive, Boca Raton, FL 33496, U.S.A. (Home).

BUDD, Sir Alan Peter, Kt., PH.D.; British economist; b. 16 Nov. 1937, Kent; s. of Ernest Budd and Elsie Budd; m. Susan Millott 1964; three s.; ed. Oundle School, London School of Economics, Cambridge Univ.; lecturer in Econs, Southampton Univ. 1966–69; Ford Foundation Visiting Prof., Carnegie-Mellon Univ., U.S.A. 1969–70; Sr. Econ. Adviser, H.M. Treasury 1970–74; Sr. Research Fellow, London Business School 1974–81, Prof. of Econs. 1981–88, Fellow 1997; Econ. Adviser, Barclays Bank 1988–91; Chief Econ. Adviser to H.M. Treasury 1991–97; mem. Bank of England Monetary Policy Cttee. 1997–; Visiting Prof., Univ. of N.S.W., Australia 1983; Grocers' Co. Scholarship; Leverhulme Undergraduate Scholarship. *Publication:* Politics of Economic Planning 1978. *Leisure interests:* music, gardening, reading. *Address:* Bank of England, Threadneedle Street, London EC2R 8AH, England. *Telephone:* 0171-601 4928 (Office).

BUDDEN, Kenneth George, M.A., PH.D., F.R.S.; British physicist; b. 23 June 1915, Portsmouth; s. of late George E. Budden and Gertrude H. Rea; m. Nicolette A. L. de Longesdon Longsdon 1947; ed. Portsmouth Grammar School and St. John's Coll. Cambridge; Telecommunications Research Establishment 1939–41; British Air Comm. Washington, D.C. 1941–44; Air Command, S.E. Asia 1945; Fellow, St. John's Coll. Cambridge 1947–; Reader in Physics, Univ. of Cambridge 1965–82, Emer. 1982–. *Publications:* four books and numerous articles in professional journals. *Leisure interest:* gardening. *Address:* 15 Adams Road, Cambridge, CB3 9AD, England. *Telephone:* (01223) 354752.

BUDDENBERG, Hellmuth, DR.RER.POL.; German business executive and economist; b. 5 May 1924, Bünde, Westphalia; s. of Friedrich and Anna (née Nehl) Buddenberg; m. Hildburg Röhr 1948; ed. Hamburg Univ.; joined OLEX (now Deutsche BP AG), Hamburg 1949, Head, Finance and Financial Accounts Dept. 1959; Man. 1960, Deputy mem. Bd. of Man. 1965–67, mem. 1967–72, Deputy Chair. with responsibility for technology, organization, planning, marketing, petrochemicals, finance, personnel 1972–76, Chair. 1976–88; Chair. Bds. numerous cos. *Leisure interests:* sport, history.

BUDGE, (John) Donald; American tennis player (retd.); b. 13 June 1915, Oakland, Calif.; s. of John Budge and Pearl Kincaid; m. 1st Deirdre Conselman 1941; m. 2nd Loriel McPherson 1967; two s. one step-s.; ed. Univ. of California at Berkeley; amateur player until 1938, when he turned professional; Triple Wimbledon Champion (singles, men's doubles and mixed doubles) 1937, 1938; U.S.A. Champion 1937, 1938; Australian Champion 1938; French Champion 1938; first player to win the Grand Slam of the world's four major titles in the same year; played Davis Cup for U.S.A. 1935, 1936, 1937, 1938; World professional champion 1939–46; Pres. Budge Enterprises Ltd. (includes Don Budge Tennis Campus, Baltimore, Md. 1964–); mem. Cttee. Int. Fed. of Tennis to name annual Men's World Champion 1977–, Bd. of Dirs. Nat. Tennis Hall of Fame. *Publications:* Budge and Tennis 1939, Don Budge: A Tennis Memoir 1969. *Leisure interests:* jazz, building stone walls, making furniture, reading, travel. *Address:* c/o The All England Club, Church Road, Wimbledon, London, S.W.19, England.

BUDIŠA, Dražen; Croatian politician; b. 25 July 1948, Drniš; m. Nada Budiša; three s.; ed. Zagreb Univ.; Pres. of Students' League of Zagreb 1971; Chair. Croatian Social Liberal Party 1990–; Minister in Croatian Govt. 1991–92; mem. House of Reps. (Parl.) of Croatia 1992, 1995–. *Publications:* Beginning of Printing in Europe 1984, Heritage of Croatian Reformers in Custody of the National and University Library 1985, Humanism in Croatia 1988, Croatian Books Published in Venice from 15th to 18th Centuries 1990. *Leisure interests:* gardening. *Address:* Galovicéva 8, 41000 Zagreb, Croatia. *Telephone:* (41) 21 57 04.

BUDOWSKI, Gerardo, PH.D.; Venezuelan agronomist and forester; b. 10 June 1925, Berlin, Germany; s. of Dr. Issar Budowski and Marguerite Wolffgang; m. Thelma T. Palma 1958; two d.; ed. Univ. Central de Venezuela, Inter-American Inst. of Agricultural Sciences, Turrialba, Costa Rica and Yale Univ. School of Forestry; Div. of Research, Ministry of Agriculture Forestry Service 1947–49, Head 1949–52; Forester, Inter-American Inst. of Agricultural Sciences, Havana 1953–55, Turrialba 1956–58, Head, Forestry Dept. 1958–67; Visiting Prof. of Geography and Forestry, Univ. of Calif., Berkeley 1967; Programme Specialist for Ecology and Conservation, UNESCO, Paris 1967–70; Dir.-Gen. Int. Union for Conservation of Nature and Natural Resources 1970–76; Head, Renewable Natural Resources Dept., Tropical Agricultural Research and Training Center, Costa Rica 1976–86; Dir. Natural Resources, Univ. for Peace, Costa Rica; Int. Co-ordinator for Agroforestry, UN Univ. (Tokyo) 1978–; Special Adviser to Worldwide Fund for Nature (WWF) 1995–; Prof. Emer., Catie, Turrialba, Costa Rica 1996–; Pres. The Ecotourism Soc. 1993–97; mem. Tech. Advisory Cttee., Consultative Group on Int. Agricultural Research 1989–93, Earth Council Advisory Cttee. 1992–; Hon. mem. Int. Union for Conservation of Nature and Natural Resources, Int. World Wide Fund for Nature; Order of the Golden Ark (Netherlands) 1976, Order Henry Pittier, 1st Class (Venezuela) 1979, IUCN Fred Packard Award 1991, Order Semper Virens (Nicaragua) 1994. *Publications:* La Conservación como instrumento para el desarrollo 1985, and more than 250 articles. *Leisure interest:* chess (several times champion of Venezuela and mem. of Olympic team). *Address:* University for Peace, P.O. Box 138, 6100 Ciudad Colón, Costa Rica (Office); P.O. Box 198, 2300 Curridabat, San José, Costa Rica (Home). *Telephone:* 225 3008. *Fax:* 2534227.

BUENAVENTURA, Enrique; Colombian playwright; b. 23 Aug. 1924, Cali; s. of Cornelio Buenaventura and Julia Emma Alder; m. Jacqueline Vidal 1961; one s.; sailor 1950–52; fmrly. painter, magazine illustrator, journalist; currently Dir. Teatro Experimental de Cali (T.E.C.) (Experimental Theatre of Cali); has written 60 plays most of which have been staged; Hon. D.Litt. and Philosophy (Valle Univ.); various nat. and int. awards. *Publications include:* Teatro 1963, A la Diestra de Dios Padre (included in Teatro Hispanoamericano Contemporáneo) 1964, La Orgía and La Maestra (included in Modern One Act Plays from Latin America) 1974. *Address:* Teatro Experimental de Cali, Calle 7, Numero 8-63, Apdo Aéreo 2050, Cali, Colombia. *Telephone:* (2) 885 38 61. *Fax:* (2) 883 26 32.

BUERO VALLEJO, Antonio; Spanish playwright; b. 29 Sept. 1916, Guadalajara; s. of Teniente Coronel Francisco Buero and Cruz Vallejo; m. Victoria Rodríguez 1959; two s.; ed. Instituto de Segunda Enseñanza de Guadalajara and Escuela de Bellas Artes de Madrid; visiting lecturer numerous Univs. in U.S.A. 1966; Hon. Fellow, Círculo de Bellas Artes, Ateneo de Madrid, American Asscn. of Teachers of Spanish and Portuguese, Soc. of Spanish and Spanish-American Studies, Modern Language Asscn., Deutscher Hispanistenverband; mem. Hispanic Soc. of America, Real Acad. Española, Int. Cttee. of the Theatre of the Nations; Premio Lope de Vega 1949; Premio Nacional de Teatro 1957, 1958, 1959, 1980; Premio María Rolland 1956, 1958, 1960; Premio March de Teatro 1959; Premio de la Crítica de Barcelona 1960; Premio Larra 1962; Premio el Espectador y la Crítica 1967, 1970, 1974, 1976, 1977, 1981, 1984, 1986; Premio Leopoldo Cano 1968, 1972, 1974, 1975, 1977; Premio Mayte 1974; Premio Foro Teatral 1974; Medalla de Oro "Gaceta Ilustrada" 1976; Premio Pablo Iglesias 1986, Premio Cervantes 1986; Medalla de Oro al mérito en las Bellas Artes. *Plays:* Historia de una Escalera 1949, Las palabras en la arena 1949, En la Ardiente Oscuridad 1950, La Tejedora de Sueños 1952, La señal que se espera 1952, Casi un Cuento de Hadas 1953, Madrugada 1953, Irene, o el Tesoro 1954, Hoy es Fiesta 1956, Las Cartas boca Abajo 1957, Un Soñador para un Pueblo 1958, Las Meninas 1960, El Concierto de San Ovidio 1962, Aventura en lo Gris 1963, El Tragaluz 1967, La doble historia del Dr. Valmy 1967, Mito 1968, El Sueño de la razón 1970, Llegada de los dioses 1971, La Fundación 1974, La Detonación 1977, Jueces en la noche 1979, El Terror Inmóvil 1979, Caimán 1981, Dialogo secreto 1984, Lázaro en el laberinto 1986, Música cercana 1989, Las Trampas del Azar 1994; *poetry:* Tentativas poéticas 1991, Obra Completa 1994; *essays:* Tres Maestros ante el público 1973; *painting:* Libro de Estampas 1993. *Leisure interest:* painting. *Address:* Calle General Díaz Porlier 36, 28001 Madrid, Spain. *Telephone:* 402-56-14.

BUFE, Uwe-Ernst, PH.D.; German business executive and chemist; b. 22 May 1944, Teschen; m.; two c.; ed. Technische Universität, Munich; with Spang and Co. 1971–74; Product Man. Degussa Frankfurt 1974, Corp. Devt. and Inorganic Chemicals 1981, mem. Bd. Degussa AG 1987, Corp. Devt. Degussa Corpn. 1977, Exec. Vice-Pres. Chemical Group 1985, Chair. Bd., C.E.O. 1996–. *Address:* Degussa AG, 60287 Frankfurt am Main, Germany. *Telephone:* 069-218-01. *Fax:* 069-218-3218.

BUFFET, Bernard; French painter; b. 10 July 1928, Paris; s. of Charles Buffet and Blanche-Emma Colombe; m. 2nd Anabelle Schwob 1958; one s. two d.; ed. Lycée Carnot, Ecole Nat. Supérieure des Beaux-Arts; annual exhbns. 1949–56 in Galerie Drouant-David, and in Galerie David & Garnier 1957–67, Galerie Maurice Garnier 1968; exhbns. in many foreign countries, including retrospective exhbns. Paris 1958, 1978, Berlin 1958, Belgium 1959, Tokyo 1963, Musée d'Unterlinden Colmar, France 1969, Wieger Deurne Holland 1977, Zürich 1983, Toulouse 1985, Musée Pouchkine, Moscow, Musée de l'Ermitage, Leningrad 1991, Château de Chenonceaux, Musée Gustave Courbet, Ornans 1993, documenta-Halle, Kassel 1994, Kaoshiung Art Gallery, Taiwan 1996; opened pvt. Bernard Buffet Museum, Japan 1973; illustrator of books, engraver, lithographer and stage designer; mem. Acad. des Beaux-Arts 1974–; Grand Prix de la Critique 1948; Officier, Légion d'honneur; Officier des Arts et des Lettres. *Address:* Galerie Maurice Garnier, 6 avenue Matignon, 75008 Paris (Office); Domaine de la Baume, Tourtour, 83690 Salernes, France (Home).

BUFFET, Marie-George; French politician; b. 7 May 1949, Sceaux (Hauts-de-Seine); d. of Paul Kossellek and Raymonde Rayer; m. Jean-Pierre Buffet 1972; two c.; joined Parti Communiste Français (PCF) 1969, elected to PCF Cen. Cttee. 1987, mem. Nat. Bureau 1994, Head Nat. Women's Cttee. 1996, elected to Nat. Secr. 1996; municipal councillor, then Deputy Mayor Châtenay-Malabry (Hauts-de-Seine) 1977–83; Nat. Ass. Deputy for Seine-Saint-Denis 1997–; Minister for Youth and Sport 1997–. *Address:* Ministry for Youth and Sport, 78 rue Olivier de Serres, 75015 Paris, France. *Telephone:* (1) 40.45.90.00. *Fax:* (1) 42.50.42.49.

BUFFETT, Warren; American investment banker; b. 30 Aug. 1930, Omaha; s. of Howard Homan and Leila Stahl; m. Susan Thompson 1952; two s. one d.; ed. Columbia Univ. Business School; Chair. Berkshire Hathaway (investment co.), Omaha, Neb., Nat. Indemnity Co., Buffalo Evening News; mem. Bd. of Dirs. Salomon Brothers 1987–, C.E.O. Aug. 1991; f. Buffet Foundation. *Address:* Berkshire Hathaway Inc., 1440 Kiewit Plaza, Omaha, NE 68131, U.S.A.

BUFI, Ylli; Albanian politician; b. 25 May 1948, Tiranë; m. Zana Bufi 1978; two d.; Minister of Foodstuff Industry 1990–91, of Food and Light Industry Feb.–May 1991, of Nutrition May–June 1991; Prime Minister of Albania June–Dec. 1991; now Minister of the Public Econ. and Privatization; mem.

Leading Cttee. of Socialist Party; mem. Parl.; Chair. Cttee. on Industry, Energetics, Transport and Telecommunications. *Address:* Ministry of the Public Economy and Privatization, c/o Këshilli i Ministrave, Tirana, Albania.

BUHARI, Maj.-Gen. Muhammadu; Nigerian government official and army officer; b. 17 Dec. 1942, Daura, Katsina Province of Kaduna; m. Safinatu Yusuf 1971; two d.; ed. Katsina Provincial Secondary School, Nigerian Mil. Training Coll., Mons Officers' Cadet School, Aldershot, England; joined Army 1962; commissioned 1963; served 2nd Bn. in Congo (now Zaire) 1963–64; Army Service Corps 1964–66; staff and command appointments in 1st and 3rd Infantry Divs.; Defence Service Staff Coll., Wellington, India 1972–73; Acting Dir. of Supply and Transport, Nigerian Army 1974–75; Mil. Gov. of North Eastern State (divided into three States Feb. 1976) 1975–76, of Borno State Feb.-March 1976; Fed. Commr. for Petroleum 1976–78; Chair. Nigerian Nat. Petroleum Corpn. 1976–80; Mil. Sec. Nigerian Army 1978; mem. Supreme Mil. Council 1976–77; overthrew govt. of Shehu Shagari (q.v.); Head of State, Chair. Supreme Mil. Council and C. in C. of Armed Forces 1983–85; detained 1985–88, released 1988; Chair. Special Trust Fund 1994–. *Leisure interests:* tennis, squash, golf. *Address:* GRA, Daura, Katsina State, Nigeria.

BÜHLER, Winfried, DR. PHIL.; German professor of classical philology; b. 11 June 1929, Münster; s. of Ottmar Bühler and Maria Michels; m. Ria Fisser 1958; one s.; ed. Univs. of Bonn and Munich; Privatdozent, Univ. of Munich 1962–66; Assoc. Prof. of Classics, Univ. of Calif. Los Angeles 1966–67; Prof. of Classical Philology and Dir. Thesaurus Linguae Graecae, Univ. of Hamburg 1967–89, Foundation for German Science Prof. 1989–91; Fellow, Göttingen Acad.; corresp. Fellow, British Acad., Bavarian Acad. of Sciences. *Publications:* Die Europa des Moschos 1960, Beiträge zur Schrift vom Erhabenen 1964, Zenobii Athoi Proverbia (Vol. 4) 1982, (Vol. 1) 1987. *Leisure interests:* music, tennis. *Address:* Stauffenbergstrasse 7/VIII, 80797 Munich, Germany. *Telephone:* (089) 303617. *Fax:* (089) 303813.

BUICAN, Denis, D.ÈS SC.NAT., D.ÈS L.ET SC.HUM.; Romanian/French professor of history of science; b. 21 Dec. 1934, Bucharest; s. of Dumitru Peligrad and Elena Buican; ed. Bucharest Univ., Faculté des Sciences de Paris, Univ. de Paris I-Sorbonne; teaching asst., Bucharest Univ. 1956–57, Prin. Scientific Researcher 1957–60, Course Leader Gen. Biology and Genetics with History of Science course 1960–69, Invited Prof. 1990–; Invited Prof. First Class, History of Sciences, Faculté des Sciences, Univ. de Paris 1969–70, Univ. de Paris-Sorbonne 1970–74, Assoc. Prof. History and Philosophy of Science 1970–74; Assoc. History and Philosophy of Science, Univ. of Dijon 1974–80; Assoc. History of Sciences, Univ. de Paris I Panthéon-Sorbonne 1980–83; Assoc. Prof. First Class, History of Sciences, Univ. de Paris X 1983–86; Invited Prof. Collège de France 1984, 1993; Prof. First Class Univ. de Paris X Nanterre 1986–. *Publications include:* Histoire de la génétique et de l'évolutionnisme en France 1984, La Génétique et l'évolution 1986, Génétique et pensée évolutionniste 1987, Darwin et le darwinisme 1987, Lyssenko et le lyssenkisme 1988, L'Evolution et les évolutionnismes 1989, La Révolution de l'évolution 1989, L'Explosion biologique, du néant au Sur-être 1991, Dracula et ses avatars de Vlad l'Empaleur à Staline et Ceausescu 1991, Charles Darwin 1992, Mendel et la génétique d'hier et d'aujourd'hui 1993, Les Métamorphoses de Dracula 1993, Biognoséologie: Evolution et révolution de la connaissance 1993, Jean Rostand 1994, Histoire de la Biologie 1994, Evolution de la pensée biologique 1995, L'Evolution aujourd'hui 1995, L'Evolution: la grande aventure de la vie 1995, Ethologie comparée 1996, Dictionnaire de la Biologie 1997. *Leisure interests:* literature and the arts. *Address:* Université de Paris X Nanterre, 92001 Nanterre (Office); 15 rue Poliveau, 75005 Paris, France (Home). *Telephone:* (1) 40-97-72-00 (Office); (1) 43-36-33-97 (Home). *Fax:* (1) 40-97-70-86 (Office).

BUIJNSTERS, Piet J.; Netherlands professor of Dutch literature; b. 18 Oct. 1933, Breda; s. of Adriaan Buijnsters and Johanna Wirken; m. Leontine Smets 1961; two s. two d.; ed. Univs. of Nijmegen and Tübingen; f. Werkgroep 18e Eeuw (with C.M. Geerars) 1968; Prof. of Dutch Literature, Univ. of Nijmegen 1971–; mem. Royal Netherlands Acad. of Arts and Sciences; Anne Frank Foundation Prize 1964, Jan Campbert Stiching Prize 1974, Menno Hertzberg Prize 1981. *Publications:* Tussen twee werelden: Rhijnvis Feith als dichter van 'Het Graf' 1963, Hieronymus van Alphen 1746–1803 1973, Nederlandse literatuur van de acht-tiende eeuw 1984, Wolff en Deken, een biografie 1984, Briefwisseling van Betje Wolff en Aagje Deken 1987, Het verzamelen van boeken 1985. *Leisure interest:* book collecting. *Address:* University of Nijmegen, Department of Language and Literature, Erasmusplein 1, 6525 GG Nijmegen (Office); Witsenburgselaan 35, 6524 TE Nijmegen, Netherlands (Home). *Telephone:* (080) 512888 (Office); (080) 225466 (Home).

BUIRA, Ariel, M.A.; Mexican economist; b. 20 Sept. 1940, Chihuahua; s. of Antonio Buira and Enriqueta Seira de Buira; m. Janet Clark 1965; two s.; ed. Univ. of Manchester, England; Lecturer, Centre for Econ. and Demographic Studies, El Colegio de México 1966–68; Prof. of Econs., Graduate School of Business, Instituto Tecnológico de Monterrey 1968–70; Economist, IMF 1970–74; Econ. Adviser to Gov., Man. for Int. Research, Banco de México, S.A. 1975–78, Deputy Dir. then Dir. for Int. Orgs. and Agreements 1982–94, Deputy Gov. and mem. Bd. of Govs. April 1994–; Del. to Conf. on Int. Econ. Co-operation (CIEC) (Financial Affairs Comm.) 1976–77; Alt. Exec. Dir., IMF 1978–80, Exec. Dir. for Mexico, Spain, Venezuela, Cen. America 1980–82; First Prize, Course on Econ. Integration, Coll. Européen des Sciences Sociales et Economiques 1963. *Publications:* 50 Años de Banca Central (jointly) 1976, LDC External Debt and the World Economy 1978, Directions for Reform—The Future of the International Monetary System (jointly) 1984, México: Crisis Financiera y Programa de Ajuste in América Latina: Deuda, Crisis y Perspectivas 1984; Is There a Need for Reform? 1984; contrib.: Politics and Economics of External Debt Crisis—The Latin American Experience 1985, Incomes Policy (ed. V. L. Urquidi) 1987, Money and Finance Vol. I (ed. R. Tandon) 1987, Adjustment with Growth and the Role of the IMF 1987, La Economía Mundial: Evolución y Perspectivas 1989, Una Evalución de la Estrategia de la Deuda 1989, Los Determinantes del Ahorro en México 1990, Evolución de la Estrategia de la Deuda 1990, International Liquidity and the Needs of the World Economy (Vol. IV) 1994, Reflections on the International Monetary System 1995, Can Currency Crises be Prevented or Better Managed? (ed. Jan Joost Teunissen) 1996, The Potential of the SDR for Improving the International Monetary System 1996, Reflections on the Mexican Crisis of 1994 1996, and numerous articles. *Leisure interests:* music, literature. *Address:* Sierra Tezonco No. 174, Lomas de Chapultepec, Delegación Miguel Hidalgo, 11000-México, D.F., Mexico. *Telephone:* 520.46.17; 540.02.37.

BUITER, Willem Hendrik, PH.D., F.B.A.; Dutch/American professor of economics; b. 26 Sept. 1949, The Hague, Netherlands; s. of Hendrien Buiter van Schooten and Harm Geert Buiter; m. 1st Jean Archer 1988; two c.; m. 2nd Anne C. Sibert 1998; ed. Cambridge Univ., Yale Univ.; Asst. Prof. of Econs. and Int. Affairs, Woodrow Wilson School, Princeton Univ. 1975–79; Prof. of Econs. Bristol Univ. 1980–82; Cassel Prof. of Econs. with Special Reference to Money and Banking, L.S.E. 1982–85; Prof. of Econs. Yale Univ. 1985–94, Juan T. Trippe Prof. of Int. Econs. 1990–94; Prof. of Int. Macroecons. Univ. of Cambridge 1994–; mem. Monetary Policy Cttee., Bank of England 1997–; Consultant IMF, IBRD, IDB 1979–; Adviser House of Commons Treasury Select Cttee., U.K. 1980–82, Netherlands Ministry of Educ. 1985–86, EC, DGII 1982–85; Corresp. Royal Netherlands Acad. of Sciences, Research Assoc. Nat. Bureau of Econ. Research, Research Fellow Centre for Econ. Policy Research. *Publications:* Temporary and Long-run Equilibrium 1979, Budgetary Policy, International and Intertemporal Trade in the Global Economy 1989, Macroeconomic Theory and Stabilization Policy 1989, Principles of Budgetary and Financial Policy 1990, International Macroeconomics 1990, Financial Markets and European Monetary Cooperation: The Lessons of the 92–93 ERM crisis (with Giancarlo Corsetti and Paolo Pesenti) 1997. *Leisure interests:* tennis, theatre, westerns, science fiction and fantasy novels, poetry. *Address:* Faculty of Economics and Politics, University of Cambridge, Sidgwick Avenue, Cambridge, CB3 9DD, England.

BUJAK, Zbigniew; Polish politician and union leader; b. 29 Nov. 1954, Łopuszno; ed. electrical eng. secondary school; worked in Polfa Pharmaceutical plant, Grodzisk Mazowiecki, then Ursus Mechanical Works 1973–81; nat. service in airborne commando div. 1974–76; organizer of strike in Ursus Works in July 1980; assoc. Workers' Cttee. for solidarity with striking coastal workers Aug. 1980; Chair. Founding Cttee. Solidarity Trade Union, Mazowsze Region 1980; mem. Nat. Consultative Comm. of Solidarity, took part in negotiations with govt. 1981; under martial law in hiding, continued union activity 1981–86; Chair. Bd. Mazowsze Region in Provisional Exec. Comm. of Solidarity 1982–86; arrested May 1986, amnestied Sept. 1986; mem. Nat. Exec. Comm. of Solidarity 1987–90; Chair. Citizens' Cttee. of Solidarity Chair. 1988–90; took part in Round Table debates and in Groups for Political Reform and for Economy and Social Policy Feb.–April 1989; Chair. Council of Warsaw Agreement of Citizens' Cttees. 1990–91; one of f. and leaders Citizens' Movt.—Democratic Action (ROAD) 1990–91; Deputy to Sejm (Parl.) 1991–97, Chair. Sejm Comm. of Admin. and Internal Affairs 1993–97; Chair. of Democratic-Social Movt. 1991; co-f. and Vice-Chair. Union of Labour (UP) 1992–98; mem. Freedom Union (UW) 1998–; fmr. mem. Socialist Rural Youth Union. *Publication:* Przepraszam za Solidarność 1991. *Address:* Unia Wolności, Al. Jerozolimskie 30, 00-024 Warsaw, Poland. *Telephone:* (22) 827 50 47. *Fax:* (22) 827 78 51.

BUJOLD, Genevieve; Canadian actress; b. 1 July 1942, Montreal; m. Paul Almond 1967 (divorced); one s.; ed. Montreal Conservatory of Drama; fmr. cinema usherette in Montreal; stage appearances include The Barber of Seville, A Midsummer Night's Dream, A House . . .A Day; TV appearances in St. Joan, Antony and Cleopatra, Mistress of Paradise, Red Earth, White Earth, Star Trek. *Films:* La guerre est finie, La fleur de l'age, Entre la mer et l'eau douce, King of Hearts, The Thief of Paris, Isabel, Anne of the Thousand Days, The Act of the Heart, The Trojan Women, The Journey, Earthquake, Alex and the Gypsy, Kamouraska, Obsession, Swashbuckler, Another Man Another Chance, Coma, Murder by Decree, Final Assignment, The Last Flight of Noah's Ark, Monsignor, Tightrope, Choose Me, Trouble in Mind, The Moderns, Dead Ringers, False Identity, Secret Places of the Heart, A Paper Wedding, Star Trek: Generations, An Ambush of Ghosts, Mon Ami Max.

BUJONES, Fernando; American ballet dancer; b. 9 March 1955, Miami, Fla.; s. of Fernando and Maria (Calleiro) Bujones; m. Marcia Kibitschek 1980; ed. School of American Ballet; joined American Ballet Theater 1972, Soloist 1973, Prin. Dancer 1974–85, Guest Prin. 1976; Guest Artist, Boston Ballet 1987–; artistic Dir. Miss. Ballet, Jackson –1994, Bay Ballet Theater, Tampa, Fla. 1994–; has danced with Nat. Ballet of Canada, Berlin Opera, Vienna State Opera, Scottish Ballet, Rome Opera and Stuttgart Ballet; appeared in film The Turning Point; has produced own dance corpn. Bujones Ltd.; choreographed Grand Pas Romantique 1985; Varna Gold Medal 1974, Dance Magazine Award 1982, Florida Prize 1986, Elliott Norton Award,

Boston Theater 1992. *Ballets:* Coppelia 1974, Swan Lake 1975, Sleeping Beauty 1976, Giselle 1977. *Address:* 401 E. Jackson Street, Suite 2355, Tampa, FL 33602, U.S.A.

BUKOVAC, Martin J., PH.D.; American professor of horticulture; b. 12 Nov. 1929, Johnston City, Ill.; s. of John Bukovac and Sadie Fak; m. Judith A. Kelley 1956; one d.; ed. Michigan State Univ.; Asst. Prof., Dept. of Horticulture, Mich. State Univ. 1957–61, Assoc. Prof. 1961–63, Prof. 1963–92, Univ. Distinguished Prof. 1992; Biological Science Collaborator, U.S.D.A./Agricultural Research Service 1982–; Postdoctoral Fellow, Univs. of Oxford and Bristol, England 1965–66; Dir. Mich. State Univ. Press 1983–91; Adviser, Eli Lilly Co. 1971–88; Pres. Martin J. Bukovac Inc. 1996–; Fellow A.A.A.S., American Soc. of Horticultural Science; mem. N.A.S., Editorial Advisory Bd. Horticultural Abstracts 1990–, Editorial Bd. Encyclopedia of Agricultural Science 1991–96, Int. Editorial Bd., Horticultural Science, Kertészetic Tudomány, Budapest 1994–; mem. Int. Advisory Bd., Life Sciences Div., Center for Nuclear Sciences, Grenoble; Hon. Dr. agr. (Bonn) 1995; Alexander von Humboldt Award for Sr. Scientist 1995 and numerous awards. *Publications:* over 300 research articles. *Leisure interests:* photography, sports. *Address:* Department of Horticulture, Michigan State University, East Lansing, MI 48824-1112; 4428 Seneca Drive, Okemos, MI 48864, U.S.A. (Home). *Telephone:* (517) 355-5207 (Office); (517) 349-1952 (Home). *Fax:* (517) 353-0890.

BUKOVSKY, Vladimir Konstantinovich, M.A.; Russian writer and scientist; b. 30 Dec. 1942, Belebey; s. of Konstantin and Nina Bukovsky; ed. Moscow State Univ., Cambridge Univ.; worked at Moscow Centre of Cybernetics; arrested for possessing banned literature 1963, confined to Leningrad Psychiatric Prison Hospital for 15 months; arrested for demonstration on behalf of Soviet writers 1965, confined for 8 months in psychiatric institutions; arrested for civil rights work 1967, on trial Sept. 1967 and sentenced to 3 years' corrective labour; arrested for delivering information on psychiatric abuse to the West 1971, on trial 1972 and sentenced to 2 years in prison, 5 in a labour camp and 5 in exile; after world-wide campaign for his release, was exchanged for Chilean Communist Party leader Luis Corvalán in Zürich Dec. 1976; citizenship restored 1992; research work, Stanford Univ., Calif. 1982–90; f. Centre for Democracy in Support of New Russia, New York; Hon. mem. several human rights orgs., several PEN clubs; Konrad Adenauer Freedom and Literature Prize 1984; lives in England. *Publications:* short stories in Russia's Other Writers 1970, and in Grani, Opposition—Eine neue Geisteskrankheit in der U.S.S.R. (German edition) 1972, A Manual on Psychiatry for Dissenters (with Semyon Gluzman) 1974, To Build a Castle: My Life as a Dissenter (in English; trans. in Swedish, Italian, Spanish, French and German) 1978, Cette lancinante douleur de la liberté 1981, The Peace Movement and the Soviet Union 1982. *Leisure interests:* the arts, architecture.

BULAI, Igor Borisovich, CAND. HIST.; Russian diplomatist; b. 17 May 1947, Moscow; m.; two c.; ed. Moscow State Inst. of Int. Relations, Inst. of U.S.A. and Canada Acad. of Sciences; jr. researcher Inst. of U.S.A. and Canada 1973–79; instructor Div. of Information Cen. Cttee. CPSU 1979–85; counsellor U.S.S.R. Embassy to U.S.A. 1985–91; with Dept. of Information U.S.S.R. Ministry of Foreign Affairs 1991–92; Head Dept. of Information and Press, Ministry of Foreign Affairs of Russia 1992–98; Consul-Gen. in Edinburgh 1998–. *Address:* Russian General Consulate, 9 Goates Crescent, Edinburgh, EH3 7AL, Scotland. *Telephone:* 0131-225 7098. *Fax:* 0131-225 9587.

BULATOVIĆ, Momir, C.ECON.SC.; Yugoslav politician; b. 1928, Montenegro; ed. Titograd Univ.; fmr. mem. League of Communists of Montenegro, then leader Republican League of Communists; Chair. Democratic Party of Socialists (DPS) 1990–; elected Pres. of Montenegro 1990–97; Prime Minister of Yugoslavia 1997–. *Address:* Vlada Savezne Republike Jugoslavije, Lenina blvd. 2, 11070 Belgrade, Yugoslavia. *Telephone:* (11) 334-281 (Office).

BULGAK, Vladimir Borisovich, DR.ECON.SC., CAND. TECH. SC.; Russian politician; b. 9 May 1941, Moscow; m.; one d.; ed. Moscow Electrotech. Inst. of Communications, Inst. of Man. of Nat. Econ., U.S.S.R. State Cttee on Science and Tech.; instructor, then sec. Moscow City Komsomol Cttee. 1963–68; for 15 years worked in Moscow radio translation network; head of depts. U.S.S.R. Ministry of Telecomunications 1983–90; Minister 1990–91; Minister of Telecommunications Russian Fed. 1991–97; Deputy Chair. Govt. of Russian Fed. 1997–98, Sept. 1998–; Minister of Science and Tech. April–Sept. 1998; mem. Int. Acad. of Informatization, Russian Acad. of Tech. Sciences, Russian Acad. of Natural Sciences; U.S.S.R. State Prize. *Address:* Government of Russian Federation, Krasnopresnenskaya nab. 2, 103274 Moscow, Russia (Office). *Telephone:* (095) 205-32-20; (095) 205-45-25 (Office).

BULGER, Roger James, M.D.; American physician; b. 18 May 1933, Brooklyn; s. of William J. Bulger and Florence D. (Poggi) Bulger; m. Ruth E. Grouse 1960; two d.; ed. Harvard Univ., Emmanuel Coll., Cambridge, Univ. of Washington and Boston Univ.; intern, Resident, Univ. of Washington Hospitals 1960–62, 1964–65; Asst. Prof., Assoc. Prof. Univ. of Washington Medical School, Seattle 1966–70; Medical Dir. Univ. Hospital, Seattle 1967–70; Prof. of Community Health Sciences, Duke Univ. Medical Center 1970–72; Exec. Officer, Inst. of Medicine, N.A.S. 1972–76; Prof. of Internal Medicine, George Washington Univ. School of Medicine 1972–76; Prof. of Internal Medicine, Family and Community Medicine, Dean, Medical School, Chancellor, Worcester Campus, Univ. of Mass. 1976–78; Pres. Univ. of Tex. Health Sciences Center, Houston 1978–88; Pres. and C.E.O. Asscn. Acad. Health Centers, Washington, D.C. Feb. 1988–; mem. numerous professional socs. etc. *Publications:* Hippocrates Revisited 1973, In Search of the Modern Hippocrates 1987, Technology, Bureaucracy and Healing 1988; articles and book chapters. *Address:* Association of Academic Health Centres # 720, 1400 Sixteenth Street, N.E., Washington, DC 20002, U.S.A.

BULIN, René Henri; French aeronautical engineer; b. 8 Aug. 1920, Langres; s. of Louis and Louise (née Walter) Bulin; m. 1st Claudine Prostot 1955; m. 2nd Catherine Tambuscio 1982; ed. Ecole Polytechnique Paris, Ecole Nationale Supérieure de l'Aéronautique; engineer responsible for setting up Centre d'Essais des Propulseurs (Fort de Villeras) 1946–53; Head Operations Dept. and Instructor, Ecole Nationale de l'Aviation Civile 1953–56; Deputy Dir., then Dir. Air Navigation Secrétariat Général de l'Aviation Civile, France 1956–61; first Dir.-Gen. European Org. for the Safety of Air Navigation (EUROCONTROL) 1961–78, responsible for having set up the Air Traffic Services Agency, Brussels and the EUROCONTROL Experimental Centre, Bretigny-sur-Orge and for establishing the Upper Area Control Centres, Maastricht, Netherlands, Karlsruhe, Germany, Shannon, Ireland, the EUROCONTROL Inst. of Air Navigation Services, Luxembourg, and the Users Charge Service, Brussels; Adviser Thomson-C.S.F. 1978–83; Special Adviser to European Community Aeronautical Comm.; Commdr., Légion d'honneur, and numerous other awards. *Address:* Altirama, avenue Frédéric Mistral, 06130, Grasse, France (Home).

BULL, Sir George, Kt., British business executive; b. 17 July 1936, London; s. of Michael Bull and Hon. Madeleine Hennessy; m. Jane Freeland 1960; four s. one d.; ed. Ampleforth Coll.; Coldstream Guards 1954–57; joined Twiss Browning & Hallowes 1958; Gilbey Vintners Ltd. 1970; Dir. Int. Distillers and Vintners (IDV) 1973; Man. Dir. IDV Europe 1977; Deputy Man. Dir. IDV Ltd. 1982; Dir. Grand Metropolitan Ltd. 1985; Chief Exec. IDV Ltd. 1987; Chair. and C.E.O. IDV Ltd. (Drinks Sector of Grand Metropolitan PLC) 1988; Chair. and C.E.O. GrandMet Food Sector 1992; Group Chief Exec. Grand Metropolitan PLC 1993, Chair. Grand Metropolitan PLC 1996–97; Co.-Chair. Diageo (after merger with Guinness PLC) 1997–98; Chair. J. Sainsbury PLC May 1998–; Dir. (non-exec.) United Newspapers 1993–; Chevalier, Légion d'honneur. *Leisure interests:* golf, photography. *Address:* J. Sainsbury PLC, Stamford House, Stamford Street, London, SE1 9LL, England (Office); The Old Vicarage, Arkesden, Saffron Walden, Essex, CB11 4HB, England (Home). *Telephone:* (0171) 921 6000 (Office); (01799) 550445 (Home).

BULLARD, Sir Julian (Leonard), G.C.M.G.; British diplomatist (retd.); b. 8 March 1928, Athens; s. of the late Sir Reader Bullard and Miriam Smith; m. Margaret Stephens 1954; two s. two d.; ed. Rugby School, Magdalen Coll., Oxford; Fellow of All Souls Coll., Oxford 1950–57, 1988–; nat. service Army 1950–52; joined H.M. Diplomatic Service 1953, served at Foreign Office 1953–54, Vienna 1954–56, Amman 1956–59, Foreign Office 1960–63, Bonn 1963–66, Moscow 1966–68, Dubai 1968–70, FCO (Head of E. European and Soviet Dept.) 1971–75; Minister, Bonn 1975–79; Deputy Under-Sec. of State 1979–84; Deputy to Perm. Under-Sec. of State and Political Dir. 1982–84; Amb. to Fed. Repub. of Germany 1984–88; Pro-Chancellor, Univ. of Birmingham 1989–94, mem. Council 1988–96; Hon. LL.D. (Birmingham) 1994. *Address:* 18 Northmoor Road, Oxford, OX2 6UR, England. *Telephone:* (01865) 512981.

BULLER, Prof. Arthur John, B.S., E.R.D., F.R.C.P., F.I.BIOL., F.R.S.A.; British physiologist; b. 16 Oct. 1923; s. of Thomas Alfred and Edith May (née Wager) Buller; m. Helena Joan Pearson 1946; one s. two d. (one deceased); ed. Duke of York's Royal Mil. School, Dover, St. Thomas's Hospital Medical School; Kitchener Scholar 1941–45; Lecturer in Physiology St. Thomas's Hospital 1946–49; Maj. R.A.M.C., Specialist in Physiology, Jr. Sec. Mil. Personnel Research Cttee. 1949–53; Lecturer in Medicine St. Thomas's Hospital 1953–57; Reader in Physiology King's Coll., London 1961–65; Gresham Prof. of Physic 1963–65; Prof. of Physiology Univ. of Bristol 1965–82 (Prof. Emer. 1982–), Dean Faculty of Medicine 1976–78; Chief Scientist (on secondment) Dept. of Health and Social Security 1978–81; Visiting Prof. Monash Univ., Australia 1972; Long Fox Memorial Lecturer, Bristol 1978; Hon. Consultant in Clinical Physiology, Bristol Dist. Hospital 1970–85; Royal Soc. Commonwealth Fellow, Canberra, Australia 1958–59; mem. Bd. of Govs. Bristol Royal Infirmary 1968–74, Avon Health Authority 1974–78, MRC 1975–81; Chair. Neurosciences and Mental Health Bd., MRC 1975–77; External Scientific Adviser, Rayne Inst. St. Thomas's Hospital 1979–85; Research Devt. Dir., Muscular Dystrophy Gp. of G.B. and N.I. 1982–90; mem. BBC, IBA Cen. Appeals Advice Cttee. 1983–88; Milroy Lecturer, Royal Coll. of Physicians 1983. *Publications:* articles in books and journals on normal and abnormal physiology. *Leisure interests:* clarets and conversation. *Address:* Lockhall, Cow Lane, Steeple Aston, Oxon., OX6 3SG, England. *Telephone:* (01869) 347502.

BULLOCK, Baron (Life Peer) cr. 1976, of Leafield in the County of Oxfordshire; **Alan Louis Charles Bullock,** Kt., F.B.A., M.A., D.LITT.; British historian and university administrator; b. 13 Dec. 1914, Trowbridge; s. of Rev. Frank A. Bullock; m. Hilda Yates Handy 1940; three s. two d. (one deceased); ed. Bradford Grammar School, Wadham and Merton Colls., Oxford; BBC European Service diplomatic and political corresp. 1940–45; Fellow, Dean and Tutor of New Coll., Oxford 1945–52; Founding Master of St. Catherine's Coll., Oxford 1960–80, Hon. Fellow 1980–; Trustee, The Observer 1957–69,

Dir. 1977–81; mem. Arts Council 1961–64, British Library Organizing Cttee. 1972–73, Cttee. of Vice-Chancellors and Principals 1969–73; Vice-Chancellor, Univ. of Oxford 1969–73; Chair. Inquiry into Teaching of Reading and Other Uses of Language 1972–74; Chair. Trustees of Tate Gallery 1973–79; Chair. Cttee. on Industrial Democracy 1975–76; Trustee, Wolfson Foundation 1974–87; Aspen Inst., Berlin; Chair. Research Cttee. and mem. Council, Royal Inst. of Int. Affairs (Chatham House) 1954–78; fmr. Chair. Nat. Advisory Council on Training and Supply of Teachers; mem. Advisory Council on Public Records to 1976; fmr. Chair. The Schools Council, Bd. of Int. Asscn. for Cultural Freedom; Joint Ed. Oxford History of Modern Europe, Int. Comm. of Historians for publication of documents on German Foreign Policy 1918–45; mem. Acad. Europaea; Foreign Mem. American Acad. of Arts and Sciences; Hon. doctorates (Aix-Marseilles, Bradford, Newfoundland, Reading, Open Univ., Leicester, Sussex, Warwick, Essex Univs.); Hon. Fellow, Merton, New Coll. Wadham, Wolfson, Linacre and St. Antony's Colls., Oxford; Hon. F.R.I.B.A.; Chevalier Légion d'honneur 1970, Grosse-dienst-kreuz, Germany. *Publications:* Hitler, a Study in Tyranny 1952, 1962, The Liberal Tradition 1956, Schellenberg Memoirs 1956, The Life and Times of Ernest Bevin, Vol. I 1960, Vol. II 1967, Vol. III 1983, The Twentieth Century (ed.) 1971, The Fontana Dictionary of Modern Thought (co-ed. with Oliver Stallybrass) 1977, 2nd Ed. (with Stephen Trombley) 1988, Faces of Europe 1979, Fontana Dictionary of Modern Thinkers (co-ed. with R. B. Woodings) 1983, The Humanist Tradition in the West 1985, Hitler and Stalin: Parallel Lives 1991. *Address:* St. Catherine's College, Oxford, OX1 3UJ; Gable End, 30 Godstow Road, Oxford, OX2 8AJ, England. *Telephone:* (01865) 271700; (01865) 513380 (Home).

BULLOCK, Peter, B.A., PH.D.; British soil scientist; b. 6 July 1937, Bridgnorth; s. of Cecil Bullock and Alice Bullock; m. Patricia Standidge 1963; one s. (deceased) one d.; ed. Birmingham, Leeds and Cornell Univs.; Scientific Officer, Soil Survey of England and Wales 1968, Sr. Scientific Officer 1970, Prin. Scientific Officer 1975, Dir. 1985; Dir. Soil Survey and Land Research Centre 1987–97; Visiting Prof. School of Agric., Food and Environment, Cranfield Univ.; Vice-Pres. British Soc. of Soil Science; mem. Govt. and Research Council Cttees. on Soil Science, Climate Change, Environmental Protection, Impacts of Environmental Change; mem. Governing Body of Inst. of Grassland and Environmental Research, Advisory Cttee. of European Soil Bureau (Chair. 1998–); Fulbright Scholar 1964–66. *Publications:* seven books on soil science; over 70 scientific papers. *Leisure interests:* sport including: football, cricket, most ball games; theatre, art, walking. *Address:* School of Agriculture, Food and Environment, Silsoe Campus, Silsoe, Beds., MK45 4DT (Office); 11 Wood End Hill, Harpenden, Herts., AL5 3EZ, England (Home). *Telephone:* (01525) 863251. *Fax:* (01525) 863253.

BULLOCK, Sandra; American actress; b. 22 July 1966; d. of John Bullock and Helga Bullock; ed. East Carolina Univ.; grew up in Germany and Washington, D.C.; frequent appearances on European stage with opera-singer mother; appeared in off-Broadway productions including No Time Flat (WPA Theatre); TV roles in The Preppy Murder (film), Lucky Chances (mini-series), Working Girl (NBC series). *Films:* Love Potion 9, The Vanishing, The Thing Called Love, When The Party's Over, Demolition Man, Wrestling Ernest Hemingway, Speed, While You Were Sleeping, Two If By Sea, Moll Flanders, A Time to Kill, In Love and War, Practical Magic, Forces of Nature; Dir. Making Sandwiches 1996, Speed 2. *Address:* UTA, 9560 Wilshire Blvd., Fl. 5, Beverly Hills, CA 90212, U.S.A.

BULLOCK, Theodore Holmes, PH.D.; American professor of neurosciences; b. 16 May 1915, Nanking, China; s. of A. Archibald and Ruth Beckwith Bullock; m. Martha Runquist 1937; one s. one d.; ed. Univ. of California, Berkeley; Sterling Fellow, Yale Univ. 1940–41; Rockefeller Fellow 1941–42; Instructor in Neuroanatomy, Yale Univ. 1942–44; Asst. Prof. of Anatomy, Univ. of Missouri 1944–46; Instructor and sometime Head, Invertebrate Zoology, Marine Biol. Lab., Woods Hole, Mass.; Asst. Prof., Assoc. Prof., Prof. of Zoology, Univ. of Calif., Los Angeles 1946–66; Prof. of Neurosciences, Univ. of Calif. San Diego School of Medicine 1966–82, Prof. Emer. 1982–; Head of Neurobiology Unit, Scripps Inst. of Oceanography; mem. American Acad. Arts and Sciences, N.A.S., American Phil. Soc., Int. Soc. for Neuroethology; fmr. Pres. American Soc. of Zoology, Soc. for Neuroscience; Dr h.c. (Frankfurt) 1988; Lashley Prize, American Philosophical Soc. 1968; Gerard Prize, Soc. for Neuroscience 1984. *Publications:* Structure and Function in the Nervous Systems of Invertebrates (with G. A. Horridge) 1965, Introduction to Nervous Systems (with R. Orkand and A. D. Grinnell) 1977, Electroreception (with W. Heiligenberg) 1986, Brain Dynamics (with E. Basar) 1989, Induced Rythms in the Brain (with E. Basar) 1992, How Do Brains Work? 1993. *Address:* Department of Neurosciences, University of California, San Diego, La Jolla, CA 92093, U.S.A. *Telephone:* (619) 534-3636.

BULMAHN, Edelgard, B.A.; German politician; b. 4 March 1951, Minden; m.; ed. Petershagen Aufbaugymnasium and Hanover Univ.; secondary school teacher for seven years, latterly at Lutherschule, Hanover; joined SPD party 1969; mem. City Dist. Council Hanover-Linden 1981–86; mem. Bundestag (SPD) 1987–, mem. Exec. Cttee. SPD Parl. Group 1991–, Exec. Cttee. SPD 1993–; Deputy Spokesman on Research and Tech. SPD Parl. Group 1990–94; Chair. Cttee. on Educ., Science, Research, Tech. and Tech. Assessment 1995–96; Fed. Minister of Educ. and Research Oct. 1998–. *Address:* Ministry of Education and Research, Heinemannstrasse 2, 53175 Bonn, Germany. *Telephone:* (49) 228 573010. *Fax:* (49) 228 573601.

BULMER-THOMAS, Victor Gerald, O.B.E., M.A., D.PHIL.; British professor of economics; b. 23 March 1948, London; s. of late Ivor Bulmer-Thomas and of Joan Bulmer; m. Barbara Swasey 1970; two s. one d.; ed. Westminster School, New Coll. and St. Antony's Coll. Oxford; Research Fellow, Fraser of Allander Inst. 1975–78; lecturer in Econs. Queen Mary Coll. London 1978–87, Reader 1987–92, Prof. of Econs. 1990–98; Dir. Inst. of Latin American Studies, Univ. of London 1992–98, Sr. Research Fellow 1998–; Emer. Prof. of Econs. Univ. of London 1998–; Dir. Schroders Emerging Countries Fund 1996–; Order of San Carlos (Colombia) 1998, Nat. Order of the Southern Cross (Brazil) 1998. *Publications:* Input-Output Analysis for Developing Countries 1982, The Political Economy of Central America Since 1920 1987, Studies in the Economics of Central America 1988, Britain and Latin America: A Changing Relationship (ed.) 1989, The Economic History of Latin America Since Independence 1994, The New Economic Model in Latin America and Its Impact on Income Distribution and Poverty (ed.) 1996, Thirty Years of Latin American Studies in the U.K. (ed.) 1997, United States Relations with Latin America: Analysis of the New Agenda (ed.) 1999. *Leisure interests:* music (viola), tennis, walking, canoeing, underwater photography. *Address:* Institute of Latin American Studies, 31 Tavistock Square, London, WC1H 9HA, England. *Telephone:* 0171-387 5671. *Fax:* 0171-388 5024.

BUMBRY, Grace; American opera singer; b. 4 Jan. 1937, St. Louis, Mo.; d. of Benjamin and Melzia Bumbry; ed. Boston and Northwestern Univs., Music Acad. of the West; début, Paris Opera as Amneris, Aida March 1960; Basel Opera 1960–63; Carmen with Paris Opera, and toured Japan; Royal Opera, Brussels; Die Schwarze Venus, Tannhäuser, Bayreuth Festival 1961 and 1962; Vienna State Opera 1963; Covent Garden 1963, 1968, 1969, 1976, 1978; Salzburg Festival 1964; Metropolitan Opera 1965–79; La Scala 1964–79, Chicago Lyric 1962–78; Porgy and Bess, N.Y. Metropolitan Opera 1985; Richard Wagner Medal 1963; Grammy Award 1979, Royal Opera House Medal 1988; Hon. D.H. (Univ. of St. Louis), (Rust Coll.); Hon. D.Mus. (Rockhurst Coll.); Hon. Citizen of Baltimore, Los Angeles, Philadelphia, St. Louis. *Leisure interests:* interior decorating, designing clothes. *Address:* c/o Columbia Artists Management, 165 West 57th Street, New York, NY 10019, U.S.A.

BUMPERS, Dale Leon, LL.D.; American politician; b. 12 Aug. 1925, Charleston, Ark.; s. of William Rufus and Lattie (née Jones) Bumpers; m. Betty Flanagan 1949; two s. one d.; ed. Univ. of Arkansas and Northwestern Law School; propr. Charleston Hardware and Furniture Co. 1951–66, Angus Breeding Farm 1966–70; Attorney, Charleston, Ark. 1951–70; Gov. of Arkansas 1971–74; Senator from Arkansas 1975–99; Democrat. *Leisure interests:* reading, tennis, hunting. *Address:* c/o 229 Dirksen Senate Office Bldg., Washington, DC 20510, U.S.A. *Telephone:* (202) 224-4843.

BUND, Karlheinz, DR.ING., DR.RER.POL.; German business executive; b. 18 March 1925, Saarlouis; m. Anni Kronenberger; Chair. Bd. of Ruhrkohle AG 1973–85; Chair. EVG and Chair. Advisory Bd. INNOTEC 1985, ENRO Energie, Rohstoff GmbH; mem. Supervisory Bd. ASEA Brown, Boveri, Deutsche Babcock Anlagen AG; Pres. World Coal Inst. (WCI); Chair. ENRO GmbH. *Address:* Huyssenallee 86-88, 45128 Essen, Germany. *Telephone:* 0201-245 360. *Fax:* 0201-245 3639.

BUNDU, Abass, PH.D.; Sierra Leonean diplomatist and lawyer; b. 3 June 1948; s. of Isatu Kallay Bundu and Pa Santigie; m. Khadija Allie 1976; two s. three d.; ed. Australian Nat. Univ., Canberra, Cambridge Univ., England; Asst. Dir., Commonwealth Secr., London 1975–82; M.P. for Port Loko N.E. 1982–90; Minister of Agric., Natural Resources and Forestry 1982–85; Exec. Sec., Econ. Community of W. African States (ECOWAS) 1989–93; Sec. of State for Foreign Affairs and Int. Co-operation 1993–95; Yorke Award, Univ. of Cambridge. *Leisure interests:* tennis, swimming. *Address:* c/o Department of Foreign Affairs, Gloucester Street, Freetown, Sierra Leone. *Telephone:* 224778.

BUNGEY, Michael, B.SC. (ECON.); British advertising executive; b. 18 Jan. 1940; s. of William F.G. Bungey and Irene E. Bungey; m. Darleen P.C. Brooks 1976; one s. two d.; ed. St. Clement Danes Grammar School and London School of Econs.; marketing with Nestlé 1961–65; Assoc. Dir. Crawfords Advertising 1965–68; Account Dir. S.H. Benson Advertising 1968–71; Chair. Michael Bungey DFS Ltd. 1972–84; Chair., C.E.O. DFS Dorland 1987, Bates Dorland 1988, Bates Europe 1989; Deputy Chair. Dorland Advertising (now Bates Dorland Advertising Ltd.) 1984–, Chair. 1987–96, C.E.O. 1987–; Chair., C.E.O. Bates Worldwide (fmrly. BSB Worldwide) 1994–; Chair. Backer Spielvogel Bates Europe 1988–, Pres., C.O.O. Backer Spielvogel Bates Worldwide 1993–, C.E.O. 1994–; Chair., C.E.O. Bates Worldwide 1994–; C.E.O. Cordiant Communications Group PLC 1997–; Dir. Saatchi & Saatchi 1995–. *Address:* c/o Bates Dorland Advertising Ltd., 121–141 Westbourne Terrace, London, W2 6JR, England.

BUNICH, Pavel Grigoryevich, DR. ECON. SC.; Russian economist; b. 25 Oct. 1929; m.; one s.; ed. Moscow Univ.; corresp. mem. U.S.S.R. (now Russian) Acad. Sciences 1970–; mem. CPSU 1956–90, mem. Cen. Cttee. 1990–91; U.S.S.R. People's Deputy 1989–91; Head of Chair. Ordzhonikidze Inst. for Man. Moscow 1976–90; Chair. All-Union Council of Scientific and Tech. Socs.; Chair., Consolidated Working Group for Collating Results of Econ. Experiment, Dept. of Econ., Russian Acad. of Sciences; Head of Problem Lab., Acad. of Nat. Economy (First Pro-Rector 1990–), Russian Council of Ministers; Pres. Union of Leaseholders and Employers of Russia 1990–; mem. Political Council, Democratic Reforms Movt. 1992–; f. Democratic

Initiative Party 1993; mem. State Duma (Parl.) Dec. 1993–; Chair. Cttee. for Property, Privatization and Econ. Activity 1996–, Int. Congress for Regional Market of Eastern Europe and Asia 1998–. *Publications:* works on man. problems in econs., and financial systems. *Address:* Academy of National Economy, Vernadskogo prosp. 82, 117571, Moscow, Russia. *Telephone:* 434 01 09 (Office); 292 39 54 (Duma); 243 33 22 (Home). *Fax:* 292 95 59 (Duma).

BUNKIN, Fedor Vasilyevich, DR. PHYS.-MATH. SC.; Russian physicist; b. 17 Jan. 1929; m.; two c.; ed. Moscow State Univ.; jr., sr. researcher, head of sector, head of lab. Physical Inst. U.S.S.R. Acad. of Sciences 1955–82; Deputy Dir. Inst. of Gen. Physics U.S.S.R. Acad. of Sciences 1982–; corresp. mem. U.S.S.R. (now Russian) Acad. of Sciences 1976, mem. 1992–; main research in quantum physics, electronics, nonlinear optics, acoustics; mem. Co-ordination Council on problem Coherent and Nonlinear Optics Russian Acad. of Sciences; U.S.S.R. State Prize. *Publications include:* 6 books, numerous articles in scientific journals. *Address:* Physical Institute, Vavilova str. 38, 117942 Moscow, Russia (Office). *Telephone:* (095) 135 8234 (Office); (095) 331 3262 (Home).

BUNNAG, Marut; Thai politician; b. 21 August 1925, Bangkok; s. of Phra Sutthikarnvinijchai and Mrs Phongsri; m. Phantipha Bunnag; two c.; ed. Thammasat Univ.; with Ministry of Justice until 1952; law practice 1952–; Minister of Justice 1979; MP 1983; Minister of Public Health 1983–86, Sept.–Dec. 1990; Minister of Education 1988; Deputy Leader, Democrat Party. *Address:* c/o House of Representatives, Bangkok, Thailand.

BUNNING, Jim, B.S.; American politician and fmr. baseball player; b. 23 Oct. 1931, Southgate, Ky.; ed. Xavier Univ.; professional baseball player 1955–71; with Detroit Tigers 1955–63, Phila. Phillies 1964–67, 1970–71, Pittsburgh Pirates 1968–69, L.A. Dodgers 1969, retd. 1971; congressman Ky. State Senate 1979–83; mem. 100th–104th Congresses from 4th Ky. Dist. 1987–99; Senator from Kentucky Jan. 1999–; Republican. *Address:* U.S. Senate, Washington, DC 20510, U.S.A.

BUNTING, Arthur Hugh, C.M.G., M.SC., D.PHIL., F.L.S., F.I.BIOL.; British botanist; b. 7 Sept. 1917, Johannesburg, S. Africa; s. of S.P. Bunting and Rebecca Bunting; m. Elsie M. Reynard 1941; three s.; ed. Univs. of Witwatersrand and Oxford, Rhodes Scholar for Transvaal 1938; Asst. Chemist, Rothamsted Experimental Station, Harpenden, Herts. 1941–45; mem. MRC Human Nutrition Research Unit 1945–46; Chief Scientific Officer, Overseas Food Corpn. (East African Groundnut Scheme, Tanganyika) 1947–51; Sr. Research Officer, Research Div. Ministry of Agric. Sudan 1951–56; Prof. of Agricultural Botany, Univ. of Reading 1956–73, Prof. of Agricultural Devt. Overseas 1974–82, Prof. Emer. 1982–; mem. numerous professional bodies etc.; Hon. LL.D. (Ahmadu Bello Univ.) 1968. *Publications:* articles in professional journals. *Leisure interests:* music, plants. *Address:* 4 Earley Gate, University of Reading, Berks., RG6 6AR (Office); 27 The Mount, Caversham, Reading, Berks., RG4 7RU, England (Home). *Telephone:* (0118) 931 8320 (Office); (0118) 947 2487 (Home). *Fax:* (0118) 975 6467.

BURBIDGE, (Eleanor) Margaret Peachey, PH.D., F.R.S.; American astronomer; b. Davenport, England; d. of Stanley John and Marjorie (née Stott) Peachey; m. Geoffrey Burbidge (q.v.) 1948; one d.; ed. Frances Holland School, London and Univ. Coll., London; Second Asst., Asst. Dir. and acting Dir. Univ. of London Observatory 1946–51; Research Fellow, Yerkes Observatory, Harvard Coll. Observatory 1951–53, Calif. Inst. of Technology 1955–57; Research Fellow and Assoc., Prof. Univ. of Chicago 1957–62; Assoc. Research Physicist, Univ. of Calif., San Diego 1962–64, Prof. 1964–, Univ. Prof. 1984–91, Emer. 1991–, Research Prof., Dept. of Physics 1990–; Dir. Royal Greenwich Observatory 1984–90; Dir. Center for Astrophysics and Space Sciences, Univ. of Calif., San Diego 1979–88; Ed. Observatory 1948–51; mem. Editorial Bd. Astronomy and Astrophysics 1969–85; Lindsay Memorial Lecture NASA 1985; mem. Royal Astronomical Soc., American Astronomical Soc. (Pres. 1978), American Acad. of Arts and Science, N.A.S., A.A.A.S. (Fellow 1981, Pres. 1982), American Philosophical Soc., Soc. Royale des Sciences de Liège, Astronomical Soc. of the Pacific, New York Acad. of Sciences; Fellow, Univ. Coll., London, Lucy Cavendish Coll., Cambridge, Girton Coll., Cambridge; numerous prizes and awards including Helen B. Warner Prize (jointly with Geoffrey Burbidge) 1959; Bruce Gold Medal, Astronomical Soc. of the Pacific 1982, Einstein Medal 1988; Hon. D.Sc. (Smith Coll., Mass., Rensselaer Political Inst. and Univs. of Sussex, Leicester, Bristol, Chicago, Mich., Mass., City Univ., Notre Dame, London and Williams Coll.). *Publications:* Quasi-Stellar Objects (with Geoffrey Burbidge) 1967; numerous articles in scientific journals. *Address:* Center for Astrophysics and Space Sciences, University of California at San Diego, Mail Code #0424, La Jolla, CA 92093, U.S.A. *Telephone:* (619) 534-4477.

BURBIDGE, Geoffrey, PH.D., F.R.S.; British physicist; b. 24 Sept. 1925; s. of Leslie and Eveline Burbidge; m. Margaret Peachey 1948 (q.v. Eleanor Margaret Peachey Burbidge); one d.; ed. Bristol Univ. and Univ. Coll., London; Asst. Lecturer, Univ. Coll. London 1950–51; Agassiz Fellow, Harvard Univ. 1951–52; Research Fellow, Cavendish Lab., Cambridge 1953–55; Carnegie Fellow, Mount Wilson and Palomar Observatories 1955–57; Asst. Prof. Dept of Astronomy, Univ. of Chicago 1957–58; Assoc. Prof. 1958–62; Assoc. Prof. Univ. of Calif. (San Diego) 1962–63, Prof. 1963–84, Prof. Emer. 1984–88, Prof. 1988–; Dir. Kitt Peak Nat. Observatory 1978–84; Phillips Visiting Prof., Harvard Univ. 1968; Pres. Astronomical Soc. of the Pacific 1974–76; Dir. Associated Univs. for Research in Astronomy 1971–74; Fellow, Univ. Coll., London; Ed. Annual Review of Astronomy and Astrophysics 1973–, Scientific Ed. Astrophysical Journal 1996–; Trustee, Associated Univs. Inc. 1973–82. *Publication:* Quasi-Stellar Objects, (with Margaret Burbidge) 1967; astrophysics papers in scientific journals. *Address:* Department of Physics, Center for Astrophysics and Space Sciences, University of California, San Diego, La Jolla, CA 92093, U.S.A. *Telephone:* (619) 534-6626.

BURBULIS, Gennady Eduardovich; Russian politician; b. 4 Aug. 1945, Pervouralsk, Sverdlovsk (now Ekaterinburg); m. Natalia Kirsahova; one s.; ed. Ural State Univ.; lecturer Ural Polytechnic Inst. 1974–83; Head of Chair., Deputy Dir. Inst. of Non-Ferrous Metals 1983–88; U.S.S.R. People's Deputy 1989–91; formed Discussion Tribune, Sverdlovsk 1988; elected to Congress of People's Deputies 1989; mem. Inter-Regional Group; Chief of Staff to Boris Yeltsin (q.v.) 1991; State Sec. RSFSR (now Russian Fed.) State Council 1991–92; First Deputy Chair. Russian Govt. 1991–92, Sec. of State Jan.–Dec. 1992; f. and Pres. Int. Humanitarian and Political Cen. Strategy 1993–; mem. State Duma (Parl.) 1993–; mem. Cttee. for Geopolitics. *Address:* Centre Strategia, Bolshaya Sadovaya 4, Moscow; State Duma, Okhotny Ryad 1, 103009 Moscow, Russia. *Telephone:* 203-72-71 (Centre); 292-83-01 (Duma).

BURCHAM, William Ernest, C.B.E., PH.D., F.R.S., F.INST.P.; British emeritus professor of physics; b. 1 Aug. 1913, Norfolk; s. of Ernest Barnard Burcham and Edith Pitcher; m. 1st Isabella Mary Todd 1942 (died 1981); two d. (one deceased); m. 2nd Patricia Newton Marson 1985; ed. City of Norwich School, Trinity Hall and Pembroke Coll., Cambridge; Scientific Officer, Ministry of Supply 1939–44; with U.K. Atomic Energy 1944–45; Lecturer, Fellow, Selwyn Coll., Univ. of Cambridge 1945–51; Demonstrator, Lecturer, Univ. of Cambridge 1945–51; Oliver Lodge Prof. of Physics, Univ. of Birmingham 1951–80, Emer. Prof. of Physics 1981–; Hon. Life Fellow, Coventry Polytechnic 1984. *Publications:* Nuclear Physics: An Introduction 1963, Elements of Nuclear Physics 1979, Nuclear and Particle Physics (with M. Jobes) 1995. *Address:* 95 Witherford Way, Birmingham, B29 4AN, England. *Telephone:* 0121-472 1226.

BURCHFIELD, Robert William, C.B.E., M.A.; author and lecturer in English language; b. 27 Jan. 1923, Wanganui, New Zealand; s. of Frederick Burchfield and Mary Blair; m. 1st Ethel May Yates 1949 (dissolved 1976); one s. two d.; m. 2nd Elizabeth Austen Knight 1976; ed. Wanganui Tech. Coll., Victoria Univ. Coll., Wellington and Magdalen Coll., Oxford; war service with Royal N.Z. Artillery 1941–46; Jr. Lecturer in English Language, Magdalen Coll., Oxford 1952–53; Lecturer in English Language, Christ Church, Oxford 1953–57; Lecturer, St. Peter's Coll., Oxford 1955–63, Tutorial Fellow 1963–79, Sr. Research Fellow 1979–90, Emer. Fellow 1990–; Ed., Notes and Queries 1959–62, A Supplement to the Oxford English Dictionary 1957–86; Chief Ed., The Oxford English Dictionaries 1971–84; Pres. English Assen. 1978–79; Hon. Sec. Early English Text Soc. 1955–68, mem. Council 1968–80; Hon. Foreign mem. American Acad. of Arts and Sciences 1977–; Hon. D.Litt. (Liverpool) 1978, Hon. Lit.D. (Victoria Univ. of Wellington) 1983; Shakespeare Prize (FVS Foundation, Hamburg) 1994; Freedom of City of Wanganui 1986. *Publications:* The Oxford Dictionary of English Etymology (with C. T. Onions and G. W. S. Friedrichsen) 1966, A Supplement of Australian and New Zealand Words (in the Pocket Oxford Dictionary) 1969, A Supplement to the Oxford English Dictionary (Vol. I) 1972, (Vol. II) 1976, (Vol. III) 1982, (Vol IV) 1986. The Quality of Spoken English on BBC Radio (with D. Donoghue and A. Timothy) 1979, The Spoken Language as an Art Form 1981, The Spoken Word 1981, The English Language 1985, The New Zealand Pocket Oxford Dictionary 1986, Studies in Lexicography 1987, Unlocking the English Language 1989, Points of View 1992, The Cambridge History of The English Language, Vol. V: English in Britain and Overseas 1994, The New Fowler's Modern English Usage 1996. *Leisure interests:* travelling, English grammar, country life. *Address:* The Barn, 14 The Green, Sutton Courtenay, Oxon., OX14 4AE, England. *Telephone:* (01235) 848645.

BURDA, Hubert, D.PHIL.; German publisher and author; b. 9 Feb. 1940, Heidelberg; s. of Dr Franz Burda and Aenne Lemminger; ed. Univ. of Munich; Man. Bild & Funk 1966–74; partner, Burda GmbH 1974, now Chair. Burda Group; co-publ. Elle-Verlag GmbH, Munich; co-f. Europe Online S.A., Luxembourg; publr. Anna, Bunte, Burda Moden, Das Haus, Elle, Elle Bistro, Elle Deco, Elle TopModel, Focus, Focus Online, Focus TV, Freundin, Freizeit Revue, Futurekids, Glücks Revue, Haus + Garten, Lisa, Lisa Kochen & Backen, Lisa Wohnen & Dekorieren, Mein schöner Garten, Meine Familie & ich, Norddeutsche Neueste Nachrichten, Schweriner Volkszeitung, Starwatch Navigation, Super Illu, Super TV, TraXXX, Verena; mem. Bd. German School of Journalism, Munich; f. Petrarca Prize (for poetry), Bambi (Media-Prize). *Address:* Arabellastrasse 23, 81925 Munich, Germany.

BURDETT-COUTTS, William Walter, M.A.; British artistic director and film and television producer; b. 17 Feb. 1955, Harare, Zimbabwe; s. of William A. F. Burdett-Coutts and Nancy C. (née Gervers) Burdett-Coutts; ed. Radley Coll., Oxford, Rhodes Univ., South Africa, Univ. of Essex; Artistic Dir. Ass. Rooms Edin. 1981–, Festival Dir. Mayfest, Glasgow 1987–90, Head of Arts Granada TV 1990–93, Dir. Riverside Studios 1993–, Exec. Producer Ass. Film and TV 1994–; Chair. Kiss 102 1993–97, Kiss 105 1996–97. *Address:* Riverside Studios, Crisp Road, London, W6 9RL, England. *Telephone:* 0181-741 2251. *Fax:* 0181-563 0336.

BUREAU, Jérôme, D.HIST.; French journalist; b. 19 April 1956, Paris; three c.; journalist with Libération 1978–81; Sr. Reporter L'Équipe Magazine

1981–87, Ed.-in-Chief 1989–93; Ed.-in-Chief Le Sport 1987–88; Editorial Dir. L'Équipe, L'Équipe-TV, L'Équipe Magazine, Vélo, XL, Tennis de France 1993–. *Publications:* L'Amour-Foot 1986, Les Géants du football 1996. *Leisure interests:* cookery, bullfighting. *Address:* 4 rue Rouget de l'Isle, 92793 Issy-les-Moulineaux, France.

BURELLI RIVAS, Miguel Angel, LL.B., DR.POL.SC.; Venezuelan diplomatist and lawyer; b. 8 July 1922; ed. Univ. de Los Andes, Bogotá, Univ. Central de Venezuela y de Ecuador, Univ. Nacional de Bogotá, Univ. de Madrid and Univ. di Firenze; pre-seminary Prof. of Political Sociology and Chief Prof. of Mining and Agrarian Legislation, Faculty of Law, Univ. de Los Andes, Bogotá, Chief Prof. of Humanities I and II, Faculty of Civil Eng., Dir. of Univ. Culture, Founder of School of Humanities, Founder-Dir. of Univ. reviews, Bibliotheca and Universitas Emeritensis; Political Dir. Ministry of the Interior; Dir.-Gen. Ministry of Foreign Affairs (nine times Acting Minister); Interim Minister of Foreign Affairs; returned to legal profession 1961; mem. Venezuelan Supreme Electoral Council 1961; Minister of Justice 1964–65; Amb. to Colombia 1965–67, U.K. 1967–69; Presidential Candidate 1968, 1973; Amb. to U.S.A. 1974–76; Minister of Foreign Affairs 1994–; numerous decorations. *Address:* Ministry of Foreign Affairs, Casa Amarilla Biblioteca Central, esq. Principal, Caracas 1010, Venezuela.

BURENGA, Kenneth L.; American publishing executive; b. 30 May 1944, Somerville, N.J.; s. of Nicholas Burenga and Louanna Chamberlin; m. Jean Case 1964; one s. one d.; ed. Rider Coll.; budget accountant, Dow Jones & Co., S. Brunswick, N.J. 1966–67, Asst. Man. data processing control 1968–69, staff asst. for systems devt. 1970–71, Man. systems devt. and control 1972–76, circulation marketing Man. 1977–78, circulation sales Dir. 1979–80, Vice-Pres. circulation and circulation Dir. 1980–86; Chief Financial Officer and Admin. Officer, Dow Jones & Co., New York 1986–88, Exec. Vice-Pres., Gen. Man. 1989–91, Pres. C.O.O. Dow Jones & Co. Inc. 1991–; Gen. Man. Wall Street Journal 1989–; mem. Bd. of Dirs. Dow Jones Courier. *Leisure interest:* cattle farming. *Address:* Dow Jones & Co. Inc., 200 Liberty St., New York, NY 10281, U.S.A.

BURGARD, Horst; German banker and company executive; b. 28 Jan. 1929; mem. Supervisory Bd., Deutsche Bank AG, Frankfurt am Main, Allianz AG, Munich, Messer Griesheim GmbH, Frankfurt. *Address:* c/o Deutsche Bank AG, 60262 Frankfurt am Main, Germany.

BURGELIN, Jean-François, L. EN D.; French civil servant; b. 17 Dec. 1936, Metz (Moselle); s. of Pierre Burgelin and Françoise Cazamian; m. Berthe du Mesnil du Buisson 1960; three s.; Deputy Public Prosecutor Nancy 1965; Premier Judge Pontoise 1973; Sec.-Gen. First Presidency Court of Appeal, Paris 1975, Solicitor-Gen. 1994–96; Prin. Pvt. Sec. (Sec. of State responsible for immigrant workers) 1976, to Minister of Work 1976; Sec. Higher Magistrate's Council 1977; Dir. Ecole Nationale de la Magistrature 1978; Vice-Pres. Tribunal, Paris 1981; Pres. Court of Appeal, Paris 1982; Dir. Office of Minister of Justice 1986; Councillor Court of Cassation 1986–94; Chief Public Prosecutor, Court of Appeal, Paris 1994; Solicitor-Gen., Court of Cassation 1996–. *Address:* Cour de Cassation, 5 quai de l'Horloge, 75001 Paris, France. *Telephone:* (1) 44.32.64.14. *Fax:* (1) 44.32.77.10.

BURGEN, Sir Arnold (Stanley Vincent), Kt., M.D., F.R.S.; British scientist; b. 20 March 1922, London; s. of the late Peter and Elizabeth (née Wolfers) Burgen; m. 1st Judith Browne 1946 (died 1993); two s. one d.; m. 2nd Olga Kennard 1993; ed. Christ's Coll., Finchley, London, Middlesex Hospital Medical School; Demonstrator, later Asst. Lecturer, Middlesex Hospital Medical School 1945–49; Prof. of Physiology, McGill Univ., Montreal 1949–62; Deputy Dir. McGill Univ. Clinic, Montreal Gen. Hospital 1957–62; Sheild Prof. of Pharmacology, Univ. of Cambridge 1962–71; Dir. Nat. Inst. of Medical Research, London 1971–82; Master Darwin Coll., Cambridge 1982–89; Deputy Vice-Chancellor, Cambridge Univ. 1983–89; mem. Medical Research Council (MRC) 1969–71, 1973–77, Hon. Dir. MRC Molecular Pharmacology Unit 1967–72; Pres. Int. Union of Pharmacology 1972–75; Foreign Sec. Royal Soc. 1981–86; Fellow, Downing Coll., Cambridge 1962–71, Hon. Fellow 1972; mem. Deutsche Akad. der Naturforscher Leopoldina 1984; mem. Bureau, European Science and Tech. Ass. 1994–; Ed. European Review 1993–; Corresp. mem. Royal Acad. of Spain 1984; Foreign Assoc. Nat. Acad. of Sciences, U.S.A.; Pres. Acad. Europaea 1988–94; Academician of Finland; Hon. D.Sc. (McGill, Leeds, Liverpool); Hon. M.D. (Zürich) 1983, (Utrecht); Hon. D. Univ. (Surrey) 1983; Hon. F.R.C.P., Canada. *Publications:* Physiology of Salivary Glands 1961, papers in journals of pharmacology and physiology. *Leisure interests:* sculpture, music. *Address:* Keelson, 8A Hills Avenue, Cambridge, CB1 4XA, England. *Telephone:* (01223) 415381. *Fax:* (01223) 334040.

BURGER, Alewyn Petrus, F.R.S.S.A., M.SC., D.SC.(TECH); South African scientist; b. 31 Jan. 1927, Middelburg, Transvaal; s. of the late D. J. Burger and M. M. Burger; m. Erica L. van der Merwe 1952; one s. four d.; ed. Univ. of Pretoria and Tech. Univ., Delft; Research Meteorologist S.A. Weather Bureau, Pretoria 1950–57; Head Dept. of Applied Math., Nat. Physics Research Lab., Council for Scientific and Industrial Research (CSIR) 1957–61; Dir. Nat. Research Inst. for Math. Sciences, CSIR 1961–73, Vice-Pres. CSIR 1973–76; Chair. Scientific Advisory Council, Scientific Adviser and Head of Science Planning 1977–81; Consultant in Atmospheric Sciences 1982–; Man. Impetus Magazine 1985–89; Dir. Inst. of World Concerns 1990–; Chair. S.A. Math. Soc. 1961–63, 1973–75; Pres. Jt. Council of Scientific Socs. 1972–73; Pres. S.A. Soc. of Atmospheric Sciences 1989–91, 1995–97; founder mem. Acad. of Science of S.A. 1996–; mem. S.A. Council for Natural Scientists 1988–91; Fellow S.A. Acad. for Sciences and Arts 1968–; Hon. Prof. of Applied Math., Univ. of Stellenbosch 1979–80; Havenga Prize for Math. Sciences 1973. *Publications:* numerous scientific articles in int. journals. *Leisure interests:* Christian work, piano, athletics, tennis. *Address:* P.O. Box 17071, Groenkloof 0027, South Africa.

BURGESS, Ian Glencross, A.O., B.SC.; Australian business executive; b. 26 Nov. 1931, Sydney; m. Barbara J. Hastie 1957; ed. The King's School, Parramatta and Univ. of N.S.W.; Man. Dir. CSR Ltd. 1987–93, Chair. 1997–; Chair. AMP Ltd. 1994– (Dir. 1989–); Dir. Western Mining Co., Deputy Chair. 1997–. *Leisure interests:* reading, golf. *Address:* AMP Ltd., Corner Phillip and Alfred Streets, Circular Quay, N.S.W. 2000, Australia.

BURGH, Sir John Charles, K.C.M.G., C.B., B.SC.(ECON.), M.A., F.R.C.M.; British administrator; b. 9 Dec. 1925, Vienna, Austria; m. Ann Sturge 1957; two d.; ed. Friends' School, Sibford, London School of Economics; Leverhulme post-intermediate Scholarship, L.S.E., Pres. of Union 1949; mem. U.K. Del. to UN Conf. on Trade Devt. 1964; Asst. Sec., Dept. of Econ. Affairs 1964; Prin. Pvt. Sec. to successive First Secs. of State and Secs. of State for Econ. Affairs 1965–68; Under-Sec., Dept. of Employment 1968–71; Deputy Chair. Community Relations Comm. 1971–72; Deputy Sec. Cabinet Office (Cen. Policy Review Staff) 1972–74, Dept. of Prices and Consumer Protection 1974–79, Dept. of Trade 1979–80; Dir.-Gen. British Council 1980–87; Pres. Trinity Coll., Oxford 1987–96; Dir. English Shakespeare Co. 1988–94; Gov. L.S.E. 1980–, Chair. 1985–87; mem. Exec., Political and Econ. Planning 1972–78, Council, Policy Studies Inst. 1978–85, Council Voluntary Service Overseas 1980–87, Wilton Park 1984–87; Chair. Assoc. Bd. Royal Coll. of Music 1987–94, Nat. Opera Co-ordinating Cttee. 1991– (Sec. 1972–91), Oxford Educational Trust for Devt. of the Arts 1991–96; Vice-Chair. Int. Student House 1985–86, Chair. 1987–92; Vice-Chair., The Yehudi Menuhin School 1995–; Hon. Fellow L.S.E., Trinity Coll. 1997; Hon. LL.D. (Bath); Hon. mem. Royal Northern Coll. of Music. *Leisure interests:* friends, music, the arts generally. *Address:* c/o Royal Over-Seas League, Over-Seas House, Park Place, London, SW1A 1LR, England.

BURGHARDT, Walter J., M.A., PH.L., S.T.L., S.T.D.; American theologian; b. 10 July 1914, New York; s. of John A. Burghardt and Mary Krupp; ed. Woodstock Coll., The Catholic University of America; Prof. Patristic (Historical) Theology, Woodstock Coll. 1946–74; Lecturer Union Theological Seminary, New York City 1971–74; Prof. Patristic Theology, The Catholic Univ. of America 1974–78, Prof. Emer. 1978–; Visiting Lecturer in Theology, Princeton Theological Seminary 1972–73; Ed. Theological Studies 1967–90, Man. Ed. 1946–67; Co-ed. Ancient Christian Writers 1958–; mem. Bd. of Patrons, Ecumenical Inst. for Advanced Theological Studies in Jerusalem (Tantur) 1981–; Chair. Cttee. on Theology and Ethics, The Catholic Health Asscn. of the U.S. 1985–89; Dir. Preaching the Just Word 1990–; mem. Corpn. Jesuit Int. Volunteers Inc. 1986–90; mem. American Theological Soc., Asscn. Int. d'Etudes Patristiques, Catholic Comm. on Intellectual and Cultural Affairs, Catholic Theological Soc. of America, Mariological Soc. of America, North American Acad. of Ecumenists, North American Patristic Soc.; Sr. Fellow Woodstock Theological Center, Washington, D.C. 1974–; Mariological Award 1958, Cardinal Spellman Award 1962; 21 hon. degrees. *Publications include:* The Image of God in Man According to Cyril of Alexandria 1957, All Lost in Wonder: Sermons on Theology and Life 1960, Saints and Sanctity 1965, Seasons That Laugh or Weep: Musings on the Human Journey 1983, Preaching: The Art and the Craft 1987, Lovely in Eyes Not His: Homilies for an Imaging of Christ 1988, To Christ I Look: Homilies at Twilight 1989, Dare to be Christ 1990, When Christ meets Christ 1993, Speak the Word with Boldness 1994, Love is a Flame of the Lord 1995, Preaching the Just Word 1996, Let Justice Roll Down Like Waters 1998; also author and ed. of many booklets, radio and TV programmes, lectures. *Leisure interests:* reading mysteries, theatre. *Address:* 19 Eye Street, N.W., Washington, DC 20001, U.S.A. *Telephone:* (202) 336-7187 (Office); (202) 336-7185 (Home). *Fax:* (202) 336-7175.

BURGIN, Victor, A.R.C.A., M.F.A.; British artist, author and lecturer; b. 24 July 1941, Sheffield; s. of Samuel Burgin and Gwendolyne A. Crowder; m. 1st Hazel P. Rowbotham 1964 (divorced 1975); m. 2nd Francette Pacteau 1988; two s.; ed. Firth Park Grammar School, Sheffield, Sheffield Coll. of Art, Royal Coll. of Art, London, and Yale Univ, U.S.A.; Sr. Lecturer, Trent Polytechnic, Nottingham 1967–73; Prof. of History and Theory of Visual Arts, Faculty of Communication, Polytechnic of Cen. London 1973–; Prof. of Art History, Univ. of Calif., Santa Cruz 1988–95, Prof. of History of Consciousness 1995–; Deutscher Akademischer Austauschdienst Fellowship 1978–79; Picker Professorship, Colgate Univ., Hamilton, New York 1980; mem. Arts Advisory Panel, Arts Council of G.B. 1971–76, 1980–81; numerous mixed and one-man exhbns. at galleries around the world since 1965. *Publications:* Work and Commentary 1973, Thinking Photography 1982, The End of Art Theory 1986, Between 1986, Passages 1991, In/Different Spaces 1996, Some Cities 1996, Venise 1998 and exhbn. catalogues. *Address:* 1223 Diamond Street, San Francisco, CA 94131, U.S.A. *Telephone:* (415) 821-4384.

BURGON, Geoffrey, G.G.S.M.; British composer and conductor; b. 15 July 1941, Hambledon; s. of Alan and Vera (née Isom) Burgon; m. 1st Janice Garwood 1963 (divorced); one s. one d.; m. 2nd Jacqueline Krofchak 1992; one s.; ed. Pewley School, Guildford, Guildhall School of Music; freelance trumpeter/composer 1964–71; conductor 1964–; full-time composer 1971–; *compositions include (dramatic works)*: Epitaph for Sir Walter Raleigh 1968, Joan of Arc 1970, The Fall of Lucifer 1977, Orpheus 1982, Hard Times (opera) 1990 (*orchestral and solo music*): Concerto for String Orchestra 1963, Gending 1968, Alleluia Nativitas 1970, Paradise Dances (Brass Band) 1994, City Adventures 1997, Singapore Vtns. 1997, Fantasia on R.E.X. 1997 (*with voices*): Acquainted with Night 1965, Think on Dredful Domesday 1969, Canciones del Alma 1975, Requiem 1976, Magnificat and Nunc dimittis 1979, The World Again 1983, Revelations 1984, Title Divine 1986, A Vision 1990, Trumpet concerto 1992, First Was the World 1993, Music's Empire 1993, Merciless Beauty 1997 (*ballet music*): The Golden Fish 1964, The Calm 1974, Running Figures/Goldberg's Dream 1975, Songs, Lamentations and Praises 1979, Mass 1984, Prometheus 1988 (*chamber music*): Four Guitars 1977, Six Studies 1980, Waiting (for solo pianoforte) 1993, Almost Peace 1995, The Wanderer 1998, Recatativo 1998 (*with voices*): Hymn to Venus 1966, Five Sonnets of John Donne 1967, Worldës Blissë 1971, Two Love Songs, Lunar Beauty 1986, Nearing the Upper Air 1988 (*choral music*): Three Elegies 1964, Short Mass 1965, Golden Eternity 1970, The Fire of Heaven 1973, Dos Coros 1975, A God and Yet a Man 1984, Prayer to St. Richard 1989, Songs of the Creation 1989, The Song of the Creatures 1989, Five Love Songs, The First World 1991 (*music for children*): Divertimento 1964, Five Studies 1965, Now Welcome Summer 1966, Beginnings 1969 (*film music*): Life of Brian 1979, Dogs of War 1980, Turtle Diary 1985, Robin Hood 1991, When Trumpets Fade 1998 (*TV music*): Dr Who 1975, Tinker Tailor Soldier Spy 1979, Brideshead Revisited 1981, Testament of Youth 1979, How Many Miles to Babylon 1981, Bewitched 1983, The Death of the Heart 1985, Happy Valley 1987, The Old Wives Tale 1988, Sophia and Constance 1988, The Chronicles of Narnia 1988–90, Children of the North 1990, A Foreign Field 1992, Martin Chuzzlewit 1994, Silent Witness 1995, Turning World 1996, Cider with Rosie 1998; recipient of Ivor Novello Awards 1980, 1981, Gold Disc 1986. *Leisure interests:* cricket, jazz, wasting money on old Bristols. *Address:* Chester Music, 8–9 Frith Street, London W1V 5TZ, England. *Telephone:* 0171-434 0066. *Fax:* 0171-287 6329.

BURKARD, Otto Michael, DR. PHIL.; Austrian academic; b. 24 Nov. 1908, Graz; s. of Otto A. Burkard; m. Herta Waidbacher 1942; three s. one d.; ed. Univ. of Graz; Prof. of Math. and Physics, Eng. School 1938; Head, Inst. of Meteorology and Geophysics, Univ. of Graz 1949–79; now Prof. Emer.; Dir. Inst. for Space Research, Austrian Acad. of Sciences 1973–84; mem. Austrian Acad. *Publications:* approximately 90 publs. on physics of the ionosphere and space. *Leisure interest:* gardening. *Address:* Grillparzerstrasse 32, 8010 Graz, Austria. *Telephone:* 0316/33-92-92.

BURKE, Bernard Flood, PH.D.; American physicist and astrophysicist; b. 7 June 1928, Boston, Mass.; s. of Vincent Paul Burke and Clare Aloyse Brine; m. Jane Chapin Pann 1953; three s. one d.; ed. Mass. Inst. of Technology; mem. of staff, Carnegie Inst. of Washington 1953–65; Chair. Radio Astronomy Section, Carnegie Inst. of Washington, Dept. of Terrestrial Magnetism 1962–65; Prof. of Physics, M.I.T. 1965–, William Burden Prof. of Astrophysics 1981–; Visiting Prof., Leiden Univ. 1971–72, Manchester Univ. 1992–93; Pres. American Astronomical Soc. 1986–88; Ed. Comments on Astrophysics 1984–87; Trustee Associated Univ. Inc. 1972–90; Trustee and Vice-Chair. N.E. Radio Observatory Corpn. 1973–82, Chair. 1982–95; Oort lecturer Leiden Univ. 1993; mem. Nat. Science Bd. 1990–(96); mem. Nat. Science Bd. American Acad. of Arts and Sciences, N.A.S.; Fellow, A.A.A.S.; Helen B. Warner Prize, American Astron. Soc. 1963, Rumford Prize, American Acad. of Arts and Sciences 1971; Sherman Fairchild Scholar, Calif. Inst. of Tech. 1984–85; Smithsonian Regents Fellow 1985; NASA Achievement Award 1989. *Publications:* Microwave Spectroscopy 1953–54, Radio Noise from Jupiter 1955–61, Galactic Structure 1959–, Very Long Baseline Interferometry 1968–, Interstellar Masers 1968–, Gravitational Lenses 1980–, Interferometry in Space 1984–, miscellaneous publs. in radio astronomy 1955–. *Leisure interests:* skiing, sailing, hiking, chamber music. *Address:* Massachusetts Institute of Technology, Department of Physics, Cambridge, MA 02139 (Office); 10 Bloomfield Street, Lexington, MA, U.S.A. (Home). *Telephone:* (617) 253-2572 (Office); (617) 862-8939 (Home).

BURKE, Hon. Brian Thomas; Australian politician and diplomatist; b. 25 Feb. 1947, Perth; s. of late Thomas Burke and of Madeleine Burke; m. Susanne May Nevill 1965; four s. two d.; ed. Marist Brothers Coll., Univ. of W. Australia; journalist W. Australian Newspapers, 6 PM and TVW Channel 7 1965–70; mem. Legis. Ass. for Balcatta (now Balga) 1973–83; Opposition Shadow Minister 1976–83, Leader 1981–83; Premier of W. Australia, State Treasurer, Minister for Women's Interests 1983–88; Minister of Tourism and Forests 1983–85; Minister Co-ordinating Econ. and Social Devt. 1983–87; Amb. to Ireland and the Holy See 1988–91; business consultant; Labor. *Leisure interests:* stamp-collecting, swimming, fishing, reading, writing poetry. *Address:* P.O. Box 668, Scarborough, WA 6019, Australia.

BURKE, Kathy; British actress; b. London; ed. Anna Scher's Theatre School, London. *TV includes:* Harry Enfield and Chums, Absolutely Fabulous, Common as Muck, Mr Woods' Virgins (Royal TV Soc. Award), Tom Jones. *Films:* Scrubbers, Nil by Mouth (Best Actress, Cannes Film Festival 1997), Elizabeth 1998, This Year's Love 1999. *Theatre includes:* Mr Thomas, London, Boom Bang-a-Bang, London (dir.).

BURKE, Philip George, C.B.E., PH.D., F.R.S., M.R.I.A.; British professor of mathematical physics; b. 18 Oct. 1932, London; s. of Henry Burke and Frances Mary Sprague; m. Valerie Mona Martin 1959; four d.; ed. Univ. Coll. of S.W. of England, Univ. Coll., Univ. of London; Research Fellow Univ. Coll., Univ. of London 1956–57, Lecturer Computer Unit 1957–59; Research Physicist, Alvarez Bubble Chamber Group, Theory Group, Lawrence Radiation Lab., Berkeley, Calif. 1959–62; Prin. Scientific Officer, then Sr. Prin. Scientific Officer, Atomic Energy Research Establishment, Harwell 1962–67; Prof. of Math. Physics Queen's Univ., Belfast 1967–98, Head Dept. of Applied Math. and Theoretical Physics 1974–77, Dir. School of Math. and Physics 1988–90; Chair. Inter-Council High Performance Computing Man. Cttee. 1996–98; Head Div. Theory and Computational Science, Science and Eng. Research Council, Daresbury Lab., Cheshire 1977–82 (jt. appointment with Queen's Univ.); mem. U.K. Science and Eng. Research Council 1989–94, Chair. Supercomputing Man. Cttee. 1991–94; mem. Council Royal Soc. 1990–92; Fellow Univ. Coll., London 1986; Hon. D.Sc. (Exeter) 1981; Inst. of Physics' Guthrie Medal and Prize 1994. *Publications:* over 300 articles in many specialist journals, author or co-author of seven books. *Leisure interests:* reading, walking, swimming, music. *Address:* Department of Applied Mathematics and Theoretical Physics, Queen's University, Belfast, Northern Ireland (Office); Brook House, Norley Lane, Crowton, Northwich, Cheshire, CW8 2RR, England (Home). *Telephone:* (01232) 335047 (Office); (01928) 788301 (Home). *Fax:* (01232) 239182 (Office).

BURKE, Ray; Irish politician; b. 30 Sept. 1943, Dublin; m. Anne Fassbender; two d.; ed. O'Connell's Co. Boys' School, Dublin; mem. Dublin County Council 1967–78, Chair. 1985–87; mem. Dail 1973–; Minister of State, Dept. of Industry and Commerce and Energy 1978–80, Minister for Environment 1980–81, 1982, for Energy and Communications 1987–88, for Industry, Commerce and Communications 1988–89, for Justice and for Communications 1989–92, for Foreign Affairs July–Oct. 1997; Fianna Fail. *Address:* Dáil Éireann, Dublin 2; Briargate, Malahide Road, Swords, Co. Dublin, Ireland (Home).

BURKE, Richard, M.A.; Irish politician and administrator; b. 29 March 1932, New York, N.Y., U.S.A.; s. of David Burke and Elisabeth Burke; m. Mary Freeley 1961; two s. three d.; ed. Christian Brothers, Thurles, Univ. College and Kings Inns, Dublin; teacher in Blackrock until 1969; mem. of the Dail for Dublin South Co. 1969–77, for West Dublin 1981–82; fmr. Chief Whip of Fine Gael; Shadow Minister for Posts and Telegraphs 1969–73; Minister for Educ. 1973–76; mem. Comm. European Communities 1977–84, Vice-Pres. 1984; Assoc. Fellow, Center for Int. Affairs, Harvard Univ. 1980–81; mem. Conseil d'Admin., FIDEPS, UNESCO, Paris, Devt. Council, HEC, Paris; Pres., C.E.O. Canon Foundation in Europe 1988–; mem. Academia Scientiarum et Artium, Salzburg 1996; Chief Burke Clan 1990–92, Hon. Life Pres. 1992–; Pro Merito Europa of European Parl. 1980; Grand Croix of Leopold II 1981, Grand Croix of Phoenix 1983. *Leisure interests:* music, golf. *Address:* 67 Ailesbury Road, Dublin 4, Ireland.

BURKE, Sir Thomas Kerry, Kt., B.A., M.P.; New Zealand politician; b. 24 March 1942, Christchurch; m. 2nd Helen Paske 1984 (died 1989); one s. (two s. from 1st m.); ed. Univ. of Canterbury, Christchurch Teachers' Coll.; general labourer in Auckland 1965–66, Factory del., Auckland Labourers' Union; teacher, Rangiora High School 1967, Chair. Rangiora Post-Primary Teachers' Asscn. 1969–71; M.P. for Rangiora 1972–75, for West Coast 1978–; teacher Greymouth High School 1975–78; Minister of Regional Devt., and of Employment and Immigration 1984–87; Speaker, New Zealand Parl. 1987–91; Labour. *Leisure interests:* skiing, swimming.

BURKE, Tom, C.B.E., B.A., F.R.S.A.; British environmental organisation administrator; b. 5 Jan. 1947, Cork, Ireland; s. of J. V. Burke and Mary Bradley; ed. St. Boniface's, Plymouth, Liverpool Univ.; Great George's Community Arts Project 1969–70; lecturer, W. Cheshire Coll. 1970–71, Old Swan Tech. Coll. 1971–73; Local Groups Co-ordinator, Friends of the Earth 1973–75, Exec. Dir. 1975–79, Dir. of Special Projects 1979–80, Vice-Chair. 1980–81; Press Officer European Environment Bureau 1979–87, mem. Exec. Cttee. 1987–91; Dir. The Green Alliance 1982–92; Sec. Ecological Studies Inst. 1987–92; Special Adviser to Sec. of State for Environment 1991–97; Adviser to Rio Tinto PLC 1996–, to BP PLC 1997–; mem. Bd. of Dirs. Earth Resources Research 1975–87, Waste Man. Advisory Council 1976–81, Packaging Council 1978–82, Exec. Cttee. Nat. Council for Voluntary Orgs. 1984–89, U.K. Nat. Cttee. European Year of the Environment 1986–88, Council, Royal Soc. for Nature Conservation 1993–, mem. Council Royal Soc. of Arts 1990–92, Overseas Cttee., Save the Children Fund 1992–; mem. High Level Advisory Group on the Environment, OECD 1996–97; stood as Social Democrat Party cand. Gen. Elections 1983, 1987; Visiting Prof. Imperial Coll. London Univ. 1997–; Visiting Fellow, Cranfield 1991–; Hon. Visiting Fellow Manchester Business School 1984; Royal Humane Soc. Testimonials on Vellum 1966, on Parchment 1968; UNEP Global 500 Laureate 1993. *Publications:* Europe: environment 1981, Pressure Groups in the Global System (jtly.) 1982, Ecology 2000 (jtly.) 1984, The Green Capitalists (jtly.) 1987, Green Pages (jtly.) 1988. *Leisure interests:* photography, birdwatching. *Address:* Studio 2, Clink Wharf, Clink Street, London, SE1 9DG, England. *Telephone:* 0171-357 9146.

BURKE, Ulick Peter, M.A., F.R.HIST.S., F.B.A.; British historian; b. 16 Aug. 1937, Stanmore; s. of John Burke and Jenny Colin; m. 1st Susan Patricia Dell 1972 (divorced 1983); m. 2nd Maria Lúcia García Pallares 1988; ed. St. Ignatius' Coll., Stamford Hill, St. John's Coll., Oxford, St. Antony's Coll., Oxford; Asst. Lecturer, then lecturer, then Reader in History (later Intellectual History) School of European Studies, Univ. of Sussex 1962–78; lecturer in History Univ. of Cambridge 1979–88, Reader in Cultural History 1988–96, Prof. of Cultural History 1996–; Fellow Emmanuel Coll. Cambridge 1979–; Visiting Prof. Univ. of São Paulo, Brazil 1986, 1987, Nijmegen Univ. 1992–93; Fellow Wissenschaftskollege, Berlin 1989–90. *Publications:* Culture and Society in Renaissance Italy 1972, Venice and Amsterdam 1974, Popular Culture in Early Modern Europe 1978, Historical Anthropology of Early Modern Italy 1987, The Fabrication of Louis XIV 1992, The Fortunes of the Courtier 1995, The European Renaissance 1998. *Leisure interests:* travel. *Address:* Emmanuel College, Cambridge, CB2 3AP (Office); 14 Warkworth Street, Cambridge, CB1 1EG, England (Home). *Telephone:* (01223) 334272.

BURKHARDT, François; Swiss architect; b. 16 April 1936, Ruschein; m. Linde Honold; ed. Haute Ecole Tech. Fed., Lausanne, Ecole Fed. d'architecture, Berne and Ecole des Beaux-Arts, Hamburg; Dir. Musée des Beaux-Arts, Hamburg 1969–71, Int. Design Centre, Berlin 1971–84; Prof. Ecole Supérieure de Design, Kiel 1970–71, Ecole des Beaux-Arts, Berlin 1980–83, Domus Acad. 1983, Ecole Polytechnique Univ. de Milan 1987, Ecole des Arts Appliqués, Vienna 1987; Dir. Nat. Council of Design, Darmstadt 1974–80, Exhbn. Council, Inst. of External Relations, Stuttgart 1977–84; mem. Deutsches Werkbund, Berlin 1972–84, Bauhaus-Archive Cttee., Berlin 1977–84. *Publications:* Produkt-Form-Geschichte 150 Jahre deutsches Design (with Ernest Fuchs) 1985, Wie ein Stil ensteht- am Beispiel von Ettore Sottsass 1986, Mésurer, adapter, mettre en forme: un processus culturel? 1986, numerous articles.

BURLATSKY, Fedor Mikhailovich, DR.PHIL.; Russian journalist, writer and politician; b. 4 Jan. 1927, Kiev; s. of Mikhail Burlatsky and Sofia Burlatsky; m. 1st Seraphyma Burlatsky 1952 (divorced 1974); two s.; m. 2nd Kyra Burlatsky 1974; one d.; ed. Tashkent Law Inst.; journalist Tashkent 1948–50; post-grad. at Inst. of State Law, U.S.S.R. Acad. of Sciences 1950–53; journalist with Kommunist 1953–59; head of section in Cen. Cttee. Dept. for Liaison with Communist and Workers' Parties of Socialist Countries 1959–65; political observer with Pravda 1965–67; Deputy Dir. of U.S.S.R. Inst. of Sociological studies 1968–72; head of section, U.S.S.R. Inst. of State and Law and head of Philosophy Dept., Inst. of Social Science, Cen. Cttee. of CPSU 1975–88; Vice-Pres. Soviet Assoc. of Political Science 1976; U.S.S.R. People's Deputy 1989–91; Chair. Subcttee. on Humanitarian, Scientific and Cultural Co-operation, Cttee. on Foreign Affairs 1989–91; political observer Literaturnaya gazeta 1983–90, Ed.-in-Chief 1990–91; Chair. of Public Comm. for Int. Co-operation on Humanitarian Problems and Human Rights 1987–90; Dir. Public Consultative Council to Chair. of State Duma 1993–96; Chief Scientific Researcher Inst. of State and Law 1992–; Visiting Prof. Heidelberg Univ. 1988, Harvard Univ. 1992, Oxford Univ. 1993; Pres. Euro-Asian Fund for Humanitarian Co-operation 1996–, Int. League for Defence of Culture; Chair., Scientific Council on Politology, Pres. Russian Acad. of Sciences 1995–; mem. Acad. of National Sciences 1993, Acad. of Socio-Political Sciences 1996; Italian Senate Prize 1988. *Publications include:* Mao Zedong (biography) 1976, The Modern State and Politics 1978, The Legend of Machiavelli 1987, New Thinking 1988, Leaders and Advisers 1990, Khrushchev and the First Russian Spring 1992, The End of the Red Empire 1993, Russian Sovereigns—Age of the Reformation 1996. *Leisure interest:* tennis. *Address:* Novovagankovsky per. 22, Apt. 90, 123022 Moscow, Russia. *Telephone:* 292-84-28 (Office); 205-28-41 (Home).

BURNET, Alastair (see Burnet, Sir J. W. A.).

BURNET, Sir James William Alexander (Alastair), Kt.; British journalist; b. 12 July 1928, Sheffield, Yorks.; s. of late Alexander and Schonaid Burnet; m. Maureen Sinclair 1958; ed. The Leys School, Cambridge, and Worcester Coll., Oxford; Sub-Ed. and Leader Writer, Glasgow Herald 1951–58, Leader Writer The Economist 1958–62; Political Ed., Independent Television News 1963–64, with ITN 1976–91, Dir. 1981–90, Assoc. Ed. ITN 1981–91; Ed. The Economist 1965–74; Ed. Daily Express 1974–76; Contributor to TV current affairs programmes, This Week, Panorama, News at Ten, etc.; Ind. Dir. Times Newspapers Holdings Ltd 1982–; mem. Council of the Banking Ombudsman 1985–96; Dir. United Racecourses Ltd. 1985–94; Hon. Vice-Pres. Inst. of Journalists 1990. *Publication:* The Time of Our Lives (with Willie Landels) 1981. *Address:* 43 Hornton Court, Campden Hill Road, London, W8 7NT, England; 33 Westbourne Gardens, Glasgow, G12 9PF, Scotland. *Telephone:* 0171-937 7563 (London); 0141-339 8073 (Glasgow).

BURNEY, Sayed Muzaffir Hussain, M.A.; Indian politician; b. 14 August 1923, Bulandshahr, Uttar Pradesh; entered Indian Admin. Service; various posts, including Jt. Sec., Ministry of Agric. 1965–72, Additional Sec. in Ministry of Petroleum and Chemicals 1973–75, Sec., Ministry of Information and Broadcasting 1975–77, Sec., Ministry of Home Affairs 1980–81; served Orissa Govt. as Divisional Commr. and Chief Sec. 1979–80; Gov. of Nagaland, Manipur and Tripura, then Haryana 1984–88. *Publications:* many articles in English and Urdu on literary subjects and public admin. *Address:* F-3/17, Vasant Vihar, New Delhi 110057, India.

BURNHAM, James B., PH.D.; American banker; b. 22 Oct 1939, New York; s. of James Burnham and Marcia Lightner; m. Anne Mullin 1964; two s. two d.; ed. Milton Acad., Princeton Univ., Washington Univ., St. Louis; Economist and special asst., Federal Reserve Bd., Washington, D.C. 1969–71; Sr. Economist, Mellon Bank, Pittsburgh, Pa. 1971–74, Vice-Pres. 1974–81, Sr. Vice-Pres. 1985–, Office of Govt. Affairs 1979–81, Chair. Country Review Cttee. 1977–81; Staff Dir. and Special Asst. to Chair., Pres.'s Council of Economic Advisers, Washington, D.C. 1981–82; U.S. Exec. Dir. IBRD, Washington, D.C. 1982–85; Fulbright Scholar, Univ. of São Paulo, Brazil 1962. *Publications:* articles on contemporary economic subjects. *Leisure interests:* canoeing, bridge. *Address:* Mellon Bank, 1 Mellon Bank Centre, Suite 0400, Pittsburgh, PA 15258, U.S.A.

BURNS, Baron (Life Peer) cr. 1998, of Pitshanger in the London Borough of Ealing, **Terence Burns,** G.C.B., B.A.ECON.; British economist; b. 13 March 1944, Durham; s. of the late Patrick O. Burns and of Doris Burns; m. Anne Elizabeth Powell 1969; one s. two d.; ed. Houghton-le-Spring Grammar School and Victoria Univ. of Manchester; held various research positions at the London Business School 1965–70, Lecturer in Econs. 1970–74, Sr. Lecturer in Econs. 1974–79, Dir. Centre for Econ. Forecasting 1976–79, Prof. of Econs. 1979; Chief Econ. Adviser to the Treasury and Head Govt. Econ. Service 1980–91; Perm. Sec. to Treasury 1991–98; Vice-Pres. Soc. of Business Economists 1985–; Fellow, London Business School 1989–; mem. Council Royal Econ. Soc. 1986–91, Vice-Pres. 1992–; Visiting Prof. Durham Univ. 1995–; Hon. D.Soc.Sc. (Manchester) 1992. *Publications:* various articles on economic matters. *Leisure interests:* Dir. Queens Park Rangers Football team, music and golf. *Address:* House of Lords, London, SW1A 0PW, England.

BURNS, Benedict DeLisle, M.R.C.S., L.R.C.P., F.R.S.; British neurophysiologist; b. 22 Feb. 1915, London; s. of C. DeLisle Burns and Margaret Hannay; m. 1st Angela Ricardo 1938; m. 2nd Monika Kasputis 1954; four s. one d.; ed. Univ. Coll. School, London, Tübingen and Cambridge Univs. and Univ. Coll. Hospital, London; operational research for Prof. S. Zuckerman 1939–45; research staff, MRC Nat. Inst of Medical Research 1945–50; Assoc. Prof. of Physiology, McGill Univ., Canada 1950–58, Prof. 1958–66, Chair. Dept. of Physiology 1965–66; Head, Div. of Physiology and Pharmacology, MRC Nat. Inst. of Medical Research 1966–76; External staff of MRC, Dept. of Anatomy, Univ. of Bristol 1976–80, Hon. Prof. of Neurobiology 1976–80; now Visitor, Div. of Neurobiology, Univ. of Newcastle upon Tyne. *Publications:* The Mammalian Cerebral Cortex 1958, The Uncertain Nervous System 1968. *Leisure interests:* painting, reading. *Address:* Division of Neurobiology, Medical School, University of Newcastle upon Tyne, NE2 4HH, England. *Telephone:* 0191-222 6948.

BURNS, Duncan Thorburn, M.R.I.A., F.R.S.EDIN.; British professor of analytical chemistry; b. 30 May 1934, Wolverhampton; s. of James Thorburn Burns and Olive Mary Constance (née Waugh) Burns; m. 1st Valerie Mary Vinton 1961 (divorced 1994); one s. two d.; m. 2nd Celia Mary Thorburn-Burns 1994; ed. Whitcliffe Mount School and Leeds Univ.; Asst. lecturer in Physical Chem., Medway Coll. of Tech. 1958–59, 1959–63; Sr. Lecturer in Analytical Chem., Woolwich Polytechnic 1963–66, Loughborough Univ. 1966–71, Reader 1971–75; Prof. of Analytical Chem., Queen's Univ., Belfast 1975–; Redwood Lecturer, Royal Soc. of Chem. 1982, Pres. Analytical Div. 1988–90; Reagents and Reactions Royal Soc. of Chemistry Medal and Award 1982, Boyle/Higgens Gold Medal, Inst. of Chem. of Ireland 1990, Ehren Nadel in Gold, Analytical Inst. Technische Univ. Wien 1990, AnalaR Gold Medal, Royal Soc. of Chem. 1990, SAC Gold Medal, Royal Soc. of Chem. 1993, Fritz Pregl Medal, Austrian Chemical Soc. 1993, Tertiary Chemical Educ. Medal and Award, Royal Soc. of Chem. 1995, Sigillum Magnum, Univ. of Bologna 1996. *Publications:* seven books and over 300 papers. *Leisure interest:* history of chemistry. *Address:* Department of Chemistry, Queen's University of Belfast, Belfast, BT9 5AG (Office); 318 Stranmillis Road, Belfast, BT9 5EB, Northern Ireland (Home). *Telephone:* (01232) 335422. *Fax:* (01232) 382117.

BURNS, John, PH.D.; American pharmacologist; b. 8 Oct. 1920, Flushing, N.Y.; ed. Queens Coll. and Columbia Univ.; Deputy Chief, Lab. of Chemical Pharmacology, Nat. Heart Inst. 1958–60; Dir. of Research, Pharmacodynamics Div. The Wellcome Research Labs. 1960–66; Vice-Pres. for Research and Devt. Hoffman-La Roche 1966–84; Adjunct Prof. Rockefeller Univ. 1984–94; Adjunct mem. Roche Inst. of Molecular Biology 1984–96; Visiting Prof. of Pharmacology, Cornell Univ. Medical Coll. 1996–; mem. N.A.S.; mem. N.A.S. Inst. of Medicine; Fellow American Inst. Chemists. *Leisure interests:* equestrian sports. *Address:* 331 Lansdowne, Westport, CT 06880, U.S.A. *Telephone:* (203) 255-6374. *Fax:* (203) 255-5508.

BURNS, John Fisher; journalist; b. 4 Oct. 1944, Nottingham, England; s. of Air Cdre. R. J. B. Burns and Dorothy Burns (née Fisher); m. 1st Jane Pequegnap 1972 (divorced); two s. one d.; m. 2nd Jane Scott-Long 1991; ed. Stowe School, McGill Univ., Canada, and Harvard Univ., U.S.A.; Foreign Corresp. New York Times 1975–; Pulitzer Prize for Int. Reporting 1993 (co-winner for reporting from Bosnia), 1997 (for coverage of the Taleban regime in Afghanistan); George Polk Prize for Foreign Correspondence 1978, 1997. *Leisure interests:* golf, music, motor racing. *Address:* New York Times, 229 W. 43rd Street, New York, NY 10036, U.S.A.

BURNS, Sir Robert Andrew, K.C.M.G., M.A.; British diplomatist; b. 21 July 1943, London; s. of Robert Burns, C.B., C.M.G. and Mary Burns (née Goodland); m. Sarah Cadogan 1973; two s. one d.; ed. Highgate School, Trinity Coll. Cambridge, School of Oriental and African Studies, London Univ.; joined Diplomatic Service 1964, served in New Delhi 1967–71, FCO, London and U.K. Del. to CSCE 1971–75, First Sec. and Head of Chancery, Bucharest 1976–78, Pvt. Sec. to Perm. Under-Sec. and Head of Diplomatic Service, FCO 1979–82, Fellow, Center for Int. Affairs, Harvard Univ., U.S.A. 1982–83,

Counsellor (Information) and Head of British Information Services, Washington, D.C. and New York 1983–86, Head S. Asian Dept., FCO 1986–88, Head News Dept. 1988–90, Asst. Under-Sec. of State (Asia), FCO 1990–92; Amb. to Israel 1992–95; Deputy Under-Sec. of State (non-Europe, Trade and Investment Promotion) 1995–97; British Consul-Gen., Hong Kong Special Admin. Region 1997–. *Publication:* Diplomacy, War and Parliamentary Democracy 1989. *Leisure interests:* music, theatre, country pursuits. *Address:* British Consulate-General, 1 Supreme Court Road, Central, Hong Kong Special Administrative Region, People's Republic of China. *Telephone:* (852) 2901-3000 (Hong Kong). *Fax:* (852) 2901-3066 (Hong Kong).

BURNS, Tom, B.A., F.B.A.; British professor of sociology; b. 16 Jan. 1913; s. of John Burns and Hannah Burns; m. Mary Elizabeth Nora Clark 1944; one s. four d.; ed. Parmiters Foundation School, and Univ. of Bristol; teacher, pvt. schools in Tunbridge Wells and Norwich 1935–39; Friends Ambulance Unit 1939–45; P.O.W., Germany 1941–43; Research Asst., W. Midland Group on Post-war Reconstruction and Planning 1945–49; lecturer, Sr. lecturer and reader, Univ. of Edin. 1949–65, Prof. of Sociology 1965–81, Visiting Prof., Harvard Univ. 1973–74; mem. Social Science Research Council 1969–70; *Publications:* Local Government and Cen. Control 1954, The Management of Innovation (with G.M. Stalker) 1961, (ed.) Industrial Man 1969, (ed. with E. Burns) Sociology of Literature and Drama 1973, The BBC: Public Institution and Private World 1977, Erving Goffman 1991, Description, Explanation and Understanding 1994, articles in a number of journals in Britain, U.S.A., France etc. *Leisure interests:* music, walking. *Address:* Inchgarvie Lodge, South Queensferry, West Lothian, EH30 9JS, Scotland.

BURNSTOCK, Geoffrey, PH.D., D.SC., F.A.A., F.R.S.; Australian university professor; b. 10 May 1929, London, England; s. of James Burnstock and Nancy Green; m. Nomi Hirschfeld 1957; three d.; ed. London and Melbourne Univs.; Nat. Inst. for Medical Research, London 1956–57; Dept. of Pharmacology, Oxford Univ. 1957–59; Dept. of Physiology, Illinois Univ. 1959; Sr. Lecturer, Dept. of Zoology, Melbourne Univ. 1959–62, Reader 1962–64, Prof. and Chair. 1964–75, Assoc. Dean (Biological Sciences) 1969–72, Prof. Emer. 1993–; Visiting Prof., Dept. of Pharmacology, Univ. of Calif. 1970; Vice-Dean, Faculty of Medical Sciences, Univ. Coll., London 1980–83, Prof. of Anatomy and Head of Dept. of Anatomy and Developmental Biology 1975–, Convenor, Centre for Neuroscience 1979–, Fellow 1996; Contract Prof., Univ. of Milan 1993–96; Visiting Prof., Royal Soc. of Medicine Foundation, New York 1988; Chair. Scientific Advisory Bd., Eisai London Ltd. 1990–; Pres., Int. Soc. for Autonomic Neuroscience 1995–; Pres. Int. Neurovegetative Soc. 1995–; Royal Soc. of Vic. Silver Medal 1970; Special Award, NIH Conf., Bethesda 1989; Hon. M.R.C.P. 1987; mem. Academia Europaea 1992; mem. Russian Soc. of Neuropathology 1993. *Publications:* Adrenergic Neurons: Their Organisation, Function and Development in the Peripheral Nervous System 1975, An Atlas of the Fine Structure of Muscle and its Innervation 1976; Ed. Purinergic Receptors 1981, Somatic and Autonomic Nerve-Muscle Interactions 1983, Nonadrenergic Innervation of Blood Vessels 1988, Peptides: A Target for New Drug Development 1990, series ed. The Autonomic Nervous System (Vols. 1–14) 1992–97; also author of over 800 publs. in scientific and medical journals and books; Ed.-in-Chief, Journal of the Autonomic Nervous System 1992–; mem. ed. bd. of over 30 journals. *Leisure interests:* wood sculpture, tennis. *Address:* Department of Anatomy and Developmental Biology, University College London, Gower Street, London, WC1E 6BT, England. *Telephone:* 0171-387 7050.

BURNYEAT, Myles Fredric, F.B.A.; British professor of philosophy; b. 1 Jan. 1939; s. of Peter James Anthony Burnyeat and Cynthia Cherry Warburg; m. 1st Jane Elizabeth Buckley 1971 (divorced 1982); one s. one d.; m. 2nd Ruth Sophia Padel 1984; one d.; ed. Bryanston School and King's Coll., Cambridge; Asst. Lecturer in Philosophy, Univ. Coll., London 1964, Lecturer 1965; Lecturer in Classics, Cambridge Univ. 1978, Lecturer in Philosophy, Robinson Coll. 1978, Fellow 1978–96; Laurence Prof. of Ancient Philosophy, Cambridge 1984–96, Sr. Research Fellow in Philosophy, All Souls Coll., Oxford 1996–; Foreign Hon. mem. American Acad. of Arts and Sciences 1992–. *Publications:* Co-Ed. Philosophy As It Is 1979, Doubt and Dogmatism 1980, Science and Speculation 1982; Ed. The Skeptical Tradition 1983, The Theaetetus of Plato 1990, Co-Ed. The Original Sceptics 1997. *Leisure interest:* travel. *Address:* All Souls College, Oxford, OX1 4AL, England.

BUROKYAVICHUS, Mikolas, DR.HIST.SC.; Lithuanian politician; b. 1927, Alitus, Lithuania; ed. Vilnius Pedagogical Inst. and CPSU Cen. Cttee. Higher Party School; mem. CPSU 1946–91; worker in plant, Udmurt A.S.S.R. 1942–44; Komsomol and party work 1944–91; sr. researcher of Cen. Cttee. of Lithuanian CP Inst. of History of the Party; Prof. of English, English Pedagogical Inst.; Sec. of Provisional Cen. Cttee. of (CPSU-based) Lithuanian CP 1989–90, First Sec. 1990–91; mem. Cen. Cttee. CPSU –1991; mem. of CPSU Politburo July 1990–91; in hiding since Aug. 1991; in exile in Moscow; arrested Jan. 1994.

BURRELL, Leroy; American athlete; b. 21 Feb. 1967, Lansdowne, Philadelphia; studying Univ. of Houston; established 'clean' world record, running 100m in 9.9 sec at U.S. Championships, New York June 1991; est. world record 100m. July 1994. *Address:* c/o U.S.A. Track and Field Press Information Department, 1 RCA Dome, Suite 140, Indianapolis, IN 46225, U.S.A.

BURRENCHOBAY, Sir Dayendranath, K.B.E., C.M.G., C.V.O., B.SC.; Mauritian administrator; b. 24 March 1919, Plaine Magnien; s. of Mohabeer Burrenchobay and Anant Coomaree Ramnath; m. Oomawati Ramphul 1957; one s. two d.; ed. Royal Coll., Curepipe, and Imperial Coll., London Univ.; grad. apprentice with British Electricity Authority 1949–50; Educ. Officer, Mauritius 1951; successively Sr. Educ. Officer, Chief Educ. Officer 1951–64; Perm. Sec. Ministry of Educ. and Cultural Affairs 1964–67; Perm. Sec. Ministry of External Affairs, Tourism and Emigration, and Prime Minister's Office 1968–76; Sec. to the Cabinet and Head of the Civil Service 1976–78; Gov.-Gen. 1978–83; Chair. Burrenchobay Ltd. 1985–; Chair. Cen. Electricity Bd. 1968–78; Chevalier, Légion d'honneur. *Leisure interests:* horticulture, history, history of science and tech., philosophy of science. *Address:* S. Ramphul Street, Eau Coulée, Mauritius. *Telephone:* 67-55-750.

BURRINGTON, Ernest; British newspaper executive; b. 13 Dec. 1926; s. of late Harold Burrington and of Laura Burrington; m. Nancy Crossley 1950; one s. one d.; reporter, Oldham Chronicle 1941–43, reporter and sub-ed. 1947–49; mil. service 1944–47; sub-ed. Bristol Evening World 1950; sub-ed. Daily Herald, Manchester 1950, night ed. 1955, London night ed. 1957; night ed. IPC Sun 1964, asst. ed. 1965; asst. ed. and night ed. News Int. Sun 1969; deputy night ed. Daily Mirror 1970; Deputy Ed. Sunday People 1971, Assoc. Ed. 1972; Ed. The People 1985–88, 1989–90; Dir. Mirror Group Newspapers 1986–92, Deputy Chair. and Asst. Publr. 1988–91, Man. Dir. 1990–91, Chair. 1991–92; Deputy Publr. Globe Communications, Montreal, Canada 1993–95, Exec. Vice-Pres. and Assoc. Publr. 1995–96; Pres. Atlantic Media 1996–98; Consultant Head of Marketing Harveys PLC, U.K. 1998–. *Leisure interests:* travel, bridge. *Address:* 17499 Tiffany Trace Drive, Boca Raton, FL 33487, U.S.A.; South Hall, Dene Park, Shipbourne Road, Tonbridge, TN11 9NS, England. *Telephone:* (561) 995-9897 (U.S.A.); (01732) 368517 (U.K.). *Fax:* (561) 995-9897 (U.S.A.); (01732) 368517 (U.K.).

BURRIS, Robert Harza, PH.D., D.SC.; American professor of biochemistry; b. 13 April 1914, Brookings, S. Dak.; s. of Edward Thomas Burris and Mable Harza Burris; m. Katherine Irene Brusse 1945; one s. two d.; ed. S. Dakota State Coll. and Univ. of Wisconsin; Research Asst., Univ. of Wis. 1936–40; Nat. Research Council Postdoctoral Fellow, Columbia Univ. 1940–41; Instructor in Bacteriology, Univ. of Wis. 1941–44, Asst. Prof. of Biochemistry 1944–46, Assoc. Prof. 1946–51, Prof. 1951–, Chair. Dept. of Biochemistry 1958–70; mem. N.A.S., American Acad. of Arts and Sciences, American Philosophical Soc., Foreign Fellow of the Indian Nat. Science Acad. 1985; Guggenheim Fellow 1954; Pres. American Soc. of Plant Physiologists 1960; Hon. D.Sc. (S. Dakota State Univ.) 1966; Merit Award of Botanical Soc. of America 1966; American Soc. of Plant Physiologists Stephen Hales Award 1968, Charles Reid Barnes Award 1977, Soc. for Industrial Microbiology Charles Thom Award 1977, American Soc. of Agronomy Edward W. Browning Award 1978, Nat. Medal of Science 1980, N.A.S. Carty Award 1984, Wolf Award 1985, American Chemical Soc. Spencer Award 1990. *Publications:* Manometric Techniques 1945, Biological Nitrogen Fixation 1992; 325 scientific papers 1936–92. *Leisure interests:* photography, lapidary, vitreous enameling. *Address:* Department of Biochemistry, University of Wisconsin, 433 Babcock Drive, Madison, WI 53706, U.S.A. *Telephone:* (608) 262-3042. *Fax:* (608) 262-3453.

BURROW, John Wyon, M.A., PH.D., F.B.A.; British professor of history; b. 4 June 1935, Southsea; s. of Charles Burrow and Alice (Vosper) Burrow; m. Diane Dunnington 1958; one s. one d.; ed. Exeter School and Christ's Coll. Cambridge; Research Fellow, Christ's Coll. Cambridge 1959–62; Fellow and Dir. of Studies in History, Downing Coll. Cambridge 1962–65; Reader, School of European Studies, Univ. of E. Anglia 1965–69; Reader in History, Univ. of Sussex 1969–82, Prof. of Intellectual History 1982–95; Visiting Fellow All Souls Coll. Oxford Univ. 1994–95, Flick Prof. of European Thought and Fellow of Balliol Coll. 1995–; Visiting Prof. Univ. of Calif. Berkeley 1981; Visiting Fellow, History of Ideas Unit, Australian Nat. Univ. 1983; Carlyle Lecturer, Oxford Univ. 1985; delivered Gauss Seminars, Princeton Univ. 1988; Hon. Dr. Sci. Pol. (Bologna) 1988; Wolfson Prize for History 1981. *Publications:* Evolution and Society 1966, A Liberal Descent 1981, That Noble Science of Politics 1983, Gibbon 1985, Whigs and Liberals 1988. *Leisure interest:* cooking. *Address:* Balliol College, Oxford, OX1 3BJ; 22 Bridge Street, Witney, Oxon. OX8 6HY, England (Home). *Telephone:* (01993) 700306.

BURROWES, Norma Elizabeth, B.A., F.R.A.M.; British opera and concert singer; b. Bangor, Co. Down; d. of Henry and Caroline Burrowes; m. 1st Steuart Bedford (q.v.) 1969 (divorced 1980); m. 2nd Emile Belcourt 1987; one s. one d.; ed. Queen's Univ., Belfast, Royal Acad. of Music; début with Glyndebourne Touring Opera singing Zerlina in Don Giovanni 1969, début with Royal Opera House, Fiakermili in Arabella 1976; roles include Blöndchen in The Abduction from the Seraglio, Oscar (Ballo in Maschera), Despina (Cosi Fan Tutte), Woodbird (Siegfried), Sophie (Der Rosenkavalier), Cunning Little Vixen, Manon (Massenet), Titania (Midsummer Night's Dream), Nanetta (Falstaff), Gilda (Rigoletto), Marie (Daughter of the Regiment), Juliet (Romeo and Juliet), Adina (Elisir d'Amore), Susanna (Nozze di Figaro), Lauretta (Gianni Schicchi); sings regularly with Glyndebourne Opera, Scottish Opera, Aldeburgh Festival, English Nat. Opera, Welsh Nat. Opera and others; abroad: Salzburg, Paris, Munich, Aix-en-Provence, Avignon, Ottawa, Montreal, New York, Vienna, Chicago, Buenos Aires; has sung with all the prin. London orchestras and on BBC radio and television; numerous recordings; Hon. D.Mus. (Queen's Univ., Belfast) 1979; Order of Worshipful Co. of Musicians. *Leisure interests:* gardening, embroidery. *Address:* c/o 56 Rochester Road, London, NW1 9JG, England.

BURROWS, Eva, A.C., B.A., M.ED.; Australian retd. Salvation Army leader; b. 15 Sept. 1929, Newcastle, Australia; d. of Robert J. Burrows and Ella M. Watson; ed. Brisbane State High School and Queensland, London and Sydney Univs.; Missionary educator, Howard Inst., Zimbabwe 1952–67; Prin. Usher Inst., Zimbabwe 1967–69; Vice-Prin. Int. Coll. for Officers, London 1970–73, Prin. 1974–75; Leader, Women's Social Services in G.B. and Ireland 1975–77; Territorial Commdr. Sri Lanka 1977–79, Scotland 1979–82, Australia 1982–86; Gen. of the Salvation Army 1986–93; Hon. Dr. Liberal Arts (Ewha Woman's Univ., Seoul) 1988; Hon. Dr. Laws (Asbury Coll., U.S.A.) 1988; Hon. Ph.D. (Queensland Univ.) 1993; Hon. D.Univ. (Griffith Univ.) 1994; Hon. LL.D. (Univ. of N.S.W.) 1996. *Leisure interests:* classical music, reading, travel. *Address:* 102 Domain Park, 193 Domain Road, South Yarra, Vic. 3141, Australia. *Telephone:* (03) 9820-9701. *Fax:* (03) 9866-5240.

BURROWS, (James) Stuart; British opera singer; b. Cilfynydd, S. Wales; s. of Albert Burrows and Irene (Powell) Burrows; m. Enid Lewis 1957; one s. one d.; ed. Trinity Coll., Carmarthen; school teacher until début Royal Opera House, Covent Garden 1967; a leading lyric tenor and has sung in world's major opera houses including San Francisco, Vienna, Paris, Buenos Aires (Théâtre Cologne) and Brussels (Théâtre de la Monnaie) as well as Covent Garden and Metropolitan Opera, New York; toured Far East with Royal Opera 1979 and sang with co. at Olympic Festival, Los Angeles 1984; four U.S. tours with Metropolitan Opera; concert appearances throughout Europe and N. America, under Solti, Barenboim, Mehta, Ozawa, Bernstein and Ormandy, including two recitals in Brahmssaal, Vienna; BBC TV series Stuart Burrows Sings every year since 1978; many recordings, including Die Zauberflöte, Don Giovanni, Die Entführung aus dem Serail, La Clemenza di Tito, La Damnation de Faust, Les Contes d'Hoffmann, Maria Stuarda, Anna Bolena, Eugene Onegin, The Midsummer Marriage, Messiah, Grande Messe des Morts (Berlioz), Les Nuits d'Eté, Das Klagende Lied, Beethoven's 9th (Choral) Symphony and single discs of Mozart arias, Operetta Favourites, German and French songs, popular ballads and Welsh songs; Pres. Save the Children, Cancer Research; Hon. D.Mus. (Wales) 1981; Dr. h.c. (Univ. Coll. of Wales, Aberystwyth). *Leisure interests:* breeding koi carp, gardening. *Address:* 'Nirvana', 35 St. Fagans Drive, St. Fagans, Cardiff, CF5 6EF, Wales.

BURSON, Harold, B.A.; American business executive; b. 15 Feb. 1921, Memphis; s. of Maurice Burson and Esther Burson; m. Bette Foster 1947; two s.; ed. Univ. of Mississippi; Acting Dir. Ole Miss News Bureau 1938–40; Reporter Memphis Commercial Appeal 1940; Asst. to Pres. and Public Relations Dir., H. K. Ferguson Co. 1941–43; operated own Public Relations Firm for six years; Chair. Burson-Marsteller 1953–, C.E.O. 1953–88; Exec. Vice-Pres. of Young and Rubicam Inc., mem. Exec. Cttee. 1979–85; Garrett Lecturer on Social Responsibility, Columbia Univ., Grad. School of Business 1973; Vice-Pres. and Mem. Exec. Cttee. Nat. Safety Council 1964–77; Int. Trustee World Wildlife Fund 1977–81; Trustee and mem. Exec. Cttee. Foundation for Public Relations Research and Educ. 1978–84; Founder and Sec. Corporate Fund, John F. Kennedy Centre for the Performing Arts 1977; Dir. Kennedy Cen. Productions Inc. 1974–89; presidential appointee to Fine Arts Comm. 1981–85; White House appointee to Exec. Cttee. Young Astronauts Co. 1984–88; Advisory Cttee., Medill School of Journalism, Northwestern Univ. 1985; Grad. School of Business, Emory Univ. 1986; Trustee Ray Simon Inst. of Public Relations, Syracuse Univ. 1985; mem. Public Relations Soc. of America, Int. Public Relations Asscn. of Business Communicators, Overseas Press Club, N.Y. Soc. of Security Analysts, Exec. Cttee., Catalyst Inc. 1977–88, Public Relations Advisory Cttee., U.S. Information Agency 1981; Assoc. mem. N.Y. Acad. of Medicine; Counsellor Nat. Press Foundation; Trustee The Economic Club of N.Y.; Chair. Jt. Council on Econ. Educ., Public Relations Seminar 1983; Hon. D. Hum. Litt. (Boston Univ.) 1988; Public Relations Professional of the Year Award (Public Relations News) 1977, Gold Anvil Award (Public Relations Soc. of America) 1980, Univ. of Mississippi Alumni Hall of Fame 1980, Silver Em Award (Mississippi Press Asscn.) 1982, Arthur Page Award, Univ. of Texas 1986, Horatio Alger Award 1986, Nat. Public Relations Achievement Award, (Ball State Univ.), Inside PR Life Achievement Award 1993. *Leisure interests:* stamp collection, West Highland White terriers. *Address:* Burson-Marsteller, 230 Park Avenue South, New York, NY 10003, U.S.A.

BURSTYN, Ellen; American actress; b. 7 Dec. 1932, Detroit, Mich.; d. of John Austin and Coriene Marie (née Hamel) Gillooly; m. 1st William C. Alexander; m. 2nd Paul Roberts; m. 3rd Neil Burstyn; one s.; ed. Cass Tech. High School, Detroit, Mich.; co-artistic dir. The Actor's Studio, New York 1982–88; Pres. Actors' Equity Asscn. 1982–88; Best Supporting Actress, The Last Picture Show (New York Film Critics Award, Nat. Soc. of Film Critics Award); Best Actress, Alice Doesn't Live Here Anymore (Acad. Award, British Acad. Award); Best Actress, Same Time Next Year (Tony Award, Drama Desk Award, Outer Critics Circle Award); dir. Judgement (off Broadway) 1981, Into Thin Air 1985. *Stage Productions include:* Fair Game 1957, Same Time Next Year 1975, 84 Charing Cross Road, Shirley Valentine 1989–90. *Film appearances (leading parts) include:* Goodbye Charlie 1964, For Those who Think Young 1965, Tropic of Cancer 1969, Alex in Wonderland 1970, The Last Picture Show 1971, The King of Marvin Gardens 1972, Thursday's Game (TV), 1973, The Exorcist 1973, Harry and Tonto 1974, Alice Doesn't Live Here Anymore 1975, Providence 1976, Dream of Passion 1978, Same Time Next Year 1978, Resurrection, Silence of the North 1980, Alamo Bay 1985, Twice in a Lifetime 1985, Hannah's War 1987, When You Remember Me (TV Film), The Colour of Evening 1990, Dying Young 1990, The Cemetery Club 1993, When a Man Loves A Woman 1994, Roommates 1994, How to Make an American Quilt 1995, The Babysitters Club 1995. *Address:* c/o CAA, 9830 Wilshire Blvd., Beverly Hills, CA 90212, U.S.A.

BURT, Peter Alexander, M.A., M.B.A., F.C.I.B.S., F.I.B. (SCOT.); British banker; b. 6 March 1944; s. of Robert W. Burt and May H. Rodger; m. Alison Mackintosh Turner 1971; three s.; ed. Merchiston Castle School, Edin., Univs. of St. Andrews and Pennsylvania; joined Hewlett Packard, Calif. 1968–70; worked for CSL, Edin. 1970–74, then Edward Bates & Sons Ltd. 1974; moved to Bank of Scotland 1975, Int. Div. 1975–88 (Head 1985), Asst. Gen. Man. 1979–84, Divisional Gen. Man. 1984–85, Jt. Gen. Man. 1985–88, Treas. and Chief Gen. Man. 1988–96, mem. Bd. of Dirs. 1995–, Chief Exec. 1996–; mem. High Constables and Guard of Honour Holyrood House, Edin.; *Leisure interests:* golf, skiing, gardening, reading. *Address:* c/o Bank of Scotland, The Mound, Edinburgh, EH1 1YZ, Scotland.

BURT, Robert Amsterdam, M.A., J.D.; American professor of law; b. 3 Feb. 1939, Philadelphia, Pa.; s. of Samuel Mathew Burt and Esther Amsterdam Burt; m. Linda Gordon Rose 1964; two d.; ed. Princeton, Oxford and Yale Univs.; Law Clerk, U.S. Court of Appeals, Dist. of Columbia Circuit 1964–65; Asst. Gen. Counsel, Exec. Office of the Pres. of U.S.A. 1965–66; Legis. Asst., U.S. Senate 1966–68; Assoc. Prof. of Law, Chicago Univ. 1968–70; Assoc. Prof. of Law, Michigan Univ. 1970–72, Prof. of Law 1972–73, Prof. of Law and Prof. of Law in Psychiatry 1973–76; Prof. of Law, Yale Univ. 1976–, Southmayd Prof. of Law 1982–93, Alexander M. Bickel Prof. 1993–; Special Master U.S. Dist. Court, Conn. 1987–92; Rockefeller Fellowship in Humanities 1976; mem. Bd. of Dirs., Benhaven School for Autistic Persons 1977–, Chair. 1983–96, Mental Health Law Project 1985–, Chair. 1990–; Dir. Yale Hillel Foundation 1996–; mem. Inst. of Medicine and N.A.S. 1976, advisory bd. Open Soc. Inst. Project on Death in America. *Publications:* Taking Care of Strangers: The Rule of Law in Doctor-Patient Relations 1979, Two Jewish Justices: Insider and Outsider in American Society 1987, The Constitution in Crisis 1992. *Leisure interests:* running, cello. *Address:* Yale Law School, P.O. Box 208215, 127 Wall Street, New Haven, CT 06520 (Office); 66 Dogwood Circle, Woodbridge, CT 06525, U.S.A. (Home). *Telephone:* (203) 432-4960 (Office); (203) 393-3881 (Home).

BURTON, Ian, M.A., PH.D., F.R.S.C.; Canadian-British environmental scientist, geographer, scholar and consultant; b. 24 June 1935, Derby, England; s. of Frank Burton and Elsie Victoria Barnes; m. 1st Lydia Demodoff 1962 (divorced 1977); one s. one d.; m. 2nd Anne V. T. Whyte 1977 (divorced 1995); one s. two d.; ed. Derby School, Univ. of Birmingham, Univ. of Chicago and Oberlin Coll., Ohio; Lecturer Univ. of Ind. 1960–61; Queen's Univ., Kingston, Ont. 1961; Consultant Ford Foundation, India 1964–66; Prof. Univ. of Toronto 1968–90, Adjunct Prof. 1990–, Dir. Inst. for Environmental Studies 1979–84; Prof. of Environmental Science Univ. of E. Anglia 1972–73; Sr. Adviser Int. Devt. Research Centre, Ottawa 1972–75; Sr. Connaught Fellow, École des Hautes Études en Sciences Sociales, Paris 1984–86; Dir. Int. Fed. of Insts. for Advanced Study 1986–92; Dir. Environmental Adaptation Research, Atmospheric Environmental Service 1990–96, Scientist Emer. 1996–; mem. Bd. of Dirs. Foundation for Int. Training 1994–; mem. Ind. World Comm. on the Oceans 1995–98; Vice-Pres. Int. Soc. of Biometeorology 1996–; numerous cttee. and consultant assignments with UNESCO, WHO, UNEP, Rockefeller Foundation, UNDP, World Bank Global Environment Facility, World Resources Inst., Intergovernmental Panel on Climate Change, European Comm., Ford Foundation, projects in Sudan and Nigeria etc.; Fellow World Acad. of Art and Sciences; Order of Zvonkova (U.S.S.R.) 1968; mem. Jury, St. Francis Environment Prize. *Publications:* co-wrote: The Human Ecology of Coastal Flood Hazard in Megalopolis 1968, The Hazardousness of a Place: A Regional Ecology of Damaging Events 1971, The Environment as Hazard 1978; co-ed.: Readings in Resource Management and Conservation 1986, Environmental Risk Assessment 1980, Living with Risk 1982, Geography, Resources and Environment 1986. *Leisure interests:* swimming, sailing, hiking, cricket. *Address:* Atmospheric Environment Service, 4905 Dufferin Street, Downsview, Ont., M3H 5T4; 72 Coolmine Road, Toronto, Ont., M6J 3E9, Canada. *Telephone:* (416) 538 2034. *Fax:* (416) 739 4297.

BURTON, Kenneth, M.A., PH.D., F.R.S.; British professor of biochemistry; b. 26 June 1926; s. of Arthur Burton and Gladys Burton; m. Hilda Marsden 1955; one s. one d.; ed. High Pavement School, Nottingham, Wath-upon-Dearne Grammar School and King's Coll. Cambridge; Asst. Lecturer in Biochemistry, Univ. of Sheffield 1949, Lecturer 1952; Research Assoc. Univ. of Chicago 1952–54; MRC Unit for Research in Cell Metabolism, Oxford 1954–66; Prof. of Biochem. Univ. of Newcastle-upon-Tyne 1966–88, Dean, Faculty of Science 1983–86, Emer. Prof. 1988–. *Publications:* articles in scientific journals. *Leisure interests:* music, hill-walking. *Address:* Byways, The Broadway, Alfriston, Polegate, East Sussex, BN26 5XH, England.

BURTON, Tim; American film director; b. 1958, Burbank, Calif.; ed. Calif. Arts Inst.; began career as animator, Walt Disney Studios (projects included The Fox and the Hound and The Black Cauldron); animator and dir. Vincent (short-length film; awards include two from Chicago Film Festival). *Films directed:* Frankenweenie (short, for Disney) 1984, Aladdin, Pee-wee's Big Adventure 1985, Beetlejuice 1988, Batman 1989, Edward Scissorhands 1991, Batman Returns 1992, Ed Wood 1994, Batman Forever 1996; dir. Mars Attacks! 1996; producer The Nightmare Before Christmas 1993, Cabin Boy

1994, James and the Giant Peach 1996. *Publication:* My Art and Films 1993. *Address:* Chapman, Bird & Grey, 1990 South Bundy Drive, Suite 200, Los Angeles, CA 90025, U.S.A.

BURWELL, Robert L., Jr., M.S., PH.D.; American professor of chemistry; b. 6 May 1912, Baltimore, Md.; s. of Robert L. and Anne H. (Lewis) Burwell; m. Elise Frank 1939; two d.; ed. St. John's Coll., Annapolis, Md. and Princeton Univ.; Instr. Trinity Coll., Hartford, Conn. 1936–39; Instructor Northwestern Univ. 1939–45, Asst. Prof. 1946, Assoc. Prof. 1946–52, Prof. 1952–70, Ipatieff Prof. 1970–80, Ipatieff Prof. Emer. 1980–; Humboldt Sr. Scientist Award, Tech. Univ. Munich 1981; Prof. Associé, Univ. Pierre et Marie Curie Paris 1982; Pres. The Catalysis Soc. 1973–77, Int. Congress on Catalysis 1980–84; mem. American Chem. Soc.; recipient of awards from American Chem. Soc. and Catalysis Soc. *Publications:* articles on heterogeneous catalysis and surface chemistry. *Leisure interests:* tennis, porcelain and history. *Address:* 5700 Williamsburg Landing Drive, Apt. 302, Williamsburg, VA 23185, U.S.A. *Telephone:* (757) 220-8984. *Fax:* (757) 565-6537.

BURWITZ, Nils, B.A.; German artist, sculptor and university professor; b. 16 Oct. 1940, Swinemünde; s. of Ulrich Burwitz and Johanna Lohse; m. Marina Schwezoff 1964; two s. one d.; ed. Univ. of Witwatersrand and postgrad. studies in London, Fribourg and Salzburg; emigrated to S. Africa 1958; settled in Balearic islands 1976; 102 one-man exhbns. including 36 Exposures 1971 and restrospective exhbn. in Sollerich Palace, Palma, Majorca 1985, Pretoria Art Museum, Pretoria 1991, Nat. Gallery 1992, Kunsthalle Munich-Germering 1995; visual concept for stage works Iconostasis 1967–68, 8 Birds 1969, 8 Beasts 1970, Gentlemen (with R. Kirby) 1972, Mobile (with V. Rodzianko), London 1972, Retalls de l'Ignorancia (with R. Esteras) 1978, Llagrimes del Vienès (with A. Ballester 1995; stained glass windows in churches of St. Philip and St. James and Sta. Eulalia, Palma de Mallorca, Monastery of Lluch and La Ermita de la Santísima Trinidad, Valldemossa, Majorca; founder, Libra Press 1984; opened Funda Art Centre, Soweto, S. Africa 1986; works in 84 public collections include: Albertina, Vienna, Ludwig Museum, Cologne, Nat. Portrait Gallery, Wash., Museum of Modern Art, Tokyo, Vic. and Albert Museum, London; has made three video documentaries in S. Africa and Namibia; corresp. mem. European Acad., Rome; numerous honours and awards including Gold Medal (Design), Johannesburg 1963, African Arts Centre Award, Durban 1971, Art Critics' Award, XI Graphic Biennale, Ljubljana 1975, Prix de la Ville de Monaco 1981, Primer Premio 'Ciutat de Palma' 1982, Merit Award, Il Biennale of Painting, Barcelona 1987; portfolios: Locust Variations 1967, It's About Time 1973, Tidal Zone 1974, Heads or Tails? 1981, 9 Terraces 1986, The Journey to Dresden 1989, The Invisible Miró 1995, Marinas Terraces 1995. *Publication:* On the Razor's Edge 1995. *Leisure interests:* swimming, diving. *Address:* Calle Rosa 22, Valldemossa, E-07170 Majorca, Spain. *Telephone:* (971) 612 838. *Fax:* (971) 612 839.

BURY, Pol; Belgian sculptor; b. 26 April 1922, Haine-St. Pierre; s. of Jules Bury and Augusta Modave; m. Velma Horne 1971; one d.; ed. Ecole St. Joseph, Haine-St. Paul, Athénée Provinciale, La Louvière and Acad. des Beaux Arts, Mons; painter 1938–; sculptor 1953–; Prof. Univ. of Calif. Berkeley 1970, Minneapolis Coll. of Art 1972, Ecole Nat. Supérieure des Beaux Arts, Paris 1983–87; one-man exhbns. in U.S.A., Germany, Netherlands, Belgium, Mexico; fountains at Univ. of Iowa 1964, Palais Royal, Paris 1985, Univ. of Yamagata 1994, etc.; mirrors at Newark Airport 1987; Dr. h.c. (Minneapolis Coll. of Art); Grand Prix Nat. de Sculpture, Paris 1985; Médaille de la Résistance; Chevalier, Légion d'honneur, Officier Ordre de la Couronne (Belgium). *Publications:* L'Art à Bicyclette et la Révolution 1972, Les Gaités de l'Esthétique 1984, Le Monochrome Bariolé 1991. *Leisure interest:* reading. *Address:* 12 Vallée de la Taupe, 78200 Perdreauville; 236 boulevard Raspail, 75014 Paris, France. *Telephone:* (1) 34.78.33.31; (1) 43.21.52.11. *Fax:* (1) 34.78.04.77.

BUSEK, Erhard, D.JUR.; Austrian politician; b. 25 March 1941, Vienna; m. Helga Busek; ed. Univ. of Vienna; Second Sec. Parly. Austrian People's Party (ÖVP); joined Fed. Exec. Cttee. of Austrian Econ. Fed. 1968, Deputy Sec.-Gen. 1969, Sec.-Gen. 1972–76; Gen. Sec. ÖVP 1975–76; mem. Parl. 1975–78; City Councillor, Vienna City Senate 1976–78, 1987–89; Deputy Mayor of Vienna 1978–87; Deputy Fed. Chair. ÖVP 1983–91, Chair. June 1991–95; Pres. Austrian Research Community; Fed. Minister of Science and Research 1989–94, of Educ. and Culture Oct. 1994–95, Vice-Chancellor 1992–95. *Publication:* Mitteleuropa: Eine Spurensicherung 1998. *Address:* c/o Austrian People's Party, Lichtenfelsgasse 7, 1010 Vienna, Austria.

BUSER, Walter Emil, DR.IUR.; Swiss government official; b. 14 April 1926, Lausen; s. of Emil and Martha Buser; m. Renée Vuille 1947; ed. Humanistic Gymnasium, Basel, Univs. of Basel and Berne; Ed. Sozialdemokratische Bundeshauskorrespondenz 1950–61; Legal Consultant 1962–64; Head, legal and information service, Fed. Dept. of Interior 1965–67; Vice-Chancellor of the Swiss Confed. 1968–81, Chancellor 1981–92; Hon. Dozent (Basel). *Publications:* Das Bundesgesetz über die Ordnung des Arbeitsverhaltnisses vom 27.6.19, Die Rolle der Verwaltung und der Interessengruppen im Entscheidungsprozess der Schweiz, Betrachtungen zum schweizerischen Petitionsrecht, Die Organisation der Rechtsetzung, in Hundert Jahre Bundesverfassung 1874–1974, Das Institut der Volksinitiative in rechtlicher und rechtspolitischer Sicht. *Address:* c/o Federal Chancellery, Swiss Confederation, 3003 Berne, Switzerland.

BUSH, Barbara Pierce; fmr. First Lady of the United States; b. 8 June 1925, Rye, N.Y.; d. of Marvin Pierce and Pauline (née Robinson) Pierce; m. George Herbert Walker Bush (q.v.) 1945; four s. one d.; ed. Smith Coll.; mem. Bd. of Dirs., Reading is Fundamental (also Hon. Chair. Advisory Bd.), Business Council for Effective Literacy; mem. advisory council, Soc. of Memorial Sloan-Kettering Cancer Center; Hon. Chair. advisory council, Literacy Volunteers of America; Pres. Ladies of the Senate 1981–88; numerous other appointments and hon. degrees; Outstanding Mother of the Year Award 1984, Distinguished Leadership Award, United Negro Coll. Fund 1986, Distinguished American Woman Award, Coll. Mt. St. Joseph 1987. *Publication:* Barbara Bush: A Memoir 1994. *Address:* 490 E. L'Enfant Plaza, S.W., Room 6125, Washington, DC 20594, U.S.A.

BUSH, George Herbert Walker, B.A. (ECONS); American politician; b. 12 June 1924, Milton, Mass.; s. of the late Prescott Sheldon Bush and of Dorothy Walker; m. Barbara Pierce 1945; four s. one d.; ed. Phillips Acad., Andover, Mass., and Yale Univ.; naval carrier pilot 1942–45 (D.F.C., three Air Medals); co-founder, Dir. Zapata Petroleum Corpn. 1953–59; founder, Pres. Zapata Offshore Co. 1956–64, Chair. 1964–66; mem. House of Reps. for 7th Dist. of Texas 1967–71; Perm. Rep. to UN 1971–72; Chair. Republican Nat. Cttee. 1973–74; Head U.S. Liaison Office, Peking (now Beijing) 1974–75; Dir. C.I.A. 1976–77; Vice-Pres. of U.S.A. Jan. 1981–89, Pres. of U.S.A. 1989–93; numerous hon. degrees; Churchill Award 1991; Hon. G.C.B. 1993. *Publication:* Looking Forward: An autobiography (with Victor Gold) 1988, A World Transformed (with Brent Scowcroft) 1998. *Leisure interests:* tennis, jogging, boating, fishing, golf. *Address:* Suite 900, 10000 Memorial Drive, Houston, TX 77024, U.S.A.

BUSH, George W., M.B.A.; American politician and business executive; b. 6 July 1946; s. of George Herbert Bush, fmr. Pres. of U.S.A. (q.v.) and Barbara Pierce (q.v.); m. Laura Bush; two d.; ed. Yale and Harvard Univs.; Founder and Man. Spectrum 7 Energy Corpn. (merged with Harken Energy Corpn. 1986), Midland, Tex.; Dir. Harken Energy Corpn.; professional baseball team exec.; Gov. of Texas Jan. 1995–; Republican. *Address:* Office of the Governor, State Capital, POB 12428, Austin, TX 78711, U.S.A.

BUSH, Kate (Katherine); British singer and performer; b. 30 July 1958, Welling; songs include: Wuthering Heights, The Man with the Child in His Eyes, Wow, Symphony in Blue, Babooshka, Army Dreamers, Breathing, Sat in Your Lap, The Dreaming, Running Up That Hill, Don't Give Up (with P. Gabriel), The Sensual World, This Woman's Work; albums: The Kick Inside, Lionheart, Never Forever, The Dreaming, The Single File, Hounds of Love, The Sensual World, The Whole Story, The Red Shoes; contributed to soundtracks of Castaway (Be Kind to My Mistakes) and She's Having a Baby (This Woman's Work); Dir. Novercia Ltd.; BPI Award for Best Vocalist 1979, 1987. *Address:* c/o EMI Records (UK), EMI House, 43 Brook Green, London, W6 7EF, England.

BUSLAEV, Yuri Aleksandrovich; Russian scientist; b. 22 Nov. 1929, Syzranj; m. 1st Margarita Rodnikova 1959 (divorced 1981); two d.; m. 2nd Elena Tsabelj 1983; two d.; ed. Moscow Chemical Technological Inst. (D.I. Mendeleev Inst.); scientific researcher 1961–; fmr. Deputy Dir. Scientific Research, Inst. of Gen. and Inorganic Chem., U.S.S.R. (now Russian) Acad. of Sciences 1959–85, Head Lab. of Fluorine Chem. 1976–, Dir. Inst. of New Chemical Problems 1985–87, Dir. Inst. of Chemical Physics 1987–88, Academician-Sec., Div. of Physico-Chem. and Tech. of Inorganic Materials 1988–; Corresp. mem. U.S.S.R. (now Russian) Acad. of Sciences 1968, mem. 1984; U.S.S.R. State Prize 1976; Chugaev Prize. *Publications:* more than 300 scientific publs., including two books, reviews, monographs. *Leisure interests:* skiing, Russian literature. *Address:* Academy of Sciences, Division of Physical Chemistry, Leninsky pr. 32a, 117071 Moscow (Office); Profsoyusnaya ul. 43, Korp. 1, Apt. 116, 117420 Moscow, Russia. *Telephone:* 938-17-67 (Office); 331-29-04 (Home).

BUSQUIN, Philippe; Belgian politician; b. 6 Jan. 1941; m.; ed. Université Libre de Bruxelles; fmr. Prof. of Biology and Physics; Deputy for Hainaut 1977–78, for Charleroi 1978–; Minister of Nat. Educ. 1980–81, of the Interior and Nat. Educ. Feb.-Dec. 1981, for the Budget and Energy (French region) 1982–85, of the Economy and Employment (French region) Feb.-May 1988, of Social Affairs 1988–92; Chair. Parti Socialiste (PS) 1992–; Vice-Pres. Socialist Int. 1992–, P.E.S. 1995–. *Address:* Maison du Parti Socialiste, Boulevard de l'Empereur 13, 1000 Brussels, Belgium. *Telephone:* (02) 548 32 11. *Fax:* (02) 548 33 80.

BUSSE, Felix; German lawyer; b. 30 April 1940, Wernigerode/Harz; s. of Max Busse and Magdalene Eicke; m. Regine Bohn; one s. one d.; ed. Oberschule, Wernigerode and Univs. of Bonn, Kiel and Berlin; legal practice in Bonn 1967–, specialist in admin. law 1988–; Sec. Deutscher Juristentag e.V. 1978–; mem. Bd. German Union of Lawyers 1978–, Vice-Pres. 1988–; Ehrenzeichen der Republik Österreich; Bundesverdienstkreuz (1st Class). *Publications:* Der Umfang des Entschädigungsanspruchs aus Enteignung, Die aussergerichtliche Tätigkeit des Anwalts in Verwaltungssachen. *Leisure interests:* music, climbing, sailing. *Address:* Oxfordstrasse 21, 53111 Bonn, Germany. *Telephone:* (0228) 983910. *Fax:* (0228) 630283.

BUSSELL, Darcey Andrea, C.B.E.; British ballet dancer; b. 27 April 1969; d. of Philip M. Bussell and Andrea Williams; m. Angus Forbes 1997; ed. Arts Educational School and Royal Ballet School; joined Sadlers Wells Royal Ballet (now Birmingham Royal Ballet) 1987; soloist, Royal Ballet 1988, first soloist 1989, prin. ballerina 1989–; appearances with Royal Ballet include leading roles in The Spirit of Fugue (created for her by David Bintley), first Royal Ballet performances of Balanchine's Rubies and Stravinsky Violin Concerto, Ashley Page's Bloodlines (creator of leading role), Swan Lake (Odette/Odile), The Nutcracker (Sugar Plum Fairy), La Bayadere (Gamzatti), The Prince of the Pagodas (created for her by Kenneth MacMillan), Manon, Cinderella, Sleeping Beauty, Elite Syncopations (MacMillan), Raymonda, Bloodlines, Romeo and Juliet and others; Prix de Lausanne 1989; Dancer of the Year, Dance and Dancers Magazine 1990; Evening Standard Award 1990. *Publication:* My Life in Dance 1998. *Leisure interests:* sketching/painting, arts. *Address:* The Royal Opera House, Covent Garden, London, WC2E 9DD; 155 New King's Road, London, SW6 4SJ, England.

BUTCHER, David John, B.A. (HONS.); New Zealand economic consultant; b. 1948, England; s. of Frank George Butcher and Dorothy May Butcher; m. Mary Georgina Hall 1980; two d.; ed. Victoria Univ. of Wellington; fmr. union field officer and research officer for Dept. of Labour, Wages Tribunal and Industrial Comm.; mem. Parl. 1978–90; fmr. Parl. Under-Sec. to Ministers of Agric., Lands and Forests; Minister of Energy, of Regional Devt. and Assoc. Minister of Finance 1987–88, of Regional Devt. 1987–90, of Commerce 1988–90, of Energy 1989–90; Man. Dir. David Butcher and Assocs. 1992–; mem. Labour Party. *Publications:* Agriculture in a More Market Economy 1985, Lessons for the Future from the Free Market Economy, A Politician's View 1987, Forum Island Countries and the Single European Market 1992 1993, and numerous speeches and articles. *Leisure interests:* tramping, reading, classical music, family history, photography. *Address:* P.O. Box 5279, Wellington, New Zealand. *Telephone:* (4) 476-9001. *Fax:* (4) 476-9001.

BUTCHER, John Charles, PH.D., D.SC., F.R.S.N.Z.; New Zealand professor of mathematics; b. 31 March 1933, Auckland; s. of Charles Hastings Butcher and Alice Lilac Cornwall (née Richards) Butcher; m. 1st Patricia Frances Nicolas 1957 (divorced 1989); two s. one d.; m. 2nd Jennifer Ann Wright (née Bowman) 1990; ed. Dargaville, Taumarunui and Hamilton High Schools, Univs. of New Zealand and Sydney; Lecturer in Applied Math., Univ. of Sydney 1959–61; Sr. Lecturer in Math., Univ. of Canterbury 1961–64; computer scientist, Stanford Linear Accelerator Center 1965–66; Prof. of Math., Univ. of Auckland 1966–79 (Head Math. Dept. 1967–73), of Computer Science 1980–88 (f. Dept. of Computer Science 1980), Head, Applied and Computational Math. Unit 1989–94, 1997–, Prof. of Math. 1989–; various visiting lectureships and professorships U.S.A., U.K., Sweden, Austria, Germany, U.S.S.R., Netherlands 1965–; Fellow Inst. of Math. and its Applications (U.K.) 1972; mem. and Past. Pres. N.Z. Math. Soc.; mem. American Math. Soc. 1966; mem. Soc. for Industrial and Applied Math. (Pa., U.S.A.); Award for Math. Research (N.Z. Math. Soc.) 1991, Hector Medal (Royal Soc. of N.Z.) 1996. *Publications:* The Numerical Analysis of Ordinary Differential Equations: Runge-Kutta and General Linear Methods 1987, papers on numerical analysis and other topics. *Leisure interests:* classical music, bridge. *Address:* Department of Mathematics and Statistics, University of Auckland, Private Bag 92019, Auckland (Office); 16 Wallace Street, Herne Bay, Auckland, New Zealand (Home). *Telephone:* (9) 3737999 (Office); (9) 3762743 (Home). *Fax:* (9) 3737457.

BUTHELEZI, Chief Mangosuthu Gatsha, B.A.; South African politician and Zulu leader; b. 27 Aug. 1928, Mahlabatini; s. of late Chief Mathole Buthelezi and Princess Magogo; m. Irene Audrey Thandekile Mzila 1952; three s. four d.; ed. Adams Coll., Fort-Hare Univ.; installed as Chief of Buthelezi Tribe 1953; assisted King Cyprian in admin. of Zulu people 1953–68; elected leader of Zululand territorial authority 1970; Chief Minister of KwaZulu 1976–94; Minister of Home Affairs (in Gov. of Nat. Unity) May 1994–; Pres. Inkatha Freedom Party; Hon. LL.D. (Zululand and Cape Town); George Meany Human Rights Award 1982; Kt. Commdr. Star of Africa (Liberia), Commdr. Ordre Nat. du Mérite 1981, and numerous other awards. *Publication:* South Africa: My Vision of the Future 1990. *Address:* Ministry of Home Affairs, Private Bag X741, Pretoria 0001, South Africa.

BUTHELEZI, Rt. Rev. Bishop Manas, S.T.M., PH.D.; South African ecclesiastic; b. 10 Feb. 1935, Mahlabathini; s. of Absalom Buthelezi and Keslinah Mkhabase; m. Grace Mhlungu 1963; two s. two d.; ed. St. Francis Coll. and Yale and Drew Univs., U.S.A.; high school teacher 1957; Visiting Prof., Heidelberg Univ., Fed. Repub. of Germany 1972, Wesley Seminary 1975; Bishop, Central Diocese, Evangelical Lutheran Church 1977–; fmr. Pres. S.A. Council of Churches 1984–91; mem. Comm. on Studies, Lutheran World Fed. 1970–77, Comm. on World Mission and Evangelism, WCC 1975–83; mem. Standing Cttee. Faith and Order Comm., Pvt. Sector Council on Urbanization, Int. Comm. on Lutheran/Catholic Dialogue, Iliff School of Theology; several hon. degrees. *Leisure interests:* music and photography. *Address:* P.O. Box 1210, Roodepoort 1725, South Africa.

BUTKEVIČIUS, Audrius; Lithuanian politician; b. 24 Sept. 1960, Kaunas; s. of Bronius Butkevičius and Nijolė Butkevičienė; m. Vilija Butkevičienė 1985; one s. one d.; ed. Kaunas Medical Inst.; when a student worked as jr. researcher lab. of psychology Kaunas Research Inst. of Cardio-Vascular Medicine; chief physician Viesintos Out-Patient Dept., Chief Narcologist Cen. Hosp. of Kaunas Region; Dir.-Gen. State Defence Dept., Govt. of Lithuania 1990–91; Signatory of Restoration of Ind. of Lithuania Act 1990; Minister of Defence 1993–94; mem. Seimas (Parl.) 1996– (membership suspended after allegation of corruption 1997). *Address:* Čiurlionio str. 86–29, Vilnius, Lithuania.

BUTLER, Alan, B.SC.; British public relations consultant; b. 6 Dec. 1940, Wallingford; s. of Albert Frederick Butler and Lilian Elizabeth Butler; m. Gail Butler 1981; two s.; ed. Raine's Foundation Grammar School, London and Univ. Coll., London; Dir. of Public Affairs, Honeywell 1970–75; Dir. Carl Byoir and Assocs. Ltd. 1970–85, Man. Dir. 1975–85; Man. Dir. Countrywide Communications (London) Ltd. 1987–89, Int. Dir. 1989–93, Deputy Chair. 1989–93, Chair. Countrywide Political Communications 1988–91; Man. Partner, Kudos Communications 1993–; Dir. YTJ Communications, Singapore; Consultant, Kudos Consulting, Dubai; mem. British Computer Soc., Marketing Soc., Int. Public Relations Assn., Int. Assn. of Business Communicators; Liveryman Worshipful Co. of Marketors; Fellow, Inst. of Dirs., Inst. of Public Relations. *Leisure interests:* sport, travel. *Address:* Kudos Communications, Little Owls, Priest Hill, Old Windsor, Berks., SL4 2JN, England. *Telephone:* (01784) 430461. *Fax:* (01784) 473204.

BUTLER, Basil Richard Ryland, C.B.E., M.A., F.ENG.; British business executive; b. 1 March 1930, Hexham; s. of Hugh Montagu Butler and Annie Isabel Wiltshire; m. Lilian Joyce Haswell 1954; one s. two d.; ed. St. John's Coll., Cambridge; Operations Man. Sinclair and BP Colombian Inc. 1968–70, Operations Man. BP Alaska Inc. 1970–72, Gen. Man. BP Petroleum Devt. Ltd. 1978–81, Chief Exec. BP Exploration Co. Ltd. 1981–86, Dir. 1986–89, Man. Dir. BP Co. PLC 1986–91; Dir. BP Solar Int. 1991–98, Chair. 1991–95; Chair. European Council of Applied Sciences and Eng. 1993–98; Dir. Brown and Root Ltd. 1991–97, Chair. 1993–97; Dir. Murphy Oil Corpn. 1991–; Gen. Man. of Kuwait Oil Co. Ltd. 1972–75, of Sullom Voe Devt. 1975–78; Chair. KS Biomedix Holdings PLC 1995–; Pres. Inst. of Petroleum 1990–92; mem. Council Royal Acad. of Eng. 1993–, Hon. Sec. Int. Activities, Sr. Vice-Pres. 1996–; Liveryman Shipwrights' Co. 1988. *Leisure interests:* sailing, music. *Address:* Royal Academy of Engineering, 29 Great Peter Street, London, SW1P 3LW, England. *Telephone:* 0171-227 0500.

BUTLER, Sir Clifford Charles, Kt., PH.D., F.R.S.; British physicist; b. 20 May 1922, Reading, Berks; s. of Charles and Olive Butler; m. Kathleen Betty Collins 1947; two d.; ed. Reading Univ.; Asst. Lecturer in Physics, Manchester Univ. 1945–47, Lecturer 1947–53; Reader in Physics, Imperial Coll., London 1953–57, Prof. 1957–70, Head, Dept. of Physics 1963–70; Dir. Nuffield Foundation 1970–75; Vice-Chancellor, Loughborough Univ. of Tech. 1975–85; Sec.-Gen. Int. Union of Pure and Applied Physics 1963–72, First Vice-Pres. 1972–75, Pres. 1975–78; Chair. Council for the Educ. and Training of Health Visitors 1977–83; Chair. Advisory Cttee. on Supply and Education of Teachers 1980–85; Chair. Educational Counselling and Credit Transfer Information Service (ECCTIS) Steering Cttee. 1982–89; Chair. ABRC/NERC Working Group on Geological Surveying 1985–87; Chair. Working Party on Research Selectivity, N. Ireland 1986–87; Vice-Chair. Open Univ. Council 1986–94; Hon. D.Sc. (Reading Univ.) 1976; Hon. D.Univ. (Open Univ.) 1986; Hon. D.Tech. (Loughborough) 1987. *Publications:* scientific papers on cosmic rays and high energy physics. *Address:* Low Woods Farm House, Low Woods Lane, Belton, Loughborough, Leics., LE12 9TR, England. *Telephone:* (01530) 223125.

BUTLER, David Edgeworth, M.A., D.PHIL., F.B.A.; British psephologist; b. 1924; s. of late Prof. Harold E. Butler and Margaret Pollard; m. Marilyn S. Evans (Marilyn Butler, q.v.) 1962; three s.; ed. St. Paul's School and New Coll. Oxford; J.E. Procter Visiting Fellow, Princeton Univ. 1947–48; student, Nuffield Coll. Oxford 1949–51, Research Fellow 1951–54, Fellow 1954–, Dean and Sr. Tutor 1956–64; Personal Asst. to British Amb. in Washington 1955–56; co-ed. Electoral Studies 1982–92; Hon. D.Univ. (Paris) 1978, (Essex) 1993; Hon. D.Sc. (Queen's Univ. Belfast) 1985; Hon. LL.D. (Plymouth) 1997. *Publications include:* The Study of Political Behaviour 1958, Elections Abroad (ed.) 1959, British Political Facts 1900–1960 (with J. Freeman), Political Change in Britain 1969, The Canberra Model 1973, Coalitions in British Politics (ed.) 1978, Policy and Politics (ed. with A.H. Halsey), Referendums (with A. Ranney) 1978, British Political Facts 1900–79 (with A. Sloman), European Elections and British Politics (with D. Marquand) 1981, Democracy at the Polls (with A. Ranney) 1981, Democracy and Elections (with V. Bogdanor) 1983, Governing without a Majority 1983, A Compendium of Indian Elections 1984, Party Strategies in Britain (with P. Jowett) 1985, British Political Facts 1900–94 (with G. Butler) 1994, Sovereigns and Surrogates (with A. Low) 1991, The British General Election of 1992 (with Dennis Kavanagh) 1992, Failure in British Government (with others) 1994, India Decides (with P. Roy) 1995, Referendums Around the World (ed. jtly) 1995, British Politics and European Elections (with Martin Westlake) 1995, The British General Election of 1997 1997; also numerous books on the British electoral system and British elections since 1945. *Address:* Nuffield College, Oxford, OX1 1NF, England. *Telephone:* (01865) 278500.

BUTLER, Frederick Guy, M.A.; South African poet and university professor; b. 21 Jan. 1918, Cradock, Cape Province; s. of E. C. Butler and Alice E. (née Stringer) Butler; m. Jean Murray Satchwell 1940; three s. one d.; ed. Rhodes Univ., Grahamstown, and Brasenose Coll., Oxford; war service Egypt, Lebanon, Italy, U.K. 1940–45; Oxford 1945–47; lecturer in English, Univ. of Witwatersrand 1948–50; Prof. of English, Rhodes Univ. 1952–; Hon. Research Fellow 1987; Hon. Life Pres. Shakespeare Soc. of Southern Africa; Hon. Life Vice-Chair. S.A. Nat. Arts Festival 1992; Hon. D.Litt. (Univ. of Natal) 1970, (Univ. of Witwatersrand) 1984 (South Africa), (Rhodes Univ.) 1994; C.N.A. Award for Literature 1973, Cape Tercentenary Award for Literature 1981, Lady Ussher Prize for Literature 1992, Freedom of City of

Grahamstown 1994. *Publications:* Stranger to Europe (poems) 1952, 1960, The Dam (play) 1953, The Dove Returns (play) 1956, A Book of South African Verse 1959, South of the Zambesi (poems) 1966, Cape Charade (play) 1968, When Boys were Men 1969, Take Root or Die (play) 1970, The 1820 Settlers (history) 1974, Selected Poems 1975, Karoo Morning (autobiog. 1918–1935) 1977, Songs and Ballads 1978, A New Book of South African Verse in English 1979 (ed. with Chris Mann), Richard Gush of Salem (play) 1982, Bursting World (autobiog. 1936–1945) 1983, The Re-interment [of Olive Schreiner] on Buffels-Kop (Diary of S. Cronwright Schreiner, ed. with N. W. Visser) 1983, A Pilgrimage to Dias Cross (poem) 1987, Out of the African Ark (ed. with David Butler) 1988, The Magic Tree (ed. with Jeff Opland) 1989, Tales of the Old Karoo 1989, Selected Poems 1989, A Rackety Colt (novel) 1989, Demea (play) 1990, South Africa: Landshapes, Landscapes, Manscapes (text for photographs by Herman Potgieter) 1990, A Local Habitation 1945–90 (autobiog.) 1991, Guy Butler: Essays and Lectures 1994, Collected Poems 1999, The Prophetic Nun (history) 1999. *Leisure interests:* African animals and rock art. *Address:* Department of English, Rhodes University, Grahamstown, 6139, South Africa. *Telephone:* 622-4874.

BUTLER, Jim; British chartered accountant; b. 15 March 1929; m. Margaret Butler; one s. two d.; ed. Marlborough Coll., Clare Coll. Cambridge; articled clerk, Peat Marwick (chartered accountants) 1952; negotiated Peat Marwick's merger with Klynveld Main Gordeler to form KPMG 1986–87; Sr. Partner, Peat Marwick McLintock (U.K. arm of KPMG) 1987–; Chair. KPMG Int. 1991–93; Dir. Camelot PLC 1994– (Deputy Chair. 1995–), Royal Opera House 1994–, Wadworth and Co. Ltd. 1994–. *Address:* Littleton House, Crawley, Winchester, Hants., SO21 2QF; Flat 8, 3 Lennox Gardens, London, SW1X 0DA, England.

BUTLER, Marilyn Speers, D.PHIL., F.R.S.L., F.R.S.A.; British academic; b. 11 Feb. 1937, Kingston-on-Thames, Surrey; d. of Trevor Evans and Margaret Evans (née Gribbin); m. David Butler (q.v.) 1962; three s.; ed. Wimbledon High School, St. Hilda's Coll. Oxford; BBC trainee and producer 1960–62; Jr. Research Fellow, St. Hilda's Coll. Oxford 1970–73; Fellow and Tutor, St. Hugh's Coll. Oxford 1973–86; King Edward VII Prof. of English Literature, Cambridge Univ. 1986–93; Fellow King's Coll. Cambridge 1987–93; Rector Exeter Coll., Oxford 1993–; British Acad. Reader 1982–85; Hon. Litt.D. (Leicester) 1992, (Birmingham) 1993, (Oxford Brookes) 1994, (Williams Coll., Mass.) 1995, (Lancaster, Warwick, Surrey) 1997, (Kingston) 1998. *Publications:* Maria Edgeworth: A Literary Biography 1972, Jane Austen and the War of Ideas 1975, Peacock Displayed 1979, Romantics, Rebels and Reactionaries 1981, Burke, Paine, Godwin and the Revolution Controversy (Ed.) 1984, Collected Works of Wollstonecraft (Ed. with J. Todd) 1989, Edgeworth's Castle Rackrent and Ennui (Ed.) 1992, Mary Shelley's Frankenstein (Ed.) 1993, Jane Austen's Northanger Abbey (Ed.) 1995, Collected Works of Edgeworth (Ed. with M. Myers) 1999. *Address:* Exeter College, Oxford, OX1 3DP, England. *Telephone:* (01865) 279647 (College); (01865) 279644 (Home). *Fax:* (01865) 279674.

BUTLER, Sir Michael Dacres, G.C.M.G.; British diplomatist (retd.); b. 27 Feb. 1927, Nairobi, Kenya; s. of Thomas D. and Beryl M. (née Lambert) Butler; m. Ann Clyde 1951; two s. two d.; ed. Winchester Coll. and Trinity Coll., Oxford; joined Foreign Office 1950; served U.K. Mission to UN 1952–56, Baghdad 1956–58, Paris 1961–65, U.K. Mission to UN at Geneva 1968–70; sabbatical year at Harvard 1970–71; served at Washington, D.C. 1971–72; Head of European Integration Dept., FCO 1972–74, Under-Sec. for European Community Affairs 1974–76, Deputy Under-Sec. for Econ. Affairs 1976–79; Perm. Rep. to European Community 1979–85; Labour Party's Special Envoy on Enlargement 1996–97; Adviser to Robin Cook on Europe 1997–98; mem. Advisory Council Foreign Policy Centre 1998–; Chair. Guide Phone Ltd. 1998–; Deputy Chair. Bd. of Trustees, Victoria and Albert Museum 1985–97; Chair. Council, Royal Coll. of Art 1991–96, Senior Fellow 1997; Dir. The Wellcome Foundation, PLC 1985–94; Exec. Dir. Hambros Bank 1986–97, Hambros PLC 1986–97, Eurosynergies (France) 1990–, Incofina (Portugal) 1990–93; Chair. Oriental Art Magazine 1987–94, European Strategy Bd. I.C.L. 1986–, European Cttee. of British Invisibles 1988–93, Editorial Advisory Panel of Treasury Man. Int. 1992–, Business Link Dorset 1994–, Halo Ltd. 1994–96, Rudolfinia Ltd. 1994–, Pathway Group Ltd. 1995–; Hon. D.B.A. (Bournemouth) 1998; Adolphe-Bentinck Prize 1987; Kt. Grand Cross of Portuguese Order of Merit 1998. *Publications:* Chinese Porcelain at the End of the Ming (O.C.S. Transactions, Vol. 48), and at the Beginning of the Qing (O.C.S. Transactions, Vol. 49), Europe—More than a Continent 1987, Seventeenth Century Porcelain from the Butler Family Collection 1990, etc. *Leisure interests:* collecting Chinese porcelain and modern Czech glass sculpture, skiing, tennis. *Address:* 36A Elm Park Road, London, SW3 6AK, England. *Telephone:* 0171-352 9360. *Fax:* 0171-351 7477.

BUTLER, Richard Edmund, A.M., A.A.S.A., C.P.A.; Australian international telecommunications policy adviser; b. 25 March 1926, Melbourne; s. of late Claude Colombia Butler and Florence Margaret Butler; m. Patricia Carmel Kelly 1951; three s. two d.; held various positions in Postmaster-General's Dept. including Chief Industrial Officer, Man. Industrial Relations Arbitration and Employment Conditions 1955–60, Exec. Officer, Deputy Asst. Dir.-Gen. (Ministerial and External Relations) 1960–68; apptd. in absentia Sec. of Australian Telecommunications Comm. 1975, later Dir. Corporate Planning Directorate; Deputy Sec.-Gen. ITU 1968–83, Sec.-Gen. 1983–89; mem. Admin. Cttee. of Co-ordination for UN and Heads of Specialised Agencies; fmr. mem. Australian Del. Int. Telecommunication Satellite Consortium, Plenipotentiary Conf. 1965; mem. Admin. Council and Planning Cttees. 1962–68; Chair. ITU Staff Pension Cttee. 1968–83; UN System Co-ordinator World Communications Year 1983; Gov. Int. Computer Communications Conf. 1975–85; ITU Rep. and Adviser, Ind. Comm. of Latin American and Caribbean Broadcasting Union (ULCRA) 1990–; mem. Advisory bd. Man. Centre for Information Tech. Research Wollongong Univ., N.S.W. 1990–, Minister's advisory cttee. Implementation of Australian Telecommunications Reform, Minister of Transport and Communications 1990–92; Pres. (desig.) Asia-Pacific Div., IC&C World Leaders Council 1993; Chair. ASIASPACE Ltd., Australia 1996; mem. Bd. Volunteers in Tech. Assistance Inc. (U.S.A.) 1993–; Fellow Royal Inst. of Public Admin., Inst. of Electronic and Telecommunication Engineers; Hon. Fellow, Inst. of Electronics and Telecommunications, India, Inaugural Fellow, Telecommunications Soc. of Australia 1995; mem. Bd. of Advisors Pacific Telecommunications Council, Hawaii 1993, mem. Man. Bd. Centre for Int. Research on Communication and Information Technologies, (CIRCIT), Melbourne 1993, mem. Advisory Bd., Telematics, India 1994; mem. MCC (Melbourne), CTA, Sydney, Royal Commonwealth Soc., Royal Overseas League; Hon. mem. Greek Soc. of Air and Space Law 1984; Grand Insignia of Order of Merit for Telecommunications (Spain) 1983, Philipp Reis Medal 1987; several other awards and decorations. *Leisure interests:* golf and reading. *Address:* 40 Barrington Avenue, Kew, 3101 Victoria, Australia. *Telephone:* (3) 9817 4231. *Fax:* (3) 9817 4231.

BUTLER, Richard Noel, PH.D., M.R.I.A., F.R.S.C.; Irish professor of chemistry; b. 24 Nov. 1942, Cork City; s. of Robert N. Butler and Celia Butler; m. Jean Keohane 1968; three s. three d.; ed. St. Finbarr's Seminary, Cork, Univ. Coll. Cork, Univ. of Leicester; Prin., Regional Technical Coll., Sligo 1970–71; lecturer, Univ. Coll. Galway 1971–76, Assoc. Prof. 1976–81, Prof. of Chem. and Head of Chem. Dept. 1981–; Chair., Nat. Cttee. for Chem. Royal Irish Acad. 1988–92; Pres. Inst. of Chem. of Ireland 1986–88; Chair., Royal Soc. Chem., Ireland Section 1993–96; 1851 Exhbn. Scholarship for Ireland 1967. *Publications:* numerous articles and chapters in scientific publs. *Leisure interests:* boating, fishing, astronomy. *Address:* Chemistry Department, University College, Galway, Ireland. *Telephone:* (091) 2441 (ext. 2478).

BUTLER, Richard William, D.UNIV.; Australian diplomatist; b. 13 May 1942; m. Barbara Evans 1974; three s. one d.; ed. Randwick Boys High School, Univ. of Sydney, Australian Nat. Univ.; Second Sec. Embassy and Perm. Mission to UN, Deputy Perm. Rep. IAEA, Vienna 1966–69; First Sec. Mission to UN, New York 1970–73; Deputy High Commr., Singapore, 1975–76; Prin. Pvt. Sec. to Leader of Opposition 1976–77; Counsellor, Bonn Embassy 1978–81; Minister Del. to OECD, Paris, Amb. and Perm. Rep. to UN (Disarmament Matters), Geneva 1983–88; Amb. to Thailand 1989–92; Amb. and Perm. Rep. to Supreme Nat. Council of Cambodia 1991–92; Amb. and Perm. Rep. to UN, New York 1992–97; Exec. Chair. UN Special Comm. on Iraqi Disarmament 1997–99. *Address:* c/o Ministry of Foreign Affairs and Trade, Locked Bag 40, QVT, Canberra, ACT 2600, Australia.

BUTLER, William Elliott, J.D., M.A., LL.M., PH.D., LL.D., F.R.S.A., F.S.A.; American professor of law; b. 20 Oct. 1939, Minneapolis, Minn.; s. of late William E. Butler and of Maxine Swan Elmberg; m. 1st Darlene Johnson (died 1989); two s.; m. 2nd Maryann Gashi 1991; ed. Hibbing Jr. Coll., The American Univ., Harvard Law School and Johns Hopkins School of Advanced Int. Studies; Research Asst. Washington Center for Foreign Policy Research, Johns Hopkins Univ. 1966–68; Research Assoc. in Law, and Assoc. Russian Research Center, Harvard Univ. 1968–70; Reader in Comparative Law, Univ. of London 1970–76, Prof. of Comparative Law 1976–, Dean, Faculty of Laws 1988–90; mem. Council, School of Slavonic and E. European Studies 1973–93; Dean, Faculty of Laws, Univ. Coll. London 1977–79, Vice-Dean 1979–81; Dir. Vinogradoff Inst. Univ. Coll. London 1994–; Dean Faculty of Law, Speranskii Prof. of Int. and Comparative Law, Moscow Higher School of Social and Econ. Sciences 1995–; partner, White & Case 1994–96; partner, Price Waterhouse Coopers (law firm) 1997–; Special Counsel, Comm. on Econ. Reform, U.S.S.R. Council of Ministers 1989–91; consultant, IBRD; adviser and consultant, Russian Fed., Belarus, Ukraine, Kirgiz Repub., Repub. of Kazakhstan, Republic of Tajikistan, Republic of Uzbekistan; Visiting scholar, Moscow State Univ. 1972, 1980, Mongolian State Univ. 1979, Inst. of State and Law, U.S.S.R. Acad. of Sciences 1976, 1981, 1983, 1984, 1988, Harvard Law School 1982; Visiting Prof. New York Univ. Law School 1978, Ritsumeikan Univ. 1985, Harvard Law School 1986–87; mem. Russian Court of Int. Commercial Arbitration 1995–2000; Academician, Russian Acad. of Natural Sciences, Acad. of Sciences of Ukraine, Int. Acad. of the Book and Art of the Book; numerous professional appts., affiliations etc.; F. F. Marten Prize 1996. *Publications:* more than 700 books, articles, reviews and translations including Basic Documents on the Soviet Legal System 1983, Soviet Law 1983, The Law of the Sea and International Shipping 1985, The Non-Use of Force in International Law 1989, Perestroika and International Law 1990, The History of International Law in Russia 1647–1917 1990, Foreign Investment Legislation in the Republics of the Former Soviet Union 1993, Russian Law of Treaties 1997, Russian Legal Texts 1998, Russian Law 1999. *Leisure interests:* book collecting and bookplate collecting. *Address:* The Vinogradoff Institute, University College London, 4–8 Endsleigh Gardens, London, WC1H 0EG (Office); 20 Ainger Road, London, NW3 3AS, England (Home). *Telephone:* 0171-391 1469 (Office); 0171-586 2454 (Home). *Fax:* 0171-483 4014.

BUTLER, William Joseph; American lawyer; b. 22 March 1924, Brighton, Mass.; s. of Patrick L. Butler and Delia Conley; m. Jane Hays 1945; one s. one d.; ed. Harvard Univ. and New York Univ. School of Law; mem. New York Bar 1950; Assoc. Hays, St. John, Abramson & Schulman, New York 1949–53; partner Butler, Jablow & Geller, New York 1953–; special counsel American Civil Liberties Union; Lecturer, Practising Law Inst. 1966; Sec., Dir., Cen. Counsel, Walco Nat. Corpn., FAO Schwarz, New York; mem. Comm. on Urban Affairs, American Jewish Congress 1965–70; mem. Bd. of Dirs. New York Civil Liberties Union, Int. League for Rights of Man; mem. Exec. Cttee. League to Abolish Capital Punishment; mem. Standing Cttee. on Human Rights, World Peace Through Law Center, Geneva; Chair. Advisory Cttee. Morgan Inst. for Human Rights; mem. Int. Comm. of Jurists, American Bar Asscn., Council on Foreign Relations, Int. Law Asscn., American Soc. of Int. Law, etc.; int. legal observer, Int. Human Rights Org. at trials in Greece, Burundi, Iran, Nicaragua, S. Korea, Philippines, Uruguay, Israel, at Int. Criminal Tribunal for fmr. Yugoslavia, The Hague 1996–; Hon. D.Hum.Litt. (Cincinnati) 1988. *Publications include:* Human Rights and the Legal System in Iran 1976, The Decline of Democracy in the Philippines 1977, Human Rights in United States and United Kingdom Foreign Policy 1977, Guatemala, a New Beginning 1987, Palau: A Challenge to the Rule of Law in Micronesia 1988, The New South Africa—The Dawn of Democracy 1994; contribs. to professional journals. *Address:* 400 Madison Avenue, New York, NY 10017 (Office); 24 E 10th Street, New York, NY 10003, U.S.A.

BUTLER OF BROCKWELL, Baron (Life Peer) cr. 1998, of Herne Hill in the London Borough of Lambeth; **(Frederick Edward) Robin Butler,** G.C.B., C.V.O.; British public servant; b. 30 Jan. 1938, Poole, Dorset; s. of Bernard Butler and Nora Butler (née Jones); m. Gillian Lois Galley 1962; one s. two d.; ed. Harrow University Coll., Oxford; with H.M. Treasury 1961–69, Private Sec. to the Financial Sec. 1964–65, Sec. Budget Cttee. 1965–69; seconded to Cabinet Office as mem. Central Policy Review Staff 1971–72; Private Sec. to Prime Minister 1972–74, 1974–75, 1982–85; Head of General Expenditure Policy Group 1977–80; Principal Establishment Officer, H.M. Treasury 1980–82; Second Perm. Sec., Public Services 1985–87; Sec. to Cabinet and Head of Home Civil Service 1988–98; Master Univ. Coll., Oxford 1998–; Chair. of Govs. Dulwich Coll. 1997–; Gov. Harrow School 1975–85 (Chair. of Govs. 1985–90); mem. Royal Comm. for Lords' Reform 1999–; Hon. Fellow, Univ. Coll. Oxford 1989; Hon. D.Sc. (Cranfield) 1994; Hon. LL.D. (Exeter) 1998. *Leisure interests:* competitive games, opera. *Address:* University College, Oxford, OX1 4BH, England.

BUTLER-SLOSS, Rt. Hon. Lady Justice, Dame (Ann) Elizabeth (Oldfield), D.B.E., P.C., F.R.S.M.; British judge; b. 10 Aug. 1933; d. of late Sir Cecil Havers, Q.C., and Enid Snelling; m. Joseph W. A. Butler-Sloss 1958; two s. one d.; ed. Wycombe Abbey School; called to Bar, Inner Temple 1955, Bencher 1979; contested Lambeth, Vauxhall as Conservative Cand. 1959; practising barrister 1955–70; Registrar, Prin. Registry of Probate, later Family Div. 1970–79; Judge, High Court of Justice, Family Div. 1979–87; Lord Justice of Appeal Jan. 1988–; a Vice-Pres. Medico-Legal Soc.; Chair. Cleveland Child Abuse Inquiry 1987–88; Pres. Honiton Agricultural Show 1985–86; Treas. Inner Temple 1998–; mem. Judicial Studies Bd. 1985–89; Hon. Fellow St. Hilda's Coll., Oxford 1988; Fellow Kings Coll., London 1991, mem. Council 1992–; Chancellor Univ. of W. of England 1993–; Hon. LL.D. (Hull) 1989, (Bristol) 1991, (Keele) 1991, (Brunel Univ.) 1992, (Exeter) 1992, (Manchester) 1995; Hon. D. Lit. (Loughborough Univ. of Tech.) 1993, Hon. D.Univ. (Univ. of Central England) 1994; Hon. mem. British Pediatric Asscn., Hon. F.R.C.P., F.R.C.PSYCH. *Publications:* Jt. Ed. Phipson on Evidence (10th ed.), Corpe on Road Haulage (2nd ed.), fmr. ed. Supreme Court Practice 1976, 1976. *Address:* c/o Royal Courts of Justice, Strand, London, WC2A 2LL, England.

BUTLER-WHEELHOUSE, Keith, B.COMM.; British business executive; b. 29 March 1946, Walsall; s. of Kenneth Butler-Wheelhouse and May Butler-Wheelhouse; m. Pamela Bosworth-Smith 1973; two s.; ed. Technicon, Port Elizabeth, Univ. of Witwatersrand and Univ. of Cape Town Grad. School of Business; Ford Motor Co. S. Africa 1965–85; Dir. of Tech. Operations, Gen. Motors S. Africa 1985–86; Chair. and C.E.O. Delta Motor Corpn. 1987–92; Pres. and C.E.O. Saab Automobile 1992–96; Chief Exec. Smiths Industries PLC 1996–. *Leisure interests:* golf, tennis, skiing, keeping fit. *Address:* Smiths Industries PLC, 765 Finchley Road, London, NW11 8DS, England. *Telephone:* 0181-458 3232. *Fax:* 0181-458 4380.

BUTLIN, Martin Richard Fletcher, C.B.E., M.A., D.LIT., F.B.A.; British museum curator and art historian; b. 7 June 1929, Birmingham; s. of K. R. Butlin and Helen M. (née Fletcher) Butlin; m. Frances C. Chodzko 1969; ed. Trinity Coll., Cambridge and Courtauld Inst. of Art., Univ. of London; Asst. Keeper, Tate Gallery, London 1955–67, Keeper of the Historic British Collection 1967–89; consultant to Christie's 1989–; Mitchell Prize (jtly.) 1978. *Publications:* works on J. M. W. Turner, William Blake, Samuel Palmer, catalogues, articles, reviews etc. *Leisure interests:* music, travel. *Address:* 74C Eccleston Square, London, SW1V 1PJ, England.

BUTOR, Michel; French writer and lecturer; b. 14 Sept. 1926, Mons-en-Baroeul, Nord; s. of Emile Butor and Anne Brajeux; m. Marie-Josephe Mas 1958; four d.; ed. Univ. of Paris; teacher at Sens (France) 1950, Minieh (Egypt) 1950–51, Manchester (England) 1951–53, Salonica (Greece) 1954–55, Geneva (Switzerland) 1956–57; Visiting Prof. Bryn Mawr and Middlebury, U.S.A. 1960, Buffalo, U.S.A. 1962, Evanston, U.S.A. 1965, Albuquerque, U.S.A. 1969–70, 1973–74, Nice and Geneva 1974–75; Assoc. Prof. Vincennes 1969, Nice 1970–73; Prof. of Modern French Literature, Geneva 1975–91; Reader Éditions Gallimard 1958–; Chevalier, Ordre national du Mérite, Ordre des Arts et des Lettres; Prix Felix Féneon 1957, Prix Renaudot 1957, Grand prix de la critique littéraire 1960. *Publications:* Novels: Passage de Milan 1954, L'emploi du temps 1956, La modification 1957, Degrés 1960, Intervalle 1973; Essays: Le Génie du lieu 1958, Répertoire 1960, Histoire extraordinaire 1961, Mobile 1962, Réseau aérien 1963, Description de San Marco 1963, Les oeuvres d'art imaginaires chez Proust 1964, Répertoire II 1964, Portrait de l'artiste en jeune singe 1967, Répertoire III 1968, Essais sur les essais 1968, Les mots dans la peinture 1969, La rose des vents 1970, Le génie du lieu II 1971, Dialogue avec 33 variations de L. Van Beethoven 1971, Répertoire IV 1974, Matière de rêves 1975, Second sous-sol 1976, Troisième dessous 1977, Boomerang 1978, Quadruple Fond 1981, Répertoire V 1982; Poetry: Illustrations 1964, 6,801.000 litres d'eau par second 1965, Illustrations II 1969, Travaux d'approche 1972, Illustrations III 1973, Illustrations IV 1976, Envois 1980, Brassée d'Avril 1982, Exprès 1983, Herbier Lunaire 1984, Mille et un plis 1985, Le Retour du Boomerang 1988, Improvisations sur Flaubert 1991, Patience, Collation 1991, Transit A, Transit B 1993, Improvisations sur Michael Butor 1994, L'Utilité Poétique 1995, le Japon depuis la France, un rêve à l'ancre 1995, Curriculum Vitae 1996 (jtly.), Gyroscope 1996, Ici et là 1997, Improvisations sur Balzac 1998. *Leisure interest:* teaching. *Address:* à l'Ecart, 74380 Lucinges, France.

BUTROS, Albert Jamil, PH.D.; Jordanian diplomatist and professor of English; b. 25 March 1934, Jerusalem; s. of Jamil Issa Butros and Virginie Antoine (Albina) Butros; m. Ida Maria Albina 1962; four d.; ed. London Univ. and Univ. of Exeter, U.K., Columbia Univ., U.S.A.; taught English and Math. in two pvt. schools, Amman 1950–55; instructor, Teachers' Coll., Amman 1958–60; lecturer in English, Hunter Coll., City Univ. of New York 1961; Instructor, Miami Univ., Oxford, Ohio 1962–63; Asst. Prof. of English, Univ. of Jordan 1963–65, Assoc. Prof. 1965–67, Prof. 1967–79, Acting Chair. Dept. of English 1964–67, Chair. 1967–73, 1974–76, Dean Research and Graduate Studies 1973–76, Prof. of English 1985–; Visiting Prof. of English, Ohio Wesleyan Univ., Delaware, Ohio 1971–72, Jordan Univ. for Women, Amman 1995–96; Dir.-Gen. and Pres. Royal Scientific Soc., Amman 1976–84; Sr. Research Fellow, Int. Devt. Research Centre, Ottawa, Canada 1983–84, Gov. 1986–; Special Adviser to H.R.H. Crown Prince Hassan of Jordan 1984–85; Amb. to U.K. 1987–91, (also accred. to Ireland 1988–91, to Iceland 1990–91); mem. Bd. of Trustees, Philadelphia Univ., Amman, 1995–; Fellow World Acad. of Art and Sciences 1990–; Istiqlal Order, First Class 1987, Order of Merit (Grande Ufficiale), Italy 1983, K.St.J. 1991. *Publications:* Leaders of Arab Thought 1969; several articles in learned journals; several translations. *Leisure interests:* reading, writing, translation, art, world affairs, walking. *Address:* P.O. Box 309, Jubeiha, Amman 11941, Jordan. *Telephone:* (6) 515 7870.

BUTT, Michael Acton, M.A., M.B.A.; British business executive; b. 25 May 1942, Thruxton; s. of Leslie Acton Kingsford Butt and Mina Gascoigne Butt; m. 1st Diana Lorraine Brook 1964; two s.; m. 2nd Zoe Benson 1986; ed. Rugby School, Magdalen Coll., Oxford and INSEAD, France; joined Bland Welch Group 1964; Dir. Bland Payne Holdings 1970; Chair. Sedgwick Ltd. 1983–87; Deputy Chair. Sedgwick Group PLC 1985–87; Chair. and C.E.O. Eagle Star Holdings PLC 1987–91; Chair. and C.E.O. Eagle Star Insurance Co. 1987–91; Dir. BAT Industries PLC 1987–91, Marceau Investissements S.A. (France) 1987–94; Dir. Phoenix Int. (Bermuda) 1992–97, Bank of N. T. Butterfield (Bermuda) 1996–; Pres. and C.E.O. Mid Ocean Ltd. 1993–98, Chair. and C.E.O. Mid Ocean Reinsurance Co. Ltd. 1993–98; Dir. Exel Ltd. 1998–; Dir. Istituto Nazionale delle Assicurazioni (INA) 1994–97; Bd. mem. Int. Advisory Council, INSEAD. *Leisure interests:* travel, tennis, opera, reading, family, the European Movt. *Address:* XL Mid Ocean Reinsurance Company Ltd., P.O. Box HM 1066, Hamilton, HM EX (Office); Leamington House, 50 Harrington Sound Road, Hamilton Parish, CR 04, Bermuda. *Telephone:* (441) 292-1358 (Office); (441) 293-1378 (Home). *Fax:* (441) 292-5226 (Office); (441) 293-851 (Home).

BUTTERFIELD, Alexander P., D.F.C., M.S.; American fmr. public official and air service and business executive; b. 6 April 1926, Pensacola, Fla.; s. of Admiral Horace Butterfield and Susan Armistead Alexander Butterfield; m. Charlotte Mary Maguire 1949 (divorced 1985); one s. two d.; ed. Univ. of Calif. at Los Angeles, Univ. of Maryland, George Washington Univ. and Nat. War Coll.; served with U.S.A.F. 1948–69; pilot; promoted to rank of Col.; fighter-gunnery instructor and weapons officer; mem. Sky Blazers, U.S.A.F. Europe jet aerobatic team; Operations Officer Fighter-Interceptor Squadron, Knoxville, Tenn.; Commdr. fighter squadron Kadena Base, Okinawa; Commdr. tactical air reconnaissance operations, S.E. Asia; F-111 Project Officer and Sr. U.S. Mil. Rep., Australia; staff positions include Aide to Commdr. Fourth Allied Tactical Air Force (NATO), Academic Instructor, Air Force Acad., Sr. Aide to C.-in-C. Pacific Air Forces, Special Air Warfare Policy Planner, Pentagon, Mil. Asst. to Special Asst. to Sec. of Defence; Deputy Asst. to Pres. Nixon and Sec. to Cabinet 1969–73; Administrator Fed. Aviation Admin. 1973–75; lecturer, 1975–76; Exec. Vice-Pres. Int. Air Service Co. Ltd. 1977–79; Pres. Calif. Life Corpn. 1979–80; Chair. GMA Corpn. 1981–82; Pres. and Chair. and C.E.O. Armistead and Alexander, Inc. 1983–94; mem. Bd. of Dirs. Aloha Airlines, Los Angeles Co. Museum of Natural History, Pres. Appointee, Bd. of Dirs. Smithsonian Inst.; Legion of Merit and other awards.

BUTTERFIELD, Baron (Life Peer) cr. 1988, of Stechford in the County of West Midlands; **(William) John (Hughes) Butterfield,** D.M., M.D., F.R.C.P., F.A.C.P.; British physician; b. 28 March 1920, Stechford, Birmingham; s. of the late William Hughes Butterfield and of Doris Butterfield (née Pritchard); m. 1st Ann West Sanders 1946 (died 1948); one s.; m. 2nd Isabel-Ann Foster Kennedy 1950; two s. one d.; ed. Solihull School, Exeter Coll. Oxford, Johns Hopkins Medical School; Royal Army Medical Corps 1946–48; scientific staff of Medical Research Council 1950–58; Prof. Guy's Hosp. 1958–70; Vice-Chancellor Univ. of Nottingham 1970–75; Regius Prof. of Physic, Cambridge Univ. 1976–87 (Deputy 1987–); Master of Downing Coll., Cambridge 1978–87; Vice-Chancellor Cambridge Univ. 1983–85; Visiting Prof. Yale Univ. 1966, Harvard Univ. 1976; Chair. East Midlands Econ. Planning Council 1974–75, Medicines Comm. 1976–81; Health Promotion Research Trust 1983–, Jardine Educ. Trust (H.K.) 1982–85, Council of Guy's and St. Thomas's United Medical and Dental Schools, London; mem. Health Educ. Council 1972–78, Inter-univ. Council for Higher Educ. Overseas 1973–, Trent Regional Health Authority 1974–76, Hong Kong Univ. and Polytechnic Grants Cttee. 1975–81, Medical Research Council 1976–80; East Anglian Regional Health Authority 1980–87, Council, St. George's House, Windsor Castle 1987–; Dir. Prudential Corpn. 1981–92; Croucher Foundation, Hong Kong 1989–; Specialist Adviser House of Lords Sub Cttee. Priorities in Medical Research; Hon. Fellow, New York Acad. of Science, Hon. LL.D. (Nottingham), (Bristol), Hon. D.Med.Sci. (Keio), Hon. D.Sc. (Florida Int. Univ.), Hon. D.M. (Chinese Univ. of Hong Kong). *Publications:* On Burns 1952, Tolbutamide after Ten Years 1966, Priorities in Medicine 1968, Health Behaviour in an Urban Community 1970, ed. Int. Dictionary of Medicine and Biology 1986, about 100 articles on diabetes, vascular disease, health care delivery, etc. *Leisure interests:* tennis, cricket, conversation, visiting Wellfleet, Mass. *Address:* 39 Clarendon Street, Cambridge, CB1 1JX, England. *Telephone:* (01223) 328854.

BUTTERWORTH, David, B.SC.(ENG.), F.ENG., F.I.CHEM.E.; British chemical engineer; b. 24 Oct. 1943; m. Pauline Morgan 1966; one s.; ed. Univ. Coll. London; Visiting Engineer, M.I.T., U.S.A. 1976–77; Group Leader, UKAEA 1977–89; Man. Dir. Heat Transfer and Fluid Flow Service 1989–95; consultant in heat transfer 1995–; Visiting Prof. Bristol Univ. 1993–, Cranfield Univ. 1996–, Aston Univ., Birmingham 1996–; Pres. UK Heat Transfer Soc. 1988–89; Gen. Sec. Aluminium Plate-Fin Heat Exchanger Mfrs. Asscn. 1995–; American Inst. of Chemical Engineers Kern Award 1986. *Publications:* Introduction to Heat Transfer 1977, Two-Phase Flow and Heat Transfer 1977 (Russian trans. 1980), Design and Operation of Heat Exchangers (Jt. Ed.) 1992, New Developments in Heat Exchangers (Jt. Ed.). *Leisure interests:* landscape painting, cooking. *Address:* 29 Clevelands, Abingdon, Oxon., OX14 2EQ, England. *Telephone:* (01235) 525955. *Fax:* (01235) 200906.

BUTTERWORTH, Ian, C.B.E., F.R.S.; British professor of physics; b. 3 Dec. 1930, Tottington; s. of Harry and Beattie Butterworth; m. Mary Therese Gough, 1964; one d.; ed. Bolton County Grammar School, Univ. of Manchester; Scientific Officer, then Sr. Scientific Officer UKAEA, Harwell A.E.R.E. 1954–58; Lecturer in Physics Imperial Coll., Univ. of London 1958–64, Sr. Lecturer 1965–68, Head High Energy Nuclear Physics Gp., Univ. Prof. of Physics 1971–91, Prof. Emer. 1991–, Head of Physics Dept. 1980–83; Visiting Physicist Lawrence Berkeley Lab., Univ. of Calif. 1964–65; Sr. Prin. Scientific Officer Rutherford Lab. 1968–71; Research Dir. C.E.R.N. (on leave of absence from Imperial Coll.) 1983–86; Prin. Queen Mary and Westfield Coll. 1989–91 (of Queen Mary Coll. 1986–89); Pro Vice-Chancellor for European Affairs, Univ. of London 1989–91; Chair. IOP Publs. Ltd. 1993–97; Vice-Pres. Inst. of Physics 1993–97; Vice-Pres. Academia Europea 1997–; Sr. Research Fellow Imperial Coll. 1991–; Fellow Imperial Coll. 1988; mem. Academia Europaea 1989; Dr. h.c. (Soka Univ.) 1989. *Publications:* numerous papers on particle physics in scientific journals. *Leisure interest:* history of art. *Address:* Blackett Laboratory, Imperial College, Prince Consort Road, London, SW7 2BZ (Office); 48 Burntwood Grange Road, London, SW18 3JX, England (Home). *Telephone:* 0171-594 7851. *Fax:* 0171-823 8830.

BUTTON, John, B.A., LL.B.; Australian politician; b. 30 June 1932, Ballarat, Vic.; m. 1st Marjorie Bowen 1960; two s.; m. 2nd Dorothy O'Neill 1985; ed. Univ. of Melbourne; former sr. partner in Melbourne law firm specializing in industrial law; mem. Senate 1974–93; Professorial Fellow, Syme Faculty of Business and Econs., Monash Univ., Vic. 1993–; Opposition Spokesman 1976–83; Deputy Leader of Opposition in Senate 1978–80, Leader 1980–83; Leader of Govt. in Senate, Minister for Industry and Commerce 1983–93, for Tech. 1984–93; Special Trade Rep. 1993–96; Labor Party. *Publications:* Flying the Kite 1994, On the Loose 1996. *Leisure interests:* skiing, languages, films, literature, theatre and the arts. *Address:* Level 33, 120 Collins Street, Melbourne, Vic. 3000, Australia.

BUXTON, Andrew Robert Fowell; British banker; b. 5 April 1939; m. Jane M. Grant 1965; two d.; ed. Winchester Coll. and Pembroke Coll. Oxford; joined Barclays Bank Ltd. 1963; Dir. Barclays Bank UK Ltd. 1978; Gen. Man. Barclays Bank PLC 1980, Vice-Chair. 1984–87, Deputy Man. Dir 1987–88, Man. Dir. 1988–91, a Deputy Chair. 1991–93, C.E.O. 1992–93, 1993–98; Pres. British Bankers' Asscn. 1997–; mem. Court, Bank of England 1997–. *Address:* c/o British Bankers' Association, Pinners Hall, 105–108 Old Broad Street, London, EC2N 1EX, England.

BUYOYA, Maj. Pierre; Burundian politician; b. 1949; ed. Royal Mil. Acad., Brussels; mem. Cen. Cttee. UPRONA party 1982–87; fmr. C.O.O. Ministry of Nat. Defence; led mil. coup against fmr. Pres. Bagaza Sept. 1987; Pres. of Third Repub. and Minister of Nat. Defence 1987–93; Chair. Mil. Cttee. for Nat. Salvation 1987–93; Pres. of Burundi July 1996–. *Address:* Office of the President, Bujumbura, Burundi.

BUZATU, Gheorghe, D.HIST.; Romanian historian; b. 6 June 1939, Sihlea, Vrancea Co.; s. of Ilie Buzatu and Maria Buzatu; m. Constanţa Huiban 1970; one s.; ed. Iaşi Univ.; Prof. Univ. of Craiova; scientific researcher and Dir. European History and Civilization Centre of Romanian Acad./Filiala, Iaşi; mem. editorial bds. Romanian Civilization, Europa XXI, Neamul Românesc, Dosarele Istoriei; Prize of the Romanian Acad. 1981, Prize of Flacăra magazine 1992, Prize of Revista de Istorie Militară 1993, 1995, 1996. *Publications include:* (in Romanian): Files of the World War 1939–45 1979, Romania and the International Oil Trusts up to 1929 1981, From the Secret History of World War II Vols. I and II 1988, 1995, Romania and World War II: A Bibliography (with others) 1981, Titulescu and the Strategy of Peace (Ed.) 1982, The Romanians in World History Vols. 1–67 (Ed.) 1986–98, Marshall Antonescu versus History, Vols. I–IV (with others) 1990–95, Forbidden History 1990, Romania with and without Antonescu 1991, The Romanians in the American Archives (Ed.) 1992, The Trial of Corneliu Zelea Codreanu (with others) 1994, Geopolitics (Vol. I) (Ed.) 1994, N. Iorga, The Man and the Word (Vols. I–II) 1971–94, Romania and the World War of 1939–1945 1995, The Romanians in the Kremlin's Archives 1995, How the Holocaust against the Romanians Began 1995, The Romanian Right (Ed.) 1996, The Secret Archives, Vols. I–II (with others) 1998, A History of Romanian Oil 1998, History of the Romanians 1918–1948 (with others) 1999; (in English): Anglo-Romanian Relations after 1821 (Ed.) 1983, N. Titulescu and Transylvania 1984, Romania's Options in June 1940 1995; (in Spanish): Breve Historia de Rumania (with others) 1982. *Address:* European History and Civilization Centre, Strada Cuza Vodă, nr. 41, etaj I, Iaşi 6600 (Office); Splai Bahlui nr. 20 A, Bloc I/1, apt. 5, Iaşi 6600, Romania (Home). *Telephone:* (032) 212441 (Office); (032) 130331 (Home).

BUZEK, Jerzy Karol; Polish politician and chemical engineer; b. 3 July 1940, Śmiłowice; m. Ludgarda Buzek; one d.; ed. Silesian Tech. Univ., Gliwice; scientific researcher and prof. Chemical Eng. Inst. Polish Acad. of Sciences, Gliwice; mem. Solidarity trade union 1980–; organiser of Solidarity underground structures in Silesia; activist of union's regional and nat. leadership; Chair. 1st, 4th, 5th and 6th Nat. Congresses of Dels.; expert and co-author economic program of the Solidarity Election Action AWS; deputy to Sejm (Parl.) 1997–; Prime Minister of Poland 1997–. *Publications including:* author of several dozen articles and monographs on mathematical modelling, desulphurisation of exhaust gases and optimalisation of processes. *Leisure interests:* poetry, theatre, horse riding, tennis. *Address:* Kancelaria Prezesa Rady Ministrów, Al.Ujazdowskie 1/3, 00-583 Warsaw, Poland. *Telephone:* (22) 694 60 00.

BUZOIANU, Cătălina; Romanian stage director; b. 13 April 1938, Brăila; d. of Roman Buzoianu and Elena Buzoianu; m. Papil Panduru 1963; one s. one d.; ed. Bucharest Theatrical and Cinematographic Art Inst.; started career at the Nat. Theatre Iaşi with Le Malade Imaginaire (Molière) 1970; at Teatrul Tineretului (Youth Theatre) in Piatra Neamţ; Prin. Dir. at Teatrul Mic, Bucharest 1978–85; has directed plays by Chekhov, Strindberg, Bulgakov, Anski, Pirandello, Shepard, Kleist and Goldoni; tours abroad and participation in int. festivals; Prof. Theatre and Cinema Institute; Dean of Theatre Dept., Theatre and Film Acad. 1990–; numerous awards including Salvo Randoni Award for whole career, and especially for Pirandello performances, Italy 1995, Prix théâtre vivant, Radio France Int. 1994, Prize for Excellence, Int. Asscn. of Critics, Romanian Section. *Publications:* Novele teatrale (essays), Meridiane (Ed.) 1987; articles and essays in various periodicals. *Address:* Bulandra Theatre, 1 Bd. Schitu Măgureanu, 70626 Bucharest (Office); C. A. Rosetti Str., Et.7, Ap.19, Sect. 1, Bucharest, Romania (Home). *Telephone:* 1.211.00.88 (Home). *Fax:* 1.312.28.97 (Office).

BYAMBASUREN, Dashiin; Mongolian politician; b. 20 June 1942, Binder somon Dist., Hentii Prov.; s. of Lombyn Dash and Tsevegeen Perenlee; m. Sanjeen Dulamlkhand 1968; three s. three d.; ed. Inst. of Economics and Statistics, Moscow, U.S.S.R.; apptd. Dept. Chief, State Statistics Bd.; Deputy Chair., then Chair. State Cttee. for Prices and Standardization 1970–76; apptd. Chair. Construction and Repair Work Trust for Auto Transport 1984, Chief Research Officer, Research Inst. of Project Drafts for Automated Man. Systems 1985, Dir. Manager Training Inst., Council of Ministers 1986; Deputy Chair. Council of Ministers 1989–90, First Deputy Chair. March–Sept. 1990, Prime Minister 1990–92; Pres. Mongolian Devt. Foundation, World Mongolian Fed. 1993; fmr. mem. Parl; Chair. Mongolian Democratic Renewal Party 1994–; Rector Inst. of Admin. and Man. 1998–. *Address:* Erh Chölööniy Gudanj 16, Ulan Bator, Mongolia. *Telephone:* 310963. *Fax:* 310963.

BYAM SHAW, Nicholas Glencairn; British publisher; b. 28 March 1934, London; s. of the late Lieut.-Commdr. David Byam Shaw and of Clarita Pamela Clarke; m. 1st Joan Elliott 1956 (divorced 1973); two s. one d.; m. 2nd Suzanne Filer 1974; m. 3rd Constance Mary Wilson (née Clarke) 1987; ed. Royal Naval Coll., Dartmouth; served R.N., retiring with rank of Lieut. 1951–56; on staff of Collins (printers and publrs.), Sales Man. 1956–64; joined Macmillan Publrs. Ltd. as Sales Man. 1964, Deputy Man. Dir. 1968, Man. Dir. 1970–90, Chair. 1990–97, Deputy Chair. 1998–; Dir. St. Martins Press 1980–, Pan Books Ltd. 1983– (Chair. 1986–); mem. British Council

Publishers' Advisory Cttee., Byam Shaw School Council. *Leisure interests:* travel, gardening, reading, music. *Address:* 9 Kensington Park Gardens, London, W11 3HB, England. *Telephone:* 0171-221 4547.

BYATT, Antonia Susan, C.B.E., B.A. (HONS.), F.R.S.L.; British author; b. 24 Aug. 1936; d. of His Honour John F. Drabble, Q.C. and late Kathleen M. Bloor; sister of Margaret Drabble (q.v.); m. 1st Ian C. R. Byatt (q.v.) 1959 (dissolved 1969); one s. (deceased), one d.; m. 2nd Peter J. Duffy 1969; two d.; ed. Sheffield High School, The Mount School, York, Newnham Coll., Cambridge, Bryn Mawr Coll., Pa., U.S.A. and Somerville Coll., Oxford; Extra-Mural Lecturer, Univ. of London 1962–71; Lecturer in Literature, Cen. School of Art and Design 1965–69; Lecturer in English, Univ. Coll., London 1972–81, Sr. Lecturer 1981–83; Assoc. Newnham Coll., Cambridge 1977–82; mem. Bd. of Creative and Performing Arts 1985–87, Bd. of British Council 1993–; Kingman Cttee. on English Language 1987–88; Man. Cttee. Soc. of Authors 1984–88 (Chair. 1986–88); broadcaster, reviewer and judge of literary prizes; Hon. D.Litt (Bradford) 1987, (Durham, York) 1991, (Nottingham) 1992, (Liverpool) 1993, (Portsmouth) 1994, (London) 1995; Irish Times-Aer Lingus Literature Prize 1990, Booker Prize for Fiction for Possession 1990. *Publications:* Shadow of the Sun 1964, Degrees of Freedom 1965, The Game 1967, Wordsworth and Coleridge in their time 1970, Iris Murdoch 1976, The Virgin in the Garden 1978, Still Life 1985, Sugar and Other Stories 1987, Possession 1990, George Eliot: Selected Essays and Other Writings 1990, Passions of the Mind (selected essays) 1991, Angels and Insects (novellas) 1992, The Matisse Stories (short stories) 1994, The Djinn in the Nightingale's Eye 1995, Imagining Characters (with Ignês Sodré) 1995, Babel Tower 1996, New Writing 6 (co-ed.) 1996, Elementals (short stories) 1998. *Leisure interests:* none. *Address:* 37 Rusholme Road, London, S.W.15, England.

BYATT, Sir Hugh Campbell, K.C.V.O., C.M.G., M.A.; British diplomatist (retd.); b. 27 Aug. 1927, Edinburgh; s. of late Sir Horace Byatt, G.C.M.G. and Lady Byatt (née Olga Campbell), M.B.E.; brother of R.A.C. Byatt (q.v.); m. Fiona M. M. Coats 1954; two s. one d.; ed. Gordonstoun and New Coll., Oxford; Royal Navy 1945–48; Nigerian political service 1952–57; Commonwealth Office 1957; subsequently served in Bombay, Lisbon; seconded Cabinet Office 1965–67; Consul-Gen. Mozambique 1972–73; Inspector H.M. Diplomatic Service 1973–75; Royal Coll. of Defence Studies 1976; Deputy High Commr. in Kenya 1977–78; First Amb. to Angola 1978–81 (also accred. to São Tomé and Príncipe 1980–81), to Portugal 1981–86; Adviser RTZ Corpn. 1986–96; Chair. of Govs., Centre for Information on Language Training and Research 1986–90; mem. Parole Bd. for Scotland 1990–92; Dir. EFM Dragon Trust PLC 1986– (Chair. 1992–98); Chair. EFM Java Trust 1990–98, Malcolm Sargent Cancer Fund for Children, Cttee. for Scotland 1990–96; Dir. EFM Japan Trust PLC 1993–97; Hon. Sheriff, Campbeltown, Argyll 1994–; Kt. Grand Cross Mil. Order of Christ 1985. *Leisure interests:* sailing, fishing, gardening, painting in watercolours. *Address:* Leargnahension, Tarbert, Argyll PA29 6YB, Scotland. *Telephone:* (01880) 820644.

BYATT, Ian Charles Rayner, B.A., D.PHIL.; British economist and government official; b. 11 March 1932, Preston; s. of Charles Rayner Byatt and Enid Marjorie Annie (née Howat) Byatt; m. 1st Antonia Susan Drabble (q.v.) 1959 (dissolved 1969); one s. (deceased) one d.; m. 2nd Dr Deirdre Kelly 1997; ed. Kirkham Grammar School, St. Edmund Hall and Nuffield Coll., Oxford, Harvard Univ.; Lecturer in Econs., Durham Coll., Univ. of Durham 1958–62, L.S.E. 1964–67; Econ. Consultant, H.M. Treasury 1962–64; Sr. Econ. Adviser, Dept. of Educ. and Science 1967–69; Dir. of Econs., Ministry of Housing and Local Govt. (and subsequently Dept. of Environment) 1969–72; Under-Sec., H.M. Treasury 1972–78, Deputy Chief Econ. Adviser 1978–89, Dir.-Gen. of Water Services 1989–; Pres. Economics and Business Educ. Assn. 1998–; mem. Econ. Policy Cttee. of EC 1978–89 (Chair. 1982–85), Bd. of Man., Int. Inst. of Public Finance 1987–90, Council, Royal Econ. Soc. 1983–90, Council of Man., Nat. Inst. of Econ. and Social Research 1996–, Governing Body of Birkbeck Coll. 1997–; Vice-Pres. Strategic Planning Soc. 1993–; Hon. D.Univ. (Brunel). *Publication:* The British Electrical Industry 1875–1914 1979. *Leisure interest:* painting. *Address:* Office of Water Services, Centre City Tower, 7 Hill Street, Birmingham, B5 4UA, England. *Telephone:* (0121) 625-1350 (Office). *Fax:* (0121) 625 1348.

BYATT, Ronald (Robin) Archer Campbell, C.M.G.; British diplomatist (retd.); b. 14 Nov. 1930; s. of late Sir Horace Byatt and Lady Byatt (née Olga Campbell); brother of Sir Hugh Byatt (q.v.); m. Ann Brereton Sharpe 1954; one s. one d.; ed. Gordonstoun, New Coll., Oxford; joined Diplomatic Service 1959; Foreign Office 1959, 1963; served in Havana 1961, Kampala 1970; with U.K. Mission to UN, New York 1966, Counsellor and Head of Chancery 1977–79; Head of Rhodesia Dept., Foreign Office 1972–75; Asst. Under-Sec. of State for Africa 1979–80; High Commr. in Zimbabwe 1980–83; Amb. to Morocco 1985–87, High Commr. in N.Z. (also accred. to Western Samoa and Gov. of Pitcairn Island) 1987–90; Visiting Fellow, Glasgow Univ. 1975–76; Civilian Dir. Royal Coll. of Defence Studies, London 1983–84; Panel Chair. Civil Service Selection Bd. 1992–95; mem. Forestry Comm. Home-Grown Timber Advisory Cttee. (Chair. Environment Sub-Cttee.) 1993–98; Trustee Beit Trust 1987–; Trustee U.K. Antarctic Heritage Trust 1993–. *Leisure interests:* birdwatching, sailing, gardening. *Address:* Drimna-Vullin, Lochgilphead, Argyll, Scotland (Home).

BYCHKOV, Aleksey Mikhailovich, D.C.T.; Russian evangelist; b. 15 July 1928; s. of Michael Bychkov and Evdokja Bychkova; m. Zoja Bychkova 1950; one s. two d.; ed. as engineer; active from early age in helping to prepare theological training material; Vice-Pres., All-Union Council of Evangelical Christian-Baptists 1969–71, 1990–, Gen. Sec. 1971–92; clergyman in Golgotha church; Vice-Pres. Russian Bible Soc. 1990–; Pres. Moscow Evangelical Christian Seminary 1995–; expanded Bible correspondence course, responsible for printing and distributing Bibles in U.S.S.R. *Leisure interest:* photography. *Address:* Muzanovskaya str. 8, 136260, Moscow 127549, Russia. *Telephone:* 4077503.

BYCHKOV, Semyon; Russian-born conductor; b. 1952, Leningrad; ed. Leningrad Conservatory (pupil of Musin); invited to conduct Leningrad Philharmonic Orchestra; left. U.S.S.R. 1975; debut with Concertgebouw, Amsterdam, and Berlin Philharmonic 1984–85; toured Germany with Berlin Philharmonic 1985; Music Dir. Buffalo Philharmonic Orchestra 1986–87, Orchestre de Paris 1989–(98); conducted Czech Philharmonic 1989–90; Prin. Guest Conductor, St. Petersburg Philharmonic 1992–, Maggio Musicale Fiorentino 1992–; Franco Abbiati Prize 1996. *Operas include:* La Finta Giardiniera 1984, Ariadne auf Naxos 1985, Rosenkavalier 1987, Aida, Lyon Opera 1987. *Address:* c/o Isabelle Barea, Orchestre de Paris, 352 Rue Saint Honoré, 75008 Paris, France; c/o IMG Artists (UK) Inc., Media House, 3 Burlington Lane, Chiswick, London, W4 2TH, England.

BYERS, Horace Robert, SC.D.; American meteorologist; b. 12 March 1906, Seattle, Wash.; s. of Charles H. Byers and Harriet E. Byers; m. Frances Clark 1927; one d.; ed. Univ. of California and M.I.T.; Research Meteorologist, U.S. Weather Bureau 1935–40; Assoc. Prof., Univ. of Chicago 1940–45, Prof. 1945–65, Chair. Dept. of Meteorology 1948–60; Distinguished Prof., Tex. A.&M. Univ. 1965–74, Dean, Coll. of Geosciences 1965–68, Vice-Pres. for Academic Affairs 1968–71; Professeur Associé, Univ. of Clermont-Ferrand, France 1975; Prof. Emer. 1975–; mem. N.A.S.; Robert M. Losey Award, Inst. of Aeronautics and Astronautics 1941; Charles F. Brooks Award, American Meteorological Soc. 1960, Cleveland Abbe Award 1972. *Publications:* General Meteorology (4th edn.) 1974, Elements of Cloud Physics 1965 and more than 75 scientific articles and monographs. *Address:* 300 Hot Springs Road, Apartment 320, Santa Barbara, CA 93108, U.S.A. *Telephone:* (805) 969-8295.

BYERS, Sir Maurice Hearne, C.B.E., Q.C.; Australian barrister; b. 10 Nov. 1917, Sydney; s. of Arthur Tolhurst and Mabel Florence (née Hearne) Byers; m. Patricia Therese Davis 1949; two s. one d.; ed. St. Aloysius Coll., Milson's Point, Sydney and Sydney Univ.; barrister-at-law 1944–, Q.C. 1960–; Solicitor-Gen. of Australia 1973–83; Vice-Pres. N.S.W. Bar Assn. 1964–65, Pres. 1965-67; Chair. N.S.W. Police Bd. 1984–88; mem. Exec. Council of the Law Council of Australia 1966–68, Australian Law Reform Comm. 1984–86; Leader, Australian del., UN Comm. on Int. Trade Law 1974, 1976–81, Australian del. to Diplomatic Conf. on Sea Carriage of Goods (Hamburg) 1979; Chair. N.S.W. Police Bd. 1983–88, Australian Constitutional Comm. 1985–88; mem. Council of Australian Nat. Univ. 1975–78. *Leisure interests:* reading, talking. *Address:* Wentworth Chambers, 180 Phillip Street, Sydney, N.S.W. 2000 (Office); 3 Kardinia Road, Clifton Gardens, N.S.W., Australia (Home). *Telephone:* 235001 (Office); 969 8257 (Home). *Fax:* (02) 221 5604.

BYFORD, Mark, LL.B.; British broadcasting executive; b. 13 June 1958, Castleford; s. of Sir Lawrence Byford and Lady Muriel Byford (née Massey); m. Hilary Bleiker 1980; two s. three d.; ed. Christ's Hospital School, Lincoln, Univ. of Leeds, Wharton Business School, Philadelphia; joined BBC as Holiday Relief Assistant 1979, Controller Regional Broadcasting 1991–94, Deputy Man. Dir. 1994–96, Dir. 1996–98; Man. Dir. BBC World Service 1998–; Royal TV Soc. Journalism Awards 1980, 1982, 1988. *Leisure interests:* soccer, cricket, family life, being with children. *Address:* BBC World Service, Bush House, Strand, London, WC2B 4PH (Office); Bolberry House, 1 Clifton Hill, Winchester, Hants., SO22 5BL, England (Home). *Telephone:* (01962) 860197 (Home). *Fax:* (01962) 860944 (Home).

BYKOV, Vasily Vladimirovich (Bykaŭ, Vasil'); Belarus writer; b. 19 June 1924, Chernovshchina, Vitebsk district; m. 1980; two s.; ed. Vitebsk School of Art; writer 1951–; U.S.S.R. People's Deputy 1989–91; mem. Belarus Democratic Movt.; Kolas Literature Prize 1964, Lenin Prize 1986, Order of the Red Star, Hero of Socialist Labour; mem. Belarus Democratic Movt., in opposition to Pres. Lukashenko. *Publications include:* The Cry of the Cranes 1960, Frontline Pages 1960, The Third Rocket 1962, Alpine Ballad 1963, The Dead Feel No Pain 1966, Cursed Height 1968, Kruglyansky Bridge 1969, Sotnikov 1972, Obelisk. Stories 1973, When You Want to Live (play) 1974, The Wolf-Pack 1975, The Mark of Doom 1982, The Sandpit 1986, In the Mist 1987, The Round-up 1988, Collected Works (6 vols.) 1992–94. *Address:* Ul. Tankova 10-132, 194292 Minsk, Belarus. *Telephone:* (17) 23-11-57.

BYRD, Harry Flood, Jr.; American newspaperman and politician; b. 20 Dec. 1914; s. of late Harry Flood Byrd; m. Gretchen B. Thomson 1941; two s. one d.; ed. John Marshall High School, Richmond, Virginia Military Inst. and Univ. of Virginia; Ed. writer Winchester Evening Star 1935, Ed. and Publr. 1935–, Ed. and Publr. Harrisonburg Daily News-Record 1937–; also active in firm of H. F. Byrd, Inc., apple growers; mem. Virginia State Senate 1947–65; mem. Democratic State Cen. Cttee. 1940–70; served U.S. N.R. 1941–46; Dir. Associated Press 1950–66; U.S. Senator from Virginia (succeeding his father, Harry Flood Byrd) 1965–83; Independent. *Address:* Rockingham Publishing Co. Inc., 2 North Kent Street, Winchester, VA 22601, U.S.A.

BYRD, Robert C., J.P.; American politician; b. 20 Nov. 1917, North Wilkesboro, N.C.; s. of Cornelius Sale and Ada Byrd; m. Erma O. James 1936; two d.; ed. George Washington Univ. Law School and Washington Coll. of Law (American Univ.); mem. West Virginia House of Delegates 1946–50, W.Va. Senate 1950–52; mem. U.S. House of Representatives rep. 6th Dist. of W.Va. 1952–58; Senator from West Virginia 1950–52, 1959–; Asst. Democratic Leader in Senate 1971–77, Majority Leader 1977–81, Minority Leader 1981–87, Majority Leader 1987–88; mem. Senate Appropriations, Judiciary and Rules and Admin. Cttees.; Democrat. *Address:* 311 Hart Senate Office Building, Washington, DC 20510, U.S.A.

BYRNE, David; American musician, composer and director; b. 14 May 1952, Dumbarton, Scotland; s. of Thomas Byrne and Emily Anderson (née Brown) Byrne; m. Adele Lutz 1987; one c.; ed. Rhode Island School of Design; performer with Talking Heads group 1975–92; musician, composer, producer 1980–; producer Index Video 1983–; *group albums:* Fear of Music 1979, Remain in Light 1980, My Life in the Bush of Ghosts 1981, Speaking in Tongues 1983, Stop Making Sense 1984, Little Creatures 1985, Naked 1988, Popular Favourites 1976–1991 1992; *solo albums include:* The Knee Plays 1985, Rei Momo 1989, The Forest 1991, Uh Oh 1992, David Byrne 1994, Feelings 1997; *film scores include:* The Last Emperor 1987 (Acad. Award winner); film appearances in Stop Making Sense 1984, True Stories (also Dir. and Co-screenwriter) 1986, Checking Out 1988; dir. videotapes 1981–; designer stage sets, lighting, LP covers and posters 1977–. *Publication:* Stay Up Late 1987, What the Songs Look Like 1987, Strange Ritual 1995.

BYRNE, Gabriel; Irish actor; b. 1950, Dublin; m. Ellen Barkin; ed. Univ. Coll. Dublin; archaeologist, then teacher, began acting in amateur productions; joined an experimental repertory co. 1980; first TV appearance in series The Riordans 1982; first cinema role in Excalibur; several roles Nat. Theatre, London; moved to New York 1987; films include Hanna K, Gothic, Julia and Julia, Siesta, Miller's Crossing, Hakon Hakenson, Dark Obsession, Cool World, A Dangerous Woman, Little Women, Usual Suspects, Frankie Starlight, Dead Man, Last of the High Kings, Mad Dog Time; co-producer In the Name of the Father.

BYRNE, John V., M.A., PH.D., F.A.A.A.S.; American academic; b. 9 May 1928, Hempstead, N.Y.; m. Shirley O'Connor 1954; one s. three d.; ed. Hamilton Coll., Clinton, N.Y., Columbia Univ. and Univ. of S. Calif., Los Angeles; research geologist, Humble Oil & Refining, Houston, Tex. 1957–60; Assoc. Prof. Oregon State Univ., Corvallis, Ore. 1960–66, Prof. of Oceanography 1966–, Chair, Oceanography 1968–72, Dean, Oceanography 1972–76, Dean, Research 1976–80, Vice-Pres. Research and Grad. Studies 1980–81, Pres. 1984–95; Program Dir. Oceanography, Nat. Science Foundation 1966–67; Exec. Dir. Kellogg Comm. on Future of State and Land Grant Univs. 1996–; Admin. Nat. Oceanic & Atmospheric Admin., Washington, D.C. 1981–84. *Leisure interests:* fishing, skiing, music. *Address:* 811 SW Jefferson, Corvallis, OR 97333, U.S.A. (Office). *Telephone:* (541) 737-3542. *Fax:* (541) 737-4380.

BYZANTINE, Julian Sarkis, A.R.C.M.; British classical guitarist; b. 11 June 1945, London; s. of Carl Byzantine and Mavis Harris; ed. Royal Coll. of Music, London and Accademia Chigiana, Siena, Italy; studied with John Williams at R.C.M., subsequently with Julian Bream and with Andrés Segovia and Alirio Diaz in Siena; taught at R.A.M. 1966–68; Sr. Lecturer in Guitar, Queensland Conservatorium of Music, Australia; has performed in 72 countries and is a regular touring artist for British Council; has performed concerts with leading British orchestras including Royal Philharmonic, City of Birmingham Symphony, Scottish Chamber, BBC Symphony; numerous radio and TV appearances; recordings: 4 solo albums for Classics for Pleasure, recording with flautist Gerhard Mallon for Walsingham Classics (Australia); awarded first A.R.C.M. for guitar 1966; Scholarships to study with Segovia from Vaughan Williams and Gilbert Foyle Trusts. *Publication:* Schotts Arrangements of Six Albéniz Piano Works for Guitar 1984. *Leisure interests:* collecting oriental art, archaeology, tennis. *Address:* Flat 1, 42 Ennismore Gardens, London, SW7 1AQ, England. *Telephone:* 0171-584 7486.

C

CAAN, James; American actor and director; b. 26 March 1940, Bronx, New York; s. of Arthur and Sophie Caan; ed. Hofstra Coll.; m. 1st DeeJay Mathis 1961 (divorced 1966); one d.; m. 2nd Sheila Ryan 1976 (divorced 1977); one s.; m. 3rd Linda O'Gara 1995; two c.; made theatre début in the off-Broadway production of La Ronde 1960; Broadway début in Blood Sweat and Stanley Poole, 1961. *Films include:* Irma La Douce 1963, Lady in a Cage 1964, The Glory Guys 1965, Countdown 1967, Games 1967, Eldorado 1967, Journey to Shiloh 1968, Submarine XI 1968, Man Without Mercy 1969, The Rain People 1969, Rabbit Run 1970, T. R. Baskin 1971, The Godfather 1972, Slither 1973, Cinderella Liberty 1975, Freebie and the Bean 1975, The Gambler 1975, Funny Lady 1975, Rollerball 1975, The Killer Elite 1975, Harry and Walter Go to New York 1976, Silent Movie 1976, A Bridge Too Far 1977, Another Man, Another Chance 1977, Comes a Horseman 1978, Chapter Two 1980, Thief 1982, Kiss Me Goodbye 1983, Bolero 1983, Gardens of Stone 1988, Alien Nation 1989, Dad 1989, Dick Tracy 1990, Misery 1991, For the Boys 1991, Dark Backward 1991, Honeymoon in Vegas 1992, Flesh and Bone 1993, The Program 1994, North Star 1995, Boy Called Hate 1995, Eraser 1996, Bulletproof 1996, Bottle Rocket 1996, This Is My Father 1997, Poodle Springs 1997, Blue Eyes 1998, The Yards 1999; Dir. and actor Hide in Plain Sight 1980, Dir. Violent Streets 1981; starred in television movie, Brian's Song, 1971; numerous TV appearances. *Address:* Licker and Ozurquich, 2029 Century Park E. # 500, Los Angeles, CA 90067, U.S.A.

CABALLÉ, Montserrat; Spanish (soprano) opera singer; b. Barcelona; m. Bernabé Marti (tenor) 1964; one s. one d.; ed. Conservatorio del Liceo; studied under Eugenia Kemeny, Conchita Badia and Maestro Annovazi; début as Mimi (La Bohème), State Opera of Basel; N. American début in Manon, Mexico City 1964; U.S. début in Lucrezia Borgia, Carnegie Hall 1965; appeared at Glyndebourne Festival as the Marschallin in Der Rosenkavalier and as the Countess in The Marriage of Figaro 1965; début at Metropolitan Opera as Marguerite (Faust) Dec. 1965; now appears frequently at the Metropolitan Opera and numerous other opera houses throughout the U.S.A.; has performed in most of the leading opera houses of Europe including Gran Teatro del Liceo, Barcelona, La Scala, Milan, Vienna State Opera, Paris and Rome Operas, Bayerische Staatsoper (Munich), etc., and also at Teatro Colón, Buenos Aires; repertoire of over forty roles; recordings of Lucrezia Borgia, La Traviata, Salomé, Aida; Most Excellent and Illustrious Doña and Cross of Isabella the Catholic, numerous hon. degrees, awards and medals, including Commdr. des Arts et des Lettres 1986.

CABANA, Marie-Claude Jeanne Blanche, LL.B.; French diplomatist; b. 19 June 1942, Montpellier; d. of late Robert Guilhaudis and of Elisabeth Grillon; m. Camille Cabana 1968; two d., three step-s. (one deceased); ed. Univ. of Paris, Institut d'Etudes Politiques, Paris, Ecole Nat. d'Administration, Paris; at Ministry of Foreign Affairs 1968–73, Deputy Dir. of Personnel 1976–78, Deputy Dir. for Cen. and E. Africa 1978–84; Rapporteur, Audit Court 1974–75; Dir. of Int. Relations Paris Town Council 1984–86; Amb., Perm. Rep. to UNESCO 1986–88, Vice-Pres. Exec. Council 1989–91; Amb., Perm. Rep. to OECD 1995–98; Magistrate, Cour des Comptes 1998–; Chevalier, Légion d'honneur, Officier, Ordre nat. du mérite; Kt. of the Equatorial Star (Gabon); Officer of the Thousand Hills (Rwanda); Officer of the Ouissam Alaouite (Morocco), Commdr. Nat. Order of Niger. *Leisure interests:* reading, theatre, travel, swimming, walking. *Address:* 13 rue Camson, 75001 Paris, France. *Telephone:* (1) 42-98-99-56.

CABANIS, José, L. ÈS L., D. EN D.; French writer; b. 24 March 1922; s. of Gaston Cabanis and Françoise de Bellomayre; one s. one d.; ed. Univ. de Toulouse; mem. Acad. Française 1990; Grand Prix de Littérature de l'Acad. Française 1976; Chevalier des Arts et des Lettres; Chevalier, Légion d'honneur. *Publications include:* novels: L'âge ingrat 1952, Juliette Bonviolle 1954, Les mariages de raison 1958, Le bonheur du jour (Prix des Critiques) 1961, Les cartes du temps (Prix des Libraires) 1962, Les jeux de la nuit 1964, La Bataille de Toulouse (Prix Théophraste Renaudot) 1966, Les jardins de la nuit 1973; Un essai sur Marcel Jouhandeau 1960, Plaisir et lectures 1964 (criticism), Plaisir et lectures II 1968, Des jardins en Espagne 1969, Le sacre de Napoléon 1970, Charles X roi ultra (Prix des Ambassadeurs) 1972, Saint-Simon l'Admirable (Grand Prix de la Critique) 1975, Les profondes années 1976, Michelet, le prêtre et la femme 1978, Petit entracte à la guerre 1981, Lacordaire et quelques autres 1983, Le Musée espagnol de Louis-Philippe Goya 1985, L'Escaladieu 1987, Pour Sainte-Beuve (essay) 1987, Chateaubriand 1988, le Crime de Torcy 1990, Fausses nouvelles 1990, Mauriac, le Roman et Dieu 1991, Dieu et la N.R.F. 1994, Le Diable et la N.R.F. 1996. *Address:* 5 rue Darquié, 31000 Toulouse; Gallimard, 5 rue Sébastien Bottin, 75007 Paris (Offices); Nollet, 31130 Balma, France (Home).

CABIALLAVETTA, Mathis; Swiss banker; ed. Univ. of Kingston, Ont., Univ. of Montréal; joined Union Bank of Switzerland econ. research dept. 1971, Head of Foreign Exchange Operations 1979, C.E.O. 1998. *Address:* c/o Union Bank of Switzerland, 45 Bahnhofstrasse, 8021 Zurich, Switzerland.

CABIBBO, Nicola; Italian professor of elementary particle physics; b. 30 April 1935, Rome; Prof. of Theoretical Physics 1965–, of Elementary Particle Physics, Univ. of Rome; Pres. Istituto Nazionale di Fisica Nucleare 1983–93, ENEA (Nat. agency for new tech. energy and the environment) 1993–, Pontifical Acad. of Sciences 1993–. *Address:* c/o ENEA, Viale Regina Margherita 125, 00198 Rome, Italy. *Telephone:* (6) 85282214. *Fax:* (6) 85282313.

CABRAL, Luís de Almeida; Guinea-Bissau politician; b. 1931, Bissau; brother of late Amílcar Cabral; founded Partido Africano da Independência da Guiné e Cabo Verde (PAIGC) with Amílcar Cabral 1956; mem. Political Bureau and Cen. Cttee., PAIGC 1956–70; fled to Senegal; Sec.-Gen. Nat. Union of Workers of Guinea-Bissau 1961; mem. PAIGC Council of War 1965–80, Perm. Comm. of Exec. Cttee., in charge of Nat. Reconstruction of the liberated areas 1970–72, Asst. Sec.-Gen. 1972–80; Pres. State Council (Head of State) of the self-proclaimed independent state of Guinea-Bissau 1973–74, Pres. of State Council of Guinea-Bissau 1974–80 (deposed in coup); under arrest 1980; released 1 Jan. 1982; went to Cuba.

CABRERA INFANTE, Guillermo; British writer; b. 22 April 1929, Gibara, Cuba; s. of Guillermo Cabrera and Zoila Infante; m. 1st Marta Calvo 1953 (divorced 1961), 2nd Míriam Gómez 1961; two d.; ed. School of Journalism, Havana; wrote first short story 1947; film critic Carteles Magazine 1954–60, Man. Ed. 1957–60; f. Cinemateca de Cuba 1950; Ed. Lunes 1959–61; diplomatist in Belgium 1962–65; film writer 1966–; scripts include Wonderwall 1967, Vanishing Point 1970, Under the Volcano (not produced) 1972, The Lost City 1990; feature writer for English, Spanish and S. American magazines and newspapers; Lecturer in U.S.A., Spain and England 1978–; Guest Dir. Telluride Film Festival 1992, Miami Film Festival 1993; mem. jury Cannes Film Festival 1994; Dr. h.c. (Fla. Int. Univ.) 1993; Biblioteca Breve Prize, Barcelona 1964, Guggenheim Fellowship Award 1970, Prix du Meilleur Livre Etranger, Paris 1971, Writer of the Year at Puterbaugh Conf., Univ. of Okla. 1987, Sancho IV Medal (Universidad Complutense, Madrid) 1993. *Publications:* Así en la paz como en la guerra (short stories) 1960, Un oficio del siglo XX (film criticism) 1963, Tres tristres tigres 1967 (novel), Vista del amancer en el trópico, O, Exorcismos de estilo 1976–77, Arcadia todas las noches 1978, La Habana para un infante difunto (novel) 1979, Holy Smoke: Smoking and the Cinema 1985, A Twentieth Century Job 1991, Mea Cuba 1992, Writes of Passage 1993, Delito por bailar el chachachá (short stories) 1995, Ella cantaba boleros (novellas) 1995, Cine o sardina (essays) 1997, Vidas para leerlas (biogs.) 1998, Todo está hecho con espejos (complete short stories) 1999, La ventana pineal (travel) 1999. *Leisure interest:* watching old and new movies and taping them. *Address:* 53 Gloucester Road, London, S.W.7, England. *Telephone:* 0171-589 4254. *Fax:* 0171-584 7370.

CACCIAVILLAN, Agostino, D.CN.L., D.C.L.; Italian ecclesiastic; b. 14 Aug. 1926, Novale; joined Holy See diplomatic service 1959, served in Philippines, Spain, Portugal; Head Documentation and Information Office, Secr. of State, Vatican City 1969–76; Apostolic Pro-Nuncio to Kenya, Apostolic Del. to Seychelles 1976–81; Apostolic Pro-Nuncio to India 1981–90, to Nepal 1985–90; Apostolic Pro-Nuncio to U.S.A., Perm. Observer to OAS 1990–. *Address:* Apostolic Nunciature, 3339 Massachusetts Avenue, N.W., Washington, DC 20008, U.S.A. *Telephone:* (202) 333-7121. *Fax:* (202) 337-4036.

CÁCERES CONTRERAS, Carlos; Chilean politician; b. 7 Oct. 1940, Valparaíso; m. Inés Consuelo Salarzano; three c.; ed. Colegio de los Sagrados Corazones, Valparaíso, Univ. Católica de Chile, Valparaíso, and Cornell Univ., Ithaca, N.Y.; Lecturer, Dept. of Econs. and Finance, Universidad Católica de Valparaíso School of Business Studies 1964, Head, Firms and Finances Dept. 1973; Visiting Lecturer, Ohio State Univ. 1971; mem. Council of State 1976; mem. Mont Pèlerin Soc. 1981; Pres. Banco Central de Chile 1982; mem. and founder, Inst. of Econ. Studies of Paris 1983; Minister of Finance 1983–84, of the Interior 1988–90.

CACHAREL, Jean, (pseudonym of Jean Léon Henri Bousquet); French politician and couturier; b. 29 March 1932, Nîmes; s. of Célestin Bousquet and Rosa Pyronnet; m. Dominique Sarrut 1965; one s. one d.; ed. Ecole Tech. de Nîmes; dress cutter, Jean Jourdan, Paris 1955–57; f. and Pres.-Dir.-Gen. Soc. Jean Cacharel 1964–, of subsidiaries abroad 1972–; Mayor of Nîmes 1983–95; Deputy from Gard (UDF), Assemblée Nat. 1986–97; mem. Radical Party 1993–; Oscar for export achievement 1969. *Leisure interests:* travel, football, golf, skiing. *Address:* Cacharel, 36 rue Tronchet, 75009 Paris, France.

CACOYANNIS, Michael, Greek film and stage director and actor; b. 11 June 1922, Limassol, Cyprus; s. of the late Sir Panayotis Cacoyannis and of Lady Cacoyannis; brother of Stella Soulioti (q.v.); ed. Greek Gymnasium, and London at Gray's Inn, Cen. School of Dramatic Art and Old Vic School; called to the Bar 1943; Producer for Overseas Service of BBC 1941–50; screen and stage producer 1950–; Hon. Doctorate (Columbia Coll., Chicago) 1981; Order of the Phoenix (Greece) 1965, Commdr. des Arts et des Lettres 1987. *Stage appearances include:* Wilde's Salomé as Herod 1947, in Camus's Caligula 1949, in Two Dozen Red Roses 1949, etc. *Directed films:* Windfall in Athens 1953, Stella 1955, A Girl in Black 1957, A Matter of Dignity 1958, Our Last Spring 1959, The Wastrel 1960, Electra 1961, Zorba the Greek 1964, The Day the Fish Came Out 1967, The Trojan Women 1971, The Story of Jacob and Joseph 1974, Attila 74 1975, Iphigenia 1977, Sweet Country

1986, Up, Down and Sideways 1992, The Cherry Orchard 1998; also a number of stage productions in Athens, New York, etc., including The Trojan Women, Paris 1965, 1995, The Devils, New York 1966, Mourning Becomes Electra, Metropolitan Opera, New York 1967, Romeo and Juliet, Paris 1968, Iphigenia in Aulis, New York 1968, La Bohème, New York 1972, King Oedipus, Dublin 1973, The Bacchae, Comédie Française, Paris 1977, Antony and Cleopatra, Athens 1979, The Bacchae, New York 1980, Zorba (musical), U.S.A. 1983, Sophocles' Electra, Epidaurus Festival 1983, Gluck's Iphigenia in Aulis and Iphigenia in Taulis, Frankfurt State Opera 1987, La Clemenza di Tito, Aix-en-Provence Music Festival 1988, Athens 1994, Cherubini's Medea, Athens 1995, The Trojan Women, Epidaurus 1997, Master Class, Athens 1998. *Publications:* translations into Greek of Shakespeare: Antony and Cleopatra 1980, Hamlet 1985, Coriolanus 1990, The Trojan Women 1995; into English: The Bacchae 1982, Collected Writings 1991, Stella (screenplay) 1991. *Address:* 15 Mouson Street, Athens 117-41, Greece. *Telephone:* 922-2054.

CADBURY, Sir (Nicholas) Dominic, Kt., M.B.A.; British business executive; b. 12 May 1940; s. of late Laurence John Cadbury and Joyce Cadbury (née Mathews); m. Cecilia Sarah Symes 1972; three d.; ed. Eton Coll., Trinity Coll. Cambridge, Stanford Univ. (U.S.A.); Chief Exec. Cadbury Schweppes PLC 1984–93, Chair. 1993–; Dir. Economist Group 1990–, Chair. 1994–; Jt. Deputy Chair. Guinness 1994–97, Deputy Chair. 1996– (Dir. 1991–); mem. Royal Mint Advisory Cttee. 1986–94, Pres.'s Cttee. CBI 1989–94, Food Asscn. 1989–, Stanford Advisory Council 1989–. *Leisure interests:* tennis, golf, shooting. *Address:* Cadbury Schweppes PLC, 25 Berkeley Square, London, W1X 6AT, England.

CADBURY-BROWN, Henry Thomas, O.B.E., T.D., R.A., F.R.I.B.A.; British architect; b. 20 May 1913; s. of Henry William Cadbury Brown and Marion Ethel Sewell; m. Elizabeth Romeyn Elwyn 1953; ed. Westminster School, Architectural Asscn. School of Architecture; pvt. practice since winning competitition for British Railway Branch Offices 1937; taught at Architectural Asscn. School 1946–49; Tutor, Royal Coll. of Art. 1952–61; architect in partnership with John Metcalfe 1962–84; Visiting Critic, School of Architecture, Harvard Univ. 1956; Prof. of Architecture, Royal Acad. 1975–88; mem. group partnership with Eric Lyons, Cunningham partnership for W. Chelsea redevt. for Royal Borough of Kensington and Chelsea; work includes: pavilions for "The Origins of the People", main concourse and fountain display, Festival of Britain; schools, housing, display and interiors; new civic centre, Gravesend; halls of residence, Birmingham Univ.; new premises for Royal Coll. of Art. (with Sir Hugh Casson (q.v.) and Prof. Robert Goodden); lecture halls, Univ. of Essex; mem. R.I.B.A. Council 1951–53, British Cttee. of Int. Union of Architects 1951–54, Modern Architectural Research group (MARS); Pres. Architectural Asscn. 1959–60; Hon. Fellow, R.C.A., Kent Inst. of Art and Design 1992. *Address:* 3 Church Walk, Aldeburgh, Suffolk, IP15 5DU, England. *Telephone:* (01728) 452591.

CADIEUX, Pierre H., B.A., LL.B., B.C.L.; Canadian politician and lawyer; b. 6 April 1948, Hudson, Quebec; s. of Antonio Cadieux and Thérèse Leduc; ed. Hudson, Collège de Valleyfield, Univ. of Montreal, McGill Univ.; Lawyer, mem. Quebec Bar Asscn., Canadian Bar Asscn., Montreal Estate Planning Council, Quebec Asscn. for Fiscal and Estate Planning; M.P. 1984–93; Minister of Labour 1986–89, for Indian Affairs and Northern Devt. 1989–90, Solicitor-Gen. for Canada 1990–91; Minister of State (Fitness Youth, Amateur Sport), Deputy Leader of the House 1991–93; now Vice-Pres. Housing Admin., Quebec; Progressive Conservative. *Address:* 1 Rue Notre-Dame Est, bureau 11.65, Montréal, Quebec, H2Y 1B6, Canada (Office).

CADOGAN, Sir John Ivan George, Kt., C.B.E., PH.D., F.R.S., F.R.S.E., C.CHEM., F.R.S.C.; British chemist; b. 1930, Pembrey, Carmarthen; s. of Alfred and Dilys Cadogan; m. 1st Margaret J. Evans 1955 (deceased 1992); one s. one d.; m. 2nd Elizabeth Purnell 1997; ed. Grammar School, Swansea, and King's Coll., London; research at King's Coll., London 1951–54; Civil Service Research Fellow 1954–56; Lecturer in Chem., King's Coll., London 1956–63; Purdie Prof. of Chem. and Head of Dept., St. Salvator's Coll., Univ. of St. Andrews 1963–69; Forbes Prof. of Organic Chem., Univ. of Edinburgh 1969–79; Chief Scientist, BP Research Centre 1979–81; Dir. of Research, British Petroleum 1981–92, C.E.O. BP Ventures 1988–92; Dir. Gen. Research Council 1994–99; Dir. BP Chemicals Int. Ltd., BP Venezuela Ltd.; Visiting Prof., Imperial Coll., London 1979–; Professorial Fellow, Univ. Coll. of Swansea, Univ. of Wales 1979–; mem. Council, Royal Inst. 1984–87, Royal Comm. on Criminal Justice 1991–93; Past Pres. Royal Soc. of Chemistry 1982–84; Gov. Jt. Research Centre, EC 1994–; mem. numerous scientific cttees. etc.; Hon. Fellow Royal Acad. of Eng. 1992; recipient of several prizes and 12 hon. degrees. *Publications:* about 300 papers in professional journals. *Leisure interest:* supporting rugby football. *Address:* Department of Chemistry, Imperial College of Science, Technology and Medicine, Prince Consort Road, London, SW7 2AY; Office of Science and Technology, Albany House, 94–98 Petty France, London SW1H 9ST, England. *Telephone:* 0171-594 5784 (Imperial Coll.); 0171-271 2030 (Office of Science and Tech.). *Fax:* 0171-271 2018.

CAGATAY, Mustafa; Cypriot politican; b. 20 April 1937, Limassol; s. of Ali Hasan and Fehime Ali; m. Tuncay Çağatay 1965; two s. one d.; ed. Nicosia Turkish Lycée; started Law Practice in Limassol 1963; elected dep. for Limassol, Turkish Communal Chamber 1970; elected mem. for Kyrenia, Legis. Assembly, Turkish Federated State of Cyprus 1976; Minister of Finance 1976, of Labour, Social Security and Health May–Dec. 1978; Prime Minister 1978–83; mem. Turkish Cypriot Cttee., Turkish and Greek Cypriot Talks on Humanitarian Issues 1974; mem. Nat. Unity Party. *Leisure interests:* reading, swimming, walking. *Address:* 6 D Kolordu Street, Kyrenia (Office); 60 Cumhuriyet Caddesi, Kyrenia, Cyprus (Home).

CAGE, Nicolas (pseudonym of Nicholas Coppola); American actor; b. 7 Jan. 1964, Long Beach, Calif.; nephew of Francis Ford Coppola (q.v.); m. Patricia Arquette (q.v.) 1995. *Films include:* Valley Girl 1983, Rumble Fish, Racing with the Moon, The Cotton Club, Birdy, The Boy in Blue, Raising Arizona, Peggy Sue Got Married, Moonstruck, Vampire's Kiss, Killing Time, The Short Cut, Queens Logic, Wild of Heart, Wings of the Apache, Zandalee, Red Rock West, Guarding Tess, Honeymoon in Vegas, It Could Happen to You, Kiss of Death, Leaving Las Vegas (Golden Globe Award for Best Actor 1996, Acad. Award for Best Actor 1996) 1996, The Rock 1996, The Funeral 1996, Con Air 1997, Face Off 1997, Eight Millimeter 1999. *Address:* Saturn Films, 9000 West Sunset Boulevard, Suite 911, West Hollywood, CA 90069, U.S.A.

CAGIATI, Andrea, LL.B.; Italian diplomatist; b. 11 July 1922, Rome; m. Sigrid von Morgen 1968; one s. one d.; ed. Univ. of Siena; entered Foreign Service 1948; Sec., Paris 1950–51; Prin. Private Sec. to Minister of State for Foreign Affairs 1951–53; Vice-Consul-Gen., New York 1953–55; Prin. Pvt. Sec. to Minister of State for Foreign Affairs, then with Dept. of Political Affairs 1955–57; Counsellor, Athens 1957–60, Mexico 1960–62; Del. Disarmament Cttee., Geneva March–Dec. 1962; mem. Italian del. to UN June 1962; Head NATO Dept. 1962–66; Minister-Counsellor, Madrid 1966–68; Amb. to Colombia 1968–71; Inst. for Diplomatic Studies 1971–72; Diplomatic Adviser to Prime Minister 1972–73; Amb. to Austria 1973–80, to U.K. 1980–86, to the Vatican 1986–88; Vice-Chair. Alitalia 1989–94 (Dir. 1987–94); Pres. Circolo Studi Diplomatici, Eurodéfence Italia; Vice-Pres. Fondazione De Gasperi; Hon. G.C.V.O. 1980. *Publications:* La Diplomazia 1945, Verso quale avvenire? 1957, I sentieri della vita 1990, Scritti di politica estera (3 vols.) 1991–93, and numerous articles on foreign policy and int. affairs. *Leisure interests:* sculpture, golf, shooting. *Address:* Largo Olgiata, 15 (49D), 00123 Rome, Italy. *Telephone:* (06) 30888135. *Fax:* (06) 30888135.

ÇAĞLAYANGIL, Ihsan Sabri; Turkish politician; b. 1908, Istanbul; s. of Saleri and Belkis Çağlayangil; m. Füruzende Çağlayangil 1933; one s. one d.; ed. School of Law, Istanbul; fmrly. with Ministry of Interior; Gov. of Antalya 1948–53; of Çannakale 1953–54, of Sivas 1954, of Bursa 1954–60; Senator for Bursa 1961; Minister of Labour Feb.-Oct. 1965, of Foreign Affairs 1965–71; Pres. Senate Foreign Affairs Cttee. 1972–79, of the Senate 1979; Minister of Foreign Affairs 1975–77, July–Dec. 1977; Acting Pres. of Turkey April–Sept. 1980; detained June–Sept. 1983, released 1983; Justice Party. *Address:* Şehit Ersan Caddesi 30/15, Çankaya, Ankara, Turkey. *Telephone:* 27-28 56.

CAHEN, Alfred; Belgian diplomatist; b. 28 Sept. 1929, Brussels; s. of Max Cahen and Rose Hazaert; m. Nicole Debeauvais 1961; one s. one d.; ed. Athénée Robert Catteau, Brussels and Université Libre de Bruxelles; Barrister at the Brussels Bar 1953–56; Attaché at Ministry of Foreign Affairs 1956; Attaché to Belgian Del. to OECD 1959–61; Sec. Embassy, Léopoldville, Congo (now Kinshasa, Zaire) 1962–64; Counsellor to Minister-Sec. of State for European Affairs in Brussels 1964–66; First Sec. to Belgian Del. to UN 1966–68; Asst. Chef de Cabinet to Minister for Foreign Trade 1968–70; Minister-Counsellor, Embassy, Kinshasa 1970–74; Minister-Counsellor, Embassy, Washington, D.C. 1974–77; Chef de Cabinet to Minister for Foreign Affairs 1977–79; Amb.-Political Dir., Ministry for Foreign Affairs, Foreign Trade and Devt. Co-operation 1979–85; Sec.-Gen. WEU 1985–89; Amb. to France 1989–96; Sec.-Gen. Atlantic Treaty Asscn. 1996–; Prof., Université Libre de Bruxelles 1980, Hon. Prof.; Chair. Study Centre on Int. Relations Univ. Libre de Bruxelles; Corresp. mem. Acad. des Sciences Morales et Politiques de l'Inst. de France, Acad. des Sciences d'Outre-mer de France; mem. Acad. Royale des Sciences d'Outre-Mer de Belgique; Hon. Prof., Nat. Inst. of Political Studies, Kinshasa; Medal for excellence in Int. Finance, School of Int. and Public Affairs, Columbia Univ., New York. *Publications:* numerous publs. on int. relations. *Leisure interest:* reading. *Address:* 10 rue Crevaux, 75116 Paris (Office); 37 square St. Charles, 75012 Paris, France; 10 rue du Magistrat, 1000 Bruxelles, Belgium (Homes). *Telephone:* (1) 45.53.28.80 (Office); (1) 43.45.42.40 (Home, Paris); (2) 647.96.33 (Home, Bruxelles). *Fax:* (1) 47.55.49.63 (Office).

CAHILL, Teresa Mary, L.R.A.M.; British opera and concert singer; b. 30 July 1944, Maidenhead, Berks.; d. of Henry D. Cahill and Florence Cahill née Dallimore; m. John A. Kiernander 1971 (divorced 1978); ed. Notre Dame High School, Southwark, Guildhall School of Music and Drama and London Opera Centre; debut at Glyndebourne 1969, Covent Garden 1970, La Scala, Milan 1976, Philadelphia Opera 1981; Prof. Royal Northern Coll. of Music, and Trinity Coll. of Music, London; Vocal Consultant Univ. of York; specializes in works of Mozart, Strauss, Mahler, Elgar and Tippett; has given concerts with all the London orchestras, Boston Symphony Orchestra, Chicago Symphony Orchestra, Berlin and Vienna Festivals, and throughout Europe, U.S.A. and the Far East; Master Classes, Dartington Festival 1984, 1986; Oxford Univ. 1995–96; recordings include works of Elgar, Strauss, Mahler; Worshipful Company of Musicians Silver Medal 1966, John Christie Award 1970. *Leisure interests:* cinema, theatre, travel, reading, and going to sales from car boots to Sothebys, photography. *Address:* 65 Leyland Road, London, SE12 8DW, England.

CAI QIJIAO; Chinese poet; b. 12 Dec. 1918, Jingjiang Cty., Fujian; s. of the late Cai Zhongsi and Chen Kuanzhi; m. Xu Jingci 1943; three s. one d.; ed. Shanghai Jinan Univ., Yan'an Lu Xun Art Coll.; participated in Dec. 9th Movement; studied in Literature Dept., Lu Xun Acad. of Literature and Art, Yan'an; army corresp., Zhangjiakou, after World War II; taught in N. China Univ.; Vice-Chair. Fujian Writers Asscn. 1959–; sent to Yong'an Mountain Area during Cultural Revolution 1969–76, returned to Fuzhou 1977. *Publications:* Prayer, Double Rainbows, Echoes 1957, A Continuation of Echoes 1958, Billow Voices, Prayer 1980, Double Rainbows, Fujian's Collections, Songs of Life 1982, Facing the Wind, Drunken Stone 1987, Translations of Sze Kungho's Poems, Selected Poems of Cai Qijiao (publ. Hong Kong) 1988, Selected Poems of Seven Chinese Poets 1993. *Leisure interests:* growing flowers, touring. *Address:* Fujian Writers Association, Fuzhou City, 350002 People's Republic of China.

CAI RUO-HONG; Chinese painter; b. 29 Jan. 1910, Jio Jang City; s. of Cai Yi-ting and Zhang Zhen-mai; m. Xia Lei 1939; three d.; ed. Art Coll. of Shanghai; caricaturist 1932–38; Prof. Lu Xun Art Inst., Yan-an 1939–45; Vice-Dir. of Art, Bureau of Ministry of Culture 1949–54; Deputy to 3rd NPC 1964–68, Deputy to 5th and 6th NPC 1978–88; Vice-Chair. Chinese Artists' Asscn. 1960–; Vice-Chair. Acad. of Chinese Painting 1981–83; mem. Standing Cttee. of China Fed. of Literary and Art Circles 1949–88. *Publications:* What Caused the Miserable Life? (album of paintings) 1954, Ruo-hong's Poems and Paintings (albums of poems) 1985, Collection of Art Theory of Cai Ruo-hong 1988, Collection of Poems of Cai Ruo-hong (Vol. II, Songs of Soul) 1997, The Ideal is More Perfect than Reality (theory of art) 1998, The Social Customs in the Small Attic in Shanghai (memoir) 1999. *Leisure interests:* reading, writing. *Address:* 9-2-2 Nan Sha Go, San Li He Street, Beijing, People's Republic of China. *Telephone:* 68523346.

CAI ZHENHUA; Chinese table tennis coach; b. 1961, Wuxi, Jiangsu Prov.; Chief Coach of Chinese Men's Table Tennis Team 1991–95; Head Coach of Chinese Table Tennis Team 1995–. *Address:* c/o State General Bureau for Physical Culture and Sports, 9 Tiyuguan Road, Chongwen District, Beijing, People's Republic of China.

CAI ZIMIN; Chinese politician; b. 1926, Zhanghua City, Taiwan Prov.; ed. in Japan; Chair. Taiwan Democratic Self-Govt. League 1988–97, Hon. Chair. 1997–; Adviser Asscn. for Relations across the Taiwan Straits (ARATS) 1991–; mem. 8th Standing Cttee. NPC 1993–98; Vice-Chair. Cttee. for Hong Kong, Macao, Taiwan and Overseas Chinese Affairs, 9th Nat. Cttee. of CPPCC 1998–. *Address:* c/o National Committee of Chinese People's Political Consultative Conference, 23 Taipingqiao Street, Beijing, People's Republic of China.

CAIN, Sir (Henry) Edney (Conrad), Kt., O.B.E.; Belizean diplomatist and chartered accountant; b. 2 Dec. 1924, Belize; s. of late Henry E. C. Cain and of Rhoda Stamp; m. Leonie E. Locke 1951; ed. St. George's and St. Michael's Colls. Belize and Balham and Tooting Coll. of Commerce, London; auditor, Audit Dept. Belize 1959; Asst. Accountant-Gen. Belize 1961, Accountant-Gen. 1963; Man. Dir. Monetary Authority of Belize 1976; Gov. Central Bank of Belize 1982–83, 1991; Amb. to U.S.A. 1983, to EC 1990–91; Financial Sec., Ministry of Finance 1985; High Commr. in U.K. 1987–90; now Chair. (non.-exec.) Bd. of Dirs Belize Bank Ltd; Dir. (non-exec.) BHI Corp. *Leisure interests:* music, travel. *Address:* 936 Orchid Gardens, P.O. Box 238, Belmopan, Belize. *Telephone:* 501-822 492.

CAIN, John, LL.B.; Australian politician; b. 26 April 1931; s. of late John Cain; m. Nancye Williams 1955; two s. one d.; ed. Northcote High School, Scotch Coll. and Melbourne Univ.; mem. Council Law Inst. of Vic. 1967–76, Exec. Law Council of Australia 1973–76; Vice-Chair. Vic. Br. Australian Labor Party 1973–75; Pres. Law Inst., Vic. 1972–73, Chair. Council 1971–72; mem. Legis. Ass. for Bundoora, Vic. 1976–92; Leader of Opposition 1981–82; Premier of Vic. 1982–90; Hon. Prof., Melbourne Univ. 1991–; Attorney-Gen. 1982–83; Minister for Fed. Affairs 1982, Minister for Women's Affairs 1982–90, for Ethnic Affairs 1990–; Treas. Law Inst., Vic. 1969–70; part-time mem. Law Reform Comm. of Australia 1975–77; mem. Commonwealth Observer Group, South African elections April 1994; Trustee, Melbourne Cricket Club 1982–; Trustee Nat. Tennis Centre 1990–94. *Leisure interests:* tennis, swimming, jogging. *Address:* 9 Magnolia Road, Ivanhoe, Vic. 3079, Australia.

CAINE, Marco, M.B., B.S., F.R.C.S., M.S., F.A.C.S.; British/Israeli urological surgeon; b. 23 May 1923, London; s. of Theodore Caine and Bella S. Federman; m. Deborah B. Binstock 1945; three s.; ed. St. Paul's School, London and St. Bartholomew's Hosp. Medical School, Univ. of London; Sr. Surgical Registrar, St. Paul's Hosp. London 1950–51; Research Asst. Inst. of Urology, Univ. of London 1951–52; Sr. Surgical Registrar, North Middx. Hosp. London 1953–59; Head, Dept. of Urology, Hadassah Univ. Hosp. Jerusalem 1959–88, Sr. Urological Surgeon 1988–; Emer. Prof. of Urology, Hebrew Univ. Jerusalem 1972–. *Publications:* The Pharmacology of the Urinary Tract 1984; book chapters and approximately 110 papers in int. scientific journals. *Leisure interests:* music, electronics. *Address:* Flat 19, 1 Itamar-Ben-Avi Street, Kiryat Shmuel, Jerusalem 92349, Israel. *Telephone:* 02-5617537. *Fax:* (02) 5617537.

CAINE, Michael, C.B.E.; British actor; b. (as Maurice Joseph Micklewhite) 14 March 1933, London; s. of late Maurice Joseph Micklewhite and of Ellen Frances Marie Micklewhite; m. 1st Patricia Haines 1954 (divorced); one d.; m. 2nd Shakira Khatoon Baksh 1973; one d.; ed. Wilson's Grammar School, Peckham; army service, Berlin and Korea 1951–53; worked at repertory theatres, Horsham and Lowestoft 1953–55; Theatre Workshop, London 1955; mem. IBA 1984–; Hon. Fellow (Univ. of London) 1994. *Acted in:* over 100 TV plays 1957–63; play: Next Time I'll Sing to You 1963; films: A Hill in Korea 1956, How to Murder a Rich Uncle 1958, Zulu 1964, The Ipcress File 1965, Alfie 1966, The Wrong Box 1966, Gambit 1966, Funeral in Berlin 1966, Billion Dollar Brain 1967, Woman Times Seven 1967, Deadfall 1967, The Magus 1968, Battle of Britain 1968, Play Dirty 1968, The Italian Job 1969, Too Late the Hero 1970, The Last Valley 1970, Kidnapped 1971, Pulp 1971, Get Carter 1971, Zee and Co. 1972, Sleuth 1973, The Black Windmill, The Marseilles Contract, Peeper, The Wilby Conspiracy 1974, Fat Chance, The Romantic Englishwoman, Harry and Walter Go to New York, The Eagle has Landed, The Man Who Would be King 1975, A Bridge Too Far, The Silver Bears 1976, The Swarm, California Suite 1977, Ashanti 1978, Beyond the Poseidon Adventure 1979, The Island 1979, Dressed to Kill 1979, Escape to Victory 1979, Deathtrap 1981, The Hand 1981, Educating Rita 1982, Jigsaw Man 1982, The Honorary Consul 1982, Blame it on Rio 1983, Water 1984, The Holcroft Covenant 1984, Sweet Liberty 1985, Mona Lisa 1985, The Whistle Blower 1985, Half Moon Street 1986, The Fourth Protocol 1986, Hannah and Her Sisters (Acad. Award for Best Supporting Actor) 1986, Surrender 1987, Without a Clue 1988, Jack the Ripper (TV mini-series) 1988 (Golden Globe Award), Dirty Rotten Scoundrels 1988, A Shock to the System 1989, Mr. Destiny 1989, Bullseye 1989, Noises Off 1991, Blue Ice 1992, The Muppet Christmas Carol 1992, On Deadly Ground 1993, World War 2—When Lions Roared (NBC TV) 1993, Bullet to Beijing 1994, Blood and Wine 1995, 20000 Leagues under the Sea 1996, Mandela and De Klerk 1996, Curtain Call, Shadowrun, Little Voice 1997, The Debtors 1998, The Cyber House Tree 1998. *Publications:* Michael Caine's File of Facts 1987, Not Many People Know This is 1988, What's It All About 1992, Acting in Film 1993. *Leisure interests:* gardening, reading. *Address:* c/o Duncan Heath, International Creative Management, Oxford House, 76 Oxford Road, London, W1R 1RB, England.

CAIO, Francesco; Italian business executive; fmrly with Omnitel Pronto Italia; Chief Exec. Olivetti and C. S.p.A., July–Sept. 1996. *Address:* c/o Olivetti & S.p.A., Via G. Jervis 77, 10015 Ivrea, Turin, Italy. *Telephone:* 125-522-428. *Fax:* 125-522-067.

CAIRD, Most Rev. Donald Arthur Richard, M.A., B.D., DIP.ED.; Irish ecclesiastic; b. 11 Dec. 1925, Dublin; s. of George R. Caird and Emily F. Dreaper; m. Nancy B. Sharpe 1963; one s. two d.; ed. Wesley Coll., Dublin Trinity Coll., Dublin and Univ. of Dublin; Curate-Asst. St. Mark's, Dundela, Belfast 1950–53, Asst. Master and Chaplain The Royal School, Portora 1953–57; Lecturer in Philosophy, Univ. of Wales 1957–60; Rector Rathmichael Parish, Co. Dublin 1960–69; Asst. Lecturer in Philosophy, Trinity Coll. Dublin 1962–63; Dean of Ossary, Kilkenny 1969–1970; Bishop of Limerick, Ardfert and Aghadoe 1970–76; of Meath and Kildare 1976–1985; Archbishop of Dublin, Primate of Ireland and Bishop of Glendalough 1985–96; Chair. Council Alexandra Coll. (Dublin); Chair. Church of Ireland Coll. of Educ.; mem. Bórd na Gaelge (Govt. Bd. for Irish Language); Patron Nat. Youth Council of Ireland; Fellow of St. Columba's Coll. (Dublin); Visiting Prof. of Anglican Studies, Gen. Theological Seminary, New York 1997; Hon. D.D. (Trinity Coll., Dublin) 1988; Hon. LL.D. (Nat. Univ. of Ireland) 1995; Sr. Exhibitioner, Foundation Scholar and Sr. Moderator, Univ. of Dublin. *Publication:* The Predicament of Natural Theology since the Criticism of Kant, in Directions 1970. *Leisure interests:* walking and swimming. *Address:* 3 Crofton Avenue, Dun Laoghaire, Co. Dublin, Ireland. *Telephone:* (01) 2807869. *Fax:* (01) 2301053.

CAIRNS, 6th Earl; **Simon Dallas Cairns,** C.B.E.; British businessman; b. 27 May 1939; s. of 5th Earl Cairns and Barbara Jeanne Harrisson; m. Amanda Mary Heathcoat Amory 1964; three s.; ed. Eton, Trinity Coll., Cambridge; Chair. Voluntary Service Overseas 1981–92 (Treas. 1974–81); mem. City Capital Markets Cttee. 1989–95; Dir. S.G. Warburg Group PLC (fmrly. Mercury Int. Group) 1985–95, Vice-Chair. 1987–91; Jt. Chair. S. G. Warburg and Co. 1987–95, C.E.O., Deputy Chair. 1991–95; Chair. Commonwealth Devt. Corpn. 1995–, BAT Industries 1996–98 (Deputy Chair. June–Dec. 1995); Chair. Allied Zurich 1998–, Vice-Chair. Zurich Allied 1998–, Zurich Financial Services 1998–; Chair. Commonwealth Business Council 1997–, Overseas Devt. Inst. 1994–; Receiver Gen. Duchy of Cornwall 1990–. *Address:* Bolehyde Manor, Allington, Nr. Chippenham, Wilts., SN14 6LW; 22 Arlington Street, London, SW1A 1RW, England. *Telephone:* 0171-317 3909.

CAIRNS, David Adam, M.A.; British journalist and musicologist; b. 8 June 1926, Loughton; s. of Sir Hugh and Barbara (née Smith) Cairns; m. Rosemary Goodwin 1959; three s.; ed. Winchester Coll., Univ. of Oxford, Princeton Univ.; Library Clerk, House of Commons 1951–53; critic, Record News 1954–56; mem. Editorial Staff, Times Educational Supplement 1955–58; music Critic, Spectator 1958–63, Evening Standard 1958–63; Asst. Music Critic, Financial Times 1963–67; Music Critic, New Statesman 1967–70; mem. staff, Philips Records, London 1968–70, Classic Programme Co-ordinator 1970–73; Asst. Music Critic, Sunday Times 1975–84, Music Critic 1985–; Visiting Prof. of Music, Univ. of Calif., Davis 1985; Leverhulme Research Fellow 1972–74; Chevalier, Ordre des Arts et des Lettres 1975, Officier 1991. *Publications:* The Memoirs of Hector Berlioz 1969 (editor and translator), Responses: Musical Essays and Reviews 1973, The Magic Flute,

Falstaff (co-author, ENO Opera Guides) 1981, 1982. *Leisure interests:* conducting, reading, walking, cinema, theatre, cricket. *Address:* c/o Sunday Times, 1 Virginia Street, London, E.1; 49 Amerland Road, London, SW18 1QA, England.

CAIRNS, H. Alan C., M.A., D.PHIL., F.R.S.C.; Canadian professor of political science; b. 2 March 1930, Galt, Ontario; s. of Hugh Cairns and Lily Cairns; m. Patricia Ruth Grady 1958; three d.; ed. Univ. of Toronto and Univ. of Oxford; Instructor Dept. of Political Science Univ. of British Columbia 1960–63, Asst. Prof. 1963–66, Assoc. Prof. 1966–70, Prof. 1971, Chair. Dept. 1973–80; Visiting Prof. Memorial Univ., Newfoundland 1970–71, of Canadian Studies Univ. of Edinburgh 1977–78, William Lyon Mackenzie King Visiting Prof. Harvard Univ. 1982–83; Brenda and David McLean Chair in Canadian Studies 1993; Dir. of Research (Insts.) Royal Comm. on Econ. Union and Devt. Prospects for Canada 1983–85; Queen's Silver Jubilee Medal 1977; Canada Council 25th Anniversary Molson Prize 1982. *Publications:* Prelude to Imperialism 1965, Constitution, Citizenship and Society (ed. with Cynthia Williams) 1986, The Politics of Gender, Ethnicity and Language in Canada (ed. with Cynthia Williams) 1986, Constitution, Government and Society in Canada: Selected Essays 1988, Disruptions: Constitutional Struggles from the Charter to Meech Lake 1991, Charter versus Federalism: The Dilemmas of Constitutional Reform 1992; many articles. *Leisure interests:* golf, theatre, swimming. *Address:* Apt. 2, 5600 Dalhousie Road, Vancouver, B.C., V6T 1W4, Canada (Home).

CAIRNS, Hugh John Forster, D.M., F.R.S.; British professor of microbiology; b. 21 Nov. 1922; m. Elspeth Mary Forster 1948; two s. one d.; ed. Univ. of Oxford; Registrar, Radcliffe Infirmary, Oxford 1945; Intern, Postgraduate Medical School, London 1946; Paediatric Intern, Royal Victoria Infirmary, Newcastle 1947; Chemical Pathologist, Radcliffe Infirmary 1947–49; Virologist, Hall Inst. Melbourne 1950–51; Virus Research Inst. Entebbe, Uganda 1952–54; Research Fellow, then Reader, Australian Nat. Univ. Canberra 1955–63; Dir. Cold Spring Harbor Lab. of Quantitative Biol. 1963–68, staff mem. 1968–; Hon. Prof. of Biology, State Univ. of N.Y. Stony Brook 1968–73; Head, Imperial Cancer Research Fund Mill Hill Labs. 1973–80; Prof. of Microbiology, Harvard School of Public Health 1980–91. *Address:* Holly Grove House, Wilcote, Chipping Norton, Oxon., OX7 3EA, England. *Telephone:* (01993) 868706.

CALABRESI, Guido, M.A., B.S., LL.B.; American judge and professor of law; b. 18 Oct. 1932, Milan, Italy; s. of Massimo Calabresi and Bianca Maria Finzi-Contini Calabresi; m. Anne Gordon Audubon Tyler 1961; one s. two d.; ed. Yale Coll., Magdalen Coll., Oxford and Yale Law School; Asst. Instr. Dept. of Econs. Yale Coll. 1955–56; Thacher & Bartlett (law firm), New York 1957; mem. Conn. Bar 1958; law clerk to Mr Justice Hugo Black, U.S. Supreme Court 1958–59; Asst. Prof. of Law, Yale Univ. School of Law 1959–61; Assoc. Prof. Yale Law School 1961–62, Prof. of Law 1962–70; John Thomas Smith Prof. of Law, Yale Univ. 1970–78, Sterling Prof. of Law 1978–95, Sterling Prof. of Law Emer. 1995–, Dean Yale Univ. Law School 1985–94; Judge, U.S. Court of Appeals (Second Circuit) 1995–; Visiting Prof. at Univs. in U.S.A. and abroad; mem. various comms., cttees. etc.; mem. Inst. of Medicine, N.A.S.; numerous hon. degrees. *Publications:* The Costs of Accidents: A Legal and Economic Analysis 1970, Tragic Choices (with P. Bobbit) 1978, A Common Law for the Age of Statutes 1982, Ideals, Beliefs, Attitudes and the Law: Private Law Perspectives on a Public Law Problem 1985. *Leisure interests:* walking, reading (especially history), gardening, travel, bridge. *Address:* United States Court of Appeals for the Second Circuit, 157 Church Street, New Haven, CT 06510 (Office); 639 Amity Road, Woodbridge, CT 06525, U.S.A. Home. *Telephone:* (203) 773-2291 (Office). *Fax:* (203) 773-2401 (Office).

CALAMIA, Pietro, D.POL.SC.; Italian diplomatist; b. 1930, Campi Salentina, Lecce; m. Marie Diane Fenelon 1956; two c.; ed. Univ. of Florence; entered Diplomatic Service 1955; various posts Rome, France, Austria, then Counsellor, Perm. Representation to EEC, Brussels; Co-ordinator for European Affairs, Rome 1973–78; Deputy Perm. Rep. to EEC, Brussels, 1978–80, Amb., Perm. Rep. 1984–90; Amb. to Yugoslavia 1980–84; Dir.-Gen. Social Affairs (emigration/immigration) 1990–93; Amb. to OECD, Paris 1993; several foreign honours. *Leisure interest:* art collecting. *Address:* c/o Ministry of Foreign Affairs, Piazzale della Farnesina 1, 00194 Rome, Italy.

CALCUTT, Sir David Charles, Kt., Q.C., M.A., LL.B., MUS.B., F.R.C.M.; British barrister; b. 2 Nov. 1930; s. of Henry Calcutt; m. Barbara Walker 1969; ed. Christ Church Oxford (chorister), Cranleigh School (music scholar), King's Coll. Cambridge (choral scholar, Stewart of Rannoch Scholar 1952); called to Bar, Middle Temple 1955 (Bencher 1981); Harmsworth Law Scholar 1956; Deputy Chair. Somerset Quarter Sessions 1970–71; a Recorder 1972–89; Fellow Commoner, Magdalene Coll. Cambridge 1980–85, Master 1986–94, Hon. Fellow 1994–; a Judge of the Courts of Appeal of Jersey and Guernsey 1978–; Chair. Civil Service Arbitration Tribunal 1979–94; Deputy Pres., Lloyd's of London Appeal Tribunal 1983–87, Pres. 1987–97; Chair. Inst. of Actuaries' Appeal Bd. 1985–94; Chair. Council of the Banking Ombudsman 1994–; conducted Falkland Islands Comm. of Inquiry 1984, Cyprus Servicemen Inquiry 1985–86, Review of Press Self-Regulation 1992–93; Chair. City Panel on Takeovers and Mergers 1989–; Chair Council of the Banking Ombudsman 1994–; mem. Criminal Injuries Compensation Bd. 1977–, Council on Tribunals 1980–86, Colliery Independent Review Body 1985–88; mem. Gen. Council of the Bar 1968–72, Senate of the Inns of Court and the Bar 1979–85, Chair. of the Senate 1984–85, Chair. of the Bar 1984–85; mem. U.K. Del., Consultative Cttee., Bars and Law Socs., EEC 1979–83, Interception of Communications Tribunal 1986– (Pres. 1996–); Chancellor of Dioceses of Exeter and Bristol 1971–, and of Gibraltar in Europe 1983–; Arbitrator Int. Centre for Settlement of Investment Disputes, Washington D.C. 1986–92; Ind. mem. Diplomatic Service Appeal Bd. 1986–92; Home Office and Ministry of Defence Assessor of Compensations for Miscarriages of Justice 1989–; Deputy Chair. RCM 1988–90; Chair. Cttee. on Privacy and Related Matters 1989–90; Fellow Winchester Coll. 1992–; Hon. mem. American Bar Asscn., Canadian Bar Asscn.; Hon. LL.D. (Exeter), (Staffs.) 1997. *Leisure interest:* hill-farming on Exmoor. *Address:* 35 Essex Street, Temple, London, WC2R 3AR, England. *Telephone:* 0171-353 6381.

CALDECOTE, 2nd Viscount, cr. 1939, of Bristol; **Robert Andrew Inskip,** K.B.E., D.S.C., D.L., M.A., F.ENG.; British chartered engineer and business executive; b. 8 Oct. 1917, London; s. of Thomas Walker Hobart Inskip, 1st Viscount Caldecote, and Lady Augusta, widow of Charles Orr Ewing; m. Jean Hamilla Hamilton 1942; one s. two d.; ed. Eton and King's Coll., Cambridge; R.N.V.R. 1939–45; Royal Naval Coll., Greenwich 1946–47; Asst. Man. Vickers-Armstrong Naval Yard, Walker-on-Tyne 1947–48; Fellow, King's Coll., Cambridge, and Lecturer, Engineering Dept., Cambridge Univ. 1948–55; Man. Dir. English Electric Aviation 1960–63; Deputy Man. Dir. British Aircraft Corpn. 1961–67; Dir. English Electric Co. 1953–69, D. Napier and Son Ltd. 1959–69, British Aircraft Corpn. (Holdings) 1960–69, Marconi Int. Marine Co. Ltd. 1960–71, Delta Group PLC 1969–82 (Chair. 1972–82); Dir. Consolidated Gold Fields Ltd. 1969–79, Cincinnati Milacron Ltd. 1969–75, Lloyds Bank Ltd. 1975–88, Lloyds Bank Int. Ltd. 1979–85; Chair. Legal and Gen. Group Ltd. 1977–80, Investors in Industry Group (3i) PLC 1980–87; Vice-Pres. Eng. Employers' Fed. 1980–83; Dir. Equity Capital for Industry 1980–86; mem. U.K. del to UN 1952; Bd. British Rail 1979–85; Chair. The Design Council 1972–80; Pres. Soc. of British Aerospace Companies 1965–66, Parl. and Scientific Cttee. 1966–69, Asscn. Int. des Constructeurs de Matériel Aérospatial (AICMA) 1966–68, Australian-British Trade Asscn. 1973–78, Fellowship of Eng. 1981–86; Pres. Royal Inst. of Naval Architects 1986–89; Chair. Econ. Devt. Cttee. for the Movement of Exports 1965–72; mem. Review Bd. for Govt. Contracts 1969–76, Inflation Accounting Cttee. 1975–76, Eng. Industries Council 1975–82, British North American Cttee. 1980–88, Advisory Council for Applied Research and Devt. 1981–84, Eng. Council 1982–85; Chair. Export Council for Europe 1970–71; Chair. Gen. Advisory Council, BBC Nov. 1982–85, Mary Rose Trust 1983–92; Pres. Dean Close School 1960–90; Chair. Industry Ventures Ltd. 1989–93, Crown Appointments Comm. 1990; Pro-Chancellor Cranfield Inst. of Tech. 1976–84; Dir. W. S. Atkins Ltd 1985–92; Hon. F.I.Mech.E., Hon. F.I.C.E., Hon. F.I.E.E.; Hon. D.Sc. (Cranfield Inst. of Tech., Aston, Bristol, City), Hon. LL.D. (London, Cambridge). *Leisure interests:* sailing, shooting, golf. *Address:* Orchard Cottage, South Harting, Petersfield, Hants., GU31 5NR, England (Home). *Telephone:* Harting (01730) 825529 (Home). *Fax:* (01730) 825763.

CALDER, Elizabeth Nicole, B.A.; British publisher; b. 20 Jan. 1938; d. of Ivor George and Florence Mary Baber; m. Richard Henry Calder 1958 (divorced 1972); one s. one d.; ed. Palmerston North Girls' High School, N.Z. and Univ. of Canterbury, N.Z.; reader Metro-Goldwyn-Mayer Story Dept. 1969–70; Publicity Man. Victor Gollancz 1971–74, Editorial Dir. 1975–78; Editorial Dir. Jonathan Cape 1979–86; Publishing Dir. Bloomsbury Publishing 1986–. *Leisure interests:* junking, thinking about gardening, reading. *Address:* Bloomsbury Publishing, 38 Soho Square, London, W1V 5DF, England. *Telephone:* 0171-494 2111.

CALDER, John Mackenzie; British publisher, critic and playwright; b. 25 Jan. 1927; m. 1st Mary A. Simmonds 1949; one d.; m. 2nd Bettina Jonic 1960 (dissolved 1975); one d.; ed. Gilling Castle, Yorks., Bishops Coll. School, Canada, McGill Univ., Montreal, Sir George Williams Coll. and Univ. of Zürich, Switzerland; f. and Man. Dir. John Calder (Publishers) Ltd. 1950–91, Calder Publs. Ltd. 1991–, Calder and Boyars Ltd. 1964–75; expanded to Edinburgh 1971; organized literature confs., Edinburgh Festival 1962, 1963, Harrogate Festival 1969; f. Ledlanet Nights (music and opera festival) Kinross-shire 1963–74; Pres. Riverrun Press Inc., New York 1978–; Prof. of Literature and Philosophy, Ecole Active Bilingue, Paris 1994–96; lecturer in History, Univ. of Paris-Nanterre 1995; acquired book-selling business of Better Books, London 1969; Chair. North American Book Clubs 1982–, Fed. of Scottish Theatres 1972–74; co-founder, Defence of Literature and the Arts Soc.; dir. of other cos. assoc. with opera, publishing etc.; Chevalier des Arts et des Lettres, Officier et Chevalier Ordre nat. du Mérite. *Publications:* A Samuel Beckett Reader, The Burroughs Reader 1981, New Beckett Reader 1983, Henry Miller Reader 1985, Nouveau Roman Reader 1986, The Defence of Literature 1991, The Garden of Eros 1992, The Philosophy of Samuel Beckett 1998. *Leisure interests:* writing, reading, chess, conversation, travelling, promoting good causes, good food and wine. *Address:* Calder Publications Ltd., 126 Cornwall Road, London, SE1 8TQ; Calder Educational Trust, 126 Cornwall Road, London, SE1 8TQ, England; Riverrun Press Inc., 1170 Broadway, Room 807, NY 10001, U.S.A.; Association Calder, 9 rue de Romainville, 93100 Montreuil, France. *Telephone:* (212) 889-6850 (U.S.A.); (1) 49.88.75.12 (France). *Fax:* (1) 48.59.66.68 (France).

CALDERA RODRÍGUEZ, Rafael; Venezuelan politician and lawyer; b. 24 Jan. 1916, San Felipe, Yaracuy; s. of Dr. Rafael and Rosa Sofia R. Caldera; m. Alicia P. Caldera 1941; three s. three d.; Sec., Cen. Council of Soc. of Venezuelan Catholic Youth 1932–34; founded U.N.E. (Nat. Union of Students) 1936; graduated as lawyer 1939; founded Acción Nacional 1942; mem. Chamber of Deputies 1942; unsuccessful Pres. Candidate for Partido Social-Cristiano (COPEI) 1947; Fellow of Acad. of Political and Social Sciences 1952, 1983; unsuccessful COPEI Pres. Candidate 1958; Pres. of Chamber of Deputies 1959–61; unsuccessful COPEI Pres. Candidate 1963, 1986; Pres. of Dem. Christian Org. of America (ODCA) 1964–69; Pres. of Venezuela 1969–74, 1994–99; Senator-for-life 1974; Pres. of Inter-Parliamentary Council 1980–83; Prof. Emer. of Sociology and Labour Jurisprudence, Univ. Cen. de Venezuela; Fellow of Venezuelan Acad. of Languages; mem. many Venezuelan and Latin American Insts. of Political Science, Spanish Language and Sociology; Dr. h.c. from more than 20 American and European univs.; numerous decorations. *Publications:* essays on legal matters, sociology and politics. *Address:* c/o Central Information Office of the Presidency, Palacio de Miraflores, Avenida Urdaneta, Caracas 1010, Venezuela. *Telephone:* (2) 81-0811.

CALDERON FOURNIER, Rafael Angel; Costa Rican politician; b. 1949, Nicaragua; s. of fmr. Pres. Rafael Calderon Guardia; lawyer; Minister of Foreign Affairs 1978–82; cand. for Pres., Social Christian Unity Party 1982, 1986, 1989; Pres. of Costa Rica 1990–94. *Address:* c/o Partido Unidad Social Cristiana, San José, Costa Rica.

CALDERON SOL, Armando; Salvadorean politician; Leader Alianza Republicana Nacionalista (ARENA); Pres. of El Salvador June 1994–. *Address:* Ministry for the Presidency, Avda. Cuba, Calle Darió González 806, Barrio San Jacinto, San Salvador, El Salvador. *Telephone:* 221-8483. *Fax:* 771-0950.

CALDICOTT, Dame Fiona, D.B.E., M.A., B.M., B.CH., F.R.C.P., F.R.C.PSYCH., F.R.C.P.I.; British psychiatrist; b. 12 Jan. 1941; d. of Joseph Maurice Soesan and Elizabeth Jane Ransley; m. Robert Gordon Woodruff Caldicott 1965; one d. (one s. deceased); ed. City of London School for Girls, Oxford Univ.; House Surgeon and Physician, Coventry Hosps. 1966–67; G.P., Family Planning and Child Welfare 1968–70; training in psychiatry 1970–76; Sr. Registrar in Psychiatry, W. Midlands Regional Training Scheme 1977–79; Consultant Psychiatrist, Univ. of Warwick 1979–85; consultant Psychotherapist Uffculme Clinic, Birmingham 1979–96; Sr. Clinical Lecturer in Psychotherapy, Univ. of Birmingham 1982–96; Unit Gen. Man., Mental Health, Central Birmingham 1989–91; Clinical Dir. Adult Psychiatric and Psychotherapy Service, Mental Health Unit, S. Birmingham 1991–94; Medical Dir. S. Birmingham Mental Health N.H.S. Trust 1994–96; mem. Sec. of State's Standing Advisory Cttee. on Medical Manpower Planning 1991–, on Post-grad. Medical Ed. 1993–; Chair. Monospecialist Cttee. for Psychiatry 1995– (Sec. 1991–95); Sec. European Bd. of Psychiatry 1992–; Sub-Dean Royal Coll. of Psychiatrists 1987–90, Dean 1990–93, Pres. 1993–96; Chair. Conf. of Medical Royal Colls. 1995–96; Prin. Somerville Coll. Oxford 1996–; mem. Union of European Medical Specialists, Broadcasting Standards Council 1996–, Czech Psychiatric Soc. 1994; Fellow Acad. of Medicine, Singapore 1994; Chevalier du Tastevin 1991. *Publications:* contrib. to Discussing Doctors' Careers (ed. Isobel Allen) 1988; papers in learned journals on psychiatry. *Leisure interests:* family, friends, reading, theatre, wine. *Address:* Somerville College, Oxford, OX2 6HD (Office); The Old Rectory, Manor Farm Lane, Balscote, Banbury, OX15 6JJ, England (Home). *Telephone:* (01295) 730293 (Home). *Fax:* (01295) 730293 (Home).

CALDWELL, John Bernard, O.B.E., PH.D., D.SC., F.ENG., F.R.I.N.A.; British professor of naval architecture; b. 26 Sept. 1926, Northampton; s. of John R. Caldwell and Doris (Bolland) Caldwell; m. Jean M. F. Duddridge 1955; two s.; ed. Bootham School, York and Univs. of Liverpool and Bristol; Prin. Scientific Officer, R.N. Scientific Service 1957–60; Asst. Prof. R.N. Coll., Greenwich 1960–66; Visiting Prof. M.I.T. 1962–63; Prof. of Naval Architecture, Univ. of Newcastle-upon-Tyne 1966–91, Emer. Prof. 1991–, Head, Dept. of Naval Architecture 1966–83, Head, School of Marine Tech. 1975–80, 1986–88, Dean, Faculty of Eng. 1983–86; Pres. Royal Inst. of Naval Architects 1984–87; Dir. Nat. Maritime Inst. Ltd. 1983–85, Marine Design Consultants Ltd. 1985–89, Marine Tech. Directorate 1986–90; mem. Eng. Council 1988–94; Gold Medal of N.E.C.I.S. 1973, Froude Medal of R.I.N.A. 1984, David Taylor Medal of S.N.A.M.E. (U.S.A.) 1987, Pres.'s Award of Eng. Council 1995. *Publications:* over 70 papers in various eng. and scientific publs. *Leisure interests:* music, walking, reading. *Address:* Barkbooth, Winster, Windermere, Cumbria, LA23 3NZ, England. *Telephone:* (015395) 68222.

CALDWELL, Philip, M.B.A.; American motor manufacturing executive; b. 27 Jan. 1920, Bourneville, Ohio; s. of Robert Clyde Caldwell and Wilhelmina (née Hemphill) Caldwell; m. Betsey Chinn Clark 1945; one s. two d.; ed. Muskingum Coll. and Harvard Univ.; served U.S. Navy, later Lieut. 1942–46; Navy Dept. 1946–53, Deputy Dir. of Procurement Policy Div. 1948–53; joined Ford Motor Co. 1953, Vice-Pres. 1968–73, Dir. 1973–90; Gen. Man. Truck Operations 1968–70; Pres. and Dir. Philco-Ford Corpn. 1970–71; Vice-Pres. of Mfg. Group 1971–72; Chair., C.E.O. and Dir. Ford Europe Inc. 1972–73; Exec. Vice-Pres. with responsiblity for int. automotive operations 1973–77, Vice-Chair. and Deputy C.E.O. 1978–79, Pres. of Ford Motor Co. 1978–80, C.E.O. 1979–85, Chair. 1980–85; also Dir. of Ford Latin America 1973–85, Ford Asia-Pacific Inc. 1973–85, Ford of Europe 1972–85, Ford Motor Credit Co. 1977–85, Ford of Canada 1977–85, Ford Mid-East and Africa Inc. 1973–85, Chase Manhatten Corpn., Chase Manhattan Bank N.A. 1982–85, Digital Equipment Corpn., Kellogg Co., Federated Dept. Stores Inc. 1984–88, Zurich Holding Co. America, Russell Reynold Assocs. Inc.; Sr. Man. Dir. Shearson Lehman Bros. Inc. 1985–; mem. Int. Advisory Cttee., Chase Manhattan Bank 1979–85, Business-Higher Educ. Forum, numerous cttees. bds. and forums; Trustee, Cttee. for Econ. Devt., Muskingum Coll. Policy Comm. Business Roundtable 1980–85; Dir. Harvard Business School Assocs 1977–93, INSEAD Int. Council 1978–81; Sec. Motor Vehicle Mfrs.' Asscn.; Dir. Detroit Symphony Orchestra; Meritorious civilian service award, U.S. Navy 1953, 1st William A. Jump memorial award 1950, Golden Plate Award, American Acad. of Achievement 1984 and several other awards; Hon. D.H. (Muskingum Coll.) 1974; Hon. D.B.A. (Upper Iowa) 1978; Hon. LL.D. (Boston Univ. 1979, Eastern Mich. Univ. 1979, Miami Univ. 1980, Davidson Coll. 1982, Lawrence Inst. of Tech. 1984, Ohio Univ. 1984). *Address:* Shearson Lehman Brothers Inc., 3 World Finance Center, American Express Tower, 200 Vesey Street, New York, NY 10285, U.S.A. (Office).

ČALFA, Marián, DR. IUR.; Czech politician and lawyer; b. 1946, Trebisov, Slovakia; m. Jiřina Čalfová; two d.; studied law in Prague, subsequently worked in legal and admin. depts. of official press agency CTK; Minister without portfolio 1988–89; resgnd. from CP of Czechoslovakia; Prime Minister of Czechoslovakia 1989–92; Chair. State Defence Council 1990–92; Deputy to House of Nations of Fed. Ass. CSFR 1990–92; official, Fed. Govt. of CSFR July–Oct. 1992; Deputy Chair. Civic Democratic Union—Public Against Violence 1991–92; Co-founder CTL Consulting, Prague 1992–95, Čalfa, Bartošík a partneři, Prague 1995–; Ed.-in-Chief Legal Adviser 1993–; Grand Cross of the Order of the Crown, Belgium 1990. *Address:* Čalfa, Bartošík a Partneři, právní kancelář Přemyslovská 28, 130 00 Prague 3, Czech Republic.

CALIFANO, Joseph Anthony, Jr., A.B., LL.B.; American lawyer, government official and writer; b. 15 May 1931, Brooklyn, New York; s. of Joseph A. Califano and Katherine Gill Califano; m. 2nd Hilary Paley Byers 1983; two s. one d. from previous marriage; one step-s. one step-d.; ed. Holy Cross Coll. and Harvard Univ.; admitted to New York Bar 1955; U.S.N.R. 1955–58; with firm Dewey Ballantine, Bushby, Palmer Wood, New York 1958–61; Special Asst. to Gen. Counsel, Dept. of Defense 1961–62; Special Asst. to Sec. of Army 1962–63; Gen. Counsel, Dept. of Army 1963–64; Special Asst. to Sec. and Deputy Sec. of Defense 1964–65; Special Asst. to Pres. 1965–69; Sec. of Health, Educ. and Welfare 1977–79; Special Counsel to House of Reps. Cttee. on Standards of Official Conduct 1982–83; admitted to U.S. District Court; U.S. Court of Appeals for 2nd Circuit; U.S. Supreme Court Bar 1966; mem. Fed. Bar Asscn., American Bar Asscn., American Judicature Soc.; mem. firm Arnold & Porter 1969–71, Williams, Connolly & Califano 1971–77, Califano, Ross & Heineman 1980–82, Dewey, Ballantine, Bushby, Palmer & Wood 1983–92; General Counsel, Democratic Nat. Cttee. 1971–72; Prof. of Public Health Policy, Schools of Medicine and Public Health, Columbia Univ. 1992–; Chair. Columbia Univ. Center on Addiction and Substance Abuse 1992–; mem. Democratic Party's Nat. Charter Comm. 1972–74; Chair. Inst. for Social Policy in the Middle East, Kennedy School of Govt., Harvard Univ.; mem. Bd. of Dirs. Chrysler Corpn., Primerica Corpn., Automatic Data Processing Inc., KMart Corpn.; Trustee, New York Univ., Kaiser Family Foundation, Urban Inst., Georgetown Univ.; Distinguished Civilian Service Medal, Dept. of Army 1964, Dept. of Defense 1968; Man of Year Award, Justinian Soc. Lawyers 1966; hon. degrees from Coll. of Holy Cross, Coll. of New Rochelle, Univ. of Michigan, Davis and Elkins Coll., Howard Univ., Univ. of Notre Dame, City Coll., New York. *Publications:* The Student Revolution, A Global Confrontation 1969, A Presidential Nation 1975, The Media and the Law (with Howard Simons) 1976, The Media and Business (with Howard Simons) 1978, Governing America: An Insider's Report from the White House and the Cabinet 1981, Report on Drug Abuse and Alcoholism 1982, America's Health Care Revolution: Who Lives? Who Dies? Who Pays? 1985; numerous articles for various newspapers and other publications. *Leisure interest:* jogging. *Address:* c/o School of Public Health, University of Columbia, Morningside Heights, New York, NY 10027, U.S.A.

CALISHER, Hortense, A.B.; American author; b. 20 Dec. 1911, New York; d. of Joseph H. Calisher and Hedwig (Lichtstern) Calisher; m. 1st. Heaton Bennet Heffelfiner 1935; one s. one d.; m. 2nd Curtis Harnack 1959; ed. Barnard Coll., New York; Adjunct Prof. of English, Barnard Coll. 1956–57; Visiting Lecturer, State Univ. of Iowa 1957, 1959–60, Stanford Univ. 1958, Sarah Lawrence Coll. Bronxville, New York 1962, 1967; Adjunct Prof. Columbia Univ., New York 1968–70, City Coll. of New York 1969; Visiting Prof. of Literature, Brandeis Univ. 1963–64, Univ. of Pa. 1965, State Univ. of New York, Purchase 1971–72; Regent's Prof. Univ. of Calif. 1976; Visiting Prof. Bennington Coll. 1978, Washington Univ., St. Louis 1979, Brown Univ. 1986; Guggenheim Fellow 1952, 1955; mem. American Acad. and Inst. Arts and Letters (Pres. 1987–90); American PEN (Pres. 1986–87); Acad. of Arts and Letters Award 1967; Nat. Council Arts Award 1967; Hon. Litt.D. (Skidmore Coll.) 1980, Hon. LL.D. (Grinnell) 1986; Kafka Prize for The Bobby Soxer, Nat. Endowment for the Arts Award For Lifetime Achievement 1988. *Publications:* In the Absence of Angels (short stories) 1951, False Entry (novel) 1961, Tale for the Mirror (short stories) 1962, Textures of Life (novel) 1963, Extreme Magic (short stories) 1964, Journal from Ellipsia (novel) 1965, The Railway Police and The Last Trolley Ride (two novellas) 1966, The New Yorkers (novel) 1966, Queenie (novel) 1971, Standard Dreaming (novel) 1972, Herself (autobiog.) 1972, Eagle Eye (novel) 1973, On Keeping Women (novel) 1977, Mysteries of Motion (novel) 1983, Saratoga, Hot 1985 (short fiction), The Bobby Soxer (novel) 1986, Age (novel) 1987,

Kissing Cousins 1988 (memoir), The Small Bang (novel) (under pseudonym Jack Fenno) 1992, In the Palace of the Movie King (novel) 1993, In the Slammer with Carol Smith 1996; several novellas and volumes of short stories, articles and reviews etc. *Leisure interests:* the other arts. *Address:* c/o Marion Boyars Publishers, 237 East 39th Street, New York, NY 10016, U.S.A.

CALLADINE, Christopher Reuben, SC.D., F.R.S., F.ENG.; British professor of structural mechanics; b. 19 Jan. 1935, Derby; s. of Reuben Calladine and Mabel (née Boam) Calladine; m. Mary Ruth Howard Webb 1964; two s. one d.; ed. Nottingham High School, Peterhouse, Cambridge, Massachusetts Inst. of Tech., U.S.A.; lecturer, Dept. of Eng., Cambridge Univ. 1963–79, Reader 1979–86, Prof. of Structural Mechanics 1986–, Fellow Peterhouse 1960–92, Sr. Fellow 1992–; Ludwig Mond Prize, Inst. of Mechanical Engineers 1966. *Publications:* Engineering Plasticity 1969, Theory of Shell Structures 1986, Understanding DNA (with H. R. Drew) 1992; many articles in eng. and biological journals. *Leisure interests:* make do and mend. *Address:* Department of Engineering, University of Cambridge, Cambridge, CB2 1PZ; 25 Almoners Avenue, Cambridge, CB1 4NZ, England. *Telephone:* (01223) 332725. *Fax:* (01223) 332662.

CALLAGHAN OF CARDIFF, Baron (Life Peer) cr. 1987, of the City of Cardiff in the County of South Glamorgan; **(Leonard) James Callaghan,** K.G., P.C.; British politician; b. 27 March 1912, Portsmouth; m. Audrey Elizabeth Moulton 1938; one s. two d.; ed. Portsmouth Northern Secondary School; Tax Officer 1929; Asst. Sec. Inland Revenue Staff Asscn. 1936–47; service in Royal Navy 1942–45; M.P. 1945–87; Parl. Sec. Ministry of Transport 1947–50; Parl. and Financial Sec., Admiralty 1950–51; Chancellor of the Exchequer 1964–67; Home Sec. 1967–70; Sec. of State for Foreign and Commonwealth Affairs 1974–76; Leader of Parl. Labour Party 1976–80; Prime Minister 1976–79; Leader of the Opposition 1979–80; mem. Consultative Assembly, Council of Europe 1948–50, 1954; Chair. Co-ordinating Advisory Cttee. on Protection of the Sea 1953–64; Consultant to Police Fed. 1955–64; mem. Nat. Exec. Cttee. Labour Party 1957–80; Treas. Labour Party 1967–76, Chair. 1973–74; Hon. Life Fellow, Nuffield Coll., Oxford 1967; Hon. Fellow (Univ. Coll. Cardiff—now Cardiff Univ.) 1978, (Portsmouth Polytechnic—now Portsmouth Univ.) 1981, (Univ. Coll. Swansea—now Swansea Univ.) 1992; Pres. U.K. Pilots' Asscn. 1963–76, Swansea Univ. Coll. Univ. of Wales (now Swansea Univ.) 1986–95; Hon. Pres. Int. Maritime Pilots' Asscn. 1971–76; Hon. LL.D. (Univ. of Wales) 1976, Hon. LL.D. (Sardar Patel Univ., India) 1978, Hon. LL.D. (Univ. of Birmingham) 1981, Hon. LL.D. (Univ. of Sussex) 1988, (Univ. of Westminster) 1993, (Open Univ.) 1996, (Liverpool) 1996; Freedom of City of Cardiff 1975, City of Sheffield 1978, City of Portsmouth 1991, City of Swansea 1993; Hon. Master of the Bench of the Inner Temple 1976; Hubert Humphrey Int. Award 1978; Grand Cross (1st Class) of the Order of Merit (Fed. Repub. of Germany) 1979. *Publications:* A House Divided 1973, Time and Chance (autobiog.) 1987. *Address:* House of Lords, London, SW1A 0PW, England.

CALLAWAY, Howard H.; American public official; b. 2 April 1927, LaGrange, Ga.; s. of Cason J. Callaway and Virginia Hand Callaway; m. Elizabeth Walton 1949; three s. two d.; ed. U.S. Military Acad.; served in Infantry, participating in Korean War in Far Eastern Command, later becoming Instructor, Infantry School, Fort Benning, Ga. 1949–52; mem. 89th Congress, rep. third district of Georgia 1965–66; Republican cand. for Gov. of Georgia 1966; Civilian Aide for Third Army Area 1970–73; Sec. of the Army May 1973–75; fmr. Campaign Man. for President Ford, 1976 Pres. Election; fmr. Chair. Interfinancial Inc. of Atlanta; Chair. Crested Butte Mountain Resort Inc., GOPAC; Chair. Colo. Republican Party; Dir. United Bank of Denver; mem. Regents Univ. System of Nat. 4-H Service Cttee. 1953–54, 1966–70, 1993–; mem. Bd. of Trustees, Nat. Recreation Asscn., Ida Cason Callaway Foundation. *Leisure interests:* skiing, sailing, tennis, trout fishing. *Address:* Callaway Gardens, Pine Mountain, CA 31822, U.S.A.

CALLEJAS, Rafael Leonardo; Honduran politician and agronomist; ed. in U.S.A.; fmr. Pres. Cen. Cttee., Partido Nacional; Minister for Agric. and Natural Resources 1978–81; cand. for Pres. 1985, 1989; Pres. of Honduras Jan. 1990–93. *Address:* c/o Partido Nacional, Tegucigalpa, Honduras.

CALLIL, Carmen Therese, F.R.S.A, B.A.; Australian publisher; b. 15 July 1938, Melbourne; d. of Lorraine Claire Allen and Frederick Alfred Louis Callil; ed. Star of the Sea Convent, Loreto Convent, Melbourne, and Melbourne Univ.; settled in England 1963; Buyer's Asst., Marks and Spencer 1963–65; Editorial Asst., Hutchinson Publishing Co. 1965–66, B. T. Batsford 1966–67, Publicity Man., Granada Publishing 1967–70, André Deutsch 1971–72; f. Carmen Callil Ltd., Book Publicity Co. and Virago Press 1972; Chairwoman and Man. Dir. Virago Press 1972–82, Chairwoman 1982–95, Man. Dir. Chatto and Windus, The Hogarth Press 1983–93; Publr.-at-Large Random House, U.K. 1993–94; Ed.-at-Large Knopf, NY 1993–94; mem. bd. Channel 4 1985–91, Random Century Bd. 1989–94; Gov. Museum of London 1992–; Chair. Booker Prize for Fiction 1996–; Hon. D.Litt. (Sheffield) 1994, (Oxford Brookes Univ.) 1995; Hon. D.Univ. (York) 1995, (Open) 1997; Distinguished Service Award (Int. Women's Writing Guild). *Leisure interests:* friends, reading, animals, films, gardening. *Address:* 30 Bedford Square, London, WC1B 3EG, England.

CALLOW, Simon Philip Hugh; British actor, director and writer; b. 15 June 1949; s. of Neil Callow and Yvonne Mary Callow; ed. London Oratory Grammar School, Queen's Univ., Belfast, Drama Centre; debut Edin. Festival 1973; repertory seasons, Lincoln and Traverse Theatre, Edin.; work at the fringe theatre, the Bush, London; joined Joint Stock Theatre Group 1977. *Stage appearances include:* Passing By 1975, Plumbers Progress 1975, Arturo Ui 1978, Titus Andronicus 1978, Mary Barnes 1978, As You Like It 1979, Amadeus 1979, Sisterly Feeling 1979, Total Eclipse 1982, Restoration 1982, The Beastly Beatitudes of Balthazar B 1982, The Relapse 1983, On The Spot 1984, Melancholy Jacques 1984, Kiss of the Spider Woman 1985, Faust 1988, Single Spies 1988, 1989, The Destiny of Me 1993, The Alchemist 1996, The Importance of Being Oscar 1997, Chimes at Midnight 1997. *Films include:* Amadeus 1983, A Room With A View 1984, The Good Father 1985, Maurice 1986, Manifesto 1987, Mr and Mrs Bridge 1991, Postcards from the Edge 1991, Soft Top Hard Shoulder 1992, Four Weddings and A Funeral 1994, Jefferson in Paris 1994, Victory 1994, Le Passager Clandestin 1995, England, my England 1995, Ace Ventura: When Nature Calls 1995, James and the Giant Peach (voice) 1996, The Scarlet Tunic 1996, Woman In White 1997, Bedrooms and Hallways 1997, Shakespeare in Love 1997, Interview with a Dead Man 1997. *Television:* Wings of Song 1977, Instant Enlightenment inc. VAT 1979, La Ronde 1980, Man of Destiny 1982, Chance in a Million 1982–84, Deadhead 1984, Handel 1985, David Copperfield 1986, Cariani and the Courtesan 1987, Old Flames 1989, Patriot Witness 1989, Trial of Oz 1991, Bye Bye Columbus 1992, Femme Fatale 1993, Little Napoleons 1994, An Audience with Charles Dickens 1996, A Christmas Dickens 1997. *Directed:* Loving Reno 1983, Passport 1985, Nicolson Fights Croydon 1986, Amadeus 1986, The Infernal Machine 1986, Così Fan Tutte 1987, Jacques and His Master 1987, Shirley Valentine (theatre production) 1988, Die Fledermaus 1988, Facades 1988, Single Spies 1988/89, Shirley Valentine 1989, Die Fledermaus 1989/90, Stevie Wants to Play the Blues 1990, The Ballad of the Sad Café (film) 1991, Carmen Jones 1991, My Fair Lady 1992, Shades 1992, The Destiny of Me 1993, Carmen Jones 1994, Il Trittico 1995, Les Enfants du Paradis (RSC) 1996, Stephen Oliver Trilogy 1996, La Calisto 1996, Il Turco in Italia 1997, HRH 1997, The Pajama Game 1998; several radio broadcasts. *Publications:* Being An Actor 1984, A Difficult Actor: Charles Laughton 1987, Shooting the Actor, or the Choreography of Confusion (with Dusan Makevejev) 1990, Acting in Restoration Comedy 1991, Orson Welles: The Road to Xanadu 1995, Les Enfants du Paradis 1996, Snowdon—On Stage 1996, The National 1997, Love is where it falls 1999; translations of works of Cocteau, Kundera, Prévert; weekly column in Sunday Express, Independent, Country Life; contrib. to The Times, The Sunday Times, The Observer, Evening Standard, etc. *Leisure interest:* 'dreaming' the future of the British theatre. *Address:* c/o Marina Martin Associates, 12/13 Poland Street, London, W1V 3DE, England. *Telephone:* 0171-734 4818.

CALLWOOD, June, O.C.; Canadian journalist, b. 2 June 1924, Chatham; d. of Harold Callwood and Gladys LaVoie; m. Trent Frayne 1944; two s. (one deceased) two d.; Columnist Toronto Globe and Mail 1983–89; Guest Lecturer on Human Rights, Univ. of Ottawa 1984; Margaret Laurence Lecture 1993; Writer-in-Residence N. York Public Library 1995–96; founding mem. and Vice-Pres. Canadian Civil Liberties Asscn. 1965–88 (Hon. Dir for Life 1988); Pres. and founder Nellie's Hostel for Women 1974-78, Dir. 1985–89, 1990–92; Pres. and founder Jessie's Centre for Teenagers 1982–83, 1987–89; Pres. and founding mem. Learnx Foundation 1977–79, Justice for Children 1979–80; Pres. and founder Casey House Hospice (for AIDS) 1988–89, Hon. Dir. 1989–; Pres. Casey House Foundation 1992–93 (Hon. Dir. 1993–), Maggie's Prostitute Community Service Org. 1990–94; Chair. The Writers' Union of Canada 1979–80 (Life mem. 1994–); mem. Council, Amnesty International (Canada) 1978–85; Dir. Canadian Inst. for Admin. of Justice 1983–84, The Electronic Rights Licensing Agency 1997–; Vice-Pres. PEN (Canada) 1987–88, Dir. 1988–89, Pres. 1989–90; Vice-Pres. Ward's Retreat 1990–91, Book and Periodical Council 1994–95 (Chair. 1995–96), Bd. of Govs. Etobicoko Gen. Hosp. 1994–98; Judge, Gov.-Gen.'s Literary Awards 1983–86; involved in many other public and humanitarian activities; Hon. D.Univ. (Ottawa) 1987; Hon. Dr. of Sacred Letters (Trinity Coll.) 1988; Hon. LL.D. (Memorial Univ., Newfoundland, Univ. of Toronto, York Univ.) 1988, (Univ. of Western Ont.) 1993, (McMaster) 1994, (Law Soc. of Upper Canada, Univ. of Calgary) 1997; Hon. Litt.D. (Carleton Univ., Univ. of Alberta) 1988, (Guelph Univ.) 1989, (Univ. of New Brunswick) 1990; Hon. D.C.L. (Acadia Univ.) 1993; Hon. D.Hum.Litt. (Mount St. Vincent Univ.) 1993; Canadian Newspaper Hall of Fame 1984, Bencher Law Soc. of Upper Canada 1987–91, Duthie Lecture (Simon Fraser Univ.) 1990, Bruce Hutchison Lecture 1998; and other awards. *Publications;* Love, Hate, Fear and Anger 1964, The Law is Not for Women 1973, Portrait of Canada 1981, Emma 1984, Emotions 1986, Twelve Weeks in Spring 1986, Jim: A Life with AIDS 1988, The Sleepwalker 1990, June Callwood's National Treasurers 1994, Trial Without End 1995, and 16 other books. *Leisure interests:* swimming, books, gliding. *Address:* 21 Hillcroft Drive, Islington, Ont., M9B 4X4, Canada. *Telephone:* (416) 231-1923. *Fax:* (416) 231-1923.

CALMAN, Sir Kenneth Charles, K.C.B., F.R.C.P., F.R.C.S., F.R.S.E.; British chief medical officer; b. 25 Dec. 1941; s. of Arthur McIntosh Calman and Grace Douglas Don; m. Ann Wilkie 1967; one s. two d.; ed. Allan Glen's School, Glasgow, Univ. of Glasgow; Hall Fellow in Surgery, Western Infirmary, Glasgow 1968; lecturer in Surgery, Univ. of Glasgow 1969, Prof. of Clinical Oncology 1974, Dean of Postgrad. Medicine and Prof. of Postgraduate Medical Educ. 1984–88; MRC Clinical Research Fellow Inst. of Cancer Research, London 1972; Chief Medical Officer, Scottish Office Home and Health Dept. 1989–91, (at Dept. of Health and Social Security) Dept. of

Educ. and Science 1991–98; Vice-Chancellor and Warden, Durham Univ. 1998–; Hon. D.Med. (Nottingham) 1994; Hon. D.Sc. (Westminster) 1996, (Glasgow) 1996, (Birmingham) 1996. *Publications:* Basic Skills for Clinical Housemen 1971, Basic Principles of Cancer Chemotherapy 1982, Invasion 1984, Healthy Respect 1987, The Potential for Health 1998. *Leisure interests:* gardening, golf, collecting cartoons, Scottish literature, sundials. *Address:* Old Shire Hall, Durham, DH1 3HP, England.

CALMES, Christian, D. EN D.; Luxembourg civil servant and lawyer; b. 11 July 1913, Oberursel, Germany; s. of Albert Calmes; m. Anne Raus 1939; three s. two d.; ed. Echternach Gymnasium, Strasbourg and Paris Univs.; called to the Bar 1938; successively Attaché, Sec., Counsellor and Minister Plenipotentiary, Ministry of Foreign Affairs 1947–52; Sec.-Gen. Special Council of Ministers of ECSC 1952–58, Council of Ministers of European Communities (ECSC, EEC, and EURATOM) 1958–73, Hon. Sec.-Gen. 1973–; Chamberlain of H.R.H. the Grand Duke 1973–; mem. historic section of Institut Grand-Ducal de Luxembourg, Hon. Minister Plenipotentiary; Marshal of the Court 1981–85, Prime Chamberlain 1986. *Publications:* L'Affaire du Luxembourg 1967, Geôles sanglantes 1947 1968, Le Luxembourg dans la guerre de 1870 1970, Au fil de l'histoire Tomã 3 1970, 1914–1919: Le Luxembourg au centre de l'annexionnisme belge 1976, Fil de l'histoire 1977, Le referendum Luxembourgeois du 28 Septembre 1919 1979, Une Banque raconte son histoire 1981, Luxembourg in the U.S.A. 1985, Jean, Grand-Duke of Luxembourg 1986, The Making of a Nation; from 1815 to the present 1988, The Schuman Plan, a plan with complex origins (also in French and German), Histoire du Grand-Duché de Luxembourg, de 1815 à nos jours 1995. *Leisure interest:* history. *Address:* Ehnen 5489, Luxembourg, Grand Duchy of Luxembourg. *Telephone:* 761 33. *Fax:* 761 33.

CALMON DE SÁ, Angelo (see Sá, Angelo Calmon de).

CALNE, Sir Roy Yorke, Kt., M.A., M.S., F.R.C.P., F.R.C.S., F.R.S.; British professor of surgery; b. 30 Dec. 1930; s. of Joseph R. Calne and Eileen Calne; m. Patricia D. Whelan 1956; two s. four d.; ed. Lancing Coll. and Guy's Hosp. Medical School, London; RAMC 1954–56; Departmental Anatomy Demonstrator, Univ. of Oxford 1957–58; Sr. House Officer, Nuffield Orthopaedic Centre, Oxford 1958; Surgical Registrar, Royal Free Hosp. 1958–60; Harkness Fellow in Surgery, Peter Bent Brigham Hosp. Harvard Medical School 1960–61; Lecturer in Surgery, St. Mary's Hosp. London 1961–62; Sr. Lecturer and Consulting Surgeon, Westminster Hosp. 1962–65; Prof. of Surgery, Univ. of Cambridge 1965–; Fellow, Trinity Hall Cambridge 1965–; Hon. Consulting Surgeon, Addenbrooke's Hosp. Cambridge 1965–; Hon. F.R.C.S. (Edin.) 1992; Hon. M.D. (Oslo) 1986, (Athens) 1990, (Hanover) 1991, (Thailand) 1993, (Belfast) 1994; Royal Coll. of Surgeons: Hallet Prize, Jacksonian Prize, Hunterian Prof. 1962, Cecil Joll Prize 1966; numerous other honours and awards including Lister Medal 1984, Hunterian Oration 1989, Cameron Prize 1990, Ellison-Cliffe Medal 1990, Ernst-Jung Prize, Gold Medal of Catalan Transplantation Soc. 1996. *Publications:* Too Many People 1994, Art, Surgery and Transplantation 1996; books and scientific papers on renal and liver transplantation and gen. surgery. *Leisure interests:* painting, tennis, squash. *Address:* 22 Barrow Road, Cambridge, England. *Telephone:* (01223) 359831.

CALOW, Peter, PH.D., F.I.BIOL., F.R.S.A.; British professor of zoology; b. 23 May 1947; two c.; ed. Univ. of Leeds; lecturer, Reader, Univ. of Glasgow 1972–84, Warden Wolfson Hall 1975–84; Prof. of Zoology, Univ. of Sheffield 1984–, Dir. Inst. of Environmental Sciences and Tech. 1991–96; Dir. Environmental Businesses Network 1998–; founding ed. Functional Ecology 1986–; Pres. SETAC (Europe) 1990–91; Chair. U.K. Govt. Advisory Cttee. on Hazardous Substances 1991–; Trustee Health and Environmental Sciences Inst. 1996–, Int. Life Sciences Inst. 1999–; mem. Council Freshwater Biology Assen. 1995–, Univ. of Buckingham 1997–. *Publications:* author, jt. author or ed. of 20 books; more than 220 articles in tech. journals. *Leisure interests:* tennis, reading. *Address:* Department of Animal and Plant Sciences, University of Sheffield, Sheffield, S10 2TN, England. *Telephone:* (0114) 222 4692. *Fax:* (0114) 278 0694.

CALVET, Jacques; French business executive and banker; b. 19 Sept. 1931, Boulogne-sur-Seine; s. of Prof. Louis Calvet and Yvonne Olmières; m. Françoise Rondot 1956; two s. one d.; ed. Paris Univ. and Nat. School of Admin.; at Cour des Comptes 1957–63; Chargé de mission to office of Valéry Giscard d'Estaing (Sec. of State for Finance) 1959–62, Dir. 1962–66; Dir. Financial Affairs, Paris Dist. 1966–68; Prin. Pvt. Sec. to Minister of Finance 1968–74; Deputy Gen. Man., Banque Nat. de Paris (BNP) 1974–75, Gen. Man. 1975–79, Chair. 1979–82, Hon. Chair. 1997–; Vice-Chair. Peugeot SA 1982–84, Pres. 1984–97; Chair. Automobiles Peugeot 1982–84, Bd. Pres. 1984–, Vice-Pres., Dir.-Gen. 1984–89, Pres. 1990–97; Pres. Citroën 1983–97; Pres. Conseil d'Admin. de la Publicité Française, de Petrofina 1991–97; Chair. European Automobiles Mfrs. Assen. 1996; Commdr., Légion d'honneur; Officier Ordre nat. du Mérite, du Mérite agricole; Chevalier des Palmes académiques. *Leisure interest:* tennis. *Address:* 31 avenue Victor Hugo, 75116 Paris, France (Home).

CALVO-SOTELO Y BUSTELO, Leopoldo, D.C.ENG.; Spanish politician and engineer; b. 14 April 1926, Madrid; s. of Leopoldo Calvo-Sotelo Bustelo and Mercedes Calvo-Sotelo Bustelo; m. Pilar Ibáñez Martín Mellado 1954; seven s. one d.; ed. Escuela de Ingenieros de Caminos, Canales y Puertos, Madrid; Pres. Spanish Railways 1967–68; Dir.-Gen. Unión Explosivos Rio Tinto 1963–67, 1968–75; Procurador 1971; Minister of Commerce 1975–76, of Public Works 1976–77; Minister for Relations with European Communities 1978–80; Second Deputy Prime Minister, Econ. Affairs 1980–81, Prime Minister of Spain 1981–82; mem. of European Parl. 1986; Pres. Union of the Democratic Centre (UCD) 1981–82. *Address:* Buho 1, Somosaguas, Madrid, Spain.

CALVOCORESSI, Peter; British writer and book publisher; b. 17 Nov. 1912, Karachi, India; s. of Pandia J. Calvocoressi and Irene (Ralli) Calvocoressi; m. Barbara Dorothy Eden 1938; two s.; ed. Eton Coll. and Balliol Coll., Oxford; called to Bar 1935; R.A.F. Intelligence 1940–45; assisted Trial of Major War Criminals, Nuremberg 1945–46; on staff, Royal Inst. of Int. Affairs 1949–54; partner Chatto & Windus, publishers 1955–65; Reader in Int. Relations, Sussex Univ. 1965–71; Ed. Dir. Penguin Books 1972, Publr. and Chief Exec. 1973–76; Chair. Open Univ. Educational Enterprises Ltd. 1979–88; mem. UN sub-comm. on the Prevention of Discrimination 1961–71; Chair. The London Library 1970–73; Hon. D.Univ. (Open Univ.) 1989. *Publications:* Nuremberg: The Facts, the Law and the Consequences 1947, Survey of International Affairs: Vols. for 1947–48, 1949–50, 1951, 1952 and 1953, Middle East Crisis (with Guy Wint) 1957, South Africa and World Opinion 1961, World Order and New States 1962, World Politics Since 1945, 1968, Total War (with Guy Wint) 1972, The British Experience: 1945–75, Top Secret Ultra 1980, A Time for Peace 1987, Who's Who in the Bible 1987, Resilient Europe 1991, Threading My Way 1994, Fall Out: World War II and the Shaping of Postwar Europe 1997. *Leisure interests:* music, walking. *Address:* 1 Queens Parade, Bath, BA1 2NJ, England. *Telephone:* (01225) 333903.

CAMARA, Assan Musa; Gambian politician; b. 1923, Mansajang; ed. St. Mary Anglican Mission School, Bathurst (now Banjul) and Anglican Mission School, Kristu Kunda; Teacher in govt. and mission schools 1948–60; mem. House of Assembly (Independent) 1960–; Minister without Portfolio 1960, of Health and Labour 1960–62, of Educ. and Social Welfare 1962–65, of Works and Communications 1965–66, of Educ., Labour and Social Welfare 1966–68, of External Affairs 1968–74, of Local Govt. and Lands 1974–77, of Educ., Youth and Sports 1977, 1981–82, of Finance and Trade 1977–79; Vice-Pres. of The Gambia 1973–77, 1978–82; Order of the Cedar of Lebanon, Commdr. Nat. Order of Senegal, Grand Band, Order of Star of Africa, Grand Cross, Brilliant Star of China. *Address:* c/o Office of the Vice-President, Banjul, The Gambia.

CÂMARA, Most Rev. Helder Pessôa; Brazilian (Roman Catholic) ecclesiastic; b. 7 Feb. 1909, Fortaleza; ordained priest 1931; consecrated Bishop 1952; Titular Bishop of Salde 1952; Titular Archbishop of Salde 1955–64; Archbishop of Olinda and Recife 1964–84, Archbishop Emer. 1985–; organized Brazilian Conf. of Bishops and co-operated in organization of CELAM (the Latin-American Conf. of Bishops); an active campaigner for social reform in Latin-America; René Sande Award 1962, Via Int. Peace Prize (Italy) 1970, Martin Luther King Jr. Award 1970, John XXII Memorial Award from Pax Christi, Spain 1970, Niwano Peace Prize 1983, Christopher Award 1987; Dr. h.c. (Univs. of St. Louis, Louvain, Münster, Fribourg and Sorbonne); People's Peace Prize 1974. *Address:* Rua Henrique Dias, 208, 50070-140 Recife, Brazil. *Telephone:* (081) 231 5341.

CAMARENA BADIA, Vicente, PH.D.; Spanish professor of mathematics; b. 26 Aug. 1941, Xativa, Valencia; s. of Vicente Camarena and Victoria Badia; m. Carmen Grau; one s. four d.; ed. Universidad de Zaragoza; Asst. Prof. of Math. Universidad de Zaragoza 1969–81, Prof. 1981–84, Rector 1984–92, Prof. of Applied Math. Dept. 1993–; mem. Spanish Royal Soc. of Math., Spanish Assen. of Math., Spanish Soc. of Gen. Systems, American Math. Soc., Soc. for Industries and Applied Math., Int. Astronomical Union. *Publications:* Curso de Mecánica 1977–78, Optimización de Trayectorias y efecto de Trampolín Lunar 1972, Formulación Sistemática de la Teoría de Perturbaciones en el Movimiento Orbital 1976, Determinación del Vector Primer de Lawden en Forma Universal y su Aplicación a Problemas de Optimización 1979–83, Elementos Orbitales y Osculadores en Teoría de Perturbaciones, Uniformización de Métodos Canónicos de Perturbaciones 1984. *Leisure interests:* cycling and swimming. *Address:* Universidad de Zaragoza, Centro Politécnico Superior, Mª Luna 3, Zaragoza 50015 (Office); Latassa 17, Zaragoza, Spain (Home).

CAMARGO, Sérgio de; Brazilian sculptor; b. 1930; ed. Academia Altamira, Buenos Aires, and Univ. de Paris à la Sorbonne; in France 1948–50, 1951–54, 1961–; visited China 1954; specializes in wood reliefs; Int. Sculpture Prize, Paris Biennale 1963; works are in permanent collections of Nat. Museum of Art, Rio de Janeiro, Museum of Art, São Paulo, Musée d'Art Moderne de la Ville de Paris, Tate Gallery, London, Galleria d'Arte Moderna, Rome, and in numerous private collections; represented in exhbns. in Paris and Brussels 1963, Mannheim, Arras, London and Paris 1964, 1974, New York 1965, and Latin-American exhbns. 1954–.

CAMBA, Erme Reamon, D.THEOL.; Philippine ecclesiastic; b. 27 Nov. 1937, Camalig, Albay; s. of Mequias Camba and Erlina Reamon-Camba; m. Eugenia D'Lunsod 1964; two d.; ed. Silliman Univ. Dumaguete City and Southeast Asia Grad. School of Theology; Church Minister, Guinobatan Evangelical Church, Guinobatan, Albay 1961–62, 1963–64, Albay Evangelical Church, Legazpi City 1964–69; Instr. in Applied Theology, Divinity School, Silliman Univ. 1970–71; Assoc. Prof. in Pastoral Theology and Social Ethics, Union Theological Seminary, Dasmariñas, Cavite (Manila) 1971–82; Jurisdictional Bishop, United Church of Christ in the Philippines (UCCP)

1982–86; Gen. Sec. UCCP 1986–94; Assoc. Prof. in Pastoral Theology, Divinity School, Silliman Univ. 1994–; co-founder and Chair. of several ecumenical orgs. in the Philippines; Chair. Nat. Council of Churches in the Philippines 1983–85; Pres. Christian Conf. of Asia 1985–90; now Co-Moderator, Unit II Comm. WCC. *Publications:* articles in church magazines. *Leisure interest:* reading. *Address:* Divinity School, Silliman University, Dumaguete City 6200, Philippines. *Telephone:* (63 35) 225-7541 (Office), (63) 0912 515-0368 (Home). *Fax:* (63 35) 225-7541.

CAMBIE, Richard Conrad, D.SC., PH.D., D.PHIL., F.R.S.N.Z.; New Zealand university professor; b. 11 Nov. 1931, Tauranga; s. of David Gilbert Carlton Cambie and Sybil Lorna Cambie; m. 1956; two s.; ed. Tauranga Coll., Auckland Univ., Oxford Univ., U.K.; jr. lecturer, Univ. of Auckland 1957, Lecturer in Chem. 1958–60, Sr. Lecturer 1961–63, Assoc. Prof. 1964–69, Prof. of Organic Chem. 1970–97, Head of Chem. Dept. 1984–91; Asst. to Vice-Chancellor (Student Services) 1978–97; Fellow N.Z. Inst. of Chem.; I.C.I. Medal (N.Z. Inst. of Chem.) 1964, Royal Soc. of N.Z. Hector Medal 1967, N.Z. Asscn. of Scientists Research Medal 1969. *Publications:* Co-author: New Zealand Medicinal Plants 1981, Economic New Zealand Plants 1988, Fijian Medicinal Plants 1994, Antifertility Plants of the Pacific 1997; 410 scientific papers on organic natural products chem. 1958–. *Leisure interest:* lawn bowling. *Address:* Chemistry Department, University of Auckland, Private Bag 92019, Auckland (Office); 21D Southern Cross Road, Kohimarama, Auckland, New Zealand (Home). *Telephone:* (09) 528-5478 (Home). *Fax:* (09) 373-7422.

CAMBITOGLOU, Alexander, A.O., PH.D., D.PHIL., F.S.A.; Australian classical archaeologist; b. Thessaloniki, Greece; s. of Anthony Cambitoglou and Helen Cambitoglou (née Antoniadou); ed. Univ. of Thessaloniki, Univs. of Manchester, London and Oxford, U.K.; Asst. Prof. Univ. of Miss., U.S.A. 1954–56; Asst. Prof., Bryn Mawr Coll., Pa. 1956–60; Sr. Lecturer in Classical Archaeology, Univ. of Sydney, Australia 1961–63, Prof. of Archaeology 1963–78, Arthur and Renee George Prof. of Classical Archaeology 1978–89, now Emer. Prof.; Curator, Nicholson Museum, Sydney 1963–; Dir. Australian Archaeological Inst. at Athens 1981–; Dir. Archaeological Expedition at Zagora, Andros 1967–77, to Torone, Chaldike 1975–; Fellow Athens Archaeological Soc., Australian Acad. of the Humanities; mem. Athens Acad.; Corresp. mem. German Archaeological Inst. *Publications:* The Brygos Painter 1968; Co-author of numerous books on the red-figured vases of Apulia and other archaeological topics; Ed.: Studies in Honour of Arthur Dale Trendall 1979. *Leisure interests:* swimming, music. *Address:* Australian Archaeological Institute at Athens, 125 Darlington Road (H5I), University of Sydney, Sydney, N.S.W. 2006, Australia; Australian Archaeological Institute at Athens, 23 Zacharitsa Street, Koukaki, 11742 Athens, Greece. *Telephone:* (2) 9351-4759 (Australia); (1) 924 3256 (Greece).

CAMBRELING, Sylvain; French conductor; b. 2 July 1948, Amiens; conducting debut with Orchestre de Lyon 1975; Prin. Guest Conductor, Ensemble Intercontemporain, Paris 1976; subsequent appearances in Paris with Orchestre de Paris, Nat. Orchestra of France and Ensemble Intercontemporain; has worked regularly at Paris Opéra since conducting Chéreau's production of Les Contes d'Hoffmann; Glyndebourne Opera debut (The Barber of Seville) 1981; Music. Dir. Nat. Opera, Théâtre Royal de la Monnaie, Brussels 1981–; debut at La Scala (Lucio Silla) 1984, Metropolitan Opera, New York (Romeo et Juliette) 1986; has also appeared at Salzburg, Aix-en-Provence and Bregenz festivals; has worked in U.K. with Halle and Royal Liverpool Philharmonic orchestras, in Germany with Berlin Philharmonic, Berlin Radio Symphony and other orchestras and in U.S.A. *Address:* c/o Frankfurt Opera, Staedtische Buennen, 60275 Frankfurt am Main, Germany.

CAMDESSUS, Michel Jean; French civil servant; b. 1 May 1933, Bayonne; s. of Alfred Camdessus and Madeleine Cassembon; m. Brigitte d'Arcy 1957; two s. four d.; ed. Notre Dame Coll., Betharram, Faculty of Law, Paris; civil servant, Treasury, Ministry of Finance 1960–66; Chief, Bureau of Industrial Affairs, Treasury, Ministry of Econ. and Finance 1969–70; Chair. "Investissements" Sub-Cttee. of Treasury 1971; Deputy Dir. of Treasury 1974–82, Dir. 1982–84; Financial Attaché, Perm. Representation, EEC, Brussels 1966–69; mem. Monetary Cttee., EEC 1978, Pres. 1982; Sec. Conseil de Direction du Fonds de Développement Economique et Social 1971; Asst. Dir. "Épargne et Crédit" Sub-Cttee. 1972; Deputy Gov. Banque de France 1984, Gov. 1984–87, Hon. Gov. 1987–; Man. Dir. IMF 1987–; Dir. Banque Européenne d'Investissements, Banque Cen. des États de l'Afrique de l'Ouest, Air France, Soc. Nat. des Chemins de fer Français, Crédit Lyonnais (all 1978); Pres. Club de Paris 1978–84; Chevalier Légion d'honneur, de l'ordre nat. du Mérite, Croix de la Valeur militaire. *Address:* International Monetary Fund, 700 19th Street, N.W., Washington, DC 20431, U.S.A. (Office); 27 rue de Valois, 75001 Paris, France (Home).

CAMERON, Averil Millicent, F.B.A., F.S.A., M.A., PH.D.; British historian of late antiquity and Byzantine studies; b. 8 Feb. 1940, Leek, Staffs.; d. of Tom Roy Sutton and Millicent Drew; m. Alan Douglas Edward Cameron 1962 (dissolved 1980); one s. one d.; ed. Somerville Coll., Oxford, Univ. Coll., London; Asst. Lecturer Classics, King's Coll., London 1965, Lecturer 1968, Reader in Ancient History 1970, Prof. 1978–88, Prof. Late Antique and Byzantine Studies 1988–94, Dir. Centre for Hellenic Studies 1989–94; Warden of Keble Coll., Oxford 1994–; Visiting Prof., Columbia Univ., New York 1967–68; Visiting mem., Inst. for Advanced Study, Princeton 1977–78, Distinguished Visitor 1992; Summer Fellow, Dumbarton Oaks 1980; Sather Prof. of Classical Literature, Univ. of Calif. 1985–86; Visiting Prof. Coll. de France 1987, Lansdowne Lecturer, Victoria, B.C. 1992; Ed. Journal of Roman Studies 1985–90; Pres. Soc. for the Promotion of Roman Studies 1995–98. *Publications:* Procopius 1967, Agathias 1970, Corippus, In laudem Iustini minoris 1976, Images of Women in Antiquity (ed.) 1983, Continuity and Change in Sixth-Century Byzantium 1981, Constantinople in the Eighth Century (ed.) 1984, Procopius and the Sixth Century 1985, 1996, History as Text (ed.) 1989, The Greek Renaissance in the Roman Empire (ed.) 1990, Christianity and the Rhetoric of Empire 1991, The Byzantine and Early Islamic Near East I (ed.) 1992, II (ed.) 1994, III (ed.) 1995, The Later Roman Empire 1993, The Mediterranean World in Late Antiquity A.D. 395–600 1993, Changing Cultures in Early Byzantium (ed.) 1996, Cambridge Ancient History vol. XIII. The Late Empire (ed.) 1997. *Address:* Keble College, Oxford, OX1 3PG, England.

CAMERON, Ian Rennell, M.A., D.M., F.R.C.P.; British professor of medicine; b. 20 May 1936, London; s. of James Cameron and Frances Cameron; m. 1st Jayne Bustard 1964 (divorced); one s. one d.; m. 2nd Jennifer Payne 1980; one s. one d.; ed. Westminster School, Corpus Christi Coll. Oxford and St. Thomas's Hosp. Medical School; jr. appts. St. Thomas's Hosp. 1961–64; lecturer, St. Thomas's Hosp. Medical School 1967, Sr. lecturer 1969, Reader 1975, Prof. of Medicine 1979–94, Dean 1986–89; Research Asst. Dept. of Physiology, Univ. Coll. London 1966–68; N.I.H. Postdoctoral Fellowship, Cedars-Sinai Medical Center, Los Angeles and Asst. Prof. Dept. of Physiology, Univ. of Calif. at Los Angeles 1968–69; Prin. United Medical and Dental Schools of Guys and St. Thomas's Hosps. 1989–92; Dir. Research and Devt. South-East Thames Health Authority 1993–94, Bro Taf Health Authority (non-exec.) 1996–; Provost and Vice-Chancellor, Univ. of Wales Coll. of Medicine 1994–. *Publications:* Respiratory Disorders (with N.T. Bateman) 1983; papers in medical and physiological journals. *Leisure interests:* collecting paintings, books and china. *Address:* University of Wales College of Medicine, Heath Park, Cardiff, CF4 4XN, Wales. *Telephone:* (01222) 742071. *Fax:* (01222) 745306.

CAMERON, James; film director and screenwriter; b. 16 Aug. 1954, Kapuskasing, Ont.; m. Linda Hamilton 1996; one d.; ed. Fullerton Jr. Coll.; formed Lightstorm Entertainment 1990, Head 1992–; C.E.O. Digital Domain 1993–. *Films:* Piranha II—The Spawning (dir.), The Terminator (dir. and screenplay) 1984, Rambo: First Blood Part II (co-screenwriter), Aliens (dir. and screenplay), The Abyss (dir. and screenplay), Terminator 2: Judgment Day (co-screenwriter, dir. and producer) 1994, Point Break (exec. producer) 1994, True Lies, Strange Days, Titanic (Acad. Award for Best Dir., film won 11 Acad Awards equalling record) 1996. *Address:* Lightstorm Entertainment, 919 Santa Monica Boulevard, Santa Monica, CA 90401, U.S.A.

CAMERON, Kenneth, C.B.E., PH.D., F.R.HIST.S., F.S.A., F.B.A.; British professor of English language (retd.); b. 21 May 1922, Burnley, Lancs.; s. of late Angus W. Cameron and E. Alice Cameron; m. 1st Kathleen Heap 1947 (died 1977); one s. one d.; m. 2nd Jean P. Russell-Gebbet 1998; ed. Burnley Grammar School and Univ. of Leeds; pilot, R.A.F. 1941–45; Asst. Lecturer in English Language, Univ. of Sheffield 1947–50; Lecturer in English Language, Univ. of Nottingham 1950–59, Sr. Lecturer 1959–62, Reader 1962–63, Prof. 1963–87, Head, Dept. of English Studies 1984–87; External Prof., Dept. of English and Drama, Univ. of Loughborough 1990–93; Emer. Fellowship, Levershulme Trust 1990–92; Hon. Dir. English Place-Name Soc. 1967–93; Hon. Fil.Dr. (Uppsala) 1977; Hon. D. Litt. (Sheffield) 1991; Jöran Sahlgren Prize, Gustav Adolfs Akademien, Sweden 1990. *Publications:* The Place-Names of Derbyshire 1959, English Place-Names 1961, 1996, Scandinavian Settlement in the Territory of the Five Boroughs 1965, The Meaning and Significance of Old English *walh* in English Place-Names 1980, The Place-Names of the City of Lincoln 1985, The Place-Names of the Wapentake of Yarborough, Lincolnshire 1991, The Place-Names of the Wapentake of Walshcroft, Lincolnshire 1992, The Place-Names of the Wapentakes of Ludborough and Haverstoe, Lincolnshire 1995, The Place-Names of the Wapentake of Bradley, Lincolnshire 1997, A Dictionary of Lincolnshire Place-Names 1998, The Place-Names of the Wapentake of Manley, Lincolnshire 1999; articles in professional journals. *Leisure interests:* sports, home. *Address:* 16 The Cloisters, Beeston, Nottingham, England. *Telephone:* (0115) 925 4503.

CAMERON, Peter Duncanson, LL.B., PH.D.; British consultant and lawyer; b. 21 June 1952, Glasgow; s. of Stewart Cameron and Margaret Cameron; ed. Bishop Vesey Grammar School, High School of Stirling and Univ. of Edinburgh; lecturer in Law, Univ. of Dundee 1977–86; Visiting Research Assoc., Oxford Univ. Centre for Socio-Legal Studies 1980, Visiting Scholar, Stanford Law School 1985; Adviser UN Centre on Transnat. Corpns. 1985–86; Dir. Int. Inst. of Energy Law, Univ. of Leiden 1986–97; Prof. of Int. Energy Law, Univ. of Dundee 1997–; Chair. Academic Advisory Group, Int. Bar Asscn. Section on Energy and Natural Resources Law 1996–; Adviser UN ESCAP 1988–89; Consultant World Bank 1990–; Visiting Prof. Univ. Autónoma de Madrid 1997–; Ed. Bd. Oil and Gas Law and Taxation Review 1989–97; Assoc. Ed. Journal of Energy and Natural Resources Law 1990–97, Jt. Ed. 1997–. *Publications:* Property Rights and Sovereign Rights: the Case of North Sea Oil 1983, Petroleum Licensing 1984, The Oil Supplies Industry: a Comparative Study of Legislative Restrictions and their Impact 1986, Nuclear Energy Law after Chernobyl (ed.) 1988, The Regulation of Gas in Europe 1995, Gas Regulation in Western and Central Europe 1998.

Leisure interest: long-distance running, travel. *Address:* Centre for Energy, Petroleum and Mineral Law and Policy, University of Dundee, Park Place, Dundee, DD1 4MN (Office); 8 Linden Avenue, Newport-on-Tay, Fife, DD6 8DU, Scotland (Home). *Telephone:* (01382) 344300 (Office); (01382) 542546 (Home). *Fax:* (01382) 322578 (Office); (01382) 542916 (Home).

CAMERON WATT, Donald, M.A., D.LITT., F.B.A., F.R.HIST.S.; British historian; b. 17 May 1928, Rugby; s. of Robert Cameron Watt and Barbara Bidwell; m. 1st Marianne R. Grau 1951 (died 1962), 2nd Felicia Cobb Stanley 1962 (died 1997); one s., one step-d.; ed. Rugby School and Oriel Coll. Oxford; asst. ed. (Foreign Office Research Dept.), documents on German foreign policy 1918–1945 1951–54; Asst. Lecturer in Political History, London School of Econs. 1954–56, Lecturer in Int. History 1957–63, Sr. Lecturer 1964–65; Reader in Int. History, Univ. of London 1966–72, Prof. in Int. History 1974–82, Stevenson Prof. in Int. History 1982–93, Emer. Prof. of Int. History 1993–; Ed. Survey of International Affairs, Royal Inst. of Int. Affairs 1962–71; historian, Cabinet Office Historical Section 1977–94; Rockefeller Fellow in Social Sciences 1960–61; Fellow Polish Acad. of Arts and Sciences, Cracow; fmr. F.R.S.A. Wolfson Prize for History 1990. *Publications:* Oxford Poetry 1950 (ed.) 1951, Britain and the Suez Canal 1956, Personalities and Policies 1965, Hitler's Mein Kampf (ed.) 1969, 1992, Too Serious a Business 1975, Succeeding John Bull 1984, How War Came 1989. *Leisure interests:* exploring London, science fiction, cats. *Address:* c/o Department of International History, London School of Economics, Aldwych, London, WC2A 2AE, England. *Telephone:* 0171-955 7924. *Fax:* 0171-955 6800.

CAMERON OF LOCHBROOM, Baron (Life Peer), cr. 1984, of Lochbroom in the District of Ross and Cromarty; **Kenneth John Cameron,** M.A., LL.B., Q.C., F.R.S.E.; British lawyer; b. 11 June 1931, Edinburgh; s. of Hon. Lord Cameron and late Eileen Dorothea Burrell; m. Jean Pamela Murray 1964; two d.; ed. The Edinburgh Acad., Corpus Christi Coll. Oxford and Univ. of Edinburgh; called to Bar 1958; Q.C. 1972; Chair. Industrial Tribunals (Scotland) 1966–81; Pres. Pensions Appeal Tribunal (Scotland) 1976–84; Chair. Cttee. for Investigation in Scotland of Agricultural Marketing Schemes 1980–84; Advocate Depute 1981–84; Lord Advocate 1984–89; Senator of Coll. of Justice in Scotland 1989–; Chair. Royal Fine Art Comm. for Scotland; Pres. Scottish Council for Voluntary Orgs. 1989–; Chancellor's Assessor, Univ. of Edin. 1997–; Hon. Bencher, Lincoln's Inn, London; Hon. Fellow, Corpus Christi Coll. Oxford, Royal Incorporation of Architects in Scotland. *Leisure interests:* fishing, sailing. *Address:* Stoneyhill House, Musselburgh, Edin., EH21 6RP, Scotland. *Telephone:* 0131-665 1081.

CAMI, Foto; Albanian party official (retd.) and academician; b. 4 Oct. 1925, Labove, Gjirokastër Dist.; s. of Premito Cami and Olimbi Cami; m. Zhaneta Cami 1960; two d.; ed. Moscow Univ.; partisan in Second World War; mem. Albanian CP 1944; propaganda dept. of Albanian Workers' Party (AWP) Cen. Cttee. apparatus 1953–66; cand. mem. AWP Cen. Cttee. 1967–71, mem. 1971–; mem. and mem. Presidium Albanian Acad. of Sciences 1972–; deputy to People's Ass. (Tirana Dist.) 1970–76, 1982–; cand. mem. Politburo 1981–86, mem. 1986; First Sec. of AWP Krujë and Shkodër Dist. Cttees. 1975–79, Tirana Dist. Cttee. 1982–85; Propaganda Sec. of AWP Cen. Cttee. 1985–; Chair. Comm. for Foreign Affairs of Albanian People's Ass. 1987–91; various orders. *Leisure interests:* politics and philosophy, fishing.

CAMILIÓN, Oscar Héctor, PH.D.; Argentinian politician; b. 6 Jan. 1930, Buenos Aires; s. of Oscar Juan Camilión and Lucía Fernández; m. Susana María Lascano 1956; two s. two d.; ed. Colegio San Salvador, Univ. Nacional de Buenos Aires; Asst., then Head of Research, Inst. of Constitutional Law, Univ. Nacional de Buenos Aires, Sec.-Gen. 1955, Prof. of Constitutional Law, concurrently at Univ. Católica de La Plata 1957; Prof. of Int. Law, Argentine Inst. of Hispanic Culture; Prof. of Int. Politics, Argentine Nat. Coll. of Defence; entered Ministry of Foreign Affairs 1958, held posts of Minister, Chief of Cabinet, Dir. of Personnel, Minister-Counsellor, Argentine Embassy, Brazil 1959–61, Under-Sec. 1961–62; mem. dels. to UN Gen. Assembly, Confs. of OAS and other regional orgs., to Conf. of Guaranteeing Countries of Peru-Ecuador Peace Protocol 1960, 1981; Chief Ed. Clarin newspaper, Buenos Aires 1965–72; Amb. to Brazil 1976–81; Minister of Foreign Affairs and Worship March–Dec. 1981, of Defence 1993–96; f. Argentine Council of Int. Relations; mem. Interamerican Dialogue, Atlantic Confs.; decorations from Brazil, Peru, Bolivia, Venezuela, Colombia, Honduras, El Salvador. *Publications:* several papers on historical, political and diplomatic subjects. *Leisure interests:* golf, classical music, history. *Address:* c/o Ministry of Defence, Avenida Paseo Colón 255, 1063 Buenos Aires; Montevideo 1597-4°, Buenos Aires 42-9557, Argentina.

CAMILLERI, Charles, MUS.BAC.; British/Maltese composer; b. 7 Sept. 1931, Malta; s. of Carmel Camilleri and Josephine Quinton; m. Doris Vella 1957; one s. one d.; ed. Lyceum High School and Toronto Univ., Canada; composer, teacher, lecturer, conductor in Malta up to 1949, Australia 1949–53, U.K. 1954–57, Toronto, conductor with CBC, Toronto 1958–63, London 1964–; apptd. Dir. Inst. of Mediterranean Music Foundation of Int. Studies, UNESCO 1987; Prof. of Music, Univ. of Malta 1990; comm. by UNESCO Songs of Infant Species for soprano and piano 1987; commissioned by Aga Khan Foundation: Mimar for piano, vibraphone and gongs 1987; visits to many countries in Far East, Europe and N. America 1949–; many Arts Council Awards. *Publications:* over 80, including Missa Mundi 1968, 2nd Piano Concerto 1969, Piano Trio 1970, String Quartet 1973, Cosmic Vixions 1974, Five Books on Improvisation 1983, 3rd Piano Concerto 1985, Interchangeable Galaxies, Diaphanion 1987, The Elements (ballet), Music of the Mediterranean 1987, Campostella (opera in two Acts) 1988, City of Brass 1989, Cello Concerto 1989, Ombras 1990. *Leisure interest:* research in primitive and folk music. *Address:* 24 Orchard Avenue, Finchley, London, N3 3NL, England. *Telephone:* 0181-349 1728.

CAMILLERI, Victor; Maltese diplomatist; b. 1942, St. Venera; m. Elizabeth B. Heaney 1967; two s.; ed. Lyceum, Malta, Univ. of Birmingham, U.K., Columbia Univ., U.S.A.; fmr. teacher, Educ. Dept.; joined External Affairs Service, Ministry of Commonwealth and Foreign Affairs 1968; First Sec., Perm. Mission to UN, New York 1974–81; Perm. Rep. to UNIDO and UNESCO 1981–84; apptd. Head Multilateral Section, Ministry of Foreign Affairs, Valletta 1984, Acting Sec. 1985–87; Amb. and Head Malta's del. to Stockholm Conf., Conf. on Security and Co-operation in Europe on Confidence and Security Bldg. Measures 1984–85; Deputy High Commr. in London 1987–90, High Commr. (also accred. to Sweden) 1991; Chef de Cabinet, Office of Pres. of 45th Session of UN Gen. Ass. 1990; Perm. Rep. to UN 1991–93; Amb. to Belgium 1997–. *Address:* Maltese Embassy, 44 rue Jules Lejeune, 1060 Brussels, Belgium.

CAMOYS, 7th Baron, (cr. 1264 called out of abeyance 1839) **(Ralph) Thomas Campion George Sherman Stonor,** G.C.V.O., P.C.; British banker; b. 16 April 1940; s. of 6th Baron Camoys and Mary Jeanne Stourton; m. Elisabeth Mary Hyde Parker 1966; one s. three d.; ed. Eton Coll., Balliol Coll., Oxford; Man. Dir. Rothschild Intercontinental Bank Ltd. 1969–75; with Amex Bank Ltd. 1975–78; Man. Dir. Barclays Merchant Bank 1978–84, Exec. Vice.-Chair. 1984–86; Dir. Barclays Bank PLC 1984–94; Chief Exec. Barclays de Zoete Wedd Holdings Ltd. 1986–87, Deputy Chair. 1987–98; Deputy Chair. Sotheby's Holdings Inc. 1994–97; Dir. 3i Group 1991–, Perpetual PLC 1994–, British Grolux Ltd. 1994–; Lord-in-Waiting to H.M. the Queen 1992–; Lord Chamberlain of H.M. Household 1998–; D.L. Oxfordshire 1994–; mem. Court of Assistants, Fishmongers' Co. 1980–; Consultor Extraordinary Section of Admin. of the Patrimony of the Holy See 1991–; Order of Gorkha Dakshina Bahu, 1st Class (Nepal). *Leisure interests:* the arts, shooting. *Address:* Stonor Park, Henley-on-Thames, Oxon., RG9 6HF; Buckingham Palace, London, SW1A 1AA, England. *Telephone:* (01491) 638644 (Oxon.); 0171-930 4832 (London).

CAMP, Jeffery Bruce, R.A.; British artist; b. 1923, Oulton Broad, Suffolk; s. of George Camp and Caroline Denny; m. Laetitia Yhap 1963; ed. Lowestoft and Ipswich Art Schools and Edinburgh Coll. of Art (under William Gillies); Andrew Grant Scholarship for travelling and study 1944, 1945, David Murray Bursary for landscape painting 1946; painted altarpiece for St. Alban's Church, Norwich 1955; lecturer Slade School of Fine Art, London 1963–88; mem. London Group 1961; one-man exhbns.: Edinburgh Festival 1950, Galerie de Seine, London 1958, 1959, Beaux Arts Gallery, London 1961, 1963, New Art Centre, London 1968, Fermoy Art Gallery, King's Lynn 1970, S. London Art Gallery 1973, Royal Shakespeare Theatre, Stratford 1974, Serpentine Gallery, London (Arts Council) 1978, Bradford City Art Gallery 1979, Browse and Darby 1984, 1993, The 29th Aldeburgh Festival 1986, Nigel Greenwood Gallery, London 1986, 1990, 1993, Royal Acad. Retrospective 1988; in numerous mixed exhbns. 1958–; works in numerous public collections in U.K., Athena Art Award 1987 *Publications:* Draw 1981, Paint 1996. *Address:* c/o Browse & Darby, 19 Cork Street, London, W1X 2LP; 27 Stirling Road, London, SW9 9EF, England.

CAMPBELL, Alastair John, M.A.; British civil servant and journalist; b. 25 May 1957; s. of Donald Campbell and Elizabeth (née Caldwell) Campbell; partner Fiona Millar; two s. one d.; ed. City of Leicester Boys School, Gonville and Caius Coll., Cambridge; trainee reporter Tavistock Times and Sunday Independent 1980–82; freelance reporter 1982–83; reporter Daily Mirror 1982–86, Political Ed. 1989–93; News Ed. Sunday Today 1985–86; political corresp. Sunday Mirror 1986–87, Political Ed. 1987–89, columnist 1989–91; Asst. Ed. and columnist Today 1993–95; Press Sec. to Leader of the Opposition 1994–97; Press Sec. to Prime Minister 1997–; Pres. Keighley Br., Burnley Football Supporters' Club. *Leisure interests:* family, bagpipes, Burnley Football Club. *Address:* Prime Minister's Office, 10 Downing Street, London, SW1A 2AA, England.

CAMPBELL, Hon. Alexander Bradshaw, P.C., Q.C., LL.B., LL.D.; Canadian politician and lawyer; b. 1 Dec. 1933, Summerside, P.E.I.; s. of late Thane A. Campbell and Cecilia Bradshaw; m. Marilyn Gilmour 1961; two s. one d.; practised law in Summerside, P.E.I. 1959–66; mem. P.E.I. Legislature 1965–78, Leader of Liberal Party for P.E.I. Dec. 1965–78; Premier of P.E.I. 1966–78; Minister of Devt. 1969–72, of Agriculture and Forestry 1972–74, Pres. Exec. Council, Minister of Justice, Attorney and Advocate-Gen. 1974–78; Justice, Supreme Court of P.E.I. 1978–94; mem. Privy Council for Canada 1967; mem. and fmr. Sec. Summerside Bd. of Trade; Past Pres. of Y's Men's Club; fmr. Vice-Pres. and Exec. mem. P.E.I. Young Liberal Assn.; Pres. Summerside Y.M.C.A. 1981–91; Elder, United Church, Summerside; Founding Pres. Summerside Area Historical Soc. 1983–88; Founding Chair. Duke of Edinburgh's Awards Cttee. (P.E.I.) 1984; Hon. LL.D. (McGill, P.E.I.). *Leisure interests:* golf, swimming, gardening. *Address:* Stanley Bridge, Kensington, R.R. # 6, Prince Edward Island, C0B 1M0, Canada. *Telephone:* (902) 886-2081.

CAMPBELL, Allan McCulloch, M.S., PH.D.; American professor of biology; b. 27 April 1929, Berkeley, Calif.; s. of Lindsay and Virginia Campbell; m. Alice Del Campillo 1958; one s. one d.; ed. Univ. of Calif. (Berkeley) and

Univ. of Ill.; Instructor in Bacteriology, Univ. of Mich. Medical School, Ann Arbor 1953–57; Research Assoc., Carnegie Inst. of Washington, Dept. of Genetics 1957–58; Asst. Prof. to Prof. of Biology, Univ. of Rochester, 1958–68; Prof. of Biological Sciences, Stanford Univ. 1968–; Fellow, American Acad. of Arts and Sciences; mem. Nat. Acad. of Sciences; Hon. D.Sc. (Univ. of Chicago) 1978, (Univ. of Rochester) 1981. *Publications:* Episomes 1969, General Virology 1978. *Address:* Department of Biological Sciences, Stanford University, Stanford, CA 94305 (Office); 947 Mears Court, Stanford, CA 94305, U.S.A. (Home). *Telephone:* 723-1170 (Office); 493-6155 (Home). *Fax:* 725-1848.

CAMPBELL, Ben Nighthorse, B.A.; American politician; b. 13 April 1933, Auburn, Calif; m. Linda Price; two c.; ed. Univ. of California, San José; educator Sacramento Law Enforcement Agency; Democrat mem. Colo. Gen. Ass. 1983–86, U.S. House of Reps. 1987–93, Senator from Colorado 1993–; fmr. Democrat, now Republican; rancher, jewellery designer; Chief Northern Cheyenne Tribe; mem. American Quarter Horse Asscn., American Indian Educ. Asscn., Aircraft Owners and Pilots Asscn. *Address:* U.S. Senate, 380 Russell Senate Office Building, Washington, DC 20510, U.S.A.

CAMPBELL, Bonnie Jean, B.A., J.D.; American lawyer; b. 9 April 1948, Norwich, N.Y.; d. of Thomas Pierce and Helen Slater; m. Edward Campbell 1974; called to Bar, Iowa 1985, U.S. Dist. (N. and S. dist.) Iowa 1985, U.S. Court of Appeals (8th circuit) 1989, U.S. Supreme Court 1989; Clerk, U.S. Dept. of Housing and Urban Devt. Washington, D.C. 1965–67, U.S. Senate Subcttee. on Intergovernmental Relations 1967–69; case-worker, Harold E. Hughes, Washington, D.C. 1969–74; Field rep. Senator John C. Culver, Des Moines 1974–80; Assoc. Wimer, Hudson, Flynn & Neugent, P.C., Des Moines 1984–89; of counsel, Belin, Harris, Helmick, Des Moines 1989–91; Attorney-Gen. State of Iowa 1991–95; Head, Agency for Combating Violence Against Women, U.S. Dept. of Justice 1995–. *Address:* Department of Justice, 10th Street and Constitution Avenue, Washington 20530, DC, U.S.A.

CAMPBELL, Carroll Ashmore, D.HUM.LITT.; American politician; b. 24 July 1940, Greenville, S.C.; s. of Carroll Ashmore Campbell Sr. and Anne Williams; m. Iris Rhodes 1959; two s.; ed. American Univ. and Sherman Coll.; Pres. Handy Park Co. 1960–78; mem. S.C. House of Reps. 1970–74, S.C. Senate 1976; Exec. Asst. to Gov. of S.C. 1975; Asst. Regional Whip to various State dels. at Repub. Convention 1976, 1980, 1984; mem. 96th–99th Congresses from S.C. 4th Dist.; Gov. of South Carolina 1987–95; mem. Advisory Council, White House Conf. on Handicapped Individuals; numerous awards including Guardian of Small Businesses Award, Watchdog of Treasury Award, Humanitarian Award, Rutledge Coll. and Leadership Award, American Security Council; Republican. *Address:* c/o Office of Governor, P.O. Box 11369, Columbia, SC, U.S.A.

CAMPBELL, Colin Kydd, F.R.S.C., F.R.S.A., F.I.E.E.E., F.E.I.C.; Canadian professor of electrical and computer engineering; b. 3 May 1927, St. Andrews, Scotland; s. of David Walker Campbell and Jean Bell Campbell; m. Vivian G. Norval 1954; two s. one d.; ed. Madras Coll. St. Andrews, Univ. of St. Andrews and Mass. Inst. of Technology; mil. service 1944–46; communications engineer, Diplomatic Wireless Service and Foreign Office, London, Washington and New York 1946–48; electronics engineer, Atomic Instrument Co., Cambridge, Mass. 1954–57; research scholar, Royal Naval Scientific Service, St. Andrews Univ. 1957–60; Asst. Prof. Electrical Eng. McMaster Univ. 1960–63, Assoc. Prof. 1963–67, Prof. of Electrical and Computer Eng. 1967–89, Emer. Prof. 1989–; Visiting Research Fellow Rand Afrikaans Univ., Johannesburg, S. Africa 1995; Invitation Fellow Japan Soc. for the Promotion of Science 1995; Eadie Medal (Royal Soc. of Canada) 1983, Hon. B.Eng., Hon. M.S., Hon. PH.D., Hon. D.Sc. *Publications:* Surface Acoustic Wave Devices and their Signal Processing Applications 1989, Surface Acoustic Wave Devices for Mobile and Wireless Communications 1998, numerous scientific and eng. publs. in professional and tech. journals with specialization in surface acoustic wave devices. *Leisure interests:* fishing, travelling. *Address:* Department of Electrical and Computer Engineering, McMaster University, 1280 Main Street West, Hamilton, Ont., L8S 4L7 (Office); 160 Parkview Drive, Ancaster, Ont., L9G 1Z5, Canada (Home). *Telephone:* (905) 525-9140 (Office); (905) 648-3867 (Home). *Fax:* (905) 523-4407.

CAMPBELL, Sir Colin Murray, Kt., LL.B.; British academic; b. 26 Dec. 1944, Aberdeen; s. of Donald Campbell and Isabel Campbell; m. Elaine Carlisle 1974; one s. one d.; ed. Robert Gordon's Coll. Aberdeen and Univ. of Aberdeen; lecturer, Faculty of Law, Univ. of Dundee 1967–69, Univ. of Edin. 1969–73; Prof. of Jurisprudence, Queen's Univ. Belfast 1973–88, Prof. Emer.; Vice-Chancellor, Univ. of Nottingham 1988–; mem. Council, Soc. for Computers and Law 1973–88, Standing Advisory Comm. on Human Rights 1977–80, Legal Aid Advisory Cttee., Northern Ireland 1978–82, Mental Health Legislation Review Cttee., Northern Ireland 1978–82, Nottingham Devt. Enterprise 1988–91, Inquiry into Police Responsibilities and Rewards 1992–93; Chair. Ind. Advisory Group on Consumers' Protection in Northern Ireland 1984, Northern Ireland Econ. Council 1987–94 (mem. 1985–94), Lace Market Devt. Co. 1989–97, Human Fertilisation and Embryology Authority 1990–94, Medical Workforce Standing Advisory Cttee. 1991–, Food Advisory Cttee. 1994–, Human Genetics Advisory Comm. 1996–; Chair. QUBIS Ltd. 1983–88, Zeton Ltd. 1990. *Publications:* Law and Society 1979 (jtly.), Do We Need a Bill of Rights (ed.) 1980, Data Processing and the Law (ed.) 1984; numerous articles in books and journals. *Leisure interests:* walking, sport, music, reading. *Address:* University of Nottingham, University Park, Nottingham, NG7 2RD, England. *Telephone:* (0115) 951 3001. *Fax:* (0115) 951 3005.

CAMPBELL, Finley Alexander, PH.D., F.R.S.C.; Canadian geologist; b. 5 Jan. 1927, Kenora, Ont.; s. of Finley McLeod Campbell and Vivian Delve; m. Barbara E. Cromarty 1953; two s. one d.; ed. Kenora High School, Portland Univ., Brandon Coll., Univ. of Manitoba, Queen's Univ. Kingston, Ont. and Princeton Univ.; exploration and mine geologist 1950–58; Asst., Assoc. Prof. Univ. of Alberta 1958–65; Prof. and Head Dept. of Geology, Univ. of Calgary 1965–69; Vice-Pres. Capital Resources, Univ. of Calgary 1969–71, Vice-Pres. (Academic) 1971–76, Prof. of Geology 1976–84, Vice-Pres. Priorities and Planning 1984–88, Prof. Emer. Dept. of Geology and Geophysics 1988–; Vice-Chair. Bd. of Dirs. Canadian Energy Research Inst.; Pres. Emer. Asscn., Univ. of Calgary; Queen's Jubilee Medal, Commemorative Medal for 125th Anniversary of Canada, Distinguished Service Award (Brandon Univ.) 1993, and other awards and distinctions. *Publications:* over 50 publs. on geological topics. *Leisure interests:* sailing, golf, music, skiing, ballet. *Address:* Department of Geology and Geophysics, University of Calgary, 2500 University Drive N.W., Calgary, T2N 1N4 (Office); 3408 Benton Drive N.W., Calgary Alta, T2L 1W8, Canada (Home).

CAMPBELL, Gordon Arden, M.A., F.ENG.; British chemical engineer; b. 16 Oct. 1946; s. of Hugh Eric Campbell and Jessie Campbell; m. Jennifer Vaughan 1970; two d.; ed. Oldershaw Grammar School, Churchill Coll., Cambridge; joined Courtaulds Research 1968; Man. Dir. British Celanese Ltd. 1980–85, Saiccor (Pty.) Ltd., S. Africa 1985–87; Dir. Courtaulds PLC 1987–, Chief Exec. 1996–; Vice-Pres. Inst. of Chemical Engineers 1992–94; Pres. Comité Int. de Rayonne at Fibres Synthetique 1995–; mem. (non-exec.) UKAEA 1993–96; Dir. (non-exec.) A.E.A. Tech. 1996–97, Argos PLC 1997–. *Leisure interests:* golf, skiing, rugby. *Address:* Courtaulds PLC, 50 George Street, London W1A 2BB, England.

CAMPBELL, Iain Donald, M.A., PH.D., F.R.S.; British biochemist; b. 24 April 1941, Perth, Scotland; s. of Daniel Campbell and Catherine Campbell (née Lauder); m. Karin C. Wehle 1967; one s. two d.; ed. Univs. of St. Andrews and Oxford; with Dept. of Physics, Univ. of Bradford 1966–67; with Physical Chemistry Lab., Univ. of Oxford 1967–70, Dept. of Biochemistry 1970–, tutor in Biochemistry and Fellow St. John's Coll. 1987–, Prof. of Structural Biology 1992–, Assoc. Head of Dept. of Biochemistry 1998–; del. to Oxford Univ. Press 1996–; mem. Wellcome Trust MC Panel 1997–; BHD Medal, Biochemical Soc. 1990. *Publications:* papers and reviews in scientific journals. *Address:* Department of Biochemistry, University of Oxford, South Parks Road, Oxford, OX1 3QU, England.

CAMPBELL, John, M.A.; Irish diplomatist; b. 23 June 1936, Dublin; s. of Ernest Campbell and Bertha Campbell (née Willan); m. Nicole Lafon 1964; two s.; ed. Trinity Coll. Dublin, Yale Univ., U.S.A.; Amb. to People's Repub. of China 1980–83, to Fed. Repub. of Germany 1983–86, to EC 1986–91, to France 1991–95; Perm. Rep. to UN, New York 1995–98. *Address:* c/o Department of Foreign Affairs, 80 St. Stephen's Green, Dublin 2, Ireland.

CAMPBELL, Juliet Jeanne d'Auvergne, C.M.G., M.A.; British fmr. diplomatist and university college head; b. 23 May 1935, London; d. of Wilfred d'Auvergne Collings and Harriet Nancy Draper Bishop; m. Alexander Elmslie Campbell 1983; ed. schools in S. Africa, Palestine, Lebanon and U.K., Lady Margaret Hall, Oxford; joined Foreign Office, London 1957, Del. to Conf. negotiating Britain's proposed entry to EC 1961–63, Second Sec., Bangkok 1964–67, First Sec. Paris (NATO) 1966, First Sec., FCO News Dept. 1967–70, Head of Chancery, The Hague 1970–74, First Sec. then Counsellor FCO 1974–77, Counsellor, Paris 1977–80, Royal Coll. Defence Studies 1981, Counsellor, Jakarta 1982–83, Head, Training Dept. 1983–87; Amb. to Luxembourg 1987–91; mem. Wilton Park Acad. Council 1992–; Mistress Girton Coll., Cambridge 1992–98; Deputy Vice-Chancellor, Cambridge Univ. 1993–98; Hon. Fellow Lady Margaret Hall Coll. (Oxford Univ.) 1992; Trustee Cambridge European Trust 1994–, Kurt Hahn Trust 1995–. *Address:* 3 Belbroughton Road, Oxford, OX2 6UZ, England.

CAMPBELL, Kim (Avril Phaedra), P.C.; Canadian politician and lawyer; b. 10 March 1947; ed. Univ. of British Columbia; lecturer in Science and History, Vancouver Community Coll., in Political Science, Univ. of B.C.; mem. B.C. Legis.; elected Progressive Conservative House of Commons 1988; Minister of State Affairs and Northern Devt. 1989–90, Minister of Justice and Attorney-Gen. of Canada 1990–93; Minister of Defence 1993; Prime Minister of Canada June–Nov. 1993; mem. Advisory Bd. Youth Option Program, Visiting Cttee. Center for Int. Affairs, Harvard Univ. 1995–; Hon. Dir. Volunteer Grandparents Asscn.; Progressive Conservative leader June–Nov. 1993; Hon. Fellow L.S.E. 1994. *Publication:* Time and Chance: A Political Memoir of Canada's First Woman Prime Minister 1996.

CAMPBELL, Naomi; British fashion model; b. 1970, London; d. of Valerie Morris; ed. Barbara Speake Stage School, Italia Conti; fashion model 1985–; recording artist with Sony Epic; released album Baby Woman 1994, Love and Tears 1994. *Publication:* Swan (novel) 1994. *Address:* c/o Elite Model Management, 40 Parker Street, London, WC2B 5PH, England.

CAMPBELL, Roderick Samuel Fisher, A.M., PH.D., D.SC., M.R.C.V.S., F.R.S.E.; Australian professor of tropical veterinary science; b. 5 June 1924, Glasgow, Scotland; s. of Robert Campbell and Harriet Hodson; m. Barbara M. Morris 1956; three s.; ed. Allan Glens School, Glasgow, McLaren High

School, Callander, and Glasgow Veterinary Coll.; Lecturer in Veterinary Pathology, Univ. of Glasgow 1948, Sr. Lecturer 1956–69; Prof. and Head, Grad. School of Tropical Veterinary Science, James Cook Univ. Townsville 1969–87, Emer. Prof. 1987–, Chair. Convocation 1992–94, Dir. Anton Breinl Centre for Tropical Health and Medicine, Townsville 1990–91; Visiting Prof. Khartoum Univ. 1964–65, Purdue Univ., U.S.A. 1967–68; Deputy Chair. Australian Veterinary Schools Acreditation Cttee. 1988–92; Project Man. Balitvet Inst. Project, Bogor, Indonesia 1981–; Consultant, Food and Agric. Org., World Bank, Australian Centre for Int. Agric. Research, Int. Devt. Program of Australian Univs., Australian Devt. Asst. Bureau, Ove Arup; Trustee, Indonesia Int. Animal Science Research and Devt. Foundation 1990–93; Fellow Australian Coll. of Veterinary Science, Australian Coll. of Tropical Medicine, Royal Coll. of Pathology; Hon. D.Sc. (James Cook); Kesteven Medal for Contrib. to Int. Veterinary Science, Pegasus Medal. *Publications:* numerous scientific papers on infectious diseases, veterinary educ., devt. assistance etc. *Leisure interests:* history, music, golf. *Address:* 21 Potts Street, Townsville, Queensland, Australia (Home). *Telephone:* (07) 4772 6249 (Home).

CAMPBELL, Steven MacMillan, B.A.; British artist; b. 19 March 1953, Glasgow; s. of George Campbell and Martha (née MacMillan) Dallas; m. Carol Ann Thompson 1975; one s. two d.; ed. Rutherglen Acad., Glasgow School of Art, Pratt Inst., N.Y.; one-man exhbns. include: Barbara Toll Fine Art 1985, Marlborough Fine Art, N.Y. 1988, 1994, Tokyo 1990, The Third Eye Centre, Glasgow 1990, Southampton City Art Gallery 1991, Talbot Rice Gallery, Edin. 1993. Major works for Hirshorn Museum, Tate Gallery, British Council, Wardsworth Atheneum, Metropolitan Museum. *Leisure interests:* angling, reading mathematics, detective novels, opera. *Address:* Marlborough Fine Art (U.K.) Ltd., 6 Albemarle Street, London, W1X 4BY; Rennies Loan, The Cross, Kippen, Stirlingshire, FK8 3DX, England. *Telephone:* 0171-629 5161 (London); (01786) 870370 (Stirling). *Fax:* 0171-629 6338 (London).

CAMPBELL OF CROY, Baron (Life Peer), cr. 1974; **Gordon Thomas Calthrop Campbell,** P.C., M.C.; British politician; b. 8 June 1921, Quetta, Pakistan; s. of Maj.-Gen. and Mrs. J. A. Campbell; m. Nicola Madan 1949; two s. one d.; ed. Wellington Coll.; served in regular army 1939–46 (Maj. 1942), wounded and disabled; diplomatic service 1946–57, mem. U.K. mission to UN 1949–52, Cabinet Office 1954–56; M.P. for Moray and Nairn 1959–74; Lord Commr. of the Treasury 1962; Parl. Under-Sec. of State for Scotland 1963–64; Sec. of State for Scotland 1970–74; Opposition Spokesman in House of Lords 1975–79; Oil Industry Consultant 1975–; Partner in Holme Rose Farms and Estate 1969–; Dir. and Chair. Scottish Bd. of Alliance and Leicester Building Soc. 1985–; Chair. Advisory Cttee. on Pollution of the Sea 1987–89; Chair. Scottish Council of Independent Schools; Chair. Stoic Insurance Services 1979–96; Chair. Scottish Cttee., Int. Year of Disabled 1981; Vice-Lord Lieut. of Nairnshire 1988; Trustee, Thomson Foundation 1977–; Pres. Anglo-Austrian Soc. 1991–; Conservative. *Publication:* Disablement: Prospects and Problems in the U.K. 1981. *Leisure interests:* music, birds. *Address:* Holme Rose, Cawdor, Nairn, Scotland. *Telephone:* (01667) 493223.

CAMPESE, David Ian; Australian rugby football player; b. 21 Oct. 1962, Queanbeyan, N.S.W.; s. of Tony Campese and Joan Campese; partner Campo's Sports Store; int. debut Australia versus N.Z. 1982; Capt. Australia team; winner World Cup 1991; world's leading try scorer with 64; scored 310 points; Australia's most capped player (represented Australia 101 times); Dir. David Campese Man. Gp. 1997–; Australian Writers Player of the Year 1991, English Rugby Writers Player of the Year 1991. *Leisure interests:* golf, cooking, music, reading. *Address:* David Campese Management Group, Suite 4, 870 Pacific Highway, Gordon, N.S.W. 2072, Australia.

CAMPION, Jane, B.A.; New Zealand film director and writer; b. Wellington; d. of Richard Campion and Edith Campion; ed. Victoria Univ., Chelsea School of Arts, London, Australian Film, TV and Radio School. *Films directed:* Peel 1981–82 (Palme d'Or, Cannes Film Festival 1986), Girls Own Story 1984 (won awards at Sydney and Melbourne Film Festivals, Australian Film Inst. Awards, Cinestud Amsterdam Film Festival), Passionless Moments 1983–84, After Hours 1984, Two Friends 1986, Sweetie (co-writer also) 1988, An Angel at my Table 1990 (voted Best Woman Dir., Best Film at Venice Film Festival 1990), The Piano (Palme d'Or, Cannes Film Festival) 1993, Portrait of a Lady 1996, Holy Smoke 1998. *Address:* c/o Hilary Linstead and Associates, Level 18 Plaza II, 500 Oxford Streeet, Bondi Junction, N.S.W. 2022, Australia.

CÁMPORA, Mario, PH.D.: Argentinian diplomatist; b. 3 Aug. 1930, Mendoza; s. of Pedro Cámpora and Ana Miralles; m. Magdalena Díaz Gavier 1972; one s. two d.; ed. Nat. Univ. of Rosario; joined Foreign Service 1955; served Geneva, Washington, D.C., The Hague, New Delhi; active in politics as mem. Justicialist Party 1971–73; resgnd. from diplomatic service 1975; following 1976 coup was active in opposition seeking restoration of civil liberties, law and order 1976–83; Amb. Argentine Special Mission for Disarmament, Geneva 1985; Asst. to presidential cand., Dr Carlos Menem (q.v.) 1988; Sec. of State, Ministry of Foreign Affairs 1989; Amb. to U.K. 1990–94, to Belgium (also accred. to Luxembourg) 1996–. *Address:* Argentinian Embassy, Avenue Louise 225, 1050 Brussels, Belgium. *Telephone:* (02) 647.78.12. *Fax:* (02) 647.93.19.

CÂNDEA, Virgil; Romanian historian; b. 29 April 1927, Focşani; s. of Lucian Cândea and of Elena Cândea; m. Alexandrina M. Anastasiu 1957; two s. one d.; ed. Bucharest Univ.; head documentation dept. of the Romanian Acad. Library 1950–61; Dir. Int. Asscn. of South-East European Studies, Bucharest 1963–68, Sec.-Gen. 1988–94; Sr. Fellow Inst. of South-East European Studies, Bucharest 1968–72; Prof. Institut Universitaire de Hautes Etudes Internationales, Geneva 1967–71; Gen. Sec. of Romania Asscn. 1972–90; Prof. Bucharest Univ.; Vice-Pres. Centro italo-rumeno di Studi Storici, Milan 1978–92; mem. Romanian Writers' Union 1971, Hellenic Soc. of Archaeology, Athens 1989–, Romanian Acad. 1992– (Pres. 1998–), European Acad. of Arts, Sciences and Humanities, Paris 1996–; Corresp. mem. Sudosteuropa Gesellschaft, Munich 1990–; Fellow Wilson Center, Smithsonian Inst. 1984; Ordre du Cèdre Award (Lebanon); Prize of Romanian Acad. *Publications:* Pagini din istoria diplomaţiei româneşti (Pages from the History of Romanian Diplomacy) 1966, co-author; Stolnicul între contemporani (The High Steward Among Contemporaries) 1971; An Outline of Romanian History 1971; Raţiunea dominantă (The Prevailing Reason) 1979; co-author: Witnesses to the Romanian presence in Mount Athos 1979, Romanian Culture Abroad 1982, Présences culturelles roumaines 1985, Mărturii româneşti peste hotare, Mică enciclopedie, I (Romanian Testimonies Abroad) 1991, Icônes grecques, melkites, russes 1993; critical edns. of works by N. Bălcescu, Al. Odobescu and D. Cantemir; Romanian translations from Nikitin, Bacon, Dante and others. *Leisure interests:* history, spirituality. *Address:* 125, Calea Victoriei, 71102 Bucharest (Office); 8 Intr. Procopie Dumitrescu, s. 2, 70262 Bucharest, Romania (Home). *Telephone:* (01) 312 53 42 (Office); (01) 619 20 63 (Home).

CANE, Louis Paul Joseph; French artist; b. 13 Dec. 1943, Beaulieu-sur-Mer; s. of Albert Cane and Andrée (née Pasquier) Cane; m. Nicole Rondinella 1970; two d.; ed. Collège des Frères Dominicains de Sorèze, Lycée Gassendi de Digne, Ecole Nationale des Arts Décoratifs, Nice, Ecole Nationale Supérieure des Arts Décoratifs, Paris; first exhbn. 1970; exhbns. Galerie Yvon, Lambert, Paris 1972, Galerie Templon, Paris, Milan 1973–75, Castelli Gallery, New York 1982, Galerie Beaubourg, Paris (sculptures) 1985–90, Musée de l'Orangerie des Tuileries 1994; regular exhbns. in Germany, Sweden, Spain, Belgium, Italy, Australia, Japan, U.S.S.R., U.K.; Officier des Arts et Lettres. *Publications:* Louis Cane, artiste-peintre 1967, Toiles découpées 1971, Toiles sol/mur 1972, Annonciations 1982, Déluges 1983, Accouchements 1983, Déjeuners sur l'herbe 1985, Trois graces 1987, 1988, Fleurs et tampons 1989, Nympheas 1992. *Leisure interests:* 18th-century France, studying 18th-century French bronzes. *Address:* 184 rue Saint Maur, 75010 Paris, France. *Telephone:* 42.03.73.31. *Fax:* 42.03.01.19.

CANELLA, Guido; Italian architect and university professor; b. 19 Jan. 1931, Bucharest, Romania; m. Laura Testori 1960; two s. two d.; ed. Polytechnic of Milan; Prof. of Architectural Composition, Polytechnic of Milan 1970–, Dir. Inst. of Architectural Composition 1970–79, Dir. Dept. of Architectural Design 1979–81; Dir. Architecture Section, Triennale of Milan 1978–82; Ed.-in-Chief Hinterland 1977–85, Zodiac 1989–; mem. S. Luca Nat. Acad. *Major Works:* Segrate Town Hall, Milan 1963, social services and Piazza, Villaggio Incis, Milan 1968, civic centres in Pieve Emanuele, Milan 1971 and Pioltello, Milan 1976, school centres in Opera, Milan 1974, Cesano Boscone, Milan 1975 and Parma 1985, residential complexes in Bollate, Milan 1974 and Peschiera Borromeo, Milan 1983, Law Courts redevelopment in Ancona 1975, town offices and law courts in Legnano, Milan 1982, social services, housing and Piazza in Monte d'Ago, Ancona 1984, theatre projects in Taranto 1988, Aosta 1989, Varese 1990, Church and housing at Casamassima, Bari 1991, auditorium, church and health complex in Peschiera Borromeo, Milan 1983–91, Italian Embassies' projects in Washington and Berlin 1992, Pescara Airport 1992; city planning projects for Milan 1991, Berlin 1992, Como 1993, Beirut 1994, Bucharest 1996; Inst. of Architects Prize 1968, Int. Cttee. of Architecture Critics Prize 1995. *Publications:* Il sistema teatrale a Milano 1966, Università: ragione, contesto, tipo 1975, articles in various specialist journals. *Address:* Via Revere 7, 20123 Milan, Italy. *Telephone:* (02) 4695222-333. *Fax:* (02) 4813704.

CANESTRI, H.E. Cardinal Giovanni; Italian ecclesiastic; b. 30 Sept. 1918, Alessandria; ordained 1941, elected to the titular Church of Tenedo 1961, consecrated Bishop 1961; transferred to Tortona 1971; prefect at the titular Church of Monterano 1975 with title of Archbishop; transferred to Cagliari 1984, Genoa 1987; cr. Cardinal 1987.

CANETE, Alfredo; Paraguayan diplomatist; b. 14 March 1942, Asunción; m.; one s.; Sec. in Paraguayan Mission to UN 1961–62, Perm. Rep. to UN 1983–92; Deputy Dir. Econ. Dept., Ministry of Foreign Affairs, then Dir. Dept. of Foreign Trade; Alt. Rep. to Latin-American Trade Asscn. 1973–78; Consul-Gen. and Chargé d'Affaires in U.K. 1978; Minister in Embassy, U.S.A. 1980–81; Amb. to Belgium, Netherlands and Luxembourg 1981–83, to Belgium 1992–97; Head of Mission to EEC (now EU) 1982–83, 1992–97; Cross of Kt., Order of Civil Merit, Spain. *Address:* c/o Ministry of Foreign Affairs, Juan O'Leary y Presidente Franco, Asunción, Paraguay.

CANGEMI, Joseph P., M.S., ED.D.; American professor of psychology; b. 26 June 1936, Syracuse, N.Y.; s. of Samuel Cangemi and Marion Cangemi; m. Amelia Elena Santalo' 1962; two d.; ed. State Univ. of New York, Oswego, Syracuse and Indiana Univs.; taught at Syracuse public schools and in Dominican Repub. 1960–64; Chair. and lecturer in psychology, State Univ. of N.Y. 1962–65; Supervisor of Educ. and of Training and Devt., U.S. Steel

Corpn., Venezuela 1965–68; Teaching Assoc., Ind. Univ., Bloomington, Ind. 1972, 1973; Asst. Prof. to Assoc. Prof., Western Ky. Univ., Bowling Green, Kentucky 1968–79, Prof. of Psychology and Full mem. Graduate Faculty 1979–; consultant to Firestone, General Motors and numerous cos.; Ed. Journal of Human Behavior and Learning 1983–90, Psychology—A Journal of Human Behavior 1977–, Organization Development Journal 1983–88; mem. Editorial Bd. Educ. and several other publs.; Fellow American Autogenic Soc.; mem. American Psychological Asscn., Nat. Vocational Guidance Asscn., Int. Asscn. for Educ. and Vocational Guidance, Nat. Asscn. of the Gifted, Inter-American Soc. of Psychology, Int. Registry of Org. Devt. Professionals; mem. Bd. of Trustees, William Woods Univ. 1988–; numerous awards including Distinguished Alumnus Award, State Univ. of N.Y. 1983, Distinguished Public Service Award, Western Ky. Univ. 1983, Diplomate in Professional Counselling, Int. Acad. of Behavioural Medicine, Counselling and Psychotherapy 1994. *Publications:* author or co-author of 18 books and monographs and 400 papers and articles. *Address:* Western Kentucky University, Department of Psychology, Bowling Green, KY 42101 (Office); 1409 Mt. Ayr Circle, Bowling Green, KY 42101, U.S.A. *Telephone:* (502) 745-2343 (Office); (502) 842-3436 (Home).

CANNADINE, David Nicholas, D.PHIL., LITT.D., F.R.HIST. S.; British professor of history; b. 7 Sept. 1950; s. of Sydney Douglas Cannadine and Dorothy Mary Hughes; m. Linda Jane Colley (q.v.) 1982; one d. (deceased); ed. King Edward's Five Ways School, Birmingham, Cambridge, Oxford and Princeton Univs.; Resident Fellow, St. John's Coll. Cambridge 1975–77, Asst. Lecturer in History 1976–80, lecturer 1980–88; Fellow, Christ's Coll. Cambridge 1977–88, Dir. of Studies in History 1977–83, Tutor 1979–81; Prof. of History, Col. Univ. 1988–92, Moore Collegiate Prof. 1992–98; Dir. Inst. of Historical Research 1998–; Prof. Univ. of London 1998–; Visiting Mem., Inst. for Advanced Study, Princeton Univ. 1980–81; Visiting Prof., Birkbeck Coll., London Univ. 1995–97; Visiting Fellow, Whitney Humanities Center, Yale Univ. 1995–96; Visiting Scholar, Pembroke Coll., Cambridge 1997; Fellow Berkeley Coll., Yale Univ. 1985, A.C.L.S. 1990–91; regular radio and TV broadcaster; Gen. Ed. Studies in Modern History 1979–, Penguin History of Britain 1989–, Penguin History of Europe 1991–, Historical Research 1998–; T. S. Ashton Prize (Econ. History Soc.) 1977, Silver Jubilee Prize (Agric. History Soc.) 1977, Dean's Distinguished Award in the Humanities, Columbia Univ. 1996. *Publications:* Lords and Landlords: the aristocracy and the towns 1774–1967 1980, (ed. and contrib.) Patricians, Power and Politics in Nineteenth-Century Towns 1982, (jt. ed. and contrib.) H. J. Dyos, Exploring the Urban Past 1982, (jt. ed. and contrib.) Rituals of Royalty: power and ceremonial in traditional societies 1987, The Pleasures of the Past 1989, (ed. and contrib.) Winston Churchill's Famous Speeches 1989, (jt. ed. and contrib.) The First Modern Society: essays in English history in honour of Lawrence Stone 1989, The Decline and Fall of the British Aristocracy (Lionel Trilling Prize) 1990, G. M. Trevelyan: A Life in History 1992, Aspects of Aristocracy: Grandeur and Decline in Modern Britain 1994, (jt. ed. and contrib.) History and Biography: essays in honour of Derek Beales 1996, History in Our Time 1998; numerous contribs. to other books and learned journals. *Leisure interests:* life, laughter. *Address:* Institute of Historical Research, Senate House, Malet Street, London, WC1E 7HU, England. *Telephone:* 0171-636 0272.

CANNELL, Melvin Gilbert Richard, PH.D., D.SC., F.R.S.E.; British research scientist; b. 12 Aug. 1944, Bungay; s. of Charles Cannell and Joyce Cannell; m. Maria Rietdijk 1966; two d.; ed. Bungay Grammar School and Univ. of Reading; research officer, coffee research station, Kenya 1966–71; Nat. Environment Research Council (NERC), Inst. of Tree Biology 1971–74; NERC Inst. of Terrestrial Ecology 1974–, now Head of Edin. Research Station; Hon. Prof. Univ. of Edin. *Publications:* jt. ed. Tree Physiology and Yield Improvement 1976, Trees as Crop Plants 1985; over 100 other scientific publs. *Address:* Institute of Terrestrial Ecology, Edinburgh Research Station, Bush Estate, Penicuik, Midlothian, EH26 0QB (Office); Cowieslinn Farmhouse, Eddleston, Tweeddale, Scotland, EH45 8QZ, Scotland (Home). *Telephone:* 0131-445 4343 (Office); (01721) 730355 (Home). *Fax:* 0131-445 3943 (Office).

CANNY, Nicholas Patrick, PH.D., F.R.HIST.S.; Irish professor of history; b. 4 Jan. 1944; s. of Cecil Canny and Helen Joyce; m. Morwena Denis 1974; one s. one d.; ed. St. Flannan's Coll., Ennis, Univ. Coll., Galway, Univ. of Pennsylvania, London, Harvard and Yale Univs.; lecturer in History, Univ. Coll., Galway 1972–79, Prof. of History 1980–; mem. Inst. for Advanced Study, Princeton 1979–80; Fellow Nat. Humanities Center, N.C. 1985–86; mem. Irish Manuscripts Comm. 1980–, Nat. Archives Advisory Council 1986–96; Chair. Irish Comm. Historical Sciences 1991–97; Distinguished Visiting Prof., New York Univ. 1995; mem. Royal Irish Acad. 1981, Academia Europaea 1995; Irish Historical Research Prize 1976. *Publications include:* The Elizabethan Conquest of Ireland 1976, The Upstart Earl: the social and mental world of Richard Boyle 1982, From Reformation to Restoration: Ireland 1534–1660 1987, Colonial Identity in the Atlantic World 1500–1800 1987, Kingdom and Colony: Ireland in the Atlantic World 1560–1800 1988, Europeans on the Move: Studies on European Migration 1500–1800 1994, The Oxford History of the British Empire (Vol. I): The Origins of Empire 1998. *Leisure interests:* reading, walking, music. *Address:* Department of History, National University of Ireland, Galway (Office); Furramelia West, Barna, Co. Galway, Ireland (Home). *Telephone:* 91-524411 (Office); 91-592351 (Home). *Fax:* 91-750556 (Office).

CANOGAR, Rafael, B.A.; Spanish painter; b. 17 May 1935, Toledo; s. of Genaro Rafael Canogar and Alfonsa Canogar; m. 1st Ann Jane McKenzie 1960; m. 2nd Purificación Chaves 1992; six c.; studied under Daniel Vázquez Díaz 1949–54; founder mem. El Paso group 1957–60; Visiting Prof. Milles Coll., Oakland, Calif. 1965–66; artist-in-residence D.A.A.D., Berlin 1972, 1974; mem. Exec. Cttee. Círculo de Bellas Artes, Madrid 1983–86, Advisory Bd. Dept. of Fine Arts, Ministry of Culture 1981–82, 1983–84, Bd. of Trustees, Museo Nac. de Arte Contemporáneo, Madrid 1983, Admin. Bd. Nat. Art Collections 1984–90, Exec. Cttee. Fundación de Gremios, Madrid 1984–87; more than 120 one-man shows and numerous group exhbns.; works in many public art collections world-wide; retrospectives include: Museo Nac. de Arte Contemporáneo, Madrid, Musée d'Art Moderne, Paris, Sonia Heine Foundation, Oslo, Lund Konsthalle, Biblioteca Nacional, Madrid, Paris Art Centre, Bochum Art Museum, Instituto di Storia dell'Arte, Parma, Museo de Bellas Artes, Bilbao; mem. Real Acad. de Bellas Artes de San Fernando 1998; Golden Palette Award, Int. Painting Festival, Cagnes-sur-Mer 1969, Special Award, São Paulo Biennale 1971, Special Award, Int. Painting Triennale, Sofia 1982, Premio Nacional de Artes Plásticas, Madrid 1982, Chevalier, Ordre des Arts et des Lettres 1985, Special Commendation, Orden de Isabel la Católica 1991. *Address:* Avenida Menéndez Pelayo 11-bis, 28009 Madrid, Spain. *Telephone:* (91) 5770315. *Fax:* (91) 5217096.

CANTACUZÈNE, Jean Michel, D.S.; French director of research; b. 15 Dec. 1933, Bucharest, Romania; s. of Dr Alexandre Cantacuzène and Marianne (née Labeyrie) Cantacuzène; m. 1st Anne-Marie Szekely 1956 (divorced); one s. one d.; 2nd Danièle Ricard 1971; one s.; ed. Ecole Supérieure Chem. Industry, Lyon, Ecole Normale Superieure, Paris; Asst. Prof., Ecole Normale Supérieure, Paris 1960–62, Deputy Dir., Lab. Chimie 1964–67; Scientific attaché, French Embassy, Moscow 1962–64, Counsellor for Science and Tech., Washington, D.C. 1977–80; Prof. Organic Chem., Univ. of Paris 1967–73, Titular Prof. 1972–; Dir. Chem. Scientific Dept., CNRS Paris 1973–77, Sr. Counsellor for Industrial Affairs 1988; Scientific Dir. Total Co. Française des Pétroles, Paris 1980–90; Counsellor for Scientific Affairs, Ministry of Foreign Affairs, Paris 1971–77; Chair. Bd. SOLEMS 1983–86, AVRIST 1982; mem. Conseil pour l'innovation industrielle 1989–91, Applications cttee. and cttee. to evaluate relations, Acad. of Science (Cadas) 1989–, exec. cttee. groupe Climents français 1990–92; mem. Advisory Comm. for Science and Tech. 1971–75, Industrial R and D Advisory Cttee., EEC, Brussels 1983–86; mem. council Nuclear Safety Cttee., 1981–90; Pres. Adit 1992–95; Le Bel Award 1968; Ordre Nat. Légion d'honneur, Chevalier 1982, Officier 1992, Ordre Nat. du Mérite, Chevalier 1973, Officier 1988, Laureate, Chem. Soc. of France. *Publications:* Chimie Organique 3 Vols. (co-author) 1971–75, America, Science and Technology in the 80s, 2 Vols. 1981, Mille Ans dans les Balkans, Chronique des Cantacuzène dans la Tourmente des Siècles 1992, over 60 papers in scientific journals. *Leisure interest:* book collecting, history. *Address:* Cadas, 23 quai de Conti, 75270 Paris cedex 06, France.

CANTARELLA, Paolo; Italian business executive; b. 1944, Varallo Sesia/Vercelli; m.; ed. graduate in eng.; began working in car components 1977; Intersectorial Coordinator, Fiat Group and Asst. to Man. Dir. Cesare Romiti 1980; joined Comau (machine tools) 1989; Man. of Supplies and Distribution, Fiat Auto S.p.A. 1989; Vice-Chair. Maserati S.p.A., Chair. 1993; Man. Dir. Fiat Auto S.p.A. 1990, Pres., C.E.O. 1990–96, Chair. 1996; Pres. C.E.O. Fiat S.p.A. 1996–; mem. Bd. Dirs. Teksid. *Address:* c/o Fiat S.p.A., 250 via Nizza, 10126 Turin, Italy. *Telephone:* 68-61111.

CANTENOT, Jean; French business executive and engineer; b. 19 Sept. 1919, Paris; s. of Joseph and Marcelle (née Tournay) Cantenot; m. Nicole Berrier 1948; two d. (one deceased); ed. Ecole Polytechnique and Ecole des Mines de Paris; dept. of iron-smelting, Ministry of Industry 1948–50; Chief Engineer, ARBED factory, Burbach-Saar 1950–57; Chief Engineer Schneider S.A. 1957, Asst. Dir. 1963–68; Man. Dir., then Chair. Droitaumont-Bruville Mining Co. 1957–69; Chair. and Man. Dir. Aciéries de Pompey 1968–82; Chair. and Man. Dir. SACILOR (Steel Co.) 1980–83; Pres. Union des industries métallurgiques et minières 1973–85, Hon. Pres. 1985, Lormines 1979–85; Pres. Centre d'Entraide des Ingénieurs (Cedi) 1988, Hon. Pres. 1994; Chevalier, Légion d'honneur, Officier nationale du Mérite; Croix de guerre. *Address:* 1 rue Perronet, 92200 Neuilly-sur-Seine, France (Home).

CANTERBURY, Archbishop of (see Carey, Most Rev. and Rt. Hon. George Leonard).

CANTONA, Eric; French football player; b. 24 May 1966, Paris; s. of Albert Cantona and Léonor Raurich; m. Isabelle Ferrer 1987; one s.; player, Auxerre 1980–88, Bordeaux, Marseille 1988–89, Montpellier 1989–90, Nimes 1992; player, Leeds United (League Champions 1992) 1992–93, Manchester United (League Champions 1993, 1994, 1995–96) 1993–97, Capt. 1996–97; announced retirement May 1997; Footballer of the Year (Football Writers' Asscn.) 1996, roles in films Le Bonheur et dans le Pré, Elizabeth. *Leisure interests:* painting. *Address:* Fédération française de football, 60 bis avenue d'Iéna, 75783 Paris cedex 16, France.

CANTONI, Giampiero Carlo; Italian banker; b. 10 Feb. 1939, Milan; m. Emilia Capponi; two c.; ed. Bocconi Univ. Milan; founded Elektropal Cantoni & Co. (electromechanical co.), Milan 1964; Chair. Italian Banking Inst. (IBI) 1982; Chair. Banca Nazionale del Lavoro BNL, Rome 1989, then Pres. –1994, also Chair. BNL Holding; Pres. Lombardia Fincapital; Assoc. Prof. and lecturer, School of Business, Bocconi Univ. Milan; Deputy Chair. Italian

Banking Asscn.; mem. Soc. for Fine Arts and Perm. Exhbn. Milan (Pres.); mem. Bd. Centre of Econ. Studies. *Leisure interests:* cultural, art and sport interests. *Address:* Via Vittorio Veneto 119, 00187 Rome, Italy.

CANTONI, Giulio L., M.D.; American laboratory chief; b. 29 Sept. 1915, Milan, Italy; s. of Umberto L. Cantoni and Nella Pesaro Cantoni; m. Gabriella S. Cantoni 1965; two d.; ed. Univ. of Milan, Italy; Instructor, New York Univ. 1943–45; Asst. Prof., Long Island Coll. of Medicine, New York 1945–48; Sr. Fellow, American Cancer Soc., New York 1948–50; Assoc. Prof., Western Reserve Univ., Cleveland, Ohio 1950–54; Chief, Lab. of Gen. and Comparative Biochemistry, Nat. Inst. of Mental Health 1956–; Distinguished Service Award, Dept. of Health and Human Services; mem. N.A.S. *Publications:* Onium compounds, in Handbook of Comparative Biochemistry (Eds. Florkin and Mason) 1960; papers in scientific journals. *Leisure interest:* chamber music. *Address:* National Institute of Mental Health, Building 36, Room 3D-06, Bethesda, MD 20892, U.S.A. *Telephone:* (301) 496-3241.

CANTOR, Charles, R., PH.D.; American molecular biologist; b. 26 Aug. 1942, New York; s. of Ida Diane Banks and Louis Cantor; ed. Columbia Coll. and Univ. of Calif., Berkeley; Asst. Prof. of Chemistry, Columbia Univ. 1966, Assoc. Prof. 1969, Prof. 1972, Chair. and Prof. of Genetics and Devt. 1981, Higgins Prof. 1988; Dir. Human Genome Center, Lawrence Berkeley Lab. 1989–90, Prin. Scientist, Department of Environment Human Genome Project 1990–92; Prof. of Molecular and Cell Biology, Univ. of Calif., Berkeley 1989–92; Prof. of Biomedical Eng. Boston Univ. 1992–, Chair. 1992–, Dir. Center for Advanced Biotech. 1995–; Prof. of Pharmacology 1995–; Pres. in the Americas Human Genome Org. 1991–, numerous professional appointments; mem. N.A.S., American Acad. of Arts and Sciences; Analytica Prize, German Soc. of Clinical Chem. *Publications:* Biophysical Chemistry (3 vols., with Paul Schimmel). *Leisure interests:* gastronomy, running, skiing. *Address:* Boston University, College of Engineering, 36 Cummington Street, Boston, MA 02216; Apt. 6, 11 Bay State Road, Boston, MA 02215, U.S.A. (Home).

CAO BOCHUN; Chinese politician; b. Nov. 1941, Zhuzhou City, Hunan Prov.; ed. Zhuzhou Aeronautical Industrial Training School; joined CCP 1966; Vice-Sec. CCP Zhuzhou City Cttee. 1983, Sec. 1984; Sec. CCP Xiangtan City Cttee. 1990; Vice-Gov. Hunan Prov. 1991; Vice-Sec. CCP Liaoning Prov. Cttee., Sec. Dalian City Cttee. 1992; alt. mem. 14th CCP Cen. Cttee. 1992; Sec. CCP Guangxi Zhuang Autonomous Regional Cttee. 1997–; mem. 15th CCP Cen. Cttee. 1997–. *Address:* Chinese Communist Party Guangxi Zhuang Autonomous Regional Committee, Naning City, Guangxi Zhuang Autonomous Region, People's Republic of China.

CAO GANGCHUAN, Gen.; Chinese army officer; b. Dec. 1935, Wuyang Co., Henan Prov.; ed. Third Artillery Tech. School, Zhengzhou City, PLA Russian Tech. School, Dalian, Artillery Mil. Eng. Acad. Moscow and PLA Univ. of Nat. Defence; joined PLA 1954; mem. CCP 1956–; Deputy Commdr. artillery troops during Sino-Vietnamese border conflict 1979; Deputy Dir. Equipment Dept. Gen. Staff H.Q. 1985; Dir. Mil. Affairs Dept. Gen. Staff H.Q. and Dir. Mil. Products Trade Office of Mil. Cttee. of Cen. Cttee. of CCP 1990; Deputy Dir. Leading Group for Placement of Demobilized Army Officers; Deputy Sec. Comm. for Disciplinary Inspection; Deputy Chief of Gen. Staff, PLA 1992–96; Minister State Comm. of Science, Tech. and Industry for Nat. Defence 1996–; mem. Cen. Mil. Comm. 1998–; Dir. PLA Gen. Equipment Dept. 1998–; rank of Gen. 1996; mem. 15th Cen. Cttee. CCP 1997–98. *Address:* c/o State Commission for Science, Technology and Industry for National Defence, Jingshanqian Jie, Beijing, People's Republic of China.

CAO QINGZE; Chinese government and party official; b. 1932, Lixian Co., Hunan Prov.; joined CCP 1952; Sec. Comm. for Discipline Inspection of CCP Sichuan Provincial Cttee. 1986–93; Minister of Supervision 1993–98; Hon. Pres. Soc. of Supervision; Deputy Sec. CCP Cen. Comm. for Inspecting Discipline 1997–. *Address:* c/o Ministry of Supervision, 35 Huayuanbei Lu, Haidan Qu, Beijing 100083, People's Republic of China.

CAO SHUANGMING, Lieut.-Gen.; Chinese army officer and party official; b. 1929, Linxian Co., Henan Prov.; joined CCP 1946; Deputy Commdr. PLA Shengyang Mil. Area Command 1987–92, Commdr. 1992–; rank of Lieut.-Gen. 1988; mem. 14th CCP Cen. Cttee. 1992–. *Address:* Shengyang Military Area Command, People's Liberation Army, Shengyang City, Liaoning Province, People's Republic of China.

CAO YUANXIN; Chinese diplomatist; b. 20 Feb. 1930, Hangzhou; s. of Cao Shiliang and Shen Zhiying; m. Zhao Yingyou 1953; two s.; Deputy Dir. Protocol Dept., Ministry of Foreign Affairs 1981, Dir (a.i.); Amb. to Spain 1984, to Liberia 1988–89; Vice-Pres. Chinese Asscn. for the Advancement of Int. Friendship. Dec. 1991–. *Leisure interests:* music, swimming. *Address:* 9, Xi Zong Bu Hutong, Beijing 100005, People's Republic of China. *Telephone:* 5121036. *Fax:* 5121040.

CAO ZHI; Chinese politician; b. 1928, Shangzhi Co., Heilongjiang Prov.; joined CCP 1947; Deputy Sec.-Gen. 7th Standing Cttee NPC 1988–92; Sec.-Gen. 8th Standing Cttee. NPC 1993–98; Vice-Chair. Standing Cttee. 9th NPC 1998–; a Vice-Chair. Cen. Cttee. for Comprehensive Man. of Social Security 1993–. *Address:* Standing Committee, National People's Congress, Tian'anmen Square, Beijing, People's Republic of China.

CAPA, Cornell, (b. Friedman); American photographer; b. 10 April 1918, Budapest, Hungary; ed. Imre Madách Gymnasium, Budapest; moved to New York 1937; began work in darkroom of Life magazine 1938; first photo story published in Picture Post, U.K. 1939; worked in U.S.A.F. Photo-Intelligence Unit and for U.S.A.F. public relations 1941–46; staff photographer Life magazine 1946–54, resident photographer in England 1950–52; returned to U.S.A. 1952, covered maj. political events for Life until 1967; mem. Magnum Photos. Inc. 1954–; extensive travel in S. America 1961–64; organizer exhbn. The Concerned Photographer shown throughout U.S.A. and in Europe and Israel 1964; covered Six-Day War in Israel 1967; photographic work in El Salvador and Honduras 1970–73, Papua New Guinea 1973; founder, Int. Center of Photography, New York 1974, Dir. 1974–. *Publications include:* Retarded Children Can Be Helped 1957, Margin of Life 1974; numerous photo-essays for Life 1946–72. *Address:* 275 5th Avenue, New York, N.Y. 10016, U.S.A.

CAPELLINO, Ally, B.A.; British fashion designer; ed. Middlesex Univ.; worked in Courtaulds Cen. Design Studio 1978–79; est. Ally Capellino Little Hat, initially selling hats and accessories 1979; developed clothing line with accessories for Moscow Olympics collection 1979–80; began selling Ally Capellino label to int. markets 1980; launched menswear collection 1986; first London fashion show 1986; opened shop in Soho, London 1988; launched Hearts of Oak sportswear collection 1990, Mini Capellino children's wear 1991; signed promotional and licensing agreement with Coats Viyella PLC 1992; launched 'ao' collection 1996; opened Ally Capellino shop, London 1997; opened flagship store Tokyo, Japan 1998. *Address:* N1R, Metropolitan Wharf, Wapping Wall, London, E1 9SS, England. *Telephone:* 0171-488 9777. *Fax:* 0171-488 9852.

CAPLIN, Mortimer M., B.S., LLB., J.S.D.; American government official, lawyer and educator; b. 11 July 1916, New York; s. of Daniel Caplin and Lillian Epstein; m. Ruth Sacks 1942; three s. one d.; ed. Univ. of Virginia and New York Univ. Law School; law Clerk to U.S. Circuit Judge 1940–41; legal practice with Paul, Weiss, Rifkind, Wharton & Garrison, New York 1941–50; U.S.N.R., Beachmaster in Normandy landings 1942–45; Prof. of Law, Univ. of Virginia 1950–61, lecturer and Visiting Prof. 1965–87, Prof. Emer. 1988–; Counsel to Perkins, Battle & Minor 1952–61; U.S. Commr. of Internal Revenue 1961–64; Sr. Partner, Caplin & Drysdale, Washington, D.C. 1964–; Chair. Nat. Civil Service League 1965–80, American Council on Int. Sports 1975–80, Nat. Citizens' Advisory Cttee. 1975–80, Asscn. of American Medical Colls.; Dir. Fairchild Corpn., Presidential Reality Corpn., Danaher Corpn.; mem. Public Review Bd., Arthur Andersen & Co. 1980–88; mem. House of Dels. 1980–92, D.C. and Fed. Bar Asscns., Va. and N.Y. State Bars, American Law Inst.; Ed.-in-Chief Virginia Law Review 1939–40; mem. Bd. of Trustees, George Washington Univ. 1964, Coll. of the Virgin Islands, Univ. of Va. Law School Foundation 1982–, Shakespeare Theatre, Wolf Trap Foundation; Hon. LL.D. (St. Michael Coll.) 1964; Order of the Coif, Raven Award, Alexander Hamilton Award, and other awards. *Publications:* Doing Business in Other States, Proxies, Annual Meetings and Corporate Democracy, and numerous articles on tax and corporate matters. *Leisure interests:* swimming, horseback riding, gardening. *Address:* One Thomas Circle, N.W., Washington, DC 20005 (Office); Apartment 18E, 5610 Wisconsin Avenue, Chevy Chase, MD 20815, U.S.A. (Home). *Telephone:* (202) 862-5050 (Office).

CAPPELLO, Carmelo; Italian sculptor; b. 21 May 1912; m. Selene Varale Cappello; one s. one d.; ed. Istituto Superiore d'Arte di Monza; sculptor 1937–; regular exhibitor at Venice Biennali, Milan Triennali and Rome Quadriennali since 1947; represented in major collections and int. exhbns. throughout the world; mem. Nat. Cttee. of UNESCO Div. of Plastic Arts; mem. Accad. Nazionale di San Luca; numerous awards. *Major works:* Freddoloso 1938, Uomo nello spazio 1955, Tempesta 1956, Cristo e i due ladroni 1955, Volo Stratosferico 1958, Il Folle 1948, Il Filosofo 1949, Tuffatori 1958, Gli Acrobati 1955, Eclisse 1959, Fughe ritmiche 1961, Involuzione del cerchio 1962, Fontana per curve d'acqua 1958, Ala 1960, Ritmi Chiusi 1963, Superficie-Spazio: Itinerario Circolare 1964, Traiet-toria Dal Piano Dello Spazio: 1965, Occhio di Cielo 1966, Cerchi in Movimento, Milan. *Address:* Bastioni Porta Nuova 11, 20121 Milan, Italy. *Telephone:* 6552431.

CAPPUCCILLI, Piero; Italian baritone opera singer; b. 9 Nov. 1929, Trieste; m. Graziella Bossi; ed. architectural studies in Rome; studied singing with Maestro Luciano Donaggio at Teatro Giuseppe Verdi, Trieste; debut as Tonio (I Pagliacci), Teatro Nuovo, Milan 1957; debut at La Scala Milan in Lucia di Lammermoor 1964; Covent Garden debut in La Traviata 1967; U.S. debut in I Due Foscari at Lyric Opera of Chicago 1969; appears at all leading Italian opera houses and major opera houses through the world; recordings include Lucia di Lammermoor (with Callas), La Gioconda, Aida, La Forza del Destino, Un Ballo in Maschera, Macbeth, Rigoletto.

CAPRA, Carlo; Italian professor of history; b. 14 Nov. 1938, Quartu S. Elena, Cagliari; s. of Agostino Capra and Maria Maxia; m. Maria Grazia Bosi 1964; one s.; ed. Univ. of Milan; teacher of English in state secondary schools until 1970; Asst. lecturer in History, Milan State Univ. 1970–72, Reader 1972–81, Assoc. Prof. 1981–86, Prof. 1986–, Head, Dept. of History 1989–92; mem. Scientific Council, Società Italiana di Studi sul XVIII Secolo. *Publications:* Giovanni Ristori da illuminista a funzionario (1755–1830) 1968, Il giornalismo nell'età rivoluzionaria e napoleonica 1976, La Lombardia austriaca nell'età delle riforme 1984, 1987; Ed.: Cesare Beccaria, Carlegio vols. IV–V of Edizione Nazionale delle Opere 1995. *Leisure interests:* music, cinema. *Address:* Istituto di Storia medievale e moderna, Via Chiaravalle 7,

Milan 20122 (Office); Corso Garibaldi 71, Milan 20121, Italy (Home). *Telephone:* (02) 58308008 (Office); (02) 86461509 (Home).

CAPRIATI, Jennifer; American tennis player; b. 29 March 1976, New York; d. of Stefano Capriati; studying Pasco High School, Fla.; coached by her father; winner, French Open Jr. 1989, U.S. Open Jr. 1989, Wimbledon and U.S. Open Jr. Doubles 1989; youngest player in Whiteman Cup 1989; competitor on pro tour 1990–Nov. 1993, 1994, 1996–; Wimbledon début 1990; semi-finalist French Open 1990, U.S. Open 1991, Wimbledon 1991 (youngest Grand Slam Finalist in tennis history), Boca Raton 1991, German Open 1991; Gold Medal (Olympic Games of 1992). *Address:* International Management Group, c/o Barbara Perry, 22 E. 71 Street, New York, NY 10021, U.S.A.

CAPRIO, H.E. Cardinal Giuseppe, J.C.D., S.T.L.; Italian ecclesiastic; b. 15 Nov. 1914, Lapio, Avellino; ed. Diocesan and Regional Seminaries, Benevento, Pontifical Gregorian Univ., Rome, Pontifical Ecclesiastical Acad., Rome; ordained Roman Catholic Priest 1938; Attaché, Secretariat of State, Vatican City 1943–47; Sec., Apostolic Nunciature, Nanking, China 1947–51; Auditor, Apostolic Nunciature, Brussels, Belgium 1952–56; Apostolic Visitor to Repub. of Viet Nam and later Regent of Apostolic Del. in Saigon 1956–59; Apostolic Nuncio to China, serving in Taiwan 1959–67; Titular Archbishop of Apollonia 1961; Apostolic Pro-Nuncio to India 1967–69; Sec. of Admin. of Patrimony of the Holy See 1969–77; Substitute of the Secretariat of State 1977–79; Pres. of Admin. of the Patrimony of the Holy See 1979–81; mem. Sacred Congregation for the Evangelization of Peoples, Pontifical Comm. for the Revision of Canon Law; created Cardinal 1979. *Address:* Piazza del S. Uffizio 11, 00193 Rome, Italy.

CAPRON, Alexander Morgan, LL.B; American professor of law; b. 16 Aug. 1944, Hartford, Conn.; s. of William M. and Margaret (Morgan) Capron; m. 1st Barbara A. Brown 1969 (divorced 1985); m. 2nd Kathleen M. West 1989; four c.; ed. Palo Alto High School, Swarthmore Coll. and Yale Law School; law clerk, U.S. Court of Appeals, D.C. Circuit 1969–70; Lecturer and Research Assoc. Yale Law School 1970–72; Asst. Prof. to Prof. of Law and Prof. of Human Genetics, Univ. of Pa. 1972–82; Exec. Dir. President's Comm. for Study of Ethical Problems in Medicine and Biomedical and Behavioural Research 1979–83; Prof. of Law, Ethics and Public Policy, Georgetown Univ. 1983–84; Topping Prof. of Law, Medicine and Public Policy, Univ. of Southern Calif. 1985–89, Univ. Prof. of Law and Medicine 1989–, Co-Dir. Pacific Center for Health Policy and Ethics 1990–; Henry W. Bruce Prof. of Law 1991–; Pres. American Soc. of Law and Medicine 1988–89; Chair. Biomedical Ethics Advisory Cttee., U.S. Congress 1988–91; mem. Nat. Bioethics Advisory Comm. 1996–; several honours and awards. *Publications:* books including Catastrophic Diseases: Who Decides What? (with J. Katz) 1975, Law, Science and Medicine (with others) 1984, Treatise on Health Care Law (with others) 1991, and 200 articles in journals and books. *Leisure interests:* gardening, films, travel. *Address:* The Law School, University of Southern California, University Park, MC 0071, Los Angeles, CA 90089-0071, U.S.A. *Telephone:* (213) 740-2557. *Fax:* (213) 740-5502.

CAPUTO, Dante; Argentinian politician, diplomatist and professor; b. 25 Nov. 1943, Buenos Aires; m. Anne Morel; three s.; ed. Salvador Univ. of Buenos Aires, Univ. of Paris, Univ. of Tuffs and Harvard, Boston; Adjunct Prof. of Political Sociology, Salvador Univ., Buenos Aires; Adjunct Prof. of Public Services and State Enterprises, Univ. of Buenos Aires; Dir. Center for Social Investigations on State and Admin. 1976; Adjunct investigator Nat. Center for Scientific Investigation, France; Minister of Foreign Affairs and of Worship 1983–88; Pres. UN Gen. Ass. 1988–89; fmr. special Rep. of UN Soc.-Gen. in Haiti. *Address:* c/o Ministerio de Relaciones Exteriores y Culto, Reconquista 1088 C.P. 1003, Buenos Aires, Argentina.

CARAMITRU, Ion; Romanian actor, theatre director and politician; b. 9 March 1942; s. of Aristide Caramitru and Maria Caramitru; m. Michaela Caracas 1975; three s.; ed. Theatre and Cinema Art Inst., Bucharest; leading actor and dir., Bulandra Theatre, Bucharest 1965; Prof. of Drama, IATC Bucharest 1976; *Principal roles include:* Romeo, Hamlet, Julius Caesar, Feste, Leonce (Büchner), Eugen Marchbanks (Bernard Shaw), Cotrone (Pirandello), Perdican (Musset), Riccardo Fontana (Rolf Hochhuth) etc. *Directed:* Remembrances (Aleksei Arbuzov), Insignificance (Terry Johnson), Dialogues (author's performance), The Third Stake (Marin Sorescu), The Shape of the Table (David Edgar), Home (David Storey); musical theatre: Eminescu (Paul Urmuzescu), My Fair Lady; opera: The Little Sweep (Benjamin Britten), Carmen (Bizet) for Belfast Opera 1993, Eugene Onegin (Tchaikovsky) for Belfast Opera 1994, Bastien and Bastienne (Mozart) for Tăndărică puppet theatre, Bucharest. *Films include:* The Treasure from Old River Bed, The City Blue Gates, Luchian, Oak—Extreme Urgency, The Purse with Dragon Flies, High-School Pupils, Civic Education Test-Write, Darkness, Citizen X, Mission Impossible. *Television appearances:* Jude City (BBC serial) 1992, An Exchange of Fire 1993, A Question of Guilt 1993, Two Deaths (BBC TV) 1994; numerous awards; mem. Exec. Bureau, Council of Nat. Salvation Front Dec. 1989–, Pres. of Cultural Cttee. 1990; Vice-Pres. of Prov. Council for Nat. Unity (responsibility for cultural and youth problems) 1990–; Pres. ITI Romanian Centre, Romanian Theatre Union (UNITER) 1990–, Artistic Dir. Bulandra Bucharest 1990–92; Minister of Culture 1996–. *Leisure interests:* collecting icons, tennis, writing, painted popular eggs. *Address:* UNITER, 2–4, George Enescu Str., Bucharest (Office); Ministry of Culture, Piaţa Presei Libere, s. 1, 71241, Bucharest; 16, Caderea Bastiliei, Sector i, Bucharest, Romania (Home). *Telephone:* (1) 311.32.14 (Office); (1) 222.33.38 (Ministry); (1) 210.63.37 (Home). *Fax:* (1) 312.09.13 (Office); (1) 223.49.51 (Ministry); (1) 210.57.83 (Home).

CARAZO ODIO, Rodrigo; Costa Rican politician; b. 27 Dec. 1926, Cartago; active mem. of Partido de Liberación Nacional (PLN) until resignation 1969, occupying posts as Dir. Nat. Inst. of Housing and Urbanization 1954–59, Adviser on Housing and Finance, Banco Obrero de Venezuela 1959–63, Dir. Banco Central de Costa Rica 1963–65; Deputy to Legislative Assembly of Costa Rica 1966, then Pres., Dir. Recope (state enterprise controlling distribution of petroleum products); founded Renovación Democrática, taking fourth place in presidential elections 1974; Leader of coalition party Unidad (Renovación Democrática, Republicano Calderonista, Unión Popular, Demócrata Cristiano) 1976–82; Pres. of Costa Rica 1978–82; Prof. of Econs., Admin., Econ. Devt. and History, visiting lecturer to U.S.A. and South America; agricultural, commercial and industrial activities. *Address:* University for Peace, Apdo 199, San José, Costa Rica.

CARDEN, Joan Maralyn, A.O., O.B.E.; Australian opera singer; b. Melbourne; d. of late Frank Carden and of Margaret Carden (née Cooke); m. William Coyne 1962 (divorced 1980); two d.; ed. schools in Melbourne, language studies in London, Trinity Coll. of Music, London and London Opera Centre; voice studies with Thea Phillips and Henry Portnoj, Melbourne and Vida Harford, London; first opera engagement, world premiere of Williamson's Our Man in Havana, Sadler's Wells; joined The Australian Opera 1971; Covent Garden debut as Gilda (Rigoletto) 1974; Glyndebourne debut as Anna (Don Giovanni) 1977; U.S. debut at Houston as Amenaide (Tancredi) 1977; Metropolitan Opera Tour as Anna (Giovanni) 1978; perf. regularly in concert repertoire of Sydney Symphony Orchestra and Australian Broadcasting Corpn.; Dame Joan Hammond Award for Outstanding Service to Opera in Australia 1987, Australia Creative Fellowship 1993. *Leisure interests:* gardening, theatre, reading. *Address:* c/o The Australian Opera, P.O. Box 291, Strawberry Hills, N.S.W. 2012, Australia.

CARDENAS CONDE, Victor Hugo, B.A.; Bolivian politician and academic; b. 4 June 1951, Achica Abajo Aymara Indian community, Omasuyos Prov., Dept. of La Paz; m. Lidia Katari 1980; one s. two d.; ed. Ayacucho High School, Universidad Mayor de San Andrés (UMSA); univ. lecturer, then prof. in educ. sciences, linguistics and languages, Faculty of Humanities and Educ., UMSA State Univ. 1975–92; Chair. First Nat. Congress for Peasant Unity 1979; consultant on educational issues UNESCO and UNICEF 1990, various other orgs. 1992; Prof. Latin American Coll. of Social Sciences 1992–93; Nat. Rep. Tupac Katari Revolutionary Movt. of Liberation party (MRTKL), Exec. Sec. (Nat. Exec. Cttee.) 1993; Pres. Nat. Congress 1993–94, Andean Parl. 1993–94, Science and Tech. Nat. Council 1993–94; Vice-Pres. of Bolivia 1993–97; mem. Culture and Educ. Comm., Bolivian Workers Union 1979, Educ. and Culture Comm., House of Reps. 1985–86, political forum of Latin American Inst. for Social Research 1992–93, Exec. Council UNESCO 1995–; Fray Bartolomé de las Casas (Spain) 1994. *Publications:* articles on culture, educ. and history in local and foreign books, journals and newspapers. *Address:* c/o Executive Council, UNESCO, 7 Place de Fontenoy, 75352 Paris, France.

CARDIFF, Jack; British film director and cameraman; b. 18 Sept. 1914; s. of John Joseph Cardiff and Florence Cardiff; m. Julia Lily Mickleboro 1940; three s.; ed. various schools, including Medburn School, Herts.; began career as child actor 1918; switched to cameras 1928; asst. to many Hollywood cameramen 1936; world travelogues 1937–39; photographer for Ministry of Information Film Unit on War Dept. films, including Western Approaches 1942; films as cameraman include: Caesar and Cleopatra 1945, A Matter of Life and Death 1946, Black Narcissus 1946 (Academy Award, Golden Globe Award 1947), The Red Shoes 1948, Scott of the Antarctic, Under Capricorn, Black Rose, Pandora and the Flying Dutchman 1951, Magic Box, African Queen, War and Peace 1956, The Vikings 1958; began to direct films 1958; *films as director include:* Intent to Kill 1958, Beyond This Place 1959, Scent of Mystery 1960, Sons and Lovers 1960, My Geisha 1962, The Lion 1963, The Long Ships 1964, Young Cassidy 1965, The Liquidator 1967, The Mercenaries 1968, Girl on a Motor Cycle (also producer) 1969, The Mutation, Penny Gold 1974, Ride a Wild Pony 1976; Dir. of photography: The Prince and the Pauper, Beyond the Iron Mask, Death on the Nile, Avalanche Express, The Awakening, The Dogs of War, Ghost Story, Last Days of Pompeii, The Wicked Lady, Conan the Destroyer, Catseyes, First Blood II, Blue Velvet, Tai-Pan, Million Dollar Mystery, Journey into Space, Magic Balloon; TV includes: The Far Pavilions; Coup de Soir (France) 1951; Film Achievement Award, Look Magazine; B.S.C. Award for War and Peace; New York Critics Award for best film direction, Golden Globe Award for outstanding dir. for Sons and Lovers, Acad. Award for Black Narcissus; Hollywood Int. Life Achievement Award 1995; British Acad. of Cinematographers Contrib. to Art of Photography Award 1996; Hon. Dr. of Art (Rome) 1953, Hon. D.Litt. (Bradford) 1996; Hon. mem. Assn. Française de Cameramen 1971. *Publication:* Autobiography 1975, Magic Hour (autobiog.) 1996. *Address:* 32 Woodland Rise, London, N.10, England.

CARDIN, Pierre; French couturier; b. 2 July 1922, San Biagio di Callatla, Italy; fmrly. worked with Christian Dior; founded own fashion house 1949; founded Espace Pierre Cardin (theatre group); Dir. Ambassadeurs-Pierre Cardin Theatre (now Espace Pierre Cardin Theatre) 1970–; Man. Société Pierre Cardin 1973; Chair. Maxims 1982–; Hon. UNESCO Amb. 1991;

exhbn. at Victoria and Albert Museum 1990; mem. Acad. des Beaux-Arts; Fashion Oscar 1985; Officier, Légion d'honneur 1997; Grand Officer, Order of Merit (Italy) 1988, Order of the Sacred Treasure (Gold and Silver Star) 1991. *Publications:* Fernand Léger, Sa vie, Son oeuvre, Son rêve 1971, Le Conte du Ver à Soie 1992 (Prix Saint-Exupéry valeurs-jeunesse 1992). *Address:* 27 avenue Marigny, 75008 Paris, France (Office).

CARDINAL, Douglas Joseph, O.C., B.ARCH., F.R.A.I.C., R.C.A.; Canadian architect; b. 7 March 1934, Calgary, Alberta; s. of Joseph Treffle Cardinal and Frances Margarete Rach; m. 1st Marilyn Zahar 1973; three s. three d.; m. 2nd Idoia Arana-Beobide 1996; ed. Univ. of Texas; design architect, Bissell & Halman, Red Deer 1963–64; Prin. Douglas Cardinal Architect, Red Deer 1964–67, Edmonton 1967–76, Douglas J. Cardinal Architect Ltd., Edmonton 1976–, Douglas Cardinal Architect, Washington, D.C. 1995–; *major works include:* St. Mary's Church, Red Deer, Alberta, Grande Prairie Regional Coll., Grande Prairie, Alberta, Ponoka Provincial Bldg., Ponoka, Alberta, St. Albert Place, St. Albert, Alberta, Canadian Museum of Civilization, Hull, Quebec, Nat. Museum of the American Indian, Washington, D.C.; awards include Honour Award, Alberta Asscn. of Architects, for St. Mary's Church 1969 and Award of Excellence, Canadian Architect Magazine, for Grande Prairie Regional Coll. 1972. *Publications:* contribs. to Of the Spirit 1977 and Human Values: A Primary Motive in Planning 1981. *Address:* Suite 4200, 490 E L'Enfant Plaza, S.W., Washington DC 20024, U.S.A.

CARDINALE, Claudia; Italian film actress; b. 15 April 1939, Tunis; d. of Franco and Yolanda Cardinale; m. Franco Cristaldi 1966; one s.; ed. Lycée Carnot and Collège Paul Cambon, Tunis; made first film 1958; awards include Nastro d'Argento, David di Donatello, Grolla d'Oro. *Films include:* 8½, The Pink Panther, The Leopard, The Professionals, Once Upon a Time in the West, Fury, The Magnificent Showman, La Scoumoune, Fitzcarraldo 1982, Le Ruffian 1982, History (TV), A Man in Love 1988, The French Revolution 1989, Hiver '54, L'abbe Pierre, Mother, 588 Rue Paradis, Son of the Pink Panther 1993, Women Only Have One Thing On Their Minds. *Address:* via Flamina Km. 17,200, I-0018 Rome, Italy.

CARDONA, Manuel, PH.D.; Spanish/American professor of physics; b. 7 Sept. 1934, Barcelona, Spain; s. of Juan Cardona and Angela Castro; m. Inge Hecht 1959; two s. one d.; ed. Univs. of Barcelona and Madrid and Harvard Univ.; Research Asst. Harvard Univ. 1956–59; mem. tech. staff, RCA Labs. Ltd., Zürich 1959–61, Princeton, N.J. 1961–64; Assoc. Prof. of Physics, Brown Univ., Providence, R.I. 1964–66, Prof. 1966–71; Scientific mem. and Dir. Max Planck Inst. for Solid State Research, Stuttgart 1971–, Business Man. Dir 1973–74; mem. various advisory bds., professional bodies, etc.; mem. N.A.S., Acad. Europaea; Fellow American Physical Soc.; A.D. Sloan Fellowship 1965–68; Guggenheim Fellowship 1969–70; Dr. h.c. (Madrid) 1985, (Barcelona) 1985, Sherbrook Univ., (Canada) 1993, (Regensburg) 1994, (Rome) 1995, (Toulouse) 1998; Prince of Asturias Prize 1988, Italgas Prize 1993, J. Wheatley Prize, American Physical Soc. 1997; Grand Cross of Alfonso X el Sabio; numerous other awards and distinctions. *Publications:* Modulation Spectroscopy 1969, Light Scattering in Solids, Vols. I–IV 1975–91, Photoemission in Solids, Vols. I–II 1978–81, Fundamentals of Semiconductors 1996. *Address:* Max-Planck-Institut für Festkörperforschung, Heisenbergstrasse 1, 70569 Stuttgart, Germany. *Telephone:* 711-689 1710.

CARDOSO, Fernando Henrique, D.SC.; Brazilian politician; b. 18 June 1931, Rio de Janeiro; ed. Univs. of São Paulo and Paris; Prof. Latin American Inst. for Econ. and Social Planning (ILPES/CEPAL), Santiago 1964–67; Prof. of Sociological Theory, Univ. of Paris-Nanterre 1967–68; Prof. of Political Science, Univ. of São Paulo 1968–69; Visiting Prof. Stanford Univ. 1972, Inst. for Econ. and Social Devt. Univ. of Paris 1977, Univ. of Calif. 1981; Simon Bolivar Prof. Univ. of Cambridge 1976; Assoc. Dir. of Studies, Inst. for Higher Studies in Social Sciences, Univ. of Paris 1980–81; many other professional appts.; Fed. Senator for State of São Paulo 1983–94; fmr. Leader, Brazilian Social Democratic Party (PSDB) in Fed. Senate; Govt. Leader in Congress 1985–86; fmr. Minister of Foreign Affairs; Minister of Economy and Finance until 1994; Pres. of Brazil Jan. 1995–; Prof. Coll. de France 1981; Dr. h.c. (Notre Dame, Ill.) 1991, (Santiago) 1993; Grand Cross, Order of Rio Branco, Chevalier, Légion d'honneur, Grand Cross, Order of Merit of Portugal. *Address:* Gabinete do Presidente, Palácio do Planalto, Praça dos Três Poderes, 70150 Brasília, Brazil.

CARDOSO E CUNHA, António José; Portuguese politician and agriculturist; b. 28 Jan. 1933; m.; four c.; ed. Inst. Superior Technico; worked in petrochem. industries, foreign trade and agric.; in Angola 1966–76; Sec. of State for Foreign Trade, Third Constitutional Govt., for Industries, Fourth Constitutional Govt.; mem. Assembly of the Repub., Social Democratic Party (PSD) Dec. 1979–; Minister of Agric. and Fisheries 1980–81; EC Commr. for Fisheries 1986–88, for Personnel and Admin., Energy, Tourism, Small and Medium-Sized Business 1989–92; Commr. Gen. EXPO '98 1993–.

CAREY, Most Rev. and Rt. Hon. George Leonard, B.D., M.TH., P.C., PH.D.; British clergyman; b. 13 Nov. 1935, London; s. of George Thomas and Ruby Catherine Carey; m. Eileen Harmsworth Hood 1960; two s. two d.; ed. Bifrons Secondary Modern School, Barking, Essex, King's Coll., London Univ.; Nat. Service, R.A.F. 1954–56; univ. studies and theological training 1957–62; Curate St. Mary's, Islington 1962–66; lecturer, Oak Hill Theological Coll. 1966–70, St. John's Coll., Nottingham 1970–75; Vicar St. Nicholas' Church, Durham 1975–82; Prin. Trinity Theological Coll., Bristol 1982–87; Bishop of Bath and Wells 1987–91; Archbishop of Canterbury 1991–; Vice-Patron RSPCA 1992–; Fellow King's Coll., London; Hon. D.Litt (Polytechnic of E. London) 1991, Hon. D.D. (Kent) 1991, (Nottingham) 1992; Hon. LL.D. (Bath) 1992; Greek, Hebrew and theological prizes; Hon. Bencher Inner Temple; Freeman City of Wells 1990. *Publications:* I Believe in Man 1978, The Great Acquittal 1981, The Church in the Market Place 1983, The Meeting of the Waters 1985, The Gate of Glory 1986, The Great God Robbery 1988, I Believe 1991, Spiritual Journey 1994, My Journey Your Journey 1996, Canterbury – Letters to the Future 1998. *Leisure interests:* walking, football, poetry, music. *Address:* Lambeth Palace, London, SE1 7JU; Old Palace, Canterbury, Kent, England. *Telephone:* 0171-928 8282.

CAREY, John, M.A., D.PHIL., F.R.S.L., F.B.A.; British literary critic and university professor; b. 5 April 1934; s. of Charles William and Winifred Ethel (née Cook) Carey; m. Gillian Mary Florence Booth 1960; two s.; ed. Richmond and East Sheen County Grammar School, St. John's Coll., Oxford; served East Surrey Regt. 1953–54; Harmsworth Sr. Scholar, Merton Coll., Oxford 1957–58; lecturer, Christ Church, Oxford 1958–59; Andrew Bradley Jr. Research Fellow, Balliol Coll., Oxford 1959–60; Tutorial Fellow, Keble Coll., Oxford 1960–64, St. John's 1964–75; Merton Prof. of English Literature, Oxford Univ. 1976–; T. S. Eliot Memorial Lecturer, Univ. of Kent 1989; Chair. Booker Prize Judges 1982, Judge, W.H. Smith Prize 1989–; Hon. Fellow St. John's Coll. Oxford 1991, Balliol Coll. Oxford 1992. *Publications:* The Poems of John Milton (Ed. with Alastair Fowler) 1968, Milton 1969, The Violent Effigy: a Study of Dickens' Imagination 1973, Thackeray: Prodigal Genius 1977, John Donne: Life, Mind and Art 1981, The Private Memoirs and Confessions of a Justified Sinner, by James Hogg (Ed.), William Golding: The Man and His Books (Ed.) 1986, Original Copy: Selected Reviews and Journalism 1987, The Faber Book of Reportage (Ed.) 1987, John Donne (Oxford Authors) (Ed.) 1990, The Intellectuals and the Masses 1992, The Faber Book of Science (Ed.) 1995; articles in Review of English Studies, Modern Language Review, etc. *Address:* Brasenose Cottage, Lyneham, Oxon., OX7 6QL; 57 Stapleton Road, Headington, Oxford, England. *Telephone:* (01865) 764304.

CAREY, Mariah; American singer and songwriter; b. 1969, Long Island, N.Y.; signed contract with Columbia Records 1989; albums include Mariah Carey 1990, Emotions 1992, MTV Unplugged 1992, Music Box 1993, Merry Christmas 1994, Daydream 1995, Butterfly 1997; over 80 million albums sold worldwide; f. Crave record label 1997; awards include two Grammy awards (Best New Artist, Best New Pop Vocal, Female) 1990, three Soul Train Music Awards (Best New Artist, Best Album, Female, Best Single, Female) 1990, four American Music Awards 1992–96, eight World Music Awards 1991–95, seven Billboard Awards 1991–96; f. Camp Mariah holiday project for inner-city children. *Address:* c/o LD Publicity Ltd., Fenton House, 55–57 Great Marlborough Street, London, W1V 1DD, England. *Telephone:* 0171-439 7222. *Fax:* 0171-734 2933.

CAREY, Peter, F.R.S.L.; Australian author; b. 7 May 1943, Bacchus March, Vic.; m. 2nd Alison Summers 1985; two s.; ed. Geelong Grammar School and Monash Univ.; fmr. partner, McSpedden Carey Advertising Consultants, Sydney; now teacher Columbia Univ. and Princeton Univ., Hon. Litt.D. (Queensland). *Publications:* The Fat Man in History (short stories) 1974 (in U.K. as Exotic Pleasures 1981), War Crimes (short stories) 1979 (N.S.W. Premier's Award), Bliss (novel) 1981 (Miles Franklin Award, Nat. Book Council Award, N.S.W. Premier's Award), Illywhacker (novel) 1985 (Age Book of the Year Award, Nat. Book Council Award, Victorian Premier's Award), Oscar and Lucinda 1988 (Booker Prize for Fiction 1988, Miles Franklin Award, Nat. Book Council Award, Adelaide Festival Award, Foundation for Australian Literary Studies Award), The Tax Inspector (novel) 1991, The Unusual Life of Tristan Smith (novel) 1994 (Age Book of the Year Award), Collected Stories 1995, The Big Bazoohley (children's novel) 1995, Jack Maggs 1997. *Screenplays* (jointly): Bliss, Until the End of the World. *Film:* Oscar and Lucinda 1998. *Address:* c/o Amanda Urban, I.C.M., 40 West 57th Street, New York, NY 10019, U.S.A.

CAREY, Sir Peter Willoughby, G.C.B.; British business executive; b. 26 July 1923, London; s. of Jack Delves Carey and Sophie Searle; m. Thelma Young 1946; three d.; ed. Portsmouth Grammar School, Oriel Coll., Oxford and School of Slavonic Studies, London; Capt. Intelligence Corps 1943–45, Information Officer, Belgrade and Zagreb 1945–46; served in Foreign Office 1947–49, Bd. of Trade, Civil Service 1949–65, Royal Coll. of Defence Studies 1965; Asst. Sec. Bd. of Trade 1963–67, Under-Sec. 1967–69; Under-Sec. Ministry of Tech. 1969–71; Deputy Sec. Cabinet Office 1971–72; Perm. Sec. Dept. of Industry 1973–83; Dir. BPB Industries PLC 1983–95, Cable and Wireless PLC 1984–94; Chair. Dalgety PLC 1986–92, Morgan Grenfell Group PLC 1987–89, Supervisory Bd. NV Philips Electronics; Hon. LL.D. (Birmingham). *Leisure interests:* music, theatre, travel, argument. *Address:* 5 Rushmere Place, Marryat Road, London, S.W.19, England (Home). *Telephone:* 0181-947 5222 (Home).

CARIDIS, Miltiades; Greek/Austrian conductor; b. 9 May 1923, Danzig; s. of Xenophon Caridis and Barbara Fuchs-Caridis; m. Sonja Caridis 1945; one d.; ed. Kreuzschule, Dresden, Dörpfeldt Gymnasium, Athens and Musikhochschule, Vienna; Opernhaus, Graz 1948–59; Opernhaus, Cologne 1959–62; Philharmonia Hungarica 1960–67; Staatsoper, Vienna 1962–69; Radio Symphony Orchestra, Copenhagen 1962–70; Oslo Philharmonic Soc. 1969–75; Duisburger Sinfoniker, Duisburg 1975–81; Tonkünstler-Orchester,

Vienna 1979–85; Artistic and Music Dir. Athens Radio Symphony Orchestra 1995–. *Address:* A-1130 Vienna, Himmelhofgasse 10, Austria. *Telephone:* 8779233. *Fax:* 8779233.

CARIGNON, Alain; French politician; b. 23 Feb. 1949, Vizille, Isère; s. of Joseph Carignon and Yvette Ramus; m. Jacqueline Bon 1987; ed. Lycée de Grenoble, Institut de l'Administration des Entreprises, Grenoble; Head of Mission to mediator Aimé Paquet 1974–75; mem. Industry Comm., Econ. and Social Council 1976–78; Head of Mission to Jérôme Monod 1978–80, Nat. Sec. RPR 1984–86; elected Deputy for Isère but gave up seat 1986, elected again June 1988, resgnd. Oct. 1988; Minister of Communications 1993–94; Deputy Chair. Nouveau Contrat Social 1986; mem. Isère Council 1976–95, Pres. 1985–95; Mayor of Grenoble 1983–95; sentenced to five years' imprisonment, two suspended, for corruption Nov. 1995; Commdr., Order of Merit (Fed. Republic of Germany). *Publications:* Jean de la Montagne 1988, Une Saison dans la Nuit 1995. *Leisure interests:* reading, music, cinema. *Address:* Conseil Général, 7 rue Fantin Latour, 38022 Grenoble cedex, France.

CARL XVI GUSTAF; King of Sweden; b. 30 April 1946; s. of Prince Gustaf Adolf and Sibylla, Princess of Saxe-Coburg and Gotha; m. Silvia Sommerlath 1976; one s., Prince Carl Philip Edmund Bertil, b. 13 May 1979; two d., Crown Princess Victoria Ingrid Alice Désirée, b. 14 July 1977, and Princess Madeleine Thérèse Amelie Josephine, b. 10 June 1982; ed. in Sigtuna and Univs. of Uppsala and Stockholm; created Duke of Jämtland; became Crown Prince 1950; succeeded to the throne on death of his grandfather, King Gustaf VI Adolf 15 Sept. 1973; Chair. Swedish Branch, World Wide Fund for Nature; Hon. Pres. World Scout Foundation; Dr. h.c. (Swedish Univ. of Agricultural Sciences, Stockholm Inst. of Tech., Åbo Acad., Finland). *Address:* Royal Palace, 111 30 Stockholm, Sweden. *Telephone:* (0) 8-402 60 00. *Fax:* (0) 8-402 60 05.

CARLIN, John William; American fmr. state governor; b. 3 Aug. 1940, Smolan, Kan.; s. of Jack W. and Hazel L. (Johnson) Carlin; m. Ramona Hawkinson 1962 (divorced 1980); one s. one d.; ed. Lindsborg High School, Kansas Univ.; farmer, dairyman, Smolan, Kan. 1962–; mem. Kan. House of Reps. for 93rd Dist. 1970–73, 73rd Dist. 1973–79, Minority Leader of House 1975–77, Speaker 1977-79; Gov. of Kansas 1979–87; Visiting Prof. of Public Admin. and Int. Trade Wichita State Univ. 1987–88; Visiting Fellow Kansas Univ. 1987–88; Archivist of the United States Nat. Archives and Records Admin. 1995–; Pres. Econ. Devt. Asscn. 1987–92, Midwest Superconductivity Inc. 1990–; fmr. Chair. Nat. Govs. Asscn.; mem. Nat. Govs. Asscn. (NGA) Exec. Cttee.; fmr. Chair. Midwestern Govs. Conf.; Hon. D.Iur. (Kansas); Democrat. *Leisure interests:* golf, swimming. *Address:* National Archives and Records Administration, 7th and Pennsylvania Avenue, Washington, D.C. 20408 (Office); 8601 Adelphi Road, Room 4200, College Park, MD 20740, U.S.A.

CARLING, William David Charles; British rugby football player; b. 12 Dec. 1965, Bradford-on-Avon, Wilts.; m. Julia Carling 1994 (divorced 1996); ed. Durham Univ.; owner Inspirational Horizons Co., Insights Ltd.; centre; fmr. mem. Durham Univ. Club; mem. Harlequins club; int. debut England versus France 1988; Capt. England team 1988–96; announced retirement from int. rugby; played 72 times for England, Capt. 59 times (world record); rugby football commentator, ITV 1997–. *Publications:* Captain's Diary 1991, Will Carling (autobiog.) 1994, The Way to Win (with Robert Heller) 1995, My Autobiography 1998. *Leisure interests:* painting and sketching. *Address:* c/o Insights Ltd., 22 Suffolk Street, London, SW1Y 4HG, England.

CARLISLE OF BUCKLOW, Baron (Life Peer) cr. 1987, of Mobberley in the County of Cheshire; **Mark Carlisle,** P.C., LL.B., Q.C.; British politician and lawyer; b. 7 July 1929; s. of Philip and Mary Carlisle; m. Sandra Des Voeux 1959, one d.; ed. Radley Coll., Manchester Univ.; called to the Bar, Gray's Inn 1953; M.P. for Runcorn 1964–83, for Warrington South 1983–87; mem. Home Office Advisory Council on the Penal System 1966–70; Joint Hon. Sec. Conservative Cttee. on Home Affairs 1965–69, Chair. 1983–87; Parl. Under-Sec. of State, Home Office 1970–72; Minister of State 1972–74; Sec. of State for Educ. and Science 1979–81; Recorder Crown Court 1976–79, 1981–98; Chair. Parole Review Cttee. 1988, Criminal Injuries Compensation Bd. 1989–, Soc. of Conservative Lawyers 1996–; Judge Courts of Appeal, Jersey and Guernsey 1990–; mem. Advisory Council, BBC 1975; Hon. Fellow, Coll. of Preceptors; Conservative. *Leisure interest:* golf. *Address:* Queen Elizabeth Building, Temple, London, EC4Y 9BS; House of Lords, Westminster, London, S.W.1 (Offices); 3 Holt Gardens, Mobberley, Cheshire, WA16 7LH, England. *Telephone:* 0171-583 5766; (0156587) 2275.

CARLOS MOCO, Marcolino José, PH.D.; Angolan politician; Prime Minister of Angola 1992–96; mem. Movimento Popular de Libertação de Angola—Partido do Trabalho (MPLA—PT). *Address:* c/o Movimento Popular de Libertação de Angola, Luanda, Angola.

CARLOT, Maxime; Ni-Vanuatu politician; Leader, Union of Moderate Parties (UMP); Prime Minister of Vanuatu Dec. 1991–95, Feb.–Sept. 1996, also fmr. Minister of Foreign Affairs, of Public Service, Planning and Statistics, of Media and Language Services; Parl. Leader, Union of Moderate Parties. *Address:* P.O. Box 698, Port Vila, Vanuatu.

CARLSON, Arne Helge, B.A.; American politician; b. 24 Sept. 1934, New York; s. of Helge William and Kerstin (Magnusson) Carlson; m. Susan Shepard 1985; one d. and one s. one d. by previous m.; ed. Williams Coll., Univ. of Minnesota; with Control Data, Bloomington, Minn. 1962–64; Councilman Minneapolis City Council 1965–67; in pvt. business, Minneapolis 1968–69; Legislator, Minn. House of Reps., St. Paul 1970–78; State Auditor, State of Minn. 1978–90, Gov. 1991–98; mem. Bd. of Dirs. Minn. Land Exchange Bd., Exec. Council St. Paul; Trustee Minn. State Bd. Investment; Sec. Minn. Housing Finance Agency 1979–91; several awards including Small Business Guardian Award, Nat. Fed. of Ind. Businesses 1994; Republican. *Leisure interests:* reading, squash, Univ. of Minn. basketball and football games. *Address:* 1006 Summit Avenue, Saint Paul, MN 55105, U.S.A. (Home).

CARLSSON, Ingvar Gösta, M.A.; Swedish politician; b. 9 Nov. 1934, Borås; m. Ingrid Melander 1957; two d.; ed. Lund Univ. and Northwestern Univ. U.S.A.; Sec. in Statsradsberedningen (Prime Minister's Office) 1958–60; Pres. Social Democratic Youth League 1961–67; Mem. Parl. 1964–; Under Sec. of State, Statsradsberedningen 1967–69; Minister of Educ. 1969–73, of Housing and Physical Planning 1973–76, Deputy Prime Minister 1982–86, Minister of the Environment 1985–86, Prime Minister 1986–91, 1994–96; Co-Chair. Comm. on Global Governance 1995–; mem. staff Lund Univ. 1989, Chicago Univ. 1991; mem. Exec. Cttee. Social Democratic Party, Chair. 1986–96. *Address:* c/o Parliament Buildings, 10012 Stockholm, Sweden.

CARLUCCI, Frank Charles; American fmr. politician and business executive; b. 18 Oct. 1930, Scranton, Pa.; s. of Frank and Roxann Carlucci; m. 1st Jean Anthony 1954 (divorced 1974); one s. two d.; m. 2nd Marcia McMillan Myers 1976; ed. Princeton Univ. and Harvard Graduate School of Business Admin.; with Jantzen Co., Portland, Ore. 1955–56; Foreign Service Officer, Dept. of State 1956; Vice-Consul, Econ. Officer, Johannesburg 1957–59; Second Sec. Political Officer, Kinshasa 1960–62; Officer in charge of Congolese Political Affairs, Zanzibar 1962–64, Consul-Gen. 1964–65; Counsellor for Political Affairs, Rio de Janeiro 1965–69; Asst. Dir. for Operations, Office of Econ. Opportunity 1969–70, Dir. OEO 1970; Assoc. Dir. Office of Management and Budget 1971–72, Deputy Dir. 1972; Under-Sec. Dept. of Health, Educ. and Welfare 1972–74; Amb. to Portugal 1974–77; Deputy Dir. CIA 1977–81, Deputy Sec. of Defense 1981–82, Sec. 1987–89; Pres. C.O.O. Sears World Trade Inc. 1983–84, Chair. and C.E.O. 1984–86; Nat. Security Adviser to Pres. of U.S.A. 1986–87; Vice-Chair. Carlyle Group, Washington 1989–93, Chair. 1993–; Hon. D.Hum.Litt.; Superior Service Award and Superior Honour Award, Dept. of State, Presidential Citizens Award, Distinguished Intelligence Medal and other awards. *Leisure interests:* tennis, swimming. *Address:* Carlyle Group, 1001 Pennsylvania Avenue, N.W., Washington, DC 20004, U.S.A.

CARLYLE, Joan Hildred; British soprano; b. 6 April 1931; d. of late Edgar J. Carlyle and Margaret M. Carlyle; m. Robert Duray Aiyar; two d.; ed. Howell's School, Denbigh, N. Wales; prin. Lyric Soprano, Covent Garden 1955; *major roles sung in U.K. include:* Oscar, Ballo in Maschera 1957–58; Sophie, Der Rosenkavalier 1958–59; Nedda, Pagliacci (Zeffirelli production) 1959, Mimi, La Bohème 1960, Titania, Midsummer Night's Dream, Britten (Gielgud production) 1960, Pamina, Magic Flute 1962, 1966, Countess, Marriage of Figaro 1963, Zdenka, Arabella (Hartman Production) 1964, Suor Angelica 1965, Desdemona, Othello 1965, Arabella 1967, Marschallin, Der Rosenkavalier 1968, Jenifer, Midsummer Marriage 1969, Donna Anna 1970, Reiza, Oberon 1970, Adrianna Lecouvreur 1970, Russalka, Elizabetta, Don Carlos 1975; *major roles sung abroad include:* Oscar, Nedda, Mimi, Pamina, Zdenka, Micaela, Donna Anna, Arabella, Elizabetta and Desdemona; has sung at La Scala Milan, Staats Oper Vienna, Munich, Berlin, Teatro Colón Buenos Aires, San Carlo Naples, Monet Monte Carlo, Nico Milan Cape Town, Brussels, Geneva, Zurich, Amsterdam, Boston, New York; several recordings including Von Karajan's production of Pagliacci as Nedda, Midsummer Marriage as Jenifer, Medea, Pagliacci from Buenos Aires, Mavra, Purcell Anthology. *Leisure interests:* gardening, travel, preservation of the countryside, interior design, cooking. *Address:* Laundry Cottage, Hanmer, North Wales, SY13 4QX. *Telephone:* (01948) 830265.

CARLYLE, Robert, O.B.E.; British actor; m. Anastasia Shirley 1997; ed. Royal Scottish Acad. of Music and Drama; dir. Rain Dog Theatre Co., productions include: Wasted, One Flew Over the Cuckoo's Nest (Paper Boat Award), Conquest of the South Pole, Macbeth (Paper Boat Award 1992); *Stage appearances include:* Twelfth Night, Dead Dad Dog, Nae Problem, City, No Mean City, Cuttin' a Rug, Othello. *Television includes:* Face, Go Now, Hamish Macbeth, Cracker, 99-1, Safe, The Advocates, Arena 'Byrne on Byrne', Taggart, The Bill. *Films include:* The Full Monty (B.A.F.T.A. Award for Best Actor), Carla's Song, Trainspotting, Priest, Marooned, Being Human, Riff Raff, Silent Scream, Apprentices, Plunkett and Macleane, The World is Not Enough.

CARLZON, Jan, M.B.A.; Swedish airlines executive; b. 25 June 1941, Nyköping; ed. Stockholm School of Econs.; began career as Product Man. at Vingressor (tour operators and SAS subsidiary from 1971) 1967–74, Man. Dir. 1974–78; Pres. Linjeflyg (the domestic airline) 1978–80; C.O.O. SAS Airline 1980, C.E.O. and Pres. SAS Group 1981–93; mem. of Bd. Linjeflyg, Enator, Pronator, Stockholms Fondkommission, Swedish Broadcasting Co.'s Friends of Music Radio, Swedish chapter of World Wildlife Fund; mem. Int. Air Transport Asscn.'s Exec. Cttee.; Pres. Swedish Br. Young Pres.'s Org.; co-owner Börsen nightclub; lectures overseas on man. and motivation issues. *Publication:* Moments of Truth. *Leisure interests:* golf, skiing, sailing. *Address:* c/o Scandinavian Airlines System, Head Office, Frösundavik Allée 1, Bromma 16187, Stockholm, Sweden.

CARMAN, George Alfred, Q.C.; British lawyer; b. 6 Oct. 1929, Blackpool; s. of late Alfred Carman and Evelyn Carman; m. 1st Ursula Groves 1955 (divorced); m. 2nd Cecelia Sparrow 1960 (divorced 1976); one s.; m. 3rd Frances Venning 1976 (divorced 1984); ed. St. Joseph's Coll. Blackpool and Balliol Coll. Oxford; Capt., Royal Army Educ. Corps. 1948–49; called to Bar, Lincoln's Inn 1953, a recorder of the Crown Court 1972–84, Bencher 1978; Q.C. 1971; appeared in courts overseas in Hong Kong, Singapore, Malaysia and Bermuda; Guest Speaker on Advocacy to Canadian Lawyers; Recorder of the Crown Court 1972–83. *Leisure interests:* theatre, travel, law reform. *Address:* New Court, Temple, London, EC4Y 9BE, England. *Telephone:* 0171-583 6166.

CARNAHAN, Mel Eugene, J.D.; American politician and lawyer; b. 11 Feb. 1934, Birch Tree, Mo.; s. of A. S. J. Carnahan and Mary Kathel (Schupp) Carnahan; m. Jean Anne Carpenter 1954; four s.; ed. George Washington Univ., Univ. of Missouri-Columbia; sr. partner Carnahan, Carnahan & Hickle, Rolla, Mo.; majority leader Mo. House of Reps. 1965–66; State Treasurer, Mo. 1980–84; Lieut.-Gov. 1988–93, Gov. of Missouri Jan. 1993–; Democrat; mem. Mo. Bar Asscn. *Address:* Office of the Governor, P.O. Box 720, Jefferson City, MO 65102 (Office); P.O. Box 698, Rolla, MO 65401, U.S.A. (Home).

CARNEGIE, Sir Roderick Howard, Kt., B.SC., M.A., M.B.A., F.T.S.; Australian mining executive; b. 27 Nov. 1932, Melbourne; s. of D. H. Carnegie; m. Carmen Clarke 1959; three s.; ed. Trinity Coll. Melbourne Univ., New Coll., Oxford, Harvard Business School; Assoc. McKinsey and Co., Melbourne and New York 1959–64, Prin. Assoc. 1964–68, Dir. 1968–70; Dir. Conzinc Riotinto of Aust. Ltd. (now CRA Ltd.) 1970, Joint Man. Dir. 1971–72, Man. Dir. and Chief Exec. 1972–74, Chair. and Man. Dir. 1974–83, Chair. and Chief Exec. 1983–86; Dir. Comalco Ltd., CRA Ltd., Rio Tinto-Zinc Corpn. Ltd.; Chair. Consultative Cttee. on Relations with Japan 1984–87; Pres. German-Australian Chamber of Industry and Commerce 1985; Pres. Business Council of Australia 1987–88; Chair. Hudson Conway Ltd. 1987–; Vice-Pres. Australian Mining Industry Council; Chair. Salvation Army Council 1992–, G10 Australia Holdings Ltd. 1992–94, Valiant Consolidated Ltd. 1993–, GPT Ltd. 1994–, Newcrest Mining Ltd. 1994–; Dir. John Fairfax Holdings Pty Ltd. 1991–, Lexmark Holdings Inc. (U.S.A.) 1994–, Adacel Techs Ltd. 1998–; mem. Int. Council Morgan Guaranty Trust, The Asia Soc., The Brookings Inst.; mem. IBM World Trade Asia/Pacific Group Bd.; Hon. D.Sc. *Address:* Hudson Conway Ltd., Level 1, 99 Queensbridge Street, Southbank, Queensland 3006, Australia.

CARNEY, Patricia, P.C., M.A.; Canadian politician and economist; b. 26 May 1935, Shanghai, China; d. of James Carney and Dora Sanders; m. 2nd Paul S. White 1998; one s. one d. from previous marriage; ed. Univ. of British Columbia; Adjunct Prof. Univ. of B.C.; fmrly. econ. journalist; f. Gemini North Ltd. (consulting firm for socio-econ. impact studies) 1970; first elected M.P. 1980; Minister of State for Finance, Minister of Finance, Energy, Mines and Resources; Minister of Energy, Mines and Resources 1984–86, of Int. Trade 1986–88; Pres. Treasury Bd. April–Oct. 1988; Chair. Cabinet Cttee. on Trade; mem. Senate 1990–; fmr. Chair. Standing Senate Cttee. on Energy, the Environment and Natural Resources; mem. Standing Senate Cttee. on Foreign Affairs; mem. Canadian Inst. of Planners, Asscn. of Professional Economists of B.C.; fmr. mem. Econ. Council of Canada; Hon. Fellow Royal Architectural Inst. of Canada 1989; Hon. LL.D. (Univ. of B.C.) 1990, (B.C. Open Univ.) 1991. *Address:* The Senate, Ottawa, Ont., K1A 0A4, Canada.

CARNLEY, Most Rev. Peter Frederick, A.O., D.D., PH.D.; Australian archbishop and theologian; b. 17 Oct. 1937, New Lambton, N.S.W.; s. of F. Carnley; m. Carol Ann Dunstan, 1966; one s. one d.; ed. St. John's Theological Coll., N.S.W., Trinity Coll., Melbourne Univ., St. John's Coll., Univ. of Cambridge; Deacon 1962; Priest 1964; Chaplain Mitchell Coll. of Advanced Educ., N.S.W. 1970–72; Research Fellow St. John's Coll., Cambridge 1971–72; Warden St. John's Coll., Univ. of Queensland 1973–81; Anglican Archbishop of Perth and Metropolitan of the Province of Western Australia 1981–; mem. Archbishop of Canterbury's Comm. on Communion and Women in the Episcopate 1988, Int. Anglican Theological and Doctrinal Comm. 1994; Visiting Prof. of Anglican Studies, Gen. Theological Seminary, New York 1993, 1996. *Publications:* The Poverty of Historical Scepticism; in Christ, Faith and History 1972, The Structure of Resurrection Belief 1987. *Leisure interests:* gardening, music. *Address:* P.O. Box W2607, Perth, WA 6846, Australia. *Telephone:* (08) 9325 7455. *Fax:* (08) 9325 6741.

ČARNOGURSKÝ, Ján, LL.D.; Slovak politician and lawyer; b. 1 Jan. 1944, Bratislava; s. of Pavol Čarnogurský and Kristína Fašungová; m. Marta Stachová 1970; two s. two d.; ed. Charles Univ., Prague 1966–69; lawyer, Bratislava 1970–81; mem. of Slovak Lawyers' Cen. Office and Czech Lawyers' Cen. Office; banned from legal profession after defence in a political trial 1981; driver, lawyer for a co. Bratislava 1982–86; unemployed, after expulsion from legal profession, continued giving legal advice to members of the political opposition and religious activists 1987–89; held in custody, released and pardoned, Aug.–Nov. 1989; First Deputy Premier, Govt. of Czechoslovakia 1989–90, Deputy Premier June 1990; Chair. Legis. Council Feb.–Aug. 1990; Chair. Christian Democratic Movt. Feb. 1990–; First Deputy Premier, Govt. of Slovak Repub. 1990–91, Prime Minister of Slovak Govt. 1991–June 1992; mem. State Defence Council 1991–92; Deputy to Slovak Nat. Council (Slovak Parl.) for KDH (Christian Democratic Movt.) 1992–98; Minister of Justice 1998–; Deputy Chair. Parl. Ass. of CSCE 1993–95; Trustee, Order of the German Kts. 1994–; Slovak Literary Fund Prize (Journalists' Section) 1992. *Publications:* The Bratislava Letters (samizdat), Suffered for the Faith 1987, Seen from Danube 1997. *Leisure interests:* history, jogging. *Address:* KDH, Žabotova 2, 811 04 Bratislava; Úrad vlády SR, Nám. Slobody 1, 813 70 Bratislava, Slovakia (Ministry). *Telephone:* (7) 35 95 111 (KDH); (7) 534 11 11 (Ministry). *Fax:* (7) 391 647 (KDH).

CARO, Sir Anthony, Kt., C.B.E., M.A.; British sculptor; b. 8 March 1924, London; s. of Alfred and Mary Caro; m. Sheila Girling 1949; two s.; ed. Charterhouse School, Christ's Coll., Cambridge, Regent St. Polytechnic and Royal Acad. Schools, London; Asst. to Henry Moore 1951–53; Part-time Lecturer St. Martin's School of Art, London 1953–79; taught at Bennington Coll. Vermont 1963–65; one-man exhbn. in Milan 1956, others subsequently in London, Washington, Toronto, New York, Houston, Hamburg, Zürich and in Netherlands, Japan, N.Z. and Australia; retrospective exhbn. Arts Council (Hayward Gallery, London) 1969, Annely Juda Fine Art 1994; works in Tate Gallery, Arts Council, Museum of Modern Art (New York), Brandeis Univ. (Boston), Albright Knox Museum, Buffalo, N.Y., Cleveland Museum Ohio, Rijksmuseum Kroller-Muller (Otterloo, Netherlands); retrospective exhbn. (1975–76) Museum of Modern Art, New York, Walker Art Center, Minneapolis, Houston Museum of Fine Art, Boston Museum of Fine Art; Arts Council of G.B. touring collection 1982–83; initiated Triangle Summer Workshop, Pine Plains, New York 1982; exhibited Galerie Lelong, Paris 1990, Baugre Palace, Antwerp 1990, Knoedler Gallery, London 1978, 1982–84, 1986, 1989, 1991, 1994, Nat. Gallery, London 1998; presented with Key of City of New York 1974; undertook comm. for new East Building, Nat. Gallery of Art, Washington, D.C., 1977; Hon. Fellow, Christ's Coll. Cambridge 1981, R.C.A., London 1986, Wolfson Coll., Oxford 1992; Foreign Hon. mem. A.A.A.S. 1988; Trustee, Tate Gallery 1982, Fitzwilliam Museum, Cambridge 1984; Hon. D.Litt. (E. Anglia, York Univ., Toronto, Cambridge), Hon. D.Univ. (Surrey) 1987, Hon. D.F.A. (Yale) 1989, Dr. h.c. (R.C.A.) 1994; Sculpture Prize, Paris Biennale 1959, David E. Bright Award, Venice Biennale 1967, Prize for Sculpture, São Paulo Biennale 1969, Imperial Prize (Japan) 1992. *Leisure interest:* listening to music. *Address:* 111 Frognal, Hampstead, London, NW3 6XR, England (Home).

CARO, David Edmund, A.O., O.B.E., M.SC., PH.D., F.INST.P., F.A.I.P., F.A.C.E.; Australian university chancellor; b. 29 June 1922, Melbourne; s. of George and Alice Caro; m. Fiona Macleod 1954; one s. one d.; ed. Geelong Grammar School, Univs. of Melbourne and Birmingham; war service, R.A.A.F. 1941–46; Demonstrator in Physics, Univ. of Melbourne 1947–49, Lecturer 1952, Sr. Lecturer 1954, Reader 1958, Prof. of Experimental Physics and Head of Dept. of Physics 1961–72, Deputy Vice-Chancellor 1972–77, Vice-Chancellor and Prin. 1982–87; Vice-Chancellor, Univ. of Tasmania 1978–82; Chair. Antarctic Research Policy Advisory Cttee. 1979–84, Australian Vice-Chancellors Cttee. 1982–83, Melbourne Theatre Co. 1982–87, UniSuper Ltd. 1984–94, Sarou Pty. Ltd. 1991–; mem. Council Asscn. Commonwealth Univs. 1982–84, Royal Melbourne Hosp. Cttee. of Man. 1982–92; Interim Vice-Chancellor, N. Territory Univ. 1988–89; mem. Council Victorian Coll. of the Arts 1989–, Pres. 1989–92; mem. Council Univ. of S. Australia 1991–94; Chancellor Univ. of Ballarat 1998– (mem. Council 1994–); Exhbn. of 1851 Overseas Research Scholar 1949–51; Hon. LL.D. (Melbourne) 1978, (Tasmania) 1982; Hon. D.Sc. (Melbourne) 1987. *Publication:* Modern Physics (co-author) 1961. *Leisure interests:* skiing, gardening, theatre. *Address:* 17 Fairbairn Road, Toorak, Vic. 3142, Australia. *Telephone:* 9827-2004.

CARON, Leslie Clair Margaret; French actress and ballet dancer; b. 1 July 1931, Boulogne-Billancourt; m. 1st George Hormel; m. 2nd Peter Reginald Frederick Hall (q.v.) 1956 (dissolved 1965); one s. one d.; m. 3rd Michael Laughlin 1969 (dissolved); ed. Convent of the Assumption, Paris, and Conservatoire de Danse; with Ballet des Champs Elysées 1947–50, Ballet de Paris 1954. *Films include:* An American in Paris, Man with a Cloak, Glory Alley, Story of Three Loves, Lili, Glass Slipper, Daddy Long Legs, Gaby, Gigi, The Doctor's Dilemma, The Man Who Understood Women, The Subterranean, Fanny, Guns of Darkness, The L-Shaped Room, Father Goose, A Very Special Favor, Promise Her Anything, Is Paris Burning?, Head of the Family, Madron, The Contract, The Unapproachable 1982, Deathly Moves 1983, Génie du Faux 1984, The Train 1987, Guerriers et Captives 1988, Courage Mountain 1988, Damage 1992, Funny Bones 1995, Let It Be Me 1995, The Reef 1996. *Plays include:* Orvet (Jean Renoir), La Sauvage (Anouilh), Gigi (Anita Loos), 13 rue de l'Amour (Feydan), Ondine (Giraudoux), Carola (Renoir), La Répétition (Anouilh), On Your Toes (Rogers and Hart), Apprends-moi Céline (Maria Pacôme) (played in English in U.S.A. as One for the Tango 1985), Grand Hotel (Vicky Baum), George Sand (Bruno Villien), Le Martyre de Saint Sébastien (Debussy), Nocturne for Lovers (Villien), Babar the Elephant (Poulenc); toured France in Apprends-moi Céline 1998–99; stage appearances in Paris, London, U.S.A., Germany and Australia. *Publication:* Vengeance 1983. *Address:* Fraser and Dunlop, 5th Floor, The Chambers, Chelsea Harbour, Lots Road, London, SW10 0KF, England; Artmedia, 10 avenue George V, 75008, France.

CARPENTER, John Howard; American film director and screenwriter; b. 16 Jan. 1948, Carthage, N.Y.; s. of Howard Ralph Carpenter and Milton Jean (née Carter) Carpenter; m. 1st Adrienne Barbeau 1979; m. 2nd Sandy King 1990; ed. Univ. of Southern California; mem. American Soc. of Composers, Authors and Publrs, Acad. of Motion Picture Arts and Sciences, Dirs. Guild of America, West, Writers Guild of America. *Films directed:* The

Resurrection of Bronco Billy 1970, Dark Star 1974, Assault on Precinct 13 1976, Someone's Watching Me, Halloween, Elvis 1978, The Fog 1979, Escape from New York 1980, The Thing 1982, Christine 1983, Starman 1984, Big Trouble in Little China 1986, Prince of Darkness 1987, They Live 1987, Memoirs of an Invisible Man 1992, Body Bags (TV) 1993, In the Mouth of Madness 1995, Village of the Damned 1995, Escape from L.A. 1996. *Leisure interests:* music, helicopter piloting. *Address:* c/o International Creative Management, 8942 Wilshire Boulevard, Beverly Hills, CA 90211, U.S.A.

CARPENTER, Leslie Arthur; British business executive; b. 26 June 1927; s. of William Carpenter and Rose Carpenter; m. 1st 1952; one d.; m. 2nd Louise Botting 1989; ed. Hackney Tech. Coll.; Dir. Country Life 1965, George Newnes 1966; Man. Dir. Odhams Press Ltd. 1968; Dir. Int. Publishing Corpn. 1972, IPC (America) Inc. 1975; Chair. Reed Holdings Inc. 1977, Reed Publishing Holdings Ltd. 1981; Chair. and Chief Exec. IPC Ltd. 1974; Dir. Reed Int. PLC 1974–, C.E.O. 1982–86, Chair. 1985–87; Dir. Watmoughs (Hldgs.) PLC 1988–. *Leisure interests:* racing, gardening. *Address:* 10 Park Square Mews, Upper Harley Street, London, NW1 4PP, England.

CARPENTIER, Jean Claude Gabriel; French aeronautical engineer; b. 13 April 1926, Haspres; m. Micheline Robinet 1950; ed. Ecole Polytechnique, Ecole Nationale Supérieure Aéronautique et Espace; service technique de l'aéronautique 1950; Direction des recherches et moyens d'essais 1961; Dir. Direction des recherches, études et techniques, Ministry of Defence 1977; Pres. Office Nat. d'études et de recherches aérospatiales (ONERA) 1984–91, Sr. Consultant 1991–; Pres. Man. Cttee. Nat. Meteorological Bureau; Pres. Comité Avion-Ozone 1992; Ed. Aerospace Research 1994–; Ed.-in-Chief Aerospace Science and Tech. 1997–; Commdr. Légion d'honneur, Ordre National du Mérite. *Publications:* Flight Mechanics 1952, Autopilots 1953, Inertial Navigation 1962. *Address:* Office National d'études et de recherches aérospatiales, 29 avenue de la Division Leclerc, P.O. Box 72, 92322 Chatillon Cedex, France. *Telephone:* 46-57-11-60.

CARPENTIER, Michel André Georges, L. EN D., L. EN SC. ECON.; French European Community official; b. 23 Oct. 1930, Billy Montigny, Pas de Calais; m. Annick Puget 1956; four s.; ed. Ecole des Hautes Etudes Commerciales, Ecole des Science Politiques and Univ. of Paris; Commissariat à l'Energie Atomique (CEA) 1958; EURATOM 1959; Dir.-Gen. Industrial, Technological and Scientific Affairs, EC Comm. 1967, Dir.-Gen. Environment 1977, Dir.-Gen. Energy 1981; mem. Task Force for Information Technologies and Telecommunications, EC Comm. 1984; Dir.-Gen. Information Technologies and Industries, and Telecommunications, EC Comm. 1986; Dir.-Gen. DG XIII, Telecommunications, Information Markets and Exploitation of Research, EC Comm. 1993–95; Hon. Dir.-Gen. and Special Advisor EC Comm.; Industrial Advisor; mem. Econ. and Social Cttee., EC Comm., Paris 1995–96; Hon. mem. Inst. of Electrical and Electronics Engs. (U.S.A.), Royal Swedish Acad. of Eng. Science; Chevalier, Légion d'honneur, Ehrenkreuz fur Wissenschaft & Forschung (Austria), Commdr. Mérite (Luxembourg); Dr. h.c. (Loughborough, Madrid). *Publications:* Telecommunications in Transition (with others) 1992. *Leisure interests:* fishing, classical music, opera, reading. *Address:* 44 Ave de la Celle St. Cloud, 92420 Vaucresson, France (Home). *Telephone:* 01.47.41.85.23. *Fax:* 01.47.41.85.23.

CARPER, Thomas Richard, M.B.A.; American politician; b. 23 Jan. 1947, Beckley, W. Va.; s. of Wallace Richard Carper and Mary Jean (Patton) Carper; m. Martha Stacy 1986; two s.; ed. Ohio State Univ., Univ. of Delaware; Commdr. U.S.N. 1968–73, Capt., Reserve 1973–91; industrial devt. specialist, then State Treasurer, State of Del., Dover 1976–83; Democrat mem. 98th–102nd Congresses from Del. 1983–93; Gov. of Delaware Jan. 1993–. *Address:* Office of the Governor, Tatnall Bldg., William Penn Street, Dover, DE 19802 (Office); 600 West Matson Run Parkway, Wilmington, DE 19802, U.S.A. (Home).

CARR, Sir (Albert) Raymond (Maillard), Kt., M.A., D.LITT., F.R.S.L., F.R.HIST.S., F.B.A.; British historian; b. 11 April 1919, Bath; s. of Reginald Henry Maillard Carr and Ethel Gertrude Marion Carr; m. Sara Ann Mary Strickland 1950; three s. one d.; ed. Brockenhurst School and Christ Church Oxford; Gladstone Research Exhibitioner, Christ Church 1941; Fellow All Souls Coll. Oxford 1946–53, New Coll. 1953–64, St. Antony's Coll. 1964–; Dir. Latin American Centre 1964–68, Chair. Soc. for Latin American Studies 1966–68; Prof. of History of Latin America, Oxford Univ. 1967–68, Warden St. Antony's Coll. 1968–87; mem. Nat. Theatre Bd. 1980; Corresp. mem. Royal Acad. of History, Madrid 1968; Hon. Fellow Christ Church Coll., Oxford; Exeter Univ.; Grand Cross of the Order of Alfonso El Sabio (for services to Spanish history) 1983. *Publications:* Spain 1808–1939 1966, Latin American Affairs 1969, The Spanish Civil War 1971, English Fox Hunting 1976, The Spanish Tragedy: the Civil War in Perspective 1977, Spain: Dictatorship to Democracy 1979, Modern Spain 1980, Fox-Hunting 1982, Puerto Rico: A Colonial Experiment 1984, ed. The Spanish Civil War 1986. *Leisure interest:* foxhunting. *Address:* Burch, North Molton, South Molton, EX36 3JU, England. *Telephone:* (01769) 550 267.

CARR, Col. Gerald Paul, D.SC.; American astronaut and engineer; b. 22 Aug. 1932, Denver, Colo.; s. of the late Thomas E. Carr and Freda L. Carr (née Wright); m. JoAnn R. Petrie 1954 (dissolved), three s. three d.; m. 2nd Dr. Patricia L. Musick 1979; ed. Univ. of S. Calif., U.S. Naval Postgraduate School and Princeton Univ.; entered U.S. Navy 1949, commissioned U.S. Marine Corps 1954; selected as NASA astronaut April 1966; mem. astronaut support crew, Apollo VIII and XII flights; commdr. of Skylab III, launched Nov. 1973 on 84-day mission; retd. from U.S. Marine Corps 1975; retd. from NASA 1977; Sr. Vice.-Pres. Bovay Engineers Inc. 1977–82; Sr. Consultant Applied Research Inc. 1982–84; Man. 7.6 m. Telescope Project, McDonald Observatory, Univ. of Tex. 1983–86; Pres. CAMUS Inc. 1984–; Dir. Nat. Space Soc., Space Dermatology Foundation; Trustee Univ. of the Ozarks; Registered Professional Engineer (Tex.); Hon. D.Sc. (Parks Coll., St. Louis Univ.); U.S. Navy D.S.M., NASA D.S.M., F.A.I. Gold Medals, Komarov Diploma, Collier Trophy, Haley Astronautics Award, inducted into Astronaut Hall of Fame 1997, other mil. decorations and numerous awards. *Leisure interests:* woodworking, fishing. *Address:* CAMUS Inc., P.O. Box 919, Huntsville, AR 72740, U.S.A. *Telephone:* (501) 559-2966.

CARR, Jack, D.PHIL., F.R.S.E.; British mathematician; b. 29 Aug. 1948, Newcastle upon Tyne; s. of John George Carr and Elizabeth Eleanor Carr; m. Teresa Nancy Thorpe 1976; one s. two d.; ed. Walbottle Secondary School, Univ. of Bath, St. Catherine's Coll., Oxford; Lecturer, Heriot-Watt Univ., Edin. 1974–83, Reader in Math. 1983–; Visiting Prof., Brown Univ., U.S.A. 1978–79, Mich. State Univ., U.S.A. 1982, Ecole Polytechnique, Lausanne, Switzerland 1983. *Publication:* Applications of Centre Manifolds 1981. *Leisure interests:* spreading urban myths, playing cricket for the W.C.C. *Address:* 42 Balgreen Avenue, Edinburgh, EH12 5SU, Scotland.

CARR, Willard Zeller Jr., B.S., J.D.; American attorney; b. 18 Dec. 1927, Richmond, Ind.; s. of Willard Z. Carr and Susan E. Brownell Carr; m. Margaret Paterson Carr 1952; two s.; ed. Purdue Univ., Indiana Univ. School of Law; Capt. Judge Advocate Gen.'s Dept. U.S.A.F. 1951–52; partner Gibson, Dunn & Crutcher, Attorneys 1952–; admitted to U.S. Supreme Court 1963; mem. Los Angeles County Bar Asscn., Calif. State Bar Asscn., American Bar Asscn., Int. Bar Asscn. (Chair. Labour Law Cttee. 1973–83); mem. Bd. of Visitors Southwestern Univ. Law School, Indiana Univ. School of Law; mem. Advisory Council Int. and Comparative Law Center, Southwestern Legal Foundation, Nat. Panel of Arbitrators, American Arbitration Asscn., World Affairs Council, Republican State Cen. Cttee. for Calif.; Chair. Calif. Chamber of Commerce; Jurisprudence Award (Anti-Defamation League) 1987. *Publications:* International Handbook on Contracts of Employment 1976, Symposium on Private Investments Abroad—Problems and Solutions in International Business 1982; numerous specialist articles. *Leisure interests:* tennis, travel. *Address:* Gibson, Dunn & Crutcher, 333 South Grand Avenue, 49th floor, Los Angeles, CA 90071 (Office); 2185 Century Hill, Los Angeles, CA 90067, U.S.A. (Home). *Telephone:* (213) 229-7238.

CARR OF HADLEY, Baron (Life Peer), cr. 1975, of Monken Hadley in Greater London; **(Leonard) Robert Carr,** P.C., M.A.; British politician and business executive; b. 11 Nov. 1916, London; s. of the late Ralph Edward and of Katie Elizabeth Carr; m. Joan Kathleen Twining 1943; one s. (deceased) two d.; ed. Westminster School and Gonville and Caius Coll., Cambridge; M.P. 1950–75, Parl. Pvt. Sec. to Sec. of State for Foreign Affairs 1951–55, to Prime Minister April-Dec. 1955, Parl. Sec. Ministry of Labour and Nat. Service 1955–58, Sec. for Tech. Co-operation May 1963–Oct. 1964; Sec. of State for Employment 1970–72; Lord Pres. of Council and Leader of House of Commons April-Nov. 1972; Sec. of State Home Dept. 1972–74; joined John Dale Ltd. 1938, Chief Metallurgist 1945–48, Dir. of Research and Development 1948–55, Chair. 1959–63 and 1965–70; Dir. Carr, Day & Martin Ltd. 1947–55, Isotope Developments Ltd. 1950–55; Deputy Chair. and Joint Man. Dir. Metal Closures Group Ltd. 1960–63, Dir. 1965–70; Dir. Scottish Union and Nat. Insurance Co. (London) 1958–63; Dir. S. Hoffnung and Co. 1963, 1965–70, 1974–80, Securicor Ltd. 1965–70, 1974–85; Norwich Union Insurance Group (London) 1965–70, 1974–76; Dir. S.G.B. Group Ltd. 1974–86; Dir. Prudential Assurance Co. 1976–85, Deputy Chair. 1979–80, Co-Chair. 1980–85; Dir. Prudential Corpn. Ltd. 1978–89, Deputy Chair. 1979–80, Chair. 1980–85; Dir. Cadbury Schweppes Ltd. 1979–87; Chair. Strategy Ventures 1988–; mem. Political Honours Scrutiny Cttee. 1977–87; Fellow, Imperial Coll., London 1985; Conservative. *Publications:* Co-author One Nation 1950, Change is our Ally 1954, The Responsible Society 1958, One Europe 1965. *Leisure interests:* lawn tennis, gardening, music. *Address:* House of Lords, Westminster, London, S.W.1 (Office); 14 North Court, Great Peter Street, London, SW1P 3LL, England (Home).

CARRARO, Franco; Italian politician and sports administrator; b. 6 Dec. 1939, Padua; graduated in econ. and commercial sciences; Chair. football team Milan Calcio 1967–71; fmr. Chair. Comm. for Amateur and Professional Football, Chair. Sub-comm. for Professional Football, UEFA; Vice-Pres. Italian Nat. Olympic Cttee. 1976–78, Pres. 1978–; mem. Int. Olympic Cttee.; Pres. Italian Football Fed. (Federazione Italiana Gioco Calcio) 1976–86, Extraordinary Commr. 1986–; Chair. Asscn. of European Olympic Cttees. 1980–; Chair. Organizing Cttee. World Cup Football Championship 1990; fmr. champion water-skier; Minister of Tourism and Performing Arts 1989–90; Mayor of Rome 1989–93.

CARRELL, Robin Wayne, M.A., PH.D., F.R.C.P., F.R.S.N.Z.; New Zealand professor of haematology; b. 5 April 1936, Christchurch; s. of Ruane George Carrell and Constance Gwendoline (née Rowe) Carrell; m. Susan Wyatt Rogers 1962; two s. two d.; ed. Christchurch Boys' High School, Univs. of Otago, Canterbury and Cambridge; mem. MRC Haemoglobin Unit, Cambridge 1965–68; Dir. Clinical Biochemistry Christchurch Hosp., N.Z. 1968–75; lecturer Clinical Biochemistry Univ. of Cambridge 1976–78, Prof. of Haematology 1986–; Prof. of Clinical Biochemistry and Dir. Molecular Research Lab. Christchurch Clinical School of Medicine, Otago Univ.

1978–86; Commonwealth Fellow St. John's Coll., Cambridge and Visiting Scientist MRC Lab. of Molecular Biology 1985; Fellow Trinity Coll., Cambridge 1987–; Gov. Imperial Coll. London 1997–; Hector Medal (Royal Soc. of N.Z.) 1986. *Publications:* articles in scientific journals on genetic abnormalities of human proteins and new protein family, serpins. *Leisure interests:* gardening, walking. *Address:* 19 Madingley Road, Cambridge, CB3 0EG, England. *Telephone:* (01223) 312 970.

CARRERAS, José; Spanish tenor; b. 5 Dec. 1947, Barcelona; s. of José Carreras and Antonia Carreras; m. Ana Elisa Carreras; one s. one d.; opera début as Gennaro in Lucrezia Borgia, Liceo Opera House, Barcelona 1970–71 season; appeared in La Bohème, Un Ballo in Maschera, I Lombardi alla Prima Crociata at Teatro Regio, Parma, Italy 1972; U.S. début as Pinkerton in Madame Butterfly with New York City Opera 1972; début Metropolitan Opera as Cavaradossi 1974; début La Scala as Riccardo in Un Ballo in Maschera 1975; appeared in film Don Carlos 1980, West Side Story (TV) 1985; has appeared at maj. opera houses and festivals including Teatro Colón, Buenos Aires, Covent Garden, London, Vienna Staatsoper, Easter Festival and Summer Festival, Salzburg, Lyric Opera of Chicago; recordings include Un Ballo in Maschera, La Battaglia di Legnano, Il Corsaro, Un Giorno di Regno, I Due Foscari, Simone Boccanegra, Macbeth, Don Carlos, Tosca, Thais, Aida, Cavalleria Rusticana, Pagliacci, Lucia di Lammermoor, Turandot, Elisabetta di Inghilterra, Otello (Rossini); Pres. José Carreras Int. Leukaemia Foundation 1988–; Hon. mem. Royal Acad. of Music 1990. *Publication:* Singing from the Soul 1991. *Address:* c/o FIJC, Muntaner 383, 2°, 08021 Barcelona, Spain.

CARRERE D'ENCAUSSE, Hélène, D. ÈS L.; French professor specializing in Soviet affairs; b. 6 July 1929, Paris; d. of Georges Zourabichvili and Nathalie von Pelken; m. Louis Carrère 1952; one s. two d.; ed. Sorbonne, Paris; fmr. Prof. Univ. of Paris (Sorbonne); now Prof. Inst. d'Etudes Politiques, Paris and Dir. of Research, Fondation Nationale des Sciences Politiques; mem. Bd. of Dirs. East-West Inst. for Security Studies; Visiting Prof. at numerous univs. in U.S.A.; mem. Acad. Française; Assoc. mem. Acad. Royale de Belgique; mem. European Parl. 1994–; Prix Aujourd'hui 1978; Prix de la Fondation Louis-Weiss 1986; Dr. h.c. (Montreal). *Publications include:* Le marxisme et l'Asie 1965, Réforme et révolution chez les musulmans de l'Empire russe 1966, L'URSS et la Chine devant les révolutions dans les sociétés pré-industrielles 1970, L'Empire éclaté 1978, Lénine: la révolution et le pouvoir 1979, Staline: l'ordre par la terreur 1979, Le pouvoir confisqué 1982, Le Grand Frère 1983, La déstalinisation commence 1984, Ni paix ni guerre 1986, Le Grand Défi: bolcheviks et nations 1917–30 1987, Le Malheur russe 1988, La Gloire des nations ou la fin de l'Empire soviétique 1991, Victorieuse Russie 1992, Nicholas II: la transition interrompue 1996. *Address:* c/o Institut de France, 23 quai de Conti, 75006 Paris, France; European Parliament, 97–113 rue Belliard, 1047 Brussels, Belgium.

CARREY, Jim; Canadian film actor; b. 17 Jan. 1962, Newmarket, Ont.; m. Melissa Worner 1986 (divorced); one d.; began performing in comedy clubs in Toronto aged 17 before moving to Hollywood; TV appearances include: In Living Colour (sit-com). *Films include:* Peggy Sue Got Married 1986, The Dead Pool 1988, Earth Girls Are Easy 1989, Ace Ventura! Pet Detective, The Mask, Dumb and Dumber, Batman Forever, The Cable Guy, The Truman Show 1998. *Address:* UTA, 9560 Wilshire Boulevard, 5th Floor, Beverly Hills, CA 90212, U.S.A.

CARRICK, Hon. Sir John Leslie, K.C.M.G., B.ECON.; Australian politician (retd.); b. 4 Sept. 1918, Sydney; s. of Arthur James and Emily Ellen (Terry) Carrick; m. Diana Margaret (Angela) Hunter 1951; three d.; ed. Sydney Technical High School, Univ. of Sydney; commissioned Univ. of Sydney Regt. 1939, served in Australian Imperial Force, Sparrow Force; P.O.W. 1942–45; mem. Citizen Mil. Force 1948–51; Gen. Sec. N.S.W. Div. of Liberal Party of Australia 1948–71; mem. Senate 1971–87; mem. Library Cttee. 1971–73, Senate Standing Cttee. on Educ., Science and the Arts 1971–75, Senate Standing Cttee. on Foreign Affairs and Defence 1971–74, Joint Cttee. on Foreign Affairs 1971–72, on Foreign Affairs and Defence 1973–75, Senate Standing Cttee. on Standing Orders 1978–83, Senate Select Cttee. on Human Embryo Experimentation Bill 1985 1985–, Standing Cttee. on Regulations and Ordinances 1983–86, Jt. Select Cttee. on Electoral Reform 1983–87; Opposition Spokesman for Federalism and Intergovernment Relations 1975; Minister for Housing and Construction, for Urban and Regional Devt. Nov.-Dec. 1975; Minister for Educ. 1975–79, Minister assisting the Prime Minister in Fed. Affairs 1975–78; Leader of Govt. in the Senate 1978–83, Vice-Pres. of Exec. Council 1978–82; Minister for Nat. Devt. and Energy 1979–83; Chair. N.S.W. State Govt. Cttee. Review of Schools 1988–89, N.S.W. Gas Council 1990–95; Pres. Univ. of Sydney Dermatology Research Foundation 1989; Chair. Gas Council of N.S.W. 1990–95; mem. N.S.W. Ministerial Advisory Council on Teacher Educ. and Quality of Teaching 1992–95, Advisory Bd. Inst. of Early Childhood, Macquarie Univ. 1992–; Hon. Fellow Australian Coll. of Educ. 1994; Hon. D. Litt. (Sydney) 1982. *Leisure interests:* swimming, running, reading. *Address:* 8 Montah Avenue, Killara, N.S.W. 2071, Australia (Home). *Telephone:* 02-498-6326 (Home).

CARRICK, Sir Roger John, K.C.M.G., L.V.O.; British diplomatist and consultant; b. 13 Oct. 1937, Middx.; s. of John Carrick and Florence Carrick; m. Hilary E. Blinman 1962; two s.; ed. Isleworth Grammar School and School of Slavonic and E. European Studies, Univ. of London; R.N. 1956–58; joined H.M. Diplomatic Service 1956; served Sofia 1962, FCO 1965, Paris 1967, Singapore 1971, FCO 1973–77; Visiting Fellow, Inst. of Int. Affairs, Univ. of Calif. Berkeley 1977–78; Counsellor, Washington, D.C. 1978; Head, Overseas Estate Dept. FCO 1982; Consul-Gen. Chicago 1985–88; Asst. Under-Sec. of State (Econ.) FCO 1988–90; Amb. to Indonesia 1990–94; High Commr. in Australia 1994–97. *Publications:* East-West Technology Transfer in Perspective 1978, RolleroundOz 1998. *Leisure interests:* sailing, reading, music, theatre, avoiding gardening. *Address:* 43 Dornden Drive, Langton Green, Tunbridge Wells, Kent, TN3 0AE, England; 9B Panners Way, Goldfield Heights, Queenstown, New Zealand.

CARRIER, George Francis, PH.D.; American professor of applied mathematics; b. 4 May 1918, Millinocket, Maine; s. of Charles Mosher Carrier and Mary Marcoux Carrier; m. Mary Casey Carrier 1946; three s.; ed. Cornell Univ.; Research Engineer, Harvard Univ. 1944–46; Asst. Prof. Brown Univ. 1946–47, Assoc. Prof. 1947–48, Prof. 1948–52; Gordon McKay Prof. of Mech. Eng., Harvard Univ. 1952–72; T. Jefferson Coolidge Prof. of Applied Math. 1972–88, Emeritus 1988–; Emer. mem. Council for Eng. Coll. Cornell Univ.; mem. N.A.S., American Philosophical Soc., Int. Soc. for Interaction of Mechanics and Math.; Fellow, American Acad. of Arts and Sciences, Nat. Acad. of Eng.; Assoc. Ed., Quarterly of Applied Math.; Hon. mem. A.S.M.E.; Hon. Fellow, Inst. for Maths. and its Applications; Pi Tau Sigma Richards Memorial Award, A.S.M.E. 1963, Von Karman Medal, American Soc. of Civil Engineers 1977, Timoshenko Medal, ASME 1978, Von Karman Prize, SIAM 1979, N.A.S. Award in Applied Math and Numerical Analysis 1980, ASME Silver Centennial Medal 1980, Fluid Dynamics Prize, American Physical Soc. 1984, Dryden Medal, A.I.A.A. 1989, Pres.'s Nat. Medal of Science 1990. *Publications:* Functions of a Complex Variable: Theory and Technique (with M. Krook and C. E. Pearson) 1966, Ordinary Differential Equations (with C. E. Pearson) 1968, Partial Differential Equations (with C. E. Pearson) 1976; numerous articles. *Address:* Harvard University, Division of Engineering and Applied Sciences, Pierce 311, Cambridge, MA 02138, U.S.A.

CARRIER, Hervé; Canadian sociologist and Jesuit; b. 26 Aug. 1921, Grand-Mère, Quebec; s. of Fortunat Carrier and Cora Gélinas; ed. Univ. de Montréal, Jesuit Faculty, Montreal, Catholic Univ. of America, Washington and Sorbonne, Paris; Prof. of Sociology, Gregorian Univ. Rome 1959–, Rector 1966–78; Pres. Int. Fed. of Catholic Univs. 1970–80, Dir. Centre for Coordination of Research 1978–82; Sec. Pontifical Council for Culture, Vatican City 1982–93; mem. Acad. des Lettres et des Sciences Humaines of Royal Soc. of Canada; Officier, Légion d'honneur; Dr. h.c. (Sogang Univ., Seoul and Fu Jen Univ., Taipei). *Publications:* Psycho-sociology of Religious Belonging 1965, Higher Education facing New Cultures 1982, Cultures: notre avenir 1985, Evangile et cultures 1987, Psico-sociologia dell'appartenenza religiosa 1988, Gospel Message and Human Cultures 1989, The Social Doctrine of the Church Revisited 1990, Evangélisation et, Développement des Cultures 1990, Lexique de la Culture 1992, Evangelizing the Culture of Modernity 1993, Diccionario de la Cultura 1994, Guide pour l'inculturation de l'Evangile 1997, Dizionario della cultura 1997. *Address:* 25 Jarry Street, W. Montreal, Quebec, H2P 1S6, Canada. *Telephone:* 514-387-2541. *Fax:* 514-387-4244.

CARRIERE, Berthold, M.MUS.; Canadian composer and musical director; b. 27 Feb. 1940, Ottawa; s. of Rolland and Berthe (Paradis) Carriere; m. Nancy Carpenter 1969; ed. Univs. of Montreal and Western Ontario Musical Dir. Banff School of Fine Arts 1968–72; Resident Musical Dir., Theatre London 1972–74, Dir. of Music 1976–77, Assoc. Dir. 1976; Dir. of Music, Stratford Shakespearean Festival 1976–83, 1985–; Musical Dir., Talk of Toronto 1980–82; Conductor/Arranger, Dominion Day Celebrations 1967; Man of the Year, City of Ottawa 1967, Guthrie Award, Stratford Shakespearean Festival 1976, Dora Mavor Moore Musical Dir. Award 1981, 1982, 1987. *Address:* Stratford Festival, Box 520, Stratford, Ont., N5A 6V2 (Office); Box 1273, St. Mary's, Ont., N0M 2V0, Canada (Home).

CARRIÈRE, Jean Paul Jacques; French author; b. 6 Aug. 1928, Nîmes; s. of Edmond Carrière and Andrée Paoli; m. 1st Michele Bollé, two s.; m. 2nd Françoise Battistini 1978, one s.; ed. Coll. Saint Stanislas, Coll. de l'Assomption and Lycée Alphonse Daudet, Nîmes; disc-jockey, Manosque 1958–63; producer, Radio Languedoc-Roussillon 1965–74; television producer, ORTF 1969–; mem. PEN Club; Prix de l'Acad. Française 1968; Prix Goncourt 1972. *Publications:* Les forêts du nouveau monde 1956, Lettre à un père sur une vocation incertaine 1956, Retour à Uzes 1968, L'Epervier de Maheux 1972, Jean Giono 1973, L'univers de Jean Carrière 1975, Noémie, Céléstin, Joseph et autres paysans d'Ardèche 1976, La Caverne des Pestiférés (two vols.) 1978, 1979, Le nez dans l'herbe 1980, Jean Giono 1985, Les années sauvages (novel) 1986, Julien Gracq 1986, Le Prix du Goncourt (novel) 1986, Le Dernier Été d'Occident 1987, Voyage d'hiver en Provence 1987, Cévennes 1988, Jean Fusaro, ou La peinture réhabilitée 1988, Un grain de beauté sur la lune (novel) 1990, Sigourney Weaver ou la Révélation 1989, Droits, Devoirs et Crocodile: essai politique (co-author) 1992, L'Indifférence des Etoiles (novel) 1994, Achigen (novel) 1995, L'Etoffe des rêves (novel) 1996, L'Empire des songes. *Leisure interests:* bicycling, walking, piano, cinema, swimming. *Address:* Les Broussanes, Domessargues, 30350 Ledignan; Le Devois, Super Camprieu, 30750 Trèves, France. *Telephone:* 66.83.30.76; 67.82.61.12. *Fax:* 66.83.33.84.

CARRILLO, Santiago; Spanish politician and journalist; b. 18 Jan. 1915, Gijón; s. of Wenceslao and Rosalía (Solares) Carrillo; m. Carmen Menéndez; three s.; Sec.-Gen. de la Juventud Socialista Unificada 1936; Councillor of Public Order, Junta de Defensa de Madrid 1936; Sec.-Gen. Partido Comunista de España 1960–82, expelled from CP 1985; mem. Congress of Deputies July 1977–, Deputy for Madrid Oct. 1982–; Dir. Ahora June 1984–; Pres. de Unidad Comunista 1985. *Publications:* Después de Franco, ¿Qué?, Nuevos enfoques a problemas de hoy, Mañana España, Eurocomunismo y Estado, El año de la Constitución, Memoria de la transición 1983, Le communisme malgré tout 1983.

CARRINGTON, Alan, C.B.E., M.A., PH.D., F.R.S.; British professor of chemistry; b. 6 Jan. 1934; s. of Albert Carrington and Constance (Nelson) Carrington; m. Noreen H. Taylor 1959; one s. two d.; ed. Colfe's Grammar School and Univs. of Southampton, Oxford and Cambridge; Asst. in Research, Univ. of Cambridge 1960, Asst. Dir. of Research 1963; Fellow, Downing Coll. Cambridge 1960; Prof. of Chem. Univ. of Southampton 1967, Royal Soc. Research Prof. 1979–84, 1987–; Royal Soc. Research Prof. and Fellow, Jesus Coll. Oxford 1984–87; Pres. Faraday Div., Royal Soc. of Chemistry 1997–99; Foreign Hon. mem. American Acad. of Arts and Sciences; Foreign Assoc. N.A.S.; Hon. D.Sc.; numerous medals and awards. *Publications:* Introduction to Magnetic Resonance (with A. D. McLachlan) 1967, Microwave Spectroscopy of Free Radicals 1974; papers in learned journals. *Leisure interests:* family, music, fishing. *Address:* 46 Lakewood Road, Chandler's Ford, Hants., SO53 1EX, England. *Telephone:* (01703) 265092.

CARRINGTON, 6th Baron; **Peter Alexander Rupert Carington,** K.G., G.C.M.G., C.H., M.C., P.C.; British politician and international administrator; b. 6 June 1919, London; s. of 5th Baron Carrington and the Hon. Sybil Marion Colville; m. Iona McClean 1942; one s. two d.; ed. Eton Coll. and Royal Military Coll., Sandhurst; Grenadier Guards 1939, served N.W. Europe; Parl. Sec. Ministry of Agriculture 1951–54, Ministry of Defence 1954–56; High Commr. in Australia 1956–59; First Lord of the Admiralty 1959–63; Minister without Portfolio (at the Foreign Office), Leader of the House of Lords 1963–64; Leader of the Opposition in the House of Lords 1964–70, 1974–79; Sec. of State for Defence 1970–74, also Minister of Aviation Supply 1971–74; Chair. Conservative Party 1972–74; Sec. of State for Energy Jan.-March 1974, for Foreign and Commonwealth Affairs 1979–82, Minister of Overseas Devt. 1979–82; Chair. GEC 1983–84; Sec.-Gen. NATO 1984–88; Chair. Christies Int. PLC 1988–93 (Dir. 1988–); Dir. The Daily Telegraph 1990–; EC Negotiating Cttee. on Yugoslavia 1992, (resgnd. Aug. 1992); Chancellor Univ. of Reading 1992–; Sec. for Foreign Correspondence and Hon. mem. R.A. of Arts 1982–; Chancellor, Order of the Garter 1994–; Chair. Bd. of Trustees, Victoria and Albert Museum 1983–88; Pres. The Pilgrims 1983–, Voluntary Service Overseas 1993–; mem. Kissinger Asscn. 1982–84, 1988–; Pres. Chiltern Open Air Museum 1983–; Dir. Int. Bd. Fiat 1995–; Hon. Bencher of the Middle Temple 1983; Hon. Fellow, St. Antony's Coll., Oxford 1982–; Hon. LL.D. (Cambridge) 1981, (Leeds) 1981, (Univ. of Philippines) 1982, (Univ. of Aberdeen) 1985, (Sussex) 1989; Hon. D.Univ. (Essex) 1983; Hon. Dr. Laws (Univ. of S.C.) 1983, (Harvard Univ.) 1986; Dr. h.c. (Buckingham) 1989; Hon. D.Lit. (Reading) 1989; Hon. D.Sc. (Cranfield) 1983; Hon. LL.D. (Nottingham) 1993, (Birmingham) 1993; Chancellor, Order of St. Michael and St. George 1984–94; Order of the Garter 1994–; Grand Officier, Légion d'honneur; Presidential Medal of Freedom 1988, Four Freedoms Award 1992, Freedom from Fear Award (Franklin Delano Inst.) 1992. *Publication:* Reflect on Things Past: The Memoirs of Lord Carrington 1988. *Address:* House of Lords, London, S.W.1; 32A Ovington Square, London, SW3 1LR; Manor House, Bledlow, Princes Risborough, Bucks., HP27 9PB, England. *Telephone:* 0171-584 1476 (London); (01844) 343499 (Bucks.). *Fax:* 0171-823 9051 (London).

CARROLL, Donal Shemus Allingham, F.C.A.; Irish banker and industrialist; b. 26 Dec. 1927, Ireland; s. of Col. J. D. Carroll and Sheila Maunsell (née Flynn); m. Monica D. M. Moran 1951; one s. one d.; ed. Glenstal Abbey School, Limerick and Trinity Coll., Dublin; joined P. J. Carroll & Co. Ltd. 1952, Dir. 1955, Chair. 1960–88 and Man. Dir. 1960–71; Chair. P. J. Carroll & Co. plc; mem. court of Dirs., Bank of Ireland 1956–88, Deputy Gov. 1962–64; Gov. 1964–70, 1982–85; Dir. Carreras Ltd. 1962, Vice-Chair. 1971–72; Dir. Rothmans Int. Ltd. 1972–, Deputy Chair. 1985–; Dir. Cen. Bank of Ireland 1970–81; Chair. Lloyds & BOLSA Int. Bank Ltd. 1971–73; mem. Public Services Advisory Council 1973–77; Dir. Dunlop Holdings Ltd. 1973–83; Dir. Irish Times Holdings, Irish Times Trust 1974–80; mem. Comm. on Taxation 1980–85; Hon. LL.D. (Dublin) 1969. *Leisure interests:* gardening, reading.

CARROLL, Kenneth Kitchener, PH.D., F.R.S.C.; Canadian professor of biochemistry; b. 9 March 1923, Carrolls, N.B.; s. of Lawrence Carroll and Sarah Della Estey; m. Margaret Aileen Ronson 1950; three s.; ed. Fredericton High School, Univs. of New Brunswick, Toronto, Western Ontario, McGill Univ. and Cambridge Univ., U.K.; Asst. Prof., Dept. of Medical Research, Univ. of Western Ont. 1954–57, Assoc. Prof. 1957–65, Prof. and Acting Head 1965–68, Prof., Dept. of Biochemistry 1968–88, Prof. Emer. 1988–; Acting Dir. Centre for Human Nutrition 1989–90, Dir. 1990–; Career Investigator, Medical Research Council of Canada 1963–94; Sec. Canadian Soc. of Nutritional Sciences 1965–67, Pres. 1978–79; Pres. Canadian Atherosclerosis Soc. 1989–91; Hon. Sec. Canadian Fed. of Biological Socs. 1967–71; Fellow American Inst. of Nutrition; Merck Fellowship 1952–53; Hon. D. Sc. (New Brunswick) 1993; Earle Willard McHenry Award, Canadian Soc. of Nutritional Sciences 1987, Lifetime Achievement Award, Canadian Section American Oil Chemists' Soc. 1995. *Publications:* about 260 original research papers, review articles and book chapters on lipid metabolism, and nutrition in relation to heart disease and cancer. *Leisure interests:* sailing, curling. *Address:* Department of Biochemistry, University of Western Ontario, London, Ont., N6A 5C1 (Office); 561 St. George Street, London, Ont., N6A 3B9, Canada (Home). *Telephone:* (519) 661-3097 (Office); (519) 438-5502 (Home). *Fax:* (519) 661-4006.

CARSBERG, Sir Bryan (Victor), Kt., M.SC., M.A.; British public servant and university professor; b. 3 Jan. 1939, London; s. of Alfred Victor and Maryllia Ciceley (née Collins) Carsberg; m. Margaret Linda Graham 1960; two d.; ed. London School of Econs.; sole practice C.A. 1962–64; Lecturer in Accounting, L.S.E. 1964–68, Arthur Andersen Prof. of Accounting 1981–87, Visiting Prof. 1987–89; Visiting lecturer, Grad. School of Business, Univ. of Chicago 1968–69; Prof. of Accounting, Univ. of Manchester 1969–78; Visiting Prof. of Business Admin. Univ. of Calif., Berkeley 1974; Asst. Dir. Research and Tech. Activities, U.S. Financial Accounting Standards Bd. 1978–81; Dir. of Research, Inst. of C.A. in England and Wales 1981–87; Dir.-Gen. of Telecommunications, Oftel 1984–92; mem. Accounting Standards Bd. 1990–94 (Vice-Chair. 1990–92); Dir.-Gen. of Fair Trading 1992–95; Sec. Gen. Int. Accounting Standards Cttee. (IASC) 1995–; Dir. Nynex Cable Comms. 1996–97, Cable & Wireless Communications 1997–; mem. Bd. Radio Communications Agency 1990–92; mem. Council Univ. of Surrey 1990–92; Hon. Fellow, L.S.E.; Hon. D.Sc. (East Anglia) 1992; Hon. D. Litt. (Loughborough) 1994; Hon. D. Univ. (Essex) 1995; Hon. LL.D. (Bath) 1990; Inst. Medal, W. B. Peat Medal and Prize (Inst. of C.A., England); Chartered Accountants Founding Socs. Centenary Award 1988, Blaew Prize for Telecommunications 1992. *Publications:* An Introduction to Mathematical Programming for Accountants 1969, Analysis for Investment Decisions 1974, Economics of Business Decisions 1975 and others. *Leisure interests:* running, theatre, music, opera. *Address:* International Accounting Standards Committee, 166 Fleet Street, London EC4A 2DY, England.

CARSON, Hampton L(awrence), A.B., PH.D.; American professor of genetics; b. 5 Nov. 1914, Philadelphia, Pa.; s. of Joseph and Edith Bruen Carson; m. Meredith Shelton 1937; two s.; Instructor in Zoology, Pa. 1938–42, Washington (St. Louis) 1943–46, Asst. Prof. 1946–49, Assoc. Prof. 1949–55, Prof. 1956–71; Prof. of Genetics, Univ. of Hawaii 1971–85, Prof. Emer. 1985–, Geneticist, Dept. of Entomology 1967–68; Visiting Prof. of Biology, Univ. of São Paulo 1951, 1977; Fulbright Research Scholar Dept. of Zoology, Univ. of Melbourne 1961; mem. American Acad. of Arts and Sciences, American Soc. of Naturalists (Pres. 1973), Genetics Soc. of America (Pres. 1982), Hawaiian Acad. of Sciences (Pres. 1975), N.A.S., Soc. for the Study of Evolution (Pres. 1971); Hon. Assoc. in Entomology and Trustee B. P. Bishop Museum 1982–88; Medal for Excellence in Research, Univ. of Hawaii 1979, Leidy Medal, Acad. of Natural Sciences, Philadelphia 1985, Charles Reed Bishop Medal, Bishop Museum, Honolulu, Hawaii 1992, George Gaylord Simpson Award (Soc. for Study of Evolution) 1996. *Publications:* Heredity and Human Life and over 280 scientific articles. *Leisure interest:* bonsai training. *Address:* Department of Genetics and Molecular Biology, 1960 East-West Road, University of Hawaii, Honolulu, HI 96822 (Office); 2001 Ualakaa Street, Honolulu, HI 96822, U.S.A. (Home). *Telephone:* (808) 956-7662 (Office); (808) 941-6319 (Home). *Fax:* (808) 956-5506.

CARSON, Johnny; American television personality; b. 23 Oct. 1925, Corning, Ia.; s. of Homer Carson and Ruth (née Hook) Carson; m. 1st Jody Wolcott 1948 (divorced 1963); three c.; m. 2nd Joanne Copeland 1963 (divorced); m. 3rd Joanna Holland 1972 (divorced 1983); m. 4th Alexis Maas 1987; ed. Univ. of Nebraska; announcer, radio station KFAB, Lincoln, Neb. 1948, then radio WOW and WOW-TV, Omaha, Neb., station KNXT, Los Angeles, Calif. 1950; TV show Carson's Cellar 1951; writer for comedian Red Skelton; introduced TV quiz show Earn Your Vacation 1954; the Johnny Carson Show, CBS 1955; introduced TV quiz show Who Do You Trust?, ABC-TV 1958–63; host Tonight programme, NBC-TV 1962–92; numerous other TV appearances; performer Las Vegas 1954–; Presidential Medal of Freedom 1992; Entertainer of Year Award, American Guild of Variety Artists. *Publication:* Happiness is a Dry Martini 1965.

CARSON, William Hunter, O.B.E.; British jockey; b. 16 Nov. 1942, Stirling, Scotland; s. of Thomas Whelan and Mary Hay (Hunter) Carson; m. 1st Carole Jane Sutton 1962 (dissolved 1979); three s.; m. 2nd Elaine Williams 1982; ed. Riverside School; apprentice with Capt. Gerald Armstrong 1957–62; rode first winner Pinker's Pond at Catterick 1962; First Jockey to Lord Derby 1968, to Bernard van Cutsem 1971–75, to Maj. Dick Hern 1977–89, to H.M. The Queen 1977; Champion Jockey 1972, 1973, 1978, 1980, 1983; rode the winners of 18 English Classics, 8 Irish Classics, and 68 English Group One races; rode 6 winners at one meeting July 1990; best horses ridden Nashwan and Dayjur; bred and rode St. Leger winner Minster Son 1988; 3,828 career winners (1997); retd. 1997; racing pundit BBC 1997–. *Publication:* Willie Carson Up Front: A Racing Autobiography 1993. *Leisure interest:* foxhunting. *Address:* Minster House, Barnsley, Cirencester, Glos., GL7 5DZ, England. *Telephone:* (01285) 658919.

CARSWELL, Rt. Hon. Sir Robert Douglas, Kt., P.C.; British judge; b. 28 June 1934, Belfast; s. of Alan E. Carswell and Nance E. Carswell; m. Romayne Winifred Ferris 1961; two d.; ed. Royal Belfast Academical Inst., Pembroke Coll. Oxford, Univ. of Chicago Law School; called to the Bar, Northern Ireland 1957, to English Bar, Gray's Inn 1972; Counsel to Attorney-Gen. for Northern Ireland 1970–71; Q.C. 1971; Sr. Crown Counsel for Northern Ireland 1979–84; Judge High Court of Justice in Northern Ireland 1984–93; Lord Justice of Appeal, Supreme Court of Judicature 1993–97;

Lord Chief Justice of Northern Ireland Jan. 1997–; Chancellor, Dioceses of Armagh and of Down and Dromore 1990–97; Chair. Council of Law Reporting for Northern Ireland 1987–97, Law Reform Advisory Cttee. for Northern Ireland 1989–97, Distinction and Meritorious Service Awards Cttee., D.H.S.S. 1995–97; Pres. Northern Ireland Scout Council 1993–; Pro-Chancellor, Chair. Council, Univ. of Ulster 1984–94; Hon. D. Litt. (Ulster) 1994. *Publications:* Trustee Acts (Northern Ireland) 1964, articles in legal periodicals. *Leisure interests:* golf, hillwalking, music, architecture, antiques and conservation, wildlife. *Address:* Royal Courts of Justice, Belfast BT1 3JF, Northern Ireland (Office). *Telephone:* (01232) 235111. *Fax:* (01232) 236838.

CARTAN, Henri Paul, D. ÈS SC.; French mathematician; b. 8 July 1904, Nancy; s. of Elie Cartan; m. Nicole Weiss 1935; two s. three d.; ed. Lycée Buffon, Lycée Hoche (Versailles) and Ecole Normale Supérieure; teacher, Lycée, Caen 1928; Lecturer, Faculty of Science, Lille Univ. 1929–31; Prof. Faculty of Science, Strasbourg Univ. 1931–40, Univ. of Paris 1940–69, Univ. de Paris-Sud (Orsay) 1969–75; Pres. French Section, European Asscn. of Teachers 1957–75; Pres. Int. Mathematical Union 1967–70; Pres. Mouvement Fédéraliste Européen (France) 1974–85; mem. Royal Acad., Denmark 1962; Corresp. Acad. des Sciences 1965, mem. 1974–; Foreign mem. Royal Soc. 1971; Foreign Hon. mem. American Acad. 1950, Foreign Assoc. Nat. Acad. of Sciences, Washington 1972, Acad. Royale Belgique 1978; Corresp. Akad. der Wissenschaften Göttingen 1971, Royal Acad. of Sciences, Madrid 1971, Bayerische Akad. der Wissenschaften 1974; hon. mem. Japan Acad. 1979; fmr. mem. Acad. Finland 1979; Foreign mem. Royal Swedish Acad. of Sciences 1981; (Polish Acad.) 1985, Hon. D.Sc. (ETH, Zurich) 1955, (Münster) 1952, (Oslo) 1961, (Sussex) 1969, (Cambridge) 1969, (Stockholm) 1978, (Oxford) 1980, (Zaragoza) 1985, (Athens) 1992; Wolf Prize in Math 1980; Commandr. Légion d'honneur. *Address:* 95 boulevard Jourdan, 75014 Paris, France. *Telephone:* (1) 45-40-51-78.

CARTELLIERI, Ulrich; German banker; b. 21 Sept. 1937; mem. Bd. Deutsche Bank AG, Frankfurt; Chair. Deutsche Bank (Asia Credit) Ltd., Singapore, DB Finance (Hong Kong) Ltd., Hong Kong; Chair. Supervisory Bd. European Asian Bank AG, Hamburg, Karstadt AG 1990–98; mem. Supervisory Bd. Deutsche Solvay-Werke GmbH, Solingen, Deutsche Telephonwerke und Kabelindustrie AG, Berlin, Euro-Pacific Finance Corpn. Ltd., Melbourne, Girmes-Werke AG, Grefrath-Oedt, Th. Goldschmidt AG, Essen, Wilhelm Karmann GmbH, Osnabrück, Thyssen Edelstahlwerke AG, Düsseldorf, G. M. Pfaff AG, Kaiserslautern. *Address:* Taunusanlage 12, 60325 Frankfurt am Main, Germany.

CARTER, Brandon, D.SC., F.R.S.; British theoretical physicist; b. 26 May 1942, Sydney, Australia; s. of Harold B. Carter and Mary Brandon-Jones; m. Lucette Defrise 1969; three d.; ed. George Watson's Coll., Edinburgh, Univ. of St. Andrews, Univ. of Cambridge (Pembroke Coll.); Research Fellow, Pembroke Coll., Univ. of Cambridge 1967–72; staff mem., Inst. of Astronomy, Cambridge 1968–72; Asst. Lecturer, Dept. of Applied Math. and Theoretical Physics, Univ. of Cambridge 1973, lecturer 1974; Maître de Recherche, Centre Nat. de la Recherche Scientifique, Paris 1975–85, Dir. of Research 1986–; Directeur-Adjoint, Group d'Astrophysique Relativiste, Observatoire de Paris-Meudon 1975–82, Directeur 1983–86; Dir. of Research Centre Nat. de la Recherche Scientifique 1986–. *Publications:* Global Structure of the Kerr Family of Gravitational Fields 1968, Black Hole Equilibrium States 1973, Large Number Coincidences and the Anthropic Principle in Cosmology 1974, The General Theory of the Mechanical Electromagnetic and Thermodynamic Properties of Black Holes 1979, The Anthropic Principle and its Implications for Biological Evolution 1983. *Address:* Centre National de la Recherche Scientifique, Observatoire de Paris-Meudon, 92190 Meudon (Office); 19 rue de la Borne au Diable, 92310 Sèvres, France (Home).

CARTER, Sir Charles Frederick, Kt., M.A., F.B.A.; British economist; b. 15 Aug. 1919, Rugby, Warwicks.; s. of Frederick William and Edith Mildred Carter; m. Janet Shea 1944; one s. two d.; ed. Rugby School and St. John's Coll., Cambridge; Lecturer in Statistics, Univ. of Cambridge 1945–51; Prof. of Applied Econs., The Queen's Univ., Belfast 1952–59; Stanley Jevons Prof. of Political Economy and Cobden Lecturer, Victoria Univ. of Manchester 1959–63; Vice-Chancellor, Univ. of Lancaster 1963–79; Chair. Research Cttee., Policy Studies Inst. 1978–88, Jt. Pres. 1988–97; Chair. Northern Ireland Econ. Council 1977–87, Goldsmiths Coll. (Univ. of London) 1988–94; Chair. various trusts; Fellow of Emmanuel Coll., Cambridge 1947–51, Hon. Fellow 1965–; Hon. Fellow Royal Irish Acad.; numerous hon. degrees. *Publications:* The Measurement of Production Movements (with W. B. Reddaway and J. R. N. Stone, qq.v.) 1948, British Economic Statistics (with A. D. Roy) 1954, Industry and Technical Progress 1957, Investment in Innovation 1958, Science in Industry 1959 (all three with B. R. Williams, q.v.), The Science of Wealth 1960, The Northern Ireland Problem (with D. P. Barritt) 1962, Wealth 1968, Higher Education for the Future 1980, Policies for a Constrained Economy (with J. H. M. Pinder) 1982, Members One of Another (on local govt.) 1996. *Leisure interest:* gardening. *Address:* 1 Gosforth Road, Seascale, Cumbria, CA20 1PU, England. *Telephone:* (019467) 28359.

CARTER, (Edward) Graydon; American magazine editor; b. 14 July 1949; s. of E. P. Carter and Margaret Ellen Carter; m. Cynthia Williamson 1982; three s. one d.; ed. Carleton Univ., Univ. of Ottawa; Ed. The Canadian Review 1973–77; writer Time 1978–83, Life 1983–86; founder, Ed. Spy 1986–91; Ed. New York Observer 1991–92; Ed. in Chief Vanity Fair 1992–; Hon. Ed. Harvard Lampoon 1989. *Leisure interest:* fly fishing. *Address:* Vanity Fair, Condé Nast Building, 350 Madison Avenue, New York, NY 10017, U.S.A.

CARTER, Elliott Cook, Jr., A.B., A.M.; American composer; b. 11 Dec. 1908, New York; s. of Elliot and Florence (née Chambers) Carter; m. Helen Frost-Jones 1939; one s.; ed. Harvard Univ., Ecole Normale de Musique, Paris; Musical Dir. Ballet Caravan 1937–39; critic Modern Music 1937–42; tutor St. John's Coll., Annapolis 1939–41; teacher of composition Peabody Conservatory 1946–48, Columbia Univ. 1948–50, Queen's Coll. (N.Y.) 1955–56; Prof. of Music, Yale Univ. 1960–61; Prof. Dept. of Composition, Juilliard School, New York 1966–82; Andrew White Prof.-at-Large, Cornell Univ. 1967; mem. Bd. of Trustees, American Acad., Rome; mem. Int. Soc. for Contemporary Music, Dir. 1946–52, Pres. American Section 1952, Nat. Inst. of Arts and Letters; mem. American Acad. of Arts and Sciences; Hon. degrees Swarthmore Coll. and Princeton Univ. 1969, Univs. of Harvard, Yale and Boston 1970, Univ. of Cambridge 1983; American Composers' Alliance Prize (for Quartet for Four Saxophones) 1943, First Prize Liège Int. Music Competition 1953, Prix de Rome 1953, Pulitzer Prize (for Second String Quartet), Sibelius Medal (Harriet Cohen Foundation) 1960, New York Critics Circle Award (for Double Concerto) 1961, Pulitzer Prize (for Third String Quartet) 1973; Ernst Von Siemens Prize, Munich 1981; Gold Medal, Nat. Inst. of Arts and Letters 1971, Handel Medallion of New York 1978, awarded Nat. Medal of Art by Pres. Reagan 1985, Commdr. des Arts et des Lettres, Gold Medal, Royal Philharmonic Soc. 1996. *Works include: (Orchestral):* Symphony No. 1 1954, Variations for Orchestra 1955, Double Concerto 1961, Piano Concerto 1965, Concerto for Orchestra 1969, Symphony of Three Orchestras 1977, Triple Duo 1982, Penthode (for 20 players) 1985, Biolin Concerto 1990; *(Chamber):* Elegy 1943, Sonata for Cello and Piano, Woodwind Quintet 1948, Sonata for Flute, Oboe, Cello and Harpsichord 1952, Brass Quintet 1974, three String Quartets 1951–71; *(Vocal):* A Mirror on Which to Dwell 1975, In Sleep In Thunder 1983, Penthode 1985, Oboe Concerto 1987, 3 Occasions of Orchestra 1989, Violin Concerto 1990; *(Choral):* The Defense of Corinth 1949; *(Instrumental):* Piano Sonata 1946, Night fantasies (piano) 1980, A Six-letter Letter (for English Horn); *(Stage Works):* Pocahontas 1939, The Minotaur 1947. *Address:* Contemporary Record Society, 724 Winchester Road, Broomall, PA 19008, U.S.A.

CARTER, H.E. Cardinal Gerald Emmett, C.C., M.A., PH.D., L.TH., D.H.L.; Canadian ecclesiastic; b. 1 March 1912, Montreal; s. of Thomas Joseph Carter and Mary (Kelty) Carter; ed. Grand Seminary, Montreal, Univ. of Montreal, Duquesne Univ.; ordained priest 1937; founder and prin. Prof. St. Joseph Teachers' Coll., Montreal 1939–61; Chaplain, Newman Club, McGill Univ. 1941–56; Charter mem. and first Pres. Thomas More Inst. of Adult Educ. 1945–61; mem. Montreal Catholic School Comm. 1948–61; Auxiliary Bishop of London, Ont. and titular Bishop of Altiburo 1961; Bishop of London, Ont. 1964–78; Archbishop of Toronto 1978–90, Archbishop Emer. 1990–; Cardinal 1979; mem. Council for studying Econ. Affairs of Holy See. 1981–, Canon Law Comm., Holy See. 1981; Chair. Episcopal Comm. on Canadian Liturgy 1966–73; mem. Consilium of Liturgy, Rome 1965; Chair. Int. Cttee. for English in Liturgy 1971; Vice-Pres. Canadian Catholic Conf. 1973, Catholic Conf. of Ont. 1971–73; Pres. Canadian Conf. of Catholic Bishops 1975; mem. Council, Synod of Bishops 1977; Hon. Canon, Cathedral Basilica, Montreal; Hon. LL.D. (Western Ont.) 1966, (Concordia) 1976, (Windsor) 1977, (McGill) 1980, (Notre Dame, Ind.) 1981; Hon. D.Lit. (St. Mary's, Halifax, N.S.) 1980. *Publications:* The Catholic Public Schools of Quebec 1957, Psychology and the Cross 1959, The Modern Challenge to Religious Education 1961, A Shepherd Speaks 1981. *Leisure interests:* fishing and swimming. *Address:* c/o Chancery Office, 1155 Yonge Street, Toronto, Ont. M4T 1W2, Canada (Office). *Telephone:* (416) 934-0606. *Fax:* (416) 934-3437.

CARTER, Jimmy (James Earl, Jr.), B.S.; American politician and farmer; b. 1 Oct. 1924, Plains, Ga.; s. of the late James Earl Carter Sr. and Lillian Gordy; m. Rosalynn Smith 1946; three s. one d.; ed. Plains High School, Georgia Southwestern Coll., Georgia Inst. of Tech., U.S. Naval Acad., Annapolis, Md.; served U.S. Navy 1946–53, attained rank of Lieut.; peanut farmer, warehouseman 1953–77, businesses Carter Farms, Carter Warehouses, Ga.; State Senator, Ga. 1962–66; Gov. of Georgia 1971–74; Pres. of U.S.A. 1977–81; Distinguished Prof., Emory Univ., Atlanta 1982–; leader int. observer teams Panama 1989, Nicaragua 1990, Dominican Repub. 1990, Haiti 1990; host peace negotiations Ethiopia 1989; visit to Democratic People's Repub. of Korea (in pvt. capacity) June 1994; negotiator in Haitian crisis Sept. 1994; visit to Bosnia Dec. 1994; f. Carter Presidential Center 1982; Chair. Bd. of Trustees, Carter Center Inc. 1986–, Carter-Menil Human Rights Foundation 1986–, Global 2000 Inc. 1986–, Council of Freely-Elected Heads of Govt. 1986–, Council of Int. Negotiation Network 1991–; mem. Sumter County, Ga., School Bd. 1955–62 (Chair. 1960–62), Americus and Sumter County Hospital Authority 1956–70, Sumter County Library Bd. 1961; Pres. Plains Devt. Corpn. 1963; Georgia Planning Asscn. 1968; Dir. Ga. Crop Improvement Asscn. 1957–63 (Pres. 1961); Chair. West Cen. Ga. Area Planning and Devt. Comm. 1964; State Chair. March of Dimes 1968–70; District Gov. Lions Club 1968–69; Chair. Congressional Campaign Cttee., Democratic Nat. Cttee. 1974; several hon. degrees; World Methodist Peace Award 1984, Albert Schweitzer Prize for Humanitarianism 1987, Onassis Foundation Award 1991, Notre Dame Univ. Award 1992, Matsunaga Medal of Peace 1993, J. William Fulbright Prize for Int. Understanding 1994, shared Houphouët Boigny Peace Prize, UNESCO 1995, UNICEF Int. Child

Survival Award (jtly. with Rosalynn Carter) 1999; Democrat. *Publications:* Why not the Best? 1975, A Government as good as its People 1977, Keeping Faith: Memoirs of a President 1982, The Blood of Abraham: Insights into the Middle East 1985, Everything to Gain: Making the Most of the Rest of Your Life 1987, An Outdoor Journal 1988, Turning Point: A Candidate, a State and a Nation Come of Age 1992, Always a Reckoning (poems) 1995, Sources of Strength 1997, The Virtues of Ageing 1998. *Leisure interests:* reading, tennis. *Address:* The Carter Center, 453 Freedom Parkway, 1 Copenhill Avenue, NE Atlanta, GA 30307, U.S.A.

CARTER-RUCK, Peter Frederick; British solicitor and commissioner for oaths; b. 26 Feb. 1914, Hove, Sussex; s. of Frederick Henry Carter-Ruck and Nell Mabel Carter-Ruck née Allen; m. Pamela Ann Maxwell 1940; one s. (deceased) one d.; ed. St. Edward's School, Oxford; qualified as solicitor of the Supreme Court of Judicature (England) 1937; served with R.A. 1939–44; Sr. Partner Oswald Hickson Collier & Co. 1945–81, Peter Carter-Ruck and Partners 1981–8, Sr. Consultant 1998–; Specialist mem. Council of Law Soc. 1971–84, Chair. Law Society Law Reform Cttee. 1980–83, mem. Intellectual Property Cttee.; Pres. City of Westminister Law Soc. 1976; Chair. Media Cttee., Int. Bar Asscn. 1983–85; mem. Council of Justice 1968–, Council of NSPCC; Hon. Consulting Solicitor, Chartered Inst. of Journalists; mem. and Past Pres. Council, Media Soc.; Gov. St. Edward's School, Oxford 1950–78; Past Chair. and Founder Gov. Shiplake Coll., Henley; mem. Livery, City of London Solicitors' Co. 1949–. *Publications:* Libel and Slander 1953, The Cyclist and the Law (with Ian Mackrill) 1953, Copyright: Modern Law and Practice (with Edmund Skone James) 1965, Memoirs of a Libel Lawyer (autobiog.) 1990. *Leisure interests:* writing, cinematography, wood-turning, ocean racing and cruising. *Address:* International Press Centre, 76 Shoe Lane, London, EC4A 3JB (Office); Latchmore Cottage, Great Hallingbury, Bishop's Stortford, Herts., CM22 7PJ, England (Home); Eilagadale, N. Ardnamurchan, Argyll, PH36 4LG, Scotland (Home). *Telephone:* 0171-353 5005 (Office); (01279) 654357 (Bishop's Stortford); (01972) 510267 (N. Ardnamurchan). *Fax:* 0171-353 5553 (Office); (01279) 504921 (Bishop's Stortford).

CARTIER, Jean-Albert; French theatre director; b. 15 May 1930, Marseilles; s. of Albert Cartier and Myriem Bordes; m. Solange Ottavy 1959; two d.; ed. Lycée Perrier, Marseilles and Ecole du Louvre; art critic, Combat and numerous reviews; artistic collaborator, France-Inter; arranged several exhbns. for Marseilles Museum; participated Paris Biennale 1959, 1961, 1963, 1965; founder and Dir. Asscn. technique pour l'action culturelle 1966–72; creator, Ballet-Théâtre contemporain, Centre chorégraphique nat. 1968; Dir. Centre chorégraphique et lyrique nat. 1972; Dir. Angers Mun. Theatre 1972–78; founder and Dir. Anjou Arts Festival; creator and Dir. Ballet-Théâtre français de Nancy 1978–87; Dir. Théâtre Musical, Paris-Châtelet 1980–88; Dir. Festival of Paris 1988; Dir. Théâtre Nat. de l'Opéra de Paris 1988, Gen. Man. 1989–91; Dir. of Music, Radio France 1991–94; Dir.-Gen. L'Opéra de Nice 1994–97; Chevalier, Légion d'honneur, Chevalier des Arts et des Lettres. *Address:* 8 rue Vernier, 06000 Nice, France.

CARTIER-BRESSON, Henri; French photographer; b. 22 Aug. 1908, Chanteloup; s. of André and Marthe (née Leverdier) Cartier-Bresson; m. 2nd Martine Franck 1970; ed. Ecole Fénelon and Lycée Condorcet, Paris; studied painting in André Lhote's studio; took up photography 1931; Asst. Dir. to Jean Renoir 1936, 1939; prisoner of war 1940–43, escaped; f. Magnum-Photos with Capa, Chim, and Rodger 1946; exhbns. Madrid, New York 1933, New York Museum of Modern Art 1946, 1968, The Louvre (Pavillon de Marsan), Paris 1954, Phillips Collection, Washington 1964, Tokyo 1965, Victoria and Albert Museum, London 1969, Grand Palais, Paris 1970, Palais de Tokyo, Paris 1985; drawing exhbns. New York, Zürich 1975, Musée d'art moderne, Paris, Museo de arte moderno, Mexico 1982; drawings, photographs and paintings exhbns. French Inst., Stockholm, Padiglione d'Arte Contemporanea, Milan, Univ. of Rome 1983, Museum of Modern Art, Oxford 1984, Palais Liechtenstein, Vienna, Salzburg 1986, Kunstverein Mannheim 1986, Museum of Modern Art, New York 1988, Printemps, Tokyo 1991, Museum of Modern Art, Taipei 1991, Parma 1992, Saragossa 1993, Minneapolis Art Inst. 1996, European Museum of Photography 1997, Musée d'art moderne, Montréal 1997; collection of 390 photographs at Menil Foundation, Houston, U.S.A., Victoria and Albert Museum, London, Univ. of Fine Arts, Osaka, Japan, and Bibliothèque Nationale, Paris, exhibited Edinburgh Festival, Hayward Gallery, London 1978; made various documentary films; CD recording Le Bon Plaisir d'HCB (interviews by Vera Feyder) 1991; mem. American Acad. of Arts and Science 1974; Grand Prix national 1981; Hasselbladt Award 1983; Overseas Press Club awards; D.Lit. h.c., Oxford Univ. 1975, Prize Novocento Palermo 1986. *Publications include:* Images à la sauvette (U.S. edition The Decisive Moment), The Europeans, From One China to the Other, The People of Moscow, Danses à Bali, The World of Henri Cartier-Bresson 1968, L'homme et la machine 1968, Vive la France 1970, Cartier-Bresson's France 1971, Faces of Asia 1972, About Russia 1974, Henri Cartier-Bresson, Photographer 1979, Photoportraits 1983, America in Passing 1991, Carnets mexicains (jtly. with Carlos Fuentes) 1996, L'Imaginaire d'après nature, Des européens (jtly. with Jean Clair) 1997, Tête-à-tête (jtly. with E. H. Gombrich (q.v.) 1998. *Address:* c/o Magnum-Photos, 5 passage Piver, 75011 Paris, France.

CARTLAND, Dame Barbara (Hamilton), D.B.E., F.R.S.A.; British author and playwright; b. 9 July 1901; d. of the late Maj. Bertram Cartland; m. 1st Alexander George McCorquodale 1927 (divorced 1933); one d.; m. 2nd Hugh McCorquodale 1936 (died 1963); two s.; author of 642 books, including sociology, philosophy, religion, poetry, biography, autobiography and romantic fiction; best-selling author in the world (Guinness Book of Records, sales number 650 million, 1996); Co. Cadet Officer St. John Ambulance Brigade, Beds. 1943–47, County Vice-Pres. 1948–50, Deputy Pres. 1978–92; County Vice-Pres. Nursing Cadets, Herts. 1951, Chair. St. John Council, Herts. 1992–; mem. many charitable bodies; numerous radio and TV appearances; mounted many pageants in aid of charity; Gold Medal of Paris 1988. *Publications include:* Jigsaw 1923, Cupid Rides Pillion (renamed Dangerous Love), A Virgin in Paris, The Irresistible Buck, The Outrageous Lady, Love and the Loathsome Leopard, The Twists and Turns of Love, Love Has His Way 1979, Kneel for Mercy, The Vibration of Love 1981, The Magic of Honey, The Incredible Honeymoon, The Romance of Food, Princess to the Rescue 1984, I Reach for the Stars, Love Solves the Problem, Metternich the Passionate Diplomat. *Address:* Camfield Place, Hatfield, Herts., AL9 6JE, England. *Telephone:* (01707) 42612.

CARTLEDGE, Sir Bryan George, K.C.M.G.; British retd. diplomatist and college principal; b. 10 June 1931; s. of Eric Cartledge and Phyllis Shaw; m. 1st Ruth Hylton Gass 1960 (dissolved), one. s. one d.; m. 2nd Freda Gladys Newcombe 1994; ed. Hurstpierpoint and St. John's Coll., Cambridge; served Queen's Royal Regt. 1950–51; Commonwealth Fund Fellow, Stanford Univ., Calif. 1956–57; Research Fellow, St. Antony's Coll., Oxford 1958–59; joined Foreign Service 1960, served Foreign Office 1960–61, British Embassy, Stockholm 1961–63, Moscow 1963–66, Diplomatic Service Admin. Office 1966–68, Teheran 1968–70, Harvard Univ. 1971–72, Counsellor, Moscow 1972–75, Head of E. European and Soviet Dept., FCO 1975–77, Pvt. Sec. (Overseas Affairs) to Prime Minister 1977–79, Amb. to Hungary 1980–83, Asst. Under Sec. of State, FCO 1983–84, Deputy Sec. of the Cabinet 1984–85, Amb. to U.S.S.R. 1985–88; Prin. Linacre Coll., Oxford 1988–96; Hon. Fellow, St. John's Coll., Cambridge 1985, St. Antony's Coll., Oxford 1987, Linacre Coll., Oxford 1996. *Publications:* Monitoring the Environment (Ed.) 1992, Energy and the Environment (Ed.) 1993, Health and the Environment (Ed.) 1994, Population and the Environment (Ed.) 1995, Transport and the Environment (Ed.) 1996, Mind, Brain and Environment (Ed.) 1997. *Address:* Jasmine House, Holton, Oxford, OX33 1PU, England.

CARTWRIGHT, Nancy Delaney, PH.D., F.B.A.; American professor of philosophy; b. 24 June 1944, Pennsylvania; d. of Claudis Delaney and Eva Delaney; m. 1st Bliss Cartwright 1966 (divorced), 2nd Ian Hacking 1974 (divorced), 3rd Sir Stuart Hampshire (q.v.) 1985; two d.; ed. Univs. of Pittsburgh and Ill.; Prof. of Philosophy, Stanford Univ. 1983–91; Prof. of Philosophy, Logic and Scientific Method, L.S.E. 1991–; Dir. Centre for the Philosophy of the Natural and Social Sciences 1993–; Macarthur Foundation Award 1993. *Publications:* How the Laws of Physics Lie 1983, Nature's Capacities and Their Measurement 1989, Otto Neurath: Between Science and Politics (with others) 1994. *Address:* Centre for the Philosophy of Natural and Social Science, London School of Economics, Houghton Street, London, WC2A 2AE, England. *Telephone:* 0171-955 7573. *Fax:* 0171-242 0392.

CARUANA, Peter R., Q.C.; Gibraltarian politician and lawyer; b. 15 Oct. 1956; m.; five c.; ed. Christian Brothers School, Grace Dieu Manor, Leicester, U.K., Ratcliffe Coll. Leicester, Queen Mary Coll. Univ. of London; joined law firm Triay & Triay, Gibraltar 1979, partner (specialising in commercial and shipping law) 1990–95; joined Gibraltar Social Democrats 1990, Leader 1991–; elected in by-election to House of Ass. 1991; Leader of Opposition 1992–96; Chief Minister of Gibraltar 1996–; Hon. Fellow Queen Mary Coll., Univ. of London. *Leisure interests:* golf, political and current affairs. *Address:* 10/3 Irish Town (Office); 6 Convent Place, Gibraltar (Home).

CARVALHO, Mário Costa Martins de; Portuguese writer and lawyer; b. 25 Sept. 1944, Lisbon; s. of Domingos Martins Carvalho and Maria Luísa Costa Carvalho; m. Maria Helena Taborda Duarte 1969; two d.; ed. Univ. of Lisbon Law School; involved in student resistance to dictatorship; received conviction for political activities; served with Army; in exile in Paris and Lund, Sweden 1973–74; returned to Portugal after revolution of 1974; involved in politics 1974–77; f. law practice 1981; mem. Bd. Portuguese Asscn. of Writers; received City of Lisbon Prize, several other awards and prizes. *Publications:* Contos da Sétima Esfera 1981, O Livro Grande de Terras, Navio e Mariana 1982, A Paixão do Conde de Fróis 1986, Os Alferes 1989, Um Deus Passeando Pela Brisa da Tarde 1995, Era Bom que Trocassemos umas Ideias sobre o Assunto 1995. *Leisure interest:* farming. *Address:* Av. Eng° Arantes e Oliveira 6-8° C, 1900 Lisbon; R. António Pereira Carrilho 27 R/C, 1000 Lisbon, Portugal. *Telephone:* (1) 8491042 (Av. Eng° Arantes e Oliveira); (1) 8460576 (R. António Pereira Carrilho). *Fax:* (1) 8464227 (R. António Pereira Carrilho).

CARVER, Baron (Life Peer), cr. 1977; **Field Marshal Richard Michael Power Carver,** G.C.B., C.B.E., D.S.O., M.C.; British army officer; b. 24 April 1915, Bletchingley, Surrey; s. of Harold Power Carver and Winifred A. G. Carver (née Wellesley); m. Edith Lowry-Corry 1947; two s. two d.; ed. Winchester Coll. and Royal Military Acad., Sandhurst; with 7th Armoured Div. 1940–42, 1st Royal Tank Regt. 1943, 4th Armoured Brigade 1944; Ministry of Supply 1947; Allied Forces, Central Europe and SHAPE 1951–54; Deputy Chief of Staff, East Africa Command 1954–56; Dir. of Plans, War Office 1958–59; Commdr. 6th Infantry Brigade 1960–62; G.O.C. 3rd Div. (Maj.-Gen.) 1962–64; Dir. Army Staff Duties 1964–66; Commdr. Far East Land Forces (Lieut.-Gen.) 1966–67; C.-in-C. Far East (Gen.) 1967–69; G.O.C.-in-C. Southern Command 1969–71; Chief of Gen. Staff 1971–73; Chief of

Defence Staff (Field-Marshal) 1973–76; Commr.-desig. for Rhodesia 1977–78; Hon. D. Litt. (Southampton) 1991. *Publications:* Second to None 1950, El Alamein 1962, Tobruk 1964, War Lords (Ed.) 1976, Harding of Petherton 1978, The Apostles of Mobility 1979, War Since 1945 1980, A Policy For Peace 1982, The Seven Ages of the British Army 1984, Dilemmas of the Desert War 1986, Twentieth Century Warriors 1987, Out of Step 1989, Tightrope Walking 1992, Letters of a Victorian Army Officer: Edward Wellesley 1840–1854 (Ed.) 1995, Britain's Army in the Twentieth Century 1998. *Leisure interests:* writing, reading, gardening. *Address:* Wood End House, Wickham, near Fareham, Hants., PO17 6JZ, England (Home). *Telephone:* (01329) 832143.

CARVER, John Henry, PH.D., F.A.A., F.T.S., F.A.I.P.; Australian physicist; b. 5 Sept. 1926, Sydney; s. of the late J. F. Carver; m. Mary Fielding 1955; two s. two d.; ed. Fort St. Boys' High School, Sydney, Univs. of Sydney and Cambridge, U.K.; Cavendish Lab., Cambridge, U.K. 1949–53; Research School of Physical Sciences, Australian Nat. Univ. 1953–61; Atomic Energy Research Establishment, Harwell, U.K. 1958–59; Elder Prof. of Physics, Univ. of Adelaide 1961–78, Emer. Prof. 1979–; Naval Research Lab., Washington, D.C., U.S.A. 1968–69; Dir. and Prof. of Physics, Research School of Physical Sciences and Eng., Australian Nat. Univ. 1978–92, Emer. Prof. 1993–, Deputy Vice-Chancellor and Dir. Inst. of Advanced Studies 1993–94; Visiting Fellow Research School of Physical Sciences and Eng. Australian Nat. Univ. 1994–; mem. Radio Research Bd. of Australia 1964–82, Australian Science and Tech. Council 1979–86, Anglo-Australian Telescope Bd. 1978–89, Australian Space Bd. 1986–92; Chair. UN Scientific and Tech. Sub-Cttee. on the Peaceful Uses of Outer Space 1970–95; mem. Int. Acad. of Astronautics; Hon. Sc.D. (Cambridge); *Publications:* numerous articles on nuclear, atomic, molecular, atmospheric and space physics in scientific journals. *Address:* Research School of Physical Sciences and Engineering, Australian National University, Canberra, A.C.T. 0200 (Office); 8 Holmes Crescent, Campbell, A.C.T, Australia (Home). *Telephone:* (02) 6249 3567 (Office); (02) 6249 8732 (Home). *Fax:* (02) 6249 0390.

CASA-DEBELJEVIC, Lisa Della (Della Casa); Swiss singer; b. 2 Feb. 1919; ed. Berne Conservatoire; Début at Zürich Opera House 1943; mem. Vienna State Opera Co. 1947–, New York Metropolitan Opera Co. 1953–; has appeared at Festivals at Salzburg 1947, 1948, 1950, 1953–58, Glyndebourne 1951, Bayreuth, Edinburgh 1952, Zürich, Lucerne, Munich 1951–58; has also appeared in London, Berlin, Paris, Milan, San Francisco and in South America, etc.; apptd. Austrian State Kammersängerin. *Address:* Schloss Gottlieben, Thurgau, Switzerland.

CASADESUS (pseudonym of Probst), **Jean Claude;** French conductor; b. 7 Dec. 1935, Paris; s. of Lucien Probst and Gisele Casadesus; m. Anne Sevestre; two s. one d.; ed. Paris Nat. Conservatoire and Ecole Normale Paris; solo timpanist, Concert Colonne 1959–68; percussion soloist, Domaine Musical (with Boulez); Conductor, Paris Opéra 1969–71; Co-Dir. Orchestre Pays de Loire 1971–76; Founder and Dir. Lille Nat. Orchestra 1976–; appears as guest conductor with leading orchestras in U.K., U.S.A., France, Germany, Norway, Russia, Czech Repub., int. music festivals etc.; Gen. Sec. Conseil Supérieur de la Musique; recordings include works by Dutilleux (1st Symphony), Berlioz, Mahler, Bizet, Stravinsky, Mozart, Beethoven, Ravel, Debussy, Poulenc, Groupe des Six, Prokofiev; Grand Prix de la S.A.C.E.M. and several other prizes and awards for recordings; Officier, Légion d'honneur, Commdr., Ordre du Mérite Nat., Commdr. des Arts et des Lettres, Chevalier, Ordre des Palmes Académiques, Commdr., Order of Orange Nassau (Netherlands), Officer, Order of Crown (Belgium). *Publication:* Le plus court chemin d'un coeur à un autre 1998. *Leisure interests:* yachting, sailing, skiing, tennis. *Address:* Orchestre National de Lille, 30 place Mendès France, B.P. 119, 59027 Lille Cedex (Office); 23 blvd. de la Liberté, 59800 Lille, France (Home). *Telephone:* 20.12.82.40 (Office).

CASANOVA, Jean-Claude, D.ECON.; French economist; b. 11 June 1934, Ajaccio, Corsica; s. of Jean Casanova and Marie-Antoinette Luciani; m. Marie-Thérèse Demargne 1962; two s.; ed. Lycée Carnot, Inst. des hautes études, Tunis, Univ. of Paris, Harvard Univ.; Asst. Fondation nat. des sciences politiques 1958; Chief of Staff to Minister of Industry 1958–61; Asst. in Law Faculty, Univ. of Dijon 1963; Sr. Lecturer then Prof. Faculty of Law and Econ. Sciences, Univ. of Nancy 1964–68; with Univ. of Paris-Nanterre 1968; with Inst. d'études politiques, Paris 1969–; Dir. of Studies and Research Fondation nat. des sciences politiques 1965–90; Tech. Adviser to Minister of Educ. 1972–74; Adviser to Prime Minister Raymond Barre 1976–81; Ed. Commentaire 1978–; leader writer l'Express 1985–95; regular contrib. to Le Figaro 1996–; mem. Econ. and Social Council 1994–, Acad. des sciences morales et politiques 1996–. *Address:* Fondation nationale des sciences politiques, 27 rue Saint-Guillaume, 75007 Paris (Office); Commentaire, 116 rue du Bac, 75007 Paris (Office); 87 boulevard Saint-Michel, 75005 Paris, France (Home).

CASAS-GONZALEZ, Antonio; Venezuelan banker; b. 24 July 1933, Mérida; m. Carmen Elena Granadino de Casas; five s. one d.; ed. George Washington Univ., Georgetown Univ.; fmrly. Prof. of Econs. at various insts.; Adviser Venezuelan Petrochemical Inst. and Asst. to Minister of Mines and Hydrocarbons 1957–59; Petroleum and Econ. Counsellor Washington Embassy 1959–61; with Interamerican Devt. Bank 1961–69; Vice-Minister of Devt. 1969; Minister for National Planning Office (CORDIPLAN) 1972; Man. Dir. Petróleos de Venezuela (UK) S.A. 1990–94; Gov. Banco Cen. de Venezuela 1994–; Vice.-Pres. Intergovernmental Group of Twenty-Four on Int. Monetary Affairs 1996–; mem. Bd. Dirs. Venezolana de Aviación (VIASA) 1970–73, Corp. Andina de Fomento 1970–73, Banco Cen. de Venezuela 1972–75, Corp. Venezolana de Guyana 1979–82, Petróleos de Venezuela S.A. 1979–90; sixteen decorations from nine countries. *Publications:* co-author América Latina y los problemas de Desarrollo 1974, Venezuela y el CIAP (jtly.) 1974, La planificación en América Latina (jtly.) 1975, World Development (jtly.) 1977, articles for various publs. *Leisure interest:* golf. *Address:* Banco Central de Venezuela, Av. Urdaneta, Esq. Las Carmelitas, Caracas 1010, Venezuela. *Telephone:* 2-801-5101, 801-5102. *Fax:* 2-835040, 2-861-1607.

CASDIN-SILVER, Harriet, A.B.; American artist; b. 2 Oct. 1925, Worcester, Mass.; d. of Samuel Casdin-Cohen and Rose Fanya Ostroff; m. Simon Silver 1952; two d.; ed. Univ. of Vermont, Vt., Columbia Univ., N.Y., New School for Social Research, Cambridge Goddard Grad. School, Mass.; artist in residence American Optical Research Labs., Framingham, Mass. 1968–73, Ukrainian Inst. of Physics, Kiev 1989; Asst. Prof. of Physics Brown Univ., R.I. 1974–78; Fellow Center for Advanced Visual Studies, M.I.T. 1976–85; consultant Rockefeller Foundation Arts Program 1980–81; visiting lecturer R.C.A., London 1992, also Univ. of Ghent; Prof. of Art Mass. Coll. of Art and Design, Boston 1999–; also independent artist. *Publications include:* My First 10 Years as Artist/Holographer 1989, Holographic Installations: Sculpting with Light 1991. *Leisure interest:* reading. *Address:* 99 Pond Avenue, D403, Brookline, MA 02445 (Home); 51 Melcher Street, 5th Floor, Boston, MA 02210, U.S.A. (Studio). *Telephone:* (617) 739-6869 (Home); (617) 423-4717 (Studio). *Fax:* (617) 739-6869 (Home).

CASE, Steve, M.A.; American business executive; b. 21 Aug. 1958, Honolulu; m. Joanne Case (divorced); three d.; ed. Williams Coll.; marketing dept. Procter & Gamble 1980–82; man. new pizza devt., Pizza Hut Div. PepsiCo 1982–83; with Control Video 1983–85; with Quantum Computer Services 1985–92; C.E.O. America Online 1992–, Chair. 1995–; Entrepreneur of the Year, Incorporated Magazine 1994. *Address:* America Online, 8619 Westwood Center Drive, Vienna, VA 22182, U.S.A.

CASEY, Gavin; British business executive; b. 1946; trained as chartered accountant; joined County NatWest 1972, latterly Deputy Chief Exec.; Finance Dir. Smith New Court (brokers) 1989, C.O.O. 1994; Chief Admin. Officer for Int. Equities, Merrill Lynch (following takeover of Smith New Court) 1994–96; Chief Exec. The Stock Exchange 1996–. *Leisure interests:* shooting, racing, theatre. *Address:* The London Stock Exchange, London, EC2N 1HP, England. *Telephone:* 0171-797-1000.

CASEY, Robert P., J.D.; American politician and lawyer; b. 9 Jan. 1932; m. Ellen T. Harding; four s. four d.; ed. Holy Cross Coll. and George Washington Univ.; Auditor Gen., Pa. 1968–77; Attorney 1977–86; Gov. of Pennsylvania 1987–95; Democrat. *Address:* c/o Office of the Governor, Main Capitol Building, Room 225, Harrisburg, PA 17120, U.S.A.

CASH, Sir Gerald Christopher, G.C.M.G., G.C.V.O., O.B.E., J.P.; Bahamian fmr. Governor-General; b. 28 May 1917, Nassau; s. of the late Wilfred Cash and the late Lillian Cash; m. Dorothy E. Long; three s. one d.; ed. Govt. High School, Nassau, Middle Temple, London; called to Bar, Bahamas 1940, London 1948; private law practice 1940–45; J.P. 1941–; general law practice 1945–76, Consultant Counsel 1989; Acting Gov.-Gen. of the Commonwealth of the Bahamas 1976–78, Gov.-Gen. 1979–88; Consultant Counsel, Cash, Fountain & Co., Nassau 1989–; Chair. Guaranty Trust Bank Ltd.; Chair. Bd. of Govs. of Govt. High School 1949–63; Chair. Labour Bd. (Bahamas) 1950–52; Chair. Nat. Cttee., United World Colls. 1977–81; Vice-Chancellor, Anglican Diocese of the Bahamas; mem. Bd. of Educ. 1950–62; mem. Immigration Cttee., Road Traffic Cttee., Air Transport Licensing Authority 1958–62; mem. Police Service Comm. 1964–69; mem. Bd. of Dirs., Cen. Bank of the Bahamas; Coronation Medal 1953, Silver Jubilee Medal 1977, Silver Medal of the Olympic Order 1983. *Address:* 4 Bristol Street, P.O. Box N-476, Nassau, Bahamas. *Telephone:* 393 4767.

CASH, J. R. (Johnny); American entertainer; b. 26 Feb. 1932, Kingsland, Ark.; s. of the late Ray and Carrie (née Rivers) Cash; m. 1st Vivian Liberto 1950; four d.; m. 2nd June Carter 1968; one s.; ed. Gardner-Webb Coll., Nat. Univ. San Diego; served with U.S.A.F. TV appearances include: The Johnny Cash Show 1969–71, Muscular Dystrophy Telethon 1972, Johnny Cash at San Quentin; documentary films: Trail of Tears, Johnny Cash, The Man, His World, His Music, United Way of America 1972; acted in films A Gunfight, North and South 1985, Stagecoach 1986; wrote, produced and narrated film The Gospel Road 1993; compositions include: I Walk the Line, Folsom Prison Blues, At Folsom Prison, Man In Black, Don't Take Your Guns to Town; composer movie sound tracks: I Walk the Line, Little Fauss and Big Halsy; albums include: Folsom and San Quentin, John R. Cash, Last Gunfighter, The Baron, Believer Sings the Truth, The Holy Land, The True West, Water from the Wells of Home, The Sun Years, Boom Chicka Boom; over 53 million albums sold.; Pres. House of Cash Inc., Song of Cash Inc.; Vice-Pres. Family of Man Music Inc.; mem. Country Music Asscn., Country Music Hall of Fame 1980; mem. Songwriters' Hall of Fame 1992, Rock and Roll Hall of Fame 1992; Grammy Living Legend Award 1993, Kennedy Center Honor 1996; Hon. D.Hum.Litt. (San Diego) 1976. *Publications:* Man in Black (autobiography) 1975, Man in White (religious novel) 1986. *Address:* House of Cash, Inc., 700 Johnny Cash Parkway, Hendersonville, TN 37077-0508, U.S.A. *Telephone:* (615) 824-5110. *Fax:* (615) 822-7332.

CASH, Pat; Australian tennis player; b. 27 May 1965; m. Emily Cash; one s. one d.; ed. Whitefriars Coll.; coached by Ian Barclay; trainer Anne Quinn; winner U.S. Open Jr. 1982, Brisbane and in winning Australian Davis Cup team 1983, in quarter-finals Wimbledon 1985, finalist Australian Open 1987, Wimbledon Champion 1987.

CASHMORE, Roger John, B.A., D.PHIL., F.R.S., F.INST.P.; British physicist; b. 22 Aug. 1944, Birmingham; s. of C. J. C. Cashmore and E. M. Cashmore; m. Elizabeth Ann Lindsay 1971; one s.; ed. Dudley Grammar School, St. John's Coll., Cambridge, Balliol Coll., Oxford; Weir Jr. Research Fellow Univ. Coll., Oxford 1967–69; 1851 Research Fellow 1968; Research Assoc. Stanford Linear Accelerator, Calif. 1969–74; Research Officer Oxford Univ. 1974–79, lecturer 1979–90, Reader in Experimental Physics 1990–91, Prof. 1991–98; Research Dir. C.E.R.N. Jan. 1999–; Boys Prize, Inst. of Physics 1983; Humboldt Research Award 1995. *Publications:* contributions to Physics Review. *Leisure interests:* sports, wine. *Address:* C.E.R.N., 1211 Geneva 23, Switzerland.

CASIDA, John Edward, M.S., PH.D., F.R.S.; American entomologist; b. 22 Dec. 1929, Phoenix, Ariz.; s. of Lester Earl Casida and Ruth Casida (née Barnes); m. Katherine Faustine Monson 1956; two s.; ed. Univ. of Winconsin; served with U.S.A.F. 1953; research asst. Univ. of Wisconsin 1951–53, tutor 1954–63, Prof. of Entomology 1959–63; Prof. of Entomology Univ. of Calif. at Berkeley 1964–, William Muriece Hoskins Chair in Chemistry and Molecular Entomology 1996–, faculty research lecturer 1998; Dir. Environmental Chemistry and Toxicology Lab. 1964–; scholar in residence Bellagio Study and Conf. Centre, Rockefeller Foundation, Lake Como, Italy 1978; Messenger Lecturer Cornell Univ. 1985; Sterling B. Hendicks lecturer USDA and A.C.S. 1992–; lecturer in Science Third World Acad. of Sciences, Univ. of Buenos Aires 1997; mem. N.A.S., A.C.S., Entomological Soc. of America, Soc. of Environmental Toxicology and Chemistry; hon. mem. Soc. of Toxicology; Haight Travelling Fellow 1958–59; Guggenheim Fellow 1970–71; Fellow of Entomological Soc. of America 1989; Hon. D.Univ. (Buenos Aires) 1997; Int. Award for Research in Pesticide Chemistry, A.C.S. 1970, Spencer Award in Agric. and Food Chemistry, A.C.S. 1978, Bussart Memorial Award, Entomological Soc. of America 1989, Wolf Prize in Agric. 1993, Founder's Award Soc. of Environmental Toxicology and Chemistry 1994, Kôrô-sho Prize Pesticide Science Soc. (Japan) 1995. *Address:* University of California Environmental Science Policy Management, Wellman Hall, Berkeley, CA 94720 (Office); 1570 La Vereda Road, Berkeley, CA 94708, U.S.A. (Home).

CASIMIR, Hendrik Brugt Gerhard, PH.D.; Netherlands physicist; b. 15 July 1909, The Hague; s. of Rommert Casimir and Teunsina Dina Borgman; m. Josina Maria Jonker 1933; one s. four d.; ed. Univs. of Leiden, Copenhagen, and at Zürich; various research positions, Leiden 1933–42; joined staff of Philips Research Labs., Eindhoven 1942, Dir. of Labs. 1946, mem. Bd. of Man. of Philips 1957–72, supervising Philips research activities in various countries; Pres. European Physical Soc. 1972–75; mem. Royal Acad. of Netherlands, now Emer. (Pres. 1973); Foreign Hon. mem. American Acad. of Arts and Sciences; mem. Royal Flemish Acad. of Science, Letters and Arts; Corresp. mem. Heidelberg Acad. of Science, Austrian Acad. of Sciences, Vienna; Foreign mem. Royal Soc., London 1970, Finnish Acad. of Technical Sciences, Helsinki, American Philosophical Soc., Philadelphia; Foreign Assoc. N.A.S., Acad. des Sciences, France, Nat. Acad. of Engineers, Washington, D.C.; Alfred Ewing Medal (London), Hon. D.Sc. Tech. Univ. Copenhagen, Louvain, Tech. Univ. Aachen, Edinburgh, Cranfield Inst. of Tech., Columbia Univ., Univ. of Paris VI, Univ. of Sussex. *Publications:* Haphazard Reality 1983, and many papers on theoretical physics, applied mathematics and low temperature physics. *Address:* De Zegge 7, 5591 TT Heeze, Netherlands. *Telephone:* 040-2862233.

ČÁSLAVSKÁ, Věra; Czech gymnast; b. 3 May 1942, Prague; d. of Václav Čáslavský and Anna Čáslavská; m. Josef Odložil 1968 (divorced 1988); one s. one d.; ed. Faculty of Physical Training and Sport, Charles Univ., Prague; signed The Two Thousand Words 1968, a declaration of the principles of anti-communist rule; coach, Sports Centre, Sparta Prague 1970–79; coach, Mexico 1979–; Adviser to Pres. of CSFR on Social Policy and mem. Pres. Havel's Advisory Bd. 1990–92; Pres. Czechoslovak Olympic Cttee. 1990–92, Czech Olympic Cttee. 1992–96; mem. Int. Olympic Cttee. 1995–; overall, vault and beam gold medals, Olympic Games, Tokyo 1964; overall, floor, asymmetric bars and vault gold medals, beam silver medal, Olympic Games, Mexico City 1968; overall and vault first place, beam and floor second place and mem. winning team World Championships, Dortmund 1966; five first places, European Championships, Sofia 1965 and Amsterdam 1967; Hiranuma Prize 1996, Pierre de Coubertine Fair Play Prize 1989, Sievert Prize 1993; Meritorious Master of Sports 1962, Order of the Republic 1968, Silver Olympic Order 1992, Medal for Merit, Czech Repub. 1995. *Publication:* Věra Čáslavská Narrates 1965. *Address:* Czech Olympic Committee, Benesovska 6, 101 00, Prague 10, Czech Republic. *Telephone:* (2) 71734734. *Fax:* (2) 71731318.

CASORATI, Francesco; Italian artist; b. 2 July 1934, Turin; s. of Felice Casorati and Daphne Maugham; m. Paola Zanetti 1959; three s.; ed. Liceo Artistico dell'Accademia di Torino; first one-man show, Milan 1954; has since exhibited at numerous int. exhbns. including Pittori Italiani, Moscow, Budapest, Prague, Sofia 1957–58, Expo, Brussels 1958, Venice Biennale, etc.; numerous one-man and group shows in various European cities; taught at Liceo Artistico di Torino 1959–75, Accad. Albertina di Torino 1970–75; holder, Chair. of Decorative Art, Accad. Albertina di Torino 1975–84. *Address:* Via Mazzini 52, Turin (Studio); C.so Kossuth 19,Turin, Italy (Home). *Telephone:* 011-831491 (Studio); 011-894950 (Home).

CASORIA, H.E. Cardinal Giuseppe; Italian ecclesiastic; b. 1 Oct. 1908, Acerra; ordained priest 1930; made Bishop 1972; Titular Archbishop of Vescovia; Prefect of the Sacred Congregation of the Sacraments; Consultant to the Sacred Congregation of the Oriental Churches; mem. Pontifical Comm. for the Interpretation of the Decrees of the Vatican Council II; cr. Cardinal 1983; Dean of S. Giuseppe in Via Trionfale 1984–. *Address:* via Pancrazio Pfeiffer 10, 00193 Rome, Italy. *Telephone:* (06) 698-4245.

CASPER, William Earl (Billy); American golfer; b. 24 June 1931, San Diego, Calif.; m. Shirley Casper; six c., five adopted c.; fmr. fruit farmer; professional golfer since 1954; winner, U.S. Open 1959, 1966; winner, Vardon Trophy for lowest scoring average 1960, 1963, 1965, 1966, 1968; winner, The Masters 1970; played eight times in Ryder Cup 1961–75; winner of 51 tournaments on pro circuit and several more on Seniors tour; won Brazilian Open twice, the Lancôme 1974, Italian Open 1975, Mexican Open 1977; U.S. PGA Player of the Year 1966, 1968, 1970.

CASPERSEN, Sven Lars, M.ECON.; Danish university rector; b. 30 June 1935, Aabenraa; s. of Jes P. Caspersen and Carla Caspersen; m. Eva Caspersen 1962; three s.; Asst. Sec. Danish Cen. Bureau of Statistics 1962–64; Deputy Chief, Cen. Statistical Centre of Danish Insurance Cos. at Danish Insurance Asscn. 1964–68; Assoc. Prof. of Statistics, Copenhagen School of Econs. and Business Admin. 1968–73, Head, Dept. of Statistics 1970–73; Prof. of Statistics, Aalborg Univ. 1973–76, Rector 1976–; Chair. Bd. Copenhagen Stock Exchange 1989–96; Chair. Liaison Cttee. of Rectors' Conferences of mem. states of the EC 1992–94; Chair. Govt. Advisory Council on EU Matters 1993–; Chair. European Capital Markets Inst. 1993–95; Vice-Pres. Fed. of Stock Exchanges of the EC 1993–95, Pres. 1995–96; Pres. (elect) Int. Asscn. of Univ. Pres.'s 1996–; Chair. Bd. Aalborg Theatre; Dr. h.c. (Vilnius Tech. Univ.) 1993; recipient, Tribute of Appreciation, U.S. Dept. of State 1981. *Leisure interests:* chess, bridge, tennis. *Address:* Aalborg University, Postboks 159, 9100 Aalborg (Office); Duebrødrevej 6, 9000 Aalborg, Denmark (Home). *Telephone:* 45 96 35 95 01 (Office). *Fax:* 45 98 15 15 22.

CASS, Sir Geoffrey (Arthur), Kt., M.A., C.I.MGT., F.R.S.A.; British publishing executive and arts and lawn tennis administrator; b. 11 Aug. 1932; s. of late Arthur and Jessie Cass; m. Olwen M. Richards 1957; four d.; ed. Queen Elizabeth Grammar School, Darlington and Jesus Coll., Oxford; Nuffield Coll., Oxford 1957–58; R.A.F. 1958–60; Ed. Automation 1960–61; Consultant, PA Man. Consultants Ltd. 1960–65; Pvt. Man. Consultant, British Communications Corpn. and Controls and Communications Ltd. 1965; Dir. Controls and Communications Ltd. 1966–69; Dir. George Allen & Unwin 1965–67, Man. Dir. 1967–71; Dir. Weidenfeld Publrs. 1972–74, Univ. of Chicago Press, U.K. 1971–86; Chief Exec. Cambridge Univ. Press 1972–92; Sec. Press Syndicate, Univ. of Cambridge 1974–92; Univ. Printer 1982–83, 1991–92; Consultant Cambridge Univ. Press 1992–; Fellow, Clare Hall, Cambridge 1979–; Hon. Fellow, Jesus Coll., Oxford 1998; Life Trustee Shakespeare Birthplace Trust 1982–; Chair. Royal Shakespeare Co. 1985–, Royal Shakespeare Theatre Trust 1983–, British Int. Tennis and Nat. Training 1985–90, Nat. Ranking Cttee.; mem. Bd. of Man., Lawn Tennis Asscn. of G.B. 1985–90, Deputy Pres. 1994–96, Pres. 1996–; mem. of Cttee. of Man., Wimbledon Championships 1989–; mem. numerous other trusts, bds., cttees. and advisory bodies particularly in connection with theatre and lawn tennis; Oxford tennis Blue, and badminton; played in Wimbledon Tennis Championships 1954, 1955, 1956, 1959; British Veterans Singles Champion, Wimbledon 1978; Companion B.I.M.; Chevalier, Ordre des Arts et des Lettres. *Publications:* articles in professional journals. *Leisure interests:* tennis, theatre. *Address:* Middlefield, Huntingdon Road, Cambridge, CB3 0LH, England.

CASSAB, Judy, A.O., C.B.E.; Australian painter; b. 15 Aug. 1920, Vienna, Austria; d. of Imre Kaszab and Ilona Kont; m. John Kampfner 1939; two s.; ed. Budapest and Prague; mem. Council for the Honours of Australia 1975–79; Trustee, Art Gallery of N.S.W. 1981–88; has held 62 individual exhbns. in galleries throughout Australia, in London and Paris since 1953 and works are in many Australian galleries including Nat. Gallery, Canberra, galleries in U.K. including Nat. Portrait Gallery, London, in U.S.A. and at Nat. Gallery of Budapest; 51 individual exhbns.; Dr. h.c. (Sydney) 1995; several prizes including Sir Charles Lloyd Jones Memorial Prize (four times), The Trustees Watercolour Prize 1994, Foundation for Australian Literary Studies Prize 1996, Nita Kibble Literary Award (for Judy Cassab Diaries) 1996. *Publications:* Ten Australian Portraits (lithographs) 1984, Judy Cassab, Places, Faces and Fantasies 1985, Artists and Friends 1988, Judy Cassab Diaries 1995, Judy Cassab, Portraits of Artists and Friend 1998. *Address:* 16C Ocean Avenue Double Bay, Sydney, N.S.W., Australia 2028. *Telephone:* (09) 326 1348.

CASSAR, Joseph, B.A., LL.D., M.P.; Maltese politician; b. 22 Jan. 1918, Qrendi; s. of late Giuseppe and Giovanna (née Magri) Cassar; m. Janie Pace 1948 (died 1989); ed. Bishop's Seminary, Gozo, the Lyceum, Malta, Univ. of Malta; with Home Guard Voluntary Force 1940–44; Barrister 1943–; mem. Council of Govt. 1945–46, Speaker, Legis. Ass. 1947–48; Minister of Justice 1949–50, 1951–53, 1955–58; Minister of Labour, Employment and Welfare 1971–74, Minister of Educ. and Culture 1974–76, Minister of Justice, Lands, Housing and Parl. Affairs 1976, Deputy Prime Minister 1976, and Deputy

Leader for Govt. Affairs 1976, 1981; Minister of Finance, Customs and People's Financial Investments 1979–81, Sr. Deputy Prime Minister and Minister of Justice and Parl. Affairs 1981–87; Perm. Rep. to UN 1993–97; mem. House of Reps. 1987–92; Labour; Companion Nat. Order of Merit (K.O.M.) 1993; *Leisure interests:* reading, swimming, travel. *Address:* Dar-is-Sliem, Tal-Ibragg Road, St. Andrew's, Malta. *Telephone:* 370045.

CASSEL, Jean-Pierre; French actor; b. 27 Oct. 1932, Paris; m. 2nd Anne Célérier 1981; two s. one d.; film debut in 1959; frequent TV appearances. *Films include:* Les Jeux de l'Amour, Le Caporal Epinglé, Paris brûle-t-il? Those Magnificent Men in Their Flying Machines, Oh What A Lovely War!, Baxter, The Discreet Charm of the Bourgeoisie, The Three Musketeers, Le Mouton Enragé, Murder on the Orient Express, That Lucky Touch, The Twist, Someone is Killing, The Great Chefs of Europe, Les Rendezvous d'Anna, From Hell to Victory, The Return of the Musketeers, Mangeclous, La Truite, Chouans, Mr. Frost, Phantom of the Opera, Theo and Vincent, The Favour, The Watch and the Very Big Fish, Amour et Petit Doigt de Pied, Pétain, Thé Noir au Citron, Casque Bleu, Prêt à Porter, La Cérémonie. *TV includes:* Love in a Cold Climate, Shillingbury Tales, Liberty, Casanova, Secret of Sahara, Matter of Convenience, Warburg, The Maid, The French Kill, Notorious, Dust and Blood, Young Indy, La 13e Voiture, Printemps de Chien, Le Fils de Paul, Le Président et la Garde Barrière 1996, Un printemps de chien, Les Tiers mondains 1996, Le Coeur et l'epée, Les Mongagnes bleues 1998. *Address:* c/o I.C.M., 388/396 Oxford Street, London, W.1, England; Art-Ciné, 36 rue de Ponthieu, 75008 Paris, France.

CASSELLS, Peter; Irish trade union official; b. 20 Oct. 1949, Co. Meath; legislation officer, Irish Congress of Trade Unions 1973–80, econ. and social affairs officer 1980–85, Asst. Gen. Sec. 1985–87, Gen. Sec. 1987–. *Address:* 19 Raglan Road, Dublin 4, Ireland. *Telephone:* (1) 668 0641. *Fax:* (1) 660 9027.

CASSELS, John William Scott, M.A., PH.D., F.R.S., F.R.S.E.; British mathematician; b. 11 July 1922, Durham City; s. of John William Cassels and Muriel Speakman Cassels (née Lobjoit); m. Constance Mabel Senior 1949; one s. one d.; ed. Neville's Cross Council School, Durham, George Heriot's School, Edinburgh, and Edinburgh and Cambridge Univs.; lecturer, Manchester Univ. 1949–50, Cambridge Univ. 1950–65; Reader in Arithmetic, Cambridge Univ. 1965–67; Sadleirian Prof. of Pure Mathematics, Cambridge Univ. 1967–84; Fellow of Trinity Coll., Cambridge 1949–. *Publications:* An Introduction to Diophantine Approximations 1957, An Introduction to the Geometry of Numbers 1959, Rational Quadratic Forms 1979, Economics for Mathematicians 1981, Local Fields 1986, Lectures on Elliptic Curves 1991, Prolegomena to a middlebrow arithmetic of curves of genus 2 (with E. V. Flynn) 1996. *Leisure interests:* The Higher Arithmetic, gardening. *Address:* Department of Pure Mathematics and Mathematical Statistics, 16 Mill Lane, Cambridge, CB2 1SB, (Office); 3 Luard Close, Cambridge, CB2 2PL, England (Home). *Telephone:* (01223) 337975 (Office); (01223) 246108 (Home).

CASSIDY, Charles Michael Ardagh, M.A., B.D., H.L.D.; South African evangelist; b. 24 Sept. 1936, Johannesburg; s. of Charles Stewart Cassidy and Mary Craufurd Cassidy; m. Carol Bam 1969; one s. two d.; ed. Parktown School, Johannesburg, Michaelhouse, Natal, Cambridge Univ., U.K., Fuller Theological Seminary, Calif., U.S.A.; Founder and Team Leader, inter-denominational evangelistic mission team African Enterprise 1962–98; conducted missions in cities including Cape Town, Johannesburg, Nairobi, Cairo, Lusaka, Gaborone, Monrovia (Liberia), Mbabane (Swaziland), etc.; initiated S.A. Congress on Mission and Evangelism 1973, Pan African Christian Leadership Ass. 1976, S.A. Christian Leadership Ass. 1979, Nat. Initiative for Reconciliation 1985; speaker at Lausanne II conf., Manila, Philippines 1989, Missionsfest 1990, N. American Renewal Conf. 1990 etc.; admitted to the Anglican Order of Simon of Cyrene 1983; Hon. H.L.D. (Azusa Pacific Univ.) 1993; Paul Harris Fellow Rotary Award 1997, Michaelhouse St. Michael's Award 1997. *Publications:* Decade of Decisions 1970, Where Are You Taking the World Anyway? 1971, Prisoners of Hope 1974, Relationship Tangle 1974, Bursting the Wineskins 1983, Chasing the Wind 1985, The Passing Summer 1989, The Politics of Love 1991, A Witness For Ever 1995, Window on the Word 1997. *Leisure interests:* music, photography, scrapbooks, sport. *Address:* African Enterprise, P.O. Box 13140, Cascades 3202 (Office); 35 Flamingo Drive, Hilton, 3245 South Africa (Home). *Telephone:* (0331) 471 911 (Office); (0331) 433886 (Home). *Fax:* (0331) 471915 (Office); (0331) 433616 (Home).

CASSIDY, Denis Patrick; British business executive; b. 2 Feb. 1933, Tyneside; various posts with British Home Stores, rising to Chair. 1969–87; Chair. Ferguson Int. Holdings 1988–, Kingsbury Group 1988–94, Boddington Group 1989–95, The Oliver Group 1992–, Liberty PLC 1995–97; Dir. (non-exec.) BAA 1986–92, Seeboard PLC 1994–96, Compass Group PLC 1994–, Newcastle United Football Club. *Leisure interests:* cricket, football. *Address:* c/o Ferguson International Holdings PLC, 75 Baker Street, London, W1M 1AH, England. *Telephone:* 0171-487 3464. *Fax:* 0171-224 3072.

CASSIDY, H.E. Cardinal Edward Idris, D.CN.L.; Australian ecclesiastic; b. 5 July 1924, Sydney; s. of Harold Cassidy and Dorothy Philipps; ed. Parramatta High School, Sydney, St. Columba's Seminary, Springwood, St. Patrick's Coll. Manly, Lateran Univ. Rome and Pontifical Ecclesiastical Acad. Rome; ordained priest 1949; Asst. Priest, Yenda, N.S.W. 1950–52; diplomatic service in India 1955–62, Ireland 1962–67, El Salvador 1967–69, Argentina 1969–70; consecrated Archbishop 1970; Titular Archbishop of Amantia 1970; Apostolic Pro-Nuncio in Taiwan 1970–79 (also accred. to Bangladesh and Burma 1973–79); Apostolic Del. to Southern Africa and Apostolic Pro-Nuncio to Lesotho 1979–84; Apostolic Pro-Nuncio to the Netherlands 1984–88; Substitute of the Secr. of State 1988–89; Pres. Pontifical Council for Promoting Christian Unity and Comm. for Religious Relations with the Jews 1989–; cr. Cardinal 1991; Cavaliere, Gran Croce dell'Ordine al Merito della Repubblica Italiana; decorations from El Salvador, Taiwan, Netherlands, Australia, France, Sweden and Germany. *Leisure interests:* tennis, golf, music. *Address:* Pontifical Council for Promoting Christian Unity, 00120 Vatican City. *Telephone:* (06) 698 84181/83071/84794. *Fax:* (06) 698 85365.

CASSIDY, Sheila Anne, B.M., B.CH., M.A.; British medical practitioner; b. 18 Aug. 1937, Lincs.; d. of late Air Vice-Marshal J. R. Cassidy and of Barbara Margaret Drew; ed. Our Lady of Mercy Coll., Parramatta, N.S.W., Univ. of Sydney and Oxford Univ.; resident posts, Radcliffe Infirmary, Oxford 1963–68, Leicester Royal Infirmary 1968–70; Medical Asst. 1970–71; Asst. Surgeon, Asistencia Pública, Santiago, Chile 1971–75; tortured and imprisoned for treating wounded guerrilla Nov.–Dec. 1975; human rights lecturing 1976–77; studied monastic life, Ampleforth Abbey, York 1977–79; novice in Bernardine Cistercian Convent 1979–80; resident in radiotherapy, Plymouth Gen. Hosp. 1980–82, Research Registrar, Dept. Radiotherapy 1982–; Medical Dir., St. Luke's Hospice, Plymouth 1982–93; Palliative Care Physician, Plymouth Gen. Hosp. 1993–96, Specialist in Psycho-social Oncology, Dept. of Oncology 1996–; Hon. D.Sc. (Exeter) 1991, Hon. D.Litt. (Council for Nat. Academic Awards) 1992; Valiant for Truth media award. *Publications:* Audacity to Believe (autobiog.) 1977, Prayer for Pilgrims 1979, Sharing the Darkness 1988, Good Friday People 1991, Light from the Dark Valley 1994, The Loneliest Journey 1995, Creation Story 1996. *Leisure interests:* writing, broadcasting, drawing, walking, swimming. *Address:* Plymouth Oncology Centre, Derriford Hospital, Plymouth, PL6 8DH (Office); 6 The Esplanade, The Hoe, Plymouth, PL1 2PJ, England (Home). *Telephone:* (01752) 777111 (Office).

CASSIERS, Juan, D.EN.D.; Belgian diplomatist; b. 11 May 1931, Middelkerke; grandson of Leon Delacroix (Prime Minister of Belgium 1918–20); m. Daisy Lannoy 1956; two s. two d.; ed. St. Jean Berchmans Coll., Brussels, Catholic Univ. of Louvain; Sec. of Embassy, Washington, D.C. 1962–67; Deputy Perm. Rep. of Belgium to OECD, Paris 1970–73, Perm. Rep. 1987–91; Fellow, Harvard Univ. 1973–74; Minister-Counsellor, Peking 1974–76; Minister-Counsellor, Bonn 1976–79; Head of Political and Mil. Affairs, Ministry of Foreign Affairs, Brussels 1979–81, Prin. Pvt. Sec. to Minister of Foreign Affairs 1981; Perm. Rep. of Belgium to NATO, Brussels 1983–87; Amb. to U.S.A. 1991–94, to the Holy See 1994–98; Grand Officier, Ordre de Léopold. *Leisure interests:* reading, writing. *Address:* 48 rue Emile Bouilliot, 1050 Brussels, Belgium.

CASSIRER, Henry R., PH.D.; American radio and television administrator; b. 2 Sept. 1911, Berlin; s. of Kurt and Eva (née Solmitz) Cassirer; m. 1st Marta Reyto (divorced); one d.; m. 2nd Arlette Freund (divorced); one s. one d.; ed. Odenwaldschule, Univs. of Frankfurt, Paris, Cologne, London School of Econs. and London Univ.; Announcer/translator, BBC European Service 1938–40; Foreign News Ed., Columbia Broadcasting System (CBS), New York 1940–44; Television News Ed., CBS 1944–49; freelance producer of TV documentary programmes 1949–52; teacher of TV Production and Public Affairs Programming, New School for Social Research, New York Univ. School of Radio Techniques; with UNESCO 1952–71, Dir. Use of Mass Media in Out-of-School Educ.; Adviser on Educational Radio/TV to Govt. of India 1957, Pakistan 1960–, Israel 1961–, Senegal 1963–, Brazil 1967–, Mali 1968–, Algeria 1969–, Singapore, United States (Alaska) 1970, Morocco 1974–, Ghana 1975, Fed. Repub. of Germany and Ford Foundation for West Africa projects 1976, Portugal for World Bank 1976; Int. Consultant communication and educ. 1971–, parent educ. 1979 (Int. Year of the Child); Visiting Prof. Ontario Inst. for Studies in Educ. 1974; Hon. Devt. Consultant Univ. of London Dept. of Extra-Mural Studies 1979–88; Communication and Educ. Consultant on Disability, UNESCO 1981–, Educ. Section Consultant 1995–; Consultant to European Space Agency 1986–88; Hon. Pres. Groupement français des personnes handicapées (G.F.P.H.) 1993–; Vice-Pres. Collectif handicap de la région Annecienne; Chevalier Ordre Nat. du Mérite 1990. *Publications:* Television, a World Survey 1954, Television Teaching Today 1960, Bildung und Kommunikation 1974; films: Man of our Age—The Sculpture of Jo Davidson, Buma-African Sculpture Speaks 1952, Television Comes to the Land 1958, Adult Education and the Media 1984, Co-operation between the Media and Adult Education Bodies, UNESCO 1985, Seeds in the Winds of Change through Education and Communication 1989, Und alles kam anders . . . 1992. *Leisure interests:* stereo photography, organic gardening. *Address:* 4 Promenade Lachenal, 74000 Annecy, France. *Telephone:* (04) 50.45.88.98. *Fax:* (04) 50.45.88.98.

CASSON, Sir Hugh Maxwell, Kt., C.H., K.C.V.O., M.A., P.R.A., F.R.I.B.A., R.D.I., HON. DES. R.C.A.; British architect; b. 23 May 1910; s. of late Randal Casson; m. Margaret Macdonald Trap 1938; three d.; ed. Eastbourne Coll., St. John's Coll., Cambridge, and Bartlett School of Architecture, Univ. Coll., London; private practice as architect 1935–; Camouflage Officer in Air Ministry 1940–44; Tech. Officer Ministry of Town and Country Planning 1944–46; Dir. of Architecture, Festival of Britain 1951; mem. MARS Group 1945–; Prof. of Environmental Design, R.C.A. 1953–75; mem. Royal Mint Advisory Cttee. 1972–; Pres. Royal Acad. of Arts 1976–84; Provost, R.C.A. 1980–86; Vice-Pres. Brighton Festival Soc. 1982–84; mem. Royal Danish Acad. 1954,

Royal Fine Art Comm. 1960–84, British Council 1977–81; Hon. LL.D. (Birmingham) 1977, (Southampton) 1977; Hon. D.Litt. (Loughborough Univ.) 1979; Dr. h.c. (Royal Coll. of Art, London) 1985; Albert Medal, Royal Soc. of Arts 1984, Order of Merit (Italy) 1980. *Publications:* Bombed Churches as War Memorials 1944, Houses: Permanence and Prefabrication (with Anthony Chitty) 1945, Homes by the Million 1945, An Introduction to Victorian Architecture 1948, Inscape: The Design of Interiors 1968, Nanny Says (with Joyce Grenfell) 1972, Diary 1981, Hugh Casson's London 1984, Hugh Casson's Oxford 1988, Japan Observed: A sketch book 1991, Hugh Casson's Cambridge 1992, The Tower of London: an artist's portrait 1993. *Leisure interest:* drawing. *Address:* 6 Hereford Mansions, Hereford Road, London, W2 5BA, England. *Telephone:* 0171-221 7774 (Office); 0171-727 2999 (Home).

CASTANEDA-CORNEJO, Ricardo Guillermo; Salvadorean public servant; b. 11 March 1938; m.; two c.; ed. Nat.Univ. of El Salvador, Princeton Univ. and Univ. of Michigan, U.S.A.; Deputy Minister for Foreign Affairs 1970–72; Head El Salvador's del. to UN Ass. 1972–76; External Dir. Banco Cuscatlan S.A. 1980–81; Pres. Nat. Cttee. and Dir. for El Salvador, Cen. American Inst. of Business Man. 1981–88; Perm. Rep. to UN 1989–. *Address:* Permanent Mission of El Salvador to the United Nations, 46 Park Avenue, New York, NY 10016, U.S.A. *Telephone:* (212) 679-1616. *Fax:* (212) 725-7831.

CASTEEN, John T., III, LL.D., PH.D.; American university administrator; b. 11 Dec. 1943, Portsmouth, Va.; s. of John T. Casteen, Jr. and Naomi Irene Casteen; two s. one d.; ed. Univ. of Va.; Asst. Prof. of English, Univ. of Calif., Berkeley 1970–75; Assoc. Prof. and Dean Univ. of Va. 1975–81; Prof. Va. Commonwealth Univ. 1982–85; Sec. of Educ., Commonwealth of Va. 1982–85; Pres. and Prof., Univ. of Conn. 1985–90; Pres. Univ. of Va. 1990–, George M. Kaufman Presidential Prof., Prof. of English 1990–; Hon. LL.D. (Shenandoah Coll.), (Bentley Coll.) 1992, (Piedmont Community Coll.) 1992, (Bridgewater Coll.) 1993; Raven Award, Univ. of Va. *Publications:* 16 stories 1982; numerous essays and articles 1970–. *Leisure interest:* sailing. *Address:* Office of the President, University of Virginia, Madison Hall, P.O. Box 9011, Charlottesville, VA 22906, U.S.A. *Fax:* (804) 924-3792.

CASTELLI, Leo; American art gallery owner; b. 4 Sept. 1907, Trieste, Italy; s. of Ernest Krauss and Bianca Castelli; m. 1st Ileana Schapira 1933 (divorced 1960); m. 2nd Antoinette Fraissex du Bost 1963 (died 1987); m. 3rd Barbara Bertozzi 1995; one s. one d.; ed. Univ. of Milan and Columbia Univ., New York; early career in int. banking; opened Galérie René Douin, Paris; worked in Knit-Goods Mfg. 1939–49; owner, Leo Castelli Gallery, New York 1957–; Hon. Pres. Modern Art Dept. Museo Revoltella, Trieste; Hon. Trustee Museum of Modern Art, N.Y. 1997; Hon. Ph.D. (School of Visual Arts, New York), Officier Legion d'honneur L.H.D. (Brenan Univ.), Officier Légion d'honneur; Butler Medal of Life Achievement in American Art 1987; and other awards. *Leisure interests:* tennis, reading. *Address:* Leo Castelli Gallery, 420 West Broadway, New York, NY 10012, U.S.A.

CASTELLINA, Luciana, LL.B.; Italian journalist; b. 9 Aug. 1929, Rome; m. (divorced); one s. one d.; ed. Univ. of Rome; Ed. Nuova Generazione (weekly) 1958–62, le Manifesto (daily) 1972–78, Pace e Guerra (weekly) then Liberazione (weekly) 1992–94; mem. Italian Parl. 1976–, European Parl. 1984–; Chair. Cultural Cttee. European Parl. 1994–96, now Chair. External Econ. Relations Cttee.; fmr. mem. Presidence Italian Women's Union, directorate Italian Communist Party. *Leisure interest:* films. *Publications:* Family and Society in Marxist Analysis 1974, Che cosa c'è in America (reports from America) 1972. *Address:* European Parliament, Brussels, Belgium. *Telephone:* (32) 2 2845151. *Fax:* (32) 2 2849151.

CASTILLO, Michel Xavier Janicot del, L. ÈS L., L. EN P.; French writer; b. 2 Aug. 1933, Madrid, Spain; s. of Michel Janicot and Isabelle del Castillo; ed. Coll. des jésuites d'Ubeba, Spain, Lycée Janson-de-Sailly, Paris; mem. Soc. des gens de lettres, PEN; Prix des Neufs 1957, Prix des Magots 1973, Grand Prix des libraires 1973, Prix Chateaubriand 1975, Prix Renaudot 1981, Prix Maurice Genevoix 1994. *Publications:* Tanguy 1957, La Guitare 1958, Le Colleur d'affiches 1959, Le Manège espagnol 1960, Tara 1962, Gerardo Laïn 1969, Le Vent de la nuit 1973, Le Silence des pierres 1975, Le Sortilège espagnol 1977, Les Cyprés meurent en Italie 1979, Les Louves de l'Escurial 1980, La nuit du décret 1981, La Gloire de Dina 1984, Nos Andalousies 1985, Le Démon de l'oubli 1987, Mort d'un poète 1989, Une Femme en Soi 1991, Le Crime des Pères 1993, Rue des Archives 1994, Mon frère l'idiot 1995, La Tunique d'infamie 1997, De père français 1998. *Address:* Editions Gallimard, 5 rue Sébastien-Bottin, 75007 Paris (Office); Le Colombier, 7 avenue Camille Martin, 30190 La Calmette, France (Home).

CASTILLO ARRIOLA, Eduardo; Guatemalan diplomatist; b. 5 Jan. 1914, Huehuetenango; m.; four s. four d.; ed. Institute Normal de Occidente, Quezaltenango and Universidad de San Carlos, Guatemala City; fmrly. Prof., Escuela Nacional de Comercio, Escuela Normal Central, Verones, School of Juridical and Social Sciences, Univ. de San Carlos; fmr. Prof. and Dir. Colegie Institute Cervantes; fmr. Vice-Pres. Colegio de Abogados; sometime Congressman and First Sec., Nat. Assembly; fmr. Chief, Legal Dept., Ministry of Foreign Affairs; has held various posts in public admin. and led Guatemalan dels. to UN Gen. Assembly 1951–54, 1967–69 and numerous int. confs.; Perm. Rep. to OAS 1971–78; Perm. Rep. of Guatemala to UN 1978–82; Minister of Foreign Affairs 1982–83. *Address:* c/o Ministry of Foreign Affairs, Guatemala City, Guatemala.

CASTILLO LARA, H.E. Cardinal Rosalio José, S.B.D.; Venezuelan ecclesiastic; b. 4 Sept. 1922, San Casimiro, Maracay; s. of Rosalio Castillo and Guillermina Lara; ordained 1949; consecrated Bishop (Titular See of Praecausa) 1973, Archbishop 1982; cr. Cardinal 1985; Pres. Admin. Patrimony of the Holy See 1989; Pres. Pontifical Comm. for Vatican City State 1990. *Address:* Palazzo del Governatorato, 00120 Città del Vaticano, Rome, Italy.

CASTLE, Michael N., J.D.; American politician and lawyer; b. 2 July 1939, Wilmington, Del.; s. of J. Manderson and Louisa B. Castle; ed. Hamilton Coll. and Georgetown Univ.; admitted Del. Bar 1964, D.C. Bar 1964; Assoc. Connolly, Bove and Lodge, Wilmington 1964–73, partner, 1973–75; Deputy Attorney-Gen. State of Del. 1965–66; Partner, Schnee & Castle 1975–80; Lieut.-Gov. State of Del. 1981–85; Prin. Michael N. Castle 1981–; Gov. of Delaware 1985–93; mem. Del. House of Reps. 1966–67, 1993–, Del. Senate 1968–76, House of Reps. from Delaware 1993–; Republican. *Address:* House of Representatives, 1207 Longworth Building, Washington, DC 20515, U.S.A.

CASTLE OF BLACKBURN, Baroness (Life Peer) cr. 1990, of Ibstone in the County of Buckinghamshire; **Barbara Anne Castle,** P.C., B.A.; British politician; b. 6 Oct. 1910, Chesterfield; d. of F. Betts and Annie Rebecca Farrand; m. Edward Castle (later Lord Castle of Islington, died 1979) 1944; ed. Bradford Girls' Grammar School, St. Hugh's Coll., Oxford Univ.; Admin. Officer, Ministry of Food 1941–44; Corresp. for Daily Mirror 1944–45; mem. St. Pancras Borough Council, London 1937–45, Metropolitan Water Bd. 1940–43; M.P. 1945–79; mem. Nat. Exec. Cttee. of Labour Party 1950–79; Chair. of Labour Party 1958–59; Minister of Overseas Devt. 1964–65; Transport 1965–68; First Sec. of State for Employment and Productivity 1968–70, for Social Services 1974–76; mem. European Parl. for Greater Manchester North 1979–84, for Greater Manchester West 1984–89 (Vice-Pres. Socialist Group 1979–85, Leader British Labour Group 1979–85); Hon. Fellow St. Hugh's Coll., Oxford 1966, UMIST 1991, Humberside Polytechnic 1991, York Univ. 1992; Hon. LL.D. (Lancaster) 1991, (Manchester) 1993, (Cambridge) 1998; Hon. D. Tech. (Bradford) 1968, (Loughborough) 1969; Hon. D.Litt. (De Montfort Leicester) 1998; Dr. h.c. (Cambridge) 1998; Cross of Order of Merit (Germany) 1990. *Publications:* The Castle Diaries 1974–76 1980, The Castle Diaries 1964–70 1984, Sylvia and Christabel Pankhurst 1987, The Castle Diaries 1964–76 1990, Fighting All the Way (autobiog.) 1993. *Leisure interests:* walking, gardening, reading. *Address:* House of Lords, London, SW1A 0PW, England.

CASTLEMAN, Christopher Norman Anthony, M.A.; British banker; b. 23 June 1941, Beaconsfield, Bucks.; s. of late S. Phillips and of J. D. S-R-Pyper; m. 1st Sarah Victoria Stockdale 1965 (died 1979); one s. one d.; m. 2nd Caroline Clare Westcott 1980; two d.; m. 3rd Susan Mary Twycross 1990; one s. one d.; ed. Harrow School and Clare Coll., Cambridge; joined M. Samuel and Co. Ltd. 1963; Gen. Man. Hill Samuel Australia 1970–72; Officer of Hill Samuel Inc., New York 1972–73; Dir. Hill Samuel and Co. Ltd., 1970–87; Man. Dir. Hill Samuel Int. Ltd. 1975–77, Hill Samuel Group (S.A.) Ltd. and Hill Samuel South Africa Ltd. 1978–80; Chief. Exec. Hill Samuel Group PLC 1980–87, Manpower PLC 1987–88, LIT Holdings PLC 1989–90, Chair. 1991–95; Financial Adviser, Christopher Castleman and Co. 1988–89; Exec. Dir. Standard Chartered Bank 1991–. *Leisure interests:* sport, travel. *Address:* 1 Aldermanbury Square, London, EC2V 7SB, England. *Telephone:* 0171-280 7008.

CASTON, Geoffrey, C.B.E., M.A., M.P.A.; British university administrator; b. 17 May 1926, Beckenham, Kent; s. of Reginald Caston and Lilian Caston; m. 1st Sonya Chassell 1956; two s. one d.; m. 2nd Judy Roizen 1983; ed. St. Dunstan's Coll., Peterhouse, Cambridge, Harvard Univ.; Sub-Lieut. R.N.V.R. 1945–47; Colonial Office 1951–58; First-Sec. U.K. Mission to UN 1958–61; Dept. of Tech. Co-operation 1961–64; Asst. Sec. Dept. of Educ. and Science 1964–66; Sec. Schools Council 1966–70; Under-Sec. Univ. Grants Cttee. 1970–72; Registrar of Univ. and Fellow of Merton Coll., Oxford 1972–79; Sec. Gen. Cttee. of Vice-Chancellors 1979–83; Vice-Chancellor, Univ. of South Pacific, Fiji 1983–92; Visiting Assoc. Center for Studies in Higher Educ., Calif. Univ. 1978–; Distinguished Lecturer in Pacific Studies, Univ. of Hawaii 1992; GAP Project Man., S. Pacific and N.Z. 1994–; Chair. Commonwealth Scholarship Comm. in the U.K. 1996–; mem. or chair. numerous dels. and cttees., nat. and int., including UN Tech. Assistance Cttee. 1962–64, Visiting Mission to Trust Territory of Pacific Islands 1961, OECD Workshops on Educational Innovation 1969, 1970, 1971, Nat. Inst. for Careers Educ. and Counselling 1975–83, Exec. Cttee. Inter-Univ. Council for Higher Educ. Overseas 1977–83, Library Advisory Council (UK) 1973–78, Council, Univ. of Papua New Guinea; Hon. LL.D. (Dundee) 1982; Hon. D.Litt. (Deakin) 1991; George Long Prize for Jurisprudence 1950. *Address:* 3 Pennsylvania Park, Exeter, EX4 6HB, England. *Telephone:* (01392) 272986. *Fax:* (01392) 421360.

CASTRILLÓN HOYOS, Cardinal Dario; Colombian ecclesiastic; b. 4 July 1929, Medellín; ordained priest 1952; Bishop 1971; Archbishop of Bucaramanga 1992–; Pro-Prefect Congregation for the Clergy; cr. Cardinal Feb. 1998. *Address:* Arzobispado, Calle 33, N. 21-18, Bucaramanga, Santander, Colombia. *Telephone:* (976) 424 387. *Fax:* (976) 421 361.

CASTRO, Amado Alejandro, B.S., A.M., PH.D.; Philippine economist; b. 29 June 1924, Manila; ed. Univ. of the Philippines and Harvard Univ., U.S.A.; Instructor in Econs., Univ. of the Philippines 1948–53, Asst. Prof. 1954–56, Assoc. Prof. 1956–62, Head of Econs. Dept. 1956–58, Acting Dean, Coll. of Business Admin. Jan.-Sept. 1958, Prof. of Econs. 1962–, Dean, School of Econs. 1965–73, Prof. of Monetary Econs. 1972; Gov. and Acting Chair. Devt. Bank of the Philippines 1962–66; Dir. Inst. of Econ. Devt. and Research

1958–66, Econ. Bureau ASEAN Secr. 1977–80. *Address:* School of Economics, University of the Philippines, Quezon City, Philippines 3041; 67 Valenzuela, San Juan, Metro Manila 3134, Philippines (Home).

CASTRO, Fidel (see Castro Ruz, Fidel).

CASTRO, Gen. Raúl (see Castro Ruz, Gen. Raúl).

CASTRO JIJÓN, Rear-Adm. Ramón; Ecuadorean politician and naval officer; b. 1915; studied naval engineering in U.S.A.; fmr. Naval Attaché, London; C.-in-C. of Navy, Ecuador; Pres. Military Junta 1963–66; in exile 1966–.

CASTRO RUZ, Fidel, D.IUR.; Cuban politician; b. 13 Aug. 1928; m. Mirta Diaz-Bilart 1948 (dissolved 1955); one s.; ed. Jesuit schools in Santiago and Havana, Univ. de la Habana; law practice in Havana; began active opposition to Batista regime by attack on Moncada barracks at Santiago 26th July 1953; sentenced to 15 years' imprisonment 1953; amnestied 1956; went into exile in Mexico and began to organize armed rebellion; landed in Oriente Province with small force Dec. 1956; carried on armed struggle against Batista regime until flight of Batista Jan. 1959; Prime Minister of Cuba 1959–76; Head of State and Pres. of Council of State 1976–, Pres. of Council of Ministers 1976–; Chair. Agrarian Reform Inst. 1965–; First Sec. Partido Unido de la Revolución Socialista (PURS) 1963–65, Partido Comunista 1965– (mem. Political Bureau 1976–), Head Nat. Defence Council 1992–; Lenin Peace Prize 1961, Muammar Gaddafi Human Rights Prize 1998; Dimitrov Prize (Bulgaria) 1980; Hero of the Soviet Union 1963; Order of Lenin 1972, 1986, Order of the October Revolution 1976, Somali Order (1st Class) 1977, Order of Jamaica 1977, Gold Star (Vietnam) 1982. *Publications:* Ten Years of Revolution 1964, History Will Absolve Me 1968, Fidel (with Frei Betto) 1987, How Far We Slaves Have Come: South Africa and Cuba in Today's World (with Nelson Mandela) 1991. *Address:* Palacio del Gobierno, Havana, Cuba.

CASTRO RUZ, Gen. Raúl; Cuban politician; b. 3 June 1931; ed. Jesuit schools; younger brother of Fidel Castro Ruz (q.v.); sentenced to 15 years' imprisonment for insurrection 1953; amnestied 1954; assisted his brother's movement in Mexico, and in Cuba after Dec. 1956; Chief of the Armed Forces 1960; First Deputy Prime Minister 1972–76; First Vice-Pres. Council of State 1976–, First Vice-Pres. Council of Ministers 1976–; Medal for Strengthening of Brotherhood in Arms 1977; Order of Lenin 1979, Order of the October Revolution 1981. *Address:* Oficina del Primer Vice-Presidente, Havana, Cuba.

CATARINO, Pedro Manuel; Portuguese diplomatist; b. 12 May 1941, Lisbon; m. Cheryl A. Steyn 1969; one s. one d.; ed. Univ. of Lisbon; served Embassy, Pretoria 1967–69; Defence Counsellor, Del. to NATO, Brussels 1974–79; Consul-Gen. Hong Kong 1979–82; mem. int. staff, NATO, Brussels 1983–89; Head, del. to negotiations for a new defence and cooperation agreement with U.S.A. 1989–92; Pres. Inter-ministerial Comm. of Macau and Head, Portuguese del. to Joint Luso-Chinese Liaison Group; Perm. Rep. to UN 1992–97. Silver Medal for Distinguished Services. *Leisure interest:* tennis. *Address:* c/o Ministry of Foreign Affairs, Largo do Rilvas, 1354 Lisbon Codex, Portugal.

CATER, Sir Jack, K.B.E.; British colonial administrator; b. 21 Feb. 1922, London; s. of Alfred F. and Pamela E. (née Dukes) Cater; m. Peggy Gwenda Richards 1950; one s. two d.; ed. Sir George Monoux Grammar School, Walthamstow; war service 1939–45, Squadron Leader, R.A.F.V.R.; British Mil. Admin., Hong Kong 1945; joined Colonial Admin. Service, Hong Kong 1946; attended 2nd Devonshire Course, Queen's Coll., Oxford 1949–50; various posts incl. Registrar of Co-operative Socs. and Dir. of Marketing, Dir. of Agric. and Fisheries, Deputy Econ. Sec.; Imperial Defence Coll. (now Royal Coll. of Defence Studies) 1966; Defence Sec., Special Asst. to Gov. and Deputy Colonial Sec. (Special Duties) 1967; Exec. Dir. Hong Kong Trade Devt. Council 1968–70; Dir. Commerce and Industry, Hong Kong 1970–72; Sec. for Information 1972, for Home Affairs and Information 1973; Founding Commr. Ind. Comm. Against Corruption 1974–78; Chief Sec., Hong Kong 1978–81 (Acting Gov. and Deputy Gov. on several occasions); Hong Kong Commr., London 1981–84; Man. Dir. Hong Kong Nuclear Investment Co. 1987–89, Consultant 1990–; Dir. Guangdong Nuclear Power Jt. Venture Co. Ltd. 1986–89 (First Deputy Gen. Man. 1985–86); Dir. TV Broadcasts Ltd., TVE (Holdings) Ltd. 1992–; Adviser to Consultative Cttee. for the Basic Law, Hong Kong 1986–90; Pres. Agency for Volunteer Service 1980–; Chair. Project Evaluation Cttee., Hong Kong Inst. of Biotech., Chinese Univ. of Hong Kong 1990–95, Oriental Devt. Co. Ltd. 1992– (Dir. 1991), H.G. (Asia) Ltd. 1992–95; Consultant Hong Kong Nuclear Investment Co. 1990–, Philips China and Hong Kong 1990–92, Int. Bechtel Ind. 1990–, DAO Heng Bank Ltd. 1996–; Dir. HKIB Syntex Ltd. 1991–95, Springfield Bank and Trust Ltd., Gibraltar 1994–; mem. Court, Univ. of Hong Kong 1982–, Hoare Govett (Asia) Ltd. 1990–92, Hong Kong Cable Communications Ltd. 1990–91; mem. Bd. of Govs., Hong Kong Baptist Univ. 1990–, School Council, St. Catharine's School for Girls, Kwun Tong 1985– (Vice-Chair. 1992–), Int. Bd. of United World Coll. 1981–92; Dir Li Po Chun United World Coll. Ltd. 1991–; Hon. D.S.Sc. (Hong Kong Univ.) 1982. *Leisure interests:* walking, bridge, reading. *Address:* Hong Kong Nuclear Investment Co. Ltd., 147 Argyle Street, Kowloon, Hong Kong Special Administrative Region (Office); 36/85 Kadoorie Avenue, Kowloon, Hong Kong Special Administrative Region, People's Republic of China (Home). *Telephone:* 27608058 (Office); 27154004 (Home).

CATHALA, Thierry Gerard, D. EN D.; French judge; b. 23 Feb. 1925, Bordeaux; s. of Jean Cathala and Juliette Monsion; m. Marie F. Mérimée 1954; two s. one d.; ed. Saint-Genes Coll., Lycée Montaigne, Faculté de droit de Bordeaux and Paris; trainee barrister Bordeaux Bar 1946–48; Deputy Judge, Bordeaux 1948–51, Examining Magistrate 1951–65; Prin. Admin. EEC Comm., Brussels 1965–73; Judge Nanterre and Paris Courts 1974–81; Chief Justice French Polynesia Court of Appeal 1981–85; Counsellor Supreme Court of Cassation 1985–94; French Rep. South Pacific Judicial Conf. 1982–84; mem. Supreme Judiciary Council 1987–91; Chair. Ninth South Pacific Judicial Conf., Tahiti 1991; mem. Comm. Informatique et Libertés 1994–; Pres. Asscn. of Friends of French Polynesia; Officier Légion d'honneur, Ordre Nat. du Mérite. *Publications:* le Contrôle de la légalité administrative par les tribunaux judiciaires 1966, numerous articles on law. *Leisure interests:* geography, travelling, religious questions. *Address:* CNIL, 21 rue Saint-Guillaume, 75340 Paris; 8 rue Ploix, 78000 Versailles, France (Home). *Telephone:* 39 50 31 98 (Home).

CATHCART, Kevin James, M.A., PH.D., M.R.I.A.; Irish professor; b. 9 Oct. 1939, Derrylin, Co. Fermanagh, N. Ireland; s. of Andrew Cathcart and Elizabeth (née Flannery) Cathcart; m. Ann McDermott 1968; two s.; ed. Salesian Coll., Cheshire, England, Mellifont Abbey, Co. Louth, Trinity Coll., Dublin, Ireland and Pontifical Biblical Inst., Rome, Italy; lecturer in Hebrew, Pontifical Biblical Inst., Rome 1968, in Near Eastern Studies, Univ. of Ottawa, Canada 1968–71, Asst. Prof. 1971–73, Assoc. Prof. 1973–74; Sr. Lecturer in Semitic Languages and Dept. Head, Univ. Coll. Dublin 1974–79; Prof. of Near Eastern Languages and Dept. Head 1979–; Visiting Fellow, St Edmund's Coll., Cambridge 1987–88, 1993–94; Visiting Academic, St. Benet's Hall, Oxford 1994; Visiting Prof., Heidelberg 1981, 1986, 1992, Ottawa 1983, Aarhus 1986, Toronto 1989, Mainz 1992; Bd. of Electors (Regius Professorship of Hebrew) Univ. of Cambridge 1989–; editorial consultant Journal of Semitic Studies 1991–; mem. Editorial Bd. Journal for the Aramaic Bible 1998–; Trustee, Chester Beatty Library, Dublin 1974–89, Chair. Bd. of Trustees 1984–86; mem. Royal Irish Acad., Royal Danish Acad. *Publications include:* Nahum in the Light of Northwest Semitic 1973, Back to the Sources: Biblical and Near Eastern Studies (with J.F. Healey) 1989, The Targum of the Minor Prophets (with R.P. Gordon) 1989, The Aramaic Bible (20 vols., co-Ed.), The Edward Hincks Bicentenary Lectures 1994, Targumic and Cognate Studies (with M. Maher) 1996. *Leisure interests:* birdwatching, medieval architecture. *Address:* Department of Near Eastern Languages, University College, Belfield, Dublin 4; 8 Friarsland Road, Clonskea, Dublin 14, Ireland.

CATHERWOOD, Sir (Henry) Frederick (Ross), Kt.; British public official and industrialist; b. 30 Jan. 1925, Castledawson, N. Ireland; s. of late Stuart and of Jean Catherwood; m. Elizabeth Lloyd-Jones 1954; two s. one d.; ed. Shrewsbury School and Clare Coll., Cambridge; Chartered Accountant 1951; Sec. Laws Stores Ltd., Gateshead 1952–54; Sec. and Controller, Richard Costain Ltd. 1954–55, Chief Exec. 1955–60; Asst. Man. Dir. British Aluminium Co. Ltd. 1960–62, Man. Dir. 1962–64; Chief Industrial Adviser, Dept. of Econ. Affairs 1964–66; mem. Nat. Econ. Devt. Council (N.E.D.C.) 1964–71, Dir. Gen. 1966–71; mem. British Nat. Export Council 1965–70; Vice-Chair. British Inst. of Man. 1972–74, Chair. 1974–76, Vice-Pres. 1976–; Chair. British Overseas Trade Bd. 1975–79; Chair. Mallinson-Denny Ltd. 1976–79 (Dir. 1974); Dir. John Laing Ltd. (Group Man. Dir. and Chief Exec. 1972–74) 1971–80, Goodyear Tyre and Rubber Co. (GB) Ltd. 1975–89; Pres. Fellowship of Ind. Evangelical Churches 1977–78; mem. European Parl. for Cambridgeshire and Wellingborough, 1979–84, for Cambridgeshire and N. Bedfordshire 1984–94, Vice-Pres. European Parl. 1989–92 (mem. Del. to U.S. Congress 1983–89, to Hungary 1989, to Canada 1991–94), Chair. Cttee. for External Econ. Relations 1979–84, Vice-Pres. European Democratic Group 1983–87, Chair. Land Use and Food Policy Inter-group 1987–92, Vice-Chair. Foreign Affairs Comm. 1992–94); mem. Council Royal Inst. of Int. Affairs 1964–77; Treas. Int. Fellowship Evangelical Students 1979–93, Vice-Pres. 1995–; Pres. Evangelical Alliance 1992–; Hon. D.Sc. (Aston) 1972, Hon. D.Sc.Econ. (Queen's Univ., Belfast) 1973, Hon. D.Univ. (Surrey) 1979. *Publications:* The Christian in Industrial Society 1964, The Christian Citizen 1969, A Better Way 1975, First Things First 1979, God's Time God's Money 1987, Pro-Europe? 1991, David: Poet, Warrior, King 1993, At the Cutting Edge (memoirs) 1995, Jobs and Justice, Homes and Hope 1997. *Leisure interests:* reading, writing, walking. *Address:* Sutton Hall, Balsham, Cambs., England. *Telephone:* (01223) 317672. *Fax:* (01223) 317671.

CATLOW, Charles Richard Arthur, M.A., D.PHIL.; British professor of natural philosophy; b. 24 April 1947, Simonstone, Lancs.; s. of R. M. Catlow and C. Aldred; m. Carey A. Chapman 1978; one s.; ed. Clitheroe Royal Grammar School and St. John's Coll. Oxford; grad. scholar, Jesus Coll. Oxford 1970–73; Research Fellow, St. John's Coll. Oxford 1970–76; lecturer, Univ. Coll. London 1976–85; Prof. of Chemistry, Univ. of Keele 1985–89; Wolfson Prof. of Natural Philosophy, Royal Inst. of G.B. 1989–. *Publications:* jtly: Computer Simulation of Solids 1982, Mass Transport in Solids 1983, Computer Simulation of Fluids, Polymers and Solids 1989, Applications of Synchrotron Radiation 1990; over 500 research papers and several monographs. *Leisure interests:* reading, walking, music. *Address:* Royal Institution of Great Britain, 21 Albemarle Street, London W1X 4BS, England. *Telephone:* 0171-409 2992. *Fax:* 0171-629 3569.

CATON-JONES, Michael; British film director; b. 1958, Broxburn, nr. Edinburgh, Scotland; ed. Nat. Film School; worked as stagehand in London

West End theatres, wrote and directed first film The Sanatorium and several other short films before being accepted by Nat. Film School; films made while a student include: Liebe Mutter (first prize European film school competition), The Making of Absolute Beginners (for Palace Productions), The Riveter; left School to make serial Brond for Channel 4 TV, then Lucky Sunil (BBC TV). *Films:* Scandal 1989, Memphis Belle 1990, This Boy's Life 1993, Rob Roy 1994.

CATTANACH, Bruce MacIntosh, PH.D., F.R.S.; British geneticist; b. 5 Nov. 1932, Glasgow; s. of James Cattanach and Margaretta May (née Fyfe) Cattanach; m. Margaret Bouchier Crewe 1966; two d.; ed. Heaton Grammar School, Newcastle-upon-Tyne, King's Coll., Univ. of Durham and Univ. of Edinburgh; Scientific Staff MRC Induced Mutagenesis Unit, Edin. 1959–62, 1964–66; N.I.H. Post-Doctoral Research Fellow Biology Div., Oak Ridge, Tenn., U.S.A. 1962–64; Sr. Scientist City of Hope Medical Centre, Duarte, Calif. 1966–69; Scientific Staff MRC Radiobiology Unit, Chilton, Oxon. 1969–86, Head of Genetics Div. 1987–96, Sr. Scientist 1997–98; retd. worker 1998–; Acting Dir. MRC Mammalian Genetics Unit, Harwell, Oxfordshire 1996–97. *Publications:* numerous papers in scientific journals. *Leisure interests:* control of inherited disease in pedigree dogs; Boxer breeding, exhibiting and judging. *Address:* Down's Edge, Reading Road, Harwell, Oxon., OX11 0JJ, England (Home). *Telephone:* (01235) 835410 (Home).

CATTO, 2nd Baron, of Cairncatto; **Stephen Gordon Catto;** British banker and company director; b. 14 Jan. 1923, s. of 1st Baron Catto and Gladys Forbes Gordon; m. 1st Josephine Innes Packer 1948, 2nd Margaret Forrest 1966; three s. three d.; ed. Eton Coll. and Cambridge Univ.; Air Force service 1943–47; fmr. Chair. Morgan Grenfell & Co. Ltd., Pres. Deutsche Morgan Grenfell Group PLC 1987–98; Chair. Yule Catto & Co. PLC 1971–; Dir. Times Newspapers Holdings and other cos.; mem. Advisory Council, Export Credits Guarantee Dept. 1959–65; Chair. Exec. Cttee. Westminster Abbey Trust –1997; part-time mem. London Transport Bd. 1962–68. *Leisure interests:* gardening, music. *Address:* First Floor, 12 Berkeley Street, London, W1X 5AD, England. *Telephone:* 0171-491 1090.

CATTO, Graeme Robertson Dawson, D.SC., M.D., F.R.C.P., F.R.S.A., F.R.S.E.; British professor of medicine; b. 24 April 1945, Aberdeen, Scotland; s. of William D. Catto and Dora E. (née Spiby) Catto; m. Joan Sievewright 1967; one s. one d.; ed. Robert Gordon's Coll., Univ. of Aberdeen; house officer Aberdeen Royal Infirmary 1969–70, Hon. Consultant Physician/Nephrologist 1977–; Research Fellow, then Lecturer Univ. of Aberdeen 1970–75, Sr. Lecturer then Reader in Medicine 1977–78, Prof. of Medicine 1988–, Dean Faculty of Clinical Medicine 1992–95, Vice-Prin., Dean 1995–; Chief Scientist, Scottish Office 1997–; Vice-Chair. Aberdeen Royal Hosp. NHS Trust 1992–; mem. Gen. Medical Council 1994–; Treas. Acad. of Medical Sciences 1998–; Chair. of Govs. Robert Gordon's Coll., Aberdeen 1995–; mem. Scottish Higher Educ. Funding Council 1996–; Harkness Fellow Commonwealth Fund of N.Y., Harvard Univ., Peter Bent Brigham Hosp., Mass. 1975–77. *Leisure interests:* curling, fresh air, France. *Publications:* chapters and books on medicine and nephrology. *Address:* Department of Medicine and Therapeutics, University of Aberdeen, Foresterhill, Aberdeen, AB9 2ZD; 4 Woodend Avenue, Aberdeen, AB15 6YL, Scotland. *Telephone:* (01224) 681818 ext. 53013; (01224) 310509. *Fax:* (01224) 699884.

CATTO, Henry Edward; American diplomatist and business executive; b. 6 Dec. 1930, Dallas; s. of Henry Edward Catto and Maureen (née Halsell) Catto; m. Jessica Oveta Hobby 1958; two s. two d.; ed. Williams Coll.; partner Catto & Catto, San Antonio 1955–; Dep. Rep. Org. of American States 1969–71; Amb. to El Salvador 1971–73; Chief of Protocol, The White House 1974–76; Amb. to the UN Office, Geneva 1976–77; Asst. Sec. of Defense, Pentagon, Washington 1981–83; Dir. Cullen-Frost Bankers, San Antonio, Nat. Public Radio, Wash.; Amb. to the U.K. 1989–91; Dir. US Information Agency 1991–93; Adjunct Prof. Univ. of Texas, San Antonio 1993–; mem. Council on Foreign Relations 1979; Vice Chair. Aspen Inst. 1993–, H and C Communications 1983–89; columnist San Antonio Light 1985–89; Hon. LL.D. (Aberdeen) 1990. *Leisure interest:* skiing. *Address:* 110 East Crockett Street, San Antonio, TX 78205, U.S.A.

CAUCHON, Martin, D.C.L.; Canadian politician and lawyer; b. 1962; m.; ed. Univ. of Ottawa, Bar School of Quebec, Univ. of Exeter, U.K.; practised as civil and commercial lawyer 1985–90; M.P. for Outremont 1993, 1997–; Vice-Chair. Public Accounts Cttee. 1994; Sec. of State (Fed. Office of Regional Devt., Quebec) 1996–; fmr. Pres. Canada-France Inter-parl. Asscn. *Publications:* articles in Revue du Barreau and Bulletin de la Société de droit int. économique. *Address:* Federal Office of Regional Development, 264 West Block, House of Commons, Ottawa, Ont., K1A 0A6, Canada.

CAULFIELD, Patrick, C.B.E., R.A.; British artist; b. 29 Jan. 1936, London; s. of Patrick Caulfield and Annie Caulfield; m. Pauline Jacobs 1968; three s.; ed. Acton Cen. Secondary Modern School, Chelsea School of Art and R.C.A.; taught at Chelsea Coll. of Art 1963–71; first exhibited, FBA Galleries 1961; one-man exhbns. include: Robert Fraser Gallery, London 1965, 1967, Robert Elkon Gallery, New York 1966, 1968, Waddington Galleries 1969, 1971, 1973, 1975, 1979, 1981, 1985, also in France, Belgium, Italy, Australia, U.S.A. and Japan; retrospective exhbn. Tate Gallery, London 1981, Serpentine Gallery, London 1992; has participated in numerous group exhbns. in U.K., Europe and New York; design for ballet Party Game, Covent Garden 1984; work in public collections include Tate Gallery, Vic. & Albert Museum, Manchester City Art Gallery and other museums and galleries in U.K., U.S.A., Australia, Germany and Japan; Sr. Fellowship, R.C.A. 1993; Hon. Fellow London Inst. 1996. *Address:* 19 Belsize Square, London, NW3 4HT; 6 Primrose Hill Studios, Fitzroy Road, London, NW1 8TR; c/o Waddington Galleries, 2 Cork Street, London, W1X 1PA, England.

CAULO, Ralph Daniel, M.A.; American publishing executive; b. 7 Jan. 1935; two s. one d.; ed. Univ. of Redlands; S.W. Regional Man. Schools Dept. Harcourt Brace Jovanovich Inc. 1974–75, Man. Gen. Sales 1975–78, Deputy Dir. 1978–79, Vice-Pres. 1979–81, Sr. Vice-Pres. 1981–83, Exec. Vice-Pres. 1983–88, Pres. and C.O.O. 1988–89, Pres. and C.E.O. 1989–90.

CAUSLEY, Charles Stanley, C.B.E., F.R.S.L.; British poet; b. 24 Aug. 1917, Launceston, Cornwall; s. of Laura and Charles Causley; ed. Horwell Grammar School, Launceston Coll., Peterborough Training Coll.; served in R.N. 1940–46; worked as a teacher for many years until 1976; Hon. D. Litt. (Exeter) 1977, Hon. M.A. (Open Univ.) 1982; Queen's Gold Medal for Poetry 1967, Cholmondeley Award 1971, shared Ingersoll Prize 1990. *Publications:* Union Street 1957, Johnny Alleluia 1961, Underneath the Water 1968, Figgie Hobbin 1971, Puffin Book of Magic Verse (Ed.) 1974, St. Martha and the Dragon (libretti, music by Phyllis Tate) 1977, Puffin Book of Salt-Sea Verse (Ed.) 1978, The Ballad of Aucassin and Nicolette 1981, The Sun, Dancing (Ed.) 1982, Secret Destinations 1984, Kings' Children (trans. German ballads) 1986, 21 Poems 1986, Early in the Morning (poems) 1986, Jack the Treacle Eater 1987, A Field of Vision 1988, Jonah (libretto, music by William Mathias) 1990, The Young Man of Cury 1991, Bring in the Holly 1991, All Day Saturday 1994, Going to the Fair (Selected Poems for Children) 1994, Collected Poems for Children 1996, Collected Poems 1951–97 1997. *Leisure interests:* theatre, cinema, foreign travel. *Address:* 2 Cyprus Well, Launceston, Cornwall, PL15 8BT, England. *Telephone:* (01566) 772731.

CAUSSE, Jean-Pierre; French scientist; b. 4 Oct. 1926, Montpellier; m. Françoise Villard; three d.; ed. Lycée de Montpellier and Ecole Normale Supérieure; Observatoire de Paris 1952–55; Physicist, Schlumberger Ltd. 1955–62; Dir. of Satellites Div., Centre Nat. d'Etudes Spatiales 1962–66, Dir. Brétigny Space Centre 1966–69; Deputy Sec.-Gen., European Launcher Devt. Org. 1969–73; Head Spacelab Programme, European Space Research Org. 1973–74; Vice-Pres. Cie. de Saint-Gobain 1974–89; Pres. European Industrial Research Man. Asscn. 1985–87; Vice-Pres. Conseil Supérieur de la recherche et de la tech. 1987–89; Pres. Int. Comm. on Glass 1988–91; mem. Conseil des Applications de l'Acad. des Sciences; Officier, Légion d'honneur. *Address:* 25 rue de l'Ouest, 75014 Paris, France. *Telephone:* (1) 43-35-02-37. *Fax:* (1) 43-35-02-37.

CAUTE, (John) David, M.A., D.PHIL.; British writer; b. 16 Dec. 1936; m. 1st Catherine Shuckburgh (divorced 1970); two s.; m. 2nd Martha Bates 1973; two d.; ed. Edinburgh Acad., Wellington, Wadham Coll., Oxford; St. Anthony's Coll. 1959; army service Gold Coast 1955–56; Henry Fellow, Harvard Univ. 1960–61; Fellow, All Souls Coll., Oxford 1959–65; Visiting Prof. New York Univ. and Columbia Univ.; 1966–67; Reader in Social and Political Theory, Brunel Univ. 1967–70; Regents' Lecturer, Univ. of Calif. 1974, Visiting Prof. Univ. of Bristol 1985; Literary Ed., New Statesman 1979–80; Co-Chair. Writers' Guild 1982. *Plays:* Songs for an Autumn Rifle 1961, The Demonstration 1969, Fallout (for radio) 1972, The Fourth World 1973, Brecht and Company (BBC TV) 1979, The Zimbabwe Tapes (BBC Radio) 1983, Henry and the Dogs (BBC Radio) 1986, Sanctions (BBC Radio) 1988, Animal Fun Park (BBC Radio) 1995. *Publications:* At Fever Pitch (novel, Authors' Club Award and John Llewelyn Rhys Prize 1960) 1959, Comrade Jacob (novel) 1961, Communism and the French Intellectuals 1914–1960 1964, The Left in Europe Since 1789 1966, The Decline of the West (novel) 1966, Essential Writings of Karl Marx (Ed.) 1967, Fanon 1970, The Confrontation: a trilogy (The Demonstration (play), The Occupation (novel), The Illusion) 1971, The Fellow-Travellers 1973, Collisions 1974, Cuba, Yes? 1974, The Great Fear 1978, Under the Skin: the Death of White Rhodesia 1983; The Baby-Sitters 1978, Moscow Gold 1980 (novels, both as John Salisbury), The K-Factor (novel) 1983, The Espionage of the Saints 1986, News from Nowhere (novel) 1986, Sixty Eight: the Year of the Barricades 1988, Veronica or the Two Nations (novel) 1989, The Women's Hour (novel) 1991, Joseph Losey: A Revenge on Life 1994, Dr. Orwell and Mr Blair (novel) 1994, Fatima's Scarf (novel) 1998. *Address;* 41 Westcroft Square, London, W6 0TA, England.

CAUTHEN, Stephen Mark "Steve"; American jockey (retd.); b. 1 May 1960, Walton, Kentucky; s. of Ronald Cauthen and Myra Cauthen; m. Amy Rothfuss 1992; rode first race 1976, first winner 1976, top jockey U.S.A. with 487 winners 1977; moved to U.K. 1979; champion jockey 1984, 1985, 1987; won Derby on Slip Anchor 1985, on Reference Point 1987; rode 1,704 winners including 10 classics 1979–93 (retd.); only jockey to have won Ky., Epsom, Irish, French and Italian Derbys; youngest person to be elected to Racing Hall of Fame; now works on family farm, Ky. and as racing commentator on TV; Seagram Prize 1977, Eclipse Award 1977.

CAUVIN, Patrick, L. ES L.; French writer; b. 6 Oct. 1932, Marseille; s. of Joseph Krotz and Victoria Cauvin; m. Evelyne Berrot 1959; two s. one d.; served in Algeria 1958–60; gave up work to concentrate on writing 1970–. *Publications include:* L'Amour aveugle, E=MC² mon amour, Monsieur Papa, Laura Brams, Ville Vanille. *Leisure interest:* football. *Address:* 59 rue Caulaincourt, 75018 Paris, France.

CAVACO SILVA, Anibal, PH.D.; Portuguese politician and university professor; b. 15 July 1939, Loulé; s. of Teodoro Silva and Maria do Nascimento

Cavaco; m. Maria Cavaco Silva 1963; one s. one d.; ed. York Univ., U.K. and Inst. of Econ. and Financial Studies; taught Public Econs. and Political Economy, Inst. of Econ. and Financial Studies 1965–67, then at Catholic Univ. 1975–, and New Univ. of Lisbon 1977–; Research Fellow, Calouste Gulbenkian Foundation 1967–77; Dir. of Research and Statistical Dept., Bank of Portugal 1977–79, 1981; Minister of Finance and Planning 1980–81; Pres. Council for Nat. Planning 1981–84; Leader, PSD 1985–95; Prime Minister of Portugal 1985–95; mem. Real Academia de Ciencias Morales y Políticas, Spain; Econ. Adviser to Cen. Bank; Social Democrat (PSD); Joseph Bech Prize 1991, Max Schmidleinz Foundation Prize. *Publications:* Budgetary Policy and Economic Stabilization 1976, Economic Effects of Public Debt 1977, The Economic Policy of Sá Carneiro's Government 1982, Public Finance and Macroeconomic Policy 1992, A Decade of Reforms 1995, Portugal and the Single Currency 1997 and over 20 articles on financial markets, public economics and Portuguese economic policy. *Leisure interests:* tennis, gardening. *Address:* c/o Bank of Portugal, Av. Almirante Reis 71, 1150 Lisbon, Portugal.

CAVALCANTI, Giacomo, Marchese di Verbicaro; Italian artist; b. 17 March 1952; s. of Bruno Cavalcanti and Angela Valente; m. Antonella De Rosa 1987; one d.; studied graphic art and photography; active in ecology, anti-drug activity and anti-vivisection movts.; writes for magazine Eco. *Publications:* La rondine da terra non sa volare 1986, Maribo 1988, Incarico Colombiano 1990, L'Aquilone innamorato, La Cicogna non porta i fratellini, L'Ippopotamo e la Farfalla 1992, Serigrafie 1993. *Leisure interests:* sport, photography, travel, horses.

CAVALIER-SMITH, Thomas, PH.D., F.R.S., F.R.S.C., F.L.S., F.I.BIOL.; British/Canadian biologist and university professor; b. 21 Oct. 1942, London; s. of Alan Hailes Spencer Cavalier-Smith and Mary Maude Cavalier-Smith (née Bratt); m. 1st Gillian Glaysher 1967 (divorced); one s. one d.; m. 2nd Ema E-Yung Chao 1991; one d.; ed. Norwich School, Gonville and Caius Coll. Cambridge, King's Coll. London; guest investigator and Damon Runyan Memorial Fellow, Rockefeller Univ., New York 1967–69; lecturer in Biophysics, King's Coll., Univ. of London 1969–82, Reader 1982–89; Prof. of Botany, Univ. of B.C. 1989–; Fellow Canadian Inst. for Advanced Research (CIAR) Evolutionary Biology Programme 1988–. *Publications:* Biology, Society and Choice (Ed.) 1982, The Evolution of Genome Size (Ed.) 1985; over 120 scientific papers. *Leisure interests:* reading, natural history. *Address:* Department of Botany, University of British Columbia, Boulevard, Vancouver, B.C., V6T 1Z4, Canada. *Telephone:* (604) 822 4906. *Fax:* (604) 822 6089.

CAVALLO, Domingo Felipe, D.ECON., PH.D.; Argentinian politician; b. 21 July 1946, San Francisco, Córdoba; m.; three s.; ed. Nat. Univ. of Córdoba and Harvard Univ.; Under-Sec. for Devt. Govt. of Prov. of Córdoba 1969–70; Vice-Pres. Bd. of Dirs. Banco de la Provincia de Córdoba 1971–72; Titular lecturer, Nat. and Catholic Univs. 1970–83; founding Dir. Inst. for Econ. Studies of Mediterranean Found. 1977–87; fmr. Pres. Argentine Cen. Bank, now Gov.; mem. Advisory Cttee. Inst. for Econ. Devt. of World Bank (IBRD) 1988; Nat. Deputy for Córdoba 1987–91; Minister of Foreign Affairs and Worship 1989–91, of the Economy 1991–92, of the Economy and Public Works 1992–96. *Publications:* Volver a Crecer 1986, El Desafío Federal 1986, Economía en Tiempos de Crisis 1989; numerous tech. publs. and articles in Argentine and foreign newspapers. *Address:* c/o Ministry of the Economy and Public Works, Hipólito Yrigoyen 250, 1310 Buenos Aires, Argentina.

CAVAZOS, Lauro Fred, PH.D.; American professor of anatomy; b. 4 Jan. 1927, King Ranch, Tex.; s. of Lauro Fred and Tomasa (Quintanilla) Cavazos; m. Peggy Ann Murdock 1954; five s. five d.; ed. Texas Tech. Univ., Iowa State Univ.; Teaching Asst., Tex. Tech. Univ., Lubbock 1949–51; Instructor in Anatomy, Medical Coll. of Va., Asst. Prof. 1956–60, Assoc. Prof. 1960–64; Prof. of Anatomy, Tufts Univ. School of Medicine, Boston 1964–80, Chair. Dept. 1964–72, Assoc. Dean 1972–73, Acting Dean 1973–75, Dean 1975–80; Pres. Health Sciences Centre, Prof. of Biological Sciences, Prof. of Anatomy, Tex. Tech. Univ. 1980–88; mem. Bd. of Dirs. Shamrock R & M Inc. 1987; Sec. of Educ. 1988–90; mem. American Asscn. of Anatomists, Endocrine Soc., Histochemical Soc., A.A.A.S., Asscn. of American Medical Colls., Pan American Asscn. of American Medical Colls., Pan American Asscn. of Anatomy. *Address:* 173 Annursnac Hill Road, Concord, MA 01742, U.S.A.

CAWLEY, Evonne Fay Goolagong, A.O., M.B.E.; Australian tennis player; b. 31 July 1951, Griffith, N.S.W.; d. of the late Kenneth Goolagong and Melinda Goolagong; m. Roger Anson Cawley 1975; one s. one d.; ed. Willoughby High School, Sydney; professional player since 1970; Wimbledon Champion 1971, 1980 (singles), 1974 (doubles); Australian Champion 1974, 1975, 1976, 1977; French Champion 1971; Italian Champion 1973; S.A. Champion 1972; Virginia Slims Circuit Champion 1975, 1976; played Federation Cup for Australia 1971, 1972, 1973, 1974, 1975, 1976; consultant to Indigenous Sports Programme; Amb. and Exec. Dir. Evonne Goolagong Sports Trust; f. Evonne Goolagong Getting Started Programme for young girls. *Publications:* Evonne Goolagong (with Bud Collins) 1975, Home: The Evonne Goolagong Story (with Phil Jarratt) 1993. *Leisure interests:* fishing, reading, researching Aboriginal heritage, movies, soccer. *Address:* c/o IMG, 281 Clarence Street, Sydney, N.S.W. 2000; P.O. Box 1347, Noosa Heads, Queensland 4567, Australia. *Telephone:* (07) 5474 0112. *Fax:* (07) 5474 0113.

CAYETANO, Benjamin J., B.A., J.D.; American politician and lawyer; b. 14 Nov. 1939, Honolulu; m. 1st Lorraine Gueco 1958; m. 2nd Vicky Tiu 1997; two s. three d.; ed. Farrington High School, Honolulu, Univ. of Calif. Los Angeles and Loyola Law School, Los Angeles; practising lawyer 1971–86; partner, Schutter Cayetano Playdon (law firm) 1983–86; mem. Hawaii State Legis. 1975–78, 1979–86; Lieut.-Gov. of Hawaii 1986–94, Gov. Dec. 1994–; numerous awards for public service; Democrat. *Address:* Office of the Governor, State Capitol, Honolulu, Hawaii 96813, U.S.A.

CAYGILL, David Francis, LL.B., M.P.; New Zealand politician and lawyer; b. 15 Nov. 1948, Christchurch; m. Eileen E. Boyd 1974; one s. three d.; ed. Univ. of Canterbury; practised law in Christchurch legal firm 1974–78; mem. Christchurch City Council 1971–80; mem. House of Reps. 1978–; Minister of Trade and Industry, Minister of Nat. Devt., Assoc. Minister of Finance 1984–87, of Health, Trade and Industry 1987–88, Deputy Minister of Finance 1988, Minister of Finance 1988–90, of Revenue 1988–89, Deputy Leader of the Opposition 1994–96; partner Buddle Findlay, Barristers and Solicitors 1996–; mem. Canterbury Regional Planning Authority 1977–80; Labour Party. *Leisure interests:* collecting classical music records, science fiction, following American politics. *Address:* c/o Buddle Findlay, P.O. Box 322, Christchurch, New Zealand.

CAYROL, Jean, L. EN D.; French author; b. 6 June 1910, Bordeaux; s. of Antoine Cayrol and Marie A. Berrogain; m. Jeanne Durand 1971; started literary review, Abeilles et Pensées 1926; later launched Les Cahiers du Fleuve; Librarian, Chamber of Commerce of Bordeaux 1937; served in navy and secret service 1939–42; prisoner-of-war 1942–45; literary adviser to Editions du Seuil 1949; collaborated with Alain Resnais in film Nuit et brouillard 1956 and wrote screenplay for Resnais' Muriel 1963; with Claude Durand produced four short films and Le coup de grâce 1964; mem. Acad. Goncourt; Prix Renaudot for Je vivrai l'amour des autres 1947; Grand Prix littéraire Prince-Pierre-de-Monaco 1968, Prix international du Souvenir 1969, Grand Prix nat. des Lettres 1984; Commdr. des Arts et des Lettres; Officier, Légion d'honneur; Croix de Guerre. *Publications:* poetic works: Ce n'est pas la mer 1935, Les Poèmes du pasteur Grimm 1936, Le Hollandais volant 1936, Les phénomènes célestes 1939, L'Age d'or 1939, Miroir de la Rédemption 1944, Poèmes de la nuit et du brouillard 1946, Passe-temps de l'homme et des oiseaux 1947, La vie répond 1948, Le charnier natal 1950, Les mots sont aussi des demeures 1952, Pour tous les temps 1955, Poésie-Journal I 1969, II 1977, III 1980, Poèmes clefs 1985, De jour en jour 1988; novels: Je vivrai l'amour des autres, La Noire 1949, Le feu qui prend 1950, Le vent de la mémoire 1952, L'espace d'une nuit 1954, Le déménagement 1956, Les corps étrangers 1959, Le froid du soleil 1963, Midi-minuit 1966, Je l'entends encore 1968, Histoire d'une prairie 1970, N'oubliez pas que nous nous aimons 1971, Histoire d'un désert 1972, Histoire de la mer 1973, Kakemono Hôtel 1974, Histoire de la fôret 1975, Histoire d'une maison 1976, L'homme dans le rétroviseur 1981, Un mot d'auteur 1983, Des Nuits Plus Blanches que Nature 1986, A Voix Haute 1990, De Vive Voix 1991, A Pleine Voix 1992, D'une voix celeste 1994, Alerte aux ombres 1997, Nuit et brouillard 1997; essays, narratives and short stories. *Address:* c/o Editions du Seuil, 27 rue Jacob, 75006 Paris, France.

CAYROL, Roland; French researcher, author and producer; b. 11 Aug. 1941, Rabat, Morocco; two s. two d.; Prof. and Researcher Nat. Foundation of Political Sciences 1968, Research Dir. 1978–; Scientific Adviser Louis Harris France 1977–86; Assoc. Dir. CSA 1986–. *Television productions include:* Portrait d'un Président: François Mitterrand (with A. Gaillard) 1985. *Publications:* François Mitterrand 1967, Le Député Français (with J. L. Parodi and C. Ysmal) 1970, La Presse écrite et audiovisuelle 1973, La télévision fait-elle l'élection? (with G. Blumler and G. Thoveron) 1974, La nouvelle communication politique 1986, Les médias 1991, Le grand malentendu, les Français et la politique 1994, Medias et démocratie: la derive 1997. *Address:* Fondation Nationale des Sciences Politiques, 10 rue de la Chaise, 75007 Paris (Office); 67 avenue André Morizet, 92100 Boulogne-Billancourt, France (Office). *Telephone:* (1) 41 86 22 00 (Office). *Fax:* (1) 41 86 22 07.

CAYZER, Baron (Life Peer), cr. 1982; **(William) Nicholas Cayzer,** Bt.; British shipowner; b. 21 Jan. 1910, Scotland; s. of the late Sir Augustus Cayzer, 1st Bt. and the late Ina Frances Stancomb; m. Elizabeth Catherine Williams 1935 (died 1995); two d.; ed. Eton and Corpus Christi Coll., Cambridge; joined Clan Line Steamers Ltd. 1931; Chair. Liverpool Steamship Owners Asscn. 1944–45; Chair. Gen. Council of British Shipping 1959; Pres. Chamber of Shipping of the U.K. 1959, Chair. British Liner Cttee. 1960–63; Mem. Ministry of Transport Shipping Advisory Panel 1962–64; Pres. Inst. of Marine Engineers 1963; Prime Warden of the Worshipful Co. of Shipwrights 1969–70; Chair. British and Commonwealth Shipping Co. PLC (later British and Commonwealth Holdings) 1958–87, Life Pres. 1987–, Union-Castle Mail Steamship Co. Ltd. 1956–87, Clan Line Steamers Ltd., Cayzer Irvine and Co. Ltd., Caledonia Investments PLC 1958–94 (now Pres. and Dir.), Scottish Lion Insurance Co. Ltd., Air Holdings Ltd. 1962–87, Air U.K. and various other cos. *Leisure interests:* gardening, golf. *Address:* The Grove, Walsham-le-Willows 263, Suffolk, IP31 3AD; 95J Eaton Square, London, SW1W 9AQ, England. *Telephone:* 0171-235 5551.

CAZALET, Sir Peter (Grenville), Kt, M.A.; British business executive; b. 26 Feb. 1929, Weymouth; s. of Vice-Admiral Sir Peter Cazalet, K.B.E., C.B., D.S.O., D.S.C., and Lady Cazalet; ed. Uppingham School, and Univ. of Cambridge; m. Jane Jennifer Rew 1957; three s.; Gen. Man. BP Tanker Co. Ltd. 1968–70, Regional Co-ordinator, Australasia and Far East, BP Trading

Ltd. 1970–72, Pres. BP North America Inc. 1972–75, Dir. BP Trading Ltd. 1975–81, Chair. BP Oil Int. Ltd. 1981–89, Man. Dir. BP 1981–89, Deputy Chair. 1986–89; Chair. APV PLC 1989–96; Chair. Armed Forces Pay Review Body 1989–93; mem. Top Salaries Review Body 1989–94; mem. Lloyds Register of Shipping Bd. 1981–86 and Gen. Cttee. 1981–; Deputy Chair. (non-exec.) GKN PLC 1989–96; Dir. Standard Oil Co., Cleveland, Ohio 1973–76, Peninsular & Oriental Steam Navigation Co. Ltd. 1980–99, De La Rue Co. PLC 1983–95, Energy Capital Investment Co. 1995–98, Seascope Shipping Holdings PLC 1997–; Chair. Hakluyt & Co. 1998–; Vice-Pres. Middle East Asscn. 1982–, China–Britain Trade Group 1993–96 (Pres. 1996–98); Trustee Wellcome Trust 1989–92, Uppingham School 1976–95; Gov. Wellcome Trust Ltd. 1992–96; Hon. Sec. King George's Fund for Sailors; mem. Liveryman, Tallow Chandlers' Co. (Master 1991–92), Shipwrights' Co. *Leisure interests:* golf, theatre, fishing. *Address:* c/o 22 Hill Street, London, W1X 7FU, England. *Telephone:* 0171-496 4423.

CAZENEUVE, Jean, D. ÈS L.; French academic; b. 1915, Ussel; s. of Charles Cazeneuve and Yvonne Renoul; m. Germaine Aladane de Paraize 1963; one s. two d.; ed. Ecole normale supérieure and Harvard Univ.; Prof. of Sociology, Paris-Sorbonne 1966–84, Prof. Emer. 1984–; Pres. and Dir.-Gen. TF1 1974–78, Hon. Pres. 1978–; Amb. to the Council of Europe 1978–80; Vice-Pres. Haut Comité de la langue française 1980–81; mem. Acad. des Sciences morales et politiques 1973–; Dr. h.c. (Univ. of Brussels); Commdr. Légion d'honneur, Commdr. Ordre de Léopold. *Publications include:* Les Dieux dansent à Cibola 1957, Bonheur et civilisation 1966, Les pouvoirs de la télévision 1970, Sociologie du rite 1971, Dix grandes notions de la sociologie 1976, La raison d'être 1981, Le mot pour rire 1989, Les hasards d'une vie 1990, Et si plus rien n'était sacré 1991, La télévision en 7 procès 1992, Du calembour au mot d'esprit 1996. *Leisure interest:* tennis. *Address:* 25 *bis* boulevard Lannes, 75116 Paris; 43 Avenue Maréchal Joffre, 14390 Cabourg, France. *Telephone:* 40.72.64.28.

CAZENOVE, Christopher de Lerisson; British actor; b. 17 Dec. 1943, Winchester; s. of Brig. Arnold Cazenove and Elizabeth L. (née Gurney) Cazenove; m. Angharad M. Rees 1974 (divorced 1993); two s.; ed. Dragon School, Oxford, and Eton Coll.; trained as actor at Bristol Old Vic Theatre School; London stage appearances in The Lionel Touch, My Darling Daisy, The Winslow Boy, Joking Apart, In Praise of Rattigan, The Life and Poetry of T. S. Eliot, The Sound of Music, An Ideal Husband; New York appearance in play Goodbye Fidel; television appearances include The Regiment (two series), The Duchess of Duke Street (two series), Jennie: Lady Randolph Churchill, The Riverman, Jenny's War, Dynasty, Hammer's House of Mystery, Lace, Windmills of the Gods, Shades of Love, Souvenir, The Lady and the Highwayman, Tears in the Rain, Ticket to Ride (A Fine Romance), To be the Best. *Films:* Zulu Dawn, East of Elephant Rock, Eye of the Needle, Heat and Dust, Until September, Mata Hari, The Fantasist, Souvenir, Hold My Hand I'm Dying, Three Men and a Little Lady, Aces: Iron Eagle III, The Proprietor, Shadow Run. *Address:* c/o Peters, Fraser & Dunlop, The Chambers, Chelsea Harbour, Lots Road, London, SW10 0XF, England. *Telephone:* 0171-344 1010.

CEBRIÁN ECHARRI, Juan Luis; Spanish writer and journalist; b. 30 Oct. 1944, Madrid; s. of Vicente Cebrián and Carmen Echarri; m. 1st María Gema Torallas 1966 (divorced); two s. two d.; m. 2nd Teresa Aranda 1988; one s. one d.; ed. Univ. of Madrid; founder-mem. of magazine Cuadernos para el Diálogo, Madrid 1963; Sr. Ed. newspapers Pueblo, Madrid 1962–67, Informaciones, Madrid 1967–69; Deputy Ed.-in-Chief, Informaciones 1969–74, 1974–76; Dir. News Programming, Spanish TV 1974; Ed.-in-Chief newspaper El País, Madrid 1976–88; C.E.O. PRISA 1988–, Canal Plus 1989–, Estructura 1989–; Publr. El País 1988–; Vice-Pres. SER 1990–; mem. Int. Press Inst. (Vice-Pres. 1982–86, Chair. 1986–88); Dr. h.c. (Iberoamericana Univ., Santo Domingo) 1988; Control Prize for Outstanding Newspaper Ed. 1976, 1977, 1978, 1979; Víctor de la Serna Prize for Journalism, Press Asscn. Fed. 1977; Outstanding Ed. of the Year (World Press Review, New York) 1980, Spanish Nat. Journalism Prize 1983; Freedom of Expression Medal, F. D. Roosevelt Four Freedoms Foundation 1986; Medal of Honour, Univ. of Miss. 1986; Trento Int. Prize for Journalism and Communication 1987; Gold Medal, Spanish Inst. New York 1988. *Publications:* La prensa y la Calle 1980, La España que Bosteza 1980, ¿Qué pasa en el mundo? 1981, Crónicas de mi país 1985, El Tamaño del elefante 1987, Red Doll 1987, La isla del viento 1990, El siglo de las sombras 1994. *Leisure interests:* music, literature. *Address:* Gran Vía 32-6a, 28013 Madrid, Spain.

CEBUC, Alexandru, PH.D.; Romanian art historian and critic; b. 5 April 1932, Păuşeşti-Măglabi; s. of Ion and Ana Cebuc; m. Florica Turcu 1958; one d.; ed. Univ. of Bucharest; Head of Dept., Museum of History of City of Bucharest 1957–69; Vice-Pres. Culture Cttee. of City of Bucharest 1969–77; Dir. Art Museum of Romania 1977–90; Gen. Man. Publishing and Printing House ARC 2000 1990–; Order of Cultural Merit, Knight of Italian Repub. *Publications:* The History of the City of Bucharest 1966, The History of Passenger Transportation 1967, Historical and Art Monuments of the City of Bucharest 1968, The Nat. Gallery 1983, Ion Irimescu (monograph) 1983, Etienne Hadju (monograph) 1984, Nicolae Grigorescu (monograph) 1985, H. H. Catargi (monograph) 1987, I. Ianchelevici (monograph) 1989, I. Irimescu—Album Drawings 1994, Encyclopaedia of Plastic Artists in Romania (Vol. I) 1994. *Leisure interest:* art. *Address:* Str. Spatarului No. 36, ET. II AP. 5, Bucharest, Romania. *Telephone:* 2118617.

CECCATO, Aldo; Italian director of music and conductor; b. 18 Feb. 1934, Milan; m. Eliana de Sabata; two s.; ed. Milan Conservatory, Hochschule für Musik Berlin; Musical Dir. Detroit Symphony 1973–77, Hamburg Philharmonic 1974–82, Norddeutsche Radio Orchestra 1985–, Bergen Symphony 1985–; guest conductor to all maj. symphony orchestras and opera houses in four continents; Hon. D. Mus. (Eastern Michigan Univ.). *Leisure interests:* tennis, stamps, books. *Address:* Chaunt da Crusch, 7524 Zuoz, Switzerland.

CECH, Thomas Robert, PH.D.; American professor of chemistry and biochemistry; b. 8 Dec. 1947, Chicago; s. of Robert Franklin Cech and Annette Marie (née Cerveny) Cech; m. Carol Lynn Martinson 1970; two d.; ed. Grinnell Coll., Univ. of Calif., Berkeley; Postdoctoral Fellow, Dept. of Biology, M.I.T., Cambridge, Mass. 1975–77; Asst. Prof., then Assoc. Prof. of Chem., Univ. of Colo., Boulder 1978–83, Prof. of Chem. and Biochem., and of Molecular, Cellular and Devt. Biology 1983–, Distinguished Prof. 1990–; Research Prof., American Cancer Soc. 1987–; investigator Howard Hughes Medical Inst. 1988–; Deputy Ed. Science; mem. Editorial Bd. Genes and Devt.; Nat. Science Foundation Fellow 1970–75; Public Health Service Research Fellow, Nat. Cancer Inst. 1975–77; Guggenheim Fellow 1985–86; mem. American Acad. of Arts and Sciences, N.A.S.; Medal of American Inst. of Chemists 1970, Research Career Devt. Award, Nat. Cancer Inst. 1980–85, Young Scientist Award, Passano Foundation 1984, Harrison Howe Award 1984, Pfizer Award 1985, U.S. Steel Award 1987, V.D. Mattia Award 1987, Heineken Prize 1988, Gairdner Foundation Award 1988, Lasker Award 1988, Warren Triennial Prize 1989, Nobel Prize for Chem. 1989, Rosenstiel Award 1989, Nat. Medal of Science 1995. *Leisure interest:* skiing. *Address:* University of Colorado, Department of Chemistry and Biochemistry, Boulder, CO 80309-0215, U.S.A. *Telephone:* (303) 492-8606. *Fax:* (303) 492-6194.

CEDAIN ZHOIMA; Chinese singer; b. 1 Aug. 1937, Xigaze, Xizang; ed. Shanghai Music Coll.; joined CCP 1961; performed in U.S.S.R. 1963; in political disgrace during Proletarian Cultural Revolution 1966–76; rehabilitated 1977; mem. Standing Cttee. 5th NPC 1978–83; Vice-Chair. 6th CPPCC Tibet Regional Cttee. 1987–; Vice-Chair. Chinese Musicians Asscn. 1979–; mem. Standing Cttee. 6th NPC 1983–88, 7th CPPCC 1988–; Exec. Vice-Chair. China Fed. of Literary and Art Circles 1988–. *Address:* Chinese Musician's Association, Beijing, People's Republic of China.

CEFIS, Eugenio; Italian business executive; b. 21 July 1921, Cividale; m. 1943; ed. Univ. of Milan; commissioned in Sardinian Grenadiers; Vice-Pres. Ente Nazionale Idrocarburi (ENI) until 1967, Pres. 1967–71; Pres. Montedison 1971–77, Chair. Montedison Int. Holdings 1977–80; Dir. Snia Viscosa 1971–.

CELA, Camilo José; Spanish writer; b. 11 May 1916; m. 2nd Marina Castaño 1991; one s. from previous m.; ed. Univ. de Madrid; fmr. Dir. and Publr. of journal Papeles de Son Armadans; mem. Real Acad. Española 1957; Premio de la crítica 1955, Nobel Prize for Literature 1989, Planeta Prize 1994. *Publications include:* La Familia de Pascual Duarte (novel) 1942, Pabellón de reposo 1943–57, Nuevas andanzas y desventuras de Lazarillo de Tormes 1944–55, Pisando la dudosa luz del día (poems) 1945, Mesa revuelta 1945 and 1957, Viaje a la Alcarria 1948, La colmena 1951, Del Miño al Bidasoa 1952, Mrs. Caldwell habla con su hijo 1953, La Catira 1955, Judíos, moros y cristianos 1956, El molino de viento (short stories) 1956, Nuevo retablo de don Cristobita 1957, Viaje al Pirineo de Lérida 1965, Diccionario Secreto I 1968, II 1971, San Camilo 1936 1969, María Sabina 1970, A vueltas con España (essays) 1973, Oficio de tinieblas 1973, Enciclopedia del Erotismo 1976–77, Vuelta de hoja 1981, Mazurca para dos muertos 1983, Cristo versus Arizona 1988, Cachondeos, escarceos y otros meneos 1991 (essays), La Sima de las penúltimas inocencias 1993 (short stories), Reloj de Sangre 1989 (poetry), Desde el Palomar de Hita 1991, El Camaleón Soltero 1992, El huero del juicio 1993, A bote pronto 1994 (all non-fiction), Memorias, entendimientos y voluntades 1993 (memoirs). *Address:* c/o Agencia Literaria Carmen Balcells, Diagonal 580, 08021 Barcelona, Spain.

CELESTE, Richard F., PH.B.; American state governor; b. 11 Nov. 1937, Cleveland, Ohio; s. of Frank Celeste; m. Dagmar Braun 1962; three s. three d.; ed. Yale Univ. and Oxford Univ.; Staff Liaison Officer, Peace Corps 1963; Special Asst. to U.S. Amb. to India 1963–67; mem. Ohio House of Reps. 1970–74, Majority Whip 1972–74; Lieut.-Gov. of Ohio 1975–79, Gov. 1983–91; Chair. Midwestern Govs.' Conf. 1987–88; Great Lakes Govs.' Asscn. 1987–89; Democrat. *Address:* c/o State Capitol, Columbus, OH 43215, U.S.A.

CELLUCCI, Argeo Paul, J.D.; American politician and lawyer; b. 24 April 1948, Marlboro, Mass.; s. of Argeo R. Cellucci and Priscilla Rose Cellucci; m. Janet Garnett 1971; two d.; ed. Boston Coll.; attorney, Kittredge, Cellucci and Moreira, Hudson, Mass. 1973–90; mem. Charter Comm. Hudson 1970–71, Selectman 1971–77; State Rep. Third Middx. Dist., Mass. 1977–84; State Senator Middx. and Worcs. Dists., Mass. 1985–90; Lieut.-Gov. of Massachusetts 1991–97, Acting Gov. 1997–98, Gov. 1998–; Capt., U.S.A.R.; mem. American Bar Asscn., Mass. Bar Asscn.; Republican. *Address:* Office of the Governor, Executive Office, State House, Boston, MA 02133, U.S.A.

CEM, İsmail; Turkish politician; fmrly. journalist; fmrly. Dir. Turkish TV network; Minister of Foreign Affairs June 1997–; mem. Democratic Left Party. *Leisure interest:* photography. *Address:* Dişişleri Bakanlığı, Yenu Hizmet Binası, 06520 Balgat, Ankara, Turkey. *Telephone:* 312-2871665. *Fax:* 312-2873689.

CENAC, Winston Francis, LL.B., Q.C.; Saint Lucia politician and lawyer; b. 14 Sept. 1925, St. Lucia; s. of Frank and Leanese (née King) Cenac; m. Flora Marie Cenac 1952; ed. St. Mary's Coll. and Univ. of London; worked as Chief Clerk in District Court, then as Deputy Registrar, Supreme Court; called to the Bar Lincoln's Inn, London 1957; Registrar, Supreme Court, St. Lucia 1957; Acting Magistrate, Southern District, St. Lucia 1958; Chief Registrar of Supreme Court of Windward and Leeward Islands 1959; Attorney-Gen. of St. Lucia 1962, of St. Vincent 1964, of Grenada 1966; del. Constitutional Conf., Little Eight Constitution, London 1962; Dir. of Public Prosecutions, Grenada 1967; pvt. practice in St. Lucia 1969; Puisne Judge of St. Vincent 1971, of Antigua 1971, of St. Kitts, Nevis and Virgin Islands 1972; returned to pvt. practice, St. Lucia 1973; Senator of St. Lucia Legis. 1978; mem. House of Ass. for Soufrière 1979–; Attorney-Gen. of Saint Lucia 1979–80, Prime Minister 1981–82; Pres. St. Lucia Bar Asscn. 1989; Chair. Org. of Eastern Caribbean States, Bar Asscn. 1989, Bd. of Appeal of Income Tax Commrs. 1989; Life mem. Commonwealth Parl. Asscn. *Publication:* Coutume de Paris to 1988: The Evolution of Land Law in Saint Lucia. *Leisure interests:* reading, gardening, music. *Address:* 7 High Street, Box 629, Castries, Saint Lucia. *Telephones:* 27919; 23891. *Fax:* 27919.

ČEPANIS, Alfreds; Latvian politician; b. 3 Aug. 1943, Kalsnava, Madona Region; m. Ilma Čepane; one d.; ed. Jaungolbene School of Agric., Higher CP School in Moscow by correspondence; Comsomol functionary 1968–74; Deputy Chair., Chair. Ventspils District Exec. Cttee. 1975–79; Sec. Preili regional cttee. Latvian CP 1979–84; First Sec. Liepaja regional CP cttee. 1983–88; Deputy Chair. Council of Ministers 1989–90; mem. Supreme Soviet of Latvia 1990–93; mem. Saeima (Parl.), Deputy Speaker 1993–95; mem. faction Demikratiska Partija Samnieks 1995, Speaker 1996–98. *Leisure interests:* hunting, literature, theatre. *Address:* Saeima, Jēkaba iela 11, 226811 Riga, Latvia. *Telephone:* 708-71-11.

CEREZO ARÉVALO, Mario Vinicio; Guatemalan politician; b. 26 Dec. 1942; s. of Marco Vinicio Cerezo; m. Raquel Blandón 1965; four c.; ed. Univ. of San Carlos; mem. Christian Democratic Party; Pres. of Guatemala 1986–91. *Address:* c/o Partido Democracia Cristiana Guatamalteca, Avda Elena 20-66, Zona 3, Guatemala City, Guatemala.

ČERNÁK, Lúdovít, DIP.TECH.; Slovak politician and industrialist; b. 12 Oct. 1951, Hliník nad Hronom; m.; three c.; ed. Univ. of Tech., Bratislava; man. training in U.K. 1990; worked for SNP Works, Žiar nad Hronom 1975–92; Minister of Economy –1993; Vice-Chair. Nat. Council 1993–94; now mem. Parl. of Slovakia; Minister of Economy 1998–; Vice-Chair. Democratic Union; mem. Int. Cttee. for Econ. Reform and Co-operation. *Leisure interests:* family, detective novels. *Address:* Democratic Union, Medená 10, 81102 Bratislava; Úrad vlády SR, Nám. Slobody 1, 813 70 Bratislava, Slovakia. *Telephone:* (7) 35 95 111 (Democratic Union); (7) 534 1111 (Ministry). *Fax:* (7) 391 647.

CÉSAIRE, Aimé Fernand, L. ÈS L.; French politician, poet and dramatist; b. 25 June 1913, Basse-Pointe, Martinique; s. of Fernand and Marie (Hermine) Césaire; m. Suzanne Roussi 1937; four s. two d.; ed. Fort-de-France (Martinique) and Lycée Louis-le-Grand (Paris), Ecole Normale Supérieure and the Sorbonne; teaching career 1940–45; mem. Constituent Assemblies 1945 and 1946; Deputy for Martinique 1946–93; Pres. Parti Progressiste Martiniquais; Mayor of Fort-de-France 1945–83, re-elected 1983 but result declared invalid by Tribunal, 1984–; Pres. Conseil régional, Martinique 1983–86; Pres. Soc. of African Culture, Paris; Grand Prize for Verse 1982. *Publications:* Verse: Cahier d'un retour au pays natal, Les armes miraculeuses, Et les chiens se taisaient, Soleil cou coupé, Corps perdu, Cadastre, Ferrements, Moi, laminaire 1982, La Poésie: Oeuvres complètes et inédits 1994; Essays: Discours sur le colonialisme; Theatre: La tragédie du roi Christophe, Une saison au Congo, Une tempête. *Address:* La Mairie, boulevard de général de Gaulle, 97200 Fort-de-France, Martinique, West Indies.

ÇETÎN, Hikmet; Turkish politician; b. 1937, Diyarbakir; m.; two c.; ed. Ankara Univ. Political Sciences Faculty, Williams Coll., U.S.A.; Sec.-Gen. Social Democratic Populist Party (SHP) (merged to form Republican People's Party), Chair. 1995; deputy from Gaziantep; fmr. Deputy Prime Minister and State Minister; Minister of Foreign Affairs 1991–95; Deputy Prime Minister and Minister of State 1995–96. *Address:* c/o Deputy Prime Minister's Office, Bakanlıkar, Ankara, Turkey.

CEWANG JIGMEI; Chinese administrator; b. 15 Sept. 1945, Xizang (Tibet); m. Zhang Tingfang 1972; two s.; ed. Beijing Normal Univ.; teacher, Tibet Teachers School, Lhasa 1972; Pres. Tibet Univ., Lhasa 1985–; Vice-Pres. Chinese Educ. Asscn. for Int. Exchange 1985–, China Tibet Education Asscn. *Address:* Tibet University, Lhasa, People's Republic of China. *Telephone:* 24375, 24786.

CHAABANE, Sadok, PH.D.; Tunisian politician and lawyer; b. 23 Feb. 1950, Sfar; s. of Jilani Chaabane; m. Dalenda Nouri 1974; one s. two d.; Prof. of Law, Univ. of Tunis 1973–; Dir. of Studies, Research and Publ. Centre 1975–82; Perm. Sec. of R.C.C. 1988; Sec. of State for Higher Educ. and Scientific Research 1989; Adviser to the President on Political Affairs 1990; Sec. of State for Scientific Research 1991; Prin. Adviser to the Pres. on Human Rights 1991; Minister of Justice 1992–97; Founder mem. Int. Acad. of Constitutional Law, Int. Law Asscn. *Publications:* The Law of International Institutions 1985, Ben Ali and The Way to Pluralism 1995. *Address:* Manan III, Rue 7114, No. 30, Tunis, Tunisia (Home). *Telephone:* 1-889-690 (Home).

CHABAN-DELMAS, Jacques Michel Pierre; French politician; b. 7 March 1915; s. of Pierre Delmas; m. 3rd Micheline Chavelet 1971; two s. two d. (from 1st m.); ed. Lycée Lakanal, Sceaux, Ecole Libre des Sciences Politiques, Paris; served army 1939–40, Brig.-Gen. 1944; nat. mil. del. responsible for co-ordination of mil. planning, Resistance 1944; Insp.-Gen. of Army Nov. 1944; Sec.-Gen. Ministry of Information 1945–46; Radical deputy for Gironde 1946–61; Mayor of Bordeaux 1947–95; leader of Gaullist group (Républicains Sociaux) in Nat. Assembly 1954–58; Minister of Public Works 1954–55; Inspecteur des Finances 1956–57; Minister of Nat. Defence 1957–58; Pres. of Nat. Ass. 1958–69, 1978–81, 1986–88; Pres. Council of the Urban Community of Bordeaux 1967, 1983, 1989–, First Vice-Pres. 1977–; Pres., Dir.-Gen. Société anonyme d'economie mixte communautaire de construction (Saemico) 1970–; Prime Minister 1969–72; Insp.-Gen. des Finances 1973; Pres. Regional Council, Aquitaine 1974–79, 1985–88; Cand. for Pres. of France May 1974; Pres. of Comm. for Regional Econ. Devt. of Aquitaine 1964–69; Pres. European Assembly of Local Authorities 1975, United Towns Org. 1985; Pres. Comité d'action pour l'Europe des Douze 1988–; Hon. Pres. Nat. Assembly 1996–; Commdr., Légion d'honneur; Croix de guerre; Compagnon de la Libération; Hon. LL.D. (Bristol) 1987. *Publications:* L'ardeur 1975, Charles de Gaulle 1980, La Libération 1984, Les Compagnons 1986, la Dame d'Aquitaine 1987, Montaigne 1992, Mémoires pour Demain 1997. *Leisure interests:* tennis, rugby, golf. *Address:* Assemblée nationale, 75355 Paris, France.

CHABROL, Claude; French film director and producer; b. 24 June 1930, Paris; s. of Yves Chabrol and Madeleine Delarbre; m. 1st Agnès Goute; two s.; m. 2nd Colette Dacheville (Stéphane Audran, q.v.); one s.; m. 3rd Aurore Pajot 1983; ed. Paris Univ., Ecole Libre des Sciences Politiques; fmrly. film critic and Public Relations Officer in Paris for 20th-Century Fox; dir. and producer 1958–; Locarno Festival Grand Prix 1958, Berlin Festival Golden Bear 1959. *Films directed include:* Le beau Serge 1957, Les cousins 1958, A double tour 1959, Les bonnes femmes 1959, Les godelureaux 1960, Ophélia 1962, L'oeil du malin 1961, Landru 1962, Les plus belles escroqueries du monde 1963, Le tigre aime la chair fraîche 1964, Le tigre se parfume à la dynamite 1965, Marie-Chantal contre le Docteur Kha 1965, Le scandale 1967, Les biches 1968, La femme infidèle 1968, Que la bête meure 1969, Le boucher 1970, La rupture 1970, Juste avant la nuit 1971, Doctor Popaul 1972, La décade prodigieuse 1972, Les noces rouges 1973, Nada 1973, Une partie de plaisir 1975, Les innocents aux mains sales 1976, Alice ou la dernière fugue 1977, Les liens de sang 1977, Violette Nozière 1978, The Twist, Blood Relations 1979, Le Cheval d'Orgueil 1980, Les fantômes du chapelier 1982, Cop au vin 1985, Inspecteur Lavardin 1986, Masques 1987, Une Affaire des Femmes 1988, Story of Women 1989, Dr M 1989, Quiet Days in Clichy 1989, Madame Bovary 1991, Betty 1991, L'Enfer 1993, La Cérémonie, Through the Eyes of Vichy, A Judgement in Stone, Rien ne va Plus 1997. *Publications:* Alfred Hitchcock (with E. Rohmer), les Noces rouges, Et pourtant je tourne. *Address:* c/o V.M.A., 40 rue François 1er, 75008 Paris; 15 Quai Conti, 75006 Paris, France.

CHADIRJI, Rifat Kamil, DIP.ARCH., F.R.I.B.A.; Iraqi architect; b. 6 Dec. 1926, Baghdad; s. of Kamil Chadirji; m. Balkis Sharara 1954; ed. Hammersmith School of Arts and Crafts, London; f. and Sr. Partner and Dir. Iraq Consult 1952–; Section Head, Baghdad Bldg. Dept. Waqaf Org. 1954–57; Dir.-Gen. Housing, Ministry of Planning, Baghdad 1958–59, Head Planning Cttee. Ministry of Housing 1959–63; returned to full-time private practice with Iraq Consult 1963–78; apptd. Counsellor to Mayoralty of Baghdad 1980–82; mem. Iraqi Tourist Bd. 1970–75; Loeb Fellow, Harvard Univ. 1983; *works include:* Council of Ministers Bldg., Baghdad 1975, Cabinet Ministers' Bldg., U.A.E. 1976, Nat. Theatre, Abu Dhabi, U.A.E. 1977, Al-Ain Public Library, U.A.E. 1978; exhbns. at Gulbenkian Hall, Baghdad 1966, Univ. of Khartoum, Sudan 1966, Ministry of Art and Culture, Accra, Ghana 1966, Kwame Nkrumah Univ. of Science and Tech., Ghana 1966, Middle East Tech. Univ., Ankara, Turkey 1966, Athens Tech. Insts., Greece 1966, American Univ. of Beirut, Lebanon 1966, Arab Engs. Conf., Jordan 1966, Amman, Jordan 1966, Hammersmith Coll. of Art 1966, Ain Shamis Univ., Cairo, Egypt 1967, Arab Engs. Conf., Kuwait 1975, Kuwait Engs. Union 1975, Iraqi Cultural Cen., London 1978, Middle East Construction Exhbn., Dubai, U.A.E. 1978, Vienna Tech. Univ., Austria 1978; many awards and prizes incl. First Prize for Council of Ministers Bldg., Baghdad 1975, First Prize New Theatre, Abu Dhabi, U.A.E. 1977, First Prize, Council of Ministers, Abu Dhabi, U.A.E. 1978. *Leisure interests:* photography and travel. *Address:* 28 Troy Court, Kensington High Street, London, W.8, England. *Telephone:* 0171-937 3715.

CHADLI, Col. Bendjedid; Algerian politician and army officer; b. 14 April 1929, Sebaa; six c.; Joined Maquisards (guerrilla forces) in fight for independence against French 1955; mem. General Staff of Col. Boumédienne's army 1961; Commdr. Constantine Mil. Region, East Algeria 1962, of Second Mil. Region (Oran) 1963–79; mem. Revolutionary Council 1965; Acting Chief of Staff 1978–79; Sec.-Gen. National Liberation Front Feb. 1979; President of Algeria, C.-in-C. of the Armed Forces 1979–91; Medal of the Resistance 1984.

CHADLINGTON, Baron (Life Peer) cr. 1996, of Dean in the County of Oxfordshire; **Peter Selwyn Gummer;** M.A.; British business executive; b. 24 Aug. 1942, Bexley; s. of Rev. Canon Selwyn Gummer and of late Sybille Gummer (née Mason); brother of John Selwyn Gummer (q.v.); m. Lucy Rachel Dudley-Hill 1982; one s., three d.; ed. King's School, Rochester,

Selwyn Coll., Cambridge; with Portsmouth & Sunderland Newspaper Group 1964–65, Viyella Int. 1965–66, Hodgkinson & Partners 1966–67, Industrial & Commercial Finance Corpn. (3i Group) 1967–74; Founder, Chair. and Chief Exec. Shandwick PLC 1974–94, Chair. 1994–; Dir. (non-exec.) CIA Group PLC 1989–94, Halifax Bldg. Soc. London Bd. 1990–94, Halifax PLC 1994–; mem. (non-exec.) Nat. Health Service Policy Bd. 1991–95, mem. Arts Council of Great Britain 1991–94, Arts Council of England 1994–96; Chair. Royal Opera House 1996–97; Chair. Understanding Industry 1991–96, Marketing Group of G.B. 1993–95, Nat. Lottery Advisory Bd. for the Arts and Film 1994–96; Inst. of Public Relations Pres.'s Medal 1988. *Publications:* articles and booklets on public relations and marketing. *Leisure interests:* opera, rugby, cricket. *Address:* International Public Relations Ltd., 61 Grosvenor Street, London, W1X 9DA, England. *Telephone:* 0171-408 2232. *Fax:* 0171-493 3048.

CHADWICK, Henry, K.B.E., F.B.A., D.D., MUS.B.; British professor of divinity; b. 23 June 1920, Bromley, Kent; s. of John Chadwick and Edith M. Chadwick; m. Margaret E. Brownrigg 1945; three d.; ed. Eton Coll. and Magdalene Coll. Cambridge; Fellow, Queens' Coll. Cambridge 1946–58, Hon. Fellow 1958–; Regius Prof. of Divinity, Univ. of Oxford 1959–69, Dean of Christ Church 1969–79; Regius Prof. of Divinity, Univ. of Cambridge 1979–83, Prof. Emer. 1983–, Fellow, Magdalene Coll. 1979–86; Master Peterhouse, Cambridge 1987–93, Hon. Fellow 1993; Del. Oxford Univ. Press 1960–79; hon. degrees from Glasgow, Leeds, Manchester, Surrey, Uppsala, Yale, Harvard, Jena and Chicago; Pour le mérite 1993. *Publications:* Origen Contra Celsum 1953, Early Christian Thought and the Classical Tradition 1966, The Early Church 1967, Priscillian of Avila 1976, Boethius 1981, History and Thought of the Early Church 1982, Augustine 1986, Heresy and Orthodoxy in the Early Church 1991, Augustine's Confessions 1991, Tradition and Exploration 1994. *Leisure interest:* music. *Address:* 46 St. John Street, Oxford, OX1 2LH, England. *Telephone:* (01865) 512814.

CHADWICK, Lynn Russell, C.B.E.; British sculptor; b. 24 Nov. 1914; s. of the late Verner Russell Chadwick and of Marjorie Brown (née Lynn) Chadwick; m. 1st Charlotte Ann Secord 1942; one s.; m. 2nd Frances Mary Jamieson (died 1964); two d.; m. 3rd Eva Reiner 1965; one s.; ed. Merchant Taylors School; works shown in London, New York, Paris, Brussels (Exposition 1958) and Venice, where he won the Int. Sculpture Prize at the Biennale 1956; 1st Prize Padua Int. Competition 1959; Hors Concours, Bienal São Paulo 1961; Premio Indebile El Circulo de Bellas Artes de Lerida, Spain 1970; mem. Acad. di San Luca, Rome, Académie Royaux de Belgique 1995; Hon. Fellow Cheltenham & Gloucester Coll. of Higher Educ. 1995; Commdr. des Arts et Lettres 1993, Order of Andres Bello (First Class) Venezuela 1988. *Address:* Lypiatt Park, Stroud, Glos., GL6 7LL, England. *Telephone:* (01452) 770 210.

CHADWICK, Michael J., M.A., PH.D.; British environmental scientist; b. 13 Sept. 1934, Leicester; s. of John Chadwick and Hilda Corman; m. Josephine Worrall 1958; one s. two d.; ed. Godalming Co. Grammar School and Univ. Coll. of N. Wales, Bangor; lecturer, Dept. of Botany, Univ. of Khartoum 1959–62; univ. demonstrator, School of Agric., Univ. of Cambridge 1962–66; lecturer, Prof. Dept. of Biology, Univ. of York 1966–91; Dir. Stockholm Environment Inst., Stockholm 1991–96; Dir. LEAD-Europe, Geneva 1996–; fmr. Sec. British Ecological Soc. *Publications:* Restoration of Land (with A. D. Bradshaw) 1980, The Relative Sensitivity of Ecosystems in Europe to Acidic Depositions (with J. C. I. Kuylenstierna) 1990. *Leisure interests:* music, gardening, travel. *Address:* LEAD-Europe, Rue de Varembé 3, C.P. 8, CH-1211 Geneva 20, Switzerland. *Telephone:* (22) 7481433. *Fax:* (22) 7481439.

CHADWICK, Owen, O.M., K.B.E., F.B.A.; British historian; b. 20 May 1916, Bromley, Kent; s. of John and Edith (née Horrocks) Chadwick; m. Ruth Hallward 1949; two s. two d.; ed. St. John's Coll., Cambridge; Fellow, Trinity Hall, Cambridge 1947–56; Master of Selwyn Coll., Cambridge 1956–83, Fellow 1983–; Dixie Prof. of Ecclesiastical History, Cambridge Univ. 1958–68, Regius Prof. of Modern History 1968–83; Vice-Chancellor of Cambridge Univ. 1969–71; Pres. British Acad. 1981–85; Chancellor Univ. of E. Anglia 1985–94; Chair. of Trustees, Nat. Portrait Gallery 1988–94; Hon. mem. American Acad. of Arts and Sciences; Wolfson Literary Award 1981; Hon. D.D. (St. Andrews) 1960, (Oxford) 1973, (Wales) 1993, Hon. D.Litt. (Kent) 1970, (Columbia Univ.) 1977, (East Anglia) 1977, (Bristol) 1977, (London) 1983, (Leeds) 1986, (Cambridge) 1987, Hon. LL.D. (Aberdeen) 1986. *Publications:* From Bossuet to Newman 1957, The Victorian Church (2 vols.) 1966–70, John Cassian (2nd edn.) 1968, The Reformation (20th edn.) 1986, The Secularization of the European Mind 1976, The Popes and European Revolution 1981, Britain and the Vatican during the Second World War 1987, Michael Ramsey: A life 1990, The Christian Church in the Cold War 1992, A History of Christianity 1995, A History of the Popes 1830–1914 1998; numerous articles and reviews in learned journals. *Leisure interests:* music and gardening. *Address:* 67 Grantchester Street, Cambridge, CB3 9HZ, England.

CHADWICK, Peter, PH.D., SC.D., F.R.S.; British scientist; b. 23 March 1931; s. of Jack Chadwick and Marjorie (Castle) Chadwick; m. Sheila G. Salter 1956; two d.; ed. Huddersfield Coll., Univ. of Manchester and Pembroke Coll. Cambridge; Scientific Officer, then Sr. Scientific Officer, Atomic Weapons Research Establishment, Aldermaston 1955–59; Lecturer, then Sr. Lecturer in Applied Math. Univ. of Sheffield 1959–65; Prof. of Math. Univ. of E. Anglia 1965–91, Emer. Prof. 1991–, Dean, School of Math. and Physics 1979–82; Visiting Prof. Univ. of Queensland 1972; Leverhulme Emer. Fellow 1991–93; mem. Exec. Cttee. Int. Soc. for Interaction of Mechanics and Math. 1983–88, British Nat. Cttee. for Theoretical and Applied Mechanics 1969–75, 1985–89; Hon. mem. British Soc. of Rheology 1991–; Hon. D.Sc. (Glasgow) 1991. *Publications:* Continuum Mechanics 1976, 1999; articles in books and learned journals. *Leisure interests:* walking, music. *Address:* 8 Stratford Crescent, Cringleford, Norwich, NR4 7SF, England. *Telephone:* (01603) 451655.

CHAFEE, John H., B.A., LL.B.; American politician and lawyer; b. 22 Oct. 1922, Providence, R.I.; s. of John Sharpe and Janet Hunter Chafee; m. Virginia Coates, 1950; four s. one d.; ed. Deerfield Acad., Yale Univ., and Harvard Law School; U.S. Marine Corps 1942–46, 1951–52; admitted to Rhode Island Bar 1951; State Rep. R.I. House 1956–62; Gov. of Rhode Island 1963–69, Senator 1977–2000; Sec. of the Navy 1969–72; Hon. LL.D. (Brown Univ., Providence Coll., Univ. of R.I.); Visiting Chubb Fellow, Yale Univ. 1965; Chair. Compact for Educ. 1965, Republican Govs'. Asscn. 1967–68, Republican Conf. 1985; Trustee, Deerfield Acad. 1970–79, Yale Univ. 1972–78; Legislator of the Year Nat. League of Women Voters 1992; inducted into Nat. Wrestling Hall of Fame 1993; Nat. Environment Quality Award, Nat. Resources Council of America 1995; Republican. *Leisure interests:* squash, tennis, sailing, skiing. *Address:* 505 Dirksen Senate Office Bldg., Washington, DC 20510, U.S.A.

CHAGAS, Carlos, M.D., SC.D.; Brazilian biophysicist; b. 12 Sept. 1910; m. Anna L. de Mello Franco Chagas 1936; four d.; ed. Colégio Rezende, Univ. do Brasil and Univ. de Paris; began career as Asst. at Inst. Oswaldo Cruz and Medical School, Univ. do Brasil; Prof. Univ. do Brasil Medical School 1937, Dir. Inst. of Biophysics 1946–64; mem. Brazilian Nat. Research Council 1950–55, UN Scientific Cttee. 1956–, WHO Scientific Advisory Cttee. 1959–61, Pan American Health Org. Scientific Advisory Cttee. 1962–; Chair. Exec. Cttee. Int. Brain Research Org.; Perm. Del. of Brazil to UNESCO; Adviser Puerto Rico Atomic Energy Comm.; mem. Brazilian Acads. of Science, Medicine and Pharmacy, Pontifical Acad. of Sciences, Assoc. Mem. Acad. de Médecine (Paris), Soc. de Biologie (Paris), London Physiological Soc.; fmr. Vice-Pres. ICSU; Dr. h.c. (Paris, Coimbra, Mexico, Recife Univs.); Premio Moinho Santista 1960; Commdr. Order of Christ (Portugal), of Merit (Italy); Officer, Légion d'honneur; Ordre de la Santé publique (France), Order of Polar Star (Sweden), Order of Rio Branco (Brazil) 1990. *Publications include:* Homems e Cousas de Ciéncia (essays) and a large number of medical and scientific papers 1936–. *Address:* 38 Francisco Otaviano, 22080-040 Rio de Janeiro, RJ, Brazil. *Telephone:* 590-5411 (Office); 227-5009 (Home). *Fax:* 280-8193 (Office).

CHAGULA, Wilbert K., M.B., CH.B., M.A.; Tanzanian public servant and administrator; b. 3 Feb. 1926, Shinyanga, Tanganyika; s. of Kiyenze Chagula; ed. Tabora Govt. School, Makerere Univ. Coll., Uganda, King's Coll., Cambridge Univ., Univ. of W. Indies, Jamaica, Yale Univ., U.S.A.; Asst. Medical Officer, Tanganyika 1952; Asst. in Dept. of Anatomy, Asst. Lecturer, Lecturer in Anatomy, Makerere Univ. Coll. 1953–61; Rockefeller Foundation Fellow in Histochemistry, Jamaica and Yale Univs. 1961–63; Registrar and Vice-Prin., Univ. Coll., Dar es Salaam 1963–65, Prin. 1965–70; Minister for Water Devt. and Power 1970–72, for Econ. Affairs and Devt. Planning 1972–75, of Water Energy and Minerals 1975–77; Minister for Finance and Admin. (East African Community) 1977–78; Amb. to the UN, Geneva, 1978–86, to the UN, New York, 1986–91; Chair. Tanzania Nat. Scientific Research Council 1972; mem. UN Advisory Cttee. for the Application of Science and Tech. to Devt. 1971– (Chair. sessions 1975–78), WHO Advisory Cttee. on Medical Research and WHO Expert Advisory Panel on Public Health Admin. 1976–77, UN Univ. Council 1977, Bd. of Trustees Int. Fed. of Science 1975, Editorial Bd. of Mazingira 1977–, E. African Acad. (Pres. 1963–, Fellow 1971), Medical Asscn. of Tanzania, Econ. Soc. of Tanzania, The Third World Forum, Tanganyika African Nat. Union Nat. Exec. Cttee. 1969–75, Tanganyika Soc. of African Culture, Tanzania Soc.; Adviser Int. Fed. of Insts. of Advanced Studies. *Publications:* books and articles on education and health. *Leisure interests:* reading, writing. *Address:* c/o Ministry of Foreign Affairs, P.O. Box 9000, Dar es Salaam, Tanzania.

CHAHINE, Youssef; Egyptian film director; b. 25 Jan. 1926, Alexandria; films include: Papa Amine 1950, Cairo Station 1953, Struggle in the Valley 1953, Saladin 1963, The Land 1969, The Choice 1970, The Sparrow 1973, Return of the Prodigal Son 1976, Alexandria . . . Why? 1978, An Egyptian Story 1982, Adieu Bonaparte 1984, Alexandria Again and Always 1990; 50th Anniversary Prize, Cannes Film Festival 1997.

CHAI SONGYUE; Chinese politician; b. Nov. 1941, Putuo Co., Zhejiang Prov.; joined CCP 1961; Vice-Gov., mem. CCP Zhejiang Provincial Cttee., Dir. Zhejiang Provincial Planning Comm. 1988; alt. mem. 14th CCP Cen. Cttee. 1992; Vice-Gov. Zhejiang Prov. 1993, Gov. 1997–; mem. 15th CCP Cen. Cttee. 1997–. *Address:* Office of the Governor, Zhejiang Provincial Government, Hangzhou City, Zhejiang Province, People's Republic of China.

CHAI ZEMIN; Chinese diplomatist; b. 1916, Shanxi Prov.; m. Li Youfeng 1948; two s. three d.; Commissar and Commdr., mil. sub-area until 1949; Sec. CCP Cttee., Beijing Suburban Work Cttee. 1949; Deputy Sec.-Gen. Municipal People's Govt., Beijing 1950, mem. Financial and Econ. Cttee. 1950; Pres. Suburban Branch, People's Court, Beijing 1950; Chair. Peasants' Cttee., Beijing 1951; Council mem. Municipal People's Govt., Beijing 1952;

Dir. Steering Cttee. of Int. Activities 1953; Sec.-Gen. Municipal People's Govt., Beijing 1955–57, Dir. Industrial and Communications Dept. 1959; mem. Municipal CCP Cttee., Beijing 1955; Amb. to Hungary 1961–64, to Guinea 1964–67, to Egypt 1970–74; Pres. Chinese People's Asscn. for Friendship with Foreign Countries 1974–76; Amb. to Thailand 1976–78; Head, Liaison Office, U.S.A. 1978; Amb. to U.S.A. 1979–82; mem. Nat. Cttee. & Deputy Dir. of Foreign Affairs Cttee. CPPCC 1978–93; Vice-Pres. Chinese People's Inst. for Foreign Affairs 1983–91; Vice-Chair. Chinese People's Asscn. for Peace and Disarmament 1984–; Pres. China Int. Public Relations Asscn. 1991–; Pres. China Asscn. for Yellow River Cultural and Econ. Devt. 1994–. *Address:* 69 Baofang Hutong, Dongcheng District, Beijing 100010, People's Republic of China. *Telephone:* (010) 65925172 (Office); 65254753 (Home). *Fax:* (010) 65925175.

CHAIGNEAU, Pascal Gérard Joël, D. ÈS L., D. EN SC. POL., D. EN SC. ECON., D. EN D.; French academic; b. 8 Feb. 1956, Paris; s. of André Chaigneau and Hélène Alexandre; m. Marie-Claude Ratsarazaka-Ratsimandresy 1983; three s.; ed. Coll. St. Michel de Picpus and Facultés de Droit et des Lettres, Paris; practical work 1974–75; Asst. 1976–78, Prof. Ecole des Hautes Etudes Internationales and Ecole Supérieure de Journalisme 1978–; Research, Fondation pour les Etudes de Défense Nationale 1980–82; in charge of course, Univ. de Paris II 1982–90; Maître de conférences, Univ. de Paris V 1990–; Dir. of Studies, Ecole des Hautes Etudes Internationales 1984–85, Dir.-Gen. 1985–90; Admin.-Gen. Ecole des Hautes Etudes Internationales, Ecole des Hautes Etudes Politiques et Sociales, Ecole Supérieure de Journalisme 1990–; Sec.-Gen. Centre de Recherches Droit et Défense, Univ. de Paris V 1985–; Founder and Dir. Centre d'Etudes Diplomatiques et Stratégiques 1986–; Advocate, Court of Appeal, Paris 1990–; Prof. Centre des Hautes Etudes sur l'Afrique et l'Asie Modernes; lecturer, Inst. des Hautes Etudes de Défense Nationale; in charge of course, Ecole des Hautes Etudes Commerciales 1990–92, Prof. 1992–; Prof. Collège Interarmées de Défense 1994–; with Bolivian Consulate in France 1994–97; Foreign Trade Counsellor 1995–; many other public appts.; mem. Acad. des Sciences d'Outre-mer, Soc. d'Economie Politique; Dr. h.c. (Nat. Univ. of Bolivia); Hon. LL.D. (Richmond, U.S.A.); Grand Prix de l'Asscn. des Ecrivains de Langue Française 1987, Prix de l'Acad. des Sciences Morales et Politiques 1993, and other prizes, awards and distinctions; Chevalier, Légion d'honneur, Chevalier, Ordre nat. du mérite, Officier, Ordre des Palmes Académiques, Commdr. des Arts et des Lettres; decorations from Bolivia, Burkina Faso, Belgium, Honduras, Chad, Madagascar, Niger, etc. *Publications:* La Stratégie soviétique 1978, La Politique militaire de la France en Afrique 1984, Rivalités politiques et socialisme à Madagascar 1985, Les Pays de l'Est et l'Afrique 1985, France-océan indien-mer rouge (with others) 1986, Pour une analyse du commerce international 1987, La Guerre du Golfe 1991, Europe: la nouvelle donne stratégique 1993, Les grands Enjeux du monde contemporain 1997, Dictionnaire des Relations Internationales 1998. *Address:* 54 avenue Marceau, 75008 Paris (Office); 68 avenue de Gravelle, 94220 Charenton-le-Pont, France (Home).

CHAILLY, Riccardo; Italian conductor; b. 20 Feb. 1953, Milan; s. of Luciano Chailly and Anna Marie Motta; m. Gabriella Terragni 1987; two s.; ed. Giuseppe Verdi and Perugia Conservatories and with Franco Caracciolo and Franco Ferrara; Asst. to Claudio Abbado, La Scala, Milan 1972–74; début as Conductor with Chicago Opera 1974; début, La Scala 1978, Covent Garden (operatic début) 1979; concert début with London Symphony Orchestra and Edin. Festival 1979; American concert début 1980; played with major orchestras 1980; début, Metropolitan Opera 1982; Prin. guest Conductor, London Philharmonic Orchestra 1982–85; début, Vienna State Opera 1983; appearances Salzburg Festival 1984, 1985, 1986; Japan début, with Royal Philharmonic Orchestra 1984; début, New York Philharmonic Orchestra 1984; Chief Conductor of Radio Symphony Orchestra Berlin 1982–89; Music Dir. Bologna Orchestra 1986–93; Prin. Conductor Royal Concertgebouw Orchestra, Amsterdam 1988–, Giuseppe Verdi, Milan 1999–. *Address:* Royal Concertgebouw Orchestra, Jacob Obrechtstraat 51, 1071 Amsterdam, Netherlands.

CHAKAIPA, Patrick Fani; Zimbabwean ecclesiastic; b. 25 June 1932, Mhondoro; ed. St. Michael's Mission, Mhondoro, Kutama Training Coll.; ordained Roman Catholic priest 1965; Titular Bishop of Rucuma and Auxiliary Bishop of Salisbury (now Harare) 1972–76; Archbishop of Salisbury (now Harare) June 1976–. *Publications:* Karikoga Gumiremiseve 1958, Pfumo Reropa 1961, Rudo Ibofu 1961, Garandichauya 1963, Dzasukwa Mwana Asina Hembe 1967. *Leisure interest:* chess. *Address:* Archbishop's House, 66 Fifth Street, Harare (Home); P.O. Box CY 330, Causeway, Harare, Zimbabwe (Office). *Telephone:* 792125 (Home); 727386 (Office). *Fax:* 721598.

CHALABI, Talal Saleem, M.B., CH.B., F.R.C.S.(E), F.A.C.S; Iraqi orthopaedic surgeon and university professor; b. 28 Feb. 1937, Baghdad; m. Selma M. Saleh 1975; two s. two d.; ed. Coll. of Medicine, Univ. of Baghdad; Consultant Orthopaedic Surgeon, Basrah Gen. Hosp. 1973; lecturer in Orthopaedic Surgery, Coll. of Medicine, Univ. of Basrah 1974, Head Dept. of Surgery 1978, Dean Coll. of Medicine 1979–85; Consultant Orthopaedic Surgeon, Al 'Yermouk Teaching Hosp., Baghdad 1985–; Prof. of Orthopaedic Surgery, Dir. of Post-Grad. Study, Coll. of Medicine, Univ. of Al-Mustansiriya 1985–. *Publications:* articles in medical journals. *Leisure interests:* classical music, reading. *Address:* College of Medicine, Al-Mustansiriya University, P.O. Box 14132, Baghdad, Iraq. *Telephone:* 5567524.

CHALANDON, Albin Paul Henri, L. ÈS L.; French politician and businessman; b. 11 June 1920, Reyrieux, Ain; s. of Pierre Chalandon and Claire Cambon; m. Princess Salomé Murat 1951; two s. one d.; ed. Lycée Condorcet, Paris; Inspecteur des Finances; Dir. Banque Nationale pour le Commerce et l'Industrie (Afrique) 1950–51; Admin. and Dir.-Gen. Banque Commerciale de Paris 1952–64, Président-Directeur Général 1964–68; M.P. 1967–76; Minister of Industry May 1968, of Public Works, Housing and Urban Devt. 1968–72, of Justice 1986–88; Special Asst., Ministry of Foreign Affairs Feb.–Aug. 1974; Treas. Cen. Cttee. Union pour la Nouvelle République (now Union des Démocrates pour la République) 1958–59, Sec.-Gen. 1959, Deputy Sec.-Gen. UDR 1974–75; Pres., Dir.-Gen. Soc. Nat. ELF Aquitaine (SNEA) 1976–83; Pres., Dir.-Gen. Texmaille 1989–; mem. Social and Econ. Council 1963–67; Officier Légion d'honneur, Croix de guerre. *Publications:* Le système monétaire international 1966, Les joueurs de flûte, Le rêve économique de la Gauche 1977, Quitte ou Double 1986. *Address:* 12 rue de Lota, 75016 Paris, France (Home). *Telephone:* 47.04.51.71.

CHALAYAN, Hussein, B.A.; fashion designer; ed. Cyprus and Cen. St. Martin's School of Art, London; student final year collection featured in Brown's window; set up own label; exhbn. of first solo collection, West Soho Galleries, London 1994; second collection shown during London Fashion Week and in Kobe and Tokyo; fourth collection received Absolut Vodka's Absolut Creation Sponsorship Award (first recipient) 1996; solo exhbn. (key pieces from past collections), The Window Gallery, Prague 1996; exhibited Buried and Path dresses, Jam (style, music and media) exhbn., Barbican Art Gallery 1996; designs selected for Cutting Edge exhbn., Victoria and Albert Museum 1997; invited to exhibit in Challenge of Materials exhbn., Science Museum 1997; talk at Tate Gallery (with Zaha Hadid, Michael Bracewell and Georgina Starr) on parallels between fashion, art and architecture 1997, Designer of the Year, London Fashion Awards 1998. *Address:* 71 Endell Rd., London, WC2 9AJ, England.

CHALFONT, Baron (Life Peer), cr. 1964; **(Arthur) Alun Gwynne Jones,** P.C., O.B.E., M.C., F.R.S.A.; British politician; b. 5 Dec. 1919, Lantarnam, Wales; s. of Arthur Gwynne Jones and Eliza Alice Hardman; m. Dr. Mona Mitchell 1948; one d. (deceased); ed. West Monmouth School; commissioned into S. Wales Borderers (24th Foot) 1940; served in Burma 1941–44, Malaya 1955–57, Cyprus 1958–59; resgnd. comm. 1961; Defence Corresp. The Times, London 1961–64; Consultant on foreign affairs to BBC TV, London 1961–64; Minister of State for Foreign Affairs 1964–70, Minister for Disarmament 1964–67, 1969–70, in charge of day-to-day negotiations for Britain's entry into Common Market 1967–69; Perm. Rep. to Western European Union 1969–70; Foreign Ed. New Statesman 1970–71; Chair. All-Party Defence Group House of Lords 1980–96, Pres. 1996–; Chair. Industrial Cleaning Papers 1979–86, Peter Hamilton Security Consultants Ltd. 1984–86, U.K. Cttee. for Free World 1981–89, European Atlantic Group 1983–, VSEL Consortium PLC 1987–93, Marlborough Stirling Group 1994–; Deputy Chair. IBA 1989–90; Chair. Radio Authority 1991–94; Pres. Hispanic and Luso Brazilian Council 1975–80, Royal Nat. Inst. for Deaf 1980–87, Llangollen Int. Music Festival 1979–90; Chair. Abington Corpn. (Consultants) Ltd. 1981–, Nottingham Building Soc. 1983–90, Southern Mining Corpn. 1996–; Dir. W. S. Atkins Int. 1979–83, IBM U.K. Ltd. 1973–90 (mem. IBM Europe Advisory Council 1973–90), Lazard Brothers and Co. Ltd. 1983–90, Shandwick PLC 1985–95, Triangle Holdings 1986–90, TV Corpn. PLC 1996–; Pres. Freedom in Sport Int.; mem. Int. Inst. of Strategic Studies, Royal Inst.; Hon. Fellow Univ. Coll. Wales, Aberystwyth 1974. *Publications:* The Sword and the Spirit 1963, The Great Commanders 1973, Montgomery of Alamein 1976; (Ed.) Waterloo: Battle of Three Armies 1979, Star Wars: Suicide or Survival 1985, Defence of the Realm 1987, By God's Will: A Portrait of the Sultan of Brunei 1989; contribs. to The Times and nat. and professional journals. *Leisure interests:* music and theatre. *Address:* House of Lords, London, SW1A 0PW, England.

CHALIDZE, Valeriy Nikolayevich; Russian writer, physicist and publisher; b. 1938, Moscow; m.; ed. Moscow Univ., then Faculty of Physics, Tbilisi Univ. 1965; head of research unit in Plastics Research Inst., Moscow 1965–70; removed from post 1970; mem. of U.S.S.R. Human Rights Cttee.; dissident activity 1969–, when started samizdat journal Obshchestvennyye problemy (Problems of Society), trip to U.S.A. to lecture on human rights in U.S.S.R., subsequently deprived of Soviet citizenship 1972; currently living in New York. *Publications* (apart from numerous samizdat articles and books) include: Ugolovnaya Rossiya (Capital Punishment in Russia) 1977, U.S.S.R.—The Workers' Movement 1978. A Foreigner in the Soviet Union. A Juridical Memoir 1980, Communism Vanquished (Stalin) 1981, The Responsibility of a Generation 1982, National Problems and Perestroika 1988, The Dawn of the Legal Reform 1990, Responsibility of the Generation 1991, A Hierarchical Man 1991.

CHALKER OF WALLASEY, Baroness (Life Peer), cr. 1992, of Leigh-on-Sea in the County of Essex; **Lynda Chalker,** P.C.; British politician; b. 29 April 1942, Hitchin, Herts.; d. of late Sidney Henry James Bates and Marjorie Kathleen Randell; m. 1st Eric Robert Chalker 1967 (divorced 1973), 2nd Clive Landa 1981; ed. Heidelberg Univ., Germany, London Univ., Cen. London Polytechnic; statistician with Research Bureau Ltd. (Unilever) 1963–69; Deputy Market Research Man., Shell Mex & BP Ltd. 1969–72; Chief Exec. Int. Div. of Louis Harris Int. 1972–74; M.P. for Wallasey 1974–92; Parl. Under-Sec. of State, Dept. of Health and Social Security 1979–82, Dept. of Transport 1982–83; Minister of State, Dept. of Transport 1983–86,

FCO 1986–97, Minister for Overseas Devt. 1989–97; ind. consultant on Africa and Devt. 1997–; Chair. Greater London Young Conservatives (GLYC) 1969–70; Nat. Vice-Chair. Young Conservatives 1970–71; Hon. Fellow Queen Mary and Westfield Coll.; mem. BBC Gen. Advisory Cttee. 1975–79; Dr. h.c. (Bradford) 1995; Conservative. *Publications:* We are Richer than We Think 1978 (co-author), Africa: turning the tide 1989. *Leisure interests:* music, cooking, theatre, driving. *Address:* House of Lords, London, SW1A 0PW, England. *Telephone:* (0118) 946 2894. *Fax:* (0118) 947 2835.

CHALMERS, Neil Robert, PH.D.; British natural history museum director; b. 19 June 1942, Surrey; s. of William King and Irene Margaret (née Pembleton) Chalmers; m. Monica Elizabeth Byanjeru Rusoke 1970; two d.; ed. King's Coll. School, Wimbledon, Magdalen Coll., Oxford, St. John's Coll., Cambridge; lecturer in Zoology, Makerere Univ. Coll., Kampala, Uganda 1966–69; Scientific Dir. Natural Primate Research Centre, Nairobi, Kenya 1969–70; lecturer, subsequently Sr. Lecturer then Reader in Biology, The Open Univ. 1970–85, Dean of Science 1985–88; Dir. The Natural History Museum, London 1988–. *Publications:* Social Behaviour in Primates 1979 and other books on animal behaviour; numerous papers in Animal Behaviour and other learned journals. *Leisure interests:* music, squash. *Address:* The Natural History Museum, Cromwell Road, London, SW7 5BD, England. *Telephone:* 0171-938 9211. *Fax:* 0171-938 8799.

CHALONER, William Gilbert, PH.D., F.R.S.; British professor of botany; b. 22 Nov. 1928; s. of late Ernest J. Chaloner and L. Chaloner; m. Judith Carroll 1955; one s. two d.; ed. Kingston Grammar School and Univ. of Reading; Lecturer and Reader, Univ. Coll. London 1956–72, Visiting Prof. 1995–; Visiting Prof. Pa. State Univ. 1961–62; Prof. Univ. of Nigeria 1965–66; Prof. of Botany, Birkbeck Coll. London 1972–79; Hildred Carlile Prof. of Botany and Head School of Life Sciences, Royal Holloway and Bedford New Coll. 1985–94 (Bedford Coll. 1979–85), Prof. Emer., Geology Dept., Royal Holloway, Univ. of London 1994–; Wilmer D. Barrett (Visiting) Prof. of Botany, Univ. of Mass., U.S.A. 1987–91; mem. Bd. of Trustees, Royal Botanic Gdns. Kew 1983–96; Pres. Linnean Soc. 1985–88; fmr. mem. Senate London Univ.; fmr. mem. National Environment Research Council; corresp. mem. Botanical Soc. of America 1987–, Associé Etranger de l'Académie des Sciences. *Publications:* papers in scientific journals. *Leisure interests:* swimming, tennis, visiting U.S.A. *Address:* 20 Parke Road, London, SW13 9NG, England. *Telephone:* 0181-748 3863.

CHAMBERLAIN, (George) Richard; American actor; b. 31 March 1935, Los Angeles; s. of Charles Chamberlain and Elsa Chamberlain; ed. Los Angeles Conservatory of Music and drama studies with Jeff Corey; stage appearances include King Lear, Hamlet, Richard II, The Lady's Not for Burning, Night of the Iguana, Cyrano de Bergerac, My Fair Lady; numerous TV appearances include Dr. Kildare 1961–65, Portrait of a Lady 1968, The Woman I Love 1973, The Count of Monte Cristo 1975, The Man in the Iron Mask 1978, Shogun 1980 (Golden Globe Award), The Thorn Birds 1983, Wallenberg: A Hero's Story 1985, Dream West 1986, The Bourne Identity 1988, Ordeal in the Arctic 1993. *Films include:* Secret of Purple Reef 1960, Thunder of Drums 1961, Twilight of Honor 1963, Joy in the Morning 1965, Petulia 1968, The Madwoman of Chaillot 1969, The Music Lovers 1971, Julius Caesar 1971, Lady Caroline Lamb 1971, The Three Musketeers 1974, Towering Inferno 1974, The Four Musketeers 1975, The Slipper and the Rose 1977, The Swarm 1978, Murder by Phone 1982, King Solomon's Mines 1985, Alan Quartermain and The Lost City of Gold 1987, The Return of the Musketeers 1989.

CHAMBERLAIN, Owen, PH.D.; American physicist; b. 10 July 1920, San Francisco; s. of Edward Chamberlain and Genevieve Lucinda (Owen) Chamberlain; m. 1st 1943 (divorced 1978); four c.; m. 2nd June Steingart Chamberlain 1980 (deceased); ed. Germantown Friends School, Dartmouth Coll., and Univ. of Chicago; Research physicist Manhattan Project, Berkeley 1942–43, Los Alamos 1943–46; graduate student (under Enrico Fermi) Univ. of Chicago 1946–48; Instructor in Physics, Univ. of Calif., Berkeley 1948–50, Asst. Prof. 1950–54, Assoc. Prof. 1954–58, Prof. 1958–89, Prof. Emer. 1989–; on leave at Univ. of Rome as Guggenheim Fellow 1957–58; Loeb Lecturer, Harvard Univ. 1959; mem. N.A.S.; Fellow, American Acad. of Arts and Sciences, American Physics Soc.; has specialized in research in spontaneous fission, proton scattering, discovery of antiproton, properties of antinucleons, etc.; shared Nobel Prize for Physics with Emilio Segre 1959, Berkeley citation, Univ. of Calif. 1989. *Address:* Department of Physics, University of California, Berkeley, CA 94720, U.S.A.

CHAMBERS, Leigh Ross, M.A.; Australian professor of French; b. 19 Nov. 1932, Kempsey, N.S.W.; s. of Cecil Edward Chambers and Beryl Alma Fayle; ed. Univ. of Sydney and Univ. of Grenoble, France; McCaughey Prof. and Head Dept. of French Univ. of Sydney 1971–75; Prof. of French Univ. of Mich., Ann Arbor 1975–85, Marvin Felheim Distinguished Univ. Prof. of French and Comparative Literature 1985; Fellow Australian Acad. of Humanities; Officier de l'Ordre des Palmes Académiques. *Publications:* Gérard de Nerval et la poétique du voyage 1969, La comédie au château 1971, L'Ange et l'automate 1971, Story and Situation 1984, Mélancholie et opposition 1987, Room for Manoeuver 1991. *Address:* c/o Department of Romance Languages, University of Michigan, Ann Arbor, MI 48109, U.S.A. (Office).

CHAMBERS, Richard Dickinson, PH.D., D.SC., F.R.S.; British professor of chemistry; b. 16 March 1935, West Stanley, Co. Durham; s. of Alfred Chambers and Elizabeth Chambers (née Allsop); m. Anne Boyd 1959; one s. one d.; ed. Stanley Grammar School, Univ. of Durham; postdoctoral research at Univ. of British Columbia, Vancouver 1959–60; lecturer Univ. of Durham 1960–69, Reader 1969–76, Prof. of Chemistry 1976–, Chair. and Head of Dept. of Chemistry 1983–86, Sir Derman Christopherson Research Fellow 1988–89; Fulbright Scholar Case Western Reserve Univ., Ohio 1966–67; Dir. (non-exec.) BNFL Fluorochemicals Ltd. 1995–; A.C.S. Award for Creative Work in Fluorine Chemistry 1991. *Publications:* Fluorine in Organic Chemistry 1973; also numerous articles in scientific journals. *Leisure interests:* opera, golf, watching soccer. *Address:* University of Durham, Department of Chemistry, Science Laboratories, South Road, Durham, DH1 3LE, England. *Telephone:* (0191) 374 3120. *Fax:* (0191) 384 4737.

CHAMBON, Pierre, M.D., L. ÈS. SC.; French professor of biochemistry; b. 7 Feb. 1931, Mulhouse; s. of Henri Chambon and Yvonne Weill; m. Brigitte Andersson 1957; two s. one d.; ed. Univ. of Strasbourg; Research Asst. Strasbourg Medical School, Assoc. Prof. 1962–66; Dept. of Biochem. Stanford Univ. Medical School 1966–67; Prof. of Biochem. Inst. de Chimie Biologique, Faculté de Médecine, Strasbourg 1967–91; Prof. Louis Pasteur Univ., Strasbourg 1974–93; Prof. Inst. Universitaire de France, Faculté de Médecine, Strasbourg 1991–; Dir. Lab. de Génétique Moléculaire des Eucaryotes (LGME), CNRS 1977–; Dir. Unité 184 de Biologie Moléculaire et de Génie Génétique, Inst. Nat. de la Santé et de la Recherche Médicale (INSERM) 1978–; Prof. Collège de France 1993–; mem. numerous scientific and editorial bds. etc.; mem. Acad. des Sciences; Foreign mem. N.A.S., Royal Swedish Acad.; Foreign hon. mem. American Acad. of Arts and Science, Acad. Royale de Médecine, Belgium; corresp. mem. Liège Acad.; hon. mem. Chinese Soc. of Genetics; Prix Rosen 1976; CNRS Gold Medal 1979; Freeman Foundation Prize of N.Y. Acad. 1981; Lounsbery Prize (N.A.S. and Acad. des Sciences) 1982, Oberling Prize 1986, Prix Griffuel 1987, King Faisal Int. Prize 1988, Krebs Medal 1990, Prix Roussel 1990, Prix Louis Jeantet 1991; other honours and awards. *Publications:* 400 articles in scientific reviews. *Address:* IGBMC, 1 rue Laurent Fries, B.P. 163, 67404 Illkirch cedex, C.U. Strasbourg, France.

CHAMORRO, Violeta Barrios de (see Barrios de Chamorro, Violeta).

CHAMOUX, François, D.ÈS.L.; French academic; b. 4 April 1915, Mirecourt; s. of Emile Chamoux and Henriette Genvot; m. 1st Lucienne Cavaye 1938 (died 1971), 2nd Christiane Humeau 1973 (died 1991); one s. one d.; ed. Ecole Normale Supérieure, Ecole française d'Athènes, Sorbonne, Paris; lecturer in Greek, Univ. of Lille 1948–49; Lecturer in Archaeology, Sorbonne 1949–51; Prof. of Archaeology, Univ. of Nancy 1952–60; Prof. of Greek Literature and Civilization, Sorbonne 1960–83, Prof. Emer. 1983–; Dir. French Archaeological Mission in Libya 1976–81; mem. Institut de France (Académie des Inscriptions et Belles-Lettres) 1981–, Acad. Royale de Belgique, Acad. Romana (Bucharest); Corresp. mem. Accad. Pontaniana (Naples); Hon. mem. Soc. for Promotion of Hellenic Studies; Dr. h.c. (Neuchâtel); Officier, Légion d'honneur, Officier, Ordre du Mérite, Commdr., Ordre des Arts et des Lettres, Croix de guerre. *Publications:* Cyrène sous la monarchie des Battiades 1953, L'Aurige de Delphes 1955, La civilisation grecque archaïque et classique 1963, Art-grec 1966, La civilisation hellénistique 1981, Marc Antoine 1986, Pausanias, Périégèse I (commentary) 1992, Diodore de Sicile (introduction) 1993; more than 150 learned articles on Greek literature, history and archaeology. *Leisure interest:* philological and historical research. *Address:* 6 avenue Paul-Appell, 75014 Paris, France. *Telephone:* 45-40-51-30.

CHAN, Heng Chee, M.A., PH.D.; Singaporean diplomatist and academic; b. 19 April 1942, Singapore; ed. Cornell Univ. and Nat. Univ. of Singapore; Asst. Lecturer, Nat. Univ. of Singapore 1967–70, lecturer 1970–75, Sr. Lecturer 1976–80, Assoc. Prof. of Political Science 1981–, Head Dept. of Political Science 1985–88, Prof. 1990; Dir. Inst. of Policy Studies, Singapore Jan.–Dec. 1988; Perm Rep. to UN 1989–91; Amb. to Mexico 1989–91; High Commr. in Canada 1989–91; Exec. Dir. Singapore Int. Foundation 1991–; Dir. Inst. of S.E. Asian Studies 1993; mem. Int. Council of Asia Soc. 1991–, Singapore Nat. Cttee. of Council for Security Co-operation in the Asia-Pacific 1993–, Int. Inst. for Strategic Studies Council, Hong Kong, 1995–, Int. Advisory Bd. of Council on Foreign Relations, New York 1995–; Nat. Book Award (non-fiction) 1978, 1986, Woman of the Year (Singapore) 1991. *Address:* Singapore International Foundation, 111 Somerset Road, 11-07 Devonshire Wing, Singapore 238164.

CHAN, Rt. Hon. Sir Julius, G.C.M.G., K.B.E., P.C.; Papua New Guinea politician; b. 29 Aug. 1939, Tanga, New Ireland; m. Stella Ahmat 1966; one d. three s.; ed. Maurist Brothers Coll., Ashgrove, Queensland and Univ. of Queensland, Australia; Co-operative Officer, Papua New Guinea Admin. 1960–62; Man. Dir. Coastal Shipping Co. Pty. Ltd.; mem. House of Assembly 1968–75, 1982–, Deputy Speaker, Vice-Chair. Public Accounts Cttee. 1968–72; Parl. Leader, People's Progress Party 1970–97; Minister of Finance and Parl. Leader of Govt. Business 1972–77; Deputy Prime Minister and Minister for Primary Industry 1977–78, Prime Minister 1980–82, Deputy Prime Minister 1986–88, Minister of Trade and Industry 1986–88, Deputy Prime Minister 1992–94, Minister for Finance and Planning 1992–94, for Foreign Affairs and Trade 1994–96; Prime Minister 1994–96; Gov. for Papua New Guinea and Vice-Chair. Asian Devt. Bank 1975–77; Fellowship mem. Int. Bankers' Asscn. Inc., U.S.A. 1976; Gov. IBRD/IMF 1992–; Hon. Dr. h.c. (Econ.), Dankook Univ., Seoul 1978; Hon. Dr. Tech., Univ. of Tech., Papua New Guinea 1983. *Address:* P.O. Box 6030, Boroto, Papua New Guinea.

CHAN FANG ON SANG, Anson; Chinese government official; b. Shanghai, China; ed. in Hong Kong; fmr. appts. include Dir. Social Welfare Dept. 1984; Sec. for Econ. Services 1987; Head (Sec.), Hong Kong Civil Service until 1993; Chief Sec. of Hong Kong Nov. 1993– (named to continue in admin. after transition). *Address:* Office of the Chief Secretary, Central Government Offices, Lower Albert Rd, Hong Kong Special Administrative Region, People's Republic of China.

CHANCE, Britton, M.S., PH.D., D.SC.; American biophysicist; b. 24 July 1913, Wilkes Barre, Pa.; s. of Edwin M. and Eleanor (Kent) Chance; m. 1st Jane Earle 1938 (divorced), 2nd Lilian Streeter Lucas 1955 (divorced); four s. four d., two step s. two step d.; ed. Univ. of Pennsylvania and Cambridge Univ.; Acting Dir. Johnson Foundation 1940–41; Investigator Office of Scientific Research and Devt. 41; staff mem. Radiation Lab., M.I.T.; Asst. Prof. of Biophysics, Univ. of Pa. 1941–46, Prof., Chair. and Dir. Johnson Foundation 1949–83, E. R. Johnson Prof. of Biophysics 1949, Prof. Emer. 1983–; Guggenheim Fellow, Nobel and Molteno Inst. 1946–48; scientific consultant, research attaché, U.S. Navy, London 1948; consultant, Nat. Science Foundation 1951–56; President's Scientific Advisory Cttee. 1959–60; NCI Working Group on Molecular Control 1973–; NIAAA Council 1971–75; Vice-Pres. Int. Union Pure and Applied Biophysics 1972–75, Pres. 1975–; Dir. Inst. for Functional and Structural Studies, Philadelphia 1982–90, Inst. for Biophysics and Biomedical Research 1990–; mem. N.A.S., American Acad. of Arts and Sciences, American Philosophical Soc., Royal Acad. of Science, Uppsala, Biochemical Soc., Biophysical Soc., Int. Soc. for Cell Biology, Royal Soc. of Arts, Royal Swedish Acad., Acad. Leopoldina, etc.; Foreign mem. Max-Planck-Inst. für Systemphysiologie und Ernährungsphysiologie, Dortmund, Royal Soc. of London 1981; Fellow, Inst. of Radio Engineers; Philip Morris Lecturer 1978; Heineken Prize 1970, Presidential Certificate of Merit 1950, Paul Lewis Award in Enzyme Chemistry, American Chemical Soc. 1950, William J. Morlock Award in biochemical electronics, Inst. of Radio Engineers 1961, Netherlands Biochemical Soc. Award 1966, Keilin Medal 1966, Franklin Medal 1966, Gairdner Award 1972, Festschrift Symposium, Stockholm 1973, Semmelweis Medal 1974, Nat. Medal of Science 1974, DaCosta Oratusi 1976, etc. *Publications:* Waveforms (with Williams, Hughes, McNichol, Sayre) 1949, Electronic Time Measurements (with Hulsizer, McNichol, Williams) 1949, Enzyme-Substrate Compounds 1951, Enzymes in Action in Living Cells 1955, The Respiratory Chain and Oxidative Phosphorylation 1956, Techniques for Assay of Respiratory Enzymes 1957, Energy-Linked Functions of Mitochondria 1963, Rapid Mixing and Sampling Techniques in Biochemistry 1964, Control of Energy Metabolism 1965, Hemes and Hemoproteins 1966, Probes of Structure and Function of Macromolecules and Enzymes 1972, Alcohol and Aldehyde (3 vols.), Tunneling in Biological Systems 1979. *Leisure interests:* yacht sailing and cruising, amateur radio. *Address:* Johnson Research Foundation, Department of Biochemistry and Biophysics, University of Pennsylvania, D 501 Richards Building, Philadelphia, PA 19104 (Office); 4014 Pine Street, Philadelphia, PA 19104, U.S.A. (Home). *Telephone:* (215) 898-4342.

CHANCELLOR, Alexander Surtees, B.A.; British journalist; b. 4 Jan. 1940, Ware, Herts.; s. of Sir Christopher Chancellor, C.M.G. and Sylvia Mary Chancellor (née Paget); m. Susanna Elizabeth Debenham 1964; two d.; ed. Eton Coll., Trinity Hall, Cambridge; Reuters News Agency 1964–74, Chief Corresp., Italy 1968–73; ITV News 1974–75; Ed. The Spectator 1975–84; Ed. Time and Tide 1984–86; Deputy Ed. Sunday Telegraph 1986; Washington Ed. The Independent 1986–88; Ed. The Independent Magazine 1988–92; The New Yorker (Ed. The Talk of the Town) 1992–93; Columnist The Times 1992–93; Assoc. Ed. The Sunday Telegraph 1994–95, The Guardian 1996–. *Address:* 1 Souldern Road, London, W14 0JE, England.

CHANDLER, Sir Colin (Michael), Kt., F.C.M.A.; British business executive; b. 7 Oct. 1939; s. of Henry John Chandler and Mary Martha Bowles; m. Jennifer Mary Crawford 1964; one s. one d.; ed. St. Joseph's Acad., Hatfield Polytechnic; commercial apprentice, De Havilland Aircraft Co. 1956–61; Contracts Officer, Hawker Siddeley Aviation 1962–66, Commercial Man. 1967–72, Exec. Dir. (Commercial) 1973–76, Exec. Dir. and Gen. Man. 1977; Div. Man. Dir. British Aerospace 1978–82, Group Marketing Dir. 1983–85; Head of Defence Export Services, Ministry of Defence 1985–89; Man. Dir. Vickers PLC 1990–, Chief Exec. 1991–96, Deputy Chair. and Chief Exec. 1996, Chair. 1997–99; Dir. (non-exec.) T.I. Group 1992, Guardian Royal Exchange 1995–; mem. Cttee., Dept. Trade and Industry Priority Japan Campaign 1992–; Chair. Overseas Project Bd. Healthcare Sector Group; Commdr. Order of Lion of Finland. *Leisure interests:* jogging, playing tennis, reading, listening to music. *Address:* c/o Vickers PLC, Vickers House, 2 Bessborough Gardens, London, SW1V 2JE, England.

CHANDLER, Kenneth A.; British journalist; b. 2 Aug. 1947, Westcliff-on-Sea, Essex; s. of Leonard Gordon Chandler and Beatrix Marie (née McKenzie) Chandler; m. Linda Kathleen Chandler 1975; one s. two d.; Man. Ed. The New York Post 1978–86, 1993–; Ed. Boston Herald 1986–93; Exec. Producer Fox TV's A Current Affair 1993. *Address:* New York Post, Suite 1910, 1211 Avenue of the Americas, Floor 10, New York, NY 10036, U.S.A.

CHANDLER, Otis; American newspaper executive; b. 23 Nov. 1927, Los Angeles; s. of Norman Chandler and Dorothy Buffum Chandler; m. 1st Marilyn Chandler 1951 (divorced 1981); m. 2nd Bettina Whitaker 1981; three s. two d.; ed. Andover Acad., Mass., and Stanford Univ.; Trainee, Times Mirror Co. 1953, Asst. to Pres. (assigned to Mirror-News) 1957, Marketing Man., Los Angeles Times 1958–60, Publr., Los Angeles Times 1960–80, Publr. and C.E.O. 1978–80; Vice-Pres. Times Mirror Co. 1961, Dir. 1962, Sr. Vice-Pres. 1966–80; Vice-Chair. Bd. Times Mirror Co. 1968–80, Chair. and Ed.-in-Chief 1981–85, Chair. of Exec. Cttee. 1986. *Leisure interests:* board surfing, hunting, fishing, photography, tennis, water skiing, track and field, sports cars. *Address:* c/o Times Mirror Square, Los Angeles, CA 90053, U.S.A. (Office).

CHANDRA, Avinash; Indian artist; b. 28 Aug. 1931, Simla; s. of Kundan Lal and Ram Parai; m. Prem Lata; one c.; ed. Delhi Polytechnic, Delhi; on staff of Delhi Polytechnic, Delhi 1953–56; in London 1956, then New York 1966; executed glass mural for Pilkington Brothers' Head Office, St. Helens, Lancs and fibreglass mural for Indian Tea Centre, London 1964; Gold Medal, Prix Européen, Ostend 1962; John D. Rockefeller Third Fund Fellowship 1965. Works in following collections: Nat. Gallery of Modern Art, New Delhi, Tate Gallery, London, Victoria and Albert Museum, London, Arts Council of Great Britain, London, Ashmolean Museum, Oxford, Ulster Museum, Belfast, City Art Gallery, Birmingham, Gulbenkian Museum, Durham, Musée National d'Art Moderne, Paris, Whitworth Art Gallery, Manchester, Museum of Modern Art, Haifa, Punjab Museum, Chandigarh, etc.; one-man exhbns. in Srinagar, New Delhi, Belfast, London, Oxford, Paris, Bristol, Arnhem, Amsterdam, Zürich, Copenhagen, Stockholm, Chicago, Toronto, Geneva, etc. *Address:* 24 Willoughby Road, Hampstead, London, N.W.3, England.

CHANDRA, Ramesh, B.SC.; Indian newspaper executive; b. 15 Aug. 1925, Najibabad, Uttar Pradesh; s. of Raibahadur Sahu Jagmandar Das and Asharfi Devi; m. Chandrakanta Jain 1948; two s.; ed. Banaras Hindu Univ.; fmr. Sr. Vice-Chair. Municipal Bd. Najibabad; joined Times of India 1959; now Exec. Dir. Bennett, Coleman & Co. Ltd. (The Times of India Group of Publs.); fmr. Chair. Press Trust of India; fmr. Pres. Indian Newspaper Soc.; Pres. Chrysanthemum Soc. of India, Int. Chrysanthemum Council, All India Digambar Jain Parishad; Trustee, Bharatiya Jnanpith; Thomson Foundation Fellow, U.K. 1968. *Publications:* articles on newspaper management in various journals. *Leisure interests:* reading, gardening, cricket, music, theatre, social work. *Address:* Bennett, Coleman & Co. Ltd., Times House, 7 Bahadurshah Zafar Marg, New Delhi 110002 (Office); C-48 Gulmohar Park, New Delhi 110049, India (Home). *Telephone:* 3312277 (Office); 6852909 (Home). *Fax:* 3715836 (Office).

CHANDRACHUD, Yeshwant Vishnu, B.A., LL.B.; Indian judge; b. 12 July 1920; s. of Vishnu Balkrishna and Indira Chandrachud; m. Prabha Chandrachud; one s. one d.; part-time Prof. of Law, Govt. Law Coll., Bombay 1949–52; practised at Bombay bar 1943–61; Govt. Pleader, Bombay High Court 1958–61, Judge 1961–72; Judge Supreme Court 1972–78, Chief Justice 1978–85; Pres. Int. Law Asscn. (India Branch) 1978, Indian Law Inst. 1978. *Address:* 7-B Samata, General Bhosale Marg, Bombay 400021; 131 Balkrishna Nivas, Budhwar Peth, Pune 411002, India.

CHANDRASEKHAR, Bhagwat Subramanya, B.SC.; Indian cricketer and bank executive; b. 17 May 1945, Mysore; m. Sandhya Rajarao 1975; one s.; ed. Nat. Educ. Soc., Bangalore; right-arm leg-spin, googly bowler; bowling arm withered by attack of polio at age of 6; played for Mysore/Karnataka 1963–64 to 1979–80; played in 58 Tests for India 1963–64 to 1979, taking 242 wickets (average 29.7); toured England 1967, 1971, 1974 and 1979; Arjuna Award; Padma Shri 1972; Hon. Life mem. MCC 1981–. *Leisure interests:* badminton, Indian classical music. *Address:* 571 31st Cross, 4th Block, Jayanagar, Bangalore 560011, India. *Telephone:* 41268.

CHANDRASEKHAR, Sivaramakrishna, PH.D., D.SC., SC.D., F.R.S.; Indian physicist; b. 6 Aug. 1930, Calcutta; s. of late S. and Sitalaxmi Sivaramakrishnan; m. Ila Pingle 1954; one s. one d.; ed. Univs. of Nagpur and Cambridge; Research Scholar, Raman Research Inst., Bangalore 1950–54; 1851 Exhbn. Scholar, The Cavendish Lab., Cambridge 1954–57; D.S.I.R. Fellow, Dept. of Crystallography, Univ. Coll., London 1957–59; Research Fellow, Royal Inst., London 1959–61; Prof. and Head, Dept. of Physics, Univ. of Mysore 1961–71; Prof. Raman Research Inst. 1971–90; Nehru Visiting Prof. and Fellow of Pembroke Coll., Cambridge 1986–87; Bhatnagar Fellow 1990–95; Dir. Centre for Liquid Crystal Research 1991–; Fellow, Indian Nat. Science Acad. etc.; Royal Medal of the Royal Soc. 1994, Niels Bohr–UNESCO Gold Medal 1998, and several Indian and int. honours for outstanding contribs. to science. *Publications*: Liquid Crystals 1992; numerous scientific articles on crystal physics and liquid crystals. *Leisure interest*: painting. *Address*: Centre for Liquid Crystal Research, P.O. Box 1329, Bangalore 560013, India. *Telephone*: (80) 8382924. *Fax*: (80) 8382044.

CHANDRASEKHAR, Sripati, M.A., M.LITT., PH.D.; Indian demographer and economist; b. 22 Nov. 1918, Rajahmundry; s. of Prof. Sripati Sarangapani and Rajamma Sarangapani; m. Dorothy Anne Downes 1947; three d.; ed. Presidency Coll., Madras, Univ. of Madras and Columbia, New York and Princeton Univ.; Visiting Lecturer, Univ. of Pa. and Asia Inst., New York 1944–46; Prof. of Econs., Annamalai Univ. 1947–50; Dir. Demographic Research, UNESCO, Paris 1947–49; Prof. of Econs. and Head of Dept., Baroda Univ. 1950–53; Nuffield Fellow, L.S.E. 1953–55; Dir. Indian Inst. for Population Studies 1956–67; mem. Rajya Sabha 1964–70; Minister of State for Health and Family Planning 1967; Minister of State in Ministry of Health, Family Planning and Urban Devt. 1967–70; Research Prof. of Demography, Univ. of Calif.; Visiting Fellow Battelle Research Centre ("Think Tank") Seattle 1971–72; Distinguished Visiting Prof. of Sociology,

Calif. State Univ., San Diego 1972–74; Prof. of Demography and Public Health Univ. of Calif., Los Angeles, 1974–75; Regents Prof., Univ. of Calif., Santa Barbara 1975–; Vice-Chancellor Annamalai Univ., Chidambaram, South India 1975–78; Ed. Population Review 1957–; Lucie Stern Trustee Prof. of Sociology, Mills Coll., Oakland, Calif. 1979–80; Visiting Prof. of Sociology, San Diego State Univ. 1981–; Visiting Prof., Univ. of Calif., Irvine 1982–; Distinguished Prof. of Demography, Univ. of Alaska, Fairbanks 1983–84, Visiting Prof. of Sociology, Univ. of Texas 1985–; Fellow, Indian Inst. of Advanced Study, Shimla 1988–89; Visiting Prof. American Grad. School of Int. Man., Ariz. 1990–; Dir. Center for the Study of Asian Indians Overseas, La Jolla 1991–; Dillingham Lecturer, East-West Centre, Honolulu 1977; Visiting Distinguished Prof. of Demography and Sociology, Univ. of North Texas 1993–94; Fellow Rockefeller Foundation 1998–(2000), Aspen Inst. 1998; Hon. D.Litt. (Redlands Univ., Kurukshetra Univ.); Hon. LL.D. (Punjabi Univ.); Hon. M.D. (Budapest); Hon. D.Sc. (Univ. of Pacific); numerous awards. *Publications:* India's Population 1946, Census and Statistics in India 1947, Indian Emigration 1948, Hungry People and Empty Lands 1952, Population and Planned Parenthood in India 1955, Infant Mortality in India 1959, China's Population 1959, Communist China Today 1961, Red China; An Asian View 1962, A Decade of Mao's China (ed.) 1963, American Aid and India's Economic Development 1965, Asia's Population Problems 1967, Problems of Economic Development 1967, India's Population: Fact, Problem and Policy 1968, Infant Mortality, Population Growth and Family Planning in India 1972, Abortion in a Crowded World: the Problem of Abortion with Special Reference to India 1974, Population and Law in India 1976, Ananda K. Coomaraswamy, A Critical Appreciation 1977, The Nagarathars of South India 1980, A Dirty Filthy Book 1981, From India to America 1983, From India to Canada 1986, From India to Mauritius 1987, The Population of Mauritius: Fact, Problem and Policy 1990, From India to Australia (ed.) 1992, India's Abortion Experience 1994, From India to Israel 1996, Norman Borlaug's Green Revolution and India's Population Problem 1997, From India to Singapore: A History of Immigration and the Indian Community 1999. *Leisure interests:* reading detective novels, listening to classical music. *Address:* 8976 Cliffridge Avenue, La Jolla, CA 92037, U.S.A. *Telephone:* (619) 455-6283. *Fax:* (619) 459-1386.

CHANDRASEKHARAN, Komaravolu, M.A., PH.D.; Indian mathematician; b. 21 Nov. 1920, Masulipatam, India; m. A. Sarada 1944; two s.; ed. Presidency Coll., Madras, and Inst. for Advanced Study, Princeton; Prof. Eidgenössische Technische Hochschule (Swiss Fed. Inst. of Tech.), Zürich 1965–; Sec. Int. Mathematical Union 1961–66, Pres. 1971–74; Vice-Pres. Int. Council of Scientific Unions 1963–66, Sec.-Gen. 1966–70; mem. Scientific Advisory Cttee, to Cabinet, Govt. of India 1961–66; Fellow Nat. Inst. of Sciences of India, Indian Acad. of Sciences; Foreign mem. Finnish Acad. of Science and Letters 1975; Hon. mem. Austrian Acad. of Sciences 1996; lectured at more than 50 univs. in the U.S.A., U.S.S.R., Europe and Asia; Padma Shri 1959, Shanti Swarup Bhatnagar Memorial Award for Scientific Research 1963, Ramanujan Medal 1966. *Publications:* Fourier Transforms (with S. Bochner) 1949, Typical Means (with S. Minakshisundaram) 1952, Lectures on the Riemann Zeta-function 1953, Analytic Number Theory 1968, Arithmetical Functions 1970, Elliptic Functions 1985, Classical Fourier Transforms 1989, Siegel's Lectures on the Geometry of Numbers (ed.) 1989, Lectures on Topological Groups 1996, Integration Theory 1996; over 70 research papers. *Leisure interests:* painting, English literature, music. *Address:* Eidgenössische Technische Hochschule, 8092 Zürich, Rämistrasse 101 (Office); Hedwigstrasse 29, 8032 Zürich, Switzerland (Home). *Telephone:* 381-96-86.

CHANEY, Frederick Michael, LL.B.; Australian politician and lawyer; b. 28 Oct. 1941, Perth; s. of Frederick Charles Chaney and Mavis Mary Bond; m. Angela Margaret Clifton 1964; three s.; ed. Univ. of Western Australia; public service, Papua New Guinea 1964–66; pvt. law practice 1966–74; Senator from Western Australia 1974–90; Senate Opposition Whip 1975, Govt. Whip 1976–78; Minister for Admin. Services 1978, Assisting the Minister for Educ. 1978–79, for Aboriginal Affairs 1978–80, Assisting the Minister for Nat. Devt. and Energy 1979–80, for Social Security 1980–83; Leader of Opposition in Senate 1983–90; Shadow Minister for Industrial Relations 1987–88, 1989–90, for the Environment 1990–92; Deputy Leader of the Opposition 1989–90; Chair. Fightback! (Co-ordination and Marketing Group) 1992–93; Researcher, lecturer Grad. School of Man., Univ of W. Australia 1993–95; Chancellor Murdoch Univ., Western Australia 1995–; mem. House of Reps. for Pearce 1990–93; mem. Nat. Native Title Tribunal 1995–; Liberal. *Leisure interests:* swimming, reading. *Address:* 5 Melville Street, Claremont, W.A. 6010, Australia.

CHANG CHIN-CHEN, PH.D.; Taiwanese computer scientist and university professor; b. 12 Nov. 1954, Taiwan; m. Ling-Hui Hwang 1981; one s. two d.; ed. Nat. Tsing Hua Univ., Hsinchu and Nat. Chiao Tung Univ., Hsinchu; Assoc. Prof., Dept. of Computer Eng., Nat. Chiao Tung Univ. 1982–83; Assoc. Prof., Dept. of Applied Math., Nat. Chung Hsin Univ. 1983–85, Prof. 1985–89; Prof. and Chair. Dept. of Computer Eng., Nat. Chung Cheng Univ. 1989–92, Prof. and Dean Coll. of Eng. 1992–95, Prof. and Dean of Academic Affairs 1995–, Acting Pres. 1996–; Ed. Journal of Information Science and Eng. 1988–93, Journal of Chinese Inst. of Engineers 1990–93, Information Science Applications 1994–; Ed.-in-Chief Information and Education 1987–; reviewer, numerous int. journals of information science; Outstanding talent in Information Science Award of Repub. of China 1984, several Distinguished Research Awards of Nat. Science Council 1986–. *Publications:* more than 300 tech. papers on database design and information security in leading scientific journals and conf. proceedings; 12 books in Chinese on database design, data structures, computer viruses, information security, cryptography etc.; Ed. Advanced Database Research and Development Series (Vols. 1, 2, 3) 1992. *Address:* Department of Computer Science and Information Engineering, National Chung Cheng University, Chiayi, Taiwan. *Telephone:* (5) 272 0405. *Fax:* (5) 272 0404.

CHANG CHONGXUAN; Chinese government official; b. 1931, Yuci City, Shanxi Prov.; m. Ni Qi Ying 1960; two s.; joined CCP 1949; Vice-Minister for Family Planning 1985–91; Vice-Pres. China Family Planning Asscn. 1992; deputy to 8th NPC, mem. Educ., Science, Culture and Public Health Cttee. *Leisure interest:* swimming. *Address:* China Family Planning Association, 1 Shenggu Beili, Yinghuayuan Xijie, Beijing 100029, People's Republic of China. *Telephone:* 4227612. *Fax:* 4227612.

CHANG DO YUNG, General; Korean army officer; b. 1923; ed. Tongyang Univ., Japan; fought in Japanese army in Second World War; further educ. in U.S.A. 1953; Deputy C.-in-C. of Gen. Staff, S. Korean Army 1956, later Commdr. Second Army; C.-in-C. of General Staff; Minister of Defence May–June 1961, Chair. Supreme Council of Nat. Reconstruction and Prime Minister May-June 1961; under house arrest July 1961; sentenced to death Jan. 1962, sentence commuted, later released 1962.

CHANG JIE; Chinese administrator; b. Feb. 1929, Liaoyang, Liaoning Prov.; ed. Northeast Zhongzheng Univ.; joined CCP 1949; Dir. Consultants' Office of State Council 1990–. *Address:* State Council, Zhongnanhai, Beijing, People's Republic of China.

CHANG, John H., B.A., M.S.; Taiwanese politician; b. 2 May 1941, Kiangsi; m. Helen Chang Huang; three c.; ed. Soochow Univ., Georgetown Univ.; Third then Second Sec., Washington Embassy 1974–78; Section Chief Dept. of N. American Affairs, Ministry of Foreign Affairs 1978, Deputy Dir. 1980–81; Sec.-Gen. Coordination Council of N. American Affairs (now TECO/TECRO) 1981–82, Dir. of Dept. 1982–86; Admin. Vice-Minister of Foreign Affairs 1986–90; Dir.-Gen. Dept. of Overseas Affairs Kuomintang Cen. Cttee. 1990; Political Vice-Minister of Foreign Affairs 1990–93; Minister Overseas Chinese Affairs Comm. and Minister of State 1993–96; Minister of Foreign Affairs 1996–97, Deputy Prime Minister 1997; mem. Kuomintang Cen. Cttee. and Cen. Standing Cttee. 1993–. *Publication:* Damansky Island Incident. *Address:* Executive Yuan, 1 Chung Hsiao E. Road, Taipei, Taiwan.

CHANG, Jung, PH.D.; British author; b. 25 March 1952, Yibin, China; d. of Shou-Yu Chang and De-hong Xia; m. Jon Halliday 1991; ed. Univ. of York; came to U.K. to study linguistics 1978; now full-time writer; Dr. h.c. (Buckingham Univ.) 1996, (Warwick, York) 1997, (Open Univ., U.K.) 1998; NCR Book Award (U.K.) 1992, U.K. Writers' Guild Best Non-Fiction Book 1992, Fawcett Soc. Book Award (U.K.) 1992, Book of the Year (U.K.) 1993, Golden Bookmark Award (Belgium) 1993, 1994, Best Book of 1993, Humo (Belgium), Bjørnsonordenen, Den Norske Orden for Literature (Norway) 1995. *Publication:* Wild Swans: Three Daughters of China 1991. *Address:* c/o Toby Eady Associates, 9 Orme Court, London, W2 4RL, England. *Telephone:* 0171-792 0092. *Fax:* 0171-792 0879.

CHANG KING-YUH, LL.M., PH.D.; Taiwanese government official; b. 27 April 1937, Hsiangtan County, Hunan; s. of Shao Chu Chang and Hsi-chen Huang; m. Grace Yu 1964; two s.; ed. Nat. Taiwan Univ., Nat. Chengchi Univ. and Columbia Univ.; lecturer, Hofstra Univ., U.S.A. 1968–69; Asst. Prof. Western Ill. Univ. 1972; Assoc. Prof. Nat. Chengchi Univ. 1972–75, Chair. Dept. of Diplomacy 1974–77, Dir. Grad. School of Int. Law and Diplomacy 1975–77, Prof. 1975–, Deputy Dir. Inst. of Int. Relations 1977–81, Dir. 1981–84, Pres. Nat. Chengchi Univ. 1989–94; Visiting Fellow, Johns Hopkins Univ. 1976–77; Distinguished Visiting Scholar, Inst. of E. Asian Studies, Univ. of Calif., Berkeley 1983; Dir.-Gen. Govt. Information Office 1984–87; Dir. Inst. of Int. Relations 1987–90; Minister of State. Exec. Yuan 1994–96. *Leisure interests:* reading, mountain climbing and sports. *Address:* 1 Chung Hsiao East Road, Sec. 1, Taipei, Taiwan. *Telephone:* (02) 356 1703. *Fax:* (02) 351 3038.

CHANG, Kwang-chih, PH.D.; American professor of anthropology; b. 15 April 1931, Peiping (now Beijing), China; s. of Chang Wo-chün and Lo Hsin-hsiang; m. Li Hwei 1957; one s. one d.; ed. Nat. Taiwan Univ., Harvard Univ.; Lecturer on Anthropology, Harvard Univ. 1960–61, Prof. 1977–96, Chair. Dept. of Anthropology 1981–84, John E. Hudson Prof. of Archaeology 1984–96, Curator of E. Asian Archaeology, Peabody Museum of Archaeology and Ethnology; Instructor in Anthropology, Yale Univ. 1961–63, Asst. Prof. 1963–66, Prof. 1969–77, Chair. Dept. of Anthropology 1970–73; Hon. M.A.; mem. Acad. Sinica (Taipei) 1974 (Vice-Pres. 1994–96), N.A.S. (Washington, D.C.) 1979–. *Publications:* The Archaeology of Ancient China 1963, Rethinking Archaeology 1967, Prehistory of Taiwan 1969, Early Chinese Civilization 1972, Shang Civilization 1980, Art, Myth and Ritual: The Path to Political Authority in Ancient China 1983, Chinese Bronze Age (Vol. I) 1983, (Vol. II) 1990. *Address:* Department of Anthropology, 57 C–D, Peabody Museum, Harvard University, Cambridge, MA 02138, U.S.A. *Telephone:* (617) 495-4389.

CHANG, Michael; American tennis player; b. 22 Feb. 1972, Hoboken, N.J.; s. of Joe Chang and Betty Chang; coached by his brother Carl and others; aged 15½ was youngest player since 1918 to compete in men's singles at U.S. Open 1987; turned professional 1988; first played at Wimbledon 1988;

winner, French Open 1989, becoming youngest known player of a Grand Slam tournament; Davis Cup debut 1989; winner Canadian Open 1990; semi-finalist, U.S. Open 1992, finalist 1996; finalist French Open 1995, semi-finalist Australian Open 1995, finalist 1996. *Address:* Advantage International, 1751 Pinnacle Drive, Suite 1500, McLean, VA 22102, U.S.A.

CHANG SHANA; Chinese artist; b. 26 March 1931, Lyon, France; one s.; ed. Dunhuang, Boston Museum of Fine Art School and New York; returned to China 1950; Asst. to architect Liang Sicheng, Qinghua Univ. 1951–56; Prof. Cen. Acad. of Arts and Design 1957–85; del. 12th Conf. CCP 1982; Pres. Cen. Acad. of Arts and Design 1985–; mem. New York Students League 1953, Cen. Acad. of Arts and Design; mem. Educ., Science, Culture and Public Health Cttee. 8th NPC. *Address:* Central Academy of Arts and Design, 34 North Dong Huan Road, Beijing 100020, People's Republic of China.

CHANG TZU-YUAN; Taiwanese business executive; fmrly. Chair. Chinese Petroleum Corp.

CHANG XIANGYU; Chinese actress; b. 1921; mem. 1st NPC 1954–58, 5th NPC 1978–83; Vice-Pres. Dramatists' Asscn. 1980–; mem. Presidium 5th NPC 1980–83, 6th NPC 1983–87, 7th NPC 1988; Pres. Henan School of Traditional Operas 1982; mem. 5th Nat. Cttee., Fed. Literary and Art Circles 1988, Hon. mem. 1996. *Address:* The Dramatists' Association, Beijing, People's Republic of China.

CHANG YUNG FA; Taiwanese business executive; b. 1927; ed. Taipei Commercial High School; joined local shipping co. as Third Officer, progressed through ranks to Capt.; est. shipping co. 1961; est. Evergreen Marine Corp. 1968, now Chair. Evergreen Group, est. EVA Airways 1991; Adviser to Pres. of Panama; Hon. D.Hum.Litt. Calif. State Univ.; Hon. D.B.A. Univ. of South Carolina; Hon. Consul-Gen. of Panama, Taipei.

CHANGEUX, Jean-Pierre, DR. ÈS SC.; French research professor; b. 6 April 1936, Domont; s. of Marcel Changeux and Jeanne Benoît; m. Annie Dupont 1962; one s.; ed. Lycées Montaigne, Louis le Grand and St. Louis, Paris, and Ecole Normale Supérieure, Ulm; research asst. 1958–60; asst. lecturer, Science Faculty, Univ. of Paris 1960–66; post-doctoral Fellow, Univ. of Calif. 1966, Columbia Univ., New York 1967; Vice-Dir. Coll. de France (Chair. of Molecular Biology) 1967; Prof. Institut Pasteur 1974–; Prof. Coll. de France 1975–; Pres. Interministerial Comm. for Preservation of Nat. Artistic Heritage 1989–, Consultative Cttee. on Ethics for Life and Medical Sciences 1992–; corresp. mem. numerous comms., Turin Acad. of Medicine, Académie des Sciences, Akademia Leopoldina, Halle, N.A.S., Swedish and Belgian acads.; Alexandre Joannidès prize (Académie des Sciences), Gairdner Foundation Award 1978, Lounsbery Prize (N.A.S., U.S.A.) 1982, Co-recipient Wolf Foundation Prize 1982, Céline Prize 1985, F.O. Schmitt Prize (Neurosciences Research Inst., New York) 1985, Fidia Neuroscience Award 1989, Bristol-Myers-Squibb Award in Neuroscience 1990; Carl-Gustav Bernhard Medal (Swedish Acad. of Sciences) 1991, Médaille d'Or (CNRS) 1992, Prix Jeantet (Geneva) 1993, Goodman and Gilman Award 1994, Camillo Golgi medal (Accad. Nazionale dei Lincei, Rome) 1994, Sir Hans Krebs medal (Helsinki) 1994; Officier Légion d'honneur, Grand Croix, Ordre nat. du mérite, Commandeur, Ordre des arts et des lettres. *Publications:* L'homme neuronal 1983, Matière à penseé 1989 (with Alain Connes), Raison et Plaisir 1994, Conversations on Mind, Matter and Mathematics (with Aida Connes) 1995, author and co-author of several research papers on allosteric proteins, on the acetylcholine receptor and on the devt. of the nervous system. *Leisure interests:* baroque paintings, organ music. *Address:* Laboratoire de Neurobiologie Moléculaire, Institut Pasteur, 25 rue du Docteur Roux, 75015 Paris (Office); 47 rue du Four, 75006 Paris, France (Home). *Telephone:* 45-68-88-05 (Office); 45-48-44-64 (Home). *Fax:* 45-68-88-36 (Office).

CHANG-HIM, Rt. Rev. French Kitchener, L.TH.; Seychelles ecclesiastic; b. 10 May 1938, Seychelles; s. of Francis Chang-Him and Amelia Zoé; m. Susan Talma 1975; twin d.; ed. Seychelles Coll., Lichfield Theological Coll., St. Augustine's Coll. Canterbury and Univ. of Trinity Coll. Toronto; primary school teacher 1958; man. of schools 1973–77; Chair. Teacher Training Coll. Bd. of Govs. 1976–77; Vicar-Gen. Diocese of Seychelles 1973–79; Archdeacon of Seychelles 1973–79; Bishop of Seychelles 1979–; Dean, Prov. of Indian Ocean 1983–84, Archbishop 1984–95; Hon. D.D. (Univ. of Trinity Coll., Toronto) 1991. *Publication:* The Seychellois: In Search of an Identity 1975. *Leisure interests:* international affairs, cooking, gardening, reading. *Address:* Bishop's House, P.O. Box 44, Victoria, Seychelles. *Telephone:* 224242. *Fax:* 224296.

CHANNING, Carol; American actress; b. 31 Jan. 1923; m. 3rd Charles Lowe 1956; one s.; Critics' Circle Award for Lend an Ear; Tony Award for Hello Dolly 1963, Golden Globe Award for Best Supporting Actress, Thoroughly Modern Millie 1967, Tony Award 1968. *Plays include:* No for an Answer, Let's Face It, So Proudly We Hail, Lend an Ear, Gentlemen Prefer Blondes, Wonderful Town, The Vamp, Hello Dolly, Lorelei. *Films include:* The First Traveling Saleslady 1956, Thoroughly Modern Millie 1967, Skidoo 1968, Sgt. Pepper's Lonely Hearts Club Band 1978, Hans Christian Andersen's Thumbelina 1994 (voice), The Line King: Al Hirschfield 1996, Homo Heights 1998. *Address:* c/o William Morris Agency, 151 S. El Camino Boulevard, Beverly Hills, CA 90212, U.S.A.

CHANNING, Stockard (b. Susan Stockard), B.A.; American actress; b. 13 Feb. 1944, New York; m. four times; ed. Harvard Univ.; performed in experimental drama with Theatre Co. of Boston 1967; numerous stage appearances include Two Gentlemen of Verona, New York, San Francisco, L.A. 1972–73, No Hard Feelings, New York 1973, Vanities, L.A. 1976, As You Like It 1978, They're Playing Our Song, Lady and the Clarinet 1983, The Golden Age 1983, A Day in the Death of Joe Egg 1985 (Tony Award for Best Actress), House of Blue Leaves 1986, Woman in Mind 1988, Love Letters 1989, Six Degrees of Separation, New York 1990 (also London stage début, Royal Court Theatre 1992), Four Baboons Adoring the Sun 1992; TV appearances include The Stockard Channing Show 1979–80 and various TV movies. *Films include:* Comforts of the Home 1970, The Fortune 1975, Sweet Revenge 1975, The Big Bus 1976, Grease 1978, The Cheap Detective 1978, Boys Life 1978, Without A Trace 1983, Heartburn 1986, Men's Club 1986, Staying Together 1987, Meet the Applegates 1987, Married to It 1993, Six Degrees of Separation 1993, Smoke 1995, Up Close and Personal, Moll Flanders, Edie and Pen. *Address:* I.C.M., 40 W. 57th Street, New York, NY 10019, U.S.A.

CHANNON, Rt. Hon. (Henry) Paul Guinness (see Kelvedon of Ongar, Baron).

CHANTURYA, Valentin Alekseyevich; Russian metallurgist; 15 Oct. 1938; m. 2nd Yelena Leonidovna Chanturya; two s. two d.; ed. Moscow Inst. of Steel and Alloys; jr., sr. researcher, head of lab. Moscow Inst. of Earth Sciences 1969–74; sr. researcher, head of lab. Inst. for Problems of Complex Devt. of Depth 1974–, deputy dir. 1993–; corresp. mem. U.S.S.R. (now Russian) Acad. of Sciences 1990, mem. 1994; research in physical and chemical aspects of processing mineral raw materials; Prize of U.S.S.R. Council of Ministers. *Publications include:* chem. of surfacial phenomena at flotation 1983. *Leisure interests:* fishing. *Address:* Institute for Problems of Complex Development of Depth, Kryukovsky tupir 4, 111020 Moscow, Russia. *Telephone:* (095) 360 0606 (Office); (095) 348 9394 (Home).

CHAO SHAO-K'ANG; Taiwanese politician; fmr. mem. Kuomintang (KMT); f. New Party Aug. 1993–. *Address:* New Party, 4th Floor, 65 Guang Fuh South Road, Taipei, Taiwan. *Telephone:* (2) 2756-2222.

CHAPIN, Schuyler Garrison; American musical impresario; b. 13 Feb. 1923, New York; s. of L. H. Paul Chapin and Leila H. Burden; m. 1st Elizabeth Steinway 1947 (died 1993); four s.; m. 2nd Catia Zoullas Mortimer 1995; ed. Longy School of Music; Spot Sales, NBC Television, New York 1947–50; Gen. Man. Tex and Jinx McCrary Enterprises, New York 1950–53; Booking Dir. Judson O'Neill and Judd Div., Columbia Artists Man. 1953–59; CBS Dir. Masterworks, Columbia Records Div. 1959–62, Vice-Pres. Creative Services 1962–63; Vice-Pres. Programming, Lincoln Center for the Performing Arts Inc. 1964–69; Exec. Producer, Amberson Productions 1969–72; Gen. Man. Metropolitan Opera Asscn. Inc. 1972–75; Dean of Faculty of Arts, Columbia Univ., New York 1976–87, Dean Emer. 1987–; Vice-Pres. Worldwide Concert & Artists Activities, Steinway & Sons 1990–92; Commr. of Cultural Affairs for City of New York 1994–; Special Consultant, Carnegie Hall Corpn. 1976–79, trustee and mem. artistic cttee. 1979–; Trustee, Naumburg Foundation 1962–; Bagby Music Lovers Foundation 1959–, mem. Bd. of Dirs., Amberson Group Inc. 1972–; mem. The Century Asscn.; Chair. Exec. Cttee. Franklin and Eleanor Roosevelt Inst. 1983–; Curtis Inst. of Music 1986–, Lincoln Center Theatre 1985; Hon. L.H.D. (New York Univ. and Hobart-William Smith Colls.) 1974; Hon. Litt.D. (Emerson Coll.) 1976, Hon. D. Mus. (Mannes Coll., New York) 1990; Air Medal 1945; N.Y. State Conspicuous Service Cross 1951; Christopher Award 1972, Emmy Awards 1972, 1976, 1980. *Publications:* Musical Chairs, A Life in the Arts 1977, Leonard Bernstein: Notes from a Friend 1992, Sopranos, Mezzos, Tenors, Basses and Other Friends 1995. *Leisure interests:* bridge, reading, swimming. *Address:* Department of Cultural Affairs, 330 West 42nd Street, New York, NY 10036 (Office); 650 Park Avenue, New York, NY 10021, U.S.A. (Home). *Telephone:* (212) 643-2101 (Office); (212) 734-5553 (Home). *Fax:* (212) 643-7780 (Office); (212) 628-8631 (Home).

CHAPLIN, Geraldine; American actress; b. 1944, Santa Monica, Calif.; d. of Charles Chaplin and Oona (O'Neill) Chaplin; one s.; ed. pvt. schools, Royal Ballet School, London, U.K. *Films include:* Doctor Zhivago 1965, Stranger in the House 1967, I Killed Rasputin 1968, The Hawaiians 1970, Innocent Bystanders 1973, Buffalo Bill and the Indians or Sitting Bull's History Lesson, The Three Musketeers 1974, The Four Musketeers, Nashville 1975, Welcome to L.A. Cria, Roseland 1977, Remember My Name, A Wedding 1978, The Mirror Crack'd 1980, Voyage en Douce 1981, Bolero 1982, Corsican Brothers, The Word, L'Amour Par Terre, White Mischief 1988, The Moderns 1988, The Return of the Musketeers, I Want To Go Home, The Children, Chaplin 1992, Jane Eyre, In the Name of God's Poor 1997, Cousin Bette 1998; TV appearances include My Cousin Rachel, A Foreign Field. *Address:* c/o Ames Cushing, William Morris Agency, 151 S. El Camino Drive, Beverly Hills, CA 90212, U.S.A.

CHAPMAN, Dennis, PH.D., F.R.S.C., F.R.S.; British professor of biophysical chemistry; b. 6 May 1927, Co. Durham; s. of George Henry Chapman and Katherine Magnus; m. 1st Elsie Margaret 1949 (died 1989); two s. one d.; m. 2nd Françoise Nioukleen 1993; ed. London, Liverpool and Cambridge Univs.; Comyns Berkeley Fellow, Gonville and Caius Coll., Cambridge Univ. 1960–63; Head of Gen. Research Div., Unilever Ltd., Welwyn 1963–69; Prof. Assoc., Biophysical Chem., Sheffield Univ. 1968–76; Sr. Wellcome Trust Research Fellow, Dept. of Chem., Chelsea Coll., Univ. of London 1976–77; Prof. of Biophysical Chem. 1977–93, now Prof. Emer., Royal Free Hosp. School of Medicine, Univ. of London, Head Div. of Basic Medical Science

1988–89, Head Dept. of Protein and Molecular Biology 1988–, Vice-Dean 1990–; f. Biocompatibles Ltd. 1984; Assoc. Dir. I.R.C. Medical Biomaterials 1991–; Langmuir Lecturer, American Chemical Soc. 1992; Hon. mem. Spanish Biophysical Soc. 1991; Hon. D.Sc. (Utrecht) 1978, (Memorial) 1980, (País Vasco) 1994, (Ancona) 1997; Hon. M.R.C.P.; Medal for Services to the School (Royal Free Hosp. School of Medicine) 1987, Interdisciplinary Award (Royal Soc. of Chemistry) 1993, Harden Medal (Biochemical Soc.) 1995. *Publications:* 14 books, 430 scientific publs. in various int. journals. *Leisure interests:* reading, painting, tennis and golf. *Address:* 10 One Tree Lane, Beaconsfield, Bucks., HP9 2BU, England. *Telephone:* (01494) 675818. *Fax:* (01494) 677718.

CHAPMAN, (F.) Ian, C.B.E., F.R.S.A., C.B.I.M.; British publisher; b. 26 Oct. 1925, St. Fergus, Aberdeenshire, Scotland; s. of late Rev. Peter Chapman and Frances Burdett; m. Marjory Stewart Swinton 1953; one s. one d.; ed. Shawlands Acad., Ommer School of Music, Glasgow; served R.A.F. 1943–44; Miner (nat. service) 1945–47; with William Collins Sons & Co. Ltd. (fmrly. W.M. Collins Holdings PLC, now Harper Collins) 1947, Man. Trainee New York br. 1950–51, Sales Man. London br. 1955; mem. main operating bd., Group Sales Dir. 1959, Jt. Man. Dir. 1967–76, Deputy Chair. 1976–81, Chair. C.E.O. 1981–89; Deputy Chair. Orion Publishing Group 1993–94, Dir. William Collins overseas cos. 1968–89: Canada 1968–89, U.S.A. 1974–89, S. Africa 1978–89, N.Z. 1978–89, William Collins Int. Ltd. 1975–89; Chair. Scottish Radio Holdings PLC (fmrly. Radio Clyde) 1972–96 (Hon. Pres. 1996–), Harvill Press 1976–89, Hatchards Ltd. 1976–89, William Collins Publrs. Ltd. 1979–81, The Listener Publs. PLC 1988–93, RadioTrust PLC 1997–, Guinness Publrs. Ltd. 1991–98; Dir. Pan Books Ltd. 1962–84 (Chair. 1973–76), Book Tokens Ltd. 1981–94, Ind. Radio News 1984–85, Stanley Botes Ltd. 1985–89, Guinness PLC. (non-exec.) 1986–91; Pres.-Dir. Gen. Guinness Media SAS, Paris 1996–; f. Chapmans Publrs. Chair. and Man. Dir. 1989–94; Trustee Book Trade Benevolent Soc. 1982–; Trustee The Publrs. Asscn.; mem. Gov. Council SCOTBIC; mem. Council Publishers Asscn. 1962–77, Vice-Pres. 1978, Pres. 1979–81; mem. bd. Book Devt. Council 1967, Ancient House Bookshop 1972–89, Scottish Opera, Theatre Royal Ltd. 1974–79, IRN Ltd. 1983–85; Chair. Advisory Bd. Strathclyde Univ. Business School 1985–88; Hon. D. Litt. (Strathclyde Univ.) 1990; Scottish Free Enterprise Award 1985. *Leisure interests:* grandchildren, music, golf, reading. *Address:* Kenmore, 46 The Avenue, Cheam, Surrey, England (Home). *Telephone:* 0181-642 1820 (Home). *Fax:* 0181-770 0225.

CHAPMAN, Orville Lamar, PH.D.; American professor of chemistry; b. 26 June 1932, New London, Conn.; m. 2nd Susan Parker Chapman 1981; two s. (from previous m.); ed. Virginia Polytechnic Inst. and Cornell Univ.; Prof. of Chem., Iowa State Univ. 1957–74, Univ. of Calif., Los Angeles 1974–; Arthur C. Cope Award (American Chem. Soc.), Texas Instrument Foundation Founders Prize, American Chem. Soc. Award in Pure Chem., Computerworld-Smithsonian Inst. Award in Educ. 1995. *Publications*: over 130 research articles. *Address*: Department of Chemistry and Biochemistry, University of California, 405 Hilgard Avenue, Los Angeles, CA 90024; 1213 Roscomare Road, Los Angeles, CA 90077, U.S.A. *Telephone*: (310) 825-4883.

CHAPMAN NYAHO, Daniel Ahmling, C.B.E., M.A.; Ghanaian public servant, teacher and business executive; b. 5 July 1909, Keta; s. of William and Jane (née Atriki) Chapman; m. Jane Abam Quashie 1941; two s. four d. (two d. deceased); ed. Bremen Mission School (Keta), Achimota Coll., Univ. of Oxford, Columbia Univ. and New York Univ.; Teacher Govt. Sr. Boys' School, Accra 1930, Achimota Coll. 1930–33, 1937–46; Gen. Sec. All-Ewe Conf. 1944–46; Area Specialist, UN Secr. Dept. of Trusteeship and Information from Non-Self-Governing Territories 1946–54; mem. Bd. of Man. of UN Int. School, New York 1950–54, 1958–59; Sec. to Prime Minister and Cabinet, Gold Coast 1954–57; Head of Ghana Civil Service 1957; Amb. to U.S.A. and Perm. Rep. to UN 1957–59; Chair. Mission of Ind. African States to Cuba, Dominican Repub., Haiti, Venezuela, Bolivia, Paraguay, Uruguay, Brazil, Argentina, Chile 1958; First Vice-Chair. Governing Council UN Special Fund 1959; Headmaster Achimota School 1959–63; Vice-Chair. Comm. on Higher Educ. in Ghana 1960–61, mem. Interim Nat. Council of Higher Educ. and Research, Ghana 1961–62; Fellow, Ghana Acad. of Arts and Sciences; mem. UN Middle East/North Africa Tech. Assistance Mission on Narcotics Control 1963; Dir. UN Div. of Narcotic Drugs 1963–66; mem. Political Cttee. of Nat. Liberation Council 1967; mem. Bd. of Trustees, Gen. Kotoka Trust Fund; Amb. Ministry of External Affairs 1967; Exec. Dir. Pioneer Tobacco Co. Ltd. (British-American Tobacco Group) 1967–70, Dir. 1970–; Dir. Standard Bank Ghana Ltd. 1970–75; Chair. Arts Council of Ghana 1968–69; Danforth Visiting Lecturer for Asscn. of American Colleges 1969, 1970; Chair. Council of Univ. of Science and Tech., Kumasi 1972–73; mem. Nat. Advisory Cttee. 1973; Dir. Ghana Film Industry Corpn. 1979–81, Ghana Nat. Honours and Awards Cttee. 1979–81; Deputy Chair. Ghana Constituent Assembly 1978–79. *Publications:* Our Homeland (Book I—A Regional Geography of South-East Gold Coast) 1945, The Human Geography of Eweland 1945. *Leisure interests:* music, walking, gardening, reading. *Address:* 7 Tenth Avenue, Tesano, Accra, Ghana (Home). *Telephone:* 227180 (Home).

CHAPPELL, Gregory (Greg) Stephen, M.B.E.; Australian cricketer and business executive; b. 7 Aug. 1948, Adelaide; s. of Arthur Martin and Jeanne Ellen (Richardson) Chappell; m. Judith Elizabeth Donaldson 1971; two s. one d.; ed. St. Leonards Primary School and Plympton High School, Adelaide, and Prince Alfred Coll., Adelaide; grandson of V. Y. Richardson (Australian Cricket Captain 1935–36); brother of I. M. Chappell (Australian Cricket Captain 1971–75); teams: S. Australia 1966–73, Somerset 1968–69, Queensland 1973–84 (Capt. 1973–77, 1979–80); 87 Tests for Australia 1970–84, 48 as Capt., scoring 7,100 runs (average 53.8) including 24 hundreds, and holding 122 catches; scored 108 on Test debut v. England, Perth 1970; only captain to have scored a century in each innings of 1st test as captain (v. West Indies, Brisbane 1975); holds record for most catches in a test match (7, v. England, Perth 1975); scored 24,535 first-class runs (74 hundreds); toured England 1972, 1975, 1977 and 1980; Australian Sportsman of the Year 1976; Hon. Life Mem. MCC 1985; Man. Dir. AD Sports Technologies (fmrly Fundamental Golf and Leisure Ltd.) 1993–95 (Dir. 1992–), Greg Chappell Sports Marketing 1995–98; State Man. of Cricket, S. Australian Cricket Asscn. 1998–. *Publication:* Greg Chappell's Health and Fitness Repair Manual 1998. *Leisure interests:* golf, tennis, reading, listening to music. *Address:* c/o South Australian Cricket Association, Adelaide Oval, North Adelaide, S.A. 5006, Australia.

CHAPPLE, Field Marshal Sir John (Lyon), G.C.B., C.B.E., M.A., F.Z.S., F.L.S., F.R.G.S.; British army officer; b. 27 May 1931; s. of C. H. Chapple; m. Annabel Hill 1959; one s. three d.; ed. Haileybury and Trinity Coll., Cambridge; joined 2nd King Edward's Own Gurkhas 1954, served Malaya, Hong Kong, Borneo; Staff Coll. 1962, Jt. Services Staff Coll. 1969; Commdr. 1st Bn. 2nd Gurkhas 1970–72; Directing Staff, Staff Coll. 1972–73; Commdr. 48 Gurkha Infantry Brigade 1976; Gurkha Field Force 1977; Prin. Staff Officer to Chief of Defence Staff 1978–79; Commdr. British Forces, Hong Kong and Maj.-Gen. Brigade of Gurkhas 1980–82; Dir. of Mil. Operations 1982–84; Deputy Chief of Defence Staff (Programmes and Personnel) 1985–87; Col. 2nd Gurkhas 1986–94; C.-in-C. U.K. Land Forces 1987–88; Aide-de-Camp Gen. to the Queen 1987–92; Chief of Gen. Staff 1988–92; Gov. and C.-in-C. Gibraltar 1993–95; Pres. Zoological Soc. of London 1991–94; Vice-Lord Lieut. of Greater London 1997–; Services Fellow Fitzwilliam Coll., Cambridge 1973; mem. Council Nat. Army Museum 1980–93; Pres. Mil. History Soc. 1991–, Soc. for Army Historical Research 1991–; Trustee World Wide Fund for Nature (U.K.) 1985–93, King Mahendra Trust for Conservation, Nepal.

CHARALAMBOPOULOS, Yannis; Greek politician; b. 1919, Psari, Messinia Pref.; m. Aga Stafila; one s. one d.; ed. Mil. Acad., Woolwich Inst., London; co. commdr. fighting invading Italians in Albania 1939; served in Greek units attached to allied armies in Middle East during World War II; teacher at Mil. Acad. 1953; Tech. Adviser, Ministry of Finance 1954–58; resigned from army 1961 and joined Centre Union Party; Deputy to Parl. 1963, 1964–67, 1974–; political prisoner 1967–72; leader, illegal Panhellenic Liberation Movt. 1972; arrested and imprisoned 1973–74; founding mem. Pasok, mem. of Cen. Cttee. and Exec. Office 1977; Pasok Parl. Rep. to European Parl. 1981; Minister of Foreign Affairs 1981–85, Deputy Prime Minister 1985–88, Minister of Defence 1986–90. *Address:* 17 Pringipos Petrou Street, 166 74 Glyfada, Greece. *Telephone:* 01-8932 333.

CHARASSE, Michel Joseph; French politician; b. 8 July 1941, Chamalières; s. of Martial Henri Charasse and Lucie Castellani; m. Daniele Bas 1978; ed. Lycée Blaise Pascal, Clermont-Ferrand, Institut d'Etudes Politiques and Faculté de Droit de Paris; mem. staff Ministry of Finance 1965–92; Asst. Sec.-Gen. Socialist group in Nat. Ass. 1962–67, 1968–81 and FGDS group 1967–68; Mayor Puy-Guillaume, Puy-de-Dôme 1977–; Regional Councillor, Auvergne 1979–87; Adviser to Pres. of the Repub. 1981–95; Senator from Puy-de-Dôme 1981–88, 1992–; Sec. of Senate 1995–; Minister-Del. for Budget 1988–92, Minister for Budget April–Oct. 1992. *Leisure interests:* hunting, fishing, reading. *Address:* Mairie, place Jean Jaurès, 63290 Puy-Guillaume; Sénat, Palais du Luxembourg, Paris 6ème, France. *Telephone:* (04) 73.94.70.49 (Puy-Guillaume); (01) 42.34.20.00 (Sénat).

CHARBONNEAU, Hubert, M.A., PH.D., F.R.S.C.; Canadian demographer; b. 2 Sept. 1936, Montreal; s. of Léonel Charbonneau and Jeanne Durand; m. Marie-Christiane Hellot 1961; one d.; ed. Univs. of Montreal and Paris; Sr. Lecturer, Univ. of Montreal 1962–68, Asst. Prof. 1968–70, Assoc. Prof. 1970–76, Prof. 1976–97; Visiting Prof. Univ. do Paraná, Brazil 1978, 1980, 1983, Univ. de Buenos Aires 1994; Killam Sr. Research Scholarship 1974, 1975, 1976; J. B. Tyrrell Historical Medal of the Royal Soc. of Canada 1990. *Publications:* author and co-author of several books on demographic topics. *Leisure interest:* genealogy. *Address:* Département de démographie, Université de Montréal, C.P. 6128, succ. "Centre-Ville", Montreal, P.Q., H3C 3J7 (Office); 19 avenue Robert, Outremont, P.Q., H3S 2P1, Canada (Home). *Telephone:* (514) 343-7229 (Office); (514) 731-5503 (Home). *Fax:* (514) 343-2309.

CHARBONNEL, Jean; French politician; b. 22 April 1927; m. Marielle Bal 1965; two s. two d.; ed. Lycées Henri IV and Louis-le-Grand, Paris, Univ. de Paris à la Sorbonne, Ecole Normale Supérieure and Ecole Nat. d'Administration; Research worker C.N.R.S.; with Cour des Comptes 1956; Prof. Inst. for Political Sciences, Paris 1957–63; Tech. Counsellor Ministry of Public Health and later Ministry of Justice 1959–62; Appeal Court Counsellor, Cour des Comptes 1962; mem. Chamber of Deputies 1962–73; Gen. Counsellor Brive-Nord area 1964–88; Mayor of Brive 1966–95; Sec. of State for Foreign Affairs (Co-operation) 1966–67; mem. nat. secretariat Union des Démocrates pour la République 1967–68, Asst. Sec.-Gen. 1968–71; Pres. Comm. des Finances, Assemblée nationale 1971–72; Minister of Industrial and Scientific Devt. 1972–73; with Cour des Comptes 1974; Pres. Fédération des républicains de progrès 1976; Délégué Gén. du R.P.R. (1980–81); Député from Corrèze 1986–93. *Publications:* L'aventure de la fidélité 1976, Comment peut-on être opposant? 1983, Le gaullisme aujourd'hui 1985, Politiques et Chrétiens, Edmond Michelet 1987, De Gaulle au présent 1990, (jtly.) Histoire de Brive et de sa région 1991, A la gauche du Général 1997. *Address:* 38 boulevard Koenig, 19100 Brive-la-Gaillarde; 14 rue Dupont-des-Loges, 75007 Paris, France.

CHAREST, Jean J., P.C., LL.B.; Canadian politician; b. 24 June 1958, Sherbrooke, Quebec; m. Michèle Dionne 1980; one s. two d.; ed. Université de Sherbrooke; mem. Sherbrooke Legal Aid Office 1981; Assoc. Beauchemin, Dussault et Charest 1981–84; Progressive Conservative M.P. for Sherbrooke 1984–; Asst. Deputy Speaker, House of Commons 1984; Minister of State (Youth) 1986–90, (Fitness and Amateur Sport) 1988–90; Deputy Govt. Leader in House of Commons 1989–90; Minister for the Environment 1991–93; Deputy Prime Minister of Canada and Minister of Industry; Leader Progressive Conservative Party 1993–98; Leader Liberal Party in Quebec 1998–; mem. numerous Cabinet Cttees.; mem. Quebec Bar Asscn., Canadian Bar Asscn. *Leisure interests:* skiing, sailing. *Address:* c/o Liberal Party of Canada, 81 Metcalfe Street, Suite 400, Ottawa, Ont., K1P 6M8, Canada.

CHARETTE DE LA CONTRIE, Hervé Marie Joseph de; French politician; b. 30 July 1938, Paris; s. of Hélion de Charette de la Contrie and Jeanne de Nolhac; m. 2nd Michèle Delor; one c. and three c. by previous m.; ed. Ecole des Hautes Etudes Commerciales, Inst. d'Etudes Politiques, Paris and Ecole Nat. d'Admin.; Deputy Sec.-Gen. Council of State 1969–72, Maître des requêtes 1973; Ministry of Labour 1973–78; Pres. Admin. Council, Nat. Immigration Office 1977; Dir. Office of Minister of Educ. 1978; Pres. Sonacotra 1980–81; Deputy Sec.-Gen. Parti Républicain 1979; returned to Council of State 1981; Deputy to Nat. Ass. 1986, 1988–93, 1997–; Asst. Minister, Office of Prime Minister 1986–88; Mayor of Saint-Florent-Le-Vieil 1989–; Vice-Pres. Union pour la Démocratie Française (UDF) 1991; Vice-Pres. Conseil Régional, Pays de la Loire 1992; Minister of Housing 1993–95, of Foreign Affairs 1995–97. *Address:* Mairie, 49410 Saint-Florent-le-Vieil; Assemblée Nationale, 75355, Paris; 8 rue Emile Acollas, 75007 Paris, France.

CHARGAFF, Erwin, DR.PHIL.; American professor of biochemistry and author; b. 11 Aug. 1905, Austria; s. of Hermann and Rosa Chargaff; m. Vera Broido 1929; one s.; ed. Maximiliansgymnasium, Vienna, and Univ. of Vienna; Research Fellow, Yale Univ. 1928–30; Asst., Univ. of Berlin 1930–33; Research Assoc., Inst. Pasteur, Paris 1933–34; Columbia Univ., N.Y. 1935–, Asst. Prof. 1938–46, Assoc. Prof. 1946–52, Prof. of Biochemistry 1952–74, Chair. Biochemistry Dept. 1970–74, Prof. Emer. of Biochemistry 1974; Visiting Prof., Sweden 1949, Japan 1958, Brazil 1959; Einstein Chair., Collège de France, Paris 1965, Cornell Univ. 1967; mem. N.A.S., American Philosophical Soc.; Fellow American Acad. of Arts and Sciences, Boston; mem. Deutsche Akad. der Naturforscher Leopoldina; Foreign mem. Royal Swedish Physiographic Soc., Lund; Guggenheim Fellow 1949, 1958; Hon. Sc.D. (Columbia) 1976, Hon. Dr.Phil. (Basel) 1976; Pasteur Medal, Paris 1949, Neuberg Medal, N.Y. 1959, Charles Leopold Mayer Prize, Acad. des Sciences, Paris 1963, Dr. H.P. Heineken Prize, Royal Netherlands Acad. of Sciences, Amsterdam 1964, Bertner Foundation Award, Houston 1965, Gregor Mendel Medal, Halle 1973, Nat. Medal of Science, Washington 1975, New York Acad. of Medicine Medal 1980, Distinguished Service Award (Columbia Univ.) 1982, Johann Heinrich-Merck Prize, Deutsche Akad. für Sprache und Dichtung 1984, Literature Prize (Vienna) 1994, Austrian Decoration of Honour for Science and Art 1994. *Publications:* Essays on Nucleic Acids 1963, Voices in the Labyrinth 1977, Heraclitean Fire: Sketches from a Life before Nature 1978, Das Feuer des Heraklit 1979, Unbegreifliches Geheimnis 1980, Bemerkungen 1981, Warnungstafeln 1982, Kritik der Zunkunft 1983, Zeugenschaft 1985, Serious Questions 1986, Abscheu vor der Weltgeschichte 1988, Alphabetische Anschläge 1989, Vorläufiges Ende 1990, Vermächtnis 1992, Über das Lebendige 1994, Ein zweites Leben 1995, Die Aussicht vom 13. Stock; Editor: The Nucleic Acids (3 vols.) 1955, 1960; numerous scientific articles and other literary work. *Address:* 350 Central Park West, Apt. 13-G, New York, NY 10025, U.S.A. *Telephone:* (212) 222-7994.

CHARKIN, Richard Denis Paul, M.A., A.M.P.; British publishing executive; b. 17 June 1949; s. of Frank Charkin and Mabel Doreen Rosen; m. Susan Mary Poole 1972; one s. two d.; ed. Haileybury and I.S.C., Cambridge and Harvard Univs.; Science Ed. Harrap & Co. 1972; Sr. Publishing Man. Pergamon Press 1973; Medical Ed. Oxford Univ. Press 1974, Head of Science and Medicine 1976, Head of Reference 1980; Man. Dir. Academic and Gen. 1984; joined Octopus Publishing Group (Reed Int. Books) 1988; Chief Exec. Reed Consumer Books 1989–94, Exec. Dir. Reed Books Int. 1988–96, Chief Exec. 1994–96; C.E.O. Current Science Group 1996–97; Chief Exec. Macmillan Ltd. 1997–; Visiting Fellow Green Coll. Oxford 1987. *Leisure interests:* music, cricket. *Address:* Macmillan Publishers Ltd., 25 Eccleston Place, London, S.W.1 (Office); 3 Redcliffe Place, London, SW10 9DB, England (Home).

CHARKVIANI, Gela; Georgian politician; b. 1 March 1939, Tbilisi, Georgia; s. of Candide Charkviani and Tamar Djaoshvili; m. Nana Toidze-Charkviani; one s. one d.; ed. Tbilisi Inst. of Foreign Languages, Univ. of Michigan; teacher Tbilisi Inst. of Foreign Languages; author and narrator TV monthly programme Globe, Georgian TV 1976–94; Vice-Pres. Georgian Soc. for Cultural Relations with Foreign Countries 1984–92; Chief Adviser to Pres. Shevardnadze on Foreign Affairs, Head of Int. Relations Georgian State Chancellery 1992–; Chair. Presidential Comm. on Peaceful Caucasus. *Publications include:* trans. of King Lear, Georgia, Transcaucasus and Beyond 1996, articles in numerous journals. *Address:* State Chancellery of Georgia, Ingorokva str. 7, Tbilisi (Office); Gamsakhurdia str. 14, Tbilisi, Georgia (Home). *Telephone:* 93 47 39 (Office); 98 96 79 (Home).

CHARLES, Caroline; British fashion designer; b. 18 May 1942, Cairo, Egypt; d. of Noel St. John Fairhurst and Helen T. Williams; m. Malcolm Valentine 1966; one s. one d.; ed. Sacred Heart Convent, Woldingham, Surrey; fashion designer since 1963; established retail outlet in London selling Caroline Charles Collection 1979; launched first Caroline Charles House of Design, London 1989, now Man. Dir.; wholesale business suppliers leading British shops and stores and exports to U.S.A., Japan, Australia and Europe; Evening Standard Design Award 1983 and other design awards. *Publication:* Weekend Wardrobe. *Leisure interests:* travel, theatre, gardening. *Address:* 170 New Bond Street, London, W1Y 9PB; 56/57 Beauchamp Place, London, SW3 1NY, England. *Telephone:* 0171-493 4733 (New Bond Street); 0171-225 3197 (Beauchamp Place).

CHARLES, Dame (Mary) Eugenia, D.B.E.; Dominican politician; b. 15 May 1919, Pointe Michel; d. of John B. and Josephine (née Delauney) Charles; mem. Inner Temple, London 1947; legal practice, Barbados, Windward and Leeward Islands; political career began 1968; co-f. and first leader Dominica Freedom Party; M.P. 1970–95; Leader of the Opposition 1975–79; Prime Minister, Minister of Finance and Devt. 1980–95; Minister of Foreign Affairs 1980–90; mem. Council Women World Leaders, John F. Kennedy School of Govt., Harvard Univ.; fmr. Minister of Tourism and Trade; Pres. Int. Federation of Women Lawyers 1990–; fmr. Dir. Dominica Co-operative Bank; fmr. mem. Bd. Dominica Infirmary. *Leisure interests:* reading, travel. *Address:* P.O. Box 121, 1 Cross Lane, Roseau, Dominica.

CHARLES, Ray (b. Ray Charles Robinson); American jazz musician; b. 23 Sept. 1930, Albany, Ga.; s. of late Bailey and Aretha Robinson; m. (divorced); nine c.; ed. St. Augustine's School, Orlando, Fla.; taught himself to play and write for every bass and wind instrument in the orchestra, specializing in piano, organ and saxophone; composes and arranges; played at Rockin' Chair Club, Seattle Elks Club, Seattle; joined Lowell Fulsom's Blues Band, toured for a year; played at Apollo, Harlem; formed group to accompany singer Ruth Brown; Leader of Maxim Trio; with Atlantic Records 1954–59, ABC Records 1959–62, formed own cos., Tangerine 1962–73, Crossover Records Co. 1973–, Columbia Records 1982–; tours with Ray Charles Revue; major albums include Ray Charles' Greatest Hits, Modern Sounds in Country and Western Music (Vols. 1 and 2), Message from the People, Volcanic Action of my Soul, Through the Eyes of Love, Would You Believe, My World, Blue and Jazz; Songwriters Hall of Fame, Rock and Roll Hall of Fame 1986; Commdr. des Arts et des Lettres 1986; Nat. Medal of Arts 1993; Kennedy Center Honor 1986; Polar Munc Prize 1998. *Address:* c/o Ray Charles Entertainment, 2107 West Washington Boulevard, Los Angeles, CA 90018, U.S.A.

CHARLES-ROUX, Edmonde; French writer; b. 17 April 1920, Neuilly-sur-Seine; d. of François Charles-Roux and Sabine Gounelle; m. Gaston Defferre 1973 (deceased); ed. Italy; served as nurse, then in Resistance Movement, during Second World War, in which she was twice wounded; Reporter, magazine Elle 1947–49; Features Ed., French edn. of Vogue 1947–54, Ed.-in-Chief 1954–66; mem. Acad. Goncourt 1983–; Prix Goncourt 1966, Grand Prix Littéraire de Provence 1977; Chevalier, Légion d'honneur 1989, Croix de guerre. *Publications:* Oublier Palerme 1966, Elle Adrienne 1971, L'irrégulière 1974, Le temps Chanel 1979, Stèle pour un bâtard, Don Juan d'Autriche: 1545–1578 1980, Une enfance sicilienne 1981, Un désir d'Orient 1988, La jeunesse d'Isabelle Eberhardt, Nomade j'étais 1995, Les années africaines d'Isabelle Eberhardt. *Leisure interests:* music, sea and sailing. *Address:* Editions Grasset, 61 rue des Saints-Pères, Paris 75006, France (Office).

CHARLTON, Jack (John), O.B.E.; British professional football manager and fmr. player; b. 8 May 1935, Ashington, Northumberland; s. of Robert Charlton and Elizabeth Charlton; brother of Sir Robert Charlton (q.v.); m. Patricia Charlton 1958; two s. one d.; ed. Hirst Park School, Ashington; player Leeds United 1952–73; 35 full England caps 1965–70; Man. Middlesbrough (Div. 2 Champions 1974) 1973–77, Sheffield Wednesday 1977–83, Newcastle United 1984–85, Repub. of Ireland (qualified for European Championships W. Germany 1988, World Cup Italy 1990) 1986–95; played with winning teams League Championship 1969, Football Asscn. Cup 1972, League Cup 1968, Fairs Cup 1968, 1971, World Cup (England v. Germany) 1966. *Publication:* Jack Charlton's American World Cup Diary 1994, Jack Charlton: The Autobiography 1996. *Address:* 1 Cairn Lodge, Dalton, Ponteland, Northumbria, England.

CHARLTON, Sir Robert (Bobby), Kt., C.B.E.; British football player; b. 11 Oct. 1937; s. of Robert Charlton and Elizabeth Charlton; brother of Jack Charlton (q.v.); m. Norma Charlton 1961; two d.; ed. Bedlington Grammar School, Northumberland; professional footballer with Manchester United 1954–73, played 751 games, scored 245 goals; F.A. Cup Winners' Medal 1963; First Div. Championship Medals 1956–57, 1964–65, 1966–67; World Cup Winners' Medal (with England) 1966; European Cup Winners' Medal 1968; 106 appearances for England 1957–73, scored 49 goals; Man. Preston North End 1973–75; Chair. N.W. Council for Sport and Recreation 1982–; Dir. Manchester United Football Club 1984–; Hon. Fellow Manchester

Polytechnic 1979; Hon. M.A. (Manchester Univ.). *Publications:* My Soccer Life 1965, Forward for England 1967, This Game of Soccer 1967, Book of European Football, Books 1–4 1969–72. *Leisure interest:* golf. *Address:* Garthollerton, Chelford Road, Ollerton, nr. Knutsford, Cheshire, WA16 8RY, England.

CHARLTON, Robert William, M.B.B.CH., M.D., F.R.C.P.E., F.R.S.S.A.; South African university vice-chancellor; b. 27 Jan. 1929, Johannesburg; s. of Robert J. W. Charlton and Marjory Thomson; m. Margaret L. D. Ritchie 1960; one s. three d.; ed. St. John's Coll. Johannesburg and Univ. of the Witwatersrand; Sr. Physician, Johannesburg Hosp. 1961–87; Prof. of Experimental and Clinical Pharmacology, Univ. of the Witwatersrand 1967–83, Dean of Medicine 1978–79, Deputy Vice-Chancellor 1980–82, Vice-Prin. 1983–87, Vice-Chancellor and Prin. 1988–98; Chair. Medicines Control Council of South Africa 1976–81. *Publications:* more than 100 articles in medical journals, mainly in the field of iron metabolism. *Leisure interests:* golf, fly fishing, music. *Address:* c/o University of the Witwatersrand, Private Bag 3, Witwatersrand 2050, Johannesburg, South Africa.

CHARMOT, Guy, M.D.; French physician; b. 1914, Toulon; s. of Ulysse Charmot and Claire Esmieu; m. Edith Dubuisson 1948; one d.; Medical Officer in forces 1938; war service in Free French Forces 1940–45; served various hospitals in French-speaking Africa: Chad, Senegal, Congo, Madagascar 1945–66; now working at Hôpital Bichat (infectious and tropical diseases), Paris; Pres. Société de Pathologie exotique; mem. Acad. des Sciences d'Outre-Mer; Commdr. Légion d'honneur, Companion de la Libération, Croix de guerre. *Publications:* numerous papers concerned chiefly with diseases of the liver and spleen, human immunodeficiency virus (HIV), hereditary anaemia, malaria and amoeba-caused diseases. *Leisure interest:* mountaineering. *Address:* 72 boulevard de Reuilly, 75012 Paris, France. *Telephone:* (01) 46-28-97-73.

CHARPAK, Georges, PH.D.; French physicist; b. 1 Aug. 1924, Dabrovica, Poland; s. of Anna Szapiro and Maurice Charpak; m. Dominique Vidal 1953; two s. one. d.; ed. Ecole des Mines de Paris; prisoner in Dachau 1943–45; physicist C.N.R.S. 1947–59, C.E.R.N. 1959–; Dir.Cogema 1993–, Fimalac 1997–; f. Soc. for Biospace Measurement 1997; mem. Higher Council of Integration 1994–; mem. French Acad. of Sciences 1985; Foreign Assoc. N.A.S. 1986; Prize of European Physics Soc.; Nobel Prize for Physics 1992. *Publications:* la Vie à fil tendu 1993 (jtly.), Feu follet et champignon nucléaire 1997, numerous papers in learned journals. *Leisure interests:* skiing, music, trekking. *Address:* C.E.R.N., Division PPE, Geneva, 1211, Switzerland (Office); 2 rue de Poissy, 75005, Paris, France (Home). *Telephone:* 767 21-44 (Office).

CHARTIER, Roger; French university professor; b. 9 Dec. 1945, Lyons; s. of Georges Chartier and Laurence Fonvielle; m. Anne-Marie Trépier 1967; one s. one d.; ed. Ecole Normale Supérieure, Saint Cloud; Prof. Lycée Louis-Le-Grand, Paris 1969–70; Asst. Prof. Univ. Paris I, Panthéon-Sorbonne 1970–75; Assoc. Prof. Ecole des Hautes Etudes en Sciences Sociales 1975–83, Dir. of Studies 1984–; Visiting Prof. Univ. of Calif. (Berkeley) 1987, Cornell Univ. 1988, Johns Hopkins Univ. 1992; Annual Award, American Printing History Asscn. 1990; Grand Prix d'Histoire, Acad. Française 1992. *Publications:* The Cultural Uses of Print in Early Modern France 1987, The Culture of Print (ed.) 1987, Cultural History: Between Practices and Representations 1988, The Cultural Origins of the French Revolution 1991. *Address:* Ecole des Hautes Etudes en Sciences Sociales, 54 boulevard Raspail, 75006 Paris, France.

CHARTRES, Rt. Rev. and Rt. Hon. Richard John Carew, D.D.; British ecclesiastic; b. 11 July 1947; s. of Richard Chartres and Charlotte Chartres; m. Caroline McLintock 1982; two s. two d.; ed. Hertford Grammar School, Trinity Coll. Cambridge, Cuddesdon Theological Coll. Oxford and Lincoln Theological Coll.; ordained deacon 1973, priest 1974; Asst. Curate, St. Andrew's Bedford 1973–75; Domestic Chaplain to Bishop of St. Albans 1975–80; Chaplain to Archbishop of Canterbury 1980–84; Vicar, St. Stephen with St. John, Westminster 1984–92; Dir. of Ordinands for London Area 1985–92; Gresham Prof. of Divinity 1986–92; Bishop of Stepney 1992–95, of London 1995–; Dean of the Chapels Royal 1996–; rep. of London Church Leaders on London Pride Partnership; Ecclesiastical Patron Prayer Book Soc.; Prelate of Imperial Soc. of Kt.'s Bachelor; Hon. Bencher, Middle Temple; Liveryman Merchant Taylors' Co.; Hon. Freeman Weavers' Co.; Prelate of O.B.E. 1995–. *Address:* The Old Deanery, Dean's Court, London, EC4V 5AA, England. *Telephone:* 0171-248 6233.

CHARUSATHIRA, Gen. Prapas; Thai politician and army officer; b. 25 Nov. 1912, Udorn Prov.; m. Khunying Sawai; one s. four d.; ed. Chulachomklao Royal Mil. Acad. and Nat. Defence Coll; Army service 1933, rose through infantry to Gen. 1960; Minister of Interior 1957–71; Deputy Prime Minister 1963–71; Army Deputy Commdr. and Deputy Supreme Commdr. 1963–64, Supreme Commdr. 1964; mem. Nat. Exec. Council and Dir. of Security Council (Defence and Interior) 1971–72; Deputy Prime Minister, Minister of Interior 1972–73; Vice-Pres. and Rector, Chulalongkorn Univ. 1961–69; in exile 1973–77, returned to Thailand Jan. 1977; numerous decorations. *Publications:* The Role of the Ministry of Interior in the Development of National Security, The Role of the Ministry of Interior in Maintenance of National Peace and Order. *Leisure interests:* sport: boxing, soccer, golf, hunting, amateur ranching, arms collecting. *Address:* 132-5 Suan Puttan Residence, Bangkok, Thailand.

CHASE, Chevy (Cornelius Crane), M.A.; American comedian, actor and writer; b. 8 Oct. 1943, New York; s. of Edward Tinsley Chase and Cathalene Crane (née Widdoes) Chase; m. 1st Jacqueline Carlin 1976 (divorced 1980), 2nd Jayni Chase; three c.; ed. Bard Coll., Inst. of Audio Research, M.I.T.; actor The Groove Tube 1967–71; writer Mad magazine 1969; TV appearances include: The Great American Machine, Smothers Brothers Show, Saturday Night Live. *Films include:* Tunnelvision 1976, Foul Play 1978, Oh Heavenly Dog 1980, Caddyshack 1980, Seems Like Old Times, Under the Rainbow 1981, Modern Problems 1981, Vacation 1983, Deal of the Century 1983, European Vacation 1984, Fletch 1985, Spies Like Us 1985, Follow that Bird 1985, The Three Amigos 1986, Caddyshack II 1988, Funny Farm 1988, Christmas Vacation 1989, Fletch Lives 1989, Memoirs of an Invisible Man 1992, Hero 1992, Last Action Hero 1993, Cops and Robbersons 1994, Man of the House 1995; mem. American Fed. of Musicians, Stage Actors Guild, Actors Equity, American Fed. of TV and Radio Artists. *Address:* PMK, Box 257, Bradford, NY 10506, U.S.A.

CHASE, Rodney F.; business executive; b. 12 May 1943; m. Diana Lyle 1968; one s. one d.; with British Petroleum PLC London, joined depts. of shipping, refining and marketing, distribution, oil trading, gas; C.E.O. BP Finance, Group Treas.; Chief Financial Officer, fmr. Exec. Vice-Pres. BP America Inc., C.E.O., Chair. 1992–; C.E.O. BP Exploration Inc. (Western Hemisphere), a Man. Dir. The British Petroleum Co. PLC 1992–, Deputy Group Chief Exec.; Dir. (non-exec.) BOC Group PLC 1995–; mem. UK Advisory Cttee. on Business and the Environment (ACBE), UK Roundtable on Sustainable Devt.; Bd. mem. World Conservation Monitoring Centre; Fellow Asscn. of Corp. Treas. *Leisure interests:* downhill skiing, golf. *Address:* British Petroleum Company PLC, Britannic House, 1 Finsbury Circus, London, EC2M 7BA, England. *Telephone:* 0171-496 4000. *Fax:* 0171-496 4574.

CHASKALSON, Arthur, S.C., LL.B.; South African judge; b. 24 Nov. 1931, Johannesburg; s. of Harry Bernard Chaskalson and Mary Dorothea (née Oshry) Bernard; m. Lorraine Diane Ginsberg 1961; two s.; ed. Univ. of Witwatersrand; admitted to bar 1956, S.C. 1971; Chair. Johannesburg Bar Council 1976, 1982 (mem. 1967–71, 1973–84); Vice-Chair. Gen. Council of S.A. Bar 1982–87, Int. Legal Aid Div., Int. Bar Asscn. 1983–93; Nat. Dir. Legal Resources Centre 1979–93; Hon. Prof. of Law Univ. of Witwatersrand 1981–; Visiting Prof. Col. Univ., N.Y. 1987–88; Chair. Rhodes Scholarship Selection Cttee. for S.A. 1988–93; consultant to Namibian Constituent Ass. (in relation to the drafting of the Namibian Constitution) 1989–90, to African Nat. Congress (ANC) 1990–; mem. Tech. Cttee. on Constitutional Issues during the Multi-Party Negotiating Process May–Dec. 1993; Pres. Constitutional Court 1994–; Commr. Int. Comm. of Jurists 1995–; Hon. mem. Bar Asscn. of N.Y. City 1985; mem. Nat. Council of Lawyers for Human Rights 1980–91, numerous other memberships; two hon. degrees; Human Rights Award (Foundation for Freedom and Human Rights, Switzerland) 1990, numerous other awards; several hon. degrees. *Address:* Constitutional Court, Private Bag X32, Braamfontein 2017, South Africa. *Telephone:* (011) 403-8032.

CHATAWAY, Rt. Hon. Sir Christopher John, Kt., P.C.; British business executive, fmr. politician and fmr. athlete; b. 31 Jan. 1931; m. 2nd Carola Walker 1976; two s.; two s. one d. from 1st m.; ed. Sherborne School and Magdalen Coll., Oxford.; rep. U.K. at Olympic Games 1952, 1956; holder of world 5,000 metres record 1954; Jr. Exec., Arthur Guinness, Son and Co. 1953–55; Staff Reporter, Ind. Television News 1955–56; Current Affairs Commentator, BBC Television 1956–59; mem. London County Council 1958–61; M.P. for Lewisham North 1959–66, for Chichester 1969–74; Parl. Private Sec. to Minister of Power 1961–62; Joint Parl. Under-Sec. of State, Dept. of Educ. and Science 1962–64; Alderman, Greater London Council 1967–70; Minister of Posts and Telecommunications 1970–72, for Industrial Devt. 1972–74; Man. Dir. Orion Royal Bank 1974–88; Chair. Civil Aviation Authority 1991–96; Dir. BET PLC 1974–96, Macquarie Securities Ltd. 1994–; Chair. U.K. Athletics 1998; Trustee ActionAid; Trustee Foundation for Sport and the Arts 1991–; Hon. D.Litt. (Loughborough) 1980; Hon. D.Sc. (Cranfield) 1955. *Address:* 66 Maida Vale, London W9 1PR, England.

CHAUDHURI, Naranarain (Sankho), B.A.; Indian sculptor; b. 25 Feb. 1916, Santhal Purganas, Bihar; s. of Narendra Narain and Kiron Moyee; m. Ira Chaudhuri; two s. one d.; ed. Armanitoba High School, Dacca and Bishwa Bharti Santiniketan, West Bengal.; freelance artist 1947–; Reader and Head Dept. of Sculpture, Univ. of Baroda 1949–50, Prof. of Sculpture 1957, Dean, Faculty of Fine Arts 1966–68; Prof. of Fine Arts, Univ. of Dar-es-Salaam 1980; mem. Lalit Kala Akademi 1956–(Sec. 1974, Chair. 1984–); Pres. Indian Sculptors' Asscn. 1964–65; mem. Indian Cttee. Int. Asscn. of Plastic Arts, All India Handicrafts Bd., Int. Jury 5th Triennale-India, Lalit Kala Acad. 1956 (Sec. 1974, Fellow 1982); exhibited São Paulo Bienal 1961, One-Man Exhbns. Bombay, New Delhi and Calcutta; numerous Indian awards; Padma Shri 1971. *Major works:* Sculptures, All India Radio, Delhi 1955, Statue of Mahatma Gandhi, Rio de Janeiro 1964, sculpture for Jyoti Ltd., Baroda 1968, brass sculpture for World Bank commissioned by Govt. of India 1976, Mahatma Gandhi, Copenhagen 1985, and works in collections in India, U.K. and U.S.A. *Address:* c/o Lalit Kala Academy, Copernicus Marg, New Delhi 110003, India.

CHAUNU, Pierre, D. ÈS L.; French professor of history; b. 17 Aug. 1923, Belleville, Meuse; m. Huguette Catella 1947; five s. (one deceased) one d.;

School of Advanced Hispanic Studies, Madrid 1948–51; C.N.R.S. 1956–59, now mem. Directorate; Univ. de Caen 1959; Prof. of Modern History, Univ. de Paris à la Sorbonne 1970–; Assoc. Prof., Faculté de Théologie Réformée, Aix-en-Provence 1974; mem. of Section, Conseil Econ. et Social 1976–77; Pres. Conseil Supérieur des Corps Universitaires 1977; Columnist Le Figaro 1982–; mem. Social and Econ. Council 1976–; mem. Scientific Cttee. (history section), C.N.R.S. 1980–, numerous other cttees.; Pres. Fed. Nat. des syndicats autonomes de l'enseignement supérieur 1988–90; mem. Acad. des Sciences morales et politiques 1982– (Pres. 1993), High Council for Integration 1994–; Chevalier, Légion d'honneur. *Publications:* forty books including: Seville et l'Atlantique (1504–1650) (12 vols.), Le Pacifique des Ibériques, Civilisation de l'Europe classique, Civilisation de l'Europe des lumières, Temps des Réformes, L'Espagne de Charles Quint, La Mort à Paris, Histoire et Prospective, La Mémoire et le sacré, Le refus de la vie, La violence de Dieu, Un futur sans avenir, La mémoire de l'éternité, Le sursis 1979, Histoire et foi, Histoire et imagination 1980, Réforme et contre-réforme, Eglise, Culture et Société, Histoire et Décadence 1981, La France 1982, Ce que je crois 1982, Le chemin des mages 1983, Combats pour l'histoire 1983, L'historien dans tous ses états 1984, L'historien en cet instant 1985, Rétrohistoire, Au coeur religieux de l'histoire, L'aventure de la réforme 1986, Une autre voie (jtly.) 1986, Du Big Bang à l'enfant 1987, L'obscure mémoire de la France 1988, Apologie pour l'histoire 1988, Le grand déclassement 1989, Journal de Jeau Héroard 1989, Trois millions d'années, Quatre-vingts millards de destins 1990, Reflets et miroir de l'histoire 1990, Colère contre Colère 1991, Dieu, Apologie 1991, L'Aventure de la Reforme, le monde de Jean Calvin 1992, Brève histoire de Dieu 1992, l'Axe du temps 1994, l'Instant éclaté 1994, Les Enjeux de la Paix 1995, l'Héritage 1995, Baptême de Clovis, baptême de la France 1996, Danse avec l'histoire 1998, Le Basculement religieux de Paris 1998; 120 articles. *Address:* Université Paris-Sorbonne, 1 rue Victor-Cousin, 75230 Paris 05; 12 rue des Cordeliers, 14300 Caen, France. *Telephone:* (1) 325-49-62 (Paris); (31) 81-61-51 (Caen).

CHAUVIRÉ, Yvette; French ballerina; b. 22 April 1917, Paris; d. of Henri Chauviré and Berthe Pinchard; ed. Paris Opera Ballet School.; joined Paris Opera Ballet 1930, Danseuse Etoile 1942; with Monte Carlo Opera Ballet 1946–47; Artistic and Technical Adviser to Admin. of Paris Opera 1963–68; Dir. Acad. int. de danse, Paris 1970; Commdr. Légion d'honneur; Commdr. des Arts et des Lettres; Grand Officier Ordre nat. du Mérite; ballets in which she has performed leading roles include Istar, Les deux pigeons, Sleeping Beauty, David triomphant, Giselle, Les créatures de Prométhée, Roméo et Juliette, L'écuyère, Les suites romantiques, Lac des cygnes, L'oiseau de feu, Petrouchka, Sylvia, La belle Hélène, Casse-Noisette, Les mirages, Le cygne, La dame aux camélias. *Films include:* Carrousal Mapolitain 1953, Le cygne 1984, Une étoile pour l'exemple. *Publication:* Je suis ballerine. *Leisure interests:* drawings, watercolours, collecting swans. *Address:* 21 Place du Commerce, 75015 Paris, France.

CHAVALIT, Gen. Yongchaiyut; Thai politician and general; fmr. Deputy Prime Minister and Minister of Defence; Leader New Aspiration Party; Prime Minister, Minister of Defence 1996–97. *Address:* New Aspiration Party, Ban Mittraphap, Thanon Rama IV, Bangkok, Thailand. *Telephone:* (2) 243-5000.

CHAVAN, Shankarrao Bhaorao, B.A., LL.B.; Indian politician; b. 14 July 1920, Paithan, Aurangabad Dist.; s. of Bhaorao and Laxmibi Chavan; m. Kusumati; one s.; ed. Univs. of Madras and Osmania; entered politics 1945; Pres. Nanded Town Municipality 1952–56; mem. Bombay Legis. Council 1956, Assembly 1957–; Deputy Minister for Revenue, Bombay Govt. 1956–60; Minister for Irrigation and Power, Maharashtra Govt. 1960–75; Deputy Leader Congress Legis. Party 1967–75, Leader 1975–; Chief Minister, Maharashtra Govt. 1975–77, 1986–88; mem. (Congress (I)) Lok Sabha 1980–; Minister of Educ. 1980–81, of Planning 1981–84, of Defence 1984–85, of Home Affairs 1985–86, 1991–96, of Finance 1988–89; Vice-Presidential cand. 1984; Vice-Pres. Nanded Co-operative Bank; Dir. Hyderabad State Co-operative Bank; mem. Exec. of Cen. Co-operative Union, Hyderabad; Exec. Cttee. of Maharashtra Pradesh Congress Cttee., A.I.C.C. *Address:* c/o Ministry of Home Affairs, Room 26, North Block, New Delhi 110 001, India.

CHAVES DE MENDONÇA, Antônio Aureliano; Brazilian politician; b. 13 Jan. 1929, Três Pontas, Minas Gerais; s. of Jose Vieira and Luzia Chaves de Mendonça; m. Vivi Sanches de Mendonça; one s. two d.; ed. Itajuba Fed. School of Eng., Fluminense Faculty of Eng., War Coll.; teaching posts at Itajuba Fed. School of Eng. and Polytech. Inst. of Catholic Univ. of Minas Gerais; Tech. Dir. ELETROBRAS 1961; Majority Leader in State Congress of Minas Gerais 1963–67; State Sec. for Educ. 1964, for Transport and Public Works 1965; Fed. Deputy 1967–75, Chair. Comm. for Mines and Energy 1971, later of Comm. for Science and Tech., also posts in various other comms.; Vice-Pres. of Brazil 1979–85, Acting Pres. Sept.–Nov. 1981; Minister of Mines and Energy 1988; mem. Brazilian Geographical Soc., Brazilian Comm. for Large Dams, Brazilian Centre for Physical Research; various Brazilian medals; Arena party. *Publications:* several text books.

CHÁVEZ FRÍAS, Hugo Rafael; Venezuelan politician; b. 28 July 1954, Sabaneta, Barinas State; s. of Hugo de los Reyes Chávez and Elena de Chávez; ed. Liceo O'Leary, Barinas State, Mil. Acad., Univ. Simón Bolívar, Caracas; f. Movimiento Bolivariano Revolucionario 1982; Lieut.-Col. Venezuelan Paratroops 1990; led failed mil. coup against Pres. Carlos Pérez (q.v.) 1992; f. Movimiento Revolucionario V República 1998; represents Patriotic Pole coalition; Pres. of Venezuela Feb. 1999–. *Address:* Central Information Office of the Presidency, Torre Oeste 18°, Parque Central, Caracas 1010, Venezuela. *Telephone:* (2) 572-7110. *Fax:* (2) 572-2675.

CHAVUNDUKA, Gordon Lloyd, M.A., PH.D.; Zimbabwean university professor and politician; b. 16 Aug. 1931, Umtali (now Mutare); s. of Solomon and Lillian Chavunduka; m. Rachel Chavunduka 1959; two s. four d.; ed. Univ. of California at Los Angeles, Univs. of Manchester and London; lecturer in Sociology, Univ. of Rhodesia, Salisbury 1966–78, Acting Head, Dept. of Sociology 1974–75, Head 1978–86; mem. Univ. Senate 1972–96; Dean, Faculty of Social Studies 1978–88, 1991–; Pro-Vice-Chancellor, Univ. of Zimbabwe 1991–92, Vice-Chancellor 1992–96; Prof. Emer. 1997–; Zimbabwe Govt. Commr. for Public Enterprises 1988–90; Sec.-Gen. African Nat. Council 1973–76; Pres. Asscn. of Univ. Teachers of Rhodesia 1974–, Zimbabwe Nat. Traditional Healers Asscn. 1980–; Chair. Traditional Medical Practitioners Council 1983–. *Publications include:* Traditional Healers and the Shona Patient, Professionalisation of African Medicine, Traditional Medicine in Modern Zimbabwe; also papers in the field of sociology and contribs. to INCIDI, The Society of Malawi Journal, etc. *Leisure interests:* gardening, boxing (spectator), football. *Address:* 40 The Chase, Mount Pleasant, Harare, Zimbabwe (Home). *Telephone:* 332958.

CHAZOT, Georges-Christian; French business executive; b. 19 March 1939, Algiers; s. of Raymond Chazot and Suzanne Monnet; m. Marie-Dominique Tremois 1962; one s. two d.; ed. Lycée Bugeaud, Algiers, Ecole Polytechnique, Harvard Int. Marketing Inst. and MSEE Univ. of Florida; electronic engineer EMR Sarasota, Florida 1962; Man., Space Electronics, Schlumberger 1965–68, Tech. Dir. for Industrial Control 1968–70, Commercial Dir. for Instruments and Systems 1970–74, Audio-professional Dir.-Gen. 1974–76; Dir.-Gen. for Alkaline Accumulators, SAFT 1976–80, Dir.-Gen. 1981–83, Pres., Dir.-Gen. 1983–88, Hon. Pres. and Admin. 1989; Pres., Dir.-Gen. Centre d'Etudes et de Services pour le Développement Industriel (CEI) 1983–86; Vice-Pres., Dir.-Gen. Télic Alcatel and Opus Alcatel 1989–90; Pres., Dir.-Gen. Alcatel Business Systems 1990–91; Pres. Business Systems Group, Vice-Pres. Alcatel NV 1990–92; Pres., Dir.-Gen. Adia France 1992–94; Group Man. Dir. Eurotunnel 1994–; numerous directorships and other business appts.; Fellow Chartered Inst. of Transport; Chevalier Légion d'honneur, Officier Ordre Nat. du Mérite. *Leisure interests:* opera, sailing. *Address:* P.O. Box 2000, Folkestone, Kent, CT18 8XY, England; 140–144 boulevard Malesherbes, 75017 Paris, France. *Telephone:* (01303) 282222 (Folkestone). *Fax:* (01303) 283909 (Folkestone).

CHAZOV, Yevgeny Ivanovich, M.D., PH.D.; Russian politician and cardiologist; b. 10 June 1929, Gorky; ed. Kiev Medical Inst.; mem. CPSU 1962–91, mem. Cen. Cttee. 1982–90; Sr. Scientific Worker, Inst. of Therapy 1959; Deputy Dir. Inst. of Therapy, U.S.S.R. Acad. of Medical Science 1963–65, Dir. Inst. of Cardiology 1965–67; Deputy Minister of Public Health 1967–87, Minister 1987–91; mem. Supreme Soviet 1974–89; Dir. Cardiology Research Centre, Acad. of Medical Science 1975–; mem. Cen. Cttee. CSPU 1982–90; mem. U.S.S.R (now Russian) Acad. of Medical Sciences 1971, U.S.S.R. (now Russian) Acad. of Sciences 1979; Pres. U.S.S.R. (now Russian) Soc. of Cardiology 1975; Co-Pres. Int. Physicians for Prevention of Nuclear War (IPPNW) 1980–87, IPPNW awarded Nobel Prize for Peace 1985; mem. Acads. of U.S.A., Germany, Hungary; Hero of Socialist Labour 1978; State Prize 1969, 1976; Lenin Prize 1982, UNESCO Peace Prize 1984. *Publications:* Myocardial Infarction (with others) 1971, Cardiac Rhythm Disorders 1972, Anti-coagulants and Fibrinolytics 1977, Health and Power (memoirs), and other monographs; over 300 articles on cardiology. *Leisure interests:* hunting, photography. *Address:* Cardiology Scientific Centre, Cherepkovskaya Str. 15A, 121552 Moscow, Russia. *Telephone:* 415-00-25.

CHECA CREMADES, Fernando, D. EN FIL. Y LETRAS, LIC. EN D.; Spanish professor of art history and arts administrator; b. 14 May 1952, Madrid; s. of Francisco Checa and Concepción Cremades; lecturer in art history, Univ. Complutense de Madrid 1976–, now Titular Prof. of Art History; specialist in Renaissance and Baroque periods; Dir. Prado Museum May 1996–; Summer Visiting Prof. Inst. of Advanced Studies, Princeton Univ. 1988; Paul Mellon Sr. Fellow Center of Advanced Studies in Visual Arts, Nat. Gallery of Art, Washington 1989; Fae Norton Prof. Okla. State Univ. 1995; fmr. mem. Ministerial Comm. for Classification of State Collections; Premio Extraordinario de Doctorado 1981. *Publications include:* Pintura y escultura del Renacimiento en España 1983, La imagen impresa en el Renacimiento y el Manierismo 1987, Carlos V y la imagen del héroe en el Renacimiento 1987, Felipe II: mecenas de las artes 1992 (Nat. History Prize, Spain), Tiziano y la Monarquía Hispánica 1994, El coleccionismo en España (jtly.) 1984, Las casas del Rey: Casas reales, cazaderos, jardines. Siglos XVI y XVII (jtly.) 1986. *Address:* Museo Nacional del Prado, Calle Ruiz de Alarcón 23, 28071 Madrid, Spain. *Telephone:* (91) 3302801.

CHECKLAND, Sir Michael, Kt., B.A., F.C.M.A.; British broadcasting executive; b. 13 March 1936, Birmingham; s. of Leslie and Ivy Florence Checkland; m. 1st. Shirley Checkland 1960 (deceased); two s. one d.; m. 2nd. Sue Zetter 1987; ed. King Edward's Grammar School, Birmingham and Wadham Coll., Oxford; Accountant, Parkinson Cowan Ltd. 1959–62, Thorn Electronics Ltd. 1962–64; Sr. Cost Accountant, BBC 1964–67, Head, Cen. Finance Unit 1967, Chief Accountant, Cen. Finance Services 1969, Chief Accountant, BBC TV 1971, Controller, Finance 1976, Controller, Planning and Resource Man., BBC TV 1977, Dir. of Resources, BBC TV 1982, Deputy Dir.-Gen. BBC

1985–87, Dir.-Gen. 1987–92, Dir. BBC Enterprises 1979–92 (Chair. 1986–87); Dir. Visnews 1980–85; Vice-Pres. RTS 1985–94, Fellow 1987–; Trustee Reuters 1994–; Pres. Commonwealth Broadcasting Asscn. 1987–88; Vice-Pres. EBU 1991–92; Chair. NCH Action for Children (fmrly. Nat. Children's Home) 1991–; Gov. Westminster Coll. Oxford 1992–97, Birkbeck Coll. London 1993–97, Brighton Univ. 1996–97; Dir. Nat. Youth Music Theatre 1991–, Nynex Cablecomms 1995–97; Chair. City of Birmingham Symphony Orchestra 1993–, Brighton Int. Festival 1993–, Higher Educ. Funding Council for England 1997–; mem. Ind. TV Comm. 1997–; numerous other appointments; Hon. Fellow Wadham Coll. Oxford 1989. *Leisure interests:* sport, music, travel. *Address:* Orchard Cottage, Park Lane, Maplehurst, West Sussex, RH13 6LL, England (Home).

CHEDID, Andrée, B.A.; French writer; b. 20 March 1920, Cairo; d. of Selim Saab and Alice K. Haddad; m. Louis A. Chedid 1942; one s. one d.; ed. French schools, Cairo and Paris, American Univ. in Cairo; has lived in Paris since 1946; Prix Louise Labé 1966, L'aigle d'or de la poésie 1972, Grand Prix des Lettres Françaises de l'Acad. Royale de Belgique 1975, Prix de l'Afrique Méditerranéenne 1975, Prix de l'Acad. Mallarmé 1976, Prix Goncourt for short story 1979, Prix de Poésie (Soc. des Gens de Lettres) 1991, Prix PEN Club Int. 1992, Prix Paul Morand, Acad. Française 1994, Prix Albert Camus 1995; Officier, Légion d'honneur, Commandeur des Arts et des Lettres. *Publications include:* poetry: Fraternité de la parole 1975, Epreuves du vivant 1983, Textes pour un poème 1949–1970, 1987, Poèmes pour un texte 1970–91, Par delà les mots 1995; novels: Le Sommeil délivré 1952, Le Sixième Jour 1960, L'Autre 1969, Nefertiti et le rêve d'Akhnaton 1974, La Maison sans racines 1985, L'Enfant Multiple 1989; plays: Bérénice d'Egypte, Les Nombres, Le Montreur 1981, Echec à la Reine 1984, Les saisons de passage 1996; short stories: les Corps et le temps 1979, Mondes Miroirs Magies 1988, A la Mort, A la Vie 1992, La Femme de Job 1993, les Saisons de passage 1996, le Jardin perdu 1997; essays, children's books. *Leisure interest:* collages. *Address:* c/o Flammarion, 26 rue Racine, 75006 Paris, France. *Telephone:* (1) 40.51.31.00.

CHEEK, James Edward, PH.D.; American university president; b. 4 Dec. 1932, Roanoke Rapids, N.C.; s. of late King Virgil Cheek and Lee Ella (Williams) Cheek; m. Celestine J. Williams 1953; one s. one d.; ed. Shaw Univ., Raleigh, N.C., Colgate-Rochester Divinity School, Drew Univ., Madison, N.J.; Teaching Asst. in Historical Theology, Drew Theological School, Madison, N.J. 1959–60; Instructor in Western History, Union Junior Coll., Cranford, N.J. 1959–61; Asst. Prof. of New Testament and Historical Theology, Virginia Union Univ. 1961–63; Pres. Shaw Univ. 1963–69; Pres. Howard Univ., Washington, D.C. 1969–88, Pres. Emer. 1989–; Dir. James S. Brady Presidential Foundation, First American Bank, N.A., Nat. Asscn. for Equal Opportunity in Higher Educ., Nat. Capital Area Council, Boy Scouts of America, Nat. Permanent Federal Savings and Loan Asscn., UNA Bd. and Advisory Cttee.; Trustee, Washington Center for Metropolitan Studies, etc.; Bd. of Dirs., Public Broadcasting Service; Bd. of Trustees, Fisk Univ. and New York Inst. of Tech.; professional memberships include American Soc. of Church History, American Asscn. of Univ. Profs., American Acad. of Religion; mem. numerous advisory boards and cttees.; Pres. Medal of Freedom 1983; numerous honorary degrees. *Address:* c/o Howard University, 2400 Sixth Street, Washington, D.C. 20012; 8035 16th Street, N.W., Washington, D.C. 20012, U.S.A. (Home).

CHEETHAM, Anthony John Valerian, B.A.; British publisher; b. 12 April 1943; s. of Sir Nicolas Cheetham; m. 1st Julia Rollason 1969 (dissolved); two s. one d.; m. 2nd Rosemary de Courcy 1979 (dissolved); two d.; ed. Eton Coll., Balliol Coll., Oxford; Editorial Dir. Sphere Books 1968; Man. Dir. Futura Publs. 1973, Macdonald Futura 1979; Chair. Century Publishing 1982–85; Man. Dir. Century Hutchinson 1985; Chair. and C.E.O. Random Century Group 1989–91; Chair. Orion Publishing Group (fmrly. Orion Books) 1991–. *Publication:* Richard III 1972. *Leisure interests:* tennis, gardening, trees, medieval history. *Address:* 20 Grove Park, London, SE5 8LH, England. *Telephone:* 0171-733 8204.

CHEF, Genia, M.A.; Russian artist; b. 28 Jan. 1954, Aktjubinsk; s. of Wladimir Scheffer and Sinaida Scheffer; m. Elke Schwab 1983; ed. Polygraphic Inst., Moscow, Acad. of Fine Arts, Vienna; painter, graphic and computer artist; has exhibited at numerous exhbns. of non-conformist artists, Moscow 1976–85, Galeria Maria Salvat, Barcelona 1989, Stuart Levy Fine Art, New York 1994, Int. Art Fair, New York 1994, Smithsonian Inst., Washington D.C. 1994, Studio Canova, Rome 1995, Zimmerly Museum, Rutgers Univ., New Jersey 1995, De Saisset Museum, Santa Clara Univ., Calif. 1995, Art Cologne 1996, Art Expo, Barcelona 1996, Avant Garde Gallery Kyra Maralt, Berlin 1997, Minnesota Univ. Art Museum 1998; has provided illustrations for publications including Edgar Allan Poe, Prose and Poetry 1983, American Romantic Tales 1984, Finger World 1993, American Alphabet 1998; Fueger Gold Prize, Acad. of Fine Arts, Vienna 1993; Delfina Studio Trust Award, New York 1994. *Publications:* Manifesto of Degeneration 1988, Manifesto of Post-Historicism 1989, Viva Canova! 1995. *Leisure interests:* music, books, collecting insects. *Address:* Leibnizstrasse 61, 10629 Berlin, Germany. *Telephone:* (030) 324 6479. *Fax:* (030) 8855 2173.

CHEIFFOU, Amadou; Niger politician and civil servant; fmr. regional official of Int. Civil Aviation Org. (ICAO); Prime Minister and Minister of Defence 1991–93; mem. Mouvement nat. pour une société de développement (MNSD). *Address:* c/o Office of the Prime Minister, Niamey, Niger.

CHEKANAUSKAS, Vitautas Edmundas; Lithuanian architect; b. 13 May 1930, Šiauliai; m. Teresa Chekanauskienė; one d.; ed. Lithuanian Art Inst., Vilnius; architect, then sr. architect, group man., sr. projects architect, Inst.of Urban Planning 1995–90; Prof. Vilnius Acad. of Arts (frmly. Inst. of Arts) 1974–; has designed exhbn. pavilion in Vilnius 1967, residential Dists. in Vilnius 1967–72, and other projects; mem. U.S.S.R. (now Russian) Acad. of Arts 1988; Lenin Prize 1974, People's Architect of U.S.S.R. 1975. *Address:* Lithuanian State Arts Academy, Maironio 6, 2600 Vilnius (Office); U. Paco 13-9, 2000 Vilnius, Lithuania (Home). *Telephone:* (3702) 619944 (Office); 721711 (Home).

CHELI, H.E. Cardinal Giovanni, M.THEOL., D.CN.L.; Italian ecclesiastic; b. 4 Oct. 1918, Turin; ed. Pontifical Lateran Univ., Pontifical Acad. for Diplomacy; ordained Roman Catholic priest 1942; Second Sec., Apostolic Nunciature in Guatemala 1952–55, First Sec., Madrid 1955–62; Counsellor, Nunciature in Rome 1962–67; served Council for Public Affairs of the Church, Vatican City 1967–73; Perm. Observer to UN 1973–86; Titular Archbishop of Santa Giusta, Apostolic Nuncio 1978–; cr. Cardinal 1998. Pres. Pontifical Council for the Pastoral Care of Migrants and Itinerant People 1986; Kt. Commdr. Orden de Isabel la Católica (Spain), Ordine al Merito della Repubblica Italiana, Verdienstkreuz der Bundesrepublik Deutschland (Germany). *Publications:* L'applicazione delle Riforme Tridentine nella diocesi di Asti 1952. *Leisure interests:* tennis, mountain climbing, reading, listening to classical music. *Address:* c/o Pontifical Council for the Pastoral Care of Migrants and Itinerant People, Piazza S. Calisto 16, 00153 Rome, Italy. *Telephone:* (06) 69887131. *Fax:* (06) 69887111.

CHELIDZE, Otar Silovanovich; Georgian author and poet; b. 8 Sept. 1925, Tbilisi, Georgia; s. of Silovan Chelidze and Sophy Chavchavadze; m. Dali Mumladze 1970; three s.; ed. Univ. of Tbilisi; Head of Dept. of Literature and Art, Georgia newspaper 1947–49; Asst. ed. Niangi magazine 1960–63; Head of Dept. of Fiction of Sabchota Sakartvelo 1964–70, Main Ed. Bd. 1974–78; Ed. the Nature of Georgia 1988–; Dir. Nakaduli, publrs. of books for children; Vazha-Pshavela Prize, Union of Writers of Georgia 1995; Medal of Honour 1995, Order of Virtue 1995. *Publications:* Ballads 1956, The Eternity 1966, Selected Poems 1972, My Magnetic Area 1973, Lust for Journey 1980, Selected Works (two vols.) 1979 and 1980, Selected Verse and Poems 1983, Earth and Georgia 1984, Buba and Medea (novel) 1992–3, The Stone Table (poems) 1993, The Ninth Floor (poems) 1994, The Golden Fireplace 1995. *Leisure interests:* chess, football, horseriding. *Address:* 380019 Marjanishvili Street 2/29, Apt. 6, Tbilisi, Georgia. *Telephone:* 96-94-11.

CHELYSHEV, Yevgeny Petrovich; Russian philologist; b. 27 Oct. 1921; m.; two d.; ed. Mil. Inst. of Foreign Languages; Head of Chair of Indian Languages Mil. Inst. of Foreign Languages, Head of Sector of Indian Philology, Head Div. of Literature Inst. of Oriental Sciences, U.S.S.R. (now Russian) Acad. of Sciences, Corresp. mem. U.S.S.R. (now Russian) Acad. of Sciences 1981, mem. 1987, Acad. Sec. Dept. of Literature and Language 1991–; mem. Bureau of Indian Soc. of Philosophy, mem. Asian Soc. in Calcutta; Merited Worker of Sciences of Russia; Int. Nehru Prize; Swami Vivekananda Prize; main research in the field of culture, comparative literary criticism, Indian philosophy. *Publications:* Modern Poetry in Hindi 1967, Contemporary Indian Literature 1981, Indian Literature Today and Yesterday 1989, Complicity in Beauty and Spirit 1991, articles in specialized periodicals. *Leisure interests:* music. *Address:* Department of Literature and Language, Russian Academy of Sciences, Leninsky prosp. 32A, 117334 Moscow, Russia. *Telephone:* (095) 938-19-36 (Office); 202-66-25 (Home).

CHEMETOV, Paul; French architect; b. 6 Sept. 1928, Paris; s. of Alexandre Chemetoff and Tamara Blumine; m. Christine Soupault 1958; one s. two d.; ed. Ecole Nationale Supérieure des Beaux Arts; participated in foundation of the Atelier d'urbanisme et l'architecture 1961; Prof. Ecole d'architecture, Strasbourg 1968–72; exhibited in the Venice Biennial 1976; Prof. of Architecture at Ecole Nationale des Ponts et Chaussées 1977–89; Vice-Pres. Plan Construction 1979–87; Prix d'architecture, Cercle d'études architecturales 1965; Grand Prix National d'architecture 1980; Officier, Légion d'honneur, Ordre du Mérite, Arts et des Lettres. *Publications:* Architectures—Paris 1848–1914 1980, Cinq projets 1979–82 1983, Monographie 1985, Paris Banlieue 1919–1939 (with B. Marrey and M. J. Dumont) 1989, la Fabrique des villes 1992, Le Territoire de L'Architecte 1995, Vingt Mille Mots pour la Ville; numerous articles in professional journals. *Address:* Chemetov-Huidobro, 4 square Masséna, 75013 Paris, France. *Telephone:* 01-45-82-85-48. *Fax:* 01-45-86-89-14.

CHEN AILIAN; Chinese dancer and choreographer; b. 24 Dec. 1939, Shanghai; d. of Chen Xi Kang and Yu Xiu Ying; m. Wei Dao Ning; two d.; ed. First Coll. of Dancing; teacher Beijing Coll. of Dancing 1959–63; Chief Actress China Opera and Dancing House 1963–; won four gold medals as a traditional dancer at 8th World Youth Festival in Helsinki 1962; now Prof. Arts Dept. Nan Kai Univ., Hainan Univ.; demonstrations and lectures in Shangdong Prov., Shaanxi Prov., Beijing Univ., Foreign Languages Inst., Post and Telegraph Inst., Light Industry Inst., and Mun. Dancers' Unions; chief dancer Chinese Art del. to U.S.S.R., U.S.A., France, Spain, Belgium, Denmark, Finland, Sweden, Italy, Norway, Hong Kong and Germany; f. Chen Ailian Artistic Troupe 1989 (first non-governmental performing org. in China); Excellent Performance Award, First Nat. Dance Concert, First Prize Ministry of Culture for Dance Soiree and Princess Wenzhen. *Perform-*

ances include: The Peony Pavilion, In the Dusk of Evening, The Oriental Melody, The Lantern Dance, Water, The Sword Dance, Ball Dance, The Song of the Serfs, Women Militia in the Grassland, The Red Silk Dance. *Publications:* articles and commentaries on dance. *Leisure interests:* literature, music, traditional opera, travel, mountain climbing. *Address:* Room 101/7, 2 Nanhuadong Street, Hufang Road, Beijing 100050, People's Republic of China. *Telephone:* 3015066.

CHEN BANGZHU; Chinese politician; b. Sept. 1934, Jiujiang City, Jiangxi Prov.; ed. Faculty of Civil Eng., Chonqing Construction Eng. Coll.; engineer at Jilin Chemical Industrial Dist. Construction Co. 1954–65; joined CCP 1975; Chief Engineer and Dept. Man. No. 4 and 9 Chemical Industrial Construction Co., Ministry of Chemical Industry 1966–80; Chief Engineer, Man. Jiuhua Bldg. Co. 1980–84; Mayor of Yueyang and Deputy Sec. CCP Yueyang City Cttee. 1983–; Vice-Gov. Hunan Prov. 1984–86, Gov. 1989–95; Minister of Internal Trade 1995–98; Vice-Minister State Econ. and Trade Comm. 1998–; Alt. mem. 13th CCP Cen. Cttee. 1987–92; Deputy Sec. CPC 6th Hunan Provincial Cttee. 1989–; mem. 14th Cen. Cttee. CCP 1992–95; a Deputy of Hunan Prov. 8th NPC 1993–95; Gov. Hunan Prov. 1993–95; Head Nat. Leading Group for Placement of Demobilised Army Officers 1995–; mem. 14th CCP Cen. Cttee. 1992–97, 15th CCP Cen. Cttee. 1997–. *Address:* c/o State Economic and Trade Commission, Beijing, People's Republic of China.

CHEN BINGDE, Lieut.-Gen.; Chinese army officer; b. July 1941, Nantong Co., Jiangsu Prov.; joined PLA 1961; joined CCP 1962; ed. PLA Mil. Acad. 1983–85; Vice-Commdr of Army Group and Chief of Staff 1985; Pres. PLA Nanchang Infantry Acad.; PLA Infantry Command Acad.; Army Group Commdr.; Chief of Staff Nanjing Mil. Area Command 1993, Vice-Commdr. 1996–; rank of Maj.-Gen. 1988, Lieut.-Gen. 1995–; mem. 15th CCP Cen. Cttee. 1997–. *Address:* Nanjing Military Area Command, Nanjing, Jiangsu Province, People's Republic of China.

CHEN, Char-Nie, M.B., M.SC., O.B.E., J.P., F.R.C. PSYCH.; British university professor and college principal; b. 19 July 1938, Fujian Prov., China; s. of the late Kam-Heng Chen and of Mei-Ai Chen-Hsu; m. Chou-May Chien 1970; one s. two d.; ed. Nat. Taiwan Univ. and Univ. Coll., London; Rotating Intern, Nat. Taiwan Univ. Hosp. 1964–65, Resident Physician, Dept. of Neurology and Psychiatry 1965–68; Sr. House Officer, Morgannwg Hosp., Wales 1968–69; Registrar, St. George's Hosp. Medical School, London 1969–71, Lecturer, Hon. Sr. Registrar 1971–72, 1973–78, Sr. Lecturer, Hon. Consultant Psychiatrist 1978–80; Prof. Dept. of Psychiatry, Chinese Univ. of Hong Kong 1981–98, Chair. of Dept. 1981–93, mem. Univ. Senate 1981, Head, Shaw Coll. 1987–94, mem. Univ. Council 1987–94; mem. Coll. Council, Hong Kong Baptist Coll. 1984–95; Pres. Hong Kong Psychiatric Asscn. 1982–84, Hong Kong Soc. of Neurosciences 1983–84, 1988–89; Exec. Chair., Hong Kong Mental Health Asscn. 1983–98; Pres. Pacific Rim Coll. of Psychiatrists 1988–90, Dir. 1990–; Chair. Action Comm. Against Narcotics 1992–98; Pres. Hong Kong Coll. of Psychiatrists 1993–98; Fellow, Royal Coll. of Psychiatrists 1985–, Royal Australian and New Zealand Coll. of Psychiatrists 1983–, Royal Soc. of Medicine 1975–, Hong Kong Acad. of Medicine 1993–, Hong Kong Soc. of Sleep Medicine (Pres. 1993–); mem. British Asscn. for Psychopharmacology 1974–, European Sleep Research Soc. 1976–, British Medical Asscn. 1979–, Collegium Internationale Neuro-psycho-pharmacologium 1981–, Hong Kong Medical Asscn. 1981–, Int. Brain Research Org. 1985–; Corresp. Fellow, American Psychiatric Asscn. 1991; Visiting Prof., St. George's Hosp. Medical School, London 1984; J.P., Hong Kong 1993–; Hon. Fellow, Hong Kong Psychological Soc. 1986–. *Publications:* over 90 scientific papers. *Leisure interests:* reading, travelling, good food. *Address:* Flat 16B, Block 3, Villa Athena, 600 Sai Sha Road, Ma On Shan, Hong Kong Special Administrative Region, People's Republic of China. *Telephone:* (852) 2633-4192. *Fax:* (852) 2633-3067.

CHEN CHI-LU, PH.D.; Taiwanese government official and university professor; b. 27 April 1923, Tainan City; s. of Chen Peng and Chen Cheng Shiu-Ming; m. Chen Chang-Jo; four s.; ed. St. John's Univ., Shanghai, Univs. of New Mexico, London and Tokyo; Research Asst. to Prof., then Head, Dept. of Archaeology and Anthropology, Nat. Taiwan Univ. 1949–69; Curator, Dept. of Anthropology, Taiwan Museum 1958–63; Visiting Prof. Michigan State Univ. 1969–70; Dir. Inst. of American Culture, Academia Sinica 1974–77; Dean, Coll. of Liberal Arts, Nat. Taiwan Univ. 1975–77; Deputy Sec.-Gen. Cen. Cttee., Kuomintang 1975–77; Minister of State 1977–81; Chair. Council for Cultural Planning and Devt., Exec. Yuan 1981; Prof. Coll. of Liberal Arts, Nat. Taiwan Univ. 1981–; mem. Academia Sinica. *Publications:* Woodcarving of the Paiwan Group of Taiwan 1961, Formosan Aboriginal Art, The Art of Paiwan Group of Southern Taiwan 1962, Material Culture of Formosan Aborigines 1968, The Aboriginal Art of Taiwan and Implication for the Cultural History of the Pacific 1972, Anthropological Studies in the Republic of China during the last three decades 1980, People and Culture 1981, over 170 books and articles. *Leisure interests:* calligraphy, painting. *Address:* 102 Ai-Kuo East Road, Taipei (Office); 7 Lane 52, Wenchow Street, Taipei, Taiwan (Home). *Telephone:* 3920059 (Office); 3512594 (Home).

CHEN DUN; Chinese business executive; b. Dec. 1928, Tianjin City; Vice-Minister for Coal 1985–90; Gen. Man. China Nat. Coal Corpn. 1993–; mem. 7th CPPCC 1987–92, 8th 1993–. *Address:* China National Coal Corporation, 21 Hepingli Xijie Street, Beijing 100713, People's Republic of China.

CHEN FU; Taiwanese politician; fmr. Minister of Foreign Affairs; apptd. mem. Kuomintang (KMT) Cen. Standing Cttee. 1994–. *Address:* c/o Ministry of Foreign Affairs, 2 Chiehshou Road, Taipei 10016, Taiwan. *Telephone:* (2) 3119292. *Fax:* (2) 3144972.

CHEN GANG; Chinese composer; b. 10 March 1935, Shanghai; s. of Chen Ge-Xin and Jin Jiao-Li; m. (divorced); two d.; ed. Shanghai Conservatory of Music; now Prof. of Composition, Shanghai Conservatory of Music; mem. Council of Chinese Musicians' Asscn.; Art Dir. Shanghai Chamber Orchestra; Guest Prof. U.S.A., France, Canada and Hong Kong; Sec. Chinese Dramatist Asscn. 1987–; Golden Record Prize (five times). *Compositions include:* Butterfly Lovers, Violin Concerto 1959, The Sun Shines on Tashikuergan, Violin Solo 1973, Morning on the Miao Mountains, Violin Solo 1975; A Moonlight Spring Night on the Flower-surrounded River, Symphonic Picture 1976, Concerto for Oboe 1985, Wang Zhaojun, Violin Concerto 1986, Chamber Music Ensemble 1989, Dragon Symphony 1991. *Leisure interests:* literature, writing. *Address:* Shanghai Conservatory of Music, 20 Fen Yang Road, Shanghai, People's Republic of China. *Telephone:* 4370689.

CHEN GUANGYI; Chinese government official; b. 7 Aug. 1933, Putian City, Fujian; s. of Chen Zhaohe and Li Muxin; m. Chen Xiuyun 1961; two s. one d.; ed. China Northeast Industry Univ.; joined CCP 1959; engineer, then section chief, div. chief, deputy Dir. Baiying Nonferrous Metal Industry Co., Gansu; mem. Gansu Metallurgy Industry Bureau, Gansu Prov. Planning Cttee.; Gov. of Gansu Prov. 1983–86; mem. of Cen. Cttee. of CCP 1985; Sec. 5th CCP Cttee., Fujian 1986; Chair. CPPCC 6th Fujian Provincial Cttee. 1988; mem. CCP 12th and 13th Cen. Cttee.; mem. 14th CCP Cen. Cttee. 1992–97, 15th CCP Cen. Cttee. 1997–; Party Cttee. Sec. and Head Civil Aviation Gen. Admin. of China 1994–98; Dir Finance Cttee. of 9th NPC 1998–. *Address:* c/o Standing Committee of National People's Congress, Beijing, People's Republic of China.

CHEN HUANYOU; Chinese administrator; b. 1934, Nantong City, Jiangsu Prov.; ed. Chinese People's Univ.; joined CCP 1954; mem. Standing Cttee. of Jiangsu Prov. CP 1983, now Chair. People's Armament Cttee.; Deputy to 8th NPC Jiangsu Prov.; Vice-Gov. Jiangsu Prov. 1984–89, Gov. 1989–94; Deputy Sec. CPC Jiangsu Prov. Cttee. 1986–93, Sec. CCP Jiangsu Prov. Cttee. 1994–; mem. 14th CCP Cen. Cttee. 1992–97, 15th CCP Cen. Cttee. 1997–; Pres. Fujian Party School 1995–. *Address:* 70 W. Beijing Road, Nanjing, Jiangsu Province, 210000, People's Republic of China. *Telephone:* 025-663 5164.

CHEN HUIGUANG; Chinese politician; b. 1939, Yulin City, Guangxi; fmr. engineer; ed. Guangxi Inst. of Coal Mining; Dongluo Mining Bureau, Guangxi, successively, Engineer, Mining Technician, Head of Production Section, Deputy Head and Head 1961–; joined CCP 1965; Sec. CCP Municipal Cttee., Nanning 1983–85; Deputy Sec. CCP Cttee., Guangxi 1983–85, (Leading) Sec. 1985–88; mem. 12th CCP Cen. Cttee. 1982–87; 13th CCP Cen. Cttee. 1987–92; Chair. Guangxi Zhuang Autonomous Region CPPCC 1988–. *Address:* 1 Minlelu Road, Nanning City, Guangxi, People's Republic of China.

CHEN JIAER; Chinese academic; b. 1934, Shanghai; ed. Jilin Univ.; Vice-Pres. Peking Univ. 1984–96, Pres. 1996–; Dir. Heavy Ion Physics Research Inst. 1986–; Fellow of Chinese Acad. of Sciences and Chair. Council of Chinese Physics Soc. 1993–. *Address:* Peking University, Beijing, People's Republic of China.

CHEN JINHUA; Chinese government official and business executive; b. 1931; Gen. Man. China Petrochemical Corpn. 1983–90; Dir. State Econ. Restructuring Comm. 1990–93; Minister in charge of State Planning Comm. 1993–98; Head Co-ordination Group for Tertiary Industries 1993–98; mem. 14th Cen. Cttee. CPC 1992–97; Vice-Chair 9th Nat. Cttee of CPPCC 1998–. *Address:* National Committee of Chinese People's Political Consultative Conference, 23 Taipingqiao Street, Beijing, People's Republic of China.

CHEN JUNSHENG; Chinese government official; b. 1927, Huanan Co., Helongjiang Prov.; mem. Standing Cttee. of Heilongjiang Prov. CP, Sec.-Gen. 1979–80, Deputy Sec. 1983–84; Sec. Qigihar City CP 1980–82; Sec. of the Fed. of T.U., Deputy Chair. Exec. Cttee. 1984–85; Vice-Pres. Fed. T.U. 1985; Sec. Gen. State Council 1985–88; Sec. CCP Cttee. of Cen. State Organs 1986–88; Head Leading Group for Econ. Devt. in Poor Areas (now Leading Group for Helping the Poor through Devt.) 1986–, for Comprehensive Agricultural Devt., for Housing System Reform; mem. 13th CCP Cen. Cttee. 1987–92; mem. 14th CCP Cen. Cttee. 1992–97; State Councillor 1988–98; Head State Flood-Control and Drought Relief H.Q.; Chair. Nat. Afforestation Cttee.; Chair. Bd. of Dirs. Nat. Office of Supply and Marketing Co-operatives 1995–98; Vice-Chair. Nat. Cttee. of CPPCC 1998–. *Address:* National Committee of Chinese People's Political Consultative Conference, 23 Taipingqiao Street, Beijing, People's Republic of China.

CHEN KAIGE; Chinese film director; b. 1954, Beijing; ed. Beijing Cinema Coll.; worker, rubber plantation, Yunnan; soldier for four years. *Films include:* The Yellow Earth (Best Film, Berlin Film Festival), Life on a String, King of the Children 1988, Farewell My Concubine 1993. *Publications:* King of the Children, The New Chinese Cinema (with Tony Raynes) 1989, Bawang bieji 1992. *Address:* Beijing Cinema College, Beijing, People's Republic of China.

CHEN KUIYUAN; Chinese party official; Sec. Tibet Autonomous Regional Cttee. Dec. 1992–; Sec. CCP Tibet Autonomous Region Cttee. 1996; mem.

14th CCP Cen. Cttee. 1992–97, 15th CCP Cen. Cttee. 1997–. *Address:* Chinese Communist Party, Beijing, People's Republic of China.

CHEN LI-AN, PH.D.; Taiwanese government official; b. 22 June 1937, Chingtien County, Chekiang; m. four s.; one d.; ed. Mass. Inst. of Tech. and New York Univ.; Eng. Honeywell Co., U.S.A. 1960–63; Prof. City Univ. of New York 1968–70; Pres Ming Chi Inst. of Tech. 1970–72; Dir. Dept. of Technological and Vocational Educ., Ministry of Educ. 1972–74; Pres, Nat. Taiwan Inst. of Tech. 1974–77; Vice-Minister, Ministry of Educ. 1977–78; Dir. Dept. of Org. Affairs, Cen. Cttee., Kuomintang 1979–80; Deputy Sec.-Gen. Cen. Cttee., Kuomintang 1980–84; Chair. Nat. Science Council, Exec. Yuan 1984–88, Minister, Ministry of Econ. Affairs 1988–90, of Nat. Defence 1990; Sec. Shaoxing City 1991–; left. Nat. Party 1995. *Address:* c/o Ministry of National Defence, Chieshou Hall, Chung-King S. Road, Taipei (Office); 120 Jen-Ai Road, Section 3, Taipei, Taiwan (Home).

CHEN LIYING; Chinese administrator; b. 1934, Changde Co., Hunan Prov.; ed. Tianjin Textile Inst.; joined CCP 1955; Deputy Chief-Engineer, Yunnan Textile Mill 1981–85; Vice-Gov. Yunnan Prov. 1989; Vice-Chair. CPPCC 7th Yunnan Provincial Cttee. 1993–. *Address:* c/o Office of Provincial Governor, Kunming City, Yunnan Province, People's Republic of China.

CHEN LUZHI; Chinese diplomatist and business executive; b. Feb. 1925, Jiangpu; fmr. Dir. Mission of People's Repub. of China at UN; fmr. Amb. to Denmark and Iceland; Dir. China-S.E. Asia Commercial Bd. 1994–.

CHEN MINGTONG; Chinese chemist and businessman; b. Aug. 1926, Nanjing City, Jiangsu Prov.; ed. Cen. Univ. of China and Zhejiang Univ.; Chief-Engineer, Shanghai Chemical Plant 1977–; visited U.S.A. 1980; Man. Gen., Shanghai Chemical Industry Corpn. 1982–; Adviser, Shantou Dist. 1986–; visited U.S.A. 1991; Chemical Prize of China.

CHEN MINGYI; Chinese administrator; b. 1940, Fuzhou City, Fujian Prov.; ed. Shanghai Jiaotong Univ. 1962; joined CCP 1960; Vice-Gov. Fujian Prov. 1985–93, Gov. 1993; Deputy Sec. CPC 6th Fujian Prov. Cttee. 1993–; alt. mem. Cen. Cttee. CPC 1992–; Sec. CCP Fujian Prov. Cttee. 1996–; Deputy to 8th NPC 1996; mem. 15th CCP Cen. Cttee. 1997–. *Address:* c/o Office of the Governor, Fujian Provincial People's Government, Fuzhou City, People's Republic of China.

CHEN MINGYUAN; Chinese linguist, computer scientist and poet; b. 5 Jan. 1941, Chongqing, Sichuan Prov.; s. of Chen Zaiwen and Shu Xiuhua; m. Guan Tinglu 1968; one s. one d.; ed. Shanghai High School, Shanghai Science and Tech. Univ., Beijing Univ.; Researcher, Electronics Inst. and Acoustics Inst., Academia Sinica, Beijing 1963–68; falsely charged with forging "Chairman Mao's Poems" and was branded a "counter-revolutionary" during the Cultural Revolution and in a labour-camp, 1968–77; rehabilitated, 1978; Researcher, Acoustics Inst., Academia Sinica 1978–81; Researcher, Committee for Reform Written Language of China, 1981–82; Lecturer, Beijing Languages Inst. 1982–; Special Correspondent of "RENWU" magazine, 1986–; Prof., Research Inst. of Buddhist Culture of China 1987–; Adviser Stone Group Co. 1988–; Dir. Chinese Poetry Soc. 1987–; Vice-Pres. Beijing Poetry Asscn. 1988–; Hon. Prize of Achievement in Languages, Science and Art 1986. *Publications:* On the Reform of Chinese Characters 1966, Poetry: Bloody Flowers 1976, Chinese Characters encoding 1978, Information Processing of Chinese Language 1981, Linguistics and Modern Science 1983, Rudiments of Chinese Phonetics 1984, Chinese Through Listening, Vol. 1-4 1984–86, Elementary Aural Comprehension 1986. *Poetry:* Underground grasses 1986, Chinese Onomastics 1987, Selected Poems of Chen Mingyuan 1988, The New Tide (with Guo Moruo) 1991, Invaluable Love 1992. Numerous articles on modern linguistics, teaching Chinese as a second language, reminiscences of Guo Moruo and Tian Han, cultural exchange between China and West, and has a patent on keyboard for Chinese information processing. *Leisure interests:* philately, music, photography, calligraphy. *Address:* Room 605, Building 919, Zhong Guan Cun, Beijing 100086, People's Republic of China.

CHEN MINZHANG; Chinese government official; b. 1931, Hangzhou, Zhejiang; ed. Shanghai No. 2 Medical Coll.; joined CCP 1954; worked as doctor at Guangci Hosp. 1955–56; Deputy Dir. of Internal Medicine and Researcher, Peking Union Medical Coll. Hosp. 1956–80; Vice-Pres. Chinese Union Medical Univ. 1980–83; Pres. Union Medical Coll. Hosp. 1983–84; Vice-Minister of Public Health 1984–87, Minister 1987–98; alt. mem. 13th CCP Cen. Cttee. 1987–92; mem. 14th CCP Cen. Cttee. 1992–97; Vice-Chair. China Asscn. for Science and Tech.; Vice-Pres. Chinese Medical Asscn. 1984–89, Pres. Feb. 1989–; Pres. Chinese Red Cross Soc. 1990–94, Hon. Vice-Chair. 1994–; Deputy Head Nat. Disaster Relief and Disease Control Group 1991–; Hon. Pres. China Venereal Disease and AIDS Prevention Asscn. 1993–; Vice-Chair. Educ., Science, Culture and Public Health Cttee. of 9th NPC 1998–. *Address:* c/o Standing Committee of National People's Congress, Beijing, People's Republic of China.

CHEN MUHUA; Chinese politician; b. 1921, Qingtian Co., Zhejiang Prov.; ed. Yanan Mil. School; joined CCP 1938; mem. 10th Cen. Cttee. of CCP 1973; Minister for Econ. Relations with Foreign Countries 1977–82, also in charge of the State Family Planning Comm. 1981–82, Minister of Foreign Trade 1982–85, a Vice-Premier 1978–82; Pres. People's Bank of China 1985–88; Dir. State Treasury Aug. 1985–; Chair. Council, People's Bank of China June 1985, Hon. Chair. Bd. of Dir. Nov. 1985–; alt. mem. Politburo 1977–87; Head Population Census Leading Group 1979–; mem. 12th CCP Cen. Cttee. 1982–87, 13th CCP Cen. Cttee. 1987–92; mem. 14th CCP Cen. Cttee. 1992–97; State Councillor 1982–; Chair. Cen. Patriotic Sanitation Campaign Cttee. Cen. Cttee. 1981–; Pres. China Greening Foundation; Chinese Gov. World Bank 1985–88, Asian Devt. Bank 1986–; Hon. Pres. Int. Econ. Co-operation Soc. 1983–, Florists' Asscn. 1984–; Pres. China Women Devt. Fund 1988–; Vice-Chair. NPC 7th Standing Cttee. 1988–93, 8th Standing Cttee. 1993–98; Pres. All-China Women's Fed. 1988–98, Hon. Pres. 1998–; Hon. Pres. China Asscn. of Women Judges 1994–, China Asscn. of Women Doctors, Asscn. for Import and Export Commodity Inspection; Advisor Nat. Co-ordination Group for Anti-Illiteracy Work 1994–, Chinese Asscn. for Promotion of the Population Culture. *Address:* c/o All-China Women's Federation, Beijing, People's Republic of China.

CHEN PO SUM; Hong Kong stockbroker; m. Choi Fook; three s.; First Vice-Pres. Exec. Council Hong Kong Stock Exchange 1988–94; Dir. several cos. in Hong Kong and People's Republ. of China; Man. Dir. Peace Hill Group.

CHEN QIQI; Chinese administrator; b. 26 April 1941, Guangdong Prov.; m. Prof. Zheng Sheu Xen; one s.; ed. Guangdong Medical School, Medical Coll. of Italy; Dr., Guangdong Leprosy Hospital 1965–75; teacher, Guangzhou Medical School 1975–81; Vice-Mayor of Guangzhou Municipality 1985; Pres. Guangdong Red Cross; Dir. China Red Cross; Vice-Pres. Guangzhou People's Asscn. for Friendship with Foreign Countries. *Address:* 1 Fuqian Road, Guangzhou, Guangdong (Office); 86 Yue Hwa Road, Guangzhou, Guangdong, People's Republic of China (Home). *Telephone:* (020) 330360 ext. 5432 (Office); 3333100 (Home). *Fax:* (020) 340347.

CHEN RONGTI (Y. T. Chen), PH.D.; Chinese professor of chemistry; b. 7 Nov. 1919, Dianjiang Co., Sichuan Prov.; m. Yang Guangyu 1947; one s. one d.; ed. Indiana Univ., U.S.A.; researcher, Northwestern Univ. and Chicago Univ. 1952–54; Prof., Nankai Univ. Tianjin 1954–; mem. Chinese Acad. of Sciences 1980–, 7th NPC 1988–93, 8th Standing Cttee. 1993–; Vice-Dir. Standing Cttee. Tianjin People's Congress 1993–; Distinguished Visiting Scholar, N.A.S. 1984; Cornell Distinguished Visiting Prof., Swarthmore Coll., U.S.A. 1988; Hon. State Prize of Science of China 1985, 1986, 1987, 1991; Chugayev Medal and Diploma, U.S.S.R. Acad. of Sciences 1987. *Publications:* Correlation Analysis in Co-ordination Chemistry 1994; over 250 articles in Chinese and foreign journals. *Leisure interests:* classical music and Beijing Opera. *Address:* Department of Chemistry, Nankai University, Tianjin 300071, People's Republic of China. *Telephone:* (86) 22-28363645. *Fax:* (86) 22-23501096. *Fax:* 22-28363645.

CHEN RUYU, PH.D.; Chinese professor of chemistry and party official; b. 1920; m. He Binlin; ed. Univ. of California, U.S.A.; researcher, Chicago Univ. 1952–56; Prof. Chemistry Dept. Nankai Univ. Tianjin 1962–96; Vice-Chair. 9th CPPCC Tianjin Municipal Cttee. 1980–; mem. Presidium 5th CPPCC 1978–82, 6th CPPCC 1983–87, 7th CPPCC 1988; mem. Dept. Chemistry, Academia Sinica 1985; mem. Standing Cttee. Tianjin Municipality CCP 1986. *Address:* c/o Department of Chemistry, Nankai University, Balitai, Tianjin, People's Republic of China.

CHEN SHINENG; Chinese administrator; b. 1938, Jiaxing Co., Zhejiang Prov.; ed. Qinghua Univ.; joined CCP 1962; Vice-Minister of Light Industry 1984–93; Gov. of Guizhou Prov. 1993; Deputy Sec., CPC 7th Guizhou Prov. Cttee. 1993, Dir. Cttee. for Comprehensive Man.; Vice-Minister of Chem. Industry 1996. *Address:* c/o Ministry of Chemical Industry, Bldg. 16, Section 4, Anhuili, Beijing 100723, People's Republic of China. *Telephone:* (10) 6491-4455. *Fax:* (10) 6421-5982.

CHEN, Shuiban; Taiwanese politician; m. Wu Shu-chen; fmr. lawyer; fmrly. active in opposition to Kuomintang; now Mayor of Taipei; mem. Democratic Progressive Party. *Address:* c/o Democratic Progressive Party, 8th Floor, 39 Pei Ping East Road, Taipei, Taiwan.

CH'EN SHUIPIAN; Taiwanese civil servant; Mayor of Taipei Dec. 1994–; mem. Democratic Progressive Party (DPP). *Address:* Democratic Progressive Party, 12th Floor, 399 Nanking East Road, Sec. 5, Taipei, Taiwan. *Telephone:* (2) 7692939. *Fax:* (2) 7658484.

CHEN SHUNLI; Chinese politician and economist; b. 1917, Fenghua Co., Zhejiang Prov.; ed. Qinghua Univ., Oxford Univ.; Prof. Shanxi Univ. 1960–; mem. Standing Cttee. of 6th CPPCC 1983–88; Pres. of Shanxi Univ. 1983–; Exec. Vice-Chair. of China Asscn. for Promoting Democracy 1983–; mem. Standing Cttee. of 7th CPPCC 1989; mem. 8th NPC Standing Cttee. 1993–, Deputy to 8th NPC Shanxi Prov. *Address:* Shanxi University, Taiyuan City, Shanxi Province, People's Republic of China.

CHEN SHUPENG; Chinese scientist; b. 14 Feb. 1920, Jiangxi; s. of Chen Yuoyuan and Lee Manlian; m. Zhang Diehua 1944; one s. one d.; ed. Zhejiang Univ.; research prof., Geography Inst. of Academia Sinica 1978–; mem. Dept. of Earth Sciences, Academia Sinica 1980–; Pres. Geographical Soc. of China 1991; Hon. Dir. Inst. of Remote Sensing Applications 1988–, Co-Chair. Space Science Application Cttee. 1990–; Fellow Third World Acad. of Sciences 1992; Hon. State Prize of Science of China 1988, State Gold Prize for Environmental Science 1993. *Publications:* Selected Works in Geo-Sciences, Vols I–IV 1990–92, Dictionary of Remote Sensing (Ed.-in-Chief) 1990, Atlas of Multidisciplinary Analysis of Meteorological Satellite Imagery in China 1992, The Start of Remote Sensing and Geo-information Systems in China 1993. *Leisure interests:* travel, field sketching, Chinese painting, Beijing opera. *Address:* Institute of Geography, Building 917, Datun Road, Beijing

100101, People's Republic of China. *Telephone:* 4914240 (Office), 2561758 (Home). *Fax:* 4911544.

CHEN SUN, PH.D.; Taiwanese politician and economist; b. 8 Nov. 1934, Pingtu County, Shantung; m.; two s.; ed. Nat. Taiwan Univ. and Univ. of Oklahoma; Assoc. Prof. of Econs. Nat. Taiwan Univ. 1968–; Vice-Chair. Econ. Planning Council, Exec. Yuan 1973–77; mem. Bd. of Reviewers on Humanities and Social Sciences, Nat. Science Council, Exec. Yuan 1974–93, Chair. 1990–; Vice-Chair. Council for Econ. Planning and Devt. Exec. Yuan 1977–84; Pres. Nat. Taiwan Univ. 1984–93, Chinese Econ. Asscn. 1985–86; Councillor, Academia Sinica, Taiwan 1987–; Minister of Nat. Defence 1993–96. *Address:* c/o Ministry of National Defence, 2nd Floor, 164 Po Ai Road, Taipei, Taiwan.

CHEN SUZHI; Chinese politician; b. 1931, Shengyang City, Liaoning Prov.; ed. Liaoning Univ.; joined the CCP 1949; factory dir. 1978; Vice-Gov. Liaoning in charge of industrial work 1982; alt. mem. 12th CCP Cen. Cttee. 1982–87, 13th Cen. Cttee. 1987; mem. Standing Cttee. CCP Prov. Cttee. Liaoning 1982; Dir. Liaoning Prov. Trade Union Council 1986; Alt. mem. CCP 12th and 13th Cen. Cttee.; mem. Standing Cttee. 7th CPC Liaoning Provincial Cttee. 1985–; Rep. to CCP 13th Nat. Congress; Vice-Gov. Liaoning Prov. 1988–; Deputy to 8th NPC Liaoning Prov.; Vice-Chair. Liaoning Provincial 8th People's Congress Standing Cttee. 1992–, Cttee. for Comprehensive Man. of Social Security; mem. NPC Internal and Judicial Affairs Cttee. *Address:* Liaoning Trade Union Offices, Shenyang, People's Republic of China.

CHEN WEI-JAO, M.D.; Taiwanese university president; b. 15 Nov. 1939, Taichung; s. of late Chen Wen-Chiang and of Chen Wu-Ping; m. Shiang Yang Tang 1970; one s. one d.; ed. Coll. of Medicine, Nat. Taiwan Univ., Postgrad. Medical School, Tohoku Univ. Japan and School of Hygiene and Public Health, Johns Hopkins Univ. U.S.A.; Resident Dept. of Surgery, Nat. Taiwan Univ. Hosp. 1966–70, Visiting Surgeon (Pediatric Surgery) 1975–, Deputy Dir. 1989–91; mem. Faculty, Coll. of Medicine Nat. Taiwan Univ. 1975–, Dean 1991–93; Pres. Nat. Taiwan Univ. 1993–, also Prof. of Surgery and Public Health; Fellow in Pediatric Surgery, Tohoku Univ. Japan 1972–75; Visiting Research Assoc. Prof. Univ. of Cincinnati 1981–82; recipient of various awards. *Publications:* Story of Separation of Conjoined Twins 1980; more than 140 scientific papers on surgery, nutrition and public health. *Leisure interest:* hiking. *Address:* 7 Chung-shan S. Road, Taipei 100; 1 Roosevelt Road, Sec. 4, Taipei 106, Taiwan. *Telephone:* (02) 23634090. *Fax:* (02) 23621877.

CHEN XIEYANG; Chinese orchestral conductor; b. 4 May 1939, Shanghai; s. of Chen Dieyi and Liang Peiqiong; m. Wang Jianying 1973; ed. Music High School, Shanghai Conservatory; Conductor, Shanghai Ballet 1965–84; studied with Prof. Otto Mueller, Yale Univ., U.S.A. 1981–82; Conductor, Aspen Music Festival, Group for Contemporary Music, N.Y., Brooklyn Philharmonia, Honolulu Symphony, Philippines State Orchestra, Hong Kong Philharmonic, Shanghai Symphony Orchestra, Cen. Philharmonic, Beijing 1981–83, Symphony Orchestra of Vilnius, Kaunas, Novosibirsk, U.S.S.R. 1985, Tokyo Symphony Orchestra 1986; Music Dir. Shanghai Symphony Orchestra; has made recording for Kuklos CBE, France 1983; Dir., China Musicians' Asscn.; Pres. Shanghai Symphonic Music Lovers' Soc.; Excellent Conducting Prize, Shanghai Music Festival 1986. *Leisure interest:* Beijing opera. *Address:* Shanghai Symphony Orchestra, 105 Hunan Road, Shanghai 200031, People's Republic of China. *Telephone:* 64333752 (Office); 62814656 (Home).

CHEN YAOBANG; Chinese politician; b. 1935, Panyu City, Guangdong Prov.; ed. Cen. China Agricultural Inst.; joined CCP 1982; Vice-Sec. CCP Wuxi City Cttee.; Vice-Minister of Farming, Husbandry and Fishery; Vice-Minister of Agric.; Minister of Forestry 1997–98, of Agric. 1998–; mem. 15th CCP Cen. Cttee. 1997–. *Address:* Ministry of Agriculture, Nongzhanguan Nan Li, Beijing 100026, People's Republic of China.

CHEN YONGNIAN; Chinese business executive; b. Dec. 1931, Changzhou City, Jiansu Prov.; Gen. Man. Baiyin Silver Corpn. 1993–; mem. 8th CPPCC 1993–; China Labour Medal. *Address:* Baiyin Silver Corporation, Baiyin City, People's Republic of China.

CHEN YUAN; Chinese banker; s. of Chen Yun; fmr. Vice-Pres. People's Bank of China; Chair. State Devt. Bank 1998–; mem. Preparatory Cttee. of Hong Kong Special Admin. Region (S.A.R.), Vice-Pres. Financial Soc.; mem. Securities Comm. of the State Council. *Address:* State Development Bank, 40 Fucheng Lu, Haidan Qu, Beijing 1000 46, People's Republic of China.

CHEN YUNLIN; Chinese politician; b. Dec. 1941, Heishan Co., Liaoling Prov.; joined CCP 1966; ed. Beijing Agric. Univ.; Vice-Sec. CCP Qiqihar City Cttee., Mayor Qiqihar City 1981; Vice-Sec. CCP Heilongjiang Prov. Cttee. 1985; Vice-Gov. Heilongjiang Prov. 1988; Deputy Dir. Cen. Office for Taiwan Affairs of State Council 1994, Dir. 1997–; alt. mem. CCP Cen. Cttee. 1992. *Address:* Central Office for Taiwan Affairs, c/o State Council, Beijing, People's Republic of China.

CHEN ZHANGLIANG; Chinese professor of chemistry; b. 1960; ed. Washington Univ.; Prof. Chemistry Dept., Beijing Univ. *Address:* Department of Chemistry, Beijing University, Haidian District, Beijing, People's Republic of China.

CHEN ZHILI; Chinese politician and academic; b. 21 Nov. 1942, Xianyou Co., Fujian Prov.; joined CCP 1961; ed. Fudan Univ., Shanghai Inst. of Ceramics, Chinese Acad. of Sciences; Visiting Scholar, Materials Research Lab., Pa. State Univ., U.S.A. 1980–82; Vice-Sec. CCP Shanghai Science Comm. Cttee. 1984; alt. mem. 13th CCP Cen. Cttee. 1987, 14th CCP Cen. Cttee. 1992; Vice-Sec. CCP Shanghai Mun. Cttee. 1989–97; Vice-Minister of State Educ. Comm. 1994–98; Minister of Educ. 1998–; mem. 15th CCP Cen. Cttee. 1997–; Hon. Pres. Shanghai Inst. of Int. Friendship. *Address:* Ministry of Education, 37 Damucang Hutong, Xicheng Qu, Beijing 100088, People's Republic of China.

CHEN ZHONGSHI; Chinese novelist; b. 1942, Xi'an, Shanxi Prov.; Vice-Chair. Shanxi Prov. Writers' Asscn.; won Mao Dun Prize for Literature (for White Deer Height) 1997. *Publications:* White Deer Height, Early Summer, Mr. Blue Gown. *Address:* Shanxi Provincial Writers' Association, Xi'an, People's Republic of China.

CHEN ZHONGWEI; Chinese surgeon; b. 1 Oct. 1929, Hangzhou City, Zhejiang Prov.; s. of B. Z. Chen and E. L. Hu; m. Dr. W. Z. Yin 1954; one s. one d.; ed. Shanghai Second Medical Coll.; succeeded in replanting the severed forearm of a worker in Shanghai—the first operation of this kind in the world 1963; Chief Orthopaedic Dept. 6th People's Hosp., Shanghai 1965–82, Deputy Dir. 1970–87; Vice-Pres. Nat. Soc. of Surgery, Chinese Medical Asscn. 1972–; Dir. Orthopaedic Dept. Zhong Shan Hosp., Shanghai Medical Univ. 1982–; Pres. Int. Soc. of Reconstructive Microsurgery 1986–89; Hon. Pres. Chinese Soc. of Reconstructive Microsurgery 1986–89; Chair. Chinese Soc. for Research in Rehabilitation of Neural Disabilities 1988–; mem. Soc. Int. de Chirurgie 1975–, Scientific Council, Chinese Acad. of Science 1980–, Third World Acad. of Science 1987–, Exec. Cttee. of Int. Soc. of Reconstructive Microsurgery 1988–. *Publications:* Salvage of the Forearm Following Complete Traumatic Amputation: Report, A Case 1963, 7 books, 108 papers. *Leisure interests:* tennis, motorcycle, fishing, violin. *Address:* Zhong Shan Hospital, Shanghai Medical University, 136 Medical College Road, Shanghai 200032, People's Republic of China.

CHEN ZIMING; Chinese dissident; imprisoned for 13 years for role in Tiananmen Square pro-democracy demonstrations 1989, released on medical parole 1994, rearrested for staging hunger strike 1995, released 1996.

CHEN ZUOHUANG, M.M., D.M.A.; Chinese orchestral conductor; b. 2 April 1947, Shanghai; s. of Chen Ru Hui and Li He Zhen; m. Zaiyi Wang 1969; one c.; ed. Cen. Conservatory of Beijing, Univ. of Michigan; Musical Dir. China Film Philharmonic 1974–76; Assoc. Prof., Univ of Kansas, U.S.A. 1985–87; Prin. Conductor Cen. Philharmonic Orchestra of China 1987–; Dir. Wichita Symphony Orchestra 1990–; Dir. Rhode Island Philharmonic Orchestra 1992–96; Artistic Dir., Conductor China Nat. Symphony Orchestra 1996–. *Address:* Wichita Symphony Orchestra, Century II Concert Hall, 225 W. Douglas Ave., Suite 207, Wichita, KS 67202, U.S.A.

CHEN ZUOLIN; Chinese politician; b. 1923, Wuwei Co., Anhui Prov.; Vice-Chair. Revolutionary Cttee., Zhejiang Prov. 1975–79; Deputy Sec. CCP Cttee., Zhejiang 1976, Sec. 1977–83; alt. mem. 11th CCP Cen. Cttee. 1977, 12th Cen. Cttee. 1982; Vice-Gov., Zhejiang 1979–83; Sec.-Gen. Cen. Comm. for Discipline Inspection 1985–87, Deputy Sec. 1987; Deputy Sec. CCP Cen. Discipline Inspection Comm. 1992–; mem. Presidium of 14th CCP Nat. Congress 1992, CPC Standing Cttee., Cen. Leading Group for Party Building Work, Internal and Judicial Affairs Cttee.; Deputy to 8th NPC Jiangxi Prov. *Address:* Zhejiang Government Office, 28 Reuminlu Road, Hangzhou, People's Republic of China. *Telephone:* (Hangzhou) 24911.

CHEN ZUTAO; Chinese business executive; b. 1928; joined CCP 1960; Gen. Man. China Nat. Automotive Industry Corpn. 1993–. *Address:* China National Automotive Industry Corporation, 12 Fuxing Menwai Street, Beijing 100860, People's Republic of China.

CHENAULT, Kenneth Irvine, J.D.; American financial services company executive; b. 2 June 1951, New York; s. of Hortensius Chenault and Anne N. (Quick) Chenault; m. Kathryn Cassell 1977; two s.; ed. Bowdoin Coll., Harvard Univ.; called to Bar, Mass. 1981; Assoc. Rogers & Wells, New York 1977–79; Consultant Bain & Co., Boston 1979–81; Dir. Strategic Planning, American Express Co., New York 1981–83, Vice-Pres. American Express Travel Related Services Co. Inc., New York 1983–84, Sr. Vice- Pres. 1984–86, Exec. Vice-Pres. Platinum Card/Gold 1986–88, Personal Card Div. 1988–89, Pres. Consumer Card and Financial Services Group 1990–93, Pres. (U.S.A.) 1993–95, Vice-Chair. American Express Co., New York 1995–97, Pres., C.O.O. 1997–; mem. Bd. of Dirs. Brooklyn Union Gas, Quaker Oats Co., New York Univ. Medical Center; mem. Council of Foreign Relations, New York 1988, A.B.A.; several hon. degrees. *Address:* American Express Company, American Express Tower, World Financial Center, 200 Vesey Street, New York, NY 10285, U.S.A.

CHENEY, Lynne V., PH.D.; American administrator and writer; b. 14 Aug. 1941, Casper, Wyo.; d. of Wayne Vincent and Edna (née Lybyer) Vincent; m. Richard Bruce Cheney (q.v.) 1964; two d.; ed. Colorado Coll., Univ. of Wisconsin; freelance writer 1970–83; lecturer George Wash. Univ. 1972–77, Wyo. Univ. 1977–78; researcher, writer Md. Public Broadcasting 1982–83; Sr. Ed. Washingtonian magazine 1983–86; Chair. Nat. Endowment for Humanities (NEH) 1986–93; W. H. Brady Fellow American Enterprise Inst. 1993–95, Sr. Fellow 1996–; Commr. US Constitution Bicentennial Comm. 1985–87; mem. Women's Forum. *Publications:* Executive Privilege 1978, Sisters 1981, Kings of the Hill (jtly.) 1983, The Body Politic 1988, Telling the Truth 1995. *Address:* American Enterprise Institute, 1150 17th Street, N.W., Washington, DC 20036, U.S.A.

CHENEY, Richard B.; American business executive and fmr. politician; b. 30 Jan. 1941, Lincoln, Neb.; s. of Richard H. Cheney and Marjorie Dickey Cheney; m. Lynne Vincent (q.v.); two d.; ed. Univ. of Wyoming, Univ. of Wisconsin; engaged on staff of Gov. of Wis. and as a Congressional Fellow on staff of a mem. of House of Reps.; also worked for an investment advisory firm; Exec. Asst. to Donald Rumsfeld 1969–71, Deputy 1971–73; Deputy Asst. to the Pres. 1974–75, Chief of White House Staff 1975–77; Congressman, At-large District, Wyoming, 1978–89; Republican Whip 1987–88; Sec. of Defense 1989–93; Sr. Fellow American Enterprise Inst. 1993–95; Chair. Bd. and C.E.O. Halliburton Co., Dallas 1995– (Pres. 1997); fmr. Chair. House Republican Policy Cttee. 1980; Republican. *Address:* Halliburton Co., 3600 Lincoln Plaza, 500 N. Akard St., Dallas, TX 75201, U.S.A.

CHENG ANDONG; Chinese politician; b. Oct. 1936, Huainan City, Anhui Prov.; ed. univ.; mem. CCP 1980–; fmr. Mayor of Pingxiang City, Jiangxi Prov., fmr. Mayor of Nanchang City; Sec. CCP Xian Municipal Cttee. 1990; mem. Standing Cttee. CCP Shaanxi Provincial Cttee. 1991; alt. mem. 14th CCP Cen. Cttee.; Gov. of Shaanxi Feb. 1995–. *Address:* Office of the Governor, Xian, Shaanxi Province, People's Republic of China.

CHENG KEJIE; Chinese government official; b. 1933, Shanglin Co., Guangxi; ed. North Jiaotong Univ.; joined CCP 1984; Vice-Chair. Self-Govt. of the Guangxi Zhuang Autonomous Region 1986–90; Chair. Guanxi Zhuang Autonomous Regional People's Govt. 1990–98; Deputy Sec. CPC 6th Guangxi Zhuang Autonomous Regional Cttee. 1989–98; mem. 14th CCP Cen. Cttee. 1992–98; Vice-Chair. Standing Cttee. of 9th NPC 1998–. *Address:* Standing Committee of National People's Congress, Beijing, People's Republic of China.

CHENG LIANCHANG; Chinese government official; b. 14 May 1931, Jilin; m. Huang Shulan; one s. one d.; ed. Jilin Industrial School, People's Univ. of China; joined CCP 1950; Vice-Minister of 7th Ministry of Machine Building 1975–82; Vice-Minister of Astronautical Ind. 1982–88; Sr. Engineer and Researcher; Exec. Vice-Minister of Personnel 1988–94; mem. State Ed. Comm.; Vice-Pres. Nat. School of Admin.; Vice-Chair. Steering Cttee. for Enterprise; Standing mem. 8th Nat. Cttee. CPCCC 1993–98, 9th Nat. Cttee. CPPCC 1998–; Prof. of China People's Univ. *Leisure interest:* swimming. *Address:* c/o Ministry of Personnel, 12 Hepingli Zhongjie, Beijing 100716, People's Republic of China.

CHENG MIAN; Chinese woodcut artist; b. 2 Nov. 1933, Shandong; s. of Cheng Qixiang and Zhang Qirong; m. Liu Qimei 1956; two s.; ed. Central Acad. of Fine Arts, Beijing; taught at the Acad. 1962; Art Ed. of Xinghua Daily 1963–78; full-time painter Jiangsu Art Gallery 1978–; one-man exhbn. in Nanjing 1984, Qidong 1984, Cité Int. des Arts, Paris 1994; mem. China Artist Asscn.; mem. and Dir. China Woodcut Artist Asscn.; Vice-Pres. Jiangsu Woodcut Artist Asscn.; mem. Selection Cttee. 13th Nat. Woodcut Exhbn.; principal works include: book illustrations for Keep the Red Flag Flying, A Doctor on Night Shift 1977, Bank of Su River, Girl Carrying Water on Back, Moon in Water, Love, Morning Market, Perpetual Blood, Song for Bride, The People of Mount Taihang (series of woodcuts), Mother (6th Int. Biennial Exhbn. of Portrait Drawings and Graphics 1990), Bridge (Prize, Woodcut Exhbn., Italy 1990), Brothers (1st Prize, Jiangsu exhbn. 1992), Sun Setting (11th China Woodcut Exhbn.), Evening Fair (13th Nat. Woodcut Exhbn.); exhibited in Australia, France, Denmark, UK and USA, woodcuts published in books and magazines; Bronze medal, 10th Domestic Woodcuts Exhbn. *Publications:* A Psychological Description of Artistic Creation; numerous articles on painting, block printing and engraving. *Leisure interests:* music and literature. *Address:* 266 Changjiang Road, Nanjing, Jiangsu, People's Republic of China. *Telephone:* (025) 6641962.

CHENG SHICAI, Lieut.-Gen.; Chinese army officer; b. Hubei Prov.; Deputy Commdr. PLA Armoured Forces 1978; mem. Standing Cttee. 5th NPC 1978–82, 6th NPC 1983–87, 7th NPC 1988–93; mem. Cen. Advisory Comm. CCP 1988–. *Address:* Headquarters of the General-Staff, Chinese People's Liberation Army, Beijing, People's Republic of China.

CHENG SHIFA; Chinese artist; b. 1921, Songjiang Cty., Jiangsu; ed. Shanghai Coll. of Fine Arts; lecturer Univ. of Hong Kong 1985; mem. Nat. Cttee. Fed. Literary and Art Circles 1983, Council Shanghai br. of Artists' Asscn.; Silver Medal Leipzig Int. Book Exhbn. (for novel The Scholars) 1959. *Publications:* A Dream of the Red Mansion, Folk Stories of the West Lake, The Twelve Beauties, The Wild Boar Forest, The True Story of Ah Q, Gall and the Sword, Tale of the Horse-headed Fiddle.

CHENG SIWEI, M.B.A.; Chinese politician, b. June 1935, Beijing; ed. East China Chemical Eng. Inst., U.C.L.A.; Vice-Chair. China Democratic Nat. Construction Asscn.; mem. Standing Cttee. 8th CPPCC 1993–98; Vice-Minister of Chemical Industry; Chair. China Democratic Nat. Construction Asscn. 1996–; Vice-Chair. Standing Cttee. of 9th NPC 1998–. *Address:* Ministry of Chemical Industry, Building 16, Section 4, Anhuili, Beijing 100723, People's Republic of China.

CHENG SIYUAN, PH.D; Chinese politician; b. 22 Aug. 1908, Binyang Co., Guangxi Prov.; m. Shi Hong 1948; ed. Rome Univ., Italy; Chief Advisor to fmr. Acting Pres. of Kuomintang Govt. Li Zongren 1965; Vice-Chair. Standing Cttee. 7th Nat. Cttee. CPPCC 1988–92; Vice-Chair. Standing Cttee. 8th NPC 1993–98, 9th NPC 1998–. *Publications include:* Li and Jiang and China 1952, Li Zongren's Last Years 1980, Political Life 1988, My Memories 1994, A Biography of General Bai Chongxi 1995. *Leisure interests:* swimming, reading, history. *Address:* Standing Committee, National People's Congress, Tian'anmen Square, Beijing, People's Republic of China.

CHENG WEIGAO; Chinese government official; b. 1933, Suzhou City, Jiangsu Prov.; joined CCP 1950; Deputy Sec. Henan Prov. CP Cttee. 1987–90; Gov. of Henan Prov. 1988–90, of Hebei Prov. 1991–93, Deputy to 8th NPC Henan Prov.; alt. mem. 14th CCP Cen. Cttee. 1992–; mem. 15th CCP Cen. Cttee. 1997–; Sec. CCP Hebei Prov. Cttee. 1993–98; Chair. Hebei Prov. People's Congress 1998–. *Address:* c/o Office of Provincial Governor, Shijiazhuang City, Hebei Province, People's Republic of China.

CHENG YANAN; Chinese sculptor; b. 15 Jan 1936, Tianjin; d. of Cheng Goliang and Liuo Shijing; m. Zhang Zuoming 1962 (died 1989); one s. one d.; ed. Cen. Acad. of Fine Arts, Beijing; sculptor Beijing Architectural Artistic Sculpture Factory 1961–84, Sculpture Studio, Cen. Acad. of Fine Arts 1984–; mem. China Artists' Asscn.; exhbns. Jia Mei Shi Museum, Aomen 1986, Hong Kong 1990, and in Japan, France, Zaire, Congo, Hungary. *Address:* 452 New Building of Central Institute of Fine Arts, No 5 Shuaifuyan Lane, East District, Beijing, People's Republic of China.

CHEPIK, Sergei; Russian artist; b. 24 June 1953, Kiev; s. of Ludmilla Sabaneyeva and Mikhail Chepik; m. Marie-Aude Albert 1992; one s.; ed. Shevchenko Art Inst., Kiev, Repin Art Inst., Leningrad; mem. Young Artists' Union 1978; studied at Mylnikov's Studio and held first exhbns. in U.S.S.R. and abroad 1978–81; moved to Paris 1988; group exhbns. include: Young Painters: Nat. Exhibition of Graduation Works, Manege, Leningrad and Moscow 1979, Young Painters, Artists' Union, Leningrad 1980, Prague Biennale 1981, Russian Painting, Tokyo 1981, Zone 1981, Manege, Leningrad 1981, Young Soviet Painters, Acad. of Arts, Moscow, Leningrad 1982, 1984, Russian Painting, Osaka, Tokyo 1982, Petersburg, Petrograd, Leningrad Manege, Leningrad 1982, Nat. Portrait Exhibition, Artists' Union, Moscow 1983, Soviet Painting Week, Tokyo 1984, Soviet Painting, Cologne 1985, Salon d'Automne, Grand Palais, Paris (Gold Medal for House of the Dead) 1988, Russian paintings, Roy Miles Gallery, London 1988, 1989, 1993, Monte Carlo Int. Exhibition of Modern Art, Rocabella (Monaco City Award for the Tree) 1989; solo exhbns. include: Russian Landscapes, Artists' Union, Leningrad 1985, Retrospective Exhbn.: Paintings, Graphic Arts, Ceramics, Youth Palace, Leningrad 1986, One Man Show and Retrospective, Roy Miles Gallery, London 1990, Recent Works, Roy Miles Gallery, London 1993, 1994, Retrospective Exhbn. Prieuré St. Maurice, Senlis 1993, Graphics, Galerie Guiter, Paris 1997, major exhbn. of works at the Catto Gallery, London 1998. *Leisure interests:* literature, ballet, ceramics, sculpture. *Address:* c/o The Catto Gallery, 100 Heath Street, London, N.W.3., England; c/o Galerie Guiter, 23 rue Guenegaud, 75006 Paris, France. *Telephone:* 0171-435 6660 (London); 43-54-30-88 (Paris). *Fax:* 0171-431 5620 (London).

CHEPURIN, Aleksander Vasilyevich; Russian diplomatist; b. 1952; ed. Moscow Inst. of Int. Relations; on staff Ministry of Foreign Affairs since 1975; various diplomatic posts abroad and in U.S.S.R. Ministry of Foreign Affairs; Deputy Head, First Deputy Head Personnel Service, Ministry of Foreign Affairs of Russia 1992–93, Dir. Dept. of Personnel 1994–; Amb. to Denmark 1996–. *Address:* Kristiansgade 5, 2100 Copenhagen, Denmark. *Telephone:* (45) 31 42 55 85 (Office).

CHER (Cherilyn Lapierre Sarkisian); American singer and actress; b. 20 May 1946, El Centro, Calif.; d. of John Sarkisian and Georgina Holt; m. 1st Sonny Bono (divorced 1975, died 1998); one d.; m. 2nd Gregg Allman (divorced); one s.; half of singing duo Sonny and Cher; Sonny and Cher Comedy Hour (TV) 1971–75; own TV variety series and night club act; *Recordings include:* I Got You Babe, The Beat Goes On, Bang Bang, You Better Sit Down Kids, We all Sleep Alone, Black Rose (album) 1980, Cher 1987, Heart of Stone 1989, It's a Man's World 1996, The Casablanca Years 1996, Believe 1998, Strong Enough 1999; has won 11 gold and 3 platinum records; Best Actress Award, Cannes Film Festival, for Mask; Acad. Award for Moonstruck 1987; acted in play Come Back to the Five and Dime, Jimmy Dean, Jimmy Dean. *Films include:* Good Times, Chastity, Come Back to the Five and Dime, Jimmy Dean, Jimmy Dean, Silkwood, Mask, Witches of Eastwick, Moonstruck, Suspect, Mermaids, Love and Understanding, Faithful. *Address:* c/o Bill Sammeth Organisation, P.O. Box 960, Beverly Hills, CA 90213, U.S.A.

CHÉREAU, Patrice; French film, theatre and opera director; b. 2 Nov. 1944; s. of Jean-Baptiste Chéreau and Marguerite Pélicier; ed. Lycée Louis-le-Grand and Faculté de Lettres, Paris; Co-Dir. Théâtre national populaire (T.N.P.) 1972–81; Dir. Théâtre des Amandiers, Nanterre 1982–90; *theatre productions include:* L'Intervention 1964, L'Affaire de la rue de Lourcine 1966, Les Soldats 1967, La Révolte au Marché noir 1968, Don Juan, Richard II, Splendeur et Mort de Joaquin Murieta 1970, La Finta Serva 1971, Lulu 1972, Massacre á Paris 1972, La Dispute 1973, Lear 1975, Peer Gynt 1981, Les Paravents 1983, Combats de Nègre et de Chiens 1983, La Fausse suivante 1985, Quai Ouest 1986, Dans la solitude des champs de coton 1987, 1995, Hamlet 1988, Le Retour au désert 1988, le Temps et la Chambre 1991; *opera productions:* L'Italiana in Algeri 1969, The Tales of Hoffmann 1974, Der Ring des Nibelungen (Bayreuth 1976–80), Lulu 1979, Lucio Silla 1984, Wozzeck 1992, Don Giovanni (Salzburg 1994–96); *films:* La Chair de l'Orchidée 1974, Judith Therpauve 1978, L'Homme blessé 1984, Hotel de France

1987, Le Temps et La Chambre 1993, Queen Margot 1994, Those Who Love Me Can Take The Train 1998. *Address:* c/o Artmedia, 10 avenue George V, 75008 Paris, France.

CHERMAYEFF, Peter, A.B., M.ARCH., F.A.I.A.; American architect; b. 4 May 1936, London; s. of Serge Ivan Chermayeff and Barbara Chermayeff; m. Andrea Petersen 1983; one s. one d. two step-s.; ed. Harvard Univ.; Prin. and Vice-Pres. Cambridge Seven Assocs. Inc., Pres. Int. Design for the Environment Assocs., Inc. (IDEA); mem. Mass. Council on Arts and Humanities 1969–72, Bd. of Advisors School of Visual Arts, Boston Univ. 1976–80, Visiting Cttee. Rhode Island School of Design, Providence 1969–75; Bd. Design Consultant Univ. of Pennsylvania, Pa. 1976–80, Bd. of Dirs. Center for Maritime Studies, Haifa, Israel 1989–91; *major works include:* Guidelines and Standards, Mass. Bay Transportation Authority 1967, U.S. Exhibition Expo 67 Montreal 1967, New England Aquarium, Boston 1969, San Antonio Museum of Art, San Antonio, Texas 1981, Nat. Aquarium, Baltimore, Maryland 1981, Ring of Fire Aquarium, Osaka, Japan 1990, Tennessee Aquarium, Chattanooga 1992, Genoa Aquarium, Italy 1992; *work in progress:* Lisbon Oceanarium, Portugal 1998; producer of films including: Orange and Blue 1962, Cheetah 1971, Wildebeest 1984; Claude M. Fuess Award, Phillips Acad., Andover 1979. *Address:* 15 East 26th Street, New York, NY 10010, U.S.A.

CHERN, Shiing-Shen, B.S., M.S., D.SC.; American (naturalized 1961) professor of mathematics; b. 26 Oct. 1911, Kashing, China; s. of Lien Chin Chern and Mei Han; m. Shih Ning Cheng 1939; one s. one d.; ed. Nankai Univ., Tientsin, Tsing Hua Univ., Peking, and Univ. of Hamburg, Germany; Prof. of Math., Tsing Hua Univ., Peking 1937–43; mem. Inst. for Advanced Study, Princeton, N.J., U.S.A. 1943–45; Acting Dir. Inst. of Math., Academia Sinica, Nanking, China 1946–48; Prof. of Math., Univ. of Chicago, U.S.A. 1949–60, Univ. of Calif. at Berkeley 1960–79, Prof. Emer. 1979–; Dir. Math. Sciences Research Inst., Berkeley 1982–84, Dir. Emer. 1984–; Dir. Nankai Inst. of Math., Tianjin, China 1984; mem. Academia Sinica, N.A.S., American Acad. of Arts and Sciences; Hon. mem. Indian Mathematical Soc.; Corresp. mem. Brazilian Acad. of Sciences; Foreign mem. Royal Soc. of London 1985–, Corresp. mem. Academia Peloritana, Messina, Sicily 1986; Hon. mem. London Math. Soc. 1986; Assoc. founding mem. Third World Acad. of Sciences 1983; Life mem. New York Acad. of Sciences 1987; mem. American Philosophical Soc. 1989; Foreign mem. Accad. Nazionale dei Lincei, Rome 1988, Académie des Sciences, Paris 1989; Hon. LL.D. (Chinese Univ. of Hong Kong) 1969; Hon. D.Sc. (Univ. of Chicago) 1969, (Univ. of Hamburg, Germany) 1971, (State Univ. of New York at Stony Brook) 1985, (Univ. of Notre Dame) 1994; Dr. h.c. (Eidgenossische Technische Hochschule, Switzerland) 1982; Hon. Dr. (Nankai Univ.) 1985; Nat. Medal of Science (U.S.A.) 1975; Chauvenet Prize (Math. Asscn. of America) 1970; Steele Prize, American Math. Soc. 1983; shared Wolf Foundation Prize, Israel 1983–84. *Publications:* S. S. Chern, Selected Papers 1978, Complex Manifolds without Potential Theory 1979, Selected Papers Vols. II, III, IV 1989, Exterior Differential Systems (with Bryant, Gardner, Goldschmidt and Griffiths) 1990. *Address:* 8336 Kent Court, El Cerrito, CA 94530, U.S.A. (Home). *Telephone:* (510) 232-4148. *Fax:* (510) 643-5340.

CHERNIN, Peter; American film company executive; fmrly. Pres. Fox Broadcasting Co.; Chair. Twentieth Century Fox Film Corpn. 1992–; now Chair. Fox Inc.; Pres., C.O.O. Fox Newscorp 1996–. *Address:* Fox Incorporated, P.O. Box 900, Beverly Hills, CA 90035, U.S.A.

CHERNOBROVKINA, Tatyana Anatolyevna; Russian ballerina; b. 14 Aug. 1965; ed. Saratov School of Choreography; soloist Saratov Theatre of Opera and Ballet 1983–87; prima ballerina Moscow Stanislavsky and Nemirovich-Danchenko Musical Theatre 1987–; prize-winner 5th Moscow Int. Competition of Ballet Dancers 1985; Merited Artist of Russia 1994. *Address:* Moscow Musical Theatre, B. Dmitrovka str. 17, 103009 Moscow, Russia (Office). *Telephone:* (095) 229 2835 (Office).

CHERNOFF, Herman, PH.D.; American professor of statistics; b. 1 July 1923, New York; s. of Max Chernoff and Pauline Markowitz; m. Judith Ullman 1947; two d.; ed. Townsend Harris High School, City Coll. of New York, Brown and Columbia Univs.; Research Assoc., Cowles Comm. for Research in Econs., Univ. of Chicago 1947–49; Asst. Prof. of Math., Illinois Univ. 1949–51, Assoc. Prof. 1951–52; Assoc. Prof. of Statistics, Stanford Univ. 1952–56, Prof. 1956–74; Prof. of Applied Math., M.I.T. 1974–85; Prof. of Statistics, Harvard Univ. 1985–97, Prof. Emer. 1997–; mem. N.A.S., American Acad. of Arts and Sciences; Dr. h.c. (Ohio State) 1983, (Technion) 1984, (Univ. of Rome, La Sapienza) 1995; Townsend Harris Prize 1982, Wilks Medal 1987. *Publications:* numerous articles in scientific journals. *Address:* Department of Statistics SC713, Harvard University, Cambridge, MA 02138; 75 Crowninshield Road, Brookline, MA 02446, U.S.A. (Home). *Telephone:* (617) 495-5462 (Office); (617) 232-8256 (Home). *Fax:* (617) 496-8057.

CHERNOMYRDIN, Viktor Stepanovich; CAND. TECH. SC; Russian politician; b. 9 April 1938, Cherny-Otrog, Orenburg Dist.; m.; two s.; ed. Kuybyshev Polytechnic; Soviet Army 1957–60; operator in oil refinery 1960–67; mem. CPSU 1961–91 (mem. Cen. Cttee. 1986–90); work with Orsk City Cttee. 1967–73; deputy chief engineer, dir. of Orenburg gas plant 1973–78; work with CPSU Cen. Cttee. 1978–82; U.S.S.R. Deputy Minister of Gas Industry, Chief of All-Union production unit for gas exploitation in Tyumen Dist. 1982–85; U.S.S.R. Minister of Gas 1985–89; Chair. Bd. Gasprom 1989–92; Deputy Prime Minister, Minister of Fuel and Energy June–Dec. 1992; Chair. Council of Ministers 1992–98; Acting Prime Minister Aug.–Sept. 1998; Deputy to U.S.S.R. Supreme Soviet 1987–89; Chair. Bd. All-Russian Movt. Our Home—Russia 1995. *Address:* c/o Our Home-Russia, Academika Sakhazova prospekt 12, 107078 Moscow, Russia.

CHERNOV, Vladimir Kirillovich; Russian baritone; b. 1956, Belorechensk; m. Olga Chernova; one s.; ed. Moscow Conservatory (pupil of Georgy Seleznev and Hugo Titz); winner of All-Union Glinka Competition, Int. Competitions: Tchaikovsky (Moscow), Voci Virdiagni (Vercelli), M. Helin (Helsinki); soloist of Kirov (now Mariinsky) Theatre 1990–; debut in U.S.A. 1988 (La Bohème, Boston), in U.K. 1990 (Forza del Destino, Glasgow); perm. soloist of Metropolitan Opera 1990–, Wiener Staatsoper 1991–; guest singer at La Scala, Chicago Lyric Opera, Mariinsky Opera, La Monnaie (Brussels) and other theatres of Europe and America; leading parts in operas Queen of Spades, Boris Godunov, Barber of Seville, La Traviata, Eugene Onegin, Don Carlos, War and Peace, The Masked Ball, Faust, Rigoletto, Falstaff; in concerts and recitals performs opera arias, song cycles of Mahler, Tchaikovsky, romances. *Address:* c/o Columbia Artists Management Inc., 165 West 57th Street, New York, NY 10019, U.S.A. *Telephone:* (212) 799-8721.

CHERNY, Gorimir Gorimirovich; Russian scientist; b. 22 Jan. 1923, Kamenets-Podol'sky; s. of the late Gorimir Cherny and Zoja Cherny; m. 1st Augusta Gubarev 1949 (died 1986); m. 2nd Alla Sebik 1989; two d.; ed. Moscow Univ.; served in Soviet Army 1941–45; worked for Cen. Inst. of Aircraft Engines 1949–58; mem. CPSU 1954–91; Prof. at Moscow Univ. 1958; Dir. Univ. Research Inst. of Mechanics 1960–92; Corresp. mem. U.S.S.R. (now Russian) Acad. of Sciences 1962–81, mem. 1981, Acad.-Sec., Div. of Eng., Mechanics and Control Processes 1990–96; Corresp. mem. Int. Acad. of Astronautics 1966, mem. 1969; State Prizes 1972, 1978, 1991, seven orders and various medals; author of numerous books and scientific articles on aerodynamics, theory of detonation and combustion, theory of gas-fired machines. *Address:* Russian Academy of Sciences, Division of Engineering, Mechanics and Control Processes, 32a Leninski prosp., Moscow, Russia. *Telephone:* (095) 938-14-04. *Fax:* (095) 938-18-44 (Office); 255-47-41 (Home).

CHERNYSHEV, Albert Sergeyevich; Russian diplomatist; b. 18 Aug. 1936, Voronezh; m.; one d.; ed. Moscow Inst. of Int. Relations; diplomatic service 1959–; asst. man., attaché, Sec. Dept. of External Policy Information, U.S.S.R. Ministry of Foreign Affairs 1959–67; Second, First Sec. Embassy Vietnam 1967–71; Counsellor of Minister of Foreign Affairs 1973–76, Chief Counsellor 1976–81, Asst. Minister 1982–87, Chief Gen. Secretariat, mem. of Bd. 1987; U.S.S.R. (later Russian) Amb. to Turkey 1987–94; Deputy Minister of Foreign Affairs 1994–96, Amb. to India 1996–. *Address:* Embassy of Russian Federation, Shantipath, Chanatyapuri, New Delhi, 110021, India. *Telephone:* (11) 687 3799.

CHEUNG, Linus; Chinese business executive; Chief Exec. Hong Kong Telecom; Chair. Companhia de Telecomunicações de Macau 1996–. *Address:* Hong Kong Telecom, Hong Kong Telecom Tower, 39/F, Taikoo Place, 979 King's Road, Quarry Bay, Hong Kong Special Administrative Region, People's Republic of China. *Telephone:* 2888-2888. *Fax:* 2877-8877.

CHEVALIER, Louis; French university professor of political science; b. 29 May 1911, Vendeé; ed. Ecole Normale Supérieure; Prof. Coll. de France; Prof. Institut d'Etudes Politiques de Paris; fmr. mem. Conseil supérieur de la Recherche Scientifique; fmr. Pres. du Conseil Scientifique du Centre Int. d'Etude des Problèmes Humains de Monaco; fmr. mem. Conseil Economique et Social du District de Paris; Hon. degree (Columbia); Commdr. Légion d'honneur. *Publications:* Les paysans, Le problème démographique nord-africain, La formation de la population parisienne, Madagascar, Démographie générale; contributor to Population, Le choléra de 1832, Classes laborieuses et classes dangereuses, Les Parisiens, Histoire anachronique des Français, L'assassinat de Paris, Montmartre du plaisir et du crime, Histoires de la nuit parisienne, Les relais de mer, Les ruines de Subure-Montmartre de 1939 aux années 80, Juanito-une Andalousie de bone et de sang. *Address:* 71 rue du Cardinal Lemoine, 75005 Paris, France.

CHEVALIER, Roger; French aeronautical engineer; b. 3 May 1922, Marseille; s. of Louis Chevalier and Marie-Louise Assaud; m. Monique Blin 1947; two s.; ed. Ecole Polytechnique and Ecole Nationale Supérieure de l'Aéronautique; Head of Dept., Aeronautical Arsenal 1948–53; Chief Engineer, Nord-Aviation 1954–60; Technical Dir. Soc. pour l'Etude et la Réalisation d'Engins Balistiques (SEREB) 1960, Dir.-Gen. 1967–70; mem. admin. council Onera 1972–; Vice-Pres. Gifas 1977–; Gen. Man. Société Nationale de l'Industrie Aérospatiale (SNIAS), Exec. Senior Vice-Pres. 1976–82, Vice-Chair. 1982–87; Pres. Asscn. Aéronautique et Astronautique de France; mem. Int. Astronautical Fed. (IAF) 1980–82, Pres. 1982–86; Vice-Pres. Aero-Club de France 1981; Pres. French Acad. for Aeronautics and Astronautics; Pres. Soc. d'études de réalisation et d'applications techniques (SERAT) 1985–91; Fellow, American Aeronautic and Astronautic Inst.; mem. Int. Acad. of Astronautics; Commdr. Légion d'honneur; Médaille de l'Aéronautique, Prix Galabert 1966, Allan D. Emil Award 1982; Commdr. Ordre national du mérite, Commdr. of Merit (Fed. Repub. of Germany) 1987. *Leisure interests:* tennis, hunting, reading. *Address:* 4 rue Edouard Detaille, 75017 Paris, France. *Telephone:* (1) 42-27-59-28.

CHEVALLAZ, Georges-André, D.LITT.; Swiss politician; b. 7 Feb. 1915, Lausanne; s. of Georges Chevallaz and Frida Chevallaz; m. Madeleine Roch

1945; two s.; ed. Univ. of Lausanne; teacher, School of Commerce 1942–55; Dir. Canton Library, Reader in Diplomatic History, Univ. of Lausanne 1955–58; Syndic de Lausanne 1957–73; Nat. Councillor 1959–73; mem. Fed. Council 1973–, Head of Finance and Customs Dept. 1974–79; Vice-Pres. of Switzerland Jan.-Dec. 1979, Pres. Jan.-Dec. 1980, Head of Fed. Military (Defence) Dept. 1980–83; Radical Democrat. *Publications:* Aspects de l'agriculture vaudoise à la fin de l'ancien régime 1949, Histoire générale de 1789 à nos jours 1957, 1967, 1973, 1990, Les grandes conférences diplomatiques 1964, La Suisse ou le sommeil du juste 1967, La Suisse est-elle gouvernable? 1984, Le Gouvernement des Suisses 1989, Le défi de la neutralité 1995, etc. *Address:* 113 Vuillettaz, 1066 Epalinges, Switzerland. *Telephone:* (021) 784.19.19. *Fax:* (021) 784.20.29.

CHEVÈNEMENT, Jean-Pierre; French politician; b. 9 March 1939, Belfort; s. of Pierre Chevènement and Juliette Garessus; m. Nisa Grünberg 1970; two s.; ed. Lycée Victor-Hugo, Besançon, Univ. de Paris, Ecole Nationale d'Admin.; joined Parti Socialiste (PS) 1964; Commercial Attaché, Ministry of Econ. and Finance 1965–68; Sec.-Gen. Centre d'études, de recherches et d'éducation socialistes 1965–71; Commercial Adviser, Jakarta, Indonesia 1969; Political Sec. Fédération socialiste de Paris 1969–70; Dir. of Studies, Soc. Eres 1969–71; Nat. Sec. PS 1971–75, 1979–80, mem. Exec. Bureau 1971–81, 1986, Steering Cttee. 1971–92; Deputy (Belfort) to Nat. Ass. 1973–81, 1986; Vice-Pres. Departmental Ass. of Franche-Comté; mem. Bd. Dirs. Repères magazine; Minister of State, Minister of Research and Tech. 1981–82, of Industry 1982–83, of Nat. Educ. 1984–86, of Defence 1988–91, of the Interior 1997–; First Asst. to Mayor of Belfort 1977–83, 1997–, Mayor 1983–; Pres. Conseil Régional de Franche-Comté 1981–82, mem. 1986–88, fmr. Vice-Pres.; f., Pres. Citizens Movt. 1992–; mem. Foreign Affairs Comm., Nat. Assembly 1986–88, Finance Comm. 1993–; Croix de la valeur militaire. *Publications:* (as Jacques Mandrin): L'enarchie ou les mandarins de la société bourgeoise 1967, Socialisme ou socialmédiocratie 1969, Clefs pour le socialisme 1973, Le vieux, la crise, le neuf 1975, Les socialistes, les communistes et les autres, Le service militaire 1977, Etre socialiste aujourd'hui 1979, Apprendre pour entreprendre 1985, Le pari sur l'intelligence 1985, Une certaine idée de la République m'amène à 1992, le Temps des citoyens 1993, Le Vert et Le Noir. Intégrisme, Pétrole, Dollar 1995, France–Allemagne: parlons franc 1996. *Leisure interest:* chess. *Address:* Ministère de l'Intérieur, place Beauvau, 75800 Paris cedex 08; Mairie de Belfort, 09020 Belfort cedex; Assemblée Nationale, 75355 Paris, France.

CHEW, Geoffrey Foucar, PH.D.; American professor of physics; b. 5 June 1924, Washington, D.C.; s. of Arthur Percy Chew and Pauline Lisette Foucar; m. 1st Ruth Elva Wright 1945 (died 1971); one s. one d.; m. 2nd Denyse Mettel 1972; two s. one d.; ed. George Washington Univ. and Univ. of Chicago; Research Physicist, Los Alamos Scientific Lab. 1944–46; Research Physicist, Lawrence Radiation Lab. 1948–49, Head of Theoretical Group 1967; Asst. Prof. of Physics, Univ. of California at Berkeley 1949–50, Prof. of Physics 1957–, Chair. Dept. of Physics 1974–78, Dean of Physical Sciences 1986–92; Asst. Prof., then Assoc. Prof. of Physics, Univ. of Illinois 1950–55, Prof. 1955–56; Fellow, Inst. for Advanced Study 1956; Overseas Fellow, Churchill Coll., Cambridge 1962–63; Scientific Associate, CERN 1978–79; Prof. Miller Inst. 1981–82; Visiting Prof., Univ. of Paris 1983–84; mem. N.A.S., American Acad. of Arts and Sciences; Hughes Prize of American Physical Soc. 1962, Lawrence Award of U.S. Atomic Energy Comm. 1969, Berkeley Citation (Univ. of Calif.) 1991. *Publications:* The S-Matrix Theory of Strong Interactions 1961, The Analytic S-Matrix 1966; over 100 scientific articles. *Leisure interests:* gardening, hiking. *Address:* Lawrence Radiation Laboratory, Berkeley, CA 94720 (Office); 10 Maybeck Twin Drive, Berkeley, CA 94708, U.S.A. (Home). *Telephone:* 642-4505 (Dept. of Physics); 486-5010, (Lawrence Radiation Lab.); 848-1830 (Home).

CHEYSSON, Claude; French politician; b. 13 April 1920, Paris; s. of Pierre Cheysson and Sophie Funck-Brentano; m. 3rd Danielle Schwartz 1969; one s. two d. (and three c. from previous m.); ed. Ecole Polytechnique and Ecole d'Administration, Paris; escaped from occupied France to Spanish prison 1943; Officer in the Free French Forces 1943–45; entered French Diplomatic Service 1948; attached to UN Mission in Palestine 1948; Head of French liaison office with Fed. German Govt., Bonn 1949–52; adviser to Prime Minister of Vietnam, Saigon 1952–54; Chef de Cabinet to French Prime Minister (Mendès-France) 1954–55; technical adviser to Minister for Moroccan and Tunisian Affairs 1955–56; Sec.-Gen. Comm. for Technical Co-operation in Africa (C.C.T.A.), Lagos 1957–62; Dir-Gen. Sahara Authority (Organisme Saharien), Algiers 1962–65; Amb. to Indonesia 1966–69; Pres. Entreprise minière et chimique and Pres. Dir.-Gen. Cie. des potasses du Congo 1970–73; mem. Bd. Le Monde 1970–81, 1985–92; Commr. for Devt. Aid, Comm. of European Communities 1973–81; Minister of External Relations 1981–84; Commr. for Mediterranean Policy and North-South Relations, Comm. of European Communities 1985–88; mem. European Parl. 1989–94; mem. Exec. Bd. Socialist Party 1989–94; Pres. Institut Mendès-France 1987–89; Pres. Fondation Arche de la Fraternité 1989–93; Town Councillor, Bargemon, France 1983–89, 1995; Dr. h.c. Univ. of Louvain; Joseph Bech Prize 1978, Prix Luderitz (Namibia) 1983; Commdr., Légion d'honneur, Croix de guerre, Grand Cross, Grand Officier, Commdr. from numerous countries. *Leisure interest:* skiing. *Address:* 52 rue de Vaugirard, 75006 Paris; La Belle Bastide, 83830 Bargemon, France. *Telephone:* 01-43.26.46.65 (Paris); 04-94.76.64.62 (Bargemon). *Fax:* 01-43.26.46.65.

CHHATWAL, H.E. Surbir Jit Singh, M.POL.SC.; Indian diplomatist; b. 1 Oct. 1931, Bannu; s. of Datar Singh Chhatwal and Rattan Kaur Chhatwal; m. Neelam Singh 1962; one s. one d.; ed. Agra Univ.; joined Foreign Service 1955; Ministry of External Affairs, including one year at Cambridge, U.K. 1955–58; Third Sec., Madrid 1958–60; Under-Sec., Ministry of External Affairs, New Delhi 1960–62; First Sec., Havana, Cuba 1962–64; Deputy Sec. (Co-ordination), Ministry of External Affairs, New Delhi 1964–66; First Sec. and Acting High Commr., Ottawa, Canada 1966–68; First Indian Consul-Gen., Seoul, S. Korea 1968–71; Dir. Ministry of Foreign Trade, New Delhi 1971–73; Chief of Protocol, Ministry of External Affairs, New Delhi 1973–75; High Commr. in Malaysia 1975–79, in Sri Lanka 1982–85, in Canada 1985–90; Amb. to Kuwait 1979–82; Visiting Prof. Jawaharlal Nehru Univ., New Delhi 1990–91; mem. and Chair. Union Public Service Comm. 1991–96. *Leisure interests:* reading, golf. *Address:* S-168, Panch Shila Park, New Delhi, India. *Telephone:* (6) 484488. *Fax:* (6) 485398.

CHI HAOTIAN, Gen.; Chinese army officer; b. 1929, Zhaoyuan Co., Shandong Prov.; m. Jiang Qingping; joined army 1944, CCP 1946; Major, unit, Nanjing Mil. Region 1958; Deputy Political Commissar, Beijing Mil. Region 1975–77; Deputy Ed.-in-Chief, People's Daily 1977–82; Deputy Chief of Staff PLA 1977–82; Political Commissar, Jinan Mil. Region 1985–87; PLA Chief of Staff Dec. 1987–; Minister of National Defence March 1993–; Chair. Drafting Cttee. for Nat. Defence Law of People's Repub. of China; mem. CCP Cen. Cttee. 1985–; mem. PRC Cen. Mil. Cttee. 1988–; rank of Gen. 1988; mem. 14th CCP Cen. Cttee. 1992–97, 15th CCP Cen. Cttee. 1997–; mem. Cen. Mil. Comm. CCP 1992–, Vice-Chair. 1995–; mem. 8th NPC 1993–, Politburo; State Councillor 1993–; Hon. Pres. Wrestling Asscn. *Address:* Ministry of National Defence, Jingshanqian Jie, Beijing, People's Republic of China.

CHIANG KAI-SHEK, Madame (Soong, Mayling), LL.D., L.H.D.; Chinese sociologist; b. 5 March 1897; m. (Pres.) Chiang Kai-shek 1927 (died 1975); ed. Wellesley Coll., U.S.A.; first Chinese woman appointed mem. of Child Labour Comm.; inaugurated Moral Endeavour Asscn.; established schools in Nanking for orphans of revolutionary soldiers; fmr. mem. Legislative Yuan; served as Sec.-Gen. of Chinese Comm. on Aeronautical Affairs; Dir.-Gen. New Life Movement; founded and directed Nat. Chinese Women's Asscn. for War Relief and Nat. Asscn. for Refugee Children; accompanied husband on mil. campaigns; Hon. Chair. American Bureau for Medical Aid to China and Cttee. for the promotion of the Welfare of the Blind; Patroness Int. Red Cross Cttee.; Hon. Chair. British United Aid to China Fund and United China Relief; First Hon. Mem. Bill of Rights Commemorative Soc.; first Chinese woman to be decorated by Nat. Govt. of China, awards include Gold Medal of Nat. Inst. of Social Sciences; L.H.D. (John B. Stetson Univ., Bryant Coll., Hobart and William Smith Colls., Nebraska Wesleyan Univ.), LL.D. (Rutgers Univ., Goucher Coll., Wellesley Coll., Loyola Univ., Russell Sage Coll., Hahnemann Medical Coll., Univs. of Michigan and Hawaii, and Wesleyan Coll., Macon); Hon. F.R.C.S. (Eng.); Hon. mem. numerous socs. *Publications:* Sian: A Coup d'Etat 1937, China in Peace and War 1939, China Shall Rise Again 1939, This is Our China 1940, We Chinese Women 1941, American Tour Speeches 1942–43, Little Sister Su 1943, The Sure Victory 1955, Madame Chiang Kai-shek: Selected Speeches 1958–59, Album of Reproductions of Paintings Vol. I 1952, Vol. II 1962, Religious Writings 1963, Madame Chiang Kai-shek: Selected Speeches 1965–66, Album of Chinese Orchid Paintings 1971, Album of Chinese Bamboo Paintings 1972, Album of Chinese Landscape Paintings 1973, Album of Chinese Floral Paintings 1974, Conversations with Mikhail Borodin 1977. *Address:* Lattingtown, Long Island, New York, U.S.A.

CHIARA, Maria; Italian opera singer; b. 24 Nov. 1939, Oderzo; m. Antonio Cassinelli; ed. Conservatorio Benedetto Marcello, Venice, with Maria Carbone; début as Desdemona in Otello, Doge's Palace, Venice, 1965, then Rome Opera début 1965; frequent performances (in Italy including Turandot with Placido Domingo, Verona 1969); débuts Germany and Austria 1970; début La Scala, Milan as Micaela, Carmen 1972; début Royal Opera House, Covent Garden, London, Turandot 1973; début Metropolitan Opera, New York in Traviata and at Lyric Opera, Chicago in Manon Lescaut 1977; sings in all major opera houses of Europe, U.S.A. and S. America; opened 1985/86 season at La Scala in Aida; has recorded Il Segreto di Susanna and a disc of operatic arias (Decca).

CHIBA, Kazuo, B.ECONS.; Japanese businessman; b. 26 March 1925, Miyagi Pref.; m. Noriko Chiba 1954; two s.; ed. Univ. of Tokyo; joined Oji Paper Co. Ltd. 1950, Dir. 1974, Mill Man. Kasugai Mill 1978, Man. Dir. 1981, Sr. Man. Dir. 1985, Exec. Vice-Pres. 1987, Pres. 1989–; Blue Ribbon Medal 1990. *Leisure interests:* golf, reading. *Address:* Umegaoka 16-32, Midori-ku, Yokohama, 227 Japan. *Telephone:* 045-971 6602.

CHIBURDANIDZE, Maiya Grigorievna; Georgian chess player; b. 17 Jan. 1961, Kutaisi, Georgia; ed. Tbilisi Medical Inst. 1978; Int. Grand Master 1977; Honoured Master of Sport 1978; U.S.S.R. Champion 1977; World Champion 1978–91; winner of numerous women's int. chess tournaments; Capt. winning Soviet team at 8th Women's Chess Olympics 1978, Georgian winning team at Chess Olympics 1994; Oscar chess prize 1984–87. *Address:* Georgian Chess Federation, Tbilisi, Georgia.

CHIEN, Rt. Rev. John Chih-Tsung, M.DIV., S.T.M.; Taiwanese ecclesiastic; b. 23 March 1940; m. Grace Chu 1963; one s. two d.; ed. Tunghai Univ., Tainan Theolgical Coll., Selly Oak Coll. U.K. and Va. Theological Seminary,

U.S.A.; St. Andrew's, Chading; Grace Church, Tainan; Good Shepherd, Taipei; Dean, St. John's Cathedral, Taipei; Bishop, Diocese of Taiwan 1988–; Trustee Tunghai Univ., St. John's and St. Mary's Inst. of Tech. *Address:* 7 Lane 105, Hangchow S. Road, Sec. 1, Taipei, Taiwan. *Telephone:* (02) 2341-1265. *Fax:* (02) 2396-2014.

CH'IEN KUO FUNG, Raymond, C.B.E., PH.D., J.P.; Chinese business executive and politician; b. 26 Jan. 1952, Tokyo, Japan; m. Whang Hwee Leng; one s. two d.; ed. schools in Hong Kong, Rockford Coll., Ill., Univ. of Pennsylvania; Group Man. Dir. Lam Soon Hong Kong Group; Chair. Industry and Tech. Devt. Council, Hong Kong Industrial Tech. Centre Corpn., Hong Kong/Japan Business Co-operation Cttee.; mem. Exec. Council 1992–97, Exec. Council Hong Kong Special Admin. Region July 1997–; mem. Bd. China Centre for Econ. Research, Beijing Univ.; Hon. Adviser China Aerospace Corpn.; Hon. Prof. Nanjing Univ. *Address:* Executive Council Secretariat, 1st Floor, Main Wing, Central Government Offices, Central, Hong Kong Special Administrative Region, People's Republic of China.

CHIEPE, Gaositwe Keagakwa Tibe, M.B.E., P.M.S., B.SC., M.A., F.R.S.A.; Botswana politician and diplomatist; b. Serowe; d. of the late T. and S. T. Chiepe (née Sebina); ed. secondary school in Tigerloof, S. Africa and Univs. of Fort Hare and Bristol; Educ. Officer, Botswana 1948, Senior Educ. Officer 1962, Deputy Dir. of Educ. 1965, Dir. of Educ. 1968; High Commr. in U.K. and Nigeria 1970–74, concurrently accredited to Sweden, Norway, Denmark, Fed. Repub. of Germany, France, Belgium and the EEC; Minister of Commerce and Industry 1974–77, of Mineral Resources and Water Affairs 1977–84, of External Affairs 1984–95, of Educ. 1995–; Patron Botswana Forestry Soc.; Hon. Pres. Kalahari Conservation Soc.; Hon. LL.D. (Bristol). *Leisure interests:* music, gardening. *Address:* Ministry of Education, Private Bag 005, Gaborone, Botswana.

CHIGYR, Mikhail Nikolayevich; Belarus politician and economist; b. 1948, Usovo, Minsk Region; m.; two c.; ed. Belarus State Inst. of Nat. Econs., Moscow Inst. of Finance and Statistics; Chief Div. of Credit, State Bank of Minsk Region, Chief Moscow Regional Br. of State Bank of Minsk 1973–80; official Belarus CP 1982–86; Dir. Minsk City Office U.S.S.R. State Bank 1986–87; First Deputy Chair. Exec. Bd. Agroprombank, Belarus Repub. 1988–91; Chair. Exec. Bd. Jt.-Stock Commercial Agricultural-Industrial Bank Belagroprombank 1991–94; Prime Minister of Belarus 1994–96 (resgnd.).

CHIHANA, Chakufwa; Malawi politician and fmr. trade union leader; b. 11 March 1939; s. of Tom Chihana and Agness Chihana; one s. two d.; Pres. Alliance for Democracy opposition party; sentenced to 9 months imprisonment for anti-govt. activities Dec. 1992, released June 1993; Second Vice-Pres. of Malawi and Minister of Irrigation and Water Devt. 1994–96; Robert F. Kennedy Memorial Human Rights Award 1993; Special Advisor Worldwide Intellectuals Asscn. for African Famine Relief, Seoul, Korea 1996–. *Address:* P.O. Box 86, Rumplii; P.O. Box 1902, Lilongwe, Malawi.

CHIHARA, Charles Seiyo, PH.D.; American professor of philosophy; b. 19 July 1932, Seattle, Wash.; s. of George Chihara and Mary Chihara; m. Carol Rosen 1964; one d.; ed. Seattle and Purdue Univs., Univ. of Washington, Oxford Univ.; Faculty mem. Univs. of Wash. 1961–62, Ill. 1962–63, Calif. at Berkeley 1963–, Prof. 1975–; Mellon Postdoctoral Fellowship 1964–65, Humanities Research Fellowship 1967–68, Nat. Endowment for the Humanities Fellowship 1985–86, 1994–95, Univ. of Calif. Pres.'s Research Fellowship in the Humanities 1996–97. *Publications:* Ontology and the Vicious-Circle Principle 1973, Constructibility and Mathematical Existence 1990, The Worlds of Possibility: Modal Realism and the Semantics of Modal Logic 1998. *Address:* 567 Cragmont Avenue, Berkeley, CA 94708, U.S.A. *Telephone:* (510) 525-4023. *Fax:* (510) 642-4164.

CHIK, Dato' Sabbaruddin, B.A., M.P.A.; Malaysian politician; b. 11 Dec. 1941, Temerloh, Penang; ed. Abu Bakar Secondary School, Temerloh, Malay Coll., Kuala Kangser, Perak, Univ. of Malaya and Inst. of Social Studies, The Hague; Asst. State Sec. Negeri Sembilan, Prin. Asst. Sec. JPM, Dir. Planning, GPU/SERU, Dir. Int. Trade, Ministry of Trade and Industry, Deputy State Sec. Salangor 1966–81; Gen. Man. Pernes Trading Sdn. Bhd. 1981–82; mem. Parl. for Temerloh 1982–; Deputy Minister of Finance 1982; Minister of Culture, Arts and Tourism 1987–; mem. UMNO Supreme Council 1984–. *Address:* Ministry of Culture, Arts and Tourism, 34th–36th Floor, POB 5-7, Menaro Dato' Onn, Putra World Trade Centre, 50694 Kuala Lumpur, Malaysia. *Telephone:* (03) 2937111 (Office). *Fax:* (03) 2910951.

CHIKANE, Rev. Frank, M.A.; South African ecclesiastic; b. 3 Jan. 1951, Soweto; s. of James Mashi and Erenia Chikane; m. Kagiso Oglobry; three s.; ed. Turfloop Univ. and Univs. of S. Africa, Durban and Pietermaritzburg; worked with Christ for All Nations 1975–76; ordained Minister 1980; part-time research officer, Inst. of Contextual Theology 1981, Gen. Sec. 1983; Gen. Sec. S. African Council of Churches 1987–94; Sr. Research Fellow Univ. of Cape Town 1995–; Hon. D.Theol. (Groningen Univ.); Diakonia Peace Prize 1986; Star Crystal Award 1987, Third World Prize 1989. *Publications include:* Doing Theology in a Situation of Conflict 1983, The Incarnation in the Life of People in South Africa 1985, Children in Turmoil: Effect of the Unrest on Township Children 1986, Kairos Document—A Challenge to Churches, No Life of my Own (autobiog.). *Leisure interests:* reading, keeping fit (mentally, spiritually, physically). *Address:* University of Cape Town, Private Bag, Rondebosch 7700; P.O. Box 4291, Johannesburg 2000; 310 Zone 7, Pimville 1808, Soweto, South Africa (Home).

CHIKAOKA, Riichiro; Japanese politician; mem. House Reps.; fmr. Parl. Vice-Minister of Health and Welfare; Dir. Gen. Science and Tech. Agency 1996. *Address:* c/o Science and Technology Agency, 2-2-1, Kasumigaseki, Chiyoda-ku, Tokyo 100, Japan (Office). *Telephone:* 3-3581-5271 (Office).

CHIKH, Slimane; Algerian politician; b. 13 July 1940, Beni Isguen; m.; four c.; ed. Coll. Sadiki de Kharznadar, Tunis and Univ. of Algiers; Dir. Inst., des Sciences politiques et de l'information, Univ. of Algiers 1975–78; Assoc. Prof., Univ. d'Aix-Marseille 1979–81; Rector Univ. of Algiers 1982–84; Prof. Univ. of Algiers 1984–88; Minister of Educ. and Training 1988–89; Assoc. Prof. Univ. Laval 1989, Institut d'Etudes Politiques, Paris 1990–91; Conseiller Présidence de la République 1992–94; Minister of Culture 1994–96, of Educ. 1996. *Address:* 8 ave de Pékin, El-Mouradia, Algiers, Algeria. *Telephone:* (2) 60-54-41.

CHIKIN, Valentin Vasilevich; Russian journalist; b. 25 Jan. 1932; ed. Moscow Univ.; literary corresp. for Moscow Komsomol newspaper 1951–58; mem. CPSU 1956–91, CP of Russian Fed. 1992–; literary corresp., Deputy Ed., Ed. of Komsomolskaya Pravda 1958–71; Deputy, First Deputy Ed.-in-Chief of Sovietskaya Rossiya 1971–84; First Deputy Pres. of State Cttee. on Publishing, Printing and the Book Trade 1984–86; Ed.-in-Chief of Sovietskaya Rossiya 1986–; Sec. of U.S.S.R. Union of Journalists 1986–90; cand. mem. of CPSU Cen. Cttee. 1986–91; mem. State Duma 1993–. *Address:* Sovietskaya Rossiya, ul. Pravdy 24, Moscow, Russia. *Telephone:* 257-27-72.

CHIKVAIDZE, Alexander Davidovich; Georgian diplomatist; b. 19 Jan. 1932, Tbilisi; m.; two s.; ed. Moscow State Univ., Acad. of Political Sciences, Diplomatic Acad.; taught int. law, Moscow State Univ., headed youth orgs. in Georgian Repub., then Head Tbilisi Region Cttee. of CPSU; Chair. Rep. Cttee. for Publishing and Book Trade 1976–79; fmr. Vice-Consul (Cultural Affairs), Bombay, First Sec. (Cultural Dept.), Embassy of U.S.S.R. in London; Consul-Gen., San Francisco 1979–83; Amb. to Kenya, and to UNEP and Habitat 1983–85; Head of Sector, CPSU Cen. Cttee. 1985–88; U.S.S.R. Amb. to Netherlands 1988–91, Russian Amb. to the Netherlands 1991–92; Minister of Foreign Affairs of Georgia 1992–95; Amb. to Greece; fmr. Chair. U.S.S.R. Chess Fed.; Lenin Centenary Medal. *Publication:* Western Countries' Foreign Policy on the Eve of the Second World War 1976. *Address:* c/o Ministry of Foreign Affairs, Chitadze str. 4, 380110 Tbilisi, Georgia. *Telephone:* (8832) 989377. *Fax:* (8832) 997249.

CHILADZE, Otar; Georgian writer; b. 20 March 1933, Signakhi, Georgia; s. of Ivane Chiladze and Tamar Chiladze; m. Nana Chiladze 1956 (died 1990); one s. one d.; ed. Tbilisi State Univ.; professional writer since 1950s; Sh. Rustaveli Prize 1983, State Prize of Georgia for play Labyrinth 1993. *Publications include:* The Trains and Passengers (collection of verses) 1959, Iron Bed, The Other Side, Remember about Life; A Man was Going by the Road (novel) 1973, Each Who Meets Me (novel) 1976, Iron Theatre (novel) 1983, March Cock (novel) 1987, Avelum 1996. *Address:* Av. of David Agmashenebeli 181, Apt. 6, 380012 Tbilisi, Georgia. *Telephone:* 34 51 84 (Home).

CHILADZE, Tamaz; Georgian writer; b. 5 March 1931, Signakhi; s. of Ivane and Tamar Chiladze; ed. Univ. of Tbilisi; first published works in 1951; mem. CPSU 1967–89; Chief Ed. Sabchota Khelovneba 1973–89; Shota Rustaveli Prize 1992, State Prize of Georgia 1997. *Publications include:* Sun Dial (poems) 1961, A Network of Stars 1961, Pony-trek 1963, The First Day 1965, Who Lives on the Stars 1970, White Smoke 1973, Memory (poems) 1978, Martyrdom of St. Shushanik (essay) 1978, Herald of Spring (essay) 1985, The Ray of the Setting Sun (novel) 1993, The Cactus Garden (novel) 1993; plays: Shelter on the Ninth Floor, Murder, Role for a Beginner Actress, Bird Fair, The Day of Appointment. *Address:* 22 Simon Chickovani Street, Flat 7, Tbilisi 380071, Georgia. *Telephone:* 33-49-87.

CHILINGAROV, Artur Nikolayevich; CAND. GEO. SC.; Russian polar explorer, traveller and politician; b. 25 Sept. 1939, Leningrad; m.; one s. one d.; ed. Adm. Makarov Higher Marine School of Eng.; worked as metalworker Baltic vessel repair plant; First Sec. Regional Comsomol Cttee. in Yakutya; headed drifting station N. Pole 19, organized station N. Pole 22, head Bellingshausen station in Antarctica, head expedition to free scientific vessel Mikhail Somol in Antarctic, expedition on bd. atomic ice-breaker Sibir; Deputy Chair. U.S.S.R. State Cttee. on Meteorology 1986–92; counsellor, Chair. Russian Supreme Soviet on problems of Arctic and Antarctic 1991–93, Asscn. of Russian Polar Researchers 1991–; mem. State Duma (Parl.) 1993–, Deputy Chair. 1994–; mem. Russian Acad. of Natural Sciences; Co-Chair. Russian Foundation of int. humanitarian aid and co-operation; Hero of the Soviet Union, U.S.S.R. State Prizes. *Leisure interest:* football. *Address:* State Duma, Okhotny ryad 1, 103009 Moscow, Russia. *Telephone:* 292-80-44.

CHILINGIRIAN, Levon, F.R.C.M.; British violinist; b. 28 May 1948, Nicosia, Cyprus; m. Susan Paul Pattie 1983; one s.; ed. R.C.M., London; f. Chilingirian string quartet 1971; has performed in N. and S. America, Africa, Australasia, Europe; Prof. R.C.M. 1985; BBC Beethoven Competition 1969, Munich Duo Competition (with Clifford Benson) 1971, Cobbett Medal 1995, Royal Philharmonic Soc. Chamber Music Award 1995. *Recordings include:* ten Mozart quartets, last three Schubert quartets, Debussy and Ravel quartets, Schubert octet and quintet, six Bartok quartets and piano quintet, late and middle Dvořák quartets, Tippett Triple Concerto; music by Panufnik, Tavener and Pärt (with Chilingirian Quartet). *Leisure interests:* reading, relaxing in warm climes, backgammon. *Address:* 7 Hollingbourne Road, London, SE24 9NB, England. *Telephone:* 0171-978 9104. *Fax:* 0171-274 5764.

CHILLIDA JUANTEGUI, Eduardo; Spanish sculptor; b. 10 Jan. 1924, San Sebastián; ed. Colegio Marianistas, San Sebastián, and Univ. de Madrid; started sculpting 1947; first one-man exhbn., Madrid 1954; numerous one-man and group exhbns. in Europe, Japan and U.S.A.; exhbn. Hayward Gallery, London 1990; has illustrated several books; Visiting Prof. Carpenter Centre, Harvard Univ. 1971; Hon. mem. Hispanic Soc. of America, New York; Corresp. mem. Bayerische Akademie der Schönen Kunste, Munich; Gran Premio Int. di Scultura, Venice Biennale 1958, Prix Kandinsky 1960, Carnegie Prize, Pittsburgh Int. 1964, 1979, North Rhine Westphalian Prize for Sculpture 1966, Wilhelm Lehmbruck Prize, Duisburg 1966, Rembrandt Prize, Basel 1975, Kaiserring Prize, City of Goslar 1985, Príncipe de Asturias de las Artes Prize, Madrid 1987, Praemium Imperiale Prize, Japan Art Asscn. 1991, and numerous other prizes; Order of Science and Art, Germany 1987. *Address:* Av. Alcade José Elósegui, 211, Villa Betania, 20015 San Sebastián, Spain. *Telephone:* (943) 271279. *Fax:* (943) 277026.

CHILUBA, Frederick J.T., M.PHIL.; Zambian politician; b. Wusakile; m. Vera Chiluba; nine c.; shop steward 1967; fmr. Chair. Zambian Congress of Trades Unions; mem. Parl. for Nkana; President of Zambia Nov. 1991–; leader Movt. for Multiparty Democracy (MMD). *Address:* Office of the President, P.O. Box 30208, Lusaka, Zambia.

CHILVER, Baron (Life Peer) cr. 1987, of Cranfield in the County of Bedfordshire; **Henry Chilver,** M.A., D.SC., F.ENG., C.I.MGT., F.R.S.; British university administrator, teacher and business executive; b. 30 Oct. 1926, Barking, Essex; s. of A. H. Chilver; m. Claudia Grigson 1959; three s. two d.; ed. Southend High School and Univ. of Bristol; Structural Eng., British Railways 1947–48; lecturer, Univ. of Bristol 1952–54, Univ. of Cambridge 1956–61, Fellow, Corpus Christi Coll., Cambridge 1958–61; Prof. of Civil Eng., London Univ. 1961–69; Dir. Centre for Environmental Studies 1967–69; Vice-Chancellor, Cranfield Inst. of Tech. 1970–89; Dir. English China Clays 1973, Chair. 1989–95; Dir. ICI 1990–93, Zeneca 1993–95; Chair. RJB Mining 1993–97, Chiroscience Group PLC 1995–98, Univs. Computer Bd. 1975–78, The Post Office 1980–81, Advisory Council for Applied Research and Devt. 1982–85, Milton Keynes Devt. Corpn. 1983–92, Plymouth Devt. Corpn. 1996–98; Dir. Univs. Funding Council 1988–91; mem. or fmr. mem. various cttees. of inquiry, review bodies etc.; Pres. Inst. of Man. Services, of Materials Man. (fmrly. Materials Handling); Hon. Fellow, Corpus Christi Coll., Cambridge; hon. degrees (Leeds, Bristol, Salford, Strathclyde, Bath, Buckingham, Cranfield, Compiègne); Telford Gold Medal 1962 and Coopers Hill War Memorial Prize 1977, Inst. of Civil Engs. *Publications:* Problems in engineering structures (with R. J. Ashby) 1958, Strength of Materials and Structures (with J. Case) 1971; papers on structural eng. and stability. *Address:* Lanlawren House, Trenewen, Looe, Cornwall, PL13 2PZ, England.

CHIN A SEN, Hendrik Rudolf; Suriname politician and physician; b. 18 Jan. 1934, Albina, Marowijne Dist.; m. Shirley Ho A Fat; three s. one d.; ed. Medical School, Paramaribo, Univ. of Utrecht, Netherlands; mem. Nat. Republican Party; medical practice as specialist in internal diseases, Nieuw Nickerie Hosp. 1969–70, joined staff of St. Vincentius Hosp., Paramaribo 1970; continued medical studies at Nanjing Univ., China Aug.–Dec. 1979; Prime Minister of Suriname and Minister for Gen. and Foreign Affairs March–Nov. 1980; Pres. 1980–82; f. Movt. for the Liberation of Suriname; in exile in the Netherlands, returned 1987; fmr. Vice-Chair. Asscn. of Medical Doctors in Suriname; fmr. Chair. Robin Hood Football Club. *Leisure interests:* music, sport.

CHINCHIAN, Zaven Osep, B.A.; Egyptian ecclesiastic; b. 1929, Aleppo, Syria; s. of Osep and Lucy Chinchian; ed. Seminary of Armenian Patriarchate, Jerusalem; teacher, Secondary Dept., Nat. School, Jerusalem 1953–56, Seminary of Jerusalem 1952–56; Vicar-Gen. in Alexandria 1958–76, in New York, U.S.A. 1977–78; Primate of Diocese of the Armenian Orthodox Church in Egypt and N. Africa 1979–; St. George's Insignia from Russian Orthodox Church 1988. *Publications:* one literary work, a book of short stories 1959, and many articles in various magazines. *Leisure interests:* studying theology and the Writings of the Church Fathers. *Address:* 179 Rameses Avenue, P.O. Box 48, Faggala, Cairo, Egypt. *Telephone:* (2) 5901385. *Fax:* (2) 5906671.

CHIPMAN, John Miguel Warwick, M.A., D.PHIL.; British/Canadian administrator and academic; b. 10 Feb. 1957, Montreal; s. of Lawrence Carroll Chipman and Maria Isabel Prados; m. Lady Theresa Manners 1997; ed. Westmount High School, Montreal, El Estudio, Madrid, Harvard Univ., London School of Econs. and Balliol Coll. Oxford; Research Assoc. Int. Inst. for Strategic Studies (IISS), London 1983–84; Research Assoc. Atlantic Inst. for Int. Affairs, Paris 1985–87; Asst. Dir. for Regional Security, IISS 1987–91, Dir. of Studies 1991–93, Dir. IISS 1993–, Founder IISS publ. Strategic Comments; mem. Bd. Aspen Inst. Italia; regular broadcaster on int. affairs; NATO Fellowship 1983. *Publications:* Cinquième République et Défense de l'Afrique 1986, French Power in Africa 1989; ed. and prin. contrib. to NATO's Southern Allies: Internal and External Challenges 1988; articles in journals and book chapters. *Leisure interests:* tennis, skiing, scuba diving, collecting travel books, music. *Address:* International Institute for Strategic Studies, 23 Tavistock Street, London, WC2E 7NQ, England. *Telephone:* 0171-379 7676. *Fax:* 0171-836 3108.

CHIPP, David Allan, M.A.; British journalist; b. 6 June 1927, Kew, London; s. of Thomas Ford Chipp and Isabel Mary Ballinger; ed. Geelong Grammar School, Australia and King's Coll. Cambridge; sports reporter, Reuters 1950–52, Corresp. S.E. Asia 1952–55, first Western Resident Corresp. in Peking 1956–58, various managerial and editorial exec. positions in Asia, Africa and U.S.A. 1958–68, Ed. 1968–69; Ed.-in-Chief, Press Asscn. 1969–1986; Chair. News World 1994–96; Dir. The Observer 1985–93, TV-am News Co. 1986–92, Reuter Foundation 1986–90, Lloyds of London Press 1990–93, Teletext U.K. 1992–, Talk Radio U.K. 1994–95. *Leisure interests:* rowing (Steward of Henley Royal Regatta), theatre, reading, music. *Address:* 2 Wilton Court, 59/60 Eccleston Square, London, SW1V 1PH, England. *Telephone:* 0171-834 5579.

CHIPP, Hon. Donald Leslie, A.O., J.P., B.COM.; Australian politician; b. 21 Aug. 1925, Melbourne, Victoria; s. of L. T. and J. S. Chipp; m. 1st Monica Lalor (divorced 1979); two s. two d.; m. 2nd Idun G. Welz 1979; two d.; ed. Northcote High School, Univ. of Melbourne; served in R.A.A.F. 1943–45; Registrar, Commonwealth Inst. of Accountants and Australian Soc. of Accountants 1950–55; Chief Exec. Officer Olympic Civic Cttee. 1955–56; Councillor, City of Kew 1955–61; mem. House of Reps. 1960–77; Senator 1977–86; Minister for Navy and Minister in charge of Tourist Activities 1966–68, Minister for Customs and Excise 1969–72; Minister assisting Minister for Nat. Devt. 1971–72; Minister for Social Security, Health, Repatriation and Compensation Nov.-Dec. 1975; Liberal to March 1977, Leader Australian Democrats Party 1977–87. *Publications:* Don Chipp—The Third Man 1978 (with J. Larkin), "Chipp" 1987 and numerous articles. *Leisure interests:* cricket, football, tennis, rafting. *Address:* 8 Patrick Court, Wheelers Hill, Vic. 3150, Australia (Home). *Telephone:* 03-9561 7574 (Home).

CHIPPERFIELD, David; British architect; b. 18 Dec. 1953; s. of Alan John Chipperfield and Peggy (née Singleton) Chipperfield; three s. one d.; ed. Architectural Asscn.; Prin. David Chipperfield Architects 1984–; Visiting Lecturer Harvard Univ. 1986–87; Visiting Prof. Univ. of Naples 1991, Univ. of Graz 1992, Ecole Polytechnique Fedérale de Lausanne 1993; Prof. Staatliche Akademie der Bildenden Künste, Stuttgart 1995–; commissions include: shops for Issey Miyake (q.v.), London and Japan 1986–87, Arnolfini Gallery, Bristol 1987, pvt. museum, Tokyo 1989, River and Rowing Museum, Henley-on-Thames 1994, Neues Museum, Berlin 1997; founder, dir. 9H Gallery, London; mem. R.I.B.A.; trustee Architectural Foundation, London; winner Premio Palladio 1993. *Publication:* Theoretical Practice 1994. *Address:* David Chipperfield Architects, 1A Cobham Mews, Agar Grove, London, NW1 9SB; 28 Cleveland Square, London, W2 6DD, England. *Telephone:* 0171-267 9422; 0171-262 3422. *Fax:* 0171-267 9347.

CHIRAC, Jacques René; French politician; b. 29 Nov. 1932, Paris; s. of François Chirac and Marie-Louise Valette; m. Bernadette Chodron de Courcel 1956; two d.; ed. Lycée Carnot, Lycée Louis-le-Grand and Ecole Nationale d'Administration; Military Service in Algeria; Auditor, Cour des Comptes 1959–62; Head of Dept., Sec.-Gen. of Govt. 1962; Head of Dept., Private Office of M. Pompidou 1962–65; Counsellor, Cour des Comptes 1965–94; Sec. of State for Employment Problems 1967–68; Sec. of State for Economy and Finance 1968–71; Minister for Parl. Relations 1971–72, for Agriculture and Rural Devt. 1972–74, of the Interior March-May 1974; Prime Minister of France 1974–1976, 1986–88; Sec.-Gen. Union des Démocrates pour la République (UDR) Jan.-June 1975, Hon. Sec.-Gen. 1975–76; Pres. Rassemblement pour la République (fmrly. UDR) 1976–94, Hon. Sec.-Gen. 1977–80; elected to Nat. Assembly 1967, 1968, 1973, 1976, 1978, 1981, 1986, 1988; mem. European Parl. 1979; Counsellor-Gen., Meymac 1968, 1970; Pres. Gen. Council, La Corrèze 1970–79; Municipal Counsellor, Sainte-Féréole 1965–77; Mayor of Paris 1977–95; Pres. of France May 1995–; Deputy for Corrèze 1981–86, 1986–88, 1993–95, mem. Comm. on Nat. Defence 1980–86; Prix Louise Michel 1986; Grand Croix, Ordre nat. du Mérite, Chevalier du Mérite agricole, des Arts et des Lettres, etc. *Publications:* Discours pour la France à l'heure du choix, La lueur de l'espérance: réflexion du soir pour le matin 1978, Une Nouvelle France, reflexion 1 1994, La France pour Tous 1995. *Address:* Palais de l'Elysée, 55–57 rue du Faubourg Saint-Honoré, 75008 Paris, France.

CHIRICĂ, Andrei; Romanian politician; b. 14 June 1939, Ploieşti; ed. Electronics and Telecommunications Coll. of Bucharest; engineer in the Radio and TV Dept. 1961–69; chief engineer with the Gen. Direction of Post and Telecommunications 1969–84, then asst. gen. dir. for matters of research and information in telecommunications, Minister of Communications 1990–94; Pres. Mobil Rom. *Publications:* specialized works. *Address:* Mobil Rom, Bucharest, Romania. *Telephone:* 2033000. *Fax:* 2033512.

CHISHOLM, Sam; New Zealand satellite television executive; b. 8 Oct. 1939; m. Ronda Chisholm 1967; one d.; ed. King's Coll. S. Auckland; fmr. salesman for Johnson's floor wax; joined Kerry Packer's (sold to Alan Bond 1987) Nine Network, Melbourne 1963, Man. Dir. 1976–90; Chief Exec. Sky Television, U.K. 1990, BSkyB 1990–97, Dir. 1997–; Deputy Chair. New Millennium Experience Co. 1997–. *Address:* Bundarbo Station, Bundarbo, N.S.W. 2726, Australia.

CHISSANO, Joaquim Alberto; Mozambican politician; b. 2 Oct. 1939, Chibuto; m. Marcelina Rafael Chissano; four c.; Asst. Sec. to Pres., Frente de Libertação de Moçambique (FRELIMO) in charge of Educ. 1963–66, Sec. to Pres., FRELIMO 1966–69; Chief Rep. FRELIMO in Dar es Salaam 1969–74; Prime Minister, Transitional Govt. of Mozambique 1974–75, Minister of Foreign Affairs 1975–86, Pres. of Mozambique and Commdr.-in-Chief of Armed Forces Nov. 1986–; Order, Augusto César Sandino (Nicaragua) 1988. *Address:* Office of the President, Avda Julius Nyerere, Maputo, Mozambique. *Telephone:* (1) 491121.

CHITANAVA, Nodari Amrosievich; Georgian politician and agricultural specialist; b. 10 March 1936, Zugdidi Region, Georgia; s. of Ambrose Chitanava and Tina Chitanava; m. Keto Dimitrovna 1964; two d.; mem. CPSU 1958–91; komsomol and party work 1959–; second sec. Adzhar obkom 1973–74; Minister of Agric. for Georgian S.S.R. 1974–79; First Deputy Chair., Georgian Council of Ministers 1979–85; Party Sec. for Agric. 1985–89; Chair. Council of Ministers, Georgian S.S.R. 1989–90; Minister of Agric. 1991–93; Dir. Econ. and Social Problems Research Inst. 1993–; Chair. Georgian Economists' Soc. *Leisure interest:* spending time in the country. *Address:* Institute for Macroeconomics, 16 Zandukeli Str., 380008 Tibilisi; Atheni str. 16, Tbilisi, Georgia (Home). *Telephone:* 93-12-55; 99-75-15 (Office); 23-37-53 (Home).

CHITTISTER, Joan D., M.A., PH.D.; American social psychologist, author and lecturer; b. 26 April 1936, Dubois, Pa.; d. of Harold C. Chittister and Loretta Cuneo Chittister; ed. St. Benedict Acad. Erie, Mercyhurst Coll. Erie, Univ. of Notre Dame and Pennsylvania State Univ.; elementary teacher, 1955–59, secondary teacher 1959–74; taught Pa. State Univ. 1969–71; Pres. Fed. of St. Scholastica 1971–78; Prioress, Benedictine Sisters of Erie 1978–90; Pres. Conf. of American Benedictine Prioresses 1974–90; Invited Visiting Fellow, St. Edmund's Coll. Cambridge, U.K. 1995–96; mem. Exec. Bd. Ecumenical and Cultural Inst. St. John's Univ. Collegeville 1976–; Exec. Dir. Benetvision; mem. Bd. of Dirs. Nat. Catholic Reporter; several awards and 7 hon degrees. *Publications include:* Climb Along the Cutting Edge: An Analysis of Change in Religious Life 1977, Women, Church and Ministry 1983, Winds of Change: Women Challenge the Church 1986, Wisdom Distilled from the Daily 1990, The Rule of Benedict: Insights for the Ages 1992, There is a Season 1995, The Fire in these Ashes: A Spirituality of Contemporary Religious Life 1995, The Psalms: Meditations for Every Day of the Year 1996, Beyond Beijing: The Next Step for Women 1996, Passion for Life: Fragments of the Face of God 1996, Songs of Joy: New Meditations on the Psalms 1997, Light in the Darkness: New Reflections on the Psalms 1998, Heart of Flesh: A Feminist Spirituality for Women and Men 1998, In Search of Belief 1999; numerous articles and lectures on religious life, peace and justice issues and women in church and society. *Leisure interests:* computers, music, reading. *Address:* St. Scholastica Priory, 355 East 9th Street, Erie, PA 16503, U.S.A. *Telephone:* (814) 454-4052. *Fax:* (814) 459-8066.

CHITTOLINI, Giorgio; Italian professor of medieval history; b. 9 Dec. 1940, Parma; s. of Gino Chittolini and Diva Scotti; m. Franca Leverotti 1977; one d.; Assoc. Prof. of History, Univ. of Pisa 1974–76, Univ. of Pavia 1976–79; Fellow at Villa I Tatti, Florence 1980; Prof. of Medieval History, Univ. of Parma 1981–84, of Medieval Insts., Univ. of Milan 1985–; mem. Bd. of Eds., Società e Storia 1979–; mem. Scientific Cttee., Istituto Storico Italo-Germanico, Trento 1989–; Pres. Centro Studi Civiltà del tardo Medioevo 1990–. *Publications:* La formazione dello stato regionale e le istituzioni del contado 1979, Gli Sforza, la chiesa lombarda e la corte di Roma (1450–1535) 1990, Comunità, Governi e Feudi nell'Italia Centrosettentrionale 1995. *Address:* Department of History, Università Degli Studi di Milano, Via Festa del Perdono 7, 20122 Milan; Via Madre Cabrini 7, 20122 Milan, Italy. *Telephone:* (02) 58.30.46.52.

CHITTY, Sir Thomas Willes, Bt., F.R.S.L. (pen name **Thomas Hinde**); British author; b. 2 March 1926, Felixstowe; s. of Sir Thomas Henry Willes Chitty; m. Susan Elspeth Hopkinson 1951; one s. three d.; ed. Winchester Coll. and Univ. Coll., Oxford; served in Royal Navy 1944–47; with Shell group 1953–60; Granada Arts Fellow, Univ. of York 1964–65; Visiting lecturer, Univ. of Illinois 1965–67; Visiting Prof. Boston Univ. 1969–70; now freelance writer. *Publications include:* Mr. Nicholas 1952, For the Good of the Company 1961, The Day the Call Came 1964, High 1968, Our Father 1975, Daymare 1980; travel: The Great Donkey Walk 1977, The Cottage Book 1979, Stately Gardens of Britain 1983, A Field Guide to the English Country Parson 1983, Forests of Britain 1984, The Domesday Book: England's Heritage, then and now 1986, Courtiers: 900 years of Court Life 1986, Tales from the Pump Room: An Informal History of Bath 1988; Sir Henry and Sons (autobiog.) 1980, Capability Brown 1986, Imps of Promise: A History of the King's School Canterbury 1990, Looking-Glass Letters (ed.) (letters of Lewis Carroll) 1991, Paths of Progress, A History of Marlborough College 1992, A History of Highgate School 1993, A History of King's College School 1994, Carpenter's Children, A History of the City of London School 1995, An Illustrated History of the University of Greenwich 1996, A History of Abingdon School 1997. *Leisure interests:* eating, drinking, talking, listening, gardening, reading, travelling. *Address:* Bow Cottage, West Hoathly, Sussex, RH19 4QF, England. *Telephone:* (01342) 810 269.

CHITVIRA, Thongyod; Thai politician; b. Suphanburi; mem. municipality Suphanburi 1949, then mayor; mem. provincial council; mem. Nat. Ass., Commerce Minister 1975; Public Health Minister 1980; Deputy Prime Minister 1981–82, Sept.–Dec. 1990; mem. Social Action Party. *Address:* c/o Social Action Party, House of Representatives, Bangkok 10300, Thailand.

CHIU CHUANG-HUAN; Taiwanese politician; b. 25 July 1925, Changhua County; ed. School of Political Science, Nat. Chengchi Univ.; Dir. 3rd Dept., Ministry of Personnel, Taiwan 1965–67; Dept. Dir. 5th Section, Cen. Cttee., Kuomintang 1967–68; Commr. Dept. of Social Affairs, Taiwan Prov. Govt. 1969–72; Dir. Dept. of Social Affairs, Cen. Cttee., Kuomintang 1972–78; Minister without Portfolio 1976–78; Deputy Sec.-Gen., Cen. Cttee., Kuomintang 1978; Minister of the Interior 1978–81; Vice-Premier Exec. Yuan, Repub. of China (Taiwan) 1981–84; Hon. Ph.D. (Youngnam Univ., Repub. of Korea). *Publications:* Thought Regarding Social Welfare in the Three Principles of the People, A Summary of the Chinese Social Welfare System.

CHIZHOV, Ludvig Aleksandrovich; Russian diplomatist; b. 25 April 1936, Radornishl, Zhitomir Region; m.; one s. one d.; ed. Moscow Inst. of Int. Relations; fmr. mem. CPSU; attaché, Embassy, Japan 1960–65, First Sec., Counsellor, 1971–77; Third Sec., Second Sec., Second Far Eastern Dept., Ministry of Foreign Affairs 1966–70; counsellor, second Far Eastern Dept. 1978–80; ministry counsellor, Embassy, Japan 1980–86; head of Pacific Ocean Countries Dept., Ministry of Foreign Affairs 1986–89; Russian Amb. to Japan 1990–96; Amb.-at-large 1996–98; Dir. 3rd European Dept., Ministry of Foreign Affairs 1998–. *Leisure interests:* fishing, reading. *Address:* Ministry of Foreign Affairs, Smolenskaya-Sennaya 32/34, Moscow, Russia.

CHKHEIDZE, Peter, PH.D.; Georgian diplomatist; b. 22 Oct. 1941, Tbilisi; s. of late Peter Chkheidze and Julia Chkheidze; m. Manana Chkheidze 1963; two s.; ed. Tbilisi Nat. Univ., Diplomatic Acad. of U.S.S.R. Ministry of Foreign Affairs and Inst. of State and Law, U.S.S.R. Acad. of Sciences; various positions, Attorney Service of Repub. of Georgia 1963–75; First Sec., Dept. of Int. Orgs., Ministry of Foreign Affairs of U.S.S.R. 1978; First Sec., Counsellor, then Chief of Dept. Perm. Mission of U.S.S.R. to UN 1978–84; leading posts in nat. state and public insts. 1984–89; Chair. Ind. Trade Unions Confed. of Repub. of Georgia 1989–91; Deputy Prime Minister of Repub. of Georgia and Perm. Rep. of Govt. of Georgia to U.S.S.R., later Russian Fed. 1991–92; Chargé d'Affaires of Repub. of Georgia in Russian Fed. 1992–93; Amb. Extraordinary and Plenipotentiary of Georgia to U.S.A., also Perm. Rep. of Georgia to UN 1993–94; Perm. Rep. of Georgia to UN 1993–; corresp. mem. Int. Informatization Acad. 1994–. *Publications:* various publs. in fields of law and int. relations 1975–95. *Leisure interests:* literature, art, horse-riding. *Address:* P.O. Box 1216, Closter Dock Road, Alpine, NJ 07620, U.S.A.; Inguri St. 3, Apt. 52, Tbilisi 380071, Georgia. *Telephone:* (212) 717-1949 (Office, U.S.A.); (201) 784-1482 (Home, U.S.A.); 33-7056 (Tbilisi). *Fax:* (212) 759-1832 (U.S.A.).

CHKHEIDZE, Revaz (Rezo) Davidovich; Georgian film director; b. 8 Dec. 1926, Kutaisi; m. Tinatin Gambashidze 1950; one s. two d.; studied acting at Tbilisi State Theatrical Inst. 1943–46; studied under Sergei Yutkevich and Mikhail Romm at VGIK (Film School) 1949–53; Dir. Georgia film studios 1972–; Deputy U.S.S.R. Supreme Soviet 1974–84; U.S.S.R. People's Artist 1980; All-Union Festival Prize 1973, 1981; Lenin Prize 1986. *Films include:* Magdana's Donkey 1956 (with T. Abuladze), Our Yard 1957, A Soldier's Father 1965, Our Youth 1970, The Seedlings 1973, Your Sun, Earth 1981, Life of Don Quixote and Sancho 1989. *Address:* Larsskaya Street 5, Apt 3, 380009 Tbilisi, Georgia. *Telephone:* (8832) 23-38-84.

CHKHEIDZE, Temur Georgyevich; Georgian theatre director; b. Nov. 1942, Tbilisi; ed. Georgian Inst. of Theatre; debut as dir. 1967; with Shota Rustaveli Drama Theatre 1969–80; Artistic Dir. Kote Mardzhanishvili Drama Theatre 1980–88; freelance 1988–; worked in Moscow Gorky Art Theatre 1983, St. Petersburg 1991; over 40 stage productions; Lenin's Prize. *Address:* Mardzhanishvili Drama Theatre, Tbilisi, Georgia (Office).

CHKHIKVADZE, Ramaz Grigorievich; Georgian actor; b. 28 Feb. 1928, Georgia; grad. Rustaveli Georgian State Drama Inst. 1951; since then with the Rustaveli Theatre, Georgia, for which he has played over 50 parts; *roles include:* Louis XIV (Bulgakov's Molière), Macheath (Brecht's Threepenny Opera), Adzhak (Caucasian Chalk Circle), Edward (King Lear), Richard (Richard III), has also acted in several films (including role of Stalin in Victory 1985); awards include Best Leading Man at VIIIth Moscow Film Festival for film Saplings, Mardzhanishvili Prize for performance of title role in Kvarkvare, 1975; Georgian State Prize 1974, 1981; U.S.S.R. State Prize 1979; U.S.S.R. People's Artist 1981, Hero of Socialist Labour 1988. *Address:* S. Chikovani Street 20, Apartment 5H, 380015 Tbilisi, Georgia. *Telephone:* (8832) 36-45-25.

CHO, Ramaswamy, B.SC., B.L.; Indian journalist, playwright, actor, lawyer; b. 5 Oct. 1934, Madras; s. of R. Srinivasan and Rajammal Srinivasan; m. 1966; one s. one d.; ed. P.S. High School, Loyola Coll., Vivekananda Coll., Madras and Madras Law Coll., Madras Univ.; started practice as lawyer, Madras High Court 1957; Legal Adviser to T.T.K. Group of Cos. 1961–; film scriptwriter and actor 1966–; theatre dir., actor and playwright 1958–; Ed. Tamil political fortnightly Thuglak 1970–; Pres. People's Union of Civil Liberties, Tamilnadu 1980–82; has acted in 180 films, written 14 film scripts, directed 4 films; written, directed and acted in 4 TV series in Tamil; Haldi Gati Award, Maharana of Mewar, for nat. service through journalism 1985, Veerakesari Award for investigative journalism 1986, B. D. Goenka Award for Excellence in Journalism, Panchajanya Award for promotion of nationalism 1998. *Publications:* 23 plays and 10 novels in Tamil; numerous articles on politics, in English and Tamil. *Leisure interest:* photography. *Address:* 46 Greenways Road, Madras, 600028, India. *Telephone:* 4936913, 4936914, 4936915, 4321313.

CHOI, Man-Duen, PH.D., F.R.S.C.; Canadian professor of mathematics; b. 13 June 1945, Nanking, China; m. Pui-Wah Ip 1972; two s. one d.; ed. Chinese Univ. of Hong Kong and Univ. of Toronto; lecturer, Dept. of Math., Univ. of Calif. Berkeley 1973–76; Asst. Prof. Dept. of Math., Univ. of Toronto 1976–79, Assoc. Prof. 1979–82, Prof. of Math. 1982–; mem. American Math.

Soc., Canadian Math Soc., Math. Asscn. of America; Israel Halperin Prize 1980. *Publications:* numerous articles in mathematical journals. *Leisure interests:* yoga, stamps. *Address:* Department of Mathematics, University of Toronto, Toronto, Ont., M5S 1A1, Canada. *Telephone:* (416) 978-3415. *Fax:* (416) 978-4107.

CHOI KYU-HAH; Korean politician; b. 16 July 1919, Wonju City, Kangwon-do; m. Kee Hong 1936; two s. one d.; ed. Kyung Gi High School, Seoul, Tokyo Coll. of Educ., Japan and Nat. Daedong Inst., Manchuria; Prof., Coll. of Educ., Seoul Nat. Univ. 1945–46; Dir. Econ. Affairs Bureau, Ministry of Foreign Affairs 1951–52; Consul-Gen. Korean Mission, Japan 1952–57, Minister 1959; Vice-Minister of Foreign Affairs 1959–60; Amb. to Malaysia 1964–67; Minister of Foreign Affairs 1967–71; Special Pres. Asst. for Foreign Affairs 1971–75; Acting Prime Minister 1975–76; Prime Minister 1976–79; Acting Pres. Oct.-Dec. 1979, Pres. 1979–80; Chief Korean del. to UN Gen. Assembly, 1967, 1968, 1969; del. to numerous int. confs. 1955–; Hon. Litt.D. (Hankook Univ. of Foreign Studies, Seoul); decorations from Ethiopia, Panama, El Salvador, Malaysia, Saudi Arabia, Tunisia and Belgium; Order of Diplomatic Service Merit. *Leisure interest:* angling.

CHOJNACKA, Elisabeth, M.A.; French harpsichordist; b. 10 Sept. 1939, Warsaw, Poland; d. of Tadeusz Chojnacki and Edwarda Chojnacka; m. Georges Lesèvre 1966; ed. Warsaw Acad. of Music, Ecole Supérieure de Musique and with Aimée van de Wiele, Paris; first recital of contemporary harpsichord, L'Arc, Paris 1971; interpreter of harpsichord works by many contemporary composers including Xenakis, Ligeti, Halffter, Donatoni, Ferrari, Busotti, Górecki, Takemitsu etc.; many works for modern harpsichord written for her and dedicated to her; soloist with Orchestre de Paris, Cleveland and Minneapolis Orchestras 1974, Suisse Romande Orchestra 1979, Orchestre National de France 1981; Prof. of Contemporary Harpsichord, Mozarteum Acad. of Music, Salzburg 1995–; numerous tours in Europe, U.S.A., Japan, and Mexico; appearances at prin. festivals of contemporary music; master classes; collaborates with choreographer Lucinda Childs 1991–; numerous recordings of classical and contemporary music; First Prize, Int. Harpsichord Competition, Vercelli, Italy 1968; Grand Prix de la SACEM 1983; Officier des Arts et des Lettres. *Publications:* articles in La Revue Musicale. *Leisure interests:* cinema, literature, dancing, genetics, astrophysics. *Address:* 17 rue Emile Dubois, 75014 Paris, France. *Telephone:* 45.65.17.20.

CHOJNOWSKA-LISKIEWICZ, Krystyna; Polish yachtswoman; b. 15 July 1936, Warsaw; d. of Juliusz and Kazimiera Chojnowski; m. Wacław Liskiewicz 1960; ed. Polytechnical Univ., Gdańsk; Shipbuilding engineer, Gdańsk 1960–; first woman to circumnavigate the world solo 28 March 1976–20 March 1978, in Yacht 'Mazurek'; Commdr. Cross of Order Polonia Restituta 1978; Hon. Medal Czechoslovakian Women's Union 1978; Prize of Minister of Foreign Affairs 1978, Slocum Award 1978, Médaille d'Argent de la Jeunesse et des Sports, France 1979, and other decorations. *Publication:* Pierwsza dookoła Świata (The First Woman Round the World) 1979. *Leisure interests:* sailing, skiing, swimming, science-fiction, music, books. *Address:* ul. Norblina 29 m. 50, 80-304 Gdańsk-Oliwa, Poland. *Telephone:* (58) 556-03-71. *Fax:* (58) 556-03-71.

CHOMSKY, (Avram) Noam, M.A., PH.D.; American theoretical linguist; b. 7 Dec. 1928, Pennsylvania; s. of William Chomsky and Elsie Simonofsky; m. Carol Schatz 1949; one s. two d.; ed. Univ. of Pennsylvania; at M.I.T. 1955–, Prof. of Modern Languages 1961–66, Ferrari Ward Prof. of Modern Languages and Linguistics 1966–, Inst. Prof. 1976–; Nat. Science Foundation Fellow, Princeton Inst. for Advanced Study 1958–59; American Council of Learned Socs. Fellow, Center for Cognitive Studies, Harvard Univ. 1964–65; mem. American Acad. of Arts and Sciences, Linguistic Soc. of America, American Philosophical Asscn., American Acad. of Political and Social Science, N.A.S., etc.; Corresp. Fellow, British Acad.; Hon. Fellow, British Psychological Soc. 1985, Royal Anthropological Inst.; Hon. D.H.L. (Chicago) 1967, (Loyola Univ., Swarthmore Coll.) 1970, (Bard Coll.) 1971, (Mass.) 1973, (Maine, Gettysburg Coll.) 1992, (Amherst Coll.) 1995, (Buenos Aires) 1996; Hon. D.Lit. (London) 1967, (Delhi) 1972, Visva-Bharati (West Bengal) 1980, (Pa.) 1984, (Cambridge) 1995; George Orwell Award, Nat. Council of Teachers of English 1987, Kyoto Prize in Basic Sciences 1988, Royal Anthropological Inst. of Great Britain Award 1989, James Killian Award (M.I.T.) 1992. *Publications include:* Syntactic Structures 1957, Current Issues in Linguistic Theory 1964, Aspects of the Theory of Syntax 1965, Cartesian Linguistics 1966, Language and Mind 1968, The Sound Pattern of English (with Morris Halle) 1968, American Power and the New Mandarins 1969, At War with Asia 1970, Problems of Knowledge and Freedom 1971, Studies on Semantics in Generative Grammar 1972, For Reasons of State 1973, The Backroom Boys 1973, Bains de Sang (trans. of Counter-revolutionary Violence) (with Edward Herman) 1974, Peace in the Middle East? 1974, Reflections on Language 1975, The Logical Structure of Linguistic Theory 1975, Essays on Form and Interpretation 1977, Human Rights and American Foreign Policy 1978, The Political Economy of Human Rights (2 Vols., with Edward Herman) 1979, Rules and Representations 1980, Lectures on Government and Binding 1981, Radical Priorities 1981, Towards a New Cold War 1982, Concepts and Consequences of the Theory of Government and Binding 1982, Fateful Triangle 1983, Knowledge of Language: Its Nature, Origins and Use 1986, Turning the Tide 1986, Barriers 1986, Pirates and Emperors 1986, On Power and Ideology 1987, Language and Problems of Knowledge 1987, Language in a Psychological Setting 1987, The Culture of Terrorism 1988, Generative Grammar 1988, Manufacturing Consent (with Edward Herman) 1988, The Chomsky Reader 1988, Necessary Illusions 1989, Language and Politics 1989, Deterring Democracy 1991, Terrorizing the Neighborhood 1991, What Uncle Sam Really Wants 1992, Chronicles of Dissent 1992, Year 501 1993, Letters from Lexington 1993, The Prosperous Few and the Restless Many 1993, Language and Thought 1994, World Orders, Old and New 1994, The Minimalist Program 1995, Powers and Prospects 1996, Class Warfare 1996; numerous lectures. *Leisure interest:* gardening. *Address:* Department of Linguistics and Philosophy, Massachusetts Institute of Technology, 77 Massachusetts Avenue, Cambridge, MA 02139 (Office); 15 Suzanne Road, Lexington, MA 02173, U.S.A. (Home). *Telephone:* (617) 253-7819 (Office); (617) 862-6160 (Home). *Fax:* (617) 253-9425 (Office).

CHONGWE, Rodger Masauso Alivas, LL.B., S.C.; Zambian lawyer; b. 2 Oct. 1940, Chipata; m. Gwenda Fay Eaton 1967; one s. one d.; ed. St. Mark's Coll., Mapanza, Choma, Munali Secondary School, Lusaka, Univ. of Western Australia School of Law, Perth; Native Courts Asst. and Dist. Asst., Govt. of Northern Rhodesia 1962–63; admitted to practise as barrister, solicitor and Proctor of the Supreme Court of Western Australia and the High Court of the Commonwealth of Australia 1968; admitted as solicitor and barrister before all courts, Zambia 1969; Asst. Solicitor, Martin & Co., Lusaka 1969–70, partner 1979; partner, Mwisiya Chongwe & Co., Lusaka 1970–77; owner, R.M.A. Chongwe & Co., Lusaka 1987–; apptd. State Counsel 1985; mem. Industrial Relations Court of Zambia 1976–87; lecturer, Law Practice Inst. 1974–83, Examiner 1975–; Dir. Tazama Pipelines Ltd. 1974–89; Local Dir. Jos Hansen & Soehne Zambia Ltd. 1983–; Dir. Standard Chartered Bank of Zambia Ltd. 1985–; mem. Int. Bar Asscn. 1978–, mem. Council 1984–86; Councillor Law Asscn. of Zambia 1979, Vice-Chair. 1980, Chair. 1981–86, Councillor 1986–, Chair. Human Rights Cttee. 1986–; Chair. African Bar Asscn. 1985–; mem. Council of Legal Educ. of Zambia 1982–; Commr. Law Devt. Comm. of Zambia 1981–; Exec. mem. Commonwealth Lawyers' Asscn. 1983–, Sec.-Gen. 1986, Pres. 1990–; Gov. Art Centre Foundation 1977–; Treasurer Int. Asscn. of Artists 1983–. *Publications:* numerous papers on legal topics, particularly concerning human rights, the legal profession and legal education. *Address:* Second Floor, Plot Number 9003, Corner Panganani and Chifinga Roads, P.O. Box 31190, Lusaka (Office); Subdivision 36, Farm Number 34A, Great East Road, Lusaka, Zambia (Home).

CHOPPIN, Purnell Whittington, M.D.; American scientist; b. 4. July 1929, Baton Rouge, La.; s. of Arthur Richard Choppin and Eunice Dolores (Bolin) Choppin; m. Joan H. Macdonald 1959; one d.; ed. Louisiana State Univ.; Intern Barnes Hosp., St. Louis 1953–54, Asst. Resident 1956–57; Postdoctoral Fellow, Research Assoc., Rockefeller Univ., New York 1957–60, Asst. Prof. 1960–64, Assoc. Prof. 1964–70, Prof., Sr. Physician 1970–85, Leon Hess Prof. of Virology 1980–85, Vice-Pres. Acad. Programs 1983–85, Dean of Graduate Studies 1985; Vice-Pres., Chief Scientific Officer, Howard Hughes Medical Inst. 1985–87, Pres. 1987–; ed. Virology 1973–82; Chair. Virology Study Section, Nat. Insts. of Health 1975–78; mem. Bd. of Dirs. Royal Soc. of Medicine Foundation Inc., New York 1978–93, Advisory Cttee. on Fundamental Research, Nat. Multiple Sclerosis Soc. 1979–84 (Chair. 1983–84), Advisory Council Nat. Inst. of Allergy and Infectious Diseases 1980–83, Sloan-Kettering Cancer Cttee., New York 1983–84, Comm. on Life Sciences, Nat. Research Council 1982-87, Council for Research and Clinical Investigation, American Cancer Soc. 1983–85; Pres. American Soc. of Virology 1985–86; Fellow A.A.A.S.; mem. N.A.S. (Chair. Class IV medical sciences 1983–86, Section 43 microbiology and immunology 1989–93), mem. Governing Bd. Nat. Research Council, N.A.S. 1990–92; mem. council Inst. of Medicine 1986–92, Exec. Cttee. 1988–91; Asscn of American Physicians, American Soc. of Microbiology, American Asscn. of Immunologists and other professional orgs.; numerous hon. degrees; Howard Taylor Ricketts Award, Univ. of Chicago 1978, Waksman Award for Excellence in Microbiology, N.A.S. 1984. *Publications:* numerous articles and chapters on virology, cell biology, infectious diseases. *Leisure interests:* fly fishing and stamp collecting. *Address:* Howard Hughes Medical Institute, 4000 Jones Bridge Road, Chevy Chase, MD 20815 (Office); 2700 Calvert Street, N.W., Washington, D.C. 20008, U.S.A. (Home).

CHOPRA, Deepak; writer. *Publications include:* Return of the Rishi 1989, Quantum Healing 1990, Perfect Health 1990, Unconditional Life 1991, Creating Health 1991, Creating Affluence 1993, Ageless Body, Timeless Mind 1993, Restful Sleep 1994, Perfect Weight 1994, The Seven Spiritual Laws of Success 1995, The Path of Love 1996.

CHORLEY, 2nd Baron, cr. 1945, of Kendal, **Roger Richard Edward Chorley,** F.C.A.; British accountant; b. 14 Aug. 1930; s. of 1st Baron Chorley and Katharine Campbell Hopkinson; m. Ann Debenham 1964; two s.; ed. Stowe School, Gonville and Caius Coll., Cambridge; joined Cooper Brothers & Co. (later Coopers & Lybrand) 1955, New York office 1959–60, Pakistan (Indus Basin Project) 1961, Partner 1967–89; Accounting Adviser to Nat. Bd.for Prices and Incomes 1965–68; Visiting Prof., Dept. of Man. Sciences, Imperial Coll. of Science and Tech., London Univ. 1979–82; mem. Royal Comm. on the Press 1975–77, Finance Act 1960 Tribunal 1974–79, Ordnance Survey Review Cttee. 1978–79, British Council Review Cttee. 1979–80, Bd. British Council 1981– (Deputy Chair. 1990–), Top Salaries Review Body 1981–90, Ordnance Survey Advisory Bd. 1983–85, House of Lords Select Cttee. on Science and Tech. 1983, 1987, 1990; Chair. The National Trust

1991–96; fmr. Pres. Cambridge Univ. Mountaineering Club, mem. expeditions Himalayas (Rakaposhi) 1954, (Nepal) 1957; Hon. Sec. Climbers' Club 1963–67; mem. Man. Cttee. Mount Everest Foundation 1968–70; Pres. Alpine Club 1983–85; mem. Council Royal Geographical Soc. 1984–, Vice-Pres. 1986–87, Pres. 1987–90; mem. Finance Cttee. Nat. Trust 1972–90, Exec. Cttee. 1989–; mem. Council, Royal Soc. of Arts 1987–89, City and Guilds of London Inst.; mem. Nat. Theatre Bd. 1980–91; Hon. D.Sc. (Reading, Kingston); Hon. LL.D. (Lancaster). *Leisure interest:* mountains. *Address:* House of Lords, London, SW1A 0PW, England.

CHORZEMPA, Daniel Walter, PH.D.; American pianist, organist, musicologist and composer; b. 7 Dec. 1944, Minneapolis; s. of Martin Chorzempa Sr. and Henrietta Reiswig; ed. Univ. of Minnesota; former church organist; Organ Instructor, Univ. of Minn. 1962–65; Fulbright Scholar, Cologne 1965–66; extensive piano and organ recitals in Germany, Denmark, Italy and U.K. etc. since 1968; J. S. Bach Prize, Leipzig 1968. *Leisure interests:* mathematics, architecture, poetry, renaissance history and literature. *Address:* 5000 Cologne 1, Grosse Budengasse 11, Germany. *Telephone:* 231271.

CHOU CHANG-HUNG, PH.D.; Taiwanese researcher and academic; b. 5 Sept. 1942, Tainan, Taiwan; s. of F. K. Chou and C. Y. Shih Chou; m. Ruth L. H. Yang Chou 1970; one s. one d.; ed. Nat. Taiwan Univ., Taipei, Univ. of Calif., Santa Barbara, U.S.A., Univ. of Toronto, Canada; Assoc. Research Fellow, Inst. of Botany, Academia Sinica, Taipei 1972–76, Research Fellow 1976–, Dir. 1989–; Prof. Dept. of Botany, Nat. Taiwan Univ. 1976–; mem. various nat. cttees. for Int. Council of Scientific Unions (ICSU) 1974–; Sec. for Int. Affairs Academia Sinica 1988–, Dir. Inst. Botany 1989–96, mem. Council Academia Sinica 1989–; mem. Council Pacific Science Asscn. 1989; mem. Cttee. for Science Educ. Ministry of Educ. 1986–, Cttee. for Environmental Educ. 1991–, Cttee. for Cultural and Natural Preservation Council of Agric. 1990, Council Taiwan Livestock Research Inst. 1976–, Taiwan Forestry Research Inst. 1989–, Council Nat. Sustainable Devt. 1997–; Dir. Life Science Research Promotion Centre Nat. Science Council 1989–; Visiting Scholar, Oklahoma Univ., Univ. of Texas, Washington State Univ. 1979–80; Pres. Botanical Soc. of the Rep. of China (Taiwan) 1983–84, Biological Soc. of Repub. of China (Taiwan) 1987–88; Chair. Nat. Cttee. Int. Union of Biological Sciences 1990–; mem. Exec. Cttee. of IUBS; Chair. SCOPE Nat. Cttee.; Vice-Pres. Int. Union of Biological Sciences 1997–; Ed. Botanical Bulletin Academia Sinica 1989–; Fellow Third World Acad. of Sciences; mem. Academia Sinica, Taipei; awards from Ministry of Educ. and Science Council of Taiwan. *Publications:* over 200 scientific papers, one univ. textbook. *Leisure interest:* listening to classical music. *Address:* 280 Yean Jiou Yuan Road, Sec. 2, Institute of Botany, Academia Sinica, Taipei, Taiwan 115. *Telephone:* (02) 2789-9590 (ext. 451); (02) 2651-0363. *Fax:* (02) 2782 7954.

CHOU CH'UEN; Taiwanese politician; founding mem. New Party Aug. 1993–; mem. Legis. Council 1995–. *Address:* New Party, 4th Floor, 65 Guang Fuh South Road, Taipei, Taiwan. *Telephone:* (2) 2756-2222.

CHOW MAN YIU, Paul; Chinese businessman; fmr. Exec. Dir. Sun Hung Kai Securities Ltd.; C.E.O. Hong Kong Securities Clearing Corpn. 1990–91; fmr. Dir. Hong Kong Stock Exchange; C.E.O. Hong Kong Stock Exchange Council 1991. *Address:* The Stock Exchange of Hong Kong Ltd., 1/F One and Two Exchange Square, Central, Hong Kong Special Administrative Region, People's Republic of China. *Telephone:* 840 3838. *Fax:* 868 1308.

CHOW YUN-FAT; Chinese film actor; b. 1956, Lamma Island; m. Jasmine Chow; began acting career at television station TVB, Hong Kong 1973, appearing in over 1,000 TV series. *Films include:* The Story of Woo Viet, A Better Tomorrow 1986, God of Gamblers 1989, The Killer, Eighth Happiness, Once a Thief 1991, Full Contact 1992, Hard Boiled 1992, Peace Hotel, Broken Arrow.

CHOWDHURY, Mizanur Rahman; Bangladeshi politician; b. 19 Oct. 1928, Chandpur; ed. Feni Coll.; m. 1955; Headmaster, Bamoni High School 1952, Teacher, Chandpur Nuria High School 1956; Vice-Chair. Chandpur Municipality 1959; elected mem. Nat. Ass. of Pakistan 1962, 1965, 1970; Organising Sec. East Pakistan Wing, Awami League 1966, Acting Gen. Sec. 1966, 1967, organized Awami League election campaign 1970, Jt. Convenor 1976; Minister of Information and Broadcasting 1972–73, Minister of Relief and Rehabilitation 1973; Minister of Posts and Telecommunications 1985–88; Prime Minister of Bangladesh 1986–88; Sr. Vice-Chair. Jatiya Dal Party 1984, Gen. Sec. 1985–86. *Leisure interest:* reading. *Address:* c/o Jatiya Dal, Dhaka, Bangladesh.

CHRAIBI, Driss; Moroccan/French novelist; b. 15 July 1926; s. of Haj Fatmi and Habiba Zwitten; m. 1st (dissolved); m. 2nd Sheena McCallion; two s.; ed. Lycée Lyautey, Casablanca, Paris; author of numerous novels including Le Passé Simple 1954, Les Boucs 1955, Une Enquête au Pays 1981, La Mère du Printemps 1983; various contributions to French radio. *Address:* c/o Editions du Seuil, 27 rue Jacob, 75261 Paris Cedex 06, France. *Telephone:* 3291215.

CHRAMOSTOVÁ, Vlasta; Czech actress and human rights activist; b. 17 Nov. 1926, Brno; m. Stanislav Milota 1971; ed. Conservatoire of Music and Performing Arts, Brno; with The Free Theatre, Brno 1945, Municipal Theatre, Olomouc 1945–46, State Theatre Brno 1946–49, Theatre in Vinohrady, Prague 1950–69; mem., ensemble, Theatre behind the Gate 1970–72; banned from acting in public; signed Charter 77, Jan. 1977; appealed to artists in the West for support for Charter 77, 1977; Charter 77 activist 1977–89; sentenced to imprisonment for 3 months, sentence suspended on one-year-probation, April 1989; mem. Nat. Theatre Ensemble Prague 1990–91; joined Drama Co. of Nat. Theatre Prague 1991–; Merited Artist 1965, Czech Theatre Artists' Award 1967, Peace Prize awarded by Paul Lauritzen Foundation 1989, Hon. mem., Masaryk Democratic Movt. 1990; Order of T. G. Masaryk 1998. *Address:* Národní divadlo, Ostrovní 1, Prague 1, Nové Město, Czech Republic.

CHRÉTIEN, Rt. Hon. Joseph Jacques Jean, P.C., B.A., LL.L.; Canadian politician and lawyer; b. 11 Jan. 1934, Shawinigan; s. of Wellie Chrétien and Marie Boisvert; m. Aline Chaîné 1957; two s. one d.; ed. Laval Univ., Quebec; Dir., Shawinigan Senior Chamber of Commerce 1962; Liberal mem. House of Commons 1963–86; Parl. Sec. to Prime Minister, 1965, to Minister of Finance 1966; Minister without Portfolio 1967–68, of Nat. Revenue Jan.-July 1968, of Indian Affairs and Northern Devt. 1968–74; Pres. Treas. Bd. 1974–76; Minister of Industry, Trade and Commerce 1976–77, of Finance 1977–79, of Justice, Attorney-Gen. of Canada and Minister of State for Social Devt. 1980–82, of Energy, Mines and Resources 1982–84, Sec. of State for External Affairs, Deputy Prime Minister June–Sept. 1984; Prime Minister of Canada Nov. 1993–; Legal Counsel, Lang, Michener, Laurence & Shaw, Ottawa, Toronto and Vancouver 1984–90; M.P. for New Brunswick 1990–; Leader Nat. Liberal Party 1990–; Hon. LL.D. (Wilfred Laurier Univ.) 1981, (Laurentian Univ.) 1982, (W. Ont.) 1982, (York Univ.) 1986, (Alberta) 1987, (Lakehead) 1988, (Ottawa) 1994, (Meiji) 1996. *Publications:* Straight from the Heart 1985, Finding a Common Ground 1992. *Leisure interests:* skiing, fishing. *Address:* Office of the Prime Minister, Langevin Block, Parliament Buildings, Ottawa, Ont. K1A 0A2, Canada.

CHRISTENSEN, Helena; Danish model; b. 25 Dec. 1968, Copenhagen; d. of Flemming Christensen and Elsa Christensen; grad. in arithmetic and sociology course; fmr. child model; began adult modelling career in Paris 1988; appeared on cover of British Vogue; has since worked as one of world's leading models in promotions for Versace, Rykiel, Chanel, Lagerfeld, Revlon, Dior, Prada etc.; has appeared on all maj. magazine covers working for photographers including Herb Ritts, Bruce Weber, Patrick DeMarchelier, Penn, Steven Meisel, Helmut Newton etc. *Leisure interests:* photography (black and white), oil/watercolour painting. *Address:* Marilyn's Agency, 4 rue de la Paix, Paris, France. *Telephone:* 53295353.

CHRISTENSEN, Kai; Danish architect; b. 28 Dec. 1916, Copenhagen; s. of late J. C. Christensen and Jenny Christensen; m. Kirsten Vittrup Andersen 1941 (died 1990); two d.; ed. Royal Acad. of Fine Arts, Copenhagen; Dir., Technical Dept. of Fed. of Danish Architects 1947–52; Man. Dir. Danish Bldg. Centre 1952–61; Attached to Danish Ministry of Housing 1961–86; Graphic Adviser to Govt. Depts. 1986–; Chief, Scandinavian Design Cavalcade 1962–69; mem. Fed. of Danish Architects 1943, The Architectural Asscn., London 1955, Danish Cttee. for Bldg. Documentation 1950–79, Danish Soc. of History, Literature and Art 1969, Cttee. mem. 1979, Vice-Pres. 1981, Pres. 1985–; Cttee. mem., Danish Soc. for Chamber Music 1989; Fellow Royal Soc. of Arts, London 1977; Sec.-Gen. Nordisk Byggedag (Scandinavian Bldg. Conf.) VIII 1961, XIII 1977; Pres. Int. Conf. of Building Centres 1960, Danish Ministries Soc. of Art 1982–87; mem. Scandinavian Liaison Cttee. concerning Govt. Bldg. 1963–72; associated Ed. Building Research and Practice/Bâtiment International (C.I.B. magazine) 1968–85; Danish Design Council's Award for Industrial Graphics 1989; awards and prizes in public competition. *Major works:* designs for arts and crafts, graphic design, exhbns., furniture for the Copenhagen Cabinet Makers' Exhbns. *Publications:* books about architecture and graphic design; articles and treatises in technical magazines and daily press. *Leisure interests:* chamber music, chess, fencing. *Address:* 100 Vester Voldgade, DK-1552 Copenhagen V, Denmark. *Telephone:* (45) 33 12 13 37.

CHRISTENSEN, Søren, LL.B.; Danish civil servant; b. 31 Oct. 1940, Copenhagen; m. Inge Rudbeck 1964; ed. Univ. of Copenhagen; sec. Secr. of Lord Mayor, Municipality of Copenhagen 1968–71, deputy office man. 1971–73; Head of Secr. Municipality of Randers 1973–78, C.E.O. 1978–86; Perm. Under-Sec. Ministry of Finance 1986–94; Head of Danish Supreme Admin. Authority, Copenhagen 1994–97; Sec.-Gen. Nordic Council of Ministers 1997–. *Publication:* Info Society Year 2000 1994. *Leisure interests:* sailing, skiing. *Address:* Nordic Council of Ministers, Store Strandstrasse 18, 1255 Copenhagen, Denmark. *Telephone:* 33.96.03.22. *Fax:* 33.93.89.55.

CHRISTESEN, Clement Byrne, O.B.E., D.LITT., F.A.H.A.; Australian editor and author; b. 28 Oct. 1911, Townsville, Queensland; s. of Patrick Christesen and Susan S. Byrne; m. Nina Maximoff 1942; ed. King's Coll. Univ. of Queensland; journalist, A.B.C. feature-writer and broadcaster, publicist for Queensland Govt. 1935–41; founder (1940) and ed./publisher, Meanjin Quarterly (literary journal) until 1974; Australian Man. William Heinemann Ltd. 1947–52; Lockie Fellow, Univ. of Melbourne 1966–74; Hon. Bibliographer, Univ. of Melbourne; Emer. Fellow, Australia Council; Hon. Fellow, Australian Acad. of Humanities; Crouch Gold Medal 1965, Britannica Award for Humanities 1970, Priestley Gold Medal 1980. *Publications:* The Hand of Memory 1970, The Gallery on Eastern Hill 1970, Having Loved 1979, The Troubled Eyes of Women 1990, Ebb-tide 1997. *Leisure interest:* painting. *Address:* Stanhope, Eltham, Victoria 3095, Australia.

CHRISTIANS, F. Wilhelm, DR.JUR.; German banker; b. 1 May 1922; fmr. Pres. Bundesverband Deutscher Banken e.V. (Fed. Asscn. of German Banks);

Chair. Supervisory Bd. Deutsche Bank AG, Mannesmann AG, Düsseldorf, VIAG 1983–93. *Address:* Königsallee 51, 40212 Düsseldorf, Germany.

CHRISTIE, Sir George William Langham, Kt.; British music administrator; b. 31 Dec. 1934; s. of John Christie, C.H. and Audrey Mildmay Christie; m. Patricia Mary Nicholson 1958; three s. one d.; ed. Eton Coll.; Asst. to Sec. of Calouste Gulbenkian Foundation 1957–62; Chair. Glyndebourne Productions 1956–; mem. Arts Council of G.B. and Chair. Music Panel 1988–92; Founder Chair. of London Sinfonietta; Hon. mem. Guildhall School of Music and Drama 1991; D.L.; Hon. F.R.C.M. 1986; Hon. F.R.N.C.M. 1986; Hon. D.Mus. (Sussex) 1990, (Keele) 1993; Hon. D.Litt. (Exeter) 1994. *Address:* Glyndebourne, Lewes, East Sussex, BN8 5UU, England. *Telephone:* (01273) 812250.

CHRISTIE, Julie Frances; British actress; b. 14 April 1940, Assam, India; d. of Frank St. John and Rosemary (née Ramsden) Christie; ed. Brighton Technical Coll., and Central School of Speech and Drama; Motion Picture Laurel Award, Best Dramatic Actress 1967, Motion Picture Herald Award 1967; Dr. h.c. (Warwick) 1994. *Films:* Crooks Anonymous 1962, The Fast Lady 1962, Billy Liar 1963, Young Cassidy 1964, Darling 1964 (Acad. Award 1966), Doctor Zhivago (Donatello Award) 1965, Fahrenheit 451 1966, Far From the Madding Crowd 1966, Petulia 1967, In Search of Gregory 1969, The Go-Between 1971, McCabe & Mrs. Miller 1972, Don't Look Now 1973, Shampoo 1974, Demon Seed, Heaven Can Wait 1978, Memoirs of a Survivor 1980, Gold 1980, The Return of the Soldier 1981, Les Quarantièmes rugissants 1981, Heat and Dust 1982, The Gold Diggers 1984, Miss Mary 1986, The Tattooed Memory 1986, Power 1987, Fathers and Sons 1988, Dadah is Death (TV) 1988, Fools of Fortune 1989, McCabe and Mrs. Miller 1990, The Railway Station 1992, Hamlet 1995. *Plays:* Old Times 1995, Suzanna Andler 1997, Afterglow 1998. *Address:* c/o International Creative Management, 76 Oxford Street, London, W1N 0AX, England.

CHRISTIE, Linford, O.B.E.; British athlete; b. 2 April 1960, St. Andrews, Jamaica; s. of James Christie and Mabel Christie; one d.; fmr. cashier Wandsworth Co-op; mem. Thames Valley Harriers; winner, U.K. 100m 1985, 1987, 200m 1985 (tie), 1988; winner, Amateur Athletics Asscn. 100m 1986, 1988, 200m. 1988; winner, European 100m record; Silver medallist, 100m, Seoul Olympic Games 1988, Winner 100m Gold Medal, Commonwealth Games 1990, Olympic Games 1992; World Athletic Championships 1993, Weltklasse Grand Prix Games 1994, European Games 1994; winner 100m. Zurich 1995; Hon. M.Sc. (Portsmouth Univ.) 1993; Male Athlete of the Year 1988, 1992; BBC Sports Personality of the Year 1993. *Publications:* Linford Christie (autobiog.) 1989, To be Honest With You 1995, A Year in the Life of Linford Christie 1996. *Leisure interests:* cooking and gardening. *Address:* "Nuff" Respect, The Coach House, 107 Sherland Road, Twickenham, Middlesex, TW9 4HB, England.

CHRISTMAN, Luther Parmalee, PH.D.; American professor of nursing and sociology; b. 26 Feb. 1915, Summit Hill, Pa.; s. of Elmer and Ellen (née Barnicott) Christman; m. Dorothy M. Black 1939; one s. two d.; ed. Pennyslvania Hosp. School, Philadelphia and Temple, Michigan State and Thomas Jefferson Univs.; Prof. of Sociology, Coll. of Arts and Sciences, Vanderbilt Univ., Nashville, Tenn. 1967–72, Dir., Nursing, Vanderbilt Univ. Hosp. 1967–72, Adjunct Prof. Vanderbilt Univ. 1991–; Vice-Pres. Nursing Affairs, Rush-Presbyterian-St. Luke's Medical Center; Dean, Coll. of Nursing, Rush Univ. 1971–77, Dean Emer. 1987–; Prof. of Sociology, Rush School of Medicine 1972–78, Dean Emer. 1977–87; Sr. Adviser, Center for Nursing, American Hosp. Asscn. 1989; Pvt. consulting service 1989–; Pres. Christman-Cornesty and Assocs. 1990–; Fellow, Nat. League for Nursing 1950–60, American Acad. of Arts and Sciences; Visiting Fellow, N.Z. Nurses' Educ. and Research Foundation 1978; Dr. h.c. H.L.D. (Thomas Jefferson Univ.) 1980, Jesse M. Scott Award, American Nurses' Asscn. 1988, Lifetime Achievement Award of Sigma Theta Tau Int. 1991, Living Legend Award, American Acad. of Nursing 1995. *Publications:* Interpersonal Behavior and Health Care (with Michael Counte) 1981, Hospital Organization and Health Care Delivery (with Michael Counte) 1981, Effects of Clinical Nursing Specialization (with Basil Georgopolous) 1990. *Leisure interest:* horticulture. *Address:* 5535 Nashville Highway, Chapel Hill, TN 37034, U.S.A. (Home).

CHRISTO (Christo Javacheff) and JEANNE-CLAUDE (Jeanne-Claude de Guillebon); American (naturalized) artists; b. 13 June 1935, Gabrovo, Bulgaria and Casablanca; one s.; Christo went to Paris 1958; works include: Wrapped Objects 1958; project for Packaging of Public Building 1961; Iron Curtain Wall of Oil Barrels blocking rue Visconti, Paris, Wrapping a Girl, London 1962; Showcases 1963; Store Front 1964; Air Package and Wrapped Tree, Eindhoven, Netherlands 1966; 42,390 cu. ft. Package, Walker Art Center, Minneapolis School of Art 1966; Wrapped Kunsthalle Bern 1968; 5,600 cu. m. Package for Kassel Documenta 4 1968; Wrapped Museum of Contemporary Art, Chicago 1969; Wrapped Coast, Little Bay, Sydney, Australia, 1 m. sq. ft. 1969; Valley Curtain, Grand Hogback, Rifle, Colorado, suspended fabric curtain 1970–72; Running Fence, Calif. 1972–76; Wrapped Roman Wall, Rome 1974; Ocean Front, Newport 1974; Wrapped Walk-Ways, Kansas City 1977–78; Surrounded Islands, Biscayne Bay, Miami, Florida 1980–83; The Pont Neuf Wrapped, Paris 1975–85; The Umbrellas, Japan-U.S.A. 1984–91; Wrapped Reichstag, Berlin 1971–95; Wrapped Trees, Fondation Beyeler and Berower Park, Riehen, Switzerland 1997–98; Praemium Imperiale 1995. *Address:* 48 Howard Street, New York, NY 10013, U.S.A. *Telephone:* (212) 966-4437 (after 10.30 a.m. NY time). *Fax:* (212) 966-2891.

CHRISTODOULOU, Anastasios, C.B.E., M.A., F.R.S.A.; British educational administrator; b. 1 May 1932, Akanthou, Cyprus; s. of Christodoulos and Maria Haji Yianni; m. Joan P. Edmunds 1955; two s. two d.; ed. St. Marylebone Grammar School and The Queen's Coll., Oxford; Infantry Signaller, Royal Sussex Regt. 1950–52; Dist. Officer, Dist. Commr. and Magistrate, H.M. Overseas Civil Service, Tanganyika Govt. 1956–62; Asst. Registrar, Univ. of Leeds 1963–66, Deputy Sec. 1966–68; Sec. Open Univ. 1969–80; Sec.-Gen. Asscn. of Commonwealth Univs. 1980–96; Exec. Sec. British Marshall Scholarships Commemoration Comm. 1980–96; Vice-Chair. Commonwealth Inst. 1982–89; Jt. Sec. U.K. Commonwealth Scholarships Comm. 1980–96; Observer U.S.-U.K. Fulbright Comm. 1980–96; Chair. Surrey Univ. and European Educ. Devt. 1990–96, Council for Educ. in the Commonwealth 1996–, Council for Educ. in the Commonwealth 1996–; mem. Comm. on Higher Educ. for Namibia; mem. Bd. of Govs. The Commonwealth of Learning 1988–93; Trustee Richmond, the American Int. Univ. in London 1988–; Chair. Int. Extension Coll. Trustees, Cambridge, Trustee Harlow Campus, Memorial Univ. of Newfoundland 1980–96; Hon. Prof. (Mauritius Univ.) 1986, Hon. Visiting Prof. Univ. of Surrey 1991; Hon. Fellow Coll. of Preceptors 1996; Hon. D.Univ. (Open Univ.) 1981, (Athabasca, Canada) 1981, (Brunel) 1996, (Ottawa) 1998; Hon. LL.D. (Auckland, Acadia) 1992. *Leisure interests:* rugby football, cricket, music, community service, growing vegetables. *Address:* 246 Lauderdale Mansions, Lauderdale Road, London, W9 1NQ, England. *Telephone:* 0171-286 0011. *Fax:* 0171-289 3309.

CHRISTOPHER, Ann, B.A., R.A., F.R.B.S., R.W.A.; British sculptor; b. 4 Dec. 1947, Watford, Herts.; d. of late William Christopher and of Phyllis Christopher; m. Kenneth Cook 1969; ed. Watford Girls' Grammar School, Harrow School of Art, West of England Coll. of Art; works include bronze sculpture, Castle Park, Bristol 1993, Corten sculpture, Marsh Mills, Plymouth 1996, Bronze Sculpture for offices of Linklaters and Paines solicitors, London 1997; works in Redfern Gallery, London, Adelson Galleries, New York; R.B.S. Silver Medal for sculpture of outstanding merit 1994. *Leisure interests:* cinema, travel, architecture. *Address:* Stable Block, Hay Street, Marshfield, Nr. Chippenham, SN14 8PF, England. *Telephone:* (01225) 891717. *Fax:* (01225) 891717.

CHRISTOPHER, Warren M.; American politician and lawyer; b. 27 Oct. 1925, Scranton, N.D.; s. of Ernest Christopher and Catharine Christopher; m. Marie Wyllis 1956; three s. one d.; ed. Univ. of Southern California, Stanford Law School; served in U.S.N.R. 1943–45; mem., O'Melveny and Myers law firm, L.A. 1950–67, 1969, partner 1958–67, 1969–76, 1981–93, Sr. Partner 1997–; special consultant on foreign econ. problems to Under-Sec. of State George Ball 1961–65; a trade negotiator in Kennedy Admin.; Deputy Attorney-Gen. in Johnson Admin.; Deputy Sec. of State in Carter Admin. (chief negotiator for Panama Canal treaties, supervisor human rights policies abroad, negotiated for release of U.S. hostages in Iran 1980) 1977–81; Chair. comm. to review conduct of L.A. Police Dept. in Rodney King case 1991; Sec. of State 1993–97; Past-Pres. L.A. Co. Bar Asscn.; fmr. Dir. L.A. World Affairs Council, mem. Trilateral Comm.; several hon. degrees; Medal of Freedom 1981. *Address:* O'Melveny and Myers, 1999 Avenue of the Stars, Floor 7, Los Angeles, CA 90067, U.S.A.

CHRISTOPHERSEN, Henning, M.ECON.; Danish politician; b. 8 Nov. 1939, Copenhagen; s. of Richard and Gretha Christophersen; m. Jytte Risbjerg Nielsen 1961; one s. two d.; ed. Univ. of Copenhagen; Head of the Economic Section of the Handicrafts Council 1965–70; mem. Folketing 1971–84, mem. of Parl. Finance Cttee. 1972–76, Vice-Chair. 1976–78, Minister of Foreign Affairs 1978–79; Deputy Leader, Danish Liberal Party 1972, Acting Party Leader 1977–78, Party Leader 1978–84; Deputy Prime Minister and Minister of Finance 1982–84; Vice-Pres. Comm. responsible for Budget, Financial Control, Personnel and Admin., Comm. of European Communities (now European Comm.) 1985–89, Econ. and Financial Affairs 1989–95, Co-ordination of Structural Funds 1989–92; a Vice Pres. of EC (now EU) 1993–95; Nat. Order of Merit. *Publications:* En udfordring for de Liberale, Taenker om Danmark i Det Nye Europa 1989, and numerous articles on economics. *Leisure interests:* genealogy, history and languages. *Address:* Avenue des Biches, 1930 Kraainem, Belgium.

CHRISTOPHERSON, Sir Derman Guy, Kt., O.B.E., S.M., D.PHIL., F.R.S., F.I.MECH.E., M.I.C.E.; British academic; b. 6 Sept. 1915, Plumstead, Kent; s. of Derman and Edith F. Christopherson; m. Frances Edith Tearle 1940 (died 1988); three s. one d.; ed. Sherborne School, Univ. Coll., Oxford and Harvard Univ.; Scientific Officer, Research and Experiments Dept., Ministry of Home Security 1941–45; Lecturer in Eng., Cambridge Univ. and Fellow and Bursar of Magdalene Coll., Cambridge 1945–49; Prof. of Mechanical Eng., Univ. of Leeds 1949–55; Prof. of Applied Science, Imperial Coll. of Science and Technology, London 1955–60; Vice-Chancellor and Warden, Univ. of Durham 1960–78; mem. Royal Fine Art Comm. 1978–85, Chair. 1980–85; Fellow, Imperial Coll. of Science and Technology 1966; Hon. Fellow, Magdalene Coll., Cambridge 1969, Master 1979–85; Hon. Fellow, University Coll., Oxford 1977; several hon. degrees; Clayton Prize, Inst. of Mechanical Engineers 1963. *Publications:* The Engineer in the University 1967, The University at Work 1973, and various articles in learned journals. *Address:* c/o 10 Hallam Road, Mapperley, Nottingham, NG3 6HA, England.

CHRISTOPHIDES, Manolis; Cypriot politician and lawyer; b. 1 Feb. 1941, Lefka; m.; two d.; ed. Pancyprian Gymnasium and Univ. of Athens; leading mem. of Youth Org. of EOKA during Cyprus liberation struggle 1955–59;

reserve officer with rank of Second. Lieut.; served in area of Morpou Lefka during Turkish invasion 1974; fmr. Chair. Nicosia Bar Asscn.; Chair. Cyprus Bar Council 1982–89; mem. Bd. Cyprus Broadcasting Corpn. 1971–79; founding mem. Democratic Rally Party, now Hon. Pres.; mem. Parl. 1981–91; Minister of Health –1995. *Address:* c/o Democratic Rally, P.O. Box 5305, 23 Pindarou Street, 1061 Nicosia, Cyprus.

CHROMY, Bronisław; Polish sculptor; b. 3 June 1925, Leńcze nr. Landskorona; m.; two d.; ed. Acad. of Fine Arts, Kraków 1956; one-man exhbns. in Poland; int. exhbns. and competitions; creator of many monuments commemorating victims of World War II; some works permanently in museums. *Leisure interests:* music, literature, nature. *Address:* ul. Halki 5, 30-228 Kraków, Poland.

CHRONOWSKI, Andrzej; Polish politician; b. 9 April 1961, Grybów, Nowy Sącz Prov.; m.; one s.; ed. Acad. of Mining and Metallurgy, Kraków; railway repair factory, Nowy Sącz 1987, production line specialist, head Employees' Council; mem. Solidarity Trade Union; Senator 1993–; Sec. Solidarity Senate Club Presidium 1993–97; mem. Nat. Econ. Cttee., Cttee. for Human Rights and Lawfulness, Cttee. of Initiatives and Legislative Work; Vice-Marshal of Senate 1997–. *Address:* Kancelaria Senatu RP, ul. Wiejska 6, 00-902 Warsaw, Poland. *Telephone:* (22) 694 24 15.

CHRYSSA; American artist; b. 1933, Athens; ed. Acad. Grand Shaumière, Paris, and San Francisco School of Fine Arts; one-woman shows, Solomon Guggenheim Museum, New York 1961, Museum of Modern Art, New York 1963, Walker Art Centre, Minneapolis 1968, Whitney Museum of Modern Art, New York 1972, Musée d'Art Contemporain, Montreal 1974, Musée d'Art Moderne de la Ville de Paris 1979, Nat. Pinacotheque Museum Alexander Soutsos, Athens 1980, Albright-Knox Gallery, Buffalo 1982, Leo Castelli Gallery 1988 and at galleries in New York, Boston, San Francisco, Paris, Cologne, Düsseldorf, Zurich, Turin and Athens since 1961; work has also appeared in many group exhbns. and belongs to numerous public collections in U.S.A. and Europe; Guggenheim Fellowship 1973; C.A.V.S., M.I.T. 1979. *Address:* c/o Albright-Knox Art Gallery, 1285 Elmwood Avenue, Buffalo, New York, NY 14222, U.S.A.

CHRYSSANTHOU, Christodoulos, LL.B.; Cypriot politician and lawyer; b. 24 May 1935, Pano Lefkara; m. Tereza Sika; one s. one d.; ed. Birmingham Univ., U.K.; admitted to Bar (Inner Temple); in pvt. practice, Nicosia 1963–; Minister of Justice 1988–90. *Address:* c/o Ministry of Justice, Nicosia, Cyprus.

CHRZANOWSKI, Wiesław Marian; Polish politician and lawyer; b. 20 Dec. 1923, Warsaw; s. of Wiesław Chrzanowski and Izabela Chrzanowska; ed. Jagiellonian Univ., Cracow; during Nazi occupation active in resistance movt., mem. Nat. Party (ed. bd. by-weekly Młoda Polska 1942–45), served Home Army 1942–44, Warsaw Uprising 1944; Pres. clandestine Law Students' Asscn. 1942–43; asst., sr. asst. Civil Law Dept. in Warsaw Univ. and Cen. School of Commerce, Warsaw 1945–48; arrested and sentenced to 8 years for attempting to overthrow regime 1948–54, acquitted and rehabilitated 1956; legal counsellor 1955–72; attorney's trainee 1957–60, attorney 1981–; researcher 1972–79, Asst. Prof. 1980–88, Prof. 1988–, Cooperative Research Inst.; Asst. Prof. Catholic Univ. of Lublin 1982–87, Prof. 1987–, Deputy Dean Canon and Secular Law Faculty 1987–90; mem. informal information group of Primate of Poland 1965–81; mem. Social Council of Primate of Poland 1983–84; mem. Episcopal Comm. for Agric. 1982–86; mem. on behalf of Episcopate of team drawing up convention between Apostolic See and Poland and Law on State-Church Relations 1987–89; mem. Solidarity Trade Union 1980– (adviser to Nat. Comm., plenipotentiary for registration by Voivodship and Supreme Court 1980–81); mem. Labour Party 1945–46, Christian-Nat. Union 1989– (Chair. Main Bd. 1989–94); Chair. Supreme Council 1995–98; Minister of Justice and Attorney-Gen. Jan.–Dec. 1991; Deputy to Sejm (Parl.) 1991–93, Marshal of Sejm 1991–93; Senator 1997. *Publications:* over 80 books and articles on civil law and cooperative law, many contribs. in underground journals and Polish journals appearing abroad. *Leisure interests:* reading, theatre, mountain hiking. *Address:* ul. Solec 79a/82, 00-402 Warsaw, Poland. *Telephone:* 629-30-88.

CHU, Chi-Ming, M.B., PH.D., F.R.C.P.; Chinese medical scientist; b. 12 Sept. 1917, Yixing, Jiansu; s. of Chu Yin-Zhi and Lu Zhi-Zhen; m. Pauline Huang 1945; one s.; ed. Nat. Medical Coll. of Shanghai, Univ. of Cambridge, England; Asst. Tech. Expert, Nat. Epidemic Prevention Bureau, Kunming 1940–45; Research Fellow, Nat. Inst. for Medical Research, London 1948–50; Chief of Control Lab. and Second Research Lab., Nat. Vaccine and Serum Inst., Beijing 1951–55; Deputy Dir. Zhangchun Inst. of Biological Products, Zhangchun 1955–63; Prof. and Deputy Dir. Inst. of Virology, Chinese Acad. of Medical Sciences 1963–80, Dir. 1981–83, Hon. Dir. 1987–; Prof. of Virology and Scientific Adviser, Chinese Acad. of Preventive Medicine 1984–; mem. NPC 1964–74, People's Political Consultative Cttee. 1978–92; mem. Standing Cttee., Medical Scientific Council and Chair. Cttee. on Viral Diseases, Ministry of Health 1963–87; Chair. Cttee. on Haemorrhagic Fever 1983–87, Sub-Cttee. for Evaluation of Biologicals 1985–92; Scientific Adviser, China Nat. Centre for Devt. of Biotechnology 1984–87; Vice-Chair. Cttee. for Evaluation of Medical Scientific Achievements 1986–88; Chair. Advisory Cttee. on Infectious Diseases 1987–92; Pres. Chinese Soc. for Microbiology 1983–87; Vice-Chair., Cttee. for Evaluation of Pharmaceuticals 1989–92; Adviser, China Int. Medical Foundation 1988–; Chair. Sub-Cttee. for Evaluation of Biotechnological Products 1992–96; mem. Cttee. for Evaluation and Supervision of High Tech. Program, State Comm. of Science and Tech. 1992–; Adviser, Consultant Cttee. for Expanded Program of Immunization 1992–; Chief Ed. Chinese Journal of Virology 1985–; mem. Chinese Acad. of Sciences 1980; at present working on expression of viral genes in mammalian cells and in vaccinia vectors. *Publications:* over 200 papers on virology, microbiology and biotechnology, especially on influenza, adeno virus, vaccinia, measles and hepatitis B. *Leisure interests:* reading history and poetry. *Address:* Institute of Virology, 100 Ying Xin Jie, Xuan Wu Qu, Beijing 100052, People's Republic of China. *Telephone:* (01) 6301-3530. *Fax:* (01) 6352-9224.

CHU, Steven, B.A., PH.D.; American physicist; b. 28 Feb. 1948, St. Louis; s. of Ju Chin Chu and Ching Chen Li; two s.; ed. Univ. of Rochester, Univ. of Calif., Berkeley; post-doctoral fellow Univ. of Calif., Berkeley 1976–78; with Bell Labs., Murray Hill, N.J. 1978–83; Head Quantum Electronics Research Dept. AT&T Bell Labs., Holmdell, N.J. 1983–87; Prof. of Physics and Applied Physics, Stanford Univ. 1987–, Frances and Theodore Geballe Prof. of Physics and Applied Physics 1990–, Chair. Physics Dept. 1990–93; Visiting Prof. Collège de France 1990; Fellow American Physics Soc. (Chair. Laser Science Topical Group 1989), Optical Soc. of America, American Acad. of Arts and Sciences; Woodrow Wilson Fellow 1970, N.S.F. Doctoral Fellow 1970–74; mem. N.A.S., Academia Sinica; awarded Herbert P. Broida Prize for laser spectroscopy 1987, King Faisal Prize for Science 1993, Schawlow Prize 1994, Meggars Award 1994, Humboldt Sr. Scientist Award 1995, Science for Art Prize 1995, shared Nobel Prize for Physics 1997 for developing methods of cooling matter to very low temperatures using lasers. *Publications:* numerous papers on atomic physics and laser spectroscopy. *Address:* Department of Physics, Stanford University, Stanford, CA 94305, U.S.A.

CHU HUY MAN, Gen.; Vietnamese politician and soldier; b. 1913, Nghe An Province; one s. three d.; Col. in Viet Nam People's Army 1950; Commdr. of Dien Bien Phu 1954; mem. Cen. Cttee. of Lao Dong Party; promoted to Maj.-Gen., Chief Commdr. in Western Highlands 1960–75; mem. Politburo of CP of Viet Nam 1976–; promoted to Gen., Dir. of Political Dept. of Viet Nam People's Army 1976–; Vice-Pres. Council of State 1981–86; promoted to four-star Gen. 1982; Adviser to Ministry of Defence 1986–. *Address:* 36 A Ly Nam De, Hanoi, Viet Nam.

CHU KAO-CHENG; Taiwanese politician; Leader New Party; mem. for Kao-hsiung, Legislative Council 1995–. *Address:* New Party, 4th Floor, 65 Guang Fuh South Road, Taipei, Taiwan. *Telephone:* (2) 2756-2222.

CHUA, Nam-Hai, PH.D., F.R.S.; Singaporean plant molecular and cell biologist; b. 8 April 1944; m. Suat-Choo Pearl Chua 1970; two d.; ed. Univ. of Singapore and Harvard Univ.; lecturer, Dept. of Biochemistry, Univ. of Singapore 1969–71; Research Assoc. Dept. of Cell Biology, Rockefeller Univ. 1971–73, Asst. Prof. Dept. of Cell Biology 1973–77, Prof. and Head, Lab. of Plant Molecular Biology 1981–, Andrew W. Mellon Prof. 1988–; consultant Shanghai Research Centre for Life Sciences, Chinese Acad. of Science 1996–, Global Tech. Centre and Nutrition, Monsanto Co. 1997–; numerous consultancies and bd. memberships. *Publications:* over 260 scientific publs. *Leisure interests:* squash, skiing. *Address:* Laboratory of Plant Molecular Biology, Rockefeller University, 1230 York Avenue, New York, NY 10021, U.S.A. *Telephone:* (212) 327-8126.

CHUA SIAN CHIN, LL.B.; Singaporean politician; b. 1933, Malacca, Malaya; m.; three c.; ed. Univs. of Malaya and London; barrister-at-law, Inner Temple, London 1959; returned to Singapore 1959 and began practice as advocate and solicitor; Chair. Univ. of Singapore Council 1967–68; mem. Parl. 1968–; Minister of Health 1968–75, of Home Affairs 1972–85, of Educ. 1975–79; Treas. People's Action Party 1970–. *Address:* c/o People's Action Party, 510 Thomson Road, 07-02 SLF Building, Singapore 1129.

CHUAN LEEKPAI, LL.B.; Thai politician; b. 28 July 1938, Trang Prov.; ed. Painting and Sculpture School and Thammasat Univ.; studied for two years with Bar Asscn. of Thailand; mem. Parl. from Trang Prov. 1969–; Minister of Justice 1975; Deputy Minister of Justice and Minister, Prime Minister's Office 1976; Minister of Justice, first Prem Govt.; Minister of Commerce 1981, of Agric. and Cooperatives 1981–83, of Educ. 1983–86, of Public Health 1988–90, of Agric. and Co-operatives 1990–91, Prime Minister of Thailand 1992–95, Nov. 1997–; Leader Democrat Party. *Address:* Office of the Prime Minister, Government House, Thanon Nakhon Pathom, Bangkok 10300, Thailand.

CHUBAIS, Anatoly Borisovich, C.ECON.SC.; Russian politician and economist; b. 16 June 1955; m.; two d.; ed. Leningrad Inst. of Tech. and Eng.; engineer and asst. of Chair. Leningrad Inst. of Econ. and Eng. 1977–82, docent 1982–90, Deputy, then First Deputy-Chair. of Leningrad Municipal Council Jan.–Nov. 1991; Minister of Russia, Chair. State Cttee. for Man. of State Property 1991–98; Deputy Prime Minister, Chair. Co-ordination Council for Privatization 1992–94; First Deputy Prime Minister 1994–96; mem. State Duma (Parl.) 1993–95; Head of Pres. Yeltsin's Admin. 1996–97; First Deputy Prime Minister 1997–98, Minister of Finance March–Nov. 1997; Head Russian Fed. Interdepartmental Comm. on Co-operation with Int. Financial and Econ. Orgs. and Group of Seven 1998; Chair. Russian Jt. Stock Co., United Power Grids of Russia May 1998–. *Address:* United Power Grids, Kitaigorodsky Proyezd 7, 103074 Moscow, Russia. *Telephone:* (095) 206-8393, 206-8223. *Fax:* (095) 206-8208.

CHUBB, Frederick Basil, D.PHIL., LITT.D., M.R.I.A.; Irish professor of political science; b. 8 Dec. 1921, Branksome, Dorset, England; s. of late Frederick

John Bailey Chubb and Gertrude May Chubb; m. 1st Margaret Gertrude Rafther 1946 (died 1984); m. 2nd Orla Mary Sheehan 1985; one d.; ed. Bishop Wordsworth's School, Salisbury, Merton Coll., Oxford; lecturer in Political Science, Trinity Coll., Dublin 1948, Fellow 1952, Reader 1955, Prof. 1960–91, Prof. Emer. 1991–, Bursar 1957–62; Chair. Comhairle na n-Ospidéal 1972–78, Employer Labour Conf. 1970–, Banking Industry Jt. Industrial Council 1981–95. *Publications:* The Control of Public Expenditure 1952, A Source Book of Irish Government 1964, 1983, The Government and Politics of Ireland 1970, 1992, The Constitution and Constitutional Change in Ireland 1978, The Politics of the Irish Constitution 1991. *Address:* 19 Clyde Lane, Ballsbridge, Dublin 4, Ireland. *Telephone:* (01) 6684625.

CHUBUK, Ion; DR. ECON; Moldovan politician; b. 1943; ed. Odessa Inst. of Agric.; First Deputy Chair. Moldovan State Planning Cttee. 1984–86; Head of Div. Research Inst. of Agric. 1986–89; Deputy Chair. Moldovan Agricultural-Industrial Council 1989–90; First Deputy Minister of Econs. 1990–91; Deputy Prime Minister, Perm. Rep. of Moldovan Govt. in U.S.S.R. Council of Ministers 1991-92; First Deputy Minister of Foreign Affairs 1992-94; First Deputy Minister of Econs. April–Dec. 1994; Chair. Moldovan Accountant Chamber 1994–97; Prime Minister of Moldova Jan. 1997–. *Address:* Office of the Prime Minister, Piata Marii Adunari Nationale 1, 277033 Chisinau, Moldova (Office). *Telephone:* (3732) 23-77-95, 23 35 72 (Office).

CHUDAKOV, Aleksandr Yevgeniyevich; Russian physicist; b. 16 June 1921, Moscow; s. of Yevgeny Chudakov; m.; two c.; ed. Moscow Univ.; Research Assoc. Lebedev Inst. of Physics, U.S.S.R. Acad. of Sciences 1946–71, Head of Lab. Inst. of Atomic Research 1971–; Corresp. mem. U.S.S.R. (now Russian) Acad. of Sciences 1966–88, mem. 1987–; Chair. Scientific Council on Cosmic Rays U.S.S.R. (now Russian) Acad. of Sciences; main works on nature and properties of cosmic rays; contributed to discovery of external radiational zones of the Earth; Lenin Prize 1960. *Publications:* works on nuclear physics. *Address:* Institute of Nuclear Research, Prospekt 60 Let Oktyabrya 7A, Moscow 117312, Russia. *Telephone:* 135 85 60 (Office); 237-43-78 (Home).

CHUDAKOVA, Marietta Omarovna, D.PHIL.; Russian academic; b. 2 Jan. 1937, Moscow; m. Alexander Pavlovich Chudakov; one d.; ed. Moscow State Univ.; school teacher in Moscow 1959–61; sr. researcher, Head Div. of Manuscripts, Head Div. of Rare Books, Head Div. of Library Research All-Union Lenin's Public Library 1965–84; teacher Inst. of Literature 1986–, Prof. 1992–; main research on history of Russian Literature (Soviet Period), archives and literary criticism; Visiting Prof. Stanford 1989, Univ. of S. Calif. 1990, Ecole Normal Superieure, Paris 1991, Geneva Univ. and European Inst. in Geneva 1991; Chair. All-Russian Mikhail Bulgakov Fund; Prize of Moscow Komsomol for research on Yuri Olesha 1970, mem. Acad. Europae. *Publications:* Effendi Kapiev (biography) 1970, Craftsmanship of Yuri Olesha 1972, Talks about Archives 1975, Poetics of Mikhail Zoshchenko 1979, Mikhail Bulgakov 1988, about 200 publs. in magazines on literary subjects and political essays. *Leisure interests:* rowing, skiing. *Address:* Miklukha-Maklai str. 39, korp. 2, Apt. 380, 117485 Moscow, Russia (Home). *Telephone:* 202 8444 (Office), 335 9257 (Home).

CHUKHRAI, Grigoriy Naumovich; Russian film director; b. 23 May 1921, Melitopol, Zaporozhye Region; s. of Naum Vladimirovich Roubanov and Klavdia Petrovna Chukhrai; m. Irina Pavlovna Penkova 1944; one s. one d.; ed. All-Union State Inst. of Cinematography 1953; Soviet Army 1939–45; mem. CPSU 1944–89; Producer Mosfilm 1955–64, 1977–; Dir. Experimental Film Studio 1965–76; Honoured Art Worker of R.S.F.S.R., People's Artist of U.S.S.R. 1981, Lenin Prize 1961, Nika Prize 1994, Order of Red Star, Order of Patriotic War, Order of Red Banner of Labour (three times), Labour Order of Hungary, Partisan Star of Czechoslovakia. *Films:* The 41st 1956, Ballad of a Soldier 1959, The Clear Sky 1961, There Lived an Old Man and Old Woman 1964, Memory 1971, Quagmire 1978, Life is Beautiful 1980, I Will Teach You to Dream 1984, Stalin and the War 1991. *Leisure interest:* the theory of economics. *Address:* Pudovkina str. 3, Apt. 60, 119285 Moscow, Russia. *Telephone:* (095) 143 34 44. *Fax:* 200-42-84.

CHUN DOO-HWAN, Gen.; Korean politician and army officer (retd.); b. 18 Jan. 1931, Kyongsangnamdo Prov.; s. of Chun Sang-Woo and Kim Jum-Mun; m. Lee Soon-Ja; three s. one d.; ed. Heedoh Primary School, Taegu, Taegu Tech. High School, Mil. Acad., Army Coll.; commissioned Second Lieut. 1955; Adjutant-Gen. School 1959; U.S. Special Forces and Psychological Warfare School 1959; U.S. Army Infantry School 1960; Acting Planning Dir., Special Warfare Bureau Army HQ, 1960–61; Domestic Affairs Sec. to Chair. of Supreme Council for Nat. Reconstruction 1961–62; Dir. Personnel Admin. Bureau, Korean CIA 1963; Exec. Officer 1st Airborne Special Forces Group 1966–67; Commdr. 30th Bn., Capital Garrison Command 1967–69; Sr. Aide to Chief of Staff 1969–70; Commdr. 29th Regt., 9th Infantry Div. (Viet Nam) 1970–71; Commdr. 1st Airborne Special Forces Group 1971; Asst. Dir. Presidential Security Office 1976; Commanding Gen. 1st Infantry Div. 1978; Commdr. Defence Security Command 1979–80; Acting Dir. Korean CIA April–June 1980; Chair. Standing Cttee. Special Cttee. for Nat. Security Measures June 1980; promoted to full Gen. Aug. 1980; retd. from army Aug. 1980; Pres. Repub. of Korea 1980–88; Pres. Democratic Justice Party 1981–87, Hon. Pres. 1987–88; in rural exile 1988–90; returned to Seoul Dec. 1990; numerous decorations; arrested and charged with orchestrating 1979 mil. coup, Dec. 1994; on hunger strike Dec. 1994–Jan. 1995; indicted on charges of taking bribes Jan. 1996; found guilty of mutiny and treason and sentenced to death Aug. 1996; sentence commuted to life imprisonment Dec. 1996. *Leisure interest:* tennis.

CHUNDER, Pratap Chandra, M.A., LL.B., PH.D.; Indian politician and lawyer; b. 1 Sept. 1919, Calcutta; s. of Nirmal and Suhasini Chunder; m. Leena Roy Chowdhury 1940; four s.; ed. Univ. of Calcutta; law practice in Calcutta since 1945; mem. Senate and Law Faculty of Calcutta Univ. 1961–68; mem. Exec. Council of Rabindra Bharati Univ. 1962–68; mem. West Bengal Legislative Ass. 1962–68; Pres. West Bengal Provincial Congress Cttee. 1967–69; Minister of Finance and Judiciary in State Govt. 1968; mem. Working Cttee. and Cen. Parl. Bd. of Org. Congress 1969–76; mem. Janata Party 1977–; mem. Lok Sabha from Calcutta North East March 1977–79; Union Minister of Education, Social Welfare and Culture 1977–79; mem. Calcutta Bar Asscn.; Pres. Int. Educ. Conf. UNESCO 1977–79, Indo-American Soc. 1984–92, 1997–, Writers' Guild of India 1985–, Bengali Literary Conf. 1987–, All India Buddhist Mission 1989–, Iran Soc. 1990–92, Indian Inst. of Social Welfare and Business Man. 1991–, World Bengali Conf. 1991, Soc. for the Deaf 1991–94, Bharatiya Vidya Bhavan Calcutta Region 1993–, Inc. Law Soc. 1995–98; Patron Mahabodhi Soc. of India 1995–; fmr. editor several Bengali literary magazines; Trustee Victoria Memorial 1990–98, Sardar V.B. Patel Memorial Trust 1991–98; Regional Grand Master of Eastern India 1990–93, Deputy Grand Master 1993–94; Hon. D.Litt., Hon. D.Sc. and Fellow, Asiatic Soc. of Calcutta 1975; Best Playwright award, Calcutta Univ. 1965; Bhalotia Prize for Best Novel 1991; Indira Gandhi Memorial Prize for Educ. 1992. *Works:* four one-man exhbns. of paintings in Calcutta and New Delhi 1982, 1984, 1985, 1987, including one on China. *Publications:* Kautilya on Love and Morals, The Sons of Mystery, Job Charnock and his Lady Fair, Socialist Legality and Indian Law, Brother Vivekananda, Facets of Freemasonry, Kautislya Arthasastra, By-ways of History, and several novels and plays. *Leisure interests:* reading, writing, painting. *Address:* 23 Nirmal Chunder Street, Calcutta 700012, India. *Telephone:* 268248.

CHUNG, (Raymond) Arthur; Guyanese judge; b. 10 Jan. 1918, Windsor Forest, West Coast, Demerara; s. of Joseph and Lucy Chung; m. Doreen Pamela Ng-See-Quan 1954; one s. one d.; ed. Modern High School, Georgetown and Middle Temple, London; land surveyor 1940; lived in England 1946–48; Asst. Legal Examiner, U.K. Inland Revenue Dept. 1947; returned to Guyana 1948; Magistrate 1954, Sr. Magistrate 1960; Registrar of Deeds of the Supreme Court 1961; Judge of the Supreme Court 1962–70; First Pres. of the Repub. of Guyana 1970–80.

CHUNG, Kyung-Wha; Korean violinist; b. 26 March 1948, Seoul; sister of Chung Myung-Whun (q.v.); m. Geoffrey Leggett 1984; two s.; ed. Juilliard School; studied under Ivan Galamian; started career in U.S.A.; winner of Leventritt Competition 1968; European debut 1970; has played under conductors such as Abbado, Barenboim, Davis, Dorati, Dutoit, Giulini, Haitink, Jochum, Kempe, Kondrashin, Leinsdorf, Levine, Maazel, Mehta, Muti, Previn, Rattle, Rozhdestvensky and Solti; has played with major orchestras including all London Orchestras, Chicago, Boston and Pittsburgh Symphony Orchestra, New York, Cleveland, Philadelphia, Berlin, Israel and Vienna Philharmonics, Orchestre de Paris; has toured world; recordings for EMI; played at Salzburg Festival with London Symphony Orchestra 1973, Vienna Festival 1981, 1984, Edinburgh Festival 1981, and at eightieth birthday concert of Sir William Walton March 1982. *Leisure interests:* arts, family. *Address:* c/o Harrison Parrott Ltd., 12 Penzance Place, London, W11 4PA, England.

CHUNG, Myung-Whun; Korean conductor and pianist; b. 22 Jan. 1953, Seoul; brother of Kyung-Wha Chung (q.v.); ed. Mannes Coll. of Music and Juilliard School, New York, U.S.A.; 2nd Prize, Tchaikovsky Competition, Moscow 1974; fmr. Asst. to Carlo Maria Giulini (q.v.), as Assoc. Conductor, Los Angeles Philharmonic; has conducted Berlin Philharmonic, Amsterdam Concertgebouw and the major orchestras of London and Paris, and the four main U.S. orchestras 1981–; Musical Dir. Radio Orchestra of Saarbrücken 1984–89; has conducted opera at Metropolitan, New York, Geneva, San Francisco and elsewhere 1986–; Guest Conductor, Teatro Comunale, Florence 1987–; Musical Dir. Opéra de la Bastille, Paris 1989–94; performs as pianist in trio with his sisters Kyung-Wha and Myung-Wha; Abbiati Prize (Italian critics). *Address:* c/o Opéra de la Bastille, 120 rue de Lyon, 75008 Paris, France.

CHUNG, Sir Sze-yuen, Kt., G.B.E., G.B.M., D.SC., D.ENG., PH.D., F.ENG., F.I.MECH.E., F.I.E.E., C.B.I.M., J.P.; Chinese business executive; b. 3 Nov. 1917; m. Nancy Cheung 1942 (died 1977); one s. two d.; ed Hong Kong and Sheffield Univs.; consulting eng. 1952–56; Gen. Man. Sonca Industries 1956–50, Man Dir. 1960–77, Chair. 1977–88; mem. Hong Kong Legis. Council 1965–74, Sr. Unofficial Member 1974–78; mem. Hong Kong Exec. Council 1972–80, Sr. Unofficial Member 1980–88; founding Chair. Hong Kong Polytechnic 1972–86, City Polytechnic of Hong Kong 1984–85, Hong Kong Univ. of Science and Tech. 1987–99, Hong Kong Hosp. Authority 1990–95; Adviser to the Govt. of Peoples' Repub. of China on Hong Kong Affairs 1992–97; f. and Pres. Hong Kong Acad. of Eng. Sciences 1994–97; mem. Chinese Govt.'s Preparatory Cttee. for the Est. of Hong Kong Special Admin. Region (HKSAR) 1996–97; Convenor HKSAR Exec. Council 1997–99; holder of many other public appts.; Order of the Sacred Treasure (Japan); Silver Jubilee Medal 1977; Hon. D.Sc. (Hong Kong) 1976 and other awards and distinctions. *Publications:* articles in professional journals. *Leisure interests:* swimming, hiking, badminton. *Address:* 128 Argyle Street, 10/F., Kowloon, Hong Kong Special Administrative Region (Office); House 25, Bella Vista, Silver Terrace Road, Clear Water Bay, Kowloon, Hong Kong Special Administrative Region, People's Republic of China (Home). *Telephone:* 2761 0281 (Office). *Fax:* 2760 7493.

CHUNG SHUI MING, B.SC., M.B.A.; Chinese government official; b. 23 Nov. 1951, Hong Kong; two c.; ed. Univ. of Hong Kong, Chinese Univ. of Hong Kong; now Chief Exec. Hong Kong Special Admin. Region Land Fund; fmr. Hong Kong Affairs Adviser to Chinese Govt.; Fellow Hong Kong Soc. of Accountants; mem. Exec. Council, Hong Kong Special Admin. Region July 1997–, Hong Kong Housing Soc. Exec. Cttee., Housing Authority Finance Cttee.; fmr. Chinese mem. Sino-British Land Comm. *Address:* Executive Council Secretariat, First Floor, Main Wing, Central Government Offices, Central, Hong Kong Special Administrative Region, People's Republic of China.

CHUNG WON SHIK; Korean politician; fmr. Minister of Educ.; Prime Minister of South Korea 1991–92; mem. Democratic Liberal Party (DLP). *Address:* c/o Office of the Prime Minister, 77 Sejong-no, Chongno-ku, Seoul, Republic of Korea.

CHURCHILL, Caryl, B.A.; British playwright; b. 3 Sept. 1938, London; d. of Robert Churchill and Jan Churchill; m. David Harter 1961; three s.; ed. Trafalgar School, Montreal, Canada, Lady Margaret Hall, Oxford Univ.; first play, Downstairs, performed at Nat. Union of Students Drama Festival 1958; numerous radio plays and several TV plays; *Stage plays include:* Having a Wonderful Time (Oxford Players, 1960), Owners (Royal Court, London) 1972, Objections to Sex and Violence (Royal Court) 1975, Vinegar Tom (Monstrous Regiment toured 1976), Light Shining in Buckinghamshire (performed by Joint Stock Co., Edin. Festival 1976, then Royal Court), Traps (Royal Court) 1977, Cloud Nine (Joint Stock Co., Royal Court) 1979, 1980, Lucille Lortel Theater, New York 1981–83), Top Girls (Royal Court) 1982, 1983, Public Theater, New York 1983, Fen (Joint Stock Co., Almeida Theatre, London 1983, Royal Court 1983, Public Theater, New York 1983), Softcops (R.S.C. 1984), A Mouthful of Birds (Joint Stock, Royal Court and tour 1986), Serious Money (Royal Court 1987, Wyndham Theatre 1987, Public Theater New York 1988), Icecream (Royal Court 1989, Public Theater New York 1990), Mad Forest (Cen. School of Drama, Nat. Theatre Bucharest, Royal Court 1990), Lives of the Great Poisoners (Second Stride Co. Riverside Studios, London and tour 1991), The Skriker (Nat. Theatre 1994), Thyestes (by Seneca, translation; Royal Court Theatre Upstairs 1994); Hotel (Second Stride Co., The Place) 1997, This Is A Chair (Royal Court) 1997, Blue Heart (Out of Joint, Royal Court) 1997. *Address:* c/o Casarotto Ramsay Ltd., National House, 60–66 Wardour Street, London W1V 3HP, England. *Telephone:* 0171-287 4450. *Fax:* 0171-734 9293.

CHURIKOVA, Inna Mikhailovna; actress; b. 5 Oct. 1945, Belibey, Bashkiria; d. of Mikhail Churikov and Yelizaveta Mantrova; m. Gleb Panfilov 1974; one s.; ed. Shchepkin Theatre School; with Moscow Youth Theatre 1965–68; with Lenin Komsomol Theatre (now Lenkom), Moscow 1973–; début in films 1961; small parts in films in 1960s; Lenin Komsomol Prize 1976; R.S.F.S.R. State Prize 1985; U.S.S.R. People's Artist 1985; Nika Prize 1993, Triumph Prize 1994, Kinotaur Festival Prize 1994, Kamaz Festival First Prize 1994. *Roles in:* No Ford Through Fire (Panfilov) 1968, The Beginning 1970, May I Speak? 1976, Valentina 1981, Vassa 1983, War-Novel 1984 (Berlin Film Festival Prize), Three Girls in Blue (theatre) 1985, The Theme 1986, Mother 1991, Adam's Rib 1991 (Critics' Prize), Sorry (theatre) 1992, Casanova's Mantle 1992, The Seagull (theatre) 1994, The Year of the Dog 1994, Sorry 1995, and many others. *Address:* Universitetsky prospekt 6, Korp. 4, Apt. 68, 117333 Moscow, Russia. *Telephone:* (095) 137-89-67.

CHURKIN, Vitaly Ivanovich, PH.D.; Russian diplomatist; b. 21 Feb. 1952; m.; one s. one d.; ed. Moscow State Inst. of Int. Relations; attaché, Translations Dept., Ministry of Foreign Affairs, Interpreter of U.S.S.R. del. to SALT II Negotiations 1974–79; Third Sec. U.S.A. Dept. of Ministry of Foreign Affairs 1979–82; Second Sec., First Sec., U.S.S.R. Embassy, Washington, D.C. 1982–87; expert, Int. Dept. of Cen. Cttee. CPSU 1987–89; Counsellor of Ministry of Foreign Affairs 1989–90; Dir. Information and Press Dept. 1990–92; rank of Amb. Extraordinary and Plenipotentiary 1990; Deputy Minister of Foreign Affairs of Russia 1992–94; Amb. to Belgium 1994–97, to Canada 1998–. *Leisure interest:* tennis. *Address:* Embassy of the Russian Federation, 285 Charlotte Street, Ottawa, Ont., K1N 8L5, Canada. *Telephone:* (613) 235-4371, 236-1413.

CHUTE, Robert Maurice, SC.D.; American professor of biology (retd.) and poet; b. 13 Feb. 1926, Bridgton, Maine; s. of James Cleveland and Elizabeth Davis Chute; m. Virginia Hinds 1946; one s. one d.; ed. Univ. of Maine, The Johns Hopkins Univ.; Instructor and Asst. Prof. Middlebury Coll. 1953–59; Asst. Prof. Northridge State Coll. 1959–61; Assoc. Prof. and Chair. of Biology, Lincoln Univ. 1961; Prof. and Chair. of Biology, then Dana Prof. of Biology, Bates Coll. 1962–93, now Emer.; Fellow A.A.A.S. *Publications:* Environmental Insight 1971; Introduction to Biology 1976, Barely Time to Study (free verse play) 1996; poetry: Quiet Thunder 1975, Uncle George Poems 1977, Voices Great and Small 1977, Thirteen Moons/Treize Lunes 1982, Samuel Sewell Sails for Home 1986, When Grandmother Decides to Die 1989, Woodshed on the Moon—Thoreau Poems, Barely Time to Study Jesus 1996, Androscoggin Too 1997, trans.: Thirteen Moons (into Micmac Maliseet—native American). *Leisure interests:* walking, reading, films. *Address:* 85 Echo Cove Lane, Poland Spring, ME 04274, U.S.A. *Telephone:* (207) 998-4338.

CHYNGYSHEV, Tursunbek; Kyrgyzstan politician and economist; b. 15 Oct. 1942, Naryn Dist; s. of Asanbek Chyngyshev and Saira Chyngysheva; m. Ludmila V. Chyngysheva 1968; one s. one d.; ed. Kyrgyz Univ., Acad.. of Social Sciences; functionary of CP of Kyrgyzstan, Head Div. of Econs., Cen. Cttee. of CP of Kirgizia; Mayor of Osh; participated in democratic movt. since late 1980s; State Sec. Kyrgyz S.S.R. 1991–92, mem. U.S.S.R. Cttee. on Operative Man. of Nat. Econ. Aug.–Dec. 1991; Prime Minister of Kyrgyzstan 1992–93, mem. Parl. Kyrgyz Repub; Gen. Man. HENFEN Ltd; Vice-Pres. Kyrgyz Nat. Oil Co. *Address:* 194 Moskovskaya Str., Bishkek 720101, Kyrgyzstan. *Telephone:* 218355. *Fax:* 218426.

CHYNOWETH, Alan Gerald, B.SC., PH.D., F.I.E.E.E., F.INST.P.; British physicist; b. 18 Nov. 1927, Harrow, Middx.; s. of James Charles Chynoweth and Marjorie Fairhurst; m. Betty Freda Edith Boyce 1950; two s.; ed. King's College, Univ. of London; Postdoctoral Fellow of Nat. Research Council of Canada, Chemistry Div., Ottawa 1950–52; mem. Tech. Staff, Bell Telephone Labs. 1953–60, Head, Crystal Electronics Dept. 1960–65, Asst. Dir. Metallurgical Research Lab. 1965–73, Dir. Materials Research Lab. 1973–76, Exec. Dir. Electronic and Photonic Devices Div. 1976–83, Vice-Pres., Applied Research, Bell Communications Research 1983–92; Survey Dir. of Nat. Acad. of Sciences Cttee. on Survey of Materials Science and Eng. 1971–73, Comm. on Mineral Resources and the Environment 1973–75; mem. of Nat. Materials Advisory Bd., Wash. 1975–79, NATO Special Programme Panel on Materials 1977–82, Consultant to NATO Advanced Study Inst. Panel 1982–89; mem. Materials Research Soc., Metallurgical Soc.; Alternate Dir. Microelectronics and Computer Tech. Corpn. 1985–92; Dir. Industrial Research Inst. 1990–92; Chair. Tech. Transfer Merit Program, N.J. Comm. on Science and Tech. 1992–; Consultant to EC Telecommunications Directorate 1995; Lecturer Electrochemical Soc. 1983; Co.-Ed. Optical Fiber Telecommunications 1979; Assoc. Ed. Solid State Comm. 1975–83; mem. visiting cttee., Cornell Univ. Materials Science Centre 1973–76, Natural Sciences Advisory Bd., Univ. of Pennsylvania 1988–92, Advisory Bd. Dept of Electrical Eng. and CS, Univ. of Calif., Berkeley 1987–, Advisory Bd., Dept. of Electrical Eng., Univ. of S. Calif. 1988–; mem. Office of Science and Tech. Policy Panel on High Performance Computing and Communications; Fellow American Physical Soc.; IEEE W. R. G. Baker Prize Award 1967, Frederik Philips Award 1992, APS George E. Pake Prize 1992, Eng. Leadership Recognition 1996. *Publications:* over 60 papers in professional journals on solid state physics, 11 patents on solid state devices, Nat. Acad. of Sciences reports: Materials and Man's Needs, Materials Conservation through Technology, Resource Recovery from Municipal Solid Wastes. *Leisure interests:* travel, boating. *Address:* 6 Londonderry Way, Summit, NJ 07901, U.S.A. (Home). *Telephone:* (908) 273-4581 (Home).

CIAMPI, Carlo Azeglio, LL.B.; Italian banker; b. 9 Dec. 1920, Livorno; s. of Pietro Ciampi and Marie Masino; m. Franca Pilla 1946; one s. one d.; ed. Scuola Normale Superiore di Pisa, Pisa Univ.; served in Italian Army 1941–44; with Banca d'Italia 1946, economist research dept. 1960–70, head research dept. 1970–73, Sec. Gen. 1973–76, Deputy Dir. Gen. 1976–78, Dir. Gen. 1978–79, Gov. 1979–93; Chair. Ufficio Italiano dei Cambi, 1979–; Prime Minister 1993–94; Minister of the Treasury and the Budget 1996–98; Chair. IMF Interim Cttee. 1998–; mem. Bd. of Govs. for Italy IBRD, IDA, IFC; mem. Cttee. of Govs. EEC; mem. Bd. of Dirs. Consiglio Nazionale delle Ricerche, BIS; mem. Istituto Adriano Olivetti di Studi per la Gestione dell'Economia e delle Aziende; Military Cross, Grand Officer, Order of Merit of the Italian Republic. *Address:* c/o International Monetary Fund, 700 19th Street, N.W., Washington, DC 20431, U.S.A.

CIEMNIEWSKI, Jerzy, LL.D.; Polish lawyer and politician; b. 2 August 1939, Warsaw; m.; one s.; ed. Warsaw Univ.; lecturer Warsaw Univ. 1962–68; scientific worker, State and Law Inst. of Polish Acad. of Sciences, Warsaw 1968–, lecturer 1972–; mem. Solidarity Independent Self-governing Trade Union 1980–; Assoc. Understanding Cttee. of Creative and Scientific Asscns. and Teachers' Solidarity, also scientific worker Social and Labour Study Centre attached to Nat. Comm. of Solidarity 1980–81; mem. Helsinki Cttee. in Poland 1983–; participant Round Table debates, mem. group for law and judicature reform, expert group for political reforms Feb.–April 1989; mem. State Election Comm. during election to the Sejm (Parl.) and Senate 1989; Under-Sec. of State in Office of the Council of Ministers, Sec. of Council of Ministers 1989–91; Deputy to Sejm 1991–98; judge Constitutional Tribunal 1998–; mem. Democratic Freedom Union 1990–94, Freedom Union 1994–; Awards of Gen. Sec. of Polish Acad. of Sciences 1974 and 1976. *Publications:* numerous scientific works, mainly on constitutional law, including Ustawa o systemie konstytucyjnym SFR Jugosławii 1976, Sejm Ustawodawczy RP (1947–1952) 1978 (co-author), Studia nad rządem 1985 (co-author), System delegacki na tle ewolucji ustroju politycznego SFR Jugosławii 1988. *Leisure interests:* family life, walking with dog, general history, painting. *Address:* Trybunał Konstytucyjny, al. J. Ch. Szucha 12A, 00-198 Warsaw, Poland. *Telephone:* (22) 6574501.

CIEŚLEWICZ, Roman; Polish graphic artist; b. 13 Jan. 1930, Lvov; m. 1st Alina Szapoeznikow; m. 2nd Chantal Petit; ed. Graphic Faculty of Acad. of Fine Arts, Kraków; graphic at Artistic Graphic Publrs., Warsaw 1956–63; artistic man. at Ty i Ja (monthly), Warsaw 1959–63; co-operation with many publrs. periodicals in Poland and France; graphic and artistic man. of Elle,

Paris 1964–69; graphic of Vogue, Paris 1965–66; Opus Internationale, Paris 1968–70; Onac Archives, Paris 1968–70; artistic man. of Madame Arnodin Foyolle Int. Agence 1969–72; Prof. Ecole Supérieure des Arts Décoratifs, Paris 1973–74; over 100 one-man exhbns.; numerous int. prizes and awards, Officier des Arts et des Lettres. *Leisure interest:* travelling. *Address:* 32 rue Victor Hugo, 92240 Malakoff, France. *Telephone:* 46 36 93 88.

ÇILLER, Tansu, PH.D.; Turkish politician; b. 1945, Istanbul; m.; two c.; ed. Robert Coll., Boğaziçi Univ., Univ. of Connecticut and Yale Univ.; Assoc. Prof. 1978, Prof. 1983; served on academic Bds. of various univs., mainly in Dept. of Econs. Boğaziçi Univ.; joined True Path Party (DYP) 1990, Leader 1993–; mem. Parl. 1991; Minister of State for the Economy 1991; Prime Minister 1993–96; Deputy Prime Minister and Minister of Foreign Affairs 1996–97. *Publications:* nine publs. on econs. *Address:* c/o True Path Party, Selanik Cod. 40, Kizilay, Ankara, Turkey. *Telephone:* (312) 4172241. *Fax:* (312) 4185657.

CILLIÉ, Petrus Johannes, B.SC.; South African journalist; b. 18 Jan. 1917, Stellenbosch; s. of late Prof. Gabriel Gideon Cillié and Maria Cillié (née Van Niekerk); m. Elizabeth Frederika Bester 1936; two d.; ed. Boys' High School, Stellenbosch, Stellenbosch Univ.; joined editorial staff Die Burger 1935, Chief Sub-Ed. 1938–44, Foreign Ed. 1944–45, Asst. Ed. 1945–54, Ed. 1954–77; Chair. Nasionale Pers Group (publishing house) 1977–92; Prof. of Journalism, Stellenbosch Univ. 1977–83; mem. Stellenbosch Univ. Council 1984–92; Hon. mem. S.A. Acad. of Science and Art; Hon. D.Litt. (Stellenbosch) 1975; Markus Viljoen Medal 1979; D.F. Malan Medal 1984; State Pres. Order for Meritorious Service (Gold) 1988; M. S. Louw Award (Afrikaans Business Inst.) 1992. *Publications:* several books of essays and political articles. *Leisure interests:* music, books. *Address:* Nasionale Pers, 40 Heerengracht, Cape Town 8001, South Africa (Office). *Telephone:* 244408 (Home).

CIMINO, Michael; American film writer and director; b. 1943, New York; screenplay writer for Silent Running 1972, Magnum Force 1973; screenplay writer and dir. Thunderbolt and Lightfoot 1974; producer, writer and dir. The Deer Hunter (Academy Award for Best Dir. 1979) 1978; writer and Dir. Heaven's Gate 1980, Prod. and Dir. Year of the Dragon 1985, Dir. The Sicilian 1987, The Last Temptation of Christ 1988, Desperate Hours 1990, The Sunchasers. *Address:* c/o Jeff Berg, ICM, 8942 Wilshire Blvd., Beverly Hills, CA 90211, U.S.A.

CIMOSZEWICZ, Włodzimierz, D.JUR.; Polish politician, lawyer and farmer; b. 13 Sept. 1950, Warsaw; m.; one s. one d.; ed. Warsaw Univ.; asst., sr. asst. in Int. Law Inst., Warsaw Univ. 1972–85; runs family farm 1985–; mem. PZPR 1971–90; deputy to Sejm (Parl.) 1989– (Vice-Chair. Cttee for Nat. and Ethnic Minorities, mem. Constitutional Cttee.); Deputy Chair. Council of Ministers and Minister of Justice and Attorney-Gen. 1993–95; Vice-Marshal (Speaker) of Sejm 1995–96; Prime Minister of Poland 1996–97; Chair. European Integration Cttee. 1996–97; Cand. Democratic Left Alliance (SLD) Pres. Election 1990. *Leisure interests:* reading, playing ping-pong, do-it-yourself. *Address:* Sejm RP, ul. Wiejska 4/6/8, 00-902 Warsaw, Poland. *Telephone:* (22) 694 25 00.

CINADER, Bernhard, O.C., PH.D., D.SC., F.R.S.C.; Canadian university professor; b. 30 March 1919, Vienna, Austria; s. of Leon and Adele (Schwarz) Cinader; one d.; ed. Univ. of London; Research Asst. Lister Inst. of Preventive Medicine, London 1945–46, Jenner Memorial Student 1946–48; Fellow of Immunochemistry, Western Reserve Univ., Cleveland, Ohio 1948–49; Beit Memorial Fellow, Lister Inst. 1949–53, Grantee of Agric. Research Council 1953–56; research work, Inst. Pasteur, Paris 1955; Prin. Scientific Officer, Inst. of Animal Physiology, Cambridge, and Hon. Lecturer, Univ. Coll., London 1956–58; Head, Subdiv. of Immunochemistry, Ont. Cancer Inst., and Assoc. Prof. Univ. of Toronto 1958–69; Prof., Dept. of Medical Cell Biology, Univ. of Toronto 1969, Dept. of Medical Genetics 1969, Dept. of Clinical Biochem. 1970, Dir. Inst. of Immunology 1971–80; mem. Gov. Council, Univ. of Toronto 1980–89, mem. Academic Board 1989–; Chair. 6th Int. Congress of Immunology, Toronto 1986; mem. numerous nat. and int. scientific orgs. and research review cttees., etc.; several honours and awards, including Médaille de la Soc. de Chimie Biologique, Paris 1954, Jubilee Medal 1977, Thomas W. Eadie Medal (Royal Soc. of Canada) 1982, Karl Landsteiner Congress Medal 1986; f. Hardi Cinader Prize (Univ. of Toronto) 1985; Bernhard Cinader Annual Lecture f. by Canadian Soc. of Immunology 1986, Commemorative Medal for 125th Anniversary of the Confed. of Canada 1992. *Publications:* 6 books and 310 scientific papers and reviews; Ed. series Receptors and Ligands in Intercellular Communication (8 vols) 1983–87, Intercellular and Intracellular Communication 1986–92. *Leisure interest:* Canadian native art. *Address:* Department of Immunology, University of Toronto, Medical Sciences Building, Toronto, Ont., M5S 1A8 (Office); 73 Langley Avenue, Toronto, Ont., M4K 1B4, Canada (Home). *Telephone:* (416) 978-6120; 463-3013 (Office); (416) 463-3013 (Home). *Fax:* (416) 978-1938.

CIOCCA, Pierluigi, D.IUR.; Italian banker; b. 17 Oct. 1941, Pescara; ed. Univ. of Rome, Fondazione Einaudi (Univ. of Turin) and Balliol Coll. Oxford; economist, Research Dept. Bank of Italy 1969–82; Asst. Cen. Man. Bank of Italy 1982–84; mem. Bd. Dirs. Italian Foreign Exchange Office 1984–95; Cen. Man. for Cen. Bank Operations, Bank of Italy 1985–88, Cen. Man. for Econ. Research 1988–95; Deputy Dir.-Gen. Bank of Italy 1995–; lecturer at univs. and research centres; mem. Soc. Italiana degli Economisti. *Publications:* books and articles on econs. and finance. *Address:* Banca d'Italia, Via Nazionale 91, 00184 Rome, Italy.

CIORBEA, Victor; Romanian politician and jurist; b. 26 Oct. 1954, Ponor Village; s. of Vasile Ciorbea and Eugenia Ciorbea; m. 1977; one d.; ed. Law School, Cluj-Napoca, Case Western Reserve Univ., Cleveland, Ohio, U.S.A.; Judge Court of Bucharest 1979–84; Prosecutor, Dept. Civil Cases, Gen. Prosecutor's Office 1984–87; Asst. to Lecturer Law School, Bucharest 1987–90; Pres. Free Trade Unions Fed. in Educ. 1990–96, CNSLR 1990–93, CNSLR-FRĂTIA 1993–94, Democratic Union Confed., Romania 1994–96; Prime Minister of Romania 1996–98; mem. Exec. Bd. ICFTU, ETUC, CES 1993–94; rep. of Romania at OIM confs; Vice-Pres. PNTCD; Mayor Bucharest 1996–98; mem. Bd. Alianta Civica 1996. *Address:* Bld. I.C. Bratianu Nr. 20, BL; 1848, Sc; ET; 4, AP; 12, Secteur; 3, Bucharest, Romania. *Telephone:* (01) 315 3862. *Fax:* (01) 315 3862.

CIOSEK, Stanisław, M.A.; Polish politician; b. 2 May 1939, Pawłowice, Radom Prov.; s. of Józef and Janina Ciosek; m. Anna Ciosek 1969; two d.; ed. Higher School of Econs., Sopot; activist in youth orgs. 1957–75; Chair. Regional Council of Polish Students' Asscn. (ZSP), Gdańsk, Deputy Chair. and Chair. Chief Council, ZSP 1957–73; Chair. Chief Council of Fed. of Socialist Unions of Polish Youth (FSZMP) 1974–75; mem. PZPR 1959–90, deputy mem. PZPR Cen. Cttee. 1971–80, First Sec. Voivodship Cttee. PZPR and Chair. Presidium of Voivodship Nat. Council, Jelenia Góra 1975–80, mem. PZPR Cen. Cttee. 1980–81, 1986–90; Deputy to Sejm 1972–85; Minister for Co-operation with Trade Unions Nov. 1980–85, for Labour, Wages and Social Affairs March 1983–84, Vice-Chair. Cttee. of Council of Ministers for Co-operation with Trade Unions 1983–85; Sec. Socio-Political Cttee. of Council of Ministers 1981–85; Sec. PZPR Cen. Cttee. 1986–88; alt. mem. Political Bureau of PZPR Cen. Cttee. 1988–89; Sec.-Gen. Nat. Council of Patriotic Movt. for Rebirth (PRON) 1988–89; Co-organiser and participant Round Table debates 1989; Amb. to U.S.S.R. 1989–91, Amb. to Russia 1991–95; Kt.'s and Commdr.'s Cross, Order of Polonia Restituta.

CIRIANI, Henri Edouard: French architect and professor of architecture; b. 30 Dec. 1936, Lima, Peru; s. of Enrique Ciriani and Caridad Suito; m. Marcelle Espejo 1962; two d.; ed. Santa Maria School, Nat. Univ. of Eng. and Town Planning Inst., Lima; Asst. Architect Dept. of Architecture, Ministry of Devt. and Public Works, Lima, Project Architect 1961–64; Pvt. Practice with Crousse and Paez 1961–63; Asst. Prof. of Design, Nat. Univ. of Eng., Lima 1962–64; emigrates to France 1964; f. Pvt. Practice 1968; Prof. Ecole des Beaux-Arts de Paris 1969–83; Prof. of Architecture, Ecole d'Architecture de Paris-Belleville 1984; Dist. Prof. Univ. Nacional de Ingeniería, Lima 1985–; Visiting Prof. Tulane Univ., New Orleans 1984, Univ. Coll., Dublin 1985, Ecole d'Architecture de Grenoble 1988, Univ. of Pennsylvania 1989 and many others; Sir Banister Fletcher Visiting Lecturer, Univ. Coll., London 1986; lectures worldwide; Nat. Grand Prix of Architecture 1983, Equerre d'Argent 1983, Palme d'Or de l'Habitat 1988, Brunner Memorial Prize 1997, Chevalier, Légion d'honneur 1997. *Public works include:* public housing at Ventanilla Matute 1963, San Felipe 1964, Rimac Mirones 1965, Marne-la-vallée Noisy II 1980, Noisy III 1981, Saint Denis 1982, Evry 1985, Lognes 1986, Charcot 1991, Bercy 1994, Colombes 1995; urban landscape at Grenoble 1968–74; public facilities at St. Denis Child-care Centre 1983; Cen. kitchen for St. Antoine Hosp., Paris 1985; Torcy Child-care Centre 1989; Museum of the First World War, Péronne 1992; extension to Ministry of Finance bldg., Paris 1993; Arles Archaeological Museum 1995; pvt. bldgs. at The Hague Apartment Tower 1995; retrospective exhbns. at Institut Français d'Architecture, Paris 1984, Figueira da Foz, Oporto and Lisbon 1985, New York 1985, Tokyo 1987, Lima 1996, New York 1997, Montréal 1997. *Publications:* Pratique de la pièce urbaine 1996, Paroles d'architecte (ed. by Jean Petit Lugano) 1997. *Leisure interests:* drawing, collecting postcards. *Address:* 61 rue Pascal, 75013 Paris, France (Office).

CIRICI, Cristian; Spanish architect; b. 26 Sept. 1941, Barcelona; s. of Alexandre Cirici and Cármen Cirici; m. Anna Bricall; thee s.; ed. Higher Tech. School of Architecture of Barcelona; partner Studio PER 1965–; partner and mem. Man. Bd. B.D. Ediciónes de Diseño; Prof. of Projects Higher Tech. School of Architecture of Barcelona 1976–78; Visiting Prof. Washington Univ. St. Louis, U.S.A. 1981, New Mexico Univ., Albuquerque; Nat. Prize for Restoration 1979, FAD Prize for the Best Decoration Work of Barcelona 1965, 1970, 1972; Prize for the Best Restoration 1979, Delta de Oro ADI-FAD 1976. *Major Works:* flats, Tokio St. Barcelona 1972, Casa Frances, Minorca 1977, restoration of Casa Thomas 1979, Casa Diaz-Morera 1981, industrial and commercial bldgs. in Tunel del Cadi area 1983, reconstruction of Mies Van der Rohe Pavilion, Barcelona 1987, extension of Zoological Museum of Barcelona 1989. *Publication:* Miró Otro (jtly.) 1968.

CIRKER, Hayward, B.S.; American book publisher; b. 1 June 1917, New York; s. of Sol Cirker and Sadie Goodman Cirker; m. Blanche Brodsky 1939; one s. one d.; ed. City Coll., New York; Founder, Owner and Pres. Dover Publs. Inc. 1943–. *Address:* Dover Publications Inc., 31 East 2nd Street, Mineola, NY 11501 (Office); 199 Woodside Drive, Hewlett, New York, NY 11557, U.S.A. *Telephone:* (516) 294-7000. *Fax:* (516) 742-5049.

CIRY, Michel; French painter, etcher and graphic artist; b. 31 Aug. 1919, La Baule; s. of Georges Ciry and Simone (née Breune) Ciry; ed. Ecole des Arts Appliqués, Paris; studied music with Nadia Boulanger; religious and secular paintings and etchings; painter 1951–; Prof. School of Fine Arts Fontainebleau 1957–58, Académie Julian 1960; fmr. mem. Conseil Supérieur de l'Enseignement des Beaux-Arts; Vice-Pres. Comité National de la Gravure 1957–; numerous exhbns. in Europe and America including Paris, London,

New York, Boston, Amsterdam, Rome and Berlin; works in Museums of Europe and America; has illustrated numerous books including books by Montherlant, Green, Claudel and Mauriac; mem. Acad. des Beaux-Arts, Florence 1964–, Belgian Acad. 1988; Prix National des Arts 1945, Grande médaille de vermeil de la Ville de Paris 1962, Prix de l'Ile de France 1964, Prix Eugène Carrière 1964, Lauréate Acad. des Beaux-Arts 1968; Prix Wildenstein 1968; Lauréat du Grand Prix Georges Baudry 1984; Officier, Légion d'honneur, Chevalier des Arts et des Lettres, Officier, Ordre Nat. du Mérite. *Major Works:* Chemin de croix 1960–64, Stabat Mater 1960, 1961, 1963, 1965, Fièvres 1965, Christ's Passion 1955, 1957, 1960, 1964, Marie-Madeleine 1961, 1963, 1965, Saint François 1950, 1954, 1959, 1960, 1964, 1965. *Compositions include:* six sacred symphonies for choir and orchestra, several chamber works. *Publications:* twenty-four vols. of autobiog., Brisons nos fers 1992. *Address:* La Bergerie, 76119 Varengeville-sur-Mer, Seine-Maritime, France.

CISNEROS, Henry G., PH.D.; American politician; b. 11 June 1947, San Antonio; m. Mary-Alice Perez; one s. two d.; ed. Texas A&M, Harvard and George Washington Univs.; fmr. Mayor of San Antonio, Tex. until 1988; f. Cisneros Asset Man. Co. 1988; fmr. mem. Bd. of Dirs. Fed. Reserve Bank of Dallas; Sec. Dept. of Housing and Urban Devt. 1993–97; Pres., C.E.O. Univision Communications Inc., L.A. 1997–. *Address:* Univision Communications Inc., 1999 Avenue of the Stars, Suite 6050, Los Angeles, CA 90067, U.S.A.

CIUHA, Jože; Slovenian artist and painter; b. 26 April 1924, Trbovlje; s. of Jože and Amalija Ciuha; m. Radmila Novak 1962; one s. one d.; ed. Acad. of Fine Arts, Ljubljana and Univ. of Rangoon, Burma (Buddhist art and philosophy); work includes painting on plexi-glass, print-making, murals, tapestry, scenography, illustrating and water colours; developed silk-screen technique; his extensive travels in Europe, Asia and S. America inspired deep interest in ancient cultures; over 100 one-man exhbns. in Europe and U.S.A.; more than 20 nat. and int. prizes. *Publications:* Petrified Smile, Conversations with Silence (based on sketchbooks from his S. American journey 1964–65), Travels to the Tenth Country (for children). *Leisure interest:* literature. *Address:* 61000 Ljubljana, Prešernova 12, Slovenia; and 4 Place de la Porte de Bagnolet, 75020 Paris, France. *Telephone:* 061/218 956 (Ljubljana) and 362 72 26 (Paris).

CIULEI, Liviu; Romanian actor, scenographer, theatre, film and opera director; b. 7 July 1923, Bucharest; ed. Bucharest Inst. of Architecture, Bucharest Conservatory of Music and Theatre; actor since 1945; stage dir. and scenographer since 1946; Dir. "Lucia Sturdza Bulandra" Theatre, Bucharest 1962–72, Hon. Dir. 1972–; Dir. Guthrie Theater, Minneapolis, Minn. 1980–84; freelance dir. and direction teacher Columbia Univ., New York; acted at Bulandra, Odeon and C. Nottara theatres in Bucharest, as Puck in A Midsummer Night's Dream, Protasov in The Children Of The Sun, Treplev in The Seagull, Dunois in St. Joan, Danton in Danton's Death; numerous roles in Romanian films 1951–75; *Plays directed include:* Night Asylum, Bucharest 1960, Munich 1976, Washington, D.C., Sydney 1977, Danton's Death, West Berlin 1967, Leonce and Lena, Bucharest 1970, Washington 1974, Vancouver 1976; Macbeth, Bucharest, Berlin 1968; As You Like It, Bucharest 1961, Gottingen 1968, Minneapolis 1982; The Tempest, Bucharest 1979, Minneapolis 1984; Richard II, Düsseldorf 1969; Hamlet, Washington 1978, New York 1987; A Midsummer Night's Dream, New York 1988; The Threepenny Opera, Bucharest 1964, Minneapolis 1986; Volpone, Berlin 1970; Macbeth, Munich 1973; Six Characters in Search of an Author, Washington 1988; Long Day's Journey into Night, Bucharest 1976; Bacchantes, Minneapolis 1988; Requiem for a Nun, Minneapolis 1984, etc. *Operas directed include:* Lady Macbeth of Mtsensk, The Gambler, Così fan tutte, Wozzeck, Falstaff, at Spoleto, Chicago, Washington, Cardiff, Amsterdam etc.; designer Prince Igor, Covent Garden, London 1990; numerous tours abroad with Romanian productions, including Budapest 1960, Leningrad and Moscow 1966, Florence 1969, 1970, Regensburg Frankfurt/Main, Essen 1970, Edinburgh Festival 1971, The Hague, Amsterdam 1972, etc.; State Prize 1962 for films; Grand Prize at the Int. Festival of Karlovy Vary 1960, for the film Valurile Dunării (The Waves of the Danube) as Dir. and interpreter; prize for the best direction at the Int. Festival at Cannes 1965, for the film Pădurea Spînzuraţilor (The Forest of the Hanged) as Dir. and interpreter. *Address:* Teatrul Bulandra, Str. Schitu Măgureanu Nr. 1, Bucharest, Romania; 400 West 119th Street, Apt. 12-0, New York, NY 10027, U.S.A. *Telephone:* 14.96.96 (Bucharest).

CIVILETTI, Benjamin R., LL.B.; American lawyer; b. 17 July 1935, Peekskill, N.Y.; s. of Benjamin C. Civiletti and Virginia I. Civiletti; m. Gaile Lundgren 1958; two s. one d.; ed. Johns Hopkins Univ., Baltimore, Md., Columbia Univ., New York, Univ. of Maryland; admitted Md. Bar 1961; law clerk to judge, U.S. District Court, Md. 1961–62; asst. U.S. attorney 1962–64; mem. firm, Venable, Baetjer & Howard 1964–77, 1981– (Chair. 1996–); Asst. Attorney-Gen., Criminal Div., U.S. Dept. of Justice 1977–79; Attorney-Gen. of U.S.A. 1979–81; Chair., Dir. Healthcorp Inc.; Dir. Beth. Steel Corpn., Wackenhut Corrections Corpn., MBNA America, MBNA International; Trustee Johns Hopkins Univ. Advisory Bd., Martindale-Lexus. *Leisure interests:* golf, gardening, antiques. *Address:* Venable, Baetjer & Howard, 1800 Merc Bank and Trust Building, 2 Hopkins Plaza, Baltimore, MD 21201; Venable, Baetjer & Howard, 1301 Pennsylvania Avenue, NW, Suite 1200, Washington, DC 20004, U.S.A. (Offices). *Telephone:* (410) 244-7600 (Baltimore), (202) 962-4843 (Washington). *Fax:* (410) 244-7742 (Baltimore), (202) 962-8300 (Washington).

CIXOUS, Hélène, D. ÈS L.; French professor of literature and author; b. 5 June 1937, Oran, Algeria; d. of Georges Cixous and Eve Klein; one s. one d.; ed. Lycée d'Alger, Lycée de Sceaux, Sorbonne; mem. staff. Univ. of Bordeaux 1962–65; asst. lecturer, Sorbonne 1965–67; lecturer, Univ. of Paris X (Nanterre) 1967–68; helped found Univ. of Paris VIII (Vincennes) 1968, Chair. and Prof. of Literature 1968–, founder and Dir. Centre d'Etudes Féminines 1974–; co-founder of journal Poétique 1969; Dr. h.c. (Queen's Univ., Kingston, Canada) 1991, (Edmonton, Canada) 1992, (York, U.K.) 1993, (Georgetown, Washington, DC, U.S.A.) 1995, (Northwestern, Chicago, U.S.A.) 1996; Prix Médicis 1969, Prix des critiques 1994 for best theatrical work of the year, Amb. of Star Awards, Pakistan 1997; Southern Cross of Brazil 1989, Légion d'honneur 1994, Officier Ordre Nat. du Mérite 1998. *Publications include:* Le Prénom de Dieu 1967, Dedans 1969, Le Troisième corps, Les Commencements 1970, Un vrai jardin 1971, Neutre 1972, Tombe, Portrait du Soleil 1973, Révolutions pour plus d'un Faust 1975, Souffles 1975, La 1976, Partie 1976, Angst 1977, Préparatifs de noces au-delà de l'abîme 1978, Vivre l'orange 1979, Anankè 1979, Illa 1980, With ou l'art de l'innocence 1981, Limonade tout était si infini 1982, Le Livre de Promethea 1983, Manne 1988, Jours de l'An 1990, L'Ange au secret 1991, Déluge 1992, Beethoven à jamais 1993, La fiancée juive 1995, Messie 1996; essays: L'exil de James Joyce 1969, Prénoms de personne 1974, La Jeune née 1975, La venue à l'écriture 1977, Entre l'écriture 1986, L'heure de Clarice Lispector 1989, Reading with Clarice Lispector 1990, Readings, the Poetics of Blanchot, Joyce, Kafka, Lispector, Tsvetaeva 1992, Three Steps on the Ladder of Writing 1993, Photos de racines 1994, Stigmata, Escaping Texts 1998; *theatre:* Portrait de Dora 1976, Le nom d'Oedipe 1978, La prise de l'école de Madhubaï 1984, L'Histoire terrible mais inachevée de Norodom Sihanouk, roi du Cambodge 1985, L'Indiade ou l'Inde de leurs rêves 1987, On ne part pas on ne revient pas 1991, Voile noire voile blanche 1994, L'Histoire qu'on ne connaîtra jamais 1994, La Ville Parjure ou le Réveil des Erinyes 1994. *Address:* c/o Myriam Diocaretz, Foreign Rights Agency, P.O. Box 10004, 1001 EA Amsterdam, The Netherlands; Editions des Femmes, 6 rue de Mézières, 75006 Paris, France. *Telephone:* (020) 6.20.39.55 (Agent). *Fax:* (020) 6.20.39.55.

CIZIK, Robert, B.S., M.B.A.; American business executive; b. 4 April 1931, Scranton, Pa.; s. of John and Anna Paraska Cizik; m. Jane Morin 1953; three s. two d.; ed. Univ. of Connecticut and Harvard Grad. School of Business Admin.; Accountant with Price, Waterhouse & Co. 1953–54, 1956; financial analyst, Exxon Co. 1958–61; joined Cooper Industries 1961, Dir. Cooper Industries 1971–96, Pres. 1973–92, C.E.O. 1975–95, Chair. Bd. 1983–96; Chair. Stanadyne Automotive 1998–; Dir. Air Products & Chemicals, Harris Corpn., Temple-Inland Inc.; Advisory Dir. Wingate Partners; Dir. American Industrial Partners 1996–98; Proprietor Cizik Interests, Houston 1996–; Hon. LL.D. (Kenyon Coll.) 1983 and other awards. *Address:* Cizik Interests, Chase Tower, 600 Travis Street, Suite 3628, Houston, TX 77002, U.S.A. *Telephone:* (713) 222-7300. *Fax:* (713) 222-7353.

CLAES, Willy; Belgian politician; b. 24 Nov. 1938, Hasselt; m. Suzanne Meynen 1965; one s. one d.; ed. Univ. Libre de Bruxelles; mem. Exec. Cttee., Belgian Socialist Party, Joint Pres. 1975–77; mem. Limbourg Council 1964; mem. Chamber of Deputies 1968–; Minister of Educ. (Flemish) 1972–73, of Econ. Affairs 1973–74, 1977–81, Deputy Prime Minister 1979–81, 1988–94, Minister of Econ. Affairs, Planning and Educ. (Flemish Sector) 1988–91, of Foreign Affairs 1991–94; Sec.-Gen. NATO 1994–95; Pres. European Socialist Party; given suspended three year prison sentence for corruption Dec. 1998. *Publications include:* Tussen droom en werkelijkheid 1979, La Chine et l'Europe 1980, Livre Blanc de l'Energie 1980, Elementen voor een nieuw energiebeleid 1980, De Derde Weg: beschouwingen over de Wereldcrisis 1987. *Address:* Berkenlaan 62, B3500 Hasselt, Belgium.

CLAIR, Louis Serge; Mauritian politician; b. 1 April 1940, Rodrigues; s. of Emmanuel Clair and Willida Clair; m. Danielle Limock 1984; two c.; studied philosophy, theology and social sciences in France and TV production in Australia; Dir. and Ed. L'Organisation (first local newspaper in island of Rodrigues) 1976–86; Leader Org. du Peuple de Rodrigues; mem. Legis. Ass. 1982–; Minister for Rodrigues and the Outer Islands 1982–89, for Rodrigues 1989–95. *Leisure interests:* sight-seeing, gardening. *Address:* Organisation du Peuple Rodriguais, Port Mathurin, Rodrigues, Mauritius.

CLANCY, H.E. Cardinal, Edward Bede, A.C.; Australian ecclesiastic; b. 13 Dec. 1923, Lithgow, N.S.W.; s. of John Bede Clancy and Ellen Lucy Clancy; ed. St. Columba's Coll., Springwood, N.S.W., St. Patrick's Coll, Manly, N.S.W., Pontifical Biblical Inst. and Propaganda Fide Univ., Rome; Auxiliary Bishop, Archdiocese of Sydney 1974–78; Archbishop, Archdiocese of Canberra and Goulburn 1979–83; Archbishop of Sydney 1983–. cr. Cardinal 1988, with the titular Church of St. Maria in Vallicella; Chancellor Australian Catholic Univ. 1992–. *Leisure interest:* golf. *Address:* Catholic Archdiocese of Sydney, Archdiocesan Chancery, 13th Floor, Polding House, 276 Pitt Street, Sydney, N.S.W. 2000, Australia. *Telephone:* (02) 9390 5100. *Fax:* (02) 9261 8312.

CLANCY, Tom; American author; b. 1947. *Publications:* The Hunt for Red October 1984, Red Storm Rising 1986, Patriot Games 1987, Cardinal of the Kremlin 1988, Clear and Present Danger 1989, The Sum of all Fears 1991, Without Remorse 1992, Submarine 1993, Debt of Honour 1994, Tom Clancy's

Op Centre (with Steve Pleczenik) 1994, Reality Check 1995, Games of Statel (with Steve Pieczenik) 1996, Tom Clancy's Op Centre II (with Steve Pieczenik) 1996, Executive Orders 1996, Into the Storm (with Fred Franks Jr.) 1997, Rainbow Six 1998, Carrier 1999. *Address:* c/o Putnam, 200 Madison Avenue, New York, NY 10016, U.S.A.

CLAPHAM, Sir Michael John Sinclair, K.B.E., M.A.; British business executive and printer; b. 17 Jan. 1912, Cambridge; s. of Sir John Clapham, C.B.E., and Lady Mary Margaret Clapham (née Green); m. Hon. Elisabeth Russell Rea (d. of 1st Baron Rea) 1935 (died 1994); three s. one d.; ed. King's Coll. Choir School, Cambridge, Marlborough Coll. and King's Coll., Cambridge; trained as printer 1933–35; joined Imperial Chemical Industries Ltd. (ICI) as Man. of Kynoch Press 1938; seconded to Tube Alloys Project (Atomic Energy) in Second World War; Dir. Metals Div., ICI (now IMI PLC) 1946–60, Chair. 1960–61, 1974–81; Dir. Main Bd. of ICI 1961–74, Deputy Chair. 1968–74; Dir. ICI of Australia and New Zealand Ltd. (renamed ICI Australia Ltd. 1971) 1961–74, Imperial Metal Industries Ltd. 1962–70, Chair. 1974–81; mem. Industrial Reorganization Corpn. April 1969–71; Chair. Council for Nat. Academic Awards 1971–77; Deputy Pres. CBI 1971–72, Pres. 1972–74, Vice-Pres. 1974–78; Dir. 1971–82 and Deputy Chair. Lloyds Bank 1974–80; Chair. BPM Holdings 1974–81; Dir. Grindlay's Bank 1975–84; Pres. Inst. of Printing 1980–82; Dir. Bell Group Int., fmrly. Associated Communications Corpn. PLC 1982–84; Dir. Stoll Moss Theatres Ltd. 1984–90, Heytesbury (U.K.) Ltd. 1988–90; mem. Court, Univ. of London 1969–86; Hon. D.Sc. (Aston) 1973, Hon. LL.D. (CNAA) 1977, (London) 1984. *Publications:* Printing in History of Technology, Vol. III 1957, Multinational Enterprises and Nation States 1975, Perishable Collections 1997. *Leisure interests:* sailing, swimming, cooking. *Address:* 26 Hill Street, London, W1X 7FU, England (Home). *Telephone:* 0171-499 1240 (Home).

CLAPTON, Eric, O.B.E.; British guitarist and songwriter; b. 30 March 1945, Ripley, Surrey; m. Patti Harrison (née Boyd) 1979 (divorced 1988); one s. (deceased) by Lori Delsanto; guitarist with groups: Roosters 1963, Yardbirds 1963–65, John Mayall's Bluesbreakers 1965–66, Cream 1966–68, Blind Faith 1969, Derek and the Dominoes 1970, Delaney and Bonnie 1970–72; solo performer 1972–; *recordings include:* Disraeli Gears 1967, Wheels of Fire 1968, Goodbye Cream 1969, Layla 1970, Blind Faith 1971, Concert for Bangladesh 1971, Eric Clapton's Rainbow Concert 1973, 461 Ocean Boulevard 1974, E.C. Was Here 1975, No Reason to Cry 1976, Slowhand 1977, Backless 1978, Just One Night 1980, Money and Cigarettes 1983, Behind the Sun 1985, August 1986, Journeyman 1989, 24 Nights 1992, Unplugged 1992; compositions include Presence of the Lord, Layla, Badge (with George Harrison); soundtrack recordings include: Tommy 1974, The Colour of Money, Lethal Weapon, Rush; appeared in film Tommy 1974; awarded six Grammys 1993; Grammy Award for best male pop vocalist 1997. *Address:* c/o Roger Forrester Management, 18 Harley House, Regents Park, London, NW1 5HE, England. *Telephone:* 0171-486 8056. *Fax:* 0171-487 5663.

CLARK, Rt. Hon. (Charles) Joseph, P.C., C.C.; Canadian politician; b. 5 June 1939, High River, Alberta; s. of Charles A. Clark and Grace R. Welch; m. Maureen Anne (née McTeer) 1973; one d.; ed. Univ. of Alberta, Dalhousie Univ.; began career as a journalist; Nat. Pres. Progressive Conservative Party of Canada (PC) Student Fed. 1963–65; First Vice-Pres. PCP Asscn. of Alberta 1966–67; Lecturer, Univ. of Alberta 1965–67; Special Asst. to Davie Fulton 1967; Exec. Asst. to PCP Leader Robert Stanfield (q.v.) 1967–70; M.P. for Rocky Mountain 1972–79, for Yellowhead 1979–93; Leader of PCP 1976–83; Prime Minister of Canada 1979–80; Sec. of State for External Affairs 1984–91, Minister responsible for Constitutional Affairs, Pres. of Queen's Privy Council 1991–93; UN Sec.-Gen.'s Special Rep. for Cyprus 1993–96; Pres. Joe Clark & Assocs.; Chair. CANOP Worldwide Corpn., SMG Canada, Canada-Korea Forum; mem. Bd. Bentall Corpn., Hughes Aircraft of Canada, Inuvaluit Energy Inc. and other resource companies, Nat. History Soc. (of Canada), Pacific Council on Int. Policy, North-South Inst.; mem. Council of Freely Elected Heads of Govt., Int. Council of the Asia Soc.; Hon. LL.D. (New Brunswick) 1976, (Calgary) 1984, (Alberta) 1985, (Univ. of King's Coll., Concordia Univ.) 1994; mem. Alberta Order of Excellence 1983, Hon. Chief Samson Cree Nation 1992. *Publication:* A Nation Too Good To Lose 1994. *Address:* c/o Joe Clark & Associates, 30th Floor, 237 4th Avenue, S.W., Calgary, Alberta, T2P 4X7, Canada. *Telephone:* (403) 268-6863. *Fax:* (403) 268-3100.

CLARK, Colin Whitcomb, PH.D., F.R.S., F.R.S.C.; Canadian mathematician; b. 18 June 1931, Vancouver; s. of George Savage Clark and Irene Clark (née Stewart); m. Janet Arlene Davidson 1955; one s. two d.; ed. Univs. of British Columbia and Washington; instructor Univ. of Calif. at Berkeley 1958–60; Asst. Prof., then Assoc. Prof., Prof. of Mathematics Univ. of British Columbia 1960–94, Emer. Prof. 1994–; Regents' Prof. Univ. of Calif. at Davis 1986; Visiting Prof. Cornell Univ. 1987, Princeton Univ. 1997. *Publications include:* Dynamic Modelling in Behavioral Ecology (with M. Mangel) 1988, Mathematical Bioeconomics 1990, Dynamic State Variable Models in Ecology (with M. Mangel) 1999. *Leisure interests:* natural history, hiking, gardening. *Address:* 9531 Finn Road, Richmond, B.C., V7A 2L3, Canada. *Fax:* (604) 822-6074.

CLARK, Rt. Hon. David George, P.C., PH.D.; British politician; b. 19 Oct. 1939; s. of George Clark and Janet Clark; m. Christine Kirkby 1970; one d.; ed. Univ. of Manchester, Univ. of Sheffield; fmr. forester, lab. asst. and student teacher; Pres. Univ. of Manchester Union 1963–64; trainee man., U.S.A. 1964; univ. lecturer 1965–70; M.P. for Colne Valley 1970–74, for S. Shields 1979–; Labour spokesman on Agric. and Food 1973–74, on Defence 1980–81, on Environment 1981–86, on Environmental Protection and Devt. 1986–87, on Food, Agric. and Rural Affairs 1987–92, on Defence, Disarmament and Arms Control 1992–97; Chancellor of Duchy of Lancaster 1997–98. *Publications:* The Industrial Manager 1966, Colne Valley: Radicalisation to Socialism 1981, Victor Grayson: Labour's Lost Leader 1985, We Do Not Want the Earth 1992. *Address:* House of Commons, London, SW1 0AA, England.

CLARK, Dick, M.A.; American politician; b. 14 Sept. 1928, Central City, Ia.; s. of Clarence and Bernice Clark; m. 1st Jean Gross 1954 (divorced 1976); one s. one d.; m. 2nd Julie Kennett 1977; one c.; ed. Lamont High School, Upper Iowa Univ. and Univ. of Iowa; U.S. Army, Germany, 1950–52; Teaching Asst., Univ. of Ia. 1956–59; Asst. Prof. of History and Political Science, Upper Ia. Univ. 1959–64, Pres. of Faculty 1962; Chair. Office of Emergency Planning in Ia., and Ia. Civil Defense Admin. 1963–64; Admin. Asst. to Congressman John C. Culver 1965–71; Senator from Iowa 1973–79; Dir. Congressional Programme, Aspen Inst., Washington 1980–; fmr. Amb.-at-large and U.S. Coordinator for Refugee Affairs; mem. Members of Congress for Peace Through Law, fmr. mem. Senate Agriculture and Foreign Relations Cttees., Special Cttee. on Aging, Rules Cttee., Democratic Steering Cttee.; mem. numerous Bds. and Advisory Councils; Nat. Oratorical and Debate Champion 1953, Sr. Fellow, Dir. Congressional Program, The Aspen Inst.; Hon. LL.D. (Upper Ia. Univ.) 1973; Hon. L.H.D. (Parsons Coll.) 1973, (Mount Mercy Coll., Drake Univ., Cornell Coll., Haverford Coll., St. Ambrose Coll.) 1977. *Leisure interests:* reading, music. *Address:* Aspen Institute, 1333 New Hampshire Avenue, N.W., Washington, DC 20036 (Office); 4424 Edmunds Street, N.W., Washington, DC 20007, U.S.A. (Home). *Telephone:* 202-736-5825. *Fax:* (202) 785 2737.

CLARK, Helen, P.C., M.A.; New Zealand politician; b. 26 Feb. 1950, Hamilton; m. Peter Davis; ed. Epsom Girls' Grammar School and Auckland Univ.; fmr. Lecturer, Dept. of Political Studies, Auckland Univ. 1973–81; M.P. for Mount Albert 1981–96, for Owairaka 1996–; Minister of Housing and Minister of Conservation 1987–89, of Health 1989–90, of Labour 1989–90; Deputy Prime Minister 1989–90; Deputy Leader of the Opposition 1990–93; Leader N.Z. Labour Party 1993–; Spokeswoman on Health and Labour 1990–93; mem. Labour Party 1971–. *Leisure interests:* tennis, film, theatre, classical music, opera, cross-country skiing. *Address:* Labour Party, 160–162 Willis Street, Wellington; Parliament House,Wellington, New Zealand. *Telephone:* (04) 471-9999. *Fax:* (04) 472-4268.

CLARK, Howard Charles, PH.D., F.R.S.C., F.C.I.C.; Canadian professor of chemistry and academic; b. 4 Sept. 1929, Auckland, N.Z.; s. of Eric Crago Clark; m. Isabel Joy Dickson-Clark 1954; two d.; ed. Takapuna Grammar School, Auckland, Univs. of Auckland, Cambridge; lecturer, Univ. of Auckland 1954–55; Fellow, Univ. of Cambridge 1955–57; Asst. Prof. then Prof., Univ. of British Columbia 1957–65; Assoc. Prof., Univ. of Western Ont. 1965–66; Prof. and Head of Chem., Univ. of Guelph 1967–76; Academic Vice-Pres. and Prof. of Chem. 1976–86; Pres., Vice-Chancellor Dalhousie Univ. 1986–95; Ed. Canadian Journal of Chemistry 1974–78; Chair. Int. Relations Cttee., Assoc. of Univs. and Colls. of Canada 1993–; Past Chair. Metro United Way Task Force; Co-Chair. NABST Oceans and Coasts Cttee. 1993–94; Dir. Corp. Higher Educ. Forum 1990–94; mem. Chem. Inst. of Canada (Pres. 1983–84), Asscn. of Atlantic Univs. 1986–, Asscn. of Univs. and Colls. of Canada 1986–, Nat. Advisory Bd. on Science and Tech. 1991–94, Commonwealth Standing Cttee. on Student Mobility and Higher Educ. Cooperation 1992–; Hon. D.Sc. (Univ. of Vic.) 1989, (Univ. of Guelph) 1993; Noranda Award of Chem. Inst. of Canada 1968. *Publications:* author or co-author of over 250 articles and chapters in professional journals. *Leisure interests:* tennis, swimming, gardening. *Address:* RR#1, Moffat, Ont., L0P 1J0, Canada.

CLARK, Ian D., D.PHIL., M.P.P.; Canadian government official and international civil servant; b. 15 April 1946, Antrim, U.K.; s. of Sidney Clark and Zella I. Stade; m. Marjorie Sweet 1968; ed. Univs. of British Columbia and Oxford and Harvard Univ.; Exec. Asst. to Minister of Urban Affairs 1972–74; Dir. then Dir.-Gen. Analysis and Liaison Br. Dept. of Regional Econ. Expansion 1974–79; Dir. then Deputy Sec. Ministry of State for Econ. Devt. 1979–82; Deputy Sec. Privy Council Office 1982–87; Deputy Minister, Dept. of Consumer and Corp. Affairs 1987–89; Sec. Treas. Bd. 1989–94, also Comptroller-Gen. of Canada 1993–94; Exec. Dir. IMF 1994–96; Partner KPMG 1996–98; Pres. Council of Ont. Univs. 1998–. *Address:* 44 Glenview Avenue, Toronto, Ont. M4R 1P6, Canada.

CLARK, Ian Robertson, C.B.E., LL.D., F.C.C.A., I.P.F.A.; British administrator; b. 18 Jan. 1939, Motherwell, Scotland; s. of Alexander and Annie Dundas (née Watson) Clark; m. Jean Scott Waddell Lang 1961; one s. one d.; ed. Dalziel High School, Motherwell; trained as certified accountant; in local govt. 1962–76, reached post of Chief Exec. Shetland Islands Council 1976; mem. Bd. British Nat. Oil Corpn. 1976–82; Jt. Man. Dir. Britoil PLC 1982–85; Chair. Sigma Resources 1986–87; Chair. and Man. Dir. Clark and Assocs. 1986–; Chair. Ventures Div., Costain PLC 1987–93, C & M (Hydraulics) Ltd. 1994–; mem Scottish Econ. Council 1978–87; mem. Glasgow Univ. Court 1980–87; Hon. LL.D. (Glasgow) 1979. *Publication:* Reservoir of Power 1980. *Leisure interests:* walking and music. *Address:* Highwood, Fir Drive, Hawley, Camberley, Surrey, GU17 9BU, England. *Telephone:* (01276) 32442.

CLARK, Sir John A., Kt.; British business executive; b. 14 Feb. 1926; s. of Sir Allen and Lady Jocelyn Clark (née Culverhouse); brother of Michael William Clark; m. 1st Deidre Waterhouse 1952 (dissolved 1962); one s. one d.; m. 2nd Olivia Pratt 1970; two s. one d.; ed. Harrow School and Cambridge Univ.; Royal Naval Volunteer Reserve, Second World War; fmrly. with Metropolitan Vickers and Ford Motor Co.; studied American electronics industry in U.S.A.; Asst. to Gen. Man., Plessey Int. Ltd. 1949; Dir. and Gen. Man. Plessey (Ireland) Ltd. and Wireless Telephone Co. Ltd. 1950; mem. Bd. of Dirs. Plessey Co. Ltd. 1953, Gen. Man. Components Group 1957, Man. Dir. and Chief Exec. 1962–70, Deputy Chair. 1967–70, Chair. and Chief Exec. 1970–90; Dir. ICL Ltd. 1968–79, Banque Nationale de Paris 1976–89; Pres. Telecommunication Engineering and Mfg. Asscn. 1964–66, 1972–74; Deputy Pres. Inst. of Works Mans.; Deputy Pres. Engineering Employers' Fed.; mem. Council and Pres.'s Cttee. of CBI Nat. Defence Industries Council; frmly. mem. Review Body on Top Salaries; Fellow Inst. of Man.; Chair. of Wavertree Technology Park Co.; Companion I.E.E.; Order of Henry the Navigator (Portugal) 1973. *Leisure interests:* shooting, swimming, riding, golf. *Address:* Redenham Park, Redenham, Nr. Andover, Hants., SP11 9AQ, England. *Telephone:* (01264) 772511. *Fax:* (01264) 772616.

CLARK, J(ohn) Desmond; C.B.E., F.B.A., F.S.A., SC.D., PH.D.; British anthropologist; b. 10 April 1916, London; s. of Thomas J. C. Clark and Catherine Wynne; m. Betty Cable Baume 1938; one s. one d.; ed. Monkton Combe School and Christ's Coll., Cambridge; Dir. Rhodes-Livingstone Museum, Livingstone, N. Rhodesia 1938–61; Prof. of Anthropology, Univ. of Calif. (Berkeley) 1961–86, Prof. Emer. 1986–, Faculty Research lecturer 1979; Mil. Service in E. Africa, Abyssinia, the Somalilands and Madagascar 1941–46; Founder mem. and Sec. N. Rhodesia Nat. Monuments Comm. 1948; Raymond Dart Lecturer, Univ. of the Witwatersrand, Johannesburg 1979; Fellow, American Acad. of Arts and Sciences 1965, Huxley Medallist, Royal Anthropological Inst., London 1972; Hon. Sc.D. (Univ. of Witwatersrand, Univ. of Cape Town) 1985; Sir Mortimer Wheeler Lecturer, British Acad. 1981; Foreign Assoc. N.A.S. 1986, mem. 1993–; Golden Mercury Int. Award 1982; Gold Medal, Soc. of Antiquaries 1985; Berkeley Citation, Univ. of Calif. 1986; Fellows' Medal, Calif. Acad. of Science 1987; Hon. Fellow Royal Soc. of S. Africa 1988; Sr. Fellow Inst. for the Study of Earth and Man, Southern Methodist Univ., Dallas 1988; Gold Medal, Archaeological Inst. of America 1989; Inaugural lecturer John Mulvaney Series Australian Nat. Univ., Canberra 1990, Distinguished Lecturer, American Anthropological Asscn. 1992, L. S. B. Leakey Foundation Prize 1996, Grahame Clark Medal, British Acad. *Publications:* The Stone Age Cultures of Northern Rhodesia 1950, The Prehistoric Cultures of the Horn of Africa 1954, The Prehistory of Southern Africa 1959, Prehistoric Cultures of Northeast Angola and their Significance in Tropical Africa 1963, Atlas of African Prehistory 1967, Kalambo Falls Prehistoric Site Vol. I 1969, Vol. II 1974, The Prehistory of Africa 1970, Ed. of and contrib. to Vol. I Cambridge History of Africa 1982, Ed. with G. R. Sharma of Palaeoenvironment and Prehistory in the Middle Son Valley, Madhya Pradesh, North Cen. India 1983, Ed. with S. A. Brandt and contrib. to From Hunters to Farmers: The Causes and Consequences of Food Production in Africa 1984; author or co-author of more than 300 papers in learned journals. *Leisure interests:* walking, photography, wood-cutting. *Address:* Department of Anthropology, University of California, Berkeley, CA 94720; 1941 Yosemite Road, Berkeley, CA 94707-1361, U.S.A. (Home). *Telephone:* (510) 642-2533 (Office).

CLARK, Johnson (John) Pepper, B.A.; Nigerian poet, dramatist and professor of English; b. 3 April 1935, Kiagbodo; s. of Fuludu Bekederemo Clark; m. Ebunoluwa Bolajoko Odutola; one s. three d.; ed. Govt. Coll. Ughelli, Univ. Coll. Ibadan, Princeton Univ.; Ed. The Horn (Ibadan) 1958; head of features, editorial writer Express Group of Newspapers, Lagos 1961–62; Research Fellow Inst. of African Studies, Univ. of Lagos 1963–64, lecturer Dept. of English 1965–69, sr. lecturer 1969–72, Prof. of English 1972–80; consultant UNESCO 1965–67; Ed. Black Orpheus (journal) 1965–78; Visiting Distinguished Fellow Center for Humanities, Wesleyan Univ., Conn. 1975–76; Visiting Research Prof. Inst. of African Studies, Univ. of Ibadan 1979–80; Distinguished Visiting Prof. of English, Writer in Residence Lincoln Univ., Pa. 1989 Visiting Prof. of English Yale Univ., Conn. 1990; Trustee, mem. Petroleum (Special) Trust Fund and Man. Bd., Abuja 1995–; mem. Nat. Council of Laureates (Nigeria) 1992; Nigerian Nat. Merit Award, Nigerian Nat. Order of Merit; Foundation Fellow Nigerian Acad. of Letters 1996. *Poetry published includes:* Poems 1962, A Reed in the Tide 1965, Casualties 1970, A Decade of Tongues 1981, State of the Union 1985, Mandela and Other Poems 1988, A Lot From Paradise 1997. *Drama includes:* Song of a Goat 1961, Three Plays 1964, Ozidi 1968, The Bikoroa Plays 1985, The Wives' Revolt. *Other publications:* America, Their America 1964, The Example of Shakespeare 1970, Transcription and Translation from the Oral Tradition of the Izon of the Niger Delta; The Ozidi Saga (trans.) 1977, The Hero as a Villain 1978. *Leisure interests include:* walking, swimming, collecting classical European and traditional African music. *Address:* G.P.O. Box 1668, Marina, Lagos; 23 Oduduwa Crescent, GRA., Ikeja, Lagos; Okemeji Place, Funama, Kiagbodo, Burutu Local Government Area, Delta State, Nigeria. *Telephone:* 01-497-8436 (Lagos). *Fax:* 01-497-8463 (Lagos).

CLARK, Jonathan Charles Douglas, PH.D.; British historian; b. 28 Feb. 1951; s. of Ronald James Clark and Dorothy Margaret Clark; m. Katherine Redwood Penovich 1996; ed. Cambridge Univ.; Research Fellow, Peterhouse, Cambridge 1977–81; Research Fellowship, The Leverhulme Trust; Fellow All Souls Coll., Oxford 1986–95, Sr. Research Fellow 1995; Joyce and Elizabeth Hall Distinguished Prof. of British History, Univ. of Kan., U.S.A. 1995–; Visiting Prof. Cttee. on Social Thought, Univ. of Chicago 1993. *Publications:* The Dynamics of Change 1982, English Society 1688–1832 1985, Revolution and Rebellion 1986; The Memoirs and Speeches of James, 2nd Earl Waldegrave (Ed.) 1988, Ideas and Politics in Modern Britain (Ed.) 1990, The Language of Liberty 1993, Samuel Johnson 1994; articles on British and American history. *Leisure interest:* history. *Address:* Hall Center for the Humanities, University of Kansas, Lawrence, KS 66045, U.S.A. *Telephone:* (785) 864-4798. *Fax:* (785) 864-3884.

CLARK, Rt. Hon. Joseph (see Clark, Rt. Hon. Charles Joseph).

CLARK, Kenneth Bancroft, PH.D.; American professor of psychology; b. 24 July 1914, Canal Zone, Panama; s. of Arthur Bancroft Clark and Miriam Hanson Clark; m. Mamie Phipps 1938 (died 1983); one s. one d.; ed. Howard Univ., Washington, D.C. and Columbia Univ., New York; Prof., Psychology Dept., City Coll., City Univ. of New York 1942–75, Prof. Emer. 1975–; Research Dir. Northside Center for Child Devt. 1946–; Founder and Dir. Harlem Youth Opportunity Unlimited, Inc. (HARYOU), New York 1964–66; Founder and Dir. Metropolitan Applied Research Center (MARC), New York 1967–75; Founder and Pres. Clark, Phipps, Clark & Harris, Inc., New York 1975–86; Pres. Kenneth B. Clark and Assocs., Inc., Hastings-on-Hudson, N.Y. 1986–; Springarn Medal 1961, Sidney Hillman Prize Book Award 1965, Kurt Lewin Award 1966, Coll. Bd. Medal of Distinguished Service to Educ. 1980; Franklin Delano Roosevelt Four Freedoms Award 1985, Nat. Medal for Liberty 1986. *Publications:* Prejudice and Your Child 1955, Dark Ghetto 1965, A Possible Reality 1972, Pathos of Power 1974, A Relevant War Against Poverty (with Jeannette Hopkins) 1968, The Negro American (Co-Ed. with Talcott Parsons) 1966, How Relevant is Education in America Today? 1970. *Leisure interests:* writing and art. *Address:* Kenneth B. Clark & Assoc., Inc., 615 Broadway, Hastings-on-Hudson, NY 10706; 17 Pinecrest Drive, Hastings on Hudson, NY 10706, U.S.A. (Home). *Telephone:* (914) 478-1010.

CLARK, Ligia; Brazilian sculptress; b. 23 Oct. 1920, Belo Horizonte; d. of Jair and Ruth Pimentel Lins; m. Alnisio Clark Ribeiro 1938; one s. two d.; ed. Sacré Coeur de Marie, Belo Horizonte, Minas Gerais, and in Paris under Fernand Léger, Dobrinsky and Arpad Szénes; Co-founder Brazilian Neo-concrete Group 1959; first exhbn. of transformable sculptures Bichos 1960; took part in Biennale 1968, Sensorial Symposium of Art, Los Angeles 1970; lectured at Sorbonne, Paris 1970–75; Exhibitions in Paris, Rio de Janeiro, New York, São Paulo, Stuttgart and London; group exhbns. in France, Argentina, Germany, U.S.A., Italy, U.K., Israel, Czechoslovakia; numerous prizes and special exhbn., São Paulo Biennal 1963. *Address:* Avenida Prado Junior 16, Apdo. 801, Copacabana, Rio de Janeiro, RJ, Brazil.

CLARK, Mary Higgins, B.A.; American author and business executive; b. 24 Dec. 1931, New York; d. of Luke Higgins and Nora Durkin; m. Warren Clark 1949 (died 1964); two s. three d.; ed. Fordham Univ.; advertising asst. Remington Rand 1946; stewardess, Pan Am 1949–50; radio scriptwriter, producer Robert G. Jennings 1965–70; Vice-Pres., partner, Creative Dir., Producer Radio Programming, Aerial Communications, New York 1970–80; Chair. Bd., Creative Dir. D.J. Clark Enterprises, New York 1980–; mem. American Acad. of Arts and Sciences, Mystery Writers of America, Authors League; Grand Prix de Littérature Policière, France 1980; several hon. degrees. *Publications:* Aspire to the Heavens, A Biography of George Washington 1969, Where Are the Children? 1976, A Stranger is Watching 1978, The Cradle Will Fall 1980, A Cry in the Night 1982, Stillwatch 1984, Weep No More, My Lady 1987, While My Pretty One Sleeps 1989, The Anastasia Syndrome 1989, Loves Music, Loves to Dance 1991, All Around the Town 1992, I'll Be Seeing You 1993, Rembember Me 1994, The Lottery Winner 1994, Let Me Call You Sweetheart 1995, Silent Night 1996, Moonlight Becomes You 1996, My Gal Sunday 1996, Pretend You Don't See Her 1997, All Through the Night 1998. *Address:* 210 Central Park S., New York, NY 10019, U.S.A.

CLARK, Petula, C.B.E.; British singer and actress; b. (as Sally Olwen) 15 Nov. 1934, Epsom; d. of Leslie Norman and Doris Olwen; m. Claude Wolff 1961; one s. two d.; started career as child singer entertaining troops during Second World War; early appearances in films under contract to Rank Organization; made numerous recordings and television appearances in both England and France; success of single Downtown started career in the U.S.; *films:* Medal for the General 1944, Murder in Reverse 1945, London Town 1946, Strawberry Roan 1947, Here Come the Huggets, Vice Versa, Easy Money 1948, Don't Ever Leave Me 1949, Vote for Huggett 1949, The Huggetts Abroad, Dance Hall, The Romantic Age 1950, White Corridors, Madame Louise 1951, Made in Heaven 1952, The Card 1952, The Runaway Bus 1954, My Gay Dog 1954, The Happiness of Three Women 1955, Track the Man Down 1956, That Woman Opposite 1957, Daggers Drawn 1964, Finian's Rainbow 1968, Goodbye Mr. Chips 1969, Second Star to the Right 1980; *stage appearances:* Sound of Music 1981, Someone Like You (also wrote) 1989, Blood Brothers (Broadway) 1993, Sunset Boulevard 1995–96; nat. tour 1994–95, Sunset Boulevard 1995; has received two Grammy Awards and ten Gold Discs. *Address:* c/o John Ashby, P.O. Box 288, Woking, Surrey, GU22 0YN, England.

CLARK, Ramsey, B.A., A.M., J.D.; American lawyer and government official; b. 18 Dec. 1927, Dallas, Tex.; s. of Thomas Campbell Clark; m. Georgia Welch 1949; one s. one d.; ed. Univs. of Texas and Chicago; Marine Corps 1945–46; admitted to Texas Bar 1951, U.S. Supreme Court 1956, New York Bar 1970; practised law, Texas 1951–61, New York 1970–; Asst. Attorney-Gen., Dept. of Justice 1961–65, Deputy Attorney-Gen. 1965–67, Attorney-Gen. 1967–69; Adjunct Prof., Howard Univ. 1969–72, Brooklyn Law School 1973–81. *Publications:* Crime in America 1970, War Crimes: A report on U.S. War Crimes against Iraq 1992. *Address:* 36 East 12th Street, 6th Floor, New York, NY 10003 (Office); 37 West 12th Street, New York, NY 10011, U.S.A. (Home). *Telephone:* (212) 475-3232 (Office); (212) 989-6613 (Home).

CLARK, Sir Robert Anthony, Kt., D.S.C.; British business executive; b. 6 Jan. 1924, London; s. of John Anthony Clark and Gladys Clark (née Dyer); m. Marjorie Lewis 1949; two s. one d.; ed. Highgate School, King's Coll., Cambridge; served in Royal Navy 1942–46; qualified as lawyer with Messrs. Slaughter and May, became partner 1953; Dir. Hill Samuel Bank Ltd. (fmrly. Philip Hill, Higginson, Erlangers Ltd., then Hill Samuel and Co. Ltd.) 1962–91, Chair. 1974–87, Chief Exec. 1974–77, also Chief Exec. Hill Samuel Group 1976–80, Chair. 1980–87; Chair. IMI PLC 1980–89, Marley 1984–89, Vodafone Group PLC 1988–, Rauscher Pierce and Clark Int. (fmrly. Rauscher Pierce and Clark) 1992–; Dir. Mirror Group Newspapers (now called Mirror Group) 1991, Chair. 1992–98; Dir. Rover Group (fmrly. BL PLC) 1977–88, Bank of England 1976–85, Shell Transport and Trading Co. 1982–94, Alfred McAlpine PLC 1957–96, SmithKline Beecham PLC 1986–95; Chair. Review Bd. on Doctors' and Dentists' Remuneration 1979–86, Charing Cross and Westminster Medical School 1982–96. *Leisure interests:* music, reading, collecting antiquarian books. *Address:* Rauscher Pierce & Clark International, 56 Green Street, London, W1Y 3RH; Munstead Wood, Godalming, Surrey GU7 1UN, England (Home). *Telephone:* (01483) 417867 (Home).

CLARK, Robin Jon Hawes, PH.D., D.SC., F.R.S.A., F.R.S.C., F.R.S.; British university professor; b. 16 Feb. 1935, Rangiora, N.Z.; s. of Reginald Hawes Clark and Marjorie Alice Clark; m. Beatrice Rawdin Brown 1964; one s. one d.; ed. Marlborough Coll., Blenheim, Christ's Coll., Christchurch, N.Z., Canterbury Univ. Coll., Univ. of N.Z., Univ. of Otago, N.Z., Univ. Coll. London; asst. lecturer in Chemistry Univ. Coll. London 1962, lecturer 1963–71, Reader 1972–81, Prof. 1982–88, Sir William Ramsay Prof. and Head Dept. of Chemistry 1989–, Dean Faculty of Science 1988–89, mem. Council 1991–94, Fellow Univ. Coll. London 1992, mem. Senate and Acad. Council Univ. of London 1988–93; mem. Dalton Council Royal Soc. of Chem. 1985–88, Vice-Pres. 1988–90; mem. S.R.C. Inorganic Chem. Panel 1977–80, S.E.R.C. Post-Doctoral Fellowships Panel 1983, S.E.R.C. Inorganic Chem. Panel 1993–94; Chair. Steering Cttee. Int. Conferences on Raman Spectroscopy 1990–92, 11th Int. Conf. on Raman Spectroscopy, London 1988, Advisory Council, Ramsay Memorial Fellowships Trust 1989– (Trustee 1994–); mem. Council, Royal Soc. 1993–94, Royal Institution 1996– (Sec. 1998–); Tilden (1983), Nyholm (1989), Thomas Graham (1991) and Harry Hallam (1993) Lecturer and Medallist Royal Soc. of Chem.; Hon. Fellow Royal Soc. of N.Z. 1989; mem. Academia Europaea 1990, Fellow Royal Soc. 1990 (mem. Council 1993–94); Joannes Marcus Marci Medal (Czech Spectroscopy Soc.) 1998. *Publications:* The Chemistry of Titanium and Vanadium 1968, The Chemistry of Titanium, Zirconium and Hafnium (jtly) 1973, The Chemistry of Vanadium, Niobium and Tantalum (jtly) 1973, Advances in Spectroscopy (co-ed.) Vols. 1–26 1975–98, Raman Spectroscopy (co-ed.) 1988, about 400 scientific papers in learned journals on topics in transition metal chemistry and spectroscopy. *Leisure interests:* golf, swimming, cycling, long distance walking, travel, bridge, music, theatre, wine. *Address:* Christopher Ingold Laboratories, University College London, 20 Gordon Street, London, WC1H 0AJ, England. *Telephone:* 0171-387 7050. *Fax:* 0171-380 7463.

CLARK, Gen. Wesley; American army officer; ed. U.S. Mil. Acad., Univ. of Oxford (Rhodes Scholar); served in Vietnam, awarded silver and bronze stars; fmr. sr. mil. asst. to Gen. Alexander Haig (q.v.); fmr. Head Nat. Army Training Centre; fmr. Dir. of Strategy Dept. of Defense; sr. mem. American negotiating team at Bosnian peace negotiations, Dayton, OH 1995; fmr. head U.S. Southern Command, Panama; NATO Supreme Allied Commdr. in Europe (SACEUR) 1997–; Head U.S. Forces in Europe 1997–. *Address:* NATO, 1110 Brussels, Belgium. *Telephone:* (2) 707-41-11. *Fax:* (2) 707-41-17.

CLARK, William, Jr., B.A.; American diplomatist; b. 12 Oct. 1930, Oakland, Calif.; s. of William Clark and Mary Edith Coady; m. Judith Lee Riley 1954; one s.; ed. San Jose State Univ., Columbia Univ., Nat. War Coll.; Dir. Liaison Dept. U.S. Civil Admin., Naha, Japan 1970–72, U.S.-Japan Trade Officer Embassy, Tokyo, Japan 1972–74, Dir. Special Trade Activities Dept. of State, Washington, DC 1974–76, Political Counsellor Embassy, Seoul, Rep. of Korea 1977–80, Dir. Japanese Affairs, Dept. of State, Washington, DC 1980–81; Minister Embassy Tokyo, Japan 1981–85, Cairo, Egypt 1985–86; Chargé d'Affaires Embassy, Egypt 1986, Deputy Asst. Sec. of State, Washington, DC 1986–89; Amb. to India 1989–92; Asst. Sec. of State East Asian and Pacific Affairs, Dept of State 1992–93; Sr. Adviser Centre for Strategic and Int. Studies 1993–95, Pres. Japan Soc. 1996–; Sr. Advisor Center for Strategic and Int. Studies, Washington 1996–; Superior Service Award 1971, Outstanding Service Award 1972, Distinguished Service Award 1985, Meritorious Service Award 1987, Distinguished Honor Award 1989. *Leisure interests:* tennis, riding, skiing, golf. *Address:* 420 E. 54th Street, Apartment 5–J, New York, NY 10022, U.S.A.

CLARK, William P.; American government official and lawyer; b. 23 Oct. 1931, Oxnard, Calif.; s. of William Pettit and Bernice (née Gregory) Clark; m. Joan Brauner 1955; three s. two d.; ed. Stanford Univ., Law School, Loyola Univ., Los Angeles; admitted to Calif. Bar 1958; Sr. Partner Clark, Cole & Fairfield, Oxnard, Calif. 1958–66; Chief of Staff to Gov. Reagan, Sacramento 1966–69; Judge, Superior Court, San Luis Obispo County, Calif. 1969–71; Justice, Court of Appeals, Los Angeles 1971–73, Supreme Court of Calif., San Francisco 1973–81; Deputy Sec. of State, Washington, D.C. 1981; Asst. to the Pres. of the U.S.A. for Nat. Security Affairs 1982–83; Sec. of Interior 1983–85; Chair. Task Group on Nuclear Weapons Program Man. 1985; mem. Comm. on Integrated Long-Term Strategy 1987–88; Counsel, Rogers & Wells Law Firm 1985–96, McCann Fitzgerald, Dublin 1990–, Sinsheimer, Schiebelhut and Baggett, San Luis Obispo 1991–; Sr. Counsel Clark, Cali and Negranti; Bd. of Dirs. Lawter Int. 1985–, Pacific Telesis Group 1985–. *Address:* Clark Company, 1031 Pine Street, Paso Robles, CA 93446, U.S.A. *Telephone:* (805) 238-7110.

CLARKE, Aidan, PH.D.; Irish professor of modern history; b. 2 May 1933, Watford, England; s. of the late Austin Clarke and of Nora Walker; m. Mary Hughes 1962; two s. two d.; ed. The High School, Dublin and Trinity Coll., Dublin; lecturer in Modern History and Politics, Magee Univ. Coll., Derry 1959–65; lecturer in Modern History, Trinity Coll., Dublin 1965–78, Assoc. Prof. 1978–86, Erasmus Smith's Prof. 1986–, Sr. Tutor 1971–73, Registrar 1974–76, Bursar 1980–81, Vice-Provost 1981–87, 1989–91, Fellow 1970–; Chair. Irish Historical Soc. 1978–80; mem. Royal Irish Acad. 1982–, Sr. Vice-Pres. 1988–89, Sec. Cttee. of Polite Literature and Antiquities 1989–90, Pres. 1990–93. *Publications include:* The Old English in Ireland 1625–42 1966, contribs. to The New History of Ireland, 111: Early Modern Ireland 1976; numerous articles and essays on early modern Irish history. *Address:* Arts Building, Trinity College, Dublin 2 (Office); 160 Rathfarnham Road, Dublin 14, Ireland (Home). *Telephone:* 01 772941 (Office).

CLARKE, Sir Arthur C. (Charles), Kt., C.B.E., B.SC.; British science writer and underwater explorer; b. 16 Dec. 1917, Minehead, Somerset; s. of Charles W. Clarke and Nora M. Willis; m. Marilyn Mayfield 1953 (divorced 1964); ed. Huish's Grammar School, Taunton, and King's Coll., London; auditor H.M. Exchequer and Audit Dept. 1936–41; R.A.F. 1941–46; Inst. of Electrical Engineers 1949–50; Technical Officer on first G.C.A. radar 1943; originated communications satellites 1945; Chair. British Interplanetary Soc. 1947–50, 1953; Asst. Ed. Physics Abstracts 1949–50; engaged on underwater exploration on Great Barrier Reef of Australia and coast of Ceylon (Sri Lanka) 1954–; has lived in Sri Lanka since 1956; Chancellor, Univ. of Moratuwa, Sri Lanka, 1979–, Int. Space Univ. 1989–; Vikram Sarabhai Prof., Physical Research Lab., Ahmedabad 1980; extensive lecturing, radio and TV, U.K. and U.S.A.; UNESCO Kalinga Prize 1961; Fellow King's Coll. London, Royal Astronomical Soc.; mem. Royal Asiatic Soc., British Astronomical Asscn.; Science Fiction Writers of America, Astronomical Soc. of the Pacific; Hon. D.Sc. (Beaver Coll.) 1971, (Moratuwa) 1979, Hon. D.Litt. (Bath) 1988, (Liverpool) 1995, (Baptist Univ. of Hong Kong) 1996; numerous prizes and awards, including Stuart Ballantine Gold Medal, Franklin Inst. 1963; A.A.A.S.—Westinghouse Science Writing Prize 1969; A.I.A.A. Aerospace Communications Award 1974; Nebula Award 1973, 1974, 1979, John Campbell Award 1974, Hugo Award 1956, 1974, 1980, Galaxy Award 1979, IEEE Centennial Medal 1984, Marconi Int. Fellowship 1982, Vidya Jyothi Medal 1986, Science Fiction Writers of America 'Grand Master' 1986, Charles A. Lindbergh Award 1987, Assoc. Fellow, Third World Acad. of Sciences 1987, Freedom of Minehead, Somerset 1992, Von Karman Award (Int. Acad. of Astronautics) 1996. *Publications:* Non-fiction: Interplanetary Flight 1950, The Exploration of Space 1951, The Young Traveller in Space 1954 (publ. in U.S.A. as Going into Space), The Coast of Coral 1956, The Making of a Moon 1957, The Reefs of Taprobane 1957, Voice across the Sea 1958, The Challenge of the Spaceship 1960, The Challenge of the Sea 1960, Profiles of the Future 1962, Voices from the Sky 1965, The Promise of Space 1968, The View from Serendip 1977, 1984: Spring 1984, Ascent to Orbit 1984, Astounding Days: A Science Fictional Autobiography 1989, How the World Was One 1992, The Snows of Olympus 1994; with Mike Wilson: Boy Beneath the Sea 1958, The First Five Fathoms 1960, Indian Ocean Adventure 1961, The Treasure of the Great Reef 1964, Indian Ocean Treasure 1964; with R. A. Smith: The Exploration of the Moon 1954; with Editors of Life: Man and Space 1964; with the Apollo XI Astronauts: First on the Moon 1970; Report on Planet Three 1972; with Chesley Bonestell: Beyond Jupiter 1972; with Simon Welfare and John Fairley: Arthur C. Clarke's Mysterious World 1980 (also TV series), Arthur C. Clarke's World of Strange Powers 1984, Arthur C. Clarke's Chronicles of the Strange and Mysterious 1987, Arthur C. Clarke's A–Z of Mysteries 1993; with Peter Hyams: The Odyssey File 1984; Fiction: Prelude to Space 1951, The Sands of Mars 1951, Islands in the Sky 1952, Against the Fall of Night 1953, Childhood's End 1953, Expedition to Earth 1953, Earthlight 1955, Reach for Tomorrow 1956, The City and the Stars 1956, Tales from the White Hart 1957, The Deep Range 1957, The Other Side of the Sky 1958, Across the Sea of Stars 1959, A Fall of Moondust 1961, From the Oceans, From the Stars 1962, Tales of Ten Worlds 1962, Dolphin Island 1963, Glide Path 1963, Prelude to Mars 1965; with Stanley Kubrick: 2001: A Space Odyssey (novel and screenplay) 1968; The Lost Worlds of 2001 1971, Of Time and Stars 1972, The Wind from the Sun 1972, Rendezvous with Rama 1973, The Best of Arthur C. Clarke 1973, Imperial Earth 1975, The Fountains of Paradise 1979, 2010: Odyssey Two 1982, The Sentinel 1984, The Songs of Distant Earth 1986, 2061: Odyssey

Three 1988, Cradle (with Gentry Lee) 1988, Rama II (with Gentry Lee) 1989, Tales from Planet Earth 1990, The Ghost from the Grand Banks 1990, The Garden of Rama (with Gentry Lee) 1991, The Hammer of God 1993, Rama Revealed (with Gentry Lee) 1993, Richter 10 (with Mike McQuay), 3001: The Final Odyssey 1997, Trigger (with Mike Kube-McDowell) 1998, "Greetings, Carbon-Based Bipeds!" 1999. *Leisure interests:* photography, table tennis, diving. *Address:* 25 Barnes Place, Colombo 7, Sri Lanka; c/o 5-8 Lower John Street, Golden Square, London, W1R 4HA, England. *Telephone:* Colombo 699757. *Fax:* (94-1) 698730.

CLARKE, Brian, F.R.S.A.; British artist; b. 2 July 1953, Oldham, Lancs.; s. of late Edward Ord Clarke and of Lilian Clarke (née Whitehead); m. Elizabeth Cecilia Finch 1972; one s.; ed. Oldham School of Arts and Crafts, Burnley School of Art, The North Devon Coll. of Art and Design; *major exhbns. include:* Festival of City of London (with John Piper and Marc Chagall) 1979, Mappin Art Gallery, Sheffield 1980, R.I.B.A., London 1981, Robert Fraser Gallery, London 1983, Seibu Museum of Art, Tokyo 1987, Hessisches Landesmuseum 1988, Deutsches Architekturmuseum Frankfurt 1980, Galerie Karsten Greve, Cologne 1989, Indar Pasricha Gallery, New Delhi 1989, Mayor Gallery, London 1990, 1993, Sezon Museum of Art, Tokyo 1990, Ingolstadt, Germany 1992, Oldham Art Gallery 1993, Tony Shafrazi Gallery, New York 1995, (with Linda McCartney) Musée Suisse du Vitrail au Château de Romont, Switzerland; *major works:* St. Gabriel's Church, Blackburn 1976, All Saints Church, Habergham 1976, Queen's Medical Centre, Nottingham 1978, Laver's & Barraud Bldg., London 1981, Olympus Optical Europa GmbH HQ Bldg., Hamburg 1981, King Khaled Int. Airport, Riyadh, Saudi Arabia 1982, Buxton Thermal Baths, Derbyshire 1987, Lake Sagami Country Club, Yamanishi, Japan (in asscn. with Arata Isozaki) 1988, New Synagogue, Darmstadt, Germany 1988, Victoria Quarter, Leeds 1989, Cibreo Restaurant, Tokyo 1990, Glaxo Pharmaceuticals, Stockley Park, Uxbridge 1990, Stansted Airport, Essex (in asscn. with Sir Norman Foster) 1991, Spindles Shopping Centre, Oldham 1991–93, España Telefónica, Barcelona 1991, Number One America Square, London 1991, 35–38 Chancery Lane, London 1991, The Carmelite, London 1992, 100 New Bridge Street, London 1992, façade of Hôtel de Ville des Bouches-du-Rhône, Marseille (with Will Alsop) 1992–94, Glass Dune, Hamburg (with Future Systems) 1992, EAM Bldg., Kassel, Germany 1992–93, New Synagogue, Heidelberg, Germany 1993, W H Smith & Sons, Abingdon 1994, SMS Lowe The Grace Bldg., New York 1994, Cliveden Hotel 1994, Schadow Arkaden, Düsseldorf 1994, Norte Shopping, Rio de Janeiro 1995, Rye Hosp., Sussex (with Linda McCartney) 1995, Pfizer Pharmaceuticals, New York 1997, Willis Corroon Bldg., Ipswich 1997, RWE Essen (refurbishment of lobby) 1997, Offenbach Synagogue 1997, Praça Norte Clock Tower 1997, Obersalbach 1997, Chicago Sinai 1997; *stage designs:* for Paul McCartney World Tour 1990, 1993, The Ruins of Time (Dutch Nat. Ballet) 1993; *design:* Hammersmith Hosp., London 1993, Crossrail, Paddington, London 1994, Q206 Berlin 1994, Frankfurter Allee Plaza, Berlin 1994, New Synagogue, Aachen 1994, Hungerford Bridge, London (with Alsop and Störmer) 1996, Center Villa-Lobos, São Paulo 1997, Future Systems Tower NEC 1997, Heidelberg Cathedral 1997, Chep Lap Kok Airport, Hong Kong 1997; Visiting Prof. Architectural Art, Univ. Coll. London 1993; mem. Council Winston Churchill Memorial Trust 1985–; Trustee and mem. Cttee. Robert Fraser Foundation 1990–; Trustee The Stained Glass Museum; the subject of six books; judge, The BBC Design Awards 1990, Royal Fine Art Comm. and Sunday Times Architecture Award 1991; Europa Nostra award 1990, Leeds Award for Architecture, Special Award for Stained Glass 1990, The European Shopping Centre Award 1995, BDA Auszeichnung guter Bauten, Heidelberg 1996; Hon. F.R.I.B.A. 1993. *Leisure interests:* reading, hoarding. *Address:* The Tony Shafrazi Gallery, 119 Wooster Street, New York, NY 10012, U.S.A. *Telephone:* (212) 274-9300. *Fax:* (212) 334-9499.

CLARKE, Bryan Campbell, M.A., D.PHIL., F.R.S.; British professor of genetics; b. 24 June 1932, Gatley, Cheshire; s. of Robert Campbell and Gladys (née Carter) Clarke; m. Ann G. Jewkes 1960; one s. one d.; ed. Fay School, Southborough, Mass., Magdalen Coll. School, Oxford and Magdalen Coll., Oxford; Nature Conservancy research student, Oxford Univ. 1956–59; Asst. in Zoology, Univ. of Edinburgh 1959–63, Lecturer 1963–69, Reader 1969–71; Prof. of Genetics, Univ. of Nottingham 1971–93, Research Prof. 1993–97, Prof. Emer. 1997–; Science Research Council Sr. Research Fellow 1976–81; Ed. Heredity 1978–85, Proc. of the Royal Society, series B 1988–93; Vice-Pres. Genetical Soc. 1981–83, Linnean Soc. 1984–86, Soc. for the Study of Evolution 1990–91; Chair. Terrestrial Life Sciences Cttee. NERC 1984–87, Biological Sciences Panel, HEFCE 1994–96; mem. Biological Sciences Cttee., SERC 1990–93, Council of Royal Soc. 1994–96. *Publications:* Berber Village 1959, about 100 scientific publications. *Leisure interests:* painting, computing. *Address:* Linden Cottage, School Lane, Colston Bassett, Nottingham, NG12 3FD, England (Home). *Telephone:* (01949) 81243 (Home).

CLARKE, Sir Cyril Astley, K.B.E., M.D., SC.D., F.R.C.P., F.R.C.P.E., F.R.C.O.G., F.R.S., F.F.C.M., F.A.C.P., F.R.C.P.I., F.I.BIOL.; British professor of medicine; b. 22 Aug. 1907, Leicester; s. of Astley V. and Ethel Mary (née Gee) Clarke; m. Frieda M. M. (Féo) Hart 1935; three s.; ed. Oundle School, Caius Coll., Cambridge, and Guy's Hosp. Medical School; house physician, Guy's Hosp., London 1932–34, Demonstrator, Dept. of Pathology and Physiology 1934–35, Chief Clinical Asst., Dept. of Dermatology 1935–36; Life Insurance Work 1936–39; Medical Specialist, R.N. 1939–45; Medical Registrar, Queen Elizabeth Hosp., Birmingham 1946; Consultant Physician, United Liverpool Hosps. and Liverpool Regional Hosp. Bd. 1946–58, Hon. Consultant Physician 1958–72; Reader in Medicine, Univ. of Liverpool 1958, Dir. Nuffield Unit of Medical Genetics 1963–72, Prof. of Medicine 1965–72; Pres. Royal Coll. of Physicians 1972–77, Harveian Soc. of London 1977–78; Dir. Medical Service Study Group, Royal Coll. of Physicians 1977–83; Dir. Research Unit, Royal Coll. of Physicians 1983–88; Nuffield Research Fellow, Dept. of Genetics, Univ. of Liverpool 1972–; Hon. Research Fellow, Dept. of Geriatric Medicine 1987–; Chair. British Heart Foundation 1982–87, British Soc. for Research on Ageing 1987–92; Fellow, Linnean Soc.; Hon. mem. Liverpool Medical Inst.; Hon. Fellow, Caius Coll., Cambridge; Chair. of Council, Bedford Coll., London Univ. 1975–85; Pres. Royal Entomological Soc. of London 1991–92; Hon. D.Sc. (Edinburgh, Leicester, East Anglia, Birmingham, Liverpool, Sussex, Hull, Wales, London, Coll. of William & Mary, Williamsburg, U.S.A.); Hon. F.R.A.C.P.; Hon. F.R.C.P.Ed.; Hon. F.R.C.Path.; Hon. Fellow Guy's and St. Thomas's Medical & Dental School 1992; Hon. mem. British Blood Transfusion Soc. 1992; BMA Essay Prize 1932, Soc. of Apothecaries of London Gold Medal for Therapeutics 1970, James Spence Medal, 1973, Fothergillian Medal, Medical Soc. of London 1977, Gairdner Award 1977, Harveian Orator, Royal Coll. of Physicians 1979, Lasker Award New York 1980, Artois-Baillet Latour Health Prize 1981, Linnean Medal Zoology 1981, Nuffield Medal, Royal Soc. of Medicine 1984, First James Blundell Award, British Blood Transfusion Society 1984, Gold Medal, Royal Soc. of Medicine 1985–86, Buchanan Medal of the Royal Soc. 1990. *Publications:* Genetics for the Clinician 1962 (2nd edn. 1964), Selected Topics in Medical Genetics 1969 (Editor), Human Genetics and Medicine 1970, 1977, 1987, Rhesus Haemolytic Disease, Selected papers and extracts (Editor) 1975, papers in professional journals. *Leisure interests:* small boat sailing, breeding butterflies. *Address:* 43 Caldy Road, West Kirby, Wirral, Merseyside, L48 2HF, England. *Telephone:* (0151) 625 8811.

CLARKE, David Stuart, A.O., B.ECON., M.B.A.; Australian business executive; b. 3 Jan. 1942; s. of Stuart Clarke and Ailsie Clarke; m. 1st Margaret Partridge 1964 (divorced 1994); two s.; m. 2nd Jane Graves 1995; ed. Knox Grammar School and Sydney and Harvard Univs.; Dir. Darling & Co. Ltd. (now Schroder Australia Ltd.) 1968–71, Babcock Australia Holdings Ltd. 1972–81, Hooker Corpn. Ltd. 1984–86, Reil Corpn. Ltd. 1986–87; Jt. Man. Dir. Hill Samuel Australia Ltd. 1971–77, Man. Dir. 1977–84, Dir. Hill Samuel & Co. Ltd. (London) 1978–84; Chair. Accepting Houses Asscn. of Australia 1974–76, Sceggs Darlinghurst Ltd. 1976–79; Exec. Chair. Macquarie Bank Ltd. 1985–; Chair. Barlile Corpn. Ltd. 1986–93, N.S.W. Rugby Union 1989–95, Wine Cttee., Royal Agricultural Soc. of N.S.W. 1990–, Brian McGuigan Wines Ltd. 1991–, Australian Wool Realization Comm. 1991–93, Menzies Research Centre 1994–97, Goodman Fielder Ltd. 1995–, Campaign Chair. Salvation Army Educ. Foundation 1996–; Deputy Chair. Australian Opera 1982–86, Chair. 1986–95, Pres. Nat. Council 1996–; Dir. Australian Rugby Union 1990–, Deputy Chair. 1997–; mem. Council Royal Agric. Soc. of New South Wales 1986– (mem. Exec. Cttee. 1991–), Bd. of Trustees, Financial Markets Foundation for Children 1989–, Sydney Advisory Bd., The Salvation Army 1990–, Corp. Citizen's Cttee. Children's Cancer Inst. of Australia 1992–, Investment Advisory Cttee., Australian Olympic Foundation 1996–, Advisory Cttee., Harvard Business School Asia 1997–. *Leisure interests:* opera, skiing, tennis, golf, bridge, philately, personal computers, ballet, wine. *Address:* 5 Keltie Bay, 15 Sutherland Crescent, Darling Point, N.S.W. 2027, Australia.

CLARKE, Sir Ellis Emmanuel Innocent, G.C.M.G., LL.B.; Trinidadian government official, lawyer and diplomatist; b. 28 Dec. 1917, Port of Spain; s. of Cecil E. I. Clarke and Elma Pollard; m. Eyrmyntrude Hagley 1952; one s. one d.; ed. St. Mary's Coll., Port of Spain, Trinidad, London Univ. and Gray's Inn, London; private law practice, Trinidad 1941–54; Solicitor-Gen. Trinidad and Tobago 1954–56; Deputy Colonial Sec. 1956–57; Attorney-Gen. 1957–61; Constitutional Adviser to the Cabinet 1961–62; Amb. to the United States 1962–73, and to Mexico 1966–73; Perm. Rep. to UN 1962–66; Rep. on Council of OAS 1967–73; Chair. of Bd., British West Indian Airways 1968–73; Gov.-Gen. and C.-in-C. of Trinidad and Tobago 1973–76, Pres. 1976–87; Awarded first Trinity Cross (T.C.) 1969, K.St.J. 1973, Hon. Master of Bench, Gray's Inn 1980. *Leisure interests:* golf, racing, cricket. *Address:* 16 Frederick Street, Port of Spain, Trinidad and Tobago.

CLARKE, Geoffrey, R.A., A.R.C.A.; British artist and sculptor; b. 28 Nov. 1924; s. of John Moulding Clarke and Janet Petts; two s.; ed. R.C.A.; exhbns. at Gimpel Fils Gallery 1952, 1955, Redfern Gallery 1965, Tranman Gallery 1975, 1976, 1982, Royal Acad. 1994, Yorkshire Sculpture Park 1994, Chappel Gallery 1994; touring exhbns. at Christchurch Mansions, Ipswich 1994, Herbert Art Gallery, Coventry and Pallant House, Chichester 1995; commissioned work includes: iron sculpture, Time Life Building, New Bond Street, cast aluminium relief sculpture, Castrol House, Marylebone Road; mosaics, Liverpool Univ. Physics Block and Basildon New Town; stained glass windows for Treasury, Lincoln Cathedral; bronze sculpture, Thorn Electric Building, Upper St. Martin's Lane; relief sculpture on Canberra and Oriana; three stained glass windows, high altar, cross and candle-sticks, the flying cross and crown of thorns, all for Coventry Cathedral, screens in Royal Mil. Chapel, Birdcage Walk; other works at Newcastle Civic Centre, Churchill Coll., Aldershot, Suffolk Police HQ, All Souls, W. London, The Majlis, Abu Dhabi, York House, N. London. *Address:* Stowe Hill, Hartest, Bury St. Edmunds, Suffolk, IP29 4EQ, England. *Telephone:* (01284) 830319.

CLARKE, Graeme Wilber, M.A., LITT.D.; Australian professor of classics; b. 31 Oct. 1934, Nelson, New Zealand; s. of Wilber P. Clarke and Marjorie E. (née Le May) Clarke; m. Nancy J. Jordan 1963; three s. one d.; ed. Sacred Heart Coll., Auckland, N.Z., Univ. of Auckland, Balliol Coll., Oxford; lecturer, Dept. of Classics, Australian Nat. Univ. 1957, 1961–63, Sr. Lecturer, Dept. of Classics and Ancient History, Univ. of Western Australia 1964–66, Assoc. Prof., Dept. of Classical Studies, Monash Univ. 1967–68, Prof. Dept. of Classical Studies, Univ. of Melbourne 1969–81, Prof. Emer. 1981–; Deputy Dir. Humanities Research Centre, Australian Nat. Univ. 1982–90, Dir. 1991–, Prof. 1991–; Fellow Australian Acad. of the Humanities 1975, Soc. of Antiquaries, London 1989; dir. archaeological excavation in N. Syria at Jebel Khalid 1984–. *Publications:* The Octavius of Marcus Minucius Felix 1974, The Letters of St. Cyprian (4 vols.) 1984–88, Rediscovering Hellenism (ed.) 1988, Reading the Past in Late Antiquity (ed.) 1990, Identities in the Eastern Mediterranean in Antiquity (ed.) 1998. *Leisure interest:* gardening. *Address:* Humanities Research Centre, Australian National University, Canberra, A.C.T. 0200 (Office); 62 Wybalena Grove, Cook, A.C.T. 2614, Australia (Home). *Telephone:* 02-62492700 (Office); 02-6251456 (Home). *Fax:* (02) 62480054 (Office).

CLARKE, John, M.A., PH.D., F.R.S.; British professor of physics; b. 10 Feb. 1942, Cambridge; s. of Victor P. Clarke and Ethel M. Clarke; m. Grethe Fog Pedersen 1979; one d.; ed. Perse School, Cambridge and Univ. of Cambridge; Postdoctoral Scholar, Dept. of Physics, Univ. of Calif. Berkeley 1968–69, Asst. Prof. 1969–71, Assoc. Prof. 1971–73, Prof. 1973–; Luis W. Alvarez Memorial Chair. in Experimental Physics 1994–(99); Prin. Investigator, Lawrence Berkeley Lab., Berkeley 1969–; Visiting Fellow Clare Hall, Cambridge 1989; Fellow, A.A.A.S., American Physical Soc.; Alfred P. Sloan Foundation Fellowship 1970–72; Adolph C. and Mary Sprague Miller Research Professorship 1975–76, 1994–95; Guggenheim Fellowship 1977–78, Calif. Scientist of the Year 1987, Fritz London Memorial Award 1987, Joseph F. Keithley Award, American Physical Soc. 1998, Cornstock Prize in Physics, Nat. Acad. of Sciences 1999, and other honours and awards. *Publications:* approx. 300 publs. in learned journals. *Address:* Department of Physics, University of California, Berkeley, CA 94720, U.S.A. *Telephone:* (510) 642-3069. *Fax:* (510) 642-1304.

CLARKE, John Kevin Aloysius, D.SC., D.I.C., M.R.I.A.; British professor of chemistry; b. 30 April 1931, Belfast, N. Ireland; s. of Daniel Clarke and Brigid Mary Fallon; m. Margaret Mary Whelan 1965; two d.; ed. St. Malachy's Coll., Belfast, Queen's Univ., Belfast, Imperial Coll., London; Sr. Scientific Officer, U.K. Dept. of Scientific and Industrial Research 1959–61; mem. Faculty of Chemistry, Nat. Univ. of Ireland at Univ. Coll., Dublin 1961, Prof. in Heterogeneous Catalysis 1981, Prof. Emer. of Inorganic Chemistry (Heterogeneous Catalysis) 1996; Gas Referee to Irish Dept. of Transport and Power 1968–81; Vice-Pres. Royal Irish Acad. 1986–87. *Publications:* numerous papers and articles on catalytic chemistry, chemical eng. science, transport properties of gases, analytical chemistry related to medicine, chemical educ. *Leisure interests:* English literature, golf, music. *Address:* 22 Leopardstown Park, Blackrock, Co. Dublin, Ireland (Home). *Telephone:* Dublin 7062291 (Office); Dublin 2881213 (Home).

CLARKE, (John) Neil, LL.B., F.C.A.; British business executive; b. 7 Aug. 1934; s. of late George P. Clarke and Norah M. Bailey; m. Sonia H. Beckett 1958; three s.; ed. Rugby School and King's Coll. London; partner, Rowley, Pemberton, Roberts & Co. 1960–69; Charter Consolidated 1969–88, Deputy Chair. and Chief Exec. 1982–88; Dir. Anglo-American Corpn. of South Africa 1976–90, Consolidated Gold Fields 1982–89, Travis Perkins 1990–, Porvair 1994–96; Chair. Johnson Matthey 1984–90; Dir. Molins 1987–91, Chair. 1989–91; Chair. Genchem Holdings 1989–, British Coal 1991–97. *Leisure interests:* music, tennis, golf. *Address:* High Willows, 18 Park Avenue, Farnborough Park, Orpington, Kent, BR6 8LL, England.

CLARKE, Rt. Hon. Kenneth Harry, Q.C., M.P., B.A., LL.B.; British politician; b. 2 July 1940; s. of Kenneth Clarke and Doris Clarke (née Smith); m. Gillian Mary Edwards 1964; one s. one d.; ed. Nottingham High School and Gonville and Caius Coll., Cambridge; called to the Bar, Gray's Inn 1963; practising mem. Midland circuit 1963–79; Research Sec. Birmingham Bow Group 1965–66; contested Mansfield, Notts. in General Elections 1964, 1966, M.P. for Rushcliffe Div. of Notts. 1970–; Parl. Pvt. Sec. to Solicitor Gen. 1971–72; an Asst. Govt. Whip 1972–74, Govt. Whip for Europe 1973–74; Lord Commr., H.M. Treasury 1974; Opposition Spokesman on Social Services 1974–76, on Industry 1976–79; Parl. Sec., Dept. of Transport, later Parl. Under Sec. of State for Transport 1979–82; Minister of State (Minister for Health), Dept. of Health and Social Security 1982–85; Paymaster-Gen. and Minister for Employment 1985–87; Chancellor of Duchy of Lancaster and Minister for Trade and Industry 1987–88, Minister for the Inner Cities 1987–88; Sec. of State for Health 1988–90, for Educ. and Science 1990–92, for the Home Dept. 1992–93; Chancellor of the Exchequer 1993–97; mem. Parl. Del. to Council of Europe and WEU 1973–74; Sec. Conservative Parl. Health and Social Security Cttee. 1974; Chair. UniChem 1997–; Dir Foreign and Colonial Investment Fund 1997–, Claverhouse Investment Trust 1997–; Co-ordinator British-American Business Network; Hon. Master of Bench, Gray's Inn; Hon. D. Iur. (Nottingham) 1989, Hon. D.Jur. (Huddersfield Univ.) 1993; Hon. D. Univ. (Nottingham) 1996. *Publication:* New Hope for the Regions 1979. *Leisure interests:* bird-watching, jazz, cricket, football. *Address:* House of Commons, London, SW1A 0AA, England.

CLARKE, Sir Robert C., Kt., M.A.; British business executive; b. 28 March 1929, Eltham; s. of Robert H. Clarke and Rose (Bratton) Clarke; m. Evelyn Mary Harper 1952; three s. one d.; ed. Dulwich Coll. and Pembroke Coll. Oxford; trainee, Cadbury Bros. Ltd. 1952; Gen. Man. John Forrest Ltd. 1954; Marketing Dir. Cadbury Confectionery 1957; Man. Dir. Cadbury Cakes Ltd. 1962; Chair. Cadbury Cakes Ltd. and Dir. Cadbury Schweppes Foods Ltd. 1969; Man. Dir. McVitie & Cadbury Cakes Ltd. 1971–74; mem. Bd. United Biscuits (UK) Ltd. 1974; Man. Dir. UB Biscuits 1977; Chair. and Man. Dir. United Biscuits (UK) Ltd. and Dir. United Biscuits (Holdings) PLC 1984–95; Group Chief Exec. United Biscuits (Holdings) PLC 1986–90, Deputy Chair. 1989, Chair. 1990–95; Dir. (non-exec.) Thames Water PLC 1988–99, Chair. 1994–99. *Leisure interests:* reading, walking, renovating old buildings and planting trees. *Address:* c/o Thames Water PLC, 14 Cavendish Place, London, W1M 9DJ, England.

CLARKE, Sir Rupert W.J., Bt., M.A., M.B.E.(MIL.); Australian company director and grazier; b. 5 Nov. 1919, Sydney; s. of late Rupert T.H. Clarke and Elsie F. Tucker; m. Kathleen Grant Hay 1947; three s. (one deceased) one d.; ed. Eton Coll., Magdalen Coll. Oxford, U.K.; Chair. United Distillers Pty. Ltd. 1958–88; Dir. P & O Australia Ltd. 1980–, Chair. 1983–96, Hon. Pres. 1996–; Chair. Nat. Australia Bank Ltd. 1986–92; Consul-Gen. of Monaco; Chair. Victory Re-Insurance Co. of Australia 1956–86, Cadbury Schweppes Australia Ltd. 1971–88, Morganite Australia Pty. Ltd. 1981–88, Legal and Gen. 1983–86; Vice-Chair. and Dir. Conzinc Riotinto of Australia Ltd. 1961–87; Dir. Howard Florey Inst. of Experimental Physiology and Medicine (Vice-Pres. 1997–); Chair. Vic. Amateur Turf Club 1973–90; Dir. Royal Humane Soc. of Australia 1955–, Pres. 1992–; Hon. Fellow Trinity Coll. Melbourne; Officier Ordre des Grimaldi (Monaco) 1975, Chevalier Légion d'honneur, Officier Ordre de Léopold. *Leisure interests:* swimming, horse breeding and racing, shooting. *Address:* Richmond House, 56 Avoca Street, South Yarra, Vic. 3141; Bolinda Vale, Clarkefield, Vic. 3430, Australia. *Telephone:* (03) 9602 3088 (South Yarra). *Fax:* (03) 9670 2629 (South Yarra).

CLARKSON, Brian Leonard, D.SC., F.ENG.; British scientist and research professor; b. 28 July 1930, Driffield; s. of L.C. Clarkson; m. Margaret Elaine Wilby 1953; three s. one d.; ed. The Grammar School, Beverley, E. Yorks, Univ. of Leeds; dynamics engineer de Havilland Aircraft Co. Ltd. 1953–57; Sir Alan Cobham Research Fellow Univ. of Southampton 1957–58, Lecturer, Dept. of Aeronautics 1958–66, Prof. of Vibration Studies 1966–82, Dir. Inst. of Sound and Vibration Research 1967–78, Dean of Eng. 1978–80, Deputy Vice-Chancellor 1980–82; Prin. Univ. Coll. of Swansea 1982–94; Vice-Chancellor Univ. of Wales 1987–89; Sec. Int. Comm. on Acoustics 1975–81; Pres. Fed. of Acoustics Socs. of Europe 1982–84; Vice-Chair. Asscn. of Commonwealth Univs. 1990–92, Chair. 1992–93; Hon. D.Sc. (Leeds) 1984, (Southampton) 1987, (Universiti Sains Malaysia) 1990; Hon. LL.D. (Wales) 1996; George Taylor Gold Medal of Royal Aeronautical Soc. 1963. *Publications:* Design of Aircraft Structures to Resist Jet Noise 1962, Noise and Acoustic Fatigue in Aeronautics (Ed.) 1967, Stochastic Problems in Dynamics (Ed.) 1977, Experimental Determination of Modal Densities of Flat Plates and Cylinders 1981, Noise and Vibration (Ed.) 1982. *Leisure interests:* travelling, walking, gardening. *Address:* Highmead, 17 Southgate Road, Southgate, Swansea, SA3 2BT, Wales. *Telephone:* (01792) 233216.

CLARKSON, Thomas William, PH.D.; professor of toxicology; b. 1 Aug. 1932, Blackburn; s. of William Clarkson and Olive Jackson; m. Winifred Browne 1957; one s. two d.; ed. Univ. of Manchester; Instructor, Univ. of Rochester School of Medicine, U.S.A. 1958–61, Asst. Prof. 1961–62, Assoc. Prof. 1965–71, Prof. 1971–, Head of Div. of Toxicology 1980–86, J. Lowell Orbison Distinguished Service Alumni Prof. 1983–, Dir. Environmental Health Sciences Center 1986–, Chair. Dept. of Environmental Medicine 1992–98; Scientific Officer, Medical Research Council, U.K. 1962–64; Sterling Drug Visiting Prof., Albany Medical Coll. 1989; Sr. Fellowship, Weizmann Inst. of Science 1964–65; Post-Doctoral Fellow, Nuffield Foundation 1956–57, and U.S. Atomic Energy Comm., Univ. of Rochester 1957–58; mem. Inst. of Medicine of N.A.S.; Dir N.A.S.A. Center in Space Environmental Health 1991–95; mem. La Academia Nacional de Medicina de Buenos Aires 1984; mem. Collegium Ramazzini 1983; Hon. Dr. Med. (Umeå) 1986; J. Lowell Orbison Distinguished Service Alumni Prof. *Publications:* over 200 published papers; co-ed. of Reproductive and Developmental Toxicology, The Cytoskeleton as a Target for Toxic Agents, Biological Monitoring of Toxic Metals, Advances in Mercury Toxicology. *Address:* Department of Environmental Medicine, University of Rochester School of Medicine, Box EHSC, Rochester, New York, NY 14642, U.S.A. *Telephone:* (716) 275-3911 (Office). *Fax:* (716) 256-2591.

CLARY, David Charles, PH.D., F.R.S., F.INST.P., F.R.S.C.; British professor of chemistry; b. 14 Jan. 1953, Halesworth, Suffolk; s. of Cecil Raymond Clary and Mary Mildred Clary (née Hill); m. Heather Ann Vinson 1975; three s.; ed. Colchester Royal Grammar School, Sussex Univ., Corpus Christi Coll., Cambridge; researcher IBM Research Lab., San Jose, Calif. 1977–78; post doctoral research at Manchester Univ. 1978–80; research lecturer in Chemistry UMIST 1980–83; Reader in Theoretical Chemistry Dept. of Chemistry, Cambridge Univ. 1983–96; Fellow Magdalene Coll., Cambridge 1983–96, Sr. Tutor 1989–93, Fellow Commoner 1996–; Prof. of Chemistry, Dir. of Centre for Theoretical and Computational Chemistry, Univ. Coll., London 1996–; mem. Int. Acad. of Quantum Molecular Science 1998; Annual Medal of Int. Acad. of Quantum Molecular Science 1998. *Publications:* research papers on chemical physics and theoretical chemistry in learned journals. *Leisure interests:* family, football. *Address:* Department of Chemistry, University College London, 20 Gordon Street, London, WC1H 0AJ, England. *Telephone:* 0171-391 1488. *Fax:* 0171-380 7463.

CLATWORTHY, Robert, R.A.; British sculptor; b. 31 Jan. 1928; s. of E. W. and G. Clatworthy; m. 1st Pamela Gordon 1954 (divorced); two s. one d.; m. 2nd Jane (née Illingworth Stubbs) 1989; ed. Dr. Morgan's Grammar School, Bridgwater, West of England Coll. of Art, Chelsea School of Art, The Slade; teacher, West of England Coll. of Art 1967–71; Visiting Tutor, R.C.A. 1960–72; mem. Fine Art Panel of Nat. Council for Diplomas in Art and Design 1961–72; Governor, St. Martin's School of Art 1970–71; Head of Dept. of Fine Art, Central School of Art and Design 1971–75; exhbns. at Hanover Gallery, Waddington Galleries, Holland Park Open Air Sculpture, Battersea Park Open Air Sculpture, Tate Gallery (British Sculpture in the Sixties), Burlington House (British Sculptors 1972), Basil Jacobs Fine Art Ltd., Diploma Galleries, Burlington House, Photographers Gallery, Quinton Green Fine Art, Chapman Gallery 1988, 1989, 1990, Austin/Desmond Fine Art, in asscn. with Keith H. Chapman 1991, 1992, 1994, 1996; work in collections of Arts Council, Contemporary Art Soc., Tate Gallery, Victoria and Albert Museum, GLC, Nat. Portrait Gallery (portrait of Dame Elisabeth Frink 1985); Monumental Horse and Rider, Finsbury Ave., London 1984. *Address:* Moelfre, Cynghordy, Llandovery, Carmarthenshire, SA20 0UW, Wales. *Telephone:* (01550) 720201.

CLAVÉ, Antoni; Spanish painter; b. 5 April 1913, Barcelona; ed. evening classes at Escuela Superior de Bellas Artes de San Jorge, Barcelona; magazine and book illustrator 1930–49; full-time painter since 1955; commenced carpet painting 1957 and metal work 1960; first one-man exhbn., Perpignan, France 1939, later in Paris, London, Oran, Gothenburg, Buenos Aires, Rome, Milan, Barcelona, Bilbao, Los Angeles, Geneva, Cologne, Luxembourg, Colmar, Toulouse, Venice and Tokyo; other exhbns.: "Thirty Years of Painting", Tokyo 1972, New York 1973, "En marge de la peinture", Centre Georges Pompidou, Paris 1978, Works 1958–78, Musée d'art moderne de la ville de Paris 1978, 1979; Musée d'Unterlinden, Colmar, peintures 1958–78, Septembre: A. H. Grafik, Stockholm, Dix Instruments étranges, gravures, Retrospective 1939–80, Museo de Arte Contemporáneo, Madrid 1980; Musée des Augustins, Toulouse, 1984, Biennale de Venise, Pavillon d'Espagne; 125 works 1958–84, paintings, sculptures, Museo de Arte contemporáneo, Madrid, 150 lithographs and carvings; exhbns in Paris and Perpignan 1985; and at Tokyo Metropolitan Teien Museum, Osaka Modern Art Museum, Yamanashi-ken Kiyoharu Museum 1986; Matarasso Prize, Biennal São Paulo 1957, UNESCO Prize, Kamakara Museum Prize. *Major works:* illustrations for La Dame de Pique, Pushkin 1946, black lithographs Candide, Voltaire 1948, Gargantua, Rabelais 1953, La Gloire des Rois, Saint-John Perse 1976.

CLAVEL, Bernard; French writer; b. 29 May 1923, Lons-le-Saunier; s. of Henri Clavel and Héloïse Dubois; m. Josette Pratte 1982; three s. (of first marriage); ed. primary school; left school aged 14 and apprenticed as pâtissier 1937; subsequently held various jobs on the land and in offices; painter and writer since age 15; has written numerous plays for radio and television and contributed to reviews on the arts and pacifist journals; Prix Eugène Leroy, Prix populiste, Prix Jean Macé, Prix Goncourt (for Les fruits de l'hiver), Grand Prix littéraire de la Ville de Paris, Prix Ardua de l'Université 1997. *Publications include:* L'ouvrier de la nuit 1956, Qui m'emporte 1958, L'espagnol 1959, Malataverne 1960, Le voyage du père 1965, L'Hercule sur la place 1966, La maison des autres 1962, Celui qui voulait voir la mer 1963, Le coeur des vivants 1964, Les fruits de l'hiver 1968, Victoire au Mans 1968, L'espion aux yeux verts 1969, Le tambour du bief 1970, Le massacre des innocents 1970, Le seigneur du fleuve 1972, Le silence des armes 1974, Lettre à un képi blanc 1975, La boule de neige 1975, La saison des loups 1976, La lumière du lac 1977, Ecrit sur la neige 1977, La fleur de sel 1977, La femme de guerre 1978; Le Rhône ou la métamorphose d'un dieu 1979, Le chien des Laurentides 1979, L'Iroquoise 1979, Marie Bon Pain 1980, La bourrelle 1980, Felicien le fantôme (with Josette Pratte) 1980, Terres de Mémoire 1980, Compagnons du Nouveau-Monde 1981, Arbres 1981, Odile et le vent du large 1981, Le Hibou qui avait avalé la lune 1981, l'Homme du Labrador 1982, Harricana 1983, L'Or de la terre 1984, Le mouton noir et le loup blanc 1984, Le roi des poissons 1984, L'oie qui avait perdu le nord 1985, Miserere 1985, Bernard Clavel qui êtes-vous? 1985, Amarok 1986, Au cochon qui danse 1986, l'Angélus du soir 1988, Le grand voyage de Quick Beaver 1988, Quand j'étais capitaine 1990, Retour au pays 1990, Meurtre sur le Grandvaux 1991, La révolte à deux sous 1992, Cargo pour l'enfer 1993, Les roses de Verdun 1994, le Carcajou 1995, Jésus le fils du charpentier 1996, Contes et légendes du Bordelais 1997, la Guinguette 1997, Le Soleil des morts 1998, and numerous essays, short stories and children's books. *Leisure interests:* sport, painting, handicraft. *Address:* Albin Michel, 22 rue Huyghens, 75014 Paris, France.

CLAVIER, Christian Jean-Marie; French actor; b. 6 May 1952, Paris; s. of Jean-Claude Clavier and Phanette Rousset-Rouard; one d. by Marie-Anne Chazel; *stage appearances include:* Ginette Lacaze, la Dame de chez Maxim's, Non Georges pas ici 1972, Ma tête est malade 1976, le Pot de terre contre le pot de vin 1977, Amours, coquillages et crustacés 1978, le Père Noël est une ordure 1979–80, Papy fait de la résistance 1981, Double Mixte 1986–88, Un fil à la patte 1989, Panique au plaza 1995. *Films include:* Que la fête commence 1974, F. comme Fairbanks 1976, le Diable dans la boîte 1976, l'Amour en herbe 1977, Des enfants gâtés 1977, Dîtes-lui que je l'aime 1977, les Bronzés font du ski (also co-writer) 1979, Cocktail Molotov 1980, Je vais craquer 1980, Clara et les chics types 1980, Quand tu seras débloqué, fais-moi signe 1981, Elle voit des nains partout 1981, le Père Noël est une ordure (also co-writer) 1982, Rock and Torah 1982, la Vengeance d'une blonde 1993, les Anges guardiens (also co-writer) 1994, Les Couloirs du temps (also co-writer) 1998. *Television includes:* l'Été 1985, Sueurs froides 1988, Palace 1988, Si Guitry m'était conté 1989, Bougez pas j'arrive 1989, Mieux vaut courir 1989, Fantôme sur l'oreiller (co-writer 1989), Charmante soirée (co-writer 1990); Chevalier Ordre nat. du Mérite, Ordre nat. des Arts et des lettres. *Leisure interests:* skiing, cycling, swimming. *Address:* 27 rue Marbeuf, 75008 Paris, France.

CLAYBURGH, Jill; American actress; b. 30 April 1944, New York; d. of Albert H. and Julia (Door) Clayburgh; m. David Rabe 1979; ed. Sarah Lawrence Coll., Bronxville, N.Y.; Broadway debut in The Rothschilds 1979: *stage appearances include:* In the Boom Boom Room, Design for Living; *film appearances include:* Portnoy's Complaint 1972, The Thief Who Came to Dinner, The Terminal Man 1974, Gable and Lombard 1976, Silver Streak 1976, Semi-Tough 1977, An Unmarried Woman 1978, La Luna 1979, Starting Over 1979, It's My Turn 1980, I'm Dancing as Fast as I Can 1982, Hannah K 1983, Shy People 1987, Beyond the Ocean, Between the Lines 1990, Naked in New York 1994, Fools Rush In 1997, Going All the Way 1997; has also appeared in television films; Best Actress Award, Cannes Film Festival, and Golden Apple Award for the best film actress for An Unmarried Woman. *Address:* c/o John Kimble, William Morris Agency, 151 El Camino Drive, Beverly Hills, CA 90212, U.S.A.

CLAYTON, Dame Barbara, D.B.E., PH.D., F.R.C.P., F.R.C.P.E., F.R.C.PATH., F.R.C.P.I.; British professor of medicine; b. 2 Sept. 1922, Liverpool; d. of William Clayton and Constance Clayton; m. William Klyne 1949; one s. one d.; ed. Bromley County School for Girls, Edinburgh Univ.; consultant Hosp. for Sick Children 1959–78 (mem. Bd. of Govs. 1968–78); Prof. Inst. of Child Health, Univ. of London 1970–78, Univ. of Southampton 1979–87 (Hon. Research Prof. 1987–); Pres. Asscn. of Clinical Biochemists 1977–78, Soc. for the Study of Inborn Errors of Metabolism 1981–82 (Hon. mem. 1988), Royal Coll. of Pathologists 1984–87, Nat. Soc. for Clean Air and Environmental Protection 1995–97; Chair. Standing Cttee. on Postgrad. Medical and Dental Educ. 1988–, Health of the Nation Task Force on Nutrition 1992–95, Medical and Scientific Panel, Leukaemia Research Fund 1988–; Dean Faculty of Medicine Univ. of Southampton 1983–86; Hon. Pres. British Dietetic Asscn. 1989–; mem. Royal Comm. on Environmental Pollution 1981–96, Gen. Medical Council 1983–87; Gov. British Nutrition Foundation; Hon. Fellow Royal Coll. of Physicians, Ireland, American Soc. of Clinical Pathologists 1987; Hon. D.Sc. (Edin.) 1987, (Southampton) 1992; Wellcome Prize (Asscn. of Clinical Biochemists) 1988, etc.; Gold Medal for Distinguished Merit (British Medical Asscn.) 1998. *Publications:* Clinical Biochemistry and the Sick Child (jtly.) 1994, numerous publs. on nutrition, pediatrics and the environment. *Leisure interests:* natural history, visiting the Arctic. *Address:* Room AC19, Level C, South Academic Block, Southampton, SO16 6YD, England. *Telephone:* (01703) 796800. *Fax:* (01703) 798554.

CLAYTON, Robert Norman, M.SC., PH.D., F.R.S.; Canadian geochemist; b. 20 March 1930; s. of Norman Clayton and Gwenda Clayton; m. Cathleen Shelbourne Clayton 1971; one d.; ed. Queen's Univ. Canada and Calif. Inst. of Tech.; Research Fellow, Calif. Inst. of Tech. 1955–56; Asst. Prof. Pa. State Univ. 1956–58; Asst. Prof. Univ. of Chicago 1958–62, Assoc. Prof. 1962–66, Prof. Depts. of Chemistry and of the Geophysical Sciences 1966–80, Enrico Fermi Distinguished Service Prof. 1980–. *Publications:* over 200 papers in geochemical journals. *Address:* 5640 South Ellis, Chicago, IL 60637 (Office); 5201 South Cornell, Chicago, IL 60615, U.S.A.

CLEARY, Jon Stephen: Australian author; b. 22 Nov. 1917, Sydney, N.S.W.; s. of Mathew Cleary and Ida F. Brown; m. Constantine E. Lucas 1946; two d. (one deceased); ed. Marist Brothers School, N.S.W.; various jobs, including bush-working and commercial art 1932–40; served Australian Imperial Forces, Middle East, New Britain, New Guinea 1940–45; full-time writer since 1945, except for 3 years as journalist, Australian News and Information Bureau, London and New York 1948–51; winner, ABC Nat. Play Competition 1945; Crouch Literary Prize 1951; Edgar Award for Best Crime Novel 1974. *Publications:* 45 novels and two books of short stories (1983), including You Can't See Round Corners 1948, The Sundowners 1952, The High Commissioner 1966, High Road to China 1977, Mask of the Andes 1971, Spearfield's Daughter 1982, The Phoenix Tree 1984, The City of Fading Light 1985, Dragons at the Party 1987, Now and Then, Amen 1988, Babylon South 1989, Murder Song 1990, Pride's Harvest 1991, Dark Summer 1992, Bleak Spring 1993, Autumn Maze 1994, Winter Chill 1995, Endpeace 1996, A Different Turf 1997, Five-Ring Circus 1998. *Leisure interests:* tennis, watching cricket, filmgoing, reading. *Address:* c/o HarperCollins, 23 Ryde Road, Pymble, N.S.W. 2073, Australia.

CLEAVER, Alan Richard, M.A.; British couturier and business executive; b. 30 May. 1952, Northampton; s. of Terence Richard Cleaver and Miriam Elanor Tomlin; ed. Wellingborough Tech. Grammar School, Northampton School of Art, Kingston Coll. of Art and R.C.A.; worked with Michael Aukett Assoc. 1973–74; freelance stylist Maison de Marie Claire, Paris 1977–79; freelance design consultant, Paris 1976–79; Co. Designer Byblos, Italy 1980–;

Man. Dir. S.R.L. Milan 1986–; External Examiner/Visiting Lecturer R.C.A. 1986–. *Leisure interests:* travel, opera, walking. *Address:* Via Vallone 11, Monte Conero, Sirolo; Bosco di San Francesco 6, Sirolo; Piazza Plebiscito 55, Ancona, Italy. *Telephone:* (071) 936 203; (071) 936 225; (071) 20-37-90.

CLEAVER, Sir Anthony Brian, Kt., M.A.; British business executive; b. 10 April 1938, London; s. of William Brian Cleaver and Dorothea Early Cleaver (née Peeks); m. Mary Teresa Cotter 1962; one s. one d.; ed. Berkhamsted School and Trinity Coll. Oxford; nat. service in Intelligence Corps 1956–58; joined IBM 1962, UK Sales Dir. 1976–77, DP Dir., mem. Bd., IBM UK (Holdings) 1977–80, Vice-Pres. of Marketing IBM Europe 1981–82, Asst. Gen. Man. IBM UK 1982–84, Gen. Man. 1984–85, Chief Exec. 1986–91, Chair. 1990–94; Chair. AEA Tech. PLC 1996–; Chair. Industrial Devt. Advisory Bd. Dept. of Trade and Industry 1993–, UKAEA 1993–96, The Strategic Partnership 1996–, Medical Research Council 1998–; Pres. Involvement and Participation Asscn. 1997–, Inst. of Man. 1998–; Dir. Nat. Computing Centre 1977–80; Dir. Gen. Accident PLC (fmrly. Gen. Accident) Fire and Life Assurance Corpn. 1988–98, Gen. Cable PLC 1994–98 (Chair. 1995–98), Smith and Nephew PLC 1993–; mem. Council, Templeton Coll. Oxford 1982–93, Asscn. for Business Sponsorship of the Arts 1985–97; mem. Bd. CEED 1985–98 (Deputy Chair. 1992–98); mem. Cttee. on Standards in Public Life 1997–, British Govt. Panel on Sustainable Devt. 1998–; Chair. Bd. of Govs., Birkbeck Coll. 1989–98; Fellow of British Computer Soc.; Hon. LL.D. (Nottingham) 1991, (Portsmouth) 1996; Hon. D.Sc. (Cranfield) 1995; Global 500 Roll of Honour (UN Environment Program) 1989. *Leisure interests:* sport, especially cricket, music, especially opera, and reading. *Address:* AEA Technology PLC, 15 Lower Regent Street, London, SW1Y 4LR, England. *Telephone:* 0171-389 6553.

CLEDWYN OF PENRHOS, Baron (Life Peer), cr. 1979, of Holyhead in the County of Anglesey; **Cledwyn Hughes,** P.C., C.H., LL.B.; British politician; b. 14 Sept. 1916, Holyhead, Anglesey; s. of Henry David Hughes and Emily Hughes; m. Jean Beatrice Hughes 1949; one s. one d.; ed. Holyhead Grammar School and Univ. Coll. of Wales, Aberystwyth; Solicitor 1940; R.A.F.V.R. 1940–46; mem. Anglesey County Council 1946–52; M.P. Anglesey 1951–79, Chair. Welsh Parl. Party 1953–54, Welsh Labour Group 1955–56, mem. Cttee. of Public Accounts 1957–64; Minister of State for Commonwealth Relations 1964–66; Sec. of State for Wales 1966–68; Minister of Agric., Fisheries and Food 1968–70; Vice-Chair. Parl. Labour Party March–Oct. 1974, Chair 1974–79; Joint Chair. TUC—Labour Party Liaison Cttee. 1974–79; Prime Minister's Emissary to Southern Africa Nov.–Dec. 1978; Pres. Univ. Coll of Wales, Aberystwyth 1976–84; Pro-Chancellor, Univ. of Wales 1985–95; mem. Cttee. of Privileges 1974–79; Commr. of House of Commons 1978–79; Deputy Leader of the Opposition, House of Lords 1981–82, Leader 1982–92; Chair. House Select Cttee. on Agric. and Food, Welsh Cttee. on Econ. Affairs 1982–84; Pres. Ass. of Welsh Counties 1990–95; Dir. Shell UK 1980–84, Anglesey Aluminium Ltd. 1980–, Holyhead Touring Ltd. 1980–; Pres. Univ. of Wales, Bangor 1995–; mem. Political Honours Cttee. 1992–98; Hon. LL.D. (Wales) 1970, (Sheffield) 1992, (Glamorgan); Hon. Freedom, Beaumaris 1972, Freeman of Anglesey 1976; Fellow Univ. Coll. of Wales Aberystwyth 1988; Labour. *Publication:* Conditions on the Island of St. Helena. *Leisure interests:* walking, reading, writing. *Address:* Penmorfa, Trearddur, Holyhead, Gwynedd, Wales. *Telephone:* (01407) 860544.

CLEESE, John Marwood, M.A.; British actor and writer; b. 27 Oct. 1939; s. of Reginald Cleese and Muriel Cleese; m. 1st Connie Booth 1968 (dissolved 1978); one d.; m. 2nd Barbara Trentham 1981 (dissolved 1990); one d.; m. 3rd Alyce Faye Eichelberger 1992; ed. Clifton Sports Acad. and Downing Coll., Cambridge; started writing and making jokes professionally 1963; first appearance on British TV 1966; appeared in and co-wrote TV series: The Frost Report, At Last the 1948 Show, Monty Python's Flying Circus, Fawlty Towers; f. and Dir. Video Arts Ltd. 1972–89; appeared as Petruchio in The Taming of the Shrew, BBC TV Shakespeare cycle 1981; appeared in Cheers, for which he received an Emmy Award; guest appearance in Third Rock From the Sun; Hon. A.D. White Prof.-at-Large, Cornell Univ. 1999–; Hon. LL.D. (St. Andrews). *Films include:* Interlude, The Magic Christian, And Now For Something Completely Different, Monty Python and the Holy Grail, Romance with a Double Bass, Life of Brian, Time Bandits, Privates on Parade, Yellowbeard 1982, The Meaning of Life 1983, Silverado 1985, Clockwise 1986, A Fish Called Wanda (BAFTA Award for Best Film Actor) 1988, Erik the Viking 1988, Splitting Heirs 1992, Mary Shelley's Frankenstein 1993, The Jungle Book 1994, Fierce Creatures 1996, The Out of Towners 1998, Isn't She Great 1998. *Publications:* Families and How to Survive Them, Life and How to Survive It (both with Robin Skynner). *Leisure interests:* gluttony, sloth. *Address:* c/o David Wilkinson, 115 Hazlebury Road, London, S.W.6, England. *Telephone:* 0171-371 5188. *Fax:* 0171-371 5161.

CLEGHORN, John E., B. COMM., C.A.; Canadian banker; b. 7 July 1941, Montreal, P.Q.; s. of H. W. Edward Cleghorn and Miriam Dunham; m. Pattie E. Hart 1963; two s. one d.; ed. McGill Univ.; Clarkson Gordon & Co. (chartered accountants) 1962–64; sugar buyer and futures trader, St. Lawrence Sugar Ltd., Montreal 1964–66; Mercantile Bank of Canada 1966–74; joined Royal Bank of Canada 1974, various sr. exec. positions 1975–83, Pres. 1983, Pres., C.O.O. 1986, Pres. C.E.O. 1994–95, Chair. C.E.O. Feb. 1995–; Dir. Royal Bank of Canada, Royal Trust; Chancellor Wilfrid Laurier Univ. 1996–; Gov. McGill Univ.; mem. Canadian and B.C. Insts. of Chartered Accountants; Fellow Ordre des Comptables Agréés du Québec, Inst. of Chartered Accountants of Ont.; Hon. D.C.L. (Bishop's Univ.) 1989, (Acadia Univ.) 1996; Hon. LL.D. (Wilfrid Laurier Univ.) 1991. *Leisure interests:* skiing, jogging, tennis, fishing. *Address:* Royal Bank of Canada, Royal Bank Plaza, 200 Bay Street, Toronto, Ont., M5J 2J5, Canada. *Telephone:* (416) 974 4049. *Fax:* (416) 974 7403.

CLELAND, Joseph Maxwell, M.A.; American politician; b. 24 Aug. 1942, Atlanta, Ga.; s. of Joseph Cleland and Juanita Kesler; ed. Stetson Univ. Deland, Fla.; mem. Ga. Senate, Atlanta 1971–75; consultant, Comm. on Veterans Affairs, U.S. Senate 1975–77; Admin. Veterans Affairs, Washington, D.C. 1977–81; Sec. of State, State of Ga. 1982–95; Senator from Georgia Jan. 1997–; Democrat; recipient of numerous awards and distinctions. *Address:* United States Senate, 461 Dirksen Senate Office Building, Washington, DC 20510, U.S.A.

CLÉMENT, Jérôme, L. EN D.; French government official; b. 18 May 1945, Paris; s. of Yves-André Clément and Raymonde Gornik; m. Marie-Christine Sterin 1974; one s. three d.; ed. Lycées Montaigne and Louis-le-Grand, Paris, Facultés de Droit et des Lettres, Paris, and Ecole Nat. d'Admin.; Ministry of Culture 1974–76, 1978–80; Cour des Comptes 1976–78; Cultural Counsellor, French Embassy, Cairo 1980–81; Counsellor, Office of Prime Minister Mauroy 1981–84; Dir.-Gen. Centre nat. de la cinématographie 1984–89; mem. Supervisory Bd. Soc. Européenne de Programmes de Télévision (La Sept) 1986–89, Pres. 1989–; Pres. Arte 1991–, la Cinquième (TV channel) 1996–; Dir. Réunion des musées nationaux, Orchestre de Paris, etc.; Chevalier, Ordre nat. du Mérite, Commdr. des Arts et des Lettres. *Publications:* Socialisme et multinationales 1976, Cahiers de l'Atelier, Un Homme en quête de Vertu 1992, Lettres à Pierre Bérégovoy 1993. *Leisure interests:* piano, music, painting, tennis, running. *Address:* La Sept–Arte, 8 avenue Marceau, 92785 Issy-les-Moulineaux cedex 9; Arte, 2a rue de la Fonderie, 67000 Strasbourg; La Cinquième, 10–14 rue Horace Vernet, 92136 Issy-les-Moulineaux cedex; 205 avenue Jean-Jaurès, 92140 Clamart, France (Home).

CLEMENT, John, C.B.I.M.; British business executive; b. 18 May 1932; s. of Frederick and Alice Eleanor Clement; m. Elisabeth Anne Emery 1956; two s. one d.; ed. Bishop's Stortford Coll.; Howards Dairies, Westcliff on Sea 1949–64; United Dairies London Ltd. 1964–69; Asst. Man. Dir. Rank Leisure Services Ltd. 1969–73; Chair. Unigate Foods Div. 1973; Chief Exec. Unigate PLC 1976–90, Chair. 1977–91; Dir. Eagle Star Holdings 1981–86; Chair. (non-exec.) The Littlewoods Org. 1982–90; Chair. Culpho Consultants 1991–, Tuddenham Hall Foods 1991–; Dir. (non-exec.) Ransomes PLC 1991–, Chair. 1993–; Dir. Anglo American Insurance Co. Ltd 1991–94, Chair. 1993–94; Dir. Jarvis Hotels Ltd. 1994–, Kleinwort 2nd Endowment Trust PLC 1993–; Chair. Nat. Car Auctions Ltd. 1995–; mem. Supervisory Bd. Nutricia N.V.; mem. Securities and Investment Bd. 1986–89. *Leisure interests:* tennis, shooting, sailing, skiing, bridge, rugby. *Address:* Tuddenham Hall, Tuddenham, Ipswich, Suffolk, IP6 9DD, England. *Telephone:* (01473) 785217.

CLEMENTE, Carmine Domenic, A.B., M.A., PH.D.; American professor of anatomy; b. 29 April 1928, Penns Grove, N.J.; s. of Ermanno Clemente and Caroline (Friozzi) Clemente; m. Juliette G. Clemente 1968; ed. Univ. of Pennsylvania and Univ. Coll. London; U.S. Public Health Service Fellow and Asst. Instr. in Anatomy, Univ. of Pa. 1950–52; Instr. in Anatomy, Univ. of Calif. Los Angeles 1952–53, Asst. Prof. 1954–59, Assoc. Prof. 1959–63, Prof. and Chair. Dept. of Anatomy 1963–73, Prof. of Anatomy 1973–94, Prof. Emer. 1994–; Prof. of Surgery (Anatomy), Charles R. Drew Postgraduate Medical School 1974– (mem. bd. 1985–), Dir. Brain Research Inst. 1976–87; John Simon Guggenheim Memorial Scholar, Nat. Inst. for Medical Research, Mill Hill, London 1988–89, 1991; Consultant in Surgical Anatomy, Martin Luther King Hosp. Los Angeles 1971; Consultant in Research Neurophysiology, Sepulveda Veterans Admin. Hosp.; mem. numerous advisory cttees. etc.; mem. Inst. of Medicine of N.A.S.; consultant Robert Wood Johnson Foundation, Princeton, N.J. 1990–; numerous awards and distinctions. *Publications:* Ed. Gray's Anatomy 1973–, numerous books, films and some 190 scientific publs. *Leisure interest:* philately. *Address:* Dept. of Neurobiology, UCLA School of Medicine, Los Angeles, CA 90095 (Office); 11737 Bellagio Road, Los Angeles, CA 90049, U.S.A. (Home). *Telephone:* (310) 825-9566 (Office); (310) 472-1149 (Home).

CLEMENTI, David Cecil, C.A.; British financial executive; b. 25 Feb. 1949, Hunts.; s. of Air Vice-Marshal Creswell Montagu Clementi and Susan Clementi (née Pelham); m. Sarah Louise (Sally) Cowley 1972; one s. one d.; ed. Winchester Coll., Lincoln Coll., Oxford, Harvard Business School; with Corp. Finance Div. Kleinwort Benson Ltd. 1975–87, Head 1989–94; Head Kleinwort Benson Securities 1987–89; Chief Exec. Kleinwort Benson Ltd. 1994–97; Vice-Chair. Kleinwort Benson Group PLC 1997; Deputy Gov. Bank of England 1997–. *Leisure interests:* sailing, athletics. *Address:* Office of the Deputy Governor, Bank of England, Threadneedle Street, London, EC2R 8AH, England. *Telephone:* 0171-601 4498. *Fax:* 0171-601 5901.

CLEMENTS, Suzanne; British fashion designer; m. Ignacio Ribeiro (q.v.) 1992; ed. Cen. St. Martin's Coll. of Art and Design; produced own range of knitwear; design consultant with husband, Brazil 1991–93; f. Clements Ribeiro with husband, London 1993; first collections launched Oct. 1993, numerous since; first solo show London Fashion Week March 1995; fashion shows since in Paris, Brazil, Japan; consultant to cos. in U.K. and Italy; winners Designer of the Year New Generation Category 1996. *Address:* Clements Ribeiro Ltd., 48 S. Molton Street, London, W1X 1HE, England. *Telephone:* 0171-409 7719. *Fax:* 0171-409 1741.

CLEMENTS, William Perry, Jr.; American fmr. politician; b. 13 April 1917, Dallas, Tex.; s. of William P. Clements and Evelyn Cammack Clements; m. Rita Crocker Clements 1975; one s. one d. (by previous marriage); ed. Highland Park High School, Dallas, and Southern Methodist Univ., Dallas; founder, Chair., C.E.O. SEDCO Inc., Dallas 1947–73, 1977, 1983–; mem. Nat. Exec. Bd., Boy Scouts of America; mem. Bd. of Trustees and Bd. of Govs., Southern Methodist Univ.; Deputy Sec. for Defense 1974–77; Gov. of Texas 1979–83, 1987–91; mem. Nat. Bipartisan Comm. of Cen. America 1983–84; Dept. of Defense Medal for Distinguished Service with Bronze Palm. *Address:* 1901 North Akard, Dallas, TX 75201, U.S.A.

CLEMET, Kristin; Norwegian politician; b. 20 April 1957; m.; ed. Norwegian School of Econs. and Business Admin.; held various posts in Conservative Party youth asscn. in Oslo and Hordaland County; Pvt. Sec. to Minister of Industry 1981–83; Group Sec. Conservative Party Parly. Group 1983–84; Information Sec. Conservative Party H.Q. 1985; Pvt. Sec. and Adviser, Office of Prime Minister 1985–86; Head, Oslo City Council Secr. 1987–88; Adviser and Head of Political Affairs Dept. Conservative Party H.Q. 1988–89; Deputy mem. Storting 1985–89, mem. 1989–93; Minister of Labour and Govt. Admin. 1989–91. *Address:* c/o Hoyre, Stortingst. 20, P.O. Box 1536, Vika, 0117 Oslo, Norway. *Telephone:* 22-82-90-90. *Fax:* 22-82-90-80.

CLEMINSON, Sir James Arnold Stacey, K.B.E., M.C., D.L.; British company director; b. 31 Aug. 1921, Hull, Yorkshire; s. of Arnold Russell and Florence Stacey Cleminson; m. Helen Juliet Measor; one s. two d.; ed. Bramcote and Rugby schools; served British Army, Parachute Regt. 1940–46; joined Reckitt Colman Overseas 1946; Dir. and later Vice-Chair. J. J. Colman Norwich 1960–69; Dir. Reckitt and Colman 1969, Chair. Food Div. 1970, CEO 1973–80, Chair. 1977–86; Vice-Chair. Norwich Union 1981–92 (Dir. 1979–92); Dir. United Biscuits Holdings 1982–89; Pres. CBI 1984–86; Pres. Endeavour Training 1984–97; Chair. British Overseas Trade Bd. 1986–90, Jeyes Hygiene PLC 1986–89, Riggs A. P. Bank 1987–91 (Dir. 1985–); Dir. Eastern Counties Newspaper Group 1986–92, J. H. Fenner PLC 1985–97 (Vice-Chair. 1993–97), Riggs Nat. Bank of Washington D.C. 1991–93; Pro-Chancellor Hull Univ. 1986–94; Hon. LL.D. (Hull) 1985; fmr. Trustee, Army Benevolent Fund; Trustee Airborne Forces Security Fund. *Leisure interests:* fishing, shooting, golf. *Address:* Loddon Hall, Hales, Norfolk NR14 6TB, England.

CLEMMESEN, Johannes, D.M.SC.; Danish pathologist; b. 14 Nov. 1908, Copenhagen; s. of Capt. Johan Clemmesen and Marie Gran; ed. Metropolitan School and Univ. of Copenhagen; Pathologist, Old People's Town 1950–55; Assoc. Prof. of Pathology, Royal Dental Coll. 1951–56; Chief Pathologist, Finsen Inst., Copenhagen 1955–78; Dir. Danish Cancer Registry 1942–80; Exec. mem. WHO Sub-cttee. on Cancer Registration and other cttees. on statistics and endemiology of cancer 1950–82; mem. Exec. Cttee. Int. Union against Cancer 1954–62; mem. Secr., Cttee. on Geographical Pathology of Cancer 1950–62, Cttees. on Tumour Nomenclature 1950–65; Chair. Co-ordinating Cttee. for Human Tumour Investigations 1973–75; Pres. Int. Asscn. for Comparative Leukemia Research 1975–77; mem. Wissenschaftliches Beirat, Deutsches Krebsforschungszentrum, Heidelberg 1977–82; mem. Int. Comm. for Protection against Environmental Mutagens and Carcinogens 1978–85; Hon. mem. Int. Asscn. Cancer Registries 1981; Chair. Danish Asscn. 1987–88; Dr. med. h.c. Aarhus 1978; Hon. mem. Danish Pathological Soc. 1996; Ramazzini Award 1988. *Publications:* X-radiation and Immunity to Heterotransplantation 1938, Statistical Studies in the Aetiology of Malignant Neoplasms 1965, 1969, 1974, 1977, Memoirs I 1986, Memoirs II 1988, Pregnancy, Smoking and Testis Cancer 1997. *Leisure interest:* history studies. *Address:* Stockholmsgade 43, Copenhagen 2100; Melbys Venge 15, Tisvildeleje 3220, Denmark (Summer). *Telephone:* 35-42-8600; 48-30-8041 (Summer).

CLEOBURY, Nicholas Randall, M.A., F.R.C.O.; British conductor; b. 23 June 1950, Bromley, Kent; s. of John Cleobury and Brenda Cleobury; m. Heather Kay 1978; one s. one d.; ed. King's School, Worcester and Worcester Coll., Oxford; Asst. organist, Chichester Cathedral 1971–72, Christ Church, Oxford 1972–76; conductor, Schola Cantorum of Oxford 1973–76; chorus master, Glyndebourne Festival Opera 1977–79; Asst. Dir. BBC Singers 1977–79; Prin. Opera Conductor, Royal Acad. of Music 1980–87; Guest Conductor, Zurich Opera House 1993–; Music Dir. Oxford Bach Choir 1997–; Artistic Dir. Aquarius 1983–92, Cambridge Symphony Soloists 1990–92, Britten Sinfonia 1992–, Sounds New 1996–; Music Dir. Broomhill 1990–94, Artistic Dir. Cambridge Festival 1992; int. conductor throughout U.K., Europe and Scandinavia 1979–; numerous recordings; Hon. R.A.M. 1985. *Leisure interests:* cricket, food, wine, reading, theatre. *Address:* China Cottage, Church Lane, Petham, Canterbury, Kent, CT4 5RD, England. *Telephone:* (01227) 700584. *Fax:* (01227) 700827.

CLEOBURY, Stephen John, M.A., B.MUS., F.R.C.M., F.R.C.O.; British director of music; b. 31 Dec. 1948, Bromley; s. of John Cleobury and Brenda (née Randall) Cleobury; m. Penelope Holloway 1971; two d.; ed. King's School, Worcester and St. John's Coll. Cambridge; organist, St. Matthew's, Northampton 1971–74; sub-organist, Westminster Abbey 1974–78; Master of Music, Westminster Cathedral 1979–82; Dir. of Music, King's Coll. Cambridge 1982–; Chief Conductor BBC Singers 1995–; Pres. Royal Coll. of Organists 1990–92; recordings of solo organ works and directing choir of King's Coll. and BBC Singers. *Address:* King's College, Cambridge, CB2 1ST, England.

CLERCQ, Willy De, LL.D.; Belgian politician and barrister; b. 8 July 1927, Ghent; s. of Frans De Clercq and Yvonne Catry; m. Fernande Fazzi 1953; two s. one d.; Barrister, Court of Appeal, Ghent 1951; with Gen. Secretariat of UN, New York 1952; mem. Chamber of Reps. for Ghent-Ekloo 1958–; Deputy Prime Minister, in charge of Budget 1966–68; Deputy Prime Minister and Minister of Finance 1973–74, Minister of Finance 1973–77, Deputy Prime Minister and Minister of Finance and Foreign Trade Dec. 1981–85; Vice-Pres. Partij voor Vrijheid en Vooruitgang (PVV 1961); Pres. PVV 1971–73, 1977–81; mem. European Parl. 1979–81, 1989–; Pres. Cttee. for External Econ. Relations; Minister of State 1985; Pres. European Fed. of Liberal and Democratic Parties (ELD) 1980–85; part-time Prof. Univs. of Ghent and Brussels; Chair. of Interim Cttee. of the IMF 1976–77, 1983–85; Commr. for External Relations and Trade Policy, Comm. of European Communities 1985–89. *Leisure interests:* sport, travel. *Address:* Cyriel Buyssenstraat 12, 9000 Ghent, Belgium (Home). *Telephone:* 091-225947; 211813.

CLERIDES, Glafcos John, B.A., LL.B.; Cypriot politician and lawyer; b. 24 April 1919, Nicosia; s. of late John Clerides and Elli Clerides; m. Lilla Erulkar 1946; one d.; ed. Pancyprian Gymnasium, Nicosia, King's Coll., London Univ.; served with R.A.F. 1939–45; called to Bar, Gray's Inn 1951; practiced law in Cyprus 1951–60; Minister of Justice 1959–60; Head Greek Cypriot Del., Jt. Constitutional Comm. 1959–60, Greek Cypriot Del., London Conference 1964, Rep. Negotiator Greek Cypriot Community Intercommunal Talks 1968; mem. House of Reps. 1960–76, 1981–93, Pres. 1960–76; Acting Pres. of Cyprus July–Dec. 1974, Pres. Feb. 1993–; Pres. Red Cross 1961–63 (Hon. Certificate and Hon. Life mem., Recognition of Distinguished Service); f. Unified Party 1969, Democratic Rally; leading mem. Unified Party, Progressive Front and Democratic Nat. Front 1976; Gold Medal (Order of Holy Sepulchre), Recognised Services and Understanding of Roman Catholic Religious Group (by approval of His Holiness Pope John XXIII); Grand Cross of the Saviour (Greece). *Address:* Presidential Palace, Nicosia; 5 Ioannis Clerides Street, Nicosia, Cyprus.

CLERMONT, Yves Wilfrid, PH.D., F.R.S.C.; Canadian professor of anatomy; b. 14 Aug. 1926, Montreal; s. of Rodolphe Clermont and Fernande Primeau; m. Madeleine Bonneau 1950; two s. one d.; ed. Univ. of Montreal, McGill Univ., Collège de France, Paris; Teaching Fellow, Dept. of Anatomy, Faculty of Medicine, McGill Univ., Montreal 1952–53, Lecturer 1953–56, Asst. Prof. 1956–60, Assoc. Prof. 1960–63, Prof. 1963–97, Chair. of Dept. 1975–85, Emer. Prof. 1997–; Vice-Pres. American Asscn. of Anatomists 1979–83; mem. Review Group and Advisory Group of Expanded Programme of Research in Human Reproduction, WHO, Geneva 1971–76, Royal Soc. of Canada 1972–; Ortho Prize, Canadian Soc. of Fertility 1958, Prix Scientifique de la Province de Québec 1963, Siegler Award, American Fertility Soc. 1966, Van Campenhout Award, Canadian Fertility Soc. 1986, J.C.B. Grant Award, Canadian Asscn. of Anatomists 1986, Distinguished Andrologist Award, American Asscn. of Andrology 1988, Osler Teaching Award, Faculty of Medicine, McGill Univ. 1990, Serono Award American Asscn. of Andrology. *Publications:* more than 140 scientific articles in journals and books in the field of biology of reproduction and cell biology. *Leisure interests:* reading history and biography, gardening, listening to classical music. *Address:* Department of Anatomy, McGill University, 3640 University Street, Montreal, Quebec, H3A 2B2 (Office); 567 Townshend, St. Lambert, Quebec, J4R 1M4, Canada (Home). *Telephone:* (514) 398-6349 (Office); (514) 671-5606 (Home). *Fax:* (514) 398-5047.

CLEVELAND, Harlan, A.B.; American administrator, educationist and government official; b. 19 Jan. 1918, New York; s. of Stanley Matthews and Marian Phelps (van Buren); m. Lois W. Burton 1941; one s. two d.; ed. Princeton and Oxford Univs.; served Allied Control Commission, Rome 1944–45; UNRRA, Rome and Shanghai 1946–48; Econ. Co-operation Admin., Washington 1948–51; Asst. Dir. for Europe, Mutual Security Agency 1952–53; Exec. Ed. The Reporter, New York 1953–55, Publr. 1955–56; Dean, Maxwell Graduate School of Citizenship and Public Affairs, Syracuse Univ. 1956–61; Asst. Sec. for Int. Organization Affairs, State Dept. 1961–65; Amb. to NATO 1965–69; Pres., Prof. of Political Science, Univ. of Hawaii 1969–74, Pres. Emer. 1974–; Dir. Aspen Program in Int. Affairs Sept. 1974–80; Chair. Weather Modification Advisory Bd. 1977–78; Distinguished Visiting Tom Slick Prof. of World Peace, LBJ School of Public Affairs, Univ. of Texas 1979; Prof. of Public Affairs and Dean Hubert H. Humphrey Inst. of Public Affairs, Univ. of Minn. 1980–87, Prof. Emer. 1988–; Pres. World Acad. of Arts and Sciences 1991; recipient of 20 hon. degrees; U.S. Medal of Freedom, Woodrow Wilson Award (Princeton Univ.), Prix de Talloires; Democrat. *Publications:* The Promise of World Tensions (ed.) 1961, The Ethic of Power (co-ed.) 1962, Ethics and Bigness (co-ed.) 1962, The Obligations of Power 1966, NATO: The Transatlantic Bargain 1970, The Future Executive 1972, The Third Try at World Order 1977; Co-author: The Overseas Americans 1960, Human Growth: An Essay on Growth, Values and the Quality of Life 1978; Energy Futures of Developing Countries (ed.) 1980, Bioresources for Development (co-ed.) 1980, The Management of Sustainable Growth (ed.) 1981, The Knowledge Executive: Leadership in an Information Society 1985, The Global Commons 1990, Birth of a New World 1993, Leadership and the Information Revolution 1997. *Leisure interests:* sailing, golf, writing. *Address:* c/o University of Minnesota, Hubert H. Humphrey Center, 301 19th Avenue South, Minneapolis, MN 55455 (Office); 46891 Grissom Street, Sterling, VA 20165, U.S.A. (Home). *Telephone:* (612) 624-5592. *Fax:* (612) 625-3513.

CLEVELAND, Paul Matthews, M.A.; American diplomatist; b. 25 Aug. 1931, Boston, Mass.; s. of Paul Cleveland and Mary E. Chestnut; m. Carter Sellwood 1953; two s. two d.; ed. Yale Univ. and Fletcher School of Law and Diplomacy; Lieut. U.S.A.F. 1953–56, Dept. of the Navy 1956–57; Man. Analyst, Dept. of State 1957, Staff Asst. 1958; Econ. Officer, Canberra 1959–61, Political Officer 1961–63; Staff Aide, Bonn 1963–65; Econ. Officer, Jakarta 1965–68; Int. Economist, Washington 1968–70; Special Asst. to Asst. Sec. of State for East Asian and Pacific Affairs 1970–73; Political Officer, Seoul 1973–75; Counsellor for Political Affairs 1975–78; Deputy Dir. of Regional Affairs, Bureau of East Asian and Pacific Affairs 1978–79, Dir. 1979; Dir. Thai Affairs 1980–81, Korean Affairs 1981–82; Minister-Counsellor and Deputy Chief of Mission, Seoul 1982–85; Amb. to New Zealand and Western Samoa 1985–89, to Malaysia 1989–92; Co-ordinator for Expert Central Policy, Dept. of State 1992–; Pres. Meritorious Service Award 1984. *Leisure interests:* golf, hiking, reading. *Address:* 989 Saigon Road, McLean, VA 22102, U.S.A. *Telephone:* (703) 356-0883.

CLEWLOW, Warren (Alexander Morton); South African business executive and chartered accountant; b. 13 July 1936, Durban; s. of Percy Edward Clewlow; m. Margaret Brokensha 1964; two s. three d.; ed. Glenwood High School, Univ. of Natal; joined Barlow Group as Co. Sec. Barlow's (OFS) Ltd. 1963; Alt. Dir. Barlow Rand Ltd. 1974, Dir. 1975; mem. Exec. Cttee. with various responsibilities Barlow Group 1978–83; C.O.O. Barlow Rand Ltd. (now Barlow Ltd.) 1983–86, Deputy Chair. and Chief Exec. 1986, Chair. 1991–; Deputy Chair. Standard Bank Investment Corpn., Standard Bank SA Ltd.; Dir. S.A. Mutual Life Assurance Soc., ISCOR Ltd., Sasol Ltd, SA Foreign Trade Org.; Pres. Keep South Africa Beautiful Asscn.; Hon. Treas. African Children's Feeding Scheme; Regional Gov. Univ. of Cape Town Foundation; Council mem. Univ. of South Africa; Chair. State Pres. Econ. Advisory Council 1985; mem. Bd. of Govs. The Urban Fund; mem. bd. Asscn. of Marketers; Hon. Prof. Business Man. and Admin., Univ. of Stellenbosch 1986; D. Econ. h.c. (Natal) 1988; Businessman of the Year, Sunday Times 1984, Marketing Man of the Year, S.A. Inst. of Marketing 1984; Dr. G. Malherbe Award, Univ. of Natal 1986, Order for Meritorious Service (Gold Class) 1988. *Leisure interests:* tennis, horticulture, fishing, historical reading. *Address:* P.O. Box 782248, Sandton, 2146, South Africa. *Telephone:* (011) 801-9111. *Fax:* (011) 444-3643.

CLIBURN, Van (Harvey Lavan, Jr.); American pianist; b. 12 July 1934, Shreveport; s. of Harvey Lavan and Rildia Bee (née O'Bryan) Cliburn; studied with mother and at Juilliard School; public appearances, Shreveport 1940; début, Houston Symphony Orchestra 1952, New York Philharmonic Orchestra 1954, 1958; concert pianist on tour U.S. 1955–56, U.S.S.R. 1958; appearances in Brussels, London, Amsterdam, Paris, etc.; Hon. H.H.D. (Baylor), M.F.A. (Moscow Conservatory) 1989, winner first Int. Tchaikovsky Piano Competition, Moscow 1958, numerous prizes. *Address:* c/o Ann Hilton, P.O. Box 470217, Fort Worth, TX 76147; Van Cliburn Foundation, 2525 Ridgmar Boulevard, Suite 307, Fort Worth, TX 76116, U.S.A.

CLIFFORD, Max; British public relations executive; b. April 1943, Kingston-upon-Thames; s. of Frank Clifford and Lilian Clifford; m. Elizabeth Clifford; one d.; ed. secondary modern school, South Wimbledon; worked in dept. store (sacked); fmr. jr. reporter Merton and Morden News; fmr. press officer EMI Records (promoted the Beatles); worked in public relations; founder Max Clifford Assocs., clients have included Muhammad Ali, Marlon Brando, David Copperfield, O.J. Simpson, Frank Sinatra, SEAT, Laing Homes. *Address:* Max Clifford Associates Ltd., 109 New Bond Street, London, W1Y 9AA, England. *Telephone:* 0171-408 2350. *Fax:* 0171-409 2294.

CLIFTON, James Albert, B.A., M.D.; American physician, investigator, teacher and administrator; b. 18 Sept. 1923, Fayetteville, N.C.; s. of the late James A. Clifton, Sr. and Flora McNair Clifton; m. Katherine Rathe 1949; two d.; ed. Vanderbilt Univ.; Asst. Prof. of Medicine, Univ. of Ia. Coll. of Medicine 1954–58, Assoc. Prof. 1958–63, Prof. 1963–76, Roy J. Carver Prof. of Medicine 1976–90, Dir. Center for Digestive Diseases 1985–90, Prof. Emer. 1991–, Interim Dean 1991–93; Chief, Div. of Gastroenterology, Univ. of Ia., Dept. of Medicine 1953–71, Prof. Emer. 1991–; Chair. Dept. of Medicine, Univ. of Ia. Coll. of Medicine 1970–76; Pres. American Coll. of Physicians 1977–78, American Gastroenterological Asscn. 1970–71; Chair. Subspecialty Bd. in Gastroenterology, American Bd. of Internal Medicine 1972–75, American Bd. of Internal Medicine 1980–81; mem. Ludwig Inst. for Cancer Research, Zürich, Switzerland 1984–95, Central Soc. for Clinical Research, American Physiological Soc., Asscn. of American Physicians, Inst. of Medicine (N.A.S.), Royal Soc. of Medicine, London, Scientific Advisory Cttee., Health Task Force Cttee. (Nat. Insts. of Health), Nat. Advisory Council, Nat. Insts. of Arthritis, Metabolism, and Digestive Diseases (Nat. Insts. of Health); consultant to numerous U.S. medical schools; Visiting Scientist, Mount Desert Island Biological Research Lab., Bar Harbor, Maine 1964; Visiting Prof. of Medicine, St. Mark's Hosp. (Univ. of London), England 1984–85; Distinguished Medical Alumnus Award, Vanderbilt Univ., Alfred Stengel Award, American Coll. of Physicians. *Publications:* numerous scientific papers on intestinal absorption of nutrients, gastrointestinal motility and numerous publs. regarding philosophy and current affairs in internal medicine. *Leisure interests:* music, photography and travel. *Address:* University of Iowa Hospital and Clinics, 4 J.C.P., Hawkins Drive, Iowa City, IA 52242; 2620 Newport Road NE, Iowa City, IA 52240, U.S.A. (Home). *Telephone:* (319) 335-8065 (Office); (319) 351-1561 (Home).

CLINTON, Bill (William) Jefferson, J.D.; American politician; b. 19 Aug. 1946, Hope, Arkansas; s. of Roger Clinton and the late Virginia Dwire; m. Hillary Rodham 1975 (q.v.); one d.; ed. Hot Springs High School, Georgetown Univ., Univ. Coll., Oxford, Yale Law School; Professor, Univ. of Arkansas Law School 1974–76; Democratic Nominee, U.S. House Third District, Arkansas 1974; Attorney-General, Arkansas 1977–79, State Gov. 1979–81, 1983–93; Pres. of U.S.A. Jan. 1993–; impeached by House of Reps. for perjury and obstruction of justice Dec. 1998; acquitted in the Senate on both counts Jan. 1999; mem. counsel firm Wright, Lindsey & Jennings 1981–83; Chair. Southern Growth Policies Bd. 1985–86; Chair. Nat. Govs.' Asscn. 1987, Co-Chair. Task Force on Educ. 1990–91; Vice-Chair. Democratic Gov's. Asscn. 1987–88, Chair. (elect) 1988–89, Chair. 1989–90; Chair. Educ. Comm. of the States 1987; Chair. Democratic Party Affirmative Action 1975, Southern Growth Policies Bd. 1980; Chair. Democratic Leadership Council 1990–91; mem. U.S. Supreme Court Bar, Bd. of Trustees, Southern Center for Int. Studies of Atlanta, Ga.; Hon. Fellow (Univ. Coll. Oxford) 1992; Hon. D.C.L. (Oxford) 1994; Hon. D.Litt. (Ulster) 1995. *Publication:* Between Hope and History 1996. *Leisure interests:* jogging, swimming, golf, reading. *Address:* The White House, 1600 Pennsylvania Avenue, Washington, DC 20500, U.S.A.

CLINTON, Hillary Rodham, M.A., D.JUR.; American First Lady and lawyer; b. 26 Oct. 1947, Chicago, Ill.; d. of Hugh Ellsworth and Dorothy Howell Rodham; m. Bill (William) Jefferson Clinton (President of U.S.A., q.v.), 1975; one d.; ed. Wellesley Coll. and Yale Univ.; joined Rose Law Firm 1977, now Sr. Partner; Legal Counsel, Nixon impeachment staff, House Judiciary Cttee. 1974; Asst. Prof. of Law, Fayetteville and Dir. Legal Aid Clinic 1974–77; lecturer in Law, Univ. of Arkansas, Little Rock 1979–80; Chair. Comm. on Women in the Profession, American Bar Asscn. 1987–91; Head Pres.'s Task Force on Nat. Health Reform 1993–94; newspaper columnist July 1995–; Co-Chair. Children's Defense Fund 1973–74; mem. Bd. Dirs. Southern Devt. Bancorpn. 1986, Nat. Center on Educ. and the Econ. 1987, Franklin and Eleanor Roosevelt Inst. 1988, Children's TV Workshop 1989, Public/Pvt. Ventures 1990, Arkansas Single Parent Scholarship Fund Program 1990; numerous awards and distinctions including One of Most Influential Lawyers in America (Nat. Law Journal) 1988, 1991, Outstanding Lawyer-Citizen Award (Arkansas Bar Asscn.) 1992, Lewis Hine Award, Nat. Child Labor Law Comm. 1993, Friend of Family Award, American Home Econs. Foundation 1993, Humanitarian Award, Alzheimer's Asscn. 1994, Elie Wiesel Foundation 1994; Hon. LL.D. (Arkansas, Little Rock) 1985, (Arkansas Coll.) 1988, (Hendrix Coll.) 1992; Hon. D.H.L. (Drew) 1996; AIDS Awareness Award 1994, Grammy Award 1996; numerous other awards and prizes. *Publications:* It Takes a Village 1996, Dear Socks, Dear Buddy 1998; numerous contribs. to professional journals. *Leisure interests:* reading, walking, tennis. *Address:* The White House, 1600 Pennsylvania Avenue, Washington, DC 20500, U.S.A.

CLINTON-DAVIS, Baron (Life Peer) cr. 1990, of Hackney in the London Borough of Hackney, **Stanley Clinton Davis,** LL.B.; British politician, solicitor and international official; b. 6 Dec. 1928, London; s. of late Sidney Davis and of Lily Davis; m. Frances J. Lucas 1954; one s. three d.; ed. Hackney Downs School, Bournemouth School, Mercers' School and King's Coll., London; fmr. Councillor and Mayor, London Borough of Hackney; mem. Parl. for Hackney Cen. 1970–83; Parl. Under-Sec. of State for Trade 1974–79; Opposition Spokesman for Trade 1979–81, for Transport, House of Lords 1990–97; Minister of State, Dept. of Trade and Industry 1997–98; Deputy Opposition Spokesman for Foreign Affairs 1981–83; Commr. of the European Communities for the Environment, Consumer Protection, Nuclear Safety, Forests and Transport Jan. 1985–86, for Environment, Transport and Nuclear Safety 1986–88; Chair. Refugee Council 1989–97, Advisory Cttee. on Protection of the Sea (ACOPS) 1989–97; Consultant on European affairs and law, S. J. Berwin & Co. 1989–97, European Cockpit Asscn. (E.C.A.) 1995–97; Pres. Asscn. of Metropolitan Authorities 1992–, Airfields Environment Fed. 1994–97, British Airline Pilots Asscn. (B.A.L.P.A.) 1995–97; Deputy Chair. Labour Finance and Industry Group 1993–; Fellow King's Coll. and Queen Mary and Westfield Coll., London Univ.; Dr. h.c. (Polytechnical Inst., Bucharest) 1993; First Medal for Outstanding Services to Animal Welfare in Europe (Eurogroup for Animal Welfare) 1988, Grand Cross, Order of Leopold II, for services to EC (Belgium) 1990; Labour. *Publication:* Good Neighbours? Nicaragua, Central America and the United States (co-author) 1982. *Leisure interests:* reading political biography, golf. *Address:* House of Lords, Westminster, London, SW1A 0PN, England.

CLOONEY, George; American actor; b. 1962; s. of Nick Clooney; m. Talia Blasam (divorced). *TV series:* E/R 1984–85, The Facts of Life 1985–86, Roseanne 1988–89, Sunset Beat 1990, Baby Talk 1991, Sisters 1992–94, ER 1994–99. *Films:* Return of the Killer Tomatoes 1988, Red Surf 1990, Unbecoming Age 1993, From Dusk Till Dawn, Batman and Robin, The Peacemaker 1998, Out of Sight 1998, The Thin Red Line 1998, Three Kings 1999. *Address:* William Morris Agency, 151 El Camino, Beverly Hills, CA 90212, U.S.A. (Office).

CLOSE, Glenn: American actress; b. 19 March 1947, Greenwich, Conn.; d. of William Close and Bettine Close; m. 1st Cabot Wade (divorced); m. 2nd James Marlas 1984 (divorced); one d. by John Starke; ed. William and Mary Coll.; joined New Phoenix Repertory Co. 1974; co-owner The Leaf and Bean Coffee House, Bozeman 1991–. *Stage appearances include:* Love for Love, The Rules of the Game, The Singular Life of Albert Nobbs, Childhood, Real

Thing (Tony Award), A Streetcar Named Desire, King Lear, The Rose Tattoo, Benefactors, Death and the Maiden, Sunset Boulevard. *Films include:* The World According to Garp 1982, The Big Chill 1983, The Natural 1984, The Stone Boy 1984, Maxie 1985, Jagged Edge 1985, Fatal Attraction 1987, Dangerous Liaisons 1989, Hamlet 1989, Reversal of Fortune 1989, The House of Spirits 1990, Meeting Venus 1990, Hamlet 1990, Immediate Family 1991, The Paper 1994, Mary Reilly 1994, Serving in Silence: The Margaret Cammermeyer Story 1995, 101 Dalmatians 1996, Mars Attacks! 1996, Air Force One 1997, Paradise Road 1997; numerous TV film appearances. *Address:* c/o C.A.A., 9830 Wilshire Boulevard, Beverly Hills, CA 90212, U.S.A.

CLOSETS, François de; French author and journalist; b. 25 Dec. 1933, Enghien-les-Bains; s. of Louis-Xavier de Closets and Marie-Antoinette Masson; m. 1st Danièle Lebrun; one s.; m. 2nd Janick Jossin 1970; one s. one d.; ed. Lycée d'Enghien, Faculté de Droit de Paris and Inst. d'Etudes Politiques, Paris; Ed. then special envoy of Agency France-Presse in Algeria 1961–65; scientific journalist, Sciences et Avenir 1964–, Acualités Télévisées 1965–68; contrib. L'Express 1968–69; Head of scientific service, TV Channel 1 1969–72; Head of scientific and tech. service of TV Channel 2 1972; contrib. to Channel 1 1974–; Asst. Ed.-in-Chief TF1; Co-producer l'Enjeu (econ. magazine) 1978–88; Dir. of econ. affairs, TFI 1987; co-producer, Médiations magazine 1987–93; Producer, illustrator Savoir Plus for France 2 1992–; Grand Prix du reportage du Syndicat des journalistes et écrivains 1966, Prix Cazes 1974, 7 d'or du meilleur journaliste 1985, Roland Dorgelès prize 1997. *Publications:* L'Espace, terre des hommes, La lune est à vendre 1969, En danger de progrès 1970, Le Bonheur en plus 1974, La France et ses mensonges 1977, Scénarios du futur (Vol. I) 1978, Le monde de l'an 2000 (Vol. II) 1979, Le Système EPM 1980, Toujours plus 1982, Tous ensemble pour en finir avec la syndicatrie 1985, La Grande Manip 1990, Tant et Plus 1992!, le Bonheur d'apprendre, et comment on l'assassine 1996, Le compte à Rebours 1998. *Address:* France 2, 7 esplanade Henri de France, 75907 Paris Cedex 15, France.

CLOTET, Lluis; Spanish architect; b. 31 July 1941, Barcelona; s. of Jaime Clotet and Concepción Clotet; ed. Higher Tech. School of Architecture; jt. f. Studio PER 1964–83; collaborator XV Triennale de Milano 1973, Festival of Fine Architecture, Paris 1978, Transformations in Modern Architecture, MOMA, New York 1979, Forum Design, Linz 1980, Biennale de Venezia 1980, The House as Image, Louisiana Museum of Modern Art 1981, The Presence of the Past, San Francisco 1982, Ten New Buildings, ICA, London 1983, Contemporary Spanish Architecture, New York 1986; Assoc. with Ignacio Paricio 1983–; Prof. in Drawing, Barcelona Higher Tech. School in Architecture 1977–84; major work includes: Banco España 1981–89, Water Cistern Ciutadella Park, Barcelona 1985–88, SIMON S.A. Bldg., Canovelles 1987–88, Museum of Art, Convent dels Angels, Barcelona (Restoration and extension plan) 1984–89, Teleport, Castellbisbal, Barcelona (plan) 1988, Sport Pavillion in Granada, 100 dwellings at the Olympic Village; numerous prizes.

CLOUDSLEY-THOMPSON, John Leonard, PH.D., F.R.E.S., C.BIOL., F.I.BIOL., F.L.S., F.Z.S., F.W.A.A.S.; British professor of zoology; b. 23 May 1921, Murree, India; s. of A. G. G. Thompson and Muriel Elaine (née Griffiths) Thompson; m. J. Anne Cloudsley 1944; three s.; ed. Marlborough Coll., Pembroke Coll., Cambridge; war service 1940–44, commissioned 4th Queen's Own Hussars 1941 transferred to 4th County of London Yeomanry (Sharpshooters); Lecturer in zoology, King's Coll., Univ. of London 1950–60; Prof. of Zoology, Univ. of Khartoum and Keeper, Sudan Natural History Museum 1960–71; Prof. of Zoology, Birkbeck Coll., Univ. of London 1972–86, Prof. Emer. 1986–; Nat. Science Senior Research Fellow, Univ. of New Mexico, Albuquerque 1969; Leverhulme Emer. Fellowship, Univ. Coll. London 1987–89; Visiting Prof. Univ. of Kuwait 1978, 1983, Univ. of Nigeria, Nsukka 1981, Univ. of Qatar 1986; Chair. British Naturalists' Asscn. 1974–83, Vice-Pres. 1985–; Chair. Biological Council 1977–82 (Medal 1985); Pres. British Arachnological Soc. 1982–85, British Soc. for Chronobiology 1985–87; Vice-Pres. Linnean Soc. 1975–76, 1977–78; Hon. mem. Royal African Soc. 1969 (Medal 1969), British Herpetological Soc. 1983 (Pres. 1991–96), Centre Int. de Documentation Arachnologique, Paris 1995; Ed.-in-Chief Journal of Arid Environments s. 1–37 1978–97; Liveryman Worshipful Co. of Skinners 1952; F.W.A.A.S., Hon. F.L.S. 1997; Hon. Fellow Linnean Soc. 1996; Hon. D.Sc. (Khartoum Univ.) and Silver Jubilee Gold Medal, 1981, Inst. of Biology Charter Award 1981, J. H. Grundy Memorial Medal, Royal Army Medical Coll. 1987, Peter Scott Memorial Award 1993. *Publications:* Spiders, Scorpions, Centipedes and Mites 1958, Animal Behaviour 1960, Rhythmic Activity in Animal Physiology and Behaviour 1961, Animal Conflict and Adaptation 1965, Animal Twilight 1967, Zoology of Tropical Africa 1969, The Temperature and Water Relations of Reptiles 1971, Desert Life 1974, Terrestrial Environments 1975, Insects and History 1976, Man and the Biology of Arid Zones 1977, The Desert 1977, Animal Migration 1978, Biological Clocks 1980, Tooth and Claw 1980, Evolution and Adaptation of Terrestrial Arthropods 1988, Ecophysiology of Desert Arthropods and Reptiles 1991, Nile Quest (novel) 1994, Predation and Defence Amongst Reptiles 1994, Biotic Interactions in Arid Lands 1996, Teach Yourself Ecology 1998, The Diversity of Amphibians and Reptiles 1999. *Leisure interests:* music, photography, travel. *Address:* 10 Battishill Street, London, N1 1TE, England.

CLOUGH, Ray William, Jr., SC.D.; American professor of structural engineering; b. 23 July 1920, Seattle; s. of Ray W. Clough, Sr. and Mildred Eva Nelson; m. Shirley Claire Potter 1942; one s. two d.; ed. Univ. of Washington, Seattle, California Inst. of Tech., Pasadena, Calif. and Massachusetts Inst. of Tech., Cambridge, Mass.; served U.S.A.F. 1942–46; joined Civil Eng. Faculty, Univ. of Calif. as Asst. Prof. of Civil Eng. 1949, Assoc. Prof. 1954, Prof. 1959–, Chair. Div. of Structural Eng. and Structural Mechanics 1967–70, Nishkian Prof. of Structural Eng. 1983–87, Prof. Emer. 1987–; Consultant in Structural Eng., specializing in structural dynamics, computer methods of structural analysis and earthquake eng. 1953–; mem. U.S. Army Corps of Engineers Structural Design Advisory Bd. 1967–; mem. N.A.S., Nat. Acad. of Eng.; Hon. mem. American Soc. of Civil Eng. 1988; Research Prize, Howard Medal, Newmark Medal, Moisieff Medal, Th. von Karman Medal (American Soc. of Civil Engineers), George W. Housner Medal 1996. *Publication:* Dynamics of Structures (with J. Penzien) 1975, 1993. *Leisure interests:* skiing (cross-country) and hiking. *Address:* P.O. Box 4625, Sunriver, OR 97707, U.S.A. (Home).

CLOUTIER, Gilles G., C.C., PH.D., F.R.S.C.; Canadian engineer and physicist; b. 27 June 1928, Quebec City; s. of late Philéas Cloutier and Valéda Nadeau; m. Colette Michaud 1954; two s. three d.; ed. Univ. Laval, Quebec and McGill Univ.; Prof. of Physics, Univ. de Montréal 1963–68; Man. of Basic Research Lab., Dir. of Research and Asst. Dir. of Inst., Research Inst. of Hydro-Quebec (IREQ) 1968–78; Pres. Alberta Research Council 1978–83; Exec. Vice-Pres. Tech. and Int. Affairs, Hydro-Quebec 1983–85; Rector, Univ. de Montréal 1985–93; Pres. Conf. of Rectors and Prins. of Quebec Univs. 1987–89; Chair. of Corporate Higher Educ. Forum 1992–93; consultant in high tech. commercialization; mem. Bd. Centre d'initiative technologique de Montréal 1985–93, Chamber of Commerce of Greater Montreal 1989–93, Asia Pacific Foundation of Canada, Bechtel Canada; mem. Bd. of Trustees of Manning Awards; five hon. doctorates (Montreal, Alberta, McGill, Lyon II and Toronto Univs.); Officier Order of Quebec, Chevalier Légion d'honneur 1991. *Address:* 2910 boulevard Edouard-Montpetit, Montreal, H3C 3J7 (Office); 4500 Promenade Paton, Apt. 1208, Laval, Quebec, H7W 4Y6, Canada (Home).

CLUFF, John Gordon (Algy); British business executive; b. 19 April 1940; s. of Harold Cluff and Freda Cluff; m. Blondel Hodge 1993; two s.; ed. Stowe School; army officer, served W. Africa, Cyprus, Malaysia 1959–64; Chief Exec. Cluff Resources (fmrly. Cluff Oil) 1971–, Chair. (and Chair. Zimbabwe) 1979–; Proprietor, The Spectator 1981–85, Chair. 1985–; Chair. Apollo Magazine Ltd. 1985; Chair., C.E.O. Cluff Mining 1996–; Pres. Société Minérales et Industrielles du Kivu 1996–; Dir. Centre for Policy Studies 1996–; mem. Bd. of Govs. Commonwealth Inst. 1995–. *Address:* 29 St. James's Place, London, SW1A 1NR, England.

CLUFF, Leighton Eggertsen, M.D.; American physician and foundation executive; b. 10 June 1923, Salt Lake City; s. of Lehi E. Cluff and Lottie (Brain) Cluff; m. Beth Allen 1944; two d.; Intern, Johns Hopkins Hosp. 1949–50, Asst. Resident 1951–52; Asst. Resident Physician, Duke Hosp. 1950–51; Visiting Investigator, Asst. Physician, Rockefeller Inst. of Medical Research 1952–54; Fellow, Nat. Foundation of Infantile Paralysis 1952–54; mem. Faculty, Johns Hopkins School of Medicine; mem. staff, Johns Hopkins Hosp. 1954–66, Prof. of Medicine 1964–66; Prof. and Chair. Dept. of Medicine, Univ. of Florida 1966–76; Exec. Vice-Pres. Robert Wood Johnson Foundation 1976–86, Pres. 1986–90, Trustee Emer. 1990–; Distinguished Physician, Dept. of Veterans' Affairs 1990–; Prof. of Medicine, Univ. of Fla. 1990–; many other professional appts. etc. *Publications:* books and articles on internal medicine, infectious diseases, clinical pharmacology. *Leisure interests:* tennis, golf, fly fishing, woodworking, writing. *Address:* 8851 S.W. 45th Boulevard, Gainesville, FL 32608, U.S.A. *Telephone:* (904) 336-0116. *Fax:* (904) 336-7821.

CLUZEL, Jean, L. EN D.; French politician; b. 18 Nov. 1923, Moulins; s. of Pierre Cluzel and Jeanne (née Dumont) Cluzel; m. Madeleine Bonnaud 1947; three s. one d.; ed. Lycée de Vichy and Univ. of Paris; Pres. and Dir.-Gen. Cluzel-Dumont 1947–71; Municipal Councillor St. Pourcain/Sioule 1959–65; Admin., later Senator, Allier 1971, 1980, 1989; Conseiller Gen. Moulins-Ouest 1967, 1973, 1979, 1985; Pres. Conseil général, Allier 1970–76, 1985–92; Senator, Allier 1971, 1980, 1989; mem. l'Union Centriste, Spokesman and Vice-Pres. Comm. des Finances du Senat; Pres. Cttee. for Econ. Expansion of Allier 1959–67; Pres. "Positions" and "L'Allier Demain", Fed. des Elus Bourbonnais 1972, Univ. Populaire de Bransat 1981, Comité Français pour l'Audiovisuel 1993; Dir. Cahiers de l'audiovisuel 1994; Council mem. Admin. du conseil mondial pour la Radio et la Télévision; Chevalier Légion d'honneur. *Publications include:* Horizons Bourbonnais 1973, Les boutiques en colère 1975, Elu de peuple 1977, Télé Violence 1978, L'argent de la télévision 1979, Finances publiques et pouvoir local 1980, Les pouvoirs publics et la transmission de la culture 1983, Les pouvoirs publics et les caisses d'épargne 1984, Les anti-monarque de la Vème 1985, Un projet pour la presse 1986, La loi de 1987 sur l'épargne 1987, La télévision après six réformes 1988, Les Finances Locales Decentralisées 1989, Le Sénat dans la société française 1990, Une ambition pour l'Allier 1992, Une Autre Bataille de France 1993, Mots pour Mots 1993, Pour qui sont ces tuyaux qui sifflent sur nos têtes? 1993, Feu d'artifices pour fin de législature 1993, L'Age de la Télévision 1993, Lettre à mes collègues représentants du peuple 1993, Education, Culture et Télévision 1994, Du modèle canadien à l'appel sud-africain 1996, L'audiovisuel en Europe centrale et orientale 1996, La télévision 1996, Presse et démocratie 1997. *Address:* 12 villa Dupont, 75116 Paris, France (Home).

CLWYD, Ann; British politician, journalist and broadcaster; b. 21 March 1937; d. of Gwilym Lewis and Elizabeth Lewis; m. Owen Roberts 1963; ed. Holywell Grammar School, The Queen's School, Chester and Univ. Coll. Bangor; fmr. BBC studio man., freelance reporter and producer; Welsh corresp. The Guardian and The Observer 1964–79; Vice-Chair. Welsh Arts Council 1975–79; mem. Royal Comm. on NHS 1976–79, Arts Council of G.B. 1975–80; various public and political appointments; mem. European Parl. for Mid and West Wales 1979–84; Opposition Front Bench Spokesperson on Women 1987–88, on Educ. 1987–88; Shadow Sec. of State on Overseas Devt. and Co-operation 1989–92, on Wales 1992, for Nat. Heritage 1992–93; Opposition Front Bench Spokesperson on Employment 1993–94, on Foreign Affairs 1994–95; mem. Select Cttee. on Int. Devt. 1997–; Chair. All-Party Group on Human Rights 1997–; mem. Parl. for Cynon Valley 1984–; Labour. *Address:* House of Commons, London, SW1A 0AA, England; 6 Deans Court, Dean Street, Aberdare, Mid Glamorgan, CF44 7BN, Wales.

CLYDE, Baron (Life Peer) cr. 1996, of Briglands in Perthshire and Kinross, **James John Clyde,** P.C., B.A., LL.B.; British judge; b. 29 Jan. 1932, Edinburgh; m. Ann Hoblyn 1963; two s.; ed. The Edinburgh Acad., Oxford Univ., Edinburgh Univ.; called to Scottish Bar 1959; Q.C. 1971; Advocate-Depute 1973–74; Judge Courts of Appeal, Jersey and Guernsey 1979–85; a Lord of Appeal in Ordinary 1996–; Chair. Medical Appeal Tribunals 1974–85, Orkney Inquiry 1991–92, St. George's School for Girls; Pres. Scottish Young Lawyers Asscn. 1988–97, Scottish Univs. Law Inst. 1991–; Vice-Pres. Royal Blind Asylum & School 1987–; Assessor to Chancellor Edin. Univ., mem. Univ. Court 1989–97, Vice-Chair. of Court 1993–96; Dir. Edin. Acad. 1978–88; leader UK del. to Consultative Comm. of the Bars of Europe 1981–84; Senator Coll. of Justice 1985–96; Chancellor to Bishop of Argyll and the Isles 1972–85; mem. Scottish Valuation Advisory Council 1972–96, Vice-Chair. 1980–87, Chair. 1987–96; Trustee Nat. Library of Scotland 1977–94, St. Mary's Music School 1978–91; Gov. Napier Polytechnic, later Univ. 1989–93. *Publication:* jt. ed. Armour on Valuation 3rd to 5th edns. *Leisure interests:* music and gardening. *Address:* House of Lords, London, SW1A 0PW, England.

CLYNE, Michael George, A.M., M.A., PH.D.; Australian professor of linguistics; b. 12 Oct. 1939, Melbourne; s. of Dr. John Clyne and Edith Clyne; m. Irene Donohoue 1977; one d.; ed. Caulfield Grammar School, Univs. of Melbourne, Bonn and Utrecht and Monash Univ.; Tutor then Sr. Tutor, Monash Univ. 1962–64, Lecturer then Sr. Lecturer 1965–71, Assoc. Prof. of German 1972–88, Prof. of Linguistics 1988–; Research Dir. Language and Soc. Centre, Nat. Languages Inst. of Australia 1990–; Pres. Australian Linguistic Soc. 1986–88, Vice-Pres. 1989–90; Fellow, Acad. of Social Sciences in Australia, Australian Acad. of Humanities; Hon. Life mem. Applied Linguistics Asscn. of Australia 1989–; other professional memberships, appts. etc.; Hon. D. Phil. (Munich); Austrian Cross of Honour for Science and the Arts (1st class) 1996. *Publications include:* Transference and Triggering 1967, Perspectives on Language Contact 1972, Deutsch als Muttersprache in Australien 1981, Multilingual Australia 1982, Language and Society in the German-Speaking Countries 1984, Australia: Meeting Place of Languages 1985, An Early Start: Second Language at the Primary School 1986, Community Languages, the Australian Experience 1991, Pluricentric Languages 1992, Inter-cultural Communication at Work 1994, Developing Second Language From Primary School 1995, The German Language in a Changing Europe 1995, Background Speakers 1997, Undoing and Redoing Corpus Planning 1997. *Leisure interests:* music, writing references. *Address:* Department of Linguistics, Monash University, 3168 (Office); 33 Quaintance Street, Mount Waverley, 3149 Australia (Home). *Telephone:* 03-9905 2291.

COAKLEY, Sarah Anne, M.A., TH.M., PH.D.; British professor of theology; b. 10 Sept. 1951, London; d. of F. Robert Furber and Anne McArthur; m. James Coakley 1975; two d.; ed. Blackheath High School for Girls, New Hall, Cambridge and Harvard Divinity School; lecturer in Religious Studies, Lancaster Univ. 1976–90, Sr. Lecturer 1990–91; Tutorial Fellow in Theology and univ. lecturer, Oriel Coll. Oxford 1991–93; Prof. of Christian Theology, The Divinity School, Harvard Univ. 1993–95, Edward Mallinckrodt, Jr. Prof. of Divinity 1995–; Harkness Fellowship 1973–75; Select Preacher, Oxford Univ. 1991; Hulsean Lecturer, Univ. of Cambridge 1991–92, Hulsean Preacher 1996; Samuel Ferguson Lecturer, Manchester Univ. 1997, Riddell Lecturer, Newcastle Univ. 1999, Tate-Wilson Lecturer, Southern Methodist Univ. 1999; Hulsean Prize, Cambridge Univ. 1977. *Publications:* Christ Without Absolutes: A Study of the Christology of Ernst Troeltsch 1988, The Making and Remaking of Christian Doctrine (co-ed. with David Pailin) 1993, Religion and the Body (ed.) 1997; contribs. to Church of England Doctrine Comm. Reports 1987, 1991; articles in theological journals. *Leisure interest:* musical activities, thinking about the garden. *Address:* The Divinity School, Harvard University, 45 Francis Avenue, Cambridge, MA 02138, U.S.A. *Telephone:* (617) 495-4518. *Fax:* (617) 495-9489.

COALES, John Flavell, O.B.E., C.B.E., M.A., SC.D., F.ENG., F.R.S.; British emeritus professor of engineering; b. 14 Sept. 1907, Birmingham; s. of John Dennis and Marion Beatrice (Flavell) Coales; m. Mary Dorothea Violet Alison 1936; two s. two d.; ed. Berkhamsted School and Sidney Sussex Coll., Cambridge; Admiralty Dept. of Scientific Research 1929–46; Research Dir. Elliott Bros. (London) Ltd. 1946–52; Asst. Dir. of Research, Eng. Dept., Cambridge Univ. 1953, lecturer 1956, Reader 1958, Prof. 1965–74, now Emer.; Fellow, Clare Hall, Cambridge 1964–74, Emer. 1974–; Mackay Visiting Prof., Univ. of California, Berkeley 1963; mem. Research and Devt. Bd. of Tube Investments Ltd. 1957–61, Eastern Electricity Bd. 1967–73; Pres. Int. Fed. of Automatic Control (IFAC) 1963–66; Chair. U.K. Automation Council 1963–66; Pres. Inst. of Electrical Engs. 1971–72; Chair. Council of Eng. Insts. 1975, Chair. Educ., Training and Qualifications Cttee. of Council 1976–77, Chair. Commonwealth Engineering Education and Training Bd. 1975–79; Deputy Chair. BSA Group Research 1963–73; mem. Exec. Cttee. of Nat. Physical Laboratory 1958–63, Gov. Body of Nat. Inst. of Agricultural Eng. 1970–75, Training and Educ. Advisory Cttee. of R.A.F. 1976–79, Court of Cranfield Inst. of Tech. 1970–82, British Library Advisory Council 1975–81; Gov. Hatfield Coll. of Tech. and Hatfield Polytechnic 1952–71; Dir. Delta Materials Research Ltd. 1974–77, Exec. Cttee., Fellowship of Engineering 1976–80; Chair. Activities Cttee. of Fellowship of Eng. 1976–80; Hon. Fellow, Hatfield Polytechnic 1971–, Hon. Fellow, Inst. of Measurement and Control 1971, Hon. Fellow Inst. of Electrical Engineers 1985; Foreign mem. Serbian Acad. of Sciences 1981; Hon. Sc.D. (City) 1970; Hon. D.Tech. (Loughborough) 1977; Hon. D.Eng. (Sheffield) 1978; Harold Hartley Medal 1971; Giorgio Quazza Medal, Int. Fed. of Automatic Control 1981; Honda Prize 1982. *Publications:* many original papers on communications, radar, magnetic amplifiers, computers, control and systems eng., econ. modelling, educ. and training in eng. *Leisure interests:* mountaineering, gardening, music, reading. *Address:* 14 Chesterford House, Southacre Drive, Cambridge, CB2 2TZ, England. *Telephone:* (01223) 363596.

COASE, Ronald; British professor of economics; b. 29 Dec. 1910, Willesden; s. of Henry Coase and Rosalie Coase; m. Marian Hartung 1937; ed. L.S.E.; Asst. lecturer, lecturer, reader L.S.E. 1935–51; Prof. Univ. of Chicago Law School 1964–82, Clifton R. Musser Prof. Emer. 1982–, also Sr. Fellow in Law and Econs.; winner Nobel Prize for Econs. 1991; numerous hon. degrees. *Publications include:* British Broadcasting a study in Monopoly 1950, The Firm, the Market and the Law 1988, Essays on Economics and Economists 1994. *Address:* University of Chicago Law School, 1111 East 60th Street, Chicago, IL 60637; 1515 N. Astor Street, Chicago, IL 60610, U.S.A. (Home).

COATES, John Henry, B.A., PH.D., F.R.S.; Australian professor of mathematics; b. 26 Jan. 1945, New South Wales; s. of J. H. Coates and B. L. Lee; m. Julie Turner 1966; three s.; ed. Australian Nat. Univ., Ecole Normale Supérieure, Paris, France, Cambridge Univ., U.K.; Asst. Prof., Harvard Univ., U.S.A. 1969–72; Assoc. Prof. (with tenure), Stanford Univ., U.S.A. 1972–75; lecturer, Cambridge Univ., U.K. 1975–77; Prof., Australian Nat. Univ. 1977–78; Prof., Université de Paris XI (Orsay)1978–85; Prof. and Dir. of Math., Ecole Normale Supérieure, Paris 1985–86; Sadleirian Prof. of Math., Cambridge Univ. 1986–, Head of Dept. of Pure Math. and Math. Statistics 1991–97; Professorial Fellow Emmanuel Coll. 1975–77, 1986–; Vice-Pres. Int. Mathematical Union 1991–95; Dr. h.c. (Ecole Normale Supérieure) 1997. *Leisure interest:* reading. *Address:* Emmanuel College, Cambridge, CB1 2EA; 104 Mawson Road, Cambridge, CB1 2EA, England.

COBURN, James; American actor; b. 31 Aug. 1928, Laurel, Nebraska; ed. Los Angeles City Coll.; studied drama with Stella Adler; m. Beverly Kelly 1959; one s. one d.; m. Paula Murad 1993; made professional theatre debut with Vincent Price in Billy Budd at the La Jolla Community Playhouse, Calif. *Films include:* Ride Lonesome 1959, Faces of a Fugitive 1959, The Magnificent Seven 1960, Hell is for Heroes, 1962, The Great Escape 1963, Charade 1963, The Americanization of Emily 1964, Major Dundee 1965, High Wind in Jamaica 1965, The Loved One 1965, Our Man Flint 1966, What Did You Do in the War Daddy? 1966, In Like Flint 1966, The President's Analyst 1967, Duffy 1968, Candy 1968, Hard Contract 1968, A Fistful of Dynamite 1971, The Carey Treatment 1972, The Honkers 1972, Pat Garrett and Billy the Kid 1973, The Last of Sheila 1973, Harry in Your Pocket 1973, Hard Times 1976, Sky Riders 1976, Midway 1976, Cross of Iron 1977, The Internecine 1979, Golden Girl 1979, Firepower 1979, The Muppet Movie 1979, Loving Couples 1980, The Baltimore Bullet 1980, High Risk 1981, Locker 1981, Death of a Soldier 1986, Phoenix Fire, Walking After Midnight, Train to Heaven, Young Guns II 1990, Hudson Hawk 1991, The Player 1992, Deadfall, Sister Act 2 1993, Maverick 1994, The Nutty Professor 1996, Eraser 1996, Keys to Tulsa 1997, Affliction (Acad. Award for Best Supporting Actor) 1998, Payback 1998; producer, The President's Analyst 1967, Waterhole No. 3 1967; owner, Panpiper Productions, Hollywood; numerous TV appearances including The Dain Curse 1978, The Hit List 1993, Profiler 1996.

COBURN, John, A.M., A.S.T.C.; Australian artist; b. 23 Sept. 1925, Ingham, Queensland; s. of Edgar L. Cockburn and Alice Beatts; m. Barbara Woodward 1953 (died 1985); two s. one d.; m. Doreen Gadsby-Wells 1991; ed. All Souls' School, Charters Towers, and East Sydney Technical Coll.; has participated in major exhbns. of Australian art in Australia and abroad, including Australian Painting, Tate Gallery 1963; first one-man exhbn. Gallery of Contemporary Art, Melbourne 1957 and has since held many others in Australian cities, in Paris and Washington 1971, New York 1977, Paris, Bologna, Istanbul and Moscow 1989; art teacher, Nat. Art School, Sydney 1959–66; lived in France 1969–72 where designed many tapestries for the Aubusson workshops including two large tapestry curtains for Sydney Opera House; Head, Nat. Art School, Sydney 1972–74; Trustee, Art Gallery of N.S.W., Sydney 1976–80; work represented in Australian Nat. Gallery, Canberra, all Australian State galleries, Vatican Museum, Graphische

Sammlung Albertina, Vienna and John F. Kennedy Center for the Performing Arts, Washington; Blake Prize for Religious Art 1960, 1977; Hon. D. Litt (James Cook), Assoc. Sydney Tech. Coll. *Leisure interests:* drawing, swimming. *Address:* 4/425 Pacific Highway, Lindfield, N.S.W. 2070, Australia.

COCHRAN, Johnnie L., Jr., B.S., J.D.; American lawyer; b. 2 Oct. 1937, Shreveport, La.; ed. Univ. of Calif. Los Angeles, Loyola Univ. and Univ. of S. Calif.; called to Bar, Calif. 1963, U.S. Dist. Court (Western Dist.) Tex. 1966, U.S. Supreme Court 1968; Deputy City Attorney, Criminal Div. City of L.A. 1963–65; Asst. Dist. Attorney, L.A. County 1978–82; fmr. Adjunct Prof. of Law, Univ. of Calif. L.A. and Loyola Univ.; lawyer rep. U.S. Dist. Court (Cen. Dist.) Calif. 1990, U.S. Court of Appeals (9th Circuit) Judicial Conf. 1990; mem. Bd. Dirs. L.A. Family Housing Corpn., Lawyers Mutual Insurance Co.; Special Counsel, Chair. Rules Cttee. Democratic Nat. Convention 1984; Special Counsel, Cttee. on Standard Official Conduct, Ethics Cttee. 99th Congress, U.S. House of Reps.; Defence Counsel in trial on charges of murder of O. J. Simpson (q.v.) 1995, of Louise Woodward 1997; Fellow, American Bar Foundation; mem. American Coll. Trial Lawyers. *Address:* 4929 Wilshire Boulevard, Ste 1010, Los Angeles, CA 90010, U.S.A.

COCHRAN, Thad; American politician; b. 7 Dec. 1937, Pontotoc, Miss.; s. of William Holmes and Emma Grace (née Berry) Cochran; m. Rose Clayton 1964; two c.; ed. Mississippi Univ. and School of Law, Univ. of Dublin, Ireland; law practice in Jackson, Miss. 1965–72; Pres. Young Lawyers' section of Miss. State Bar, Chair. Miss. Law Inst.; mem. U.S. House of Reps. 1973–78, mem. Agric. Nutrition and Forestry Cttee., Appropriations Cttee., Govt. Affairs Cttee., Rules and Admin. Cttee. and Select Cttee. on Indian Affairs; Senator from Mississippi 1979–; Sec. Republican Conf. in U.S. Senate 1985–90, Chair. Republican Conf., U.S. Senate 1990–. *Address:* Senate Office Building, Washington, DC 20510, U.S.A.

COCHRAN, William, PH.D., F.R.S.; British professor of natural philosophy; b. 30 July 1922, Scotland; s. of James Cochran and Margaret W. Baird; m. Ingegerd Wall 1953; one s. two d.; ed. Boroughmuir School, Edinburgh and Univ. of Edinburgh; Asst. in Physics, Univ. of Edinburgh 1943–46; Research Asst., Univ. Demonstrator, Lecturer, Reader, Cavendish Lab., Cambridge 1946–64; Fellow, Trinity Hall, Cambridge 1953–64; Hon. Fellow 1982–; Prof. of Physics, later of Natural Philosophy, Univ. of Edinburgh 1964–87, Dean, Faculty of Science 1978–81, Vice-Principal 1983–87; Hon. D.Sc. (Heriot-Watt) 1992, (Edin.) 1994; Hughes Medal, Royal Soc. 1978. *Publications:* The Crystalline State, Vol. III (with H. S. Lipson) 1966, Dynamics of Atoms in Crystals 1973. *Leisure interests:* family history, Scots verse and light verse. *Address:* Department of Physics, The University, King's Buildings, Edinburgh, EH9 3JZ (Office); 3 Rustic Cottages, Colinton Road, Edinburgh, EH13 0LD, Scotland (Home).

COCKBURN, William, C.B.E., T.D., F.C.I.T.; British business executive; b. 28 Feb. 1943; entered Post Office 1961, Personal Asst. to Chair. 1971–73, Asst. Dir. of Planning and Finance 1973–77, Dir. Cen. Finance Planning 1977–78, Dir. Postal Finance 1978–79, Dir. London Postal Region 1979–82, mem. Bd. 1981–95, Man. Dir. Royal Mail 1986–92, Chief Exec. The Post Office 1992–95; Chair. Int. Post Corpn. 1994–95; Group Chief Exec., W H Smith Group PLC 1996–97; Group Man. Dir. British Telecommunications PLC 1997–; Dir. (non-exec.) Watkins Holdings Ltd. 1985–93, Lex Service PLC 1993–, Centrica PLC 1996–; Dir. Business in the Community 1990–. *Address:* BT Centre, 81 Newgate Street, London, EC1A 7AJ, England.

COCKER, Jarvis Branson; British singer; ed. St Martin's Coll. of Art and Design; singer with Pulp (fmrly. named Arabacus Pulp) 1981–; made videos for Pulp, Aphex Twin, Tindersticks; co-producer "Do You Remember The First Time?" (TV). *Singles include:* My Legendary Girlfriend 1991, Razzmatazz 1992, O.U. 1992, Babies 1992, Common People 1995, Disco 2000 1996. *Albums include:* It, Freaks, Separations, PulpIntro: The Gift Recordings, His 'N' Hers, Different Class 1995, This is Hardcore 1998. *Address:* c/o Savage and Best Limited, 79 Parkway, London, NW1 7PP, England. *Telephone:* 0171-482 7166. *Fax:* 0171-482 7216.

COCKERELL, Sir Christopher (Sydney), Kt., C.B.E., M.A., F.R.S.; British engineer; b. 4 June 1910, Cambridge; s. of Sir Sydney Cockerell and Florence Kingsford; m. Margaret E. Belsham 1937; two d.; ed. Gresham's, Holt and Peterhouse, Cambridge; radio research Cambridge 1933–35; joined Marconi's 1935, in charge Airborne Devt. Section 1937, Airborne Div. and Navigational Research 1946–48, research 1948–50; started boat-building business later known as Ripplecraft Co. Ltd. 1948, Chair. 1950–79; inventor of Hovercraft 1954, formed Hovercraft Ltd. 1957; consultant to Ministry of Supply on Hovercraft Project 1957–58; consultant Hovercraft Devt. Ltd. 1958–70, Dir. 1959–66; Chair. Wavepower Ltd. 1974–82; mem. Ministry of Technology's Advisory Cttee. for Hovercraft 1968–70; f. and Pres. Int. Air Cushion Eng. Soc. 1969–71 (Vice-Pres. 1971–); Pres. U.K. Hovercraft Soc. 1972–; Fellow, Royal Soc. of Arts 1960–70, Hon. Fellow 1978–, Soc. of Engineers, Manchester Univ. of Science and Technology, Swedish Soc. of Aeronautics; Hon. Fellow, Downing Coll., Cambridge 1969, Fellow of the Royal Soc. 1967, Southampton Chamber of Commerce 1967; Hon. Fellow, Peterhouse, Cambridge 1974; Trustee, Nat. Portrait Gallery 1967–79; Hon. D.Sc. (Leicester and Heriot-Watt Univs.), Hon. D.Sc. (Royal Coll. of Art) 1968, (London Univ.) 1975; Royal Medal, Royal Soc. 1966; Royal Designer for Industry (RDI) 1987; numerous medals. *Leisure interests:* fishing, gardening, visual arts. *Address:* 16 Prospect Place, Hythe, Southampton, Hants., SO45 6AU, England. *Telephone:* (01703) 842931.

COCKFIELD, Baron (Life Peer), cr. 1978, of Dover in the County of Kent; **(Francis) Arthur Cockfield,** Kt., LL.B., B.SC.(ECON.).; British business executive; b. 28 Sept. 1916; s. of Lieut. Charles Cockfield and Louisa James; m. Aileen Monica Mudie 1970 (died 1992); ed. Dover Grammar School, London School of Economics; called to Bar, Inner Temple 1942; Inland Revenue Dept. of Civil Service 1938; Asst. Sec. Bd. of Inland Revenue 1945, Commr. 1951–52, also Dir. of Statistics and Intelligence to Bd. of Inland Revenue 1945–52; Finance Dir. Boots Pure Drug Co. Ltd. 1953–61, Man. Dir. and Chair. Exec. Man. Cttee. 1961–67; mem. Nat. Econ. Devt. Council (N.E.D.C.) 1962–64, 1982–83; Special Adviser on Taxation to the Chancellor of the Exchequer 1970–73; Chair. Price Comm. 1973–77; Minister of State, Treasury 1979–82; Sec. of State for Trade 1982–83, Chancellor of the Duchy of Lancaster 1983–84; Commr. for Internal Market, Tax Law and Customs, Comm. of European Communities and a Vice-Pres. of the Comm. 1985–88; Adviser to Peat, Marwick McLintock 1989–93; Hon. Fellow, L.S.E. 1972; Hon. LL.D. (Fordham, N.Y.), (Sheffield) 1990; Dr. h.c. (Surrey) 1989. *Publication:* The European Union: creating the single market 1994. *Address:* House of Lords, London, SW1A 0PW, England.

COCKING, Edward Charles Daniel, PH.D., D.SC., F.I.BIOL., F.R.S.; British professor of botany; b. 26 Sept. 1931, London; s. of late Charles Cocking and of Mary (Murray) Cocking; m. Bernadette Keane 1960; one s. one d.; ed. Buckhurst Hill Co. High School, Essex and Univ. of Bristol; Civil Service Comm. Research Fellow, 1956–59; Lecturer in Plant Physiology, Univ. of Nottingham 1959–66, Reader 1966–69, Prof. of Botany and Head, Dept. of Botany 1969–97, Prof. Emer. 1997–; Trustee, Royal Botanic Gardens, Kew 1983–93; mem. Governing Body British Soc. for Horticultural Research 1987–89, Council, Royal Soc. 1986–88; Royal Soc. Assessor AFRC 1988–90; Leverhulme Trust Research Fellow 1995–; mem. Lawes Agricultural Trust Cttee. (Rothamsted Experimental Station) 1987–91, Forestry Comm. Advisory Cttee. on Forest Research 1987–95. *Publications:* Introduction to the Principles of Plant Physiology (with W. Stiles); articles in professional journals. *Leisure interests:* walking, travelling, chess. *Address:* Centre for Crop Nitrogen Fixation, School of Biological Sciences, University of Nottingham, University Park, Nottingham, NG7 2RD (Office); 30 Patterdale Road, Woodthorpe, Notts., NG5 4LQ, England (Home). *Telephone:* 0115-951 5151, ext. 8502 (Office); 0115-926 2452 (Home).

COCKS OF HARTCLIFFE, Baron (Life Peer) cr. 1987, of Chinnor in the County of Oxfordshire, **Michael Francis Lovell Cocks,** P.C.; British politician; b. 19 Aug. 1929; m. 1st Janet Macfarlane 1954; two s. two d.; m. 2nd Valerie Davis 1979; ed. Bristol Univ.; fmr. lecturer at Bristol Polytechnic; M.P. for Bristol South 1970–87; Asst. Govt. Whip 1974–76, Parl. Sec. to Treasury and Govt. Chief Whip 1976–79, Opposition Chief Whip 1979–85; Vice-Chair. Bd. of Govs. BBC 1993–98; Labour. *Publication:* Labour and the Benn Factor 1989. *Address:* c/o House of Lords, Westminster, London, SW1A 0PW, England.

CODRON, Michael Victor, C.B.E., M.A.; British impresario; b. 8 June 1930, London; s. of I. A. Codron and Lily (née Morgenstern) Codron; ed. St Paul's School, Worcester Coll., Oxford; Dir. Aldwych Theatre, Hampstead Theatre, Royal Nat. Theatre; Cameron Mackintosh Prof. Oxford Univ. 1993; independent theatrical producer; has produced over 300 shows in West End, London including: The Birthday Party 1958, The Caretaker 1960, The Killing of Sister George, Little Malcolm and his Struggle against the Eunuchs, Big Bad Mouse 1966, The Boyfriend (revival) 1967, A Voyage Round My Father, The Homecoming (revival), Dr Faustus, The Dresser, Three Sisters, Uncle Vanya, The Cherry Orchard 1989, Man of the Moment, Private Lives 1990, The Rise and Fall of Little Voice 1992, Time of My Life, Jamais Vu 1993, Kit and the Widow, Dead Funny, Arcadia, The Sisters Rosensweig 1994, Indian Ink, Dealer's Choice 1995, The Shakespeare Revue 1996, A Talent to Amuse 1996, Tom and Clem 1997, Silhouette 1997, Heritage 1997, Things We Do For Love 1998. *Film:* Clockwise 1986. *Leisure interest:* collecting Caroline of Brunswick memorabilia. *Address:* c/o Aldwych Theatre, Aldwych, London, WC2B 4DF, England. *Telephone:* 0171-240 8291. *Fax:* 0171-240 8467.

COE, Sebastian Newbold, O.B.E., B.SC.; British athlete; b. 29 Sept. 1956, London; s. of Peter Coe and Angela Coe; m. Nicola Susan Elliott 1990; two s. one d.; ed. Loughborough Univ.; competed Olympic Games, Moscow 1980, winning Gold Medal at 1500 m. and Silver Medal at 800 m., and repeated this in Los Angeles 1984; European Junior Bronze Medallist at 1500 m. 1975; European Bronze Medallist at 800 m. 1978; European Silver Medallist at 800 m. 1982; European 800 m. Champion 1986; has held world records at 1500 m. and mile; world record holder at 800 m. and 1000 m.; est. new records at 800 m., 1000 m. and mile 1981; mem. 4 × 400 m. world record relay squad 1982; only athlete to hold world records at 800 m., 1000 m., 1500 m. and mile simultaneously; Pres. first athletes' del. to IOC, Baden-Baden 1981, and mem. first athletes' comm. set up after Congress by IOC 1981–; Conservative M.P. for Falmouth and Camborne 1992–97; mem. Employment Select Cttee. 1992–94, Nat. Heritage Select Cttee. 1995–97; Parl. Pvt. Sec. to Chancellor of Duchy of Lancaster 1994–95, to Michael Heseltine 1995–96; Jr. Govt. Whip 1996–97; Deputy Chief of Staff then Parl. Pvt. Sec. to William Hague, Leader of the Opposition 1997–; Chair. Diadora UK 1987–, ADT Health Quest Charitable Trust 1991–; Vice-Chair. Sports

Council 1986–89, Sports Aid Trust 1987; mem. Health Educ. Authority 1987–92, Health Educ. Council 1986–87; Vice-Patron Sharon Allen Leukemia Trust 1987–, Olympic Cttee. Medical Comm. 1987–95, Sport for All Comm. 1997–; Admin. Steward, British Boxing Bd. of Control 1995–; BBC Sports Personality of 1979; Sir John Cohen Memorial Award 1981; Príncipe de Asturias Award (Spain) 1987; Hon. D. Tech. (Loughborough) 1985, Hon. D.Sc. (Hull) 1988, Hon. LL.B. (Sheffield) 1991. *Publications:* Running Free (with David Miller) 1981, Running for Fitness 1983, The Olympians 1984, More Than a Game 1992, Born to Run (autobiog.) 1992. *Leisure interests:* jazz, theatre, reading, some writing. *Address:* c/o Conservative Central Office, 32 Smith Square, London, SW1P 3HH, England.

COELHO, Paulo; Brazilian author; b. 1947, Rio de Janeiro; fmr. playwright, theatre director, hippie and popular songwriter; imprisoned for alleged subversive activities against Brazilian Govt. 1974. *Publications include:* The Pilgrimage 1987, The Alchemist 1988, Brida 1990, The Valkyries 1992, Maktub 1994, By The River Piedra I Sat Down and Wept 1994, The Fifth Mountain 1998, Veronica Decides to Die 1999. *Address:* c/o HarperCollins, 77–85 Fulham Palace Road, Hammersmith, London, W6 8JB, England. *Telephone:* 0181-741 7070.

COËME, Guy; Belgian politician; b. 21 Aug. 1946, Waremme; m.; two c.; ed. Univ. of Liège; mem. Nat. Office, Parti Socialiste (PS) 1970–74, Vice-Pres. PS 1983–; Deputy Mayor, Waremme 1971–74, 1982–87; Prov. Councillor, Liège 1971–74; Deputy, Liège 1974–81, Huy-Waremme 1982–; Burgomaster, Waremme 1987–; Sec. of State for the Wallonne Region, with responsibility for the Environment and Planning 1981–82; Minister-Pres. Wallonne Regional Exec., with responsibility for Water, Rural Devt., Conservation and Admin. Feb-May 1988; Minister of Nat. Defence 1988–92, Deputy Prime Minister and Minister of Communications and Public Services 1992–94; Pres. Soc. for the Regional Devt. of Wallonne 1978; Vice-Pres. Socialist Party 1983; Admin. Soc. for Regional Investment in Wallonne 1979. *Address:* c/o Parti Socialiste, 13 boulevard de l'Empereur, 1000 Brussels, Belgium.

COEN, Ethan; American film producer and screenwriter; b. 1958, St. Louis Park, Minn.; s. of Ed Coen and Rena Coen; brother of Joel Coen (q.v.); m.; ed. Princeton Univ.; screenwriter (with Joel Coen) Crime Wave (fmrly. XYZ Murders); producer, screenplay, ed. Blood Simple 1984. *Other films* (with Joel Coen): Raising Arizona 1987, Miller's Crossing 1990, Barton Fink 1991 (Palme d'Or, Cannes Festival), The Hudsucker Proxy 1994, Fargo 1996. *Publication:* Gates of Eden 1998. *Address:* c/o U.T.A., 9560 Wilshire Boulevard, Beverly Hills, CA 90212, U.S.A.

COEN, Joel; American film director and screenwriter; b. 1955, St. Louis Park, Minn.; s. of Ed Coen and Rena Coen; brother of Ethan Coen (q.v.); m. (divorced); ed. Simon's Rock Coll. and New York Univ., Asst. Ed. Fear No Evil, Evil Dead; worked with rock video crews; screenwriter (with Ethan Coen) Crime Wave (fmrly. XYZ Murders). *Other films* (with Ethan Coen): Blood Simple 1984, Raising Arizona 1987, Miller's Crossing 1990, Barton Fink 1991 (Palme d'Or, Cannes Festival), The Hudsucker Proxy 1994, Fargo 1996 (Best Dir. Award, Cannes Int. Film Festival 1996). *Address:* c/o U.T.A., 9560 Wilshire Boulevard, Beverly Hills, CA 90212, U.S.A.

COETSEE, Hendrik Jacobus, B.A., LL.B.; South African politician; b. 19 April 1931, Ladybrand, O.F.S.; m. Helena Elizabeth Malan 1956; two s. three d.; ed. Free State Univ.; lectured in law; qualified as attorney; practised, Bloemfontein –1972; called to the Bar 1972; M.P. for Bloemfontein West 1968–94; mem. Exec. Cttee. Nat. Party, O.F.S. 1968–76, Chair. Congress 1979–85; Leader, Nat. Party, O.F.S. 1985–94; Deputy Minister of Defence and Nat. Security 1978–80; Minister of Justice 1980–94, of Defence, of Nat. Intelligence Service 1993–94; Senator O.F.S. 1994–; Pres. of the Senate 1994; Order for Meritorious Service (Gold) 1990, Justice Medal 1990. *Leisure interests:* small scale mixed farming, fishing, clay pigeon shooting. *Address:* P.O. Box 15, Cape Town 8000, South Africa.

COETZEE, John M., M.A., PH.D.; South African writer and academic; b. 9 Feb. 1940, South Africa; one s. one d.; ed. Univ. of Cape Town, Univ. of Texas; Asst. Prof. of English, State Univ. of New York 1968–71; Lecturer, Univ. of Cape Town 1972–76, Sr. lecturer 1977–80, Assoc. Prof. 1981–83, Prof. of General Literature 1984–; Hon. Dr. (Strathclyde) 1985, (State Univ. of New York) 1989, (Cape Town) 1995; CNA Literary Award 1977, 1980, 1983, Geoffrey Faber Prize 1980, James Tait Black Memorial Prize 1980, Booker-McConnell Prize 1983, Prix Femina Etranger 1985 (for Life and Times of Michael K), Jerusalem Prize 1987, Sunday Express Book of the Year Prize (for Age of Iron) 1990, Premio Mondello (for The Master of Petersburg) 1994, Irish Times Int. Fiction Prize (for the Master of Petersburg) 1995. *Publications:* Dusklands 1974, In the Heart of the Country 1977, Waiting for the Barbarians 1980, Life and Times of Michael K 1983, Foe 1986, White Writing 1988, Age of Iron 1990, Doubling the Point: Essays and Interviews (ed. by David Atwell) 1992, The Master of Petersburg 1994, Giving Offence: Essays on Censorship 1996, Boyhood 1997, The Lives of Animals (lecture) 1999. *Address:* P.O. Box 92, Rondebosch 7700, South Africa.

COEY, John Michael David, D.SC.; Irish professor of physics; b. 24 Feb. 1945, Belfast; s. of David S. Coey and Joan E. Newsam; m. Wong May 1973; two s.; ed. Tonbridge School, Jesus Coll. Cambridge and Univ. of Manitoba; Chargé de Recherches, CNRS, Grenoble 1974–78; lecturer/Prof. Trinity Coll. Dublin 1978–, Prof. of Experimental Physics 1987–, Head, Dept. of Physics 1989–92; Visiting Scientist, IBM Research Center, Yorktown Heights, N.Y. 1976–77, 1988, Univ. of Bordeaux 1984, Centre d'Etudes Nucléaires de Grenoble 1985–86, Johns Hopkins Univ. Applied Physics Lab. 1986, Univ. de Paris 7 1992, Univ. of Calif. San Diego 1997, Fla. State Univ. 1998; co-inventor, thermopiezic analyser 1986, nitromag 1990; Chief Coordinator, Concerted European Action on Magnets 1987–94; Dir. Magnetic Solutions Ltd.; mem. Academic Cttee. Magnetism Lab. Inst. of Physics, Beijing 1988–; mem. Royal Irish Acad., Vice-Pres. 1989; Fulbright Fellow 1997–98; Charles Chree Prize and Medal, Inst. of Physics London. *Publications:* Magnetic Glasses (with K. Moorjani) 1984, Structural and Magnetic Phase Transitions in Minerals (with S. Ghose and E. Salje) 1988, Rare-Earth Iron Permanent Magnets 1996, Permanent Magnetism (with R. Skomski) 1999; numerous papers on magnetic and electronic properties of solids. *Address:* Department of Physics, University of Dublin Trinity College, Dublin 2; Hillbrook House, Castleknock, Dublin 15, Ireland.

COFFEY, Rev. David Roy, B.A.; British Baptist leader and minister of religion; b. 13 Nov. 1941; s. of Arthur Coffey and Elsie Maud Willis; m. Janet Anne Dunbar 1966; one s. one d.; ed. Spurgeon's Coll., London; ordained to Baptist ministry 1967; Minister Whetstone Baptist Church, Leicester 1967–72, N. Cheam Baptist Church, London 1972–80; Sr. Minister Upton Vale Baptist Church, Torquay 1980–88; Sec. for Evangelism, Baptist Union of G.B. 1988–91, Gen. Sec. 1991–; Pres. Baptist Union 1986–87; Vice-Pres. European Baptist Fed. 1995–, Pres. 1997–. *Publication:* Build that Bridge: a Study in Conflict and Reconciliation 1986. *Leisure interests:* music, soccer, bookshops. *Address:* Baptist House, P.O. Box 44, 129 Broadway, Didcot, Oxon, OX11 8RT, England. *Telephone:* (01235) 517700. *Fax:* (01235) 517715.

COFFEY, Shelby, III; American journalist; m. Mary Lee Coffey; ed. Univ. of Virginia; with Washington Post 1968–85, latterly Asst. Man. Ed. for nat. news and Deputy Man. Ed. for features; Ed. U.S. News and World Report 1985–86; Ed. Dallas Times Herald 1986; Deputy Assoc. Ed. Los Angeles Times, subsequently Exec. Ed. 1986–89, Ed. and Exec. Vice-Pres. 1989; Nat. Press Foundation Ed. of the Year 1994. *Address:* c/o Los Angeles Times, Times Mirror Co., Times Mirror Square, Los Angeles, CA 90053, U.S.A.

COFFEY, Thomas (see Ó Cofaigh, Tomás).

COFFIN, Frank Morey; American government official and lawyer; b. 11 July 1919, Lewiston, Maine; s. of Herbert and Ruth Coffin; m. Ruth Ulrich 1942; one s. three d.; ed. Bates Coll., and Harvard Univ.; admitted to Maine Bar 1947, legal practice 1947–56; mem. U.S. House of Reps. 1957–61; Man. Dir. Devt. Loan Fund, Dept. of State 1961; Deputy Admin., Agency for Int. Devt. 1961–62; Deputy Admin. for Operations 1962–64; U.S. Rep. to Devt. Assistance Cttee., Org. for European Co-operation and Devt. (OECD), Paris 1964–65; U.S. Circuit Judge, Court of Appeals for First Circuit 1965–89, Chief Judge 1972–83; Sr. Judge 1989–; Adj. Prof., Univ. of Maine School of Law 1986–89; Dir. Governance Inst. 1987–; mem. American Acad. of Arts and Sciences. *Publications:* Witness for Aid 1964, The Ways of a Judge 1980, A Lexicon of Oral Advocacy 1984, On Appeal 1994. *Leisure interests:* sculpture, painting, boating. *Address:* United States Court of Appeals, 156 Federal Street, Portland, ME 04101, U.S.A.

COGGAN, Baron (Life Peer), cr. 1980, of Canterbury and of Sissinghurst in the County of Kent; **Rt. Rev. and Rt. Hon. (Frederick) Donald Coggan,** D.D.; British ecclesiastic; b. 9 Oct. 1909, London; s. of Cornish and Fannie Coggan; m. Jean Strain 1935; two d.; ed. Merchant Taylors' School, St. John's Coll., Cambridge and Wycliffe Hall, Oxford; Asst. lecturer in Semitic Languages and Literature, Manchester Univ. 1931–34; Curate, St. Mary, Islington 1934–37; Prof. at Wycliffe Coll. Toronto 1937–44; Prin., London Coll. of Divinity 1944–56; Bishop of Bradford 1956–61; Archbishop of York 1961–74, of Canterbury 1974–80; Prelate Order of St. John of Jerusalem 1967–80; Life Pres. Church Army 1981–; Chaplain of the Merchant Taylors' Co. 1980–81; Freedom of City of Canterbury 1976. *Publications:* A People's Heritage 1944, The Ministry of the Word 1945, The Glory of God 1950, Stewards of Grace 1958, Five Makers of the New Testament 1962, Christian Priorities 1963, The Prayers of the New Testament 1967, Sinews of Faith 1969, Word and World 1971, Convictions 1975, On Preaching 1978, The Heart of the Christian Faith 1978, Sure Foundation 1981, Mission to the World 1982, Paul: Portrait of a Revolutionary 1984, The Sacrament of the Word 1987, Cuthbert Bardsley: Bishop, Evangelist, Pastor 1989, God of Hope 1991, The Voice from the Cross 1993, The Servant-Son: Jesus Then and Now 1995, A New Day for Preaching 1996, Meet Paul 1998, Psalms 1–72 1998. *Leisure interests:* tapestry, music. *Address:* 28 Lions Hall, St. Swithun Street, Winchester, SO23 9HW, England. *Telephone:* (01962) 864289.

COHAN, Robert Paul, C.B.E.; British choreographer; b. 27 March 1925; s. of Walter and Billie Cohan; ed. Martha Graham School, New York; Partner, Martha Graham School 1950, Co-Dir. Martha Graham Co. 1966; Artistic Dir. Contemporary Dance Trust Ltd., London 1967–; Artistic Dir. and Prin. Choreographer, London Contemporary Dance Theatre 1969–87, Founder-Artistic Dir. 1987–89; Artistic Adviser, Batsheva Co., Israel 1980–89; Dir. York Univ., Toronto Choreographic Summer School 1977, Gulbenkian Choreographic Summer School, Univ. of Surrey 1978, 1979, 1982 and other int. courses; Gov. Contemporary Dance Trust; Ed.-in-Chief, Choreography and Dance (journal); Chair. Robin Howard Foundation; with London Contemporary Dance Theatre has toured Europe, S. America, N. Africa, U.S.A.; major works created: Cell 1969, Stages 1971, Waterless Method of Swimming Instruction 1974, Class 1975, Stabat Mater 1975, Masque of Separation 1975, Khamsin 1976, Nympheas 1976, Forest 1977, Eos 1978, Songs, Lamentations and Praises 1979, Dances of Love and Death 1981, Agora 1984, A Mass for Man 1985, Ceremony 1986, Interrogations 1986, Video Life 1986, Phantasmagoria 1987, A Midsummer Night's Dream 1993, The Four Seasons 1996; Hon. Fellow York Univ., Toronto; Hon. D.Litt. (Exeter Univ.) 1993; Dr. h.c. (Middx.) 1994; Evening Standard Award for outstanding achievement in ballet 1975; Soc. of W. End Theatres Award for outstanding achievement in ballet 1978. *Publication:* The Dance Workshop 1986. *Leisure interest:* dancing. *Address:* The Place, 17 Dukes Road, London, WC1H 9AB, England. *Telephone:* 0171-387 0161.

COHEN, Abby Joseph, M.A.; American financial executive; b. 29 Feb. 1952, New York; d. of Raymond Joseph Cohen and late Shirley (Silverstein) Joseph; m. David M. Cohen 1973; two d.; ed. Martin Van Buren High School, Cornell Univ., George Washington Univ.; Jr. Economist, Fed. Reserve Bd., Washington, D.C. 1973–76; economist/analyst, T. Rowe Price Assocs., Baltimore, Md. 1976–83; investment strategist, Drexel Burnham Lambert, New York 1983–90, BZW, New York 1990, Goldman, Sachs & Co. 1990–, Man. Dir. 1996–; Chair. Inst. of Chartered Financial Analysts; mem. Bd. of Govs. Nat. Economists Club, New York Soc. of Security Analysts; Vice-Chair. Asscn. for Investment Man. Research; mem. Nat. Asscn. of Business Economists; Trustee/Fellow Cornell Univ.; Woman Achiever (Woman of the Year) Award, YWCA, New York 1989. *Address:* Goldman, Sachs & Co., 85 Broad Street, New York, NY 10004, U.S.A.

COHEN, Alexander H.; American theatre and television producer; b. 24 July 1920, New York; s. of Alexander H. and Laura (Tarantous) Cohen; m. 1st Jocelyn Newmark 1942 (divorced); m. 2nd Hildy Parks 1956; two s. one d.; ed. New York Univ.; Producer, Broadway 1941–, London 1963–; has designed numerous theatres; New York productions include Anna Christie, Comedians, Ulysses in Nighttown, Good Evening, Home, Marlene Dietrich, John Gielgud's Ages of Man, Black Comedy, Victor Borge, Hamlet, Beyond the Fringe, The Devils, The School for Scandal, The Unknown Soldier and his Wife, At the Drop of a Hat, Little Murders, Maurice Chevalier, The Homecoming, Mike Nichols and Elaine May, Baker Street, I Remember Mama, A Day in Hollywood/A Night in The Ukraine, 84 Charing Cross Road, Ben Kingsley as Edmund Kean, the Peter Brook production of Carmen, Memory; London productions include Applause, The Happy Apple, Who Killed Santa Claus, Halfway Up the Tree, 1776, Plaza Suite, Mixed Doubles, The Price, Ivanov, Man and Boy, The Rivals, Come As You Are, The Doctor's Dilemma, You Never Can Tell, The Merchant of Venice, The Unknown Soldier and His Wife, The Herbal Bed, Life Support; productions for television: Annual Antoinette Perry (Tony) Awards 1967–87, CBS: On The Air (A Celebration of Fifty Years) 1978, The Emmy Awards 1978, Applause, Night of 100 Stars, Night of 100 Stars II, 1982, 1990, Parade of Stars 1983, The Best of Everything 1983, Happy Birthday Hollywood 1987, Sam Found Out 1988.

COHEN, Bernard Woolf, D.F.A.; British artist; b. 28 July 1933, London; m. Jean Britton 1959; one s. one d.; ed. South West Essex School of Art, St. Martin's School of Art, London and Slade School of Fine Art, London; held teaching appts. at several art schools 1957–67; teacher of painting and drawing, Slade School of Fine Art 1967–73, 1977; Visiting Prof. Univ. of New Mexico 1969–70, faculty alumni 1974; guest lecturer, Royal Coll. of Art 1974–75; Visiting Artist, Minneapolis School of Art 1964, 1969, 1971, 1975, Ont. Coll. of Art 1971, San Francisco Art Inst., Univ. of Vic., B.C. 1975; has lectured at several Canadian univs. since 1969; fmrly. Principal lecturer (Painting), Wimbledon School of Art; Slade Prof., Chair. of Fine Art Univ. of London 1988–; Fellow, Univ. Coll. London 1992; one-man exhbns. at various London galleries since 1953, Venice Biennale 1966, Betty Parsons Gallery, N.Y. 1967, Hayward Gallery, London (retrospective) 1972, Studio La Città, Verona 1972, 1975, Galleria Anunciata, Milan 1973, Tate Gallery, London (print retrospective) 1976, (paintings) 1995, Gallery Omana, Osaka 1979, Flowers East, London 1998, Flowers West, Los Angeles 1999; has participated in numerous group exhbns. in London, Europe, Japan and U.S.A. since 1953. *Publications:* articles and statements in journals and catalogues. *Leisure interests:* music, cinema, travel. *Address:* Slade School of Fine Art, University College London, Gower Street, London, WC1E 6BT, England. *Telephone:* 0171-380 7040. *Fax:* 0171-380 7801.

COHEN, Gerald Allan, M.A., B.PHIL., F.B.A.; Canadian academic; b. 14 April 1941, Montreal; s. of Bella Lipkin and Morrie Cohen; m. Margaret Florence Pearce 1965 (divorced 1996); one s. two d.; ed. Morris Winchewsky Jewish School, Strathcona Acad. and McGill Univ., Montreal and New Coll. Oxford, England; lecturer in Philosophy, Univ. Coll. London 1963–78, Reader 1978–84; Chichele Prof. of Social and Political Theory and Fellow of All Souls, Oxford Jan. 1985–; Isaac Deutscher Memorial Prize. *Publications:* Karl Marx's Theory of History: A Defence 1978, History, Labour, and Freedom: Themes from Marx 1988, Self-Ownership, Freedom, and Equality 1995. *Leisure interests:* Guardian crossword puzzles, American popular music 1920–60, painting and architecture, the politics of India. *Address:* All Souls College, Oxford, England. *Telephone:* (01865) 279339.

COHEN, Laurence Jonathan, M.A., D.LITT., F.B.A.; British university teacher (retd.); b. 7 May 1923, London; s. of Israel and Theresa Cohen; m. Gillian M. Slee 1953; three s. one d.; ed. St. Paul's School, London and Balliol Coll., Oxford; served Naval Intelligence to Lieut., R.N.V.R. 1942–45; Asst. Dept. of Logic and Metaphysics, Edinburgh Univ. 1947–50; lecturer in Philosophy, Univ. of St. Andrews at Dundee 1950–57; Fellow and Praelector, Queen's Coll., Oxford 1957–90, British Acad. Reader in the Humanities 1982–84, Sr. Tutor 1985–90, Fellow Emer. 1990; Commonwealth Fund Fellow, Princeton and Harvard Univs. 1952–53; Visiting Prof., Columbia Univ. 1967–68, Yale Univ. 1972–73; Visiting Fellow, Australian Nat. Univ. 1980, Visiting Prof., Northwestern Univ. Law School 1988; Hon. Prof. North Western Univ., Xian, China 1987; Pres. British Soc. for Philosophy of Science 1977–79; Co-Pres. Int. Union of History and Philosophy of Science 1987–91; Chair. Philosophy Section, British Acad. 1993–96; Sec.-Gen. ICSU 1993–96; mem. Nat. Exec. Cttee. of Council for the Protection of Rural England 1992–95. *Publications:* The Principles of World Citizenship 1954, The Diversity of Meaning 1962, The Implications of Induction 1970, The Probable and the Provable 1977, The Dialogue of Reason 1986. An Introduction to the Philosophy of Induction and Probability 1989, An Essay on Belief and Acceptance 1992, (Gen. Ed.) Clarendon Library of Logic and Philosophy 1970–. *Leisure interests:* gardening, walking. *Address:* The Queen's College, Oxford, OX1 4AW, England.

COHEN, Leonard, O.C.; Canadian singer and songwriter; b. 21 Sept. 1934, Montreal; ed. McGill Univ.; two c.; f. country-and-western band, The Buckskin Boys 1951; initially wrote poetry, winning McGill Literary Award for first collection, Let Us Compare Mythologies; moved to New York in early 1960s; *recordings include:* Songs of Leonard Cohen, Songs From A Room, Various Positions 1985, I'm Your Man 1988, The Future, Cohen Live 1994. *Address:* c/o Kelley Lynch, 419 North Larchmont Blvd., Suite 91, Los Angeles, CA 90004, U.S.A.

COHEN, Marvin Lou, PH.D.; American (b. Canadian) professor of physics; b. 3 March 1935, Montreal, Canada; s. of Elmo Cohen and Molly Zaritsky; m. 1st Merrill Leigh Gardner 1958 (died 1994); one s. one d.; m. 2nd Suzy R. Locke 1996; ed. Univs. of California (Berkeley) and Chicago; mem. Tech. Staff, Bell Labs., Murray Hill, N.J. 1963–64; Asst. Prof. of Physics, Univ. of Calif. (Berkeley) 1964–66, Assoc. Prof. 1966–68, Prof. 1969–95, Univ. Prof. 1995–; Prof. Miller Inst. Basic Research in Science, Univ. of Calif. 1969–70, 1976–77, 1988, Chair. 1977–81, Univ. Prof. 1995–, Faculty research Prof., lecturer 1997–; Chair. Gordon Research Conf. on Chem. and Physics of Solids 1972; U.S. Rep., Semiconductor Comm., Int. Union of Pure and Applied Physics 1975–81; Visiting Prof., Cambridge Univ., U.K. 1966, Univ. of Paris 1972–73 etc., Univ. of Hawaii 1978–79, Technion, Haifa, Israel 1987–88; Alfred P. Sloan Fellow, Cambridge Univ. 1965–67; Guggenheim Fellow 1978–79, 1990–91; Fellow, American Physics Soc. Exec. Council 1975–79, Chair. 1977–78; mem. N.A.S. 1980, American Acad. of Arts and Sciences, Oliver E. Buckley Prize Comm. 1980–81, Chair. 1981; mem. Selection Cttee. for Presidential Young Investigator Awards 1983; mem. Cttee. on Nat. Synchotron Radiation Facilities 1983–84; Chair. 17th Int. Conf. on the Physics of Semiconductors 1984; mem. Govt.-Univ.-Industry Research Round Table 1984–, Vice-Chair. Working Group on Science and Eng. Talent 1984–, Advisory Bd. Texas Center for Superconductivity 1991–(mem. 1988–90); mem. Research Briefing Panels N.A.S. on Funding and on High Temperature Superconductivity 1987, U.S.-Japan Workshop on Univ. Research 1988–89, Science Policy Bd. Stanford Synchrotron Radiation Lab. 1990–92, Visiting Cttee. The Ginzton Lab., Stanford Univ. 1991, American Acad. of Arts and Sciences 1993, Scientific Policy Cttee., Stanford Linear Accelerator Center 1993–95; Chair. Comstock Prize Cttee. N.A.S.; Assoc. Ed. Materials Science and Eng. 1987; mem. Advisory Bd. Int. Journal of Modern Physics B 1987–, Editorial Bd. Perspectives in Condensed Matter Physics 1987–, A.A.A.S. 1993–, American Physical Society Lilienfeld Prize Cttee. 1994–95; Oliver E. Buckley Prize for solid state physics 1979; Dept. of Energy Award 1981, 1990, Lawrence Berkeley Lab. Certificate of Merit 1991, Julius Edgar Lilienfeld Prize (American Physical Soc.) 1994. *Publications:* over 600 articles on research topics. *Leisure interests:* music (clarinet), running. *Address:* Department of Physics, University of California, Berkeley, CA 94720, U.S.A. *Telephone:* 510-642-4753. *Fax:* 510-643-9473.

COHEN, Sir Philip, Kt., PH.D., F.R.S., F.R.S.E.; British research biochemist; b. 22 July 1945, Edgware, Middx.; s. of Jacob Davis Cohen and Fanny Bragman; m. Patricia T. Wade 1969; one s. one d.; ed. Hendon County Grammar School and Univ. Coll. London; SERC/NATO Postdoctoral Fellow, Univ. of Washington, Seattle 1969–71; lecturer in Biochemistry, Univ. of Dundee 1971–78, Reader 1978–81, Prof. of Enzymology 1981–84, Royal Soc. Research Prof. 1984–; Dir. Wellcome Trust Bldg., Univ. of Dundee 1996–; Dir. MRC Protein Phosphorylation Unit 1990–; Dir. Wellcome Trust Bldg. 1997–; Fellow, Univ. Coll. London 1993–; mem. Discovery Advisory Bd. SmithKline Beecham Pharmaceutical Co. 1993–97; mem. European Molecular Biology Org., Academia Europaea; Crooman Lecturer, Royal Soc. 1998; Colworth Medal 1977, CIBA Medal 1992, British Biochemical Soc.; Prix Van Gysel, Belgian Royal Acads. of Medicine 1992; Bruce Preller Prize, Royal Soc. of Edin. 1993, Louis Jeantet Prize for Medicine 1997, etc. *Publications:* Control of Enzyme Activity 1976; over 350 articles in scientific journals. *Leisure interests:* bridge, chess, golf, natural history. *Address:* Medical Research Council Protein Phosphorylation Unit, Department of Biochemistry, University of Dundee, Dundee, DD1 4HN (Office); Inverbay II, Invergowrie, Dundee, DD2 5DQ, Scotland (Home). *Telephone:* (01382) 344238 (Office); (01382) 562328 (Home). *Fax:* (01382) 223778.

COHEN, Robert; British cellist; b. 15 June 1959, London; s. of Raymond Cohen and Anthya Rael; m. Rachel Smith 1987; three s.; ed. Purcell School and Guildhall School of Music, cello studies with William Pleeth, André Navarra, Jacqueline du Pré and Mstislav Rostropovich; started playing cello at age of 5; Royal Festival Hall début (Boccherini Concerto), aged 12; London recital début, Wigmore Hall, aged 17; Tanglewood Festival, U.S.A. 1978; recording début (Elgar concerto) 1979; concerts U.S.A., Europe and Eastern Europe 1979; since 1980, concerts world-wide with maj. orchestras and with conductors who include Muti, Abbado, Dorati, Sinopoli, Mazur, Davis, Marriner and Rattle; Dir. Charleston Manor Festival, E. Sussex 1989–; regular int. radio broadcasts and many int. TV appearances; plays on the "Ex-Roser' David Tecchler of Rome cello dated 1723; winner Young Concert Artists Int. Competition, N.Y. 1978, Píatigorsky Prize, Tanglewood Festival 1978; winner UNESCO Int. Competition, Czechoslovakia 1981. *Recordings include:* Elgar concerto (new Elgar concerto 1993), Dvořák concerto, Tchaikovsky Rococo Variations, Rodrigo Concierto en modo Galante, Beethoven Triple concerto, Grieg sonata, Franck sonata, Virtuoso Cello Music record, Dvořák Complete Piano trios with Cohen Trio, Schubert String Quintet with Amadeus Quartet, Complete Bach solo cello Suites, Howard Blake Diversions, Bliss Concerto 1992, Walton Concerto 1995, Britten Cello Suites 1997, Morton Feldman Concerto 1998, Britten Cello Symphony 1998. *Leisure interests:* photography, squash, cars, computers. *Address:* c/o Intermusica Artists' Management, 16 Duncan Terrace, London, N1 8BZ, England. *Telephone:* 0171-278 5455.

COHEN, Stanley, B.A., PH.D.; American professor of biochemistry; b. 17 Nov. 1922, Brooklyn, New York; s. of Louis Cohen and Fruma Feitel; m. 1st Olivia Larson 1951; m. 2nd Jan Elizabeth Jordan 1981; three s.; ed. Brooklyn and Oberlin Colls., Univ. of Michigan; Teaching Fellow, Dept. of Biochemistry, Univ. of Mich. 1946–48; Instructor, Depts. of Biochemistry and Pediatrics, Univ. of Colo. School of Medicine, Denver 1948–52; Postdoctoral Fellow, American Cancer Soc., Dept. of Radiology, Washington Univ., St. Louis 1952–53; Research Prof. of Biochem. American Cancer Soc. Nashville 1976–; Asst. Prof. of Biochemistry, Vanderbilt Univ. School of Medicine, Nashville 1959–62, Assoc. Prof. 1962–67, Prof. 1967–86, Distinguished Prof. 1986–; mem. Editorial Bds. Excerpta Medica, Abstracts of Human Developmental Biology, Journal of Cellular Physiology; mem. N.A.S., American Soc. of Biological Chemists, Int. Inst. of Embryology, American Acad. of Arts and Sciences; Hon. D.Sc. (Chicago) 1985; Nobel Prize for Physiology and Medicine 1986 and many other prizes and awards. *Leisure interests:* camping, tennis. *Address:* Department of Biochemistry, Vanderbilt University School of Medicine, 607 Light Hall, Nashville, TN 37232, U.S.A.

COHEN, Stanley, M.D.; American pathologist; b. 4 June 1937, New York; s. of Herman Joseph Cohen and Eva Lapidus; m. Marion Doris Cantor 1959; two s. one d.; ed. Stuyvesant High School, Columbia Coll. and Columbia Univ. Coll. of Physicians and Surgeons; Internship and Residency, Albert Einstein Medical Center and Harvard-Mass. Gen. 1962–64; Instructor, Dept. of Pathology, New York Univ. Medical Center 1965–66; Captain, M.C., U.S.A., Walter Reed Inst. of Research 1966–68; Assoc. Prof., State Univ. of New York at Buffalo 1968–72, Assoc. Dir., Center for Immunology 1972–74, Prof. of Pathology 1972–74; Assoc. Chair. Dept. of Pathology, Univ. of Conn. Health Center 1976–80, Prof. of Pathology 1974–87; Prof., Chair. Bd. Hahnemann Univ., Philadelphia 1987–94; Chair. Dept. of Pathology, Hahnemann Medical Center 1986–94; Prof., Chair. Univ. Medicine and Dentistry, N. J. Medical Center 1994–; Kinne Award 1954; Borden Award 1961; Parke-Davis Award in Experimental Pathology 1977; Outstanding Investigator Award, Nat. Cancer Inst. 1986; Co-Chair. Int. Lymphokine Workshop 1979, 1982 and 1984. *Publications:* 175 scientific articles on cellular immunity, ed. 7 books including Mechanisms of Cell-Mediated Immunity 1977, Mechanisms of Immunopathology 1979, The Biology of the Lymphokines 1979, Interleukins, Lymphokines and Cytokines 1983, Molecular Basis of Lymphatic Action 1986, The Role of Lymphatics in the Immune Response 1989. *Leisure interests:* music, photography, karate. *Address:* 611 Bryn Mawr Avenue, Narberth, PA 19072, U.S.A. (Home).

COHEN, Stanley Norman, B.A., M.D.; American professor of genetics; b. 17 Feb. 1935, Perth Amboy, N.J.; s. of Bernard and Ida (Stolz) Cohen; m. Joanna Lucy Wolter 1961; one s. one d.; ed. Rutgers Univ., New Brunswick, N.J. and Univ. of Pennsylvania School of Medicine, Philadelphia, Pa.; intern, The Mount Sinai Hosp., New York 1960–61; Asst. Resident in Medicine, Univ. Hosp., Ann Arbor, Mich. 1961–62; Clinical Assoc., Arthritis and Rheumatism Branch, Nat. Inst. of Arthritis and Metabolic Diseases 1962–64; Sr. Resident in Medicine, Duke Univ. Hosp., Durham, N.C. 1964–65; American Cancer Soc. Postdoctoral Research Fellow, Dept. of Molecular Biology and Dept. of Developmental Biology and Cancer, Albert Einstein Coll. of Medicine, Bronx, New York 1965–67, Asst. Prof. 1967–68; Asst. Prof. of Medicine, Stanford Univ. School of Medicine 1968–71, Head, Div. of Clinical Pharmacology 1969–78, Assoc. Prof. of Medicine 1971–75, Prof. of Genetics 1977 and Prof. of Medicine 1975–, Chair. Dept. of Genetics 1978–86, K.-T. Li Prof. of Genetics 1993–; mem. N.A.S.; Fellow American Acad. of Arts and Sciences, American Acad. of Microbiology; Kinyoun Lecturer 1981, Wolf Prize in Medicine 1981, Marvin J. Johnson Award, American Chemical Soc. 1980, Albert Lasker Basic Medical Research Award 1980, Nat. Medal of Science 1988, Cetus Award 1988, Nat. Biotech. Award 1989, Nat. Medal of Tech. 1989, American Chem. Soc. Special Award 1992, and numerous other prizes and awards. *Address:* Department of Genetics M-320, Stanford University School of Medicine, Stanford, CA 94305, U.S.A. *Telephone:* (415) 497-5315.

COHEN, Sydney, C.B.E., M.D., PH.D., F.R.C.PATH., F.R.S.; British professor of medicine; b. 18 Sept. 1921, Johannesburg, S. Africa; s. of Morris and Pauline Cohen; m. June Bernice Adler 1950; one s. one d.; ed. King Edward VII School, Witwatersrand Univ., Johannesburg, Univ. of London; Emergency Medical Service, U.K. 1944–46; lecturer, Dept. of Physiology, Univ. of Witwatersrand 1947–53; mem. Scientific Staff, Nat. Inst. for Medical Research, London 1954–60; Reader, Dept. of Immunology, St. Mary's Hosp., London 1960–65; Prof. of Chemical Pathology, Guy's Hosp. Medical School, London 1965–86, now Prof. Emer.; mem. MRC 1974–76, Chair. Tropical Medicine Research Bd. 1974–76, Assessor 1983–85; Chair. WHO Scientific group on Immunity to Malaria 1976–81; mem. Council, Royal Soc. 1981–83; Nuffield Dominion Fellow in Medicine 1954; Founding Fellow, Royal Coll. of Pathologists 1964; Hon. D.Sc. (Witwatersrand) 1987. *Publications:* papers and books on immunology and parasitic infections. *Leisure interests:* golf, gardening, hill-farming. *Address:* 4 Frognal Rise, London, NW3 6RD, England; Hafodfraith, Llangurig, SY18 6QG, Wales (Homes). *Telephone:* (0171) 435 6507 (London Home).

COHEN, William S., B.A., LL.B.; American politician; b. 28 Aug. 1940, Bangor, Maine; s. of Reuben and Clara (née Hartley) Cohen; two s.; ed. Bangor High School, Bowdoin Coll., Boston Univ. Law School; admitted to Maine Bar, Mass. Bar, Dist. of Columbia Bar; partner Prairie, Cohen, Lynch, Weatherbee and Kobritz 1966–72; Asst. Attorney, Penobscot County, Maine 1968–70, instructor Univ. of Maine at Orono 1968–72; mem. Bd. of Overseers, Bowdoin Coll. 1973–85; City Councillor, Bangor 1969–72, Mayor 1971–72; elected to Congress 1972, re-elected 1974, 1976, Senator from Maine 1979–96; fmr. mem. numerous cttees. and subcttees.; Sec. of Defense Dec. 1996–; Fellow of John F. Kennedy Inst. of Politics, Harvard 1972; award for Distinguished Public Service, Boston Univ. Alumni Asscn. 1976, L. Mendel Rivers Award, Non-Commissioned Officers' Asscn. 1983, President's Award, New England Asscn. of School Superintendents 1984, Silver Anniversary Award, Nat. Collegiate Athletic Asscn. 1987, Nat. Asscn. Basketball Coaches, U.S. 1987, numerous other awards. *Publications:* Of Sons and Seasons 1978, Roll Call 1981, Getting the Most Out of Washington 1982 (with Prof. Kenneth Lasson), The Double Man 1985 (with Senator Gary Hart), A Baker's Nickel 1986, Men of Zeal (with Senator George Mitchell) 1988, One-Eyed Kings 1991, Murder in the Senate (with Thomas B. Allen) 1993. *Leisure interests:* poetry, sport. *Address:* Secretary of Defense, The Pentagon, Washington, DC 20301, U.S.A. *Telephone:* (202) 697-5737.

COHEN-TANNOUDJI, Claude Nessim, D. ÈS SC.; French academic; b. 1 April 1933, Constantine; s. of Abraham Cohen-Tannoudji and Sarah Sebbah; m. Jacqueline Veyrat 1958; two s. one d.; ed. Ecole Normale Supérieure; Research Assoc. C.N.R.S. 1962–64; Maître de Conférences, then Prof. Faculté des Sciences, Paris 1964–73; Prof. Coll. de France 1973–; mem. Acad. des Sciences; Foreign Assoc. N.A.S.; Foreign Hon. mem. American Acad. of Arts and Sciences; Fellow, American Physical Soc.; Dr. h.c. (Uppsala); recipient of several awards including Ampère Prize (Acad. des Sciences) 1980, Lilienfeld Prize (American Physical Soc.), Charles Townes Award (Optical Soc. of America) 1993; Harvey Prize (Technion, Haifa); CNRS Gold Medal 1996; Nobel Prize for Physics 1997; Commdr. Ordre nat. du Mérite; Officier Légion d'honneur. *Publications:* in collaboration: Optique et Electronique Quantiques 1965, Mécanique Quantique (2 Vols.) 1973, Photons et Atomes, Introduction à l'Electrodynamique Quantique 1987, Processus d'Interaction entre Photons et Atomes 1988, Atoms in Electromagnetic Fields 1994. *Leisure interest:* music. *Address:* 38 rue des Cordelières, 75013 Paris, France. *Telephone:* 33 1 45 35 02 18.

COHN, Haim; Israeli lawyer; b. 11 March 1911, Lübeck, Germany; s. of Zeev Cohn and Miriam Cohn (née Carlebach); m. 1st Else Benjamin 1933; m. 2nd Michal Smoira 1966; one s. one d.; ed. Univs. of Munich, Hamburg and Frankfurt-on-Main, Germany, Hebrew Univ. of Jerusalem and Govt. Law School, Jerusalem; admitted to Bar of Palestine 1937; Sec. Legal Council Jewish Agency for Palestine, Jerusalem 1947; State Attorney, Ministry of Justice, Hakirya 1948, Dir.-Gen. 1949; Attorney-Gen., Govt. of Israel 1950; Minister of Justice and Acting Attorney-Gen. 1952; Attorney-Gen., later Justice, Supreme Court of Israel 1960–81; mem. Perm. Court of Arbitration, The Hague 1962–89, UN Comm. on Human Rights 1957–59, 1965–67; Deputy Chair. Council of Higher Educ., Israel 1958–71; fmr. mem. Bd. of Govs., Int. Inst. of Human Rights, Strasbourg; fmr. Chair. Exec. Council Hebrew Univ. of Jerusalem; Visiting Prof. Emer. of Law, Univ. of Tel-Aviv; Visiting Prof. Emer. of Jurisprudence, Hebrew Univ. of Jerusalem; Hon. mem. Int. Comm. of Jurists; Hon. Pres. Int. Asscn. of Jewish Lawyers and Jurists 1969–89, Israel Civil Rights Asscn. 1981–89; Hon. Pres. Int. Center for Peace in the Middle East 1982–; Haim Cohn Chair of Human Rights, Hebrew Univ. of Jerusalem; LL.D. h.c. John Jay Coll. of Criminal Justice, City Univ. of N.Y. 1980, Georgetown Univ., Washington 1981, Univ. of Aberdeen 1981, Hon. D.Litt. (Hebrew Union Coll., Cincinnati) 1982, Hon. D.Sc. (Weizmann Inst. of Science, Rehovot) 1982. *Publications:* The Foreign Laws of Marriage and Divorce (English) 1937, Glaube und Glaubensfreiheit (German) 1967, The Trial and Death of Jesus (Hebrew) 1968, The Trial and Death of Jesus (English) 1971, Jewish Law in Ancient and Modern Israel (English) 1972, Human Rights in Jewish Law 1983, The Law (Hebrew) 1991, Selected Essays (English and Hebrew) 2 vols. 1992. *Address:* 27 Bet Hakeren Street, Jerusalem 96343, Israel. *Telephone:* (2) 6540883. *Fax:* (2) 6540883.

COHN, Mildred, M.A., PH.D.; American professor of biochemistry and biophysics; b. 12 July 1913, New York City; d. of Isidore M. Cohn and Bertha Klein; m. Henry Primakoff 1938; one s. two d.; ed. Hunter Coll. and Columbia Univ.; Cornell Univ. Medical Coll., New York 1938–46; Washington Univ. Medical School, St. Louis, Mo. 1946–60; Prof. of Biophysics and Biophysical Chem., Univ. of Pa. School of Medicine 1961–75, Prof. of Biochemistry and Biophysics 1975–82; Benjamin Rush Prof. of Physiological Chem. 1978–82, Prof. Emer. 1982–; Visiting Prof. Univ. of Calif., Berkeley 1981, Johns Hopkins Univ. Medical School 1982–91; Career Investigator, American Heart Asscn. 1964–78; Sr. mem. Inst. for Cancer Research 1982–85; mem. American Acad. of Arts and Sciences, N.A.S., American Philosophical Soc.; Hon. Sc.D. (Women's Medical Coll. of Pennsylvania) 1966, (Radcliffe Coll.) 1978, (Washington Univ.) 1981, (Brandeis, Hunter Coll., Univ. of Pennsylvania) 1984, (N. Carolina) 1985, (Miami) 1990; Hon. Ph.D. (Weizmann Inst. of Science) 1988; Cresson Medal, Franklin Inst. 1975, Garvan Medal, American Chem. Soc, Nat. Medal for Science 1982, Chandler Medal, Columbia Univ. 1986, Distinguished Service Award, Coll. of Physicians, Phila. 1987, Remsen Award, Maryland Section, American Chemical Soc. 1988, Pa. Gov.'s Award for Excellence in Science 1993, Stein-Moore Award, Protein Soc. 1997. *Publications:* articles in professional journals, etc. *Leisure interests:* hiking, writing, history of science. *Address:* Department of Biochemistry and Biophysics, University of Pennsylvania School of Medicine, Philadelphia, PA 19104-6089 (Office); 226 W. Rittenhouse Square #1806, Philadelphia, PA 19103, U.S.A. (Home). *Telephone:* (215) 898-8404 (Office); (215) 546-3449 (Home). *Fax:* (215) 898-1806.

COHN, Norman, M.A., D.LITT., F.B.A.; British author and historian; b. 12 Jan. 1915, London; s. of August Cohn and Daisy Cohn (née Reimer); m. Vera Broido 1941; one s.; ed. Gresham's School, Holt and Christ Church Oxford; served in Queen's Royal Regt. and Intelligence Corps 1940–46; lecturer in French, Glasgow Univ. 1946–51; Prof. of French, Magee Univ. Coll. (then associated with Trinity Coll. Dublin), Ireland 1951–60; Prof. of French, King's Coll., Durham Univ. 1960–63; changed career to become Dir. Columbus Centre, Sussex Univ. and Gen. Ed. of Centre's Studies in Persecution and Extermination 1966–80; Professorial Fellow, Sussex Univ. 1966–73, Astor-Wolfson Prof. 1973–80, Prof. Emer. 1980–; Visiting Prof. King's Coll., London 1986–89; Adviser, Montreal Inst. for Genocide Studies 1986–; Hon. LL.D. (Concordia, Canada); Anisfield-Wolf Award in Race Relations 1967. *Publications:* Gold Khan and other Siberian Legends 1946, The Pursuit of the Millennium: Revolutionary Millenarians and Mystical Anarchists of the Middle Ages 1957, Warrant for Genocide: the Myth of the Jewish World-conspiracy and the Protocols of the Elders of Zion 1967, Europe's Inner Demons: an Enquiry Inspired by the Great Witch-hunt 1975, Cosmos, Chaos and the World to Come: the Ancient Roots of Apocalyptic Faith 1993, Noah's Flood: The Genesis Story in Western Thought 1996. *Leisure interests:* travel, walking, looking at pictures, butterfly-watching. *Address:* Orchard Cottage, Wood End, Ardeley, Herts., SG2 7AZ, England. *Telephone:* (01438) 869-247.

COHN, Paul Moritz, PH.D., F.R.S.; British professor of mathematics; b. 8 Jan. 1924, Hamburg, Germany; s. of James and Julia (née Cohen) Cohn; m. Deirdre S. Sharon 1958; two d.; ed. Trinity Coll., Cambridge; Chargé de Recherches, Nancy, France 1951–52; lecturer, Univ. of Manchester 1952–62; Visiting Prof., Yale Univ. 1961–62; Reader, Queen Mary Coll., London 1963–67; Visiting Prof, Univ. of Chicago 1964; Prof. and Head, Dept. of Math., Bedford Coll., London 1967–84; Prof., Univ. Coll., London 1984–89, Astor Prof. of Mathematics 1986–89, Prof. Emer. and Hon. Research Fellow 1989–; Pres. London Mathematical Soc. 1982–84; mem. Math. Cttee., S.R.C. 1977–80, Council, Royal Soc. 1985–87, Nat. Cttee. for Math. 1985–89 (Chair. 1988–); L.R. Ford Award 1972, Berwick Prize 1974. *Publications include:* Free Rings and Their Relations 1971, Algebra 1, 2 1974, 1982, Algebra (2nd Edn. in 3 vols.) 1982–90, Algebraic Numbers and Algebraic Functions 1991, Elements of Linear Algebra 1994, Skew Fields 1995; research papers in algebra. *Leisure interest:* language in all its forms, genealogy. *Address:* Department of Mathematics, University College London, Gower Street, London, WC1E 6BT, England. *Telephone:* (0171) 387 7050.

COHN-SHERBOK, Dan, PH.D., D.D., M.A.H.L., M.LITT.; American rabbi and university professor; b. 1 Feb. 1945, Denver, Colo.; s. of Bernard Sherbok and Ruth Sherbok; m. Lavinia C. Heath 1976; ed. Williams Coll., Hebrew Union Coll. and Univ. of Cambridge; rabbi in U.S.A., U.K., Australia and South Africa 1968–74; Univ. lecturer in Theology, Univ. of Kent 1975–97, Dir. Centre for Study of Religion and Society 1982–90; Visiting Prof. of Judaism, Univ. of Wales at Lampeter 1995–97, Prof. 1997–; Visiting Prof. Univ. of Essex 1993–94, Middx. Univ. 1994–, Univ. of St. Andrews 1995–96, St. Andrews Biblical Theological Coll. Moscow 1996; Fellow, Hebrew Union Coll., Acad. of Jewish Philosophy. *Publications:* The Jewish Heritage 1988, The Crucified Jew 1992, The Jewish Faith 1993, Not a Nice Job for a Nice Jewish Boy 1993, Judaism and Other Faiths 1994, The Future of Judaism 1994, The American Jew 1994, Jewish and Christian Mysticism 1994, Modern Judaism 1995, Jewish Mysticism 1995, The Hebrew Bible 1996, Biblical Hebrew for Beginners 1996, The Liberation Debate 1996, Atlas of Jewish History 1996, Medieval Jewish Philosophy 1996, Fifty Key Jewish Thinkers 1996, The Jewish Messiah 1997, After Noah: Animals and the Liberation of Theology 1997. *Leisure interests:* keeping cats, walking, drawing cartoons. *Address:* Department of Theology and Religious Studies, University of Wales, Lampeter, Ceredigion, SA48 7ED, Wales. *Telephone:* (01570) 424708. *Fax:* (01570) 423641.

COING, Helmut, DR. JUR.; German jurist; b. 28 Feb. 1912; s. of Herman and Elisabeth (Krüger) Coing; m. Hilde Knetsch 1941; one d.; ed. Hanover, Lille, Kiel, Munich and Göttingen; Prof. of Jurisprudence, Goethe Univ., Frankfurt (Main) 1940, Ord. Prof. 1948, Faculty Dean 1950–51, Univ. Rector 1955–57; Pres. West German Conf. of Rectors 1956–57, Wissenschaftsrat 1958–61; Chair. Wissenschaftlicher Beirat, F. Thyssen-Stiftung 1961–; Dir. Max Planck Inst. for History of European Law 1964–80; Vice-Pres. Max Planck Gesellschaft zur Förderung der Wissenschaften e.V., Munich 1978–84; Chancellor of Order of Merit für Wissenschaften und Künste 1973, 1984; mem. Bayerische Akad. der Wissenschaften, Accademia delle Scienze dell'Istituto di Bologna 1965; corresp. mem. Accademia Nazionale dei Lincei 1984; foreign mem. numerous acads. and socs.; Commendatore Ordine al Merito (Italy); Stern zum Grossen Verdienstkreuz des Verdienstordens der Bundesrepublik Deutschland, Officier de la Légion d'honneur (France), Premio Galileo Galilei (Italy) 1980, etc.; Dr. Iur. h.c. Lyon, Montpellier, Vienna, Aberdeen, Brussels, Milano and Uppsala. *Publications:* Die Rezeption des römischen Rechts in Frankfurt am Main 1939, Die obersten Grundsätze des Rechts 1947, Grundzüge der Rechtsphilosophie 1950, 1969, 1976, 1985, Lehrbuch des Erbrechts 1953, Staudinger-Kommentar zum Allgemeinen Teil des BGB 1957 and 1978–80, Römisches Recht in Deutschland (contribution to Ius Romanum Medii Aevi) 1964, Epochen d. Rechtsgeschichte in Deutschland 1967, 1971, Rechtsformen der privaten Vermögensverwaltung insbesondere durch Banken in U.S.A. und Deutschland 1967, Die Treuhand, kraft privaten Rechtsgeschäfts 1973, Gesammelte Aufsätze zu Rechtsgeschichte, Rechtsphilosophie und Zivilrecht 1982; Ed. Handbuch der Quellen und Literatur der neueren europäischen Privatrechtsgeschichte Vol. I 1972, Vols. II/1 and II/2 1976/7, III/1 and III/2 1982, Aufgaben des Rechtshistorikers 1978, Europäisches Privatrecht 1500–1800 1985, 1800–1914 1989. *Leisure interests:* history, architecture. *Address:* Feldbergstrasse 13–15, 61476 Kronberg Germany. *Telephone:* 06173-312512.

COINTAT, Michel; French politician and agronomist; b. 13 April 1921, Paris; s. of Lucien Cointat and Marie-Louise Adam; m. Simone Dubois 1942; two s.; ed. Ecole Nat. des Eaux et Forêts; Insp. of water and forests, Uzès, Gard 1943–49; Insp. forests of Haute-Marne 1950–58; Dir. Gen. Soc. for Devt. of waste ground and scrub lands of the East 1948–61, Pres. 1961–71; Dir. du Cabinet, Ministry of Agriculture 1961–62, Dir. Gen. of Production and Supply 1962–67; Pres. Special Agricultural Cttee. to EEC 1965; Minister of Agriculture 1971–72, of External Trade 1980–81; Deputy Rassemblement pour la République (fmrly. Union Démocratique pour la République) for Ille-et-Vilaine 1967–71, 1981–93; mem. European Parl. 1968–71, 1974–79; Mayor of Fougères 1971–83; Pres. Financial Comm. in Regional Council of Brittany; Pres. Special Comm. to examine proposed land law; Dir. Editions Ufap 1975–83; Questeur (Admin. Official) Assemblée Nat. 1988–90; Pres. Paneurope France 1990–92; mem. Acad. d'agriculture de France and various local socs.; Officier, Légion d'honneur; Officier de l'Ordre national du Mérite; Commandeur du Mérite agricole; Officier des Palmes académiques; Chevalier de l'Economie nationale; Grand Officier du Mérite (Fed. Repub. of Germany); Grand Officier de l'Ordre de Victoria; Commandeur du Mérite Italien; Grand Officier de l'Ordre de la Haute-Volta; Grand Officier du Rio Branco; Mérite Européen. *Publications:* about 500 articles on agriculture, forestry, fishing and related subjects; collections of poems: Souvenirs du temps perdu 1957, Poèmes à Clio 1965, Les heures orangées 1974, les Moments inutiles 1983, le Neveu de Jules Ferry: Abel 1987, 1789: Sept députés bretons à Versailles 1988, Souvenirs de l'Uzège 1992, Poèmes en fleurs 1996. *Address:* 89 rue du Faubourg Saint-Denis, 75010 Paris, France.

COKER, Peter Godfrey, R.A., A.R.C.A.; British artist; b. 27 July 1926; m. Vera J. Crook 1951; one s. (deceased); ed. St. Martin's School of Art, Royal Coll. of Art; one-man exhbns. include Zwemmer Gallery, 1956, 1957, 1959, 1964, 1967, Thackeray Gallery, London 1950, 1972, 1974, 1975, 1976, 1978, Gallery 10, London 1980, 1982, 1984–86, 1988–, Flying Colours Gallery, Edin. 1990; retrospective exhbn. Royal Acad. 1979; has participated in numerous group shows including Tate Gallery 1958, 1992, Royal Coll. of Art 1952–62, Royal Acad. Bicentenary Exhbn. 1968, British Painting 1952–77, Royal Acad. and at other galleries in U.K., Austria and Canada; works in numerous perm. collections in U.K. including Tate Gallery, Arts Council, Chantrey Bequest, Victoria & Albert Museum, British Museum, Nat. Portrait Gallery, Nat. Maritime Museum etc.; Arts Council Award 1976. *Publication:* Etching Techniques 1976. *Address:* The Red House, Mistley, Manningtree, Essex, CO11 1BX, England.

COLASUONNO, H.E. Cardinal Francesco; Italian ecclesiastic; b. 2 Jan. 1925, Grumo Appula; ordained priest 1947; Archbishop, See of Tronto, Truentum 1975; also apptd. Apostolic Nuncio in Italy and San Marino 1975; cr. Cardinal Feb. 1998. *Address:* Apostolic Nunciature, Via Po, 27–29, 0198 Rome, Italy.

COLBERT, Edwin Harris, A.M., D.SC., PH.D.; American vertebrate palaeontologist; b. 28 Sept. 1905, Clarinda, Iowa; s. of George H. and Mary A. Colbert; m. Margaret Matthew 1933; five s.; ed. Univ. of Nebraska and Columbia Univ.; Student Asst. Univ. of Nebraska 1926–29; Univ. Fellow Columbia Univ. 1929–30; Research Asst. American Museum of Natural History 1930–32, Asst. Curator 1933–42, Curator and Chair. Dept. of Amphibians and Reptiles 1944–45, Chair. Dept. of Geology and Palaeontology

1958–60; Dept. of Vertebrate Palaeontology 1960–66, Curator 1966–70, Curator Emer. 1970–; Prof. Vertebrate Palaeontology, Columbia Univ. 1945–69, Prof. Emer. 1969–; Assoc. Curator, Acad. of Natural Sciences of Philadelphia 1937–48; Research Assoc., Museum of N. Ariz. 1954–68, Hon. Curator of Vertebrate Palaeontology 1970–; mem. N.A.S.; Pres. Soc. of Vertebrate Palaeontology 1946–47, Soc. for Study of Evolution 1958; Vice-Pres. Palaeontological Soc. 1963–; Daniel Giraud Elliot Medal (N.A.S.), American Museum of Nat. History Medal 1970, Romer-Simpson Medal, Soc. of Vertebrate Paleontology 1989, Hayden Medal, Acad. of Natural Sciences Pa. 1996. *Publications:* The Dinosaur Book 1951, Evolution of the Vertebrates 1955, 1969, 1980, 1991 (with Michael Morales) Millions of Years Ago: Prehistoric Life in North America 1958, Dinosaurs 1961, Stratigraphy and Life History (with Marshall Kay) 1965, The Age of Reptiles 1965, Men and Dinosaurs 1968, Wandering Lands and Animals 1973, The Year of the Dinosaur 1977, A Fossil Hunter's Notebook 1980, Dinosaurs, An Illustrated History 1983, Digging into the Past 1989, William Diller Matthew, Paleontologist 1992, The Little Dinosaurs of Ghost Ranch 1995, and over 300 papers, etc. *Leisure interests:* history, travel. *Address:* c/o The Museum of Northern Arizona, Route 4, Box 720, Flagstaff, AZ 86001, U.S.A. *Telephone:* 602-774-5213.

COLCLEUGH, D. W. (Dave), PH.D.; Canadian business executive; b. Fort Erie, Ont.; m.; two c.; ed. Univs. of Toronto and Cambridge; research engineer DuPont Canada, Kingston 1963–68, polymer tech. supervisor, Fibres Div. 1968–73, tech. superintendent, Explosives Div., North Bay 1973–75, Tech. and Planning Man., Explosives Div., Montreal 1975–79, Rubber Industry Man., Tyre and Industrial Div. 1979–82, Man. of Gen. Products, Mississauga 1982–85, prin. consultant Corp. Planning Div., Wilmington April–Dec. 1985, Gen. Man. of Finishes, Toronto 1985–89, Dir. of Corp. Planning and Devt. April–Nov. 1989, Vice-Pres. of Mfg. and Eng. 1989–92, Sr. Vice-Pres. with responsibility for Fibres and Intermediates, Eng. Polymers Units and Mfg. and Eng. 1992–94; Vice-Pres., Gen. Man. of Nylon, DuPont Asia-Pacific 1994–95, Pres. 1995–97; Pres., C.E.O. DuPont Canada Inc. 1997–, Chair of Bd. 1998–. *Address:* Office of the President and Chief Executive Officer, DuPont Canada Inc., P.O. Box 2200, Mississauga, Ont., L5M 2H3, Canada.

COLE, Sir (Alexander) Colin, K.C.B., K.C.V.O., O.ST.J., T.D., B.C.L., M.A., F.H.S.; British fmr. Garter Principal King of Arms and barrister; b. 16 May 1922, London; s. of Capt. Edward Harold and Blanche Ruby Lavinia (Wallis) Cole; m. Valerie Card 1944; four s. three d.; ed. Dulwich Coll. and Brasenose Coll. Oxford; Capt., Coldstream Guards 1939–45; barrister-at-law Inner Temple 1949, Hon. Bencher 1988; rank of Major, Honourable Artillery Co. (TA); Lieut.-Col. Queen's Regt. (TA) RARO 1973; Hon. Col. 6/7th Bn. Queen's Regt. 1983–87; Fitzalan Pursuivant of Arms Extraordinary 1953; Portcullis Pursuivant of Arms 1957; Windsor Herald of Arms 1966–78, Garter Principal King of Arms 1978–92; Kt. Prin., Imperial Soc. of Knights Bachelor 1983–94; mem. Court of Common Council, City of London 1964–, Sheriff of City of London 1976–77; Master, Scriveners Co. of London 1978–79; Pres. Royal Soc. of St. George 1982–98; fmr. mem. Int. Acad. of Heraldry; Cruz Distinguida (1st Class), Orden de San Raimundo de Peñafort. *Publications:* numerous articles; illustrator: Visitation of London 1568, Visitation of Wiltshire 1623. *Leisure interests:* architecture, wine-tasting, archaeology. *Address:* Holly House, Burstow, Surrey, RH6 9RG, England.

COLE, Natalie Maria, B.A.; American singer; b. 6 Feb. 1950, Los Angeles; d. of Nathaniel Adam Cole (Nat 'King' Cole) and Maria Hawkins; m. 1st Marvin J. Yancy 1976 (divorced); m. 2nd Andre Fisher (divorced); ed. Univ. of Massachusetts; recordings of albums and singles 1975–; albums include: Inseparable 1975, Natalie 1976, Unpredictable 1977, Thankful 1977, Live 1978, I Love You So 1979, We're The Best Of Friends 1979, Don't Look Back 1980, Happy Love 1981, I'm Ready 1983, Unforgettable – A Tribute to Nat 'King' Cole (with Johnny Mathis) 1983, Dangerous 1985, Everlasting 1987, Good To Be Back 1989, Unforgettable 1991, Too Much Weekend 1992, Take A Look 1993, Holly and Ivy 1994; recipient of several Grammys and other music awards. *Address:* c/o Jennifer Allen, PMK, 995 S. Carrillo Drive, Suite 200, Los Angeles, CA 90048, U.S.A.

COLEGATE, Isabel, F.R.S.L.; British writer; b. 10 Sept. 1931, London; d. of Arthur Colegate and Winifred Colegate; m. Michael Briggs 1953; two s. one d.; ed. Runton Hill School, Norfolk; literary agent Anthony Blond Ltd., London 1952–57; Dr. h.c. (Bath) 1988. *Publications include:* The Blackmailer 1958, A Man of Power 1960, The Great Occasion 1962, Statues in a Garden 1964, The Orlando Trilogy 1968–72, News From the City of the Sun 1979, The Shooting Party 1980 (W. H. Smith Literary Award; filmed 1985), A Glimpse of Sion's Glory 1985, Deceits of Time 1988, The Summer of the Royal Visit 1991, Winter Journey. *Address:* c/o Peters, Fraser and Dunlop, 503/4 The Chambers, Chelsea Harbour, London, SW10 0XF, England. *Telephone:* 0171-344 1000. *Fax:* 0171-352 7356.

COLE-HAMILTON, David John, PH.D., F.R.S.C., F.R.S.E.; British professor of chemistry; b. 22 May 1948, Bovey Tracey; s. of A.M. Cole-Hamilton and the late M.M. Cartwright; m. Elizabeth A. Brown 1973; two s. two d.; ed. Haileybury & Imperial Service Coll. and Univ. of Edinburgh; Research Asst. and temporary lecturer, Imperial Coll. London 1974–78; lecturer, Univ. of Liverpool 1978–83, Sr. lecturer 1983–85; Irvine Prof. of Chemistry St. Andrews Univ. 1985–, Chair. of Chem. 1985–90; Sir Edward Frankland Fellowship 1985; Corday Morgan Medal and Prize 1983. *Publications:* 205 articles on homogeneous catalysis and organometallic chemistry. *Address:* School of Chemistry, University of St. Andrews, St. Andrews, Fife, KY16 9ST (Office); St. Rule, Boarhills, By St. Andrews, Fife, KY16 8PP, Scotland (Home). *Telephone:* (01334) 463805 (Office). *Fax:* (01334) 463808.

COLEMAN, Robert John, J.D.; British civil servant and lawyer; b. 8 Sept. 1943; m. Malinda Tigay Cutler 1966; two d.; ed. Devonport High School for Boys, Plymouth, Jesus Coll. Oxford and Univ. of Chicago Law School; lecturer in Law, Univ. of Birmingham 1967–70; called to the Bar 1969; in practice as barrister-at-law, London 1970–73; Admin., subsequently Prin. Admin., EC 1974–82, Deputy Head of Div. 1983, Head of Div. 1984–87, Dir. Public Procurement 1987–90, Dir. Approximation of laws, freedom of establishment and freedom to provide services, the professions 1990–91, Dir.-Gen. Transport, European Comm. 1991–; Visiting Prof. Univ. of East London 1997–. *Publications:* articles in professional journals. *Address:* 114 rue des Deux Tours, 1030 Brussels, Belgium. *Telephone:* (2) 218.38.65.

COLEMAN, Sidney, PH.D.; American physicist and teacher; b. 7 March 1937, Chicago; s. of Harold Coleman and Sadie (Shanas) Coleman; m. Diana Teschmacher 1982; ed. Illinois Inst. of Tech. and California Inst. of Tech.; mem. Physics Dept., Harvard Univ. 1961–, Donner Prof. of Science 1980–; Trustee Aspen Center for Physics; Fellow American Physical Soc., N.A.S., American Acad. of Arts and Sciences; J. Murray Lack Award (N.A.S.) 1989, Distinguished Alumnus Award (Calif. Inst. of Tech.), Dirac Medal (Int. Centre for Theoretical Physics) 1990. *Publications:* numerous tech. papers on high-energy physics; Aspects of Symmetry 1985. *Address:* Physics Department, Harvard University, Cambridge, MA 02138; 1 Richdale Avenue, Unit 12, Cambridge, MA 02140, U.S.A. (Home). *Telephone:* (617) 495-3763 (Univ.); (617) 492 3491 (Home). *Fax:* (617) 496-8396.

COLEMAN, Terry (Terence Francis Frank), LL.B.; British reporter and author; b. 13 Feb. 1931; s. of Jack Coleman and D. I. B. Coleman; m. 1st Lesley Fox-Strangeways Vane 1954 (dissolved); two d.; m. 2nd Vivien Rosemary Lumsdaine Wallace 1981; one s. one d.; ed. 14 schools and Univ. of London; fmr. Reporter Poole Herald; fmr. Ed. Savoir Faire; fmr. Sub-Ed. Sunday Mercury, Birmingham Post; Reporter then Arts Corresp. The Guardian 1961–70, Chief Feature Writer 1970–74, 1976–79, New York Corresp. 1981, Special Corresp. 1982–89; Special Writer with Daily Mail 1974–76; Assoc. Ed. The Independent 1989–91; Columnist The Guardian 1992–; Feature Writer of the Year, British Press Awards 1982, Journalist of the Year (What the Papers Say Award) 1988. *Publications:* The Railway Navvies 1965 (Yorkshire Post Prize for best first book of the year), A Girl for the Afternoons 1965, Providence and Mr Hardy (with Lois Deacon) 1966, The Only True History: collected journalism 1969, Passage to America 1972, An Indiscretion in the Life of an Heiress (Hardy's first novel) (Ed.) 1976, The Liners 1976, The Scented Brawl: collected journalism 1978, Southern Cross 1979, Thanksgiving 1981, Movers and Shakers: collected interviews 1987, Thatcher's Britain 1987, Empire 1994, W. G. Grace: a biography 1997. *Leisure interests:* cricket, opera and circumnavigation. *Address:* c/o A. D. Peters, The Chambers, Chelsea Harbour, London, SW10 0XF, England. *Telephone:* 0171-720 2651 (Home).

COLERIDGE, David Ean; British business executive; b. 7 June 1932; s. of Guy Cecil Richard Coleridge and Katherine Cicely Stewart Smith; m. Susan Senior 1955; three s.; ed. Eton Coll.; with Glanvill Enthoven 1950–57; joined R. W. Sturge & Co. 1957, Dir. 1966–; Chair. A. L. Sturge (Holdings) Ltd. (now Sturge Holdings PLC) 1978–95; mem. Cttee. of Lloyd's Underwriting Agents Asscn. 1974–82, Chair. 1981–82; mem. Council and Cttee. of Lloyd's 1983–86, 1988–92; Deputy Chair. Lloyd's 1985, 1988, 1989, Chair. 1991–92; Dir. Wise Speke Holdings Ltd. 1987–94, Ockham Holdings PLC 1996–. *Leisure interests:* golf, racing, gardening, family. *Address:* Spring Pond House, Wispers, nr. Midhurst, West Sussex, GU29 0QH; 37 Egerton Terrace, London, SW3 2BU, England. *Telephone:* (01730) 813277; 0171-581 1756 (London). *Fax:* 0171-591 0637 (London).

COLERIDGE, Nicholas David; British publisher and journalist; b. 4 March 1957; s. of David Ean Coleridge (q.v.) and Susan (Senior) Coleridge; m. Georgia Metcalfe 1989; two s. one d.; ed. Eton, Trinity Coll., Cambridge; Assoc. Ed. Tatler 1979–81; columnist Evening Standard 1981–84; Features Ed. Harpers and Queen 1985–86, Ed. 1986–89; Editorial Dir. Condé Nast Publs. 1989–91, Man. Dir. 1992–; mem. Council R.C.A. 1995–; Young Journalist of the Year, British Press Awards 1983. *Publications include:* Tunnel Vision 1982, Around the World in 78 Days 1984, Shooting Stars 1984, The Fashion Conspiracy 1988, How I Met My Wife and Other Stories 1991, Paper Tigers 1993, With Friends Like These 1997. *Address:* 39 Kensington Park Gardens, London, W11 2QT, England. *Telephone:* 0171-221 4293.

COLES, Anna L. Bailey, PH.D.; American professor of nursing; b. 16 Jan. 1925, Kansas City; d. of Lillie Mai Buchanan and Gordon A. Bailey; m. 1953 (divorced 1980); three d.; ed. Freedmen's Hosp. School of Nursing, Washington, D.C., Avila Coll., Kansas City, Mo. and Catholic Univ. of America; Instructor, Veterans Admin. Hosp., Topeka, Kan. 1950–52; Supervisor, Veterans Admin. Hosp., Kansas City 1952–58; Asst. Dir. In-Service Educ., Freedmen's Hosp. 1960–61, Admin. Asst. to Dir. 1961–66, Assoc. Dir. Nursing Service 1966–67, Dir. of Nursing 1967–69; Prof. and Dean, Howard Univ. Coll. of Nursing 1968–86, Dean Emer. 1986–, retd. 1986; Dir. Minority Devt., Univ. of Kansas School of Nursing 1991–95; Pres. Societas Docta, Inc. 1996–; mem. Inst. of Medicine; Meritorious Public Service Award, D.C. 1968; Lifetime Achievement Award Asscn. of Black Nursing Faculty in Higher Educ. 1993, numerous other awards. *Publications:* articles in professional journals; contrib. to Fundamentals of Stroke Care 1976; Nurses, in Encyclopedia of Black America 1981. *Leisure interests:* reading, outdoor cooking and travelling. *Address:* 15107 Interlachen Drive, #205, Silver Spring, MD 20906, U.S.A.

COLES, Sir (Arthur) John, G.C.M.G.; British diplomatist; b. 13 Nov. 1937; s. of Arthur S. Coles and Doris G. Coles; m. Anne M. S. Graham 1965; two s. one d.; ed. Magdalen Coll. School, Brackley and Magdalen Coll. Oxford; joined H.M. Diplomatic Service 1960; Middle Eastern Centre for Arabic Studies, Lebanon 1960–62; Third Sec. Khartoum 1962–64; Asst. Political Agent, Trucial States (Dubai) 1968–71; Head of Chancery, Cairo 1975–77; Counsellor, U.K. Perm. Mission to EEC 1977–80; Head of S. Asian Dept. FCO 1980–81; Pvt. Sec. to Prime Minister 1981–84; Amb. to Jordan 1984–88; High Commr. in Australia 1988–91; Deputy Under-Sec. of State, FCO 1991–94; Perm. Under-Sec. of State and Head of H.M. Diplomatic Service 1994–97; Dir. B.G. PLC 1998–; Visiting Fellow All Souls Coll. Oxford 1998–. *Leisure interests:* walking, cricket, bird-watching, reading, music. *Address:* All Souls College, Oxford, OX1 4AL, England.

COLES, John Morton, M.A., PH.D., SC.D., F.B.A., F.S.A., F.R.S.A.; archaeologist; b. 25 March 1930, Canada; s. of John L. Coles and Alice M. Brown; m. 1st Mona Shiach 1958 (divorced 1985); two s. two d.; m. 2nd Bryony Orme 1985; ed. Univs. of Toronto, Edinburgh and Cambridge; Univ. Lecturer and Reader, Univ. of Cambridge 1960–80, Prof. of European Prehistory 1980–86; Fellow, Fitzwilliam Coll. Cambridge 1963–; mem. Academia Europaea 1989–, Royal Comm. on Ancient and Historical Monuments of Scotland 1992–; Hon. Prof. Exeter and Hull univs.; Dr. h.c. (Uppsala) 1997; Grahame Clark Medal, British Acad. 1995. *Publications:* The Archaeology of Early Man (with E. Higgs) 1969, Field Archaeology in Britain 1972, Archaeology by Experiment 1973, The Bronze Age in Europe (with A. Harding) 1979, Experimental Archaeology 1979, Prehistory of the Somerset Levels (with B. Orme) 1980, The Archaeology of Wetlands 1984, Sweet Track to Glastonbury (with B. Coles) 1986, Meare Village East: the excavations of A. Bulleid and H. St. George Gray 1932–1956 1987, People of the Wetlands (with B. Coles) 1989, Images of the Past 1990, From The Waters of Oblivion 1991, Arthur Bulleid and the Glastonbury Lake Village 1892–1992 (with A. Goodall and S. Minnitt) 1992, Fenland Survey (with D. Hall) 1994, Rock Carvings of Uppland 1995, Industrious and Fairly Civilised: the Glastonbury Lake Village (with S. Minnitt) 1995, Enlarging the Past (with B. Coles) 1996, Lake Villages of Somerset (with S. Minnitt) 1996, Changing Landscapes: the ancient Fenland (with D. Hall) 1998; numerous papers on European prehistory, field archaeology, experimental archaeology. *Leisure interests:* music, travel. *Address:* Fursdon Mill Cottage, Thorverton, Devon, EX5 5JS, England. *Telephone:* (01392) 860125. *Fax:* (01392) 861095.

COLES, Robert Martin, A.B., M.D.; American child psychiatrist; b. 12 Oct. 1929, Boston, Mass.; s. of Philip W. Coles and Sandra (Young) Coles; m. Jane Hallowell 1960; three s.; ed. Harvard Coll. and Columbia Univ.; Intern, Univ. of Chicago clinics 1954–55; Resident in Psychiatry, Mass. Gen. Hosp., Boston 1955–56, McLean Hosp., Belmont 1956–57; Resident in Child Psychiatry, Judge Baker Guidance Center, Children's Hosp., Roxbury, Mass. 1957–58, Fellow 1960–61; mem. psychiatric staff, Mass. Gen. Hosp. 1960–62; Clinical Asst. in Psychiatry, Harvard Univ. Medical School 1960–62; Research Psychiatrist in Health Services, Harvard Univ. 1963–, lecturer in Gen. Educ. 1966–, Prof. of Psychiatry and Medical Humanities, Harvard Univ. Medical School 1977–; numerous other professional appts.; mem. American Psychiatric Asscn.; Fellow, American Acad. of Arts and Sciences etc.; awards include Pulitzer Prize for Vols. II and III of Children of Crisis 1973, Sara Josepha Hale Award 1986. *Publications:* Harvard Diary 1988, Times of Surrender: Selected Essays 1989, The Spiritual Life of Children, numerous books and articles in professional journals. *Leisure interests:* tennis, bicycle riding, skiing. *Address:* Harvard Health Services, Harvard University, 75 Mt. Auburn Street, Cambridge, MA 02138 (Office); 81 Carr Road, Concord, MA 01742, U.S.A. (Home). *Telephone:* 617-495-3736 (Office); 617-369-6498 (Home).

COLGAN, Michael Anthony, B.A.; Irish theatre, film and television producer; b. 17 July 1950, Dublin; s. of James Joseph Colgan and Josephine Patricia (née Geoghegan) Colgan; m. Susan Mary FitzGerald 1975; one s. two d.; ed. Trinity Coll. Dublin; Theatre Dir. Abbey Theatre, Dublin 1974–78; Co. Man. Irish Theatre Co., Dublin 1977–78; Man. Dublin Theatre Festival 1978–80, Artistic Dir. 1981–83, mem. Bd. of Dirs. 1983–; Artistic Dir. Gate Theatre, Dublin 1984–; Exec. Dir. Little Bird Films, Dublin and London 1986–; Artistic Dir. Parma Festival, Italy 1982; mem. Irish Arts Council 1989–93; plays produced: I'll Go On (Samuel Beckett), Dublin, Paris, London, Edin., Bari, Jerusalem, Brussels, Amsterdam, Chicago, New York; Juno and the Paycock (Sean O'Casey), Dublin, Jerusalem, Edin., New York; Salome (Oscar Wilde), Dublin, Edin., Charleston, S.C.; Three Sisters, Dublin and Royal Court Theatre, London; Molly Sweeney (Brian Friel), Dublin, London and New York; The Beckett Festival, Dublin and New York; The Pinter Festival, Dublin; Executive Producer for Two Lives (series of television plays) for RTE; Gov. Dublin City Univ. 1998–; Arts Award, Irish Independent 1985, 1987. *Address:* Gate Theatre, Cavendish Row, Dublin 1 (Office); 25 Orwell Park, Dublin 6, Ireland (Home). *Telephone:* (01) 8744368, 8744085 (Office).

COLLARD, Jean Philippe; French solo pianist; b. 27 Jan. 1948, Mareuil S/AY (Marne); s. of Michel Collard and Monique (Philipponnat) Collard; m. 2nd Ariane de Brion; one s. and two s. from a previous marriage; ed. Conservatoire National de Musique de Paris; *numerous recordings:* music by Bach, Brahms, Debussy, Fauré, Franck, Rachmaninov, Ravel, Saint-Saëns, Schubert Chopin, Mozart; Chevalier Ordre des Arts et des Lettres, Chevalier Ordre nat. du Mérite. *Leisure interests:* windsurfing, tennis. *Address:* Musicaplotz, 11 rue Le Verrier, 75006 Paris, France. *Telephone:* (1) 42.34.53.40 (Office). *Fax:* (1) 40.46.93.77.

COLLENETTE, David Michael, B.A.; Canadian politician; b. 1946, London, England; s. of David H. Collenette and Sarah M. Collenette; m. Penny Collenette 1975; one s.; ed. Glendon Coll., York Univ.; fmrly. worked in life insurance, plastics and exec. recruitment; fmr. Exec. Vice-Pres. Mandrake Man. Consultants; elected to House of Commons 1974, 1980, 1993; fmr. Minister of State (Multiculturalism), Parl. Sec. to Postmaster-Gen. and to Pres. of Privy Council; Minister of Nat. Defence and Minister of Veterans Affairs 1993–96, of Transport July 1997–; Liberal Party. *Leisure interests:* squash, soccer, swimming, classical music and theatre. *Address:* Transport Canada Bldg., 330 Sparks Street, Ottawa, Ont., K1A 0N5; House of Commons, Ottawa, Ont., K1A 0A6, Canada.

COLLET, Bernt Johan; Danish politician; b. 23 Nov. 1941; s. of Harald Collett; m. Catharina Collet; two s. one d.; ran family estate, Lundbygaard; First Lieut. of the Reserve, Den Kongelige Livgarde 1964–; elected to Folketing 1981; Minister of Defence 1987–88; Conservative People's Party. *Address:* c/o Conservative People's Party, Nyhavn 4, P.O. Box 1515, 1020 Copenhagen K, Denmark.

COLLEY, Linda Jane, PH.D., F.R.HIST.S.; British professor of history; b. 13 Sept. 1949; d. of Roy Colley and Marjorie Colley (née Hughes); m. David Nicholas Cannadine (q.v.) 1982; one d. (deceased); ed. Bristol and Cambridge Univs.; Eugenie Strong Research Fellow, Girton Coll., Cambridge 1975–78; Fellow Newnham Coll., Cambridge 1978–79, Christ's Coll., Cambridge 1979–81; Asst. Prof. of History Yale Univ. 1982–85, Assoc. Prof. 1985–90, Prof. of History 1990–92, Richard M. Colgate Prof. of History 1992–98, Dir. Lewis Walpole Library 1982–96; Prof. School of History, L.S.E. 1998–, Leverhulme Personal Research Prof., European Inst. 1998–; Anstey Lecturer Univ. of Kent 1994; William Church Memorial Lecturer, Brown Univ. 1994, Distinguished Lecturer in British History, Univ. of Texas at Austin 1995, Trevelyan Lecturer Cambridge Univ. 1997, Wiles Lecturer, Queen's Univ. Belfast; mem. Women's Forum. *Publications:* In Defiance of Oligarchy: The Tory Party 1714–60 1982, Namier 1989, Crown Pictorial: Art and the British Monarchy 1990, Britons: Forging the Nation 1707–1837 1992 (Wolfson Prize 1993); numerous articles and reviews in U.K. and American learned journals. *Leisure interests:* travel, looking at art. *Address:* European Institute, London School of Economics, Houghton Street, London, WC2A 2AE; c/o Curtis Brown, Haymarket House, 28–29 Haymarket, London, SW1 4SP, England.

COLLIER, Lesley Faye, C.B.E.; British ballet dancer; b. 13 March 1947; d. of Roy Collier and Mavis Collier; twin s.; ed. The Royal Ballet School, White Lodge, Richmond; joined Royal Ballet 1965, prin. dancer 1972–95, ballet mistress 1995–; has danced most of the prin. roles in the repertory; Evening Standard Ballet Award 1987. *Address:* c/o Royal Ballet Company, 155 Talgarth Road, London, W14 9DE, England.

COLLIGNON, Stefan Colin, PH.D.; German economist; b. 11 Dec. 1951, Munich; s. of Klaus Collignon and Rosemarie Collignon; m. Judith Zahler 1984; ed. Institut d'Etudes Politiques, Paris, Free Univ. of Berlin, Univ. of Dar es Salaam, Tanzania, Queen Elizabeth House, Oxford, U.K., London School of Econs.; Financial Analyst, First Nat. Bank in Dallas, Paris 1975–76; teacher, Lindi Secondary School, Deutscher Entwicklungsdienst (Germany Volunteer Service), Tanzania 1977–79; Man. Dir. and Chair. Dorcas Ltd., London 1981–88; Dir. Research and Communication, Asscn. for the Monetary Union of Europe, Paris 1989–; lecturer, Teaching Seminar on EMU, Institut d'Etudes Politiques, Paris 1990–; Pres. Asscn. France-Birmanie 1990–. *Publications:* Droits de l'Homme, Monnaie et développement économique 1992, Europe's Monetary Future (Vol. I) 1994, The Monetary Economics of Europe: Causes of the EMS Crisis (Vol. II) 1994, European Monetary Policy (ed.) 1997; numerous articles and book chapters on monetary union. *Address:* Association for the Monetary Union of Europe, 26 rue de la Pépinière, 75008 Paris (Office); 11 rue d'Ormesson, 75004 Paris, France (Home).

COLLINS, Bob; Australian politician; b. Newcastle, N.S.W.; m.; three c.; worked as extension officer, N.T. Dept. of Agric., market gardener, Arnhem Land, tech. officer, Wildlife Research Div., CSIRO 1967–77; elected as mem. for Arnhem, House of Reps. 1977, subsequently mem. for Arafura; Parl. Leader Australian Labor Party 1981–86; elected Senator for N.T. 1987–98; Minister for Shipping, Aviation Support and Minister Assisting the Prime Minister for Northern Australia 1990–92, Minister for Transport and Communications 1992–93, Minister for Primary Industries and Energy 1993–96; Shadow Minister for Primary Industries and for Northern Australia and Territories 1996–97. *Address:* 7th Floor, Hooker Bldg., Mitchell Street, Darwin, N.T. 0800, Australia.

COLLINS, Christopher Douglas, F.C.A.; British business executive; b. 19 Jan. 1940, Welwyn; s. of Douglas Collins and Patricia Collins; m. Susan Lumb 1976; one s. one d.; ed. Eton Coll.; articled clerk, Peat Marwick Mitchell 1958–64; Man. Dir. Goya Ltd. 1968–75, Dir. 1975–80; amateur steeplechase jockey 1965–75; rep. G.B. in three-day equestrian events 1974–80; Steward, Jockey Club 1980–81; mem. Horse Race Betting Levy

Board 1982–84; Chair. Aintree Racecourse Ltd. 1983–88, Nat. Stud 1986–88; joined Hanson PLC 1989, Dir. 1991, Vice-Chair. 1995, Deputy Chair. 1997, Chair. 1998–. *Leisure interests:* riding, skiing. *Address:* 1 Grosvenor Place, London, SW1X 7JH, England. *Telephone:* 0171-245 1245. *Fax:* 0171-235 3455.

COLLINS, Gerry; Irish politician; b. 16 Oct. 1938, Abbeyfeale, Co. Limerick; m. Hilary Tattan; ed. Univ. Coll. Dublin; fmr. vocational teacher; mem. Dáil 1967–; Acting Gen. Sec. Fianna Fáil Party 1964–67; Parl. Sec. to Minister for Industry and Commerce and to Minister for the Gaeltacht 1969–70; Minister for Posts and Telegraphs 1970–73; mem. Consultative Ass. of Council of Europe 1973–75; Limerick County Council 1974–77; Minister for Justice 1977–81, 1987–89, for Foreign Affairs March–Dec. 1982, 1989–93; Chair. Parl. Cttee. on EEC Affairs 1983–87; mem. European Parl. 1994–, Leader Fianna Fáil Group, Vice-Pres. Union for Europe Group, Pres. European Parl. Del. to S. Africa; Fianna Fáil. *Address:* The Hill, Abbeyfeale, Co. Limerick, Ireland (Home). *Telephone:* 068 31126 (Home).

COLLINS, Jackie; British novelist. *Publications:* The World is Full of Married Men 1968, The Stud 1969, Sunday Simmons and Charlie Brick 1971, Lovehead 1974, The World is Full of Divorced Women 1975, Lovers and Gamblers 1977, The Bitch 1979, Chances 1981, Hollywood Wives 1983, Lucky 1985, Hollywood Husbands 1986, Rock Star 1988, Lady Boss 1990, American Star 1993, Hollywood Kids 1994, Vendetta–Lucky's Revenge 1996, Thrill 1998, L.A. Connections (four-part serial novel) 1998, Dangerous Kiss 1999. *Mini-series:* Hollywood Wives (ABC TV), Lucky Chances (NBC TV), Lady Boss (NBC TV). *Screenplays:* Yesterday's Hero, The World is Full of Married Men, The Stud. *Address:* c/o Simon and Schuster, 1230 Avenue of the Americas, New York, NY 10020, U.S.A. *Fax:* (310) 278-6517.

COLLINS, James Franklin; American diplomatist; Dir. for Intelligence Policy, Nat. Security Council, Washington; Deputy Exec. Sec. Europe and Latin America, U.S. Dept. of State, Washington; Vice-Counsel Izmir, Turkey; Political Counsellor Amman, Jordan; Deputy Chief of Mission, American Embassy Moscow 1990–93, Coordinator for Regional Affairs for New Ind. States, U.S. Dept. of State 1993–94, Sr. Co-ordinator Office of Amb.-at-Large for New Ind. States 1994–97; Amb. to Russia 1997–. *Address:* United States Embassy, 121099 Moscow, Novinski bul. 19/23, Russia. *Telephone:* (095) 252 24 51. *Fax:* (095) 956 41 61.

COLLINS, Joan, O.B.E.; British actress; b. 23 May 1933, London; d. of Joseph William and Elsa (née Bessant) Collins; m. 1st Maxwell Reed (divorced); m. 2nd Anthony Newley (divorced); one s. one d.; m. 3rd Ronald S. Kass 1972 (divorced); one d.; m. 4th Peter Holm 1985 (divorced 1987); *Films include:* I Believe in You 1952, Our Girl Friday 1953, The Good Die Young 1954, Land of the Pharaohs 1955, The Virgin Queen 1955, The Girl in the Red Velvet Swing 1955, The Opposite Sex 1956, Island in the Sun 1957, Sea Wife 1957, The Bravados 1958, Seven Thieves 1960, Road to Hong Kong 1962, Warning Shot 1966, The Executioner 1969, Quest for Love 1971, Revenge 1971, Alfie Darling 1974, The Stud 1979, The Bitch 1980, The Big Sleep, Tales of the Unexpected, Neck 1983, Georgy Porgy 1983, Nutcracker 1984, Decadence 1994, In the Bleak Midwinter 1995, Hart to Hart 1995, Annie: A Royal Adventure 1995, The Clandestine Marriage 1998; numerous TV appearances including Dynasty (serial) 1981, Cartier Affair 1985, Sins 1986, Monte Carlo 1986, Tonight at 8.30 (TV) 1991, Pacific Palisades (serial) 1997; *Plays include:* Private Lives London 1990, Broadway 1991. *Publications:* Past Imperfect 1978, The Joan Collins Beauty Book 1980, Katy, A Fight for Life 1982, Prime Time 1988, Love and Desire and Hate 1990, My Secrets 1994, Too Damn Famous 1995, Second Act 1996, My Friends' Secrets 1999. *Leisure interests:* cinema, antiques, reading, collecting. *Address:* c/o Paul Keylock, 16 Bulbecks Walk, South Woodham Ferrers, Essex, CM3 5ZN, England. *Fax:* (01245) 328367.

COLLINS, Joseph; American communications executive; b. 27 July 1944; s. of Mark Francis Collins and Olive Elizabeth Collins (née Jameson); m. Maura McManmon 1972; one s. three d.; with American TV and Communications Corpn. 1964–84, 1988–90, fmrly. Chair., C.E.O.; Pres. HBO 1984–88; Chair., C.E.O. Time Warner Cable 1990–. *Address:* Time Warner Cable, 290 Harbor Drive, Stamford, CT 06902, U.S.A.

COLLINS, Larry, B.S.; American author; b. 14 Sept. 1929, Hartford, Conn.; s. of John L. Collins and Helen Cannon Collins; m. Nadia Hoda Sultan 1966; two s.; ed. Loomis Inst., Windsor, Conn. and Yale Univ.; Advertising Dept., Proctor and Gamble, Ohio 1951–53; U.S. Army Supreme HQ, Paris 1953–55; Correspondent, United Press Paris 1956, Rome 1957, Middle East, Beirut 1957–59, Newsweek Magazine, Beirut 1959–61, Chief of Bureau, Newsweek, Paris 1961–65; Deauville Film Festival Literary Award 1985. *Publications:* Is Paris Burning? 1965, Or I'll Dress you in Mourning 1968, O Jerusalem 1972, Freedom at Midnight 1975, The Fifth Horseman 1980, Fall from Grace 1985, Maze 1989, Black Eagles 1993, Le Jour du Miracle: D-Day Paris 1994, Tomorrow Belongs to Us 1998. *Leisure interests:* tennis, skiing. *Address:* La Biche Niche, 83350 Ramatuelle, France.

COLLINS, Martha Layne, B.S.; American politician; b. 7 Dec. 1936, Shelby County, Ky.; d. of Everett Larkin and Mary Lorena (Taylor) Hall; m. Bill Collins 1959; one s. one d.; ed. Lindenwood Coll. and Univ. of Kentucky; fmr. high school teacher; Lieut. Gov. State of Ky. 1979–83, Gov. 1983–87; Exec.-in-Residence Univ. Louisville School of Business 1988–; Pres. Martha Layne Collins & Assocs. 1988–; Pres. St. Catherine Coll., Ky. 1990–; mem. Woodford County (Ky.) Democratic Exec. Cttee.; mem. Democratic Nat. Cttee. 1972–76; Chair. Nat. Gov's. Task Force on Drug and Substance Abuse 1986; mem. Credentials Cttee. Democratic Nat. Cttee., Vice-Presidential Selection Process Comm.; mem. Ky. Democratic Cen. Exec. Cttee.; Sec. Ky. Democratic Party; elected Clerk of Court of Appeals 1975, then Clerk of Supreme Court, Ky. *Address:* Office of the President, Saint Catherine College, KY 40061, U.S.A.

COLLINS, Michael; American fmr. astronaut and museum official; b. 31 Oct. 1930, Rome, Italy; m. Patricia M. Finnegan 1957; one s. two d.; ed. U.S. Military Acad. and Harvard Univ.; commissioned by U.S.A.F., served as experimental flight test officer, A.F. Flight Test Center, Edwards A.F. Base, Calif.; selected by NASA as astronaut Oct. 1963; backup pilot for Gemini VII mission 1965; pilot of Gemini X 1966; command pilot, Apollo XI mission for first moon landing July 1969; Asst. Sec. for Public Affairs, Dept. of State 1970–71; Dir. Nat. Air and Space Museum 1971–78, Under-Sec. Smithsonian Inst 1978–80; Maj.-Gen. U.S.A.F. Reserve; Vice-Pres. LTV Aerospace and Defense Co. 1980–85; Pres. Michael Collins Assocs. 1985–; Fellow, Royal Aeronautical Soc., American Inst. of Aeronautics and Astronautics; mem. Int. Acad. of Astronautics, Int. Astronautical Fed.; Exceptional Service Medal (NASA), D.S.M. (NASA), Presidential Medal of Freedom, D.C.M. (U.S.A.F.), D.F.C., F.A.I. Gold Space Medal. *Publications:* Carrying the Fire 1974, Flying to the Moon and Other Strange Places 1976, Liftoff 1988, Mission to Mars 1990.

COLLINS, Pauline; British actress; b. 3 Sept. 1940, Exmouth, Devon; m. John Alderton; two s. one d.; ed. Central School of Speech and Drama; *Stage appearances:* A Gazelle in Park Lane (stage debut, Windsor 1962), Passion Flower Hotel, The Erpingham Camp, The Happy Apple, The Importance of Being Earnest, The Night I Chased the Women with an Eel, Come as You Are, Judies, Engaged, Confusions, Romantic Comedy, Woman in Mind, Shirley Valentine (Olivier Award for best actress, London, Tony, Drama Desk and Outer Critics' Circle awards, New York), Shades, Albery 1992; *Films:* Shirley Valentine 1989, City of Joy 1992, My Mother's Courage 1997, Paradise Road 1997; *TV:* Sarah in series Upstairs, Downstairs, Thomas and Sarah, Forever Green, No—Honestly, Tales of the Unexpected, Knockback, Tropical Moon over Dorking, The Ambassador 1998. *Publication:* Letter to Louise 1992. *Address:* c/o James Sharkey Associates, 21 Golden Square, London, W1R 3PA, England.

COLLINS, Phil, L.V.O.; British pop singer, drummer and composer; b. 1951; s. of Greville Collins and June Collins; m. 1st 1976 (divorced); one s. one d.; m. 2nd Jill Tavelman 1984 (divorced 1995); one d.; ed. Barbara Speake stage school; former child actor appearing as the Artful Dodger in London production of Oliver; joined rock group Genesis as drummer 1970, lead singer 1975–96; albums with Genesis include: Selling England by the Pound 1973, Invisible Touch 1986, We Can't Dance 1991; has also made own solo albums, including No Jacket Required, But Seriously, Face Value, Hello I Must be Going, Dance into the Light 1996 and sound-track singles; appeared in films Buster 1988, Frauds 1993; Trustee Prince of Wales's Trust 1983–97 awards include: Grammy (seven), Ivor Novello (six), Brit (four), Variety Club of GB (two), Silver Clef (two) and Elvis awards. *Address:* c/o Hit & Run Music, 30 Ives Street, London, SW3 2ND, England.

COLLINSON, Patrick, C.B.E., PH.D., F.B.A.; British professor of history; b. 10 Aug. 1929, Ipswich; s. of William Cecil Collinson and Belle Hay Collinson (née Patrick); m. Elizabeth Albinia Susan Selwyn 1960; two s. two d.; ed. King's School, Ely, Pembroke Coll., Cambridge and Univ. of London; Research Asst., Univ. Coll. London 1955–56; Lecturer in History, Univ. of Khartoum, Sudan 1956–61; Lecturer in Ecclesiastical History, King's Coll. London 1961–69; Prof. of History, Univ. of Sydney, Australia 1969–75; Prof. of History, Univ. of Kent at Canterbury 1976–84; Prof. of Modern History, Univ. of Sheffield 1984–88; Regius Prof. of Modern History, Univ. of Cambridge 1988–96, now Emer.; Fellow Trinity Coll., Cambridge 1988–; Chair. Advisory Ed. Bd. Journal of Ecclesiastical History 1982–93; Pres. Ecclesiastical History Soc. 1985–86, Church of England Record Soc. 1991–; mem. Council British Acad. 1986–89; Ford's Lecturer in English History, Oxford Univ. 1979; Hon. D.Univ. (York) 1988, Hon. D.Litt. (Kent) 1989, (Trinity Coll. Dublin) 1992, (Sheffield) 1994, (Oxford) 1997; Medlicott Medal, Historical Assen. 1998. *Publications:* The Elizabethan Puritan Movement 1967, Archbishop Grindal 1519–1583: the Struggle for a Reformed Church 1979, The Religion of Protestants: the Church in English Society 1559–1625 (The Ford Lectures 1979) 1982, Godly People: Essays on English Protestantism and Puritanism 1984, English Puritanism 1984, The Birthpangs of Protestant England: religious and cultural change in the 16th and 17th centuries 1988, Elizabethan Essays 1993, A History of Canterbury Cathedral (jtly.) 1995, The Reformation in English Towns (jtly.). *Leisure interests:* mountain walking and music. *Address:* The Winnats, Cannon Fields, Hathersage, Sheffield, S30 1AG, England (Home). *Telephone:* (01433) 650333 (Home).

COLLMAN, James Paddock, PH.D.; American professor of chemistry; b. 31 Oct. 1932, Beatrice, Neb.; s. of Perry G. Collman and Frances Dorothy Palmer; m. Patricia Tincher 1955; four d.; ed. Univs. of Nebraska and Illinois; Instructor, Univ. of N.C. 1958–59, Asst. Prof. 1959–62, Assoc. Prof. 1962–66, Prof. of Organic and Inorganic Chem. 1966–67; Prof., Stanford Univ. 1967–, George A. and Hilda M. Daubert Prof. of Chem. 1980–; mem. N.A.S., American Acad. of Arts and Sciences; Alfred P. Sloan Foundation

Fellow 1963–66; Nat. Science Foundation Sr. Postdoctoral Fellow 1965–66; Guggenheim Fellow 1977–78, 1985–86; Churchill Fellow (Cambridge) 1977–; Hon. Dr. (Univ. of Nebraska) 1988; Dr. h.c. (Univ. de Bourgogne) 1988; American Chemical Soc. (ACS) Award in Inorganic Chem. 1975, Calif. Scientist of the Year Award 1983, Arthur C. Cope Scholar Award (ACS) 1986, Pauling Award 1990, ACS Award for Distinguished Service in the Advancement of Inorganic Chem. 1991, LAS Alumni Achievement Award, Coll. of Liberal Arts and Sciences Univ. of Ill. 1994. *Publications:* Principles and Applications of Organo-transition Metal Chemistry (with Louis S. Hegedus) 1980, 1987 and 255 scientific papers. *Leisure interest:* fishing. *Address:* Department of Chemistry, Stanford University, Stanford, CA 94305, U.S.A. (University); 794 Tolman Drive, Stanford, CA 94305, U.S.A. (Home). *Telephone:* (415) 723-4648 (University); (415) 493-0934 (Home).

COLLOMB, Bertrand Pierre Charles, PH.D.; French business executive; b. 14 Aug. 1942, Lyon; s. of Charles Collomb and Hélène Traon; m. Marie-Caroline Collomb 1967; two s. one d.; ed. Ecole Polytechnique, Paris, Univ. of Texas, Austin, U.S.A; worked with French govt., f. and man. Center for Man. Research, Ecole Polytechnique 1972–75; joined Lafarge Coppée as Regional Man. 1975, later Pres. and C.E.O. Ciments Lafarge France; C.E.O. Orsan (Biotechnology Co. of the Lafarge Group) 1983; C.E.O. Lafarge Corp. 1987–88; Vice-Chair. and C.E.O. Lafarge 1989, Chair., and C.E.O. Aug. 1989–. *Leisure interests:* horse riding, tennis, hunting. *Address:* Lafarge, 61 rue des Belles Feuilles, 75116 Paris (Office); 4 rue de Lota, 75116 Paris, France (Home). *Telephone:* (1) 44-34-12-02 (Office); 45-53-02-86 (Home). *Fax:* (1) 44-34-12-07.

COLLOR DE MELLO, Fernando; Brazilian politician; b. 1949, Rio de Janeiro; m. 1st Lilibeth Monteiro de Carvalho 1975 (divorced 1981); two s.; m. 2nd Rosane Malta 1984; ed. Univ. of Brasilia; joined family media group becoming Pres. in 1978; Mayor of Maceió, Alagoas state 1979; Fed. Deputy from Alagoas 1982; Gov. of Alagoas 1986; formed Nat. Reconstruction Party 1989; Pres. of Brazil 1990–92; found guilty of official misconduct and officially removed from office by the Senate Dec. 1992; charged with corruption June 1993; banned from political activity until year 2000; brought to trial Dec. 1994; acquitted of all charges by High Court Dec. 1994.

COLLUM, Hugh Robert, F.C.A.; British business executive; b. 29 June 1940, Tavistock; m. Elizabeth Noel Stewart 1965; two d.; with Coopers & Lybrand 1959–64; Finance Dir. Courage Ltd. 1973–81; Deputy Finance Dir. Cadbury Schweppes PLC 1981–83, Finance Dir. 1983–86; Finance Dir. Beecham PLC 1987–89, Exec. Vice-Pres. and Chief Financial Officer, SmithKline Beecham PLC 1989–98; Chair. Hundred Group of Finance Dirs. 1990–92; Non-exec. Chair Chiroscience Group PLC 1998–; Non-Exec. Dir. Sedgwick Group PLC 1987–92, M & G Group PLC 1992–98, Ladbroke Group PLC 1994–96, Whitehead Mann Group PLC 1997–, Safeway PLC 1997–, Siebe PLC 1998–; mem. Cadbury Cttee. on Financial Aspects of Corporate Governance 1991–95. *Leisure interests:* sport, opera. *Address:* 33 Chester Row, London, SW1W 9JE, England. *Telephone:* 0171-823 6304. *Fax:* 0171-823 6312.

COLLYEAR, Sir John Gowen, Kt., B.SC., F.ENG., F.I.M., F.I.E.E., F.R.S.A., C.INST.M.; British engineer; b. 19 Feb. 1927, Bushey; s. of John Robert and Amy Elizabeth (née Gowen) Collyear; m. Catherine Barbara Newman 1953; one s. two d.; ed. Watford Grammar School, Univs. of Manchester and Leeds; with Glacier Metal Co. Ltd. 1953, Jt. Man. Dir. 1969, Man. Dir. 1970–73; Man. Dir. Bearings Div., Assoc. Engineering Ltd. (AE PLC) 1973–75, Group Man. Dir. 1975–81, Chair. 1981–86; Chair. M.K. Electrics Group 1987–88, Fulmer Research Ltd 1987–91, United Texon PLC 1987–95; Pres. MIRA 1987–97, Inst. of Materials 1992–94; Hon. F.I.Mech.E. *Publications:* Management Precepts 1975, The Practice of First Level Management 1976. *Leisure interests:* golf, bridge, music. *Address:* Walnut Tree House, Nether Westcote, Oxon., OX7 6SD, England. *Telephone:* (01993) 831247. *Fax:* (01993) 830794.

COLMAN, Sir Michael Jeremiah, 3rd Bt., cr. 1907; British business executive; b. 7 July 1928, London; s. of Sir Jeremiah Colman, 2nd Bt. and Edith Gwendolyn Tritton; m. Judith Jean Wallop (née William-Powlett) 1955; two s. three d.; ed. Eton; Capt. Yorks Yeomanry 1967; Dir. Reckitt and Colman PLC 1970–95, Chair. 1986–95; First Church Estates Commr. 1993–; Dir. Foreign and Colonial Ventures Advisors Ltd. 1988–; Trade Affairs Bd. Chemical Industries Asscn. 1978–84, Council 1983–84; Council Mem. Royal Warrant Holders Asscn. 1977–, Pres. 1984; Assoc. of Trinity House, mem. Lighthouse Bd. 1985–94; mem. Bd. UK Centre for Econ. and Environmental Devt. 1985–; mem. of the Court of Skinners' Co. 1985– (Master 1991–92); mem. Council of Scouts Asscn. 1985–; Assoc. Trustee, St. Mary's Hosp., London 1988–; Hon. LL.D. (Hull) 1993. *Leisure interests:* farming, shooting, forestry, golf. *Address:* Malshanger, Basingstoke, Hants., RG23 7EY (Home); 40 Chester Square, London, SW1W 9HT, England. *Telephone:* (01256) 780241 (Home).

COLOMBANI, Jean-Marie; French journalist; b. 7 July 1948, Dakar, Senegal; m. Catherine Sénès 1976; five c.; ed. Lycée Hoche, Versailles, Lycée La Pérouse, Nouméa, New Caledonia, Univ. of Paris II-Assas, Univ. of Paris I Panthéon-Sorbonne, Inst. d'Etudes Politiques, Paris and Inst. d'Etudes Supérieures de Droit Public; journalist, ORTF, later Office of FR3, Nouméa 1973; Ed. Political Service, Le Monde 1977, Head of Political Service 1983, Ed.-in-Chief 1990, Deputy Editorial Dir. 1991; Man. Dir. S.A.–Le Monde March–Dec. 1994, Chair. of Bd. and Dir. of Publs. Dec. 1994–. *Publications:* Contradictions: entretiens avec Anicet Le Poro 1984, L'utopie calédonienne 1985, Portrait du président ou le monarque imaginaire 1985, Le mariage blanc (co-author) 1986, Questions de confiance: entretiens avec Raymond Barre 1987, Les héritiers (co-author), La France sans Mitterrand 1992, La gauche survivra-t-elle aux socialistes? 1994, Le Double Septennat de François Mitterrand, Dernier Inventaire (jtly.) 1995, De la France en général et de ses dirigeants en particulier 1996. *Address:* Le Monde, 21 bis rue Claude Bernard, Paris Cedex 05 (Office); 5 rue Joseph Bara, 75006 Paris, France (Home).

COLOMBO, Emilio; Italian politician; b. 11 April 1920; ed. Rome Univ.; took active part in Catholic youth orgs.; fmr. Vice-Pres. Italian Catholic Youth Asscn.; Deputy, Constituent Assembly 1946–48, Parl. 1948–; Under-Sec. of Agriculture 1948–51, of Public Works 1953–55; Minister of Agriculture 1955–58, of Foreign Trade 1958–59, of Industry and Commerce 1959–60, March-April 1960, July 1960–63, of the Treasury 1963–70, Feb.-May 1972; Prime Minister 1970–72; Minister without Portfolio in charge of Italian representation of UN 1972–73; Minister of Finance 1973–74, of the Treasury 1974–76, of Foreign Affairs 1980–83, 1992–93, of Budget and Econ. Planning 1987–88, of Finance 1988–89; mem. European Parl. 1976–80 (Pres. 1977–79); Pres. Nat. Cttee. for Nuclear Research 1961; mem. Cen. Cttee. Christian Democratic Party 1952, 1953. *Address:* Via Aurelia 239, Rome, Italy.

COLOMBO, John Robert, B.A.; Canadian editor, author and consultant; b. 24 March 1936, Kitchener, Ont.; m. Ruth F. Brown 1959; two s. one d.; ed. Kitchener-Waterloo Collegiate Inst., Waterloo Coll. and Univ. of Toronto; editorial asst. Univ. of Toronto Press 1957–59; Asst. Ed. The Ryerson Press 1960–63; Consulting Ed. McClelland & Stewart 1963–70; Editor-at-Large 1970–; General Ed. The Canadian Global Almanac 1992–, Centennial Medal 1967; Hon. D.Litt. (York Univ., Toronto) 1998; Order of Cyril and Methodius 1979; Esteemed Kt. of Mark Twain 1979; Harbourfront Author's Prize 1985. *Publications:* over 100 books of poetry, prose, reference, science fiction anthologies and translations including Colombo's Canadian Quotations 1974, Colombo's Canadian References 1976, Colombo's Book of Canada 1978, Canadian Literary Landmarks 1984, 1,001 Questions about Canada 1986, Off Earth 1987, Colombo's New Canadian Quotations 1987, Mysterious Canada 1988, Extraordinary Experience 1989, Songs of the Great Land 1989, Mysterious Encounters 1990, The Dictionary of Canadian Quotations 1991, Mackenzie King's Ghost 1991, UFOs over Canada 1991, Dark Visions 1992, Worlds in Small 1992, The Mystery of the Shaking Tent 1993, Walt Whitman's Canada 1993, Luna Park 1994, Voices of Rama 1994, Canadian Global Almanac 1995, Close Encounters of the Canadian Kind 1995, Ghost Stories of Ontario 1995, Haunted Toronto 1996, Iron Curtains 1996, The New Consciousness 1997, Semicertainties 1998. *Leisure interest:* reading. *Address:* 42 Dell Park Avenue, Toronto, Ont., M6B 2T6, Canada. *Telephone:* (416) 782-6853. *Fax:* (416) 782-0285.

COLOMBO, Umberto, SC.D.; Italian public enterprise executive; b. 20 Dec. 1927, Livorno; s. of Eugenio Colombo and Maria Eminente Colombo; m. Milena Piperno 1951; two d.; ed. Univ. of Pavia, Massachusetts Inst. of Tech., U.S.A.; Dir. Montedison's G. Donegani Research Centre 1967–70, Dir.-Gen. for Research and Corp. Strategies, Montedison 1971–78; Chair. Italian Atomic Energy Comm. 1979–82; Chair. ENEA (Italian Nat. Agency for New Tech., Energy and the Environment) 1982–93; Pres. European Science Foundation 1991; Minister for Univs. and Scientific Research 1993–94; Hon. Trustee Aspen Inst. of Humanistic Studies; fmr. mem. Council, UN Univ.; fmr. Chair. European Communities' Cttee. on Science and Tech. (CODEST), UN Advisory Cttee. on Science and Tech. for Devt., OECD Cttee. on Scientific and Tech. Policy, European Industrial Research Man. Asscn.; mem. Accademia Nazionale dei Lincei; Foreign mem. Swiss, Swedish, Japanese and U.S. Acads. of Eng. Sciences, American Acad. of Arts and Sciences, Fellowship of Eng. (U.K.); Conrad Schlumberger Prize 1958, Roncaglia Mari Prize 1977, Honda Prize for Ecotechnology 1984. *Publications:* (Co-Author): Beyond the Age of Waste 1976, WAES Report Italy 1978, La Speranza Tecnologica 1979, Il Secondo Pianeta 1982, Scienza e Tecnologia verso il XXI Secolo 1988, Le Frontiere della Tecnologica 1990. *Leisure interests:* music, farming. *Address:* ENEA, Viale Regina Margherita 125, 00198 Rome (Office); Via San Martino ai Monti 26 *bis*, 00184 Rome, Italy (Home). *Telephone:* (39-6) 854 1007 (Office); (39-6) 482 7265 (Home).

COLOMER VIADEL, Vicente; Spanish professor; b. 30 April 1946, Valencia; s. of Antonio Colomer de Figueroa and Vicenta Viadel Haro; m. Carmen Zafra García 1981; two d.; ed. Colegio Blay de Valencia, Colegio Cervantes de Valencia, Univ. Complutense de Madrid; Assoc. Prof. of Electricity and Magnetism, Univ. Complutense de Madrid 1978–79; Asst. Prof., Univ. of Córdoba 1979, Head of Physics Dept. 1979–84, Prof. 1980–, Rector 1984–90; Visiting Scientist, M.I.T. 1980; Visiting Prof. Univ. de Paris-Sud 1983; Pres. Roger Garaudy 1992–; Dir. Torre Calahorra Centre; Premio Extraordinario de doctorado; Visitante distinguido Univ. Córdoba, Argentina. *Publications:* 50 scientific papers on plasma physics and electromagnetism. *Leisure interests:* reading, travelling, solving mathematical problems. *Address:* Torre Calahorra, Puente Ramano s/n. 14009 Córdoba; Profesor Julian Rivera Tarraco 1 (El Brillante), 14012 Córdoba, Spain. *Telephone:* 293929; 282078. *Fax:* 202677.

COLOTKA, Peter, J.U.DR., DR.SC.; Slovak politician and lawyer; b. 10 Jan. 1925, Sedliacka Dubová; ed. Comenius Univ., Bratislava; asst. lecturer Law Faculty, Comenius Univ. 1950–56, Asst. Prof. 1956–64, Prof., Vice-Dean 1956–57, Dean 1957–58, Pro-Rector 1958–61; mem. Int. Court of Arbitration,

The Hague 1962–70; Commr. for Justice Slovak National Council 1963–68; Deputy to Slovak Nat. Council 1963–88, mem. Presidium 1963–68; Deputy Premier 1968–69; Deputy Premier Fed. Govt. 1969–88; mem. Cen. Cttees. CP of Slovakia and CP of Czechoslovakia 1966–88, mem. Presidiums' Cen. Cttees. 1969–88; Deputy to House of Nations Fed. Ass. 1968–89, Pres., mem. Presidium Jan.–April 1969; Premier Slovak Socialist Republic 1969–88; Amb. to France 1989–90; expelled from CP Feb. 1990; tried for abuse of office, fraud and other offences, Bratislava 1991–94, acquitted April 1994; Dr. h.c. Nicolaus Copernicus Univ., Toruń, Poland 1973; Distinction for Merit in Construction 1965; Order of Labour 1969; J.A. Comenius Univ. Gold Medal 1969; Order of Victorious Feb. 1973; Order of the Repub. 1975. *Publications:* Personal Property 1956, Our Socialist Constitution 1961, scientific articles in collaboration with Dr. Matoušek. *Address:* Podtatranského 1, 811 05 Bratislava, Slovakia.

COLSON, Charles Wendell, J.D.; American lay preacher and author; b. 16 Oct. 1931, Boston; s. of Wendell Colson and Inez Ducrow; m. 1st Nancy Billings 1953; two s. one d.; m. 2nd Patricia Hughes 1964; ed. Brown Univ. and George Washington Univ.; Asst. to Asst. Sec. Navy 1955–56; admin. asst. to Senator L. Saltonstall 1956–61; Sr. partner, Gadsby & Hannah 1961–69; Special Counsel to Pres. Nixon 1969–72; partner, Colson & Shapiro, Washington, D.C. 1973–74; received seven month gaol sentence for role in Watergate scandal; Assoc. Fellowship House, Washington 1975–76, Prison Fellowship 1976–; Distinguished Sr. Fellow Coalition for Christian Colls. and Univs. 1997; Templeton Prize 1993; recipient of several hon. degrees and other awards. *Publications:* Born Again 1975, Life Sentence 1979, Crime and The Responsible Community 1980, Loving God 1983, Who Speaks for God? 1985, Kingdoms in Conflict 1987, Against the Night 1989, The God of Stones and Spiders 1990, Why America Doesn't Work (with J. Eckerd) 1991, The Body 1992, A Dance with Deception 1993, A Dangerous Grace 1994, Gideon's Torch 1995, Burden of Truth 1997. *Leisure interests:* writing, fishing. *Address:* Prison Fellowship, P.O. Box 17500, Washington, DC 20041, U.S.A. *Telephone:* (703) 478-0100. *Fax:* (703) 834-3658.

COLSON, Elizabeth Florence, PH.D.; American anthropologist; b. 15 June 1917, Hewitt, Minn.; d. of Louis Henry Colson and Metta Damon Colson; ed. Wadena Public High School, Univ. of Minnesota, Radcliffe Coll.; Sr. Research Officer Rhodes-Livingstone Inst. 1946–47, Dir. 1948–51; Sr. lecturer Manchester Univ., U.K. 1951–53; Assoc. Prof. Goucher Coll. 1954–55; Assoc. Prof. and Research Assoc., Boston Univ. 1955–59; Prof. Brandeis Univ. 1959–63; Prof. Univ. of Calif., Berkeley 1964–84, Prof. Emer. June 1984–, mem. N.A.S., American Acad. of Arts and Science; Fellow Center for Advanced Study in the Behavioral Sciences, Stanford Univ.; Fairchild Fellow Calif. Inst. of Technology; Hon. Fellow Royal Anthropological Soc., U.K.; Rivers Memorial Medal; Dr.h.c. (Brown, Rochester, Univ. of Zambia). *Publications:* The Makah 1953, Marriage and the Family among the Plateau Tonga 1958, Social Organization of the Gwembe Tonga 1962, Social Consequences of Resettlement 1971, Tradition and Contract 1974; (with Thayer Scudder) Secondary Education and the Formation of an Elite 1980, People in Upheaval (sr. ed.) 1987, For Prayer and Profit 1988; (with Lemore Raiston and James Anderson) Voluntary Efforts in Decentralized Management 1983. *Address:* c/o Department of Anthropology, University of California, Berkeley, CA 94720, U.S.A. *Telephone:* (510) 642-3391.

COLTRANE, Robbie; British actor; ed. Glasgow School of Art; dir. and producer, Young Mental Health (documentary) 1973; stage appearances include: Waiting for Godot, End Game, The Bug, Mr Joyce is Leaving, The Slab Boys, The Transfiguration of Benno Blimpie, The Loveliest Night of the Year, Snobs and Yobs, Your Obedient Servant (one-man show) 1987, Mistero Buffo; TV: The Comic Strip Presents . . . ., Five Go Mad In Dorset, The Beat Generation, War, Summer School, Five Go Mad in Mescalin, Susie, Gino, Dirty Movie, The Miner's Strike, The Supergrass (feature film), The Ebb-tide, Alice in Wonderland; numerous other TV appearances include guest roles in The Young Ones, Kick Up the Eighties, The Tube, Saturday Night Live, Lenny Henry Show, Blackadder; TV series: Tutti Frutti, Coltrane in a Cadillac, Cracker; TV film: Boswell and Johnson's Tour of the Western Isles. *Films include:* Mona Lisa, Subway Riders, Britannia Hospital, Defence of the Realm, Caravaggio, Eat The Rich, Absolute Beginners, The Fruit Machine, Slipstream, Nuns On The Run, Huckleberry Finn, Bert Rigby, You're A Fool, Danny, Champion of the World, Henry V, Let It Ride, The Adventures of Huckleberry Finn, Goldeneye, Buddy, Montana, Frogs for Snakes, Message in a Bottle. *Address:* c/o C.D.A., 19 Sydney Mews, London, SW3 6HL, England. *Telephone:* 0171-581 8111.

COLVILLE OF CULROSS, 4th Viscount, cr. 1902; 14th Baron (Scotland), cr. 1604; 4th Baron (U.K.), cr. 1885; **His Honour Judge The Viscount John Mark Alexander Colville,** Q.C., M.A.; British judge; b. 19 July 1933; s. of late Viscount Colville of Culross and Kathleen Myrtle Gale; m. 1st Mary Elizabeth Webb-Bowen 1958 (divorced 1973); four s.; m. 2nd Margaret Birgitta, Viscountess Davidson (née Norton) 1974; one s.; ed. Rugby School, New Coll. Oxford; called to Bar, Lincoln's Inn 1960, Bencher 1986, Q.C. 1978, a Recorder 1990–93, Circuit Judge 1993–; Minister of State, Home Office 1972–74; U.K. Rep., UN Human Rights Comm. 1980–83, mem. UN Working Group on Disappeared Persons 1980–84 (Chair. 1981–84), Special Rapporteur on Human Rights in Guatemala 1983–86, mem. UN Human Rights Cttee. 1996–; Dir. Securities and Futures Authority (fmrly. Securities Asscn.) 1987–93; Chair. Mental Health Act Comm. 1983–88, Alcohol Educ. and Research Council 1984–90, Parole Bd. for England and Wales 1988–92; author of reports for Govt. on Prevention of Terrorism Act and Northern Ireland Emergency Powers Act 1986–93; Chair. Norwich Information and Tech. Centre 1983–85; Dir. Rediffusion TV Ltd. 1961–68, British Electric Traction Co. Ltd. 1968–72, 1974–84 (Deputy Chair. 1980–81); mem. CBI Council 1982–84; Gov. BUPA 1990–93; Hon. Fellow New Coll. Oxford; mem. Royal Co. of Archers (Queen's Body Guard for Scotland). *Address:* House of Lords, London, SW1A 0PW, England.

COLVIN, Sir Howard Montagu, Kt., C.V.O., C.B.E., M.A., F.B.A., F.R.HIST.S., F.S.A.; British architectural historian; b. 15 Oct. 1919; s. of late Montagu Colvin; m. Christina E. Butler 1943; two s.; ed. Trent Coll. and Univ. Coll. London (UCL); served in R.A.F. 1940–46; Asst. lecturer, UCL 1946–48; Fellow, St. John's Coll. Oxford 1948–87, now Emer., Tutor in History 1948–78, Librarian 1950–84; Reader in Architectural History, Univ. of Oxford 1965–87; Fellow, UCL 1974; mem. Historic Bldgs. Council for England 1970–84, Historic Bldgs. and Monuments Comm. 1984–85, Historic Bldgs. Advisory Cttee. 1984–99, Royal Comm. on Ancient and Historical Monuments of Scotland 1977–89, Royal Comm. on Historical Manuscripts 1981–88, Royal Fine Art Comm. 1962–72, Royal Comm. on Historical Monuments, England 1963–76, etc.; Hon. F.R.I.B.A.; Hon. F.S.A. (Scotland); Wolfson Literary Award 1978; D. Univ. (York) 1978. *Publications include:* The White Canons in England 1951, A Biographical Dictionary of English Architects 1660–1840 1954, The History of the King's Works (gen. ed. and part author) 1963–82, A History of Deddington 1963, Building Accounts of King Henry III 1971, Unbuilt Oxford 1983, Calke Abbey, Derbyshire 1985, The Canterbury Quadrangle, St. John's College, Oxford 1988, All Souls: an Oxford college and its buildings (with J. S. G. Simmons) 1989, Architecture and the After-Life 1991, A Biographical Dictionary of British Architects 1600–1840 1995, Essays in English Architectural History 1999; catalogues; articles in learned journals. *Leisure interest:* gardening. *Address:* 50 Plantation Road, Oxford, OX2 6JE, England. *Telephone:* (01865) 557460.

COLWELL, Rita Rossi, PH.D.; American professor of microbiology; b. 23 Nov. 1934, Mass.; d. of Louis Rossi and Louise DiPalma; m. Jack H. Colwell 1956; two d.; ed. Purdue Univ. and Univ. of Wash.; Research Asst. Purdue Univ. 1956–57; Research Asst. Univ. of Wash. 1957–58, Predoctoral Assoc. 1959–60, Asst. Research Prof. 1961–64; Asst. Prof. of Biology Georgetown Univ. 1964–66, Assoc. Prof. 1966–72; Prof. of Microbiology Univ. of Md. 1972–, Dir. Sea Grant Coll. 1977–83, Dir. Center of Marine Biotech. 1987–91, Dir. Md. Biotech. 1987–91, Pres. Md. Biotech. Inst. 1991–; numerous professional appointments; six hon. doctorates; Gold Medal, Canterbury (U.K.) 1990, Purkinje Gold Award (Prague) 1991, Civic Award 1991, Barnard Medal, Col. Univ. 1996; numerous other awards. *Publications:* 18 books, 500 articles in journals, book chapters, abstracts. *Leisure interests:* gardening, sailing. *Address:* University of Maryland, Maryland Biotechnology Institute, Suite 550, 4321 Hartwick Road, Suite 550, College Park, MD 20740 (Office); 5010 River Hill Road, Bethesda, MD 20816, U.S.A. (Home). *Telephone:* (301) 403-0501 (Office); (301) 229-5129 (Home). *Fax:* (301) 454-8123.

COMANECI, Nadia; Romanian gymnast; b. 12 Nov. 1961, Onești, Bacău County; m. Bart Connor 1996; ed. Coll. of Physical Educ. and Sports, Bucharest; overall European Champion Skien 1975, Prague 1977, Copenhagen 1979; overall Olympic Champion, Montreal 1976; overall World Univ. Games Champion, Bucharest 1981; Gold Medals European Championships, Skien 1975 (vault, asymmetric bars, beam), Prague 1977 (bars), Copenhagen 1979 (vault, floor exercises), World Championships, Strasbourg 1978 (beam), Fort Worth 1979 (team title), Olympic Games, Montreal 1976 (bars, beam), Moscow (beam, floor), World Cup, Tokyo 1979 (vault, floor); World Univ. Games, Bucharest 1981 (vault, bars, floor and team title); Silver Medals European Championships, Skien 1975 (floor), Prague 1977 (vault), World Championships, Strasbourg 1978 (vault), Olympic Games, Montreal 1976 (team title), Moscow 1980 (individual all-round, team title), World Cup, Tokyo 1979 (beam); Bronze Medal Olympic Games, Montreal 1976 (floor); retd. May 1984, jr. team coach 1984–89; granted refugee status in U.S.A. 1989; with Bart Connor Gymnastics Acad.; performs as dancer, gymnastics entertainer and promotes commercial products.

COMBS, Thomas Neal, J.D.; American lawyer; b. 30 Nov. 1942, Dallas, Tex.; s. of Thomas J. Combs and Edith Gibson; m. Dorothy E. Bell 1965; three s.; ed. Southern Methodist Univ.; admitted D.C. Bar 1968, U.S. Supreme Court Bar 1975, Mich. Bar 1976; Assoc. Alston, Miller & Gaines, Washington 1968–70, Marmet & Webster, Washington 1970–73; Assoc. then partner, Webster, Kilcullen & Chamberlain, Washington 1973–75; Vice-Pres., Gen. Counsel, Sec. Fruehauf Corpn., Detroit 1975–85, Exec. Vice-Pres. Finance and Legal, Chief Financial Officer, Sec. 1985–86, Pres., Chief Admin. and Financial Officer 1986–88, Vice-Chair., C.E.O. 1988–89; fmr. mem. bd., Pres., C.E.O. Fruehauf Trailer Operations, Detroit 1989–91; mem. Bd. of Dirs Fruehauf Corpn., Fruehauf Int. Ltd., Fruehauf Canada. *Publications:* articles in professional journals.

COMENDANT, Grigory Ivanovich; Ukrainian ecclesiastic; b. 1946, Ukraine; ed. Hamburg Theological Seminary; minister, sr. minister of Ukraine 1971–90; Chair. Union of Evangelic Christian Baptists 1990–; Chair. Bd. of Union of Evangelic Christian Baptists, Pres. Fed. of Union of Evangelic Christian Baptists 1992–. *Address:* Union of Evangelic Christian Baptists, Trechsvyatski per. 3, 109028 Moscow, Russia. *Telephone:* 917-51-61.

COMFORT, Alexander, M.A., M.B., D.SC., M.R.C.S., L.R.C.P., D.C.H.; British writer and medical biologist; b. 10 Feb. 1920; s. of Alexander Charles Comfort and Daisy Elizabeth Fenner; m. 1st Ruth M. Harris 1943 (divorced 1973); one s.; m. 2nd Jane Tristram Henderson 1973 (died 1991); ed. Highgate School, Trinity Coll., Cambridge, and The London Hospital; medical and hospital practice 1944–48; lecturer in Physiology, The London Hospital 1948–51; Nuffield Research Asst. Univ. Coll., London 1951–54, Nuffield Research Fellow in Biology of Senescence 1954–63; Dir. Medical Research Council Research Group in Ageing, Univ. Coll., London 1963–70; Dir. of Research, Gerontology, Univ. Coll., London 1970–73; Clinical lecturer, Dept. Psychiatry, Stanford Univ. 1974–83; Prof. Dept. Pathology, Irvine Medical Coll., Univ. of Calif. 1976–78; Adjunct Prof., Dept. Psychiatry, Univ. of Southern Calif. 1977–81; Adjunct Prof. Neuropsychiatric Inst. UCLA 1980–; Consultant, Geriatric Psychiatry, VA Hospital, Brentwood, Calif. 1977–82, Ventura Co. Medical Hosp. 1981–92. *Publications:* Novels: No Such Liberty 1941, The Almond Tree 1943, The Powerhouse 1945, On This Side Nothing 1948, A Giant's Strength 1952, Come out to Play 1961, Tetrarch (science fiction trilogy) 1981, Imperial Patient 1987, The Philosophers 1989; Verse: A Wreath for the Living 1942, Elegies 1944, The Signal to Engage 1946, And All but he Departed 1952, Haste to the Wedding 1962, Poems for Jane 1979, Mikrokosmos 1994; Stories: Letters from an Outpost 1947; Essays: Art and Social Responsibility 1946, The Novel and Our Time 1948, The Pattern of the Future 1951, Darwin and the Naked Lady 1961, What is a Doctor? 1980, Writings against Power and Death 1993; Other: Barbarism and Sexual Freedom 1948, Sexual Behaviour in Society 1949, First-Year Physiological Technique 1949, Authority and Delinquency in the Modern State 1950, The Biology of Senescence 1956, Sex in Society 1963, Ageing 1964, The Koka Shastra (trans.) 1964, The Process of Ageing 1964, Nature and Human Nature (essays) 1966, The Anxiety Makers 1967, The Joy of Sex 1972, More Joy 1973, A Good Age 1976, Sexual Consequences of Disability (ed.) 1978, I and That: the Biology of Religion 1979, The Facts of Love (with Jane Comfort) 1979, Practice of Geriatric Psychiatry 1980, Reality and Empathy 1983, What About Alcohol 1983, The New Joy of Sex 1991, Mikrokosmos 1994. *Address:* Chacombe House, Chacombe, Banbury, Oxon., OX17 3SL, England.

COMISKEY, Brendan, M.SC., D.D.; Irish ecclesiastic; b. 13 Aug. 1935, Tasson, Co. Monaghan; ed. Ireland and U.S.A., post-graduate educ. Catholic Univ. of America, Lateran Univ., Rome, Trinity Coll. Dublin; teacher and Dean Damien High School, La Verne, Calif; Chair. of Dept. Washington (D.C.) Theological Union; elected Prov., Anglo-Irish Prov. of the Congregation of the Sacred Hearts and Sec.-Gen. Conference of Maj. Religious Superiors 1974; Auxiliary Bishop of Dublin 1979–84, Bishop of Ferns 1984–; Chair. Bishops' Comm. for Communications; Pres. Catholic Communications Inst. of Ireland; Chair. Irish Churches Council for TV and Radio Affairs; mem. Nat. Episcopal Conf., Bishops' Comm. for Ecumenism, Jt. Comm. of Bishops and Religious Superiors, Comm. for Youth; mem. Standing Cttee. of Glenstal Ecumenical Conf.; Patron Wexford Festival Opera; Trustee St. Patrick's Coll., Maynooth; Freeman Wexford Town 1990; Conventual Chaplain ad Honorem of Order of Malta. *Address:* Bishop's House, Wexford, Ireland. *Telephone:* (053) 22177. *Fax:* (053) 23436.

COMPAGNON, Antoine Marcel Thomas; French university professor and writer; b. 20 July 1950, Brussels, Belgium; s. of Gen. Jean Compagnon and Jacqueline Terlinden; ed. Lycée Condorcet, The Maret School, Washington, D.C., U.S.A., Prytanée Militaire, La Flèche, Ecole Polytechnique, Paris, Ecole Nationale des Ponts et Chaussées, Paris, Univ. of Paris VII; with Fondation Thiers and Research Attaché, Centre National de la Recherche Scientifique 1975–78; Asst. Lecturer, Univ. of Paris VII 1975–80; Asst. Lecturer, Ecole des Hautes Etudes en Sciences Sociales, Paris 1977–79; Lecturer, Ecole Polytechnique, Paris 1978–85; teacher at French Institute, London 1980–81; Lecturer, Univ. of Rouen 1981–85; Prof. of French, Columbia Univ., New York 1985–91; Visiting Prof., Univ. of Pa. 1986, 1990; Prof., Univ. of Le Mans 1989–90; Blanche W. Knopf Prof. of French and Comparative Literature, Columbia Univ. New York 1991–; Prof. Univ. of Paris IV-Sorbonne 1994–; Guggenheim Fellow 1988; Visiting Fellow, All Souls Coll. Oxford 1994; Fellow American Acad. of Arts and Sciences 1997. *Publications:* La Seconde Main ou le travail de la citation 1979, Le Deuil antérieur 1979, Nous, Michel de Montaigne 1980, La Troisième République des lettres, de Flaubert à Proust 1983, Ferragosto 1985, critical edn. of Marcel Proust, Sodome et Gomorrhe 1988, Proust entre deux siècles 1989, Les Cinq Paradoxes de la modernité 1990, Chat en poche: Montaigne et l'allégorie 1993, Connaissez-vous Brunetière? 1997, Le Démon de la théorie 1998; numerous articles on French literature and culture. *Address:* Columbia University, New York, NY 10027 (Office); 29 Claremont Avenue, New York, NY 10027, U.S.A.; 36 rue de Moscou, 75008 Paris, France (Home). *Telephone:* (212) 854-5528 (Office); (212) 222-2550 (Home, New York); 1-43-87-71-48 (Paris).

COMPAORÉ, Blaise; Burkinabè politician and army officer; fmr. second in command to Capt. Thomas Sankara whom he overthrew in a coup in Oct. 1987; Chair. Popular Front of Burkina Faso and Head of Govt. Oct. 1987–, Interim Head of State June–Dec. 1991, President of Burkina Faso Dec. 1991–. *Address:* Office of the President, Ougadougou, Burkina Faso.

COMPER, Francis Anthony, B.A.; Canadian banker; b. 24 April 1945, Toronto, Ont.; m. Elizabeth Comper 1971; ed. Univ. of Toronto; Vice-Pres., Systems Devt., Bank of Montreal 1978–82, Sr. Vice-Pres., Personal Banking 1982, Sr. Vice-Pres. and Sr. Operations Officer, Treasury Group 1982–84, and Man., London, U.K. Branch 1984–86, and Sr. Marketing Officer, Corp. and Govt. Banking 1986–87, Exec. Vice-Pres., Operation 1987–89, Chief Gen. Man. and C.O.O. 1989–90, Pres., C.O.O. and Dir. 1990–; Chair. Governing Council Univ. of Toronto, Campaign for the Univ. of Toronto 1997–(2002); Hon. Chair. Bd. of Govs. The Yee Hong Centre for Geriatric Care; Dir. Harris Bancorp, Inc., Harris Trust and Savings Bank, St. Michael's Hosp., Toronto, C. D. Howe Inst., Canadian Club, Nesbitt Burns Corpn. Ltd., Catalyst, N.Y.; mem. Exec. Council, Canadian Bankers' Asscn. *Leisure interests:* golf, tennis, theatre, arts, reading. *Address:* Bank of Montreal, First Bank Tower, First Canadian Place, Toronto, Ont., M5X 1A1 (Office); PHI, Suite 1101, 40 Rosehill Avenue, Toronto, Ont., M4T 1G5, Canada (Home). *Telephone:* (416) 867-7650 (Office); (416) 923-1161 (Home). *Fax:* (416) 867-7061.

COMPTON, Rt. Hon. John George Melvin, P.C., L.L.B.; Saint Lucia politician; b. 1926, Canouan, St. Vincent and the Grenadines; m.; five c.; ed. London School of Econs.; called to the Bar (Gray's Inn); private practice in St. Lucia 1951–; independent mem. Legis. Council 1954; joined Labour Party 1954; Minister for Trade and Production 1957; Deputy Leader Labour Party 1957–61; resgnd. 1961; formed Nat. Labour Movt. 1961 (later became United Workers' Party); Leader, United Workers' Party 1964; Chief Minister of St. Lucia 1964, Premier 1967–79, Prime Minister Feb.-July 1979, 1982–96, also Minister of Foreign Affairs, Planning and Finance 1982–88, of Planning, Finance, Statistics, Devt. and Home Affairs 1988–92, of Finance, Planning and Devt. 1992–96, Sr. Minister 1996–97. *Address:* P.O. Box 149, Castries, Saint Lucia.

CONABLE, Barber B., B.A., LL.B.; American politician and official; b. 2 Nov. 1922, Warsaw, New York; s. of Barber B. Conable and Agnes Gouinlock; m. Charlotte Williams 1952; four c.; ed. Cornell Univ.; admitted to New York Bar 1948, practice in Buffalo 1948–50, Batavia 1952–64; served with U.S. Marine Corps. Reserve 1942–46, 1950–51; mem. New York State Senate 1963–64; mem. House of Reps. 1964–84; fmr. mem. House Cttee. on Ways and Means; Pres. Govt. Comm. on Defence Man. 1985; Prof. Univ. of Rochester 1985–86; Pres. and Chair. Exec. Dirs. The World Bank 1986–91. *Address:* c/o The World Bank, 1818 H Street, N.W., Washington, DC 20433, U.S.A. *Telephone:* (202) 477-2001.

CONACHER, Desmond John, PH.D., F.R.S.C.; Canadian professor of classics; b. 27 Dec. 1918, Kingston; s. of William M. Conacher and Madeline M. (née Cashel) Conacher; m. Mary Smith 1952; one s. one d.; ed. Queen's Univ., Kingston, Univ. of Chicago; Master Upper Canada Coll., Toronto 1943–46; Lecturer in Classics Dalhousie Univ., Halifax 1946–47; Asst. Prof. Classics Univ. of Saskatchewan 1947–52, Assoc. Prof. 1952–58; Assoc. Prof. Trinity Coll., Univ. of Toronto 1958–65, Prof. 1965–84, Prof. Emer. 1984–, Head Dept. of Classics 1966–72, Chair. 1972–75; Bonsall Visiting Prof. Classics Dept. Stanford Univ. 1981, Visiting Prof. Princeton Univ. 1987, Univ. of Texas at Austin 1989, Univ. of Canterbury, N.Z. 1993; Nuffield Research Fellow, Oxford 1957–58; Dir. American Philological Asscn. 1974–77; Hon. LL.D. (Dalhousie), (Queen's); Hon. D.Litt. (Univ. of Victoria, B.C.), (Univ. of Sask.); Hon. Pres. Classical Asscn. of Canada 1990–. *Publications:* Euripidean Drama 1967, Aeschylus' Prometheus Bound: A Literary Commentary 1980, Aeschylus' Oresteia: A Literary Commentary 1987, Euripides Alcestis (ed. with trans., introduction and commentary) 1988, Sources of Dramatic Theory (ed. M. Sidnell): Introduction and Notes on Plato, Aristotle, Horace 1991, Aeschylus: The Earlier Plays and Related Studies 1996, Euripides and the Sophists 1998; articles on ancient Greek Tragedy in various classical journals. *Address:* Trinity College, University of Toronto, Toronto, M5S 1H8 (Office); 126 Manor Road E., Toronto, Ont., M4S 1P8, Canada (Home). *Telephone:* (416) 978-3608 (Office); (416) 487-0777 (Home).

CONDE CONDE, Mario; Spanish businessman; b. 14 Sept. 1948, Tuy, Pontevedra; m. Lourdes Arroyo; two s.; ed. Univ. of Deusto; Head State Law Dept., Toledo 1973, Head of Studies Gen. State Admin. Ministry of Finance 1974–76; Man. Dir. and Co. Sec. various family cos. 1976–81; set up own law firm 1981; Vice-Pres. and Man. Dir. Antibióticos S.A. Group 1983–87; Pres. Penibérica S.A. 1984–87, Inst. of Biology and Serum Therapy IBAS S.A. 1985–87; Vice-Pres. Alergia e Inmunología S.A. 1986–87; Pres. Banco Español de Crédito (Banesto) 1987–93; Pres. Unión y el Fénix Español S.A., La Corporación Industrial y Financiera de Banesto; mem. Bd. Hidroeléctrica Española, Petróleos del Mediterráneo (Petromed); mem. Admin. Bd. and Exec. Bd. Montedison; Perm. mem. Gen. Comm. for Codification; Gov. Foundation for the Support of Culture; Mercurio de oro "ad personam" 1987, Encomienda de Número de la Orden del Mérito Agrícola; indicted on charges of embezzling funds 1996, convicted March 1997, sentenced to six years' imprisonment; charged with fraud Dec. 1997. *Publication:* El Sistema 1994.

CONDE de SARO, Francisco Javier, M.L.; Spanish diplomatist; b. 13 March 1946, Madrid; s. of Francisco Javier Conde and María Jesús de Saro; m. Ana Martínez de Irujo; one s. two d.; ed. Univ. of Madrid, Diplomatic School, Madrid; Dir.-Gen. for Int. Econ. Relations, Ministry of Foreign Affairs 1971; Asst. Dir.-Gen. for Int. Relations, Directorate of Maritime Fisheries 1976; Dir. of Political Affairs for Africa and Asia, Ministry of Foreign Affairs 1978; counsellor Ministry of Transport, Tourism and Communications 1978; Econ. and Commercial Counsellor, Spanish Embassy, Rabat 1979–83, Buenos Aires 1983–86; Dir.-Gen. Juridical and Institutional Co-ordination, Sec. of State for EU, Ministry of Foreign Affairs 1986–90, Sec.-Gen. 1994;

Amb. of Spain to Algeria 1990–94; Perm. Rep. of Spain to NATO 1996–; Kt. Commdr. of Civil Merit (Spain), of Isabel la Católica (Spain), of Mayo Order (Argentina), of Order of the Lion (Senegal); Kt. of Order of El Ouissam El Mohammadi (Morocco); Grand Cross for Naval Merit (Spain), Grand Cross of Merit (Austria). *Address:* Boulevard Leopold III, 1110 Brussels (Office); Clos des Taillis 1, 1150 Brussels, Belgium (Home). *Telephone:* 707.65.00 (Office); 772.82.81 (Home). *Fax:* 726.47.16 (Office).

CONDON, Sir Paul, Kt., Q.P.M.; British police officer; b. Dorset; m.; two s. one d.; ed. St. Peter's Coll. Oxford; joined Metropolitan Police 1967; Asst. Chief Constable of Kent 1984; Deputy Asst. Commr. Metropolitan Police 1987; Asst. Commr. Metropolitan Police 1988; Chief Constable of Kent 1989–92; Commr., Metropolitan Police 1993–. *Address:* New Scotland Yard, Broadway, London, SW1H 0BG, England. *Telephone:* 0171-230 1212.

CONLON, James, B.MUS.; American conductor; b. 18 March 1950, New York; s. of Joseph and Angeline Conlon; m. Jennifer Ringo; two d.; ed. High School of Music and Art, New York and Juilliard School; fmr. faculty mem. Juilliard School of Music; since making début with New York Philharmonic has conducted every major U.S. and European orchestra and many leading European orchestras; Conductor New York Philharmonic Orchestra 1974–, Metropolitan Opera, New York 1979–; début at Metropolitan Opera 1976, Covent Garden 1979, Paris Opéra 1982, Lyric Opera of Chicago 1988, La Scala, Milan 1993–, Kirov Opera 1994–; Music Dir. Cincinnati May Festival 1979–, Berlin Philharmonic Orchestra 1979–, Rotterdam Philharmonic Orchestra 1983–91; Musical Adviser to Dir. Paris Opera 1995– (Prin. Conductor 1996–); conducted opening of Maggio Musicale, Florence 1985; Chief Conductor, Cologne Opera 1989; Gen. Music Dir. City of Cologne 1990–; has conducted at major int. music festivals and with numerous leading orchestras; Grand Prix du Disque for recording of Poulenc Piano Concertos (Erato); numerous recordings of works by Mozart, Liszt, Poulenc etc; Officier, Ordre des Arts et des Lettres 1996–. *Address:* Shumen Associates, 120 W. 58th Street, New York, NY 10019, U.S.A.

CONNELL, Elizabeth, B.MUS.; Irish opera singer; b. 22 Oct. 1946, South Africa; d. of the late (Gordon) Raymond Connell and (Maud) Elizabeth Connell (née Scott); ed. Univ. of the Witwatersrand and Johannesburg Coll. of Educ., S.A. and London Opera Centre; début at Wexford Festival, Ireland as Varvara in Katya Kabanova 1972; Australian Opera 1973–75; English Nat. Opera 1975–80; début Royal Opera House, Covent Garden, London as Viclinda in I Lombardi 1976; Ortrud in Lohengrin, Bayreuth Festival 1980; Electra in Idomeneo, Salzburg Festival 1984; début Metropolitan Opera, New York as Vitellia in La Clemenza di Tito 1985; début Vienna State Opera as Elisabeth in Tannhäuser 1985; début Glyndebourne, England as Electra in Idomeneo 1985; début La Scala, Milan as Ortrud in Lohengrin 1981; sang full range of dramatic mezzo repertoire until 1983 when moved into dramatic soprano field; sings worldwide, freelance in opera, oratorio, concert and recital work; Maggie Teyte Prize 1972. *Leisure interests:* reading, theatre, concerts, cooking, embroidery, writing and composing. *Address:* c/o I.M.G. Artists, Media House, 3 Burlington Lane, London, W4 2TH, England. *Telephone:* 0181-233 5800. *Fax:* 0181-233 5801.

CONNERY, Sean; Scottish actor; b. 25 Aug. 1930; s. of Joseph and Euphamia Connery; m. 1st Diane Cilento 1962 (dissolved 1974); one s. one step-d.; m. 2nd Micheline Boglio Roquebrun 1975; served in Royal Navy; Dir. Tantallon Films Ltd. 1972–; Hon.D.Litt. (Heriot-Watt) 1981, (St. Andrews) 1988; Acad. Award, Best Supporting Actor 1988; Fellow, Royal Scottish Acad. of Music and Drama 1984; Freeman City of Edin. 1991; mem. Scottish Nat. Party 1992; Commdr. Ordre des Arts et des Lettres 1987, American Cinematique Award 1991, Rudolph Valentino Award 1992, Nat. Board of Review Award, Légion d'honneur, BAFTA Lifetime Achievement Award 1990, BAFTA Fellowship 1998; numerous awards and prizes. *Films include:* No Road Back 1955, Time Lock 1956, Action of the Tiger 1957, Another Time, Another Place, Hell Drivers, 1958, Darby O'Gill and the Little People 1959, Tarzan's Greatest Adventure 1959, On the Fiddle 1961, The Longest Day 1962, The Frightened City 1962, Woman of Straw 1964, Marnie 1964, The Hill 1965, A Fine Madness 1966, Shalako 1968, The Molly Maguires 1968, The Red Tent 1969, The Anderson Tapes 1970, The Offence 1973, Zardoz 1974, Murder on the Orient Express 1974, Ransom 1974, The Wind and the Lion 1975, The Man Who Would Be King 1975, Robin and Marian 1976, A Bridge Too Far 1977, The Great Train Robbery 1978, Meteor 1978, Cuba 1979, Outland 1981, The Man with the Deadly Lens 1982, The Untouchables 1986, The Name of the Rose 1987, The Presidio 1988, Rosencrantz and Guildenstein are Dead, A Small Family Business, Indiana Jones and the Last Crusade 1989, Hunt for Red October 1989, The Russia House 1989 (BAFTA Award 1990), Mutant Ninja Turtles 1990, Highlander 2 1990, Medicine Man 1992, Rising Sun 1993, A Good Man in Africa 1994, First Knight 1994, Just Cause 1994, The Rock 1996, Dragonheart 1996, The Avengers 1998; as James Bond in Dr. No 1963, From Russia with Love 1964, Goldfinger 1965, Thunderball 1965, You Only Live Twice 1967, Diamonds are Forever 1971, Never Say Never Again 1983. *Publication:* Neither Shaken Nor Stirred 1994.

CONNICK, Harry, Jr.; American jazz musician, actor and singer; b. 1968, New Orleans, La.; m. Jill Goodacre 1994; ed. New Orleans Center for the Creative Arts, Hunter Coll. and Manhattan School of Music; studied with Ellis Marsalis. *Albums include:* Harry Connick Jr. 1987, 20 1989, We Are In Love 1991, Lofty's Roach Soufflé 1991, Blue Light, Red Light 1991, Eleven 1992, 25 1992, When My Heart Finds Christmas 1993, She 1994; contrib. to music for film When Harry Met Sally. *Films (actor):* Memphis Belle, Little Man Tate 1991, Independence Day, Excess Baggage, Hope Floats; Band Leader Harry Connick's Big Band; Grammy Award. *Address:* Columbia Records, c/o Anita Nanko, 51/12, P.O. Box 4450, New York, NY 10101, U.S.A.

CONNICK, Robert Elwell, B.S., PH.D.; American professor of chemistry; b. 29 July 1917, Eureka, Calif., s. of Arthur E. Connick and Florence Robertson Connick; m. Frances Spieth 1951; two s. four d.; ed. Univ. of California; Prof. of Chem. Univ. of Calif., Berkeley 1952–88, Emer. 1988–, Chair. Dept. of Chem. 1958–60, Dean of Coll. of Chem. 1960–65, Vice-Chancellor for Academic Affairs 1965–67, 1969–71; mem. N.A.S. *Publications:* numerous articles in Journal of American Chem. Soc., Journal of Chem. Physics, Inorganic Chem., etc. *Leisure interest:* Indian petroglyphs. *Address:* 50 Marguerita Road, Berkeley, CA 94707, U.S.A. (Home).

CONNOLLY, Billy; British comedian, actor, playwright and presenter; b. 24 Nov. 1942; m. 1st Iris Connolly (dissolved 1985); one s. one d.; m. 2nd Pamela Stephenson 1990; three d.; worked as apprentice welder; performed originally with Gerry Rafferty and The Humblebums; first play, The Red Runner, staged at Edinburgh Fringe 1979. *Theatre:* The Great Northern Welly Boot Show, The Beastly Beatitudes of Balthazar B 1982. *Television includes:* Androcles and the Lion 1984, Return to Nose and Beak (Comic Relief), South Bank Show Special (25th Anniversary Commemoration) 1992, Billy, Billy Connolly's World Tour of Scotland (6 part documentary) 1994, The Big Picture 1995, Billy Connolly's World Tour of Australia 1996. *Films include:* Absolution 1979, Bullshot 1984, Water 1984, The Big Man 1989, Pocahontas 1995, Treasure Island (Muppet Movie) 1996, Deacon Brodie (BBC Film) 1996, Mrs Brown 1997, Ship of Fools 1997, Still Crazy 1998, Debt Collector 1998; numerous video releases of live performances including Bite Your Bum 1981 (Music Week and Record Business Award 1982), An Audience with Billy Connolly 1982; numerous albums including The Great Northern Welly Boot Show (contains no. 1 hit DIVORCE), Pick of Billy Connolly (Gold Disc) 1982. *Publications include:* Gullible's Travels 1982. *Address:* c/o Tickety-boo Limited, The Boathouse, Crabtree Lane, London, SW6 6LU, England. *Telephone:* 0171-610 0122.

CONNOR, Joseph E., A.B., M.S.; American international official and accountant; b. 23 Aug. 1931, New York; s. of Joseph E. Connor; m. 1st Cornelia B. Camarata 1958 (died 1983); two s. one d.; m. 2nd Sally Howard Johnson 1992; ed. Univ. of Pittsburgh and Columbia Univ.; joined Price Waterhouse & Co., New York 1956, Partner 1967–, Man. Partner, Western region, Los Angeles 1976–78, Chair. Policy Bd. 1978–88, Chair. World Firm 1988–92; Pres. ICC 1990–92; Under-Sec. Gen. UN, New York 1994–; Distinguished Prof. of Business, Georgetown Univ. 1992–94; Consultant Foreign Direct Investment Programme, U.S. Dept. of Commerce; mem. Pres.'s Man. Advisory Council, Pres.'s Private Sector Survey on Cost Control. *Address:* United Nations, United Nations Plaza, New York, NY 10017, U.S.A.

CONNORS, James Scott (Jimmy); American lawn tennis player; b. 2 Sept. 1952, East St Louis, Ill.; s. of James Scott Connors I and Gloria Thompson Connors; m. Patti McGuire 1978; one s. one d.; ed. Univ. of California at Los Angeles; amateur player 1970–72, professional since 1972; Australian Champion 1974; Wimbledon Champion 1974, 1982; U.S.A. Champion 1974, 1976, 1978, 1982, 1983; S.A. Champion 1973, 1974; WCT Champion 1977, 1980; Grand Prix Champion 1978; commentator for NBC; played Davis Cup for U.S.A. 1976, 1981; BBC Overseas Sports Personality 1982. *Address:* Tennis Management Inc., 109 Red Fox Road, Belleville, IL 62223; RHB Ventures/Nuveen Tour, Suite 175, 1205 Westlakes Drive, Berwyn, PA 19312, U.S.A.

CONOMBO, Joseph Issoufou; Burkinabè fmr. politician; b. 9 Feb. 1917, Kombissiri, Upper Volta (now Burkina Faso); s. of Ousman Conombo and Tassombedo Timpoko; m. 2nd Genevieve Nuninger di Illfurth 1978; two s. three d.; ed. Ecole Primaire et Supérieure, Bingerville, Ecole Normale "William Ponty", Dakar, Senegal; participated in World War II; Co-founder of Union Voltaïque 1946; medical practitioner 1946–48; Consultant to Union Française 1948–51; Del. to Assemblée Nat. in Paris 1951–59; mem. Nat. Assembly 1952–80; Mayor of Ouagadougou 1960–65; Dir.-Gen. for Public Health 1966–68; Minister of Foreign Affairs 1971–73; Prime Minister 1978–80; Sec. Gen. for Overseas Relations Asscn. Seuloguin-Developpement, Kombissiri Prov.; mem. Rassemblement Démocratique Africain 1959–80; Pres. Upper Volta Red Cross Soc. 1961–80. *Publications include:* M'Ba Tinga 1989, Souvenirs de guerre d'un Tirailleur Sénégalais 1989, Bouda François Timpiga de Manga 1995. *Address:* 2033 Avenue de la Liberté, BP 613, Ouagadongou, Burkina Faso. *Telephone:* 334912.

CONQUEST, (George) Robert (Acworth), C.M.G., O.B.E., M.A., D.LITT., F.B.A., F.R.S.L.; British/American author and scholar; b. 15 July 1917, Malvern, England; s. of Robert F.W. Conquest and Rosamund A. Acworth; m. 1st Joan Watkins 1942 (divorced 1948); two s.; m. 2nd Tatiana Milhailova 1948 (divorced 1962); m. 3rd Caroleen Macfarlane 1964 (divorced 1978); m. 4th Elizabeth Neece 1979; ed. Winchester Coll., Univ. of Grenoble and Magdalen Coll. Oxford; mil. service 1939–46; H.M. Foreign Service 1946–56; Sydney and Beatrice Webb Research Fellow, London School of Econs. 1956–58; Visiting Poet, Univ. of Buffalo 1959–60; Literary Ed. The Spectator 1962–63; Sr. Fellow, Columbia Univ. Russian Inst. 1964–65; Fellow, Woodrow Wilson Int. Center, Washington, D.C. 1976–77; Sr. Research Fellow, Hoover Inst. Stanford Univ. 1977–79, 1981–; Distinguished Visiting

Fellow, Heritage Foundation 1980–81; Adjunct Fellow Center for Strategic and Int. Studies 1983–. *Publications:* Power and Policy in the U.S.S.R. 1961, The Great Terror 1968, V.I. Lenin 1972, Kolyma: The Arctic Death Camps 1978, The Harvest of Sorrow 1986, New and Collected Poems 1988, Tyrants and Typewriters 1989, Stalin and the Kirov Murder 1989, The Great Terror Reassessed 1990, Stalin; Breaker of Nations 1991. *Address:* c/o Hoover Institution, Stanford, CA 94305, USA. *Telephone:* (415) 493-5152. *Fax:* (415) 723-1687.

CONRAD, Donald Glover, B.S., M.B.A.; American insurance company executive; b. 23 April 1930, St. Louis; s. of Harold Armin and Velma Glover (Morris) Conrad; m. M. Stephania Shimkus 1980; one d. one step-d.; one s. two d. by previous marriage; ed. Wesleyan and Northwestern Univs. and Univ. of Michigan; with Exxon Co. 1957–70; Financial Adviser, Esso Natural Gas, The Hague, Netherlands 1965–66, Treasurer Esso Europe, London 1966–70; Sr. Vice-Pres. Aetna Life & Casualty Co., Hartford, Conn. 1970–72, fmr. Exec. Vice-Pres. and Dir.; Dir. Terra Nova Insurance Co., Federated Investors Inc.; owner Hartford Whalers Hockey Club 1988–92; U.S. Senate Vice-Chair. Ind. Energy Corpn. 1989–; Sr. Adviser to the Pres., World Bank 1995–; mem. Bd. and Exec. Cttee., American Council for the Arts.

CONRAD, Kent, M.B.A.; American politician; b. 12 March 1948, Bismarck, N.D.; m. Lucy Calautti 1987; one d.; ed. Univ. of Missouri, Stanford Univ. and George Washington Univ.; Asst. to tax commr. State of N.D. Tax Dept. Bismarck 1974–80, tax commr. 1981–86; Senator from North Dakota 1987–; Democrat. *Address:* U.S. Senate, 530 Hart Senate Office Bldg., Washington, DC 20510, U.S.A.

CONRAN, Jasper Alexander Thirlby; British fashion designer; b. 12 Dec. 1959, London; s. of Sir Terence Conran (q.v.) and Shirley Conran (q.v.); ed. Bryanston School, Dorset, Parsons School of Art and Design, New York; Fashion Designer, Man. Dir. Jasper Conran Ltd. 1978–; theatre costumes, Jean Anouilh's The Rehearsal, Almeida Theatre 1990, My Fair Lady 1992; Sleeping Beauty, Scottish Ballet 1994, The Nutcracker Sweeties, Birmingham Royal Ballet 1996; Fil d'Or (Int. Linen Award) 1982, 1983, British Fashion Council Designer of the Year Award 1986–87, Fashion Group of America Award 1987, Laurence Olivier Award for Costume Designer of the Year 1991, British Collections Award (in British Fashion Awards) 1991. *Address:* Jasper Conran Ltd., 2 Munden Street, London, W14 0RH, England. *Telephone:* 0171-603 6668.

CONRAN, Shirley Ida; British designer and author; b. 21 Sept. 1932; d. of Ida and W. Thirlbey Pearce; m. 1st Sir Terence Conran (q.v.) (divorced 1962); two s.; ed. St. Paul's Girls' School and Portsmouth Art Coll.; Press Officer, Asprey Suchy (jewellers) 1953–54; Publicity Adviser to Conran Group Cos. 1955; org. and designed several kitchen and design exhbns.; ran Conran Fabrics Ltd. 1957; started Textile Design Studio 1958; Home Ed., Daily Mail 1962, Women's Ed. 1968; Women's Ed. The Observer Colour Magazine and contrib. to Woman's Own 1964; Fashion Ed. The Observer 1967, columnist and feature writer 1969–70; columnist Vanity Fair 1970–71, Over 21 1972; has made numerous TV and radio appearances. *Publications:* Superwoman 1974, Superwoman Yearbook 1975, Superwoman in Action 1977, Futures 1979, Lace 1982, The Magic Garden 1983, Lace 2 1984, Savages (novel) 1987, Down with Superwoman 1990, The Amazing Umbrella Shop 1990, Crimson 1991, Tiger Eyes 1994, The Revenge of Mimi Quinn1998. *Leisure interests:* long distance swimming, yoga. *Address:* 39 avenue Princess Grace, MC 98000, Monaco.

CONRAN, Sir Terence Orby, Kt.; British designer and retailing executive; b. 4 Oct. 1931, Esher, Surrey; s. of Rupert Conran and Christina Halstead; m. 1st Brenda Davison (divorced); m. 2nd Shirley Conran (q.v.) (divorced 1962); two s.; m. 3rd Caroline Herbert 1963 (divorced 1996); two s. one d.; ed. Bryanston School and Cen. School of Art and Design, London; Chair. Conran Holdings Ltd. 1965–68; Jt. Chair. Ryman Conran Ltd. 1968–71; Chair. Habitat Group Ltd. 1971–88, Habitat/Mothercare PLC 1982–88; Chair. Habitat France SA 1973–88, Conran Stores Inc. 1977–88, J. Hepworth & Son Ltd. 1981–83 (Dir. 1979–83), Richard Shops 1983; Chair. Storehouse PLC 1986–90, C.E.O. 1986–88, non-exec. Dir. 1990; Chair. The Conran Shop Ltd. 1976–, Conran Roche 1980–, Jasper Conran 1982–, Butlers Wharf 1984–90, Bibendum Restaurant 1986–, Benchmark Ltd. 1989–, Blueprint Café 1989–, Terence Conran Ltd. 1990–, Conran Shop Holdings 1990–, The Conran Shop SNC 1990–, Le Pont de la Tour 1991–, Quaglino's Restaurant Ltd. 1991–, The Butler's Wharf Chop-House Ltd. 1992–; C.D. Partnership 1993–, Conran Restaurants Ltd. 1994–, Bluebird Store Ltd. 1994–, Mezzo Ltd. 1995–, Conran Shop Marylebone 1995–, Conran Shop Germany 1996–, Coq d'Argent Ltd. 1997–, Orrery Ltd. 1997–; Vice-Pres. FNAC 1985–89; Dir. Conran Ink Ltd. 1969–, The Neal Street Restaurant, Electra Risk Capital 1981–84, Conran Octopus Ltd. 1983–, Heal & Son Ltd. 1983–87, Savacentre 1986–88, British Home Stores 1986–88, Michelin House Investment Co. Ltd. 1989–; f. Conran Foundation, Butler's Wharf; mem. Royal Comm. on Environmental Pollution 1973–76; mem. Council, Royal Coll. of Art 1978–81, 1986–; mem. Advisory Council, Victoria & Albert Museum 1979–83, Trustee 1984–90; Trustee Design Museum 1989–, Chair. 1992–; R.S.A. Bicentenary Medal 1982, Commdr. Ordre des Arts et des Lettres 1991 and other awards for design, Dr. h.c. (R.C.A.) 1996, Hon. D.Litt. (Portsmouth) 1996. *Publications:* The House Book 1974, The Kitchen Book 1977, The Bedroom & Bathroom Book 1978, The Cook Book (with Caroline Conran) 1980, The New House Book 1985, The Conran Directory of Design 1985, The Soft Furnishings Book 1986, Plants at Home 1986, Terence Conran's France 1987, Terence Conran's D.I.Y. by Design 1989, D.I.Y. in the Garden 1991, Terence Conran's Toys and Children's Furniture 1992, Terence Conran's Kitchen Book 1993, The Essential House Book 1994, Terence Conran on Design 1996, The Essential Garden Book 1998. *Leisure interests:* gardening, cooking. *Address:* 22 Shad Thames, London, SE1 2YU, England. *Telephone:* 0171-378 1161. *Fax:* 0171-403 4309.

CONROY, Pat; American author; b. 26 Oct. 1945, Atlanta, Ga.; s. of Col. Donald Conroy and Frances (Peg) Dorothy Conroy; m. 1st Barbara Bolling 1969 (divorced 1977); m. 2nd Lenore Gurewitz 1981 (divorced 1995); one s. five d.; ed. The Citadel; all novels have been filmed, with the film Conrack based on his non-fiction work The Water Is Wide; Ford Foundation Leadership Devt. Grant 1971, Nat. Endowment for the Arts Award for Achievement in Educ. 1974, S.C. Hall of Fame, Acad. of Authors 1988, Golden Plate Award, American Acad. of Achievement 1992, Ga. Comm. on the Holocaust Humanitarian Award 1996, Lotos Medal of Merit for Outstanding Literary Achievement 1996 and many others. *Publications:* non-fiction: The Boo 1970, The Water Is Wide 1972; novels: The Great Santini 1976, The Lords of Discipline 1980, The Prince of Tides 1986, Beach Music 1995; screenplays: Invictus 1988 (TV film), The Prince of Tides (with Becky Johnson) 1991, Beach Music 1997. *Address:* c/o Nan A. Talese/Doubleday, 1540 Broadway, New York, NY 10036, U.S.A.

CONSAGRA, Pietro; Italian sculptor; b. 4 Oct. 1920, Mazara; two s. two d.; ed. Acad. of Fine Arts, Palermo; one-man shows: Rome 1947, 1949, 1951, 1959, 1961; Milan 1958, 1961; Venice 1948; Brussels 1958; Paris 1959; Zürich 1961; São Paulo Bienal 1955, 1959; Venice Biennale 1956, 1960, New York 1962, Buenos Aires 1962, Boston 1962; Works in following museums: Tate Gallery, London; Nat. Museum and Middleheim Park, Antwerp; Museums of Modern Art, São Paulo, Paris, Rome, New York, Buenos Aires, Caracas, Zagreb, Helsinki; Guggenheim Museum, New York; Art Inst., Chicago; Carnegie Inst., Pittsburgh; Inst. of Fine Arts, Minneapolis and Houston; Grand Prize for Sculpture, Venice Biennale 1960. *Address:* Via Cassia 1162, Rome, Italy. *Telephone:* 6995119.

CONSALVI, Simón Alberto; Venezuelan diplomatist; b. 7 July 1929; m.; two c.; ed. Univ. Central de Venezuela; mem. Nat. Congress 1959–64, 1974–; Amb. to Yugoslavia 1961–64; Dir. Cen. Office of Information for the Presidency 1964–67; Pres. Nat. Inst. of Culture and Art 1967–69; Dir. Nat. Magazine of Culture; Int. Ed. El Nacional newspaper 1971–74; Minister of State for Information 1974; Perm. Rep. to UN 1974–77; Minister of Foreign Affairs 1977–79, 1985–88; fmr. Sec.-Gen. of Presidency; mem. Nat. Congress Foreign Relations Comm. *Address:* c/o Ministerio de Relaciones Exteriores, Casa Amoville, esq. Principal, Caracas, Venezuela.

CONSIDINE, Frank William; American business executive; b. 15 Aug. 1921, Chicago; s. of Frank J. Considine and Minnie Regan; m. Nancy Scott 1948; ed. Loyola Univ. Chicago; partner, F.J. Hogan Agency, Chicago 1945–47; Asst. to Pres. Graham Glass Co. Chicago 1947–51; owner, F.W. Considine Co., Chicago 1951–55; Vice-Pres. Metro Glass Div. Kraftco, Chicago 1955–60; Vice-Pres. and Dir. Nat. Can Corpn. (now American Nat. Can Co.), Chicago 1961–67, Exec. Vice-Pres. 1967–69, Pres. 1969–88, C.E.O. 1973–88, Chair. 1983–90, Hon. Chair. and Chair. Exec. Cttee. 1990–; Vice-Chair. Triangle Industries Inc. (parent corpn.) 1985–88; mem. Bd. of Dirs. Encyclopaedia Britannica, First Chicago Corpn., First Nat. Bank of Chicago, Helene Curtis Industries Inc., Ill. Power Co., Schwitzer Inc., Scotsman Industries, Maytag Co., Tribune Co., IMC Fertilizer Group Inc.; Hon. LL.D. (Loyola) 1986, Hon. L.H.D. (Northwestern) 1987. *Address:* c/o American National Can Co., 8770 W. Bryn Mawr, Chicago, IL 60631, U.S.A.

CONSTÂNCIO, Vitor; Portuguese banker; b. 12 Oct. 1943, Lisbon; s. of António Francisco Constâncio and Ester Ribeiro Vieira Constâncio; m. Maria José Pardana Constâncio 1968; one s. one d.; ed. Instituto Superior de Ciências Económicas e Financeiras, Lisbon and Bristol Univ.; Asst. Prof. Faculty of Econs. 1965–73 and 1989–; Dir. of Global Planning Studies, Planning Research Centre 1973; Sec. of State for Planning and Budget 1974–75; Head of Econ. Research Dept., Banco de Portugal 1975; mem. Parl. 1976, 1980-82, 1987–89; Chair. Parl. Comm. of Econ. and Finance 1976; Pres. of Comm. formed to negotiate with EEC 1977; Vice-Gov. Banco de Portugal 1977 and 1979–85, Gov. 1985, Adviser 1989–95; Minister of Finance and Planning 1978; Sec.-Gen. Socialist Party 1986–89; Prof. of Econs. Tech. Univ. of Lisbon 1989; mem. Bd. Banco BPI 1998–; Int. Consultant with missions to Poland and Czechoslovakia for I.F.C. and to Angola for S.I.D.A. *Address:* rua Vasco da Gama 8, 2780 Oeiras, Portugal. *Telephone:* 44 25 383. *Fax:* 44 26 458.

CONSTANT, Paule, D. ÈS L.; French author; b. 25 Jan. 1944, Gan; s. of Yves Constant and Jeanne Tauzin; m. Auguste Bourgeade 1968; one s. one d.; ed. Univ. of Bordeaux and Univ. of Paris (Sorbonne); Asst. Lecturer in French Literature, Univ. of Abidjan 1968–75; Maître-assistant, then Maître de Conférences in French Literature and Civilization, Univ. of Aix-Marseille III 1975–90, Inst. of French Studies for Foreign Students 1986–95; Prof. Université Aix-Marseille III 1995–; diarist, Revue des Deux Mondes, Paris; Prix Valéry Larbaud 1980, Grand Prix de l'Essai, Acad. Française 1987, Prix François Mauriac 1990, Grand Prix du Roman, Acad. Française 1990, Prix Goncourt 1998; Chevalier, Légion d'honneur, France; Ordre de l'Educ. Nat. de Côte d'Ivoire. *Publications:* novels: Ouregano 1980, Propriété privée 1981, Balta 1983, White Spirit 1989, Le Grand Ghâpal 1991, La Fille du

Gobernator 1994, Confidence pour confidence 1998; Un monde à l'usage des demoiselles (essay) 1987. *Leisure interest:* bibliophile (18th and 19th century works on educ.). *Address:* 29 rue Cardinale, 13100 Aix-en-Provence, France. *Telephone:* 04 42 38 45 08.

CONSTANTINE II; former King of the Hellenes; b. 2 June 1940; m. Princess Anne-Marie of Denmark 1964; three s. two d.; ed. Anavryta School and Law School, Athens Univ.; Military Training 1956–58; visited United States 1958, 1959; succeeded to throne March 1964; left Greece Dec. 1967; deposed June 1973; Monarchy abolished by Nat. Referendum Dec. 1974; deprived of Greek citizenship, remaining property in Greece nationalized April 1994; Gold Medal, Yachting, Olympic Games, Rome 1960. *Address:* 4 Linnell Drive, Hampstead Way, London, N.W.11, England.

CONSTANTINESCU, Emil, PH.D.; Romanian politician, jurist, and geologist; b. 19 Nov. 1939, Tighina (now Repub. of Moldova); m. Nadia Ileana; one s. one d.; ed. Bucharest Univ.; asst. lecturer Bucharest Univ. 1966, lecturer 1980, sr. lecturer 1990, Pro-rector 1990, Prof. 1991, Pres. 1992, Hon. Chair. Senate 1996–; founder and Vice-Pres. Civic Alliance; acting Chair. Romanian Antitotalitarian Forum 1991; Pres. Democratic Convention 1992–96; Pres. of Romania 1996–; Grigore Cobălcescu Prize, Romanian Acad. 1980; mem. and hon. mem. Socs. for Mineralogy and Geology, U.S.A., U.K., Germany, Greece, S. Africa, Australia; mem. NY Acad. of Sciences; numerous hon. degrees and awards; European Statesman of the Year, Inst. for East-West Studies, New York 1998; Order of the Sun (Peru) 1998; Order of the White Rose (Finland) 1998. *Publications:* 10 books and over 60 studies published in various periodicals. *Address:* Office of the President, 76258 Cotroceni Palace, Bucharest, Romania.

CONTAMINE, Claude Maurice; French television executive; b. 29 Aug. 1929, Metz, Moselle; s. of late Henry Contamine and Marie-Thérèse Dufays; m. Renée Jaugeon (deceased); one s.; ed. Lycée Malherbe, Caen, Facultés de Droit, Caen and Paris and Ecole Nat. d'Administration; public servant until 1964; Asst. Dir.-Gen. O.R.T.F. and Dir. of TV 1964–67; Pres. Dir.-Gen. Union générale cinématographique (U.G.C.) 1967–71; Consul-Gen. Milan 1971–72; Asst. Dir.-Gen. in charge of external affairs and co-operation, O.R.T.F. 1973–74; Minister plenipotentiary 1974; mem. Haut Conseil de l'Audovisuel 1973–80; Pres. France-Régions (F.R.3) 1975–81; Conseiller Maître, Cour des Comptes 1981; Pres. Télédiffusion de France (T.D.F.) 1986; Pres. Dir.-Gen. Société nat. de programme Antenne 2 1986–89; Pres. Conservatoire Européen d'Ecriture Audiovisuelle 1996; mem. Conseil Supérieur de la Magistrature 1998–; Officier, Légion d'honneur, Commandeur, Ordre Nat. du Mérite, Officier des Arts et des Lettres. *Address:* 12 rue de Bassano, 75116 Paris, France.

CONTAMINE, Philippe, D. ÈS L.; French university professor; b. 7 May 1932, Metz; s. of Henry Contamine and Marie-Thérèse Dufays; m. Geneviève Bernard 1956; two s. one d.; ed. Lycée Malherbe, Caen, Lycée Louis-le-Grand, Paris, Sorbonne; History and Geography teacher, Lycée, Sens 1957–60, Lycée Carnot, Paris 1960–61; Asst. Prof. of Medieval History, Sorbonne 1962–65; Asst. lecturer, lecturer then Prof. of Medieval History, Univ. of Nancy 1965–73; Prof. of Medieval History, Univ. of Paris (Nanterre) 1973–89; Prof. of Medieval History, Univ. of Paris (Sorbonne) 1989–; Dir. Dept. of History 1976–79; Sec. to Soc. de l'histoire de France 1984–; mem. Institut de France (Académie des Inscriptions et Belles-Lettres) 1990, Acadaemia Europea 1993; Corresp. Fellow Royal Historical Soc. *Publications:* La Guerre de cent ans 1968, Guerre, Etat et Société à la fin du Moyen Age 1972, La Vie quotidienne en France et en Angleterre pendant la guerre de cent ans 1976, La guerre au Moyen Age 1980, La France aux XIVe et XVe siècles 1981, La France de la fin du XVe siècle (co-ed.) 1985, L'Etat et Les Aristocraties (Ed.) 1989, L'histoire militaire de la France 1992, Des pouvoirs en France 1300–1500 1992, L'Economie Mediévale 1993, De Jeanne d'Arc aux guerres d'Italie 1994, La Noblesse au royaume de France de Philippe Le Bel à Louis XII 1997, Guerre et concurrence entre les Etats européens du XIVe au XVIIIe siècle (Ed.) 1998. *Address:* 1 rue Victor Cousin, 75005 Paris; 11–15 rue de l'Amiral Roussin, 75015 Paris, France.

CONTE, Arthur; French politician, journalist and broadcasting executive; b. 31 March 1920, Salses, Pyrénées-Orientales; s. of Pierre Conte and Marie-Thérèse Parazols; m. Colette Lacassagne 1951; one s. one d.; ed. Montpellier Univ.; foreign leader writer, Indépendant de Perpignan 1945; later worked for Paris Match; subsequently leader-writer for Les Informations and contributor to Le Figaro, Historia, Les Nouvelles Littéraires; Sec. Socialist Party Fed. for Pyrénées-Orientales; Deputy to Nat. Assembly 1951–62, 1968–72; Sec. of State for Industry and Commerce 1957; Mayor of Salses 1947–72; Del. to Assembly of Council of Europe 1956–62; Pres. WEU Assembly 1961–62; Chair. and Dir.-Gen. ORTF 1972–73. *Publications:* La légende de Pablo Casals, Les étonnements de Mister Newborn, Les promenades de M. Tripoire, Les hommes ne sont pas des héros, La vigne sous le rempart, Yalta ou le partage du monde, Bandoung, tournant de l'histoire, Sans de Gaulle, Lénine et Staline, Les frères Burns, Hommes libres, L'épopée mondiale d'un siècle (5 vols.), Le premier janvier 1900, Le premier janvier 1920, Le premier janvier 1940, Le premier janvier 1960, Le premier janvier 1983, L'aventure européenne (2 vols.), L'homme Giscard, L'Après-Yalta, Karl Marx face à son temps, Les dictateurs du vingtième siècle, Les présidents de la cinquième république, Les premiers ministres de la Ve république, Verdun, Le 1er janvier 1789 1988, Billaud Varenne, géant de la Révolution 1989, Joffre 1991, L'Epopée coloniale de la France 1992, Nostalgies Françaises 1993, Au Village de Mon Enfance 1994, L'Epopée des chemins de fer français 1996, C'était la IVe république 1998. *Leisure interest:* golf. *Address:* 94 avenue de Suffren, 75015 Paris, France. *Telephone:* (1) 47 83 23 45.

CONTÉ, Gen. Lansana; Guinean politician and army officer; fmr. mil. commdr. of Boké Region, W. Guinea; Pres. Repub. of Guinea after mil. coup, April 1984–, also Minister of Defence, Security, Planning and Co-operation, and Information; Chair. Comité militaire de redressement nat. (CMRN) April 1984–90, Comité transitoire de redressement national (CTRN) 1991–92. *Address:* Office du Président, Conakry, Guinea.

CONTI, Rt. Rev. Mario Joseph Conti, PH.L., S.T.L., F.R.S.E.; British ecclesiastic; b. 20 March 1934, Elgin; s. of Louis Joseph Conti and Josephine Quintilia Panicali; ed. Blairs Coll., Aberdeen, Pontifical Scots Coll. and Gregorian Univ., Rome; ordained Priest 1958; apptd. Curate St Mary's Cathedral, Aberdeen 1959, ordained Bishop of Aberdeen 1977; apptd. Parish Priest St. Joachim's Wick 1962; Pres.-Treas. Scottish Catholic Int. Aid Fund 1978–84; Pres. Nat. Liturgy Comm. 1981–85, Nat. Comm. for Christian Doctrine and Unity 1985–; Vice-Pres. Comm. for Migrant Workers and Tourism 1978–84, Scottish Catholic Heritage Comm. 1980–; mem. Council for Promotion of Christian Unity (Rome) 1984–, Int. Comm. for English in the Liturgy 1978–87, Pontificial Comm. for Cultural Heritage of the Church, Rome 1994–; Convener, Action of Churches Together in Scotland 1990–93; Co-Moderator of Jt. Working Group, R.C. Church and World Council of Churches 1995; Hon. D.D. (Aberdeen) 1989; Order of Merit of the Italian Repub. 1982, Kt. Commdr of Holy Sepulchre 1989, Principal Chaplain to British Asscn. of the Order of Malta 1995. *Publications:* occasional articles and letters in nat. and local press. *Leisure interests:* walking, travel, swimming, music and the arts. *Address:* Bishop's House, 3 Queen's Cross, Aberdeen, AB15 4XU, Scotland. *Telephone:* (01224) 319154. *Fax:* (01224) 325570.

CONTI, Tom; British actor and director; s. of Alfonso Conti and Mary McGoldrick; m. Kara Wilson 1967; one d.; ed. Royal Scottish Acad. of Music; *London Theatre includes:* Savages (Christopher Hampton) 1973, The Devil's Disciple (Shaw) 1976, Whose Life is it Anyway? (Brian Clarke) 1978, They're Playing Our Song (Neil Simon/Marvin Hamlisch) 1980, Romantic Comedy (Bernard Salde), An Italian Straw Hat 1986, Two Into One, Treats 1989, Jeffrey Bernard is Unwell 1990, The Ride Down Mt. Morgan 1991, Present Laughter (also dir.) 1993, Chapter Two 1996, Jesus My Boy 1998; *Films include:* Flame, Full Circle, Merry Christmas Mr. Lawrence, Reuben, American Dreamer, Saving Grace, Miracles, Heavenly Pursuits, Beyond Therapy, Roman Holiday, Two Brothers Running, White Roses, Shirley Valentine, Chapter Two, Someone Else's America, Crush Depth, Something to Believe In 1996, Out of Control 1997; *Television work includes:* Madame Bovary, Treats, The Glittering Prizes, The Norman Conquests, The Beate Klarsfield Story, Fatal Dosage, The Quick and the Dead, Blade on the Feather, Wright Verdict. *Directed:* Last Licks, Broadway 1979, Before the Party 1980, The Housekeeper 1982, Treats 1989; West End Theatre Managers' Award; Royal Television Soc. Award, Variety Club of Great Britain Award 1978, Tony Award of New York 1979. *Leisure interest:* music. *Address:* c/o Chatto & Linnit, 123A King's Road, London, SW3 4PL, England.

CONTOGEORGIS, George, M.A., PH.D.; Greek professor of political science; b. 14 Feb. 1947, Greece; s. of Dimitri Contogeorgis and Elia Contogeorgis; m. Catherine Kampourgiannidou 1972; two d.; ed. Univ. of Athens, Univ. of Paris II, Ecole Pratique des Hautes Etudes, Ecole des Hautes Etudes en Sciences Sociales; Prof. of Political Science, Panteion Univ. Athens 1983–, Rector 1984–90; Gen. Dir. ERT S.A. (Hellenic Broadcasting Corpn.) 1985, Pres.-Gen. Dir. 1989; Minister, Ministry of the Presidency (State Admin., Communication, Media), Govt. Spokesman 1994; Dir. European Masters Programme in Political Science; founder mem. and Sec.-Gen. Greek Political Sciences Asscn. 1975–80; leader writer in Athenian daily newspapers; mem. High Council and Research Council, European Univ. Florence 1986–94; mem. High Council, Univ. of Europe, Paris and Centre of Regional Studies, Montpellier; Visiting Prof. Inst. d'Etudes Politiques, Paris, Univ. Libre de Bruxelles, Univ. Catholique de Louvain, Univs. of Montpellier, Tokyo, etc.; Prof. Franqui Chair. Univ. of Brussels; mem. Council Pôle Sud, Political Science Review, Revue Internationale de Politique Comparée; mem. French Political Science Asscn, I.P.S.A. and other int. asscns. *Publications:* The Theory of Revolution in Aristotle 1975, The Popular Ideology. Socio-political Study of the Greek Folk Song 1979, Political System and Politics 1985, Social Process and Political Self-government. The Greek City-State Under the Ottoman Empire 1982, The Local Government in the State 1985, Nuclear Energy and Public Opinion in Europe 1991, History of Greece 1992, Système de communication et système d'échange: La télévision 1993, After Communism (in collaboration) 1993, Greek Society in 20th Century 1995, Democracy in the Technological Society 1995, Society and Politics 1996, The Greek Cosmosystem 1997. *Address:* Panteion University of Athens, 136 Sygrou Avenue, Athens 176 71; 7 Tassopoulou Street, Athens 153 42, Greece. *Telephone:* (01) 6399662; 6081780; *Fax:* (01) 6081780.

CONWAY, John Horton, M.A., PH.D., F.R.S.; British mathematician; ed. Gonville and Caius Coll., Cambridge; Lecturer in Pure Math., Cambridge Univ. 1973, Reader in Pure Math. and Math. Statistics 1973–83, Prof. of Math. 1983; John von Neumann Prof. of Math., Princeton Univ.; Fellow Sidney Sussex Coll., Cambridge 1963–68, Gonville and Caius Coll., Cambridge 1968; Polya Prize London Mathematical Soc. 1987. *Publications:* Regular Algebra and Finite Machines 1971, On Numbers and Games 1976,

Atlas of Finite Groups 1985. *Address:* Department of Mathematics, Princeton University, Fine Hall, Washington Road, Princeton, NJ 08544, U.S.A.

COOBAR, Abdulmegid; Libyan politician; b. 1909; ed. Arabic and Italian schools in Tripoli, and privately; with Birth Registration Section, Tripoli Municipal Council and later its Section Head, Adviser on Arab Affairs for the Council 1943–44; resigned from Govt. Service 1944; mem. Nat. Constitutional Assembly 1950, and mem. its Cttee. to draft the Libyan Constitution; M.P. for Eastern Gharian 1952–55, Pres. of Parl. Assembly 1952–55; Deputy Prime Minister and Minister of Communications 1955–56; again elected for Eastern Gharian to the new Chamber of Deputies 1955, Pres. 1956; mem. of Council of Viceroy 1956; Deputy Prime Minister and Minister of Foreign Affairs 1957; Prime Minister 1957–60; concurrently Minister for Foreign Affairs 1958–60; Independence Award (1st Class).

COOK, Sir Alan Hugh, Kt., M.A., PH.D., SC.D., F.R.S., F.R.S.E., F.INST.P.; British professor of natural philosophy; b. 2 Dec. 1922, Felstead; s. of Reginald Thomas Cook and Ethel (née Saxon) Cook; m. Isabell Weir Adamson 1948; one s. one d.; ed. Westcliff High School, Corpus Christi Coll., Cambridge; scientist Nat. Physical Lab., Teddington 1952–69; First Prof. of Geophysics, Univ. of Edin. 1969–72; Jacksonian Prof. of Natural Philosophy, Univ. of Cambridge 1972–90; Master of Selwyn Coll., Cambridge 1983–93; Visiting Fellow, Jt. Inst. for Lab. Astrophysics, Univ. of Colorado 1965–66; Visiting Prof. Univ. of Calif. at Los Angeles, Berkeley and San Diego 1981–82, Center for Theological Enquiry, Princeton 1993; Ed. Geophysical Journal 1958–85, Notes and Records of the Royal Soc. 1996–; Pres. Royal Astronomical Soc. 1977–79; Foreign Fellow Acad. Nazionale Lincei, Rome, C.V. Boys Prize, Charles Chree Medal and Prize 1993. *Publications:* Gravity and the Earth 1969, Global Geophysics 1970, Interference/Electromagnetic Waves 1971, Physics of the Earth and Planets 1973, Celestial Masers 1977, Interiors of the Planets 1980, The Motion of the Moon 1988, Gravitational Experiments in the Laboratory 1993, Observational Foundations of Physics 1994, Edmond Halley 1997, and many contributions to learned journals. *Leisure interests:* travel, painting, listening to music. *Address:* 8 Wootton Way, Cambridge, CB3 9LX, England.

COOK, Beryl, O.B.E.; British artist; b. 10 Sept. 1926, Egham, Berks.; d. of Adrian S. Barton-Lansley and Ella M. Farmer-Francis; m. John V. Cook 1948; one s.; ed. Kendrick Girls School, Reading; exhbns. at Plymouth Arts Centre 1975, Whitechapel Art Gallery 1976, Walker Art Gallery, Liverpool 1979, Musée de Cahors 1981, Chelmsford Museum 1982, Glasgow 1992, New York 1992, Plymouth Arts Centre (20th anniversary exhbn.) 1995; retrospective travelling exhbns., Plymouth, Stoke-on-Trent, Preston, Nottingham, Edin. 1988–89, Blackpool, Durham, Hartlepool, Stoke-on-Trent 1998; Kate Greenaway Medal 1980. *Publications:* The Works 1978, Private View 1980, Seven Years and a Day (illustrations) 1980, One Man Show 1981, Bertie and the Big Red Ball (illustrations) 1982, My Granny (illustrations) 1983, Beryl Cook's New York 1985, Beryl Cook's London 1988, Mr Norris Changes Trains (illustrations) 1990, Bouncers 1991, The Loved One (illustrations) 1993, Happy Days 1995, illustrations for Folio Soc.'s edn. of The Prime of Miss Jean Brodie 1998. *Leisure interests:* reading, travel. *Address:* The Coach House, 1A Camp Road, Clifton, Bristol, BS8 3LW, England.

COOK, Brian (Robert) Rayner, B.A., A.R.C.M.; British professional singer (baritone); b. 17 May 1945, London; s. of Robert Cook and Gladys Soulby; m. Angela M. Romney 1974; one s. one d.; ed. Univ. of Bristol, Royal Coll. of Music and privately with Alexander Young (vocal studies) and Helga Mott (repertoire); church organist and choirmaster at age 15; major conducting début (opera) 1966; professional singing début 1967; has appeared as soloist in oratorio, recitals, music-theatre and opera throughout the U.K. and Europe, in U.S.A., Canada, S. America, the Middle East, the Far East and N. Africa and broadcasts frequently in U.K. and Europe; has given first performances of various works written for him by distinguished composers; Dir. singers' workshops and jury mem. int. singing competitions; Visiting Tutor in Vocal Studies, Birmingham Conservatoire 1980–, fmrly. Tutor Welsh Coll. of Music and Drama, Cardiff, Specialist Univ. Music Assessor, Higher Educ. Funding Councils of England and Wales 1994–95; Kathleen Ferrier Memorial Scholarship 1969 and many other major singing prizes; recordings include opera, oratorio and song ranging from Schütz and Charpentier to Fauré, Dvorak, Elgar, Delius, Butterworth, Vaughan Williams, Havergal Brian and Ferguson. *Leisure interests:* news, current affairs and scientific devts., practical healing, colour photography, major comedy figures of the 20th century, historic recordings, messing about in boats. *Address:* The Quavers, 53 Friars Avenue, Friern Barnet, London, N20 0XG, England. *Telephone:* 0181-368 3010.

COOK, Christopher Paul, M.A.; British artist and poet; b. 24 Jan. 1959, Great Ayton, N. Yorks.; s. of E. P. Cook and J. Leyland; m. Jennifer Jane Mellings 1982; two s.; ed. Univ. of Exeter, Royal Coll. of Art; Italian Govt. scholar to Accad. di Belle Arti, Bologna 1986–89; Fellow in Painting Exeter Coll. of Art 1989–90; guest artist Stadelschule, Frankfurt 1991; Visiting Fellow Ruskin School, Univ. of Oxford 1992–93; Distinguished Visiting Artist Calif. State Univ., Long Beach 1994; Visiting Artist to Banaras Hindu Univ., Varanasi, India 1994, 1996; Reader in Painting Univ. of Plymouth 1997–; has exhibited at Camden Arts Centre 1985, Benjamin Rhodes Gallery, London 1988, 1990, 1993, 1996, Cleveland Gallery, Middlesbrough 1989, Museum van Rhoon, Rotterdam 1992, Northern Centre for Contemporary Art 1993, Helmut Pabst Gallery, Frankfurt 1995, Haugesund Kunstforening, Norway 1997, De Beyerd Museum, Breda 1999, Heidelberger Kunstverein 1999. *Publications include:* Dust on the Mirror 1997, For and Against Nature 1999. *Leisure interest:* the outdoors. *Address:* 12 Archibald Road, Exeter, EX1 1SA, England. *Telephone:* (01392) 426843; (01392) 475108. *Fax:* (01392) 475063.

COOK, Gordon Charles, M.D., D.SC., M.R.C.S., F.R.C.P., F.R.A.C.P., F.L.S.; British physician; b. 17 Feb. 1932, Wimbledon; s. of Charles F. Cook and Kate (née Grainger) Cook; m. Elizabeth J. Agg-Large 1963; one s. three d.; ed. Wellingborough Grammar School, Kingston-upon-Thames, Raynes Park Grammar Schools and Royal Free Hospital School of Medicine, Univ. of London; junior appts. Royal Free Hosp., Brompton Hosp. and Royal Northern Hosp. 1958–60; medical specialist, R.A.M.C. and Royal Nigerian Army 1960–62; Lecturer in Medicine, Royal Free Hosp. School of Medicine 1963–65, 1967–69, Makerere Univ. Coll., Uganda 1965–67; Prof. of Medicine, Univ. of Zambia 1969–74, Univ. of Riyadh, Saudi Arabia 1974–75; Visiting Prof. of Medicine, Univs. of Basrah and Mosul, Iraq 1976; Sr. Lecturer in Clinical Tropical Medicine, London School of Hygiene and Tropical Medicine 1976–97; Consultant Physician, Univ. Coll. London Hosps. and Hosp. for Tropical Diseases, London 1976–97; Prof. of Medicine and Chair. Clinical Sciences Dept., Univ. of Papua New Guinea 1978–81; Hon. Sr. Lecturer in Medicine Univ. Coll. London 1981–; Hon. Consultant Physician, St. Luke's Hosp. for the Clergy 1988–; Visiting Prof. of Medicine, Doha, Qatar 1989; Hon. Lecturer in Clinical Parasitology, Medical Coll. of St. Bartholomew's Hosp., London 1992–; Research Assoc., Wellcome Inst. for the History of Medicine 1997–; Chair. Erasmus Darwin Foundation, Lichfield 1994–; Chair. Medical Writers Group, Soc. of Authors 1997–99; Vice-Pres. Royal Soc. of Tropical Medicine and Hygiene 1991–93, Pres. 1993–95; Vice-Pres., History of Medicine Section, Royal Soc. of Medicine 1994–96, Fellowship of Postgrad. Medicine 1996–; Examiner, Royal Coll. of Physicians, Univs. of London and Makerere, Uganda; Ed. Journal of Infection 1995–97; mem. Editorial Bd. Transactions of Royal Soc. of Tropical Medicine, The Postgrad. Medical Journal; Consultant Adviser, HelpAge 1992; mem. Jt. Cttee. on Higher Medical Training, Exec. Cttee. and examiner Faculty of History and Philosophy of Medicine and Pharmacy, The Worshipful Soc. of Apothecaries 1997–; Medical Adviser, Overseas Devt. Admin. and Int. Book Devt.; mem. Code of Practice Cttee., Asscn. of British Pharmaceutical Industry; mem. Asscn. of Physicians of G.B. and Ireland 1973–; numerous other medical and scientific socs.; Trustee Educational Low-Priced Sponsored Texts (ELST) 1996–; Charlotte Brown Prize, Cunning and Legg Awards, Frederick Murgatroyd Memorial Prize, Royal Coll. of Physicians, London 1973. *Publications:* Acute Renal Failure (jointly) 1964, Tropical Gastroenterology 1980, Communicable and Tropical Diseases 1988, Parasitic Disease in Clinical Practice 1990, From the Greenwich Hulks to Old St. Pancras: a history of tropical disease in London 1992; Ed. 100 Clinical Problems in Tropical Medicine (jointly) 1987, Travel-associated Disease 1995, Gastroenterological Problems from the Tropics 1995, Manson's Tropical Diseases (20th edn.) 1996; over 400 papers on physiology, gastroenterology, tropical medicine, nutrition and medical history. *Leisure interests:* cricket, walking, medical history, African and Pacific artefacts. *Address:* Infectious Diseases Unit, Windeyer Bldg., 46 Cleveland Street, London, W1P 6DB; Wellcome Institute for the History of Medicine, 183 Euston Road, London, NW1 2BE (Offices); 11 Old London Road, St. Albans, Herts., AL1 1QE, England (Home). *Telephone:* 0171-504 9311; 0171-611 8615 (Offices); (01727) 869000 (Home).

COOK, Michael John, A.O., LL.B.; Australian diplomatist; b. 28 Oct. 1931, Burma; s. of H.J.M. Cook and Maureen H. Taylor; m. 1st Helen Ibbitson 1957 (divorced 1970); one s. three d.; m. 2nd Catriona Matheson 1970; one s. one d.; ed. Geelong Grammar School, Univ. of Melbourne, Canberra Univ. Coll. and Imperial Defence Coll.; joined Australian Dept. of Foreign Affairs 1954; Amb. to Vietnam 1973–74; C.E.O. Pvt. Office of Prime Minister 1979–81; Dir.-Gen. Office of Nat. Assessments 1981–89; Amb. to U.S.A. 1989–93; Distinguished Visiting Fellow Menzies Centre, Univ. of London 1993–94. *Leisure interests:* tennis, history, Bach.

COOK, Peter Frederick Chester, A.A.DIP., R.I.B.A., B.D.A., F.R.S.A., M.E.A.S.A.; British architect and professor of architecture; b. 22 Oct. 1936, Southend-on-Sea; s. of late Maj. Frederick William Cook and Ada Alice Cook (née Shaw); m. 1st Hazel Aimée Fennell 1960 (divorced 1990); m. 2nd Yael Reisner 1990; one s.; ed. Bournemouth Coll. of Art, Architectural Asscn. (A.A.), London; Architectural Asst., James Cubitt & Partners, London 1960–62; Asst. Architect, Taylor Woodrow Design Group, London 1962–64; taught at A.A. 1964–89; Partner, Archigram Architects 1964–75, Cook and Hawley Architects, London 1976–; Bartlett Prof. of Architecture, Bartlett School of Architecture and Planning, Univ. Coll. London 1990–; Prof. of Architecture, HBK Frankfurt, Germany 1984–; visiting critic many schools of architecture U.S.A., and abroad; Visiting Prof. Oslo Architecture School 1982–83, R.I. School of Design 1981, 1984; Architect of "Plug-in-City", "Instant City", etc. and of the Lutlowplatz Housing, Berlin 1990 (with Christine Hawley); works featured in several books; Graham Foundation Award 1970, Monte Carlo Competition 1st Prize 1970, Landstuhl Housing Competition 1st Prize 1980, L.A. Prize (A.I.A.) 1988, Int. Competition for Historic Museum 1st Prize, Austria 1995, Jean Tschumi Prize (U.I.A.) 1996 and various other prizes. *Leisure interests:* listening to music, talking to young architects, restaurants. *Publication:* Primer 1996. *Address:* Bartlett School of Architecture and Planning, University College, Gower Street,

London WC1E 6BT (Office); 54 Compayne Gardens, London, NW6 3RY, England (Home). *Telephone:* 0171-380 7504 (Univ.); 0171-372 3784 (Home). *Fax:* 0171-380 7453 (Univ.).

COOK, Robert Manuel, M.A., F.B.A.; British academic (retd.); b. 4 July 1909, Sheffield; s. of Charles Robert and Mary Manuel Cook; m. Kathleen Porter 1938 (died 1979); ed. Marlborough Coll. and Cambridge Univ.; Asst. Lecturer in Classics, Manchester Univ. 1934–38, Lecturer 1938–45; Laurence Reader in Classical Archaeology, Cambridge Univ. 1945–62, Laurence Prof. 1962–76; Chair. British School at Athens 1983–87; O.M. Deutsches Archäologisches Institut. *Publications:* Greek Painted Pottery 1960, The Greeks till Alexander 1961, Southern Greece: an Archaeological Guide (with Kathleen Cook) 1968, Greek Art 1972, Clazomenian Sarcophagi 1981, East Greek Pottery (with P. Dupont) 1998. *Address:* 15 Wilberforce Road, Cambridge, CB3 0EQ, England. *Telephone:* (01223) 352863.

COOK, Rt. Hon. Robert (Robin) Finlayson, P.C., M.A., M.P.; British politician; b. 28 Feb. 1946; s. of Peter Cook and Christina Cook (née Lynch); m. 1st Margaret K. Whitmore 1969 (divorced 1998); two s.; m. 2nd Gaynor Regan 1998; ed. Aberdeen Grammar School and Univ. of Edinburgh; Tutor-Organiser with Workers' Educ. Asscn. 1970–74; Labour M.P. for Edinburgh Cen. 1974–83, for Livingston 1983–; Chair. Scottish Asscn. of Labour Student Orgns. 1966–67; Sec. Edin. City Labour Party 1970–72; mem. Edin. Corpn. 1971–74, Chair. Housing Cttee. 1973–74; an Opposition Treasury Spokesman 1980–83; Opposition Spokesman on Trade 1986–87; Opposition Front Bench Spokesman on European and Community Affairs 1983–86, on Health and Social Security 1987–89, on Health 1989–92, on Trade and Industry 1992–94, on Foreign and Commonwealth Affairs 1994–97; Sec. of State for Foreign and Commonwealth Affairs May 1997–; Labour's Campaign Co-ordinator 1984–86; Chair. Labour Party 1996–97; mem. Tribune Group. *Leisure interests:* eating, reading and talking. *Address:* House of Commons, London, SW1A 0AA, England. *Telephone:* 0171-219 5120.

COOK, Stanton R., B.S.; American newspaper publisher; b. 3 July 1925, Chicago, Ill.; s. of Rufus M. Cook and Thelma M. Borgerson; m. Barbara Wilson 1950 (died 1994); ed. Northwestern Univ.; Dist. sales rep. Shell Oil Co. 1949–51; Production Eng. Chicago Tribune Co. 1951–60, Asst. Production Man. 1960–65, Production Man. 1965–67, Production Dir. 1967–70, Dir. Operations 1970, Gen. Man. 1970–72, Publr. 1973–90, Pres. 1972–74, Chief Officer 1974–76, Chair. 1974–81; Dir. Tribune Co. Chicago 1972–96, Pres. and C.E.O. 1974–88, Chair. 1989–91; Chair. Chicago Nat. League Ball Club (Chicago Cubs) 1990–94; Dir. A.P. 1975–84; Deputy Chair. and Dir. Fed. Reserve Bank of Chicago 1980–83, Chair. 1984–85; numerous trusteeships. *Address:* 224 Raleigh Road, Kenilworth, IL 60043, U.S.A.

COOK, Stephen Arthur, PH.D., F.R.S.C., F.R.S.; Canadian/American university professor; b. 14 Dec. 1939, Buffalo, N.Y.; s. of Gerhard A. Cook and Lura Lincoln Cook; m. Linda Craddock 1968; two s.; ed. Univ. of Michigan and Harvard Univ.; Asst. Prof. of Math., Univ. of Calif. at Berkeley 1966–70; Assoc. Prof. of Computer Science, Univ. of Toronto, Canada 1970–75, Prof. 1975–85, Univ. Prof. 1985–; E.W.R. Staecie Memorial Fellowship 1977–78; Killam Research Fellow, Canada Council 1982–83; Turing Award, Assoc. Computing Machinery 1982; mem. N.A.S., American Acad. of Arts and Science; Killam Prize 1997. *Publications:* numerous articles in professional journals on theory of computation. *Leisure interests:* sailing, playing violin. *Address:* Department of Computer Science, University of Toronto, Toronto, Ont., M5S 3G4 (Office); 6 Indian Valley Crescent, Toronto, Ont., M6R 1Y6, Canada (Home).

COOKE, (Alfred) Alistair; American (b. British) writer and broadcaster; b. 20 Nov. 1908, Manchester, England; s. of Samuel Cooke and Mary Elizabeth Byrne; m. 1st Ruth Emerson 1934; m. 2nd Jane White Hawkes; one s. one d.; ed. Jesus Coll., Cambridge, Yale and Harvard Univs.; Film Critic, BBC 1934–37; London Corresp. Nat. Broadcasting Co. 1936–37; Special Corresp. on American Affairs, The Times 1938–41; Commentator on American Affairs BBC 1938–, wrote and narrated America: a Personal History of the United States, BBC TV 1972–73; American feature writer, Daily Herald 1941–44; UN Corresp. The Manchester Guardian (now The Guardian) 1945–48, Chief Corresp. in U.S.A. 1948–72; host T.V. Masterpiece Theatre 1971–92; Hon. Fellow Jesus Coll. Cambridge 1989; Hon. LL.D. (Edinburgh, Manchester), Hon. Litt.D. (St. Andrews) 1975, Hon. D.Lit. (Cambridge) 1988; Peabody Award 1952, 1972, Writers' Guild Award for best documentary 1972, Dimbleby Award 1973, four Emmy Awards (Nat. Acad. of TV Arts and Sciences, U.S.A.) 1973, Benjamin Franklin Award 1973, Medal for Spoken Language (American Acad. of Arts and Letters) 1983; Hon. K.B.E. 1973; BAFTA Award 1991. *Publications:* Garbo and the Night Watchmen (edited) 1937, Douglas Fairbanks 1940, A Generation on Trial: U.S.A. v. Alger Hiss 1950, One Man's America (English title Letters from America) 1952, Christmas Eve 1952, A Commencement Address 1954, The Vintage Mencken (edited) 1955, Around the World in Fifty Years 1966, Talk about America 1968, Alistair Cooke's America 1973, Six Men 1977, The Americans: Fifty Letters from America on Our Life and Times 1979, Above London (with Robert Cameron), Masterpieces 1982, The Patient has the Floor 1986, America Observed: The Newspaper Years of Alistair Cooke 1989, Fun and Games with Alistair Cooke 1994. *Leisure interests:* biography, music, playing golf, watching tennis. *Address:* 1150 Fifth Avenue, New York, NY 10028; Nassau Point, Cutchogue, NY 11935, U.S.A.

COOKE, Herbert Basil Sutton, D.SC., F.R.S.S.AF.; Canadian professor of geology; b. 17 Oct. 1915, Johannesburg, S.A.; s. of Herbert Sutton Cooke and Edith Mary Sutton; m. Dorothea Winifred Hughes 1943; two s.; ed. King Edward VII School, Johannesburg, Cambridge Univ. and Univ. of the Witwatersrand; geologist Cen. Mining and Investment Corpn., Johannesburg 1936–38; Jr. Lecturer, Lecturer in Geology, Univ. of the Witwatersrand 1938–47, Sr. Lecturer and Reader 1953–61; served S.A. Air Force 1941–46; Prin. Geologist Univ. of Calif. African Expedition 1947–48; Pvt. Geological Consultant, Johannesburg 1948–53; Prof. of Geology, Dalhousie Univ. N.S. 1961–81, Emer. Prof. 1981–, Dean Faculty of Arts and Science 1963–68; Geological Consultant B.C. 1981–85; Pres. S.A. Geographical Soc. 1949–50, S.A. Archaeological Soc. 1950–51, Nova Scotian Inst. of Science 1967–68, Royal Commonwealth Soc. 1985–91; Hon. LL.D. (Dalhousie) 1981; Hon. D.Sc. (Witwatersrand, S.A.) 1998; Canadian Centennial Medal 1967. *Publications:* Geology for South African Students (with G. N. Hamilton) 1939, Science in South Africa 1949, The Contribution of C. Van Riet Lowe to Prehistory in Southern Africa (ed. with B. D. Malan) 1962, Evolution of African Mammals (ed. with V. J. Maglio), over 100 scientific monographs and papers. *Leisure interests:* travel, photography. *Address:* 2133-154th Street, White Rock, B.C., V4A 4S5, Canada. *Telephone:* (604) 536 0363.

COOKE, Jean Esme Oregon, R.A.; British artist; b. 18 Feb. 1927, Lewisham, London; d. of Arthur Oregon Cooke and Dorothy E. Cranefield; m. John Bratby 1953 (divorced 1977, died 1992); three s. one d.; ed. Blackheath High School, Cen. School of Arts and Crafts, Camberwell, City & Guilds School, Goldsmiths' Coll. School of Art and Royal Coll. of Art; pottery workshop 1950–53; lecturer in Painting, Royal Coll. of Art 1964–74; mem. Council, Royal Acad. 1983–85, 1992–94, Academic Bd. Blackheath School of Art 1986–; Gov. Cen. School of Art and Design 1984; mem. tertiary educ. bd. Greenwich 1984; Life Pres. Friends of Woodlands Art Gallery 1990–; numerous solo shows in London and throughout Britain 1963–; works exhibited annually at Royal Acad. and in other group exhbns.; made TV film for B.B.C. Portrait of John Bratby 1978. *Publications:* Contemporary British Artists, The Artist 1980, The Artist's Garden 1989. *Leisure interests:* ungardening, talking, shouting, walking along the beach. *Address:* 7 Hardy Road, Blackheath, London, SE3 7NS, England. *Telephone:* 0181-858 6288.

COOKE OF THORNDON, Baron (Life Peer) cr. 1996, of Wellington in New Zealand and of Cambridge in the County of Cambridgeshire; **Robin Brunskill Cooke,** K.B.E., P.C., M.A., PH.D., Q.C.; New Zealand judge; b. 9 May 1926, Wellington; s. of Hon. Philip Brunskill Cooke, M.C. and Valmai Digby Gore; m. Phyllis Annette Miller 1952; three s.; ed. Victoria Univ. Coll., Wellington, Clare Coll., Cambridge, Gonville & Caius Coll., Cambridge; called to Bar 1954; practised at N.Z. Bar 1955–72; Judge of Supreme Court 1972–76, of Court of Appeal 1976–86, now of Hong Kong Court of Final Appeal, Supreme Court of Fiji, Court of Appeal of Samoa; Visiting Fellow All Souls Coll., Oxford 1990; Chair. Comm. of Inquiry into Housing 1970–71; Ed.-in-Chief The Laws of N.Z.; Life mem. Lawasia; comm. mem. Int. Comm. of Jurists 1993–; Hon. Fellow Legal Research Foundation, N.Z. 1993; Special status mem. American Law Inst. 1993–; Research Fellow Gonville & Caius Coll. 1952–56, Hon. Fellow 1982; Hon. Bencher, Inner Temple 1985; Sultan Azlan Shah Law Lecturer, Malaysia 1990, Peter Allan Memorial Lecturer, Hong Kong 1994, Hamlyn Lecturer, U.K. 1996; Patron Wellington Cricket Asscn. 1995–; Hon. LL.D. (Vic. Univ. of Wellington) 1989, (Cambridge) 1990; Hon. D.C.L. (Oxford) 1991; Yorke Prize 1954. *Publications:* Ed. Portrait of a Profession (Centennial Book of N.Z. Law Soc.) 1969, Turning Points of the Common Law 1997; articles in law reviews. *Leisure interests:* The Times crossword, watching cricket. *Address:* 4 Homewood Crescent, Karori, Wellington 5, New Zealand; House of Lords, London SW1A 0PW, England. *Telephone:* 476-8059 (New Zealand).

COOKSON, Richard Clive, PH.D., F.R.S.C., F.R.S.; British chemist; b. 27 Aug. 1922, Hexham, Northumberland; s. of Clive and Marion (James) Cookson; m. Ellen Fawaz 1948; two s.; ed. Harrow School and Trinity Coll. Cambridge; Research Fellow, Harvard Univ. 1948; Research Chemist, Glaxo Labs. Ltd. 1949–51; Lecturer, Birkbeck Coll. London 1951–57; Prof. of Chem. Univ. of Southampton 1957–85, Prof. Emer. 1985–; Dir. Cookson Chemicals Ltd. 1986–; Chair. Tocris Cookson Ltd. 1994–. *Publications:* research papers. *Address:* Northfield House, Stratford Tony Road, Coombe Bissett, Salisbury, Wilts., SP5 4JZ, England.

COOLEY, Denton Arthur, B.A., M.D.; American surgeon; b. 22 Aug. 1920, Houston, Tex.; s. of Ralph C. Cooley and Mary Fraley Cooley; m. Louise Goldsborough Thomas 1949; five d.; ed. Univ. of Texas and Johns Hopkins Univ. School of Medicine; Intern Johns Hopkins School of Medicine, Baltimore 1944–45, Instructor surgery 1945–50; Sr. Surgical Registrar Thoracic Surgery, Brompton Hospital for Chest Diseases, London 1950–51; Assoc. Prof. of Surgery Baylor Univ. Coll. of Medicine, Houston 1954–62, Prof. 1962–69; Surgeon-in-Chief (founder) Texas Heart Inst., Houston 1962–; Clinical Prof. of Surgery, Univ. of Texas Medical School, Houston 1975–; served Capt., Chief Surgical Service, Army Medical Corps, Linz, Austria 1946–48; has performed numerous heart transplants; implanted first artificial heart 1969; Hon. Fellow Royal Coll. of Physicians and Surgeons 1980, Royal Coll. of Surgeons 1984, Royal Australasian Coll. of Surgeons 1986; mem. numerous socs. and asscns.; Hon. Doctorem Medicinae (Turin) 1969; numerous awards and prizes include: Hoktoen Gold Medal 1954, Grande Médaille, Univ. of Ghent, Belgium 1963, René Leriche Prize, Int. Surgical Soc. 1965–67, Billings Gold Medal, American Medical Asscn. 1967, Semmelweis Medal 1973, St. Francis Cabrini Gold Medal (first recipient) 1980, Theodore Roosevelt Award, Nat. Collegiate Athletic Asscn. 1980, Presidential Medal of Freedom 1984; Knight Commdr., Order of Merit of Italian Repub., Order of the Sun, Peru and others. *Publications:* Surgical Treatment of Congenital Heart Disease 1966, Techniques in Cardiac Surgery 1975, Techniques in Vascular Surgery 1979, Techniques in Cardiac Surgery 1984, Essays of Denton A. Cooley—Reflections and Observations 1984; over 1,000 scientific articles. *Leisure interests:* golf, tennis, ranching. *Address:* Texas Heart Institute, P.O. Box 20345, 6621 Fannin Street, Houston, TX 77225, U.S.A. *Telephone:* (713) 791-4900 (Office).

COOLIDGE, Martha; American film director, producer and writer; b. 17 Aug. 1946, New Haven, Conn.; d. of Robert Tilton Coolidge and Jean McMullen; m. Michael Backes; one s.; ed. Rhode Island School of Design, Columbia Univ. and New York Univ. Inst. of Film and TV Grad. School; producer, dir. and writer of award-winning documentaries including Passing Quietly Through, David: Off and On, Old Fashioned Woman; wrote and produced daily children's TV show Magic Tom, Canada; other work for TV includes The Twilight Zone, Sledge Hammer (pilot), House and Home (pilot), Trenchcoat in Paradise (film), Bare Essentials, Crazy in Love; author of original story filmed as The Omega Connection; dir. Bimbo (short film); Blue Ribbon Award, American Film Festival for first feature film Not a Pretty Picture. *Feature films include:* The City Girl, Valley Girl, Joy of Sex, Glory Days, Real Genius, Plain Clothes, Rambling Rose, Lost in Yonkers, Angie, Three Wishes, Out to Sea. *Leisure interest:* breeding Paso-Fino horses. *Address:* c/o Beverly Magid Guttman Associates, 118 South Beverly Drive, Suite 201 Beverly Hills, CA 90212, U.S.A.

COOMBE, George William, Jr., B.A., LL.B.; American lawyer; b. 1 Oct. 1925, Kearny, N.J.; s. of Geroge W. Coombe and Laura Montgomery; m. Marilyn Coombe 1949; one s. two d.; ed. Rutgers Univ. and Harvard Law School; pvt. practice, New York 1949–53; Asst. Gen. Counsel and Corporate Sec. Gen. Motors Corpn. 1953–75; Exec. Vice-Pres. and Gen. Counsel, Bank of America, San Francisco 1975–90; partner Graham and James 1991–; Sr. Fellow Stanford Law School 1995–. *Address:* 2190 Broadway Street, Apartment 2E, San Francisco, CA 94115, U.S.A. (Home).

COOMBS, Douglas Saxon, PH.D., F.R.S.N.Z.; New Zealand professor of geology; b. 23 Nov. 1924, Dunedin; s. of Leslie D. Coombs and Nellie Véra Coombs; m. Anne G. Tarrant 1956; two s. one d.; ed. King's High School, Dunedin, Univ. of Otago, Emmanuel Coll., Cambridge; Asst. Lecturer in Geology, Univ. of Otago 1947–48, Lecturer 1949, 1952–55, Prof. 1956–90; 1851 Exhbn. Scholar, Emmanuel Coll., Cambridge 1949–52; Visiting Prof. Pa. State Univ. 1960, Yale Univ. 1967–68, Geneva Univ. 1968, 1975, Univ. of Calif. at Santa Barbara 1982; Chair. Bd. of Govs., King's High School 1979–88; Life Fellow Mineralogical Soc. of America; Foreign Assoc. N.A.S. 1977; Hon. Fellow Geological Soc. of London 1968, Geological Soc. of America 1983; Hon. mem. Mineralogical Soc. of Great Britain and Ireland 1986; Hon. D.Sc. (Geneva); McKay Hammer Award, Geological Soc. of N.Z. 1961, Hector Medal, Royal Soc. of N.Z. 1969. *Publications:* numerous scientific papers. *Leisure interests:* cricket, fishing, walking. *Address:* Geology Department, University of Otago, P.O. Box 56, Dunedin (Univ.); 6 Tolcarne Avenue, Dunedin, New Zealand (Home). *Telephone:* (03) 479 7505 (Office); (03) 467 5699 (Home). *Fax:* (64-3) 479 7527.

COOMBS, Philip H.; American educator and economist; b. 15 Aug. 1915, Holyoke, Mass.; s. of Chas and Nellie Coombs; m. Helena Brooks 1941; one s. one d.; ed. Holyoke Public Schools, Amherst Coll., Univ. of Chicago and Brookings Inst.; Instructor in Econs., Williams Coll., Mass. 1940–41; Economist, Office of Price Admin. 1941–42; mem. U.S. Army and Econ. Adviser, Office of Strategic Services 1942–45; Econ. Adviser to Dir. of Office of Econ. Stabilization 1945–46; Deputy Dir. Veterans Emergency Housing Program 1946–47; Prof. of Econs., Amherst Coll. 1947–49; Econ. Advisor to Gov. Chester Bowles, Conn., Exec. Dir. President's Materials Policy Comm. (Paley Comm.) 1951–52; Sec. and Dir. of Research, Fund for Advancement of Educ. (Ford Foundation) 1952–61, Program Dir., Educ. Div., Ford Foundation 1957–61; Asst. Sec. of State for Educational and Cultural Affairs, Dept. of State 1961–62; Fellow Council on Foreign Relations 1962–63; Dir. Int. Inst. for Educational Planning (UNESCO), Paris 1963–68, Dir. of Research 1969–70; Visiting Prof., Harvard Univ. Grad. School of Educ. 1969–70; Co-founder Center for Educational Enquiry 1970; Vice-Chair. Int. Council for Educational Devt. 1970–, Chair. 1990–95; Faculty mem. Inst. of Social and Policy Studies, Yale Univ. 1970–72; Visiting Scholar, Univ. of London Inst. of Educ. 1983–86; Hon. Visiting Prof., Beijing Normal Univ., P.R. China 1987, 1988; mem. Council on Foreign Relations; official numerous educational orgs.; Hon. L.H.D. (Amherst Coll.), LL.D. (Brandeis Univ. and Monmouth Coll.); Legion of Merit 1944. *Publications:* The Fourth Dimension of Foreign Policy 1964, Education and Foreign Aid 1965, The World Educational Crisis—A Systems Analysis 1968, Managing Educational Costs 1972, New Paths to Learning: for Rural Children and Youth 1973, Attacking Rural Poverty: How Nonformal Education Can Help 1974, Education for Rural Development: Case Studies for Planners 1975, Meeting the Basic Needs of the Rural Poor: The Integrated, Community-Based Approach 1980, Future Critical World Issues in Education 1981, New Strategies for Improving Rural Family Life 1981, The World Crisis in Education: The View from the Eighties 1985, Cost Analysis: A Tool for Educational Policy and Planning 1987, The Spanish University Reform—An Assessment Report 1987, A Strategy to Improve the Quality of Mexican Higher Education 1992, A Productive Future for the Benemérita Universidad Autónoma de Puebla (Mexico) 1994. *Leisure interests:* sailing, fishing, swimming, reading, touring, house repairs, community service. *Address:* 127 River Road, Essex, CT 06426, U.S.A. (Home). *Telephone:* (860) 767-2726. *Fax:* (860) 767-2726.

COOMBS, Robert Royston Amos, SC.D., F.R.S., F.R.S.M., F.R.C.PATH.; British professor of immunology; b. 9 Jan. 1921; s. of Charles R. and Edris (née Coombs) Amos; m. Anne M. Blomfield 1952; one s. one d.; ed. Diocesan Coll., Cape Town, South Africa, Univs. of Edinburgh and Cambridge; Stringer Fellow, King's Coll., Cambridge 1947; Asst. Dir. of Research, Dept. of Pathology, Univ. of Cambridge 1948, Reader in Immunology 1963–66, Quick Prof. of Biology and Head, Immunology Div. Dept. of Pathology 1966–88, Prof. Emer. 1988–; Fellow, Corpus Christi Coll. Cambridge 1962–; Foreign Hon. mem. Royal Acad. of Medicine of Belgium, Hon. Fellow, American Coll. of Allergists; four hon. degrees and other awards and prizes. *Publications:* Serology of Conglutination and its relation to disease (co-author) 1960, Clinical Aspects of Immunology 1963; numerous papers on immunology. *Leisure interests:* retreat to the country. *Address:* 6 Selwyn Gardens, Cambridge, CB3 9AX, England. *Telephone:* (01223) 352681.

COON, Minor Jesser, PH.D.; American professor of biological chemistry; b. 29 July 1921, Englewood, Colo.; s. of Minor Dillon Coon and Mary (née Jesser) Coon; m. Mary Louise Newburn 1948; one s. one d.; ed. Univ. of Colorado, Univ. of Illinois at Urbana; Postdoctoral Fellow, Univ. of Ill. 1946–47; Asst. Prof. of Physiological Chem., Univ. of Pa. 1949–53, Assoc. Prof. 1953–55; Research Fellow Dept. of Pharmacology, Univ. of New York 1952–53; Prof. Dept. of Biological Chem., Univ. of Mich. 1955, Chair. Dept. 1970–90, Victor Vaughan Distinguished Prof. of Biological Chem. 1983; Foreign Adjunct Prof. Karolinska Inst., Stockholm 1992–; Special Research Fellow, Nat. Cancer Inst., U.S. Public Health Service 1952–53, Nat. Inst. of Gen. Medical Science 1961–62; Research Fellow Laboratorium für Organische Chemie, Eidgenössische Technische Hochschule, Zürich 1961–62; Plenary Lecturer Int. Symposium on Microsomes, Drug Oxidations and Drug Toxicity, Tokyo 1981; Pres. Asscn. of Medical School Depts. of Biochemistry 1974–75; elected Fellow New York Acad. of Sciences 1977; mem. N.A.S. 1983, American Acad. of Arts and Sciences 1984; Sr. mem. Inst. of Medicine 1987; awards include American Chemical Soc. Award in Enzyme Chemistry 1959; William C. Rose Award in Biochemistry 1978; Bernard B. Brodie Award in Drug Metabolism 1980; Mich. Scientist of the Year Award (Science Museum, Lansing) 1988; Hon. D.Sc. (Northwestern) 1983, (Northeastern Ohio Univ. Coll. of Medicine) 1987, Hon. M.D. (Karolinska Inst., Stockholm) 1991; Distinguished Achievement Award (Mich. Univ., Medical Center Alumni Soc.) 1993. *Publications:* over 300 scientific papers and reviews; ed. of numerous books. *Leisure interest:* art. *Address:* 1901 Austin Avenue, Ann Arbor, MI 48104, U.S.A. (Home). *Telephone:* (313) 769-0783 (Home).

COONEY, Patrick, LL.B.; Irish politician and solicitor; b. 2 March 1931, Dublin; s. of Mark Aloysius Cooney and Margaret Blake; m. Brigid McMenamin; three s. one d.; ed. Castleknock Coll., Univ. Coll., Dublin; Fine Gael T.D. for Longford and Westmeath 1970–77; Minister of Justice 1973–77, of Transport, Posts and Telegraphs 1981–82, of Defence 1982–86, of Educ. 1986–87; Senator 1977–81; Deputy 1987–89; M.E.P. 1989–94. *Address:* Garnafailagh, Athlone, Co. Westmeath, Ireland (Home). *Telephone:* (0902) 75531 (Home). *Fax:* (0902) 73339.

COOPER, Imogen; British concert pianist; b. 28 Aug. 1949, London; d. of the late Martin Du Pré Cooper and of Mary Stewart; m. John Batten 1982; ed. Paris Conservatoire and pvtly. under Alfred Brendel, Vienna; TV début at Promenade Concerts, London 1975, has appeared regularly since then; first British pianist, and first woman pianist in South Bank Piano series, Queen Elizabeth Hall, London; broadcasts regularly for BBC; performances in Australia, Austria, France, Germany, Iceland, Japan, the Netherlands, Portugal, S. America, Spain, Scandinavia, U.S.A., N.Z.; Premier Prix, Paris Conservatoire 1967, Mozart Memorial Prize 1969; recordings: Schubert four-hand piano music (with Anne Queffélec), Schubert Schwannengesang, Winterreise, Die Schöne Mullerin and Lieder (with Wolfgang Holzmair), Mozart two- and three-piano concertos (with Alfred Brendel and Acad. of St. Martin in the Fields and Neville Marriner) 1985, Schubert cycle: "The Last Six Years" 1986–90, Schumann Heine Lieder (with Wolfgang Holzmair). *Leisure interests:* visual arts, reading, hill-walking. *Address:* c/o Van Walsum Management Ltd., 4 Addison Bridge Place, London, W14 8XP, England. *Telephone:* 0171-371 4343. *Fax:* 0171-371 4344.

COOPER, Jilly; British writer; b. 21 Feb. 1937, Essex; d. of Brig. W.B. Sallitt, O.B.E. and Mary Elaine Whincup; m. Leo Cooper 1961; one s. one d.; ed. Godolphin School, Salisbury; reporter Middx. Ind. 1957–59; account exec.; copy writer; publr.'s reader; receptionist; puppy fat model; switchboard wrecker; temp. typist 1959–69; columnist The Sunday Times 1969–82, Mail on Sunday 1982–87. *Publications:* 35 books, include: Class 1979, Intelligent and Loyal 1981, The Common Years 1984, Riders 1985, Rivals 1988, Polo 1991, The Man who Made Husbands Jealous, Araminta's Wedding 1993, Apassionata 1996, How to Survive Christmas 1996, Score! 1999. *Leisure interests:* merry-making, mongrels, music, wild flowers. *Address:* c/o Desmond Elliott, 38 Bury Street, St. James's, London, SW1Y 6AU, England. *Telephone:* 0171-930 0097. *Fax:* 0171-321 0190.

COOPER, John Allen Dicks, M.D., PH.D.; American physician and medical educator; b. 22 Dec. 1918, El Paso, Tex.; s. of John Allen Dicks Cooper and Cora (Walker); m. Mary Jane Stratton 1944; two s. two d.; ed. New Mexico

State and Northwestern Univs.; Instructor in Biochem., Northwestern Univ., Evanston, Ill. 1943–47, Asst. Prof. 1947–51, Assoc. Prof. 1951–57, Prof. 1957, 1969, Assoc. Dean of the Medical School 1959–63, Dir. Integrated Program in Medical Educ. 1960–68, Dean of Sciences 1963–69, Assoc. Dean of Faculties 1963–69; mem. Faculty Georgetown Univ. 1970, Baylor Coll. of Medicine, Houston 1987–96; Pres. Asscn. of American Medical Colls., Washington D.C. 1969–86; mem. Inst. of Medicine 1972–; Distinguished Physician Veterans Asscn. 1988–; Fellow A.A.A.S.; Hon. mem. American Hosp. Asscn.; selected by Eds. of U.S. News and World Report as one of the five most influential leaders in field of health 1977–81; Bd. of Trustees' Award, American Medical Asscn. 1985; numerous hon. degrees. *Publications:* over 250 articles in professional journals. *Address:* 800 Caledonian Way, Birmingham, AL 35242, U.S.A.

COOPER, John Philip, C.B.E., PH.D., F.R.S.; British professor of genetics; b. 16 Dec. 1923, Buxton, Derbys.; s. of Frank Edward Cooper and Nora Goodwin Stubbs; m. Christine Mary Palmer 1951; one s. three d.; ed. Univs. of Reading and Cambridge; Research Asst., Welsh Plant Breeding Station, Aberystwyth 1946–50; lecturer, Dept. of Agricultural Botany, Univ. of Reading 1950–54; Plant Geneticist, Welsh Plant Breeding Station 1954–59, Head Dept. of Developmental Genetics 1959–75, Dir. Welsh Plant Breeding Station and Prof. of Agricultural Botany, Univ. Coll. of Wales, Aberystwyth 1975–83, Emer. Prof., Univ. of Wales 1984–; Visiting Prof., Dept. of Agric., Univ. of Reading 1983–89; mem. Int. Bd. for Plant Genetic Resources 1981–86; Hon. Research Fellow, Inst. for Grassland and Environmental Research, Aberystwyth 1992–. *Publications:* Potential Crop Production (with P. F. Wareing) 1971, Photosynthesis and Productivity in Different Environments 1975; over 100 papers on the genetics and physiology of crop plants. *Leisure interests:* gardening, grandchildren. *Address:* 31 West End, Minchinhampton, Glos., GL6 9JA, England. *Telephone:* (01453) 882533.

COOPER, Joseph, O.B.E., M.A., A.R.C.M.; British pianist and lecturer; b. 7 Oct. 1912; s. of Wilfrid Needham and Elsie (Goodacre) Cooper; m. 1st Jean Greig 1947 (died 1973); m. 2nd Carol Borg 1975 (died 1996); ed. Clifton Coll. (music scholarship), Keble Coll., Oxford (organ scholarship), studied piano under Egon Petri 1937–39; served in Royal Artillery 1939–46; solo pianist début, Wigmore Hall 1947; concerto début, Philharmonia Orchestra 1950; BBC début, Promenade Concerts, Royal Albert Hall 1953; tours specializing in lecture recitals in British Isles, Europe, Africa, India, Canada; Chair. BBC TV programme Face the Music 1966–84; Liveryman, Worshipful Co. of Musicians 1963–; mem. Music Panel of Arts Council and Chair. piano sub-cttee. 1966–71; mem. Council, Musicians Benevolent Fund 1987–89; Trustee Countess of Munster Musical Trust 1975–80; Gov. Clifton Coll.; Ambrose Fleming Award 1961, Royal TV Soc. 1971. *Publications:* Hidden Melodies 1975, Arrangement of Vaughan Williams Piano Concerto for 2 pianos (in collaboration with composer), Facing the Music (autobiog.) 1979; numerous recordings. *Leisure interests:* walking, church architecture. *Address:* Octagon Lodge, Ranmore, Nr. Dorking, Surrey, RH5 6SX, England.

COOPER, Leon N., D.SC., PH.D.; American professor of physics; b. 28 Feb. 1930, New York; s. of Irving Cooper and Anna Zola; m. Kay Anne Allard 1969; two d.; ed. Columbia Univ.; mem. Inst. for Advanced Study 1954–55; Research Assoc., Univ. of Ill. 1955–57; Asst. Prof., Ohio State Univ. 1957–58; Assoc. Prof. Brown Univ. 1958–62, Prof. 1974, Thomas J. Watson, Sr. Prof. of Science 1974–, Dir. Center for Neural Science 1978–90, Inst. for Brain and Neural Systems 1991–; Visiting Lecturer, Varenna, Italy 1955; Visiting Prof., Brandeis Summer Inst. 1959, Bergen Int. School of Physics, Norway 1961, Scuola Internazionale Di Fisica, Erice, Italy 1965, L'Ecole Normale Supérieure, Centre Universitaire Int., Paris 1966, Cargèse Summer School 1966, Radiation Lab., Univ. of Calif., Berkeley 1969, Faculty of Sciences, Quai St. Bernard, Paris 1970, 1971, Brookhaven Nat. Lab. 1972; Consultant for various industrial and educational orgs.; Chair. of Math. Models of Nervous System Fondation de France 1977–83; mem. Conseil supérieur de la Recherche Univ. René Descartes, Paris 1981–88; mem. Defence Science Bd. 1989–93; Nat. Science Foundation Post-doctoral Fellow 1954–55; Alfred P. Sloan Foundation Research Fellow 1959–66; John Simon Guggenheim Memorial Foundation Fellow 1965–66; Fellow, American Physical Soc., American Acad. of Arts and Sciences; Sponsor, American Fed. of Scientists; mem. N.A.S., American Philosophical Soc.; Hon. D.Sc. (Columbia, Sussex), 1973, (Illinois, Brown) 1974, (Gustavus Adolphus Coll.) 1975, (Ohio State Univ.) 1976, (Univ. Pierre et Marie Curie, Paris) 1977; Comstock Prize, N.A.S. 1968; Nobel Prize 1972; Award in Excellence (Columbia Univ.) 1974; Descartes Medal, Acad. de Paris, Univ. René Descartes 1977; John Jay Award (Columbia Coll.) 1985. *Publications:* An Introduction to the Meaning and Structure of Physics 1968, Structure and Meaning 1992, How We Learn, How We Remember 1995; numerous scientific papers. *Leisure interests:* skiing, music, theatre. *Address:* Box 1843, Physics Department, Brown University, Providence, RI 02912 (Office).

COOR, Lattie Finch, PH.D.; American academic; b. 26 Sept. 1936, Phoenix, Ariz.; s. of Lattie F. Coor and Elnora (née Witten) Coor; m. Elva Wingfield 1994; three c.; ed. N. Arizona Univ., Washington Univ., St. Louis, American Coll., Greece; admin. asst. to Gov. of Mich. 1961–62; asst to Chancellor, Washington Univ., St. Louis 1963–67, Asst. Dean, Grad. School of Arts and Sciences 1967–69, Dir. Int. Studies 1967–69, Asst. Prof. of Political Science 1967–76, Vice-Chancellor 1969–74, Univ. Vice-Chancellor 1974–76; Pres., Univ. of Vt., Burlington 1976–89, Ariz. State Univ. 1990–; consultant for Dept. of Health, Educ. and Welfare; special consultant to U.S. Commr. for Educ. 1971–74; Chair., Cttee. on governmental relations, American Council on Educ. 1976–80; Dir. New England Bd. of Higher Educ. 1976–; mem. Pres.'s Comm., Nat. Coll. Athletic Asscn., Nat. Asscn. State Univs. and Land Grant Colls. (Chair. Bd. 1991–92). *Address:* Arizona State University, Office of the President, Administration Building, Tempe, AZ 85287-2203, U.S.A.

COORE, David Hilton, B.A., B.C.L., Q.C., M.P.; Jamaican politician; b. 22 Aug. 1925, St. Andrew; s. of Clarence Reuben Coore and Ethlyn Maud Hilton; m. Rita Innis 1949; three s.; ed. Jamaica Coll., McGill Univ., Exeter Coll., Oxford; practised as barrister-at-law in Jamaica 1950–72; mem. Legis. Council 1960–62; Opposition Spokesman on Finance 1967–72; Chair. People's Nat. Party 1969–78; mem. Parl. 1972–; Deputy Prime Minister 1972–78, also Minister of Finance 1972–78, of Planning Jan. 1977–78, of Foreign Affairs and Foreign Trade 1989, of Legal Affairs and Attorney Gen. 1993–95; Leader Govt. Business 1989; Chair. Bd. of Govs. Caribbean Devt. Bank 1972–73, Inter-American Devt. Bank 1973–74; Queen's Counsel 1961. *Leisure interests:* reading, swimming, golf. *Address:* c/o Ministry of Legal Affairs, 12 Ocean Boulevard, Kingston Mall, Kingston 10, Jamaica.

COPE, Jonathan; British ballet dancer; b. 1963; m. Maria Almeida; ed. White Lodge Royal Ballet School; joined Royal Ballet 1982, Prin. 1987–90; set up property devt. business 1990–92; returned to Royal Ballet 1992. *Leading roles (with Royal Ballet) include:* Prince in Swan Lake, The Sleeping Beauty and The Nutcracker, Romeo and Juliet (partnering Sylvie Guillem and Darcey Bussell), Solor in La Bayadère, Albrecht in Giselle, Le Baiser de la Fée, The Prince of the Pagodas, Cinderella, Palemon in Ondine, Serenade, Agon, Apollo, Opus 19/The Dreamer, The Sons of Horus, Young Apollo, Galanteries, The Planets, Still Life at the Penguin Café, The Spirit of Fugue, Concerto, Gloria, Requiem, A Broken Set of Rules, Pursuit, Piano, Grand Pas Classique, Monotones, Crown Prince Rudolph in Mayerling, Woyzeck in Different Drummer, Second Friend in The Judas Tree, Beliaev in A Month in the Country, Birthday Offering, La Valise, Air Monotones II, Fox in Renard, Fearful Symmetries, Symphony in C (partnering Sylvie Guillem), Duo Concertant, If This Is Still a Problem, Des Grieux in Manon, Illuminations. *Address:* The Royal Ballet, Royal Opera House, London, WC2E 9DD, England. *Telephone:* 0171-240 1200. *Fax:* 0171-212 9121.

COPE, Wendy Mary, M.A., F.R.S.L.; British writer; b. 21 July 1945, Erith; d. of Fred Stanley Cope and Alice Mary Cope (née Hand); ed. Farringtons School, St. Hilda's Coll., Oxford Univ., Westminster Coll. of Educ., Oxford; primary school teacher, London 1967–86; professional writer 1986–; Cholmondley Award for Poetry 1987, Michael Braude Award, American Acad. of Arts and Letters 1995. *Publications:* Making Cocoa for Kingsley Amis (poetry) 1986, Serious Concerns (poetry) 1992. *Leisure interest:* music. *Address:* c/o Faber and Faber, 3 Queen Square, London, WC1N 3AU, England. *Telephone:* 0171-465 0045.

COPPEL, Ronald Lewis, A.M., F.C.A.; Australian stock exchange official and accountant; b. 19 Dec. 1933, Belfast; s. of Marcus Coppel and Mabel Coppel; m. Valerie K. Bentley 1960; two s. one d.; ed. Royal Belfast Academical Inst. and Belfast Coll. of Tech.; partner, Coppel & Coppel (chartered accountants), Belfast 1957–63; Sr. Accountant, C.P. Bird & Assocs. Perth, W. Australia 1963–67; partner, Crowther, Bird & Spillsbury (public accountants), Perth 1967–70; Gen. Man. The Stock Exchange of Perth Ltd. 1970–74; Exec. Dir. Australian Associated Stock Exchanges 1974–87; Exec. Dir. and Deputy Man. Dir. Australian Stock Exchange Ltd. 1987–94; Chair. ASX Clearing Corpn. Ltd. 1994–; mem. Accounting Standards Review Bd. 1986–90. *Leisure interests:* current affairs, walking, music, theatre. *Address:* 137 Koola Avenue, Killara, N.S.W. 2071, Australia.

COPPENS, Yves; French professor of palaeoanthropology and prehistory; b. 9 Aug. 1934, Vannes; s. of René Coppens and Andrée Coppens; m. Françoise Le Guennec 1959; ed. Univ. of Rennes, Univ. of Paris (Sorbonne); Research Asst. C.N.R.S., Paris 1956–69; Assoc. Prof., then Prof. Nat. Museum of Natural History 1969–83; Prof. of Palaeoanthropology and Prehistory, Collège de France 1983–; mem. Acad. of Sciences, Nat. Acad. of Medecine, Royal Acad. of Sciences (Belgium); Dr. h.c. (Bologne Univ.) 1988, (Liège Univ.) 1992; prizes include Silver Medal C.N.R.S., Kalinga Prize for Popularization of Science (UNESCO) 1984, Glaxo Prize 1978; Chevalier, Légion d'honneur, Officier, Ordre Nat. du Mérite, Officier Ordre Nat. des Palmes Académiques, Officier, Ordre Nat. des Arts et des Lettres, Officier, Ordre Nat. Tchadien. *Publications:* c. 400 scientific papers; ed., author or jt. author of over 20 books on palaeontology, anthropology and prehistory. *Address:* Collège de France, 11 place Marcelin Berthelot, 75005 Paris; 4 rue du Pont-aux-Choux, 75003 Paris, France (Home). *Telephone:* 44-27-10-23.

COPPERFIELD, David (b. Kotkin); American magician; b. 1956, Metuchen, N.J.; ed. Fordham Univ.; Prof. of Magic, New York Univ. 1974; appeared in musical Magic Man 1974; presenter, The Magic of ABC; performer, dir., producer, writer, The Magic of David Copperfield 1978–; creator, founder, Project Magic 1982; levitated across Grand Canyon 1984; walked through Great Wall of China 1986; escaped from Alcatraz prison 1987; made Statue of Liberty disappear 1989; went over Niagara Falls 1990; made Orient Express disappear 1991; introduced flying illusion 1992; escaped from burning ropes 13 storeys above ground, Caesar's Palace 1993; appearances in Taiwan 1987, Mexico City 1987, Hong Kong, Singapore, Kuala Lumpur, Brazil 1988, Germany 1993; first U.K. tour 1994; European tour 1995; Golden Rose Award, Montreux Film Festival 1987; recipient of numerous

Emmy awards and nominations; Bambi award 1993, etc. *Film:* Terror Train 1980.

COPPERWHEAT, Lee; British fashion designer; ed. Tresham Coll., Northampton, London Coll. of Fashion; fmrly. tailor with Aquascutum; est. design room and fmr. man. of sampling and production Passenger sportswear; freelance design projects for numerous clients; fmr. teacher menswear tailoring Brighton Univ.; fmr. lecturer St. Martin's School of Art, London; formed Copperwheat Blundell with Pamela Blundell (q.v.); Young Designer of the Year 1994 (with Pamela Blundell). *Address:* Copperwheat Blundell, 14 Cheshire Street, London, E2 6EH, England. *Telephone:* 0171-613 0651. *Fax:* 0171-729 8600.

COPPOCK, John Terence, C.B.E., F.B.A., F.R.S.E., F.R.S.A.; British professor of geography; b. 2 June 1921, Cardiff; s. of the late Arthur Leslie Coppock and Margaret Valerie Coppock (née Phillips); m. Sheila Mary Burnett 1953 (died 1990); one s. one d.; ed. Penarth County School, Queens' Coll., Cambridge; civil servant, Lord Chancellor's Dept., Ministry of Works and Bd. of Customs and Excise 1938–47; war service in Army 1939–46; Departmental Demonstrator, Dept. of Geography, Univ. of Cambridge 1949–50; Asst. Lecturer in Geography, Univ. Coll. London 1950–52, Lecturer 1952–64, Reader 1964–65; Ogilvie Prof. of Geography, Univ. of Edin. 1965–86, Prof. Emer. 1987–; Visiting Sr. Lecturer, Dept. of Geography, Univ. of Ibadan, Nigeria 1963–64; Visiting Prof., Univ. of Tech., Loughborough 1986–89, Birkbeck Coll., London 1986–96; Sec. and Treasurer Carnegie Trust for the Univs. of Scotland 1986–; mem. England Cttee., Nature Conservancy 1965–71; Specialist Adviser, Select Cttee. on Scottish Affairs 1971–72; Pres. Inst. of British Geographers 1973–74; mem. Ordnance Survey Review Cttee. 1978–79; Chair. British Nat. Cttee. for Geography 1979–84; mem. Scottish Sports Council 1976–87; Chair. British Library/British Acad. Review Panel on Information Needs in the Humanities 1990–92; Ed. Int. Journal of Geographical Information Systems 1986–93; Murchison Grant, Royal Geographical Soc. 1971, Victoria Medal 1985, Fellow Royal Scottish Geographical Soc. *Publications:* The Changing Use of Land in Britain (with R. H. Best) 1962, An Agricultural Atlas of England and Wales 1964, An Agricultural Geography of Great Britain 1971, An Agricultural Atlas of Scotland 1976, Recreation in the Countryside (with B. S. Duffield) 1975, Agriculture in Developed Countries 1984, Institutional Innovation in Water Management: The Scottish Experience (with W. R. D. Sewell and A. Pitkethly) 1986, Geography, Planning and Policy Making (Ed. with P. T. Kivell) 1986, and 15 other books; 140 articles. *Leisure interests:* walking, natural history, listening to music, travel, reading. *Address:* Carnegie Trust for the Universities of Scotland, Cameron House, Abbey Park Place, Dunfermline, Fife, KY12 7PZ; Flat 45, 14 Maxwell Street, Edinburgh, EH10 5HU, Scotland (Home); *Telephone:* (01383) 622148 (Office); (0131) 447 3443 (Home). *Fax:* (01383) 622149 (Office).

COPPOLA, Francis Ford; American film director and writer; b. 7 April 1939, Detroit, Michigan; s. of Carmine and Italia Coppola; m. Eleanor Neil; two s. (one deceased) one d.; ed. Hofstra Univ., Univ. of California. *Films include:* Dementia 13 1963, This Property is Condemned 1965, Is Paris Burning? 1966, You're A Big Boy Now 1967, Finian's Rainbow 1968, The Rain People 1969, Patton 1971, The Godfather 1972, American Grafitti 1973, The Conversation 1974, The Godfather Part II 1975, The Great Gatsby 1974, The Black Stallion (produced) 1977, Apocalypse Now 1979, One from the Heart 1982, Hammett (produced) 1982, The Escape Artist 1982, The Return of the Black Stallion 1982, Rumble Fish 1983, The Outsiders 1983, The Cotton Club 1984, Peggy Sue Got Married 1986, Gardens of Stone 1986, Life without Zoe 1988, Tucker: The Man and His Dream 1988, The Godfather Part III 1990, Dracula 1991, My Family/Mi Familia 1995, Don Juan De Marco 1995, Jack 1996, The Rainmaker 1997; exec. producer The Secret Garden 1993, Mary Shelley's Frankenstein 1994, Buddy 1997; theatre direction includes Private Lives, The Visit of the Old Lady, San Francisco Opera Co. 1972; Artistic Dir. Zoetrope Studios 1969–; owner Niebaum-Coppola Estate, Napa Valley; Cannes Film Award for The Conversation 1974; Director's Guild Award for The Godfather; Acad. Award for Best Screenplay for Patton, Golden Palm (Cannes) 1979 for Apocalypse Now, also awarded Best Screenplay, Best Dir. and Best Picture Oscars for The Godfather Part II; U.S. Army Civilian Service Award; Commandeur, Ordre des Arts et des Lettres. *Address:* Zoetrope Studios, 916 Kearny Street, San Francisco, CA 94133; c/o CAA, 9830 Wilshire Boulevard, Beverly Hills, CA 90212, U.S.A.

COPPS, Sheila Maureen, P.C., B.A.; Canadian politician; b. 27 Nov. 1952, Hamilton, Ont.; d. of Victor Kennedy and Geraldine Florence (Guthro) Copps; one d.; ed. Univ. of Western Ont., Univ. of Rouen, France, McMaster Univ.; journalist, Ottawa Citizen 1974–76, Hamilton Spectator 1977; Constituency Asst. to Leader Liberal Party Ont. 1977–81; M.P.P. for Hamilton Centre 1981–84; Deputy Leader Fed. Liberal Party; Deputy Prime Minister 1993–97, Environment Minister 1993–96, Heritage Minister 1996–. *Publication:* Nobody's Baby 1986. *Address:* Ministry of Canadian Heritage, Immeuble Jules Léger, 25 rue Eddy, Hull, Quebec, K1A 1K5, Canada. *Telephone:* (819) 997-0055. *Fax:* (819) 953-5382.

CORBALLY, John Edward, PH.D.; American university administrator; b. 14 Oct. 1924, South Bend, Wash.; s. of John E. and Grace Williams Corbally; m. Marguerite Walker 1946; one s. one d.; ed. Univs of Washington and California, Berkeley; High School Teacher and principal, State of Wash. 1947–53; College of Educ. Faculty, Ohio State Univ. 1955–61, Dir. Personnel Budget 1959–61, Exec. Asst. to Pres. 1961–64, Vice-Pres. for Admin. 1964–66, Vice-Pres. for Academic Affairs and Provost 1966–69; Chancellor and Pres. Syracuse Univ. 1969–71; Pres. Univ. of Illinois 1971–79, Pres. Emer. 1979–, Distinguished Prof. of Higher Educ. 1979–82, Prof. Emer. 1982–; Dir. John D. and Catherine T. MacArthur Foundation 1979–, Pres. 1980–89, Chair. 1995–; Consultant Heidrik & Struggles 1989–90; Chair. Nat. Council on Educational Research 1973–79; Hon. LL.D. (Univ. of Md. 1971, Blackburn Coll. 1972, Ill. State Univ. 1977, Univ. of Akron 1978, Ohio State Univ. 1980). *Publications:* co-author: Educational Administration: The Secondary School 1961, School Finance 1962, An Introduction to Educational Administration 1984. *Leisure interests:* gardening, travel. *Address:* 1507 151st Place, S.E. Mill Creek, WA 98012, U.S.A.

CORBEIL, Jean, P.C.; Canadian politician; b. 7 Jan. 1934, Montreal, Quebec; s. of Lionel Corbeil and Beatrice Montbriand; m. 1st Pierrette Beauchemin 1956; m. 2nd Madeleine Tremblay 1988; four s.; Progressive Conservative M.P. for Anjou-Rivière-des-Prairies 1988–93; Minister of Labour 1989–91, of Transport 1991–93; Minister of State (Transport) 1990–91; Pres. Jean Corbeil & Assocs. Consultants Inc. 1994–, Pi[3] (Privatised Int. Infrastructures Inc.). *Leisure interests:* reading, golfing. *Address:* 7013 Giraud, Anjou, Que., H1J 2H2, Canada. *Telephone:* (514) 354-4647. *Fax:* (514) 351-1636.

CORBETT, Michael McGregor, B.A., LL.B.; South African judge; b. 14 Sept. 1923, Pretoria; s. of Alan Frederick Corbett and Johanna Sibella McGregor; m. Margaret Murray Luscombe 1949; two s. two d.; ed. Univ. of Cape Town, Trinity Hall Cambridge, England; enlisted in S.A. Army 1942, active service 1943–44; admitted as advocate and commenced practice at Cape Bar, Cape Town 1948, appointed Q.C. 1961, Judge of Cape Prov. Div. of Supreme Court 1963, Judge of Appeal 1974, Chief Justice of S.A. 1989–96; Hon. LL.D. (Cape Town) 1982, (O.F.S.) 1990, (Rhodes) 1990, (Pretoria) 1993, (Witwatersrand) 1994, (Stellenbosch) 1996; Hon. Bencher Lincoln's Inn 1991; Hon. Fellow Trinity Hall, Cambridge 1992; Hon. mem. American Bar Assen. 1997; Order for Meritorious Service 1996. *Publications:* The Quantum of Damages in Bodily and Fatal Injury Cases (jtly.) 1960, The Law of Succession in South Africa (jtly.) 1980. *Leisure interests:* tennis, walking. *Address:* 18 Ladies Mile Extension, Constantia, Cape Town 7800, South Africa (Home).

CORBETT, Robert Edward, PH.D., F.R.S.N.Z.; New Zealand academic; b. 13 June 1923, Port Chalmers; s. of Walter Corbett and Margaret Whitehead Corbett; m. Enid Mary Carter 1949; one s. one d.; ed. Otago Boys' High School, Univ. of Otago, Dunedin, Cambridge Univ., U.K.; Asst. Lecturer in Chem., Univ. of Otago 1945, Lecturer 1950, Sr. Lecturer 1955, Reader 1960–65, Prof. 1966–71, Mellor Prof. of Chem. and Chair. Dept. of Chem. 1972–83, Emer. Prof. 1983–; Fellow N.Z. Inst. of Chem. (Pres. 1973); mem. Council, Univ. of Otago 1975–79; Hon. Sec. Nuffield N.Z. Advisory Cttee. 1951–92; mem. Bd. of Govs. Columba Coll. 1969–88; N.Z. Research Scholarship 1947, Carnegie Travel Award 1950; Easterfield Medal for Research, Royal Inst. of Chem. 1956. *Publications:* numerous papers in chemical journals including Journal of the Chemical Soc., Tetrahedron Letters 1950–. *Leisure interests:* fly fishing, gardening. *Address:* 106 Taipari Street, Maungatapu, Tauranga, New Zealand.

CORBIN, Raymond Pierre Louis; French sculptor and professor; b. 23 April 1907, Rochefort-sur-Mer; s. of Georges Corbin and Hélène (née Boyau) Corbin; m. Charlotte Canale 1934; one s. three d.; ed. Ecole des Arts Appliqués de Paris and Ecole nat. supérieure des Beaux Arts de Paris; Prof. of Medal Engraving Ecole nat. supérieure des Beaux Arts de Paris 1955–77, Hon. Prof. 1977–; mem. Acad. des Beaux Arts 1970, Comité du Salon des Tuileries; Exhbns. Monnaie de Paris 1986, Cabinet des Médailles de Munich 1987, Corderie Royale de Rochefort 1989, Musée Denon à Châlon-sur-Saône 1992, Musée Colette à Saint-Sauver 1998; *Sculptures and medals include:* portraits of Charles Nodier, L. P. Fargue, Marcel Pagnol, Roland Dorgelès, Gérard de Nerval, Marie Curie, Colette, Guillaume Budé, Louis Pergaud; stone statue Ville de Borges; numerous exhbns. at Poitiers, Strasbourg, Algiers, Paris, Rochefort, Munich, Châlon-sur-Saône; High Relief, Monument of Mount Valérien; Chevalier Légion d'honneur, Officier des Arts et Lettres; Prix Blumenthal 1936, Prix Germain Pilon 1969. *Address:* 32 rue Alphonse Bertillon, 75015 Paris (Office); 3 rue des Arts, 92100 Boulogne-Billancourt, France (Home).

CORBO, Vittorio, PH.D.; Chilean economist; b. 22 March 1943, Iquique; s. of Gerardo Corbo and Maria Lioi; m. Veronica Urzua 1967; one s. one d.; ed. Universidad de Chile and Massachusetts Inst. of Tech.; Asst. Prof. Concordia Univ. 1972–74, Assoc. Prof. 1974–78, Prof. of Econs. 1979–81; Prof. of Econs. Pontificia Univ. Católica de Chile 1981–84, 1991–; Sr. adviser, IBRD 1984–87, Div. Chief. 1987–91; econ. adviser, Santander Group 1991–. *Publications include:* Inflation in Developing Countries 1974. *Leisure interest:* the sky. *Address:* Instituto de Economia, Pontificia Universidad Católica de Chile, Casilla 114–D, Santiago, Chile.

CORBY, Sir (Frederick) Brian, Kt., M.A., F.I.A.; British company executive and actuary; b. 10 May 1929, Raunds, Northants.; s. of Charles Walter and Millicent Corby; m. Elizabeth Mairi McInnes 1952; one s. two d.; ed. Kimbolton School and St. John's Coll., Cambridge; joined Prudential Assurance Co. Ltd. 1952, Asst. Gen. Man. (Overseas) 1968–73, Deputy Gen. Man. 1974–75, Gen. Man. 1976–79, Chief Actuary 1980–81, Group Gen. Man., Prudential Corpn. PLC 1979–82, C.E.O. 1982–90, Chair. 1990–95; Chief

Gen. Man. Prudential Assurance Co. Ltd. 1982–85, Chair. 1985–90; Deputy Pres. CBI 1989–90, Pres. 1990–92; Pres. Nat. Inst. for Econ. and Social Research 1994–; Vice-Pres. Inst. of Actuaries 1979–83; Chair. South Bank Bd. 1990–98; Deputy Chair. British Insurance Asscn. 1984–85; Chair. Asscn. of British Insurers 1985–87; Dir. Bank of England 1985–93, Pan-Holding 1993–, Montanaro Small Cos. Investment Trust PLC (Chair.) 1995–, Mid-Ocean Reinsurance 1995–98, Brockbank Holdings Ltd. (Chair.) 1995–99, Moorfield Estates PLC (Chair.) 1996–, Exel Ltd. 1998–; Chancellor Univ. of Herts. 1992–96. *Publications:* articles in Journal of Inst. of Actuaries. *Leisure interests:* reading, golf, gardening. *Address:* Fairings, Church End, Albury, Ware, Herts., SG11 2JG.

CORCUERA CUESTA, José Luis; Spanish politician; b. 2 July 1945, Pradoluengo, Burgos Prov.; m.; two d.; joined Partido Socialista Obrero Español 1973; joined Unión Gen. de Trabajadores (UGT) 1973, Org. Sec. Metalworking Fed., UGT, later Gen. Sec. 1977; mem. UGT Exec. Cttee. 1980–85, Exec. Sec. Fed. Exec. Cttee. 1986, Sec. for Inst. Policy 1988; Deputy for Vizcaya 1979, 1982–94; Minister of the Interior 1989–93. *Address:* c/o PSOE, Ferraz 68 y 70, 28008 Madrid, Spain.

CORDEN, Warner Max, M.COMM., M.A., PH.D.; Australian professor of international economics; b. 13 August 1927, Breslau, Germany (now Wrocław, Poland); s. of late Ralph S. Corden; m. Dorothy Martin 1957; one d.; ed. Melbourne Boys High School, Univ. of Melbourne and L.S.E.; lecturer, Univ. of Melbourne 1958–61; Nuffield Reader in Int. Econ. and Fellow of Nuffield Coll., Oxford 1967–76; Professorial Fellow, Australian Nat. Univ. 1962–67, Prof. of Econs. 1976–88; Prof. of Int. Econ., Paul H. Nitze School of Advanced Int. Studies, Johns Hopkins Univ. 1989–; Visiting Prof., Univ. of Calif. (Berkeley) 1965, Univ. of Minn. 1971, Princeton Univ. 1973, Harvard Univ. 1986; Sr. Adviser, IMF 1986–88; Pres. Econ. Soc. of Australia and New Zealand 1977–80; mem. Group of Thirty 1982–90; Foreign Hon. mem. American Econ. Asscn. 1986; Hon. Dr. (Melbourne) 1995; Bernard Harms Prize 1986, Distinguished Fellow, Econ. Soc. of Australia 1995. *Publications:* The Theory of Protection 1971, Trade Policy and Economic Welfare 1974, Inflation, Exchange Rates and the World Economy 1977, Protection, Growth and Trade 1985, International Trade Theory and Policy 1992, Economic Policy, Exchange Rates and the International System 1994, The Road to Reform 1997. *Address:* School of Advanced International Studies, 1740 Massachusetts Avenue, N.W., Washington, DC 20036, U.S.A. *Telephone:* (202) 663 5679 (Office). *Fax:* (202) 663-7718.

CORDOBA, José ("Pepe"); Mexican public servant; b. Paris, France; ed. Sorbonne, Paris, Stanford Univ., U.S.A.; naturalized Mexican 1985; Chef de Cabinet, Pres.'s Office 1988–. *Address:* Oficina del Presidente, Los Pinos, México, D.F., Mexico.

CORDOVEZ, Diego; Ecuadorean diplomatist and lawyer; b. 3 Nov. 1935, Quito; s. of Luis Cordovez-Borja and Isidora Zegers de Cordovez; m. Maria Teresa Somavia 1960; one s.; ed. Univ. of Chile; admitted to bar 1962; foreign service of Ecuador until 1963; joined UN as Econ. Affairs Officer 1963; political officer on special missions to Dominican Repub. 1965, Pakistan 1971; Dir. UN Econ. and Social Council Secr. 1973–78, Asst. Sec.-Gen. for Econ. and Social Matters, UN 1978–81; Special Rep. of UN Sec.-Gen. on Libya-Malta dispute 1980–82; Sec.-Gen.'s rep. on UN Comm. of Inquiry on hostage crisis in Teheran 1980; sr. officer responsible for efforts to resolve Iran/Iraq war 1980–88; Under-Sec.-Gen. for Special Political Affairs 1981–1988; Special Envoy to Grenada 1983; UN Mediator, Afghanistan 1982–88, Rep. for implementation of Geneva Accords 1988–89; Minister for Foreign Affairs 1988–92; Pres. World Trade Center (Ecuador) 1993–; Special Counsel Le Boeuf, Lamb, Greene and Macrae 1993–; Special Adviser to UN Sec. Gen. for Cyprus 1997–; mem. American Soc. of Int. Law; Order of Merit (Ecuador), Légion d'honneur, Grand Cross (Spain, Portugal, Brazil, Argentina, Chile, Peru, Colombia, Venezuela). *Publications:* UNCTAD and Development Diplomacy 1971, Out of Afghanistan: The Inside Story of the Soviet Withdrawal (jtly.) 1995. *Leisure interests:* reading, carpentry. *Address:* Calle Afganistán 1988, El Bosque, Quito, Ecuador. *Fax:* (5932) 440289.

CORELL, Hans, LL.B.; Swedish diplomatist and lawyer; b. 7 July 1939, Västermo; s. of Alf Corell and Margit Norrman; m. Inger Peijfors 1964; one s. one d.; ed. Univ. of Uppsala; court clerk, Eksjö Dist. Court and Göta Court of Appeal 1962–67; Asst. Judge, Västervik Dist. Court 1968–72; Legal Adviser, Ministry of Justice 1972, 1974–79; Additional mem. and Assoc. Judge of Appeal, Svea Court of Appeal 1973; Asst. Under-Sec. Div. for Constitutional and Admin. Law, Ministry of Justice 1979–81; Judge of Appeal 1980; Under-Sec. for Legal Affairs, Ministry of Justice 1981–84; Amb. and Under-Sec. for Legal and Consular Affairs, Ministry of Foreign Affairs 1984–94; mem. Perm. Court of Arbitration, The Hague 1990–; Under-Sec.-Gen. for Legal Affairs, The Legal Counsel of the UN 1994–; Hon. LL.D. (Stockholm) 1997. *Publications:* Sekretesslagen (co-author) 1992, Proposal for an International War Crimes Tribunal for the Former Yugoslavia (CSCE Report) (co-author) 1993; various legal publs. *Leisure interests:* art, music (Piper of the Caledonian Pipes and Drums of Stockholm 1975–84), ornithology. *Address:* UN Secretariat, Room S-3427, New York, NY 10017 (Office); 249 East 48th Street, New York, NY 10017, U.S.A. (Home). *Telephone:* (212) 963-5338 (Office); (212) 753-1160 (Home).

CORELLI, Franco; Italian tenor; b. Ancona; ed. Pesaro Conservatory, Maggio Musicale, Florence; first appearance as Don José in Carmen, Spoleto; appeared in Spontini's La Vestale, La Scala, Milan 1954, Teatro San Carlo, Naples 1955, Cavaradossi, Covent Garden, London 1956, Rome 1957, 1958, Naples 1958, La Scala (with Maria Callas) 1960; Metropolitan Opera début as Manrico in Il Trovatore 1961; has sung major parts in Andrea Chénier, La Bohème, Turandot, Tosca, Ernani, Aïda, Don Carlos, Forza del Destino, Cavalleria Rusticana, I Pagliacci, etc.; performs regularly on American TV; recital tour with Renata Tebaldi; 1st Prize Spoleto Nat. Competition.

COREN, Alan, M.A.; British editor, author and broadcaster; b. 27 June 1938, London; s. of Samuel Coren and Martha (née Coren) Coren; m. Anne Kasriel 1963; one s. one d.; ed. East Barnet Grammar School, Wadham Coll., Oxford, Univ. of California, Berkeley and Yale Univ.; Asst. Ed. Punch 1963–66, Literary Ed. 1966–69, Deputy Ed. 1969–77, Ed. 1977–87; Ed. The Listener 1988–89; Columnist The Times 1971–78, 1988–, Daily Mail 1972–76, Mail on Sunday 1983–92, Era 1983–, Sunday Express 1992–96; contrib. to Observer, Listener, Sunday Times, Atlantic Monthly, TV Guide, Tatler, Times Literary Supplement, London Review of Books, Daily Telegraph, The Spectator, Playboy, Guardian; Commonwealth Fellowship 1961–63; Rector St. Andrew's Univ. 1973–76; Hon. D.Litt. (Nottingham) 1993, British Soc. of Magazine Eds. Ed. of the Year 1986. *Publications:* The Dog it was that Died 1965, All Except the Bastard 1969, The Sanity Inspector 1974, The Collected Bulletins of Idi Amin 1974, Golfing for Cats 1975, The Further Bulletins of Idi Amin 1975, The Arthur Books (12 novellas) 1976–80, The Lady from Stalingrad Mansions 1977, The Peanut Papers 1977, The Rhinestone as Big as the Ritz 1979, Tissues for Men 1980, The Cricklewood Diet 1982, Bumf 1984, Something for the Weekend 1986, Bin Ends 1987, Seems Like Old Times 1989, More Like Old Times 1990, A Year in Cricklewood 1991, Toujours Cricklewood? 1993, Sunday Best 1993, Animal Passions 1994, A Bit on the Side 1995, The Alan Coren Omnibus 1996, The Cricklewood Dome 1998. *Leisure interests:* bridge, tennis, riding. *Address:* c/o Robson Books, Bolsover House, Clipstone Street, London, W1P 7EB, England.

COREY, Elias James, PH.D.; American professor of chemistry; b. 12 July 1928, Methuen, Mass.; s. of Elias J. Corey and Tina Hasham; m. Claire Higham 1961; two s. one d.; ed. Massachusetts Inst. of Tech.; Instructor in Chem., Univ. of Ill. 1951–53, Asst. Prof. of Chem. 1953–55, Prof. 1956–59; Prof. of Chem., Harvard Univ. 1959–, Chair. Dept. of Chem. 1965–68, Sheldon Emery Prof. 1968–; Alfred P. Sloan Foundation Fellow 1955–57, Guggenheim Fellow 1957, 1968–69; mem. American Acad. of Arts and Sciences 1960–68, N.A.S. 1966; Hon. A.M., Hon. D.Sc.; Pure Chem. Award of American Chemical Soc. 1960, Fritzsche Award of American Chemical Soc. 1967, Intra-Science Foundation Award 1967, Harrison Howe Award, American Chemical Soc. 1970, Award for Synthetic Organic Chem. 1971, CIBA Foundation Award 1972, Evans Award, Ohio State Univ. 1972, Linus Pauling Award 1973, Dickson Prize in Science, Carnegie Mellon Univ. 1973, George Ledlie Prize, (Harvard) 1973, Remsen Award, Arthur C. Cope Award 1976, Nichols Medal 1977, Buchman Memorial Award (Calif. Inst. of Tech.) 1978, Franklin Medal 1978, Scientific Achievement Award Medal 1979, J. G. Kirkwood Award (Yale) 1980, C. S. Hamilton Award (Univ. of Nebraska) 1980, Chemical Pioneer Award (American Inst. of Chemists) 1981, Rosenstiel Award (Brandeis Univ.) 1982, Paul Karrer Award (Zurich Univ.) 1982, Medal of Excellence (Helsinki Univ.) 1982, Tetrahedron Prize 1983, Gibbs Award (American Chem. Soc.) 1984, Paracelsus Award (Swiss Chem. Soc.) 1984, V. D. Mattia Award (Roche Inst. of Molecular Biology) 1985, Wolf Prize in Chemistry (Wolf Foundation) 1986, Silliman Award (Yale Univ.) 1986, U.S. Nat. Medal of Science 1988, Japan Prize 1989, Nobel Prize for Chemistry 1990 and numerous others. *Publications:* approx. 700 chemical papers. *Leisure interests:* outdoor activities and music. *Address:* Department of Chemistry, Harvard University, 12 Oxford Street, Cambridge, MA 02138 (Office); 20 Avon Hill Street, Cambridge, MA 02140, U.S.A. (Home). *Telephone:* (617) 495-4033 (Office); (617) 864-0627 (Home).

CORFIELD, Rt. Hon. Sir Frederick Vernon, Kt., P.C., Q.C.; British politician and barrister-at-law; b. 1 June 1915, London; s. of Brig. Frederick A. Corfield, D.S.O. and Mary Vernon; m. Ruth Taylor 1945; ed. Cheltenham Coll. and Royal Military Acad., Woolwich; regular army 1935–45, prisoner-of-war 1940–45; called to Bar, Middle Temple 1945; Judge Advocate Gen.'s Branch, War Office 1945–46; farming 1946–56; Conservative M.P. for S. Glos. 1955–74; Jt. Parl. Sec. Ministry of Housing and Local Govt. 1962–64; Minister of State, Bd. of Trade June-Oct. 1970; Minister of Aviation Supply 1970–71, Minister for Aerospace, Dept. of Trade and Industry 1971–72; mem. British Waterways Bd. 1974–83, Vice-Chair. 1980–83; Dir. Mid-Kent Water Co. 1974–91; Recorder 1979–87; Bencher, Middle Temple 1980; Pres. Cheltenham Coll. Council 1985–88. *Publications:* Corfield on Compensation 1959, A Guide to the Community Land Act 1975, Compulsory Acquisition and Compensation (joint author) 1978. *Leisure interest:* gardening. *Address:* Wording's Orchard, Sheepscombe, Stroud, Glos., GL6 7RE, England.

CORFIELD, Sir Kenneth George, Kt., C.E., F.ENG., F.I.E.E., F.I.MECH.E.; British company executive and engineer; b. 27 Jan. 1924, Rushall; s. of Stanley Corfield and Dorothy Elisabeth (née Mason); m. Patricia Jean Williams 1960; one d.; ed. Elmore Green High School, South Staffs. Coll. of Advanced Tech.; Tech. Officer, ICI Ltd. 1947–50; Chief Exec., K.G. Corfield Ltd., camera mfrs. 1950–61; Exec. Dir. Parkinson Cowan Ltd. 1962–67; Vice-Pres., Dir. ITT Europe Inc. 1967–70; Man. Dir. Standard Telephones and Cables Ltd. 1970–85, Deputy Chair. 1974–79, Chair. and C.E.O. 1979–85; Chair. Standard Telephones and Cables (N. Ireland) 1974–85; Vice-Pres. Int. Standard Electric Corpn., ITT Sr. Officer in U.K. 1974–84; Chair. Nat. Econ. Devt. Cttee. for Ferrous Foundries Industry 1975–78;

Vice-Chair. British Inst. of Man. 1978–84; Vice-Pres. Inst. of Marketing 1980–; Chair. Eng. Council 1981–85, Distributed Information Processing Ltd. 1987–, Octagon Investment Man. 1987–96, Gandolfi Ltd. 1987–, Tanks Consolidated Investments 1990, Linhof & Studio Ltd. 1993–; Dir. Midland Bank Group 1979–91, Britoil 1982–88, Vice-Pres. Eng. Employers Fed. –1985; mem. Pres.'s Cttee. and Council, CBI –1985; mem. Council, Inst. of Dirs. 1981–85 (Pres. 1984–85); mem. Advisory Council, Science Museum 1975–83, Trustee 1984–92; mem. Advisory Council for Applied Research and Devt. 1981, Nat. Econ. Devt. Cttee. for Electronics 1981; Hon. Fellow, Sheffield City Polytechnic 1983, Wolverhampton Polytechnic 1986; Dr. h.c. (Surrey), (Open Univ.) 1985, Hon. D.Sc. (City Univ.) 1981, (Bath) 1982, (Queen's, Belfast) 1982, (Loughborough) 1982, (Aston) 1985, Hon. LL.D. (Strathclyde) 1982, Hon. D.Sc. (Eng.) Univ. of London 1982, Hon. D.Eng. (Bradford) 1983; Hon. F.I.E.E. *Publications:* Report on Product Design for NEDC 1979, No Man an Island 1982, Patterns of Change: Collected Essays 1983. *Leisure interests:* shooting, Hi Fi, photography, cinema. *Address:* 10 Chapel Place, Rivington Street, London, EC2A 3DQ, England.

CORISH, Patrick Joseph, M.A., D.D.; Irish historian (retd.); b. 20 March 1921, Co. Wexford; s. of Peter William Corish and Brigid Mary O'Shaughnessy; ed. St. Peter's Coll., Wexford and Nat. Univ. of Ireland (St. Patrick's Coll., Maynooth and Univ. Coll., Dublin); ordained as Priest 1945; Prof. of Ecclesiastical History Pontifical Univ., Maynooth 1947–75; Prof. of Modern History, Maynooth, N.U.I. 1975–88; mem. Royal Irish Acad. 1956; Sec. Catholic Record Soc. of Ireland 1948, ed. Soc.'s journal Archivium Hibernicum 1948–77; mem. Irish Manuscripts Comm. 1949; Domestic Prelate 1967. *Publications:* A History of Irish Catholicism (ed. and contrib.) 1967–71, The Catholic Community in the Seventeenth and Eighteenth Centuries 1981, The Irish Catholic Experience 1985, Maynooth College: a bicentenary history 1995. *Leisure interest:* gardening. *Address:* St. Patrick's College, Maynooth, Co. Kildare, Ireland. *Telephone:* 01-6285222. *Fax:* 01-6289063.

CORMAN, Roger William, A.B.; American film director and producer; b. 5 April 1926, Detroit, Mich.; m. Julie Ann Halloran; two s. two d.; ed. Stanford Univ. Calif., Oxford Univ., England; dir. Five Guns West 1955; Founder, Pres. New World Pictures 1970–83, Concorde-New Horizons Corpn. 1983–. *Produced films:* over 200 including Monster from the Ocean Floor 1953, Grand Theft Auto, I Never Promised You a Rose Garden, Thunder and Lightning, Avalanche, Deathsport, Piranha, Rock 'n' Roll High School Forever, Deathrace 2000, Transylvania Twist, Nightfall, Roger Corman Presents (13 horror/science fiction films for TV). *Films as producer and director include:* The Day the World Ended 1956, The Fall of the House of Usher 1960, The Little Shop of Horrors 1960, The Pit and the Pendulum 1961, The Intruder 1962, The Raven 1963, Masque of the Red Death 1964, The Secret Invasion 1964, The Wild Angels 1966, The Saint Valentine's Day Massacre 1967, The Trip 1967, Bloody Mama 1970, Gas-s-s 1970, Frankenstein Unbound 1989; dir. Von Richthofen and Brown 1971; produced Dracula Rising 1991; exec. producer Hollywood Boulevard, Rock and Rol High School, Apollo 13, Philadelphia; play: Little Shop of Horrors 1982. *Film appearances include:* The Silence of the Lambs, The Godfather, Part III; distributed films including: Cries and Whispers, Amarcord, Fantastic Planet, The Story of Adele H, Small Change, The Tin Drum; mem. Producers' Guild of America, Directors' Guild of America. *Address:* c/o Concorde-New Horizons Corpn., 11600 San Vincente Blvd., Los Angeles, CA 90049, U.S.A.

CORNEA, Doina; Romanian philologist; b. 30 May 1929, Braşov; m.; one d.; ed. Faculty of Philology, Univ. of Cluj; Asst. Lecturer in French Literature, Univ. of Cluj; dismissed for writing an open letter to Those Who Haven't Ceased to Think 1983; held for interrogation for five weeks Nov. 1987; under house arrest 1988–89; mem. Romanian Nat. Salvation Front 1989–90, Memory Foundation; founder mem. of Social Dialogue Group (G.D.S.) 1989, of Civil Alliance; co-founder of Antitotalitarian Forum of Romania 1990; Dr. h.c. (Brussels) 1989; int. awards for activities in furtherance of human rights. *Publications:* Liberté? 1990, Opened Letters and Other Texts 1991, translations from French. *Address:* Str. Alba Iulia Nr. 16, Cluj 3400, Romania. *Telephone:* (064) 198460. *Fax:* (064) 432571.

CORNEILLE (see Beverloo, Cornelis Van).

CORNELIS, François; Belgian oil company executive; b. 25 Oct. 1949, Uccle, Brussels; m. Colette Durant 1973; two s. two d.; ed. Univ. of Louvain; joined Petrofina S.A. as a systems engineer, subsequently Co-ordinator of Supply and Refining Operations, Brussels, Supply and Shipping Man., Petrofina, U.K., London, Vice-Pres., Special Asst. to Pres., American Petrofina, Dallas, Tex., U.S.A. 1983–84, Gen. Man. and Asst. to Pres., Petrofina 1984–86, Exec. Dir., Office of the Chair. 1986–90, C.E.O. Vice-Chair. 1990–; Chair. Fina Inc. 1998–. *Address:* Petrofina S.A., Rue de l'Industrie 52, B-1040 Brussels, Belgium.

CORNESS, Sir Colin (Ross), Kt., M.A.; British business executive; b. 9 Oct. 1931, Chorlton; s. of Thomas Corness and Mary Evlyne Corness; ed. Uppingham School, Magdalene Coll., Cambridge, Grad. School of Business Admin., Harvard; Dir. Taylor Woodrow Construction Ltd. 1961–1964; Man. Dir. Redland Tiles Ltd. 1965–70, Group Man. Dir. Redland PLC 1967–82, Deputy Chair. and Man. Dir. 1974–77, Chair. 1977–95; C.E.O. 1977–91; Chair. Nationwide Bldg. Soc. 1991–96; Dir. Chubb and Son PLC 1974–84, W.H. Smith and Son Holdings PLC 1980–87, S.E. Region, Nat. Westminster Bank PLC 1982–86, Courtaulds PLC 1986–, Gordon Russell PLC 1985–89, Bank of England 1987–95, S. G. Warburg Group PLC 1987–95, Unitech PLC 1987–95, Union Camp Corpn. 1991–, Chubb Security PLC 1992–97, Glaxo Wellcome PLC 1994–97 (Chair. 1995–97, Chair. Pension Trustees 1995–), Taylor Woodrow PLC 1997–; Chair. Bldg. Centre 1974–77; mem. Econ. Devt. Cttee. for Bldg. 1980–84, Ind. Devt. Advisory Bd. 1982–84, U.K. Advisory Bd. of the British-American Chamber of Commerce 1987–. *Leisure interests:* travel, music. *Address:* Glaxo Wellcome PLC, 34 Berkeley Square, London, W1X 6JT, England. *Telephone:* 0171-408 8489. *Fax:* 0171-408 8921.

CORNFORTH, Sir John Warcup, Kt., A.C., C.B.E., D.PHIL., F.R.S.; Australian research scientist; b. 7 Sept. 1917, Sydney; s. of J. W. Cornforth and Hilda Eipper; m. Rita H. Harradence 1941; one s. two d.; ed. Univs. of Sydney and Oxford; Scientific Staff, Medical Research Council 1946–62; Dir. Milstead Lab. of Chemical Enzymology, Shell Research Ltd. 1962–75; Assoc. Prof. Univ. of Warwick 1965–71; Visiting Prof. Univ. of Sussex 1971–75; Royal Soc. Prof. Univ. of Sussex 1975–82; Foreign Hon. mem. American Acad. 1973–; Corresp. mem. Australian Acad. of Science 1977–; Foreign Assoc. U.S. Nat. Acad. of Sciences 1978–; Foreign mem. Royal Netherlands Acad. of Sciences 1978–; Hon. Fellow St. Catherine's Coll., Oxford 1976–; Hon. Prof. Beijing Medical Univ. 1986–; Hon. D.Sc. (ETH Zurich) 1975, (Oxford, Dublin, Liverpool, Warwick Univs.) 1976, (Aberdeen, Hull, Sussex, Sydney Univs.) 1977; Corday-Morgan Medal, Chem. Soc. 1953, Flintoff Medal, Chem. Soc. 1966, Ciba Medal, Biochem. Soc. 1966, Stouffer Prize 1967, Davy Medal, Royal Soc. 1968, Ernest Guenther Award, American Chemical Soc. 1969, Prix Roussel 1972, Nobel Prize for Chemistry 1975, Royal Medal, Royal Soc. 1976, Copley Medal, Royal Soc. 1982. *Publications:* The Chemistry of Penicillin (part author) 1949, and numerous papers on chemical and biochemical topics. *Leisure interests:* tennis, gardening, chess. *Address:* Saxon Down, Cuilfail, Lewes, East Sussex, BN7 2BE, England.

CORNILLET, Thierry Pierre Fernand, D. ÈS SC.POL.; French politician; b. 23 July 1951, Montélimar, Drôme; s. of Col. Jean-Baptiste Cornillet and Inès Genoud; m. Marie-France Rossi 1983; one s. one d.; ed. Lycée Alain Borne, Montélimar, Univs. of Lyon II, Lyon III and Paris I—Panthéon Sorbonne; Head of Dept., Office of Dir. of Civil Security at Ministry of Interior 1977–81; Head of Dept., Office of Minister of External Trade, then of Admin. Reform 1980–81; Export Man., Lagarde S.A.., Montélimar 1981–83; Dir. Office of Deputy Mayor of Nancy 1983–85; Legal Adviser to Jr. Minister, Ministry of Interior 1985–86, Chef de Cabinet 1986–88; Head of Dept., Cie. nationale du Rhône 1988–93; Municipal Councillor, Montélimar 1983, Mayor 1989–; mem. Gen. Council of Drôme 1985–93, Vice-Chair. 1992–93; mem. and Sec. Regional Council of Rhône-Alpes 1986; Deputy from Drôme for Union pour la démocratie française et du Centre (UDF) 1993–97; Vice-Chair. Parti Radical 1988–97, Chair. 1997–; Sec. Assemblée nationale 1993–95; Chevalier Ordre nat. du Mérite. *Address:* Mairie, BP 279, 26216 Montélimar, France.

CORNISH, Robert Francis, C.M.G., L.V.O.; British diplomatist; b. 18 May 1942, Bolton; m. Alison Jane Cornish (née Dundas) 1964; three d.; ed. Charterhouse School, Royal Mil. Acad., Sandhurst; commissioned 14th/20th King's Hussars and served in Libya, U.K. and Germany, becoming Adjutant 1966; joined H.M. Diplomatic Service 1968, served in Kuala Lumpur and Jakarta before becoming Head, Greek Dept., London; First Sec. (EEC), Bonn 1976–80; apptd. Asst. Pvt. Sec. to Prince of Wales 1980, also worked for Princess of Wales –1983; High Commr. to Brunei 1983–86; Dir. of Public Diplomacy, Washington, D.C. and Head, British Information Services, New York 1986; Head News Dept. FCO, London and Spokesman for the Foreign Sec. 1990–93, Sr. British Trade Commr., Hong Kong 1993, first Consul Gen. Hong Kong 1997. *Leisure interests:* riding, hill walking. *Address:* c/o Foreign and Commonwealth Office, King Charles Street, London, S.W.1, England.

CORNISH, William Rodolph, LL.B., B.C.L., F.B.A.; barrister; b. 9 Aug. 1937, S. Australia; s. of Jack R. Cornish and Elizabeth E. Cornish; m. Lovedy E. Moule 1964; one s. two d.; ed. St. Peter's Coll., Adelaide, Adelaide Univ. and Oxford Univ., England; Lecturer in Law, L.S.E. 1962–68; Reader in Law, Queen Mary Coll., London Univ. 1969–70; Prof. of English Law, L.S.E. 1970–90; Prof. of Law, Cambridge Univ. 1990–95, Dir. Centre for Euro Legal Studies 1991–94, Herchel Smith Prof. of Intellectual Property Law, Univ. of Cambridge 1995–; Fellow, Magdalene Coll. 1990–; Academic Dir. British Law Centre, Warsaw Univ. 1996–; Hon. Q.C. 1997. *Publications:* The Jury 1968, Intellectual Property 1981, Encyclopaedia of U.K. and European Patent Law (with others) 1978, Law and Society in England 1750–1950 1989; numerous articles in legal periodicals. *Address:* Magdalene College, Cambridge, CB3 0AG, England. *Telephone:* (01223) 332132. *Fax:* (01223) 363637.

CORNWELL, David John Moore (pseudonym John le Carré); British writer; b. 19 Oct. 1931, Poole, Dorset; s. of Ronald Thomas Archibald Cornwell and Olive Glassy; m. 1st Alison Ann Veronica Sharp 1954 (divorced 1971); three s.; m. 2nd Valerie Jane Eustace 1972; one s.; ed. St. Andrew's Preparatory School, Pangbourne, Sherborne School, Berne Univ., and Lincoln Coll., Oxford; Teacher, Eton Coll. 1956–58; in Foreign Service (Second Sec., Bonn, then Political Consul Hamburg) 1959–64; Hon. Fellow Lincoln Coll. Oxford; Hon. D. Litt. (Exeter) 1990; Somerset Maugham Award 1963, James Tait Black Award 1977. *Publications:* Call for the Dead 1961 (filmed as The Deadly Affair 1967), Murder of Quality 1962 (filmed), The Spy Who Came in From the Cold 1963 (filmed), The Looking Glass War 1965, A Small Town in Germany 1968, The Naive and Sentimental Lover 1971, Tinker, Tailor, Soldier, Spy 1974 (made into TV series), The Honourable Schoolboy

1977 (made into TV series), Smiley's People 1979 (made into TV series), The Quest for Carla (collected edn. of previous three titles) 1982, The Little Drummer Girl 1983 (filmed), A Perfect Spy 1986, The Russia House 1989 (filmed), The Secret Pilgrim 1991, The Night Manager 1993, Our Game 1995, The Tailor of Panama 1996. *Address:* c/o David Higham Associates, 5–8 Lower John Street, Golden Square, London, W1R 4HA, England.

CORR, Edwin Gharst, M.A.; American diplomatist; b. 6 Aug. 1934, Edmond, Okla.; s. of E. L. Corr and Rowena Gharst; m. Susanne Springer 1957; three d.; ed. Univ. of Okla. and Texas; officer Dept. of State, Foreign Office 1961–62; sent to Mexico 1962–66; Dir. Peace Corps, Cali, Colombia 1966–68; Panama Desk Officer, Dept. of State 1969–71; Program Officer InterAmerican Foundation 1971; Exec. Asst. to Amb., Embassy, Bangkok 1972–75; Counsellor Political Affairs, Embassy, Ecuador 1976; Deputy Chief of Mission 1977–78; Deputy Asst. Sec. Int. Narcotics Matters, State Dept. 1978–80; Amb. to Peru 1980–81, Bolivia 1981–85, El Salvador 1985–88; State Dept. Diplomat-in-Residence, Univ. of Okla. 1988–90, Prof. of Political Science 1990–96, Dir. Energy Inst. of the Americas and Assoc. Dir. of Int. Program Center 1996–; Nat. Order of Merit (Ecuador), Condor of the Andes (Bolivia), Pres.'s Performance Award (USA), Award for Superior Performance (USA), Distinguished Service Award (USA), Jose Matias Delgado Decoration (El Salvador). *Publications:* The Political Process in Colombia 1971, Low-Intensity Conflict: Old Threats in a New World (co-editor) 1992, numerous articles in English and Spanish. *Leisure interests:* ranching, reading, public speaking, writing, exercise. *Address:* Energy Institute of the Americas, Sarkeys Energy Center, University of Oklahoma, Norman, OK 73019 (Office); 544 Shawnee, Norman, OK 73071, U.S.A. (Home). *Telephone:* (405) 325-6621 (Office); (405) 321-7036 (Home).

CORREA, Charles M., M.ARCH.; Indian architect and planner; b. 1 Sept. 1930, Hyderabad; s. of Carlos Marcos Correa and Ana Florinda de Heredia; m. Monika Sequeira 1961; one s. one d.; ed. Univ. of Michigan and M.I.T.; Pvt. Practice 1958–; Chief Architect New Bombay 1971–74; Chair., Nat. Comm. on Urbanization, Steering Cttee. Aga Khan Award for Architecture 1977–86; Hon. Fellow, American Inst. of Architecture 1977, Finnish Asscn. of Architects 1992, R.I.B.A. 1993, American Acad. of Arts and Sciences 1993; Hon. Dr. (Univ. of Mich.) 1980; Padma Shri, Pres. of India 1972; R.I.B.A. Gold Medal 1984, Gold Medal, Indian Inst. of Architects 1987, Gold Medal, Int. Union of Architects 1990, Praemium Imperiale for Architecture, Japan Art Asscn. 1994. *Major works include:* Mahatma Gandhi Memorial Museum, Sabarmati Ashram, Ahmedabad, Kovalam beach Devt., Kerala, Kanchanjunga apartments, Bombay, Cidade de Goa, Dona Paula, New India Centre, Delhi, performing arts centre, Kala Acad., Goa, Previ low-income housing, Peru, Bharat Bhavan, Bhopal, Jawahar Kala Kendra, Jaipur, Nat. Crafts Museum, Delhi, British Council, Delhi, IUCCA, Pune Univ. *Publication:* The New Landscape 1985. *Leisure interests:* model railways, old films, swimming. *Address:* 9 Mathew Road, Bombay 400.004 (Office); Sonmarg, Nepean Sea Road, Bombay 400006, India (Home). *Telephone:* 3633307/3611858 (Office); 3633306 (Home).

CORREIA, Carlos; Guinea-Bissau politician; mem. Partido Africano da Indepêndencia da Guiné e Cabo Verde (PAIGC); fmr. Minister of State for Rural Devt. and Agric.; Prime Minister of Guinea Bissau 1991–94, 1997–98; fmr. Perm. Sec. Council of State. *Address:* c/o Office of the Prime Minister, Bissau, Guinea-Bissau.

CORRELL, A.D. (Pete), M.S.; American paper industry executive; b. 28 April 1941, Brunswick, Ga.; s. of Alston Dayton Correll and Elizabeth Correll (née Flippo); m. Ada Lee Fulford 1963; one s. one d.; ed. Univs. of Georgia and Maine (Orono); tech. service engineer, Westvaco 1963–64; instructor, Univ. of Maine (Orono) 1964–67; various positions in pulp and paper man., Weyerhaeuser Co. 1967–77; Div. Pres., Paperboard, Mead Corpn. 1977–80, Group Vice-Pres. 1980–83, Sr. Vice-Pres., Forest Products 1983–88; Sr. Vice-Pres., Pulp and Printing Paper, Ga. Pacific Corpn. 1988–89, Exec. Vice-Pres., Pulp and Paper 1989–91, now Pres., C.O.O. 1991–93, C.E.O. 1993–, Chair. 1993–; mem. Bd. of Dirs. Univ. of Maine Pulp and Paper Foundation (Vice-Pres.), Engraph Inc., Trust Co. Bank of Atlanta, Trust Co. of Ga., Atlanta Chamber of Commerce, Atlanta Symphony Orchestra, Robert W. Woodruff Arts Center. *Address:* Georgia-Pacific Corporation, P.O. Box 105605, 133 Peachtree Street, N.E., Atlanta, GA 30303, U.S.A. *Telephone:* (404) 521-4000.

CORRIGAN, E. Gerald, PH.D.; American banker and economist; b. 1941, Waterbury, Conn.; ed. Fairfield and Fordham Univs.; Group Vice-Pres. (Man. and Planning) Fed. Reserve Bank of New York 1976–80, Pres. 1985–93; Special Asst. to Chair., Bd. of Govs. Fed. Reserve System 1979–80; Pres. Fed. Reserve Bank of Minneapolis 1981–84; Chair. int. advisers, Goldman Sachs & Co. 1994–96, Man. Dir. 1997–; now partner Man. Dir.; Chair. Bd. of Dirs. Russian-American Enterprise Fund 1993–; Trustee, Macalester Coll., St. Paul, Minn. 1981–, Jt. Council Econ. Educ. 1981–, Fairfield Univ., Fairfield, Conn. 1985–; mem. Trilateral Comm. 1986–; Pres. B.R.I. 1991–. *Address:* Goldman Sachs & Co., 85 Broad Street, New York, NY 10004, U.S.A.

CORRIGAN, (Francis) Edward, PH.D., F.R.S.; British professor of mathematics; b. 10 Aug. 1946, Birkenhead; s. of Anthony Corrigan and Eileen Corrigan (née Ryan); m. Jane Mary Halton 1970; two s. two d.; ed. St. Bede's Coll., Manchester, Christ's Coll. Cambridge; Addison Wheeler Fellow, Durham Univ. 1972–74; C.E.R.N. Fellow, C.E.R.N. Geneva 1974–76; lecturer Univ. of Durham 1976, Reader 1987, Prof. of Math. 1992–; Adrian-Daiwa Prize 1998. *Publications:* over 75 articles in learned journals and conf. proceedings. *Leisure interests:* music, squash, walking. *Address:* University of Durham, Mathematical Sciences, South Road, Durham, DH1 3LE (Office); 40 St. John's Road, Durham, DH1 4NU, England (Home). *Telephone:* (0191) 374 2372 (Office); (0191) 384 8029 (Home). *Fax:* (0191) 374 7388.

CORRIGAN-MAGUIRE, Mairead; Northern Irish human rights activist; b. 27 Jan. 1944, Belfast; d. of Andrew Corrigan and Margaret Corrigan; m. 2nd Jackie Maguire 1981; two s. three step-c.; ed. St. Vincent's Primary School, Belfast, Miss Gordon's Commercial Coll.; works as shorthand typist; Jt. recipient of Nobel Peace Prize for launching the Northern Ireland Peace Movement (later renamed Community of the Peace People) 1976, Chair. 1980–81; Carl von Ossietzky Medal for Courage (Berlin Section, Int. League of Human Rights); Hon. LL.D. (Yale Univ.) 1976. *Leisure interests:* swimming, walking. *Address:* Community of the Peace People, 224 Lisburn Road, Belfast, BT9 6GE, Northern Ireland. *Telephone:* (01232) 663465. *Fax:* (01232) 683947.

CORRIPIO AHUMADA, H.E. Cardinal Ernesto; Mexican ecclesiastic; b. 29 June 1919, Tampico; ordained priest 1942; Titular Bishop of Zapara 1953–56; Bishop of Tampico 1956–67; Archbishop of Antequera 1967–76, of Puebla de los Angeles 1976–77; Archbishop of Mexico City and Primate of Mexico 1977–94, Archbishop Emer. 1994–; cr. Cardinal 1979; mem. Sacred Congregation for the Sacraments and Divine Worship, Pontifical Comm. for Latin America; entitled L'Immacolata al Tiburtino. *Address:* Apolinar Nieto, 40 Col. Tetlameya, 04730 México, Mexico.

CORSARO, Frank Andrew; American theatre and opera director; b. 22 Dec. 1924, New York; s. of Joseph and Marie (née Quarino) Corsaro; m. Mary Cross Bonnie Lueders 1971; one s.; ed. Yale Univ.; began career as actor 1948, appearing since in productions including Mrs. McThing, Broadway 1951; first film appearance in Rachel, Rachel 1967; dir. of numerous plays including A Hatful of Rain, Broadway 1955–56, The Night of the Iguana 1961–62, Tremonisha 1975, 1600 Pennsylvania Avenue 1976, Cold Storage, Lyceum 1977–, Whoopee! 1979, Knockout 1979; directed and acted in numerous TV productions; one-man art show 1976; dir. numerous operas with New York City Opera 1958–, Washington Opera Soc. 1970–74, St. Paul Opera 1971, Houston Grand Opera 1973–77, Assoc. Artistic Dir. 1977–; Artistic Dir., The Actors Studio 1988–; Drama Dir. Juilliard Opera Centre 1989; productions include La Traviata, Madame Butterfly, Faust, Manon Lescaut, A Village Romeo and Juliet, L'Incoronazione di Poppea, The Angel of Fire, Hugh the Drover, Rinaldo, Love for Three Oranges (Glyndebourne 1983), La Fanciulla del West (Deutsches Oper Berlin 1983), Rinaldo (Metropolitan Opera 1983), Fennimore and Gerda (Edinburgh Festival 1983), Where the Wild Things Are, Higgeldy, Piggeldy, Pop (Glyndebourne 1985), Alcina (Spitalfields 1985), (L.A. Opera Centre 1986), L'Enfant et les Sortilèges, L'heure Espagnol, Glyndebourne Festival 1987, Hansel and Gretel (Houston, Toronto, Zurich 1997–98), Kuhlhandel (Juilliard 1998). *Publications include:* L'histoire du soldat (adaptation), La Bohème (adaptation), A Piece of Blue Sky (play), Maverik 1978, Libretto: Before Breakfast (music by Thomas Pasatieri), Libretto: Heloise and Abelard (music by Steven Paulus). *Leisure interests:* painting, piano playing, writing. *Address:* 33 Riverside Drive, New York, NY 10023, U.S.A. *Telephone:* (212) 874-1048.

CORSON, Dale R., PH.D.; American physicist and university administrator; b. 5 April 1914, Pittsburg, Kan.; s. of the late Harry R. Corson and of Alta Hill Corson; m. Nellie E. Griswold 1938; three s. one d.; ed. Coll. of Emporia, Univs. of Kansas and California; with Los Alamos Scientific Lab. 1945–46; Asst. Prof. of Physics, Cornell Univ. 1946–47, Assoc. Prof. 1947–52, Prof. 1952–56, Chair., Dept. of Physics 1956–59, Dean, Coll. of Eng. 1959–63, Univ. Provost 1963–69; Pres. Cornell Univ. 1969–77, Chancellor 1977–79, Pres. Emer. and Prof. Emer. 1979–; Fellow American Acad. of Arts and Sciences; mem. Nat. Acad. of Eng.; Public Welfare Medal, N.A.S.; Arthur M. Breche Medal, N.A.E. *Publications:* Introduction to Electromagnetic Fields and Waves (with Lorrain), Electromagnetism (with Lorrain). *Leisure interests:* hiking, mountain climbing, canoeing, photography, sailing. *Address:* 615 Clark Hall, Cornell University, Ithaca, NY 14853, U.S.A.

CORSTEN, Severin, DR.PHIL.; German librarian: b. 8 Dec. 1920, Heinsberg/Rheinland; s. of Leo and Gertrud (née Heusch) Corsten; m. Dr. Margret Loenartz 1952; one s. two d.; ed. Univ. of Bonn; Librarian, Library of Ministry of Foreign Affairs, Bonn 1954–63; Deputy Dir. Universitäts- und Stadtbibliothek, Cologne 1963–71, Dir. 1971–85; Hon. Prof. Univ. of Cologne 1975–; Kt. of the Papal Order of St. Gregory; Verdienstkreuz am Bande des Verdienstordens. *Publications:* Das Domanialgut im Amt Heinsberg 1953, Die Anfänge des Kölner Buchdrucks 1955, Das Heinsberger Land im frühen Mittelalter 1959, Die Bibliothek des Auswärtigen Amtes 1961, Die Kölnische Chronik von 1499 1982, Studien zum Kölner Frühdruck 1985, Der Buchdruck im. 15. Jahrhundert, (Vols. 1, 2) 1988–93, Untersuchungen zum Buch- und Bibliothekswesen 1988. (Ed.), Handbuch der historischen Buchbestände in Deutschland (Vols. 3, 4) 1992–93. *Leisure interest:* music. *Address:* Breslauer Strasse 14, D-53175 Bonn, Germany. *Telephone:* 0228-375320.

CORTAZZI, Sir (Henry Arthur) Hugh, G.C.M.G.; British diplomatist (retd.); b. 2 May 1924, Sedbergh, Yorks. (now Cumbria); s. of F. E. M. Cortazzi and M. Cortazzi; m. Elizabeth Esther Montagu 1956; one s. two d.; ed. Sedbergh School, Univ. of St. Andrews and Univ. of London; served R.A.F. 1943–48; joined Foreign Office 1949; Third Sec., Singapore 1950–51; Second Sec., Tokyo 1951–54; Foreign Office, London 1954–58; First Sec.,

Bonn 1958–60, Tokyo 1961–65 (Head of Chancery 1963); Foreign Office 1965–66; Counsellor (Commercial), Tokyo 1966–70; Royal Coll. of Defence Studies 1971; Minister (Commercial), Washington 1972–75; Deputy Under-Sec. of State FCO 1975–80; Amb. to Japan 1980–84 (retd.); apptd. Dir. Hill Samuel and Co. Ltd. (now Hill Samuel Bank Ltd.), Foreign and Colonial Pacific Investment Trust 1984–, G. T. Japan Investment Trust 1984–, Thornton Pacific Investment Trust S.A. 1986–; apptd. Adviser (with Lady Cortazzi) to Mitsukoshi Dept. Store, Tokyo, Japan 1984; Sr. Adviser NEC Corpn., Japan 1992–, Dai-Ichi Kangyo Bank, Japan 1992–, Bank of Kyoto 1992–, Wilde Sapte, solicitors 1992–; mem. Econ. and Social Research Council 1984–90; Grand Cordon, Order of the Sacred Treasure (Japan) 1995. *Publications:* trans. of Japanese short stories by Keita Genji 1972, A Diplomat's Wife in Japan: Sketches at the Turn of the Century (Ed.) 1982, Isles of Gold: Antique Maps of Japan 1983, Higashi No Shimaguni, Nishi No Shimaguni 1984, Dr. Willis in Japan (1862–1877) 1985, Mitford's Japan (Ed.) 1985, Zoku Higashi No Shimaguni, Nishi No Shimaguni (Ed.) 1987, Victorians in Japan: in and around the Treaty Ports 1987, Kipling's Japan (Ed.) 1988, The Japanese Achievement, A Short History of Japan and Japanese Culture 1990, Themes and Personalities 1991, Modern Japan: a concise survey 1993; ed.: A British Artist in Meiji Japan 1991, Building Japan 1968–1876 1991, co-ed. Britain and Japan 1859–1991 1991, Textbooks for Japanese students of English: Thoughts from a Sussex Garden 1985, Second Thoughts 1986, Japanese Encounter 1987, Caught In Time: Japan 1995. *Leisure interests:* the arts, especially literature and Japanese studies. *Address:* Ballsocks, Vines Cross, Heathfield, East Sussex, TN21 9ET, England (Home).

CORTES, Joaquín; Spanish dancer; b. 1970, Madrid; joined Spanish Nat. Ballet 1985, Prin. Dancer 1987–90; now appears in own shows, blending gypsy dancing, jazz blues and classical ballet; appeared in Pedro Almodóvar's film The Flower Of My Secret.

CORWIN, Norman; American writer-producer-director of radio, television, stage and cinema; b. 3 May 1910, Boston, Mass.; s. of Samuel H. Corwin and Rose Ober; m. Katherine Locke 1947; one s. one d.; Newspaperman 1929–38; writer, director, producer for Columbia Broadcasting System 1938–48; Chief, Special Projects, UN Radio 1949–53; mem. Faculty of Theatre Arts Univ. of Calif., L.A.; Regents Lecturer Univ. of Calif., Santa Barbara; Visiting Prof. School of Journalism, Univ. of Southern Calif. 1981–; writer in residence, Univ. of N. Carolina; Patten Memorial Lecturer, Indiana Univ. 1981; Co-Chair. Scholarship Cttee. of Acad. of Motion Picture Arts and Sciences; Chair. Documentary Awards Cttee. of Acad. of Motion Picture Arts and Sciences 1964–81; Distinguished Visiting Lecturer, San Diego State Univ. 1978; Chair. Writers Exec. Cttee. of Acad. of Motion Picture Arts and Sciences and mem. Bd. of Govs. 1979–88, Chair. Documentary Awards Comm. 1967–82, 1985–94, Sec. Acad. Foundation 1983–88; mem. Bd. of Dirs. Writers Guild of America, Selden Ring Journalism Award 1994–, Bette Davis Foundation 1997–; Trustee Filmex; writer, Dir. and host TV series, Norman Corwin Presents, Westinghouse Broadcasting Co.; radio series More by Corwin, Nat. Public Radio 1996–97; Sec. Acad. of Arts and Sciences Foundation 1983; First Vice-Pres. Acad. of Motion Picture Arts and Sciences 1988; Stasheff Lecturer, Univ. of Mich. 1984; papers acquired by Thousand Oaks Library Foundation 1993; subject of 90-minute TV documentary 1995; three hon. degrees; Peabody Medal, Edward Bok Medal, Award of American Acad. of Arts and Sciences 1942, American Newspaper Guide Page One Award 1944, 1945, Wendell Wilkie One-World Award 1946, PEN Award 1986, inducted Radio Hall of Fame 1993, Dupont Award, Columbia Univ. 1996, and other awards. *Publications:* They Fly through the Air 1939, Thirteen by Corwin 1942, More by Corwin 1944, On a Note of Triumph (both as a book and album of recordings) 1945, Untitled, and Other Dramas 1947, Dog in the Sky 1952, Overkill and Megalove 1962, Prayer for the 70's 1969, Holes in a Stained Glass Window 1978, Jerusalem Printout 1978, Greater than the Bomb 1981, A Date with Sandburg 1981, Trivializing America 1984, Network at Fifty 1984, CONartist 1993, Norman Corwin's Letters 1994, Years of the Electric Ear 1994; *Films:* The Blue Veil, The Grand Design, Lust for Life, The Story of Ruth, Yamashita, The Tiger of Malaya; *Cantatas:* The Golden Door, Yes Speak Out Yes (commissioned by UN 1968); *Stage plays:* The Rivalry, The World of Carl Sandburg, The Hyphen, Cervantes, Together Tonight 1975, The Strange Affliction 1995, Fifty Years After 14 August (on surrender of Japan) 1995. *Leisure interests:* mineralogy, music, painting, chess. *Address:* 1840 Fairburn Avenue, Los Angeles, CA 90025, U.S.A.

CORZINE, Jon Stevens, M.B.A.; American banker; b. 1 Jan. 1947, Taylorville, Ill.; s. of Roy Allen Corzine and Nancy June (née Hedrick) Corzine; m. Joanne Dougherty 1968; two s. one d.; ed. Univs. of Chicago and Illinois; bond officer Continental Ill. Nat. Bank 1970; Asst. Vice-Pres. BancOhio Corpn. 1974–75; joined Goldman, Sachs & Co. 1975, Vice-Pres. 1977, partner 1980–98, man. consultant 1985, Co-Head Fixed Income Div. 1988, Sr. Partner, Chair. Man. Cttee., C.E.O. 1994–98; mem. Bd. Dirs. NY Philharmonic 1996–, Public Securities Asscn. (Vice-Chair. 1985, Chair. 1986). *Address:* c/o Goldman, Sachs and Co., 85 Broad Street, New York, NY 10004, U.S.A.

COSBY, Bill, M.A., ED.D.; American actor; b. 12 July 1937, Philadelphia; s. of William Cosby and Anna Cosby; m. Camille Hanks 1964; five c. (one s. deceased); ed. Temple Univ. and Univ. of Mass.; served U.S.N.R. 1956–60; Pres. Rhythm and Blues Hall of Fame 1968–; TV appearances include: The Bill Cosby Show 1969, 1972–73, I Spy, The Cosby Show 1984–92, Cosby Mystery Series 1994–; recitals include: Revenge, To Russell, My Brother, With Whom I Slept, Top Secret, 200 M.P.H., Why Is There Air, Wonderfulness, It's True, It's True, Bill Cosby is a Very Funny Fellow: Right, I Started Out as a Child, 8:15, 12:15, Hungry, Reunion 1982, Bill Cosby . . . Himself 1983, Those of You With or Without Children, You'll Understand; numerous night club appearances; Exec. Producer A Different Kind of World (TV series) 1987–; recipient of four Emmy Awards and eight Grammy Awards. *Films include:* Hickey and Boggs 1972, Man and Boy 1972, Uptown Saturday Night 1974, Let's Do It Again 1975, Mother, Jugs and Speed 1976, Aesop's Fables, A Piece of Action 1977, California Suite 1978, Devil and Max Devlin 1979, Leonard: Part VI 1987, Ghost Dad 1990, The Meteor Man 1993, Jack 1996. *Publications:* The Wit and Wisdom of Fat Albert 1973, Bill Cosby's Personal Guide to Power Tennis, Fatherhood 1986, Time Flies 1988, Love and Marriage 1989, Childhood 1991. *Address:* c/o The Brokaw Co., 9255 Sunset Boulevard, Los Angeles, CA 90069, U.S.A.

COSGRAVE, Liam; Irish politician; b. 13 April 1920, Templeogue, Co. Dublin; s. of the late William T. Cosgrave (Pres. of the Exec. Council of the Irish Free State, 1922–32) and Louise Flanagan; m. Vera Osborne 1952; two s. one d.; ed. Christian Brothers' Schools, Dublin, St. Vincent's Coll., Castleknock, Co. Dublin and Kings Inns; called to the Bar 1943; Sr. Counsel 1958; served in Army, pvt.; T.D., Dublin Co. 1943–48, Dún Laoghaire and Rathdown 1948–81; Leader, Fine Gael Party 1965–77; Parl. Sec. to the Prime Minister and to Minister for Industry and Commerce 1948–51; Minister for External Affairs 1954–57; Prime Minister 1973–77; Minister for Defence 1976; Chair. and Leader of first Irish Del. to UN Gen. Ass. 1956; Hon. LL.D. (Duquesne Univ., St. John's Univ.) 1956, (De Paul Univ.) 1958, (Nat. Univ. of Ireland and Dublin Univ.) 1974; Kt. Grand Cross of Pius IX (Ordine Piaro). *Address:* Beechpark, Templeogue, Co. Dublin, Ireland.

ĆOSIĆ, Dobrica; Serbian politician and writer; b. 29 Dec. 1921, Velika Drenova; ed. Belgrade Univ., Higher Party School; war service 1941–45; worked as journalist, then as freelance writer; corresp. mem. Serbian Acad. of Arts and Sciences 1970, mem. 1976; expelled from League of Communists of Yugoslavia (LCY), prosecuted; resumed active political activity 1980s; initiator of Programme of Revival of Serbia by Serbian Acad. of Sciences; Pres. of Repub. of Yugoslavia 1992–93. *Publications:* The Sun is Far 1951, Roots 1954, Sections 1961, The Time of Death (Vols. 1–4) 1972–79, The Time of Evil: Sinner (Vols. 1-4) 1985, Apostate 1986, Believer 1990. *Address:* Serbian Academy of Sciences and Art, Knez Mikailova str. 35, Belgrade, Yugoslavia.

COSMOS, Jean; French playwright; b. Jean Louis Gaudrat, 14 June 1923, Paris; s. of Albert Gaudrat and Maria Maillebuau; m. Alice Jarrousse 1948; one s. two d.; ed. Inst. St. Nicholas, Igny, Coll. Jean-Baptiste Say, Paris; songwriter 1945–50, writer for radio 1952–60, for TV 1964–; mem. Comm. Soc. des auteurs dramatiques 1971–. *Plays:* author or adapter of numerous plays for the theatre including la Fille du roi 1952, Au jour le jour 1952, les Grenadiers de la reine 1957, Macbeth 1959, 1965, le Manteau 1963, la Vie et la Mort du roi Jean 1964, Arden de Faversham 1964, Monsieur Alexandre 1965, la Bataille de Lobositz 1969, Major Barbara 1970, le Marchand de Venise 1971, Sainte Jeanne des Abattoirs 1972, Ce sacré Bonheur 1987; author of numerous TV plays including les Oranges (Albert Ollivier prize) 1964, le Pacte 1966, Un homme, un cheval 1968, la Pomme oubliée (after Jean Anglade), l'Ingénu (after Voltaire), Bonsoir Léon, la Tête à l'envers, le Trêve, le Coup Monté, Aide-toi, Julien Fontanes, magistrat (TV Series 1980–89); with Jean Chatenêt: 16 à Kerbriant, Ardéchois coeur fidèle (Critics' choice) 1975, Les Yeux Bleus, la Lumière des Justes (after Henri Troyat); with Gilles Perrault: le Secret des dieux, la Filière, Fabien de la Drôme, seven-part serial of Julien Fontanes, Magistrat, regular contrib. to les Cinq dernières minutes; *films:* La dictée 1984, La vie et rien d'autre 1989, Le Colonel Chabert 1994, La Fille de d'Artagnan 1994, Capitaine Conan 1996, Le Bossu 1997; co-librettist Goya 1996 (opera); TV, Soc. des auteurs et compositeurs prizes 1970. *Address:* Artmédia, 10 avenue George V, 75008 Paris (Office); 57 rue de Versailles, 92410 Ville d'Avray, France (Home).

COSSIGA, Francesco, LL.D.; Italian politician; b. 26 July 1928, Sassari; m. Giuseppa Sigurani 1960; two s.; joined Democrazia Cristiana (DC) 1945, Provincial Sec. 1956–58, mem. Nat. Council 1956–85; M.P. for Sassari 1958–85; Under-Sec. of State for Defence 1966–70; Minister for Public Admin. 1974–76, of the Interior 1976–78; Prime Minister 1979–80; Pres. of Senate 1983–85; Pres. of Italy 1985–92; Life-term Senator (Ind. Group) 1992–; Dr. h.c. (Oxford) 1987. *Address:* c/o Palazzo Giustiniani, Via della Dogana Vecchia 29, 00186 Rome, Italy. *Telephone:* (39-6) 6706-2012. *Fax:* (39-6) 6706-3658.

COSSINS, Edwin Albert, PH.D., D.SC., F.R.S.C.; Canadian professor of botany; b. 28 Feb. 1937, Havering, U.K.; s. of A.J. Cossins; m. Lucille J. Salt 1962; two d.; ed. Clark's Coll. Romford, S.E. Essex Tech. Coll., Chelsea Coll., Univ. of London and Purdue Univ.; Research Assoc. Purdue Univ. 1961–62; Asst. Prof. Univ. of Alberta 1962–65, Assoc. Prof. 1965–69, Prof. of Botany (Plant Biochemistry) 1969–94, of Biological Sciences 1994–96, Assoc. Dean of Science 1983–88, Prof. Emer. 1996–; Visiting Prof. Univ. of Geneva 1972–73, Univ. of Calif., Berkeley 1989; Pres. Canadian Soc. of Plant Physiologists 1976–77; other professional appts.; Centennial Medal, Govt. of Canada 1967, Gold Medal, Canadian Soc. of Plant Physiologists 1998. *Publications:* co-author of three books and author of over 100 publs. in scientific journals. *Leisure interests:* golf, gardening, cross-country skiing. *Address:* Department of Biological Sciences, University of Alberta, Edmonton, Alta., T6G 2E9 (Office); 99 Fairway Drive, Edmonton, Alta., T6J 2C2, Canada (Home). *Telephone:* (403) 492-3991 (Office); (403) 434-7613 (Home). *Fax:* (403) 492-9234.

COSSONS, Sir Neil, Kt., O.B.E., M.A., F.S.A.; British museum director; b. 15 Jan. 1939, Nottingham; s. of Arthur Cossons and Evelyn Cossons (née Bettle); m. Veronica Edwards 1965; two s. one d.; ed. Univ. of Liverpool; Curator of Tech., Bristol City Museum 1964; Deputy Dir., City of Liverpool Museums 1969; Dir. Ironbridge Gorge Museum 1971; Dir. Nat. Maritime Museum, Greenwich 1983; Dir. Science Museum, London 1986–; Commr. Historic Buildings and Monuments Comm. for England (English Heritage) 1989–95; mem. Royal Coll. of Art Council 1989–, Design Council 1990–94, British Waterways Bd. 1995–; mem. Council Foundation for Mfg. and Industry 1993–98; Fellow and Past Pres. of the Museums Asscn.; Comité scientifique, Conservatoire National des Arts et Métiers 1991–; Hon. Fellow R.C.A.; Hon. D.Soc.Sc. (Birmingham) 1979; Hon. D.Univ. (Open Univ.) 1984, (Sheffield Hallam) 1995, (York) 1998; Hon. D.Litt. (Liverpool) 1989, (Bradford) 1991, (Nottingham Trent) 1994, (Univ. of West of England) 1995, (Bath) 1997; Hon. D.Sc. (Leicester) 1995; Hon. D.Arts (De Montfort) 1997; Companion, Inst. of Man. 1996; Norton Medlicott Medal (Historical Asscn.) 1991, President's Medal (Royal Acad. of Eng.) 1993. *Publications:* Industrial Archaeology of the Bristol Region (with R.A. Buchanan) 1968, Industrial Archaeology 1975, Transactions of the First International Congress on the Conservation of Industrial Monuments (Ed.) 1975, Rees's Manufacturing Industry (Ed.) 1975, Ironbridge—Landscape of Industry (with H. Sowden) 1977, The Iron Bridge—Symbol of the Industrial Revolution (with B.S. Trinder) 1979, The Management of Change in Museums (Ed.) 1985, Making of the Modern World (Ed.) 1992. *Leisure interests:* travel, industrial archaeology. *Address:* The Science Museum, London, SW7 2DD (Office); The Old Rectory, Rushbury, Shropshire, SY6 7EB, England (Home). *Telephone:* 0171-938 8003 (Office); (01694) 771603 (Home).

COSSUTTA, Carlo; Italian opera singer; b. 8 May 1932, Trieste; ed. in Argentina; tenor range; began career at the Teatro Colon, Buenos Aires; début in Europe at Teatro San Carlo, Lisbon in Simon Boccanegra 1962; Royal Opera House, Covent Garden in Rigoletto 1964; Metropolitan Opera, New York in Norma 1973; Trovatore at Paris Opera 1973; Fanciulla del West and I Pagliacci at Lyric Opera of Chicago 1978; has recorded La Vida Breve, Verdi Requiem and Otello.

COSTA, Antonio Maria, PH.D.; Italian economist; b. 16 June 1941, Mondovi; s. of Francesco Costa and Maria Costa; m. Patricia Agnes Wallace 1971; two s. one d.; ed. Univ. of California, Berkeley, Acad. of Sciences of the U.S.S.R. and Univ. of Turin; Visiting Prof. of Econs., Moscow Univ. and Acad. of Sciences of the U.S.S.R. 1965–67; Instructor of Econs., Univ. of Calif., Berkeley 1968–70; Prof. of Econs., New York Univ., 1976–83; Sr. Econ. Adviser to the UN 1970–83; Special Counsellor in Econs. to the Sec.-Gen. of OECD 1983–87; Dir. Gen. Econ. and Financial Affairs, EC 1987–90. *Publications:* articles on econs. and politics. *Leisure interest:* work. *Address:* c/o Ministry of Finance, Viale Americane, EUR, 00144 Rome, Italy.

COSTA, Manuel Pinto da; São Tomé e Príncipe politician; b. 5 Aug. 1937, Água Grande; Founded Movement for the Liberation of São Tomé and Príncipe (MLSTP) 1972; Sec.-Gen., MLSTP, based in Gabon 1972–75, Pres. 1978; Pres. of São Tomé and Príncipe 1975–91; Minister of Agric., Land Reform and Defence 1975–78, of Labour and Social Security 1977–78, of Territorial Admin. 1978–82, of Defence and Nat. Security 1982–86, fmr. Minister of Planning and Econs.; Prime Minister 1978–88; visited China and N. Korea Dec. 1975; Dr. h.c. (Berlin); José Marti Medal, Cuba. *Address:* c/o Office of the President, C.P. 38, São Tomé, São Tomé e Príncipe.

COSTA-GAVRAS, Kostantinos; French (Greek-born) film director; b. 13 Feb. 1933, Arcadia; s. of Panayotis and Panayota Gavras; m. Michele Ray 1968; three c.; ed. Sorbonne, Inst. d'Etudes Cinématiques, Paris; worked as Asst. to film Dirs. Yves Allegret, Jacques Demy, René Clair, René Clément; Pres. Cinémathèque Française 1982–87. *Films directed include:* The Sleeping Car Murder (also writer) 1965 (MWA Award), Un Homme de Trop 1966 (Moscow Film Festival Prize), Z (co-writer) 1969 (Jury Award, Cannes, Award for Best Foreign-Language Film), L'Aveu (co-writer) 1970, State of Siege (co-writer) 1973 (Louis Delluc Prize), Section Spéciale (co-writer) 1975 (Best Dir., Cannes), Clair de Femme (writer) 1979, Missing (co-writer) 1982 (Gold Palm, Cannes, Academy Award, best screenplay, British Acad. best screenplay), Hanna K (co-writer) 1983, Family Business (writer) 1985, Betrayed 1988 (ACLUF Award), Music Box 1989 (Golden Bear, Berlin), The Little Apocalypse (dir. and co-writer) 1993, Mad City 1996; directed opera Il Mondo della Luna (Joseph Haydn), Teatro San Carlo, Naples 1994; Prix Académie Française for Life Achievement 1998; Chevalier Légion d'honneur; Commdr. Arts et Lettres. *Address:* c/o Artmédia, 10 avenue George V, 75008 Paris, France.

COSTEDOAT, Maj.-Gen. Pierre-Jacques; French army officer; b. 27 Jan. 1942, Casablanca, Morocco; s. of René Costedoat and Marguerite Bosc; m. Anne-Marie Delamare 1965; four d.; ed. Saint-Cyr-Coëtquidan mil. acad.; Second Lieut., 74th Artillery Regt. 1964, Lieut. 1966; Capt., 1st Artillery Regt. 1972, then Battery C.O.; Maj., 11th Artillery Regt. 1977, Lieut.-Col. 1981, Col. 1984; attended as auditeur Centre des hautes études militaires and Institut des hautes études de défense nationale 1987–88; C.O. 93rd Mountain Artillery Regt., then Staff 1988–89, at Direction Générale de la Sécurité extérieure (DGSE) 1989–95; Brig. 1992; C.O. Saint-Cyr Coëtquidan Mil. Acad. 1995–; rank of Maj.-Gen. 1995; Officier Légion d'honneur, Officier Ordre nat. du Mérite. *Leisure interests:* skiing, tennis, golf. *Address:* La Résidence, Ecoles de Coëtquidan, 56381 Guer, France.

COSTELLO, Elvis (Declan Patrick McManus); British singer and songwriter; b. 25 Aug. 1954, London; s. of Ross McManus; m. Cait O'Riordan 1986; one c. by previous m.; concert appearances, U.K. and U.S.A. 1978–; albums include: My Aim is True 1977, This Year's Model 1978, Armed Forces 1979, Get Happy 1980, Trust 1980, Almost Blue 1981, Taking Liberties, Imperial Bedroom 1982, Goodbye Cruel World 1984, Punch the Clock 1984, The Best Of 1985, Blood and Chocolate 1986, King of America 1986, Spike 1989, Mighty Like a Rose 1991, The Juliet Letters (with the Brodsky Quartet) 1993, Brutal Youth (with Steve Nieve, Pete Thomas, Bruce Thomas and Nick Lowe) 1994; songs composed include: Alison 1977, Watching the Detectives 1977, Crawling to the U.S.A. 1978, Radio, Radio 1978, Stranger in the House 1978, Girls Talk 1979, Oliver's Army 1979, (I Don't Want To Go To) Chelsea 1979, Boy With a Problem 1982, Every Day I Write the Book 1983. *Film:* Americathon 1979. *Address:* c/o Warner Bros. Records, 3300 Warner Boulevard, Burbank, CA 91510, U.S.A.

COSTELLO, Peter Howard, B.A., LL.B.; Australian politician; b. 14 Aug. 1957; s. of R. J. Costello and M. A. Costello; m. Tanya Costello 1982; one s. two d.; ed. Carey Grammar School, Monash Univ.; solicitor, Mallesons, Melbourne 1981–84; tutor (part-time) Monash Univ. 1984–86; mem. Victorian Bar 1984–90; M.P. for Higgins, Vic., 1990–; Shadow Minister for Corp. Law Reform and Consumer Affairs 1990–92; Shadow Attorney-Gen. and Shadow Minister for Justice 1992–93, for Finance 1993–94; Deputy Leader of the Opposition and Shadow Treas. 1994–96; Deputy Leader Liberal Party 1996–, Commonwealth of Australia Treas. March 1996–; Liberal Party. *Publication:* Arbitration in Contempt (jtly.) 1986. *Leisure interests:* swimming, football, reading. *Address:* Parliament House, Canberra, A.C.T. 2600, Australia.

COSTELLOE, Paul; Irish fashion designer and artist; b. 23 June 1945, Dublin; m. 1982; six s. one d.; ed. Blackrock Coll. Dublin, design coll. in Dublin and Chambre Syndical Paris; design asst. Jacques Esterel, Paris 1969–71; designer, Marks & Spencer 1972; chief house designer, A. Rinascente, Milan 1972–74; designer, Anne Fogerty, New York, Pennaco, New York and Trimfit, Philadelphia 1974–79; established own design house, Paul Costelloe Int. Ltd., in conjunction with business partner Robert Eitel 1979–; merchandise sold in U.K., Ireland, Europe, Scandinavia and N. America under Paul Costelloe Collection and Dressage labels; opened flagship store, Knightsbridge 1994; designer of new British Airways uniform 1994; Fil d'Or award, Int. Linen Council, 1987, 1988, 1989; British Designer of the Year 1989 and other awards; Hon.D.Litt. (Ulster) 1996. *Leisure interests:* rugby, tennis, golf. *Address:* Moygashel Mills, Dungannon, BT71 7PB, Northern Ireland; 27 Cheval Place, London, SW7 1EW, England. *Telephone:* (018687) 22291 (N.I.); 0171-589 9484 (London). *Fax:* (01868) 726433 (N.I.); 0171-589 9481 (London).

COSTNER, Kevin; American actor; b. 1955; m. Cindy Silva (divorced); one s. two d.; one s. by Bridget Rooney; ed. California State Univ. Fullerton; directing début in Dances with Wolves 1990 (Acad. Award for Best Picture 1991). *Film appearances include:* Frances 1982, The Big Chill 1983, Testament 1983, Silverado 1985, The Untouchables 1987, No Way Out 1987, Bull Durham 1988, Field of Dreams 1989, Revenge 1989, Robin Hood: Prince of Thieves 1990, JFK 1991, The Bodyguard 1992, A Perfect World 1993, Wyatt Earp 1994, Waterworld 1995, Tin Cup 1996, Message in a Bottle 1998; co-producer Rapa Nui; co-producer China Moon. *Leisure interest:* golf. *Address:* TIG Productions, Producers' Building 5, 4000 Warner Boulevard, Burbank, CA 91523; c/o William Morris Agency, 151 El Camino Drive, Beverly Hills, CA 90212, U.S.A.

COT, Jean-Pierre; French politician and academic; b. 23 Oct. 1937, Geneva, Switzerland; s. of Pierre Cot and Luisa Phelps; m.; three c.; Prof., then Dean, Faculty of Law, Amiens 1968; Prof. of Int. Law and Political Sociology, Univ. of Paris I (Panthéon-Sorbonne) 1969, Dir. Disarmament Research and Study Centre (CEREDE); mem. Steering Cttee., Parti Socialiste (PS) 1970, 1973, mem. Exec. Bureau 1976; Mayor of Coise-Saint-Jean-Pied-Gauthier 1971–; Deputy (Savoie) to Nat. Ass. 1973–81; Gen. Councillor, Savoie 1973–81; PS Nat. Del. for matters relating to the European Communities 1976–79; mem. European Parl. 1978–79, 1984–, Pres. Budget Cttee. 1984–87, Chair. Socialist Group 1989–94, Vice-Pres. 1997–; Minister-Del. for Co-operation, attached to Minister for External Relations 1981–82; mem. Exec. Council UNESCO 1983–84. *Publication:* A l'épreuve du pouvoir: le tiers-mondisme, pour quoi faire? 1984, and numerous works on int. law and political science. *Address:* European Parliament, rue Wiertz, 1047 Brussels, Belgium; Coise-Saint-Jean-Pied-Gauthier, 73800 Montmélian, France (Home).

COTRUBAŞ, Ileana; Romanian opera and concert singer (retd.); b. 1939, Galaţi; d. of Maria and Vasile Cotrubaş; m. Manfred Ramin 1972; ed. Conservatorul Ciprian Porumbescu, Bucharest; Lyric soprano range; début as Yniold in Pelléas et Mélisande at Bucharest Opera 1964; Frankfurt Opera 1968–70; Glyndebourne Festival 1968; Salzburg Festival 1969; Staatsoper Vienna 1969; Royal Opera House, Covent Garden 1971; Lyric Opera of Chicago 1973; Paris Opera 1974; La Scala, Milan 1975; Metropolitan Opera, New York 1977; operatic roles include Susanna, Pamina, Norina, Gilda,

Traviata, Manon, Antonia, Tatyana, Mimi, Mélisande; concerts with all major European orchestras; Lieder recitals at Musikverein Vienna, Royal Opera House, Covent Garden, Carnegie Hall, New York, La Scala; First Prize, Int. Singing Competition, Hertogenbosch, Netherlands 1965, First Prize, Munich Radio Competition 1966; Austrian Kammersängerin 1981; Grand Officer, Order of Sant' Iago da Espada (Portugal) 1990; Hon. Citizen of Bucharest 1995. *Recordings:* Bach Cantatas, Mozart Masses, Brahms Requiem, Mahler Symphonies 2, 8; complete operas including Le Nozze di Figaro, Die Zauberflöte, Hänsel und Gretel, Calisto, Louise, L'Elisir d'amore, Les Pêcheurs de perles, La Traviata, Rigoletto, Alzira, Manon. *Publication:* Opernwahrheiten 1998.

COTTA, Michèle; L. ÈS L., DR. ÈS SC.POL.; French journalist; b. 15 June 1937, Nice; d. of Jacques Cotta and Helène Scoffier; m. 1st Claude Tchou (divorced); one s. (deceased) one d.; m. 2nd Phillipe Barret 1992; ed. Lycée de Nice, Faculté de Lettres de Nice and Inst. d'études politiques de Paris; Journalist with L'Express 1963–69, 1971–76; Europ I 1970–71, 1986; political diarist, France-Inter 1976–80; Head of political service, Le Point 1977–80, Reporter 1986; Chief Political Ed. R.T.L. 1980–81; Pres. Dir.-Gen. Radio France 1981–82; Pres. Haute Autorité de la Communication Audiovisuelle 1982–86; Producer Faits de Société on TF 1 1987, Dir. of Information 1987–92, Pres. Sofica Images Investissements 1987; producer and presenter La Revue de presse, France 2 1993–95; political ed. Nouvel Economiste 1993–96; producer and presenter Polémiques, France 2 1995–; editorial writer R.T.L. 1996–; mem. Coll. de la prévention des risques technologiques 1989–; Chevalier, Légion d'honneur. *Publications:* La collaboration 1940–1944, 1964, Les elections présidentielles 1966, Prague, l'été des Tanks 1968, Le VIème République 1974, Les miroirs de Jupiter 1986, Les Secrets d'une Victoire 1995. *Address:* R.T.L., 22 rue Bayard, 75008 Paris; France 2, 22 avenue Montaigne, 75387 Paris Cedex 08, France.

COTTERILL, Rodney Michael John, PH.D., D.SC.; British/Danish biophysicist; b. 27 Sept. 1933, Bodmin, U.K.; s. of Herbert Cotterill and Aline Le Cerf; m. Vibeke Nielsen 1959; two d.; ed. Cowes and Newport High Schools, Isle of Wight, Univ. Coll. London, Yale Univ. and Emmanuel Coll. Cambridge; R.A.F. 1952–54; Assoc. Scientist, Argonne Nat. Lab. 1962–67; Prof. Tech. Univ. of Denmark (now Danish Tech. Univ.) 1967–; Visiting Prof. Tokyo Univ. 1978, 1985; Fellow, Royal Danish Acad. of Sciences and Letters, Danish Acad. of Tech. Sciences, Inst. of Physics (U.K.); Kt., Order of the Dannebrog (First Class) 1994; Ellen and Hans Hermer Memorial Prize 1978. *Publications:* The Cambridge Guide to the Material World 1985, Computer Simulation in Brain Science (ed.) 1988, No Ghost in the Machine 1989, Models of Brain Function (ed.) 1989, Neural Network Dynamics (co-ed.) 1992, Brain and Mind (ed.) 1994, Autism, Intelligence and Consciousness 1994,Enchanted Looms 1998; articles on topics in physics, biology and medicine. *Leisure interests:* sailing, choral singing, writing. *Address:* Danish Technical University, Building 307, 2800 Lyngby, Denmark. *Telephone:* 45-25-32-03. *Fax:* 45-93-23-99.

COTTI, Flavio; Swiss politician; b. 18 Oct. 1939, Muralto; m. Renata Naretto; one d.; ed. Univ. of Freiburg; barrister and public notary in Locarno 1965–75; mem. Locarno Communal Council 1964–75; mem. of cantonal Parl. of Ticino 1967–75; mem. of govt., canton of Ticino, Head Dept. of Home Affairs, Econ. Affairs, Justice and Mil. Matters 1975–83; mem. Nat. Council 1983–; mem. Fed. Council Dec. 1986–; Head Fed. Dept. of Home Affairs 1987–91; Pres. of Switzerland and Pres. Fed. Dept. of Home Affairs 1991–92, 1998–, of Foreign Affairs 1992–98; Pres. Bd. of Dirs., Ticino Cantonal Tourist Office 1976–84; Pres. Christian Democratic People's Party (CDPP) of Ticino 1981, CDPP 1984; Chair. Org. for Security and Co-operation in Europe (OSCE) 1996. *Address:* c/o Christian Democratic People's Party, Klaraweg 6, Postfach 5835, 3001 Bern, Switzerland.

COTTINGHAM, Robert; American artist; b. 26 Sept. 1935, Brooklyn, New York; s. of James and Aurelia Cottingham; m. Jane Weismann 1967; three d.; ed. Brooklyn Tech. High School, Pratt Inst.; army service 1955–58; Art Dir. with Young and Rubicam Advertising Inc., New York 1959–64, Los Angeles 1964–68; left advertising to paint 1968–; taught at Art Centre Coll. of Design, Los Angeles 1969–70; moved to London 1972–76; returned to U.S.A. 1976–; Nat. Endowment for the Arts 1974–75; numerous one-man exhbns. 1968–; works in many public galleries in U.S.A. and also in Hamburg Museum, Tate Gallery, London and Utrecht Museum; MacDowell Colony Residency 1993, 1994; Walter Gropius Fellowship, Huntington Museum of Art 1992; mem. Nat. Acad. of Design. *Publications:* numerous print publs. (lithographs, etchings). *Leisure interests:* travel, music, history. *Address:* P.O. Box 604, Blackman Road, Newtown, CT 06470, U.S.A. *Telephone:* (203) 426-4072.

COTTON, Frank Albert, PH.D.; American chemist; b. 9 April 1930, Philadelphia, Pa.; s. of Albert Cotton and Helen M. Taylor; m. Diane Dornacher 1959; two d.; ed. Drexel Inst. of Tech., Temple and Harvard Univs.; Asst. Prof. Mass. Inst. of Tech. (M.I.T.) 1955–60, Assoc. Prof. 1960–61, Prof. 1961–71; Robert A. Welch Distinguished Prof., Texas A & M Univ. 1971–; Dir. Lab. for Molecular Structure and Bonding 1983–; Consultant Union Carbide, New York 1964–; mem. Nat. Science Bd. 1986–92; mem. N.A.S. (Chair. Physical Sciences 1985–88), American Acad. of Arts and Sciences, Göttingen Acad. of Sciences, Royal Danish Acad. of Sciences and Letters, Indian Acad. of Sciences, Indian Nat. Science Acad., Royal Soc. of Edin.; American Chem. Soc. Awards in Inorganic Chem. 1962, 1974, Baekeland Award (N.J. section) 1963, Dwyer Medal (Univ. of N.S.W.) 1966, Centenary Medal (Chemical Soc. London) 1974, Nichols Medal (New York section) 1975, Harrison Howe Award (Rochester section) 1975, Edgar Fahs Smith Award (Philadelphia section) 1976, Pauling Medal (Oregon and Puget Sound Sections) 1976, Kirkwood Medal (Yale Univ.) 1978, Willard Gibbs Medal (Chicago Section, ACS) 1980, Nyholm Medal (Royal Soc. Chem.) 1982, Nat. Medal of Science 1982, Award in Physical and Mathematical Sciences (New York, Acad. Sciences), T. W. Richards Medal (New England Section, American Chem. Soc.), King Feisal Int. Prize in Science 1990, Chemical Sciences Award, N.A.S.; numerous hon. degrees. *Publications:* Advanced Inorganic Chemistry (with G. Wilkinson, F.R.S.) 5th edn. 1988, Chemical Applications of Group Theory 3rd edn. 1990, Chemistry, An Investigative Approach 2nd edn. 1973, Basic Inorganic Chemistry (with G. Wilkinson) 2nd edn. 1987, Multiple Bonds between Metal Atoms (with R. A. Walton) 1982, approx. 1120 research papers. *Leisure interests:* equitation, conservation. *Address:* Department of Chemistry, Tex. A & M University, College Station, TX 77843 (Office); 4101 Sand Creek Road, Bryan, TX 77803; Twaycliffe Ranch, Route 2, Box 285, Bryan, TX 77803, U.S.A. (Homes). *Telephone:* (409) 845-4432 (Office); (409) 589-2501 (Home).

COTTON, Hon. Sir Robert Carrington, K.C.M.G., A.O., F.C.P.A.; Australian politician; b. 29 Nov. 1915, Broken Hill, N.S.W.; s. of H. L. Carrington and Muriel Cotton; m. Eve MacDougall 1937; one s. two d.; ed. St. Peter's Coll., Adelaide; fmr. Federal Vice-Pres. Liberal Party of Australia; State Pres. N.S.W. 1957–60, Acting Pres. 1965; Senator for N.S.W. 1965–78; leader Del. of Fed. Parl. to meetings of IPU in Majorca and Geneva 1967; Minister of State for Civil Aviation 1969–72, Minister of Mfg. Industry, Science and Consumer Affairs Nov.-Dec. 1975, of Industry and Commerce 1975–77; Consul-Gen., New York 1978–81; Amb. to U.S.A. 1982–85; Chair. Kleinwort Benson Australian Income Fund (New York) 1986–; Deputy Chair. Allders Int. Pty. Ltd.; Dir. Reserve Bank of Australia 1981–82, Hill and Knowlton Inc. 1986–91, Capital Television Holdings Ltd., Thomson—CSF Pacific Holdings Pty. Ltd. 1996–; Chair. Australian Taiwan Business Council 1987–89, Australian Photonics Cooperative Research Centre, Nat. Gallery of Australia Foundation 1991–94, Australian Medical Asscn. Enquiry 1986–87. *Leisure interests:* photography, writing. *Address:* Apartment 47, Southern Cross Gardens, 2 Spruson Street, Neutral Bay, N.S.W. 2089, Australia.

COTTON, William (Bill) Frederick, C.B.E.; British television administrator; b. 23 April 1928; s. of William (Billy) Edward Cotton and Mabel Hope; m. 1st Bernadine Maud Sinclair 1950 (died 1964); three d.; m. 2nd Ann Bucknall 1965 (divorced 1989); one step-d.; m. 3rd Kathryn Mary Burgess 1990; ed. Ardingly Coll.; Jt. Man. Dir. Michael Reine Music Co. 1952–56; BBC-TV producer, Light Entertainment Dept. 1956–62, Asst. Head of Light Entertainment 1962–67, Head of Variety 1967–70, Head of Light Entertainment Group 1970–77; Controller BBC 1 1977–81; Deputy Man. Dir. TV, BBC 1981–82, Dir. of Programmes, TV and Dir. of Devt., BBC 1982; Man. Dir., TV, BBC 1984–87; Chair. BBC Enterprises 1982–87; Dir. Noel Gay Org. 1988–97, Chair. Noel Gay TV 1988–97; Non-exec. Dir. Alba PLC 1988–; Deputy Chair. Meridian Broadcasting 1991– (Chair. 1996–); Dir. Billy Marsh Assocs. 1998–. *Leisure interest:* golf. *Address:* 52 Warwick Square, London, SW1V 2AJ, England.

COTTRELL, Sir Alan (Howard), Kt., PH.D., SC.D., F.ENG., F.R.S.; British scientist and professor of physical metallurgy; b. 17 July 1919, Birmingham; s. of Albert and Elizabeth Cottrell; m. Jean Elizabeth Harber 1944; one s.; ed. Moseley Grammar School, Univ. of Birmingham, Univ. of Cambridge; lecturer in Metallurgy, Univ. of Birmingham 1943–49, Prof. of Physical Metallurgy 1949–55; Deputy Head, Metallurgy Div., A.E.R.E., Harwell, Berks. 1955–58; Goldsmiths' Prof. of Metallurgy, Cambridge Univ. 1958–65; Deputy Chief Scientific Adviser (Studies), Ministry of Defence 1965–67, Chief Adviser 1967; Deputy Chief Scientific Adviser to H.M. Govt. 1968–71, Chief Scientific Adviser 1971–74; Master, Jesus Coll., Cambridge 1974–86, Vice-Chancellor, Cambridge Univ. 1977–79; Part-time mem. UKAEA 1962–65, 1983–87; Dir. Fisons PLC 1979–90; mem. Advisory Council on Scientific Policy 1963–64, Cen. Advisory Council for Science and Technology 1967–, Exec. Cttee. British Council 1974–87, Advisory Council, Science Policy Foundation 1976–, U.K. Perm. Security Comm. 1981–92; Hon. mem. American Soc. for Metals 1972, Fellow 1974; Hon. mem. The Metals Soc. 1977, Japan Inst. of Metals 1981; Foreign Assoc. N.A.S., U.S.A. 1972, Nat. Acad. of Eng., U.S.A. 1976; Foreign Hon. mem. American Acad. of Arts and Sciences 1960; Fellow Royal Soc., (Vice-Pres. 1964, 1976, 1977), Royal Swedish Acad. of Sciences 1970; mem. Academia Europaea 1991; Hon. Fellow Christ's Coll., Cambridge 1970 (Fellow 1958–70), Jesus Coll., Cambridge 1986, Imperial Coll., London 1991, Inst. of Metals 1989; Hon. D.Sc. (Columbia) 1965, (Newcastle) 1967, (Liverpool) 1969, (Manchester) 1970, (Warwick) 1971, (Sussex) 1972, (Bath) 1973, (Strathclyde and Aston in Birmingham) 1975, (Cranfield Inst. of Tech.) 1975, (Oxford) 1979, (Essex) 1982, (Birmingham) 1983; Hon. D.Eng. (Tech. Univ. of Nova Scotia) 1984; Sc.D. (Cambridge) 1976; LL.D. (Cambridge) 1996; Rosenhain Medal, Inst. of Metals, Hughes Medal, Royal Soc. 1961, Réaumur Medal, Soc. Française de Métallurgie 1964; Inst. of Metals (Platinum) Medal 1965, James Alfred Ewing Medal, ICE 1967, Holweck Medal, Soc. Française de Physique 1969, Albert Sauveur Achievement Award, American Soc. for Metals 1969, James Douglas Gold Medal, American Inst. of Mining, Metallurgy and Petroleum Engineers 1974, Rumford Medal, Royal Soc. 1974, Harvey Prize (Technion, Israel) 1974, Acta Metallurgica Gold Medal 1976, Guthrie Medal and Prize,

Inst. of Physics 1977, Gold Medal, American Soc. for Metals 1980, Brinell Medal, Royal Swedish Acad. of Eng. Sciences 1980, Kelvin Medal, ICE 1986, Holloman Award, Acta Metallurgica 1990, Copley Medal, Royal Soc. 1996, Von Hippel Award, Materials Res. Soc. 1996. *Publications:* Theoretical Structural Metallurgy 1948, Dislocations and Plastic Flow in Crystals 1953, The Mechanical Properties of Matter 1964, Theory of Crystal Dislocations 1964, An Introduction to Metallurgy 1967, Portrait of Nature 1975, Environmental Economics 1978, How Safe is Nuclear Energy? 1981, Introduction to the Modern Theory of Metals 1988, Chemical Bonding in Transition Metal Carbides 1995, Concepts in the Electron Theory of Alloys 1998 and scientific papers in various learned journals. *Leisure interest:* music. *Address:* 40 Maids Causeway, Cambridge, CB5 8DD, England. *Telephone:* (01223) 63806.

COUCHEPIN, François; Swiss lawyer; b. 19 Jan. 1935, Martigny; s. of Louis Couchepin and Andrée Couchepin; m. Anne Marie Cottier 1957; six c.; ed. Univ. of Lausanne; legal practitioner at law firm of Rodolphe Tissières 1959–64; own legal practice in Martigny 1964–; elected to Cantonal Council of Canton Valais 1965, re-elected 1969, 1973, 1977; Sec. Radical Group 1965–77, Pres. 1977–79; Head, French Section, Cen. Language Service, Fed. Chancellery 1980; Vice-Chancellor responsible for gen. admin. of Fed. Chancellery 1981; Chancellor of the Swiss Fed. 1991–; mem. Defence Staff; mem. numerous comms. etc. *Address:* c/o Federal Chancellery, Bundeshaus-West, 3003 Berne, Switzerland. *Telephone:* (31) 3222111. *Fax:* (31) 3223706.

COULOMB, Jean; French physicist; b. 7 Nov. 1904, Blida, Algeria; s. of Charles Coulomb and Blanche d'Izalguier; m. Alice Gaydier 1928 (died 1994); two s. two d.; ed. Ecole Normale Supérieure; Dir. Institut de Physique du Globe Algiers 1937–41; Dir. Institut de Physique du Globe Paris 1941–56; Prof. at the Sorbonne 1941–72; Visiting Prof. Istanbul Univ. 1954–55; Pres. Int. Assen. of Terrestrial Magnetism and Electricity 1951–54; Dir.-Gen. Centre Nat. de la Recherche Scientifique 1956–62; mem. of Cttee. for Int. Geophysical Year 1957–59; Pres. of Centre Nat. d'Etudes Spatiales 1962–67; Pres. Int. Union of Geodesy and Geophysics 1967–71; Pres. Bureau des Longitudes 1966–69; Vice-Pres. Int. Council of Scientific Unions 1968–72, Pres. 1972–74; mem. French Acad. of Sciences 1960– (Pres. 1977–78), Royal Danish Acad. 1969, Acad. Royale de Belgique 1971, Romanian Acad. 1991; Grand Croix, Légion d'honneur, Grand Croix de l'ordre nat. du Mérite, Officier du Mérite Saharien. *Publications:* La physique des nuages (in collaboration) 1940, La constitution physique de la terre 1952, Physical Constitution of the Earth (in collaboration) 1963, Expansion des fonds océaniques 1969, Sea Floor Spreading and Continental Drift 1972, Traité de géophysique interne, Vol. I 1973, Vol. II 1975 (in collaboration). *Address:* 4–6 rue Emile Dubois, 75014 Paris, France. *Telephone:* (1) 45.88.43.01.

COUPLES, Frederick Stephen (Fred); American golfer; b. 3 Oct. 1959, Seattle, Wash.; ed. Univ. of Houston; turned professional 1980; won Kemper Open 1984, Tournament Players Championship 1984, Byron Nelson Golf Classic 1987, Nissan Los Angeles Open 1990, Federal Express St. Jude Classic B.C. Open, Johnnie Walker World Championship 1991, Nissan Los Angeles Open, Nestlé Int., Masters 1992, Honda Classic 1993, Buick Open 1994, World Cup 1994, Dubai Desert Classic, Johnnie Walker Classic 1995, The Players' Championship 1996, Bob Hope Chrysler Classic 1998, Memorial Tournament 1998; PGA Tour Player of the Year 1991, 1992. *Leisure interests:* tennis, all sports, antiques, bicycling, vintage cars. *Address:* c/o PGA Tour, 100 Avenue of the Champions, P.O. Box 109601, Palm Beach Gardens, FL 33410, U.S.A.

COURANT, Ernest D., PH.D.; American (naturalized) physicist; b. 26 March 1920, Göttingen, Germany; s. of Richard Courant and Nina Runge; m. Sara Paul 1944; two s.; ed. Swarthmore Coll. and Univ. of Rochester, U.S.A.; Scientist Nat. Research Council (Canada), Montreal 1943–46; Research Assoc. in Physics, Cornell Univ. 1946–48; Physicist Brookhaven Nat. Lab., Upton, N.Y. 1948–60, Sr. Physicist 1960–89, Distinguished Scientist Emer. 1990–; Prof. (part-time) Yale Univ. 1961–67, State Univ. of N.Y., Stony Brook 1967–85; Visiting Prof. Univ. of Mich. 1989–; co-discoverer of Strong-focusing principle, particle accelerators; mem. N.A.S. 1976; Fellow A.A.A.S. 1981; Hon. D.Sc. (Swarthmore Coll.) 1988; Pregel Prize, New York Acad. of Sciences 1979, Fermi Prize 1986, R. R. Wilson Prize 1987. *Publications:* various articles; contrib. to Handbuch der Physik 1959, Annual Review of Nuclear Science 1968. *Address:* 109 Bay Avenue, Bayport, NY 11705, U.S.A. (Home). *Telephone:* (516) 472-0510 (Home).

COURCHENE, Thomas Joseph, PH.D., F.R.S.C.; Canadian professor of economics; b. 16 Sept. 1940, Wakaw, Sask.; m. Margareta Strohhofer 1962; two s. one d.; ed. Univ. of Sask., Princeton Univ. and Univ. of Chicago; Prof. of Econs. Univ. of Western Ontario 1965–88; Sr. Fellow, Howe Research Inst. 1981; Dir. School of Policy Studies, Queen's Univ. 1988, now Jarislowsky-Deutch Prof. of Econ. and Financial Policy; Chair. Ont. Econ. Council 1982–85; Robarts Prof. of Canadian Studies (York Univ.) 1987–88; Visiting Prof. Univ. of Toronto 1970–71, Grad. Inst. of Int. Studies Geneva 1975–76, Queen's Univ. (Canada) 1982–83; Pres. Canadian Econ. Assen. 1991–92; Ed. Bell Canada Papers on Econ. and Public Policy (Vols 1–5) 1993–97. *Publications include:* Money, Inflation and the Bank of Canada (Vol. I) 1976, (Vol. II) 1981, Equalization Payments: Present and Future 1984, Economic Management and the Division of Powers 1986, Social Policy: The Mandate for Reform 1987, Les offrandes des rois-mages 1987, What Does Ontario Want? 1989, Social Canada in the Millennium 1994, Redistributing Money and Power 1995, Celebrating Flexibility 1996. *Address:* School of Policy Studies, Queen's University, Kingston, Ont., K7L 3N6, Canada.

COURIER, Jim; American tennis player; b. 17 Aug. 1970; ed. Nick Bollettieri Tennis Acad.; coached by José Higueras; winner, French Open 1991, Indian Wells (doubles) 1991, Australian Open 1993; runner-up, U.S. Open 1991, ATP World Championship 1991; semi-finalist Australian Open 1994, French Open 1994; quarter-finalist, Wimbledon Championship 1991; Winner Australian Open 1992–93, Italian Open 1993. *Address:* International Management Group, Suite 300, 1 Erieview Place, Cleveland, OH 44114; U.S. Tennis Association, 70 West Red Oak Lane, White Plains, NY 10604, U.S.A.

COURRÈGES, André; French couturier; b. 9 March 1923, Pau (Pyrénées-Atlantiques); s. of Lucien Courrèges and Céline Coupe; m. Jacqueline Barrière 1966; one d.; ed. Ecole Supérieure Technique; studied eng.; moved to Paris and spent year as fashion designer 1945; went to Balenciaga's workrooms 1948 and served 11 years apprenticeship; f. Société André Courrèges 1961, Founder Dir., then Chair. and Man. Dir. 1966; Founder Dir. and Admin, Sport et Couture Amy Linker 1969; Founder Dir. Société Courrèges design 1981; launched his "Couture-Future" 1967; "Couture-Future" distributed by stores all over the world and by 45 exclusive boutiques in 10 countries including U.S.A., Canada, Japan, Australia; architecture and industrial design 1986. *Leisure interests:* Basque pelota, physical fitness. *Address:* 40 rue François 1er, 75008 Paris (Office); 27 rue Delabordère, 92200 Neuilly-sur-Seine, France (Home).

COURT, Hon. Sir Charles (Walter Michael), Kt., A.K., K.C.M.G., O.B.E. (MIL.), F.C.A., F.C.I.S., F.A.S.A.; Australian politician (retd.); b. 29 Sept. 1911, Crawley, Sussex, England; s. of late W. J. Court and Rose R. Court; m. 1st Rita Steffanoni 1936 (died 1992); five s.; m. 2nd Judith Butt 1997; ed. Perth Boys' School, W.A.; Founder Partner, Hendry, Rae & Court, chartered accountants 1938–70; served Australian Imperial Forces 1940–46, rising to rank of Lieut.-Col.; Liberal mem. Legis. Ass. for Nedlands, Parl. W.A. 1953–82, Deputy Leader of Opposition 1956–59; Minister for Railways 1959–67, for Industrial Devt. and the N.W. 1959–71, for Transport 1965–66; Deputy Leader of Opposition 1971–72, Leader 1972–74; Premier, State Treas., Minister Co-ordinating Econ. and Regional Devt., W.A. 1974–82; State Registrar (W. Australia) Inst. of Chartered Accountants in Australia 1946–52; Senator Jr. Chamber Int. 1971; Nat. Pres. Order of Australia Assen. 1986–89; Hon. Col. W. Australia Univ. Regt. 1969–74, S.A.S. Regt. (A.M.F.) 1976–80; Fellow Inst. of Chartered Accountants in Australia, Inst. of Chartered Secs. and Admins.; Life mem. Australian Soc. of Accountants; Life mem. Inst. of Chartered Accountants 1982; Hon. F.A.I.M. 1980; Patron or Vice-Patron numerous musical, sporting and other bodies; Hon. LL.D. (W. Australia) 1969; Hon. D.Tech. (W.A. Inst. of Tech.); Dr. h.c. (Murdoch Univ. of W.A.) 1995; Mfrs.' Export Council Award 1969, Industrial Design Council of Australia Award 1978 and numerous other awards; Knight of the Order of Australia; First Class Order of the Sacred Treasure, Japan; Kt. Commdr., Order of Merit, Italy; Order of Brilliant Star, Taiwan. *Publications:* many papers on industrial, economic and resource development matters. *Leisure interests:* music, various cultural and sporting interests. *Address:* 6th Floor, 256 St. George's Terrace, Perth, WA 6000 (Office); 18 Peel Parade, Coodanup, WA 6210, Australia (Home). *Telephone:* (8) 9481 1448 (Office); (8) 9535 5983 (Home). *Fax:* (8) 9535 5641.

COURT, Rev. Margaret, M.B.E.; Australian fmr. lawn tennis player; b. (as Margaret Smith) 16 July 1942, Albury, N.S.W.; m. Barry Court 1967; one s. three d.; ed. Albury High School; amateur player 1960–67; professional 1968–77; Australian Champion 1960, 1961, 1962, 1963, 1964, 1965, 1966, 1969, 1970, 1971, 1973; French Champion 1962, 1964, 1969, 1970, 1973; Wimbledon Champion 1963, 1965, 1970; U.S.A. Champion 1962, 1965, 1969, 1970, 1973; holds more major titles in singles, doubles and mixed doubles than any other player in history; won two Grand Slams, in mixed doubles 1963, and singles, 1970; played Federation Cup for Australia 1963, 1964, 1965, 1966, 1968, 1969, 1971. *Publications:* The Margaret Smith Story 1964, Court on Court 1974, Winning Faith (with Barbara Oldfield) 1993. *Address:* 21 Lowanna Way, City Beach, Perth, WA 6010, Australia.

COURTENAY, Tom; British actor; b. 25 Feb. 1937; s. of Henry Courtenay and late Anne Eliza Quest; m. 1st Cheryl Kennedy 1973 (dissolved 1982); m. 2nd Isabel Crossley 1988; ed. Kingston High School, Hull, Univ. Coll., London, Royal Acad. of Dramatic Art; started acting professionally 1960; stage performances in Billy Liar 1961–62, The Cherry Orchard 1966, Macbeth 1966, Hamlet 1968, She Stoops to Conquer 1969, Charley's Aunt 1971, Time and Time Again (Variety Club of G.B. Stage Actor Award) 1972, Table Manners 1974, The Norman Conquests 1974–75, The Fool 1975, The Rivals 1976, Clouds 1978, Crime and Punishment 1978, The Dresser (Drama Critics Award and New Standard Award for Best Actor) 1980, 1983, The Misanthrope 1981, Andy Capp 1982, Jumpers 1984, Rookery Nook 1986, The Hypochondriac 1987, Dealing with Clair 1988, The Miser 1992, Moscow Stations Edin. 1993, London 1994, Poison Pen Manchester 1993, Uncle Vanya, New York 1995, Art, London 1996. *Films include:* The Loneliness of the Long Distance Runner 1962, Private Potter 1962, Billy Liar 1963, King and Country 1964, Operation Crossbow 1965, King Rat 1965, Doctor Zhivago 1965, The Night of the Generals 1966, The Day the Fish Came Out 1967, A Dandy in Aspic 1968, Otley 1969, One Day in the Life of Ivan Denisovitch 1972, Catch Me a Spy, The Dresser, The Last Butterfly, Redemption (TV), Let Him Have It 1991, Redemption, The Boy from Mercury. *Address:* c/o Garrick Club, Garrick Street, London, W.C.2, England.

COUTARD, Raoul; French film maker; b. 1924, Paris; with French mil. Information Service, Vietnam, subsequently civilian photographer for Time and Paris-Match; worked in photographic labs. during 2nd World War; f. production co. making documentary films; cameraman with French New Wave dirs. including Godard and Truffaut; later with Costa-Gavras; films include: Au bout de souffle, Shoot the Pianist, Lola, Jules et Jim, Baie des Anges, Les Carabiniers, Alphaville, La Peau Douce, Pierrot Le Fou, La 317ème Section, Weekend, Sailor from Gibraltar, The Bride Wore Black, Z, Carmen, Dangerous Moves, La Garce, Let Sleeping Cops Lie, Bethune: the Making of a Hero.

COUTINHO, Vice-Admiral António Alba Rosa; Portuguese naval officer (retd.); b. 14 Feb. 1926, Lisbon; s. of António Rodrigues Coutinho and Ilda dos Prazeres Alva Rosa Coutinho; m. Maria Candida Maldonado 1950; three s. one d.; ed. Portuguese Naval Acad., Libson Univ., Scripps Inst. of Oceanography, U.S.A.; commissioned in Portuguese Navy 1947; served on board naval vessels and attended naval courses 1948–54; Hydrographic Engineer, Chief of Hydrographic Mission, Angola 1959–61; in prison in Zaire 1961; several commissions and naval courses 1962–64; Dir. of Dredging Services, Mozambique 1964–72; Commdg. Officer of Frigate Admiral P. Silva 1973–74; mem. Portuguese Armed Forces Movt. 1974, mem. Mil. Junta 1974–75, mem. Supreme Revolutionary Council March-Nov. 1975; Pres. Angola Gov. Junta 1974, High Commr. in Angola 1974–75; accused of violating human rights Jan. 1977, acquitted by supreme discipline council July 1977, forced to retire by navy chief of staff Aug. 1977, reintegrated on active duty by decision of supreme mil. court Feb. 1978, retd. (on his own request) Dec. 1982; Distinguished Services Medal, Mil. Merit; Knight Aviz Order; Commdr. Order of Henry the Navigator; Vasco da Gama Naval Medal; Kt. of Spanish Naval Merit. *Leisure interests:* big game hunting, angling, sailing. *Address:* Rua Carlos Malheiro Dias 18, 3° esq., 1700 Lisbon, Portugal. *Telephone:* 883638.

COUTTS, Ronald Thomson, PH.D., D.SC., F.R.S.C., F.R.S.(C.); Canadian professor of medicinal chemistry; b. 19 June 1931, Glasgow, Scotland; s. of Ronald Miller Coutts and Helen Alexanderina Crombie; m. Sheenah Kirk Black 1957; two s. one d.; ed. Woodside Secondary School, Glasgow, Univ. of Strathclyde, Glasgow Univ. and Chelsea Coll., London; lecturer in Medicinal Chem. Sunderland Tech. Coll., England 1959–63; Asst. then Assoc. Prof. Univ. of Saskatchewan, Canada 1963–66; Prof. Univ. of Alberta 1966–97, Distinguished Univ. Prof. 1984–, Pres. Faculty Asscn. 1978–79, mem. Bd. of Govs. 1982–85, Hon. Prof. of Psychiatry 1979–, Prof. Emer. 1997–; McCalla Prof. Univ. of Alberta 1985–86; Pres. Xenotox Services Ltd. 1978–; Scientific Ed. Canadian Journal of Pharmaceutical Sciences 1967–72; mem. Ed. Bd. Asian Journal of Pharmaceutical Sciences 1978–85; Ed. Journal of Pharmacological Methods 1984–98; Ed. Bd. Chirality 1989–95; Pres. Asscn. of Faculties of Pharmacy of Canada 1994–96; Fellow, Pharmaceutical Soc. of G.B., Canadian Inst. of Chemistry, American Asscn. of Pharmaceutical Scientists; McNeil Research Award 1982; McCalla Prof. Univ. of Alberta 1985–86; Canadian Coll. of Neuropsychopharmacology Medal 1992. *Publications:* 333 research manuscripts and reviews; several textbooks and chapters in textbooks. *Leisure interests:* golf, cross-country skiing, squash and music (playing and listening). *Address:* University of Alberta, Faculty of Pharmacy and Pharmaceutical Sciences, Edmonton, Alta., T6G 2N8 (Office); 4724-139 Street, Edmonton, Alta., Canada (Home). *Telephone:* (403) 492-3362 (Office); (403) 436-4313 (Home).

COUVE DE MURVILLE, (Jacques) Maurice; French politician; b. 24 Jan. 1907, Rheims; m. Jacqueline Schweisguth 1932; three d.; ed. Paris Univ.; Gen. Sec. to Gen. Giraud, Algiers March–June 1943; mem. French Cttee. for Nat. Liberation June-Nov. 1943; Italian Advisory Council 1944; Amb. to Italy 1945; Dir.-Gen. Political Affairs, Foreign Office 1945–50; Amb. to Egypt 1950–54, to U.S.A. 1955–56, to Fed. Repub. of Germany 1956–58; Minister of Foreign Affairs 1958–68, of Finance May-July 1968; Prime Minister July 1968–June 1969; Pres. N. Atlantic Council 1967–68; Inspector-Gen. of Finance 1969; elected to Nat. Ass. 1968, 1973, 1978, 1981; Pres. Foreign Affairs Cttee. of Nat. Ass. 1973–81; Senator 1986–95; mediator in Lebanon civil war 1975; Commdr. Légion d'honneur. *Publications:* Une politique étrangère 1958–69 1973, Le Monde en Face 1989. *Address:* 44 rue du Bac, 75007 Paris, France. *Telephone:* 42-22-98-10.

COUVE DE MURVILLE, Maurice Noel Leon, M.A., M.PHIL., S.T.L.; British ecclesiastic; b. 27 June 1929, St. Germain-en-Laye, France; s. of Noel Couve de Murville and Marie Souchon; ed. Downside School, Trinity Coll., Cambridge, Inst. Catholique, Paris and School of Oriental and African Studies, London; ordained priest for diocese of Southwark 1957; Curate, Dartford, Kent 1957–60; Priest-in-Charge St. Francis, Moulscoomb 1961–64; Catholic Chaplain Univ. of Sussex 1961–77; Sr. Catholic Chaplain Univ. of Cambridge 1977–82; Archbishop of Birmingham 1982–; Order of Malta Grand Cross Coventual Chaplain ad honorem 1982, D.Univ. h.c. (Open Univ.) 1994; Hon. D.D. (Birmingham Univ.) 1996. *Publications:* Catholic Cambridge (with Philip Jenkins) 1983, John Milner 1752–1826 1986. *Leisure interests:* walking, gardening, local history. *Address:* Archbishop's House, 8 Shadwell Street, Birmingham, B4 6EY, England. *Telephone:* (0121) 236 9090. *Fax:* (0121) 212 0171.

COUZENS, Sir Kenneth (Edward), K.C.B.; British public official; b. 29 May 1925; s. of Albert and May (née Biddlecombe) Couzens; m. Muriel Eileen Fey 1947; one s. (deceased) one d.; ed. Portsmouth Grammar School, Univ. of London and Caius Coll., Cambridge; served in R.A.F. 1943–47; Inland Revenue 1949–51; Private Sec. to Financial Sec., H.M. Treasury 1952–55, to Chief Sec. 1962–63; Asst. Sec. Treasury 1963–69; Under-Sec. Civil Service Dept. 1969–70, Treasury 1970–73; Deputy Sec. Incomes Policy and Public Finance 1973–77; Second Perm. Sec. (Overseas Finance), Treasury 1977–82; Vice-Chair. Monetary Cttee. of the EEC 1981–82; Perm. Under-Sec. of State, Dept. of Energy 1982–85; mem. U.K. Advisory Bd., Nat. Econ. Research Associates 1986–98; Deputy Chair. British Coal 1985–88; Chair. Coal Products Ltd 1988–92; Dir. Crédit Lyonnais Capital Markets 1989–98, Chair. 1991–96 (non-exec, Vice-Chair. 1996–98); Commr., Local Govt. Comm. for England 1993–95. *Address:* Coverts Edge, Woodsway, Oxshott, Surrey, KT22 0ND, England. *Telephone:* (01372) 843207.

COVELL, Roger David, A.M., PH.D., F.A.H.A.; Australian professor of music, critic, composer and conductor; b. 1 Feb. 1931, Sydney; s. of Harold Covell and Margaret Bardsley; m. 1st Sue Catling 1953 (divorced 1964); one s. one d.; m. 2nd Merle Berriman 1965 (divorced 1976); two s.; m. 3rd Patricia Brown 1976; ed. Brisbane High School and Univs. of Queensland and N.S.W.; Chief Music Critic, The Sydney Morning Herald 1960–; Sr. lecturer and Head, Dept. of Music, Univ. of N.S.W. 1966, Assoc. Prof. 1973, Prof. 1984, Head School of Music and Music Educ. 1993–96; Artistic Dir. Univ. of N.S.W. Opera 1968; co-founder, Australia Ensemble 1980; mem. Australia Council 1977–83; Pres. Australian Soc. for Music Educ. 1978–81; Pres. Musicological Soc. of Australia 1983–84; Challender Memorial Lecture 1994; mem. Council, Australian Acad. of Humanities 1986–88; Geraldine Pascall Prize for Music Criticism 1993. *Publications:* Australia's Music: Themes of a New Society 1967, Music in Australia: Needs and Prospects 1970, Folk Songs of Australia, Vol. 2 (with J. Meredith and P. Brown) 1987; ed. of baroque opera scores. *Leisure interests:* cycling, bird-watching. *Address:* 9 Kubya Street, Blackheath, N.S.W. 2785, Australia (Home). *Telephone:* 047-87 6182 (Home).

COVENEY, James, D.D'UNIV., B.A.; British university professor of French; b. 4 April 1920, London; s. of James and Mary Coveney; m. Patricia Yvonne Townsend 1955; two s.; ed. St. Ignatius Coll., London, and Univs. of Reading and Strasbourg; served in R.A.F. as Pilot (Flight-Lieut.), World War II; Lecturer, Univ. of Strasbourg 1951–53; Lecturer in medieval French, Univ. of Hull 1953–58; Asst. Dir., Civil Service Comm. 1958–59; UN Secretariat 1959–61; NATO Secretariat 1961–64; Sr. Lecturer, Head of Modern Languages, Univ. of Bath 1964–68, Prof. of French 1969–85, now Prof. Emer.; Visiting Prof. Ecole Nat. d'Admin., Paris 1974–85, Univ. of Buckingham 1974–86, Bethlehem Univ. 1985; Consultant, Univ. of Macau 1988, Int. Communications, Inc., Tokyo 1991–94; Corresp. mem. Acad. des Sciences, Agric., Arts et Belles-lettres, Aix-en-Provence 1975; Chevalier, Ordre des Palmes Académiques 1978; Officier, Ordre Nat. du Mérite 1986. *Publications:* La Légende de l'Empereur Constant 1955; Co-author: Glossary of French and English Management Terms 1972, Le français pour l'ingénieur 1974, Guide to French Institutions 1978, French Business Management Dictionary 1993. *Address:* 40 Westfield Close, Bath, BA2 2EB, England. *Telephone:* (01225) 316670. *Fax:* (01225) 400090.

COVERDELL, Paul Douglas, B.A.; American politician; b. 20 Jan. 1939; m. Nancy Nally; ed. Univ. of Missouri; mem. Ga. Senate 1970–89, minority leader 1974–89; Chair. Fulton del. 1974–84; Senator from Georgia 1993–; Dir. Peace Corps Washington 1989–91; fmr. Pres., C.E.O. Coverdell & Co. Inc.; Chair. Ga. Republican Party; mem. Senate Agric. Cttee., Small Business Cttee. *Address:* U.S. Senate, 200 Russell Senate Building, Washington, DC 20510, U.S.A.

COWAN, William Maxwell, M.A., D.PHIL., B.M., B.CH., F.R.S.; British biologist; b. 27 Sept. 1931, Johannesburg, South Africa; s. of Adam and Jessie (née Sloan) Cowan; m. Margaret Sherlock 1956; two s. one d.; ed. High School, S. Africa, Witwatersrand Univ., Oxford Univ.; Departmental Demonstrator in Anatomy, Oxford Univ. 1953–58, Univ. lecturer in Anatomy 1958–66; Fellow, Pembroke Coll., Oxford Univ. 1958–66; Assoc. Prof. of Anatomy, Univ. of Wis., U.S.A. 1966–68; Prof. and Head, Dept. of Anatomy and Neurobiology, Wash. Univ. School of Medicine 1968–80; Dir. Div. of Biology and Biomedical Sciences, Wash. Univ. 1975–80, Provost and Exec. Vice-Chancellor 1986–87; Non-Resident Fellow, Salk Inst. for Biological Studies 1977–80; Prof. and Dir. Weingart Lab. for Developmental Neurobiology, Salk Inst. for Biological Studies 1980–86; Vice-Pres. Salk Inst. 1981–86; Vice-Pres. and Chief Scientific Officer, Howard Hughes Medical Inst. 1988–; Fellow American Acad. of Arts and Sciences; Foreign Assoc. U.S. N.A.S. *Publications include:* Studies in Developmental Neurobiology 1981; numerous articles in scientific journals; Ed.: Annual Reviews of Neuroscience (Vol. I) 1978, (Vols 2–20) 1979–96, Journal of Comparative Neurology 1969–80, Journal of Neuroscience 1981. *Leisure interests:* photography, reading, travel. *Address:* Howard Hughes Medical Institute, 4000 Jones Bridge Road, Chevy Chase, MD 20815, U.S.A. *Telephone:* (301) 215-8803 (Office).

COWDREY OF TONBRIDGE, Baron (Life Peer), cr. 1997, of Tonbridge, in the County of Kent; **(Michael) Colin Cowdrey,** C.B.E.; British cricketer and businessman; b. 24 Dec. 1932, Bangalore, India; s. of late Ernest Arthur Cowdrey and Kathleen Mary Cowdrey (née Taylor); m. 1st Penelope Susan Chiesman 1956 (divorced 1985); three s. one d.; m. 2nd Baroness Herries of Terregles 1985; ed. Homefield, Sutton, Tonbridge and Brasenose Coll., Oxford; youngest cricketer (13) to appear in an important match at Lord's; played for Kent 1950–76 (Capt. 1957–71), Oxford Univ. 1952–54 (Capt. 1954); played in 114 Tests for England 1954–55 to 1974–75, 27 as Capt., scoring 7,624 runs (average 44.0) including 22 hundreds, and holding 120 catches; firt to appear in 100 Test matches (v. Australia at Edgbaston July 1968, when he scored 104); scored 42,719 first-class runs (107 hundreds); toured Australia 1954–55, 1958–59, 1962–63, 1965–66 and 1970–71; mem. MCC Cttee. 1970–; Dir. Whitbread Fremlins 1974–85; Exec. Barclays Int. 1975–, local Dir. Barclays, Maidstone, then Brighton, consultant Barclays Bank PLC 1991–; Dir. Master Skinners Co.; mem. Council, Winston Churchill Memorial Trust 1971–88, Britain Australia Soc. 1975–; Chair. Cook Soc. 1986, Int. Cricket Council 1993–95; Dir. Bilton PLC 1995–. *Publications:* Cricket Today 1957, Tackle Cricket This Way 1960, Time for Reflection 1963, Incomparable Game 1969, MCC: Life of a Cricketer 1975. *Leisure interests:* golf, reading. *Address:* Angmering Park, Littlehampton, West Sussex, BN16 4EX, England.

COWEN, Brian, B.C.L.; Irish politician; b. 10 Jan. 1960, Tullamore; s. of late Bernard Cowen and of Mary Cowen; m. Mary Molloy 1990; two d.; ed. Univ. Coll. Dublin and Inc. Law Soc. of Ireland; solicitor; mem. Offaly Co. Council 1984–93; mem. Dáil 1984; Minister for Labour 1993–94, for Health and Children June 1997–; fmrly. Opposition Spokesperson on Agric. and Food; Fianna Fáil. *Leisure interests:* sport, reading, music. *Address:* Department of Health, Hawkins House, Hawkins Street, Dublin 2; Ballard, Tullamore, Co. Offaly, Ireland. *Telephone:* (1) 6354148 (Office); (0506) 52047 (Home).

COWEN, Rt. Hon. Sir Zelman, P.C., A.K., G.C.M.G., G.C.V.O., Q.C.; Australian academic; b. 7 Oct. 1919, Melbourne; s. of late Bernard Cowen and of Sara Granat; m. Anna Wittner 1945; three s. one d.; ed. Scotch Coll., Melbourne, Univ. of Melbourne, Univ. of Oxford; served in Royal Australian Naval Volunteer Reserve 1940–45; consultant to Mil. Govt. in Germany 1947; Australian Dominion Liaison Officer to Colonial Office 1951–66; Dean of Faculty of Law, Prof. of Public Law, Univ. of Melbourne 1951–66; Vice-Chancellor, Univ. of New England, N.S.W. 1967–70, Univ. of Queensland 1970–77; Gov.-Gen. of Australia 1977–82; Provost of Oriel Coll., Oxford 1982–90; Pro-Vice Chancellor of Oxford Univ. 1988–90; Chair. John Fairfax Holdings Ltd. 1992–94 (Dir. 1994–96); Visiting Prof., Univ. of Chicago 1949, Harvard Law School and Fletcher School of Law and Diplomacy 1953–54, 1963–64, Univ. of Utah 1954, Ill. 1957–58, Wash. 1959, Univ. of Calcutta, India 1975; Menzies Scholar in Residence, Univ. of Va., 1983; Pres. Adult Educ. Asscn. of Australia 1968–70; mem. and (at various times) Chair. Victorian State Advisory Cttee. to Australian Broadcasting Comm.; mem. Devt. Corpn. of N.S.W. 1969–70, Bd. of Int. Asscn. for Cultural Freedom 1970–75; Academic Gov. of Bd. of Govs., Hebrew Univ. of Jerusalem 1969–77, 1982–; mem. Club of Rome 1974–77; Pres. Australian Inst. of Urban Studies 1973–77; Chair. Bd. of Govs., Utah Foundation 1975–77; Law Reform Commr., Commonwealth of Australia 1976–77; Chair. Australian Vice-Chancellor's Cttee. 1977, Australian Studies Centre Cttee. (London) 1982–90, Press Council (U.K.) 1983–88, Nat. Council of Australian Opera 1983–, Victoria League for Commonwealth Friendship 1986–89, of Trustees, Visnews Ltd. 1986–91, Bd. of Dirs., Sir Robert Menzies Memorial Foundation 1990–97, Australian Nat. Acad. of Music 1995–; Dir. Australian Mutual Provident Soc. 1982–90; mem. Nat. Council of Australian Opera (Chair. 1983–95); Trustee Sydney Opera House 1969–70, Queensland Overseas Foundation 1976–77, Sir Robert Menzies Memorial Trust (U.K.), Winston Churchill Memorial Trust (U.K.), Van Leer Inst. of Jerusalem (Chair. 1988–95, Hon. Chair. 1995–); Pres. Order of Australia Asscn. 1992–95; Nat. Pres. Australia-Britain Soc. 1993–95; Foreign Hon. Mem. American Acad. of Arts and Sciences; Fellow, Royal Soc. of Arts, Acad. of Social Sciences in Australia, Australian Coll. of Educ., Australian and N.Z. Asscn. for the Advancement of Science (now Hon. Fellow); Hon. Fellow New Coll., Oxford, Univ. House, Australian Inst. of Architects, Australian Acad. of Social Sciences, Australian Coll. of Educ., Univ. House of Australia, Nat. Univ., Australian Acad. of Technological Sciences, Royal Australasian Coll. of Physicians, Royal Australian Coll. of Medical Administrators, Royal Australian Coll. of Obstetricians and Gynaecologists, Australian Acad. of the Humanities, Australian Soc. of Accountants, Australian Inst. of Chartered Accountants, Australian Coll. of Rehabilitation Medicine; Hon. Master, Gray's Inn Bench 1976, Q.C. of the Queensland Bar, mem. Victorian Bar and Hon. Life mem. N.S.W. Bar Asscn.; Hon. Fellow, Trinity Coll., Dublin, Oriel Coll., Oxford; Hon. LL.D. (Univs. of Hong Kong, Queensland, Melbourne, W.A., Turin, Australian Nat. Univ., Tasmania, Victoria Univ. of Tech.), Hon. D.Litt. (Univs. of New England, Sydney, Oxford, James Cook Univ. of N.Queensland), Hon. D.H.L. (Hebrew Union Coll., Cincinnati), (Univ. of Redlands, Calif.), Hon. D.Univ. (Newcastle, Griffith), Hon. D.Phil. (Hebrew Univ. of Jerusalem, Univ. of Tel Aviv); Kt., Order of Australia, Kt. Grand Cross, Order of St. Michael and St. George, Royal Victorian Order, K.St.J., Kt. Grand Cross, Order of Merit, Italy. *Publications:* Specialist Editor, Dicey: Conflict of Laws 1949, Australia and the United States: Some Legal Comparisons 1954, (with P. B. Carter) Essays on the Law of Evidence 1956, American-Australian Private International Law 1957, Federal Jurisdiction in Australia 1959, (with D. Mendes da Costa) Matrimonial Causes Jurisdiction 1961, The British Commonwealth of Nations in a Changing World 1964, Sir John Latham and Other Papers 1965, Sir Isaac Isaacs 1967, The Private Man (A.B.C. Boyer Lectures 1969), Individual Liberty and the Law (Tagore Law Lectures 1975), The Virginia Lectures 1984, Reflections on Medicine, Biotechnology and the Law (Pound Lectures, Neb. Univ.) 1986, A Touch of Healing 1986. *Leisure interests:* music, performing and visual arts. *Address:* 4 Treasury Place, East Melbourne, Vic. 3002, Australia. *Telephone:* (03) 96500299. *Fax:* (03) 96500301.

COWLEY, Alan H., PH.D., F.R.S.; British professor of chemistry; b. 29 Jan. 1934, Manchester; s. of Herbert Cowley and Dora Cowley; m. Deborah Elaine Cole 1975; two s. three d.; ed. Univ. of Manchester; Postdoctoral Fellow, then Instr. Univ. of Fla., U.S.A. 1958–60; Tech. Officer, Exploratory Group, ICI (Billingham Div.), U.K. 1960–61; Asst. Prof. of Chem., Univ. of Tex. at Austin 1962–67, Assoc. Prof. 1967–70, Prof. 1970–84, George W. Watt Centennial Prof. of Chem. 1984–88, Richard J.V. Johnson Regent's Prof. of Chem. 1989–91; Robert A. Welch Prof. of Chem., Univ. of Texas at Austin 1991–; Sir Edward Frankland Prof. of Inorganic Chem., Imperial Coll., London 1988–89; Vice-Chair. Bd. of Trustees, Gordon Research Confs. 1993–94 (Chair. 1994–95); Ed.-in-Chief Inorganic Syntheses Vol. 31 1990–; mem. several editorial bds.; Guggenheim Fellowship 1976–77, Centenary Medal and Lectureship, Royal Soc. of Chem. 1986, Chemical Pioneer Award, American Inst. of Chemists 1994, Von Humboldt Prize 1996, Chevalier, Ordre des Palmes Académiques and several other awards. *Publications:* more than 400 articles in learned journals. *Leisure interests:* squash, sailing, classical music, literature. *Address:* Department of Chemistry and Biochemistry, University of Texas at Austin, Austin, TX 78712, U.S.A. *Telephone:* (512) 471-7484. *Fax:* (512) 471-6822.

COWLEY, John Maxwell, PH.D., F.A.A., F.R.S.; Australian professor of physics; b. 18 Feb. 1923, Australia; s. of Alfred E. Cowley and Doris R. Cowley; m. Roberta Beckett 1951; two d.; ed. Univ. of Adelaide and M.I.T., U.S.A.; Research Officer, Commonwealth Scientific and Industrial Research Org., Australia 1945–62; Chamber of Mfrs. Prof. of Physics, Univ. of Melbourne 1962–70; Galvin Prof. of Physics, Arizona State Univ., U.S.A. 1970–94, Dir. Facility for High Resolution Electron Microscopy 1983–90, Regents' Prof. 1988–94, Prof. Emer. 1994–; B.E. Warren Award, American Crystallographic Asscn. 1976, Distinguished Award, Electron Microscopy Soc. of America 1979, Ewald Award, Int. Union of Crystallography 1987; Fellow American Physical Soc. *Publications:* Diffraction Physics 1975, Modulated Structures—1979 (Ed.) 1979, Electron Diffraction Techniques (Ed.) 1992, approximately 400 scientific articles in journals. *Leisure interests:* painting and hiking. *Address:* Department of Physics and Astronomy, Box 871504, Arizona State University, Tempe, AZ 85287-1504, U.S.A. *Telephone:* (602) 965-6459. *Fax:* (602) 965-7954.

COWLEY, Roger A., F.R.S., F.R.S.E.; British professor of physics; b. 24 Feb. 1939, Essex; s. of C. A. Cowley; m. Sheila Joyce Wells 1964; one s. one d.; ed. Brentwood School and Univ. of Cambridge; Fellow of Trinity Hall, Cambridge 1962–64; Research Officer. Atomic Energy of Canada Ltd. 1964–70; Prof. of Physics, Univ. of Edinburgh 1970–88; Dr. Lee's Prof. of Experimental Philosophy and Fellow of Wadham Coll., Univ. of Oxford 1988–, Chair. of Physics 1993–96; Max Born Medal and Prize 1973, Holweck Medal and Prize 1990. *Publications:* approx. 300 scientific publs. *Address:* Oxford Physics Clarendon Laboratory, Parks Road, Oxford OX1 3PU (Office); Tredinnock, Harcourt Hill, Oxford OX2 9AS, England (Home). *Telephone:* (01865) 272224 (Office); (01865) 247570 (Home).

COWLING, Maurice, M.A.; British academic; b. 6 Sept. 1926, London; s. of R. F. Cowling and May Cowling (née Roberts); m. P. M. Gale (née Holley) 1996; ed. Battersea Grammar School, Jesus Coll., Cambridge; served in British and Indian Armies 1944–47; Fellow Jesus Coll., Cambridge 1950–53, 1961–63, Peterhouse, Cambridge 1963–93; on editorial staff The Times and Daily Express 1955–59; County Councillor, Cambs. 1966–70; Literary Ed. The Spectator 1970–71; Visiting Prof. Adelphi Univ. 1993–97. *Publications include:* The Nature and Limits of Political Science 1963, Mill and Liberalism 1963, 1867: Disraeli, Gladstone and Revolution 1967, The Impact of Liberalism 1971, The Impact of Hitler 1975, Religion and Public Doctrine in Modern England 1981. *Address:* 9A Redcliffe Caswell Bay, Swansea, SA3 3BT, Wales. *Telephone:* (01792) 367934.

COX, Archibald, A.B., LL.B.; American lawyer; b. 17 May 1912, Plainfield, N.J.; s. of Archibald Cox and Frances B. Perkins; m. Phyllis Ames 1937; one s. two d.; ed. St. Paul's School, Concord, and Harvard Univ.; admitted to Mass. Bar 1937; in practice with Ropes, Gray, Best, Coolidge and Rugg, Boston 1938–41; Attorney, Office of Solicitor-Gen., U.S. Dept. of Justice 1941–43; Assoc. Solicitor, Dept. of Labor 1943–45; lecturer on Law, Harvard Univ. 1945–46, Williston Prof. of Law 1946–76; Carl M. Loeb Univ. Prof. 1976–84, Prof. Emer. 1984–; Visiting Prof. of Law, Boston Univ. 1984–97; Chair. Wage Stabilization Bd. 1952, Advisory Panel to Senate Cttee. on Educ. and Labour 1958–59; Solicitor-Gen. of U.S. 1961–65; Prosecutor, Watergate Investigation 1973; Pitt Prof. of American History and Insts., Cambridge Univ. 1974–75; Chair. Common Cause 1980–93; mem. American Bar Asscn., American Acad. of Arts and Sciences, Bd. of Overseers, Harvard Univ. 1962–65. *Publications:* Cases on Labor law 1948, Law and the National Labor Policy 1960, Civil Rights, the Constitution and the Courts 1967, The Warren Court 1968, The Role of the Supreme Court in American Government 1976, Freedom of Expression 1981, The Court and the Constitution 1987, and articles in legal periodicals. *Address:* Harvard Law School, Cambridge, MA 02138 (Office); 34 Old Connecticut Path, PO Box 393, Wayland, MA 01778, U.S.A. (Home).

COX, Barry Geoffrey, B.A.; British executive and journalist; b. 25 May 1942, Guildford; m. 1st Pamela Doran 1967 (divorced 1977); m. 2nd Kathryn Kay 1984 (divorced 1992); two s. two d.; ed. Tiffin School, Kingston, Surrey and Magdalen Coll. Oxford; reporter, The Scotsman 1965–67; feature writer, Sunday Telegraph 1967–70; producer/dir. World in Action, Granada TV

1970–74; Controller of Features and Current Affairs, London Weekend Television 1974–87, Dir. of Corp. Affairs 1987–94, Special Adviser to Chief Exec. 1994–95; Dir. Ind. Television Asscn. 1995–; Fellow, Royal TV Soc. *Publications:* Civil Liberties in Britain 1975, The Fall of Scotland Yard 1977. *Leisure interests:* tennis, walking, theatre. *Address:* ITV Association, 200 Gray's Inn Road, London, WC1X 8HF, England. *Telephone:* 0171-843 8000. *Fax:* 0171-843 8150.

COX, Courteney; American actress; b. 15 June 1964, Birmingham, Ala.; d. of Richard Lewis and Courteney (Bass-Copland) Cox; modelling career New York; appeared in Bruce Springsteen music video Dancing in the Dark 1984. *Films:* Down Twisted 1986, Masters of the Universe 1987, Cocoon: The Return 1988, Mr. Destiny 1990, Blue Desert 1990, Shaking the Tree 1992, The Opposite Sex 1993, Ace Ventura, Pet Detective 1994, Scream 1996, Commandments 1996. *Television series:* Misfits of Science 1985–86, Family Ties 1987–88, The Trouble with Larry 1993, Friends 1994–. *Television films include:* Roxanne: The Prize Pulitzer 1989, Till We Meet Again 1989, Curiosity Kills 1990, Morton and Hays 1991, Topper 1992, Sketch Artist II: Hands That See 1995. *Address:* c/o Creative Artists Agency, 9830 Wilshire Boulevard, Beverly Hills, CA 90212, U.S.A.

COX, Sir David (Roxbee), Kt., PH.D., F.R.S.; British statistician; b. 15 July 1924, Birmingham; s. of Sam R. Cox and Lilian (née Braines) Cox; m. Joyce Drummond 1948; three s. one d.; ed. Handsworth Grammar School, Birmingham, and St. John's Coll. Cambridge; at Royal Aircraft Establishment 1944–46; Wool Industries Research Asscn. 1946–50; Statistical Lab., Univ. of Cambridge 1950–55; with Dept. of Biostatistics, Univ. of N. Carolina 1955–56, Birkbeck Coll., London 1956–66; Bell Telephone Labs. 1965; Prof. of Statistics, Imperial Coll. of Science and Tech., London 1966–88; Warden Nuffield Coll., Oxford 1988–94; Science and Eng. Research Council Sr. Research Fellow 1983–88; Ed. Biometrika 1966–91; Pres. Int. Statistics Inst. 1995–97; Fellow Imperial Coll.; Hon. Fellow St. John's Coll. Cambridge, Inst. of Actuaries, Nuffield Coll. Oxford, British Acad.; Hon. D.Sc. (Reading, Bradford, Heriot Watt, Helsinki, Limburg, Queen's, Kingston, Ont., Waterloo, Neuchâtel, Padua, Minn., Dundee, Toronto, Abertay Dundee, Crete, Bordeaux 2, Athens Univ. of Econs.); Hon. Foreign mem.: U.S. Acad. of Arts and Sciences, Royal Danish Acad., N.A.S., American Philosophical Soc.; Guy Medals in silver and gold, Royal Statistical Soc., Weldon Medal, Univ. of Oxford, Derning Medal, ASQC, Kettering Medal and Prize, Gen. Motors Cancer Research Foundation, Max Planck Prize. *Publications:* several books on statistics, articles in Journal of the Royal Statistical Soc., Biometrika etc. *Address:* c/o Nuffield Coll., Oxford, OX1 1NF, England.

COX, Glenn A., B.B.A.; American business executive; b. 6 Aug. 1929, Sedalia, Mo.; s. of Glenn A. Cox and Ruth L. Atkinson; m. Veronica M. Martin 1953; two s. one d.; ed. Southern Methodist Univ. and Central Methodist Coll.; served as pilot, U.S.A.F. 1951–55; began career with Phillips Petroleum Co., in Treasury Dept. 1956, Asst. to Chair. of Operating Cttee. 1973, elected Vice-Pres. Man. Information and Control 1974, elected Exec. Vice-Pres. with responsibility for all corpn. financial matters 1980, elected mem. Bd. of Dirs. and Exec. Cttee. 1982, Pres. and C.O.O. 1985–91; Dir. The Williams Cos., Thermon Industries, Bank of Oklahoma, Helmerich and Payne Inc.; mem. Nat. Exec. Bd. Boy Scouts of America; Trustee Cen. Methodist Coll.; Order of the Ivory Coast. *Publication:* "Financing an Oil Company" in Energy Finance. *Leisure interests:* reading, flying and jogging. *Address:* Reda Bldg., 401 S. Dewey Avenue, Suite 318, Bartlesville, OK 74003, U.S.A.

COX, Paul; Australian film director; b. (as Paulus Cox) 16 April 1940, Venlo, The Netherlands; ed. Melbourne Univ.; two s. one d.; settled in Australia 1965; photographic exhbns. in Australia, The Netherlands, Germany, Japan, India and U.S.A.; taught photography and cinematography for several years; f. Illumination Films with Tony Llewellyn-Jones and Bernard Eddy 1977; directed: (shorts) Mantuta 1965, Time Past 1966, Skindeep 1968, Marcel 1969, Symphony 1969, Mirka 1970, Phyllis 1971, Island 1975, We are All Alone My Dear 1975, Ways of Seeing 1977, Ritual 1978; (feature length) The Journey 1972, Illuminations 1976, Inside Looking Out 1977, Kostas 1978, Lonely Hearts 1981, Man of Flowers 1983, Death and Destiny (A Journey into Ancient Egypt) 1984, My First Wife 1984, Cactus 1986, Vincent 1988, Island 1989, Golden Braid 1990, A Woman's Tale 1991, The Nun and the Bandit 1992, Exile 1993, Lust and Revenge 1996, The Hidden Dimension 1997, Molokai – the true story of Father Damien 1998, Innocence 1998; (documentaries) Calcutta 1970, All Set Backstage 1974, For A Child Called Michael 1979, The Kingdom of Nek Chand 1980, Underdog 1980, Death and Destiny 1984, Handle with Care 1985; (for Children's TV) The Paper Boy 1985, The Secret Life of Trees 1986, The Gift 1988, Exile 1993. *Address:* Illumination Films, 1 Victoria Avenue, Albert Park, Vic. 3208, Australia. *Telephone:* (03) 9690-5266 (Office). *Fax:* (03) 9696-5625.

COX, Philip Sutton, A.O., B.ARCH.; Australian architect; b. 1 Oct. 1939, Killara, Sydney; s. of Ronald Albert Cox and Lilian May Cox; m. Virginia Louise Gowing 1972; two d.; ed. Sydney Church of England Grammar School, Sydney Univ.; worked in New Guinea 1962; apptd. Tutor in Architecture, Univ. of Sydney 1963; est. Ian McKay & Philip Cox pvt. practice with Ian McKay 1963; est. Philip Cox and Assocs. 1967; Architect Sydney Olympics, Stage I; Tutor in Architecture, Univ. of N.S.W. 1971, 1973, 1978, Prof. 1989–; Founding mem. The Australian Acad. of Design 1990–; Life Fellow Royal Australian Inst. of Architects, Chair. Educ. Bd., Fed. Chapter; Vice-Chair. Architecture and Design Panel, Visual Arts Bd., Australia Council; Vice-Pres. Cancer Patients Assistance Soc. of N.S.W.; Hon. F.A.I.A.; Fellow Australian Acad. of Humanities; Commonwealth Scholarship 1956; numerous awards and prizes including Royal Australian Inst. of Architects Gold Medal and Merit Awards, Commonwealth Asscn. of Architects Sir Robert Matthew Award, Blacket Award, Sir John Sulman Medal. *Publications:* several books including The Australian Homestead (with Wesley Stacey) 1972, Historic Towns of Australia (with Wesley Stacey) 1973, Restoring Old Australian Houses and Buildings, an Architectural Guide (with others) 1975, Australian Colonial Architecture (with Clive Lucas), The Functional Tradition (with David Moore) 1987. *Leisure interests:* gardening, swimming, walking, painting. *Address:* Cox Richardson Architects and Planners, Level 1, 469 Kent Street, Sydney, N.S.W. 2000, Australia.

COX, Stephen Joseph; British artist; b. 16 Sept. 1946, Bristol; s. of Leonard John Cox and Ethel Minnie May McGill; m. Judith Atkins 1970; two d.; ed. St. Mary Redcliffe, Bristol, West of England Coll. of Art, Bristol and Cen. School of Art and Design, London; lives and works in London, Italy, India and Egypt; many one-man exhbns. in London (Lisson Gallery, Nigel Greenwood Gallery, Tate Gallery, Royal Botanic Gardens, Michael Hue-Williams Fine Art, Dulwich Picture Gallery), Bath Festival Artsite, Bristol (Arnolfini Gallery), Nottingham (Midland Group Gallery), Oxford (Museum of Modern Art), Glyndebourne Festival Opera, Amsterdam, Bari, Milan, Rome, Spoleto (1982 Festival), Florence, Geneva, Basle, Paris, Cairo and New Delhi; numerous group exhbns. in several countries, including Paris Biennale 1977, British Sculpture in 20th Century, Whitechapel Art Gallery, London 1981, Venice Biennale 1982, 1986, New Art, Tate Gallery, London 1983, Int. Garden Festival, Liverpool 1984 and Int. Survey of Painting and Sculpture 1984, M.O.M.A., New York, Forty Years of Modern Art 1945–85, Tate Gallery (new display 1992), Origins, Originally and Beyond, Sydney Biennale, Prospekt '86, Frankfurt, 19th Sculpture Biennale, Middlehiem, Belgium, British Art in the 1980s, Museum of Modern Art, Brussels, 20th Century British Sculpture, Schloss Ambross, Innsbruck, Austria; works in collections of Tate Gallery, Victoria and Albert Museum, British Museum, Arts Council of G.B., British Council, Walker Art Gallery, Liverpool, Henry Moore Centre for Sculpture, Leeds City Gallery, Fogg Museum, U.S.A., Groningen Museum, Netherlands, Peter Ludwig Collection, Fed. Repub. of Germany, Uffizi Gallery, Florence, and pvt. collections in U.S.A. and Europe; numerous public sculptures in England, India, Egypt and Australia; Sr. Research Fellow, Wimbledon School of Art 1995–96; Gold Medal Indian Triennale, Arts Council Major Awards 1978, 1980, British Council Bursaries 1978, 1979, Hakone Open Air Museum Prize, Japan 1985, Goldhill Sculpture Prize, Royal Acad. 1988. *Address:* 154 Barnsbury Road, Islington, London, N1 0ER, England. *Telephone:* 0171-278 4184.

COX, Warren Jacob, B.A., M.ARCH., F.A.I.A.; American architect; b. 28 Aug. 1935, New York; s. of Oscar Sydney Cox and Louise Bryson (Black) Cox; m. Claire Christie-Miller 1975; one s. one d.; ed. The Hill School, Yale Univ., Yale Univ. School of Architecture; partner Hartman-Cox Architects, Washington D.C. 1965–; Visiting Architectural Critic, Yale Univ. 1966, Catholic Univ. of America 1967, Univ. of Va. 1976; Dir. Center for Palladian Studies in America 1982–; lecturer numerous architectural schools and insts., juror for design awards programs; mem. Editorial Bd. Guide to the Architecture of Washington, D.C. 1965, 1974; A.I.A. Architectural Firm Award 1988, A.I.A. Nat. Honor Awards 1970, 1971, 1981, 1983, 1989, 1994, Louis Sullivan Prize 1972, and over 90 other awards. *Work includes:* Euram Bldg., Nat. Perm. Bldg., Sumner Square, Market Square, Mount Vernon Coll. Chapel, Folger Shakespeare Library Additions, Immanuel Presbyterian Church, Washington, D.C.; Winterthur Museum New Exhbn. Bldg., Wilmington, Del.; Chrysler Museum, Norfolk, Va.; John Carter Brown Library Addition, Providence, R.I.; H.E.B. Corp. HQ, San Antonio, Tex.; Nat. Humanities Center, Raleigh, N.C.; U.S. Embassy, Malaysia; Law School, Washington Univ.; Law School, Tulane Univ.; Library, Addition and Residence Hall, Georgetown Univ.; Law Center, Washington; Library, Case Western Reserve Univ., Cleveland, Ohio; Law Library, Univ. of Conn., Hartford, Conn. *Address:* Hartmann Cox Architects, 1074 Jefferson Street, N.W., Washington, DC 20007 (Office); 3111 N Street, N.W., Washington, DC 20007, U.S.A. (Home).*Telephone:* (202) 333-6446 (Home).

COXETER, Harold Scott MacDonald, C.C., PH.D., LL.D., D.MATH., D.SC., F.R.S., F.R.S.C.; British mathematician; b. 9 Feb. 1907, London; s. of Harold Samuel Coxeter and Lucy (née Gee) Coxeter; m. Hendrina Johanna Brouwer 1936; one s. one d.; ed. King Alfred School, London, St. George's School, Harpenden, and Trinity Coll., Cambridge; Rockefeller Foundation Fellow, Princeton 1932–33; Procter Fellow, Princeton 1934–35; Asst. Prof., Toronto 1936–43, Assoc. Prof. 1943–48, Prof. of Math. 1948–80, Prof. Emer. 1980–; Visiting Prof., Notre Dame 1947, Columbia Univ. 1949, Dartmouth Coll. 1964, Univ. of Amsterdam 1966, Univ. of Edin. 1967, Univ. of E. Anglia 1968, Australian Nat. Univ. 1970, Univ. of Sussex 1972, Univ. of Warwick 1976, Calif. Inst. of Tech. 1977, Univ. of Bologna 1978; foreign mem. Koninklijke Nederlandse Akademie van Wetenschappen; Hon. mem. Mathematische Gesellschaft in Hamburg, London Mathematical Soc., etc. *Publications:* Non-Euclidean Geometry 1942, 1997, Regular Polytopes 1948, 1973, The Real Projective Plane 1949, 1992, Introduction to Geometry 1961, 1969, Projective Geometry 1946, 1987, Twelve Geometric Essays 1968, Regular Complex Polytopes 1974, 1991, Kaleidoscopes 1995. *Leisure interest:*

music. *Address:* 67 Roxborough Drive, Toronto M4W 1X2, Ont., Canada. *Telephone:* (416) 9625665.

COZ, Steve; American editor and publishing executive; b. 26 March 1957, Grafton, Mass.; s. of Henry Coz and Mary Coz; m. Valerie Virga 1987; ed. Harvard Univ.; freelance writer various U.S. publs. 1979–82; reporter Nat. Enquirer, Fla. 1982–95, Ed.-in-Chief 1995–; American celebrity analyst BBC Radio 1995–96; Edgar Hoover Memorial Award for Distinguished Public Service 1996; Haven House Award of Excellence for Outstanding Reporting on Domestic Violence Issues 1996. *Address:* National Enquirer, 600 South East Coast Avenue, Lantana, FL 33464, U.S.A.

CRABTREE, Robert H., M.A., D.SC., D.PHIL.; British/American professor of chemistry; b. 17 April 1948, London; s. of Arthur Crabtree and Marguerite M. Vaniere; ed. Brighton Coll. and Univs. of Oxford and Sussex; Attaché de Recherche, CNRS, France 1975–77; Asst. Prof. of Chem. Yale Univ. 1977–82, Assoc. Prof. 1982–85, Prof. 1985–; A.P. Sloan Fellow 1981; Dreyfus Teacher-Scholar 1982; Corday-Morgan Medal 1984; Royal Soc. of Chem. Organometallic Chem. Award 1991, American Chem. Soc., Organometallic Chem. Award 1993. *Publication:* The Organometallic Chemistry of the Transition Metals 1994. *Leisure interest:* travel. *Address:* 97 Fairwood Road, Bethany, CT 06524, U.S.A.

CRACKNELL, Ruth Winifred, A.M.; Australian actor and writer; b. 6 July 1925, Maitland, N.S.W.; d. of Charles Cracknell and Winifred Watts; m. Eric Charles Harry Phillips 1957; one s. two d.; ed. The North Sydney Girls' High School; joined John Alden Co. 1948; with BBC, London 1953–54. *Theatre includes:* Murder in the Cathedral, A Delicate Balance, The Chalk Garden, King Oedipus, Trelawny of the Wells, Arsenic and Old Lace, The Seagull, Habeas Corpus, School for Scandal, The Cherry Orchard, Bedroom Farce, The Dresser, The Way of the World, Nicholas Nickleby, All's Well that Ends Well, Tom and Viv, Medée (with Australian Opera), The Importance of Being Earnest 1988/89, 1990/91, Lettice and Lovage 1990, Lost in Yonkers 1992, Three Tall Women 1995, A Little Night Music 1996/97, Vita and Virginia 1997/98; numerous TV and film roles; mem. Bd. of Dirs. Sydney Theatre Co., Christian Children's Fund; Hon. D.Litt. (Sydney Univ., Queensland Univ. of Tech.). *Publication:* A Biased Memoir (autobiog.) 1997. *Leisure interest:* peace and quiet. *Address:* c/o International Casting Service and Associates, 147A King Street, Sydney, N.S.W. 2000, Australia. *Telephone:* (02) 232 6955. *Fax:* (02) 221 4091.

CRADOCK, Rt. Hon. Sir Percy, P.C., G.C.M.G.; British diplomatist; b. 26 Oct. 1923; m. Birthe Marie Dyrlund 1953; joined FCO 1954; First Sec. Kuala Lumpur, Malaya 1957–61, Hong Kong 1961–62, Beijing 1962–63; Foreign Office 1963–66; Counsellor and Head of Chancery, Beijing 1966–68, Chargé d'affaires 1968–69; Head of FCO Planning Staff 1969–71; Asst. Under-Sec. of State and Head of Cabinet Office Assessments Staff 1971–76; Amb. to German Democratic Repub. 1976–78, concurrently Leader U.K. Mission to Comprehensive Test Ban Negotiations, Geneva 1977–78; Amb. to People's Repub. of China 1978–83: Leader of Negotiating Team with China over Hong Kong 1982–83; Deputy Under-Sec. with special responsibility for negotiations with China over Hong Kong 1983–85; Foreign policy adviser to the Prime Minister 1984–92; Dir. South China Morning Post 1996–; Hon. Fellow St. John's, Cambridge 1982. *Publications:* Experiences of China 1993, In Pursuit of British Interests 1997. *Address:* c/o The Reform Club, 104 Pall Mall, London, S.W.1, England.

CRAGG, Anthony Douglas, M.A.; British sculptor; b. 9 April 1949, Liverpool; s. of Douglas R. Cragg and Audrey M. Rutter; m. 1st Ute Oberste-Lehn 1977; two s.; m. 2nd Tatjana Verhasselt 1990; one s. one d.; ed. Cheltenham and Wimbledon Schools of Art and Royal Coll. of Art; teacher, Düsseldorf Kunstakademie 1979–, Prof. and Co-Dir. 1988–; one-man exhbns. include Lisson Gallery 1979, 1980, 1985, 1991, 1992, Whitechapel Gallery, London 1981, Kanrasha Gallery, Tokyo 1982, 1984, 1989, 1990, Kunsthalle, Bern 1983, Palais de Beaux-Arts, Brussels 1985, Staatsgalerie Moderner Kunst, Munich 1985, Musée d'Art Contemporain, Paris 1985, Brooklyn Museum 1986, Hayward Gallery, London 1986, Houston Contemporary Art Museum 1991, Whitechapel Art Gallery 1997; group exhbns. include Venice Biennale 1980–86, São Paulo Bienale 1983, Sydney Bienale 1984, 1990; Turner Prize 1988; Chevalier des Arts et des Lettres 1992. *Leisure interests:* walking, geology. *Address:* Adolf-Vorwerk-Str. 24, 5600 Wuppertal 2, Germany.

CRAIG, David Parker, A.O., D.SC., F.R.S., F.R.S.A., F.A.A.; Australian professor of chemistry; b. 23 Nov. 1919, Sydney; s. of Andrew Hunter Craig and Mary Jane Parker; m. Veronica Bryden-Brown 1948; three s. one d.; ed. Univ. of Sydney and Univ. Coll. London; Capt., Australian Imperial Force 1941–44; lecturer in Chem., Univ. of Sydney 1944–46, Prof. of Physical Chem. 1952–56; Turner and Newall Research Fellow 1946–49; lecturer in Chem., Univ. Coll. London 1949–52, Prof. 1956–67, Visiting Prof. 1968–; Prof. of Chem., Australian Nat. Univ. 1967–85, Prof. Emer. 1985–, Dean, Research School of Chem. 1970–73, 1977–81; Firth Visiting Prof., Univ. of Sheffield 1973; Visiting Prof., Univ. Coll. Cardiff 1975–89; Visiting Foreign Prof., Univ. of Bologna 1984; part-time mem. Exec. CSIRO 1980–85; Pres. Australian Acad. of Science 1990–94; Hon. D.Sc. (Sydney), (Bologna); Hon. F.R.S.C.; Fellow, Univ. Coll. London; H. G. Smith Memorial Medal, Leighton Medal. *Publications:* Excitons in Molecular Crystals—Theory and Applications (co-author) 1968, Molecular Quantum Electrodynamics: An Introduction to Radiation-Molecule Interactions (co-author) 1984; original papers on chemistry in scientific journals. *Leisure interest:* tennis. *Address:* 199 Dryandra Street, O'Connor, A.C.T. 2602, Australia.

CRAIG, George; American publishing executive; Dir. Production, Honeywell Computers Scotland 1965–74; Vice-Chair. and Group Man. Dir. William Collins, U.K. 1974–87; Pres. and C.E.O. Harper & Row Publrs. Inc. (now HarperCollins Publs.), New York 1987–96; mem. Bd. of Dirs. The News Corpn. Ltd.; mem. Editorial Advisory Bd. Publrs. Weekly Int. *Address:* c/o HarperCollins Publishers, 10 East 53rd Street, New York, NY 10022, U.S.A. *Telephone:* (212) 207-7000. *Fax:* (212) 207-7759.

CRAIG, Ian Jonathan David, PH.D.; British astrophysicist; b. 30 Aug. 1950, Sheffield; s. of Ronald W. Craig and Beatrice I. Craig; m. Fiona M. Jardine 1979; one s. one d.; ed. Chesterfield Coll. of Tech. and Westfield and Univ. Colls. London; Research Fellow, Dept. of Astronomy, Univ. of Glasgow 1974–76, 1977–79; Research Assoc. Inst. for Plasma Research, Stanford Univ. 1976–77; lecturer in Math. Univ. of Waikato, N.Z. 1979–85, Sr. Lecturer 1985–93, Assoc. Prof. 1993–; research astronomer, Inst. for Astronomy, Univ. of Hawaii 1990–91; guest investigator on Skylab 1977; mem. Int. Astronomical Union. *Publications include:* Inverse Problems in Astronomy—A Guide to Inversion Strategies For Remotely Sensed Data (with J. C. Brown) 1986. *Leisure interests:* cycling, swimming, skiing, windsurfing; wood: growing it, working it and burning it. *Address:* Department of Mathematics, University of Waikato, Private Bag, Hamilton (Office); 25 Cranwell Place, Hamilton, New Zealand (Home).

CRAIG, Larry Edwin, B.A.; American politician; b. 20 July 1945, Council, Ida.; s. of Elvin Craig and Dorothy Craig; m. Suzanne Thompson 1983; two s. one d.; ed. Univ. of Idaho and George Washington Univ.; farmer, rancher, Midvale area, Ida.; mem. Ida. Farm Bureau 1965–79; mem. N.R.A., Future Farmers of America; Pres. Young Republican League, Ida. 1976–77; mem. Ida. Republican Exec. Cttee. 1976–78; mem. Ida. Senate 1974–80; mem. 97th–100th Congresses from 1st Dist. of Ida. 1981–91; Senator from Idaho 1991–; Republican. *Leisure interest:* gardening. *Address:* United States Senate, 313 Hart Senate Building, Washington, DC 20510, U.S.A.

CRAIG, Mary, M.A.; British author and broadcaster; b. 2 July 1928, St. Helens, Lancs.; d. of William Joseph Clarkson and Anne Mary Clarkson; m. Francis John Craig 1952 (died 1995); four s. (one deceased); ed. Notre Dame Convent, St. Helens, Liverpool Univ., St. Anne's Coll., Oxford Univ.; N.-W. Organizer, Sue Ryder Trust 1962–68; TV Critic, Catholic Herald 1971–76; presenter and features writer (freelance) with BBC Radio 1969–77; interviewer, Thames TV, Southern TV (freelance); freelance journalist and book reviewer; The Christopher Book Award (for Blessings), U.S.A. 1979, John Harriott Award 1993, and other awards; Officer's Cross of Order of Polonia Restituta 1987. *Publications:* Longford 1978, Woodruff at Random 1978, Blessings 1979, Man from a Far Country 1979, Candles in the Dark 1983, The Crystal Spirit 1986, Spark from Heaven 1988, Tears of Blood: A Cry for Tibet 1992, Kundun: The Dalai Lama, His Family and His Times 1997, The Last Freedom: A Journal 1997; *for children:* Pope John Paul II 1982, Mother Teresa 1984, Lech Wałęsa 1989. *Leisure interests:* reading modern history and biography, logic puzzles, listening to music, travel. *Address:* c/o Peters Fraser and Dunlop, 503/4 The Chambers, Chelsea Harbour, London, SW10 0XF, England. *Telephone:* 0171-344 1000.

CRAIG, Michael; British actor; b. 1928 India; appeared in The Homecoming, New York 1967–68; frequent appearances on stage in Australia; actor and scriptwriter for TV plays and films in Australia; TV appearances in U.K. *Films include:* The Love Lottery, Passage Home, The Black Tents, To the Night, Eyewitness, House of Secrets, High Tide at Noon, Campbell's Kingdom, The Silent Enemy, Nor the Moon by Night, The Angry Silence, Doctor in Love, The Mysterious Island, Payroll, No My Darling Daughter, A Life for Ruth, The Iron Maiden, Captive City, Summer Flight, Of a Thousand Delights, Life at the Top, Modesty Blaise, Funny Girl, Royal Hunt of the Sun, Twinky, Country Dance, Royal Hunt of the Sun, The Second Mrs Anderson, Inn of the Damned, A Sporting Proposition, The Irishman, Turkey Shoot, Stanley, The Timeless Land, Appointment with Death. *Address:* c/o Shanahans, P.O. Box 478, Kings Cross, Sydney, N.S.W. 2033, Australia.

CRAIG-MARTIN, Michael, M.F.A.; Irish artist; b. 28 Aug. 1941, Dublin; s. of Paul F. Craig-Martin and Rhona Gargan Craig-Martin; m. Janice Hashey 1963 (divorced); one d.; ed. Yale Univ.; lecturer British Acad. of Art 1966–69; artist in residence King's Coll., Cambridge 1970–72; sr. lecturer Goldsmith's Coll., Univ. of London 1974–88, Millard Prof. of Fine Art 1994–; Trustee Tate Gallery 1989–99. *Exhibitions include:* "The New Art", Hayward Gallery, London 1972, Retrospective 1968–1989, Whitechapel Art Gallery, London, 1989, "Always Now", Kunstverein, Hannover 1998. *Address:* c/o Waddington Galleries, 11 Cork Street, London, W1X 1PD, England. *Telephone:* 0171-437 8611. *Fax:* 0171-734 4146.

CRAIG OF RADLEY, Baron (Life Peer) cr. 1991, of Helhoughton in the County of Norfolk; **Marshal of the R.A.F. David Brownrigg Craig,** G.C.B., O.B.E., M.A.; British air force officer; b. 17 Sept. 1929; s. of Maj. Francis Brownrigg Craig and Olive Craig; m. Elizabeth June Derenburg 1955; one s. one d.; ed. Radley Coll. and Lincoln Coll., Oxford; commissioned in R.A.F. 1951, Commanding Officer R.A.F. Cranwell 1968–70; ADC to The Queen 1969–71; Dir. Plans and Operations, HQ Far East Command 1970–71, Commanding Officer R.A.F. Akrotiri 1972–73, ACAS (Ops) Ministry of

Defence 1975–78, Air Officer Commanding No. 1 Group R.A.F. Strike Command 1978–80, Vice-Chief of the Air Staff 1980–82, Air Officer, C.-in-C., R.A.F. Strike Command and C.-in-C. U.K. Forces 1982–85, Chief of Air Staff 1985–88, Chief of Defence Staff 1988–91; Air ADC to The Queen 1985–88; Chair. Council of King Edward VII Hosp. for Officers 1998–; Deputy Chair. R.A.F. Benevolent Fund 1996–; mem. House of Lords Select Cttee. on Science and Tech. 1993–; Hon. Fellow Lincoln Coll. Oxford 1984. *Leisure interests:* fishing, shooting, golf. *Address:* c/o House of Lords, London, SW1A 0PW, England.

CRAIK, Fergus Ian Muirden, PH.D., F.R.S.C.; British/Canadian professor of psychology; b. 17 April 1935, Edinburgh; s. of George Craik and Frances Crabbe; m. Anne Catherall 1961; one s. one d.; ed. George Watson's Boys' Coll. Edinburgh and Univs. of Edinburgh and Liverpool; mem. scientific staff, MRC Unit for Research on Occupational Aspects of Ageing, Univ. of Liverpool 1960–65; lecturer in Psychology, Birkbeck Coll. London 1965–71; Assoc. Prof. then Prof. of Psychology, Univ. of Toronto 1971–, Chair. Dept. of Psychology 1985–90; Fellow, Center for Advanced Study in Behavioral Sciences, Stanford Univ. 1982–83; Killam Research Fellowship 1982–84; Guggenheim Fellowship 1982–83; Fellow, Soc. of Experimental Psychologists, Canadian Psychological Asscn., American Psychological Asscn.; D. O. Hebb Award; William James Fellow Award. *Publications:* Levels of Processing in Human Memory (ed. with L. S. Cermak) 1979, Aging and Cognitive Processes (ed. with S. Trehub) 1982, Varieties of Memory and Consciousness (ed. with H. L. Roediger III) 1989, The Handbook of Aging and Cognition (ed. with T. A. Salthouse) 1992. *Leisure interests:* reading, walking, tennis, music. *Address:* Department of Psychology, University of Toronto, 100 St. George Street, Toronto, Ont., M5S 1A1, Canada. *Telephone:* (416) 978-7815. *Fax:* (416) 978-4811.

CRAINZ, Franco, M.D., F.R.C.O.G.; Italian university professor; b. 18 May 1913, Rome; s. of the late Silvio Crainz and Ada Fanelli Crainz; ed. Rome Univ.; Prof. and Head of Dept., School for Midwives, Novara 1956–64; Prof. and Head, Dept. of Obstetrics and Gynaecology, Univ. of Cagliari 1964–66, of Messina 1966–67, of Bari 1967–72; Prof. of Obstetrics and Gynaecology, Rome Univ. 1972–88, Prof. Emer. 1988–; Vice-Pres. Italian Soc. of the History of Medicine; Hon. Pres. Italian Soc. of Obstetrics and Gynaecology (Pres. 1977–80); Hon. mem. European Soc. of Gynaecology and of the Austrian, Portuguese, Romanian, Spanish and Swiss socs., Corresp. mem. German Soc. *Publications:* An Obstetric Tragedy–The Case of H.R.H. the Princess Charlotte Augusta 1977, The Birth of an Heir to the 5th Duke of Devonshire 1989, Dr. Matthew Baillie 1995; over 100 medical papers. *Leisure interests:* history of medicine, music, archaeology, history, gardening. *Address:* Via P. Mascagni 124, 00199, Rome, Italy. *Telephone:* (06) 8610433.

CRAM, Donald James, M.S., PH.D.; American professor of chemistry; b. 22 April 1919, Chester, Vt.; s. of Joanna Shelley and William Moffet Cram; m. Jane Maxwell 1969; ed. Rollins College Fla., Univ. of Nebraska and Harvard Univ.; Researcher, Merck & Co., Rahway, N.J. 1942–45; Instructor, American Chem. Soc. Fellowship, Univ. of Calif., L.A. 1947–48, Asst. Prof. 1948–51, Assoc. Prof. 1951–56, Prof. 1956–90, Prof. Emer. 1990–, S. Winstein Prof. 1985–95; mem. N.A.S., American Acad. of Arts and Sciences; Dr. h.c. (Uppsala Univ., Sweden) 1977, (Univ. of S. Calif.) 1983, (Rollins Coll.) 1988, (Neb.) 1989, (W. Ont.) 1989, (Sheffield, England) 1991; A.C.S. Cope Award in Organic Chem. 1974, McCoy Award for Contribs. to Chem. 1965, 1975; Calif. Scientist of the Year 1974; several American Chemical Soc. Awards, including Roger Adams Award 1985, Gibbs Medal (Chicago Section) 1985, Tolman Medal (Southern Calif. Section) 1985, shared Nobel Prize in Chemistry 1987, Seaborg Award 1989, N.A.S. Award in the Chemical Sciences 1993, Nat. Medal of Science 1993. *Publications:* Organic Chemistry (with Prof. George Hammond, Prof. James Hendrickson and Prof. Stanley Pine), Elements of Organic Chemistry (with Prof. John Richards and Prof. George Hammond), Essence of Organic Chemistry (textbook with Jane M. Cram) 1977, From Design to Discovery 1990, Molecular Container Chemistry (co-author) 1994, monograph Carbanions, 424 research papers in Journal of American Chemical Society and other chemical journals from 1943. *Leisure interests:* tennis, surfing, skiing, guitar. *Address:* Department of Chemistry, University of California, 405 Hilgard Avenue, Los Angeles, CA 90024 (Office); (1 May to 1 Nov.) 25 Monarch Bay Drive, Dana Point, CA 92629; (1 Nov. to 1 May) 72935 Carriage Trail Drive, Palm Desert, CA 92260, U.S.A. (Homes). *Telephone:* (310) 825-1562 (Office); (714) 499-6980 (Dana Point), (760) 568-0389 (Palm Desert) (Homes). *Fax:* (714) 499-6980 (Dana Point), (760) 568-0389 (Palm Desert) (Homes).

CRAMER, Jan or Mars; Netherlands economist and statistician; b. 26 April 1928, The Hague; s. of P. J. S. Cramer and A. P. van Deventer; m. Mathilde van Gogh 1953; four c.; ed. Univ. of Amsterdam; Cen. Planning Bureau 1953–56, Dept. of Applied Econs., Cambridge 1956–59; CREDOC, Paris 1959–62; Prof. of Econometrics, Univ. of Amsterdam 1962–95, Dir. Inst. of Econ. Research 1985–92, Dean Faculty of Econs. and Econometrics 1992–95. *Publications:* Empirical Econometrics 1968, Econometric Applications of Maximum Likelihood Methods 1986, The Logit Model 1991. *Leisure interests:* reading, gardening. *Address:* Baambrugse Zuwe 194, 3645 AM Vinkeveen, The Netherlands. *Telephone:* (0294) 29 30 60. *Fax:* (0294) 29 18 99.

CRAMOND, William Alexander, A.O., O.B.E., M.D., F.R.C.PSYCH., F.R.A.N.Z.C.P., F.R.A.C.P., F.R.S.E.; British/Australian professor of clinical psychiatry; b. 2 Oct. 1920, Aberdeen; s. of W. J. Cramond, M.B.E. and May Battisby; m. Bertine J. C. Mackintosh 1949; one s. one d.; ed. Robert Gordon's Coll. Aberdeen and Univ. of Aberdeen; Physician Supt., Woodilee Hosp. Glasgow 1955–61; Dir. of Mental Health, S. Australia 1961–65; Foundation Prof. of Mental Health, Univ. of Adelaide 1963–71; Prin. Medical Officer in Mental Health, Scottish Home and Health Dept. 1971–72; Foundation Dean, Faculty of Medicine, Univ. of Leicester 1972–75; Prin. and Vice-Chancellor, Univ. of Stirling 1975–80; Dir. of Mental Health, Health Comm. N.S.W. 1980–83; Prof. of Clinical Psychiatry, Univ. of Sydney 1980–83, The Flinders Univ. of S. Australia 1983–92; Emer. Prof. 1993–; Chair. Bd. of Dirs. S.A. Mental Health Services 1993–95; Hon. D. Univ. (Stirling). *Leisure interests:* reading, theatre. *Address:* 28 Tynte Street, North Adelaide, South Australia 5006. *Telephone:* (08) 82671600.

CRANBORNE, Viscount, Rt. Hon. Robert Michael James Cecil, P.C., D.L.; British politician; b. 30 Sept. 1946; s. of 6th Marquess of Salisbury; m. Hanna Anne Stirling 1970; two s. three d.; ed. Eton Coll., Oxford Univ.; M.P. for Dorset S. 1979–87; mem. House of Lords 1992–; Parl. Under-Sec. of State for Defence 1992–94; Lord Privy Seal 1994–97; Shadow Leader of House of Lords 1997–98; Pres. Herts. Agric. Soc. 1998–; D.L. Dorset 1987; Conservative. *Address:* Manor House, Cranborne, Wimborne, Dorset, BH21 5PP, England.

CRANBROOK, 5th Earl of (cr. 1892); **Gathorne Gathorne-Hardy,** M.A., PH.D., C.BIOL., D.L.; British biologist; b. 20 June 1933, London; m. Caroline Jarvis 1967; two s. one d.; ed. Eton Coll., Corpus Christi Coll. Cambridge and Univ. of Birmingham; lecturer, Sr. lecturer in Zoology, Univ. of Malaya 1961–70; Ed. Ibis (journal of British Ornithologists' Union) 1973–80; mem. Royal Comm. on Environmental Pollution 1981–92; Trustee, Natural History Museum 1982–86; mem. Natural Environment Research Council 1982–88; mem. Nature Conservancy Council 1990–91; Chair. English Nature 1991–98, ENTRUST 1996–; Dir. Anglian Water (non-exec.) 1989–98; mem. Broads Authority, Harwich Haven Authority 1988–98; mem. Bd. Foundation for European Environmental Policy 1987–98, Chair. 1990–98; Vice-Pres. Nat. Soc. for Clean Air and Environmental Protection; also partner in family farming business in Suffolk. *Publications include:* Mammals of Borneo 1965, Riches of the Wild: Mammals of South East Asia 1987, Belalong: a tropical rain forest (jtly.) 1994, Wonders of Nature in South East Asia 1996. *Address:* ENTRUST, Acre House, 2 Market Square, Sale, M33 7WZ, England. *Telephone:* 0161-972 0044. *Fax:* 0161-972 0055.

CRANDALL, Robert Lloyd, B.A.; American business executive; b. 6 Dec. 1935, Westerly, R.I.; s. of Lloyd Evans Crandall and Virginia (née Beard) Crandall; m. Margaret Jan Schmults 1957; two s. one d.; ed. William and Mary Coll., Univ. of Rhode Island, Wharton School, Univ. of Pennsylvania; Dir. of Credit and Collections, then Vice-Pres. Data Services TWA 1967–73; C.O.O. 1973–85 and Sr. Vice-Pres. (Finance), American Airlines 1973–74, Sr. Vice-Pres. Marketing 1974–80, Dir. 1976–, Pres. 1980–95, Chair., CEO Jan. 1985–; Pres., Chair. and C.E.O. AMR Corpn. 1985–98; Dir. of several cos. *Leisure interests:* skiing, tennis, running, reading. *Address:* c/o AMR Corporation, 4333 Amon Carter Boulevard, Fort Worth, TX 76155, U.S.A.

CRANE, Peter Robert, PH.D., F.R.S.; British professor of paleontology; b. 18 July 1954, Kettering; s. of Walter Robert Crane and Dorothy Mary Crane (née Mills); m. Elinor Margaret Hamer 1986; one s. one d.; ed. Reading Univ.; lecturer Dept. of Botany, Reading Univ. 1978–82; post-doctoral research scholar, Dept. of Biology, Ind. Univ. 1981–82; Curator Dept. of Geology, The Field Museum, Chicago 1982–92, Vice-Pres. Center for Evolutionary and Environmental Biology 1992–93, Vice-Pres. Academic Affairs and Dir. The Field Museum 1994–; Bicentenary Medal, Linnean Soc. 1984. *Publication:* The Origin and Early Diversification of Land Plants (with P. Kenrick). *Address:* The Field Museum, Academic Affairs, Roosevelt Road at Lake Shore Drive, Chicago, IL 60625, U.S.A. *Telephone:* (312) 922-9410 ext. 559. *Fax:* (312) 360-9858.

CRANFIELD, Rev. Charles Ernest Burland, M.A., F.B.A.; British professor of theology; b. 13 Sept. 1915, London; s. of Charles Ernest Cranfield and Beatrice Mary Cranfield (née Tubbs); m. Ruth Elizabeth Gertrude Bole 1953; two d.; ed. Mill Hill School, Jesus Coll., Cambridge and Wesley House, Cambridge; research in Basle until outbreak of Second World War; Probationer in Methodist Church 1939; ordained 1941; Minister in Shoeburyness 1940–42; Chaplain to the Forces (from end of hostilities worked with German Prisoners of War, was first staff chaplain to P.O.W. Directorate in War Office) 1942–46; Minister in Cleethorpes 1946–50; admitted to Presbyterian Church of England (now part of United Reformed Church) 1954; Lecturer in Theology, Univ. of Durham 1950–62, Sr. Lecturer 1962–66, Reader 1966–78, Prof. of Theology (personal) 1978–80, Emer. Prof. 1980–; Jt. Gen. Ed., new series of International Critical Commentary 1966–; Hon. D.D. (Aberdeen) 1980; Burkitt Medal for Biblical Studies 1989. *Publications:* The First Epistle of Peter 1950, The Gospel according to Saint Mark 1959, I and II Peter and Jude 1960, A Critical and Exegetical Commentary on the Epistle to the Romans, Vol. 1 1975, Vol. 2 1979, Romans: a Shorter Commentary 1985, The Bible and Christian Life: a Collection of Essays 1985, If God Be For Us: a Collection of Sermons 1985, The Apostles' Creed: a Faith to Live By 1993, On Romans and Other Essays 1998. *Address:* 30 Western Hill, Durham City, Durham, DH1 4RL, England. *Telephone:* (0191) 3843096.

CRANSTON, Alan; American politician; b. 19 June 1914, Palo Alto, Calif.; s. of William MacGregor and Carol (née Dixon) Cranston; m. 1st Geneva

McMath 1940 (divorced 1977); two s.; m. 2nd Norma Weintraub 1978 (divorced 1986); ed. Mount View High School, Los Altos, Pomona Coll., Univ. of Mexico, and Stanford Univ.; Int. News Service, England, Germany, Italy, Ethiopia 1937–38; Chief, Foreign Language Div., Office of War Information 1940–44; U.S. Army 1944–45; Nat. Pres. United World Federalists 1949–52; Pres. Calif. Democratic Council 1953–58; State Controller of Calif. 1958; re-elected 1962; business career in land investment and home construction; U.S. Senator from Calif. 1969–93; Chair. U.S.-Kyrgyz Business Council 1993–96 (Hon. Chair. 1997); Sr Int. Adviser, Schooner Capital Corpn., Boston, Mass. 1993–96; Democratic Whip in the Senate 1977–93. *Publications:* co-author The Big Story (play) 1940, The Killing of the Peace 1945, and numerous articles in newspapers and periodicals. *Leisure interests:* painting in oils, running. *Address:* 27080 W. Fremont Road, Los Altos, CA 94022, U.S.A.

CRAPO, Michael Dean, J.D., B.A.; American politician and lawyer; b. 20 May 1951, Idaho Falls; s. of George Lavelle Crapo and Melba (née Olsen) Crapo; m. Susan Diane Hasleton 1974; two s. three d.; ed. Brigham Young, Utah and Harvard Univs.; called to Bar Calif. 1977, Idaho 1979; law clerk to U.S. Court of Appeals San Diego 1977–78; assoc. attorney Gibson, Dunn & Crutcher 1978–79; attorney Holden, Kidwell, Hahn & Crapo 1979–92, partner 1983–92; mem. Idaho State Senate 1984–93, asst. majority leader 1987–88, Pres. Pro Tempore 1989–92; mem. U.S. House of Reps. from 2nd Idaho Dist. 1992–99; Senator from Idaho Jan. 1999–; mem. numerous cttees. and bds.; numerous awards; Republican. *Address:* U.S. Senate, Washington, DC 20510, U.S.A.

CRAVEN, Sir John Anthony, Kt., B.A.; Canadian/British merchant banker; b. 23 Oct. 1940; m. 2nd Jane Frances Stiles-Allen 1970; three s.; one s. one d. from 1st m.; ed. Michaelhouse, S. Africa, Jesus Coll., Cambridge, Queen's Univ., Kingston, Ont.; with Clarkson & Co., Toronto 1961–64, Wood Gundy Bankers 1964–67; Dir. S. G. Warburg & Co. 1967–73, Vice-Chair. 1979; Chief Exec. White Weld & Co. Ltd. 1973–78; Founder and Chair. Phoenix Securities Ltd. 1981–89; C.E.O. Morgan Grenfell Group 1987–89, Chair. 1989–97; mem. Bd. Man. Dirs. Deutsche Bank AG, Frankfurt 1990–96, Supervisory Bd. Société Générale de Surveillance Holding, Geneva 1989–98, (non-exec.) Tootal Group 1985–91, (non-exec.) Lonrho 1997–; Dir. Securities and Investment Bd. 1990–93; Dir. Rothmans Int. PLC 1991–; Dir (non-exec.) Reuters 1997–; mem. Ont. Inst. of Chartered Accountants, Canadian Inst. of Chartered Accountants. *Leisure interests:* hunting, shooting, skiing. *Address:* 20 Cheyne Walk, London, SW3 5RA, England. *Telephone:* 0171-352 9104. *Fax:* 0171-349 0592.

CRAWFORD, Bryce, Jr., PH.D.; American professor of chemistry; b. 27 Nov. 1914, New Orleans, La.; s. of Bryce Low Crawford and Clara Hall Crawford; m. Ruth Raney 1940; two s. one d.; ed. Stanford Univ.; Nat. Research Council Fellow, Harvard Univ. 1937–39; Instructor, Yale Univ. 1939–40; Asst. Prof., Univ. of Minn. 1940–43, Assoc. Prof. 1943–46, Prof. 1946–82, Regents' Prof. 1982–85, Prof. Emer. 1985–, Chair. Dept. of Chem. 1955–60, Dean, Graduate School 1960–72; Fulbright Prof., Oxford Univ. 1951, Tokyo Univ. 1966; Ed. Journal of Physical Chem. 1970–80; Chair. Council of Graduate Schools 1962–63; Pres. Asscn. of Graduate Schools 1970, Graduate Record Examinations Bd. 1968–72; mem. N.A.S. (Council 1975–78), Home Sec. 1979–87; mem. American Acad. of Arts and Sciences 1977; American Chem. Soc. (Bd. of Dirs. 1969–77), Coblentz Soc., American Philosophical Soc.; Fellow, American Physical Soc.; Presidential Certificate of Merit 1946; Guggenheim Fellowships 1950, 1972; Fulbright Professorship 1951, 1966; Minn. Award, American Chem. Soc. 1969, Pittsburgh Spectroscopy Award 1977, Ellis Lippincott Award 1978, Priestley Medal 1982. *Publications:* Articles in scientific journals. *Address:* Dept. of Chemistry, University of Minnesota, 207 Pleasant Street SE, Minneapolis, MN 55455 (Office); 1545 Branston, St. Paul, MN 55108, U.S.A. (Home). *Telephone:* (612) 625-5394.

CRAWFORD, Cindy; American fashion model; b. 1966; m. 1st Richard Gere (q.v.) 1991 (divorced); m. 2nd Rande Gerber 1998; promotes Revlon (cosmetics) and Pepsi Cola; presents own fashion show on MTV (cable and satellite); has appeared on numerous covers for magazines; model for numerous fashion designers; has released several exercise videos. *Film:* Fair Game 1995. *Publication:* Cindy Crawford's Basic Face 1996. *Address:* c/o Wolf-Kasteler, 132 S. Rodeo Drive, Suite 300, Beverly Hills, CA 90212, U.S.A.

CRAWFORD, Sir Frederick William, Kt., D.L., D.SC., F.ENG., F.I.E.E.E., F.I.E.E., F.INST.P., F.I.M.A.; British scientist; b. 28 July 1931, Birmingham; s. of William Crawford and Victoria Maud Crawford; m. Béatrice Madeleine Jacqueline Hutter 1963; one s. (deceased) one d.; ed. George Dixon Grammar School, Birmingham, Univ. of London, Univ. of Liverpool; Research Trainee, J. Lucas Ltd. 1948–52; scientist, Nat. Coal Bd. Mining Research Establishment 1956–57; Sr. Lecturer in Electrical Eng., Birmingham Coll. of Advanced Tech. 1958–59; Stanford Univ., Calif 1959–82; Prof. (Research), Inst. for Plasma Research 1964–67, Assoc. Prof. 1967–69, Prof. 1969–82, Chair. 1974–80; Dir. Centre for Interdisciplinary Research 1973–77; Visiting Prof., Math. Inst. 1977–78, Visiting Fellow, St. Catherine's Coll., Oxford 1977–78, 1996–97; Vice-Chancellor, Aston Univ. 1980–96; Chair., U.S. Nat. Comm., Union Radio-Scientifique Internationale 1975–78, Chair. Int. Comm. 1978–81, U.K. Rep. 1982–84; Chair. Int. Scientific Cttee., Int. Conf. on Phenomena in Ionised Gases 1979–81; mem. U.S.-U.K. Educ. Comm. 1981–84, British North-American Cttee. 1987–, Franco-British Council 1987–98; Chair. Birmingham Civic Soc. 1983–88, Criminal Cases Review Comm. 1996–; High Sheriff, W. Midlands Co. 1995; Freeman, City of London 1986; Master, Worshipful Co. of Engineers 1996; Hon. Bencher, Inner Temple 1996; Hon. D.Sc. (Buckingham) 1996. *Publications:* numerous papers on plasma physics in scientific books and journals. *Address:* 47 Charlbury Road, Oxford, OX2 6UX, England.

CRAWFORD, James Richard, D.PHIL.; Australian professor of international law; b. 14 Nov. 1948, Adelaide; s. of James Crawford and Josephine Bond; m. 1st Marisa Luigina Ballini 1971 (divorced 1990); m. 2nd Patricia Hyndman 1992 (divorced 1998); four d.; ed. Brighton High School and Univs. of Adelaide and Oxford; lecturer, Sr. lecturer, Reader, Prof. of Law, Univ. of Adelaide 1974–86; mem. Australian Law Reform Comm. 1982–84, part-time 1984–90; Challis Prof. of Int. Law, Univ. of Sydney 1986–92, Dean, Faculty of Law 1990–92; Whewell Prof. of Int. Law, Univ. of Cambridge 1992–; Dir. Lanterpacht Research Centre for Int. Law 1997–; barrister, Sr. Counsel (N.S.W., Australia) 1997; mem. U.N. Int. Law Comm. 1992. *Publications:* The Creation of States in International Law 1979, The Rights of Peoples (ed. 1988), Australian Courts of Law (3rd edn.) 1993. *Leisure interests:* reading, cricket, walking. *Address:* Lanterpacht Research Centre for International Law, 5 Cranmer Road, Cambridge, CB3 8AL, England. *Telephone:* (01223) 335358. *Fax:* (01223) 311668.

CRAWFORD, Michael, O.B.E.; British actor and singer; b. (as Michael Dumbell-Smith) 19 Jan. 1942; ed. St. Michael's Coll., Bexley, Oakfield School, Dulwich; actor 1955–; films for Children's Film Foundation; hundreds of radio broadcasts; appeared in original productions of Noyes Fludde and Let's Make an Opera by Benjamin Britten; has toured in U.K., U.S.A. and Australia. *Stage Roles include:* Travelling Light 1965, the Anniversary 1966, No Sex Please, We're British 1971, Billy 1974, Same Time, Next Year 1976, Flowers for Algernon 1979, Barnum 1981–83, 1984–86, Phantom of the Opera, London 1986–87, Broadway 1988, Los Angeles 1989. *Films include:* Soap Box Derby 1950, Blow Your Own Trumpet 1954, Two Living One Dead 1962, The War Lover 1963, Two Left Feet 1963, The Knack 1965, A Funny Thing Happened on the Way to the Forum 1966, The Jokers 1966, How I Won the War 1967, Hello Dolly 1969, The Games 1969, Hello Goodbye 1970, Alice's Adventures in Wonderland 1972, Condor Man 1980. *TV appearances include:* Sir Francis Drake (series) 1962, Some Mothers Do 'Ave 'Em (several series), Chalk and Cheese (series), Sorry (play) 1979; Tony Award 1988. *Address:* c/o ICM Ltd., Oxford House, 76 Oxford Street, London, W1R 1RB, England. *Telephone:* 0171-636 6565.

CRAWFORD, Michael Hewson, M.A., F.B.A.; British university teacher; b. 7 Dec. 1939, Twickenham, Middx.; s. of Brian Hewson Crawford and Margarethe Bettina Crawford (née Nagel); ed. St. Paul's School, London and Oriel Coll. Oxford; Research Fellow, Christ's Coll. Cambridge 1964–69; Univ. Lecturer, Cambridge 1969–86; Jt. Dir. Excavations of Fregellae 1980–86, Valpolcevera Project 1987–94, Velleia Project 1994–95, S. Martino Project 1996–; Visiting Prof. Pavia Univ. 1983, Ecole Normale Supérieure, Paris 1984, Padua Univ. 1986, Sorbonne, Paris 1989, San Marino Univ. 1989, Milan Univ. 1990, L'Aquila Univ. 1990, Pavia Univ. 1992, Ecole des Hautes Etudes, Paris 1997; Prof. of Ancient History, Univ. Coll. London 1986–; Foreign mem. Istituto Lombardo; mem. Academia Europaea. *Publications:* Roman Republican Coinage 1974, The Roman Republic 1978, La Moneta in Grecia e a Roma 1981, Sources for Ancient History 1983, Coinage and Money under the Roman Republic 1985, L'Impero romano e la struttura economica e sociale delle province 1986, Medals and Coins from Budé to Mommsen (with C. Ligota and J. B. Trapp) 1990, Antonio Agustín between Renaissance and Counter-reform 1993, Roman Statutes (Ed.) 1995. *Address:* Department of History, University College London, Gower Street, London, WC1E 6BT, England. *Telephone:* 0171-380 7396.

CRAWFORD, William Avery; American diplomatist; b. 14 Jan. 1915, New York; s. of John Raymond and Pauline Avery Crawford; m. 1st Barbara Gardner 1940; two s. three d.; m. 2nd Gudrun Hadell 1980; ed. Haverford Coll., Haverford, Pa., Centro de Estudios Históricos, Madrid, Ecole Libre des Sciences Politiques, Paris, Harvard Coll., Columbia Univ. and Nat. War Coll., Washington, D.C.; Foreign Service 1941–, Havana 1941–44, Dept. of State 1944–45, Moscow 1945–47, Dept. of State 1947–50, Paris 1950–54, Dept. of State 1954–57, Prague 1957–59; Dir. Office of Research and Analysis for Sino-Soviet Bloc, Dept. of State 1959–61; Minister to Romania 1961–64, Amb. 1964–65; Special Asst. for Int. Affairs to Supreme Allied Commdr., Europe, NATO 1965–67; Sr. Foreign Service Insp. 1967–70; Editorial Dir. Scholarly Resources Inc. 1970–73; Dir. WJS, Inc. 1974–83; Dir. Foreign Bondholders Protective Council, Inc. 1975–92. *Address:* 9707 Old Georgetown Road, Apt. 1514, Bethesda, MD 20814, U.S.A. *Telephone*: (301) 897-0307.

CRAWLEY, Frederick William, C.B.E., F.C.I.B.; British banker; b. 10 June 1926, London; s. of William Crawley and Elsie Crawley; m. Ruth E. Jungman 1951; two d.; entered Lloyds Bank 1942, Chief Accountant 1969, Asst. Gen. Man. 1973, Exec. Dir. Lloyds Bank Int. 1975, Asst. Chief Gen. Man. 1977, Deputy Chief Gen. Man. 1978–82, 1983–84, Vice-Chair. and C.E.O. Lloyds Bank Calif. 1982–83, Chief Gen. Man. Lloyds Bank PLC 1984–85, Deputy Group Chief Exec. 1985–87; Chair. Black Horse Agencies Ltd. 1985–88; Deputy Chair. Girobank PLC 1991, Chair. 1991–94; Chair. Betta Stores PLC 1990–92, Alliance & Leicester Bldg. Soc. 1991–94, Legal and Gen. Recovery Investment Trust PLC 1994–98; Dir. Lloyds Bank 1984–88, Lloyds

Devt. Capital Ltd. 1987–92, FS Assurance Ltd. 1988–89, FS Investment Mans. Ltd. 1988–89, FS Investment Services Ltd. 1988–89, Barratt Devts. Ltd. 1988–96, Alliance & Leicester Estate Agents Ltd. 1988–92, Legal and Gen. Bank Ltd. 1997–; Consultant Anglo-Airlines Ltd. 1988–92; Hon. Treas. R.A.F. Benevolent Fund 1988–, Deputy Chair. R.A.F. Benevolent Fund Enterprises Ltd. 1988–; Fellow St. Andrews Man. Inst. 1996–97. *Leisure interests:* aviation, shooting, photography. *Address:* 4 The Hexagon, Fitzroy Park, London, N6 6HR, England. *Telephone:* 0181-341 2279.

CRAXI, Bettino; Italian politician, journalist and writer; b. 24 Feb. 1934, Milan; m. Anna Maria Moncini 1959; one s. one d.; active in Socialist Youth Movement and working on socialist daily and scientific review during 1950s; promoted "autonomist tendency" within Socialist Youth Movement, worked on Energie nuove (publ. of autonomist tendency) 1956–; Pres. Nat. Union of Students 1957; mem. Cen. Cttee. of Italian Socialist Party (PSI) 1957; mem. Community Council of Milan 1960–70; Pres. Inst. for Science of Public Admin. 1964; Provincial Sec. Milan Fed. of PSI and mem. PSI Nat. Exec. 1965; mem. Chamber of Deputies 1968; faced corruption charges 1994; sentenced to eight and a half years in prison for fraud July 1994, in absentia; sentenced to a further 18 years imprisonment for corruption in absentia 1996; ordered to stand trial with Silvio Berlusconi (q.v.) 1996; on trial for siphoning cash from Third World projects Nov. 1996; sentenced to four years' imprisonment in absentia and fined 8 million lire July 1997 for breaking political party funding laws; Deputy Sec. PSI 1970–76; Gen. Sec. Socialist Party of Italy (PSI) 1976–93; Vice-Pres. Socialist Int. 1977; Prime Minister of Italy 1983–87. *Publications:* Socialismo e realtà 1973, Nove lettere da Praga 1973, Socialismo da Santiago a Praga 1976, Costruire il futuro 1977; co-author Inequality in the World 1977 (contributions by Willy Brandt, q.v., Felipe González, q.v., Carlos Andrés Pérez, q.v., Léopold Sédar Senghor, q.v.). *Leisure interests:* Italian history, especially Garibaldi. Lives in Tunisia.

CRAXTON, John Leith, R.A.; British artist; b. 3 Oct. 1922; s. of late Harold Craxton and Essie Craxton; ed. Betteshanger, Kent, Westminster School of Art, London, Cen. School of Art, London, Goldsmiths' Coll., London; has designed sets for Royal Ballet, London; solo exhbns. include Leicester Galleries, London 1944, 1951, 1954, 1956, 1961, 1966, St. George's Gallery, London 1945, Galerie Gasser, Zürich 1946, British Council, Athens 1946, 1949, 1985, Mayor Gallery, London 1950, Crane Gallery, Manchester 1955, Whitechapel Art Gallery 1967, Hamet Gallery, London 1971, Christopher Hull Gallery, London 1982, 1985, 1987, 1993, Chrysostomos Gallery, Hania, Crete 1985; works in Tate Gallery, London, Victoria and Albert Museum, London, British Museum, London, Gallery of Modern Art, Edin., Nat. Museum of Wales, Arts Council, British Council, British Govt. Picture Collection, Nat. Gallery, Melbourne, Metropolitan Museum, N.Y.; H.M. Consular Corresp., Hania, Crete. *Address:* 14 Kidderpore Avenue, London, NW3 7SU, England.

CREAN, Hon. Frank, B.A., B.COM.; Australian politician and accountant; b. 28 Feb. 1916, Hamilton, Victoria; s. of John and Alison Crean; m. Mary Isabella Findlay 1946; three s.; ed. state schools, Melbourne Univ.; Income Tax Assessor for ten years; mem. Victoria Legis. Ass. for Albert Park 1945–47, for Prahan 1949–51; M.P. for Melbourne Ports 1951–77; mem. Fed. Parl. Labor Party Exec. 1956–72; Deputy Leader 1975–76; mem. Privileges Cttee. 1967–77, Jt. Cttee. on Defence Forces Retirement Benefits Legislation 1970–72; Treas. 1972–74; Minister for Overseas Trade 1974–75; Deputy Prime Minister July-Nov. 1975; mem. several Parl. dels. abroad; Pres. Victoria Br., Australian Inst. for Int. Affairs 1983–86; Labor Party. *Publication:* Government and Politics (with W. Byrt) 1973. *Leisure interests:* walking, reading. *Address:* 31/27 Queens Road, Melbourne, 3004 Vic., Australia. *Telephone:* (03) 9867 7996.

CREAN, Simon, LL.B.; Australian trade union official; b. 26 Feb. 1949, Melbourne; s. of Frank Crean and Mary Crean; m. Carole Lamb 1973; two d.; ed. Middle Park Cen. School, Melbourne High School and Monash Univ.; Research Officer, Federated Storemen and Packers' Union of Australia 1970–74, Asst. Gen. Sec. 1974–79, Gen. Sec. 1979–85; Minister of Science and Tech. 1990–91, of Employment, Educ. and Training 1993–96; Man. Opposition Business, Shadow Minister for Industry and Regional Devt. 1996–; Pres. Australian Council of Trades Unions 1985–90; mem. House of Reps. (for Hotham, Vic.) 1990–; mem. Econ. Planning Advisory Council, Nat. Labor Consultative Council, ILO Governing Body, Qantas Bd., Transport Industry Advisory Council, Business Educ. Council. *Leisure interest:* tennis. *Address:* 401 Clayton Road, Clayton, Vic. 3168, Australia.

CREECH, Wyatt (W.B.), B.A.; New Zealand politician, accountant and vineyard developer; b. 1946, Oceanside, Calif., U.S.A.; m.; three c.; ed. Massey and Victoria Univs.; mem. Martinborough Council 1980–86; M.P. for Wairarapa 1988–; Minister of Revenue, Customs, in Charge of the Public Trust Office and responsible for Govt. Superannuation Fund 1990–91, Minister of Revenue, in Charge of the Public Trust Office and responsible for Govt. Superannuation Fund and Sr. Citizens, Assoc. Minister of Finance and Social Welfare 1991–93, Minister of Revenue and Employment, Deputy Minister of Finance 1993–96, Minister of Educ., for Courts, for Ministerial Services, and Leader of the House 1996–, Deputy Prime Minister 1998–; Deputy Leader Nat. Party; Chair. Cabinet Social Policy Cttee., Cabinet Legislation Cttee.; Nat. Party. *Address:* House of Representatives, Wellington, New Zealand.

CREELEY, Robert White, M.A.; American writer and professor of English; b. 21 May 1926, Arlington, Mass.; s. of Oscar Slade and Genevieve (Jules) Creeley; m. 1st Ann McKinnon 1946 (divorced 1955); two s. one d.; m. 2nd Bobbie Louise Hall 1957 (divorced 1976); three d.; m. 3rd Penelope Highton 1977; one s. one d.; ed. Univ. of New Mexico and Harvard Univ.; Instructor Black Mountain Coll. 1954–55; Visiting Lecturer Univ. of New Mexico, Albuquerque 1961–62, Lecturer in English 1963–66, Visiting Prof. 1968–69, 1978, 1979, 1980; lecturer Univ. of B.C., Vancouver 1962–63; Prof. of English, State Univ. of N.Y., Buffalo 1967–, Gray Prof. of Poetry and Letters 1978–89, Dir. Poetics Program 1991–92; Capen Prof. of Poetry and the Humanities 1989–; Visiting Prof., San Francisco State Coll. 1970–71; Bicentennial Chair. of American Studies, Helsinki Univ. 1988–89; Ed. Black Mountain Review 1954–57; American Field Service 1944–45; mem. American Acad. of Arts and Letters; D. H. Lawrence Fellow 1960, Guggenheim Fellow 1964, 1971; Rockefeller Grantee 1965; Hon. D.Litt. (Univ. of New Mexico) 1993; Levinson Prize of Poetry Magazine 1960, Blumenthal-Leviton Award of Poetry Magazine 1965, Union League Civic and Arts Foundation Prize, Poetry Magazine 1967, Shelley Memorial Award of Poetry Soc. of America 1981, Nat. Endowment for the Arts Grant in Writing 1982, DAAD Grant 1983, 1987, Leone D'Oro Premio Speciale 1985, Frost Medal, Poetry Soc. of America 1987, SUNY Distinguished Prof. 1989, State Poet of N.Y. 1989–91, Horst Bienek Lyric Prize (Munich) 1993, Lila Wallace-Reader's Digest Writers Award 1995. *Publications:* Le Fou 1952, The Immoral Proposition 1953, The Kind of Act of 1953, The Gold Diggers 1954, revised edn. 1965, All That is Lovely in Men 1955, If You 1956, The Whip 1957, A Form of Women 1959, For Love, Poems 1950–60 1962, The Island 1963, Words 1967, Numbers 1968, Pieces 1969, The Charm 1969, A Quick Graph 1970, The Finger 1970, St. Martins 1971, A Day Book 1972, Listen 1972, A Sense of Measure 1973, His Idea 1973, Contexts of Poetry 1973, Thirty Things 1974, Backwards 1975, Presences (with Marisol) 1976, Selected Poems 1976, Mabel: A Story 1976, Myself 1977, Hello 1978, Was That a Real Poem and Other Essays 1979, Corn Close 1979, Later 1979, Robert Creeley and Charles Olson: The Complete Correspondence, vols. 1 & 2, 1980, vol. 3 1981, vol. 4 1982, vol. 5 1983, vol. 6 1985, vols. 7 and 8 1987, vol. 9 1990, Mother's Voice 1981, Echoes 1982, Collected Poems 1945–75, 1983, Mirrors 1983, The Collected Prose 1984, Memory Gardens 1986, The Company 1988, Collected Essays 1989, Windows 1990, Autobiography 1990, Echoes 1994, So There, Poems 1976–1983 1998, Life & Death 1998; Edited: New American Story (with Donald M. Allen) 1965, The New Writing in the U.S.A. (with Donald M. Allen) 1967, Selected Writings of Charles Olson 1967, Whitman: Selected Poems 1972, The Essential Burns 1989, Selected Poems (revised) 1991, Selected Poems of Charles Olson (ed.) 1993, Tales out of School, Selected Interviews 1993. *Address:* Clemens 313, State University of New York, Buffalo, NY 14260, U.S.A. (Office). *Telephone:* (716) 645-2575 ext. 1018 (Office).

CREMONA, Hon. John Joseph, K.M., LL.D., D.LITT., PH.D., DR.JUR.; Maltese jurist, historian and writer; b. 6 Jan. 1918, Gozo; s. of Dr. Antonio Cremona and Anne Camilleri; m. Beatrice Barbaro Marchioness of St. George 1949; one s. two d.; ed. Malta, Rome, London, Cambridge and Trieste Univs.; Crown Counsel 1947; Lecturer in Constitutional Law, Royal Univ. of Malta 1947–65; Attorney Gen. 1957–64; Prof. of Criminal Law, Univ. of Malta 1959–65; Prof. Emer. 1965–; Pres. of Council 1972–75; Crown Advocate-Gen. 1964–65; Vice Pres. Constitutional Court and Court of Appeal 1965–71; Judge, European Court of Human Rights 1965–92, Vice-Pres. 1986–92; Pro-Chancellor, Univ. of Malta 1971–74; Chief Justice of Malta, Pres. the Constitutional Court, the Court of Appeal and the Court of Criminal Appeal 1971–81; mem. UN Cttee. on Elimination of Racial Discrimination 1984–88, Chair. 1986–88; Judge, European Tribunal in Matters of State Immunity 1986–92, Vice-Pres. 1986–92; fmr. Acting Gov.-Gen., Acting Pres. of Malta; Chair. Human Rights Section, World Asscn. of Lawyers; Chair. Public Broadcasting Services Ltd. 1996–; Pres. Malta Human Rights Asscn.; Vice-Pres. Int. Inst. of Studies Documentation and Information for the Protection of the Environment 1980–; mem. Int. Inst. of Human Rights 1992; mem. Editorial Bd. several human rights journals in Europe and America; Fellow, Royal Historical Soc.; Hon. Fellow, L.S.E.; Hon. mem. Real Academia de Jurisprudencia y Legislación (Madrid); Kt. of Magisterial Grace, Sovereign Mil. Order of Malta; Kt. Grand Cross Order of Merit (Italy); Kt. Grand Cross, Constantine St. George; Kt. Order of St. Gregory the Great; Kt. Most Venerable Order of St. John of Jerusalem; Companion of the Nat. Order of Merit (Malta); Chevalier, Légion d'honneur. *Publications include:* The Treatment of Young Offenders in Malta 1956, The Malta Constitution of 1835 1959, The Legal Consequences of a Conviction in the Criminal Law of Malta 1962, The Constitutional Development of Malta 1963, From the Declaration of Rights to Independence 1965, Human Rights Documentation in Malta 1966, Selected Papers (1946–89) 1990, The Maltese Constitution and Constitutional History 1994, Malta and Britain: The Early Constitutions 1996; three volumes of poetry; articles in French, Italian, German, Portuguese and American law reviews. *Address:* Villa Barbaro, Main Street, Attard, Malta. *Telephone:* 440818.

CRÉPEAU, Paul-André, C.C., Q.C., L.PH., LL.L., B.C.L., D.EN.D.; Canadian professor of law; b. 20 May 1926, Gravelbourg, Sask.,; s. of J. B. Crépeau and Blanche Provencher; m. Nicole Thomas 1959; two s. one d.; ed. Univs. of Ottawa, Montreal, Oxford and Paris; Pres. Civil Code Revision Office 1965–77; Prof. of Civil Law 1966–94, McGill Univ. Wainwright, Chair. of Civil Law 1976–94; Dir. Inst. of Comparative Law 1975–84, now Prof. Emer.;

Dir. Quebec Research Centre of Private and Company Law 1975–96; Pres. Int. Acad. of Comparative Law 1990–98; LL.D., h.c. (Ottawa) 1971, (York) 1984, (Dalhousie) 1989, (Strasbourg) 1990, (Montréal) 1994; Chevalier de L'Ordre du Mérite (France); Kt., Order of St. John, Jerusalem (Malta). *Publications:* La responsabilité civile du médecin et de l'établissement hospitalier 1956, Rapport sur le Code civil 1978, Code civil, Edition historique et critique 1966–1980 1981, L'intensité de l'obligation juridique 1989, L'Affaire Daigle et la Cour Suprême du Canada ou la Méconnaissance de la tradition civiliste in Mélanges Brière 1993, Lecture du message législatif in Mélanges Beetz 1995, Les Principes d'Unidroit et le Code civil du Québec: Valeurs partagées? 1998. *Leisure interests:* reading, gardening. *Address:* Quebec Research Centre of Private and Comparative Law, 3647 Peel Street, Montreal, Que. H3A 1X1 (Office); 5 Place du Vésinet, Montreal, Que., H2V 2L6, Canada, (Home). *Telephone:* (514) 398-2770 (Office); 272-5941 (Home). *Fax:* (514) 398-7145.

CRESPIN, Régine; French soprano; b. 23 Feb. 1927, Marseilles; d. of Henri and Marguerite (née Meirone) Crespin; m. Lou Bruder 1962; ed. Conservatoire Nat. d'Art Dramatique; Singer, Opéra, Paris; has sung in prin. concert houses, Europe and America; Prof. of Music, Higher Nat. Conservatory of Music 1976–92; Commdr. Légion d'honneur, Grand Officier Ordre national du Mérite, Commdr. Ordre des Arts et Lettres. *Publication:* A la scène, à la ville (memoirs) 1997. *Address:* 3 avenue Frochot, 75009 Paris, France.

CRESSON, Edith; French politician; b. 27 Jan. 1934, Boulogne-sur-Seine; d. of Gabriel and Jacqueline Campion; m. Jacques Cresson 1959; two d.; Nat. Sec. Parti Socialiste; Youth Organizer, Parti Socialiste 1975; Mayor, then Deputy Mayor, Châtellerault 1983–97; Gen. Counsellor Chatellerault-Ouest 1982–; mem. European Parl. 1979; Minister of Agric. 1981–83, of Foreign Trade and Tourism 1983–84, of Industrial Redeployment and Foreign Trade 1984–86, of European Affairs 1988–90; Prime Minister of France 1991–92; Pres. L'Association démocratique des français de l'étranger 1986; Pres. SISIE 1992–94; European Commr. for Educ., Research, Science and Devt. 1994–; mem. Nat. Ass. for Vienne 1986–88; mem. Nat. Secr. Parti Socialiste 1987, Chevalier Légion d'honneur. *Publication:* Avec le soleil 1976. *Address:* Mairie, 86108 Châtellerault cedex, France.

CRETNEY, Stephen Michael, Q.C., M.A., D.C.L., F.B.A.; British professor of law; b. 25 Feb. 1936, Witney, Oxon.; s. of Fred Cretney and Winifred Cretney; m. Rev. Antonia L. Vanrenen 1973; two s.; ed. Manchester Warehousemen and Clerks' Orphan Schools, Cheadle Hulme and Magdalen Coll., Oxford; Partner, Macfarlanes (Solicitors), London 1964–65; Lecturer, Kenya School of Law, Nairobi 1966–67, Southampton Univ. 1968–69; Fellow and Tutor in Law, Exeter Coll., Oxford 1969–78; mem. Law Comm. for England and Wales 1978–83; Prof. of Law (Dean of Faculty 1984–88), Univ. of Bristol 1984–93; Fellow All Souls Coll. Oxford 1993–. *Publications:* Enduring Powers of Attorney (4th edn.) 1996, Elements of Family Law (3rd edn.) 1997, Principles of Family Law (6th edn.) 1997, Law, Law Reform and the Family 1998. *Address:* All Souls College, Oxford, OX1 4AL (Office); The Vicarage, 3 Drake's Farm, Peasemore, Berks., RG20 7DF, England (Home). *Telephone:* (01865) 279379 (Office); (01635) 248925 (Home). *Fax:* (01865) 279299.

CREUTZ, Edward Chester, PH.D.; American physicist and consultant; b. 23 Jan. 1913, Beaver Dam, Wis.; s. of Lester Raymond Creutz and Grace Smith; m. 1st Lela Marie Rollefson 1937; m. 2nd Elisabeth Butler Cordle 1974; two s. one d.; ed. Univ. of Wisconsin; Instructor in Physics, Princeton Univ. 1939–42; Group Leader Manhattan Project 1942–46; Assoc. Prof. Carnegie Inst. of Tech. 1946–48, Prof. Physics and Head Dept. 1948–55; Vice-Pres. Research and Devt. Gen. Atomic Corpn. 1955–70; Asst. Dir. Research Nat. Science Foundation 1970–77; Dir. Bernice Pauali Bishop Museum, Honolulu 1977–84, Hon. Consultant 1984–; mem. N.A.S. *Publications:* Resonance Absorption of Neutrons in Uranium, Proton Scattering, Artificial Radioactivity, Flow of Gases through Porous Media, Fabrication of Uranium and Beryllium. *Leisure interests:* orchid growing, computer programming, radio-controlled model boats. *Address:* P.O. Box 2757, Rancho Santa Fe, CA 92067, U.S.A. *Telephone:* (619) 756-4980.

CREWE, Albert Victor, PH.D.; American physicist and professor; b. 18 Feb. 1927, Bradford, England; s. of Wilfred and Edith Fish (née Lawrence) Crewe; m. Doreen Crewe; one s. three d.; ed. Liverpool Univ.; Asst. Lecturer, Liverpool Univ. 1950–52, lecturer 1952–53; Research Assoc. Chicago Univ. 1955–56, Asst. Prof. of Physics 1956–59, Assoc. Prof. 1959–63; Dir. Particle Accelerator Div., Argonne Nat. Lab. 1958–61, Dir. 1961–67; Prof. Dept. of Physics and Biophysics Enrico Fermi Inst. 1963–71, Univ. of Chicago 1963–71, Dean, Physical Sciences Div. 1971–81, William E. Wrather Distinguished Service Prof. 1977–96, Prof. Emer. 1996–; Pres. Orchid One Corp. 1987–90; constructed England's first diffusion cloud chamber with Dr. W. H. Evans at Liverpool Univ.; directed construction of large magnetic spectrometer for Chicago Univ.'s synchrocyclotron; consultant Sweden, Argentina; directed much of design and construction of Argonne's Zero Gradient Synchrotron; as Dir. Argonne Nat. Lab., developed relationships with U.S. Atomic Energy Comm., Argonne Univ. and Chicago Univ., expressed in Tripartite Agreement; invented the scanning transmission electron microscope; obtained first atom images 1971; Fellow, American Physical Soc., American Nuclear Soc.; mem. N.A.S., American Acad. of Arts and Sciences, Scientific Research Soc. for America, Electron Microscopy Soc. of America, Chicago Area Research and Devt. Council (Chair. 1964), Gov.'s Science Advisory Cttee. for State of Ill.; Hon. Fellow, Royal Microscopical Soc. 1984; Immigrant's Service League's Annual Award for Outstanding Achievement in the Field of Science 1962; "Industrial Research Man of the Year 1970"; Michelson Medal (Franklin Inst.) 1978; Ernst Abbe Award New York Microscope Soc. 1979; Duddell Medal, Inst. of Physics, U.K. 1980. *Leisure interests:* sculpture, painting. *Address:* 8 Summit Drive, Dune Acres, Chesterton, IN 46304, U.S.A. (Home).

CRICHTON, (John) Michael (pseudonyms Jeffrey Hudson and John Lange, joint pseudonym with Douglas Crichton as Michael Douglas); American writer, film director and physician; b. 23 Oct. 1942, Chicago; m. 4th Anne-Marie Martin 1987; one d.; ed. Harvard Medical School; lecturer in anthropology Cambridge Univ. 1965; Post-Doctoral Fellow Salk Inst., La Jolla 1969–70; Visiting Writer M.I.T. 1988; creator and co-exec. producer TV series ER 1994–. *Films directed:* The Great Train Robbery, Coma, Runaway. *Publications include:* (as Michael Douglas) Dealing: or, The Berkeley to Boston Forty-Brick Lost-Bag Blues 1972; (as Jeffrey Hudson) A Case of Need 1968, The Andromeda Strain 1969; (as John Lange) Odds On 1966, Scratch One 1967, Easy Go 1968, Zero Cool 1969, The Venom Business 1969, Drug of Choice 1970, Grave Descend 1970, Five Patients: The Hospital Explained 1970, Binary 1972, The Terminal Man 1972, Westworld (screenplay) 1973, The Great Train Robbery 1975, Eaters of the Dead 1976, Jasper Johns 1977, Congo 1980, Looker (screenplay) 1981, Electronic Life: How to Think About Computers 1983, Runaway (screenplay) 1984, Sphere 1987, Travels 1988, Jurassic Park 1990, Rising Sun 1992, Disclosure 1994, The Lost World 1995, The Terminal Man 1995, Airframe 1996. *Address:* Constant Productions, 194 Katonah Avenue, #246, Katonah, NY 10536, U.S.A.

CRICHTON-BROWN, Sir Robert, K.C.M.G., C.B.E., T.D.; Australian business executive; b. 23 Aug. 1919, Melbourne; s. of L. Crichton-Brown; m. Norah I. Turnbull 1941; one s. one d.; ed. Sydney Grammar School; Man. Dir. Security and Gen. Insurance Co., Ltd. 1952; Chair. Security Life Assurances Ltd. 1961–85, NEI Pacific Ltd. 1961–85, Edward Lumley Ltd. (Group), Australia 1974–89 (Man. Dir. 1952–82, Dir. 1989), The Commercial Banking Co. of Sydney Ltd. 1976–82, Commercial and General Acceptance Ltd. 1977–82, Westham Dredging Co. Pty. Ltd. 1975–85, Rothmans of Pall Mall (Australia) Ltd. 1981–85 (Exec. Chair. 1985–88); Vice-Chair. Nat. Australia Bank Ltd. 1982–85, Custom Credit Corpn. Ltd. 1982–85; Dir. Daily Mail & General Trust Ltd. (U.K.) 1979–95; Exec. Chair. Rothmans Int. PLC 1985–88; Underwriting mem. Lloyd's 1946–97; Dir. Royal Prince Alfred Hosp. 1970–84; Fed. Pres. Inst. of Dirs. in Australia 1967–80; Fed. Hon. Treas. Liberal Party of Australia 1973–85; Nat. Co-ordinator, Duke of Edinburgh's Award Scheme in Australia 1980–85; mem. or official of numerous professional and charitable orgs. in Australia; mem. Australia's winning Admiral's Cup Team (Balandra) 1967; winner, Sydney-Hobart Yacht Race (Pacha) 1970. *Leisure interest:* sailing.

CRICK, Francis Harry Compton, O.M., F.R.S., PH.D.; British neuroscientist; b. 8 June 1916, Northampton; m. Odile Speed 1949; one s. (by previous marriage) two d.; ed. Univ. Coll., London, and Cambridge Univ.; Scientist, Admiralty, 1940–47; Medical Research Council (M.R.C.) Student, Strangeways Lab. Cambridge 1947–49; M.R.C. Lab. of Molecular Biology, Cambridge 1949–76; Kieckhefer Distinguished Research Prof., The Salk Inst., La Jolla, Calif. 1977–, Pres. 1994–95; Adjunct Prof. of Psychology, Univ. of Calif., San Diego; Fellow, Churchill Coll., Cambridge 1960–61, Hon. Fellow 1965; Fellow Univ. Coll., London 1962; Hon. Fellow, Caius Coll., Cambridge 1976; Fellow A.A.A.S. 1966; Fellow, Indian Nat. Science Acad. 1982; Foreign Assoc. N.A.S. 1969; Assoc. Académie Française 1978; mem. German Acad. of Science 1969; Foreign mem. American Phil. Soc., Philadelphia 1972; Foreign Hon. mem. American Acad. of Arts and Sciences 1962; Hon. mem. American Soc. Biological Chem. 1963, Hellenic Biochemical and Biophysical Soc. 1974; Hon. MRIA 1964; Hon. F.R.S.E. 1966; Hon. Fellow Inst. of Biology 1995; Hon. Fellow Tata Inst. of Fundamental Research, Bombay 1996; Nobel Prize for Medicine (with J. D. Watson and M. H. F. Wilkins, qq.v.) 1962; Royal Medal, Royal Soc. 1972; Copley Medal, Royal Soc. 1975, Michelson-Morley Award, Cleveland, U.S.A. 1981; numerous memorial lectures and other awards. *Publications:* numerous papers and articles on molecular and cell biology and on neurobiology; Of Molecules and Men 1967, Life Itself 1981, What Mad Pursuit 1988, The Astonishing Hypothesis 1994. *Leisure interests:* gardening, swimming. *Address:* The Salk Institute for Biological Studies, P.O. Box 85800, San Diego, CA 92186–5800 (Office); 1792 Colgate Circle, La Jolla, CA 92037, U.S.A. (Home).

CRICK, Ronald Pitts, F.R.C.S., F.R.C.OPHTH.; British ophthalmic surgeon; b. 5 Feb. 1917, Toronto, Canada; s. of Owen John Pitts Crick and Margaret Daw; m. Jocelyn Mary Grenfell Robins 1941; four s. one d.; ed. Latymer Upper School, London, King's Coll. Hosp. Medical School, London; surgeon, Merchant Navy 1939–40; Surgeon-Lieut., R.N.V.R. 1940–46; Ophthalmic Registrar, King's Coll. Hosp., London 1946–48; Surgical First Asst., Royal Eye Hosp., London 1947–50, Surgeon 1950–69; Ophthalmic Surgeon, Belgrave Hosp. for Children 1950–66; Consultant Ophthalmic Surgeon, King's Coll. Hosp. 1950–82, Hon. Consultant 1982; Recognized Teacher in Ophthalmology, Univ. of London 1960–82, Lecturer Emer., School of Medicine and Dentistry, King's Coll. 1982–; Visiting Research Fellow Sussex Univ. 1976–; Chair. Ophthalmic Training Cttee., S.E. Thames Regional Health Authority 1973–82; Fellow and Vice-Pres. Ophthalmology Section, Royal Soc. of Medicine 1964; Charter mem. Int. Glaucoma Congress of American Soc. of Contemporary Ophthalmology 1977–; Chair. Int. Glaucoma Asscn. 1974–;

Open Science Scholarship, King's Coll. Hosp. Medical School 1934; Fellow Royal Coll. of Ophthalmologists; Sir Stewart Duke-Elder Glaucoma Award (Int. Glaucoma Congress) 1985; Alim Memorial Lecturer, Ophthalmological Soc. of Bangladesh 1991. *Publications:* All About Glaucoma (with W. Leydhecker) 1981, A Text Book of Clinical Ophthalmology (with R. Trimble) 1987; numerous articles in ophthalmic books and journals. *Leisure interests:* natural history, motoring, sailing, designing ophthalmic instruments. *Address:* King's College Hospital, Denmark Hill, London, SE5 9RS (Office); Sandbanks House, 2 Panorama Road, Sandbanks, Poole, Dorset BH13 7RD, England. *Telephone:* 0171-737-3265 (Office); (01202) 707560 (Sandbanks). *Fax:* 0171-346 5929 (Office); (01202) 707560 (Home).

CRICKHOWELL, Baron (Life Peer), cr. 1987, of Pont Esgob in the Black Mountains and County of Powys, **(Roger) Nicholas Edwards,** P.C., M.A.; British politician; b. 25 Feb. 1934; s. of late Ralph Edwards and Marjorie Brooke; m. Ankaret Healing 1963; one s. two d.; ed. Westminster School, Trinity Coll., Cambridge; mem. Lloyd's 1965–; M.P. for Pembroke 1970–87; Opposition Spokesman on Welsh Affairs 1975–79; Sec. of State for Wales 1979–87; Chair. Nat. Rivers Authority 1989–96, IT Net PLC 1997–; Pres. Univ. of Wales, Cardiff 1988–98, Contemporary Art Soc. for Wales 1988–93; Dir. HTV Ltd. 1987– (Chair. 1997–), Anglesey Mining PLC 1988– (Deputy Chair. 1997–), Associated British Port Holdings PLC 1988–; mem. Cttee. Automobile Asscn. 1997–98; Conservative. *Publication:* Opera House Lottery 1997. *Leisure interests:* gardening, fishing. *Address:* 4 Henning Street, London, SW11 3DR, England; Pont Esgob Mill, Fforest Coal Pit, Nr. Abergavenny, Mon., NP7 7LS, Wales.

CRISTIANI BURKARD, Alfredo; Salvadorean politician and businessman; b. *c* 1948; m. Margarita Cristiani; ed. Georgetown Univ., Washington, D.C., U.S.A.; fmr. exec. in family pharmaceutical, coffee and cotton businesses; Leader, Republican Nationalist Alliance (ARENA) 1985; mem. Nat. Assembly 1988–; Pres. of El Salvador 1989–94. *Address:* National Assembly, San Salvador, El Salvador.

CRISTOL, Stanley Jerome, PH.D.; American professor of chemistry; b. 14 June 1916, Chicago, Ill.; s. of Myer J. and Lillian (Young) Cristol; m. Barbara Wright Swingle 1957; one s. one d.; ed. Northwestern Univ. and Univ. of California, Los Angeles; Asst. in Chem., Univ. of Calif. at Los Angeles (UCLA) 1937–38, 1941–42; Research Chemist, Standard Oil Co. of Calif. 1938–41; Instructor, UCLA 1942–43; Post-doctoral Fellow, Univ. of Ill. 1943–44; Research Chemist, Bureau of Entomology and Plant Quarantine U.S. Dept. of Agric. 1944–46; Univ. of Colo., Asst. Prof. 1946–49, Assoc. Prof. 1949–55, Prof. 1955–, Chair. Dept. of Chem. 1960–62, Joseph Sewall Distinguished Prof. of Chem. 1979–, Dean, Graduate School 1980–81; mem. N.A.S., American Chem. Soc.; Guggenheim Fellow 1955–56, 1981–82; Fellow, A.A.A.S. (Councillor 1986–92), Chem. Soc., London; Robert L. Stearns Award 1971, James Flack Norris Award of the American Chemical Soc. 1972, Colo. Univ. Medal 1984, Northwestern Univ. Alumni Merit Award 1987. *Publications:* Organic Chemistry 1966 (with L. O. Smith, Jr.), numerous articles in scientific journals. *Leisure interests:* skiing, fishing. *Address:* Department of Chemistry and Biochemistry, University of Colorado, Boulder, CO 80309-0215 (Office); 2918 Third Street, Boulder, CO 80304, U.S.A. (Home). *Telephone:* (303) 492-6661 (Office); (303) 443-1781 (Home).

CROCKER, Chester Arthur, PH.D.; American government official; b. 29 Oct. 1941, New York; s. of Arthur and Clare Crocker; m. Saone Baron 1965; three d.; ed. Ohio State Univ., Johns Hopkins Univ.; editorial asst. Africa Report 1965–66, News Ed. 1968–69; lecturer American Univ. 1969–70; staff officer Nat. Security Council 1970–72; Dir. Master of Science, Foreign Service Programme, Georgetown Univ. 1972–78, Dir. African Studies, Center for Strategic and Inst. Studies 1976–81; Asst. Sec. of State for African Affairs 1981–89; Research Prof., Georgetown Univ. 1989–; Chair. African working group, Reagan Campaign 1980; Chair. Bd. U.S. Inst. of Peace; Int. Consultant; mem. Bd. Minorco, SA, mem. Bd. ASA Ltd., Corp. Council on Africa; Presidential Citizen's medal, Sec. of State's Distinguished Service Award. *Publications:* South Africa's Defense Posture 1982, South Africa into the 1980s 1979, High Noon in Southern Africa 1992, African Conflict Resolution 1995, Managing Global Chaos 1996; numerous articles. *Address:* Room 813, Intercultural Center, School of Foreign Service, Georgetown University, Washington, DC 20057, U.S.A. *Telephone:* (202) 687-5074. *Fax:* (202) 687-2315.

CROCKETT, Andrew Duncan, M.A.; British banker; b. 23 March 1943; s. of Andrew Crockett and Sheilah Stewart; m. Marjorie Hlavacek 1966; two s. one d.; ed. Queens' Coll. Cambridge and Yale Univ.; Bank of England 1966–72, Exec. Dir. 1989–93; IMF 1972–89; Gen. Man. BIS Jan. 1994–. *Publications:* Money: Theory, Policy, Institutions 1973, International Money: Issues and Analysis 1977; contribs. to professional journals. *Leisure interests:* reading, golf, tennis. *Address:* Bank for International Settlements, Centralbahnplatz 2, 4002 Basel, Switzerland.

CROFF, Davide; Italian banker; b. 1 Oct. 1947; ed. in Venice, Pembroke Coll. Oxford; Asst. Prof. of Political Econ., Univ. of Padua 1971–72; Research Dept. Officer Banca d'Italia, Rome 1974–79; Foreign and Financial Affairs Dept. Fiat S.p.A., Turin 1979–83, in charge of Int. Treasury Dept. 1982, Finance Man. 1983–86, Sr. Vice-Pres. 1986–89; C.E.O. Finance and Int., Banca Nazionale del Lavoro, Rome 1989–90, Man. Dir. 1990–. *Address:* Banca Nazionale del Lavoro, Via Vittorio Veneto 119, Rome, Italy.

CROHAM, Baron (Life Peer), cr. 1978, of the London Borough of Croydon; **Douglas Albert Vivian Allen,** G.C.B.; British civil servant; b. 15 Dec. 1917, Surrey; s. of Albert Allen and Elsie Maria Allen (née Davies); m. Sybil Eileen Allegro 1941 (died 1994); two s. one d.; ed. Wallington County Grammar School and London School of Econs.; Asst. Prin., Bd. of Trade 1939; served Royal Artillery 1940–45; Prin., Bd. of Trade 1945, Cabinet Office 1947, Treasury 1948; Asst. Sec., Treasury 1949–58; Under-Sec., Ministry of Health 1958–60, Treasury 1960–62; Third Sec., Treasury 1962–64; Deputy Under-Sec. of State, Dept. of Econ. Affairs 1964–66, Second Perm. Under-Sec. of State 1966; Perm. Under-Sec. of State, Dept of Econ. Affairs 1966–68; Perm. Sec., Treasury 1968–74; Head Home Civil Service, Perm. Sec. Civil Service Dept. 1974–77; Chair. Econ. Policy Cttee., OECD 1972–77, Deputy Chair. BNOC 1978–82, Chair. 1982–86; Adviser to Gov., Bank of England 1978–83; Dir. (non-exec.) Pilkington PLC 1978–92; Trustee, Anglo-German Foundation 1977–, Chair. 1982–98; Pres. Inst. of Fiscal Studies 1978–92; Chair. Inst. of Man. Econ. and Social Affairs Cttee. 1982–85, Trinity Insurance 1988–92; Dir. (non-exec.) Guinness Peat Group 1983–87, Chair. 1983–86; Dir. (non-exec.) Guinness Mahon and Co. Ltd. 1989–92. *Leisure interests:* woodwork, bridge. *Address:* 9 Manor Way, South Croydon, Surrey, England (Home). *Telephone:* 0181-688 0496 (Home).

CROISSIER, Luis Carlos; Spanish politician; b. 1950, Arucas, Las Palmas; m.; two s.; ed. Complutense Univ. of Madrid, Sorbonne, Paris; mem. Socialist Party (PSOE) 1974–; Sec.-Gen. Socialist Group of Majadahonda; Deputy Dir.-Gen. Office for Budgeting in Industry, Rep. of Ministry of Industry in Cttee. for Elaboration of Plan for Public Investments and in Inter-Ministerial Comm. for Rationalisation and Decentralisation of Public Expenditure 1980; Deputy Sec., Ministry of Industry 1982–84; then Pres. of Instituto Nacional de Industria (INI); Minister for Industry and Energy 1986–88. *Address:* c/o Partido Socialista Obrero Español, Ferraz 68 y 70, 28008 Madrid Spain.

CROMBIE, Leslie, C.CHEM., PH.D., D.SC., F.R.S.C., F.R.S.; British organic chemist; b. 10 June 1923, York; s. of Walter Leslie Crombie and Gladys May (née Clarkson) Crombie; m. Winifred Mary Lovell Wood 1953; two s. two d.; ed. Portsmouth Municipal Coll., King's Coll., London; Scientist Admiralty Chem. Lab., Portsmouth Naval Dockyard 1941–46; Lecturer Imperial Coll., London 1950–58; Reader in Organic Chem., King's Coll., London 1958–63; Prof. of Organic Chem., Univ. Coll., Cardiff 1963–69; Sir Jesse Boot Prof. of Organic Chem., Univ. of Nottingham 1969–88, Emer. Prof. 1988–, Dean of Science 1980–83; Fellow King's Coll., London 1978; Pres. Chemical Soc. Perkin Div. 1976–79, British Asscn., Section B; Vice-Chair. Phytochemical Soc. of Europe 1984–86, 1988–90, Chair. 1986–88; mem. Jt. Chem. Educ. Cttee. 1981–82 (Chair. 1983–87), SERC Chem. Cttee. 1970–75, Enzyme Cttee. 1973–75, Univ. Grants Physical Science Sub-Cttee. 1978–85, Royal Soc. Educ. Cttee. 1983–91 (Chair. 1984–91); Hon. Fellow Portsmouth Univ. 1983; Trustee Uppingham School 1994–97; Tilden Lecturer 1970, Simonsen Lecturer 1975, Hugo Muller Lecturer 1977, Pedler Lecturer 1982, Robert Robinson Lecturer 1992; Council mem. Chem. Soc. 1962–64, 1972–81; mem. Royal Inst. of Chem. 1975–78, Royal Soc. 1984–86; Royal Soc. of Chem. Natural Products Chem. Award 1980; Flintoff Medal 1984; Phytochemical Soc. Medal 1990; Int. Award for Research in Agrochemicals (A.C.S.) 1998. *Publications:* numerous scientific papers. *Leisure interests:* gardening, reading. *Address:* 153 Hillside Road, Bramcote, Beeston, Nottingham, England. *Telephone:* (0115) 9259412.

CROMME, Gerhard, DR. JUR.; German business executive; b. 25 Feb. 1943, Vechta/Oldenburg; m.; four d.; ed. Münster, Lausanne, Paris and Harvard Univs.; joined Compagnie de Saint-Gobain 1971, latterly Deputy Del.-Gen. for Fed. Repub. of Germany and Chair. Man. Bd. VEGLA/Vereinigte Glaswerke GmbH, Aachen; Chair. Man. Bd. Krupp Stahl AG, Bochum 1986; mem. Exec. Bd. Fried. Krupp GmbH, Essen 1988 (now Fried. Krupp AG Hoesch-Krupp), Chair. 1989–, also C.E.O.; C.E.O. Thyssen Krupp AG 1998–; mem. several supervisory bds. and advisory councils. *Address:* Fried. Krupp AG, Altendorfer Strasse 103, 45143 Essen, Germany. *Telephone:* 0201/188-1. *Fax:* 0201/188-4100.

CRONE, Christian, M.D., SC.D.; Danish professor of physiology; b. 1 Feb. 1926, Copenhagen; s. of F. L. Crone and Betty Bredsdorff; m. Monna Nyeborg 1949; two s. three d.; ed. Univ. of Copenhagen, Univ. of Cambridge, England; Lieut. Royal Danish Navy 1952; Internship, Copenhagen City Hospitals 1953–56; Research Assoc., Dept. of Physiology, Univ. of Copenhagen 1957–66, Prof. of Physiology 1967; Chair. Int. Comm. for Micro-circulation 1977–86, Nat. Cttee. for Physiology 1977–88; Vice-Pres. Int. Union of Physiological Sciences (IUPS) 1983–89; mem. Royal Danish Acad. of Sciences 1968–, Hon. Sec. 1980–85; mem. Bd. of Dirs. Carlsberg Foundation 1971–80; Visiting Prof., Faculty of Medicine, Paris 1984–85; Hon. mem. American Physiological Soc. 1989; mem. Academia Europea 1989; Dr. h.c. (Sorbonne, Paris) 1989; Christian Bohr Award, Copenhagen 1963, Zweifach Int. Award, U.S.A. 1979, Novo Prize, Denmark 1983, Lucian Prof., McGill Univ., Montreal 1982; Malpighi Award 1986; Fernstrom Research Award (Lund Univ.) 1986. *Publications:* Diffusion of Organic Nonelectrolytes from Blood to Brain 1961, Capillary Permeability 1970, History of Capillary Physiology 1974, American Handbook of Physiology (Contrib.) 1984; numerous articles on capillary physiology and the blood-brain barrier. *Leisure interest:* music (active flautist).

CRONENBERG, David; Canadian film director; b. 15 March 1943, Toronto; ed. Univ. of Toronto; has directed fillers and short dramas for TV; directed:

(shorts) Transfer 1966, From the Drain 1967; (feature length) Stereo 1969, Crimes of the Future 1970, The Parasite Murders/Shivers 1974, Rabid 1976, Fast Company 1979, The Brood 1979, Scanners 1980, Videodrome 1982, The Dead Zone 1983, The Fly 1986, Dead Ringers 1988, The Naked Lunch 1991, Crash 1996; acted in Nightbreed 1990, The Naked Lunch (wrote screenplay), Trial by Jury, Henry and Verlin. *Publications:* Crash 1996, Cronenberg on Cronenberg 1996. *Address:* David Cronenberg Productions Ltd., 217 Avenue Road, Toronto, Ont., M5R 2J3, Canada; c/o William Morris Agency, 151 South El Camino Drive, Beverly Hills, CA 90212, U.S.A.

CRONIN, Anthony; Irish author; b. 23 Dec. 1928, Co. Wexford; s. of John Cronin and Hannah Barron; m. Thérèse Campbell 1955; two d.; ed. Blackrock Coll., Univ. Coll., Dublin and Kings Inns, Dublin; Assoc. Ed. The Bell 1952–54; Literary Ed. Time and Tide 1956–58; Visiting lecturer in English, Univ. of Montana, U.S.A. 1966–68; writer-in-residence, Drake Univ., Ia. 1968–70; columnist, Irish Times 1973–80; cultural and artistic adviser to the Prime Minister of Ireland 1980–83, 1987–92; Martin Toonder Award for contrib. to Irish literature 1983. *Publications include:* Poems 1958, The Life of Riley 1964, A Question of Modernity 1966, Dead as Doornails 1976, Identity Papers 1980, New and Selected Poems 1982, Heritage Now 1982, An Irish Eye 1985, No Laughing Matter, The Life and Times of Flann O'Brien 1989, The End of the Modern World 1989, Relationships 1994, Samuel Beckett: The Last Modernist 1996. *Leisure interests:* reading, walking, travelling, watching horse-racing. *Address:* 9 Rainsford Avenue, Dublin 8, Ireland. *Telephone:* 4545954. *Fax:* 4545954.

CRONIN, James Watson, PH.D.; American professor of physics; b. 29 Sept. 1931, Chicago, Ill.; s. of James Farley Cronin and Dorothy Watson Cronin; m. Annette Martin 1954; one s. two d.; ed. Southern Methodist Univ., Univ. of Chicago; Nat. Science Foundation Fellow 1952–55; Assoc. Brookhaven Nat. Lab. 1955–58; Asst. Prof. of Physics, Princeton Univ. 1958–62, Assoc. Prof. 1962–64, Prof. 1964–71; Prof. of Physics, Univ. of Chicago 1971–; Loeb Lecturer in Physics, Harvard Univ. 1976; mem. N.A.S., American Acad. of Arts and Sciences, American Physical Soc.; Research Corpn. Award 1968; Ernest O. Lawrence Award 1977; John Price Wetherill Medal, Franklin Inst. 1975; shared Nobel Prize for Physics 1980 with Prof. Val Fitch (q.v.) for work on elementary particles; Hon. D.Sc. (Leeds) 1996. *Publications:* numerous articles on physics. *Address:* Enrico Fermi Institute, University of Chicago, 5630 South Ellis Avenue, Chicago, IL 60637 (Office); 5825 South Dorchester Avenue, Chicago, IL 60637, U.S.A. *Telephone:* (312) 962-7102 (Office).

CRONKITE, Eugene Pitcher, M.D.; American physician (retd.); b. 11 Dec. 1914, Los Angeles; s. of Anita P. Cronkite and Clarence E. Cronkite; m. Elizabeth E. Kaitschuk 1940; one d.; ed. Univ. of California at Los Angeles and Stanford Univ. Medical School; Medical Officer U.S.N. 1942–54; Head of Haematology, Naval Medical Research Inst., Bethesda, Md. 1946–54; Head of Experimental Haematology, Medical Dept., Brookhaven Nat. Lab., Upton, New York 1954–67, Chair. Medical Dept. 1967–79, Chair. Emer. and Sr. Scientist 1979–95; Prof. of Medicine, State Univ. of New York, Stony Brook 1979–95; Medical Corps, U.S.N.R. (retd. as Rear Adm.) 1954–74; Ed. Experimental Hematology 1985–91; mem. N.A.S.; Dr. Med. h.c. (Ulm) 1987, (Parma) 1991; Sir Henry Wellcome Prize, Alfred Benzon Award (Denmark), L. Heilmeyer Gold Medal (Fed. Repub. of Germany), Semmelweis Medal (Hungary), Alexander von Humboldt Award (Fed. Repub. of Germany), DeVilliers Award (Leukemia Soc. of U.S.A.) 1989, Medal for Distinguished Achievement 1998. *Publications:* over 400 publs. on radiation biology, leukaemia, cell proliferation, effects of radiation on humans. *Leisure interests:* tennis, photography and fishing. *Address:* c/o Medical Department, Brookhaven National Laboratory, Upton, NY 11973, U.S.A. *Telephone:* (516) 344-5311. *Fax:* (516) 344-7538.

CRONKITE, Walter Leland, Jr.; American television correspondent; b. 4 Nov. 1916, St. Joseph, Missouri; s. of the late W. L. Cronkite and of Helene Fritsche; m. Mary Elizabeth Maxwell 1940; one s. two d.; ed. Univ. of Texas; News writer and Editor, Scripps-Howard & United Press, Houston, Kansas City, Dallas, Austin, El Paso and New York; United Press War Corresp. 1942–45, later Foreign Corresp., Chief Corresp. Nuremberg War Crimes Trials, Bureau Man., Moscow 1946–48; lecturer 1948–49; CBS, news corresp. 1950–81; Anchorman and Man. Ed., CBS Evening News with Walter Cronkite 1962–81, CBS News Special Corresp. 1981–, mem. Bd. of Dirs. CBS Inc.; Chair. The Cronkite Ward Co. 1993–; several hon. degrees; Emmy Award (several times), Acad. TV Arts and Sciences 1970, George Polk Journalism Award 1971, Jefferson Award 1981, Presidential Medal of Freedom 1981, and other awards. *Publications:* Challenges of Change 1971; co-author South by Southeast 1983, A Reporter's Life 1996. *Leisure interest:* yachting. *Address:* c/o CBS Inc., 51 West 52nd Street, New York, NY 10019, U.S.A.

CRONYN, Hume, O.C.; Canadian actor and director; b. 18 July 1911, London, Ont.; s. of Hume Blake and Frances A. (née Labatt) Cronyn; m. Jessica Tandy 1942 (died 1994); one s. two d.; ed. Ridley Coll., St. Catharine's, Ont., McGill Univ., New York School of Theatre, Mozarteum, Salzburg, and American Acad. of Dramatic Art, New York; after amateur experience with an acting group in Montreal, joined Cochran's Stock Co., Wash., D.C.; professional début in Up Pops the Devil 1931; made first film, Shadow of a Doubt 1943; dir. several Actor's Lab. productions 1946–57; staged (with Norman Lloyd) and co-starred in Phoenix Theatre's production Madam Will You Walk 1953; staged successful production of The Fourposter 1952, on tour 1951–53; inaugurated NBC radio series The Marriage 1953; has appeared in several films including Cleopatra 1963, Rollover 1981, Garp 1981, Impulse 1983, Cocoon 1985, Batteries Not Included 1987, Age Old Friends 1990, Cocoon: The Return, The Pelican Brief 1994, Camilla, Marvin's Room, and numerous plays and has toured extensively with his productions; has appeared in many major U.S. TV drama series; TV films include To Dance With the White Dog 1993, Alone 1996, Twelve Angry Men 1997, Sea People 1998; mem. Bd. Dirs. Stratford Festival (first actor) 1978; nominated for Acad. Award for performance in The Seventh Cross 1944; Comoedia Matinee Club's Award for The Fourposter 1952, American Theatre Wings' Antoinette Perry Play Award (The Fourposter) 1952, Barter Theatre Award 1961, Delia Austria Medal, New York Drama League (Big Fish Little Fish) 1961, Antoinette Perry (Tony) Award and won Variety New York Drama Critics Poll for Polonius (Hamlet) 1964, Herald Theater Award for Tobias (A Delicate Balance), L.A. Drama Critics Circle Award for best actor (Caine Mutiny Court Martial) 1972, 1972–73 Obie Award (Krapp's Last Tape), Brandeis Univ. Creative Arts Awards for distinguished achievement 1978, L.A. Critics' Award (Gin Game) 1979, elected to American Hall of Fame 1979, Kennedy Center Honor 1986, Nat. Medal Arts 1990; Antoinette Perry Lifetime Achievement Award (with Jessica Tandy) 1994; Hon. LL.D. (Univ. of Western Ont.) 1974. *Publications:* A Terrible Liar (autobiog.) 1991, Birdhouse Contributions (poetry) 1993, Voices of Oppression (jtly.) 1995. *Address:* 63-23 Carlton Street, Rego Park, New York, NY 11374, U.S.A.

CROSBIE, John Carnell, B.A., B.L., M.P.; Canadian politician; b. 30 Jan. 1931, St. John's, Newfoundland; m. Jane Furneaux; one s. two d.; ed. St. Andrew's Coll., Aurora, Ont., Queen's Univ., Ont., Dalhousie Law School, Univ. of London, L.S.E.; called to Newfoundland Bar 1957; Prov. Minister of Municipal Affairs and Housing 1966, mem. Newfoundland House of Ass. 1966, 1971–76; Minister of Finance, Econ. Devt., Fisheries, Inter-Govt. Affairs, Mines and Energy and Pres. of the Treasury Bd., Leader of House of Ass. 1975; mem. House of Commons 1976–93; Minister of Finance 1979; Minister of Justice and Attorney-Gen. of Canada 1984–86, of Transport 1986–89 , of Int. Trade 1989–91, of Fisheries and Oceans for the Atlantic Opportunities Agency 1991–93; Counsel to Patterson Palmer Hunt Murphy 1994–; Chancellor Memorial Univ. of Newfoundland 1994–; Dir. Canadian Helicopters Ltd. 1993–; fmr. Chair. of Caucus Cttee. on Energy, Caucus spokesperson for Finance, External Affairs, Industry, Trade and Commerce; f. Newfoundland and Labrador Housing Corpn.; Progressive Conservative Party. *Address:* 235 Water Street, St. John's, Newfoundland, A1C 5L3; P.O. Box 23119, St. John's, Newfoundland A1B 4J9, Canada.

CROSS, George Alan Martin, PH.D., F.R.S.; British professor of molecular parasitology; b. 27 Sept. 1942, Cheshire; s. of George Bernard Cross and Beatrice Mary Horton; m. Nadia Nogueira 1986; one d.; ed. Univ. of Cambridge; Scientist, Biochemical Parasitology, MRC 1969–77; Head, Dept. of Immunochem. and Molecular Biology, Wellcome Foundation Research Labs. 1977–82; Andre and Bella Mayor Prof. of Molecular Parasitology, Rockefeller Univ. 1982–, Dean Grad. and Postgrad. Studies 1995–; Fleming Prize, Soc. for Gen. Microbiology 1978, Chalmers Medal, Royal Soc. of Tropical Medicine and Hygiene 1983, Paul Ehrlich and Ludwig Darmstaedter Prize 1984. *Address:* The Rockefeller University, 1230 York Avenue, New York, NY 10021, U.S.A. *Telephone:* (212) 327-7571. *Fax:* (212) 327-7845.

CROSSLAND, Sir Bernard, Kt., C.B.E., D.SC., M.R.I.A., F.ENG., F.R.S.; British professor of mechanical engineering; b. 20 Oct. 1923, Sydenham; s. of Reginald F. and Kathleen M. (née Rudduck) Crossland; m. Audrey E. Birks 1946; two d.; ed. Simon Langton Grammar School, Derby Tech. Coll. and Nottingham Univ. Coll.; eng. apprentice, Rolls-Royce, Derby 1940–41, Tech. Asst. 1943–45; Asst. Lecturer, Lecturer, Sr. Lecturer in Mech. Eng., Univ. of Bristol 1946–59; Prof. and Head, Dept. of Mechanical and Industrial Eng., Queen's Univ., Belfast 1959–82, Dean, Faculty of Eng. 1964–67, Pro-Vice–Chancellor 1978–82, Special Research Prof. 1982–84, Emer. Prof. 1984–; Consulting Eng. 1984–; Chair., N. Ireland Manpower Council 1981–86; Pres. Inst. of Mechanical Engineers 1986–87, Past Pres. 1987–91; Pres. The Welding Inst. 1995–98; mem. Industrial Devt. Bd. for N. Ireland 1982–87, N. Ireland Econ. Council 1981–85; mem. Agricultural and Food Research Council 1981–87, Engineering Council 1983–88; Chair. Postgrad. Advisory Bd. to Dept. of Educ. for Northern Ireland 1982–95, Bd. for Engineers Registration 1983–86, Hazards Forum 1991–93, Bilsthorpe Colliery Accident Public Hearing 1994; Non-exec. Dir. Gilbert Assocs. (Europe) Ltd. 1991–94; Assessor to King's Cross Underground Fire Investigation; Hon. mem. A.S.M.E.; Founder Fellow Irish Acad. of Eng. 1998; Hon. Fellow Welding Inst., Inst. of Engineers of Ireland, Inst. of Mechanical Engineers; Thomas Lowe Gray Lecture, Inst. of Mechanical Eng. 1999; Hon. D.Sc. (Ireland) 1984, (Dublin) 1985, (Edin.) 1987, (Aston) 1988, (Queen's Univ., Belfast) 1988, (Cranfield Inst. of Tech.) 1989, Hon. D. Eng. (Bristol) 1992, (Limerick) 1993, (Liverpool) 1993; Hon. Fellowship (Univ. of Luton) 1994; George Stephenson Research Prize and Thomas Hawksley Gold Medal of Inst. of Mech. Eng., Kelvin Medal of Inst. of Civil Eng. 1992. *Publications:* An Introduction to Mechanics of Machines 1964, Explosive Welding of Metals 1982, Industry's Needs in the Education and Training of Engineers (report); numerous papers on high-pressure eng. and explosive welding in int. journals. *Leisure interests:* walking, reading, travel. *Address:* The Queen's University, Belfast BT7 1NN; (Office); 16 Malone Court, Belfast, BT9 6PA,

Northern Ireland. *Telephone:* (01232) 247303 (Office); (01232) 667495 (Home).

CROW, James F(ranklin), PH.D.; American geneticist; b. 18 Jan. 1916, Phoenixville, Pa.; s. of H. E. Crow and Lena Whitaker Crow; m. Ann Crockett 1941; one s. two d.; ed. Friends Univ. (Wichita, Kan.) and Univ. of Texas; Instructor and Asst. Prof. Dartmouth Coll. 1941–48; Asst. Prof., Assoc. Prof., Prof., Dept. of Genetics, Univ. of Wis., 1948–86, Prof. Emer. 1986–; Chair. of Dept. 1959–63, 1965–72, 1975–77; Acting Dean, Medical School, Univ. of Wis. 1963–65; mem. N.A.S.; Pres. Genetics Soc. of America 1959, American Soc. of Human Genetics 1961. *Publications:* Introduction to Population Genetics Theory 1970, Genetics Notes (8th edn.) 1982, Basic Concepts in Population, Quantitative and Evolutionary Genetics 1986. *Leisure interest:* orchestral and chamber music. *Address:* Department of Medical Genetics, University of Wisconsin, Madison, WI 53706; 24 Glenway, Madison, WI 53706, U.S.A. (Home). *Telephone:* (608) 263-4438 (Office); (608) 233-6709 (Home). *Fax:* (608) 262-2976.

CROW, John W., B.A.; Canadian banker; b. 22 Jan. 1937, London, England; s. of John Cornell Crow and Mary Winifred (née Weetch) Crow; m. Ruth Kent 1963; one s. one d.; ed. Oxford Univ.; Economist IMF 1961–70; Chief N. American Dept., IMF 1970–73; Deputy Chief Research Dept. Bank of Canada 1973, Chief Dept. 1974, Adviser 1979–81, Deputy Gov. 1981–84, Sr. Deputy Gov. 1984–87, Gov. 1987–94; Chair. G10 Cen. Bank Govs. 1993–94; Chair. Investment Cttee., Canada Council; Dir. Midland Walwyn; Sr. Adviser American Int. Group; Adjuct. Prof. of Econs., Univ. of Toronto. *Leisure interests:* reading, gardening. *Address:* 191 Ellis Avenue, Toronto, Ont., M6S 2X4, Canada. *Telephone:* (416) 760-7142; (416) 760-0812.

CROWE, Martin David, M.B.E.; New Zealand cricketer; b. 22 Sept. 1962, Auckland; s. of David Crowe and Audrey Crowe; m. Simone Curtice 1991 (separated 1996); ed. Auckland Grammar School; right-hand batsman, slip fielder; played for Auckland 1979–80 to 1982–83, Cen. Dists. 1983–84 to 1989–90 (Capt. 1984–85 to 1989–90), Somerset 1984–88, Wellington 1990–91 to 1994–95 (Capt. 1993–94); played in 77 Tests for N.Z. 1981–82 to 1995–96, 16 as Capt., scoring 5,444 runs (average 45.36) with 17 hundreds, including N.Z. record 299 v. Sri Lanka, Wellington, Feb. 1991); scored 19,608 first-class runs (71 hundreds); toured England 1983, 1986, 1990 and 1994; 143 limited-overs internationals; N.Z. Sportsman of the Year 1991; selected World Cup Champion Cricketer 1992. *Publication:* Out on a Limb 1996. *Leisure interests:* tennis, golf, wine. *Address:* P.O. Box 109302, Newmarket, Auckland, New Zealand. *Fax:* (09) 6304824.

CROWE, Adm. William James, Jr., PH.D.; American diplomatist and naval officer; b. 2 Jan. 1925, La Grange, Ky.; s. of William J. Crowe and Eula Russell; m. Shirley M. Grennell 1954; two s. one d.; ed. U.S. Naval Acad., and Stanford and Princeton Univs.; commissioned ensign, U.S. Navy 1946; Commanding Officer U.S.S. Trout 1960–62; Commdr. Submarine Div. 31, San Diego 1966–67; Sr. Adviser, Vietnamese Navy Riverine Force 1970–71; Deputy to Pres.'s Special Rep. for Micronesian Status Negotiations 1971–73; Dir. E. Asia and Pacific Region, Office of Sec. of Defense, Washington until 1976; Commdr. Middle East Force, Bahrain 1976–77; Deputy Chief of Naval Operations, Dept. of Navy, Washington 1977–80; C.-in-C. Allied Forces, Southern Europe 1980–83; C.-in-C. Pacific 1983–85; Chair. Joint Chiefs of Staff 1985–89; Prof. of Geopolitics, Univ. of Okla. 1989–94; Chair. Foreign Intelligence Advisory Bd. 1993–94; Amb. to U.K. 1994–97; partner Bioport Corpn.; Counsellor, Center for Strategic and Int. Studies; Bd. Dirs. Texaco, Merrill Lynch, Pfizer, Gen. Dynamics, Norfolk and So. Co.; numerous decorations. *Publications:* The Line of Fire (with David Chanoff) 1992, Reducing Nuclear Danger: The Road Away from the Brink (with McGeorge Bundy and Sidney Drell) 1993.

CROZIER, Brian Rossiter; British writer and journalist; b. 4 Aug. 1918; s. of R. H. Crozier and Elsa (McGillivray) Crozier; m. Mary Lillian Samuel 1940 (died 1993); one s. three d.; ed. Lycée, Montpellier, Peterborough Coll., Harrow, Trinity Coll. of Music, London; music and art critic, London 1936–39; reporter and sub-ed., Stoke-on-Trent, Stockport, London 1940–41; aeronautical inspection 1941–43; sub-ed., Reuters 1943–44, News Chronicle 1944–48, sub-ed. and writer Sydney Morning Herald, Australia 1948–51; corresp., Reuters-AAP 1951–52; features ed., Straits Times, Singapore 1952–53; leader writer and corresp., The Economist 1954–64; BBC commentator, English, French and Spanish overseas services 1954–66, Chair. Forum World Features 1965–74; Ed., Conflict Studies 1970–75; Co-founder and Dir. Inst. for the Study of Conflict 1970–79, Consultant 1979–; Columnist, Now!, London 1980–81, Nat. Review, New York 1978– (contributing ed. 1982–), The Times 1982–84, The Free Nation, London 1982–89; Adjunct Scholar, The Heritage Foundation 1983–95; Distinguished Visiting Scholar, Hoover Inst., Stanford, Calif., U.S.A. 1996–. *Publications:* The Rebels 1960, The Morning After 1963, Neo-Colonialism 1964, South-East Asia in Turmoil 1965, The Struggle for the Third World 1966, Franco 1967, The Masters of Power 1969, The Future of Communist Power (in U.S.A.: Since Stalin) 1970, De Gaulle (vol. I) 1973, (vol. II) 1974, A Theory of Conflict 1974, The Man Who Lost China (Chiang Kai-shek) 1977, Strategy of Survival 1978, The Minimum State 1979, Franco: Crepúsculo de un hombre 1980, The Price of Peace 1980, Socialism Explained (co-author) 1984, This War Called Peace (co-author) 1984, The Andropov Deception (novel) (under pseudonym John Rossiter) 1984, The Grenada Documents (ed.), 1987, Socialism: Dream and Reality 1987, The Gorbachev Phenomenon 1990, Communism: Why Prolong its Death Throes? 1990, Free Agent: The Unseen War 1993, The KGB Lawsuits 1995, Le Phénix rouge (co-author) 1995, and contributions to journals in numerous countries. *Leisure interests:* taping stereo, piano. *Address:* 1AA Carlisle Place, London, SW1P 1NP (Office); 18 Wickliffe Avenue, Finchley, London, N3 3EJ, England (Home). *Telephone:* 0171-931-8046 (Office); 0181-346 8124 (Home).

CRUICKSHANK, Donald Gordon, M.B.A., C.A.; British government official; b. 17 Sept. 1942; s. of Donald C. Cruickshank and Margaret Morrison; m. Elizabeth B. Taylor 1964; one s. one d.; ed. Univ. of Aberdeen and Manchester Business School; consultant, McKinsey & Co. 1972–77; Gen. Man. Sunday Times, Times Newspapers 1977–80; Pearson PLC 1980–84; Man. Dir. Virgin Group 1984–89; Chair. Wandsworth Health Authority 1986–89; Chief Exec. Nat. Health Service in Scotland 1989–93; Dir.-Gen. of Telecommunications 1993–98; Chair. Action 2000 1997–. *Leisure interests:* sport, golf, opera. *Address:* Action 2000, 1 Victoria Street, London, SW1H 0ET, England.

CRUICKSHANK, Durward William John, M.A., SC.D., C.CHEM., F.R.S.C., F.R.S.; British professor of chemistry; b. 7 March 1924; s. of William Durward Cruickshank and Margaret Ombler (née Meek) Cruickshank; m. Marjorie Alice Travis 1953 (died 1983); one s. one d.; ed. St. Lawrence Coll., Ramsgate, Loughborough Coll., Univ. of Cambridge, Univ. of Leeds; Eng. Asst. War Office and Admiralty 1944–46; Research Asst. Chemistry Dept., Leeds Univ. 1946–47, Lecturer 1950–57, Reader in Math. Chemistry 1957–62; Joseph Black Prof. of Chem., Glasgow Univ. 1962–67; Prof. of Chem. UMIST 1967–83, Deputy Prin. 1971–72, Hon. Professorial Research Fellow 1983–; Treas. Int. Union of Crystallography 1966–72, Gen. Sec. 1970–72; Fellow St. John's Coll., Cambridge 1953–56; Companion of UMIST 1992; Bragg Lecture 1997; Chem. Soc. Award for Structural Chem. 1978, Dorothy Hodgkin Prize, British Crystallographic Asscn. 1991. *Publications:* numerous scientific papers. *Leisure interests:* golf, genealogy. *Address:* Chemistry Department, University of Manchester Institute of Science and Technology, Manchester, M60 1QD (Office); 105 Moss Lane, Alderley Edge, Cheshire, SK9 7HW, England (Home). *Telephone:* (01625) 582656 (Home).

CRUISE, Tom (Thomas Cruise Mapother IV); American actor; b. 3 July 1962, Syracuse, N.Y.; m. 1st Mimi Rogers 1987 (divorced 1990); m. 2nd Nicole Kidman 1990; one adopted d. one adopted s. *Films include:* Endless Love 1981, Taps 1981, All the Right Moves 1983, Losin' It 1983, The Outsiders 1983, Risky Business 1983, Legend 1984, Top Gun 1985, The Color of Money 1986, Rain Man 1988, Cocktail 1989, Born on the Fourth of July 1989, Daytona, Rush, Days of Thunder 1990, Sure as the Moon 1991, Far and Away 1992, A Few Good Men 1992, The Firm 1993, Interview with the Vampire 1994, Jerry Maguire 1996, Mission Impossible 1996, Jerry McGuire 1996, Eyes Wide Shut 1997; producer Without Limits 1998.

CRUMB, George, B.M., M.M., D.M.A.; American composer; b. 24 Oct. 1929, Charleston, W. Va.; s. of George Henry and Vivian Reed; m. Elizabeth Brown 1949; two s. one d.; ed. Mason Coll. of Music, Univ. of Illinois, Univ. of Michigan, Hochschule für Musik (Berlin); Prof., Univ. of Colorado 1959–63; Creative Assoc., State Univ. of New York at Buffalo 1963–64; Prof., Univ. of Pa. 1971–, Annenberg Prof. 1983–; Pulitzer Prize for Music 1968; Koussevitsky Int. Recording Award 1971; 1968; Prince Pierre de Monaco Prize 1989. *Publications:* Ancient Voices of Children, Black Angels, Eleven Echoes of Autumn, 1965, Songs, Drones and Refrains of Death, Makrokosmos Vols. I–III, Music for a Summer Evening, Five Pieces for Piano, Night of the Four Moons, Night Music I, Echoes of Time and the River, Four Nocturnes, Star-child, Dream Sequence, Celestial Mechanics, Apparition, A Little Suite for Christmas 1979, Gnomic Variations, Pastoral Drone, Processional, A Haunted Landscape, The Sleeper, An Idyll for the Misbegotten, Federico's Little Songs for Children, Zeitgeist, Easter Dawning for Carillon. *Leisure interest:* reading. *Address:* 240 Kirk Lane, Media, PA 19063, U.S.A. *Telephone:* (215) 565-2438.

CRUMPTON, Michael Joseph, C.B.E., PH.D., F.R.S.; British biochemist and immunologist; b. 7 June 1929; s. of Charles E. Crumpton and Edith Crumpton; m. Janet Elizabeth Dean 1960; one s. two d.; ed. Poole Grammar School, Univ. Coll., Southampton and Lister Inst. of Preventive Medicine, London; joined scientific staff Microbiological Research Establishment, Porton, Wilts. 1955–60; Deputy Dir. Research Labs., Imperial Cancer Research Fund Labs., London 1979–91, Dir. 1991–93; Dir. Imperial Cancer Research Tech. Ltd. 1989– (C.O.O. 1993–94); Visiting Scientist Fellowship, Nat. Insts. of Health, Bethesda, Md., U.S.A. 1959–60; Research Fellow, Dept. of Immunology, St. Mary's Hosp. Medical School, London 1960–66; mem. scientific staff Nat. Inst. for Medical Research, Mill Hill 1966–79, Head of Biochemistry Div. 1976–79; Visiting Fellow, John Curtin School for Medical Research, Australian Nat. Univ., Canberra 1973–74; mem. Cell Bd. MRC 1979–83, Science Council, Celltech Ltd. 1980–90, EMBO 1982–, W.H.O. Steering Cttee. for Encapsulated Bacteria 1984–91 (Chair. 1988–91), Sloan Cttee. Gen. Motors Research Foundation 1986–88 (Chair. 1988), Council Royal Inst. 1986–90 (mem. Davy Faraday Lab. Comm. 1985–90, Chair. 1988–90), MRC 1986–90, Royal Soc. 1990–92, Scientific Advisory Comm., Lister Inst. 1986–91, MRC AIDS Directed Prog. Steering Cttee. 1987–91, Scientific Cttee. Swiss Inst. for Experimental Cancer Research 1989–96; Chair. Scientific Advisory Bd. Biomedical Research Centre, Univ. of British Columbia 1987–91, Health and Safety Exec./Dept. of Health Advisory Comm. on Dangerous Pathogens 1990–; Dir. (non-exec.) Amersham Int. PLC 1990–97, Amersham Pharmacia 1997–; mem. Governing Body B.P.M.F.

1987–95, Academia Europea 1996–, Governing Body Imperial Coll. 1994; mem. numerous Editorial Bds.; Biochemistry Soc. Visiting Lecturer, Australia 1983; Trustee EMF Biological Research Trust 1995–, Breakthrough Breast Cancer 1997–. *Publications:* numerous scientific papers. *Leisure interests:* gardening, reading. *Address:* 33 Homefield Road, Radlett, Herts., WD7 8PX, England. *Telephone:* (01923) 854675.

CRUTZEN, Paul; Netherlands scientist; b. 1933, Amsterdam; ed. Stockholm Univ.; Dir. Atmospheric Chemistry Div. Max-Planck Inst. for Chem.; mem. Royal Swedish Acad. of Sciences, Royal Swedish Acad. of Eng. Sciences, Academia Europaea; shared Nobel Prize in Chem. 1995. *Address:* Max-Planck Institute for Chemistry, Jon.-Joachim-Becher-Weg 27, 55128 Mainz, Germany. *Telephone:* (6131) 3050. *Fax:* (6131) 305388.

CRUYFF, Johan; Netherlands footballer; b. 25 April 1947, Amsterdam; played for Ajax 1964–73; top scorer in Dutch League, with 33 goals 1967; moved to Barcelona, now Coach of Barcelona; captained Netherlands 1974 World Cup final; retd. 1978; started playing again, signed for Los Angeles Aztecs; played for Washington Diplomats 1979–80, for Levante, Spain 1981, then for Ajax and Feyenoord 1982; Man. Ajax 1985–87, winning European Cup-Winners' Cup 1987; fmr. Man. Barcelona, winning Cup-Winners' Cup 1989, European Cup 1992, Spanish League title 1991, 1992, 1993, Spanish Super Cup 1992.

CRUZ, Celia; Cuban singer; b. 21 Oct. 1929, Havana; d. of Simón Cruz and Catalina Alfonso; m. Pedro Knight 1962; performed salsa music with various artists including: La Sonora Matancera, Ray Barretto, Willie Colón and Tito Puente; appeared in film The Mambo Kings 1992; Grammy award for Latin Tropical Performance (with Ray Barretto) 1974; Nat. Medal of Arts 1994. *Address:* c/o Ralph Mercado Management, Inc., 568 Broadway, Room 806, New York, NY 10012, U.S.A.

CRUZ-DIEZ, Carlos; Venezuelan painter; b. 17 Aug. 1923; ed. School of Plastic and Applied Arts, Caracas; Dir. of Art. Venezuelan subsidiary of McCann-Erickson Advertising Agency 1946–51; Teacher, History of Applied Arts, School of Arts, Caracas 1953–55; in Barcelona and Paris working on physical qualities of colour now named *Physichromies* 1955–56; opened studio of visual arts and industrial design, Caracas 1957; Prof. and Asst. Dir. School of Arts, Caracas 1959–60; moved to Paris 1960; First one-man exhbn., Caracas 1947, later in Madrid, Genoa, Turin, London, Paris, Cologne, Munich, Oslo, Brussels, Ostwald Museum, Dortmund, Bottrop (Fed. Repub. of Germany), New York, Bogotá, Rome, Venice and Essen; Retrospective exhbns. at Signals, London and Galerie Kerchache, Paris 1965; represented at numerous Group exhbns.; works in Museo de Bellas Artes, Caracas, Victoria and Albert Museum, Tate Gallery, London, Casa de las Américas, Havana, Städtisches Museum, Leverkusen, Germany, Museum of Modern Art, N.Y., Museum of Contemporary Art, Montreal, Museum des 20. Jahrhunderts, Vienna, Univ. of Dublin, Museo Civico di Torino, Wallraf-Richartz Museum, Cologne, Musée de Grenoble, Centre Georges Pompidou, Musée d'Art Moderne, Paris, Neue Pinakothek, Munich; Grand Prix at 3rd Biennale, Córdoba, Argentina; Prix Int. de Peinture à la IX Biennale de São Paulo. *Address:* 23 rue Pierre Semard, Paris 75009, France.

CRVENKOVSKI, Branko; Macedonian politician and engineer; b. 12 Oct. 1962, Sarajevo; m.; one s. one d.; ed. Skopje Univ.; computer eng. SEMOS Co. 1987–90; Chair. Social-Democratic Union of Macedonia 1990–92; Chair. Cabinet of Ministers (Prime Minister) Repub. of Macedonia 1992–98. *Address:* c/o Social Democratic Union of Macedonia, Prihačka str. 8, 91000 Skopje, Republic of Macedonia.

CRVENKOVSKI, Stevo; Macedonian politician and film director; b. 18 March 1947, Skopje; ed. Acad. of Theatre, Film, Radio and TV, Belgrade; film dir. Vardarstudio (Skopje), later concurrently Dir. 1970–92; in independence movt. since 1990; Deputy Chair. Macedonian Govt. 1992–93; Minister of Foreign Affairs 1993–96; Amb. to U.K. 1997–. *Address:* Macedonian Embassy, 10 Harcourt House, 19A Cavendish Square, London, W1M 9AD, England.

CRYSTAL, Billy; American actor and comedian; b. 14 March 1947, Long Beach, N.Y.; s. of Jack Crystal and Helen Crystal; m. Janice Crystal (née Goldfinger); two d.; ed. Marshall Univ., Nassau Community Coll., New York Univ.; mem. of the group 3's Company; solo appearances as a stand-up comedian; TV appearances include: Soap 1977–81, The Billy Crystal Hour 1982, Saturday Night Live 1984–85, The Love Boat, The Tonight Show; TV films include: Breaking up is Hard to do 1979, Enola Gay, The Men, The Mission, The Atomic Bomb 1980, Death Flight; *feature films include:* The Rabbit Test 1978, This is Spinal Tap 1984, Running Scared 1986, The Princess Bride 1987, Throw Momma from the Train 1987, When Harry Met Sally . . . 1989, City Slickers 1991, Mr Saturday Night (also Dir. Producer, co-screen-play writer) 1993, Forget Paris 1995, Hamlet, Father's Day, Deconstructing Harry, My Grant 1998, Analyse This 1998. *Publication:* Absolutley Mahvelous 1986.

CSÁSZÁR, Ákos; Hungarian mathematician; b. 26 Feb. 1924, Budapest; s. of Károly Császár and Gizella Szücs; m. Klára Cseley; ed. Budapest Univ.; Prof. Loránd Eötvös Univ. Budapest 1957–94, Prof. Emer. 1994–; Dir. Inst. of Mathematics, Loránd Eötvös Univ. 1983–86; Visiting Prof. Technische Universität Stuttgart 1975, Università di Torino 1979, Technische Universität Graz 1983; fmr. mem. Editorial Bd., Periodica Mathematica Hungarica, Studia Mathematica Hungarica; mem. Editorial Bd. Applied Categorical Structures; Chief Ed. Acta Mathematica Hungarica 1996, Annales Univ. Scientiarum Budapestinensis Sectio Mathematica; Gen. Sec. János Bolyai Mathematical Soc. 1966–80, Pres. 1980–90, Hon. Pres. 1990–; corresp. mem. Hungarian Acad. of Sciences 1970, full mem. 1979–; Kossuth Prize 1963. *Leisure interests:* music, botany, bridge. *Publications:* Foundations of General Topology 1960, General Topology 1974, Valós analízis (Real Analysis) 1983 (2 vols.); articles in int. mathematical periodicals. *Address:* 1052 Budapest, Párizsi utca 6/a, Hungary. *Telephone:* 36/1/318-5172.

CSIKÓS-NAGY, Béla; Hungarian economist; b. 9 Sept. 1915, Szeged; s. of Dr. József Csikós-Nagy and Jolán Jedlicska; m. Dr. Livia Kneppó 1944; two d.; ed. Szeged Univ. and Univ. of Pécs; joined Hungarian CP 1945; Chair. Hungarian Bd. of Prices and Materials 1957–84; Exec. Co-Chair. Council of Industrial Policy 1984–90; lecturer on Price Theory at Karl Marx Univ. of Econ. Sciences, Budapest 1959–90, title of Univ. Prof. 1964, Dr. of Econ. Sc. 1967; Under-Sec. of State 1968–84; Pres. Hungarian Econ. Assn. 1970–90, Hon. Chair. 1994–; mem. Exec. Cttee. Int. Econ. Assn. 1971–77, 1983–86; Hon. Prof. Univ. of Vienna, mem. Oxford Energy Club 1977, Corresp. mem. Austrian Acad. of Sciences; mem. Hungarian Acad. of Sciences 1982–; Hon. Chair. Int. Soc. of Econs.; Pres. Hungarian Bridge Fed. 1983–90; Hungarian State Prize 1970, Banner Order of Hungarian People's Repub. *Publications:* Pricing in Hungary 1968, General and Socialist Price Theory 1968, Hungarian Economic Policy 1971, Socialist Economic Policy 1973, Socialist Price Theory and Price Policy 1975, Towards a New Price Revolution 1978, On Hungarian Price Policy 1980, Economic Policy 1982, The Price Law in Socialist Planned Economy 1983, Topical Issues of Hungarian Price Policy 1985, Socialist Market Economy 1987, Price and Power (with Peter S. Elek) 1995, Hungarian Economic Policy in the 20th Century 1996. *Leisure interest:* card patience. *Address:* Budapest 1245, Pf. 1044 (Office); Budapest XII, Varosmajor u. 26/c, Hungary (Home). *Telephone:* 331-6906 (Office); 3554-081 (Home). *Fax:* 331-6906 (Office).

CSIKSZENTMIHALYI, Mihaly, PH.D.; American professor of psychology; b. 29 Sept. 1934, Fiume, Italy; s. of Alfred Csikszentmiha'lyi and Edith (Jankovich de Jessenice) Csikszentmiha'lyi; m. Isabella Selega 1961; two s.; ed. Univs. of Illinois and Chicago; went to U.S.A. in 1956; Assoc. Prof. and Chair., Dept. of Sociology and Anthropology, Lake Forest Coll. 1965–71; Prof. of Human Devt., Univ. of Chicago 1971, Chair. Dept. of Behavioral Sciences 1985–87; mem. Bd. of Advisers, Encyclopaedia Britannica 1985–; Consultant, The J.P. Getty Museum, Malibu 1985–; Sr. Fulbright Scholar, Brazil 1984, New Zealand 1990; Fellow American Acad. of Arts and Sciences, Hungarian Acad. of Sciences, Nat. Acad. of Educ., Nat. Acad. of Leisure Sciences, World Economic Forum, Center for Advanced Study in the Behavioral Sciences. *Publications:* Beyond Boredom and Anxiety 1975, The Creative Vision 1976, The Meaning of Things 1981, Being Adolescent 1984, Optimal Experience 1988, Flow—The Psychology of Optimal Experience 1990, Television and the Quality of Life 1990, The Art of Seeing 1990, Talented Teenagers 1993, The Evolving Self 1993, Creativity 1996, Finding Flow in Everyday Life 1997, contrib. to several other books. *Leisure interests:* mountain climbing, chess and history. *Address:* 5848 South University Avenue, Chicago, IL 60637 (Office); 5333 South Hyde Park Boulevard, Chicago, IL 60615, U.S.A. (Home). *Telephone:* (312) 493-4681 (Home).

CSOÓRI, Sándor; Hungarian poet and writer; b. 3 Feb. 1930, Zámoly, Co. Fejér; Contrib. to Irodalmi Újság (monthly) 1954–55; ed. Új hang (monthly) 1955–56; drama critic Mafilm Studio 1968; joined opposition movt. 1980; participated in political discussions of Monor 1985 and Lakitelek 1987; founding mem. Hungarian Democratic Forum 1987, presidium mem. 1988–92; Chair. Illyés Gyula Foundation 1990–94; Pres. World Fed. of Hungarians 1991–; Attila József Prize 1954, Herder Prize 1981, Kossuth Prize 1990, Eeva Joenpelto Prize 1995. *Publications:* selected poems: Fölröppen a madár (Up Flies the Bird) 1954, Ördögpille (Demon Butterfly) 1957, Knives and Nails 1981, Memory of Snow 1983, Várakozás a tavaszban (Waiting in the Spring) 1983, Menekülés a magányból (Escape from Loneliness) 1962, Hattyúkkal ágyútűzben (In Cannon Fire with Swans) 1995, Ha volna életem (If I Had a Life) 1996; sociographies: Tudósítás a toronyból (Report From the Tower) 1963, Kubai utinapló (Cuban Travel Diary) 1965; essay volumes: Faltól falig (From Wall to Wall) 1968, Nomád napló (Nomadic Diary) 1979, Félig bevallott élet (Half Confessed Life) 1984, Készülődés a számadásra (Preparation for Final Reckoning) 1987, Nappali hold (Daytime Moon) 1991, Tenger és diólevél I. II. (The Sea and Nut Leaves) 1994, Száll alá a poklokra (Descent into Hell) 1997; Film scripts: Tízezer nap (Ten thousand days), Földobott kő (The thrown-up stone), 80 huszár (Eighty Hussars), Tüske a köröm alatt (A Thorn under the Fingernail). *Address:* 1068 Budapest, Benczúr u. 15, Hungary.

CUBAS GRAU, Raúl, Ing.; Paraguayan politician; b. 23 August 1943, Asunción; m. Mirta Gusinsky de Cubas; two d.; ed. Universidade Católica do Rio de Janeiro; Man. C.I.E. SRL 1977, 1979; Dir. CONCRET-MIX S.A. 1970–88; Legal Rep. 14 de Julio S.A. 1980–1993; Dir. COPAC VIAL S.A. 1987–91; Legal Rep. of consortium OCHO A S.A.C.I.–14 Julio S.A.–CONPASA 1992; Exec. Minister of State for Ministry of Econ. and Social Planning and Devt. 1994–96; Minister of Finance 1996; Pres. of Paraguay 1998–99.

CUBILLOS SALLATO, Hernán; Chilean government official and company director; b. 25 Feb. 1936, Viña del Mar; s. of Hernán Cubillos Leiva and María Graciela Sallato; m. Marcela Sigall 1960 (separated); three s. one d.;

ed. Colegio de los Sagrados Corazones in Viña del Mar and Santiago, Oratory School, Bournemouth, England, Arturo Prat Naval Coll., Valparaíso; Officer, Chilean Navy 1953–61; Empresas Industriales El Melón S.A. 1961–62; Empresa Periodística El Mercurio, S.A.P. 1963–74; Pres. Revista Qué Pasa 1974–78, Santillana del Pacífico S.A. de Ediciones 1974–78, Compañía de Inversiones La Transandina, S.A. 1974–78, Transamerica S.A. de Comercio Exterior, Banco de Crédito e Inversiones 1981, Cía. Inversiones Transandina S.A., Transat S.A.; Minister of Foreign Affairs 1978–80; mem. Superior Council of Foreign Affairs; Dir. Inter-American Press Asscn. 1974–77; mem. Int. Press Inst.; Presidential Medal, Medal of City of Santiago 1953, Abdón Calderón Medal (Ecuador), Antonio Nariño Medal (Colombia), Grand Cross of Order of the Sun (Peru), Bicentenario del General Bernardo O'Higgins Award (Chile), Decoration for Services to the Nation (Chile). *Leisure interests:* yachting, photography. *Address:* Av. Dag-Hammarskjold 3081 Dp. 111, Vitacura, Santiago, Chile. *Telephone:* (2) 2071531; (2) 2060036. *Fax:* (2) 2073466.

CUBITT, Sir Hugh (Guy), Kt., C.B.E., F.R.I.C.S., J.P., D.L., F.R.S.A.; British business executive; b. 2 July 1928; s. of late Col. the Hon. Guy Cubitt and Rosamond M.E. Cholmeley; m. Linda I. Campbell 1958; one s. two d.; ed. Royal Naval Colls. Dartmouth and Greenwich; R.N. 1949–53; partner, Rogers, Chapman & Thomas 1958–67, Cubitt & West 1962–79; Chair. The Housing Corpn. 1980–90, Lombard North Cen. PLC 1980–91; Chair., Commr. London Advisory Cttee., English Heritage 1988–94; Chair. Anchor Group of Housing Assocs. 1991–98; Chair. Rea Brothers Group PLC 1996–98; Dir. Property Security Investment Trust PLC (now PSIT PLC) 1962–97; Dir. Nat. Westminster Bank 1977–90, mem. U.K. Advisory Bd. 1990–91; Gov. Peabody Trust 1991– (Chair. 1998); mem. Westminster City Council 1963–78; Lord Mayor of Westminster 1977–78; Pres. London Chamber of Commerce 1988–91; High Sheriff of Surrey 1983–84; Chair. Rea Bros. Group PLC 1995–; other professional and civic appts.; Hon. F.R.A.M.; Chief Hon. Steward, Westminster Abbey 1997–. *Leisure interests:* country sports, travel, photography. *Address:* Chapel House, West Humble, Dorking, Surrey, RH5 6AY, England. *Telephone:* (01306) 882994.

CUCKNEY, Baron (Life Peer), cr. 1995, of Millbank in the City of Westminster; **John Graham Cuckney,** Kt., M.A.; British business executive; b. 12 July 1925, India; s. of late Air Vice-Marshal E. J. Cuckney; m. 2nd Muriel Boyd 1960; ed. Shrewsbury School, Univ. of St. Andrews; Civil Asst., Gen. Staff, War Office 1949–57; Dir. of various industrial and financial cos. 1957–72 incl. Lazard Bros. & Co. 1964–70, J. Bibby & Sons 1970–72; Chair. Standard Industrial Trust 1966–70, Mersey Docks and Harbour Bd. 1970–72, Bldg. Econ. Devt. Cttee. 1976–79; Ind. mem. Railway Policy Review Cttee. 1966–67; Special mem. Hops Marketing Bd. 1971–72; Chief Exec. (Second Perm. Sec.), Property Services Agency 1972–74; Sr. Crown Agent and Chair. of Crown Agents for Oversea Govts. and Administrations 1974–78; Chair. (part-time) Int. Mil. Services Ltd. 1974–85, Port of London Authority 1977–79, The Thomas Cook Group Ltd. 1978–87; Dir. Midland Bank PLC 1978–88; Dir. Royal Insurance PLC 1979; Deputy Chair. 1982–85, Chair. 1985–94; Dir. Brooke Bond Liebig Ltd. (now Brooke Bond Group PLC) 1978–84, Vice-Chair. 1980–81, Chair. 1981–84; Dir. John Brown PLC 1981–86, Deputy Chair. 1982–83, Chair. 1983–86; Chair. Westland Group PLC 1985–89, The Orion Publishing Group Ltd. 1994–97; Dir. and Deputy Chair. TI Group PLC 1985–90; Dir. Brixton Estate PLC 1985–96, Lazard Brothers & Co. Ltd. 1988–90; Dir. Investors in Industry Group PLC (now 3i Group PLC) 1986–92, Chair. 1987–92; Dir. Glaxo Holdings PLC 1990–95 (Vice-Chair. 1993–95); Chair. Int. Maritime Bureau 1981–85; Founder Chair. Maxwell Pensioners' Trust 1992–95; Adviser to Sec. of State for Social Security on the Maxwell pensions affair 1992–95; Elder Brother of Trinity House 1980. *Address:* House of Lords, London, SW1A 0PW, England. *Telephone:* 0171-219-3000.

CUCU, Vasile, Romanian geographer; b. 7 April 1927, Igiroasa, Mehedinţi county; s. of Sălică Cucu and Maria Cucu; m. Ana Popova 1954; two d.; ed. Coll. of Geography, Sverdlovsk Univ., U.S.S.R. 1954; Univ. lecturer Coll. of Geography, Bucharest Univ. 1965–69, Prof. 1969–; Pro-Rector, Bucharest Univ. 1968–74, of the Cen. Inst. of the Specialization of Teaching Staff 1972–74; Chair. Geography Dept., Bucharest Univ. 1975–89, Head Dept. Human and Econ. Geography, Geography Faculty 1990–; Dean Walachia Univ., Tîrgovişte 1996–; Ed.-in-Chief of geographical periodicals: Terra 1956–, Buletinul Societăţii de Ştiinţe Geografice 1972–, Analele Universităţii din Bucureşti 1977–; mem. Int. Union of Geography Cttees. on Population 1966–, Town Planning 1968–86, Nat. Demography Dept. 1971–89; mem. Bd. of Geographical Sciences of the S.R. Romania 1956–, Vice-Pres. 1970–. *Publications:* Romania's Geography (in collaboration) 1966, 1977, 1987, Romania's Cities 1970, The Geography of Population and Human Settlements 1974, 1980, Geography and Urbanization 1976, The Systematization of Romania's Territory and Localities 1977, Millionaire Cities (in collaboration) 1983, Romania—A Geographical Synthesis 1984, Romania's Cities and Towns 1989, Insula Serpilor (The Snakes' Island) 1991, Romania—Geopolitical Aspects—Terra 1992–93, Romania's Human Geography 1994, Romania's Economic and Political Geography 1996, Human Geography - Population 1997, Human Geography - Geography of Settlements 1998, Romania, Human and Economic Geography 1998. *Address:* Facultatea de geografie, Bd. Nicolae Bălcescu No. 1, Bucharest 70111; Walachia University of Tîrgovişte, Calea Domneasca No. 236, Jud. Dâmboviţa; 2 Bitolia str., Flat 14, Sector 1, Bucharest, Romania. *Telephone:* (1) 230 4217 (Bucharest); (45) 210 275, 611 042 (Tîrgovişte). *Fax:* (45) 217 692.

CUEVAS, José Luis; Mexican painter; b. 26 Feb. 1934, México, D.F.; s. of Alberto Cuevas and María Regla; m. Bertha Riestra 1961; three d.; ed. Univ. de México, School of Painting and Sculpture "La Esmeralda", Mexico; over forty one-man exhbns. in New York, Paris, Milan, Mexico, Buenos Aires, Toronto, Los Angeles, Washington, etc.; Group Exhbns. all over N. and S. America, Europe, India and Japan; works are in Museum of Modern Art, Solomon R. Guggenheim Museum, Brooklyn Museum (New York), Art Inst. Chicago, Phillips Collection, Washington, D.C., Museums of Albi and Lyons, France, etc.; First Int. Award for Drawing, São Paulo Bienal 1959, First Int. Award, Mostra Internazionale di Bianco e Nero de Lugano, Zürich 1962, First Prize, Bienal de Grabado, Santiago, Chile 1964, First Int. Prize for engraving, first Biennial of New Delhi, India 1968, Nat. Fine Arts Award Mexico 1981; has illustrated following books: The Worlds of Kafka and Cuevas 1959, The Ends of Legends String, Recollections of Childhood 1962, Cuevas por Cuevas (autobiog.) 1964, Cuevas Charenton 1965, Crime by Cuevas 1968, Homage to Quevedo 1969, El Mundo de José Luis Cuevas 1970, Cuaderno de Paris 1977, Zarathustra 1979, Les Obsessions Noirs 1982, Letters to Tasenda 1982. *Publications:* Cuevas by Cuevas 1964, Cuevario 1973, Confesiones de José Luis Cuevas 1975, Cuevas por Daisy Ascher 1979. *Address:* Galeana 109, San Angel Inn, México 20, D.F., Mexico; c/o Tasende Gallery, 820 Prospect Street, La Jolla, CA 92037, U.S.A. *Telephone:* 548-78-20; 548-90-54 (both México, D.F.)

CUEVAS CANCINO, Francisco; Mexican diplomatist; b. 7 May 1921, Mexico City; m. Ana Hilditch 1946; two s. one d.; ed. Free School of Law, Mexico City, McGill Univ., Montreal, Ottawa, London and Columbia Univs.; Third Sec., London 1946–49; served UN Secr. 1950–53; Adviser to Minister of Foreign Affairs 1954; Asst. Dir. of Int. Orgs., Ministry of Foreign Affairs and Head, Tech. Assistance Programme in Mexico 1956–57; Legal Counsellor, Perm. Mission of Mexico at UN 1959–60; Dir. Centre for Int. Studies, Mexico City 1961; Alt. Rep. of Mexico at UN 1962, Perm. Rep. 1965–70, 1978; Perm. Del. of Mexico to UNESCO, Paris 1970–76, mem. Exec. Bd. UNESCO 1971–74; Consul Gen., Paris 1977; mem. Mexican del. to UN Gen. Ass. 1955–70; Amb. to EEC 1981–83, to U.K. 1983–86, to Austria 1986–90; Perm. Rep. to UNIDO and IAEA 1986–. *Publications:* books on law, international affairs and history. *Address:* Secretariat of State for Foreign Affairs, Ricardo Flores Magón, 1 Tlatelolco, 06995, México D.F., Mexico.

CUI NAIFU; Chinese politician; b. 8 Oct. 1928, Beijing; s. of Cui Yu Lian and Chang Wei Fung Cui; m. 1955; one s. one d.; joined CCP 1948; Dir. Propaganda Dept. and Dean of Studies, Lanzhou Univ.; Vice-Chair. Lanzhou Univ. Revolutionary Cttee.; Vice-Minister of Civil Affairs 1981, Minister 1982–93; mem. 12th Cen. Cttee. CCP 1982–87, 13th Cen. Cttee. CCP 1987–92, 14th Cen. Cttee. 1992–; mem. 8th NPC 1993–, NPC Deputy Jiangxi Prov.; Deputy Head, Group for Resettlement of Ex-Servicemen and Retired Officers 1983–88, Head 1988–; Research Soc. for Theory of Civil Admin. and Social Welfare 1985; Chair. China Org. Comm. of UN Decade of Disabled Persons 1986; Hon. Pres. China Asscn. of Social Workers 1991–; Deputy Dir. China Org. Comm. of Int. Decade of Natural Disaster Reduction 1991–; Hon. Dir. China Welfare Fund for the Handicapped 1985–; Hon. Pres. China Asscn. for the Blind and Deaf Mutes 1984; Pres. China Charity Fed. 1994–. *Leisure interest:* calligraphy. *Address:* No. 9, Xi Huang Cheng Gen Street, Beijing 100032, People's Republic of China. *Telephone:* 6601-7240. *Fax:* 6601-7240.

CUISIA, Jose L., B.A., B.SC., M.B.A.; Philippine banker; b. 16 July 1944, Manila; s. of Jose Cuisia and Magdalena (née Lampe) Cuisia; m. Maria Victoria Jose Cuisia 1973; five d.; ed. De la Salle Univ., The Wharton School, Pa. Univ.; Exec. Vice-Pres; C.E.O. Filinvest Credit Corpn. Jan.–Aug. 1980, Insular Bank of Asia and America 1980–84, Pres. C.E.O. 1984–85; Admin. Social Security System 1986–90; Chair. Barcelon Roxas Securities Inc. 1986, Union Bank of the Philippines 1986–90, Monetary Bd.; Vice-Chair. Century Bank 1986, Philippine Business for Social Progress; Gov. Cen. Bank of the Philippines 1990; Chair. Bd. Paraclete Foundation; Gov. Cen. Monetary Authority; mem. Bd. of Trustees, Asian Man. Inst., Makati Medical Center, Pres. Philippine Financial Exec. Inst. 1984, Philippine Man. Asscn. 1984. *Address:* 626 Adelfa Street, New Ayala Alabang Village, Muntinlupa, Manila, Philippines (Home).

CULHANE, John Leonard, PH.D., F.R.S.; Irish university professor; b. 14 Oct. 1937, Dublin; s. of John Thomas Culhane and Mary Agnes Culhane (née Durkin); m. Mary Brigid Smith 1961; two s.; ed. Univ. Coll. Dublin, Univ. Coll. London; lecturer in Physics Univ. Coll. London 1967–69, 1970–76, Reader 1976–81, Prof. 1981–; research scientist Lockheed Palo Alto Lab. 1969–70; Dir. Mullard Space Science Lab. Univ. Coll. London 1983–, Head Dept. of Space and Climate Physics 1993–; U.K. Del. and Vice-Pres. European Space Agency Science Programme Cttee. 1989–; Chair. British Nat. Space Centre Space Science Programme Bd. 1989–; Dir. (non-exec.) Satellites Int. Ltd. U.K. 1988–; mem. Advisory Panel European Space Agency Space Science Dept. 1995–. *Publications:* X-Ray Astronomy, over 200 papers on Solar and Cosmic X-Ray Astronomy, X-Ray Instrumentation and Plasma Spectroscopy. *Leisure interests:* music, motor racing. *Address:* 24 Warnham Road, Horsham, W. Sussex, RH12 2QU, England. *Telephone:* (01483) 274111 (Office).

CULKIN, Macaulay; American actor; b. 26 Aug. 1980, New York; s. of Christopher "Kit" Culkin and Pat Culkin; m. Rachel Milner 1998; ed. St. Joseph's School of Yorkville, New York and George Balanchine's School of Ballet, New York. *Films:* Rocket Gibraltar 1988, Uncle Buck 1989, See You

In The Morning 1989, Jacob's Ladder 1990, Home Alone 1990, My Girl 1991, Only the Lonely 1991, Home Alone 2: Lost in New York 1992, The Nutcracker, The Good Son 1993, The Pagemaster, Getting Even With Dad, Richie Rich 1995, Body Piercer 1998. *Address:* c/o Brian Gersh, William Morris Agency, 151 S. El Camino Drive, Beverly Hills, CA 90212, U.S.A.

CULLBERG, Brigit Ragnhild; Swedish choreographer; b. 3 Aug. 1908, Nyköping; d. of Carl Cullberg and Elna Westerström; m. Anders Ek 1942 (divorced); two s. one d.; ed. Univ. of Stockholm, Jooss School of Dance, Lilian Karina Ballet School; Choreographer, Swedish Opera Ballet 1951–57; Guest Choreographer, Royal Danish Ballet 1957–61, 1975, American Ballet Theatre 1958–64, New York City Ballet 1958, Nat. Ballet of Santiago de Chile, City Ballets of Cologne, Munich, Düsseldorf, Zürich, Dortmund, Oslo, Helsinki, Antwerp, Geneva, Warsaw, Teheran and West Berlin; Dir. Cullberg Ballet, The Swedish Nat. Theatre Centre 1967–85; choreography includes: Miss Julie, Medea, Moon-reindeer, The Evil Queen (Prix d'Italia 1961), Lady from the Sea, Adam and Eve, Eurydice is Dead, Romeo and Juliet, Red Wine in Green Glasses (Prix d'Italia 1971), Revolt, Rapport (The 7th Symphony of Allan Pettersson), War Dances (9th Symphony), Dreams of Love and Death, Medea's Children, Pulcinella (in collaboration with Giuseppe Carbone). *Publication:* Ballet and Us 1954. *Leisure interests:* theatre, art, political and social problems, peace. *Address:* Cullberg Ballet, c/o The Swedish National Theatre Centre, Rasunderagen 150, Solna, Sweden. *Telephone:* 8-652387.

CULLEN, Alexander Lamb, O.B.E., D.SC.(ENG.), F.ENG., F.R.S.; British professor of electrical engineering; b. 30 April 1920, London; s. of R.H. Cullen and J. Cullen; m. Margaret Lamb 1940; two s. one d.; ed. Lincoln School and Imperial Coll., London; Lecturer, Univ. Coll., London 1946–55, Pender Prof. of Electrical Eng. 1967–80, Sr. Research Fellow 1980–83, Hon. Research Fellow 1983–; Prof. of Electrical Eng. and Head, Dept. of Electrical Eng., Sheffield Univ. 1955–67; Prof. Emer., Univ. of London; Hon. Fellow Univ. Coll. London 1994; Hon D.Eng. (Sheffield) 1985; Hon. D.Sc. (Chinese Univ. of Hong Kong) 1981, (Kent) 1986. *Publications:* Microwave Measurements 1950; numerous articles in scientific journals. *Leisure interest:* music. *Address:* Department of Electronic and Electrical Engineering, University College London, Torrington Place, London, WC1E 7JE; 3 Felden Drive, Hemel Hempstead, Herts., HP3 0BD, England. *Telephone:* (01442) 258277. *Fax:* (01442) 258277.

CULLEN, Michael John, M.A., PH.D.; New Zealand politician; b. 1945, London, England; m. Anne Lowson Collins; two d.; ed. Christ's Coll. Christchurch, Canterbury Univ. and Univ. of Edinburgh; Asst. Lecturer, Canterbury Univ., Tutor Univ. of Stirling, Sr. Lecturer in History, Univ. of Otago (Dunedin) and Visiting Fellow, Australian Nat. Univ. 1968–81; mem. Parl. 1981–; Minister of Social Welfare 1987–90; Assoc. Minister of Finance 1987–88, of Health 1988–90, of Labour 1989–90; Opposition Spokesperson on Finance 1991, Deputy Leader of Opposition 1996–; Labour Party. *Leisure interests:* music, reading, house renovation, golf. *Address:* Parliament House, Wellington; P.O. Box 2294, Harrington Point Road, Dunedin, New Zealand. *Telephone:* 471 9876. *Fax:* 472 4268.

CULLINAN, Brendan Peter; Irish judge; b. 24 July 1927, Dublin; s. of Patrick J. Cullinan and Elizabeth Kitchen; one s. (one deceased) two d.; ed. Christian Bros. School, Dublin, Univ. Coll. Dublin, Nat. Univ. of Ireland, King's Inns, Dublin and Irish Mil. Coll.; mil. service 1946–65; mem. Irish contingent, Equestrian Games of XVIth Olympiad, Stockholm 1956; called to Irish Bar 1963; legal officer, army Legal Service, Dublin 1963–65; seconded to Inst. of Public Admin. Dublin for service in Zambia and designated under Overseas Service Aid Scheme (OSAS) of Ministry of Overseas Devt. (now Overseas Devt. Admin.), London 1965–68; lecturer, Sr. Lecturer and Acting Head of Law School, Lusaka, Zambia 1965–68; legal officer, Army Legal Service, Dublin 1968–69; Resident Magistrate and Deputy Registrar, High Court, Lusaka 1969–70, Sr. Resident Magistrate and Registrar 1970–73; admitted to practice as legal practitioner in Zambia 1971; Puisne Judge Dec. 1973; called to Bar, Lincoln's Inn, London 1977; frequently Acting Judge of Supreme Court, Lusaka 1976–80, Judge of Supreme Court 1980; Dir. of Legal Services Corpn. Lusaka 1982–83; Puisne Judge of Supreme Court of Fiji, Lautoka and Suva 1984–87; Chief Justice of Lesotho 1987–95, Judge of Court of Appeal (ex officio) and Chair. Judicial Services Comm. *Leisure interests:* golf, swimming, gardening. *Address:* 16 Oak Park Gardens, London, S.W.19, England. *Telephone:* 0181-785 2260.

CULLINAN, Edward Horder, C.B.E., R.A.; British architect; b. 17 July 1931, London; s. of Edward Revil Cullinan and Dorothea Joy Horder; m. Rosalind Sylvia Yeates 1961; one s. two d.; ed. Ampleforth Coll., Cambridge Univ., Architectural Asscn., Univ. of Calif., Berkeley, U.S.A.; with Denys Lasdun 1958–65; est. Edward Cullinan Architects 1965; numerous professorships include Bannister Fletcher Prof. London Univ. 1978–79; Graham Willis Prof., Sheffield Univ. 1985–87; George Simpson Prof., Univ.of Edin. 1987–; designed and built Horder House, Hampshire 1959–60, Minster Lovell Mill, Oxfordshire 1969–72, Parish Church of St. Mary, Barnes 1978–84, Lambeth Community Care Centre 1979–84, R.M.C. Int. H.Q. 1985–90, Visitor Centre and Landscape at Fountains Abbey and Studley Royal 1988–92, Media Bldg. Cheltenham Art Coll. 1990–93, Library St. John's Coll. Cambridge 1991–94, Archaeolink Visitor Centre, Aberdeenshire 1996–97; now bldg. Faculties of Math. and Divinity, Cambridge Univ., and Docklands Campus, Univ. of E. London; numerous prizes and awards including Financial Times Architecture at Work Award for R.M.C. 1991. *Publications:* Edward Cullinan Architects 1984, Edward Cullinan Architects 1995, Master Plan for the University of North Carolina at Charlotte 1995, contribs. to journals. *Leisure interests:* horticulture, cycling, surfing, Arctic and Sahara travel, history, building, geography. *Address:* 1 Baldwin Terrace, London, N1 7RU, England. *Telephone:* 0171-704 1975.

CULLMANN, Oscar, DR. THEOL., DR. PHIL., D.D.; French professor of theology; b. 25 Feb. 1902, Strasbourg; s. of Georges Cullmann and Frédérique (née Mandel) Cullmann; ed. Univ. of Strasbourg, Sorbonne, Paris, Ecole des Hautes Etudes, Paris; Dir. of Protestant Seminary, Strasbourg 1925–30; Prof. New Testament and Ancient History of Christianity, Univ. of Strasbourg 1930–38, Univ. of Basle 1938–72; Rector Univ. of Basle 1968–69; Prof. Ecole des Hautes Etudes, Paris and Sorbonne 1948–72; Guest Lecturer U.S.A., U.K., Scandinavia, Finland, Greece, Romania, Italy, Netherlands 1948–85; Prof. Emer. Sorbonne and Basle Univs. 1972; mem. Institut de France; Corresp. mem. British Acad., Akademie Mainz, Royal Netherlands Acad.; Dr. h.c. Lausanne, Edinburgh, Lund, Manchester, Basle, Debrecen; Int. Paul VI Prize 1993; Commdr. Légion d'honneur. *Publications:* over 100 titles, including Christus und die Zeit (trans. English, French, Swedish, Greek, Italian) 1946, Petrus, Jünger, Apostel, Martyrer 1972, Der Staat in Neuen Testament 1956, Die Christologie des Neuen Testaments 1957, Der Johanneische Kreis 1975, Einheit durch Vielheit 1986, Ursprung des Weihnachtsfests und des Weihnachtsbaums 1990, Das Gebet im neuen Testament 1994 (trans. into seven languages). *Leisure interest:* gardening. *Address:* Rue Ravignan 20, 75018 Paris, France. *Telephone:* (1) 42-54-99-12.

CULVER, David M., C.C., B.SC., M.B.A.; Canadian business executive; b. 5 Dec. 1924, Winnipeg, Man.; s. of Albert Ferguson and Fern Elizabeth (Smith) Culver; m. Mary Cecile Powell 1949; three s. one d.; ed. McGill Univ., Montreal, Harvard Graduate School of Business Admin., Centre d'Etudes Industrielles, Geneva; served Canadian Infantry Corps 1942–45; joined Alcan Aluminium Ltd. 1949–, later Chair. and C.E.O., retd. 1989; Chair. CAI Capital Corpn., Montreal, D. Culver and Co. Investments 1989–; Hon. Chair. Business Council on Nat. Issues; Dir. American Express Co., Hon. Dir. The Seagram Co. Ltd.; mem. Canadian Advisory Bd., Banque Julius Baer (Zurich); Gov. Joseph H. Lauder Inst. of Man. and Int. Studies, Univ. of Pa., mem. Int. Advisory Council Inst. for Int. Studies, Stanford Univ., Advisory Council, Centre of Canadian Studies, Johns Hopkins Univ. School of Advanced Int. Studies; Gov. Joseph H. Lauder Inst. of Man. and Int. Studies, Univ. of Penn.; mem. Bd. of Trustees, Lester B. Pearson Coll. of the Pacific; Canadian Chair., Canada-Japan Business Cttee. 1977–88; Hon. LL.D. (McGill Univ., York Univ., Toronto); Hon. D.Sc. App. (Univ. of Sherbrooke); Officer, Order of Quebec, Grand Cordon, Order of the Sacred Treasure of Japan. *Address:* 3429 Drummond Street, Montreal, H3G 1X6, Canada (Office).

CUMING, Frederick George Rees, R.A.; British painter; b. 16 Feb. 1930; s. of Harold and Grace Cuming; m. Audrey Cuming 1962; one s. one d.; ed. Univ. School, Bexley Heath, Sidcup Art School, Royal Coll. of Art; travelling scholarship to Italy; Exhbns. Redfern, Walker, New Grafton, Thackeray, Fieldborne Galleries; group shows at R.A., John Moore's London Group; one man exhbns. at Thackeray Gallery, and in Chichester, Lewes, Eastbourne, Guildford, Durham, Chester, Folkestone, Canterbury, New York; works in collections including Dept. of the Environment, Treasury, Chantrey Bequest, R.A., Kendal Museum, Scunthorpe Museum, Bradford, Carlisle, Nat. Museum of Wales, Brighton and Hove Museum, Maidstone Museum, Towner Gallery, Eastbourne, Monte Carlo Museum, Farringdon Trust, Worcester Coll. Oxford, St. John's Coll. Oxford, W. H. Smith, Thames TV, Nat. Trust Foundation for Art, etc.; works in galleries in Canada, France, Germany, Greece, Holland. *Leisure interests:* tennis, golf, snooker. *Address:* The Gables, Wittersham Road, Iden, Nr. Rye, E. Sussex TN31 7WY, England. *Telephone:* (01797) 280322.

CUMMINGS, Constance, C.B.E.; British actress; b. (as Constance Halverstadt) 15 May 1910, Seattle, U.S.A.; m. Benn W. Levy 1933 (died 1973); one s. one d.; ed. St. Nicholas School, Seattle; first appeared on the stage in Sour Grapes, since then in many stage, film and television roles; mem. Arts Council 1965–70; Chair. of Arts Council Young People's Theatre Panel 1965–74; mem. Royal Soc. of Arts 1975; mem. Council, English Stage Co. 1978–; Antoinette Perry Award for Best Actress (in Wings). *Plays include:* Emma Bovary, The Taming of the Shrew, Romeo and Juliet, St. Joan, Lysistrata, Coriolanus, Long Day's Journey into Night, The Cherry Orchard, The Bacchae, Mrs. Warren's Profession, Wings (U.S.A.) 1978–79, Hay Fever 1980, Chalk Garden (New York) 1982, (London) 1992, The Old Ladies (BBC TV) 1983, Eve 1984, The Glass Menagerie 1985, Fanny Kemble at Home 1986, Crown Matrimonial 1987, Tête-à-Tête 1990, The Chalk Garden 1992, Uncle Vanya 1996. *Films include:* Busman's Honeymoon 1940, Blithe Spirit 1945, John and Julie 1955, The Intimate Stranger 1956, The Battle of the Sexes 1959, Sammy Going South 1962, In the Cool of the Day 1963. *Leisure interests:* needlework, gardening. *Address:* 68 Old Church Street, London, S.W.3, England. *Telephone:* 0171-352 0437.

CUMMINGS, Ralph W., PH.D.; American agriculturist; b. 13 Dec. 1911, Reidsville, N.C.; s. of William and Sarah Elizabeth (née Huffines) Cummings; m. 1st Mary Catherine Parrish 1936 (died 1989); three s. one d.; m. 2nd Eunice G. Perkinson 1993; ed. N. Carolina State Univ., Ohio State Univ.; Asst. and Assoc. Prof. Cornell Univ. 1937–42; Prof. Head of Agronomy, N.

Carolina State Univ. 1942–47, Asst. Dir. of Agricultural Research 1945–47, Dir. 1948–54, Admin. Dean for Research 1968–71, Emer. Prof. of Soil Science 1977–; Chief N. Carolina Agricultural Research Mission in Peru 1955–56; Field Dir., Chief Rep. in India, Rockefeller Foundation 1957–66, Assoc. Dir. for Agricultural Sciences 1963–68; Agric. Programme Adviser in Asia and the Pacific, Ford Foundation 1971–72; Dir. Int. Rice Research Inst., Philippines June-Nov. 1972, Int. Crops Research Inst. for the Semi-Arid Tropics, Hyderabad 1972–77; Chair. Tech. Advisory Cttee. Consultative Group on Int. Agric. Research 1977–82; Chair. Govt. of India Cttee. on Agricultural Univs. 1960–64; Consultant Agricultural Research Org., Indonesia 1970; Vice-Chair. Cttee. on Study of African Agricultural Research Capabilities, N.A.S., U.S.A. 1970–73; Acting Dir.-Gen. Int. Irrigation Man. Inst. 1983–84; Fellow, American Acad. of Arts and Sciences, American Soc. for Agronomy; mem. American Chem. Soc., Soil Science Soc. of America; Trustee Int. Council for Research in Agroforestry 1985–91, Int. Livestock Center for Africa 1986–92 (Chair. 1987–91); Sr. Consultant World Bank, West African Agric. Research 1985–87; numerous consultancies and advisory missions on int. agric. research and educ.; many hon. degrees; Int. Agronomy Award, Soc. of Agronomy 1970, Presidential End Hunger Award 1988, Distinguished Service Award, Soil Science Soc. of America 1992, Meritorious Service Award (N.C. State Univ. Alumni Asscn.) 1991, Alumni Medallist (Ohio State Univ.) 1993, Watanga Medallist (N.C. State Univ.) 1995. *Address:* 812 Rosemont Avenue, Raleigh, NC 27607, U.S.A. (Home). *Telephone:* (919) 833-1863. *Fax:* (919) 833-0842.

CUNHAL, Alvaro; Portuguese politician; b. 10 Nov. 1913, Coimbra; s. of Avelino Cunhal and Mercedes Cunhal; ed. Lisbon Univ.; mem. of Portuguese Communist Party 1931–; Sec.-Gen. Fed. of Communist Youth Movts. 1935; mem. PCP Cen. Cttee. 1936–, Cen. Cttee. Secr. 1942–49, 1960–92; active in party reorganization and devt. of links with int. communist movt. 1942–49; imprisoned for political activities 1937–38, 1940, 1949–60 (escaped from gaol 1960); Sec.-Gen. PCP 1961–92, Chair. Nat. Council 1992–96; Minister without Portfolio 1974–75; elected M.P. 1975, 1976, 1979, 1980, 1983, 1985, 1987; mem. Council of State 1983–91; mem. many PCP dels. abroad. *Publications:* numerous vols. concerning Portuguese social and econ. history and political tracts; novels under the pseudonym Manuel Tiago. *Leisure interests:* drawing and painting. *Address:* Partido Comunista Português, Rua Soeiro Pereira Gomes, 3, 1699 Lisbon, Portugal.

CUNNINGHAM, Edward Patrick, M.AGR.SC., PH.D.; Irish professor of animal genetics and international public servant; b. 4 Aug. 1934, Dublin; s. of Eugene Cunningham and Kathleen Moran; m. Catherine Dee 1965; four s. two d.; ed. Clongowes Wood Coll., Univ. Coll. Dublin and Cornell Univ.; Housemaster, Albert Agricultural Coll. Dublin 1956–57; Research and Teaching Asst., Univ. Coll. Dublin 1957–58, Cornell Univ., Ithaca, N.Y. 1960–62; Research Officer, The Agricultural Inst., Dublin 1962, Head Dept. of Animal Breeding and Genetics 1970, Deputy Dir. Agricultural Inst. 1980–88; Prof. of Animal Genetics, Trinity Coll., Dublin 1974–; Dir. Animal Production and Health Div., FAO, Rome 1990–93, Dir. Screwworm Emergency Centre for N. Africa 1990–92; Visiting Prof. Agricultural Univ. of Norway 1968–69, Econ. Devt. Inst., IBRD 1988; mem. Royal Irish Acad., Royal Swedish Acad. of Agriculture and Forestry, Royal Norwegian Acad. of Science and Letters, Russian Acad. of Agricultural Sciences, Acad. d'Agriculture de France; A. M. Leroy Fellowship 1991; Hon. D.Agric. h.c. (Agric. Univ., Norway) 1997; Hon. Sc.D. (Dublin Univ.) 1997; Chevalier, Ordre du Mérite Agricole; Golden Egg Int. Award, Verona 1983. *Publications:* Animal Breeding Theory 1969, Development Issues in the Livestock Sector 1992. *Leisure interests:* farming, history. *Address:* Department of Genetics, Trinity College, Dublin 2 (Office); Vesington House, Dunboyne, Co. Meath, Ireland (Home). *Telephone:* (1) 608 1064 (Office); (1) 825 5350 (Home). *Fax:* (1) 679 8558 (Office); (1) 825 5350 (Home).

CUNNINGHAM, Rt. Hon. John A. (Jack), P.C., PH.D., M.P.; British politician; b. 4 Aug. 1939; s. of Andrew Cunningham; m. Maureen Cunningham 1964; one s. two d.; ed. Jarrow Grammar School and Univ. of Durham; former Research Fellow in Chem. Univ. of Durham; school teacher; trades union officer; mem. Parl. for Whitehaven, Cumbria 1970–83, for Copeland 1983–; Parl. Pvt. Sec. to Rt. Hon. James Callaghan 1972–76; Parl. Under-Sec. of State, Dept. of Energy 1976–79; Opposition Spokesman on Industry 1979–83, on Environment 1983–89, Shadow Leader of the House and Campaigns Co-ordinator 1989–92, Opposition Spokesman on Foreign and Commonwealth Affairs 1992–94, on Trade and Industry 1994–95, on Nat. Heritage 1995–97; Minister of Agric., Fisheries and Food 1997–98, for the Cabinet Office and Chancellor of the Duchy of Lancaster July 1998–; D.L. (Cumbria) 1991; Labour. *Leisure interests:* fell walking, fly fishing, gardening, classical and folk music, reading, listening to other people's opinions. *Address:* House of Commons, London, SW1A 0AA, England.

CUNNINGHAM, Merce; American choreographer and dancer; b. 16 April 1919, Centralia, Wash.; s. of Mr. and Mrs. C. D. Cunningham; ed. Cornish School, Seattle and Bennington Coll. School of Dance; soloist with Martha Graham Dance Co. 1939–45; began solo concerts 1942; on faculty of School of American Ballet, New York 1948, 1950–51; formed own company 1953; opened his own dance school in New York 1959; Hon. mem. American Acad. and Inst. of Arts and Letters 1984; Guggenheim Fellowships 1954, 1959; MacArthur Fellowship 1985; Hon. D.Litt. (Univ. of Ill.) 1972; Hon. D.F.A., Wesleyan Univ., Conn. 1995; Wexner Prize, Ohio State Univ. 1993; Dance Magazine Award 1960, Soc. for Advancement of The Dance in Sweden Gold Medal 1964, Gold Star for Choreographic Invention Paris 1966, New York State Award 1975, Capezio Award 1977, Wash. State Award 1977, Samuel H. Scripps American Dance Festival Award 1982, Mayor of New York's Award of Honor for Arts and Culture 1983, Kennedy Center Honors 1985, Laurence Olivier Award 1985, Algur H. Meadows Award (Southern Methodist Univ., Dallas) 1987, Digital Dance Premier Award 1990, Nat. Medal of Arts 1990, Medal of Honor, Universidad Complutense of Madrid 1993, Dance and Performance Award, London 1993, Golden Lion of Venice Biennale 1995, Nellie Cornish Arts Archievement Award, Seattle 1996; Ordre des Arts et des Lettres 1982, Légion d'honneur 1989. *Works include:* The Seasons 1947, 16 Dances for Soloist and Company of Three 1951, Septet 1953, Minutiae 1954, Springweather and People 1955, Suite for Five 1956, Nocturnes 1956, Antic Meet 1958, Summerspace 1958, Rune 1959, Crises 1960, Aeon 1961, Story 1963, Winterbranch 1964, Variations V 1965, How to Pass, Kick, Fall and Run 1965, Place 1966, Scramble 1967, RainForest 1968, Walkaround Time 1968, Canfield 1969, Second Hand 1970, Tread 1970, Signals 1970, Un Jour ou Deux 1973, Sounddance 1975, Rebus 1975, Torse 1976, Squaregame 1976, Travelogue 1977, Inlets 1977, Fractions 1978, Exchange 1978, Locale 1979, Duets 1980, Channels/Inserts 1981, Gallopade 1981, Trails 1982, Quartet 1982, Coast Zone 1983, Roaratorio 1983, Pictures 1984, Doubles 1984, Phrases 1984, Native Green 1985, Arcade 1985, Grange Eve 1986, Points in Space 1986, Carousal 1987, Five Stone Wind 1988, Cargo X 1989, Field and Figures 1989, Inventions 1989, August Pace 1989, Polarity 1990, Neighbors 1991, Trackers 1991, Beach Birds 1991, Loosestrife 1991, Change of Address 1992, Enter 1992, Doubletoss 1993 CRWDSPCR 1993, Breakers 1994, Ocean 1994, Ground Level Overlay 1995, Windows 1995, Rondo 1996, Installations 1996, Scenario 1997, Pond Way 1998. *Publications:* Changes: Notes on Choreography 1969, The Dancer and the Dance, Conversations with Jacqueline Lesschaeve 1985. *Address:* Cunningham Dance Foundation, 55 Bethune Street, New York, NY 10014, U.S.A. (Office). *Telephone:* (212) 255-8240. *Fax:* (212) 633-2453.

CUNNINGHAM, William Hughes, M.B.A., PH.D.; American professor of marketing; b. 5 Jan. 1944, Detroit, Mich.; m.; one s.; ed. Michigan State Univ.; Asst. Prof. of Marketing, Univ. of Texas at Austin 1971–73, Assoc. Prof. 1973–79, Prof. 1979–, Foley's/Sanger Harris Prof. of Retail Merchandising 1982–83, Dean, Coll. of Business Admin./Grad. School of Business 1983–85, Regents Chair in Higher Educ. Leadership 1985–92, James L. Bayless Chair. for Free Enterprise 1988–; Pres. Univ. of Texas at Austin 1985–92; Chancellor, Univ. of Texas System 1992–, Lee Hage and Joseph D. Jamail Regents Chair in Higher Educ. Leadership 1992–; dir. numerous cos.; Hon. LL.D. (Michigan State Univ.) 1993 and other distinctions. *Publications:* with others: The Personal Force in Marketing 1977, Consumer Energy Attitudes and Behavior in the Southwest 1977, Effective Selling 1977, Métodos Efectivos de Ventas 1980, Marketing: A Managerial Approach 1987, Grondslagen van het Marketing Management 1984, Introduction to Business 1988, Business in a Changing World 1992. *Leisure interests:* golf, tennis, raquetball, horseback riding. *Address:* Chancellor's Office, University of Texas System, 601 Colorado Street, Austin, TX 78701 (Office); 1909 Hills Oak Court, Austin, TX 78703, U.S.A. (Home). *Telephone:* (512) 499-4201 (Office); (512) 499-0488 (Home). *Fax:* (512) 499-4215 (Office).

CUNY, Jean-Pierre, M.SC.; French business executive; b. 8 April 1940, Menton; s. of Robert Cuny and Marie-Louise Marchal; m. Anne-Marie Fousse 1968; two d.; ed. Ecole Centrale, Paris and Mass. Inst. of Tech.; engineer Serete 1968, Information Man. 1973; Project Man. CGA 1976; Cost Controller Placoplatre 1977, Production Dir. 1978, Marketing Dir. 1982, Gen. Man. 1985, Chair. and Chief Exec. 1986, Dir. BPB PLC (parent co. of Placoplatre) 1988, Deputy Chair. Gypsum Div. 1988, Chief Exec. 1994–. *Leisure interests:* skiing, theatre, reading, music, film. *Address:* BPB PLC, Langley Park House, Uxbridge Road, Slough, Berks., SL3 6DU, England; 50 Avenue de Saxe, 75015 Paris, France. *Telephone:* (01753) 898839 (England); (1) 47-83-54-13 (France).

CUOMO, Andrew, B.A., J.D.; American politician; s. of Mario Cuomo (q.v.); m. Kerry Cuomo; one d.; ed. Fordham Univ., Albany Law School; fmr. Asst. Dist. Attorney, Manhattan; fmr. partner Blutrich, Falcone and Miller, NY; Chair. N.Y. Comm. on the Homeless 1991–93; Asst. Sec. Community Planning and Devt., Dept. of Housing and Urban Devt. 1993–97, Sec. of Housing and Urban Devt. 1997–. *Address:* Department of Housing and Urban Development, 451 7th Street, S.W., Washington, DC 20410, U.S.A.

CUOMO, Mario Matthew, LL.B.; American state governor; b. 15 June 1932, Queen's County N.Y.; s. of Andrea and Immaculata Cuomo; m. Matilda Raffa; two s. (including Andrew Cuomo, (q.v.)) three d.; ed. St. John's Coll., and St. John's Univ.; admitted to N.Y. Bar 1956, Supreme Court Bar 1960; Confidential Legal Asst. to Hon. Adrian P. Burke, N.Y. State Court of Appeals 1956–58; Assoc., Corner, Weisbrod, Froeb and Charles, Brooklyn 1958–63, partner 1963–75; Sec. of State, N.Y. 1975–79; Lieut.-Gov. of New York State 1979–82, Gov. 1983–95; partner Wilkie Farr and Gallagher 1995–; mem. Faculty St. John's Univ. Law School 1963–75; Counsel to community groups 1966–72; N.Y. Rapallo Award, Columbia Lawyers' Asscn. 1976, Dante Medal, Italian Govt./American Asscn. of Italian Teachers 1976, Silver Medallion, Columbia Coalition 1976, Public Admin. Award, C. W. Post Coll. 1977; Democrat. *Publications include:* Forest Hills Diary: The Crisis of Low-Income Housing 1974, Maya 1984, Lincoln on Democracy (jtly.) 1990, The New York Idea 1994, Common Sense 1995, Reason to Believe

1995; articles in legal journals. *Address:* 50 Sutton Place South, New York, NY 10036, U.S.A.

CUPITT, Rev. Don, M.A.; British ecclesiastic and university lecturer; b. 22 May 1934, Oldham; s. of Robert Cupitt and Norah Cupitt; m. Susan Marianne Day 1963; one s. two d.; ed. Charterhouse, Trinity Hall, Cambridge, Westcott House, Cambridge; ordained 1959; Vice-Prin., Westcott House, Cambridge 1962; Dean of Emmanuel Coll., Cambridge 1966–91; Stanton Lecturer, Univ. of Cambridge 1968–71; lecturer, Univ. of Cambrige 1973–96; Life Fellow Emmanuel College 1996; Hon. D.Litt. (Bristol) 1985. *Publications:* Christ and the Hiddenness of God 1971, Crisis of Moral Authority 1972, The Leap of Reason 1976, The Debate about Christ 1979, Jesus and the Gospel of God 1979, Taking Leave of God 1980, The World to Come 1982, The Sea of Faith 1984, Only Human 1985, Life Lines 1986, The Long-Legged Fly 1987, The New Christian Ethics 1988, Radicals and the Future of the Church 1989, Creation out of Nothing 1990, What is a Story? 1991, The Time Being 1992, After All 1994, The Last Philosophy 1995, Solar Ethics 1995, After God: The Future of Religion 1997, Mysticism after Modernity 1997, The Religion of Being 1998, The Revelation of Being 1998. *Leisure interests:* hill-walking, the arts. *Address:* Emmanuel College, Cambridge, CB2 3AP, England. *Telephone:* (01223) 334200. *Fax:* (01223) 334426.

CURIEN, Hubert, D. ÈS SC.; French politician and scientist; b. 30 Oct. 1924, Cornimont, Vosges; s. of Robert Curien; m. Anne-Perrine Dumézil 1949; three s.; ed. Lycée d'Epinal, Coll. de Remiremont, Lycée Saint-Louis, Ecole Normale Supérieure and Faculté des Sciences, Paris; Prof., Faculté des Sciences, Paris 1956–95; Scientific Dir. Centre Nat. de la Recherche Scientifique (CNRS) 1966–69, Dir.-Gen. 1969–73, Gen. Del. of Scientific and Tech. Research 1973–76, Pres. Admin. Council, Institut de biologie physico-chimique 1975–; Pres. Centre Nat. Etudes Spatiales 1976–84; Minister of Research and Technology 1984–86, 1988–93; Pres. Scientific Council of Defence 1986–93; Pres. European Science Foundation 1979–84; Vice-Pres. Soc. of French Engineers and Sciences 1987–89; Chair. Council, European Space Agency 1981–84; Chair. Council, CERN, European Lab. for Particle Research 1994–96; Chair. Acad. Europaea 1994–97; fmr. Pres. Soc. Française de Minéralogie et Cristallographie; mem. Acad. des Sciences; Prize, Acad. des Sciences, Honda Prize 1998; Grand Officier, Légion d'honneur, Commdr., Ordre nat. du Mérite, Commdr., Palmes académiques; Military Medal. *Publications:* scientific articles on solid state physics and mineralogy. *Address:* 24 rue des Fossés Saint-Jacques, 75005 Paris, France (Home). *Telephone:* (1) 46-33-26-36 (Home).

CURMAN, Johan; Swedish agronomist (retd.) and landowner; b. 10 Oct. 1919, Ed, Sweden; s. of Carl G. Curman and Birgitta Palme; m. Britt Ekelund 1945; two s. two d.; ed. Royal Swedish Agricultural Coll.; Vice-Pres. Upplands Vaesby Property Admin. Co. 1956–79; Sec. C. F. Lundstrom Foundation 1957–92; Pres. Bd. of Swedish Plant Protection Inst. 1968–76; Pres. Swedish Employers' Asscn. for Forestry and Agric. 1970–85, Swedish Soc. of Agricultural Eng. 1973–80, Royal Swedish Acad. of Agric. and Forestry 1980–83; mem. Bd. Swedish Employers' Asscn. 1979–85; Patron of Royal Uppsala Univ., Chorus of Sweden. *Publications:* Leaf-fodder Husbandry and Coppice Woods 1993, An Early European: C. F. Lundstrom 1996. *Address:* Edsby, 194 91 Upplands Vaesby, Sweden. *Telephone:* (08) 59030401.

CURNOW, (Thomas) Allen (Monro), O.N.Z., C.B.E., LITT.D.; New Zealand poet and journalist; b. 17 June 1911, Timaru; s. of Tremayne Curnow and Jessie Curnow (née Gambling); m. 1st Elizabeth LeCren 1936 (divorced); m. 2nd Jenifer Mary Tole 1965; two s. one d.; ed. Univs. of Canterbury and Auckland, Coll. of St. John the Evangelist, reporter, sub-ed. The Press, Christchurch, N.Z. 1936–48, The Chronicle, London 1949; Carnegie Visitor to U.S.A. 1950; lecturer, then Assoc. Prof. of English Univ. of Auckland 1951–76; Fulbright Fellow 1961; British Commonwealth Poetry Prize 1988, Cholmondeley Award for Poets 1992, Queen's Gold Medal for Poetry 1989. *Publications include:* The Penguin Book of New Zealand Verse (ed.) 1960, Four Plays 1972, Collected Poems 1933–1973 1974, Look Back Harder, Critical Writings 1935–1984 1987, Selected Poems 1940–1989 1990, Early Days Yet, New and Collected Poems 1941–1997 1997. *Address:* 62 Tohunga Crescent, Parnell, Auckland, New Zealand. *Telephone:* (09) 373215.

CURRAN, Charles E., S.T.D.; American professor of moral theology and ecclesiastic; b. 30 March 1934, Rochester, N.Y.; s. of John F. Curran and Gertrude L. Beisner; ed. St. Bernard's Coll. Rochester, Gregorian Univ. Rome and Accademia Alfonsiana, Rome; ordained Roman Catholic priest 1958; Prof. of Moral Theology, St. Bernard's Seminary, Rochester, N.Y. 1961–65; Asst. Prof., Assoc. Prof., Prof. of Moral Theology, Catholic Univ. of America, Washington, D.C. 1965–89; Sr. Research Scholar, Kennedy Center for Bio-Ethics, Georgetown Univ. 1972; External Examiner in Christian Ethics, Univ. of W.I. 1982–86; Visiting Prof. of Catholic Studies Cornell Univ. 1987–88; Visiting Brooks and Firestone Prof. of Religion, Univ. of S. Calif 1988–90; Visiting Eminent Scholar in Religion, Auburn 1990–91; Elizabeth Scurlock Univ. Prof. of Human Values, Southern Methodist Univ. 1991–; Pres. Catholic Theological Soc. of America 1969–70, Soc. of Christian Ethics 1971–72; Pres. American Theological Soc. 1989–90; Dr. h.c. (Charleston, W. Va.) 1987, (Concordia Coll., Portland, Ore.) 1992; J. C. Murray Award (Catholic Theol. Soc.) 1972, Building Bridges Award, New Ways Ministry 1992. *Publications:* numerous books, articles, lectures and addresses. *Leisure interests:* reading, golf. *Address:* Southern Methodist University, 317 Dallas Hall, Box 750317, Dallas, TX 75275-0317, U.S.A. *Telephone:* (214) 768-4073. *Fax:* (214) 768-4129.

CURRIE, Edwina, M.A., M.SC.; British politician and writer; b. 13 Oct. 1946; m. Raymond F. Currie 1972 (separated); two d.; ed. Liverpool Inst. for Girls, St. Anne's Coll., Oxford, London School of Econs. and Political Science; teacher and lecturer in econs., econ. history and business studies 1972–81; mem. Birmingham City Council 1975–86; Conservative M.P. for Derbyshire S. 1983–97; Parl. Pvt. Sec. to Sec. of State for Educ. and Science 1985–86; Parl. Under-Sec. of State for Health 1986–88; mem. Parl. Select Ctte. on Social Services 1983–86; Jt. Chair. Conservative Group for Europe 1995–97; Vice-Chair. European Movt. 1995–; Jt. Chair. Future of Europe Trust 1995–97, Dir. 1996–; Speaker of the Year, Asscn. of Speakers' Clubs 1990, 1994 Campaigner of the Year, The Spectator/Highland Park Parliamentarian of the Year Awards. *Publications:* Life Lines 1989, What Women Want 1990, Three Line Quips 1992, A Parliamentary Affair (novel) 1994, A Woman's Place (novel) 1996, She's Leaving Home (novel) 1997. *Leisure interests:* keeping fit, family, theatre. *Address:* c/o Little, Brown (U.K.) Ltd., Brettenham House, Lancaster Place, London, WC2E 7EN, England. *Telephone:* 0171-911 8000.

CURRIE, James, M.A.; British civil servant and European Union official; b. 17 Nov. 1941, Kilmarnock; s. of David Currie and Mary Smith; m. Evelyn MacIntyre 1968; one s. one d.; ed. St. Joseph's School, Kilmarnock, Blairs Coll., Aberdeen, Royal Scots Coll., Valladolid, Univ. of Glasgow; Admin. trainee Scottish Office, Edin. 1968–72; Prin. Scottish Educ. and Devt. Depts. 1972–77; Asst. Sec. Scottish Industry Dept. 1977–82; Transport and Environment Counsellor U.K. Perm. Representation to EC 1982–86; Dir. of Programmes Directorate-Gen. XVI Regional Policy 1987–88; Chief of Staff to Competition Policy Commr. Sir Leon Brittan 1989–93; Deputy Head of Del., Washington, D.C. 1993–96; Dir.-Gen. Customs and Indirect Taxation 1996–97, Environment, Nuclear Safety and Civil Protection 1997–. *Leisure interests:* golf, guitar, good food. *Address:* Directorate-General XI, European Commission, rue de la Loi 200, BU5, 3/3, 1040 Brussels, Belgium. *Telephone:* (2) 2961170. *Fax:* (2) 2991105.

CURRIE OF MARYLEBONE, Baron (Life Peer), cr. 1996, of Marylebone, in the City of Westminster; **David Anthony Currie,** PH.D., M.SOC.SC., D.LITT.; British university professor; b. 9 Dec. 1946, London; s. of Kennedy Moir Currie and Marjorie (née Thompson); m. 1st Shaziye Gazioglu 1965 (divorced); two s.; m. 2nd Angela Mary Piers Dumas 1995; ed. Battersea Grammar School, Univs. of Manchester, Birmingham, London; Economist Hoare Govett 1971–72, Sr. Economist Econ. Models 1972; lecturer in Econs. Queen Mary Coll., Univ. of London 1972–79, Reader 1979–81, Prof. 1981–88; Prof. of Econs. London Business School 1988–, Dir. Centre for Econ. Forecasting 1988–95, Research Dean 1989–92, Deputy Prin. 1992–95; Houblon-Norman Research Fellow Bank of England 1985–86, Visiting Scholar IMF 1987; mem. Advisory Bd. to Research Councils 1992–93, Retail Price Index Advisory Cttee. 1992–93, Treasury's Panel of Ind. Forecasters 1992–95; Trustee Joseph Rowntree Reform Trust 1991–; Dir. Int. Schools of Business Man.; Gov. London Business School 1989–95. *Publications:* Advances in Monetary Economics 1985, The Operation and Regulation of Financial Markets (jtly.) 1986, Macroeconomic Interactions Between North and South (jtly.) 1988, Macroeconomic Policies in an Interdependent World (jtly.) 1989, Rules, Reputation and Macroeconomic Policy Co-ordination (jtly.) 1993, European Monetary Union: Problems in the Transition to a Single European Currency (jtly.) 1995, North-South Linkages and International Macroeconomic Policy (jtly.) 1995, The Pros and Cons of EMU 1997, Will the Euro Work? 1998. *Leisure interests:* music, literature, running. *Address:* London Business School, Regents Park, London, NW1 4SA, England. *Telephone:* 0171-262 5050. *Fax:* 0171-402 0718.

CURTEIS, Ian Bayley; British playwright; b. 1 May 1935, London; m. 1st Dorothy Joan Armstrong 1964 (dissolved); two s.; m. 2nd Joanna Trollope (q.v.) 1985; two step-d.; ed. London Univ.; dir. and actor in theatres throughout U.K., and BBC TV script reader 1956–63; BBC and ATV staff dir. (drama) 1963–67; Chair. Cttee. on Censorship, Writers' Guild of Great Britain 1981–85, Pres. of Guild 1998–. *Plays for TV:* Beethoven, Sir Alexander Fleming (BBC entry, Prague Festival 1973), Mr. Rolls and Mr. Royce, Long Voyage out of War (trilogy), The Folly, The Haunting, Second Time Round, A Distinct Chill, The Portland Millions, Philby, Burgess and Maclean (British entry, Monte Carlo Festival 1978, BAFTA nomination Best Play of the Year), Hess, The Atom Spies, Churchill and the Generals (Grand Prize for Best Programme of 1981, New York Int. Film and TV Festival and BAFTA nomination Best Play of the Year), Suez 1956 (BAFTA nomination Best Play of the Year), Miss Morison's Ghosts (British entry Monte Carlo Festival), BB and Lord D.; writer of numerous television series; screenplays: La condition humaine (André Malraux), Lost Empires (adapted from J. B. Priestley), Eureka, Graham Greene's The Man Within (TV) 1983, The Nightmare Years (TV) 1989, The Zimmerman Telegram 1990, Yalta 1991, The Choir (BBC 1); numerous articles and speeches on the ethics and politics of broadcasting. *Publications:* Long Voyage out of War (trilogy) 1971, Churchill and the Generals 1980, Suez 1956, 1980, The Falklands Play 1987. *Leisure interest:* avoiding television. *Address:* c/o Coutts and Co., 1 Cadogan Place, London, SW1X 9PX, England. *Fax:* (01285) 750551.

CURTIS, David Roderick, A.C., M.B., B.S., PH.D., F.R.A.C.P., F.A.A., F.R.S.; Australian professor of pharmacology; b. 3 June 1927, Melbourne; s. of E. D. and E. V. Curtis; m. Lauris Sewell 1951; one s. one d.; ed. Melbourne High School, Univ. of Melbourne, and Australian Nat. Univ., Canberra; resident medical positions 1950–53; Research Scholar, Australian Nat. Univ.

1954–56, Research Fellow 1956–57, Fellow 1957–59, Sr. Fellow 1959–62, Professorial Fellow 1962–65, Prof. of Pharmacology 1966–68, Prof. of Neuropharmacology 1968–73; Prof. and Head, Dept. of Pharmacology, John Curtin School of Medical Research, Australian Nat. Univ. 1973–89, Dir. and Howard Florey Prof. of Medical Research 1989–92, Univ. Fellow 1993–95, Emer. Prof. 1997–; Visiting Fellow, John Curtin School 1995–; Burnet Lecturer 1983; Pres. Australian Acad. of Science 1986–90; Chair. Inaugural Australia Prize Cttee. 1989–90. *Publications:* scientific papers on various topics concerned with neurophysiology and neuropharmacology. *Leisure interests:* gardening, turning wood, wombling. *Address:* 7 Patey Street, Campbell, A.C.T. 2612, Australia. *Telephone:* (2) 6248 5664. *Fax:* (2) 6248 5664.

CURTIS, Jamie Lee; American actress; b. 22 Nov. 1958, Los Angeles, Calif.; d. of Tony Curtis (q.v.) and Janet Leigh; m. Christopher Guest; one c.; ed. Choate School, Conn., Univ. of the Pacific, Calif.; *films include:* Halloween, The Fog, Terror Train, Halloween II, Road Games, Prom Night, Love Letters, Trading Places, The Adventures of Buckaroo Banzai: Across the 8th Dimension, Grandview, USA, Perfect, 8 Million Ways to Die, Amazing Grace and Chuck, A Man in Love, Dominick and Eugene, A Fish Called Wanda, Blue Steel, My Girl, Forever Young, My Girl 2; *TV:* She's In The Army Now, Dorothy Stratten: Death of a Centrefold, Operation Petticoat, The Love Boat, Columbo, Quincy, Charlie's Angels, Anything but Love, Money on the Side, As Summers Die, Mother's Boys, True Lies, My Girl 2, True Lies 1994 (Golden Globe Award for Best Actress in a musical or comedy), House Arrest 1996, Fierce Creatures 1996, Halloween H20 1998, Virus 1998. *Publications:* When I Was Little 1993, Today I Feel Silly and Other Moods That Make My Day 1999. *Address:* c/o Rick Kurtzmann, CAA, 9830 Wilshire Blvd., Beverly Hills, CA 90212, U.S.A.

CURTIS, Tony (Bernard Schwarz); American film actor; b. 3 June 1925, New York; s. of Manuel and Helen (née Klein) Schwarz; m. 1st Janet Leigh 1951 (divorced 1962); two d.; m. 2nd Christine Kaufmann 1963 (divorced 1967); two d.; m. 3rd Leslie Allen 1968; two s.; m. 4th Lisa Deutsch 1993; ed. New School of Social Research; served in U.S. Navy; Kt. Order of the Repub. of Hungary 1996. *Films include:* Houdini 1953, Black Shield of Falworth 1954, So This is Paris? 1954, Six Bridges to Cross 1955, Trapeze 1956, Mister Cory 1957, Sweet Smell of Success 1957, Midnight Story 1957, The Vikings 1958, Defiant Ones 1958, Perfect Furlough 1958, Some Like It Hot 1959, Spartacus 1960, The Great Imposter 1960, Pepe 1960, The Outsider 1961, Taras Bulba 1962, Forty Pounds of Trouble 1962, The List of Adrian Messenger 1963, Captain Newman 1963, Paris When It Sizzles 1964, Wild and Wonderful 1964, Sex and the Single Girl 1964, Goodbye Charlie 1964, The Great Race 1965, Boeing, Boeing 1965, Arriverderci, Baby 1966, Not with My Wife You Don't 1966, Don't Make Waves 1967, Boston Strangler 1968, Lepke 1975, Casanova 1976, The Last Tycoon 1976, The Manitou 1978, Sextette 1978, The Mirror Crack'd 1980, Venom 1982, Insignificance 1985, Club Life 1986, The Last of Phillip Banter 1988, Balboa, Midnight, Lobster Man from Mars, The High-Flying Mermaid, Prime Target, Center of the Web, Naked in New York, The Reptile Man, The Immortals 1995, The Celluloid Closet 1995, Louis et Frank 1997, Brittle Glory 1997. *Television includes:* Third Girl from the Left 1973, The Persuaders 1971–72, The Count of Monte Cristo 1976, Vegas 1978, Mafia Princess 1986, Christmas in Conneticut 1992, A Perry Mason Mystery: The Case of the Grimacing Governor. *Publications:* Kid Andrew Cody and Julie Sparrow 1977, The Autobiography 1993. *Leisure interest:* painting. *Address:* c/o William Morris Agency, 151 S. El Camino Drive, Beverly Hills, CA 90212, U.S.A.

CUSACK, John; American actor; b. 28 June 1966, Evanston, Ill.; s. of Richard Cusack and Nancy Cusack; mem. Piven Theatre Workshop, Evanston from age 9–19; f. New Criminals Theatrical Co., Chicago. *Films:* (actor): Class 1983, Sixteen Candles 1984, Grandview USA 1984, The Sure Thing 1985, Journey of Natty Gann 1985, Better Off Dead 1985, Stand By Me 1985, One Crazy Summer 1986, Broadcast News 1987, Hot Pursuit 1987, Eight Men Out 1988, Tapeheads 1988, Say Anything 1989, Fatman and Little Boy 1989, The Grifters 1990, True Colors 1991, Shadows and Fog 1992, Roadside Prophets 1992, The Player 1992, Map of the Human Heart 1992, Bob Roberts 1992, Money for Nothing 1993, Bullets Over Broadway 1994, The Road to Wellville 1994, City Hall 1995, Anastasia 1997, Con Air 1997, Hellcab 1997, Midnight in the Garden of Good and Evil 1997, This is My Father 1998, The Thin Red Line 1989, Pushing Tin 1998; (actor, dir., writer): Grosse Pointe Blank 1997; (producer, actor): Arigo 1998; (actor, writer): High Fidelity 1997, The Cradle Will Rock 1999. *Address:* c/o Gaby Margeman, William Morris Agency, 151 South El Camino Drive, Beverly Hills, CA 90212, U.S.A.

CUSACK, Sinead Mary; Irish actress; b. 1948; d. of late Cyril Cusack and Maureen Kiely; m. Jeremy Irons (q.v.) 1977; two s.; appearances with RSC include Lady Amaranth in Wild Oats, Lisa in Children of the Sun, Isabella in Measure for Measure, Celia in As You Like It, Evadne in The Maid's Tragedy, Lady Anne in Richard III, Portia in The Merchant of Venice, Ingrid in Peer Gynt, Kate in The Taming of the Shrew, Beatrice in Much Ado About Nothing, Lady Macbeth in Macbeth, Roxanne in Cyrano de Bergerac; other stage appearances at Oxford Festival, Gate Theatre, Dublin, Royal Court etc.; numerous appearances in TV drama. *Films:* Alfred the Great, Tamlyn, Hoffman 1969, David Copperfield 1970, Revenge 1971, The Devil's Widow 1971, Horowitz in Dublin Castle, The Last Remake of Beau Geste 1977, Rocket Gibraltar, Venus Peter, Waterland, God on the Rocks 1992, Bad Behaviour 1993, The Cement Garden 1993, The Sparrow, Flemish Board, Stealing Beauty. *Address:* c/o Markham & Froggatt Ltd., 4 Windmill Street, London, W1P 1HF, England. *Telephone:* 0171-636 4412. *Fax:* 0171-637 5233.

CUSSLER, Clive (Eric); American novelist; b. 1931; s. of Eric Cussler and Amy Hunnewell; m. Barbara Knight 1955; three c.; owner Bestgen & Cussler Advertising, Newport Beach, Calif. 1961–65; Copy Dir. Darcy Advertising, Hollywood, Calif. and Instr. in Advertising Communications, Orange Coast Coll. 1965–67; Advertising Dir. Aquatic Marine Corpn., Newport Beach, Calif. 1967–79; Vice-Pres. and Creative Dir. of Broadcast, Meffon, Wolff and Weir Advertising, Denver, Colo. 1970–73. *Publications:* The Mediterranean Caper 1973, Iceberg 1975, Raise the Titanic 1976, Vixen O-Three 1978, Night Probe 1981, Pacific Vortex 1983, Deep Six 1984, Cyclops 1986, Treasure 1988, Dragon 1990, Sahara 1992, Inca Gold 1994, Shock Wave 1995, Sea Hunters 1996, Flood Tide 1997. *Leisure interest:* discovering shipwrecks. *Address:* 5539 E. Sanna Street, Paradise Valley, AZ 85253, U.S.A.

CUTAYAR, Egidio; Egyptian banker; b. 22 Dec. 1937, Alexandria; m.; one d.; joined Barclays Bank Int. 1961, Asst. Rep., Milan 1970, Asst. Man. Banca Barclays Castillini S.p.A., Milan 1975, Man. 1976, Asst. Gen. Man. Europe Barclays Bank PLC Head Office, London 1986, Sr. Gen. Man., Milan, Vice-Chair. Barclays Financial Services Italia S.p.A., Milan 1986, Jt. Man. Dir. Banque du Caire Barclays Int. S.A.E., Cairo 1988–, Vice-Chair. Loans and Participations Cttee. Hellenic Mutual Fund Man. Co. S.A., Greece 1979, Vice-Pres. Egyptian British Businessmen Asscn., Dir. Barclays Leasing Int., Milan 1978, Bd. mem. Hellenic Investment Bank, Hellenic Mutual Fund Man. Co. S.A., Greece 1979, Italian Chamber of Commerce, Egyptian British Friendship Soc., mem. American Chamber of Commerce, German Chamber of Commerce. *Address:* Banque du Caire Barclays International S.A.E., 12 Midan El Sheikh Youssef, Garden City, Cairo, Egypt. *Telephone:* 202-354 0686.

CUTHBERT, Alan William, PH.D., F.R.S.; British professor of pharmacology; b. 1932, Peterborough; s. of Thomas William and Florence Mary (née Griffin) Cuthbert; m. Harriet Jane Webster 1957; two s.; ed. Deacons Grammar School, Peterborough, Leicester Coll. of Tech., Univs. of St. Andrews and London; Reader in Pharmacology, Univ. of Cambridge 1973–79, Sheild Prof. of Pharmacology 1979–; Master, Fitzwilliam Coll. Cambridge 1991–; Chair. Editorial Bd. British Journal of Pharmacology 1974–82; mem. Academia Europaea, Acad. Royale de Médecine de Belgique; Fellow, Jesus Coll. Cambridge 1968–91, Hon. Fellow 1991–; Hon. D.Sc.; Hon. LL.D. *Publications:* numerous articles on physiology, pharmacology and biology. *Leisure interests:* painting, sculpture, photography, gardening, travel. *Address:* Department of Pharmacology, University of Cambridge, Tennis Court Road, Cambridge, CB2 1QJ (Office); The Master's Lodge, Fitzwilliam College, Cambridge, England (Home). *Telephone:* (01223) 334004 (Office); (01223) 332053 (Home). *Fax:* (01223) 334040.

CUTLER, Sir (Arthur) Roden, V.C., A.K., K.C.M.G., K.C.V.O., C.B.E., K.ST.J., B.EC.; Australian diplomatist and public servant; b. 24 May 1916, Sydney; s. of Arthur and Ruby (née Pope) Cutler; m. 1st Helen Morris 1946 (died 1990); four s.; m. 2nd Joan Edith Goodwin 1993; ed. Sydney High School and Univ. of Sydney; Justice Dept. N.S.W. (Public Trust Office) 1935–42; 2/5th Field Regt., A.I.F., Middle East 1940–42; State Sec. Retd. Servicemen's League N.S.W. 1942–43, State Pres. Retd. Servicemen's League A.C.T. 1957–58; mem. of Aliens' Classification and Advisory Cttee. to advise Commonwealth Govt. 1942–43; Asst. Deputy Dir. of Security Service N.S.W. 1943; Commonwealth Asst. Commr. of Repatriation 1943–46; High Commr. in N.Z. 1946–52, in Ceylon 1952–55; Minister to Egypt 1955–56; Sec.-Gen. SEATO 1957; Chief of Protocol, Dept. of External Affairs, Canberra 1957; Australian High Commr. in Pakistan 1959–61; Australian Rep. to the Independence of the Somali Repub. 1960; Australian Consul-Gen., New York 1961–65; Del. to UN Gen. Ass. 1963–64; Australian Amb. to the Netherlands 1965–66; Gov. N.S.W. 1966–81; Chair. State Bank of N.S.W. 1981–86, Air N.S.W. 1982–93 (from 1989 Ansett Express Airlines), First Australian Prime Fund Investment Co. Ltd. 1986–96 (mem. Bd. 1996–), First Australia Fund 1985–96 (mem. Bd. 1996–), First Australia Prime Income Fund 1986–, Rothmans Foundation 1987–93, Occidental Life Insurance Co. of Australia 1987–90, First Commonwealth Fund 1992–96 (mem. Bd. 1996–); Dir. Rothmans Holdings Ltd., Permanent Trustee Co. 1981–92; Pres. Scout Asscn. of N.S.W.; Hon. Col. Royal N.S.W. Regt. and Sydney Univ. Regt. 1966–85; Hon. Air Commodore R.A.A.F. 1981–; Hon. F.C.A.; Hon. LL.D. (Sydney), Hon. D.Litt. (New England Univ., Univ. of Wollongong), Hon. D.Sc. (Univ. of N.S.W., Univ. of Newcastle). *Leisure interests:* sailing, swimming, photography. *Address:* 22 Ginahgulla Road, Bellevue Hill, N.S.W. 2023, Australia. *Telephone:* (02) 9326-1233. *Fax:* (02) 9326-1233.

CUTLER, Walter Leon, M.A.; American diplomatist; b. 25 Nov. 1931, Boston, Mass.; s. of Walter Leon Cutler and Esther Dewey; m. 1st Sarah Gerard Beeson 1957 (divorced 1981); two s; m. 2nd Isabel Kugel Brookfield 1981; ed. Wesleyan Univ. and Fletcher School of Int. Law and Diplomacy; Vice-Consul, Yaoundé, Cameroon 1957–59; Staff Asst. to Sec. of State 1960–62; Political-Econ. Officer, Algiers 1962–65; Consul, Tabriz, Iran 1965–67; Political-Mil. Officer, Seoul, Repub. of Korea 1967–69; Political Officer, Saigon, Repub. of Viet Nam 1969–71; Special Asst., Bureau of Far Eastern Affairs, Dept. of State 1971–73, mem. Sr. Seminar on Foreign Policy 1973–74, Dir. Office of Cen. Africa 1974–75; Amb. to Zaire 1975–79, to Iran 1979; Deputy Asst. Sec. of State for Congressional Relations 1979–81; Amb.

to Tunisia 1981–83, Amb. to Saudi Arabia 1983–87, 1988–89; Pres. Meridian Int. Center, Wash. 1989–; Sr. Advisor Trust Co. of the West, L.A. 1990–; Research Prof. of Diplomacy, Georgetown Univ. 1987–88; Special Emissary for Sec. Gen. of UN New York 1994; mem. Council on Foreign Relations, New York, American Acad. of Diplomacy, Washington Inst. of Foreign Affairs; Wilbur J. Carr Award 1989, Dir.-Gen.'s Cup, Dept. of State 1993; Order of the Leopard (Repub. of Zaire) 1979; King Abdulaziz Decoration (Saudi Arabia) 1985. *Leisure interests:* sports, ornithology. *Address:* Meridian International Center, 1630 Crescent Place, N.W. Washington, DC 20009, U.S.A.

CUTTS, Simon; British artist, poet and publisher; b. 30 Dec. 1944, Derby; s. of George Tom Cutts and Elizabeth Purdy; m. 1st Annira Uusi-Illikainen (divorced 1973); one s.; m. 2nd Margot Hapgood (died 1985); ed. Herbert Strutt Grammar School, Belper, Derbyshire, Nottingham Coll. of Art, Trent Polytechnic; travel and miscellaneous employment including The Trent Bookshop, Nottingham 1962–69; Jt. Ed. Tarasque Press 1964–72; publishing, lecturing and writing 1972–74; Dir. and Co-Partner Coracle Press Books (now Coracle Production and Distribution) 1975–87; Dir., Coracle Press Gallery 1983–86; Dir. Victoria Miro Gallery 1985–; org. of exhbns. in Europe and New York. *Publications:* numerous publs. including Quelque Pianos 1976, Pianostool Footnotes 1983, Petits-Airs for Margot 1986, Seepages 1988. *Leisure interests:* walking, running, cooking, eating, drinking and the nostalgia of innocence. *Address:* Victoria Miro, 21 Cork Street, London, W.1 (Office); 4/16 Courtfield Gardens, London, S.W.5, England (Home). *Telephone:* 0171-734 5082 (Office); 0171-370 4301 (Home).

CYWIŃSKA, Izabella, M.A.; Polish theatre producer and director; b. 22 March 1935, Kamień; d. of Andrzej Cywiński and Elżbieta Cywińska; m. Janusz Michałowski 1968; ed. Warsaw Univ., State Acad. of Drama, Warsaw; Asst., Rural Architecture Faculty, Warsaw Univ. of Tech. 1956–58; Stage Dir., Theatre in Cracow-Nowa Huta 1966–68, Polski Theatre, Poznań 1966–68; Dir. and Artistic Man. Wojciech Bogusławski Theatre, Kalisz 1969–73, Nowy Theatre, Poznań 1973–88; Vice-Pres. Understanding Cttee. of Creative Circles, Poznań 1980–81; Minister of Culture and Art 1989–91; founder and Vice-Pres. Culture Foundation 1991–93; artistic dir. 50th Anniversary of the Revolt in the Warsaw Ghetto; mem. Polish Stage Artists' Asscn., Presidential Council for Culture 1992–95, Gen. Ass. European Cooperation Foundation, Brussels. Awards: First Prize for "Beauty" Int. TV Festival, Plovdiv, Bulgaria 1997; All-Poland Drama Festivals, Kalisz 1970, 1973, 1980, Opole 1976, Wrocław 1976, Minister of Culture and Art Award (2nd class) 1977; Kt.'s Cross Order of Polonia Restituta, Medal Kalos Kagathos, Gold Cross of Merit, Nat. Educ. Comm. Medal and other decorations. *Plays directed include:* Iphigenie auf Tauris 1968, The Morals of Mrs. Dulska 1970, The Death of Tarelkin 1973, I giganti della montagna 1973, Lower Depths 1974, They 1975, Wijuny 1976, Bath-house 1978, Judas from Karioth 1980, The Accused: June '56 1981, Enemy of the People 1982, Dawn 1986, Virginity 1986, Cementeries 1988, Tartuffe 1989, Antygona in New York 1993, God's Lining (TV series) 1997; also dir. in U.S.A. and U.S.S.R. *TV film:* Frédéric's Enchantment (about Chopin) 1998. *Publication:* Nagłe zastępstwo 1992. *Leisure interests:* foreign travel, politics. *Address:* ul. Piwna 7A m. 5, 00-265 Warsaw, Poland (Home). *Telephone:* (22) 635 32 33.

CZIBERE, Tibor; Hungarian politician and engineer; b. 16 Oct. 1930, Tapolca; s. of Jozsef Czibere and Maria Loppert; m. Gabriella Nagy 1956; two d.; ed. Tech. Univ. of Heavy Industry, Miskolc; engineer with Ganz-MÁVAG Machine Works 1956; rejoined Miskolc Univ. and active as lecturer 1963, Prof. and Dean of Mechanical Eng. Faculty 1968, Rector 1978–86, Prof. 1986–88, 1989–; Minister of Culture 1988–89; Corresp. mem. Hungarian Acad. of Sciences 1976, mem. 1985–, mem. of Parl. 1983–85, 1988–90; Vice-Pres. Nat. Council of Patriotic People's Front 1985–89; Kossuth Prize 1962, Labour Order of Merit 1971, Star Order of the People's Repub. 1986, Szetgyörgyi Albert Prize 1996. *Address:* University of Miskolc, 3515-Miskolc-Egyetemváros, Hungary. *Telephone:* (46) 365-111.

D

DA COSTA, Manuel Saturnino; Guinea-Bissau politician; Sec. Gen. Partido Africano da Independência da Guiné e Cabo Verde (PAIGC); Prime Minister 1994–97. *Address:* c/o Partido Africano da Independência da Guiné e Cabo Verde. C.P. 106, Bissau, Guinea-Bissau.

DA CRUZ VILAÇA, José Luís, D.ECON.; Portuguese judge and lawyer; b. 20 Sept. 1944, Braga; s. of Fernando da Costa Vilaça and Maria das Dores G. Cruz Vilaça; m. Marie-Charlotte Olitz 1995; two s. two d. (three c. from previous m.); ed. Univs. of Coimbra and Paris; Asst. Faculty of Law, Univ. of Coimbra 1966, Prof. of Fiscal Law and Community Law 1979; mil. service, Naval Legal Dept. 1969–72; mem. Parl. 1980–86; Sec. of State for Home Affairs 1980, for Presidency of Council of Ministers 1981, for European Affairs 1982; Advocate-Gen. Court of Justice of EC 1986–89; Prof. of European Economy and Int. Orgs. and Dir. Inst. for European Studies, Lusiada Univ. Lisbon 1988; Pres. Court of First Instance of EC 1989–95; Visiting Prof. Nat. Inst. of Admin., Lisbon; Gran Croce del Ordine di Merito (Italy). *Publications:* A empresa cooperativa 1969, L'économie portugaise face à l'intégration économique européenne 1978, Introdução ao estudo da Economia 1979, Modelo económico da CEE e modelo económico português 1984, As consêquencias da adesão de Portugal à CEE no sector cultural 1984, The Court of First Instance of the European Communities: A Significant Step towards the Consolidation of the European Community as a Community Governed by the Rule of Law 1993, Y-a-t-il des limites matérielles à la révision des traités instituant les communautés européennes ? 1993, The Development of the Community Judicial System before and after Maastricht 1994. *Leisure interests:* tennis, gardening, literature. *Address:* Pereira and Associates, Rua Silva Carvalho, 234, 1250 Lisbon, Portugal.

DA SILVA, Luis Inácio (Lula); Brazilian trades unionist; b. 1946; m.; two s.; metal-worker, São Bernardo do Campo 1968–, organized strike 1977 and became union leader; imprisoned 1977 and freed later that year; arrested 1981; f. and Pres. Central Unica dos Trabalhadores (PT) 1980–87, Presidential Cand. of PT 1994. *Address:* c/o Central Unica dos Trabalhadores, Rua São Bento 405, Edif. Martinelli, 7° andar, 01011 São Paulo, SP, Brazil.

DA SILVEIRA GODINHO, José António; Portuguese diplomatist and economist; b. 16 Oct. 1943, Lisbon; s. of Raúl Catarino Godinho and Angela Maria da Silveira Godinho; m. Isabel Maria Segura de Faria da Silveira Godinho 1972; three s.; ed. Lisbon School of Econs. and Tech. Univ. of Lisbon; Asst. Prof. Lisbon School of Econs. 1967–77; Sr. Vice-Pres. Bank of Portugal 1975–79; Sec. of State, Ministry of Finance and Planning 1980; Sec. of State for Finance 1981; mem. Bd. Dirs. Banco Pinto & Sotto Mayor 1979, 1981–82, Banco Espírito Santo e Comercial de Lisboa 1982–93; Sec. of State for Nat. Defence 1986–87; Minister for Internal Affairs 1987–90; Amb. and Perm. Rep. of Portugal to OECD 1993. *Leisure interests:* music, reading, sport. *Address:* c/o Ministry of Foreign Affairs, Largo do Rilvas, 1354 Lisbon Codex, Portugal.

DAANE, James Dewey; American banker and educator; b. 6 July 1918, Grand Rapids, Mich.; s. of Gilbert L. and Mamie (née Blocksma) Daane; m. 1st Blanche M. Tichenor 1941 (dissolved); one d.; m. 2nd Onnie B. Selby 1953 (deceased); m. 3rd Barbara W. McMann 1963; two d.; ed. Duke Univ. and Harvard Univ.; Fed. Reserve Bank of Richmond 1939–60, Monetary Economist 1947, Asst. Vice-Pres. 1953, Vice-Pres., Dir., Research Dept., 1957; Chief, IMF Mission to Paraguay 1950–51; Vice-Pres., Econ. Adviser, Fed. Reserve Bank of Minneapolis May-July 1960; Asst. to Sec. of U.S. Treasury, Prin. Adviser to Under-Sec. for Monetary Affairs 1960–61; Deputy Under-Sec. of Treasury for Monetary Affairs and Gen. Deputy to Under-Sec. for Monetary Affairs 1961–63; mem. Bd. of Govs., Fed. Reserve System 1963–74; Vice-Chair. Commerce Union Bank 1974–78; Vice-Chair. Tennessee Valley Bancorp 1975–78; Chair. Int. Policy Cttee., Sovran Financial Corpn./Cen. South 1978–87; Dir. Nat. Futures Asscn., Ill. 1983–; Chair. money market cttee. S. Sovran Bank 1988–90; Frank K. Houston Prof. of Banking and Finance, Graduate School of Man., Vanderbilt Univ. 1974–85, Valere Blair Potter Prof. of Banking and Finance 1985–89, Prof. Emer. 1989–; Alan R. Holmes Prof. of Econs. Middlebury Coll. 1991–93; Dir. Whittaker Corpn. 1974–89, Chicago Bd. of Trade 1979–82; mem. American Finance Asscn., American Econ. Asscn. *Address:* Vanderbilt University, Owen Graduate School of Management, 401 21st Avenue, South Nashville, TN 37203 (Office); 102 Westhampton Place, Nashville, TN 37205, U.S.A. (Home).

DABO, Bakary Bunja, B.A.; Gambian politician; b. 10 Aug. 1946, Dumbutto; s. of Bunja Dabo and Fatoumatta Saidykhan; m. Awa Kainde Dabo 1972; three d.; ed. Methodist Boys' High School and Gambia High School, Banjul, Univs. of Ibadan, Nigeria and Abidjan, Ivory Coast; Asst. Commr., Basse 1967–68; Asst. Sec. Prime Minister's Office, Ministry of External Affairs 1968–70, Commr., Kerewan 1970–71; Dir. Econ. and Tech. Affairs, Senegambian Perm. Secr. 1971–74; Man. Commercial Banking Operations, Gambia Commercial and Devt. Bank 1974–79; High Commr. in Repub. of Senegal, also accred. to Mali, Guinea-Bissau, Cape Verde, Mauritania and Morocco 1979–81; nominated mem. of Parl. and apptd. Minister of Information and Tourism 1981–82; Vice-Pres. 1982–92, Hon. Treas., mem. Cen. Cttee. of People's Progressive Party 1982–; Minister of Educ., Youth, Sports and Culture 1987–92, of Finance and Econ. Affairs 1992–94 (in mil. govt. July–Oct. 1994). *Leisure interests:* reading, theatre.

DACHEVILLE, Colette (pseudonym Stéphane Audran); French actress; b. 8 Nov. 1932, Versailles; d. of Corneille Dacheville and Jeanne Rossi; m. 1st Jean-Louis Trintignant; m. 2nd Claude Chabrol 1964; one s.; ed. Lycée Lamartine, Paris, Cours Charles Dullin; studied drama under Tania Balachova and Michel Vitold. *Films include:* Les bonnes femmes 1959, L'oeil du malin 1961, Landru 1962, Ligne de Démarcation 1966, Champagne Murders 1966, Les biches 1968 (Best Actress, Berlin), La femme infidèle 1968, La peau de torpedo 1969, La dame dans l'auto avec les lunettes et un fusil 1969, Le boucher 1970 (Best Actress, San Sebastián), La rupture 1970, Aussi loin que l'amour 1970, Juste avant la nuit 1971, Without Apparent Motive 1971, Un meurtre est un meurtre 1972, Dead Pigeon on Beethoven Street 1972, Discreet Charm of the Bourgeoisie 1972 (Best Actress, Soc. of Film and TV Arts), Les noces rouges 1973, Comment réussir dans la vie quand on est con et pleurnichard 1973, Le cri du coeur 1974, Ten Little Indians 1974, B Must Die 1974, The Black Bird 1975, Vincent, François, Paul and Others 1975, Folies bourgeoises 1976, Silver Bears 1976, Devil's Advocate 1976, Violette Nozière 1978, Le Soleil en face 1979, The Big Red One 1980, Coup de Torchon 1981, Boulevard des assassins 1982, Le choc 1982, On ira tous au paradis, Le sang des autres 1983, Poulet au vinaigre 1984, Babette's Feast 1988 (Best Actress, Taormina), La Cage aux Folles III: The Wedding, Manika: The Girl Who Lived Twice 1989, Quiet Days in Clichy 1989, Betty 1991. *TV appearances in:* Brideshead Revisted 1981, Mistral's Daughter 1984, The Sun Also Rises 1984, Poor Little Rich Girl 1986, Tecx 1989, Cry No More My Lady. *Address:* c/o 2F De Marthod, 11 rue Chanez, Paris 75016, France. *Telephone:* 47 43 13 14.

DACIE, Sir John (Vivian), Kt., M.D., F.R.C.P., F.R.C.PATH., F.R.S.; British professor of haematology; b. 20 July 1912, Putney, London; s. of John C. Dacie and Lilian M. Dacie; m. Margaret K. V. Thynne 1938; three s. two d.; ed. King's Coll. School, Wimbledon, King's Coll., London and King's Coll. Hosp.; various appts. King's Coll. Hosp., Postgrad. Medical School and Manchester Royal Infirmary 1936–39; Pathologist, Emergency Medical Service 1939–42; RAMC 1943–46, rank of Maj. then Lieut.-Col.; Sr. Lecturer in Clinical Pathology, then Reader in Haematology, Postgrad. Medical School 1946–56; Prof. of Haematology, Royal Postgrad. Medical School, Univ. of London 1957–77, Prof. Emer. 1977–. *Publications:* Practical Haematology 1950, Haemolytic Anaemias (3rd edn.) Vols 1-5 1985–99; papers on anaemia in medical journals. *Leisure interests:* music, entomology, gardening. *Address:* 10 Alan Road, Wimbledon, London, SW19 7PT, England. *Telephone:* 0181-946 6086.

DACKO, David; Central African Republic politician; b. 24 March 1930, M'Baiki; ed. Ecole Normale, Brazzaville; Minister of Agriculture, Stockbreeding, Water and Forests, Cen. African Govt. Council 1957–58; Minister of Interior, Economy and Trade, Cen. African Provisional Govt. 1958–59; Premier, Cen. African Repub. 1959–66, Minister of Nat. Defence, Guardian of the Seals 1960–66; Pres. of Cen. African Repub. 1960–66 (deposed by mil. coup); mem. Mouvement pour l'Evolution Sociale de l'Afrique Noire (MESAN); under house arrest for several years; appointed Personal Adviser to Pres. (later Emperor) 1976; Pres. of restored Repub. 1979–81; ousted in coup Sept. 1981; Pres. UDEAC 1979; Ind. Cand., Presidential Elections Oct. 1992; Head Provisional Nat. Political Council March–May 1993; f., Leader Mouvement pour la Démocratie et le Développement (MDD) 1993–. *Address:* Mouvement pour la démocratie et le développement, Bangui, Central African Republic.

DACOSTA, Claude Antoine; Republic of the Congo politician and agronomist; Prime Minister of the Congo 1992–93; Chair. Devt. Cttee. 1993.

DACRE, Paul Michael, B.A.; British newspaper editor; b. 14 Nov. 1948, London; s. of Joan Dacre (née Hill) and Peter Dacre; m. Kathleen Thomson 1973; two s.; ed. Univ. Coll. School, London, Leeds Univ.; reporter, feature writer, Assoc. Features Ed., Daily Express 1970–76, Washington and New York Corresp. 1976–79; New York Bureau Chief, Daily Mail 1980, News Ed., London 1981–85, Asst. Ed. (News and Foreign) 1986, Asst. Ed. (Features) 1987, Exec. Ed. 1988, Assoc. Ed. 1989–91, Ed. 1992–, Ed.-in-Chief Assoc. Newspapers 1998–; Ed. Evening Standard 1991–92; Dir. Associated Newspaper Holdings 1991–. *Address:* Daily Mail, Northcliffe House, 2 Derry Street, London, W8 5TT, England. *Telephone:* 0171-938 6000. *Fax:* 0171-937 7977.

DACRE OF GLANTON, Baron (Life Peer), cr. 1979, of Glanton, in the County of Northumberland; **Hugh Redwald Trevor-Roper,** F.B.A.; British historian; b. 15 Jan. 1914, Glanton, Northumberland; s. of the late Dr. B. W. E. Trevor-Roper and of Mrs. Trevor-Roper; m. The Lady Alexandra Haig 1954 (died 1997); ed. Charterhouse and Christ Church, Oxford; Research Fellow, Merton Coll., Oxford 1937–39; Student of Christ Church, Oxford 1945–57; Regius Prof. of Modern History of Oxford 1957–80; Master of Peterhouse, Cambridge 1980–87; Dir. Times Newspapers Ltd. 1974–88; Chevalier, Légion d'honneur 1976. *Publications:* Archbishop Laud 1940, The

Last Days of Hitler 1947, Hitler's Table Talk (Ed.) 1953, The Gentry 1540–1640 1954, The Poems of Richard Corbett (Ed. with J. A. W. Bennett) 1955, Historical Essays 1957 (American title, Men and Events 1958), Hitler's War Directives (Ed.) 1964, The Rise of Christian Europe 1963, Religion, the Reformation and Social Change 1967 (American title The Crisis of the 17th Century 1968), The Philby Affair 1968, The European Witch-Craze in the 16th and 17th Centuries 1970, Queen Elizabeth's First Historian 1971, Princes and Artists: Patronage and Ideology at Four Habsburg Courts 1976, A Hidden Life: The Enigma of Sir Edmund Backhouse 1976, Goebbels Diaries, The Last Days (Ed.) 1978, Renaissance Essays 1985, Catholics, Anglicans and Puritans 1987, From Counter-Reformation to Glorious Revolution (essays) 1992; ed. The Golden Age of Europe: From Elizabeth to the Sun King 1987. *Address:* The Old Rectory, Didcot, Oxon., OX11 7EB, England. *Telephone:* (01235) 818568.

DADDAH, Moktar Ould, L. EN D.; Mauritanian politician; b. 20 Dec. 1924, Boutilmit; ed. secondary school, Senegal and Paris; Interpreter; studied law; with firm Boissier Palun, Dakar; territorial councillor 1957; Premier, Islamic Repub. of Mauritania 1958–78; Pres. of the Repub. 1961–78; under house arrest 1978–79; left Mauritania, sentenced in absentia to hard labour for life Nov. 1980; Pres. Org. Commune Africaine et Malgache 1965; Chair. OAU 1971–72; fmr. Sec.-Gen. Parti du Peuple Mauritanien.

DAFALLAH, Gizouli; Sudanese politician and physician; b. Dec. 1935, Blue Nile Prov.; two d.; ed. Khartoum Medical Coll.; Chair. Alliance of the Nat. Forces April 1985 (after overthrow of Pres. Gaafar al-Nemery (q.v.) in coup); Chair. Doctors' Union; Prime Minister of Sudan 1985–86. *Address:* c/o Office of the Prime Minister, Khartoum, Sudan.

DAFOE, Willem; American actor; b. 22 July 1955, Appleton, Wis. s. of William Dafoe; one s.; ed. Wisconsin Univ. *Films include:* The Loveless 1981, New York Nights 1981, The Hunger 1982, Communists are Comfortable (and three other stories) 1984, Roadhouse 66 1984, Streets of Fire 1984, To Live and Die in L.A. 1985, Platoon 1986, The Last Temptation of Christ 1988, Saigon 1988, Mississippi Burning 1989, Triumph of the Spirit 1989, Born on the 4th of July 1990, Flight of the Intruder 1990, Wild at Heart 1990, The Light Sleeper 1991, Body of Evidence 1992, Far Away, So Close 1994, Tom and Viv 1994, The Night and the Moment 1994, Clear and Present Danger 1994, The English Patient 1996, Basquiat 1996, Speed 2: Cruise Control 1997, Affliction 1997, Lulu on the Bridge 1998, Existenz 1998, American Psycho 1999.

DAGENAIS, Marcel Gilles, M.A., PH.D., F.R.S.C.; Canadian economist; b. 22 Feb. 1935, Montreal; s. of Emilien Dagenais and Antoinette Girard; m. Denyse Laberge 1958; two s. one d.; ed. Coll. Jean-de-Brébeuf, Univ. de Montréal and Yale Univ.; Asst. Prof. Univ. de Montréal 1961–66, Visiting Prof. 1972–73, Prof. of Econs. 1973–97, Assoc. Fellow Centre de recherche et dévt. en écon. 1987–, Prin. Investigator, Center for Interuniversity Research and Analysis on Orgs. 1994–, Prof. Emer. 1997–; Consulting economist, AMSTEC Inc. 1998–; Visiting Prof. Ecole des Hautes Etudes Commerciales de Montréal 1966–67, Assoc. Prof. 1967–70, Prof. 1970–72; Special Prof. Sir George Williams Univ. 1969–73; Assoc. Ed., Journal of Econometrics 1980–; Consultant Nat. Ass. of Quebec 1991–92; mem. Ed. Bd. Advanced Studies in Theoretical & Applied Econometrics 1982–, Kluwer Acad. Publs.; mem. Advisory Cttee. on Nat. Accounts, Statistics, Canada; Woodrow Wilson Hon. Fellowship; Award of Soc. Canadienne de sciences écon.; Killam Research Fellow; Prix du Statisticien d'Expression Française, Soc. de Statistique de Paris 1990, Prix Marcel Vinlent, Asscn. Française pour L'Avancement des Sciences 1991. *Publications:* numerous papers in economic journals. *Address:* 60 Berlioz, Apt. 1002, Ile des Soeurs, Québec, H3E 1M4, Canada. *Telephone:* (514) 766-0473 (Home).

DAGHESTANI, Najib Abu Al Alaa, M.SC; Syrian engineer, technical and investment analyst; b. 26 June 1940, Damascus; s. of Dr Kazem Daghestani and Inaam Al Azem; m. Moira Beaton 1972 (divorced 1987); two s.; ed. Enfield Coll. of Tech. London and Univ. of Strathclyde; geotechnical engineer, U.K. 1968–72; counterpart to ILO expert, geotechnical engineer (Ministry of Communication), Syria 1972–74; civil and material engineer Saudi Arabia 1974–78; project man., jt. gen. man. Sultanate of Oman 1978–81; contracts man. Libya 1981–82; promotion and devt. man (Middle East and Africa), Cyprus, U.A.E., Saudi Arabia, Yemen 1982–86; consultant, Daghestani Eng. Services, Portugal 1996–. *Publication:* Ground Engineering 1970. *Leisure interests:* water sports, hiking, painting, reading. *Address:* 62 Mahdi Ben Barakeh Avenue, Damascus, Syria; P.O. Box 428, 8500 Portimão, Portugal. *Telephone:* (11) 3334544 (Damascus); (82) 424050 (Portimão).

DAGWORTHY PREW, Wendy Ann, DIP.A.D.; British fashion designer; b. 4 March 1950, Gravesend; d. of Arthur S. Dagworthy and Jean A. Stubbs; m. Jonathan W. Prew 1973; two s.; ed. Medway Coll. of Design and Middx. Polytechnic; started own design co., designer and Dir. Wendy Dagworthy Ltd. 1972–; Dir. London Designer Collections 1982; consultant to C.I.Y.A.A. Fashion/Textiles Bd. 1982–; Course dir. Fashion, B.A. Hons. Degree, Cen. St. Martin's Coll. of Art and Design 1989–; Prof. of Fashion, Royal Coll. of Art 1998–; Judge, Royal Soc. of Arts Bd.; judge of art and design projects for various manufacturers; participating designer in Fashion Aid and many charity shows; exhibits seasonally in London, Milan, New York and Paris; Lecturer and External Assessor at numerous polytechnics and colls. of art and design; frequent TV appearances; Fil d'Or Int. Linen Award 1986. *Leisure interests:* dining out, cooking, reading, painting, horse racing. *Address:* 18 Melrose Terrace, London, W.6, England (Home). *Telephone:* 0171-602 6676 (Home).

DAHAB, Field Marshal Abdul-Rahman Swar al-; Sudanese politician and army officer; b. 1934, Omdurman; m.; two s. three d.; joined Sudanese Mil. Acad. 1954; trained at mil. acads. in Jordan, Britain and Egypt; Minister of Defence, C.-in-C. Sudanese Army March 1985–86; led. mil. coup April 1985; Chair. Transitional Mil. Council 1985–86; rank of Field Marshal 1987. *Address:* c/o Ministry of Defence, Khartoum, Sudan.

DAHL, Birgitta, B.A.; Swedish politician; b. 20 Sept. 1937, Råda; d. of Anna-Brita Axelsson and Sven Dahl; m. Enn Kokk; one s. two d.; ed. Univ. of Uppsala; teacher, clerical officer, Scandinavian Inst. of African Studies, Uppsala 1960–65; Sr. Admin. Officer, Dag Hammarskjold Foundation 1965–68, Swedish Int. Devt. Authority 1965–82; mem. Parl. 1968; mem. Bd. of Dirs. Nat. Housing Bd.; mem. Advisory Council of Foreign Affairs; del. to UN Gen. Ass.; mem. Exec. Cttee. Social Democratic Party 1975–96; Minister with special responsibility for Energy Issues, Ministry of Energy 1982–86, for the Environment and Energy 1987–90, for the Environment 1990–91; Spokesperson on Social Welfare; Chair. Environment Cttee. of Socialist Int. 1986–93, Confed. of Socialist Parties of EC 1990–94, Chair. High Level Advisory Bd. on Sustainable Devt. to Sec.-Gen. 1996–97; Speaker of Swedish Parl. 1994–. *Address:* Riksdag, 100 12 Stockholm (Office); Idrottsgt 12, 753 35, Uppsala, Sweden (Home). *Telephone:* (8) 786 4000 (Office). *Fax:* (8) 786 6143 (Office).

DAHL, Robert Alan, PH.D.; American professor of political science; b. 17 Dec. 1915, Inwood, Iowa; s. of Peter I. Dahl and Vera Lewis Dahl; m. 1st Mary Louise Barlett 1940 (died 1970); three s. one d.; m. 2nd Ann Goodrich Sale 1973; ed. Univ. of Washington, Div. of Econ. Research, Nat. Labor Relations Bd. and Yale Univ.; Man. Analyst, U.S. Dept. of Agric. 1940; Economist, Office of Production Man., O.P.A.C.S. and War Production Bd. 1940–42; U.S. Army 1943–45; Yale Univ., successively Instructor, Asst. Prof., Assoc. Prof. and Sterling Prof. of Political Science 1964–86; Chair. Dept. of Political Science 1957–62; Ford Research Prof. 1957; Lecturer in Political Science, Flacso, Santiago, Chile 1967; Guggenheim Fellow 1950 and 1978; Fellow, Center for Advanced Study in the Behavioral Sciences 1955–56 and 1967; Pres. American Political Science Asscn. 1967; Fellow, American Acad. of Arts and Sciences, American Philosophical Soc., N.A.S.; fmr. Trustee, Center for Advanced Study in the Behavioral Sciences; fmr. mem. Educ. Advisory Bd., Guggenheim Foundation; Hon. LL.D. (Mich.) 1983, (Alaska) 1987; D.Hum.Litt. h.c. (Georgetown) 1993; Woodrow Wilson Prize 1963, Talcott Parsons Prize 1977, and other prizes; Bronze Star Medal with Cluster, Cavaliere of Repub. of Italy. *Publications:* Congress and Foreign Policy 1950, Domestic Control of Atomic Energy (with R. Brown) 1951, Politics, Economics and Welfare (with C. E. Lindblom) 1953, A Preface to Democratic Theory 1956, Social Science Research on Business (with Haire and Lazarsfeld) 1959, Who Governs? 1961, Modern Political Analysis 1963, Political Oppositions in Western Democracies 1966, Pluralist Democracy in the United States 1967, After the Revolution 1970, Polyarchy: Participation and Opposition 1971, Regimes and Opposition 1972, Democracy in the United States 1972, Size and Democracy (with E. R. Tufte) 1973, Dilemmas of Pluralist Democracy 1982, A Preface to Economic Democracy 1985, The Control of Nuclear Weapons: Democracy *v* Guardianship 1985, Democracy, Liberty and Equality 1986, Democracy and the Critics 1989, Towards Democracy: A Journey 1997, Reflections (1940–1997) 1997, On Democracy 1999. *Leisure interests:* tennis, sailing, fly-fishing. *Address:* 17 Cooper Road, North Haven, CT 06473, U.S.A. (Home). *Telephone:* (203) 288 3126. *Fax:* (203) 432 6196.

DAHL, Sophie; British fashion model; b. 1978; granddaughter of Patricia Neal (q.v.) and the late Roald Dahl; discovered as a model by Isabella Blow (q.v.) who saw her crying in the street; has worked with fashion photographers Nick Knight, David La Chapelle, Karl Lagerfeld, David Bailey, Enrique Badulescu, Herb Ritts and Ellen Von Unwerth; has appeared in I.D., The Face, Arena, Elle, Esquire, Scene magazines and advertising campaigns for Lainey Keogh, Bella Freud, Printemps, Nina Ricci, Karl Lagerfeld, Oil of Ulay, Hennes; music videos for U2, Elton John and Duran Duran; contribs. to The Telegraph, The Sunday Times, Tatler and Elle magazine; cameo appearance in films Mad Cows and Best 1999; stage appearance in The Vagina Monologues, The Old Vic 1999. *Address:* c/o Storm Model Management, 5 Jubilee Place, London, S.W.3, England. *Telephone:* 0171-352 2278.

DAHLBECK, Eva; Swedish actress and author; b. 8 March 1920, Nacka; d. of Edvard Dahlbeck and Greta Österberg; m. Col. Sven Lampell 1944; two s.; ed. Royal Dramatic Theatre School, Stockholm. *Films acted in include:* The Counterfeit Traitor 1961, Biljett till Paradiset 1961, För att inte tala om alla dessa Kvinnor 1964, Alskande par 1964, Kattorna 1965, Les créatures 1965, Den Röda Kappan 1966. *Plays acted in include:* Candida 1961, Ändå älskar vi varavdra 1963, Tchin-Tchin 1963, The Balcony 1964, Doctors of Philosophy 1964. *Publications:* Dessa mina minsta (play) 1955, Hem till Kaos (novel) 1964, S'is'ta Spegeln (novel) 1965, Den S'junde Natten (novel) 1966, Domen (novel) 1967, Med Seende Ögon (novel) 1972, Hjrätslagen (novel) 1974, Saknadens Dal (novel) 1976, Maktspråket 1978, I Våra Tomma Rum 1980. *Leisure interests:* reading, music.

DAHLERUP, Troels, D.THEOL.; Danish professor of modern history; b. 3 Dec. 1925, Frederiksberg; s. of Nicolai Frederik Bjerre Dahlerup and Inger

Dahlerup; m. Merete Valt 1958 (died 1998); three s.; ed. St. Jørgen Grammar School and Univ. of Copenhagen; grammar school teacher 1953; archivist Rigsarkivet 1956; Prof. of Modern History, Univ. of Aarhus 1968–92; mem. Kongelige Danske Selskab for Faedrelandets Historie, Kongelige Danske Videnskabernes Selskab; Kt. 1st Degree Order of Dannebrog. *Publications:* Studier i Senmiddelalderlig dansk Kirkeorganisation 1963, Det danske Sysselprovsti i Middelalderen 1968; with A. E. Christensen, Aasum herreds Tingbog 1640–48 1956–62, Det Kongelige Rettertings Domme og Rigens Forfølgninger I-II 1959–69, De fire Staender (Danmarks Historie VI, 1400–1500) 1989. *Address:* Aarhus Universitet, Ndr. Ringgade, 8000 Aarhus C (Office); Kildevangen 15, 8382 Hinnerup, Denmark. *Fax:* 89 42 20 47 (Office).

DAHLFORS, John Ragnar, M.C.E.; Swedish engineer; b. 31 Dec. 1934, Stockholm; s. of Mats Dahlfors and Astrid Dahlfors; m. 1st Anita Roger 1962 (dissolved); one s. two d.; m. 2nd Ing-Britt Schlyter 1998; ed. Royal Inst. of Tech., Stockholm; engineer with Gränges AB Liberia project 1962–66, Sales Man. Gränges Hedlund AB 1967–68, Pres. 1970–74, Tech. Man. Gränges Construction AB 1969, Pres. Gränges Aluminium AB 1974–78; Pres. Boliden AB 1978–86; man. consultant at SEVENCO; mem. Bd., Latour, Plymovent, Nordbanken Alfa, Trust & Olympia Fund, ABA of Sweden, Perten Instruments, EIAB, Vemdalsfjäll and ACB Group, Swedish Chamber of Commerce; mem. Industrial Advisory Bd. to the Swedish Acad. of Eng. Sciences. *Leisure interests:* sailing, golf, tennis, hunting. *Address:* Sävstigen I, 133 35 Saltsjöbaden, Sweden (Home). *Telephone:* 08-619-5200 (Office); 08-717-2800 (Home). *Fax:* 08-130288 (Office); 08-717-6798 (Home).

DAHLLÖF, Urban Sigurd, D.PHIL.; Swedish professor; b. 11 Nov. 1928, Göteborg; s. of Sigurd Dahllöf and Karin Hansson; m. Tordis Larsson 1950; two s. one d.; ed. Uppsala Univ. and Univ. of Stockholm; Research Asst., Stockholm School of Educ. 1963–66; Asst. Prof., Univ. of Göteborg 1960–62, Assoc. Prof. 1966–72, Prof. of Educ. 1972–76; Prof. of Educ., Uppsala Univ. 1976–83; Research Dir. (part-time) Univ. of Trondheim 1991–; Adjunct Prof. Møre Research/Volda Coll., Volda, Norway 1994–; Head of Bureau, Nat. Bd. of Educ., Stockholm 1962–63, Office of the Swedish Chancellor of the Univs., Stockholm 1973–75; Visiting Prof., Univ. of Melbourne 1984; Sr. Consultant, Interior Univ. Soc., Prince George, B.C. 1988; Chair. Study Group on Evaluation in Higher Educ., OECD, Paris 1988–90; Chair. Swedish School Research Cttee. 1978–80, Swedish Secondary School Planning Cttee. 1979–81; Pres. Swedish Psychological Asscn. 1966–68; mem. Swedish Royal Acad. of Sciences, Swedish Acad. of Letters, History and Antiquities; Sidney Suslow Award for Outstanding Research, Asscn. for Inst. Research 1989. *Publications include:* Demands on the Secondary School 1963, Ability Grouping, Content Validity and Curriculum Process Analysis 1971, Reforming Higher Education and External Studies in Sweden and Australia 1977, Regional Universities in a Comparative Western Perspective 1988, Dimensions of Evaluation in Higher Education (jtly.) 1991, New Universities and Regional Context (jtly.) 1994, Expanding Colleges and New Universities (jtly.) 1996. *Leisure interest:* train timetables. *Address:* Östra Ågatan 17, 753 22 Uppsala, Sweden (Home). *Telephone:* (18) 14-16-94 (Home). *Fax:* (18) 18-16-51 (Office).

DAHRENDORF, Baron (Life Peer) cr. 1993, of Clare Market in the City of Westminster, **Ralf (Gustav) Dahrendorf,** K.B.E., F.B.A., DR.PHIL., PH.D.; British (b. German) sociologist, politician and university administrator; b. 1 May 1929, Hamburg; s. of Gustav Dahrendorf and Lina Witt; m. Ellen Joan de Kadt 1980; ed. Hamburg Univ. and London School of Econs.; Asst., Univ. of Saar, Saarbrücken 1954, Privatdozent in sociology 1957; Fellow, Center for Advanced Study in the Behavioral Sciences, Palo Alto, U.S.A. 1957–58; Prof. of Sociology, Hamburg 1958, Tübingen 1960, Constance 1966 (on leave since 1969); Visiting Prof. at several European and U.S. Univs.; Vice-Chair. Founding Cttee. Univ. Constance 1964–66, First Dean Faculty of Social Science 1966–67; Adviser on educational questions to the Land Govt. of Baden-Württemberg 1964–68; mem. German Council of Educ. 1966–68; Chair. Comm. on Comprehensive Univ. Planning 1967–68; mem. Free Dem. Party (FDP) 1967, Fed. Exec. 1968–74; mem. Land Diet of Baden-Württemberg and Vice-Chair. FDP Parl. Party 1968–69; mem. Fed. Parl. (Bundestag) and Parl. Sec. of State in Foreign Office 1969–70; mem. Comm. of the European Communities 1970–74; Chair. Royal Univ. of Malta Comm. 1972–74; mem. Hansard Soc. Comm. for Electoral Reform 1975–76, Royal Comm. on Legal Services 1976–78, Cttee. to Review the Functioning of Financial Insts. 1977–80; Dir. European Centre for Research and Documentation in Social Sciences 1966–82, L.S.E. 1974–84; BBC Reith Lecturer 1974; Visiting Scholar, Russell Sage Foundation, New York 1986–87; Warden, St. Antony's Coll. Oxford 1987–97; Pres. German Sociological Soc. 1967–70; Hon. Presidium Anglo-German Soc. 1973–; Chair. Social Science Council of the European Science Foundation 1976–77, Newspaper Publishing 1992–93; Trustee Ford Foundation 1976–88; Chair. Bd. Friedrich-Naumann-Stiftung 1982–87; dir. (non-exec.) Bankges. Berlin (UK) PLC 1996–; mem. Council, British Acad. 1980–81, Vice-Pres. 1982–84; mem. German PEN Centre 1971–; Foreign Assoc., N.A.S. 1977; Foreign mem. American Philosophical Soc., Phila. 1977; Hon. mem. Royal Irish Acad. 1974; Foreign Hon. mem. American Acad. of Arts and Sciences 1975; Hon. mem. Royal Coll. of Surgeons 1982; Fellow Imperial Coll., London 1974, Royal Soc. of Arts 1977, British Acad. 1977; Hon. Fellow L.S.E. 1973; Hon. D.Litt (Reading) 1973, (Malta) 1992, Hon. LL.D. (Manchester) 1973, Hon. D.Sc. (Ulster) 1973, (Bath) 1977, Hon. D.Univ. (Open Univ.) 1974, Hon. D.H.L. (Kalamazoo Coll.) 1974, (Maryland) 1978, (Johns Hopkins Univ.) 1982, Hon. Litt.D. (Trinity Coll., Dublin) 1975, Hon. Dr. (Univ. Catholique de Louvain) 1977, (Univ. of Buenos Aires) 1993, Hon. LL.D. (Wagner Coll., Staten Is., New York, Columbia Univ., N.Y.), Hon. D. Univ. (Surrey) 1978, Hon. LL.D. (York, Ontario Univs.) 1979, Dr. Social Sc. (Queen's Belfast), (Birmingham); Hon. D.Pol.Sci. (Bologna) 1991; Dr. h.c. (Urbino) 1993, (Univ. René Descartes) 1994; Hon.Ph.D. (Univ. of Haifa) 1994; Hon. LL.D. (Westminster) 1996; Journal Fund Award for Learned Publications 1966; Agnelli Prize 1992; Grand Croix de l'Ordre du Mérite du Sénégal 1971, Grand Croix de l'Ordre du Mérite du Luxembourg 1974, Grosses Bundesverdienstkreuz mit Stern und Schulterband (Feb. Repub. of Germany) 1974, Grosses goldenes Ehrenzeichen am Bande (Austria) 1975, Grand Croix de l'Ordre de Léopold II (Belgium) 1975. *Publications include:* Marx in Perspective 1953, Industrie- und Betriebssoziologie 1956, Homo Sociologicus 1958, Soziale Klassen und Klassenkonflikt 1957 and 1959, Die angewandte Aufklärung 1963, Gesellschaft und Demokratie in Deutschland 1965, Pfade aus Utopia 1967, Essays in the Theory of Society 1968, Konflikt und Freiheit 1972, Plädoyer für die Europäische Union 1973, The New Liberty: Survival and Justice in a Changing World (Reith Lectures) 1975, A New World Order? (Ghana Lectures 1978) 1979, Life Chances (also in German) 1979, On Britain (BBC TV Lectures) 1982/83, Reisen nach innen und aussen 1984, Law and Order 1985, The Modern Social Conflict 1988, Reflections on the Revolution in Europe 1990, History of the London School of Economics and Political Science 1895–1995 1995, Liberale und Andere; Portraits 1995, After 1989: Morals, Revolution and Civil Society 1997. *Address:* House of Lords, London, SW1A 0PW, England.

DAI AILIAN; Chinese choreographer and dancer; b. 1916, Trinidad, W. Indies; m. Ye Qianyu (divorced); studied in London 1931; worked with Modern Dance Co. of Ernst and Lotte Berk; studied at Jooss-Leeder Dance School, and with Anton Dolin, Margaret Craske, Marie Rambert; went to China 1941; teacher Nat. Opera School, Nat. Inst. of Social Educ. and Yucai School; since 1949 has been leader dance team attached to N. China Univ., Cen. Theatrical Inst., leader Cen. Song and Dance Ensemble, Artistic Dir. dance drama troupe, Cen. Experimental Opera Theatre; Pres. Beijing Dancing Acad., China Ballet Soc., China Labanotation Soc.; Hon. Chair. Chinese Dancers' Asscn.; Adviser Cen. Ballet; mem. Int. Jury, Int. Youth Festival, Bucharest 1953, Moscow 1957, Choreography Competition, Turin 1983, 3rd U.S.A. Int. Ballet Competition, Jackson 1986, 2nd Int. Ballet Competition 1987, New York, 3rd Int. Ballet Competition, Paris 1988, 3rd Tokyo Ballet Competition for Asia and Pacific 1987, New York Int. Ballet Competition 1990; Chair. China Nat. Ballet Competition 1984, New York 1987, Chair. of Jury, 1st Shanghai Int. Ballet Competition 1998; Lecture-demonstrations on Chinese Ethnic Folk Dance at CEO China Forum, Beijing, UNESCO, Paris, Dartington Coll. of Arts, Devon 1988–89; lectur-demonstrations on Chinese Dance History, Univ. of Calif., Univ. of San Francisco, Asian Museum, Inst. of Arts, U.S.A. 1993; Sr. Consultant, China Asscn. for the Advancement of Int. Friendship; Cttee. mem. Int. Dance Council UNESCO, Vice-Chair. 1982–86, 1986; Consultant London Chinese Cultural Centre 1989, Int. Folk Arts Org. Mödling, Austria 1990; Hon. Chair. Chinese Dancers' Assn. 1991–; mem. Int. Labanotation Council; Lecture on Labanotation in China, Laban Centre, London 1988; Patron Language of Dance Centre, London 1992, Laban Inst., Univ. of Surrey 1992; mem. Cttee. China Int. Cultural Exchange Centre; mem. Beijing Int. Soc.; mem. Standing Cttee. CPPCC; mem. Presidium 6th CPPCC Nat. Cttee. 1983, 8th 1993–; Hon. mem. China Fed. of Literary and Art Circles 1996; Fellow Hong Kong Acad. of Arts 1996; Guest Lecturer Univs. of Toronto, Ottawa and Vancouver, Canada 1997. *Works include:* Lotus Dance, The Old Carries the Young, Flying Apsaras, The Women Oil-drillers' Dance, Tears of Pear Blossoms. *Address:* Apt. 2-16 Hua Qiao Gong Yu, Hua Yuan Cun, Hai Dian, Beijing 100044, People's Republic of China. *Telephone:* (10) 6841 4163.

DAI BINGGUO; Chinese diplomatist; b. 1941, Yinjiang Co., Guizhou Prov.; ed. Sichuan Univ.; joined CCP 1973; Dir. Dept. of U.S.S.R. and Eastern European Affairs, Ministry of Foreign Affairs; Vice-Minister of Foreign Affairs; Dir. Int. Liaison Dept. of CCP Cen Cttee. 1997–; mem. 15th CCP Cen. Cttee. 1997–. *Address:* International Liaison Department of Chinese Communist Party Central Committee, Beijing, People's Republic of China.

DAI JIE; Chinese administrator; b. 1928, Shengyang Co., Liaoning Prov.; Commercial attaché at the embassy in Yugoslavia 1971; Dir. Import and Export Bureau under the Ministry of Foreign Econ. Relations and Trade 1982; Dir.-Gen. Admin. of Customs 1985; Vice-Chair. Tariff Regulations Cttee. 1988; Deputy Head Interministry Co-ordination Group for GATT Negotiations 1988; mem. 8th NPC 1993–, Deputy to 8th NPC Guangdong Prov.; Chair. China-Germany Friendship Group 1994–. *Address:* The Customs General Administration, Beijing 100730, People's Republic of China.

DAI QIANDING, M.A.; Chinese government official; b. 21 March 1925, Sichuan; m. Ye Zhiqing 1953; one s. two d.; ed. Central Univ., China and Michigan Univ., U.S.A.; Deputy Man., People's Bank of China 1950–71, Deputy Man., Research Dept. 1972–80, Dir. Research Inst. of Int. Finance 1983–84, Gen. Man., Bank of China, London 1985–86, Dir. of Bd. 1985–; Alt. Exec. Dir. Int. Monetary Fund for China 1980–82, Exec. Dir. 1986–91; Man. Dir. China Int. Finance Soc. 1992–. *Publications:* The IMF and the World Bank 1978; numerous articles on int. finance. *Leisure interests:* travel, music, arts. *Address:* 62 Xi Jiao Min Xiang, 2-1006, Beijing 100031, People's Republic of China.

DAI XIANGLONG; Chinese banker and economist; b. Oct. 1944, Yizheng City, Jiangsu Prov.; ed. Cen. Inst. of Finance and Banking; mem. CCP

1973–; Deputy Section Chief, People's Bank of China (PBC), Jiangsu Prov. br. 1978; Deputy Section Chief and Deputy Head of Dept. Agricultural Bank of China (ABC), Jiangsu br., Vice-Gov. 1983; Sec. CCP Group, Communications Bank of China (CBC), also Gen. Man. and Vice-Chair. Bd. CBC 1989; Chair. Bd. China Pacific Insurance Co. Ltd. 1990–93; Vice-Gov. People's Bank of China 1993–95, Gov. 1995–; alt. mem. 14th CCP Cen. Cttee. 1992–97; mem. 15th CCP Cen. Cttee. 1997–. *Address:* People's Bank of China, 32 Chengfang Jie, Xicheng Qu, Beijing, People's Republic of China. *Telephone:* (1) 6015522. *Fax:* (1) 6016704.

DAIANU, Daniel, PH.D.; Romanian economist and politician; b. 30 Aug. 1952, Bucharest; ed. Acad. of Econ. Studies, Bucharest, Acad. of Sciences, Bucharest and Harvard Business School; Visiting Scholar Russian Research Center, Harvard Univ. 1990–92; Deputy Minister of Finance Feb.–Aug. 1992; Chief Economist Cen. Bank of Romania 1992–97; Minister of Finance 1997–98; Visiting Scholar, Woodrow Wilson Center, Washington, DC 1992, IMF, Washington, DC 1993; Visiting Sr. Fellow NATO Defense Coll., Rome 1995; Visiting Prof. Berkeley Univ. 1998; Acad of Sciences Award for Econs. 1994. *Publications:* Transformation of Economies as a Real Process 1998, Economic Vitality and Viability 1996. *Leisure interests:* reading, football, basketball. *Address:* Negro Voda Street, Block C3, Floor 3, apt. 9, Sector 3, Bucharest, Romania. *Telephone:* (1) 2300723. *Fax:* (1) 3127192.

DAIBER, Hans Joachim, D.PHIL.; German professor of Arabic; b. 1 April 1942, Stuttgart; s. of Otto Daiber and Martha Daiber; m. Helga Brosamler 1971; one s. one d.; ed. Theological Seminaries of Maulbronn and Blaubeuren, Univs. of Tübingen and Saarbrucken; lecturer in Arabic, Univ. of Heidelberg 1975–77; Prof. of Arabic, Free Univ. Amsterdam 1977–95; Prof. of Oriental Philology and Islam, Univ. of Frankfurt a.M. 1995–; Special Visiting Prof., Univ. of Tokyo 1992; mem. Royal Netherlands Acad. of Arts and Sciences; mem. German Oriental Inst., Beirut 1973–75, German Oriental Soc., American Oriental Soc., Oosters Genootschap, Soc. Int. pour l'étude de la philosophie médiévale, Union Européenne d'Arabisants et d'Islamisants; ed. Aristoteles Semitico-Latinus, Islamic Philosophy, Theology and Science. *Publications:* Die arabische Übersetzung der Placita philosophorum 1968, Ein Kompendium der aristotelischen Meteorologie in der Fassung des Hunain Ibn Ishaq 1975, Das theologisch-philosophische System des Muammar Ibn Abbad as-Sulami 1975, Gott, Natur und menschlicher Wille im fruehen islamischen Denken 1978, Aetius Arabus 1980, The Ruler as Philosopher: a new interpretation of al-Farabi's view 1986, Wasil Ibn Ata' als Prediger und Theologe 1988, Catalogue of Arabic Manuscripts in the Daiber Collection Vol. I 1988, (Vol. II) 1996, Naturwissenschaft bei den Arabern im 10 Jahrhundert n. Chr. 1993, Neuplatonische Pythagorica in arabischem Gewande 1995, The Islamic Concept of Belief in the 4th/10th Century 1995; numerous articles in journals on Islamic philosophy, theology, history of sciences, Greek heritage in Islam. *Address:* University of Frankfurt a.M., Department of Oriental Studies, P.B.111932, 60054 Frankfurt a.M. (Office); Am Huettenhof 10, 40489 Düsseldorf, Germany (Home). *Telephone:* (0211) 403714 (Home). *Fax:* (0211) 403725 (Home).

DAICHES, David, C.B.E., M.A. (EDIN.), D.PHIL (OXON.), PH.D. (CANTAB.), F.R.S.L., F.R.S.E.; British writer and university professor; b. 2 Sept. 1912, Sunderland; s. of Dr. Salis and Flora (née Levin) Daiches; m. 1st Isobel J. Mackay 1937 (died 1977); one s. two d.; m. 2nd Hazel Neville 1978 (died 1986); ed. George Watson's Coll., Edinburgh, Edinburgh Univ. and Balliol Coll., Oxford; Bradley Fellow, Balliol Coll., Oxford 1936–37; Asst. Prof. of English, Univ. of Chicago 1940–43; Second Sec. British Embassy, Washington 1944–46; Prof. of English, Cornell Univ. 1946–51; Univ. Lecturer in English, Cambridge Univ. 1951–61, Fellow of Jesus Coll., Cambridge 1957–62; Dean, School of English Studies, Univ. of Sussex 1961–67, Prof. of English 1961–77, Prof. Emer. 1977–; Dir. Inst. for Advanced Studies in the Humanities, Edinburgh Univ. 1980–86, Gifford Lecturer 1983; Sr. Fellow, Nat. Humanities Center, U.S.A. 1987–88; Hon. Litt.D. (Brown, Edinburgh, Sussex, Glasgow and Guelph Univs.); Dr. h.c. (Sorbonne, Bologna), Hon. D.Univ. (Stirling); many awards and prizes. *Publications:* 45 books including: The Novel and the Modern World 1939, A Study of Literature 1948, Robert Burns 1950, Two Worlds 1956, Critical Approaches to Literature 1956, Literary Essays 1956, Milton 1957, A Critical History of English Literature 1960, More Literary Essays 1968, Scotch Whisky 1969, Sir Walter Scott and his World 1971, A Third World (autobiography) 1971, Robert Burns and his World 1971, Prince Charles Edward Stuart 1973, Robert Louis Stevenson and his World 1973, Was 1975, Moses 1975, James Boswell and His World 1976, Scotland and the Union 1977, Glasgow 1977, Edinburgh 1978, Fletcher of Saltoun: Selected Political Writings and Speeches (Ed.) 1979, Literature and Gentility in Scotland 1982, God and the Poets 1984, Edinburgh: A Traveller's Companion 1986, A Weekly Scotsman and Other Poems 1994. *Leisure interests:* music, talking. *Address:* 22 Belgrave Crescent, Edinburgh, EH4 3AL, Scotland.

DAINBA GYAINCAN; Chinese government official; b. 1940, Lhasa, Tibet; joined CCP 1964; Mayor of Lhasa Municipality 1993–. *Address:* Government of Xizang Autonomous Region, Lhasa City, People's Republic of China.

DAINTITH, Terence Charles, M.A.; British professor of law; b. 8 May 1942, Coulsdon; s. of Edward Daintith and Irene M. Parsons; m. Christine Bulport 1965; one s. one d.; ed. Wimbledon Coll. and St. Edmund Hall, Oxford; called to Bar, Lincoln's Inn 1966; Assoc. in Law, Univ. of Calif. Berkeley 1963–64; lecturer in Constitutional and Admin. Law, Univ. of Edinburgh 1964–72; Prof. of Public Law, Univ. of Dundee 1972–83, Dir. Centre for Petroleum and Mineral Law Studies 1977–83; Prof. of Law, European Univ. Inst., Florence 1981–87, External Prof. 1988–; Prof. of Law, Univ. of London 1988–, Dir. Inst. of Advanced Legal Studies 1988–95, Dean Univ. of London Insts. of Advanced Study 1991–94, School of Advanced Study 1994–; mem. Conseil d'Admin. Asscn. Int. de Droit Econ. 1985–94; Trustee, Petroleum and Mineral Law Educ. Trust 1988–95, Hamlyn Trust 1988–98; Ed. Journal of Energy and Natural Resources Law 1983–92; mem. Academia Europaea (Chair. Law Cttee. 1993–96, Social Sciences Section 1996–98). *Publications:* The Economic Law of the United Kingdom 1974, United Kingdom Oil and Gas Law (with G. D. M. Willoughby) 1977, Energy Strategy in Europe (with L. Hancher) 1986, The Legal Integration of Energy Markets (with S. Williams) 1987, Law as an Instrument of Economic Policy 1988, Harmonization and Hazard (with G. R. Baldwin) 1992, Implementation of EC Law in the United Kingdom 1995. *Address:* School of Advanced Study, Senate House, Malet Street, London, WC1E 7HU, England; Pouzols, Josat, 43230 Paulhaguet, France. *Telephone:* 0171-862 8659 (London). *Fax:* 0171-862 8657 (London).

DAJANY, Musa I. R., M.A., LL.B.; Jordanian broadcasting executive; b. 1924, Jerusalem; m. Nadia Dajany 1947; one s. three d.; chief announcer, Near East Arab Broadcasting Station 1944, Controller of Programmes, Palestine Broadcasting Dept. 1946, Head of Programmes Operations 1952, Deputy Dir. of Programmes, Cyprus 1956; Controller of Programmes, Jordan Broadcasting Dept. 1957; Asst. Dir. Bahrain Broadcasting 1958; Expert in Radio Production, Libyan Broadcasting Dept. 1959; Controller of Special Programmes, Kuwait Broadcasting 1960; Information Adviser, Arab Student Aid Int., U.S.A. 1989; currently Adviser and Man. Dir. The Broadcasters Est.; Prize from Japan Broadcasting NHK; Independence Decoration. *Publications:* Fifty Years with Arab Broadcasting 1996; articles on various topics in Arabic press. *Leisure interests:* reading, theatre, music. *Address:* P.O. Box 5517, Zahran, Amman 11183, Jordan. *Telephone:* (6) 5534815. *Fax:* (6) 695273.

DAKOV, Mako; Bulgarian politician; b. 5 Dec. 1920, Pleven; m. 1st Milka Stefanova 1951 (deceased); two d.; m. 2nd Nadka Lazarova 1979; one s.; ed. studies in forestry engineering; Dir. of Scientific Research, Inst. of Forestry 1950–51; Prof. Higher Forestry and Tech. Inst. 1951–57; Deputy Minister of Agric. and Forestry 1957, subsequently Chair. Cttee. for Forestry; Minister for Forestry and Forest Industry 1966–71; Deputy Chair. Council of Ministers 1971–78; mem. Bulgarian Acad. of Sciences, Vice-Pres. 1978–88. *Publications:* more than 200 publications on politics, economics and forestry. *Leisure interest:* sport (especially tennis). *Address:* c/o Bulgarian Academy of Sciences, 7th November Street 1, 1040 Sofia, Bulgaria. *Telephone:* 8-41-41.

DALAI LAMA, The (Tenzin Gyatso); temporal and spiritual head of Tibet; Fourteenth Incarnation; b. 6 July 1935, Taktser, Amdo Prov., N.E. Tibet; s. of Chujon Tsering and Tsering Dekyi; born of Tibetan peasant family in Amdo Province; enthroned at Lhasa 1940; rights exercised by regency 1934–50; assumed political power 1950; fled to Chumbi in S. Tibet after abortive resistance to Chinese 1950; negotiated agreement with China 1951; Vice-Chair. Standing Cttee., mem. Nat. Cttee. CPPCC 1951–59; Hon. Chair. Chinese Buddhist Asscn. 1953–59; Del. to Nat. People's Congress 1954–59; Chair. Preparatory Cttee. for the "Autonomous Region of Tibet" 1955–59; fled Tibet to India after suppression of Tibetan national uprising 1959; Dr. of Buddhist Philosophy (Monasteries of Sera, Drepung and Gaden, Lhasa) 1959; Supreme Head of all Buddhist sects in Tibet (Xizang); Memory Prize 1989, Congressional Human Rights Award 1989, Nobel Peace Prize 1989, Freedom Award (U.S.A.) 1991. *Publications:* My Land and People 1962, The Opening of the Wisdom Eye 1963, The Buddhism of Tibet and the Key to the Middle Way 1975, Kindness, Clarity, and Insight 1984, A Human Approach to World Peace 1984, Freedom in Exile (autobiog.) 1990, The Good Heart 1996, Ethics for the New Millennium 1998. *Leisure interests:* gardening, mechanics. *Address:* Thekchen Choeling, McLeod Ganj 176219, Dharamsala, Himachal Pradesh, India.

DALBERTO, Michel; French pianist; b. 2 June 1955, Paris; s. of Jean Dalberto and Paulette Girard-Dalberto; ed. Lycée Claude Bernard, Lycée Racine, Conservatoire National Supérieur de Musique, Paris; prin. teacher at Conservatoire: Vlado Perlemuter; started professional career 1975; concerts in major musical centres and at int. festivals; Artistic Dir. Festival des Arcs 1991–; Pres. of the Jury Clara Haskil Competition 1991–; Clara Haskil Prize 1975; First Prize Leeds Int. Pianoforte Competition 1978; Acad. Charles Gros Award 1980 and Acad. Disque Français Award 1984, for recordings; Chevalier Ordre nat. du Mérite. *Leisure interests:* skiing, scuba diving, parachuting. *Address:* c/o IMG Artists, Media House, 3 Burlington Lane, London, W4 2TH, England. *Telephone:* 0181-233 5800. *Fax:* 0181-233 5801.

DALBORG, Hans Folkeson, M.B.A., PH.D.; Swedish banker; b. 21 May 1941, Säter; m. Anna Ljungqvist 1965; one s. two d.; ed. Univ. of Uppsala and Stockholm School of Econs.; teacher and admin. Stockholm School of Econs. 1967–72; joined Skandia 1972, Deputy Man. Dir. responsible for int. business 1981–83, Pres. and C.O.O. Skandia Int. Insurance Corpn. 1983–89, Sr. Exec. Vice-Pres., C.O.O. Skandia Group and C.E.O. Skandia Int. Insurance Corpn. 1989–91; Pres. and C.E.O. Nordbanken AB 1991–97; Pres., C.E.O. MeritaNordbanken Abp 1998–. *Address:* MeritaNordbanken SE-105 71 Stockholm, Sweden. *Fax:* 46-8 614 78 10.

DALDRY, Stephen; British theatre director; b. 2 May 1960, Dorset; f. Metro Theatre Fringe Co.; fmr. Dir., Sheffield Crucible's studio; Dir. Gate Fringe Theatre, London 1989–91; Artistic Dir. English Stage Co., Royal Court Theatre, London 1992–99; Dir. Stephen Daldry Pictures 1998–. *Producer:* Six Degrees of Separation, Oleanna, An Inspector Calls, Machinal, Judgement Day, Ingoldstadt, Figaro Gets Divorced, Rat in the Skull. *Address:* c/o Royal Court Theatre, Sloane Square, London, SW1W 8AS, England.

DALE, Jim; British actor; b. 15 Aug. 1935 (as James Smith); m.; three s. one d.; appearances in nine Carry On films began in 1960s; later appeared with Nat. Theatre and Young Vic; appeared in London's West End in The Card 1973; host, Sunday Night at the London Palladium (TV show) 1994; with Young Vic appeared on Broadway in The Taming of the Shrew and Scapino 1974; Broadway appearances: Barnum (Tony Award) 1980, Joe Egg 1985, Me and My Girl 1987–88, Candide 1997; other stage appearances include: Privates on Parade (New York), Travels With My Aunt (off-Broadway) 1995, Fagin in Oliver! (London Palladium) 1995–97; lyricist for film Georgy Girl. *Films include:* Carry on Cowboy, Carry On, Follow That Camel, Carry On Spying, Carry On Columbus 1992, Pete's Dragon, Hunchback of Notre Dame 1997. *Address:* c/o Mark Sendroff, 139 West 82nd Street, New York, NY 10024, U.S.A; c/o Janet Glass, 28 Berkeley Square, London, W1X 6HD, England.

D'ALEMA, Massimo; Italian politician and journalist; b. 20 April 1949, Rome; Sec. Partido Democratico de la Sinistra (PDS); mem. Camera dei Deputati for Apulia; fmr. mem. Progressisti Federativo; fmr. mem. Budget Comm.; Prime Minister of Italy Oct. 1998–. *Address:* Office of the Prime Minister, Palazzo Chigi, Piazza Colonna 370, 00187 Rome, Italy.

DALES, Richard Nigel, C.M.G., M.A.; British diplomatist; b. 26 Aug. 1942, Woodford, Essex.; s. of late Major K. Dales and of O.M. Dales; m. Elizabeth M. Martin 1966; one s. one d.; ed. Chigwell School, Essex and St. Catharine's Coll. Cambridge; joined Foreign Office 1964; Third Sec. Yaoundé, Cameroon 1965–67; FCO 1968–70; Second Sec., later First Sec. Copenhagen 1970–73; Asst. Pvt. Sec. to Sec. of State for Foreign and Commonwealth Affairs 1974–77; Head of Chancery, Sofia 1977–81; FCO 1981–82; Head of Chancery, Copenhagen 1982–86; Deputy High Commr. in Zimbabwe 1986–89; Head of Southern Africa Dept. FCO 1989–91; seconded to Civil Service Comm. 1991–92; High Commr. in Zimbabwe 1992–95; Dir. (Africa and Commonwealth), FCO 1995–98; Amb. to Norway 1998–. *Leisure interests:* music, walking, reading. *Address:* Foreign and Commonwealth Office (Oslo 19736), King Charles Street, London, SW1A 2AH, England. *Telephone:* 23 13 27 00 (Norway). *Fax:* 23 13 27 89 (Norway).

DALEY, Richard M.; American politician and lawyer; b. 24 April 1942, Chicago, Ill.; s. of the late Richard J. Daley and of Eleanor Guilfoyle; m. Margaret Corbett 1972; one s. (and one s. deceased), two d.; ed. De La Salle High School, Providence Coll. R.I., and DePaul Univ. Chicago; Asst. Corpn. Counsel, City of Chicago 1969; del. Ill. Constitutional Convention 1970; briefly formed law practice with Raymond F. Simon; subsequently joined father's law firm; mem. Ill. State Senate 1972; State Attorney, Cook County, Ill. 1980–89; Mayor of Chicago 1989–; Democrat. *Leisure interests:* cinema, reading. *Address:* Office of the Mayor, City Hall, Room 507, 121 N. LaSalle Street, Chicago, IL 60602, U.S.A.

DALGARNO, Alexander, PH.D., F.R.S., M.R.I.A.; British professor of astronomy; b. 5 Jan. 1928, London; s. of William Dalgarno and Margaret Dalgarno; m. 1st Barbara Kane 1957 (divorced 1972); two s. two d.; m. 2nd Emily Izsák 1972 (divorced 1987); ed. Univ. Coll. London; mem. Faculty, Applied Math., Queen's Univ. of Belfast 1951–67; Prof. of Astronomy, Harvard Univ. 1967–77, Chair. Dept. of Astronomy 1971–76, Dir. Harvard Coll. Observatory 1971–72, Phillips Prof. of Astronomy 1977–; mem. Smithsonian Astrophysical Observatory 1967–; Ed. Astrophysical Journal Letters 1973–; Spiers Memorial Lecturer, Royal Soc. of Chem. 1992; Hon. D.Sc. (Queen's, Belfast) 1972; Medal of Int. Acad. of Quantum Molecular Science 1969; Hodgkins Medal, Smithsonian Inst. 1977; Davisson-Germer Prize, American Physical Soc. 1980; Meggers Award, Optical Soc. of America 1986, Gold Medal, Royal Astronomical Soc. 1986, Fleming Medal, American Geophysical Union 1995. *Publications:* numerous scientific papers in journals. *Address:* 27 Robinson Street, Cambridge, MA 02138, U.S.A. (Home).

DALGLISH, Kenneth (Kenny) Mathieson, M.B.E.; British football manager; b. 4 March 1951; played for Celtic, Scottish League Champions 1972–74, 1977, Scottish Cup Winners 1972, 1974, 1975, 1977, Scottish League Cup winners 1975; played for Liverpool, European Cup Winners 1978, 1981, 1984, FA Cup Winners 1986, 1989, League Cup Winners 1981–84, Man. 1986–91; Man. Blackburn Rovers 1991–97, Newcastle United 1997–98; 102 full caps for Scotland; Freeman of Glasgow.

DALHOUSIE, 16th Earl of; **Simon Ramsay,** K.T., G.C.V.O., G.B.E., M.C., LL.D.; British fmr. Governor-General and politician; b. 17 Oct. 1914; s. of the late 14th Earl of Dalhousie and Lady Mary Adelaide Heathcote Drummond Willoughby; m. Margaret Elizabeth Stirling 1940 (died 1997); three s. two d.; ed. Eton Coll., and Oxford Univ.; served in Black Watch 1936–45; M.P., 1945–50; Conservative Whip 1946–48; Gov.-Gen. Fed. of Rhodesia and Nyasaland 1957–63; Lord Lieut. District of Angus 1965–89; Lord Chamberlain to H.M. Queen Elizabeth, the Queen Mother 1965–92; Chancellor of Dundee Univ. 1977–92; Hon. LL.D. (Dundee Univ.) 1967. *Address:* Brechin Castle, Brechin, Angus, DD9 6SH, Scotland; 199 Cranmer Court, Sloane Avenue, London, SW3 3HG, England. *Telephone:* (01356) 622176 (Brechin); 0171-589 8938 (London).

DALITZ, Richard Henry, PH.D., F.R.S.; British research physicist; b. 28 Feb. 1925, Dimboola, Australia; s. of Frederick W. and Hazel Blanche (née Drummond) Dalitz; m. Valda Suiter 1946; one s. three d.; ed. Tooronga Rd. Cen. School and Scotch Coll., Melbourne, Ormond Coll., Univ. of Melbourne and Trinity Coll., Cambridge; Research Asst. in Physics, Univ. of Bristol 1948–49; lecturer in Math. Physics, Univ. of Birmingham 1949–55; Reader 1955–56; Prof. of Physics, Enrico Fermi Inst. for Nuclear Studies, Univ. of Chicago 1956–66; Royal Soc. Research Prof., Univ. of Oxford 1963–90; Prof. Emer. 1990–; Fellow, All Souls Coll., Oxford 1964–90; Emer. Fellow 1990–; Hon. D.Sc. (Melbourne) 1991; Maxwell Medal, Inst. of Physics, London 1966, Bakerian Lecture and Jaffe Prize, Royal Soc. 1969, Hughes Medal, Royal Soc. 1975; J. Robert Oppenheimer Memorial Prize, Univ. of Miami 1980, Royal Medal, Royal Soc. 1982, Harrie Massey Prize (jtly. Inst of Physics, London and Australian Inst. of Physics) 1990. *Publications:* Strange Particles and Strong Interactions 1962, Nuclear Interactions of the Hyperons 1965, Nuclear Energy Today and Tomorrow (co-author) 1971, A Breadth of Physics (co-author) 1988, The Collected Papers of P. A. M. Dirac 1924–1948 1995, Selected Scientific Papers of Sir Rudolf Peierls (co-ed.) 1997, The Foundations of Newtonian Scholarship (co-ed.) 1999; numerous papers on theoretical physics, in scientific journals. *Leisure interests:* study of the history of the Wends and their emigration to the New World, walking, travelling hopefully and finding out why. *Address:* Department of Theoretical Physics, University of Oxford, 1 Keble Road, Oxford, OX1 3NP, England. *Telephone:* (01865) 273966. *Fax:* (01865) 273947.

dalla CHIESA, Romeo; Italian banker; b. 15 Oct. 1924, Livorno, Italy; s. of Gen. Romano dalla Chiesa and Maria L. Bergonzi; m. Ebba Tamm (divorced); four c.; ed. Torquato Tasso School, Florence, Orazio Flacco School, Bari, American Univ. of Washington, Rome Univ., with cen. admin. of Bank of Italy, Rome 1943–49; Economist, Econ. Consultant to Panamanian and Thai Govts., Loan Officer (Far East Dept.) IBRD-World Bank, Wash. DC 1949–58; Gen. Man. for Loans to EC, EIB, then Hon. Dir. 1958–81; Gen. Financial Consultant, Banca Nazionale del Lavoro, Rome 1981–82; Pres. Banco di Roma, Rome 1983–88; FINROMA 1983–88; Consultant Foreign Interests of Banco di Roma, Italian Banking Asscn. (ABI), ASSO-NIME (Asscn. for Italian Share Cos.), NOMISMA (stock market research and analysis), to Italian-Soviet Chamber of Commerce, to Economia Italiana (journal), to Banco di Roma Int. SA, Luxembourg; Dir. Rominvest Int. Fund SA, Luxembourg, Banco di Roma Caribbean Co. Ltd., George Town; mem. Int. Council for New Initiatives in E.-W. Co-operation, Vienna; mem. Advisory Bd. Int. Inst. for Applied Systems Analysis; Pres. Social Devt. Fund of the Council of Europe, Paris 1993–95; Grande Ufficiale della Repub. Italiana, Grosses Verdienstkreuz mit Stern (Germany). *Publications:* articles and papers on economics, finance and banking. *Leisure interests:* fine arts, literature, chess. *Address:* 63 Piazza di Pietra, 00186 Rome, Italy.

DALLARA, Charles H., PH.D., M.A., M.A.L.D.; American international finance official; b. 1948; m. Carolyn Gault; one s. one d.; ed. Univ. of S. Carolina and Fletcher School of Law and Diplomacy; int. economist, U.S. Treasury Dept. 1976–79; Special Asst. to Under-Sec. for Monetary Affairs 1979–80; Guest Scholar Brookings Inst. 1980–81; Special Asst. to Asst. Sec. for Int. Affairs 1981–82; Alt. Exec. Dir. IMF 1982–83; Deputy Asst. Sec. for Int. Monetary Affairs, U.S. Treasury Dept. 1983–85; Exec. Dir. IMF 1984–89; Asst. Sec. for Policy Devt. and Sr. Advisor for Policy 1988–89; Asst. Sec. for Internal Affairs 1989–93; Man. Dir. J. P. Morgan 1991–93; Man. Dir. Inst. of Int. Finance 1993–. *Address:* IIF, 200 Pennsylvania Avenue, Washington, DC 20003, U.S.A.

DALLE, François Léon Marie-Joseph, L. EN D.; French business executive; b. 18 March 1918, Hesdin; s. of Joseph and Jeanne (Dumont) Dalle; three s. two d.; ed. Saint-Joseph de Lille, Faculty of Law, Paris; fmr. advocate, Court of Appeal, Paris 1941–42; Plant Man., then Asst. Gen. Man., Monsavon Co. 1945–48, Marketing Man., l'Oréal 1948–50, Asst. Gen. Man. 1950–57, Pres., Dir.-Gen. L'Oréal 1957–84, Pres. Strategy Cttee. 1984–90; Pres. L'Oréal Soc. 1957–84; Pres. Saipo 1957–; Dir. Philips (France), Banque Nat. de Paris 1973–82, Editions Masson, Union des Annonceurs, Dir. and mem. bd. Nestlé S.A. 1975– (Vice-Pres. 1986–90), fmr. Dir. Lancôme; Vice-Pres. Institut Pasteur 1970–78; Hon. Dir. 1978–; Pres. Exec. Cttee. Humanisme et Entreprise 1968; mem. staff, Conseil Nat. du Patronat Français 1968, Exec. Council 1972–75; Founder and Pres. Asscn. Entreprise et Progrès 1969, mem. Exec. Cttee. 1971–; mem. Grandes Entreprises Françaises Asscn. (AGREF) 1977–82; mem. Futuribles Int. Asscn., INSEAD, council Centre d'Etudes Littéraires et Scientifiques Appliquées (CELSA), (Pres. 1989–), Vice-Pres. Institut de l'Entreprise 1975–; fmr. Pres. Mennen-France, Dir. Centre Européen d'Educ. Permanente; Pres. Comm. Nat. de l'Industrie 1984; Lauréat de la faculté de droit de Paris; Commdre. Légion d'honneur, Ordre nat. du Mérite, Médaille de la Résistance, Commdr. des Palmes académiques, Commendatore della Repubblica Italiana. *Publications:* L'entreprise du futur (with Jean Bounine Cabalé) 1971, Quand l'entreprise s'éveille à la conscience sociale (with Jean Bounine Cabalé) 1975, Dynamique de l'auto-reforme de l'entreprise (with Nicolas Thiéry) 1976, L'Education en entreprise: contre le chômage des jeunes (jtly.) 1993, le Sursaut (jtly.) 1994. *Leisure interests:* writing, hunting. *Address:* Villa Clairefontaine, 14 chemin du Nant d'Argent, CH-1223 Cologny, (Geneva), Switzerland.

DALLI, John, C.P.A., M.B.I.M.; Maltese politician and accountant; b. 5 Oct. 1948, Qormi; s. of Carmelo Dalli and Emma Bonnici; m. Josette Callus; two d.; ed. Malta Coll. of Arts, Science and Tech.; posts in financial admin. and gen. man., Malta and Brussels; Man. Consultant; M.P., Nationalist Party 1987–; Parl. Sec. for Industry 1987–90; Minister for Econ. Affairs 1990–92, of Finance 1992–96, 1998–; Shadow Minister and Opposition Spokesman for Finance 1996–98. *Address:* Ministry of Finance, Cavalier House, 158 Old Mint Street, Valletta, CMR 02, Malta. *Telephone:* 232646; 251349. *Fax:* 242609.

D'ALMEIDA, Armindo Vaz; São Tomé e Príncipe politican; Prime Minister 1995–96. *Address:* c/o Office of the Prime Minister, Praça Yon Gato, CP 302, São Tomé, São Tomé e Príncipe.

DALMIA, Vishnu Hari; Indian industrialist; b. May 1924; s. of J. Dalmia; fmr. Chair. Dalmia Dairy Industries Ltd., GTC Industries Ltd., The Shree Meenakshi Mills Ltd.; Advisor Dalmia Cement (Bharat) Ltd.; Dir. Dalton Int. Ltd., U.K.; Dir. Export-Import Bank of India 1983–85; Pres. Cement Mfrs. Asscn. 1968–70, Indian Sugar Mills Asscn. 1969–70, All India Distillers' Asscn. 1963–64, Indian Nat. Cttee. of Int. Chamber of Commerce 1976–77; mem. Tourism Advisory Bd. 1984–86, Nat. Integration Council, Crime Prevention Soc.; Man. Trustee Dalmia Charitable Trust.; Vice-Pres. Indian Fed. of UN Asscns. *Address:* 11th Floor, Hansalaya, 15 Barakhamba Road, New Delhi 110001 (Office); 18 Golf Links, Archbishop Makarios Marg, New Delhi 110003, India (Home). *Telephone:* 3315476, 3310121 (Office); 4644930 (Home). *Fax:* 3313303.

DALRYMPLE, Frederick Rawdon, A.O.; Australian diplomatist; b. 6 Nov. 1930, Sydney; s. of Frederick Dalrymple and Evelyn Dalrymple; m. Ross E. Williams 1957; one s. one d.; ed. Sydney Church of England Grammar School and Univs. of Sydney and Oxford; lecturer in Philosophy, Univ. of Sydney 1955–57; joined Dept. of External Affairs 1957; served Bonn, London 1959–64; Alt. Dir. Asian Devt. Bank, Manila 1967–69; Minister, Djakarta 1969–71; Amb. to Israel 1972–75, to Indonesia 1981–85, to U.S.A. 1985–89, to Japan 1989–93; Chair ASEAN Focus Group Pty. Ltd. 1994–; Pres. Australian Centre for American Studies 1995–; Visiting Prof. Univ. of Sydney 1994. *Publications:* Looking East and West from Down Under 1992; articles in journals. *Leisure interests:* reading, golf. *Address:* 34 Glenmore Road, Paddington, N.S.W. 2021, Australia.

DALSAGER, Poul Christian; Danish politician; b. 5 March 1929, Hirtshals; s. of the late Verner and Carla (née Svendsen) Dalsager; m. Betty Jørgensen 1951; two s.; mem. Folketing (Parl.) 1964–81; del. to UN Gen. Ass. 1969, 1971; Chair. Common Market Cttee., Parl. 1971–73; Minister of Agric. and Fisheries 1975–77, 1979–81; Minister of Agric. 1977–78; Vice-Pres. EEC Parl. 1973–74; EEC Commr. for Agric. 1981–84; Deputy Mayor, Hjørring 1986, Mayor 1990–95; Chair. Social Democratic Group in Parl. 1978; Pres. East of England Agric. Soc. 1983. *Address:* Nørregade 4-3, 9800 Hjørring, Denmark. *Telephone:* 98 90 10 08.

DALTON, Timothy; British actor; b. 21 March 1946; ed. Royal Acad. of Dramatic Art; joined Nat. Youth Theatre; first London appearance at Royal Court Theatre; toured with Prospect Theatre Co.; guest artist with R.S.C. *Film appearances include:* The Lion in Winter, Le Voyeur (France), Cromwell, Wuthering Heights, Mary, Queen of Scots, Permission to Kill, The Man Who Knew Love (Spain), Sextette, Agatha 1978, Flash Gordon 1979, Chanel Solitaire 1980, The Doctor and the Devils 1985, Brenda Starr, role of Ian Fleming's James Bond in The Living Daylights 1987 and Licence to Kill 1989, Hawks 1987, The King's Whore 1989, The Rocketeer 1990, The Informant 1996, The Reef 1996, The Beautician and the Beast 1996. *Stage appearances include:* King Lear, Love's Labour's Lost, Henry IV, Henry V (all with Prospect Theatre Co.), Romeo and Juliet (R.S.C.), The Samaritan, Black Comedy and White Liars, The Vortex, The Lunatic, the Lover and the Poet 1980, The Romans 1980, Henry IV, Part I (R.S.C.) 1981, Antony and Cleopatra 1986, The Taming of the Shrew 1986, A Touch of the Poet 1988. *Television appearances include:* Centennial 1979, Jane Eyre, The Master of Ballantrae, Mistral's Daughter 1984, Florence Nightingale 1984, Sins 1985, Framed 1992, Scarlett 1994, Salt Water Moose 1995. *Address:* James Sharkey Associates, 21 Golden Square, London, W1R 3PA, England. *Telephone:* 0171-434 3801.

DALY, Brendan; Irish politician; b. 2 Feb. 1940, Cooraclare; m. Patricia Carmody; two s. one d.; ed. Kilrush Co. Boys' School; mem. Dáil 1973–; Minister of State, Dept. of Labour 1980–81; Minister for Fisheries and Forestry March–Dec. 1982, for the Marine 1987–89, for Defence Feb.–Nov. 1991, for Social Welfare 1991–92; Minister of State, Dept. of Foreign Affairs 1992–93; elected to Seanad Éireann 1993–; mem. Northern Ireland Peace Forum 1994; mem. Irish Parl. Foreign Affairs Cttee. 1993–; Fianna Fáil. *Address:* Cooraclare, Kilrush, Co. Clare, Republic of Ireland (Home). *Telephone:* 065 59040.

DALY, H.E. Cahal Brendan, M.A., D.D.; Irish ecclesiastic; b. 1 Oct. 1917, Loughguile, Co. Antrim; s. of Charles Daly and Susan Connolly; ed. St. Malachy's Coll., Belfast, Queen's Univ., Belfast, St. Patrick's Coll., Maynooth, Institut Catholique, Paris; Classics Master St. Malachy's Coll. 1945–46; Lecturer in Scholastic Philosophy, Queen's Univ., Belfast 1946–63, Reader 1963–67; Bishop of Ardagh and Clonmacnois 1967–82; Bishop of Down and Connor 1982–90; Archbishop of Armagh and Primate of All Ireland Nov. 1990–96, now Archbishop Emer.; cr. Cardinal 1991; mem. Congregation for Clergy, for Evangelization of the Peoples; mem. Pontifical Council for the Union of Christians; Hon. D.D. (Queen's Univ. of Belfast) 1990. *Publications:* Morals, Law and Life 1962, Natural Law Morality Today 1965, Violence in Ireland and Christian Conscience 1973, Theologians and the Magisterium 1977, Peace and the Work of Justice 1979, Communities Without Consensus: The Northern Irish Tragedy 1984, Renewed Heart for Peace 1984, Cry of the Poor 1986, The Price of Peace 1991, Tertullian: the Puritan and his Influence 1993, Moral Philosophy in Britain from Bradley to Wittgenstein 1996, Steps on my Pilgrim Journey 1998, contrib. to various philosophical works. *Address:* 23 Rosetta Court, Ormeau Road, Belfast, BT7 3HW, Northern Ireland.

DALY, Rt. Rev. Edward Kevin, B.PHIL., S.T.L., D.D.; Irish ecclesiastic; b. 5 Dec. 1933, Co. Donegal; s. of Thomas Daly and Susan Flood; ordained as Priest 1957; Curate, Castlederg, Co. Tyrone 1957–62; St. Eugene's Cathedral, Derry 1962–74, Bishop of Derry 1974–93 (retd.); Religious Adviser to Radio Telefís Éireann (RTE) 1973–74. *Leisure interests:* theatre, angling. *Address:* 9 Steelstown Road, Derry BT48 8EU, Northern Ireland. *Telephone:* (01504) 359809. *Fax:* (01504) 371960.

DALY, John Patrick; American golfer; b. 28 April 1966, Carmichael, Calif.; ed. Univ. of Arkansas; m.; two c.; turned professional 1987; won Missouri Open 1987, Ben Hogan Utah Classic 1990, PGA Championship, Crooked Stick 1991, B.C. Open 1992, BellSouth Classic 1994, British Open 1995. *Leisure interests:* sports. *Address:* c/o PGA America, 100 Avenue of the Champions, Palm Beach Gardens, FL 33418, U.S.A.

DALY, Robert Anthony; American film executive; b. 8 Dec. 1936; s. of James Daly and Eleanor Daly; two s. one d.; ed. Brooklyn Coll.; Dir. business affairs, then Vice-Pres. business affairs, then Exec. Vice-Pres. CBS TV Network 1955–80; Pres. CBS Entertainment Co. 1977–; Chair. and Co-C.E.O. Warner Bros., Burbank, Calif. 1980, Chair., C.E.O. 1982–, Chair. and Co-C.E.O. 1994, Chair. and Co-C.E.O. Warner Music Group 1995–; mem. Bd. Dirs. American Film Inst., Museum of TV and Radio; mem. Acad. of Motion Picture Arts and Sciences, Nat. Acad. of TV Arts and Sciences. *Address:* Warner Bros., 4000 Warner Boulevard, Burbank, CA 91522, U.S.A.

DAM, Kenneth W., J.D.; American lawyer and university professor; b. 10 Aug. 1932, Marysville, Kan.; s. of Oliver W. and Ida L. Dam; m. Marcia Wachs 1962; one s. one d.; ed. Univs. of Kansas and Chicago; law clerk, Mr. Justice Whittaker, U.S. Supreme Court 1957–58; Assoc., Cravath, Swaine & Moore, New York 1958–60; Asst. Prof., Univ. of Chicago Law School 1960–61, Assoc. Prof. 1961–64, Prof. 1964–71, 1974–76, Harold J. & Marion F. Green Prof. of Int. Legal Studies 1976–85; Max Pam Prof. of American and Foreign Law 1992–; Provost, Univ. of Chicago 1980–82; Consultant, Kirkland & Ellis, Chicago 1961–71, 1974–80, 1993–; Exec. Dir. Council on Econ. Policy 1973; Asst. Dir. for Nat. Security and Int. Affairs, Office of Man. and Budget 1971–73; Deputy Sec. of State 1982–85; Vice-Pres., Law and External Relations, IBM Corp. 1985–92; Pres., C.E.O. United Way America 1992; Dir. Alcoa 1987–; Dir. America-China Soc., Brookings Inst., Council on Foreign Relations, Chicago Council on Foreign Relations; mem. American Acad. of Arts and Sciences, American Acad. of Diplomacy, American Bar Asscn., American Law Inst., German-American Academic Council. *Publications:* Federal Tax Treatment of Foreign Income (with L. Krause) 1964, The GATT: Law and International Economic Organization 1970, Oil Resources: Who Gets What How? 1976, Economic Policy Beyond the Headlines (with George P. Shultz) 1978, The Rules of the Game: Reform and Evolution in the International Monetary System 1982, Cryptography's Role in Securing the Information Society 1996 (co-ed.); numerous articles on legal and economic issues. *Address:* University of Chicago Law School, 1111 East 60th Street, Chicago, IL 60637, U.S.A.

D'AMATO, Alfonse M., B.A., LL.B.; American politician and lawyer; b. 1 Aug. 1937, Brooklyn, New York; m. Penelope Ann Collenburg 1960 (divorced); two s. two d.; ed. Syracuse Univ.; Receiver of Taxes, Town of Hempstead 1971–72, Supervisor, Hempstead 1972–78, Presiding Supervisor 1978–81; Senator from N.Y. State 1981–98, on Banking, Housing and Urban Affairs Cttee. (Chair. 1995) and Finance Cttee; Republican. *Publications:* Power, Pasta and Politics (autobiog.) 1995. *Address:* c/o 520 Hart Senate Office Building, Washington, DC 20510 (Office); Island Park, NY 11558, U.S.A. (Home).

DAMON, Matt; American actor. *Film appearances include:* Rising Son 1990, School Ties 1992, Geronimo: An American Legend 1993, Good Will Hunting 1997, Saving Private Ryan 1998, Rounders 1998. *Address:* United Talent Agency, 9560 Wilshire Boulevard, 5th Floor, Beverly Hills, CA 90212, U.S.A.

DANCE, Charles; British actor; b. 10 Oct. 1946, Rednal, Worcs.; m. Joanna Haythorn 1970; one s. one d.; formerly worked in industry; with RSC 1975–80, 1980–85; *Television appearances include:* The Fatal Spring, Nancy Astor, Frost in May, Saigon–The Last Day, Thunder Rock (drama), Rainy Day Women, The Jewel in the Crown (nominated for Best Actor BAFTA Award), The Secret Servant, The McGuffin, The Phantom of the Opera 1989, Rebecca 1996, In the Presence of Mine Enemies, Hilary and Jackie 1998. *Films include:* For Your Eyes Only, Plenty, The Golden Child, White Mischief, Good Morning Babylon, Hidden City, Pascali's Island 1988, China Moon 1990, Alien III 1991, Limestone 1991, Kabloonak, Century, Last Action Hero, Exquisite Tenderness 1993, Short Cut to Paradise 1993, Undertow,

Michael Collins, Space Truckers. *Theatre:* Coriolanus (title role) (R.S.C.) 1989, Irma La Douce, Turning Over, Henry V, Three Sisters 1998; Good 1999. *Address:* c/o I.C.M., Oxford House, 76 Oxford Street, London, W1N 0AX, England. *Telephone:* 0171-636 6565.

D'ANCONA, Hedy, D.SC.; Netherlands politician; b. 1 Oct. 1937; former journalist and broadcaster; mem. Senate 1974; State Sec. for Female Emancipation 1981–82; mem. European Parl. 1984–89; Minister of Welfare, Public Health and Culture 1989–94; Partij van de Arbeid. *Address:* c/o Partij van de Arbeid, Nicolaas Witsenkade 30, 1017 ZT Amsterdam; P.O. Box 1310, 1000 BH Amsterdam, Netherlands.

DANCZOWSKA, Kaja; Polish violinist; b. 25 March 1949, Cracow; one d.; ed. State Higher Music School in Cracow, Moscow Conservatory; Prof. Acad. of Music, Cracow 1977–; Prof. at courses of interpretation in Poland and abroad 1984–86; Ordinary Prof. 1997; mem. of jury int. violin competitions in Poznań, Munich, New York and Tokyo 1986–; participation in the greatest violin festivals; co-operation with the greatest conductors and orchestras; numerous awards include Queen Elizabeth Prize, Brussels 1976 (Silver Medal), Individual Prize of Minister of Culture and Art 1991, Prize of Minister of Culture and Art 1998; Excellence in Teaching Award, U.S.A. 1998, Polish Culture Foundation Award 1998; recordings for Wifon, Polskie Nagrania, Deutsche Grammophon, Philips. *Leisure interests:* film, literature. *Address:* Polska Agencja Artystyczna "Pagart", pl. Piłsudskiego 9, 00-078 Warsaw, Poland. *Telephone:* (22) 827 44 63.

DANDAVATE, Madhu; Indian politician and fmr. professor of physics; b. 21 Jan. 1924, Ahmed Nagar, Maharashtra; ed. Royal Inst. of Science, Bombay; participated in Independence Movement, later in Quit India Movement 1942; leader of passive resistance in Goa Campaign 1955; took part in Samyukta Maharashtra Movt. for formation of Maharashtra state; joined Praja Socialist Party (PSP) 1948, Chair. Maharashtra State Unit of PSP, later Jt. Sec. of All-India PSP; participated in Land Liberation Movt. 1969; associated with Maharashtra Citizens' Defence Cttee. during conflicts with People's Repub. of China and Pakistan; mem. Maharashtra Legis. Council 1970–71; mem. Lok Sabha from Rajapur 1971–79, 1980–; Vice-Prin. and Head of Physics Dept., Siddhartha Coll. of Arts and Science, Bombay until 1971; mem. Janata Party 1977–; Minister of Railways 1977–80, of Finance 1989–90. *Publications:* Gandhiji's Impact on Socialist Thinking, Three Decades of Indian Communism, Evolution of Socialist Policies, Kashmir—a Test for Secularism, Myth and Mystery of Congress Socialism, Bharatiya Swarajwad (in Marathi). *Address:* Sharadashram, Bhawani Shankar Road, Dadar, Bombay 400028, India.

DANELIUS, Hans Carl Yngve; Swedish diplomatist and lawyer; b. 2 April 1934, Stockholm; s. of Sven and Inga (née Svensson) Danelius; m. Hanneke Schadee 1961; three s. one d.; ed. Dept. of Legal Studies, Stockholm Univ.; law practice in Swedish courts 1957–64; mem. Secr., European Comm. of Human Rights, Strasbourg 1964–67, mem. European Comm. of Human Rights 1983–; Asst. Judge, Svea Court of Appeal 1967–68; Adviser, Ministry of Justice 1968–71; Deputy Head, Legal Dept., Ministry for Foreign Affairs 1971–75, Head 1975–84, rank of Amb. 1977–84; Amb. to Netherlands 1984–88; Judge, Supreme Court of Sweden 1988–; mem. Perm. Court of Arbitration at the Hague 1982–; mem. Court of Conciliation and Arbitration of Org. for Security and Co-operation in Europe (OSCE) 1995–; mem. Constitutional Court of Bosnia and Herzegovina 1996–; Chief Ed. Svensk Juristtidning (Swedish Law Journal) 1973–84; Dr. h.c. (Stockholm) 1988; Swedish and foreign decorations. *Publications:* Mänskliga Rättigheter (Human Rights) 1975, The United Nations Convention against Torture 1988, Mänskliga Rättigheter i Europeisk Praxis (Human Rights in European Practice) 1997; numerous articles in Swedish and foreign journals. *Address:* Supreme Court, Box 2066, S-10312 Stockholm (Office); Roslinvägen 33, S-16851 Bromma, Sweden (Home). *Telephone:* 8-6176400 (Office); 8-373491 (Home).

DANELIYA, Georgy Nikolayevich; Georgian film director; b. 25 Aug. 1930, Tbilisi; m. Galina Daneliya; one s. one d.; ed. Moscow Inst. of Architecture, Higher Courses of Film Dir.; worked Inst. for City Designing; Prof. All-Russian Inst. of Cinematography 1975–85; film dir. studio Mosfilm; State Prizes of U.S.S.R. and Russia; U.S.S.R. People's Artist; more than 70 prizes in int. film festivals. *Films include:* Serezha 1960, I am Wailing About Moscow 1963, Thirty Three 1965, Don't Grieve 1969, Aphonya 1975, Mimino 1978 (Gold Prize Avelino Festival, Italy), Autumn Marathon 1979 (Grand Prix San Sebastian Festival, Spain, Grand Prix Chambourci Festival, France), Gentlemen of Luck 1981, Tears were Dropping 1982, Kin-Dza-Dza 1987, Passport 1989, White Dance 1992, Nastya 1993, On the First Breath or Heads or Tails? 1995. *Address:* Makarenko 1/19 apt. 15, 103062 Moscow, Russia. *Telephone:* (095) 921-4374.

DANES, Claire; American film actress; b. 12 April 1979, New York; ed. performing arts school, N.Y. and Lee Strasberg Studio; first acting roles in off-Broadway theatre productions: Happiness, Punk Ballet and Kids on Stage. *Films:* Dreams of Love (debut) 1992, Thirty (short) 1993, The Pesky Suitor (short), Little Women 1994, Romeo and Juliet 1996, To Gillian on Her 37th Birthday 1996, Polish Wedding, U-Turn 1997, The Rainmaker 1997, Les Misérables 1998. *TV:* My So-Called Life (series), No Room for Opal (film), The Coming Out of Heidi Leiter. *Address:* c/o Addis/Wechsler Associates, 955 Carrillo Drive, Los Angeles, CA 90048, U.S.A.

DANFORTH, John Claggett, A.B., B.D., LL.B.; American politician and lawyer; b. 5 Sept. 1936, St. Louis; s. of Donald and Dorothy Danforth; m. Sally B. Dobson 1957; one s. four d.; ed. Princeton and Yale Univs.; admitted to N.Y. bar 1963, Mo. bar 1966; Davis Polk and others, law firm 1963–66, Bryan Cave and others, law firm 1966–68, 1995–; Attorney-Gen. of Mo. 1969–76; Senator from Missouri 1976–95; mem. Senate Cttees. on Finance; Commerce, Science and Transportation; Select Cttee. on Intelligence; ordained priest, Episcopal Church 1964; asst. or assoc. rector of churches in New York City, St. Louis, Jefferson City; assoc. rector Church of the Holy Communion, Univ. City, Mo. 1995–; Hon. Assoc. St. Alban's Church, Washington; awards include Presidential World Without Hunger Award, Legislative Leadership Award of Nat. Comm. against Drunk Driving, Brotherhood and Distinguished Missourian awards of Nat. Conf. of Christians and Jews; Republican. *Publication:* Resurrection: The Confirmation of Clarence Thomas 1994. *Address:* Bryan Cave LLP, 1 Mel Nor Lane, Suite 3600, Saint Louis, MO 63125, U.S.A.

DANIEL, Jean, L. ÈS L.; French journalist and author; b. 21 July 1920, Blida, Algeria; m. Michèle Bancilhon 1965; one d.; Cabinet of Felix Gouin, Pres. Council of Ministers 1946; founder and Dir. Caliban (cultural review) 1947–51; Prof. of Philosophy, Oran 1953; Asst. Ed.-in-Chief, subsequently Ed.-in-Chief, L'Express 1955–64; corresp., New Repub., Washington 1956–65; Associate, Le Monde 1964; Ed.-in-Chief Le Nouvel Observateur 1964–, Ed. Dir. 1965–, Dir. 1978–; fmr. mem. Supervisory Council, Agence-France-Presse; Admin. Louvre Museum 1992–; mem. Conseil supérieur de la langue française 1989–94; Chevalier, Légion d'honneur, Croix de Guerre, Commdr. Arts et Lettres. *Publications:* L'Erreur 1953, Journal d'un journaliste, Le Temps qui reste 1973, Le Refuge et la source 1977, L'Ère des ruptures 1979, De Gaulle et l'Algérie 1985, Les religions d'un président 1988, Cette grande lueur à l'Est 1989, La Blessure suivi de le Temps qui vient 1992, L'ami anglais 1994, Voyage au bout de la Nation (essay) 1995, Dieu, est-il fanatique? 1996. *Leisure interest:* tennis. *Address:* Le Nouvel Observateur, 10–12 place de la Bourse, 75002 Paris, France. *Telephone:* 44.88.34.10. *Fax:* 44.88.34.28.

DANIEL, Sir John Sagar, Kt., M.A., D. ÈS SC; British/Canadian university administrator; b. 31 May 1942, Banstead, U.K.; s. of John Edward Daniel and Winifred Sagar; m. Kristin Anne Swanson 1966; one s. two d.; ed. Christ's Hosp., Sussex, St. Edmund Hall, Univ. of Oxford, Univ. of Paris; Assoc. Prof. Ecole Polytechnique, Univ. de Montréal 1969–73; Dir. des Etudes, Télé-Univ., Univ. de Québec 1973–77; Vice-Pres. Athabasca Univ., Alberta 1977–80; Acad. Vice-Rector Concordia Univ., Montreal 1980–84; Pres. Laurentian Univ., Sudbury 1984–90; Vice-Chancellor Open Univ., U.K. July 1990–; mem. Council of Foundation, Int. Baccalaureate 1992– (Vice-Pres. 1996–99), British North American Cttee. 1995–; mem. Council Open Univ., Hong Kong 1996–, Confed. of British Industry 1996–; Trustee Carnegie Foundation for the Advancement of Teaching 1993–; Forum Fellow, World Econ. Forum, Switzerland 1998; Hon. Fellow St. Edmund Hall, Oxford; Hon. D.Litt. (Deakin Univ., Australia), (Univ. of Lincs. and Humberside) 1996; Hon. D.Sc. (Coll. Mil. Royale, Saint-Jean), (Open Univ. of Sri Lanka) 1994; Hon. D.Ed. (C.N.A.A.); Hon. LL.D. (Waterloo, Canada); Hon. D.Univ. (Univ. Aberta, Portugal, Humberside, Anadolu Univ., Turkey); Hon. D.Hum.Lit. (Thomas Edison State Coll., U.S.A., Richmond, American Int. Univ. in London); Individual Award of Excellence, Commonwealth of Learning 1995; Officier, Ordre des Palmes Académiques. *Publications:* over 100 articles, and books including Learning at a Distance: A World Perspective 1982, Developing Distance Education (jt. ed.) 1988, Mega-universities and Knowledge Media: Technology Strategies for Higher Education 1996. *Leisure interests:* walking, boating, reading. *Address:* The Open University, Milton Keynes, MK7 6AA, England. *Telephone:* (01908) 653214.

DANIEL, Paul; British conductor; m. Joan Rodgers (q.v.) 1988; two d.; mem. music staff English Nat. Opera (ENO), London 1982–87, Music Dir. 1997–; Music Dir. Opera Factory 1987–90, Opera North, Leeds 1990–97; operas conducted include: (ENO) The Mask of Orpheus, Akhnaten, Tosca, Rigoletto, Carmen, Figaro's Wedding, King Priam, Flying Dutchman, From the House of the Dead, Tales of Hoffman, Falstaff, Manon, Otello, Boris Godunov, La Traviata, The Carmelites; (Opera North) Ariane et Barbe-Bleue, Attila, King Priam, Don Giovanni, Der Ferne Klang, Boris Godunov (also at BBC Proms 1992), Rigoletto, Don Carlos, Wozzeck, Gloriana, Baa Baa Black Sheep (world premiere), Playing Away, Il Trovatore, Pelléas et Mélisande, Jenufa, Luisa Miller; (Royal Opera Covent Garden) Mitridate; has also conducted opera productions in Nancy, Munich, Brussels, Geneva; Prin. Conductor English Northern Philharmonia 1990–97; has conducted all the maj. London orchestras and most of the regional U.K. orchestras, and orchestras in U.S.A., Germany, Netherlands, France and Australia. Olivier Award for Outstanding Achievement in Opera 1997. *Address:* c/o Ingpen and Williams, 26 Wadham Road, London, SW15 2LR, England.

DANIEL-LESUR, J. Y.; French composer; b. 19 Nov. 1908, Paris; s. of Robert and Alice (née Thiboust) Lesur; m. Simone Lauer 1943; one s. one d.; ed. Paris Conservatoire; Musical Adviser to Radiodiffusion-Télévision Française; Prin. Insp. of Music at Ministry of Cultural Affairs; Admin. de la Réunion des Théâtres Lyriques Nationaux; Insp.-Gen. of Music, Ministry of Cultural Affairs; Pres. Acad. Charles Cros 1978–84, Hon. Pres. 1984–; contrib. to Arts, La Gazette des Lettres, Polyphonie, La Revue Musicale and other publs.; teaches and writes film music; Dir. hon. Schola Cantorum; French Comm. UNESCO; membre de l'Institut (Acad. des Beaux-Arts) 1982;

Assoc. Mem. Acad. Royale des Sciences, des Lettres et des Beaux-Arts, Belgium 1984; mem. Acad. Européenne des Sciences, des Arts et des Lettres; Grand Prix du Conseil Général de la Seine, Grand Prix de Paris, Lauréat Acad. des Beaux Arts, Grand Prix Musical de la Soc. des Auteurs et Compositeurs de Musique, Prix Int. Maurice Ravel 1994; Grand Officier Légion d'honneur, Commdr. Ordre nat. du Mérite, Commdr. Ordre des Arts et des Lettres. *Works include:* Suite française pour orchestre 1935, Passacaille 1937, Pastorale pour petit orchestre 1938, Ricercare pour orchestre 1939, Quatre lieder pour chant et orchestre 1933–39, Trio d'Anches 1939, Trois poèmes de Cécile Sauvage 1939, Quatuor à cordes 1941, L'enfance de l'art 1942, Variations pour piano et orchestre à cordes 1943, Clair comme le jour 1945, Suite pour trio à cordes et piano 1943, Suite médiévale pour flûte, harpe et trio à cordes 1944, Chansons cambodgiennes 1946, Berceuses à tenir éveillé (chant) 1947, Pastorale variée pour piano 1947, Ballade pour piano 1948, Andrea del Sarto (symphonic poem) 1949, Dix chansons populaires à trois voix égales 1950, Ouverture pour un festival 1951, Chansons françaises à quatre voix mixtes 1951, L'annonciation (cantata) 1952, Cantique des cantiques, pour 12 voix mixtes 1953, Concerto da camera pour piano et orchestre de chambre 1953, Cantique des colonnes pour ensemble vocal féminin et orchestre 1954, Sérénade pour orchestre à cordes 1954, Le bal du destin (ballet), Elégie pour deux guitares 1956, Symphonie de danses 1958, Messe du jubilé pour choeur mixte, orchestre et orgue 1960, Fantaisie pour deux pianos, Trois études pour piano 1962, Chanson de mariage pour choeur de voix de femmes 1964, Deux chansons de marins pour choeur d'hommes 1964, Deux chansons de bord pour choeur mixte 1964, Andrea del Sarto (2-act opera) 1968, Contre-fugue pour deux pianos 1970, Symphonie 1974, Nocturne pour hautbois et orchestre à cordes 1974, Berceuse pour piano 1975, Intermezzo pour violon et piano, Novelette pour flûte et piano 1977, Marine pour harpe 1978, Air à danser pour piano 1980, Ondine, opera in three acts 1981, La reine morte, opera in three acts 1987, Dialogues dans la nuit 1988, Encore un instant de bonheur (Cantata) 1989, Le voyage d'automne, A la lisière du temps, Permis de séjour for singer and orchestra 1990, Dialogues imaginaires 1991, Stele 1991, Mélodrame 1991, Fantaisie concertante (for cello and orchestra) 1992, Le vert paradis 1993, Duo concertant pour flûte et harpe 1993, Impromptu pour flûte, harpe et cordes 1994, Lamento (for harp and orchestra) 1995. *Leisure interest:* Racing Club de France. *Address:* 101 rue Sadi Carnot, 92800 Puteaux, France. *Telephone:* (1) 47-67-01-17.

DANIELL, Robert F.; American business executive; m.; ed. Boston Univ. Coll. of Industrial Tech.; joined Sikorsky as design eng. 1956, program man. for S-61, S-62 and S-58 commercial helicopter programs 1968, Commercial Marketing Man. 1971, Vice-Pres. (Commercial Marketing) 1974, Vice-Pres. (Marketing) 1976, Exec. Vice-Pres. 1977, later Pres. and C.E.O. until 1982; Vice-Pres. United Technologies Corpn. 1982, Sr. Vice-Pres. (Defense Systems) 1983, Pres., C.O.O. and Dir. 1984–92, C.E.O. 1986–94, Chair. 1987–97; Dir. Travelers Corpn., Hartford, Shell Oil Co., Houston; Fellow, Univ. of Bridgeport; Hon. D.Sc. (Bridgeport); Hon. LL.D. (Trinity Coll. and Boston Univ.). *Address:* c/o United Technologies Corporation, United Technologies Building, One Financial Plaza, Hartford, CT 06101, U.S.A.

DANIELS, Henry Ellis, M.A., PH.D., SC.D., F.R.S.; British professor of mathematical statistics; b. 2 Oct. 1912, London; s. of Morris Daniels and Hannah Daniels; m. Barbara E. Pickering 1950; one s. one d.; ed. Sciennes School, Edinburgh, George Heriot's School, Edinburgh, Edinburgh Univ. and Clare Coll., Cambridge; statistician, Wool Industries Research Asscn. 1935–47; Ministry of Aircraft Production 1942–45; Lecturer in Math. Univ. of Cambridge 1947–57; Prof. of Mathematical Statistics Univ. of Birmingham 1957–78, Prof. Emer. 1978–; Fellow, King's Coll., Cambridge 1975–76; Pres. Royal Statistical Soc. 1974–75; Fellow, Inst. of Mathematical Statistics; Hon. mem. Int. Statistical Inst. 1993; Hon. Fellow Clare Coll., Cambridge 1992; Freeman Clockmakers Co. 1981, Liveryman 1984; Guy Medal (Silver) 1957, (Gold) 1984, Royal Statistical Soc.; Sc.D. (Cantab.) 1983. *Publications:* papers in learned journals. *Leisure interests:* playing the English concertina, repairing watches. *Address:* 12 Kimberley Road, Cambridge, CB4 1HH, England. *Telephone:* (01223) 313402.

DANIELS, Jeff; American actor; b. 19 Feb. 1955, Athens, Ga.; ed. Cen. Michigan Univ.; apprentice Circle Repertory Theatre, New York; f. Purple Rose Theatre Co., Chelsea, Mich. *Theatre:* The Farm 1976, Brontosaurus 1977, My Life 1977, Feedlot 1977, Lulu 1978, Slugger 1978, The Fifth of July 1978, Johnny Got His Gun 1982 (Obie Award), The Three Sisters 1982–83, The Golden Age 1984, Redwood Curtain 1993, Short-Changed Review 1993, Lemon Sky. *Films:* Ragtime 1981, Terms of Endearment 1983, The Purple Rose of Cairo 1985, Marie 1985, Heartburn 1986, Something Wild 1986, Radio Days 1987, The House on Carroll Street 1988, Sweet Hearts Dance 1988, Grand Tour 1989, Checking Out 1989, Arachnophobia 1990, Welcome Home, Roxy Carmichael 1990, Love Hurts 1990, The Butcher's Wife 1992, Gettysburg 1993, Speed 1994, Dumb and Dumber 1994, Fly Away Home 1996, Two Days in the Valley 1996, 101 Dalmatians 1996, Trial and Error 1997. *TV:* (films) A Rumor of War 1980, Invasion of Privacy 1983, The Caine Mutiny Court Martial 1988, No Place Like Home 1989, Disaster in Time 1992, Redwood Curtain 1995, Teamster Boss: The Jackie Presser Story; (specials) Fifth of July, The Visit (Trying Times). *Plays (author):* Shoeman 1991, The Tropical Pickle 1992, The Vast Difference 1993, Thy Kingdom's Coming 1994, Escanaba in da Moonlight 1995.

DANIELS, William B., PH.D., M.S.; American professor of physics; b. 21 Dec. 1930, Buffalo, N.Y.; s. of William C. Daniels and Sophia P. Daniels; m. Adriana A. Braakman 1958; two s. one d.; ed. Univ. of Buffalo and Case Inst. (now Case-Western Reserve Univ.); Asst. Prof. of Physics, Case Tech. 1957–59; Research Scientist, Union Carbide Corpn. 1959–61; Asst. Prof. Princeton Univ. 1961–63, Assoc. Prof. 1963–66, Prof. of Mechanical Eng. 1966–72; Unidel Prof. of Physics, also of Astronomy Univ. of Del. 1972–, Chair. Physics Dept. 1977–80; Fellow, American Physical Soc.; John Simon Guggenheim Memorial Fellow 1976–77; Humboldt Sr. Award 1982, 1992. *Publications:* more than 100 articles on the physics of solids at high pressures. *Leisure interests:* sailing, mountaineering. *Address:* Physics Department, University of Delaware, Newark, DE 19716 (Office); 283 Dallam Road, Newark, DE 19711, U.S.A. (Home). *Telephone:* (302) 451-2667 (Office). *Fax:* (302) 831-1637.

DANIELSSON, Bengt Emmerik, PH.D.; Swedish anthropologist and writer; b. 6 July 1921, Krokek; s. of Emmerik Danielsson and Margareta Källgren; m. Marie-Thérèse Sailley 1948; one adopted s. one d. (died 1972); ed. Univ. of Uppsala, Sweden and Univ. of Washington, Seattle; field research among Jibaro Indians, Upper Amazonas 1946–47, in Tuamotu Archipelago, French Polynesia 1949–51, Australia 1955–56; mem. Kon-Tiki Expedition 1947; Assoc. Anthropologist Bernice P. Bishop Museum Honolulu, 1952–; mem. Pacific Science Bd. expedition to Tuamotu Archipelago 1952; Leader George Vanderbilt expedition to Soc. Islands 1957, Swedish TV expedition to S. Seas 1962; tech. adviser for film Mutiny on the Bounty 1961; Producer TV series Terry's South Sea Adventures 1962, Captain Cook's Voyages 1986; Swedish Consul, French Polynesia 1960–78; Dir. Nat. Museum of Ethnography, Stockholm 1967–71; Corresp. for Pacific Islands Magazine 1978–88. *Publications:* The Happy Island 1951, The Forgotten Islands of the South Seas 1952, Love in the South Seas 1954, Work and Life on Raroia 1955, From Raft to Raft 1959, What Happened on the Bounty 1962, Gauguin in the South Seas 1965, La découverte de la Polynésie 1972, Moruroa, mon amour 1974, Mémorial Polynésien (6 vols.) 1976–80, Tahiti autrefois 1981, New Horizons in the Pacific 1986, Poisoned Reign 1986, In the Wake of Captain Cook 1991; Children's Books: Terry in the South Seas 1957, Terry in Australia 1958, Terry's Kon-Tiki Adventure 1963. *Address:* Papehue, Paea; Box 558, Papeete, Tahiti. *Telephone:* (689) 534474. *Fax:* (689) 534474.

DANILOV-DANILYAN, Victor Ivanovich, DR. ECON.; Russian politician; b. 9 May 1938, Moscow; m.; three s.; ed. Moscow State Univ.; jr. researcher, engineer, sr. engineer Computation Cen. Moscow State Univ. 1960–64; researcher, leading engineer, Head of lab. Cen. Inst. of Math. and Econs. U.S.S.R. Acad. of Sciences 1964–76; Head of lab., Prof. All-Union Research Inst. of System Studies U.S.S.R. Acad. of Sciences 1976–80; Head of lab., Chair Acad. of Nat. Econ. U.S.S.R. Council of Ministers 1980–91; Deputy Minister of Nature and Environment of U.S.S.R. Aug.–Nov. 1991; Minister of Ecology and Natural Resources Russian Fed. 1991–96; Chair. State Cttee. on Ecology Russian Fed. Aug. 1996–; mem. State Duma (parl.) 1993–96. *Address:* State Committee on Ecology, B. Gruzinskaya str. 4/6, 123812 Moscow, Russia (Office). *Telephone:* (095) 254 7683, 254 8072 (Office).

DANINOS, Pierre; French writer; b. 26 May 1913, Paris; m. 1st Jane Marrain 1942; m. 2nd Marie-Pierre Dourneau 1968; one s. two d.; ed. Lycée Janson de Sailly; began as journalist 1931; liaison agent to the British Army, Flanders 1940; Columnist for Le Figaro. *Publications:* Les carnets du bon Dieu (Prix Interallié) 1947, Sonia, les autres et moi (Prix Courteline) 1952, Les carnets du Major Thompson 1954, Vacances à tous prix 1958, Un certain Monsieur Blot 1960, Le jacassin 1962, Snobissimo 1964, Le 36e dessous 1966, Les touristocrates 1974, Made in France 1977, La composition d'histoire 1979, Le veuf joyeux 1981, La galerie des glaces 1983, La France dans tous ses états 1985, Profession: Écrivain 1988, Candidement vôtre 1992, 40 ans de vacances 1993. *Leisure interests:* loafing, tennis, collecting British hobbies. *Address:* 15 rue Chauveau, 92200 Neuilly-sur-Seine, France.

DANKERT, Pieter (Piet); Netherlands politician; b. 1934; m.; mem. European Parl. 1977–; Pres. European Ass. 1982–84; fmr. mem. Parl. Ass. of Council of Europe, Ass. of WEU; mem. Parl.; State Sec. for Foreign Affairs 1989; Labour Party. *Address:* c/o Ministry of Foreign Affairs, P.O. Box 20061, 2500 EB The Hague, Netherlands.

DANKWORTH, John Philip William, C.B.E., F.R.A.M.; British musician; b. 20 Sept 1927, London; m. Cleo Laine (q.v.) 1958; one s. one d.; ed. Monoux Grammar School, Royal Acad. of Music; f. large jazz orchestra 1953; with Cleo Laine f. Wavendon Stables (performing arts centre) 1970; Pops Music Dir. London Symphony Orchestra 1985–90; *compositions include:* Improvisations (with Matyas Seiber) 1959, Escapade (commissioned by Northern Sinfonia Orchestra) 1967, Tom Sawyer's Saturday, for narrator and orchestra (commissioned by Farnham Festival) 1967, String Quartet 1971, Piano Concerto (commissioned by Westminster Festival) 1972, Grace Abounding (for Royal Philharmonic Orchestra) 1980, The Diamond and the Goose (for City of Birmingham Choir and Orchestra) 1981, Reconciliation (for Silver Jubilee of Coventry Cathedral) 1987, Woolwich Concerto (clarinet concerto for Emma Johnson) 1995, Double Vision 1997, Dreams '42 (string quartet for Kidderminster Fesival) 1997; *film scores include:* Saturday Night and Sunday Morning, Darling, The Servant, Morgan, Accident; numerous record albums, most recent include Echoes of Harlem, Misty, Symphonic Fusions, Moon Valley; Hon. M.A. (Open Univ.) 1975; Hon. D.Mus. (Berklee School of Music) 1982, (York) 1993; Variety Club of G.B. Show Business

Personality Award (with Cleo Laine) 1977. *Publication:* Sax from the Start 1996, Jazz in Revolution 1998. *Leisure interests:* driving, household maintenance. *Address:* The Old Rectory, Wavendon, Milton Keynes, MK17 8LT, England. *Fax:* (01908) 584414.

DANNEELS, H.E. Cardinal Godfried; Belgian ecclesiastic; b. 4 June 1933, Kanegem, Bruges; ordained priest 1957; Bishop of Antwerp 1977; Archbishop of Malines-Brussels 1979–; Castrene Bishop of Belgium 1980–; Pres. Episcopal Conf. of Belgium, Pax Christi Int.; mem. Synod of Bishops, Sacred Congregation for Evangelization, Council for the Public Affairs of the Church, Congregation of Catholic Educ., Congregation of Divine Worship, Secr. for Non-believers, Congregation for the Oriental Churches; cr. Cardinal 1983. *Address:* Aartsbisdom, Wollemarkt 15, 2800, Mechelen, Belgium. *Telephone:* (015) 216501. *Fax:* (015) 209485.

DANSEREAU, Pierre, C.C., G.O.Q., D.SC., F.R.S.C.; Canadian professor of ecology; b. 5 Oct. 1911, Montreal; s. of J.-Lucien Dansereau and Marie Archambault; m. Françoise Masson 1935; ed. Collège Sainte-Marie, Montreal, Institut Agricole d'Oka, Univ. of Geneva, Switzerland; Asst. Dir. of Tech. Services, Montreal Botanical Garden 1939–42; Dir. Service de Biogéographie, Montreal 1943–50; Assoc. Prof. of Botany, Univ. of Mich., Ann Arbor, U.S.A. 1950–55; Dean of Faculty of Science and Dir. of Botanical Inst., Univ. of Montreal 1955–61; Asst. Dir. and Head, Dept. of Ecology, The New York Botanical Garden, Bronx, 1961–68; Prof., Inst. of Urban Studies, Univ. of Montreal 1968–71; Prof. and Scientific Dir., Centre de Recherches Ecologiques de Montréal, Univ. of Quebec 1971–72, Prof. of Ecology attached to Centre de Recherches en Sciences de l'Environnement 1972–76, Emer. Prof. and Prof. of Ecology in Master's Programme in Environmental Sciences 1976–, doctoral programme 1987–; many visiting professorships; Commonwealth Prestige Fellowship, Univ. of N.Z. 1961; numerous hon. degrees; 1st Prize (Prix David) Quebec, science section 1959, Massey Medal, Royal Canadian Geographical Soc. 1973, Molson Prize 1974, Canada Council 1975, Izaak Walton Killam Prize, Canada Council 1985, Lawson Medal, Canadian Botanical Asscn. 1986, Dawson Medal, Royal Soc. of Canada 1995 and numerous other prizes and awards; Grand Officier, Ordre nat. du Québec. *Publications include:* Biogeography: an ecological perspective 1957, Contradictions & Biculture 1964, Dimensions of Environmental Quality 1971, Inscape and Landscape 1973, La Terre des Hommes et le Paysage Intérieur 1973, Harmony and Disorder in the Canadian Environment 1975, EZAIM: Écologie de la Zone de l'Aéroport International de Montréal-Le cadre d'une recherche écologique interdisciplinaire 1976, Essai de Classification et de Cartographie Ecologique des Espaces 1985, Les dimensions écologiques de l'espace urbain 1987, Interdisciplinary perspective on production-investment-control processes in the environment 1990, L'envers et l'endroit: le désir, le besoin et la capacité 1994, Postface: la voie forestière, la vérité biologique, la vie durable 1994. *Leisure interests:* swimming, travel, theatre. *Address:* Université du Québec à Montréal, B.P. 8888, Succ. Centre-Ville, Montreal, Quebec, H3C 3P8 (Office); 205 chem. Côte-Sainte-Catherine, apt. 104, Outremont, Montreal, Quebec H2V 2A9, Canada (Home). *Telephone:* (514) 987-3000 ext. 3045 (Office). *Fax:* (514) 987-4054 (Office).

DANSON, Ted; American actor; b. 29 Dec. 1947, San Diego, Calif.; s. of Edward Danson and Jessica McMaster; m. 1st Randall L. Gosch 1970 (divorced 1977); m. 2nd Cassandra Coates 1977; two d.; ed. The Kent School, Connecticut and Stanford and Carnegie-Mellon Univs.; teacher, The Actor's Inst. Los Angeles 1978; star, NBC-TV series Cheers (American Comedy Award 1991) 1982–93; C.E.O. Anasazi Productions (fmrly. Danson/Fauci Productions); Off-Broadway plays include: The Real Inspector Hound 1972, Comedy of Errors; actor and producer of TV films including: When the Bough Breaks 1986, We Are The Children 1987; exec. producer TV films: Walk Me to the Distance 1989, Down Home 1989, Mercy Mission: The Rescue of Flight 771 1993, On Promised Land 1994; other appearances in TV drama, etc. *Films include:* The Onion Field 1979, Body Heat 1981, Creepshow 1983, A Little Treasure 1985, A Fine Mess 1986, Just Between Friends 1986, Three Men and a Baby 1987, Cousins 1989, Dad 1989, Three Men and a Little Lady 1990, Made in America 1992, Getting Even With Dad 1993, Pontiac Moon 1993, Gullivers' Travels (TV) 1995, Loch Ness 1996. *Address:* c/o Creative Artists Agency, 9830 Wilshire Boulevard, Beverly Hills, CA 90212, U.S.A.

DANTON, J. Periam, M.A., PH.D.; American professor and librarian; b. 5 July 1908, Palo Alto, California; s. of George Henry and Annina Periam; m. Lois King 1948 (divorced 1973); one s. one d.; ed. Leipzig, Columbia and Chicago Univs., and Oberlin and Williams Colls.; served in N.Y. Public Library 1928–29; Williams Coll. Library 1929–30, American Library Asscn. 1930–33; Librarian and Assoc. Prof. Colby Coll. Library 1935–36, Temple Univ. 1936–46; Del. Int. Fed. of Library Asscns. meetings 1939, 1964, 1966–72; Visiting Prof., Univs. of Chicago 1942 and Columbia 1946; Lt., Lt.-Commdr., U.S.N.R. 1942–45; Prof. Librarianship, Calif. Univ. 1946–76, Dean, School of Librarianship 1946–61, Prof. Emer. 1976–; Pres. Asscn. American Library Schools 1949–50; Fulbright Research Scholar (Univ. Göttingen) 1960–61, (Vienna) 1964–65; Guggenheim Fellow 1971–72; U.S. Dept. of State, American Specialist, Ethiopia 1961; Ford Foundation Consultant on Univ. Libraries in Southeast Asia 1963; UNESCO Library Consultant, Jamaica 1968; Surveyor and Consultant, numerous libraries; Dir. U.S. Dept. of State—American Library Asscn. Multi-Area Group Librarian Program 1963–64; Guest lecturer, The Hague 1961, Univ. Toronto 1963, Hebrew Univ. Jerusalem 1965, 1985, Univs. Belgrade, Ljubljana and Zagreb 1965, Univ. of British Columbia 1968, McGill Univ. 1969, Univ. Puerto Rico 1970, Univ. of N. Carolina 1977, Univ. of Tex. 1978, Southern Ill. Univ. 1979; mem. Bd. of Editors Asscn. of Coll. and Research Libraries Monographs 1966–70, Library Quarterly 1968–90, International Library Review 1968–75; Hon. mem. Vereinigung Österreichischer Bibliothekare, Verein Deutscher Bibliothekare; Hon. Research Fellow, Univ. London 1974–75; Berkeley Citation 1976; mem. American Library Asscn., Asscn. of American Library Schools, Calif. Library Asscn. *Publications:* Library Literature, 1921–32 1934, Education for Librarianship 1949, United States Influence on Norwegian Librarianship 1890-1940 1957, The Climate of Book Selection: Social Influences on School and Public Libraries 1959, Book Selection and Collections: A Comparison of German and American University Libraries 1963, Jamaica: Library Development 1968, Index to Festschriften in Librarianship 1970, Between M.L.S. and Ph.D.: A Study of Sixth-Year Specialist Programs in Accredited Library Schools 1970, The Dimensions of Comparative Librarianship 1973, Index to Festschriften in Librarianship 1967–75, 1978. *Leisure interests:* classical music, swimming, travel. *Address:* School of Information Management and Systems, 104 South Hall #4600, Berkeley, CA 94720-4600, U.S.A. *Telephone:* (510) 642-1464. *Fax:* (510) 642-5814.

DANTZIG, George Bernard, PH.D.; American professor of operations research and computer science; b. 8 Nov. 1914, Portland, Ore.; s. of Tobias and Anja G. Dantzig; m. Anne Shmuner 1936; two s. one d.; ed. Univs. of Maryland, Michigan and California (Berkeley); Statistician, U.S. Bureau of Labor Statistics 1937–39; Chief, Combat Analysis Branch, U.S.A.F. HQ Statistical Control 1941–46; Math. Adviser, U.S.A.F. HQ 1946–52; Research Mathematician, Rand Corpn., Santa Monica, Calif. 1952–60; Chair. Operations Research Center and Prof., Univ. of Calif. (Berkeley) 1960–66; Prof. of Operations Research and Computer Science, Stanford Univ. 1966; Int. Inst. for Applied Systems Analysis, Head of Methodology Project 1973–74; mem. N.A.S., Nat. Acad. of Eng.; Fellow, American Acad. of Arts and Sciences; Hon. mem. Inst. Electrical and Electronics Engineers; numerous Hon. degrees; Nat. Medal of Science, U.S.A. 1975, Harvey Prize 1985, Silver Medal Operational Research Soc., G.B. 1986, COORS American Ingenuity Award 1989. *Publications:* Linear Programming and Extensions 1963, Compact City (with Thomas L. Saaty) 1973; over 150 published technical papers. *Leisure interests:* planning future cities, writing science fiction. *Address:* 821 Tolman Drive, Stanford, CA 94305, U.S.A. (Home). *Telephone:* (415) 493-0578.

DANTZIG, Rudi Van; Netherlands choreographer; b. 4 Aug. 1933, Amsterdam; s. of Murk van Dantzig and Berendina Hermina Homburg; ed. High School and Art Coll.; took ballet lessons with Sonia Gaskell; joined Sonia Gaskell's co. Ballet Recital (later Netherlands Ballet), soloist 1959; won Prix de la Critique (Paris) for choreography in Night Island 1955; with Netherlands Dance Theatre 1959–60, artistic dir. and prin. choreographer Netherlands Nat. Ballet 1968–91; has also worked for London Dance Theatre, Ballet Rambert, The Royal Ballet, Harkness Ballet (New York), Bat-Dor (Tel-Aviv), Ballet d'Anvers (Antwerp), Nat. Ballet of Washington, Royal Danish Ballet, American Ballet Theater, Nat. Ballet of Canada, Ballets of Munich and Cologne, Viennese Opera Ballet, Royal Winnipeg Ballet, Houston Ballet, Hungarian State Ballet, Finnish Opera Ballet, Pacific South-West Ballet (Seattle), Paris Opera Ballet, Royal N.Z. Ballet, Cape Town Ballet (S.A.), Lyriki Skini Ballet (Athens, Royal Ballet of Stockholm, Classical Ballet of Israel); Officer Oranje-Nassau 1969, Verdienstkreuz (Germany). *Choreography for:* Night Island 1955, Jungle 1961, Monument for a Dead Boy 1965, Romeo and Juliet 1967, Moments 1968, Epitaaf 1969, Astraal 1969, The Ropes of Time 1970, On Their Way 1970, Painted Birds 1971, Are Friends Delight or Pain 1972, The Unfinished 1973, Orpheus 1974, Ramifications 1974, Blown in a Gentle Wind (with Wade Walthall, for Rudolf Nureyev) 1975, Ginastera 1976, Gesang der Jünglinge 1977, Vier letzte Lieder 1978, Ulysses (for Nureyev) 1979, Life (with Toer van Schayk) 1979, Voorbÿ Gegaan 1979, About a Dark House 1978, Dialogues 1980, Underneath My Feet 1981, Room at the Top 1982, No-Mans Land 1982, I Just Simply Hold my Breath 1983, In Praise of Folly 1983, For We Know Not What We Are Doing 1986, To Bend or to Break 1987, Sans armes, Citoyens! 1987 (for the Paris Opera), Swan Lake (with Toer van Schayk) 1988, Archangels Paint Red the Sky 1990, Memories from the Lower Depths 1991, Memories of the Lower Depths 1991, Refuge 1994, Tables d'Amour 1995. *Publications:* Nureyev, Aspects of the Dancer, Spectrum jaarboek 1979, Voorbÿ Gegaan—the making of a Pas-de-deux, Olga de Haas: A Memory, For a Lost Soldier (novel) 1986, Rudolf Nureyev, The Trail of a Comet 1993, Abyss (short stories) 1996; articles in Ballet and Modern Dance; film appearances in Van Dantzig—Portrait of a Choreographer (by Jan Vrÿman), The Making of a Ballet. *Leisure interests:* literature, politics. *Address:* Het Nationale Ballet, Het Muziek theater, Waterlooplein 22, 1011 PG Amsterdam (Office); Emma-Straat 27, Amsterdam, Netherlands (Home). *Telephone:* 551-82-25 (Office); 679-83-31 (Home).

DAOUDI, Riad, PH.D.; Syrian lawyer and professor of law; b. 22 July 1942, Damascus; s. of Rashad Daoudi and Adallat Daoudi; m. Viviane Collin 1978; two s. one d.; ed. Institut des Hautes Etudes Internationales, Paris; Prof. of Int. Law, Damascus Law School 1978–91; Dean Asst. for Academic Affairs, Faculty of Law, Univ. of Damascus 1980–82; lawyer, mem. Syrian Bar 1982–; Registrar, Judicial Tribunal of Org. of Arab Petroleum Exporting Countries (OAPEC) 1983–; Legal Adviser to Ministry of Foreign Affairs 1991–; Lauréat, best doctoral thesis, Univ. of Paris 1977–78. *Publications:*

Parliamentary Immunities: comparative study in Arab constitutions (in Arabic) 1982, Peace Negotiations – Treaty of Versailles (textbook for law students, in Arabic) 1983, Arab Commission for Human Rights, in Encyclopedia of Public International Law (in English) 1985; articles and contribs. to books on int. affairs and int. law. *Leisure interests:* tennis, reading. *Address:* The Judicial Tribunal of the OAPEC, P.O. Box 20501, Safat 13066, Kuwait. *Telephone:* 481 82 89; 245 78 58. *Fax:* 481 82 74.

DARBINYAN, Armen Razmikovich, CAND. ECON.; Armenian politician; b. 23 Jan. 1965, Gioumri, Armenia; m.; one d.; ed. Moscow State Univ.; lecturer, Moscow State Univ. 1986–89; sr. expert, Head of dept., Perm. Mission of Armenia to Russian Fed., Plenipotentiary Rep., Intergovt. Comm. on debts of Vnesheconombank 1989–92; Dir.-Gen. Armenian Foreign Trade Co. Armenintorg 1992–94; First Deputy Chair. Cen. Bank of Armenia 1994–97; Minister of Finance 1997, of Finance and Econs. 1997–98; Prime Minister of Armenia April 1998–. *Address:* Parliament Buildings, Square of Republic, 375010 Yerevan, Armenia. *Telephone:* (374) 52 03 60 (Office).

DARBOVEN, Hanne; German artist; b. 29 April 1941, Munich; ed. Hochschule für Bildende Künste, Hamburg; one-man exhbns. in Düsseldorf 1967, 1968, 1970, 1971, 1975, Munich 1969, Cologne 1970, 1980, Amsterdam 1970, 1972, 1974, 1975, 1976, Leo Castelli Gallery, New York 1973, 1974, 1976, 1977, 1978, 1980, 1982; and in Paris, Brussels, Oxford, Turin, Milan, Bologna, Zürich, Basle, Houston, etc.; has participated in numerous group exhbns. of contemporary art in galleries in Europe, U.S.A., Canada, São Paulo Biennale 1973, Venice Biennale 1982. *Publications:* books including: El Lissitzky, Hosmann, Hamburg und Yves Gevaert 1974, Atta Troll Kunstmuseum 1975, Baudelaire, Heine, Disecpolo, Maizi, Flores, Kraus: Pour écrire la liberté 1975, New York Diary 1976, Ein Jahrhundert, Vol. 1 1971–77. *Address:* Am Burgberg 26, D-21 Hamburg 90, Germany. *Telephone:* 040/763-3033.

D'ARCEVIA, Bruno; Italian painter and sculptor; b. 21 Oct. 1946, Arcevia, Ancona; s. of Benedetto Bruni and Amelia Filippini; m. Maria Falconetti 1972; one s. one d.; worked in France and Venezuela 1975–78; co-f. Nuova Maniera Italiana Movt. 1982–83; solo exhbns. include Mayer Swarz Gallery, Beverly Hills, L.A. 1988–90, Koplin Gallery, Santa Monica, Calif. 1993, Caldwell-Snyder Gallery, San Francisco and New York 1996–; group exhbns. include Profili, Rome 1990; one of 20 Italian artists included in ArToday review, London 1996; Gold San Valentino award, named Marchigiano dell'Anno 1998; Commendatore Ordine della Repubblica Italiana. *Leisure interests:* underwater fishing. *Address:* Via dei Campi Sportivi 2A, 00197 Rome (Office); Via Luigi Angeloni 29, 00149 Rome, Italy (Home). *Telephone:* (06) 8070185 (Office); (06) 5503637 (Home). *Fax:* (06) 8070185.

D'ARCY, Margaretta; Irish playwright and author; m. John Arden (q.v.) 1957; five c. (one deceased); Artistic Dir. Corrandulla Arts and Entertainment Club 1973–, Galway Women's Entertainment 1982, Galway Women's Sceal Radio, Radio Pirate-Woman 1986. *Plays produced:* The Happy Haven 1961, Business of Good Government 1962, Ars Longa Vita Brevis 1964, The Royal Pardon 1966, Friday's Hiding 1967, The Hero Rises Up 1969, Keep These People Moving 1972, The Island of the Mighty 1974, The Non-Stop Connolly Show 1975, Vandaleur's Folly 1978, The Little Gray Home in the West 1978, The Making of Muswell Hill 1979, The Manchester Enthusiasts 1984, Whose Is the Kingdom? 1988, A Suburban Suicide 1994 (all with John Arden), A Pinprick of History 1977; TV documentary (with John Arden) Profile of Sean O'Casey 1973. *Publications:* Tell Them Everything (Prison Memoirs) 1981, Awkward Corners (with John Arden) 1988, Galway's Pirate Women, a Global Trawl 1996. *Address:* c/o Casarotto Ramsay, 60–66 Wardour Street, London, W1V 3HP, England.

DARGIE, Sir William Alexander, Kt., C.B.E., F.R.S.A., F.R.A.S.; Australian artist and administrator; b. 4 June 1912, Melbourne; s. of late A. Dargie; m. Kathleen Howitt 1937; one s. one d.; official war artist with Australian Imperial Forces, Royal Australian Air Force, Royal Australian Navy; Head. Nat. Gallery, Vic. Art School 1946–53; Chair. Commonwealth Art Advisory Bd. 1969–73; mem. Interim Council, Nat. Gallery, Canberra 1968–73, Nat. Capital Planning Advisory Cttee. 1970–73, Aboriginal Arts Advisory Cttee. 1969–71, Council, Nat. Museum of Vic. 1978–83; Trustee, Native Cultural Reserve, Port Moresby, Papua New Guinea 1969–75, Museum and Art Gallery, Papua New Guinea 1970–73; Chair. Bd. of Trustees, McLelland Gallery 1981–87; has painted portraits of H.M. Queen Elizabeth II, H.R.H. Duke of Gloucester, H.R.H. the late Princess Royal, H.R.H. the late Princess Marina, H.R.H. Princess Alexandra and many individuals distinguished in arts, sciences and politics in Australia, N.Z. and U.K.; exhibitor, Royal Acad. and Royal Soc. of Portrait Painters; M.A. (h.c.); Woodward and McPhillimy Awards 1940, Archibald Prize (eight times) N.S.W., MacKay Prize 1942. *Leisure interests:* tennis, folklore, material culture of Melanasia. *Address:* 19 Irilbarra Road, Canterbury, Vic. 3126, Australia. *Telephone:* (3) 836 3396.

DARIDA, Clelio; Italian politician; b. 3 May 1927, Rome; joined Christian Democrat party (D.C.) 1946, elected mem. Rome Cttee. 1947, Dir. Propaganda Office 1954–55; M.P. for Rome 1963–69; Mayor of Rome 1969–76; M.P. for Rome 1976–; fmr. Under-Sec. of State, Ministry of Interior then fmr. Minister of Post and Telecommunications, of Public Admin. of Justice; Minister of State-owned Industries 1985–87. *Address:* c/o Ministry of State Industry, Via Sallustiana 53, 00187 Rome, Italy.

DARLING, Rt. Hon. Alistair Maclean, P.C.; British politician and lawyer; b. 28 Nov. 1953; m. Margaret McQueen Vaughan 1986; one s. one d; ed. Aberdeen Univ.; fmr. advocate; mem. Lothian Regional Council 1982–87 (Chair. Transport Cttee. 1986–87), Lothian and Borders Police Bd. 1982–86; M.P. for Edin. Cen. 1987–; Shadow Chief Sec. to Treasury 1996–97; Chief Sec. to Treasury 1997–98; Sec. of State for Social Security 1998–. *Address:* House of Commons, London, SW1A 0AA, England.

DARMAN, Richard Gordon, M.B.A.; American government official and investor; b. 10 May 1943, Charlotte; m. Kathleen Emmet 1967; three. s.; ed. Harvard Univ.; Deputy Asst. Sec. Dept. of Health, Educ. and Welfare, Wash., D.C. 1971–72, Asst. to Sec., Dept. of Defense 1973, Special Asst. to Attorney-Gen. 1973; Asst. Sec. Dept. of Commerce 1976–77; Asst. to Pres. 1981–85; Deputy Sec. Treasury Dept. 1985–87; Dir. Office of Man. and Budget (Cabinet post) 1988–93; Man. Dir. The Carlyle Group 1993–; Prof. JFK School of Govt., Harvard Univ. 1998–; Prin. Dir. ICF Inc., Wash., D.C. 1975, 1977–80; lecturer in Public Policy and Man., Harvard Univ. 1977–80; Man. Dir. Shearson Lehman Brothers Inc., New York 1987–88; Asst. to fmr. Pres. Reagan 1981–85; Vice-Chair. Del. to UN Conf. on Law of Sea 1977; mem. Ocean Policy Cttee., N.A.S. 1978–80, Bd. of Dirs. Frontier Ventures Corpn., Telcom Ventures, Sequana Therapeutics, The New England Funds, Council on Excellence in Govt.; Ed. Harvard Educ. Review 1970, Contributing Ed. U.S. News and World Report 1987–88; trustee Brookings Inst. 1987–88. *Publication:* Who's in Control? 1996. *Address:* The Carlyle Group, 1001 Pennsylvania Avenue, N.W., Washington, DC 20004, U.S.A.

DARMON, Marco; French lawyer; b. 26 Jan. 1930, Tunis; m. Elsa Lévy 1958; one s. one d.; magistrate in Brittany 1957–59; joined Ministry of Justice 1959; Tech. Counsellor, Office of the Keeper of the Seals 1973–74; subsequently Vice-Pres. Tribunal de Grande Instance, Paris; Asst. Dir. Office of Keeper of the Seals 1981–82; Pres. of Chamber, Cour d'Appel, Paris; Dir. of Civil Affairs and of the Seal of Ministry of Justice 1982; Advocate-Gen., European Court of Justice, Luxembourg 1984–94. *Address:* c/o Court of Justice of the European Communities, 2925 Luxembourg.

DARNTON, Robert Choate, D.PHIL.; American professor of history; b. 10 May 1939, New York, N.Y.; s. of the late Byron Darnton and Eleanor Darnton; m. Susan Lee Glover 1963; one s. two d.; ed. Harvard Univ., Oxford Univ., U.K.; reporter, The New York Times 1964–65; Jr. Fellow, Harvard Univ., 1965–68; Asst. Prof., subsequently Assoc. Prof., Prof., Princeton Univ. 1968–, Shelby Cullom Davis Prof. of European History 1984–, Dir. Program in European Cultural Studies 1987–; fellowships and visiting professorships including: Ecole des Hautes Etudes en Sciences Sociales, Paris 1971, 1981, 1985, Netherlands Inst. for Advanced Study 1976–77, Inst. for Advanced Study, Princeton 1977–81, Oxford Univ. (George Eastman Visiting Prof.) 1986–87, Collège de France; Pres. Int. Soc. for Eighteenth-Century Studies 1987–91; mem. Bd. of Dirs., Voltaire Foundation, Oxford, Social Science Research Council 1988–91; mem. Bd. of Trustees Center for Advanced Study in the Behavioral Sciences 1992–, Oxford Univ. Press, U.S.A. 1993–, The New York Public Library 1994–; mem. various editorial bds.; Fellow American Acad. of Arts and Sciences, American Philosophical Soc., American Antiquarian Soc.; Beirat, Wissenschafts-Kolleg zu Berlin 1994–; Foreign mem. Academia Europaea, Acad. Royale de Langue et de Littérature Françaises de Belgique; Guggenheim Fellow 1970; Dr. h.c. (Neuchâtel) 1986, (Lafayette Coll.) 1989, (Univ. of Bristol) 1991; MacArthur Prize 1982 and several other awards; Officier Ordre des Arts et des Lettres 1995. *Publications:* Mesmerism and the End of the Enlightenment in France 1968, The Business of Enlightenment 1979, The Literary Underground of the Old Regime 1982, The Great Cat Massacre 1984, Edition et sédition 1991, Berlin Journal, 1989–1900 1991, Gens de lettres, gens du livre 1992, The Forbidden Best-Sellers of Pre-Revolutionary France 1995, The Corpus of Clandestine Literature 1769–1789 1995. *Leisure interests:* squash, travel. *Address:* Department of History, Princeton University, Princeton, NJ 08540 (Office); 6 McCosh Circle, Princeton, NJ 08540, U.S.A. (Home). *Telephone:* (609) 924-6905 (Home).

DARRIEUX, Danielle; French actress; b. 1 May 1917, Bordeaux; d. of Jean and Marie-Louise (née Witkowski) Darrieux; m. 3rd Georges Mitsinkides 1948; one s.; ed. Paris Univ.; First appeared in films 1931; in theatre 1937; Chevalier, Légion d'honneur, Commdr., Ordre des Arts et des Lettres, César d'honneur 1985, Prix de l'Amicale des Cadres de l'Industrie Cinématographique 1987. *Film appearances include:* Le bal, Mayerling, Un mauvais garçon, Battement de coeur, Premier rendez-vous, Ruy Blas, Le plaisir, Madame de ..., Le rouge et le noir, Bonnes à tuer, Le salaire du péché, L'amant de Lady Chatterley, Typhon sur Nagasaki, La ronde, Alexander the Great, Marie Octobre, L'homme à femmes, Les lions sont lâchés, Le crime ne paie pas, Le diable et les dix commandements, Le coup de grâce, Patate, Greengage Summer, Les demoiselles de Rochefort, 24 heures de la vie d'une femme, Divine, L'année sainte, En haut des marches, Le lieu du crime, Corps et biens, Quelques jours avec moi, Bille en tête, le Jour des rois, les Mamies; *Plays:* La robe mauve de Valentine 1963, Gillian 1965, Comme un oiseau 1965, Secretissimo 1965, Laurette 1966, CoCo 1970, Ambassador (musical) 1971, Folie douce 1972, les Amants terribles 1973, Boulevard Feydau 1978, L'intoxe 1981, Gigi 1985, Adorable Julia 1987, Adelaïde 90 1990, George et Margaret 1992, les Mamies 1992, Harold et Maude 1995, Ma petite fille, mon amour 1998; numerous TV film appearances. *Address:* Agence Nicole Cann, 1 rue Alfred de Vigny, 75008 Paris, France.

DASCHLE, Thomas Andrew, B.A.; American politician; b. 9 Dec. 1947, Aberdeen, S. Dak.; m. Linda Hall Daschle; one s. two d.; ed. S. Dak. State

Univ.; served to 1st Lieut., U.S.A.F. 1969–72; Chief Legis. Aide and then Field Co-ordinator to U.S. Senator 1973–77; mem. 96th–97th Congresses from 1st S. Dak. Dist., 98th Congress 1977–87; Senator from S. Dakota Jan. 1987–; Senate Minority Leader 104th Congress 1995; Democrat. *Address:* U.S. Senate, 509 Hart Senate Building, Washington, DC 20510, U.S.A.

d'ASCOLI, Bernard Jacques-Henri Marc; French concert pianist; b. 18 Nov. 1958, Aubagne; one s.; ed. Marseille Conservatoire; became blind 1962; took up music 1970; youngest Baccalauréat matriculate of France 1974; first public appearances on both piano and organ 1974; elected as most talented French artist of the year (Megève) 1976; began int. professional career 1982, following débuts at major London concert halls with Royal Philharmonic Orchestra and first recording; toured Australia with Chamber Orchestra of Europe 1983; début Amsterdam Concertgebouw 1984, U.S.A., with Houston Symphony Orchestra 1985, Musikverein, Vienna 1986, Henry Wood Promenade Concerts, London 1986, Tokyo Casals Hall and Bunka Kaikan Hall 1988, with Boston Symphony Orchestra 1992; recordings of Chopin and Schumann; first prize Int. Maria Casals competition, Barcelona 1979; prizewinner, Leipzig Bach competition and Warsaw Chopin competition 1980; 3rd prize, Leeds Int. piano competition 1981. *Address:* c/o Clarion/Seven Muses, 47 Whitehall Park, London, N19 3TW, England. *Telephone:* 0171-272 4413.

DASGUPTA, Partha Sarathi, PH.D., F.B.A.; Indian professor of economics and philosophy; b. 17 Nov. 1942, Dacca; s. of the late Prof. Amiya Dasgupta and Shanti Dasgupta; m. Carol M. Meade 1968; one s. two d.; ed. Univs. of Delhi and Cambridge; lecturer in Econs. London School of Econs. 1971–75, Reader 1975–78, Prof. of Econs. 1978–85; Prof. of Econs. Univ. of Cambridge and Fellow, St. John's Coll. Cambridge 1985– (Frank Ramsey Prof. of Econs. 1994–); Prof. of Econs. and Prof. of Philosophy and Dir. of Program on Ethics in Society, Stanford Univ. 1989–92; Chair. Beijer Int. Inst. of Ecological Economics, Stockholm; Fellow, Econometric Soc.; Foreign hon. mem. American Acad. of Arts and Sciences; Foreign mem. Royal Swedish Acad. of Sciences; Hon. Fellow, L.S.E. *Publications:* books and articles on econs. of environmental and natural resources, technological change, normative population theory, political philosophy, devt. planning and the political economy of destitution. *Address:* 1 Dean Drive, Holbrook Road, Cambridge, England. *Telephone:* (01223) 212179.

DASH-YONDON, Budragchaagiin, PH.D.; Mongolian politician; b. 17 Feb. 1946, Huvsgul; s. of Jugnaa Budragchaa and Sengee Chogjmoo; m. Choijamts Batjargal; one s. two d.; ed. Mongolian State Univ., State Univ. of Kiev, U.S.S.R.; Prof., Mongolian State Univ. 1968–74; officer at Scientific and Educational Dept, MPRP Cen. Cttee. 1978–79; Vice-Chancellor, Higher Party School, MPRP Cen. Cttee. 1979–85; Deputy Head and Head of Dept, MPRP Cen. Cttee. 1985–90; First Sec.-Gen., MPRP Ulan Bator City Party Cttee. 1990–91; MPRP Sec.-Gen. 1991–96; Political Adviser to Pres. 1997–. *Leisure interests:* reading, chess. *Address:* Mongolian People's Revolutionary Party, Central Building of the MPRP, Baga toiruu 37/1, Ulaanbaatar-11, Mongolia.

DASSAULT, Serge; French engineer; b. 4 April 1925, Paris; s. of the late Marcel Dassault and Madeleine Minckès; m. Nicole Raffel 1950; three s. one d.; ed. Lycée Janson-de-Sailly, Ecole Polytechnique, Ecole Nat. Supérieure de l'Aéronautique, Centre de Perfectionnement dans l'Administration des Affaires, Inst. des Hautes Etudes de la Défense Nationale; Dir. of Flight Testing, Avions Marcel Dassault 1955–61, Export Dir. 1961–63; Dir.-Gen. Société Electronique Marcel Dassault 1963–67, Pres. Dir.-Gen. 1967–86; Admin. Avions Marcel Dassault-Breguet Aviation 1967, Pres. Dir.-Gen. 1986–; Vice-Pres. Société de Gestion de Participations Aéronautiques (SOGEPA); Admin. Dassault Belgique Aviation 1968; Town Councillor, Corbeil-Essonnes 1983–95, Mayor 1995–; Regional Councillor, Ile de France 1986–95; Gen. Councillor Essonne 1988–; mem. Comité de direction du Groupement des industries électroniques 1968–, Groupement des Industries Françaises Aéronautiques et Spatiales 1968–; Hon. Pres. Fondation des Oeuvres Sociales de l'Air 1968; Commissaire Général des Salons Internationaux de l'Aéronautique et de l'Espace 1974–93; Chief Engineer Armaments 1974; Pres. Asscn. Française pour la Participation dans les Entreprises 1972; Pres. working group, Participation active dans l'entreprise, Nat. Council, Patronat Français 1985; Pres. of Section Asscn. européene des constructeurs de matérial spatial (AECMA) 1987–, Groupement des Industries Françaises Aéronautiques et Spatiales (Gifas) 1993–97, Council of French Defence Industry 1994–96; Chevalier, Légion d'honneur; Médaille de l'Aéronautique, Officier de l'Ordre national du Mérite ivoirien. *Publications:* la Gestion participative, J'ai choisi la vérité 1983. *Leisure interests:* golf, hunting, fishing. *Address:* 27 rue du Professeur Victor Pauchet, 92420 Vaucresson; Mairie, place Galignani, 91100 Corbeil-Essonnes, France. *Telephone:* (1) 47.41.79.21.

DASSIN, Jules; American film director; b. 18 Dec. 1911, Middletown, Conn.; s. of Samuel and Berthe (née Vogel) Dassin; m. 1st Béatrice Launer (divorced); one s. (deceased) two d.; m. 2nd Melina Mercouri (deceased) 1966; ed. Morris High School; attended drama school in Europe 1936; Asst. Dir. to Alfred Hitchcock 1940; films directed in U.S. include Brute Force 1947, Naked City 1948, Thieves' Highway 1949; settled in France 1954 and directed Rififi (also acted) 1954, Celui qui doit mourir 1956, Never on Sunday (also acted) 1960, Phaedra 1961, Topkapi 1963, 10.30 p.m. Summer 1966, Up Tight 1968, Promise at Dawn 1970, The Rehearsal 1974, A Dream of Passion 1978, Circle of Two; plays directed: Ilya, Darling, Medicine Show, Magdalena, Joy to the World, Isle of Children, Two's Company, Heartbreak House, Threepenny Opera, Sweet Bird of Youth, A Month in the Country, Who's Afraid of Virginia Woolf?, The Road to Mecca, Death of A Salesman; Director's Prize, Cannes Film Festival 1955 for Rififi; Commdr. Légion d'honneur, Commdr. Ordre des Arts et Lettres. *Address:* Melina Mercouri St. 8, Athens 11521, Greece. *Telephone:* (1) 723 2300. *Fax:* (1) 723 2042.

DATARS, William Ross, PH.D., F.R.S.C.; Canadian professor of physics; b. 14 June 1932, Desboro; s. of Albert J. Datars and Leona A. Fries; m. Eleanor R. Wismer 1959; three s.; ed. McMaster Univ. and Univ. of Wisconsin; Scientific Officer, Defence Research Board 1959–62; Asst. Prof. McMaster Univ. 1962–65, Assoc. Prof. 1965–69, Prof. of Physics 1969–96, Prof. Emer. 1996–; E.W.R. Steacie Research Fellow 1968–70; Fellow, American Physical Soc. *Publications:* 175 scientific papers. *Leisure interests:* farming, skiing, jogging. *Address:* McMaster University, Faculty of Science, Hamilton, Ont., L8S 4L8; 3365 Powerline Road, R.R. 2, Lynden Ont., L0R 1T0, Canada. *Telephone:* (519) 647-2327.

DAUBE, David, D.IUR., PH.D., D.C.L., F.B.A.; university professor; b. 8 Feb. 1909, Freiburg-im-Breisgau, Germany; s. of Jakob Daube and Selma Daube (née Ascher); m. 1st 1936 (divorced 1964); three s.; m. 2nd Helen Smelser (née Margolis) 1986; ed. Berthold-Gymnasium, Freiburg, and Univs. of Freiburg, Göttingen and Cambridge; Fellow of Caius Coll., Cambridge 1938–46; lecturer in Law, Cambridge 1946–51; Prof. of Jurisprudence, Aberdeen 1951–55; Regius Prof. of Civil Law, Oxford, and Fellow of All Souls Coll. 1955–74, Emer. Regius Prof. 1970–, Emer. Fellow 1980; Dir. Robbins Hebraic and Roman Law Collections and Prof.-in-Residence, School of Law, Univ. of Calif., Berkeley 1970–80, Emer. 1981–; mem. Academic Bd., Inst. of Jewish Studies, London 1953–; Sr. Fellow, Yale Univ. 1962; Gifford Lecturer, Edin. 1962, 1963; Olaos Petrie lecturer at Uppsala Univ. 1963; Ford Prof. of Political Science, Univ. of Calif., Berkeley 1964; Riddell Lecturer, Newcastle 1965; Gray Lecturer, Cambridge 1966; Pope John XXIII lecturer, Catholic Univ. of America, Wash. 1966, Lionel Cohen lecturer, Jerusalem 1970; Messenger Lecturer, Cornell Univ. 1971; Visiting Prof., Univ. of Constance 1966–78, Hon. Prof. 1980–; Charles Inglis Romson Prof. of Law, Univ. Colorado 1974; Fellow, British Acad., American and World Acad. of Arts and Sciences, American Acad. of Jewish Research; Pres. Soc. Int. des Droits de l'Antiquité 1957; Pres. Classical Asscn. of G.B. 1976–77, Jewish Law Asscn. 1983–85; Hon. Fellow, Oxford Univ. Centre for Postgraduate Hebrew Studies 1973, Gonville and Caius Coll., Cambridge 1974, American Soc. for Legal History; Founder-Pres. Oxford B'nai B'rith 1961; Corresp. mem. Göttingen and Bavarian Acads. of Sciences, Royal Irish Acad.; Hon. LL.D. (Edinburgh, Leicester, Cambridge and Aberdeen); Dr. h.c. (Paris, Sorbonne, Munich); Hon. D.H.L. (Hebrew Union Coll.); Dr. Phil. h.c. (Göttingen); Grad. Theological Union, Berkeley. *Publications:* Studies in Biblical Law 1947, The New Testament and Rabbinic Judaism 1956, Forms of Roman Legislation 1956, The Exodus Pattern in the Bible 1963, The Sudden in the Scriptures 1964, Collaboration with Tyranny in Rabbinic Law 1965, Roman Law 1969, Civil Disobedience in Antiquity 1972, Duty of Procreation 1977, Typologie im Werk des Flavius Josephus 1977, Ancient Jewish Law 1981, Ursprung der Detektivgeschichte 1983, Sons and Strangers 1984, Das Alte Testament im Neuen 1984, Witnesses in Bible and Talmud (with C. Carmichael) 1986, Appeasement or Resistance and other essays on New Testament Judaism 1987; Festschriften: Daube Noster (Ed. A. Watson) 1974, Studies in Jewish Legal History (Ed. B. S. Jackson) 1974, Donum Gentilicium (Ed. E. Bammel, C. K. Barrett and W. D. Davies) 1978. *Address:* School of Law, University of California, Berkeley, CA 94720, U.S.A.

DÄUBLER-GMELIN, Herta, DR.JUR.; German politician; b. 12 Aug. 1943, Bratislava, Slovakia; m. Wolfgang Däubler 1969; one s. one d.; ed. Univs. of Tübingen and Berlin; mem. Social Democratic Party of Germany (SPD) 1965–, Chair. Tübingen Dist. br. 1971–72, State Chair. Asscn. of Social Democrat Women Baden-Württemberg 1971–76, mem. State Exec. Baden-Württemburg, elected to Fed. Exec. Cttee. 1979, Deputy Chair. Bundestag Parl. Group 1983, 1991–93, elected mem. Party Presidium 1984, 1997, Deputy Chair. 1988–, legal adviser to Parl. Group 1994, elected to Party Exec. Cttee. 1997; Fed. Minister of Justice 1998–; Chair. working group on Equality for Women 1983, Bundestag Legal Affairs Cttee. 1980–83, Legal Policy Working Group 1994; Dr. h.c. (Freie Univ. Berlin). *Publications:* numerous books, articles in political journals and newspapers. *Address:* Ministry of Justice, Heinemannstrasse 6, 53175 Bonn; Geierweg 20, 72114 Dusslingen, Germany. *Telephone:* (228) 580 (Bonn). *Fax:* (228) 58-45-25 (Bonn).

DAUD, Datuk Dr. Sulaiman bin Haj, B.D.S.; Malaysian politician; b. 4 March 1933, Kuching, Sarawak; m.; four c.; ed. Otago Univ., New Zealand and Univ. of Toronto; teacher 1954–56; Dental Officer, State Govt. of Sarawak 1963–68; State Dental Officer, Brunei 1971; Political Sec. Ministry of Primary Industries 1972; Minister for Land and Mineral Resources, Sarawak 1973–74; mem. Parl. 1974–; Deputy Minister of Land Devt. 1974–75, of Land and Mines 1975–76, of Land and Regional Devt. 1976–77, of Health 1978–81; Minister of Fed. Territory March 1981; Minister of Educ. July 1981, of Sport, Youth and Culture 1984–86, of Land and Regional Devt. 1986–89; Minister in the Prime Minister's Dept. 1989–90; Vice-Pres. Party Pesaka Bumiputra Bersatu, Sarawak; other public appts. and leader of Malaysian dels. to int. confs.; Johan Bintang Sarawak; Panglima Negara

Nintang Sarawak. *Address:* c/o Parti Pesaka Bumiputra Bersatu, Jalan Satok/Kulas, 93400 Kuching, Sarawak, Malaysia.

DAUDISS, Imants; Latvian politician; b. 15 Aug. 1945, Riga; m.; one d.; ed. Ivanovo Inst. of Chem. Eng.; Head of lab., Riga Chem. Eng. plant 1968–70; Head of Dept., Sec., Riga Comsomol City Cttee. 1970–76; Sec. Riga Dist. CP Cttee. 1976–80; First Deputy Chair. State Publishing, Printing and Book Sale Cttee. 1980–86; Sec., head of dept. Riga City CP Cttee. 1986–89; Sec. of Presidium, Supreme Soviet Latvian S.S.R. 1989–90; Sec. Supreme Council Latvian Repub. 1989–93; Sec. Saeima (Parl.) 1993–97; Amb. to Russia 1998–. *Address:* Latvian Embassy, Chaplygina str. 3, 103062 Moscow, Russia. *Telephone:* (095) 925 0052. *Fax:* (095) 923 2525.

DAUGNY, Bertrand, L.ÈS SC.; French business executive and engineer; b. 5 Jan. 1925, Paris; s. of Pierre-Marie Daugny and Suzanne Hauser; m. 1st Nicole Wolff (deceased); one s. one d.; m. 2nd Elisabeth Joussellin 1958; two d.; ed. Faculté des Sciences, Paris, and Ecole Supérieure d'Electricité; engineer, later Head of Dept. Cie. Française Thomson-Houston 1948–54; founder, Electronic Dept., Avions Marcel Dassault 1954; Admin. Deputy and Man. Dir. Electronique Marcel Dassault (now Dassault Electronique) 1963, Admin. and Man. Dir. 1967, Vice-Chair. and Man. Dir. Electronique Serge Dassault 1983–86; Chair. and C.E.O. Dassault Electronique 1986–; mem. Bd. of Dirs. Dassault Industries 1990, Dassault Aviation 1991, Dassault Automatismes et Télécommunications 1991; Commdr. Légion d'honneur; Médaille Militaire; Chevalier Ordre nat. du Mérite; Croix de Guerre, Médaille Aéronautique. *Address:* Dassault Electronique, 55 quai Marcel Dassault, 92210 Saint-Cloud, France. *Telephone:* (1) 49.11.80.00.

DAUSSET, Jean Baptiste Gabriel, M.D.; French doctor; b. 19 Oct. 1916, Toulouse; s. of Henri Pierre Jules Dausset and Elisabeth Brullard; m. Rosa Mayoral Lopez 1962; one s. one d.; ed. Lycée Michelet, Faculty of Medicine, Paris; internship, Paris hosps. 1941; Asst. Faculty of Medicine, Univ. of Paris 1946; Dir. Lab., Nat. Blood Transfusion Cen. 1950–63; Chief, Immunohaematology Lab., Inst. de Recherches sur les Leucémies et les Maladies du Sang, Paris 1961; Chief Biologist Service d'Hématologie-Serologie-Immunologie, Hôpital Saint-Louis, Paris 1963; Dir. of Research Unit on Immunogenetics of Human Transplantation, of Inst. Nat. de la Santé et la Recherche Médicale 1968–84; Prof. of Immunohaematology, Head Dept., Faculty of Medicine, Univ. of Paris 1968–77; Prof. of Experimental Medicine, Collège de France 1978–87; mem. French Acads. of Science and Medicine 1977–87; Dir. Human Polymorphism Study Center 1984–; mem. N.A.S., Washington 1980; shared Nobel Prize for Physiology and Medicine 1980 with Dr. Baruj Benacerraf (q.v.) and Dr. George Snell for work on histocompatibility antigens; Honda Prize 1987; Grand Croix Légion d'honneur, Commdr. des Palmes Academiques, Grand Croix Ordre Nat. du Mérite; numerous other awards. *Publications:* Immuno-hématologie biologique et clinique 1956, numerous articles. *Leisure interest:* modern art. *Address:* CEPH, 27/29 rue Juliette Dodu, 75010 Paris (Office); 9 rue de Villersexel, 75007 Paris, France (Home). *Telephone:* 42-49-98-50 (Office); 42-22-18-82 (Home).

DAUZIER, Pierre Marie, B.A., LL.B.; French advertising executive; b. 31 Jan. 1939, Périgueux; s. of late Maurice Dauzier and of Marie Faucher; m. Erle Fleischmann 1968; one s. one d.; ed. Ecole Bossuet, Lycée Henri IV, Univs. of Clermont-Ferrand and Paris and Inst. of Higher Advertising Studies; Account Exec. Havas Conseil (Advertising Agency) 1963–65, Sr. Account Exec. 1965–66, Head, Commercial Dept. 1966–68, Man. 1968–70, Gen. Man. 1972–75, Chair. Supervisory Bd. 1975–79, Chair. of Man. Bd. of Dirs. 1979, Chair. and C.E.O. 1982, Hon. Pres. 1982–86; Man. Rep. at Needham Harper & Steers, New York 1970–72, Gen. Man. 1972–75, Pres. and C.E.O. Univas 1975–79, Chair. and C.E.O. 1980–82; Gen. Man. Havas 1982–86, Chair. and C.E.O. 1986–98; Chair. and C.E.O. Information & Publicité 1986–93; Chair. and C.E.O. Eurocom 1988–89, CLMM (Cie. Luxembourgeoise Multi Média) 1994–97; Deputy Chair. Supervisory Bd. ODA 1994; Chevalier, Ordre Nat. du Mérite; Officier Légion d'honneur. *Publications include:* Le Marketing de l'apocalypse 1998. *Address:* 68 rue du Faubourg Saint-Antoine, 75012 Paris, France (Office).

DAVAR, Dharmendar Nath, M.A., B. COM., S.A.S., C.A.I.I.B.; Indian financial official; b. 8 Aug. 1934; s. of Daryai Lal and Smt. Bhagwanti; m. Santash Dawar 1960; one s. one d.; Man., Sr. Man. at various branches and head office of Punjab Nat. Bank 1960–68; Man. Industrial Finance Corpn. of India 1968–74, Gen. Man. 1980–82, Exec. Dir. 1982–84; Chair. 1984–95; Fellow, Econ. Devt. Inst. of IBRD; mem. Bd. of Govs., Man. Devt. Inst.; mem. Advisory Council, Devt. Banking Centre; Trustee Risk Capital Foundation, mem. Bd., Industrial Devt. Bank of India, Industrial Reconstruction Corpn. of India, Int. Devt. Inst. of India. *Address:* Industrial Finance Corporation of India, Bank of Baroda Building, 16 Sansad Marg, Post Box No. 363, New Delhi 110001, India. *Telephone:* (11) 2027012 (Office); 606757 (Home).

DAVENPORT, (Arthur) Nigel, M.A.; British actor; b. 23 May 1928, Shelford, Cambridge; s. of Arthur H. Davenport and Katherine L. Meiklejohn; m. 1st Helena White 1951 (deceased); one s. one d.; m. 2nd Maria Aitken 1972 (divorced); one s.; ed Cheltenham Coll. and Trinity Coll. Oxford; entered theatrical profession and worked mainly in theatre 1951–61; since 1961 has starred in more than 30 films, notably High Wind in Jamaica 1964, Man for All Seasons 1966, Play Dirty, Virgin Soldiers, Villain, No Blade of Grass, Nighthawks, Chariots of Fire, Greystoke, Caravaggio, Hotel Shanghai; frequent TV appearances; Pres. British Actors Equity Assn. 1986–92. *Leisure interests:* gardening, travel.

DAVENPORT, Paul Theodore, PH.D.; Canadian university president; b. 24 Dec. 1946, Summit, N.J.; s. of Theodore Davenport and Charlotte Lomax Paul; m. Josette Brotons 1969; one s. two d.; ed. Stanford Univ. and Univ. of Toronto; Assoc. then full Prof. Dept. of Econs. McGill Univ. 1973; Assoc. Dean, Faculty of Grad. Studies and Research, McGill Univ. 1982–86; Vice-Prin. (Planning and Computer Services), McGill Univ. 1986–89; Pres., Vice-Chancellor Univ. of Alberta 1989–94, Univ. of Western Ont. 1994–; Chair. Asscn. of Univs. and Colleges of Canada, Council of Ontario Univs. *Publication:* Reshaping Confederation: The 1982 Reform of the Canadian Constitution (ed. with R. Leach) 1984. *Leisure interests:* biking, Impressionist painting, modern jazz, photography. *Address:* Office of the President, Stevenson-Lawson Building, University of Western Ontario, London, Ont., N6A 5B8 (Office); 1836 Richmond Street, London, Ont., N6A 4B6, Canada (Home). *Telephone:* (519) 661-3106 (Office); (519) 660-0178 (Home). *Fax:* (519) 661-3139.

DAVEY, Grenville, B.A.; British sculptor and artist; b. 28 April 1961, Launceston, Cornwall; ed. Exeter Coll., Goldsmith's Coll., London; one-man exhbns. include: Lisson Gallery, London 1987, Primo Piano, Rome 1989, Stichting De Appel Foundation, Amsterdam 1990, Galerie Crousel-Robelin Bama, Paris 1991, Galleria Franz Paludetto, Turin 1992, Chisenhale Gallery, London 1992, Château Rochechouart and Crypt, Limoges 1993, Henry Moore Foundation 1994, Museum of Modern Art, Vienna 1996, Kunstverein, Hanover 1996; Group exhbns. include: Centre Nat. d'Art Contemporain de Grenoble 1988, Fondation Cartier, Paris 1989, Galeria Grita Insam, Vienna 1989, Nat. Museum of Modern Art, Tokyo 1989–90, Leeds City Art Gallery 1990, Hayward Gallery, London 1990, Fundacio Caixa de Pensions, Barcelona 1991, Palacio Velázquez, Madrid 1991–92, Whitechapel Art Gallery, London 1992, Tate Gallery, London 1992, Killerton House, Exeter 1993; Turner Prize (Tate Gallery) 1992. *Leisure interest:* work. *Address:* Lisson Gallery, 67 Lisson Street, London, NW1 5DA, England.

DAVEY, Kenneth George, O.C., PH.D., F.R.S.C.; Canadian professor, scientist and educator; b. 20 April 1932, Chatham, Ont.; s. of William Davey and Marguerite (Clark) Davey; m. Jeannette Isabel Evans 1959 (separated 1989); one s. two d.; ed. McKeough Public School, Chatham, Chatham Collegiate Inst., Univ. of Western Ontario, Cambridge Univ.; N.R.C. Fellow (Zoology), Univ. of Toronto 1958–59; Drosier Fellow, Gonville and Caius Coll., Cambridge 1959–63; Assoc. Prof. of Parasitology, McGill Univ., Montreal 1963–66, Dir. Inst. of Parasitology 1964–74, Prof. of Parasitology and Biology 1966–74; Prof. of Biology, York Univ., Toronto 1974–, Chair. of Biology 1974–81, Dean of Science 1982–85, Distinguished Research Prof. of Biology 1984–, Vice-Pres. (Academic Affairs) 1986–91; Ed. Int. Journal of Invertebrate Reproduction and Devt. 1979–85, Canadian Journal of Zoology 1995–; Assoc. Ed. Encyclopedia of Reproduction 1996–; mem. Bd. of Dirs. Huntsman Marine Lab. 1978–80, 1982–85, Pres. and Chair. of Bd. 1977–80; Pres. Biological Council of Canada 1979–82, Canadian Soc. of Zoologists 1981–82; Sec. Acad. of Science, Royal Soc. of Canada 1979–85; mem. Council, Royal Canadian Inst. 1996– (Vice-Pres. 1998–); Fellow Entomological Soc. of Canada, Gold Medal 1981, Fry Medal (Canadian Soc. of Zoologists) 1987, Gold Medal (Biological Council of Canada) 1987, Distinguished Biologist Award (Canadian Council of Univ. Biology Chairs) 1992. *Publications:* Reproduction in Insects 1964; 180 articles on insect endocrinology. *Leisure interests:* handweaving, food and wine. *Address:* 4700 Keele Street, Downsview, Ont., M3J 1P3; Department of Biology, York University, North York, Ont., M3J 1P3 (Office); 96 Holm Crescent, Thornhill, Ont., L3T 5J3, Canada (Home). *Telephone:* (416) 736-2100 (Office); (905) 882-5077 (Home). *Fax:* (416) 736-5698.

DAVID, Edward Emil, Jr., SC.D.; American scientist; b. 25 Jan. 1925, Wilmington, N.C.; s. of the late Edward Emil and Beatrice Liebman David; m. Ann Hirshberg 1950; one d.; ed. Georgia Inst. of Tech. and Mass. Inst. of Tech. (M.I.T.); joined Bell Telephone Labs. 1950; specialized in field of underwater sound and communication acoustics 1950–63, in research in computing science 1963–70; Science Adviser to Pres. Nixon and Dir. Office of Science and Tech. (Exec. Office of the Pres.) 1970–73; Exec. Vice-Pres. Gould Inc. 1973–77; Pres. Gould Labs. 1973–77, Edward E. David, Inc., Chicago, Ill. 1977, Bedminster, N.J. 1986–, Exxon Research and Eng. Co. 1977–86; Vice-Pres. Science and Tech., Exxon Corpn. 1978–80; Vice-Pres. Washington Advisory Group 1997–; fmr. U.S. Rep. to NATO Science Cttee.; mem. Bd. of Dirs. Int. Media Research Foundation, Lord Corpn., Intermagnetics Gen. Corpn., Protein Polymer Technologies Inc., Spacehab, Inc., On-Line Computer Library Center, InterVU, Aquasearch; Life-mem. Corpn., M.I.T.; Chair. Bd. of Trustees, Aerospace Corpn. 1975–81; mem. Bd. of Trustees, 20th Century Fund, Scientists' Inst. for Public Information, John Simon Guggenheim Memorial Foundation, Carnegie Inst., Washington; mem. N.A.S., American Asscn. for the Advancement of Science (Pres. 1977–78), Nat. Acad. of Eng.; Fellow, American Acad. of Arts and Sciences, Acoustical Soc. of America, Audio Eng. Soc., Inst. of Electrical and Electronics Engineers; hon. degrees, (Stevens Inst. of Tech., Polytechnic Inst. of Brooklyn, Carnegie-Mellon Univ., Univ. of Mich. etc.). *Publications:* Co-author of Man's World of Sound 1958, Waves and the Ear 1960, The Man-made World 1969; over 100 technical articles. *Leisure interests:* tennis, mineral collections, photography. *Address:* EED Inc., Box 435, Bedminster, NJ 07921, U.S.A. (Office). *Telephone:* 908-234-9319. *Fax:* 908-234-2956.

DAVID, George Alfred Lawrence, M.B.A.; American business executive; b. 7 April 1942, Bryn Mawr, Pa.; s. of Charles Wendell David and Margaret

Simpson; m. Barbara Osborn 1965; one s. two d.; ed. Harvard Univ. and Univ. of Virginia; Asst. Prof. Univ. of Va., Charlottesville 1967–68; Vice-Pres. Boston Consulting group 1968–75; Sr. Vice-Pres. (Corpn. Planning and Devt.) Otis Elevator Co. New York 1975–77, Sr. Vice-Pres. and Gen. Man. Latin American Operations, West Palm Beach, Fla. 1977–81, Pres. N. American Operations, Farmington, Conn. 1981–85, Pres. and C.E.O. Otis Elevator Co. 1985–89; Exec. Vice-Pres. and Pres. (Commercial/Industrial) United Technologies Corpn. (parent co.) 1989–92, Pres., C.O.O. 1992–, C.E.O. 1994–, Chair. 1997–. *Address:* United Technologies Corporation, United Technologies Building, Hartford, CT 06101, U.S.A.

DAVID, Jacques-Henri; French business executive; b. 17 Oct. 1943, Ygrande (Allier); s. of André David and Suzanne Dupeyrat; m. Isabelle Lamy 1967; one d.; ed. Lycée Louis-le-Grand, Paris, Ecole Polytechnique, Inst. d'Etudes Politiques, Paris and Ecole Nat. Supérieure de la Statistique et des Études Economiques (Insee), Paris; Admin. Insee 1967–68; Head, econometric studies service, Banque de France 1969–75; Deputy Sec.-Gen. Conseil Nat. du Crédit 1973–75; Prof. Inst. d'Etudes Politiques 1975; Insp. of Finance, Ministry of Econ. and Finance 1975–79; Adviser, Office of Minister of Econ. 1979, Deputy Dir. 1980, Dir. 1980–81; Sec.-Gen. Conseil Nat. du Crédit 1981–84; Finance Dir. Cie. Saint-Gobain 1984–86, Dir.-Gen. 1986–89; Pres. Banque Stern 1989–92; Pres. Centre de Recherche pour l'expansion de l'économie (Rexecode) 1989–96, Ipécode 1989; Dir.-Gen. Compagnie Gen. des Eaux 1993–95; Pres. CEPME 1995–, Sofaris 1996–, Bank for Devt. of Small and Medium-Sized Businesses 1997–; mem. Social and Econ. Council 1996–; Chevalier Légion d'honneur, Officier Ordre nat. du Mérite. *Publications:* La Politique monétaire 1974, Réévaluation et verité des bilans 1977, La Monnaie et la politique monétaire 1983, Crise financière et relations monétaires internationales 1985, Le Financement des opérations à risque dans les PME 1997. *Leisure interests:* piano, skiing, tennis, yachting. *Address:* Sofaris, 4 rue Cambon, 75008 Paris, France.

DAVIDOVICH, Bella; American (U.S.S.R. born) pianist; b. 16 July 1928, Baku, Azerbaijan; m. Julian Sitkovetsky 1950 (died 1958); one s.; ed. Moscow Conservatory; studied with Konstantin Igumnov and Jakob Flier; First Prize, Chopin Competition, Warsaw 1949; soloist with Leningrad Philharmonic for 28 consecutive seasons; toured Europe; went to U.S.A. 1978; mem. faculty Juilliard School of Music, N.Y. 1982–; became U.S. citizen 1984; has performed with world's leading conductors in U.S.A., Europe and Japan; recordings for Philips and Orfeo; Prof., Juilliard School of Music; Deserving Artist of the Soviet Union. *Address:* c/o Columbia Artists Management, Sheldon Division, 165 West 57th Street, New York, NY 10019, U.S.A. *Telephone:* (212) 315-2430.

DAVIDSON, Basil; British historian; b. 9 Nov. 1914, Bristol; m. Marion Ruth Young 1943; three s.; served British Army 1940–45, Lieut.-Col. 1945; journalist with The Economist, The Star, The Times, New Statesman, Daily Herald, Daily Mirror, 1938–62; Visiting Prof. in African History, Univ. of Ghana 1964, Univ. of Calif., L.A. (UCLA) 1965; Regent's Lecturer in African History, UCLA 1971; Montague Burton Visiting Prof. of Int. Relations, Univ. of Edin. 1972; Hon. Research Fellow, Univ. of Birmingham 1974; Simon Sr. Research Fellow, Univ. of Manchester 1975–76; Agnelli Visiting Prof., Univ. of Turin 1990; Hon. Fellow, S.O.A.S. (Univ. of London) 1989; Hon. D.Litt. (Univ. of Ibadan) 1975, (Dar es Salaam) 1985, (Univ. of Western Cape, S.A.) 1997; Hon. D.Univ. (Open Univ.) 1980, (Edin.) 1981; Mil. Cross; Bronze Star, U.S. Army; Zasluge za Narod, Yugoslav Army; Freeman City of Genoa 1945; Haile Selassie Award for African Research 1970; Medalha Amílcar Cabral 1976. *Publications:* principal works: Old Africa Rediscovered 1959, Black Mother—The African Slave Trade 1961 (revised 1980), The African Past 1964, History of West Africa to 1800 1965, History of East and Central Africa to the Late Nineteenth Century 1967, Africa in History: Themes and Outlines 1967, The Africans: A Cultural History 1969, The Liberation of Guiné 1969 (revised 1981), In the Eye of the Storm: Angola's People 1972, Black Star 1973, Can Africa Survive? 1975, Africa in Modern History, The Search for a New Society 1978, Special Operations Europe—Scenes from the anti-Nazi War 1980, The People's Cause: A History of Guerrillas in Africa 1981, Modern Africa 1982, Africa (TV series) 1984, The Story of Africa 1984, The Fortunate Isles 1988, The Black Man's Burden 1992, The Search for Africa—History, Politics, Culture 1994. *Leisure interests:* planting trees, watching wild birds. *Address:* Old Cider Mill, North Wootton, Somerset, BA4 4HA, England.

DAVIDSON, Donald, PH.D.; American professor of philosophy; b. 6 March 1917, Springfield, Mass.; s. of Clarence H. Davidson and Grace C. Anthony; m. 2nd Marcia Cavell 1984; one d.; ed. Harvard Univ.; Asst. in Philosophy, Harvard Univ. 1941–42, 1946; Instructor, Queen's Coll., New York 1947–50; Asst. Prof., Stanford Univ. 1951–56, Assoc. Prof. 1956–60, Prof., 1960–67; Prof., Princeton Univ. 1967–70, lecturer with the rank of Prof. 1970–75; Prof. Rockefeller Univ. 1970–76; Univ. Prof., Univ. of Chicago 1976–81; Prof. Univ. of Calif., Berkeley 1981–, Willis S. Marion Slusser Prof. of Philosophy 1986; numerous visiting professorships; Ed. Synthese Library 1966–; Consulting Ed. Behaviorism 1972–, Philosophia 1970–, Dialectica 1982–, The Thoreau Quarterly 1986–; mem. American Philosophical Asscn., Pres. 1985–86; mem. American Acad. of Arts and Sciences, Inst. Int. de Philosophie, American Philosophical Soc., Norwegian Acad. of Science and Letters; Corresp. Fellow, British Acad.; F.A.A.A.; Hon. D.Litt. (Oxford) 1995; Hegel Prize 1991. *Publications include:* Decision-Making: An Experimental Approach (with Patrick Suppes) 1957, Reasons and Causes 1963, Essays on Actions and Events 1982, Inquiries into Truth and Interpretation 1984, Plato's Philebus 1990, Structure and Content of Truth 1990, numerous essays and articles in philosophical journals. *Leisure interests:* gliding, skiing, music. *Address:* Department of Philosophy, University of California, Berkeley, CA 94720, U.S.A. *Telephone:* (415) 642-2722 (Office).

DAVIDSON, Inger; Swedish politician; m.; three c.; school teacher 1969–87; Political Sec. Christian Democratic Party 1987–88, Party Sec. 1989–91, mem. Bd. and Exec. Cttee., Vice-Chair. County of Stockholm Dist. Bd.; Minister of Public Admin. 1991–94; mem. Parochial Church Council. *Leisure interests:* travelling, reading. *Address:* c/o Kristdemokraterna, Målargt. 7, P.O. Box 451, 101 29 Stockholm, Sweden.

DAVIDSON, Janet Marjorie, O.N.Z.M., M.A., D.SC., F.R.S.N.Z.; New Zealand archaeologist and ethnologist; b. 23 Aug. 1941, Lower Hutt; m. Bryan Foss Leach 1979; one d.; ed. Hutt Valley High School and Univ. of Auckland; Field Assoc. Bernice P. Bishop Museum, Honolulu 1964–66; E. Earle Vaile Archaeologist Auckland Inst. and Museum 1966–79; Hon. lecturer in Anthropology, Univ. of Otago 1980–86; ethnologist Nat. Museum of New Zealand 1987–91; Curator (Pacific) Museum of New Zealand Te Papa Tongarewa 1991–; extensive archaeological field work in New Zealand and the Pacific; Rhodes Visiting Fellow, Lady Margaret Hall, Oxford 1974–76. *Publications:* Archaeology on Nukuaro Atoll 1971, The Prehistory of New Zealand 1984, numerous articles on the archaeology and prehistory of New Zealand and various Pacific Islands. *Leisure interests:* music, theatre, opera, ballet, cooking. *Address:* Museum of New Zealand, Cable Street, Box 467, Wellington 1 (Office); 5 Hillview Crescent, Paparangi, Wellington 4, New Zealand (Home).

DAVIDSON, John Macdonald, A.M., B.ARCH., L.F.R.A.I.A., R.I.B.A.; Australian architect; b. 21 Oct. 1926, Sydney; s. of the late John H. Davidson and of Daisy Macdonald; m. Helen M. King 1954; two s. one d.; ed. Geelong Coll. and Univ of Melbourne; Assoc. Godfrey and Spowers (architects) 1954–61, Partner, later Dir. 1961, Chair. Godfrey and Spowers Australia Pty. Ltd. 1979–91; Pres. Royal Australian Inst. of Architects 1978–79; mem. Expert Panel in Arch. (COPQ) 1978–; mem. Int. Council, Int. Union of Architects (UIA) 1981–85, Vice-Pres. UIA 1985–87; Chair. Metropolitan Strategy Consultative Cttee. 1984–89, South Yarra Collaborative Pty. Ltd. 1983–89; Partner, Catalyst Design Group 1992–; Hon. Fellow American Inst. of Architects. *Publication:* The Awarding and Administration of Architectural Contracts 1961. *Leisure Interests:* music, art, writing, fly fishing. *Address:* 4/6 Lennox Street, Hawthorn, Vic. 3122; 252 Church Street, Richmond, Vic. 3121, Australia. *Telephone:* (03) 9428 6352. *Fax:* (03) 9428 6897.

DAVIDSON, Norman Ralph, PH.D.; American professor of molecular biology; b. 5 April 1916, Chicago, Ill.; s. of Bernard R. Davidson and Rose Lefstein; m. Annemarie Behrendt 1942; three s. one d.; ed. Univ. of Chicago and Oxford Univ.; Prof. of Chem., Calif. Inst. of Tech. 1957–82, Chandler Prof. of Chemical Biology 1982–86, Prof. Emer. 1986–, Interim Chair. Biology 1990, Exec. Officer Biology 1990; Sr. Consultant Amgen 1992–; mem. N.A.S. *Publications:* Statistical Mechanics 1962, and numerous scientific articles. *Address:* Division of Biology, 154-29, California Institute of Technology, 156–29 Pasadena, CA 91125 (Office); 318 East Laurel Avenue, Sierra Madre, CA 91024, U.S.A. (Home). *Telephone:* (818) 395-6055 (Office); (818) 355-1969 (Home).

DAVIDSON, Ralph P.; American magazine publisher; b. 17 Aug. 1927, Santa Fe, N.M.; s. of William Clarence and Doris Parsons Davidson; m. Jeanne Skidmore 1951 (divorced); two s.; ed. Stanford Univ.; with CIA 1952–54; Advertising Salesman Life Magazine 1954–56; European Advertising Dir. Time Magazine, London 1956–62; European Advertising Dir. Time-Life Int., London 1964, Man. Dir. Time-Life Int., New York 1967–78; Asst. Publr. Time 1968, Assoc. Publr. 1969, Publr. 1972–78; Chair. Bd. Time Inc. 1972–88; Pres., C.E.O. Kennedy Center for Performing Arts, Washington 1988–90. *Leisure interests:* reading, tennis, skiing.

DAVID-WEILL, Michel; French banking executive; b. 23 Nov. 1932, Paris; s. of late Pierre David-Weill and of Berthe Haardt; m. Hélène Lehideux 1956; four d.; ed. Lycée français, New York and Inst. d'études politiques, Paris; Lazard Frères & Co. LLC, N.Y. 1961–65, Sr. Partner 1977–; Gen. Partner Lazard Frères & Cie., Paris 1965, Maison Lazard & Cie 1976–; Gen. Partner and Chair. Lazard Partners Ltd. Partnership 1984–; Chair. Lazard Brothers & Co. Ltd., London 1990–92, Deputy Chair. 1992; Chair. Eurafrance 1972–; mem. Man. Bd., Sovac 1972–, Chair. 1982–95; mem. Bd. of Dirs., Danone, later Vice-Chair.; mem. Man. Bd. Publicis; Dir. La France S.A., La France I.A.R.D., La France-Vie, La France Participations et Gestion, S.A. de la Rue Impériale de Lyon, Fonds Partenaires-Gestion (F.P.G.), Fiat S.p.A., Pearson PLC, Euralux, Exor Group, I.T.T. Corp., The Dannon Co., Inc.; Chair. Artistic Council, Réunion des Musées Nationaux, Paris, Metropolitan Museum Council, New York, New York Hosp. Morgan Library; mem. Inst. (Acad. des Beaux Arts, Paris); Officier, Légion d'honneur, Officier, Ordre Nat. du Mérite, Commdr. des Arts et des Lettres. *Address:* 121 boulevard Haussmann, 75008 Paris, France (Office); 30 Rockefeller Plaza, New York, NY 10020 (Office); Viking's Cove, Peacock Lane, Locust Valley, NY 11560, U.S.A. (Home).

DAVIE, Alan, C.B.E.; British painter, jazz musician and jeweller; b. 1920, Grangemouth, Stirlingshire; s. of James W. Davie and Elizabeth Turnbull; m. Janet Gaul 1947; one d.; ed. Edinburgh Coll. of Art; Gregory Fellowship,

Leeds Univ. 1956–59; first one-man exhbn. Edinburgh 1946; numerous one-man exhbns. in Europe and U.S.A. 1949–, at Gimpel Galleries in London, New York and Zürich 1949–98, ACA Gallery, New York 1993, 1997, Cohon Gallery, Chicago, Brighton Univ. 1993, FIAC, Paris 1994, 1995, Porto, Almada, Portugal 1994–95, Pallant House, Chichester, Mappin Gallery, Sheffield 1996, Inverness Gallery 1997, Art Fair, Nice 1997, Pier Arts Centre, Orkney 1998; rep. at Dunn Int. Exhbn., London 1963; Prize for the best foreign painter at his one-man exhbn. at the 7th Bienal de São Paulo, Brazil 1963; Gulbenkian Painting and Sculpture of a Decade Exhbn., Tate Gallery, London 1964; several exhbns. at the Salon de Mai; exhbn. Paintings 1956–88, touring Scotland, Helsingborg 1988; retrospective exhbns. Edinburgh Festival, R.S.A. Galleries 1972; exhbn. Tapestries, Paris 1977; Sr. Fellow R.C.A. Lectures Colour Conf. Bristol 1991; retrospective exhbn. McLellan Gallery Glasgow, Talbot Rice Gallery, Edin. 1992, British Council touring exhbn., Edin., Brussels, S. America 1992–95, Australia 1995–97; Kilkenny Castle, Ireland 1993, Barbican Gallery, London 1993, Chicago 1994; tapestry design executed by Tapestry Workshop, Vic., Australia, exhibited London 1995; retrospective exhbn. of drawings, Scottish Nat. Gallery of Modern Art, Brighton Univ. 1997, of oils and gouache, ACA Gallery, New York 1997, mixed exhbn. Pallant House, Chichester, Ricard Gallery, New York 1997, Scottish Art 1945–2000, Aberdeen, Dundee 1999; exhbn. Works on Paper, Faggionata Fine Arts Gallery, London 1998; Visiting Prof. Univ. of Brighton 1993–; first public music recital, Tate Gallery and Gimpel Fils, London 1971; four recordings 1972–86; music concerts 1972, concerts and broadcasts 1974; Hon. mem. Royal Scottish Acad. 1977; Hon. D.Litt. (Heriot-Watt) 1994, (Herts.) 1995; Saltire Award, Mosaic Scotland 1976. *Publications:* Monograph: Alan Davie 1992, The Quest for the Miraculous, Alan Davie 1993. *Leisure interests:* gliding, music, photography, underwater swimming. *Address:* Gamels Studio, Rush Green, Hertford, SG13 7SB, England. *Telephone:* (01920) 463684. *Fax:* (01920) 484406.

DAVIES, A. Michael, M.A., F.C.A.; British company director; b. 23 June 1934; s. of Angelo Henry Davies and Clarice Mildred Davies; m. Jane Priscilla Davies 1962; one s. (deceased) one d.; ed. Shrewsbury School, Queens' Coll., Cambridge; Chair. Tozer Kemsley & Millbourne 1982–86, Bredero Properties 1986–94, Worth Investment Trust 1987–95, Calor Group 1989–97 (Dir. 1987–97), Perkins Foods 1987–, Berk 1988–95, Wiltshier 1988–95, Nat. Express Group PLC, Simon Group 1993–; Deputy Chair. T.I. Group 1990–93 (Dir. 1984–93), Manpower 1987–91, AerFi 1993–; Dir. Imperial Group 1972–82, Littlewoods Org. 1982–88, TV-am 1982–88, British Airways 1983–, Worcester Group 1991–92. *Address:* Little Woolpit, Ewhurst, Cranleigh, Surrey, GU6 7NP; 7 Lowndes Close, London, S.W.1, England. *Telephone:* (01483) 277344.

DAVIES, David, B.A.; British designer; ed. Kingston Coll. of Art; with designer Stuart Baron launched own multi-disciplinary design consultancy David Davies Assocs. 1982, now Creative and Man. Dir. Davies/Baron; work includes retail and graphic identity for Next, creation of all brand identities for British Airways and int. store design for Valentino, Italy; consultant to many leading cos. including British Airways, Royal Bank of Scotland, Marks & Spencer, Mothercare, Malaysia Airlines, Sonae (Portugal), Coin (Italy), Austrian Airlines, Air N.Z.; has designed lines of clothing, furniture and products for the 'Davies' label; consultant to Marks & Spencer Home Furnishings; Channel 4 TV commission to create design series Eye to Eye. *Address:* Davies/Baron, 12 Goslett Yard, London, WC2H 0EE, England. *Telephone:* 0171-437 9070. *Fax:* 0171-734 0291.

DAVIES, Sir David E. N., Kt., C.B.E., PH.D., F.I.E.E., F.I.E.R.E., F.ENG., F.R.S.; British electrical engineer; b. 28 Oct. 1935, Cardiff; s. of D. E. Davies and Sarah Samuel; m. 1st Enid Patilla 1962 (died 1990); two s.; m. 2nd Jennifer E. Rayner 1992; ed. Univ. of Birmingham; Lecturer, then Sr. Lecturer in Electrical Eng., Univ. of Birmingham 1961–67; Asst. Dir. Research Dept., British Railways Bd. 1967–71; Visiting Industrial Prof. of Electrical Eng. Loughborough Univ. 1969–71; Prof. of Electrical Eng. Univ. Coll. London 1971–88, Pender Prof. of Electrical Eng. 1985–88, Vice-Provost Univ. Coll. 1986–88; Dir. Strategy Ltd. 1974–79, Gaydon Tech. 1986–88, Loughborough Consultants 1988–93, Inst. Consumer Ergonomics 1988–93; Vice-Chancellor Loughborough Univ. of Tech. 1988–93; Chief Scientific Adviser, Ministry of Defence 1993–; Chair. Defence Scientific Advisory Council 1992–93; Pres. Inst. of Electrical Engineers 1994–95; Vice-Pres. Royal Acad. of Eng. 1995–96, Pres. 1996–; Fellow Univ. of Wales, Coll. of Cardiff; Hon. D.Sc. (Birmingham) 1994, (Loughborough) 1994, (South Bank) 1994, (Bradford) 1995, (Surrey) 1996, (Warwick) 1997, (Bath) 1997; Rank Prize for Optoelectronics 1984; I.E.E.E. Centennial Medal 1984, I.E.E. Faraday Medal 1987 and other awards. *Publications:* about 120 publications on antennas, radar and fibre optics. *Address:* Ministry of Defence, Whitehall, London, SW1A 2HB, England. *Telephone:* 0171-218 6588. *Fax:* 0171-218 6552.

DAVIES, David Reginald, D.PHIL.; American X-ray crystallographer and researcher; b. 22 Feb. 1927, Camarthen, Wales; s. of Theophilus Howel Davies and Gwladys Evelyn Evans (Hodges) Davies; m. 1st Cynthia Margaret Seaman 1951 (divorced 1981); two d.; m. 2nd Monica Walters 1985; ed. Magdalen Coll., Oxford, England, California Inst. of Tech., Pasadena, U.S.A.; Research Assoc., Albright & Wilson Ltd., Birmingham, England 1954–55; Visiting Scientist Nat. Insts. of Health, Bethesda, Md., U.S.A. 1955–61, Chief, Section on Molecular Structure 1961–; Visiting Scientist, MRC Lab. Molecular Biology 1963–64; mem. Study Section on Molecular Biology, Nat. Science Foundation 1969–77; mem. American Acad. of Arts and Sciences, N.A.S., American Soc. of Biological Chemists, American Crystallographic Asscn., Biophysical Soc. (Council 1960–65, 1973–78); Presidential Meritorious Exec. Award 1982, Presidential Rank Award 1988. *Publications:* articles in scientific journals. *Leisure interests:* tennis, sailing. *Address:* National Institutes of Health, NIDDK, Laboratory of Molecular Biology, 9000 Rockville Pike, Bethesda, MD 20892; 4224 Franklin Street, Kensington, MD 20895, U.S.A. (Home). *Telephone:* (301) 496-4295 (Office).

DAVIES, Emrys, C.M.G.; British diplomatist (retd.); b. 8 Oct. 1934, London; s. of Evan Davies and Dinah Davies; m. Angela May 1960; one s. two d.; ed. Parmiter's Foundation School, London, Univs. of Tours and Grenoble, France, School of Slavonic Studies, Cambridge Univ., School of Oriental and African Studies, London Univ.; served in R.A.F. 1953–55; joined H.M. Diplomatic Service 1955, Attaché, Chargé d'Affaires Office, Peking 1956–59, Northern Dept. (Soviet and E. European Affairs), FCO 1959–60, Third Sec. British Political Residency, Bahrain 1960–62, mem. U.K. Del. UN Gen. Ass. (Econ. Cttee.) 1962, Desk Officer, Econ. Affairs, UN Dept., FCO 1962–63, Asst. Political Adviser Govt. of Hong Kong 1963–68, First Sec. (Political), High Comm., Ottawa 1968–72, Asst. Head N. American Dept., FCO 1972–74, Asst. Head Financial Relations Dept., FCO 1974–76, Commercial Counsellor, Embassy Peking (Chargé 1976 and 1978) 1976–78, NATO Defense Coll. Rome 1979, Deputy High Commr. Ottawa 1979–82, Overseas Inspector H.M. Diplomatic Service 1982–84, Deputy Head U.K. Del. (and Counsellor Econ. and Financial Affairs) OECD Paris 1984–87, Amb. to Vietnam 1987–90, High Commr. in Barbados, Grenada, St. Vincent, St. Lucia, Dominica, Antigua and St. Kitts 1990–94; Head U.K. Del. to EC Monitor Mission to fmr. Yugoslavia, Zagreb 1995, Sarajevo 1998–99; Sec.-Gen. Tripartite Comm. for Restitution of Monetary Gold, Brussels 1995–98. *Leisure interests:* golf, visual arts, walking, reading. *Address:* Taringa, 1 Bloomfield Park, Bath, BA2 2BY, England.

DAVIES, Gavyn, O.B.E., B.A.; British economist; b. 27 Nov. 1950; s. of W. J. F. Davies and M. G. Davies; m. Susan Jane Nye 1989; two s. one d.; ed. St. John's Coll., Cambridge and Balliol Coll., Oxford; Econ. Adviser, Policy Unit, 10 Downing Street 1974–79; economist Phillips and Drew 1979–81; Chief U.K. Economist Simon & Coates 1981–86, Goldman Sachs 1986–93, partner 1988–, Head of Investment Research (London) 1991–93, Chief Int. Economist and Head of European Investment Research 1993–97; Visiting Prof. of Econs. L.S.E. 1988–; Prin. Econs. commentator, The Independent 1991–; mem. H.M. Treasury's Ind. Forecasting Panel 1993–; Hon. D.Sc.S. (Southampton) 1998. *Leisure interest:* Southampton Football Club. *Address:* Peterborough Court, 133 Fleet Street, London, EC4A 2BB, England. *Telephone:* 0171-774 1161.

DAVIES, Sir Graeme John, Kt., F.ENG., F.R.S.E., M.A., SC.D., B.E., PH.D.; British university vice-chancellor; b. 7 April 1937, New Zealand; s. of Harry J. Davies and Gladys E. Davies; m. Florence I. Martin 1959; one s. one d.; ed. Univ. of Auckland; lecturer Univ. of Cambridge 1962–77, Fellow, St. Catharine's Coll. 1967–77; Prof. Dept. of Metallurgy, Univ. of Sheffield 1978–86; Vice-Chancellor, Univ. of Liverpool 1986–91; Chief Exec. Univs. Funding Council 1991–93, Polytechnics and Colleges Funding Council 1992–93, Higher Educ. Funding Council for England 1992–95; Prin., Vice-Chancellor Univ. of Glasgow 1995–; Hon. Fellow Royal Soc. of N.Z.; Freeman City of London, Freeman and Burgess Holder City of Glasgow; Hon. D.Sc. (Nottingham) 1995; Hon. D.Met. (Sheffield) 1995; Hon. LL.D. (Liverpool) 1991; Hon. D.Eng. (Manchester Metropolitan) 1996. *Publications:* Solidification and Casting 1973, Textures and Properties of Materials 1976, Hot Working and Forming Processes 1980, Superplasticity 1981, Essential Metallurgy for Engineers 1985. *Leisure interests:* cricket, birdwatching. *Address:* The Principal's Lodging, University of Glasgow, Glasgow, G12 8QQ, Scotland.

DAVIES, Howard John, M.A., M.S.; British administrative official; b. 12 Feb. 1951; s. of Leslie Davies and Marjorie Davies; m. Prudence Keely 1984; two s.; ed. Manchester Grammar School, Merton Coll. Oxford and Stanford Grad. School of Business; Foreign Office 1973–74; Pvt. Sec. to British Amb. in Paris 1974–76; H.M. Treasury 1976–82; McKinsey & Co. Inc. 1982–87; Controller, Audit Comm. 1987–92; Dir. GKN PLC 1990–95; numerous other directorships; Dir.-Gen. Confed. of British Industry (CBI) 1992–95; Deputy Governor Bank of England 1995–97; Chair. Financial Services Authority (fmrly. Securities and Investments Bd.) 1997–; Dir. (non-exec.) Bank of England 1998–; mem. NatWest Int. Advisory Bd. 1992–95; Pres. Age Concern England 1994–. *Leisure interests:* cricket, writing for publication. *Address:* c/o Financial Services Authority, 25 The North Colonnade, Canary Wharf, London, E14 5HS, England.

DAVIES, John Arthur, M.A., PH.D., F.R.S.C.; Canadian research scientist; b. 28 March 1927, Prestatyn, Wales; s. of Francis J. Davies and Doris A. Edkins; m. Florence Smithson 1950; three s. three d.; ed. St. Michael's Coll. High School and Univ. of Toronto; Asst., later Assoc. Research Officer, Atomic Energy of Canada 1950–65, Sr. Research Officer 1965–70, Prin. Research Officer 1970–85; Part-time Prof. of Eng. Physics, McMaster Univ. 1970–92, Dir. McMaster Accelerator Lab. 1989–92, Prof. Emer. 1992–; Adjunct Prof., Dept. of Electrical Eng, Univ. of Salford (U.K.) 1972–92; Visiting Prof., Nobel Inst. of Physics, Stockholm, Sweden 1962, Univ. of Aarhus, Denmark 1964–65, 1969–70, 1994, Univ. of Osaka, Japan 1972; mem. Royal Danish Acad. of Arts and Sciences, Böhmische Physical Soc., Chemical Inst. of Canada; D.Sc. h.c. (Royal Roads Mil. Coll.) 1984, (Univ. of

Salford) 1993; Noranda Award (Chem. Inst. of Canada) 1965; First T. D. Callinan Award (Electrochem. Soc.) 1968, W. B. Lewis Medal 1998. *Publications:* co-author of over 250 research articles and five books in the fields of ion implantation, ion channelling and ion beam analysis. *Leisure interests:* canoeing, cross-country skiing. *Address:* Box 224, 7 Wolfe Avenue, Deep River, Ont., K0J 1P0, Canada.

DAVIES, John Thomas, F.C.I.B.; British banker (retd.); b. 9 Feb. 1933; s. of Joseph Robert Davies and Dorothy Mary Davies; m. Margaret Ann Johnson 1957; two s. three d.; ed. King Edward's Grammar School, Birmingham; joined Lloyds Bank 1949, brs. Man. 1963–78, Gen. Man. 1978–89, Dir. Int. Banking Div. 1989–91, Dir. 1990–98, Asst. Chief Exec. 1991–92, Deputy Chief Exec. 1992–94, Deputy Chair. 1995–98, Deputy Chair. Lloyds TSB Group PLC 1995–98; Deputy Chair. TSB Bank PLC 1995–98; served R.A.F. 1951–53. *Leisure interests:* gardening, reading, walking. *Address:* Lloyds Bank PLC, 71 Lombard Street, EC3P 3BS, England.

DAVIES, Jonathan, M.B.E.; British rugby union player; b. 24 Oct. 1962; s. of the late Leonard Davies and of Diana Davies (née Rees); m. Karen Marie Davies 1984 (died 1997); two s. one d. Gwendraeth Grammar School; rugby union outside-half; played for the following rugby union clubs: Trimsaran, Neath, Llanelli; turned professional in 1989; with Cardiff 1995–97; played for Welsh nat. team (v. England) 1985, World Cup Squad (6 appearances) 1987, Triple Crown winning team 1988, tour N.Z. (2 test appearances) 1988, 29 caps, sometime Capt.; also played for Barbarians Rugby Football Club; rugby league career; played at three-quarters; Widnes (world record transfer fee) 1989, Warrington 1993–95 (free transfer); reverted to rugby union in 1995; Welsh nat. team; British nat. team, tour N.Z. 1990, 6 caps, fmr. Capt. *Publication:* Jonathan 1989. *Leisure interest:* any sport. *Address:* c/o Cardiff Rugby Football Club, Cardiff Arms Park, Westgate Street, Cardiff, Wales.

DAVIES, Kay Elizabeth, C.B.E., M.A., D.PHIL.; British geneticist; b. 1 April 1951, Stourbridge; d. of Harry Partridge and Florence Partridge; m. Stephen Graham Davies 1973; one s.; ed. Somerville Coll. Oxford; Guy Newton Jr. Research Fellow, Wolfson Coll. Oxford 1976–78; Royal Soc. European Postdoctoral Fellow, Service de Biochimie, Centre d'études nucléaires de Saclay, Gif-sur-Yvette, France 1978–80; Cystic Fibrosis Research Fellow, Biochem. Dept., St. Mary's Hosp. Medical School, London 1980–82, MRC Sr. Research Fellow, 1982–84; MRC Sr. Research Fellow, Nuffield Dept. of Clinical Medicine, John Radcliffe Hosp., Oxford 1984–86, MRC External Staff 1986–89, Molecular Genetics Group, Inst. of Molecular Medicine 1989–92, MRC Research Dir., Royal Postgrad. Medical School 1992–94, Head of Molecular Genetics Group, Inst. of Molecular Medicine 1994–95; Prof. of Molecular Genetics, Univ. of London 1992–94; Prof. of Genetics, Dept. of Biochem., Univ. of Oxford 1995–97; Dr. Lee's Prof. of Anatomy, Univ. of Oxford 1997–; Univ. Research Lecturer, Nuffield Dept. of Clinical Medicine, John Radcliffe Hosp. 1989–92; Fellow Green Coll. Oxford 1989–92, 1994–95; Fellow Keble Coll. Oxford 1995–; Fellow Hertford Coll. Oxford 1997–. *Publications:* numerous papers in scientific journals. *Leisure interests:* tennis, music, general keep-fit. *Address:* Department of Human Anatomy and Genetics, University of Oxford, South Parks Road, Oxford, OX1 3QX, England.

DAVIES, Laura, M.B.E.; British golfer; b. 5 Oct. 1963, Coventry; d. of David Thomas Davies and Rita Ann Davies (née Foskett); turned professional 1985; won Belgian Open 1985, British Women's Open 1986, U.S. Women's Open 1987, AGF Biarritz Open 1990, Wilkinson Sword English Open 1995, Irish Open 1995, French Masters 1995, LPGA Championship 1996, Danish Open 1997; rep. England in World Team Championship, Taiwan 1992, Europe in Solheim Cup 1990, 1992, 1994; Rookie of the Year 1985; Order of Merit winner 1985, 1986, 1992. *Leisure interest:* fast cars. *Address:* c/o Women's Professional Golf European Tour, The Tytherington Club, Dorchester Way, Tytherington, Macclesfield, SK10 2JP, England.

DAVIES, Sir Peter Maxwell, Kt., C.B.E., MUS.B., F.R.C.M., F.R.S.A.M.D.; British composer; b. 8 Sept. 1934, Manchester; s. of Thomas Davies and Hilda (née Howard) Davies; ed. Leigh Grammar School, Royal Manchester Coll. of Music, Manchester Univ.; studied with Goffredo Petrassi, Rome 1957 and with Roger Sessions, Milton Babbitt, Earl Kim, Princeton Univ., N.J., U.S.A. (Harkness Fellow) 1962–64; Dir. of Music, Cirencester Grammar School 1959–62; lecture tours in Europe, Australia, U.S.A., Canada, Brazil; Visiting Composer, Univ. of Adelaide 1966; Prof. of Composition, Royal Northern Coll. of Music, Manchester 1965–80 (Fellow 1978); Pres. Schools Music Asscn. 1983–, Composers' Guild of G.B. 1986–, Nat. Fed. of Music Socs. 1989–, Cheltenham Art Festival 1994–96, Soc. for Promotion of New Music 1995–; Visiting Fromm Prof. of Composition, Harvard Univ. 1985; f. and Co-Dir. (with Harrison Birtwistle, q.v.), Pierrot Players 1967–71; f. and Artistic Dir. The Fires of London 1971–87; f. and Artistic Dir. St. Magnus Festival, Orkney Islands 1977–86, Pres. 1986–; Artistic Dir. Dartington Summer School of Music 1979–84; Assoc. Conductor and Composer Scottish Chamber Orchestra 1985–94, Composer Laureate 1994–; Conductor/Composer, BBC Philharmonic Orchestra (Manchester) 1992–; Assoc. Conductor/Composer Royal Philharmonic Orchestra 1992–; mem. Accademica Filarmonia Romana 1979, Royal Swedish Acad. of Music 1993, Bayerische Akad. der Schönen Künste 1998; Hon. mem. Royal Acad. of Music 1979, Guildhall School of Music and Drama 1981, Royal Philharmonic Soc. 1987; Hon. Fellow Royal Incorporation of Architects in Scotland 1994; several hon. degrees including Hon. D.Mus. (Edin.) 1979, (Manchester) 1981, (Bristol) 1984, (Open Univ.) 1986, (Glasgow) 1993, (Durham) 1994; Hon. D.Litt. (Warwick) 1986; Olivetti Prize 1959; Koussevitsky Award 1964, Koussevitsky Recording Award 1966, Cobbett Medal for services to chamber music 1989, First Award of Asscn. of British Orchestras, for contribs. to orchestras and orchestral life in U.K. 1991, Gulliver Award for Performing Arts in Scotland 1991, Nat. Fed. of Music Socs. Charles Groves Award for outstanding contrib. to British Music 1995, Royal Philharmonic Soc. Award for Large-scale Composition (for Symphony No. 5) 1995; Officier, Ordre des Arts et des Lettres 1988. *Compositions include:* Sonata for trumpet and piano 1955, Alma redemptoris mater for ensemble 1957, St. Michael sonata for 13 wind instruments 1957, Prolation for orchestra 1958, Five Motets for soli, chorus and ensemble 1959, O Magnum Mysterium for chorus, instruments and organ 1960, String Quartet 1961, Leopardi Fragments for soprano, contralto and chamber ensemble 1961, First Fantasia on John Taverner's In Nomine for orchestra 1962, Veni Sancte Spiritus for chorus and orchestra 1963, Seven In Nomine 1963–65, Second Fantasia on John Taverner's In Nomine 1964, Shepherd's Calendar for young singers and instrumentalists 1965, Ecce Manus Tradentis for mixed chorus and instruments 1965, Revelation and Fall for soprano and instrumental ensemble 1966, Antechrist for chamber ensemble 1967, Missa super L'Homme Armé for speaker and ensemble 1968, revised 1971, Stedman Caters for instruments 1968, St. Thomas Wake-Foxtrot for orchestra 1968, Worldes Blis 1969, Vesalii Icones 1969, Eram quasi Agnus (instrumental motet) 1969, Eight Songs for a Mad King for male singer ensemble 1969, Vesalii Icones for dancer and ensemble 1969, Taverner (opera) 1970, From Stone to Thorn for mezzo-soprano and instrumental ensemble 1971, Blind Man's Buff (masque) 1972, Hymn to Saint Magnus for chamber ensemble and soprano 1972, Stone Litany for mezzo-soprano and orchestra 1973, Miss Donnithorne's Maggot for mezzo-soprano and chamber ensemble 1974, Ave Maris Stella for chamber ensemble 1975, Three Studies for Percussion 1975, Five Klee Pictures for percussion, piano and strings, revised 1976, Stevie's Ferry to Hoy (beginner's piano solo) 1976, Three Preludes for Organ 1976, Kinloche His Fantassie (Kinloch/Davies) 1976, Anakreontika (Greek songs for mezzo-soprano) 1976, The Blind Fiddler for soprano and chamber ensemble 1976, Orchestral Symphony No. 1 1976, The Martyrdom of St. Magnus (chamber opera) 1976, Westerlings (unaccompanied part songs) 1977, A Mirror of Whitening Light for chamber ensemble 1977, Le Jongleur de Notre Dame (Masque) 1978, The Two Fiddlers 1978, Black Pentecost (for voices and orchestra) 1979, Solstice of Light (for Tenor, Chorus and Organ) 1979, A Welcome to Orkney (chamber ensemble) 1980, Orchestral Symphony No. 2 1980, Little Quartet (string quartet) 1980, The Yellow Cake Revue (for voices and piano) 1980, Piano Sonata 1981, Little Quartet No. 2 (for string quartet) 1981, Lullabye for Lucy 1981, Salome 1981, Brass Quintet 1981, Songs of Hoy (Masque for children's voices and instruments) 1981, Sea Eagle (for horn solo) 1982, Image, Reflection, Shadow (for chamber ensemble) 1982, Sinfonia Concertante (for chamber orchestra) 1982, Into the Labyrinth (tenor and chamber orchestra) 1983, Sinfonietta Academica (chamber orchestra) 1983, Guitar Sonata 1984, The No. 11 Bus 1984, One Star, At Last (carol) 1984, Symphony No. 3 (for orchestra) 1985, Violin Concerto 1985, An Orkney Wedding, with Sunrise 1985, Oboe Concerto 1986, Resurrection (opera in one act with prologue) 1987, Cello Concerto 1988, Mishkenot (chamber ensemble) 1988, Trumpet Concerto 1988, The Great Bank Robbery 1989, Symphony No. 4 1989, Concerto No. 3 for horn and trumpet 1989, No. 4 for clarinet 1990, Caroline Mathilde (ballet) 1990, Tractus 1990, The Spiders' Revenge 1991, First Grace of Light 1991, Dangerous Errand (for tenor soli and chorus) 1991, Strathclyde Concerto No. 5 for violin and viola, No. 6 for flute 1991, Ojai Festival Overture 1991, A Selkie Tale (music-theatre work for performance by children) 1992, The Turn of the Tide (for orchestra and children's chorus and instrumental groups) 1992, Strathclyde Concerto No. 7 (for double bass) 1992, Sir Charles his Pavan 1992, Strathclyde Concerto No. 8 (for bassoon) 1993, A Spell for Green Corn: The MacDonald Dances 1993, Symphony No. 5 1994, Cross Lane Fair (for orchestra) 1994, Strathclyde Concerto No. 9 (for six woodwind instruments) 1994, The Three Kings (for chorus, orchestra and soloists) 1995, The Beltane Fire (choreographic poem) 1995, The Doctor of Myddfai (opera) 1995, Symphony No. 6 1996, Strathclyde Concerto No. 10 (for orchestra) 1996, Piccolo Concerto 1996, Job (oratorio for chorus, orchestra and soloists) 1997, Mavis in Las Vegas—Theme and Variations 1997, Sails in St. Magnus I: Fifteen keels laid in Norway for Jerusalem-farers 1997, The Jacobite Rising (for chorus, orchestra and soloists) 1997, Piano Concerto 1997, Sails in St. Magnus II: In Kirkwall, the first red Saint Magnus stones 1997, A Reel of Seven Fishermen 1998, Sea Elegy (for chorus, orchestra and soloists) 1998, Rome Amor Labyrinthus 1998; has written music for films: The Devils, The Boyfriend, for the ballet Salome 1978, Cinderella (pantomime opera for young people) 1979, The Lighthouse (chamber opera) 1979 and many piano pieces, works for choir, instrumental works and realisations of fifteenth and sixteenth century composers. *Address:* c/o Judy Arnold, 50 Hogarth Road, London, SW5 0PU, England. *Telephone:* 0171-370 2328. *Fax:* 0171-373 6730.

DAVIES, Rodney Deane, C.B.E., PH.D., F.R.S.; British radio astronomer; b. 8 Jan. 1930, Balaklava, S. Australia; s. of Holbin James Davies and Rena Irene (neé March) Davies; m. Valda Beth Treasure 1953; two s. (one deceased), two d.; ed. Univs. of Adelaide and Manchester; Research Officer Radio Physics Div., CSIRO Sydney 1951–53; lecturer Univ. of Manchester 1953–63, Sr. lecturer 1963–67, Reader 1967–76, Prof. of Radio Astronomy 1976–; Sec. Royal Astronomical Soc. 1978–86, Pres. 1987–89; Dir. Nuffield

Radio Astronomy Labs., Jodrell Bank 1988–97. *Publications:* Radio Studies of the Universe (with H. P. Palmer) 1959, Radio Astronomy Today (with H. P. Palmer and M. I. Large) 1963. *Leisure interests:* fell-walking, gardening. *Address:* University of Manchester, Nuffield Radio Astronomy Laboratories, Jodrell Bank, Macclesfield, Cheshire, SK11 9DL; Park Gate House, Fulshaw Park Road, Wilmslow, Cheshire, SK9 1QG, England. *Telephone:* (01477) 571321 (Office); (01625) 523592 (Home). *Fax:* (01477) 571618.

DAVIES, Rt. Hon. Ronald, P.C.; British politician; b. 6 Aug. 1946; s. of late Ronald Davies; m. Christina Elizabeth Rees 1981; one d.; ed. Bassaleg Grammar School, Portsmouth Polytechnic, Univ. Coll. of Wales, Cardiff; schoolteacher 1968–70; Workers' Educ. Asscn. Tutor/Organiser 1970–74; Further Educ. Adviser, Mid-Glamorgan Local Educ. Authority 1974–83; mem. Rhymney Valley Dist. Council 1969–84 (fmr. Vice-Chair.); M.P. for Caerphilly 1983–; Opposition Whip 1985–87; Labour Spokesman on Agric. and Rural Affairs 1987–92, on Wales 1992–97; Sec. of State for Wales 1997–98; elected leader of Labour Group in Nat. Ass. for Wales Sept. 1998, resgnd. Oct. 1998. *Publications:* pamphlets on Welsh devolution. *Leisure interests:* walking, gardening, sport. *Address:* Bedwas Community Council Offices, Newport Road, Bedwas, NP1 8YB, Wales. *Telephone:* (01222) 852477. *Fax:* (01222) 866022.

DAVIES, Ryland; Welsh opera and concert singer (tenor); b. 9 Feb. 1943, Cwm Ebbw Vale, Monmouthshire (now Gwent); s. of Joan and Gethin Davies; m. 1st Anne Howells (q.v.) 1966 (divorced 1981); m. 2nd Deborah Rees 1983; one d.; ed. Royal Manchester Coll. of Music (Fellow 1971); voice teacher Royal Northern Coll. of Music 1987–94; début as Almaviva in The Barber of Seville, Welsh Nat. Opera 1964, subsequent appearances including Tamino in The Magic Flute 1974, Yenick in Bartered Bride 1989; Glyndebourne Festival Chorus 1964–66, taking parts including Belmonte in The Abduction from the Seraglio, Ferrando in Così fan tutte, Flamand in Capriccio, Lysander in A Midsummer Night's Dream, The Prince in Love of Three Oranges, Lensky in Eugene Onegin; appearances with Scottish Opera as Ferrando and as Fenton in Falstaff and as Nemorino in L'Elisir d'Amore; with Sadler's Wells Opera as Almaviva, Essex in Britten's Gloriana; with Royal Opera as Hylas in The Trojans, Don Ottavio in Don Giovanni, Ferrando, Cassio in Otello, Nemorino in L'Elisir d'Amore, Ernesto in Don Pasquale, Lysander in A Midsummer Night's Dream, and Almaviva; with English Nat. Opera as Eisenstein in Die Fledermaus; overseas appearances include Salzburg Festival, at San Francisco, Chicago, Paris, at Metropolitan Opera, New York, Hollywood Bowl, Paris Opera, Geneva, Brussels, Lyons, Amsterdam, Mannheim, Israel, Buenos Aires, Stuttgart, Nice, Nancy, Philadelphia, Berlin, Hamburg; returned to Covent Garden 1994, Welsh Nat. Opera 1994, New York Metropolitan Opera 1994, 1995, Glyndebourne 1997, New Israeli Opera 1997, Chicago Lyric Opera 1998, Santa Fe Opera 1998, 1999, New Israeli Opera 1998, Netherlands Opera 1998, 1999, English Nat. Opera 1999. *Recordings include:* The Abduction from the Seraglio, L'Amore dei Tre Re (Montemezzi), La Navarraise (Massenet), The Trojans, Saul, Così fan tutte, Thérèse, Monteverdi Madrigals, Idomeneo, The Seasons (Haydn), Messiah, L'Oracolo (Leone), Judas Maccabaeus, Pulcinella, Il Matrimonio Segreto. *Video Films include:* Don Pasquale, A Midsummer Night's Dream, Die Entführung aus dem Serail, Love of Three Oranges, Trial by Jury, Kata Kabanava. *Leisure interests:* art, cinema, sport. *Address:* c/o IMG Artists, 3 Burlington Lane, London, W4 2TH, England.

DAVIES, Stephen Graham, M.A., D.PHIL.; British research chemist; b. 24 Feb. 1950; s. of Gordon W.J. Davies and June M. Murphy; m. Kay E. Partridge 1973; one s.; ICI Postdoctoral Fellow, Oxford 1975–77; NATO Postdoctoral Fellow, Oxford 1977–78; Attaché de Recherche, CNRS, Paris 1978–80; Fellow, New Coll. Oxford 1980–; Univ. lecturer in Chem. Univ. of Oxford 1980–; Dir. Oxford Asymmetry Ltd. 1991–; mem. various cttees., editorial bds. etc.; Hickinbottom Fellowship 1984; Pfizer Award for Chem. 1985, 1988; Corday Morgan Medal 1984; Royal Soc. of Chem. Award for Organometallic Chem. 1989; Bader Award, Royal Soc. of Chem. 1989. *Publications:* Organometallic Chemistry: Applications to Organic Chemistry 1982; more than 250 papers in learned journals. *Leisure interest:* chemistry. *Address:* Dyson Perrins Laboratory, University of Oxford, South Parks Road, Oxford, OX1 3QY, England. *Telephone:* (01865) 275646. *Fax:* (01865) 275633.

DAVIES, (Stephen) Howard; British theatre director; b. 26 April 1945; s. of Thomas Davies and late Hilda Bevan; m. Susan Wall; two d.; ed. Christ's Hosp. and Univs. of Durham and Bristol; Theatre Dir., Assoc. Dir. Bristol Old Vic 1971–73; founder mem. Avon Touring Co.; Asst. Dir. RSC 1974, Assoc. Dir. 1976–86; Founder and Dir. The Warehouse RSC (productions include Piaf, Good, Les Liaisons Dangereuses) 1977–82; freelance dir. 1974–76; Assoc. Dir. Nat. Theatre (productions include The Shaughraun, Cat on a Hot Tin Roof, The Secret Rapture) 1987–88; Assoc. Dir. Royal Nat. Theatre (productions include Hedda Gabler, Cat on a Hot Tin Roof, The Crucible, Piano, A Long Day's Journey Into Night) 1989–; dir. Who's Afraid of Virginia Woolf? 1996, The Italian Girl in Algiers, ENO 1997. *Leisure interests:* travel, hill-walking, watching rugby. *Address:* c/o Royal National Theatre, South Bank, London, SE1 9PX, England. *Telephone:* 0171-928 2033. *Fax:* 0171-620 1197.

DAVIES, Susan Elizabeth, O.B.E.; British gallery director (retd.); b. 14 April 1933, Iran; d. of late Stanworth Adey and Joan Charlsworth; m. John R.T. Davies 1954; two d.; ed. Nightingale Bamford School, New York, Eothen School, Surrey and Triangle Secretarial Coll.; Municipal Journal 1953–54; Artists' Placement Group 1966–67; I.C.A. 1967–70; founder and Dir. The Photographers' Gallery, London 1971–91; photography consultant and writer 1991–; Progress Medal, Royal Photographic Soc. 1982; Kulturpreis, German Photographic Soc. 1990. *Leisure interests:* jazz, gardening, grandchildren. *Address:* 53/55 Britwell Road, Burnham, Bucks., SL1 8DH, England. *Telephone:* (01628) 662677. *Fax:* (01628) 662677.

DAVIES, Terence; British screenwriter and film director; b. 1945, Liverpool; ed. Coventry Drama School and Nat. Film School; articled clerk in shipping office; later worked for 12 years in an accountancy practice. *Films:* Children 1977, Madonna and Child 1980, Death and Transfiguration 1983, Distant Voices, Still Lives (Int. Critics Prize, Cannes Film Festival) 1988, Movie Masterclass 1990, The Long Day Closes 1992, The Neon Bible 1995. *Publications:* Hallelujah Now, Travels in Celluloid. *Address:* c/o Nigel Britten Management, Garden Studios, 11–15 Betterton Street, Covent Garden, London, WC2H 9BP, England.

DAVIGNON, Viscount Etienne, LL.D.; Belgian business executive; b. 4 Oct. 1932, Budapest, Hungary; m. Françoise de Cumont 1959; one s. two d.; Head of Office of Minister of Foreign Affairs 1963, Political Dir. 1969–76; Chair. Gov. Bd., Int. Energy Agency 1974–76; Commr. for Industry and Int. Markets, Comm. of European Communities 1977–81, Vice-Pres. for Industry, Energy and Research Policies 1981–85; C.E.O. SIBEKA 1986–; Man. Dir. Société Générale de Belgique 1985–, Exec. Chair. Bd. of Dirs. March 1989–; Chair. Union Minière; Vice-Chair. Petrofina 1990–; Chair. Spaak Foundation, Union Minière 1993–; Dir. (non-exec.) Minorco 1990–; Dir. ICL 1991–, Suez Lyonnaise des Eaux, BASF 1998–; mem. Steering Cttee. European Round Table of Industrialists 1998–; Hon D. Hum. Litt. (American Coll. in Paris) 1988. *Leisure interests:* golf, skiing, tennis. *Address:* 12 avenue des Fleurs, 1150 Brussels, Belgium.

DAVIS, Sir Andrew, Kt., C.B.E.; British conductor; b. 1944; m. Gianna Rolandi 1989; one s.; ed. Royal Coll. of Music, King's Coll., Cambridge; studied conducting with Franco Ferrara, Rome; continuo player with Acad. of St. Martin-in-the-Fields and English Chamber Orchestra; Festival Hall début conducting BBC Symphony Orchestra Nov. 1970; Asst. Conductor Philharmonia Orchestra 1973–77, Prin. Guest Conductor Royal Liverpool Philharmonic Orchestra 1974–77; Music Dir. Toronto Symphony 1975–88, Conductor Laureate 1988–; Musical Dir. Glyndebourne Festival Opera 1988–; Chief Conductor BBC Symphony Orchestra 1989–, tours with orchestra: Far East 1990, Europe 1992, Japan 1993, 1997, U.S.A. 1995, 1998; has conducted London Philharmonic, London Symphony, Royal Philharmonic, Boston, Chicago, Cleveland, Los Angeles Philharmonic, New York Philharmonic, Pittsburg Symphony, Orchestre Nat. de France, Frankfurt Radio Orchestra, Royal Concertgebouw Orchestra, Tonhalle Orchestra, Stockholm Philharmonic Orchestra, Israel Philharmonic, Bavarian Radio Symphony and Berlin Philharmonic orchestras and London Sinfonietta; has conducted at Glyndebourne Festival Opera, Covent Garden Opera, Metropolitan Opera, Washington, D.C., Chicago Lyric Opera, Bavarian State Opera, Paris Opéra, La Scala, Milan, Sir Henry Wood Promenade Concerts, major British and European music festivals; tours of People's Republic of China 1978, Europe 1983 with Toronto Symphony Orchestra; recordings for CBS include Duruflé's Requiem (Grand Prix du Disque 1978), cycle of Dvořák symphonies and, for EMI, Tippett's The Mask of Time (won a Gramophone Record of the Year Award 1987, Grand Prix du Disque 1988); currently recording for Teldec Classics (has completed Vaughan Williams symphony cycle). *Address:* c/o Askonas Holt Ltd., Lonsdale Chambers, 27 Chancery Lane, London, WC2A 1PF, England. *Telephone:* 0171-400 1700.

DAVIS, Most Rev. Brian Newton, M.A., L.TH.; New Zealand ecclesiastic; b. 28 Oct. 1934, Stratford, N.Z.; s. of Leonard L. Davis and Ethel M. Davis; m. Marie L. Waters; four d.; ed. Ardmore Teachers Training Coll., Auckland Univ., Victoria Univ. of Wellington, Christchurch Theological Coll.; ordained Deacon 1960, Priest 1961; Asst. Curate St. Mark's, Wellington 1960–62, Parish of Karori and Makara 1962–64; Vicar of Makara and Karori West 1964–67, of Dannevirke 1967–73, of Cathedral Parish of St. John the Evangelist and Dean of Waiapu 1973–80; Vicar Gen. of Waiapu 1979–80; Bishop of Waikato 1980–86; Primate and Archbishop of Aotearoa, N.Z. and Polynesia 1986–97, Bishop of Wellington 1986–97. *Publication:* The Way Ahead: Anglican Change and Prospect in New Zealand 1995. *Leisure interests:* tennis, water colour painting, reading, wood turning, writing. *Address:* 1 Wells Place, Tamatea, Napier, New Zealand.

DAVIS, Carl, B.A.; American composer and conductor; b. 28 Oct. 1936, New York; s. of Isadore Davis and Sara Davis; m. Jean Boht 1971; two d.; ed. New England Conservatory of Music, Bard Coll.; Asst. Conductor, New York City Opera 1958; Assoc. Conductor, London Philharmonic Orchestra 1987–88; Prin. Conductor, Bournemouth Pops 1984–87; Prin. Guest Conductor Munich Symphony Orchestra 1990–; Artistic Dir. and Conductor, Royal Liverpool Philharmonic Orchestra, Summer Pops 1993–. *Musical theatre:* Diversions (Obie Prize Best Review) 1958, Twists (Arts Theatre London) 1962, The Projector and Cranford (Theatre Royal Stanford East), Pilgrim (Edin. Festival), The Wind in the Willows (Haymarket) 1985, Alice in Wonderland (Hammersmith) 1987, The Vackees (Haymarket) 1987. *Incidental music for theatre includes:* Prospect Theatre Co., The Nat Theatre, R.S.C. *Ballet:* A Simple Man 1987, Lipizzaner 1988, Liaisons Amoureuses (Northern Ballet Theatre) 1988, Madly, Badly, Sadly, Gladly, David and Goliath, Dances of Love and Death (London Contemporary Dance Theatre),

The Picture of Dorian Gray (Sadler's Wells Royal Ballet), A Christmas Carol (Northern Theatre Ballet) 1992, The Savoy Suite (English Nat. Ballet) 1993, Alice in Wonderland (English Nat. Ballet) 1995. *Music for TV includes:* The Snow Goose 1971, The World at War (Emmy Award) 1972, The Naked Civil Servant 1975, Our Mutual Friend 1978, Hollywood 1980, Churchill: The Wilderness Years 1981, Silas Marner 1985, Hotel du Lac 1986, The Accountant (BAFTA Award) 1989, The Secret Life of Ian Fleming 1989, Separate but Equal 1991, The Royal Collection 1991, A Year in Provence 1992, Fame in the 20th Century: Clive James 1992, Ghengis Cohn 1993, Thatcher: The Downing Street Years 1993, Pride and Prejudice 1995, Oliver's Travels 1995, Eurocinema: The Other Hollywood 1995. *Operas for TV:* The Arrangement, Who Takes You to The Party?, Orpheus in the Underground, Peace. *Film music:* The Bofors Gun 1969, The French Lieutenant's Woman (BAFTA award) 1981, Champions 1984, The Girl in a Swing 1988, Rainbow 1988, Scandal 1988, Frankenstein Unbound 1989, The Raft of the Medusa 1991, The Trial 1992, Voyage 1993, Widow's Peak 1994; series of Thames Silents including Napoleon, The Wind, The Big Parade, Greed, The General, Ben Hur, Intolerance, Safety Last, The Four Horsemen of the Apocalypse 1992, Wings 1993, Waterloo 1995, Phantom of the Opera 1996. *Concert works:* Music for the Royal Wedding, Variations on a Bus Route, Overture on Australian Themes, Clarinet Concerto 1984, Lines on London Symphony 1984, Fantasy for Flute and Harpsichord 1985, The Searle Suite for Wind Ensemble, Fanfare for Jerusalem 1987, The Glenlivet Fireworks Music 1988, Norwegian Brass Music 1988, Variations for a Polish Beggar's Theme 1988, Pigeons Progress 1988, Jazz Age Fanfare 1989, Everest 1989, Landscapes 1990, The Town Fox (text by Carla Lane) 1990, A Duck's Diary 1990, Paul McCartney's Liverpool Oratorio (with Paul McCartney) 1991. *Recordings include:* Christmas with Kiri (with Kiri Te Kanawa) 1986, Beautiful Dreamer (with Marylin Horne) 1986, The Silents 1987, Ben Hur 1989, A Simple Man 1989, The Town Fox and Other Musical Tales (text by Carla Lane) 1990, Paul McCartney's Liverpool Oratorio 1991, Leeds Castle Classics, Liverpool Pops at Home 1995; Hon. Fellowship (Liverpool Univ.) 1992; Hon. D.A. (Bard, New York) 1994; Chevalier des Arts et des Lettres (France) 1983. *Publications:* sheet music of television themes. *Leisure interests:* reading, gardening, playing chamber music, cooking. *Address:* c/o Paul Wing, 16 Highland Road, Amersham, Bucks., HP7 9AW, England. *Telephone:* (01494) 431667. *Fax:* (01494) 431714.

DAVIS, Sir Colin Rex, Kt., C.B.E.; British musician; b. 25 Sept. 1927, Weybridge, Surrey; s. of Reginald George Davis and Lilian Colbran; m. 1st April Cantelo 1949 (dissolved 1964); one s. one d.; m. 2nd Ashraf Naini 1964; three s. two d.; ed. Christ's Hospital and Royal Coll. of Music; Asst. Conductor, BBC Scottish Orchestra 1957–59; Conductor, Sadler's Wells Opera House 1959, Musical Dir. 1961–65; Chief Conductor, BBC Symphony Orchestra 1967–71, Chief Guest Conductor 1971–75; Artistic Dir. Bath Festival 1969; Musical Dir. Royal Opera House, Covent Garden 1971–86; Prin. Guest Conductor, Boston Symphony Orchestra 1972–84; Prin. Guest Conductor, London Symphony Orchestra 1975–95, Prin. Conductor 1995–; Prin. Guest Conductor, New York Philharmonic Orchestra 1998–; Music Dir. and Prin. Conductor, Bavarian State Radio Orchestra 1983–92; Hon. Conductor Dresden Staatskapelle 1990–; Grosser Deutscher Schallplattenpreis 1978; Grammy Award 'Opera Recording of the Year' 1980, Royal Philharmonic Soc. Gold Medal 1995; Commendatore of the Repub. of Italy 1976, Légion d'honneur 1982, Commdr.'s Cross of the Order of Merit, Fed. Repub. of Germany 1987; Commdr. Ordre des Arts et des Lettres 1990, Order of the Lion of Finland (Commdr. 1st Class) 1992, Bayerischen Verdienstorden 1993, Distinguished Musician Award (I.S.M.) 1996, Grammy Award 'Best Orchestral Recording' 1997, Sibelius Birth Place Medal 1998; Freedom of the City of London 1992. *Leisure interests:* poetry, tree-planting, knitting. *Address:* c/o Alison Glaister, 39 Huntingdon Street, London, N1 1BP, England. *Telephone:* 0171-609 5864. *Fax:* 0171-609 5866.

DAVIS, Don H., M.B.A.; American business executive; ed. Texas A & M Univ.; joined Allen-Bradley Co. 1963, Pres. 1989; fmrly. Exec. Vice-Pres., C.O.O. Rockwell Automation and Semiconductor Systems, Pres. Automation, Rockwell Int. Corpn. 1993, Sr. Vice-Pres. 1993, C.O.O. 1995–97, Pres. July 1995–, C.E.O. Oct. 1997–, Chair. Feb. 1998–; Dir. Ingram Micro Inc., Sybron Corpn.; mem. bd. numerous orgs. *Address:* Rockwell International Corporation, World Headquarters, 600 Anton Boulevard, Suite 700, P.O. Box 5090, Costa Mesa, CA 92628, U.S.A.

DAVIS, Geena, B.F.A.; American actress; b. 21 Jan. 1957, Wareham, Mass.; m. 1st Richard Emmolo 1981 (divorced 1983); m. 2nd Jeff Goldblum (q.v.) (divorced 1990); m. 3rd Renny Harlin 1993; ed. Boston Univ.; mem. Mount Washington Repertory Theatre Co.; worked as a model. *TV appearances include:* Buffalo Bill 1983, Sara 1985, The Hit List. *Films include:* Tootsie 1982, Fletch 1984, Transylvania 6-5000 1985, The Fly 1986, The Accidental Tourist 1988 (Acad. Award for Best Supporting Actress), Earth Girls are Easy 1989, Quick Change, The Grifters, Thelma and Louise, A League of Their Own, Hero, Angie, Speechless (also producer), Cutthroat Island, The Long Kiss Goodnight. *TV appearances include:* Buffalo Bill, Sara, Family Ties, Remington Steele. *Address:* c/o William Morris Agency, 151 S. El Camino Boulevard, Beverly Hills, CA 90212, U.S.A.

DAVIS, George Kelso, PH.D.; American nutrition biochemist; b. 2 July 1910, Pittsburgh, Pa.; s. of Ross I. Davis and Jennie (Kelso) Davis; m. Ruthanna Wood 1936; two s. four d.; ed. Pennsylvania State Univ. and Cornell Univ.; Research Asst. Cornell Univ. 1932–37; Research Asst. Prof. of Chem. Mich. State Univ. 1937–42; Prof. of Nutrition, Animal Nutritionist, Univ. of Fla., Gainesville 1942–79, Distinguished Prof. Emer. 1979–, Dir. Nuclear Sciences 1960–65, Dir. Biological Sciences 1965–70, Dir. Research 1970–75; Prof. of Nutrition, Univ. of Hawaii 1985; numerous other professional appts.; mem. N.A.S. and other professional socs.; Borden Award 1964, Elvehjem Award 1985, Distinguished Achievement Award, Univ. of Fla. 1996, Hixson Award 1998 and other honours and distinctions. *Publications:* articles in professional journals and book chapters. *Address:* 2903 S.W. 2nd Court, Gainesville, FL 32601, U.S.A. *Telephone:* (904) 376-6732.

DAVIS, Gray, J.D., B.A.; American politician; b. 26 Dec. 1942; m. Sharon Ryer 1983; ed. Stanford and Columbia Univs.; chief of staff to Gov. of Calif. 1974–81, state rep. 1982–86, State Controller 1986–94, Lieut. Gov. 1994–99, Gov. of California Jan. 1999–; mem. various bds.; f. Calif. Foundation for the Protection of Children; Democrat. *Address:* Governor's Office, State Capitol, Sacramento, CA 95814, U.S.A.

DAVIS, James Othello, M.D., PH.D.; American physician; b. 12 July 1916, Tahlequah, Okla.; s. of Zemry and Villa (Hunter) Davis; m. Florrilla L. Sides 1941; one s. one d.; ed. Univ. of Missouri and Washington Univ. School of Medicine, St. Louis, Mo.; Intern and Fellow, Barnes Hospital, St. Louis 1946; Investigator, Gerontology Unit, Nat. Heart Inst., Bethesda, Md. and Baltimore City Hospital 1947–49; Investigator, Lab. of Kidney and Electrolyte Metabolism 1949–57; Chief, Section on Experimental Cardiovascular Disease, Nat. Heart Inst., Bethesda, Md. 1957–66; Prof. and Chair. Dept. of Physiology, Univ. of Missouri School of Medicine 1966–82, Prof. Emer. 1982–; discovered and defined the important relationship of the renin-angiotensin system to the control of aldosterone secretion; mem. N.A.S. and numerous other professional socs. and orgs.; several awards and honours; James O. Davis Distinguished Lecturership in Cardiovascular Science est. in his honour 1995. *Publications:* more than 260 scientific publications. *Leisure interests:* trout fishing, travel. *Address:* 612 Maplewood Drive, Columbia, MO 65203, U.S.A.

DAVIS, John Horsley Russell, PH.D., F.B.A.; British professor of social anthropology; b. 9 Sept. 1938; s. of William Davis and Jean Horsley; m. Dymphna Hermans 1981; three s.; ed. Univ. Coll. Oxford and Univ. of London; lecturer, Sr. lecturer, Reader in Social Anthropology, then Prof. Univ. of Kent 1966–90; Prof. of Social Anthropology, Univ. of Oxford 1990–95; Warden, All Souls Coll. Oxford 1995–; Chair. European Assсn. of Social Anthropologists 1993–94; Pres. Royal Anthropological Inst. 1997–(99). *Publications:* Land and Family in Pisticci 1973, People of the Mediterranean 1977, Libyan Politics: tribe and revolution 1987, Exchange 1992. *Leisure interests:* gardens, music. *Address:* All Souls College, Oxford, OX1 4AL, England.

DAVIS, Judy; Australian actress; b. 23 April 1956, Perth; m. Colin Friels; one s. one d.; films include: My Brilliant Career, High Tide, Kangaroo, A Woman Called Golda, A Passage to India, Impromptu, Alice, Barton Fink, Where Angels Fear To Tread, Naked Lunch, Husbands and Wives, The Ref, The New Age, Children of the Revolution, Blood and Wine, Absolute Power, Deconstructing Harry. *Address:* c/o Shanahan Management Pty Ltd., P.O. Box 478, Kings Cross, N.S.W. 2011, Australia.

DAVIS, Leonard Andrew; Australian engineer and business executive; b. 3 April 1939, Port Pirie; s. of Leonard Harold Davis and Gladys Davis; m. Annette Brakenridge 1963; two d.; ed. S. Australian Inst. of Tech.; Man. Dir. Pacific Coal 1984–89; Group Exec. CRA Ltd. 1989–91; Mining Dir. RTZ Corpn. 1991–94; Man. Dir., Chief Exec. CRA Ltd. 1994–95; Deputy Chief Exec., C.O.O. RTZ–CRA 1996; C.E.O. Rio Tinto PLC 1996–. *Address:* Rio Tinto PLC, 6 St. James's Square, London, SW1Y 4LD, England. *Telephone:* 0171-930 2399. *Fax:* 0171-930 3249.

DAVIS, Martin S.; American investment company executive; b. 5 Feb. 1927, New York; ed. City Univ., New York, New York Univ.; with Samuel Goldwyn Productions 1947–55; with Allied Artists Corpn. 1955–58; with Paramount Pictures Corpn. 1958–69 (C.O.O. 1966–69); Sr. Vice-Pres. Paramount Communications Inc. (fmrly. Gulf & Western Inc.) 1969–74, Exec. Vice-Pres. 1974–83, Chair. Exec. Cttee., C.E.O. 1983–94; C.E.O., Man. Partner Wellspring Man. L.L.C. 1994–; Chair. New York City Chapter Nat. Multiple Sclerosis Soc., Montefiore Medical Center; Trustee Carnegie Hall, Thomas Jefferson Memorial Foundation, Inc.; mem. Bd. of Dirs. Western NIS Enterprise Fund, National Amusements, Inc. *Address:* Wellspring Capital Management L.L.C., 620 5th Avenue, New York, NY 10020, U.S.A. (Office). *Telephone:* (212) 332-7555.

DAVIS, Nathaniel, PH.D.; American diplomatist; b. 12 April 1925, Boston, Mass.; s. of Harvey Nathaniel Davis and Alice Marion Rohde; m. Elizabeth Kirkbride Creese 1956; two s. two d.; ed. Phillips Exeter Acad., Brown Univ., Fletcher School of Law and Diplomacy, Cornell Univ., Middlebury Coll., Columbia Univ., Univ. Central de Venezuela; Asst. in History, Tufts Univ. 1947; Lecturer in History, Howard Univ. 1962–65, 1966–68; Third Sec., U.S. Embassy, Prague 1947–49; Vice-Consul, Florence 1949–52; Second Sec., Rome 1952–53, Moscow 1954–56; Deputy Officer-in-Charge, Soviet Affairs, Dept. of State 1956–60; First Sec., Caracas 1960–62; Special Asst. to Dir. of Peace Corps 1962–63, Deputy Assoc. Dir. 1963–65; Minister to Bulgaria 1965–66; Senior Staff, Nat. Security Council, White House 1966–68; Amb. to Guatemala 1968–71, to Chile 1971–73; Dir.-Gen. U.S. Foreign Service 1973–75; Asst. Sec. of State for African Affairs April-Dec. 1975; Amb.

to Switzerland 1975–77; State Dept. Adviser, Naval War Coll. 1977–83; Alexander and Adelaide Hixon Prof. of Humanities, Harvey Mudd Coll., Claremont, Calif 1983–; lecturer Naval War Coll., San Diego 1991–; Del., Democratic Nat. Convention 1988, 1992, 1996; Fulbright Scholar 1996–97; mem. Exec. Bd. Calif. Democratic Party; mem. American Acad. of Diplomacy 1990–; Hon. LL.D. (Brown Univ.) 1970; Hartshorn Premium 1942, Caesar Misch Premium 1942; Cinco Aguilas Blancas Alpinism Award 1962, U.S. Navy's Distinguished Public Service Award 1983, Elvira Roberti Award for Outstanding Leadership, L. A. County Democratic Party 1995. *Publications:* The Last Two Years of Salvador Allende 1985, Equality and Equal Security in Soviet Foreign Policy 1986, A Long Walk to Church 1995. *Leisure interests:* skiing, mountain climbing, white water canoeing, water-colour painting. *Address:* 1783 Longwood Ave., Claremont, CA 91711, U.S.A. *Telephone:* (909) 607-3384 (Office); (909) 624-5293 (Home). *Fax:* (909) 621-8360.

DAVIS, Sir Peter J., Kt., F.R.S.A.; British business executive; b. 23 Dec. 1941, Heswall, Cheshire; s. of John S. Davis and Adriaantje (de Baat) Davis; m. Susan J. Hillman 1968; two s. one d.; ed. Shrewsbury School, Inst. of Marketing; man. trainee, The Ditchburn Org., Lytham, Lancs. 1959–65; Gen. Foods Ltd., Banbury, Oxon 1965–72; Marketing Dir. Key Markets 1973; Man. Dir. David Grieg and Group Man. Dir. Key Markets, David Grieg 1975–76; Departmental Dir. (non-foods) J. Sainsbury PLC 1976, mem. Bd. responsible for marketing 1977, Asst. Man. Dir. Buying and Marketing and Dir. Sava Centre 1979–86; Dir. then Deputy Chair. Homebase Ltd. 1983–86; Dir. Shaws Supermarkets, U.S.A. 1984–86; Deputy Chief Exec. Reed Int. PLC 1986, Chief Exec. 1986–94, Chair. 1990–94, C.E.O. and Deputy Chair. of Reed Elsevier 1993 (following merger Jan. 1993), Co-Chair. 1993–94; Vice-Pres. Chartered Inst. of Marketing 1991–; Chair. Nat. Advisory Council for Educ. and Training Targets 1993–97, Basic Skills Agency 1991–97, New Deal Task Force 1997–; Deputy Chair. Business in the Community 1991–97 (Chair. 1997–); Founder and Bd. mem. Marketing Council 1994–; Dir. (non-exec.) Granada Group 1987–91; Dir. British Satellite Broadcasting (BSB) 1988–90; Dir (non-exec.) Boots Co. 1991–, Prudential Corpn. 1994–95 (Group Chief Exec. 1995–); Trustee Royal Opera House 1994–, Victoria and Albert Museum 1994–96. *Leisure interests:* sailing, opera, reading, wine. *Address:* Prudential Corporation PLC, 142 Holborn Bars, London, EC1N 2NH, England.

DAVIS, Raymond, Jr., PH.D.; American nuclear chemist; b. 14 Oct. 1914, Washington, D.C.; s. of Raymond Davis and Ida Rogers Davis; m. Anna Marsh Torrey 1948; three s. two d.; ed. Univ. of Maryland and Yale Univ.; Dow Chemical Co. 1937–38; served U.S.A.F. 1942–46; Monsanto Chemical Co. (Mound Lab.) 1946–48; Brookhaven Nat. Lab. 1948–84; Research Prof., Dept. of Physics and Astronomy, Univ. of Pa. 1985–; Boris Pregel Prize (with O. A. Schaeffer), New York Acad. of Sciences 1957; Comstock Award, N.A.S. 1978; American Chem. Soc. Award for Nuclear Chem. 1979; Tom Banner Prize (American Physical Soc.) 1988, W.K.H. Panofsky Prize (American Physical Soc.) (jtly.) 1991, Beatrice Tinsley Prize (American Astronomical Soc.) 1994, George Ellory Hale Prize (American Astronomical Soc.) 1996. *Publications:* Several articles on neutrinos and lunar rock study. *Leisure interests:* sailing and tennis. *Address:* Department of Physics and Astronomy, University of Pennsylvania, Philadelphia, PA 19104; 28 Bergen Lane, Blue Point, NY 11715, U.S.A. (Home). *Telephone:* (215) 898-8176 (Office); (516) 363-6521 (Home). *Fax:* (516) 344-5815 (Office, Brookhaven).

DAVIS, Steve, M.B.E.; British snooker player; b. 22 Aug. 1957, Plumstead, London; s. of Harry George Davis and Jean Catherine Davis; m. Judith Lyn Greig 1990; two s.; ed. Alexander McLeod Primary School, Abbey Wood School, London; became professional snooker player 1978; has won 70 titles; in 93 tournament finals (1995); major titles include: U.K. Professional Champion 1980, 1981, 1984, 1985, 1986, 1987; Masters Champion 1981, 1982, 1988, 1997; Int. Champion 1981, 1983, 1984; World Professional Champion 1981, 1983, 1984, 1987, 1988, 1989; Winner Asian Open 1992, European Open 1993, Welsh Open 1994; mem. bd. World Professional Billiards and Snooker Asscn. 1993–; BBC Sports Personality of the Year 1989, BBC TV Snooker Personality of the Year 1997. *Publications:* Steve Davis, World Champion 1981, Frame and Fortune 1982, Successful Snooker 1982, How to be Really Interesting 1988, Steve Davis Plays Chess 1996. *Leisure interest:* collecting R & B and soul records, chess. *Address:* 10 Western Road, Romford, Essex, RM1 3JT, England. *Telephone:* (01708) 782200.

DAVIS, Sir Thomas Robert Alexander Harries, K.B.E., M.D.; Cook Islands politician (retd.); b. 11 June 1917, Ruatonga, Rarotonga; s. of Sydney Thomes Davis and Maryanne Harries; m. 1st Myra Lydia Henderson 1940; three s.; m. 2nd Pa Tepaeru Ariki 1979; three s.; ed. Otago Univ. and Medical School, Univ. of Sydney, Harvard School of Public Health; Medical Officer and Surgeon Specialist, Cook Islands Medical Service 1945–48; Research mem. Dept. of Nutrition, Harvard School of Public Health 1952; Head of Dept. of Environmental Medicine, Arctic Aero-medical Laboratory, Fairbanks, Alaska 1955–56; U.S. Army Medical Research Laboratory, Fort Knox, Ky. 1956–61; Dir. of Research, U.S. Army Research Inst. of Environmental Medicine 1961–63; employed by Arthur D. Littlem Inc. 1963–71; returned to Cook Islands 1971, formed Democratic Party; also runs medical practice in Rarotonga; Prime Minister of Cook Islands 1978–87 (numerous other portfolios); designed and built two Polynesian canoes 1991–95; Fellow, Royal Soc. of Tropical Medicine and Hygiene, Royal Soc. of Medicine; mem. N.Z. Medical Asscn., Cook Islands Medical and Dental Asscn., Visitors' Bd. of Dirs., Bishop Museum, Hawaii; Chair. Voyaging Canoe Building Cttee., Library and Museum Devt. Cttee.; Pres. Library, Museum Soc. 1991–92; Hon. mem. Alaska Territorial Medical Asscn.; Patron Rarotonga Sailing Club, Auatiu Sports Club; Silver Jubilee Medal 1977, Order of Merit, Fed. Repub. of Germany, Papua New Guinea Independence Medal. *Publications:* Doctor to the Islands 1954, Makutu 1956, Island Boy 1992, Vaka 1992, and over 100 scientific and other publications. *Leisure interests:* big game fishing, ham radio, music, planting vegetables, yachting, traditional canoeing. *Address:* P.O. Box 116, Aremango, Rarotonga, Cook Islands. *Telephone:* 27-400.

DAVISON, Edward Joseph, M.A., PH.D., SC.D., F.I.E.E.E., F.R.S.C.; Canadian professor of engineering; b. 12 Sept. 1938, Toronto; s. of Maurice J. Davison and Agnes E. Quinlan; m. Zofia M. Perz 1966; four c.; ed. Royal Conservatory of Music, Toronto and Univs. of Toronto and Cambridge; Asst. Prof. Dept. of Electrical Eng., Univ. of Toronto 1964–66, 1967–68, Assoc. Prof. 1968–74, Prof. Dept. of Electrical Eng. 1974–; Asst. Prof. Univ. of Calif., Berkeley 1966–67; Pres. I.E.E.E. Control Systems Soc. 1983 (Distinguished mem. 1984–); Chair. Int. Fed. of Automatic Control (IFAC) Theory Cttee. 1987–90, mem. IFAC Council 1991–93, 1993–96, Vice-Chair. IFAC Tech. Bd. 1991–93, Vice-Chair. IFAC Policy Cttee. 1996–(99); Dir. Electrical Eng. Assocs. Ltd., Toronto 1977–, Pres. 1997–; Consulting Engineer Asscn. of Professional Engineers of Prov. of Ontario 1979–; Killam Research Fellowship 1979, 1981, E.W.R. Steacie Research Fellowship 1974, Athlone Fellowship 1961; Hendrik W. Bode Lecture Prize (I.E.E.E. Control Systems Soc.) 1997; I.E.E.E. Centennial Medal 1984, Hon. Prof. Beijing Inst. of Aeronautics and Astronautics 1986, IFAC Quazza Medal 1993, IFAC Outstanding Service Award 1996. *Publications:* more than 300 research papers in numerous journals. *Leisure interests:* backpacking, skiing. *Address:* Department of Electrical Engineering, University of Toronto, Toronto, Ont. M5S 1A4, Canada. *Telephone:* (416) 978-6342. *Fax:* (416) 978-0804.

DAVISON, Ian Frederic Hay, B.SC., F.C.A.; British business executive and accountant; b. 30 June 1931; s. of late Eric Hay Davison and the late Inez Davison; m. Maureen Patricia Blacker 1955; one s. two d.; ed. Dulwich Coll., L.S.E. and Univ. of Mich., U.S.A.; mem. Inst. of Chartered Accountants (mem. Council 1975–); Man. Partner Arthur Andersen & Co., Chartered Accountants 1966–82, Adviser 1986–88; Ind. mem. NEDC for Bldg. Industry 1971–77; mem. Price Comm. 1977–79; Chair. Review Bd. for Govt. Contracts 1981; Chief Exec. and Deputy Chair. Lloyd's 1983–86; Dept. of Trade Insp., London Capital Securities 1975–77; Insp. Grays Bldg. Soc. 1978–79; Chair. Accounting Standards Cttee. 1982–84; Chair. The Nat. Mortgage Bank PLC 1992–, Roland Berger Ltd. 1996–; Chair. (non-exec.) MDIS (fmrly. McDonnell Information Systems) 1993– (Dir. 1986–94), Douglas Information Systems Newspaper Publrs. 1993–94; Gov. L.S.E. 1982–; Chair. Monteverdi Trust 1979–84, Sadler's Wells Trust 1995–, Sadler's Wells Foundation 1995–; Chair., Pro Provost Royal Coll. of Art 1996–; Crédit Lyonnais Capital Markets 1988–91, Charterrail 1991–; Dir. Morgan Grenfell Asset Man. 1986–88, Midland Bank PLC 1986–88, The Independent 1986–, Storehouse PLC 1988– (Chair. 1990–96), Chloride PLC 1988–, Cadbury Schweppes PLC 1990–, CIBA PLC 1991–96; Trustee, Victoria and Albert Museum 1984–; Dir. and Trustee, Royal Opera House, Covent Garden 1984–86. *Publication:* Lloyds: A View of the Room 1987. *Leisure interests:* music, theatre, squash, skiing. *Address:* 40 Earlham Street, London, WC2H 8LN, England.

DAVISON, Rt. Hon. Sir Ronald Keith, G.B.E., C.M.G., P.C., LL.B.; New Zealand judge and lawyer; b. 16 Nov. 1920, Kaponga; s. of late Joseph James and late Florence Minnie Davison; m. Jacqueline May Carr 1948; two s. (one deceased) one d.; ed. Te Kuiti Dist. High School, Auckland Univ.; served in Army, reaching rank of lieut., 1940–46; Flying Officer, R.N.Z.A.F., Europe; called to bar 1948; partner, Milne, Meek and Davison 1948–53; private practice 1953–; Q.C. 1963–; Chief Justice of N.Z. 1978–89; Chair. Legal Aid Bd. 1969–78; Chair. Environmental Council 1969–74; Chair. Aircrew Industrial Tribunal 1971–78; Chair. Montana Wines Ltd. 1972–78; mem. Auckland Dist. Law Soc. Council 1959–65, Pres. 1965–66; Dir., N.Z. Insurance Co. Ltd. 1975–78; mem., Auckland Electric Power Bd. 1958–71; mem., N.Z. Law Soc. Council 1964–66; fmr. mem. Torts and Gen. Law Reform Cttee.; Church Advocate, Auckland Diocese 1973–78; Vicar's Warden, St. Mark's Church, Remuera 1974–78. *Leisure interests:* golf, fishing. *Address:* 1 Lichfield Road, Parnell, Auckland, New Zealand.

DAVYDOV, Oleg Dmitriyevich; Russian politician; b. 25 May 1940, Moscow; m.; three c.; ed. Moscow Inst. of Construction Eng.; st-mem. Inst. Hydroproject 1953–63; counsellor on foreign econ. activities in U.S.S.R. Trade Missions in Finland, Libya and other countries, supervised construction of energy plants abroad; Deputy Chair. U.S.S.R. State Cttee. on Econ. Relations 1985–88, Deputy Minister of Foreign Econ. Relations 1988–91; mem. Bd. of Dirs. and Exec. Bd. NIPEC Oil Corpn., consultant Dagwig Bureau Consulting Co. 1991–92; First Deputy Minister of Foreign Econ. Relations of Russia Jan.–Sept. 1993, Minister 1993–97; Deputy Prime Minister 1994–97; First Deputy Chair. Co-ordinating Cttee., Interdepartmental Council for Mil. Tech. Policy (KMS) 1996–97; Counsellor Immatrom Voyma Co. 1997–.

DAVYDOV, Yuri Vladimirovich; Russian author; b. 20 Nov. 1924, Moscow; m. Bronislava Taroshchina; two s.; served in Soviet Navy 1942–49; first works published 1945; political prisoner 1949–54; mem. Russian PEN Centre; U.S.S.R. State Prize 1987, Triumph Prize 1995, A. Sakharov Literary Prize 1995. *Publications include:* On Seas and Journeys 1949, The Southern

Cross 1957, The Captains Are Looking for the Way 1959, About Your Friends, Africa 1962, The Dead Spell of the Fall 1972, The Straw Guard 1987, Volunteer for Freedom 1988, An Evening at Kholmov 1989, The Blue Tulips 1990, The Three Admirals 1991, Zorovavel 1993, The Zionists Plot 1993, Selected Works (Vols. 1–3) 1996, The Bestseller (novel) 1998. *Address:* 103104 Moscow, Malaya Bronnaya 12, Apt. 46, Russia. *Telephone:* 290 1027.

DAWAGIV, Luvsandorj; Mongolian diplomatist; b. 15 May, 1943, Uyanga soum, Uburkhangai aimak (Prov.); s. of Luvsandorj Doljin and Dolgorgiv Seree; m. Maya Jagdal 1971; one s. two d.; ed. Moscow State Inst. of Int. Relations, Diplomatic Acad., Moscow; joined Foreign Service of Mongolia in 1971; Attaché, London 1974; Deputy Head, Head of Dept. 1984–90; Head of European and American Dept. 1990–; Amb. in U.S.A. 1991–95; Head of Law, Treaty and Archives Dept. 1995–; Deputy Dir. First Dept. (Asia and America) 1996–97, Ministry of External Relations, Dir. 1997–. *Leisure interests:* hunting, travelling. *Address:* Peace Avenue 7a, Ulan Bator 13, Mongolia. *Telephone:* 311311. *Fax:* (1) 322127.

DAWE, Donald Bruce, A.O., M.LITT., PH.D.; Australian writer; b. 15 Feb. 1930, Geelong; s. of Alfred John Dawe and Mary Ann Amelia Dawe; m. Gloria Desley Dawe (née Blain) 1964 (died 1997); two s. two d.; ed. Northcote High School, Univs. of Melbourne, New England and Queensland; Educ. Section, R.A.A.F. 1959–68; teacher, Downlands Sacred Heart Coll., Toowoomba, Queensland 1969–71; lecturer, Sr. Lecturer, Assoc. Prof., Faculty of Arts, Univ. of Southern Queensland 1971–93; Hon. D.Litt. (Univ. of Southern Queensland) 1995, (Univ. of N.S.W.) 1997; Ampol Arts Award 1967, Patrick White Award 1980. *Publications:* Condolences of the Season: Selected Poems 1971, Over Here, Hark! and Other Stories 1983, Essays and Opinions 1990, Mortal Instruments 1995, Sometimes Gladness: Collected Poems 1954–97 1997. *Leisure interests:* gardening, watching Australian Rules football. *Address:* 30 Cumming Street, Toowoomba, Queensland 4350, Australia. *Telephone:* (7) 4632 7525.

DAWKINS, (Clinton) Richard; British biologist; b. 26 March 1941, Nairobi, Kenya; s. of Clinton John Dawkins and Jean Mary Vyvyan (née Ladner) Dawkins; m. Hon. Lalla Ward 1992; one d. (by previous marriage); Asst. Prof. of Zoology Univ. of Calif., Berkeley 1967–69; lecturer Oxford Univ. 1970–89, Reader in Zoology 1989–95, Charles Simonyi Reader in the Public Understanding of Science 1995–96, Professor of the Public Understanding of Science 1996–; Fellow New College, Oxford 1970–; Hon. D.Sc. (Westminster) 1997; numerous awards. *Publications include:* The Selfish Gene, The Blind Watchmaker, River Out of Eden, Climbing Mount Improbable, Unweaving the Rainbow 1998. *Address:* Oxford University Museum, Parks Road, Oxford, OX1 3PW, England. *Telephone:* (01865) 514103.

DAWKINS, John Sydney, B.E.C., DIP.AGR.; Australian politician, economist and business advisor; b. 2 March 1947, Perth; m. 1st (divorced); one s. one d.; m. 2nd Maggie Dawkins 1987; one d. one step-s.; ed. Scotch Coll., Roseworthy Agricultural Coll.; fmr. mem. Senate, Univ. of W. Australia; worked for Bureau of Agricultural Econs. and Dept. of Trade and Industry 1971–72; M.P., House of Reps., Seat of Tangney, W.A. 1974–75, Seat of Fremantle, W.A. 1977–94; Minister for Finance and Minister Assisting the Prime Minister for Public Service Matters 1983–84, Minister for Trade and Minister Assisting the Prime Minister for Youth Affairs 1984–87, for Employment, Educ. and Training 1987–91, Treasurer 1991–93; Chair. Cairns Group of Agricultural Exporting Countries 1985–87, OECD Ministerial Council 1993, John Dawkins and Co. 1994–, M. and C. Saatchi (Australia) 1996–, Impac (Australia) 1996–, Medical Corpn. of Australasia 1997–, Indian Ocean Centre; mem. Bd. Sealcorp Holdings, Fred Hollows Foundation; fmr. mem. Nat. Exec., Australian Labor Party, Party Vice-Pres. 1982–83; Australian Govt. Special Investment Rep. 1994–95; Press Officer, W.A. Trades and Labor Council 1976–77; Hon. D.Univ. (Univ. of South Australia, Queensland Univ. of Tech.) 1997; Hon. D.Sc. (Westminster) 1998. *Leisure interests:* farming, viticulture, travel. *Address:* 25th Floor, 91 King William Street, Adelaide, S.A. 5000 (Office); 75 Church Terrace, Walkerville, S.A. 5081, Australia (Home). *Telephone:* (8) 82123667. *Fax:* (8) 82124228.

DAWSON, Sir Daryl Michael, A.C., K.B.E., C.B., LL.M.; Australian judge; b. 12 Dec. 1933, Melbourne; s. of Claude Charles Dawson and Elizabeth May Dawson; m. Mary Thomas 1971; ed. Canberra High School and Melbourne and Yale Univs.; admitted to Bar, Vic. 1957; lecturer, Council of Legal Educ. 1962–74; mem. Ormond Coll. Council 1965–73 (Chair. 1992–93); Q.C. 1971; mem. Victoria Bar Council 1971–74; admitted to Tasmania Bar 1972; Solicitor-Gen. State of Victoria 1974–82; mem. Australian Motor Sport Appeal Court 1974–86; Judge, High Court of Australia 1982–97; Judge, Hong Kong Court of Final Appeal 1997–; Adjunct Prof. Monash Univ. 1998–; Professorial Fellow Univ. of Melbourne 1998–; Fulbright Scholar 1955. *Leisure interest:* gardening. *Address:* P.O. Box 147, East Melbourne, Vic. 3002, Australia. *Telephone:* (03) 9417-4499. *Fax:* (03) 9417-4499.

DAWSON, Sandra Jane Noble, B.A.; British college principal and professor of management studies; b. 4 June 1946; d. of Wilfred Denyer and Joy Denyer (née Noble); m. Henry R. C. Dawson 1969; one s. two d.; ed. Dr. Challoner's Grammar School, Amersham, Univ. of Keele; research officer Govt. Social Survey 1968–69; research officer, then lecturer, sr. lecturer Industrial Sociology Unit, Dept. of Social and Econ. Studies, Imperial Coll. of Science, Tech. and Medicine 1969–90, Prof. of Organizational Behaviour, Man. School 1990–95; KPMG Peat Marwick Prof. of Man. Studies and Dir. Judge Inst. of Man. Studies, Univ. of Cambridge 1995–, also Fellow Jesus Coll.; Master Sidney Sussex Coll., Cambridge 1998–; Chair Riverside Mental Health Trust 1992–95; Dir. (non.-exec.) Riverside Health Authority 1990–92, Cambridge Econometrics 1996–, Fleming Claverhouse Investment Trust 1996–; mem. Research Strategy Bd., Offshore Safety Div., Health and Safety Exec. 1991–95, Strategic Review Group, Public Health Lab. Service 1994, Sr. Salaries Review Body 1997–. *Publications include:* Analysing Organisations 1986, Safety at Work: The Limits of Self Regulation 1988, Managing the NHS 1995, papers on man. in learned journals. *Leisure interests:* music, walking, family. *Address:* Judge Institute of Management Studies, Trumpington Street, Cambridge, CB2 1AG; Sidney Sussex College, Cambridge, CB2 3HU, England. *Telephone:* (01223) 339700 (Judge Institute); (01223) 338800 (Sidney Sussex College).

DAWSON, Thomas C., II, M.B.A.; American economist; b. 9 March 1948, Washington, D.C.; s. of Allan Duval Dawson and Jane Dodge Dawson; m. Moira Jane Haley 1974; two s. one d.; ed. Stanford Univ., Woodrow Wilson School of Public and Int. Affairs at Princeton Univ.; fmrly. economist, U.S. Consulate Gen., Rio de Janeiro for U.S. State Dept.; fmr. Consultant, McKinsey and Co.; Deputy Asst. Sec. for Developing Nations, Treasury Dept. 1981–84; Asst. Sec. for Business and Consumer Affairs, Treasury Dept. 1984–85; fmr. Deputy Asst. to the Pres. and Exec. Asst. to Chief of Staff, the White House; fmr. Special Asst. to Asst. Sec. for Int. Affairs, Treasury Dept.; Exec. Dir. IMF 1989–93; First Vice-Pres. Merrill Lynch and Co. 1993–94, Dir. 1995–. *Address:* World Finance Center, North Tower, New York, NY 10281 (Office); 50 Portland Road, Summit, NJ 07901, U.S.A. (Home).

DAY, Sir Derek (Malcolm), K.C.M.G.; British diplomatist; b. 29 Nov. 1927; s. of late Alan W. Day; m. Sheila Nott 1955; three s. one d.; ed. Hurstpierpoint Coll. and St. Catharine's Coll. Cambridge; R.A. 1946–48; entered diplomatic service 1951; served Tel Aviv 1953–56, Rome 1956–59, Washington, D.C. 1962–66, Nicosia 1972–75; Amb. to Ethiopia 1975–78; Asst. Under-Sec. of State FCO 1979, Deputy Under-Sec. of State 1980, Chief Clerk 1982–84; High Commr. in Canada 1984–87; Commr. Commonwealth War Graves Comm. 1987–92; Vice-Chair. British Red Cross 1988–94; Dir. Monenco Ltd., Canada 1988–92; Chair. Crystal Palace Sports and Leisure Ltd. 1992–97; Chair. Govs. Hurstpierpoint Coll. 1987–97; Gov. Bethany School 1987–. *Address:* Etchinghill, Goudhurst, Kent, England.

DAY, Doris (Doris von Kappelhoff); American actress and singer; b. 3 April 1924, Cincinnati, Ohio; d. of Frederick Wilhelm and Alma Sophia von Kappelhoff; m. 1st Al Jorden 1941 (divorced 1943); one s.; m. 2nd George Weilder 1946 (divorced 1949); m. 3rd Marty Melcher 1951 (died 1968); professional dancing appearances, Doherty and Kappelhoff, Glendale, Calif.; singer Karlin's Karnival, radio station WCPO; singer with bands, Barney Rapp, Bob Crosby, Fred Waring, Les Brown; singer and leading lady, Bob Hope radio show (NBC) 1948–50, Doris Day Show (CBS) 1952–53; singer for Columbia Records 1950–; with Warner Bros. film studio. *Films include:* Romance on the High Seas 1948, My Dream is Yours 1949, Young Man With a Horn 1950, Tea for Two 1950, West Point Story 1950, Lullaby of Broadway 1951, On Moonlight Bay 1951, I'll See You in My Dreams 1951, April in Paris 1952, By the Light of the Silvery Moon 1953, Calamity Jane 1953, Lucky Me 1954, Yankee Doodle Girl 1954, Love Me or Leave Me 1955, The Pajama Game 1957, Teacher's Pet 1958, The Tunnel of Love 1958, It Happened to Jane 1959, Pillow Talk 1959, Please Don't Eat the Daisies 1960, Midnight Lace 1960, Lover Come Back 1962, That Touch of Mink 1962, Jumbo 1962, The Thrill of It All 1963, Send Me No Flowers 1964, Do Not Disturb 1965, The Glass Bottom Boat 1966, Caprice 1967, The Ballad of Josie 1968, Where Were You When the Lights Went Out? 1968, With Six You Get Egg Roll 1968, Sleeping Dogs, Hearts and Souls 1993, That's Entertainment III 1994; TV series The Doris Day Show 1968–72; appearance on TV in The Pet Set 1972. Address: c/o Doris Day Animal League, 227 Massachusetts Avenue, N.E., Washington, D.C. 20002, U.S.A.

DAY, Sir (Judson) Graham, Kt., LL.B.; Canadian business executive; b. 3 May 1933; s. of Frank C. Day and Edythe G. née Baker; m. Leda A. Creighton 1958; one s. two d.; ed. Queen Elizabeth High School, Halifax, N.S. and Dalhousie Univ., Halifax; pvt. law practice, Windsor, N.S. 1956–64; Canadian Pacific Ltd., Montreal and Toronto 1964–71; Deputy Chair. Org. Cttee. for British Shipbuilders and Deputy Chair. and Chief Exec. desig., British Shipbuilders 1975–76; Prof. of Business Studies and Dir. Canadian Marine Transportation Centre, Dalhousie Univ. 1977–81; Vice-Pres. Shipyards and Marine Devt., Dome Petroleum Ltd. 1981–83; Chair. and C.E.O. British Shipbuilders 1983–86; Chair. The Rover Group (fmrly. BL) PLC 1986–91, C.E.O. 1986–88; Dir. Cadbury Schweppes plc 1988–93, Chair. 1989–93; Deputy Chair. MAI 1989–93; Chair. British Aerospace 1991–92; Chair. PowerGen 1990–93, Dir. 1990–93; Special Consultant to Ashurts Morris Crisp 1994–; Dir. The Laird Group PLC 1985–, Bank of N.S. (Canada) 1989–, NOVA Corpn. of Alberta 1990–; Dir. (non-exec.) Ugland Int. Holdings (Deputy Chair. 1997–); Pres. Inc. Soc. of British Advertisers 1991–; Fellow Univ. of Wales, Coll. of Cardiff 1990–; Dr. h.c. (Humberside) 1992. *Leisure interests:* reading, lakeside chalet in Canada. *Address:* 18 Avon Street, Hantsport, N.S., B0P 1P0, Canada.

DAY, Peter, D.PHIL., F.R.S.; British scientist and academic; b. 20 Aug. 1938, Wrotham, Kent; s. of Edgar Day and Ethel Hilda Day (née Russell); m. Frances Mary Elizabeth Anderson 1964; one s. one d.; ed. Maidstone Grammar School, Wadham Coll., Oxford; Cyanmid European Research Inst., Geneva 1962; Jr. Research Fellow St. John's Coll., Oxford 1963–65, Tutor

1965–91; Departmental Demonstrator Univ. of Oxford 1965–67, lecturer in Inorganic Chemistry 1967–89; Oxford Univ. Prof. Associé de Paris-Sud 1975; Guest Prof. Univ. of Copenhagen 1978, Visiting Fellow Australian Nat. Univ. 1980; Du Pont lecturer Indiana Univ. 1988; Sr. Research Fellow S.R.C. 1977–82; mem. Neutron Beam Research Cttee. Science and Eng. Research Council 1983–88, Chem. Cttee. 1985–88, Molecular Electronics Cttee. 1987–88, Nat. Cttee. on Superconductivity 1987–88, Materials Comm. 1988–90; Vice-Pres. Dalton Div. Royal Soc. of Chemistry 1986–88; Dir. Inst. Laue-Langevin, Grenoble 1988–91; Dir. Royal Inst. and Davy Faraday Research Lab. 1991–, Fullerian Prof. of Chemistry 1994–; Visiting Prof. Univ. Coll., London 1991, Royal Inst. Research Fellow 1995–; mem. Academia Europaea; Hon. Foreign mem. Indian Acad. of Science; Hon. Fellow Wadham Coll. 1991, St. John's Coll. 1996; Hon. D.Sc. (Newcastle); Corday-Morgan Medal 1971, Solid State Chem. Award 1986. *Publications:* Physical Methods in Advanced Inorganic Chemistry (jtly.) 1968, Electronic States of Inorganic Compounds 1974, Emission and Scattering Techniques 1980, Electronic Structure and Magnetism of Inorganic Compounds (Vols. 1–7) 1972–82, numerous papers on inorganic chem. in learned journals. *Leisure interest:* driving slowly through rural France. *Address:* The Royal Institution of Great Britain, 21 Albemarle Street, London, W1X 4BS (Office); 16 Dale Close, Oxford, OX1 4TU, England (Home). *Telephone:* 0171-409 2992 (Office). *Fax:* 0171-629 3569.

DAY, Peter Rodney, PH.D.; American (b. British) agricultural scientist; b. 27 Dec. 1928, Chingford, Essex; s. of Roland Percy Day and Florence Kate (née Dixon); m. Lois Elizabeth Rhodes 1950; two s. one d.; ed. Chingford County High School and Birkbeck Coll., Univ. of London; John Innes Inst. 1946–63; Assoc. Prof., Ohio State Univ., Columbus, U.S.A. 1963–64; Chief, Genetics Dept., Conn. Agricultural Experiment Station, New Haven 1964–79; Dir. Plant Breeding Inst., Cambridge, England 1979–87; Dir. Center for Agricultural Molecular Biology, Rutgers Univ., N.B. 1987–, Rutgers Univ. Prof. of Genetics 1987–; Special Professorship, Univ. of Nottingham 1981–87; Sec. Int. Genetics Fed. 1984–93; Pres. British Soc. for Plant Pathology 1985; Chair. Cttee. on Managing Global Genetic Resources, N.A.S., U.S.A. 1986–94; mem. Exec. Cttee., Norfolk Agricultural Station 1980–1987, Cttee. on Genetic Experimentation, Int. Council of Scientific Unions 1984–93, Bd. of Trustees, Int. Centre for Maize and Wheat Improvement, 1986–92, panel mem. Int. Food Biotechnology Council 1988–90, mem. Scientific Advisory Bd. DNA Plant Technology; Fellow American Phytopathological Soc.: Frank Newton Prize, Birkbeck Coll., Univ. of London 1950; Commonwealth Fund Fellow, Univ. of Wis. 1954–56; John Simon Guggenheim Memorial Fellow, Univ. of Queensland 1972; non-resident Fellow Noble Foundation, Ardmore, Okla. 1991–97. *Publications:* Fungal Genetics (with J. R. S. Fincham) 1963, Genetics of Host-Parasite Interactions 1974; more than 100 scientific papers. *Leisure interests:* music, Scottish country dancing. *Address:* Biotechnology Center for Agriculture and the Environment, P.O. Box 231, Foran Hall, Cook College, Rutgers University, New Brunswick, NJ 08903 (Office); 394 Franklin Road, North Brunswick, NJ 08902, U.S.A. (Home). *Telephone:* (732) 932-8165 (Office). *Fax:* (732) 932-6535.

DAY, Sir Robin, Kt.; British television and radio journalist; b. 24 Oct. 1923, London; s. of William and Florence Day; m. Katherine Mary (née Ainslie) 1965 (divorced 1986); two s.; ed. Bembridge School, St. Edmund Hall, Oxford Univ.; Army Service 1943–47; Pres. Oxford Union 1950; called to the Bar 1952, Hon. Bencher 1990; BBC radio journalist 1954–55; Independent Television News newscaster and political corresp. 1955–59; BBC TV political interviewer and reporter specializing in current affairs 1959–; BBC radio World at One presenter 1979–87; introducer of Panorama 1967–72; Chair. Question Time, BBC 1979–89, The Elder Statesmen 1992, 1997; with British Satellite Broadcasting 1990; interviewer The Parliament Programme 1991; mem. Phillimore Cttee. on Law of Contempt 1971–74; Chair. Hansard Soc. for Parl. Govt. 1981–83, mem. Council 1977–; Richard Dimbleby Award, Soc. of Film and TV Arts 1974; Broadcasting Press Guild Award (for Question Time) 1980; RTS Judges Award for 30 years TV journalism 1985; Hon. LL.D. (Exeter) 1986, (Keele) 1988; Hon. Fellow St. Edmund Hall, Oxford 1989, Sr. Fellow R.C.A. 1991. *Publications:* Television—A Personal Report 1961, The Case for Televising Parliament 1963 (pamphlet), Troubled Reflections of a TV Journalist (article in "Encounter") May 1970, Day by Day 1975, Grand Inquisitor (memoirs) 1989, . . . But With Respect—Memorable Interviews 1993. *Leisure interests:* talking, skiing, reading. *Address:* c/o BBC Studios, Lime Grove, London, W.12, England.

DAY-LEWIS, Daniel; Irish actor; b. 20 April, London; s. of the late Cecil Day-Lewis and of Jill Balcon; m. Rebecca Miller 1996; one s. by Isabelle Adjani; ed. Sevenoaks School, Sherington, S.E. London, Bedales and Bristol Old Vic Theatre School; plays: Class Enemy, Funny Peculiar, Bristol Old Vic; Look Back in Anger, Dracula, Little Theatre, Bristol and Half Moon Theatre, London; Another Country, Queen's Theatre; Futurists, Nat. Theatre; Romeo, Thisbe, R.S.C., Hamlet 1989; television: A Frost in May, How Many Miles to Babylon?, My Brother Jonathan, Insurance Man; films: My Beautiful Laundrette, A Room with a View, Stars and Bars, The Unbearable Lightness of Being, My Left Foot 1989 (Acad. Award for Best Actor, B.A.F.T.A. Award, Best Actor), The Last of the Mohicans 1991, In the Name of the Father 1993, The Age of Innocence 1992, The Crucible 1995, The Boxer 1997. *Address:* c/o Julian Belfrage Associates, 46 Albemarle Street, London, W1X 4PP, England.

DÉ, Shoba; Indian author; m. 1st (divorced); m. 2nd Dilip Dé; six c.; ed. Queen Mary's School, Bombay; fmr. model; later copy-writer; launched India's first gossip magazine Stardust; also launched magazines Society, Celebrity; TV soap-opera Swabhimaan launched 1995. *Publications include:* English-language novels: Socialite Evenings, Strange Obsessions, Snapshots; Small Betrayals (short stories); articles and columns in newspapers and magazines. *Address:* c/o Penguin Books, 27 Wrights Lane, London, W8 5TZ, England.

DEACON, Richard, C.B.E.; British sculptor; b. 15 Aug. 1949, Bangor, Wales; s. of Group Capt. Edward William Deacon and the late Joan Bullivant Winstanley; m. Jacqueline Poncelet 1977; one s. one d.; ed. Somerset Coll. of Art, St. Martin's School of Art, R.C.A., Chelsea School of Art; *works include:* What Could Make Me Feel This Way?, Struck Dumb, Doubletalk, Body of Thought No 2, The Back of My Hand, Distance No Object No 2, Dummy, Under My Skin, Breed, Skirt; *exhbns. include:* Whitechapel Art Gallery (a retrospective), Hanover Kunstverein 1993, Orangerie in the Herrenhäuser Gärten, Hanover 1993, Tate Gallery, Liverpool 1999; recipient of Turner Prize 1987; toured S. America 1996–97; Maastricht Visiting Prof. Chelsea School of Art 1992–; mem. British Council, Arts Council of England Architecture Advisory Group 1996–; Turner Prize 1987; Chevalier Ordre des Arts et des Lettres. *Address:* c/o Lisson Gallery, 67 Lisson Street, London, NW1 5DA, England.

DEAN, Antony Musgrave, O.B.E., F.R.S.A.; British broadcaster; b. 7 Jan. 1921, Loose, Kent; s. of Arthur Edis Dean, C.B.E., M.A., M.LITT. and Elsie Georgina Dean (née Musgrave-Wood); m. 1st Anne Virginia Batcup 1943; m. 2nd Sheila Francis Whittingham 1956; three s. three d.; ed. The King's School, Canterbury; Commissioned Queen's Bays (2nd Dragoon Guards) 1941, wounded Western Desert 1942; Forces Broadcasting Service Kenya 1945–46; Recording, feature film work and BBC news stringer 1947–52; Broadcasting Officer, Kenya Govt. 1952–59; Controller of Programmes, Kenya Broadcasting Service 1959–61, Operations Exec. 1962–64; Dir. of Radio Programme Dept., Sec. Radio Programme Cttee., European Broadcasting Union 1964–86; Media Consultant, Council of Europe 1986–90; Hon. Citizen of Catalunya. *Leisure interests:* music, wine. *Address:* 36 chemin de la Pie, CH-1292 Chambésy, Geneva, Switzerland; 6 The Carriage House, Lees Court, Sheldwich Lees, Faversham, Kent, ME13 0NQ, England. *Telephone:* (022) 7583348 (Switzerland); (01795) 535581 (England).

DEAN, Christopher, M.B.E.; British ice skater; b. 27 July 1958, Nottingham; s. of the late Colin Dean and Mavis (née Pearson) Dean; m. 1st Isabelle Duchesnay 1991 (divorced 1993); m. 2nd Jill Ann Trenary 1994; police constable 1974–80; British Ice Dance Champion (with Jayne Torvill, q.v.) 1978–83, 1993; European Ice Dance Champion (with Jayne Torvill, q.v.) 1981, 1982, 1984, 1994; World Ice Dance Champion (with Jayne Torvill, q.v.) 1981–84, World Professional Champions 1984–85, 1990, 1995–96; Olympic Ice Dance Champion (with Jayne Torvill, q.v.) 1984; choreographed Encounters for English Nat. Ballet 1996; BBC Sportsview Personality of the Year (with Jayne Torvill, q.v.) 1983–84; Hon. M.A. 1994. *Leisure interests:* theatre, ballet, fast cars. *Publications:* Torvill and Dean's Face the Music and Dance (with Jayne Torvill) 1993, Torvill and Dean: An Autobiography (with Jayne Torvill) 1994, Facing the Music (with Jayne Torvill) 1996. *Address:* 124 Ladies Mile Road, Brighton, E. Sussex, BN1 8TE, England. *Telephone:* (01273) 330798.

DEAN, Howard, B.A., M.D.; American state governor; b. 17 Nov. 1948; s. of Howard Brush Dean and Andrea Maitland; m. Judith Steinberg; one s. one d.; ed. Yale Univ. and Albert Einstein Coll. of Medicine; Intern, then res. in internal medicine, Medical Center Hosp. Vermont 1978–82; internal medicine specialist medical practice in Shelburne, Vt.; mem. Vermont House of Reps. 1983–86, Asst. minority leader 1985–86; Lieut. Gov. State of Vermont 1986–91; Gov. of Vermont 1991–; Democrat. *Address:* Office of the Governor, Pavilion Office Building, 109 State Street, Montpelier, VT 05609, U.S.A.

DEAN, John Gunther, PH.D.; American diplomatist; b. 24 Feb. 1926, Germany; s. of Dr. Joseph and Lucy Dean; m. Martine Duphénieux 1952; two s. one d.; ed. Harvard Coll., Harvard and Paris Univs.; entered Govt. Service 1950; diplomatic posts in France, Belgium, Viet Nam, Laos, Togo, Mali and in U.S. Dept. of State; Dir. Pacification Program in Mil. Region 1, Viet Nam 1970–72; Deputy Chief Mission, American Embassy, Laos 1972–74; Amb. to Khmer Repub. 1974–75, to Denmark 1975–78, to Lebanon 1978–81, to Thailand 1981–85, to India 1985–88; mem. bd. of dirs. of corpns. and academic insts. in U.S., Europe and Asia; currently Personal Rep. of Dir.-Gen. of UNESCO for Cambodia; various U.S. and foreign decorations. *Leisure interest:* tennis. *Address:* 29 boulevard Jules Sandeau, 75116 Paris, France. *Telephone:* (1) 45-04-71-84. *Fax:* (1) 45-04-78-57.

DEAN, Stafford Roderick; British opera and concert singer; b. 20 June 1937, Surrey; s. of Eric E. Dean and Vera S. Bathurst; m. 1st Carolyn J. Lambourne 1963; four s.; m. 2nd Anne E. Howells 1981; one s. one d.; ed. Epsom Coll., Royal Coll. of Music and pvtly. with Howell Glynne and Otakar Kraus; Opera for All 1962–64; Glyndebourne Chorus 1963–64, Prin. début as Lictor in L'Incoronazione di Poppea 1963; under contract to Sadlers Wells Opera/English Nat. Opera 1964–70; Royal Opera House, Covent Garden 1969–, début as Masetto in Don Giovanni; int. début as Leporello in Don Giovanni, Stuttgart 1971; guest appearances with Metropolitan Opera, New York, Chicago Lyric, San Francisco, Berlin, Munich, Hamburg, Cologne, Frankfurt, Vienna, Paris, Turin operas etc.; specializes in Mozart bass repertoire; bass soloist in world premier of Penderecki Requiem, Stuttgart 1984; concert appearances in choral works by Beethoven, Shostakovich, Verdi. *Leisure interests:* family life, tennis, garden. *Address:* c/o IMG Artists, Media House, 3 Burlington Lane, London, W4 2TH, England. *Telephone:* 0181-233 5800. *Fax:* 0181-233 5801.

DEAN, Winton (Basil), M.A., F.B.A.; British musicologist and author; b. 18 March 1916, Birkenhead; s. of Basil Dean and Esther (née Van Gruisen); m. Hon. Thalia Mary Shaw 1939; one s. (two d. deceased) one adopted d.; ed. Harrow, King's Coll., Cambridge; mem. Music Panel, Arts Council of G.B. 1957–60; Ernest Bloch Prof. of Music, Univ. of Calif., Berkeley, U.S.A. 1965–66, Regent's Lecturer 1977; mem. Council, Royal Musical Assen. 1965–98 (Vice-Pres. 1970–98, Hon. mem. 1998–); mem. Vorstand, G.F. Händel-Gesellschaft, Halle 1980– (Vice-Pres. 1991–), Kuratorium, Göttinger Händel-Gesellschaft 1982–97, Hon. mem. 1997–; Hon. mem. R.A.M.; Corresp. mem. American Musicological Soc.; Hon. Mus.Doc. (Cambridge) 1996; City of Halle Handel Prize 1995. *Publications:* Bizet 1948, Carmen 1949, Handel's Dramatic Oratorios and Masques 1959, Shakespeare and Opera 1964, Handel and the Opera Seria 1969, The New Grove Handel 1982, Handel's Operas 1704–1726 (with J. M. Knapp) 1987, 1995, Essays on Opera 1990; maj. contribs. to New Oxford History of Music, vol. VIII 1982 and Grove's Dictionary of Music and Musicians, 5th and 6th edns. 1954, 1980. *Leisure interests:* shooting, naval history. *Address:* Hambledon Hurst, Godalming, Surrey, GU8 4HF, England. *Telephone:* (01428) 682644.

DEANE, Derek; British artistic director; b. 18 June 1953, Cornwall; s. of Mr and Mrs W. G. Shepherd; ed. Royal Ballet School; entered Royal Ballet Co. 1972 reaching rank of Premier Dancer; Asst. Dir. Rome Opera 1990–92; Artistic Dir. English Nat. Ballet 1993–. *Leisure interests:* tennis, gardening, reading, dinner parties. *Address:* English National Ballet, Markova House, 39 Jay Mews, London, SW7 2ES, England. *Telephone:* 0171-581 1245. *Fax:* 0171-225 0827.

DEANE, Phyllis Mary, M.A., F.B.A., F.R.HIST.S.; British professor of economic history; economic historian; b. 13 Oct. 1918; d. of John Edward Deane and Elizabeth Jane Brooks; ed. Chatham County School, Hutcheson's Girls' Grammar School, Glasgow and Univ. of Glasgow; Carnegie Research Scholar 1940–41; Research Officer, Nat. Inst. of Econ. and Social Research 1941–45; Colonial Research Officer 1946–48; Research Officer, Colonial Office 1948–49; Dept. of Applied Econs., Cambridge Univ. 1950–61, Lecturer, Faculty of Econs. and Politics 1961–71, Reader in Econ. History 1971–81, Prof. 1981–82, now Prof. Emer.; Fellow of Newnham Coll. 1961–83, Hon. Fellow 1983; Ed. Economic Journal 1968–75; Pres. Royal Econ. Soc. 1980–82; Hon. D. Litt. (Glasgow) 1989. *Publications:* The Future of the Colonies (with Julian Huxley) 1945, The Measurement of Colonial National Incomes 1948, Colonial Social Accounting 1953, British Economic Growth 1688–1959 (with W. A. Cole) 1962, The First Industrial Revolution 1965, The Evolution of Economic Ideas 1978, The State and the Economic System 1989, papers and reviews in econ. journals. *Leisure interests:* walking and gardening. *Address:* 4 Stukeley Close, Cambridge, CB3 9LT, England.

DEANE, Seamus Francis, PH.D.; Irish professor of English and American literature; b. 9 Feb. 1940; s. of Winifred Deane and Frank Deane; m. Marion Treacy 1963; three s. one d.; ed. Queen's Univ., Belfast, Cambridge Univ.; Fulbright and Woodrow Wilson Scholar, Visiting Lecturer, Reed Coll., Portland, Ore. 1966–67; Visiting Lecturer, Univ. of Calif., Berkeley 1967–68, Visiting Prof. 1978; lecturer, Univ. Coll., Dublin 1968–77, Sr. Lecturer 1978–80, Prof. of English and American Literature 1980–93; Visiting Prof., Univ. of Notre Dame, Indiana 1977, Keough Prof. of Irish Studies 1993–; Walker Ames Prof., Univ. of Washington, Seattle 1987, Jules Benedict Distinguished Visiting Prof., Carleton Coll., Minn. 1988; Dir. Field Day Theatre Co. 1980–; mem. Royal Irish Acad. 1982; Hon. D.Litt. (Ulster) 1998; AE Memorial Award for Literature 1972; Ireland/America Fund Literary Award 1988; Guardian Fiction Prize 1996; Irish Times Int. Fiction Prize 1997, Irish Times Irish Literature Prize 1997; Ruffino Antico Fattore Int. Literary Award (Florence, Italy) 1998. *Publications:* Celtic Revivals 1985, Short History of Irish Literature 1986, Selected Poems 1988, The French Revolution and Enlightenment in England 1789–1832 1988, Field Day Anthology of Irish Writing 550–1990 1991, Reading in the Dark 1996, Strange Country 1997. *Address:* Institute of Irish Studies, 1145 Flanner Hall, University of Notre Dame, IN 46556, U.S.A.

DEANE, Hon. Sir William Patrick, A.C., K.B.E., B.A., LL.B., Q.C.; Australian Governor-General and fmr. judge; b. 4 Jan. 1931, St. Kilda; s. of late C. A. Deane, M.C.; m. Helen Russell 1965; one s. one d.; ed. St. Joseph's Coll. Sydney, Sydney Univ. and Trinity Coll. Dublin, Ireland; barrister 1957; Justice, Supreme Court, N.S.W. 1977, Fed. Court of Australia 1977–82; Pres. Australian Trade Practices Tribunal 1977–82; Justice, High Court of Australia 1982–95, Gov.-Gen. of Australia Feb. 1996–. *Address:* Government House, Canberra, A.C.T. 2600, Australia.

DEARING, Baron (Life Peer), cr. 1998, of Kingston upon Hull in the County of the East Riding of Yorkshire, **Ronald Ernest Dearing,** Kt; C.B., B.SC.ECON., C.B.I.M., F.INST.M.; British civil servant and business executive; b. 27 July 1930, Hull; s. of E. H. A. and M. T. (née Hoyle) Dearing; m. Margaret Patricia Riley 1954; two d.; ed. Malet Lambert High School, Doncaster Grammar School, Hull Univ., London Business School; Ministry of Labour and Nat. Service 1946–49; Ministry of Power 1949–62; Treasury 1962–64; Ministries of Power and Tech. and Dept. of Trade and Industry 1965–72; Regional Dir. Dept. of Trade and Industry 1972–74; Under Sec. Dept. of Industry 1974–76, Deputy Sec. for Nationalized Industry Matters 1976–80, Chair. of Nationalized Industries' Chairmen's Group 1983–84; Deputy Chair. Post Office 1980–81, Chair. 1981–87; Chair. C.N.A.A. 1987–88, Review Cttee. on Accounting Standards 1987–88, Co. Durham Devt. Co. 1987–90, Polytechnics and Colleges Funding Council 1988–92, Financial Reporting Council 1990–93, Northern Devt. Co. 1990–94, Univs. Funding Council 1991–92, Higher Educ. Funding Council (England) 1992–93, Schools Curriculum and Assessment Authority 1993–96, Camelot Group PLC 1993–95, Nat. Cttee. of Inquiry into Higher Educ. 1996–97, Write Away 1997–; Pres. Inst. of Direct Marketing 1994–97; Chancellor Univ. of Nottingham 1993–; mem. Cadbury Cttee. on Financial Aspecs of Corporate Governance 1991–92; Dir. (non-exec.) Whitbread 1987–90, Prudential Corpn. 1987–91, I.M.I. PLC, British Coal 1988–91, Thorn Ericsson Ltd., SDX Business Systems Ltd.; Fellow of London Business School; Hon. Fellow Sunderland Univ., Royal Acad. of Eng.; Hon. D.Sc.(Econ.) (Hull) 1986, Hon. D. Tech. (C.N.A.A.), Hon. D.C.L. (Durham) 1992, Hon. LL.D. (Nottingham) 1993, (Exeter) 1998. *Leisure interests:* gardening, reading, car boot sales. *Address:* London Institute, 65 Davies Street, London, W1Y 2DA, England.

DEARNLEY, Christopher Hugh, L.V.O., M.A., D.MUS., F.R.C.O., F.R.S.C.M.; British organist; b. 11 Feb. 1930, Wolverhampton; s. of Rev. Charles Dearnley and Gertrude Dearnley (née Smith); m. Bridget Wateridge 1957; three s. one d.; ed. Cranleigh School and Worcester Coll., Oxford; Asst. Organist, Salisbury Cathedral 1954–57, Organist and Master of the Choristers 1957–68; Organist and Dir. of Music, St. Paul's Cathedral, London 1968–90; Acting Dir. of Music Christ Church St. Lawrence, Sydney 1990–91, Organist (locum tenens) St David's Cathedral, Hobart 1991; Dir. of Music, Trinity Coll., Melbourne 1992–93; Organist and Master of the Choristers, St. George's Cathedral, Perth 1993–94; Acting Organist and Master of the Choristers, St. Andrew's Cathedral, Sydney 1995; Acting Organist and Choirmaster, Christ Church Cathedral, Newcastle 1996; Pres. Inc. Assen. of Organists 1968–70; Chair. Friends of Cathedral Music 1971–90 (Vice-Pres. 1990–), Percy Whitlock Trust 1982–89 (Pres. 1989–); mem. Council, Royal Coll. of Organists 1980–89; Dir. English Hymnal Co. 1970–96, Harwich Festival 1981–89 (Pres. 1989–); Patron Nat. Accordion Org. 1989–94, Organ Historical Trust of Australia 1990–; Hon. Gov. Corpn. of the Sons of the Clergy 1989–; Hon. Dr. of Fine Arts (Westminster Coll., Fulton, U.S.A.) 1989. *Publications:* The Treasury of English Church Music Vol. III 1965, English Church Music 1650–1750 1970, various church music. *Leisure interests:* sketching, gardening. *Address:* P.O. Box 102, Wilberforce, N.S.W. 2756, Australia. *Telephone:* (02) 4575 0453.

DEASY, Austin, T.D.; Irish politician; b. 26 Aug. 1936, Dungarvan, Co. Waterford; s. of Michael Deasy and Geraldine Deasy; m. Catherine Keating 1961; two s. two d.; ed. Dungarvan Christian Brothers' School, and Univ. Coll., Cork; former secondary school teacher; mem. Waterford County Council and Dungarvan Urban Council 1967–; mem. Seanad Éireann 1973–77; mem. Dáil Éireann 1977–, Vice-Chair. Foreign Affairs Cttee. 1997–; Minister for Agric. 1982–87; Leader, Irish Del. to Council of Europe 1997–; Fine Gael. *Leisure interests:* golf, gardening, horse-racing. *Address:* Kilrush, Dungarvan, Co. Waterford, Ireland. *Telephone:* (058) 43003. *Fax:* (058) 45315.

DEAVER, Michael Keith, B.A.; American fmr. government official; b. 11 April 1938, Bakersfield, Calif.; m. Carolyn Deaver; two c.; ed. San José State Univ.; worked as Cabinet Sec. and Asst. to Ronald Reagan as Gov. of Calif. in 1960s; active in Reagan's presidential campaign 1980; Deputy Chief of Staff, White House, Washington, D.C. 1981–85; set up own lobbying firm 1985; later convicted of lying to Congress about his lobbying activities; Republican.

DeBAKEY, Michael Ellis, B.S., M.D., M.S.; American surgeon; b. 7 Sept. 1908, Lake Charles, Louisiana; s. of Shaker M. DeBakey and Raheeja Zorba; m. 1st Diana Cooper 1936 (died 1972); four s.; m. 2nd Katrin Fehlhaber 1975; one d.; ed. Tulane Univ., New Orleans; Instructor Tulane Univ. 1937–40, Asst. Prof. of Surgery 1940–46, Assoc. Prof. 1946–48; War Service, Colonel, ultimately Dir. Surgical Consultant Div., Office of the Surgeon Gen. 1942–46; U.S. Army Surgical Consultant to Surgeon-Gen. 1946–; Prof. and Chair. Dept. of Surgery, Baylor Coll. of Medicine, Houston, Texas 1948–93, Pres. 1969–79, Chancellor 1978–96, Chancellor Emer. 1996–; Dir. Nat. Heart and Blood Vessel Research and Demonstration Center, Baylor Coll. of Medicine 1976–84; Dir. DeBakey Heart Center 1985–; Surgeon-in-Chief, Ben Taub Gen. Hosp.; Senior Attending Surgeon, Methodist Hosp. and Consultant in Surgery, Veterans Administration Hospital, Houston; consultant surgeon to many hospitals in Texas; mem. Nat. Advisory Heart Council 1957–61, Program, Planning Cttee. and Cttee. on Training 1961–, Nat. Advisory Council on Regional Medical Programs 1965–, Advisory Council, Inst. for Advanced Research in Asian Science and Medicine, Brooklyn, New York 1978–, Advisory Council, Nat. Heart, Lung and Blood Inst. 1957–61, 1974–77, 1982–86, Tex. Science and Tech. Council 1984–86; Chair. Pres. Comm. on Heart Disease, Cancer and Stroke 1964–66; Pres. Southern Surgical Assen. 1989–90; Hon-Pres. Int. Soc. for Rotary Blood Pumps 1994; implanted first artificial heart in man April 1966; editorial boards of numerous medical journals and editor of General Surgery: Vol. II, History of World War II, co-editor American Lectures in Surgery, ed. Journal of Vascular Surgery 1983–88; Fellow Biomaterials Science and Eng., Soc. for Biomaterials 1994–; mem. numerous American and foreign medical socs. and asscns. and holder of numerous advisory appointments; many hon.

degrees; Encyclopaedia Britannica Achievement in Life Award 1980 and many other American and foreign awards including Albert Lasker Award for Clinical Research 1963, Harris County Hospital District 30-year Service Award 1978, Clemson Award 1983, Presidential Medal of Freedom with Distinction 1969, Distinguished Service Award (American Surgical Asscn.) 1981, Theodore E. Cummings Memorial Prize for Outstanding Contribs. in Cardiovascular Disease 1987, Nat. Medal of Science 1987, Distinguished Service Award, American Legion 1990, Lifetime Achievement Award, Foundation for Biomedical Research 1991, Jacobs Award, American Task Force for Lebanon 1991, Maxwell Finland Award, Nat. Foundation for Infectious Diseases 1992, Royal Coll. of Physicians and Surgeons of U.S.A. Hon. Distinguished Fellow 1992, Founding Fellow American Inst. of Medical and Biological Eng. 1993; Giovanni Lorenzini Foundation Prize for the Advancement of Biomedical Sciences 1994, Lifetime Achievement Award, American Heart Asscn. 1994, Dean's Award for Distinguished Service in the Health Sciences, Columbia Univ. Coll. of Physicians and Surgeons 1995; Commdr.'s Cross, Order of Merit (Germany) 1992, Order of Independence Medal (First Class), U.A.E. 1992, Ellis Island Medal of Honor 1993, Boris Petrovsky Int. Surgeon's Award, First Laureate of the Petrovsky Gold Medal, Russian Mil. Acad. 1997, and other honours. *Publications:* numerous chapters in medical textbooks and a number of books including: The Living Heart 1977, The Living Heart Diet 1984; over 1,500 articles. *Address:* Baylor College of Medicine, Texas Medical Center, 1 Baylor Plaza, Houston, TX 77030, U.S.A. (Office). *Telephone:* (713) 797-9353.

DEBBASCH, Charles, D. EN D.; French professor of public law; b. 22 Oct. 1937, Tunis; s. of Max Debbasch; m. Odile Peyridier 1959; three s. two d.; tutorial asst. 1957; junior lecturer, law faculty, Aix-en-Provence Univ. 1959–62, Prof. of Law, Grenoble Univ. 1962–63, Aix-en-Provence 1963–67; Chair of Public Law, Faculty of Law and Econ. Sciences, Aix-en-Provence 1967, Dir. Centre of Research into Legal Admin. 1966–, Centre of Research and Study on Mediterranean Societies 1969–71; Head of Research Comm., Ministry of Educ. 1968–69; Dir. Teaching and Research Unit attached to faculty of Law and Pol. Sciences, Aix-Marseille Univ. 1966, Dean, Faculty of Law and Pol. Sciences 1971–73; Pres. Nat. Asscn. of Pres. of Univs. specializing in law and politics and Deans of law faculties 1971–78; Prof. Coll. of Europe, Bruges 1975–81; Pres. Consultative Cttee. public law univs. 1978; tech. adviser Gen. Secr. French presidency 1978–81; Pres. Fondation Vasarely 1981; Dir. and Dir.-Gen. of Press Group, Dauphiné Libéré 1984–89; Pres. Agence générale d'information 1985–89; Pres. Supervisory Council of Dauphiné Libéré 1989–94, Observatoire int. de la démocratie 1994–; Dir. Inst. Int. du droit de l'audiovisuel 1989–; Officier, Ordre nat. du Mérite, Chevalier, Légion d'honneur, Chevalier des Palmes Académiques, Grand Officer of the Aztec Eagle (Mexico), Commdr. Order of Tunisian Repub., Officer of Merit, Senegal. *Publications:* Procédure administrative contentieuse et procédure civile 1962, la République tunisienne 1962, Institutions administratives 1975, Traité du droit de la radio-diffusion 1967, le Droit de la radio et de la télévision 1970, l'Administration au pouvoir 1970, l'Université désorientée 1971, Droit administratif 1973, Science administrative 1980, la France de Pompidou 1974, Introduction à la politique 1982, Contentieux administratif 1985, les Chats de l'émirat 1976, Institutions et droit administratifs (4 vols., 1980–98), l'Etat civilisé 1979, L'Elysée dévoilé 1982, Lexique de politique 1984, Les constitutions de la France 1983, Droit constitutionnel 1986, Le Droit de l'audiovisuel 1984, Les Associations 1985, la Ve République 1985, La Disgrace du socialisme 1985, Les recettes de la cuisine politique 1986, La réussite politique 1987, La Cohabitation froide 1988, Le Droit de l'audiovisuel 1988, La société française 1989, Les Grands arrêts du droit de l'audiovisuel 1991, Mémoires du Doyen d'Aix-en-Provence 1997, Droit des médias 1998, contrib. to numerous other works. *Address:* Centre de recherches administratives, Université de Droit, d'Economie et des Sciences, 3 avenue Robert Schuman, 13628 Aix-en-Provence (Office); 25 avenue Mozart, 75116 Paris, France (Home). *Telephone:* (1) 45-20-45-72 (Office).

de BEAUCÉ, Thierry; French government official; b. 14 Feb. 1943, Lyon; s. of Bertrand Martin de Beauce and Simone de la Verpillère; two d.; ed. Univ. of Paris and Ecole Nat. d'Admin.; civil admin., Ministry of Cultural Affairs 1968–69; seconded to Office of Prime Minister 1969–73; Tech. Adviser, Pvt. Office of Pres. of Nat. Ass. 1974; seconded to Econ. Affairs Directorate, Ministry of Foreign Affairs 1974–76; Cultural Counsellor, Japan 1976–78; Second Counsellor, Morocco 1978–80; Vice-Pres. for Int. Affairs Société Elf Aquitaine 1981–86; Dir.-Gen. of Cultural, Scientific and Tech. Relations, Ministry of Foreign Affairs 1986–87; State Sec. attached to Minister of Foreign Affairs 1988–91; Adviser to Pres. on African Affairs 1991–94; Vice-Pres. Conf. on Yugoslavia 1992; Amb. to Indonesia 1995–97; Dir. of Int. Affairs, Vivendi 1997–; Chevalier, Légion d'honneur. *Publications:* Les raisons dangéreuses (essay) 1975, Un homme ordinaire (novel) 1978, L'Ile absolue (essay) 1979, Le desir de guerre 1980, La chute de Tanger (novel) 1984, Nouveau discours sur l'universalité de la langue française 1988, Le livre d'Esther 1989, la République de France 1991, La Nonchalence de Dieu 1995. *Address:* Vivendi, 52 rue d'Anjou, 75008 Paris (Office); 73 avenue F. D. Roosevelt, Paris 8, France (Home). *Telephone:* (1) 45.63.22.37 (Home).

De BEER, Zacharias Johannes, M.B., CH.B.; South African retd. politician, physician and business executive; b. 11 Oct. 1928, Woodstock, Cape; s. of the late Dr. Z. J. De Beer and Jean De Beer; m. 1st Maureen Strauss 1952; m. 2nd Mona Schwartz 1965; one s. two d.; ed. Diocesan Coll., Rondebosch and Univ. of Cape Town; House Surgeon, Groote Schuur Hosp. 1952; Medical Practitioner 1953–59; mem. Parl. 1953–61, 1977–80 (Progressive Fed. Party, Leader 1988–89); Jt. Leader Democratic Party 1989–90, Leader 1990–94; Amb. to Netherlands 1994–96; Dir. P. N. Barrett Co. (S. African Advertising Contractors) 1962–67; joined Anglo American Corpn. of S. Africa 1968, Man. 1970–72, mem. Bd. 1974–88; Chair. Anglo American Corpn. of Cen. Africa Ltd. 1972–80, Anglo-American Properties 1980–88; Chair. LTA Ltd. 1975–88; Deputy Chair. Southern Life Asscn. Ltd. 1984–85, Chair. 1985–88; Exec. Dir. Anglo American Corpn. (South Africa) Ltd. 1974–88. *Publication:* Multi-Racial South Africa: the Reconciliation of Forces 1960. *Leisure interests:* bridge, politics, tennis. *Address:* 10 Clifton Breakers, 27 Victoria Road, Clifton 8001, South Africa. *Telephone:* (021) 4381316. *Fax:* (021) 4380378.

De BENEDETTI, Carlo; Italian company executive; b. 14 Nov. 1934, Turin; m. Margherita Crosetti 1960; three s.; ed. Turin Polytechnic; Chairman and C.E.O. Gilardini 1972–76; Dir. Euromobiliare Finance Co. 1973–, Vice-Chair. 1977–; Vice-Chair. and C.E.O. Compagnia Industriali Riunite (CIR) 1976–95, Chair. 1995–; with FIAT 1976; C.E.O. 1978–96, Vice-Chair. 1978–83 Ing. C. Olivetti & Co. S.p.A., Chair. 1983–96, Hon. Chair. 1996–; Dir. SMI S.p.A. 1983–; Vice-Chair. and C.E.O. Compagnia Finanziaria De Benedetti (Cofide) 1985, C.E.O. 1991–95, Chair. 1995–; Chair. Cerus (Paris) 1986–; Vice-Pres. Confindustria 1984–; mem. Int. Council, Morgan Guaranty Trust 1980–; Chair. Fondiara 1989–; controlled Editore Arnoldo Mondadori 1990, half-share 1991–; Co-Chair. Council for U.S.A. and Italy; mem. Centre for Strategic and Int. Studies; Hon. LL.D. (Wesleyan Univ., Conn., U.S.A.) 1986; Cavaliere del Lavoro 1983, Officier, Légion d'honneur 1987; to go on trial for fraudulent bankruptcy 1991–; under house arrest after questioning on corruption charges Nov. 1993, released Nov. 1993; sentenced to six years and four months' imprisonment, sentence reduced to four and a half years July 1996; cleared of fraud charges connected with collapse of Banco Ambrosiano Veneto Aug. 1998. *Publications:* lectures and articles in business journals. *Address:* CIR SpA, Via Ciovassino 1, 20121 Milan, Italy; Olivetti SpA, Via Jervis 77, 10015 Ivrea, Italy. *Telephone:* (2) 722701 (Milan); (125) 522011 (Ivrea).

DE BONIS, Donato; Italian ecclesiastic; b. 13 April 1930, Potenza; s. of Domenico De Bonis and Maria Vincenzina De Bonis; ed. Lateran Univ.; ordained priest 1953; at the service of the Holy See 1953–; Prelate, Inst. for Religious Works 1989; Bishop, Kts of Malta 1993; Gen. Treasurer of Apostolic Admin. *Address:* Vatican City, 00193 Rome, Italy.

de BONO, Edward Francis Charles Publius, D.PHIL., PH.D.; British author and academic; b. 19 May 1933; s. of the late Prof. Joseph de Bono and of Josephine de Bono; m. Josephine Hall-White 1971; two s.; ed. St. Edward's Coll., Malta, Royal Univ. of Malta and Christ Church, Oxford; Research Asst., Univ. of Oxford 1958–60, Jr. Lecturer in Medicine 1960–61; Asst. Dir. of Research, Dept. of Investigative Medicine, Cambridge Univ. 1963–76, Lecturer in Medicine 1976–83; Dir. Cognitive Research Trust, Cambridge 1971–; Sec.-Gen. Supranational Independent Thinking Org. 1983–; f. Edward de Bono Nonprofit Foundation; Hon. Registrar St. Thomas' Hosp. Medical School, Harvard Medical School; Hon. Consultant Boston City Hosp. 1965–66; creator of two TV series: The Greatest Thinkers 1981, de Bono's Thinking Course 1982. *Publications include:* The Use of Lateral Thinking 1967, The Five-Day Course in Thinking 1968, The Mechanism of Mind 1969, Lateral Thinking: a textbook of creativity 1970, The Dog Exercising Machine 1970, Technology Today 1971, Practical Thinking 1971, Lateral Thinking for Management 1971, Children Solve Problems 1972, Po: Beyond Yes and No 1972, Think Tank 1973, Eureka: a history of inventions 1974, Teaching Thinking 1976, The Greatest Thinkers 1976, Wordpower 1977, The Happiness Purpose 1977, The Case of the Disappearing Elephant 1977, Opportunities: a handbook of Business Opportunity Search 1978, Future Positive 1979, Atlas of Management Thinking 1981, de Bono's Thinking Course 1982, Conflicts: a better way to resolve them 1985, Six Thinking Hats 1985, Letter to Thinkers 1987, I am Right You are Wrong 1990, Positive Revolution for Brazil 1990, Six Action Shoes 1991, Serious Creativity 1992, Teach Your Child to Think 1992, Water Logic 1993, Parallel Thinking 1994, Teach Yourself to Think 1995, Mind Pack 1995, Edward de Bono's Textbook of Wisdom 1996, How to be More Interesting 1997, Simplicity 1998 and numerous publs. in Nature, Lancet, etc. *Leisure interests:* travel, toys, thinking. *Address:* L2 Albany, Piccadilly, London, W1V 9RR, England. *Telephone:* (353-1) 8250466. *Fax:* (353-1) 8250467.

DEBONO, Giovanna, B.A.; Maltese politician; b. 25 Nov. 1956; d. of late Coronato Attard and of Anna Attard (née Tabone); m. Anthony Debono; one s. one d.; ed. Univ. of Malta; teacher Educ. Dept. 1981–87; M.P., Nationalist Party 1987–; Parl. Sec. Ministry for Social Devt. 1995–96; Minister for Gozo 1998–. *Address:* Ministry for Gozo, St. Francis Square, Victoria, CMR 02, Gozo, Malta. *Telephone:* 563202/3. *Fax:* 561755.

DE BONT, Jan, cinematographer and director; b. 22 Oct. 1943; Netherlands; ed. Amsterdam Film Acad. *Cinematography:* Turkish Delight, Keetje Tippel, Max Heuelaar, Soldier of Orange, Private Lessons (American debut) 1981, Roar, I'm Dancing as Fast as I Can, Cujo, All the Right Moves, Bad Manners, The Fourth Man, Mischief, The Jewel of the Nile, Flesh and Blood, The Clan of the Cave Bear, Ruthless People, Who's That Girl, Leonard Part 6, Die Hard, Bert Rigby—You're A Fool, Black Rain, The Hunt for Red October, Flatliners, Shining Through, Basic Instinct, Lethal Weapon 3. *TV (photography):* The Ray Mancini Story, Split Personality (episode of Tales from the Crypt). *Films directed:* Speed (debut) 1994, Twister, Speed 2: Cruise Control (also screenplay and story). *Address:* c/o David Gersh, The Gersh Agency, 232 North Canon Drive, Beverly Hills, CA 90210, U.S.A.

DE BORTOLI, Ferruccio; Italian journalist; b. 20 May 1953, Milan; s. of Giovanni De Bortoli and Giancarla Soresini; m. Elisabetta Cordani 1982; one d.; ed. Univ. of Milan; journalist 1973–; mem. editorial staff, Corriere d'Informazione 1975–78; econs. ed. Corriere della Sera 1978–85; Ed.-in-Chief, L'Europeo (magazine) 1985–86; Ed.-in-Chief, Econs. Section, Corriere della Sera 1987–93; Deputy Ed. Corriere della Sera 1993–. *Leisure interests:* reading, music, skiing. *Address:* Via Solferino 28, 20122 Milan (Office); Via Donatello 36, 20131 Milan, Italy (Home).

DEBRAY, Régis; French author and government official; b. 2 Sept. 1940, Paris; s. of Georges Debray and Janine Alexandre; m. Elisabeth Burgos 1968; one d.; ed. Ecole normale supérieure de la rue d'Ulm; colleague of Che Guevara, imprisoned in Bolivia 1967–70; Co-Ed., Comité d'études sur les libertés 1975; Adviser on foreign affairs to François Mitterrand; responsible for Third World Affairs, Secr.-Gen. of Presidency of Repub. 1981–84; Office of Pres. of Repub. 1984–85, 1987–88; Maître des requêtes, Conseil d'Etat 1985–93; Sec.-Gen. Conseil du Pacifique Sud 1986–; Prix Fémina 1977. *Publications:* La Critique des armes 1973, La Guerilla du Che 1974, Entretiens avec Allende 1971, Les Epreuves du fer 1974, L'Indésirable 1975, La Neige brûle 1977, Le Pouvoir intellectuel en France 1979, Le Scribe, Critique de la raison politique, La Puissance et les rêves 1984, Les Empires contre l'Europe 1985, Comète, ma comète 1986, Eloges 1986, Masques 1987, Que vive la République 1988, A demain de Gaulle 1990, Cours de médiologie générale 1991, Christophe Colomb, le visiteur de l'aube; les traités de Tordesillas 1992, Vie et Mort de l'Image: une histoire du regard en Occident 1992. *Address:* Editions Gallimard, 5 rue Sébastien Bottin, 75007 Paris, France.

DEBRÉ, Bernard André Charles Robert, D. EN MED.; French politician and surgeon; b. 30 Sept. 1944, Toulouse; s. of Michel Debré and Anne-Marie Lemaresquier; m. Véronique Duron 1971; three s. one d.; ed. Lycée Janson de Sailly and Faculté de Médecine, Paris; hosp. doctor 1965–1980; hosp. surgeon 1980; Prof. Faculté de Médecine, Paris 1985; Head of Urology, Hôpital Cochin 1990; other professional appts.; Deputy (R.P.R.) to Nat. Assembly 1986–94; Mayor of Amboise 1992–; Minister of Cooperation 1994–95. *Publications:* La France malade de sa santé 1983, Un traité d'urologie (4 vols.) 1985, Le Voleur de vie (la bataille du Sida) 1989, L'Illusion humanitaire 1997, Le Retour de Mwami 1998; articles in French and foreign journals. *Leisure interests:* travel, collecting antique plates, sports. *Address:* Mairie, 37402 Amboise cedex; Paris, France.

DEBRÉ, Jean-Louis, D. EN D.; French politician and magistrate; b. 30 Sept. 1944, Toulouse; s. of Michel Debré (fmr. Prime Minister of France, (q.v.)) and Anne-Marie Lemaresquier; m. Ann-Marie Engel 1971; two s. one d.; ed. Lycée Janson-de-Sailly, Inst. d'Etudes Politiques, Faculté de Droit, Paris and Ecole Nat. de la Magistrature; Asst. Faculté de Droit, Paris 1972–75; Adviser, Office of Jacques Chirac 1974–76; Deputy Public Prosecutor, Tribunal de Grande Instance, Evry 1976–78; Magistrate, Cen. Admin. of Ministry of Justice 1978; Chef de Cabinet to Minister of Budget 1978; Examining Magistrate, Tribunal de Grande Instance, Paris 1979; RPR Deputy to Nat. Ass. 1986–95, 1997–; Town Councillor, Evreux 1989; Conseiller Gén. Canton de Nonancourt 1992–; Deputy Sec.-Gen. and Spokesman for Gaullist Party 1993; Minister of the Interior 1995–97; Vice-Pres. Gen. Council of the Euro 1998–; Chevalier du Mérite Agricole. *Publications:* Les idées constitutionnelles du Général de Gaulle 1974, La constitution de la Ve République 1974, Le pouvoir politique 1977, Le Gaullisme 1978, La justice au XIXe 1981, Les républiques des avocats 1984, Le curieux 1986. *Leisure interests:* riding, tennis. *Address:* Assemblée nationale, 75355 Paris (Office); 123 rue de Lille, 75340 Paris, France (Home).

de BREE, Jr., Simon; Netherlands business executive; b. 14 April 1937, Koudekerke; s. of Cornelis de Beer and Leintje Minderhoud; m. Judith Rijkée 1963; one s. one d.; ed. Univ. of Tech. Delft; research scientist, DSM NV 1966–69, Acquisition Dept. 1969–73, Sales and Marketing, Plastics Div. 1973–80, Man. Polymers Group 1980–83, Pres. Polymers Group 1983–86; mem. Man. Bd. DSM NV 1986–93, Chair. Man. Bd. 1993–; Knight, Order of Netherlands Lion. *Leisure interests:* skiing, skating, cycling. *Address:* DSM NV, P.O. Het Overloon 1, 6411 TE Heerlen, The Netherlands. *Telephone:* (45) 578-2423. *Fax:* (45) 574-0680.

DEBREU, Gerard, D.SC; American (b. French) professor of economics and mathematics; b. 4 July 1921, Calais, France; s. of Camille and Fernande (née Decharne) Debreu; m. Françoise Bled 1945; two d.; ed. Ecole Normale Supérieure, Paris, and Univ. of Paris; naturalized U.S. citizen 1975; Research Assoc. C.N.R.S. 1946–48; Cowles Comm. for Research in Econs., Univ. of Chicago 1950–55; Assoc. Prof. of Econs. Cowles Foundation for Research in Econs. Yale Univ. 1955–61; Prof. of Econs., Univ. of Calif., Berkeley 1962–, also of Mathematics 1975–, Faculty Research Lecturer 1984–85, Univ. Prof. 1985, Class of 1958 Chair. 1986, Prof. Emer.; Guggenheim Fellow, Visiting Prof., Univ. of Louvain, Belgium 1968–69; Overseas Fellow, Churchill Coll. Cambridge, U.K. 1972; several visiting professorships; Frisch Memorial Lecturer, Fifth World Congress of Econometric Soc., Cambridge, Mass. 1985; mem. Editorial Bd. Journal Econ. Theory 1972–, Games and Econ. Behaviour 1989–; Assoc. Ed. Int. Econ. Review 1959–69; mem. Advisory Bd. Journal of Math. Econs. 1974–; Corresp. The Mathematical Intelligencer 1983–84; mem. Editorial Bd. Journal of Complexity 1985, Econ. Theory 1991–; Fellow A.A.A.S., American Acad. of Arts and Sciences; mem. N.A.S. (Chair. Section of Econ. Sciences 1982–85, mem. Cttee. on Human Rights 1984–90, Class V Chair. (Behavioral and Social Sciences), mem. Council 1993–96), American Philosophical Soc.; Pres. Econometric Soc. 1971; Distinguished Fellow, American Econ. Asscn. 1982; (Pres. 1990); Foreign Assoc. French Acad. of Sciences; Dr.h.c. (Bonn, Lausanne, Northwestern Univ., Toulouse, Yale, Bordeaux, Keio (Japan)); Nobel Prize for Econ. Sciences 1983; Officier, Légion d'honneur, Commdr. de l'Ordre Nat. du Mérite. *Publications:* Theory of Value: An Axiomatic Analysis of Economic Equilibrium 1959, Mathematical Economics. Twenty Papers of Gerard Debreu 1983. *Address:* Department of Economics, University of California, 549 Evans Hall, Berkeley, CA 94720-3880, U.S.A. *Telephone:* (510) 642-7284; (510) 642-1966. *Fax:* (510) 642-6615.

de BROGLIE, Prince Gabriel Marie Joseph Anselme; French administrator; b. 21 April 1931, Versailles; s. of Prince Edouard de Broglie and Princess Hélène Le Bas de Courmont; m. Diane de Bryas 1953; one s. one d.; ed. Ecole Saint-Martin de France, Faculté de droit de Paris and Inst. d'études politiques; Auditor Conseil d'Etat 1960, Counsel 1967; Legal Adviser to Sec.-Gen., Interdepartmental Cttee. on matters of European econ. cooperation 1964; Tech. Adviser, Ministry of Social Affairs 1966–68, to Prime Minister 1968–69, Minister of State for Cultural Affairs 1970; Sec.-Gen. Office de Radiodiffusion-Télévision Française 1971, Asst. Dir.-Gen. 1973; Dir. Radio-France 1975–77, Dir.-Gen. 1978–; Pres. Inst. nat. de l'audiovisuel 1979–1981; mem. Haut Conseil de l'Audiovisuel 1972; Pres. Univ. Radiophonique et Télévisuelle Int. 1976–87, Hon. Pres. 1987; Vice-Pres., later Pres. TV Historical Cttee. 1980; mem. Comm. Nat. de la Communication et des Libertés 1986–89, Pres. 1986; Pres. Soc. des Bibliophiles Français; mem. Acad. des Sciences Morales et Politiques 1997; Officier, Légion d'honneur, Ordre nat. du Mérite, Commdr. des Arts et Lettres. *Publications include:* Le Général de Valence ou l'insouciance et la gloire 1972, Ségur sans cérémonie, ou la gaieté libertine 1977, L'histoire politique de la Revue des Deux Mondes 1979, L'Orléanisme, la ressource libérale de la France 1981, Une image vaut dix mille mots 1982, Madame de Genlis (Gobert Prize) 1985, Le français, pour qu'il vive 1986, Guizot (Amb.'s Prize) 1990, Le XIXe siècle, l'éclat et le déclin de la France 1995. *Leisure interest:* books. *Address:* 96 rue de Grenelle, 75007 Paris, France (Home).

De BURGH, Chris; British singer and songwriter; b. 15 Oct. 1948, Argentina; m. Diane Patricia Morley; two s. one d.; ed. Trinity Coll. Dublin; albums include: Far Beyond These Castle Walls 1975, Spanish Train & Other Stories 1975, End Of A Perfect Day 1977, Crusader 1979, Eastern Wind 1980, Best Moves 1981, Man On The Line 1984, Very Best of 1984, Into the Light (including No. 1 U.K. hit song The Lady In Red) 1986, Beautiful Dreams 1995, The Love Songs Album 1997. *Address:* Mismanagement, 754 Fulham Road, London, SW6 5SH, England. *Telephone:* 0171-731 7074. *Fax:* 0171-736 8605.

DEBY, Idriss; Chadian politician; fmr. C.-in-C. of Armed forces; fmr. mil. adviser to Pres. Hissène Habré (q.v.), overthrew him in coup Dec. 1990; Chair. Interim Council of State, Head of State 1990–91; Pres. of Chad March 1991–, also C.-in-C. of Armed Forces. *Address:* Office of the President, N'Djamena, Chad. *Telephone:* 51-44-37.

de CASTELLA, (François) Robert, M.B.E., B.SC.; Australian athlete, biophysicist, company director and consultant; b. 27 Feb. 1957, Melbourne; s. of Rolet François de Castella and Ann M. Hall; m. Gayelene J. Clews 1980 (separated 1998); two s. one d.; ed. Xavier Coll., Kew, Monash Univ. and Swinburne Inst. of Tech.; winner, Fukuoka Marathon (world's fastest for out-and-back course) 1981; Marathon Champion, Commonwealth Games, Brisbane 1982; winner Rotterdam Marathon 1983; World Marathon Champion, Helsinki 1983; winner Boston Marathon 1986; winner Commonwealth Games 1986; Dir. Australian Inst. of Sport 1990–95; Chair. Health Promotions Bd. A.C.T. (Healthpact) 1996–; Dir. Decorp Pty. Ltd. 1995–, Action Potential 1996–, RWM Publs. 1996–; Man. Dir. Smart Start (Australia) Pty. Ltd. 1997–; mem. Bd. Australian Sports Comm. *Publications:* de Castella on Running 1984, Deek, Australia's World Champion 1984, Smart Sport 1996. *Leisure interests:* music, relaxation, motorcycling, tennis, golf, Scuba diving. *Address:* Smart Start (Australia) Pty. Ltd., P.O. Box 3808, Weston, A.C.T. 2611, Australia. *Telephone:* (2) 6288-0361. *Fax:* (2) 6287-1461.

DECAUX, Alain; French historian and TV producer; b. 23 July 1925, Lille; s. of Francis Decaux and Louise Tiprez; m. 1st Madeleine Parisy 1957; one d.; m. 2nd Micheline Pelletier 1983; one s. one d.; ed. Lycée Faidherbe, Lille, Lycée Janson-de-Sailly, Paris, and Univ. of Paris; journalist 1944–; historian 1947–; Minister Del. attached to the Minister for Foreign Affairs: Francophone Countries 1988–91; cr. radio programme La tribune de l'histoire with André Castelot, Colin-Simard, and later Jean-François Chiappe 1951; created T.V. programmes: La caméra explore le temps with Stellio Lorenzi and André Castelot 1956, Alain Decaux raconte 1969, L'histoire en question 1981, Le dossier d'Alain Decaux 1985; f. magazine L'histoire pour tous 1960; Pres. Groupement syndical des auteurs de télévision 1964–66, 1971–72; Vice-Chair. Société des auteurs et compositeurs dramatiques 1965–67, 1969–71, Chair. 1973–75; Dir. Société Técipress 1967–91; Vice-Chair. Syndicat nat. des auteurs et compositeurs 1968–73; Dir. Librairie Plon 1969–72; Dir. Historia Magazine 1969–71; worked on various periodicals, including Les nouvelles littéraires, Le Figaro littéraire, Historia, Histoire pour tous, Miroir de l'histoire, Lecture pour tous; Chair. Centre d'animation culturelle des Halles et du Marais (Carré Thorigny) 1971–73; mem. Conseil supérieur des lettres 1974; mem. Man. Cttee. Centre nat. des lettres 1974–75; Minister of Francophone Affairs 1988–91; Policy Co-ordinator, French Overseas TV 1989; elected to Académie Française 1979; Chair. Centre d'action culturelle de Paris 1981–; Chair. Société des amis d'Alexandre Dumas; Pres. Coll. des conservateurs 1998–; prix d'histoire, Académie Française 1950, grande médaille d'or, Ville de Versailles 1954, grand prix du disque for Révolution française 1963, prix Plaisir de lire 1968, Oscar de la télévision et de la radio 1968, 1973, prix de la Critique de Télévision 1972, médaille de vermeil de la Ville de Paris 1973, prix littéraire de la Paulée de Meursault 1973; Commdr., Légion d'honneur, Commdr. Ordre National du Mérite, Ordre des Arts et des Lettres. *Publications:* Louis XVII 1947, Letizia, mère de l'empereur 1949, La conspiration du général Malet 1952, La Castiglione, dame de coeur de l'Europe 1953, La belle histoire de Versailles 1954, De l'Atlantide à Mayerling 1954, Le prince impérial 1957, Offenbach, roi de Second Empire 1958, Amours Second Empire 1958, L'énigme Anastasia 1960, Les heures brillantes de la Côte d'Azur, Les grands mystères du passé 1964, Les dossiers secrets de l'histoire 1966, Grands secrets, grandes énigmes 1966, Nouveaux dossiers secrets 1967, Les Rosenberg ne doivent pas mourir (play) 1968, Grandes aventures de l'histoire 1968, Histoire des Françaises (2 vols.) 1972, Histoire de la France et des Français (with André Castelot, 13 vols.) 1970–74, Le cuirassé Potemkine (co-writer, play) 1975, Blanqui 1976, Les face à face de l'histoire 1977, Alain Decaux raconte (4 vols.) 1978, 1979, 1980, 1981, L'Histoire en question (2 vols.) 1982–83, Notre-Dame de Paris (co-writer, play) 1978, Danton et Robespierre (co-writer, play) 1979, Un homme nommé Jésus (co-writer, play) 1983, Victor Hugo (biog.) 1984, Les Assassins 1986, Le Pape pélerin 1986, Destins fabuleux 1987, Alain Decaux raconte l'Histoire de France aux enfants 1987, l'Affaire du Courrier de Lyon 1987, Alain Decaux raconte la Révolution Française aux enfants 1988, La Liberté ou la mort (co-writer) 1988, la Révolution racontée aux enfants 1988, Alain Decaux racontre Jésus aux enfants 1991, Jésus était son nom 1991 (adapter), le Tapis rouge 1992, Je m'appelais Marie-Antoinette (co-writer, play) 1993, Histoires Extraordinaires 1993, Nouvelles histoires extraordinaires 1994, L'abdication 1995, C'était le XXe siècle 1996, Alain Decaux raconte la Bible aux enfants 1996, Monaco et ses princes 1997, La course à l'abîme 1997, La Guerre absolue 1998. *Address:* 86 boulevard Flandrin, 75116 Paris, France.

de CECCO, Marcello, B.A., LL.B.; Italian professor of economics; b. 17 Sept. 1939, Rome; s. of Vincenzo de Cecco and Antonietta de Cecco; m. Julia Maud Bamford; two s.; ed. Univ. of Parma, Cambridge Univ., England; Asst. Lecturer, Univ. of E. Anglia, England 1967–68; Prof. of Econs., Univ. of Siena 1968–79, European Univ. Inst., Florence 1979–86, Univ. of Rome "La Sapienza" 1986–, Prof. of Monetary Econs. 1989–; Exec. Dir. Monte dei Paschi di Siena 1978–83; Dir. Crediop, Rome 1979–81, Italian Int. Bank, London 1980–83. *Publications:* Money and Empire 1976, International Economic Adjustment 1981, Changing Money 1985, A European Central Bank 1990. *Address:* Dipartimento di Economia Pubblica, Via Castro Laurenziano 9, Rome, Italy. *Telephone:* (06) 49766358.

De CONCINI, Dennis, LL.B.; American politician and lawyer; b. 8 May 1937, Tucson, Ariz.; s. of Evo and Ora DeConcini; m. Susan Margaret Hurley 1959; one s. two d.; ed. Univ. of Arizona and Univ. of Arizona Coll. of Law; Committeeman, Pima County 1958–76; worked with family law practice 1963–65; special counsel to Gov. of Ariz. 1965, Admin. Asst. to Gov. 1965–67; Partner, DeConcini & McDonald, law firm 1968–73; Pima County Attorney 1973–76; Admin., Ariz. Drug Control District 1975–76; fmr. mem. Ariz. Democratic Exec. Cttee., Vice-Chair. 1964, 1970; Senator from Arizona 1977–95, mem. judiciary cttee., appropriations cttee., Rules cttee., Special Select Cttee. on Indian Affairs, Veterans' Affairs Cttee.; mem. Select Cttee. on Intelligence, Senate Caucus on Int. Narcotics Control; law practice Perry-Romani Assocs., Washington, D.C. 1995–, De Concini, McDonald, Yetwin & Lacy, Tucson 1995–; Dir. Nat. Center for Missing and Exploited Children 1995–; mem. Académie Française 1993–; Chair. Comm. on Security and Co-operation in Europe; served U.S. Army 1959–60, Judge Advocate Gen. Corps. 1964–67; mem. Pima County Bar Asscn., Ariz. Bar Asscn., American Bar Asscn., American Judicature Soc., American Arbitration Asscn., Nat. District Attorneys' Asscn.; mem. Ariz. County Attorneys' and Sheriffs' Asscn., Sec.-Treas. 1975, Pres. 1976. *Leisure interests:* tennis, golf, boating.

DeCRANE, Alfred C., Jr.; American business executive; b. 11 June 1931, Cleveland, Ohio; s. of Alfred Charles DeCrane and Verona (Marquard) DeCrane; m. Joan Elizabeth Hoffman 1954; one s. five d.; ed. Notre Dame and Georgetown Univs.; attorney, Texaco Inc., Houston and New York 1959, Asst. to Vice-Chair. 1965, to Chair. 1967, Gen. Man. Producing Dept., Eastern Hemisphere 1968, Vice-Pres. 1970, Sr. Vice-Pres. and Gen. Counsel 1976, mem. Bd. of Dirs. 1977–96, Exec. Vice-Pres. 1978–83, Pres. 1983–86, Chair. of Bd. 1987–96, C.E.O. 1993–96; Hon. Dir. American Petroleum Inst.; mem. Bd. of Dirs., CIGNA Corpn., Bestfoods, Corn Products Int., Harris Corpn., Birmingham Steel Corpn.; mem. Advisory Bd. Morgan Stanley Int.; mem. Bd. of Trustees Univ. of Notre Dame; Hon. DHL (Manhattanville Coll.) 1990. *Address:* Two Greenwich Plaza, P.O. Box 1247, Greenwich, CT 06836, U.S.A. *Telephone:* (203) 863-6580.

DE CUENCA Y CUENCA, Luis Alberto; Spanish philologist, poet, translator and writer; b. 1950, Madrid; ed. Universidad Autónoma de Madrid; Prof. Philology Inst. of Council for Scientific Research, Publs. Dir.; literary critic for several publs. including El País; Dir. Biblioteca Nacional (Nat. Library) 1996–; Premio Nacional de Literatura Infantil y Juvenil 1989. *Publications include:* El cantar de Valtario (The Song of Valtario) (translation), El héroe y sus máscaras (The Hero and his Masks). *Address:* Biblioteca Nacional, Paseo de Recoletos 20, 28071 Madrid, Spain. *Telephone:* (1) 580-78-00. *Fax:* (1) 577-56-34.

DE DEO, Joseph E. (Joe), B.A.; American advertising executive; b. 18 Sept. 1937, Newark; s. of Joseph De Deo and Clara Veneziano; m. Esther Ellen Dadigan 1969; one s.; ed. The Delbarton School, Princeton Univ.; joined Young and Rubicam (Y & R) as man. trainee, New York 1961, Account Exec. 1963, Account Supervisor 1967, Vice-Pres. 1968, Chair. Australian operations, opening agencies Sydney, then Adelaide and Melbourne 1969–79, Sr. Vice-Pres. and Area Dir. for Asia/Pacific Region 1971, set up Y & R cos. Tokyo 1972, Hong Kong 1974, Chair. U.K. group, London and Regional Dir. for U.K., France, Belgium and Netherlands 1974–77, Area Dir. for Europe and the Middle East 1977–80, Pres. Y & R Europe 1980–90, Pres. and C.E.O. Young and Rubicam Advertising Worldwide 1990–92, Vice-Chair., Chief Creative Officer Young & Rubicam Inc., N.Y. 1992–93, Corp. Vice-Chair. 1993–. *Leisure interests:* skiing, reading, antique collecting. *Address:* Young & Rubicam Inc., 285 Madison Avenue, New York, NY 10017, U.S.A.

DEDEURWAERDER, Jose Joseph, B.S.(ENG.); Belgian business executive; b. 31 Dec. 1932, Halle; s. of Louis and Philippine (Paternot) Dedeurwaerder; m. Nelly Clemens 1955; one d.; ed. Ecole Technique Supérieure de Schaerbeek; Man. Dir. Renault Belgium 1958–67; Industrial Dir. Renault Argentina 1967–73; C.E.O. Renault Mexico 1973–76; Dir. Douai (France) ass. plant 1976–81; Exec. Vice-Pres., Dir. American Motors Corpn., Southfield, Mich. 1981–82, Pres. and C.O.O. 1982–84, Pres. and C.E.O. 1984–.

DÉDÉYAN, Charles, D. ÈS L; French university professor; b. 4 April 1910, Smyrna, Turkey; s. of Prince and Princess Dédéyan (née Emma Elisabeth Ekisler); m. Phyllis Sivrisarian 1938; four s. one d.; ed. Coll. Notre Dame de Ste. Croix, Neuilly and Sorbonne; Reader in French Literature, Univ. of Rennes 1942; Prof. of French and Comparative Literature, Univ. of Lyons 1945; Prof. of Comparative Literature at the Sorbonne 1949–; Sec.-Gen. Int. Fed. of Modern Languages and Literatures 1946–54; Dir. Inst. of Comparative Modern Literature, Sorbonne 1955–68, 1971; ed. of Encyclopédie permanente Clartés 1961, and Revue des Etudes Gaulliennes. *Publications:* La "Sophonisbe" de Mairet 1945, Montaigne chez ses amis anglo-saxons 1946, Essai sur le journal de voyage de Montaigne 1946, Le journal de voyage de Montaigne 1947, Argile 1947, Studies in Marivaux, Stendhal, Du Fail, Balzac, V. Hugo 1950–53, Le thème de Faust dans la littérature européenne 1954–67, Madame de Lafayette, La nouvelle Héloïse, Stendhal et les Chroniques italiennes 1955, Voltaire et la pensée anglaise 1956, Le "Gil Blas" de Le Sage 1956, 1965, Gérard de Nerval et l'Allemagne 1957–59, L'Angleterre dans la pensée de Diderot 1959, Dante en Angleterre 1958–66, "Le Roman Comique" de Scarron 1959, Rilke et la France 1961, L'influence de Rousseau sur la sensibilité européenne à la fin du XVIIIe. siècle 1961, Stendhal chroniqueur 1962, Victor Hugo et l'Allemagne 1963, 1965, 1967, L'Italie dans l'oeuvre romanesque de Stendhal 1963, Le cosmopolitisme littéraire de Charles Du Bos 1968–70, Racine et sa "Phèdre" 1968, Le nouveau mal du siècle de Baudelaire à nos jours 1968–72, Une guerre dans le mal des hommes 1971, Chateaubriand et Rousseau 1972, Le cosmopolitisme européen sous la Révolution et l'Empire 1976, L'Arioste en France 1975–76, Lamartine et la Toscane 1978, Giorgione dans les lettres françaises 1979, Le drame romantique en Europe 1982, Dante dans le romantisme anglais 1983, Le roman comique de Scarron 1983, Le critique en voyage 1985, Diderot et la pensée anglaise 1986, Montesquieu ou l'Alibi persan 1987, Le retour de Salente ou Voltaire et l'Angleterre 1988, La nouvelle Héloïse ou l'éternel retour 1990, Montesquieu ou les lumières d'Albion 1990, Télémaque ou la liberté de l'esprit 1991, Polyeucte ou le coeur et la grâce 1992, Lorelei ou l'enchanteur enchanté 1993, De l'Amadis est née l'Astrée 1994, Quand Guarini franchit les Alpes 1995, N'allez pas au théâtre 1997, En écoutant Stendhal 1997, Stendhal captivé et captif ou le mythe de la prison 1998, Le critique en voyage: esquisse d'une histoire littéraire comparée 1998. *Leisure interest:* fine arts. *Address:* 90 bis rue de Varenne, 75007 Paris; Manoir de La Motte, 35780 La Richardais, France. *Telephone:* (1) 01.45.51.07 (Paris); (2) 99.88.52.50 (La Richardais).

de DUVE, Christian René, M.D., M.SC.; Belgian scientist; b. 2 Oct. 1917, Thames Ditton, England; s. of Alphonse de Duve and Madeleine Pungs; m. Janine Herman 1943; two s. two d.; ed. Univ. of Louvain; Prof. of Physiol. Chemistry, Univ. of Louvain Medical School 1947–85, now Emer.; Prof. of Biochemical Cytology, Rockefeller Univ., New York City 1962–88, now Emer.; founder-mem., Pres. Int. Inst. of Cellular and Molecular Pathology, Brussels 1974–91; mem. Royal Acad. of Medicine (Belgium), Royal Acad. of Belgium, American Chem. Soc., Biochem. Soc., American Soc. of Biol. Chem., Pontifical Acad. of Sciences, American Soc. of Cell Biology, Deutsche Akademie der Naturforschung, Leopoldina, Koninklijke Akademie voor Geneeskunde van België, etc.; Foreign mem. American Acad. of Arts and Sciences, Royal Soc., London, Royal Soc. of Canada; Foreign assoc. N.A.S., U.S.A.; Hon. D.Sc. (Keele Univ.) 1981; Prix des Alumni 1949; Prix Pfizer 1957; Prix Francqui 1960; Prix Quinquennal Belge des Sciences Médicales 1967; Gairdner Foundation Int. Award of Merit (Canada) 1967; Dr. H. P. Heineken Prijs (Netherlands) 1973; Nobel Prize for Medicine 1974. *Leisure interests:* tennis, skiing, bridge. *Address:* Le Pré St. Jean, 239 rue de Weert, 1390 Nethen, Belgium; 80 Central Park West, New York, NY 10023, U.S.A. *Telephone:* (10) 866628 (Belgium); (212) 724-8048 (New York).

DEECH, Ruth Lynn, M.A.; British university administrator and lawyer; b. 29 April 1943, London; d. of Josef Fraenkel and Dora Rosenfeld; m. John Deech

1967; one d.; ed. St. Anne's Coll. Oxford and Brandeis Univ. U.S.A.; called to Bar, Inner Temple 1967; Legal Asst. Law Comm. 1966–67; Asst. Prof. Univ. of Windsor Law School, Canada 1968–70; Fellow and Tutor in Law, St. Anne's Coll. Oxford 1970–91, Vice-Prin. 1988–91, Prin. 1991–; mem. Oxford Univ. Hebdomadal Council 1986–; Chair. Oxford Univ. Admissions Cttee. 1993–97; Gov. Oxford Centre for Hebrew and Jewish Studies 1994–; Trustee, Jewish Continuity 1994–; Chair. Human Fertilization and Embryology Authority 1994–; Rhodes Trustee 1997–; Hon. Bencher, Inner Temple 1996–; Visiting Prof. Osgoode Hall Law School, Canada 1978. *Publications:* Divorce Dissent 1994; articles on family law, property law, autobiog. etc. *Leisure interests:* music, after-dinner speaking. *Address:* St. Anne's College, Oxford, OX2 6HS, England. *Telephone:* (01865) 274820. *Fax:* (01865) 274895.

DEEDES, Baron (Life Peer), cr. 1986, of Aldington in the County of Kent; **William Francis Deedes,** P.C., M.C.; British fmr. politician and newspaper editor; b. 1 June 1913, Aldington, Kent; m. Evelyn Hilary Branfoot 1942; two s. (one deceased) three d.; ed. Harrow School; M.P. for Ashford (Kent) 1950–74; Parl. Sec., Ministry of Housing and Local Govt. 1954–55; Parl. Under-Sec. Home Dept. 1955–57; Deputy Lieut., Kent 1962; Minister without Portfolio (Information) July 1962–64; mem. Advisory Cttee. on Drug Dependence 1967–74; Chair. Select Cttee. on Immigration and Race Relations 1970–74; Ed. Daily Telegraph 1974–86; Special Award, British Press Awards 1992; Hon. D.C.L. (Kent) 1988. *Publication:* Dear Bill: W. F. Deedes Reports 1997. *Address:* New Hayters, Aldington, Kent, TN25 7DT, England. *Telephone:* (01233) 720269.

DEER, William Alexander, M.SC., PH.D., F.R.S.; British mineralogist and petrologist; b. 26 Oct. 1910, Manchester; s. of William Deer and the late Davina Cunningham; m. 1st Margaret Marjorie Kidd 1939 (died 1971); m. 2nd Rita Tagg 1973; two s. one d.; ed. Central High School, Manchester, Univs. of Manchester and Cambridge; lecturer, Univ. of Manchester 1937–39; Senior 1851 Research Fellow 1939–40; Research Fellow, St. John's Coll., Cambridge 1939–47; served War of 1939–45, Royal Engs. (Lieut.-Col.); Demonstrator, Mineralogy Dept., Cambridge Univ. 1946–50; Tutor, St. John's Coll. 1948–50; Prof. of Geology, Manchester Univ. 1950–61; Prof. of Mineralogy and Petrology, Cambridge Univ. 1961–78, Prof. Emer. 1978–; Master of Trinity Hall, Cambridge 1966–75; Vice-Chancellor, Cambridge Univ. 1971–73; mem. Natural Environment Research Council 1968–71; Pres. Mineralogical Soc. 1968–70; Pres. Geological Soc. 1969–71; Greenland expeditions 1935, 1936, 1953, 1966; Hon. Fellow, St. John's Coll., Cambridge, Trinity Hall, Cambridge; Trustee, British Museum 1966–75; Hon. D.Sc. (Aberdeen) 1983; Daniel Pigeon Prize and Murchison Medal of Geological Soc., London; Bruce Medal of Royal Soc. of Edinburgh. *Publications:* Carsphairn Igneous Complex 1935, Petrology of the Skaergaard Intrusion, East Greenland (with L. R. Wager) 1939, Rock Forming Minerals, 5 vols. (with R. A. Howie and J. Zussman) 1962–63, 1978–98, Petrology and Mineralogy of the Kangerdlugssuaq Alkaline Intrusion (with Dr. C. Kempe) 1970. *Leisure interests:* bassoon, music. *Address:* 12 Barrington House, Southacre Park, Chaucer Road, Cambridge, CB2 2TY, England.

de FERRANTI, Sebastian Ziani, D.L.; British electrical engineer; b. 5 Oct. 1927, Alderley Edge, Cheshire; s. of late Sir Vincent and of Lady de Ferranti (née Wilson); brother of late Basil Ziani de Ferranti; m. 1st Mona Helen Cunningham 1953; one s. two d.; m. 2nd Naomi Angela Rae 1983; ed. Ampleforth Coll.; served 4th/7th Dragoon Guards 1947–49; Brown Boveri, Switzerland and Alsthom, France 1948–50; Transformer Dept., Ferranti Ltd. 1950, Dir. 1954–82, Man. Dir. 1958–75, Chair. 1963–82; Dir. GEC PLC 1982–97; Pres. BEAMA 1969–70, Manchester and Region Centre for Educ. in Science, Educ. and Tech. 1972–78; Chair. Int. Electrical Assen. 1970–73; Vice-Pres. R.S.A. 1980–84; Commr. Royal Comm. for Exhbn. of 1851 1984–97; Dir. Nat. Nuclear Corpn. 1984–88; mem. Nat. Defence Industries Council 1969–77; Trustee, Tate Gallery 1971–78; Chair. North-West Civic Trust 1978–83; Chair. Hallé Concerts Soc. 1988–96, Pres. 1997–; High Sheriff of Cheshire 1988–89; Hon. mem. Royal Northern Coll. of Music 1997; Hon. Fellow, Manchester Univ. Inst. of Science and Tech.; Granada Guildhall Lecture 1966; Royal Inst. Discourse 1969; Louis Blériot Lecture, Paris 1970; Faraday Lecture 1970, 1971; Hon. D.Sc. (Cranfield Inst. of Tech.) 1973, (Salford Univ.). *Address:* Henbury Hall, Macclesfield, Cheshire, SK11 9PJ, England (Home). *Telephone:* (01625) 422101.

DEFLASSIEUX, Jean Sébastien; French banker; b. 11 July 1925, Cap d'Ail; s. of Alexis Deflassieux and Thérèse Dalmasso; m. Christiane Orabona 1950 (deceased); one s.; ed. HEC, Law Faculty, Paris, London School of Econs., Ecole d'organisation scientifique du travail; analyst, Div. of financial studies, Crédit Lyonnais 1948–54; attached to Cabinet of Jean Filippi (Sec. of State for the Budget) 1956–57 and of Arthur Conte (Sec. of State for Industry) 1957; Insp. of Paris br. offices, Crédit Lyonnais 1958; Sub-Dir. Haute Banque 1959–69, Dir of External Commerce 1969–72, of Int. Affairs 1972–, in charge of the Cen. Man. of Int. Affairs 1978–82; Gen. Admin. 1982, Chair. and C.E.O. Crédit Lyonnais 1982–86, Hon. Chair. 1986–; Chair. Banque des Echanges Internationaux, Paris 1987–96, Monacrédit (Monaco) 1980; Dir. ABC Int. Bank PLC, London 1990 and of other banks and cos.; Pres. European League for Econ. Co-operation (French Section) 1983; Pres. (French Section) Int. Vienna Council (East–West) 1985–96; Admin. Arab Banking Corpn. Int. Bank 1991–; Officier, Légion d'honneur, Commandeur Ordre Nat. du Mérite, Croix de Guerre 1939–45, Palmes Académiques. *Leisure interest:* swimming. *Address:* 9 boulevard du Jardin exotique, Monaco; 41 rue Vineuse, 75116 Paris, France (Homes).

DEGENHARDT, Johannes Joachim, DR.THEOL.; German ecclesiastic; b. 31 Jan. 1926, Schwelm; s. of Julius and Elfriede Degenhardt; ed. Albrecht Dürer Gymnasium, Hagen, and theological studies in Paderborn, Munich, Münster and Würzburg; ordained in Paderborn 1951; subsequently student chaplain, Pädagogische Hochschule, Paderborn, and Bezirksdekan, Hochstift Paderborn; Bishop of Paderborn 1968, Archbishop 1974–; Chair. of Educ. Comm., Conf. of German Bishops. *Publications:* Lukas, Evangelist der Armen 1966, Ein Segen sollt ihr sein 1984; Ermutigung zum Glauben 1989. *Address:* Kamp 38, 33098 Paderborn, Germany. *Telephone:* 20 73 27.

DEGENHART, Bernhard, DR. PHIL.; German art historian; b. 4 May 1907, Munich; s. of Max Degenhart and Matilde (née Raila) Degenhart; m. Annegrit Schmitt-Degenhart 1987; ed. Univs. of Munich, Vienna, Berlin; with Munich State Museums 1931–32; Asst. Bibliotheca Hertziana, Rome 1933–39; with Kustos Museum Albertina, Vienna 1940–46; Keeper Staatliche Graphische Sammlung (Print Room Munich) 1949–71; mem. Accademia Nazionale di San Luca, Rome 1973, Akademie der Schönen Künste, Munich 1973, Accademia Marchigiana di scienze ed arti, Ancona 1979, Accademia degli Intronati, Siena 1980, Bayerischer Maximiliansorden für Kunst und Wissenschaft 1984, Bayerische Akademie der Wissenschaften 1985, Accademia Ateneo Veneto, Venice 1986; Dr. h.c. (Munich) 1972; prizes include Medaglia ai Benemeriti della Cultura, Rome 1957, Premio Internazionale Galileo Galilei, University Pisa 1976. *Publications:* Corpus der ital. Zeichnungen 1300–1450 (with Annegrit Schmitt), Parts 1–12 1968–90, Graphologie der ital. Handzeichnung 1937, Pisanello 1941, Europäische Handzeichnungen 1943, Jacopo Bellini 1984, Pisanello und Bono da Ferrara (with Annegrit Schmitt) 1995. *Leisure interest:* Italian drawings. *Address:* Staatliche Graphische Sammlung, Meiserstrasse 10, 80333 Munich, Germany. *Telephone:* (089) 5591497.

DE GENNES, Pierre-Gilles, PH.D.; French professor; b. 24 Oct. 1932, Paris; s. of Robert De Gennes and Yvonne Morin-Pons; m. Anne-Marie Rouet 1954; two s. one d.; ed. Ecole Normale; Research Engineer, Commissariat Energie Atomique 1955–59; Prof. Univ. Orsay 1961–71; Prof. Coll. de France 1971–; Dir. Ecole de Physique et Chimie industrielles 1976–; Wolf Prize 1990, Nobel Prize for Physics 1991. *Publications:* Superconductivity of Metals and Alloys 1966, The Physics of Liquid Crystals 1974, Scaling Concepts in Polymer Physics 1979, Simple Views on Condensed Matter 1992, Les objets fragiles 1994. *Leisure interests:* hiking, windsurfing and drawing. *Address:* 11 place Marcelin-Berthelot, 75005 Paris (Office); 10 rue Vauquelin, 75005 Paris, France (Home). *Telephone:* (1) 40-79-45-00 (Home).

DE GIORGI, H. E. Cardinal Salvatore; Italian ecclesiastic; b. 6 Sept. 1930, Vernole; ordained priest 1953; Bishop 1973, Archbishop, See of Oria 1978, of Foggia 1981, of Taranto 1987, of Palermo 1996; cr. Cardinal Feb. 1998. *Address:* Curia Arcivescovile, Corso Vittorio Emanuele 461, 90134 Palermo, Italy.

DE GROOT, Albert; Netherlands publisher; b. 3 May 1945, Rotterdam; s. of Albertus A. De Groot and Cornelia A. Hess; m. Janetta C. Pasman 1964; one s. one d.; no formal educ.; Production Man. Rotterdam Univ. Press 1963, Sales Man. 1967; Ed., Elsevier Nederland 1969, Ed.-in-Chief 1972, Vice-Man. 1974; Man. Dir. Veen, Luitingh-Sijthoff, Kosmos, Contact 1979, Uitgeverij L. J. Veen BV; now Dir. Veen Uitgevers Groep. *Address:* Veen Uitgevers Groep, St. Jacobsstraat 125, P.O. Box 14095, 3508 SC Utrecht, Netherlands.

DEGUARA, Louis, M.D.; Maltese politician and doctor; b. 18 Sep. 1947, Naxxar; m. Maria Fatima Mallia; one s. one d.; ed. St. Aloysius Coll., Birkikara, Univ. of Malta; medical practitioner 1973; fmrly. houseman St. Luke's, Sir Paul Boffa and Gozo General Hospitals, Prin. Medical Officer of Health, Northern Region; Gen. Practitioner 1977–; M.P., Nationalist Party 1981–; Parl. Sec. Ministry for Social Devt. 1995–96; Shadow Minister and Opposition Spokesman for Health 1996–98; Minister of Health 1998–. *Address:* Ministry of Health, Palazzo Castellania, 15 Merchant Street, Valletta, CMR 02, Malta. *Telephone:* 224071–7. *Fax:* 252574.

DE HAAN, Hendrik, PH.D.; Netherlands professor of international economics; b. 8 April 1941, Nijmegen; m. Adriana Annie Kramer 1966; two s. one d.; ed. Univ. of Groningen, Netherlands, Catholic Univ. of Louvain, Belgium; Prof. of Int. Econs., Univ. of Groningen 1971–; consultant to UNCTAD 1975; consultant-expert to UN on econ. and social consequences of the arms race 1977, 1982, 1987; consultant to UN on relationship between disarmament and devt. 1985–87; Foreign Policy Adviser to Christian Democratic Party 1989–. *Publications:* Het Moderne Geldwezen (Modern Money); several other books on econ. topics; numerous articles in scientific journals. *Address:* Department of Economics, P.O. Box 800, 9700 AV Groningen (Office); Hoofdstraat 173, 9827 PB Lettelbert, Netherlands (Home). *Telephone:* 050-633710 (Office); 05945-18238 (Home). *Fax:* 050-637337.

DEHAENE, Jean-Luc; Belgian politician; b. 7 Aug. 1940, Montpellier; m. Celie Verbeke 1965; four c.; ed. Univ. of Namur; adviser to various govt. ministries 1972–81; Minister of Social Affairs and Institutional Reforms 1981–88; Deputy Prime Minister and Minister of Communications and Institutional Reforms 1988–92; Prime Minister of Belgium March 1992–. *Address:* Office of the Prime Minister, 16 rue de la Loi, 1000 Brussels; Berkendallaan 52, 1800 Vilvoorde, Belgium. *Telephone:* (2) 5010211 (Brussels).

de HAVILLAND, Olivia Mary; American (b. British) actress; b. 1 July 1916, Tokyo, Japan; d. of Walter Augustus de Havilland and Lilian Augusta (née Ruse); m. 1st Marcus Aurelius Goodrich 1946 (divorced 1953); one s.; m. 2nd Pierre Paul Galante 1955 (divorced 1979); one d.; ed. Saratoga Grammar School, Notre Dame Convent, Los Gatos Union High School; stage début in A Midsummer Night's Dream 1934, film début in screen version 1935; Pres. Cannes Film Festival 1965; on lecture tours in U.S.A. 1971–80; mem. Bd. of Trustees of American Coll. in Paris 1970–71, of American Library in Paris 1974–81; mem. Altar Guild, Lay Reader, American Cathedral in Paris 1971–81; numerous awards include: Acad. Award 1946, 1949; New York Critics Award 1948, 1949; Look Magazine Award 1941, 1946, 1949; Venice Film Festival Award 1948; Filmex Tribute 1978; American Acad. of Achievement Award 1978; American Exemplar Medal 1980, Golden Globe 1988; Dr. h.c. (American Univ. of Paris) 1994. *Films include:* Captain Blood 1935, Anthony Adverse 1936, The Adventures of Robin Hood 1938, Gone with the Wind 1939, Hold Back the Dawn 1941, Princess O'Rourke 1942, To Each His Own (Acad. Award) 1946, The Dark Mirror 1946, The Snake Pit 1947, The Heiress (Acad. Award) 1949, My Cousin Rachel 1952, Not as a Stranger 1954, The Proud Rebel 1957, The Light in the Piazza 1961, Lady in a Cage 1963, Hush Hush Sweet Charlotte 1964, The Adventurers 1968, Airport '77 1976, The Swarm 1978, The Fifth Musketeer. *Plays:* Romeo and Juliet 1951, Candida 1951–52, A Gift of Time 1962. *TV:* Noon Wine 1966, Screaming Woman 1972, Roots, The Next Generations 1979, Murder is Easy 1981, Charles and Diana: A Royal Romance, 1982, North and South II 1986, Anastasia 1986 (Golden Globe Award), The Woman He Loved 1987. *Publications:* Every Frenchman Has One 1962, Mother and Child (contrib.) 1975. *Leisure interests:* crossword puzzles, reading tales of mystery and imagination, painting on Sunday. *Address:* B.P. 156-16, 75764 Paris Cedex 16, France.

DEHEM, Roger Jules, PH.D., F.R.S.C.; Belgian professor of economics; b. 24 July 1921, Wemmel; s. of Charles Dehem and Elise (née Masschelein) Dehem; m. Gertrude Montbleau 1950; two s. four d.; ed. Univ. of Louvain; Lecturer McGill Univ. 1947–49, Prof. Univ. of Montreal 1948–58; Prin. Admin. OEEC 1958–59; Economist Adv. Fabrimétal, Brussels 1959–60; Prof. Economics Laval Univ., Quebec 1961–95, Prof. Emer. 1995–; Fellow Rockefeller Foundation 1946–48; Pres. Canadian Econ. Asscn. 1973–74. *Publications:* L'efficacité sociale du système économique 1952, Traité d'analyse économique 1957, L'utopie de l'économiste 1969, L'équilibre économique international 1970, De l'étalon sterling à l'étalon dollar 1972, Précis d'économique internationale 1982, Histoire de la pensée économique 1984, Les Economies capitalistes et socialistes 1988, Capitalismes et Socialismes 1989. *Address:* 2000 rue Chapdelaine, Sainte-Foy, Quebec, G1V 1M3, Canada (Home). *Telephone:* (418) 681-9593.

DEHENNIN, Baron Herman, LL.D.; Belgian diplomatist; b. 20 July 1929, Lier; s. of Alexander Dehennin and Flora Brehmen; m. Margareta-Maria Donvil 1954; two s.; ed. Catholic Univ. of Leuven; Lieut. in Royal Belgian Artillery 1951–53; entered Diplomatic Service 1954, Second Sec. The Hague 1956–59, First Sec. New Delhi 1960–63, Commercial Counsellor, Madrid 1964–65, Chargé d'Affaires, Congo 1965–66, Amb. to Rwanda 1966–70, EC Minister of Belgium in Washington, DC 1970–74, Deputy Admin. to Dir.-Gen. Foreign Econ. Relations, Brussels 1974–77, Grand Marshal of the Belgian Royal Court 1981–85; Amb. to Japan 1978–81, to U.S.A. 1985–90, to U.K. 1991–94; Grand Cross of Order of Leopold, Grand Cross of Order of the Crown. *Leisure interests:* jogging, hiking, tennis, fishing, hunting, reading (history and philosophy).

DEHMELT, Hans Georg, DR.RER.NAT.; American physicist; b. 9 Sept. 1922, Görlitz, Germany; s. of Georg Dehmelt and Asta Klemmt; m. Diana Dundore 1989; one s. from a previous marriage; ed. Gymnasium Zum Grauen Kloster, Berlin, Breslau Tech. Univ., Göttingen Univ. and Inst. of Hans Kopfermann; served as private in German army 1940–46, P.O.W. 1945–46; Deutsche Forschungs-Gemeinschafts Fellow, Inst. of Hans Kopfermann 1950–52; co-discovered nuclear quadrupole resonance 1949; postdoctoral work in microwave spectroscopy lab., Duke Univ., U.S.A. 1952–55; Visiting Asst. Prof., Univ. of Washington, Seattle, U.S.A. 1955–56, Asst. Prof. 1956–58, Assoc. Prof. 1958–61, Prof. 1961–, also research physicist; with others, achieved the most precise electron magnetic moment determination to date, through work on geonium 1976–; became U.S. citizen 1961; Fellow American Physical Soc.; mem. N.A.S., American Acad. of Arts and Sciences; Dr. Rer. Nat. h.c. (Ruprecht Karl Univ., Heidelberg) 1986, Hon. D.Sc. (Chicago) 1987; Davisson-Germer Prize, American Physical Soc. 1970, Alexander von Humboldt Prize 1974, Award in Basic Research, Int. Soc. of Magnetic Resonance 1980, Count Rumford Prize, American Acad. of Arts and Sciences 1985, Nobel Prize in Physics 1989 for measurement on isolated Subatomic particle and atomic particle at rest, Nat. Medal of Science 1995. *Publication:* Radiofrequency Spectroscopy of Stored Ions 1967. *Address:* Department of Physics, FM 15, University of Washington, Seattle, WA 98195, U.S.A.; 1600 43rd Avenue E., Seattle, WA 98112, U.S.A. (Home).

DE HOOP, Adrianus Teunis, PH.D.; Netherlands professor of electromagnetic theory and applied mathematics; b. 24 Dec. 1927, Rotterdam; ed. Delft Univ. of Tech.; Research Asst., Delft Univ. of Tech. 1950–52, Asst. Prof. 1953–56, Assoc. Prof. 1957–60, Prof. 1960–96, Prof. Emer. 1996–; Reserve Officer, Royal Netherlands Navy 1952–53; Research Asst., Univ. of Calif., Los Angeles 1956–57; Visiting Research Scientist, Philips Research Labs., Eindhoven 1976–77, Consultant 1977–89; mem. Royal Netherlands Acad. of Arts and Sciences 1989, Royal Acad. of Arts and Sciences of Belgium 1998; Hon. Ph.D. (Ghent) 1982; awards from Stichting Fund for Science, Tech. and Research 1986, 1989, 1990, 1993, 1994, Gold Research Medal, Royal Inst. of Eng. 1989. *Publications:* Handbook of Radiation and Scattering of Waves 1995; numerous articles in journals. *Leisure interest:* playing the piano. *Address:* Faculty of Information Technology and Systems, Delft University of Technology, P.O. Box 5031, 2600 GA Delft (Office); Korenmolen 17, 2661 LE Bergschenhoek, Netherlands (Home). *Telephone:* (15) 2785203 (Office); (10) 5220049 (Home). *Fax:* (15) 2786194.

DEIGHTON, Len; British author; b. 1929, London. *Publications:* The Ipcress File 1962 (also film), Horse under Water 1963, Funeral in Berlin 1964 (also film), Où est le Garlic 1965, Action Cook Book 1965, Cookstrip Cook Book (U.S.A.) 1966, Billion Dollar Brain 1966 (also film), An Expensive Place to Die 1967, Len Deighton's London Dossier (guide book) 1967, The Assassination of President Kennedy (co-author) 1967, Only When I Larf 1968 (also film), Bomber 1970 (also radio dramatization), Declarations of War (short stories) 1971, Close-Up 1972, Spy Story 1974 (also film), Yesterday's Spy 1975, Twinkle, Twinkle, Little Spy 1976, Fighter: the True Story of the Battle of Britain 1977, SS-GB 1978, Airshipwreck (co-author) 1978, Blitzkrieg 1979, Battle of Britain (co-author) 1980, XPD 1981, Goodbye Mickey Mouse 1982, Berlin Game 1983, Mexico Set 1984, London Match 1985, Winter: a Berlin Family 1899–1945 1987, Spy Hook 1988, ABC of French Food 1989, Spy Line 1989, Spy Sinker 1990, Basic French Cookery Course 1990, Mamista 1991, City of Gold 1992, Violent Ward 1993, Blood, Tears and Folly 1993, Faith 1994, Hope 1995, Charity 1996. *Address:* c/o Jonathan Clowes Ltd., 10 Iron Bridge House, Bridge Approach, London, NW1 8BD, England.

DEINEKIN, Piotr Stepanovich, Gen., DR.MIL.SC.; Russian army officer; b. 14 Dec. 1937, Morozovsk, Rostov Region; m.; three c.; ed. Balashov Military Aviation School, Yuri Gagarin Air Force Acad., Gen. Staff Acad.; pilot, army air force 1957–69, commdr. aviation regt., div. 1969–82, Deputy Commander Army Air Force 1982–85, Commdr. 1985–90, First Vice-C.-in-C. of U.S.S.R. Air-Force 1990, C.-in-C. and Deputy Minister of Defence of U.S.S.R. (now Russia) 1991–98; Head Pres. Yeltsin's Admin. Dept. on the Cossack Problem Sept. 1998–; Hero of Russian Fed. 1997. *Address:* Staraya pl. 4, entr. 1, Moscow, Russia. *Telephone:* (095) 206-35-73 (Office).

DE IRALA, Xabier; Spanish business executive; b. 1947, New York; ed. France and the Philippines; Vice-Pres. Gen. Electric France, mem. Bd. of Dirs.; Exec. Vice-Pres. Asean Brown Boveri España 1990–96, adviser 1991–96; Pres. Iberia July 1996–. *Address:* IBERIA, Líneas Aéreas de España, SA, Velázquez 130, 2006 Madrid, Spain. *Telephone:* (1) 5878787. *Fax:* (1) 5857682.

De JAGER, Cornelis; Netherlands astronomer; b. 29 April 1921, Den Burg, Texel; s. of Jan de Jager and Cornelia Kuyper; m. Duotje Rienks 1947; two s. two d.; ed. Univ. of Utrecht; Asst. in theoretical physics, Univ. of Utrecht 1946; Asst. in Astronomy, Univ. of Leiden; Asst. Astron. Inst., Utrecht; Assoc. Prof. of Stellar Astrophysics, Univ. of Utrecht 1957, Ordinary Prof. in Gen. Astrophysics 1960–86; Extraordinary Prof., Univ. of Brussels and founder, Space Research Lab., Utrecht and Astron. Inst., Brussels 1961; Man. Dir. Utrecht Astron. Inst. 1963–78, Chair. Inst. Council 1978–83; Asst. Gen. Sec. Int. Astron. Union 1967–70, Gen. Sec. 1970–73; Pres. Netherlands Astron. Comm. 1975–83; mem. Exec. Council Cttee. on Space Research (COSPAR) 1970–72, Pres. 1972–78, 1982–86; mem. Exec. Council, ICSU 1970–82, Vice-Pres. 1976–78, Pres. 1978–80; Chair. Skepsis (for critical evaluation of the paranormal) 1987–97; European Council of Sceptical Orgs. 1995–; Aggregate Prof., Univ. of Brussels 1970–86; mem. Royal Netherlands Acad. of Art and Sciences (Foreign Sec. 1985–90), Royal Belgium Acad. of Art and Sciences, Acad. Europe (Paris and London); Assoc. mem. Royal Astron. Soc. (London); Corresp. mem. Soc. Royale de Science, Liège; mem. Int. Acad. Astronautics, Chair. Basic Sciences Section 1984–92; Foreign mem. Deutsche Akademie Leopoldina, Halle; Hon. mem. Netherlands Soc. Astronomy and Meteorology 1996; Foreign Fellow Indian Nat. Scientific Acad.; Dr. h.c. Univ. of Wrocław, Poland 1975, Observatoire de Paris 1976; Yuri Gagarin Medal (U.S.S.R.) 1984, J. Janssen Medal (France) 1984, Ziolkowski Medal, U.S.S.R. Acad. of Sciences; Kt., Order of the Dutch Lion 1983; Gold Medal Royal Astronomical Soc., London 1988; Hale Medal, American Astronomical Soc. 1988; COSPAR Medal for Int. Co-operation in Space Science 1988, Gold Medal Royal Netherlands Acad. Arts and Sciences, Gold Medal Netherlands Soc. Astronomy and Meteorology, In Praise of Reason Award CSICOP, Buffalo, NY 1990, Von Karman Award of Int. Acad. of Astronautics 1993. *Publications:* About 550 publications including: The Hydrogen Spectrum of the Sun 1952, Structure and Dynamics of the Solar Atmosphere 1959, The Solar Spectrum 1965, Solar Flares and Space Research (with Z. Svestka) 1969, Sterrenkunde 1969, Reports on Astronomy 1970, 1973, Highlights in Astronomy 1970, Ontstaan en Levensloop van Sterren (with E. van den Heuvel), 2nd edn. 1973, Image Processing Techniques in Astronomy (with H. Nieuwenhuyzen) 1975, The Brightest Stars 1980, Instabilities in evolved super- and hypergiants 1992, Bolwerk van de Sterren 1993, Tien Opmerkelijke Sterrekundige Ontdekkingen 1995, Kannibalen bij de grenzen van het heelal 1996. *Leisure interests:* birds, plants, jogging, history. *Address:* Space Research Laboratory, Sorbonnelaan 2, 3584 CA Utrecht (Office); Zonnenburg 1, 3512 NL Utrecht, Netherlands (Home). *Telephone:* (30) 2535723 (Office); (30) 2314253 (Home). *Fax:* (30) 2540860.

DEJMEK, Kazimierz; Polish theatre producer, director and actor; b. 17 May 1924, Kowel; s. of Henryk and Włodzimiera Dejmek; m. 1st Irena

Dejmek 1945; m. 2nd Danuta Dejmek 1954; m. 3rd; one s. one d; ed. State Theatrical Acad., Łódź 1949; Actor, Rzeszów, Jelenia Góra Companies 1944–46; Actor, Teatr Wojska Polskiego Łódź 1946–49; Founder and Gen. Dir. Teatr Nowy, Łódź 1949–61, 1974–79; Gen. Man. and Artistic Dir., Teatr Narodowy, Warsaw 1962–68; Gen. Man. and Artistic Dir., Teatr Polski, Warsaw 1980–93; mem. Consultative Council attached to Chair. of Council of State; Pres. Polish Artists' Asscn. 1988–89; Minister of Culture and Art 1993–96; numerous decorations incl. Commdr. Cross (with Star) of Order Polonia Restituta, Order of Banner of Labour (2nd class); State Prizes (1st, 2nd & 3rd class), Alfred Jurzykowski Foundation Award 1975, Gottfried von Herder Prize 1979. *Principal productions:* Baths (Mayakovsky) 1954, Winkelried's Day (Andrzejewski and Zagórski) 1956, Measure for Measure (Shakespeare) 1956, Darkness Covers the Earth (Andrzejewski) 1957, The Life of Joseph (Rej) 1958, 1965, Three Sisters (Chekhov) 1960, Julius Caesar (Shakespeare) 1960,The Frogs (Aristophanes) 1961, 1963, The Story of the Glorious Resurrection of Our Lord (Nicolai of Wilkowiecko) 1961, 1962, Word about Jacob Szela (Bruno Jasieński) 1962, Agamemnon (Aeschylus) 1963, Electra (Euripides) 1963, Controller (Gogol) 1964, 1989, Kordian (Słowacki) 1965, 1966, Der Stellvertreter (Hochhuth) 1965, 1973, Dziady (A. Mickiewicz) 1967, Uncle Vanya (Chekhov) 1968, Jeux de Massacre (Ionesco) 1971, La Passione (anon.) 1972, opera Henry VI at the Chase (Karol Kurpiński-Dobrzański) 1973, opera Magic Flute (Mozart) 1973, Electra (Giraudoux) 1973, opera Devils of Loudun (Penderecki) 1974, Operetka (Gombrowicz) 1975, Dialogus de Passione (anon.) 1975, 1998, opera Franc-tireur (Carl Maria von Weber) 1978, Vatzlav (Mrożek) 1978, 1982, Portret (Mrożek) 1987, Drzewo (Myśliwski) 1988, opera Halka (Moniuszko) 1960, 1984, Wesele (Wyspiański) 1990. *Leisure interests:* literature, music. *Address:* ul. Rajców 8 m. 1, 00-220 Warsaw, Poland.

DE JONG, Jan Willem, PH.D.; Netherlands academic; b. 15 Feb. 1921, Leiden; s. of late Dirk Cornelis de Jong and Johanna Elisabeth van Biemen; m. Gisèle Fernande Bacquès 1949; one s. two d.; Gymnasium, Leiden, Univ. of Leiden, Harvard Univ. and Univ. of Paris; Prof. of Tibetan and Buddhist Studies Univ. of Leiden 1956–65; Prof. of S. Asian and Buddhist Studies Australian Nat. Univ., Canberra 1965–86, Visiting Fellow Dept. of East Asian History 1987–92; Co-Founder and Co-Ed. Indo-Iranian Journal 1956–; Corresp. mem. Royal Netherlands Acad. of Arts and Sciences 1978; Fellow Australian Acad. of the Humanities 1970; Hon. D.Litt. (Nava Nalanda Mahavihara, India) 1983. *Publications:* Cinq chapitres de la Prasannapadā 1949, Mi la ras pa'i rnam thar, Texte tibétain de la vie de Milarepa 1959, A Brief History of Buddhist Studies in Europe and America 1976, Textcritical Remarks on the Bodhisattvāvadānakalpalatā 1979, Buddhist Studies 1981, The Story of Rama in Tibet 1989, Tibetan Studies 1994. *Leisure interests:* tennis, walking. *Address:* 4 Jansz Crescent, Griffith, A.C.T. 2603, Australia. *Telephone:* (2) 62953750.

de JONGH, Eduard, S.; Netherlands art historian; b. 7 June 1931, Amsterdam; m. Lammijna Oosterbaan 1977; two s. one d.; ed. Baarns Lyceum, Baarn and Univ. of Utrecht; journalist and art critic, Het Parool and Vrij Nederland 1954–74; Librarian, Inst. for Art History, Univ. of Utrecht 1963–66; Ed. Openbaar Kunstbezit (radio course) 1963–73; Ed. Simiolus (art history quarterly) 1966–77; mem. staff, Centrum Voortgezet Kunsthistorisch Onderzoek, Univ. of Utrecht 1966–73; Asst. Prof. Inst. for Art History, Univ. of Utrecht 1973–76, Prof. of Art History 1976–89, Prof. Emer. 1989–; Ed. Kunstschrift 1990–; Visiting scholar, Getty Center for History of Art and Humanities 1987; mem. Royal Netherlands Acad.; foreign mem. Royal Belgian Acad.; Karel van Mander Award. *Publications:* Zinne- en minnebeelden in de schilderkunst van de zeventiende eeuw 1967, Tot Lering en Vermaak. Betekenissen van Hollandse genrevoorstellingen uit de zeventiende eeuw 1976, Still Life in the Age of Rembrandt 1982, Portretten van echt en trouw. Huwelijk en gezin in de Nederlandse kunst van de zeventiende eeuw 1986, Kunst en het vruchtbare misverstand 1993, Faces of the Golden Age: Seventeenth-Century Dutch Portraits 1994, Kwesties van betekenis. Thema en motief in de Nederlandse schilderkunst van de zeventiende eeuw 1995, The Mirror of Everyday Life. Genre Prints in The Netherlands 1550–1700 (with Ger Luijten) 1997; many articles on iconological and art theoretical subjects. *Address:* Frederick Hendrikstraat 29, 3583 VG Utrecht, Netherlands.

DE KEERSMAEKER, Anne Teresa; Belgian choreographer; b. 11 June 1960, Wemmel; one s. one d.; ed. Mudra, School of Maurice Béjart, Brussels and Tisch School of the Arts, New York Univ.; presented first work, Asch in Brussels 1980; founded Rosas Dance Co. 1983; Rosas became co.-in-residence, Théâtre de la Monnaie, Brussels with herself as resident choreographer 1992; choreographic works: Asch 1980, Fase: four movements to music of Steve Reich 1982, Rosas danst Rosas 1983, Elena's Aria 1984, Bartók/Aantekeningen 1986, Verkommenes Ufer/Medeamaterial/Landschaft mit Argonauten 1987, Mikrokosmos-Monument/Selbstporträt mit Reich und Riley (und Chopin ist auch dabei)/Im zart fliessender Bewegung-Quatuor Nr. 4 1987, Ottone, Ottone 1988, Stella 1990, Achterland 1990, ERTS 1992, Mozart/Concert Arias, un moto di gioia 1992, Toccata 1993, Kinok 1994, Amor Constante más allá de la muerte 1994, Verklärte Nacht 1995, Woud 1996, Just Before 1997; directed opera Bluebeard (Bartók) 1997; artistic dir. at P.A.R.T.S. school; has also directed work for video; recipient of numerous int. dance awards. *Address:* Rosas VZW, Van Volxemlaan 164, 1190 Brussels, Belgium. *Telephone:* (32) (2) 344.55.98. *Fax:* (32) (2) 343.53.52.

DEKKER, W.; Netherlands business executive; b. 26 April 1924, Eindhoven; joined Philips, S.E. Asia Regional Bureau 1948, Man. 1956–59, with Indonesian Philips co. 1948–66, Man. Far East Regional Bureau 1959–66, Gen. Man. Philips in Far East, Tokyo 1966–72, mem. Bd. British Philips 1972, Chair. and Man. Dir. 1972–76, mem. Bd. of Man. N.V. Philips' Glœilampenfabrieken 1976–82, Pres. 1982, Chair. 1982–94; mem. Supervisory Bd. Dresdner Bank, Germany, AMRO Bank, Netherlands; mem. Int. Advisory Bd. Allianz Versicherungs AG, Germany, Volvo, Sweden; mem. Bd. Fiat, Italy; mem. Int. Advisory Cttee. Chase Manhattan Bank, New York; mem. Advisory Bd. Montedison, Italy; mem. Advisory Cttee. for Investments of Foreign Cos. in the Netherlands to Minister of Econ. Affairs; mem. Atlantic Advisory Council, United Technologies Corp., U.S.A.; Chair. Supervisory Bd. Maatschappij voor Industriële Projecten; mem. European Advisory Cttee. New York Stock Exchange; mem. Special Advisory Group, UNIDO; Prof. of Int. Man., Univ. of Leiden; mem. Tinbergen Inst., Rotterdam; Co-founder European Roundtable of Industrialists 1983, Chair. 1988–; Hon. LL.D. (Univ. of Strathclyde) 1976, Dr. h.c. (Tech. Univ. of Delft) 1987; Hon. C.B.E.; Goldenes Ehrenzeichen für Verdienste um das Land Wien (Vienna); Commdr., Order of Orange Nassau; Commdr., Order of Belgian Crown; Kt., Order of Dutch Lion; Commdr. Légion d'honneur; Cavaliere di Gran Croce dell'Ordine al Merito, Italy.

de KLERK, Albert; Netherlands organist and composer; b. 4 Oct. 1917; ed. Amsterdamsch Conservatorium under Dr. Anthon van der Horst; Organist St. Joseph's Church, Haarlem 1934–; City Organist Haarlem 1956–82; Dir. of Catholic Choir, Haarlem 1946–91; Prof. of Organ and Improvization, Sweelinck Conservatorium, Amsterdam 1964–85; numerous gramophone records for Telefunken, C.B.S., E.M.I.-Bovema, etc.; Prix d'Excellence, Amsterdam 1941, Prix du Disque, Prix Edison (for Die Kleinorgel) 1962. *Compositions:* several works for organ including three concertos for organ and orchestra, chamber-music, and liturgical music (seven masses); Netherlands Choir Music Prize 1991. *Address:* Crayenesterlaan 22, Haarlem, Netherlands.

de KLERK, Frederik Willem, LL.B.; South African politician; b. 18 March 1936, Johannesburg; s. of J. de Klerk; m. 1st Marike Willemse 1959 (divorced 1998); two s. one d.; m. 2nd Elita Georgiadis 1998; ed. Monument High School, Krugersdorp, Potchefstroom Univ.; in law practice 1961–72; mem. House of Assembly 1972; Information Officer Nat. Party, Transvaal 1975; Minister of Posts and Telecommunications and Social Welfare and Pensions 1978, subsequently Minister of Posts and Telecommunications and of Sport and Recreation 1978–79, of Mines, Energy and Environmental Planning 1979–80, of Mineral and Energy Affairs 1980–82, of Internal Affairs 1982–85, of Nat. Educ. and Planning 1984–89; Acting State Pres. of South Africa Aug.–Sept. 1989, State Pres. of South Africa 1989–94; Exec. Deputy Pres., Govt. of Nat. Unity 1994–96; Leader of the Official Opposition 1996–97; mem. Nat. Party, Transvaal Leader 1982–89, Leader 1989–97; also fmr. Chair. of the Cabt. and C.-in-C. of the Armed Forces; fmr. Chair. Council of Ministers; shared Nobel Prize for Peace with Nelson Mandela (q.v.) 1993; jt. winner Houphouet Boigny Prize (UNESCO) 1991; Asturias Prize 1992, Liberty Medal (S.A.) 1993. *Publications:* The Last Trek: A New Beginning (autobiography) 1999, various articles and brochures for the Nat. Party Information Service. *Leisure interests:* golf. *Address:* 7 Eaton Square, London, S.W.1, England; Private Bag X999, Cape Town 8000, South Africa. *Telephone:* (21) 418 2202 (Cape Town). *Fax:* (21) 418 2626 (Cape Town).

DE KORTE, Rudolf Willem, DR.RER.NAT.; Netherlands politician; b. 8 July 1936, The Hague; m.; two c.; ed. Maerlant Gymnasium, The Hague, Leiden Univ., Harvard Business School; employed in industry, Hong Kong 1964–66, Ethiopia 1967–68; Gen. Sales Man. Unilever-Emery NV 1969–71, Dir. 1972–77; Sec. People's Party for Freedom and Democracy (VVD) 1971–78; M.P. 1977, Minister for Home Affairs March–July 1986, Deputy Prime Minister and Minister for Econ. Affairs 1986–89; mem. (VVD) Lower House of Parl. 1989–; mem. Wassenaar Municipal Council 1978–82; People's Party for Freedom and Democracy (VVD). *Address:* c/o Tweede Kamer der Staten-Generaal, P.O. Box 20018, 2500 EA The Hague, Netherlands.

de la BARRE de NANTEUIL, Luc, L. ÈS L.; French diplomatist; b. 21 Sept. 1925, Lhommaize; s. of Jean de la Barre de Nanteuil and Marguerite de Beauchamp; m. 1st Philippa MacDonald; one s.; m. 2nd Hedwige Frèrejean de Chavagneux; one s. one d.; ed. Faculty of Arts and Letters, Paris and Ecole Nat. d'Administration; Ministry of Foreign Affairs 1950–59; First Sec. Embassy London 1959–64; Asst. Dir. African and Middle East Affairs Dept., Paris 1964–70; promoted to rank of Minister Plenipotentiary 1969; Head, Econ. Co-operation Service, Directorate of Econ. Affairs 1970–76; Amb. to Netherlands 1976–77; Amb. Perm. Rep. to EEC, Brussels 1977–81, 1984–86; Amb. Perm. Rep. to UN Security Council and Head., Perm. Mission to UN, N.Y. 1981–84; Diplomatic Adviser 1986; Amb. to U.K. 1986–91; Chair. Groupe de Presse Les Echos 1991–; Officier, Légion d'honneur, Commdr., Ordre Nat. du Mérite. *Publication:* a book on the painter Jacques-Louis David. *Leisure interests:* economics and arts. *Address:* Les Echos, 46 rue La Boétie, 75008 Paris, France. *Telephone:* 49-53-65-65.

de la BILLIÈRE, Gen. Sir Peter (Edgar de la Cour), K.C.B., K.B.E., D.S.O., M.C. (and bar); British army officer (retd.); b. 29 April 1934, Plymouth; s. of Surgeon Lieut.-Commdr. Claude de Labillière and Frances C. W. Lawley; m. Bridget C. M. Goode 1965; one s. two d.; ed. Harrow School, Staff Coll. and Royal Coll. of Defence Studies; joined King's Shropshire Light Infantry

1952; commissioned, Durham Light Infantry; served Japan, Korea, Malaya (despatches 1959), Jordan, Borneo, Egypt, Aden, Gulf States, Sudan, Oman, Falkland Islands; Commdg. Officer, 22 Special Air Service (SAS) Regt. 1972–74; Gen. Staff Officer 1 (Directing Staff), Staff Coll. 1974–77; Commdr. British Army Training Team, Sudan 1977–78; Dir. SAS and Commdr. SAS Group 1978–83; Commdr. British Forces, Falkland Islands and Mil. Commr. 1984–85; Gen. Officer Commdg. Wales 1985–87; Gen. Officer commanding Col. Comdt. Light Div. 1986–90; Lieut.-Gen. S.E. Dist. 1987–90; Commdr. British Forces in Middle East Oct. 1990–91; rank of Gen. 1991 after Gulf War, Ministry of Defence Adviser on Middle East 1991–92; retd. from army June 1992; Pres. SAS Asscn. 1991–96, Army Cadet Force 1992–; mem. Council Royal United Services Inst. 1975–77; Chair. Jt. Services Hang Gliding 1986–88; Cdre. Army Sailing Asscn. 1989–90; Commr. Duke of York's School 1988–90; Trustee Imperial War Museum 1992–; Dir. (non-exec.), Middle East and Defence Adviser, Robert Fleming Holdings 1992–; Jt. Vice-Chair. Dirs. FARM Africa 1995–; D.L. Hereford and Worcester 1993; Hon. Freeman Fishmongers' Co. 1991; Hon. D.Sc. (Cranfield) 1992; Hon. D.C.L. (Durham) 1993; Legion of Merit Chief Commdr. (USA), Order of Abdul Aziz 2nd Class (Saudi Arabia), Meritorious Service Cross (Canada), Kuwait Decoration of the First Class, Order of Qatar Sash of Merit, Freeman City of London 1991. *Publications:* Storm Command 1992, Looking for Trouble 1994. *Leisure interests:* family, squash, apiculture, farming, sailing. *Address:* c/o Robert Fleming Holdings, 25 Copthall Avenue, London, EC2R 7DR, England. *Telephone:* 0171-638 5858. *Fax:* 0171-256 8592.

DELACÔTE, Jacques; French conductor; s. of Pierre Delacôte and Renée Wagner Delacôte; m. Maria Lucia Alvares-Machado 1975; ed. Music Conservatoire, Paris, Acad. of Music, with Prof. Hans Swarowsky, Vienna; was asst. of Darius Milhaud and Leonard Bernstein; among the orchestras conducted: Orchestre de Paris, Orchestre Nat. de France, New York Philharmonic, Vienna Philharmonic, Vienna Symphony, Israel Philharmonic, Orchestre Nat. de Belgique, London Symphony Orchestra, San Francisco, Cleveland Orchestra, Scottish Chamber, Scottish Nat., RIAS Berlin, WDR Cologne, SF Stuttgart, SWF Baden-Baden, Bavarian Radio, Munich, English Chamber, BBC, London, London Philharmonic, Japan Philharmonic, Yomiuri Symphony, Royal Opera House Covent Garden (including Far East tour, Korea and Japan), English Nat. Opera, Scottish Opera, Opernhaus Zürich, Teatro Real Madrid, Vienna State Opera, Deutsche Oper Berlin, Pittsburgh Opera, Welsh Nat. Opera, Teatro Liceo Barcelona, Opéra de Paris, Teatro Colón Buenos Aires, Canadian Opera Co., Royal State Opera Copenhagen, State Opera Hamburg, State Opera Munich; also recordings with EMI and Philips London; 1st Prize and Gold Medal Mitropoulos Competition, New York 1971. *Leisure interest:* chess. *Address:* Dr Hilbert Maximilianstr. 22, 80539 Munich, Germany.

DE LA MADRID HURTADO, Miguel; Mexican politician and lawyer; b. 1935; m. Paloma C. de la Madrid; five c.; ed. Harvard Univ., U.S.A.; successively with Bank of Mexico, Petróleos Mexicanos (PEMEX) (Asst. Dir. of Finances 1970–72); Dir. Public Sector Credit, later Under-Sec., Ministry of Finance; Sec. for Planning and Fed. Budget, Govt. of Mexico 1979–80; Institutional Revolutionary Party (PRI) cand. to succeed López Portillo as Pres. of Mexico Sept. 1981; Pres. of Mexico 1982–88; Pres. Nat. Asscn. of Lawyers 1989–, Mexican Inst. of Culture 1989–; Dir.-Gen. Fondo de Cultura Económica 1990–. *Address:* Parras 46, Barrio Sta. Catarina, Deleg. Coyoacán, 04010, México, D.F., Mexico. *Telephone:* (525) 658 4459.

de la MORENA, Felipe, LL.D.; Spanish diplomatist; b. 22 Oct. 1927, Málaga; s. of Felipe de la Morena and Luisa Calvet; m. María Teresa Casado Bach 1958; two s. two d.; ed. Universidad Complutense de Madrid, Univ. of Grenoble, France, Univ. of Oxford, U.K.; entered Diplomatic Service 1957, Sec., Embassy, Beirut 1959–61, Embassy, Berne 1961–65, First Sec., Embassy, Washington, D.C. 1965–71; Dir. E. European Desk, Ministry of Foreign Affairs 1971–73; Asst. Rep., Conf. on Security and Co-operation, Helsinki 1973–74; Dir. Tech. Office, Minister of Devt. Planning 1974–75; Minister-Counsellor, Embassy in Lisbon 1976–78; Amb. to People's Repub. of China 1978–82; Dir.-Gen. of Foreign Policy for Latin America 1982–83; Amb. to Syria (also accred. to Cyprus) 1983–87, to Tunisia 1987–90, to the U.K. 1990–92; Chair. British Hispanic Foundation, Madrid 1993–; Alfonso X el Sabio, Mérito Civil, Isabel la Católica and Carlos III awards, Grand Cross, Mérito Naval. *Leisure interest:* golf. *Address:* Fundación Hispano-Británica, Maestro Lasalle 46, 28016 Madrid, Spain.

DE LA PEÑA, Javier, M.S.; Spanish petrochemical industry executive; b. 13 May 1940, Cortes, Navarra; s. of Juan-Jesus de la Peña and Julia de la Peña; m. Katherine Zegarra 1969; one s. three d.; ed. Univ. of Valencia and Univ. of Kansas, U.S.A.; joined Phillips Petroleum group 1965, Dept. of Eng. (Okla.) and Int. Dept. (New York), U.S.A. 1965–67, Marketing, Phillips Calatrava Ventas, Madrid 1967–68, Man. in charge of Projects for Latin America (New York) 1968–70, Marketing Man. Phillips Calatrava Ventas, Madrid 1970–72, Gen. Man. 1972–74, Devt. Man. Phillips Petroleum Chemicals, Brussels 1975–77, Vice-Pres., Devt. and Licensing 1978–82, Vice-Pres. and Man. Dir. for Petrochemicals (Olefins and Aromatics) of Phillips Petroleum Chemicals 1982–85; Vice-Pres. REPSOL PETROLEO, S.A., in charge of Petrochemical Group; REPSOL Rep. in Asscn. of European Petrochemical Producers 1985; Pres. REPSOL QUIMICA, S.A. 1986; Fulbright Scholar 1963–64. *Leisure interests:* sports, piano and music.

DE LA QUADRA-SALCEDO Y FERNANDEZ DEL CASTILLO, Tomás, PH.D.; Spanish politician; b. 1946, Madrid; m.; two c.; ed. Complutense Univ. of Madrid; Asst. Lecturer in Administrative Law, Faculty of Law, Complutense Univ. of Madrid 1977–81 (Temporary Lecturer 1968), in Audio-visual Media, Information Sciences Faculty 1981–; mem. Lawyers' Asscn. of Madrid 1968–; Minister of Territorial Admin. 1982–85, of Justice 1985–93; Pres. Council of State 1985. *Publications:* various articles and books. *Address:* c/o PSOE, Ferraz 68 y 70, 28008 Madrid, Spain. *Telephone:* 1-582-0444. *Fax:* 1-582-0422.

de la RENTA, Oscar; Dominican Republic fashion designer; b. 22 July 1932, Santo Domingo; m. 1st Françoise de Langlade 1967 (died 1983); one adopted s.; m. 2nd Anne E. de la Renta 1989; ed. Santo Domingo Univ., Academia de San Fernando, Madrid; staff designer, under Cristobal Balenciaga, AISA couture house, Madrid; asst. to Antonio Castillo, Lanvin-Castillo, Paris 1961–63; designer, Elizabeth Arden couture and ready-to-wear collection, New York 1963–65; designer and partner, Jane Derby Inc. New York 1965; after her retirement firm evolved into Oscar de la Renta, Inc. which was purchased by Richton Int. 1969; Chief Exec. Richton's Oscar de la Renta Couture, Oscar de la Renta II, Oscar de la Renta Furs, Oscar de la Renta Jewelry and mem. Bd. of Dirs. Richton Int. 1969–73; f. Oscar de la Renta, Ltd. 1973, C.E.O. 1973–; couturier for Balmain, Paris Nov. 1992–; produces about 80 different product lines including high-fashion clothing, household linens, accessories and perfumes for shops in U.S.A., Canada, Mexico and Japan; owner, Oscar de la Renta shop, Santo Domingo 1968–; recipient of numerous fashion awards; Caballero, Order of San Pablo Duarte, Order of Cristobal Colon. *Address:* Oscar de la Renta Ltd., 550 7th Avenue, 8th Floor, New York, NY 10018, U.S.A.

de LAROSIÈRE de CHAMPFEU, Jacques Martin Henri, Marie, L. ÈS L., L. EN D.; French banking executive; b. 12 Nov. 1929, Paris; s. of Robert de Larosière and Hugayte de Champfeu; m. France du Bos 1960; one s. one d.; ed. Lycée Louis-le-Grand, Inst. d'études politiques de Paris and Ecole nat. d'admin.;. Asst. Inspector of Finances 1958, Inspector 1960, chargé de mission, inspection gen. des Finances 1961, Dir. des Finances extérieures 1963, attached to the Treasury 1965, Deputy Dir. 1967, Dir. 1974–78; Asst. Dir. then Dept. Head, Ministry of Economy and Finance 1971, Dir. Jan.–May 1974; Admin. Nat. Man., Renault 1971–74, Banque nat. de Paris 1973–78, Air France 1974–78, SNCF 1974–78, Soc. nat. industrielle aérospatiale 1976–78; Censeur, Comptoir des entrepreneurs 1973–75, Crédit nat. 1974–78, Banque de France 1974–78, Crédit foncier de France 1975–78; Vice-Pres. Caisse nat. des télécommunications 1974–78; Pres. Group of Ten, OECD 1976–78, Chair. Cttee of Govs. 1990–93; Pres. E.B.R.D. 1993–98; Man. Dir. IMF 1978–87; Gen. Inspector of Finance 1981–; Gov. Banque de France 1987–93, Hon. Gov. 1993–; Officier, Légion d'honneur, Chevalier, ordre nat. du Mérite (Cincinnati); numerous other decorations. *Address:* 5 rue de Beaujolais, 75001 Paris, France.

de la TOUR, Frances; British actress; b. 30 July 1944, Bovingdon, Herts.; d. of Charles de la Tour and Moyra (née Fessas); m. Tom Kempinski 1972 (divorced 1982); one s. one d.; ed. Lycée français de Londres, Drama Centre, London; with the R.S.C. 1965–71. *Stage appearances include:* As You Like It 1967, The Relapse 1969, A Midsummer Night's Dream 1971, The Man of Mode 1971, Small Craft Warnings (Best Supporting Actress, Plays and Players Award) 1973, The Banana Box 1973, The White Devil 1976, Hamlet (title role) 1979, Duet for One (Best Actress, New Standard Award, Best Actress, Critics Award, Best Actress, Soc. of W. End Theatres—SWET Award) 1980, Skirmishes 1981, Uncle Vanya 1982, Moon for the Misbegotten (Best Actress, SWET Award) 1983, St. Joan 1984, Dance of Death 1985, Brighton Beach Memoirs 1986, Lillian 1986, Façades 1988, King Lear 1989, When She Danced (Olivier Award) 1991, The Pope and the Witch 1992, Greasepaint 1993, Les Parents Terribles (Royal Nat. Theatre) 1994, Three Tall Women 1994–95, Blinded by the Sun (Royal Nat. Theatre) 1996, The Play About the Baby (Almeida Theatre) 1998, The Forest (Royal Nat. Theatre) 1998–99, Antony and Cleopatra (RSC) 1999. *Films include:* Our Miss Fred 1972, To the Devil a Daughter 1976, Rising Damp (Best Actress, Standard Film Award) 1980, Murder with Mirrors 1984, Bejewelled 1990, Genghis Cohn 1994, The Cherry Orchard 1998. *Television appearances include:* Crimes of Passion 1973, Rising Damp 1974, 1976, Cottage to Let 1976, Flickers 1980, Skirmishes 1982, Duet for One 1985, Partners 1986, Clem 1986, A Kind of Living (series) 1987/88, Downwardly Mobile (series) 1994, Cold Lazarus 1996, Tom Jones 1997. *Address:* c/o Kate Feast Management, 10 Primrose Hill Studios, Fitzroy Road, London, NW1 8TR, England. *Telephone:* 0171-586 5502. *Fax:* 0171-586 4092.

De LAURENTIIS, Dino; Italian film producer; b. 8 Aug. 1919, Torre Annunziata, Naples; s. of Aurelio and Giuseppina (née Salvatore) De Laurentiis; m. Silvana Mangano 1949; one s. (deceased) three d.; founded Real Ciné, Turin 1941; Exec. Producer Lux Film 1942; acquired Safir Studios and f. Teatri della Farnesina 1948; co-founder Ponti-De Laurentiis S.p.A. 1950; Prin. De Laurentis Entertainment Group Inc. 1986–88, Prin., founder Dino De Laurentiis Comm. 1988–; now Chair. Bd.; numerous awards and prizes include Oscars for La Strada 1957, Le Notti di Cabiria 1958, Golden David Awards for Le Notti di Cabiria 1958, The Tempest 1959, Silver Ribbon (Italian Film Critics) for La Strada 1954, Venice Silver Lion for Europa 51 1952. *Films produced include:* La Figlia del Capitano, Il Bandito, Molti Sogni per la Strada, Anna, Bitter Rice, La Strada, Le Notti di Cabiria, Ulysses, War and Peace, The Tempest, This Angry Age, Europa 51, The Gold of Naples, The Great War, Five Branded Women, I Love, You Love, The Best of Enemies, Barabbas, To Bed or not to Bed, The Bible, The Three

Faces of a Woman, Barbarella, A Man Called Sledge, Waterloo, The Valachi Papers, Serpico, Mandingo, Lipstick 1976, Buffalo Bill and the Indians 1976, Drum 1976, King Kong 1976, Hurricane 1979, Flash Gordon 1980, Ragtime 1981, Conan the Barbarian 1982, Firestarter 1984, The Bounty 1984, Dune 1984, Year of the Dragon 1985, Blue Velvet 1986, Trick or Treat 1986, King Kong Lives 1986, Crimes of the Heart 1986, Weeds 1987, Dracula's Widow 1987, Adult Education 1987, The Desperate Hours, Kuffs, Once Upon a Crime, Body of Evidence, Army of Darkness, Unforgettable, Assassins, Dragonheart. *Address:* De Laurentiis Entertainment Group, 8670 Wiltshire Boulevard, Beverly Hills, CA 90211, U.S.A.

DELEBARRE, Michel Stephane Henry Joseph; French politician; b. 27 April 1946, Bailleul (Nord); m. Janine Debeyre 1969; one d.; Asst. Sec.-Gen. Cttee. for the Expansion of the Nord-Pas de Calais area 1968–71, Sec.-Gen. 1971–74; Cabinet Dir. for Pres. of Nord-Pas de Calais Regional Council 1974–78; Gen. Del. for Devt. for City of Lille 1977–80; Sec.-Gen. City of Lille 1980; Pres. regional fund for contemporary art 1982; mem. of Cabinet of Prime Minister 1981–82; Cabinet Dir. 1982–84; unassigned prefect 1983; Minister of Labour, Employment and Professional Training 1984–86; Socialist Mem of Parl. for Nord 1986, 1988–93, 1997–98; mem. Exec. Bd. Socialist Party 1987; Minister of Transport and Marine Affairs 1989; Minister of State, Minister of Town and Physical Planning 1990–91; Minister of State, Minister of Civil Service and Public Admin. Enhancement 1991–92; Adviser for Urban and Regional Planning; Chair. Cttee. of Experts advising Lionel Jospin, Leader Socialist Party 1995; First Deputy Pres., Regional Council for Nord-Pas de Calais 1986, 1992–(98); Mayor of Dunkirk 1989–; Pres. Urban Community of Dunkirk 1995–, Regional Council of Nord-Pas de Calais 1998–. *Address:* Conseil Régional Nord-Pas de Calais, Hôtel de Région, Centre Rihour, 59555 Lille Cedex; Hôtel de Ville, place Charles Valentin, 59140 Dunkirk, France.

De LEEUW, Ton; Netherlands composer; b. 16 Nov. 1926, Rotterdam; m. Arlette Reboul 1952; one s. three d.; ed. musical colls. in Netherlands and France and under Jaap Kunst, Amsterdam; with Radio Hilversum 1954–, responsible for annual radio programmes of Contemporary and non-Western Music 1956–; Prof. Composition Conservatoires of Amsterdam and Utrecht 1959–, lecturer, Univ. of Amsterdam 1962–; Dir. Conservatoire of Amsterdam 1972; Study of Indian classical music and dance 1961; numerous prizes including Prix Italia 1956 and Prix des Jeunesses Musicales 1961. *Compositions:* Hiob (Radiophonic Oratorio) 1956, Mouvements Rétrogrades 1957, First String Quartet 1958, Antiphonie (chamber music with 4 electronic sound-tracks) 1960, Symphonies for Wind Instruments 1963, The Dream (Opera) 1963, Men go their ways (piano) 1964, Second String Quartet 1965, Syntaxis I (Electronic) 1966, Spatial music I-IV 1966–68, Haiku II (Sopr. and orch.) 1968, Lamento Pacis (vocal and instr.) 1969, Litany of our Time (Television play) 1970, Music for Strings 1970 and works for electronic instruments, Mountains (bass clarinet and tape) 1977, The Birth of Music 1978, Chronos (Electronic) 1980, Car nos Vignes sont en Fleur (Mixed Voices) 1980, And They Shall Reign Forever (vocal and instr.) 1981, Clair-Obscur (Electronic) 1982. *Publication:* The Music of the 20th Century 1964 and numerous articles on cultural interaction. *Address:* Costeruslaan 4, Hilversum, Netherlands. *Telephone:* 02150-15783.

de LEON CARPIO, Ramiro, LIC. EN DER.; Guatemalan politician, lawyer and professor; b. Guatemala City; m.; Prof. Legal and Social Sciences Faculty, Political and Social Sciences Faculty, Rafael Landívar Univ., asst. consultant Ministry of Econ., consultant Common Market div. 1967–69; Sec. Perm. Comm. of Tariffs 1968–70, Nat. Comm. of Econ. Integration 1970; Sec.-Gen. State Council 1974–78; legal consultant 1978–81; Gen. Man. Sugar Asscn. of Guatemala 1981–83; co-f. Unión del Centro Nacional (Union of Nat. Centre) Party 1983, Sec.-Gen. 1983–86; mem. Constituent Nat. Ass. 1984–86, Alt. Pres. 1984–86; Pres. of Guatemala 1993–96; founder, Pres. Inst. de Investigación y Capacitación Atanasio Tzul (ICAT); Pres. Council for Cen. American Civil Soc. for Peace (COCEPAZ). *Address:* c/o Office of the President, Palacio Nacional, Guatemala City, Guatemala.

DELEURAN, Aage; Danish journalist; b. 11 Oct. 1925, Korsør; s. of Holger Johannes and Agnete (née Lorentsen) Deleuran; m. Birthe Braae 1955; Staff reporter Korsør Avis 1942, Berlingske Aftenavis 1945; Paris Corresp. Berlingske Tidende 1952–56, Asst. Ed.-in-Chief 1961, Exec. Ed. 1967, Ed.-in-Chief 1970–92; Dir. Berlingske House 1975–92; Chair. Soc. of Danish Press History 1966–92, Ritzau's News Agency 1971–76, 1980–90, Asscn. of Danish Newspapers 1972–79, Vice-Chair. 1979–85, Chair. 1985–89; Commdr. of the Order of Dannebrog; Officier, Légion d'honneur. *Publication:* April 40 1965. *Address:* Nøjsomhedsvej 2, 2100 Copenhagen Ø, Denmark (Home).

DELFIM NETTO, Antônio, D.ECON.; Brazilian economist; b. 5 May 1928, São Paulo; s. of José Delfim and Maria Delfim; ed. School of Econs. and Management, Univ. de São Paulo; Univ. de São Paulo, Asst. Prof. 1952–54, Assoc. Prof. 1954–59, Prof. 1963; fmr. Dir. Insts. of Man. and Econ. Research, School of Econs. and Man.; mem. São Paulo State Planning Comm. for Devt. 1965; Sec. of Finance, São Paulo State Govt. 1966–67; Minister of Finance 1967–74, of Planning 1979–85; Consultant and Technical Adviser to several orgs. in São Paulo; Order of Merit of the Brazilian Armed Forces; Order of Boyaca (Colombia); Order of Christ (Portugal); Ordine del Merito (Italy); Légion d'honneur (France). *Publications:* O Mercado de Açúcar no Brasil 1958, O Problema do Café no Brasil 1959, O Trigo no Brasil 1960, Alguns Aspectos da Inflação Brasileira 1963, Agricultura e Desenvolvimento 1966, Planejamento para o Desenvolvimento 1966. *Leisure interest:* reading.

DELGADO, Alvaro; Spanish artist; b. 9 June 1922, Madrid; m. Mercedes Gal Orendain; one s.; ed. pupil of Vazquez Diaz 1936–39, Benjamin Palencia 1939–42; mem. Real Acad. de Bellas Artes, Real Acad. de San Fernando; Acad. Delegado de la Calcografia; Commdr. Order of Ethiopia; First Prize, Concurso Nacional de Carteles Para Teatro 1939; First Prize, Proyecto Para Figurines y Decorados 1940; Cuba Prize for Painting, IIa Bienal Arte Hispano Americano 1952; Grand Prize for Painting, Bienal de Arte Mediterraneo, Alejandria 1955; Grande Prize for Painting, Exposición Int., Alicante 1960; Primera Medalla de Dibujo, Exposición Nacional Bellas Artes 1960; Gold Medal, Salon Nacional del Grabado 1962; Vocal del Patronato del Museo del Prado, Madrid 1970. *Leisure interest:* constant travel. *Address:* Biarritz 5, Parque de las Avenidas, Madrid 28028, Spain.

DELIBES, Miguel, D.IUR.; Spanish writer and university teacher; b. 17 Oct. 1920, Valladolid; s. of Adolfo and Maria Delibes; m. Angeles de Castro 1946 (died 1974); seven c.; ed. School of Higher Studies, Bilbao, Univ. of Valladolid, School of Journalism, Bilbao; Prof. Univ. of Valladolid 1945–85; Dir. El Norte de Castilla (newspaper) 1956–62; mem. Real Acad. de la Lengua 1973; recipient Premio Nadal, Premio Nacional de Literatura, Premio Príncipe de Asturias; Miguel de Cervantes Prize 1993; Dr. h.c. (Madrid, Valladolid, Saarbrücken). *Publications include:* La sombra del ciprés es alargada 1948, El camino 1950, Las ratas 1962, El libro de la caza menor 1964, Cinco horas con Mario 1966, Parábola del náufrago 1969, El disputado voto del señor Cayo 1978, Los santos inocentes 1981, El tesoro 1985, Pegar la hebra 1990, El conejo 1991, El último coto 1992, Diario de un jubilado 1995. *Leisure interests:* hunting, fishing, tennis. *Address:* c. Dos de Mayo No. 10, 47004 Valladolid, Spain. *Telephone:* 983/300250.

DeLILLO, Don; American writer; b. 20 Nov. 1936; Award in Literature, American Acad. and Inst. of Arts and Letters 1984. *Publications:* Americana 1971, End Zone 1972, Great Jones Street 1973, Ratner's Star 1976, Players 1977, Running Dog 1978, The Names 1982, White Noise 1985 (Nat. Book Award 1985), Libra 1988 (Int. Fiction Prize 1989), Mao II 1991 (Pen Faulkner Award 1992), Underworld 1996. *Address:* c/o Wallace Literary Agency, 177 E. 70th Street, New York, NY 10021, U.S.A.

DELL, Rt. Hon. Edmund, P.C., M.A.; British fmr. politician, author and businessman; b. 15 Aug. 1921, London; s. of Reuben and Frances Dell; m. Susanne Gottschalk 1963; ed. Owen's School, London, The Queen's Coll., Oxford; Lecturer, The Queen's Coll., Oxford 1947–49; Exec. Imperial Chemical Industries Ltd., 1949–63; mem. Manchester City Council 1953–60, Pres. Manchester and Salford Trades Council 1958–61; M.P. for Birkenhead 1964–79; Parl. Sec. Ministry of Tech. 1966–67, Parl. Under-Sec. of State, Dept. of Econ. Affairs 1967–68, Minister of State, Bd. of Trade 1968–69, Minister of State, Dept. of Employment 1969–70, Chair. Public Accounts Cttee. of House of Commons 1972–74, Paymaster-Gen. 1974–76; Sec. of State for Trade 1976–78; apptd. by the European Council as mem. of Cttee. of Three to report on mechanisms and procedures of the Institutions of the EEC 1978–79; Dir., Chair. Guinness Peat Group 1979–82; Founder-Chair. Channel Four TV Co. 1980–87; Chair. Public Finance Foundation 1984–91, Prison Reform Trust 1988–93; Deputy Chair. of Council, London Chamber of Commerce and Industry 1988–90, Chair. 1990–92, Pres. 1991–92; Deputy Chair. Bd. of Govs., Imperial Coll., Univ. of London 1988–91; Dir. (non-exec.) Shell Transport and Trading 1979–92; Hon. Sr. Research Fellow, Univ. Coll. London 1998–; Hon. Fellow Fitzwilliam Coll., Cambridge. *Publications:* Political Responsibility and Industry 1973; Report on European Institutions (with B. Biesheuvel and R. Marjolin) 1979, The Politics of Economic Interdependence 1987, A Hard Pounding: Politics and Economic Crisis 1974–76 1991, Britain and the Origins of the European Monetary System 1994, The Schuman Plan and the British Abdication of Leadership in Europe 1995, The Chancellors: A History of the Chancellors of the Exchequer 1945–90 1996. *Leisure interest:* listening to music. *Address:* 4 Reynolds Close, London, NW11 7EA, England. *Telephone:* 0181-455 7197.

DELL, Michael S.; American business executive; b. 1965, Houston, Tex.; s. of Alexander Dell and Lorraine Dell; m. Susan Lieberman 1989; two d.; ed. Univ. of Texas 1983–84; founder Dell Computer Corpn. (fmrly. PC's Ltd.), Austin, Tex. 1984, now Chair. and C.E.O.; Entrepreneur of the Year Award (Inc. magazine) 1990, J.D. Power Customer Satisfaction Award 1991, 1993; C.E.O. of the Year (Financial World magazine) 1993. *Address:* Dell Computer Corporation, 1 Dell Way, Round Rock, TX 78682, U.S.A. (Office).

DELLA CASA-DEBELJEVIC, Lisa (see Casa-Debeljevic, Lisa Della).

DELL'OLIO, Louis; American fashion designer; b. 23 July 1948, New York; ed. Parsons School of Design, New York; asst. designer to Dominic Rompello of Teal Traina, New York 1969–71; Chief Designer, Georgini div. of Originala, New York 1971–74; design collaborator with Donna Karan (q.v.), Anne Klein & Co. 1974–93; Chief Designer 1984–93; mem. Fashion Designers of America; Coty Awards 1977, 1981.

DELON, Alain; French actor; b. 8 Nov. 1935, Sceaux; m. Nathalie Delon (dissolved); one s.; one s. one d. by Rosalie Van Breemen; with French Marine Corps 1952–55; independent actor-producer under Delbeau (Delon-Beaume) Productions 1964–; Pres., Dir.-Gen. Adel Productions 1968–87, Leda Productions 1987–; Chevalier, Légion d'honneur, Commdr. des Arts et des Lettres. *Films include:* Christine 1958, Faibles femmes 1959, Le chemin des écoliers 1959, Purple Noon 1959, Rocco and His Brothers 1960, Eclipse 1961, The Leopard 1962, Any Number Can Win 1962, The Black Tulip 1963, The Love

Cage 1963, L'insoumis 1964, The Yellow Rolls Royce 1964, Once a Thief 1964, Les centurions 1965, Paris brûle-t-il? 1965, Texas Across the River 1966, Les adventuriers 1966, Le samourai 1967, Histoires extraordinaires 1967, Diaboliquement votre 1967, Adieu l'ami 1968, Girl on a motorcycle 1968, La piscine 1968, Jeff 1968, Die Boss, Die Quietly 1969, Borsalino 1970, Madly 1970, Doucement les basses 1970, Le cercle rouge 1971, L'assassinat de Trotsky 1971, La veuve Couderc 1971, Un flic 1972, Le professeur 1972, Scorpio 1972, Traitement de choc 1972, Les granges brûlées 1973, Deux hommes dans la ville 1973, Borsalino & Co. 1973, Les seins de glace 1974, Creezy 1975, Zorro 1975, Le gitan 1975, Mr. Klein 1975, Le gang 1977, Mort d'un pourri 1977, Armaguedon 1977, L'homme pressé 1977, Attention, les enfants regardent 1978, Le toubib 1979, Trois hommes à abattre 1980, Pour la peau d'un flic 1981, Le choc 1982, Le battant 1982, Un Amour de Swann 1984, Notre Histoire (César, Best Actor 1985) 1984, Parole de flic 1985, Le passage 1986, Ne réveillez pas un flic qui dort, Nouvelle Vague 1989, Dancing Machine 1990, le Retour de Casanova 1992, Un Crime 1993, L'Ours en peluche 1994, Le Jour et La Nuit 1996, Une Chance sur deux 1998. *Stage performances:* 'Tis Pity She's a Whore 1961, 1962, Les yeux crevés 1967, Variations énigmatiques 1996; also television appearances. *Address:* c/o Leda Productions, 4 rue Chambiges, 75008 Paris, France.

DELORS, Jacques Lucien Jean; French politician and economist; b. 20 July 1925, Paris; s. of Louis Delors and Jeanne Rigal; m. Marie Lephaille 1948; one s. (deceased) one d. (Martine Aubry, q.v.); ed. Lycée Voltaire, Paris, Lycée Blaise-Pascal, Clermont-Ferrand, Univ. of Paris; Head of Dept., Banque de France 1945–62, attached to staff of Dir.-Gen. of Securities and Financial Market 1950–62, mem. Gen. Council 1973–79; mem. Planning and Investments Section, Econ. and Social Council 1959–61; Head of Social Affairs Section, Commissariat général du Plan 1962–69; Sec.-Gen. Interministerial Cttee. for Vocational Training and Social Promotion 1969–73; Adviser to Jacques Chaban-Delmas (q.v.) 1969, Chargé de mission 1971–72; mem. Bd. of Dirs. Banque de France 1973–79; Assoc. Prof. of Co. Man., Univ. of Paris IX 1973–79; f. Club Echange et Projets 1974; Dir. Labour and Soc. Research Centre 1975–79; Parti Socialiste Nat. Del. for int. econ. relations 1976–81; elected mem. Ass. of the European Communities 1979, Chair. Econ. and Monetary Cttee. 1979–81; Minister for the Economy and Finance 1981–83, for the Economy, Finance and Budget 1983–84; Mayor of Clichy 1983–84; Pres. Comm. of the European Communities (now European Commission) 1985–94, Commr. for Monetary Affairs 1979–81; also for Forward Planning and Legal Service, for Gen. Admin. and Co-ordination of Structural Funds 1985–89; Columnist Europe 1 1987–; Pres. Int. Comm. on Educ. for the Twenty-First Century, UNESCO 1994–; Pres. Conseil d'admin. Collège d'Europe, Bruges 1996–; f. Notre Europe 1996; Onassis Foundation Award 1992; Hon. LL.D. (Univ. of Glasgow), (L.S.E.) 1997; Dr. h.c. (Edin.) 1992; Hon. D.Univ. (York) 1996; Chevalier, Légion d'honneur, Charles V Prize (Spain) 1995. *Publications:* Les indicateurs sociaux 1971, Changer 1971, En sortir ou pas (jtly.) 1985, La France par l'Europe (jtly.) 1988, le Nouveau concert Européen 1992, Our Europe: The Community and National Development 1993, Pour Entrer dans le XXIe Siècle 1994, Combats pour l'Europe 1996; numerous articles; reports for UN on French planning (1966) and long-term planning (1969). *Address:* Association Notre Europe, 44 rue Notre Dame des Victoires, 75002 Paris (Office); 19 boulevard de Bercy, 75012 Paris, France (Home).

de los ANGELES, Victoria; Spanish soprano singer; b. (as Victoria Gómez Cima) 1 Nov. 1923, Barcelona; m. Enrique Magriñá 1948 (deceased); two s.; ed. Univ. and Conservatoire of Barcelona; Barcelona début 1945, Paris Opera and La Scala, Milan 1949, Royal Opera House, Covent Garden, London 1950, Metropolitan Opera House, New York 1951, Vienna State Opera 1957; numerous appearances at other opera houses, concert tours and recordings; Dr h.c. (Barcelona); 1st Prize, Geneva Int. Competition 1947; Cross of Lazo de Dama of the Order of Isabel the Catholic, Condecoración Banda de la Orden Civil de Alfonso X (El Sabio), Spain and numerous other orders and decorations. *Address:* Avenida de Pedralbes 57, 08034 Barcelona, Spain.

DELPY, Julie; French film actress; b. 21 Dec. 1969; ed. New York Univ. Film School. *Films include:* Detective 1985, Mauvais Sang 1986, La Passion Béatrice 1987, L'Autre Nuit 1988, La Noche Oscura 1989, Europa Europa 1991, Voyager 1991, Warszawa 1992, Young and Younger 1993, The Three Musketeers 1993, When Pigs Fly 1993, The Myth of the White Wolf 1994, Killing Zoe 1994, Mesmer 1994, Trois Couleurs Blanc 1994, Trois Couleurs Rouge 1994, Before Sunrise 1995, An American Werewolf in Paris 1997.

De LUCCHI, Michele; Italian architect; b. 8 Nov. 1951, Ferrara; s. of Alberto De Lucchi and Giuliana Zannini; ed. Liceo Scientifico Enrico Fermi, Padua, Faculty of Architecture, Univ. of Florence; founder mem., Cavart (avant-garde design and architecture group) 1973–76; Asst. Prof., Univ. of Florence 1976–77; worked with Gaetano Pesce, Superstudio, Andrea Branzi, Ettore Sottsass 1977–80; Consultant, Centrokappa Noviglio, Milan 1978; Consultant, Olivetti Synthesis, Massa 1979–, Olivetti SpA, Ivrea 1984–; freelance designer, several furniture mfrs. 1979–; founder mem., Int. Designer Group Memphis 1981–. *Publication:* Architetture Verticali 1978. *Leisure interest:* travel photography. *Address:* Via Cenisio 40, 20154 Milan, Italy (Home). *Telephone:* (02) 314636 (Home).

DeLUISE, Dom; American comedian and actor; b. 1 Aug. 1933, Brooklyn, New York; ed. Tufts Coll.; m. Carol Arthur; three s.; spent two seasons with Cleveland Playhouse; TV debut on the Garry Moore Show. *Theatre includes:* Little Shop of Horrors, Die Fledermaus (New York Metropolitan Opera), Peter and the Wolf. *Films include:* Fail Safe, Blazing Saddles, Hot Stuff (also dir.), The Best Little Whorehouse in Texas. *Television:* (series): The Entertainers, The Dean Martin summer Show, Dom DeLuise Show, The Barrum-Bump Show, The Glenn Campbell Goodtime Show, The New Candid Camera, Fievel's American Tails (voice); (films): Evil Roy Slade, Only With Married Men, Happy (also exec. producer), Don't Drink the Water, The Tin Soldier.

DELVALLE, Eric Arturo; Panamanian politician; b. 2 Feb. 1937, Panama; m. Mariela Díaz de Delvalle; one s. two d.; ed. Colegio Javier, Panama City, Louisiana State Univ. and Soulé Coll. of Accountancy; fmr. Chair. and Dir. of several pvt. commercial enterprises; mem. Bd. of Dirs. Inst. for Econ. Promotion 1963; mem. Games Control Bd. 1960–64; Del. to Nat. Ass. 1968; Vice-Pres. Nat. Ass. 1968; Leader, Repub. Party; Vice-Pres. of Panama 1984, Pres. 1985–88 (removed from office for alleged drug-trafficking).

DEL VALLE ALLIENDE, Jaime; Chilean politician and lawyer; b. 2 July 1931, Santiago; m. Paulina Swinburn Pereira; four c.; ed. Escuela de Derecho de la Universidad Católica de Chile; taught at Catholic Univ. Law School from 1955, appt. Dir. 1969, Dean 1970; various posts in Supreme Court 1958–64; Public Prosecutor 1964–74; Pro-Rector, Pontificia Univ. Católica de Chile 1974; Dir.-Gen. nat. TV channel 1975–78; mem. Bd. Colegio de Abogados 1981–, Pres. 1982–83; Minister of Justice Feb.–Dec. 1983; Minister of Foreign Affairs 1983–87. *Address:* c/o Ministerio de Asuntos Exteriores, Palacio de la Moneda, Santiago, Chile. *Telephone:* 6982501.

de MADARIAGA, Isabel, PH.D., F.B.A., F.R.HIST.S.; British professor of Russian studies; b. 27 Aug. 1919, Glasgow, Scotland; d. of Salvador de Madariaga and Constance Archibald; m. Leonard B. Schapiro 1943 (divorced 1976); ed. Ecole Internationale, Geneva, Switzerland, Headington School for Girls, Oxford, Instituto Escuela, Madrid, London Univ.; BBC Monitoring Service 1940–43; Cen. Office of Information London 1943–47; Econ. Information Unit., Treasury 1947–48; Editorial Asst., Slavonic and East European Review 1951–64; Part-time lecturer in History, L.S.E. 1953–66; lecturer in History, Univ. of Sussex 1966–68; Sr. Lecturer in Russian History, Lancaster Univ. 1968–71; Reader in Russian Studies, School of Slavonic and East European Studies, London Univ. 1971–81, Prof. 1981–84, Emer. Prof. 1984–; Corresp. mem. Royal Acad. of History, Spain. *Publications:* Britain, Russia and the Armed Neutrality of 1780 1963, Opposition (with G. Ionescu) 1965, Russia in the Age of Catherine the Great 1981, Catherine II: A Short History 1990, Politics and Culture in Eighteenth-Century Russia 1998; many scholarly articles. *Leisure interest:* music. *Address:* 25 Southwood Lawn Road, London, N6 5SD, England. *Telephone:* 0181-341 0862.

de MAIZIÈRE, Lothar; German politician and lawyer; b. 2 March 1940, Nordhausen; m.; three d.; mem. Christian Democratic Union, Leader 1989–90; Deputy Prime Minister and Spokesman on Church Affairs 1989–90; Prime Minister German Democratic Republic and Minister of Foreign Affairs March–Oct. 1990; Minister without Portfolio 1990–91, Deputy Chair. CDU, Chair Brandenburg CDU Oct.-Dec. 1990, 1991; leader Lutheran Church Council; resgnd. as CDU deputy 1991. *Address:* Am Kupfergraben 6/6A, 10117 Berlin, Germany.

de MAIZIÈRE, General Ulrich; German army officer (retd.); b. 24 Feb. 1912, Stade; s. of Walther de Maizière and Elisabeth Dückers; m. Eva Werner 1944; two s. two d.; ed. Humanistisches Gymnasium, Hanover; army service 1930, commissioned 1933; Battalion and Regimental Adjutant, 50th Infantry Reg.; Gen. Staff Coll., Dresden 1940; during Second World War Gen. Staff Duties with 18th Motorized Infantry Div., G3 and Chief of Staff of 10th Mechanized Div., wounded 1944, at end of war Deputy Chief of Operations Div. Army Gen. Staff; Prisoner-of-war 1945–47; dealer in books and sheet music 1947–51; Office of Fed. Commr. for Nat. Security Affairs 1951; Col. and Chief of Ops. Branch, Fed. Armed Forces Staff 1955; Commdr. of Combat Team A1 and Commdr. 2nd Brigade 1958; Deputy Commdr. 1st Armoured Infantry Div. 1959; Commdt. Fed. Armed Forces School for Leadership and Character Guidance 1960–62, Fed. Armed Forces Command and Staff Coll. 1962–64; Chief of Army Staff 1964–66; Chief of Fed. Armed Forces Staff 1966–72; Hon. Pres. Claüsewitz Gesellschaft; Commdr., Légion d'honneur 1962, Freiherr-von-Stein-Preis 1964, Commdr. Legion of Merit 1965, 1969, Grand Officier, Légion d'honneur 1969, Grosses Bundesverdienstkreuz mit Stern und Schulterband 1970, Hermann-Ehlers-Preis 1986. *Publications:* Die Landesverteidigung im Rahmen der Gesamtverteidigung 1964, Soldatische Führung heute 1966, Bekenntnis zum Soldaten 1971, Führen im Frieden 1974, Verteidigung in Europa—Mitte 1975, In Der Pflicht (autobiog.) 1989. *Leisure interests:* classical music, literature, contemporary history. *Address:* 53177 Bonn, Tulpenbaumweg 20, Germany. *Telephone:* (0228) 9524459.

DE MARCO, Guido, K.O.M., B.A., LL.D., M.P.; Maltese politician; b. 22 July 1931, Valletta; s. of Emmanuele de Marco and Giovanna Raniolo; m. Violet Saliba; one s. two d.; ed. St. Aloysius Coll. and Royal Univ. of Malta; Crown Counsel 1964–66; mem. Parl. 1966–; Deputy Prime Minister 1987–96, Minister for Internal Affairs and Justice 1987–91, of Foreign Affairs 1991–96, 1998–; Shadow Minister and Opposition Spokesman on Foreign Affairs 1996–98; Pres. Gen. Ass. of U.N. 1990–91; Nationalist Party. *Publications:* A Presidency With a Purpose 1991, A Second Generation United Nations 1995. *Leisure interests:* reading and travel. *Address:* Ministry of Foreign

Affairs, Palazzo Parisio, Merchants Street, Valletta, CMR 02, Malta. *Telephone:* 242853. *Fax:* 237822.

DEMARCO, Richard, O.B.E.; British professor of European cultural studies; b. 9 July 1930, Edinburgh; s. of Carmine DeMarco and Elizabeth Valentine Fusco; m. Anne C. Muckle 1956; ed. Holy Cross Acad., Edinburgh Coll. of Art, Moray House Coll. and Royal Army Educ. Corps.; art master, Duns Scotus Acad. Edinburgh 1956–67; Vice-Chair. Founding Cttee. and Vice-Chair. Bd. Dirs. Traverse Theatre, Edinburgh 1963–67; Dir. Sean Connery's Scottish Int. Educ. Trust (S.I.E.T.) 1972–73; Dir. Richard DeMarco Gallery 1966–; Trustee Kingston DeMarco European Cultural Foundation 1993–; Prof. of European Cultural Studies, Kingston Univ. 1994–; Artistic Adviser European Youth Parl. 1992–; mem. Royal Scottish Soc. of Painters in Watercolours; Hon. Fellow, Royal Incorporation of Architects; Hon. LL.D. (Dundee); Cavaliere della Repubblica Italiana, Chevalier des Arts et des Lettres (France). *Publications:* The Artist as Explorer 1978, The Road to Meikle Seggie 1978, A Life in Pictures 1995, Art = Wealth 1995. *Leisure interest:* exploring the road to Meikle Seggie in the footsteps of Roman legionnaires, Celtic saints and scholars, respectful of the Rule of St. Benedict. *Address:* Kingston University, Millennium House, 21 Eden Street, Kingston-upon-Thames, Surrey, KT1 2EE, England (Office); DeMarco European Cultural Institute, St. Mary's School, Albany Street, Edin.; 23A Lennox Street, Edin., EH4 1PY, Scotland (Home). *Telephone:* 0181-547 7780 (Kingston); 0131-557 0707 (Edin.); 0131-343 2124 (Home). *Fax:* 0181-547 7789 (Kingston); 0131-557 5972 (Edin.); 0131-343 3124 (Home).

de MARIA y CAMPOS, Mauricio, M.A.; Mexican international civil servant and economist; b. 13 Oct. 1943, Mexico D.F.; s. of Mauricio de María y Campos and Teresa Castello; m. Patricia Meade 1981; two s. one d.; ed. Nat. Univ. of Mexico, Univ. of Sussex; Head Planning and Policy Unit Mexican Nat. Science and Tech. Council 1971–72; Deputy Dir. Evaluation Dept. Tech. Transfer Ministry of Trade and Industry 1973–74, Dir. Gen. Foreign Investment 1974–77, Vice-Minister Industrial Devt. 1982–89; Dir. Gen. Tax Incentives and Fiscal Promotion Ministry of Finance 1977–82; Exec. Vice-Pres. Banco Mexicano SOMEX 1989–92; Deputy Dir. Gen. UNIDO 1992–93, Dir. Gen. 1993–97; Amb. at Large and Special Adviser on UN Affairs, Ministry of Foreign Affairs 1998–; mem. Int. Club of Rome 1998– (Pres. of Mexican Chapter 1998–); Grand Commendateur Ordre nat. du Mérite, Order of Francisco de Miranda (Venezuela); Great Decoration in Gold on the Sash for Services Rendered to the Republic of Austria; Grand Ordre du Mono (Togo). *Publications:* Challenges and Opportunities for Scientific and Technological Collaboration Between the E.E.C. and Mexico 1990, The Transformation of the Mexican Automobile Industry during the 1980s 1992; various publs. on industrial and technological policy and on regional devt. *Leisure interests:* classical music, writing, reading, swimming, jogging, dancing, journalism. *Address:* Tiburcio Montiel 75, San Miguel Chapultepec, México, D.F. 11850, Mexico. *Telephone:* (5) 271-8958, 515-1605. *Fax:* (5) 593-2686.

DEMAS, William Gilbert, M.A.; Trinidadian civil servant and economist; b. 14 Nov. 1929, Port-of-Spain; s. of late Herman and Audrey (née Walters) Demas; m. Norma Taylor 1958; one d.; ed. Queen's Royal Coll., Trinidad and Emmanuel Coll., Cambridge; Adviser to W. Indies Trade Comm. U.K. 1957–58; Head, Econ. Planning Div., Govt. of Trinidad and Tobago 1959–66; Perm. Sec. Ministry of Planning and Devt. 1966–68; Econ. Adviser to the Prime Minister 1968–69; Sec.-Gen. Commonwealth Caribbean Regional Secr. 1970–74; Pres. Caribbean Devt. Bank 1974–88; Dir. Cen. Bank; Chair. Multi-Sectoral Planning Task Force (Trinidad and Tobago) 1985–; Humming Bird Gold Medal (for public service). *Publications:* Economics of Development in Small Countries 1965, Planning and the Price Mechanism in the Context of Caribbean Economic Integration 1966. *Leisure interests:* films, listening to all kinds of music.

DEMEL, Herbert, PH.D.; Austrian business executive; b. 14 Oct. 1953, Vienna; ed. Vienna Tech. Univ.; Robert Bosch GmbH, Stuttgart 1984–90; Audi AG, Ingolstadt 1990–, mem. Man. Bd. in charge of Research and Devt. 1993, Speaker of Man. Bd. and C.E.O. responsible for Research and Devt. and Sales and Marketing 1994, Chair. Man. Bd. 1995–97.

DE MELO, Eurico; Portuguese politician and chemical engineer; b. Sept. 1925; worked in the Textile industry; taught Textile Chem. at Faculty of Engineering, Oporto; mem. Popular Democratic Party (PPD, now PSD) May 1974–; Chair. District Political Cttee. of Braga; Civil Gov. of Braga 1975–76; Minister of the Interior 1980–81, of State and of Internal Admin. 1986–87; Deputy Prime Minister and Minister of Defence 1987–90; mem. Social Democratic Party (PSD) Nat. Political Cttee. *Address:* c/o Partido Social Democrata, Rua de São Caetano 9, 1296 Lisbon Codex, Portugal.

DEMERITTE, Richard C., C.A., F.A.I.A., F.C.G.A., F.B.I.M., F.R.S.A.; Bahamian diplomatist; b. 27 Feb. 1939, Nassau; s. of Richard and Miriam (née Whitfield) Demeritte; m. Ruth Smith 1966; one s. (deceased) two d.; ed. Eastern Secondary School, Bahamas School of Commerce, Metropolitan Coll., London, and Century Univ., U.S.A.; Deputy Treas. Treasury Dept. 1956–79; Auditor-Gen. Commonwealth of the Bahamas 1980–84, 1988–96; High Commr. in U.K. 1984–87; Amb. to EEC 1986–88, to Belgium, France, Fed. Repub. of Germany 1987–88; now Man. Partner Richard C. Demeritte & Co., Chartered Accountants; Pres. Certified Gen. Accountants Asscn. of the Bahamas, Caribbean Asscn. of Certified Gen. Accountants; fmr. Pres. Asscn. of Int. Accountants; mem. Bahamas Inst. of Chartered Accountants; mem. Bahamas Inst. of Chartered Accountants. *Leisure interests:* golf, chess, billiards, gardening, research, computer technology. *Address:* P.O. Box CB-11001, Nassau, Bahamas. *Telephone:* 327-5729 (Office); 327-8193 (Home). *Fax:* 327-0288 (Office); 327-8861 (Home).

DEMESSINE, Michelle; French politician; b. 18 June 1947, Frelinghien (Nord); m.; one c.; ed. Valentine Labbé Tech. Lycée, Lille; worked as sec. 1964–75; elected a union del. 1968, apptd. mem. Département Exec. Cttee. of Conféd. Générale du Travail 1973; Dept. Br. Sec. Union des Femmes Françaises 1976–90, now Hon. Chair.; joined Parti Communiste Français (PCF) 1970, elected mem. Nord Département Cttee. 1977, mem. PCF Bureau 1977–; mem. Regional Econ. and Social Cttee. 1983–95; Senator for Nord 1992–97; Vice-Chair. Social Affairs Cttee., study group on combating drug trafficking and addiction, fact-finding mission on women in public life; municipal councillor for Houplines 1995–; Sec. of State for Tourism 1997–. *Publication:* Femmes d'ici (co-author) 1985. *Address:* Secretariat d'Etat au Tourisme, 40 rue du Bac, 75700 Paris, France.

DE MEYER, Jan Carl Hendrika Oswald, D.JUR.; Belgian judge; b. 21 Feb. 1921, Malines; s. of Oswald De Meyer and Anna Maria Gysbrechts; m. Rita Smets 1949 (died 1986); one s. four d.; ed. St. Rombout's Coll. Malines, Faculté St. Louis, Brussels and Univ. of Louvain; mem. Bar at Malines 1944–48, 1952–86; Substitute Auditor, Council of State 1948–49, mem. Coordination Office 1949–52, Assessor 1962–80; lecturer, Univ. of Louvain 1951–56, Ordinary Prof. 1956–86, Prof. Emer. 1986–, Head, Dept. of Political and Social Sciences 1964–67, Dean, School of Law 1971–74; mem. Belgian Senate 1980–81; Judge, European Court of Human Rights 1986–98. *Address:* Kerselarenweg 1, B-3020 Herent, Belgium; Faculteit Rechtsgeleerdheid, Tiensestraat 41, B-3000 Louvain, Belgium. *Telephone:* (32) 16226384.

DE MICHELIS, Gianni; Italian politician and professor of chemistry; b. 26 Nov. 1940, Venice; Prof. of Chem., Univ. of Padua; Lecturer in Chem., Univ. of Venice; Nat. Chair. Unione Goliardica Italiana 1962–64; Councillor, Venice 1964–76; mem. Cen. Cttee. Italian Socialist Party (PSI) 1969–76, mem. Nat. Exec. 1976–; M.P. for Venice 1976–; fmr. Minister for State-owned Industries; Minister of Labour and Social Security 1986–87; Deputy Prime Minister 1988–89; Minister of Foreign Affairs 1989–92; Deputy Leader PSI 1992; charged with fraud May 1995; sentenced to 4 years imprisonment for corruption July 1995; on trial for siphoning cash from Third World projects 1996. *Address:* c/o Socialisti Italiani, Via del Corso 476, 00186 Rome, Italy.

DEMIDOVA, Alla Sergeyevna; Russian actress; b. 29 Sept. 1936, Moscow; d. of S. Demidov and A. Kharchenko; m. Vladimir Valutsky 1961; ed. Moscow Univ. and Shchukin Theatre School; acted with Taganka Theatre, Moscow 1964–; in films since 1957–; f. own Little Theatre "A" 1993; People's Artist of R.S.F.S.R. 1984, U.S.S.R. State Prize 1977. *Film roles include:* Olga (Day Stars) 1968, Maria Spiridonova (The Sixth of July) 1968, Zhenya (A Degree of Risk) 1969, Julia von Meck (Tchaikovsky) 1970, Lesya Ukrainka (I Come to You) 1972, Arkadina (The Seagull), 1975, Liza (The Mirror) A. Tarkovsky, 1975, the Soothsayer (The Little Scarlet Flower) 1978, Pashenka (Father Sergius) 1978, Duchess of Marlborough (A Glass of Water) TV 1979, Lebiadkina (Demons) 1993. *Theatre roles include:* Ranevskaya (Cherry Orchard), Gertrud (Hamlet), Fedra (Fedra M. Tsvetaeva), Melentyeva (Wooden Horses); also performed Akhmatova's Requiem. *Publications:* works on the art of theatre including The Second Reality, The Shadows behind the Mirrors; numerous articles. *Leisure interests:* philosophy, painting, gardening, her animals (two dogs and a cat). *Address:* Tverskaya str. 8, korp. 1 Apt. 83, 103009 Moscow, Russia. *Telephone:* (095) 229-04-17.

DEMIREL, Süleyman; Turkish politician and engineer; b. 1924; ed. Istanbul Technical Univ.; researcher in irrigation and electrification, Bureau of Reclamation 1949–50; Engineer, Electrical Survey Admin.; Head of Dams Dept. 1954–55; Exchange Fellowship scholar, several pvt. cos. and public depts. U.S.A. 1954–55; Dir.-Gen. Hydraulic Works, Turkey 1955–60; pvt. contractor, engineer, and Lecturer, Middle East Tech. Univ. 1962–64; Chair. Justice Party (AP) 1965–80; Isparta Deputy 1965–80; Deputy Prime Minister Feb.-Oct. 1965; Prime Minister (led AP govt.) 1965–71, (four coalition govts.) 1977–78; Opposition Leader 1978–80; Prime Minister 1979–80; banned from politics 1980–87; Chair. True Path Party (DYP) 1987–93; Deputy for Isparta 1987–93; Prime Minister 1991–93; Pres. of Turkey May 1993–. *Address:* Office of the President, Cumhurbaş-Kanliği Köşkü, Çankaya, Ankara, Turkey.

De MITA, Luigi Ciriaco; Italian politician; b. 2 Feb. 1928, Fusco, Avellino; fmr. mem. Catholic Action; mem. Chamber of Deputies for Benevento-Avellino-Salerno 1963, 1972–; Nat. Counsellor Partito Democrazia Cristiana (Christian Democrats) (DC) 1964, later Political Vice-Sec.; Under-Sec. for the Interior; Minister of Industry and Commerce 1973–74, of Foreign Trade 1974–76; Minister without Portfolio with responsibility for the Mezzogiorno July 1976–79; Sec.-Gen. DC 1982–88, Pres. 1989, 1991–92; Prime Minister of Italy 1988–89; Head Parl. Comm. for Constitutional Reform –1993. *Address:* c/o Partito Democrazia Cristiana, Piazza del Gesù 46, 00186 Rome, Italy.

DEMME, Jonathan; American director, producer and writer; b. 22 Feb. 1944, Rockville Centre, N.Y.; m. Joanne Howard; two c.; ed. Univ. of Florida; worked in publicity dept. United Artists, Embassy Pictures, Pathe Contemporary Films; writer for Film Daily 1966–68. *Films directed:* Hot Box (also co-screenwriter), Caged Heat 1974, Crazy Mama 1975, Fighting Mad 1976, Citizens Band 1977, Last Embrace 1979, Melvin and Howard 1980, Swing

Shift 1983, Something Wild 1986, Married to the Mob 1988, Swimming to Cambodia, The Silence of the Lambs (Acad. Award for Best Film 1992), Cousin Bobby 1992, Philadelphia 1993, Mandela 1996, That Thing You Do 1996, Beloved 1998; exec. producer Devil in a Blue Dress 1995; Who am I this Time (for TV) 1982, Stop Making Sense (documentary) 1984, Konbir (video) 1989, Konbir: Burning Rhythms of Haiti (recording) 1989; producer Miami Blues 1990. *Address:* c/o Bob Bookman, Creative Artists Agency, 9830 Wilshire Boulevard, Beverly Hills, CA 90212; Clinico Estelico, 127 W. 24th St. #7, New York, NY 10011, U.S.A.

DE MORNAY, Rebecca; American film and television actress; b. 29 Aug. 1962, Los Angeles, Calif.; m. Bruce Wagner 1989 (divorced); ed. in Austria and at Lee Strasberg Inst. in Los Angeles; apprenticed at Zoetrope Studios. *Theatre includes:* Born Yesterday 1988, Marat/Sade 1990. *Films include:* One from the Heart 1982, Risky Business 1983, Testament 1983, The Slugger's Wife 1985, Runaway Train 1985, The Trip to Bountiful 1985, Beauty and The Beast 1987, And God Created Woman 1988, Feds 1988, Dealers 1989, Backdraft 1991, The Hand that Rocks the Cradle (Best Actress, Cognac Crime Film Festival 1992), Guilty as Sin 1993, The Three Musketeers 1993, Never Talk to Strangers, The Winner. *TV appearances include:* The Murders in the Rue Morgue 1986, By Dawn's Early Light 1990, An Inconvenient Woman 1992, Blind Side 1993, Getting Out 1994, The Shining.

DEMPSEY, Noel, B.A.; Irish politician; b. Jan. 1953, Trim, Co. Meath; m. Bernadette Rattigan; two s. two d.; ed. St. Michael's Christian Bros.' School, Trim, Univ. Coll., Dublin, St. Patrick's Coll., Maynooth; fmr. career guidance counsellor; Nat. Sec. Local Authority Mems. Asscn. 1984–89; Chair. Meath Co. Council 1986–87; fmr. mem. numerous local govt. cttees.; mem. Dáil Éireann Feb. 1987–; mem. Dáil Public Accounts Cttee. 1987–89, 1990–92; fmr. Chair. Backbench Cttee. on Tourism, Transport and Communications; fmr. Sec. Backbench Cttee. on the Environment; fmr. Dir. Midland East Regional Tourism Org.; Minister of State at Depts. of Taoiseach, Defence and Finance, Govt. Chief Whip 1992–94; fmr. Opposition Spokesperson on Environment; Fianna Fáil Co-ordinator on Forum for Peace and Reconciliation; Nat. Treasurer Fianna Fáil; Minister for the Environment June 1997–. *Leisure interests:* Gaelic football, reading, golf. *Address:* Department of the Environment, Custom House, Dublin 1 (Office); Newtown, Trim, County Meath, Ireland (Home). *Telephone:* (1) 6793377 (Office). *Fax:* (1) 8742710 (Office).

DEMSZKY, Gábor; Hungarian politician and sociologist; b. 4 Aug. 1952, Budapest; s. of Rudolf Demszky and Irén Király; m. Vera Révai; four c.; ed. Eötvös Loránd Univ.; contrib. to periodical Világosság (Lucidity) 1977; founder Paupers Relief Fund 1979; founder AB Independent Publishing House 1980; Ed. illegal Hirmondó (Courier) 1983; founding mem. Network of Free Initiatives and Alliance of Free Democrats 1989; mem. Parl. 1989–90 (resgnd.), 1998; Chair. Cttee. of Nat. Security 1990; mem. Exec. Bd. Alliance of Free Democrats 1994–; founder Children's Rescue Soc.; negotiator in Moscow talks on Soviet troops withdrawal, and on Hungary's leaving the Warsaw Pact; Mayor of Budapest 1990–; Vice-Pres. Standing Conf. of Local and Regional Authorities, Council of Europe 1992–94, Congress of Local and Regional Authorities 1994–96; Freedom to Publish Prize, Int. Asscn. of Publishers 1984. *Leisure interests:* sailing, riding, water-skiing. *Address:* 1052 Budapest, Városház-utca 9/11, Hungary. *Telephone:* (36) 1 327-1022.

DEMUS, Jörg; Austrian concert pianist; b. 2 Dec. 1928, St. Pölten, Lower Austria; s. of Dr. Otto and Erika (Budik) Demus; ed. Vienna State Acad. of Music and studies with various musicians; début at age 14; Gesellschaft der Musikfreunde, Vienna; débuts in London and Switzerland 1950, tour of Latin America 1951, Paris 1953, New York 1955, Japan 1961; has performed in almost all important musical centres; has made over 350 LP records; Dr. h.c. (Amherst Univ.); Premier Busoni at Int. Piano Competition, Bolzano 1956; Harriet Cohen Bach-Medal 1958; Hon. Prof. of Austria 1977; Beethoven Ring, Vienna Beethoven Soc. 1977; Mozart Medal, Mozartgemeinde, Vienna 1979; several Edison Awards and Grand Prix du Disque. *Publications:* Abenteuer der Interpretation (essays); co-author of a book on Beethoven's piano sonatas. *Leisure interests:* antiques, nature, collecting and restoring historic keyboard instruments. *Address:* Döblinger Hauptstrasse 77A, A-1190 Vienna, Austria. *Telephone:* (0222) 366238.

DEMUTH, Richard H., A.B., LL.B.; American financier and lawyer; b. 11 Sept. 1910, New York; s. of Leopold and Dora Holzman Demuth; m. Eunice Burdick 1947; one d.; ed. Princeton Univ. and Harvard Law School; Law Clerk to Fed. Circuit Judge 1934–35; practised law in New York with firm of Simpson, Thacher and Bartlett 1935–39; Special Asst. to U.S. Attorney-Gen., Office of Solicitor-Gen. 1939–42; Asst. to Chief of Procurement Div., Air Technical Service Command 1942–45; Legal Adviser, Industry Division, U.S. Mil. Govt. in Germany, mem. Cen. German Admin. Depts. (Economic) Cttee. Allied Control Council 1945–46; Asst. to Pres., IBRD 1946–47, Asst. to Vice-Pres. 1947–51, Dir. Tech. Assistance and Liaison 1951–61, Dir. Devt. Services Dept. 1961–73; Asst. to Pres. Int. Finance Corpn. 1956–57; Partner law firm of Surrey & Morse, Washington 1973–81, Counsel 1982–83; led IBRD missions to Brazil 1949, Suriname 1951, Burma 1953, Spain 1958, Turkey 1965; mem. of President's Council; Chair. Int. Bd. for Plant Genetic Resources 1974–81, Chair. Emer. 1982; Chair. Bd. Genetic Resources Communications Systems, Inc. 1987–91; fmr. Vice-Chair. Montgomery Co. Citizens' Housing Advisory Cttee.; fmr. Chair. Consultative Group on Int. Agricultural Research; fmr. mem. Governing Bd., Int. Inst. for Educational Planning. *Leisure interest:* golf. *Address:* 5404 Bradley Boulevard, Bethesda, MD 20814, U.S.A. (Home). *Telephone:* (301) 652-8439.

DENARD, Col. Bob (Robert) (b. Gilbert Bourgeaud); French mercenary; b. 1929, Nr. Bordeaux; m. Amina Denard; two c.; joined French colonial army, quartermaster to a commando regt. Indo-China, Algeria; charged with an assassination attempt on Pierre Mendès-France 1954, acquitted 1955; mercenary for Moise Tshombe's breakaway Congo State of Katanga 1960; mercenary activities Biafra, Gabon, Yemen 1960s; backed coup to depose Pres. Abdallah of the Comoros Repub. 1976 (after Abdallah had declared independence from France 1975), Pres. Soilih installed; Minister of Defence Comoros Govt. of Pres. Soilih (as Col. Said Mustapha M'hadju); undertook failed coup attempt against Mathieu Kérékou's (q.v.) regime Benin 1977; supported reinstatement of Pres. Abdallah following the assassination of Pres. Soilih 1978, apptd. Chief of the Presidential Guard; took refuge in South Africa following charges of responsibility for the assassination of Pres. Abdallah 1989; charged with involvement in abortive coup in Benin 1991, received five-year sentence in absentia, prison term commuted to suspended sentence 1993; returned to France Feb. 1993; launched attempted coup in Comoros Sept. 1995; arrested by French special forces who put down coup Oct. 1995, released from prison Aug. 1996.

DENCH, Dame Judith (Judi) Olivia, D.B.E.; British actress; b. 9 Dec. 1934, York; d. of Reginald Arthur and Eleanora Olave (née Jones) Dench; m. Michael Williams 1971; one d.; ed. The Mount School, York, Central School of Speech Training and Dramatic Art; played in Old Vic seasons 1957–61, appearing in parts including Ophelia (Hamlet), Katherine (Henry V), Cecily (The Importance of Being Earnest), Juliet (Romeo and Juliet), appeared with Old Vic Co. at two Edinburgh Festivals, Venice, on tour to Paris, Belgium and Yugoslavia, and on tour to U.S.A. and Canada; appearances with R.S.C. 1961–62, including parts as Anya (The Cherry Orchard), Titania (A Midsummer Night's Dream), Dorcas Bellboys (A Penny for a Song), Isabella (Measure for Measure); on tour to W. Africa with Nottingham Playhouse 1963; mem. Bd. Nat. Theatre 1988–91; subsequent roles include Irina (The Three Sisters), and Doll Common (Alchemist), Oxford Playhouse 1964–65, title-role in Saint Joan, and Barbara (The Astrakhan Coat), Nottingham Playhouse 1965, Amanda (Private Lives), Lika (The Promise) 1967, Sally Bowles (Cabaret) 1968, Grace Harkaway (London Assurance) 1970, 1972, Barbara Undershaft (Major Barbara) 1970; Assoc. Mem. R.S.C. 1969–, appearing as Bianca (Women Beware Women), Viola (Twelfth Night), Hermione and Perdita (Winter's Tale), Portia (Merchant of Venice), Duchess (Duchess of Malfi), Beatrice (Much Ado About Nothing), Lady Macbeth (Macbeth), Adriana (Comedy of Errors), also on tour with R.S.C. to Japan and Australia 1970, Japan 1972; other performances include Vilma (The Wolf), Oxford and London 1973, Miss Trant (The Good Companions), 1974, Sophie Fullgarney (The Gay Lord Quex) 1975, Nurse (Too True to be Good) 1975, 1976, Millament (Way of the World) 1978, Cymbeline 1979, Juno and the Paycock 1980–81, Lady Bracknell (The Importance of Being Earnest) 1982, Deborah (A Kind of Alaska) 1982, Pack of Lies 1983, Mother Courage 1984, Waste 1985, Mr. and Mrs. Nobody 1986, Antony and Cleopatra 1987, Entertaining Strangers 1987, Hamlet 1989, The Cherry Orchard 1989, The Sea 1991, The Plough and the Stars 1991, Coriolanus 1992, The Gift of the Gorgon 1993, The Seagull (Royal Nat. Theatre) 1994, The Convent 1995, Absolute Hell (Royal Nat. Theatre) 1995, A Little Night Music (Royal Nat. Theatre) 1995, Amy's View (Royal Nat. Theatre) 1997, (New York) 1999, Filumena 1998; 1997 Dir. Much Ado About Nothing 1988, Look Back in Anger 1989, The Boys from Syracuse 1991. *Films include:* A Study in Terror 1965, He Who Rides a Tiger 1966, Four in the Morning 1966, A Midsummer Night's Dream (R.S.C. Production) 1968, The Third Secret 1978, Dead Cert, Wetherby 1985, Room with a View 1986, 84 Charing Cross Road 1987, A Handful of Dust 1988, Henry V 1989, Goldeneye 1995, Mrs. Brown 1996, Tea with Mussolini 1998, Shakespeare in Love (Acad. Award for Best Supporting Actress) 1998, The World is Not Enough 1999. *TV appearances in:* Major Barbara, Pink String and Sealing Wax, Talking to a Stranger, The Funambulists, Age of Kings, Jackanory, Hilda Lessways, Luther, Neighbours, Parade's End, Marching Song, On Approval, Days to Come, Emilie, Comedy of Errors, Macbeth, Langrishe Go Down, On Giants Shoulders, Love in a Cold Climate, A Fine Romance, The Cherry Orchard, Going Gently, Saigon—Year of the Cat 1982, Ghosts 1986, Behaving Badly 1989, Absolute Hell, Can You Hear Me Thinking?, As Time Goes By; mem. Bd., Nat. Theatre 1988–; Hon. D.Litt. (Warwick) 1978, (York) 1983, (Keele) 1989, (Birmingham) 1989, (Loughborough) 1991, (Open Univ.) 1994, (London) 1994; Dr. h.c. (Surrey) 1996; Hon. Fellow Royal Holloway Coll. London; numerous awards including Paladino d'Argentino (Venice Festival Award for Juliet) 1961, Best Actress of Year (Variety London Critics for Lika in The Promise) 1967, Most Promising Newcomer (British Film Acad. for Four in the Morning) 1965, Best Actress of the Year (Guild of Dirs. for Talking to a Stranger) 1967, Soc. West End Theatre Award (for Lady Macbeth) 1977, Best Actress New Standard Drama Awards (for Juno and the Paycock) 1980, (for Lady Bracknell in The Importance of Being Earnest and Deborah in A Kind of Alaska) 1983, (for Cleopatra in Antony and Cleopatra) 1987, Olivier Award for Best Actress in Antony and Cleopatra 1987; BAFTA Award for Best Television Actress 1981, for Best Supporting Actress (for A Room with a View) 1987 and (for A Handful of Dust) 1988, Golden Globe and BAFTA Best Actress Award for Mrs. Brown. *Publications:* Judi Dench: A Great Deal of Laughter (biog.), Judi Dench: With a Crack in Her Voice 1998. *Leisure interests:*

painting, drawing, swimming, sewing, catching up with letters. *Address:* c/o Julian Belfrage Associates, 46 Albemarle Street, London, W1X 4PP, England.

DENENBERG, Herbert Sidney, PH.D., J.D., LL.M.; American consumer reporter, lawyer and educator; b. 20 Nov. 1929, Omaha, Neb.; s. of David Aaron Denenberg and Fannie Molly (Rothenberg) Denenberg; m. Naomi Glushakow 1958; ed. Omaha Cen. High School, Johns Hopkins and Creighton Univs., Harvard Law School and Univ. of Pennsylvania; lawyer, Denenberg & Denenberg, Attorneys-at-Law 1954–55; lawyer, U.S. Army Judge Advocate Gen. Corps. 1955–58; Prof., Wharton School, Univ. of Pa. 1962–71; Insurance Commr., State of Pa. 1971–74; Special Adviser to Gov. of Pa. on Consumer Affairs 1974; Commr., Pa. Public Utilities Comm. 1974–75; Consumer Reporter, WCAU-TV (NBC), Philadelphia 1975-, Consumer Columnist Philadelphia Daily News 1979-81, Philadelphia Journal 1981–82, Delaware Co. Daily and Sunday Times 1987–89, Burlington Co. Daily Times 1987–89, Reading Eagle 1989–, Doylestown Patriot 1991–, and other newspapers; mem. Advisory Bd. The People's Doctor 1988–91; Trustee Center for Proper Medication Use; mem. Inst. of Medicine (N.A.S.); Hon. LL.D. (Allentown Coll.) 1989, Hon. D.H.L. (Spring Garden Coll.) 1992; numerous awards from Nat. Press Club, Consumer Fed. of America and Nat. Acad. of TV Arts and Sciences, B'nai B'rith Beber Award, Consumer Fed. of America Outstanding Media Service Award. *Publications include:* Risk and Insurance (textbook) 1964, Insurance, Government and Social Policy (textbook) 1969, Herb Denenberg's Smart Shopper's Guide 1980, The Shopper's Guidebook 1974, Life Insurance And/Or Mutual Funds 1967, Mass Marketing of Property and Liability Insurance 1970, The Insurance Trap 1972, Getting Your Money's Worth 1974, Cover Yourself 1974, Shoppers Guide to Medical Equipment 1990; hundreds of articles, govt. reports and statutes. *Leisure interests:* reading, photography. *Address:* WCAU-TV, City Avenue and Monument Road, Philadelphia, PA 19131 (Office); P.O. Box 7301, St. David's, PA 19087-7301, U.S.A. (Home). *Telephone:* (610) 668-5645. *Fax:* (610) 668-5649.

DENEUVE, Catherine (Catherine Dorléac); French actress; b. 22 Oct. 1943, Paris; d. of Maurice Dorléac and Renée Deneuve; m. David Bailey (q.v.) 1965 (divorced); one s. by Roger Vadim; one d. by Marcello Mastroianni; ed. Lycée La Fontaine, Paris; Film début in Les petits chats 1959; Pres., Dir.-Gen. Films de la Citrouille 1971–79; f. Société Cardeva 1983; Co.-Chair UNESCO Campaign to protect the World's Film Heritage 1994–; Hon. Golden Bear, Berlin Film Festival. *Films include:* Les portes claquent 1960, L'homme à femmes 1960, Le vice et la vertu 1962, Et Satan conduit le bal 1962, Vacances portugaises 1963, Les parapluies de Cherbourg 1963 (Palme d'Or, Festival de Cannes 1964), Les plus belles escroqueries du monde 1963, La chasse à l'homme 1964, Un monsieur de compagnie 1964, La Costanza della Ragione 1964, Repulsion 1964, Le chant du monde 1965, La vie de château 1965, Liebes Karusell 1965, Les créatures 1965, Les demoiselles de Rochefort 1966, Belle de jour 1967 (Golden Lion at Venice Festival 1967), Benjamin 1967, Manon 70 1967, Mayerling 1968, La chamade 1966, Folies d'avril 1969, Belles d'un soir 1969, La sirène du Mississippi 1969, Tristana 1970, Peau d'âne 1971, Ça n'arrive qu'aux autres 1971, Liza 1971, Un flic 1972, L'évènement le plus important depuis que l'homme a marché sur la lune 1973, Touche pas la femme blanche 1974, La femme aux bottes rouges 1975, La grande bourgeoisie 1975, Hustle 1976, March or Die 1977, Coup de foudre 1977, Ecoute, voir . . . 1978, L'argent des autres 1978, A nous deux 1979, Ils sont grands ces petits 1979, Le dernier métro 1980, Je vous aime 1980, Le choix des armes 1981, Hôtel des Amériques 1981, Le choc 1982, L'africain 1983, The Hunger 1983, Le bon plaisir 1984, Paroles et musiques 1984, Le lieu du crime 1986, Pourvu que ce soit une fille 1986, Drôle d'Endroit pour une rencontre 1989, La reine blanche 1991, Indochine 1992 (César award for Best Actress 1993), Ma saison Préférée 1993, La Partie d'Echecs 1994, The Convent 1995, les Cent et une nuits 1995, les Voleurs 1995, Genéalogie d'un crime 1997. *Address:* c/o Artmedia, 10 avenue George-V, 75008 Paris, France.

DENG LIQUN; Chinese politician; b. 1914, Guidong Co., Hunan Prov.; m. Luo Liyun; one s.; ed. Beijing No. 26 Middle School; mem. CCP 1936–; Dir. Educ. Dept. Marxism-Leninism Inst.; Dir. Propaganda Dept. CCP Jibei Pref. Cttee.; Deputy Dir. Gen. Office of Finance and Econ. Comm. of North-East China; Dir. Policy Research Office of CCP Liaoning Provincial Cttee.; after founding of People's Repub. of China in 1949 served as Chair. Cultural and Educ. Cttee. of Xinjiang Regional People's Cttee.; Dir. Propaganda Dept. of Xinjiang Bureau under CCP Cen. Cttee.; Ed. and Deputy Ed.-in-Chief, Red Flag; branded as counter-revolutionary revisionist and purged during Cultural Revolution; Vice-Pres. Acad. of Social Sciences 1978; Dir. Policy Research Section under CCP Cen. Cttee. 1981; Adviser to Soc. for Study of Econ. of Minority Areas 1981, to Soc. of Labour Science 1982, to Soc. for Study of Workers' Political and Ideological Work; Dir. CCP Cen. Cttee. Propaganda Dept. 1982–85; mem. 12th CCP Cen. Cttee. 1982, also mem. Secr. 1982–87; Vice-Chair. Nat. Cttee. for Promoting Socialist Ethics 1983; Head, CCP Cen. Leading Group for Educ. of Cadres 1985; mem. CCP Cen. Advisory Comm. 1987; Deputy Head, CCP Cen. Cttee. Party Bldg. Group 1990–; Hon. Pres. Soc. for Studies on Party Mems. 1991–; Deputy Head, CCP Cen. Cttee. Leading Group for Party History Work 1994–. *Address:* c/o Central Committee of Chinese Communist Party, Beijing, People's Republic of China.

DENG PUFANG; Chinese politician; b. 1943; s. of late Deng Xiaoping and Zhuo Lin; ed. Beijing Univ.; Deputy Dir.-in-Chief of the Welfare Fund for Handicapped 1984, Dir.-in-Chief, 1985–; Ed.-in-Chief Spring Breeze (Journal) 1984–; visited France on invitation of Danielle Mitterrand, Aug. 1985; Vice-Chair. of China Organizing Comm. of UN's Decade of Disabled Persons 1986–90, Chair. 1990–; Vice-Chair. Cttee. for Coordination of Work for the Disabled; Pres. Chinese Fed. for the Disabled 1988–; Advisor China Asscn. for Int. Friendly Contacts 1991–; alt. mem. 15th CCP Cen. Cttee. 1997. *Address:* China Welfare Fund for Handicapped, Beijing, People's Republic of China.

DENG YAPING; Chinese table tennis player; b. Feb. 1973, Zhengzhou, He'nan Prov.; mem. of Chinese Women's Table Tennis Team 1988; won over 20 gold medals in various world championships; mem. Sports Cttee. of IOC. *Address:* c/o State General Bureau for Physical Culture and Sports, 9 Tiyuguan Road, Chongwen District, Beijing, People's Republic of China.

DENG YOUMEI; Chinese writer; b. 1931, Tianjin; messenger in CCP-led New 4th Army 1945; entered Cen. Research Inst. of Literature 1952; in political disgrace 1957–77; Sec. Secr., Sec. Chinese Writers' Asscn. 1985–96, Vice-Chair. 1996–. *Publications:* On the Precipice, Our Army Commander, Han the Forger, Tales of Taoranting Park, Snuff Bottles, Na Wu, Moon Over Liangshan Mountain. *Address:* Chinese Writers' Association, 25 Dongtucheng Road, Beijing 100013, People's Republic of China. *Telephone:* (10) 64261554.

DENHAM, Susan Gageby, B.A., LL.M.; Irish judge; b. 22 Aug. 1945, Dublin; d. of R.J.D. Gageby and Dorothy Lester; m. Brian Denham 1970; three s. one d.; ed. Alexandra Coll. Dublin, Trinity Coll. Dublin, King's Inns, Dublin and Columbia Univ. New York; called to Irish Bar 1971; mem. Midland Circuit 1971–91; called to Inner Bar 1987; Judge, High Court 1991–92, Supreme Court 1992–; Pro-Chancellor Univ. of Dublin Trinity Coll. 1996–; Chair. Working Group on a Courts Comm. 1995–98; fmr. mem. Free Legal Advice Centres, Garda Siochana Complaints Bd., Adoption Bd. *Leisure interests:* horses, gardens. *Address:* The Supreme Court, The Four Courts, Dublin 7, Ireland. *Telephone:* (1) 8725555 (Ext. 519).

DENHARDT, David Tilton, PH.D., F.R.S.C.; American professor of biological sciences; b. 25 Feb. 1939, Sacramento, Calif.; s. of David B. Denhardt and Edith E. Tilton; m. Georgetta Louise Harrar 1961; one s. two d.; ed. Swarthmore Coll., Pa. and Calif. Inst. of Tech. Pasadena; Instructor Biology Dept. Harvard Univ. 1964–66, Asst. Prof. 1966–70; Assoc. Prof. Biochemistry Dept. McGill Univ., Montreal 1970–76, Prof. 1976–80; Dir. Cancer Research Lab. and Prof. of Biochem., Microbiology and Immunology, Univ. of W. Ont. 1980–88; Chair. Biological Sciences, Rutgers Univ. 1988–95, Dir. Bureau of Biological Research 1988–95, Prof. of Biological Sciences 1988–, Chair. Biology Dept. 1988–95; ed. Journal Virology 1977–87, GENE 1985–93, Experimental Cell Research 1994–; Assoc. ed. Journal of Cell Biochemistry 1994–; mem. numerous ed. bds. *Leisure interests:* travel, reading, canoeing, skiing, camping. *Address:* Nelson Biological Laboratories, Rutgers University, 604 Allison Road, Piscataway, NJ 08855, U.S.A. *Telephone:* (908) 445-4569 (Office); (908) 704-0279 (Home). *Fax:* (908) 445-0104.

DENHOLM, Sir Ian (John Ferguson), Kt., C.B.E., J.P., D.L.; British shipowner; b. 8 May 1927, Glasgow; s. of Sir William and Lady Denholm (née Ferguson); m. Elizabeth Murray Stephen 1952; two s. two d.; ed. Loretto School, Midlothian; Chair. Denholm Group of Companies 1974–98; Deputy Chair. P & O Steam Navigation Co. 1980–83; Pres. Chamber of Shipping of U.K. 1973–74; Chair. North of England Protecting & Indemnity Asscn. 1976–78, Murray Group Investments Trusts 1985–93, Murray Man. Ltd. 1985–92; Dir. Fleming Mercantile Investment Trust PLC 1984–94; Pres. Gen. Council of British Shipping 1988–89, B.I.F.A. 1990–91, B.I.M.C.O. 1991–93; mem. Nat. Ports Council 1974–77, Scottish Transport Group 1975–82, London Bd. of Bank of Scotland 1982–91, West of Scotland Bd. of Bank of Scotland 1991–95; D.L. Renfrewshire 1980; Hon. Norwegian Consul in Glasgow 1975–97. *Leisure interest:* fishing. *Address:* Newton of Belltrees, Lochwinnoch, Renfrewshire, PA12 4JL, Scotland. *Telephone:* (01505) 842406.

DENIAU, Jean François, D. EN D., L. ÈS L.; French politician, diplomatist and economist; b. 31 Oct. 1928, Paris; s. of Marc Deniau and Marie-Berthe Loth-Simmonds; m. 1st Dominique de Mirbeck 1958; one s. one d.; m. 2nd Frédérique Dupuy 1971; ed. Inst. d'Etudes Politiques de Paris, Ecole Nat. d'Admin.; Ecole Nat. d'Admin. 1950–52; Finance Insp. 1952–55; Sec.-Gen. Inter-Ministerial Cttee. on European Econ. Co-operation 1955–56; Del. to OEEC 1955–56; Del. to Inter-Govt. Conf. on the Common Market and Euratom 1956; Head of Mission, Cabinet of Pres. of Counsel 1957–58; Tech. Adviser, Ministry of Industry and Commerce 1958–59; Dir. Comm. on countries seeking asscn. with EEC 1959–61; Head of Del., Conf. with States seeking membership of EEC 1961–63; Dir. External Econ. Relations, Ministry of Finance and Econ. Affairs (France) 1963; Amb. to Mauritania 1963–66; Pres. Comm. Franco-Soviétique pour la télévision en couleur; mem. Combined Comm. of EEC, ECSC, and Euratom 1967–73; Commr. for Devt. Aid, European Communities 1969–73; Sec. of State for Foreign Affairs 1973–74, for Agricultural and Rural Devt. 1974, for Agric. 1975–76; Amb. to Spain 1976–77; Sec. of State for Foreign Affairs 1977–78; Minister of Foreign Trade 1978–80; Minister Del. to the Prime Minister in Charge of Admin. Reforms 1980–81; lost seat in Nat. Ass. 1981, re-elected Deputy for Cher 1986, 1988; mem. European Parl. 1979–86, Vice-Pres. Political Comm., Vice-Pres. Sub-Comm. on Human Rights; Pres. Conseil Général, Cher 1981–85, re-elected 1985, 1988, 1993; Pres. Féd. Nat. des Clubs Perspective et Réalité 1982–84; Vice-Pres. Nat. Ass. Comm. on Foreign Affairs, 1986; Titular Judge High Court of Justice 1993–; elected to Acad. Française 1992;

Grand Prix de Littérature, Acad. Française 1990; Commdr. Légion d'honneur, Croix de guerre, Commdr. du Mérite Agricole. *Publications:* Le marché commun 1958, 1960, La mer est ronde (Prix de la Mer) 1976, L'Europe interdite 1977, Deux heures après minuit 1985, La Désirade 1988, Un héros très discret 1989, L'empire nocturne 1990, Ce que je crois 1992, le Secret du Roi des Serpents 1993, Mémoires de 7 Vies 1994 (Vol. II Croire et oser 1997), L'Atlantique mon désert 1996, le bureau des secrets perdus 1998. *Leisure interest:* sailing. *Address:* 3 avenue Octave Gréard, 75007 Paris, France. *Telephone:* (1) 44-38-41-58.

DE NIRO, Robert; American actor; b. 1943, New York; s. of the late Robert De Niro and of Virginia Admiral; m. Diahnne Abbott 1976; one s. one d.; two c. by Toukie Smith; f. and Pres. Tri Beca Productions 1989–; Commdr. Ordre des Arts et des Lettres. *Films include:* The Wedding Party 1969, Jennifer On My Mind 1971, Bloody Mama, Born to Win 1971, The Gang That Couldn't Shoot Straight 1971, Bang the Drum Slowly 1973, Mean Streets 1973, The Godfather, Part II 1974 (Acad. Award for Best Supporting Actor), The Last Tycoon, Taxi Driver 1976, New York, New York, 1900 1977, The Deer Hunter 1978, Raging Bull (Acad. Award Best Actor) 1980, True Confessions 1981, The King of Comedy 1982, Once Upon a Time in America 1984, Falling in Love 1984, Brazil 1984, The Mission 1985, Angel Heart 1986, The Untouchables 1987, Letters Home from Vietnam, Midnight Run 1988, We're No Angels 1989, Stanley and Iris 1989, Good Fellas 1989, Jacknife 1989, Awakenings 1990, Fear No Evil 1990, Backdraft 1990, Cape Fear 1990, Guilty of Suspicion 1991, Mistress 1992, Night and the City 1992, Mad Dog and Glory 1992, This Boy's Life 1993, Mary Shelley's Frankenstein 1993, A Bronx Tale (also dir., co-produced) 1993, Sleepers 1996, The Fan 1996, Marvin's Room 1996, Sleepers 1996, Great Expectations 1997, Jackie Brown 1998, Ronin 1998, Analyse This 1999; producer Thunderheart 1992. *Address:* C.A.A., 9830 Wilshire Boulevard, Beverly Hills, CA 90212, U.S.A.

DENISSE, François-Jean; French astronomer, b. 16 May 1915, Saint-Quentin, Aisne; s. of Jean Julien Denisse and Marie Nicolas; m. Myriam Girondot 1948; two d., ed. Ecole Normale Supérieure; Teacher at Lycée, Dakar 1942–45; Attaché at Centre Nat. de la Recherche Scientifique (C.N.R.S.) 1946–47; Guest Worker, Nat. Bureau of Standards, U.S.A. 1948–49; Head of Research of C.N.R.S. at Ecole Normale Supérieure 1950–51, Dir. of Studies, Inst. des Hautes Etudes, Dakar 1952–53; Asst. Astronomer, Paris Observatory 1954–56, Astronomer 1956–63, Dir. 1963–68; Chair. of Bd. of Nat. Space Research Centre 1968–73; Dir. Institut Nationale d'Astronomie et de Géophysique 1968–71; Pres. Bureau des Longitudes 1974–75; mem. Atomic Energy Comm. 1970–75, Head of Research at the Ministry of Universities 1976–81; Pres. Council of the European Southern Observatory 1977–81; Pres. Cttee. for Space Research (COSPAR) 1978–82; mem. Acad. des Sciences 1967, Int. Acad. of Astronautics 1968–; Commdr., Légion d'honneur, Commdr., Ordre national du Mérite. *Leisure interest:* golf. *Address:* 48 rue Monsieur Le Prince, 75006 Paris, France (Home). *Telephone:* (1) 43-29-48-74.

DENKTAŞ, Rauf R.; Cypriot politician; b. 27 Jan. 1924, Ktima, Paphos; s. of Judge M. Raif bey; m. Aydin Munir 1949; two s. (one deceased) two d.; ed. The English School, Nicosia, and Lincoln's Inn, London; law practice in Nicosia 1947–49; Jr. Crown Counsel 1949, Crown Counsel 1952; Acting Solicitor-Gen. 1956–58; Pres. Fed. of Turkish Cypriot Asscns. 1958–60; Pres. Turkish Communal Chamber 1960, re-elected 1970; Pres. "Turkish Federated State of Cyprus" 1975–83; Pres. "Turkish Repub. of Northern Cyprus" Nov. 1983–. *Publications:* Secrets of Happiness 1943, Hell Without Fire 1944, A Handbook of Criminal Cases 1955, Five Minutes to Twelve 1966, The AKRITAS Plan 1972, A Short Discourse on Cyprus 1972, The Cyprus Problem 1973, A Discourse with Youth 1981, The Cyprus Triangle 1982. *Leisure interests:* reading, writing, sea sports, shooting, photography. *Address:* The Office of the President, "Turkish Republic of Northern Cyprus", Lefkoşa, via Mersin 10, Turkey. *Telephone:* 9052071444.

DENMAN, Sir Roy, K.C.B., C.M.G., M.A.; British civil servant and administrator; b. 12 June 1924, Liverpool; s. of Albert Edward and Gertrude Ann Denman; m. Moya Lade 1966; one s. one d.; ed. Harrow Grammar School and St. John's Coll., Cambridge; Asst. Prin., Bd. of Trade 1948, Asst. Pvt. Sec. to successive Pres. 1950–52; First Sec., Embassy, Bonn, Fed. Repub. of Germany 1957–60; mem. del., Geneva 1960–61; Counsellor, Geneva 1965–67; mem. negotiating del. with European Communities 1970–72; Deputy Sec. Dept. of Trade and Industry 1970–75; Second Perm. Sec., Cabinet Office 1975–77; Dir.-Gen. of External Relations Comm. of EEC 1977–82; Head of EEC Del. to Washington 1982–89; Business Fellow, John F. Kennedy School of Govt., Harvard 1989–90; Consultant in Int. Trade. *Publication:* Missed Chances: Britain and Europe in the 20th Century 1996. *Address:* c/o Coutts & Co., 2 Lower Sloane Street, London, SW1W 8BJ, England.

DENNEHY, Brian; American actor; b. 9 July 1939, Bridgeport, Conn.; m. 2nd Jennifer Dennehey; three c. (from previous marriage); ed. Chaminade High School, Columbia and Yale Univs.; served with U.S. Marine Corps for five years. *Films include:* Semi-Tough 1977, F.I.S.T. 1978, Foul Play 1978, Butch and Sundance: the Early Days 1979, 10 1979, Little Miss Marker 1980, Split Image 1982, First Blood 1982, Never Cry Wolf 1983, Gorky Park 1983, Twice in a Lifetime 1985, Silverado 1985, Cocoon 1985, F/X 1986, Legal Eagles 1986, Best Seller 1987, The Belly of an Architect 1987, Return to Snowy River 1988, Cocoon: The Return, The Last of the Finest, Presumed Innocent, FX2, Gladiator, Seven Minutes, Midnight Movie 1993, Gilligan's Island 1997, Tommy Boy, The Stars Fell on Henrietta, Romeo and Juliet, Deep River, Finders Keepers, Looking for Mr. Goodbar. *TV Appearances in:* Big Shamus, Little Shamus, Star of the Family, Birdland 1993, numerous TV films and stage appearances. *Address:* c/o Susan Smith and Associates, 121 North San Vicente Boulevard, Beverly Hills, CA 90211, U.S.A. *Telephone:* (213) 852-4777 (Office).

DENNETT, Daniel Clement, D.PHIL.; American philosopher, university professor and author; b. 28 March 1942, Boston; s. of Daniel C. Dennett, Jr. and Ruth M. Leck; m. Susan Bell 1962; one s. one d.; ed. Phillips Exeter High School, Harvard Univ., Oxford Univ.; Asst. Prof. of Philosophy, Univ. of Calif., Irvine 1965–70, Assoc. Prof. 1971; Assoc. Prof., Tufts Univ. 1971–75, Prof. 1975–85, Distinguished Arts and Sciences Prof., Dir. Center for Cognitive Studies, Tufts 1985–; Visiting Prof., Harvard 1973–74, Pittsburgh 1975, Oxford 1979, Ecole Normale Supérieure, Paris 1985; Visiting Fellow, All Souls Coll. Oxford 1979; John Locke Lecturer, Oxford 1983, Gavin David Young Lecturer, Adelaide, Australia 1984; Woodrow Wilson Fellow 1963, Guggenheim Fellow 1973, 1986, Fulbright Fellow 1978; Fellow Center for Advanced Study in Behavioral Sciences 1979, American Acad. of Arts and Sciences 1987. *Publications:* Content and Consciousness 1969, Brainstorms 1978, The Mind's I (with Douglas Hofstadter) 1981, Elbow Room 1984, The Intentional Stance 1987, Consciousness Explained 1991, Darwin's Dangerous Idea 1995, Kinds of Minds 1996, Brain Children 1998; numerous articles in professional journals. *Leisure interests:* sculpture, farming, cider-making, sailing, choral singing. *Address:* Center for Cognitive Studies, Tufts University, Medford, MA 02155 (Office); 20 Ironwood Road, North Andover, MA 01845, U.S.A. (Home). *Telephone:* (617) 627-3297 (Office); (508) 689-7460 (Home). *Fax:* (617) 627-3952 (Office); (508) 685-8420 (Home).

DENNIS, Bengt, M.A.; Swedish banker; b. 5 Jan. 1930, Grengesberg; m. Turid Stroem 1962; one s. one d.; ed. Columbia Univ., N.Y.; econ. journalist 1959–67; Head of Dept., Ministry of Finance 1967–70; Under-Sec. of State, Ministry of Commerce 1970–76; Amb., Ministry of Foreign Affairs 1977–80; Ed.-in-Chief, Dagens Nyheter 1981–82; Gov. Cen. Bank of Sweden 1982–92; Chair. Bd. of Dirs. BIS 1990–93; Sr. Adviser Skandinaviska Enskilda Banken 1994–. *Leisure interests:* sailing, skiing, skating. *Address:* Maria Sandels Gränd 3, 11269 Stockholm, Sweden. *Telephone:* 08-6510432.

DENNIS, Donna Frances; American sculptor and teacher; b. 16 Oct. 1942, Springfield, Ohio; d. of Donald P. and Helen Hogue Dennis; ed. Carleton Coll., Northfield, Minn, Paris and New York; teaching positions at Skowhegan School 1982, Boston Museum School (Visiting artist) 1983, State Univ. of N.Y., Purchase Coll. 1984–86, 1988–, School of Visual Arts, New York 1983–90, Princeton Univ. (Visiting Artist) 1984, S.U.N.Y. Purchase Coll. (Assoc. Prof.) 1990–96, Prof. 1996–; one-woman exhbns. include West Broadway Gallery, New York 1973, Holly Solomon Gallery, New York 1976, 1980, 1983, 1998, Contemporary Arts Center, Cincinnati 1979, Locus Solus Gallery, Genoa 1981, Neuberger Museum, State Univ. of N.Y., Purchase Coll. 1985, Univ. Gallery, Univ. of Mass. at Amherst 1985, Brooklyn Museum, New York 1987, Richard Green Gallery, New York 1987, Del. Art Museum, Wilmington 1988, Muhlenberg Coll. Center for the Arts, Allentown, Pa. 1988, Madison Art Center, Madison, Wis. 1989, Indianapolis Museum of Art 1991–98, Sculpture Center, New York 1993; group exhbns. include Walker Art Center, Minneapolis 1977, Biennial Exhbn. Whitney Museum 1979, Hirshhorn Museum, Washington, D.C. 1979, 1984, Developments in Recent Sculpture, Whitney Museum 1981, Venice Biennale 1982, 1984, New Art at the Tate, Tate Gallery, London 1983, Storm King Art Center, Mountainville, NY 1991, 42nd St. Art Project 1994, Katonah Museum, N.Y. 1994, Neuberger Museum, State Univ. of N.Y., Purchase Coll. 1997, Asheville Art Museum, Asheville, N.C. 1998; perm. comms.: Dreaming of Faraway Places: The Ships come to Washington Market, P.S. 234, New York, Klapper Hall, Queens Coll., C.U.N.Y. 1995, Anmerican Airlines Terminal, J.F.K. Int. Airport, N.Y. 1996; Fellow Nat. Endowment for the Arts 1977, 1980, 1986, 1994; recipient of several awards, including Distinguished Achievement Award, Carleton Coll. 1989, Bard Award, City Club of New York 1989; Bessie Award for Set Design 1992, NEA Fellowship (4 times). *Publication:* 26 Bars (with Kenward Elmslie) 1987. *Leisure interests:* exotic cooking, reading fiction, swing dancing. *Address:* 131 Duane Street, New York, NY 10013, U.S.A. *Telephone:* (212) 233-0605.

DENNIS, Michael Mark, LL.M.; Canadian property developer; b. 4 March 1942, Toronto; ed. Osgoode Hall Law School and Univ. of Calif. (Berkeley); Asst. Prof. Osgoode Hall Law School 1965–67; Consultant, Nat. Planning Comm. Philippines 1968–69; Chair. Fed. Govt. Task Force on Housing 1970–72; Special Asst. to Mayor of Toronto 1973; Commr. of Housing City of Toronto 1974–79; Exec. Vice-Pres. Olympia & York Properties (U.S.A.) 1985–; Exec. Dir. Olympia & York Canary Wharf Ltd. 1987–90. *Publication:* Programs in Search of a Policy (with Susan Fish) 1973. *Leisure interests:* literature, travel, sports, music. *Address:* 101 Woodlawn Avenue, W. Toronto, Ont., M4V 1G6, Canada.

DENNISTON, Rev. Robin Alastair, M.A., B.LIT.HUM.; British publisher and ecclesiastic; b. 25 Dec. 1926, London; s. of late Alexander Guthrie Denniston and Dorothy Mary Gilliat; m. 1st Anne Alice Kyffin Evans 1950 (died 1985); one s. two d.; m. 2nd Dr. Rosa Susan Penelope Beddington 1987; ed. Westminster School and Christ Church, Oxford; Ed. Collins 1950–59; Man. Dir. Faith Press 1959–60; Ed. Prism 1959–61; Promotion Man. Hodder

& Stoughton Ltd. 1960–64, Editorial Dir. 1966, Man. Dir. 1968–72, also Dir. Mathew Hodder Ltd. and subsidiary cos.; Deputy Chair. George Weidenfeld & Nicolson (and subsidiary cos.) 1973; Chair. (non-exec.) A. R. Mowbray & Co. 1974–88; Chair. Sphere Books 1975–76, Thomas Nelson & Sons (and subsidiary cos.) 1975, Michael Joseph Ltd. 1975, George Rainbird Ltd. 1975; Dir. Thomson Publs. Ltd. 1975, Hamish Hamilton Ltd. 1975, (non-exec.) W. W. Norton 1989–; Academic Publr. Oxford Univ. Press 1978, Sr. Deputy Sec. to the Dels. 1984–88, Oxford Publr. 1984–88; Student of Christ Church 1978; ordained Deacon 1978, Priest 1979; Hon. Curate Parish of Clifton-on-Teme 1978; New with S. Hinksey 1985; Non-Stipendiary Minister, Great with Little Tew 1987–90, Burntisland and St. Columba's Aberdour, Fife 1990–93; Priest-in-charge Great with Little Tew and Over Worton with Nether Worton 1995–. *Publications:* The Young Musicians 1956, Partly Living 1967, Part Time Priests? (Ed.) 1960; co-ed. Anatomy of Scotland 1992. *Leisure interests:* music, farming, walking. *Address:* The Vicarage, Great Tew, Oxon., OX7 4AG; 112 Randolph Avenue, London, W9 1PQ, England.

DENNY, Floyd Wolfe, Jr., M.D.; American professor of pediatrics; b. 22 Oct. 1923, South Carolina; s. of Floyd W. Denny and Marion P. Denny; m. Barbara Horsefield 1946; two s. one d.; ed. Wofford Coll. and Vanderbilt Univ. School of Medicine; Asst. Prof. of Pediatrics, Univ. of Minn. 1951–53, Vanderbilt Univ. 1953–55; Asst. Prof. of Pediatrics and Preventive Medicine, Case Western Reserve Univ. 1955–60, Assoc. Prof. of Preventive Medicine 1960; Prof. of Pediatrics, Univ. of N.C. 1960–, Alumni Distinguished Prof. of Pediatrics 1973–, Chair. Dept. of Pediatrics 1960–81, Dir. Program on Health Promotion and Disease Prevention 1985–93; Lasker Award; Hon. D.Sc. (Wofford Coll.) 1985. *Publications:* over 100 articles in medical journals on rheumatic fever, streptococcal infections, acute respiratory infections and sarcoidosis. *Leisure interests:* gardening, reading. *Address:* 358, Wing C, CB No. 7225, University of North Carolina, Chapel Hill, NC 27599 (Office); 9210 Dodsons Crossroads, Chapel Hill, NC 27516, U.S.A. (Home). *Telephone:* (919) 966-2504 (Office); (919) 929 2359 (Home).

DENNY, Robyn (Edward M. F.), A.R.C.A.; British artist; b. 3 Oct. 1930, Abinger, Surrey; s. of Sir Henry Denny, Bt. and Joan, Lady Denny; m. 1st Anna Teasdale (divorced); m. 2nd Marjorie Abéla; two s. one d.; ed. Clayesmore School, Dorset, St. Martin's School of Art and Royal Coll. of Art, London; first one-man exhbns. in London at Gallery One and Gimpel Fils 1958; has since given one-man exhbns. throughout Britain, Europe and U.S.A.; retrospective exhbn. Tate Gallery, London 1973; has represented Britain at Biennales in Paris, Tokyo, Milan, Brussels, U.S.A. and Australia and at 33rd Venice Biennale; works in numerous public collections; has received many public commissions for murals; teaching assignments have included Slade School, Univ. of London and Minn. Inst. of Fine Art; fmr. adviser, Arts Council of G.B., Inst. of Contemporary Arts, London; recipient of several awards and prizes. *Publications:* articles and criticism in int. publs. *Address:* Unit 4B, 20/30 Wilds Rents, London, SE1 4QG, England.

DENT, Sir John, Kt., C.B.E., F.ENG., F.R.AE.S., F.I.MECH.E., F.I.E.E.; British business executive and engineer; b. 5 Oct. 1923, Burton-on-Trent, Staffs.; s. of Harry F. Dent; m. Pamela A. Bailey 1954; one s.; ed. Burton-on-Trent Grammar School, King's Coll., London; with Admiralty Gunnery Establishments, Teddington and Portland 1944–55; Chief Eng., Guided Weapons Dept., Short Bros. and Harland Ltd., Belfast 1955–60; Chief Eng., Armaments Div., Armstrong Whitworth Aircraft Ltd., Coventry 1961–63; Dir. and Chief Eng., Hawker Siddeley Dynamics Ltd. 1963–67, Dir. and Div. Man., Guided Weapons Equipment and Systems 1967; Dir. Eng. Group, Dunlop Ltd. 1968–75; Dir. Dunlop Holdings Ltd. 1970–82; Man. Dir. Dunlop Ltd. 1978–82; Dir. Industrie Pirelli SpA 1978–80, Pirelli Gen. PLC 1980–92, Pirelli Ltd. 1985–92; Chair. Civil Aviation Authority 1982–86; Pres. Eng. Employers' Fed. 1974–76, Inst. of Travel Mans. 1986–93, Int. Fed. of Airworthiness 1987–89. *Leisure interests:* cabinet making, fishing, gardening, *Address:* Helidon Grange, Helidon, Daventry, Northants., NN11 6LG, England. *Telephone:* (01327) 260589.

DENTON, Charles Henry, B.A., F.R.S.A.; British television executive; b. 20 Dec. 1937; s. of Alan Denton; ed. Reading School and Univ. of Bristol; m. Eleanor Mary Denton (née Player) 1961; one s. two d.; worked as deckhand 1960; trainee advertising 1961–63; with BBC 1963–68; freelance TV producer Granada, ATV and Yorkshire TV cos. 1969–70; Dir. Tempest Films Ltd. 1969–71; Man. Dir. Black Lion Films 1979–81; Head of Documentaries ATV 1974–77, Controller of Programmes 1977–81; Dir. of Programmes Cen. Independent TV 1981–84; Dir. Cen. Independent Television PLC 1981–87; Chief Exec. Zenith Productions 1984–93, Chair. Zenith North Ltd. 1988–93; Head of Drama BBC 1993–96; Chair. PACT –1993; Gov. BFI 1993–; mem. Arts Council of England; Fellow Royal TV Soc. *Address:* British Film Institute, 21 Stephen Street, London, W1P 2LN, England. *Telephone:* 0171-255 1444.

DENTON, Derek Ashworth, M.M., B.S., F.A.A., F.R.A.C.P., F.R.C.P.; Australian research physiologist; b. 27 May 1924, Launceston, Tasmania; s. of A. A. Denton; m. Dame Margaret Scott 1953; two s.; ed. Launceston Grammar School and Univ. of Melbourne; Haley Research Fellow, Walter & Eliza Hall Inst. of Medical Research 1948; Overseas Nat. Health and Medical Research Council (NH & MRC) Fellow, Cambridge 1952–53; Medical Research Fellow, later Sr. Medical Research Fellow, Nat. Health and Medical Research Council 1949–63, Prin. Research Fellow, Admin. Head and Chief Scientist 1964–70; Dir. and originating Bd. mem. Howard Florey Inst. of Experimental Physiology and Medicine 1971–89, Emer. Dir. 1990–; Visiting Prof., British Heart Foundation and Balliol Coll. Oxford, U.K.; Adjunct Scientist, Southwest Foundation for Biomedical Research, San Antonio, Tex., U.S.A.; Dir. The David Syme Co. Ltd. 1984–, Australian Ballet Foundation 1983–, Sydney Dance Co. 1994–; First Vice-Pres. Int. Union of Physiological Sciences 1983–89; Chair. Nommating Cttee. of Council, Int. Union of Physiological Sciences 1986–89; Chair. Cttee. to Review Comms. of Int. Union of Physiological Sciences 1986–95; Foreign Assoc. N.A.S. (U.S.A.); Foreign Medical mem. Royal Swedish Acad. of Sciences; mem. Jury of Basic and Clinical Medical Awards, Albert and Mary Lasker Foundation 1979–89; Hon. Foreign Fellow, American Acad. of Arts and Sciences; Hon. Foreign mem. American Physiology Soc. *Publications:* The Hunger for Salt 1982, The Pinnacle of Life 1993; 300 articles and reviews. *Leisure interests:* tennis, fishing, ballet, music, wine. *Address:* 816 Orrong Road, Toorak, Vic. 3142, Australia (Home). *Telephone:* (03) 9827-2640 (Home).

DENTON, Sir Eric James, Kt., C.B.E., F.R.S.; British physiologist; b. 30 Sept. 1923, Doncaster; s. of George Denton and Mary Anne Ogden; m. Nancy Emily Wright 1946; two s. one d.; ed. Doncaster Grammar School, St. John's Coll., Cambridge, University Coll., London; Lecturer, Dept. of Physiology, Univ. of Aberdeen 1948–56; Physiologist, Marine Biological Asscn. Lab., Plymouth 1956–64, Sec. of Asscn. and Dir. of Lab. 1974–87; Royal Soc. Research Prof., Univ. of Bristol 1964–74; Royal Medal, Royal Soc. 1987, Frink Medal, Zoological Soc. of London 1987, Int. Prize for Biology, Japan Soc. for Promotion of Science 1989. *Publications:* numerous papers since 1948 in Journal of Marine Biological Asscn., Journal of Physiology and other scientific journals. *Leisure interest:* gardening. *Address:* The Laboratory, Citadel Hill, Plymouth, PL1 2PB (Office); Fairfield House, St. Germans, Saltash, Cornwall, PL12 5LS, England (Home). *Telephone:* 01752-633100 (Office); 01503-230204 (Home).

DENTON, Frank Trevor, M.A., F.R.S.C.; Canadian professor of economics; b. 27 Oct. 1930, Toronto; s. of Frank W. Denton and Kathleen M. Davies; m. Marilyn J. Shipp 1953; three s. one d.; ed. Univ. of Toronto; economist, Govt. of Ont. 1953–54, Govt. of Canada 1954–59, 1961–64, Philips Electronics Industries Ltd. 1959–60, Senate of Canada cttee. staff 1960–61; Dir. of Econometrics, Dominion Bureau of Statistics 1964–68; Consultant, Econ. Council of Canada 1964–68; Prof. of Econs. McMaster Univ. 1968–96, Prof. Emer. 1996–; Dir. McMaster Program for Quantitative Studies in Econs. and Population 1981–96; various other consulting appts.; Fellow, American Statistical Asscn., Royal Statistical Soc.; mem. Int. Statistical Inst., Int. Union for Scientific Study of Population. *Publications:* Growth of Manpower in Canada 1970; Co-author: Population and the Economy 1975, Working-Life Tables for Canadian Males 1969, Historical Estimates of the Canadian Labour Force 1967, The Short-Run Dynamics of the Canadian Labour Market 1976, Unemployment and Labour Force Behaviour of Young People: Evidence from Canada and Ontario 1980, Pensions and the Economic Security of the Elderly 1981; numerous monographs, articles, technical papers. *Address:* Department of Economics, McMaster University, Hamilton, Ont., L8S 4M4 (Office); 382 Blythewood Road, Burlington, Ont., L7L 2G8, Canada (Home). *Telephone:* (905) 525-9140 Ext. 24595 (Office); (905) 639-9361 (Home). *Fax:* (905) 521-8232.

DENTON, Richard Michael, PH.D., F.R.S.; British biochemist; b. 16 Oct. 1941, Sutton Coldfield; s. of the late Arthur Benjamin Denton and of Eileen Mary Denton (née Evans); m. Janet Mary Jones 1965; one s. two d.; ed. Wycliffe Coll., Stonehouse, Glos., Christ's Coll., Cambridge; lecturer in Biochemistry Univ. of Bristol 1973–78, Reader 1978–87, Prof. (Personal Chair) 1987–, Head of Biochemistry Dept. 1995–; MRC Research Fellowship 1984–88; Founder Fellow Acad. of Medical Sciences. *Publications:* over 220 research papers in various int. research journals, with maj. topic the molecular basis of the control of metabolism by insulin and other hormones. *Leisure interests:* family, fell walking, keeping fit, cooking. *Address:* Department of Biochemistry, University of Bristol School of Medical Sciences, University Walk, Bristol, BS8 1TD, England.

DÉON, Michel; French writer; b. 4 Aug. 1919, Paris; s. of Paul Déon and Alice de Fossey; m. Chantal d'Arc 1963; one s. one d.; ed. Lycée Janson-de-Sailly and Faculty of Law, Paris; journalist with l'Action française, Marie-Claire 1942–56; publisher 1954; writer 1956–; mem. Acad. Française 1978–; Officier, Légion d'honneur; Officier des Arts et des Lettres; Prix Interallié 1970, Grand Prix du Roman 1973, Grand Prix Jean Giono 1996. *Publications:* novels: Je ne veux jamais l'oublier 1950, La Corrida 1952, Le Dieu pâle 1954, Les trompeuses espérances 1956, Les gens de la nuit 1957, Tout l'amour du monde 1959, Un parfum de jasmin 1966, Les poneys sauvages 1970, Un taxi mauve 1973, Le jeune homme vert 1976, Mes arches de Noé 1978, Un déjeuner de soleil 1981, Louis XIV par lui-même 1983, Je vous écris d'Italie 1984, Bagages pour Vancouver 1985, La Montée du Soir, Ma Vie n'est plus un Roman (drama), Un Souvenir 1990, le Prix de l'amour 1992, Parlons en . . . 1993, Ariane (drama) 1993, Pages grecques (essays) 1993, Une longue amitié 1995, Je me suis beaucoup promené 1995, La Cour des Grands 1996, Madame Rose et Pages grecques 1998. *Leisure interests:* shooting, sailing. *Address:* The Old Rectory, Tynagh, Co. Galway, Ireland; 33 rue Claude Bernard, 75005 Paris, France. *Telephone:* (0509) 45.143 (Ireland). *Fax:* (0509) 45.376 (Ireland).

DE PALACIO DEL VALLE-LERSUNDI, Loyola; Spanish politician; ed. Univ. Complutense de Madrid; Deputy for Segovia (Partido Popular); Minister of Agric., Fisheries and Food. *Address:* Ministry of Agriculture, Fisheries and Food, paseo. Infanta Isabel 1, 28071 Madrid, Spain.

DE PALMA, Brian, M.A.; American film director; b. 11 Sept. 1940, Newark, N.J.; s. of Anthony Fredrick De Palma and Vivienne (née Muti) De Palma; m. Gale Ann Hurd 1991; one d.; ed. Sarah Lawrence Coll., Bronxville and Columbia Univ.; directed (short films) Icarus 1960, 660124: The Story of an IBM Card 1961, Wotan's Wake 1962; (feature length) The Wedding Party 1964, The Responsive Eye (documentary) 1966, Murder à la Mod. 1967, Greetings 1968, Dionysus in '69 (co-dir.) 1969, Hi Mom! 1970, Get to Know Your Rabbit 1970, Sisters 1972, Phantom of the Paradise 1974, Obsession 1975, Carrie 1976, The Fury 1978, Home Movies 1979, Dressed to Kill 1980, Blow Out 1981, Scarface 1983, Body Double 1984, Wise Guys 1985, The Untouchables 1987, Casualties of War 1989, Bonfire of the Vanities 1990, Raising Cain 1992, Carlito's Way 1993, Mission Impossible 1996, Snake Eyes 1998. *Address:* Paramount Pictures, Lubitsch Annex #119, 5555 Melrose Avenue #119, W. Hollywood, CA 90038, U.S.A.

DE PALMA, Rossy (b. Rosa Elena García); Spanish actress; b. Palma de Mallorca; fmrly. singer with punk band Peor Imposible; fashion model in Spain and for John-Paul Gaultier, Paris. *Films include:* Law of Desire, Women on the Verge of a Nervous Breakdown, Kika, Las Hetairas, Prêt à Porter.

DEPARDIEU, Gérard; French actor and vineyard owner; b. 27 Dec. 1948, Chateauroux; s. of René Depardieu and Alice Depardieu (née Marillier); m. Elisabeth Guignot 1970; one s. one d.; ed. Ecole communale, Cours d'art dramatique de Charles Dullin and Ecole d'art dramatique de Jean Laurent Cochet; Pres. Jury, 45th Cannes Int. Film Festival 1992; Chevalier, Ordre national du Mérite; numerous nat. and int. awards; *appeared in short films:* le Beatnik et le minet 1965, Nathalie Granger 1971; *feature films include:* Les gaspards 1973, Les valseuses 1973, Pas si méchant que ça 1974, 1900 1975, La dernière femme 1975, Sept morts sur ordonnance 1975, Maîtresse 1975, Barocco 1976, René la Canne 1976, Les plages de l'Atlantique 1976, Baxter vera Baxter 1976, Dites-lui que je l'aime 1977, Le camion 1977, Préparez vos mouchoirs 1977, Rêve de singe 1977, Le sucre 1978, Buffet froid 1979, Loulou 1979, Le dernier métro 1980 (César award Best Actor, France), Le choix des armes 1981, La femme d'à côté 1981, La chèvre 1981, Le retour de Martin Guerre 1981 (Best Actor Award, American Society of Film Critics), Danton 1981, Le grand frère 1982, La lune dans le caniveau 1983, Les compères 1983, Fort Saganne 1983, Tartuffe (also Dir.) 1984, Rive Droite, Rive Gauche 1984, Police 1984, One Woman or Two 1985, Jean de Florette 1985, Tenue de soirée 1985, Rue du départ 1986, Les fugitifs 1986, Sous le Soleil de Satan 1986, Camille Claudel 1987, Drôle d'endroit pour une rencontre 1988, Je veux rentrer à la maison 1988, Trop belle pour toi 1988, Cyrano de Bergerac 1989 (César award Best Actor), Uranus 1990, Green Card (Golden Globe for Best Comedy Actor), Mon Père Ce Héros 1991, 1492: Conquest of Paradise 1991, Tous les matins du monde 1991, Germinal 1992, A Pure Formality 1993, Le Colonel Chabert 1993, La Machine 1994, Elisa, Les Cents et Une Nuits, Les Anges Gardiens, Le Garçu (all 1994), Bogus, Unhook the Stars, Secret Agent 1995, Vatel 1997, The Man in the Iron Mask 1997, Les Portes du Ciel 1999, Asterix et Obelix 1999; *plays:* Boudu sauvé des eaux 1968, les Garçons de la bande 1969, Une fille dans ma soupe 1970, Galapagos 1971, Saved 1972, Home 1972, Ismé 1973, Isaac 1973, la Chevauchée sur le lac de Constance 1974, les Gens déraisonnables sont en voie de disparition 1977, Tartuffe (also Dir.) 1983, Lily Passion 1986; *TV series:* l'Inconnu 1974. *Publication:* Lettres volées 1988. *Address:* Art Média, 10 avenue George V, 75008 Paris, France.

DEPARDON, Raymond; French photographer; b. 6 July 1942, Villefranche-sur-Saône; s. of Antoine Depardon and Marthe Bernard; m. Claudine Nougaret 1987; two s.; ed. primary school in Villefranche; apprentice to Louis Foucherand, Paris 1958, asst. 1959; copy ed. then photographic reporter, Dalmas agency 1960; co-founder Gamma agency 1967; mem. Magnum Agency, Paris and New York 1978; one-man exhbn. Correspondance new yorkaise, San Clemente, Paris 1984, Lausanne 1985; participant in group exhbns. in Paris, New York etc.; recipient of several film awards. *Films include:* Ian Pallach, Tibesti Tou (short) 1974, Numéros zéro 1977, Reporters 1981, Faits divers: les Années déclic 1983, Empty Quarter 1985, Urgences 1987, la Captive du désert 1990, la Colline des Anges 1993, Délits flagrants 1994, Sida propos 1995, Afriques: Comment ça va avec la douleur 1995, Paris 1998. *Publications:* photographic albums: Tchad 1978, Notes 1979, Correspondance new yorkaise 1981, Le Désert américain 1983, San Clemente 1984, Les Fiancées de Saigon 1986, Hivers 1987, Depardon cinéma 1993, Return to Vietnam (with Jean-Claude Guillebaud) 1994, la Ferme du Garet 1995, la Porte des Larmes (with Jean-Claude Guillebaud) 1995, En Afrique 1995, Voyages 1998, Silence rompu 1998. *Address:* Magnum, 5 Passage Piver, 75011 Paris (Office); 18 bis rue Henri Barbusse, 75005 Paris, France (Home).

DE PERETTI, Jean-Jacques; French politician; b. 21 Sept. 1946, Clermont-Ferrand; m.; two c.; ed. Inst. des Hautes Etudes Internationales; Asst. lecturer, St.-Maur Faculty of Law and Univs. of Orléans and Paris I 1969–84; Chargé de Mission, Cabinet of Pierre Messmer 1972; Dir. de Cabinet to Pres. of Paris Region 1974; Chargé de Mission to André Bord, Sec.-Gen. of Union des Démocrates pour la République (UDR) 1976; Chargé de Mission, Cabinet of Antoine Rufenacht, Sec. of State to Prime Minister; Sec. of State to Minister for Industry, Trade and Craft Trades; Man. Exec. IBM until 1986; Adviser to Prime Minister Jacques Chirac 1986; Mayor of Sarlat 1989–; fmr. mem. Regional Council and Deputy to Nat. Ass. for Dordogne Dept's. 4th constituency; Departmental Councillor for Dordogne 1992; Nat. Sec. Rassemblement pour la République (RPR) 1990–93, Deputy Sec.-Gen. 1994–95; Minister for Overseas France May–Nov. 1995; Minister-Del. to Prime Minister with responsibility for Overseas France 1995–97. *Address:* Mairie, 24200 Sarlat-la-Canéda, France.

DE PEYER, Gervase, F.R.C.M.; British clarinettist and conductor; b. 11 April 1926, London; s. of Esme Everard Vivian de Peyer and Edith Mary Bartlett; m. 1st Sylvia Southcombe 1950 (divorced 1971), one s. two d.; m. 2nd Susan Rosalind Daniel 1971 (divorced 1979); m. 3rd Katia Perret Aubry 1980; ed. King Alfred's School, London, Bedales School, and Royal Coll. of Music, London; studied in Paris 1949; Int. soloist 1949–; Founder-mem. and Dir. Melos Ensemble; Prin. Clarinet, London Symphony Orchestra 1955–72; Founder and Conductor Melos Sinfonia; Dir. London Symphony Wind Ensemble; Assoc. Conductor Haydn Orchestra of London; solo clarinettist, Chamber Music Soc. of Lincoln Center, N.Y. 1969–; Resident Conductor Victoria Int. Festival, BC, Canada; Co-founder and Artistic Dir. Innisfree Music Festival, Pa., U.S.A.; mem. Faculty, Mannes Coll. of Music, N.Y.; f. Melos Sinfonia of Washington 1992, also conductor; recording artist with all major companies (most recorded solo clarinettist in the world); gives recitals and master classes throughout the world; Gold Medallist Worshipful Co. of Musicians 1948, Charles Gros Grand Prix du Disque 1961, 1962, Plaque of Honor for Acad. of Arts and Sciences of America for recording of Mozart concerto 1962. *Leisure interests:* theatre, good food, anything dangerous. *Address:* Porto Vecchio 109, 1250 S. Washington Street, Alexandria, VA 22314, U.S.A.; 42 Tower Bridge Wharf, St. Katherine's Way, London, E1 9UR, England. *Telephone:* (703) 739-0824 (U.S.A.); 0171-265 1110 (England). *Fax:* (703) 739-0572 (U.S.A.); 0171-265 1110 (England).

DEPP, Johnny; American actor; b. 9 June 1963, Owensboro, Ky.; m. Lori Anne Allison (divorced); fmr. rock musician; TV appearances include 21 Jump Street. *Films include:* A Nightmare on Elm Street, Platoon, Slow Burn, Cry Baby, Edward Scissorhands 1990, Benny and Joon 1993, What's Eating Gilbert Grape 1993, Arizona Dream, Ed Wood, Don Juan de Marco 1994, Dead Man, Nick of Time, Divine Rapture, The Brave 1997 (also writer and dir.), Donnie Brasco 1997, Fear and Loathing in Las Vegas 1998, The Astronaut's Wife 1998. *Address:* c/o Tracy Jacobs, ICM, 8942 Wilshire Boulevard, Beverly Hills, CA 90211; 500 S. Sepulveda Boulevard, Suite 500, Los Angeles, CA 90049, U.S.A.

DE PRÉMONVILLE, Myrène Sophie Marie; French designer; b. 1 April 1949, Hendaye; d. of Jean-Marie de Prémonville and Monique Arnault; m. (divorced); one d.; gained degree in decorative arts; Asst., Pronostyl 1970–75; freelance designer 1975–83; f. Myrène de Prémonville SARL 1983, Myrène de Prémonville S.A. 1986. *Leisure interests:* art, cinema, travel. *Address:* 180 rue de Grenelle, 75007 Paris, France. *Telephone:* 47.05.44.10.

DE PURY, David (see Pury, David de).

DEQUAE, André, L. ÈS SC.ECON.; Belgian politician; b. 3 Nov. 1915, Kortrijk; s. of F. Paul and M. Elodie Soen; m. Agnes Vandemoortele 1940; three s. three d.; ed. Louvain Univ.; mem. Chamber of Reps. 1946–77, Vice-Pres. 1958–60, First Vice-Pres. 1965–74, Pres. 1974–77; Minister of Reconstruction 1950, of Colonies 1950–54, of External Trade 1958, of Econ. Co-ordination 1960–61, of Finance 1961–65; Pres. Chamber of Deputies 1973–77; Pres. of Belgian Farmers' Union 1977–81; Chair. and Pres. Bd. of Banque Bruxelles Lambert 1981–86; Pres. Confédération Internationale du Lin et du Chanvre; mem. Council of Europe 1965–77, and WEU 1965–77; Christian Social Party; Grand Cordon de l'Ordre de Léopold, Médaille de la Résistance, Médaille du Souvenir. *Leisure interests:* books, swimming. *Address:* Dam 77 Bus 12, 8500 Kortrijk, Belgium. *Telephone:* 056-200899.

de RACHEWILTZ, Igor, PH.D., F.A.H.A.; Italian historian and philologist; b. 11 April 1929, Rome; s. of Bruno Guido and Antonina Perosio; m. Ines Adelaide Brasch 1956; one d.; ed. St. Gabriel's Coll., Rome Univ. and A.N.U.; Research scholar A.N.U. 1956–60, Sr. Lecturer Faculty of Asian Studies 1963–65, Fellow Inst. of Advanced Studies 1965–67, Sr. Fellow 1967–94, Visiting Fellow 1995–; Lecturer in Asian Civilization, Canberra Univ. Coll. 1960–62; Visiting Prof. Bonn Univ. 1979, Rome Univ. 1996; mem. Sonderforschungsbereich 12, 1979–; Vice-Pres. Int. Assn. for Mongol Studies 1992–; Hon. Pres. Int. Centre for Genghis Khan Studies, Mongolia. *Publications:* The Hsi-yu lu by Yeh-lü Ch'u-ts'ai 1962, Papal Envoys to the Great Khans 1971, Index to the Secret History of the Mongols 1972, The Preclassical Mongolian Version of the Hsiao-ching 1982, The Secret History of the Mongols 1971–86, Repertory of Proper Names in Yüan Literary Sources 1988–96, text edn. and word-index of Erdeni-yin tobci 1990–91, In the Service of the Khan 1993, Le matériel mongol du Houa i i iu de Houng-ou (1389): Commentaires 1995, The Mongolian Tanjur version of the Bodhicaryāvatāra 1996; numerous articles on Sino-Mongolian topics, medieval history and Altaic philology. *Leisure interests:* botany, travel. *Address:* c/o Division of Pacific and Asian History, Australian National University, Canberra A.C.T. 0200 (Univ.); 9 Ridley Street, Turner, A.C.T. 2612, Australia (Home). *Telephone:* (02) 6249-3171 (Univ.); (02) 6248-0557 (Home). *Fax:* (02) 6249-5525.

DERBYSHIRE, Sir Andrew George, Kt., M.A., A.A.DIP., F.R.I.B.A., F.R.S.A.; British architect; b. 7 Oct. 1923; s. of late Samuel Reginald and Helen Louise Puleston (née Clarke) Derbyshire; m. Lily Rhodes (née Binns); three s. one d.; ed. Chesterfield Grammar School, Queens' Coll., Cambridge, Architectural Assn., London; Admiralty Signals Establishment and Bldg. Research Station 1943–46; Farmer and Dark (Marchwood and Belvedere power stations) 1951–53; W. Riding Co. Architect's Dept. 1953–55; Asst. City Architect, Sheffield 1955–61; mem. Research Team, R.I.B.A. Survey of Architects' Offices 1960–62; mem. Robert Matthew, Johnson-Marshall and Partners 1961–, Chair. 1983–89, Pres. RMJM Group 1989–98; involved with devt. of Univ. of York 1962–, Cen. Lancs. New Town, N.E. Lancs. Impact Study, Univ. of Cambridge, W. Cambridge Devt. and New Cavendish Lab., Preston Market and Guildhall, London Docklands Study, Hillingdon Civic Centre, Cabtrack and Minitram feasibility studies, Suez Master Plan Study, Castle Peak Power Station, Hong Kong, Harbour reclamation and urban devt., Hong Kong; mem. R.I.B.A. Council 1950–72, 1975–81, Sr. Vice-Pres. 1980–81; mem. Bldg. Industry Communications Research Cttee. 1964–66; mem. Ministry of Transport Urban Research and Devt. Group 1967; mem. Inland Transport Research and Devt. Council 1968; mem. Dept. of the Environment Planning and Transport Research Advisory Council 1971–76; mem. Comm. on Energy and the Environment 1978–81; mem. (part-time) Cen. Electricity Generating Bd. 1973–84; mem. of Bd., Property Services Agency 1975–79; mem. Bd. London Docklands Devt. Corpn. and Chair. of Planning Cttee. 1983–88; mem. Construction Industry Sector Group of Nat. Econ. Devt. Council 1988–92; mem. Construction Industry Council, Chair. Research Cttee. 1989–94; Chair. Art for Architecture Project, R.S.A. 1994–98; Hoffman Wood Prof. of Architecture, Univ. of Leeds 1978–80; External Prof., Dept. of Civil Eng., Univ. of Leeds 1981–85; Gresham Coll. Prof. of Rhetoric 1990–92; Hon. Fellow Inst. of Structural Eng. 1992, Inst. of Advanced Architectural Studies, Univ. of York 1994; Hon. D.Univ. (York) 1972. *Publication:* The Architect and His Office 1962 and numerous publs. on planning, energy conservation and scientific research. *Leisure interests:* family, garden. *Address:* 4 Sunnyfield, Hatfield, Herts., AL9 5DX (Home); 83 Paul Street, London, EC2A 4NQ, England (Office). *Telephone:* (01707) 265903. *Fax:* (01707) 275874.

DERINGER, Arved; German lawyer; b. 4 June 1913, Neustuttgart; s. of Nicolai Deringer and Gertrud von Toerne; m. Erika Stapff 1950; two s. three d.; ed. Univs. of Tübingen, Kiel, Berlin and Geneva; mem. Bundestag 1957–69; mem. European Parl. 1958–70; mem. Bar of Cologne 1962–; Sr. Partner Deringer, Tessin, Herrmann and Sedermund, Cologne; Adviser to Antimonopoly Cttee. of Ukraine 1993–; mem. Int. Bar Asscn., British Inst. for Int. and Comparative Law, and various other legal asscns.; Bundesverdienstkreuz; Ordine al Merito della Repubblica Italiana; Hon. Prof. Baden-Württenburg. *Publications:* Commentary on European Competition Law 1962–68; over 200 articles on German and European law, especially anti-trust law, European Community law, and Media Law. *Leisure interests:* photography, gardening. *Address:* Freibadstrasse 93, 70563 Stuttgart, Germany (Home). *Telephone:* 711-7354643 (Home). *Fax:* 711-7354543.

de RIVOYRE, Christine Berthe Claude Denis, L. ÈS L.; French author and journalist; b. 29 Nov. 1921, Tarbes, Hautes-Pyrénées; d. of François de Rivoyre and Madeleine Ballande; ed. Insts. du Sacré-Coeur of Bordeaux and Poitiers, Faculté des lettres de Paris and School of Journalism, Syracuse Univ., N.Y.; journalist with Le Monde 1950–55; Literary Ed. of Marie-Claire 1955–65; mem. Haut comité de la langue française 1969–, Jury of Prix Médicis 1970–; Chevalier, Légion d'honneur, Chevalier des Arts et des Lettres; Prix Interallié (for Le petit matin) 1968; Prix des Trois Couronnes (for Boy) 1973; Grand Prix de la ville de Bordeaux 1973; Grand Prix littéraire Prince Rainier de Monaco 1982; Prix Paul Morand 1984. *Publications:* L'alouette au miroir 1956, La mandarine 1957, La tête en fleurs 1960, La glace à l'ananas 1962, Les sultans 1964, Le petit matin 1968, Le seigneur des chevaux (with Alexander Kalda) 1969, Fleur d'agonie 1970, Boy 1973, Le voyage à l'envers 1977, Belle alliance 1982, Reine-mère 1985, Crépuscule taille unique 1989, Racontez-moi les flamboyants 1995. *Address:* Onesse-Laharie, 40110 Morcenx, France.

DERN, Laura; American actress; b. 10 Feb. 1967, Los Angeles; d. of Bruce Dern and Diane Ladd; film debut aged 11 in Foxes 1980; TV appearances include: Happy Endings, Three Wishes of Billy Greer, Afterburn, Down Came a Blackbird. *Films:* Teachers, Mask, Smooth Talk, Blue Velvet, Haunted Summer, Wild of Heart, Rambling Rose, Jurassic Park, A Perfect World, Devil Inside, Citizen Ruth 1996.

DERNESCH, Helga; Austrian opera singer; b. 3 Feb. 1939, Vienna; two c.; sang many operatic roles in Berne 1961–63, Wiesbaden 1963–66, Cologne 1966–69; freelance guest appearances at all maj. opera houses in Europe 1969–; regular appearances at Bayreuth Festival 1965–69, at Salzburg Easter Festival 1969–73; since 1979 has sung as mezzo-soprano; regular appearances at San Francisco Opera 1981–; début Metropolitan Opera, New York 1985; has sung in operas and concerts throughout Europe, N. and S. America, Japan; many recordings. *Leisure interests:* films, people, literature. *Address:* Neutorgasse 2/22, A-1013 Vienna, Austria.

De ROBERTIS, Eduardo Diego Patricio, M.D.; Argentinian histologist, cytologist and embryologist; b. 11 Dec. 1913, Buenos Aires; s. of Francisco and Emilia De Robertis; m. Nelly Armand Ugon; one s. one d.; ed. Univ. de Buenos Aires; Rockefeller Fellow, Chicago and Johns Hopkins Univs. 1940, 1944; at Biophysical Laboratory, Rio de Janeiro 1943; Dir. Dept. of Cellular Ultrastructure, Inst. de Investigaciones de Ciencias Biológicas 1946; Lecturer in Physiology, Texas Univ. 1952; Walker-Ames Prof. Univ. of Washington (Seattle) 1953; Prof. Histology, Univ. de Buenos Aires 1957, now Prof. Emer. and Dir. of Research; Pres. Int. Union of Biological Sciences 1979–82; mem. Argentine Acad. of Sciences, Argentine Acad. of Medicine, Argentine Research Council, American Acad. of Neurology, American Soc. for Neurochemistry; Fellow, New York Acad. of Sciences; Mitre Inst. Award, Van Meeter Award, Argentine Nat. Prize, Buenos Aires Gold Medal, Shell Foundation Prize 1969, Prize of Cuenca Villoro Foundation 1976, of Eugenio Rodríguez Pascuel Foundation 1977, Bunge and Born Prize 1984, Houssay Prize of the OAS 1985; Dr. h.c. (Loyola Univ.); Hon. mem. American Coll. of Physicians, Pan American Medical Asscn. *Publications:* Citología General 1946, 1952, 1955 (English trans. 1948, 1954, Japanese trans. 1955, Russian trans. 1962; since 1965 appears as Cell Biology); Histophysiology of Synapses and Neurosecretion 1946 (French trans.), Cell and Molecular Biology 7th edn. (translated into Spanish, Italian, Russian, Hungarian, Polish), Synaptic Receptors: Isolation and Molecular Biology, Modern Pharmacology-Toxicology, Vol. 4 1975, Essentials of Cell and Molecular Biology 1981; more than 300 papers on cytology, thyroid gland, electromicroscopy, neurology and neuro-chemistry. *Address:* Galileo 2442 8B, 1425 Buenos Aires, Argentina. *Telephone:* 801-9643.

DE ROMILLY, Jacqueline, D. ÈS L.; French academic; b. 26 March 1913, Chartres; d. of Maxime David and Jeanne Malvoisin; m. Michel Worms de Romilly 1940 (divorced 1973); ed. Ecole Normale Supérieure, Univ. of Paris; Prof. of Ancient Greek, Univ. of Lille 1949–57, Univ. of Paris-Sorbonne 1957–73; Prof. Coll. de France 1973–84, Hon. Prof. 1984; mem. Acad. des Inscriptions et Belles Lettres, Inst. de France 1975–, Acad. Française 1988–; Corresp. mem. 8 Acads.; several French Acad. Prizes; Commdr. Légion d'honneur, des Palmes académiques, Ordre des Arts et des Lettres; Grand Officier Ordre nat. du mérite; Commdr. Order of the Phoenix (Greece); Insignia of Honour for Science and Art (Austria). *Publications:* L'enseignement en détresse 1984, Sur les chemins de Ste. Victoire 1987, Ouverture à coeur 1990, Pourquoi la Grèce? 1992, les Oeufs de Pâques 1993, Lettres aux Parents sur les Choix Scolaires 1993, Tragédies grecques au fil des ans 1995, Rencontres avec la Grèce antique 1995, Alcibiade ou les dangers de l'ambition 1995, Jeux de lumière sur l'Hellade 1996, Hector 1997, Le Trésor des savoirs oubliés 1998, and about twenty books on classical Greek literature. *Address:* 12 rue Chernoviz, 75016 Paris, France. *Telephone:* (1) 42-24-59-07.

DERR, Kenneth T., M.B.A.; American business executive; b. 1936; m. Donna Mettler 1959; three c.; ed. Cornell Univ.; with Chevron Corpn. (formerly Standard Oil Co. of Calif.) 1960–, Vice-Pres. 1972–85; Pres. Chevron U.S.A. Inc. 1978–84; Head, merger program, Chevron Corpn. and Gulf Oil Corpn. 1984–85; Vice-Chair. Chevron Corpn. 1985–88, Chair., C.E.O. 1989–; mem. Bd. of Dirs. Citicorp, AT&T, Potlatch Corpn.; Dir. American Petroleum Inst., now Chair. *Address:* Chevron Corporation, P.O. Box 7643, 575 Market Street, San Francisco, CA 94105, U.S.A.

DERRIDA, Jacques; French philosopher; b. 15 July 1930, El Biar, Algiers; s. of Aimé Derrida and Georgette Safar; m. Marguérite Aucouturier 1957; two s.; ed. Ecole Normale Supérieure, Paris; taught at Sorbonne 1960–64, at Ecole Normale Supérieure 1965–84; Hon. D.Litt. (Cambridge) 1992. *Publications include:* La voix et le phénomène 1967, De la grammatologie 1967, L'écriture et la différence 1967, Marges 1972, La dissémination 1972, GLAS 1974, La vérité en peinture 1979, La carte postale 1980, Psyché 1987, De l'esprit 1987, Mémoires—Pour Paul De Man 1988, Du droit à la philosophie 1990, Mémoires d'aveugle 1990, Le problème de la genèse dans la philosophie de Husserl 1990, L'autre cap 1991, Donner le temps 1991, Qu'est-ce que la poésie? 1991, Spectres de Marx 1993, Politiques de l'amitié 1994, Mal d'Archive 1995, Adieu à Emmanuel Levinas 1997, De l'hospitalité 1997. *Address:* Ecole des Hautes Etudes en Sciences Sociales, 54 boulevard Raspail, 75006 Paris, France.

DERSHOWITZ, Alan Morton, LL.B.; American professor of law; b. 1 Sept. 1938; s. of Harry Dershowitz and Claire Ringel; m. Carolyn Cohen; two s. one d.; ed. Brooklyn Coll. and Yale Univ.; admitted D.C. Bar 1963, Mass. Bar 1968, U.S. Supreme Court 1968; Law clerk to Chief Judge David Bazelon, U.S. Court of Appeal 1962–63, to Justice Arthur Goldberg, U.S. Supreme Court 1963–64; mem. Faculty, Harvard Coll. 1964–, Prof. of Law 1967–; Fellow, Center for Advanced Study of Behavioural Sciences 1971–72; consultant to Dir. Nat. Inst. for Mental Health (NIMH) 1967–69, (Pres.'s Comm. on Civil Disorders) 1967, (Pres.'s Comm. on Causes of Violence) 1968, (Nat. Asscn. for Advancement of Colored People Legal Defense Fund) 1967–68, President's Comm. on Marijuana and Drug Abuse 1972–73, (Ford Foundation Study on Law and Justice) 1973–76; rapporteur, Twentieth Century Fund Study on Sentencing 1975–76; Guggenheim Fellow 1978–79; mem. Comm. on Law and Social Action, American Jewish Congress 1978; Dir. American Civil Liberties Union 1968–71, 1972–75, Ass. of Behavioral and Social Sciences N.A.S. 1973–76; Chair. Civil Rights Comm. New England Region, Anti-Defamation League, B'nai B'rith 1980; Hon. M.A. (Harvard Coll.) 1967; Hon. LL.D. (Yeshiva) 1989. *Publications:* Psychoanalysis, Psychiatry and the Law 1967, Criminal Law: Theory and Process 1974, The Best Defense 1982, Reversal of Fortune: Inside the von Bülow Case 1986, Taking Liberties: A Decade of Hard Cases, Bad Laws and Bum Raps 1988, Chutzpah 1991, Contrary to Popular Opinion 1992, The Abuse Excuse 1994, The Advocate's Devil 1994, Reasonable Doubt 1996, The Vanishing American Jew 1997; articles in legal journals. *Address:* Harvard University Law School, Cambridge, MA 02138, U.S.A.

de RUITER, Hendrikus; Netherlands business executive; b. 3 March 1934, The Hague; m. Theodora O. van der Jagt 1957; one s. two d.; ed. Technological

Univ. of Delft; Research Chemist, Koninklijke/Shell Laboratorium Amsterdam (KSLA) 1956; Chief Technologist, Berre Refinery, Compagnie de Raffinage Shell-Berre 1965–67; returned to KSLA 1967; joined Shell Int. Petroleum Co. Ltd. (SIPC), London 1969; Man. Dir. Shell Co. of Thailand and Pres. Société Shell du Laos 1972; Coal Production and Trading Co-ordinator, SIPC 1975; Pres. Shell Int. Trading Co. 1979; Dir. Shell Internationale Petroleum Maatschappij B.V. 1981; Man. Dir. N.V. Koninklijke Nederlandsche Petroleum Maatschappij, mem. Presidium, Bd. of Dirs., Shell Petroleum N.V. and Man. Dir. The Shell Petroleum Co. Ltd. 1983–; mem. Supervisory Bd. Royal Dutch Petroleum Co. 1994–; Dir. Shell Petroleum N.V. 1994–, The Shell Petroleum Co. Ltd. 1994–. *Address:* c/o Royal Dutch Petroleum Company, Carel van Bylandtlaan 30, P.O. Box 162, 2501 AN The Hague, Netherlands. *Telephone:* 070-3774504.

de RUITER, Jacob (Job); Netherlands politician and lawyer; b. 1930; ed. Univ. of Utrecht; Judge, later Dist. Judge, Court of Zutphen; Prof. of Civil Law, Vrije Universiteit, Amsterdam, Rector 1976; Minister of Justice 1977–82, of Defence 1982–86; Attorney-Gen., Amsterdam 1986; mem. Christian Democratic Appeal. *Address:* c/o Christian Democratic Appeal, Dr. Kuyperstraat 5, 2514 BA The Hague, Netherlands.

DERYABIN, Yuri Stepanovich; Russian diplomatist; b. 3 Jan. 1932, Karachelka, Kurgan Region; m.; two d.; ed. Moscow Inst. of Int. Relations; diplomatic service 1954–; Third, then Second Sec. Dept. of Scandinavian Countries, Ministry of Foreign Affairs 1959–62; Second Sec. Embassy, Norway 1962–65, First Sec. U.S.S.R Embassy, Finland 1968–73, Counsellor 1973–75; Counsellor-Envoy 1980–83; Deputy Chief Second European Dept., Ministry of Foreign Affairs 1986–87; Chief Dept. of Problems of Security and Cooperation in Europe 1987–90; Deputy Minister of Foreign Affairs 1991–92; Russian Amb. to Finland 1992–96; Deputy Sec., Security Council of Russia 1997–98; *Address:* c/o Security Council, Ipat'yevski per. 4/10, Suite 6, Moscow, Russia. *Telephone:* (095) 206-43-96.

DERYCKE, Erik, LL.M.; Belgian politician and lawyer; b. 28 Oct. 1949, Waregem; m.; two c.; ed. Rijksuniversiteit Gent; barrister in Kortrijk 1972–; Provincial Councillor for W. Flanders 1975–84; Rep. for Kortrijk, Belgian Chamber of Reps. 1984–; Municipal councillor for Waregem 1989–; Sec. of State for Science Policy 1990–91; Minister for Devt. Aid and Deputy Minister for Science Policy 1991–92; Sec. of State for Devt. Aid 1992–95; Minister for Foreign Affairs and Devt. Co-operation March–June 1995; Minister for Foreign Affairs June 1995–; Hon. Pres. Socialist Party of Waregem; mem. Socialist Party Bureau. *Address:* Ministry of Foreign Affairs, 2 rue des Quatre Bras, 1000 Brussels, Belgium.

DESAI, Anita; Indian author; b. 24 June 1937; d. of Toni Nimé and D.N. Mazumbar; m. Ashvin Desai 1958; two s. two d.; ed. Queen Mary's School, Delhi and Miranda House, Univ. of Delhi. *Publications:* Cry, The Peacock 1963, Voices in the City 1965, Bye-Bye Blackbird 1971, Where Shall We Go This Summer? 1973, Fire on the Mountain 1978, Games at Twilight 1979, Clear Light of Day 1980, The Village by the Sea 1983, In Custody (filmed 1994) 1984, Baumgartner's Bombay 1988, Journey to Ithaca 1995. *Address:* c/o Deborah Rogers Ltd., 20 Powis Mews, London, W11 1JN, England.

DESAI, Baron (Life Peer) cr. 1991, of St Clement Danes in the City of Westminster, **Meghnad Jagdishchandra Desai,** PH.D.; British (b. Indian) economist; b. 10 July 1940, Baroda, India; s. of Jagdishchandra Desai and Mandakini Desai, (née Majmundar); m. Gail Wilson 1970 (separated 1995); one s. two d.; ed. Univ. of Bombay, Univ. of Pennsylvania, U.S.A.; Assoc. Specialist, Dept. of Agricultural Econs., Univ. of Calif. at Berkeley, U.S.A. 1963–65; lecturer, L.S.E. 1965–77, Sr. Lecturer 1977–80, Reader 1980–83, Prof. of Econs. 1983–; Head Devt. Studies Inst. 1990–95; Dir. Centre for the Study of Global Governance, L.S.E. 1992–; Consultant at various times to FAO, UNCTAD, Int. Coffee Org., World Bank, UNIDO, Ministries of Industrial Devt. and Educ., Algeria, British Airports Authority and other bodies; Co-Ed. Journal of Applied Econometrics 1984–; mem. Editorial Bds. Int. Review of Applied Econs. and several other journals; mem. Council, Royal Econ. Soc. 1988; mem. Exec. Cttee. Asscn. of Univ. Teachers in Econs. 1987– (Pres. 1987–90); mem. Univ. of London Senate representing L.S.E. 1981–89; Chair. Econ. Research Div., L.S.E. 1983–; mem. Nat. Exec. of Council for Academic Freedom and Democracy 1972–83, Speaker's Comm. on Citizenship 1989–, Berndt Carlson Trust; mem. or fmr. mem. Governing Body of Courtauld Inst., British Inst. in Paris, Cen. School of Arts, Polytechnic of N. London; Chair. Holloway Ward (Islington Cen.) Labour Party 1977–80, Islington S. and Finsbury Labour Party 1986; Dr. h.c. (Kingston Univ.) 1992. *Publications:* Marxian Economic Theory 1974 (trans. in several languages), Applied Econometrics 1976, Marxian Economics 1979, Testing Monetarism 1981; Ed. several books; numerous papers and contribs. to books and journals. *Address:* Centre for the Study of Global Governance, London School of Economics, Houghton Street, London, WC2A 2AE (Office); 606 Collingwood House, Dolphin Square, London, SW1V 3NF, England (Home). *Telephone:* 0171-955 7489 (Office); 0171-798 8673 (Home). *Fax:* 0171-955 7591.

DESAI, Nitin Dayalji, B.A., M.SC.; Indian international official, economist and civil servant; b. 5 July 1941, Bombay; s. of Dayalji M. Desai and Shantaben Desai; m. Aditi Gupta 1979; two s.; ed. Univ. of Bombay and London School of Econs.; lecturer in Econs. Univ. of Liverpool 1965–67, Univ. of Southampton 1967–70; consultant, Tata (India) Econ. Consultancy Services 1970–73; consultant/adviser, Planning Comm. Govt. of India 1973–85; Sr. adviser, Brundtland Comm. 1985–87; Special Sec. Planning Comm. India 1987–88; Sec./Chief Econ. Adviser, Ministry of Finance 1988–90; Deputy Under-Sec.-Gen. UNCED, Geneva 1990–92; Under-Sec.-Gen. of Dept. for Policy Co-ordination and Sustainable Devt. UN 1993–97, now Under-Sec.-Gen. for Econ. and Social Affairs. *Address:* United Nations, Room DC2–2320, New York, NY 10017 (Office); 330 East 33 Street Apt. 12M, New York, NY 10016, U.S.A. (Home). *Telephone:* (212) 532-0028 (Home).

DESAILLY, Jean; French actor; b. 24 Aug. 1920, Paris; m. Ginette Nicolas (divorced); two d.; ed. Paris Ecole des Beaux Arts; Pensionnaire, Comédie Française 1942–46; mem. Renaud-Barrault Company 1947–68; Dir. Théâtre Jacques Hébertot 1972–; mem. Council for Cultural Devt. 1971–73; Co-Dir., Théâtre de la Madeleine 1980–; mem. du Haut Comité de la langue française 1969–; Chevalier, Légion d'honneur, Officier, Ordre nat. du Mérite, Chevalier, Palmes Académiques, Commdr., Arts et Lettres. *Plays include:* La nuit du diable, Le bossu, Malatesta, Le procès, On ne badine pas avec l'amour, Le château, Madame Sans-Gène, Tête d'or, La cerisaie, Le marchand de Venise, Comme il vous plaira, Hamlet, Andromaque, Le soulier de satin, Il faut passer par les nuages, Le mariage de Figaro, Brève rencontre, Un ami imprévu, Double jeu, Le légume, Dis-moi Blaise, Amphitryon 38 1976, Un ennemi du peuple 1977, Le Cauchemar de Bella 1978, Siegfried 1980, Arsenic et vieilles dentelles 1981, La dixième de Beethoven 1982, Sodome et Gomorrhe 1982, L'amour fou 1983, Les oeufs de l'autruche 1984, Un otage 1984, Comme de mal entendu 1985, Le silence éclaté 1986, les Pieds dans l'eau 1987, la Foire d'empoigne 1988, le Cardinal d'Espagne 1993; Co-Dir. Tout dans le jardin. *Films include:* Le père Goriot, La symphonie pastorale, Le point du jour, Occupe-toi d'Amélie, Si Versailles m'était conté, Les grandes manoeuvres, Maigret tend un piège, Les grandes familles, Le baron de l'ecluse, Plein soleil, La mort de belle, Un soir sur la plage, Les sept péchés capitaux, Les amours célèbres, L'année du bac, La peau douce, Le doulos, Les deux orphelines, Le franciscain de Bourges, L'Ardoise, Comptes à rebours, L'assassinat de Trotsky, Un flic, L'ironie du sort, Le professionnel 1981, Le fou du roi 1984; numerous TV appearances. *Address:* c/o Babette Pouget, 9 Square Villaret de Joyeuse, 75017 Paris, France.

DE SANCTIS, Roman William, M.D.; American cardiologist; b. 30 Oct. 1930, Cambridge Springs, Pa.; s. of Vincent De Sanctis and Marguerita De Sanctis; m. Ruth A. Foley 1955; four d.; ed. Univ. of Arizona, Harvard Medical School; Resident in Medicine Mass. Gen. Hosp. 1958–60, Fellow in Cardiology 1960–62, Dir. Coronary Care Unit 1967–80, Dir. Clinical Cardiology 1980–98, Dir. Emer. 1998–; Physician 1970–; mem. Faculty of Medicine, Harvard Medical School 1964–, Prof. 1973–; U.S. Navy Consultant and Asst. to Attending Physician to U.S. Congress 1956–58; Master, American Coll. of Physicians 1995; Fellow, American Coll. of Cardiology, Inst. of Medicine; Distinguished Clinical Teaching Award, Harvard Medical School 1980; Gifted Teacher Award (American Coll. of Cardiologists), Hon. D.Sc. (Wilkes Coll.). *Publications:* author and co-ed. of over 130 scientific papers. *Leisure interests:* travel, music. *Address:* Massachusetts General Hospital, 15 Parkman Street, Suite 467, Boston, MA 02114 (Office); 5 Thoreau Circle, Winchester, MA 01890, U.S.A. (Home). *Telephone:* (617) 7262889 (Office); (617) 729-1453 (Home). *Fax:* (617) 726-5271.

DESARIO, Vincenzo, B.A.; Italian banker; b. 11 June 1933, Barletta; m.; three c.; ed. Univ. of Bari; joined Bank of Italy, Foggia br. 1960; Banking Supervision Inspectorate, Bank of Italy head office, Rome 1968; Cen. Man. for Banking and Financial Supervision, Bank of Italy 1983; Bank of Italy del. to Interbank Deposit Protection Fund 1991; Deputy Dir.-Gen. Bank of Italy 1993–94, Dir.-Gen. 1994–. *Address:* Banca d'Italia, Via Nazionale 91, 00184 Rome, Italy. *Telephone:* (6) 47921. *Fax:* (6) 47922983.

de SAVARY, Peter John; British entrepreneur; b. 11 July 1944, Essex; m. 3rd Lucille Lana Paton; three d. and two d. from previous marriage; ed. Charterhouse; commercial activities in finance, energy, leisure and property; British challenger for America's Cup 1983, 1987; Tourism Personality of the Year (English Tourist Bd.) 1988; Chair. The Carnegie Club, Scotland. *Leisure interest:* sailing. *Address:* Skibo Castle, Dornoch, Sutherland, IV25 3RQ, Scotland.

DESCHÊNES, Hon. Jules, C.C., Q.C., LL.D., F.R.S.C.; Canadian judge; b. 7 June 1923, Montréal; s. of Wilfrid Deschênes and Berthe (Bérard) Deschênes; m. Jacqueline Lachapelle 1948; three s. two d.; ed. Ecole St.-Jean Baptiste Montréal, Coll. André-Grasset, Coll. de Montréal and Seminaire de Philosophie, Univ. of Montréal; called to Bar of Québec 1946; Q.C. 1961; practised as barrister and solicitor 1946–72; Sr. Partner Deschênes, de Grandpré, Colas, Godin & Lapointe 1966–72; Justice, Court of Appeal, Québec 1972–73; Chief Justice, Superior Court of Québec 1973–83; Lecturer in Private Int. Law, Univ. of Montréal 1962–69; mem. Exec. Cttee. Canadian Judicial Council 1977–83; Pres. Comm. of Inquiry on War Criminals 1985–86; Consultant, U.N. Centre for Social Devt. and Humanitarian Affairs, Vienna 1983–85; Judge, Int. Criminal Tribunal for the fmr. Yugoslavia 1993–97; Pres. World Asscn. of Judges' Cttee. on Expanding Jurisdiction of Int. Court of Justice 1977–82, Québec Bar Admission School 1988–90, Royal Soc. of Canada 1990; mem. Council, World Peace Through Law Center 1980–82; mem. Int. Law Asscn., Int. Comm. of Jurists, Canadian Council on Int. Law; Order of Malta 1978. *Publications:* The Sword and the Scales 1979, Les plateaux de la balance 1979, L'école publique confessionnelle au Québec 1980, Ainsi parlèrent les Tribunaux . . . Conflits linguistiques au Canada 1968–80 1981, Justice et Pouvoir 1984, Ainsi parlèrent les Tribunaux II 1985, Co-author L'Université; son rôle, le rôle de ses composantes, les relations entre ses composantes 1969, Maîtres chez eux 1981, Judicial Independence: The Contemporary Debate 1985, Sur la ligne de feu (autobiog.) 1989, and numerous articles. *Address:* 300 Place Juge-Desnoyers, Apt. C-911, Laval, Québec, H7G 4R1, Canada (Home). *Telephone:* (514) 669-6363. *Fax:* (514) 669-3416.

de SCHOUTHEETE de TERVARENT, Philippe (Baron); Belgian diplomatist; b. 21 May 1932, Berlin, Germany; m. Bernadette Joos de Ter Beerst 1956; two s.; joined Belgian diplomatic service; served Paris 1959–61, Cairo 1962–65, Madrid 1968–72, Bonn 1972–76; Chef de Cabinet to Minister of Foreign Affairs 1980–81; Amb. to Spain 1981–85; Political Dir. 1985–87; Perm. Rep. to EU 1987–97; Guest Prof. Univ. of Louvain la Neuve 1990–; mem. Bd. Général de Banque; mem. Acad. Royale de Belgique; Grand Officer, Order of Leopold. *Publications:* La coopération politique européenne 1986, Une Europe pour tous. *Address:* avenue de Broqueville 99, 1200 Brussels, Belgium.

D'ESCOTO BROCKMANN, Miguel; Nicaraguan politician; b. 5 Feb. 1933, Hollywood, U.S.A.; s. of Miguel D'Escoto Muñoz and Rita Brockmann Meléndez; ed. Instituto Pedagógico La Salle, Managua, Nicaragua, St. Mary's Coll., Moraga, Calif., Manhattan Coll., New York, State Univs. of New York and Columbia Univs. Sur le ligne de Feu 1988, New York, (studied philosophy, theology, educ. and political economy); Sub-Dir. Dept. of Social Communications, Maryknoll, New York, U.S.A. 1962–63; worked for Brazilian and Mexican church in slums of Belo Horizonte, Rio de Janeiro, Brazil and Mexico D.F. 1963–69, Dir. 1970–79; founder and Pres. Fundación Nicaragüense Pro-Desarrollo Comunitario Integral, León, Nicaragua 1973; became involved with Frente Sandinista de Liberación Nacional from 1975; f. Grupo de los 12, a group of professionals and intellectuals supporting the Sandinista Front 1977; Minister of Foreign Affairs 1979–90; elected mem. of Sandinista Ass. 1980. *Address:* c/o Ministerio del Exterior, Detrás de Los Ranchos, Managua, JR, Nicaragua.

DESHPANDE, Shashi, B.A., M.A., B.L.; Indian author; b. 19 Aug. 1938, Dharwad; d. of Adya Rangacharya and Sharada Adya; m. D. H. Deshpande 1962; two s.; ed. Univs. of Bombay and Mysore; fmrly. worked for a law journal and magazine; full-time writer 1970–; mem. Sahitya Akademi Bd. for English 1989–94; received Thirumathi Rangammal Prize, Sahitya Akademi Award for a Novel, Nanjangud Thirumalamba Award. *Publications:* The Dark Holds No Terrors 1980, Roots and Shadows 1983, That Long Silence 1988, The Binding Vine 1993, A Matter of Time 1996, The Intrusion and Other Stories 1994. *Leisure interests:* reading, music. *Address:* 409 41st Cross, Jayanagar V Block, Bangalore 560041, India. *Telephone:* (080) 6636228. *Fax:* (080) 6641137.

DESIO, Ardito, DR.RER.NAT., F.D.S., F.R.G.S., F.M.G.S.; Italian geologist, geographer and explorer; b. 18 April 1897, Palmanova, Udine; s. of Antonio Desio and Caterina Zorzella; m. Aurelia Bevilacqua 1932; one s. one d.; ed. Dept. of Natural Science, Univ. of Florence; Lecturer of Geology, Univ. of Milan 1927–31; Prof. of Geology, Univ. of Milan 1931; Dir. Inst. of Geology, Univ. of Milan, now Prof. Emer.; led 20 overseas exploratory expeditions and scientific missions in Libya, Sahara, Ethiopia, Jordan, Iran, Afghanistan, Pakistan (Karakoram), India, Nepal (Himalaya), Philippines, Burma, Antarctica; discovered the first petroleum accumulations in subsurface of Libya 1938, and Mg and K deposits; leader of the first successful ascent of K2 (28,250 feet), second highest peak in the world 1954; organized expeditions for gauging height of K2 and Everest 1987, for geophysical and geological investigation in Shaksgam Valley and Sinkiang 1988, and multidisciplinary researches on the south slope of Everest 1989, Hindu Kush, Karakorum, Nepal, Himalayas 1990, 1991; mem. Acad. Nazionale dei Lincei; Hon. mem. Italian Geog. Soc., Geol. Soc., London, Gesellschaft für Erdkunde, Berlin, Soc. Belge de Géologie, Indian Palaeontological Soc., Faculty of Sciences, Univ. of Chile; Patron's Medal Royal Geographical Soc. (U.K.), Antarctic Service Medal (U.S.A.), Gold Medal of Pakistan, Knight Grand Cross (Italy); numerous other awards. *Publications:* 445 publs. including a number of vols. about the geology and geography of Libya, Aegean Islands, Eastern Alps, Karakoram Range (Pakistan), Hindu Kush Range (Afghanistan), a monograph on the glaciers of Ortles-Cevedale massif, a treatise of geology applied to engineering, a vol. on the geology of Italy, nine vols. of scientific reports on expeditions to Karakoram and Hindu Kush, seven to Libyan Sahara, one on Antarctica, etc. *Leisure interests:* mountaineering, photography. *Address:* Via S. Andrea delle Fratte 38/A, 00187 Rome, Italy. *Telephone:* (06) 6792806.

DESKUR, H.E. Cardinal Andrzej Maria; Polish ecclesiastic; b. 29 Feb. 1924, Sancygniów, Kielce; ordained 1950; consecrated Bishop (Titular See of Thenae) 1974, Archbishop 1980; cr. Cardinal 1985; Hon. Chair. Pontifical Council for Social Communications; Pres. Pontifical Acad. of the Immaculate Conception. *Address:* Palazzo S. Carlo, 00120 Città del Vaticano, Rome, Italy. *Telephone:* (06) 69883597.

DESLONGCHAMPS, Pierre, F.C.I.C., O.C., PH.D., F.R.S.C., F.R.S.; Canadian professor of chemistry; b. 8 May 1938, St.-Lin, Québec; s. of Rodolphe Deslongchamps and Madeleine Magnan; m. 1st Micheline Renaud 1960 (divorced 1975); two s.; m. 2nd Shirley E. Thomas 1976 (divorced 1983); m. 3rd Marie-Marthe Leroux 1987; ed. Montréal Univ., Univ. of New Brunswick; Post-doctoral Fellow Harvard Univ. 1965–66; Asst. Prof. Montréal Univ. 1966–67, Asst. Prof. Sherbrooke Univ. 1967–68, Assoc. Prof. 1968–72, Prof. 1972–; A.P. Sloan Fellowship 1970–72, E.W.R. Steacie Fellowship 1971–74; mem. Canadian Cttee. of Scientists and Scholars 1993–, Société française de Chimie 1995, Foreign Asst. mem. Acad. des Sciences de Paris 1995; fellow numerous academic socs., A.A.A.S.; Fellow Guggenheim Foundation, 1979; several hon. degrees; Scientific Prize of Québec 1971, E.W.R. Steacie Prize 1974, Médaille Vincent (ACFAS) 1975, Izaak Walton Killam Memorial Scholarships 1976–77, Merck, Sharp and Dohme Lectures Award (CIC) 1976, Médaille Parizeau (ACFAS) 1979, Marie-Victorin Prize 1987, Alfred Bader Award (CSC) 1991, Canada Gold Medal for Science and Eng. 1993, R.U. Lemieux Award for Organic Chem. (Chemical Soc. for Chem.) 1994; Officer Ordre Nat. du Québec. *Publications:* over 170 publs. in the area of organic synthesis and the development of the concept of stereoelectronic effects in organic chemistry, Stereoelectronic Effects in Organic Chemistry 1983. *Leisure interests:* reading, fishing, hunting, canoeing. *Address:* Département de chimie, Faculté des Sciences, Université de Sherbrooke, Sherbrooke, Québec, J1K 2R1 (Office); RR 1, 11 Church McFarland, North Hatley, Québec J0B 2C0, Canada (Home). *Telephone:* (819) 821-7002 (Office); (819) 842-4238 (Home). *Fax:* (819) 821-7910.

DESMEDT, John E., M.D., PH.D.; Belgian neurologist; b. 19 Feb. 1926, Wavre; Prof. and Dir. Univ. of Brussels Brain Research Unit 1962–; fmr. Chair. Dept. of Physiology and Pathophysiology, Univ. of Brussels Medical Faculty; Pres. Int. Fed. for Clinical Neurophysiology 1985–; mem. Acad. Royale de Médecine de Belgique, Acad. Royale de Belgique; foreign mem. Accademia Nazionale dei Lincei (Italy), Acad. Nat. de Médecine (France); Fellow, New York Acad. of Sciences, Royal Soc. of Medicine, A.A.A.S. and mem. or hon. mem. of numerous other professional socs., int. scientific orgs. etc.; Francqui Prize 1972, Dautrebande Prize for Pathophysiology 1979, Maisin Prize (Fonds National de la Recherche Scientifique) 1985; Dr. h.c. (Palermo) 1975, (Strasbourg) 1981; Grand Officier, Ordre de Léopold. *Publications:* New Developments in Electromyography and Clinical Neurophysiology (3 vols.) 1973, Motor Control Mechanisms in Health and Disease 1983. *Leisure interests:* horse-riding, jogging, fishing. *Address:* Brain Research Unit, University of Brussels, 20 rue Evers, Brussels 1000, Belgium. *Telephone:* (02) 538-08-44. *Fax:* (02) 538-29-05.

DESMOND, Barry, M.COMM.; Irish politician; b. May 1935, Cork; s. of late Senator Con Desmond; m. Stella Murphy; four s.; ed. Presentation Brothers, Coláiste Chriost Rí, Cork, School of Commerce, Cork and Univ. Coll., Cork; mem. Dáil Éireann for Dun Laoghaire 1969–89; Labour Party spokesman on Social Welfare 1972–73; Labour Party Chief Whip 1973–81; Minister of State, Dept. of Finance 1981–82; Minister for Health and Social Welfare 1982–86, for Health 1986–87; mem. Council of State 1973–91; Deputy Leader Labour Party 1982–89, Chair. 1987–88; mem. European Parl. 1989–94; Vice-Pres. Socialist Group, Econ. and Monetary Cttee. 1989–94; mem. European Court of Auditors 1994–; Irish Council of the European Movt.; Fellow Inst. of Industrial Engineers. *Address:* Court of Auditors, 12 rue Alcide de Gasperi, 1615 Luxembourg (Office); 2 Taney Avenue, Dublin 14, Ireland (Home). *Telephone:* 4398-45370 (Office); 2985719 (Home). *Fax:* 4398-46493 (Office).

DE SOTO, Alvaro; Peruvian diplomatist; b. 16 March 1943, Argentina; m. Irene Philippi 1981 (divorced); two s. one d.; ed. Int. School, Geneva, Catholic Univ. Lima, San Marcos Univ. Lima, Diplomatic Acad. Lima and Inst. of Int. Studies Geneva; Acting Dir. Maritime Sovereignty Div. Ministry of Foreign Affairs 1975–78; Deputy Perm. Rep. of Peru at UN, Geneva 1978–82; Special Asst. to UN Sec.-Gen. 1982–86; Asst. Sec.-Gen. and Exec. Asst. to UN Sec.-Gen. 1987–91; Personal Rep. of UN Sec.-Gen. in El Salvador Peace Negotiations 1990–91; Asst. Sec.-Gen. UN Office for Research and Collection of Information 1991; Sr. Political Adviser to UN Sec.-Gen. 1992–94; Asst. Sec.-Gen. for Political Affairs 1995–. *Address:* United Nations, Room S-3527 A, New York, NY 10017, U.S.A. *Telephone:* (212) 963-5034.

DESPIĆ, Aleksandar; DR.PHYS.CHEM.; Serbian electrochemist; b. 6 Jan. 1927, Belgrade; s. of Ranko Despić and Vukosava Despić (née Kalimančić); m. Zorica Despić (née Vukadinović) 1954; served World War II; ed. Belgrade Univ., London Univ.; teacher, Prof. of Physical Chem. Belgrade Univ. 1951–92; worked in Pa. Univ. 1957–59, 1967–68; Chair. Serbian Chemical Soc. 1973–77; Chair. Union of Chemical Socs. of Yugoslavia 1978–81; mem. Serbian Acad. of Sciences and Arts, Vice-Pres., Pres. 1994–; mem. Croatian and Slovenian Acads. of Sciences and Arts, European Acad. of Sciences and Arts; Hon. Chair. Serbian Chemical Soc. 1979–; Dir. Museum of Science and Tech. in Belgrade; Chair. Exec. Bd. Repub. Found. for Devt. of Scientific and Artistic Youth; Head of Div. of Surface Tech. and Energy Inst. of Tech. Sciences, Serbian Acad. of Sciences; October Prize 1968, 7 July Prize 1990. *Publications:* over 160 scientific works, 22 invention patents, over 15 monographs and textbooks including On Theory of Mechanisms of Chem. Reactions 1965, On Theory of Dendritic Growth 1968, Aluminium-Air Battery with Salt Solution 1976, Electrochemical Deposition of Alloys and Composites 1995; numerous articles in Yugoslavian and foreign scientific periodicals. *Leisure interest:* gardening. *Address:* Serbian Academy of Sciences and Arts, Knez Mihailova str. 35, 11000 Belgrade, Yugoslavia. *Telephone:* (11) 634-055. *Fax:* (11) 638-792.

de STRYCKER, Cecil A. J. F. J. M., D.S.C.; Belgian banker; b. 2 Feb. 1915, Derby, England; s. of Joseph de Strycker and Jeanne André Dumont; m. Elisabeth Braffort 1948; Hon. Gov. Banque Nationale de Belgique; Grand Officier de l'Ordre de Léopold, Grand Officier de l'Ordre de la Couronne. *Leisure interest:* gardening. *Address:* 14 avenue Bois du Dimanche, B-1150 Brussels, Belgium. *Telephone:* 2770-3572 (Home).

de THÉ, Guy Blaudin, M.D., PH.D.; French cancer research specialist; b. 5 May 1930, Marseilles; s. of François Blaudin de Thé and Madeleine du Verne; m. Colette Pierrard de Maujouy 1958 (died 1991); one s. two d.; ed. Faculty of Medicine, Marseilles, Univ. of Paris, Sorbonne; Research Asst. Duke Univ. Medical Center, U.S.A. 1961–63; Visiting Scientist, Laboratory of Viral Oncology, Nat. Cancer Inst., N.I.H., U.S.A. 1963–65; Head of Unit of Electron Microscopy, Centre Nat. de Recherche Scientifique 1965–67; Chief, Unit of Biological Carcinogenesis, WHO Int. Agency for Research on Cancer, Lyons 1967–78; Dir. of Research C.N.R.S., Faculty Med. A. Carrel, Lyon and Cancer Research Inst., Villejuif, Paris 1979–90; Head Unit of Epidemiology of Oncogenic Viruses and Prof. Pasteur Inst., Paris 1990–97, Prof. Emer. 1998–; Visiting Prof. Faculty of Public Health, Harvard Univ. 1981–; Fogarty Scholar-in-Residence, N.I.H., Bethesda U.S.A. 1992–96; mem. Scientific Council, Ligue nat. française contre le cancer 1972–74; mem. Nat. Acad. Médecine, Soc. française de Microbiologie, American Soc. for Cell Biology, American Asscn. for Cancer Research, A.A.A.S., European Asscn. for Cancer Research; Corresp. mem. Acad. des Sciences, Inst. de France; Scientific Prize, Acad. of Sciences 1971, Medical Research Foundation 1979, Collège de France 1981, Silver Medal, C.N.R.S 1981, Life Sciences Inst. Paris 1991; Officier, Ordre nat. du Mérite. *Publications:* many publs. on the cell virus relationship in avian and murine leukaemia viruses, and role of viruses in human tumours (Burkitt's lymphoma in Africa, Nasopharyngeal carcinoma in South-East Asia); Sur la piste du cancer (popular scientific book) 1984, Modes de vie et cancers 1988. *Leisure interest:* arts. *Address:* Institut Pasteur, Unité d'Epidémiologie des virus oncogènes, 28 rue Dr. Roux, 75015 Paris (Office); 14 rue Le Regrattier, 75004 Paris, France (Home). *Telephone:* (1) 45-68-89-30 (Office); (1) 43-54-01-22 (Home). *Fax:* (1) 45-68-89-31 (Office); (1) 40-51-05-15 (Home).

de TRAFFORD, Sir Dermot Humphrey, Bt., M.A.; British business executive; b. 19 Jan. 1925; s. of Sir Rudolph de Trafford and June Lady Audley Chaplin; m. 1st Patricia Mary Beeley 1946 (divorced 1973); three s. six d.; m. 2nd Xandra Caradini Walter 1973; ed. Harrow School, Christ Church, Oxford; trained as man. consultant, Clubley Armstrong & Co. Ltd and Orr & Boss and Partners 1949–52; Man. Dir. GHP Group Ltd. 1961, Chair. 1965–77; Dir. Low & Bonar PLC 1977–80, Deputy Chair. 1980–82, Chair. 1982–90; Chair. Calor Gas Holding 1974–88; Dir. Investment Trust; Chair. Council, Inst. of Dirs 1990–93, Vice-Pres. 1993–95. *Leisure interests:* golf. *Address:* The Old Vicarage, Appleshaw, Andover, Hants., SP11 9BH, England. *Telephone:* (01264) 772357.

DETTORI, Lanfranco; Italian flat race jockey; b. 15 Dec. 1970; s. of Gianfranco Dettori and Iris Maria Niemen; m. Catherine Allen 1997; has ridden races in England, France, Germany, Italy, U.S.A., Dubai, Australia, Hong Kong and other countries in the Far East 1992–; 1,000 rides and 215 wins in U.K. 1995; horses ridden include Lamtarra, Barathea, Vettori, Mark of Distinction, Balanchine, Moonshell, Lochsong, Classic Cliché; maj. race victories include St Leger (twice), The Oaks (twice), The Breeders Cup Mile, Arc de Triomphe, French 2000 Guineas, Queen Elizabeth II Stakes, Prix L'Abbaye; rode winners of all seven races at Ascot on 28 Oct. 1996; Jockey of the Year 1994, 1995. *Publication:* A Year in the Life of Frankie Dettori 1996. *Address:* c/o Peter Burrell, The School Office, 47 The Street, Kirtling, Newmarket, Suffolk, CB8 9AF, England. *Telephone:* (01638) 731071. *Fax:* (01638) 731095.

DETWEILER, David Kenneth, V.M.D., M.S.; American professor of physiology; b. 23 Oct. 1919, Philadelphia, Pa.; s. of David Rieser Detweiler and Pearl I. (Overholt) Detweiler; two s. four d.; ed. Univ. of Pennsylvania; Asst. Instructor Veterinary School, Univ. of Pa. 1942–43, Instructor 1943–45, Assoc. Instructor 1945–47, Asst. Prof. 1947–51, Assoc. Prof. 1951–62, Prof. of Physiology and Head of Physiology Lab. 1962–90, Dir. Comparative Cardiovascular Studies Unit 1960–90, Prof. Emer. 1990–; Guggenheim Fellow 1955–56; mem. Inst. of Medicine, N.A.S.; mem. Nat. Acads. of Practice 1989; Hon. D.Sc. (Ohio State Univ.) 1966; Hon. M.V.D. (Vienna) 1968; Hon. D.M.V. (Turin) 1969; Gaines Award and Medal, American Veterinary Asscn. 1960; Distinguished Veterinarian Award, Pa. Veterinary Medical Asscn. 1989; elected to Hon. Roll American Veterinary Asscn. 1990; D. K. Detweiler Prize for Cardiology established by German-speaking group of World Veterinary Medicine Asscn. 1982; David K. Detweiler Conf. Room dedicated in School of Veterinary Medicine, Univ. of Pa. 1993, School's Centennial Medal 1994. *Publications:* some 170 publications on cardiology and cardiovascular physiology. *Leisure interests:* art, music, languages. *Address:* School of Veterinary Medicine, University of Pennsylvania, 3800 Spruce Street, Philadelphia, PA 19104 (Office); Waverly Heights, Apt. A212, 1400 Waverly Road, Gladwyne, PA 19035, U.S.A. (Home). *Telephone:* (610) 645-8964. *Fax:* (610) 645-8719.

DEUBA, Sher Bahadur, M.A.; Nepalese politician; b. 12 June 1946, Angra, Dadeldhura Dist.; ed. Tribhuvan Univ.; Chair. Far Western Students Cttee. Kathmandu 1965; served a total of nine years imprisonment for political activities 1966–85; founder mem. Nepal Students' Union 1970; Research Fellow, L.S.E. 1988–90; active in Popular Movt. for Restoration of Democracy in Nepal 1991; mem. Parl. 1991–; Minister of Home Affairs; Leader, Parl. Party, Nepali Congress 1994; Prime Minister 1995–97. *Address:* c/o Office of the Prime Minister, Central Secretariat, Singha Durbar, Kathmandu, Nepal.

DEUKMEJIAN, George, J.D.; American state governor; b. 6 June 1928, Albany, N.Y.; s. of C. George and Alice (née Gairdan) Deukmejian; m. Gloria M. Saatjian 1957; one s. two d.; ed. Siena Coll. and St John's Univ.; admitted to N.Y. State Bar 1952, Calif. Bar 1956, Supreme Court Bar 1970; partner Riedman, Dalessi, Deukmejian & Woods, Long Beach, Calif. –1979; mem. Calif. Ass. 1963–67, Calif. Senate (Minority Leader); Attorney-Gen., Calif. 1979–82; Gov. of California 1983–90; partner Sidley and Austin 1991–; Republican. *Address:* Sidley and Austin, 555 West 5th Street, 40th Floor, Los Angeles, CA 90013, U.S.A.

DEUTCH, John, PH.D.; American professor of chemistry; b. 27 July 1938, Brussels, Belgium; s. of Michael J. and Rachel Fischer Deutch; m. Pat Lyons; three s.; ed. Amherst Coll. and M.I.T.; Systems Analyst, Office of Sec. for Defense 1961–65; Fellow, N.A.S./N.R.C. Nat. Bureau of Standards 1966–67; Asst. Prof. Princeton Univ. 1967–70; mem. Faculty, M.I.T. 1970–, Prof. of Chemistry 1971–; Chair. Dept. of Chem. 1976–77, Dean, School of Science 1982–85, Provost 1985–90, Inst. Prof. 1990–; Dir. of Energy Research, Dept. of Energy 1977–79, Acting Asst. Sec. 1979, Under-Sec. 1979–80; Under Sec. for Acquisition and Tech. Dept. of Defense 1993–94, Deputy Sec. 1994–95; Dir CIA 1995–96; mem. White House Science Council 1985–89; mem. Bd. of Dirs. Citicorp, CMS Energy, Parkin-Elmer Corpn., Schlumberger, Science Applications Inc.; other professional and public appts.; mem. American Physics Soc., American Chem. Soc., American Acad. of Arts and Sciences, Council on Foreign Relations, President's Foreign Intelligence Advisory Cttee. 1990–, Trilateral Comm. 1991; Sloan Fellow 1969–71; Guggenheim Fellow 1974; recipient of awards from Dept. of State and Dept. of Energy; D.Sc. h.c. (Amherst Coll.) 1978; D.Phil. h.c. (Lowell) 1986. *Publications:* research articles. *Address:* Massachusetts Institute of Technology, 77 Massachusetts Avenue, Cambridge, MA 02139, U.S.A.

DEUTEKOM, Cristina; opera singer; b. 28 Aug. 1938, Amsterdam; one d.; first major appearance at Munich State Opera 1966, then at Vienna Festwochen; sang at Metropolitan Opera, New York 1967; has sung in all the major opera houses in Europe, especially Italy, and U.S.A.; specializes in bel canto operas by Rossini, Bellini and Donizetti and the great Verdi operas; recordings for EMI, Decca and Philips; Grand Prix du Disque 1969, 1972. *Leisure interests:* driving round the world, singing, shopping (especially for shoes).

DEUTSCH, André, C.B.E.; British publisher; b. 15 Nov. 1917, Budapest; s. of late Bruno Deutsch and Maria (Havas) Deutsch; ed. Budapest, Vienna and Zürich; first publishing job with Nicholson & Watson 1942; independent publisher under imprint Allan Wingate (Publrs.) Ltd. 1945; formed André Deutsch Ltd. 1951, Chair. and Man. Dir. 1951–84, Co.-Chair. and Co-Man. Dir. 1984–87, Pres. 1987–91; f. African Univs. Press, Lagos 1962, E. Africa Publishing House, Nairobi 1964; Dir. Libra Books, Budapest 1991–; Chair. Aurum Press 1992–. *Leisure interests:* travel (preferably by train), publishing, talking. *Address:* 5 Selwood Terrace, London, SW7 3QN, England.

DEV, Kapil (see Kapil Dev).

de VALOIS, Dame Ninette, O.M., C.H., D.B.E.; British choreographer; b. 6 June 1898, Baltiboys, Blessington, Co. Wicklow, Ireland; d. of Lieut.-Col. T. R. A. Stannus, D.S.O.; m. Dr. A. B. Connell 1935; Prima Ballerina, Royal Opera Season, Covent Garden 1919 and 1928; British Nat. Opera Co. 1918; mem. The Diaghileff Russian Ballet 1923–26; Choreographic Dir. to the Old Vic. Festival Theatre, Cambridge, and the Abbey Theatre, Dublin 1926–30; Founder and Dir. The Royal Ballet and the Royal Ballet School 1931–63, now Gov. Royal Ballet; fmr. Pres. London Ballet Circle; Hon. Mus. Doc. (London) 1947; Hon. D.Mus. (London, Sheffield, Trinity Coll. Dublin, Durham, Cambridge); Hon. D.Litt. (Reading, Oxford, New Univ., Ulster); Hon. D.F.A. (Smith Coll. Mass.) 1957; Hon. LL.D. (Aberdeen, Sussex) 1958; Chevalier, Légion d'honneur 1950; Erasmus Prize 1974; Irish Community Award 1980. *Choreographic works include:* Job, The Rake's Progress, Checkmate, The Prospect Before Us, Don Quixote. *Publications:* Invitation to the Ballet 1937, Come Dance with Me 1957, Step by Step 1977. *Address:* c/o The Royal Ballet School, 153 Talgarth Road, London, W14, England.

DEVAN NAIR, Chengara Veetil; Singaporean politician and trade unionist; b. 5 Aug. 1923, Malacca, Malaysia; s. of I.V.K. Nair and Sri Devi; m. Avadai Dhanam 1953; three s. one d.; ed. Victoria Secondary School, Singapore; teacher, St. Andrew's School, Singapore 1949–51; Gen. Sec. Singapore Teachers' Union 1949–51; detained 1951–53; Convenor and mem. Cen. Exec. Cttee, People's Action Party (PAP) 1954–56; Sec. Singapore Factory and Shopworkers Union 1954–56; detained 1956–59; Political Sec. Ministry of Educ. 1959–60; Chair. Prisons Inquiry Comm. 1960; Chair. Adult Educ. Bd. 1960–64; Sec. Nat. Trades Union Congress (NTUC) and Dir. of its Research Unit, Singapore 1964–65; mem. House of Reps., Malaysia 1964–69; Founder and First Sec.-Gen. Democratic Action Party, Malaysia 1964–69; Dir. NTUC Research Unit 1969–81; Sec.-Gen. NTUC 1969–79, Pres. 1979–81; Pres. ICFTU Asian Regional Org. 1975–81; M.P. for Anson, Singapore 1979, re-elected 1980; resgnd. as M.P. and Pres. NTUC Oct. 1981; Pres. of Repub. of Singapore 1981–85; Consultant to AFL-CIO 1985–87; Fellow Inst. of Advanced Study, Ind. Univ. U.S.A. 1985–87; Fellow Southeast Asia Program Cornell Univ., U.S.A.; Hon. D.Litt. (Univ. of Singapore) 1976; Public Service Star, Singapore 1963. *Publications:* Singapore Socialism that Works, Who Lives if Malaysia Dies?, Tomorrow—The Peril and the Promise, Asian Labour and the Dynamics of Change, Not By Wages Alone, Singapore: Reflective Essays, Singapore: The Promise and the Breach. *Leisure interests:* swimming, reading, music. *Address:* 176 Buckingham Drive, Hamilton, Ont. L9C 2G7, Canada. *Telephone:* (905) 575-0739. *Fax:* (905) 575-7973.

DEVE GOWDA, Haradanahalli; Indian politician; m.; six c.; ed. govt. polytechnic inst.; trained as civil eng.; ran contracting business; elected to Karnataka State Legis. in 1960s; imprisoned during state of emergency in 1970s; Minister of Public Works and Irrigation, Karnataka until 1980; Chief Minister of Karnataka 1995–96; fmr. mem. Lok Sabha; leader multiparty United Front 1996; Prime Minister, Minister of Home and Agric., Science and Tech., Personnel and Atomic Energy 1996–97. *Address:* c/o Office of the Prime Minister, New Delhi, India.

DEVESI, Sir Baddeley, G.C.M.G., G.C.V.O.; Solomon Islands politician and administrator; b. 16 Oct. 1941, East Tathiboko, Guadalcanal; s. of Mostyn Tagabasoe Norua and Laisa Otu; m. June Marie Barley 1969; four s. three d. (one d. deceased); ed. St. Mary's School, Maravovo, King George VI School, Solomon Islands, Ardmore Teachers' Training Coll., Auckland, New Zealand; Teacher, Melanesian Mission schools, Solomon Islands 1965–66; elected mem. British Solomon Islands Legis. and Exec. Councils 1967–68; lecturer, Solomon Islands Teachers' Coll. 1970–72, Asst. Sec. for Social Services 1972, Internal Affairs 1972; Dist. Officer, S. Malaita 1973–75; Perm. Sec. Ministry of Works and Public Utilities 1976, Ministry of Transport and Communications 1977; Gov.-Gen. of Solomon Islands 1978–88; Minister for Foreign Affairs and Trade Relations 1989–91; Deputy Prime Minister and Minister for Home Affairs 1990–92, for Health and Medical Sciences 1992; Deputy Prime Minister and Minister for Transport, Works, Communications and Aviation 1996–; Chancellor, Univ. of S. Pacific 1980–83; Hon. D. Univ.; K.St.J. *Leisure interests:* swimming, lawn tennis, cricket, reading, snooker. *Address:* Office of Deputy Prime Minister, Honiara, Solomon Islands.

DEVI, Phoolan; Indian politician; b. 1959; m. 1st 1970; m. 2nd Vickram Mallah (deceased); m. 3rd; known as the "Bandit Queen"; imprisoned for murder of twenty high-caste men whom she alleges raped her 1983–94; mem. Lok Sabha (Parl.) for Mirzapur, Uttar Pradesh 1996–; mem. Samajwadi Party (Socialist); film "Bandit Queen" made of her life 1995. *Publication:* I, Phoolan Devi: The Autobiography of India's Bandit Queen (jtly.) 1996. *Address:* Lok Sabha, New Delhi, India.

DE VICENZO, Roberto; Argentinian golfer; b. 14 April 1923, Buenos Aires; professional golfer since 1938; won Argentine PGA and Open 1944; subsequently won Argentine PGA six more times by 1952 and Open eight more times, finally in 1974; represented Argentina in numerous World Cups, twice individual winner; winner, Chilean, Colombian, Brazilian and Panama Opens; first appeared in Britain 1948; winner, British Open, Hoylake 1967.

de VIRION, Tadeusz Józef; Polish diplomatist and lawyer; b. 28 March 1926, Warsaw; s. of Jerzy de Virion and Zofia de Virion; m. Jayanti de Virion 1985; two d.; educ. Warsaw Univ.; served in Home Army during Nazi occupation 1943–45, took part in Warsaw Uprising 1944; qualified as judge 1948; qualified as attorney 1950, since then on Warsaw Bar, counsel for the defence in criminal cases; judge in State Tribunal 1989–90 (resgnd.), 1993–; Amb. to U.K. 1990–93 (also accred. to Ireland until Oct. 1991); Kt. Sovereign Order of Kts. of Malta, Commdr. Gold Cross of Merit of Polonia Restituta, Order Grand'Ufficiale dell'Ordine al Merito Meliteriese. *Address:* ul. Długa 8/14, 00 328 Warsaw, Poland. *Telephone:* (22) 831 12 63.

DeVITO, Danny; American actor and director; b. 1944, New Jersey; m. Rhea Perlman 1982; two s. two d.; ed. American Acad. of Dramatic Arts, Wilfred Acad. of Hair and Beauty Culture; worked for a year as a hairdresser. *Stage appearances include:* The Man with a Flower in his Mouth, Down the Morning Line The Line of Least Existence, The Shrinking Bride, Call me Charlie, Comedy of Errors, Merry Wives of Windsor, Three by Pirandello, One Flew Over the Cuckoo's Nest. *Film appearances include:* Lady Liberty, Scalawag, Hurry Up or I'll be 30, One Flew Over the Cuckoo's Nest, Deadly Hero, Car Wash, The Van, The World's Greatest Lover, Goin' South, Going Ape, Terms of Endearment, Romancing the Stone, Johnny Dangerously, Head Office, Jewel of the Nile, Wiseguys, Ruthless People, My little Pony (voice), Tin Men, Throw Momma from the Train (also dir.), Twins, War of the Roses (also dir.), Hoffa (also dir.), Other People's Money 1991, Batman Returns 1992, Hoffa (also producer, dir.) 1992, Renaissance Man 1994, Junior 1994, Get Shorty (also co-producer), Matilda (also dir., co-producer), Mars Attacks 1997, The Rainmaker 1997, L.A. Confidential 1997; producer Feeling Minnesota 1996, Gattaca 1997; *TV work includes:* Taxi (also dir.), Mary (dir. only), Valentine, The Rating Game (dir.), All the Kids Do It, A Very Special Christmas Party, Two Daddies? (voice), The Selling of Vince DeAngelo (dir.), Amazing Stories (also dir.), The Simpsons (voice). *Address:* c/o Fred Specktor, Creative Artists Agency, 9830 Wilshire Boulevard, Beverly Hills, CA 90212, U.S.A.

DEVLIN, Dean; American actor, screenplay writer and producer; numerous film and TV appearances; stage role in There Must Be a Pony (Broadway); joined Centropolis Films (f. by Roland Emmerich). *Films:* Moon 44, Universal Soldier (screenplay), Stargate (co-writer and producer), Independence Day (co-writer and producer). *TV:* (series) The Visitor (producer) 1997. *Address:* c/o Creative Artists Agency, 9830 Wilshire Boulevard, Beverly Hills, CA 90212, U.S.A.

DEVLIN, Stuart Leslie, A.O., C.M.G.; Australian goldsmith, silversmith and designer; b. 9 Oct. 1931, Geelong; s. of Richard and Jesse Devlin; m. 1st Kim Hose 1962; m. 2nd Carole Hedley-Saunders 1986; ed. Gordon Inst. of Tech., Geelong, Royal Melbourne Inst. of Tech. and Royal Coll. of Art; art teacher, Victoria Educ. Dept. 1950–58; Royal Coll. of Art 1958–60; Harkness Fellow, New York 1960–62; lecturer, Prahan Tech. Coll., Melbourne 1962; Inspector of Art in Tech. Schools, Victoria Educ. Dept. 1964–65; working as goldsmith, silversmith and designer in London 1965–; exhbns. of gold and silver in numerous cities in U.K., U.S.A., Australia, Middle East, etc.; has executed many commissions for commemorative coins in gold and silver for various countries; designed and made cutlery for State Visit to Paris 1972, Duke of Edinburgh Trophy for World Driving Championship 1973, silver to commemorate opening of Sydney Opera House 1973, Grand National Trophy 1975 and Regalia for Order of Australia 1975–76; Centrepiece for Royal Engs. to commemorate their work in Northern Ireland 1984; Bas-relief portrait H.R.H. Princess of Wales for Wedgwood 1986; devised and executed Champagne Diamond Exhbn. 1987; granted Royal Warrant (goldsmith and jeweller to H.M. Queen Elizabeth II) 1982; mem. Court of Wardens, Goldsmiths' Co. 1992, Prime Warden, 1996–97; Vice-Chair. Intergraph Graphics Users' Group, U.K. 1996–. *Leisure interests:* work, wind-surfing, tennis. *Address:* 33 Coastal Road, Angmering-on-Sea, West Sussex, BN16 1SJ, England. *Telephone:* (01903) 858939.

DEVONS, Samuel, PH.D., F.R.S.; British professor of physics; b. 30 Sept. 1914, Bangor, N. Wales; s. of David I. Devons and Edith Edlestein; m. Celia Ruth Toubkin 1938; four d.; ed. Trinity Coll., Cambridge; Scientific Officer, Air Ministry 1939–45; Fellow, Dir. of Studies, Lecturer in Physics, Trinity Coll., Cambridge 1946–49; Prof. of Physics, Imperial Coll. of Science 1950–55, Acting Dir. of Laboratory 1953–54; Langworthy Prof. of Physics and Dir. of Physical Laboratories, Manchester Univ. 1955–60; Visiting Prof. of Physics, Columbia Univ. New York 1959–60, Prof. 1960–85, Prof. Emer. 1985–, Chair. Dept. of Physics 1963–67; Visiting Prof., Barnard Coll., Columbia Univ., History of Physics 1969, Dir. History of Physics Lab.; mem. UNESCO Technical Aid, Argentina 1957; Royal Soc./Leverhulme Visiting Prof., India 1968–69; Racah Visiting Prof., Hebrew Univ., Jerusalem 1973–74; Balfour Visiting Prof., Weizmann Inst., Rehovot 1973; Rutherford Memorial Lecturer, Royal Soc. (Australia) 1989; Bd. of Govs. Weizmann Inst. 1971–; Founder and Convenor, The Joseph Priestley Assn. 1986–; Rutherford Prize and Medal, Physical Soc. 1970. *Publications:* Excited States of Nuclei 1949, Biology and the Physical Sciences (Ed.) 1969, High Energy Physics and Nuclear Structure (Ed.) 1970. *Leisure interests:* writing, theatre. *Address:* Nevis Laboratory, Columbia University, P.O. Box 137, Irvington-on-Hudson, NY 10533 (Office); 34 Lewis Road, Irvington, New York, NY 10533, U.S.A. (Home). *Telephone:* (914) 591-2860 (Office); (914) 591-7681 (Home). *Fax:* (914) 591-7080.

DEVONSHIRE, 11th Duke of, cr. 1694; **Andrew Robert Buxton Cavendish,** K.G., P.C., M.C.; British politician and landowner; Baron Cavendish, Earl of Devonshire, Marquess of Hartington, Earl of Burlington, Baron Cavendish (U.K.); b. 2 Jan. 1920; s. of 10th Duke of Devonshire and Lady Mary Cecil; m. Hon. Deborah Vivian Freeman-Mitford 1941; one s. two d.; ed. Eton and Trinity Coll. Cambridge; served Coldstream Guards 1939–45; Conservative parl. cand. 1945, 1950; succeeded father 1950; Pres. Bldg. Socs. Assn. 1954–61; Parl. Under-Sec. of State for Commonwealth Relations 1960–62; Minister of State, Commonwealth Relations Office 1962–64, and for Colonial Affairs 1963–64; Chancellor of Manchester Univ. 1965–86; Steward, Jockey Club 1966–69; mem. Horserace Totalisator Bd. 1977–86; Trustee, Nat. Gallery 1960–68; Pres. Royal Hosp. and Home, Putney 1954–91, Lawn Tennis Assn. 1955–61, Royal Nat. Inst. for Blind 1979–85, Nat. Assn. for Deaf Children 1978–95; Vice-Pres. London Library 1993–; Chair. Grand Council, British Empire Cancer Campaign 1956–81, Thoroughbred Breeders' Assn. 1978–81; Hon. LL.D. (Manchester, Sheffield, Liverpool); Hon. LL.D. (Newfoundland). *Publication:* Park Top: A Romance of the Turf 1976. *Address:* Chatsworth, Bakewell, Derbyshire DE45 1PP; 4 Chesterfield Street, London, W1X 7HG, England. *Telephone:* (01246) 582204; 0171-499 5803.

DE VRIES, Bert, D.ECON; Netherlands politician; b. 29 March 1938; ed. Groningen Univ. and Amsterdam Free Univ.; formerly worked in tax service, with Philips and as lecturer, Erasmus Univ. Rotterdam; mem. Parl. 1982–; Parl. Leader, Christian Democratic Appeal 1982; Minister of Social Affairs and Employment 1989–94. *Address:* c/o Christian Democratic Appeal, Dr. Kuyperstraat 5, 2514 BA The Hague, Netherlands.

DEVRIES, William Castle, M.D.; American surgeon; b. 19 Dec. 1943, Brooklyn; s. of Hendrik Devries and Cathryn L. Castle; seven c.; ed. Univ. of Utah; intern Duke Univ. Medical Center 1970–71; Resident in cardiovascular and thoracic surgery 1971–79; Asst. Prof. of Surgery, Univ. of Utah until 1984; Chief of Thoracic Surgery, Salt Lake Hosp., Va. until 1984; Pres. De Vries & Assocs. 1988–. *Address:* Devries & Associates, PSC 906 Woodland Drive, 202 Elizabethtown, KY 42701, U.S.A.

DE WAAL, Marius Theodorus, B.SC., B.ING.; South African business executive; b. 12 March 1925, Paarl Dist.; s. of Pieter de Waal; m. Kitty du Plessis 1949; three s. one d.; ed. Univs. of Stellenbosch and Delft and Harvard Advanced Man. Programme, Swansea; town engineer, Bellville 1947–60; with Industrial Devt. Corpn. of S.A. Ltd. 1961–90; Chair. Iscor Ltd. 1988–95, Transnet 1990–, Siemens Ltd.; Dir. S.A. Reserve Bank, BMW; Hon. D.Eng., Hon. D.Com., Hon. D.B.A. *Leisure interest:* tennis. *Address:* c/o Iscor Ltd., P.O. Box 450, Pretoria 0001, South Africa.

de WAART, Edo; Netherlands conductor; b. 1 June 1941, Amsterdam; s. of M. de Waart and J. Rose; one s. one d. from 1st marriage; ed. Amsterdam Music Lyceum; Asst. Conductor, Concertgebouw Orchestra, Amsterdam

1966; Perm. Conductor, Rotterdam Philharmonic 1967, Musical Dir. and Prin. Conductor 1973–79; Prin. Guest Conductor, San Francisco Symphony Orchestra 1975–77, Music Dir. 1977–85; Music Dir. Minn. Orchestra 1986–95; Artistic Dir., Netherlands Radio Philharmonic Orchestra 1989–; Prin. Guest Conductor, Santa Fe Opera 1991–92; Chief Conductor, Dutch Radio Philharmonic Orchestra 1989–; Artistic Dir. and Chief Conductor, Sydney Symphony Orchestra 1993–; First Prize Dimitri Mitropoulos Competition, New York 1964. *Address:* RFO No. 8—Muziekcentrum Van, de Omroep Postbus 10, 1200 JB Hilversum, The Netherlands; Sydney Symphony Orchestra, P.O. Box 4338, Sydney, N.S.W. 2001, Australia.

DEWAR, Rt. Hon. Donald Campbell, P.C., M.A., LL.B., M.P.; British politician and lawyer; b. 21 Aug. 1937; s. of Alasdair Dewar; m. Alison McNair 1964 (divorced 1973); one s. one d.; ed. Glasgow Acad. and Univ. of Glasgow; solicitor, Ross Harper & Murphy, Glasgow; mem. Parl. for S. Aberdeen 1966–70, for Glasgow, Garscadden 1978–97, for Glasgow, Anniesland 1997–; Parl. Pvt. Sec. to Pres. of Bd. of Trade 1967; Chair. Select Cttee. on Scottish Affairs 1979–81; Shadow Spokesman on Scottish Affairs 1981–92, on Social Security 1992–95; Chief Whip 1995–97; mem. Shadow Cabinet 1984–97; Sec. of State for Scotland and Lord Keeper of the Great Seal of Scotland May 1997–; Labour. *Address:* 23 Cleveden Road, Glasgow, G12 0PQ, Scotland; House of Commons, London, SW1A 0AA, England.

de WECK, Philippe; Swiss banker; b. 2 Jan. 1919, Fribourg; s. of Pierre and Lucie (Glasson) de Weck; m. Alix de Saussure 1944; two s. five d.; ed. Fribourg Grammar School, Univ. of Fribourg; joined law firm of Mr. Bourgknecht (later Fed. Councillor) 1948–51; partner in Bank Weck, Aeby and Cie, Fribourg 1951–54; Man. Fribourg Branch Office, Union Bank of Switzerland 1954–56, Man. Geneva Branch Office 1956–62, Gen. Man. Head Office, Zürich 1964, Chair. Bd. 1976–80. *Leisure interests:* skiing, sailing, mountain climbing, history. *Address:* c/o Union Bank of Switzerland, rue St.-Pierre 1, 1701 Fribourg, Switzerland. *Telephone:* 026-350 4111. *Fax:* 026-322 2809.

DE WEERDT, Hon. Mark Murray, Q.C., M.A., LL.B.; Canadian judge and lawyer (retd.); b. 6 May 1928, Cologne, Germany; s. of Hendrik Eugen de Weerdt and Ina Dunbar Murray; m. Linda Anne Hadwen 1956; four s.; ed. Glasgow Univ., Univ. of B.C., Vancouver; Constable, Royal Canadian Mounted Police 1950–52; barrister and solicitor, B.C. 1956–70, 1973–81, N.W.T. 1958–81; Crown Attorney, N.W.T. 1958–63; City Solicitor, Yellowknife, N.W.T. 1959–71; Magistrate and Juvenile Court Judge, N.W.T. 1971–73; Gen. Solicitor, Insurance Corpn. of B.C. 1974–76; Sr. Counsel, Dept. of Justice of Canada, Vancouver 1976–79, Gen. Counsel and Dir. 1979–81; Sr. Judge of the Supreme Court of the N.W.T. 1981–96; Justice of Appeal, Court of Appeal of the N.W.T. 1981–97, Court of Appeal of the Yukon Territory 1981–97; Chair. Judicial Council of the N.W.T. 1981; mem. Nat. Council Canadian Foundation for Human Rights; Dir. Canadian Inst. for the Admin. of Justice; mem. Canadian Bar Asscn.; Q.C. (Canada) 1968; mem. Int. Comm. of Jurists (Canadian Sec.), Advisory Council, Canadian Human Rights Inst., The Osgoode Soc., The Selden Soc. *Leisure interest:* general reading. *Address:* 5459 Crown Street, Vancouver, B.C., V6N 4K1, Canada (Home).

DEWEY, John Frederick, M.A., PH.D., D.SC., F.R.S., F.G.S.; British professor of geology; b. 22 May 1937, London; s. of John Edward Dewey and Florence Nellie Mary Dewey; m. Frances Mary Blackhurst 1961; one s. one d.; ed. Bancroft's School, Univ. of London; lecturer, Univ. of Manchester 1960–64, Univ. of Cambridge 1964–70; Prof. Univ. of Albany, N.Y. 1970–82; Prof. Univ. of Durham 1982–86; Prof. of Geology Univ. of Oxford 1986–, Fellow Univ. Coll. 1986–; mem. Academia Europaea 1990; Foreign mem. Nat. Acad. of Sciences 1997; Lyell Medal, Geological Soc. of London, T.N. George Medal, Univ. of Glasgow, Penrose Medal, Geological Soc. of America, Arthur Holmes Medal, European Union of Geosciences. *Publications:* 112 papers in scientific journals. *Leisure interests:* skiing, tennis, cricket, model railways, water-colour painting. *Address:* Department of Earth Sciences, Parks Road, Oxford, OX1 3PR; University College, Oxford, OX1 4BH; Sherwood Lodge, Bagley Wood Road, Kennington, Oxford, OX1 5NA, England (Home).

DEWINE, R. Michael, B.S., J.D.; American politician; b. 5 Jan. 1947, Springfield, Ohio; s. of Richard DeWine and Jean DeWine; m. Frances Struewing 1967; four s. four d.; ed. Miami Univ. Oxford, Ohio and Ohio Northern Univ.; admitted to Bar, Ohio 1972, U.S. Supreme Court 1977; Asst. prosecuting attorney, Green County, Xenia, Ohio 1973–75, prosecuting attorney 1977–81; mem. Ohio Senate 1981–82; mem. U.S. House of Reps. 1983–90; Lieut.-Gov. of Ohio 1991–94; Senator from Ohio 1995–; Republican. *Address:* U.S. Senate, Washington, DC 20510 (Office); 2587 Conley Road, Cedarville, OH 45314, U.S.A. (Home).

DEWOST, Jean-Louis; French European Community official; b. 6 Sept. 1937, Dunkirk; m. Agnès Huet 1967; one s. two d.; ed. Univ. de Paris, Inst. d'Etudes Politiques de Paris and Ecole Nat. d'Admin.; jr. official, Conseil d'Etat 1967–69; Asst. Man. Industrial Affairs, European Org. for Devt. and Construction of Space Vehicle Launchers (CECLES/ELDO) 1962–72, Dir. Finance and Econ. Planning 1972–73; Maître des Requêtes, Conseil d'Etat 1972; legal adviser EC Council Legal Service 1973–85, Jurisconsulte 1986–87; Conseiller d'Etat 1986; Dir.-Gen. EC Comm. Legal Service 1987–; Chevalier, Légion d'honneur, Chevalier, Ordre nat. du Mérite, Order of White Rose of Finland. *Publications:* several publs. on law and EC law. *Leisure interests:* tennis, swimming, opera. *Address:* Director-General of the Legal Service, Commission of the European Communities, 200 rue de la Loi, 1049 Brussels (Office); 484 avenue Molière, 1050 Brussels, Belgium (Home). *Telephone:* (2) 296.24.12 (Office). *Fax:* (2) 296.30.86 (Office).

DEXTER, Colin, M.A.(CANTAB), M.A.(OXON); British author; b. 29 Sept. 1930, Stamford, Lincs.; s. of Alfred Dexter and Dorothy Dexter; one s. one d.; ed. Stamford School, Christ's Coll., Cambridge; nat. service (Royal Signals) 1948–50, taught Classics 1954–66; Sr. Asst. Sec. Oxford Delegacy of Local Examinations 1966–88; Gold Dagger, Crime Writers' Asscn. (twice), Silver Dagger (twice), Cartier Diamond Dagger. *Publications:* Last Bus to Woodstock 1975, Last Seen Wearing 1977, The Silent World of Nicholas Quinn 1977, Service of All the Dead 1979, The Dead of Jericho 1981, The Riddle of the Third Mile 1983, The Secret of Annexe 3 1986, The Wench is Dead 1989, The Jewel that was Ours 1991, The Way through the Woods 1992, Morse's Greatest Mystery and Other Stories 1993, The Daughters of Cain 1994, Death is Now my Neighbour 1996. *Leisure interests:* reading, music, crosswords (fmr. nat. crossword champion). *Address:* 456 Banbury Road, Oxford, OX2 7RG, England.

DEZZA, H.E. Cardinal Paolo, B.A., D.PHIL., D.THEOL.; Italian ecclesiastic; b. 13 Dec. 1901, Parma; s. of Giovanni and Carla Riccadonna Dezza; ed. Milan, Barcelona, Innsbruck, Naples; Prof. of Philosophy, Pontifical Gregorian Univ., Rome 1929–33, 1941–62, Rector 1941–51; Rector Faculty of Aloisian Philosophy 1934–35; Provincial Superior of the Jesuit Prov. of Milan 1935–39; Asst. Gen., Soc. of Jesus 1965–75; Adviser various congregations of the Holy See 1929–91; Pres. Pontifical Inst. Regina Mundi 1954–66; Papal Del. of the Co. of Jesus 1981–83; cr. Cardinal 1991; Dr. h.c. (Univ. of Santiago, Chile); Commdr. Order of Alfonso the Wise, Spain. *Publications:* Alle origini del Neotomismo 1940, I Neotomisti italiani del secolo XIX 1942–44, Metaphysica Generalis 1962, Filosofia 1988, Esercizi Ignaziani 1987. *Address:* Borgo Santo Spirito 4, Rome, Italy. *Telephone:* 689-771.

DHANABALAN, Suppiah, B.A. (HONS.); Singaporean politician; b. 8 Aug. 1937; m. Tan Khoon Hiap 1963; one s. one d.; ed. Victoria School and Univ. of Malaya, Singapore; Asst. Sec. Ministry of Finance 1960–61; Sr. Industrial Economist, Deputy Dir. (Operations and Finance) Econ. Devt. Bd. 1961–68; Vice-Pres., Exec. Vice-Pres. Devt. Bank of Singapore 1968–78; M.P. 1976–; Sr. Minister of State, Ministry of Nat. Devt. 1978–79, Ministry of Foreign Affairs 1979–80; Minister of Foreign Affairs 1980–88, for Culture 1981–84, for Community Devt. 1984–86, also Minister for Nat. Devt. 1987–92; Chair. Parameswara Holdings 1994–; with Singapore Indian Chamber of Commerce 1992–; Minister, Ministry of Trade and Industry 1992–93; Sr. Adviser, Nuri Holdings (S) Pte. Ltd 1994–; fmrly. Chair. Singapore Airlines Ltd.; Chair. Devt. Bank of Singapore 1998–. *Leisure interests:* reading, squash, golf. *Address:* Development Bank of Singapore, 6 Shenton Way, DBS Building, Tower One, Singapore 068809. *Telephone:* 2201111. *Fax:* 2211306.

DHANIN CHEARAVANONT: Thai business executive; b. Bangkok; ed. secondary school, Shantou, China and commercial school, Hong Kong; Chair. CP Group (conglomerate of 250 cos. involved in agribusiness, petrochemicals, motorcycles, autoparts, telecommunications, etc. and owner of TM Int. Bank, Shanghai (first foreign-owned bank with head office in China); adviser to Chinese Govt. during Hong Kong negotiations with Britain. *Address:* CP Group, Bangkok, Thailand.

DHAR, Bansi, F.I.M.A., A.M.P.; Indian business executive; b. 7 March 1930, Delhi; s. of late Murli Dhar and Swaroop Devi; m. 1st Urmila Bansidhar 1953 (deceased); m. 2nd Suman Bansidhar 1976; three s.; ed. Delhi Univ., Harvard Univ.; trainee, eng. dept. DCM Ltd. 1952, various man. appts., Chair. of Bd. and Man. Dir. DCM Shriram Industries Ltd. 1990–; Chair. Bd. Daurala Organics Ltd., DCM Shriram Leasing & Finance Ltd., Indital Tintoria Ltd., DCM Hyundai Ltd., Hindustan Vacuum Glass Ltd., DCM Remy Ltd.; mem. Bd. Dirs. several cos.; mem. Exec. Cttee., Fed. Indian Chambers of Commerce and Industry (and fmr. Pres.), Indian Chemical Mfrs. Asscn.; Vice-Chair. Shriram Scientific and Industrial Research Foundation; Dir. Indian Trade Promotion Org.; Chair. Delhi Asscn. of the Deaf; Pres. Delhi Badminton Asscn.; fmr. Pres. All India Org. of Employers, Indian Sugar Mills Asscn., Delhi Factory Owners Asscn., Indian Council of Arbitration. *Leisure interests:* badminton, gardening, philately, photography, Indian classical music, theatre, bridge. *Address:* DCM Shriram Industries Ltd., Kanchenjunga Building, 18 Barakhamba Road, New Delhi 110001 (Office); 27 Sardar Patel Marg., New Delhi 110021, India (Home). *Telephone:* 3314641 (Office). *Fax:* 3315424.

DHARMASAKTI, Sanya; Thai judge and lawyer; b. 5 April 1907, Bangkok; s. of Phaya Dharmsaravedya and Lady Dharmasaravedya; m. Panga Benjati 1935; two s.; ed. Bangkok and London; fmr. Chief Justice of Thailand; fmr. Rector, Thammasat Univ.; Prime Minister 1973–75; Pres. Privy Council 1976; Pres. World Fellowship of Buddhists 1984–88. *Leisure interests:* gardening, reading. *Address:* 15 Sukhumvit Road, Soi 41, Bangkok, Thailand. *Telephone:* 251-1151 (Office); 258-8891 (Home).

DHARSONO, Gen. Hartono; Indonesian politician and army officer; fmr. Sec. Gen. of ASEAN; arrested Nov. 1984, sentenced to 10 years' imprisonment 1986, reduced to 7, released Sept. 1990; launched Forum for the Purification of People's Sovereignty (FPPS) 1991.

d'HAUTERIVES, Arnaud Louis Alain; French artist; b. 26 Feb. 1933, Braine (Aisne); s. of Louis and Germaine (née Hincelin) d'Hauterives; m. Renée Delhaye 1959; two s. one d.; ed. Ecole des Beaux Arts, Reims, Ecole Supérieure des Beaux Arts, Paris; started painting as a career 1957;

illustrator of some art books; Jt. Pres. Soc. Int. des Beaux Arts 1985, Hon. Pres. La Critique Parisienne 1984–; Pres. Acad. des Beaux Arts 1987–92, Life Sec. 1996–; mem. Inst. de France (Vice-Pres. 1987), Acad. des Sciences d'outre mer, Russian Acad. of Fine Arts; exhbns. in France, Belgium, U.S.A., China, Japan, Italy, Spain, U.S.S.R.; Chevalier Légion d'honneur, des Palmes Académiques, Officier Ordre nat. du Merite, Ordre des Arts et des Lettres; Premier Grand Prix de Rome 1957, Prix de la Critique 1967. *Leisure interest:* lithography, gliding. *Address:* Musée Marmottan-Claude Monet, 2 rue Louis Boilly, 75016 Paris; Académie des Beaux Arts, 23 Quai de Conti, 75006 Paris, France.

DHLOMO, Oscar Dumisani, D.ED.; South African politician; b. 28 Dec. 1943, Umbumbulu, Natal; s. of late Isaac Dhlomo; m. Nokukhanya V. Ntshingila 1966; three s. one d.; ed. Sibusiswe Secondary School, Amanzimtoti Coll., Univ. of S.A. and Univ. of Zululand; teacher, Umlazi 1967–72; secondary school headmaster, Umlazi 1973–74; lecturer in Educ. Univ. of Zululand 1974–77; mem. KwaZulu Legislative Ass. 1978–90; Sec.-Gen. Inkatha 1978–90; Minister of Educ. and Culture, KwaZulu Govt. until 1990; First Chair. KwaZulu Nat. Jt. Exec. Authority 1988–89; Chair. Bd. KwaZulu Training Trust, Emandleni-Matleng Training Camp; Co-convenor, KwaZulu-Natal Indaba, Chair. 1988–90; Dir. Devt. Bank of Southern Africa 1990–; Founder, Exec.-Chair. Inst. for Multiparty Democracy 1991–; Dir. Standard Bank Investment Corpn. 1991–, Anglovaal Ltd. 1991–, The Natal Witness Printing and Publishing Co. (Pty) Ltd. 1991–, Shell S.A. (Pty) Ltd. 1992–, Southern Life 1994–, and several other cos.; mem. Buthelezi Comm. 1982. *Publications:* co-author of two books on social studies; educ. papers. *Leisure interests:* music, reading. *Address:* Private Bag X04, Ulundi 3838, South Africa.

DIA, Mamadou; Senegalese politician; b. 18 July 1910, Kombole; ed. William Ponty School, Dakar; Councillor, Senegal 1946–52; Grand Councillor, French West Africa 1952–57; Founder mem. Bloc Démocratique Sénégalais (BDS), later Sec.-Gen; Senator for Senegal 1949–55; Deputy to Nat. Ass., Paris 1956–59; Deputy to Legis. Ass., Senegal 1959; Vice-Pres., Council of Ministers, Senegal 1957–58, Pres. 1958–59; Vice-Pres., Mali Fed. 1959–60; Pres. Council of Ministers, Senegal 1960–62, concurrently Minister of Defence and Security 1962; Govt. overthrown Dec. 1962, sentenced to life detention May 1963, sentence reduced to 20 years imprisonment 1972, released 1974; political rights restored 1976; co-founder and Ed. of Ande Soppi (perodical) July 1977; Chevalier, Palmes académiques. *Publications:* Réflexions sur l'économie de l'Afrique noire 1953, Contributions à l'étude du mouvement coopératif en Afrique noire 1957, L'économie africaine 1957, Nations africaines et solidarité mondiale 1960, Africa's Management in the 1990s and beyond 1996. *Address:* Dakar, Senegal.

DIALLO, Absa Claude, B.A.; Senegalese diplomatist; b. 1942, Hanoi, Vietnam; ed. Univ. of Dakar and Nat. School of Admin. Senegal; Head, Geographical Div. Office of Political, Cultural and Social Affairs, Ministry of Foreign Affairs 1964; Adviser, Office of Minister for Foreign Affairs 1965–72; Minister-Counsellor, Bonn (also accred. to Austria and Switzerland) 1972–77; Perm. Del. of Senegal at UNESCO 1977–80; roving Amb. 1980–81; Dir. of Political and Cultural Affairs, Ministry of Foreign Affairs 1981–88; Perm. Rep. to UN 1988–91, to UN Security Council 1988–89; Chair. UN Cttee. on the exercise of the inalienable rights of the Palestinian People 1988–91; UN ad hoc Cttee. on Cambodia 1988–90; Amb. to Sweden 1992–93, to Norway 1993, to Russia 1993–95 (also accred. to Bulgaria, Romania, Hungary, Ukraine, Poland, Czech Repub., Slovakia); Amb. and Perm. Rep. to UN and other int. orgs. in Geneva 1996–. *Address:* Ministry of Foreign Affairs and Sengalese Abroad, place de l'Indépendance, Dakar, Senegal.

DIAMOND, Baron (Life Peer), cr. 1970, of the City of Gloucester; **John Diamond,** F.C.A.; British politician; b. 30 April 1907, Leeds; s. of Solomon Diamond and Henrietta Beckerman; m.; two s. two d.; ed. Leeds Grammar School; Chartered Accountant; Labour M.P. for Blackley, Manchester 1945–51, Gloucester 1957–70; mem. Gen. Nursing Council and Chair. of its Finance and Gen. Purposes Cttee. 1947–53; Hon. Treas. Fabian Soc. 1950–64; Dir. Sadler's Wells Trust 1957–64; Hon. Treas. Labour Cttee. for Europe 1961–64; Chief. Sec. to the Treasury 1964–70; mem. Cabinet 1968–70; Hon. Treas. The European Movt.; Deputy Chair. of Cttees., House of Lords 1974; Chair. Royal Comm. on Distribution of Income and Wealth 1974–79, Prime Minister's Advisory Cttee. on Business Appts. of Crown Servants 1975–88; Privy Councillor; Chair. Industry and Parl. Trust 1977–82; Trustee, S.D.P. 1981–82, Leader S.D.P. in House of Lords 1982–88; LL.D. h.c. 1978. *Publications:* Public Expenditure in Practice 1975, co-author: Socialism the British Way 1948. *Leisure interests:* music. *Address:* House of Lords, London, S.W.1; Aynhoe, Doggetts Wood Lane, Chalfont St. Giles, Bucks., HP8 4TH, England. *Telephone:* (01494) 763229.

DIAMOND, Abel J., O.C., D.ENG., M.ARCH, M.A., F.R.A.I.C. A.R.I.B.A., R.C.A.; Canadian architect; b. 8 Nov. 1932, S. Africa; s. of Jacob Diamond and Rachel Zipporah Diamond (née Werner); m. Gillian Mary Huggins 1959; one s. one d.; ed. Univs. of Cape Town, Oxford and Pennsylvania; Asst. Prof. of Architecture and Architectural Asst. to Louis Kahn, Philadelphia 1963–64; Assoc. Prof., Univ. of Toronto 1964–69; Prof., Univ. of York 1969–72; Adjunct Prof., Univ. of Texas at Arlington 1980–81; Sr. Partner A. J. Diamond, Donald Schmitt and Co. 1975–; Chair. Nat. Capital Comm., Design Advisory Comm., Ottawa; Advisory Bd., School of Architecture, Univ. of Toronto 1987–; Commr. Ont. Human Rights Comm. 1986–89; Bd. of Govs., Mount Sinai Hosp., Toronto 1988–; Graham Prof. of Architecture, Univ. of Pa. 1996; mem. Royal Acad. of Arts (Canada), R.I.B.A., Canadian Inst. of Planners, American Inst. of Planners; Hon. Fellow A.I.A.; 29 design prizes; Toronto Arts Award 1990. *Works include:* Ontario Medical Asscn. HQ 1970, Univ. of Alberta Long Range Plan 1970, Alcan HQ Office, Toronto 1972, Montreal 1978, Cleveland 1982, Queen's Univ. Housing, Kingston, Ont. 1976, Citadel Theatre, Edmonton, Alberta 1976 (with B. Myers and R. L. Wilkin), Nat. Ballet School Stage Training Facility, Toronto 1983, Burns Bldg. Renovation, Calgary 1983, Berkeley Castle Renovation, Toronto 1983, Metro Toronto Central YMCA 1984, Ont. Arts Council HQ Offices, Toronto 1985, Four Seasons HQ Offices, Toronto 1985, Imperial Theatre, Saint John, N.B. 1988, Earth and Sciences Center, Univ. of Toronto 1988, Curtiss Hall, Toronto 1988, Sunny Brook Hosp., Newcastle Town Hall 1989, York Univ. Student Centre 1991, Lois Hancsey Aquatic Center 1991, Jerusalem City Hall 1992, Richmond Hill Cen. Library 1992, HQ Toronto Historic Bd. 1993, Israeli Foreign Ministry, Jerusalem 1996. *Leisure interest:* watercolour painting. *Address:* 2 Berkeley Street, Toronto, Ont. M5A 2W3, Canada (Office). *Telephone:* (416) 862-8800.

DIAMOND, Jared Mason, PH.D.; American biologist; b. 10 Sept. 1937, Boston; s. of Louis K. Diamond and Flora K. Diamond; m. Marie M. Cohen 1982; ed. Harvard Coll., Univ. of Cambridge, U.K.; Fellow Trinity Coll., Univ. of Cambridge 1961–65, Jr. Fellow Soc. of Fellows, Harvard Coll. 1962–65; Assoc. in Biophysics, Harvard Medical School 1965–66; Assoc. Prof. of Physiology, Univ. of Calif. Medical School, Los Angeles 1966–68, Prof. 1968–; Research Assoc. Dept. of Ornithology American Museum of Natural History; mem. N.A.S., Fellow American Acad. of Arts and Sciences; Burr Award of Nat. Geographical Soc. *Publications:* contrib. Discover magazine; The Avifauna of the Eastern Highlands of New Guinea 1972, Ecology and Evolution of Communities 1975, Community Ecology 1985, Guns, Germs and Steel: The Facts of Human Societies (Pulitzer Prize) 1998, several hundred research papers on physiology, ecology and ornithology. *Address:* Department of Physiology, University of California at Los Angeles Medical School, Los Angeles, CA 90024, U.S.A. *Telephone:* (310) 825-6177.

DIAMOND, Neil Leslie; American pop singer and composer; b. 24 Jan. 1941, Brooklyn; m. Marcia Murphey 1975, two c.; also two c. by previous m.; ed. New York Univ.; frmly. with Bang Records, Uni, MCA Records, Los Angeles; now recording artist with Columbia Records; guest artist, TV network shows; songs include Solitary Man, Cherry, Cherry, Kentucky Woman, I'm a Believer, September Morn, Sweet Caroline, Holly Holy, A Little Bit Me, A Little Bit You, Longfellow Serenade, Song Sung Blue, America, I Am, I Said; numerous albums 1966–; 19 platinum albums; 28 Gold albums; composer of film scores, Jonathan Livingston Seagull (Grammy Award) 1973, Every Which Way but Loose 1978, The Jazz Singer (also actor) 1980. *Address:* c/o Columbia Records, 2100 Colorado Avenue, Santa Monica, CA 90404, U.S.A.

DIANOV, Yevgeniy Mikhailovich; Russian physicist; b. 31 Jan. 1936, Tula; m. Helen Zagorovskaya 1968; one s. one d.; ed. Moscow State Univ.; researcher, Lebedev Inst. U.S.S.R. Acad. of Sciences 1960–72, sr. researcher 1972–80, Head of Lab. 1980–83; Head of Lab. Gen. Physics Inst. of U.S.S.R. Acad. of Sciences 1983–85, Head of Dept. of Gen. Physics 1985–88; Prof. Physical-Technical Inst. 1985–88; Deputy Dir. of Gen. Physics Inst. Acad. of Sciences of Russia 1988–93, Dir. Fibre Optics Research Centre, Gen. Physics Inst. 1993–; Corresp. mem. U.S.S.R. (now Russian) Acad. of Sciences 1987, mem. 1994; U.S.S.R. State Prize 1974; Popov Prize, U.S.S.R. Acad. of Sciences 1988. *Publications:* over 300 papers on quantum electronics, fibre and integrated optics. *Leisure interest:* jogging. *Address:* Fibre Optics Research Centre, General Physics Institute, RAS, 38 Vavilova Street, 117942 Moscow (Office); Leninsky Prospekt 13, Apt. 139, 117071 Moscow, Russia (Home). *Telephone:* (095) 135-05-66 (Office); (095) 237-32-76 (Home). *Fax:* (095) 135-81-39; (502) 224-71-34.

DIAZ, Cameron; American actress; b. 30 Aug. 1972, Long Beach, Calif.; d. of Emilio Diaz and Billie Diaz; fmr. model. *Films include:* The Mask, The Last Supper, Feeling Minnesota, She's the One, A Life Less Ordinary, There's Something About Mary 1998, Very Bad Things 1998. *Address:* c/o International Creative Management, 8942 Wilshire Boulevard, Beverly Hills, CA 90211, U.S.A.

DIBA, Farah (see Pahlavi, Farah Diba).

DIBDIN, Michael John, M.A.; British writer; b. 21 March 1947, Wolverhampton; s. of Frederick John Dibdin and Peigi Taylor; m. 1st Benita Mitbrodt 1971 (divorced 1986); m. 2nd Sybil Sheringham 1987 (divorced 1995); m. 3rd Kathrine Beck 1997; two d.; ed. Friends' School, Lisburn, N. Ireland, Univs. of Sussex and Alberta, Canada; CWA Gold Dagger Award 1988, Prix des Romans Policiers 1993. *Publications:* The Last Sherlock Holmes Story 1978, A Rich Full Death 1986, Ratking 1988, The Tryst 1989, Vendetta 1990, Dirty Tricks 1991, Cabal 1992, The Dying of the Light 1993, Dead Lagoon 1994, Dark Spectre 1995, Così fan Tutti 1996, A Long Finish 1998. *Leisure interests:* wine, music, travel. *Address:* c/o Pat Kavanagh, Peters, Fraser & Dunlop, 503/4 The Chambers, Chelsea Harbour, London, SW10 0XF, England. *Telephone:* 0171-344 1000.

DIBELA, Sir Kingsford, G.C.M.G., K.ST.J.; Papua New Guinea politician and teacher; b. 16 March 1932; s. of Norman Dibela and Edna Dalauna; m. Winifred Tomalarina 1952; two s. four d.; ed. St. Paul's Primary School,

Dogura; qualified as primary school teacher, teacher 1949–63; Pres. Weraura Local Govt. Council 1963–77; M.P. 1975–82, Speaker of Nat. Parl. 1977–80; Gov.-Gen. 1983–89. *Leisure interests:* golf, sailing and cricket. *Address:* P.O. Box 113, Port Moresby, Papua New Guinea.

DI BELGIOJOSO, Lodovico Barbiano; Italian architect; b. 1 Dec. 1909, Milan; s. of Alberico Barbiano and Margherita (née Confalonieri) di Belgiojoso; m. Carolina Cicogna Mozzoni 1934; two s. two d.; ed. School of Architecture, Milan; Architect 1932; Prof. of Architecture 1949; Prof. Venice Univ. Inst. of Architecture 1956–63; Prof. of Architectural Composition, School of Architecture, Milan Polytechnic 1963; private practice with Peressutti and Rogers in town planning, architecture, interior decoration and industrial design; mem. Nat. Council of Italian Town Planning Inst.; mem. Acad. di S. Luca, Rome; *works include* houses, factories, pavilions; Italian Merchant Navy Pavilion, Paris Int. Exhbn. 1937; health resort for children, Legnano 1939; Post Office, Rome 1939; monument to the dead in German concentration camps, Milan cemetery 1946; U.S. Pavilion at Triennale 1951; Olivetti Showroom, Fifth Avenue, New York, and Labyrinth at the Tenth Triennale 1954; restoration and re-arrangement of Castello Sforzesco Museums 1956; skyscraper Torre Velasca, Milan 1957; Canadian Pavilion, Venice Biennale; collaborator Italian Pavilion, Brussels Exhbn. 1958; Hispano Olivetti Building, Barcelona 1965; consultant motorways throughout Italy 1970; Messina Univ. 1973; Gratosoglio housing devt., Milan 1976; Renovation of Royal Palace as Museum, Milan 1978, Galleria Sabanda Museum, Turin 1983, Stock Exchange, Milan 1985, 19th century bldg. for offices, Milan 1986; Designer, Extension of Law Courts, Messina 1988; Extension of Messina Univ. 1989. *Publications:* (in collaboration with Banfi, Peressutti and Rogers): Piano regolatore della Val d'Aosta 1937, Piano A.R. 1946, Stile 1936, etc. *Leisure interests:* arts, poetry. *Address:* Studio Architetti B.B.P.R., 2 via dei Chiostri, 20121 Milan (Office); 8 via Perugia, 20121 Milan, Italy. *Telephone:* 86463085 (Office); 784362 (Home).

DIBIAGGIO, John A., D.D.S., M.A.; American university administrator; b. 11 Sept. 1932, San Antonio; s. of Ciro DiBiaggio and Acidalia DiBiaggio; m. Nancy Cronemiller 1989; one s. two d. (from previous marriage); ed. E. Mich. Univ., Univ. of Detroit and Univ. of Mich.; gen. dentistry practice, New Baltimore, Mich. 1958–65; Asst. Prof. School of Dentistry, Univ. of Detroit 1965–67; Asst. Dean Student Affairs, Univ. of Ky. 1967–70; Prof., Dean, School of Dentistry, Va. Commonwealth Univ. Richmond 1970–76; Vice-Pres. for Health Affairs, Exec. Dir. Health Center, Univ. of Conn. Farmington 1976–79; Pres. Univ. of Conn. Storrs 1979–85, Mich. State Univ. E. Lansing 1985–92, Tufts Univ., Medford, Mass. 1992–; mem. numerous comms. and professional socs.; six hon. degrees; Order of Merit (Italy), Pierre Fauchard Gold Medal Award 1987, 1989. *Publications:* Applied Practice Management: A Strategy for Stress Control (with others) 1979; articles in professional journals. *Leisure interest:* tennis. *Address:* Tufts University, Office of the President, Medford, MA 02155, U.S.A. (Office).

DiCAPRIO, Leonardo; American actor; b. 11 Nov. 1974, Hollywood; s. of George DiCaprio and Irmelin DiCaprio. *Films include:* Critters III 1991, Poison Ivy 1992, This Boy's Life 1993, What's Eating Gilbert Grape 1993, The Quick and the Dead 1995, The Basketball Diaries 1995, William Shakespeare's Romeo and Juliet 1996, Titanic 1996, Man in the Iron Mask 1997. *TV series include:* Parenthood 1990, Growing Pains 1991. *Address:* c/o Addis Wechsler and Associates, 955 Carrillo Drive, Floor 3D, Los Angeles, CA 90048, U.S.A.

DICHTER, Misha, B.S.; American concert pianist; b. 27 Sept. 1945, Shanghai, China; s. of Leon Dichter and Lucy Dichter; m. Cipa Dichter 1968; two s.; ed. Juilliard School of Music under Rosina Lhevinne; winner, Silver Medal, Tchaikovsky Int. Competition, Moscow 1966; since then has performed with leading orchestras and at festivals and given recitals worldwide; also performs with wife as piano duo. *Publications:* articles in New York Times, Ovation and Keyboard magazines. *Leisure interests:* tennis, jogging, drawing, sketching. *Address:* c/o CAMI, Mushalla Division, 165 W. 57th Street, New York, NY 10019, U.S.A.

DICK, Paul Wyatt, Q.C., B.A., B.C.; Canadian politician and barrister; b. 27 Oct. 1940, Kapuskasing, Ont.; s. of William Wyatt Dick and Constance Grace Harrison; m. Judith Ann Parish 1971; two s.; ed. Trinity Coll. School, Univ. of Western Ont., Univ. of New Brunswick; early career as a barrister and solicitor; Asst. Crown Attorney, Carleton Co. 1969–72; Chair. Ont. Fed. Progressive Conservative Caucus 1974–78; Q.C. 1981; Sr. Partner Dick and Nichols, Ottawa; Ont. Opposition Deputy House Leader 1983–84, Parl. Sec. to Govt. House Leader 1984, Parl. Sec. to Pres. of Queen's P.C. 1985; M.P. 1972–93, Parl. Sec. to Pres. of Treasury Bd. 1985; Assoc. Minister of Nat. Defence 1986–89, Minister for Supply and Services 1989–93, of Public Works and Govt. Services 1993; financial consultant Merrill Lynch Canada Inc. 1994–; Progressive Conservative. *Address:* Merrill Lynch Canada Incorporated, Suite 800-50, O'Connor Street, Ottawa, Ont., K1P 6L2 (Office); 75 Shaughnessy Crescent, Kanata, Ont., K2K 2N1, Canada (Home).

DICKENS, Arthur Geoffrey, C.M.G., M.A., D.LIT., D.LITT., LITT.D., F.B.A., F.S.A.; British university administrator (retd.) and professor of history; b. 6 July 1910, Hull, Yorks.; s. of Arthur J. Dickens and Gertrude H. (Grasby) Dickens; m. Molly Bygott 1936 (died 1978); two s.; ed. Hymers Coll., Hull and Magdalen Coll. Oxford; Fellow, Keble Coll. Oxford 1933–49; served R.A. 1940–45, rank of Capt.; Prof. of History and Head of Dept., Univ. of Hull 1949–62, Pro-Vice-Chancellor 1959–62; Prof. of History and Head of Dept., King's Coll. London 1962–67; Dir. Inst. of Historical Research, Univ. of London 1967–77, Prof. Emer. 1977–; Foreign Sec. British Acad. 1967–77; mem. numerous cttees. and holder of various nat. and int. offices; five hon. degrees; Norton Medlicott Medal (Historical Asscn.) 1985; Commdr.'s Cross, Order of Merit (Fed. Repub. of Germany) 1980. *Publications:* Lübeck Diary 1947, Lollards and Protestants 1959, The English Reformation 1964, Reformation and Society in Europe 1966, The Age of Humanism and Reformation 1972, The German Nation and Martin Luther 1974, The Reformation in Historical Thought (with J. M. Tonkin) 1985, Erasmus the Reformer (jtly.) 1994, Late Monasticism and the Reformation 1994; numerous articles in learned journals. *Leisure interests:* art history, especially English painting 1890–1950. *Address:* 401 Carole House, Oldfield Estate, Fitzroy Road, London, NW1 8UA, England.

DICKIE, Brian James; British opera director; b. 23 July 1941; s. of the late Robert Kelso and of Harriet Elizabeth (née Riddell) Dickie; m. 1st Victoria Teresa Sheldon (née Price) 1968; two s. one d.; m. 2nd Nancy Gustafson 1989; ed. Trinity Coll., Dublin; Admin. Asst. Glyndebourne Opera 1962–66; Admin. Glyndebourne Touring Opera 1967–81; Opera Man. Glyndebourne Festival Opera 1970–81, Gen. Admin. 1981–89; Artistic Dir. Wexford Festival 1967–73; Artistic Advisor Théâtre Musical de Paris 1981–87; Gen. Dir. Canadian Opera Co. 1989–93; Artistic Counsellor Opéra de Nice 1994–97; Gen. Dir. EU Opera 1997–; Chair. London Choral Soc. 1978–85, Theatres Nat. Cttee. Opera Cttee. 1976–85; Vice-Chair. Theatres Nat. Cttee. 1980–85; Vice-Pres. Theatrical Man. Assoc. 1983–85; mem. Bd. Opera America 1991–. *Address:* 6A Pont Street, London, SW1X 9EL, England. *Telephone:* 0171-235 7671.

DICKIE, Lloyd M., PH.D., F.R.S.C.; Canadian ecologist; b. 6 March 1926, Kingsport, N.S.; s. of Ebenezer Cox Dickie and Pearl (née Sellars) Dickie; m. Marjorie C. Bowman 1952; one s. two d.; ed. Acadia Univ., Yale Univ., Univ. of Toronto; research scientist, Fisheries Research Bd., N.B. 1951–62, Great Lakes Inst., Toronto 1962–65; Dir. Marine Ecology Lab., Bedford Inst. Oceanography, Dartmouth, N.S. 1965–74; Chair. and Prof. of Oceanography, Dalhousie Univ., Halifax 1974–77, Dir. Inst. of Environmental Studies, Dalhousie Univ. 1974–76; Research Scientist, Marine Ecology Lab. and Marine Fish Div., Bedford Inst. of Oceanography, Dartmouth, N.S. 1976–87, Sr. Research Scientist Biological Sciences Br., Dept. of Fisheries and Oceans 1987–93, participant in Ocean Production Enhancement Network 1991–92, Scientist Emer. 1994–; Oscar-Sette Memorial Award (American Fish Soc.) 1991. *Publications:* Ad Mare: Canada Looks to the Sea (with R. W. Stewart) 1971; some 80 scientific papers. *Address:* c/o Bedford Institute of Oceanography, P.O. Box 1006, Dartmouth, N.S., B2Y 4A2 (Office); 7 Lakewood Court, Dartmouth, N.S., B2X 2R6, Canada (Home). *Telephone:* (902) 426-7368 (Office); (902) 435-1545 (Home).

DICKINSON, Angie (pseudonym of Angeline Brown); American actress; b. 30 Sept. 1931, Kulm, N.D.; ed. Immaculate Heart Coll., Glendale Coll. *Films:* Lucky Me 1954, Man With the Gun, The Return of Jack Slade, Tennessee's Partner, The Black Whip, Hidden Guns, Tension at Table Rock, Gun the Man Down, Calypso Joe, China Gate, Shoot Out at Medicine Bend, Cry Terror, I Married a Woman, Rio Bravo, The Bramble Bush, Ocean's 11, A Fever in the Blood, The Sins of Rachel Cade, Jessica, Rome Adventure, Captain Newman M.D., The Killers, The Art of Love, Cast a Giant Shadow, The Chase, The Poppy is Also a Flower, the Last Challenge, Point Blank, Sam Whiskey, Some Kind of a Nut, Young Billy Young, Pretty Maids All in a Row, The Resurrection of Zachary Wheeler, The Outside Man, Big Bad Mama, Klondike Fever, Dressed to Kill, Charlie Chan and the Curse of the Dragon Queen, Death Hunt, Big Bad Mama II, Even Cowgirls Get the Blues, The Maddening, Sabrina, The Sun—The Moon and The Stars. *Television series:* Police Woman, Cassie & Co. *Television films:* The Love War, Thief, See the Man Run, The Norliss Tapes, Pray for the Wildcats, A Sensitive Passionate Man, Overboard, The Suicide's Wife, Dial M for Murder, One Shoe Makes it Murder, Jealousy, A Touch of Scandal, Stillwatch, Police Story: The Freeway Killings, Once Upon a Texas Train, Prime Target, Treacherous Crossing, Danielle Steel's Remembrance; mini-series: Pearl, Hollywood Wives, Wild Palms.

DICKINSON, Christopher John, M.A., M.SC., D.M., F.R.C.P., F.R.S.A., A.R.C.O.; British professor of medicine and physician; b. 1 Feb. 1927, Sydney, Australia; s. of Reginald Ernest Dickinson and Margaret Dickinson; m. Elizabeth Patricia Farrell 1953; two s. two d.; ed. Berkhamsted School, Oxford Univ., Univ. Coll. Hosp. Medical School, London; jr. medical posts, Univ. Coll. Hosp., London 1953–54; R.A.M.C., jr. medical specialist 1955–56; Registrar and Research Fellow, Middx. Hosp., London 1957–60; Rockefeller Travelling Fellow, Cleveland Clinic, U.S.A. 1960–61; Lecturer, Sr. Lecturer and Consultant, Univ. Coll. Hosp. and Medical School, London 1962–75; Prof. of Medicine and Chair. Dept. of Medicine, St. Bartholomew's Hosp. Medical Coll., London 1975–92, now Prof. Emer.; Visiting Prof. Wolfson Inst., St. Bartholomew's Hosp. Medical Coll.; Sr. Censor and Sr. Vice-Pres., Royal Coll. of Physicians of London 1982–83; mem. MRC 1986–90; Vice-Chair. Council British Heart Foundation 1995–; Medical Adviser Jules Thorn Charitable Trust 1994–. *Publications:* Electrophysiological Technique 1950, Clinical Pathology Data 1951, Clinical Physiology 1959, Neurogenic Hypertension 1965, Computer Model of Human Respiration 1977, Software for Educational Computing 1980, Neurogenic Hypertension 1991. *Leisure interests:* theatre, opera, playing the organ. *Address:* Wolfson Institute of Preventive Medicine, Charterhouse Square, London, EC1M 6BQ (Office); Griffin Cottage, 57 Belsize

Lane, London, NW3 5AU, England (Home). *Telephone:* 0171-982 6219 (Office); 0171-431 1845 (Home). *Fax:* 0171-982 6270.

DICKSON, Jennifer, O.C., R.A.; Canadian artist and photographer; b. 17 Sept. 1936, S. Africa; d. of the late John L. Dickson and Margaret J. (Turner) Dickson; m. Ronald A. Sweetman 1962; one s.; ed. Goldsmiths' Coll. School of Art, Univ. of London; Assoc. Atelier 17 (graphic workshop), Paris 1960–65; teacher, Brighton Coll. of Art 1961–68, Univ. of W. Indies, Jamaica 1968, Univ. of Wis. 1972, Saidye Bronfman Centre, Montreal 1970–71, 1982–83, Ohio Univ., Athens 1973, 1979, Univ. of S. Ill. 1973, Calif. State Univ., Sacremento 1974, Denison Univ. 1976, Univ. of Ottawa 1980–83 (Sessional Instructor 1980-85); lecturer, History of Art, Montreal Museum of Fine Arts 1988–91; visiting artist at many univs., colls. etc.; has held more than 55 one-woman exhbns. in six countries and participated in more than 350 group exhbns; works in numerous public collections in Canada, U.S.A., U.K., Europe, New Zealand, Australia and S. Africa including Nat. Gallery of Canada, Metropolitan Museum, New York, British Museum, London and Hermitage Museum, Leningrad; Fellow, Royal Soc. of Painter-Etchers and Engravers; Hon. LL.D. (Univ. of Alberta) 1988; awards include Prix de Jeunes Artistes pour Gravure, Biennale de Paris 1963, Special Purchase Award, World Print Competition, San Francisco Museum of Art 1974, Biennale Prize, 5th Norwegian Int. Print Biennale 1980. *Publications:* The Hospital for Wounded Angels 1987, The Royal Academy Gardener's Journal 1991, and suites of original prints and photographs. *Leisure interests:* historic gardens, opera, films. *Address:* 20 Osborne Street, Ottawa, Ont., K1S 4Z9, Canada. *Telephone:* (613) 233-2315 (Studio); (613) 730-2083 (Home). *Fax:* (613) 730-1818 (Home).

DICKSON, Peter George Muir, D.LITT., F.B.A.; British professor of history; b. 26 April 1929, London; s. of William Muir Dickson and Regina Dowdall-Nicolls; m. Ariane Flore Faye 1964; one d.; ed. St. Paul's School, London, Worcester Coll., Oxford; Fellow Nuffield Coll., Oxford 1954–56; Tutor, St. Catherine's Soc., Oxford 1956–60, Fellow St. Catherine's Coll. 1960–96, Emer. Fellow 1996–, Univ. Reader in Modern History 1978–89, Prof. of Early Modern History 1989–96, Emer. Prof. 1996–. *Publications:* The Sun Insurance Office 1710–1960 1960, The Financial Revolution in England 1688–1756 1967, Finance and Government under Maria Theresia 1740–1780 1987. *Leisure interests:* tennis, swimming, cinema, art. *Address:* Field House, Iffley, Oxford, OX4 4EG, England (Home). *Telephone:* (01865) 271700 (Office); (01865) 779599 (Home).

DICKSON, Robert George Brian, P.C., C.C., K.ST.J., LL.B., D.CN.L., C.D.; Canadian lawyer; b. 25 May 1916, Yorkton, Sask.; s. of Thomas Dickson and Sarah Elizabeth Gibson; m. Barbara Melville 1943; three s. one d.; ed. Regina Collegiate Inst., Univ. of Manitoba and Manitoba Law School; served with Royal Canadian Artillery 1940–45; called to Man. Bar 1940; Lawyer, Aikins, MacAuley & Co. 1945–63; Lecturer, Man. Law School 1948–54; apptd. to Court of Queen's Bench, Man. 1963, Court of Appeal 1967, Justice, Supreme Court of Canada 1973–84, Chief Justice of Canada 1984–90, Deputy Gov.-Gen.; Life Bencher, Law Soc., Man.; Hon. Bencher, Lincoln's Inn 1984, Law Soc. of Upper Canada 1997; Hon. Fellow, American Coll. of Trial Lawyers; Hon. Prof., Univ. of Man. 1985; Chancellor, Diocese of Rupert's Land, Anglican Church of Canada 1960–71; mem. Bd. of Trustees, the Sellers Foundation; Hon. LL.D. (Man.) 1973, (Sask.) 1978, (Ottawa) 1979, (Queen's) 1980, (Dalhousie) 1983, (York) 1985, (B.C.) 1986, (Toronto) 1986, (Laurentian) 1986, (Yeshiva) 1987, (McGill) 1987, (Carleton) 1988, (Mount Allison) 1989, (Brock) 1990, (Winnipeg) 1991, (Western) 1992, (Law Soc. of Upper Canada) 1993, (Univ. of Victoria) 1993; K.St.J. 1985, Commandeur, Ordre ynat. du Mérite 1994, Kt. Marshall Mil. and Hospitaller Order of St. Lazarus of Jerusalem 1996, Vimy Award 1997. *Leisure interest:* riding. *Address:* 360 Berry Side Rd., Dunrobin, Ontario, Canada.

DIDION, Joan, B.A.; American writer; b. 5 Dec. 1934, Sacramento; d. of Frank Reese Didion and Eduene (née Jerrett) Didion; m. John G. Dunne 1964; one d.; ed. Univ. of California, Berkeley; Assoc. Features Ed. Vogue magazine 1956–63; fmr. columnist Saturday Evening Post, fmr. contributing ed. Nat. Review; now freelance writer; awarded 1st Prize Vogue's Prix de Paris 1956, Morton Dauwen Zabel prize (American Asscn. of Arts and Letters) 1978, Edward McDowell Medal 1996. *Publications: novels* Run River 1963, Play It as It Lays 1970, A Book of Common Prayer 1977, Democracy 1984, The Last Thing He Wanted 1996; *essays:* Slouching Towards Bethlehem 1969, The White Album 1978, After Henry 1992; *non-fiction* Salvador 1983, Miami 1987, After Henry 1992. *Screenplays for films:* The Panic in Needle Park 1971, A Star is Born 1976, True Confessions 1981, Up Close and Personal 1996. *Address:* c/o Janklow & Nesbit, 598 Madison Avenue, New York, NY 10022, U.S.A.

DIEBOLD, John, M.B.A., LL.D., SC.D., D.ENG.; American management consultant; b. 8 June 1926, Weehawken, N.J.; s. of William and Rose (Theurer) Diebold; m. 1st Doris Hackett 1951 (divorced 1975); one d.; m. 2nd Vanessa von der Porten 1982; one s. one d.; ed. Swarthmore Coll. and Harvard Business School; with Griffenhagen & Assocs., management consultants, New York City, also Chicago 1951–57, owner 1957–, merged with Louis J. Kroeger and Assocs. to become Griffenhagen-Kroeger Inc., Chair. Bd. 1960–; established Diebold Group Inc., New York City 1954, Pres., Chair. Board Chicago 1954–; est. Urwick Diebold Ltd., England 1958, Co-Chair. 1958–79; est. Raadgevend Bur. Berenschot-Diebold, N.V. 1958, Diebold Europe, S.A., Pres. 1960–91; Chair. Diebold Computer Leasing Inc. 1967–76, Gemini Computer Systems Inc. 1968–76, INTERMODAL Transport Systems Inc. 1969–76; Dir. Genesco 1969–; U.S. Council Trusteeship, Int. Chamber of Commerce 1972–; Dir. Acad. for Educ. Devt. 1972–; Dir. Prentice-Hall Inc. 1981–85; Trustee Nat. Planning Asscn. 1973–, Carnegie Inst., Washington 1975–, Overseas Devt. Council 1974–82 (mem. Advisory Bd. 1982–), Lehigh Univ. June 1987–; Fellow, Int. Acad. of Man. 1983–; Chair. Int. mem. Advisory Bd., Inst. of French Studies, N.Y. Univ. 1984, Advisory Comm. Deutsches Museum, Munich 1984–; Pres. World Man. Council (CIOS) 1986–89; Order of Merit, Italy; Grand Cross 1971; Chevalier, Légion d'honneur; several hon. degrees; coiner of word automation. *Publications:* Automation—The Advent of the Automatic Factory 1952, Beyond Automation 1964, Man and the Computer Technology as an Agent of Social Change 1969, Business Decisions and Technological Change 1970, The Role of Business in Society 1983; Ed. World of the Computer 1973, Making the Future Work 1984, Business in the Age of Information 1985, Managing Information: The Challenge and the Opportunity 1985, The Innovators 1990. *Address:* J.D. Consulting Group Inc., P.O. Box 515, Bedford Hills, NY 10507, U.S.A. (Office).

DIEL, Rolf; German banking executive; b. 20 Sept. 1922, Bochum; fmr. Chair. Supervisory Bd. Dresdner Bank AG. *Address:* Theodor-Andersen-Strasse 1, 4000 Düsseldorf, Germany. *Telephone:* 432723 (Office).

DIENER, Theodor Otto, D.SC.; American plant virologist; b. 28 Feb. 1921, Zürich, Switzerland; s. of Theodor E. Diener and Hedwig R. Baumann; m. Sybil Mary Fox 1968; three s. (from previous m.); ed. Swiss Fed. Inst. of Tech., Zürich; Plant Pathologist, Swiss Fed. Agricultural Research Station, Waedenswil 1948–49; Asst. Prof. of Plant Pathology Rhode Island State Univ., Kingston, U.S.A. 1950; Asst.-Assoc. Plant Pathologist, Wash. State Univ., Prosser 1950–59; Research Plant Pathologist, Plant Virology Lab., Agricultural Research Service, U.S. Dept. of Agric., Beltsville, Md. 1959–88; Collaborator, Agricultural Research Service, U.S. Dept. of Agric., Beltsville, Md. 1988–97; Prof., Center for Agric. Biotech. and Dept. of Botany, Univ. of Md., College Park 1988–, Acting Dir. Center for Agric. Biotech. 1991–92; Distinguished Univ. Prof. 1994–; Distinguished Prof. Univ. of Md. Biotech. Inst. 1998–; discovered and named viroids, smallest known agents of infectious disease; mem. N.A.S., American Acad. of Arts and Sciences, Leopoldina (German Acad. of Nat. Scientists); Fellow N.Y. Acad. of Sciences, American Phytopathological Soc.; Campbell Award, American Inst. of Biological Sciences 1968; Superior Service Award, U.S. Dept. of Agric. 1969, Distinguished Service Award 1977; Alexander von Humboldt Award (Fed. Repub. of Germany) 1975; Wolf Prize (Israel) 1987, E. C. Stakman Award, Univ. of Minn. 1988; Nat. Medal of Science (U.S.A.) 1987; Science Hall of Fame, Agricultural Research Service, U.S. Dept. of Agriculture 1989. *Publications:* Viroids and Viroid Diseases, Ed. The Viroids 1987, numerous chapters in scientific books and more than 200 scientific papers. *Leisure interest:* private pilot. *Address:* Center for Agricultural Biotechnology, Univ. Maryland, College Park, MD 20742 (Office); 11711 Battersea Drive, P.O. Box 272, Beltsville, MD 20705, U.S.A. (Home). *Telephone:* (301) 504-6202 (Office). *Fax:* (301) 504-5449.

DIENSTBIER, Jiři; Czech politician, journalist and writer; b. 20 April 1937, Kladno; s. of Jiři Dienstbier and Anna Dienstbierova; one s. three d.; ed. Charles Univ., Prague; ed., Czechoslovak Broadcasting 1959; foreign correspondent in Far East, U.S.S.R., Germany, France, U.K., Yugoslavia 1960–68; U.S.A. 1968–69; dismissed from broadcasting 1970; worked in archives of an eng. company; expelled from Czechoslovak CP and Journalists' Union 1969; signed Charter 1977, spokesman 1979; sentenced to three years in prison 1979–82; boilerman 1982–89; spokesman for Charter 77 1985–86; ed. of Čtverec (The Square), a periodical on int. politics 1979–; co-founder of Lidové Noviny (The People's Newspaper) 1988–; Czechoslovak Minister for Foreign Affairs 1989–92; mem. Council of State 1990–92, Deputy Prime Minister CFSR 1990–92, Deputy to House of People Fed. Ass. 1990–92, Chair. Council of the Civic Movt. 1991–; Chair. Free Democrats Party (fmrly. Civic Movt.) 1993–95 (merged with Liberal Nat. Social Party 1995); Chair. Liberal Nat. Social Party 1995–96 (left Party 1997); Chair. Czech Council on Foreign Relations; mem. Comm. on Global Governance; mem. UN Cttee. for Solving Global Problems 1995–; Special Envoy to Gen. Ass. of UN 1995; lecturer 1998–; Special Rapporteur of the UN Comm. on Human Rights for Bosnia and Herzegovina, Croatia and Yugoslavia 1998–; Dr. h.c. (Univ. du Bourgogne) 1993; Humanist of the Year (U.S.A.) 1979; Grand Cross of Order for Merit (Order of Kt.'s of Malta) 1990, Francesco Cossiga Medal (Italy) 1991, Pro Merito Medal, Parl. Ass. Council of Europe 1991. *Publications include:* The Night Began at Three in the Morning 1967, Before We Roast Young Pigs 1976, Christmas Present 1977, Guests 1978; Charter 77—Human Rights and Socialism 1981, Dreaming of Europe 1990, From Dreams to Reality 1999; stage plays, articles and essays in samizdat. *Leisure interests:* reading, music, history. *Address:* Apolinářská 6, 12800 Prague 2, Czech Republic. *Telephone:* (2) 292534. *Fax:* (2) 292534.

DIEPGEN, Eberhard; German politician; b. 13 Nov. 1941, Berlin; m. Monika Adler 1975; one s. one d.; ed. Free Univ. of Berlin; joined CDU 1962, later Chair., W. Berlin CDU; mem. Berlin Chamber of Deputies 1971–81; mem. Bundestag (Parl.) as W. Berlin Rep. 1980–81; Mayor of Berlin 1984–89, 1991–. *Leisure interests:* soccer, European history. *Address:* Berliner Rathaus, 10173 Berlin, Germany. *Telephone:* (030) 2401 3000.

DIESEL, John Phillip, B.S.; American business executive; b. 10 June 1926, St. Louis, Mo.; s. of John Henry and Elsa A. (Poetting) Diesel; m. Rita Jan Meyer 1949; one s. three d.; ed Washington Univ., St. Louis, Mo.; Exec. Asst.

Div. Man., McQuay-Norris Mfg. Co., St. Louis 1951–57; Partner Booz, Allen and Hamilton Inc., Chicago 1957–61; Vice-Pres. Operations, Operations Research Inc., Santa Monica, Calif. 1961–62; Vice-Pres., Treas. and Dir. Management Technology Inc., Los Angeles 1962–63; Dir. Marketing and Planning, A. O. Smith Corpn., Milwaukee, Wis. 1963–65, Dir. Mfg. and Engineering 1965–67, Vice-Pres. Mfg. and Planning 1967–70, Group Vice-Pres. 1970–72; Chair. Armor Elevator Can. Ltd. 1970–72; Chair. and Pres. Armor Elevator Co. Inc. 1970–72; Pres., C.E.O., Newport News (Va.) Shipbuilding and Dry Dock Co. 1972–78, Chair. 1976–78; Exec. Vice-Pres. Tenneco Inc. 1976–79, Pres. 1979–89; Chair. Bd. of Albright and Wilson Ltd. (London, England) 1981–89; Dir. Tenneco Inc., Aluminum Co. of America, Cooper Industries Inc., First City Bancorpn. of Texas Inc., Poclain S.A., Allied Stores Corpn. *Address:* 327 Longwoods Lane, Houston, TX 77024, U.S.A. (Home).

DIEZ de VELASCO, Manuel, D. EN D.; Spanish judge and professor of international law; b. 22 May 1926, Santander; s. of Faustino Manuel Diez de Velasco and Mercedes Vallejo; m. Josefina-Tomasa Abellan y Vota 1959; ed. Valladolid, Madrid and Rome Univs., Int. Law Acad., The Hague; Prof. of Int. Law, Univ. of Granada 1959–61, Univ. of Barcelona 1961–71, Univ. Autónoma de Madrid 1971–74, Complutense Univ. of Madrid 1974–; Judge Constitutional Court 1980–86, Court of Justice, EEC 1988–; mem. Inst. de Droit Int.; Dir. Revista de Inst. Europeas; Pres. Spanish Asscn. of Profs. of Int. Law and Int. Relations. *Publications include:* Curso de Derecho Internacional Público, Vol. 1 1963, La Protection diplomatique des sociétés et des actionnaires 1974, Instituciones de Derecho Internacional, and numerous papers on aspects of int. law. *Address:* c/o Palais de la Cour de Justice, 2925 Luxembourg.

DIFORIO, Robert G., B.A.; American publishing executive; b. 19 March 1940, Mamaroneck, N.Y.; s. of Richard John Diforio Sr. and Mildred Kuntz; m. Birgit Rasmussen 1983; one s. one d.; ed. Williams Coll., Mass. and Harvard Business School; Vice-Pres. Kable News Co. 1970; Vice-Pres. and Sales Man. New American Library (NAL) 1972, Sr. Vice-Pres. and Marketing Dir. 1976, Pres. and Publisher 1980–81, C.E.O. and Chair. Bd. NAL/E. P. Dutton 1983–89; Prin. D4EO Unlimited Inc. 1991–. *Leisure interests:* reading, children, golf. *Address:* 7 Indian Valley Road, Weston, CT 06883, U.S.A. (Home).

DIJOUD, Paul Charles Louis; French politician; b. 25 July 1938, Neuilly-sur-Seine; s. of Jules-Raoul Dijoud and Andrée Claquin; m. Catherine Cochaux 1968 (divorced 1983); one s. one d.; m. 2nd Maryse Dolivot 1988; ed. Lycée Condorcet, Faculté de Droit de Paris, Inst. d'Etudes politiques de Paris; Student at Ecole Nat. d'Admin. 1964–66; Commercial attaché, dept. of external econ. relations in Ministry of Econ. and Finance; elected to Nat. Ass. 1967, 1968, 1973, 1978, defeated 1981; Asst. Sec.-Gen. Ind. Republican Party 1967–69; Conseiller Général for canton of Embrun 1968–88; Pres. Ind. Republican Exec. Cttee. for Provence-Côte d'Azur 1968–88; Mayor of Briançon 1971–83; Sec. of State attached to Prime Minister's Office 1973–74, later to Minister of Cultural Affairs and the Environment, to Minister of Employment with Responsibility for Immigrant Workers 1974, Secretary of State for Sport 1977, for Overseas Depts. and Territories 1978; Commercial Adviser to cen. admin. Ministry of Economy and Finance 1981; Man. Dir. Cie. Commerciale Sucres et Denrées 1982–84; Pres. Comidex 1984; Pres. Conseil d'administration du parc national des Ecrins 1973; Plenipotentiary Minister 1988; Amb. to Colombia 1988–91, to Mexico 1992–94; Minister of State with responsibility for the principality of Monaco 1994–97; Amb. to Argentina 1997–. *Address:* French Embassy, Cerrito 1399, Buenos Aires, Argentina.

DIKSHIT, Uma Shankar; Indian politician and journalist; b. 12 Jan. 1901, Ugoo Dist., Uttar Pradesh; s. of late Ram Swarup and Jwala Devi Dikshit; m. Shiva Pyari Dikshit 1915; two s.; ed. Govt. School and Christchurch Coll., Kanpur; Sec. Kanpur City Congress Cttee. and mem. Uttar Pradesh Congress Cttee. 1920–25; imprisoned for participation in Non-Co-operation Movt. 1921–23; Pres. Uttar Bharatiya Sabha and Hindi Bhashi Sammendan 1925–30; active in underground movt. 1932, imprisoned 1930–31, 1931–33; Hon. Sec. Hindustani Prachar Sabha, Bombay 1934–41; joined Quit India Movt. 1942, detained until 1944; Custodian Evacuee Property, New Delhi 1948–52; Hon. Adviser, Nat. Small Industries Corpn. 1956; Man. Dir. Associated Journals Ltd., Lucknow 1957–71; mem. Rajya Sabha 1961–76; mem. All India Congress Cttee., mem. and Hon. Treas. Indian Nat. Congress 1969–76, Gen. Sec. 1971–72; Minister of Works and Housing, later also of Health and Family Planning 1971–73, of Home Affairs 1973–74, without Portfolio 1974–75, of Shipping and Transport Feb.-Nov. 1975; Gov. of Karnataka 1976–77, resgnd. and rejoined working Cttee., All India Congress Cttee. Aug. 1977; Gov. West Bengal 1984–86; re-appointed mem. Congress Working Cttee. 1987; Chair. two Congress Organizational Cttees. 1987. *Leisure interests:* reading, swimming, badminton.

DILENSCHNEIDER, Robert, M.A.; American business executive; b. 21 Oct. 1943, New York; s. of Sigmund J. Dilenschneider and Martha Witucki; m. Janet Hennessey 1969; two s.; ed. Univ. of Notre Dame and Ohio State Univ.; Account Supervisor, Hill and Knowlton Inc., New York 1967–70, Vice-Pres. 1970–73, Sr. Vice-Pres. 1973–80, Exec. Vice-Pres., Chicago 1980–84, Pres. and C.O.O., Chicago 1984–86, Pres. and C.E.O. Hill and Knowlton, New York 1986–91; Prin. The Dilenschneider Group Inc., New York 1991–; mem. U.S. Japan Business Council, Public Relations Soc. of America, Int. Public Relations Asscn.; mem. Advisory Bd. New York Hosp., Cornell Medical Center, Coll. of Business Admin. at Univ. of Notre Dame; recipient, New York's Big Apple Award. *Publications:* Power and Influence: A Briefing for Leaders 1991, On Power 1993. *Address:* Dilenschneider Group Inc., 200 Park Avenue, New York, NY 10166, U.S.A.

DILIBERTO, Oliviero; Italian politician and professor of law; b. 13 Oct. 1956, Cagliari; s. of Marco Diliberto and Mariadonella Reale; m. Gabriella Serrenti 1997; ed. in Cagliari, Rome, Frankfurt and Paris; Prov. Sec. Juvenile Fed. of Italian Communist Party 1978; mem. Prov. Sec.'s Office, Italian Communist Party 1982; mem. Nat. Sec.'s Office, Reconstructed Communism Party 1994, Dir. Liberazione (party journal) 1994, leader Parl. Group 1995, now Pres. Progressive Parl. Group; fmrly. mem. Third Perm. Cttee. on Foreign and EC Affairs, Ninth Perm. Cttee. on Transport, Post and Telecommunications; Minister of Justice 1998–; also Prof. of Roman Law, Univ. of Cagliari. *Address:* Ministry of Justice, Via Arenula 70, 00186 Rome, Italy. *Telephone:* (06) 8897790.

DILIGENSKY, German Germanovich; Russian sociologist and historian; b. 22 Feb. 1930, Moscow; s. of German Diligensky and Natalia Diligensky; m. Maia Isayevna Novinskaya; one s.; ed. Moscow Univ.; grad. research, Inst. of History, U.S.S.R. Acad. of Sciences 1952–63; on staff of Inst. of World Econ. and Int. Relations (IMEMO) 1969–; Ed.-in-Chief of inst. journal ME i MO 1988–; Dir. Centre of Comparative Socio-economic and Socio-political Studies (CESPI) 1992–; mem. Int. Acad. of Informatization 1994–; mem. Bd., Moscow br. Inst. of Open Soc., U.S.S.R. State Prize 1977. *Publications:* North Africa in the 4th–5th Centuries 1961, Sozialpsychologie und Klassenbewusstsein der Arbeiterklasse im Heutigen Kapitalismus 1978, Search for Meaning and Aim 1986, Socio-political Psychology 1994. *Leisure interests:* reading, classical music, tourism, skiing, cycling. *Address:* Institute of World Economics and International Relations, Profsoyuznaya 23, 117859 Moscow (Office); B. Afanasyevski per. 17, 29 Moscow 121019, Russia (Home). *Telephone:* 128-47-09 (Office); 203-30-20 (Home).

DILKS, David Neville, B.A., F.R.S.L.; British professor of international history; b. 17 March 1938, Coventry; s. of Neville Ernest and Phyllis Dilks; m. Jill Medlicott 1963; one s.; ed. Royal Grammar School, Worcester, Hertford Coll. and St. Antony's Coll., Oxford; Asst. lecturer, lecturer LSE 1962–70; Prof. of Int. History, Univ. of Leeds 1970–91, Chair. School of History 1974–79, Dean Faculty of Arts 1975–77; Vice-Chancellor Univ. of Hull 1991–; Visiting Fellow All Souls' Coll., Oxford 1973; Chair. and Founder Commonwealth Youth Exchange Council 1968–73; mem. Advisory Council on Public Records 1977–85, Inst. of Contemporary British History 1986–, Univs. Funding Council 1988–91; Trustee Edward Boyle Memorial Trust 1982–96, Imperial War Museum 1983–91, Lennox-Boyd Trust 1984–91, Royal Commonwealth Soc. Library Trust 1987–91; Pres. Int. Cttee. for the History of the Second World War 1992–; Curzon Prize, Univ. of Oxford 1960; Liveryman, Goldsmiths Co. 1984; Prix du rayonnement de la langue française 1994; Médaille de Vermeil Acad. Française; Dr. h.c. (Russian Acad. of Sciences) 1996. *Publications:* Curzon in India (Vol. 1 & 2) 1969, 1970, The Diaries of Sir Alexander Cadogan (ed.) 1971, Retreat from Power (ed.) 1981, Neville Chamberlain: Pioneering & Reform, 1869–1929 1984, Barbarossa 1941—The Axis, The Allies and World War—Retrospect, Recollection, Revision (jt. ed.), Grossbritannien und der deutsche Wiederstand (jt.ed.) 1994, and numerous articles in learned journals. *Leisure interests:* ornithology, steam railways, organ music, Bentley cars. *Address:* Office of the Vice-Chancellor, Hull University, Cottingham Road, Hull HU6 7RX, England. *Telephone:* (01482) 465131. *Fax:* (01482) 466557.

DILLARD, Annie, M.A.; American author; b. 30 April 1945, Pittsburgh, Pa.; d. of Frank Doak and Gloria Lambert; m. 1st R. H. W. Dillard 1965; m. 2nd Gary Clevidence 1979; m. 3rd Robert D. Richardson, Jr. 1988; one d. two step.-d.; ed. Hollins College; contributing editor, Harper's Magazine 1974–85; Distinguished Visiting Prof. Wesleyan Univ. 1979–83, Adjunct Prof. 1983–, writer in residence 1987–; mem. Bd. of Dirs. Writers' Conf. 1984– (Chair. 1991–); mem. Nat. Cttee. on U.S.-China Relations, Century Asscn.; Pulitzer Prize (for Pilgrim at Tinker Creek) 1974, Nat. Endowment for the Arts (Literature) Grant 1981, John Simon Guggenheim Memorial Grant 1985, Gov.'s of Conn.'s Award 1993, The Campion Award 1994, The Milton Prize 1994. *Publications:* Tickets for a Prayer Wheel (poetry), Pilgrim at Tinker Creek (prose) 1974, Holy the Firm 1978, Living by Fiction 1982, Teaching a Stone to Talk 1982, Encounters with Chinese Writers 1984, An American Childhood 1987, The Writing Life 1989, The Living (novel) 1992, The Annie Dillard Reader 1994, Mornings Like This (poetry) 1995. *Address:* c/o Timothy Seldes, Russell and Volkering, 50 W. 29th New York, NY 10001, U.S.A.

DILLER, Barry; American entertainment executive; b. 2 Feb. 1942, San Franscisco; s. of Michael Diller and Reva (née Addison) Diller; Vice-Pres. feature films and movies of week ABC network 1971–74; Chair. Bd. Paramount Pictures Corpn. 1974–84; Pres. Gulf and Leisure Time Group 1983–84; Chair. and C.E.O. Twentieth Century Fox Film Corpn., Los Angeles 1984–92, Fox Inc. 1985–92; Chair., C.E.O. TCF Holdings Inc. 1984–85, QVC Network 1992–95, Silver King Communications 1995–; Chair. (desig.) Home Shopping Network (HSN) 1995–; mem. Bd. Dirs. News Corp Ltd.; mem. American Film Inst., Variety Clubs Int., Hollywood Radio and TV Soc., Acad. of Motion Picture Arts and Sciences. *Address:* Home Shopping Network, P.O. Box 9090, Clearwater, FL 33758, U.S.A.

DILLON, Brendan, M.A.; Irish diplomatist; b. 30 Nov. 1924, Dublin; s. of William Dillon and Pauline Kerrigan; m. Alice O'Keeffe 1949; four s. one d.; ed. Blackrock Coll. and Univ. Coll., Dublin; Chief of Protocol, Ministry of Foreign Affairs 1968; Amb. to Denmark, concurrently to Norway and Iceland 1970; Asst. Sec.-Gen., Ministry of Foreign Affairs 1972; Amb., Perm. Rep. to European Communities 1973–81, to France, concurrently to OECD 1981–86, to Holy See 1986–89; Grand Cross, Order of Leopold II (Belgium), Grand Cross, Order of Merit (Luxembourg). *Address:* c/o Department of Foreign Affairs, 80 St. Stephen's Green, Dublin 2, Ireland.

DILLON, C. Douglas, A.B.; American diplomatist (retd.) and investment banker; b. 21 Aug. 1909, Geneva; s. of the late Clarence and of Anne (Douglass) Dillon; m. 1st Phyllis Elsworth 1931 (died 1982); two d.; m. 2nd Susan S. Sage 1983; ed. Groton School and Harvard Coll.; mem. New York Stock Exchange 1931–36; with U.S. and Foreign Securities Corpn. and U.S. and Int. Securities Corpn. 1937–53, Pres. 1946–53, Pres. U.S. and Foreign Securities Corpn. 1967–71, Chair. of Bd. 1971–84, Dir. 1938–53, 1967–71; Dir. Dillon, Read & Co. Inc. 1938–53, Chair. of Bd. 1946–53, Dir. 1971–81; served as Ensign, advancing to Lieut.-Commdr. U.S.N.R. 1941–45; awarded Air Medal, Legion of Merit with Combat Device; Amb. to France 1953–57; Under-Sec. of State for Econ. Affairs 1957–59; Under-Sec. of State 1959–61; Sec. of the Treasury 1961–65; Chair. Rockefeller Foundation, Brookings Inst.; Pres. Bd. of Overseers Harvard Univ. 1968–72, Metropolitan Museum of Art 1970–78, Chair. 1978–83; mem. Cttee. to Fight Inflation 1980; Hon. LL.D. (Harvard, Columbia, New York, Hartford, Rutgers, Pennsylvania and Princeton Univs., Lafayette, Williams and Middlebury Colls.); Presidential Medal of Freedom 1989; Republican. *Address:* 27th Floor, 1330 Avenue of the Americas, New York, NY 10019, U.S.A. *Telephone:* (212) 315-8353.

DILLON, Matt; American actor; b. 18 Feb. 1964, New Rochelle, N.Y.; s. of Paul Dillon and Mary Ellen Dillon. *Films include:* Over the Edge 1979, Little Darlings 1980, My Bodyguard 1980, Liar's Moon 1982, Tex 1982, The Outsiders 1983, Rumble Fish 1983, The Flamingo Kid 1984, Target 1985, Rebel 1985, Native Son 1986, The Big Town (The Arm) 1987, Kansas 1988, Drugstore Cowboy 1989, A Kiss Before Dying 1991, Singles 1992, The Saint of Fort Washington, Mr. Wonderful 1993, Golden Gate 1994, To Die For, Frankie Starlight, Beautiful Girls, Grace of My Heart, Albino Alligator, In and Out 1997, There's Something About Mary 1998; several TV appearances. *Address:* c/o Elaine Goldsmith, 40 W. 57th Street, New York, NY 100119, U.S.A.

DIMBLEBY, David, M.A.; British broadcaster and newspaper proprietor; b. 28 Oct. 1938, London; s. of the late Richard Dimbleby and of Dilys Thomas; m. Josceline Gaskell 1967; one s. two d.; ed. Charterhouse, Christ Church, Oxford, Univs. of Paris and Perugia; presenter and interviewer BBC Bristol 1960–61: *Broadcasts include:* Quest (religious programme), What's New? (children's science), People and Power 1982–83; General Election Results Programmes 1979, 1983, 1987, various programmes for the Budget, by-elections, local elections etc.; presenter Question Time BBC 1993–. *Documentary films include:* Ku-Klux-Klan, The Forgotten Million, Cyprus: The Thin Blue Line 1964–65, South Africa: The White Tribe 1979 (Royal TV Soc. Supreme Documentary Award), The Struggle for South Africa 1990 (U.S. Emmy Award, Monte Carlo Golden Nymph), U.S.-U.K. Relations: An Ocean Apart 1988, David Dimbleby's India 1997; live commentary on many public occasions including: State Opening of Parliament, Trooping the Colour, Wedding of H.R.H. Prince Andrew and Sarah Ferguson, H.M. The Queen Mother's 90th Birthday Parade (Royal TV Soc. Outstanding Documentary Award), Funeral of Diana, Princess of Wales 1997, Memorial services including Lord Olivier (Royal TV Soc. Outstanding Documentary Award); Chair. Dimbleby and Sons Ltd. 1986–, fmrly. Man. Dir 1967; Richard Dimbleby Award B.A.F.T.A. 1998. *Publication:* An Ocean Apart (with David Reynolds) 1988. *Address:* 14 King Street, Richmond, Surrey, TW9 1NF, England.

DIMBLEBY, Jonathan; British broadcaster, journalist and author; b. 31 July 1944; s. of the late Richard Dimbleby and of Dilys Dimbleby; m. Bel Mooney 1968; one s. one d.; ed. Univ. Coll. London; reporter, BBC Bristol 1969–70, BBC Radio, World at One 1970–71; reporter, This Week, Thames TV 1972–78, 1986–88, TV Eye 1979; reporter, Yorkshire TV, Jonathan Dimbleby in Evidence: The Police (series), The Bomb 1980, The Eagle and the Bear 1981, The Cold War Game 1982, The American Dream 1984, Four Years On—The Bomb 1984; Assoc. Ed./Presenter, First Tuesday 1982–86; Presenter/Ed. Jonathan Dimbleby on Sunday, TV-am 1985–86, On the Record, BBC TV 1988–93, Charles: the Private Man, the Public Role, Central TV 1994, Jonathan Dimbleby, London Weekend Television 1995–; Presenter, Any Questions?, BBC Radio 4 1987–, Any Answers? 1989–; writer/presenter The Last Governor, Central TV 1997; Pres. Voluntary Service Overseas 1999–, Soil Asscn. 1997–; Vice-Pres. Council for Protection of Rural England 1997–; Chair. Bath Festivals Trust 1998–; Richard Dimbleby Award 1974. *Publications:* Richard Dimbleby 1975, The Palestinians 1979, The Prince of Wales: A Biography 1994, The Last Governor 1997. *Leisure interests:* music, sailing, tennis, farming. *Address:* c/o David Higham Associates, Ltd., 5 Lower John Street, London, W1R 4HA, England.

DIMÉNY, Imre, DR.AGR.SC.; Hungarian agropolitician and agronomist; b. 3 Aug. 1922, Komolló; s. of János Dimény and Anna Illyés; m. Margit Erzsébet Buzgó 1947; one d.; agronomic engineer; rural, county and ministry official 1945–55; Dept. Head, later Vice-Pres. Nat. Planning Bureau 1955–62; Alt. mem. Cen. Cttee. and Leader Agricultural Dept. Hungarian Socialist Workers' Party 1962–66; Minister of Agric. and Food 1967–75; Prof., Univ. of Horticulture, Budapest 1975–95, Rector 1975–86, Prof. Emer. 1995–; mem. Hungarian Acad. of Sciences 1982–; Dr. h.c. (Univ. of Agricultural Sciences Gödöllő) 1994, (Univ. of Horticulture and Food Ind., Pannon Univ. of Agric.) 1997. *Leisure interest:* reading, gardening. *Address:* University of Horticulture and Food Industry, Budapest XI, Villányi út 35–41, 1118 (Office); 1026 Budapest, Szilágyi Erzsébet fasor 79, 111/2, Hungary (Home). *Telephone:* (36) 3-566-580.

DIMITROV, Aleksander; Macedonian politician and lawyer; b. 1949, Skopje; ed. Skopje Univ.; mem. Man. Bd., Air Service Skopje, Sec. Forum for Int. Relations; ed. Forum (newspaper) 1969–71; ed. Mlad Borac (newspaper) 1972–78; Sec. Council for Foreign Relations 1979–82; Under-Sec. Cttee. for Int. Relations 1982–92; Dir. for Int. Affairs, Dir. Office of Palair 1993–96; Minister of Foreign Affairs of Macedonia 1998–. *Address:* Ministry of Foreign Affairs, Dame Grueva 14, 9100 Skopje, Macedonia. *Telephone:* (91) 23 63 11 (Office).

DIMITROV, Filip; Bulgarian politician; b. 1955; ed. St. Kliment Ohridsky Univ., Sofia; fmr. lawyer; leader Bulgarian Union of Democratic Forces; Prime Minister of Bulgaria 1991–92. *Publication:* For They Lived Lord 1991. *Address:* c/o Union of Democratic Forces, 134 Rakovsky Street, Sofia 1000, Bulgaria.

DIMITROVA, Ghena; Bulgarian opera singer; b. 6 May 1941, Beglej; ed. Bulgarian State Conservatoire (with Christo Bumbarov); début as Abigaille in Nabucco, Sofia Opera; Singer Laureate, Int. Competition, Treviso, Italy for interpretation of Amelia, Un Ballo in Maschera 1972; appearances France, Italy and Spain, early 1970s; appeared in Cen. and S. America and at Bolshoi, Moscow 1975–78; début Vienna Opera 1978; début Verona in La Gioconda 1980, several subsequent appearances there 1980–; début London, concert performance of La Gioconda at Barbican 1983; in Turandot, La Scala 1983; Macbeth, Salzburg Festival 1984; début Royal Opera House, Covent Garden in Turandot 1984; appears in opera houses of Vienna, Munich, Paris, Hamburg, Berlin, Madrid, Barcelona, Naples, Zürich, Rome, N.Y., San Francisco, Chicago; opened La Scala 1985/86 season in Aida; Gold Medal and First Prize, Fourth Int. Competition for Young Singers, Sofia 1970; People's Artist 1979; Golden Archer and Giovanni Zenatello Prizes (Rome and Verona) 1981; has recorded Nabucco and Oberto, Conte di San Bonifacio and discs of opera arias and Puccini arias.

DINCERLER, M. Vehbi; Turkish politician; b. 2 Aug. 1940, Gaziantep; s. of Esat and Şefika Dincerler; m.; three s. one d.; ed. Depts of Eng., Istanbul Tech. Univ., Business Inst., Istanbul Univ., Graduate School, Univ. of Syracuse, N.Y.; worked for State Planning Org.; joined Project Studies for Turkey at World Bank, studied economy of Ireland; academic at Middle East Tech. Univ., Gaziantep Campus; mem. Nat. Assembly 1983–, Minister of Educ., Youth and Sports 1983–85, Minister of State 1985–87; Chair. Nat. Ass. Foreign Relations Cttee. 1988–90; Minister of State 1989–91; mem. Constitutional Cttee. 1991–, N. Atlantic Ass.; Motherland Party. *Leisure interests:* music, social activities. *Address:* Ahmet Hasim Cad. 67/U Dikmen, Ankara, Turkey, 06460. *Telephone:* (312) 441 5361. *Fax:* (312) 438 1555.

DINE, James; American artist; b. 16 June 1935, Cincinnati, Ohio; m. Nancy Minto 1957; three s.; ed. Cincinnati Art Acad.; first one-man exhbn. Reuben Gallery, New York 1960; has subsequently held numerous one-man exhbns. in U.S.A. and throughout Europe including Palais des Beaux Arts, Brussels 1963, 1970, Sidney Jannis Gallery, New York 1963, 1964, 1967, Robert Fraser Gallery, London 1965, 1966, 1969, Stedelijk Museum, Amsterdam (drawings) 1967, Museum of Modern Art, Munich 1969, Berlin Festival, Sonnabend Gallery, New York, and Whitney Museum of American Art, New York 1970; exhbn. of Designs for A Midsummer Night's Dream, Museum of Modern Art, New York 1967; has participated in numerous group exhbns. including Painting and Sculpture of a Decade, Tate Gallery, London 1964, Venice Biennale 1964, A Decade of American Drawings 1965, Young America 1965, and Art of the United States 1670-1966 1966 (all three at Whitney Museum of American Art), U.S. Pavilion, Expo 1967, Montreal, and Hayward Gallery, London 1969; work appears in many public collections including Guggenheim Museum, Moderna Museet, Stockholm, Museum of Modern Art, New York, Dallas Museum of Fine Arts, Tate Gallery, and Whitney Museum of Modern American Art. *Publications:* Welcome Home, Lovebirds 1969 (also illustrator); co-author and illustrator The Adventures of Mr. and Mrs. Jim & Ron 1970; illustrator The Poet Assassinated 1968, Drawing from the Glypothek 1993. *Address:* c/o The Pace Gallery, 32 East 57th Street, New York, NY 10022, U.S.A.

DING FENGYING; Chinese party official; b. 1943, Luotian Co., Hubei Prov.; ed. Huazhong Teachers Coll.; joined CCP 1961; Chair. Hubei Branch, Chinese Women's Fed. 1973; Vice-Chair. Revolutionary Cttee., Hubei Prov. 1978–79; alt. mem. 12th CCP Cen. Cttee. 1982–87; First Sec. CCP Cttee., Huangguang Pref. 1983–; Deputy Sec. CCP Cttee., Hubei Prov. 1986, mem. CPC 5th Hubei Prov. Cttee. 1988–, Sec. Comm. for Discipline Inspection, Hubei Prov. 1988–; mem. CCP Cen. Discipline Inspection Comm. 1992–. *Address:* Hubei Dangwei, 1 Beihuanlu Road, Shuiguohu, Wuchang City, Hubei Province, People's Republic of China. *Telephone:* (Wuchang) 813351.

DING GUANGEN; Chinese state official; b. Sept. 1929, Wuxi Co., Jiangsu Prov.; ed. Jiaotong Univ. of Shanghai; joined CCP. 1956; Deputy Sec.-Gen.

Standing Comm. NPC 1983–85; Minister of Railways 1985–88; Vice-Minister State Planning Comm. 1988; Dir. Taiwan Affairs Office 1988; mem. 12th CCP Cen. Cttee. 1985–87, 13th CCP Cen. Cttee. 1987–92; Sec. Secr. 14th CCP Cen. Cttee. 1992–; alt. mem. Political Bureau 1987, mem. 1992–; Head United Front Work Dept. of CCP 1990–92; Head CCP Propaganda Dept. 1992–; Head Cen. Leading Group for Propaganda and Thought 1994–; mem. 15th CCP Cen. Cttee. 1997–. *Address:* Central Committee of the Chinese Communist Party, Zhongnanghai, Beijing, People's Republic of China.

DING GUANGXUN (Bishop K. H.); Chinese theologian and church leader; b. 20 Sept. 1915; ed. St. Johns Univ., Shanghai, and New York Union Theological Seminary, ordained 1942, Sec. Student Christian Movt. of Canada, Student World Christian Fed., Geneva; returned to China 1951; Pres. Nanking Theological Seminary 1952, consecrated Bishop 1955; Vice-Chair. Three-Self Patriotic Cttee. Movt. of the Protestant Churches of China 1961, Chair. 5th Cttee. 1980–97, Hon. Chair. 1997–; Pres. Christian Council of China; Hon. Pres. Chinese People's Asscn. for Peace and Disarmament 1985–; a Deputy Chair. Chinese People's Political Consultative Conf. 1989–; Vice-Chair. CPPCC 7th Nat. Cttee. 1989–93, Religious Cttee. 1991–; Vice-Chair. CPPCC 8th Nat. Cttee. 1993–98, 9th Nat. Cttee. 1998–; Chinese Religious Peace Cttee. 1994–; Sec. of Secr. CCP Cen. Cttee. 1992–. *Address:* Nanjing Theological Seminary, Nanjing 210029; 378 Mo Chou Road, Nanjing 210004, People's Republic of China.

DING HENGGAO, Gen.; Chinese politician and scientist; b. 1931, Nanjing Co., Jiangsu Prov.; ed. Nanjing Univ., and in U.S.S.R.; m. Nie Lili (d. of Marshal Nie Rongzhen); Minister of State Comm. of Science, Tech. and Industry for Nat. Defence 1985, Party Cttee. Sec. 1989–; rank of Lieut.-Gen. PLA 1988, Gen. 1994; mem. 13th CCP Cen. Cttee. 1989–92, 14th CCP Cen. Cttee. 1992–, Nat. Leading Group for Science and Tech. Chinese Acad. of Eng., Minister in charge of Comm. of Science, Tech. and Industry for Nat. Defence 1993–96. *Address:* c/o Commission of Science, Technology and Industry for National Defence, Beijing, People's Republic of China.

DING JIEYIN; Chinese sculptor; b. 4 Feb. 1926, Yinxian, Zhejiang; d. of Ding Yong-sen and Gao Yu-ding; m. Hong Bo 1952; one d.; ed. Cen. Acad. of Fine Arts, Beijing; Asst. Researcher, Sculpture Studio, Cen. Acad. of Fine Arts; Ed. China Sculpture; Chief Ed. supplement Chinese Art, New Evening newspaper, Hong Kong; Vice-Dir. Longshan Art Acad., Rizhao 1992–; mem. China Artists' Asscn.; about 60 pieces of sculpture; works exhibited at China Art Gallery, Beijing 1991, 1992, and commissioned by various cities. *Publications:* Clay Figures in the Temples of Da Tong 1982, The Art of Colour Clay Sculpture in Jin Ancestral Temple 1988; articles in Meishu, Art Research, People's Daily and Chinese Art supplement, New Evening (Hong Kong). *Leisure interests:* literature, basketball. *Address:* Xiao-Wei-Hu-Tong 68, Beijing 100005, People's Republic of China. *Telephone:* 5136377.

DING SHISUN; Chinese university administrator and mathematician; b. 5 Sept. 1927, Shanghai; s. of Ding Rounong and Liu Huixian; m. Gui Linlin 1956; two s.; ed. Math. Dept., Tsing-hua Univ.; Asst. Tsing-hua Univ. 1950–52; joined staff Beijing Univ. 1952, promoted to Prof. of Math. 1979, Vice-Chair. Math. Dept. 1978–80, Chair. 1981–82, Pres. Beijing Univ. 1984–89; Pres. Math. Soc. of Beijing 1986–88; Vice-Pres. Chinese Math. Soc. 1988–91; visited Math. Dept., Harvard Univ., U.S.A. 1983; specializes in fields of algebra and number theory; Exec. Vice-Chair. China Democratic League Cen. Cttee. 1987, Chair. 1997; mem. CPPCC 8th Nat. Cttee. 1993–98; Vice-Chair. Educ. and Culture Cttee.; Vice-Chair. Standing Cttee. of 9th NPC 1998–; Hon. Dr. (Soka, Japan) 1985; Hon. D.Sc. (Nebraska) 1988. *Publications:* several books and papers. *Leisure interest:* classical music. *Address:* Mathematics Department, Beijing University, Haidian, Beijing, 100871, People's Republic of China.

DING TINGMO; Chinese party official; b. 1936, Puding Co., Guizhou Prov.; ed. Guizhou Univ.; joined CCP 1956; Deputy Sec. Prov. CCP Cttee. Guizhou 1985, CPC 6th Guangxi Zhuang Autonomous Regional Cttee. 1990–; alt. mem. Cen. Cttee. 1985–. *Address:* Central Committee of the Chinese Communist Party, Zhongnanhai, Beijing, People's Republic of China.

DING WENCHANG, Maj.-Gen.; Chinese party official and army officer; b. 1933, Suxian Co., Anhui Prov.; joined CCP 1956; Dir. Political Dept., PLA Air Force 1988, Political Commissar 1992–, Party Cttee. Sec.; rank of Maj.-Gen. 1988, Gen. of Air Force 1996; mem. 14th CCP Cen. Cttee. 1992–97; mem. 15th CCP Cen. Cttee. 1997–. *Address:* Political Department of Air Force, Beijing, People's Republic of China.

DING XIAQI; Chinese mathematician and research professor; b. 25 May 1928, Yiyang Co., Hunan Prov.; m. Luo Peizhu 1957; three d.; ed. Dept. of Math., Wuhan Univ.; Research Asst., Assoc., Assoc. Prof., Prof. Inst. of Math., Acad. Sinica 1951–79; Research Prof., Inst. of Systems Sciences, Acad. Sinica 1979–91; Research Prof., Inst. of Applied Math., Acad. Sinica 1991–; Prof. Dir. Wuhan Inst. of Math., Acad. Sinica 1985–94, Dr. Wuhan Inst. of Mathematical Physics; Academician, Chinese Acad. of Sciences 1991–; mem. Cttee. Math. Soc. of China; Standing mem. Cttee. of Chinese Soc. of Systems Eng.; Prize Award, Nat. Science Conf., Beijing 1978, Prize of Chinese Acad. of Sciences 1978, 1st Class Prize, Chinese Acad. of Science 1988, 2nd Class Prize Natural Science Prize of People's Repub. of China 1989. *Publications:* more than 80 papers on PDE, functions spaces, number theory and numerical analysis; 4 monographs. *Leisure interests:* mathematics. *Address:* Institute of Applied Mathematics, Academia Sinica, Beijing 100080, People's Republic of China. *Telephone:* 6256293910 (Office); 62561754 (Home). *Fax:* 62541689.

DINI, Lamberto; Italian politician and banker; b. 1 March 1931, Florence; m.; one d.; ed. Univ. of Florence, Univs. of Minnesota and Michigan, U.S.A.; economist, IMF, Washington D.C., then various posts to Deputy Dir. Africa Dept. 1959–76, mem. Bd. Exec. Dirs. 1976–78, now Alt. Gov. for Italy; joined Banca d'Italia (cen. bank) as Asst. Gen. Man. 1979, now Gen. Man.; mem. Monetary Cttee. of EU, Bd. Dirs. BIS; Minister of the Treasury 1994–95; Prime Minister of Italy 1995–96, Minister of Foreign Affairs 1996–98; Fulbright Scholar. *Address:* c/o Ministry of Foreign Affairs, Piazzale della Farnesia 1, 00194 Rome, Italy.

DINI AHMED, Ahmed; Djibouti politician; b. 1932, Obock; Vice-Pres., Territorial Assembly, French Somaliland (now Repub. of Djibouti) 1959–60; Minister of Production 1963–64, of the Interior 1967–72; joined Ligue Populaire Africaine pour l'Indépendance 1972; Pres. Nat. Ass. of French Territory of the Afars and the Issas May-June 1977, of Repub. of Djibouti June-July 1977; Prime Minister July-Dec. 1977; Pres. Front pour la restauration de l'unité et de la démocratie (insurgent movement) 1992–94, split into two factions March 1994, leader of faction favouring a continuation of mil. activities.

DINKINS, David, B.S.; American politician and lawyer; b. 10 July 1927, Trenton, N.J.; m. Joyce Burrows 1953; one s. one d.; ed. Howard Univ., Washington, D.C. and Brooklyn law school; joined Harlem law firm 1956; elected to New York State Ass. 1965; Pres. Bd. of Elections, New York 1972; City Clerk, New York 1975–85; Manhattan Borough Pres. 1986; contested Democratic Primary, defeating Mayor Edward Koch (q.v.) Sept. 1989; Mayor of New York 1990–93; Prof. Columbia Univ.'s School of Int. and Public Affairs 1993. *Leisure interest:* tennis. *Address:* Columbia University, Morningside Heights, New York, NY 10027, U.S.A.

DION, Céline, O.Q.; Canadian singer; b. 30 March 1968, Charlemagne, Quebec; d. of Adhémar Dion and Thérèse Dion; m. René Angélil 1994; winner, Gold Medal, Yamaha World Song Festival, Tokyo 1982; became first Canadian to win Gold Disc in France with single D'amour ou d'amitié which sold over 700,000 copies 1983; winner, Eurovision song contest, Dublin 1988; first English-language album Unison (including single Where Does My Heart Beat Now) released 1990; other albums include Dion chante Plamondon 1991, Sleepless in Seattle 1993, The Colour of My Love 1993, D'eux 1995 (best-selling French-language album of all time) 1995, Falling Into You 1996, Let's Talk About Love 1998; singles include: Beauty and the Beast (Acad. Award for Best Song Written for a Motion Picture or TV 1992, Grammy Award 1993), If You Asked Me To, Nothing Broken But My Heart, Love Can Move Mountains, When I Fall In Love, The Power of Love, Misled, Think Twice, Because You Loved Me; performed anthem The Power of the Dream at opening ceremony of Olympic Games, Atlanta 1996; Female Vocalist of the Year, Juno Awards 1991, 1992, 1993 and many other awards; Medal of Arts (France) 1996. *Leisure interests:* swimming, cooking. *Address:* Les Productions Feeling, 2540 boulevard Daniel-Johnson, Porte 755, Laval, Quebec H7T 2S3, Canada.

DION, Stéphane, P.C., M.SC.; Canadian politician and academic; b. 1955; m.; one d.; ed. Laval Univ., Inst. d'études politiques de Paris; Prof. of Political Science, Univ. of Montréal 1984–96; Minister of Intergovernmental Affairs and Pres. Queen's Privy Council for Canada 1996–; Guest Scholar, Brookings Inst., Washington, D.C. 1990–91, Laboratoire d'économie publique de Paris 1994–95; Research Fellow, Canadian Centre for Man. Devt. 1990–91; Co-Ed. Canadian Journal of Political Science 1990–93; mem. Aid to Scholarly Publs. Cttee. of Social Sciences Fed. of Canada, Advisory Council of Inst. of Intergovernmental Relations, Queen's Univ. *Address:* Privy Council Office, Langeuin Block, 80 Wellington Street, Ottawa, Ont., K1A 0A3, Canada

DIONNE, Joseph Lewis, B.A., M.S.; American publisher; b. 29 June 1933, Montgomery, Ala.; s. of Antonio Ernest Joseph Dionne and Myrtle Mae (Armstrong) Dionne; m. Joan F. Durand 1954; two s. one d.; ed. Hofstra Univ., Columbia Univ.; Guidance Counsellor, L.I. public schools 1956–61; Asst. Prof., Hofstra Univ., Hempstead, N.Y. 1962–63; Dir. of Instruction, Project Dir. Ford Foundation School Improvement, Brentwood, N.Y. public schools 1963–66; Vice-Pres. (Research and Devt.) Educational Devt. Labs., Huntington, N.Y. 1966–68; Vice-Pres. and Gen. Man. CTB/McGraw-Hill, Monterey, Calif. 1968–73, Sr. Vice-Pres. (Corp. Planning) McGraw-Hill Inc., New York 1973–77, Pres. McGraw-Hill Information Systems Co., New York 1977–79, Exec. Vice-Pres. (Operations) McGraw Hill Inc. 1979–81, Pres. 1981–93, C.E.O. 1983–98, Chair. 1988–; mem. Bd. of Dirs., Equitable Life Insurance Co. of America, Utd. Telecommunications Inc.; Trustee Harris Corpn., Teachers' Coll., Columbia Univ., Hofstra Univ. *Address:* McGraw-Hill Inc., 1221 Avenue of the Americas, New York, NY 10020 (Office); 198 North Wilton Road, New Canaan, CT 06840, U.S.A. (Home).

DIOP, Majhemout; Senegalese politician and pharmacist; b. 30 Sept. 1922, St. Louis; ed. Ecole Africaine de Médecine et de Pharmacie (Dakar), Paris Univ. and African Inst., Univ. of Moscow; Hospital pharmacist, Senegal and Gabon 1947–50; Pres. Senegalese students' asscn. in France 1951; studied Marxism at Bucharest 1953–56; Sec.-Gen. Parti Africain de l'Indépendance (PAI) 1957–76, Pres 1976–; exiled from Senegal 1961–76; engaged in research in political sociology at Inst. of Human Sciences, Mali 1968–76; dispensary pharmacist, Dakar 1977–. *Publications:* Contribution à l'Etude des problèmes politiques en Afrique Noire 1959, Classes et idéologies de classe au Sénégal 1963, Notes sur la classe ouvrière sénégalaise 1965, Histoire des classes sociales dans l'Afrique de l'Ouest (Vol. I) 1971, (Vol. II) 1972, Etude sur le Salariat 1975, Essai sur l'esclavage en Afrique de l'Ouest (to be published); and many articles in review and journals. *Address:* Parti Africain de l'Indépendance (PAI), P.O. Box 820, Dakar; 153 Avenue du Président Lamine Gueye, Dakar (Offices); 210 HCM, Guediawaye, Dakar, Senegal (Home).

D'IORIO, Antoine, O.C., PH.D.; Canadian university rector and vice-chancellor; b. 22 April 1925, Montréal; s. of Giuseppe D'Iorio and Assunta (Torino) D'Iorio; m. 1st Ghislaine Chatel 1950 (deceased); three s. four d.; m. 2nd Doreen Steele 1990; ed. Univs. of Montréal, Wisconsin and Oxford; Asst. Prof. of Physiology, Univ. of Montréal 1949–55, Assoc. Prof. 1956–61; Prof. of Biochem. and Chair. of Dept., Univ. of Ottawa 1961–69, Dean, Faculty of Science and Eng. 1969–76, Vice-Rector, Academic 1976–84, Rector and Vice-Chancellor 1984–90; Pres. Canadian Mediterranean Inst. 1990–93; mem. Société médicale de Montréal; Ciba Award 1974, Parizeau Medal ACFAS 1974, Ottawa Biological Biochemical Soc. 1976, Queen Elizabeth II Silver Jubilee Medal 1978, Ordre du Mérite national (France) 1988. *Publications:* about 90 research papers in field of biological sciences. *Leisure interests:* photography, reading. *Address:* 405–15 Murray Street, Ottawa, Ont., K1N 9M5, Canada (Home). *Telephone:* (613) 241 8549.

DIOUF, Abdou, L. EN D., L. ÈS SC.; Senegalese politician; b. 7 Sept. 1935, Louga; m. 1963; ed. Lycée Faidherbe, St. Louis, Dakar and Paris Univs.; Dir. of Technical Co-operation and Minister of Planning Sept.-Nov. 1960; Asst. Sec.-Gen. to Govt. 1960–61; Sec.-Gen. Ministry of Defence June-Dec. 1961; Gov. Sine-Saloum Region 1961–62; Dir. de Cabinet of Minister of Foreign Affairs 1962–63, of Pres. of Repub. 1963–65; Sec.-Gen. to Pres.'s Office 1964–68; Minister of Planning and Industry 1968–70; Prime Minister 1970–80; Pres. of Senegal Jan. 1981–, of Confed. of Senegambia 1982–89; Chair. OAU 1985–86; mem. Nat. Assembly for Longa Département 1973–; mem. Sengalese Progressive Union (U.P.S.) 1961–, later Asst. Sec.-Gen.; fmr. Asst. Sec.-Gen. Parti Socialiste Sénégalais (P.S.), now Sec.-Gen; jt. winner Africa Prize for Leadership 1987. *Address:* Office of the President, avenue Roume, BP 168, Dakar, Senegal.

DIOUF, Jacques; Senegalese international civil servant and agronomist; b. 1 Aug. 1938, Saint-Louis; m. Aissatou Seye 1963; one s. four d.; ed. Lycée Faidherbe, Saint-Louis, Ecole Nat. d'Agriculture, Paris/Grignon, Ecole Nat. d'Application d'Agronomie Tropicale, Paris/Nogent, and Sorbonne, Paris; Exec. Sec. African Groundnut Council, Lagos 1965–71; Exec. Sec. West African Rice Devt. Asscn., Monrovia 1971–77; Sec. of State for Science and Tech., Govt. of Senegal, Dakar 1978–83; mem. Nat. Ass., Chair. Foreign Relations Comm. and elected Sec., Dakar 1983–84; Sec. Gen. Banque centrale des états de l'Afrique de l'ouest, Dakar 1985–90; Perm. Rep. of Senegal to UN 1991; Dir.-Gen. F.A.O. Jan. 1994–; led Senegalese dels. to UN Confs. on Science and Tech., Vienna 1979 (Chair. of 1st Comm.), Industrial Devt., New Delhi 1980, New and Renewable Energy Sources, Nairobi (Vice-Chair.) 1981, Peaceful Use of Space, Vienna 1982; African Rep., Consultative Group on Int. Agricultural Research, Washington; mem. Bd. of Dirs. I.S.N.A.R., The Hague, IITA Lagos, IIRSDA Abidjan, I.C.R.A.F., Nairobi, Int. Foundation for Science, Stockholm, African Capacity Building Foundation, Harare, World Inst. for Devt. Econs. Research, Helsinki, Council of African Advisors of the World Bank, Washington D.C.; Chair. S.I.N.A.E.S., Dakar; mem. Consultative Cttee. on Medical Research, WHO, Geneva; Officier Légion d'honneur, des Palmes Académiques (France); Grand Commdr., Order of the Star of Africa (Liberia). *Publications:* La détérioration du pouvoir d'achat de l'Arachide 1972, Les fondements du dialogue scientifique entre les civilisations Euro-occidentale et Négro-Africaine 1979, The Challenge of Agricultural Development in Africa 1989. *Leisure interests:* reading, music, sports. *Address:* Food and Agriculture Organization of the United Nations, Viale delle Terme di Caracalla, 00100 Rome, Italy.

DIPICO, Manne Emsley, B.A.; South African civil servant and trade unionist; b. 21 April 1959, Kimberley; ed. Univ. of Fort Hare; joined African Nat. Congress (ANC) 1982; Nat. Educ. Co-ordinator Nat. Union of Mineworkers; Azanian Students' Org. (AZASO) rep. for United Democratic Front (UDF) Exec. Border Region, AZASO Treas. Univ. of Fort Hare; mem. UDF N. Cape 1985–86; detained Ciskei 1984, detained under state of emergency, Kimberley 1986, arrested and sentenced to five years for furthering the aims of a banned org. through terrorist activities 1987–90, released before end of sentence; Regional Sec. ANC 1991–92, Regional Chair. N. Cape 1992–; Regional Elections Co-ordinator 1993–94; Premier N. Cape Prov. Legislature 1994–. *Address:* Private Bag X5016, Kimberley 8301 (Office); 5248 Magashula Street, P.O. Mankurwane, Galeshawe-Kimberley 8345, South Africa (Home).

DI PIETRO, Antonio; Italian lawyer and politician; b. 2 Oct. 1950, Montenero di Bisaccia; m. 1st Isabella Ferrara; one s.; m. 2nd Susanna Mazzoleni 1995; studied law at evening classes; fmrly. worked as factory hand, Germany; fmr. police officer; fmr. magistrate, Bergamo; prosecutor, Milan 1984–94; uncovered bribery of officials, Milan March 1992, led Operation Clean Hands exposing high levels of political corruption in Italy 1992–94; univ. teacher and parl. consultant 1995–96; Minister of Public Works 1996. *Address:* c/o Ministry of Public Works, Piazza Porta Pia 1, 00198 Rome, Italy.

DIRKSEN, Gebhard, DR.JUR.; German banker and lawyer; b. 29 June 1929, Göttingen; s. of Wilhelm and Magdalene (née Güthenke) Dirksen; m. Renate Pöhl 1971; one s. two d.; ed. at schools in Gutersloh/Westfalen and Univs. of Mainz, Freibourg and Göttingen; articled in Göttingen, Hanover and Celle; Deputy Chair. Bd. of Dirs Norddeutsche Landesbank Girozentrale 1959–94. *Address:* Westpreussenufer 4, 30659 Hannover, Germany. *Telephone:* 64 787 46.

DI ROSA, Antonio, B.SC.; Italian journalist; b. 17 April 1951, Messina; s. of Calogero Rossetti and Anna Rossetti; partner; one s. two d.; began career at Giornale di Calabria 1974–78; moved to Gazzetta del Popolo 1978, Deputy Head Home News 1979–81, Head 1981–84; joined La Stampa 1984, Head Home News April–July 1988; Deputy Cen. Ed.-in-Chief Corriere della Sera 1988, Cen. Ed.-in-Chief 1993, Deputy Ed. Jan. 1996–; Premio Senigallia 1983. *Leisure interests:* books, cinema, travel. *Address:* Via G. Morelli 1, Milan, Italy (Home). *Telephone:* (39) 2 781199.

DISANAYAKA, Heen Banda, B.A.; Sri Lankan banker; b. 28 Aug. 1937, Talawa; m. Wasantha Wijekoon 1963; one s. two d.; ed. Univ. of Sri Lanka; Dir.-Gen. of Customs 1976; Alt. Exec. Dir. Asian Devt. Bank 1987; Deputy Sec. to Treasury 1989; Gov. Cen. Bank of Sri Lanka 1992–95, also fmr. Chair. of Monetary Bd; Alt. Dir. IMF, Washington DC 1996–98. *Address:* 84/1 Old Kottawa Road, Mirihana, Nugegoda, Sri Lanka. *Telephone:* 852199.

DISNEY, Anthea; British business executive; b. 13 Oct. 1946, Dunstable; d. of Alfred Leslie and Elsie Wale; m. Peter Robert Howe 1984; ed. Queen's Coll.; New York corresp. London Daily Mail 1973–75, Features Ed. 1975–77, New York Bureau Chief 1977–79; columnist London Daily Express, New York 1979–84; Managing Ed. New York Daily News 1984–87; Ed. Sunday Daily News 1984–87; Ed. US magazine 1987–88; Ed.-in-Chief Self magazine 1988–89; magazine developer Murdoch magazines 1989–90; exec. producer A Current Affair, Fox TV 1990–91; Ed.-in-Chief TV Guide magazine 1991–95; Editorial Dir. Murdoch Magazines 1994–95; Pres. and C.E.O. HarperCollins Publrs. 1996–97; Chair., C.E.O. News America Publishing 1997–. *Address:* News America Publishing Group, 1211 Avenue of the Americas, New York, NY 10036, U.S.A.

DISTEL, Sacha; French singer and songwriter; b. 29 Jan. 1933, Paris; s. of Léon and Andrée (née Ventura) Distel; m. Francine Breaud 1963; two s.; ed. Lycée Claude-Bernard, Paris; voted best guitarist by Jazz Hot magazine, and in critics poll 1957, 58, 59; acted in films, Les Mordus 1960, Nous irons à Deauville 1962, La Bonne Soupe 1964, Le Voyou 1970, Sans mobile apparent 1971; has sung more than 200 songs in French, English, Italian, German; TV presenter in France, England and Germany; producer of TV shows Sacha Show, Top à Sacha Distel 1973, Sacha's in Town (U.K.) 1972; producer and performer La Belle Vie TV programme 1984–85; Chevalier des Arts et des Lettres 1987, Chevalier, Légion d'honneur 1997, numerous awards. *Publication:* Les Pendules à l'heure 1985. *Leisure interests:* swimming, skiing and tennis. *Address:* c/o Charley Marouani, 37 rue Marbeuf, 75008 Paris, France.

DITYATIN, Aleksandr Nikolayevich; Russian gymnast; b. 7 Aug. 1957, Leningrad; s. of Nikolai Konstantinovich Dityatin and Fedocya Kudinovna Dityatin; m. Elena Evgenievna Dityatin 1979; one s.; ed. Leningrad Lesgaft Inst. of Physical Culture; many times Soviet champion and cup winner; overall champion Soviet Summer Games 1975, 1979, World Cup 1978, 1979; team and rings silver medals, Montreal Olympic Games 1976; overall bronze medallist world championships 1978; overall world champion 1979; overall gold medallist, team gold medal, rings gold medal, vault, parallel bars, pommel horse and horizontal bar silver medals, Moscow Olympic Games 1980; now coach of young gymnasts; works at Pulkovo Int. Airport 1985–. *Address:* Nevski prosp. 18, Apt. 25, St Petersburg, Russia. *Telephone:* (812) 312-66-57.

DIXIT, Jyotindranath, M.A.; Indian diplomatist; b. 8 Jan. 1936, Madras; m. Vijaya Sundaram 1958; three s. two d.; ed. Univ. of Delhi; served in different capacities in Indian embassies in Mexico, Chile, Bhutan, Japan, Austria 1958–69; at Ministry of External Affairs dealing with China, Pakistan and UN Affairs 1961–63, 1969–72; first Amb. (acting) to Bangladesh 1972–75; Minister Indian Embassy, Washington, U.S.A. 1975–78; Chief Spokesman on Foreign Policy, Govt. of India 1978–82; Amb. to Afghanistan 1982–85, to Pakistan 1989; High Commr. to Sri Lanka 1985–89, to Pakistan 1989–91; Foreign Sec. to the Govt. of India 1991–94. *Publication:* Self in Autumn (poems) 1982. *Leisure interests:* reading, swimming, rowing, hiking. *Address:* AJH-102-A, Aryun rang, DLF Dunkirk Enclave phase 1, Gurgaon-122002, Haryana, India.

DIXON, (David) Jeremy, R.I.B.A.; British architect; b. 31 May 1939; s. of Joseph L. Dixon and Beryl M. Braund; m. Fenella Clemens 1964; one s. two d.; ed. Merchant Taylors' School and Architectural Asscn. School of Architecture; pvt. practice with Fenella Dixon 1975–90; formed partnership of Jeremy Dixon/BDP with William Jack (for extension to Royal Opera House, Covent Garden) 1984; Prin. Jeremy Dixon–Edward Jones 1990–; other projects include: competition for Tate Gallery restaurant; shop for Clifton Nurseries; competition for Northants. county offices; housing projects in London; study centre for Darwin Coll., Cambridge; work for J. Sainsbury PLC, Henry Moore Foundation. *Leisure interests:* walking in English landscape, contemporary sculpture and painting, music. *Address:* 41 Shelton Street, London, WC2H 9HJ, England (Office).

DIXON, Frank James, M.D.; American medical scientist; b. 9 March 1920, St. Paul, Minnesota; s. of Frank James and Rose Augusta (née Kuhfeld)

Dixon; m. Marion Edwards 1946; one s. one d.; ed. Univ. of Minnesota, U.S. Naval Hospital, Great Lakes, Illinois; Research Asst., Dept. of Pathology, Harvard Medical School 1946–48; Instructor, Dept. of Pathology, Washington Univ. Medical School 1948–50; Asst. Prof. Dept. of Pathology 1950–51; Prof. and Chair. Dept. of Pathology, Univ. of Pittsburgh School of Medicine 1951–61, Chair. Biomedical Research Depts. 1970–74; Chair. Dept. of Experimental Pathology, Scripps Clinic and Research Foundation 1961–74, Dir. Research Inst. 1974–86, Dir. Emer. 1986–; Prof. in Residence, Dept. of Biology, Univ. of Calif. at San Diego 1965–68, Adjunct Prof. Dept. Pathology 1968–96; mem. N.A.S., Asscn. American Physicians, A.A.A.S. and numerous other professional orgs.; Hon. Dr. Sc. (Medical Coll. of Ohio); Harvey Society Lecturer 1962; mem. numerous editorial bds. and advisory cttees.; Theobald Smith Award in Medical Sciences from A.A.A.S. 1952, Parke-Davis Award from the American Soc. for Experimental Pathology 1957, Award for Distinguished Achievement from Modern Medicine 1961, Martin E. Rehfuss Award in Internal Medicine 1966, Von Pirquet Medal from Annual Forum on Allergy 1967, Bunim Gold Medal from the American Rheumatism Asscn. 1968, Mayo Soley Award from the Western Soc. for Clinical Research 1969, Gairdner Foundation Award 1969, Dickson Prize in Medicine, Univ. of Pittsburgh 1975, Albert Lasker Basic Medical Research Award 1975, Pahlavi Lecturer, Ministry of Science and Higher Educ., Iran 1976, Homer Smith Award in Renal Physiology, New York Heart Asscn. 1976, Rous-Whipple Award of the American Asscn. of Pathologists 1979, First award in Immunology from Kaiser Permanente Medical Group, Los Angeles, Calif. 1979, Distinguished Service Award, Lupus Foundation 1987, Paul Klemperer Award 1989, Jean Hamburger Award 1990. *Publications:* Ed. Advances in Immunology, and over 450 papers. *Leisure interests:* running, tennis, art collecting. *Address:* Scripps Research Institute, 10550 North Torrey Pines Road, La Jolla, CA 92037 (Office); 2355 Avenida de la Playa, La Jolla, CA 92037, U.S.A. (Home). *Telephone:* (619) 455-8100.

DIXON, Gordon Henry, O.C., PH.D., F.R.S.C., F.R.S.; Canadian university professor; b. 25 March 1930, Durban, S.A.; s. of Walter James Dixon and Ruth Nightingale; m. Sylvia Weir Gillen 1954; three s. one d.; ed. Cambridgeshire High School for Boys, Trinity Coll., Cambridge, Univ. of Toronto, Canada; Asst. Prof., Dept. of Biochemistry, Univ. of Washington, Seattle, U.S.A. 1954–58; mem. staff MRC Unit for research in cell metabolism, Univ. of Oxford 1958–59; Research Assoc., Connaught Medical Research Lab., Univ. of Toronto 1959–60, Asst. Prof., Dept. of Biochemistry 1961–62, Assoc. Prof. 1962–63; Assoc. Prof., Dept. of Biochemistry, Univ. of B.C., Vancouver, Canada 1963–66, Prof. 1966–72; Prof. and Head, Biochemistry Group, Univ. of Sussex, England 1972–74; Prof. of Medical Biochemistry, Faculty of Medicine, Univ. of Calgary 1974–94, Head of Dept. 1983–88, Prof. Emer. 1994–; Visiting Fellow Commoner, Trinity Coll., Cambridge 1979–80; Pres. Canadian Biochemical Soc. 1982–83; Pres. Pan-American Asscn. of Biochemical Socs. 1987–90, Vice-Pres. 1984–87; Chair. Canadian Nat. Cttee. for Int. Union of Biochem. 1984–86, Exec. Cttee. Int. Union of Biochem. 1988–94; Assoc. Ed. Journal of Molecular Evolution, Biochemistry Int.; Ayerst Award, Canadian Biochem. Soc. 1966, Steacie Prize 1966, Flavelle Medal, Royal Soc. of Canada 1980, Izaak Walton Killam Memorial Prize 1991 and other awards. *Publications:* more than 200 articles in scientific journals. *Leisure interests:* hiking, gardening. *Address:* 4402 Shore Way, Vic., BC V8N 3T9, Canada. *Telephone:* (250) 721-2078. *Fax:* (250) 721-2078.

DIXON, Kenneth Herbert Morley, B.A.(ECON.); British business executive; b. 19 Aug. 1929, Stockport; s. of Arnold Morley Dixon and Mary Jolly; m. Patricia Oldbury Whalley 1955; two s.; ed. Cranbrook School, Sydney, Manchester Univ.; joined Rowntree & Co. Ltd. 1956, Dir. 1970, Chair. U.K. Confectionery Div. 1973–78; Deputy Chair. Rowntree Mackintosh Ltd. 1978–81; Chair. Rowntree Mackintosh PLC (now Rowntree PLC) 1981–89; Vice-Chair. Legal and General Group 1986–94; Deputy Chair. Bass PLC 1990–96; mem. Council Inc. Soc. of British Advertisers 1971–79, Council Cocoa, Chocolate and Confectionery Alliance 1972–79, Council Advertising Asscn. 1976–79, CBI Cos. Cttee. 1979–84, Council CBI 1981–90, B.I.M. Econ. and Soc. Affairs Cttee. 1980–84, Food and Drink Fed. Exec. Cttee. 1986–89 (mem. Council 1986–87); mem. Council York Univ. 1983–, Pro-Chancellor 1987–, Chair. 1990–; Dr. h.c. (York Univ.) 1993. *Leisure interests:* reading, music, fell walking. *Address:* c/o Fairfax House, Castlegate, York, YO1 1RN, England.

DIXON, Richard Newland, SC.D., F.R.S.; British professor of chemistry; b. 25 Dec. 1930, Borough Green; s. of Robert T. Dixon and Lilian Dixon; m. Alison M. Birks 1954; one s. two d.; ed. Judd School, Tonbridge, King's Coll. London and St. Catharine's Coll. Cambridge; Scientific Officer, U.K.A.E.A. Aldermaston 1954–56; Postdoctoral Fellow, Univ. of Western Ont. 1956–57, Nat. Research Council, Ottawa 1957–59; ICI Fellow, Univ. of Sheffield 1959–60, Lecturer in Chemistry 1960–69; Prof. of Chemistry, Univ. of Bristol 1969–96, Alfred Capper Pass Prof. of Chemistry 1990–96, Prof. Emer. 1996–, Leverhulme Emer. Fellow 1996–98, Univ. Sr. Research Fellow 1996–, Dean, Faculty of Science 1979–82, Pro-Vice Chancellor 1989–92; Sorby Research Fellow, Royal Soc. 1964–69; mem. Council, Faraday Div. Royal Soc. of Chem. 1985–98 (Vice-Pres. 1989–98), Cttees. of S.E.R.C., 1980–83, 1987–90; Corday Morgan Medal and Spectroscopy Awards, and Liversidge Lecturer, Royal Soc. of Chem.; Harkins Lecturer, Univ. of Chicago, U.S.A. 1994; Dir. non-exec. United Bristol Healthcare N.H.S. Trust 1994–, Vice-Chair. 1995–. *Publications:* Spectroscopy and Structure 1965, Theoretical Chemistry, Vol. I 1972, Vol. II 1974, Vol. III 1977; numerous research articles in scientific journals. *Leisure interests:* mountain walking, photography, gardening, theatre-going. *Address:* School of Chemistry, University of Bristol, Cantock's Close, Bristol, BS8 1TS (Office); 22 Westbury Lane, Coombe Dingle, Bristol, BS9 2PE, England (Home). *Telephone:* (0117) 9287661 (Office); (0117) 9681691 (Home). *Fax:* (0117) 9251295.

DIXON, Thomas F., B.S.ENG., B.S. AND M.S. CHEM.ENG., M.S.AERO.ENG.; American executive and aerospace engineer; b. 15 March 1916, Nashville, Tenn.; s. of Sam J. and Katherine Dixon; m. Margaret Ann Donovan 1943; two s. two d.; ed. Vanderbilt and Michigan Univs., and California Inst. of Technology; Research Engineer, N. American Aviation 1946–54, Dir. Propulsion Center, Rocketdyne Div. N. American Aviation 1954–55, Chief Engineer 1955–60, Vice-Pres. Research and Eng. 1960–63, Vice-Pres. 1963–68; Deputy Assoc. Administrator Nat. Aeronautics and Space Admin. 1961–63; Chair. of the Bd., Airtronics Inc. 1967–69, 1973–, Pres. 1969–73; Exec. Vice-Pres. Teledyne McCormick Selph 1975–76, Pres. 1976–82; Pres. Calif. Capital Tech. Resources, Inc. 1984–87, Destech Co. 1987–98; Dir. Maine Space Application Inst. 1989–98; Pres. Int. Space Inst. 1995; Prof. Emery-Riddle Univ. of Space 1995; Bd. mem. State of Maine Center of Tech. Transfer and NASA Maine Consortium; Fellow, American Rocket Soc., A.I.A.A.; Robert M. Goddard Memorial Award 1957; shared Louis W. Hill Space Transportation Award 1961. *Leisure interests:* tennis, collecting antiques. *Address:* 1761 Cuba Island Lane, Hayes, VA 23072, U.S.A. (Home). *Telephone:* (804) 642-1761 (Home).

DIZ, Adolfo César, C.P.A., D.ECON., M.A., D.PHIL.; Argentinian economist; b. 12 May 1931, Buenos Aires; s. of Agustín Diz and Elisa Aristizábal; m. Martha Solari 1959; five s.; ed. Univ. de Buenos Aires and Univ. of Chicago; Instructor of Statistics, Univ. de Buenos Aires 1951–55, 1958–59; Prof. of Statistics, Univ. Nacional de Tucumán 1959–60, Dir. Inst. of Econ. Research 1959–65, Prof. of Statistics and Econometrics 1960–61, 1964, Prof. of Monetary Theory 1962, 1965–66; Exec. Dir. Int. Monetary Fund (IMF) 1966–68; Envoy extraordinary and Minister plenipotentiary, Argentine Financial Rep. in Europe 1969–73; Dir. Center for Latin American Monetary Studies 1973–76; Pres. Banco Central de la República Argentina 1976–81; Dir. Per Jacobsson Foundation 1976–; Econ. Consultant 1981–; mem. of Argentine socs., American Econ. Asscn. and Econometric Soc. *Publications:* Money and Prices in Argentina 1935–62, in Varieties of Monetary Experience (Ed. D. Meiselman), Money Supply Models (in Spanish), and numerous economic articles. *Address:* Callao Avenida 2049-P6 (1024), Buenos Aires, Argentina.

DJERASSI, Carl, A.B., PH.D.; American chemist, educator, author; b. 29 Oct. 1923, Vienna; s. of Dr. Samuel Djerassi and Dr. Alice Friedmann; m. 1st Virginia Jeremiah (divorced 1950); m. 2nd Norma Lundholm (divorced 1976); one s. one d. (deceased); m. 3rd Diane W. Middlebrook 1985; ed. Kenyon Coll. and Univ. of Wisconsin; Research Chemist, Ciba Pharmaceutical Co., Summit, N.J. 1942–43, 1945–49; Assoc. Dir. of Research, Syntex, S.A., Mexico City 1949–51, Research Vice-Pres. 1957–60, Pres. Syntex Research 1968–72; Assoc. Prof. of Chem., Wayne State Univ., Detroit 1952–54, Prof. 1954–59, Stanford Univ. 1959–; Pres. of the Bd. Zoecon Corpn. (renamed Sandoz Crop Protection Corpn.) 1968–83, Chair. 1968–88; Djerassi Foundation Resident Artists Program; Royal Chemical Soc. Centenary Lecturer 1964; Royal Swedish Acad. of Eng. Sciences thirteenth Chemical Lecturer 1969; Swedish Pharmaceutical Soc. Scheele Lecturer 1972; mem. Editorial Bd. Journal of the American Chemical Society 1968–76, Journal of Organic Chemistry 1955–58, Tetrahedron 1958–92, Steroids 1963–, Proceedings of Nat. Acad. of Sciences 1964–70; mem. Nat. Acad. of Sciences Bd. on Science and Tech. for Int. Devt. 1967–76, Chair. 1972–76; mem. American Pugwash Cttee. 1967–1981; mem. Nat. Acad. of Sciences, N.A.S. Inst. of Medicine, Brazilian Acad. of Sciences, American Acad. of Arts and Sciences; Foreign mem. German Acad. of Natural Scientists (Leopoldina), Royal Swedish Acad. of Sciences 1973, Bulgarian Acad. of Sciences 1979, Royal Swedish Acad. of Eng. Sciences 1984; Hon. Fellow Royal Chemical Soc. 1968, American Acad. of Pharmaceutical Science; numerous hon. degrees; Award in Pure Chemistry 1958, Baekeland Medal 1959, Fritzsche Medal 1960, Creative Invention Award 1973, Award in the Chemistry of Contemporary Technological Problems 1983, Esselen Award for Chemistry in the Public Interest 1989, American Chemical Soc.; Intra-Science Research Award 1969, Freedman Foundation Patent Award 1971, Chemical Pioneer Award 1973, Perkin Medal 1975, American Inst. of Chemists; Nat. Medal of Science 1973 (for synthesis of first oral contraceptive), Wolf Prize in Chemistry 1978, Bard Award in Medicine and Science 1983, Roussel Prize (Paris) 1988, Nat. Acad. of Science Award for the Industrial Application of Science 1990, Nat. Medal of Tech. 1991, Priestley Medal (American Chem. Soc.) 1992, Nevada Medal 1992, Thomson Gold Medal (Int. Mass Spectrometry Soc.) 1994, Prince Mahidol Award (Thailand) 1996, Willard Gibbs Medal 1997. *Publications:* (author or co-author) Optical Rotatory Dispersion 1960, Steroid Reactions 1963, Interpretation of Mass Spectra of Organic Compounds 1964, Structure Elucidation of Natural Products by Mass Spectrometry (2 vols.) 1964, Mass Spectrometry of Organic Compounds 1967, The Politics of Contraception 1979, 1981, The Futurist and Other Stories (fiction) 1988, Cantor's Dilemma (novel) 1989–, Steroids Made It Possible (autobiog.) 1990, The Clock Runs Backward (poetry) 1991, The Pill, Pygmy Chimps and Degas' Horse (autobiog.) 1992, Bourbaki Gambit (novel) 1994, From the Lab into the World (collected essays) 1994; Marx, deceased (novel) 1996, Menachem's Seed (novel) 1997, NO (novel) 1998; ICSI (play) 1998; of numerous scientific articles, also poems, memoirs and short stories. *Leisure interests:*

skiing, modern art, opera, theatre. *Address:* Department of Chemistry, Stanford University, Stanford, CA 94305-5080, U.S.A. *Telephone:* 415-723-2783.

DJIMASTA, Koibla; Chadian politician; mem. Union pour la démocratie et la République (UDR); Prime Minister of Chad 1995–97. *Address:* c/o Union pour la démocratie et la République, N'Djamena, Chad.

DJINDJIĆ, Zoran, DR.PHIL.SC.; Yugoslav politician and philosopher; b. 1 Aug. 1952, Bosanski Samac; s. of Dragan Djindjić and Mila Djindjić; m. Ruzica Djindjić; one s. one d.; ed. Belgrade Univ., Univ. in Konstanz (Germany); sr. researcher Cen. of Phil. and Social Theory in Belgrade 1985–; Prof. Novi Sad Univ.; Ed.-in-Chief Journal of Philosophical Soc. Teorija; political activities since late 1980s; one of founders Democratic Party of Serbia 1989, Chair. 1994–; mem. Narodna Skuptsina (Parl.) of Serbia 1990–; one of leaders of opposition, bloc Zajedno 1996–97; Mayor of Belgrade Feb.–Sept. 1997. *Publications:* Subjectiveness and Violence 1984, Autumn of Dialectics 1986, Yugoslavia as Incompleted State 1987, Serbia Between East and West 1996, trans. into Serbian works of W. Dilthey, I. Loyola, P. Kropotkin. *Leisure interest:* antiques. *Address:* Demokratska stranka, Krunska 69, 11000 Belgrade, Yugoslavia. *Telephone:* (11) 344-3003. *Fax:* (11) 344-2946.

DJOHAR, Said Ahmed; Comoran politician; leader Union comorienne pour le progrès (UDZIMA); Acting Pres. of the Comoros Nov. 1989–March 1990; elected Pres. 1990–95; stripped of exec. power; returned to Comoros Jan. 1996; Interim Pres. Jan.–March 1996; Pres. cand. March 1996.

DJOUSSOUF, Abbass; Comoran politician; leader Forum pour le redressement national (FRN); Prime Minister of Comoros Nov. 1998–. *Address:* Office of the Prime Minister, Moroni, Comoros.

DJUKANOVIĆ, Milo; Yugoslav politician and economist; b. 15 Feb. 1962, Nikšić, Montenegro; ed. Titograd Univ.; joined League of Communists of Yugoslavia (LCY) 1979 (mem. Cen. Cttee. 1986–89) later named Democratic Party of Socialists (DPS); Prime Minister of Montenegro 1991–97, Pres. 1997–. *Address:* Office of the President, Podgorica, Montenegro, Yugoslavia.

DLAMINI, Barnabas Sibusiso; Swazi politician; Minister of Finance 1984–93; fmr. Exec. Dir. IMF; Prime Minister of Swaziland July 1996–. *Address:* Office of the Prime Minister, P.O. Box 395, Mbabane, Swaziland. *Telephone:* 42251. *Fax:* 43943.

DLAMINI, Prince Bhekimpi Alpheus; Swazi politician, soldier and administrator; served with Eighth Army 1937-45; mem. Swazi Nat. Council, participated in constitutional talks 1963; Asst. Minister of Admin. 1966, then Deputy Minister, Deputy Prime Minister's Dept.; Prime Minister of Swaziland 1983–86; found guilty of treason and sentenced to 15 years' imprisonment March 1988; granted pardon July 1988.

DLAMINI, Obed Mfanyana; Swazi politician; b. 4 April 1937, Mhlosheni Area, Shiselweni Dist.; ed. Sincen Primary School, Hlatikulu Primary School, Swaziland Nat. High School, U.N.I.S.A.; teacher and Boarding Master Manzini Nazarene High School 1961–64; cost clerk, later Asst. Personel Officer Roberts Construction (Swaziland) (Pty) Ltd. 1964–66; clerk Standard Chartered Bank of Swaziland 1966, Asst. Man. Admin. –1981; fmr. Training and Independent Relations Man. Swaziland Fruit Canners (Pty) Ltd.; fmr. Gen. Sec. Swaziland Fed. of Trade Unions, mem. Labour Advisory Bd., Training and Localisation Council, Wages Advisory Bd., Man. Training Council, Regional Educ. Advisory Bd., Workers' Educ. Group; Prime Minister of Swaziland 1989–93; Senator 1993–. *Leisure interests:* soccer, wrestling, tug-of-war, jazz, music. *Address:* The Senate, Mbabane, Swaziland.

DLAMINI, Sotsha; Swazi politician; fmr. Asst. Police Commr.–1984; Prime Minister of Swaziland 1986–89. *Address:* c/o Office of the Prime Minister, Mbabane, Swaziland.

DLAMINI, Timothy Lutfo Lucky, M.T.S., PH.D.; Swazi diplomatist; b. 1952, Swaziland; m.; one d.; ed. Botswana, Lesotho and Swaziland Univ., McCormick Theological Seminary, and Pittsburg Univ.; Teacher, Swazi Nat. High School 1973–75; Lecturing Asst., Dept. of Theology and Religious Studies, Univ. of Botswana, Lesotho and Swaziland (later renamed Univ. of Swaziland) 1975–76, Lecturer 1976–82 and part-time Lecturer, Faculty of Educ. 1976–83, Head of Dept., Theology and Religious Studies 1982–83; Private Sec. to Minister of Foreign Affairs 1983–85; Perm. Rep. to the UN 1985–94. *Address:* c/o Ministry of Foreign Affairs, P.O. Box 518, Mbabane, Swaziland.

DLAMINI-ZUMA, Nkosazana C., M.B., CH.B.; South African politician and doctor; b. 27 Jan. 1949; m.; four c.; ed. Amanzintoti Training College, Univ. of Zululand, Univ. of Natal, Univ. of Bristol, Univ. of Liverpool; Research Technician Medical School, Univ. of Natal 1972; Vice-Pres. S.A. Students Org. 1975–76; Chair. ANC Youth Section G.B. 1977–78; House Officer Frenchay Hosp. Bristol 1978–79; House Officer Canadian Red Cross Memorial Hosp., Berks. 1979–80; Medical Officer-Pediatrics Mbabane Govt. Hosp. Swaziland 1980–85; Pediatric attachment Wittington Hosp. 1987–89; Vice Chair. Regional Political Cttee. of ANC G.B. 1978–88, Chair. 1988–89; ANC Health Dept. Lusaka 1989–90; Research Scientist Medical Research Council, Durban 1991–94; Minister of Health 1994–; Dir. Health Refugee Trust, Health and Devt. Org., England 1988–90; Chair. S. Natal Region Health Cttee. of ANC 1990–92; mem. Exec. Cttee. S. Natal Region of ANC 1990–93; Chair. S. Natal Region ANC Women's League 1991–93; mem. Steering Cttee. National AIDS Coordinating Cttee. 1992–; mem. Bd. Centre for Social Devt. Studies Univ. of Natal, Durban 1992–; Trustee Health Systems Trust 1992–. *Address:* Ministry of Health, 2027 Civitas Bldg., Cnr. Andries and Struben Sts., Pretoria 0002; Private Bag X399, Pretoria; 602 Stretten Bay, St Andrews Street, Durban 4001, South Africa (Home). *Telephone:* 326-8081, 328-4773, 021-45-7407. *Fax:* 325-5526.

DLOUHÝ, Vladimír, C.SC.; Czech politician and economist; b. 31 July 1953, Prague; one s. one d.; ed. Prague School of Econs., Charles Univ. Prague and Catholic Univ., Louvain; fmr. teacher, Prague School of Econs.; scientist, Inst. of Econ. Forecasting, Czechoslovak Acad. of Sciences 1983–89, latterly Deputy Dir.; Deputy Prime Minister and Chair. State Planning Comm. 1989–90; Minister of the Economy 1990–92; Minister of Trade and Industry of Czech Repub. 1992–97; Int. Adviser, Goldman Sachs 1997–; Adviser to Exec. Man., ABB 1997–, Chair. Supervisory Bd. ABB (Czech Rep.) 1997–; mem. Civic Democratic Alliance 1991–98, Vice-Pres. March–Oct. 1992, Third Deputy Chair. 1993–; mem. State Defence Council 1993; Chair. Council of Customs Union 1994–, Bd. of Supervisors Stock Co. Unipetrol 1996–; Deputy Chair. Bd. of Supervisors, Volkswagen-Skoda Group, Mladá Boleslav 1994–95; mem. Parl. 1996–98; Grand Croix, Ordre de Léopold II (Belgium). *Publications:* Ekonometrický model čs. obchodní bilance 1985, Models of Disequilibrium and Shortage in Centrally Planned Economies 1989; articles in Czechoslovak and int. econ. journals. *Leisure interest:* music. *Address:* Pachtův palác, Anenské naměstí 4, 110 00 Prague 1, Czech Republic. *Telephone:* (02) 2163-5351. *Fax:* (02) 2163-5350.

DMITRIYEVA, Tatyana Borisovna, DR. MED.; Russian politician; b. 21 Feb. 1951, Ivanovo; m. Aleksander Sergeyevich Dmitriyev; ed. Ivanovo Inst. of Medicine; psychiatrist Ivanovo Region Psychiatric Hosp. 1975–76; jr., sr. researcher All-Union Serbsky Research Inst. of Gen. and Judicial Psychiatry 1976–86, Head of Clinical Dept., Deputy Dir. 1986–90; Dir. Serbsky State Scientific Centre of Social and Judicial Psychiatry 1990–; concurrently Prof., Head of Chair. Moscow Sechenov Acad. of Medicine; Minister of Public Health 1996–98. *Address:* Serbsky Scientific Centre, Kropotkinsky per. 23, 119839 Moscow, Russia. *Telephone:* (095) 201 5262.

DMITRIYEVSKY, Anatoly Nikolayevich; Russian engineer; b. 6 May 1937; m.; two d.; ed. Gubkin Moscow Inst. of Oil and Gas; sr. teacher Gubkin Moscow Inst. of Oil and Gas; Pro-rector, Chair Algerian Nat. Int. of Oil, Gas and Chem.; Dir. Inst. of Problems of Oil and Gas Russian Acad. of Sciences; Pres. Union of Scientific and Eng. Org. of Russia; mem. of bd. Int. Gas Union; mem. Russian Acad. of Sciences 1991; U.S.S.R. State Prize, Gubkin Prize. *Publications include:* Study of Natural Oil Reservoirs 1976, Fundamental Basis of Oil and Gas Geology 1991. *Leisure interests:* tennis, mountain skiing, photography. *Address:* Institute of Problems of Oil and Gas, Leninsky pr. 63/2, 117296 Moscow, Russia (Office). *Telephone:* (095) 135 8076 (Office).

DO AMARAL, Diogo Freitas, PH.D.; Portuguese politician and university professor; b. 21 July 1941, Póvoa de Varzim; s. of Duarte P. C. Freitas do Amaral and Maria Filomena Campos Trocado; m. Maria José Salgado Sarmento de Matos 1965; two s. two d.; Prof. of Administrative Law, Lisbon Univ. 1968, Head Dept. of Juridical and Political Sciences, Prof. Portuguese Catholic Univ. 1978; mem. Council of State 1974–75, Parl. 1975–82, 1992–93; Pres. Centre Democrat Party (CDS) 1974–82, 1988–91; Pres. European Union of Christian Democrats 1981–82; Deputy Prime Minister and Minister for Foreign Affairs 1980–81, Deputy Prime Minister and Minister of Defence 1981–83; Presidential cand. 1986; Pres. 50th Gen. Ass. of UN 1995–96; Pres. Fundação Portugal Século XXI, PETROCONTROL; Calouste Gulbenkian Prize (twice); Henry the Navigator Prize. *Publications:* A Utilização do Domínio Público Pelos Particulares 1965, A Execução das Sentenças dos Tribunais Administrativos 1967, Conceito e natureza do recurso hierárquico 1981, Uma Solução para Portugal 1985, Curso de Direito Administrativo I, 1986, 1994, O Antigo Regime e a Revolução (Memórias Políticas—1941–76) 1995. *Leisure interests:* music, horses. *Address:* Av. Fontes Pereira de Melo 35 13A, 1050 Lisbon, Portugal.

DO MUOI; Vietnamese politician; b. 1917, Hanoi; joined movement against French colonial rule 1936; imprisoned by French; escaped in 1945 and took part in anti-Japanese uprising in Ha Dong Prov.; political and mil. leader in provs. of Red River delta during struggle against French 1951–54; Alt. mem. Cen. Cttee. Communist Party of Viet Nam (CPV) March 1955–60, mem. 1960–; Alt. mem. Political Bureau CPV 1976–82, now mem. Gen. Sec. of Cen. Cttee. CPV 1987–; Deputy to Nat. Ass. 2nd, 4th, 5th, 6th, 7th and 8th Legislatures; Minister of Commerce 1969; Deputy Prime Minister and Minister of Bldg. 1976–87; Vice-Chair. Council of Ministers in charge of Economy 1987–; Prime Minister 1988–91; Sec. Gen. CPV 1991–98; Vice-Chair. Nat. Defense Council Dec. 1989; Order of the October Revolution (U.S.S.R.) 1987 and several Vietnamese decorations. *Address:* Communist Party of Viet-Nam, 1 Hoang Van Thu, Hanoi; Council of Ministers, Hanoi, Viet Nam.

DOBBS, Mattiwilda; American singer; ed. Spelman Coll., Atlanta, and Columbia Univ.; m. 1st Luis Rodríguez García 1953 (died 1954); m. 2nd Bengt Janzon 1957; studied with Lotte Leonard 1946–50; Marian Anderson scholarship, soloist at Mexico Univ. Festival 1947; studied at Mannes Music School and Berkshire Music Center 1948, with Pierre Bernac, Paris 1950–52; 1st Voice Prize, Geneva Int. Competition 1951; concert tour Netherlands, France and Sweden 1952; debut La Scala (Milan) in L'Italiana in Algeri 1953; sang at Glyndebourne 1953, 1954, 1956, 1961, Royal Opera House,

Covent Garden (London) 1954, 1955, 1956, 1959, San Francisco Opera 1955, Metropolitan Opera (New York) 1956–; Stockholm Royal Opera 1957–; Hamburg State Opera 1961–63; concert appearances in Europe, U.S.A., Mexico, Israel, Australia, New Zealand and U.S.S.R.; Order of the North Star (Sweden). *Address:* 1101 South Arlington Ridge Road., Apt. 301, Arlington, VA 22202, U.S.A. *Telephone:* (703) 892-5234.

DOBBS, Michael John, PH.D., M.A.L.D., M.A.; British author; b. 14 Nov. 1948; m. Amanda L. Collingridge 1981; two s.; ed. Christ Church, Oxford and Fletcher School of Law and Diplomacy, U.S.A.; U.K. Govt. Special Adviser 1981–87; Chief of Staff, U.K. Conservative Party 1986–87, Deputy Chair. 1994–95; Deputy Chair. Saatchi & Saatchi 1983–91; Jt. Deputy Chair. Conservative Party 1994–95; Chair. Spirit Advertising 1998–. *Publications:* House of Cards 1989, Wall Games 1990, Last Man to Die 1991, To Play the King 1993, The Touch of Innocents 1994, The Final Cut 1995, Goodfellowe M.P. 1997, The Buddha of Brewer Street 1998. *Address:* Ashcott House, Bath Road, Ashcott, Nr. Bridgwater, Somerset, TA7 9QJ, England. *Telephone:* (0836) 201967 (mobile).

DOBESCH, Gerhard, DR.PHIL.; Austrian professor of Roman history, archaeology and epigraphy; b. 15 Sept. 1939, Vienna; s. of Dr. Carl Dobesch and Gustave Dobesch; ed. Univ. of Vienna; lecturer in Ancient History 1967–73; Prof. of Greek and Roman History, Univ. of Graz 1973–76; Prof. of Roman History, Archaeology and Epigraphy, Univ. of Vienna 1976–; corresp. mem. Austrian Archaeological Inst. 1972–, mem. 1998–; corresp. mem. Austrian Acad. of Sciences 1980, mem. 1984–. *Publications:* Caesars Apotheose zu Lebzeiten und sein Ringen um den Königstitel 1966, Der panhellen: Gedanke und der Philippos des Isokrates 1968, Wurde Caesar zu Lebzeiten in Rom als Staatsgott anerkannt?, 1971, Nochmals zur Datierung des grossen Senatskonsultes 1971, Nikolaos von Damaskus und die Selbstbiographie des Augustus 1978, Die Kelten in Österreich nach den ältest 1980, Die Kimbern in den Ostalpen und die Schlacht bei Noreia 1982, Zu Caesars Sitzenbleiben vor dem Senat 1988, Zur Einwanderung die Kelten in Oberitalien 1989, Caesar als Ethnograph 1989, Zu zwei Daten d. Gesch. Galliens 1989, Europa in d. Reichskonzeption 1989, Autonomie des Menschen und Werthaftigkeit in der Antike 1990, Die Kelten als Nachbarn der Etrusker 1992, J. K. Newman u. Catull 1992, 100 Jahre Kleinasiat. Komm. 1993, Principis dignationem 1993; Vom äusseren Proletariat zum Kulturträger 1994, Phokion und der Korinthische Bund 1994, Aus der Vor-und Nachgeschichte der Markomannenkriege 1994, Das europäische "Barbaricum" und die Zone der Mediterrankultur 1995, Der Ostalpenraum als Kultur- und Machtgrundlage in keltischer und römischer Zeit 1996, Würdigung Fritz Schachermeyr 1996, Die römische Kaiserzeit—eine Fortsetzung des Hellenismus? 1996; numerous specialist articles. *Leisure interests:* literature, art history. *Address:* Universität Wien, Institut für Alte Geschichte, Dr. Karl Lueger-Ring 1, A-1010 Vienna (Office); Spitalgasse 29/10, A-1090 Vienna, Austria (Home). *Telephone:* 4277-40520 (Office); 407 95 22 (Home). *Fax:* 4277-9405 (Office).

DOBRETSOV, Nikolai Leontyevich, D.GEOLOGY; Russian geologist; b. 15 Jan. 1936; ed. Leningrad Inst. of Mines; m.; five c.; chief Altai Mining expedition, jr. then sr. researcher; Head of Lab. Inst. of Geology and Geophysics, Siberian br. of U.S.S.R. (now Russian) Acad. of Sciences in Novosibirsk; Head of Lab. Inst. of Tectonics and Geophysics, U.S.S.R. Acad. of Sciences in Khabarovsk; Dir. Buryat Inst. of Geology, Chair. Presidium of Buryat Research Cen. Siberian br. of U.S.S.R. Acad. of Sciences, Dir. United Inst. of Geology, Geophysics and Mineralogy; Corresp. mem. U.S.S.R. (now Russian) Acad. of Sciences 1984, mem. 1987, mem. Presidium 1991–; now Pres. of Siberian Br., Vice-Pres. Russian Acad. of Sciences. *Publications include:* Introduction to Global Petrology 1980, Global Petrological Processes 1981, Deep-level Geodynamics 1994; papers on tectonics and petrography. *Leisure interests:* books, fishing. *Address:* United Institute of Geology, Geophysics and Mineralogy, Prospect Acad. Koptyuga 3, 630090 Novosibirsk, Russia (Office). *Telephone:* 35 46 50, 35 05 67 (Office). *Fax:* 35 26 92 (Office).

DOBRYNIN, Anatoliy Fedorovich, M.SC.; Russian diplomatist (retd.); b. 16 Nov. 1919, Krasnaya Gorka, Moscow Region; ed. technical coll.; engineer at aircraft plant, Second World War; joined diplomatic service 1946; Counsellor, later Minister-Counsellor, Soviet Embassy, Washington 1952–55; Asst. Minister of Foreign Affairs 1955–57; Under-Sec.-Gen. for Political and Security Council Affairs UN 1957–59, Head American Dept., U.S.S.R. Ministry of Foreign Affairs 1959–61; Amb. to U.S.A. 1962–86; Consultant to Russian Ministry of Foreign Affairs 1992–; mem. CPSU 1945–, Cand. mem., CPSU Cen. Cttee. 1966–71, mem. 1971–90, Sec. Cen. Cttee. for Foreign Affairs 1986–88; Head Int. Dept. 1986–88; Deputy of U.S.S.R. Supreme Soviet 1986–89; Adviser to Pres. Gorbachev (q.v.) 1988–91; Hero of Socialist Labour 1982, Order of Lenin (five times), Order of Red Banner and other decorations. *Publication:* In Confidence (memoirs) 1995. *Address:* c/o Ministry of Foreign Affairs, Smolenskaya Sennaya 32/34, Moscow, Russia.

DOBSON, Rt. Hon. Frank Gordon, P.C., B.SC.ECON., M.P.; British politician; b. 15 March 1940; s. of James W. Dobson and Irene S. Dobson; m. Janet M. Alker 1967; three c.; ed. Archbishop Holgate's Grammar School, York and London School of Econs.; admin. appts. with Cen. Electricity Generating Bd. 1962–70, Electricity Council 1970–75; mem. Camden Borough Council 1971–76, Leader 1973–75; Asst. Sec. Comm. for Local Admin. 1975–79; M.P. for Holborn and St. Pancras South 1979–83, for Holborn and St. Pancras 1983–; Opposition Spokesman on Educ. 1981–83, on Health 1983–87, on Energy 1989–92, on Employment 1992–93, on Transport and London 1993–94, on Environment and London 1994–97; Sec. of State for Health May 1997–; Shadow Leader of the House of Commons 1987–89; Gov. L.S.E. 1986–, Inst. of Child Health 1987–92; Labour. *Address:* House of Commons, London, SW1A 0AA; 22 Great Russell Mansions, Great Russell Street, London, WC1B 3BE, England. *Telephone:* 0171-242 5760.

DOCHANASHVILI, Guram; Georgian writer; b. 1939, Tbilisi, Georgia; s. of Petre Dochanashvili and Gulnara Emukhvari; m.; one d.; ed. Tbilisi State Univ.; worked in Dept. of Archaeology Inst. of History Georgian Acad. of Sciences 1962–75; Head. Div. of Prose Mnatobi (magazine) 1975–85; Deputy Dir. Gruzia Film Studio 1985–; Ivane Dzhavakhishvili Medal, Tbilisi State Univ. 1984, State Prize of Georgia 1994. *Publications include:* There, Behind the Mountain 1966. *Address:* c/o Georgian Union of Writers, Machabeli str. 13, 380000 Tbilisi, Georgia.

DOCHERTY, David, B.A., PH.D.; British broadcasting executive; b. 10 Dec. 1956, Scotland; s. of David Docherty and Anna Docherty; m. Kate Stuart-Smith 1992; two d.; ed. Univ. of Strathclyde, L.S.E.; Research Fellow Broadcasting Research Unit, London 1984–88; Dir. of Research Broadcasting Standards Council 1988–89; Head of Broadcasting Analysis BBC TV 1990–92, Head of TV Planning and Strategy BBC Network TV 1992–96, Dir. of Strategy and Channel Devt. BBC Broadcast 1996–97, Deputy Dir. of TV BBC Broadcast 1997–; mem. bd. BBC America UKTV. *Publications:* The Last Picture Show?: Britain's Changing Film Audience 1987, Keeping Faith?: Channel 4 and Its Audience 1988, Running the Show: 21 Years of London Weekend Television 1990, Violence in Television Fiction 1991. *Leisure interest:* writing. *Address:* BBC TV, Wood Lane, London, W.12, England. *Telephone:* 0181-743-8000.

DOCTOROW, Edgar Lawrence, A.B.; American novelist; b. 6 Jan. 1931, New York; s. of David Richard and Rose (Levine) Doctorow; m. Helen Esther Setzer 1954; one s. two d.; ed. Kenyon Coll., Gambier, Ohio; served with U.S. army 1953–55; Ed. New American Library, New York 1960–64; Ed.-in-Chief Dial Press., New York 1964–69, Publr. 1969; writer-in-residence Univ. of Calif., Irvine 1969–70; mem. faculty Sarah Lawrence Coll., Bronxville, N.Y. 1971–78; mem. Authors Guild (Dir.), American P.E.N. (Dir.), Writers Guild of America East, Century Assen.; Creative Writing Fellow Yale School of Drama 1974–75; Creative Artists Program Service Fellow 1973–74; Visiting Sr. Fellow Council on Humanities, Princeton Univ. 1980; Gluckman Prof. of American and English Letters, New York Univ. 1982–; Guggenheim Fellow 1973; Hon. L.H.D. (Kenyon Coll.) 1976, (Hobart Coll.) 1979; Arts and Letters Award (American Acad. and Nat. Inst. Art) 1976, Nat. Book Critics Circle Award 1976, 1990, Guggenheim Fellow 1973, American Book Award 1986, Howells Medal, American Acad. of Arts and Letters 1990, PEN/Faulkner Prize 1990, Nat. Humanities Medal 1998. *Publications:* Welcome to Hard Times 1960, Big as Life 1966, The Book of Daniel 1971, Ragtime 1975, Drinks before Dinner (play) 1975, Loon Lake 1980, Lives of the Poets: Six Stories and a Novella 1984, World's Fair 1985, Billy Bathgate 1988, The Waterworks 1994, Poets and Presidents: Selected Essays 1994. *Address:* English Department, New York University, New York, NY 10003; c/o Random House Publishers, 210 E 50th Street, New York, NY 10022, U.S.A. (Office).

DODD, Christopher J., B.A., J.D.; American politician; b. 27 May 1944, Willimantic, Conn.; s. of Thomas J. and Grace (Murphy) Dodd; ed. Providence Coll., R.I., and Univ. of Louisville, Ky.; Volunteer with Peace Corps, Dominican Repub. 1966–68; admitted to Conn. Bar 1973; mem. House of Reps. 1975–81 from 2nd Dist. Conn.; Senator from Connecticut 1980–; Democrat. *Address:* U.S. Senate, 444 Russell Senate Building, Washington, DC 20510, U.S.A.

DODD, John Newton, M.SC., PH.D.; New Zealand physicist; b. 19 April 1922, Hastings; s. of John H. Dodd and Eva E. Weeks; m. Jean P. Oldfield 1950; three s. one d.; ed. Otago Boys' High School and Univs. of Otago and Birmingham; lecturer, Sr. Lecturer, Reader in Physics, Otago Univ. 1952–65, Prof. of Physics 1965–88 (Beverly Prof. 1968–88); Pres. Royal Soc. of N.Z. 1989–94; 1851 Exhibition Scholarship; Nuffield Fellowship; Hector Medal (R.S.N.Z.). *Publications:* Einstein (with A. E. Musgrave), Atoms and Light 1991; scientific papers in field of atomic and optical physics. *Leisure interests:* music, gardening, reading, theatre, snooker, croquet. *Address:* Royal Society of New Zealand, P.O. Box 398, Wellington; 13 Malvern Street, Dunedin, New Zealand. *Telephone:* 4679757.

DODIN, Lev Abramovich; Russian stage director; b. 14 May 1944, Leningrad; ed. Leningrad Theatre Inst.; lecturer in drama, Leningrad Theatre Inst., 1963–83; with Leningrad Youth Theatre 1967– (now Chief Dir.), Dir. of Leningrad Maly Drama Theatre 1983–; Prof., St. Petersburg Acad. of Dramatic Art; R.S.F.S.R. Merited Artist 1986; U.S.S.R. State Prize 1986, State Prize of Russia 1992, Stanislavsky Prize 1996. *Productions include:* Live and Remember (V. Rasputin); The House (F. Abramov) 1980; Brothers and Sisters (F. Abramov) 1985, Stars in the Morning Sky (A. Galin) 1988, Stroybat 1990, The Demons (Dostoyevsky) 1992, Claustrophobia (V. Yerofeev) 1994. *Address:* Maly Drama Theatre, Rubinstein Str. 18, St. Petersburg, Russia. *Telephone:* 113-21-08.

DODSON, Sir Derek Sherborne Lindsell, K.C.M.G., M.C., D.L.; British diplomatist (retd.); b. 20 Jan. 1920, Cambridge; s. of Charles Sherborne Dodson and Irene Frances Lindsell; m. 1st Julie Maynard Barnes 1952 (died 1992); one s. one d.; m. 2nd Ourania Massourides (née Papadam) 1997; two step-s.; ed. Stowe School, Royal Mil. Coll., Sandhurst; commissioned in Royal

Scots Fusiliers 1939; Mil. Asst. to British Commr., Allied Control Comm. for Bulgaria 1945–46; Second Sec., Foreign Office 1947–48; Vice-Consul, Salonika, Greece 1948–50; in British Embassy to Spain 1950–53; at Foreign Office 1953–58; Head of Chancery, Embassy to Czechoslovakia 1958–62; Consul, Elisabethville (now Lubumbashi), Zaire 1962–63; Head of Central Dept., FCO 1963–66; Counsellor, Embassy to Greece 1966–69; Amb. to Hungary 1970–73, to Brazil 1973–77, to Turkey 1977–80; Special Rep. of Foreign and Commonwealth Sec. 1981–95; a Gov. United World Coll. of the Atlantic 1982–95; Chair. Anglo-Turkish Soc. 1982–95, Beaver Guarantee Ltd. 1984–86; Dir. Benguela Railway Co. 1984–92, Consultant 1992–; Deputy Lieut. for Lincolnshire 1988–; Grand Cross of Cruzeiro do Sul (Brazil). *Leisure interests:* reading history, walking. *Address:* 47 Ovington Street, London, S.W.3; Gable House, Leadenham, Lincoln, England.

DOERING, William von Eggers, PH.D.; American professor of chemistry; b. 22 June 1917, Fort Worth, Tex.; s. of Carl Rupp Doering and Antoinette Mathilde von Eggers; m. 1st Ruth Haines 1947 (divorced 1954); two s. one d.; m. 2nd Sarah Cowles 1969 (divorced 1981); ed. Shady Hill School, Mass., Belmont Hill School, Mass. and Harvard Univ.; with Office of Scientific Research and Devt. 1941, Nat. Defense Research Cttee. 1942, Polaroid Corpn. 1943 (all in Cambridge, Mass.); Instructor, Columbia Univ. 1943–45, Asst. Prof. 1945–48, Assoc. Prof. 1948–52; Prof. Yale Univ. 1952–56, Whitehead Prof. of Chem. 1956–67; Prof. Harvard Univ. 1967–68, Mallinckrodt Prof. of Chem. 1968–86, Prof. Emer. 1986–; Chair. Council for a Livable World, Washington, D.C. 1964–73, Pres. 1973–78; U.S. Dir. People's Repub. of China-U.S.A. Chem. Graduate Program 1982–86; mem. N.A.S., American Acad. of Arts and Sciences; Hon. Prof. Fudan Univ., Shanghai 1980; John Scott Award 1945, American Chem. Soc. Award in Pure Chem. 1953, A. W. von Hoffman Medal (Gesellschaft Deutscher Chemiker) 1962, William C. DeVane Medal 1967, Theodore William Richards Medal 1970, James Flack Norris Award 1989, and other awards from American Chem. Soc.; Robert A. Welch Award in Chemistry 1990; Kosolapoff Award, Auburn Univ. 1995; Hon. D.Sc. (Texas Christian Univ.); Hon. D. Nat. Sci. (Karlsruhe) 1987. *Publications:* Quinine 1944, Tropolone 1950, Tropylium Ion 1954, Carbenes 1954, Bullvalene 1962, Thermal Rearrangements 1966. *Leisure interests:* music, theatre, tennis, hiking. *Address:* Harvard University, Dept. of Chemistry, 12 Oxford Street, Cambridge, MA 02138 (Office); 53 Francis Avenue, Cambridge, MA 02138, U.S.A. (Home). *Telephone:* 617-495-4263 (Office).

DOGRAMACI, Ihsan, M.D., LL.D., L.H.D., F.R.C.P., F.A.A.P.; Turkish paediatrician and educator; b. 3 April 1915, Erbil; s. of Ali Dogramaci and Ismet Kirdar; m. Ayser Hikmet Suleyman 1941; two s. one d.; ed. Istanbul, Harvard and Washington Univs.; Asst. Prof. of Pediatrics, Ankara Univ. 1947–49, Assoc. Prof. 1949–54, Prof. and Head of Dept. 1954–63; Dir. Research Inst. of Child Health, Ankara 1958–81; Prof. of Pediatrics and Head of Dept., Hacettepe Faculty of Medicine 1963–81, Dean of Faculty June–Nov. 1963; Pres. Ankara Univ. 1963–65; Chair. Bd. of Trustees Middle East Tech. Univ. 1965–67; Pres. Hacettepe Children's Medical Centre, Ankara 1965–81; Rector, Hacettepe Univ. 1967–75; Pres. UNICEF Exec. Bd. 1967–70; Pres. Int. Pediatric Assen. 1968–77, Dir.-Gen. 1977–93, Hon. Pres. 1992–; Pres. Bd. of Trustees, Bilkent Univ. 1985, Pres. Bilkent Univ. 1992–; Pres. Union of Middle-Eastern and Mediterranean Pediatric Socs. 1971–73, Turkish and Int. Children's Center, Ankara 1980–, Higher Educ. Council of Turkey 1981–92; mem. of Standing Conf. of Rectors and Vice-Chancellors of the European Univs. 1969–81; Hon. Pres. Int. Conf. for Higher Educ. 1992–; Hon. Fellow, American Acad. Pediatrics 1959; Hon. mem. American Pediatric Soc., Deutsche Gesellschaft für Kinderheilkunde 1973, Soc. de Pédiatrie de Paris 1958, British Ped. Assen. 1964, Finnish Pediatric Assen. 1971, etc.; Corresp. mem. Acad. Nat. de Médecine, France 1973; Léon Bernard Foundation Prize 1981; Maurice Pate Award (UNICEF) 1995; Hon. LL.D. (Nebraska) 1965; Dr. h.c. (Nice) 1973; hon. degrees also from Univs. of Glasgow, Anatolia, Bosporus, Baghdad, Marmara, Ain Shams, Soka, Devlet Tib (Baku), E. Mediterranean, De Montfort and Istanbul; Fellow, Royal Coll. of Physicians (London) 1971; Grand Officier, Duarte, Sánchez y Mella 1976, Officier, Légion d'honneur 1978, Christopherson Award 1986, Commdr., Order of the Lion of Finland (First Class), Commdr. Order of Merit of Poland 1989, Gran Cruz Placa de Plata de la Orden Heráldica de Cristóbal Colón (Dominican Rep.) 1990, State Medal for Outstanding Merit 1995, State Medal (Romania) 1997, Health-For-All Gold Medal (WHO) 1997. *Publications:* Annenin Kitabi—Mother's Handbook on Child Care 1952–84, Premature Baby Care 1954, ed. Turkish Journal of Paediatrics. *Address:* Bilkent University Board of Trustees, P.O. Box 126 Bahçelievier, 06533 Ankara, Turkey. *Telephone:* (90-312) 266 4596-8. *Fax:* (90-312) 266 4678.

DOHNÁNYI, Christoph von (see von Dohnányi, Christoph).

DOHNANYI, Klaus von (see von Dohnanyi, Klaus).

DOI, Takako; Japanese politician; b. 30 Nov. 1928, Kobe; ed. Doshisha Univ.; fmr. univ. lecturer on Japanese constitution; mem. Lower House (Diet) 1969–; Leader, Japan Socialist Party (JSP) 1986–91; Speaker, House of Reps. 1993–96; Chair Social Democratic Party of Japan 1996–. *Leisure interest:* singing. *Address:* Social Democratic Party of Japan, 1-8-1 Nagatacho, Chiyoda-ku, Tokyo 100, Japan. *Telephone:* (3) 3580-1171. *Fax:* (3) 3580-0691.

DOINAŞ, Ştefan Augustin; Romanian writer; b. 26 April 1922, Caporal Alexa, Arad County; s. of Augustin Popa and Florita Popa; m. Silvia Lia Voicu 1958; ed. Coll. of Philology and Philosophy, Cluj Univ.; teacher 1948–55; Ed. of periodicals: Teatrul 1956–57, Lumea 1963–66, Secolul 20 1969–90; Deputy Ed.-in-chief of Secolul 20; Hon. Pres. Romanian Writers' Union 1990–; Corresp. mem. Romanian Acad. 1990–, mem. 1992–; awards for poetry from the Romanian Writers' Union, Prize of the Romanian Acad., Goethe medal for translations, Prize for European Literature, KOV (Yugoslavia). *Works include:* vols of poetry: Man with Compass 1966, Laocoön's Descendants 1967; Hypostases 1968, Hesperia 1980, Falcon Hunting 1985, Lamentations 1992, The Adventures of Proteus 1995, Psalms 1997 and others; Brutus and His Sons (tragedy); essays; translations from Goethe, Dante, Hölderlin, Mallarmé and others. *Address:* 35 Bulevardul I.C. Brătianu, Bucharest 70051, Romania. *Telephone:* 6.14.61.19.

DOJE CEDAIN; Chinese government official; b. 1924; m. Gesang Zhuoga; ed. Beijing Normal Univ.; Gov. of Xizang (Tibet) Autonomous Region 1983–85; Researcher, Inst. of Research on World Religions, Chinese Acad. of Social Sciences 1985–; Adviser United Front Work Dept. under CCP Cen. Cttee. 1986–; mem. Standing Cttee 6th NPC 1986–88, Standing Cttee. 7th 1988–93, 8th 1993–; Vice-Chair. Educ., Science, Culture and Public Health Cttee. under the NPC 1986; Deputy Head China-Spain Friendship Group 1986. *Address:* Chinese Academy of Social Sciences, 5 Jianguomen Nei Da Jie, Beijing, People's Republic of China.

DOJE CERING; Chinese government official; b. 1939, Xiahe Co., Gansu Prov.; worked in Tibet 1959; joined CCP 1960; country magistrate in Tibet 1962; mem. Tibet Autonomous Region CCP 1974–90; mem., Standing Cttee. Tibet CCP 1977–90; First Sec., Xigaze Municipality CCP 1979–82; Vice-Chair. Tibet Autonomous Region 1983–85, Acting Admin. Head 1986–88, Chair. 1988–90; deputy for Tibet Autonomous Region, 7th NPC 1988–; Vice-Minister of Civil Affairs 1990–93, Minister March 1993–; Vice-Chair. China Cttee. Int. Decade for Nat. Disaster Reduction; mem. 8th NPC 1993; mem. 14th CCP Cen. Cttee. 1992–97, 15th CCP Cen. Cttee. 1997–; Dir. Leading Group for Placement of Demobilized Army Officers 1993–; Deputy Head Leading Group for the Work of Supporting the Army, Giving Preferential Treatment to the Families of Armymen and Martyrs, supporting the Govt. and Cherishing the People, State Council Leading Group on Boundary Delimitation. *Address:* Ministry of Civil Affairs, Beijing, People's Republic of China.

DOKTOR, Martin; Czech canoeist; b. 21 May 1974, Policka; s. of Josef Doktor and Zuzana Doktorová; ed. Charles Univ., Prague; Silver Medals 500m. and 1000m. Canoeing World Championships, Duisburg, Germany; Gold Medals 500m. and 1000m. Olympic Games, Atlanta, U.S.A. 1996; Silver Medals 200m. and 1000m., Gold Medal 500m. Canoeing World Championships, Dartmouth, Canada 1997; Silver Medal 500m., Gold Medal 1000m. European Championships, Plovdiv, Bulgaria 1997; World Cup Winner 1998; Gold Medal 200m. World Championships, Szeged, Hungary 1998, Silver Medal 1000m.; Best Czech Sportsman of the Year 1996. *Leisure interests:* skiing, music, cycling. *Address:* Canoe Club Prosport Sezemice, Slunecní 627, Sezemice 533 04, Czech Republic. *Telephone:* (40) 6931417. *Fax:* (60) 3560030.

DOLAN, Beverly Franklin; American business executive; b. 1927, Augusta, Ga.; m.; ed. Univ. Georgia and Harvard Univ.; served with U.S. army 1952–54; Pres. and co-founder E–Z Go Car Corpn. 1954–60; joined Textron Inc. 1960, Pres. Homelit Div. 1976–79, Corpn. Exec. Vice-Pres. (Operations) 1979–80, Pres. and C.O.O. 1980–85, Pres., C.E.O. 1985, Chair. 1986–92, also Dir.; Dir. First Union Corpn., Alledale Mutual Insurance Co.

DOLAN, Charles F.; American cable television executive; b. 16 Oct. 1926, Cleveland, Ohio; m. Helen Burgess; three s. three d.; ed. John Carroll Univ.; served in U.S.A.F.; jtly. with wife est. co. producing and distributing sports and industrial films; subsequently f. Teleguide Inc. (providing information services via cable to New York hotels) and Sterling Manhattan Cable (first urban cable TV co. in U.S.A.), Home Box Office Inc.; Founder and Chair. Cablevision Systems Corp. 1985–; co-owner Madison Square Garden Properties; Dir. Cold Spring Harbor Lab., St. Francis Hosp., Long Island; Chair. Nat. Acad. of TV Arts and Sciences; a Man. Dir. of Metropolitan Opera, New York; Trustee Fairfield Univ., Conn.; mem. Bd. of Govs. Nat. Hockey League. *Address:* Cablevision Systems Corporation, 1 Media Crossways, Woodbury, NY 11797, U.S.A.

DOLAN, James; American business executive; m.; five c.; fmrly. Asst. Gen. Man. Cablevision Chicago, Vice-Pres. for Advertising Sales Cablevision; Man. WKNR-AM radio station, Cleveland; Corp. Dir. Advertising Rainbow Programming Holdings, C.E.O. 1992–95; C.E.O. Cablevision Systems Corp. Oct. 1995–. *Leisure interests:* yachting, music. *Address:* Cablevision Systems Corporation, 1 Media Crossways, Woodbury, New York, NY 11797, U.S.A.

DOLE, Elizabeth Hanford, M.A., J.D.; American administrator; b. 29 July 1936, Salisbury, N.C.; d. of John Van Hanford and Mary E. Cathey; m. Robert J. Dole (q.v.) 1975; ed. Duke and Harvard Univs. and Univ. of Oxford; called to Bar, Dist. of Columbia 1966; Staff Asst. to Asst. Sec. for Educ., Dept. of Health, Educ. and Welfare 1966–67; practising lawyer, Washington, D.C. 1967–68; Assoc. Dir. Legis. Affairs, then Exec. Dir. Pres.'s Comm. for Consumer Interests 1968–71; Deputy Asst. Office of Consumer Affairs, The White House, Washington, D.C. 1971–73; Commr. Fed. Trade. Comm. 1973–79; Asst. to Pres. for Public Liaison 1981–83; Sec. of Transport 1983–87; Trustee Duke Univ. 1974–88; mem. Visiting Comm., John F. Kennedy School of Govt. 1988–; Sec. of Labor 1989–90; Pres. American Red Cross 1991–98;

mem. Comm. Harvard School of Public Health 1992–, Bd. of Overseers, Harvard Univ. 1989–95. *Address:* c/o American Red Cross, 8111 Gatehouse Road, Falls Church, VA 22042, U.S.A.

DOLE, Robert J.; American politician: b. 22 July 1923, Russell, Kan.; s. of Mr. and Mrs. Doran R. Dole; m. 2nd Elizabeth Hanford Dole (q.v.) 1975; one d.; ed. Russell public schools, Univ. of Kansas and Washbourn Municipal Univ.; mem. Kansas Legislature 1951–53; Russell County Attorney 1953–61; mem. House of Reps. 1960–68; U.S. Senator from Kansas 1969–96; Senate Majority Leader 1995–96; Senate Republican leader 1987–96; House Majority Leader 1985–87, Minority leader 1987; Chair. Republican Nat. Cttee. 1971–72; Vice-Presidential Cand. 1976, Presidential Cand. 1996; Chair. Senate Finance Cttee. 1981–84, Dole Foundation; Dir. Mainstream Inc.; Adviser, U.S. Del. to FAO Conf., Rome 1965, 1974, 1977; mem. Congressional del. to India 1966, Middle East 1967; mem. U.S. Helsinki Comm., del. to Belgrade Conf. 1977; Trustee, William Allen White Foundation, Univ. of Kan.; mem. Nat. Advisory Cttee., The John Wesley Colls.; mem. American Bar Asscn.; mem. Nat. Advisory Cttee. on Scouting for the Handicapped, Kan. Asscn. for Retarded Children, Advisory Bd. of United Cerebral Palsy, Kan.; Hon. mem. Advisory Bd. of Kidney Patients Inc.; Presidential Medal of Freedom 1997; Distinguished Service Award 1997; Republican. *Publication:* Great Political Wit (co.ed.) 1999. *Leisure interests:* politics, watching the news. *Address:* Suite 410, 901 15th Street, N.W., Washington, DC 20005, U.S.A.

DOLGEN, Jonathan L., J.D.; American film executive; ed. Cornell Univ., New York. Univ. Law School; lawyer Fried, Frank, Harris, Shriver & Jacobson 1969–76; Asst. Gen. Counsel then Deputy Gen. Counsel Columbia Pictures Industries 1976–85, Sr. Vice-Pres. World Business Affairs 1979, Exec. Vice-Pres. 1980; Pres. Columbia's Pay Cable & Home Entertainment Group 1983; Sr. Exec. Vice-Pres. Fox Inc. 1985–90; Pres. T.V. Div. Twentieth Century Fox Inc. 1985–88, Pres. 1988–93; Chair. Twentieth T.V. 1988–90; Pres. Columbia Pictures 1990–94; Chair. and C.E.O. Viacom Entertainment Group 1994–; f. Friends of Cornell Univ. Arts Center, founder mem. Educ. First; mem. Alumni Council New York Univ. Law School; mem. Bd. Dirs. Sony Pictures; Fellow Claremont Univ. Center and Grad. School. *Address:* Viacom Entertainment Group, Paramount Pictures, 5555 Melrose Avenue, Los Angeles, CA 90038, U.S.A.

DOLGUSHIN, Nikita Aleksandrovich; Russian choreographer; b. 8 Nov. 1938, Leningrad; ed. Leningrad School of Choreography; soloist, Kirov (now Maryinsky) Theatre of Opera and Ballet 1959–61; leading dancer, Novosibirsk Theatre of Opera and Ballet 1961–66, 1968–83; soloist, Leningrad Maly Opera and Ballet Theatre; Head of Ballet Chair, St. Petersburg Conservatory 1983–, head of ballet group, Musical Theatre of Conservatory; Prof., Paris Univ. of Dance; U.S.S.R. People's Artist. *Leading roles include:* Satire (Spartacus), Albert (Giselle), Romeo (Romeo and Juliet), Prince (Nutcracker), Prince Igor (Yaroslavna). *Address:* St. Petersburg State Conservatory, Teatralnaya pl. 3, St. Petersburg, Russia. *Telephone:* (812) 312 2507 (Office).

DOLL, Sir (William) Richard (Shaboe), Kt., C.H., O.B.E., F.R.S., M.D., D.SC., F.R.C.P.; British epidemiologist and medical researcher; b. 28 Oct. 1912, Hampton; s. of William and Kathleen Doll; m. Joan Faulkner (née Blatchford) 1949; one s. one d.; ed. Westminster School and St. Thomas's Hospital Medical School, Univ. of London; Military Service 1939–45; with Medical Research Council's Statistical Research Unit 1948–69, Dir. 1961–69; mem. Advisory Cttee. on Medical Research WHO 1963, Council of Int. Epidemiological Asscn. 1961, Scientific Cttee. Int. Agency for Cancer Research 1965–70, 1975–78, Hebdomadal Council, Oxford Univ. 1975–81, Comm. on Environment and Health, WHO 1990–91; Regius Prof. of Medicine, Oxford 1969–79, Warden Green Coll. 1979–83; Hon. Consultant, Imperial Cancer Research Fund, Cancer Studies Unit, Radcliffe Infirmary, Oxford 1983–; mem. Royal Comm. on Environmental Pollution 1973–79; Comm. on Energy and the Environment 1978–81; Foreign Hon. mem. Norwegian Acad. of Sciences 1976, New York Acad. of Arts and Sciences 1977; Hon. Assoc. Physician Central Middx. Hospital 1949–69; David Anderson Berry Prize, Royal Soc. of Edin. (jointly) 1958, Bisset Hawkins Medal, Royal Coll. of Physicians, London 1962, UN Award for Cancer Research 1962, Rock Carling Fellow, Nuffield Provincial Hospitals Trust, London 1967, Gairdner Award 1970, Buchanan Medal, Royal Soc. 1972, Presidential Award, New York Acad. of Sciences 1975, Prix Griffuel, Paris 1975, John Snow Award, Epidemiology Section, American Public Health Asscn. 1976, Gold Medal, Royal Inst. of Public Health 1977, Charles S. Mott Prize for Prevention of Cancer 1979, Nat. Award, American Cancer Soc. 1981, Gold Medal, B.M.A. 1983, Wilhelm Conrad Röntgen Prize, Accademia dei Lincei 1984, Johann-Georg-Zimmermann Preis, Hanover 1985, Founders' Award, Chemical Inst. of Toxicology 1986, Royal Medal, Royal Soc. 1986, Alton Ochsner Award (jtly) 1988, Helmut Horten Award (jtly.) 1991, first Prince Mahidol Award (Bangkok) 1992; Hon. D.Sc. (Newcastle) 1969, (Belfast) 1972, (Reading) 1973, (Newfoundland) 1973, (Stony Brook) 1988, (Harvard) 1988, (London) 1988, (Oxford) 1989, (Oxford Brookes) 1994, (Kingston) 1996; D.M. (Tasmania) 1975, (Birmingham) 1994, (Bergen) 1996. *Publications:* Articles on causes of cancer, aetiology of lung cancer, leukaemia, epidemiology, effects of ionizing radiations, oral contraceptives, treatment of gastric ulcers, etc. *Leisure interests:* conversation, good food. *Address:* 12 Rawlinson Road, Oxford, OX2 6UE, England. *Telephone:* (01865) 558887.

DOLLERY, Sir Colin (Terence), Kt., F.R.C.P.; British physician; b. 14 March 1931; s. of Cyril R. Dollery and Thelma M. Dollery; m. Diana M. Stedman 1958; one s. one d.; ed. Lincoln School and Univ. of Birmingham; House Officer, Queen Elizabeth Hosp. Birmingham, Hammersmith Hosp. and Brompton Hosp. 1956–58; Medical Registrar, Hammersmith Hosp. 1958–60, Sr. Registrar and Tutor in Med. 1960–62; Consultant Physician 1962–96; lecturer in Medicine Royal Postgrad. Medical School, Univ. of London 1962–65, Prof. of Clinical Pharmacology 1965–87, Prof. of Medicine 1987–91, Dean 1991–96, Pro Vice-Chancellor for Medicine 1992–96; mem. Medical Research Council 1982–84, Univ. Funding Council (fmrly. Univ. Grants Cttee.) 1984–91; hon. mem. Asscn. of American Physicians; Chevalier, Ordre Nat. du Mérite. *Publications:* The Retinal Circulation 1971, Therapeutic Drugs 1991; papers in scientific journals. *Leisure interests:* travel, amateur radio, work. *Address:* 101 Corringham Road, London, NW11 7DL, England. *Telephone:* 0181-458 2616.

DOLLEZHAL, Nikolay Antonovich; Russian power engineering scientist; b. 27 Oct. 1899, Omelnik, Ukraine; s. of the late Anton Ferdinandovitch and Barbara Vladimirovna; m. Alexandra Grigorievna Savvakina 1943; one d.; ed. Moscow Higher Tech. School; Lecturer, Inst. of Nat. Economy, and Moscow Higher Tech. School 1923–32; Tech. Dir. Leningrad Inst. of Nitrogen Production Equipment 1932–34; Chief Eng. Kiev "Bolshevik" plant 1935–38; Dir. Moscow Research Inst. of Chemical Machinery 1942–53; Dir. Power Eng. Inst. of the U.S.S.R. (now Russian) State Atomic Energy Cttee. 1953–89, Adviser to Pres. 1989–; mem. Bureau of Dept. of Physico-Tech. Problems of Energy of U.S.S.R. Acad. of Sciences 1953–62; corresp. mem. U.S.S.R. (now Russian) Acad. of Sciences 1953–62, mem. 1962–; Chief constructor first nuclear power-station reactor; State Prize (five), Lenin Prize 1957, Hero of Socialist Labour 1949, 1984, Order of Lenin (six), Hammer and Sickle Gold Medal, etc. *Publications:* The Principles of Designing Steam Operated Power Units 1933, Theory of Compressor Valves 1941, Reactor of Atomic Power Station of U.S.S.R. Academy of Sciences 1956; Uranium-graphite reactors in power stations with steam heating 1957, At The Outset (The Designer's Notes) 1989, On the Uranium–Graphite Reactor and on One Version of the Chernobyl Atom Power Station Accident of 26 April 1986 1995. *Leisure interest:* philately, classical music. *Address:* Lenynsky prospect 13, apt. 140, 117071 Moscow, Russia. *Telephone:* (095) 237-34-96. *Fax:* (095) 236-44-28.

DOLLFUS, Audouin, D. ÈS SC.; French astronomer; b. 12 Nov. 1924, Paris; s. of Charles Dollfus and Suzanne Soubeyran; m. Catherine Browne 1959; four c.; ed. Univ. de Paris; joined Observatoire de Meudon (astrophysical div. of Observatoire de Paris) 1946, Head of Lab. for Physics of the Solar System; Astronomer, Observatoire de Paris 1965, now Emer.; mem. Int. Acad. of Astronautics (Trustee 1975–81), Société Astronomique de France (Pres. 1979–81), Aéro-club de France (Trustee 1995–), French Asscn. for the Advancement of Science (Pres. 1993–95); Hon. mem. Royal Astronomical Soc. of Canada, Astronomy and Geophysics Soc. of U.S.S.R.; Assoc. Royal Astronomical Soc., London, Soc. French Explorers, Explorers Club U.S.A., Soc. Philomatique de Paris; Grand Prix of Acad. des Sciences, Int. Award Galabert for Astronautics, Diploma Tissandier, Int. Fed. Astronautics. *Publications:* 350 scientific publications on astrophysics. *Leisure interest:* ballooning (holds three official world records with gas balloons: duration, distance, altitude). *Address:* 77 rue Albert Perdreaux, 92370 Chaville, France. *Telephone:* 01-47-50-97-43.

DOMARCAS, Juozas; Lithuanian conductor; b. 28 July 1936, Varkaliai, Plunge Dist.; m. (wife deceased); two s.; ed. Klaipeda Simkus College of Music, Lithuanian State Conservatory, Leningrad State Conservatory; asst. conductor, Vilnius Band 1957–60; Artistic Dir. and Chief Conductor Lithuanian Nat. Orchestra (NLO) 1964–; participated in numerous nat. and int. festivals; teacher, sr. teacher, Assoc. Prof. Lithuanian State Conservatory 1968–93; Chair and Prof. Lithuanian Acad. of Music 1993–; several decorations. *Address:* Lietuvos Nacionaline Filharmonija, Ausros Vartu 5, LT-2001, Vilnius (Office); Jogalios 16-5, LT-2001 Vilnius, Lithuania (Home). *Telephone:* (370) 62 70 47 (Office); (370) 62 56 10 (Home). *Fax:* (370) 62 28 59 (Office).

DOMB, Cyril, M.A., PH.D., F.R.S.; British-Israeli professor of physics; b. London; s. of Joel and Sarah (née Wulkan) Domb; m. Shirley Galinsky 1957; three s. three d.; ed. Hackney Downs School, London, Pembroke Coll., Cambridge; Fellow, Clarendon Lab., Oxford 1949–52; Univ. Lecturer in Mathematics, Cambridge 1952–54; Prof. of Theoretical Physics, London Univ. 1954–81; Prof. of Physics, Bar Ilan Univ., Israel 1981–89, Prof. Emer. 1989–; Academic Pres. Jerusalem Coll. of Technology 1985–94; Rayleigh Prize 1947, Max Born Prize 1981. *Publications:* Co-operative Phenomena in Crystals, in Advances in Physics 1960, Phase Transitions and Critical Phenomena, Vols. 1–6 (ed. with M. S. Green), vols. 7–17 (ed. with J. L. Lebowitz), Memories of Kopul Rosen (ed.) 1970, Challenge—Torah views on science and its problems (ed. with A. Carmell) 1976, The Critical Point 1996; scientific papers. *Leisure interests:* walking, swimming. *Address:* c/o Department of Physics, Bar Ilan University, 52 100 Ramat Gan, Israel; 28 St. Peter's Court, Queen's Road, London, N.W.4, England.

DOMENICI, Pete V., B.S., LL.B.; American senator; b. 7 May 1932, Albuquerque; s. of Cherubino Domenici and Alda Domenici; m. Nancy Burk 1958; two s. six d.; ed. Univs of Albuquerque, New Mexico, Denver; elected to Albuquerque City Comm. 1966, Chair. 1967; mem. Nat. League of Cities Revenue and Finance Steering Cttee. and the Resolutions Cttee. of the 1969 Annual Conf. of Mayors; served on Governor's Policy Bd. for Law

Enforcement and on Middle Rio Grande Conf. of Govts.; U.S. Senator from New Mexico 1972–; Chair. Senate Budget Cttee. 1981, 1995–, Senate Indian Affairs Cttee.; Public Sector Leadership Award 1996; numerous other awards and several hon. degrees; Republican. *Leisure interests:* hunting, fishing. *Address:* U.S. Senate, 328 Hart Senate Office Building, Washington, DC 20510 (Office); 120 3rd Street, N.E., Washington, DC 20002; 135 East 50th Street, 5L, New York, NY 10022, U.S.A. (Homes).

DOMINGO, Placido, F.R.C.M.; Spanish opera singer; b. 21 Jan. 1941, Madrid; s. of the late Placido and Pepita (Embil) Domingo; m. Marta Ornelas; three s.; ed. Nat. Conservatory of Music, Mexico City; operatic début at Monterrey, Mexico 1961; début at Metropolitan Opera, New York, 1968; British début in Verdi's Requiem at Festival Hall 1969; Covent Garden début in Tosca 1971, returned to sing in Aïda, Carmen 1973, La Bohème 1974, Un ballo in maschera 1975, La Fanciulla del West; has taken leading roles in about 50 operas; with New York City Opera 1965–; Artistic Dir. Washington Opera 1994–; Artistic Adviser and Prin. Guest Conductor Los Angeles Opera; Fellow, Royal N. Coll. of Music; Dr. h.c. (Royal Coll. of Music) 1982, (Univ. Complutense de Madrid) 1989; Commdr. Légion d'honneur; recent engagements include Tosca (conducting), Romeo and Juliet at Metropolitan Opera, New York, N.Y., Aïda, Il Trovatore in Hamburg, Don Carlos in Salzburg, I vespri siciliani and La forza del destino in Paris, Turandot in Barcelona, Otello in Paris, London and Hamburg, Carmen in Edinburgh, Turandot at the Metropolitan, New York; film: Madame Butterfly with Von Karajan, La Traviata 1982, Carmen 1984, Otello 1986; stage debut in My Fair Lady 1988; recent recordings include: Aïda, Un ballo in maschera, Tosca. *Publication:* My First Forty Years (autobiog.) 1983. *Address:* c/o Metropolitan Opera Company, Lincoln Center Plaza, New York, NY 10023, U.S.A.

DOMINIAN, Jacobus, M.B.E., D.S.C., F.R.C.P.(E.), F.R.C.PSY.; British psychiatrist; b. 25 Aug. 1929, Athens, Greece; s. of Charles Dominian and Mary Scarlato; m. Edith Mary Smith 1955; four d.; ed. St. Mary's School, Bombay, Stamford Grammar School, England, Fitzwilliam Coll., Cambridge, Exeter Coll., Oxford and Inst. of Psychiatry, London; Sr. House Officer United Oxford Hosps. 1955–58; Registrar Maudsley Hosp., London 1958–61, Sr. Registrar 1961–64; Sr. Consultant Psychiatrist Cen. Middx. Hosp., London 1965–88, Hon. Consultant 1988–; Dir. One Plus One (Marriage and Partnership Research) 1971–; Hon. D.Sc. (Lancaster) 1976. *Publications:* Christian Marriage 1967, Marital Breakdown 1968, Depression 1976, Proposals for a New Sexual Ethic 1976, Authority 1976, Marital Pathology 1980, Marriage, Faith and Love 1981, The Capacity to Love 1985, Sexual Integrity: the answer to AIDS 1987, Passionate and Compassionate Love—A Vision for Christian Marriage 1991, The Everyday God (with Edmund Flood) 1993, Marriage 1995. *Leisure interests:* swimming, theatre, music and reading. *Address:* Pefka, The Green, Croxley Green, Rickmansworth, Herts., WD3 3JA, England. *Telephone:* 0923-720972.

DOMITIEN, Elisabeth; Central African Republic politician; fmr. mem. Mouvement d'évolution sociale de l'Afrique noire (MESAN), Vice-Pres. 1975–79; Prime Minister of Central African Repub. 1975–76.

DOMLJAN, Žarko; Croatian politician; b. 14 Sept. 1932, Imotski; m. Iva Marijanovic; one d.; ed. Zagreb Univ., Music Coll.; mem. Croatian Nat. Theatre Orchestra 1955–57; Ed.-in-Chief, Deputy Dir., Editorial Dept of Lexicographical Inst. 1968–86; Ed.-in-Chief Yugoslav Encyclopedia of Art and Encyclopedia of Croatian Art 1985–96; Life of Art Journal 1967–73; research advisor Inst. of Art History 1987–90; mem. and Pres. Parl. of Croatian Repub. 1990–92; mem. Chamber of Reps. of Croatian Parl. 1992, Vice Pres. 1992–; Chair. Foreign Policy Bd.; mem. State Council of Defence and Nat. Security and of Presidential Council. *Publications:* Architect Hugo Erlich 1979, Modern Architecture in Yugoslavia 1986. *Leisure interests:* tennis, mountain trekking. *Address:* Kukuljevićeva 32, 10000 Zagreb, Croatia (Home). *Telephone:* (1) 4851011 (Office).

DOMMISSE, Ebbe, B.A., M.SC.; South African newspaper editor; b. 14 July 1940, Riversdale; s. of Jan Dommisse and Anna Dommisse; m. Daléne Laubscher 1963; two s. one d.; ed. Paarl Boys High School, Univ. of Stellenbosch and Grad. School of Journalism, Columbia Univ.; reporter, Die Burger, Cape Town 1961, Chief sub-ed. 1968, News Ed. 1971; Asst. Ed. and political commentator, Beeld, Johannesburg (founder mem. of new Johannesburg daily) 1974; Asst. Ed. Die Burger 1979, Sr. Asst. Ed. 1984, Ed. 1990–; Exec. mem. Nasionale Koerante; Trustee Helpmekaarfonds; mem. Akad. vir Wetenskap en Kuns; Nieman Travel Fellowship 1987. *Publications:* with Alf Ries: Broedertwis 1982, Leierstryd 1990. *Leisure interests:* reading, the arts, ecology, tennis. *Address:* Die Burger, 40 Heerengracht, Cape Town, South Africa (Office). *Telephone:* 021-406-2222.

DOMOTO, Hisao; Japanese painter; b. 1928; ed. Kyoto Acad. of Fine Arts; First Prize, Acad. of Japan 1951 and 1953; studied in France, Italy and Spain 1952; settled in Paris 1955; abandoned traditional Japanese style and exhibited abstract paintings Salon des Indépendants, Salon de Mai, Paris 1956, 1957; rep. at Rome/New York Art Foundation first exhbn. Rome, "Otro Arte" Exhbn. Madrid, Facchetti and Stadler Galleries, Paris 1957; First Prize of Musée d'Art Moderne for foreign painters in Paris 1958; one-man exhbn. Martha Jackson Gallery, New York 1959.

DONABEDIAN, Avedis, B.A., M.D.; American professor of public health and physician; b. 7 Jan. 1919, Beirut, Lebanon; s. of Samuel Donabedian and Maritza (née Der Hagopian) Donabedian; m. Dorothy Salibian 1945; three s.; ed. Friends' Boys' School, Ramallah (Palestine), American Univ. of Beirut and Harvard Univ. School of Public Health, U.S.A.; Teaching Fellow in Pharmacology, American Univ. of Beirut 1938–40; Physician, then Acting Supt., English Mission Hosp., Jerusalem 1945–47; Instructor in Physiology, Clinical Asst. in Venereology, American Univ. of Beirut 1948–50, Physician, then Dir. Univ. Health Service 1951–54; Medical Assoc., Medical Care Evaluation Studies, United Community Services of Metropolitan Boston, Mass., U.S.A. 1955–57; Research Assoc., then Visiting Lecturer, Harvard School of Public Health 1955–57; Asst. Prof., then Assoc. Prof. of Preventive Medicine, New York Medical Coll. 1957–61; Assoc. Prof. of Public Health Econs., then Prof. of Public Health Econs., then Prof. of Medical Org., Univ. of Mich. School of Public Health 1961–79; Nathan Sinai Distinguished Prof. of Public Health, Univ. of Mich. 1979–89, Prof. Emer. 1989–; Hon. Pres. Avedis Donabedian Foundation 1990–; mem. Inst. of Medicine; Hon. Fellow Royal Coll. of Gen. Practitioners, London 1991; Hon. mem. Nat. Acad. of Mexico 1992; several awards including Award in Recognition of a Distinguished Career in Health Services Research, Asscn. for Health Services Research 1985, Baxter American Foundation Prize 1986, Ernest A. Codman Award (Jt. Comm. on Accreditation of Healthcare Orgs.) 1997. *Publications:* A Guide to Medical Care Administration: Vol. II, Medical Care Appraisal 1969, Aspects of Medical Care Administration 1973, Benefits in Medical Care Programs 1976, The Definition of Quality and Approaches to its Assessment 1980, The Criteria and Standards of Quality 1982, The Methods and Findings of Quality Assessment and Monitoring 1985. *Leisure interests:* gardening, photography, languages, literature and music. *Address:* Department of Health Management and Policy, School of Public Health, The University of Michigan, 109 South Observatory Street, Ann Arbor, MI 48109; 1739 Ivywood Drive, Ann Arbor, MI 48103, U.S.A. (Home). *Telephone:* (313) 764-5433 (Office); (313) 665-4565. *Fax:* (313) 764-4338.

DONAHUE, Phil; American broadcaster; b. 5 Dec. 1935; m. 1st Marge Cooney 1958 (divorced 1975); four s. one d.; m. 2nd Marlo Thomas 1980; ed. Univ. of Notre Dame; host. Donahue (fmrly. The Phil Donahue Show), Dayton, Ohio 1967–74, Chicago 1974–85, New York 1985–96; Co-host Donahue/Pozner Show; regular appearances on the Today show 1979–; recipient of four Emmy Awards. *Publications:* Donahue 1979, The Human Animal 1985. *Address:* Donahue Multimedia Entertainment, 1 Penn Plaza #2225-35, New York, NY 10119, U.S.A.

DONAHUE, Thomas Michael, PH.D.; American professor and atmospheric scientist; b. 23 May 1921, Healdton, Okla.; s. of Robert E. Donahue and Mary J. Lyndon; m. Esther McPherson 1950; three s.; ed. Rockhurst Coll. and Johns Hopkins Univ.; Asst. Prof., Prof. of Physics, Univ. of Pittsburgh 1951–74, Dir. Space Research Lab. 1966–74; Prof. of Atmospheric and Oceanic Science Univ. of Mich. 1974–87, Edward H. White II Distinguished Univ. Prof. of Planetary Science 1987–94, Prof. Emer. 1994–, Prof. of Physics 1989–, Dir. Program for the Integrated Study of Global Change 1990–94; mem. Visiting Cttee. Max Planck Soc., Lindau; mem. N.A.S., Chair. Space Science Bd. 1982–88; mem. NASA Advisory Council 1982–88; Chair. Science Steering Group, Pioneer Venus Mission 1974–93; Chair. Cttee. on Solar Terrestial Research 1972–75; Chair. Atmospheric Sciences Advisory Panel 1968–72; mem. Cttee. on Atmospheric Science 1960–72, Rocket Research Cttee. 1966–69, Geophysics Research Forum (fmrly Bd.) 1972–75, 1982–, Climate Bd. 1979–82, Physical Science Cttee. 1972–76, Solar System Exploration Cttee. 1980–82; Chair. Cttee. for U.S.–U.S.S.R. Workshop on Planetary Sciences 1988–91, Space Science in the 21st Century Study 1985–88, Space Telescope Inst. Visiting Cttee. 1987–89, Cttee. on Public Affairs, American GEO Physical Union 1990–93; participated in Voyager Missions to Outer Planets 1977, Galileo Mission to Jupiter 1995; Henry Russel Lectureship, Univ. of Mich. 1986; mem. NASA Science Center Assessment Study 1987–88; Fellow, American Physical Soc., A.A.A.S., American Geophysical Union (Pres. Solar Planetary Relations Section 1974–76); mem. American Astronomical Soc., Bd. of Trustees, Upper Atmosphere Research Corpn. 1968–80 (Chair. 1972), Univ. Space Research Corpn. for Atmospheric Research 1976–83 (Sec. 1978–89, Vice-Chair. 1980-83), Int. Acad. of Astronautics 1987–; mem. ARECIBO Advisory Bd. 1971–75, 1987–89 (Chair. 1989); NASA Public Service Award 1977, Distinguished Public Service Medal 1980; Henry Arctowski Medal (N.A.S.) 1981; Fleming Medal, American Geophysical Union 1981; winner Space Science Award, American Inst. of Aeronautics and Astronautics 1987, Space Science Award (Nat. Space Club) 1989, Attwood Award (Coll. of Eng., Mich. Univ.) 1994; Guggenheim Fellow (at Observatoire de Meudon, France) 1960; Hon. D.Sc. (Rockhurst Coll.) 1981. *Publications:* numerous scientific papers. *Leisure interests:* tennis, wine, music (classical and traditional), Irish history. *Address:* 1781 Arlington Boulevard, Ann Arbor, MI 48104, U.S.A. (Home). *Telephone:* (313) 763-2390. *Fax:* (313) 764-5137.

DONALD, Sir Alan (Ewen), K.C.M.G., LL.M.; British diplomatist (retd.); b. 5 May 1931, Inverurie, Aberdeenshire, Scotland; s. of Robert T. Donald and Louise Turner; m. Janet H.T. Blood 1958; four s.; ed. Aberdeen Grammar School, Fettes Coll. Edin. and Trinity Hall, Cambridge; mil. service 1949–50; joined diplomatic service 1954; Third Sec. Beijing 1955–57; Pvt. Sec. to Parl. Under Sec. of State, Foreign Office 1958–61; U.K. Del. to NATO, Paris 1961–64; First Sec. Beijing 1964–66; Counsellor, Athens 1971–73; Political Adviser to Gov. of Hong Kong 1974–77; Amb. to Zaire, Rwanda and Burundi 1977–80, to People's Republic of Congo 1978–80, to Indonesia 1984–88, to

People's Repub. of China 1988–91; Adviser on Chinese Affairs Rolls-Royce 1991–; Dir. Fleming Far Eastern Investment Co. 1991–97, China Fund Inc. 1992–, Batey, Burn Ltd. 1992–98, HSBC China Fund Ltd. 1994–, Pacific Rim Investments Ltd. 1994–, China Aeronautical Tech. Fund 1994–97, Fleming Asian Investment Co. 1997–; Adviser to Willis, Faber and Dumas Ltd. 1994–; Hon. LL.D. (Aberdeen) 1991. *Leisure interests:* music, military history, water colour sketching, films. *Address:* Applebys, Chiddingstone Causeway, nr. Tonbridge, Kent, TN11 8JH, England. *Telephone:* (01892) 870598. *Fax:* (01892) 870490.

DONALDSON, Charles Ian Edward, M.A., F.B.A., F.R.S.E., F.A.H.A.; British professor of English; b. 6 May 1935, Melbourne, Australia; s. of Dr. William Edward Donaldson and Elizabeth (née Weigall) Donaldson; m. 1st Tamsin Jane Procter 1962 (divorced 1990); one s. one d.; m. 2nd Grazia Maria Therese Gunn 1991; ed. Melbourne Grammar School, Melbourne Univ., Magdalen Coll., Oxford, Merton Coll., Oxford; Sr. Tutor in English, Melbourne Univ. 1958; Fellow and lecturer in English, Wadham Coll., Oxford 1962–69; CUF Lecturer in English, Oxford Univ. 1963–69; Chair. Oxford English Faculty 1968–69; Prof. of English, A.N.U. 1969–91, Dir., Humanities Research Centre 1974–90; Regius Prof. of Rhetoric and English Literature Edin. Univ. 1991–95; Grace 1 Prof. of English and Fellow, King's Coll., Cambridge Univ. 1995–; visiting appointments at Univ. of Calif., Santa Barbara 1967–68, Gonville and Caius Coll., Cambridge 1985, Cornell Univ. 1988, Folger Shakespeare Library 1988. *Publications:* The World Upside Down: Comedy From Jonson to Fielding 1970, Ben Jonson: Poems (ed.) 1975, The Rapes of Lucretia: A Myth and its Transformations 1982, Jonson and Shakespeare (ed.) 1982, Transformations in Modern European Drama 1983, Seeing the First Australians (ed., with Tamsin Donaldson) 1985, Ben Jonson 1985, Shaping Lives (Co-Ed.) 1992, Jonson's Walk to Scotland 1993, The Death of the Author and the Life of the Poet 1995, Jonson: Selected Poems (ed.) 1995, Jonson's Magic Houses 1997. *Address:* King's College, Cambridge, CB2 1ST (Office); 11 Grange Road, Cambridge, CB3 9AS, England (Home). *Telephone:* (01223) 331100 (Office); (01223) 321683 (Home). *Fax:* (01223) 462449 (Home).

DONALDSON, Dame (Dorothy) Mary, G.B.E., J.P.; British local government official; b. 29 Aug. 1921, Wickham, Hants.; d. of late Reginald George Gale Warwick and Dorothy Alice Warwick; m. John Francis Donaldson (q.v.) 1945; one s. two d.; ed. Portsmouth High School of Girls, Wingfield Morris Orthopaedic Hosp., Middlesex Hosp., London; Chair. Women's Nat. Cancer Control Campaign 1967–69; Vice-Pres. British Cancer Council 1970; served on numerous other medical and community bds. and Cttees.; Alderman, City of London (Ward of Coleman Street) 1975–91, Sheriff 1981–82, first woman Lord Mayor of London 1983–84; Chair. Interim Licensing Authority for In-vitro Fertilisation and Human Embryology 1985–91; Chair. Council responsible for Ombudsman in Banking 1985–94; mem. Press Complaints Comm. 1991–94; Hon. Fellow, Girton Coll.; Order of Oman 1982; Order of Bahrain 1984; Grand Officier, Ordre national du mérite (France) 1984; Pres.'s Medal of Inst. of Public Relations 1984; Hon. D.Sc. (City Univ.) 1983; F.C.R.O.G. ad eundem 1991. *Leisure interests:* sailing, gardening, skiing. *Address:* 171 Andrewes House, Barbican, London, EC2Y 8BA, England. *Telephone:* 0171-588 6610 (Home).

DONALDSON, Roger; New Zealand (b. Australian) film director; b. 15 Nov. 1945, Ballarat, Australia; emigrated to N.Z. aged 19; established still photography business, then started making documentary films. *Television:* Winners and Losers (series of short dramas). *Films:* Sleeping Dogs (also producer), Smash Palace (also producer), The Bounty, Marie, No Way Out, Cocktail, Cadillac Man (also producer), White Sands, The Getaway, Species, Dante's Peak.

DONALDSON, Samuel Andrew, B.A.; American journalist; b. 11 March 1934, El Paso, Texas; s. of Samuel A. Donaldson and Chloe Hampson; m. 1st Billie K. Butler 1963; three s. one d.; m. 2nd Janice C. Smith 1983; ed. Univ. of Texas, El Paso and Univ. of S. Calif.; radio/TV news reporter/anchorman, WTOP, Washington 1961–67; Capitol Hill/corresp., ABC News, Washington 1967–77, White House Corresp. 1977–89, anchor Prime Time Live 1989–; panelist This Week With David Brinkley 1981–96; co-anchor This Week 1996–. *Publication:* Hold on Mr President 1987. *Address:* Prime Time Live, 1717 DeSales Street, N.W., Washington, DC 20036, U.S.A.

DONALDSON, Simon Kirwan, D.PHIL; British professor of mathematics; b. 20 Aug. 1957, Cambridge; s. of Peter Donaldson and Jane Stirland; m. Ana Nora Hurtado 1986; one s. one d.; ed. Sevenoaks School, Kent, Pembroke Coll., Cambridge; Jr. Research Fellow, All Souls Coll., Oxford 1983–85; Wallis Prof. of Math., Oxford Univ. 1985–98; Fellow St. Anne's Coll., Oxford 1985–98; Prof. of Mathematics Univ. of Bristol 1998–; Hon. Fellow Pembroke Coll., Cambridge 1992; Fields Medal 1986, Crafoord Prize 1994. *Publications:* The Geometry of Four-manifolds (with P. B. Kronheimer) 1990; numerous papers in mathematical journals. *Leisure interest:* sailing. *Address:* Department of Mathematics, University of Bristol, Senate House, Tyndall Avenue, Bristol, BS8 1TH, England.

DONALDSON OF LYMINGTON, Baron (Life Peer), cr. 1988, of Lymington in the County of Hampshire; **John Francis Donaldson,** Kt.; British judge; b. 6 Oct. 1920, London; s. of Dr. M. Donaldson and Mrs. E. M. H. Maunsell; m. Dorothy M. Warwick 1945; one s. two d.; ed. Charterhouse School and Trinity Coll., Cambridge; called to the Bar, Middle Temple 1946; Judge of the High Court of Justice, Queen's Bench Div. 1966–79; Pres. Nat. Industrial Relations Court (NIRC) 1971–74; Pres. British Maritime Law Asscn. 1979–95; Lord Justice of Appeal 1979–82; Chair. Advisory Council on Public Records 1982–92; Master of the Rolls 1982–92; Chair. Financial Law Panel 1992–, Inquiry into Coastal Pollution from Merchant Shipping 1993–94, Lord Donaldson's Assessment (Derbyshire) 1995; Pres. British Insurance Law Asscn. 1979–81, Chartered Inst. of Arbitrators 1980–83; Dr. h.c. (Essex) 1983, Hon. LL.D. (Sheffield) 1984, (Nottingham Trent) 1992, (Southampton) 1998. *Leisure interest:* sailing. *Address:* House of Lords, London, SW1A 0PW, England.

DO NASCIMENTO, H.E. Cardinal Alexandre; Angolan ecclesiastic; b. 1 March 1925, Malanje; s. of Antonio André do Nascimento and Maria Ana Alves da Rocha; ed. Gregoriana Univ., Rome, Faculty of Laws, Lisbon; ordained priest 1952; Bishop of Malanje 1975; Archbishop of Lubango 1977–86, of Luanda 1986–; Apostolic Admin. of Onjiva; mem. Sacred Congregation for the Propagation of the Faith and the Evangelization of the People; cr. Cardinal 1983; Pres. Caritas Internationalis; Preacher, Retreat of the Holy Father and the Roman Curia 1984; mem. Sacred Congregation Pro Culto Divino 1985. *Leisure interests:* reading, music. *Address:* Arcebispado, C.P. 87, 1230–C, Luanda, Angola. *Telephone:* (2) 334640. *Fax:* (2) 334433.

DO NASCIMENTO, Edson Arantes (see Pelé).

DONATH, Helen; American opera and concert singer; b. 10 July 1940, Corpus Christi, Tex.; d. of Jimmy Erwin and Helen Hamauei; m. Klaus Donath 1965; one s.; ed. Roy Miller High School, Del Mar Coll., Texas; studied with Paola Novikova, later with husband Klaus Donath (by whom all song-recitals are accompanied); début at Cologne Opera House 1962, at Hanover Opera House 1963–68, Bayerische Staatsoper, Munich 1968–72; guest appearances in London (Covent Garden), Vienna, Milan, San Francisco, Lisbon, New York, etc.; has given concerts in all major European and American cities; major roles include, Pamina in Die Zauberflöte, Zerlina in Don Giovanni, Eva in Die Meistersinger, Sophie in Der Rosenkavalier, Susanna in Le Nozze de Figaro, Anne Trulove in the Rake's Progress, Ilia in Idomeneo, Micaela in Carmen; over 100 recordings 1962–; Pope Paul Medal, Salzburg 50 Year Anniversary Medal, Bratislava Festival Award, Deutscher Schallplattenpreis and Grosses Lob for her first song recital recording, Lower Saxony Prize for Culture 1990. *Leisure interests:* family, gardening, cooking, swimming, filming. *Address:* Bergstrasse 5, 30900 Wedemark, Germany.

DONATONI, Franco; Italian professor of musical composition; b. 9 June 1927, Verona; s. of Silvio Donatoni and Dolores Stefannucci; m. Susan Park 1958; one s. one d.; ed. Bologna and Rome; Prof. of Composition, Bologna 1953–55, Milan 1955–67, Turin 1967–69, Milan 1969; Docente, Advanced Course in Composition, Accad. Chigiana di Siena 1970; Marzotto Prize 1966, Koussevitsky Prize 1968 and other prizes for composition. *Works include:* Puppenspiel 1951, Sezioni 1960, Per Orchestra 1962, Quartetto IV 1963, Asar 1964, Puppenspiel (2) 1965, Souvenir 1967, Etwa ruhiger im Ausdruck 1967, Doubles II 1969–70, Questo 1970. *Address:* Via Bassini 39, 20133 Milan, Italy. *Telephone:* (02) 293408.

DONDELINGER, Albert Marie Joseph, D.JUR.; Luxembourg banker; b. 22 March 1934, Redange, Attert; s. of Jean Dondelinger and Simone Lamborelle; m. Francine Dondelinger-Gillen; three d.; ed. Coll. St. Michel, Brussels, Catholic Univ. of Louvain, Belgium; Alt. Gov. for Luxembourg, IBRD 1967–76; mem. European Monetary Cttee. 1971–76, Bd. of Belgium-Luxembourg Exchange Inst. 1972–76; Adviser to Group of Twenty and Assoc. mem. IMF Interim Cttee. 1972–76; mem. Bd. European Monetary Co-operation Fund and mem. Govs. Cttee., EEC Cen. Banks 1973–76; Govt. Commr. to State Savings Bank 1974–76; Co-Chair. Comm. for Financial Affairs of Conf. for Int. Econ. Co-operation (North-South Dialogue, Paris) 1975–76; Chair. Luxembourg Bankers' Asscn. 1977–78; Man. Dir. and Chair. Exec. Bd., Banque Internationale à Luxembourg 1977–90, Hon. Chair. 1990–; independent economic and business man. consultant 1990–; Pres. European League for Econ. Co-operation (Luxembourg Bureau); Vice-Pres. Foundation Prince Henri-Princesse Maria Teresa; Vice-Chair. SOS-Sahel; Pres. Cercle Artistique de Luxembourg; mem. Bd. Inst. Régional Intracommunautaire; mem. Inst. Int. d'Etudes Bancaires 1978–; Commdr. Order of Couronne de Chêne (Luxembourg); Commdr. Order of the Crown (Belgium), the Nat. Order (Ivory Coast); Officier, Ordre Nat. du Mérite, Order of Merit (Luxembourg). *Publication:* Le secret bancaire au Grand-Duché de Luxembourg 1972. *Leisure interests:* photography, bibliophily, golf, skiing, swimming.

DONDELINGER, Jean, D. EN. D., B.LITT.; Luxembourg diplomatist and international official; b. 4 July 1930, Luxembourg; m.; one s.; ed. Faculties of Law, Nancy and Paris and St. Antony's Coll. Oxford; barrister/solicitor, Luxembourg Bar 1954–58; legal adviser to major oil co.; Asst. to Head of Int. Econ. Relations Service, Dept. of Foreign Affairs 1958–61; Deputy Perm. Rep. of Luxembourg to the EEC 1961–70, Amb. and Perm. Rep. 1970–84; Sec.-Gen. Ministry of Foreign Affairs 1984; Rep. of Pres. of Govt. on ad hoc Cttee. on Institutional Affairs (Dooge Cttee.) 1984–85; Chair. Negotiating Group on Single Act 1986; Vice-Pres. ITU World Conf. on fixing of orbital frequencies of satellites (ORB 88) 1988; Govt. Commr. to Cie. Luxembourgeoise de Télédiffusion 1984; Co-Chair. Belgo-Luxembourg Admin. Comm. 1984; Chair. Coordinating Cttee. for Installation of Community Insts. and Depts. in Luxembourg 1984; Chair. Warehouse Service Agency 1984; EEC Commr. for Cultural Affairs, Audiovisual Affairs, Information, Citizens'

Europe and Publs. 1989–92. *Address:* c/o Ministry of Foreign Affairs, 5 rue Notre Dame, 2911 Luxembourg.

DONDOUX, Jacques; French telecommunications engineer and politician; b. Dec. 1931; ed. Ecole supérieure des télécommunications; engineer, Centre nat. d'études des télécommunications (CNET) 1956–68, Asst. Dir. 1968–71, Dir. 1971–74; Production Dir. Gen. Telecommunications Directorate 1974–75; Special Adviser, Postal Services and Telecommunications Inspectorate 1975–81, Telecommunications Dir.-Gen. 1981–86; Mayor of Saint-Agrève 1995–; Minister of State attached to Minister for the Economy, Finance and Industry, with responsibility for Foreign Trade 1997–. *Address:* Ministry of the Economy, Finance and Industry, 139 rue de Bercy, 75572 Paris cédex 12 (Office); 49 rue de Boulainvilliers, 75016 Paris, France (Home). *Telephone:* (1) 40.04.04.04 (Office). *Fax:* (1) 43.43.75.97 (Office).

DONE, Kenneth Stephen, A.M.; Australian artist; b. 29 June 1940, Sydney; s. of Clifford Wade Done and Lillian Maureen Done; m. Judith Ann Walker; one s. one d.; ed. Katoomba and Mosman High Schools, Nat. Art School, Sydney; Chair. Ken Done Group of Cos. 1979–; Creative Dir. Advertising Samuelson Talbot, Sydney, J. Walter Thompson 1960–78; solo exhbn. Paris 1996; group exhbn., Baltimore 1997; numerous solo and group exhbns. throughout Australia and Japan; Goodwill Amb. UNICEF Australia; Paul Harris Fellow, Rotary Int., N.S.W. Tourism Award 1986, Rotary Award for Excellence 1993, Spirit of Australia Award 1993, Cannes Gold Lion Award and many others. *Publications:* Ken Done: Paintings and Drawings 1975–87, Craftsman House 1992, Ken Done Paintings (1990–1994) 1994, Ken Done: The Art of Design. *Leisure interests:* golf, swimming, diving, travelling. *Address:* 28 Hopetoun Avenue, Mosman, N.S.W. 2088, Australia. *Telephone:* 96988555. *Fax:* 93193374.

DONEN, Stanley; American film producer and director; b. 13 April 1924, Columbia, S.C.; s. of Mortie and Helen Donen; ed. Univ. of South Carolina; Dir. of films including Fearless Fagan, Give the Girl a Break, Royal Wedding, Love is Better Than Ever, Deep in My Heart, Seven Brides for Seven Brothers, Funny Face, Kiss Them for Me; co-dir. Singin' in the Rain, It's Always Fair Weather, On the Town; producer-dir. Pajama Game, Indiscreet, Damn Yankees, Once More with Feeling, Surprise Package, The Grass is Greener, Charade, Arabesque, Two for the Road, Bedazzled, Staircase, The Little Prince, Lucky Lady, Movie, Movie, Saturn 3, Blame it on Rio 1984, Red Shoes 1993. *Address:* c/o Directors' Guild of America, 7950 West Sunset Boulevard, Hollywood, CA 90046, U.S.A.

DONG FUREN; Chinese economist; b. 26 July 1927, Ningbo, Zhejiang Prov.; s. of Dong Junmin and Zhao Jueying; m. Liu Ainian 1957; one s. one d.; ed. Wuhan Univ. and Moscow Nat. Inst. of Econs. of the Soviet Union; Teacher Dept. of Econs., Wuhan Univ. 1950–52, Lecturer 1957–58; Asst. Researcher Econs. Inst., Chinese Acad., and Deputy Head Group on Balance of Nat. Economy 1959–77; Deputy Dir. Econs. Inst., Chinese Acad. of Social Sciences 1978–85, Dir. 1985–89, Hon. Dir. 1989–; Sr. Researcher and Vice-Chair. Academic Cttee. Inst. of Econs. 1979–85; Prof., Beijing Univ. 1979–, Wuhan Teachers' Coll. 1980–, Wuhan Univ. 1986–, Chinese People's Univ.; Deputy to NPC of People's Republic of China 1988–, mem. Standing Cttee. of NPC 1988–, Vice-Chair. Financial and Econ. Cttee. of NPC 1988–; mem. Academic Cttee. Inst. of Marxism and Mao Zedong Thought, Chinese Acad. of Social Sciences 1980–88; Gen. Sec. Union of Chinese Socs. for Econ. Research 1981–87; Vice-Pres. Graduate School of Chinese Acad. of Social Sciences 1982–85; mem. Academic Senate of Chinese Acad. of Social Science 1982–85; Chair. Acad. Cttee. Inst. of Econs. 1985–88; Econ. Consultant, China Int. Trust and Investment Corpn. (CITIC), Dir. CITIC Research Int. 1991–93; Consultant, Environment Protection Cttee., State Council 1991–, Environment Protection Bureau 1991–; mem. Nat. Cttee. of CPPCC 1998–, also Vice-Chair. CPPCC Econ. Cttee.; Short-term Consultant, The World Bank 1985; Visiting Prof. St. Antony's Coll. and Wolfson Coll., Univ. of Oxford 1985, Duisberg Univ. 1988; Chief Ed. Journal of Econ. Research 1985–88; Officier, Ordre des Palmes Académiques 1987. *Publications:* Dynamic Analysis of the Soviet National Income 1959, Problems of the Socialist Reproduction and the National Income 1980, Socialist Economic Institution and its Superiority (ed.) 1981, Theoretical Problems of the Chinese Economy in the Great Transformation 1981, On Sun Yefang's Socialist Economic Theory 1983, Selected Works of Dong Fureng 1985, On Economic Devt. Strategies 1988, Industrialization and China's Rural Modernization 1992, Reform and Development—On the Chinese Economy in the Great Transformation 1995, On Economic Reform 1995, On China's Economy 1996, Studies On Economic Development 1997, On Socialist Market Economy 1998, Talking on Economy 1998, Studies on the Chinese Economy (Co-Ed. with Peter Nolan) and over 120 essays on the Chinese economy. *Leisure interests:* arts, reading. *Address:* Institute of Economics (CASS), 2 Beixiaojie, Yuetan, Beijing 100836, People's Republic of China (Office). *Telephone:* 6803 2473 (Office). *Fax:* 6803 2473.

DONG JICHANG; Chinese party official; b. 1930, Hancheng Co., Shaanxi Prov.; joined CCP 1949; alt. mem. 12th CCP Cen. Cttee. 1982–87, mem. 13th Cen. Cttee. 1987–; Deputy Sec. CCP Cttee., Shaanxi Prov. 1983–90, a Vice-Chair. 1990–; Sec. CCP Cttee., Xian 1984; Vice-Chair. Shaanxi Prov. Ctte. of CPPCC 1990–; Pres. Econ. Promotion Asscn. for Lonhai-Lanxin Area 1987–. *Address:* Shaanxi Provincial Chinese Communist Party, Xian, Shaanxi, People's Republic of China.

DONG KEJUN; Chinese woodcut artist; b. 18 Feb. 1939, Chongqing, Sichuan; s. of Dong Xueyuan and Gue Ximing; m. Lü Hengfen 1969; one s.; Dir. of Chinese Artistic Asscn.; Standing Dir. Chinese Woodcut Asscn.; Vice-Chair. Guizhow Artistic Asscn.; Chair. Guiyang Artistic Asscn.; Vice-Pres. Acad. of Painting and Calligraphy; mem. Standing Cttee. of Guizhou br. of Chinese People's Political Consultative Conf.; Vice-Chair. Guizhou Prov. Br. Artists' Assoc. 1988–; Chair. Artists' Assoc. Guiyang Br. 1988–; council mem. Artists' Assoc. 1988–; works on view at nat. exhbns. 1965–, also in Japan, U.S.A., France, Sweden, Germany, Africa and Australia; works include: Spring Returns to the Miao Mountain 1979, A Close Ball 1979, An Illustration of the Continuation of Feng Xuefeng's Fables (a hundred pieces) 1980, Company 1981, Go Back Drunkenly 1982, Lively Spring 1983, The Miao Nat. Sisters in Their Splendid Costume 1985, Contemporary Totem-1 1986, Mountain Breath 1986, A White Cottage 1987, Sunny Rain 1988, A Hundred Pieces of Coloured Inkwash Drawings 1991–92, The Big Sleep 1993, The Bird Market 1993, Illusion 1993, Eagle 1994, Man and Horse 1995, Going to Market 1995; Prizewinner, 9th Nat. Woodcut Exhbn. 1986. *Publications:* Dong Kejun Woodcut Works, Selected Paintings of Dong Kejun 1992, Selected Chinese Coloured Inkwash Paintings 1995. *Leisure interests:* literature, music, film and dance. *Address:* Guiyang Artistic Asscn., 27 Road Shizi, Guiyang, Guizhou Prov., People's Republic of China.

DONG ZHENG; Chinese research professor and physician; b. 3 Nov. 1926, Gaoyang Co., Hebei Prov.; s. of Dong Mingxun and Dong Wangshi; m. Li Qun 1953; two s.; ed. Bethune Medical Univ., Northwest China Univ.; Chief Physician, Inst. of Acupuncture and Moxibustion 1955–70; 2nd Nat. Training Course of Traditional Medicine 1958–59; Research Prof. and Dir. Dept. of Medicine, Guanganmen Hosp. 1983–95; Research Prof. Tung Shin Hosp., Malaysia 1993–96; mem. Acupunture and Moxibustion Asscn., Traditional Chinese Medicine Research Asscn., Specialist Group, China Scientific and Tech. Asscn.; specializes in use of combined Chinese traditional medicine and Western medicine; has conducted studies of asthma, eczema, emphysema, bronchitis, allergic diseases, immunopathy, diseases of connective tissues and nerve system. *Publications:* Male Sex Disorders 1959, A Short Course in Acupuncture and Moxibustion 1960, A Short Course in Traditional Chinese Herbs 1960, The Surface of the Body connects with the Viscera 1992, External Qigong in the Treatment of Disease, Smoking is Harmful to Health, and numerous articles concerning connection between Yinyang theory and modern medicine, effect of external Qigong on human body. *Leisure interests:* traditional Chinese painting, Chinese qigong and taiji box. *Address:* Guanganmen Hospital, Academy of Traditional Medicine, Bei-xin-Ge, Guang An Men, Beijing 100053, People's Republic of China. *Telephone:* 3013311 (ext. 359).

DÖNHOFF, Gräfin (Countess) **Marion,** DR. RER. POL.; German journalist; b. 2 Dec. 1909, Friedrichstein, East Prussia; d. of August Graf Dönhoff and Ria (née von Lepel); ed. in Potsdam, Königsberg, Frankfurt/Main and Basel Univ.; engaged in admin. of various agricultural estates in East Prussia 1936–45; joined Die Zeit 1946, Political Ed. 1955, Chief Ed. of Die Zeit 1968–72, Herausgeber (Publr.). 1972; Hon. Trustee Aspen Inst. for Humanistic Studies, U.S.A.; Hon. Dr. (Smith Coll., U.S.A., Columbia Univ., New York, New School for Social Research, New York, Toruń, Poland); Joseph E. Drexel Prize 1964, Theodor Heuss Prize 1966, Peace Prize of German Book Trade 1971, Wolfgang-Döring Medal 1984, Preis Louise-Weiss-Stiftung, Paris 1985, Heinrich-Heine-Preis 1988, Roosevelt-Freiheitspreis 1994. *Publications:* Namen, die keiner mehr nennt 1962, Die Bundesrepublik in der Ära Adenauers 1963, Reise in ein fernes Land (co-author) 1964, Welt in Bewegung 1965, Deutsche Aussenpolitik von Adenauer bis Brandt 1970, Menschen, die wissen, worum es geht 1976, Hart am Wind, The Political Career of Helmut Schmidt 1978 (Ed.), Von Gestern nach Übermorgen-zur Geschichte der Bundesrepublik Deutschland 1981, Amerikanische Wechselbäder 1983, Weit ist der Weg nach Osten 1985, Südafrikanischer Teufelkreis 1987, Preussen-Mass und Masslosigkeit 1987, Kindheit in Ostpreussen 1988, Bilder, die langsam verblassen 1989, Gestalten Unserer Zeit: Politische Porträts 1990. *Leisure interest:* art (painting and graphic art).

DONLEAVY, James Patrick; American author; b. 23 April 1926, New York City; s. of Patrick and Margaret Donleavy; m. 1st Valerie Heron (divorced 1969); one s. one d.; m. 2nd Mary Wilson Price (divorced 1989); one s. one d.; ed. Preparatory School, New York, and Trinity Coll., Dublin; served in the U.S.N. during the Second World War; Brandeis Univ. Creative Arts Award, Evening Standard Drama Award, American Acad. and Nat. Inst. of Arts and Letters Award, AAAL Grantee 1975, Worldfest Houston Gold Award 1992, Cine Golden Eagle Writer and Narrator 1993. *Publications: novels:* The Ginger Man 1955, A Singular Man 1963, The Beastly Beatitudes of Balthazar B 1968, The Onion Eaters 1971, A Fairy Tale of New York 1973, The Destinies of Darcy Dancer, Gentleman 1977, Schultz 1979, Leila 1983,Wrong Information Is Being Given Out at Princeton 1998; *plays:* The Ginger Man 1959, Fairy Tales of New York 1960, A Singular Man 1964, The Saddest Summer of Samuel S 1968, The Plays of J. P. Donleavy 1972, The Beastly Beatitudes of Balthazar B 1981, Are You Listening Rabbi Low 1987, That Darcy, That Dancer, That Gentlemen 1990; *short stories and sketches:* Meet My Maker the Mad Molecule 1964, An Author and His Image 1997; *novella:* The Saddest Summer of Samuel S 1966; also: The Unexpurgated Code: A Complete Manual of Survival and Manners 1975, De Alfonce Tennis, The Superlative Game of Eccentric Champions. Its History, Accoutrements, Rules, Conduct and Regimen. A Legend 1984, J. P. Donleavy's Ireland: In

All Her Sins and in Some of Her Graces 1986, A Singular Country 1989, The History of the Ginger Man 1993, The Lady Who Liked Clean Rest Rooms 1995, The Wrong Information is Being Given Out at Princeton 1998. *Leisure interests:* De Alfonce Tennis, dry stone walling. *Address:* Levington Park, Mullingar, Co. Westmeath, Ireland.

DONNELLAN, Declan; British theatre and opera director; b. 1953, Manchester; ed. Univ. of Cambridge; freelance productions include Don Giovanni (Scottish Opera Go Round), A Masked Ball (Opera 80), Rise and Fall of the City of Mahagonny (Wexford Festival), Macbeth and Philoctetes (Nat. Theatre of Finland); with designer Nick Ormerod founded Cheek By Jowl (production co.) 1981, artistic dir. 1981–; productions with Cheek By Jowl include Racine's Andromache, Corneille's The Cid, Twelfth Night, A Midsummer Night's Dream, Hamlet, As You Like It, Measure for Measure, Martin Guerre 1996 and his own translations of Musset's Don't Fool With Love and The Blind Men; also wrote and dir. Lady Betty and Sara Sampson; Assoc. Dir. Nat. Theatre (NT) 1989–97; work for NT includes Fuente Ovejuna 1989, Peer Gynt, Sweeney Todd 1993, Angels in America, Perestroika 1993, School for Scandal 1998; writer and dir. The Big Four (Channel Four TV); recipient of six Olivier Awards; dir. Mahoganny (opera) 1995; Time Out Award (with Nick Ormerod) for Angels in America 1992. *Address:* Cheek by Jowl Theatre Company, Alford House, Aveline Street, London, SE11 5DQ, England. *Telephone:* 0171-793 0153. *Fax:* 0171-735 1031.

DONNELLY, Christopher Nigel, B.A., T.D.; British military specialist; b. 10 Nov. 1946, Rochdale, Lancs.; s. of late Anthony Donnelly and of Dorothy M. Morris; m. Jill Norris 1971; one s. one d.; ed. Cardinal Langley School, Middleton, Lancs. and Univ. of Manchester; Instr. Royal Mil. Acad. Sandhurst (RMAS) 1969–72; Sr. lecturer, Soviet Studies Research Center, RMAS 1972–79, Dir. 1979–89; Territorial Army Officer (Int. Corps) 1970–93; Adjunct Prof. Carnegie Mellon Univ. 1985–89, Georgia Tech. Univ. 1989–93; Special Adviser for Cen. and E. European Affairs to Sec.-Gen. of NATO 1989–. *Publications:* Red Banner 1989, War and the Soviet Union 1990, Gorbachev's Revolution 1991. *Leisure interests:* shooting, fishing. *Address:* Office of the Secretary-General, HQ NATO, Avenue Leopold III, 1110 Brussels, Belgium. *Telephone:* (32) 2-707-4521. *Fax:* (32) 2-707-3586.

DONNELLY, James; Canadian atomic power administrator; b. 22 March 1931, Wishaw, Lanarkshire, Scotland; s. of Peter and Mary (née Morris) Donnelly; m. Brenda Marks 1956; three s. one d.; ed. Royal Tech. Coll., Glasgow; exec. posts, Gen. Electric Co. (GEC), England, and English Electric Co. 1954–74; Project Man. Hinkley Point and Sizewell nuclear power stations, U.K.; fmr. Man. Power Station Projects, GEC, and Commercial Dir. Turbine Generators; joined Int. Systems and Controls Corpn., Montreal 1974, Vice-Pres. Forestry Products 1974–78; Pres. and C.E.O. Atomic Energy of Canada Ltd. 1978–89; Dir. Canadian Nat. Cttee.-World Energy Conf.; Pres. James Donnelly & Assoc.; mem. World Energy Council Programme Cttee.; Assoc. Royal Tech. Coll., Glasgow; mem. Inst. of Electrical Engineers, U.K. *Leisure interests:* tennis, skiing, theatre, golf. *Address:* Benson Lake, Elgin, Ont., Canada (Home). *Telephone:* (613) 761-9365.

DONNER, Andreas Matthias, D.IUR.; Netherlands jurist; b. 15 Jan. 1918; s. of Jan Donner and Golida van den Burg; m. Dina A. Mulder 1946; three s. six d.; ed. Amsterdam Free Univ.; Legal Adviser Assoc. of Christian Schools in the Netherlands 1941–45; Prof. of Constitutional Law, Free Univ. of Amsterdam 1945–58; Pres. Court of Justice of the European Communities 1958–64, Judge 1964–79, alt. Pres. of First Chamber; Prof. Constitutional Law Univ. of Groningen 1979–85, Prof. Emer. 1985–; mem. European Court of Human Rights 1986–88; Hon. Dr. Iur. (Louvain, Edinburgh, Freiburg); fmr. Pres., Royal Netherlands Acad. of Arts and Sciences. *Publications:* Nederlands Bestuursrecht (Netherlands Administrative Law) 5th edn. 1986, Handboek van het Nederlandse Staatsrecht 11th edn. 1983. *Address:* c/o Univ. of Groningen, Broerstraat 5, P.O. Box 72, 9700 AB Groningen, Netherlands. *Telephone:* (050) 639111.

DONNER, Clive; British film and theatre director; b. 21 Jan. 1926, London; s. of Alex Donner and Deborah Donner (née Taffel); m. Jocelyn Rickards 1971; Asst. film editor, Denham Studios 1942; free-lance film director 1956–; work has included documentary films for British television and direction of theatrical productions in London and New York; recipient of various awards at int. film festivals, incl. Silver Bear (Berlin Film Festival) for The Caretaker. *Films include:* Some People 1962, The Caretaker 1963, Nothing but the Best 1963, What's New Pussycat? 1965, Luv 1967, Here We Go Round the Mulberry Bush 1967, Alfred the Great 1969, Rogue Male 1976, She Fell Among Thieves 1978, The Three Hostages 1978, The Nude Bomb 1980, Oliver Twist 1981, The Scarlet Pimpernel, Arthur the King, To Catch a King, A Christmas Carol, Dead Man's Folly 1986, Babes in Toyland 1986, Best Kept Secret (Silver Award, Motor Neurone Asscn.) 1986, Stealing Heaven 1988, Not a Penny More, Not a Penny Less 1989, Coup de Foudre, Arrivederci Roma, First Love Second Chance, Gumshoe Waltz 1990, For Better or Worse 1992, Charlemagne 1993. *Leisure interests:* classical music (particularly opera), popular music, reading, walking anywhere from the streets of London to the Australian sea shore. *Address:* 20 Thames Reach, 80 Rainville Road, London, W6 9HS, England.

DONNER, Jörn Johan, B.A.; Finnish film director and writer; b. 5 Feb. 1933, Helsinki; s. of Dr. Kai Donner and Greta von Bonsdorff; m. 1st Inga-Britt Wik 1954 (divorced 1962); m. 2nd Jeanette Bonnier 1974 (divorced 1988); m. 3rd Bitte Westerlund 1995; five s. one d.; ed. Helsinki Univ.; worked as writer and film dir. in Finland and Sweden, writing own film scripts; contributor and critic to various Scandinavian and int. journals; Dir. Swedish Film Inst., Stockholm 1972–75, Exec. Producer 1975–78, Man. Dir. 1978–82; Chair. Bd. Finnish Film Foundation, 1981–83, 1986–89, 1992–95; Man. Dir. Jörn Donner Productions; mem. Bd. Marimekko Textiles and other cos.; mem., Helsinki City Council 1969–1972, 1984–92; M.P. 1987–95; Vice-Chair. Foreign Affairs Cttee. 1991–95; Chair. Finnish EFTA Parliamentarians 1991–95; Consul-Gen. of Finland, Los Angeles 1995–96; mem. European Parl. 1996–99; Opera Prima Award Venice Film Festival 1963, Vittorio de Sica Prize, Sorrento 1978. *Films:* A Sunday in September 1963, To Love 1964, Adventure Starts Here 1965, Rooftree 1967, Black on White 1968, Sixtynine 1969, Portraits of Women 1970, Anna 1970, Images of Finland 1971, Tenderness 1972, Baksmalla 1974, Three Scenes (with Ingmar Bergman), The Bergman File 1975–77, Men Can't Be Raped 1978, Dirty Story 1984, Letters from Sweden 1987. *Publications:* 43 books including: Report from Berlin 1958, The Personal Vision of Ingmar Bergman 1962. *Leisure interests:* fishing, cooking. *Address:* Pohjoisranta 12, 00170 Helsinki, Finland. *Telephone:* (9) 1356060 (Office); (19) 202033, (9) 1357112 (Home). *Fax:* (9) 1357568 (Office); (19) 202150 (Home).

DONNER, Richard; American director and producer; b. 1939, New York; actor off-Broadway; collaborated with dir. Martin Ritt on TV adaptation of Somerset Maugham's Of Human Bondage; moved to Calif. and began directing commercials, industrial films and documentaries. *Films:* X-15 1961, Salt and Pepper 1968, Twinky 1969, The Omen 1976, Superman 1978, Inside Moves 1981, The Toy 1982, Ladyhawke 1985, The Goonies 1985, Lethal Weapon 1987, Scrooged 1988, Lethal Weapon 2 1989, Radio Flyer 1991, The Final Conflict (exec. producer) 1991, The Lost Boys (exec. producer) 1991, Delirious (exec. producer) 1991, Lethal Weapon 3 1992, Free Willy (co-exec. producer) 1993, Maverick 1994, Assassins 1995, Free Willy 3: The Rescue. *TV:* (films) Portrait of a Teenage Alcoholic, Senior Year, A Shadow in the Streets, Tales from the Crypt presents Demon Knight (co-exec. producer); (series episodes) Have Gun Will Travel, Perry Mason, Cannon, Get Smart, The Fugitive, Kojak, Bronk, Lucas Tanner, Gilligan's Island, Man From U.N.C.L.E., Wild Wild West, Twilight Zone, The Banana Splits, Combat, Two Fisted Tales, Conspiracy Theory. *Address:* Richard Donner Productions, 4000 Warner Boulevard, Bldg. 102, Burbank, CA 91522; c/o 9830 Wilshire Boulevard, Beverly Hills, CA 90212, U.S.A.

DONOGHUE, Denis, PH.D.; Irish literary critic; b. 1 Dec. 1928; ed. Univ. Coll., Dublin; Admin. Office, Irish Dept. of Finance 1951–54; Asst. Lecturer, Univ. Coll., Dublin 1954–57, Coll. lecturer 1957–62, 1963–64, Prof. of Modern English and American Literature 1965–79; Visiting Scholar, Univ. of Pa. 1962–63; Univ. lecturer, Cambridge Univ., and Fellow, King's Coll. 1964–65; Henry James Prof. of Letters, New York Univ. 1979–; mem. Int. Cttee. of Asscn. of Univ. Profs. of English; BBC Reith Lecturer 1982. *Publications:* The Third Voice 1959, Connoisseurs of Chaos 1965, The Ordinary Universe 1968, Emily Dickinson 1968, Jonathan Swift 1969, Yeats 1971, Thieves of Fire 1974, Sovereign Ghost: studies in Imagination 1978, Ferocious Alphabets 1981, The Arts Without Mystery 1983, We Irish: Essays on Irish Literature and Society 1987, Walter Pater: Lover of Strange Souls 1995; contribs. to reviews and journals and ed. of three vols. *Address:* New York University, 19 University Place, New York, NY 10003, U.S.A.; Gaybrook, North Avenue, Mount Merrion, Dublin, Ireland.

DONOHOE, Amanda; British actress; b. 1962; ed. Francis Holland School for Girls, London, Cen. School of Speech & Drama, London; mem. Royal Exchange Theatre, Manchester; Broadway debut, Uncle Vanya 1995. *Films:* Foreign Body, Castaway, The Lair of the White Worm, The Rainbow, Tank Malling, Diamond Skulls (Dark Obsession), Paper Mask, The Madness of King George, Liar Liar. *Television:* (series): L.A. Law (Golden Globe Award); (films): Married to Murder, Shame, It's Nothing Personal (also co-exec. producer), The Substitute, Shame II: The Secret (also co-exec. producer); (special): Game, Set and Match.

DONOHOE, Peter; British pianist; b. 18 June 1953, Manchester; s. of Harold Donohoe and Marjorie (née Travis) Donohoe; m. Elaine Margaret Burns 1980; one d.; ed. Royal Manchester Coll. of Music, teachers include Derek Wyndham and Yvonne Loriod, Paris; professional solo pianist 1974–; appears several times each season with major symphony orchestras in London and rest of U.K. and performs regularly at the Promenade Concerts 1979–; performances with the L.A. Philharmonic, Chicago, Pittsburgh, Cincinnati, Dallas, Detroit and Cleveland orchestras, and in Europe with Berlin Philharmonic and Symphony, Leipzig Gewandhaus, Dresden Philharmonic, Swedish Radio and Radio France Philharmonic orchestras, and Maggio Musicale Fiorentino; has also performed at Edin. Festival, Schleswig-Holstein Music Festival and Festival of the Ruhr; recordings include Messiaen's Turangalila Symphony (EMI) 1986, Dominic Muldowney Piano Concerto 1986, and Tchaikovsky's Piano Concerto No. 2 1986 (Gramophone magazine's Concerto of the Year) 1988, Brahms Piano Concerto No. 1, Liszt, Berg and Bartok Sonatas, Beethoven, Diabelli Variations and Sonata Opus 101, Rachmaninov Preludes; Hon. D.Mus. (Birmingham) 1992; Hon. D.Litt. (Warwick) 1996; winner Moscow Int. Tchaikovsky Competition 1982. *Leisure interests:* golf, helping young musicians, jazz. *Address:* c/o Askonas Holt Ltd., Lonsdale Chambers, 27 Chancery Lane, London, WC2A 1PF, England. *Telephone:* 0171-400 1700. *Fax:* 0171-400 1799.

DONOVAN, Jason Sean; Australian actor and singer; b. 1 June 1968, Melbourne; s. of Terence Donovan and Susan Menlove; first appearance,

Skyways, Network 7, Australia 1979; subsequently appeared in I Can Jump Puddles, Australian Broadcasting Corpn. 1979, Neighbours (series) 1985–89, Heroes 1988, Shadows of the Heart 1990; appeared as Joseph in Joseph and the Amazing Technicolor Dreamcoat, London Palladium 1991–92; concert tours throughout Australia, Far East and Europe; hit singles include: Nothing Can Divide Us 1988, Especially for You (duet with Kylie Minogue) 1988, Too Many Broken Hearts 1989, Sealed With A Kiss 1989, Everyday 1989, Hang On To Your Love 1990, Another Night 1990, Rhythm of the Rain 1990, Doing Fine 1990, Any Dream Will Do 1991, Happy Together 1991, Rough Diamonds 1994; Platinum Disc for album Ten Good Reasons 1989; other albums include Between the Lines 1990, Joseph and the Amazing Technicolor Dreamcoat 1991; recipient of numerous show business awards. *Leisure interests:* surfing, biographies. *Address:* c/o Jonathan Altaras Associates Ltd., 13 Shorts Gardens, London, WC2H 9AT, England. *Telephone:* 0171-836 8722. *Fax:* 0171-836 6066.

DOOB, Joseph Leo, M.A., PH.D.; American professor of mathematics; b. 27 Feb. 1910, Cincinnati, Ohio; s. of Leo and Mollie Doerfler Doob; m. Elsie Haviland Field 1931 (died 1991); two s. one d.; ed. Harvard Univ.; Univ. of Illinois 1935–78, Prof. of Maths 1945–78, Prof. Emer. 1979–; mem. N.A.S., American Acad. of Arts and Sciences; Foreign Assoc. French Acad. des Sciences; Nat. Medal of Science. *Publications:* Stochastic Processes, Classical Potential Theory and its Probabilistic Counterpart, Measure Theory. *Leisure interest:* recorder. *Address:* 101 West Windsor Road, No. 1104, Urbana, IL 61801, U.S.A. (Home).

DOOB, Leonard W., PH.D.; American psychologist; b. 3 March 1909, New York; s. of William and Florence Doob; m. Eveline Bates 1936; three s.; ed. Dartmouth Coll., Duke Univ., Univ. of Frankfurt, and Harvard Univ.; Dept. of Psychology, Yale University 1934–77, Prof. of Psychology 1950–77, Emer. 1977–94, Assoc. Dir. South African Research Programme 1977–94, Sr. Research Scientist 1978–; Psychologist, War Dept., 1942–43; Policy Coordinator, Overseas Branch, Office of War Information 1944–45; Chair. Council of African Studies, Yale Univ. 1961–67, 1972; Visiting Research Prof. Univ. Coll. of Dar es Salaam, Tanzania 1967–68, Univ. of Ghana 1971; Dir. of Social Sciences, Yale 1963–66; Ed. Journal of Social Psychology 1965–; Fellow John Simon Guggenheim Foundation 1960–61. *Publications:* Propaganda 1935, Frustration and Aggression 1939, The Plans of Men 1940, Public Opinion and Propaganda 1948, Social Psychology 1952, Becoming More Civilised 1960, Communication in Africa 1961, Patriotism and Nationalism 1964, Ants Will Not Eat Your Fingers 1966, A Crocodile Has Me by the Leg 1967, Resolving Conflict in Africa 1970, Patterning of Time 1972, Pathways to People 1975, Ezra Pound Speaking 1978, Panorama of Evil 1978, The Pursuit of Peace 1981, Personality, Power and Authority 1983, Slightly Beyond Skepticism 1987, Inevitability 1988, Hesitation 1990, Intervention 1993, Sustainers and Sustainability 1995. *Leisure interests:* music, cycling, gardening. *Address:* c/o Department of Psychology, Yale University, P.O. Box 208205, New Haven, CT 06520 (Office), 6 Clark Road, Woodbridge, CT 06525, U.S.A. (Home). *Telephone:* (203) 387-2266.

DOODY, Margaret Anne, D.PHIL.; Canadian professor of English; b. 21 Sept. 1939, St. John, N.B.; d. of Rev. Hubert Doody and Anne Ruth Cornwall; ed. Centreville Regional High School, Dalhousie Univ., Halifax, Lady Margaret Hall, Oxford; Instructor in English 1962–64; Asst. Prof., English Dept. Vic. Univ. 1968–69; lecturer, Univ. Coll. of Swansea, Wales 1969–77; Visiting Assoc. Prof. of English, Univ. of Calif. at Berkeley 1976–77, Assoc. Prof. 1977–80; Prof. of English, Princeton Univ. 1980–89; Andrew W. Mellon Prof. of Humanities and Prof. of English, Vanderbilt Univ., Nashville 1989–, Dir. Comparative Literature 1992–; Commonwealth Fellowship 1960–62; Canada Council Fellowship 1964–65; Imperial Oil Fellowship 1965–68; Guggenheim Foundation Fellowship 1978; Hon. LL.D. (Dalhousie) 1985; Rose Mary Crawshay Prize 1986. *Publications:* A Natural Passion: A Study of the Novels of Samuel Richardson 1974, Aristotle Detective 1978, The Alchemists 1980, The Daring Muse 1985, Frances Burney: The Life in the Works 1988, Samuel Richardson: Tercentenary Essays (ed. with Peter Sabor) 1989, The True Story of the Novel 1996. *Leisure interests:* travel, looking at ancient paintings and mosaics, reading detective fiction, swimming in the sea, music (Mozart, bluegrass). *Address:* English Department, Vanderbilt University, Nashville, TN 37235 (Office); 2710 Fairfax Avenue, Nashville, TN 37212, U.S.A. (Home). *Telephone:* (615) 343-3192 (Office); (615) 292-3724 (Home). *Fax:* (615) 343-6141.

DOOGE, James Clement Ignatius, M.E., M.SC.; Irish politician and engineer; b. 30 July 1922, Birkenhead, England; s. of Denis Patrick and Veronica Catherine (née Carroll) Dooge; m. Veronica O'Doherty 1946; two s. three d.; ed. Christian Brothers' School, Dún Laoghaire, Univ. Coll., Dublin, Iowa, U.S.A.; Jr. Civil Engineer, Irish Office of Public Works 1943–46; Design Engineer, E.S.B. 1946–58; Prof. of Civil Eng., Univ. Coll., Cork 1958–70, Univ. Coll., Dublin 1970–81, 1982–84, now Prof. Emer.; Minister for Foreign Affairs 1981–82; Leader Irish Senate 1983–87; consultant UN specialized agencies, EC; Pres. Royal Irish Acad. 1987–90, Int. Asscn. for Hydrological Sciences 1975–79; mem. Exec. Bureau Int. Union for Geodesy and Geophysics 1979–87; Pres. ICSU 1993–96; Hon. Agric. Science Degree 1978, Hon. D.Tech. 1980, Hon. D.Sc. (Birmingham), Hon. Sc.D. (Dublin) 1988; Horton Award 1959, Bowie Medal (American Geophysical Union) 1986; Kettle Plaque 1948, 1985, and Mullins Medal 1951, 1962 (Institution of Engineers of Ireland), John Dalton Medal 1998. *Address:* 2 Belgrave Road, Monkstown, Ireland (Home). *Telephone:* 7067399 (Home). *Fax:* 2806583 (Home).

DOOLITTLE, James H., B.A.; American communications executive; ed. High Point Coll.; System Man. American TV and Communications Corpn. 1970–72, Regional Man. 1972–77, E. Div. Man. of N.C. and mid-states regions 1977–80, Vice-Pres. Eastern Operations 1980–82, Sr. Vice-Pres. Cable Operations 1982–84, Exec. Vice-Pres. 1984–85, with Pres.'s office 1985–87, Exec. Vice-Pres., C.O.O. 1987–; Pres. Time Warner Cable. *Address:* American TV and Communications Corpn., 300 First Stamford Place, Stamford, CT 06902; Time Warner Cable, 290 Harbor Drive, Stamford, CT 06902, U.S.A.

DORAZIO; Italian artist; b. 1927, Rome; ed. Rome, Paris; played major role in the revival of Italian Futurist and Abstractionist tradition, published manifesto Forma I 1947; has exhibited throughout Europe, U.S.A., S. America and Australia; est. Fine Arts Dept. of School of Fine Arts, Univ. of Pa. 1960–61, Prof. 1960–69; included in main avant-garde exhbns. of 1950s and 1960s; one-man exhbns. mainly in Venice Biennale 1960, 1966, Düsseldorf 1961, San Marino Int. 1967, Bennington, U.S.A., Cologne, Berlin 1969, Museum of Modern Art, Belgrade 1970, and at Marlborough Galleries in Rome 1964, 1968, 1972, New York 1965, 1969, London 1966; Venice Biennale Prize 1960, Paris Biennale Prize 1961, Prix Kandinsky 1961, Premio Int. Lissone 1965, Int. Prize, Cracow 1970.

DORE, Ronald Philip, C.B.E., B.A.; British university professor; b. 1 Feb. 1925, Bournemouth; s. of Philip H. B. Dore and Elsie C. King; m. Nancy MacDonald 1957; two s. one d.; ed. School of Oriental and African Studies, London Univ.; Asst. Prof. then Assoc. Prof., Univ. of B.C. 1956–60; Reader, L.S.E. 1961, Hon. Fellow 1980; Prof., L.S.E. and S.O.A.S. 1964–69; Prof. and Fellow, Inst. of Devt. Studies, Sussex Univ. 1970–81; Tech. Change Centre, London 1982–86; Dir. Japan-Europe Industry Research Centre, Imperial Coll., London 1986–91; Research Assoc., Centre for Econ. Performance, L.S.E. and Political Science 1991–; Visiting Prof. Imperial Coll. of Science, Tech. and Medicine, London Univ. 1982, of Sociology, Harvard Univ. 1987; Adjunct Prof., M.I.T. 1989–94; mem. British Acad. 1975–; Japan Foundation Prize 1977; Foreign Hon. Fellow, American Acad. of Arts and Sciences 1978, Hon. Foreign Fellow Japan Acad. 1986–; Order of the Rising Sun (Third Class) Japan. *Publications:* City Life in Japan 1958, Land Reform in Japan 1959, Education in Tokugawa Japan 1965, British Factory/Japanese Factory 1973, The Diploma Disease 1976, Shinohata Portrait of a Japanese Village 1978, Flexible Rigidities, Industrial Policy and Structural Adjustment in Japanese Economy 1986, Taking Japan Seriously: A Confucian Perspective on Leading Economic Issues 1987, Japan and World Depression, Then and Now (Essays) (Jt. Ed.) 1987, How the Japanese learn to work (with Mari Sako) 1988, Corporatism and Accountability: organized interests in British public life (Jt. Ed.) 1990, Will the 21st Century be the Age of Individualism? 1991, The Japanese Firm: the source of competitive strength (Jt. Ed.) 1994, Japan, Internationalism and the UN 1997. *Address:* Centre for Economic Performance, London School of Economics and Political Science, Houghton Street, London, WC2A 2AE; 157 Surrenden Road, Brighton, East Sussex, BN1 6ZA, England. *Telephone:* 0171-955 7788 (Office); (01273) 501 370 (Home).

DORENSKY, Sergey Leonidovich; Russian pianist and piano teacher; b. 3 Dec. 1931, Moscow; m. Nina Tserevitinova; one s.; ed. Moscow State Conservatory (pupil of Grigory Ginzburg); winner Int. Competitions Warsaw 1955, Rio de Janeiro 1958; concert tours in U.S.S.R., Brazil, Japan, Italy, Germany, Australia, N.Z., S. Korea; teacher Moscow Conservatory 1957–, Prof. 1981, Dean Piano Faculty 1978–97; mem. jury of more than 65 major int. competitions, including Tchaikovsky (Moscow), Van Cliburn (Fort Worth), Mozart (Salzburg), UNISA (Pretoria); People's Artist of Russia 1988; mem. Russian Acad. of Arts 1995, Order of Friendship 1997. *Address:* Bryusov per. 8/10, Apt. 75, 103009 Moscow, Russia (Home). *Telephone:* 229 2224 (Home).

DORF, Stephen; American actor; b. 29 July 1973; started acting aged 9. *Films:* The Gate, The Power of One, An Ambush of Ghosts, Judgment Night, Rescue Me, BackBeat, S.F.W., Reckless, Innocent Lies, I Shot Andy Warhol, City of Industry. *Television films:* I Know My First Name is Steven, Always Remember I Love You, Do You Know the Muffin Man?, A Son's Promise; *Television series:* What a Dummy.

DORFMAN, Ariel; Chilean writer; b. Argentina; Research Prof. of Literature and Latin American Studies, Duke Univ., N.C. 1992–; won Time Out and Olivier Prize for Death and the Maiden. *Publications include:* Death and the Maiden (play, also screenplay), My House is on Fire (short stories), Konfidenz, Reader (play).

DORGAN, Byron Leslie, M.B.A.; American politician; b. 14 May 1942, Dickinson, N.D.; s. of Emmett P. Dorgan and Dorothy (Bach) Dorgan; m. Kimberly Olsen Dorgan; four c. (one deceased); ed. Univ. of North Dakota, Univ. of Denver; Exec. Devt. trainee, Martin Marietta Corpn., Denver 1966–67; Deputy Tax Commr., then Tax Commr., State of N.D. 1967–80; Democrat mem. 97th–101st Congress from North Dakota 1981–93, mem. Ways and Means Cttee. 1981–93; Senator from North Dakota Jan. 1993–, Asst. Democratic Floor Leader 1996–, Vice-Chair. Special Cttee. on Ethics, mem. Govt. Affairs Cttee. *Address:* U.S. Senate, 713 Hart Senate Office Bldg., Washington, DC 20510, U.S.A.

DORIN, Bernard J., G.C.V.O.; French diplomatist; b. 25 Aug. 1929, Beauvais; s. of Gen. Robert Dorin and Jacqueline Dorin (née Goumard); m. Christine du Bois de Meyrignac 1971; two s. two d.; ed. Univs. of Paris, Lyon, Harvard, Institut d'Etudes Politiques, Paris, Ecole Nationale d'Admin.; Attaché Embassy, Ottawa 1957–59; Political Directorate Ministry of Foreign Affairs 1959–63, Adviser to Sec.-Gen. 1963–64; Tech. Adviser to Pvt. Office of Minister of Information 1964–66, of Minister Del. with responsibility for Scientific Research and Nuclear and Space Questions 1966–67, of Minister of Nat. Educ. 1967–68, of Minister with responsibility for Scientific Research 1968–69; Chargé de Mission responsible to the Personnel and Gen. Admin. Dir. Ministry of Foreign Affairs 1970–71; Amb. to Haiti 1972–75; Head Francophone Affairs Dept. Ministry of Foreign Affairs 1975–78, of American Div. 1981–84; Amb. to S. Africa 1978–81, to Brazil 1984–87, to Japan 1987–90, to U.K. 1991–93; Ambassadeur de France dignitaire 1992–; Conseiller d'Etat 1993–; Officier Légion d'honneur, Officier Ordre Nat. du Mérite; Chevalier Order of Malta. *Leisure interests:* mountaineering, heraldry, naive painting. *Address:* 98 rue de Sèvres, 75116 Paris (Office); 6 rue Guy de Maupassant, 75116 Paris, France (Home).

DORIN, Françoise Andrée Renée; French actress, novelist and playwright; b. 23 Jan. 1928, Paris; d. of late René Dorin and of Yvonne Guilbert; m. Jean Poiret (b. Poiré) (divorced); one d.; at Théâtre des Deux-Ânes, then du Quartier Latin (Les Aveux les plus doux 1957), then La Bruyère (Le Chinois 1958); Presenter TV programme Paris-Club 1969; playwright and author 1967–. *Publications:* novels include Virginie et Paul, La Seconde dans Rome, Va voir Maman, Papa travaille 1976, Les lits à une place 1980, les miroirs truqués 1982, Les jupes-culottes 1984, Les corbeaux et Les renardes 1988, Nini patte-en-l'air 1990, Au nom du père et de la fille 1992, Pique et Coeur 1993, la Mouflette 1994, les Vendanges tardives 1997; *songs include:* Que c'est triste Venise, N'avoue jamais, Faisons l'humour ensemble, les miroirs truqués 1982; *plays include:* Comme au théâtre 1967, la Facture 1968, Un sale égoiste, les Bonshommes 1970, le Tournant 1973, le Tube 1974, l'Autre Valse 1975, Si t'es beau, t'es con 1976, le Tout pour le tout 1978, l'Intoxe 1980, les Cahiers Tango 1987, Et s'il n'en restait qu'un 1992; lyrics for Vos gueules les mouettes 1971, Monsieur Pompadour 1972, l'Etiquette 1983, Les jupes-culottes 1984, La valise en carton (musical comedy) 1986, L'âge en question 1986, La Retour en Toupaine 1993, Monsieur de Saint-Futile (Vaudeville) 1996; Chevalier, Légion d'honneur, Officier, Ordre nat. du Mérite, Arts et Lettres; trophée Dussane 1973, Grand Prix du théâtre (for l'Etiquette) 1981. *Address:* c/o Artmedia, 10 avenue George-V, 75008 Paris, France.

DORIVAL, Bernard, D. ÈS L.; French professor and writer; b. 14 Sept. 1914; s. of André Dorival and Suzanne Beurdeley; m. Claude de la Brosse 1944; three s. one d.; ed. Lycées Carnot and Condorcet, Paris and Ecole normale supérieure; Prof. Ecole du Louvre 1941–; Curator Musée Nat. de l'Art Moderne, Paris 1941–65, Chief Curator 1967–68; Curator Musée Nat. des Granges de Port-Royal 1955–68; Chargé de recherches at Centre Nat. de la Recherche Scientifique 1968–72; Prof. Univ. of Paris (Sorbonne) 1972–83, Prof. Emer. 1983–; mem. Société Royale d'Art et Archéologie de Belgique; Chevalier, Légion d'honneur, Officier des Arts et des lettres. *Publications:* La peinture française 1942, Les étapes de la peinture française contemporaine 1943–46, Du côté de Port-Royal 1946, Les peintres du XXe siècle 1955, L'école de Paris au Musée National de l'Art Moderne 1961; Robert Delaunay 1975, Sonia Delaunay 1980; monographs on Cézanne, Philippe de Champaigne, Jean-Baptiste de Champaigne and Rouault, 2 vols. (with Isabelle Ronalt), numerous works on painting. *Address:* 78 rue Notre-Dame-des-Champs, 75006 Paris, France. *Telephone:* 01.43.54.69.12.

DORMANDY, John Adam, D.SC., M.D., F.R.C.S.; British surgeon; b. 5 May 1937, Hungary; s. of Paul Szeben and Clara Szeben; m. Klara Dormandy 1982; one s. one d.; ed. St. Paul's School, London and London Univ.; Resident in Surgery, St. George's Hosp. Medical School 1963–65, Lecturer in Applied Physiology 1970–74, Sr. Lecturer in Surgery 1975–80, Prof. of Vascular Sciences 1995–; Consultant Vascular Surgeon, St. James' and St. George's Hosp. 1973–; Pres. of Section of Clinical Medicine, Royal Soc. of Medicine 1978; Pres. Venous Forum 1984; Chair. Int. Soc. of Haemorheology 1982; Examiner in Physiology, Royal Coll. of Surgeons 1984, Hunterian Prof. 1970; Hamilton Bailey Prize in Surgery 1973; Fahreus Medal 1983. *Publications:* numerous articles in books and scientific journals. *Leisure interests:* tennis, skiing. *Address:* Department of Vascular Surgery, St. George's Hospital, St James' Wing, London SW17 0QT, England. *Telephone:* 0181-767 8346. *Fax:* 0181-682 2550.

DORN, Dieter; German theatre director; b. 31 Oct. 1935, Leipzig; ed. Theaterhochschule, Leipzig and Max-Reinhardt-Schule, Berlin; actor, producer and dir. in Hannover 1958–68; dir. in Essen and Oberhausen 1968–70; Dir. at Deutsches Schauspielhaus, Hamburg 1971, Burgtheater, Vienna 1972, 1976; Dir. at Staatliche Schauspielbühnen, Berlin 1972–75, Salzburg Festival 1974, 1982, 1986; Chief Dir. Münchner Kammerspiele (producing works by Lessing, Goethe, Büchner, Shakespeare etc.) 1976–83, Man. (Intendant) 1983–; has also dir. opera productions in Vienna, Munich, Kassel and at Salzburg and Ludwigsburg festivals; mem. Akademie der Künste, Berlin, Bayerische Akademie der Schönen Künste. *Address:* Münchner Kammerspiele, Postfach 221613, 80506 Munich, Germany, *Telephone:* 23-72-10.

DORNBUSCH, Rudiger, PH.D.; American (b. German) professor of economics and international management; b. 8 June 1942, Krefeld, Germany; s. of Paul Dornbusch and Josephine Dornbusch (née Buhner); ed. Univ. of Geneva, Switzerland, Univ. of Chicago, U.S.A.; Prof. Univ. of Rochester, U.S.A. 1972–73, Univ. of Chicago, U.S.A. 1974–75, Fundação Getulio Vargas, Rio de Janeiro, Brazil 1979–80; Assoc. Prof. of Econs. M.I.T. 1975–77, Prof. 1977–, now Fort Int. Prof. of Econs.; adviser Inst. Int. Econs., Washington 1982–; Fellow Econometric Soc., American Acad. of Arts and Sciences; Dr. h.c. Univ. of Basle, Switzerland; Hon. Prof. Universidad del Pacífico, Lima, Peru. *Publications:* Macroeconomics 1977, Open Economy Macroeconomics (jtly.) 1980, Dollars, Debts and Deficits 1987, Exchange Rates and Inflation 1988, Stabilization, Debt and Reform 1993. *Leisure interest:* modern painting. *Address:* Department of Economics, Massachusetts Institute of Technology, E52-357, Cambridge, MA 02139, U.S.A. *Telephone:* (617) 253-3648. *Fax:* (617) 253-4096.

DORONINA, Tatyana Vasiliyevna; Russian actress; b. 12 Sept. 1933, Leningrad; d. of Vasiliy Ivanovich Doronin and Anna Ivanovna Doronina; m. Robert Dimitrievich Takhnenko; ed. Studio School of Moscow Art Theatre; Leningrad Lenin Komsomol State Theatre 1956–59; Leningrad Maxim Gorky State Bolshoi Drama Theatre 1959–66; Moscow Art Theatre 1966–71; Moscow Mayakovski Theatre 1971–83; Moscow Arts Theatre 1983–, Artistic Dir. Moscow Gorky Arts Theatre 1987–; works as actress and stage dir.; People's Artist of the U.S.S.R. 1981. *Main roles include:* theatre: Zhenka Shulzhenko (Factory Girl by Volodin), Lenochka (In Search of Happiness by Rozov), Sophia (Wit Works Woe by Griboyedov), Nadya Rozoyeva (My Elder Sister by Volodin), Nadezhda Polikarpovna (The Barbarians by Gorky), Lushka (Virgin Soil Upturned by Sholokov), Nastasya Filippovna (The Idiot by Dostoyevsky), Valka (Irkutsk Story by Arbuzov), Oxana (Loss of the Squadron by Korneichuk), Masha (Three Sisters by Chekhov), Grushenka (Brothers Karamazov by Dostoyevsky), Arkadina (The Seagull by Chekhov); films: Nadya (Elder Sister by Volodin), Natasha (Again about Love by Radzinskiy), Zoya (First Echelon), Klava (Horizon), Nika (Roll Call), Shura (Stepmother); also acted in TV films. *Address:* Moscow Gorky Arts Theatre, 22 Tverskoi Blvd., 119146 Moscow, Russia. *Telephone:* 203-74-66.

DORR, Noel, M.A., B. COMM.; Irish diplomatist; b. 1 Nov. 1933, Limerick; s. of John Dorr and Bridget Clancy; m. Caitríona Doran 1983; ed. St. Nathy's Coll., Ballaghderreen, Nat. Univ. of Ireland, Georgetown Univ., Washington, D.C.; Third Sec., Dept. of Foreign Affairs, Dublin 1960–62, Embassy, Brussels 1962–64, First Sec. Embassy, Washington, D.C. 1964–70, Dept. of Foreign Affairs, Dublin 1970–72, Counsellor (Press and Information) 1972–74, Asst. Sec. and Political Dir. 1974-77, Deputy Sec. and Political Dir. 1977–80, Perm. Rep. to UN 1980–83; Amb. to U.K. 1983–87; Sec. Dept. of Foreign Affairs 1987–95; Personal Rep. of Minister for Foreign Affairs, EU Intergovernmental Conference 1996–. *Leisure interests:* reading, swimming. *Address:* Department of Foreign Affairs, Iveagh House, 76–78 Harcourt Street, Dublin 2, Ireland.

DORRELL, Rt. Hon. Stephen James, B.A.; British politician; b. 25 March 1952; s. of Philip Dorrell; m. Penelope Anne Wears Taylor 1980; two s. one d.; ed. Uppingham School, Brasenose Coll. Oxford; Conservative M.P. for Loughborough 1979–97, for Charnwood 1997–, Parl. Pvt. Sec. to Sec. of State for Energy 1983–87, Asst. Govt. Whip 1987–88, a Lord Commr. of Treasury 1988–90, Parl. Under-Sec. of State, Dept. of Health 1990–92, Financial Sec. to Treasury 1992–94; Sec. of State for Nat. Heritage 1994–95, for Health 1995–97; Bd. mem. Christian Aid 1985–87. *Leisure interests:* aviation, reading. *Address:* House of Commons, London, SW1A 0AA, England.

DORSEN, Norman, B.A., LL.B.; American professor of law and civil libertarian; b. 4 Sept. 1930, New York; s. of Arthur Dorsen and Tanya Stone; m. Harriette Koffler 1965; three d.; ed. Bronx High School of Science, Columbia Coll., Harvard Law School and London School of Econs.; law clerk to Chief Judge Calvert Magruder, U.S. Court of Appeals, First Circuit 1956–57, to Justice John M. Harlan, U.S. Supreme Court 1957–58; pvt. law practice, New York 1958–60; Assoc. Prof. of Law, New York Univ. Law School 1961–65, Prof. 1965–78, Stokes Prof. 1978–; mem. Bd. of Dirs. American Civil Liberties Union 1965–91, Gen. Counsel 1969–76, Pres. 1976–91; Founding Pres. Soc. of American Law Teachers 1972–74, U.S. Asscn. of Constitutional Law; Vice-Chair. U.S. Dept. of Health, Educ. and Welfare Review Panel on New Drug Regulation 1975–76, Chair. 1976–77; mem. Bd. of Dirs. Lawyers Comm. for Human Rights 1978–, Chair. 1995–; Bd. Dirs. Thomas Jefferson Center for Protection of Free Expression 1990–; Dir. Global Law School Program 1994–, Chair. 1996–; mem. Council on Foreign Relations; consultant, NYC Landmarks Conservancy, Americans for Religious Liberty; Fellow American Acad. of Arts and Sciences; various awards for civil rights; Hon. LL.D. (Ripon Coll., John Jay Coll. of Criminal Justice). *Publications include:* Political and Civil Rights in the U.S. (with others) 1967, Frontiers of Civil Liberties 1968, ACLU Handbooks Series (Gen. Ed.) 1971–95, Disorder in the Court (co-author) 1973, The Evolving Constitution 1987, Human Rights in Northern Ireland (with others) 1991; articles on constitutional law and civil liberties. *Leisure interests:* country living, aerobics. *Address:* 40 Washington Square South, New York, NY 10012, U.S.A. *Telephone:* (212) 998-6233. *Fax:* (212) 995-4030.

DORST, Tankred; German author; b. 19 Dec. 1925, Sonneberg; s. of Max and Elisabeth Dorst; m. Ursula Ehler-Dorst; mem. German PEN Centre, Bayerische Akad. der schönen Künste, Deutsche Akad. der darstellenden Künste, Deutsche Akad. für Sprache und Dichtung; several prizes including Gerhart Hauptmann Prize, Georg-Büchner Prize 1990. *Works include:* around 30 plays for stage and television including Toller, Eiszeit, Merlin oder das wüste Land, Herr Paul, Was sollen wir tun, Fernando Krapp hat mir diesen Brief geschrieben, Die Legende vom Armen Heinrich; ; several opera libretti; author and dir. of films including Klaras Mutter, Mosch, Eisenhans. *Address:* Karl Theodor Strasse 102, 80796 Munich, Germany. *Telephone:* 3006432.

DOSHI, Balkrishna Vithaldas, A.R.I.B.A.; Indian architect; b. 26 Aug. 1927, Pune (Poona); s. of Vithaldas Gokuldas and Radhaben Vithaldas; m. Kamala Savailal Parikh 1955; three d.; ed. Sir J.J. Coll. of Arts, Bombay; Sr. Designer, Le Corbusier Studio, Paris 1951–55; Prin., Vastu-Shilpa Architecture and Planning Firm, Ahmedabad 1956–77; f. mem. and First Hon. Dir. School of Architecture, Ahmedabad 1962–72, School of Planning, Ahmedabad 1972–81; Dean, Centre for Environmental Planning and Tech. 1972–79, Dean Emer. 1981–; founder and Hon. Dir. Kanoria School of Arts Ahmedabad 1984–; Vice-Pres. Council of Architecture, Govt. of India 1973–74; mem. Advisory Bd., Architecture and Urbanism Publishing Co., Tokyo 1972–, Bldg. Inst., London 1972–76, Int. Jury Panel, Competition for Urban Environment in Developing Countries, Manila 1975–76; Sr. Partner, Messrs. Stein Doshi & Bhalla, New Delhi, Ahmedabad 1977–; f. mem.-trustee and Dir. Vastu-Shilpa Foundation for Studies and Research in Environmental Design, Ahmedabad 1978–; Chair. Centre for Environmental Planning and Tech., Study Cell 1978–81; Chair. Panel of Juries, Int. Architectural Design Competition for the Indira Gandhi Nat. Centre for Arts 1987–; Fellow, Indian Inst. of Architects; Hon. Fellow, A.I.A. 1971; Acad., Int. Acad. of Architecture 1989; awards include Padmashree award, Govt. of India 1976; Pan Pacific Architectural Citation award, Hawaii Chapter of A.I.A. 1981, Baburao Mhatre Gold Medal (Indian Inst. of Architects) 1988, Architect of the Year Award 1991. *Major works include:* Campus for Centre for Environmental Planning and Tech., Ahmedabad 1966, townships for Gujarat State Fertilizer Co. Ltd., Baroda 1968, Electronics Corpn. of India Ltd., Hyderabad 1972, Dept. of Atomic Energy, Govt. of India, Kota 1972, Indian Farmers' Fertilizer Co-op. Ltd., Kalol 1973, Indian Inst. of Man., Bangalore 1977, Nat. Inst. of Fashion Tech., New Delhi 1989, Kharghar Node, New Bombay 1992, Office Complex for Bharat Diamond Bourse, Bombay, Husain-Doshi Gufa Museum 1992. *Publications:* numerous articles and contributions to architectural journals. *Leisure interests:* photography, studies of philosophy. *Address:* 14, Shree Sadma Society, Navrangpura, Ahmedabad–380009, India. *Telephone:* 491610 (Office); 429344 (Home).

DOSHI, Vinod, M.SC. (ENG.); Indian business executive; b. 20 March 1932; ed. Albion Coll., Mich., U.S.A. and Univ. of Mich.; man. trainee, Cooper Eng. Ltd. (now amalgamated with Walchandnagar Industries Ltd.) 1958, Dir. in charge of operations 1960, Man. Dir. 1970–75; Vice-Chair. and Man. Dir. Walchandnagar Industries Ltd. 1975, now Chair.; mem. Bd. of Dirs. The Premier Automobiles Ltd. 1972–, Chair. of Bd. 1982–, now Chair. and Man. Dir.; Chair. and Dir. numerous cos.; mem. or fmr. mem. of numerous govt. bodies etc. *Leisure interests:* colour photography, music and sound recording, amateur theatre and commercial cinema. *Address:* 92/93 Maker Towers, F Cuffe Parade, Mumbai, 400005, India.

DOS SANTOS, H.E. Cardinal Alexander José Maria, O.F.M.; Mozambican ecclesiastic; b. 18 March 1924, Inhambane; ordained 1953, elected to Church in Lourenço Marques, (now Maputo) 1974, consecrated Bishop 1975; cr. Cardinal 1988; Archbishop of Maputo 1976–. *Address:* Paço Arquiepiscopal, Avenida Eduardo Mondlane 1448, C.P. 258, Maputo, Mozambique. *Telephone:* 426240. *Fax:* 421873.

DOS SANTOS, José Eduardo; Angolan politician; b. 28 Aug. 1942, Luanda; s. of Eduardo Avelino dos Santos and Jacinta José Paulino; ed. Liceu Salvador Correia; joined Movimento Popular de Libertação de Angola (MPLA) 1961; went into exile 1961 and was a founder mem. and Vice-Pres. of MPLA Youth based in Léopoldville, Congo (now Kinshasa, Zaire); first Rep., MPLA, Brazzaville 1961; sent with group of students for training in Moscow 1963; graduated as Petroleum Engineer, Inst. of Oil and Gas, Baku 1969; then military course in telecommunications; returned to Angola and participated in war against Portuguese 1970–74; Second in Command of Telecommunications Services, MPLA Second Politico-Military Region, Cabinda; mem. Provisional Readjustment Cttee., Northern Front 1974; mem. MPLA Cen. Cttee. and Political Bureau 1974–; Chair. MPLA; Minister of Foreign Affairs, Angola 1975; Co-ordinator, MPLA Foreign Relations Dept. 1975; Sec. Cen. Cttee. for Educ., Culture and Sport, then for Nat. Reconstruction, then Economic Devt. and Planning 1977–79; First Deputy Prime Minister, Minister of Planning and Head of Nat. Planning Comm. 1978–79; Pres. of Angola and Chair. of Council of Ministers Sept. 1979–; C.-in-C. of FAPLA (Armed Forces of MPLA). *Address:* Gabinete do Presidente, Luanda, Angola.

DOS SANTOS, Manuel, B.SC.(ECONS.); Mozambican diplomatist; b. 7 May 1944; s. of Armando Augusto dos Santos and Luisa Chapassuca; m. Dabanga Diana dos Santos 1966; mem. Mozambique Liberation Front Exec. Cttee. 1967–77, Nat. Treasurer, Sec. for Econ. Affairs 1967–73; mem. FRELIMO-Cen. Cttee. 1967–91; Public Relations Officer to Prime Minister's Office 1974–75; Dir. Foreign Trade at Ministry for Industry and Trade 1975–76; Gen. Sec. Ministry of Foreign Affairs 1977–78; Minister for Internal Trade 1978–80; Amb. to Tanzania 1980–83; Amb. and Perm. Rep. of Mozambique to UN 1983–89; Pres. Econ. and Soc. Council UN 1986; mem. Nat. Ass. 1972–; Deputy Minister for Foreign Affairs 1989–. *Address:* c/o Ministry for Foreign Affairs, Avda. Julius Nyerere 4, Maputo, Mozambique. *Telephone:* 744061.

DOS SANTOS, Marcelino; Mozambican nationalist leader and poet; b. 1931, Lourenço Marques; ed. Lisbon and Paris; Sec. of External Affairs, Presidential Council of Frente de Libertação de Moçambique (FRELIMO) 1969–75; Vice-Pres. FRELIMO (now Frelimo Party) 1970–78, mem. Political Bureau FRELIMO, Sec. for Econ. Affairs 1980; Minister of Devt. and Econ. Planning 1975–78, for the Nat. Comm. of the Plan 1978–80; fmr. Gov. Sofala Province. *Address:* c/o FRELIMO, Rua Pereiro do Lago, Maputo, Mozambique.

DOST, Shah Mohammad; Afghanistan politician; b. 1929, Kabul; ed. Kabul Univ.; mem. People's Democratic Party of Afghanistan 1963, mem. Cen. Cttee. 1979; fmr. Deputy Foreign Minister and Foreign Minister of the Democratic Rep. of Afghanistan; mem. Revolutionary Council; Minister of State for Foreign Affairs 1986–88; Perm. Rep. to U.N. 1988–90; Order of People's Friendship. *Address:* c/o Ministry of Foreign Affairs, Shah Mahmoud Ghazi Street, Shar-i-Nau, Kabul, Afghanistan.

DOTRICE, Roy; British actor; b. 26 May 1925, Guernsey, Channel Islands; s. of Louis Dotrice and Neva Wilton; m. Kay Newman 1946; three d.; ed. Dayton and Intermediate Schools, Guernsey; air gunner, R.A.F. 1940; P.O.W. 1942–45; acted in repertory 1945–55; formed and directed Guernsey Theatre Co. 1955; Royal Shakespeare Co. 1957–65 (playing Caliban, Julius Caesar, Hotspur, Firs, Puntila, Edward IV, etc.); World War 2½, New Theatre, London 1966; Brief Lives (one-man play), Criterion (over 400 performances, world record for longest-running solo performance) 1969, toured England, Canada, U.S.A. 1973, Mayfair (over 150 performances) 1974; Broadway season 1974; Australian tour 1975; Peer Gynt, Chichester Festival 1970; One At Night, Royal Court 1971; The Hero, Edinburgh 1970; Mother Adam, Arts 1971; Tom Brown's Schooldays, Cambridge 1972; The Hollow Crown, seasons in U.S.A. 1973 and 1975, Sweden 1975; Gomes, Queen's 1973; The Dragon Variation, Duke of York's 1977; Australian tour with Chichester Festival 1978; Passion of Dracula, Queen's 1978; Oliver, Albery 1979; Mr. Lincoln (one-man play), New York 1980, Fortune 1981, A Life, New York 1981, Henry V, Stratford, Conn. 1981, Falstaff (American Shakespeare Co.) 1982, Kingdoms, Broadway 1982, Churchill, Washington and Los Angeles 1983, The Genius, Los Angeles 1984, Enemy of the People, New York 1985, Hay Fever, New York and Washington 1985–86, The Homecoming 1991, New York, The Best of Friends, New York 1993, The Woman In Black, U.S.A. 1995. *Films include:* The Heroes of Telemark 1965, A Twist of Sand 1968, Lock up Your Daughters 1969, Buttercup Chain, Tomorrow, One of Those Things 1971, Nicholas and Alexandra 1971, Amadeus, The Corsican Brothers 1983, The Eliminators 1985, Shaka Zulu 1985, Young Harry Houdini 1986, Camila, L-Dopa, The Lady Forgets, The Cutting Edge, The Scarlet Letter, Swimming with Sharks. *TV appearances include:* Dear Liar, Brief Lives, The Caretaker (Emmy Award), Imperial Palace, Misleading Cases, Clochemerle, Dickens of London, Stargazy on Zummerdown; numerous American TV appearances including Remington Steel, Hart to Hart, Family Reunion, Magnum P.I., Fairy Tale Theatre, Beauty and the Beast, Tales of Gold Monkey, The Wizard, A Team, Tales from the Dark Side, Beauty and the Beast, Going to Extremes, The Good Policeman; TV Actor of the Year Award 1968. *Leisure interests:* baseball, fishing, riding. *Address:* 98 St. Martin's Lane, London, W.C.2, England. *Telephone:* 0171-836-7054.

DOTY, Paul Mead, B.S., M.A., PH.D.; American biochemist and specialist in science policy and arms control; b. 1 June 1920, Charleston, W. Va.; s. of Paul Mead and Maud Stewart Doty; m. 1st 1941; m. 2nd 1954; four c.; ed. Pennsylvania State Coll., Columbia and Cambridge Univs.; Instructor and Research Assoc. Polytechnic Inst., Brooklyn 1943–45, Asst. Prof. Chemistry 1945–46; Asst. Prof. Chemistry, Univ. de Notre Dame 1947–48; Asst. Prof. Harvard 1948–50, Assoc. Prof. Chemistry 1950–56, Prof. 1956, Pres. Science Advisory Cttee. 1961–65, Mallinckrodt Prof. of Biochemistry 1968–88, Prof. of Public Policy 1988–90, Emer. Prof. of Biochemistry 1988–, Emer. Prof. of Public Policy 1990–; Sr. Fellow Harvard 1973–91; Dir. of Center for Science and Int. Affairs, Harvard Univ. 1973–85; Consultant to the Arms Control and Disarmament Agency, Nat. Security Council; mem. Gen. Advisory Cttee. on Arms Control 1977–81; mem. Bd. MITRE Corpn. 1975–92, Int. Science Foundation 1992–; Founder, Ed. Int. Security 1975–85; Sr. Fellow, Aspen Inst. Berlin (mem. Bd. 1973–); Fellow, American Acad. of Arts and Science, N.A.S., Philosophical Soc., Rockefeller Fellow, Cambridge Univ. 1946–47. *Leisure interests:* reading, travel, computing. *Address:* c/o John F. Kennedy School of Government, Harvard University, 79 JFK Street, Cambridge, MA 02138 (Office); 4 Kirkland Place, Cambridge, MA 02138, U.S.A. (Home). *Telephone:* (617) 495-1401 (Office). *Fax:* (617) 864-6679 (Office).

DOUGLAS, Barry; Irish concert pianist; b. 23 April 1960, Belfast, Northern Ireland; s. of Barry Douglas and Sarah Jane (née Henry) Douglas; m. Deirdre O'Hara; two s. one d.; ed. Royal Coll. of Music, London; pvt. study with Maria Curcio; London début, Wigmore Hall 1981; toured Europe 1986–; regularly performs in U.S.A.; other concerts in Japan, U.S.S.R., Australia, Iceland, Czechoslovakia; recital début in Carnegie Hall, New York 1988; winner of Tchaikovsky Piano Competition, Moscow 1986; Hon. D.Mus. (Belfast); Diploma Royal Coll. of Music. *Recordings include:* Tchaikovsky Concertos Nos. 1, 2 and 3, Sonata in G, Brahms Concerto No. 1, Piano Quintet in F Minor, Liszt concertos and Sonata in B Minor, Beethoven, Mussorgsky, Prokofiev, Rachmaninov Concerto No. 2, Berg, Reger, Strauss, Debussy, Britten, Corigliano. *Leisure interests:* driving, reading, food and wine. *Address:* c/o IMG Artists, Media House, 3 Burlington Lane, London W4 2TH, England.

DOUGLAS, James Buster; American boxer; b. 1960; s. of Billy Douglas; m. (separated); two c.; ed. Coffeyville Jr. Coll., Kansas, Sinclair Community Coll., O. and Mercyhurst Coll., Erie, Pa.; 30 wins, four losses, one draw; became World Heavyweight Champion, on defeating Mike Tyson (q.v.) in Tokyo Feb. 1990; lost World title fight to Evander Holyfield (q.v.) Oct. 1990; returned to boxing June 1996.

DOUGLAS, Kirk, A.B.; American actor; b. 9 Dec. 1916, Amsterdam, N.Y.; s. of Harry and Bryna (née Sanglel) Danielovitch; m. 1st Diana Dill (divorced 1950); two s.; m. 2nd Anne Buydens 1954; two s.; ed. St. Lawrence Univ., and American Acad. of Dramatic Arts; Pres. Bryna Productions 1955–; Dir. Los Angeles Chapter, UN Asscn.; Acad. Awards 1948, 1952, 1956; New York Film Critics Award, Hollywood Foreign Press Award, Commdr., Ordre des Arts et Lettres 1979, Légion d'honneur 1985, Presidential Medal of Freedom 1981, American Film Inst.'s Lifetime Achievement Award 1991, Kennedy Center Honors 1994, Hon. Acad. Award 1996, Lifetime Achievement Award Screen Actors' Guild 1999. *Broadway stage appearances:* Spring Again, Three Sisters, Kiss and Tell, The Wind is Ninety, Alice in Arms, Man Bites Dog, The Boys of Autumn (not on Broadway). *Films include:* The Strange Love of Martha Ivers, Letter to Three Wives, Ace in the Hole, The Bad and the Beautiful, 20,000 Leagues under the Sea, Ulysses, Lust for Life, Gunfight at O.K. Corral, Paths of Glory, The Vikings, Last Train from Gun Hill, The Devil's Disciple, Spartacus, Strangers When We Meet, Seven Days in May, Town without Pity, The List of Adrian Messenger, In Harms Way, Cast a Giant Shadow, The Way West, War Waggon, The Brotherhood, The Arrangement, There Was a Crooked Man, Gunfight 1971, Light at the Edge of the World, Catch Me a Spy, A Man to Respect 1972, Cat and Mouse, Scalawag (dir.) 1973, Once Is Not Enough 1975, Posse (prod., actor) 1975, The Moneychangers (TV) 1976, Holocaust 2000 1977, The Fury 1977, Villain 1978, Saturn 3 1979, The Final Countdown 1980, The Man from Snowy River, Tough Guys 1986, Queenie (TV mini series) 1987, Oscar, Welcome to Veraz, Greedy 1994. *Publications:* The Ragman's Son: An Autobiography 1988, Dance with the Devil (novel) 1990, The Secret (novel) 1992, The Gift (novel) 1992, Last Tango in Brooklyn (novel) 1994, Climbing the Mountain: My Search for Meaning 1997. *Address:* The Bryna Company, 141 S. El Camino Drive, Beverly Hills, CA 90212; 805 N. Rexford Drive, Beverly Hills, CA 90210, U.S.A. *Telephone:* (213) 274-5294 (Office).

DOUGLAS, Margaret Elizabeth, O.B.E.; British broadcasting executive; b. 22 Aug. 1934, London; d. of Thomas Douglas and Dorothy Douglas (née Jones); ed. Parliament Hill School for Girls; joined BBC 1951, fmrly. sec., researcher dir., ed. in current affairs TV, Chief Asst. to Dir.-Gen. 1983, Chief Political Adviser 1987; Supervisor of Parl. Broadcasting, Palace of Westminster 1993–. *Address:* House of Commons, London, SW1A 0AA, England. *Telephone:* 0171-219 5849. *Fax:* 0171-219 2573.

DOUGLAS, Michael Kirk, B.A.; American actor and film producer; b. 25 Sept. 1944, New Brunswick, N.J.; s. of Kirk Douglas (q.v.) and Diana Douglas; m. Diandra Mornell Luker 1977 (separated); one s.; Acad. Award for Best Actor (for Wall Street) 1988. *Film appearances:* It's My Turn, Hail Heroll 1969, Summertime 1971, Napoleon and Samantha 1972, Coma 1978, Running 1979, Star Chamber 1983, Romancing the Stone 1984, A Chorus Line 1985, Jewel of the Nile 1985, Fatal Attraction 1987, Wall Street 1987, Heidi 1989, Black Rain 1989, The War of the Roses 1990, Shining Through 1990, Basic Instinct 1992, Falling Down 1993, The American President 1995, The Ghost and the Darkness 1996, The Game 1997. *Films produced include:* One Flew Over the Cuckoo's Nest (Academy Award for Best Film 1975), The China Syndrome, Sarman (exec. producer), Romancing the Stone, Jewel of the Nile, Flatliners 1990, Made in America (co-exec. producer), Disclosure 1994, A Perfect Murder 1998; appeared in TV series Streets of San Francisco. *Address:* c/o Creative Artists Agency Inc., 9830 Wilshire Boulevard, Beverly Hills, CA 90212, U.S.A.

DOUGLAS, Sir Roger Owen, Kt.; New Zealand politician and accountant; b. 5 Dec. 1937, Auckland; s. of Norman V. and Jennie Douglas; m. Glennis June Anderson 1961; one s. one d.; ed. Auckland Grammar School, Auckland Univ.; entered House of Reps. as Labour mem. for Manukau 1969 (now Manurewa); Minister of Broadcasting 1973–75, of the Post Office 1973–74, of Housing (with State Advances, Housing Corpn.) 1974–75; Minister of Finance and Minister in Charge of the Inland Revenue Dept. and of Friendly Socs. 1984–87, of Finance 1988, of Police and Immigration 1989–90; Dir. Brierley Investments 1990–98 (Chair. (interim) 1998); John Fairfax Ltd. 1997–, Aetna Health (N.Z.) Ltd. 1997–, Tasman Inst. 1997–; fmr. Pres. Auckland Labour Regional Council, Manukau Labour Cttee; Max Schmidheiny Freedom Prize, Switzerland 1995, Ludwig Erhard Foundation Prize, Germany 1997. *Publications:* There's Got to be a Better Way 1980, Toward Prosperity 1987, Unfinished Business 1993, Completing the Circle 1996; several papers on int. and econ. affairs. *Leisure interests:* cricket, rugby, rugby league, reading. *Address:* 411 Redoubt Road, R.D. Papatoetoe, Auckland, New Zealand. *Telephone:* (9) 2639596. *Fax:* (9) 2636928.

DOUSTE-BLAZY, Philippe Jean Georges Marie, D. EN MED.; French politician and doctor; b. 1 Jan. 1953, Lourdes; s. of Louis Douste-Blazy and Geneviève Béguère; m. Marie-Yvonne Calazel 1977; ed. Lycée Pierre de Caousou, Toulouse and Univ. Paul Sabatier, Toulouse; Intern, Toulouse hosps. 1976–82; Head of Cardiology Clinics and Asst. to Toulouse hosps. 1982–86; Univ. Prof. 1988–; Dir. Arcol 1988–; mem. European Parl. 1989; Regional Councillor for Midi-Pyrénées 1992–; Deputy to Nat. Ass. (Union pour la Démocratie Française) 1993, 1997–; Minister of Social Affairs, of Health and the City 1993–95; Minister of Culture 1995–97; Pres. Union pour la démocratie françaisê group, Nat. Ass. 1998–; mem. New York Acad. of Sciences and numerous medical orgs. *Leisure interests:* classical music, golf. *Address:* Assemblée nationale, 75355 Paris; Hôtel de Ville, B.P. 309, 65115 Lourdes cedex (Offices); 1 rue de Bagnères, 65100 Lourdes, France (Home).

DOVE, Rita Frances, B.A., M.F.A.; American author and professor of English; b. 28 Aug. 1952, Akron, Ohio; d. of Ray Dove and Elvira Dove (née Hord); m. Fred Viebahn 1979; one d.; ed. Miami Univ., Ohio, Univ. of Tübingen, Germany, and Univ. of Iowa; Asst. Prof. Ariz. State Univ. Tempe 1981–84, Assoc. Prof. 1984–87, Prof. 1987–89; Prof. Univ. of Va. Charlottesville 1989–93, Commonwealth Prof. of English 1993–; U.S. Poet Laureate 1993–95; Writer-in-residence, Tuskegee Inst. Ala. 1982; literary panellist, Nat. Endowment for Arts, Washington, D.C. 1984–86; Judge Pulitzer Prize in Poetry 1991, Nat. Book Award in Poetry 1991 and other awards; numerous hon. degrees; numerous prizes and awards including Pulitzer Prize (for Thomas and the Beulah) 1987. *Publications include:* The Yellow House on the Corner (poetry) 1980, Museum (poetry) 1983, Fifth Sunday (short stories) 1985, Thomas and the Beulah (poetry) 1986, Grace Notes (poetry) 1989, Through the Ivory Gate (novel) 1992, Selected Poems 1993, Darker Face of the Earth (verse drama) 1994, Mother Love (poetry) 1995, The Poet's World (essays) 1995. *Address:* Department of English, University of Virginia, Charlottesville, VA 22903, U.S.A. *Telephone:* (804) 924-6618 (Office).

DOVER, Sir Kenneth James, Kt., M.A., D.LITT., F.R.S.E., F.B.A.; British classical scholar; b. 11 March 1920, Croydon; s. of Percy Henry James and Dorothy Valerie Anne (Healey) Dover; m. Audrey Ruth Latimer 1947; one s. one d.; ed. St. Paul's School, Balliol and Merton Colls., Oxford; served Royal Artillery 1940–45; Fellow and Tutor of Balliol Coll., Oxford 1948–55; Prof. of Greek, Univ. of St. Andrews 1955–76, Chancellor 1981–; Pres. Corpus Christi Coll. Oxford 1976–86, Hon. Fellow 1986–; Visiting Lecturer, Harvard Univ. 1960; Visiting Prof. Univ. of Calif., Berkeley 1967; Prof.-at-Large Cornell Univ. 1983–88; Prof. Stanford Univ. 1987–92; F.B.A. 1966–, Pres. 1978–81; Hon. Fellow, Balliol Coll. 1977–, Merton Coll. 1980–, Pres. Hellenic Soc. 1971–74, Classical Asscn. 1975; Foreign mem. Royal Netherlands Acad. 1979–; Foreign hon. mem. American Acad. of Arts and Sciences 1979–; Hon. LL.D. (Birmingham) 1979, Hon. D.Litt. (Bristol and London) 1980, (Liverpool) 1983, (Durham) 1984, Hon. LL.D. and D. Litt. (St. Andrews) 1981, Hon. D.H.L. (Oglethorpe) 1984; Kenyon Medal, British Acad. 1993. *Publications:* Greek Word Order 1960, Clouds (Aristophanes) 1968, Lysias and the Corpus Lysiacum 1968, (with A. W. Gomme and A. Andrewes) Historical Commentary on Thucydides, vol. IV 1970, vol. V 1981, Theocritus, Select Poems 1971, Aristophanic Comedy 1972, Greek Popular Morality in the Time of Plato and Aristotle 1974, Greek Homosexuality 1978, The Greeks 1980, Ancient Greek Literature (with M. L. West and others) 1980, Greek and the Greeks 1987, The Greeks and their Legacy 1989, Frogs (Aristophanes) 1993, Marginal Comment 1994, The Evolution of Greek Prose Style 1997. *Leisure interests:* gardening, historical linguistics. *Address:* 49 Hepburn Gardens, St. Andrews, Fife, KY16 9LS, Scotland. *Telephone:* (01334) 473589.

DOVGAN, Vladimir Viktorovich, CAND. ECON.; Russian business executive; b. 1964; ed. Polytech. Inst., Tolyaffi; master, head of section Tech. Centre Volzhsky automobile factory 1986–92; f., Dir.-Gen. Co. Doka Pizza 1992–; Pres. Jt. Stock Co. Doka-Khleb 1993–; Head Dovgan Corpn. 1996–. *Leisure interests:* kayak-paddling, oriental wrestling, classical music, painting. *Address:* Dovgan Corporation, Kotelnicheskaya nab. 33, Bldg. 1, Moscow, Russia (Office). *Telephone:* (095) 967 1740 (Office). *Fax:* (095) 915 8950 (Office).

DOWDESWELL, Elizabeth; Canadian international administrative official; Exec. Dir. UN Environment Programme 1993–98. *Address:* c/o United Nations Environment Programme, P.O. Box 30552, Nairobi, Kenya.

DOWELL, Sir Anthony James, Kt., C.B.E.; British ballet dancer; b. 16 Feb. 1943, London; s. of Arthur H. Dowell and late Catherine E. Dowell; ed. Royal Ballet School; Prin. dancer, The Royal Ballet 1966, Sr. Prin. dancer 1967–; joined American Ballet Theatre 1978; created roles in the following ballets: The Dream 1964, Romeo and Juliet 1965, Shadow Play 1967, Monotones 1969, Triad 1972, Manon 1974; narrator in Oedipus Rex, Metropolitan Opera House, New York 1981; created role of Prospero in Nureyev's The Tempest, Royal Opera House, London 1982; Asst. to Dir. Royal Ballet 1984–85, Dir. 1986–. *Address:* c/o The Royal Ballet, Covent Garden, London, WC2E 7QA, England. *Telephone:* 0171-240 1200.

DOWELL, John Derek, PH.D., C.PHYS., F.INST.P., F.R.S.; British professor of elementary particle physics; b. 6 Jan. 1935, Ashby de la Zouch; s. of William E. Dowell and Elsie D. Dowell; m. Patricia Clarkson 1959; one s. one d.; ed. Coalville Grammar School, Leics. and Univ. of Birmingham; Research Fellow, Univ. of Birmingham 1958–60; Research Assoc. CERN, Geneva 1960–62; Lecturer, Univ. of Birmingham 1962–70, Sr. Lecturer 1970–74, Reader 1974–80, Prof. of Elementary Particle Physics 1980–97, Poynting Prof. of Physics 1997–; Visiting Scientist, Argonne Nat. Lab. U.S.A. 1968–69; Scientific Assoc. CERN 1973–74, 1985–87; Chair. SERC Particle Physics Cttee. 1981–85; mem. CERN Scientific Policy Cttee. 1982–90, 1993–96; mem. European Cttee. for Future Accelerators 1989–93, BBC Science Consultative Group 1992–94, DESY Extended Scientific Council 1992–98; Chair. CERN

LEP Cttee. 1993–96; mem. CERN Research Bd. 1993–96; Chair. ATLAS Collaboration Bd. 1996–98; mem. U.K. Particle Physics and Astronomy Research Council 1994–97; mem. Court of Univ. of Warwick 1993–; mem. Council, Royal Soc. 1997–98, also Vice-Pres.; mem. American Physical Soc.; Rutherford Medal and Prize, Inst. of Physics 1988. *Publications:* numerous papers in physics journals. *Leisure interests:* piano, amateur theatre, skiing, squash. *Address:* 57 Oxford Road, Moseley, Birmingham, B13 9ES, England. *Telephone:* (0121) 449-3332.

DOWIYOGO, Bernard; Nauruan politician; b. 14 Feb. 1946; ed. local schools and Australian Nat. Univ.; Lawyer; M.P. 1973–; Sec. Nauru Gen. Hosp. and Gen. Man. Nauru Co-operative Soc.; Pres. of Nauru 1976–78, 1989–95, 1996–; Minister of Justice 1983, also of External Affairs, Devt. and Industry, Public Service and Civil Aviation; Chair. Bank of Nauru 1985; fmr. Leader Nauru Party. *Address:* Office of the President, Yaren, Nauru.

DOWLING, James Hamilton, B.J.; American public relations executive; b. 20 Oct. 1931, Chicago; s. of Joseph H. Dowling and Margaret Hamilton; m. Julie A. Pastor 1958; two s. one d.; ed. Univ. of Montana; writer and ed., UPI, New Orleans 1957, Newsweek, Atlanta and New York 1958–59, AP, Chicago and New York 1960–63; mem. public relations staff, Mobil Oil Corpn., New York 1963; with Burson-Marsteller Inc. 1964–; Gen. Man. Burson-Marsteller Inc., New York 1968–70, Chicago 1970–75; Pres. Burson-Marsteller, New York 1975–, C.E.O. 1988–; mem. Public Relations Soc. of America. *Address:* Burson-Marsteller, 230 Park Avenue S., New York, NY 10003, U.S.A.

DOWLING, John Elliott, PH.D.; American professor of biology and neurobiologist; b. 31 Aug. 1935, Rhode Island; s. of Joseph Leo Dowling and Ruth W. (Tappan) Dowling; m. 1st Susan Kinney (divorced 1974); two s.; m. 2nd Judith Falco 1975; one d.; ed. Harvard Univ.; Instructor, Harvard Univ. 1961, Asst. Prof. 1961–64; Assoc. Prof., Johns Hopkins Univ. 1964–71; Prof. of Biology, Harvard Univ. 1971–87, Assoc. Dean 1980–84, Master, Leverett House 1981–98, Maria Moors Cabot Prof. of Natural Science 1987–, Pres. of Corpn. Marine Biological Lab. 1998–; mem. N.A.S., American Acad. of Arts and Sciences, American Philosophical Soc.; Hon. M.D. (Lund, Sweden) 1982; Friedenwald Medal 1970, Retinal Research Award 1981, Prentice Medal 1991, Von Sallman Prize 1992. *Publications:* 214 publs. in professional journals and ed. of 5 vols; The Retina: An Approachable Part of the Brain 1987, Neurons and Networks 1992, Creating Mind: How the Brain Works 1998. *Leisure interests:* sailing, squash and music. *Address:* The Biological Laboratories, Harvard University, 16 Divinity Avenue, Cambridge, MA 02138 (Office); 135 Charles Street, Boston, MA 02114, U.S.A. (Home).

DOWLING, Patrick Joseph, PH.D., F.C.G.I., F.ENG., F.R.S.; Irish university vice-chancellor; b. 23 March 1939, Dublin; s. of John Dowling and Margaret McKittrick; m. Grace Lobo 1966; one s. one d.; ed. Christian Bros. School, Dublin, Univ. Coll. Dublin and Imperial Coll. London; sr. demonstrator in Civil Eng. Univ. Coll. Dublin 1960–61; Bursar in Structural Steelwork, Imperial Coll. London 1961–62, research on Steel Bridge Decks 1962–65; bridge engineer British Constructional Steelwork Asscn. 1965–68; Research Fellow, Imperial Coll. London 1968–74, Reader in Structural Steelwork 1974–79, Prof. of Steel Structures 1979–94, British Steel Prof. and Head, Dept. of Civil Eng. 1985–94; Vice-Chancellor, Univ. of Surrey Oct. 1994–; partner Chapman and Dowling Consulting Engineers 1981–94; Chair. Surrey Satellite Tech. Ltd. 1994–; Pres. Inst. of Structural Engineers 1994–95; Telford Premium, Inst. of Civil Engs. 1976; Fellow Imperial Coll. 1997; Gustave Trasenster Medal, Asscn. des Ingénieurs Sortis de l'Univ. de Liège 1984; Hon. LL.D (Nat. Univ. of Ireland) 1995; Dr. h.c. (Vilnius Tech. Univ. Lithuania) 1996; several awards from Inst. of Structural Engs. *Publications:* Steel Plated Structures 1977, Buckling Shells in Offshore Structures 1982, Structural Steel Design 1988; over 200 refereed papers. *Leisure interests:* travelling, sailing, reading, good company. *Address:* University of Surrey, Guildford, Surrey, GU2 5XH, England. *Telephone:* (01483) 259249. *Fax:* (01483) 259518.

DOWLING, Vincent, D.F.A.; American (b. Irish) actor, director, producer and playwright; b. 7 Sept. 1929, Dublin; s. of Mai Kelly Dowling and William Dowling; m. Olwen Patricia O'Herlihy 1975; one s. four d.; ed. St. Mary's Coll., Rathmines, Dublin, Brendan Smith Acad. of Acting; with Standard Life Insurance Co., Dublin 1946–50; Brendan Smith Productions, Dublin 1950–51; Roche-David Theatre Productions 1951–53; actor, dir., Deputy Artistic Dir., Lifetime Assoc., Abbey Theatre, Dublin 1953–76, Artistic Dir. 1987–89; Producing Dir. Great Lakes Shakespeare Festival, Cleveland, Ohio 1976–84; Artistic and Producing Dir. Solvang Theaterfest 1984–86; Prof. of Theatre, Coll. of Wooster, Ohio 1986–87; Producing Dir., Abbey Theatre 1989–90; founding Dir. Miniature Theatre of Chester 1990–; Co-founder, Jacob's Ladder Trail Business Asscn.; Dr. h.c. (Westfield State Coll., John Carroll Univ., Cleveland, Ohio); Outstanding Producer, Cleveland Critics Circle Award 1982 for The Life and Adventures of Nicholas Nickelby; Irishman of the Year 1982; TV Emmy Award, for Playboy of the Western World 1983, Loyola-Mellow Humanitarian Award 1989. *Original plays:* Do Me A Favorite, or The Fit-Ups 1978, Acting is Murder 1986, A Day in the Life of an Abbey Actor 1990, Wilde About Oscar, Another Actor at the White House (one-man show), The Upstart Crow (A Two-Person Play about Will Shakespeare) 1995. *Leisure interests:* fly fishing, collecting paintings and sculpture, canoeing, travel abroad on house-swaps. *Address:* 322 East River Road, Huntington, MA 01050, U.S.A. *Telephone:* (413) 667-3906. *Fax:* (413) 667-3906.

DOWN, Sir Alastair Frederick, Kt., O.B.E., M.C., T.D., C.A.; British oil executive; b. 23 July 1914, Kirkcaldy, Fife, Scotland; s. of Frederick Edward Down and Margaret Isobel Hutchison; m. Bunny Mellon 1947; two s. two d.; ed. Marlborough Coll.; British Petroleum (then Anglo-Iranian Oil Co.) 1938–; Army Service 1940–45; with BP in Iran 1945–47, London 1947–54; Chief Rep. of BP, Canada 1954, later Pres. The British Petroleum Co. of Canada Ltd., BP Canada Ltd., BP Refinery Canada Ltd., BP Exploration Co. of Canada Ltd.; Man. Dir. The British Petroleum Co. Ltd. 1962–75, Deputy Chair. 1969–75; Chair., Burmah Oil Co. Ltd. 1975–83, Chief Exec. 1975–80; Chair. British-North American Research Asscn. 1980–84, London American Energy, N.V., 1981–; Dir. TRW Inc., Ohio 1977–, Scottish American Investment Co. Ltd., Edinburgh 1980–, Royal Bank of Canada, Montreal, 1981–; mem. Soc. of Chartered Accountants of Scotland; Chair. Council of Marlborough Coll.; Fellow, British Inst. of Man., Businessman of the Year Award 1980; Cadman Memorial Medal, Inst. of Petroleum 1981. *Leisure interests:* golf, fishing, shooting. *Address:* Greystones, 91 Newland, Sherbourne, Dorset, DT9 3AG, England.

DOWNER, Alexander John Gosse, B.A.; Australian politician and fmr. diplomatist; b. 9 Sept. 1951; s. of Sir Alexander Downer; m. Nicola Robinson 1978; one s. three d.; ed. Geelong Grammar School, Vic., Radley Coll. and Univ. of Newcastle-upon-Tyne, U.K.; mem. Australian Diplomatic Service 1976–81, Australian Mission to European Communities, Embassy to Belgium and Luxembourg 1977–80; Sr. Foreign Affairs Rep., S. Australia 1981; Political Adviser to Prime Minister 1982–83; Dir. Australian Chamber of Commerce 1983–84; Liberal Mem. House of Reps. for Mayo, S. Australia 1984–; Shadow Minister for Arts, Heritage and Environment 1987, for Housing, Small Business and Customs 1988–89, for Trade and Trade Negotiations 1990–92, for Defence 1992–93; Fed. Shadow Treasurer 1993–94; Leader Liberal Party 1994–95; Shadow Minister for Foreign Affairs 1995–96; Minister of Foreign Affairs 1996–. *Leisure interests:* reading, music, tennis. *Address:* Department of Foreign Affairs and Trade, Locked Bag 40, QVT, Canberra, A.C.T. 2600; 76 Mount Barker Road, Stirling, SA 5152, Australia. *Telephone:* (2) 6261-9111. *Fax:* (2) 6261-3111.

DOWNES, Sir Edward, Kt.; British conductor; b. 17 June 1924; studied with Herman Scherchen; professional conducting debut in U.K. with Carl Rosa Co.; conductor at Royal Opera House, Covent Garden 1952–69; Musical Dir. Australian Opera 1970; Chief Guest Conductor, BBC Philharmonic Orchestra 1979, Prin. Conductor 1980–91; Chief Conductor, Netherlands Radio Orchestra until 1983; Assoc. Music Dir. and Prin. Conductor, Royal Opera House, Covent Garden 1991–; regular appearances abroad as guest conductor; Hon. D. Mus. (Birmingham) 1994; Evening Standard Opera Award for production of Verdi's Attila at Covent Garden 1991. *Address:* Royal Opera House, Covent Garden, London, WC2E 7QA, England. *Telephone:* 0171-240 1200.

DOWNEY, Sir Gordon (Stanley), K.C.B., B.SC.ECON.; British public servant; b. 26 April 1928, London; s. of Stanley William and Winifred Downey; m. Jacqueline Goldsmith 1952; two d.; ed. Tiffin's School, London School of Econs.; comm. Royal Artillery 1946–48; Ministry of Works 1951; entered Treasury 1952; Asst. Private Sec. to Chancellor of Exchequer 1955–57; Asst. Sec. 1965, Under-Sec. 1972; Head of Cen. Unit., Treasury 1975; Deputy Sec. 1976; Deputy Head of Cen. Policy Review Staff (on secondment) 1978–81; Comptroller and Auditor-Gen. 1981–87; Special Adviser to Ernst and Young 1988–90; Complaints Commr. for Securities Asscn. 1989–90; Chair. Delegacy, King's Coll. Medical and Dental School 1989–91; Chair. Financial Intermediaries, Mans. and Brokers Regulatory Asscn. (FIMBRA) 1990–93, Personal Investment Authority 1992–93; Parl. Commr. for Standards 1995–; Readers' Rep. The Independent 1990–95; mem. Bd., Business Performance Group, L.S.E. 1989–94. *Leisure interests:* reading, tennis, visual arts. *Address:* 137 Whitehall Court, London, SW1A 2EP, England. *Telephone:* 0171-321 0914.

DOWNEY, James, O.C., PH.D.; Canadian professor of English and administrator; b. 20 April 1939; s. of Ernest and Mimy Ann (Andrews) Downey; m. Laura Ann Parsons 1964; one s. one d.; ed. Memorial Univ. of Newfoundland, Univ. of London; Asst. Prof. of English, Carleton Univ. 1966–69, Assoc. Prof. 1969–75, Prof. 1975–80, Chair. Dept. of English 1972–75, Acting Dean, Faculty of Arts 1975, Dean 1976–78, Vice-Pres. (Acad.) 1978–80, Pres. pro tempore 1979; Pres. and Vice-Chancellor Univ. of New Brunswick 1980–90, Prof. of English 1980–; Pres. and Vice-Chancellor Univ. of Waterloo 1993–; Co-Chair. Comm. on Excellence in Educ. in N.B. 1991–92; Hon. D. Hum. Litt. (Maine) 1987; Hon. D.Litt (Newfoundland) 1991; Hon. LL.D. (New Brunswick) 1991, (Toronto) 1998; Fellow, Univ. of Georgia 1985. *Publications:* The Eighteenth Century Pulpit 1969, Fearful Joy 1974 (co-ed.). *Address:* Office of the President, University of Waterloo, Waterloo, Ont., N2L 3G1; 272 Mary Street, Waterloo, Ont., N2J 1S6, Canada.

DOWNEY, Robert, Jr.; American actor; b. 4 April 1965, New York; s. of Robert Downey; m. Deborah Falconer; one c.; sentenced to probation for possession of cocaine; imprisoned for further drugs offence breaching terms of probation Dec 1997; released to serve 6 months at rehabilitation centre 1998. *Films include:* Pound (début) 1970, Firstborn, Weird Science, To Live and Die in L.A., Back to School, The Pick-Up Artist, Johnny B. Good, True Believer, Chances Are, Air America, Soapdish, Chaplin (BAFTA Award), Heart and Souls, Short Cuts, The Last Party, Natural Born Killers, Only You, Restoration, Mussolini: The Untold Story (TV mini-series), Restoration, Danger Zone, Home for the Holidays, Richard III, Bliss Vision 1997, The

Gingerbread Man 1997, Two Girls and a Guy 1998. *Address:* c/o C.A.A., 9830 Wilshire Boulevard, Beverly Hills, CA 90212, U.S.A.

DOWNIE, Leonard, Jr., M.A.; American newspaper editor; b. 1 May 1942, Cleveland, Ohio; s. of Leonard Downie Sr. and Pearl Evenheimer; m. 1st Barbara Lindsey 1960 (divorced 1971); two s.; m. 2nd Geraldine Rebach 1971 (divorced 1997); one s. one d.; m. 3rd Janice Galin 1997; ed. Ohio State Univ.; joined The Washington Post 1964, became investigative reporter in Washington, specializing in crime, housing and urban affairs, helped to supervise coverage of Watergate affair, Asst. Man. Ed. Metropolitan news 1974–79; London Corresp. Washington Post 1979–82, Nat. Ed. 1982–84, Man. Ed. 1984–91; Exec. Ed. 1991–; Dir. L.A. Times—Washington Post News Service 1991–, Int. Herald Tribune 1996–; Alicia Patterson Foundation Fellow 1971–72; two Washington-Baltimore Newspaper Guild Front Page Awards, American Bar Assen. Gavel Award for legal reporting, John Hancock Award for business and financial writing. *Publications:* Justice Denied 1971, Mortgage on America 1974, The New Muckrakers 1976. *Leisure interests:* ballet, classical music, travel, sports. *Address:* The Washington Post, 1150 15th Street N.W., Washington, DC 20071, U.S.A. (Office). *Telephone:* (202) 334-7512 (Office).

DOWNIE, Robert Silcock, M.A., B.PHIL., F.R.S.E.; British professor of moral philosophy; b. 19 April 1933, Glasgow; s. of Robert M. Downie and Margaret M. Brown; m. Eileen Dorothea Flynn 1958; three d.; ed. Glasgow Univ., Queen's Coll., Oxford; Tutor, Worcester Coll., Oxford 1958–59; Lecturer in Moral Philosophy, Glasgow Univ. 1959–68, Sr. Lecturer 1968–69, Prof. 1969–; Visiting Prof. Syracuse Univ., U.S.A. 1963–64, Dalhousie Univ., Nova Scotia 1976. *Publications:* Government Action and Morality 1964, Respect for Persons 1969, Roles and Values 1971, Education and Personal Relationships 1974, Caring and Curing 1980, Healthy Respect 1987, Health Promotion: Models and Values 1990, The Making of a Doctor 1992, The Healing Arts 1994, Francis Hutcheson: Selected Writings 1994, Palliative Care Ethics 1996, Medical Ethics 1996. *Leisure interest:* music. *Address:* Department of Philosophy, Glasgow University, Glasgow, G12 8QQ, Scotland. *Telephone:* (0141) 339 8855 Ext. 4273. *Fax:* (0141) 330 4112.

DOWNS, Sir Diarmuid, C.B.E., F.R.S., F.ENG.; British chartered engineer; b. 23 April 1922, Kilburn, Middx.; s. of John Downs and Ellen McMahon; m. Mary C. Chillman 1951; one s. three d.; ed. Gunnersbury Catholic Grammar School and Univ. of London; joined Ricardo Consulting Engineers 1942, Dir. 1957, Man. Dir. 1967, Chair. and Man. Dir. 1976, Chair. Ricardo Consulting Engineers PLC 1984–87; Pres. Inst. of Mechanical Engs. 1978–79, Fed. Int. des Socs. d'Ingénieurs des Techniques de l'Automobile 1978–80; mem. Advisory Council for Applied Research and Devt. 1976–80, Science and Eng. Research Council 1981–84, Design Council 1981–89; mem. Bd. of Dirs. Soc. of Automotive Engs. Inc. 1983–86, British Council 1988–93; Foreign Assoc. Nat. Acad. of Eng., U.S.A.; Dir. Gabriel Communications (fmrly. Universe Publs.) Ltd. 1986–93; Chair. Council of Surrey Univ. 1989–91, Pro-Chancellor 1992–94; Hon. mem. Hungarian Acad. of Sciences 1988; J. A. Ewing Medal (Inst. of Civil Engs.); Kt. of St. Gregory 1993. *Publications:* papers on internal combustion engines in British and int. journals. *Leisure interests:* theatre, literature. *Address:* 143 New Church Road, Hove, Sussex, England. *Telephone:* (01273) 419357.

DOWSON, Duncan, C.B.E., PH.D., F.ENG., F.I.MECH.E., F.R.S., F.R.S.A.; British professor of mechanical engineering; b. 31 Aug. 1928; s. of Wilfrid Dowson and Hannah Dowson; m. Mabel Strickland 1951; one s. (and one s. deceased); ed. Lady Lumley's Grammar School, Pickering and Univ. of Leeds; research eng. Sir W.G. Armstrong Whitworth Aircraft Co. 1953–54; lecturer in Mechanical Eng. Univ. of Leeds 1954, Sr. Lecturer 1963, Reader 1965, Prof. of Eng. Fluid Mechanics and Tribology 1966–93, now Prof. Emer., Hon. Fellow and Research Prof.; Hon. Prof. Univ. of Hong Kong; Hon. Prof. Univ. of Bradford 1996–; Dir. Inst. of Tribology, Dept. of Mech. Eng. 1967–87, Head, Dept. of Mech. Eng. 1987–93, Pro-Vice-Chancellor 1983–85, Dean for Int. Relations 1987–93; Pres. Inst. of Mechanical Engineers 1992–93; Chair. Yorks. Region, Royal Soc. of Arts 1992–97; Foreign mem. Royal Swedish Acad. of Eng. Sciences; Fellow, American Soc. of Mechanical Eng. (ASME), American Soc. of Lubrication Engs. (ASLE); recipient of numerous awards from Inst. of Mech. Eng., ASME, ASLE etc.; Hon. D. Tech. (Chalmers Univ. of Tech. Göteborg); Hon. D.Sc. (Inst. Nat. des Sciences Appliquées, Lyon); Dr. h.c. (Liège) 1996; James Clayton Fund Prize, Thomas Hawksley Gold Medal, Tribology Gold Medal 1979, James Alfred Medal 1988, Sarton Medal (Belgium) 1998. *Publications:* Elastohydrodynamic Lubrication: the fundamentals of roller and gear lubrication (jointly) 1966, History of Tribology 1979, An Introduction to the Biomechanics of Joints and Joint Replacement (jtly.) 1981, Ball Bearing Lubrication: The Elastohydrodynamics of Elliptical Contacts (jtly.) 1981; papers in professional journals. *Leisure interests:* travel, astronomy. *Address:* 23 Church Lane, Adel, Leeds, LS16 8DQ, England. *Telephone:* (0113) 2678933.

DOWSON, Graham Randall; British business executive; b. 13 Jan. 1923, Southend; s. of late Cyril James and late Dorothy Celia Dowson (née Foster); m. 1st Fay Valerie Weston 1954 (dissolved 1974); two d.; m. 2nd Denise Joy Shurman 1975; ed. City of London School, Ecole Alpina, Switzerland; war service 1939–45, Pilot, Squadron Leader R.A.F. 1941–46; Sales, U.S. Steel Corpn. (Columbia Steel), Los Angeles 1946–49; Mid-South Network (MBS), Radio U.S.A. 1949–52; Dir. A. C. Nielsen Co., Oxford 1953–58, Southern T.V. Ltd., London 1958–74, Paravision (U.K.) Ltd 1988–, Grovewood Securities PLC 1990–91; Dir. Rank Org. 1960, Deputy Chief Exec. 1972, Chief Exec. 1974–75; Partner Graham Dowson and Assocs. 1975–; Chair. Mooloya Investments 1975–78, Erskine House Investments 1975–83, Pincus Vidler Arthur Fitzgerald 1979–83, Dowson Shurman (fmrly. Dowson Salisbury, Assocs. Ltd.) 1988–, Nash Industries PLC 1988–89; Chair. and Chief Exec., Teltech Marketing Services Ltd. 1984–87; Dir. Carron Holdings Ltd. 1976–, Carron Investments Ltd. 1976–, Nimslo Ltd. 1979–87 (Dir. 1978), PPR Securities Ltd. 1976–82, RCO Holdings PLC 1979–, Filmbond PLC 1985–88, Fairhaven Int. 1988–95; Deputy Chair. Nimslo Int. Ltd., Nimslo European Holdings Ltd., Nimslo Corpn. 1979–88, Nat. Playing Fields Assen. 1974–; Jt. Pres. British Section, European League for Econ. Co-operation 1972–83, Jt. Pres. 1983; Chair. Migraine Trust 1985–88, Premier Speakers 1987–; mem. Court of Common Council, Corpn. of London 1993–95. *Leisure interest:* sailing. *Address:* 193 Cromwell Tower, Barbican, London, EC2Y 8DD, England.

DOWSON, Sir Philip (Manning), Kt., C.B.E., P.R.A., R.I.B.A.; British architect; b. 16 Aug. 1924, Johannesburg, S. Africa; s. of Robert Dowson and Ina Cowen; m. Sarah Crewdson 1950; one s. two d.; ed. Gresham's School, Univ. Coll., Oxford, Clare Coll., Cambridge; Lieut. R.N.V.R. 1943–47; Cambridge 1947–50; Architectural Assen. 1950–53; joined Ove Arup & Partners 1953; Founder, Architectural Partner, Arup Assocs. 1963; Sr. Partner, Ove Arup Partnership 1969–90, Consultant 1990–; Pres. Royal Acad. of Arts 1993–; mem. Royal Fine Art Comm. 1971–97, Craft Advisory Cttee. 1972–75; Gov. St. Martin's School of Art 1975–80; Trustee, Thomas Cubitt Trust 1978–, Royal Botanic Gardens, Kew 1983–95, The Armouries, HM Tower of London 1984–89, Nat. Portrait Gallery 1993–, Coram Foundation 1993–; Hon. F.A.I.A.; Hon. Fellow, Duncan of Jordanstone Coll. of Art 1985, Royal Coll. of Art 1989, Clare Coll., Cambridge 1992; Royal Gold Medal for Architecture 1981. *Works include:* urban and univ. devt. and coll. buildings: Oxford, Cambridge, Birmingham, Leicester; housing; schools; new uses for old buildings; buildings for music and industrial and office devts. *Publications:* articles in technical press. *Leisure interest:* sailing. *Address:* Royal Academy of Arts, Piccadilly, London, W1V 0DS, England. *Telephone:* 0171-300 5690. *Fax:* 0171-300 5642

DOYLE, Brian André, B.A., LL.B.; Zambian (b. British) judge; b. 10 May 1911, Moulmien, Burma; m. Nora Slattery 1937 (died 1992); one s. one d.; ed. Douai School and Trinity Coll., Dublin; Magistrate, Trinidad and Tobago 1937; Resident Magistrate Uganda 1942; Solicitor-Gen. Fiji 1948, Attorney-Gen. 1949; Attorney-Gen. N. Rhodesia 1956, Attorney-Gen. and Minister of Legal Affairs 1959–65; Justice of Appeal, Zambia 1965; Chief Justice of Zambia 1969–75; Dir. Law Devt. Comm. 1975–79; Judge Botswana Court of Appeal 1973–79, 1988–91; Chair. Delimitation Comm., Botswana 1981–82. *Address:* 26 Choumert Square, Peckham Rye, London, SE15 4RE, England.

DOYLE, Frederick Bernard, B.SC., M.B.A., C.ENG., F.I.C.E., C.B.I.M.; British civil engineer; b. 17 July 1940, Manchester; s. of James Hopkinson and Hilda Mary (née Spotsworth) Doyle; m. Ann Weston 1963; two s. one d.; ed. St. Bede's Coll., Manchester, Victoria Univ. of Manchester, Harvard Business School; Resident Civil Engineer, British Rail 1961–65; Man. Consultant, Arthur D. Little Inc. 1967–72; with Booker McConnell Ltd. 1973–81, Sec. to Exec. Cttee. 1973, Dir. Eng. Div. 1974, Chair. Gen. Eng. Div. 1976, Chair. and Chief Exec. Booker McConnell Eng. Ltd. Jan. 1979, Dir. of parent co. Jan. 1979; Chief Exec. Social Democratic Party Sept. 1981–83, Welsh Water Authority 1983–87; Dir. Public Sector Operations, MSL Int. 1988–90, Dir. 1994–96, Man Dir. 1997–; Man. Dir. Hamptons 1990–92; Gen. Man. Bristol and West Bldg. Soc. 1992–94; NATO Fellowship 1965. *Leisure interests:* walking, theatre, reading, travel. *Address:* 38A West Road, Bromsgrove, Worcs., B60 2NQ, England. *Telephone:* (01527) 873565.

DOYLE, Roddy; Irish writer; b. 1958, Dublin; Booker Prize (for Paddy Clarke Ha Ha Ha) 1993. *Publications:* The Commitments 1987 (filmed 1991), The Snapper 1990 (filmed 1992), The Van 1991, Paddy Clarke Ha Ha Ha 1993, The Woman Who Walked into Doors 1996. *Address:* c/o Secker and Warburg, Michelin House, 81 Fulham Road, London, SW3 6RB, England. *Telephone:* 0171-581 9393. *Fax:* 0171-581 6243.

DRABBLE, Margaret, C.B.E.; British author; b. 5 June 1939, Sheffield; d. of the late J. F. Drabble and Kathleen (née Bloor) Drabble; sister of A. S. Byatt (q.v.); m. 1st Clive Swift 1960 (divorced 1975); two s. one d.; m. 2nd Michael Holroyd (q.v.) 1982; ed. Newnham Coll., Cambridge; Chair., Nat. Book League 1980–82; Ed. The Oxford Companion to English Literature 1979–84; Vice-Patron, Child Psychotherapy Trust 1987–; Hon. D.Litt. (Sheffield) 1976, (Bradford) 1988, (Hull) 1992; Hon. Fellow, Sheffield City Polytechnic 1989; E. M. Forster Award, American Acad. of Arts and Letters 1973. *Publications:* A Summer Bird-Cage 1963, The Garrick Year 1964, The Millstone 1965 (John Llewelyn Rhys Memorial Prize 1966), Jerusalem the Golden 1967, The Waterfall 1969, The Needle's Eye 1972, Arnold Bennett: A Biography 1974, The Realms of Gold 1975, The Genius of Thomas Hardy (Editor) 1976, The Ice Age 1977, For Queen and Country: Britain in the Victorian Age 1978, A Writer's Britain 1979, The Middle Ground (novel) 1980, The Oxford Companion to English Literature (Ed.) 1985, The Radiant Way (novel) 1987, A Natural Curiosity 1989, Safe as Houses 1990, The Gates of Ivory 1991, Angus Wilson: A Biography 1995, The Witch of Exmoor (novel) 1996. *Leisure interests:* walking and talking. *Address:* c/o A. D. Peters, Fifth Floor, The Chambers, Chelsea Harbour, Lots Road, London SW10 0XF, England. *Telephone:* 0171-344 1000.

DRABINSKY, Garth Howard, O.C., LL.B.; Canadian impresario; b. 27 Oct. 1949, Toronto, Ont.; s. of Philip Drabinsky and Ethel (Waldman) Drabinsky; m. Pearl Kaplan 1971; one s. one d.; ed. Univ. of Toronto; practised as lawyer in entertainment business; produced numerous films; co-f. Cineplex cinema chain; Chair Livent Inc., Toronto 1989. *Productions include:* The Phantom of the Opera, Toronto 1988–, Kiss of the Spider Woman, Joseph and the Amazing Technicolor Dreamcoat, Show Boat, Sunset Boulevard, Aspects of Love, The Music of Andrew Lloyd Webber in Concert, Ragtime, The Musical; mem. Bd. of Dirs. Mount Sinai Hosp., Hollinger Inc., Bd. of Govs. Baycrest Center for Geriatric Care, Advisory Bd., Center for Research in Neurodegenerative Diseases, Univ. of Toronto; Founder United Way, The Tomorrow Fund 1995, B'nai B'rith Int. Garth H. Drabinsky Lecture Series 1989; mem. Acad. of Motion Picture Arts and Sciences, Acad. of Canadian Cinema and TV, Canadian Tourism Comm., Variety Club of Ont.; Hon. Fellow York Univ. Faculty of Fine Arts, Toronto and several other honours and awards. *Publications:* Motion Pictures and the Arts in Canada: The Business and the Law 1976; Closer to the Sun (autobiog., co-author). *Address:* Livent Inc., 165 Avenue Road, Suite 600, Toronto, Ont., M5R 3S4, Canada.

DRACH, Ivan Fyodorovich; Ukrainian politician and writer; b. 17 Oct. 1936, Telizhentsy, Kiev Oblast; ed. Univ. of Kiev, Moscow State Univ.; author of several novels and books of poetry, fmrly. worked on Literaturnaya Ukraina and Witczyna newspapers; joined CP 1959, resgnd. 1990; f. mem. Narodny Rukh (Ukrainian nationalist opposition movt.), leader, then Co-Chair. 1989–92; Chair. Bd. Ukraina Soc. 1992–; mem. Ukrainian Supreme Soviet 1990–; Ukrainian State Prize 1976, U.S.S.R. State Prize 1983. *Publications:* Sun Flower 1962, Ballads of Everyday Life 1967, I Come to You 1970, Poems 1972, The Kievan Sky 1976, The Sun and the Word (poetry) 1978. *Address:* Gorky str. 18, Apt. 7, 252005 Kiev, Ukraine. *Telephone:* (044) 27-24-01.

DRACHEVSKY, Leonid Vadimovich; Russian diplomatist; b. 5 April 1942; ed. Mendeleyev Inst. of Chemical Tech., Diplomatic Acad. Ministry of Foreign Affairs; on staff Ministry of Foreign Affairs since 1992; Consul (rank of Counsellor) Gen. Consulate of Russian Fed., Barcelona, Spain 1992; Head of Div., Dir. Dept. on Problems of C.I.S. 1993–94; Dir. First Dept. of C.I.S. Countries 1994–96; Amb. to Poland 1996–98; Deputy Minister of Foreign Affairs 1998–. *Address:* Ministry of Foreign Affairs, Smolenskaya-Sennaya pl. 32/34, 121200 Moscow, Russia. *Telephone:* (095) 244 16 06. *Fax:* (095) 244 32 76.

DRAKE, Frank Donald, B.ENG.PHYS., M.A., PH.D.; American astronomer; b. 28 May 1930, Chicago; s. of Richard C. Drake and Winifred Thompson Drake; m. 1st Elizabeth B. Bell 1953 (divorced 1977); three s.; m. 2nd Amahl Shakhashiri 1978; two d.; ed. Cornell and Harvard Univs.; U.S.N. 1952–55; Harvard Radio Astronomy Project 1955–58; Ewen-Knight Corpn. 1957–58; Scientist, Head Scientific Services and Telescope Operations on Nat. Radio Astron. Observatory 1958–63; Chief, Lunar and Planetary Science Section, Jet Propulsion Laboratory 1963–64; Prof. of Astronomy, Cornell Univ. 1964–85, Goldwin Smith Prof. of Astronomy 1976–85; Dir. Arecibo Ionospheric Observatory 1966–68; Assoc. Dir. Center for Radiophysics and Space Research, Cornell Univ. 1967–75; Chair. Dept. of Astronomy, Cornell Univ. 1968–71; Dir. Nat. Astronomy and Ionosphere Center 1971–81; Prof. of Astronomy, Univ. of Calif., Santa Cruz 1984–95, Prof. Emer. 1995–, Dean Div. of Natural Sciences 1984–88; Pres. Astronomical Soc. of the Pacific 1988–90; mem. A.A.A.S., N.A.S. 1972, The Explorers Club, Advisory Bd. The World Book Encyclopedia, Int. Astronomical Union, Int. Scientific Radio Union, American Astronomical Soc.; Fellow, American Acad. of Arts and Sciences; Pres. SETI Inst. *Publications:* Intelligent Life in Space 1962, Murmurs of Earth 1979, (with Dava Sobel) Is Anyone Out There? 1992 and over 135 papers and articles. *Leisure interests:* snorkelling, horticulture, lapidary. *Address:* c/o Department of Astronomy and Astrophysics, Univ. of California, Santa Cruz, CA 95064, U.S.A. *Telephone:* (408) 459 4885.

DRAPER, Kenneth, M.A., R.A.; British painter and sculptor; b. 19 Feb. 1944, Killamarsh, Sheffield; s. of Albert Draper and Dorothy Rosa Anne Lamb; m. 1st Heather Lieven Beste 1965 (divorced); one s.; m. 2nd Nadiya Jinnah 1972 (divorced); partner Jean Macalpine; ed. Chesterfield Coll. of Art, Kingston School of Art, R.C.A.; solo exhbns. include Redfern Gallery, London 1969, Warwick Arts Trust, London 1981, Galerie Nouvelles Images, Den Haag, Holland 1984, Austin Desmond, London 1991, Adelson Gallery, New York 1993, Friends Room, R.A. 1993, Hart Gallery, London 1994, 1996, 1998, Peter Bartlow Gallery, Chicago 1995; group exhbns. include British Sculptors 1972, R.A. 1972, Silver Jubilee Exhbn. Contemporary British Sculpture, Battersea Park 1977, The British Art Show, Mappin, Sheffield 1980, British Sculpture in the Twentieth Century, Whitechapel Art Gallery 1981; work in public collections of Arts Council of G.B., Contemporary Arts Soc., Courtauld Inst., London, Ashmolean Museum, Oxford, Usher Gallery, Lincoln; Mark Rothko Memorial Award 1971. *Leisure interests:* reading, chess, sport, travel. *Address:* Carrer D'es Port 2, Apto. 6, 07720 Es Castell, Minorca, Balearic Is., Spain. *Telephone:* (971) 35 34 57. *Fax:* (971) 35 34 57.

DRAPER, William Henry, III, M.B.A.; American government official; b. 1 Jan. 1928, White Plains, N.Y.; s. of William Henry Draper and Katherine Baum; m. Phyllis Culbertson 1953; one s. two d.; ed. Yale and Harvard Univs.; with Inland Steel Co., Chicago 1954–59; Draper, Gaither & Anderson, Palo Alto, Calif. 1959–62; Pres. Draper & Johnson Investment Co. Palo Alto 1962–65; founder, gen. partner, Sutter Hill Capital Co., Palo Alto 1965–70, Sutter Hill Ventures, Palo Alto 1970–81; Pres., Chair. Export-Import Bank U.S., Washington, D.C. 1981–86; Admin., C.E.O. UNDP 1986–93; Man. Dir. Draper Int., San Francisco 1994–; numerous directorships etc.; Trustee Yale Univ. 1991–, George Bush Library Foundation 1993–; Hon. LL.D. (Southeastern Univ.); Republican. *Address:* Draper International, 50 California Street, Suite 2925, San Francisco, CA 94111 (Office); 91 Tallwood Court, Atherton, CA 94027, U.S.A. (Home).

DRAŠKOVIĆ, Vuk; Serbian politician, journalist and writer; b. 29 Nov. 1946, Mezha Banat Region, Vojvodina; m. Danika Drašković (née Bošković); moved to Herzegovina; ed. Belgrade Univ.; as student took part in demonstrations 1968; mem. staff Telegraph Agency of Yugoslavia TANJUG 1969–78, worked in Lusaka, Zambia; dismissed from post of correspondent for disinformation 1978; Adviser Council of Trade Unions of Yugoslavia 1978–80; Ed. Rad (newspaper) 1980–85; freelance journalist and writer 1985–; f. and Chair. Serbian Renewal Movt. (SRM) 1990–; candidate for Presidency of Yugoslavia 1990, 1992, of Serbia 1997; mem. Nat. Ass.; detained, released from detention July 1993; leader of mass protests against Pres. Milošević from Nov. 1996. *Publications:* 8 books, including novels: Judge, Knife, Prayer 1, Prayer 2, Russian Consul, Night of the General, Polemics, Answers as well as numerous articles and collections of articles. *Address:* Serbia Renewal Movement, André Nikolića 1–3, 11000 Belgrade, Yugoslavia. *Telephone:* (11) 687223.

DRAVINS, Dainis, PH.D.; Swedish professor of astronomy; b. 10 Sept. 1949, Lund; m. Christina (née Hedqvist) Dravins 1982; one s.; ed. Lund and Uppsala Univs. and Calif. Inst. of Tech., Calif., U.S.A.; Prof. of Astronomy, Lund Univ. 1984–; mem. Royal Swedish Acad. of Sciences 1987; Foreign mem. Latvian Acad. of Sciences 1992. *Publications:* numerous articles on astronomy. *Address:* Lund Observatory, Box 43, 22100 Lund, Sweden. *Telephone:* (46) 222 7297; (46) 222 7000.

DRAWICZ, Andrzej; Polish writer, critic and essayist; b. 20 May 1932, Warsaw; s. of Józef Drawicz and Krystyna Drawicz; m. Vera Drawicz 1963; ed. Univ. of Warsaw; published works 1950; led Koła Młodych ZLP, Warsaw 1953–54; dir. Student Theatre of Satire 1954–64; research work in Polish-Soviet Inst., Warsaw 1955–57; lecturer, Dept. of Literature, Inst. of Russian Philology, Cracow 1981–91, Asst. Prof. 1989–; Prof., Slavonic Inst., Polish Acad. of Sciences 1991–, Slavonic Inst., Univ. of Warsaw 1992–; interned 1981–82; mem. Polish Writers' Union (ZLP) 1969–83, Solidarity Independent Trade Union 1980–, Asscn. of Polish Writers (SPP) 1989–; Chair. Cttee. for Radio and TV 1989–91. *Publications include:* Soviet Literature 1917–67, 1968, Konstanty Ildefons Gałczyński 1968, Konstanty Paustowski 1972, Zaproszenie do podróży 1974, Pytania o Rosję 1981, Spór o Rosję 1988, Pocałunek na mrozie (Ayckbourn and Frayn Award, Independent Journalists' Award) 1989, and numerous articles on Russian literature. *Leisure interests:* Mazurian Lakes, walking in the forests. *Address:* ul. Sonaty 6 m. 631, 02-744 Warsaw, Poland. *Telephone:* (022) 43-57-27.

DRAY, William Herbert, M.A., D.PHIL., LL.D., F.R.S.C.; Canadian professor of philosophy; b. 23 June 1921, Montreal, P.Q.; s. of William J. Dray and Florence E. Jones; m. Doris K. Best 1943; one s. one d.; ed. Univ. of Toronto and Balliol and Nuffield Colls. Oxford; R.C.A.F. 1941–46, Active Reserve (Wing Commdr., retd.) 1956–66; lecturer in Philosophy, Univ. of Toronto 1953–55, Asst. Prof. to Prof. 1955–68; Prof. Trent Univ. 1968–76, Chair. Dept. of Philosophy 1968–73; Prof. of Philosophy with cross-appt. to History, Univ. of Ottawa 1976–86, Prof. Emer. 1986–; visiting appts. at Ohio State Univ. 1959, Case Inst. 1966, Harvard Univ. 1967, 1973, Stanford Univ. 1962, Duke Univ. 1973; ACLS Fellowship 1960–61, Killam Research Fellowship 1980–81, Nat. Humanities Center Fellowship 1983–84; Molson Prize of the Canada Council 1986. *Publications:* Laws and Explanation in History 1957, Philosophy of History 1964, 1993, Philosophical Analysis and History (ed.) 1966, Perspectives on History 1980, Substance and Form in History (ed., with L. Pompa) 1981, La philosophie de l'histoire et la pratique historienne d'aujourd'hui (ed. with D. Carr et al.) 1982, On History and Philosophers of History 1989, History as Re-enactment 1995. *Address:* Apt. 818, 32 Clarissa Drive, Richmond Hill, Ont., L4C 9R7, Canada. *Telephone:* (905) 883-1995.

DREIER, Ralf, DR.JUR.; German professor of law; b. 10 Oct. 1931, Bad Oeynhausen; s. of Heinrich and Martha (née Volkmann) Dreier; ed. legal studies; Asst. Lecturer, Kommunalwissenschaftliches Inst., Univ. of Münster 1963–70; Lecturer, later Prof. Univ. of Münster 1970–73; Prof. of Gen. Legal Theory, Univ. of Göttingen 1973–; mem. Akad. der Wissenschaften, Göttingen; Pres. Int. Asscn. for Philosophy of Law and Social Philosophy. *Publications:* Zum Begriff der 'Natur der Sache' 1965, Das kirchliche Amt 1972, Recht-Moral-Ideologie 1981, Rechtsbegriff und Rechtsidee 1986, Recht-Staat-Vernunft 1991, Juristische Vergangenheitsbewältigung 1995. *Address:* Juristisches Seminar der Universität Göttingen, Platz der Göttinger Sieben 6, 37073 Göttingen; Wilhelm-Weber Strasse 4, 37073 Göttingen, Germany. *Telephone:* 5-91-14.

DREIFUSS, Ruth; Swiss politician; b. 9 Jan. 1940, St. Gall; ed. Ecole d'Etudes Sociales, Geneva and Univ. of Geneva; Sec. 1958–59; Ed. Coopération, Swiss Union of Cooperatives, Basle 1961–64; asst. sociologist, Centre Psycho-Social Universitaire, Geneva 1965–68; Asst. in Nat. Accounting, Faculty of Econ. and Social Sciences, Univ. of Geneva 1970–72; civil servant, Swiss Devt. Corpn. Fed. Ministry of Foreign Affairs 1972–81; Sec. Swiss Fed. of Trade Unions 1981–93; elected to Swiss Fed. Council March 1993; Head, Fed. Dept. of Home Affairs April 1993–; Pres. of Switzerland 1999–.

Address: Federal Department of Home Affairs, Bundeshaus, Inselgasse, 3003 Berne, Switzerland.

DRELL, Sidney David; American professor of physics; b. 13 Sept. 1926, Atlantic City, N.J.; s. of Tulla and Rose White Drell; m. Harriet Stainback 1952; one s. two d.; ed. Princeton Univ. and Univ. of Illinois; Research Assoc. Univ. of Illinois 1949–50; Physics Instructor Stanford Univ. 1950–52; Research Assoc. M.I.T. 1952–53, Asst. Prof. 1953–56; Assoc. Prof. Stanford Univ. 1956–60, Prof. of Physics 1960–63, Lewis M. Terman Prof. and Fellow 1979–84; Prof. Stanford Linear Accelerator Center 1963–, Deputy Dir. 1969–98, Exec. Head of Theoretical Physics 1969–86; Prof. Emer. 1998–; Sr. Fellow Hoover Inst. 1998–; Adjunct Prof. Dept. of Eng. and Public Policy, Carnegie Mellon Univ. 1989–96; Visiting Scientist and Guggenheim Fellow, CERN 1961–62; Visiting Prof. and Loeb Lecturer, Harvard Univ. 1962, 1970; Consultant to Los Alamos Scientific Lab. 1956–, Office of Science and Tech., Exec. Office of the Pres. 1960–73; consultant Arms Control and Disarmament Agency 1969–81, Office of Tech. Assessment, U.S. Congress 1975–91, Office of Science and Tech. Policy 1977–82, Nat. Security Council 1973–81; Consultant, Senate Select Cttee. on Intelligence 1978–83; Co-Dir. Stanford Centre for Int. Security and Arms Control 1984–89; consultant House Armed Services Cttee. 1990–91, Senate Select Cttee. on Intelligence 1990–93; Chair. Int. Advisory Bd. Inst. of Global Conflict and Cooperation, Univ. of Calif. 1990–93; mem. High Energy Physics Advisory Panel to DOE 1974–86 (Chair. 1974–82); mem. JASON Div. (Mitre Corpn.) 1960–; mem. Bd. The Arms Control Asscn., Washington 1971–93; mem. Council on Foreign Relations 1980–; mem. Advisory Cttee. M.I.T. Physics Dept. 1974–90; mem. President's Science Advisory Cttee. 1966–70; Visiting Schrodinger Prof., Theoretical Physics, Univ. of Vienna 1975; mem. Bd. of Trustees, Inst. for Advanced Study, Princeton, N.J. 1974–83; Bd. Gov. Weizmann Inst. of Science, Rehovoth, Israel 1970–; Bd. Dir. Annual Reviews Inc. 1976–97; mem. numerous advisory cttees. and editorial boards, including M.I.T. Lincoln Lab. Advisory Bd. 1985–90, Aspen Strategy Group 1984–91, Carnegie Comm. on Science, Tech. and Govt. 1988–93, Scientific and Academic Advisory Cttee. on Nat. Labs., Univ. of Calif. 1988–92, Pres.'s Foreign Intelligence Advisory Bd. 1993–, Comm. on Maintaining U.S. Nuclear Weapons Expertise; Chair. Pres.'s Council on the Nat. Labs. 1992–; Fellow American Physical Soc. (Pres. 1986); mem. N.A.S., American Acad. of Arts and Sciences, American Philosophical Soc. 1987–, Academia Europaea; Guggenheim Fellow, Rome 1972; Richtmeyer Memorial Lecturer to American Asscn. of Physics Teachers 1978; Visiting Fellow, All Souls Coll., Oxford Univ. 1979; Danz Lecturer, Univ. of Washington 1983; I. I. Rabi Visiting Prof. Columbia Univ. 1984; Hon. D.Sc. (Univ. of Ill., Chicago Circle) 1981; E. O. Lawrence Memorial Award 1972, Univ. of Ill. Alumni Award for Distinguished Service in Engineering 1973, Leo Szilard Award for Physics in the Public Interest 1980, MacArthur Fellowship Award 1984–89, Univ. of Ill. Achievement Award 1988, Hans Bethe Lecturer, Cornell Univ. 1988, Hilliard Roderick Prize in Science, Arms Control and Int. Security (AAAS) 1993, Co-recipient Ettore Majorana-Erice Science for Peace Prize 1994, Woodrow Wilson Award for Distinguished Achievement in the Nation's Service, Princeton Univ. 1994, Gian Carlo Wick Commemorative Award I.C.S.C. World Lab. 1996, Distinguished Assoc. Award of U.S. Dept. of Environment 1997; I. Ya. Pomeranchuk Prize (Moscow) 1998. *Publications include:* Relativistic Quantum Mechanics, Relativistic Quantum Fields (both with J. D. Bjorken), and numerous papers on theoretical physics; Facing the Threat of Nuclear Weapons 1983 (updated 1989), The Reagan Strategic Defense Initiative: A Technical, Political, and Arms Control Assessment (co-author) 1984, Sidney Drell on Arms Control 1988, Reducing Nuclear Danger (co-author) 1993, In the Shadow of the Bomb: Physics and Arms Control 1993, and other books on arms control. *Leisure interest:* music. *Address:* Stanford Linear Accelerator Center, P.O. Box 4349, Stanford, CA 94309 (Office); 570 Alvarado Row, Stanford, CA 94305, U.S.A. (Home).

DRENTH, Pieter Johan Diederik, PH.D.; Netherlands professor of work and organisational psychology; b. 8 March 1935, Appelscha; s. of Gerrit Drenth and Froukje Wouda; m. Maria Annetta Elizabeth de Boer 1959; three s.; ed. Vrije Univ., Amsterdam; served in Royal Dutch Navy 1955–60; Research Fellow Social Science Research Div., Standard Oil Co., New York 1960–61; Sr. lecturer in Psychometrics and Industrial Psychology, Vrije Univ., Amsterdam 1962–67, Prof. of Work and Organisational Psychology 1967–; Vice-Chancellor 1983–87; Dean Faculty of Psychology and Educ. 1998–; Visiting Prof. Washington Univ. St. Louis 1966, Univ. of Washington, Seattle 1977; Pres. Royal Netherlands Acad. of Arts and Sciences 1990–96; mem. Royal Netherlands Acad. of Arts and Sciences 1980; mem. Supervisory Bd. Shell-Nederland B.V.; Dr. h.c. (Ghent) 1980, (Paris V) 1996; Heymans Award for Outstanding Contrib. to Psychology 1986, Kt. Order of the Lion 1991, Aristotle award for outstanding contribs. to European psychology 1995, Commdr. Order of Oranje Nassau 1996. *Publications:* Mental Tests and Cultural Adaptation (Ed.) 1972, Inleiding in de testtheorie 1976, Decisions in Organizations 1988, Advances in Organizational Psychology (Ed.) 1988, New Handbook Work and Organizational Psychology (Ed.) 1989, Testtheorie 1990, Gardening in Science 1996, numerous scientific papers and psychological tests. *Leisure interests:* cycling, music, literature. *Address:* Vrije Universiteit, Department of Work and Organizational Psychology, V.d. Boechorstraat 1, 1081 BT Amsterdam; Royal Netherlands Academy of Arts and Sciences, Kloveniersburgswal 27-29, 1000 GC Amsterdam (Office); Pekkendam 6, 1081 HR Amsterdam, Netherlands (Home). *Telephone:* (020) 4448701 (Office); (020) 6465954 (Home). *Fax:* (20) 444 8702.

DRESE, Claus Helmut, DR.PHIL.; German theatre director; b. 25 Dec. 1922, Aachen; s. of Karl Drese and Helene Drese; m. Helga Lautz 1950; two c.; studied German studies, philosophy and history in Cologne, Bonn and Marburg; Theatre Literary Man., Mannheim 1952–59; Theatre Dir., Heidelberg 1959–62, Wiesbaden 1962–68, Cologne 1968–75, Zurich 1975–; Dir. Vienna State Opera 1986–91. *Publications:* various contributions to newspapers, radio and television.

DRETSKE, Frederick Irwin, PH.D.; American philosopher; b. 9 Dec. 1932, Ill.; s. of Hattie Walschlager and Frederick E. Dretske; m. 1st Virginia Lord 1954; m. 2nd Brenda Peters 1965; m. 3rd Judith Fortson 1988; one s. one d.; ed. Purdue Univ., Univ. of Minnesota; Asst. Prof. to Prof., Univ. of Wis. 1960–90; Prof. of Philosophy Stanford Univ. 1990–; American Council of Learned Socs. Fellowship 1965, Nat. Endowment for the Humanities Fellowships 1975, 1980; Pres. American Philosophical Asscn. (Cen. Div.) 1984–85. *Publications:* Seeing and Knowing 1969, Knowledge and the Flow of Information 1981, Explaining Behavior 1988, Naturalizing the Mind 1995. *Leisure interests:* carpentry, travel. *Address:* 2431 Ramona, Palo Alto, CA 94301, U.S.A. *Telephone:* (415) 326 6952.

DREW, John Sydney Neville, M.A., A.M., M.B.A.; British academic; b. 7 Oct. 1936, Hornchurch; s. of late John Drew and Kathleen Wright; m. Rebecca Usher 1962; two s. one d.; ed. King Edward's School, Birmingham, St. John's Coll. Oxford, Tufts Univ. and London Business School; H.M. Diplomatic Service 1960–73; Dir. of Marketing and Exec. Programmes, London Business School 1973–79; Dir. of Corporate Affairs, Rank Xerox 1979–84; Dir. of European Affairs, Touche Ross Int. 1984–86; Head, U.K. Offices, Comm. of EC 1987–93; Dir. Research Inst. for Study of Change, Visiting Prof. of European Business, Durham Univ.; Dir. Europa Times 1993–94, Change Group Int. 1996–; Deputy Chair. Enterprise Support Group 1993–94; Pres. Inst. of Linguists 1993–; Assoc. Fellow, Templeton Coll. Oxford 1982–86; Visiting Prof. Imperial Coll. London 1987–91, Open Univ. 1992–; Hon. Ed. European Business Journal 1987–; Hon. M.B.A. (Northumbria) 1991. *Publications:* Doing Business in the European Community 1979, Networking in Organizations 1986, Developing an Active Company Approach to the European Market 1988, Readings in International Enterprise (Ed.) 1995, articles on European integration and man. devt. *Leisure interests:* travel, golf, personal development. *Address:* 49 The Ridgeway, London, NW11 8QP, England (Home). *Telephone:* 0181-455 5054 (Office). *Fax:* 0181-455 4516 (Office).

DREWS, Juergen, M.D.; German research director and physician; b. 16 Aug. 1933, Berlin; m. Dr. Helga Eberlein 1963; three d.; ed. Berlin, Innsbruck, Heidelberg and Yale Univs.; Head, Chemotherapy Section, Sandoz Research Inst., Vienna 1976–79, Head, Sandoz Research Inst. 1979–82, Int. Pharmaceutical R&D, Sandoz, Basel 1982–85; Dir. Pharmaceutical Research, F. Hoffmann-La Roche Ltd., Basel 1985–86, Chair. Research Bd. and mem. Exec. Cttee. 1986–90, Pres. Int. R&D and mem. Exec. Cttee. Roche Group, Hoffmann-La Roche Inc., Nutley, N.J. 1991–95, Pres. global research, mem. exec. Cttee. 1996–97. *Publications:* Chemotherapie 1979, Immunpharmakologie, Grundlagen und Perspektiven 1986, Immunopharmacology 1990, Die verspielte Zukunft 1998; more than 200 scientific papers. *Leisure interests:* skiing, climbing, literature, piano. *Address:* c/o Hoffmann-La Roche Inc., Nutley, NJ 07110, U.S.A.

DREYFUS, George, A.M.; composer; b. 22 July 1928, Wuppertal, Germany; m.; two s. one d.; ed. Vienna Acad. of Music; Composer-in-residence, Tienjin, China 1983, Shanghai 1987, Nanjing 1991; Henry Lawson Award 1972; Prix de Rome 1976; Mishkenot Sha'ananim, Jerusalem 1980; Don Banks Fellowship 1992. *Compositions include:* Garni Sands, The Gilt-Edged Kid (operas): Symphonies Nos. 1 & 2; Symphonie Concertante 1977; Jingles . . . & More Jingles; Reflections in a Glasshouse; The Illusionist; The Grand Aurora Australis Now Show; Galgenlieder; Songs Comic & Curious; Music in the Air; From within Looking out; The Seasons; Ned Kelly Ballads; Quintet after the Notebook of J.-G. Noverre; Sextet for Didjeridu & Wind Instruments; Old Melbourne; several pieces for young people; The Sentimental Bloke (musical) 1985, Lifestyle 1988, Song of Brother Sun 1988 (choral pieces), Rathenau (opera) 1993, Die Marx Sisters (opera) 1994. *Publications:* The Last Frivolous Book (autobiog.) 1984, Being George—And Liking It! 1998. *Leisure interests:* swimming, gardening. *Address:* 3 Grace Street, Camberwell, Vic. 3124, Australia. *Fax:* (3) 9809-2671.

DREYFUSS, Richard Stephan; American actor; b. 29 Oct. 1947, New York; s. of Norman Dreyfuss and Gerry D. Student; m. Jeramie Dreyfuss 1983; two s. one d.; ed. San Fernando Valley State Coll.; alternative mil. service Los Angeles County Gen. Hosp. 1969–71; mem. American Civil Liberties Union Screen Actors Guild, Equity Asscn., American Fed. of TV and Radio Artists, Motion Picture Acad. Arts and Sciences; Golden Globe Award 1978, Acad. Award for Best Actor in The Goodbye Girl 1978. *Stage appearances include:* Julius Caesar 1978, The Big Fix (also producer) 1978, Othello 1979, Death and the Maiden 1992, The Prisoner of Second Avenue 1999. *Films include:* American Graffitti 1972, Dillinger 1973, The Apprenticeship of Duddy Kravitz 1974, Jaws 1975, Inserts 1975, Close Encounters of the Third Kind 1976, The Goodbye Girl 1977, The Competition 1980, Whose Life Is It Anyway? 1981, Down and Out in Beverly Hills 1986, Stakeout 1988, Moon over Parador 1989, Let it Ride, Always 1989, Rosencrantz and Guildernstern are Dead, Postcards from the Edge 1990, Once Around 1990, Randall and Juliet 1990, Prisoners of Honor 1991,

What About Bob? 1991, Lost in Yonkers 1993, Another Stakeout 1993, The American President, Mr Holland's Opus 1995, Mad Dog Time 1996, James and the Giant Peach 1996, Night Falls on Manhattan 1997, The Call of the Wild 1997; TV movie Oliver Twist 1997; Dir., producer Nuts 1987, Hamlet (Birmingham) 1994. *Publication:* The Two Georges (with Harry Turtledove) 1996. *Address:* c/o ICM, 8942 Wilshire Blvd., Beverly Hills, CA 90211, U.S.A.

DRICKAMER, Harry George, B.S.E., M.S., PH.D.; American professor of chemistry, physics and chemical engineering (retd.); b. 19 Nov. 1918, Cleveland, Ohio; s. of George H. and Louise S. Drickamer; m. Mae Elizabeth McFillen 1942; two s. three d.; ed. Univ. of Michigan; Pan American Refining Corpn., Texas City 1942–46; Asst. Prof. of Chemical Eng., Univ. of Illinois 1946–49, Assoc. Prof. 1949–53, Prof. 1953–90, Prof. Emer. 1990–, Head, Div. of Chemical Eng. 1955–58, mem. Center for Advanced Study 1963; mem. Nat. Acad. of Eng., N.A.S., American Acad. of Arts and Sciences, American Philosophical Soc.; Dr. h.c. (Russian Acad. of Science) 1994; numerous awards including Allan P. Colburn Award, American Inst. of Chemical Engineers 1947, Ipatieff Prize, American Chem. Soc. 1956, Oliver E. Buckley Solid State Physics Award, American Physical Soc. 1967, William Walker Award, American Inst. of Chemistry 1972, Langmuir Award in Chemical Physics, American Chemical Soc. 1974, P. W. Bridgman Award, Int. Asscn. for the Advancement of High Pressure Research and Tech. 1977, Michelson-Morley Award, Case-Western Reserve Univ. 1978, John Scott Award, City of Philadelphia 1984, A. von Humboldt Award, Fed. Repub. of Germany 1986, W. K. Lewis Award, American Inst. of Chemical Engs. 1986, Peter Debye Award in Physical Chem., American Chemical Soc. 1987, Welch Award in Chem., R.A. Welch Foundation 1987, Distinguished Professional Achievement Award, Univ. of Mich. 1987, Elliot Cresson Medal (Franklin Inst.) 1988, Nat. Medal of Science 1989, Gold Medal American Inst. of Chemists 1996. *Publications:* Over 400 papers in scientific journals. *Leisure interests:* reading of Roman, medieval and 18th century history, walking. *Address:* 304 East Pennsylvania Street, Urbana, IL 61801, U.S.A. (Home).

DRINAN, Robert F., M.A., LL.M., TH.D.; American politician, professor and writer; b. 15 Nov. 1920, Boston; s. of James J. Drinan and Ann Flanagan; ed. Boston Coll., Georgetown Univ. and Gregorian Univ., Rome; ordained Jesuit Priest 1953; Dean Boston Coll. Law School 1956–70; mem. U.S. Congress from Mass. 1971–81; Prof. Georgetown Univ. Law Center 1980–; mem. A.B.A., Chair. Section on Individual Rights and Responsibilities 1990–91; Fellow, American Acad. of Arts and Sciences; 21 hon. degrees from American univs. *Publications:* Religion, the Courts and Public Policy 1963, Democracy, Dissent and Disorder 1969, Vietnam and Armaggedon 1970, Honor the Promise 1977, Beyond the Nuclear Freeze 1983, God and Caesar on the Potomac 1985, Cry of the Oppressed 1987, Stories from the American Soul 1990, The Fractured Dream 1991. *Address:* Georgetown University Law Center, 600 New Jersey Avenue, N.W., Washington, DC 20001, U.S.A. *Telephone:* (202) 662-9073. *Fax:* (202) 662-9412.

DRISS, Rachid; Tunisian diplomatist and journalist; b. 27 Jan. 1917, Tunis; m. Jeanine Driss 1953; one s.; ed. Sadiki Coll., Tunis; joined Neo-Destour party 1934; journalist exiled in Cairo, and with Pres. Bourguiba founder mem. Bureau du Maghreb Arabe; returned to Tunisia 1955; Ed. El Amal; Deputy, Constitutional Assembly 1956; Sec. of State Post Office and Communications 1957–64; mem. Nat. Assembly 1958, 1969; Amb. to the U.S.A. and Mexico 1964–68; mem. Political Bureau of Council of the Repub. 1969–; Perm. Rep. to UN 1970–76; Vice-Pres. Econ. and Soc. Council 1970, Pres. 1971; mem. Conseil Constitutionnel 1987–92; Special Emissary of Arab League to Kuwait and Iraq 1992; Founder, Pres. Asscn. des Etudes Internationales 1981–, Arab Bd. for Child Devt.; Pres. Presidential Comm. on Human Rights 1991–; Dir. Etudes Int. (quarterly); Grand Cordon de l'Ordre de l'Indépendance de la République Tunisienne and many foreign decorations. *Publications:* From Bab Souika to Manhattan 1980, Diaries from the Maghreb Office in Cairo 1981, A l'aube la lanterne 1981, From Djakarta to Carthage 1985, Errances (poems) 1990, Feuilles d'insomnie (novel) 1990, Report on Human Rights in Tunisia 1992. *Address:* Rue St. Cyprien, 2016 Carthage, Tunisia.

DRIVER, Minnie (Amelia); British actress; b. 1970; ed. Bedales School, Hants. *Television appearances include:* God on the Rocks, Mr. Wroe's Virgins, The Politician's Wife. *Film appearances include:* Circle of Friends, Goldeneye, Baggage, Big Night, Sleepers, Grosse Point Blank, Good Will Hunting, The Governess, Hard Rain, An Ideal Husband. *Address:* c/o Lou Coulson, 1st Floor, 37 Berwick Street, London, W1V 3LF, England. *Telephone:* 0171-734 9633.

DRNOVŠEK, Janez, D.ECON.; Slovenian politician; b. 17 May 1950, Celje; ed. Maribor Univ.; worked as Dir. Zagorje Construction Co., Chief Exec. Trbovlje br. of Ljubljanska Bank, adviser on econ. affairs in Yugoslavian Embassy, Egypt; elected to Slovenian Parl. (Skupščina) of Yugoslavia 1986; Slovenian mem. of Collective Presidency of Yugoslavia 1989; Pres. of Presidency 1989–90; Head of Non-Allied Movt., Chair. Summit Conf. Sept. 1989; one of initiators of introduction of multi-party system in Yugoslavia; f. and Pres. Liberal Democracy of Slovenia (LDS) Party 1991; leader of Ind. Movt.; Prime Minister of Slovenian Repub. 1992–; Hon. D.Jur. (Boston Univ.) 1994. *Publications:* numerous articles on loans, monetary policy and int. financial relations. *Address:* Office of the Prime Minister, Gregorčičova St. 20, 61000 Ljubljana, Slovenia. *Telephone:* (61) 1259280 (Office).

DROIT, Michel; French writer and journalist; b. 23 Jan. 1923, Vincennes; s. of Jean Droit and Suzanne Plisson; m. Janine Bazin 1947; one s. one d.; ed. Lycée Louis le Grand, Paris, Univ. of Paris, and Ecole Libre des Sciences Politiques; Resistance Movement 1942–44; War Correspondent and Reporter for press, radio and TV 1944–56; Foreign Affairs Commentator, French TV 1956–60; Ed.-in-Chief Tribunes et Débats, French TV 1960–61, Le Figaro Littéraire 1961–71; Advisory Ed. to La Librairie Plon 1968; Reporter France-Inter 1969–81; leader writer, Man. Adviser to Le Figaro and Le Figaro Magazine 1971–; Producer TV Programme A propos 1962–74; writer and dir. Ces Années Là 1975, Cela s'appelait l'Empire 1980; co-produced Le XIXe siècle ou la peinture en liberté 1981; mem. Académie française 1980; Prix Max Barthou 1955, Prix Carlos de Lazerme 1961, Grand Prix du Roman de l'Académie Française (for Le retour) 1964; Officier, Légion d'honneur, Médaille militaire, Croix de guerre, Officier, Ordre nat. du Mérite. *Publications include:* novels: L'écorché, Pueblo, Le retour, Les compagnons de la Forêt-Noire, L'Orient perdu, La ville blanche, La mort du connétable, Les Feux du crépuscule, La rivière de la guerre 1985, Nous Parlerons de Rome 1992, le Temps d'apprendre à vivre 1993 (first vol. of memoirs) le Temps qui tient au coeur 1996 (second vol. of memoirs); travel: Jours et nuits d'Amérique du sud, J'ai vu vivre le Japon, Panoramas mexicains, Les clartés du jour, Les lueurs de l'aube, Une plume et un micro; Ordres et décorations de France, le Rendez-Vous d'Elchingen; essays: André Maurois, La Camargue; biography: De Lattre Maréchal de France, L'homme du destin (5 vols.), Le fils unique 1988, Le Rendez-vous d'Elchingen 1990; short stories: La fille de l'ancre bleue; film: Un Français libre. *Leisure interests:* big game hunting, karate, skin-diving. *Address:* 76 rue Spontini, 75116 Paris, France.

DROMER, Jean; French banker; b. 2 Sept. 1929, Paris; s. of Henri Dromer and Fortunée Sayag; m. Eliane Dhombres 1952; one s. four d.; ed. Ecole Libre des Sciences Politiques and Ecole Nationale d'Administration; Insp.-Gen. des Finances; Sec.-Gen. Rueff-Armand Cttee. on econ. expansion 1958; Tech. Counsellor, Office of Minister of Foreign Affairs 1961–64; Counsellor for Financial, Econ. and Social Affairs to Pres. de Gaulle 1964–67; Sec.-Gen. responsible for Econ. and European Co-operation 1967; Jt. Man. Dir. Banque Nationale de Paris 1968–; Pres. Cie. Financière France-Afrique Natio-bail 1970–, 1973–87; Admin. Banque Internationale pour l'Afrique Occidentale 1968–, Chair. 1975–86; Pres. C.I.C. de Paris 1986, Compagnie Financière du C.I.C. 1986, Banque de l'Union Européene 1986, L'Union des Assurances de Paris 1987–88, UAP-INT. 1987, French Asscn. of Banks; Pres. Planinter 1989, Médecins sans frontières foundation 1990, Louis Vuitton 1990–, SMEG 1990–, Fondation de France 1996–; Admin. Soudure autogène française, Compagnie int. pour le développement Interfinexa 1971–, Compagnie navale Worms 1972–, Philips (Compagnie française) 1986–, and to numerous other cos.; Int. Vice-Pres. Conseil Nat. du patronat français (CNPF) 1992; mem. bd. dirs. Banque pour l'expansion industrielle (Banexi) 1969–; mem. Council Société Nat. industrielle aérospatiale (Snias) 1974–; mem. numerous councils etc.; Chevalier, Légion d'honneur; Commdr., Ordre nationale du Mérite. *Address:* Financière Agache, 11 rue François 1er, 75008 Paris; Fondation de France, 40 avenue Hoche, 75008 Paris (Offices); 39 boulevard de Montmorency, 75016 Paris, France (Home). *Telephone:* 42.60.33.40 (Office); 525.72.73 (Home).

DRONKE, (Ernst) Peter (Michael), M.A., F.B.A.; British medieval Latin scholar and author; b. 30 May 1934; s. of A. H. R. Dronke and M. M. Dronke (née Kronfeld); m. Ursula Miriam Brown 1960; one d.; ed. Victoria Univ., N.Z. and Magdalen Coll. Oxford; Research Fellow, Merton Coll. Oxford 1958–61; Lecturer in Medieval Latin, Cambridge Univ. 1961–79, Reader in Medieval Latin Literature 1979–89, Prof. 1989–, Fellow of Clare Hall 1964–; Visiting Prof. of Medieval Studies, Westfield Coll. London 1981–86; Carl Newell Jackson Lecturer, Harvard Univ. 1992; Corresp. Fellow, Real Academia de Buenas Letras, Royal Dutch Acad.; Hon. Pres., Int. Courtly Literature Soc.; Co-Ed. Mittellateinisches Jahrbuch 1977–; Premio Internazionale Ascoli Piceno 1988. *Publications:* Medieval Latin and the Rise of European Love-Lyric (2 vols.) 1965–66, The Medieval Lyric 1968, Poetic Individuality in the Middle Ages 1970, Fabula 1974, Abelard and Heloise in Medieval Testimonies 1976, Barbara et antiquissima carmina (with Ursula Dronke) 1977, Bernardus Silvestris, Cosmographia (Ed.) 1978, Introduction to Francesco Colonna, Hypnerotomachia 1981, Women Writers of the Middle Ages 1984, The Medieval Poet and his World 1984, Dante and Medieval Latin Traditions 1986, Introduction to Rosvita, Dialoghi Drammatici 1986, Ed. A History of Twelfth-Century Western Philosophy 1988, Hermes and the Sibyls 1990, Latin and Vernacular Poets of the Middle Ages 1991, Intellectuals and Poets in Medieval Europe 1992, Verse with Prose: From Petronius to Dante 1994, Nine Medieval Latin Plays 1994, (Ed.) Hildegard of Bingen, Liber divinorum operum 1996, Sources of Inspiration 1997, Dante's Second Love (lectures) 1997, Introduction to Alessandro nel medioevo occidentale 1997, Growth of Literature: the Sea and the God of the Sea (with Ursula Dronke) 1998; Etienne Gilson's Letters to Bruno Nardi (Ed.) 1998, Hildegard of Bingen: The Context of Her Thought and Art (Jt. Ed.) 1998; essays in learned journals and symposia. *Leisure interests:* music, film and Brittany. *Address:* 6 Parker Street, Cambridge, CB1 1JL, England. *Telephone:* (01223) 359942.

DROSSOYIANNIS, Anthony; Greek politician and former army officer; b. 1922, Athens; m.; one s.; ed. Mil. Acad.; during 2nd world war, active service with Ieros Lochos (Sacred Battalion) in Middle East under Allied Command, took part in liberation of Samos 1943, of islands of Aegean and Dodecanese as Commdr. of commando units of Ieros Lochos 1944; subsequently in Third Army Corps, and Instructor, Mil. Acad. until 1947, Co. Commdr. of Tactical Staff and Deputy Commdr. of a commando unit, Civil War 1947–50, served with commando and infantry units 1950–67 rank of Bn. Commdr.; banished, and imprisoned several times during mil. dictatorship; promoted to rank of Maj.-Gen. after return to democracy; M.P. 1985; Minister of Public Order 1986–88; Gold Medal of Bravery with Mil. Cross, Medal of Merit (several times). *Address:* 42 Pipinou Street, 112 51, Athens, Greece.

DROZ, Georges André Léopold, D. EN D.; French international official; b. 4 May 1931, Algiers; s. of Albert Droz and Denise Droz (née Dupré); m. 1st Danièle Frison-Roche 1952 (died 1986); one s. three d.; m. 2nd Alida Brans 1991; ed. Algiers and Paris; mil. service, French Air Force 1955–57; Sec. Hague Conf. on Private Int. Law 1957, First Sec. 1965, Deputy Sec.-Gen. 1968, Sec.-Gen. 1978; Assoc. Prof., Paris I, Panthéon-Sorbonne Univ. 1975–76; Lecturer, Hague Acad. of Int. Law 1974, 1980, 1991; Dr. h.c. (Nijmegen, Fribourg); Commdr. Order of Orange-Nassau; Officer, Nat. Order of Merit of Luxembourg. *Publications:* Compétence judiciaire et effets des jugements dans le Marché Commun 1972, Pratique de la Convention de Bruxelles du 27 septembre 1968 1973, Les Régimes matrimoniaux en droit international privé comparé 1974, Regards sur le droit international privé comparé 1992; one hundred articles in French and foreign legal publs. *Leisure interests:* mountaineering. *Address:* c/o Hague Conference on Private International Law, 6 Scheveningseweg, 2517 KT The Hague, Netherlands. *Telephone:* (70)-3633303. *Fax:* (70) 3604867.

DROZDOVA, Margarita Sergeyevna; Russian ballerina; b. 7 May 1948; ed. Moscow Choreographic School, State Inst. of Theatre Art (GITIS); danced with Stanislavsky Musical Theatre Ballet Co., Moscow 1967–91, coach 1991–; mem. CPSU 1980–91; Anna Pavlova Award, Paris 1968; R.S.F.S.R. State Prize 1980, People's Artist of U.S.S.R. 1986. *Roles include:* Odette-Odile, Gayané, The Commissar (M. Bronner's 'Optimistic Tragedy'), Medora (A. Adam's 'Corsaire'), Swanilda (Delibes' 'Coppélia'), Cinderella (Prokofiev). *Address:* Stanislavsky and Nemirovich Danchenko Musical Theatre, Pushkinskaya str. 17, Moscow, Russia. *Telephone:* 299-31-36 (Home).

DRUCKER, Daniel Charles, PH.D.; American engineer; b. 3 June 1918, New York; s. of Moses Abraham Drucker and Henrietta Weinstein; m. Ann Bodin 1939; one s. one d.; ed. Columbia Univ., New York; Instructor Cornell Univ., Ithaca, N.Y. 1940–43; Supervisor Armour Research Foundation 1943–45; Asst. Prof. Ill. Inst. of Tech., Chicago 1946–47; Assoc. Prof., then Prof. Brown Univ., Providence, R. I. 1947–64, Chair. Div. of Eng. 1953–59, L. Herbert Ballou Univ. Prof. Brown Univ. 1964–68; Pres. Soc. for Experimental Stress Analysis 1960–61, American Acad. of Mechanics 1972–73, American Soc. of Mechanical Eng. 1973–74, Int. Union of Theoretical and Applied Mechanics 1980–84, Vice-Pres. 1984–88; Pres. American Soc. for Eng. Educ. 1981–82; Dean of Eng., Univ. of Ill. at Urbana-Champaign 1968–84; Graduate Research Prof. of Eng. Sciences, Univ. of Florida 1984–94, Grad. Research Prof. Emer. 1994–; mem. Nat. Acad. of Eng.; Foreign mem. Polish Acad. of Sciences; mem. Nat. Science Bd. 1988–94; Hon. mem. Ill. Soc. of Professional Engineers; Fellow American Acad. of Arts and Sciences, American Acad. of Mechanics, American Soc. of Civil Engineers, American Soc. for Eng. Educ., American Soc. of Mechanical Engineers (also Hon. mem.), Soc. for Experimental Mechanics (also Hon. mem.); Fellow, A.A.A.S.; Guggenheim Fellow 1960–61, NATO Sr. Science Fellow 1968, Charter Fellow, American Soc. for Eng. Educ. 1983; Murray Lecturer, Soc. for Experimental Stress Analysis 1967, Marburg Lecturer, American Soc. for Testing and Materials 1966; Hon. D.Eng. (Lehigh, Univ. Bethlehem, Pa.) 1976; Dr. h.c. Technion, Israel Inst. of Tech. 1983; Hon. Dr. Sc. (Brown Univ.) 1984, (Northwestern Univ.) 1985, (Univ. of Illinois) 1992; M. M. Frocht Award, Soc. for Experimental Stress Analysis, 1971, Illig Medal, Columbia Univ. 1938, Lamme Medal, American Soc. for Eng. Educ. 1967, von Karman Medal, American Soc. of Civil Eng. 1966, Thomas Egleston Medal, Columbia Univ. School of Eng. and Applied Science 1978, Gustave Trasenster Medal, Univ. of Liège, Belgium 1979, William Prager Medal, Soc. of Eng. Science 1983, Timoshenko Medal, American Soc. of Mechanical Engineers 1983, John Fritz Medal, Founder Eng. Socs. 1985, 1986 Thurston Lecturer and Distinguished Lecturer 1987–89, American Soc. of Mechanical Engineers, Nat. Medal of Science 1988, ASME Medal 1992, American Soc. for Eng. Educ. Hall of Fame 1993. *Publications:* Introduction to the Mechanics of Deformable Bodies 1967, and over 200 technical articles. *Address:* 231 Aerospace Engineering Building, University of Florida, Gainesville, FL 32611, U.S.A. *Telephone:* (352) 392-9699.

DRUCKER, Jean Maurice; French television executive; b. 12 Aug. 1941, Vire (Calvados); s. of Abraham Drucker and Lola Schafler; m. Véronique Siney 1973; one d.; ed. Inst. d'Etudes Politiques de Paris, Ecole Nat. d'Admin.; Chargé de mission, Ministry of Cultural Affairs 1968–70; Tech. Adviser to Gen. Man. Office de radiodiffusion télévision française (ORTF) 1970–71; Asst. Man. First TV network 1971–75; Chargé de mission to Pres.-Dir.-Gen., Soc. Française de Production (SFP), then Dir. 1975–78, Dir.-Gen. 1978–80; Asst. Dir.-Gen. Compagnie Luxembourgeoise de télédiffusion, Vice-Pres. Dir.-Gen. Radio Télé Luxembourg (RTL) 1980–85; Pres.-Dir.-Gen. Antenne 2 1985–87, Metropole Télévision (M6) 1987–; Prof. of Media Man., Inst. d'Etudes Politiques de Paris 1982. *Address:* Metropole Télévision, 89–91 avenue Charles de Gaulle, 92575 Neuilly-sur-Seine (Office); 7 bis rue de Monceau, 75008 Paris, France (Home). *Telephone:* 42.56.66.66 (Office).

DRUCKER, Peter Ferdinand, LL.D.; American management consultant and teacher; b. 19 Nov. 1909, Vienna, Austria; s. of Adolph and Caroline Drucker; m. Doris Schmitz 1937; one s. three d.; ed. Gymnasium, Vienna and Univ. of Frankfurt; Prof. of Political Philosophy, Bennington Coll., Bennington, Vt. 1942–49; Prof. of Management, Graduate School of Business Admin., New York 1950–72; Clarke Prof. of Social Science, Claremont Grad. School, Claremont, Calif. 1971; Prof. and Lecturer in Oriental Art, Pomona Coll., Claremont 1980–85; Godkin Lecturer, Harvard Univ. 1994; Man. Consultant (own firm) 1945–; Fellow, A.A.A.S., American Acad. of Management, Int. Acad. of Man.; Hon. Fellow, British Inst. of Management; 22 hon. degrees from univs. in U.S.A., U.K., Japan, Belgium, Spain, and Switzerland; Britannica Award 1987. *Publications:* The End of Economic Man 1939, The Future of Industrial Man 1942, Concept of the Corporation 1946, The New Society 1950, The Practice of Management 1954, America's Next Twenty Years 1957, Landmarks of Tomorrow 1959, Managing for Results 1964, The Effective Executive 1966, The Age of Discontinuity 1969, Technology, Management and Society 1970, The New Markets and other essays 1971, Management: Tasks, Responsibilities, Practices 1974, The Unseen Revolution; How Pension Fund Socialism came to America 1976, People and Performance 1977, Management, an Overview 1978, Adventures of a Bystander 1979, Song of the Brush, Japanese Paintings 1979 (co-author), Managing in Turbulent Times 1980, Toward the Next Economics and other essays 1981, The Changing World of the Executive 1982, The Last of All Possible Worlds (fiction) 1982, The Temptation to Do Good (fiction) 1984, Innovation and Entrepreneurship 1985, Frontiers of Management 1986, The New Realities 1989, Managing the Non-Profit Organization 1990, Management for the Future 1991, Social Ecology 1992, Post Capitalist Society 1993, Managing in a Time of Great Change 1995, Drucker on Asia: A Dialogue with Tsao Nagauchi 1997, and educational films. *Address:* c/o Claremont Graduate School, Claremont, CA 91711, U.S.A. (Office).

DRUK, Mirchea; Moldovan politician and economist; b. 1941, Pochumbeuts, Moldova; ed. Leningrad State Univ., Moscow State Univ., U.S.S.R. Acad. of Sciences; worked in educ. insts. and research centers; mem. Supreme Soviet of Moldova 1989–; Dir.-Gen. Moldovan Center of Econ. Co-operation with Foreign Countries 1989–90; Prime Minister of Moldova 1990–91; mem. Pres.'s Council 1990–91; Chair. Nat. Council for Reunification with Romania 1991–93; Chair. Christian Democratic Front of Moldova 1992. *Publications:* articles on man., and psychology of man.

DRUMMOND, Sir John Richard Gray, Kt., M.A., F.R.S.A., F.R.C.M.; British arts administrator; b. 25 Nov. 1934; s. of late Capt. A.R.G. Drummond and of Esther Pickering; ed. Canford School, Trinity Coll. Cambridge; joined BBC 1958, Asst. Head, Music and Arts, Controller of Music 1985–91, Controller Radio 3 1987–91, Dir. BBC Promenade Concerts 1985–95. *Programmes produced include:* Tortelier Master Classes 1964, Leeds Piano Competition 1966, Diaghilev 1967, Kathleen Ferrier 1968, Music Now 1969, Spirit of the Age 1975, The Lively Arts 1976–78; Dir. Edin. Int. Festival 1978–83, European Arts Festival 1992; Vice-Chair. British Arts Festivals Asscn. 1981–83 (Vice-Pres. 1994–); Pres. Kensington Soc. 1985–97; Chair. Nat. Dance Co-ordinating Cttee. 1986–95; Gov. Royal Ballet 1986–97; mem. Theatres Trust 1989–. *Publications:* A Fine and Private Place (with Joan Bakewell) 1977, The Turn of the Dance (with N. Thompson) 1984, Speaking of Diaghilev 1997. *Address:* 61c Campden Hill Court, London, W8 7HL, England. *Telephone:* 0171-937 2257.

DRUON, Maurice Samuel Roger Charles; French author; b. 23 April 1918, Paris; m. Madeleine Marignac 1968; ed. Lycée Michelet, Ecole des Sciences Politiques, Faculté des Lettres de Paris; War Corresp. Allied Armies 1944–45; mem. Académie Française 1966, Perpetual Sec. 1986; Minister for Cultural Affairs 1973–74; mem. French Parl. 1978–81, mem. European Parl. 1979–80, mem. Académie Royale du Maroc 1980, assoc. mem. Académie d'Athènes 1981; mem. Franco-British Council 1973–74; Pres. Assn. France-Italie; Assoc. mem. Lisbon Acad. of Sciences, Brazilian Acad.; hon. mem. Romanian Acad. 1996; Dr. h.c. (York Univ., Ont.) 1987, (Boston) 1997; Prix Goncourt for novel Les grandes familles 1948, Prix de Monaco 1966; Hon. C.B.E.; Grand Officier, Légion d'honneur, Commdr. des Arts et Lettres, Commdr., Order of Phoenix (Greece), Commdr. Ordre de la Républíque de Tunisie, Grand Cross of Merit (Italy), Grand Officier ordre du Lion du Sénégal, Grand Cross of the Aztec Eagle (Mexico), Grand Officer, Order of Merit (Malta), Ordre du Mérite culturel (Monaco), Ordre de l'Honneur de Grèce, du Ouissam Alaouite, Grand Cross of the Christ (Portugal), Grand Officier Orden de Mayo (Argentina). *Publications:* Lettres d'un Européen 1943, La dernière brigade 1946, La fin des hommes (3 vols. Les grandes familles 1948, La chute des corps 1950, Rendez-vous aux enfers 1951), La volupté d'être 1954, Les rois maudits 1955–77 (7 vols. Le roi de fer, La reine étranglée, Les poisons de la couronne, La loi des mâles, La louve de France, Le lis et le lion, Quand un Roi perd la France), Tistou les pouces verts 1957, Alexandre le Grand 1958, Des seigneurs de la plaine à l'hôtel de Mondez 1962, Les mémoires de Zeus (2 vols. L'aube des dieux 1963, Les jours des hommes 1967), Bernard Buffet 1964, Paris, de César à Saint Louis 1964, Le pouvoir 1965, Les tambours de la mémoire 1965, Le bonheur des uns ... 1967, Discours de réception à l'Académie française 1968, L'avenir en désarroi 1968, Vézelay, colline éternelle 1968, Nouvelles lettres d'un européen 1943–70, Une église qui se trompe de siècle 1972, La parole et le pouvoir 1974, Oeuvres complètes 1974–79, Attention la France 1981, Réformer la démocratie 1982, La culture et l'état 1985, Lettre aux français sur leur langue et leur âme 1994, Circonstances 1997, Circonstances Politiques 1998; plays: Mégarée 1942, Un voyageur 1953, La Contessa 1962. *Leisure interests:* riding, travel. *Address:* Académie Française, 23 quai Conti, 75006 Paris (Office); Palais Mazarin, 1 rue de Seine, 75006 Paris; Abbaye de Faise, 33570 Les Artigues de Lussac, France (Homes).

DRURY, David J., B.SC.; American finance executive; b. Iowa; ed. Iowa State Univ.; joined The Prin. Financial Group as asst. actuary 1970, Vice-Pres. 1985, Vice-Pres. and Chief Actuary 1987, Sr. Vice-Pres. and Chief Actuary 1989, Exec. Vice-Pres. 1992, Pres. 1993, Chair. and C.E.O. 1994–. *Address:* The Principal Financial Group, 711 High Street, Des Moines, IA 50309, U.S.A. *Telephone:* (515) 247-5111. *Fax:* (515) 246-5475.

DRURY, Very Rev. John Henry, M.A.; British ecclesiastic and university administrator; b. 23 May 1936, Clacton; s. of Henry Drury and Barbara Drury; m. Clare Nineham 1972; two d.; ed. Bradfield and Trinity Hall, Cambridge; Curate, St. John's Wood Church, London 1963; Chaplain, Downing Coll. Cambridge 1966; Chaplain and Fellow, Exeter Coll. Oxford 1969; Canon of Norwich Cathedral 1973; lecturer, Univ. of Sussex 1979; Dean, King's Coll. Cambridge 1981; Dean, Christ Church, Oxford 1991–; Hon. Fellow Exeter Coll., Oxford 1992, Trinity Hall, Cambridge 1997; Hussey Lecturer Univ. of Oxford 1997. *Publications:* Angels and Dirt 1972, Luke 1973, Tradition and Design in Luke's Gospel 1976, Parables in the Gospels 1985, Critics of the Bible 1724–1873 1989, The Burning Bush 1990. *Leisure interests:* drawing, walking, carpentry. *Address:* The Deanery, Christ Church, Oxford, OX1 1DP, England. *Telephone:* (01865) 276161. *Fax:* (01865) 276238.

DRUT, Guy Jacques; French athlete and politician; b. 6 Dec. 1950, Oignies (Nord); s. of Jacques Drut and Jacqueline Wigley; m. 2nd Véronique Hardy 1984; one d. and one d. by first m.; ed. Lycée de Douai, Lycée d'Henin-Liétard, Lycée Roubaix, Ecole Normale Supérieure d'Education Physique et Sportive and Inst. Nat. des Sports; French Jr. record-holder, 110m hurdles, pole vault and decathlon; French 110m hurdles champion 1970–76, 1981; European 100m hurdles champion, Rome 1974; European 110m hurdles record, Rome 1974, world record, Berlin 1975; Silver Medal, 110m hurdles, Munich Olympics 1972, Gold Medal, Montreal Olympics 1976; Bronze Medal, 50m hurdles, European Championships 1981; retd. from competition 1981; Chief of Staff to Prime Minister Jacques Chirac 1975–76; mem. Nat. Council UDR, Cen. Cttee. R.P.R.; Deputy Mayor of Paris responsible for Youth and Sport 1985–89; R.P.R. Deputy from Seine-et-Marne to Nat. Ass. 1986–95; Town Councillor, Meaux 1989–92; Regional Councillor, Ile-de-France 1992–; Mayor of Coulommiers 1992–; Minister of Youth and Sport May–Nov. 1995, Minister del. 1995–97; elected Deputy for Seine-et-Marne (Groupe du Rassemblement pour la République) 1997–; mem. IOC 1996–; Chevalier, Ordre Nat. du Mérite. *Publications:* L'or et l'argent 1976, Jacques Chirac: la victoire du sport (jtly) 1988, J'ai deux mots à vous dire 1997. *Leisure interest:* golf. *Address:* Mairie, 77120 Coulommiers; Assemblée nationale, 75355 Paris, France.

DRUTSE, Ion; Moldovan writer; b. 3 Sept. 1928, Horodişte; s. of Panteleimon Drutse and Sofia Drutse; m. Rosina Era Samuilovna; two d.; ed. Higher Literary School of Writers' Union, Moscow; first works published in 1950s, People's Writer of Moldova 1988; U.S.S.R. People's Deputy 1989–91; mem. U.S.S.R. Supreme Soviet 1989–91; mem. Acad. of Sciences of Moldova, Romanian Acad. of Sciences. *Publications:* short stories and novels including Leaves of Melancholy 1957, Burden of Our Kindness 1968, A Return to One's Own Circle, A White Church 1982, The Samaritan 1989, Saturday in Nazareth 1994, The Apostle Paul 1994; plays Kasa Mare 1960, Birds of Our Youth 1972, Holy of Holies 1976, The Falling of Rome 1996. *Leisure interest:* sport. *Address:* Lomonosovsky prospekt 19, Apt. 107, 117311 Moscow, Russia. *Telephone:* (095) 930-11-96.

DRUZHININ, Igor Petrovich; Russian hydrologist; b. 10 Feb. 1929; m.; ed. Moscow Energy Inst.; jr. researcher section of scientific devt. of water problems U.S.S.R. Acad. of Sciences 1955–57; head of lab. Inst. of Energetics and Water Kyrgyz Acad. of Sciences 1957–61; sr. researcher, head of lab., Deputy Dir., head of div. Energy Inst. Siberian br. U.S.S.R. Acad. of Sciences 1961–85; Vice-Pres. E. Siberian br. U.S.S.R. Acad. of Sciences 1978–87; Dir. Inst. of Water and Ecology Problems Far E. br. 1987–96; adviser Russian Acad. of Sciences 1996–; corresp. mem. U.S.S.R. (now Russian) Acad. of Sciences 1987, mem. 1994; research in long-term prognosis of evolution of nature processes, ecology. *Publications:* Solar Activity and Crises of the Evolution of Nature Processes on the Earth 1969, Long-term Analysis and Information 1987, numerous articles in scientific journals. *Leisure interests:* horticulture, gardening. *Address:* Russian Institute of Water and Ecology Problems, Kim Yu Chen str. 65, 630063 Khabarovsk, Russia. *Telephone:* (095) 711-17-99.

DRYSDALE, Andrew; South African journalist; b. 19 Oct. 1935, Duiwelskloof, Transvaal; s. of Andrew Patarson Drysdale; ed. Parktown High School; Ed. The Argus; Fellow, Harvard Univ., U.S.A. *Leisure interests:* golf, tennis. *Address:* P.O. Box 56, Cape Town 8000, South Africa.

DRYUKOV, Anatoly Matveyevich; Russian diplomatist; b. 4 Sept. 1936, Voronezh; m.; two d.; ed. Moscow Inst. of Int. Relations; diplomatic service 1960–; attaché Embassy, Pakistan 1962–64; mem. Dept. of South-East Asia, U.S.S.R. Ministry of Foreign Affairs 1964–66; mem. Secr. of Deputy Minister 1966–69; First Sec. Embassy, Zambia 1969–73; Asst. Deputy Minister 1973–78, expert, Deputy Chief Dept. of South-East Asia 1978–86, Deputy Chief Dept. of Socialist Countries of Asia 1986–87; with Embassy, Singapore 1987–90; Chief Main Dept. of Staff and higher educ. establishments of U.S.S.R. Ministry of Foreign Affairs 1990–91; Russian Amb. to India 1991–96, Gen. Insp. Ministry of Foreign Affairs 1996–98; Amb. to Armenia 1998–. *Address:* Russian Embassy, Pionerskaya str. 72, 375015 Yerevan, Armenia. *Telephone:* 52-45-22, 52-45-24. *Fax:* 52-13-78.

D'SOUZA, Most Rev. Eugene, B.A., B.ED.; Indian ecclesiastic; b. 15 Nov. 1917, Nagpur; s. of Ignatius Charles D'Souza; mem. Congregation of Missionaries of St. Francis de Sales 1935; ordained priest 1944; consecrated first native Bishop of Nagpur 1951, first Archbishop 1953; est. St. Francis de Sales Coll. of Arts & Science and St. Charles Seminary, Nagpur 1956; Archbishop of Bhopal 1963–94, Archbishop Emer. 1994–; est. Bhopal School of Social Sciences, Univ. Coll., Univ. of Bhopal 1965; est. Asha Niketan, Rehabilitation Centre for handicapped and deaf children 1967; mem. Catholic Bishops' Conf. of India, mem. Standing Cttee. 1953–; mem. Governing Bd. St. John's Medical Coll., Bangalore; active participant Vatican Council II and several int. conventions; Nat. Award for Distinguished Service in Educ. and Rehabilitation of the Handicapped 1976. *Address:* c/o Archbishop's House, 33 Ahmedabad Palace Road, Bhopal, M.P. 462 001, India.

DU DAOZHENG; Chinese journalist; b. Nov. 1923, Dingxiang Co., Shanxi Prov.; s. of Du Xixiang and Qi Luaying; m. Xu Zhixian 1950; one s. four d.; ed. Middle School, Dingxiang, Shanxi and Beijing Marx-Lenin Coll.; joined CCP 1937; Chief of Hebei and Guangdong Bureau, Xinhua News Agency 1949–56; Ed.-in-Chief Yangchen Wanbao 1956–69; Dir. Home News Dept., Xinhua News Agency 1977–82; Ed.-in-Chief Guangming Daily 1982; Dir. Media and Publs. Office 1987–88; Hon. Pres. Newspaper Operation and Man. Assoc. 1988–; Deputy 7th NPC 1988–; Dir. State Press and Publs. Admin. 1988–89; winner of the Nat. News Prize 1979. *Publications:* Explore Japan (co-author), Interviews with Famous Chinese Journalists. *Leisure interest:* photography.

DU MINGXIN; Chinese composer and university professor; b. Aug. 1928, Qianjiang Co., Hubei Prov.; ed. Tchaikovsky State Conservatoire U.S.S.R. 1954–58; Prof. of Composition, Cen. Conservatory of Music 1978–; Exec. Dir. Chinese Musicians' Asscn.; mem. 11th CPPCC 1997–. *Compositions include:* Great Wall Symphony, Luoshen Symphony, two violin concertos, two piano concertos, music (with others) for ballets Mermaid, The Red Detachment of Women, piano trio, string quartet. *Address:* Central Conservatory of Music, 43 Baojia Street, Beijing 100031, People's Republic of China.

DU QINGLIN; Chinese politician; b. Nov. 1946, Panshi Co., Jilin Prov.; joined CCP 1966; Sec. Communist Youth League Jilin City Cttee. 1978; Vice-Sec. Communist Youth League Jilin Provincial Cttee., mem. Communist Youth League Cen. Cttee. 1979; Vice-Sec. CCP Changchun City Cttee. 1984; Vice-Sec. CCP Jilin Provincial Cttee. 1988; Vice-Sec. CCP Hainan Provincial Cttee. 1992–; alt. mem. 14th CCP Cen. Cttee. 1992–97; Chair. Standing Cttee. of Hainan Provincial People's Congress 1993–; mem. 15th CCP Cen. Cttee. 1997–. *Address:* Standing Committee of Hainan Provincial People's Congress, Haikou City, Hainan Province, People's Republic of China.

DU RUNSHENG; Chinese politician and economist (retd.); b. 8 Aug. 1913, Taigu, Shanxi; ed. Beijing Teachers Univ.; involved in revolutionary activities in early 1930s; commdr. guerrilla forces Taihang Mountains; mem. of a border region govt., Deputy Gov. Taihang Pref. 1937–45; Sec.-Gen. Cen.-Plains Bureau, CPC 1946–49; Sec.-Gen. Cen.-South Bureau, CPC, Vice-Chair. Land Reform Cttee. of Cen.-South Region 1949; Sec.-Gen. Cen. Dept. of Rural Work, CPC and Deputy Dir. Agric. and Forestry Office of State Council 1953; Sec.-Gen. Acad. of Sciences 1956–79; in disgrace during Cultural Revolution 1967–76; Deputy Dir. State Agric. Comm. in charge of Policy Study on Rural Reform 1979–82; Dir. Rural Policy Research Office of Secr., CPC and Pres. Rural Devt. Research Centre, State Council; in charge of Policy Study on Rural Econ. Reform and Devt. 1982; Pres. Soc. of Land Econ. 1994–; mem. Cen. Advisory Cttee., CPC 1983–, Deputy Head Leading Group for Educ. of Cadres, CCP Cen. Cttee. 1985–, Deputy to NPC, mem. Finance and Econ. Cttee., NPC 1983–88; mem. Leading Group for Finance and Economy of CCP Cen. Cttee. 1988–89; Pres. China Agricultural Econs. Soc. 1988–; Vice-Chair. Nat. Agricultural Zoning Cttee. 1983–; Deputy Head Leading Group for Devt. of Rural Energy 1984–; Dir. Rural Policy Research Centre of CCP Cen. Cttee. 1988; Pres. Friendship Asscn. for the Mentally Handicapped 1993–; a Vice-Pres. Chinese Fed. for the Disabled 1993–; Hon. Prof. Beijing Agricultural Univ. 1949–, especially since 1979; Guest Prof. Chinese People's Univ. *Publications:* Rural Economic Reform in China (collection of articles) 1985, many articles on rural devt. in China. *Leisure interest:* tennis. *Address:* State Council's Research Center for Rural Development, 9 Xihuangchenggen Nanjie, Beijing 100032, People's Republic of China. *Telephone:* 665254.

DU TIEHUAN; Chinese government official; Asst. Dir. PLA Gen. Political Dept. 1993–94; Political Commissar Ji'nan Mil. Region 1994–96; Political Commissar, Beijing Mil. Area Command 1996–; rank of Lieut.-Gen; mem. 15th CCP Cen. Cttee. 1997–. *Address:* Political Commissar's Office, Beijing Military Area Command, Beijing, People's Republic of China.

DU YUZHOU; Chinese government official; b. 1942, Qiqihar, Heilongjiang; ed. Qinghua Univ.; joined CCP 1965; technician, Changde Textile Machinery Plant, Hunan 1968–70, Deputy Workshop Head, then Deputy Section Chief 1970–73; engineer, Deputy Dir. then Dir. Design Inst. of Ministry of Textile

Industry 1978–85; Vice-Minister of Textiles 1985–93; a Vice-Chair. Chinese Gen. Asscn. of Textile Industry 1993–. *Address:* Chinese General Association of Textile Industry, 12 East Changan Street, Beijing 100742, People's Republic of China.

DU ZIWEI, M.D.; Chinese neurosurgeon and administrator; b. 1932, Tokyo, Japan; ed. Keio Univ.; returned to China 1972; Prof. of Suzhou Medical Univ.; mem. 5th, 6th, 7th Standing Cttee. NPC 1978–92. *Address:* Suzhou Medical University, Suzhou City, Jiangsu Province, People's Republic of China.

DUBAI, Ruler of (see Maktoum, Rashid al-).

DUBENETSKY, Yakov Nikolayevich; Russian economist and banker; b. 26 Oct. 1938, Belarus; m.; one s.; ed. Moscow State Univ.; Deputy Chair. Stroybank of the U.S.S.R. 1985–87; First Deputy Chair. Bank for Industry and Construction of the U.S.S.R. (Pomstroybank of the U.S.S.R.) 1987–91; Chair. Bd. Russian Jt. Stock Investment and Commercial Bank for Industry and Construction (Pomstroybank of Russia) 1991–; Chair. Bd. Bank Asscn. Russia 1995–; Vice-Pres. Asscn. of Russian Banks 1995–; mem. Political Consultative Council of Pres. of Russian Fed. 1996–, Nat. Banking Council 1996–, Int. Acad. of Man. 1997–. *Address:* Russian Joint Stock Investment and Commercial Bank for Industry and Construction, 13 Tverskoy blvd., Moscow 103867, Russia. *Telephone:* (095) 200 7860; (095) 200 7287. *Fax:* (096) 200 6507.

DUBININ, Sergey Konstantinovich, DR.ECON.; Russian business executive; b. 10 Dec. 1950, Moscow; m.; two c.; ed. Moscow State Univ.; on staff Moscow State Univ. 1974–, sr. teacher 1977–81, docent 1981–88, sr. researcher 1988–91, Prof. 1992–; mem. Pres. Mikhail Gorbachev's Admin. 1991; Deputy Chair. Russian State Cttee. for co-operation with C.I.S. 1992–93; First Deputy Minister of Finance, Acting Minister of Finance 1993–94; Deputy Chair. Exec. Bd. Commercial Bank Imperial Oct. 1994–95; mem. Exec. Bd. Jt. Stock co. Gazprom 1995; Chair. Cen. Bank of Russia 1995–98; Russian Rep. to IBRD 1996–98; Chair. Interstate Monetary Cttee. C.I.S. 1996–98; Deputy Chair. Bd. Gazprom Co. 1998–. *Address:* Gazprom RAO, Nametkina str. 16, 117884 Moscow, Russia. *Telephone:* (095) 719-3001.

DUBININ, Yuri Vladimirovich, DR. HIST. SC.; Russian diplomatist; b. 17 Oct. 1930, Nalchik; m. Liana Khatchatrian 1953; three d.; ed. Moscow Inst. for Int. Relations; mem. CPSU 1954–91; Asst. in Embassy to France trans. with UNESCO; mem. Diplomatic Service 1955–; mem. Apparat U.S.S.R. Ministry of Foreign Affairs 1960–63, 1968–78; First Sec., Embassy Counsellor, Embassy in France 1963–68; Amb. to Spain Oct. 1978–86, to U.S.A. 1986–90, to France 1990–91; Perm. Rep. to UN 1986; Amb.-at-Large 1991–; Amb. to Ukraine 1996–; Head of Russian del. on negotiations with fmr. Soviet Repubs'.; Hon. D. Hist. (George Washington Univ.) 1990. *Publications:* U.S.S.R.–France: Experience of Co-operation 1979, Soviet-Spanish Relations 1983, Representing Perestroika in the West 1989. *Address:* Russian Embassy, Kutuzova str. 8, Kiev, Ukraine. *Telephone:* 294-63-89. *Fax:* 294-79-36.

DUBOIS, Jacques-Emile, D.SC.; French university professor; b. 13 April 1920, Lille; s. of Paul Dubois and Emilienne Chevrier; m. Bernice Claire Shaaker 1952; one s. one d.; ed. Univs. of Lille and Grenoble; Mem. Liberation Cttee., Isère 1944; Ramsay Fellow, Univ. Coll., London 1948–50; Scientific Adviser to French Cultural Counsellor, London 1948–50; Prof. of Physical Chemistry and Petrochemistry, and Dir. of Chemistry Inst., Univ. of Saar 1949–57, Dean of Science Faculty 1953–57; Prof. of Physical Organic Chemistry, Univ. of Paris 1957–; Research Fellow, Columbia Univ., New York 1956; Guest Prof. of Physical Chemistry, Univ. of Saar 1958; Scientific Adviser to French Minister of Educ. 1962–63; Joint Dir. of Higher Educ. 1963–65; Dir. of Research for Ministry of Defence 1965–77; Co-Dir. Curie Foundation 1977–80; Dir. French Nat. Univ. Agency for Scientific and Tech. Documentation and Information (AUDIST) 1978–81; Scientific Dir. Cie. Générale d'Electricité 1979–83; Chair. IUPAC Interdivisional Cttee. on Machine Documentation 1970–77; Founding Pres., Asscn. for Research and Devt. in Chem. Informatics (ARDIC) 1971–; Vice-Pres. French Physical Chem. Soc. 1972–74, Pres. 1974–76; Vice-Pres. CNIC (Nat. Centre for Chemical Information) 1972–89; French Nat. Del. to CODATA, Vice-Chair. 1980–88, Chair. CODATA Artificial Intelligence and Graphics Task Group 1988–, Pres. CODATA Int. 1994–98; mem. Directorate Nat. Research Council 1963–71, 1975–; mem. Council French Chemical Soc. 1965–67, Faraday Soc.; Dr. h.c. (Regensburg); Commdr., Légion d'honneur, Commdr. Ordre national du Mérite, Médaille de la Résistance, Commdr. des Palmes académiques, Jecker Prize and Berthelot Medal (Acad. of Sciences), Le Bel and Ancel Prizes (French Chemical Soc.), Stas Medal (Belgian Chemical Soc.), Grand Prix Technique, City of Paris 1975, Bruylants Chair. and Medal (Louvain Univ.) 1982, Grand prix du Festival d'Angers 1986, C.A.O.C. Medal 1991, Herman Skolnik Award for Chemical Information 1992. *Publications:* coed. Data and Knowledge in a Changing World 1996, works in field of kinetics, fast reaction rates, electro-chemistry, automation applied to chemistry and author of the DARC topological system used for on-line information systems and for computer-assisted design in chemistry. *Leisure interest:* skiing. *Address:* 100 rue de Rennes, 75006 Paris, France. *Telephone:* (1) 42-22-45-16. *Fax:* (1) 45.49.27.46.

DUBOWITZ, Victor, M.D., PH.D., F.R.C.P., F.R.C.P.C.H., D.C.H.; British professor of pediatrics; b. 6 Aug. 1931, Beaufort West, S. Africa; s. of late Charley Dubowitz and Olga Schattel; m. Lilly M. S. Sebok 1960; four s.; ed. Central High School, Beaufort West and Univs. of Cape Town and Sheffield; intern, Groote Schuur Hospital, Cape Town 1955; Sr. House Officer, Queen Mary's Hosp. for Children 1957–59; Research Assoc. Royal Postgraduate Medical School 1958–59; Lecturer in Clinical Pathology, Nat. Hosp. for Nervous Diseases, London 1960; Lecturer in Child Health, Univ. of Sheffield 1961–65, Sr. Lecturer 1965–67, Reader 1967–72; Research Assoc. Inst. for Muscle Disease and Asst. Pediatrician, Cornell Medical Coll., New York 1965–66; Prof. of Pediatrics, Royal Postgraduate Medical School, Univ. of London 1972–96, Emer. Prof. 1996–; Consultant Pediatrician, Hammersmith Hosp. 1972–; Dir. Jerry Lewis Muscle Research Centre, Royal Postgrad. Medical School 1975–96; Pres. European Pediatric Neurology Soc. 1994–97; World Muscle Soc. 1995–, Medical Art Soc. 1996–; Curator of Art, Royal Coll. of Paediatrics and Child Health; recipient of several awards etc. *Publications:* The Floppy Infant 1969, Muscle Biopsy: A Modern Approach (with M. H. Brooke) 1973, Gestational Age of the Newborn (with L. M. S. Dubowitz) 1977, Muscle Disorders in Childhood 1978, The Neurological Assessment of the Pre-term and Full-term Newborn Infant (with L. M. S. Dubowitz) 1981, A Colour Atlas of Muscle Disorders in Childhood 1989, A Colour Atlas of Brain Disorders in the Newborn (with L. de Vries, L. Dubowitz and J. Penock) 1990, Muscle Disorders in Childhood 2 1995, Ed.-in-Chief Neuromuscular Disorders, European Journal of Pediatric Neurology. *Leisure interests:* sculpting, hiking, photography, antique glass. *Address:* Department of Pediatrics, Hammersmith Hospital, Du Cane Road, London, W12 0HS (Office); 25 Middleton Road, Golders Green, London, NW11 7NR, England (Home). *Telephone:* 0181-383 3295 (Office); 0181-455 9352 (Home). *Fax:* 0181-740 8281 (Office); 0181-905-5922.

DUBY, Jean Jacques, PH.D.; French mathematician and scientist; b. 5 Nov. 1940, Paris; s. of Jean Duby and Lucienne (née Lacomme) Duby; m. Camille Poli 1963; one d.; ed. Ecole Normale Supérieure, Paris; research staff mem., Thomas J. Watson Research Center, U.S.A. 1963–64; Systems Engineer IBM France 1965–66, Man. Application Systems IBM Mohansic Lab. 1974–75, Exec. Asst. to Vice-Chair. IBM Corpn. 1975–76, Br. Office Man. IBM France 1977–78, Special Assignment IBM Communications Div. 1979, Dir. Switching Systems IBM Europe 1980–82, Dir. Science and Tech. IBM France 1986–88, Group Dir. Science and Tech. IBM Europe 1988–91; Man. Grenoble Scientific Centre 1967–69; Assoc. Prof. European Systems Research Inst. and Univ. of Geneva 1970–71; Project Man. Paris Stock Exchange 1972–73; Scientific Dir. C.N.R.S. 1982–86; Scientific Dir. Union d'assurances de Paris (UAP) 1991–97; Pres. Inst. Nat. de recherche sur les transports et leur securité 1992–96; Chair. Bd. of Dirs. Ecole Normale Supérieure de Cachan 1994–; Dir.-Gen. Ecole Supérieure d'Electricité 1995–; Officier Ordre Nat. du Mérite (France), Chevalier Ordre Nat. de la Côte d'Ivoire. *Leisure interests:* skiing, mountaineering. *Address:* Ecole supérieure d'électricité, Plateau de Moulon, 91192 Gif-sur-Yvette, France.

du CANN, Col. the Rt. Hon. Sir Edward Dillon Lott, P.C., K.B.E., M.A., F.R.S.A.; British politician and businessman; b. 28 May 1924, Beckenham; s. of late C. G. L. du Cann and Janet (née Murchie) du Cann; m. 1st Sallie Murchie 1962 (divorced 1989); one s. two d.; m. 2nd Jenifer Patricia Evelyn (Lady Cooke) née King 1990 (died 1995); ed. Woodbridge School, Suffolk, and St. John's Coll., Oxford; M.P. 1956–87; Founder and Chair. Unicorn Group of Unit Trusts 1957–62, 1964–72, 87; Founder mem. Asscn. Unit Trust Mans. 1961, Chair. 1961; Econ. Sec. to the Treasury 1962–63; Minister of State, Bd. of Trade 1963–64; Chair. of Conservative Party 1965–67, Pres. 1981–82; Chair. 1922 Cttee. 1972–84; First Chair. Select Cttee. on Public Expenditure 1971–73, Public Accounts Cttee. 1974–79; mem. Cttee. of Privileges 1972–87; First Chair. Treasury and Civil Service Cttee. 1979–83, Liaison Cttee. of Select Cttee. Chairs. 1979–83; Vice-Chair. British-American Parl. Group 1977–81; Pres. of Conservative Parl. European Community Reform Group 1985–87; Founder Chair. All-Party Maritime Affairs Parl. Group 1984–87; First Chair. Public Accounts Comm. 1984–87; led parl. del. to U.S.A. 1978, 1979, first British Parl. del. to China 1982; Chair. Keyser Ullmann Ltd. 1972–75, Cannon Assurance Ltd. 1972–80, Lonrho PLC 1984–91 (Dir. 1972–92); Dir. Martins Bank 1967–69, Barclays Bank (London Bd.) 1969–72; Visiting Fellow, Univ. of Lancaster Business School 1970–82; Patron, Asscn. of Insurance Brokers 1973–77, Human Ecology Foundation 1987; Gov. Hatfield Coll., Durham Univ. 1988–92; Master Fruiterers Co. 1990; Pres. Inst. of Freight Forwarders 1988–89; Hon. Vice-Pres. British Insurance Brokers Asscn. 1978–; Chair. Templeton Foundation Awards Ceremony 1984 (mem. Panel of Judges 1984–); mem. of Man. Council of the G.B.-SasaKawa British-Japanese Foundation 1984–93; First Hon. Freeman Borough of Taunton Deane 1977; Hon. Col. 155 Regiment (Wessex) Volunteers 1972–82, Hon. Life mem. of the Inst. of RCT; Admiral, House of Commons Yacht Club 1974–87. *Publications:* Investing Simplified 1959, How to Bring Government Expenditure under Parlimentary Control 1979, A New Competition Policy 1984, Hoist the Red Ensign 1987, Two Lives 1995, The Wellington Caricatures 1997. *Leisure interests:* sailing, gardening. *Address:* 6 Old Pye House, 15–17 St Ann's Street, London, SW1P 2DE, England; Fort Corblets, Alderney, GY9 3YG, Channel Islands.

DUCCI, Roberto, LL.D.; Italian fmr. diplomatist and professor of diplomacy; b. 8 Feb. 1914, Florence; s. of Adm. of the Fleet Gino Ducci and Virginia Boncinelli; m. Wanda Matyjewicz 1951; two s.; ed. Rome Univ.; entered Foreign Service 1937; served Ottawa 1938, Newark N.J. 1940; Italian Del. to Peace Conf. 1946, Warsaw 1947, Rio de Janeiro 1949, Italian Del. to N.A.T.O. and O.E.E.C. 1950–55; mem. Del. Brussels Six-Power Conf.

1955–57; Chair. Drafting Cttee. Rome Treaties 1956–57; Asst. Dir.-Gen. Econ. Affairs 1955–57; Amb. to Finland 1958–62; Head, Italian Del. to Brussels U.K.-EEC Conf. 1961–63; Deputy Dir.-Gen. for Political Affairs 1963–64, Dir.-Gen. 1970–75; Amb. to Yugoslavia 1964–67, to Austria 1967–70, to U.K. 1975–80; State Councillor 1980–84; Prof. of Political Science, Rome Univ. 1982; mem. Bd., European Investment Bank 1958–68; Vice-Pres. Mattiotti Foundation; Grand Cross, Italian Order of Merit. *Publications:* Prima età di Napoleone 1933, Questa Italia 1948, L'Europa Incompiuta 1971, D'Annunzio Vivente 1973, I Contemporanei 1976, L'Innocenza (poems) 1978, Libro di Musica (poems) 1980, I'Capintesta 1982, Candidato a Morte 1983 and numerous political essays and articles. *Leisure interests:* riding, collecting antique glass. *Address:* Via Belsiana 35, 00187, Rome, Italy (Home). *Telephone:* (06) 678 0183.

DUCHOVNY, David; American film actor; b. 7 Aug. 1960, New York; s. of Amram Duchovny and Meg Duchovny; m. Tea Leoni (q.v.) 1997; ed. Yale and Princeton Univs.; stage appearances include off-Broadway plays, The Copulating Machine of Venice, California and Green Cuckatoo; appears in TV series, The X Files (film 1998). *Films include:* New Year's Day 1989, Julia has Two Lovers 1990, The Rapture 1991, Don't Tell Mom the Babysitter's Dead 1991, Chaplin 1992, Red Shoe Diaries 1992, Ruby 1992, Kalifornia 1993, Venice, Venice, Apartment Zero, Close Enemy, Loan, Independence Day, Playing God. *Address:* c/o William Morris Agency, 151 S. El Camino Drive, Beverly Hills, CA 90212, U.S.A.

DUCKWORTH, Marilyn, O.B.E.; New Zealand writer; b. 10 Nov. 1935, Auckland; d. of Cyril John Adcock and Irene Robinson; m. 1st Harry Duckworth 1955 (dissolved 1964); m. 2nd Ian Macfarlane 1964 (dissolved 1972); m. 3rd Daniel Donovan 1974 (died 1978); m. 4th John Batstone 1985; four d.; ed. Queen Margaret Coll., Wellington and Victoria Univ., Wellington; 10 writers' fellowships 1961–96 including Katherine Mansfield Fellowship, Menton 1980, Fulbright Visiting Writer's Fellowship, U.S.A. 1987, Victoria Univ. Writing Fellowship, Hawthornden Writing Fellowship, Scotland 1994, Sargeson Writing Fellowship, Auckland 1995, Auckland Univ. Literary Fellowship 1996; N.Z. Literary Fund Award for Achievement 1963, N.Z. Book Award for Fiction 1985. *Publications:* thirteen novels including A Gap in the Spectrum 1959, A Barbarous Tongue 1963, Disorderly Conduct 1984, Married Alive 1985, Pulling Faces 1987, A Message from Harpo 1989, Unlawful Entry 1992, Seeing Red 1993, Leather Wings 1995, Studmuffin 1997; short stories: Explosions on the Sun 1989. *Leisure interest:* playing the violin. *Address:* 41 Queen Street, Mt. Victoria, Wellington 6001, New Zealand.

DUCORNET, Rikki, B.A.,; American/French writer; b. 19 April 1943, U.S.A.; s. of Gerard De Gré and Muriel Harris; one s.; Novelist in Residence, Univ. of Denver 1988–; Lannan Literary Fellowship 1993. *Publications:* (novels) The Stain 1984, Entering Fire 1986, The Fountains of Neptune 1989, The Jade Cabinet 1993, Phosphor in Dreamland 1995; (short fiction) The Word Desire 1997. *Address:* Department of English, University of Denver, Denver, CO 80208, U.S.A.

DUCZMAL, Agnieszka; Polish conductor; b. 7 Jan. 1946, Krotoszyn; m.; three c.; ed. Acad. of Music, Poznań; creator and Dir. Radio Amadeus Chamber Orchestra 1968–; asst. conductor Poznań Nat. Philharmonic, conductor of Poznań Opera; performs in Europe, N. and S. America and Asia; Silver Medal of Herbert von Karajan at the Meeting of Young Orchestras, West Berlin 1976; La Donna del Mondo Award of Saint Vincent Int. Culture Centre, Rome 1982. *Leisure interests:* dogs, mountains, literature, gardening. *Address:* Polish Radio Amadeus Chamber Orchestra, al. Marcinkowskiego 3, 61-745 Poznań, Poland. *Telephone:* (61) 851 66 86. *Fax:* (61) 851 66 87.

DUDA-GRACZ, Jerzy; Polish painter; b. 20 March 1941, Czestochowa; s. of Adam Duda-Gracz and Pelagia Stepniewska; m. Wilma Dudek 1969; one d.; ed. Acad. of Fine Arts in Krakow 1968; lecturer, Acad. of Fine Arts in Katowice, Silesian Univ. and European Acad. of Arts, Warsaw; 147 one-man and 291 gen. exhbns. in Poland, Europe, America and Asia; perm. exhbn. Duda-Gracz Author's Gallery; numerous awards including Prime Minister Prize (2nd Class) 1979, Minister of Culture and Art Prize (1st Class) 1985, Minister of Foreign Affairs Prize (1st Class) 1988, Kt.'s Cross of Polonia Restituta 1988, Commdr.'s Cross 1996. *Address:* ul. Dazyńskiego 24, 40-834 Katowice, Poland.

DUDBRIDGE, Glen, PH.D., F.B.A.; British academic; b. 2 July 1938, Clevedon, Somerset; s. of George Victor Dudbridge and Edna Kathleen Dudbridge (née Cockle); m. Sylvia Lo Fung-young 1965; one s. one d.; ed. Bristol Grammar School, Magdalene Coll. Cambridge (Scholar, then Bye-Fellow) and New Asia Inst. of Advanced Chinese Studies, Hong Kong; Research Fellow, Magdalene Coll. 1965; Lecturer in Modern Chinese, Oxford Univ. 1965–85; Prof. of Chinese, Cambridge Univ. 1985–89; Shaw Prof. of Chinese, Oxford Univ. 1989–; Fellow, Wolfson Coll. Oxford 1966–85, Emer. Fellow 1985–; Fellow, Magdalene Coll. Cambridge 1985–89; Fellow, Univ. Coll. Oxford 1989–; Visiting Prof., Yale Univ., U.S.A. 1972–73, Univ. of Calif., Berkeley, U.S.A. 1980, 1998; Hon. mem. Chinese Acad. of Social Sciences 1996. *Publications:* The Hsi-yu chi (a study of antecedents to the sixteenth-century Chinese novel) 1970, The Legend of Miao-shan 1978, The Tale of Li Wa (study and critical edition of a Chinese story from the ninth century) 1983, Religious Experience and Lay Society in T'ang China (A reading of Tai Fu's Kuang-I Chi) 1995, Sanguo Dian Lüe Ji Jiao 1998. *Address:* Institute for Chinese Studies, Walton Street, Oxford, OX1 2HG, England. *Telephone:* (01865) 280389. *Fax:* (01865) 280431.

DUDERSTADT, James J., PH.D.; American professor of engineering and university president; b. 5 Dec. 1942, Madison, Iowa; s. of Mack Henry Duderstadt and Katharine Sydney Johnson Duderstadt; m. Anne Marie Lock 1964; two d.; ed. Yale Univ., California Inst. of Tech.; U.S. Atomic Energy Comm. Postdoctoral Fellow, California Inst. of Tech. 1968; Asst. Prof. of Nuclear Eng., Univ. of Mich. 1969, Assoc. Prof. 1972, Prof. 1976–81, Dean Coll. of Eng. 1981, Provost and Vice-Pres. for Academic Affairs 1986, Pres. 1988–96, Pres. Emer. and Prof. of Scientific Eng. 1996–; Dir. Millennium Project 1996–; mem. U.S. Nat. Science Bd. 1985–96 (Chair. 1991–94), NAE Council 1997–, of Advisory Councils of Cornell Univ. and M.I.T., Nat. Acad. of Eng.; Compton Award, American Nuclear Soc. 1985, Lawrence Award, U.S. Dept. of Energy 1986. *Publications:* Nuclear Reactor Analysis (with L. J. Hamilton) 1976, Transport Theory (with W. R. Martin) 1979, Inertial Confinement Fusion (with G. A. Moses) 1982, numerous tech. publs. on nuclear reactor theory, radiation transport, statistical mechanics and kinetic theory, plasma physics and computer simulation. *Address:* Millennium Project, The University of Michigan, 2001 Media Union, Ann Arbor, MI 48109, U.S.A. *Telephone:* (313) 647-7300. *Fax:* (313) 647-6814.

DUDINSKAYA, Natalya Mikhailovna; Russian ballerina and choreographer; b. 21 Aug. 1912, Kharkov, Russia; d. of Mikhail Dudinskiy and Natalya Grippenberg; m. Konstantin Sergeyev 1947 (deceased); ed. Leningrad School of Choreography; Prima Ballerina Kirov Academic Opera and Ballet Theatre, Leningrad; theatre coach in the Kirov Theatre 1951–71, Head of Classical Dance 1993–; lecturer Vaganova Ballet Acad., Leningrad (now St. Petersburg) 1964–, Head, Faculty of Classical Dance 1997–. *Principal parts include:* all ballets by Tchaikovsky, Raimonda by Glazunov, Giselle, Les Sylphides, Don Quixote and The Bayadere by Mincous; has created leading roles in: Laurencia by Krein, Gayane by Khachaturyan, Cinderella by Prokofiev, The Bronze Horseman by Gliere, Shuralé by Yarullin, the Polish Maiden in Taras Bulba by Soloviev-Sedoy 1956, Sarie in The Path of Thunder by Kara Karayev 1958, Baroness Strahl in The Masquerade by Laputin 1960, Titania in A Midsummer Night's Dream 1963, The Wicked Fairy in the film The Sleeping Beauty 1964, The Spanish Suite by Viana López Gerardo 1966, Miniature by Krein 1967, Pacquita 1968; *choreographic work:* (as asst. to K. Sergeyev): Hamlet 1970, Le Corsair 1973, The Left-Hander 1976, Beethoven Apassionata 1977, Class-Concert 1981, Swan Lake (Boston Ballet, U.S.A.) 1989, The Fairy Doll by Bayer (after Legat) 1990, Cinderella (Osaka, Japan) 1991, Giselle (Osaka, Japan) 1992, Le Corsaire (Bolshoi, Moscow) 1992, (Boston Ballet, U.S.A.) 1997; as sole choreographer: Sleeping Beauty (Boston Ballet) 1993, Symphony of St. Petersburg (Osaka) 1994; guest artist in many foreign countries; People's Artist of U.S.S.R. 1957; State Prizewinner 1941, 1947, 1949, 1951 and other decorations. *Leisure interests:* swimming, diving. *Address:* 2 Gogol Street, Apt. 13, St. Petersburg 191184, Russia. *Telephone:* (812) 314.71.72.

DUDLEY, Hugh Arnold, C.B.E., CH.M., F.R.C.S., F.R.A.C.S.; British professor of surgery; b. 1 July 1925, Dublin, Eire; s. of Walter Dudley and Ethel Smith; m. Jean Bruce Lindsay Johnston 1947; two s. one d.; ed. Edinburgh and Harvard Univs.; Lecturer in Surgery, Edin. Univ. 1954–58; Sr. Lecturer in Surgery, Aberdeen Univ. 1958–63; Foundation Prof. of Surgery, Monash Univ., Melbourne 1963–72; Prof. of Surgery, St. Mary's Hosp., London 1973–88, Prof. Emer. 1988–; Ed. Operative Surgery 1976–94, Consulting Ed. 1994–; Chair. Ethics Cttee., Army Personnel Research Establishment 1989–94, Chemical and Biological Research Establishment, Porton Down 1988–96 (mem. Council 1992–94); fmr. Pres. of Surgical Research Soc. of Australasia, and of G.B. and Ireland, of Biological Eng. Soc. and of British Journal of Surgery Soc.; Hon. Fellow American Surgical Asscn. 1986, S.A. Coll. of Surgeons 1987. *Publications:* Principles of General Surgical Management 1958, Communication in Medicine and Biology 1977; Ed. Emergency Surgery 1979, 1986, Guide for House Surgeons 1974, 1982, 1987, Practical Procedures for House Officers 1988, The People's Hosp. of North East Scotland (jtly.) 1992. *Leisure interests:* shooting, surgical history. *Address:* House of Broombrae, Glenbuchat, Aberdeenshire, AB36 8UA, Scotland (Home). *Telephone:* (01975) 641341. *Fax:* (01975) 641201.

DUE, Ole; Danish lawyer; b. 10 Feb. 1931, Korsør; s. of H. P. Due and Jenny (née Jensen) Due; m. Alice Maud Halkier Nielsen 1954; three s. one d.; ed. Univ. of Copenhagen; civil servant Ministry of Justice Copenhagen 1955, Head of Div. 1970, Head of Dept. 1975, Acting Appeal Court Judge 1978; Judge Court of Justice, EEC 1979–94, Pres. 1988–94; Arbitrator OSCE Court of Conciliation and Arbitration 1995–; Chair. Danish Inst. of Int. Affairs; Hon. Bencher Gray's Inn, London, King's Inns, Dublin; Hon. Prof. (Copenhagen Univ.); Hon. Dr. (Stockholm Univ.); Grand Cross Order of Dannebrog, Ordre de la Couronne (Belgium), Ordre de la Couronne de Chêne (Luxembourg). *Publications include:* articles on Community law, private int. law and legal technique. *Address:* University of Copenhagen, Institute of Legal Science, A, Skindergade 14, 3rd Floor, 1159 Copenhagen K, Denmark. *Telephone:* 35 32 31 20. *Fax:* 35 32 40 00.

DUERR, Hans-Peter Emil, PH.D.; German physicist; b. 7 Oct. 1929, Stuttgart; s. of Dr. Rupert and Eva (née Kraepelin) Duerr; m. Carol Sue Durham 1956; two s. two d.; ed. Univs. of Stuttgart and California, Berkeley; Research Asst. Dept. of Physics, Berkeley 1956–57, Max-Planck Inst. für Physik, Göttingen and Munich 1958–62; Visiting Assoc. Prof., Berkeley and Inst. of Mathematical Sciences, Madras, India 1962–63; Visiting Prof., Berkeley 1968–69; Prof. Univ. of Munich 1969; mem. Directorate Max-Planck Inst. für Physik, München, Chair. 1971–72, 1977–80, 1987–92, Vice-Chair.

1981–86, 1993–95; Man. Dir. Max-Planck-Inst. für Physik und Astrophysik 1978–80; mem. Bd. Vereinigung Deutscher Wissenschaftler 1980–86, mem. Advisory Bd. 1986–91, Chair. Bd. 1991–; Chair. Advisory Cttee. Wissenschaftszentrum München 1984–; mem. Bd. Greenpeace Germany 1985–91, Co-Chair. Exec. Cttee. 1988–89; Chair. Bd. Global Challenges Network 1987–; mem. Pugwash Council 1987–, Club of Rome 1991–; mem. Bd. Int. Foundation for the Survival and Devt. of Humanity 1988–93, Moscow, Chair. Bd. German br., Munich 1988–93; mem. Bd. and Scientific Advisory Cttee. Internationale Akademie für Zukunftsfragen, Vienna 1990–; Chair. Kuratorium Umweltakademie-Umwelt und Man., Oberpfaffenhofen, 1990–; mem. Kuratorium E.F.-Schuhmacher-Gesellschaft 1980-, City Energy Cttee., Munich 1983-, Int. Advisory Council Econ. Devt. of Hainan, China 1990-93, Council Int. Network of Engineers and Scientists for Global Responsibility, Hamburg 1991-, Ständiges Wissenschaftsforum der Sozialdemokratie, Bonn 1994-, Scientific Advisory Cttee. Institut für Zukunftsstudien und Technologiebewertung, Berlin 1995-, and other cttees. and advisory bds.; Pres. Bd. of Trustees European Trust for Natural and Cultural Wealth, Prague; mem. Bd. Dir. Bulletin of Atomic Scientists, Chicago 1993–, Academia Scientarium et Artium Europaea, Salzburg; Advisory Cttee. Int. Judicial Org. for Environment and Devt. IJO 1991–, Advisory Council Int. Center of Integrative Studies, New York 1993–, Scientific Advisory Bd. Potsdam Inst. for Climate Impact Research; Trustee Muhammad Abdus Salam Foundation, London 1994–; mem. Deutsche Akademie der Naturforscher Leopoldina Halle; Right Livelihood Award 1987, Waldemar von Knoeringen Award 1989, Natura Obligat Medal 1991, Elise and Walter Haas Int. Award 1993. *Publications:* more than 200 publs. on nuclear physics, elementary particle physics, gravitation, epistemology, peace and disarmament, energy, ecology, econs., politics. *Address:* Rheinlandstrasse 14A, 80805 Munich, Germany.

DUFF, Michael James, PH.D.; British professor of physics; b. 28 Jan. 1949, Manchester; s. of Edward Duff and Elizabeth Duff (née Kaylor); m. Lesley Yearling 1984; one s. one d.; ed. De La Salle Coll., Salford, Queen Mary Coll. and Imperial Coll., London Univ.; Post-doctoral Fellowships in Theoretical Physics, Int. Centre for Theoretical Physics, Trieste, Italy, Oxford Univ., King's Coll. and Queen Mary Coll., London Univ., Brandeis Univ., U.S.A. 1972–79; Faculty mem. Imperial Coll. London 1979–88, Sr. Physicist, CERN, Geneva 1984–87; Prof. of Physics, Texas A&M Univ., U.S.A. 1988–92, Distinguished Prof. of Physics 1992–; Fellow American Physical Soc. *Publications:* Observations on Conformal Anomalies 1977, Kaluza-Klein Supergravity 1986, Strings from Fivebranes 1991; numerous articles on unified theories of the elementary particles. *Leisure interests:* scuba diving, golf. *Address:* 907 Carmel Place, Southwood Forest, College Station, TX 77845, U.S.A. *Telephone:* (409) 693-7346 (Home); (409) 845-7799 (Office).

DUFFEY, Joseph Daniel, PH.D.; American administrator and professor; b. 1 July 1932, Huntington, West Virginia; s. of Joseph I. Duffey and Ruth Wilson Duffey; m. Anne Wexler 1974; four s.; ed. Marshall Univ., Andover Newton Theological School, Yale Univ. and Hartford Seminary Foundation; Assoc. Prof. and Acting Dean, Hartford Seminary Foundation 1960–70; Adjunct Prof. and Fellow, Calhoun Coll. 1970–74; Gen. Sec. and Spokesman American Assen. of Univ. Prof., Washington, D.C. 1974–76; Asst. Sec. of State, U.S. Dept. of State 1977; Chair. Nat. Endowment for the Humanities, U.S. Govt. 1977–82; Chancellor Univ. of Mass. 1982–90, Pres. 1990–91; Pres. American Univ. Washington 1991–93; Head U.S. Information Agency 1993–; Order of Leopold II (Belgium); Tree of Life Award, American Jewish Congress. *Publications include:* Lewis Mumford's Quest 1979, U.S. Global Competitiveness 1988, Looking Back and Looking Forward: The U.S. and the World Economy 1989. *Address:* United States Information Agency, 301 Fourth Street, S.W., Washington, DC 20547, U.S.A.

DUFFIELD, Vivien Louise, C.B.E., M.A.; British philanthropist; b. 26 March 1946; d. of Sir Charles Clore and Francine Halphen; m. John Duffield 1969 (divorced 1976); one s. one d.; ed. Cours Victor Hugo, Paris, Lycée Français de Londres; Heathfield School, Lady Margaret Hall, Oxford; Dir. Royal Opera House Trust 1985–, Royal Opera House 1990–; Vice-Chair. Great Ormond Street Hosp. Wishing Well Appeal 1987, Royal Marsden Hosp. Cancer Appeal 1990; mem. N.S.P.C.C. Centenary Appeal Cttee. 1983, Financial Devt. Cttee. 1985; mem. Royal Ballet Bd. 1990–; Trustee Dulwich Collection Picture Gallery 1993–; Hon. D.Litt. (Buckingham) 1990; Hon. D.Phil. (Weizmann Inst.) 1985; Hon. R.C.M. 1987. *Leisure interests:* skiing, opera, ballet, shooting. *Address:* c/o Clore Foundation, 3 Chelsea Manor Studios, Flood Street, London, SW3 5SR, England. *Telephone:* 0171-351 6061.

DUFFY, Maureen Patricia, B.A., F.R.S.L.; British author; b. 1933; d. of Grace Rose Wright; ed. Trowbridge High School for Girls, Sarah Bonnell High School for Girls, King's Coll., London Univ.; staged pop art exhbn. with Brigid Brophy 1969; Chair. Greater London Arts Literature Panel 1979–81, Authors Lending and Copyright Soc. 1982–94, Copyright Licensing Agency 1996–99 (Vice-Chair. 1994–96); Pres. Writers' Guild of G.B. 1985–88 (Jt. Chair. 1977–78); Co-Founder Writers' Action Group 1972–79; Vice-Pres. European Writers Congress 1992–, Beauty without Cruelty 1975–, British Copyright Council 1998– (Vice-Chair. 1981–86, Chair. 1989–98). *Publications:* That's How It Was 1962, The Single Eye 1964, The Microcosm 1966, The Paradox Players 1967, Lyrics for the Dog Hour (poetry) 1968, Wounds 1969, Rites (play) 1969, Love Child 1971, The Venus Touch 1971, The Erotic World of Faery 1972, I Want to Go to Moscow 1973, A Nightingale in Bloomsbury Square (play) 1974, Capital 1975, Evesong (poetry) 1975, The Passionate Shepherdess 1977, Housespy 1978, Memorials of the Quick and the Dead (poetry) 1979, Inherit the Earth 1980, Gorsaga 1981 (adapted for TV 1988), Londoners: An Elegy 1983, Men and Beasts 1984, Collected Poems 1949–84 1985, Change 1987, A Thousand Capricious Chances: Methuen 1889–1989 1989, Illuminations 1991, Occam's Razor 1993, Henry Purcell (biography) 1994, Restitution 1998. *Address:* 18 Fabian Road, London, SW6 7TZ, England. *Telephone:* 0171-385 3598.

DUFFY, Michael John, O.N.Z., B.L.; Australian politician; b. 2 March 1938, Mildura, Vic.; m. Carolyn Adams 1965; one s. two d.; ed. Christian Brothers' Coll., Albury, N.S.W., Newman Coll., Univ. of Melbourne; worked as solicitor; mem. House of Reps. for Holt, Vic. 1980–96; Minister for Communications and Minister assisting the Minister for Defence 1983–87, for Trade Negotiations, Minister Assisting the Minister for Industry, Tech. and Commerce and Minister Assisting the Minister for Primary Industries and Energy 1987–90; Attorney Gen. 1990–93; Chair. Trade Sub-Cttee. of Jr. Standing Cttee. on Foreign Affairs, Defence and Trade 1994–96; consultant Mallesons Stephen Jacques, Melbourne 1996–; del. to Victoria Labor Party State Conf. 1971–80, Nat. Conf. 1982, 1984; mem. Labor Party Victorian Branch Admin. Cttee. 1973–76; mem. House of Reps. Jt. Cttee. of Public Accounts 1980–83. *Leisure interests:* cricket, football, horse racing, reading and music. *Address:* 42B Milan Street, Mentone, Vic. 3194, Australia. *Telephone:* (03) 95802506.

DUFOIX, Georgina, D.ÈS SC. ECON.; French politician; b. 16 Feb. 1943, Paris; d. of Alain Negre and Antoinette Pallier; m. Antoine Dufoix 1963; two s. two d.; ed. Lycée de Nîmes and Univs. of Montpellier and Paris; mem. Man. Cttee. Parti Socialiste 1979; Sec. of State for Family Affairs 1981–83, for Family Affairs, Population and Immigrant Workers 1983–84; Minister for Social Affairs and Nat. Solidarity 1984–86; Conseiller gen. for Gard 1982–, Socialist Deputy 1986–88; Sec. of State for Family Affairs, for Women's Rights, and for Repatriates May–June 1988; Chargée de mission auprès du Président 1988–92; Pres. Admin. Council, French Red Cross 1989–92; Del. Fight against Drugs 1989–93; mem. UNRISD Bd.; Communications Co. Vera. *Leisure interest:* her vineyard. *Address:* 35 rue des Blancs-Manteaux, 75004 Paris, France (Home).

DUFOUR, Bernard, M.SC.; French aviation official; b. 14 Feb. 1933, France; s. of Jean Dufour and Denise (née Penot) Dufour; m. Bernadette de Villepin 1956; five c.; ed. Ecole Ozsnam, Limoges, Lycée Janson de Sailly, Paris; Engineer Sud Aviation 1956–61, Dir. (helicopter production) 1961–64, St. Nazaire 1964–65, Toulouse 1965–76, Usine Belfort Alsthom 1977–89, GEC Alsthom (Electromechanic Div.) 1989–94; Jt. Dir.-Gen. (Tech. and Production) Ste. Aerospatiale 1976–77; Pres., Dir.-Gen. SNECMA 1994–96; Chevalier, Ordre nat. du Mérite. *Leisure interests:* cycling, horses, sailing, skiing. *Address:* 4 rue Henri Heine, 75016 Paris, France.

DUFOURCQ, Bertrand Charles Albert, L. EN D.; French diplomatist; b. 5 July 1933, Paris; s. of Norbert Dufourcq and Marguerite-Odette Latron; m. Elisabeth Lefort des Ylouses 1961; two s. two d.; ed. Lycées Montaigne and Louis-le-Grand, Paris, Faculté de Droit, Paris, Inst. d'Etudes Politiques, Paris and Ecole Nat. d'Admin.; Sec. for Foreign Affairs 1961; Chef de Cabinet to Prefect/Admin.-Gen. of City of Algiers 1961; Ministry of Foreign Affairs 1962; Cultural Counsellor, Tokyo 1964; Counsellor for Foreign Affairs 1967; various posts at Ministry of Foreign Affairs and Ministry of Industrial and Scientific Devt. 1967–69; Head of Cultural, Scientific and Tech. Service, Embassy, Moscow 1969–72; Ministry of Foreign Affairs 1972–76, 1978–79; Amb. to People's Repub. of Congo 1976–78; European Dir. Ministry of External Relations 1979–84; Dir. Office of M. Claude Cheysson 1984; special attachment to Minister of External Relations 1984–85; Admin. Ecole Nat. d'Admin. 1980–83; Amb. to Vatican 1985–88; Dir. of Political Affairs, Ministry of Foreign Affairs 1988–91; Amb. to U.S.S.R. 1991, to Russia 1992 (also accred. to Mongolia 1991–92), to Germany 1992–93; Sec.-Gen. Ministry of Foreign Affairs 1993–98; Officier, Légion d'honneur, Ordre nat. du Mérite, Amb. de France. *Address:* 48 rue Madame, 75006 Paris, France (Home).

DUGGER, John Scott; American artist and designer; b. 18 July 1948, Los Angeles, Calif.; s. of Dr. James Attwood Dugger, M.D. and Julian Marie Riddle; ed. Loy Norrix High School, Kalamazoo, Mich., Gilmore Inst. of Art, Mich., School of the Art Inst. of Chicago, Ill.; created Perennial (first Ergonic Sculpture), Paris 1970; Delegation Leader, Soc. for Anglo-Chinese understanding Delegation to China 1972; Founder-Dir. Banner Arts, London 1976; mem. Exec. Cttee. Art Services Grants Ltd. (Artists' Housing Charity) 1980–85; Chair. Assen. of Space Artists, London 1984, 1985; Vice-Chair. Int. Artists Assen., U.K. Cttee. 1986–87; maj. works include Documenta 5, People's Participation Pavilion, Kassel, Fed. Repub. of Germany 1972, Monumental Strip-Banner Installation, Trafalgar Square, London 1974, Sports Banner Exhbn., Inst. of Contemporary Arts, London 1980; Major Award, Arts Council of G.B. 1978, Calouste Gulbenkian Foundation Awards 1979, 1980, Original Art Banners commissioned for H.M. the Queen's 60th Birthday, Buckingham Palace 1986, Tibet Mountainscape Banner for His Holiness the XIV Dalai Lama—Int. Year of Tibet 1991; Int. Certified Master Fabric Craftsman, I.F.A.I. (Industrial Fabric Assen.) 1992, Int. Achievement Award 1993; works on display at Arts Council of G.B., Tate Gallery, London. *Leisure interests:* oriental art, mountaineering, martial arts.

DUIGAN, John, M.A.; Australian film director, screenwriter and author; b. England; ed. Univ. of Melbourne; fmr. lecturer, Univ. of Melbourne and Latrobe Univ.; co-dir. Vietnam (TV mini-series); wrote and dir. TV documentaries: Fragments of War: The Story of Damien Parer 1988, Bitter Rice 1989. *Films written and directed include:* Trespassers, Mouth to Mouth, Winter of

Our Dreams 1981, Far East, The Year My Voice Broke 1987 (Australian Acad. Award for Best Dir.), Romero (dir. only), Flirting 1991, Wide Sargasso Sea 1993, Sirens (actor, dir. only) 1994, The Journey of August King, The Leading Man (dir. only) 1996, Lawn Dogs (dir. only). *Publications:* novels: Badge, Players, Room to Move.

DUISENBERG, Willem Frederik, D.ECONS.; Netherlands economist; b. 9 July 1935, Heerenveen; m. Gretta Nieuwenhuizen 1987; two s. one d.; ed. State Univ. of Groningen; Scientific Asst., State Univ., Groningen 1961–65; with IMF 1966–69; Special Adviser De Nederlandsche Bank N.V. 1969–70; Prof. of Macro-econs., Univ. of Amsterdam 1970–73; Minister of Finance 1973–77; Pres. De Nederlandsche Bank 1982; Chair. EC Bank Govs.; Pres. European Cen. Bank May 1998–; Chevalier Légion d'honneur. *Publications:* Economic Consequences of Disarmament 1965, The IMF and the International Monetary System 1966, The British Balance of Payments 1969, Some Remarks on Imported Inflation 1970. *Leisure interests:* sailing, tennis, photography. *Address:* European Central Bank Kaiserstrasse 29, D-60311, Frankfurt, Germany. *Telephone:* (69) 13440.

DUKAKIS, Michael Stanley; American politician; b. 3 Nov. 1933, Brookline, Mass.; s. of Dr. Panos Dukakis and Euterpe Dukakis; m. Katharine Dickson; one s. two d.; ed. Brookline High School, Swarthmore Coll., Harvard Law School; Army service in Korea 1955–57; mem. Town Meeting, Brookline 1959, Chair. Town Cttee. 1960–62; Attorney Hill & Barlow, Boston 1960–74; alt. Del. Democratic Nat. Convention 1968; mem. Mass. House of Reps. for Brookline 1962–70, later Chair. Cttee. on Public Service and mem. Special Comm. on Low Income Housing; founded a research group for public information 1970; moderator of television public affairs debate programme The Advocates; Gov. of Massachusetts 1975–79, 1983–91; teacher Fla. Atlantic Univ., Boca Raton 1992; Democratic Cand. for Pres. 1988; lecturer and Dir. of Inter-Governmental Studies, John F. Kennedy School of Govt., Harvard Univ. 1979–82; Gold Medal, City of Athens, Greece 1996. *Publication:* Creating the Future: Massachusetts comeback and its promise for America (with Rosabeth Moss Kanter) 1988. *Address:* 85 Perry Street, Brookline, MA 02146, U.S.A. (Home).

DUKAKIS, Olympia, M.A.; American actress; m. Louis Zorich; three s.; ed. Boston Univ.; teacher of drama at New York Univ. grad. programme for 15 years; founding mem. The Charles Playhouse, Boston, Whole Theatre, Montclair, N.J.; appeared in more than 100 regional theatre productions; subsequently appeared in off-Broadway shows including Mann Ish Mann, The Marriage of Bette and Boo, Titus Andronicus, Peer Gynt, The Memorandum, The Curse of the Starving Class, Electra; has appeared in Broadway productions of Abraham Cochrane, The Aspern Papers, The Night of the Iguana, Who's Who in Hell, Mike Nichols' Social Security; numerous TV appearances; mem. Bd. Nat. Museum of Women in the Arts, Washington, D.C. and other arts orgs.; Acad. Award for Best Supporting Actress for Moonstruck 1988; recipient of two Obie Awards. *Films include:* The Idolmaker, John Loves Mary, Death Wish, Rich Kids, Made for Each Other, Working Girl, Moonstruck, Dad, Look Who's Talking, Steel Magnolias, In the Spirit, Look Who's Talking Too, The Cemetery Club, Digger, Over the Hill, Look Who's Talking Now, Naked Gun 33⅓: The Final Insult (cameo), I Love Trouble, Jeffrey, Mighty Aphrodite, Mr Holland's Opus, Picture Perfect; TV includes: Tales of the City (series). *Address:* William Morris Agency, 151 S. El Camino Drive, Beverly Hills, CA 90212; 222 Upper Mountain Avenue, Montclair, NJ 07043, U.S.A. (Home).

DUKES, Alan M., M.A.; Irish politician; b. 22 April 1945, Dublin; s. of James Dukes and Margaret Moran; m. Fionnuala Corcoran 1968; two d.; ed. Scoil Colmcille and Colaiste Mhuire, Dublin, and Univ. Coll., Dublin; Chief Econ., Irish Farmers Asscn. 1967–72; Dir. Irish Farmers Asscn., Brussels 1973–76; Personal Adviser to Commr. of EEC 1977–80; mem. Dáil Éireann for Kildare 1981–; Opposition Spokesperson on Agric. March–Dec. 1982; Minister of Agric. 1981–82, for Finance 1982–86, for Justice 1986–87; Leader and Pres. Fine Gael 1987–90; mem. Council of State 1987–90; Minister for Transport, Energy and Communications 1996–97; Opposition Spokesperson on Environment and Local Govt. 1997–; Pres. Irish Council of the European Movt. 1987–91, Chair. 1997–; Vice-Pres. Int. European Movt. 1991–96; Adjunct Prof. of Public Admin., Man. Univ. of Limerick 1991–; Vice-Pres. European People's Party 1987–96; Chair. Jt. Olreachtas Cttee. on Foreign Affairs 1995–96. *Address:* Dáil Éireann, Dublin 2, Ireland. *Telephone:* 01-6183729. *Fax:* 01-6184159.

DULBECCO, Renato; American virologist; b. 22 Feb. 1914, Cantanzaro, Italy; s. of Leonardo and Maria Dulbecco; m. 1st Guiseppina Salva 1940 (divorced 1963); m. 2nd Maureen Muir 1963; one d. (one s. deceased); ed. Università degli Studi, Turin; Asst. Prof. of Pathology, Univ. of Turin 1940–46, of Experimental Embryology 1947; Research Assoc. Dept. of Bacteriology, Indiana Univ. 1947–49; Senior Research Fellow Calif. Inst. of Tech. 1949–52, Assoc. Prof. 1952–53, Prof. 1954–63; Senior Fellow, Salk Inst. for Biological Studies 1963–72; Asst. Dir. of Research, Imperial Cancer Research Fund Labs. (London) 1972–74, Deputy Dir. 1974–77; Distinguished Research Prof., Salk Inst., La Jolla, Calif. 1977–, Pres. 1989–92, Pres. Emer. 1993–; Chair. Int. Physicians for Prevention Nuclear War Inst., American-Italian Foundation for Cancer Research; mem. American Asscn. for Cancer Research, N.A.S., American Acad. of Arts and Sciences; Foreign mem. Royal Soc., London 1974, Accad. Nazionale dei Lincei; Hon. mem. Accademia Ligure di Scienze e Lettere; Trustee, La Jolla County Day School; Hon. LL.D. (Glasgow) 1970, Hon. D.Sc. (Yale) 1968, Dr. h.c. (Vrije Univ., Brussels) 1978; several awards, including Ehrlich Prize, Ludovic Gross Horwitz Prize 1973, Selman A. Waksman Award in Microbiology, N.A.S., 1974, Nobel Prize in Medicine (Physiology) 1975; Mandel Gold Medal (Czechoslovak Acad. of Sciences) 1982. *Address:* 7525 Hillside Drive, La Jolla, CA 92037, U.S.A. (Home).

DUMAS, Jean-Louis Robert Frédéric, L. EN D.; French business executive; b. 2 Feb. 1938, Paris; s. of Robert Dumas and Jacqueline Hermès; m. Rena Gregoriadès 1962; one s. one d.; ed. Lycée Janson-de-Sailly, Faculté de Droit de Paris and Inst. d'Etudes Politiques, Paris; Asst. buyer, Bloomingdales, New York 1963; joined gen. man. Hermès 1964, Dir., Gen. Man. 1971–78, Chair. and Man. Dir. Hermès, Holding Hermès 1978–95, Pres. Groupe Hermès 1995–, Man. Hermès Int. 1995–, Saint-Louis Glassworks 1997–; Pres. Sport-Soie 1978; Vice-Pres. Comité Colbert 1978–88, Pres. 1988–91; Dir. Orfèvrerie Christofle 1988, Banque française du commerce extérieur de la France 1989–, Gaumont 1991; Nat. adviser on foreign trade 1973–. *Leisure interest:* photography. *Address:* Hermès, 24 rue du Faubourg St. Honoré, 75008 Paris, France (Office).

DUMAS, Pierre, L. ÈS D.; French politician; b. 15 Nov. 1924; m. Janine Berenfeld 1992; one d.; ed. Ecole Libre des Sciences Politiques; Sales Man. Box Co., La Rochette; Deputy 1958–62, 1967, 1968, 1969–73; Sec. of State for Public Works April-Oct. 1962, Sec. of State for Relations with Parl., responsible for Tourism 1962–67; Sec. of State to Prime Minister, in charge of Tourism 1967–68; Sec. of State for Social Affairs 1968–69; Chair. Comm. on Foreign Affairs, Nat. Ass. 1986; Senator 1986–95; Pres. Soc. française pour le Tunnel Routier du Fréjus 1962–; Pres. Office Nat. des Forêts 1973–83; Mayor of Chambéry 1959–77, 1983–89; Officier, Légion d'honneur; Rassemblement pour la République. *Address:* 22 rue Benoît Molin, 73000 Chambéry, France (Home).

DUMAS, Rhetaugh Etheldra Graves, M.S., PH.D., R.N., F.A.A.N.; American health and higher education administrator and nurse; b. 26 Nov. 1928, Natchez, Miss.; d. of Rhetaugh Graves and Josephine (Clemmons) Graves Bell; m. A. W. Dumas, Jr. 1950; one d.; ed. Dillard Univ., New Orleans, Yale Univ. School of Nursing and Union Graduate School, Yellow Springs, Ohio; Dir. Student Health Center, Dillard Univ. 1957–59; Yale-New Haven Hosp. 1960; Instr. in Psychiatric Nursing, Dillard Univ. 1961; Research Asst. and Instr. Yale Univ. School of Nursing 1962–65, Asst. Prof. 1965–66, Assoc. Prof. 1966–72; Dir. of Nursing, Conn. Medical Health Center, Yale-New Haven Medical Center 1966–72; Chief, Psychiatric Nursing Educ. Branch, Div. of Manpower and Training 1972–75; Deputy Dir. Div. of Manpower and Training Programs, Nat. Inst. of Mental Health 1976–79; Deputy Dir. Nat. Inst. of Mental Health, Alcohol, Drug Abuse and Mental Health Admin., U.S. Public Health Service 1979–81; Dean Univ. of Mich. School of Nursing, Ann Arbor 1981, Prof. 1981, Vice-Provost for Health Affairs, Univ. of Mich. 1994–97, Cole Prof., School of Nursing 1994–, Vice-Provost Emer. 1997–, Dean Emer. 1997–; Pres. American Acad. of Nursing 1987–89; Pres. Nat. League of Nursing 1995–; mem. N.A.S. Inst. of Medicine; Hon. D.Hum.Litt. (Yale) 1989 and several other hon. degrees and awards. *Publications:* numerous articles in professional journals and book chapters. *Leisure interests:* reading, music, singing. *Address:* The University of Michigan, 400 N. Ingalls Street, Room 4320, Ann Arbor, MI 48109 (Office); 6 Eastbury Court, Ann Arbor, MI 48105, U.S.A. (Home). *Telephone:* (313) 936-6213 (Office); (313) 668-6103 (Home). *Fax:* (313) 764-4546.

DUMAS, Roland, L. EN D.; French politician, lawyer and journalist; b. 23 Aug. 1922, Limoges; s. of Georges and Elisabeth (née Lecanuet) Dumas; m. 2nd Anne-Marie Lillet 1964; two s. one d.; ed. Lycée de Limoges, Univs. of Paris and London; called to the Bar, Paris 1950, and has practised as a lawyer ever since; journalist with AGEFI, Socialiste Limousin; Political Dir. La Corrèze républicaine et socialiste 1967–; mem. Nat. Assembly 1956–58, 1967–68, 1981–83, 1986–93, Vice-Pres. 1968; Minister for European Affairs 1983–84, for Foreign Affairs 1984–86, 1988–93; Govt. Spokesman July–Dec. 1984; Pres. Nat. Ass. Comm. on Foreign Affairs 1986–87; Chair. Constitutional Court 1995–99; Officier, Légion d'honneur, Croix de guerre, Croix du combattant volontaire, grand-croix de l'ordre d'Isabelle la Catholique (Spain), Ordre du Mérite (Germany). *Publications:* J'ai vu vivre la Chine, Les Avocats, Le Droit de l'information et de la presse, Plaidoyer pour Roger-Gilbert Lecomte, Le droit de la Propriété Littéraire et Artistique. Le peuple assemblé 1989, Le fil et la pelote—Mémoires 1996. *Address:* 19 quai de Bourbon, 75004 Paris, France.

DUMBUTSHENA, Enoch, B.A., B.ED.; Zimbabwean judge; b. 25 April 1920, Chegutu; s. of the late Job Dumbutshena and Sarah Chendzira Dumbutshena; m. 1st Alphosina Mahlangu 1948 (divorced, died 1989); one s. one d.; m. 2nd Miriam Masango 1964 (divorced, then deceased); one s. two d.; ed. Adams Coll., Natal, South Africa, Univ. of South Africa, Gray's Inn, London; worked as teacher, journalist and legal practitioner; Legal Adviser to African Nat. Congress (ANC), Vic. Falls Constitutional Negotiations, S. Rhodesia 1975, to UANC, Geneva Constitutional Conf. 1976, Int. Constitutional Conf. 1978; M.P. for Zimbabwe Democratic Party 1979; Judge 1980; mem., Judicial Service Comm. 1980–90; Judge Pres., High Court of Zimbabwe 1983; Chief Justice of Zimbabwe 1984–90; Judge of Appeal, Transkei, S.A. 1991–93; Acting Judge of Appeal, Supreme Court of Namibia 1993–; apptd. by UN Sec.-Gen. as independent jurist to inquire into case of detainees in Somalia 1993; Leader Forum Party of Zimbabwe 1993–97; Pres. Zimbabwe Conservation Trust; Chair. Law Review Comm. 1988–90, Omay Devt. Trust, Art

Printers Employees' Trust, Modus Publs., Legal Resources Foundation, Child Protection Soc.; Founder-mem. Judicial Colloquium 1988–; mem. Advisory Cttee. Interrights 1992–; Vice-Pres. Int. Comm. of Jurists 1992–; Hon. Bencher of Hon. Soc. of Gray's Inn; Hon. Vice-Pres. Zimbabwe Law and Population Studies Project; Trustee, Prince Edward School; mem., Bd. of Trustees, Chisipite Jr. School, Bd. of Govs., Arundel School; Hon. Citizen of Atlanta, Ga. 1981; Hon. D.C.L. (Oxford) 1990. *Publication:* Zimbabwe Tragedy 1976. *Leisure interests:* reading, writing, walking, climbing not-very-high mountains. *Address:* P.O. Box CH 70, Chisipite, Harare; 11 Cromlet Road, Valleydale Township, Arcturus, Zimbabwe (Home).

DUMMETT, Sir Michael Anthony Eardley, KT., M.A., D.LITT.; British professor of philosophy; b. 27 June 1925, London; s. of George Herbert Dummett and Mabel Iris Dummett (née Eardley-Wilmot); m. Ann Chesney 1951; three s. two d.; ed. Sandroyd School, Winchester Coll., Christ Church, Oxford; served army 1943–47; Asst. lecturer in Philosophy, Univ. of Birmingham 1950–51; Prize Fellow, All Souls Coll., Oxford 1950–57, Research Fellow 1957–61; Harkness Foundation Fellow, Univ. of Calif., Berkeley 1955–56; Reader in Philosophy of Mathematics, Oxford Univ. 1961–74; Sr. Research Fellow, All Souls Coll., Oxford 1974–79, Sub-Warden 1974–76; Visiting lecturer Univ. of Ghana 1958, Stanford Univ., Calif., U.S.A. 1960–66, Univ. of Minn. 1968, Princeton Univ. 1970, Rockefeller Univ., New York 1973; William James Lecturer in Philosophy, Harvard Univ. 1976; Wykeham Prof. of Logic, Univ. of Oxford 1979–92; Fellow, New College, Oxford 1979–92, Emer. Fellow 1992–98, Hon. Fellow 1998–; Fellow, British Acad. 1967–84 (resgnd.), Sr. Fellow 1995–; Emer. Fellow, All Souls College, Oxford 1979–; Chair. Joint Council for the Welfare of Immigrants 1970–71; mem. unofficial cttee. of enquiry into events in Southall, 1979–80, Shadow Bd. Barclays Bank 1981; Foreign Hon. mem. American Acad. of Arts and Sciences; Hon. Ph.D. (Nijmegen) 1983; Hon. D.Litt. (Caen) 1993, (Aberdeen) 1993; Lakatos Award 1994, Rolf Shock Prize in Philosophy and Logic 1995. *Publications:* Frege: Philosophy of Language 1973, The Justification of Deduction 1973, Elements of Intuitionism 1977, Truth and other Enigmas 1979, Immigration: where the Debate goes wrong 1978, Catholicism and the World Order 1979, The Game of Tarot 1980, Twelve Tarot Games 1980, The Interpretation of Frege's Philosophy 1981, Voting Procedures 1984, The Visconti-Sforza Tarot Cards 1986, Ursprünge der Analytischen Philosophie 1988, The Logical Basis of Metaphysics 1991, Frege and other Philosophers 1991, Frege: Philosophy of Mathematics 1991, Grammar and Style 1993, The Seas of Language 1993, Origins of Analytical Philosophy 1993, Il Mondo e l'Angelo 1993, I Tarocchi Siciliani 1995, Principles of Electoral Reform 1997. *Leisure interests:* history of card games and playing cards. *Address:* 54 Park Town, Oxford, OX2 6SJ, England. *Telephone:* (01865) 558698. *Fax:* (01865) 558698.

DUNAWAY, Dorothy Faye; American actress; b. 14 Jan. 1941, Bascom, Florida; d. of John and Grace Dunaway; m. 1st Peter Wolf 1974; m. 2nd Terry O'Neill (q.v.) 1981; one s.; ed. Univs. of Florida and Boston; spent three years with Lincoln Center Repertory Co. in New York, appearing in A Man For All Seasons, After the Fall and Tartuffe; Off-Broadway in Hogan's Goat 1965; appeared at the Mark Taper Forum, L.A. in Old Times, as Blanche du Bois in A Streetcar Named Desire 1973, The Curse of an Aching Heart 1982; *films include:* Hurry Sundown 1967, The Happening 1967, Bonnie and Clyde 1967, The Thomas Crown Affair 1968, A Place For Lovers 1969, The Arrangement 1969, Little Big Man 1970, Doc 1971, The Getaway 1972, Oklahoma Crude 1973, The Three Musketeers 1973, Chinatown 1974, Three Days of the Condor 1975, The Towering Inferno 1976, Voyage of the Damned 1976, Network 1976, The Eyes of Laura Mars 1978, The Champ 1979, The First Deadly Sin 1981, Mommie Dearest 1981, The Wicked Lady 1982, Supergirl 1984, Barfly 1987, Burning Secret 1988, The Handmaid's Tale 1989, On a Moonlit Night 1989, Up to Date 1989, Scorchers 1991, Faithful 1991, Three Weeks in Jerusalem, The Arrowtooth Waltz 1991, Double Edge, Arizona Dream, The Temp, Dun Juan DeMarco 1995, Drunks, Dunston Checks In, Albino Alligator, The Chamber. *Television includes:* After the Fall 1974, The Disappearance of Aimee 1976, Hogan's Goat, Mommie Dearest 1981, Evita!—First Lady 1981, 13 at Dinner 1985, Beverly Hills Madame 1986, The Country Girl, Casanova, The Raspberry Ripple, Cold Sassy Tree, Silhouette, Rebecca; Academy Award Best Actress for Network. *Publication:* Looking For Gatsby (autobiog., with Betsy Sharkey) 1995. *Address:* c/o ICM, 8942 Wilshire Boulevard, Beverly Hills, CA 90211, U.S.A.

DUNBAR, Adrian; British actor; b. Enniskillen, N. Ireland; m. Anna Nygh; one d.; one step s.; ed. Guildhall School of Music and Drama, London; numerous stage appearances including Ourselves Alone (Royal Court Theatre) 1985, King Lear (Royal Court). TV appearances include: Reasonable Force (BBC TV), Cracker. *Films include:* The Fear, A World Apart, Dealers, My Left Foot, Hear My Song 1992, The Crying Game 1993.

DUNCAN, Archibald Alexander McBeth, M.A., F.R.S.E., F.B.A.; British professor of history; b. 17 Oct. 1926, Pitlochry; s. of Charles George Duncan and Christina Helen McBeth; m. Ann Hayes Sawyer 1954; two s. one d.; ed. George Heriot's School, Edinburgh, Univ. of Edinburgh, Balliol Coll., Oxford; Lecturer, Balliol Coll. 1950–51, Queen's Univ., Belfast 1951–53, Univ. of Edin. 1953–62; Prof. of Scottish History, Univ. of Glasgow 1962–93, Clerk of Senate 1978–83. *Publications:* Scotland, The Making of the Kingdom 1975, ed. and revised W. C. Dickinson, Scotland from the Earliest Times to 1603, 1977, Ed. Acts of Robert I, 1306–29, vol. V., Regesta Regum Scottorum 1988, Ed. The Bruce by John Barbour 1997. *Leisure interest:* swimming. *Address:* 17 Campbell Drive, Bearsden, Glasgow, G61 4NF, Scotland. *Telephone:* (0141) 942 5023.

DUNCAN, Daniel Kablan; Côte d'Ivoirian politician; b. 1943, Ouelle; ed. Inst. Commercial, Nancy and Inst. de Commerce Int. Paris; Ministry of Economy and Finance 1970; in-house training, IMF, Washington, D.C. 1973; joined Cen. Bank of W. African States (BCEAO); with Caisse Nat. de Prévoyance Sociale; returned to BCEAO HQ, Dakar 1989; Minister Del. responsible for Econ., Finance and Planning, Office of Prime Minister 1990–93; Prime Minister of Côte d'Ivoire 1993–, also fmr. Minister of Economy, Finance and Planning, Minister of Planning and Industrial Devt. *Address:* Office of the Prime Minister, Abidjan, Côte d'Ivoire.

DUNHAM, Katherine; American dancer and choreographer; b. 22 June 1909, Ill.; m. 1st Jordis McCoo 1931 (divorced); m. 2nd John Thomas Pratt 1941 (died 1986); one d.; ed. Chicago and Northwestern Univs.; début, Chicago World's Fair 1934; with Chicago Opera Co. 1935–36; Julius Rosenwald Travel Fellowship 1936–37; Dance Dir. Labor Stage 1939–40; has appeared in numerous films 1941–; founded Katherine Dunham School of Cultural Arts and Katherine Dunham Dance Co. 1945; numerous tours and personal appearances in North and South America and Europe. *Publications:* Journey to Accompong, Form and Function in Primitive Dance, Form and Function in Educational Dance, etc. *Address:* 532 North 10th Street, East St. Louis, IL 62201, U.S.A.

DUNHAM, Sir Kingsley C., KT., PH.D., F.R.S., F.ENG., F.R.S.E., S.D.; British geologist; b. 2 Jan. 1910, Sturminster Newton, Dorset; s. of Ernest Pedder and Edith Agnes Dunham; m. Margaret Young 1936; one s. (deceased); ed. Johnston School, Durham, Univ. of Durham and Harvard Univ.; Temp. Geologist, New Mexico Bureau Mines 1935; Geologist, Geological Survey of Great Britain 1935–45, Head of Petrographical Dept. 1946–50; Prof. of Geology and Head of Dept. Univ. of Durham 1950–66, Sub-Warden 1959–61, Prof. Emer. 1968–; Consulting Geologist, Laporte Industries Ltd. 1953–66, Consolidated Gold Fields Ltd. 1954–66; Geological Adviser ICI Ltd. 1961–66; Dir. Inst. of Geological Sciences (Natural Environment Research Council) 1966–75; Chair. Council for Environmental Science and Eng. 1972–75; Pres. Yorks. Geological Soc. 1958–60, British Asscn. for the Advancement of Science (Section C 1961, Asscn. 1972–73), Inst. of Mining and Metallurgy 1963–64, Geological Soc. of London 1966–68, Int. Union of Geological Sciences 1969–72, Mineralogical Society 1976–78; Dir. Weardale Holdings Ltd., Weardale Minerals Ltd. 1982–86; mem. Council, Royal Soc. 1964–66, Foreign Sec., Vice-Pres. 1971–76; Chair. Int. Geological Correlation Project of IUGS/UNESCO 1972–76; mem. Council for Scientific Policy, Dept. of Educ. and Science 1964–66; U.K. mem. Council Int. Inst. for Applied Systems Analysis 1973–77, Hon. Scholar 1977; Pres. Probus Clubs of Durham 1982–, Friends of Killhope 1985–; Fellow of Imperial Coll. 1976; Hon. Fellow St. John's Coll., Durham 1991; D.Sc. h.c. (Durham, Liverpool, Birmingham, Illinois, Leicester, Michigan, Kent, Edinburgh, Exeter, Hull); Hon. Sc.D. (Cambridge); D.Univ. (Open Univ.); Bigsby Medal of Geological Soc. 1954, Gold Medal of Inst. of Mining and Metallurgy 1968, Murchison Medal of Geological Soc. 1966, Royal Medal of the Royal Soc. 1970, Wollaston Medal 1976, Haidinger Medal, Austrian Geological Survey 1976; Leopold von Buch Medal, German Geological Soc. 1981, Aberconway Medal, Inst. of Geology 1986. *Publications:* Geology of the Organ Mountains of New Mexico 1936, Geology of the Northern Pennine Orefield (Vol. I) 1949, 1990, (Vol. II with A. A. Wilson) 1985, Fluorspar 1952, Geology of North Skye (with F. W. Anderson) 1966, Geology and Hematite Deposits of South Cumbria (with W. C. C. Rose) 1977; Ed. Symposium on the Paragenesis and Reserves of the Ores of Lead and Zinc 1948. *Leisure interests:* music, gardening. *Address:* Charleycroft, Quarryheads Lane, Durham, DH1 3DY, England. *Telephone:* 0191-384 8977.

DUNITZ, Jack David, F.R.S.; British professor of chemistry; b. 29 March 1923, Glasgow, Scotland; s. of William (Wulfi) Dunitz and Mildred Dunitz; m. Barbara Steuer 1953, two d.; ed. Hutchesons' Grammar School, Glasgow, Univ. of Glasgow; Research Fellowships at Univ. of Oxford 1946–48, 1951–53; at Calif. Inst. of Tech. 1948–51, 1953–54; Visiting Scientist, U.S. Nat. Insts. of Health 1954–55; Sr. Research Fellow, Davy-Faraday Research Lab., Royal Inst., London 1956–57; Visiting appointments at Ia. State Univ. 1965, Univ. of Minn. 1966, 1983, Tokyo Univ. 1967, Technion, Haifa 1970, Cornell Univ. 1976, Calif. Inst. Tech. 1985, Cambridge Univ. 1990, Univ. of N. Carolina at Chapel Hill 1991, Harvard Univ. 1992; Overseas Fellow, Churchill Coll., Univ. of Cambridge 1968; Prof. of Chemical Crystallography, Eidgenössische Technische Hochschule (Swiss Fed. Inst. of Tech.), Zürich 1957–90; mem. and fellow, several foreign acads., including Academia Europaea; Centenary Medal, Chem. Soc., London 1977, Havinga Medal, Leiden Univ. 1980, Tishler Prize, Harvard Univ. 1985, Paracelsus Prize, Swiss Chemical Soc. 1986, Bijvoet Medal, Utrecht Univ. 1989, Aminoff Prize, Royal Swedish Acad. of Sciences 1990, Buerger Award (American Crystallographic Asscn.) 1991, Cape Scholar Award (American Chemical Soc.) 1997; Hon. D.Sc. (Technion, Israel) 1990, Hon. Ph.D. (Weizmann Inst. of Science) 1992. *Publications:* X-Ray Analysis and the Structure of Organic Molecules 1979, Reflections on Symmetry in Chemistry . . . and Elsewhere (with E. Heilbronner) 1993, Structure Correlation (Ed. with H. B. Bürgi); about 300 papers on various aspects of crystal and molecular structure. *Address:* Laboratory of Organic Chemistry, ETH-Zentrum, CH-8092 Zürich (Office); Obere Heslibachstrasse 77, CH-8700 Küsnacht, Switzerland (Home). *Telephone:* 01-632-2892 (Office).

DUNKEL, Arthur, B.SC.ECON.; Swiss consultant and fmr. international civil servant; b. 28 Aug. 1932, Lisbon, Portugal; m. Christiane Müller-Serda

1957; one s. one d.; ed. French Lycée, Lisbon, Business School, Lausanne, Coll. St. Michel, Fribourg, Univ. of Lausanne; joined Swiss Fed. Office for Foreign Econ. Affairs, Bern 1956, Head, section for OECD matters 1960–64, for co-operation with developing countries 1964–71, for world trade policy 1971–73; Perm. Rep. to GATT 1973–76; Del. of Fed. Council for Trade Agreements with rank of Amb. 1976–80; Dir.-Gen. GATT 1980–93; Vice-Chair. and Rapporteur UNCTAD Inter-Governmental Group on Supplementary Financing 1968, Rapporteur UNCTAD Bd. 1969, Chair. Cttee. on Balance-of-Payments Restrictions 1972–75; Chair. UN Conf. on New Wheat Agreement 1978; Asst. Lecturer, Inst. of Journalism, Univ. of Fribourg 1974–78; Sr. Lecturer on Int. Econs., Univs. of Geneva and Fribourg 1983–; Arthur Dunkel Consultancy 1993–; mem. Bd. of Dirs. various cos.; Pres. Swiss Trade Initiative for the Middle East and N. Africa; Chair. Council, Lausanne School of Art, Foundation 'A Future for Geneva'; Hon. Dr. (Fribourg) 1980, (Basle) 1992; Freedom Prize, Max Schmidheiny Foundation (Switzerland) 1989, Consumers for World Trade Award (U.S.A.) 1990, Fed. of Swiss Industrial Holding Cos. Award 1993, Max-Petitpierre Award (Switzerland) 1993, Médaille d'Or, Foundation Jean Monnet for Europe (Switzerland) 1995. *Address:* Boulevard du Théâtre 6-4, 1204 Geneva, Switzerland.

DUNKLEY, Carlyle Anthony; Jamaican politician; b. 29 Jan. 1939, Portland; m. 2nd Beverley Erica Woung 1989; three s. one .d.; ed. Kingston Coll. and Univ. of West Indies; radio news ed. and also ed. Pelican magazine 1963–78; research officer, Caribbean Bauxite Mine and Metal Workers' Fed. 1966–70; Supervisor (Chief Negotiator), Nat. Workers' Union 1970, Pres. 1973–78; lecturer, Trade Union Inst. Univ. of W.I. 1975–82, Dept. of Man., Univ. of W.I. 1982–89; mem. Nat. Exec. Council, People's Nat. Party (PNP) 1966–; Govt. Senator and Deputy Pres. of Senate 1972–78; mem. Parl. 1978–80; Minister of Public Utilities and Transport 1979–80, Minister of Nat. Security 1980; Opposition Senator 1980–83; Shadow Minister of Educ. 1984–89; Senator 1989–; Minister of Educ. 1989–91; Minister of Industry, Tourism and Commerce 1992–95. *Publications include:* Collective Bargaining: Some Problems in Jamaican Aluminium Industry and the Caribbean Connexion, A Manual for Trade Union Officers; articles on personnel man. and industrial relations. *Leisure interests:* reading, swimming, music, tennis. *Address:* c/o People's National Party, 89 Old Hope Road, Kingston 5, Jamaica.

DUNLOP, Frank, B.A., C.B.E.; British theatre director; b. 15 Feb. 1927, Leeds; s. of Charles Norman Dunlop and Mary Aarons; ed. Kibworth Beauchamp Grammar School, Univ. Coll. London, Old Vic School, London; served R.A.F. 1946–49; f. and Dir. Piccolo Theatre Co. 1954–; Assoc. Dir. Bristol Old Vic 1955–59; Dir. Plays W. End of London and Mermaid Theatre 1959–; Theatre Dir. Brussels, including Theatre Nat. Belge 1959–; Dir. Nottingham Playhouse 1961–64; f. Dir. Pop Theatre 1966–; Assoc. Dir. and Admin. Nat. Theatre London 1967–71; Founder and Dir. Young Vic Theatre 1970–78, 1980–83; Theatre Dir. U.S.A. (Broadway, L.A.) 1974–; Dir. Edin. Festival 1983–91; Fellow Univ. Coll., London 1979; Hon. D.Univ. (Heriot-Watt) 1989, (Edin.) 1990. *Publication:* Scapino 1975. *Leisure interests:* work and doing nothing. *Address:* c/o Piccolo Theatre Co., 6 Langley Street, London W.C.2, England; c/o E. Nives, 157 W. 57 Street, Suite 700, New York, NY 10019, U.S.A. *Telephone:* 0171-379 1084 (London); (212) 265 8787 (U.S.A.). *Fax:* 0171 379 1087 (London); (212) 265-8873 (U.S.A.).

DUNLOP, John T., A.B., PH.D., LL.D.; American industrial relations expert and economist; b. 5 July 1914, Placerville, Calif.; s. of John and Antonia Dunlop (née Forni); m. Dorothy Webb 1937; two s. one d.; ed. Univs. of California and Cambridge, England; Instructor Harvard Univ. 1938, Assoc. Prof. 1945, Chair. Wertheim Cttee. on Industrial Relations 1945–, Prof. 1950–, Chair. Dept. of Econs. 1961–66, Dean Faculty of Arts and Sciences 1970–73; Chair. Bd. for Settlement of Jurisdictional Disputes 1948–57; mem. Atomic Energy Labor Relations Panel 1948–53; mem. Sec. Labor's Advisory Cttee. on Labor-Management Relations in Atomic Energy Installations 1954–57; mem. Kaiser Steelworkers' Commission 1960–68, Presidential Railroad Comm. 1960–62, Missiles Sites Labor Comm. 1961–67; Chair. Nat. Manpower Policy Task Force 1968–69; mem. President's Nat. Comm. on Productivity 1970–73, Chair. 1973–75; Chair. Manpower Inst. 1970–73; Dir. Cost of Living Council 1973–74; Co-ordinator President's Labor-Man. Cttee. 1974–76; U.S. Sec. of Labor 1975–76; Chair. Construction Industry Joint Conf. 1959–68; mem. Construction Industry Collective Bargaining Comm. 1969–71; Chair. U.S. Labor Man. Group 1976–95; Chair. Construction Industry Stabilization Cttee. 1971–73, mem. 1973–74; Chair. Pay Advisory Cttee. 1979–80; Chair. Comm. on Future of Worker-Man. Relations 1993–95, Int. Competition Policy Advisory Cttee. to Attorney Gen. 1997–; Pres. Industrial Relations Research Asscn. 1960, Int. Industrial Relations Research Asscn. 1973–76; mem. American Acad. of Arts and Sciences, American Philosophical Soc., Inst. of Medicine; Louis K. Comstock Award, Nat. Electrical Contractors' Asscn. 1974, Housing Hall of Fame 1986, Murray-Green-Meany Award 1987; Hon. Life Mem. Nat. Acad. of Arbitrators 1991. *Publications:* Wage Determination under Trade Unions 1944, Cost Behaviour and Price Policy 1943, Collective Bargaining: Principles and Cases (with James J. Healy) 1949, The Wage Adjustment Board. (with Arthur D. Hill) 1950, The Theory of Wage Determination (Ed. 1957, Industrial Relations Systems 1958, 1993, Industrialism and Industrial Man 1960, Potentials of the American Economy (Ed.) 1961, Economic Growth in the United States (Ed.) 1961, Automation and Technological Change (Ed.) 1962, Frontiers of Collective Bargaining (Ed.) 1967, Labor and the American Community (with Derek Bok) 1970, Inflation and Incomes Policies: the Political Economy of Recent U.S. Experience 1974, Industrialism and Industrial Man Reconsidered 1975, The Lessons of Wage and Price Controls—The Food Sector 1978, Business and Public Policy 1980, Dispute Resolution, Negotiation and Consensus Building 1984, The Management of Labor Unions 1990, Mediation and Arbitration of Employment Disputes (with A. Zack) 1997. *Leisure interest:* walking. *Address:* 509 Pleasant Street, Belmont, MA 02178, U.S.A.

DUNMORE, Helen; British poet and novelist; b. 1953, Yorks.; m.; one s. one d. one step-s. *Publications:* (poetry): The Sea Skater (Poetry Soc.'s Alice Hunt Bartlett Award), The Raw Garden (Poetry Book Soc. Choice), Secrets (Signal Poetry Award 1995); (novels): Zennor in Darkness (McKitterick Prize 1994), Burning Bright, A Spell of Winter (Orange Prize for Women Writers of Fiction 1996), Talking to the Dead 1996, Love of Fat Men (short stories) 1998, Your Blue-Eyed Boy 1998; also children's novels. *Address:* c/o Caradoc King, A. P. Watt Ltd., 20 John Street, London, WC1N 2DR, England. *Telephone:* 0171-405 6774. *Fax:* 0171-831 2154.

DUNN, Baroness (Life Peer), cr. 1990, of Hong Kong Island in Hong Kong and of Knightsbridge in the Royal Borough of Kensington and Chelsea; **Lydia Selina Dunn;** Hong Kong business executive; b. 29 Feb. 1940; d. of Yenchuen Yeh Dunn and Chen Yin Chu; m. Michael David Thomas, C.M.G., Q.C. 1988; ed. St. Paul's Convent School, Coll. of Holy Names, Oakland, Calif., U.S.A. and Univ. of California, Berkeley; Exec. Dir. John Swire & Sons Ltd. 1996–; Dir. John Swire & Sons (HK) Ltd. 1978–, Swire Pacific Ltd. 1981–, Cathay Pacific Airways Ltd. 1985– (Adviser to Bd. 1997–), Volvo 1991–93 (mem. Int. Advisory Bd. 1985–91), Christie's Int. PLC 1996–, Gen. Electric Co. PLC 1997–; Deputy Chair. Hong Kong & Shanghai Banking Corpn. 1992–96 (Dir. 1981–86), HSBC Holdings PLC (fmrly. Hong Kong and Shanghai Banking Corpn. Holdings—London) 1992–96 (Dir. 1990–); mem. Hong Kong Legis. Council 1976–88 (Sr. mem. 1985–88); mem. Hong Kong Exec. Council 1982–95 (Sr. mem. 1988–95); Chair. Lord Wilson Heritage Trust 1993–95; mem. Hong Kong/Japan Business Co-operation Cttee. 1983–95, Chair. 1988–95; mem. Hong Kong/U.S. Econ. Co-operation Cttee. 1984–93; Chair. Hong Kong Trade Devt. Council 1983–91; Hon. LL.D. (Chinese Univ. of Hong Kong) 1984, (Univ. of Hong Kong) 1991, (Univ. of B.C., Canada) 1991, (Leeds) 1994; Hon. D.Sc. (Buckingham) 1995; Prime Minister of Japan's Trade Award 1987, U.S. Sec. of Commerce's Award to Peace and Commerce 1988. *Publication:* In the Kingdom of the Blind 1983. *Leisure interest:* study of antiques. *Address:* John Swire & Sons Ltd., Swire House, 59 Buckingham Gate, London, SW1E 6AJ, England.

DUNN, Douglas Eaglesham, F.R.S.L.; British poet; b. 23 Oct. 1942; s. of William D. Dunn and Margaret McGowan; m. 1st Lesley B. Wallace 1964 (died 1981); m. 2nd Lesley Jane Bathgate 1985; one s. one d.; ed. Univ. of Hull; full-time writer 1971–91; Writer-in-residence Duncan of Jordanstone Coll. of Art and Dundee Dist. Libraries 1987–; Fellow in Creative Writing, Univ. of St. Andrews 1989–91, Prof. 1991–; Dir. St. Andrews Scottish Studies Inst. 1992–, Head School of English 1994–; Hon. Visiting Prof. Dundee Univ. 1987–89; Hon. Fellow, Humberside Coll. 1987; Hon. LL.D. (Dundee) 1987; Hon. D. Litt. (Hull) 1995; Cholmondeley Award 1989. *Publications:* Terry Street 1969 (Somerset Maugham Award 1972), The Happier Life 1972, New Poems 1972–73 (ed.) 1973, Love or Nothing 1974 (Faber Memorial Prize 1976), A Choice of Byron's Verse (ed.) 1974, Two Decades of Irish Writing (criticism) 1975, The Poetry of Scotland (ed.) 1979, Barbarians 1979, St. Kilda's Parliament 1981 (Hawthornden Prize 1982), Europa's Lover 1982, A Rumoured City: New Poets from Hull (ed.) 1982, To Build a Bridge: A Celebration of Humberside in Verse (ed.) 1982, Elegies 1985 (Whitbread Poetry Award and Whitbread Book of the Year 1986), Secret Villages (short stories) 1985, Selected Poems 1986, Northlight 1988, New and Selected Poems 1989, Poll Tax: The Fiscal Fake 1990, Andromache 1990, The Essential Browning (ed.) 1990, Scotland. An Anthology (ed.) 1991, Faber Book of Twentieth Century Scottish Poetry (ed.) 1992, Dante's Drum-Kit 1993, Boyfriends and Girlfriends (short stories) 1995, Oxford Book of Scottish Short Stories (Ed.) 1995. *Leisure interests:* playing the clarinet and saxophone, listening to jazz, gardening, philately. *Address:* School of English, The University, St. Andrews, Fife, KY16 9AL, Scotland. *Telephone:* (01334) 462666. *Fax:* (01334) 462655.

DUNN, Hugh Alexander, A.O., D.UNIV., M.A.; Australian diplomatist and academic; b. 20 Aug. 1923, Rockhampton; s. of James M. Dunn and Mary E. Miller; m. 2nd Margaret J. Anderson 1968; one d. from previous marriage; ed. Brisbane Boys' Coll., Queensland Univ., Univ. of Oxford; journalist, Brisbane Courier-Mail 1953; Lecturer, East Asiatic Studies, Toronto Univ., Canada 1953–54; joined foreign service 1952, served in Japan, Repub. of Korea, U.S.A., India and Viet Nam; Amb. to Repub. of China (Taiwan) 1969–72, to Argentina (also accred. to Uruguay and Paraguay) 1973–76; High Commr. in Kenya (also accred. to Uganda, Seychelles and Ethiopia) 1978–80; Amb. to People's Repub. of China 1980–84; Paul Martin Prof. of Int. Relations, Canada 1991; Hon. Prof. Griffiths Univ. 1985–95; mem. Australia-China Council 1985–88. *Publications:* Cao Zhi, The Life and Works of a Royal Chinese Poet 1983, Sino-Australian Relations: The Record 1972–85, (jtly. 1988), The Shaping of a Sinologue of Sorts 1987, The Teaching of Chinese Language and its Application (Co-Ed.) 1987–, Conversations about Tibet with H. H. the Dalai Lama and Chinese Officials 1987, Conversations about Taiwan in Taipei and Beijing 1988. *Leisure interests:* golf, trout fishing, writing.

DUNN, John Montfort, B.A., F.B.A., F.S.A.; British professor of political theory; b. 9 Sept. 1940, Fulmer; s. of Brig. Henry G.M. Dunn and Catherine M. Kinloch; m. 1st Susan D. Fyvel 1965; m. 2nd Judith F. Bernal 1971; m. 3rd Ruth Ginette Scurr 1997; two s. (one deceased), one d.; ed. Winchester Coll., Millfield School, King's Coll. Cambridge and Harvard Univ.; Grad. School of Arts and Sciences; Official Fellow in History, Jesus Coll. Cambridge 1965–66; Fellow, King's Coll. Cambridge 1966–, Coll. lecturer, Dir. of Studies in History 1966–72; Lecturer in Political Science, Univ. of Cambridge 1972–77, Reader in Politics 1977–87, Prof. of Political Theory 1987–; Visiting Lecturer, Univ. of Ghana 1968–69; Chair. Section P (Political Studies), British Acad. 1994–97, Bd. of Consultants, Kim Dae-Jung Peace Foundation for the Asia-Pacific Region 1994–. *Publications:* The Political Thought of John Locke 1969, Modern Revolutions 1972, Dependence and Opportunity (with A. F. Robertson) 1973, Western Political Theory in the Face of the Future 1979, Political Obligation in its Historical Context 1980, Locke 1984, The Politics of Socialism 1984, Rethinking Modern Political Theory 1985, The Economic Limits to Modern Politics (ed.) 1990, Interpreting Political Responsibility 1990, Storia delle dottrine politiche 1992, Democracy: the unfinished journey (Ed.) 1992, Contemporary Crisis of the Nation State? (Ed.) 1994, The History of Political Theory 1995, Great Political Thinkers (21 vols.) (co-ed.) 1997. *Leisure interests:* watching birds and animals, opera, travel. *Address:* King's College, Cambridge, CB2 1ST (Office); The Merchant's House, 31 Station Road, Swavesey, Cambridge, CB4 5QJ, England (Home). *Telephone:* (01223) 331258 (Office); (01954) 231451 (Home). *Fax:* (01223) 331315.

DUNROSSIL, 2nd Viscount (cr. 1959); **John William Morrison,** C.M.G.; British diplomatist (retd.); b. 22 May 1926, London; s. of 1st Viscount Dunrossil, G.C.M.G., M.C., P.C., Q.C.; m. 1st Mavis Spencer-Payne 1951 (dissolved 1969), three s. one d.; m. 2nd Diana M. Cunliffe 1969, two d.; ed. Fettes Coll., Edinburgh, and Oriel Coll., Oxford; joined Commonwealth Service 1951, served in Canberra, Dhaka, Pretoria, Cape Town; External Relations Officer, IMCO 1968–70; Counsellor and Head of Chancery, Ottawa 1970–74; Counsellor, Brussels 1974–78; High Commr. in Fiji 1978–82, concurrently accred. to Nauru and Tuvalu, and alt. U.K. del. to S. Pacific Comm.; High Commr. in Barbados 1981–83, concurrently accred. to Grenada, Saint Lucia, Dominica, Saint Vincent and the Grenadines, later to Antigua and Barbuda, and British Govt. Rep. to St. Christopher and Nevis; Gov. and Commdr.-in-Chief of Bermuda 1983–88; Lord Lieut., Western Isles 1993–94, 1996–; Chair. Bison Books Ltd. 1990–95; Deputy Chair. Bank of Bermuda (Luxembourg) SA 1990–; K.St.J. *Address:* Dunrossil House, Trunisgarry, North Uist, Hebrides, HS6 5AY, Scotland. *Telephone:* (01876) 500213.

DUNSTAN, (Andrew Harold) Bernard, R.A.; British artist; b. 19 Jan. 1920; s. of late Dr. A. E. Dunstan; m. Diana M. Armfield 1949; three s.; ed. St. Paul's School, Byam Shaw School and Slade School; has exhibited at Royal Acad. since 1945; exhibits regularly at Agnews, London; numerous one-man exhbns.; works in many public and pvt. collections including Museum of London, Nat. Portrait Gallery, Nat. Gallery of New Zealand; mem. Royal Acad., Royal West of England Acad., New English Art Club; Chair. Artists' Gen. Benevolent Inst. 1987–91; Trustee R.A. 1989–95. *Publications:* Learning to Paint 1970, Painting in Progress 1976, Painting Methods of the Impressionists 1976, The Paintings of Bernard Dunstan 1993. *Leisure interest:* music. *Address:* 10 High Park Road, Kew, Richmond, Surrey, TW9 4BH, England. *Telephone:* 0181-876 6633.

DUNSTAN, Gordon Reginald, C.B.E., M.A., F.S.A.; British university professor (retd.); b. 25 April 1917, Plymouth; s. of Frederick John Menhennet Dunstan and Winifred Amy Orchard; m. Ruby Maud Fitzer 1949; two s. one d.; ed. Leeds Univ.; Minor Canon, St. George's Chapel, Windsor Castle 1955–59; Minor Canon, Westminster Abbey 1959–67; Canon Theologian, Leicester Cathedral 1966–82; Prof. of Moral and Social Theology, King's Coll., London Univ. 1967–82, Prof. Emer. 1982–; Hon. Research Fellow, Univ. of Exeter 1982–; Chaplain to H.M. the Queen 1976–87; Founder Fellow Acad. of Medical Sciences 1998; mem. Nuffield Council on Bioethics 1990–95; Hon. D.D. (Exeter) 1973, Hon. LL.D. (Leicester) 1986; Hon. F.R.S.M. 1984, Hon. M.R.C.P. 1987, Hon. F.R.C.P. 1995, Hon. mem. British Paediatric Assen. 1990, Hon. F.R.C.O.G. 1991, Hon. F.R.C.G.P. 1993, Hon. F.R.C.P. 1997. *Publications:* The Family Is Not Broken 1962, The Register of Edmund Lacy, Bishop of Exeter 1420–1455, 5 vols. 1963–72, A Digger Still 1968, Not Yet the Epitaph 1968, The Sacred Ministry 1970, The Artifice of Ethics 1974, A Moralist in the City 1974, Consent in Medicine (Co-Ed. with M. J. Seller) 1983, The Moral Status of the Human Embryo (Co-Ed. with M. J. Seller) 1988, Biomedical Ethics: An Anglo-American Dialogue (Co.-Ed. with D. Callahan) 1988, Doctors' Decisions: Ethical Conflicts in Medical Practice (Co.-Ed. with E. A. Shinebourne) 1989, The Human Embryo: Aristotle and the Arabic and European Traditions (Ed.) 1990, Euthanasia: Life, Death and the Medical Duty 1996. *Leisure interests:* small islands, *domus* and *rus*. *Address:* 9 Maryfield Avenue, Pennsylvania, Exeter, EX4 6JN, Devon, England. *Telephone:* (01392) 214 691.

DUNWOODY, Richard, M.B.E.; Irish jockey; b. 18 Jan. 1964, Belfast, Northern Ireland; s. of George Dunwoody and Gillian Dunwoody (née Thrale); m. (separated); ed. Rendcomb Coll.; rode winner Grand Nat. (West Tip) 1986, (Minnehoma) 1994, Cheltenham Gold Cup (Charter Party) 1988, Champion Hurdle (Kribensis) 1990; Champion Nat. Hunt Jockey 1992–93, 1993–94, 1994–95. *Publications:* Hell For Leather (with Marcus Armytage), Dual (with Sean Magee), Hands and Heels (with Marcus Armytage). *Leisure interest:* motor sport. *Address:* 14 St. Maur Road, Fulham, London, SW6 4DP, England. *Telephone:* (01638) 663029 (Agent).

DUPLAT, Jean-Louis; Belgian judge; Pres. Tribunal de Commerce until 1989; Chair. Belgian Banking Comm. 1989–. *Address:* Commission Bancaire et Financière, 99 ave Louise, 1050 Brussels, Belgium.

DU PLESSIS, Barend Jacobus, B.SC.; South African politician; b. 1 Jan. 1940, Johannesburg; m. Antoinette Van Den Berg 1962; three s. one d.; ed. Voortrekker High School, Boksburg, Potchefstroom Univ. for Christian Higher Educ., Potchefstroom Coll. of Educ.; teacher 1962, joined S. A. Broadcasting Corpn., then worked in pvt. sector; elected to Roodepoort City Council 1972, subsequently Deputy Mayor, then Mayor; M.P. for Florida 1974–94; served on numerous cttees. and select groups; Deputy Minister of Foreign Affairs 1982; Minister for Educ. and Training 1983, Minister of Finance 1984–92.

DU PLESSIS, Christian; British freelance opera singer; b. 2 July 1944, Vryheid, South Africa; ed. Potchefstroom and Bloemfontein Univs.; début in Pretoria 1967; British début in Andrea Chenier at Theatre Royal, Drury Lane 1970; prin. baritone, English Nat. Opera 1973–81; U.S.A. début in Les Pêcheurs de Perles, Texas 1984; Covent Garden début in Rigoletto 1984; recipient, Ernest Oppenheimer Bursary 1968, 1969, 1970; maj. roles with cos. in U.K., U.S.A., France, Holland, Hong Kong, Ireland; major recordings for Opera Rara, EMI, Decca and ABC Dunhill. *Leisure interest:* Dir. of Fine Arts gallery. *Address:* c/o Performing Arts, 1 Hinde Street, London, W1M 5RH, England.

DU PLESSIS, Daniel Jacob, M.B., CH.B., M.CH., F.R.C.S.; South African surgeon and university vice-chancellor; b. 17 May 1918, Paarl; s. of Daniel J. du Plessis and Louisa M. (Carstens) du Plessis; m. Louisa S. Wicht 1946; two s.; ed. Paarl Boys' High School, Univs. of Cape Town and the Witwatersrand; Capt. S. African Medical Corps 1942–46; postgraduate studies, Cape Town, Johannesburg, Oxford and London 1946–52; Surgeon, Univ. of Cape Town and Groote Schuur Hosp. 1952–58; Prof. of Surgery, Univ. of the Witwatersrand, Johannesburg 1958–77, Vice-Chancellor 1978–83; Nuffield Scholarship 1951–52, Carnegie Fellowship 1963; Hon. Fellowship American Coll. of Surgeons 1974, American Surgical Assen. 1981, Assen. of Surgeons of G.B. and Ireland 1979, Coll. of Surgeons of S.A. 1982; Pres. Southern Transvaal Br., Medical Assen. of S.A. 1986–87; mem. Advisory Council for Univs. and Technikons 1984–92; Hon. Life Vice-Pres. Surgical Research Soc. of S.A., Assen. of Surgeons of S.A. 1984; Chair. of Council, B. G. Alexander Nursing Coll. 1985–95; Natalspruit (now Bonalesedi) Nursing Coll. 1986–92; mem. Council, Medical Univ. of Southern Africa 1986–94, Johannesburg Coll. of Educ. 1986–92, Univ. of Transkei 1989–92; mem. Bd. of Govs., American Coll. of Surgeons 1988–(94); Trustee, S.A. Blood Transfusion Service 1985–; Hon. LL.D. (Witwatersrand) 1984; Hon. M.D. (Cape Town) 1986; Hon. Ph.D. (Medical Univ. of Southern Africa) 1995; Paul Harris Rotary Award 1983; Order for Meritorious Service (Gold) 1989. *Publications:* Principles of Surgery 1968, Synopsis of Surgical Anatomy 1975 and articles in professional journals. *Leisure interests:* walking, reading. *Address:* 17 Chateau Road, Richmond, Johannesburg 2092, South Africa (Home).

du PONT, Pierre Samuel, IV, LL.D.; American politician and lawyer; b. 22 Jan. 1935, Wilmington, Del.; s. of Pierre S. du Pont III and Jane (née Holcomb) du Pont; m. Elise R. Wood 1957; three s. one d.; ed. Philips Exeter Acad., Princeton Univ., and Harvard Univ.; mem. Delaware House of Reps. 1968–70; U.S. House of Reps. 1970–76, serving on Int. Relations Cttee. and Merchant Marine and Fisheries Cttee.; Gov. of Delaware 1977–85; attorney Richards, Layton and Finger 1985–; "Watchdog of the Treasury" Award; Republican. *Address:* Richards, Layton and Finger, One Rodney Square, P.O. Box 551, Wilmington, DE 19899 (Office); Patterns, Rockland, DE 19732, U.S.A. (Home).

DU PUIS, George Bonello, LL.D.; Maltese politician and notary; b. 24 Jan. 1928; m. Iris Gauci Maistre; three c.; ed. St. Catherine's High School, Sliema, the Lyceum and Univ. of Malta; practising notary 1952; mem. Parl. 1971–96; mem. Nationalist Party, Spokesman on Finance, State Industry, Tourism, Trade and Industry; Minister of Finance 1987–92, for Economic Services 1992–95; fmr. Chair. Parl. Standing Cttee on Foreign Affairs, EU Malta Jt. Parl. Cttee; High Commr. to U.K. 1999–. *Address:* 36–38 Piccadilly, London, W1V 0PQ, England. *Telephone:* 0171-292 4800. *Fax:* 0171-734 1831.

DUQUESNE, Jacques Henri Louis, L. EN D.; French journalist and author; b. 18 March 1930, Dunkirk; s. of Louis Duquesne and Madeleine Chevalier; m. Edith Dubois 1954; one s. one d.; ed. Coll. Jean-Bart, Dunkirk and Faculté de Droit, Paris; reporter, La Choix 1957–64; Deputy Dir. Panorama Chrétien 1964–70, head of investigations 1967; Asst. Ed.-in-Chief, L'Express 1970–71; Co-founder and Asst. Ed.-in-Chief, Le Point 1972–74, Ed.-in-Chief 1974–77, Pres.-Dir.-Gen. 1985–90; Dir.-Gen. La Vie Catholique group of publs. 1977–79; news reporter, Europe No. 1 1969–, La Croix 1983–, Midi Libre 1997–; Chair. Bd. L'Express 1997–; Dir. TFI, Editions du Seuil; mem. Jury, Prix Interallié 1986–; Chevalier, Légion d'honneur. *Publications:* L'Algérie ou la guerre des mythes 1959, Les 16–24 ans 1964, Les prêtres 1965, Les catholiques français sous l'occupation 1966, Demain une Eglise sans prêtres 1968, Dieu pour l'homme d'aujourd'hui 1970, La gauche du Christ 1972, Les 13–62 ans 1974, La grande triche 1977, Une voix, la nuit 1979, La rumeur de la ville 1981, Maria Vadamme 1983, Alice Van Meulen 1985,

Saint-Eloi 1986, Au début d'un bel été 1988, les Vents du Nord m'ont dit 1989, Catherine Courage 1990, Jean Bart 1992, Laura C. 1994, Jésus 1994, Théo et Marie 1996, les Années Jean-Paul II 1996 (jtly.), Le Dieu de Jésus 1997. *Address:* 13 rue de Poissy, 75005 Paris, France (Home).

DURACK, David Tulloch, M.B., D.PHIL., F.R.C.P., F.R.A.C.P., F.A.C.P.; American professor of medicine; b. 18 Dec. 1944, W. Australia; s. of Reginald W. Durack and Grace E. Tulloch; m. Carmen E. Prosser 1970; three s. one d.; ed. Scotch Coll. Perth and Univs. of W. Australia and Oxford; Rhodes Scholar; intern Radcliffe Infirmary, Oxford; further training at Royal Postgrad. Medical School, London; fmr. Chief, Div. of Infectious Diseases and Int. Health, Duke Univ. 1977–; Chair. Dept. of Medicine and Chief, Div. of Infectious Diseases, Health Care Int. (Scotland) 1994–95; now Vice-Pres. of Medical Affairs, Becton Dickinson Microbiology Systems; Fellow, American Coll. of Physicians. *Publications:* more than 170 articles and 30 textbook chapters. *Leisure interest:* flying. *Address:* Becton Dickinson Microbiology Systems, 7 Loveton Circle, Sparks, MD 21152; 1411 Wine Spring Lane, Ruxton, MD 21204, U.S.A. (Home). *Telephone:* (410) 316-4824; (410) 321-6643 (Home). *Fax:* (410) 316-4126.

DURAFOUR, Michel André François; French politician and writer; b. 11 April 1920, Saint-Etienne, Loire; s. of Antoine Durafour and Olga Durafour (née Gaillard); m. Maryse Forissier 1973; one s. one d.; ed. Lycée de St. Etienne and Law Faculty of Paris Univ.; assignment in office of Minister of Information 1944–46; journalist, writer, Deputy Mayor 1947–65, Mayor of St.-Etienne 1965–77; mem. Senate for Loire, Independent 1965–67; Deputy to Nat. Assembly for St.-Etienne N.-E., N.-W. 1967–68, 1973–74, 1978–81; Minister of Labour 1974–76, Minister attached to PM with responsibility for Econ. and Finance 1976–77, of the Civil Service and Admin. Reform 1988–91, of State 1989–91; mem. Secretariat Parti Radical-Socialiste; mem. Nat. Bureau of Mouvement Réformateur 1971–; Chair. Groupe des Réformateurs (social democratic group) in Nat. Assembly 1973–74; Pres. Comm. de la Production et des échanges de l'Assemblée Nat.; Assoc. Prof. Univ. of Paris IX 1980–81; Prof. Univ. of Lyon III 1981–; Pres. Conseil Régional (Rhône-Alpes) 1980–81, Regional Councillor and Gen. Chair. Budget 1986–; mem. Senate for Loire, Social Democratic group 1983–; Vice-Prés. de la Commission des Affaires Culturelles du Sénat 1985, de la Commission des Finances du Sénat 1986–88; Ministre d'Etat in charge of civil service and admin. reforms 1988–91; Conseiller d'Etat (on special service) 1992–96; Grand Prix du Théâtre for Les Démoniaques 1950, Grand Prix du Roman d'Aventure for Agnès et les vilains Messieurs 1963. *Publications:* Les Démoniaques 1950, Notre rêve qui êtes aux cieux (film entitled Les fruits sauvages), Bettina Colonna, Les hommes sont comme ça, Le juif du ciel, Les moutons du ciel, Agnès et les vilains Messieurs (under pseudonym Pierre Jardin), Dites-le avec des pastèques, Pascaline, La Baïonnette de Mirabeau, and others. *Address:* 62 rue de Ponthieu, 75008 Paris, France.

DURÁN, Roberto; Panamanian boxer; b. 16 June 1951, Chorrillo; m. Felicidad Durán; four c.; ed. primary school; professional boxer March 1967–; won world lightweight title from Ken Buchanan June 1972; made record number of championship defences (12) before relinquishing title to box as welterweight from Feb. 1979; won World Boxing Council version of world welterweight title from Ray Leonard (q.v.), Montreal June 1980: lost it to Leonard, New Orleans Nov. 1980, retained it 1989; won WBC version of world middleweight title against Ian Barkley, Atlantic City Feb. 1989, relinquished it to challenge Ray Leonard to WBC super-middleweight title: lost to Leonard, Las Vegas Dec. 1989; exempt from all taxes, receives monthly pension for life from Govt. *Leisure interest:* cars. *Address:* Nuevo Reperto El Carmen, Panama.

DURAN BALLEN, Sixto; Ecuadorean politician; b. 14 July 1921, Boston, Mass., U.S.A.; s. of Sixto E. Duran Ballen and Maria E. Duran Ballen; m. Josephine Villa Lobos 1945; three s. six d.; ed. Columbia Univ.; practised as architect; fmr. Mayor of Quito; fmr. official of Inter-American Devt. Bank, Washington D.C.; Pres. of Ecuador 1992–96; mem. Partido Conservador Ecuatoriano (PCE), M.P. 1998–. *Address:* P.O. Box 3122, Quito, Ecuador.

DURAND-RIVAL, Pierre J. H.; French steel industry executive; b. 1 July 1930, Chambéry; s. of Eugène and Marie (née Callet) Durand-Rival; m. Nicole Guyot 1953; three d.; ed. Ecole Polytechnique, Ecole Nat. des Ponts et des Chaussées; mil. service 1951–52; Engineer Ministry of Public Works, Corsica 1954–58, Bas-Rhin 1958–61; Engineer Ministry of Public Health 1961–63; iron and steel engineer SACILOR steel makers, constructing and operating new mills 1963–66, Man., then Gen. Man. 1966–70, Chair. and Man. Dir. 1976–80; Gen. Man. and mem. Bd. SOLMER steel makers 1971–76; Admin. Marine-Wendel 1977; Chair. and Man. Dir. Cie. générale d'automatismes (CGA-Alcatel) 1983; Chair. Chief Exec. Carnaud-Basse Indre; Deputy Chief Exec. and Dir. Eurotunnel 1986–89, Tech. Adviser 1989. *Leisure interests:* skiing, walking. *Address:* 6 rue des Gates Ceps, 92210 Saint-Cloud; Le Pradon, 83320 Carqueiranne, France (Homes).

DURANTE, Viviana Paola; Italian ballet dancer; b. 8 May 1967, Rome; joined Royal Ballet Co., London 1984, became soloist 1987, prin. 1989, guest artist 1997; repertory includes: Ondine, Juliet, Nikiya (La Bayadère), Odette-Odile (Swan Lake), Aurore (Sleeping Beauty), Cinderella, Princess Rose (Prince of Pagodas), Anastasia, Mary Vetzera (Mayerling); also roles in My Brother and My Sisters, Requiem, Don Quixote, Manon, Nutcracker, Rhapsody, Capriccio, Anna Karenina; Premio Positano Award (Italy) 1991, Evening Standard Award, Time Out Award. *Leisure interests:* yoga, reading, life. *Address:* Royal Ballet Company, Royal Opera House, Covent Garden, London, WC2E 9DD, England.

DURÃO BARROSO, José Manuel, M.POL.SC.; Portuguese politician; b. 23 March 1956, Lisbon; m.; three c.; ed. Univs. of Lisbon and Geneva; lecturer, Faculty of Law, Univ. of Lisbon, Dept. of Political Science, Univ. of Geneva; Visiting Scholar, Univ. of Georgetown, Washington, D.C.; mem. Parl. 1985–; fmr. Sec. of State for Home Affairs and for Foreign Affairs and Co-operation; Minister of Foreign Affairs 1992–95; mem. Nat. Council Social Democratic Party (PSD). *Publications:* Governmental System and Party System (co-author) 1980, Le Système Politique Portugais face à l'Intégration Européenne 1983, Política de Cooperação 1990; several studies on political science and constitutional law in collective works, encyclopaedias and int. journals. *Address:* c/o Social Democratic Party, Rua de São Caetano 9, 1296 Lisbon Codex, Portugal.

DURBIN, Richard Joseph, J.D.; American politician; b. 21 Nov. 1944, East St. Louis, Ill.; s. of William Durbin and Ann Durbin; m. Loretta Schaefer 1967; one s. two d.; ed. Georgetown Univ.; called to bar, Ill. 1969; legal practice 1969–; Chief legal counsel to Lieut. Gov. Paul Simon of Ill. 1969; mem. staff, minority leader, Ill. State Senate 1972–77, parliamentarian 1969–77; Assoc. Prof. Medical Humanities, S. Ill. Univ. 1978–; mem. 98th–103rd Congress 1983–97; Senator from Illinois 1997–; Democrat. *Address:* United States Senate, 364 Russell Senate Office, Washington, DC 20510, U.S.A.

DURHAM, Sir Kenneth, Kt., B.SC., C.B.I.M.; British company director; b. 28 July 1924, Blackburn, Lancs.; s. of George and Bertha (née Aspin) Durham; m. Irene Markham 1946; one s. one d.; ed. Queen Elizabeth Grammar School, Blackburn, Univ. of Manchester; Flight Lieut. in R.A.F. 1943–46; joined Atomic Research Establishment, Harwell, then Unilever Research Lab., Port Sunlight 1950, Head of Lab. 1961; Head of Lab., Colworth 1965; Chair. BOCM Silcock Ltd. 1971; Dir. Unilever Ltd. and Unilever NV 1974–86; Vice-Chair. Unilever Ltd. (now Unilever PLC) 1978–82, Chair. 1982–86; Dir. British Aerospace Ltd. 1980–90, Deputy Chair. 1986–90; Dir. Woolworth Holdings (now Kingfisher, plc) 1985–90, Chair. 1986–90; Dir. Morgan Grenfell Holdings 1986–90; Chair. Trade Policy Research Centre 1982; Vice-Pres. Liverpool School of Tropical Medicine 1982–, Help the Aged 1986–; Gov. London Business School 1982; Advisory Council Chase Manhattan Bank NA 1983; mem. Int. Advisory Cttee. of United Technologies Corpn. 1983; Chair. Econ. and Financial Policy Cttee., CBI 1983–86; Trustee Leverhulme Trust 1974; Hon. D.Sc. (Loughborough) 1984; Order of Orange Nassau (Netherlands) 1985; Hon. F.B.A. 1997. *Publications:* Surface Activity and Detergency 1960, various scientific papers. *Leisure interests:* walking, golf.

DURLACHER, Nicholas, C.B.E., B.A.; British business executive; b. 20 March 1946, Plaxtol; s. of John Sidney Durlacher and Alma Gabriel Adams; m. Mary McLaren 1971; one s.; ed. Stowe School, Buckingham, Magdalene Coll., Cambridge; fmrly. Chair. London Int. Financial Futures and Options Exchange; now Chair. Securities and Futures Authority; Dir. BZW, Investor's Compensation Scheme; mem. Takeover Panel; Sr. Adviser to Office of Electricity Regulation; Trustee British Brain and Spine Foundation. *Leisure interests:* skiing, golf, tennis. *Address:* c/o Securities and Futures Authority, Cottons Centre, Cottons Lane, London, SE1 2QB (Office); 10 Rutland Street, London, SW7 1EH, England (Home).

DUROV, Lev Aleksandrovich; Russian actor; b. 23 Dec. 1931, Moscow; m. Irina Nikolayevna Kirichenko; one d.; ed. Studio School of Moscow Art Theatre; actor and stage dir. Cen. Children's Theatre 1954–63, Lenkom Theatre 1963–67, Malaya Bronnaya Theatre 1967–; Theatre-School of Contemporary Plays 1993–; as stage dir. produced over 20 plays. *Plays include:* Chebutykin, Medvedenko, Molière, Sganarelle, Yago, Zhevakin, Alyosha; in cinema since 1953. *Films include:* Farewell, Leap Year, Don't be Afraid, I'm with You, Three Musketeers, Success, Orphan of Kazan; as stage dir. over 20 theatre productions; People's Artist of Russian Fed. 1982, U.S.S.R. People's Artist 1990. *Address:* Frunzenskaya nab. 3b, Apt. 206, 119146 Moscow, Russia (Home). *Telephone:* (095) 242 4346 (Home).

DÜRR, Heinz; German industrialist; b. 16 July 1933, Stuttgart; s. of Otto Dürr; m. Heide Dürr; three d.; ed. Tech. Hochschule, Stuttgart; Man. and Man. Dir. Dürr GmbH (fmrly. Otto Dürr GmbH), Stuttgart 1957–80; Chair. Bd. of Dirs. AEG Aktiengesellschaft, Berlin and Frankfurt 1980–; mem. Bd. of Dirs. Daimler-Benz AG, Stuttgart 1986–, Chair. 1991; Chair. Supervisory Bd. Olympia AG, Wilhelmshaven 1980–, AEG KABEL 1980–, Telefunken Electronic GmbH, Heilbronn 1989–, AEG Austria, Vienna 1989–, Exec. Bd. Deutsche Bank AG 1994–; Chair. Bd. Deutschen Bahn Aktienges 1997–; mem. Supervisory Bd. Frankfurter Allianz-AG, Frankfurt 1981–; Pres. Metal Industry Asscn., Stuttgart 1975–80; mem. Advisory Council Dresdner Bank, Frankfurt 1980–; mem. Cen. Asscn. Electrical and Electronics Industry of Germany; Chair. Supervisory Bd. of Dirs. Deutsche Bundesbahn; Chair. Bd. Deutsche Reichsbahn. *Leisure interests:* tennis, golf, theatre. *Address:* Charlottenstrasse 57, 10117 Berlin, Germany.

DURR, Kent D. Skelton; South African fmr. politician, diplomatist and business executive; b. 28 March 1941, Cape Town; s. of Dr. John M. Durr and Diana Skelton; m. Suzanne Wiese 1966; one s. two d.; ed. S.A. Coll. School, Cape Town Univ.; Dir. family publishing co. 1966–68; Founder and later Man. Dir. Durr Estates 1968–84; Chair. Clean Diesel Technologies Inc.

1995–97, Fuel-Tech N.V. 1995–97; Exec. Chair. Commonwealth Investment Guarantee Agency Ltd. 1997–, active in est. of CIGA Africa Rep. Office, Cape Town 1998–; elected to Prov. Council of Cape 1974, M.P. for Maitland 1977–91, Deputy Minister (Trade and Industry) 1984–86, (Finance) 1984–88; Minister of Budget and Public Works 1988–89; Cabinet Minister of Trade and Industry and Tourism 1989–91; Amb. to U.K. 1991–94, High Commr. in U.K. 1994–95; mem. S.A. Nat. Foundation for Conservation of Coastal Birds 1985 (Award of Honour 1987), Freeman City of London 1995. *Leisure interests:* field sports, mountaineering, conservation. *Address:* Commonwealth Investment Guarantee Agency Ltd., 67 Pall Mall, London, SW1Y 5PA, England; CIGA Africa, P.O. Box 289, Yzerfontein 7351, Cape, South Africa. *Telephone:* 0171-930 9310 (Office); 0171-730 8250 (Home). *Fax:* 0171-930 9311 (Office); 02245-352 (Home).

DURRANT, Jennifer Ann; British artist; b. 17 June 1942, Brighton; d. of Caleb John Durrant and Winifred May Wright; m. William A. H. Henderson 1964 (divorced 1976); ed. Varndean Grammar School for Girls, Brighton, Brighton Coll. of Art and Crafts, Slade School of Fine Art, Univ. Coll., London; part-time art teacher various colls. 1965–74; part-time Lecturer on Painting, St. Martin's School of Art, London 1974–87, R.C.A. 1979–, Chelsea School of Art 1987–, Royal Acad. Schools 1991–; Exhbn. Selector, Northern Young Contemporaries, Whitworth Gallery, Manchester, TV S.W. Arts; Painting Faculty mem. The British School at Rome 1979–83; Newham Hosp. Comm. (in asscn. with Greater London Arts Asscn. and King Edward's Hosp. Fund), Towner Art Gallery, Eastbourne; Abbey Minor Travelling Scholarship 1964; Arts Council Award 1976; Arts Council Maj. Award 1978; Artist-in-Residence, Somerville Coll., Oxford 1979–80; Greater London Arts Asscn. Award 1980; one-person exhbns. at Univ. of Surrey, Guildford 1975, Arnolfini Gallery, Bristol 1979, Museum of Modern Art, Oxford 1980, Nicola Jacobs Gallery, London 1982, 1985, Arcade Gallery, Harrogate 1983, Northern Centre for Contemporary Art, Sunderland 1986; Serpentine Gallery, London 1987, Newlyn-Orion, Penzance 1988, Lynne Stern Assocs., London 1989; numerous group exhbns. in London, Liverpool, Reykjavik, Boston, U.S.A., Edmonton, Canada, New York, Aachen, Fed. Repub. of Germany, Pittsburg, U.S.A., Birmingham, Stoke-on-Trent, Sheffield 1988, Newcastle 1989, London, Lincoln 1990; works in collections of Arts Council of G.B., British Council, Contemporary Art Soc., Tate Gallery, London, Museum of Fine Arts, Boston, U.S.A., Neue Gallery, Aachen etc. and in pvt. collections; Athena Art Award 1988. *Leisure interests:* classical music, including opera, archaeology, visiting museums, looking at paintings and sculpture. *Address:* 9-10 Holly Grove, London, SE15 5DF, England. *Telephone:* 0171-639 6424.

DUSSAULT, René, LL.L., PH.D., F.R.S.C.; Canadian judge; b. 23 Nov. 1939, Quebec; s. of Daniel Dussault and Madeleine Pelletier; m. Marielle Godbout 1967; two s.; ed. Laval Univ. and London School of Econs. and Political Science; lecturer in Law, Laval Univ. 1966–70; legal counsel, Quebec Health and Welfare Inquiry Comm.; Special Adviser to Minister of Social Affairs of Quebec 1970–73; Chair. Quebec Professions Bd. 1973–77; Deputy Minister of Justice, Quebec 1977–80; Prof. Nat. School of Public Admin. 1981–89; Laskin Chair in Public Law, Osgoode Hall Law School 1983–84; legal consultant, Kronström, McNicoll & Assocs., Quebec City; Judge, Quebec Court of Appeal 1989–; Co-Chair. Royal Comm. on Aboriginal Peoples 1991–96; Quebec Bar Asscn. Medal 1987, Vanier Medal of Inst. of Public Admin. of Canada 1998; Quebec Interprofessional Council Prize 1991; Hon. LL.D. (York) 1992, (Dalhousie) 1997. *Publications:* Le contrôle judiciaire de l'administration au Québec 1969, Traité de droit administratif, Vols. I & II 1974 (also co-author of subsequent vols.), Administrative Law: A Treatise, Vols. I-V 1985–90. *Address:* 300 Jean-Lesage Boulevard (R. 438), Quebec, P.Q. G1K 8K6 (Office); 1332 James-LeMoine Avenue, Sillery, P.Q. G1S 1A3, Canada (Home). *Telephone:* (418) 649-3425 (Office); (418) 527-6332 (Home). *Fax:* (418) 643-4154 (Office).

DUTILLEUX, Henri; French composer; b. 22 Jan. 1916, Angers; s. of Paul and Thérèse (née Koszul) Dutilleux; m. Geneviéve Joy 1946; ed. Conservatoire Nat. de Musique, Paris; career devoted to music 1945–; Dir. service Créations Musicales Radiodiffusion française 1945–63; Prof. of Composition Ecole Normale de Musique, Paris 1961–, Pres. 1969–74; Assoc. Prof. Conservatoire Nat. Supérieur de Musique, Paris 1970–71; fmr. mem. UNESCO Music Council; Hon. mem. American Acad. and Inst. of Arts and Letters, Accad. di Santa Cecilia; Assoc. mem. Royal Acad. of Belgium; Hon. mem. R.A.M., London; 1st Grand Prix de Rome 1938, Grand Prix du Disque 1957, 1958, 1966, 1968, 1976, 1978 and 1984, Grand Prix National de la Musique 1967, Prix de la Ville de Paris 1974, Koussevitzky Int. Recording Award 1976, World Record Award (Montreux) 1983; Prix Int. Maurice Ravel 1987, Grand Prix, Music Council UNESCO 1987, Praemium Imperiale Japan 1994; Grand Officier, Légion d'honneur, Commdr. Ordre Nat. du Mérite, des Arts et des Lettres, du Mérite Culturel de Monaco. *Compositions:* Sonata for Piano 1948, First Symphony 1951, Le Loup (Ballet) 1953, Second Symphony (Le Double) 1959, Métaboles (for orchestra) 1964, Cello Concerto: Tout un monde lointain 1970, Figures de Résonances (for two pianos) 1971, Preludes for Piano 1974, Ainsi la Nuit (for string quartet) 1976, Timbres, Espace, Mouvement (for orchestra) 1978, 3 Strophes sur le nom de Sacher (for cello) 1981, L'Arbre des Songes (violin concerto) 1985, Le Jeu des contraires (for piano) 1988, Mystère de l'instant (for 24 strings and cymbalum) 1989, Les Citations (for oboe, harpsicord, double-bass and percussion) 1991, The Shadows of Time (for orchestra) 1997. *Address:* 12 rue St.-Louis-en-l'Isle, 75004 Paris, France. *Telephone:* 43-26-39-14.

DUTOIT, Charles E.; Swiss conductor and music director; b. 7 Oct. 1936; s. of Edmond Dutoit and Berthe Dutoit (Laederman); m. Marie-Josée Drouin 1982; one s. one d.; ed. Conservatory of Lausanne, Accademia Musicale Chigiana, Siena, Italy, Conservatorio Benedetto Marcello, Venice, Italy and Berks. Music Center, Tanglewood, U.S.A.; Conductor Berne Symphony Orchestra (Assoc. Conductor 1964, Music Dir. 1966–68), Radio Zurich Orchestra, Nat. Symphony Orchestra of Mexico (Music Dir.), Gothenberg Symphony Orchestra, Sweden (Music Dir.) Montreal Symphony Orchestra (Music Dir.) 1977–, Minn. Orchestra (Prin. Guest Conductor 1983–84, 1985–86); Artistic Dir. and Prin. Conductor Philadelphia Orchestra 1990, 1991; Music Dir. Orchestre Nat. de France 1990–, Nat. Symphony Orchestra of Mexico; Prin. Conductor NHK Symphony Orchestra, Tokyo 1996; many recordings including 24 for Decca since 1980; début Royal Opera House Covent Garden (conducting Faust) 1983; D.Mus. h.c. (Montreal) 1984, (Laval) 1985; Grand Prix de l'Académie du disque français, High Fidelity Int. Record Critics' Award, Montreux Record Award, Grand Prix du Prés. de la République (France), Japan Record Acad. Award, Artist of the Year (Canada Music Council) 1982. *Address:* Orchestre Symphonique de Montréal, 260 Boulevard Maisonneuve Ouest, Montréal, Quebec H2X 1Y9, Canada.

DUTTON, Geoffrey Piers Henry, A.O.; Australian writer; b. 2 Aug. 1922, Anlaby, S. Australia; s. of Henry Hampden Dutton and Emily Dutton (née Martin); m. 1st Ninette Clarice Florence Trott 1944 (divorced 1985); two s. one d.; m. 2nd Robin Lucas 1985; ed. Geelong Grammar School, Vic., Univ. of Adelaide, Magdalen Coll., Oxford; Pilot, R.A.A.F. 1941–45; Sr. Lecturer in English, Univ. of Adelaide 1954–62; Commonwealth Fellow, Univ. of Leeds, England 1960; Visiting Prof., Kansas State Univ., U.S.A. 1962; Founding Ed. Australian Letters, Australian Book Review, Penguin Australia 1955–65; Co-founder and Dir. Sun Books 1965–; Ed. The Bulletin Literary Supplement 1980–85, Ed. The Australian Literary Quarterly 1985–89; mem. Australian Council for the Arts, Commonwealth Literary Fund, Literature Bd., Australia Council 1968–78; mem. Council, Australian Nat. Univ. 1976–80. *Publications:* 51 books of poetry, biography, fiction, literary and art criticism, travel, children's; they include Nightflight and Sunrise 1944, Antipodes in Shoes 1958, Walt Whitman 1961, Patrick White 1961, Russell Drysdale 1964, The Literature of Australia 1964, Poems Soft and Loud 1967, Tamara 1969, Australia's Censorship Crisis (with M. Harris) 1970, Findings and Keepings 1970, New Poems to 1972, Australian Verse from 1805–1976, A Body of Words 1978, Patterns of Australia 1980, The Australian Heroes 1981, S. T. Gill's Australia 1981, The Eye-Opener 1982, In Search of Edward John Eyre 1982, The Prowler 1982, Snow on the Saltbush 1984, The Australian Collection 1985, The Innovators 1986, Kanga Creek 1989, The Picador Henry Lawson 1990, The Enigma of a Poet—Kenneth Slessor 1990, Flying Low 1992, New and Selected Poems 1993, Out in the Open: An Autobiography 1994. *Leisure interest:* swimming. *Address:* c/o Curtis Brown Ltd., P.O. Box 19, Paddington, N.S.W. 2021, Australia. *Telephone:* 02-331 5301.

DUȚU, Alexandru, PH.D.; Romanian historian and author; b. 2 Sept. 1928, Bucharest; s. of Nicolae Duțu and Elisabeta Negoescu; m. Angela Dăscălescu 1958 (died 1986); one d., one s.; ed. Coll. of Modern Philology and Coll. of Law; researcher, Inst. for South East European Studies 1963–90, Dir. 1990–97; Prof., Int. School for Political Sciences 1990–; Dir. French-Romanian Seminar (Bucharest) 1990–95; Dir. Centre for the Study of European Mentalities 1994–; Visiting Prof., E.H.E.S.S. (Paris) 1990, Collège de France 1995; ed. Revue des études sud-est européennes; Deputy Ed. Synthesis; Deputy Ed. Mentalities 1984–; Prize of the Romanian Acad., of the Int. Asscn. for South-East European Studies; Fellowship Great Britain 1968–69, U.S.A. 1986; Vice-Chair. Int. Asscn. for Comparative Literature 1979–85; mem. Scientific Council of Coll. of European Citizenship (Council of Europe) 1997–; mem. French, Austrian, Spanish socs. for the study of 18th century culture; mem. Romanian Writers' Union; Corresp. mem. Foundation for Hellenic Culture; Chevalier des Palmes Académiques 1997. *Publications include:* Shakespeare in Romania, 1964, Les livres de sagesse dans la culture roumaine 1971, Romanian Humanists and the European Culture 1977, European Intellectual Movements and the Modernization of the Romanian Culture 1981, Humanisme, baroque, lumières—l'exemple roumain 1984, The Human Dimension of History. Trends in the History of Mentalities 1986, L'état des lieux en sciences sociales 1993, Culture et Politique 1995, Y a-t-il une Europe orthodoxe? 1997, Political Models and National Identities in 'Orthodox Europe' 1998. *Leisure interests:* skiing, travelling. *Address:* Calea 13 Septembrie 13, C.P. 22.159, Bucharest (Office); Str. C. C. Arion 6, 78144 Bucharest, Romania (Home). *Telephone:* (1) 314.49.96 (Office). *Fax:* (1) 312 41 34.

DUVALIER, Jean-Claude; Haitian politician; b. 3 July 1951, Port-au-Prince; s. of late Pres. François Duvalier and late Simone (née Ovide) Duvalier; m. Michele Bennett 1980 (divorced 1990); one s.; ed. Coll. of St. Louis de Gonzague, Port-au-Prince and faculty of law, Univ. of Haiti; named political heir to Pres. François Duvalier Jan. 1971; Life Pres. 1971–86 (overthrown in coup); now living in Mougins, France; extradition requested by Haitian Govt. Dec. 1998.

DUVALL, Robert; American actor; b. 1931, San Diego; s. of William H. Duvall; m. 1st Gail Youngs (divorced); m. 2nd Sharon Brophy 1991; ed. Principia Coll. Ill.; student, Neighborhood Playhouse, New York; stage appearances include: A View from the Bridge 1965 (Obie Award), Wait Until Dark 1966, American Buffalo; Acad. Award for Best Actor in Tender Mercies

1984; recipient of other film awards. *Films include:* To Kill a Mockingbird 1963, Captain Newman, M.D. 1964, The Chase 1965, Countdown 1968, The Detective 1968, Bullitt 1968, True Grit 1969, The Rain People 1969, M*A*S*H 1970, The Revolutionary 1970, The Godfather 1972, Tomorrow 1972, The Great Northfield, Minnesota Raid 1972, Joe Kidd 1972, Lady Ice 1973, The Outfit 1974, The Conversation 1974, The Godfather Part II 1974, Breakout 1975, The Killer Elite 1975, Network 1976, The Eagle Has Landed 1977, The Greatest 1977, The Betsy 1978, Apocalypse Now 1979, The Great Santini 1980, True Confessions 1981, Angelo My Love (actor and dir.) 1983, Tender Mercies 1983, The Stone Boy 1984, The Natural 1984, The Lightship 1986, Let's Get Harry 1986, Belizaire the Cajun 1986, Colors 1988, Convicts, Roots in a Parched Ground, The Handmaid's Tale 1990, A Show of Force 1990, Days of Thunder 1990, Rambling Rose 1991, Newsies 1992, The New Boys 1992, Stalin 1992, The Plague, Geronimo, Falling Down 1993, The Paper 1994, Wrestling Ernest Hemingway 1994, Something To Talk About, The Stars Fell on Henrietta, The Scarlet Letter, A Family Thing (also co-producer), Phenomenon 1996, The Apostle 1997, Gingerbread Man 1997, A Civil Action 1999; dir. film We're Not the Jet Set; several TV films and appearances. *Address:* c/o William Morris Agency, 151 S. El Camino Drive, Beverly Hills, CA 90212, U.S.A.

DUVALL, Shelley; American actress and producer; b. 7 July 1949, Houston, Tex.; f. TV production co. Think Entertainment. *Films:* (actress): Brewster McCloud, McCabe and Mrs. Miller, Thieves Like Us, Nashville, Buffalo Bill and the Indians, Three Women (Cannes Festival Prize 1977), Annie Hall, The Shining, Popeye, Time Bandits, Roxanne, Suburban Commando, The Underneath, Portrait of a Lady, Changing Habits. *Television:* (actress): Bernice Bobs Her Hair, Lily, Twilight Zone, Mother Goose Rock 'n' Rhyme, Faerie Tale Theatre (Rumpelstiltskin, Rupunzel), Tall Tales and Legends (Darlin' Clementine); (exec. producer): Faerie Tale Theatre, Tall Tales and Legends, Nightmare Classics, Dinner at Eight (film), Mother Goose Rock 'n' Rhyme, Stories from Growing Up, Backfield in Motion (film), Bedtime Stories, Mrs. Piggle-Wiggle.

DUVERGER, Maurice; French political scientist; b. 5 June 1917, Angoulême; s. of Georges and Anne (née Gobert) Duverger; m. Odile Batt 1949; ed. Bordeaux Univ; contrib. to Le Monde 1946–; Prof. of Political Sociology, Paris Univ. 1955–85, Prof. Emer. 1985–; f. and Pres. Inst. of Research into Insts. and Cultures of Europe (IRICE); mem. European Parl. 1989-95; mem. American Acad. of Arts and Sciences; Grand Officier Légion d'honneur. *Publications:* Les partis politiques 1951, Demain, la république . . . 1959, De la dictature 1961, La Sixième république et le régime présidentiel 1961, Introduction to the Social Sciences 1964, Introduction à la politique 1964, La démocratie sans le peuple 1967, Institutions politiques 1970, Janus: les deux faces de l'Occident 1972, Sociologie de la politique 1973, La monarchie républicaine 1974, Lettre ouverte aux socialistes 1976, L'autre coté des choses 1977, Echec au roi 1978, Les orangers du lac Balaton 1980, La République des Citoyens 1982, Bréviaire de la cohabitation 1986, La Cohabitation des Français 1987, La nostalgie de l'impuissance 1988, le Lièvre libéral et la tortue européenne 1990, Europe des hommes 1994, L'Europe dans tous ses Etats 1995. *Leisure interest:* theatre. *Address:* 24 rue des Fossés-Saint-Jacques, 75005 Paris; Mas du Grand Côté, 13100 Le Tholonet, France (Homes).

DUVILLARD, Henri; French politician; b. 3 Nov. 1910, Luxeuil-les-Bains; s. of Benoit Duvillard and Emilie Mougenot; m. Germaine Grandjean 1933; journalist; Dir. La Dépêche du Loiret 1947–52; on staff of Gen. Koenig (Minister of Nat. Defence) 1954–55; on staff of Henri Ulver (Minister of Industry and Commerce) 1955–56; on staff of Maurice Lemaire (Sec. of State for Industry and Commerce) 1956–58; Deputy for Loiret 1958–63, 1963–67, 1973–78; fmr. Vice-Pres. U.N.R. Group in Nat. Assembly; fmr. Public Relations Officer, Papeteries de France; Minister for Ex-Servicemen 1967–72; Pres. Comité Nat. du Mémorial du Gen. de Gaulle; mem. Inst. Charles du Gaulle; Hon. Deputy; Légion d'honneur, Médaille militaire, Croix de guerre (1939–45), Médaille de la Résistance. *Address:* 12 rue du Grenier-à-sel, 45000 Orléans, France.

DUWAISAN, Khaled Abdulaziz al-, B.A. (COMM.); Kuwaiti diplomatist; b. 15 Aug. 1947; s. of Abdulaziz Saud Al-Duwaisan and Sabeka Abdullah Al-Duwaisan; m. Dalal Al-Humaizi 1980; one s. one d.; ed. Cairo Univ., Univ. of Kuwait; joined Ministry of Foreign Affairs 1970, Diplomatic Attaché 1974, Embassy, Washington, D.C. 1975; Amb. to Netherlands 1984 (also accred. Amb. to Romania 1988); Chair. Kuwaiti del. for supervision of de-militarized zone between Iraq and Kuwait and Chief Co-ordinator Comm. for Return of Stolen Property 1991; Amb. to U.K. 1993– (also accred. to Repub. of Ireland, Norway, Sweden and Denmark); Hon. G.C.V.O. (U.K.). *Leisure interests:* tennis, swimming. *Address:* Kuwaiti Embassy, 2 Albert Gate, London, SW1X 7JU (Office); 22 Kensington Palace Gardens, London, W.8, England (Home). *Telephone:* 0171-590 3400 (Office); 0171-221 7374 (Home). *Fax:* 0171-259 5087.

DVORSKÝ, Peter; Slovak opera singer; b. 25 Sept. 1951, Partizánske, Topol'čany Dist.; s. of Vendelín Dvorský and Anna Dvorská; m. Marta Varšová 1975; two d.; ed. State Conservatoire, Bratislava; studied with R. Carossi and M. di Luggo, Milan 1975–76; opera soloist, Slovak Nat. Theatre, Bratislava 1972–96, 1999; sang at Metropolitan Opera, New York 1977, Covent Garden, London 1978, Bolshoi Theatre, Moscow 1978, La Scala, Milan 1979; regularly at Bratislava, Vienna State Opera, Covent Garden, La Scala, New York Metropolitan Opera, Munich, Berlin, Prague, Geneva and Paris; also in many other cities throughout the world; numerous radio and TV performances; many recordings; Chair. Council of Slovak Music Union 1991–; Pres. Harmony Foundation 1991–; awards include Tchaikovsky Competition, Geneva (5th Prize 1974, 1st Prize 1975), Leoš Janáček Memorial Medal 1978, Giuseppe Verdi Medal 1979, Artist of Merit 1981, Nat. Artist 1984, Kammersänger, Vienna 1986, Francisco Cilea Prize 1991, Wilhelm Furtwängler Prize 1992. *Leisure interests:* hunting, music, piano, family. *Address:* Peter Dvorský Secretariat, Bradlianska ulica 11, SK-811 03 Bratislava, Slovakia.

DWEK, Raymond Allen, D.PHIL., D.SC., F.R.S., F.R.S.C.; British scientist and university professor; b. 10 Nov. 1941, Manchester; s. of Victor Joe Dwek and Alice Liniado; m. Sandra Livingstone 1964; two s. two d.; ed. Carmel Coll., Manchester Univ., Lincoln Coll., Oxford, Exeter Coll., Oxford; research lecturer in Physical Chem., Christ Church, Oxford 1966–68, in Biochem. 1975–76; lecturer in Inorganic Chem., Christ Church, Oxford 1968–75, in Biochem., Trinity Coll., Oxford 1976–84; Fellow Exeter Coll., Oxford 1974–88, Professorial Fellow 1988–; Dir. Oxford Glycobiology Inst., Prof. of Glycobiology Univ. of Oxford 1988–; Assoc. Head of Dept. of Biochem., Dir. for Grad. Training; mem. Oxford Enzyme Group 1971–88; founder mem. Oxford Oligo-saccharide Group 1983; Oxford Univ. Non-exec. Dir. Glycosciences Ltd. (fmrly. Glycosystems Ltd.); Dir. and f. scientist IgX, Oxford 1998; Visiting Royal Soc. Research Fellow Weizmann Inst., Rehovot, Israel 1969; Royal Soc. Locke Research Fellow 1974–76; Visiting Prof. Duke Univ., NC; Hon. Life/Founder mem. Swedish Biophysical Soc. 1979–, mem. European Molecular Biological Org. (EMBO) 1988–, Advisory Panel, The Foundation for Ethnobiology 1994–, Scientific Advisory Bd., Hepatitis Foundation U.S.A. 1994–; Judge, Millennium Fund Competition, The Daily Telegraph 1994; Dr. h.c. (Catholic Univ. of Louvain) 1996; Wellcome Trust Award for Research in Biochemistry Related to Medicine 1994; Scientific Leadership Award Hepatitis B Foundation, Philadelphia; Delaware Valley Coll. Centennial Award 1997. *Publications:* Nuclear Magnetic Resonance (NMR) in Biochemstry 1973, Physical Chemistry Principles and Problems for Biochemists (jtly.) 1975, NMR in Biology (jtly.) 1977, Biological Spectrosocopy (jtly.) 1984. *Leisure interests:* family, patent law, sport, sailing, listening to music. *Address:* Glycobiology Institute, South Parks Road, Oxford, OX1 3QU (Office); Exeter College, Oxford, OX1 3DP; Ambleside, Vernon Avenue, North Hinksey, Oxford, OX1 3QU, England. *Telephone:* (01865) 275344 (Office). *Fax:* (01865) 275771.

DWORKIN, Andrea; American author; b. 26 Sept. 1946, Camden, N.J., U.S.A.: d. of Harry Spiegel and Sylvia Spiegel; ed. Bennington Coll.; has worked as a waitress, receptionist, factory worker. *Publications include:* Woman Hating 1974, Out Blood: Prophecies and Discourses on Sexual Politics (Essays) 1976, The New Woman's Broken Heart 1980, Take Back the Night: Women on Pornography 1980, Pornography: Men Possessing Women 1981, Right-wing Women 1983, Ice and Fire (novel) 1986, Letters from a War Zone 1976–1987, 1989, Mercy 1990, Life and Death 1996.

DWORKIN, Ronald Myles, F.B.A.; American professor of law; b. 11 Dec. 1931; s. of David Dworkin and Madeline Talamo; m. Betsy Celia Ross 1958; one s. one d.; ed. Harvard Coll., Oxford Univ., U.K., Harvard Law School; Legal Sec. to Judge Learned Hand 1957–58; Assoc., Sullivan & Cromwell, New York 1958–62; Assoc. Prof. of Law, Yale Law School 1962–65, Prof. 1965–68, Wesley N. Hohfeld Prof. of Jurisprudence 1968–69; Prof. of Jurisprudence, Oxford Univ. 1969–98, now Emer., Fellow Univ. Coll. 1969–98, now Emer.; Quain Prof. of Jurisprudence, Univ. Coll., London 1998–; Visiting Prof. of Philosophy, Princeton Univ. 1974–75; Prof. of Law, New York Univ. Law School 1975–; Prof.-at-Large, Cornell Univ. 1976–80; Visiting Prof. of Philosophy and Law, Harvard Univ. 1977, of Philosophy 1979–82; mem. Council, Writers and Scholars Educational Trust 1982–, Programme Cttee., Ditchley Foundation 1982–; Co-Chair. U.S. Democratic Party Abroad 1972–76; Fellow American Acad. of Arts and Sciences 1979; Hon. LL.D. (Williams Coll.) 1981, (John Jay Coll. of Criminal Justice) 1983, (Claremont Coll.) 1987, (Kalamazoo Coll.) 1987. *Publications:* Taking Rights Seriously 1977, The Philosophy of Law (Ed.) 1977, A Matter of Principle 1985, Law's Empire 1986, Philosophical Issues in Senile Dementia 1987, A Bill of Rights for Britain 1990, Life's Dominion 1993, Freedom's Law 1996; articles in legal and philosophical journals. *Address:* 17 Chester Row, London, SW1W 9JF, England.

DWURNIK, Edward; Polish painter; b. 19 April 1943, Radzymin; m.; one d.; ed. Acad. of Fine Arts, Warsaw; over 150 one-man exhbns. including Warsaw 1971, 1974, 1975, 1977, 1980 (Norwid Prize), 1990, Toruń 1980, Lublin 1982, Wrocław 1987, Olsztyn 1988, Bydgoszcz 1997, Bytom 1997, exhbns. abroad: Darmstadt 1977, Moscow 1978, Goteborg 1981, Eindhoven 1985, Lindgen 1986, London 1987, 1991–92, Stuttgart 1994; numerous Polish and int. awards. *Leisure interests:* driving, travelling, opera, films. *Address:* ul. Podgorska 5, 02-921 Warsaw, Poland. *Telephone:* 42 98 79.

DYACHENKO, Tatyana Borisovna; Russian politician; b. 17 Jan. 1960, Sverdlovsk; d. of Pres. Boris Yeltsin (q.v.) and Naina Yeltsin; m. Valery Mikhailovich Okulov; two s.; ed. Moscow State Univ.; engineer Construction Bureau Salut 1982–94, Construction Bureau Larya Urula, Moscow 1994–95; mem. Boris Yeltsin Election Campaign 1996; counsellor to Pres. 1997–. *Leisure interest:* tourism. *Address:* Office of the President, Ipatyevsky per. 4/10, entr. 6, Moscow, Russia (Office). *Telephone:* (095) 206 5874 (Office).

DYADKOVA, Larissa; Russian singer; b. 9 March 1952, Zelenodolsk; m. Alexandre Kogan 1985; one d.; ed. Leningrad Conservatory class of J. Levando; soloist Mariinsky Theatre 1978–; toured with Mariinsky Theatre in European countries, guest soloist Metropolitan-Opera, La Scala, Communale Theatre, Florence, Berlin Opera, Arena de Verona, San Francisco Opera, New Israeli Opera; performs Verdi's Requiem in concerts, vocal series by Mussorgsky and Mahler, cantatas by Prokofiev; works with conductors Levine, Rostropovich, Mehta, Abbado, Temirkanov, Gergiev. *Address:* Mariinsky Theatre, Teatralnaya pl. 1, St. Petersburg, Russia (Office). *Telephone:* (812) 114-3039. *Fax:* (812) 114-3039.

DYAKOV, Dumitru; Moldovan politician and journalist, b. 10 Feb. 1952, Kargopole, Kurgan Region, Russia; m.; two d.; ed. Belarus State Univ.; Sec. Comsomol Cttee., Moldovan State TV and Radio; corresp., Komsomolskaya Pravda in Moldova –1976; on Comsomol Cen. Cttee., on Moldovan CP Cen. Cttee.; Head TASS Bureau in Romania 1989–93; Sec. Moldovan Embassy, Moscow 1993–94; M.P. 1994–; Chair. Parl. Comm. on Foreign Policy 1994–95; Deputy Speaker 1995–97, Speaker 1998–; f. Movt. for Democratic and Flourishing Moldova 1997. *Address:* Parliament Buildings, Stefan Chelmari prosp. 105, 277073 Chişinău, Moldova. *Telephone:* (373) 23 35 28 (Office).

DYBA, Karel, PH.D.; Czech politician and economist; b. 21 Oct. 1940, Prostějov; m. Blanka Kozlová 1969; one s. one d.; ed. Prague School of Econs. and Univ. of Alberta; teacher, Prague School of Econs.; later Research Fellow and Sr. Research Fellow, Inst. of Econs. and Inst. of Forecasting of Czechsolovak Acad. of Sciences; Dir. Econ. Inst. Czechoslovak Acad. of Sciences and Econ. Adviser to Fed. Govt. of Czechoslovakia; Pres. Czech Econ. Asscn.; Minister for Econ. Policy and Devt. of Czech Republic 1990–92; Minister of Economy Czech Repub. 1992–96; Chair. Cttee. for the State System of Information of Czech Govt. 1992–, Czech Econ. Soc. of Czechoslovak Acad. of Sciences; mem. Civic Democratic Party 1991–; mem. State Defence Council 1992–; Reader in Econs. 1992; econ. adviser to Prime Minister Václav Klaus 1997; now pvt. consultant; mem. Exec. Cttee. Int. Econ. Asscn, State Defence Council 1992. *Publications:* articles on Czechoslovak economy in int. journals; co-author of several books. *Leisure interests:* tennis, skiing. *Address:* Národní 37, 110 00 Prague 1, Czech Republic. *Telephone:* 242 37 303. *Fax:* 242 37 303.

DYBKJAER, Lone; Danish politician; b. 23 May 1940, Copenhagen; two d.; ed. Tech. Univ. of Denmark; Sec., Acad. of Tech. Sciences 1964–66, Medico-Tech. Cttee. 1966–70; Head Information Secr., Tech. Univ. of Denmark 1970–77; Adviser, Geotechnical Inst. 1978–79; mem. Folketing (Parl.) 1973–77, 1979–; Chair. Parl. Energy Policy Cttee. 1984–87, Parl. nine-mem. Cttee. on Tech. Bds. 1986–; Social Liberal Party Spokesperson on Energy, Labour Market and Environmental Questions 1987–88; Minister of the Environment 1988–90; M.E.P. 1994–. *Leisure interest:* tennis. *Address:* European Parliament, Centre Européen, Plateau de Kirchberg, 2929 Luxembourg; Christiansborg, 1240 Copenhagen K, Denmark.

DYER, Alexander Patrick, B.S., M.B.A.; American business executive; b. 30 Aug. 1932, Santa Rosa, Calif.; s. of John Dyer and late Amie M. Moore; m. Shirley Shine 1954; one s. (and one s. deceased); ed. U.S. Mil. Acad. and Harvard Business School; Exec. Vice-Pres. Air Products and Chemicals, BOC Group PLC 1987–89, Man. Dir. Gases and C.E.O. 1989–93, Deputy Chair. 1993–95, C.E.O. 1993–96; Deputy Chair. Bunzl PLC 1996– (Chair. 1993–96); Non-exec. Dir. AMEC PLC. *Leisure interests:* golf, skeet, antique collecting. *Address:* 1803 Apple Tree Lane, Bethlehem, PA 18105, U.S.A.

DYKA, Zbigniew; Polish politician and barrister; b. 5 Oct. 1928, Warsaw; m.; one d.; ed. Jagellonian Univ., Cracow; during Nazi occupation soldier of underground Grey Ranks of Polish Pathfinders' Union; barrister, Cracow 1952–; Adviser to Solidarity of Individual Farmers' Independent Self-governing Trade Union 1980–81; mem., Pres. Bar Council 1986–, Deputy Pres. 1989–92; mem. Christian Nat. Union (ZChN); Deputy to Sejm (Parl.) 1991–93; Minister of Justice, Attorney-Gen. 1992–93. *Address:* Naczelna Rada Adwokacka, ul. Swiętojerska 16, 00-202 Warsaw, Poland (Office) *Telephone:* 635-40-63.

DYKE, Greg, B.A.; British television executive; b. 20 May 1947; two s. two d.; ed. Univ. of York and Harvard Business School; man. trainee, Marks & Spencer; reporter on local paper; campaigner for Community Relations Council, Wandsworth; researcher, The London Programme, London Weekend Television (LWT), later founding producer, The Six O'Clock Show; joined TV-AM 1983; Dir. of Programmes, LWT 1987–91; Group Chief Exec. LWT (Holdings) PLC 1991–94; Chair. GMTV 1993–94; Chair. C.E.O. Pearson TV 1995–; Chair. Channel 5 Broadcasting 1997–; fmr. TVB Hong Kong; Dir. BSkyB 1995, Phoenix Pictures Inc., New York, Pearson PLC 1996 and others; Dir. (non-exec.) Manchester United 1997–; Trustee Science Museum 1996–, English Nat. Stadium Trust 1997–. *Address:* Pearson Television Ltd., 1 Stephen Street, London, W1P IPJ, England. *Telephone:* 0171-691 6000.

DYLAN, Bob; American composer and singer; b. Robert Zimmerman 24 May 1941, Duluth, Minn.; m. Sarah Lowndes (divorced 1978); four c. one adopted d.; ed. Univ. of Minnesota; best known for composition and interpretation of pop, country and folk music; self-taught on harmonica, guitar, piano, autoharp; performer numerous tours and concerts 1960–66, 1971, 1974, 1975, 1976, 1978–80, 1981; devised and popularized folk-rock 1965; f. new group The Travelling Wilburys 1988. *Numerous songs include:* Blowin' in the Wind, Don't Think Twice It's All Right, A Hard Rain's A-gonna Fall, She Belongs to Me, It's All over Now Baby Blue, The Times They Are A-changing, Just Like a Woman, I'll Be Your Baby Tonight, I Shall Be Released, Lay, Lady, Lay, If Not for You, Mr. Tambourine Man, Like a Rolling Stone, Simple Twist of Fate, Forever Young, Mozambique, Hurricane, Knockin' on Heaven's Door, Gotta Serve Somebody, etc.; albums include: Blonde on Blonde, The Freewheelin' Bob Dylan, Highway 61 Revisited, Nashville Skyline, New Morning, Blood on the Tracks, Desire, Slow Train Coming, Infidels, Empire Burlesque, Knocked out Loaded, Down in the Groove 1988, Dylan and the Dead (with Grateful Dead) 1989, Oh Mercy 1989, Blonde on Blonde, Under The Red Sky 1990, Vol. 3 (with Travelling Wilburys) 1990, The Bootleg Series 1990, Good as I Been to You 1992, World Gone Wrong 1993, Unplugged 1995, Time Out of Mind (Grammy Award 1998) 1998; has acted in films Eat the Document, Pat Garrett and Billy the Kid, Renaldo and Clara (also directed), Hearts of Fire 1986 and Concert for Bangladesh; Hon. D.Mus. (Princeton) 1970, Commdr. Ordre des Arts et des Lettres, named to Rock and Roll Hall of Fame 1988. *Publications:* Tarantula 1966, 1971, Writings and Drawings 1973, The Songs of Bob Dylan 1966–1975, Lyrics 1962–1985, Drawn Blank 1994; Highway 61 Revisited (interactive CD-ROM). *Address:* P.O. Box 870, New York, NY 10276; c/o Columbia Records, 550 Madison Avenue, New York, NY 10022, U.S.A.

DYSON, Freeman John, F.R.S.; American physicist; b. 15 Dec. 1923, Crowthorne, England; s. of late Sir George Dyson and Lady Mildred (Atkey) Dyson; m. 1st Verena Huber 1950 (divorced 1958); m. 2nd Imme Jung 1958; one s. five d.; ed. Cambridge and Cornell Univs; Fellow of Trinity Coll., Cambridge 1946; Warren Research Fellow, Birmingham Univ. 1949; Prof. of Physics, Cornell Univ. 1951–53; Prof., Inst. for Advanced Study, Princeton 1953–94, Prof. Emer. 1994–; Chair. Fed. of American Scientists 1962; mem. N.A.S. 1964–; Foreign Assoc. Acad. des Sciences, Paris 1989; Hon. D.Sc. (City Univ., U.K.) 1981 (Oxford) 1997; Gifford Lecturer, Aberdeen 1985; Heineman Prize, American Inst. of Physics 1965, Lorentz Medal, Royal Netherlands Acad. 1966, Hughes Medal, Royal Soc. 1968, Max Planck Medal, German Physical Soc. 1969, Harvey Prize, Israel Inst. of Tech. 1977, Wolf Prize (Israel) 1981, Matteucci Medal, Rome 1990, Fermi Award (U.S.A.) 1994. *Publications:* Disturbing the Universe 1979, Weapons and Hope 1984, Origins of Life 1986, Infinite in All Directions 1988, From Eros to Gaia 1992, Imagined Worlds 1997; papers in The Physical Review, Journal of Mathematical Physics, etc. *Address:* 105 Battle Road Circle, Princeton, NJ 08540, U.S.A.

DYSON, James, F.C.S.D., M.DES.; British designer; b. 2 May 1947; s. of Alec Dyson and Mary (née Bolton) Dyson; m. Deirdre Hindmarsh 1967; two s. one d.; ed. Gresham's School, Royal Coll. of Art; Dir. Rotork Marine 1970–74; Man. Dir. Kirk Dyson 1974–79; developed and designed Dyson Dual Cyclone vacuum cleaner 1979–93; f., Chair. Prototypes Ltd. 1979–; Dyson Appliances Ltd. 1992–; Chair. Bath Coll. of Higher Educ. 1990–92; mem. Design Council 1997–; Hon. D.Litt. (Staffordshire) 1996; Hon. D.Sc. (Oxford Brookes) 1997; numerous design awards and trophies. *Publications include:* Doing a Dyson 1996, Against the Odds (autobiog.) 1997. *Leisure interests:* running, garden design, music, fishing, cricket, tennis. *Address:* Kingsmead Mill, Little Somerford, Wilts., SN15 5JN, England. *Telephone:* (01666) 827203.

DYVIK, Helge Julius Jakhelln, DR.PHILOS.; Norwegian professor of general linguistics; b. 23 Dec. 1947, Bodø; s. of late Einar Dyvik and Harriet Dyvik (née Jakhelln); m. Eva Sætre 1973 (divorced 1996); one s. one d.; ed. Univ. of Bergen, Univ. of Durham, U.K.; Research Asst. (Old Norse), Univ. of Bergen 1974–75, lecturer 1976, Project Asst. (Old Norwegian syntax) 1976–81, Research Fellow (Vietnamese syntax project) 1981–83, Prof. of Gen. Linguistics 1983–; Pres. Nordic Asscn. of Linguists 1993–; Fridtjof Nansen Award for Eminent Research, Norwegian Acad. of Letters and Science 1987. *Publications:* Grammatikk og Empiri 1981, Categories and Functions in Vietnamese Classifier Constructions 1983, Semantic Mirrors 1998. *Leisure interests:* play reading, choral singing. *Address:* Department of Linguistics and Comparative Literature, Linguistic Studies Section, University of Bergen, Sydnespl. 7, 5007 Bergen (Office); Straumevn. 13, 5042 Bergen-Fjøsanger, Norway (Home).

DZASOKHOV, Aleksandr Sergeyevich, CAND.HIST.SC.; Russian politician; b. 3 April 1934, Ordzhonikidze, North-Ossetian A.S.S.R.; m. Farisa Borissovna 1959; two s.; ed. North Caucasian Mining-Metallurgical Inst. and CPSU Higher Party School; mem. CPSU 1957–91; First Sec. Ordzhonikidze Komsomol City Cttee. 1957–61; Sec. of U.S.S.R. Cttee. of Youth Orgs. 1961–64; leader of young Soviet specialists to Cuba 1964–65; First Sec., Pres. of U.S.S.R. Youth Orgs. 1965–67; Deputy Chair., Chair. of Soviet Cttee. for Solidarity with Countries of Asia and Africa 1965–86; U.S.S.R. Amb. to Syria 1986–88; First Sec. of North Ossetian CPSU Dist. Cttee. (obkom) 1988–90; U.S.S.R. People's Deputy 1989–91; Chair. Cttee. of U.S.S.R. Supreme Soviet on Int. Affairs 1990–91; mem., Sec. of Cen. Cttee. CPSU, mem. of CPSU Politburo 1990–91; People's Deputy of Russia, mem. Supreme Soviet of Russian Fed. 1992–93; Chair. Sub-Cttee. on Asia and the Pacific; mem. State Duma (Parl.) 1993–98; elected Pres. of Repub. of N. Ossetia (Alania) 1998–; Deputy Chair. Inter-Parl. Group of Russian Fed. 1993, Chair. 1996–; mem. Acad. of Creative Endeavours. *Publications:* several books on problems of post-colonialism in third-world countries. *Address:* House of Soviets, Office of the President, Svobody pl. 1, Vladikavkaz; Council of the Russian Federation, Bolshaya Dmitrovka 26, 103426 Moscow, Russia. *Telephone:* (8672) 53-35-24 (Vladikavkaz); (095) 292-1150 (Moscow).

DZHANIBEKOV, Maj.-Gen. Vladimir Aleksandrovich; Russian cosmonaut (retd.); b. 13 May 1942, Iskander, Tashkent Region, Uzbekistan; m. Lilya Munirovna Dzhanibekova; two d.; mem. CPSU 1970–91; ed. Yeisk High Mil. Aviation School; mil. pilot-instr. 1965–70; mem. Cosmonauts' team 1970–; 5 space flights including Soviet-Mongolian on spaceship Salut 6-Soyuz 39; Commdr. Cosmonauts' team Yuriy Gagarin Centre of Cosmonauts' Training 1985–88; Head Dept. of Theoretical and Research Educ. of Cosmonauts 1988–98; Hero of Soviet Union 1978, 1981; Hero of Mongolian Repub. 1981; Officier Légion d'honneur 1982. *Address:* Yuriy Gagarin Centre for Cosmonauts' Training, Zvezdny Gorodok, Moscow Region, Russia. *Telephone:* (095) 526-28-70.

DZHELEPOV, Venedikt Petrovich; Russian nuclear physicist; b. 12 April 1913, Moscow; s. of Petr Dzhelepov and Nadezhda Ivanova; m. Tatiana Zinovieva 1941; ed. Leningrad Polytech. Inst; Soviet Army Lieut. 1938–41; mem. CPSU 1949–91; mem. of staff at U.S.S.R. Acad. of Sciences Inst. of Physics and Tech. 1941–43; at Inst. of Atomic Energy 1943–48; Deputy Dir. of U.S.S.R. Acad. of Sciences Inst. of Nuclear Problems 1948–56; Dir. of Lab. for Nuclear Problems at Jt. Inst. for Nuclear Research, Dubna 1956–88, Hon. Dir. 1989–; work in accelerator physics and tech., work on high energy particle physics and muon catalyzed fusion on applications of nuclear physics to medicine (proton therapy for cancer 1967–); Corresp. mem. of U.S.S.R. (now Russian) Acad. of Sciences 1966–; Dr. h.c. (Univs. in Germany and Slovakia); U.S.S.R. State Prize 1951, 1953, Kurchatov Gold Medal, Order of Lenin, Orders of Red Banner of Labour, Order of October Revolution and many other awards. *Leisure interest:* travelling. *Address:* Joint Institute for Nuclear Research, 141980 Dubna, Russia. *Telephone:* 926-22-20 (Office); 926-22-73 (Home, Dubna); 196-07-16 (Home, Moscow).

DZHEMILEV, Mustafa (Abdul-Dzhemil); Ukrainian/Crimean Tatar activist; b. 1943; suffered continual harrassment from Soviet authorities, when he attempted to form a youth movt. in Tashkent 1962–; subsequently, imprisonment or exile for activity: 1966–67, 1969–72, 1974–75, 1975–77, 1979–82, 1983–86; continued to organise Crimean Tatar protest actions in Cen. Asia and Moscow; returned to Crimea 1989; Chair. Crimean Tatar Majlis 1991–; Pres. Crimea Foundation 1991–; mem. Ukrainian Parl. 1998–. *Address:* Parliament Buildings, 2 Simferopol Street, Crimea, Ukraine.

DZHIGARKHANIAN, Armen Borisovich; Armenian/Russian stage and film actor; b. 3 Oct. 1935, Yerevan; m. Tatiana Vlasova 1967; one s.; ed. Yerevan Theatre Inst.; actor with Stanislavsky Russian Drama Theatre in Yerevan 1955–67; with Moscow Lenin Komsomol Theatre 1967–69, with Mayakovsky Theatre 1969–; Armenian S.S.R. State Prize 1975, 1979; R.S.F.S.R. People's Artist 1973; U.S.S.R. People's Artist 1985. *Roles include:* Levinson in Fadeev's Thunder, Stanley in Tennessee Williams' Streetcar Named Desire, Socrates and Nero in Radzinsky's Chats with Socrates and the Theatre in the time of Nero and Seneca, Big Daddy in Tennessee Williams' Cat on a Hot Tin Roof, Nelson in Rattigan's Vivat Regina!; has also starred in a number of films. *Leisure interests:* reading, listening to classical music, playing with pet Siamese cat. *Address:* 37 Starokonysheny per., Apt. 9, 121002 Moscow, Russia. *Telephone:* 203-30-79.

DZIUBA, Andrzej Franciszek, D.D.; Polish ecclesiastic and university professor; b. 10 Oct. 1950, Pleszew; s. of Stanisław Dziuba and Ludwika Szlachciak; ed. Primatial Priests' Seminary, Gniezno, Pontifical Theological Faculty, Poznań, Catholic Univ. Lublin, Acad. Alfonsiana, Rome and Univ. Italiana per Stranieri, Perugia; ordained priest, Gniezno 1975; asst. parish priest, Łobżenica 1975–76; studies in Lublin 1976–79, Rome 1979–81; Sec. to Primate of Poland 1981–98, Dir. Secr. 1984–98; asst. parish priest, St. Martin's Church, Warsaw 1981–98, St. Barbara's Church, Warsaw 1998–; Prof. Catholic Univ. Lublin 1989–, Acad. of Catholic Theology, Warsaw 1995–, Primatial Priest's Seminary, Gniezmo 1998–; Hon. Chaplain to His Holiness Pope John Paul II 1990, Prelate 1996; Primate of Poland Foundation in G.B. 1991; Hon. Conventual Chaplain of Order of Malta 1998–; Kt. Commdr. of Equestrian Order of Holy Sepulchre of Jerusalem 1996, Cross with Gold Star of Merit of Holy Sepulchre of Jerusalem 1996. *Publications:* Mikołaj z Mościsk, teolog moralista XVII w. 1985, Jan Azor, teolog-moralista 1988, Informator Katoliki 89/90 1990, Droga Krzyżowa 1991, Różaniec święty 1992, Kościół katolicki w Polsce. Informator 1993, Jezus nam przebacza. Przygotowanie do sakramentu pojednania 1994, Matka Boża z Guadalupe 1995, Kościół katolicki w Polsce. Informator 1995, Orędzie moralne Jezusa Chrystusa 1996 Dynamika wiary 1997, Kościół katolicki w Polsce. Informator 1997, Droge krzyżowa 1998, biography of Cardinal Józef Glemp 1998; numerous articles on theological ethics, church history, Catholic social sciences. *Address:* ul. Nowogrodzka 49/11, 00-695 Warsaw, Poland. *Telephone:* 621 35 10. *Fax:* 635 87 45.

DZUMAGULOV, Apas Dzumagulovich; Kyrgyzstan politician; b. 19 Sept. 1934, Arashan, Kyrgyz S.S.R., m.; two. s.; ed. Moscow Gubkin Inst. of Oil; mem. CPSU 1962–91; worked at Complex S., Geological Expedition U.S.S.R. Acad. of Sciences 1958–59; sr. geologist oil field Changar-Tash, Head. Cen. Research Lab., Chief Geologist Drilling Div., Chief Eng. Oil Co. Kyrghizneft Osh District 1959–73; Head Industrial-Transport Div. Cen. Cttee. CP of Kyrgyz S.S.R. 1973–79; Sec. Cen. Cttee. CP of Kirgyzia 1979–85; First Sec. Issyk-Kul Dist. Cttee. 1985–86; Chair. Council of Ministers Kyrgyz S.S.R. 1986–91; Chair. Org. Cttee., then Chair. Regional Soviet of Deputies, Head of Admin. Chuysk Region 1991–93; Deputy to U.S.S.R. Supreme Soviet 1984–89; U.S.S.R. People's Deputy 1989–91; People's Deputy of Kyrgyzstan; mem. Revision Comm. CPSU 1986–91; Prime Minister of Kyrgyz Repub. 1993–97.

DZURINDA, Mikuláš, PH.D.; Slovak politician; b. 4 Feb. 1955, Spišský Štvrtok; m.; two c.; ed. Univ of Transport and Communications, Žilina, econ. researcher Transport Research Inst., Žilina 1979–80; information tech. officer Czechoslovak Railways Regional Directorate, Bratislava 1980–88, head of Automated Control Systems Dept. 1988–91; Deputy Minister of Transport and Postal Service of Slovak Repub. 1991–92, 1994; Vice-Chair. for Econ. Christian Democratic Movt. 1993–; spokesman Slovak Democratic Coalition 1997–98, Chair. 1998–; Premier Govt. of Slovak Repub. 1998–; mem. Nat. Council of Slovak Repub. (NCSR) 1992–. *Leisure interests:* family, sport. *Address:* Office of the Government of the Slovak Republic, Nám. Slobody 1, 813 70 Bratislava 1, Slovakia. *Telephone:* (7) 534-1111.

DZYUBA, Ivan Mykhailovych; Ukrainian literary critic; b. 26 July 1931, Mykolaivka, Ukraine; s. of Mykhailo Dzyuba and Olga Dzyuba; m. Marta Lenets 1963; one d.; ed. Donetsk Pedagogical Inst., research at Shevchenko Inst. of Literature; Ed. various journals published by Ukrainian State Publishing House; published An Ordinary Man or a Petit-Bourgeois as well as numerous samizdat articles in 1960s; expelled from Writers' Union 1972 after publication of Internationalism or Russification? (numerous edns.); arrested 1972, sentenced to 5 years' imprisonment 1973; recanted and released Nov. 1973; Writers' Union membership restored 1980s; mem. Ukrainian Acad. of Sciences 1992–; Minister of Culture Dec. 1992–94; Sr. Researcher, T. Shevchenko Inst. of Literature 1994–; Ed.-in-Chief Sučasnist (magazine); Laureate Shewtchenko's Award 1991. *Publications:* 16 books including Between Politics and Literature 1998 and numerous articles on history and devt. of Ukrainian literature and writers of former U.S.S.R. *Leisure interests:* gardening, mushrooming. *Address:* Antonova str. 7, Apt. 60, 252186 Kiev, Ukraine. *Telephone:* 276-10-19.

E

EABORN, Colin, F.R.S.; British scientist and professor of chemistry; b. 15 March 1923, Cheshire; s. of Tom Stanley Eaborn and Caroline Eaborn; m. Joyce Thomas 1949; ed. Ruabon Grammar School, Clwyd, Univ. Coll. of N. Wales, Bangor; worked at Univ. of Leicester 1947–62 (Asst. Lecturer 1947–50, Lecturer 1950–57, Reader in Chem. 1957–62); at Univ. of Sussex 1962–, Prof. of Chem. 1962–, Dean of School of Molecular Sciences 1964–68, 1978–79, Pro-Vice Chancellor (Science) 1968–73; Research Assoc., Univ. of Calif. at Los Angeles 1950–51; Robert A. Welch Visiting Scholar, Rice Univ., Tex. 1961–62, Erskine Fellow, Univ. of Canterbury, N.Z. 1965; Distinguished Prof. of Chem., New Mexico State Univ. 1973, Commonwealth Fellow and Visiting Prof. of Chem., Univ. of Victoria, B.C., Canada 1976, Riccoboni Lecture, Univ. of Padua 1977; Gilman Lecturer, Iowa State Univ. 1978; Hon. Sec., Chemical Soc. 1964–71; mem. Council Royal Soc. 1978–80, 1988–89; Regional Ed., Journal of Organometallic Chem. 1963–95; Hon. D.Sc. (Sussex) 1990; F. S. Kipping Award for Organosilicon Chem. (American Chem. Soc.) 1964, Award for Organometallic Chem. 1974, Ingold Medal 1976, Award for Main Group Chemistry 1989 (all Royal Soc. of Chem.). *Publications:* Organosilicon Compounds 1960, The Synthesis and Reactions of the Carbon-Silicon Bond (in Organometallic Compounds of the Group IV Elements, Pt. 1) 1968, over 500 research papers in scientific journals. *Address:* School of Chemistry, Physics and Environmental Science, University of Sussex, Brighton, BN1 9QJ, England (Office). *Telephone:* (01273) 606755. *Fax:* (01273) 677196.

EAGLEBURGER, Lawrence Sidney, M.S.; American government official; b. 1 Aug. 1930, Milwaukee, Wis.; s. of late Dr. Leon S. and Helen M. Eagleburger; m. Marlene Ann Heinemann 1966; three s.; ed. Univ. of Wisconsin; joined U.S. foreign service 1957; Third Sec., Tegucigalpa, Honduras 1957–59; Dept. of State 1959–62; Second Sec., Belgrade, Yugoslavia 1962–65; Dept. of State 1965–66; mem. Nat. Security Council staff 1966–67; Special Asst. to Under-Sec. of State 1967–68; Exec. Asst. to Asst. to Pres. for Nat. Security affairs 1969; Politicial Adviser, U.S. Mission to NATO 1969–71; Dept. Asst. Sec. of Defense, Internal Security Affairs 1971–72, Acting Asst. Sec. of Defense, Internal Security Affairs 1973, Exec. Asst. to Sec. of State 1973–77; Deputy Asst. to Pres. for Nat. Security Operations 1973; Deputy Under-Sec. of State for Man., Exec. Asst. to Sec. of State 1975–77; Amb. to Yugoslavia 1977–81; Asst. Sec. of State for European Affairs 1981–82, Under-Sec. of State for Political Affairs 1982–84; Deputy Sec. of State 1989–92 (Envoy to Israel during Gulf Conflict 1991); Acting Sec. of State Aug.–Dec. 1992, Sec. of State Dec. 1992–Jan. 1993; Prof. (part-time) Univ. of S. Carolina 1984 (Distinguished Visiting Prof. of Int. Studies 1984), Univ. of Va. (part-time) 1993–; Pres. Kissinger Assocs. Inc. July 1984–; mem. Bd. ITT Corpn. 1984–, Josephson Int. Mutual Life Insurance Co. of N.Y., LBS Bank; Hon. LL.D. (South Carolina) 1985, (George Washington Univ.) 1986; President's Award for Distinguished Civil Service, Dept. of Defence Distinguished Service Medal; Hon. K.B.E. 1995. *Address:* c/o University of Virginia, University Station, P.O. Box 9011, Charlottesville, VA 22906, U.S.A.

EAGLETON, Terence Francis, PH.D.; British professor of English literature; b. 22 Feb. 1943; s. of Francis Paul Eagleton and Rosaleen Riley; m. Elizabeth Rosemary Galpin 1966; two s.; ed. Trinity Coll., Cambridge; Fellow in English Jesus Coll., Cambridge 1964–69; Tutorial Fellow Wadham Coll., Oxford 1969–89; lecturer in Critical Theory and Fellow of Linacre Coll., Oxford 1989–92; Thomas Warton Prof. of English Literature and Fellow of St. Catherine's Coll., Oxford Oct. 1992–; Hon. D.Litt. (Salford). *Publications:* Criticism and Ideology 1976, Marxism and Literary Criticism 1976, Literary Theory: an Introduction 1983, The Function of Criticism 1984, The Ideology of the Aesthetic 1990, The Crisis of Contemporary Culture 1993, Heathcliff and the Great Hunger 1995, The Illusions of Postmodernism 1996, Literary Theory 1996, Crazy John and the Bishop, and other Essays on Irish Culture 1998. *Leisure interest:* Irish music. *Address:* St. Catherine's College, Oxford, OX1 3UJ, England. *Telephone:* (01865) 271700.

EAGLETON, Thomas Francis, LL.B.; American politician and lawyer; b. 4 Sept. 1929; ed. Amherst Coll. and Harvard Univ.; admitted to Mo. Bar 1953; pvt. law practice, St. Louis 1953–56; Circuit Attorney, St. Louis 1957–60; Attorney-Gen., State of Mo. 1961–65, Lieut.-Gov. 1965–68; Senator from Missouri 1969–87; selected as candidate for Vice-Presidency but later resigned 1972; Democrat.

EAGLING, Wayne John; Canadian ballet dancer and choreographer; s. of Eddie Eagling and Thelma Eagling; ed. P. Ramsey Studio of Dance Arts, Royal Ballet School; Sr. Prin. Royal Ballet 1975–91; Artistic Dir. Dutch Nat. Ballet 1991–; has danced lead roles in Sleeping Beauty, Swan Lake, Cinderella and other major classics; created roles include: Young Boy in Triad, Solo Boy in Gloria, Ariel in The Tempest, Woyzeck in Different Drummer; choreographed The Hunting of the Snark and Frankenstein, The Modern Prometheus, Ruins of Time 1993, Symphony in Waves 1994, Alma Mahler (for La Scala, Milan) 1994, Duet 1995, Lost Touch 1995, Nutcracker and Mouseking (with Toer Van Schayk) 1996, The Last Emperor (for Hong Kong Ballet) 1998. *Publication:* The Company We Keep (with Ross MacGibbon and Robert Jude) 1981. *Leisure interests:* golf, scuba diving, tennis. *Address:* Dutch National Ballet, Het Muziektheater, Waterlooplein 22, 1011 PG Amsterdam; Postbus 16486, 1001 RN Amsterdam, Netherlands. *Telephone:* (20) 551 8138. *Fax:* (20) 551 8070.

EAMES, Baron (Life Peer), cr. 1995, of Armagh in the County of Armagh; **Most Rev. Robert Henry Alexander Eames,** PH.D.; British ecclesiastic; b. 27 April 1937; s. of William E. Eames and Mary E. T. Eames; m. Ann C. Daly 1966; two s.; ed. Methodist Coll., Belfast, Queen's Univ., Belfast and Trinity Coll., Dublin; Research Scholar and Tutor, Faculty of Laws, Queen's Univ., Belfast 1960–63; Curate Asst., Bangor Parish Church 1963–66; Rector, St. Dorothea's, Belfast 1966–74; Examining Chaplain to Bishop of Down 1973; Rector, St. Mark's, Dunelda 1974–75; Bishop of Derry and Raphoe 1975–80; Bishop of Down and Dromore 1980–86; Archbishop of Armagh and Primate of All Ireland 1986–; Select Preacher, Oxford Univ. 1986–87, Cambridge Univ. 1989; Irish Repub., Anglican Consultative Council 1984, mem. Standing Cttee. 1985; Chair. Archbishop of Canterbury's Comm. on Communion and Women in the Episcopate 1988–, Comm. on Inter-Anglican Relations 1988–, Anglican Int. Doctrinal Comm. (USA) 1991; Gov. Church Army 1985–; Hon. LL.D. (Queen's Univ. of Belfast) 1989, (Trinity Coll. Dublin) 1992; Dr. h.c. (Cambridge) 1994; Hon. LL.D. (Lancaster) 1994. *Publications:* A Form of Worship for Teenagers 1965, The Quiet Revolution—Irish Disestablishment 1970, Through Suffering 1973, Thinking through Lent 1978, Through Lent 1984, Chains to be Broken 1992 and contributions to New Divinity, Irish Legal Quarterly, Criminal Law Review, Northern Ireland Legal Quarterly, Univ. Review and The Furrow. *Address:* The See House, Cathedral Close, Armagh, BT61 7EE, Northern Ireland.

EANES, Gen. António dos Santos Ramalho; Portuguese politician and army officer; b. 25 Jan. 1935, Alcains; s. of Manuel dos Santos Eanes and Maria do Rosario Ramalho; m. Maria Manuela Duarte Neto Portugal 1970; two s.; ed. High School, Castelo Branco, Higher Inst. of Applied Psychology, Lisbon Faculty of Law; enlisted in Army School 1953; Commissioned to Portuguese India 1958–60, Macau, Mozambique 1962–64, Operations Officer of Light Infantry Battalion, Mozambique 1966–67, Information Officer, Portuguese Guinea (Guinea-Bissau) 1969–73, Angola 1973–74; Physical Education Instructor, Mil. Acad. 1968; Dir. of Dept. of Cultural and Recreational Affairs 1973; rank of Second Lieut. 1957, Lieut. 1959, Capt. 1961, Major 1970, Gen. 1978; involved in leadership of mil. movements finally contesting mil. apparatus and colonial wars 1968–74; after April Revolution named to first 'Ad-hoc' Cttee. for mass media June 1974; Dir. of Programmes of Portuguese TV June-Sept. 1974, Chair. of Bd. of Dirs. of TV co., resigned after accusation of 'probable implication' in abortive counter-coup March 1975, cleared after inquiry; rank of Lieut.-Col.; mem. Cttee. restructuring 5th Div., Gen. Staff Armed Forces; Army Chief of Staff (with temporary rank of Gen.) 1975–76; mem. of Mil. Cttee. of Council of Revolution; responsible for Constitutional Law approved Dec. 1975; Col. 1976; Pres. of Portugal 1976–86; Chair. of Council of Revolution; C.-in-C. of Armed Forces 1976–80, 1980–81; Leader, Portuguese Democratic Renewal Party 1986–87; mem. Council of State; War Cross 2nd class, Silver Medal for Distinguished Services with Palm, Silver Medal for Exemplary Behaviour, Commemorative Medal of the Portuguese Armed Forces, Degree of Knight of Mil. Order of Avis. *Address:* c/o Partido Renovador Democrático, Travessa do Fala Só 9, 1200 Lisbon, Portugal. *Telephone:* 323997.

EASON, Henry, C.B.E., J.P., B.COM.; British banking administrator; b. 12 April 1910, Middlesbrough; s. of late H. and F.J. Eason; m. Florence Isobel Stevenson 1939 (died 1992); one s. two d.; ed. Yarm and King's Coll., Univ. of Durham; Barrister, Gray's Inn; Lloyds Bank Ltd. until 1939; R.A.F. (Wing Commdr.), Second World War; Sec.-Gen. Inst. of Bankers 1959–71, Vice-Pres. 1969–75, Hon. Fellow 1971. *Leisure interests:* golf, travel, reading. *Address:* 12 Redgate Drive, Hayes Common, Bromley, Kent, BR2 7BT, England.

EAST, Paul; New Zealand politician and lawyer; b. 1946, Opotiki; m.; three c.; ed. Univ. of Virginia School of Law; law clerk, Morpeth Gould & Co., Auckland 1968–70; partner, East Brewster Solicitors, Rotorua 1974–; fmr. Rotorua City Councillor and Deputy Mayor; Nat. Party M.P. for Rotorua 1978–96; Attorney-Gen., Minister responsible for Serious Fraud Office and Audit Dept. 1990–97, Leader of the House 1990–93, Minister of Crown Health Enterprises 1991–96, for Defence and War Pensions 1996–97. *Address:* 23 Sophia Street, Rotorua, New Zealand.

EASTCOTT, Harry Hubert Grayson, M.S., F.R.C.S., F.R.C.O.G.; British surgeon; b. 17 Oct. 1917, Montreal, Canada; s. of Henry George Eastcott and Gladys (née Tozer) Eastcott; m. Doreen Joy Mittell 1941; four d.; ed. Latymer School, London and Medical Schools at St. Mary's Hosp., London, Middlesex Hosp., London and Harvard; jr. resident appointments 1941–43; Surgeon Lieut. R.N.V.R. 1944–46; Sr. Surgical Registrar St. Mary's Hosp., London 1947–50, Asst. Dir. Surgical Unit of Medical School 1950–54, Consultant Surgeon 1955–82, Emer. 1982–; Consultant Surgeon Royal Masonic Hosp., London 1964–80; King Edward VII Hosp. for Officers, London 1965–87; in Surgery and Vascular Surgery R.N. 1957–82; Pres. Medical Soc., London 1976 (Sec. 1963, Trustee 1987), Section of Surgery, Royal Soc. of Medicine 1977 (Sec. 1963), United Services Section 1980–82, Int. Vascular Symposium,

London 1981; Sr. Vice-Pres. Royal Coll. of Surgeons 1982 (mem. Ct. of Examiners 1964–70, mem. Council 1971–83, Jr. Vice-Pres. 1981–83, mem. Court of Patrons 1997); fmr. Examiner in Surgery Univs. of London, Cambridge, Lagos and Queen's, Belfast; Hunterian Professorship R.C.S. 1953; Editorial Sec. British Journal of Surgery 1972–78; Hon. mem. Soc. for Vascular Surgery, U.S.A. 1974, Purkinje Soc., Czechoslovakia 1984, Int. Union of Angiology 1995, European Soc. for Vascular Surgery 1995; Hon. mem. and Hippocratic Orator Hellenic Medical Soc. 1986; Hon. F.A.C.S. 1977, Hon. F.R.A.C.S. 1978, Hon Fellow American Surgical Asscn. 1981, Int. Union of Angiology 1995, European Soc. for Vascular Surgery 1995; several memorial lectures; Fothergillian Gold Medal (Medical Soc. of London) 1974, Cecil Joll Prize (Royal Coll. of Surgeons) 1983, Galen Medal of Worshipful Soc. of Apothecaries 1993. *Publications:* Arterial Surgery 1969, 1973, 1993, A Colour Atlas of Operations upon the Internal Carotid Artery 1984, contrib. to Lancet. *Leisure interests:* music, travel and aeronautics. *Address:* 47 Chiltern Court, Baker Street, London, NW1 5SP, England. *Telephone:* 0171-935 2020. *Fax:* 0170-486 4084.

EASTMAN, Dean Eric, PH.D.; American physicist, science policy consultant, and data processing executive; b. 21 Jan. 1940, Oxford, Wis.; m. Ella Mae Staley 1979; Research Staff mem. IBM, Yorktown Heights, N.Y. 1963–74, Man. Surface Physics and Photo-emission 1971–82, Dir. Advanced Packaging Tech. Lab. and Sr. Man. III-V Semi-conductor Packaging Tech. & Systems Dept. and GaAs Devices and Tech. Dept. 1982–85, STD Dir. of Devt. and Product Assurance 1985–86, IBM Research Vice-Pres. of System Tech. and Science 1986–94, IBM Dir. Hardware Devt. Re-eng. 1994–95, IBM Server Group Vice-Pres. Devt. Re-eng. and Tech. Strategy 1996–98; Prof. of Physics Univ. of Chicago 1996–; Govt. Adviser to numerous science orgs.; Fellow American Physical Soc.; mem. N.A.S., Nat. Acad. of Eng.; IBM Fellow 1974–; APS Oliver E. Buckley Prize 1980. *Publications:* numerous articles on solid state physics in professional journals. *Address:* Department of Physics, University of Chicago, 5801 S. Ellis Avenue, Chicago, IL 60637 (Office); 806 Pines Bridge Road, Ossining, NY 10562, U.S.A. (Home).

EASTMAN, Ernest, M.I.A.; Liberian politician and diplomatist; b. 27 March 1930, Monrovia; s. of H. Nathan Eastman and Adeliue Payne; m. Salma Mohammedali; four s. five d.; ed. Coll. of West Africa, Oberlin Coll., Ohio, Columbia Univ., New York; Dir. Bureau of Afro-Asian Affairs (Dept. of State) 1957–64; Under-Sec. of State for Admin. 1964–67; Under Sec. of State 1968–72; Amb. to East Africa (Kenya, Lesotho, Madagascar, Tanzania, Uganda, Zambia) 1972–74; Amb. to the Far East (Japan, Repub. of Korea, Democratic People's Repub. of Korea, Philippines, Indonesia, India) 1974–77; Sec.-Gen. Mano River Union (Economic and Customs Union for the Repubs. of Liberia, Sierra Leone and Guinea) 1977–83; Minister of Foreign Affairs 1983–85; mem. special missions to the Presidents of Dahomey, Niger, Guinea, Ivory Coast, Gambia, and U.S.A.; mem. official del. to several int. confs. of the O.A.U., U.N. and Non-Aligned Movement; several decorations including Knight Great Band, Humane Order of African Redemption, several European and African decorations. *Publications:* A History of the State of Maryland in Liberia 1957, many newspaper articles on international affairs. *Address:* c/o Ministry of Foreign Affairs, P.O.B. 9002, Monrovia, Liberia.

EASTMAN, John; American lawyer; b. 1940, New York; s. of late Lee Eastman; brother-in-law of Paul McCartney (q.v.); m. Jodie Eastman; one s. one d.; ed. Stanford Univ. and Univ. of New York; worked for Senate Commerce Cttee. 1963; Office of U.S. Attorney, New York; took part in Robert Kennedy's 1968 presidential election campaign; with father founded Eastman & Eastman (law firm); specializes in contract and copyright law; represents many leading showbusiness and media personalities. *Leisure interests:* collecting pictures, 19th-century English literature.

EASTON, David, B.A., PH.D., F.R.S.C.; professor of political science; b. 24 June 1917, Toronto; s. of Albert Easton and Mary Easton; m. Sylvia Johnstone 1942; one s.; ed. Univ. of Toronto and Harvard Univ.; Teaching Fellow Dept. of Govt. Harvard Univ. 1944–47; Asst. Prof. Dept. of Political Science Univ. of Chicago 1947–53, Assoc. Prof. 1953–55, Prof. 1955–, Andrew MacLeish Distinguished Service Prof. 1969–82, Prof. Emer. 1982–; Sir Edward Peacock Prof. of Political Science Queen's Univ., Kingston, Ont. 1971–80; Distinguished Prof. of Political Science Univ. of Calif., Irvine 1981–; Pres. American Political Science Asscn. 1968–69; Int. Cttee. on Social Science Documentation 1969–71; Chair. Bd. of Trustees Acad. of Ind. Scholars 1979–81; Co-Chair. Western Center, American Acad. of Arts and Sciences 1984–90, Vice-Pres. of Acad. 1984–90; Fellow Center for Advanced Study in the Behavioral Sciences, Stanford 1957–58, American Acad. of Arts and Sciences 1962–; Ford Prof. of Governmental Affairs 1960–61; Hon. LL.D. (McMaster) 1970, (Kalamazoo) 1972. *Publications:* The Political System: An Inquiry into the State of Political Science 1953, A Framework for Political Analysis 1965, A Systems Analysis of Political Life 1965, Varieties of Political Theory (Ed.) 1966, Children in the Political System: Origins of Political Legitimacy (with J. Dennis) 1969, The Analysis of Political Structure 1990, Divided Knowledge: Across Disciplines, Across Cultures (Co-Ed.) 1991, The Development of Political Science (Ed. with others) 1991, Regime and Discipline (Ed. with others) 1995, plus several reports of educ. cttees. chaired by him. *Address:* University of California, School of Social Sciences, Irvine, CA 92697, U.S.A. *Telephone:* (949) 856-6132. *Fax:* (949) 856-8762; (949) 854-5180.

EASTON, Sheena; British singer; b. 27 April 1959, Bellshill; ed. Royal Scottish Acad. of Music and Drama; career launched by appearance on TV show The Big Time; has collaborated with Prince (q.v.); Grammy Award for Best New Artist 1981. *Songs include:* 9 to 5, Modern Girl, For Your Eyes Only (theme of James Bond film), Sugar Walls, U Got the Look (with Prince). *Albums include:* Take My Time 1981, You Could Have Been with Me 1981, Madness, Money and Music 1982, Best Kept Secret 1983, A Private Heaven 1984, The Lover in Me 1988, Greatest Hits (jtly.) 1989, Me gustas tal como eres (Grammy Award for Mexican-American Performance) 1984. *TV appearance:* Miami Vice (series). *Musical:* Man of La Mancha. *Address:* c/o Harriet Wasserman Management, 5954 Wilkinson Avenue, N. Hollywood, CA 91607, U.S.A.

EASTWICK-FIELD, Elizabeth, F.R.I.B.A.; British architect; b. 21 Nov. 1919, London; d. of Philip Gee and Georgia Urban Smith; m. John Eastwick Field 1942; three s. one d.; ed. pvtly. Hampstead in London, Schule der Angewandte Kunst, Munich, Cen. School of Arts and Crafts, London and Univ. Coll. London Bartlett School of Architecture; lecturer in sciography, Bartlett School of Architecture 1940–41; freelance architectural design and draughting 1947–54; partner, Stillman and Eastwick-Field, architects 1954–86, consultant 1986–; recipient of several architectural awards; illustrator of various architectural books and papers. *Leisure interests:* landscape gardening and horticulture; video-filming. *Address:* Low Farm, Low Road, Denham, Eye, Suffolk, IP21 5ET, England.

EASTWOOD, Clint; American actor and film director; b. 31 May 1930, San Francisco; s. of Clinton and Ruth Eastwood; m. 1st Maggie Johnson 1953 (divorced); one s. one d.; one d. by Frances Fisher 1993; m. 2nd Dina Ruiz 1996; one d.; ed. Los Angeles City Coll.; worked as lumberjack, Ore.; army service; appeared in TV series Rawhide 1959–65; owner Malpaso Productions 1969–; Co-Chair. UNESCO Campaign to protect the world's film heritage; mem. Nat. Arts Council 1973; Mayor of Carmel 1986–88; Acad. Award for Best Film and Best Dir. for The Unforgiven, 1993; Fellow B.F.I. 1993; Irving G. Thalberg Award 1995; Légion d'honneur, Commdr. Ordre des Arts et des lettres, American Film Inst.'s Life Achievement Award 1996. *Films appeared in include:* Revenge of the Creature 1955, Francis in the Navy 1955, Lady Godiva 1955, Tarantula 1955, Never Say Goodbye 1956, The First Travelling Saleslady 1956, Star in the Dust 1956, Escapade in Japan 1957, Ambush at Cimarron Pass 1958, Lafayette Escadrille 1958, A Fistful of Dollars 1964, For a Few Dollars More 1965, The Good, the Bad and the Ugly 1966, The Witches 1967, Hang 'Em High 1968, Coogan's Bluff 1968, Where Eagles Dare 1969, Paint Your Wagon 1969, Kelly's Heroes 1970, Two Mules for Sister Sara 1970, The Beguiled 1971, Play Misty for Me (also dir.) 1971, Dirty Harry 1971, Joe Kidd 1972, High Plains Drifter (also dir.) 1973, Magnum Force 1973, Thunderbolt and Lightfoot 1974, The Eiger Sanction (also dir.) 1975, The Outlaw Josey Wales (also dir.) 1976, The Enforcer 1976, The Gauntlet (also dir.) 1978, Every Which Way But Loose 1978, Escape from Alcatraz 1979, Bronco Billy (also dir.) 1980, Any Which Way You Can 1980, Firefox (also dir.) 1982, Honky Tonk Man (also dir.) 1982, Sudden Impact (also dir.) 1983, Tightrope 1984, City Heat 1984, Pale Rider 1985 (also dir.), Heartbreak Ridge 1986 (also dir.), dir. film Breezy 1973, Bird 1988 (Golden Globe Award for Best Dir. 1989), The Dead Pool 1988, Pink Cadillac 1989, White Hunter, Black Heart (also dir.) 1989, The Rookie (also dir.) 1990, Unforgiven (also dir.) 1992, In the Line of Fire 1993, A Perfect World (also dir.) 1993, The Bridges of Madison County (also dir., producer) 1995, The Stars Fell on Henrietta (co-producer only), Absolute Power (also dir.) 1997, True Crime 1998; dir. Midnight in the Garden of Good and Evil 1997. *Address:* c/o William Morris Agency, 151 S. El Camino Drive, Beverly Hills, CA 90212, U.S.A.

EATON, Fredrik Stefan, O.C., B.A., LL.D.; Canadian diplomatist and business executive; b. 26 June 1938, Toronto; s. of late John David Eaton and Signy Hildur Stephenson; m. Catherine Martin 1962; one s. one d.; ed. New Brunswick Univ.; joined The T. Eaton Co. Ltd. and held various positions in Victoria, London, Toronto 1962–67, Dir. 1967–69, Chair., Pres., C.E.O. 1977–88, Chair. 1988–91; Pres., Dir. Eaton's of Canada (parent co. of the other Eaton cos.) 1969–77, Chair. Exec. Cttee. 1994–97; High Commr. in U.K. 1991–94; Chancellor Univ. of New Brunswick 1993–; Hon. LL.D. (New Brunswick) 1983; Man. Award 1987 (McGill Univ.). *Leisure interests:* art, music, reading, shooting, yachting. *Address:* Eaton's of Canada, 250 Yonge Street, 15th Floor, Toronto, Ont., M5B 1C8, Canada.

EATON, George, F.C.A.; Irish management consultant; b. 11 Jan. 1942, Cork; s. of Thomas J. V. Eaton and Catherine Hannon; m. Ellen Patricia O'Grady 1966; one d.; ed. Christian Brothers Coll., Cork, The Inst. of Chartered Accountants, Ireland; with Touche Ross, Chartered Accountants, Cork 1960–66; Chief Accountant, Seafield Fabrics, Youghal 1966–67; Deputy Man. Dir. General Textiles 1967–75; Sr. Partner Eaton Dowd, Man. Consultants 1976–; Chair. Portuguese Irish Chamber of Commerce 1987–89; Pres. The Chambers of Commerce of Ireland 1985–87; Hon. Consul of Hungary 1990–. *Publication:* Introducing Ireland 1989. *Leisure interests:* history, genealogy, reading, writing. *Address:* McConnell House, Charlemont Place, Dublin 2; Custume Place, Athlone, Ireland. *Telephone:* (353) 902-78531. *Fax:* (353) 902-74691.

EATON, Robert J., B.S.; American motor industry executive and engineer; b. 13 Feb. 1940, Buena Vista; s. of Gene Eaton and Mildred Eaton; m. Connie Drake 1964; two s.; ed. Univ. of Kansas; joined Gen. Motors (Chevrolet Motor Div.) 1963, transferred to Eng. staff 1971, Exec. Engineer 1974, Chief Engineer, Corp. Car Programs 1976, Asst. Chief Engineer and Dir. of

Reliability at Oldsmobile 1979, Vice-Pres. in charge of Tech. Staffs 1986, Pres. Gen. Motors Europe 1988–92; C.O.O. Chrysler Motors Corporation 1992–93, Chair., C.E.O. 1993–, now Co.-Chair., Co.-C.E.O. Daimler Chrysler; Chair. Bd. Dirs. Saab Auto 1990–; mem. Bd. Dirs. Group Lotus 1986–; mem. Industrial Advisory Bd. Stanford Univ.; Fellow, Soc. of Automotive Engineers, Eng. Soc. of Detroit; mem. Nat. Acad. of Eng.; Chevalier du Tastevin 1989. *Leisure interests:* skiing, golf, hunting. *Address:* Daimler Chrysler, 12000 Chrysler Drive, Highland Park, MI 48288, U.S.A.

EATWELL, Baron (Life Peer), cr. 1992, of Stratton St. Margaret in the County of Wiltshire; **John Leonard Eatwell,** PH.D.; British academic; b. 2 Feb. 1945; s. of Harold Jack Eatwell and Mary Eatwell; m. Hélène Seppain 1970; two s. one d.; ed. Headlands Grammar School, Swindon, Queens' Coll. Cambridge, Harvard Univ., U.S.A.; Teaching Fellow Grad. School of Arts and Sciences, Harvard Univ. 1968–69; Research Fellow Queens' Coll. Cambridge 1969–70; Fellow Trinity Coll. Cambridge 1970–96, Asst. Lecturer Faculty of Econs. and Politics, Cambridge Univ. 1975–77, Pres. Queens' Coll. 1997–; Visiting Prof. of Econs. New School for Social Research, New York 1982–96; Econ. Adviser to Neil Kinnock, Leader of Labour Party 1985–92; Opposition Spokesman on Treasury Affairs and on Trade and Industry, House of Lords 1992–93, Prin. Opposition spokesman on Treasury and Econ. Affairs 1993–97; Trustee Inst. for Public Policy Research 1988–95, Sec. 1988–97, Chair. 1997–; Dir. (non-exec.) Anglia TV Group 1994–, Cambridge Econometrics Ltd. 1996–; Chair. Extemporary Dance Theatre 1990, Crusaid 1993–, British Screen Finance Ltd. 1997– and assoc. cos.; Gov. Contemporary Dance Trust 1991–95; Dir. Arts Theatre Trust, Cambridge 1991–98, Bd., Securities and Futures Authority 1997–; mem. Bd. Royal Opera House 1998–; Chair. Royal Ballet 1998–. *Publications:* An Introduction to Modern Economics (with Joan Robinson) 1973, Whatever Happened to Britain? 1982, Keynes's Economics and the Theory of Value and Distribution (ed. with Murray Milgate) 1983, The New Palgrave: A Dictionary of Economics, 4 vols. 1987, The New Palgrave Dictionary of Money and Finance, 3 vols. 1992 (both ed. with Murray Milgate and Peter Newman), Transformation and Integration: Shaping the Future of Central and Eastern Europe (jtly.) 1995, Global Unemployment: Loss of Jobs in the '90s (ed.) 1996, Not "Just Another Accession": The Political Economy of EU Enlargement to the East (jtly.) 1997; articles in scientific journals. *Leisure interests:* classical and contemporary dance, Rugby Union football. *Address:* The President's Lodge, Queens' College, Cambridge, CB3 9ET, England. *Telephone:* (01223) 335556. *Fax:* (01223) 335566.

EBAN, Abba, M.A.; Israeli politician; b. (as Aubrey Solomon) 2 Feb. 1915, Cape Town, South Africa; s. of Avram Solomon and Alida Solomon; m. Susan Ambache 1945; one s. one d.; ed. Queens' Coll., Cambridge; Research Fellow and Tutor for Oriental Languages, Pembroke Coll. 1938; apptd. Liaison Officer of Allied H.Q. with the Jewish population in Jerusalem for training volunteers 1942; Chief Instructor at the Middle East Arab Centre in Jerusalem 1944; entered service of Jewish Agency 1946; apptd. Liaison Officer with UN Special Comm. on Palestine 1947; apptd. by the Provisional Govt. of Israel as its rep. in the UN 1948, Perm. Rep. 1949–59, Vice-Pres. Gen. Assembly 1953; Amb. to U.S.A. 1950–59; mem. Knesset 1959–88; Minister without Portfolio 1959–60, Minister of Educ. and Culture 1960–63, Deputy Prime Minister 1963–66, Minister of Foreign Affairs 1966–74; Guest Prof. Columbia Univ. 1974; on-screen Commentator and Chief Consultant, TV series Civilization and the Jews 1984; Pres. Weizmann Inst. of Science 1958–66; Vice-Pres. UN Conf. on Science and Tech. in Advancement of New States 1963, mem. UN Advisory Cttee. on Science and Tech. for Devt.; mem. Inst. for Advanced Study, Princeton Univ. 1978; Fellow World Acad. of Arts and Sciences, Fellow American Acad. of Arts and Sciences, Hon. L.H.D., Hon. Ph.D., Hon. Dr. (Univs. of New York, Boston, Maryland, Cincinnati, Temple, Brandeis, Yeshiva, etc.). *Publications:* The Modern Literary Movement in Egypt 1944, Maze of Justice 1946, The Toynbee Heresy 1955, Voice of Israel 1957, Tide of Nationalism 1959, Chaim Weizmann: A Collective Biography 1962, Reality and Vision in the Middle East (Foreign Affairs) 1965, My People 1968, My Country 1973, Autobiography 1978, The New Diplomacy 1983, Heritage, Civilization and the Jews 1985, Personal Witness 1993, Diplomacy for the Next Century 1998; numerous articles in English, French, Hebrew and Arabic. *Address:* P.O. Box 394, Herzliya, Israel.

EBASHI, Setsuro, M.D., PH.D.; Japanese biophysicist and pharmacologist; b. 31 Aug. 1922, Tokyo; s. of Haruyoshi Ebashi and Hisaji Ebashi; m. Fumiko Takeda 1956; ed. Univ. of Tokyo; Prof. of Pharmacology, Faculty of Medicine, Univ. of Tokyo 1959–83, Prof. of Biophysics, Faculty of Science 1971–83, Prof. Emer. 1983–; Prof. Nat. Inst. for Physiological Science 1983–86, Dir.-Gen. 1985–91, Prof. Emer. 1993–; Prof. Grad. Univ. for Advanced Studies 1988, Prof. Emer. 1993–; Pres. Okazaki Nat. Research Inst. 1991–93; Visiting Prof. Univ. of Calif. 1963, Harvard Univ. 1974; Pres. Int. Union of Pure and Applied Biophysics 1978–81, Int. Union of Pharmacology 1990–94; mem. Japan Acad.; Foreign mem. Royal Soc., Academia Europaea; Foreign Assoc. N.A.S.; Asahi Prize 1968; Imperial Prize, Japan Acad. 1972; Peter Harris Award 1986; Order of Cultural Merit (Bunka-Kunsho), Grand Cordon of Order of the Sacred Treasure. *Publications:* articles in scientific journals. *Address:* 17-503, Nagaizumi Myodaiji, Okazaki 444, Japan (Home).

EBBERS, Bernard J.; American (b. Canadian) communications executive; b. 27 Aug. 1941, Edmonton, Alberta, Canada; ed. Mississippi Coll., Clinton, Miss., U.S.A.; jr. high school science teacher and physical educ. coach, then man. of a clothing warehouse; started hotel business 1974; f. Best Western hotel chain; invested in telecommunications co. Long Distance Discount Service (LDDS – renamed LDDS Communications Inc. 1993, WorldCom Inc. 1995), Jackson, Miss. 1983, Pres. 1985, now Pres. and C.E.O.; mem. Promise Keepers (Christian men's org.); Trustee Miss. Coll. *Address:* WorldCom Inc., 515 East Amite Street, Jackson, MS 39201, U.S.A.

EBEN, Petr; Czech composer; b. 22 Jan. 1929, Žamberk; s. of Vilém Eben and Marie Ebenová-Kahlerová; m. Šárka Ebenová (née Hurníková) 1953; three s.; ed. Acad. of Music Arts, Prague; Music Dir., TV, Prague 1954; début as pianist, Prague 1954; lecturer, Inst. for Musicology, Charles Univ., Prague 1955–, Assoc. Prof. –1990; Prof. of Composition, Acad. of Music, Prague 1990–96; lecturer at Royal Northern Coll. of Music (RNCM), (Manchester, U.K.) 1978, sr. lecturer in theory of music 1988; Pres. Prague Spring music festival 1990–96; mem. Union of Composers, Prague; Pres. Czech Soc. for Spiritual Music, Endowment of Prague Nat. Theatre; Hon. Fellow RNMC 1992; Hon. Dr. (Charles Univ.) 1994; Czech Music Fund Prize 1991, 1992, Stamitz-Preis, Künstlergilde 1993; Chevalier Ordre des Arts et des Lettres; Order of Cyril and Methodius. *Compositions include:* (church opera) Jeremias; (ballet) Curses and Blessings; (oratorios) Apologia Socratus, Sacred Symbols; (symphonic works) Vox clamantis, Prague Nocturne, Night Hours, Improperia; (concertos) for organ and orchestra, for piano and orchestra; (music for organ) Sunday Music, Laudes, Mutationes, Faust, Job, Biblical Dances, Labyrinth of the World and Heart's Paradise 1997, Chagall Windows (for trumpet and organ); (cantatas) Pragensia, Bitter Earth; also song cycles, piano trio, string quartet, quintets, many choral works. *Publications:* Score-Reading and Playing (co-author), contributions to journals. *Address:* Hamsíkova 19, 150 00 Prague 5, Czech Republic. *Telephone:* (2) 558441.

EBERHART, Richard, M.A., LITT.D.; American poet; b. 5 April 1904, Austin, Minn.; s. of the late Alpha La Rue Eberhart and Lena Lowenstein; m. Helen Elizabeth Butcher 1941; one s. one d.; ed. Univ. of Minnesota, Dartmouth Coll., St. John's Coll., Cambridge, England and Harvard Univ.; U.S.N.R. World War II, rose to Lieut.-Commdr.; Asst. Man. Butcher Polish Co. 1946, now Hon. Vice-Pres. and mem. of Bd. of Dirs.; Master of English, St. Mark's School, Southborough, Mass. 1933–41, Cambridge School, Kendal Green, Mass. 1941–42; Visiting Prof. of English and Poet in residence, Univ. of Washington 1952–53; Prof. of English, Univ. of Connecticut 1953–54; inaugural Visiting Prof. of English, Poet in residence, Wheaton Coll., Norton, Mass. 1954–55; Resident Fellow in Creative Writing, Christian Gauss Lecturer, Princeton 1955–56; Prof. of English, Poet in residence, Dartmouth 1956–, Class of 1925 Prof. 1968–70, Emer. 1970–; Distinguished Visting Prof., Univ. of Fla., Gainesville 1974–, Visiting Prof. 1975–86; Adjunct Prof., Colombia Univ. 1975; Regents' Prof., Univ. of Calif., Davis 1975; Fla. Amb. of the Arts 1984–; Hon. Fellow, St. John's Coll. Cambridge 1986; mem. Advisory Cttee. on Arts for Nat. Cultural Center, Washington (now John F. Kennedy Center for Performing Arts) 1959; Consultant in Poetry, Library of Congress 1959–61; mem. Nat. Inst. Arts and Letters (now American Acad. and Inst. of Arts and Letters) 1960 (mem. American Acad. 1982), Peace Corps Mission to Kenya Aug. 1966, American Acad. Arts and Sciences 1967; Founder and Pres. Poets' Theatre Inc., Cambridge, Mass. 1951; Fellow of Acad. of American Poets 1969; Consultant in American Letters 1963–66; Hon. Pres. Poetry Society of America 1972, London Poetry Int. 1973, Third World Congress of Poets, Baltimore 1976; D.Lit. (Dartmouth) 1954, (Skidmore) 1966, (Wooster) 1969, (Colgate) 1974, D.H.L. (Franklin Pierce) 1978, (St. Lawrence Univ.) 1985; Harriet Monroe Memorial Prize 1950, Shelley Memorial Prize 1951, Bollingen Prize 1962, Pulitzer Prize 1966, Nat. Book Award 1977, Pres.'s Medallion, Univ. of Fla. 1977; Poet Laureate of New Hampshire 1979; New York quarterly Poetry Award 1980, Diploma of World Acad. of Arts and Culture, Repub. of China 1981, Sarah Jolepha Hale Award 1982; honoured by proclamation of Richard Eberhart Day (Rhode Island 14 July 1982, Dartmouth Coll. 14 Oct. 1982), Robert Frost Medal, Poetry Soc. of America 1986. *Publications:* A Bravery of Earth 1930, Reading the Spirit 1937, Song and Idea 1942, Poems New and Selected 1944, Burr Oaks 1947, Brotherhood of Men 1949, An Herb Basket 1950, Selected Poems 1951, Undercliff 1953, Great Praises 1957, Collected Poems 1930–60 1960, Collected Verse Plays 1962, The Quarry 1964, Selected Poems 1930–65 1965, New Directions 1965, Thirty One Sonnets 1967, Shifts of Being 1968, Fields of Grace 1972, Collected Poems 1930–1976 1976, Collected Poems 1930–1986 1986, Poems to Poets 1976, To Eberhart from Ginsberg 1976, Survivors 1979, Of Poetry and Poets (criticism) 1979, Ways of Light 1980, New Hampshire/Nine Poems 1980, Four Poems 1980, A Celebration 1980, Chocorua 1981, Florida Poems 1981, The Long Reach 1984, Negative Capability 1986, Maine Poems 1988, New and Collected Poems 1990. *Leisure interests:* cruising on coast of Maine and swimming. *Address:* 80 Lyme Road, Apartment 161, Hanover, NH 03755, U.S.A.

EBERLE, Adm. Sir James Henry Fuller, G.C.B.; British naval officer (retd.); b. 31 May 1927, Bristol; s. of Victor Fuller Eberle, M.C. and Joyce May Eberle; m. Ann Patricia Thompson 1950 (died 1988); one s. two d.; ed. Clifton Coll. and Royal Naval Coll., Dartmouth; served in Second World War at home, East Indies and Pacific 1944–45; served in Korean War, H.M.S. Belfast and Fleet Staff Officer 1952–53; sr. officer, 100 Minesweeping Squadron 1958–59; Capt. H.M.S. Intrepid 1968–70; Defense Fellow, Univ. Coll., Oxford 1970; Flag Officer, Carriers and Amphibious Ships, and Commdr. NATO Striking Group Two 1975–76; mem. Admiralty Bd. 1977–78; Commdr.-in-Chief Fleet, Allied C.-in-C. Eastern Atlantic, C.-in-C. Channel 1979–80; C.-in-C. Naval Home Command 1981–82; retd. 1983, rank of Adm.; rank of

Rear Adm. 1990–94, Vice-Adm. 1994–97; Dir. Royal Inst. of Int. Affairs 1984–90; Dir. UK-Japan 2000 Group 1986; Hon. LL.D. (Bristol) 1989, (Sussex) 1992; Freeman of Bristol 1946, London 1982; Vice-Adm. of the U.K. 1993–97. *Leisure interests:* tennis, field sports. *Publications:* Management in the Armed Forces 1972, Jim, First of the Pack 1982, Britain's Future in Space 1988. *Address:* c/o Chatham House, St. James Square, London, SW1Y 4LE, England.

EBERT, James David, PH.D.; American embryologist; b. 11 Dec. 1921, Bentleyville, Pa.; s. of Alva Charles Ebert and Anna Frances Brundege; m. Alma Christine Goodwin 1946; one s. two d.; ed. Washington and Jefferson Coll. and Johns Hopkins Univ.; Faculty, M.I.T. 1950–51, Indiana Univ. 1951–55; Dir. Dept. of Embryology at Carnegie Inst. of Washington 1956–76; Hon. Prof. of Biology at Johns Hopkins Univ. and Hon. Prof. of Embryology at Johns Hopkins Univ. School of Medicine 1956–86; Dir. Marine Biological Lab. 1970–75, 1977–78, Pres. 1970–78, 1991–98, Hon. Trustee 1998–; Pres. Carnegie Inst. of Washington 1978–87; Dir. Chesapeake Bay Inst., Johns Hopkins Univ. 1987–92; Chair. Assembly of Life Sciences 1973–77; mem. N.A.S. (Vice-Pres. 1981–93); mem. Philosophical Soc.; Fellow, American Acad. of Arts and Sciences; Hon. Sc.D. (Yale, Indiana, Duke and Washington and Jefferson Coll.), Hon. LL.D. (Moravian Coll.); First Distinguished Service Award, Washington and Jefferson Coll. 1965, Eminent Scientist Award, Japan Soc. for the Promotion of Science 1972, Pres. Medal, American Inst. of Biological Sciences 1972; *Publications:* The Biology of Ageing (Co-ed.) 1960, Interacting Systems in Development (Co-author) 1965, 1970, Biology (Co-author) 1973, Tests of Teratogenicity in Vitro (Co-ed.) 1976, Mechanisms of Cell Change (Co-ed.) 1979, This Our Golden Age (Ed.) 1994; professional articles. *Address:* 4100 North Charles Street, Baltimore, MD 21218, U.S.A. (Home).

EBERT, Peter; British (naturalized) opera director; b. 6 April 1918, Frankfurt-am-Main, Germany; s. of late Carl Ebert and Lucie Oppenheim; m. 1st Kathleen Havinden 1944; two d.; m. 2nd Silvia Ashmole 1951; five s. three d.; ed. Salem School, Germany, and Gordonstoun, Scotland; Intendant, Stadttheater Bielefeld, Germany 1973–75, Wiesbaden State Theatres 1975–77; Dir. of Productions, Scottish Opera 1965–76, Gen. Admin. 1977–80; Producer, Guild Opera Co., Los Angeles 1962–76; Hon. D.Mus. (St. Andrew's) 1979. *Leisure interest:* building walls. *Address:* Col di Mura, Lippiano, 06010, Italy.

ECCLESTON, Christopher; British actor; b. 16 Feb. 1964, Salford; s. of Joseph Ronald Eccleston and Elsie Lavinia Eccleston. *Film appearances:* Let Him Have It 1991, Shallow Grave 1995, Jude 1996, Elizabeth 1998, A Price Above Rubies 1998, Heart 1999, Old New Borrowed Blue 1999, Existenz 1999. *Television appearances:* Cracker 1993–94, Hearts and Minds 1995, Our Friends in the North 1996, Hillsborough 1996. *Leisure interest:* supporting Manchester United Football Club. *Address:* Hamilton Asper Management, Ground Floor, 24 Hanway Street, London, W1P 9DD, England. *Telephone:* 0171-636 1221. *Fax:* 0171-636 1226.

ECCLESTONE, Bernie, B.SC.; British business executive; b. Oct. 1930; m. 1st; one d.; m. 2nd Slavica Ecclestone; two d.; ed. Woolwich Polytechnic, London; est. car and motorcycle dealership, Bexley, Kent; racing-car driver for short period; set up Brabham racing team 1970; owner Formula One Holdings, now controls Formula One Constructors' Asscn., representing all the top car-racing teams; Deputy Chief Officer Fed. Int. de l'Automobile (FIA) (racing's int. governing body); homes in Corsica, Gstaad and the French Riviera. *Address:* Formula One Administration Limited, 6 Prince's Gate, London, SW7 1QJ, England.

ECEVIT, Bülent, B.A.; Turkish politician and journalist; b. 28 May 1925, Istanbul; s. of late Prof. Fahri Ecevit, M.P. and Nazli Ecevit; m. Rahşan Ecevit 1946; ed. Robert Coll., Istanbul, Ankara, London and Harvard Univs.; govt. official 1944–50, Turkish Press Attaché's Office, London 1946–50; Foreign News Ed., Man. Ed., later Political Dir. Ulus (Ankara) 1950–61, Political Columnist, Ulus 1956–61; M.P. (Republican People's Party) 1957–60, 1961–80; mem. Constituent Assembly 1961; Minister of Labour 1961–65; Deputy Prime Minister and Minister of State 1997–98; Prime Minister of Turkey 1998–; Political Columnist Milliyet 1965; Prime Minister Jan.–Nov. 1974, June–July 1977, 1978–79 (resigned Oct. 1979); Sec.-Gen. Republican People's Party 1966–71, Chair. 1972–80; detained after coup Sept. 1980, released Oct. 1980, imprisoned by mil. régime Dec. 1981–Feb. 1982, rearrested April 1982, imprisoned again Aug.–Oct. 1982; Chair. Democratic Left Party Jan. 1989–; mem. Turkish Philosophical Soc., Turkish Language Asscn., Ankara Journalists' Asscn. *Publications:* Ortanin Solu (Left of Centre) 1966, Bu Düzen Değismelidir (The System Must Change) 1968, Atatürk ve Devrimcilik (Atatürk and Revolution) 1970, Sohbet (conversations), Demokratik Sol (Democratic Left) 1974, Dis Politika (Foreign Policy) 1975, Işçi-Köylü Elele (Workers and Peasants Together) 1976, Şiirler (Poems) (German, Russian, Serbian, Danish and Romanian trans.) 1976; Translations into Turkish: Gitanjali (R. Tagore) 1941, Straybirds (R. Tagore) 1943, Cocktail Party (T. S. Eliot) 1963. *Leisure interests:* art and literature. *Address:* Office of the Prime Minister, Başbakanlık, Bakanlıklar, Ankara; Demokratik Sol Parti (DSP) (Democratic Left Party), Fevzi Çakma Cad. 17, Ankara; Or-an Şehri 69/5, Ankara, Turkey (Home). *Telephone:* (312) 419-1621. *Fax:* (312) 419-1547.

ECHANDI JIMÉNEZ, Mario, LL.D.; Costa Rican politician and diplomatist; b. 1915; ed. Univ. de Costa Rica; legal career 1938–47; Sec.-Gen. Partido Unión Nacional 1947; Amb. to U.S.A. 1950–51, 1966–68; Minister for Foreign Affairs 1951–53; Pres. of Costa Rica 1958–62; defeated candidate in Pres. election Feb. 1970. *Address:* San José, Costa Rica.

ECHEVARRIA, Most Rev. Javier, PH.D.; Spanish ecclesiastic; b. 14 June 1932; ed. Univ. of Madrid, Pontifical Univ. of St. Thomas, Rome, Pontifical Lateran Univ., Rome; moved to Rome 1950; ordained priest 1955; lecturer in Moral Theology, Collegio Romano della Santa Croce 1960, Collegio Romano di Santa Maria 1964; apptd. personal sec. to Josemaría Escrivá (founder of Opus Dei) 1957, mem. Gen. Council Opus Dei 1966–75, Sec.-Gen. 1975–82, Vicar-Gen. 1982–94, Prelate of Opus Dei April 1994–; consecrated Bishop 1995; mem. Sacred Congregation for the Causes of Saints 1981–, Sacred Congregation for the Clergy 1995–. *Address:* Curia of the Prelature, 73 Viale Bruno Buozzi, 00197 Rome, Italy. *Telephone:* 80-89-61. *Fax:* 80-89-64-20.

ECKHARDT, Sándor; Hungarian oncologist; b. 14 March 1927, Budapest; s. of Sándor Eckhardt and Irén Huszár; m. Mária Petrányi; three s.; ed. Semmelweis Medical Univ. Budapest; specialist in internal medicine 1955; training course of malignant diseases in children, Villejuif, France 1969; MRC Fellow, Chester Beatty Inst., London, 1961; Eleanor Roosevelt Cancer Research Fellow, Bethesda 1964–65; Chair. Drug Devt. Program, Hungary 1966–70; Dir. Nat. Inst. of Oncology, Budapest 1971–92; Prof. Clinical Oncology, Postgrad. Univ. Medical School, Budapest 1977–; mem. Hungarian Acad. of Sciences 1984–; Chair. Trial Centre of East European countries and Program Co-ordinator of drug research 1979–; mem. Union Int. Contre le Cancer (UICC) Exec. Cttee. 1978–86, Treas. 1986–90, Pres. 1990–94, Past. Pres. 1994–; Sec. Gen. 14th Int. Cancer Congress 1982–86; adviser WHO Cancer Unit 1971–; mem. Medical Advisory Cttee. WHO Euro Office, Copenhagen 1974–82; mem. Scientific Council Int. Agency for Research on Cancer 1976–80, Chair. 1979–; mem. American Asscn. of Cancer Research 1976–, Medical Acad. of Moscow 1979–, American Soc. of Clinical Oncology 1987–, European Soc. of Medical Oncology 1985–; Chief ed. Antitumour Drug Therapy, Budapest 1977–; Clinical ed. Oncology 1978–, Onkologie 1980–; Labour Order of Merit 1975, State Prize 1980. *Publications:* include Drug Therapy of Cancer (WHO Geneva) 1973; Dibromodulcitol 1982; Drug Development in Eastern Europe 1987; co-ed. Proceedings of the 14th International Cancer Congress, Budapest (13 vols.) 1986, Cancer, Annals of Oncology, Cancer Surveys 1994. *Address:* National Institute of Oncology, 1525 Budapest, Ráth György utca 7/9, Hungary. *Telephone:* (1) 224-8751. *Fax:* (1) 224-8620.

ECO, Umberto; Italian author and university professor; b. 5 Jan. 1932; s. of Giulio Eco and Giovanna Bisio; m. Renate Ramge 1962; two c.; ed. Univ. degli Studi, Turin; with Italian Television 1954–59; Asst. Lecturer in Aesthetics, Univ. of Turin 1956–63, Lecturer 1963–64; Lecturer Faculty of Architecture, Univ. of Milan 1964–65; Prof. of Visual Communications, Univ. of Florence 1966–69; Prof. of Semiotics, Milan Polytechnic 1970–71, Univ. of Bologna 1971–; Visiting Prof. New York Univ. 1969–70, 1976, Northwestern Univ. 1972, Yale Univ. 1977, 1980, 1981, Columbia Univ. 1978, 1984; Columnist on L'Espresso 1965; Ed. VS 1971–; mem. European Acad. 1998–; Hon. D.Litt. (Glasgow) 1990, (Kent) 1992; Medici Prize 1982, McLuhan Teleglobe Prize 1985. *Publications:* Il Problema Estetico in San Tommaso 1956 (as The Aesthetics of Thomas Aquinas 1988), Sviluppo dell'Estetica Medioevale 1959 (as Art and Beauty in the Middle Ages 1986), Opera Aperta 1962, Diario Minimo 1963, Apocalittici e Integrati 1964, L'Oeuvre Ouverte 1965, La Struttura Assente 1968, Il Costume di Casa 1973, Trattato di Semiotica Generale 1975, A Theory of Semiotics 1976, The Role of the Reader 1979, Il Nome della Rosa (novel) 1981, Semiotics and the Philosophy of Language 1984, Sette anni di desiderio 1977–83 1984, Il pendolo di Foucault 1988, The Open Work 1989, The Limits of Interpretation 1990, Misreadings 1993, How to Travel with a Salmon and Other Essays 1994, The Search for the Perfect Language 1995, The Island of the Day Before (novel) 1995. *Address:* Piazza Castello 13, 20121 Milan, Italy.

EDA, Satsuki, LL.B.; Japanese politician and lawyer; b. 22 May 1941, Okayama; s. of Saburo Eda and Mitsuko Eda; m. Kyoko Eda 1967; two s. one d.; ed. Univs. of Tokyo and Oxford; Asst. Judge, Tokyo, Chiba and Yokohama Dist. Court 1968–77; Attorney-at-law 1977; mem. House of Councillors 1977; mem. House of Reps. 1983–; Pres. United Social Democratic Party 1985; Minister of State for Science and Tech. 1993–94. *Publications:* Shuppatuno Tameno Memorandamu (autobiography) 1978, Kokkaigiin 1985. *Leisure interests:* swimming, calligraphy.

EDBERG, Stefan; Swedish tennis player; b. 19 Jan. 1966, Vastervik; m. Annette Edberg; one d.; won Jr. Grand Slam 1983, Milan Open 1984, San Francisco, Basle and Memphis Opens 1985, Gstaad, Basle and Stockholm Opens 1986, Australian Open 1986, 1987, Wimbledon 1988, 1990, finalist 1989, U.S. Open 1991, Masters 1989, German Open 1992, U.S. Open 1992; Winner (with Anders Jarryd) Masters and French Open 1986, Australian and US Opens 1987; semi-finalist in numerous tournaments; mem. Swedish Davis Cup Team 1984, 1987. *Address* c/o ATP Tour 200, ATP Tour Boulevard, Ponte Vedra Beach, FL 32082, U.S.A.

EDDY, Don, M.F.A.; American artist; b. 4 Nov. 1944, Long Beach, Calif.; m. Leigh Behnke 1995; one d.; ed. Fullerton Jr. Coll., Univ. of Hawaii, Honolulu, Univ. of California at Santa Barbara; solo exhbns. at Ewing Krainin Gallery, Honolulu 1968, Molly Barnes Gallery, L.A. 1970, 1971, Esther Bear Gallery, Santa Barbara 1970, Galerie M.E. Thelen, Essen/Cologne 1970, French and Co., New York 1971, Galerie Petit, Paris 1973, Nancy Hoffman Gallery, New

York 1974, 1976, 1979, 1983, 1986, 1990, 1992, 1994, 1996, Williams Coll. Museum of Art, Williamstown, Mass. 1975, The Art Gallery, Miami-Dade Community Coll., Miami 1976, Univ. of Hawaii at Manoa, Honolulu 1982, Scarabb Gallery, Cleveland, Ohio 1994, The Huntington Museum of Art, West Virginia 1996; has participated in numerous group exhbns. 1970–; represented in numerous public collections. *Address:* 543 Broadway, New York, NY 10012, U.S.A. *Telephone:* (212) 925-3124.

EDELMAN, Gerald Maurice, M.D., PH.D.; American molecular biologist; b. 1 July 1929, New York; s. of Edward and Anna Freedman Edelman; m. Maxine Morrison 1950; two s. one d.; ed. Ursinus Coll., Univ. of Pennsylvania, and The Rockefeller Univ.; Medical House Officer, Mass. Gen. Hospital 1945–55; Capt., U.S. Army Medical Corps. 1955–56; Asst. Physician, Hospital of The Rockefeller Univ. 1957–60; Asst. Prof. and Asst. Dean of Grad. Studies, The Rockefeller Univ, 1960–63, Assoc. Prof. and Assoc. Dean of Grad. Studies 1963–66, Prof. 1966–74; Vincent Astor Distinguished Prof. 1974–92, Assoc. Neurosciences Research Program, Scientific Chair. 1980; Dir. Neurosciences Inst., Neurosciences Research Program 1981–; mem. The Scripps Research Inst. La Jolla, Calif., Chair. Dept. of Neurobiology 1992–, Chair. Dept. of Neurobiology 1992–; mem. Biophysics and Biophysical Chemistry Study Section, N.I.H. 1964–67, Scientific Council, Centre for Theoretical Studies 1970–72, The Harvey Society 1974–, Pres. 1975–76; mem. N.A.S. American Acad. of Arts and Sciences, American Philosophical Soc., Genetics Soc., American Chem. Soc., American Soc. of Biological Chemists, American Asscn. of Immunologists, American Soc. for Cell Biology, Soc. for Developmental Biology, Alpha Omega Alpha Hon. Medical Soc., Council on Foreign Relations, A.A.A.S.; Hon. mem. Japanese Biochemical Soc., Pharmaceutical Soc. of Japan; Foreign mem. Acad. des Sciences; Fellow, N.Y. Acad. of Sciences; Trustee, Rockefeller Brothers Fund 1972–82; Non-Res. Fellow and mem. Bd. of Trustees, Salk Inst. for Biological Studies; Fellow, New York Acad. of Medicine; mem. Bd. of Overseers Faculty of Arts and Sciences, Univ. of Pa.; mem. Bd. Scientific Overseers, The Jackson Laboratory; mem. Bd. of Trustees, Carnegie Inst. of Washington, mem. Advisory Cttee.; mem. Advisory Bd., The Basel Inst. for Immunology 1970–77, Chair. 1975–77; mem. Bd. of Governors, Weizmann Inst. of Science, Israel; Hon. D.Sc. (Univ. of Pa.) 1973, (Adolphus Coll., Minn.) 1975, (Georgetown) 1989, (Tulane) 1991, (Miami) 1995, (Adelphi) 1995; Hon. Sc.D. (Ursinus Coll.) 1974, (Williams Coll.) 1976; Hon. M.D. (Siena) 1974; Dr. h.c. (Paris, Cagliari) 1989, (Naples) 1990; Annual Alumni Award, Ursinus Coll. 1969, Eli Lilly Award in Biological Chem., American Chemical Soc. 1965, Spencer Morris Award, Univ. of Pa. 1954, Nobel Prize for Physiology or Medicine 1972 (with R. Porter q.v.), Albert Einstein Commem. Award of Yeshiva Univ. 1974, Buchman Memorial Award, Calif. Inst. of Tech. 1975, Rabbi Shai Shaknai Mem. Prize in Immunology and Cancer Research, Hebrew Univ.-Hadassah Medical School, Jerusalem 1977, Regents Medal of Excellence, New York 1984, Cécile and Oskar Vogt Award (Düsseldorf) 1988, Distinguished Grad. Award, Univ. of Pa. 1990, and many other awards and prizes. *Publications:* Neural Darwinism 1987, Topobiology 1988, The Remembered Present 1989, Bright Air, Brilliant Fire 1992; about 400 articles in professional journals. *Leisure interests:* violin, chamber music. *Address:* Department of Neurobiology, SBR 14, The Scripps Research Institute, 10550 North Torrey Pines Road, La Jolla, CA 92037, U.S.A. *Telephone:* (619) 784-2600. *Fax:* (619) 784-2646.

EDELMANN, Otto Karl; Austrian opera singer; b. 5 Feb. 1917, Vienna; m. Ilse-Maria Straub 1960; two s. one d.; ed. Realgymnasium and State Acad. of Music, Vienna; first opera appearances 1938; P.O.W. in U.S.S.R. two years during Second World War; mem. Vienna State Opera 1948–; with Salzburg Festival 1948–; perm. mem. Metropolitan Opera New York 1954–; took part in first Bayreuth Festival 1951; world-famous as Sachs in Die Meistersinger; Kt. Order of Dannebrog, Austrian Gold Cross of Honour for Sciences and Arts. *Leisure interests:* painting and boxing. *Address:* Wien-Kalksburg 1238, Breitenfurterstrasse 547, Austria.

EDELSTEIN, Victor; British couturier and artist; b. 10 July 1945, London; m. Anna Maria Succi 1973; trainee designer Alexon 1962, Asst. Designer and Pattern Cutter to Biba 1967, designer Salvador 1971, Christian Dior 1975; f. Victor Edelstein Ltd. 1978–93; designed ballet of Rhapsody in Blue for Rambert Dance Co. 1989; pantomime Cinderella, Richmond Theatre 1991, black pas de deux, Swan Lake, Covent Garden 1991; exhbns. include Sotheby's, London 1996, Hopkins Thomas Gallery, Paris 1999. *Leisure interests:* opera, gardening, collecting old master drawings, skiing.

EDELSTEIN, Yuli; Israeli politician; b. 1958, Ukraine; m.; two c.; ed. Moscow Inst. for Teacher Training; fmr. Hebrew teacher, Moscow; emigrated to Israel 1987; fmr. teacher Melitz Centre for Jewish-Zionist Educ., School for Educational Inst., Jerusalem; Adviser to Opposition Leader Benjamin Netanyahu 1993–94; a founder of Yisrael Ba-Aliya party 1995; headed party's election campaign; mem. Knesset (Parl.) 1996–, Minister of Immigration and Absorption 1996–. *Address:* Ministry of Immigration and Absorption, P.O. Box 883, 2 Rehov Kaplan, Kiryat Ben-Gurion, Jerusalem 91006, Israel. *Telephone:* 2-752691. *Fax:* 2-669244.

EDEN OF WINTON, Baron (Life Peer), cr. 1983, of Rushyford in the County of Durham; **John Eden,** Bt., P.C.; British politician; b. 15 Sept 1925; m. 1st Belinda Jane Pascoe 1958 (divorced 1974); two s. two d.; m. 2nd Margaret Ann, Viscountess Strathallan 1977; M.P. for Bournemouth West 1954–83; Minister of State, Ministry of Technology July-Oct. 1970; Minister for Industry, Dept. of Trade and Industry 1970–72; Minister of Posts and Telecommunications 1972–74; Del. to Council of Europe and WEU 1960–62, NATO Parliamentarians' Conf. 1962–66; mem. House of Commons Expenditure Cttee. 1974–76; Pres. Independent Schools' Asscn. 1969–71; Chair. House of Commons Select Cttee. on European Legislation 1976–79; Chair. Select Cttee. on Home Affairs 1981–83; Chair. Lady Eden's Schools Ltd. 1960–, Wonderworld PLC 1982–98, Gamlestaden PLC 1987–92, Bricom Group Ltd, 1990–93, British Lebanese Asscn. Ltd. 1990–98, Royal Armouries 1986–94; Conservative. *Address:* 41 Victoria Road, London, W8 5RH, England.

EDGAR, David, B.A.; British writer; b. 26 Feb. 1948, Birmingham; s. of Barrie Edgar and Joan Edgar; m. Eve Brook 1979; two s.; ed. Manchester Univ.; Fellow in Creative Writing, Leeds Polytechnic 1972–74; Resident Playwright, Birmingham Repertory Theatre 1974–75; Lecturer in Playwrighting, Univ. of Birmingham 1975–78, Prof. 1995–; U.K./U.S. Bicentennial Arts Fellow resident in U.S.A. 1978–79; Literary Consultant, R.S.C. 1984–88; Bd. mem., Birmingham Repertory Theatre 1985–; Hon. Sr. Research Fellow, Univ. of Birmingham 1988–92, Hon. Prof. 1992–; Hon. M.A. (Bradford) 1986; Dr. h.c. (Univ. of Surrey) 1993; Fellow Birmingham Polytechnic 1991; Soc. of West End Theatres Best Play Award 1980, New York Tony Best Play Award 1981. *Plays:* Dick Deterred 1974, O Fair Jerusalem 1975, Saigon Rose 1976, Blood Sports 1976, Destiny (for R.S.C.) 1976, Wreckers 1977, The Jail Diary of Albie Sachs (for R.S.C.) 1978, Mary Barnes 1978–79, Teendreams 1979, Nicholas Nickleby (adaptation for R.S.C.) 1980, Maydays (for R.S.C.) 1983, Entertaining Strangers 1985, That Summer 1987, The Shape of the Table 1990, Dr. Jekyll and Mr Hyde (adaptation for R.S.C.) 1991, Pentecost 1994, Other Place 1994, Young Vic 1995. *TV Plays:* I Know What I Meant 1974, Baby Love 1974, Vote for Them 1989, Buying a Landslide 1992, Citizen Locke 1994. *Radio:* Ecclesiastes 1977, A Movie Starring Me 1991. *Film:* Lady Jane 1986. *Leisure interests:* fine art, cookery. *Address:* c/o Michael Imison, 28 Almeida Street, London N1 1TD, England.

EDGAR, James; American politician; b. 22 July 1946, Vinita, Okla.; m. Brenda Smith; one s. one d.; ed. Eastern Ill. Univ., Univ. of Ill. and Sangamon State Univ.; key asst. to Speaker, Ill. House of Reps. 1972–73; aide to Pres. Ill. Senate 1974, to House Minority Leader 1976; mem. Ill. House of Reps. 1977–91; Dir. Legis. Affairs, Gov. of Ill. 1979–80; Sec. of State of Ill. 1981–91; Gov. of Illinois 1991–99; Chair. Nat. Govt.'s Asscn. Comm. Econ. Devt. and Tech. Innovation 1991, Strategic Planning Review Task Force 1991; Republican. *Address:* c/o Office of the Governor, 207 State House, Springfield, IL 62706, U.S.A.

EDGE (THE), (David Evans); Irish musician; b. 8 Aug. 1961; s. of Garvin Evans and Gwenda Evans; ed. Mount Temple School; guitarist and founder mem. U2 1978–; toured Australasia, Europe and USA 1980–84, Live Aid Wembley 1985, Self Aid Dublin, A Conspiracy of Hope (Amnesty Int. Tour) 1986, world tour of 100 performances Europe and USA 1987, toured Australia 1989, New Year's Eve concert Point Depot Dublin (broadcast live to Europe and U.S.S.R.) 1989, World tour 1992–93, Dublin Concert 1993; albums with U2: Boy 1980, October 1981, War 1983, Under a Blood Red Sky 1983, The Unforgettable Fire 1984, The Joshua Tree 1987, Rattle and Hum 1988, Achtung Baby 1991, Zooropa 1993, Pop 1997; singles with U2 include With or Without You, I Still Haven't Found What I'm Looking For and Where the Streets Have No Name (all reached number 1 in U.S. charts) 1987, Desire (first U.K. number 1 single) 1988, Stay 1993 (U.K. number 1 single), Discotheque 1997 (entered UK charts at number 1), Gold disc for War (U.S.A.), Platinum disc for Under a Blood Red Sky (U.K.), Band of the Year (Rolling Stone Writers' poll) 1984, (Readers' poll) 1986, Grammy Awards: Album of the Year (The Joshua Tree) 1987, Best Rock Performance (Desire) 1989, Best Video (Where the Streets Have No Name) 1989, Best Live Act BPI Awards 1993. *Address:* c/o Regine Moylet Publicity, First Floor 145a Ladbroke Grove, London, W10 6HJ, England. *Telephone:* 0171-221 0554. *Fax:* 0171-221 8532.

EDGLEY, Michael Christopher, M.B.E.; Australian entrepreneur; b. 17 Dec. 1943, Melbourne; s. of the late Eric Edgley and of Edna Edgley (née Luscombe); m. Jeni King 1972; one s. three d.; ed. Trinity Coll., Perth; Chair. Edgley Ventures Pty. Ltd. 1962–, promoting a wide range of cultural, artistic and sporting events throughout Australia, N.Z., the U.K. and Asia; Citizens of the Year Award for W.A. 1976. *Leisure interests:* jogging, tennis. *Address:* Edgley International, 2 Chapel Street, Richmond, Vic. 3121, Australia.

EDINBURGH, H.R.H. The Prince Philip, Duke of, K.G., K.T., O.M., G.B.E.; Prince of the United Kingdom of Great Britain and Northern Ireland, Earl of Merioneth, Baron Greenwich; b. 10 June 1921, Corfu, Greece; s. of Prince Andrew of Greece and Denmark and Princess Alice of Battenberg; m. H.R.H. Princess Elizabeth (now H.M. Queen Elizabeth II, q.v.) 20 Nov. 1947; children: Prince Charles Philip Arthur George, Prince of Wales (q.v.) b. 14 Nov. 1948, Princess Anne Elizabeth Alice Louise, The Princess Royal (q.v.) b. 15 Aug. 1950, Prince Andrew Albert Christian Edward, Duke of York (q.v.) b. 19 Feb. 1960, Prince Edward Antony Richard Louis (q.v.) b. 10 March 1964; ed. Cheam, Salem and Gordonstoun Schools, Royal Naval Coll., Dartmouth; renounced right of succession to thrones of Greece and Denmark, naturalised British subject 1947, adopting surname Mountbatten; served Royal Navy 1939–51, served in Indian Ocean, Mediterranean, North Sea, Pacific Ocean during Second World War; Personal ADC to King George VI 1948–52; P.C. 1951–; ranks of Adm. of the Fleet, Field Marshal, Marshal of the Royal Air Force, Captain-Gen. Royal Marines 1953–; Chancellor, Univs.

of Wales 1948–76, Edin. 1952–, Salford 1967–91, Cambridge 1977–; Pres., Patron or Trustee numerous orgs. including: Nat. Playing Fields Asscn. 1948–, Nat. Maritime Museum 1948–, London Fed. of Clubs for Young People 1948–, Automobile Asscn. 1948–, Royal Yachting Asscn. 1948–, Variety Clubs Int. 1951–, City & Guilds of London Inst. 1951–, Cen. Council of Physical Recreation 1951–, Design Council 1952–, Royal Soc. of Arts 1952–, English-Speaking Union of the Commonwealth 1952–, Outward Bound Trust 1952–, Trinity House 1952–, R.C.A. 1955–, Commonwealth Games Fed. 1955–90, Duke of Edinburgh's Award Scheme 1956–, Duke of Edinburgh's Commonwealth Study Confs. 1956–, Royal Agric. Soc. of the Commonwealth 1958–, Voluntary Service Overseas 1961–, World Wildlife Fund U.K. 1961–82, Int. Equestrian Fed. 1964–86, Maritime Trust 1969–, British Commonwealth Ex-Services League 1974–, Royal Acad. of Eng. 1976–; Pres. World Wide Fund for Nature 1981–96, Pres. Emer. 1997–; numerous awards, decorations and hon. degrees worldwide. *Publications:* 12 publications 1957–94. *Address:* Buckingham Palace, London, SW1A 1AA, England.

EDMOND, John Marmion, PH.D., F.R.S.; American professor of marine geochemistry; b. 27 April 1943, Glasgow, Scotland; s. of late Andrew J. S. Edmond and Christina M. Edmond; m. Massoudeh Vafai 1978; two s.; ed. Univ. of Glasgow, Univ. of Calif. at San Diego and Scripps Inst. of Oceanography; Asst. Prof. Mass. Inst. of Tech. 1970, Assoc. Prof. 1975, Prof. of Marine Geochemistry 1981–; Mackelwane Award, American Geophysical Union 1976. *Publications:* more than 150 scientific papers in professional journals. *Leisure interests:* reading, gardening. *Address:* M.I.T., E34-201, Cambridge, MA 02139 (Office); 21 Robin Hood Road, Arlington, MA 02174, U.S.A. *Telephone:* (617) 253-5739 (Home). *Fax:* (617) 253-8630.

EDMONDS, John Walter, M.A.; British trade union official; b. 28 Jan. 1944, London; s. of Maude Rose Edmonds and Walter Edgar Edmonds; m. Janet Lindon 1967; two d.; ed. Oriel Coll. Oxford; Research Asst., General, Mun. and Boilermakers' Union Trade Union 1965, Deputy Research Officer 1967, Regional Organiser 1968, Nat. Officer 1972, Gen. Sec. 1986–; Hon. LL.D. (Sussex). *Leisure interests:* cricket, carpentry. *Address:* General, Mun. and Boilermakers' Union, 22–24 Worple Road, Wimbledon, London, SW19 4DD (Office); 50 Graham Road, Mitcham, Surrey, CR4 2AJ, England (Home). *Telephone:* 0181-947 3131 (Office); 0181-648 9991 (Home).

EDSALL, John Tileston, A.B., M.D.; American professor of biological chemistry; b. 3 Nov. 1902, Philadelphia; s. of David Linn Edsall and Margaret Harding Tileston; m. Margaret Dunham 1929 (died 1987); three s. (one deceased); ed. Harvard Coll., Harvard Medical School and Cambridge Univ.; Asst. Prof. of Biological Chem., Harvard Univ. 1932–38, Assoc. Prof. 1938–51, Prof. 1951–73, Prof. Emer. 1973–; Guggenheim Fellow, Calif. Inst. of Tech. 1940–41; Ed.-in-Chief Journal of Biological Chemistry 1958–67; Visiting Fulbright Lecturer, Cambridge 1952, Tokyo 1964; Visiting Prof., Coll. de France, Paris 1955; Spiers Memorial Lecturer, Faraday Soc., Cambridge 1952; Visiting Lecturer, Australian Nat. Univ., Canberra 1970; Scholar Fogarty Int. Center, Nat. Insts. of Health, Bethesda, Md. 1970–71; Pres. American Soc. of Biological Chemists 1957–58, Sixth Int. Congress of Biochemistry, New York 1964; Chair. Survey of Sources for the History of Biochemistry and Molecular Biology 1975–80; Visiting Prof., Univ. of Calif., Los Angeles 1977, Univ. of Calif., Riverside 1980; mem. Interunion Biothermodynamics Comm. 1973–78, Nat. Acad. of Sciences, American Philosophical Soc., American Acad. of Arts and Sciences, Deutsche Akad. der Naturforscher (Leopoldina), Royal Danish Acad. of Sciences; mem. Cttee. on Scientific Freedom and Responsibility, American Asscn. for the Advancement of Science 1976–82, Chair. 1979–81; Foreign mem. Royal Swedish Acad. of Sciences; Hon. Dr. Phil. Univ. of Göteborg 1972, Hon Sc.D. (Western Reserve Univ., New York Medical Coll. and Univs. of Chicago and Mich.); Passano Foundation Award for Medical Research 1966, Willard Gibbs Medal (American Chemical Soc.) 1972, Philip Hauge Abelson Award (A.A.A.S.) 1989. *Publications:* Proteins, Amino Acids and Peptides (with E. J. Cohn) 1943, Biophysical Chemistry (with J. Wyman) Vol. 1 1958, Aspects actuels de la biochimie des acides aminés et des proteines 1958, Advances in Protein Chemistry (Co-Ed.) Vols. 1–49 1944–96, Archival Sources for the History of Biochemistry and Molecular Biology (Co-Ed.) 1980, Biothermodynamics (with H. Gutfreund) 1983; numerous papers on chemistry of amino acids, proteins, and enzymes in Journal of American Chemical Soc., Journal of Biological Chemistry, etc. *Leisure interests:* travel, photography, walking. *Address:* Department of Molecular and Cellular Biology, Harvard University, 7 Divinity Avenue, Cambridge, MA 02138 (Office); 985 Memorial Drive, Apartment 503, Cambridge, MA 02138, U.S.A. (Home). *Telephone:* (617) 495-2314 (Office); (617) 876-5007 (Home). *Fax:* (617) 495-8308.

EDSTRÖM, Jan-Erik, M.D.; Swedish professor of molecular genetics; b. 21 April 1931; s. of Erik Edström and Vera (née Henriksson) Edström; m. 1st Karin Ivarsson 1955 (divorced 1968); three s.; m. 2nd Elisabet Ericson 1980; two s. two d.; Assoc. Prof. of Histology, Univ. of Gothenburg 1962–64; Prof. of Histology, Univ. of Umeå 1964–65, Karolinska Inst., Stockholm 1965–79; Sr. Scientist, European Molecular Biology Lab., Heidelberg 1979–85; Prof. of Molecular Genetics, Univ. of Lund 1985–; M.D. h.c. (Karolinska Inst.) 1968; mem. Royal Acad. of Science. *Publications:* publs. on molecular genetics. *Address:* Högviltsgränd 8, 22652 Lund, Sweden.

EDWARD, H.R.H. The Prince; Edward Antony Richard Louis, C.V.O., B.A.; b. 10 March 1964; s. of Queen Elizabeth II (q.v.) and Prince Philip, Duke of Edinburgh (q.v.); engagement to Sophie Rhys-Jones announced 6 Jan. 1999; ed. Heatherdown Prep. School, Gordonstoun School, Jesus Coll., Cambridge; fmrly. Second Lieut. Royal Marines; worked in theatre production with Theatre Div., Really Useful Theatre Co.; f. Ardent Productions Ltd. 1993, also Dir. of Production; opened Commonwealth Games, Auckland 1990; Pres. Commonwealth Games Fed. 1990–; U.K. and Int. Trustee, Duke of Edin. Award Scheme; Patron Nat. Youth Music Theatre and Royal Exchange Theatre, Manchester, Nat. Youth Orchestra of Scotland, City of Birmingham Symphony Orchestra and Chorus, Ocean Youth Club, Scottish Badminton Union; Gold Duke of Edin. Award Scheme 1986. *Leisure interests:* the arts, horse-riding, sailing, skiing, badminton, Real Tennis. *Address:* Buckingham Palace, London, S.W.1, England.

EDWARD, David Alexander Ogilvy, C.M.G., Q.C., M.A., LL.D., F.R.S.E.; British public servant; b. 14 Nov. 1934, Perth; s. of John O. C. Edward and Margaret I. MacArthur; m. Elizabeth Young McSherry 1962; two s. two d.; ed. Sedbergh School, Univ. Coll., Oxford and Edinburgh Univ.; advocate 1962–, Clerk Faculty of Advocates 1967–70, Treas. 1970–77; Pres. Consultative Cttee., Bars and Law Socs. of the EEC 1978–80; Salvesen Prof. of European Insts. and Dir. Europa Inst., Univ. of Edinburgh 1985–89, Hon. Prof. 1990; Judge of the Court of First Instance of the European Communities 1989–92, Judge of EC Court of Justice 1992–; Pres. Scottish Council for Int. Arbitration; fmr. Specialist Adviser to House of Lords Select Cttee. on the EEC; fmr. Chair. Continental Assets Trust PLC; fmr. Dir. Adam & Co. PLC, Harris Tweed Asscn. Ltd.; fmr. mem. Law Advisory Cttee. British Council, Panel of Arbitrators, Int. Centre for Settlement of Investment Disputes; fmr. mem. Gründungssenat, Europa.-Univ. Viadrina, Frankfurt/Oder; fmr. Trustee, Nat. Library of Scotland; Trustee Trier Acad. of European Law, Industry and Parl. Trust, Hopetoun House Trust, Carnegie Trust for the Univs. of Scotland; Hon. Bencher, Gray's Inn; Hon. Fellow Univ. Coll. Oxford; Hon. LL.D. (Univ. of Edin.) 1993, (Aberdeen) 1997, (Napier) 1998. *Publications:* The Professional Secret, Confidentiality and Legal Professional Privilege in the EEC 1976, European Community Law: an introduction (with R. C. Lane) 1995; articles in legal journals. *Address:* Court of Justice of the European Communities, L-2925 Luxembourg *Telephone:* 4303 2203. *Fax:* 4303 2040.

EDWARDES, Sir Michael Owen, Kt., B.A., F.B.I.M.; British company executive; b. 11 Oct. 1930, South Africa; s. of Denys Owen Edwardes and Audrey Noel (née Copeland); m. 1st Mary Margaret Finlay 1958 (divorced); three d.; m. 2nd Sheila Ann Guy 1988; ed. St. Andrew's Coll., Grahamstown, S.A., Rhodes Univ., S.A.; joined Chloride Group in S.A. as management trainee 1951, mem. Man. Bd. 1969, Chief Exec. 1972, Exec. Chair. 1974–77, non-Exec. Deputy Chair. 1977–82, Chair. (non-exec.) 1982–88 (acting Chief Exec. 1985–87); Chair. and Chief Exec. BL PLC 1977–82; Dir. (non-exec.) Hill Samuel Group PLC 1980–87, Standard Securities 1984–87, Minerals and Resources Corpn. 1984–, Flying Pictures Ltd. 1987–; Chair. Mercury Communications Ltd. 1982–83, ICL PLC 1984; Chair. and Chief Exec. Dunlop Holdings 1984–85; Chair. Charter Consolidated PLC 1988–96, Tryhorn Investments Ltd. 1987–, Porth Group PLC 1991–95, ARC Int. Ltd. 1991–93; Exec. Dir. Minorco 1984, Strand Partners 1994–, Syndicated Services Co. Inc. 1995–; Deputy Chair. R. K. Carvill Int. Holdings Ltd.; Dir. (non-exec.) Int. Man. Devt. Inst., Washington 1978–, Hi-Tec Sports 1993–; Pres. Comité des Constructeurs d'Automobile du Marché Commun 1979–80; Trustee Thrombosis Research Inst. 1991–; mem. Nat. Enterprise Bd. 1975–77, CBI Council 1974 (mem. President's Cttee. 1981–), Review Cttee. for Queen's Award for Industry; Young Businessman of the Year 1975; Hon. D.Iur. Rhodes Univ., S.A. 1980; Hon. Fellow, Inst. of Mechanical Engineers. *Publication:* Back From the Brink 1983. *Leisure interests:* water skiing, sailing, squash, tennis.

EDWARDS, Anthony; American actor; b. 19 July 1962, Santa Barbara, Calif.; ed. R.A.D.A., London; joined Santa Barbara Youth Theatre, in 30 productions aged 12–17; working in commercials aged 16; stage appearance in Ten Below, New York 1993. *Films:* Fast Times at Ridgemont High 1982, Heart Like a Wheel 1982, Revenge of the Nerds 1984, The Sure Thing 1985, Gotcha! 1985, Top Gun 1985, Summer Heat 1987, Revenge of the Nerds II 1987, Mr. North 1988, Miracle Mile 1989, How I Got into College 1989, Hawks 1989, Downtown 1990, Delta Heat, The Client 1994, Us Begins with You 1998, Don't Go Breaking My Heart 1999. *TV:* (series) It Takes Two 1982–83, Northern Exposure 1992–93, ER 1994–, Soul Man; (films) The Killing of Randy Webster 1981, High School U.S.A. 1983, Going for the Gold: The Bill Johnson Story 1985, El Diablo 1990, Hometown Boy Makes Good 1990; (specials) Unpublished Letters, Sexual Healing. *Address:* c/o United Talent Agency, 9560 Wilshire Boulevard, Suite 500, Beverly Hills, CA 90212, U.S.A.

EDWARDS, Blake; American film director and screen writer; b. (as William Blake McEdwards) 26 July 1922, Tulsa, Okla.; m. Julie Andrews (q.v.) 1969; ed. high school; Served U.S. Coast Guard Reserve W.W.II.; wrote for radio shows Johnny Dollar, Line-Up; writer and creator of Richard Diamond; creator TV shows Dante's Inferno, Peter Gunn, Mr. Lucky; *writer and co-producer:* Panhandle 1947, Stampede 1948; *writer:* All Ashore 1952, Sound Off 1952, Cruisin' Down the River 1953, Drive a Crooked Road 1954, My Sister Eileen (musical version) 1955, Operation Mad Ball 1957, Notorious Landlady 1962; writer and dir. of films including: Bring Your Smile Along 1955, He Laughed Last 1955, Mr. Cory 1956, This Happy Feeling 1958; *films directed:* Operation Petticoat 1959, High Time 1960, Breakfast at Tiffany's 1961, Days of Wine and Roses 1962, The Carey Treatment 1972; producer, co-writer, dir.: The Soldier in the Rain 1963, The Pink Panther

1964, A Shot in the Dark 1964, What Did You Do in the War, Daddy? 1966, Peter Gunn 1967, The Party 1968, Darling Lili 1969, Wild Rovers 1971, The Tamarind Seed 1974, The Return of the Pink Panther 1975, The Pink Panther Strikes Again 1976, Revenge of the Pink Panther 1978, 10 1979, S.O.B. 1980, Victor/Victoria 1981, Trail of the Pink Panther 1982, Curse of the Pink Panther 1983, The Man Who Loved Women 1983, Micki and Maude 1984, That's Life 1986, Blind Date 1986, Sunset 1988, Skin Deep 1989, Switch 1991, Son of the Pink Panther 1993; *producer and dir.:* Experiment in Terror 1962; *co-writer, dir.:* The Great Race 1964; *writer, dir. and co-producer:* Victor/Victoria (stage musical), Broadway 1995. *Address:* c/o Blake Edwards Company, 11777 San Vincente Boulevard, Suite 501, Los Angeles, CA 90049, U.S.A. *Telephone:* (310) 571-2828. *Fax:* (310) 571-2832.

EDWARDS, Edwin Washington, LL.D.; American politician; b. 7 Aug. 1927, Marksville, La.; s. of Clarence W. Edwards and Agnes Brouillette Edwards; m. 1st Elaine Schwartzenburg 1949 (divorced 1989); two d. two s.; m. 2nd Candace Picou 1994; ed. Louisiana State Univ.; naval cadet 1945–46; practised law in Crowley, La. 1949–80, sr. partner in law firm of Edwards, Edwards and Broadhurst; practised in Baton Rouge, La. 1980–; pvt. practice 1988–; mem. Crowley City Council 1954–62, La. State Senate 1964–66; House of Reps. 1965–72, Public Works Cttee. 1965–68, Whip to La. and Miss. Dels., Judiciary Cttee. and Cttee. on Internal Security; Gov. of Louisiana 1972–80, 1984–88, 1992–96; Chair. Interstate Oil Compact Comm. 1974, Ozarks Regional Comm. 1974, Educ. Comm. of Task Force on State, Institutional and Fed. Responsibilities May 1975–; mem. Nat. Resources and Environmental Man. Cttee. of Southern Govs.' Conf., Rural and Urban Devt. Cttee. of Nat. Govs.' Conf.; mem. Crowley Chamber of Commerce, Crowley Industrial Foundation, American Legion; Democrat.

EDWARDS, Gareth Owen, M.B.E.; British rugby union player (retd.) and businessman; b. 12 July 1947; s. of Thomas Granville Edwards and Annie-Mary Edwards; m. Maureen Edwards 1972; two s.; ed. Pontardawe Tech. School, Millfield School, Cardiff Coll. of Educ.; Welsh Secondary Schools Rugby int. 1965–66; English Schools 200 yards hurdles Champion 1966 (U.K. under 19 record holder); Welsh nat. team: 53 caps 1967–78, Capt. 13 times, youngest captain (aged 20) 1968; played with following clubs: Cardiff 1966–78, Barbarians 1967–78, British Lions 1968, 1971, 1974; Jt. Dir. Euro-Commercials (South Wales) Ltd. 1982–, Players (UK) Ltd. 1983–88; Chair. Hamdden Ltd. 1991–; Chair. Regional Fisheries Advisory Cttee., Welsh Water Authority 1983–89. *Publications:* Gareth—An Autobiography 1978, Rugby Skills 1979, Rugby Skills for Forwards 1980, Gareth Edwards on Fishing 1984, Gareth Edwards on Rugby 1986, Gareth Edwards' 100 Great Rugby Players 1987. *Leisure interests:* fishing, golf. *Address:* Hamdden Ltd., Plas y Ffynnon, Cambrian Way, Brecon, Powys, LD3 7HP; 211 West Road, Nottage, Porthcawl, Mid-Glamorgan, CF36 3RT, Wales. *Telephone:* (01874) 614657 (Brecon); (01656) 785669 (Porthcawl).

EDWARDS, Sir George Robert, Kt., O.M., C.B.E., F.R.S.; British aeronautical executive and designer; b. 9 July 1908; m. Marjorie Annie Thurgood 1935 (died 1994); one d.; ed. London Univ.; design staff, Vickers Armstrong, Weybridge 1935, Experimental Man. 1940, Chief Designer 1945, Gen. Man. and Chief Engineer 1953; Man. Dir. British Aircraft Corpn. Ltd. 1960–75; Pro-Chancellor Univ. of Surrey 1964–79, Pro-Chancellor Emer. Sept. 1979–; mem. Royal Inst. 1971–; Hon. F.R.Ae.S., Hon. F.A.I.A.A.; Trustee R.A.F. Museum; Hon. D.Sc. (Southampton) 1962, (Salford) 1967, (Cranfield Inst. of Tech.) 1970, (City Univ.) 1975, (Stirling) 1979, (Surrey) 1979; Hon. D.Sc.(Eng.) (London) 1970; Hon. LL.D. (Bristol) 1973; British Gold Medal for Aeronautics 1952, Daniel Guggenheim Medal 1959, Taylor Gold Medal, Albert Medal 1972, Royal Soc. Royal Medal 1974, D.L. Surrey 1981. *Address:* Albury Heights, White Lane, Guildford, Surrey, GU4 8PR, England.

EDWARDS, James Burrows, D.M.D., F.A.C.D., F.I.C.D.; American university president and oral surgeon; b. 24 June 1927, Hawthorne, Fla.; s. of O. M. Edwards and Bertie R. Hieronymus Edwards; m. Ann Norris Darlington 1951; one s. one d.; ed. Coll. of Charleston, Univ. of Louisville and Univ. of Pa. Graduate Medical School; oral surgery residency, Henry Ford Hosp., Detroit, Mich. 1958–60; dentistry practice, specializing in oral and maxillofacial surgery, Charleston, S.C. 1960–; Clinical Assoc. in Oral Surgery, Coll. of Dental Medicine, Medical Univ., S.C. 1967–77, Clinical Prof. of Oral Surgery and Community Dentistry 1977-82, Prof. of Oral and Maxillofacial Surgery 1982, Pres. of Univ. 1982–; Fellow American Coll. of Dentists, Int. Coll. of Dentists; mem. Federation Dentaire Internationale, British Asscn. of Oral and Maxillofacial Surgeons, Int. Soc. of Oral and Maxillofacial Surgeons and numerous dental orgs. in U.S.; Chair. of Charleston County Republican Cttee. 1964–69; Chair. of First Congressional District Republican Cttee. 1970; mem. S.C. Statewide Steering Cttee. for Republican Party; mem. S.C. State Senate 1972–74; Governor of South Carolina 1975–78; U.S. Sec. of Energy 1981–82; mem. Bd. of Dirs. Wachovia Bank of S.C., Phillips Petroleum Co., William Benton Foundation, Brendle's Inc., SCANA Corpn., Encyclopaedia Britannica Inc., Imo Delaval Inc., Harry Frank Guggenheim Foundation, and numerous others; several hon. degrees. *Leisure interests:* hunting, fishing, sailing, water skiing. *Address:* Office of the President, Medical University of South Carolina, 171 Ashley Avenue, Charleston, SC 29425, U.S.A.

EDWARDS, James Griffith, C.B.E.; British psychiatrist; b. 3 Oct. 1928, India; s. of the late J. T. Edwards and C. A. Edwards; m. Susan Frances Stables 1981; one s. one d.; ed. Andover Grammar School, Balliol Coll., Oxford; Dir. Addiction Behaviour Unit 1967–94; fmrly. Chair. Nat. Addiction Centre; Emer. Prof. of Addiction Behaviour 1994–. *Publications:* papers on scientific and clinical aspects of addiction. *Address:* National Addiction Centre, 4 Windsor Walk, London, SE5 8AF, England. *Telephone:* 0171-919 3452. *Fax:* 0171-703 5787.

EDWARDS, John Coates, C.M.G., M.A.; British diplomatist; b. 25 Nov. 1934, Tunbridge Wells, Kent; s. of Herbert J. Edwards and Doris M. Edwards (née Starzacher); m. Mary Harris 1959; one s. one d.; ed. Skinners' Company School, Tunbridge Wells and Brasenose Coll. Oxford; Lieut. R.A. 1953–55; Colonial Office 1960–62; Nature Conservancy Council 1962–64; Ministry of Overseas Devt. 1965–68, 1976–78; First Sec. Bangkok and Perm Rep. to ECAFE 1968–71; Head, E. Africa Devt. Div. British High Comm. Nairobi 1972–75; Head, British Devt. Div. in the Caribbean, Barbados, and U.K. Dir. Caribbean Devt. Bank 1978–81; Head, W. Indian and Atlantic Dept. FCO 1981–84; Deputy High Commr. in Kenya 1984–88; High Commr. in Lesotho 1988–91, in Botswana 1991–94; Head U.K. Del., EC Monitoring Mission in fmr. Yugoslavia 1995, 1996, 1997, 1998. *Leisure interests:* bird-watching, fishing. *Address:* Fairways, Back Lane, Ightham, Sevenoaks, Kent. TN15 9AU, England. *Telephone:* (01732) 883556.

EDWARDS, John Hilton, M.B., B.CHIR., F.R.S., F.R.C.P.; British consultant in genetics and professor; b. 26 March 1928, London; s. of late Harold Clifford Edwards and of Ida Margaret (Phillips) Edwards; m. Felicity Clare Toussaint 1956; two s. two d.; ed. Univ. of Cambridge, Middlesex Hospital, London; Medical Officer, Falklands Islands Dependancy Survey 1952–53; with MRC Unit on Population Genetics, Oxford 1958–60; Geneticist, Children's Hospital of Philadelphia, Pa. 1960–61; Lecturer, Univ. of Birmingham, subsequently Sr. Lecturer and Reader, 1961–67, Prof. of Human Genetics 1969–79; Investigator, New York Blood Center 1967–68; Consultant in Human Genetics, Univ. of Iceland 1967–, in Clinical Genetics, Nat. Health Service; Prof. of Genetics, Univ. of Oxford 1979–95, Prof. Emer. 1995–; Visiting Prof. of Paediatrics, Cornell Univ., Ithaca, N.Y., U.S.A. 1967–68; Hon. Consultant Paediatrician, Birmingham Regional Bd. 1967–79. *Publications:* numerous publications on paediatrics, clinical genetics and mathematical genetics; Human Genetics 1978. *Leisure interests:* gliding, skiing, walking. *Address:* 78 Old Road, Headington, Oxford, England. *Telephone:* (01865) 60430.

EDWARDS, Jonathan, M.B.E.; British athlete; b. 10 May 1966, London; s. of Andrew David Edwards and Jill Caulfield; m. Alison Joy Briggs; two s.; ed. West Buckland, Devon; Bronze Medal, World Championships 1993; Gold Medal, Fifth Athletics World Championships, Gothenburg 1995 (twice breaking own world record for triple jump, clearing 18.29m.); Silver Medal, Olympic Games, Atlanta 1996, World Championships 1997; Gold Medal European Championships 1998, European Indoor Championships 1998, Goodwill Games 1998. *Address:* MTC, 10 Kendall Place, London, W1H 3AH, England. *Telephone:* 0171-935 8000. *Fax:* 0171-935 8066.

EDWARDS, Kenneth John Richard, PH.D.; British university vice-chancellor; b. 12 Feb. 1934; s. of John Edwards and Elizabeth M. Edwards; m. Janet M. Gray 1958; two s. one d.; ed. Market Drayton Grammar School, Univ. of Reading and Univ. Coll. of Wales, Aberystwyth; Fellow, Univ. of Calif. 1961–62; A.R.C. Fellow, Welsh Plant Breeding Station, Aberystwyth 1962–63, Sr. Scientific Officer 1963–66; Lecturer in Genetics, Univ. of Cambridge 1966–84, Head, Dept. of Genetics 1981–84; Lecturer, St. John's Coll. Cambridge 1971–84, Fellow 1971–87, Tutor 1981–84; Sec.-Gen. of Faculties, Univ. of Cambridge 1984–87; Vice-Chancellor, Univ. of Leicester 1987–; Chair. Cttee. of Vice-Chancellors and Prins. 1993–95; mem. Marshall Aid Commemoration Comm. 1991–, Council ACU 1994–, Comm. for Racial Equality 1994–; Chair. Governing Body, Inst. of Grassland and Environmental Research 1994–; Hon LL.D. (Reading) 1994. Visiting Lecturer, Birmingham 1965; Visiting Prof., Buenos Aires 1973; Leverhulme Research Fellow, Univ. of Calif. 1973; Hon. D.Sc. (Reading) 1995, (Loughborough) 1995. *Publications:* Evolution in Modern Biology 1977; articles on genetics in scientific journals. *Leisure interests:* music, gardening. *Address:* Knighton Hall, Leicester, LE2 3WG, England. *Telephone:* (0116) 2706677.

EDWARDS, Philip Walter, PH.D., F.B.A.; British professor of English literature; b. 7 Feb. 1923, Barrow-in-Furness; s. of the late R. H. Edwards and B. Edwards; m. 1st Hazel Valentine 1947 (died 1950); m. 2nd Sheila Wilkes 1952; three s. one d.; ed. King Edward's High School, Birmingham, Univ. of Birmingham; Lecturer in English, Univ. of Birmingham 1946–60, Prof. of English Literature, Trinity Coll. Dublin 1960–66, Visiting Prof., Univ. of Mich. 1964–65, Prof. of Literature, Univ. of Essex 1966–74, Visiting Prof., Williams Coll., Mass. 1969, Visiting Fellow, All Souls Coll., Oxford 1970–71, King Alfred Prof. of English Literature, Univ. of Liverpool 1974–90, Visiting Prof., Univ. of Otago, New Zealand 1980, Int. Christian Univ., Tokyo 1989. *Publications:* Sir Walter Ralegh 1953, The Spanish Tragedy (ed.) 1959, Shakespeare and the Confines of Art 1968, Massinger, Plays and Poems (ed. with C. Gibson) 1976, Pericles Prince of Tyre (ed.) 1976, Threshold of a Nation 1979, Hamlet Prince of Denmark (ed.) 1985, Shakespeare: A Writer's Progress 1986, Last Voyages 1988, The Story of the Voyage 1994, Sea-Mark: The Metaphorical Voyage, Spenser to Milton 1997. *Leisure interest:* calligraphy. *Address:* High Gillinggrove, Gillinggate, Kendal, Cumbria, LA9 4JB, England. *Telephone:* (01539) 721298.

EDWARDS, Robert Geoffrey, C.B.E., M.A., PH.D., F.R.S.; British professor of human reproduction; b. 27 Sept. 1925; s. of Samuel Edwards and Margaret Edwards; m. Ruth E. Fowler 1956; five d.; ed. Manchester Cen. High School and Univs. of Wales and Edinburgh; Research Fellow, Calif. Inst. of Tech. 1957–58; scientist, Nat. Inst. of Medical Research, Mill Hill 1958–62; Glasgow Univ. 1962–63; Dept. of Physiology, Univ. of Cambridge 1963–89; Ford Foundation Reader in Physiology 1969–85; Prof. of Human Reproduction, Univ. of Cambridge 1985–89, Prof. Emer. 1989–; Fellow, Churchill Coll. Cambridge, now Extraordinary Fellow; Scientific Dir. Bourn Hallam Clinics, Cambs. and London; Chair. European Soc. of Human Reproduction and Embryology 1984–86; Visiting Scientist, Johns Hopkins Univ. 1965, Univ. of N.C. 1966, Free Univ. Brussels 1984; Hon. Pres. British Fertility Soc. 1988–; Hon. mem. French Soc. for Infertility; Life Fellow, Australian Fertility Soc.; Chief Ed. Human Reproduction 1986–; Hon. Citizen of Bordeaux; Hon. F.R.C.O.G.; Hon. M.R.C.P.; Hon. D.Sc. (Hull, York, Free Univ. Brussels); Gold Medal, Spanish Fertility Soc. 1985; King Faisal Award 1989. *Publications:* A Matter of Life (with P.C. Steptoe) 1980, Conception in the Human Female 1980, Mechanisms of Sex Differentiation in Animals and Man (with C.R. Austin), Human Conception in Vitro (with J.M. Purdy) 1982, Implantation of the Human Embryo (with J.M. Purdy and P.C. Steptoe) 1985, In Vitro Fertilization and Embryo Transfer (with M. Seppälä) 1985, Life Before Birth 1989; numerous articles in scientific and medical journals. *Leisure interests:* farming, politics, music. *Address:* Duck End Farm, Dry Drayton, Cambridge, CB3 8DB, England. *Telephone:* (01954) 780602.

EDWARDS, Robert John, C.B.E.; British journalist; b. 26 Oct. 1925, Farnham, Surrey; s. of Gordon and Margaret (née Grain) Edwards; m. 1st Laura Ellwood 1952 (dissolved 1972); two s. two d.; m. 2nd Brigid Segrave 1977; ed. Ranelagh School; Ed. Tribune 1951–55; Deputy Ed. Sunday Express 1957–59; Ed. Daily Express 1961–62, 1963–65; Ed. Evening Citizen (Glasgow) 1962–63; Ed. Sunday People (fmrly. The People) 1966–72; Ed. Sunday Mirror 1972–84; Dir. Mirror Group Newspapers 1976–86, Sr. Group Ed. 1984–85, Non-exec. Deputy Chair. 1985–86; Ombudsman to Today newspaper 1990–95. *Leisure interest:* boating. *Publication:* Goodbye Fleet Street 1988. *Address:* Williamscot House, Nr. Banbury, Oxon., OX17 1AE, England. *Telephone:* (01295) 750809. *Fax:* (01295) 750826.

EDWARDS, (Roger) Nicholas (see Crickhowell, Baron).

EDWARDS, Sir Sam(uel Frederick), Kt., F.R.S., F.INST.P., F.I.M.A., F.R.S.C., C.CHEM., C.PHYS., C.MATH.; British physicist and administrator; b. 1 Feb. 1928, Swansea; s. of Richard and Mary Jane Edwards; m. Merriell E. M. Bland 1953; one s. three d.; ed. Swansea Grammar School, Gonville and Caius College, Cambridge, Harvard Univ.; member, Inst. for Advanced Study, Princeton 1952–53; staff mem. Birmingham Univ. 1953–58, Manchester Univ. 1958–72; Prof. of Theoretical Physics, Manchester Univ. 1963–72; John Humphrey Plummer Prof. of Physics, Cambridge Univ. 1972–84, Cavendish Prof. 1984–95, Pro Vice-Chancellor 1992–95, Prof. Emer. 1995–; mem. Council, Inst. of Physics 1967–73, Vice-Pres. of Inst. 1970–73, Chair. Publ. Div. 1970–73; mem. Science Bd., Science Research Council 1970–73, mem. Physics Cttee. 1968–70, Polymer Science Cttee. 1968–73, Chair. Physics Cttee. 1970–73, Science Research Council 1973–77; Dir. Lucas Industries 1981–93, Steetley PLC 1985–92; mem. Council European Physical Soc. 1969–71, Univ. Grants Cttee. 1971–73, Scientific Advisory Council, Min. of Defence 1973–81, 1988– (Chair. 1978–81), Advisory Bd. for the Research Councils, Dept. of Ed. and Science 1973–77, Metrology and Standards Requirements Bd., Dept. of Industry 1974–77, Advisory Council on Research and Devt., Dept. of Energy 1974–77 (Chair. 1983–88), U.K. Del. NATO Science Cttee. 1974–78, Senatsausschuss für Forschungspolitik und Forschungsplanung der Max Planck Gesellschaft 1975–77, Council Inst. of Mathematics and its Applications 1976– (Pres. 1980–81), European Council for Research and Devt. 1975–79, Scientific Advisory Cttee. Allied Corpn. 1980–84; Chair. Council British Asscn. for Advancement of Science 1977–82, Pres. 1988–89, Council Royal Soc. 1981–83 (Vice-Pres. 1982–83); Chief Scientific Adviser, Dept. of Energy 1983–88; Chair. Sr. Advisory Group of Unilever PLC 1992–96; mem. Research Advisory Group BP 1993–; Fellow Gonville and Caius Coll., Cambridge 1972–; Foreign mem. Acad. des Sciences 1989, N.A.S. 1996; Hon. Fellow Inst. of Physics, French Physical Soc.; Hon. mem. European Physical Soc.; Hon. D.Tech. (Loughborough) 1975; Hon. D.Sc. (Edinburgh, Salford, Bath, Birmingham, Wales, Strasbourg, Sheffield, Dublin, Leeds) 1994, (Swansea) 1994, (E. Anglia) 1995; Maxwell and Guthrie Medals and Prizes, Inst. of Physics 1974, 1987, American Physical Soc. Prize for High Polymer Physics 1982, Davy Medal, Royal Soc. 1984, Gold Medallist, Inst. of Math. 1986, Gold Medallist Rheology Soc. 1990, LVMH Science pour l'Art Prize 1993, Boltzmann Medal, Int. Union of Pure and Applied Physics 1995. *Publications:* Technological Risk 1980, Theory of Polymer Dynamics (with M. Doi) 1986, Networks of Liquid Crystal Polymers (with S. Aharoni) 1994. *Address:* 7 Penarth Place, Cambridge, CB3 9LU, England (Home). *Fax:* (01223) 366610 (Home).

EDWARDS, Sian; British conductor; ed. Royal Northern Coll. of Music, Manchester; studied with Sir Charles Groves, Norman Del Mar and Neeme Järvi, and with Prof. I.A. Musin, Leningrad Conservatoire 1983–85; won first Leeds Conductors' Competition 1984; has worked with many leading orchestras in U.K. including London Philharmonic (LPO), Royal Liverpool Philharmonic, Royal Scottish Orchestra, City of Birmingham Symphony, Halle, BBC Philharmonic, English Chamber orchestras and London Sinfonietta; also with Los Angeles Philharmonic Orchestra, The Cleveland Orchestra, The Ensemble Modern, Rotterdam Philharmonic Orchestra, and other orchestras; operatic debut, Mahagonny, Scottish Opera 1986; other operatic productions include La Traviata and L'Heure Espagnol (Glyndebourne) 1987–88, Kat'a Kabanova, New Year (Glyndebourne Touring Opera) 1988–90, The Knot Garden, Rigoletto, Il Trovatore (Royal Opera House, Covent Garden) 1988–91, world premiere Greek (Mark Anthony Turnage), Munich Biennale 1988, Edin. Festival 1988, The Gambler (English Nat. Opera—ENO) 1990, Khovanschina (ENO) 1994, Mahagonny 1995, La Clemenza di Tito 1998; Music Dir. ENO 1993–95; recordings include Tchaikovsky orchestral music (Royal Liverpool Philharmonic Orchestra), and Peter and the Wolf, Young Person's Guide to the Orchestra, Tchaikovsky's 5th symphony, (LPO). *Address:* c/o Ingpen and Williams, 14 Kensington Court, London, W8 5DN; 70 Twisden Road, London, NW5 1DN, England.

EELSEN, Pierre Henri Maurice, L. EN D.; French administrator and company executive; b. 12 July 1933, Montmorency, Val-d'Oise; s. of Maurice Eelsen and Jacqueline Robert; m. 1st; two s. one d.; m. 2nd Danièle Mesle, 1980; one s.; ed. Lycée Jacques-Decour, Paris, Univ. de Paris; at Renault 1958–84, responsible for econ. studies Renault Eng. 1959, attached to Dir. of Relations 1965, Head Dept. Agric. Machinery 1967, attached to Gen. Secretariat 1969, Asst. to Sec.-Gen. 1971, Jt. Sec.-Gen. 1975, Gen. Del. 1979, mem. Exec. Cttee. 1981; Head Dept. Int. Affairs Chambre syndicale des constructeurs d'automobiles 1962; mem. European Econ. and Social Cttee. 1982–84; Pres. Nat. Asscn. for devt. of Overseas depts. 1982–85; Admin. Ecole nat. d'admin. 1983; Pres.-Dir.-Gen. Air Inter 1984–90; Pres. Agence Nationale pour le Développement de l'Education Permanente (ADEP) 1985–91, Centre nationale d'enseignement à distance 1988–, Admin. council Institut régional d'admin. de Nantes 1988, French Div. of Centre européen de l'entreprise publique 1989, Chambre Syndicale des Transporteurs Aériens 1986–90; Pres. Nord-Pas de Calais Développement 1991–94, Observatoire Nat. du Tourisme 1991–96, L'Institut européen de recherche et de formation supérieure du tourisme 1992–94; Man. Ed Consultants 1994–; Officier, ordre nat. du Mérite, Officier, Légion d'honneur. *Address:* Ed Consultants, 5 Allée Hélène Boucher, Orlytech, 91781 Wissous (Office); 33 rue Lhomond, 75005 Paris; Domaine de Camarat, 83350 Ramatuelle, France. (Homes). *Telephone:* 0141730908.

EFFERT, Sven, DR.MED.; German professor of medicine; b. 31 March 1922, Aachen; s. of Edgar Effert and Else Philips; m. Ilse Tutscheck 1946; two s. one d.; ed. Univs. of Bonn, Freiburg and Düsseldorf; Asst. Prof. Univ. of Düsseldorf, Faculty of Medicine 1964–66; Prof. of Internal Medicine, Faculty of Medicine, Rheinisch-Westfälische Technische Hochschule Aachen 1966–, Head of Dept. for Internal Medicine I 1966–, Dir. Helmholtz-Inst. for Biomedical Eng. 1970–; Pres. Soc. of German Natural Researchers and Physicians 1979–; German Soc. of Cardiology 1981–; mem. Deutsche Akad. der Naturforscher (Leopoldina); Int. Fellow of the Council of the American Heart Asscn.; Verdienstkreuz 1st Class. *Publications:* numerous publs. and contribs. to books since 1948. *Address:* Helmholtz-Institute for Biomedical Engineering, RWTH Aachen, Pauwelsstrasse 30, Aachen (Office); Rotbendenstrasse 14, 52076 Aachen, Germany (Home). *Telephone:* 0241-80 88 760 (Office); 0241-6 10 58 (Home).

EFHOLM, Mogens; Danish business executive; b. 20 May 1910, Copenhagen; s. of Christian Christensen and Ingeborg Ohlsson; m. Birgitte Jensen 1947; ed. univ., and commercial studies in England, Germany and France; Copenhagen trade agencies 1930–45; Man. Dir. Emil Warthoe & Soenner A/S 1945–50, Nordisk Andelsforbund (Scandinavian Co-operative Wholesale Soc.) 1951–64, "National" Co. 1953–57, Nordisk Andels-Eksport (Scandinavian Co-operative Export) 1954–64; mem. Cen. Cttee. Int. Co-operative Alliance, London 1961–64; mem. Maritime and Commercial Court 1961–81; Chair. Nordisk Andelsforbund, Calif., Inc., San Francisco 1962–64; Sec.-Gen. European Co-operative Wholesale Cttee. for Developments in Production and Marketing Fields 1963–64; Commercial Adviser 1964–; Kt., first rank Order of Dannebrog. *Leisure interests:* literature and philosophy. *Address:* 65B Strandvejen, Copenhagen Ø, Denmark. *Telephone:* 39-29-36-46.

EFI, The Hon. Taisi Tupuola Tufuga; Samoan politician; b. 1938; s. of Tupua Tamasese Mea'ole; ed. St. Joseph's Coll., Apia, Western Samoa and Victoria Univ., Wellington, N.Z.; elected to Western Samoan Parl. 1965–91; Minister of Works, Civil Aviation, Marine and Transport 1970–73; Prime Minister 1976–82, fmr. Minister of Foreign Affairs, Local and Dist. Affairs and Police; Jt. Leader Samoa Nat. Devt. Party (SNDP). *Address:* Samoa National Development Party, Apia, Samoa.

EFIMOV (see Yefimov).

EGAL, Mohamed Ibrahim; Somali politician; b. 1928, Berbera; s. of Haji Ibrahim Egal and Hajia Khadija Mohamed Osman; m. Aasha Saeed Abby 1946; three s. two d.; ed. Koranic School, Sheikh Intermediate School, and in U.K.; Sec. Berbera Branch, Somali Nat. League Party 1956; Sec.-Gen. Somali Nat. League Party 1958–60; Prime Minister of Somaliland 1960; Minister of Defence, Somali Repub. 1960–62, of Educ. 1962–63; resgnd. from cabinet 1963; f. SNC Party 1963; re-elected to Parl. March 1964; Leader of Parl. Opposition 1963–65; resgnd. leadership 1965; mem. Somali Youth League Party 1966; Prime Minister and Minister of Foreign Affairs, Somali Repub. 1967–69; in detention following coup 1969, released Oct. 1975; apptd. Amb. to India July 1976, rearrested Oct. 1976, released Feb. 1982; Chair. Chamber of Commerce, Industry and Agric.; Pres. self-proclaimed Repub. of Somaliland (N.-Western Somalia) 1993–98. *Leisure interests:* golf, reading and films.

EGAN, Sir John Leopold, Kt., M.SC., B.SC.ECON., F.I.C., F.I.M.I.; British business executive; b. 7 Nov. 1939, Rawtenstall, Lancs.; s. of James Edward

Egan; m. Julia Emily Treble 1963; two d.; ed. Bablake School, Coventry, Imperial Coll., London, London Business School; petroleum engineer, Shell Int. 1962–66; Gen. Man. A.C. Delco Replacement Parts Operation, Gen. Motors 1968–71; Man. Dir. Unipart, Parts and Service Dir., Leyland Cars 1971–76; Corp. Parts Dir. Massey Ferguson 1976–80; Chair. Jaguar Cars Ltd. 1980–84, Chair and Chief Exec., Chief Exec. and Man. Dir. Jaguar PLC 1984–85, Chair. and Chief Exec. Jaguar PLC 1985–90; Chief Exec. BAA PLC 1990–, Dir. 1990–; Dir. Legal and Gen. Group 1987–97, Chair. 1993–97, Pres. 1998–; mem. Bd. British Tourist Authority 1994–97; Sr. Fellow R.C.A.; Hon. Prof., Dept. of Eng., Univ. of Warwick 1990; Dr. h.c. (Cranfield Inst.) 1986, Hon. Dr. Tech. (Loughborough) 1987, Hon. LL.D. (Bath) 1988; Castrol Gold Medal, Inst. of Motor Industry Award 1982, Int. Gold Medal, Inst. of Production Engineers, City and Guilds of London Hon. Insignia Award for Tech. 1987 and several other awards. *Leisure interests:* skiing, squash, walking, music. *Address:* BAA PLC, 130 Wilton Road, London, SW1V 1LQ, England. *Telephone:* 0171-932 6707.

EGDAHL, Richard H., M.D., PH.D.; American professor of surgery; b. 13 Dec. 1926, Eau Claire, Wis.; s. of Harry I. Egdahl and Rebecca (née Ball) Egdahl; m. Cynthia H. Taft 1983; three s. one d. (by previous m.); ed. Dartmouth Coll., Harvard Medical School and Univ. of Minnesota; Prof. of Surgery and Dir. of Research Labs. Medical Coll. of Va. 1957–64; Chair. Div. of Surgery, Boston Univ. Medical Center 1964–73; Prof. of Surgery, Boston Univ. School of Medicine 1964–73, Prof. of Public Health 1983; Dir. Boston Univ. Medical Center 1973–96; Academic Vice-Pres. for Health Affairs, Boston Univ. 1973, Dir. Health Policy Inst. 1975, Dir. Center for Industry and Health Care 1976. *Publications:* 250 publs. *Leisure interest:* tennis. *Address:* 333 Commonwealth Avenue, Apt. 23, Boston, MA 02115, U.S.A. (Home).

EGERSZEGI, Krisztina; Hungarian swimmer; b. 1974; Gold Medallist 200m. Backstroke, Olympic Games, Seoul 1988 (youngest Olympic swimming champion) and Barcelona 1992; Bronze Medallist 400m. Individual Medley, Olympic Games, Atlanta 1996. *Address:* Budapest Spartacus, 1103 Budapest, Kőér u 1/a, Hungary.

EGERTON, Sir Stephen Loftus, K.C.M.G., M.A.; British fmr. diplomatist and business consultant; b. 21 July 1932, Indore, India; s. of William Egerton and Angela D. (née Bland) Egerton; m. Caroline Cary-Elwes 1958; one s. one d.; ed. Eton Coll., Trinity Coll., Cambridge; served with 60th Rifles 1951–53; joined Foreign Office 1956; served in Lebanon, Kuwait, Baghdad, New York, Tripoli, Rio de Janeiro; Amb. to Iraq 1980–82; Asst. Under-Sec. of State for Middle Eastern Affairs FCO 1982–86; Amb. to Saudi Arabia 1986–89, to Italy 1989–92, to Albania (non-resident) May–July 1992; consultant, Enterprise Oil PLC 1992–; Dir. St. Andrew's Trust, Lambeth Palace 1994–99; Pres. Soc. for Libyan Studies 1995–98; Vice-Pres. British School of Archaeology in Iraq and Mesopotamia 1995–; First Class, Order of Feisal bin Abdul Aziz 1987; Grand Cross of Merit of the Italian Repub. 1990. *Leisure interests:* conversation, topiary. *Address:* c/o Barclays Bank, 8 High Street, Eton, Windsor SL4 6AU, England. *Telephone:* (01508) 558360 (Home). *Fax:* (01508) 558360.

EGGLETON, Arthur C. (Art); Canadian politician; fmr. accountant; mem. Toronto City Council and Metropolitan Toronto Council 1969–93; Mayor of Toronto 1980–91; mem. Parl. 1993–; Pres. Treas. Bd. and Minister responsible for Infrastructure 1993–96; Minister for Int. Trade 1996–97, of Nat. Defence 1997–; Civic Award of Merit, Toronto 1992. *Address:* Ministry of National Defence, Major-General George R. Pearkes Building, 101 Colonel By Drive, Ottawa, Ont., K1A 0K2, Canada.

EGILSSON, Ólafur; Icelandic diplomatist and lawyer; b. 20 Aug. 1936, Reykjavík; s. of Egill Kristjánsson and Anna Margrjet Thurídur Ólafsdóttir Briem; m. Ragna Sverrisdóttir Ragnars 1960; one s. one d.; ed. Commercial College of Iceland and Iceland Univ.; journalist with newspapers Vísir 1956–58, Morgunblad¯id¯ 1959–62; Publishing Exec. 1963–64; Head, NATO Regional Information Office, Reykjavík 1964–66; Gen.-Sec. Icelandic Asscn. for Western Co-operation 1964–66; Political Div., Icelandic Foreign Ministry 1966–69; First Sec., then Counsellor, Icelandic Embassy, Paris 1969–71; Deputy Perm. Rep. OECD, UNESCO and Council of Europe 1969–71; Deputy Perm. Rep. N. Atlantic Council, Deputy Head, Icelandic Del. to EEC, Counsellor, Embassy in Brussels 1971–74; Counsellor, then Minister Counsellor, Political Div. of Foreign Ministry 1974–80; Chief of Protocol (with rank of Amb.) 1980–83; Acting Prin. Pvt. Sec. to Pres. of Iceland 1981–82; Deputy Perm. Under Sec. and Dir.-Gen. for Political Affairs, Foreign Ministry 1983–87; Amb. to U.K. (also accred. to Ireland, Netherlands and Nigeria) 1986–89; Amb. to U.S.S.R., later Russia 1990–94; Amb. to Denmark (also accred. to Japan, Italy, Israel, Lithuania and Turkey) 1994–96; in charge of Arctic co-operation 1996–98 (also accred. to Holy See, Turkey, Australia and N.Z.); Amb. to China 1998– (also accred. to Australia, Japan, Repub. of Korea, N.Z. and Viet Nam); Chair., Bd. of Govs. Icelandic Int. Devt. Agency 1982–87; Exec. mem. Bible Soc. of Iceland 1977–87, History Soc. 1982–88; Commdr. Icelandic Order of the Falcon and decorations from Finland, France, Norway, Spain, Sweden and Luxembourg. *Publications:* Co-author: Iceland and Jan Mayen 1980, NATO's Anxious Birth—The Prophetic Vision of the 1940's 1985; Ed. Bjarni Benediktsson 1983. *Leisure interests:* history, skiing, music (classical, opera). *Address:* Icelandic Embassy, 1-12-2 Ta Yuan Diplomatic Office Building, 100600 Beijing, China. *Telephone:* (10) 6532-6882. *Fax:* (10) 6532-6882.

EGLI, Alphons, D.JUR.; Swiss politician; b. 8 Oct. 1924, Lucerne; s. of Gotthard Egli; m.; three c.; ed. legal studies in Zurich, Berne and Rome; private legal practice in Lucerne 1952–82; mem. Lucerne Municipal Council 1963–67, Lucerne Cantonal Parl. 1967–75; mem. Council of States 1975, Leader, Christian Democratic Group 1979; Fed. Councillor 1982–; Head, Fed. Dept. of the Interior 1982–85, 1986, Pres. of Swiss Confed. and Head of State Jan.–Dec. 1986. *Address:* c/o Federal Chancellery, Bundeshaus-West, Bundesgasse, 3003 Berne, Switzerland.

EGLIN, Colin Wells; South African politician and quantity surveyor; b. 14 April 1925, Cape Town; s. of Carl Eglin and Elsie May Wells; three d.; ed. De Villiers Graaff High School and Univ. of Cape Town; army service in Egypt and Italy 1943–45; mem. Pinelands Municipal Council 1951–54, Cape Prov. Council 1954–58; mem. Parl. 1958–61, 1974–; Leader Progressive Party 1970–75; Leader Progressive Reform Party 1975–77, Progressive Federal Party 1977–79, 1986–88; (Official Opposition Leader 1977–79, 1986–87); Chair. Democratic Party Caucus, Democratic Party Spokesman on Foreign Affairs 1989–; Co-Chair. Transitional Exec. Council 1993–94; Chief DP Constitutional Negotiator; Vice-Pres. Liberal Int. 1990–; mem. Man. Cttee. Constitutional Ass. 1994–96; Sec.-Gen. Org. of African Liberal Parties 1995–; Partner, Bernard James and Partners (Quantity Surveyors) 1952–; Hon. LL.D. (Cape Town) 1997. *Publications:* Betrayal of Coloured Rights, Forging Links in Africa, Priorities for the Seventies, New Deal for the Cities, Africa—A Prospect of Reconciliation, Pacesetter for Political Change, Security Through Negotiation. *Leisure interests:* golf, travel. *Address:* Democratic Party, P.O. Box 15, Cape Town 8000 (Office); 2 Cassandra, 42 Victoria Road, Clifton, Cape, South Africa (Home). *Telephone:* (021) 4387278 (Home).

EGLINTON, Geoffrey, PH.D., D.SC., F.R.S.; British professor of organic geochemistry; b. 1 Nov. 1927, Cardiff; m. Pamela J. Coupland 1955; two s. one d. (deceased); ed. Sale Grammar School and Univ. of Manchester; Post-doctoral Fellow, Ohio State Univ. 1952; Lecturer in Organic Chem., Univ. of Glasgow 1954–64; Visiting Fellow, Univ. of Calif. (Berkeley) 1964; Sr. Lecturer in Organic Chem., Univ. of Glasgow 1964–67, Reader 1967; Sr. Lecturer in Organic Geochem. and Head, Organic Chem. Unit, Univ. of Bristol 1967, Reader in Organic Geochem. 1968–73, Prof. and Head of Organic Geochem. Unit 1973–93, Prof. Emer. 1993–, Dir. Biogeochemistry Centre 1991–97, Sr. Research Fellow 1995–; Visiting Scholar Woods Hole Oceanographic Inst., Mass. 1986, Adjunct Scientist 1991–; Geochemistry Fellow of Geochemical Soc. and European Asscn. for Geochemistry 1996; NASA Gold Medal 1973, Hugo Muller Silver Medal (Chem. Soc.) 1974, Alfred E. Treibs Medal 1981, Melvin Calvin Lectureship (Univ. of Calif., Berkeley) 1985, Major Edward Fitzgerald Coke Medal of the Geological Soc. 1986, H. Burr Steinbach Visiting Scholar, Woods Hole Oceanographic Inst. 1986; Harold C. Urey Award, European Asscn. of Geochemists 1997; Royal Medal, Royal Soc. 1997. *Publications:* over 490 articles and books. *Leisure interests:* hiking, sailing. *Address:* Oldwell, 7 Redhouse Lane, Westbury-on-Trym, Bristol, BS9 3RY, England (Home). *Telephone:* (0117) 9683833 (Home).

EGON, Nicholas, British painter; b. 15 Nov. 1921, Brno, Czechoslovakia; m. 1st Diana Horton 1948; m. 2nd Matti Xylas 1980; ed. pvt. tutors, Birkbeck Coll., London Univ., Oxford Univ.; served with army in Middle East 1942–46; taught painting and history of art, Sir John Cass Coll., lectured at Nat. Gallery, London, and Oxford and Cambridge 1946–50; 10 one-man exhbns. London 1950–90; portraits, landscapes and abstracts in nat., royal and pvt. collections, U.S.A., U.K., France, Italy, Greece, Spain, Jordan, Saudi Arabia, Morocco, Oman and Switzerland; Chair. of Patrons, Centre for Hellenic Studies, King's Coll., London Univ. 1989–. *Publications:* Some Beautiful Women (portraits) 1952, Paintings of Jordan 1986. *Leisure interests:* travel, history, music, archaeology. *Address:* Villa Aëtos, Katakali, 20100 Corinthias (Studio); Deinokratous 81, 115 21 Athens, Greece; 34 Thurloe Square, London, SW7 2SR, England. *Telephone:* 0741 33442 (Corinthias); 01 729 1774 (Athens); 0171-589 0700 (London). *Fax:* 0741 33640 (Corinthias); 0171-589 0620 (London).

EGOYAN, Atom, B.A.; film director; b. 19 July 1960, Cairo; s. of Joseph Egoyan and Shushan Devletian; m. Arsinee Khanjian; one c.; ed. Univ. of Toronto; Dir. Ego Film Arts, Toronto 1982–; films shown at int. film festivals around the world; writer, dir. and producer feature films: Next of Kin 1984 (Gold Ducat award, Mannheim Int. Film Week 1984), Family Viewing 1987 (Int. Critics Award 1988, Best Feature Film Award, Uppsala, Prix Alcan, Festival du Nouveau Cinéma, Montréal), Speaking Parts 1989 (Best Screenplay Prize, Vancouver Int. Film Festival), The Adjuster 1991 (Special Jury Prize, Moscow Film Festival, Golden Spike Award, Valladolid Film Festival), Calendar 1993 (prize at Berlin Int. Film Festival), Exotica 1994 (Int. Film Critics Award, Cannes Film Festival 1994, Prix de la Critique award for Best Foreign Film 1994), Salome Canadian Opera Co. 1996, Houston Grand Opera 1997, The Sweet Hereafter 1997 (Grand Prix, Int. Critics Prize, Cannes Film Festival 1997), Elsewhereless 1998, Dr. Ox's Experiment 1998; numerous other awards for films. *Leisure interest:* classical guitar. *Address:* Ego Film Arts, 80 Niagara Street, Toronto, Ont., M5V 1C5, Canada.

EGUIAGARAY UCELAY, Juan Manuel, B.A., PH.D.; Spanish politician; b. 25 Dec. 1945, Bilbao; m.; one s.; ed. Univ. of Deusto, Univ. of Nancy, France; mem. PSE-PSOE (Workers' Socialist Party of Spain) 1977–; counsellor Town Council, Bilbao 1979, Provincial Deputy, Vizcaya 1979–81, mem. Juntas Generales Vizcaya 1979–83, Deputy and Spokesman for Socialist Party of

Basque Parliament 1980–88, mem. Exec. Cttee. PSE-PSOE 1979–, Vice-Sec. Gen. Basque Socialists 1985–88, Govt. Del. for Autonomous Community of Murcia, then for Autonomous Community of the Basque Country 1988–89; Exec. Sec. PSOE Fed. Exec. Comm. 1990; Minister for Public Admin. 1991–93, of Industry and Energy 1993–96; Nat. Deputy for Murcia 1996–(99); Fed. Sec. for the Economy (34th Fed. Congress of PSOE), fmrly. PSOE Nat. Parl. Spokesman, now PSOE Nat. Parl. Spokesman for Econ. Affairs. *Address:* c/o PSOE, c/Ferraz 68 y 70, 28008 Madrid, Spain. *Telephone:* (1) 582-0444. *Fax:* (1) 582-0422.

EHLERMANN, Claus-Dieter, DR. IUR.; German lawyer; b. 15 June 1931, Scheessel; s. of Kurt Ehlermann and Hilde (née Justus) Ehlermann; m. Carola Grumbach 1959; two d.; ed. Univs. of Marburg/Lahn and Heidelberg, Univ. of Michigan Law School, Ann Arbor; Research Asst. Fed. Constitutional Court, Karlsruhe 1959–61; Legal Adviser, Legal Service of the Comm. of European Communities 1961–73, Dir. and Deputy Financial Controller 1973–77, Dir.-Gen. of the Legal Service 1977–87; Spokesman of the Comm. of the European Communities and of its Pres. Jacques Delors (q.v.) 1987–90, Dir.-Gen. of Directorate-Gen. for Competition 1990–95; Prof of Econ. Law, European Univ. Inst., Florence; mem. Appellate Body of WHO, Geneva; Hon. Prof. Univ. of Hamburg. *Publications:* numerous documents on the European Community and its legal order. *Leisure interests:* reading, skiing. *Address:* Istituto Universitario Europeo, Badia Fiesolana, Via dei Roccettini 9, 50016 San Domenico di Fiesole (Firenze), Italy; Centre William Rappard, Ruede Lausanne 154, Case postale, CH-1211 Geneva 21, Switzerland. *Telephone:* (55) 4685798 (Italy); (22) 739-51-11 (Switzerland). *Fax:* (55) 4685776 (Italy); (22) 739-57-86 (Switzerland).

EHRLICH, Paul Ralph, M.A., PH.D.; American population biologist; b. 29 May 1932, Philadelphia, Pa.; s. of William and Ruth (Rosenberg) Ehrlich; m. Anne Fitzhugh Howland 1954; one d.; ed. Univs. of Pennsylvania and Kansas; Assoc. investigator, U.S.A.F. research project, Alaska and Univ. of Kansas 1956–57; Research Assoc. Chicago Acad. of Sciences and Univ. of Kansas Dept. of Entomology 1957–59; mem. Faculty, Stanford Univ. 1959, Prof. of Biology 1966–, Bing Prof. of Population Studies 1976–; Pres. Centre for Conservation Biology 1988–; Corresp. NBC News 1989–92; Fellow A.A.A.S.; mem. N.A.S.; Hon. D.Hum.Litt. (Univ. of the Pacific) 1970. *Publications:* How to Know the Butterflies 1961, Population Resources, Environment 1970, 1972 (both with A. H. Ehrlich); The Population Bomb 1968, 1971; How to be a Survivor (with R. L. Harriman) 1971; co-editor: Man and the Ecosphere (with J. P. Holdren and R. W. Holm) 1971; Global Ecology (with J. P. Holdren) 1971, Human Ecology (with A. H. Ehrlich and J. Holdren) 1973, Ark II (with D. Pirages) 1974, The Process of Evolution (with R. W. Holm and D. R. Parnell) 1974, The End of Affluence (with A. H. Ehrlich) 1974; Biology and Society (with R. W. Holm and I. Brown) 1976, The Race Bomb (with S. Feldman) 1977, Ecoscience: Population, Resources, Environment (with A. H. Ehrlich and J. P. Holdren) 1977, Introduction to Insect Biology and Diversity (with H. V. Daly and J. T. Doyen) 1978, The Golden Door: International Migration, Mexico and the U.S. (with D. L. Bilderback and A. H. Ehrlich) 1979, Extinction: The Causes and Consequences of the Disappearance of Species (with A. H. Ehrlich) 1981, Machinery of Nature 1986, Earth (with A. H. Ehrlich) 1987, The Birder's Handbook (with D. Dobkin and D. Wheye) 1988, New World/New Mind (with R. Ornstein) 1989, The Population Explosion (with A. H. Ehrlich) 1990, Healing the Planet (with A. H. Ehrlich) 1991, Birds in Jeopardy 1992, The Stork and the Plow (with A. H. Ehrlich and G. C. Daily) 1995, Betrayal of Science and Reason (with A. H. Ehrlich) 1996, and other books; over 500 scientific and popular articles. *Leisure interest:* collecting primitive art. *Address:* Department of Biological Sciences, Stanford University, Stanford, CA 94305, U.S.A. *Telephone:* (415) 723-3171.

EHRLICH, S. Paul, Jr., M.P.H., M.D.; American physician; b. 4 May 1932, Minn.; s. of S. Paul Ehrlich and Dorothy E. Fiterman; m. Geraldine McKenna 1959; three d.; ed. Univs. of Minnesota and Calif.; Staff Physician, Grants and Training Branch, Nat. Heart Inst., Nat. Insts. of Health, Bethesda 1959–60; Chief, Epidemiology Field Training Station, Heart Disease Control Program, Wash., D.C. 1961–66, Deputy Chief Heart Disease Control Program 1966–67; Lecturer in Epidemiology, School of Public Health, Univ. of Calif. 1961–63; Clinical Assoc. Prof., Dept. of Community Medicine and Int. Health, Georgetown Univ. School of Medicine, Wash., D.C. 1967; Adjunct Prof. of Int. Health, Univ. of Texas; Deputy Dir. Pan American Health Org., Washington 1979–83; Assoc. Dir. for Bilateral Programs, Office of Int. Health, 1967–68; Deputy Dir. Office of Int. Health 1968–69; Acting Dir. Office of Int. Health, Dept. of Health, Educ. and Welfare Dec. 1969–70, Dir. 1970–77; Asst. Surgeon-Gen., USPHS 1970, Acting Surgeon-Gen. 1973–77, Deputy Surgeon-Gen. 1976-77; U.S. Rep. to World Health Org. (WHO) 1969–72, 1973–76; Diplomate, American Bd. of Preventive Medicine; Chair. Exec. Bd. of WHO 1972; Sr. Adviser American Asscn. of World Health 1984–86, Health Consultant 1984–. *Publications:* Articles on Chronic Disease Control, Coronary Disease Risk Factors, and the Relationship of the Stroke to Other Cardiovascular Diseases. *Address:* 6512 Lakeview Drive, Falls Church, VA 22041, U.S.A.

EHRLICH, Thomas, LL.B.; American university president and professor of law; b. 4 March 1934, Cambridge, Mass.; m. Ellen Rome Ehrlich; two s. one d.; ed. Harvard Coll. and Harvard Law School, Cambridge, Mass.; law clerk, U.S. Court of Appeals, New York 1959–60; Assoc., Foley, Sammond & Lardner law practice, Milwaukee, Wis. 1960–62; Special Asst. to Legal Adviser, Dept. of State, Washington, D.C. 1962–65, to Under-Sec. of State George W. Ball 1964–65; Prof., Stanford Univ. Law School, Stanford, Calif. 1965–71, Dean and Richard E. Lang Prof. 1971–75; Pres. Legal Services Corpn., Washington, D.C. 1976–79; Dir. Int. Devt. Co-operating Agency, Washington, D.C. 1979–80; Guest Scholar, The Brookings Inst. 1981; Provost and Prof. of Law, Univ. of Pa., Phila., Pa. 1982–87; Pres. Ind. Univ. 1987–94; Visiting Prof. Stanford Law School 1994–; Distinguished Univ. Scholar, Calif. State Univ., San Francisco 1995–; sr. scholar Carnegie Foundation for the Advancement of Tech. 1997–; Arbitrator, U.S.-France Int. Aviation Dispute, Geneva, Switzerland; mem. American Asscn. for Higher Educ., American Bar Asscn. Special Comm. on Professional Standards, Council of Ten (Council of Pres., Big Ten Univs.), Council on Foreign Relations, Exec. Cttee. American Soc. of Int. Law, Bd. of Dirs. Center for Law and Social Policy, and many other bodies; Hon. LL.D. (Univ. of Pa) 1987, (Villanova) 1979, (Notre Dame) 1980. *Publications:* The International Legal Process (with Abram Chayes and Andreas F. Lowenfeld), (3 vols.) 1968, Supplement 1974, New Directions in Legal Education (with Herbert L. Packer) 1972, International Crises and the Role of Law, Cyprus 1958–67 1974, International Law and the Use of Force (with Mary Ellen O'Connell) 1993, The Courage to Inquire 1995; numerous articles, reviews and other publs. *Address:* San Francisco State University, Diagnostic Center D25, 1600 Holloway Avenue, San Francisco, CA 94132, U.S.A.

EHRMAN, John Patrick William, M.A., F.B.A., F.S.A., F.R.HIST.S.; British historian; b. 17 March 1920, London; s. of Albert Ehrman and Rina Ehrman; m. Elizabeth Susan Anne Blake 1948; four s.; ed. Charterhouse and Trinity Coll. Cambridge; served R.N. 1940–45; Fellow of Trinity Coll. 1947–52; Historian, Cabinet Office 1948–56; Lees Knowles Lecturer, Cambridge Univ. 1957–58; James Ford Special Lecturer, Oxford Univ. 1976–77; Hon. Treas. Friends of the Nat. Libraries 1960–77; Trustee, Nat. Portrait Gallery 1971–85; Chair. Nat. Manuscripts Conservation Trust 1989–94; mem. Reviewing Cttee. on the Export of Works of Art 1970–76, Royal Comm. on Historical Manuscripts 1973–94; Chair. Advisory Cttee. to British Library Reference Div. (later Humanities and Social Sciences) 1975–84. *Publications:* The Navy in the War of William III 1953, Grand Strategy 1943–45 (2 vols.: U.K. Official Military Histories of the Second World War) 1956, Cabinet, Government and War 1890–1940 1958, The British Government and Commercial Negotiations with Europe 1783–1793 1962, The Younger Pitt (Vol. I) 1969, (Vol. II) 1983, (Vol. III) 1996 (Yorkshire Post Book of the Year Award). *Address:* The Mead Barns, Taynton, Nr. Burford, Oxon, England.

EIBL-EIBESFELDT, Irenäus, DR.PHIL.; Austrian professor of zoology; b. 15 June 1928, Vienna; s. of Anton and Maria (von Hauninger) Eibl-Eibesfeldt; m. Eleonore Siegel 1950; one s. one d.; ed. Univs. of Vienna and Munich; Research Assoc., Biol. Station, Wilhelminenberg, nr. Vienna 1946–49, Max Planck Inst. of Behavioural Physiology 1951–69; Head of ind. research unit on human ethology, Max Planck Inst. 1970–; Prof. Univ. of Munich 1963; Corresp. mem. Deutsche Akad. der Naturforscher Leopoldina; Dr. h.c. (Salamanca) 1994; Wilhelm Bölsche Gold Medal 1971, Burda Prize for Communications research 1980, Philip Morris Research Prize 1988, Gold Medal of Honour (City of Vienna) 1989; Grosses Verdienstkreuz des Verdienstordens (Germany) 1995; Schwenk'scher Umweltpreis 1996, Haackert Medal 1997, Bayerischer Verdienstorden 1997, Jahrespreis von STAB, Zurich 1997. *Publications:* Galapagos, die Arche Noah im Pacific 1960, Im Reich der tausend Atolle 1964, Grundriss der vergleichenden Verhaltensforschung 1967, Liebe und Hass 1970, Der vorprogrammierte Mensch 1973, Menschenforschung auf neuen Wegen 1976, Der Hai: Legende eines Mörders (with H. Hass) 1977, Die Malediven. Paradies im Indischen Ozean 1982, Die Biologie des menschlichen Verhaltens, Grundriss der Humanethologie 1984, Der Mensch—das riskierte Wesen 1988, Human Ethology 1989, Das verbindende Erbe 1991, Und grün des Lebens göldner Baum 1992, Im Banne der Angst (co-author) 1992, Wider die Misstrauens-gesellschaft 1994. *Leisure interests:* skin diving, skiing, arts. *Address:* Max Planck Gesellschaft, Von-der-Tann-Strasse 3-5, D-82348 Andechs (Office); Fichtenweg 9, 82319 Starnberg, Germany (Home). *Telephone:* (08152) 37357; 37359. *Fax:* (08152) 37370.

EICHEL, Hans; German politician; b. 24 Dec. 1941, Kassel; m.; two c.; ed. Univs. of Marburg and Berlin; fmr. schoolmaster; mem. Kassel City Council 1968–75, Chair. Social Democratic Party (SDP) Group 1970–75; mem. Nat. Exec. of Young Socialists 1969–72; Chief Mayor of Kassel 1957–91; mem. SDP Nat. Exec. and Spokesman on Local Govt. 1984; Chair. SDP Asscn. Hesse 1989; Minister-Pres. of Hesse 1991–99; Minister of Finance 1999. *Address:* Ministry of Finance, 53117 Bonn, Graurheindorfer Str. 108, Germany. *Telephone:* (228) 6820. *Fax:* (228) 6824420.

EICHELBAUM, Rt. Hon. Sir (Johann) Thomas, G.B.E., P.C.; New Zealand judge; b. 17 May 1931, Koenigsberg, Germany; s. of Dr. Walter Eichelbaum and Frida M. Eichelbaum; m. Vida Beryl Franz 1956; three s.; ed. Hutt Valley High School and Victoria Univ. Coll.; admitted solicitor 1953, barrister 1954; partner, Chapman Tripp & Co. 1958–78; Q.C. 1978; barrister 1978–82; Pres. N.Z. Law Soc. 1980–82; Judge, High Court of N.Z. 1982; Chief Justice of N.Z. 1989–. *Publication:* Mauet's Fundamentals of Trial Techniques (Ed.-in-Chief). *Leisure interests:* reading, bush-walking. *Address:* Chief Justice's Chambers, High Court of New Zealand, P.O. Box 1091, Wellington, New Zealand. *Telephone:* (4) 915-8139. *Fax:* (4) 915-8136.

EICHER, Lawrence D., PH.D.; American administrator and scientist; b. 3 Nov. 1938, Colorado; m. Nancy Darby 1960; one s. two d.; ed. Univ. of

Northern Colorado, Univ. of California (Berkeley), Texas A & M Univ.; science teacher 1960–64; Sr. Data Analyst, Thermodynamics Research Center, Texas A & M Univ. 1967–72; Program Man., Scientific and Tech. Data Systems, Nat. Science Foundation 1972–74; Asst. to Dir., Inst. for Applied Tech., Nat. Bureau of Standards 1974–76, Chief, Office of Standards Information, Analysis and Devt., Nat. Eng. Lab., NBS 1975–79, Dir. Office of Eng. Standards, NBS 1979–80; Asst. Sec.-Gen., Int. Org. for Standardization (ISO), Geneva 1980–86, Sec.-Gen. 1986–. *Publications:* Finding and Building Agreement for the Technology of a Better World (ISO) 1984, Standards for Expanding Markets—the ISO/IEC Approach (review) 1987, Technical Regulations and Standards (World Bank Handbook) 1987, over forty scientific and educational papers. *Address:* International Organization for Standardization, Case Postale 56, CH-1211 Geneva 20, Switzerland (Office); Joli Crêt C, 1275 Chéserex, Switzerland (Home). *Telephone:* (022) 749-01-11 (Office); (022) 369 24 49 (Home).

EICHHORN, Lisa; American film actress; b. 2 April 1952, Glen Falls, N.Y.; ed. Queen's Univ. Ontario, St. Peter's Coll. Oxford and Royal Acad. of Dramatic Art; stage appearances include roles in British Shakespearean productions, A Doll's House, A Golden Boy, The Speed of Darkness, The Summer Winds, The Common Pursuit, The Hasty Heart, Pass/Fair, Arms and the Man, Misfits 1996. *Films include:* Yanks 1979, The Europeans 1979, Why Would I Lie? 1980, Cutter and Bone (Cutter's Way) 1981, The Weather in the Streets 1983, Wildrose 1984, Opposing Force (Hell Camp) 1987, Grim Prairie Tales, Moon 44 1989, King of the Hill 1993, The Vanishing 1993, Mr 247 1994, A Modern Affair.

EIFMAN, Boris Yakovlevich; Russian balletmaster; b. 22 July 1946, Rubtsovsk, Altai Region; s. of Iankel Borisovich Eifman and Klara Markovna Kuris; m. Valentina Nikolayevna Morozova; one s.; ed. Kishinev School of Choreography, Leningrad State Conservatory; balletmaster Leningrad School of Choreography 1970–77; concurrently ballet productions in professional theatres including Firebird (Kirov Theatre 1975); f. and artistic dir. Leningrad Ensemble of Ballet 1977 (now St. Petersburg Ballet Theatre Boris Eifman) 1977–; numerous productions of ballets including Before Firebird—Gayaney 1972, Idiot (Tchaikovsky's 6th Symphony) 1980, Marriage of Figaro 1982, The Legend 1982, Twelfth Night 1984, The Duel (after Kuprin) 1986, Master and Margarita (after Bulgakov) 1987, Thérèse Requin 1991, Requiem (Mozart) 1991, Tchaikovsky 1993, Don Quixote or Madman's Fantasy (Minkus) 1994, Brothers Karamazov (after Dostoyevsky) 1995, Red Giselle 1997; Triumph Prize 1995, Golden Baton Prize 1995, 1996, Golden Mask Prize 1996. *Address:* St. Petersburg Ballet Theatre Boris Eifman, Liza Chaikina str. 2, St. Petersburg, 197198, Russia. *Telephone:* (812) 232-23-70 (Office), (812) 164-01-88 (Home). *Fax:* (812) 232-23-70.

EIGEN, Manfred, DR. RER. NAT.; German physical chemist; b. 9 May 1927, Bochum; s. of Ernst Eigen and Hedwig Feld; m. Elfriede Müller; one s. one d.; ed. Georg-August-Univ. zu Göttingen; Max-Planck Inst. of Physical Chem., Göttingen, as Asst., later as Prof. and Head of Dept. 1953–, Dir. 1964; Hon. Prof. Technical Univ., Göttingen 1971–; Pres. Studienstiftung des Deutschen Volkes 1983–; Otto Hahn Prize 1967, Nobel Prize for Chem. (with Norrish and Porter) for investigation of extremely rapid chemical reactions by means of disturbing the (molecular) equilibrium by the action of very short energy pulses 1967; mem. Akad. der Wissenschaften, Göttingen; Foreign hon. mem. American Acad. of Arts and Sciences, Foreign Assoc. mem. Nat. Acad. of Sciences, U.S.A.; Foreign mem. Royal Soc., U.K., Acad. Française 1978; Hon. Dr. Univ. of Washington, St. Louis Univ., Harvard Univ. and Cambridge Univ. and numerous other hon. degrees. *Address:* Georg-Dehio-Weg 14, 37075, Germany.

EILTS, Hermann Frederick, M.A., LL.D.; American (b. German) diplomatist (retd.) and academic; b. 23 March 1922, Weissenfels/Saale, Germany; s. of Friedrich A. Eilts and Meta D. Eilts; m. Helen Brew Eilts 1948; two s.; ed. Ursinus Coll., Johns Hopkins Univ., Univ. of Pennsylvania; several diplomatic posts in Teheran 1947–48, Jeddah 1948–51, Aden 1951–54, Baghdad 1954–56, Washington, D.C. 1956–61; First Sec., American Embassy, London 1962–64; Counsellor, Deputy Head of Mission, American Embassy, Tripoli 1964–65; Amb. to Saudi Arabia 1965–70; Diplomatic Adviser to U.S. Army War Coll. 1970–73; Amb. to Egypt 1973–79; Dist. Univ. Prof. of Int. Relations, Boston Univ. 1979–, Dir. Center for Int. Relations 1982, Chair. Dept. of Political Science 1982–87, Dept. of Int. Relations 1989–93; Academic Coordinator, Mil. Educ. Div. 1990–93, Prof. Emer. 1993–; Middle East Consultant 1993–; Arthur Fleming Award for Distinguished Govt. Service, U.S. Army Decoration for Distinguished Civilian Service, Joseph C. Wilson Award for Achievement in International Affairs 1979, Dept. of State Distinguished Service Award 1979, American Foreign Service Cup 1992; Egyptian Collar of The Nile (First Class) 1979. *Leisure interests:* coins, stamps, reading, hiking, tennis. *Address:* 67 Cleveland Road, Wellesley, MA 02181, U.S.A. *Telephone:* (617) 235-5480.

EINARSSON, Sveinn; Icelandic theatre director and author; b. 18 Sept. 1934, Reykjavik; s. of Einar Ól Sveinsson and Kristjana Thorsteinsdóttir; m. Thora Kristjánsdóttir 1964; one d.; ed. Univ. of Stockholm and Sorbonne, Paris; Artistic Dir. Reykjavik Theatre Co. 1963–72; Prin. Reykjavik Theatre School 1963–70; Gen. Man. and Artistic Dir. Nat. Theatre of Iceland 1972–83; Head of Programme Production, Icelandic State TV 1989–93; Counsellor, Ministry of Culture 1983–89, 1993–; Chair. Icelandic Nat. Comm. for UNESCO 1994–; Artistic Dir. Reykjavik Arts Festival 1998–; Vice-Pres. Int. Theatre Inst. 1979–81; mem. (part-time) Faculty, Univ. of Iceland 1970–; now freelance director and author; has directed about 70 productions on stage and TV in Iceland and other Nordic countries; productions also presented in U.K., Germany, Venezuela, Canada, the Baltic States and Korea (Theatre of Nations); hon. mem. of several socs. etc.; Order of White Rose of Finland, Order of Merit (Norway), Children's Book of Year Award 1986; Clara Lachmann Prize 1990; First Prize, Short Story Competition, 50th Anniversary of Repub. of Iceland 1994; Jón Sigurdsson Prize 1997. *Publications include:* on theatre: Theatre By the Lake 1972, My Nine Years Down There 1987, Íslensk Leiklist (History of Icelandic Theatre, Vol. I) 1991, Vol. II 1996; plays: Egg of Life 1983, I am Gold and Treasures 1984, Bukolla 1991, Bandamannasaga 1992, The Amlodi Saga 1996, The Daughter of the Poet 1998; novel: The Electricity Man 1998; children's books: Gabriella in Portugal 1985, Dordingull 1994; several TV and radio plays. *Leisure interests:* music, skiing. *Address:* Tjarnargata 26, 101 Reykjavik, Iceland. *Telephone:* 551-4032. *Fax:* 562-2350.

EIRIKSSON, Gudmundur, LL.M., B.S., A.B.; Icelandic judge; b. 26 Oct. 1947, Winnipeg, Canada; s. of Rev. Eirikur Sverrir Brynjolfsson and Gudrun Gudmundsdottir; m. Thorey Vigdis Olafsdottir 1973; one s. three d.; ed. Rutgers Coll., U.S.A., King's Coll., Univ. of London, U.K., Columbia Univ., U.S.A.; Law of the Sea Office and Consultant, UN, New York 1974–77; Asst. Legal Adviser, legal adviser, Ministry of Foreign Affairs, Iceland 1977–96, Amb. 1988–96; Rep. of Iceland to Third UN Conf. on Law of the Sea 1978–82; mem. UN Int. Law Comm. 1987–96; Judge, Int. Tribunal for the Law of the Sea 1987–; Visiting Scholar Univ. of Va. Law School, U.S.A. 1984–85; lecturer Univ. of Iceland 1987–96; Visiting Prof. of Law, Univ. of New Mexico School of Law 1994–95; Pres. Council of N. Atlantic Salmon Conservation Org. 1984–88; Grand Kt., Order of the Icelandic Falcon. *Address:* International Tribunal for the Law of the Sea, Wexstrasse 4, 20355 Hamburg, Germany.

EISELE, Lieut.-Gen. Manfred S.; German army officer; b. 17 March 1938, Wilhelmshaven; s. of Wilhelm Eisele and Gertrud Eisele-Meyer; m. Elke Krümpelmann 1962; two d.; ed. Blankenese High School, Mil. Acad., Gen. Staff Acad., Hamburg, U.S.A. Command and Gen. Staff Coll. and Royal Coll. of Defence Studies; Commdg. Officer, Artillery-Bn. 125, Bayreuth 1977–78; Chef de Cabinet/Chief of Gen. Staff, Bonn 1978–80; Head of Public Information, Ministry of Defence 1980–81; Commdg. Officer, Mechanized Infantry Brigade 17, Hamburg 1984–88; Chief, Combat Requirements Brigade, Supreme H.Q. Allied Forces Europe (SHAPE), Mons, Belgium 1988–91; Dir. Politico-Military Affairs, Ministry of Defence, Bonn 1991–92; Commdg. Officer, 12th Panzer Div. Würzburg 1992–94, Armed Forces Office, Bonn 1994; Asst. Sec.-Gen. UN Dept. of Peace-Keeping Operations 1994; Bundesverdienstkreuz, Legion of Merit, U.S.A., Grand Cross, Rider of Vadar, Bulgaria. *Leisure interests:* international politics, history, music, sport. *Address:* Ravensburgstrasse 2A, 97209 Veitshöchheim, Germany. *Telephone:* (931) 9500055. *Fax:* (931) 9500042.

EISEN, Herman N(athaniel), A.B., M.D.; American immunologist and microbiologist; b. 15 Oct. 1918, Brooklyn, N.Y.; s. of Joseph M. Eisen and Lena M. (Karush) Eisen; m. Natalie Aronson 1948; three s. two d.; ed. New York Univ.; Prof. of Medicine (Dermatology), Washington Univ., St. Louis 1955–61, Prof. of Microbiology and Head of Dept. 1961–73; Dermatologist-in-Chief, Barnes Hosp. 1995–61, 1978–90; Prof. of Immunology, M.I.T. 1973–89, Whitehead Inst. Prof. of Immunology 1982–89, Prof. Emer. 1989–; mem. Bd. Scientific Advisors Mass. Gen. Hospital, Boston 1977–, Boston Children's Hospital 1976–, Howard Hughes Medical Inst., Sharp & Dohme Research Laboratories, Rahway 1976–; Harvey Lecturer 1964; Consultant to Surgeons-Gen. of Public Health Service, Dept. of the Army; Chair. Study Section for Allergy and Immunology, Nat. Insts. of Health 1964–68; mem. editorial boards of Journal of Immunology, Bacteriological Reviews, Physiological Reviews, Proceedings of the Nat. Acad. of Sciences of U.S.A.; mem. Bd. of Scientific Advisors, Mass. Gen. Hosp., Boston; mem. Bd., Merck, Sharpe and Dohme, Howard Hughes Medical Inst.; mem. American Soc. for Clinical Investigation (Vice-Pres. 1963–64), American Asscn. of Immunologists (Pres. 1968–69), American Soc. for Biological Chemists, American Asscn. of Physicians, Inst. of Medicine, N.A.S., American Acad. of Arts and Sciences; New York Univ. Medical Science Achievement Award 1978, Dupont Award, Clinical Ligand Soc. 1987, Outstanding Investigator Award, Nat. Cancer Inst. 1986, Behring-Heidelberger Award (American Asscn. of Immunologists) 1993. *Publications:* Methods in Medical Research Vol. 10 (Ed.) 1964, Microbiology (co-Author) 1967–90, Immunology 1974–90, Contemporary Topics in Molecular Immunology Vol. 5 (Ed.) 1976; over 200 scientific articles. *Leisure interests:* landscape gardening, tennis. *Address:* Center for Cancer Research, Massachusetts Institute of Technology, BE 17R, 128 77 Massachusetts Avenue, Cambridge, MA 02139 (Office); 9 Homestead Street, Waban, MA 02168, U.S.A. (Home). *Telephone:* (617) 253-6406. *Fax:* (617) 258-6172.

EISENBERG, Leon, M.D., M.A.; American physician and professor of psychiatry; b. 8 Aug. 1922, Philadelphia; s. of Morris Eisenberg and Elizabeth Sabreen; m. 1st Ruth Bleier 1947 (divorced 1967); m. 2nd Carola Guttmacher 1967; one s. one d.; ed. Univ. of Pennsylvania, Mt. Sinai Hosp., New York, Sheppard Pratt Hosp., Baltimore, Johns Hopkins Hosp., Baltimore; Capt. U.S. Army Medical Corps 1948–50; Instructor in Psychiatry and Pediatrics, Johns Hopkins Medical School 1954, Asst. Prof. 1955–58, Assoc. Prof. 1958–61, Prof. of Child Psychiatry 1961–67; Chief of Psychiatry Massachusetts Gen. Hosp. 1967–74; Prof. of Psychiatry, Harvard Medical School 1967–93, Prof. Emer. 1993–, Chair. of Exec. Cttee., Dept. of Psychiatry

1974–80, Presley Prof., Dept. of Social Medicine and Health Policy 1980–93, Prof. Emer. 1993–; Royal Soc. of Medicine Visiting Prof. 1983; Queen Elizabeth II Lecturer, Canadian Pediatric Soc. 1986; Consultant, Div. of Mental Health, WHO 1980; Lilly Lecturer, Royal Coll. of Psychiatrists 1986; Dir. WHO/Harvard Collaborating Center for Research and Training in Psychiatry 1986–; mem. Inst. of Medicine N.A.S. 1974–; WHO expert advisory panel on Mental Health 1984–; Consultant, Child Mental Health, Pan American Health Org., Uruguay 1991; William Potter Lecturer, Thomas Jefferson Univ. 1992; mem. American Acad. of Arts and Sciences; Hon. Sc.D. (Manchester) 1973, (Massachusetts) 1991; Hon. Fellow Royal Coll. of Psychiatrists 1985; Theobald Smith Award 1979, Aldrich Award 1980, Samuel T. Orton Award 1980, Dale Richmond Award, A.A.P. 1989, Special Presidential Commendation, American Psychiatric Asscn. 1992, numerous other awards. *Publications:* many medical publications. *Leisure interests:* classical music, theatre, reading. *Address:* Harvard Medical School, Department of Social Medicine, 641 Huntington Avenue, Boston, MA 02115; 9 Clement Circle, Cambridge, MA 02138, U.S.A. *Telephone:* (617) 432-1710 (Office); (617) 868-0112 (Home). *Fax:* (617) 432-2565.

EISENHOWER, John Sheldon Doud, B.S., M.A.; American author and diplomatist; b. 3 Aug. 1922, Denver, Colo.; s. of late Gen. Dwight D. Eisenhower (President of the U.S.A. 1953–61) and Mamie (Doud) Eisenhower; m. 1st Barbara Jean Thompson 1947 (divorced 1986); one s. three d.; m. 2nd Joanne Thompson 1990; ed. Stadium High School, Tacoma, Wash., U.S. Military Acad., West Point, Columbia Univ. and Armored Advance Course and General Staff Coll., U.S. Army; assigned to First Army, Second World War; Instructor in English, U.S. Mil. Acad., West Point 1948–51; served as Battalion Operations Officer, Div. Asst. Operations Officer and Div. Intelligence Officer, Korea; Joint War Plans Div., Army Staff, Pentagon 1957–58; Asst. Staff Sec. in White House 1958–61; researcher and editor on Eisenhower memoirs The White House Years; Amb. to Belgium 1969–71; Consultant to President Nixon; Chair. Interagency Classification Review Cttee. 1972–73; Brig.-Gen. U.S. Army Reserve 1974; mem. Nat. Archives Advisory Cttee. 1974–77; Chair. Pres.'s Advisory Cttee. on Refugees 1975; Legion of Merit, Bronze Star, Army Commendation Ribbon, Combat Infantry Badge, Grand Cross, Order of the Crown (Belgium). *Publications:* The Bitter Woods 1969, Strictly Personal 1974, Allies 1981, So Far From God 1989, Intervention! 1993, Agent of Destiny 1997. *Leisure interest:* aviation. *Address:* P.O. Box 778, Kimberton, PA 19442, U.S.A. (Home).

EISENSTADT, Shmuel N., M.A. PH.D.; Israeli professor of sociology; b. 10 Sept. 1923, Warsaw, Poland; s. of Michael Eisenstadt and Rosa Baruchin; m. Shulamit Yaroshevski 1948; two s. one d.; ed. Hebrew Univ., Jerusalem and London School of Econs. and Political Science; Chair. Dept. of Sociology, Hebrew Univ., Jerusalem 1951–69, Prof. of Sociology 1959–, Dean, Faculty of Social Sciences 1966–68; Fellow, Center for Advanced Studies in the Behavioral Sciences, Stanford Univ., U.S.A. 1955–56; Visiting Prof., Univ. of Oslo 1958, Univ. of Chicago 1960, Harvard Univ. 1966, 1968–69, 1975–80, Michigan 1970, Chicago 1971, Zürich 1975, Stanford 1984, 1986, 1987, 1988; Carnegie Visiting Prof., Mass. Inst. of Technology 1962–63, Simon Visiting Prof., Univ. of Manchester 1977; Research Fellow, Hoover Inst. 1986; Hon. Research Fellow, Australian Nat. Univ. 1977; Tanner Lecturer on Human Values, Univ. of Calif. 1988; Distinguished Visiting Prof., Univ. of Alberta, Canada 1989; Prof. Univ. of Chicago Cttee. on Social Thought 1990–93; Max Weber Prof., Univ. of Heidelberg; Chair. Council on Community Relations, Israel 1962–64, Israeli Sociological Soc. 1969–72; mem. Advisory Bd. International Encyclopedia of the Social Sciences; mem. Scientific Cttee. Centro Gino Germani, Rome; Hon. Fellow, London School of Econs.; Foreign Fellow American Anthropological Asscn.; Fellow Netherlands Inst. of Advanced Studies 1973; mem. Israel Acad. of Sciences and Humanities, Int. Sociological Soc., American Sociological Asscn., New York Acad. of Sciences; Foreign mem.American Philosophical Soc.; Foreign Hon. mem. American Acad. of Arts and Sciences; Foreign Assoc. N.A.S.; Dr. h.c. (Helsinki) 1986, Hon. LL.D. (Harvard); Hon. D.Hum.Litt. (Hebrew Union Coll. Jewish Inst. of Religion); Hon. D. Phil. (Tel Aviv); McIver Award, American Sociological Asscn. 1964, Rothschild Prize in the Social Sciences 1969, Israel Prize in the Social Sciences 1973, Int. Balzan Prize in Sociology 1988, Max Planck Research Award 1994. *Publications:* The Absorption of Immigrants 1954, From Generation to Generation 1956, Essays on Sociological Aspects of Economical and Political Development 1961, The Political Systems of Empires 1963, (new edn. with special introduction) 1993, Essays on Comparative Institutions 1965, Modernization, Protest and Change 1966, Israeli Society 1968, The Protestant Ethic and Modernization 1968, Political Sociology of Modernization (in Japanese) 1968, Comparative Perceptives on Social Change (Ed.) 1968, Charisma and Institution Building: Selections from Max Weber (Ed.) 1968, Ensayos sobre el Cambio social y la Modernización (Spanish) 1969, Modernização e Mudança Social (Portuguese) 1969, Political Sociology (Ed.) 1970, Social Differentiation and Stratification 1971, Collection of Essays in Japanese 1971, Tradition, Change and Modernity 1973, Collection of Essays in Spanish 1973, Post-traditional Societies (Ed.) 1974, The Form of Sociology: Paradigms and Crises (with M. Curelaru) 1976, Macrosociology (with M. Curelaru) 1977, Revolutions and Transformation of Societies 1978, Patrons, Clients and Friends (with L. Roniger) 1984, Transformation of Israeli Society 1985, Origins and Diversity of Axial Age Civilizations (Ed.) 1986, Society, Culture and Urbanisation (with A. Shachar) 1987, The Origins of the State Reconsidered (with M. Abitbol and N. Chazan) 1986, European Civilization in Comparative Perspective 1987, Center Formation, Protest Movements and Class Structure in Europe and the U.S. (with L. Roniger and A. Seligman) 1987, Patterns of Modernity I and II 1987, Kulturen der Achsenzeit (trans.) 1987, Die Transformation der Israelichen Gesellschaft (trans.) 1987, The Early State in African Perspective 1988, Knowledge and Society: Studies in the Sociological Culture, Past and Present (Co-ed. with I. Silber) 1988, Japanese Models of Conflict Resolution (Co-ed. with Eyal Ben-Ari) 1990, Martin Buber on Intersubjectivity and Cultural Creativity (Ed.), Jewish Civilization — The Jewish Historical Experience in a Comparative Perspective 1992, The Political Systems of Empires 1993, Power, Trust and Meaning 1995, Japanese Civilization — A Comparative View 1996, Modernità, Modernizzazione e Oltré 1997. *Address:* The Hebrew University, Mount Scopus, Jerusalem (Office); 30 Radak Street, Jerusalem, Israel (Home). *Telephone:* (2) 5605222 (Office); 5632467. *Fax:* (2) 5619293.

EISNER, Michael Dammann, B.S.; American entertainment executive; b. 7 March 1942, Mt. Kisco, N.Y.; m. Jane Breckenridge 1967; three s.; ed. Lawrenceville School, Denison Univ.; Sr. Vice-Pres., prime-time production and devt., ABC Entertainment Corpn. 1973–76; Pres. and C.O.O. Paramount Pictures Corpn. 1976–84; Chair. and C.E.O. The Walt Disney Co. 1984–; Chevalier, Légion d'honneur. *Leisure interests:* spectator sports. *Address:* Walt Disney Co., 500 South Buena Vista Street, Burbank, CA 91521, U.S.A. *Telephone:* (818) 560-1000.

EISNER, Thomas, B.A., PH.D.; American professor of biology; b. 25 June 1929, Berlin, Germany; s. of Hans E. Eisner and Margarete Heil-Eisner; m. Maria L. R. Löbell 1952; three d.; ed. High School and Preparatory School, Montevideo, Uruguay, Champlain Coll., Plattsburgh, N.Y. and Harvard Univ; Research Fellow in Biology, Harvard Univ. 1955–57; Asst. Prof. of Biology, Cornell Univ. 1957–62, Assoc. Prof. 1962–66, Prof. of Biology 1966–76, Jacob Gould Schurman Prof. of Chemical Ecology 1976–, Dir. Cornell Inst. for Research in Chemical Ecology 1992–; Sr. Fellow Cornell Center for the Environment 1994–; Consultant, World Environment and Research Programme MacArthur Foundation 1987–92; Lalor Fellow 1954–55, Guggenheim Fellow 1964–65, 1972–73; mem. Nat. Council for Nature Conservancy 1969–74, Council Fed. American Scientists 1977–81, External Scientific Advisory Cttee., MBL, Woods Hole 1989–91, 1996–; foreign mem. Royal Soc. 1997; Dir. National Audubon Soc. 1970–75; Pres. American Soc. of Naturalists 1988; mem. N.A.S. 1969, American Philosphical Soc. 1986, Akademie Naturforscher Leopoldina 1986; Fellow, American Acad. of Arts and Sciences 1969, Animal Behaviour Soc. 1971, American Entomological Soc. 1987, Club of Earth 1986–, Zero Population Growth (Dir. 1969–70); Chair. Biology Section, A.A.A.S. 1980–81, mem. Cttee. for Scientific Freedom and Responsibility 1980–87, Chair. Subcttee. on Science and Human Rights 1981–87; mem. Steering Cttee. on Consequences of Nuclear War 1983–87, Scientific Advisory Council, World Wildlife Fund 1983–90, N.A.S. Cttee. on Human Rights 1987–90, Advisory Council, Monell Chemical Senses Center 1988–; World Resources Inst. 1988–95; mem. Task Force for the 90s, A.I.B.S. 1990–, Scientific Advisory Council, Xerces Soc. (Pres. 1992–), Scientific Advisory Cttee., Cttee. for Nat. Inst. for the Environment 1991–, Entomology Soc. of America Standing Cttee. on Fellows 1993–94, Bd. of Dirs. Union of Concerned Scientists 1993–; Chair. Endangered Species Coalition 1994–96, Advisory Council, Center for Biodiversity and Conservation, American Museum of Natural History 1995–; Hon. Ph.D. (Würzburg, Zürich, Göteborg, Drexel); Newcomb-Cleveland Prize (with E. O. Wilson) of A.A.A.S. 1967, Founders Memorial Award of Entomological Soc. of America 1969, Prof. of Merit, Cornell Univ. 1973, Archie F. Carr Medal 1983, four awards for film Secret Weapons, BBC TV 1984; Proctor Prize 1986, Karl Ritter von Frisch Medal 1988, Centennial Medal, Harvard Univ. 1989, Tyler Prize 1990, Esselen Award 1991, Silver Medal, Int. Soc. of Chemical Ecology 1991, Nat. Medal of Science 1994, Green Globe Award 1997; numerous other awards. *Publications:* over 350 technical papers and seven books on animal behaviour, chemical ecology, comparative physiology, chemical communication in animals, conservation. *Leisure interests:* photography, cinematography, orchestra conducting, piano. *Address:* Section of Neurobiology and Behaviour, Division of Biological Sciences, W347 Mudd Hall, Cornell University, Ithaca, NY 14853, U.S.A. *Telephone:* (607) 255-4464. *Fax:* (607) 255-6186.

EITAN, Lieut.-Gen. Raphael; Israeli army officer; b. 1929, Tel Adashim; m.; four c.; ed. Tel-Aviv and Haifa Univs.; joined Palmach when 17; Deputy Co. Commdr. 1948; various posts with paratroops 1950–53; Commdr. Paratroop Unit, Sinai campaign 1956; Deputy Commdr. Paratroop Brigade 1958, Commdr. 1964–67; Commdr. Jordan Valley Brigade 1967–68; Chief Paratroop and Infantry Officer, rank of Brig.-Gen. 1968–73; Commdr. Div. on Golan Heights, rank of Maj.-Gen., Yom Kippur War 1973–74; C.O. Northern Command 1974–77; Chief of Gen. Staff Branch 1977–78; Chief of Gen. Staff 1978–83; mem. Ministerial Defence Cttee. 1990–; Minister of Agric. 1990–91, 1996–; Deputy Prime Minister, Minister of Environment 1996–. *Address:* Ministry of Agriculture, P.O. Box 7011, 8 Arania Street, Tel-Aviv 61070, Israel. *Telephone:* (3) 697-1444. *Fax:* (3) 696-7891.

EITEL, Tono, DR.IUR.; German diplomatist; b. 5 June 1933, Münster; m.; ed. Univs. of Berlin, Bonn, Hamburg, Münster, New York; practical legal training 1957–61; joined Foreign Service 1963; with Mission to European Communities, Brussels 1963–64; at Fed. Foreign Office 1964–66, 1969–70, 1973–74, 1977–82, Head of Working Staff on UN Conf. on Law of the Sea 1980–82, Dir. Legal Dept. 1987–92, Dir.-Gen. Legal Affairs and Legal Adviser 1992–95; with Embassy, Kingston, Jamaica 1966–69; with Fed. Chancellery

1970–73; with Embassy, Bern 1974–77; Amb. to Lebanon 1982–87; Perm. Rep. to UN 1995; Hon. Prof. 1991. *Address:* c/o Ministry of Foreign Affairs, Adenauerallee 99–103, 53115 Bonn, Germany.

EIZENSTAT, Stuart E., LL.B.; American diplomatist, lawyer and government official; b. 15 Jan. 1943, Chicago; s. of Leo Eizenstat and Sylvia Eizenstat; m. Frances Taylor 1967; two s.; ed. Univ. of North Carolina and Harvard Univ.; admitted Ga. Bar 1967, D.C. Bar 1981; mem. White House staff 1967–68; mem. nat. campaign staff for Hubert M. Humphrey 1968; law clerk, U.S. Dist. Court, Ga. 1968–70; partner, Powell, Goldstein, Frazer & Murphy, Washington, D.C. 1970–77, 1981–93, Chair. Washington Office 1991–93; Asst. to Pres. of U.S.A. for domestic affairs and policy 1977–81, Dir. Domestic Policy Staff 1977–81; Amb. to European Union 1993–96; Under-Sec. of Commerce 1996–97; Special Envoy Property Restitution in Cen. Europe 1993–96, Dept. of State Property Claims in Cen. Europe 1995–97; Under-Sec. of Econ., Business and Agricultural Affairs 1997–; State Dept. Special Envoy on Property Claims in Cen. Europe; Adjunct lecturer, J. F. Kennedy School of Govt. Harvard Univ. 1981–93; guest scholar, Brookings Inst. Washington 1981; mem. Presidential Task Force on U.S. Int. Broadcasting 1991; mem. Bd. of Dirs. Hercules Inc. Wilmington, Israel Discount Bank of New York, P.S.I. Holdings Inc. Indianapolis; numerous other public appts.; Democrat. *Publications include:* The Path to History (with A. Young) 1973, Environmental Auditing Handbook 1984; articles in newspapers and professional journals. *Leisure interest:* tennis. *Address:* Department of Commerce, Suite 3805, 14th Constitution Avenue, N.W., Washington, DC 20011 (Office); 9107 Brierly Road, Chevy Chase, MD 20815, U.S.A. (Home).

EKANGAKI, Nzo; Cameroonian politician; b. 22 March 1934, Nguti; ed. Bali Coll., Hope Waddle Training Inst., Calabar, Nigeria and Univs. of Ibadan, Nigeria, London, Oxford and Bonn; served in several posts in Cameroon Admin. 1959–60; Deputy Minister of Foreign Affairs 1962–64; Minister of Public Health and Population 1964–65, of Labour and Social Welfare 1965–72; Sec.-Gen. Org. of African Unity 1972–74; Adviser to Presidency, Yaoundé 1985–; Sec.-Gen. Kamerun Nat. Democratic Party (KNDP) 1962–66; mem. of Political Bureau, Cameroon Nat. Union Party (CNU) 1966–75; mem. Parl. S. Cameroon 1961–62, mem. first Nat. Federal Assembly 1962–65, 1965–71; del. to many int. confs., to WHO Conf., Geneva 1964, to several Int. Labour Confs.; rep. on many missions abroad. *Publications:* An Introduction to East Cameroon 1956, To the Nigerian People 1958. *Address:* c/o Presidency of the Republic, Yaoundé, Cameroon.

EKEUS, Carl Rolf; Swedish diplomatist; b. 7 July 1935, Kristinehamn; s. of Axel Eriksson and Margit Johansson; m. Kerstin C. Oldfelt 1970; three s. three d.; ed. Univ. of Stockholm; law practice, Karlstad 1959–62; Legal Div. Ministry of Foreign Affairs 1962–63; Sec. Swedish Embassy, Bonn 1963–65; First Sec. Nairobi 1965–67; Special Asst. to Minister of Foreign Affairs 1967–73; First Sec., Counsellor, Perm. Mission to UN, New York 1974–78; Counsellor, The Hague 1978–83; Amb. and Perm. Rep. to Conf. on Disarmament, Geneva 1983–89, Chair. Cttee. on Chemical Weapons 1984, 1987; Amb. and Head of Swedish Del. to CSCE, Vienna 1989–93; Chair. Cttee. on Principles Chapter of Charter of Paris 1991; Chair. CSCE Vienna Group 1993; Exec. Chair. UN Special Comm. on Iraq 1991–97; Amb. to U.S.A. 1997–; mem. Canberra Comm. on the Elimination of Nuclear Weapons, advisory bd. Center for Non-Proliferation, Monetary Inst., Tokyo Forum on Non-Proliferation and Disarmament; mem. advisory bd. of UN Sec.-Gen. on Disarmament Matters 1999. *Publications:* several articles on foreign policy, int. economy, nuclear non-proliferation, disarmament and arms control, chemical weapons, European security, Iraq and weapons of mass destruction. *Leisure interests:* piano playing, tennis. *Address:* Swedish Embassy, 1501 M Street, N.W., Washington, DC 20005, U.S.A. *Telephone:* (202) 467-2600. *Fax:* (202) 467-2699.

EKLUND, (Arne) Sigvard, D.S.; Swedish nuclear physicist; b. 19 June 1911, Kiruna; s. of Severin Eklund and Vilhelmina Pettersson; m. Anna-Greta Johansson 1941; one s. two d.; ed. Univ. of Uppsala; Nobel Inst. for Physics 1937–45; Asst. Prof. of Nuclear Physics, Royal Inst. of Technology, Stockholm 1946, Senior Scientist, Research Inst. for Nat. Defence Stockholm 1946–50; Dir. of Research AB Atomenergi, Stockholm 1950–56, Deputy to Man. Dir. 1950–61, Dir. of Reactor Devt. Div. 1957–61; Sec.-Gen. Second UN Conf. on Peaceful Uses of Atomic Energy 1958; Dir.-Gen. Int. Atomic Energy Agency (IAEA) 1961–81; Dir.-Gen. Emer. 1981–; mem. Royal Swedish Acad. of Eng. Sciences 1953, Royal Swedish Acad. of Sciences 1972; Fellow, American Nuclear Soc. 1961; Hon. mem. British Nuclear Eng. Soc. 1963, Asscn. for Nuclear Technique, Stockholm 1992; Hon. Lifetime mem. American Nuclear Soc. 1992; Foreign Assoc. Nat. Acad. of Engineering (U.S.A.) 1979; Dr. h.c. (Graz) 1968, (Acad. Mining and Metallurgy, Cracow) 1971, (Bucharest) 1971, (Chalmers Inst. of Tech., Gothenburg, Sweden) 1974, (Moscow State Univ.) 1977, (Columbia) 1977, (Buenos Aires) 1977, (Budapest Tech. Univ.), (Tech. Univ. Dresden) 1978, (Yon-Sei Univ., Seoul) 1978, (National Agrarian Univ., La Molina, Peru) 1979, (Royal Inst. of Tech., Stockholm) 1980; Hon. Senator (Vienna Univ.) 1977; Atoms for Peace Award 1968; Gold Medal, Province of Vienna 1971; Swedish Energy Prize 1991; Grand Cordon, Order of the Sacred Treasure (Japan) 1991. *Address:* International Atomic Energy Agency, P.O. Box 200, A-1400 Vienna (Office); Krapfenwaldgasse 48, 1190 Vienna, Austria (Home). *Telephone:* 2360-1515 (Office); 320-24-24 (Home). *Fax:* 320-84-92.

EKSTEEN, Jacobus Adriaan, M.A.; South African diplomatist, broadcasting executive (retd.) and political consultant; b. 31 Oct. 1942, Volksrust; s. of Jacobus Adriaan and Helena Barendina Hendrika (née Baard) Eksteen; m. Ria Hofmeyr 1991; three s. (previous marriage); ed. Univs. of Pretoria and South Africa; entered Civil Service 1961; mem. S.A. legal team at Int. Court of Justice in South West Africa (Namibia) cases 1966; Third Sec., Second Sec., then First Sec., Embassy, U.S.A. 1968–73; served in Head Office of Dept. of Foreign Affairs as Head of UN and S.W.A. sections 1973–76; Counsellor and Deputy Perm. Rep. at S.A. Perm. Mission to UN 1976, Minister 1978, Acting Perm. Rep. 1977–79, Perm. Rep. and Amb. 1979–81; Head of Planning Div., Ministry of Foreign Affairs 1981–83; mem. S.A. Del. to Patent Cooperation Treaty, Washington 1970, to INTELSAT Conf., Washington 1971, to UN Gen. Assembly 1972, 1979, 1981; involved in all discussions on Namibia 1977–83; presented South Africa's case in UN Security Council Aug. 1981; Dir.-Gen. (desig.) South African Broadcasting Corp. 1983, Dir.-Gen. 1984–88; S.A. Rep. in Namibia 1990–91; Amb. and Perm. Rep. to UN and Special Agencies in Geneva 1992–95; Amb. to Turkey (also accred. to Azerbaijan, Kyrgyzstan, Turkmenistan, Uzbekistan) 1995. *Leisure interests:* reading, walking, stamp collecting, hunting. *Address:* c/o Ministry of Foreign Affairs, Union Buildings, East Wing, Government Avenue, Pretoria 0002, South Africa.

EKWENSI, Cyprian; Nigerian author and pharmacist; b. 26 Sept. 1921, Minna, Northern Nigeria; ed. Govt. Coll., Ibadan, Achimota Coll., Ghana, School of Forestry, Ibadan, Higher Coll., Yaba, Chelsea School of Pharmacy, Univ. of London, Iowa Univ.; Lecturer in Biology, Chem. and English, Igbobi Coll., Lagos 1947–49; Lecturer, School of Pharmacy, Lagos 1949–56; Pharmacist, Nigerian Medical Service 1956; Head of Features, Nigerian Broadcasting Corpn. 1956–61; Dir. of Information, Fed. Ministry of Information, Lagos 1961–66; Dir. of Information Services, Enugu 1966; Chair. East Cen. State Library Board, Enugu 1971–75; Man. Dir. Star Printing and Publishing Co. Ltd. 1975–79, Niger Eagle Press 1981–; Visiting Lecturer, Iowa Univ.; mem. Pharmaceutical Socs. of Great Britain and Nigeria, Nigerian Arts Council, Soc. of Nigerian Authors, Inst. Public Relations Nigeria and U.K.; Dag Hammarskjöld Int. Award for Literary Merit 1968. *Publications:* When Love Whispers, Ikolo the Wrestler 1947, The Leopard's Claw 1950, People of the City 1954, Passport of Mallam Ilia, The Drummer Boy 1960, Jagua Nana 1961, Burning Grass, An African Night's Entertainment, Yaba Round about Murder 1962, Beautiful Feathers 1963, Great Elephant Bird, Rainmaker 1965, Lokotown, Juju Rock, Trouble in Form VI, Iska, Boa Suitor 1966, Coal Camp Boy 1973, Samankwe in the Strange Forest 1974, Samankwe and the Highway Robbers, Restless City, Christmas Gold 1975, Survive the Peace 1976, Divided We Stand 1980, Motherless Baby 1980, Jaguanana's Daughter 1986, For a Roll of Parchment 1986, Beneath the Convent Wall 1987, Restless City and Xmas Gold, Behind the Convent Wall 1988, Death at Mile Two 1988, Lagos Love Deal 1988, Masquerade Time 1991, King Forever 1992. *Leisure interests:* photography, Adire Tie-Die. *Address:* Hillview Crescent, Independence Layout, P.O. Box 317, Enugu, Nigeria (Home).

EKWUEME, Alex Ifeanyichukwu, PH.D.; Nigerian politician and architect; b. 21 Oct. 1932, Oko; ed. King's Coll., Lagos, Univ. of Washington, Seattle, Univ. of Strathclyde, Glasgow; est. Ekwueme Associates (architects) 1958; fmr. Pres. Architectural Registration Council of Nigeria; Vice-Pres. candidate with Alhaji Shehu Shagari in Presidential elections Aug. 1979; Vice-Pres. of Nigeria 1979–83; arrested 1984, released August 1986; fmr. mem. Nat. Exec. of banned Nat. Party of Nigeria; Chair. All Nigeria Politicians Summit Conf. 1995. *Address:* Oko, Anambra State, Nigeria. *Telephone:* (42) 454815. *Fax:* (42) 456667.

EL ADM, Khaled Charles, B.SC.; Egyptian library consultant and information adviser; b. 29 April 1957, Alexandria; ed. St. Mark's Coll., Faculty of Science and Technology, Paris, Alexandria Univ.; scientific reporter, Al-Ahram daily newspaper; Exec. Vice-Pres. Egyptian Scientific Clubs 1971–84; library science consultant and reference librarian, pvt. and govt. sectors 1979–; Project Man., Solid Waste Project, El-Mokattam Dist., Cairo 1987; f. 43 scientific clubs in Egypt 1972–83, Cultural Heritage Asscn. in Africa 1982, Nubian and Historical Heritage Asscn. 1990; mem. Alexandria Planetarium project cttee. 1982, numerous int. library science and other asscns. *Publications:* 34 scientific and library science articles in Arab and foreign journals. *Leisure interests:* landscape photography, history of the ancient world, tennis, basketball, volleyball, reading, classical music, plastic arts. *Address:* P.O. Box 37, Ibrahimieh (21321), Alexandria; P.O. Box 421, Ibrahimieh (21321) Alexandria, Egypt. *Telephone:* (3) 59 75 238.

ELARABY, Nabil A.; Egyptian diplomatist and international arbitrator; b. 15 March 1935; m.; two s. one d.; ed. Cairo Univ., New York Univ. Law School; fmr. Rep. of Egypt to various UN bodies, including Gen. Ass., Security Council, ECOSOC, Comm. on Human Rights, Conf. on Disarmament; Legal Adviser to Egyptian del. to UN Middle East Peace Conf., Geneva 1973–75; Dir. Legal and Treaties Dept., Ministry of Foreign Affairs 1976–78, 1983–87; led Egyptian Del. to Taba talks 1986–89; Deputy Perm. Rep. to UN, New York 1978–81, Perm. Rep. 1991–; Perm. Rep., UN Office at Geneva 1987–91; Judge, Judicial Tribunal of Org. of Arab Petroleum Exporting Countries (OAPEC) 1990–; mem. Int. Law Comm. 1994–; appt. by ICC as Arbitrator in a dispute concerning Suez Canal 1989; fmr. Chair. numerous UN cttees. and working groups. *Leisure interest:* tennis. *Address:* Permanent Mission of Egypt to the United Nations, 304 East 44th Street, New York, NY 10017, U.S.A. *Telephone:* (212) 503-0300. *Fax:* (212) 949-5999.

ELBARADEI, Mohamed Mostafa, J.S.D.; Egyptian international civil servant; b. 17 June 1942, Cairo; m. Aida ElKachef 1975; one s. one d.; ed. Cairo Univ. and New York Univ.; with Ministry of Foreign Affairs, Dept. of Int. Orgs. 1964–67; mem. Perm. Mission to UN, New York 1967–71; Sr. Fellow Center for Int. Studies, New York Univ. 1973–74; Special Asst. to Foreign Minister, Ministry of Foreign Affairs 1974–78; mem. Perm. Mission to UN, Geneva and Alt. Rep. Cttee. on Disarmament 1978–80; Adjunct Prof. of Int. Law New York Univ. 1981–87; Sr. Fellow and Dir. Int. Law and Orgs. Programme, UN Inst. for Training and Research, New York 1980–84; Rep. of Dir. Gen. of IAEA to UN, New York 1984–87, Dir. Legal Div. and Legal Adviser IAEA, Vienna 1987–91, Dir. of External Relations 1991–93, Asst. Dir. Gen. for External Relations 1993–97, Dir. Gen. IAEA 1997–; rep. to numerous cttees.; has lectured widely on int. law and orgs.; mem. Int. Law Asscn., American Soc. of Int. Law, Nuclear Law Asscn. *Publications:* The International Law Commission: The Need for a New Direction 1981, Model Rules for Disaster Relief Operations 1982, The Role of international Atomic Energy Agency Safeguards in the Evolution of the Non-Proliferation Regime 1991, The International Law of Nuclear Energy 1993, On Compliance with Nuclear Non-Proliferation Obligations (Security Dialogue) 1996 and articles in int. law journals. *Address:* International Atomic Energy Agency (IAEA), Wagramerstrasse 5, P.O. Box 100, A-1400 Vienna, Austria. *Telephone:* 2600 21111. *Fax:* 2600 29805.

ELBEGDORJ, Tsahiagiyn; Mongolian politician; b. 30 March 1963, Zereg Som, Hovd Prov.; m.; two c.; machinist Erdenet copper mine 1981–82; army service 1982; mil. reporter Mil. School, Lvov, Ukraine 1983–88; journalist Ulaan-Od (Ministry of Defence newspaper) 1988–90; mem. Co-ordinating Council of Mongolian Democratic Union (MDU) 1989, leader 1990; deputy to People's Great Hural 1990–92, also mem. State Little Hural; mem. State Great Hural 1992–94, 1996, Vice-Chair. July 1996–; mem. Gen. Council Mongolian Nat. Democratic Party 1994, Leader 1996–, also Leader Democratic Union coalition in State Great Hural; Prime Minister of Mongolia April–Dec. 1998. *Address:* Mongolian National Democratic Party, Chingisiyn Örgön Chölöö 1, Ulan Bator, Mongolia. *Telephone:* 372810. *Fax:* 372810.

ELDEM, M. Necat; Turkish politician; b. 1928, Mardin; m.; two c.; ed. Erzurum Lycée, Faculty of Political Sciences, Istanbul Univ.; Jr. Gov. in various towns in Anatolia; Admin. Insp. 1961–74; Gov. of Çankin 1974, Burdur and Yozgat –1978; Minister of Justice 1983–86. *Address:* c/o Adalet Bakanlığı, Bakanlıklar, Ankara, Turkey. *Telephone:* (41)185260.

ELDER, Mark Philip, C.B.E., M.A.; British music director; b. 2 June 1947; s. of John Elder and Helen Elder; m. Amanda Jane Stein 1980; one d.; ed. Bryanston School and Corpus Christi Coll., Cambridge; music staff Wexford Festival 1969–70; Chorus Master and Asst. Conductor Glyndebourne 1970–71; music staff Covent Garden 1970–72, Staff Conductor Australian Opera 1972–74, English Nat. Opera 1974, Assoc. Conductor 1977, Music Dir. 1979–93; Prin. Guest Conductor London Mozart Players 1980–83; BBC Symphony Orchestra 1982–85; Music Dir., Rochester Philharmonic Orchestra, N.Y. 1989–94; Olivier Award for Outstanding Contribution to Opera 1990; Prin. Guest Conductor London Mozart Players 1980–83, BBC Symphony Orchestra 1982–85, City of Birmingham Symphony Orchestra 1991–95. *Address:* c/o Ingpen & Williams, 26 Wadham Road, London, SW15 2LR, England.

ELDER, Murdoch George, D.SC., M.D., F.R.C.S., F.R.C.O.G.; British professor of obstetrics and gynaecology; b. 4 Jan. 1938, Calcutta, India; s. of late A. J. Elder and L. A. C. Elder; m. Margaret McVicker 1964; two s.; ed. Edinburgh Acad. and Edinburgh Univ.; lecturer, Royal Univ. of Malta 1969–71; Sr. lecturer and Reader, Univ. of London, Charing Cross Hosp. Medical School 1971–78; Prof. of Obstetrics and Gynaecology, Univ. of London at Hammersmith Hosp. 1978–98; Dean, Royal Postgrad. Medical School Inst. of Obstetrics and Gynaecology 1985–95; Chair. Div. of Paediatrics, Obstetrics and Gynaecology, Imperial Coll. School of Medicine, Univ. of London 1996–98; Visiting Prof. U.C.L.A. 1984, 1986, 1997, Univ. of Singapore 1987, Univ. of Natal 1988; consultant to WHO and other int. orgs. etc.; mem. WHO Scientific and Ethics Research Group; External Examiner to Univs. of Edin., Cambridge, Oxford, London, Leeds, Bristol, Glasgow, Dundee, Malta, Malaya, Malaysia, Helsinki, Rotterdam, Cape Town, Singapore; Silver Medal, Hellenic Obstetrical Soc. 1984. *Publications include:* Human Fertility Control (co-author) 1979, Preterm Labor (co-ed.) 1996; more than 220 original publs. in field of biochemistry of reproduction and clinical high risk obstetrics. *Leisure interests:* travel, golf. *Address:* Easter Calzeat, Broughton, Biggar, ML12 6HQ, Scotland. *Telephone:* (01899) 830359.

ELDIN, Gérard; French civil servant and banker; b. 21 March 1927, Cannes; s. of Charles and Elise Eldin; m. Marie-Cécile Bergerot 1960; two s. two d.; ed. Bethany Coll., U.S.A., Univ. d'Aix-en-Provence and Ecole Nationale d'Administration; Insp. of Finances 1954–58; served in the Treasury 1958–63; Adviser to Minister of Finance and Econ. Affairs 1963–65; Deputy Dir. Dept. of Planning 1965–70; Deputy Sec.-Gen. OECD 1970–80; Deputy Gov. Crédit Foncier de France 1980–86; Chair. Foncier-Investissement 1982–86, Crédit-Logement 1986–87; Chair. Banque centrale de compensation 1987–90; Pres. Foncier-court terme Sicav 1988–96; Chair. Société d'études immobilières et d'expertises foncières (Foncier-Expertise) 1990–96; Dir. Compagnie foncière de France 1980–93, Société immobilière Paix-Daunou 1987–93, Société des Immeubles de France 1993–; Chevalier Légion d'honneur; Commdr. Ordre national du Mérite. *Leisure interests:* music, local history, archaeology. *Address:* 32 rue des Archives, 75004 Paris, France (Home). *Telephone:* (1) 44-54-09-83 (home).

ELDON, David Gordon, F.C.I.B.; British banker; b. 14 Oct. 1945, Inverness; s. of Leslie Eldon and Mary Eldon; m. Maria (Monsé) Martinez-Col 1975; two s. one d.; ed. Duke of York's Royal Mil. School; with Commercial Banking Co. of Sydney 1964–68; with the British Bank of the Middle East 1968–79; joined Hongkong and Shanghai Banking Corpn. 1979, Sr. Man. Int. Corporate Accounts 1987–88, C.E.O. Malaysia 1988–90, Gen. Man. Malaysia 1990–92, Gen. Man. Int. 1992–94, Exec. Dir. 1994–96, C.E.O. 1996–, Chair. 1999–; Deputy Man. Dir. The Saudi British Bank 1984–87; Chair. Resource Man. Bd. Hong Kong Arts Devt. Council 1993–; Pres. Soc. for the Relief of Disabled Children 1993–; Dir. Hang Seng Bank Ltd. 1996–, Hong Kong Bank of Australia Ltd. (non-exec.) 1993–; mem. Gen. Cttee. Hong Kong Gen. Chamber of Commerce 1995–, Council Hong Kong Acad. for Performing Arts 1993–; Steward Hong Kong Jockey Club 1996–. *Address:* The Hongkong and Shanghai Banking Corporation Ltd., Level 34, 1 Queen's Road Central, Hong Kong Special Administrative Region, People's Republic of China. *Telephone:* 2822-1370. *Fax:* 2596-0646.

ELDON, Rt. Rev. Michael Hartley, C.M.G., M.A.; Bahamian ecclesiastic; b. 8 Aug. 1931; ed. Univ. of Cambridge, St. Stephen's House, Oxford; ordained deacon 1954; ordained priest 1955; Asst. Master, St. John's Coll. Nassau 1954–62; Curate, St. Agnes Parish, Nassau 1954; Asst. Priest, St. Matthew's Parish, Nassau 1955–62; Parish Priest of Grand Bahama 1962; Rural Dean of Northern Bahamas 1965; Archdeacon of Grand Bahama 1967; Bishop Suffragan of New Providence 1971; Bishop of Nassau and the Bahamas 1972. *Address:* c/o Bishop's Lodge, P.O. Box N-7107, Nassau, Bahamas.

ELFMAN, Danny; American film music composer; b. 29 May 1953; lead singer, rhythm guitarist and chief songwriter for Oingo Bongo (eight-piece rock band); Music for films including: Fast Times at Ridgemont High, Weird Science, Ghostbusters II, Something Wild; numerous scores for TV programmes. *Film scores include:* Pee-Wee's Big Adventure, Batman, Dick Tracy, Midnight Run, Darkman, Edward Scissorhands, Beetlejuice, Article 99, Nightbreed, Batman Returns, Sommersby, March of the Dead Theme (Army of Darkness) 1993, The Nightmare Before Christmas 1993, Black Beauty 1994, Dolores Claiborne 1995, To Die For 1995, Dead Presidents 1995, Mission Impossible 1996, The Frighteners 1996, Mars Attacks! 1996, Men In Black 1997.

ELGEE, Neil Johnson, M.D.; American clinical professor of medicine; b. 3 April 1926, Nova Scotia, Canada; s. of William Harris Elgee and Lucile Nevers Elgee; m. Leona Karlson 1951; one s. four d.; ed. New Brunswick and Rochester Univs.; Intern in Medicine, Peter Bent Brigham Hosp., Boston 1950–51; Asst. Resident in Medicine, Strong Memorial Hosp., Rochester 1951–52; Research Fellow in Endocrinology, Univ. of Wash. 1952–54, Chief Resident in Medicine 1954–55, Clinical Faculty 1957–, Clinical Prof. of Medicine 1968–93, Emer. Clinical Prof. 1993–; Pres. Ernest Becker Foundation; Gov. American Coll. of Physicians 1965–71, Regent 1974–78; Inst. of Medicine 1978–; Master American Coll. of Physicians. *Publications:* contribs. to several scientific journals; writings on Becker. *Leisure interests:* squash, writing. *Address:* 3621 72nd Avenue S.E., Mercer Island, WA 98040, U.S.A. *Telephone:* 206 232 2994.

EL GOULLI, Salah Eddine, D.IUR.; Tunisian business executive and fmr. diplomatist; b. 22 June 1919, Sousse; m. M. J. Zeineb Larre 1958; one d.; ed. Univ. of Paris (Sorbonne); Consul Gen., Marseilles 1956–57; Minister, Embassy, Washington, D.C. 1958–61; Amb. to Belgium (also accred. to Netherlands, Luxembourg, EEC), UN 1962–69, to U.S.A. (also accred. to Venezuela and Mexico) 1970–73, to Netherlands 1976–78; Adviser to Minister of Foreign Affairs 1973–75, 1979–81; Pres. Philips Electronics 1981–90, World Trade Centre, Tunis 1990–; Grand Cordon of the Repub. of Tunisia; Grand Cross of Leopold and Grand Cross Crown of Belgium; Grand Cross Chene and Grand Cross Nassau, Luxembourg. *Publications:* lectures on political and econ. matters in U.S.A., Europe and Middle East; numerous articles in European press. *Leisure interests:* golf, reading, swimming. *Address:* 2 rue des Roses, 2070 La Marsa, Tunisia. *Telephone:* 774 307. *Fax:* 792 373.

ELIADES, Elias; Cypriot politician; b. 24 Oct. 1947, Paphos; m. Irene Chalkiadaki; one d.; ed. Athens Univ., Greece; practised as lawyer, Paphos 1973–82; Chair. Paphos Greek Co-operative Savings Bank 1973; mem. Bd. of Dirs. Land Devt. Org.; Minister of Defence 1985–88.

ELIASSEN, Kjell, LL.D.; Norwegian diplomatist (retd.); b. 18 Aug. 1929, Mosjoen; s. of Carl August Eliassen and Bergljot Store; m. Vesla Skretting 1953; one s. one d.; ed. Oslo Univ.; entered Foreign Service 1953, Counsellor, Embassy Moscow 1967–70, Deputy Dir.-Gen., Ministry of Foreign Affairs 1970–72, Dir.-Gen. 1972–77; Amb. to Yugoslavia 1977–80; Perm. Under-Sec., Ministry of Foreign Affairs 1980–84; Amb. to the U.S.A. 1984–89, to the U.K. 1989–94, to Germany 1994–98. *Address:* Generallunden 21, 0382 Oslo, Norway.

ELIASSON, Jan, M.A.; Swedish international official and diplomatist; b. 17 Sept. 1940, Göteborg; s. of John H. Eliasson and Karin (née Nilsson) Eliasson; m. Kerstin Englesson 1967; one s. two d.; ed. School of Econs., Gothenburg; entered Swedish Foreign Service 1965; Swedish OECD Del., Paris 1967; at

Swedish Embassy, Bonn 1967–70; First Sec. Swedish Embassy, Washington 1970–74; Head of Section, Political Dept., Ministry for Foreign Affairs, Stockholm 1974–75; Personal Asst. to the Under-Sec. of State for Foreign Affairs 1975–77; Dir. Press and Information Div., Ministry for Foreign Affairs 1977–80, Asst. Under-Sec., Head of Div. for Asian and African Affairs, Political Dept. 1980–82; Foreign Policy Adviser, Prime Minister's Office 1982–83; Amb., Under-Sec. for Political Affairs, Stockholm 1983–87; Perm. Rep. of Sweden to UN, New York 1988–92; Under-Sec.-Gen. for Humanitarian Affairs, UN 1992–94; Chair. Minsk Conf. on Nagornyi Karabakh 1994; State Sec. for Foreign Affairs 1994–; Sec. to Swedish Foreign Policy Advisory Bd. 1983–87; Expert, Royal Swedish Defence Comm. 1984–86; Chair. UN Trust Fund for S.A. 1988–92; Personal Rep. to Sec.-Gen. on Iran-Iraq 1988–92; Dir. Inst. for East-West Security Studies, New York 1989–93; Dir. Int. Peace Acad. 1989–; Vice-Pres. ECOSOC 1991–92. *Leisure interests:* art, literature, sports. *Address:* c/o Ministry of Foreign Affairs, Gustav Adolfstorg 1, P.O. Box 16121, 10323 Stockholm, Sweden.

ELIEL, Ernest L., PH.D.; American professor of chemistry; b. 28 Dec. 1921, Cologne, Germany; s. of Oskar Eliel and Luise Tietz; m. Eva Schwarz 1949; two d.; ed. Univs. of Edinburgh, Havana and Illinois; Asst. Laboratorios Vieta-Plasencia 1943–46; Instructor to Assoc. Prof., Univ. of Notre Dame 1948–60, Prof. 1960–72, Head Dept. of Chem. 1964–66; W. R. Kenan Jr. Prof. of Chem., Univ. of N. Carolina, Chapel Hill 1972–93, Prof. Emer. 1993–; Nat. Science Foundation Senior Post-doctoral Fellow, Harvard Univ. 1958, Calif. Inst. of Technology 1958–59, Eidgenössische Technische Hochschule, Zürich 1967–68; Guggenheim Fellow 1975–76, 1983–84; mem. Nat. Acad. of Sciences, American Acad. of Arts and Sciences, American Chemical Soc. (Chair. 1987–89, Pres. 1992); Hon. D.Sc. (Duke Univ.) 1983, (Notre Dame) 1990, (Babes-Bolyai Univ., Cluj, Romania) 1993; Lavoisier Medal 1968, N. Carolina Award in Science 1986, Priestley Medal 1996, N.A.S. Award for Chemistry in Service to Society 1997 and other awards. *Publications:* Stereochemistry of Carbon Compounds 1962, Conformational Analysis (co-author) 1965, Elements of Stereochemistry 1969, Stereochemistry of Organic Compounds (co-author) 1994, and over 300 articles in professional journals; co-editor: Topics in Stereochemistry 1967–94. *Leisure interests:* photography, travel, swimming, hiking. *Address:* 725 Kenmore Road, Chapel Hill, NC 27514, U.S.A. (Home). *Telephone:* (919) 929-7966 (Home).

ELINSON, Jack, PH.D.; American professor of sociomedical sciences; b. 30 June 1917, New York; s. of Sam Elinson and Rebecca Block Elinson; m. May Gomberg 1941; three s. one d.; ed. Coll. of the City of New York and George Washington Univ.; scientific aide, U.S. Govt. Food and Drug Admin., Soil Conservation Service, Nat. Bureau of Standards 1937–41; statistician, War Dept. 1941–42; Social Science Analyst, Dept. of Defense, Armed Forces Information and Educ. Div., Attitude Research Br. 1942–51; Sr. Study Dir. Nat. Opinion Research Center, Univ. of Chicago 1951–56; Prof. of Sociomedical Sciences, Columbia Univ. 1956–86, Emer. 1986–; Visiting Prof. of Behavioral Sciences, Univ. of Toronto 1969–75, Distinguished Visiting Prof., Inst. for Health Care Policy, Rutgers Univ. 1986–89, Distinguished Sr. Scholar 1990–; Visiting Prof. Graduate Program in Public Health, Robert Wood Johnson Medical School 1986–; Consultant, Medical and Health Research Asscn. of New York City 1986–; Service Fellow, Nat. Center for Health Statistics, U.S. Public Health Service 1977–81; numerous professional appts., honours and distinctions. *Publications:* Chronic Illness in a Rural Area (with R. E. Trussell) 1959, Family Medical Care under Three Types of Health Insurance (with J. J. Williams and R. E. Trussell) 1962, Public Image of Mental Health Services (with E. Padilla and M. E. Perkins) 1967, Health Goals and Health Indicators (with A. Mooney and A.E. Siegmann) 1977, Sociomedical Health Indicators (with A.E. Siegmann) 1979, Assessment of Quality of Life in Clinical Trials of Cardiovascular Therapies (with N. K. Wenger, M. E. Mattson and C. D. Furberg) 1984; articles in professional journals. *Address:* c/o Columbia University, School of Public Health, Division of Sociomedical Sciences, 600 West 168th Street, New York, NY 10032 (Office); 1181 E. Laurelton Parkway, Teaneck, NJ 07666, U.S.A. *Telephone:* (201) 836-9222.

ELION, Gertrude Belle, M.S.; American pharmacologist; b. 23 Jan. 1918, New York; d. of Robert Elion and Bertha Cohen; ed. Hunter Coll. and New York Univ.; Lab. Asst. Biochem. New York Hosp. School of Nursing 1937; Research Asst. Denver Chemical Manufacturing Co., New York 1938–39; schoolteacher, New York 1940–42; food analyst, Quaker Maid Co. Brooklyn 1942–43; Research Asst. Johnson & Johnson, New Brunswick, N.J. 1943–44; Biochemist, Wellcome Research Labs., Tuckahoe, New York 1944–50, Sr. Research Chemist 1950–55, Head of Experimental Therapy 1966–83, Scientist Emer. 1983–; Adjunct Prof. of Pharmacology and Experimental Medicine, Duke Univ. 1970, Research Prof. of Pharmacology 1983–; Adjunct Prof. Pharmacology Univ. of N.C., Chapel Hill 1973; consultant, U.S. Public Health Service 1960–64; mem. Bd. of Scientific Counselors, Nat. Cancer Inst. 1980–84; mem. Council, American Cancer Soc. 1983–86; Fellow, New York Acad. of Sciences; mem. N.A.S., American Acad. of Arts and Sciences, Inst. of Medicine and numerous professional asscns.; Foreign mem. Royal Soc.; Hon. D.M.Sc. (Brown Univ.) 1969; Hon. D.Sc. (George Washington Univ.) 1969, (Univ. of Mich.) 1983, (N.C. State Univ., Hunter Coll., N.Y. Univ., Polytechnic Univ., Ohio State Univ.) 1989, (Univ. of N.C. at Chapel Hill, Russell Sage Coll., Duke Univ.) 1991, (Columbia and McMaster Univs., State Univ. of N.Y. at Stony Brook) 1992, (Washington Coll., S. Florida, Wisconsin, Eastern Carolina) 1993, (Utah State Univ., Wake Forest Univ.) 1994, (Phila. Coll. of Pharmacy, Albany Coll. of Pharmacy) 1996, (Harvard) 1998; Hon. M.D. (Chieti Univ., Italy) 1995; Hon. D.H.L. (Rochester Inst. of Tech.) 1996; Garvan Medal 1968, President's Medal, Hunter Coll. 1970, Judd Award Memorial Sloan-Kettering Cancer Center 1983, Cain Award, American Asscn. for Cancer Research 1984, Nobel Prize in Medicine (with G. H. Hitchings and Sir James Black) 1988, Discoverers Award, Pharmaceutical Mfg. Asscn. 1990, Medal of Honor, American Cancer Soc. 1990, Nat. Medal of Science 1991, Eng. and Science Hall of Fame 1992, Lemelson/M.I.T. Lifetime Achievement Award 1997, Women in Tech. Hall of Fame 1998, Arthritis Foundation Lifetime Achievement Award 1998, and other awards; Dame, Order of St. John of Jerusalem. *Publications:* articles in professional journals. *Leisure interests:* photography, travel. *Address:* Glaxo Wellcome Inc., 5 Moore Drive, Durham, NC 27701 (Office); 1 Banbury Lane, Chapel Hill, NC 27514, U.S.A. (Home). *Telephone:* (919) 483-1664 (Office). *Fax:* (919) 315-5819.

ELIOT, Charles William John, O.C., PH.D.; Canadian professor of classics; b. 8 Dec. 1928, Rawalpindi; s. of William E. C. Eliot and Ann Catherine Gertrude Eliot; m. D. P. Mary Williamson 1954; three s. two d. (one deceased); ed. Ashbury Coll., Ottawa, Trinity Coll., Univ. of Toronto, American School of Classical Studies; Instructor, then Prof., Univ. of British Columbia 1957–71; Prof. of Archaeology, American School of Classical Studies, Athens 1971–76; Prof. of Classics, Mount Allison Univ., Sackville 1976–85, Academic Vice-Pres. 1981–83; Pres. and Vice-Chancellor, Univ. of P.E.I. 1985–95, Pres. Emer. 1996–; Hon. D.C.L. (Univ. of King's Coll., Halifax). *Publications:* The Athenian Agora, a Guide to the Excavations (with M. Lang) 1954, Coastal Demes of Attika: A Study of the Policy of Kleisthenes 1962, Discipline and Discovery, a Proposal to the Faculty of Arts at the University of British Columbia (jt. author) 1965, numerous articles and chapters in journals. *Leisure interest:* collecting books by John Galt. *Address:* c/o 13 Water Street, Apt. 4, Charlottetown, P.E.I., C1A 1A3 (Office); P.O. Box 33, Dorchester, N.B., E0A 1M0, Canada (Home).

ELIZABETH II (Elizabeth Alexandra Mary); Queen of Great Britain and Northern Ireland and of Her other Realms and Territories (see under Reigning Royal Families at front of book for full titles); b. 21 April 1926, London; d. of H.R.H. Prince Albert, Duke of York (later H.M. King George VI), and Duchess of York (now H.M. Queen Elizabeth The Queen Mother, q.v.); succeeded to The Throne following Her father's death, 6 Feb. 1952; married, 20 Nov. 1947, H.R.H. The Prince Philip, Duke of Edinburgh, b. 10 June 1921; children: Prince Charles Philip Arthur George, Prince of Wales (heir apparent, q.v.), b. 14 Nov. 1948; Princess Anne Elizabeth Alice Louise, The Princess Royal (q.v.) b. 15 Aug. 1950; Prince Andrew Albert Christian Edward, Duke of York (q.v.) b. 19 Feb. 1960; Prince Edward Antony Richard Louis (q.v.) b. 10 March 1964. *Address:* Buckingham Palace, London, SW1A 1AA; Windsor Castle, Berkshire, SL4 1NJ, England; Palace of Holyroodhouse, Edinburgh, Scotland; Balmoral Castle, Aberdeenshire, AB35 5TB, Scotland; Sandringham House, Norfolk, PE35 6EN, England.

ELIZABETH ANGELA MARGUERITE; H.M. Queen Elizabeth the Queen Mother, Lady of the Order of the Garter, Lady of the Order of the Thistle, C.I., G.C.V.O., G.B.E., Lord Warden of the Cinque Ports; member of the British Royal Family; b. 4 Aug. 1900; d. of the 14th Earl of Strathmore and Kinghorne; m. 1923 H.R.H. The Duke of York, later H.M. King George VI (died 1952); reigned as Queen 1936–52. *Address:* Clarence House, London, SW1A 1AA; Royal Lodge, Windsor Great Park, Berks., England; Castle of Mey, Caithness, Scotland.

EL-KADDOUR, Mohammed Ghassan; Syrian civil engineer; b. 1952, El-Bab; m. Myriam Koudsi; one s. two d.; ed. Univ. of Aleppo; with Milihouse Corpn. 1976–80; in business 1981–83; Chair.-Dir. Gen. Syrian Railways 1983–. *Leisure interest:* sport. *Address:* Syrian Railways Administration, P.O. Box 182, Aleppo, Syria. *Telephone:* (21) 2213900/01/02. *Fax:* (21) 2228480, 2225697.

ELKIN, Alexander, C.M.G., DR.JUR., LL.M.; British international law consultant (retd.); b. 2nd Aug. 1909, St. Petersburg; s. of Boris Elkin and Anna Elkin; m. Muriel Solomons 1937; ed. Grunewald Gymnasium, Russian Academic School, Berlin, and Univs. of Berlin, Kiel and London; called to Bar, Middle Temple 1937; practised at English Bar 1937–39; B.B.C. Monitoring Service 1939–42; govt. service 1942–45; UN Service 1945–48 (Assoc. Chief, Legal Service, Interim Secr., Asst. Dir. UN European Office, Geneva); Deputy Legal Adviser, later Legal Adviser OEEC (later OECD), Paris 1949–61; Legal Consultant, formation of AfDB 1962–64; Acting Gen. Counsel AfDB 1964–65; UNDP Legal Consultant, formation of Caribbean Devt. Bank 1967–68; Special Adviser on European Community Law, FCO 1970–79; other legal consultancies for int. orgs.; Ford Foundation Leadership Grant 1960; lecturer at int. seminars etc. and Univ. of Bradford 1979–84, Univ. of Bath 1979–96; Hon. LL.D. (Univ. of Bath). *Publications:* articles in yearbooks, professional journals etc. *Leisure interests:* reading, visiting art collections, travel. *Address:* 70 Apsley House, Finchley Road, London NW8 0NZ, England. *Telephone:* 0171-483 2475.

ELLEMANN-JENSEN, Uffe, M.A.; Danish politician; b. 1 Nov. 1941; s. of Jens Peter Jensen; m. Alice Vestergaard 1971; two s. two d.; ed. Univ. of Copenhagen; Danish Defence staff 1962–64; Sec. Meat Producers' Asscn. 1964–67; journalist on Berlingske Aftenavis 1967–70; Econ. and political corresp. Danish television 1970–75; Ed.-in-Chief and mem. Bd. daily newspaper Borsen 1975–76; mem. Parl. 1977– (Liberal); Party spokesperson, political affairs 1978–82; Chair. Parl. Market Cttee. 1978–79; mem. Exec. Cttee. Liberal Party 1979, Chair. 1984–98; mem. Bd. Cen. Bank 1978–81, 1996–, Index Figures' Bd. 1979–81, Inter-Parl. Union 1979–; Minister of Foreign Affairs 1982–93; Vice-Pres. European Liberal Party 1985–95, Pres. 1995–; Chair. Foreign Policy Soc., Denmark 1993–, Baltic Devt. Forum 1998–; Robert Schuman Prize 1987. *Publications:* De nye millionaerer (The New Millionaires) 1971, Det afhaengige samfund (The Dependent Society) 1972, Hvad gør vi ved Gudenåen (We ought to do something about Gudenåen) 1973, Den truede velstand (The Threatened Wealth) 1974, Økonomi (Economy) 1975, Da Danmark igen sagde ja til det falles (When Denmark Repeated its Yes to Europe) 1987, Olfert Fischer 1991, Et lille land—og dog (A Small Country—And Yet) 1991, Din egen dag er kori (Short is your own day) 1996; numerous articles in newspapers and periodicals. *Leisure interests:* fishing, hunting, opera. *Address:* Folketinget, Christiansborg, 1240 Copenhagen, Denmark. *Telephone:* 33 37 55 00. *Fax:* 33 37 54 93.

ELLIOTT, Rev. Charles Middleton, M.A., D.PHIL.; British ecclesiastic; b. 9 Jan. 1939, Wakefield; s. of Joseph W. Elliott and Mary E. Elliott; m. Hilary M. Hambling 1962; three s. one d. (deceased); ed. Repton, Lincoln and Nuffield Colls. Oxford and Scholae Cancellarii, Lincoln; lecturer in Econs. Univ. of Nottingham 1962–65; Reader in Econs. Univ. of Zambia 1965–69; Asst. Sec. Jt. Cttee. on Soc., Devt. and Peace, Vatican/WCC, Geneva 1969–72; Sr. Lecturer in Econs. Univ. of E. Anglia 1972–77; Prof. of Devt. Studies, Univ. of Wales 1977–82; Dir. Christian Aid 1982–84; Benjamin Meaker Prof. Univ. of Bristol 1985–86; Visiting Prof. King's Coll. London 1987–88; Prebendary of Lichfield Cathedral 1987–96; Fellow, Chaplain and Dean, Trinity Hall, Cambridge 1990–, Affiliated Lecturer in Theology, Univ. of Cambridge 1991–, in Social and Political Sciences 1993–; Sec. Inst. of Contemporary Spirituality 1988–92; Pres. Feed the Minds 1991–; Chair. Univ. Bd. of Electors to Livings 1997–; Collins Religious Book Prize 1985. *Publications:* Patterns of Poverty in the Third World 1975, Praying the Kingdom 1985, Praying through Paradox 1987, Comfortable Compassion 1987, Signs of Our Times 1988, Sword and Spirit: Christianity in a Divided World 1989, Memory and Salvation 1995, Strategic Planning for Churches: An Appreciative Approach 1997; numerous articles in learned journals. *Leisure interests:* walking, gardening, fly-fishing, sailing. *Address:* Trinity Hall, Cambridge, CB2 1TJ; 11 Perowne Street, Cambridge, CB1 2AY, England. *Telephone:* (01223) 332525 (Office); (01223) 69233 (Home). *Fax:* (01223) 332537.

ELLIOTT, James Philip, PH.D., F.R.S.; British professor of theoretical physics; b. 27 July 1929; s. of James Elliott and Dora K. Smith; m. Mavis R. Avery 1955; one s. two d.; ed. Univ. Coll. Southampton; Sr. Scientific Officer, Atomic Energy Research Est. Harwell 1951–58; Visiting Assoc. Prof. Univ. of Rochester, U.S.A. 1958–59; Lecturer in Math. Univ. of Southampton 1959–62; Reader in Theoretical Physics, Univ. of Sussex 1962–69, Prof. 1969–. *Publications:* Symmetry in Physics 1979; papers in learned journals. *Leisure interests:* gardening, sport, music. *Address:* 36 Montacute Road, Lewes, Sussex, BN7 1EP, England. *Telephone:* (01273) 474783.

ELLIOTT, Sir John Huxtable, Kt., F.B.A.; British professor of history; b. 23 June 1930, Reading, Berks.; s. of Thomas Charles Elliott and Janet Mary Payne; m. Oonah Sophia Butler 1958; ed. Eton Coll. and Trinity Coll., Cambridge; Asst. Lecturer in History, Univ. of Cambridge 1957–62, Lecturer 1962–67; Prof. of History, King's Coll., Univ. of London 1968–73; Prof., School of Historical Studies, Inst. for Advanced Study, Princeton, N.J. 1973–90; Regius Prof. of Modern History, Oxford Univ., and Fellow of Oriel Coll., Oxford 1990–97; Fellow, Trinity Coll., Cambridge 1954–67, Royal Acad. of History, Madrid, American Acad. of Arts and Sciences, American Philosophical Soc, King's Coll., Univ. of London 1998; Hon. Fellow Trinity Coll., Cambridge 1991, Oriel Coll., Oxford 1997; mem. Scientific Cttee., Prado Museum 1996; Dr. h.c. (Universidad Autónoma de Madrid) 1983, (Genoa) 1992, (Portsmouth) 1993, (Barcelona) 1994, (Warwick) 1995, (Brown) 1996, (Valencia) 1998; Visitante Ilustre of Madrid 1983, Wolfson Literary Award for History and Biography 1986, Medal of Honour, Universidad Int. Menéndez y Pelayo 1987, Gold Medal for Fine Arts (Spain) 1991, Eloy Antonio de Nebrija Prize (Univ. of Salamanca) 1993, Prince of Asturias Prize in Social Sciences 1996; Commdr. of the Order of Alfonso X El Sabio 1984, Commdr. Order of Isabel la Católica 1987, Grand Cross of the Order of Alfonso X, El Sabio 1988, Grand Cross of Order of Isabel la Católica 1996–, Gold Medal, Spanish Inst., New York 1997. *Publications:* Imperial Spain, 1469–1716 1963, The Revolt of the Catalans 1963, Europe Divided, 1559–1598 1968, The Old World and the New, 1492–1650 1970, Ed. (with H. G. Koenigsberger) The Diversity of History 1970, A Palace for a King (with J. Brown) 1980, Memoriales y Cartas del Conde Duque de Olivares 1978–80, Richelieu and Olivares 1984, The Count-Duke of Olivares 1986, Spain and Its World 1500–1700 1989, The Hispanic World (Ed.) 1991, The World of the Favourite (Ed. jtly.) 1999. *Leisure interest:* looking at paintings. *Address:* 122 Church Way, Iffley, Oxford, OX4 4EG, England. *Telephone:* (01865) 716703.

ELLIOTT, Marianne, D. PHIL., F.R.HIST.S.; Irish historian; b. 25 May 1948, N. Ireland; d. of Terence J. Burns and Sheila O'Neill; m. Prof. Trevor Elliott 1975; one s.; ed. Dominican Convent, Fort William, Belfast, Queen's Univ. Belfast and Lady Margaret Hall, Oxford; French Govt. research scholar in Paris 1972–73; other research in Ireland, U.K., France, Netherlands and U.S.A.; Lecturer in History, W. London Inst. of Higher Educ. 1975–77; Research Fellow, Univ. Coll. Swansea 1977–82; Visiting Prof. Ia. State Univ. 1983, Univ. of S. Carolina 1984; Research Fellow, Univ. of Liverpool 1984–87; Simon Fellow, Univ. of Manchester 1988–89; lecturer Birkbeck Coll., Univ. of London 1991–93; Andrew Geddes and John Rankin Prof. of Modern History and Dir. Inst. of Irish Studies, Univ. of Liverpool 1993–; mem. Opsahl Comm. on Northern Ireland; Leo Gershoy Award for History 1983; Sunday Independent/Irish Life Award for Biography 1989, James Donnelly Sr. Award for History (American Conf. for Irish Studies) 1991. *Publications:* Partners in Revolution. The United Irishmen and France 1982, Watchmen in Sion. The Protestant Idea of Liberty 1985, The People's Armies (translation) 1987, Wolfe Tone. Prophet of Irish Independence 1989, A Citizens' Inquiry: The Report of the Opsahl Commission on Northern Ireland 1993, A History of the Catholics in Ulster 1998. *Address:* Department of History, University of Liverpool, P.O. Box 147, Liverpool, L69 3BX, England. *Telephone:* 0151-794 3831. *Fax:* 0151-794 3836.

ELLIOTT, Michael, C.B.E., D.SC., C.CHEM., PH.D., F.R.S.C., F.R.S.; British organic research chemist; b. 30 Sept. 1924, London; s. of Thomas W. and Isobel C. (Burnell) Elliott; m. Margaret O. James 1950; two d.; ed. The Skinners' Co. School, Tunbridge Wells, Univ. of Southampton and King's Coll., London; Scientific Officer Dept. of Insecticides and Fungicides, Rothamsted Experimental Station 1948–53, Sr. Scientific Officer 1953–61, Prin. Scientific Officer 1961–70, Sr. Prin. Scientific Officer 1970–79, Deputy Chief Scientific Officer 1979–84, Head of Dept. of Insecticides and Fungicides and Deputy Dir. Rothamsted Experimental Station 1979–84; Visiting Lecturer, Univ. of Calif. (Berkeley) 1969, 1974; Visiting Prof., Imperial Coll., London 1979–85; Fellow, King's Coll., London 1984–; consultant on chem. of insecticides 1984–; Visiting Research Scientist, Pesticide Chem. and Toxicology Lab., Univ. of Calif. (Berkeley) 1985–88; Lawes Trust Sr. Fellow, Rothamsted Experimental Station 1989–; Foreign Assoc. N.A.S. 1996; Hon. D.Sc. (Southampton) 1985; Mullard Medal, Royal Soc. 1982, Wolf Foundation Prize in Agriculture 1989, Prix de la Fondation de la Chimie 1989, The SCI Environment Medal 1993, and other awards and prizes. *Publications:* more than 200 scientific articles. *Leisure interest:* photography. *Address:* 45 Larkfield, Ewhurst, Cranleigh, Surrey, GU6 7QU, England. *Telephone:* (01483) 277506.

ELLIOTT, Osborn, A.B.; American journalist; b. 25 Oct. 1924, New York City; s. of John and Audrey N. (Osborn) Elliott; m. 1st Deirdre M. Spencer 1948 (divorced 1972); three d.; m. 2nd the fmr. Mrs. Inger A. McCabe; one step s. two step d.; ed. The Browning School (N.Y.), St. Paul's School (Concord) and Harvard Univ.; served with U.S.N.R. 1944–46; Reporter N.Y. Journal of Commerce 1946–49; Contributing Ed. Time 1949–52, Assoc. Ed. 1952–55; Senior Business Ed. Newsweek 1955–59, Man. Ed. 1959–61, Ed., Editor-in-Chief, Pres., C.E.O., Chair. of Bd. 1961–76; Deputy Mayor for Econ. Devt., New York 1976–77; Dean Graduate School of Journalism, Columbia Univ., New York 1979–86; Prof. Columbia Univ. 1979–94; fmr. Dir. Washington Post Co.; fmr. Trustee, American Museum of Natural History, Asia Soc., Lincoln Center Theatre, New York Public Library, St. Paul's School, Winston Churchill Foundation of the U.S. Ltd.; mem. Council on Foreign Relations, Pulitzer Prize Bd. 1979–86; mem. Bd. of Overseers of Harvard Coll. 1965–71; Chair. Citizens' Cttee. for New York City 1975–80, 1990–; Organiser Save Our Cities! Save Our Children! march, Washington, D.C. May 1992; Fellow American Acad. of Arts and Sciences; numerous awards and hon. degrees. *Publications:* Men at the Top 1959, The World of Oz 1980; Ed. The Negro Revolution in America 1964. *Leisure interests:* boating, fishing. *Address:* 36 E. 72nd Street, New York, NY 10021, U.S.A.

ELLIOTT, Sir Roger (James), Kt., M.A., D.PHIL., F.R.S.; British physicist and publisher; b. 8 Dec. 1928, Chesterfield; s. of James Elliott and Gladys Elliott (née Hill); m. Olga Lucy Atkinson 1952; one s. two d.; ed. Swanwick Hall School, Derbyshire and New Coll., Oxford; Research Assoc. Univ. of Calif., Berkeley 1952–53; Research Fellow, Atomic Energy Research Est., Harwell 1953–55; lecturer, Univ. of Reading 1955–57; Lecturer, Oxford Univ. 1957–65, Reader 1965–74, Fellow, St. John's Coll. 1957–74, New Coll. 1974–96, Wykeham Prof. of Physics 1974–89, Prof. of Physics 1989–96, now Emer. Prof.; Sec. to Dels. and Chief Exec., Oxford Univ. Press 1988–93; Visiting Prof. Univ. of Calif., Berkeley 1960–61; Miller Visiting Prof. Univ. of Ill., Urbana 1966; Visiting Distinguished Prof. Fla. State Univ. 1981, Mich. State Univ. 1997–; Del. OUP 1971–88, Chair. Computer Bd. 1983–87; Physical Sec. and Vice-Pres. Royal Soc. (London) 1984–88; Treas. Publrs. Asscn. 1990–92, Pres. 1992–93; Chair. ICSU Press 1997–, Disability Information Trust 1998–; mem. Bd. (part-time) UKAEA 1988–94, British Council 1990–98, Blackwells Ltd. 1996–; Hon. D.Sc. (Paris) 1983, Bath (1991), (Essex) 1993; Maxwell Medal (Physical Soc.) 1968, Guthrie Medal 1989. *Publications:* Magnetic Properties of Rare Earth Metals 1972, Solid State Physics and its Applications 1973, articles in learned journals. *Address:* 11 Crick Road, Oxford, OX2 6QL, England (Home). *Telephone:* (01865) 273997. *Fax:* (01865) 273947.

ELLIS, Alice Thomas (see Haycraft, Anna Margaret).

ELLIS, Charles Richard, M.A.; American publishing executive; b. 20 July 1935, New York; s. of Charles Ellis and Ruth Allen; m. 1st Nathalie Likwas 1957 (divorced 1963); one s.; m. 2nd Jeanne Laurent 1963; four step-s.; ed. Princeton and Columbia Univs.; teacher, Barnard School, New York 1958–63; Man. Scientific Research Assocs. Chicago 1963–68; Exec. Ed. D.C. Heath, Boston 1968–70; Chair. and Man. Dir. D.C. Heath Ltd., U.K. 1970–75; Co-Man. Dir. Pergamon Press, U.K. 1975–78; Marketing Dir. Elsevier Publishing, Amsterdam 1978–81; Pres. Elsevier Scientific Publishing Co. New

York 1981–88; Exec. Vice-Pres. John Wiley & Sons, New York 1988–90, Pres., C.E.O. 1990–97, sr. adviser 1998–; Pres. Bd. of Trustees, Princeton Univ. Press. 1987–; Chair. Asscn. of American Publrs. 1992–94. *Address:* John Wiley & Sons, 605 Third Avenue, New York, NY 10158 (Office); 300 East 54th Street, New York, NY 10022, U.S.A (Home). *Telephone:* (212) 850-6000 (Office). *Fax:* (212) 850-6088 (Office).

ELLIS, Gavin Peter; New Zealand journalist; b. 6 March 1947, Auckland; s. of Peter Fisher Dundass Ellis and Catherine Ellis (née Gray); m. 1st Janine Laurette Sinclair 1969; m. 2nd Jennifer Ann Lynch 1991; one s.; ed. Mount Roskill Grammar School and Auckland Univ.; on staff of Auckland Star paper 1965–70; public relations consultant 1970–71; joined New Zealand Herald 1972, Asst. Ed. 1987–96, Ed. 1996–; Brittain Memorial Fellow 1980. *Leisure interests:* medieval history, opera. *Address:* 46 Albert Street, Auckland, New Zealand. *Telephone:* (09) 379-5050. *Fax:* (09) 377-1568.

ELLIS, George Francis Rayner, F.R.A.S., PH.D.; British/South African professor of astrophysics and applied mathematics; b. 11 Aug. 1939, Johannesburg; s. of George Rayner Ellis and Gwen Hilda (née MacRobert) Ellis; m. 1st Sue Parkes 1963; m. 2nd Mary Wheeldon 1978; one s. one d.; ed. Michaelhouse, Univ. of Cape Town and Cambridge Univ.; Fellow Peterhouse, Cambridge 1965–67; Asst. Lecturer, lecturer Cambridge 1967–73; Prof. of Applied Math., Univ. of Cape Town 1974–88, 1990–; Prof. of Cosmic Physics, SISSA, Trieste 1988–92; G. C. MacVittie Visiting Prof. of Astronomy, Queen Mary Coll., London 1987–; Chair. GR1O Scientific Cttee. 1988; Pres., Int. Soc. of Gen. Relativity and Gravitation 1989–92; mem. cttee. (and Vice-Pres.) Royal Soc. of S.A. 1990–, Pres. 1992–96; Founding mem., mem. Council, Acad. of Science of S.A. 1995–; Fellow Inst. of Maths and its Applications; mem. Int. Cttee. on Gen. Relativity and Gravitation; Chair. Quaker Service, West Cape 1976–86, Quaker Peacework Cttee. 1978–86, 1990–95, S.A. Inst. of Race Relations, West Cape 1985–87; Clerk S.A. Yearly Meeting of Quakers 1986–88; Fellowship of Univ. of Cape Town; Hon. D.Sc. (Haverford Coll.) 1996; Herschel Medal of Royal Soc. of S.A.; Gravity Research Foundation 1st Prize 1979. *Publications:* The Large Scale Structure of Space-Time (with S. W. Hawking q.v.) 1973, The Squatter Problem in the Western Cape (with J. Maree, D. Hendrie) 1976, Low Income Housing Policy (with D. Dewar) 1980, Flat and Curved Space-Times (with R. Williams) 1988, Before the Beginning 1993, The Renaissance of General Relativity and Cosmology 1993, The Dynamical Systems Approach to Cosmology (co-ed.) 1996, The Density of Matter in the Universe (with P. Coles) 1996, On the Moral Nature of the Universe: Cosmology, Theology and Ethics (with M. Murphy) 1996. *Leisure interests:* climbing, gliding. *Address:* Department of Applied Mathematics, University of Cape Town, Rondebosch 7700, Cape Town (Office); 3 Marlow Road, Cape Town 7700, South Africa (Home). *Telephone:* (21) 650-2340 (Office); (21) 7612313 (Home). *Fax:* (21) 650-2334.

ELLIS, John Martin, PH.D.; American professor; b. 31 May 1936, London, England; s. of John Albert Ellis and Emily Ellis; m. Barbara Rhoades 1978; two s. two d.; ed. City of London School and Univ. Coll., London; Royal Artillery 1954–56; Tutorial Asst. in German, Univ. of Wales, Aberystwyth 1959–60; Asst. lecturer in German, Univ. of Leicester 1960–63; Asst. Prof. of German, Univ. of Alberta, Canada 1963–66; Assoc. Prof. of German Literature, Univ. of Calif., Santa Cruz 1966–70, Prof. 1970–94, Prof. Emer. 1994, Dean Graduate Div. 1977–86; Literary Ed. Heterodoxy 1992–; Sec.-Treas. Asscn. of Literary Scholars and Critics 1994–99; Guggenheim Fellowship, Nat. Endowment for the Humanties Sr. Fellowship; Nat. Asscn. of Scholars' Peter Shaw Memorial Award (for Literature Lost). *Publications include:* Narration in the German Novelle 1974, The Theory of Literary Criticism: A Logical Analysis 1974, Heinrich von Kleist 1979, One Fairy Story Too Many: The Brothers Grimm and Their Tales 1983, Against Deconstruction 1989, Language, Thought and Logic 1993, Literature Lost: Social Agendas and the Corruption of the Humanities 1997. *Leisure interests:* birdwatching, golf. *Address:* 144 Bay Heights, Soquel, CA 95073, U.S.A. *Telephone:* (831) 476 1144. *Fax:* (831) 476-1144.

ELLIS, Jonathan Richard (John), M.A., PH.D., F.R.S., F.INST.P.; British physicist; b. 1 July 1946, Hampstead; s. of Richard Ellis and Beryl Lilian (née Ranger) Ellis; m. Maria Mercedes Martinez Rengifo 1985; one s. one d.; ed. Highgate School, King's Coll., Univ. of Cambridge; Post-doctoral Research Fellow, Stanford Linear Accelerator Center 1971–72; Richard Chase Tolman Fellow, Calif. Inst. of Technology 1972–73; Research Fellow, C.E.R.N. 1973–74, Staff mem. 1974–, Leader, Theoretical Physics Div. 1988–94, Sr. Staff Physicist 1994–; Maxwell medal (Inst. of Physics) 1982. *Publications:* over 390 scientific publs. *Leisure interests:* literature, music, travel, hiking. *Address:* Theory Division, C.E.R.N., CH-1211 Geneva 23 (Office); 5 Chemin du Ruisseau, Tannay, 1295 Mies, Vaud, Switzerland (Home). *Telephone:* (767) 4142 (Office); (776) 4858 (Home).

ELLIS, Osian Gwynn, C.B.E., F.R.A.M.; British harpist; b. 8 Feb. 1928, Ffynnongroew, Flintshire, Wales; s. of Rev. T. G. Ellis; m. Rene Ellis Jones 1951; two s.; ed. Denbigh Grammar School, Royal Acad. of Music; Prin. Harpist London Symphony Orchestra 1960–94; mem. Melos Ensemble; Prof. of Harp Royal Acad. of Music 1959–89; recitals and concerts worldwide; radio and TV broadcasts; works written for him include harp concertos by Hoddinott 1957, Mathias 1970, Jersild 1972, Robin Holloway 1985, and solos and chamber music by Gian Carlo Menotti 1977, William Schuman 1978 and Harp Suite in C, Op. 83 by Britten; Hon. D.Mus. (Wales) 1970; Grand Prix du Disque, French Radio Critics' Award and other awards. *Publication:* Story of the Harp in Wales 1991. *Address:* 90 Chandos Avenue, London, N20 9DZ, England; Arfryn, Ala Road, Pwllheli, Gwynedd, LL53 5BN, Wales. *Telephone:* 0181-445 7896 (London); (01758) 612501 (Wales).

ELLIS, Reginald John, PH.D., F.R.S.; British professor of biological sciences; b. 12 Feb. 1935, Newcastle-under-Lyme; s. of Francis Gilbert Ellis and Evangeline Gratton Ellis; m. Diana Margaret Warren 1963; one d.; ed. Highbury Grove Grammar School, London and King's Coll., Univ. of London; Agricultural Research Council Fellow, Dept. of Biochemistry, Univ. of Oxford 1961–64; Lecturer, Depts. of Botany and Biochemistry, Univ. of Aberdeen 1964–70; Sr. Lecturer, Univ. of Warwick 1970–73, Reader 1973–76, Prof. of Biological Sciences 1976–96, Prof. Emer. 1996–; Sr. Research Fellow, Science and Eng. Research Council 1983–88; mem. EMBO 1986–; Sr. Visiting Research Fellow, St. John's Coll. Oxford 1992–93; Academic Visitor, Oxford Centre for Molecular Sciences 1996–99; Tate & Lyle Award 1980. *Publications:* 140 papers on plant and microbial biochemistry in the scientific literature; Chloroplast Biogenesis (Ed.) 1984, Molecular Chaperones (Ed.) 1993, The Chaperonins (Ed.) 1996. *Address:* Department of Biological Sciences, University of Warwick, Coventry, West Midlands, CV4 7AL (Office); 44 Sunningdale Avenue, Kenilworth, Warwicks., CV8 2BZ, England (Home). *Telephone:* 01203-523509 (Office); 01926-856382 (Home).

ELLISON, Harlan Jay; American author; b. 27 May 1934, Cleveland; s. of Louis Laverne Ellison and Serita (née Rosenthal) Ellison; m. 1st Charlotte Stein 1956 (divorced 1959); m. 2nd Billie Joyce Sanders 1961 (divorced 1962); m. 3rd Lory Patrick 1965 (divorced 1965); m. 4th Lori Horwitz 1976 (divorced 1977); m. 5th Susan Toth 1986; ed. Ohio State Univ.; part-time actor, Cleveland Playhouse 1944–49; f. Cleveland Science-Fiction Soc. 1950, and Science-Fantasy Bulletin; served U.S. Army 1957–59; ed. Rogue magazine, Chicago 1959-60, Regency Books, Chicago 1960–61; lecturer at Colls. and Univs.; voice-overs for animated cartoons; book critic, L.A. Times 1969–82; Editorial Commentator Canadian Broadcasting Co. 1972–78; Instructor Clarion Writers Workshop, Michigan State Univ. 1969–77; Pres. The Kilimanjaro Corpn. 1979–; TV writer for Alfred Hitchcock Hour, Outer Limits, The Man from U.N.C.L.E., Burkes Law; Film writer for The Dream Merchants, The Oscar, Nick the Greek, Best By Far, Harlan Ellison's Movie: scenarist: I, Robot 1978, Bug Jack Barron 1982–83; creative consultant, writer and dir. The Twilight Zone 1984–85; conceptual consultant Babylon 5 1993–98; mem. American Writers Guild and American Science Fiction Writers; Hugo Awards 1967, 1968, 1973, 1974, 1975, 1977, 1986; Special Achievement awards 1968–72, Certificate of merit, Trieste Film Festival 1970, Edgar Allan Poe award, Mystery Writers 1974, 1988, American Mystery Award 1988, Bram Stoker Award, Horror Writers 1988, 1990, 1994; World Fantasy Award 1989, George Melies Award for cinematic achievement 1972, 1973, PEN Award for journalism 1982; Americana Annual American Literature: Major Works 1988, World Fantasy 1993 Life Achievement Award. *Publications:* A Boy and His Dog (novella) 1975, Stalking the Nightmare 1982, An Edge in My Voice 1985, The Essential Ellison 1987, Angry Candy (short stories) 1988, Harlan Ellison's Watching 1989, The Harlan Ellison Hornbook 1990, Harlan Ellison's Movie 1990, Mefisto in Onyx 1993, Mind Fields (33 stories inspired by the art of Jacek Yerka) 1994, Robot: The Illustrated Screenplay 1994, City on the Edge of Forever (screenplay) 1995, Slippage 1996, Edgeworks: The Collected Ellison (4 Vols.) 1996–97. *Address:* c/o HERC, P.O. Box 55548, Sherman Oaks, CA 91413, U.S.A.

ELLISON, Lawrence, J., B.S.; American computer software executive; b. 1944; with Amdahl Inc., Calif. 1967–71; Pres. Omex Corpn., Systems Div. 1972–77; with Oracle Corpn., Calif. 1977–, Pres., C.E.O. 1978–, mem. Bd. of Dirs.; mem. Bd. of Dirs. Apple Computer Inc. 1997. *Address:* Oracle Corporation, 500 Oracle Parkway, Redwood City, CA 94065, U.S.A.

ELLWOOD, Peter Brian, F.C.I.B., F.R.S.A.; British banker; b. 15 May 1943, Bristol; s. of late Isaac Ellwood and Edith Trotter; m. Judy Windsor 1968; one s. two d.; ed. King's School, Macclesfield; joined Barclays Bank 1961; worked in London and Bristol; in charge of Barclaycard operations 1983; Chief Exec. Barclaycard 1985; Chief Exec. Cen. Retail Services Div. Barclays Bank; Dir. On-Line Card Services Ltd., Barclays Bank (U.K.) Ltd.; Chief. Exec. Retail Banking, TSB Bank PLC; Dir. TSB Group PLC 1992–; Chief Exec. 1992–95; Chief Exec. TSB Bank PLC 1992–; Deputy Chief Exec. Lloyds TSB Group PLC 1996–97, Chief Exec. 1997–; Chair. Visa Europe, Middle East and Africa 1992–96, Visa Int. 1994–, fmr. Chair. United Dominions Trust (UDT); Dir. (non.-exec.) Sears PLC 1994–96, Royal Philharmonic Orchestra 1996–; Trustee Royal Theatre, Northampton; mem. Nene Coll. Court; Hon. LL.D. (Leicester) 1994; Dr. h.c. (Univ. of Cen. England) 1995. *Leisure interests:* music, theatre. *Address:* 71 Lombard Street, London, EC3P 3BS, England. *Telephone:* 0171-356 2072 (Office). *Fax:* 0171-356 2049.

ELMANDJRA, Mahdi, PH.D.; Moroccan university professor; b. 13 March 1933, Rabat; s. of M'Hamed Elmandjra and Rabia Elmrini; m. Amina Elmrini 1956; two d.; ed. Lycée Lyautey, Casablanca, Putney School, Vermont, U.S.A., Cornell Univ., London School of Economics and Faculté de Droit, Univ. de Paris; Head of Confs., Law Faculty, Univ. of Rabat 1957–58; Adviser, Ministry of Foreign Affairs, and to Moroccan Del. to UN 1958–59; Dir.-Gen., Radiodiffusion Télévision Marocaine 1959–60; Chief of African Div., Office of Relations with Mem. States, UNESCO 1961–63; Dir. Exec. Office of Dir.-Gen. of UNESCO 1963–66; Asst. Dir.-Gen. of UNESCO for Social Sciences, Human Sciences and Culture 1966–69; Visiting Fellow, Centre of Int. Studies, London School of Econs. and Political Science 1970; Asst. Dir.-Gen. of

UNESCO for Pre-Programming 1971–74; Special Adviser to Dir.-Gen. of UNESCO 1975–76; Prof. Univ. Mohamed V, Rabat 1977–; Co-ordinator, Conf. on Tech. Co-operation between Developing Countries (UNDP) 1979–80; Senior Adviser, UN Int. Year of Disabled Persons 1980–81; mem. Consultative Cultural Council of the Inst. of the Arab World (Paris); fmr. Pres. World Future Studies Fed. (WFSF), Futuribles Int.; mem. Club of Rome, Acad. of the Kingdom of Morocco; Vice-Pres. Asscn. Maroc-Japon; mem. World Acad. of Art and Science, Exec. Cttee., Soc. for Int. Devt., Exec. Cttee., African Acad. of Sciences, Pugwash Conferences, Founding Pres. Moroccan Asscn. of Human Rights; Master Jury Aga Khan Award for Architecture 1986, Albert Einstein Int. Foundation Medal for Peace 1990; Officier Arts et Lettres (France), Order of the Rising Sun (Japan) and numerous other decorations. *Publications include:* Africa 2000 1980, The New Age of Culture and Communication 1981, The Future of Humor 1982, Maghreb 2000 1982, L'Interpellation du Tiers Monde 1982, Les Aspects économiques du dialogue Euro-Arabe 1982, Information and Sovereignty 1983, The Conquest of Space: Political, Economic and Socio-Cultural Implications 1984, Casablanca 2000 1984, Development and Automation 1985, Communications, Information and Development 1985, Tomorrow's Habitat 1985, Learning Needs in a Changing Society 1986, Media and Communications in Africa 1986, The Future of International Cooperation 1986, The Financing of Research and Development in the Third World 1986, Maghreb et Francophonie 1988, Three Scenarios for The Future of International Cooperation 1988, The Place of Arab Culture in the World of Tomorrow 1988, Social Change and Law 1988, China in the 21st Century 1989, Fusion of Science and Culture: Key to the 21st Century 1989, Human Rights and Development 1989, How to Construct a Positive Vision of the Future 1990, Gulf Crisis: Prelude to the North-South Confrontation 1990, Western Discrimination in the Field of Human Rights 1990, Africa: The Coming Upheaval 1990, La Première Guerre Civilisationnelle 1991, Retrospective des Futurs 1992, Nord-Sud: Prélude à l'Ere Post-coloniale 1992, The Agreements Concerning Gaza and Jericho 1993, Biodiversity: Cultural and Ethical Aspects 1994, Cultural Diversity: Key to Survival in the 21st Century 1994, The New Challenges Facing the United Nations 1995, Dialogue de la Communication 1996, Al Quds (Jerusalem): Symbole et mémoire 1996, La décolonisation culturelle: défi majeur du 21e siècle 1996, Immigration as a Cultural Phenomenon 1997, The Path of a Mind 1997. *Leisure interests:* reading, swimming, music. *Address:* B.P. 53, Rabat, Morocco. *Telephone:* Rabat 774-258. *Fax:* 757-151.

ELMER, Michael B.; Danish lawyer; b. 26 Feb. 1949, Copenhagen; s. of Poul Chr. B. Elmer and Etly (née Andersson) Elmer; m. Lise Skovby 1993; ed. Univ. of Copenhagen; civil servant Ministry of Justice 1973–76, 1977–82, Head of Div. 1982–87, 1988–91, Deputy Perm. Sec., Head of Community Law and Human Rights Dept. 1991–94; Assoc. Prof. Univ. of Copenhagen 1975–85; Deputy Judge, Hillerød 1976–77; Asst. Public Prosecutor 1980–81; Judge Court of Ballerup 1981–82; external examiner Danish law schools 1985–; High Court Judge (a.i.) Eastern High Court, Copenhagen 1987–88; Vice-Pres. (a.i.) Maritime and Commercial Court, Copenhagen 1988, Vice Pres. 1997–; Rep. EC Court of Justice, Luxembourg 1991–94; Advocate-Gen. EC Court of Justice 1994–97; mem. governing council UNIDROIT, Rome 1999–; Chair. and mem. numerous govt. and int. orgs. cttees. *Publications:* several books and articles on civil law (especially property law), penal law and community law. *Leisure interests:* travelling, collecting antiques. *Address:* Só-og Handelsretten, Bredgade 70, DK-1260, Copenhagen, Denmark. *Telephone:* 33479222. *Fax:* 33145677.

ELS, Ernie; South African golfer; b. 17 Oct. 1969, Kempton Park; s. of Nils Els and Hettie Els; won South African Open 1992, 1996, US Open, 1994, 1997, Toyota World Matchplay Championships 1994, 1995, 1996, South African PGA Championship 1995, Byron Nelson Classic 1995, Buick Classic 1996, 1997, Johnny Walker Classic 1997, Bay Hill Invitational 1998, named South African Sportsman of the Year 1994. *Address:* 46 Chapman Road, Klippoortjie 1401, South Africa.

ELSÄSSER, Hans Friedrich, DR.RER.NAT.; German astronomer; b. 29 March 1929, Aalen/Württemberg; s. of Jakob Elsässer and Margarete Elsässer-Vogelgsang; m. Ruth Abele 1953; two s. one d.; ed. Univ. of Tübingen; Asst. Prof., Univ. of Tübingen 1957, Univ. of Göttingen 1959; Prof. of Astronomy, Univ. of Heidelberg 1962–; Dir. State Observatory, Heidelberg-Königstuhl 1962–75; Dir. Max Planck Inst. for Astronomy, Heidelberg-Königstuhl 1968–, Calar Alto Observatory, Spain; mem. Acad. of Sciences of Heidelberg, Halle, Helsinki and Vienna; planet Elsässer named after him; Comendador de la Orden de Isabel la Católica (Spain), Bundesverdienstkreuz. *Publications:* about 150 articles in astronomical journals and three textbooks, two with H. Scheffler. *Leisure interest:* tennis. *Address:* Max-Planck-Institut für Astronomie, Königstuhl, 69117 Heidelberg, Germany. *Telephone:* 06221/528 200.

ELSON, Bill; American music agent; Head, Music Div. Int. Creative Man. (ICM); clients have included Janis Joplin, the Doors, Jefferson Airplane, Def Leppard, Paul McCartney, Bob Dylan, Metallica.

ELSTEIN, David Keith, M.A.; British broadcasting executive; b. 14 Nov. 1944; s. of the late Albert Elstein and Millie Cohen; m. Jenny Conway 1978; one s.; ed. Haberdashers' Aske's School, Gonville and Caius Coll. Cambridge; producer (BBC) The Money Programme, Panorama, Cause for Concern, People in Conflict 1964–68; (Thames TV) This Week, The Day Before Yesterday, The World At War 1968–72; (London Weekend) Weekend World 1972; Ed. This Week (Thames TV) 1974–78; f. Brook Productions 1982; Exec. Producer A Week in Politics 1982–86, Concealed Enemies 1983; Man. Dir. Primetime TV 1983–86; Dir. of Programmes Thames TV 1986–92; Head of Programmes BSkyB 1993–96; Chief Exec. Channel 5 Broadcasting 1996–; Chair. Nat. Film and TV School 1996–. *Leisure interests:* theatre, cinema, bridge, politics, reading. *Address:* Channel 5 Broadcasting Ltd., 22 Long Acre, London, WC2E 9LY, England.

ELTIS, Walter Alfred, M.A., D.LITT.; British economist; b. 23 May 1933, Warnsdorf, Czechoslovakia; s. of Rev. Martin Eltis and Mary Schnitzer; m. Shelagh M. Owen 1959; one s. two d.; ed. Wycliffe Coll., Emmanuel Coll. Cambridge and Nuffield Coll. Oxford; Research Fellow in Econs. Exeter Coll., Oxford 1958–60; lecturer in Econs., Univ. of Oxford 1961–88; Fellow and Tutor in Econs., Exeter Coll. Oxford 1963–88, Fellow Emer. 1988–; Econ. Dir. Nat. Econ. Devt. Office 1986–88, Dir.-Gen. 1988–92; Chief Econ. Adviser to the Pres. of Bd. of Trade 1992–95; Visiting Reader in Econs., Univ. of W. Australia 1970–71; Visiting Prof. Univ. of Toronto 1976–77, European Univ. Florence 1979, Univ. of Reading 1992–; Gresham Prof. of Commerce, Gresham Coll. London 1993–96; Adam Smith Prize, Cambridge 1956. *Publications:* Growth and Distribution 1973, Britain's Economic Problem: Too Few Producers (with R. Bacon) 1976, The Classical Theory of Economic Growth 1984, Keynes and Economic Policy (with P. Sinclair) 1988, Classical Economics, Public Expenditure and Growth 1993, Britain's Economic Problem Revisited 1996, Condillac: Commerce and Government (ed. with S. M. Eltis) 1998. *Leisure interests:* chess, music, *Address:* Danesway, Jarn Way, Boars Hill, Oxford, OX1 5JF, England. *Telephone:* (01865) 735440.

ELTON, 2nd Baron, cr. 1934, of Headington; **Rodney Elton,** M.A., T.D.; British politician and company director; b. 2 March 1930, Oxford; s. of Godfrey Elton, 1st Baron and Dedi Hartmann; m. 1st Anne Frances Tilney 1958 (dissolved 1979); one s. three d.; m. 2nd Susan Richenda Gurney 1979; ed. Eton Coll. and New Coll., Oxford; fmr. Capt. Queen's Own Warwicks. and Worcs. Yeomanry; fmr. Maj. Leics. and Derbyshire Yeomanry; farming 1957–73; Asst. Mastership in History Loughborough Grammar School 1962–67, Fairham Comprehensive School for Boys 1967–69; contested Loughborough div. of Leics. 1966, 1970; Lecturer Bishop Lonsdale Coll. of Educ. 1969–72; Opposition Whip House of Lords 1974–76, a Deputy Chair. of Cttees. 1997–; an Opposition Spokesman 1976–79; Parl. Under-Sec. of State for N. Ireland 1979–81, Dept. of Health and Social Security 1981–82, Home Office 1982–84, Minister of State 1984–85; Minister of State Dept. of Environment 1985–86; Chair. Financial Intermediaries' Mans.' and Brokers' Regulatory Asscn. (FIMBRA) 1987–90; Dir. Andry Montgomery Ltd. 1977–79, Deputy Chair. 1986–; Dir. Overseas Exhbns. Ltd. 1977–79, Bldg. Trades Exhbn. Ltd. 1977–79; mem. Panel on Takeovers and Mergers 1987–90; Chair. Independent Enquiry into Discipline in Schools (Report 1989); Chair. Intermediate Treatment Fund 1990–93; Chair. DIVERT Trust 1993–; Quality and Standards Cttee., City and Guilds of London Inst. 1999–; Deputy Chair. Asscn. of Conservative Peers 1986–93; Vice-Pres. Inst. of Trading Standards Admins. 1990–; mem. House of Lords Select Cttee. on the Scrutiny of Delegated Powers 1993–97; mem. council Rainer Foundation 1990–96, City and Guilds of London Inst. 1991–97; fmr. Trustee City Parochial Foundation and Trust for London; Hon. Vice-Pres. Inst. of Trading Standards Officers; Conservative. *Leisure interest:* painting. *Address:* House of Lords, London, SW1A 0PW, England. *Telephone:* 0171-219 3165.

ELTON, Sir Arnold, Kt., C.B.E., M.S., F.R.C.S., F.R.S.M.; British surgeon; b. 14 Feb. 1920; s. of late Max Elton and of Ada Elton; m. Billie Pamela Briggs 1952; one s.; ed. Univ. Coll., London, Univ. Coll. Hosp. Medical School, London; House Surgeon, House Physician, Casualty Officer Univ. Coll. Hosp. 1943–45; Sr. Surgical Registrar, Charing Cross Hosp. 1947–51; Consultant Surgeon Northwick Park Hosp. and Clinical Research Centre 1970–, British Airways 1981–; Consultant Surgeon Harrow Hosp. 1951–70, Mount Vernon Hosp. 1960–70; First Chair. Medical Staff Cttee.; Chair. Surgical Div. and Theatre Cttee.; mem. Ethical Cttee. Northwick Park Hosp., Govt. Working Party on Breast Screening for Cancer 1985–; Surgical Tutor Royal Coll. of Surgeons 1970–82; Nat. Chair. Conservative Medical Soc. 1975–92 (Chair. European Group, Pres. 1992–, European Rep. 1994–), Ed. European Bulletin 1994–; examiner Gen. Nursing Council, Royal Coll. of Surgeons 1971–83; medical dir. Man. of Medical Innovation; medical advisor Virgin Fitness Clubs; Chair. Medical and Science Div., World Fellowship Duke of Edin. Award; Fellow Asscn. of Surgeons of G.B., Hunterian Soc., Int. Coll. of Surgeons; f. mem. British Asscn. of Surgical Oncology; mem. Court of Patrons Royal Coll. of Surgeons 1986–, Int. Medical Parliamentarians Org. (Chair UK Div.), European Soc. of Surgical Oncology, World Fed. of Surgical Oncological Socs., European Fed. of Surgeons, Tricare Europe Preferred Provider Network (U.S. Armed Forces and Families), Breast and Thyroid Surgery 1997–; mem. council and advisor on int. affairs World Fed. of Surgical Oncology Socs. *Leisure interests:* tennis, music. *Address:* The Consulting Rooms, Wellington Hospital, Wellington Place, London, NW8 9LE; 58 Stockleigh Hall, Prince Albert Road, London, NW8 7LB, England (Home). *Telephone:* 0171-935 4101. *Fax:* 0171-483 0297.

ELTON, Benjamin Charles (Ben), B.A.; British author and performer; b. 3 May 1959; s. of Prof. Lewis Richard Benjamin Elton and Mary Elton (née Foster); m. Sophie Gare 1994; ed. Godalming Grammar School, South Warwickshire Coll. of Further Educ., Manchester Univ.; first professional appearance Comic Strip Club 1981; numerous tours as 'stand-up comic' 1986–. *writer for TV:* Happy Families 1985, Filthy Rich and Catflap 1986;

(jtly.): The Young Ones 1983, Blackadder II 1987, Blackadder the Third 1988, Blackadder Goes Forth 1989, The Thin Blue Line 1995–96; *writer and performer:* Friday Live 1987–88, Saturday Live 1987, The Man from Auntie 1990, 1994, Stark 1993; *theatre (writer and dir.):* Gasping 1990, Silly Cow 1991, Popcorn 1997; *actor:* Much Ado About Nothing (film) 1993. *Publications:* (novels) Stark 1989, Gridlock 1991, This Other Eden 1993, Popcorn 1996; (plays) Gasping 1990, Silly Cow 1991, Popcorn 1996. *Leisure interests:* walking, reading, socializing. *Address:* c/o Phil McIntyre, 2nd Floor, 35 Soho Square, London, W1V 5DG, England.

ELVIN, Herbert Lionel, M.A.; British educationalist; b. 7 Aug. 1905, Buckhurst Hill, Essex; s. of Herbert Henry Elvin and Mary Jane Elvin; m. Mona Bedortha Dutton 1934; one s.; ed. Trinity Hall, Cambridge, and Yale Univ; Fellow of Trinity Hall, Cambridge, and mem. of Faculty of English, Cambridge, 1930–45; temporary civil servant, Air Ministry 1940–42, Ministry of Information (American Div.) 1942–45; Principal, Ruskin Coll., mem. Faculty of English, Oxford 1945–50; mem. Univ. Grants Cttee. 1946–50; Dir. Dept. of Education, UNESCO 1950–56; Prof. Education (Tropical Areas) London Univ., Inst. of Education 1956–58; Dir. Inst. of Education, London Univ. 1958–73; Chair. Commonwealth Educ. Liaison Cttee. 1965–73; mem. Govt. of India Educ. Comm. 1965–66; Hon. Fellow, Trinity Hall, Cambridge 1979, London Univ. Inst. of Educ. 1992; Emer. Prof. of Educ. (London). *Publications:* Men of America 1941, An Introduction to the Study of Poetry 1949, Education and Contemporary Society 1965, The Place of Commonsense in Educational Thought 1977, The Educational Systems in the European Community (Ed.) 1982, Encounters with Education 1987. *Leisure interest:* reading. *Address:* 4 Bulstrode Gardens, Cambridge, England. *Telephone:* (01223) 358309.

ELVIN, Violetta (Violetta Prokhorova); British ballerina; b. 3 Nov. 1925, Moscow; d. of Vassili Prokhorov and Irena T. Grimusinskaya; m. 1st Harold Elvin 1944 (divorced 1952); m. 2nd Siegbert J. Weinberger 1953; m. 3rd Fernando Savarese 1959; one s.; ed. Bolshoi Theatre School, Moscow; Mem. Bolshoi Theatre Ballet 1942, evacuated to Tashkent 1943; ballerina, Tashkent State Theatre; rejoined Bolshoi Theatre as soloist 1944; joined Sadler's Wells Ballet, Royal Opera House, Covent Garden (now the Royal Ballet) as guest soloist 1946, and later as regular mem., prima ballerina 1951–56; guest artist, Stanislavsky Theatre, Moscow 1944, Sadler's Wells Theatre 1947; guest prima ballerina, La Scala 1952–53; guest artist, Cannes 1954, Copenhagen 1954, Teatro Municipal, Rio de Janeiro 1955, Festival Hall 1955; guest prima ballerina, Royal Opera House, Stockholm 1956; Royal Opera House, Covent Garden 1956 (concluded her stage career); Dir. Ballet Co. San Carla Opera, Naples 1985–87; film appearances: The Queen of Spades, Twice Upon a Time, Melba. *Leisure interests:* reading, walking, swimming. *Address:* Marina di Equa, 80066 Seiano, Bay of Naples, Italy. *Telephone:* (81) 8798520.

ELWORTHY, Sir Peter (Herbert), Kt.; New Zealand business executive and farmer; b. 3 March 1935; s. of Harold Herbert Elworthy and June Mary Elworthy (née Batchelor); m. Fiona Elizabeth McHardy 1960; two s. two d.; ed. Christ's Coll., Lincoln Agric. Coll.; Chair. Ravensdown Co-op 1977–82, Timaru Port Co. 1988–, N.Z. Advisory Cttee. on Overseas Aid 1988–89 (mem. 1986–89), N.Z. Farmlands Ltd. 1989–92, Electricity Distribution Reform Unit 1990–92, The Power Co. 1990–97, Rural Electrical Reticulation Council 1990–96, Southland Electric Power Supply 1990–97, QEII Nat. Trust 1987–93, N.Z. Rural Property Trust 1988–89, Opihi (SC) River Devt. Co. 1992–; Sky City Ltd. (Auckland) 1992–, N.Z. Rural Properties Ltd. 1992–, Seabil (NZ) Ltd. 1994–96, Salvation Army Inaugural Community Support Cttee. 1994–96; Pres. N.Z. Deer Farmers Asscn. 1974–81, Federated Farmers of N.Z. 1984–87; Dir. Reserve Bank of N.Z. 1985–, Landcorp 1986–88, BP NZ Ltd. 1986–, Ascot Man. Corp. (NZ) Ltd. 1991–94, Enerco NZ Ltd. 1992–95, Huttons Kiwi Ltd. 1992–96, Skellerup Group Ltd. 1993–96; Trustee Lincoln Univ. Foundation 1989–, Waitaingi Foundation 1990–, N.Z. Inst. of Econ. Research Inc. 1991–, Alan Duff Charitable Foundation 1994–; Fellow N.Z. Inst. of Agric. Sciences; Patron Int. Organic Agric. Conf., Lincoln 1994–; Nuffield Scholarship, UK 1970, McMeekan Memorial Award 1978, Bledisloe Award, Lincoln 1987, N.Z. Commemoration Medal 1990. *Leisure interests:* riding, fishing, flying, tennis, reading. *Address:* Craigmore Farm, Maungati, 2RD, Timaru, New Zealand. *Telephone:* (3) 6129809.

EMAN, J. H. A. (Henny); Aruban politician and lawyer; leader Arubaanse Volkspartij (AVP); Prime Minister of Aruba and Minister of Gen. Affairs 1986–89. *Address:* Arubaanse Volkspartij, Oranjestad, Aruba.

EMANUEL, Elizabeth Florence, M.A., R.C.A., F.C.S.D.; British fashion designer; b. 5 July 1953, London; d. of Samuel Charles Weiner and Brahna Betty Weiner; m. David Leslie Emanuel 1975 (separated 1990); one s. one d.; ed. City of London School for Girls, Harrow Coll. of Art; opened London salon 1978; designed wedding gown for H.R.H. Princess of Wales 1981, costumes for Andrew Lloyd Webber's Song and Dance 1982, sets and costumes for ballet Frankenstein, The Modern Prometheus, Royal Opera House London, La Scala Milan 1985, costumes for Stoll Moss production of Cinderella 1985, costumes for film Diamond Skulls 1990, The Changeling 1995, uniforms for Virgin Atlantic Airways 1990, Britannia Airways 1995; launched int. fashion label Elizabeth Emanuel 1991; launched Bridal Collection for Berkertex Brides U.K. Ltd. 1994; launched bridal collection in Japan 1994. *Publication:* Style for All Seasons (with David Emanuel) 1982. *Leisure interests:* ballet, cinema, environmental and conservation issues. *Address:* 42A Warrington Crescent, Maida Vale, London, W9 1EP, England. *Telephone:* 0171-266 1055.

EMBUREY, John Ernest; British cricketer; b. 20 Aug. 1952, Peckham, London; s. of John Emburey and Rose Emburey; m. 2nd Susie Emburey 1980; two d.; ed. Peckham Manor Secondary School; right-hand late-order batsman, off-break bowler, slip or gully fielder; teams: Middx. 1973–95, Western Prov. 1982–84, Northants. 1996–98 (player/chief coach and Man.), retd. from playing 1997; 64 Tests for England 1978–1995, 2 as Capt., scoring 1,713 runs (average 22.5) and taking 147 wickets (average 38.4); scored 12,021 runs (7 hundreds) and took 1,608 wickets in first-class cricket; toured Australia 1978–80, 1986–88; 61 limited-overs internationals; winner 7 County Championships Middx. (1976, 1977, 1980, 1982, 1985, 1990, 1993). *Publications:* Emburey—A Biography 1987, Spinning in a Fast World 1989. *Leisure interests:* golf, squash, reading. *Address:* Northants. County Cricket Club, Wantage Road, Northampton, NN1 4TJ. *Telephone:* (01604) 32917.

EMENEAU, Murray Barnson, M.A., PH.D.; American professor; b. 28 Feb. 1904, Lunenburg, Nova Scotia, Canada; s. of Archibald and Ada Emeneau; m. Katharine Fitch Venter 1940; two step-d.; ed. Dalhousie, Oxford and Yale Univs.; Instructor in Latin, Yale Univ. 1926–31; Fellowships, Yale Univ. and American Council of Learned Socs. 1931–40; research in India 1935–38; Asst. Prof. of Sanskrit and Gen. Linguistics, Univ. of Calif., Berkeley 1940–43, Assoc. Prof. 1943–46, Prof. 1946–71, Prof. Emer. 1971–, Faculty Research Lecturer 1955–56, Chair. Dept. of Linguistics 1953–58, Chair. Dept. of Classics 1959–62; Guggenheim Fellowship 1949, 1956–57, 1958; Vice-Pres. Linguistic Soc. of America 1949, Pres. 1950; Assoc. Ed. American Oriental Soc. 1940–47, Ed. 1947–52, Pres. 1954–55, Western Branch 1964–65; Hermann Collitz Prof. of Indo-European Comparative Linguistics, Indiana Univ. 1953; Rhodes Scholar (Nova Scotia; Balliol Coll. Oxford) 1923–26; mem. American Philosophical Soc. 1952; Hon. mem. Nat. Inst. of Humanistic Sciences, Vietnam 1957, Linguistic Soc. of India 1964, Linguistic Research Group of Pakistan 1971; Hon. Fellow Royal Asiatic Soc. 1969; mem. American Acad. of Arts and Sciences 1970; Vice-Pres. Int. Asscn. for Tamil Research 1966; Hon. Pres. 6th World Sanskrit Conf. 1984; Presented with Studies in Indian Linguistics by Centres of Advanced Study in Linguistics, Deccan Coll. and Annamalai Univ., and Linguistic Soc. of India 1968; Berkeley Fellow 1993; Corresp. Fellow British Acad. 1993; Hon. L.H.D. (Chicago) 1968, Hon. LL.D. (Dalhousie) 1970, Hon. D. Litt (Hyderabad) 1987; Berkeley Citation 1971; Lucius Wilbur Cross Medal Yale Graduate School Asscn. 1969. *Publications:* Jambhaladatta's Version of the Vetālapañcavinšati 1934, A Union List of Printed Indic Texts and Translations in American Libraries 1935, Kota Texts 1944–46, Studies in Vietnamese (Annamese) Grammar 1951, Kolami, a Dravidian Language 1955; Vedic Variants Vol. III (with M. Bloomfield & F. Edgerton) 1934; A Dravidian Etymological Dictionary (with T. Burrow) 1961, 1984, Dravidian Borrowings from Indo-Aryan (with T. Burrow) 1962, Brahui and Dravidian Grammar 1962, Kālidāsa's Sakuntalā translated from the Bengali Recension 1962, Dravidian Linguistics, Ethnology and Folktales (collected papers) 1967, A Dravidian Etymological Dictionary: Supplement (with T. Burrow) 1968, Toda Songs 1971, Ritual Structure and Language Structure of the Todas 1974, Language and Linguistic Area 1980, Toda Grammar and Texts 1984, Sanskrit Studies 1988, Dravidian Studies 1994. *Leisure interests:* ballet, opera, travel. *Address:* Department of Linguistics, University of California, Berkeley, CA 94720 (Office); 909 San Benito Road, Berkeley, CA 94707, U.S.A. (Home).

EMERSON, Michael, M.A., F.C.A.; British economist and European public servant; b. 12 May 1940, Bordeaux, France; s. of James and Priscilla Emerson; m. Barbara Brierley 1966; one s. two d.; ed. Hurstpierpoint Coll., Sussex, Balliol Coll. Oxford, Harvard Univ. Centre for Int. Affairs; with Price Waterhouse & Co., London 1962–65; various positions including Head Gen. Econs. Div., OECD, Paris 1966–73; joined staff EC, Brussels 1973, Econ. Adviser to Pres. (Roy Jenkins) 1977–78; Dir. Macro-economic Forecasting and Policies 1978–85, Dir. Econ. Evaluation of Community Policies 1986–90, Amb., Head of Del. of EC to Commonwealth of Independent States 1991–96; Hon. LL.D. (Keele) 1993; Hon. D.C.L. (Kent) 1993. *Publications:* Europe's Stagflation (Ed.) 1984, What Model for Europe? 1988, The Economics of 1992 1988, One Market, One Money 1991, The ECU Report 1991. *Address:* 128 avenue de Tervuren, 1150 Brussels, Belgium. *Telephone:* (2) 7361283.

EMERTON, Rev. John Adney, M.A., D.D., F.B.A.; British ecclesiastic and academic; b. 5 June 1928, Winchmore Hill; s. of Adney S. Emerton and Helena M. (née Quin) Emerton; m. Norma E. Bennington 1954; one s. two d.; ed. Minchenden Grammar School, Southgate, Corpus Christi Coll., Oxford and Wycliffe Hall, Oxford; ordained deacon 1952, priest 1953; Asst. lecturer in Theology, Birmingham Univ. 1952–53; curate, Birmingham Cathedral 1952–53; lecturer in Hebrew and Aramaic, Univ. of Durham 1953–55; lecturer in Divinity, Univ. of Cambridge 1955–62; Fellow, St. Peter's Coll. and Reader in Semitic Philology, Univ. of Oxford 1962–68; Regius Prof. of Hebrew, Univ. of Cambridge 1968–95, Prof. Emer. 1995–; Fellow St. John's Coll. Cambridge 1970–; Sec., Int. Org. for Study of Old Testament 1971–89, Pres. 1992–95; Hon. Canon, St. George's Cathedral, Jerusalem 1984–; mem. Ed. Bd. Vetus Testamentum 1971–97; Visiting Fellow, Inst. for Advanced Studies, Hebrew Univ. of Jerusalem 1983; visiting professorships at various overseas univs. etc.; Corresp. mem. Göttingen Akademie der Wissenschaften 1990; Hon. D.D. (Edin.); Burkitt Medal for Biblical Studies, British Acad. 1991. *Publications:* The Peshitta of the Wisdom of Solomon 1959, The Old

Testament in Syriac—The Song of Songs 1966; articles in journals. *Address:* 34 Gough Way, Cambridge, CB3 9LN, England.

EMERY, Alan Eglin Heathcote, M.D., PH.D., D.SC., F.R.C.P., F.R.C.P.(E.), F.R.S.M., F.L.S., F.R.S.E.; British physician and professor of human genetics; b. 21 Aug. 1928, Manchester; s. of Harold Heathcote Emery and Alice Eglin; m. Marcia Lynn Miller 1988; three s. three d.; ed. Manchester Grammar School, Chester Coll., Manchester Univ. and Johns Hopkins Univ., U.S.A.; Postdoctoral Research Fellow, Johns Hopkins Univ., Baltimore 1961–64; Lecturer, then Reader in Medical Genetics, Manchester Univ. 1964–68; Foundation Prof. and Chair., Dept. of Human Genetics, Edin. Univ. 1968–83, Prof. Emer. and Hon. Fellow 1983–; Hon. Visiting Fellow, Green Coll., Oxford 1985–; Research Dir. European Neuromuscular Centre and Chair. Research Cttee. 1990–; Pres. British Clinical Genetics Soc. 1980–83; Visiting Prof. univs. of New York, Heidelberg, U.C.L.A., Padua, Beijing, Duke, Cape Town, Warsaw, Royal Postgrad. Medical School, London, etc.; Harveian, Boerhave, Jenner Lecturer, etc.; mem. Scientific Cttees. of Int. Congress of Neuromuscular Disorders and World Fed. of Neurology; Hon. Fellow Univ. of Edin. 1990–; mem. Royal Soc. of Literature; Hon. Fellow Gaetano Conte Acad. (Italy) 1991; Hon. F.A.C.M.G.; M.D. h.c. (Naples, Würzburg); Int. Award for Genetic Research (U.S.A.) and other awards. *Publications:* Psychological Aspects of Genetic Counselling 1984, Introduction to Recombinant DNA (2nd edn. with S. Malcolm) 1995, Methodology in Medical Genetics, (2nd edn.) 1986, Principles and Practice of Medical Genetics (2nd edn.) 1991, Elements of Medical Genetics (8th edn.) 1992, Duchenne Muscular Dystrophy (2nd edn.) 1993; Muscular Dystrophy: The Facts 1994, The History of a Genetic Disease: Duchenne Muscular Dystrophy or Meryon's Disease 1995, Diagnostic Criteria for Neuromuscular Disorders (2nd edn.) 1997, Neuromuscular Disorders; Clinical and Molecular Genetics 1998; 300 scientific papers. *Leisure interests:* marine biology, oil painting, fly fishing. *Address:* 2 Ingleside Court, Upper West Terrace, Budleigh Salterton, Devon, EX9 6NZ, England (Home). *Telephone:* (01395) 445847.

EMERY, Kenneth O., PH.D.; American oceanographer; b. 6 June 1914, Saskatchewan, Canada; s. of Clifford A. and Agnes B. Emery; m. 1st Caroline Alexander 1941 (died 1984); two d.; m. 2nd Phyllis Z. Williams 1985 (divorced 1987); m. 3rd Joy S. Travis 1993 (died 1995); m. 4th Alice G. Williston 1995; ed. N. Texas Agricultural Coll., Arlington, Univ. of Illinois and Scripps Inst. of Oceanography; Assoc. Geologist, Ill. State Geological Survey 1941–43; Assoc. Marine Geologist, Univ. of Calif. Div. of War Research 1943–45; Asst., Assoc. and Prof. of Geology, Univ. of S. Calif. 1945–62; Geologist, U.S. Geological Survey (summer only) 1946–60; Senior Scientist, Woods Hole Oceanographic Inst. 1962–79, Emer. 1979–, Dean of Educ. 1967, Henry Bryant Bigelow Chair., Oceanography 1975; Guggenheim Fellowship 1959; mem. Nat. Acad. of Sciences, American Acad. of Arts and Sciences, American Asscn. of Petroleum Geologists, Geological Soc. of America, Royal Swedish Acad. of Sciences; Hon. D.Sc. (Univ. of S. Calif.) 1990; Shepard Prize in Marine Geology 1969, Médaille Commémorative du Prince Albert Ier de Monaco, Compass Distinguished Achievement Award 1974, A.A.A.S.—Rosenstiel Award in Oceanography 1975, Illinois Achievement Award (Univ. of Ill.) 1977, Maurice Ewing Award for Geophysics 1985, W. H. Twenhofel Medal for Sedimentary Geology 1989. *Publications:* Bikini and Adjacent Atolls 1954, The Sea off Southern California 1960, The Dead Sea 1967, Oyster Pond 1970, The Western North Atlantic Ocean (with Elazar Uchupi) 1972, The Geology of the Atlantic Ocean (with Elazar Uchupi) 1984, Eighteenth-century Gunflints from Fort Michilimackinac and other colonial sites (with T. M. Hamilton) 1987, Mediterranean Coasts of Israel and Sinai: Holocene Tectonism from Geology, Geophysics and Archaeology (with D. Neev and N. Bakler) 1987, Sea Levels, Land Levels and Tide Gauges (with D. A. Aubrey) 1991, Morphology of Rocky Members of the Solar System (with Elazar Uchupi) 1993, Geology, Climatology and Archaeology of Sodom, Gomorrah and Jericho (with David Neev) 1995, Oceanography Illustrated by Coins. *Leisure interest:* stock market. *Address:* Woods Hole Oceanographic Institute, Department of Geology, Woods Hole, MA 02543; 35 Horseshoe Lane, North Falmouth, MA 02556, U.S.A. *Telephone:* (508) 548-7592.

EMERY, Lin, B.A.; American sculptor; b. 20 May 1958, New York City; d. of Cornell Emery and Jean Weill; m. S. B. Braselman 1962; one s.; ed. Univs. of Chicago and Sorbonne, Paris; worked in studio of Ossip Zadkine, Paris 1950; 46 solo exhbns. in U.S. museums and galleries 1957–98; int. exhbns. in Tokyo, Hong Kong, Manila, Sofia, Paris, London, Berlin, Brisbane, Kyoto and Frankfurt 1961–98; public sculpture erected in Civic Center, New Orleans 1966–70, Fidelity Center, Oklahoma City 1972, Humanities Center, Columbia, S.C. 1974, Federal Plaza, Houma, La. 1997, Marina Centre, Singapore 1986, City of Oxnard, Calif. 1988, Osaka Dome, Japan 1997 etc.; Visiting Prof. Tulane School of Architecture, New Orleans 1969–70, Newcomb School of Art, New Orleans 1980; Visiting Artist and lecturer Art Acad. of Cincinnati, La. State Univ., Univ. of New Orleans, Univ. of Tex. at Austin, Univ. of Maine 1985–88; Chair. 9th Int. Sculpture Conf. 1976, Co-Chair. Mayor's Steering Cttees., New Orleans 1979–80; Studio Chair. Coll. Art Asscn. 1979; mem. Bd. Contemporary Arts Center, New Orleans 1997–; mem. Loyola Univ. Visiting Cttee. 1996–99; adviser Artists Guild, New Orleans 1997–99; mentor Center for Creative Arts, New Orleans 1998; Mayor's Award for Achievement in the Arts, La. 1980, Lazlo Aranyi Award for Public Art, Va. 1990, Delgado Award for Artistic Excellence, La. 1997, Grand Prix for Public Sculpture (Japan) 1997. *Address:* 7520 Dominican Street, New Orleans, LA 70118, U.S.A. *Telephone:* (504) 866-7775. *Fax:* (504) 866-0144.

EMILIANI, Vittorio; Italian journalist; b. 1 Dec. 1935, Predappio, Forlì; s. of Nicola Emiliani and Lina Bartoletti; m. Silvana Forni 1960; one s. one d.; ed. High School and Univ.; began reporting career with Olivetti journal Comunità; then contributor to Il Mondo and L'Espresso; Sub-Ed. and Special Corresp. of Milan daily Il Giorno with emphasis on social and econ. matters and devt. of urban environment mid-1960s–1974; Special Corresp., then Chief Political Commentator of Rome daily Il Messaggero 1974–80, Ed.-in-Chief 1980. *Publications:* Ravenna, una capitale 1965, Gli anarchici 1973, L'Italia mangiata 1977 and contributions to Enciclopedia europea Garzanti; wrote inquiry for TV on Italian minor industries. *Leisure interests:* cycling, tennis, skiing, cooking and wine tasting. *Address:* Il Messaggero, Via del Tritone 152, Rome 00187 (Office); Viale delle Medaglie d'Oro, Rome, Italy (Home).

EMIN, Tracey; British artist; b. 1964, Margate; ed. John Cass School of Art, London, Maidstone Coll. of Art, Royal Coll. of Art; f. Tracey Emin Museum, London 1996. *Exhibitions include:* White Cube Gallery, London 1992, Minky Manky 1995, My Major Retrospective, Part of What Made Me What I Am. *Films include:* Why I Never Became a Dancer. *Leisure interests:* writing poetry, watching sunsets. *Address:* The Tracey Emin Museum, 221 Waterloo Road, London, S.E.1, England. *Telephone:* 0171-261 1116.

EMMANUELLI, Henri Joseph; French politician; b. 31 May 1945, Eaux-Bonnes, Pyrénées-Atlantiques; s. of late Louis Emmanuelli and of Julie Chourre; m. Antonia Gonzalez 1967; one s. one d.; ed. Lycée Louis-Barthou, Pau, Institut d'études politiques de Paris; mem. staff Banque de l'Union Parisienne, then Compagnie financière de banque 1969–78; Deputy for Landes 1978–82, 1986–93; Chair. Conseil général, Landes 1982–; Sec. of State for Overseas Territories and Depts. 1981–83, for Budget 1983–86; Chair. Finance Comm. of Nat. Ass. 1991–93, Pres. Nat. Ass. 1992–93, Pres. Comm. for Finances, Gen. Econs. and Planning 1997–; mem. Nat. Secr. Parti Socialiste 1987–, Leader 1994–95. *Publication:* Plaidoyer pour l'Europe 1992. *Leisure interests:* skiing, swimming. *Address:* Assemblée nationale, 75355 Paris; Parti Socialiste, 10 rue de Solférino, 75333 Paris Cedex; 22-24 rue Victor Hugo, 40000 Mont-de-Marsan, France (Office).

EMMENS, Clifford Walter, PH.D., D.SC., F.S.S., C.BIOL., , F.I.BIOL., F.A.A.; Australian university professor; b. 9 Dec. 1913, London; s. of Walter J. Emmens and Narcissa L. Pugh; m. Muriel E. Bristow 1937; two s. two d.; ed. Purley County School and Univ. Coll., London; demonstrator in Zoology, Univ. Coll., London 1936–37; research biologist MRC 1937–48, seconded to Ministry of Home Security and R.A.F. 1941–46; Head Dept. of Veterinary Physiology, Univ. of Sydney 1948–78, seconded part-time as officer-in-charge, CSIRO Sheep Biology Lab., later Div. of Animal Physiology 1952–54; Chair. various cttees. of CSIRO, Nat. Health and Medical Research Council etc.; Fellow Inst. of Biology; Hon. Fellow Australian Coll. of Veterinary Scientists; mem. numerous professional socs.; Hon. D.V.Sc., Hon. F.A.C.V.Sc.; Oliver Bird Medal and Prize (U.K.) 1961; Istituto Spallanzani Medal (Italy) 1964. *Publications:* author and co-author of numerous books and more than 200 scientific papers. *Leisure interests:* aquarium keeping, history of science.

EMMERICH, Roland; director, screenplay writer and executive producer; b. Germany; ed. film school in Munich; film produced as a student The Noah's Ark Principle shown at 1984 Berlin Film Festival and sold to more than twenty countries; f. Centropolis Film Productions. *Films:* Making Contact (Joey) (dir. only), Ghost Chase, Eye of the Storm (producer only), Moon 44, Universal Soldier, Stargate, Independence Day. *TV:* (series) The Visitor (producer) 1997. *Address:* c/o Creative Artists Agency, 9830 Wilshire Boulevard, Beverly Hills, CA 90212, U.S.A.

EMMET, Dorothy Mary, M.A., D.LITT.; British university professor; b. 29 Sept. 1904, London; d. of late Rev. Cyril W. Emmet and late Gertrude Julia Emmet (née Weir); ed. Lady Margaret Hall, Univ. of Oxford; adult education work Maesyrhaf Settlement 1927–28, 1931–32; Commonwealth Fellowship in U.S. 1928–30; Research Fellow, Somerville Coll., Oxford 1930–31; Lecturer in Philosophy, King's Coll., Newcastle-on-Tyne 1932–38; Lecturer in Philosophy of Religion, Univ. of Manchester 1938–45, Reader in Philosophy 1945–46; Sir Samuel Hall Prof. of Philosophy, Univ. of Manchester 1946–66, Emer. Prof. 1966–; Hon. Fellow Lady Margaret Hall, Oxford; Emer. Fellow Lucy Cavendish Coll., Cambridge; Hon. D.Litt. (Glasgow, Leicester); Dr. h.c. (Open Univ.). *Publications:* Whitehead's Philosophy of Organism 1932, Philosophy and Faith 1936, The Nature of Metaphysical Thinking 1945, Function, Purpose and Powers 1958, Rules, Roles and Relations 1966; Ed. (with A. MacIntyre) Sociological Theory and Philosophical Analysis 1970, The Moral Prism 1979, The Effectiveness of Causes 1984, The Passage of Nature 1992, The Role of the Unrealisable 1994, Philosophers and Friends 1996, Outward Forms, Inner Springs 1998. *Address:* Hope Residential and Nursing Care Home, Brooklands Avenue, Cambridge, CB2 2BQ, England. *Telephone:* (01223) 359087.

EMMONS, Howard Wilson, M.E., M.S., SC.D.; American professor of mechanical engineering; b. 30 Aug. 1912, Morristown, N.J.; s. of Peter Emmons and Margaret Lang Emmons; m. Dorothy Allen 1937; two s. one d.; ed. Stevens Inst. of Technology and Harvard Univ.; Research Eng., Westinghouse Electric and Manufacturing Co. 1938–39; Prof., Univ. of Pa. 1939–40; Prof., Harvard Univ. 1940–83, Prof. Emer. 1983–; Chair. Fire Research Cttee.,

Nat. Acad. of Sciences 1968–70, *ad hoc* Fire Panel, Nat. Bureau of Standards 1971–75, Engineering Evaluation Panel; mem. N.A.S. Nat. Acad. of Engineering, Cttee. on Fire and Smoke Resistant Materials for Commercial Aircraft Interiors 1993–95; Hon. mem. American Soc. of Mechanical Eng.; Hon. Dr. Eng. (Stevens Inst. of Technology), Dr. h.c. (Worcester Polytechnic Inst.); Gold Medal Int. Combustion Symposium; Centenary Award Stevens Inst. of Technology; Timoshenko Medal ASME, Fluid Dynamics Award, American Physical Soc., Man of the Year Award, Soc. of Fire Protection Engineers 1982, Guise Award 1986. *Publications:* numerous articles in scientific journals. *Leisure interests:* tennis, town government. *Address:* 1010 Waltham Street, Apt. 443B, Lexington, MA 02173, U.S.A. (Home). *Telephone:* (781) 862-8821 (Home). *Fax:* (781) 863-9944 (Home).

EMMOTT, William John (Bill), B.A.; British journalist; b. 6 Aug. 1956; s. of Richard Emmott and Audrey Emmott; m. 1st Charlotte Crowther 1982 (divorced); m. 2nd Carol Barbara Mawer 1992; ed. Latymer Upper School, Hammersmith and Magdalen and Nuffield Colls. Oxford; Brussels corresp. The Economist 1980–82, Economics corresp. 1982–83, Tokyo corresp. 1983–86, Finance Ed. 1986–89, Business Affairs Ed. 1989–93, Ed. 1993–; Editorial Dir. Economist Intelligence Unit. May–Dec. 1992. *Publications:* The Pocket Economist (with R. Pennant-Rea q.v.) 1983, The Sun Also Sets 1989, Japanophobia 1993, Kanryo no Taizai 1996. *Address:* The Economist, 25 St. James's Street, London, SW1A 1HG, England. *Telephone:* 0171-839 7061. *Fax:* 0171-925 0651.

EMOVON, Emmanuel Uwumagbuhunmwun, PH.D.; Nigerian professor of chemistry and government minister; b. 24 Feb. 1929, Benin City; s. of late Gabriel A. Emovon and Oni Emovon; m. Princess Adesuwa C. Akenzua 1959; three s. three d.; ed. Baptist School, Benin City, Edo Coll., Benin City, Univ. Coll., Ibadan, Univ. Coll., London Univ., U.K.; Lecturer in Chem., Univ. Coll. Ibadan 1959; Prof. of Chem., Univ. of Benin 1971; Vice-Chancellor Univ. of Jos 1978; Fed. Minister of Science and Tech. 1985–89; Co-ordinator, Sheda Science and Technology Complex 1990–; invested Chief Obayagbona of Benin 1991; fmr. mem. numerous Govt. Cttees. and Bds.; fmr. external examiner; Fellow Science Asscn. of Nigeria, Nigerian Acad. of Science; nat. mem. ICSU 1986. *Publications:* numerous scientific papers. *Leisure interest:* photography, gardening, long and table tennis, cricket and football. *Address:* Sheda Science and Technology Complex, Ministry of Science and Technology, P.M.B. 186, Garki, Abuja, Nigeria. *Telephone:* (09) 5233918 (Office); (09) 2340667 (Home). *Fax:* (09) 5233919.

EMSLIE, Rt. Hon. Lord; George Carlyle Emslie, M.B.E., P.C., M.A., LL.B., F.R.S.E.; British judge; b. 6 Dec. 1919, Glasgow; s. of late Alexander Emslie and Jessie B. Carlyle; m. Lilias A. M. Hannington 1942; three s.; ed. High School of Glasgow and Univ. of Glasgow; mil. service 1940–46; Advocate 1948; Advocate-Depute (Sheriff Courts) 1955–57; Q.C. (Scotland) 1957; Sheriff of Perth and Angus 1963–66; Dean, Faculty of Advocates 1965–70; Senator, Coll. of Justice in Scotland 1970–72; Lord Justice-Gen. of Scotland and Lord Pres. Court of Session 1972–89; Chair. Scottish Agric. Wages Bd. 1969–73; mem. Council on Tribunals (Scottish Cttee.) 1962–70; Hon. Bencher, Inner Temple 1974; Inns of Court of N. Ireland 1981; Hon. LL.D. (Glasgow) 1973. *Leisure interests:* golf, reading. *Address:* 47 Heriot Row, Edinburgh, EH3 6EX, Scotland. *Telephone:* 0131-225 3657.

ENAHORO, Chief Anthony; C.FR.; Nigerian politician, journalist, newspaper publisher and company director; b. 22 July 1923, Uromi Ishan, Bendel State; s. of late Chief Okotako Enahoro and Princess Inibokun Okoje; m. Helen Ediae 1954; four s. one d.; ed. Govt. Schools Uromi and Owo, King's Coll. Lagos; journalist 1942–52; Ed. Southern Nigerian Defender 1944–45, Daily Comet 1945–49; Assoc. Ed. West African Pilot; Ed.-in-Chief Nigerian Star 1950–52; foundation mem. Action Group Party, later Acting Gen. Sec. and Fed. Vice-Pres.; Chair. Uromi Dist. Council and Ishan Div. Council; mem. Western House of Assembly and Fed. House of Reps. and Party Chief Whip 1951–54; Dir. Nat. Coal Bd. 1953–56; Minister of Home Affairs, Transport, Information and Midwest Affairs and Leader of the House (Western Region) 1954–59; Fed. M.P. and Opposition Spokesman on Foreign Affairs, Internal Affairs and Legislature Affairs 1959–63; moved motion for self-govt. and attended all constitutional talks preceding independence in 1960; detained during Emergency period Western Region 1962, fled to Britain, extradited and imprisoned in Nigeria for treasonable felony; released by Mil. Govt. 1966; Leader, Midwest State del. to Constitutional Conf. and mem. Constitutional Cttee. 1966; Fed. Commr. for Information, Culture, Youth, Sports, Co-operatives and Labour 1967–75; mem. Nat. Democratic Coalition (NADECO); Fed. Commr. for Special Duties 1975; Pres. World Black and African Festival of Arts and Culture 1972–75; State Chair. Nat. Party of Nigeria 1978–80; Chair. Cttees. Edo State Movt. 1981–, Nigerian Shippers Council 1982; detained Aug.–Dec. 1994; Hon. D.Sc. (Benin) 1972. *Publication:* Fugitive Offender (autobiography). *Leisure interests:* golf, reading, travel. *Address:* Rainbow House, 144 Upper Mission Road, P.M.B. 1425, Benin City, Nigeria. *Telephone:* 20080-3 (Office); 052-243770 (Home).

ENDARA GALIMANY, Guillermo; Panamanian politician and lawyer; m. 1st (died 1989); m. 2nd Ana Mae Díaz 1990; labour lawyer; aide to fmr. Pres. of Panama, Arnulfo Arias Madrid; leader Alianza Democrática Oposicionista y Civilista (ADOC); mem. Nat. Democratic Coalition (NADECO); Pres. of Panama 1989–94. *Address:* c/o Oficina del Presidente, Palacio Presidencial, Valija 50, Panamá 1, Panama..

ENDELEY, E. M. L., O.B.E.; Cameroonian politician and medical doctor; b. 10 April 1916, Buea (then in Nigeria); s. of late Chief Mathias Liffafe Endeley and of Mariana Mojoko Liombe; m. 1st Ethel Mina Green (divorced 1961); m. 2nd Fanny Ebenye Njoh 1965; nine s. three d.; ed. Buea Govt. School, Catholic Mission, Bojongo, Govt. Coll. Umuahia, Higher Coll., Yaba; qualified as doctor 1942; entered Govt. service 1943; served Lagos, Port Harcourt, etc.; in charge of Cottage Hospital, Buea; trade union leader 1947; formed Cameroons Nat. Fed. (afterwards Kamerun Nat. Congress) 1949; mem. House of Reps. and Council of Ministers 1952–54, Minister without Portfolio, Minister of Labour; First Premier, Southern Cameroons 1955–59; Pres. Bakweri Co-op. Marketing Union 1955; led South Cameroons Del. to Constitutional Conf., London 1957; first Premier of South Cameroons 1958–59; Leader of the Opposition 1959–61; Leader Nat. Convention Party (later Cameroon People's Nat. Convention Party), West Cameroon 1961–66; Asst. Treas. and mem. Cameroon Nat. Union (now Cameroon People's Democratic Movt.) Political Bureau 1966–74, mem. Cen. Cttee. 1975–; mem. Nat. Ass., Yaoundé 1973–; Chair. House Cttee. on Production, Town Planning, Agriculture, Stockfarming, Rural and Civil Engineering. *Leisure interests:* mountaineering, gardening, wild game hunting, farming. *Address:* P.O. Box 5, Buea, Southwest Province, Cameroon. *Telephone:* Buea 32-42-26.

ENDERBY, John Edwin, C.B.E., PH.D., F.R.S.; British scientist; b. 16 Jan. 1931, Grimsby; s. of late Thomas Edwin Enderby and late Rheita Rebecca Hollinshead Enderby; m. Susan Bowles; one s. two d.; one s. (deceased) one d. from previous marriage; ed. Chester Grammar School, Westminster Coll., Birkbeck Coll., Univ. of London; lecturer then Reader Univ. of Sheffield 1960–69; Prof. and Head of Dept. Univ. of Leicester 1969–76; Prof. of Physics Univ. of Bristol 1976–81; H.O. Wills Prof. 1981–96, Prof. Emer. 1996–, Head of Dept., Dir. H. H. Wills Lab. 1981–94; Directeur-Adjoint Inst. Laue-Langevin, Grenoble, France (on secondment) 1985–88; Ed. Proc. of the Royal Soc.'A' 1989–93; Ed.-in-Chief Journal of Physics: Condensed Matter 1997–; mem. Council PPARC 1994–98; Distinguished Argonne Fellow (U.S.A.); Guthrie Medal and Prize, Inst. of Physics 1995. *Publications:* numerous papers on liquids in learned journals. *Address:* 7 Cotham Lawn Road, Bristol, BS6 6DU (Home); H. H. Wills Physics Laboratory, Tyndall Avenue, Bristol, BS8 1TL, England (Office). *Telephone:* (0117) 9288737 (Office); (0117) 9733411 (Home). *Fax:* (0117) 9255624.

ENDERBY, Keppel Earl, Q.C., LL.M.; Australian politician and lawyer; b. 25 June 1926, Dubbo, N.S.W.; s. of Alfred Charles and Daisy Kathleen Enderby; m.; two c.; ed. Dubbo High School, Univs. of Sydney and London; N.S.W. singles and Australian foursomes amateur golf champion 1946; practising barrister 1955–62, 1976–82; Lecturer, Examiner in Commercial Law, Sydney Technical Coll. 1955–62; Senior Lecturer in Law, Australian Nat. Univ. 1963–65; mem. Nat. Exec. Australian Labor Party 1971–75; M.P. for A.C.T. 1970–74, for Canberra 1974–75; Minister for A.C.T. and Northern Territory 1972–73; Minister for Supply and for Secondary Industry 1973–74, for Mfg. Industry 1974–75; Attorney-Gen. Feb.–Nov. 1975, Minister for Customs and Excise Feb.–June 1975; Judge Supreme Court, N.S.W. 1982–92; mem. Privileges Cttee. of House of Representatives 1973–75, Chair. 1975; Councillor, N.S.W. Branch, Australian Inst. of Int. Affairs 1980–94, Pres. 1983–85; Nat. Pres. Australia-U.S.S.R. Soc. (now Australia-Russia and Affiliates Friendship Soc.) 1986–92; Vice.-Pres. Australian Esperanto Asscn. 1988–90, Nat. Pres. 1991–98; Vice-Pres. N.S.W. Br., Council for Civil Liberties 1993–94, councillor 1998–; Pres. N.S.W. Soc. of Labor Lawyers 1993–95, Int. Esperanto Jura Asscn. 1994–, Universal Esperanto Asscn. 1998–; Chair. N.S.W. Serious Offenders Review Council (SORC) 1997–. *Publications:* articles in Federal Law Review 1964, Australian Quarterly 1976. *Leisure interests:* reading, farming, flying, golf, sailing, Esperanto. *Address:* 2 Phoebe Street, Balmain, Sydney, Australia. *Telephone:* 98104227.

ENESTAM, Jan-Erik, M.POL.SC.; Finnish politician; b. 12 March 1947, Västanfjärd; m. Solveig V. Dahlqvist 1970; travel researcher, Åland Provincial Govt. 1972–74; researcher, Finnish Tourist Bd. 1974; Head of Office, Åland Provincial Govt. 1974–78; Municipal Man. Västanfjärd 1978–83; Project Man. Nordic Council of Ministers 1983–91; mem. Parl. 1981–; Chair. Västanfjärd Municipal Council 1989–; Special Adviser to Minister of Defence 1990–91; Minister of Defence and Minister at Ministry of Social Affairs and Health Jan.–April 1995; Minister of the Interior April 1995–; Swedish People's Party (RKP). *Address:* Ministry of the Interior, Kirkkokatu 12, 00170 Helsinki, Finland. *Telephone:* (90) 1601.

ENGEL, Johannes K.; German journalist and editor; b. 29 April, 1927, Berlin; s. of Karl and Anna (née Helke) Engel; m. Ruth Moter 1951; one s. one d.; journalist Int. News Service and Der Spiegel magazine 1946–, Office Man., Frankfurt-am-Main 1948, Dept. Head 1951, Ed.-in-Chief, Hamburg 1961. *Address:* Kirchenredder 7, 22339 Hamburg, Germany. *Telephone:* 3007-1 (Office).

ENGELBRECHT, Jüri; Estonian physicist and mathematician; b. 1 Aug. 1939, Tallinn; m.; two c.; ed. Tallinn Tech. Univ.; sr. lecturer Tallinn Tech. Univ.; sr. researcher, head of dept., Deputy Dir. Inst. of Cybernetics Estonian Acad. of Sciences 1968–94; part-time assoc., then Prof. Tallinn Tech. Univ. 1974–92, 1994–; Adjunct Prof. Helsinki Univ. of Tech.; mem. Estonian Acad. of Sciences 1990, Pres. 1994–; Chair. Estonian Cttee. for Mechanics 1991–; mem. numerous socs. and cttees; Ed.-in-Chief Proc. of the Estonian Acad. of Sciences 1991–95; ed. Research Reports in Physics 1988–93; mem. Ed. Bd. Prikladnaya Mekhanika; mem. Estonian Soc. for Physics, New York

Acad. of Sciences, European Acad. of Sciences and Arts, Accademia Peloritana dei Pericolanti (Italy), Latvian Acad. of Sciences, Hungarian Acad. of Sciences; Estonian Science Prize, Humboldt Research Award 1993; Kt. White Rose 1st Class (Finland). *Publications:* Nonlinear Deformation Waves 1981, Nonlinear Wave Processes of Deformation in Solids 1983, Nonlinear Evolution Equations 1986, An introduction to Asymmetric Solitary Waves 1991, Nonlinear Dynamics and Chaos 1993, Nonlinear Wave Dynamics: Complexity and Simplicity 1997 and over 200 scientific articles. *Address:* Institute of Cybernetics, Estonian Academy of Sciences, Akadeemia tee 21, Tallinn EE0026, Estonia. *Telephone:* (372) 644 21 29 (Office). *Fax:* (372) 645 18 05.

ENGELHARD, Hans Arnold; German politician and lawyer; b. 16 Sept. 1934, Munich; m.; studied law in Erlangen and Munich; in legal practice, Munich 1963–; joined Free Democratic Party (FDP) 1954; City Councillor, Munich 1970–72; FDP Chair., Munich 1970–82; mem. FDP State Exec., Bavaria 1971–, FDP Fed. Exec. 1977–82; mem. Deutscher Bundestag 1972–, Deputy Chair. FDP Parl. Group 1977–82; Fed. Minister of Justice 1982–90. *Address:* Unsöldstrasse 14, 80538 Munich, Germany. *Telephone:* 089-297379.

ENGELHARDT, Klaus, D.THEOL.; German ecclesiastic; b. 11 May 1932, Schillingstadt; s. of Wilhelm and Therese (née Nell) Engelhardt; m. Dorothea Schlink 1960; two s. one d.; ed. Univs. of Göttingen, Basel, Heidelberg; curate, Evangelische Landeskirche (Protestant Church), Baden 1960–62; student priest, Karlsruhe 1962–65; Prof. of Theology, Päd. Hochschule 1965–80; Bishop of the Protestant Church of Baden 1980–97, Landesbischof 1997–; Chair. Evangelical Church in Germany 1991–97. *Address:* Herrenhäuser Str. 12, 30419 Hannover, Germany.

ENGELL, Hans; Danish politician; b. 8 Oct. 1948, Copenhagen; s. of Knud Engell Anderson; ed. Coll. of Journalism; journalist for Berlingske newspaper consortium 1968–78; Head of Press Service of Conservative People's Party 1978–82; M.P. 1984–, Minister for Defence 1982–87, of Justice 1989–93; Chair. Conservative Parl. Group 1987–89; Leader Conservative People's Party 1995–97. *Address:* c/o Conservative People's Party, Nyhavn 4, P.O. Box 1515, 1020 Copenhagen K; Mørdrupvej 16, 3060 Espergaerde, Denmark.

ENGEN, René Léopold Alexis; Belgian civil engineer; b. 13 Dec. 1918, Brussels-Etterbeek; s. of Léopold Engen and Louise Etienne; ed. Free Univ. of Brussels; engineer with ACEC 1942–45; Eng. Verreries de Momignies 1945, Chief Eng. 1949, Dir. 1950; Dir. Verreries Réunies Val St. Lambert et Momignies 1954; Gen. Man. Verlica-Momignies 1960, Man. Dir. 1961, Admin. Dél. 1968–81; Dir. Bouteilleries Belges Réunies 1967, Vice-Pres. 1968–73; Gen. Man. Electrorail 1969–81, Schneider 1972–80 (Vice-Pres. and Gen. Man. 1979–81); fmr. Dir. Spie-Batignolles, Jeumont-Schneider, Jeumont-Industrie, Cie. Financière pour le Développement des Entreprises, Creusot-Loire (Pres. 1975–81), Arbed, Salem, Banque de l'Union Européenne, Intercom, Merlin Gerin, Interrelax (Pres. 1969), Fondation Industrie Université, Marine Schneider, CFUE, Ceca, Elican Devt. Co. etc.; Pres. Exec. Cttee. Creusot-Loire; Officier Ordre de la Couronne, Ordre de Léopold, Officier Légion d'honneur, Citoyen d'honneur de Momignies, Médaille de la Résistance, Médaille Civique (1st Class), Insigne d'honneur d'or de lauréat de travail de Belgique and numerous other decorations. *Address:* Villa L'Aulnaie, Avenue François Pelletier, F-83990 Saint-Tropez, France.

ENGHOLM, Björn, DIPL.-POL.; German politician; b. 9 Nov. 1939, Lübeck; m.; two d.; ed. Acad. of Econs. and Politics, Hamburg, and Univ. of Hamburg; apprentice printer 1959–62, Journeyman's Certificate 1962; joined SPD 1962, mem. governing bd. 1984–; lecturer and freelance journalist 1964–69; mem. Bundestag 1969–82; Parl. State Sec. Ministry of Educ. and Science 1977–81, Minister 1981–82, Opposition leader Landstag of Schleswig-Holstein 1983–88, Minister-Pres. 1988–93; Chair. S.D.P. 1990–93. *Address:* Jürgen-Wullenwever-Str. 9, 23566 Lübeck, Germany.

ENGL, Walter L., DR.RER.NAT., F.I.E.E.E.; German professor of engineering; b. 8 April 1926, Regensburg; ed. Technical Univ. of Munich; Siemens Instrument and Control Div. 1950–63, latterly Head of Research Div.; Prof. Tech. Univ. of Aachen 1963–91, Dean Faculty of Eng. 1968–69; Visiting Prof. Univ. of Arizona 1967, Stanford Univ. 1970, Univ. of Tokyo 1972, 1980; Hon. Prof. Univ. of Kiel 1992; mem. Acad. of Science of North Rhine-Westphalia; mem. Int. Union of Radio Science; Foreign Assoc. mem. Eng. Acad. of Japan; VDE-Ehrenring (highest award of German Electrical Engineers Soc.). *Publications:* 100 publs. *Address:* Zum Heider Busch 5, 52134 Herzogenrath, Germany (Home).

ENGLAND, Glyn, F.ENG., F.I.E.E., F.I.MECH.E., J.P.; British engineer and administrator; b. 19 April 1921, Tonyrefail, South Wales; s. of Charles Thomas and Alice England; m. Tania Reichenbach 1942; two d.; ed. Queen Mary Coll. and London School of Econs., London Univ.; Research Asst. 1939–40; war service in R.E.M.E. 1942–47; variety of field work in electricity supply industry 1947–58; Devt. Engineer (Policy), Cen. Electricity Generating Bd. (CEGB) 1958–66, Chief Operations Engineer 1966–71, Dir.-Gen. of S.-W. Region 1971–73; Chair. of S.-W. Electricity Bd. 1973–77; Chair. CEGB 1977–82; Chair. Council for Environmental Conservation (now The Environment Council) 1983–88; Dir. U.K. Centre for Econ. and Environmental Devt. 1984–96; Vice-Pres. Int. Union of Producers and Distributors of Electrical Energy; fmr. Labour mem. Hertfordshire County Council, Council of Magistrates' Asscn.; Freeman of the City of London; Dir. F. H. Lloyd (Holdings) 1982–87, Triplex Lloyd PLC 1987–90; Chair. Dartington Inst. (now Silvanus Trust) 1985–94, Windcluster Ltd. 1991–96; Dir. The Wind Fund PLC 1994–; Pres. Mendip Soc.; Hon. D.Sc. (Bath). *Publications:* The Electricity Supply Industry and Economic Growth 1964, Security of Supply in the Design and Operation of the Grid System in England and Wales 1968, Efficiency Audit and Public Enterprise, Landscape in the Making (jointly). *Leisure interest:* active enjoyment of the countryside. *Address:* Woodbridge Farm, Ubley, Bristol, BS40 6PX, England. *Telephone:* (01761) 462479.

ENGLAND, Richard, B.ARCH.; Maltese architect, university professor and artist; b. 3 Oct. 1937; s. of Edwin England Sant Fournier and Ina Desain; m. Myriam Borg Manduca 1962; one s. one d.; ed. St. Edward's Coll., Univ. of Malta, Politecnico, Milan, Italy; student-architect in Gio Ponti's studio, Milan 1960–62; Dir. England & England, Architects 1962–; Dean Faculty of Architecture, Head Dept. of Architecture, Univ. of Malta 1987–89; Prof. Int. Acad. of Architecture 1987–, Academician 1991–; subject of several monographs; Fellow Inst. of Professional Designers (London); Hon. Prof. Univ. of Ga., Inst. of Advanced Studies, Univ. of N.Y., Univ. of Malta; Hon. Fellow Univ. of Bath, England; Interarch 1985 and 1991 Laureate Prizes, Commonwealth Asscn. of Architects Regional Awards 1985, 1987, Gold Medal City of Toulouse 1985, Comité des Critiques d'Architecture Silver Medal 1987, U.S.S.R. Biennale Laureate Prize 1988, IFRAA Prize (U.S.A.) 1991, Int. Prize, Costa Rica Bienale 1996; Officer, Order of Merit (Malta) 1993. *Publications:* Walls of Malta 1973, White is White 1973, Contemporary Art in Malta 1974, Carrier-Citadel Metamorphosis 1974, Island: A Poem for Seeing 1980, In Search of Silent Spaces 1983, Octaves of Reflection 1987, Eye to I (selected poems) 1994, Sacri Luogi 1995, Mdina, Citadel of Memory 1996, Fraxions 1996, Gozo—Island of Oblivion 1997. *Leisure interests:* music and art in general. *Address:* 26/1 Merchants Street, Valletta, VL10 (Office); 8 Oleander Street, The Gardens, St. Julians, STJ 12, Malta (Home). *Telephone:* 356 240894/245187 (Office); 356 330171 (Home). *Fax:* 356 241174 (Office); 356 334263 (Home).

ENGLER, John Mathias, J.D.; American politician; b. 12 Oct. 1948, Mt. Pleasant, Mich.; s. of Mathias Engler and Agnes Neyer; m. Michele Engler; three d.; ed. Mich. State Univ. and Thomas M. Cooley Law School; mem. Mich. House of Reps. 1971–78; mem. Mich. Senate 1979–90, Republican leader 1983, majority leader 1984–90; state senator 1979–90; Gov. of Michigan 1990–; Hon. LL.D. (Alma Coll.) 1984, (W. Mich.) 1991. *Address:* Office of the Governor, State Capitol Building, P.O. Box 30013, Lansing, MI 48909, U.S.A.

ENGLISH, Bill, B.COMM., B.A.; New Zealand politician; b. 1961; m.; five c.; ed. Otago Univ., Victoria Univ. of Wellington; fmr. policy analyst and farmer; M.P. for Wallace 1990–93, for Clutha-Southland 1993–; Parl. Under-Sec. for Health and Crown Health Enterprises 1993–96, Minister of Crown Health Enterprises, Assoc. Minister of Educ., subsequently Minister of Health and Assoc. Minister of Revenue 1996–, Assoc. Treasurer 1998–; Nat. Party. *Address:* Ministry of Health, P. O. Box 5013, Wellington, New Zealand. *Telephone:* (04) 496-2000. *Fax:* (04) 496–2340.

ENGLISH, Joseph Thomas, M.D.; American psychiatrist; b. 21 May 1933, Philadelphia, Pa.; s. of Thomas J. English and Helen Gilmore English; m. Ann Carr Sanger 1969; two s. one d.; ed. Jefferson Medical Coll.; Resident in Psychiatry, Inst. of Pa. Hospital, Philadelphia 1959–61, Nat. Inst. of Mental Health, Bethesda, Md. 1961–62; Chief Psychiatrist, U.S. Peace Corps. 1962–66; Dir. Office of Econ. Opportunity, Office of the Pres. 1966–68; Admin., Health Services and Mental Health Admin. U.S. Dept. of Health, Educ. and Welfare 1968–70; Pres. New York City Health and Hosps. Corpn. 1970–73; Adjunct Prof. Cornell Univ. School of Medicine 1975–; Assoc. Dean and Prof. of Psychiatry, New York Medical Coll. 1979–; Chair. Dept. of Psychiatry, St. Vincent's Hosp., New York 1973–; Visiting Fellow, Woodrow Wilson Nat. Fellowship Foundation 1979–; Trustee Sarah Lawrence Coll. 1986–90, Menninger Foundation 1993–; Pres. American Psychiatric Asscn. 1992–93, mem. World Psychiatric Soc. (Chair. section on religion and psychiatry 1994–). *Address:* St. Vincent's Hospital and Medical Center, 203 West 12 Street, New York, NY 10011, U.S.A. *Telephone:* (212) 604-8252. *Fax:* (212) 604-8794.

ENGLISH, Sir Terence Alexander Hawthorne, K.B.E., D.L., M.A., F.R.C.S., F.R.C.P.; British surgeon; b. 3 Oct. 1932, Pietermaritzburg, South Africa; s. of Arthur Alexander English and the late Mavis Eleanor Lund; m. Ann Margaret Smart Dicey 1963; two s. two d.; ed. Witwatersrand Univ. and Guy's Hosp. Medical School, London; Intern, Demonstrator in Anatomy, Junior Surgical Registrar, Guy's Hosp. 1962–65; Resident Surgical Officer, Bolingbroke Hosp. 1966; Surgical Registrar, Brompton Hosp. 1967; Sr. Surgical Registrar, Nat. Heart and London Chest Hosps. 1968–72; Research Fellow, Cardiac Surgery, Ala. Univ. 1969; Consultant Cardiothoracic Surgeon to Papworth and Addenbrooke Hosps. 1973–95; Dir. British Heart Foundation Heart Transplant Research Unit, Papworth Hosp. 1980–89; Consultant Cardiac Adviser, Humana Hosp. Wellington, London 1983–89; Master of St. Catharine's Coll. Cambridge 1993–; D.L. Cambridgeshire; Pres. Int. Soc. for Heart Transplantation 1984–85; Pres. Royal Coll. of Surgeons 1989–92; mem. Jt. Consultants Cttee. 1989–92, Standing Medical Advisory Cttee. 1989–92, Audit Comm. 1993–; Pres. B.M.A. 1995–96; Gov. The Leys School 1993–; Hon. Fellow St. Catharine's Coll., Cambridge; Hon. F.R.C.P. & S. (Canada); Hon. F.R.A.C.S., Hon. F.R.C.A., Hon. F.A.C.S., Hon. F.R.C.S. (Ireland), Hon. F.R.C.S. (Glasgow), Hon. Fellow U.M.D.S.; Hon. D.Sc. (Sussex, York); Hon. M.D. (Nantes); Man. of the Year, Royal Asscn. for

Disability and Rehabilitation 1980, Clement Price Thomas Award, Royal Coll. of Surgeons 1986. *Publications:* over 100 articles in scientific journals. *Leisure interests:* reading, hill walking, South African history. *Address:* The Master's Lodge, St. Catharine's College, Cambridge, CB2 1RL, England. *Telephone:* (01223) 368744.

ENGO, Paul Bamela; Cameroonian diplomatist; b. 5 Oct. 1931, Ebolowa; s. of Frederick Engo Mimbe and Elizabeth Ekoto Engo; m. 1st Beatrice Viola Engo 1958 (deceased); m. 2nd Ruth Bamela Engo 1974; seven c. and one adopted d.; ed. Middle Temple Inn, London; Crown Counsel, Legal Depts. of Nigeria and Cameroon 1959–61; Magisterial Bench for Southern Cameroon 1961–63; mem. Cameroon's Fed. Judicial Comm. 1961–64; Minister Counsellor, Embassy in Bonn, Fed. Repub. of Germany 1964–65, in Washington D.C. 1965–68, of the Cameroon Perm. Mission to the UN 1968, Minister Plenipotentiary 1969; Vice-Chair. Sixth Cttee. UN Gen. Ass. 1969, Chair. 1970; Perm. Rep. of Cameroon to the UN 1984–90; Tech. Adviser to Minister for Foreign Affairs 1973–84; Personal Rep. of Pres. for Law of the Sea and Chair. of its Nat. Comm. 1973–84; Lecturer, English Common Law, Nat. School of Admin. and Magistrature 1973–84; Vice-Pres. Bd. of UNICEF 1989; Chair. CM3, VN Disarmament Comm.; Chair. Bd. of Dirs. CamAfric Int. Inc. (consultants). *Leisure interests:* photography, video filming, music, encouraging young people to understand nation-building. *Address:* P.O. Box 6382, Yaoundé, Cameroon. *Telephone:* 31-4916. *Fax:* 31-4916.

ENGSTRÖM, Odd, B.A.; Swedish politician; b. 20 Sept. 1941, Skillingmark, Värmland Co.; m. Gunilla Engström; one s. one d.; ed. Univ. of Uppsala; Admin. Officer, Cabinet Office 1965–67, Ministry of Finance 1967–68; Prin. Admin. Officer, Nat. Bd. of Health and Welfare 1968–70; Deputy Asst. Under-Sec., Asst. Under- Sec. Ministry of Finance 1970–77; Sec. to Parly. Group, Social Democratic Party 1977–82; Under-Sec. of State, Cabinet Office 1982–84; Dir. of Finance, Stockholm City Admin. 1984–86; Dir.-Gen. Nat. Audit Bureau 1986; Political Adviser, Cabinet Office 1986–88; Minister with responsibility for the budget, Ministry of Finance 1988–89; Deputy Prime Minister 1989–91, M.P. 1991–93; Chair. Bank Support Group 1993–; Dir. Gen. Ministry of Finance 1993–. *Address:* c/o Ministry of Finance, Drottninggt. 21, 103 33 Stockholm, Sweden.

ENHSAYHAN, Mendsayhany; Mongolian politician; fmrly. worked as economist; fmr. Chief of Staff to Pres. Ochirbat; Prime Minister of Mongolia 1997–98; Pres. Premier Int. Inc. 1998–; mem. Democratic Alliance. *Address:* c/o Great Hural, Ulan Bator, Mongolia.

ENKHSAIKHAN, Jargalsaihany, PH.D.; Mongolian diplomatist; b. 4 Sept. 1950, Ulan Bator; m. 1st Tuul Myagmarjavyn 1976 (divorced 1993); m. 2nd Batgerel Batjavyn 1994; two s. four d.; ed. Moscow State Inst. for Int. Relations; Sec. of Legal Dept., Ministry of Foreign Affairs 1974–79; Mongolian Rep. at UN Conf. on Law of the Sea 1976–82; Sec. Mongolian Mission to UN, N.Y. 1979–86; Acting Head Legal and Policy Planning Depts. Ministry of Foreign Affairs 1986–88; Minister-Counsellor Mongolian Embassy, Moscow 1988–92; Adviser to Pres. of Mongolia 1992–93; Exec. Sec. to Mongolian Nat. Security Council, Nat. Security Adviser to Pres. of Mongolia 1994–96; Perm. Rep. of Mongolia to UN Aug. 1996–; Rapporteur Legal (Sixth) Cttee. of UN Gen. Ass. 1983, Vice-Chair. 1984; Vice-Chair. Special Cttee. on non-use of force in int. relations 1983; Chair. Group of Land-Locked States at UN 1997–; Vice-Pres. 52nd session UN Gen. Ass. 1997; Vice-Chair. Disarmament Comm. 1997; Mongolian State Order of the Polar Star. *Publications:* articles on int. relations and int. law. *Address:* 6 East 77th Street, New York, NY 10021, U.S.A. *Telephone:* (212) 861-9460.

ENNACEUR, Mohamed, PH.D.; Tunisian diplomatist and politician; b. 21 March 1934, El Djem; m. Siren Möenstre; three s. two d.; ed. Univ. of Tunis, Univ. of Paris (Sorbonne); fmrly. practised as lawyer; Gov. of Sousse 1972–73; Minister of Labour and Social Affairs 1974–77, 1979–85; Pres. Econ. and Social Council of Tunisia 1985–91; Amb., Perm. Rep. of Tunisia to UN and other int. orgs., Geneva 1991–96; barrister 1997–; Chair. World Employment Conf. (ILO) 1976, 71st session of Int. Labour Conf. (ILO) 1985, 49th session of Human Rights Comm. (UN) 1993; Ed. Tunisian Social Law Review; Grand Cordon of Order of Independence, Grand Cordon of Order of the Repub.; several awards and decorations from France, Britain, Germany, Belgium, Netherlands, Luxembourg, Ivory Coast. *Publications:* Human Rights after the Vienna Conference 1993; articles on labour law, human rights and social policy in Int. Studies Review, Tunisian Social Law Review, Int. Review of the Red Cross and other publs. *Leisure interests:* sports, music. *Address:* 10 rue du Mali, 1002 Tunis (Office); 15 rue Othman Kaak, 2026 Sidi Bousaid, Tunisia (Home). *Telephone:* (1) 848439 (Office); (1) 741127 (Home). *Fax:* (1) 847943 (Office).

ENO, Brian; British composer, artist and keyboardist; b. 15 May 1948, Woodbridge, Suffolk; s. of late William Arnold Eno and of Maria Alphonsine Eno (née Buslot); m. 1st Sarah Grenville 1967; one d.; m. 2nd Anthea Norman-Taylor 1988; two c.; educ. St. Mary's Convent, St. Joseph's Coll., Ipswich School of Art, Winchester Coll. of Art; founder mem. Roxy Music; worked with guitarist Robert Fripp 1975–76; invented 'ambient music' 1975; singles include: Seven Deadly Finns 1974; co-writer Talking Heads hit single Once In A Lifetime 1981; albums include: Here Come The Warm Jets 1974, Taking Tiger Mountain (By Strategy), Discreet Music, Another Green World, Music for Airports, Music for Films, Apollo, Before And After Science, Ambient 4 On Land, Neroli and The Drop; three albums with David Bowie 1977–79; three albums with Talking Heads 1978–80; My Life In The Bush of Ghosts (with David Byrne); co-producer U2 The Unforgettable Fire 1984; Joshua Tree 1987; Zooropa 1993; Bright Red (Laurie Anderson) 1995, Outside (David Bowie) 1996; over 70 exhbns. of video artworks worldwide; Visiting Prof. R. C. A. 1995–; BRIT Award for Best Producer 1994. *Publications include:* Swollen Appendices 1996. *Address:* OPAL Ltd., 3 Pembridge Mews, London, W11 3EQ, England. *Telephone:* 0171-727 8656. *Fax:* 0171-221 4901.

ENRIGHT, Dennis Joseph, O.B.E., C.LIT.; British teacher and writer; b. 11 March 1920, Leamington Spa, Warwicks.; s. of George and Grace (née Cleaver) Enright; m. Madeleine Harders 1949; one d.; ed. Leamington Coll., and Downing Coll., Cambridge; Lecturer in English, Farouk I Univ. Alexandria 1947–50; Org. Tutor, Birmingham Univ. Extra-Mural Dept. 1950–53; Visiting Prof. Konan Univ. (Japan) 1953–56; Gastdozent, English Seminar, Berlin Free Univ. 1956–57; British Council Prof. Chulalongkorn Univ. Bangkok 1957–59; Johore Prof. of English, Univ. of Singapore 1960–70; Co-editor Encounter Magazine 1970–72; Editorial adviser, Chatto and Windus 1972–74, Dir. 1974–82; Dr. h.c., (Surrey, Warwick); Univ. of Surrey, Univ. of Warwick, Queen's Gold Medal for Poetry 1981. *Publications:* poetry: The Laughing Hyena and Other Poems 1953, Bread rather than Blossoms: Poems 1956, The Poetry of Living Japan: An Anthology 1957, Some Men are Brothers: Poems 1960, Addictions: Poems 1962, The Old Adam 1965, Unlawful Assembly 1968, Daughters of Earth 1972, The Terrible Shears 1973, Rhyme Times Rhyme 1974, A Choice of Milton's Verse 1975, Sad Ires 1975, Paradise Illustrated 1978, A Faust Book 1979, Collected Poems 1981, Instant Chronicles 1985, Collected Poems 1987, Selected Poems 1990, Under the Circumstances 1991, Old Men and Comets 1993, Collected Poems 1948–98 1998; essays and literary criticism: The Apothecary's Shop: Essays on Literature 1957, Conspirators and Poets: literary criticism 1966, Man is an Onion 1972, A Mania for Sentences 1983, The Alluring Problem: An Essay On Irony 1986, Fields of Vision: Essays On Literature, Language and Television 1988, Interplay: A Kind of Commonplace Book 1995, Play Resumed: A Journal 1999; children's novels: The Joke Shop 1976, Wild Ghost Chase 1978, Beyond Land's End 1979; also: Academic Year 1955, The World of Dew: Aspects of Living Japan 1956, Heaven Knows Where 1957, Insufficient Poppy 1960, Figures of Speech 1965, Memoirs of a Mendicant Professor 1969, Shakespeare and the Students 1970, The Way of the Cat 1992; Editor: Samuel Johnson: The History of Rasselas, Prince of Abyssinia 1976, Oxford Book of Contemporary Verse 1945–1980 1980, Oxford Book of Death 1983, Fair of Speech: The Uses of Euphemism 1985, Faber Book of Fevers and Frets 1989, Oxford Book of Friendship (with David Rawlinson) 1991, Oxford Book of the Supernatural 1994, The Sayings of Goethe 1996. *Address:* 35A Viewfield Road, London, SW18 5JD, England. *Telephone:* 0181-874 8908.

ENRILE, Juan Ponce (see Ponce Enrile, Juan).

ENRIQUEZ SAVIGNAC, Antonio, M.A.; Mexican politician; b. 12 Sept. 1948, Querétaro; s. of Salvador Hernandez and Laura Enriquez Savignac; one s. one d.; loan official, IDB 1960–63; Adviser to Dir.-Gen., Bank of Mexico 1964–73; Dir.-Gen. Nat. Fund for Devt. of Tourism 1969–76; Under-Sec. of Planning, Ministry of Tourism 1976–77; Dir. Industrial Devt., Nat. Bank of Mexico 1977–81; Asst. Dir. of Finance, Petróleos Mexicanos 1981–82; Under-Sec. Ministry of Finance 1982; Minister of Tourism 1982–89. *Leisure interest:* reading. *Address:* c/o Secretaría de Turismo, Avenida Presidente Masaryk No. 172, 8° piso, Col. Chapultepec Morales, CP 11587, México, D.F., Mexico.

ENTHOVEN, Marius, M.SC.; Netherlands civil servant and international official; b. 23 Nov. 1940, Baarn; s. of Emil S. Enthoven and Anna G. Schouten; m. Lidwine Kolfschoten 1965; four d.; ed. Delft Tech. Univ., Princeton Univ.; scientist with Dutch Aerospace Labs. (NLR) 1967–72; Head Noise Abatement Dept. Ministry for Environment 1972–77, Dir. Scientific Affairs 1977–80, Chief Insp. Environmental Protection 1980–88, Dir.-Gen. Environmental Protection 1988–94; Dir.-Gen. Environment, Nuclear Safety and Civil Protection, Directorate-Gen. XI, European Comm. 1994–97; Special Adviser to Sec.-Gen., European Comm. Nov. 1997–; Kt. Order of the Dutch Lion. *Publications:* books and articles on environmental man. issues. *Leisure interests:* literature, theatre, music, tennis. *Address:* European Commission, rue de la Loi 200, 1049 Brussels, Belgium. *Telephone:* 2299-4949. *Fax:* 2295-7338.

ENTOV, Revold Mikhailovich, PH.D.; Russian economist; b. 23 March 1931, Kiev; m. Galina Gorvitz 1962; one s. one d.; ed. Kharkov Univ. and Inst. for World Econ. and Int. Relations (IMEMO); Asst. Prof. Bashkirian Agricultural School 1954–57; research worker, IMEMO 1961, now Head of Section; Prof. Univ. of Moscow 1970–; mem. Comm. Evaluating Projects of Econ. Reform in U.S.S.R. (now Russia) 1990–91; mem. Russian Acad. of Sciences 1994; U.S.S.R. State Prize 1977. *Publications:* Public Credit of the U.S. 1967, Theories of Prices 1982, Movements of Capital and the Profit Rate 1987; numerous articles on econ. theory and the U.S. econ. *Leisure interest:* history of psychology. *Address:* Institute for World Economy and International Relations, 117859 Moscow, Profsoyuznaya 23 (Office); 113149 Moscow, Azovskaya 4, Apt. 44, Russia. (Home). *Telephone:* 128-29-07 (Office); 310-17-67 (Home).

ENTREMONT, Philippe; French pianist and conductor; b. 7 June 1934, Reims; s. of Jean and Renée (Monchamps) Entremont; m. Andrée Ragot 1955; one s. one d.; ed. Institution Notre-Dame à Reims, Conservatoire National Supérieur de Musique de Paris; has performed with all major orchestras of world 1953–; Pres. of Acad. Int. de Musique Maurice Ravel,

Saint-Jean-de-Luz 1973–80; Musical Dir. and Permanent Conductor, Vienna Chamber Orchestra 1976–; Dir. New Orleans Symphony Orchestra 1980–86; Principal Conductor Denver Symphony Orchestra 1986–88, Paris Orchestre Colonne 1987–90, Netherlands Chamber Orchestra 1993–, Israel Chamber Orchestra 1995–; Officier de l'Ordre nat. du Mérite, Chevalier, Légion d'honneur; Österreichisches Ehrenkreuz für Wissenschaft und Kunst; Harriet Cohen Piano Medal 1951, Grand Prix International Concours Marguerite Long-Jacques Thibaud 1953, 4 Grand Prix du Disque Awards, Edison Award 1968; Grammy Award 1972. *Leisure interest:* golf. *Address:* 10 rue de Castiglione, 75001 Paris, France; Schwarzenbergplatz 10/7, A-1040 Vienna, Austria. *Telephone:* 42.86.06.08, 42.86.86.61 (Paris).

ENYA; Irish singer and composer; b. 1961, Gweedore, Donegal; d. of Leo Bhraonain and Maire Bhraonain; keyboard and background vocals with family group Clannad (traditional Irish music) for two years; later started to write and record with Nicky and Roma Ryan; wrote music for film The Frog Prince and soundtrack for the BBC TV series The Celts (with Nicky and Roma Ryan); number one single Orinoco Flow and four best-selling albums, Paint the Sky with Stars 1997; two Grammy awards. *Address:* Ayesha Castle, Co. Dublin, Ireland.

ENZENSBERGER, Hans Magnus, DR. PHIL.; German poet and writer; b. 11 Nov. 1929, Kaufbeuren; m. 3rd Katharina Bonitz 1986; two d.; ed. Univs. of Erlangen, Freiburg im Breisgau, Hamburg and Paris; Third Programme Editor, Stuttgart Radio 1955–57; Lecturer, Hochschule für Gestaltung, Ulm 1956–57; Literary Consultant to Suhrkamp's (publishers), Frankfurt 1960–; mem. "Group 47", Ed. Kursbuch (review) 1965–75, Publisher 1970–90; Ed. TransAtlantik (monthly magazine) 1980–82; Publisher and Ed., Die Andere Bibliothek 1985–; Hugo Jacobi Prize 1956, Kritiker Prize 1962, Georg Büchner Prize 1963, Premio Pasolini 1982, Heinrich Böll Prize 1985, and others. *Publications:* poetry: Verteidigung der Wölfe 1957, Landessprache 1960, Blindenschrift 1964, Poems for People Who Don't Read Poems (English edn.) 1968, Gedichte 1955–1970 1971, Mausoleum 1975; essays: Clemens Brentanos Poetik 1961, Einzelheiten 1962, Politik und Verbrechen 1964; also: Deutschland, Deutschland unter Anderen 1967, Das Verhör von Habana (play) 1970, Freisprüche 1970, Der kurze Sommer der Anarchie (novel) 1972, Gespräche mit Marx und Engels 1973, Palaver 1974; Edited Museum der Modernen Poesie 1960, Allerleirauh 1961, Andreas Gryphius Gedichte 1962, Edward Lears kompletter Nonsense (translation) 1977, Raids and Reconstruction (essays, English edn.), Der Untergang der Titanic (epic poem) 1978, Die Furie des Verschwindens 1980, Politische Brosamen 1982, Critical Essays 1982, Der Menschenfreund 1984, Ach Europa! 1987, Mittelmass und Wahn 1988, Requiem für eine romantische Frau 1988, Der Fliegende Robert 1989, Zukunftsmusik (poems) 1991, Die grosse Wanderung 1992, Aussideren auf den Bürgerkrieg 1993, Diderots Schatten 1994, The Palace (libretto) 1994, Civil War (English edn.) 1994, Selected Poems (English edn.) 1994, Kiosk (poems) 1995, English edn. 1997, Voltaires Neffe (play) 1996, Der Zahlenteufel 1997, Zickzack 1997, Wo warst du, Robert? (novel) 1998, Leichter als Luft (poems) 1999, Mediocrity and Delusion (English edn.) 1992. *Address:* c/o Lindenstr. 29, 60325 Frankfurt am Main, Germany.

ENZI, Michael Bradley, M.B.A.; American politician; b. 1 Feb. 1944, Bremerton, Wash.; s. of Elmer Enzi and Dorothy Bradley; m. Diana Buckley 1968; one s. two d.; ed. George Washington Univ. and Denver Univ.; Pres. NZ Shoes, Inc. Gillette, Wyoming 1969–95, NZ Shoes of Sheridan, Inc. Wyoming 1983–91; Acting Man. Dunbar Well Services, Gillette 1985–97; Chair. Bd. Dirs. First Wyoming Bank, Gillette 1978–88; mem. Bd. Dirs. Black Hill Corpn.; Mayor of Gillette 1975–82; mem. Wyoming House of Reps. Cheyenne 1987–91, Wyoming State Senate 1991–97; Senator from Wyoming 1997–; Republican. *Address:* United States Senate, Washington, DC 20510, (Office); 431 Circle Drive, Gillette, WY 82716, U.S.A. (Home).

EÖTVÖS, Peter; German (b. Hungarian) composer and conductor; b. 2 Jan. 1944, Székelyudvarhely, Hungary; s. of László Eötvös and Ilona Szücs; m. 1st Piroska Molnár 1968; one s.; m. 2nd Pi-Hsien Chen 1976; one d.; m. 3rd Maria Mezei; ed. Budapest Acad. and Musikhochschule, Cologne; played in Stockhausen's Ensemble, Cologne 1966–76; composer and producer at WDR Electronic Music Studio, Cologne 1971–79; Conductor and Musical Dir. Ensemble. Intercontemporain, Paris 1979–91; Prin. Guest Conductor BBC Symphony Orchestra, London 1985–88; First Guest Conductor, Budapest Festival Orchestra 1992–95; Chief Conductor Netherlands Radio Chamber Orchestra 1994–; Prof., Musikhochschule Karlsruhe, Germany 1992–98, Cologne 1998–; f. Int. Eötvös Inst. for Young Conductors; mem. Akad. der Kunst, Berlin, Szechenyi Acad. of Art, Budapest; Officier, Ordre des Arts et des Lettres 1986; Bartok Award, Budapest 1997. *Compositions include:* (for orchestra) Chinese Opera, Shadows, Psychokosmos, Atlantis, Two Monologues, Replica; (for ensemble) Intervalles-Intérieures, Windsequenzen, Steine, Triangel; (for string quartet) Korrespondenz; (for vocal ensemble) Three comedy madrigals; (for percussion) Psalm 151, (for musical theatre/ opera) Radames, Harakiri, Three Sisters. *Leisure interests:* pipe, jazz, walking. *Address:* Naarderweg 56, 1261 BV Blaricum, Netherlands. *Telephone:* (35) 5313265. *Fax:* (35) 5313265.

EPERON, Alastair David Peter, F.R.S.A.; British corporate affairs consultant; b. 17 Nov. 1949, Kent; s. of Stanley A. Eperon and Patricia Woodrow; m. Ruth Tabbenor 1976; two d.; ed. Ramsden School for Boys, Orpington, Kent; worked as journalist; Press Officer, Surrey Co. Council 1972-74; Head of Public Affairs, The Housing Corpn. 1974–78; Sr. Consultant, Shandwick 1978–80; Dir., then Deputy Man. Dir. Ogilvy & Mather Public Relations, then Chief Exec. Ogilvy & Mather Corporate Financial 1980–86; Dir. McAvoy Wreford Bayley 1986–, Man. Dir. 1988–89, Chief Exec. McAvoy Bayley 1989–91; Dir. Valin Pollen Int. 1989–90; Dir. of Group Corporate Affairs, The Boots Co. PLC 1991–; Deputy Chair. British Retail Consortium; Chair. CBI Distributive Trades Panel; Fellow Inst. of Public Relations. *Leisure interests:* gardening, countryside. *Address:* The Boots Company PLC, Group Headquarters, Nottingham, NG2 3AA, England. *Telephone:* (0115) 968 7023. *Fax:* (0115) 968 7161.

EPHRON, Nora, B.A.; American author and scriptwriter; b. 19 May 1941, New York; d. of Henry Ephron and Phoebe (née Wolkind) Ephron; m. 1st Dan Greenburg (divorced); m. 2nd Carl Bernstein (divorced); two s.; m. 3rd Nicholas Pileggi; ed. Wellesley Coll.; reporter, New York Post 1963–68; freelance writer 1968–; Contributing Ed. and columnist, Esquire Magazine 1972–73, Sr. Ed. 1974–78; Contributing Ed., New York Magazine 1973–74; mem. American Writers' Guild, Authors' Guild, PEN, Acad. of Motion Picture Arts and Sciences. *Film appearances:* Crimes and Misdemeanors, Husbands and Wives. *Publications:* Wallflower at the Orgy 1970, Crazy Salad 1975, Scribble, Scribble 1978, Heartburn 1983, Nora Ephron Collected 1991. *Screenplays:* Silkwood (with Alice Arlen) 1983, Heartburn 1986, When Harry Met Sally. . . 1989, Cookie 1989 (co-exec. producer, co-screenwriter), My Blue Heaven 1990, This is My Life 1992 (dir., screenwriter, with Delia Ephron), Sleepless in Seattle (also dir.) 1993, Mixed Nuts (also dir.), Michael (also dir.) 1996. *Address:* c/o Sam Cohn International Creative Management, 40 West 57th Street, New York, NY 10019, U.S.A.

EPP, Jake, B.A., B.ED., M.P.; Canadian politician; b. 1 Sept. 1939, St. Boniface, Man.; m. Lydia Martens; one d.; ed. Univ. of Manitoba; teacher Steinbach Coll. Inst., Man.; mem. House of Commons 1972–74, 1988; Minister of Indian Affairs and Northern Devt. 1979; Minister of Nat. Health and Welfare 1984–89, of Energy, Mines and Resources Jan. 1989–93; Chair. Caucus Cttee. on Fed. Prov. Relations 1980, of Health and Welfare 1983; mem. House Standing Cttee. on Labour, Manpower and Immigration and of Special Jt. Cttee. on Immigration; mem. Canadian Parl. Asscn., Canada-U.S.A. Inter-parl. Group; Town Councillor, Steinbach 1970–72; Sr. Vice-Pres. Transcanada Pipelines Ltd. 1993–; Progressive Conservative Party. *Address:* 111 5th Avenue S.W., P.O. Box 1000, Stn. M, Calgary, Alta. T2P 4K5 (Office); 1108 4th Street N.W., Calgary, Alta. T2M 2Y4, Canada (Home).

EPSTEIN, Emanuel, PH.D.; American professor of plant nutrition and plant physiologist; b. 5 Nov. 1916, Duisburg, Germany; s. of Harry Epstein and Bertha Epstein (née Löwe); m. Hazel M. Leask 1943; two c. (one deceased); ed. Univ. of California (Davis and Berkeley); served U.S. Army 1943–46; Plant Physiologist, U.S. Dept. of Agric., Beltsville, Md. 1950–58; Lecturer and Assoc. Plant Physiologist, Univ. of California (Davis) 1958–65, Prof. of Plant Nutrition and Plant Physiologist 1965–87, Prof. Emer. (active) 1987–; Prof. of Botany 1974–87, Prof. Emer. (active) 1987–; Faculty Research Lecturer 1980; Consultant to Govt. agencies, private orgs. and publrs. at various times; Guggenheim and Fulbright Fellowships; mem. N.A.S.; Gold Medal, Pisa (Italy) Univ. 1962; Pres. Pacific Div., A.A.A.S. 1990–91; Charles Reid Barnes Life Membership Award, American Soc. of Plant Physiologists 1986. *Publications:* Mineral Nutrition of Plants: Principles and Perspectives 1972, The Biosaline Concept: An Approach to the Utilization of Underexploited Resources (co-ed.) 1979, Saline Agriculture: Salt-Tolerant Plants for Developing Countries (co-ed.) 1990, research papers, reviews and articles. *Leisure interests:* hiking, photography and history. *Address:* Department of Land, Air and Water Resources, Soils and Biogeochemistry, University of California, Davis, CA 95616-8627, U.S.A. *Telephone:* (530) 752-0197. *Fax:* (530) 752-1552.

EPSTEIN, Gabriel, F.R.I.B.A., S.A.D.G.; British architect and planning consultant; b. 25 Oct. 1918, Duisburg, Germany; s. of Dr. Harry Epstein and Bertha Loewe; m. Josette A. Glonneau 1955; two s. one d.; ed. schools in Germany, Switzerland and Israel and Architectural Asscn. School of Architecture, London; officer in Royal Engineers in World War II; Partner, Shepheard, Epstein & Hunter 1955–86; Prof. of Architecture and Dir. of Inst. of Public Bldgs. and Design, Univ. of Stuttgart 1978–88; Prof. Centre for Infrastructure Planning, Univ. of Stuttgart 1984–; consultant, and mem. competition juries Stuttgart, Paris, Brussels, Leipzig, Berlin, Erfurt, etc. 1992–96; Pres. Architectural Asscn., London 1963–64, Franco-British Union of Architects 1976–77; mem. Berlin Acad. of Arts and Letters; Dr.h.c. (Lancaster). *Works include:* master plan and bldgs., Univ. of Lancaster; master plans for Open Univ. (U.K.), Univ. of Tlemcen (Algeria) and Univ. of Ghana; town-planning consultant for London Docks (Wapping) 1976–81, for New Univ., Paris Region 1992, for European Parl. Complex, Brussels 1992–; many housing projects in London and schools and colleges in England 1950–85. *Publications:* Planning Forms for Twentieth Century Cities 1976, Well-Being In Cities: The Low Energy City 1979, Energy Use and City Form 1981. *Leisure interest:* painting. *Address:* 3 rue André Mazet, 75006 Paris, France. *Telephone:* (01) 43.25.89.59. *Fax:* (01) 43.26.57.42.

EPSTEIN, Matthew; American opera administrator; ed. Univ. of Pa; Artistic Dir. Brooklyn Acad. of Music 1987–91; consultant for the opera cos. of Chicago and Santa Fe; Artistic Dir. Welsh Nat. Opera 1991–94, Vice-Pres. Columbia Artists Man. 1973–. *Address:* c/o Columbia Artists Management, 165 West 57th Street, New York, NY 10019, U.S.A.

EPSTEIN, Sir (Michael) Anthony, Kt., C.B.E., M.D., D.SC., PH.D., F.R.C.PATH., F.R.S.; British virologist; b. 18 May 1921, London; ed. St. Paul's School, London, Trinity Coll., Cambridge, and Middlesex Hosp. Medical School, London; House Surgeon, Middlesex Hosp. and Addenbrooke's Hosp., Cambridge 1944; commissioned R.A.M.C. 1945–47; Asst. Pathologist, Bland Sutton Inst., Middlesex Hosp. Medical School 1948–65; Berkeley Travelling Fellow and French Govt. Exchange Scholar, Inst. Pasteur, Paris 1952–53, Visiting Investigator, Rockefeller Inst., New York 1956; Reader in Experimental Pathology, Middlesex Hosp. Medical School, and Hon. Consultant in Experimental Virology, Middlesex Hosp. 1965–68; Prof. of Pathology, Univ. of Bristol 1968–85, Head of Dept. and Hon. Consultant Pathologist, Avon Area Health Authority (Teaching) 1968–82; Emer. Prof. of Pathology, Univ. of Bristol at Nuffield Dept. of Clinical Medicine, Univ. of Oxford 1985–; Extraordinary Fellow, Wolfson Coll., Oxford 1986–; mem. MRC Cell Bd. 1979–84, Chair. 1982–84; Chair. CRC/MRC Jt. Cttee. for Inst. of Cancer Research 1982–87; mem. MRC 1982–86, Chair. MRC Tropical Medicine Research Bd. 1985–88, Medical and Scientific Advisory Panel, Leukaemia Research Fund 1982–85, Council of Royal Soc. 1983–85, 1986–91; mem. UK Co-ordinating Cttee. on Cancer Research 1983–87, Scientific Advisory Cttee., The Lister Inst. of Preventive Medicine 1984–86; Scientific Adviser, Charing Cross Medical Research Centre 1984–87; Foreign Sec. and Vice-Pres. Royal Soc. 1986–91, MRC Assessor 1987–91; mem. Expert Working Party on Bovine Spongiform Encephalopathy, Dept. of Health 1988, mem. Exec. Bd. Int. Council of Scientific Unions 1990–93, Chair. Cttee. for Science in Cen. and Eastern Europe 1992–95; mem. Exec. Council European Science Foundation 1990–93; Special Rep. of Dir.-Gen., UNESCO, for Science in Russia, Moscow 1992; mem. Programme Advisory Group, World Bank China Key Studies Project 1992–96; Fellow Univ. Coll. London 1991; Hon. Prof. Zhongshan Medical Univ., People's Repub. of China 1981, Chinese Acad. of Preventive Medicine 1988; Hon. Fellow Queensland Inst. of Medical Research 1983; Hon. mem. Belgian Soc. for Study of Cancer 1979, Pathological Soc. 1987; Hon. F.R.S.E. 1991; Hon. F.R.C.P. 1986; Hon. F.R.C.P.A. 1995; Hon. M.D. (Edin.) 1986, (Charles Univ., Prague) 1998; Hon. D.Sc. (Birmingham) 1996; Leeuwenhoek Prize Lecturer, Royal Soc. 1983; Markham Skerritt Prize (Univ. of Bristol) 1977, Paul Ehrlich and Ludwig Darmstaedster Prize and Medal (Frankfurt) 1973, Bristol-Myers Award (New York) 1982, Prix Griffuel (Paris) 1986, Gairdner Foundation Int. Award (Toronto) 1988, S. Weiner Distinguished Visitor Award (Univ. of Manitoba) 1988, Royal Medal, The Royal Soc. 1992. *Publications:* over 220 scientific papers in international journals. *Address:* Nuffield Department of Clinical Medicine, Oxford University, John Radcliffe Hospital, Headington, Oxford, OX3 9DU, England. *Telephone:* (01865) 221334. *Fax:* (01865) 222901.

ERBAKAN, Necmettin; Turkish politician; b. 1926, Sinop; ed. Inst. of Mechanics, Technical Univ. of Istanbul and Technische Universität, Aachen, Germany; Asst. lecturer, Inst. of Mechanics, Technical Univ. of Istanbul 1948–51; Engineer, Firma Deutz 1951–54; Prof. Technical Univ. of Istanbul 1954–66; Chair. Industrial Dept., Turkish Asscn. of Chambers of Commerce 1966–68, Chair. of Asscn. 1968; mem. Nat. Assembly 1969–80; f. Nat. Order Party 1970 (disbanded 1971); Chair. Nat. Salvation Party Oct. 1973 (disbanded 1981); Deputy Prime Minister and Minister of State Jan.-Sept. 1974; Deputy Prime Minister 1975–77, July-Dec. 1977; detained 1980–81; now leader Refah Partisi (Welfare Party, f. 1983); Prime Minister of Turkey 1996–98. *Address:* c/o Office of the Prime Minister, Basbakanlik, Ankara, Turkey.

ERBSEN, Claude Ernest, B.A.; American journalist; b. 10 March 1938, Trieste, Italy; s. of Henry M. Erbsen and Laura Treves Erbsen; m. 1st Jill J. Prosky 1959; m. 2nd Hedy M. Cohn 1970; two s. one d.; ed. Amherst Coll. Mass.; reporter and printer, Amherst Journal Record 1955–57; staff reporter, El Tiempo, Bogotá 1960; with Associated Press (AP) in New York and Miami 1960–65; reporter to Chief of Bureau, AP Brazil 1965–69; Exec. Rep. for Latin America, AP 1969–70; Business Man. and Admin. Dir. AP-Dow Jones Econ. Report, London 1970–75; Deputy Dir. AP World Services, New York 1975–80, Vice-Pres., Dir. 1986–; Vice-Pres., Dir. AP-Dow Jones News Services 1980–87; mem. Bd. Dirs. World Press Inst. St. Paul; mem. Int. Press Inst., Council on Foreign Relations; San Giusto d'Oro award, City of Trieste 1995. *Leisure interests:* reading, travel. *Address:* Associated Press, 50 Rockefeller Plaza, New York, NY 10020, U.S.A. *Telephone:* (212) 621-1750.

ERÇEL, Gazi; Turkish banker; b. 20 Feb. 1945, Gelibolu; m. Zeynel Erçel; one d.; ed. Ankara Univ., Vanderbilt Univ., Tenn.; bank examiner Ministry of Finance 1967–77; Deputy Dir.-Gen. of Treasury 1977–82; asst. to Exec. Dir. IMF, Washington D.C. 1982–86; Dir.-Gen. of Treasury and Foreign Trade 1987–89; Vice-Chair., mem. bd. Yaşar Holding A.Ş. 1989–94; C.E.O. and Man. Dir. Tütünbank A.Ş. 1994–96; Gov. Cen. Bank of Turkey 1996–; Chair. Express Trade Bank GmbH, Berlin, Tütün Leasing, Tütün Factoring, Yadaş, Batı Sigorta 1994–96; mem. bd. Tourism Bank, Ereğli Iron and Steel Co. 1987–88; auditor European Resettlement Fund, Paris 1988–89; deputy IDA 1989. *Address:* Türkiye Cumhuriyet Merkez Bankasi AS, Istiklal Cad. 10, 06100 Ulus, Ankara, Turkey. *Telephone:* 312-309 3131. *Fax:* 312-311 6685; 312-310 9121.

ERDEM, Kaya; Turkish government official; b. 1928, Zonguldak; s. of Hilmi and Pakize Erdem; m. Sevil Şibay 1956; two d.; ed. High School of Commerce, Univ. of Marmara; mem. faculty, Anatolian Univ. 1959–65; Finance Dir. Sugar Corpn. 1960–62; Asst. Dir.-Gen. State Treasury 1963–72; mem. Cttee. for Reorganization of State Econ. Enterprises 1971–72; Dir.-Gen. State Treasury 1972–73; Chief Financial Counsellor, Turkish Embassy, London 1973–76; Sec.-Gen. Ministry of Finance 1978–80; Minister of Finance 1980–82, Deputy Prime Minister, Minister of State 1983–89; prominent in drafting and implementation of econ. stabilization programme 1980. *Publications:* State Economic Enterprise 1966, and numerous articles on cost and managerial accountancy. *Leisure interests:* bridge, tennis. *Address:* c/o Office of the Deputy Prime Minister, Basbakan yard. ve Devlet Bakani, Bakanlıklar, Ankara, Turkey.

ERDENECHULUUN, Luvsangiin; Mongolian diplomatist; b. 10 Oct. 1948, Ulan Bator; s. of Sonomyn Luvsan and Lhamsurengiin Baimanhand; m. Sukh-Ochiryn Solongo 1969; two s. one d.; ed. State Inst. of Int. Relations, Moscow and Diplomatic Acad. Moscow; officer, Dept. of Int. Relations, Ministry of Foreign Affairs 1972–80; First Sec. Perm. Mission of Mongolia at UN 1980–84; Head, Press and Information Dept. Ministry of Foreign Affairs 1985–86, Head, Dept. of Int. Orgs. 1988–90; Deputy Perm. Rep. to UN 1990, Perm. Rep. 1992–96; adviser to Pres. of Mongolia 1996–97; scholar of int. relations 1998–; Distinguished Service Medal, Order of Polar Star. *Address:* Chingeltein duureg, 1-r horoo, Mergejiltnii 100 ailyn bair, 4–421, Ulan Bator, Mongolia. *Telephone:* 372-966.

ERDŐS, André; Hungarian diplomatist; b. 1941, Algiers; s. of Gusztáv Erdős and Márta Czeichner; m. Katalin Pintér 1965; one d.; ed. Moscow State Inst. for Int. Relations, Budapest School of Political Sciences; joined Hungarian Ministry of Foreign Affairs 1965; Attaché, Morocco 1968–72; staff mem. CSCE Dept. Ministry of Foreign Affairs 1972–78; assigned to Perm. Mission of Hungary at UN, New York 1978–83; del. to UN Gen. Ass. 1984, 1985, 1989; Adviser to Minister of Foreign Affairs of Hungary 1984–86; Head of Hungary's del. to Vienna CSCE follow-up meeting 1986–89; Perm. Rep. to UN 1990–94, 1997–; Hungarian rep. UN Security Council 1992–93; Deputy State Sec. for Multilateral Affairs, Ministry of Foreign Affairs 1994–97. *Publications:* Co-operation in the United Nations between Socialist and Developing Countries 1981, Soviet-German Relations 1939–41 1984, The Circumstances of the Birth of the 1941 Soviet-German Non-Aggression Pact 1987; numerous articles on int. affairs. *Leisure interests:* philately, numismatics, collecting postcards, making video movies. *Address:* 227 East 52nd Street, New York, NY 10022, U.S.A. *Telephone:* (212) 752-0209. *Fax:* (212) 755-5395.

ERDRICH, Karen Louise, M.A.; American writer and poet; b. 7 June 1954, Little Falls, Minn.; d. of Ralph Louis Erdrich and Rita Joanne (Gourneau) Erdrich; m. Michael Anthony Dorris 1981 (died 1997); six c. (one s. deceased); ed. Dartmouth Coll., Johns Hopkins Univ.; Visiting Poetry Teacher, N.D. State Arts Council 1977–78; Teacher of Writing, Johns Hopkins Univ., Baltimore 1978–79; Communications Dir., Ed., Circle-Boston Indian Council 1979–80; Textbook Writer Charles Merrill Co. 1980; mem. PEN (mem. Exec. Bd. 1985–); Guggenheim Fellow 1985–86; numerous awards including Nelson Algren Award 1982, Pushcart Prize 1983, Nat. Magazine Fiction Award 1983, 1987, First Prize O. Henry Awards 1987. *Publications:* Imagination (textbook) 1981, Jacklight (poems) 1984, Love Medicine (novel; trans. in more than 18 languages; numerous awards including Nat. Book Critics' Circle Award for best work of fiction 1984) 1984, The Beet Queen 1986, Tracks 1988, The Crown of Columbus (jtly.) 1991, The Bingo Palace 1994, The Bluejay's Dance 1995; short stories, essays and poems publ. in magazines. *Address:* c/o Rambar and Curtis, 19 West 44th Street, New York, NY 10036, U.S.A.

EREDIAUWA, Omo N'Oba N'Edo Uku-Akpolokpolo, B.A.; Oba of Benin; Nigerian traditional monarch; b. 24 June 1923; ed. Edo Coll., Benin, Govt. Coll., Ibadan, Yaba Coll., Lagos, Cambridge Univ., England; followed career in Civil Service; retd. 1973 as Perm. Sec. in Fed. Ministry of Health; Civil Commr. for Bendel State 1975–77; succeeded to throne of Benin March 1979; mem. Council of State 1979–. *Address:* The Palace, Box 1, Benin City, Bendel State, Nigeria. *Telephone:* (052) 240001.

ERH DONGQIANG; Chinese photographer; b. Shanghai; m. (divorced); freelance photo-journalist 1981–; co-founder, with Tess Johnston, Old China Press 1993; work appears in China Tourism monthly, airline magazines and other publs.; noted for pictures of architecture, especially images of Shanghai; has turned his home into pvt. Folk Art Museum containing memorabilia from old Shanghai and Southern China. *Publications:* with Tess Johnston: A Last Look, Near to Heaven. *Address:* c/o Old China Hand Press, Hong Kong Special Administrative Area, People's Republic of China.

ERICKSON, Arthur Charles, C.C., B.ARCH., F.R.A.I.C., A.R.C.A.; Canadian architect; b. 14 June 1924, Vancouver; s. of late Oscar and of Myrtle Erickson; ed. Univ. of British Columbia, McGill Univ.; travel study in Mediterranean countries and N. Europe 1950–53; private practice 1953–62; Asst. Prof. Univ. of Oregon 1955–56; Instructor and Asst. Prof. Univ. of British Columbia 1957–60, Assoc. Prof. 1961; Canada Council Fellowship for architectural research in Asia 1961; with Erickson, Massey 1963–72; Prin. Arthur Erickson Architects 1972–91, Arthur Erickson Architectural Corpn. 1991–; mem. many architectural insts., asscns.; mem. Science Council of Canada Cttee. on Urban Devt. 1971, Bd. Canadian Conf. of the Arts 1972, Canadian Council on Urban Research, Bd. of Trustees, Inst. for Research on Public Policy, fmr. mem. Design Council of Portland Devt. Comm.; mem. Int. Cttee. of Museums of Modern Art, Americas Soc.; Life mem. Vancouver Art Gallery; Hon. Fellow, American Inst. of Architects 1978; Hon. D. Eng., (Nova Scotia Technical Coll.) 1971, Hon. LL.D. (Simon Fraser Univ.) 1973, (McGill Univ.) 1975,

(Univ. of Manitoba) 1978, (Lethbridge Univ.) 1981; Hon. D.Litt. (British Columbia) 1985; Hon. F.A.I.A.; Hon. M.R.I.B.A.; won First Prize in competition for Simon Fraser Univ., First Prize for design of Canadian Pavilion at Expo '70, Osaka, Pan Pacific Citation, American Inst. of Architects, Hawaiian Chapter 1963, Molson Prize, Canada Council for the Arts 1967, Architectural Inst. of Japan Award for Best Pavilion Expo '70, Royal Bank of Canada Award 1971, American Architectural Fraternity 1973, Auguste Perret Award, Int. Union of Architects 1974, Canadian Housing Design Council Awards for Residential Design 1975, President's Award of Excellence, American Soc. of Landscape Architects 1979, Grande Medaille d'Or Académie d'Architecture de France 1984, Gold Medal Royal Architectural Inst. of Canada 1984, Gold Medal, American Inst. of Architects 1986. *Publications:* The Architecture of Arthur Erickson 1975, Seven Stones by Edith Iglaner, The Architecture of Arthur Erickson 1988. *Address:* 1672 West 1st Avenue, Vancouver, B.C., V6J 1G1, Canada.

ERICKSON, John, F.R.S.E., F.B.A., F.R.S.A.; British academic (retd.); b. 17 April 1929, South Shields; s. of Henry Erickson; m. Ljubica Petrović 1957; one s. one d.; ed. South Shields High School and St. John's College, Cambridge; Research Fellow, St. Antony's Coll. Oxford 1955–58; lecturer, Univ. of St. Andrews 1958–61; lecturer, Sr. lecturer, Reader, Univ. of Manchester 1962–67; Reader, Prof. Univ. of Edinburgh 1967–88, Univ. Endowment Fellow, Dir. Centre for Defence Studies 1988–96, Hon. Fellow Defence Studies and Prof. Emer. 1996–. *Publications:* The Soviet High Command 1918–1941 1962, Storia dello stato Maggiore Sovietico 1963, The Military-Technical Revolution 1966, The Armed Forces and Society 1969, Soviet Military Power 1971, Soviet Military Thought in the Nuclear Era 1972, Zum Frühstück in München: Möglichkeit der sowietischen Militärpolitik 1972, The Road to Stalingrad 1973, Soviet Military Power and Performance 1979, The Road to Berlin 1983, Soviet Ground Forces: An Operational Assessment 1986, Barbarossa 1994, The Soviet Armed Forces 1918–22; a research guide to Soviet sources 1996. *Leisure interest:* model making. *Address:* 13 Ravelston House Road, Edin., EH4 3LP, Scotland.

ERIKSSON, Göran Olof, M.A.; Swedish theatre director, author and translator; b. 7 March 1929; s. of Walfrid Eriksson and Ebba Renck; m. 1st Lill-Inger Ingman 1953; m. 2nd Jane Friedmann 1982; one s. one d.; ed. Uppsala Univ.; Literary Ed. Göteborgs Handels-och Sjöfarts-Tidning 1956–62; Chief Cultural Ed. Stockholms-Tidningen 1962–66; theatre critic, Dagens Nyheter 1966–68; Dir. Stockholms Stadsteater 1967–69, 1975–90; Prin. Dramatiska Institutet 1969–73; Artistic Leader, Ländsteatern i Dalarna 1974–77; now freelance author and dir.; Swedish Theatre Critics' Award 1985; Elsa Thulin Prize 1990. *Publications:* I samma plan (essays) 1966; plays: Volpone 1969, Pariserliv 1975, En Skandal i Wien 1978, Freden 1987; essays; radio plays; translations of about 100 plays by Shakespeare, Molière, Racine, Beckett, etc.

ERIKSSON, Per-Olof, M.SC.ENG.; Swedish business executive; b. 1 March 1938, Seglora; s. of Gunhild Eriksson and Herbert Eriksson; m. Helena Eriksson Joachimsson 1962; two s. one d.; ed. Royal Inst. of Tech., Stockholm; Dir. and Head of Production and Materials Control, Sandvik Coromant 1975; Pres. Seco Tools AB 1976; Pres. and C.E.O. Sandvik AB 1984–94; mem. Bd. Sandvik AB, Skanska AB, SKF AB, Custos AB, Volvo AB, Sv. Handelsbanken AB, Swedish Steel AB, Preem Petroleum AB, Sphinx-Gustavsberg NV; Chair. Swedish Nat. Grid; Hon. Dr. Tech. *Leisure interests:* orienteering, skiing, hunting and sailing. *Address:* Sandvik AB, S-811 81 Sandviken; Hedåsvägen 57, S-811 61 Sandviken, Sweden (Home). *Telephone:* 26 26 10 01 (Office); 26 27 02 02 (Home).

ERKEBAYEV, Abdygany, DR. PHIL. SC.; Kyrgyzstan politician; b. 1953, Kara-Tent, Osh Region; m.; two s. one d.; ed. Kyrgyz State Univ.; jr. researcher, Inst. of World Literature U.S.S.R. Acad. of Sciences 1976–82; sr. teacher Kyrgyz Women's Pedagogical Inst. 1982–85; Deputy Ed. Kyrgyzstan Madanyaty (newspaper), Dir., Inst. of Language and Literature Kyrgyz Acad. of Sciences 1985–90; Deputy Supreme Soviet Kyrgyz S.S.R. 1990–91; Minister of Press and Information Kyrgyz Repub. 1991–92; Vice-Prime Minister 1992–93; Head, Osh Region Admin. 1993–95; mem. Ass. of People's Repub. of Zhokorgu Kenesh, Chair. Cttee. on Social Problems 1995–97; Chair. 1997–; Chair. Interparl. Cttee. of Russia, Belarus, Kazakhstan, Kyrgyzstan (Union of Four); mem. Nat. Acad. of Sciences Kyrgyz Repub. *Publications:* 4 books and over 100 articles and reviews on problems of literature, arts and politics. *Address:* Zhokorgu Kenesh, 720003 Bishkek, Kyrgyzstan. *Telephone:* (996) 21 89 35 (Office).

ERKMEN, Hayrettin, D.ECON.S.; Turkish economist and politician; b. 19 April 1915, Giresun; s. of Ali and Rahime Erkmen; m. Münire Babaoglu 1955; two s.; ed. Ankara School of Political Sciences, Geneva School of Econs. and Lausanne School of Law; Reporter, Bd. of Financial Research, Ministry of Finance 1948; Asst. Prof. of Econs. Univ. of Istanbul 1949; M.P. 1950–60, Minister of Labour 1953–55, 1957–58, of Commerce 1958–60, of Reconstruction (acting) 1959–60, of Foreign Affairs 1979–80; mem. Nat. Assembly (Dem. Party) before 1960; mem. Senate (Justice Party) 1975–80; Chair. Bd. Import-Export Bank of Turkey 1984; Leader Democrat Party 1992; arrested after mil. coup 1960, found guilty on political charges 1961. *Publication:* La participation des salariés à la gestion de l'entreprise 1948. *Address:* Arifi Paşa Korusu 11/5, 80810 Bebek, Istanbul, Turkey.

ERLANDE-BRANDENBURG, Alain; French museum curator; b. 2 Aug. 1937, Luxeuil les Bains; s. of Gilbert Erlande and Renée Pierra; m. Anne-Bénédicte Mérel 1980; four c.; Curator musée de Cluny and musée d'Ecouen 1967, Chief Curator 1981; Dir. of Studies école pratique des hautes études 1975; Prof. école du Louvre; Assoc. Prof. Ecole Nationale des Chartes 1991; Asst. Dir. Musées de France 1987–92; Head Musée Nat. du Moyen-Age 1991–94; Assoc. Prof. Ecole Nationale des Chartes 1991–; Pres. Soc. française d'archéologie; Dir. French Archives, Ministry of Culture and the French Language 1994–98; Pres. French Soc. of Archaeology 1985–94, Nat. Soc. of French Antique Dealers 1995–; Officier Ordre nat. du mérite, Légion d'honneur, Officier des arts et lettres. *Publications:* Paris monumental 1974, Le roi est mort 1975, Les rois retrouvés 1977, La Dame à la licorne 1978, La cathédrale d'Amiens 1982, L'abbaye de Cluny 1982, L'art gothique 1984, Chartres 1986, La conquête de l'Europe 1260–1380 1987, La cathédrale 1989, Notre-Dame de Paris 1991, Quand les cathédrales étaient peintes 1993, Histoire de l'architecture française: Du Moyen Age à la Renaissance 1995. *Address:* 10 bis rue du Pré-aux-clercs, 75007 Paris; Impasse de l'abbaye, 77120 Beautheil, France.

ERLO, Louis Jean-Marie (pseudonym of Louis Camerlo); French theatre director; b. 26 April 1929, Lyons; one s.; ed. Ecole de la Martinière and Ecole Nat. Professionnelle, Lyons; Asst. producer, Opéra de Lyon 1951, producer 1953, Dir. 1969–; Dir. Opéra-Studio, Paris 1973–79; mem. Conseil de développement culturel 1971–73; Dir. Aix-en-Provence Festival 1982; has produced operas in many of the maj. houses of Europe and in San Francisco and Buenos Aires and also for TV (especially works by Wagner); Chevalier, Légion d'honneur, Ordre nat. du Mérite, Commdr. des Arts et des Lettres. *Address:* Théâtre de l'Opéra, 69001 Lyon, France.

ERNAUX, Annie; French writer; b. 1 Sept. 1940, Lillebonne, Seine-Maritime; d. of the late Alphonse Duchesne and Blanche Dumenil; m. Philippe Ernaux 1964; two s.; ed. Lycée Jeanne-d'Arc, Rouen, Univs. of Rouen, Bordeaux and Grenoble; teacher of literature Annecy, Haute-Savoie 1965–75, higher educ.), Leroy 1975–; Prix Renaudot 1984. *Publications include:* Les armoires violes 1974, La femme gelée 1984, La place 1984, Une femme 1988, Passion simple 1992, La honte 1997. *Address:* 23 rue des Lozères, 95000 Cergy, France. *Fax:* (1) 30.31.27.74.

ERNI, Hans; Swiss painter; b. 21 Feb. 1909, Lucerne; m. Doris Kessler 1949; one s. two d.; ed. Académie Julien, Paris and Vereinigte Staatsschulen für freie und angewandte Kunst, Berlin; mem. Groupe Abstraction-Création, Paris; mem. S.W.B.; exhbns. Lucerne, Paris, Basel, Oxford, Liverpool, London, Cambridge, Leicester, Zürich, Milan, Rotterdam, Prague, Stockholm, Chicago, New York, Rome, Copenhagen, Tokyo, San Francisco, Los Angeles, Washington, Mannheim, Cologne; abstract mural picture Swiss section Triennale Milan, frescoes Lucerne; great mural Switzerland for Swiss Nat. Exhbn. Zürich 1939; Great Murals Exposition internationale de l'Urbanisme et de l'Habitation Paris 1947, Mural in Bernese hospital Montana; mem. Alliance Graphique Int.; Int. Prize at the Biennale del Mare 1953; great mural at the Musée Ethnographique, Neuchâtel 1954; has illustrated bibliophile edns. of classics by Plato, Pindar, Sophocles, Virgil, Buffon, Renard, Valéry, Homer (Odyssey), Albert Schweitzer (La Paix), Voltaire (Candide), Paul Eluard, etc.; murals for Int. Exhbn. in Brussels 1958; mosaics for the Abbey of St. Maurice 1961, for Swiss T.V. and Radio Building, Berne 1964; Engraved glass panels "Day and Night" and "Towards a Humanistic Future" for the Société des Banques Suisses, Geneva, 1963; exhbns. in Japan and Australia 1963, 1964, Pro Juventute stamps 1965; murals in Rolex Foundation, Union de Banques Suisses, Sion 1966, for Swissair Zürich, and La Placette Geneva 1967; exhbns. in Chicago, New York, Geneva 1966–68. *Publications:* Wo steht der Maler in der Gegenwart? 1947, Erni en Valais 1967, Israel Sketchbook 1968. *Leisure interest:* art. *Address:* 6045 Meggen, Lucerne, Switzerland. *Telephone:* 041-371382.

ERNST, Richard R., DR.SC.TECH.; Swiss professor of physical chemistry; b. 14 Aug. 1933, Winterthur; s. of Robert Ernst and Irma Brunner; m. Magdalena Kielholz 1963; one s. two d.; ed. Edgenössische Technische Hochschule Zürich (ETH-Z); Scientific Collaborator, Physical-Chem. Lab., ETH-Z 1962–63; Scientist, Varian Assocs., Palo Alto, Calif., U.S.A. 1963–68; tutor, then Asst. Prof., Assoc. Prof., ETH-Z 1968–76, Prof. of Physical Chem. 1976–; mem. Editorial Bd. various journals on magnetic resonance; Pres. Research Council of ETH-Z 1990–94; Vice-Pres. Bd. Spectrospin AG, Fällanden 1989–; Fellow American Physical Soc.; mem. Schweizer Chemikerverband, Int. Soc. of Magnetic Resonance, Schweizerische Chemische Gesellschaft, Deutsche Akademie der Naturforscher Leopoldina, Academia Europaea, Schweizerische Akademie der Technischen Wissenschaften, N.A.S. (U.S.A.), Royal Soc. London; Dr. h.c. (ETH-Lausanne) 1985, (Zürich) 1994, (Antwerp) 1997; Hon. Dr.rer.nat. (Munich Tech. Univ.) 1989; several awards including Benoist Prize 1986, John Gamble Kirkwood Medal, Yale Univ. 1989, Ampere Prize 1990, Wolf Prize for Chem., Jerusalem 1991, Nobel Prize for Chem. 1991. *Leisure interests:* music, Tibetan art. *Address:* Laboratorium für Physikalische Chemie, ETH-Zentrum, 8092 Zürich (Office); Kurlistr. 24, 8404 Winterthur, Switzerland (Home). *Telephone:* (052) 2427807 (Home); (01) 6324368 (Office). *Fax:* (01) 6321257 (Office).

EROĞLU, Derviş, PH.D.; Turkish-Cypriot politician; b. 1938, Ergazi Magosa Dist.; four c.; ed. Univ. of Istanbul; fmr. urologist, Ankara; mem. Parl. 1976–; Chair. Ulusal Birlik Partisi (Nat. Unity Party) 1981–; Prime Minister, "Turkish Repub. of Northern Cyprus" 1985–93, Aug. 1996–. *Address:* Office of the Prime Minister, Lefkoşa (Nicosia), Mersin 10; National Unity Party, 9 Atatürk Meydanı, Lefkoşa (Nicosia), Mersin 10, "Turkish Republic of Northern Cyprus".

ERRERA, Gérard; French diplomatist; b. 30 Oct. 1943, Brive; s. of Paul Errera and Bella Montekio; m. Virginie Bedoya-Calvo; three c.; ed. Inst. d'Etudes Politiques and Ecole Nat. d'Admin. Paris; First Sec. Washington, D.C. 1971–75; Special Adviser to Minister of Foreign Affairs 1975–77, 1980–81; Political Counsellor, Madrid 1977–80; Consul-Gen. San Francisco 1982–85; Dir. of Int. Relations, French Atomic Energy Comm. and Gov. for France, IAEA 1985–90; Amb. to Conf. on Disarmament, Geneva 1991–95; Amb. and Perm. Rep. to NATO, Brussels 1995–98; Jt. Sec.-Gen. and Dir.-Gen. of Political Affairs and Security, Ministry of Foreign Affairs 1998–; Chevalier, Ordre Nat. du Mérite. *Leisure interests:* skiing, tennis, guitar. *Address:* Director of Political Affairs and Security, Ministry of Foreign Affairs, 37 quai d'Orsay, 75007 Paris, France.

ERRINGTON, Stuart Grant, C.B.E., M.A.; British financier and business executive; b. 23 June 1929, Liverpool; s. of Sir Eric Errington Bt., and Lady (Marjorie) Errington; m. Anne Baedeker 1954; two s. one d.; ed. Rugby School, Trinity Coll., Oxford; nat. service 1947–49; Man., Ellerman Lines Ltd. 1952–59; various positions, to Jt. Man. Dir., Astley Industrial Trust Ltd. 1959–70; various positions, to Chair. and Chief Exec., Mercantile Credit Co. Ltd. (now Mercantile Group PLC) 1970–89; Dir. Kleinwort Overseas Investment Trust PLC 1982–, Northern Electric PLC 1989–96, Nationwide Building Soc. (mem. 1989–, Vice-Chair. 1995–); Chair. Equipment Leasing Asscn. 1976–78, Finance Houses Asscns. 1982–84, Europe Fed. of Leasing Asscns. 1978–80; Chair. Nat. Asscn. of Citizens' Advice Bureaux 1989–94; mem. Council Royal Holloway 1989– (Vice-Chair. 1995–). *Leisure interests:* fishing, golf, reading. *Address:* Earleywood Lodge, Ascot, Berks., SL5 9JP, England.

ERRO, Gudmundur; Icelandic artist; b. 19 July 1932, Olafsvik; s. of Gudmundur Einarsson and Soffia Kristiansdottir; m. Bat Yosef 1958 (divorced 1969); one c.; ed. Oslo, Ravenna, Florence; painter since 1956, over 135 personal exhbns. and has participated in over 250 jt. exhbns.; Gold Medal (Sweden), Falcon Medal (Iceland), Officier d'arts et lettres. *Leisure interests:* travelling (Far East), food, Cuban cigars. *Address:* 39 rue Fondary, 75015 Paris, France. *Telephone:* 01-45-75-26-33. *Fax:* 01-45-75-26-33.

ERROLL OF HALE, 1st Baron (cr. 1964) of Kilmun in the County of Argyll; **Frederick James Erroll,** P.C., M.A. C.ENG., F.I.E.E., F.I.MECH.E.; British politician; b. 27 May 1914, London; s. of late George Murison Erroll; m. Elizabeth Sowton Barrow 1950; ed. Oundle School and Trinity Coll., Cambridge; served in engineering industry 1936–39; war service, Tank Div., reached rank of Col. 1939–45; M.P. for Altrincham and Sale 1945–64; Parl. Sec. Ministry of Supply 1955–56, Bd. of Trade 1956–58; Econ. Sec. Treasury 1958–59; Minister of State, Bd. of Trade 1959–60; Privy Counsellor 1960–; Pres. Bd. of Trade 1961–63; Minister of Power 1963–64; mem. Nat. Econ. Development Council 1962–63; Chair. Bowater Corpn. 1973–84, Consolidated Gold Fields 1976–82 (Pres. 1982–89); Chair and Dir. of several other cos. 1965–; Pres. London Chamber of Commerce 1966–69, Vice-Pres. 1969–; mem. of the Council of Inst. of Dirs. 1949–55, 1965, Chair. 1973–76, Pres. 1976–84, Chancellor 1984–87; Deputy Chair. Decimal Currency Bd. 1966–71; Pres. of the British Export Houses Asscn. 1968–72, Hispanic and Luso-Brazilian Councils 1969–73, U.K.-S.A. Trade Asscn. 1979–84; Vice-Pres. Inst. of Marketing 1983–92; Chair. Cttee. on Liquor Licensing 1971–72, Automobile Asscn. 1974–86 (Vice-Pres. 1986–); Conservative. *Address:* House of Lords, London, SW1A 0PW, England.

ERSBØLL, Niels, LL.M.; Danish diplomatist; b. 9 April 1926, Copenhagen; m. Birgitte Ullerup; two s. five d.; joined Ministry of Foreign Affairs 1955, Head of Div. 1964–67, Dir. Secr. for Econ. Affairs 1967–73, State-Sec. for Econ. Affairs 1977–78; Embassy Sec. Del. to NATO, Paris 1958–60, Mission to EFTA and GATT, Geneva 1963–64, Amb. Perm. Rep. to EC, Brussels 1973–77; served in the EFTA Secr., Geneva 1960–63; Chair. Govt. Bd. Int. Energy Agency 1978–80; Sec.-Gen. EU (fmrly EC) Council, Brussels 1980–94; Hon. K.C.M.G.; numerous mil. awards. *Address:* Rungstedvej 36, 2970 Hørsholm, Denmark; Gachard, Montfaucon, 46240 La Bastide Murat, France.

ERSHAD, Lieut.-Gen. Hossain Mohammad; Bangladeshi politician and fmr. army officer; b. 1 Feb. 1930, Rangpur; s. of the late Maqbul Hussain and of Begum Majida Khatun; m. Raushan Ershad 1956; one s. one adopted d.; ed. Univ. of Dacca, Officers' Training School, Kohat, Pakistan; first appointment in 2nd East Bengal Regt. 1952; several appointments in various units including Adjutant, East Bengal Regt. Centre, Chittagong 1960–62; completed staff course, Quetta Staff Coll. 1966; promoted Lieut.-Col. 1969; Commdr. 3rd East Bengal Regt. 1969–70, 7th East Bengal Regt. 1971–72; Adjutant-Gen. Bangladesh Army; promoted Col. 1973; attended Nat. Defence Coll., New Delhi, India 1975; promoted Brig. 1975, Maj.-Gen. 1975; Deputy Chief of Army Staff 1975–78, Chief 1978–86; rank of Lieut.-Gen. 1979; led mil. takeover in Bangladesh March 1982; Chief Martial Law Administrator and Pres. Council of Ministers 24 March 1982, adopted title of Prime Minister Oct. 1982, of Pres. of Bangladesh Dec. 1983, elected Pres. of Bangladesh Oct. 1986, resigned Dec. 1990; also Minister of Defence 1986–90, of Information 1986–88; fmrly. in charge of several ministries including Home Affairs; Chief Adviser Bangladesh Freedom Fighters' Asscn.; Chair. Bangladesh Olympic Asscn., Bangladesh Lawn Tennis Fed.; UN Population Award 1987; sentenced to ten years' hard labour on charges of keeping unlicensed firearms, acquitted after appeal 1995; to a further ten years for illegally amassing money 1992; to seven years' imprisonment for graft 1993. *Leisure interests:* golf, writing poems, art, literature and oriental music.

ERSKINE, Ralph, C.B.E., A.R.I.B.A., A.M.T.P.I., S.A.R.; British architect; b. 24 Feb. 1914, Mill Hill, London; s. of George and Mildred (née Gough) Erskine; m. Ruth Monica Francis 1939; one s. two d.; ed. Friends' School, Saffron Walden, Essex, Regent Street Polytechnic, London, and Konst. Akad., Stockholm; own practice in Sweden 1939–, branch office in Byker, Newcastle upon Tyne 1969–; engaged in city renewals plans, new library for Stockholm Univ., town planning, designs for flats, private houses, housing estates, industrial buildings, churches, shopping centres, and homes for the elderly; designed Hall of Residence, Clare Coll., Cambridge, England; studies and research in architectural problems on building in subarctic regions; sketches: town site, Resolute, N.W.T., Canada; Guest Prof. at Technical School, Zürich; lectures in Netherlands, Japan, Canada, Sweden, Finland, Poland, Denmark, Switzerland, Austria, Germany, Norway, Russia, England, France, Italy and America; has participated in exhbns. in Sweden, Canada, Netherlands, Denmark, Norway and Switzerland; foreign mem. Royal Swedish Acad. of Arts; Hon. A.I.A., Dr.Tech. (Lund Univ.) 1970; Hon. D.Litt. (Heriot Watt Univ., Edinburgh) 1982; Kasper Salin Prize (Sweden), Ytong Prize 1974; medal: litteris et artibus 1980; Gold Medal (Royal Architecture Inst. of Canada) 1982; Wolf Prize for Architecture 1984; Royal Gold Medal (Royal Inst. of British Architects) 1987. *Publications:* contrib. to architectural magazines, etc. *Leisure interests:* skiing, skating, sailing. *Address:* Box 156, Gustav III's väg 4, 17802 Drottingholm, Sweden.

ERTL, Josef; German politician; b. 7 March 1925, Oberschleissheim; s. of Adolf Ertl and Magdalena Wagner; m. Paula Niklas 1953; three s.; ed. Technical Univ. of Munich; nat. labour service, mil. service as pilot in support aviation wing (cadet); agric. labourer and apprentice; joined Bavarian State Ministry of Food, Agric. and Forests 1952; Dir. Youth Advisory Service until 1959; Head, Agricultural School, Miesbach 1959; Dir., Office of Agric., Miesbach 1960; Sr. Agricultural Counsellor 1960; mem. Bundestag 1961–87; Land Vice-Chair. 1963; Fed. Minister of Food, Agric. and Forestry 1969–83; Vice-Chair. Parl. Free Democrats 1971–83 (retd.), Hon. Pres. 1983–; Pres. German Agricultural Soc. 1984–; Chair. Bavarian FDP 1971–83; Hon. Chair. 1983–; Hon. Senator Univ. of Soil Culture, Vienna; Dr. h.c. (Tokyo); Grosskreuzverdienstorden; numerous foreign decorations; Free Democrat. *Publications:* 1000 Fragen für den jungen Landwirt, Agrarpolitik Ohne Illusionen. *Leisure interests:* skiing, hunting, sailing, swimming, historical literature and biographies, classical music, painting. *Address:* Auerstrasse 20, 83707 Bad Wiessee/Obb, Germany. *Telephone:* (08022) 8870.

ERWA, Lieut.-Gen. Elfaith Mohamed; Sudanese diplomatist; b. 11 May 1950, Khartoum; m. Kawther Amin Mohamed 1973; seven c.; ed. Sudan Military Coll.; fmr. pilot; Adviser to Pres. of Repub. 1989–90; State Minister in the Presidency for Nat. Security 1990–95, for Nat. Defence 1995–96; Amb., Perm. Rep. to UN July 1996–; Order of Bravery. *Leisure interests:* flying, reading, computers. *Address:* 655 Third Avenue, Suite 500-10, New York, NY 10021, U.S.A. *Telephone:* (212) 573-6033. *Fax:* (212) 573-6160.

ERWIN, Alexander, B. ECON. (HONS.); South African politician, academic and trade union official; b. 17 Jan. 1948; ed. Durban High School, Univ. of Natal; lecturer Dept. of Econs., Univ. of Natal 1971–78; visiting lecturer Centre of Southern African Studies, Univ. of York 1974–75; Gen. Sec. Trade Union Advisory and Co-ordinating Council 1977–79; Gen. Sec. Fed. of S.A. Trade Unions 1979–81; Br. Sec. Nat. Union of Textile Workers 1981–83; Educ. Sec. Fed. of S.A. Trade Unions 1983–85; Educ. Sec. Congress of S.A. Trade Unions 1986–88; Nat. Educ. Officer Nat. Union of Metalworkers 1988–93; Interim Exec. mem. ANC S. Natal Region 1989; Br. Exec. mem. ANC Western Areas Br. 1990–91; fmr. mem. Devt. and Reconstruction Cttee., Natal Peace Accord; fmr. Congress of S.A. Trade Unions rep. at Nat. Econ. Forum; fmr. Ed. ANC Reconstruction and Devt. Programme; Deputy Minister of Finance 1994; Minister of Trade and Industry 1996–. *Address:* Ministry of Trade and Industry, 11th Floor, Prinsloo Street, Pretoria 0002; Private Bag X274, Pretoria 0001, South Africa (Office). *Telephone:* 12-322-7677 (Office). *Fax:* 12-322-7851 (Office).

ERZEN, Jale Nejdet, M.F.A., PH.D.; Turkish art historian and artist; b. 12 Jan. 1943, Ankara; d. of Nejdet Erzen and Selma Erzen; ed. Art Center Coll. of Design, L.A.; mem. staff Faculty of Architecture Middle East Tech. Univ. 1974–, Prof. of History of Art and Aesthetics 1992–; Ed. Boyut Fine Arts Journal 1980–84; f., Pres. SANART Asscn. (for promotion of visual arts in Turkey) 1991–; Sec.-Gen. Int. Asscn. for Aesthetics 1995; also consultant for various architectural journals; Chevalier, Ordre des Arts et des Lettres. *Publications include:* books on Sinan, Sabri Berkel, Erol Akyavas, Mehmet Aksoj; various articles on aesthetics, modern art, Ottoman architecture. *Leisure interests:* gardening, horse-riding, poetry. *Address:* Faculty of Architecture, Middle East Technical University, Ankara 06531 (Office); Kennedy Cad. 42/A, K. Esat 06660, Ankara, Turkey (Home).

ESAKI, Leo, PH.D.; Japanese scientist; b. 12 March 1925, Osaka; s. of Soichiro Esaki and Niyoko Ito; m. 1st Masako Araki 1959; one s. two d.; m. 2nd Masako Kondo 1986; ed. Univ. of Tokyo; with Sony Corpn. 1956–60, conducted research on heavily-doped Ge and Si which resulted in the discovery of tunnel diode; with IBM Corpn., U.S.A. 1960–92, IBM Fellow 1967–92, IBM T. J. Watson Research Center, New York, 1960–92, Man. Device Research 1962–92; Dir. IBM-Japan 1976–92, Yamada Science Foundation 1976–; Pres. Univ. of Tsukuba, Ibaraki, Japan 1992–98; Chair. Science and Tech. Promotion Foundation of Ibaraki 1998–; Sir John Cass Sr. Visiting Research Fellow, London Polytechnic 1981; major field of research is nonlinear transport and optical properties on semiconductors, junctions, thin films, etc., currently involved on man-made semiconductor quantum structures grown by an advanced ultra-high vacuum evaporation system: a computer-controlled molecular-beam epitaxy; mem. Japan Acad. 1975, American Philosophical Soc. 1991, Max-Planck Gesellschaft 1984; Foreign Assoc. N.A.S. 1976, American Nat. Acad. of Engineering 1977; Nishina Memorial Award 1959, Asahi Press Award 1960, Toyo Rayon Foundation Award 1961, Morris N. Liebmann Memorial Prize 1961, Stuart Ballantine Medal, Franklin Inst. 1961, Japan Acad. Award 1965, Nobel Prize for Physics 1973, Order of Culture, Japanese Govt. 1974, U.S.-Asia Inst. Science Achievement Award 1983, American Physical Soc. Int. Prize for New Materials (with others) 1985, I.E.E.E. Medal of Honor 1991, Japan Prize 1998, Grand Cordon Order of Rising Sun (First Class) 1998. *Publications:* numerous articles in professional journals. *Address:* Science and Technology Promotion Foundation of Ibaraki, 2-1-6 Tsukuba, Ibaraki 305 (Office); 2484 Uenomuro, Tsukuba, Ibaraki 305, Japan (Home). *Telephone:* 0298 60 6801 (Office); 0298 57 7171 (Home). *Fax:* 0298 60 6802 (Office); 0298 50 6262 (Home).

ESCHENBACH, Christoph; German conductor and concert pianist; b. 20 Feb. 1940, Breslau (now Wrocław, Poland); ed. Musikhochschulen, Cologne and Hamburg; Musical Director of Philharmonic Orchestra, Ludwigshafen 1979–83; Leader and Chief Artistic Dir. Tonhalle Orchestra, Zürich 1982–86; 1st Prize, Steinway Piano Competition 1952, Munich Int. Competition 1962, Clara Haskil Competition 1965; has appeared with Vienna Symphony, London Philharmonic, Royal Philharmonic and Tonhalle Orchestras, Radio Orchestras of Hamburg, Munich, Stuttgart, Israel Philharmonic and Israel Chamber Orchestras, NHK Orchestra Tokyo, Houston Symphony, Atlanta Symphony and Houston Opera Orchestras, Musical Dir. Houston Symphony Orchestra 1988–, Ravinia Festival 1994–; Prin. Conductor NDR Symphony Orchestra 1998–. *Address:* c/o Columbia Artists Management Inc., 165 West 57th Street, New York, NY 10019, U.S.A.

ESCHENMOSER, Albert, DR. SC. NAT.; Swiss chemist; b. 5 Aug. 1925, Erstfeld; s. of Alfons and Johanna (née Oesch) Eschenmoser; m. Elizabeth Baschnonga 1954; two s. one d.; ed. Collegium Altdorf, Kantonsschule St. Gallen, Swiss Federal Inst. of Technology, Zürich; Privatdozent, Organic Chemistry, Swiss Fed. Inst. of Technology 1956, Assoc. Prof. of Organic Chemistry 1960, Prof. Organic Chemistry 1965; Prof. Skaggs Inst. for Chemical Biology, La Jolla, Calif. 1996; Foreign Hon. mem. American Acad. of Arts and Sciences 1966; Foreign Assoc. Nat. Acad. of Sciences, U.S.A. 1973; mem. Deutsche Akademie der Naturforscher Leopoldina (Halle) 1976; Hon. Fellow, Royal Soc. Chem. (London) 1981; Foreign mem. Royal Soc. 1986, Pontifical Acad. (Vatican) 1986, Akad. der Wissenschaften (Göttingen) 1986, Acad. Europaea 1988, Croatian Acad. of Sciences and Arts 1994; Hon. mem. Gesellschaft Oesterreichischer Chemiker 1997; Hon. Dr. rer. nat. (Fribourg) 1966, Hon. D.Sc. (Chicago) 1970, (Edinburgh) 1979, (Bologna) 1989, (Frankfurt) 1990, (Strasbourg) 1991, (Harvard) 1993; Kern Award, Swiss Fed. Inst. of Technology 1949, Werner Award, Swiss Chemical Soc. 1956, Ruzicka Award, Swiss Fed. Inst. of Technology 1958, Fritzsche Award, American Chemical Soc. 1966, Marcel Benoist Prize (Switzerland) 1973, R. A. Welch Award in Chemistry (Houston, Texas) 1974, Kirkwood Medal (Yale) 1976, A.W.V. Hofmann-Denkmünze, GDCh 1976, Dannie-Heinemann Prize (Akademie der Wissenschaften, Göttingen) 1977, Davy Medal (Royal Soc., London) 1978; Tetrahedron Prize (Pergamon Press) 1981, G. Kenner Award (Univ. of Liverpool) 1982, Arthur C. Cope Award (American Chemical Soc.) 1984, Wolf Prize in Chemistry (Israel) 1986, Cothenius Medal (Akad. Leopoldina) 1991, Nakanishi Prize, Chemical Soc. of Japan 1998; Orden pour le mérite für Wissenschaften und Künste (Bonn) 1992, Österreich. Ehrenzeichen für Wissenschaften und Kunst (Vienna) 1993. *Publications:* numerous articles on organic synthesis in professional journals. *Address:* Bergstrasse 9, 8700 Küsnacht (ZH), Switzerland. *Telephone:* 9107392.

ESCHERICH, Rudolf Johann, DR.RER.POL; German business executive; b. 27 Oct. 1923, Wegscheid, Bavaria; m. Helga Koch 1959; one s. one d.; ed. Univ. of Munich; Chair. Man. Bd. Vereinigte Aluminium-Werke AG 1976–85, Chair. Supervisory Bd. 1986–91 (mem. 1991–), Man. Bd. VIAG 1975–. *Leisure interests:* flying, golf, tennis, skiing. *Address:* Drachenfelsstrasse 13, 53757 St. Augustin, Germany (Home). *Telephone:* St. Augustin 22596 (Home).

ESCOBAR CERDA, Luis; Chilean economist; b. 10 Feb. 1927; m. 2nd Helga Koch 1973; five c.; ed. Univ. de Chile and Harvard Univ.; Dir. School of Econs., Univ. de Chile 1951–55, Dean of Faculty of Econs. 1955–64; Minister of Econ. Devt. and Reconstruction 1961–63; mem. Inter-American Cttee. for Alliance for Progress 1964–66; Exec. Dir. Int. Monetary Fund 1964–66, 1968–70, IBRD 1966–68; Special Rep. for Inter-American Orgs. IBRD 1970–75; Trustee of Population Reference Bureau 1968–73; mem. Advisory Cttee. on Population and Devt. OAS 1968–73, Council Soc. for Int. Devt. 1969–72; Deputy Exec. Sec. Joint Bank/Fund Devt. Cttee. 1975–79; Prof. Georgetown Univ. 1975–79, George Washington Univ. 1977, Dept. of Econs., American Univ. 1978–79; C.E.O. private banks 1979–84; Minister of Finance 1984–85; Amb. to UN and Int. Orgs. in Geneva 1986–90; Consultant on Econ. and Financial Matters 1990–; Prof. Univ. of Chile 1990–, Dean, Faculty of Business Admin., Iberoamerican Univ. for Sciences and Tech. 1997–; Vice-Pres. Partido Radical Social Democrata 1994–95. *Publications:* The Stock Market 1959, Organization for Economic Development 1961, A Stage of the National Economic Development 1962, Considerations on the Tasks of the University 1963, Organizational Requirements for Growth and Stability 1964, The Role of the Social Sciences in Latin America 1965, The Organization of Latin American Government 1968, Multinational Corporations in Latin America 1973, International Control of Investments 1974, External Financing in Latin America 1976, 1978, Mi Testimonio 1991, Financial Problems of Latin American Economic Integration 1992; articles in newspapers. *Address:* 1724 Sánchez Fontecilla, Santiago 10, Chile. *Telephone:* (2) 2080227. *Fax:* (2) 6716920.

ESCOBEDO, Helen (Elena), A.R.C.A.; Mexican sculptor; b. 28 July 1934, Mexico City; d. of Manuel G. Escobedo and Elsie Fulda Escobedo; m. 1st Fredrik Kirsebom (divorced 1982); one s. one d.; m. 2nd Hans-Jürgen Rabe 1995; ed. Univ. of Motolinia, R.C.A.; Dir. of Fine Arts Nat. Univ. of Mexico 1961–74, Dir. of Museums and Galleries 1974–78; Tech. Dir. Nat. Museum of Art, Mexico 1981–82; Dir. Museum of Modern Art, Mexico 1982–84; mem. Espacio Escultorico design team 1978–79; Guggenheim Fellowship; assoc. mem. Acad. Royale de Belgique; Tlatilco Prize for Sculpture. *Designs include:* Gateway to the Wind, Olympic Highway 68, 1968, Signals, Auckland Harbour 1971, Jerusalem Cone, Jerusalem 1986. *Publication:* Mexican Monuments, Strange Encounters 1989. *Leisure interests:* reading, writing. *Address:* Mühlenberger Weg 16, 22587 Hamburg, Germany (March–Sept.); 1A Cerrada de San Jerónimo 19, Mexico 10200 D.F., Mexico (Oct.–Feb.). *Telephone:* (40) 86-16-90 (Hamburg); (5) 595-0941 (Mexico). *Fax:* (5) 683-4699 (Mexico).

ESCOVAR SALOM, Ramón; Venezuelan politician; b. 1926, Lara State; mem. Nat. Congress 1947; Minister of Justice; Rep. to Lara State Legis. Assembly; mem. Senate; Sec.-Gen. of the Presidency 1974–75; Minister of Foreign Affairs 1975–77; Amb. to France 1986–89; Attorney-Gen. of Venezuela 1989–95; Perm. Rep. to UN 1997–. *Address:* Permanent Mission of Venezuela to United Nations, 335 E. 46th Street, New York, NY 10017, U.S.A.

ESKÉNAZI, Gérard André, M.B.A.; French business executive; b. 10 Nov. 1931, Paris; s. of Roger Eskénazi and Léone Blanchard; m. Arlette Gravelin 1964; three s. one d.; ed. studies in law and business admin.; joined Banque de Paris et des Pays-Bas (now Banque Paribas) 1957, Pres. Cie Financière de Paribas 1978–82; Chair. of Bd. and Chair. Exec. Cttee. of Pargesa S.A. 1985–90; Deputy Chair. and Pres. Groupe Bruxelles Lambert S.A. 1982–90; Chair. Parfinance 1986–90; Deputy Chair. Banque Bruxelles Lambert 1982–90; Chair. Compagnie Industrielle Pallas (COMIPAR) 1991–95; Chair. Banque Pallas Stern 1993–95; mem. Bd. Pallas Invest; Chevalier, Légion d'honneur and Ordre nat. du mérite. *Leisure interest:* horse riding. *Address:* 68 rue de Faubourg Saint-Honoré, 75008 Paris (Office); 7 rue Maurice Ravel, 92210 Saint Cloud, France (Home). *Telephone:* (1) 53.05.28.30 (Office).

ESKOLA, Antti Aarre, PH.D.; Finnish professor of social psychology; b. 20 Aug. 1934, Urjala; m. Riti Laakso 1958; one s. one d.; ed. Univ. of Helsinki; Prof. of Sociology, Univ. of Turku 1965; Prof. of Social Psychology, Univ. of Tampere 1966; Research Prof., Acad. of Finland 1982–87. *Publications:* Social Influence and Power in Two-Person Groups 1961, Blind Alleys in Social Psychology 1988, several other studies, textbooks, essay collections and a novel. *Address:* c/o University of Tampere, Department of Sociology and Social Psychology, P.O. Box 607, 33101 Tampere, Finland.

ESMENARD, Francis; French publisher; b. 8 Dec. 1936, Paris; s. of Robert Esmenard and Andrée Michel; one s.; Pres., Dir.-Gen. Éditions Albin Michel 1982–, Paris; Vice-Pres. Nat. Publishing Syndicat 1979–. *Address:* Éditions Albin Michel, 22 rue Huyghens, 75014 Paris, France (Office). *Telephone:* 42-79-10-00. *Fax:* 43-27-21-58.

ESPERT ROMERO, Nuria; Spanish actress and director; b. 11 June 1935, Hospitalet (Barcelona); m. Armando Moreno 1955; two d.; professional actress since 1947; first maj. success in Medée aged 19; created her own co. 1959; has appeared in works by Calderón, Shakespeare, O'Neill, Cope, De Vega, Genet, Lorca, Espriu, Valle Inclán, Sartre etc.; dir. The House of Bernarda Alba (Lorca) with Glenda Jackson and Joan Plowright, London 1986 (Evening Standard Drama Award); has also dir. operas Madame Butterfly, Elektra, Rigoletto, La Traviata and Carmen at Covent Garden and in Scotland, Brussels, Israel and Japan; more than 100 Spanish honours and awards; 17 int. awards. *Publications:* numerous int. theatre publications. *Leisure interests:* resting, thinking, reading. *Address:* Pavia 2, 28013 Madrid, Spain. *Telephone:* (1) 5414851; (64) 412239.

ESPINASSE, Jacques Paul, M.B.A.; French business executive; b. 12 May 1943, Ales; s. of Gustave Espinasse and Andrée Bernadel; m. Daniele Samat 1964; one s. one d.; ed. Univ. of Michigan; financial analyst, London and Brussels 1967–70; Consultant, Science Man. Int. 1970–73; Head, Control Dept. Renault Véhicules Industriels 1973–78, Commercial Man. in charge of export in Europe 1979; Head, Int. Treasury Dept. Régie Renault 1980; Financial Officer, Sommer Allibert 1981–82; Chief Financial Officer, CEP Communication 1982–85; Chief Financial Officer, Havas 1985–87, Exec. Vice-Pres. 1987–93; Consultant 1994–. *Leisure interest:* golf. *Address:* 29 boulevard Suchet, 75016 Paris, France. *Telephone:* (1) 45.27.86.65. *Fax:* (1) 45.24.23.78.

ESPY, Mike; American politician; b. 1953, Yazoo City, Miss.; m. (divorced); one s. one d.; ed. Howard Univ., Washington, D.C., Univ. of Santa Clara Law School, Calif.; fmrly. attorney with Cen. Miss. Legal Services and Asst. Sec. of public lands div. of Miss.; Asst. Attorney-Gen., Miss. 1984–85; elected to U.S. House of Reps. 1986; fmr. mem. House Agric. Cttee., Budget Cttee. and Select Cttee. on Hunger; Sec. of Agric. 1993–94; mem. Nat. Rifle Asscn.

Address: c/o U.S. Department of Agriculture, 14th Street and Independence Avenue, S.W., Washington, DC 20520, U.S.A.

ESQUIVEL, Manuel, P.C.; Belizean politician and teacher; b. 2 May 1940, Belize City; s. of John and Laura Esquivel; m. Kathleen Levy 1971; one s. two d.; ed. Loyola Univ., U.S.A., Univ. of Bristol, England; teacher at St. John's Junior Coll., Belize City–1984; f. United Democratic Party 1973, Chair. 1976–82; fmr. Councillor, Belize City Council; mem. Senate 1979–84; Prime Minister of Belize 1984–89, 1993–98, also Minister of Finance, fmrly. of Defence and of Econ. Devt.; Leader of the Opposition 1989–93; Dr. h.c. (Loyola Univ., U.S.A.) 1986. *Address:* c/o United Democratic Party, 19 King Street, P.O. Box 1143, Belize City, Belize.

ESSAAFI, M'Hamed; Tunisian diplomatist; b. 26 May 1930, Kelibia; m. Hedwige Klat 1956; one s. one d.; ed. Sorbonne, Paris; First Sec., London 1956; Counsellor, then Minister plenipotentiary, Ministry of Foreign Affairs 1960–64; Amb. to U.K. 1964–69; Sec.-Gen. Ministry of Foreign Affairs 1969–70, 1976–78; Amb. to U.S.S.R. 1970–74, to Fed. Germany 1974–76, to Belgium, Luxembourg and EEC 1978–79; Perm. Rep. to UN Jan.–Aug. 1980; UN Sec.-Gen.'s Special Rep. for Humanitarian Affairs in S.E. Asia 1980–81; Chef de Cabinet of UN Sec.-Gen. Jan.–June 1982; UN Under-Sec.-Gen. and Disaster Relief Co-ordinator 1982–92; Grand Officier, Ordre de la République tunisienne; Chevalier, Ordre de l'Indépendance. *Address;* c/o Ministère des Affaires Etrangères, Tunis, Tunisia.

ESSBERGER, Ruprecht; German television director and writer; b. 8 March 1923, Berlin; s. of Eduard Essberger and Hedwig Schülthes; m. 1st Alexandra Massenberg 1949 (divorced 1962); two s.; m. 2nd Merle Insanali 1969; one d.; ed. Univs. of Hamburg and Göttingen; asst. television dir. North German Rundfunk 1950, television dir. 1953; freelance television dir. and writer 1957–. *television series include:* Familie Schölermann 1955–60, Das Fernsehgericht tagt 1960–78, Ehen vor Gericht 1970–83, 1989–96, Verkehrsgericht 1983–95, Bundesverdienstkreuz 1989; Golden Screen, Golden Rose and Golden Camera awards. *Leisure interests:* music, sailing. *Address:* Agnesstrasse 2, 22301 Hamburg, Germany.

ESSER, Otto; German business executive; b. 1 June 1917; Partner and Man. E. Merck, Darmstadt; Vice-Chair. Fed. of Employers, German Chem. Industry; Pres. Confederation of German Employers' Asscns. (BDA) 1977–86. *Address:* Am Forstweg 1, 63906 Erlenbach, Germany.

ESSEX, David, O.B.E.; British singer, actor and composer; b. 23 July 1947, London; s. of Albert and Doris Cook; m. Maureen Neal 1971; one s. one d.; started in music industry 1965; TV debut on Five O'Clock Club; has since made numerous TV appearances in U.K., Europe and U.S.A., including own BBC series 1977, The River BBC1 Series 1988; appeared on stage in repertory and later in Godspell 1971, Evita 1978, Childe Byron, Mutiny! (also wrote music) 1985, with Sir Peter Hall's Co. in She Stoops to Conquer tour and Queen's Theatre, London 1993–94; wrote score for Russian All Stars Co.'s Beauty and the Beast 1995–96; albums include: Rock On 1974, All the Fun of the Fair 1975, Out on the Street 1976, Gold and Ivory 1977, Imperial Wizard 1979; Hot Love 1980, Be Bop the Future 1981, Stage Struck 1982, The Whisper 1983, This One's For You 1984 (all solo); Under Different Skies (album of musicians from developing countries); War of the Worlds (with Jeff Wayne, Richard Burton and others), From Alpha to Omega (with Cat Stevens) 1978, Silver Dream Racer (film soundtrack: composer/producer) 1979, Centre Stage 1986, Touching the Ghost 1989, David Essex Greatest Hits 1991, Cover Shot 1993, Back to Back 1994; first concert tour of U.K. 1974, subsequent tours 1975 (including Europe, U.S.A. and Australia), 1976, 1977, 1978, 1979 (including Europe and U.S.A.), 1980, 1987, 1988, 1989/90 (World Tour); films include: Assault, All Coppers Are . . . 1971, That'll Be The Day (Variety Club Award) 1973, Stardust 1974, Silver Dream Racer 1979, Shogun Mayeda 1991; numerous gold and silver discs for LP and single records in Europe and U.S.A.; voted Best Male Singer and Outstanding Music Personality in Daily Mirror poll 1976; Variety Club of G.B. Award for Show Business Personality of the Year (joint) 1978 ASCAP Award 1989; BASCA Award for Composer 1994; Amb. for Voluntary Service Overseas 1990–92; Pres. Stanstead Park Cricket Club. *Leisure interests;* motorcycling, cricket, squash, flying helicopters. *Address:* c/o London Management, 2–4 Noel Street, London, W1V 3RB, England. *Telephone:* 0171-287 9000. *Fax:* 0171-287 3036.

ESSWOOD, Paul Lawrence Vincent, A.R.C.M.; British counter-tenor singer; b. 6 June 1942, Nottingham; s. of Alfred W. Esswood and Freda Garatt; m. 1st Mary L. Cantrill 1966 (dissolved 1990); two s.; m. 2nd Aimée Désirée Blattmann 1990; one s. one d.; ed. West Bridgford Grammar School and Royal Coll. of Music; Lay Vicar, Westminister Abbey 1964–71; Prof. Royal Coll. of Music 1973–85, Royal Acad. of Music 1985–; co-founder, Pro Cantione Antiqua—A Cappella 1967; opera debut, L'Erismena, Univ. of Calif., Berkeley 1968; debut at La Scala, Milan with Zürich Opera in L'Incoronazione di Poppea and Il Ritorno d'Ulisse 1978; Scottish opera debut in Dido and Aeneas 1978; world premiere, Penderecki's Paradise Lost, Chicago Lyric Opera 1979, Philip Glass's Akhnaton, Stuttgart 1984, Herbert Will's Schlafes Bruder, with Zurich Opera 1996; world première, Schnittke's Faust Cantata, Vienna, 1986; Handel's Riccardo Primo, Covent Garden, 1991; has appeared at many maj. int. festivals; specialist in performance of baroque music and has made many recordings of works by Bach, Handel, Purcell, Monteverdi, Cavalli, Britten (Abraham and Isaac), folksongs etc.; Prof. at "Maîtrise de Notre Dame", Paris; Hon. R.A.M. 1990; Handel Prize (Germany) 1992. *Leisure interests:* gardening, apiculture. *Address:* Jasmine Cottage, 42 Ferring Lane, Ferring, West Sussex, BN12 6QT, England. *Telephone:* (01903) 504480. *Fax:* (01903) 504480.

ESSY, Amara; Côte d'Ivoirian diplomatist; b. 20 Dec. 1944, Bouake; m. Lucie Essy 1971; three s. three d.; head, Div. of Econ. Relations 1970; First Counsellor, Ivory Coast Embassy, Brazil 1971–73, Ivory Coast Mission to the UN 1973–75; Perm. Rep. to the UN Office, Geneva 1975–81, to UNIDO, Vienna 1975–81; Amb. to Switzerland 1978–81; Perm. Rep. to the UN, New York 1981–91; Pres. UN Security Council 1990–91; Minister of Foreign Affairs 1990–; Pres. 49th Session UN Gen. Ass.; participated in the following UN confs.: Law of the Sea (Caracas, Geneva, New York), Int. Women's Year (Mexico City), Econ. Co-operation among Developing Countries, UNCTAD (Nairobi, Manila) and of the codification of int. law; meetings of the Econ. and Social Council and Comm. on Human Rights. *Address:* Ministry of Foreign Affairs, BP V109, Abidjan, Côte d'Ivoire. *Telephone:* 22-71-50. Fax: 33-23-08.

ESTEFAN, Gloria Maria; American singer and composer; b. 1 Sept. 1957, Havana, Cuba; d. of Jose Fajardo and Gloria Garcia; m. Emilio Estefan 1979; one s. one d.; ed. Univ. of Miami; went to U.S.A. 1959; composer of popular songs: Anything for You 1987, Live for Loving You 1991, Can't Forget You 1991, Coming Out of the Dark 1991, Always Tomorrow 1992, Go Away 1993; *albums include:* Primitive Love 1986, Let it Loose 1987, Cuts Both Ways 1990, Coming Out of the Dark 1991, Greatest Hits 1992, Mi Terra 1993, Destiny 1996; performed songs at Olympic Games, Seoul, S. Korea 1988, World Series Baseball, St Louis 1987, Pan American Games 1988, Superbowl Halftime, Minneapolis 1992; American Music Award 1987. *Address:* Estefan Enterprises Inc., 6205 Bird Road, Miami, FL 33155, U.S.A.

ESTERHÁZY, Péter; Hungarian writer and essayist; b. 14 April, 1950; s. of Mátyás Esterházy and Lili Mányoky; m. Gitta Reén; two s. two d.; ed. Budapest Univ.; full-time writer since 1978; Füst Milán, Déry, Kossuth, József Attila, Krúdy, Aszu, Vilenica awards. *Publications:* short stories: Pápai vizeken ne kalózkodj! 1977; Novels: Fancsikó és Pinta 1976, Termelési regény 1979, Függő 1981, Ki szavatol a lady biztonságáért? 1982, Kis magyar pornográfia 1984, A sziv segédigéi 1985, Bevezetés a szépirodalomba 1986, Tizenhét hattyúk (as Csokonai Lili) 1987, Hrabal könyve 1990, Hahn-Hahn grófnő pillantása (The Glance of Countess Hahn-Hahn Down the Danube) 1991, Egy nő (She Loves Me) 1995; Essays: A kitömött hattyú 1988, Az elefántcsonttoronyból 1991, A halacska csodálatos élete 1991, Egy kékharisnya följegyzéseiből 1994, Egy kék haris 1996. *Leisure interests:* football, mathematics. *Address:* c/o Hungarian Writers Federation, 1062 Budapest, Bajza-utca 18, Hungary. *Telephone:* 36 (1) 322-8840.

ESTES, William K., PH.D.; American behavioural scientist; b. 17 June 1919, Minneapolis, Minn.; s. of Dr. George D. Estes and Mona Kaye; m. Katherine Walker 1942; two s.; ed. Univ. of Minnesota; Medical admin. officer U.S. Army 1944–46; Faculty mem. Indiana Univ. 1946–62; Prof. of Psychology Stanford Univ. 1962–68; Ed. Journal of Comparative and Physiological Psychology 1962–68, Psychological Review 1977–82, Psychological Science 1990–94; Prof., Rockefeller Univ. 1968–79; Prof., Harvard Univ. 1979–89, Prof. Emer. 1989–; Pres. Experimental Div., American Psychological Asscn. 1958; Chair. Office of Scientific and Eng. Personnel, Nat. Research Council 1982–85; Chair., Cttee. on Contribs. of the Behavioral and Social Sciences to the Prevention of Nuclear War, N.A.S. 1985–89; Guggenheim Fellow 1985–86; Chair. Psychonomic Soc. 1972, Soc. for Math. Psychology 1984; mem. Soc. of Experimental Psychologists, N.A.S., American Acad. of Arts and Sciences, etc.; Distinguished Scientific Contribution Award of American Psychological Asscn. 1962, Warren Medal for Psychological Research 1963, Gold Medal for Lifetime Achievement in Psychological Science (American Psychological Foundation) 1992, Nat. Medal of Science (U.S.A.) 1997. *Publications:* An Experimental Study of Punishment 1944, Modern Learning Theory (with S. Koch and others) 1954, The Statistical Approach to Learning Theory 1959, Studies in Mathematical Learning Theory (with R. R. Bush) 1959, Stimulus Sampling Theory (with E. Neimark) 1967, Learning Theory and Mental Development 1970, Handbook of Learning and Cognitive Processes (ed.) 1975, Models of Learning, Memory, and Choice 1982, Statistical Models in Behavioral Research 1991, Classification and Cognition 1994. *Leisure interest:* music. *Address:* 95 Irving Street, Cambridge, MA 02138, U.S.A.

ESTEVE-COLL, Dame Elizabeth, D.B.E., B.A., F.R.S.A.; British fmr. museum director and university vice-chancellor; d. of P. W. Kingdon and Nora Kingdon; m. José Alexander Timothy Esteve-Coll 1960 (died 1980); ed. Birkbeck Coll., Univ. of London; librarian, London Borough of Merton, Kingston Coll. of Art, Kingston Polytechnic 1968–77; Head, Dept. of Learning Resources, Kingston Polytechnic 1977–82; Univ. Librarian Univ. of Surrey, Chair. Arts Cttee. 1982–85; Chief Librarian, Nat. Art Library, Victoria & Albert Museum 1985–87; Dir. Victoria & Albert Museum 1988–95; Vice-Chancellor Univ. of E. Anglia 1995–97; Assoc. Library Asscn.; Hon. Litt.D. (E. Anglia) 1997. *Publication:* The Victoria and Albert Museum (with others) 1992. *Address:* 27 Ursula Street, London, SW11 3DW, England. *Telephone:* 0171-652 3744.

ESTEVEZ, Emilio; American actor; b. 12 May 1962, New York; s. of Martin Sheen (q.v.); m. Paula Abdul (q.v.) 1992 (divorced 1994); one s. one d. *Films include:* Tex 1982, Nightmares 1983, The Outsiders 1983, The Breakfast Club 1984, Repo Man 1984, St. Elmo's Fire 1984, That was then . . . This is

Now 1985, Maximum Overdrive 1986, Wisdom 1986 (also wrote and dir.), Stakeout 1987, Men at Work 1989, Freejack 1992, Loaded Weapon 1993, Another Stakeout 1993, Champions II 1993, Judgement Night 1993, D2: the Mighty Ducks 1994, The Jerky Boys (co-exec. producer only), Mighty Ducks 3, Mission Impossible 1996, The War at Home 1996. *Address:* c/o UTA, 5th Floor, 9560 Wilshire Boulevard, Beverly Hills, CA 90212, U.S.A.

ESTIER, Claude; French journalist and politician; b. 8 June 1925, Paris; s. of Henri Ezratty and Luice Bernerbe; ed. Lycée Carnot, Paris; Political Ed. Le Populaire 1947; Ed. L'Observateur, France-Observateur, then le Nouvel Observateur 1950–; Ed. Le Monde 1955–58; Ed.-in-Chief Libération 1958–64, Dire 1968; mem. Nat. Assembly 1967–68, 1981–86; Pres. Comm. for Foreign Affairs 1983–86; mem. Paris City Council 1971–89; Nat. Press Sec. Socialist Party 1971–79; Editorial Dir. L'Unité (Socialist Party Weekly) 1972–86; mem. European Parl. 1979–81; Senator 1986; Pres. Senate Socialist Group 1988–. *Publications:* Pour l'Algérie 1963, L'Egypte en révolution 1965, Journal d'un Fédéré 1969, La plume au poing 1977, Mitterrand Président 1981, Veridique histoire d'un Septennat (with Veronique Neiertz) 1987, De Mitterand à Jospin: Trente ans de campagnes présidentielles 1995. *Address:* Palais du Luxembourg, 75291 Paris cedex 06, France.

ESTLEMAN, Loren Daniel, B.A.; American writer; b. 15 Sept. 1952, Ann Arbor, Mich.; s. of Leauvett C. Estleman and Louise A. Estleman; m. Deborah Ann Green 1993; one step-s. one step-d.; ed. Eastern Mich., Univ.; police reporter, Ypsilanti Press 1972–73; Ed.-in-Chief, Community Foto News 1975–76; Special Writer, Ann Arbor News 1976; staff writer, Dexter Leader 1977–80; full-time novelist 1980–; Western Writers of America Spur Award, Best Historical Novel 1981, Spur Award, Best Short Fiction 1986, 1996, Private Eye Writers of America Shamus Award, Best Novel 1984, Shamus Award, Best Short Story 1985, 1988, Mich. Foundation of the Arts Award for Literature 1987, Mich. Library Asscn. Authors Award 1997. *Publications: novels:* The Oklahoma Punk 1976, The Hider, Sherlock Holmes vs. Dracula 1978, The High Rocks 1979, Dr. Jekyll and Mr. Holmes, Stamping Ground, Motor City Blue 1980, Aces and Eights, Angel Eyes, The Wolfer 1981, Murdock's Law, The Midnight Man 1982, Mister St. John, The Glass Highway 1983, This Old Bill, Sugartown, Kill Zone, The Stranglers 1984, Every Brilliant Eye, Roses Are Dead, Gun Man 1985, Any Man's Death 1986, Lady Yesterday 1987, Bloody Season, Downriver 1988, Silent Thunder, Peeper 1989, Sweet Women Lie, Whiskey River 1990, Sudden Country, Motown 1991, King of the Corner 1992, City of Widows 1994, Edsel 1995, Stress 1996, Never Street, Billy Gashade 1997, The Witchfinder, Journey of the Dead, Jitterbug 1998, The Rocky Mountain Moving Picture Association 1999; *non-fiction:* The Wister Trace 1987; *collections:* General Murders 1988, The Best Western Stories of Loren D. Estleman 1989, People Who Kill 1993. *Leisure interests:* collecting books, records and old films on tape, hunting. *Address:* 5552 Walsh Road, Whitmore Lake, MI 48189, U.S.A.

ESTRADA, Joseph Marcelo Ejercito; Philippine politician; b. 19 April 1937, Tondo, Manila; Mayor of San Juan 1969–85; mem. Senate 1987, Vice-Pres. 1992; Chair. Partido ng Masang Pilipino (PMP); Pres. of the Philippines June 1998–. *Address:* Office of the President, Malacanang Palace Compound, J. P. Laurel Street, San Miguel, Metro Manila, Philippines. *Telephone:* (2) 5212301. *Fax:* (2) 7421641.

ESZTERHAS, Joseph A.; American scriptwriter; b. 23 Nov. 1944, Csakanydoroszlo, Hungary; s. of Stephen Eszterhas and Maria Biro; m. 1st Geraldine Javer 1972 (divorced 1994); one s. one d.; m. 2nd Naomi Baka 1994; one s.; ed. Ohio State Univ.; reporter, Plain Dealer, Cleveland; staff writer, Man. Ed. Rolling Stone, San Francisco 1971–75; screenwriter 1975–; writer and producer, Checking Out 1980, Betrayed 1989; recipient of various awards. *Publications:* books: Thirteen Seconds: Confrontation at Kent State 1970, Charlie Simpson's Apocalypse 1974, Nark! 1974, Fist 1977; screenplays: Fist 1978, Flashdance 1983, Jagged Edge 1985, Big Shots 1987, The Music Box 1990, Basic Instinct 1991, Sliver 1993, Showgirls 1995, Telling Lies in America 1997, Original Sin 1997, One Night 1997. *Leisure interest:* reading. *Address:* c/o McElwaine International Creative Management, 8942 Wilshire Boulevard, Beverly Hills, CA 90211, U.S.A.

ETAIX, Pierre; French film director and actor; b. 23 Nov. 1928, Roanne; s. of Pierre and Berthe (née Tacher) Etaix; m. 2nd Annie Fratellini 1969; ed. lycée; apprenticed as stained-glass designer; Asst. film producer 1949–55; small part in Robert Bresson's Pickpocket 1959; leading role in Jacques Tati's Jour de Fête, Paris Olympia 1960; Chevalier, Ordre nat. du Mérite, Ordre des Arts et des Lettres; directed first short film Rupture 1961; other short films; Heureux anniversaire 1962 (Acad. Award ("Oscar") for best short film 1963), Insomnie (First Prize, Oberhausen Festival 1965); full-length films: Le soupirant 1963 (Prix Louis Delluc, Prize for best humorous film, Moscow Festival 1963), Yoyo 1964 (Grand Prix de l'O.C.I.C., Grand Prix pour la Jeunesse, Cannes 1965), Tant qu'on a la santé 1966 (Coquille d'Argent, Saint-Sebastian Festival), Le grand amour 1969 (Grand Prix du Cinéma Français, Grand Prix de l'O.C.I.C. 1969), Les clowns 1970, Pays de cocagne 1971, Sérieux comme le plaisir 1975, Max mon amour 1986, L'âge de Monsieur est avancé (dir., wrote screenplay, actor). *Publications:* Vive la pub. 1984, Stars System 1986 (both jtly.). *Address:* Cirque Fratellini, 2 rue de la Clôture, 75019 Paris, France.

ETAYO MIQUEO, José Javier; Spanish professor of mathematics; b. 28 March 1926, Pamplona; s. of Nicolás Etayo and María Miqueo; m. Laura Gordejuela 1956; four s.; ed. Univs. of Valladolid, Zaragoza and Madrid; Prof. Univ. of Madrid 1952–61; Full Prof. Univ. of Zaragoza 1961–63; Full Prof. of Math. Univ. Complutense of Madrid 1963–91, Emer. Prof. 1991–; Vice-Dean Faculty of Sciences, Univ. of Madrid 1971–75; Pres. Real Soc. Matemática Española 1976–82; mem. Consejo Superior de Investigaciones Científicas 1969, Spanish Cttee. Int. Math. Union 1979–85; mem. Real Acad. de Ciencias de Madrid 1983–. *Publications:* Gen. math. and geometry textbooks, various math. research papers, especially in differential geometry. *Leisure interests:* reading, music, theatre, cinema. *Address:* Av. Reina Victoria, 70, 4 B, 28003 Madrid, Spain (Home). *Telephone:* 5541173 (Home).

ETCHEGARAY, A. E. Cardinal Roger, D.IUR.UTR.; French ecclesiastic; b. 25 Sept. 1922, Espelette; s. of Jean-Baptiste Etchegaray and Aurélie Dufau; ed. Petit Séminaire, Ustaritz, and Grand Séminaire, Bayonne; ordained priest 1947, served diocese of Bayonne 1947–60; Asst. Sec., then Sec.-Gen. French Episcopal Conf. 1961–70, Pres. 1975–81; Archbishop of Marseilles 1970–84; Pres. Council of European Episcopal Confs. 1971–79; Prelate, Mission of France 1975–81; cr. Cardinal 1979; Pres. Comm. Justice and Peace 1984–; Pres. Council Cor Unum 1984–95; Special Papal Emissary to Togo 1993; Pres. Cttee. for Grand Jubilee of Year 2000; Officier, Légion d'honneur, Commdr. l'Ordre nat. du Mérite. *Publications:* Dieu à Marseille 1976, J'avance comme un âne 1984, L'évangile aux couleurs de la vie 1987. *Address:* Piazza San Calisto, Vatican City. *Telephone:* 698 71 91.

ETCHEGARAY AUBRY, Alberto; Chilean politician and civil engineer; b. 5 May 1945; s. of Alberto Etchegaray and Odette Etchegaray; m.; five s., two d.; Univ. Prof. of Business Administration; Dir. Dept. of Studies, Unión Social de Empresarios Cristianos; co-ordinator of visit of Pope John Paul II to Chile; Dir. Hogar de Cristo; mem. Council, Semanas Sociales de Chile (initiative of Episcopal Conf. of Chile); Minister of Housing and Urban Devt. 1990–94; Pres. Nat. Council against Poverty 1994–98. *Address:* Canada 185-A, Providencia, Santiago, Chile.

ETCHEVERRY, Michel Adrien; French actor; b. 16 Dec. 1919, Saint-Jean-de-Luz; s. of Paul and Marie (née Manton) Etcheverry; m. Jacqueline Hebel 1947; one s. one d.; ed. Teacher Training Coll., Gironde, Conservatoire d'Art Dramatique, Bordeaux, Conservatoire National Supérieur d'Art Dramatique; began career as teacher, Saint-Sulpice-de-Faleyrens 1940; actor with Louis Jouvet 1945–51, appearing in productions including L'école des femmes, Knock, Le Diable et le bon Dieu, Pygmalion, L'alouette, Le journal d'Anne Frank, L'annonce faite à Marie; assoc. mem. Comédie-Française 1961–63, mem. 1963–, appearing in productions including Nicomède, Cinna, Polyeucte, L'avare, Marie Stuart, Le maître de Santiago, Le Cardinal d'Espagne, La reine morte, Le Cid, Le carrosse du Saint Sacrement, La Rabouilleuse, La soif et la faim, L'otage, L'école des femmes, Dom Juan, Malatesta, Le bourgeois gentilhomme, Georges Dandin, Un fil à la patte, L'impromptu de Marigny, C'est la guerre Monsieur Gruber, La nostalgie, Camarade, Le légataire universel, Le médecin malgré lui, La Célestine, La nuit des rois, Cinna, Monsieur le Trouhadec saisi par la débauche, La poudre aux yeux, On ne badine pas avec l'amour, Meurtre dans la cathédrale, Met en scène les Fausses Confidences. *Films include:* Le fils de Caroline Chérie, Notre-Dame de Paris, Le salaire du péché, C'est arrivé à Aden, Michel Strogoff, Recours en grâce, Vers l'extase, Le passage du Rhin, Le puits aux 3 vérités, Le petit garçon de l'ascenseur, Amours célèbres, Mathias Sandorf, Le tigre se parfume à la dynamite, Paris brûle-t-il?, Perceval le Gallois, I . . . comme Icare; numerous TV appearances including Les loups, La dévotion à la croix, Quatre-vingt treize, L'île mystérieuse, Un bourgeois de Calais, Cinna, Le Cid, Le roi Lear, Le fil rouge, Un bourgeois de Paris, Georges Dandin, Le Maître de Santiago, Le deuil sied à Electre, Le légataire universel, Le jeu de l'amour et du hasard 1976; Pres. French Actors' Union 1959, Membre du Droit 1963; Chevalier de la Légion d'honneur, Officier des Arts et des Lettres. *Address:* 47 rue du Borrégo, 75020 Paris, France.

ETEKI MBOUMOUA, William-Aurélien, LIC. EN DROIT; Cameroonian politician; b. 20 Oct. 1933, Douala; s. of Joseph Mboumoua and Mana Katta; m. Naimi Betty Eyewe; one s. one d.; ed. Ecole Nat. de la France d'Outremer, Paris; Prefect for Nkam 1959, for Sanage Maritime 1960–61; Minister of Educ., Youth and Culture 1961–68; mem. Exec. Council, UNESCO 1962–68, Pres. of Conf., UNESCO 1968–70; Special Adviser, with rank of Minister, to Pres. of United Republic of Cameroon 1971–74, 1978–80; Minister charged with Special Functions at the Presidency 1978; Co-Minister in charge of Missions 1980–84, Minister of Foreign Affairs 1984–87; Sec.-Gen. OAU 1974–78; Special Rep. of UN Sec.-Gen. on Small Arms Proliferation in West Africa; Nat. Pres. Cameroon Red Cross Soc.; Commdr. des Palmes académiques, and many other decorations. *Publications:* Un certain humanisme 1970, Démocratiser la culture 1974, and many articles on education and African culture. *Leisure interests:* literature, poetry, painting, tennis, football, swimming. *Address:* P.O. Box 1155, Yaoundé, Cameroon. *Telephone:* (237) 224177. *Fax:* (237) 231596.

ETIANG, Paul Orono, B.A.; Ugandan diplomatist; b. 15 Aug. 1938, Tororo; s. of Kezironi Orono and Mirabu Adacat Adeke; m. Zahra A. Foum 1967; two s. two d.; ed. Busoga Coll. and Makerere Univ. Coll.; District Officer, Provincial Admin. 1962–64; Asst. Sec., Ministry of Foreign Affairs 1964–65, Third Sec. 1965–66; Second Sec., Uganda Embassy, Moscow 1966–67; First Sec. Uganda Mission to UN 1967–68; First Sec. 1968; High Commr. to U.K. 1969–71; Chief of Protocol and Marshal of Diplomatic Corps, Uganda 1971–; Perm. Sec. Ministry of Foreign Affairs 1971–73, Acting Minister of Foreign Affairs May-Oct. 1973; Minister of State for Foreign Affairs 1973–74, Minister of State 1974–76, of Transport and Communications 1976–78, of Transport 1978–79, for Regional Co-operation 1988–89, of Commerce 1989–91, of Information 1996, Third Deputy Prime Minister 1996–, also Minister of Labour and Social Services 1996, Minister of Disaster Preparedness and Refugees 1998–; Asst. Sec.-Gen. OAU 1978–87. *Leisure interests:* billiards, badminton, music, theatre. *Address:* c/o Ministry of Labour and Social Services, P.O. Box 7009, Kampala, Uganda. *Telephone:* 242837.

ETIEMBLE, René, D. ÈS L.; French writer and professor of literature; b. 26 Jan. 1909, Mayenne; m. 2nd Jeannine Kohn 1963; one d.; ed. Lycée de Laval, Lycée Louis le Grand, Ecole Normale Supérieure and Fondation Thiers; Faculté de droit, Ecole des langues orientales; Prof. Univ. of Chicago 1937–43, Univ. of Alexandria, Egypt 1944–48, Univ. of Montpellier 1949–55; Prof. of Gen. and Comparative Literature, Univ. of Paris (Sorbonne) 1956–78, Hon. Prof. 1979; mem. Istituto Veneto di Scienze, Lettere ed Arti; Prix de la Première Pièce 1948, Prix de l'Essai, Acad. Française, Prix Int. du Livre 1981, Prix de l'Union Rationaliste 1982, Ecrivain de 1986, P.E.N. Club français, Prix Balzan-Comparatisme 1988. *Publications include:* Rimbaud (with Y. Gauclère) 1936, L'enfant de choeur 1937, Peaux de couleuvre 1948, Le mythe de Rimbaud (3 vols. 1952, 1955, 1958 Prix Sainte-Beuve de la Critique), Supervielle 1960, Blason d'un corps 1961, Parlez-vous franglais? 1964, Hygiène des lettres (5 vols.) 1952–67, Le nouveau singe pèlerin 1958, Le jargon des sciences 1966, Le sonnet des voyelles 1968, Retours du monde 1969, Mes contre-poisons 1974; on China: Confucius 1956, Le nouveau singe pèlerin 1958, Connaissons-nous la Chine 1964, Les Jésuites en Chine 1966, Yun Yu, l'érotique chinoise 1969, Essais de littérature (vraiment) générale 1974, Quarante ans de mon maoïsme 1976, Colloque sur la traduction poétique 1978, Philosophes Taoïstes 1980, Comment lire un roman japonais 1980, Trois femmes de race 1981, Quelques essais de litterature universelle 1982, Rimbaud: systéme solaire ou trou noir 1983, Le coeur et la cendre, soixante ans de poésie 1984, Racismes 1986, Confucius 551–1985, 1986, Goliath ou la marche du fascisme (trans.) 1986, L'Europe chinoise (2 vols.) 1987, 1989, Romanciers du XVIIIe siècle (2nd edn.) 1988, Ouverture(s) pour un comparatisme planétaire 1988, Lignes d'une Vie 1989, Le Meurtre du Petit Père 1990, Vingt-cinq ans après 1991, Parlez-vous franglais? 1992, Nouveaux essais de littérature universelle 1992. *Address:* La Paletière, 4 rue de la Paletière-Vigny, 28500 Vernouillet, France. *Telephone:* 37-38-38-26.

ETKIND, Efim Grigorievich; Russian literary scholar; b. 26 Feb. 1918, Petrograd (now St. Petersburg); s. of Grigori Etkind and Polina Spivak; m. Katherina Zvorykina 1940; two d.; ed. Leningrad Univ.; served in Soviet army in Second World War on Karelian and Ukrainian fronts; Candidate of Philol. Sc. 1947 (dissertation on Novels of Zola in 1860s); taught in Faculty of Romance Langs., Leningrad Pedagogical Inst. 1947–74; Dr. Philol. Sc. 1965 (dissertion on Theory of Translation); degrees and title of Prof. removed and expelled from U.S.S.R. Union of Writers for defence of various poets 1974; left U.S.S.R. Oct. 1974; Docteur d'État 1975 (Sorbonne; dissertation on Theory of Poetic Translation); now lives in Paris, and teaches at Université de Paris X; Corresp. mem. Bayerischen Akademie der Schönen Künste, Akad. der Wissenschaften und der Literatur zu Mainz, Deutschen Akad. für Sprache und Dichtung, Darmstadt. *Publications include:* Poetry and Translation 1963; Russian Poet-Translators from Trediakovsky to Pushkin 1973, The Substance of Verse and the Problems of the Theory of Translation 1974, Notes of a Non-Conspirator 1977 (Paris), Form as Content (articles) 1977 (Würzburg); Un art en crise (Essai d'une poétique de la traduction poétique) 1981; Russische Lyrik aus drei Jahrhunderten 1981, Anna Achmatowa 1982, Poésie russe (anthology) 1983, Russische Lyrik des 20. Jahrhunderts 1984, The Trial of Josef Brodsky 1988, Symmetrical Compositions by Pushkin 1988. *Address:* 31 Jardins Boieldieu, 92800 Puteaux, France.

ETO, Seishiro; Japanese politician; fmr. Parl. Vice-Minister of Agric., Forestry and Fisheries; mem. House of Reps. (fmr. Chair. Cttee. on Finance), fmrly. mem. House of Councillors; fmr. Sec.-Gen. LDP; Minister of State; Dir-Gen. Defence Agency 1995–96. *Address:* c/o Defence Agency, 9-7-45, Akasaka, Minato-ku, Tokyo 107, Japan.

ETO, Takami; Japanese politician; b. 1925; fmr. mem. Miyazaki Prefectural Ass., elected mem. House of Reps. for 1st Constituency Miyazaki Prefecture 1969; fmrly. Dir. House of Reps. Rules and Admin. Cttee., Parl. Vice-Minister of Agric., Forestry and Fisheries; Deputy Chair. Liberal Democratic Party Policy Research Council, Chair. Diet Affairs Cttee. 1984; Minister of Construction 1985–86, of Transport 1989–90; Dir.-Gen. Man. and Co-ordination Agency Aug.–Nov. 1995; Liberal Democratic Party. *Address:* c/o Liberal Democratic Party, 1-11-23, Nagata Cho, Chiyoda-ku, Tokyo 100, Japan.

ETOUNGOU, Simon Nko'o; Cameroonian diplomatist and politician; b. 14 Feb. 1932; ed. secondary and post-secondary schools, and diplomatic training in France; Head of Office in Ministry of Econ. Planning 1956–57; Cabinet Attaché, Ministry of Finance 1958–59; First Sec., Cameroon Embassy, Paris 1960; Minister-Counsellor 1960–61; Amb. to Tunisia 1961–64; led numerous Cameroon dels. 1963–64; concurrently Amb. to Algeria July-Nov. 1964, to U.S.S.R. 1964–65; Minister of Foreign Affairs 1965–66, 1968–70, Minister of Finance 1966–68; Amb. to Belgium, Netherlands and Luxembourg and Perm. Rep. to EEC 1971–79; Amb. to Algeria 1985–88, to France 1988–96; Kt. of Nat. Order of Merit (Cameroon), and decorations from Senegal, Tunisia, Fed. Repub. of Germany and Gabon. *Address:* c/o Ministry of Foreign Affairs, Yaoundé, Cameroon.

ETROG, Sorel, C.M.; Canadian sculptor; b. 29 Aug. 1933, Jassy, Romania; s. of Moshi Etrog and Toni Etrog; ed. Jassy High School and Tel Aviv Art Inst.; Brooklyn Museum Art School Scholarship 1958; first one-man show 1958; Canadian rep. Venice Biennale 1966; comms. include Los Angeles Co. Museum 1966, Canadian Pavilion, Expo 67, Olympic Centre, Toronto 1972, Bow Valley Square, Calgary 1975, SunLife Canada. Toronto 1984, Olympic Park, Seoul 1988; works now in numerous public collections including Nat. Gallery of Canada, Tate Gallery, London, Musée d'Art Moderne, Paris, Museum of Modern Art, New York, Stratford Shakespeare Festival Theatre, Stratford, Ont., etc.; one-man exhbns. in Montreal, Toronto, New York, Paris, London, Chicago, Los Angeles, Geneva, Amsterdam, Venice, Milan, Rome; designer and illustrator of books; wrote and dir. film Spiral (CBC) 1975; mem. Royal Canadian Acad., Arts and Letters Club; Hon. Fellow, Univ. Coll. of Swansea 1990; Chevalier des Arts et des Lettres. *Publications include:* Dream Chamber 1982, Hinges (play) 1983, The Kite 1984, Images from the film Spiral 1987. *Address:* Box 67034, 2300 Yonge Street, Toronto, Ont. M4P 1E0, Canada. *Telephone:* (416) 480-0109. *Fax:* (416) 480-2914.

ETTL, Harald; Austrian politician; b. 7 Dec. 1947, Gleisdorf, Styria; m.; two c.; ed. Higher Fed. Teaching and Experimental Coll. for Textile Industry, Vienna; Asst. to Works Man. Eybl carpet factory, Ebergassing; Sec., subsequently Cen. Sec. Textile, Garment and Leather Workers' Trade Union, Chair. 1984–; Minister for Health and the Civil Service 1989–92; fmr. Chair. Gen. Accident Insurance Scheme; Pres. Accident Insurance Cttee., Fed. of Austrian Social Insurance Bodies; Chair. Working Group for Integration in Austrian Trade Union Confed. *Address:* Textile, Garment and Leather Workers' Trade Union, Hohenstanfengasse 10, 1010 Vienna I, Austria. *Telephone:* (1) 534-44. *Fax:* (1) 534-44-498.

ETZWILER, Donnell Dencil, B.A., M.D.; American paediatrician; b. 29 March 1927, Mansfield, Ohio; s. of Donnell S. Etzwiler and Berniece J. Etzwiler; m. Marion Grassby Etzwiler 1952; one s. three d.; m. 2nd Helen B. Etzwiler 1989; ed. Indiana and Yale Univs.; Intern, Yale-Grace New Haven Community Hosp. 1953–54; Resident, New York Hosp., Cornell Medical Center 1954–55, N.I.H. Fellowship in Metabolism 1955–56; Instructor, Cornell Univ. Medical Coll., New York 1956–57; Clinical Prof., Univ. of Minn. School of Medicine 1957–; Pediatrician, Park Nicollet Medical Center, Minn. 1957–96; Medical Dir., Camp Needlepoint 1960–85; Pediatrician, Project Hope, Peru 1962; Founder, Pres. Int. Diabetes Center 1967–96, Pres. Emer. 1996–; Vice-Pres. Int. Diabetes Fed. 1979–85; Commr., Nat. Comm. on Diabetes 1975–76; Pres. American Diabetes Asscn. 1976–77; Dir. Diabetes Collaborating Center, WHO 1985–, Chair. 1988–94; Founder and mem. Bd. Compass Project Foundation, Pres. 1998–; mem. Bd., Park Nicollet Medical Foundation 1976–96, Diabetes Research Educational Foundation 1983–93, Diabetes Center Inc. 1985–, Int. Research and Educ. 1996–; Co-Dir. Int. Diabetes Programme (Russia) 1989–; Fellow, All India Inst. of Diabetes, Bombay 1979, Inst. of Medicine, N.A.S. 1982; Hon. mem. American Dietetic Asscn. 1980, American Asscn. of Diabetes Educators 1993, Russian Nat. Diabetes Fed. 1995; Banting Medal 1977, Upjohn Award 1983, Beckton Dickinson Camp Award 1979, Diabetes in Youth Award, American Diabetes Asscn. 1976, N.I.H. Certificate of Approval 1993; Peace Award (Russia) 1994, Charles H. Best Medal for Distinguished Service (American Diabetes Asscn.) 1994. *Publications:* Education Management of the Patient with Diabetes 1973, Diabetes Manual; Health Education for Living Program 1976, Living Well With Diabetes 1985; Ed. First International Workshop on Diabetes and Camping 1974, How to Live with Diabetes (in Russian) 1991; over 200 scientific articles in medical journals. *Leisure interests:* tennis, photography, travel. *Address:* 7611 Bush Lake Drive, Minneapolis, MN 55438, U.S.A. *Telephone:* (612) 942-8489. *Fax:* (612) 944-2537.

EUBANK, Chris; British middleweight boxer; b. 8 Aug. 1966, Dulwich; WBC Int. Middleweight Boxing Champion March–Nov. 1990 two defences; WBO Middleweight Boxing Champion Nov. 1990–Aug. 1991 three defences; WBO World Super-Middleweight Boxing Champion Sept. 1991–March 1995 fourteen defences, lost title to Steve Collins, Cork Sept. 1995, failed to regain title against Joe Calzaghe, Sheffield Oct. 1997; unsuccessful fights for WBO Cruiserweight title against Carl Thompson, Manchester April 1998, Sheffield July 1998. *Address:* 9 The Upper Drive, Hove, East Sussex, BN3 6GR, England.

EUSTACE, Sir Joseph Lambert; Saint Vincent and the Grenadines politician; b. 1908; b. 28 Feb. 1908; m. Faustina Gatherer 1945; one s. one d.; teacher; Man. St. Vincent Cotton Ginnery 1952–59; factory man.; M.P. for South Leeward 1966–71; Speaker House of Ass. 1972–74; Gov.-Gen. of St. Vincent and the Grenadines 1985–89. *Address:* c/o Government House, Montrose, Saint Vincent and the Grenadines, West Indies.

EVANGELISTA, Linda; Canadian fashion model; b. St. Catherine, Toronto; m. Gerald Marie (divorced 1993); endorses Diet Coke (French TV); face of Yardley Cosmetics; numerous catwalk fashion shows. *Address:* c/o Elite Model Management, 40 Parker Street, London, WC2B 5PH, England; Elite Model Management Corporation, 111 E. 22nd Street, Floor 2, New York, NY 10010, U.S.A. *Telephone:* 0171-333 0888 (London).

EVANGELOU, Alecos C.; Cypriot politician and lawyer; b. 23 July 1939, Kato Lakatamia; s. of Costas Evangelou and Theano A. Tsiappa; m. Nicoulla Protopapa 1965; one s. two d.; called to the bar, Gray's Inn, London 1967; worked in Nicosia Dist. Admin., later at Ministry of Finance; law officer, Attorney, Office of Attorney-Gen. 1972–93; fmr. Chair. Appropriate Authority for Intellectual Property; fmr. Pres. Supreme Sports Tribunal; Minister of Justice and Public Order 1993–97; now sr. partner Alecos Evangelou and Co. (law firm). *Leisure interest:* gardening. *Address:* P.O. Box 9238, Nicosia 1623; 16 Kyriacos Matsis Avenue, Eagle Star House, 7th Floor, Nicosia 1082, Cyprus.

EVANS, Chris; British broadcaster; b. 1966; Warrington; m. Carol McGiffin 1991 (divorced); after leaving school aged 16 had numerous jobs including shoeshop asst., forklift truck driver; fmr. broadcasting asst., Piccadilly Radio, Manchester, producer, GLR Radio, London, presenter, BSB satellite TV, TV-am, Don't Forget Your Toothbrush, co-presenter The Big Breakfast, Channel 4 TV; presenter BBC Radio 1 Breakfast Show 1995–97, Virgin Radio Breakfast Show 1997–; f. Ginger Productions 1992, took over Virgin Radio 1997; presenter TFI Friday, Channel 4 TV, Tee Time. *Address:* Ginger Productions, 131–151 Great Titchfield Street, London, W1P 8DP, England. *Telephone:* 0171-577 7100.

EVANS, Daniel Jackson, M.S.; American politician; b. 16 Oct. 1925, Seattle, Wash.; s. of Daniel Lester and Irma (Ide) Evans; m. Nancy Ann Bell 1959; three s.; ed. Roosevelt High School, Seattle, and Univ. of Washington; U.S.N.R. 1943–46; Lieut. on active duty Korean War 1951–53; Asst. Man. Mountain Pacific Chapter, Assoc. Gen. Contractors 1953–59; State Rep. King County 1956–64; Partner, Gray and Evans, structural and civil engineers 1959–64; Gov. Washington State 1965–77; Chair. Western Govs. Conf. 1968–69, Nat. Govs. Conf. 1973–74; Senator from Washington 1983–89; now involved with environmental work; mem. Advisory Comm. on Intergovernmental Relations 1972, Trilateral Comm. 1973; Keynote Speaker Republican Nat. Convention 1968; mem. Pres.'s Vietnamese Refugee Comm. 1974; mem. Nat. Center for Productivity and Quality of Working Life 1975–76; mem. Carnegie Council on Policy Studies in Higher Educ. 1977; Trustee Urban Inst. 1977, The Carnegie Foundation for the Advancement of Teaching 1977; Pres. Evergreen State Coll. 1977–83; Consultant Daniel J. Evans & Assocs., Seattle; Dir. Puget Sound Power and Light, Tera Computer Co., Burlington Northern/Santa Fe, Inc., Flow Int., WA Mutual Bank; Regent Univ. of Wash. 1993–; several hon. degrees; Nat. Municipal League Distinguished Citizen Award 1977; Republican. *Leisure interests:* skiing, sailing, mountain climbing. *Address:* Daniel J. Evans & Assocs., 1111 3rd Avenue, Suite 3400, Seattle, WA 98101, U.S.A.

EVANS, David (see The Edge).

EVANS, David Wyke, M.A.; Australian diplomatist; b. 13 March 1934, Adelaide; s. of Dr Mervyn W. Evans and Phyllis E. Evans; m. Pamela R. Stratmann 1959; two s. one d.; ed. Prince Alfred Coll., Adelaide, and Univs. of Adelaide and Oxford; joined Australian Commonwealth Public Service 1959; Third (later Second) Sec., Embassy in Jakarta 1962–65; First Sec. Australian Mission to UN, New York 1968–70; Counsellor, Belgrade 1970–72; High Commr. in Ghana (and Amb. to Senegal and Ivory Coast) 1974–77; Head of Information Branch, Dept. of Foreign Affairs 1977–79, Head of Europe, Americas and N.Z. Div. 1980; Amb. to U.S.S.R. (also accred. to Mongolia) 1981–83, to Turkey 1994–98; High Commr. in Malaysia 1984–87, in India 1990–94; Deputy High Commr. in U.K. 1987–90; Rhodes Scholar 1957. *Leisure interests:* tennis, golf. *Address:* 16 MacDonald Street, Paddington, N.S.W. 2021, Australia.

EVANS, Edwin C., B.S., M.D.; American physician; b. 30 June 1917, Milledgeville, Ga.; s. of Watt Collier and Bertha (Chambers) Evans; m. Marjorie Wood 1945; one s. five d.; ed. Univ. of Georgia, Johns Hopkins Univ. School of Medicine; Intern Hartford (Connecticut) Hosp. 1940–42; Medical Corps, U.S. army 1942–46; Chief Resident in Medicine, Baltimore City Hosp. 1946–47; Fellow in Pathology, Hosp. of Univ. of Pa. 1947-48; pvt. practice of Internal Medicine in Atlanta, Georgia 1948–87; Clinical Assoc. Prof. of Medicine, Emory Univ. School of Medicine, Atlanta 1972–87, Prof. Emer. 1987–; Adjunct Prof. of Medicine, Mercer Univ. School of Pharmacy, Atlanta 1980–87; Dir. of Geriatrics, Georgia Baptist Medical Center 1987–91; mem. N.A.S. Inst. of Medicine, and numerous medical asscns. *Publications:* a number of contributions to medical journals. *Leisure interest:* photography. *Address:* 500 Westover Drive, N.W., Atlanta, GA 30305, U.S.A. (Home). *Telephone:* (404) 355-2203 (Home).

EVANS, Gareth John, Q.C., M.A., LL.B.; Australian politician; b. 5 Sept. 1944, Melbourne; s. of late Allan O. Evans and of Phyllis Evans (née Le Boeuf); m. Merran Anderson 1969; one s. one d.; ed. Melbourne High School, Univ. of Melbourne, Magdalen Coll., Oxford; lecturer and Senior lecturer in Law, Univ. of Melbourne 1971–76; mem. Australian Reform Comm. 1975; Barrister-at-Law 1977–; Senator for Victoria 1978–96; 'Shadow' Attorney-Gen. 1980–83; Attorney-Gen. 1983–84; Minister for Resources and Energy, Minister Assisting the Prime Minister and Minister Assisting the Minister for Foreign Affairs 1984–87; Minister for Transport and Communications 1987–88, for Foreign Affairs 1988–96; Deputy Leader of Govt. in the Senate 1987–93, Leader 1993–96; MP for Holt, Vic. 1996–; Deputy Leader of Opposition, Shadow Treasurer 1996–98. *Publications:* Labor and the Constitution 1972–75 (Ed.) 1977, Law, Politics and the Labor Movement (Ed.) 1980, Labor Essays 1980, 1981, 1982 (Co-Ed.), Australia's Constitution—Time for Change? 1983 (Co-author), Australia's Foreign Relations 1991 (Co-author), Co-operating for Peace 1993. *Leisure interests:* reading, golf, tennis, travel. *Address:* Parliament House, Canberra, A.C.T. 2600, Australia.

EVANS, Gwynfor, M.A., LL.D.; Welsh politician; b. 1 Sept. 1912, Barry; s. of Dan and Catherine (née Richard) Evans; m. Rhiannon Prys Thomas 1941; four s. three d.; ed. Barry County School, Univ. Coll. of Wales, Aberystwyth, St. John's Coll., Oxford; qualified as solicitor 1939; Hon. Sec. Heddychwyr Cymru (Welsh Pacifist Movement) 1939–45; Chair. Union of Welsh Independents 1954; M.P. (Plaid Cymru), Carmarthen 1966–70, 1974–79; Pres. Plaid Cymru (Welsh Nationalist Party) 1945–81; mem. Carmarthen County Council 1949–74; past mem. Welsh Broadcasting Council; Fellow, Univ. Coll. Aberystwyth, Trinity Coll. Carmarthen; Hon. LL.D. (Univ. of Wales) 1973; Hon. Pres. Plaid Cymru. *Publications:* Plaid Cymru and Wales 1950, Rhagom i Ryddid 1964, Aros Mae 1971, Wales can Win 1973, Land of My Fathers 1974, A National Future for Wales 1975, Diwedd Prydeindod, Bywyd Cymro 1982, Seiri Cenedl 1986, Welsh Nation Builders 1988, Pe Bai Cymru'n Rhydd 1989, Fighting for Wales 1991, Heddychiaeth Gristnogol Yng Nghymru 1991, For the Sake of Wales 1996. *Address:* Talar Wen, Pencarreg, Llanybydder, Camarthenshire, Wales. *Telephone:* (01570) 480907.

EVANS, Harold J., PH.D.; American plant physiologist; b. 19 Feb. 1921, Franklin, Ky.; s. of James H. and Allie Evans; m. Elizabeth Dunn 1946; two d.; ed. Univ. of Kentucky and Rutgers Univ.; Asst. Prof., Assoc. Prof., Prof. of Botany, N. Carolina State Univ. 1950–60; Post-doctoral Fellow, Johns Hopkins Univ. 1952; Prof. of Plant Physiology, Oregon State Univ. 1961–89, Dir. Lab. for Nitrogen Fixation 1978–89, Distinguished Prof. of Plant Physiology Emer. 1989–; Visiting Prof. Univ. of Sussex 1967; George A. Miller Visiting Prof. Univ. of Illinois 1973; mem. Editorial Bd. Biofactors 1989–; Pres. American Soc. of Plant Physiologists 1971, mem. Bd. of Trustees 1977; mem. N.A.S. 1971–; Fellow American Acad. of Microbiology 1992; Hoblitzelle Nat. Award 1965, Oregon State Univ. Alumni Distinguished Prof. Award 1973, Univ. of Kentucky Distinguished Alumnus Award 1975, Milton Harris Research Award, George Ferguson Distinguished Prof. Award 1983, Charles Ried Barnes Award, American Soc. of Plant Physiologists 1985, Senior Humboldt Fellowship 1991. *Publications:* Nitrogen Fixation Research Progress (Co-ed.) 1985, Biology of Nitrogen Fixation (Co-Ed.) 1992; numerous articles in professional journals. *Leisure interests:* fishing, travelling, woodwork. *Address:* 14151 Redwood Court, Lake Oswego, OR 97034, U.S.A. *Telephone:* (503) 635-3870. *Fax:* (541) 737-3573.

EVANS, Harold Matthew, M.A.; American (b. British) publisher and fmr. newspaper editor and writer; b. 28 June 1928, Manchester, England; s. of Frederick and Mary Evans; m. 1st Enid Parker 1953 (divorced 1978); one s. two d.; m. 2nd Tina Brown (q.v.) 1982; one s. one d.; ed. Durham Univ.; Commonwealth Fund Fellow, Univ. of Chicago 1956–57; Ed. Sunday Times, London 1967–81, The Times 1981–82; mem. Bd. Times Newspapers Ltd., Dir. 1978–82; Int. Press Inst. 1974–80; Dir. Goldcrest Films and Television 1982–85; Ed.-in-Chief Atlantic Monthly 1984–86, Contributing Ed. 1986–, Editorial Dir. and Vice-Chair. 1998–; Ed. Dir. U.S. News and World Report 1984–86, Contributing Ed. 1986–, Editorial Dir. and Vice-Chair. 1998–; Vice-Pres. and Sr. Ed. Weidenfeld and Nicolson 1986–87; Adviser to Chair. Condé Nast Publications 1986–; Founding Ed.-in-Chief, Condé Nast Traveler 1986–90; Pres. and Publr. Random House Adult trade group 1990–97; Editorial Dir. Mortimer Zuckerman's media properties 1997–; Editorial Dir. and Vice-Chair. New York Daily News Inc. 1998–, Fast Co. 1998–; Hon. Visiting Prof. of Journalism City Univ. 1978–; Fellow, Soc. Industrial Artists, Inst. of Journalists; Dr. h.c. (Stirling); Journalist of the Year Prize 1973, Int. Ed. of the Year Award 1975, Inst. of Journalists Gold Medal Award 1979; Design and Art Dir., Pres.'s Award 1981, Ed. of Year Award, Granada 1982, Hood Medal, Royal Photographic Soc. 1981, Press Photographers of G.B. Award 1986. *Publications:* Active Newsroom 1964, Editing and Design, Newsman's English 1970, Newspaper Design 1971, Newspaper Headlines 1973, Newspaper Text 1973, We Learned to Ski (co-author) 1974, Freedom of the Press 1974, Pictures on a Page 1978, Suffer the Children (co-author), How We Learned to Ski 1983, Good Times, Bad Times 1983, Front Page History 1984, The American Century 1998. *Leisure interests:* music, table tennis, skiing. *Address:* U.S. News and World Report, 450 West 33rd Street, New York, NY 10001, U.S.A.

EVANS, John David Gemmill, PH.D., M.R.I.A.; British professor of philosophy; b. 27 Aug. 1942, London; s. of John Desmond Evans and Babette Evans; m. Rosemary Ellis 1974; ed. St Edward's School, Oxford, Queen's Coll., Cambridge; Research Fellow, Sidney Sussex Coll., Cambridge 1964–65, Fellow and lecturer 1965–78; Visiting Prof., Duke Univ., N. C. 1972–73; Dean of Arts Faculty, Queen's Univ., Belfast 1986–89, Prof. of Logic and Metaphysics 1978–, Dir. of School of Philosophical and Anthropological Studies 1987–; Bd. mem. Arts Council of Northern Ireland 1991–94; Council mem. Royal Inst. of Philosophy 1991–; Chair. U.K. Nat. Cttee. for Philosophy 1994–; mem. Exec. Cttee. Int. Fed. of Philosophical Socs. (FISP) 1988–. *Publications:* Aristotle's Concept of Dialectic 1977, Aristotle 1987, Moral Philosophy and Contemporary Problems 1987, Teaching Philosophy on the Eve of the Twenty-First Century 1997. *Leisure interests:* mountaineering, astronomy, travel, gardening. *Address:* 57 Ballynagarrick Road, Carryduff, Belfast, Northern Ireland, BT8 8JD.

EVANS, Leo Henry 'Rusty', B.A., B.ADMIN.; South African diplomatist; b. 12 Dec. 1943, Durban; s. of John Evans and Dorothy Redstone; m. 1st Kathleen Barbour 1967 (divorced 1989); three s. one d.; m. 2nd Gerda van Tonder 1989; one d.; ed. Christian Brothers' Coll. Kimberley and Univs. of Natal and S. Africa; entered Dept. of Foreign Affairs 1966; Third Sec. Lisbon 1967–70; Consul, Rio de Janeiro 1972; Consul-Gen. São Paulo 1976–78; Minister, Washington, D.C. 1980, London 1982; Dir. Ministry of Foreign Affairs 1986, Chief Dir. 1988, Deputy Dir.-Gen. Africa 1989, Deputy Dir.-

Gen. Overseas Countries 1991; Dir.-Gen. Dept. of Foreign Affairs 1992–; Order of Dom Infante Henriques (Portugal). *Leisure interests:* yachting, hunting. *Address:* c/o Department of Foreign Affairs, Private Bag X152, Pretoria 0001, South Africa. *Telephone:* (012) 325 0200 (Office). *Fax:* (012) 351 0257.

EVANS, Lloyd Thomas, A.O., M.AGR.SCI., D.PHIL., D.SC.; Australian botanist; b. 6 Aug. 1927, Wanganui, New Zealand; s. of Claude Evans and Gwendolyn Fraser; m. Margaret Newell 1954; two s. two d. (one deceased); ed. Wanganui Collegiate School, Univ. of Canterbury, New Zealand, and Brasenose Coll., Oxford; Rhodes Scholar 1951–54; Commonwealth Fund Fellow, Calif. Inst. of Tech. 1954–56; Research Scientist, Div. of Plant Industry, Commonwealth Scientific and Industrial Research Org. (CSIRO) 1956–, Chief 1971–78, now Hon. Research Scientist; N.A.S. Pioneer Research Fellow, U.S. Dept. of Agric., Beltsville, U.S.A. 1963–64; Overseas Fellow, Churchill Coll., Cambridge 1969–70; Visiting Fellow, Wolfson Coll., Cambridge 1978; Pres. Australian Soc. of Plant Physiologists 1971–73, Australian and New Zealand Asscn. for Advancement of Science 1976–77, Australian Acad. of Science 1978–82 (Fellow); mem. Bd. of Trustees, Int. Foundation for Science, Stockholm 1982–87, Int. Rice Research Inst., Philippines 1984–89, Int. Centre for Improvement of Wheat and Maize 1990–95; mem. Norwegian Acad. of Science and Letters; Hon. mem. Royal Soc., N.Z., Royal Agric. Soc., England; Hon. LL.D. (Canterbury) 1978; Fellow, Royal Soc., U.K.; Bledisloe Medal 1974, Farrer Medal 1979, other awards and prizes. *Leisure interests:* windsurfing, chopping wood, Charles Darwin. *Publications:* Environmental Control of Plant Growth 1963, The Induction of Flowering 1969, Crop Physiology 1975, Day-length and the Flowering of Plants 1975, Wheat Science—Today and Tomorrow 1981, Policy and Practice: Essays in Honour of Sir John Crawford 1987, Crop Evolution, Adaptation and Yield 1993, Feeding the Ten Billion: Plants and Population Growth 1998, over 150 research papers. *Address:* 3 Elliott Street, Campbell, Canberra, A.C.T. 2601, Australia. *Telephone:* (062) 477815.

EVANS, Martin John, PH.D., F.R.S.; British professor of mammalian genetics; b. 1 Jan. 1941, Stroud, Glous.; s. of Leonard Evans and Hilary Redman; m. Judith Evans 1966; two s. one d.; ed. St. Dunstan's Coll. Catford and Christ's Coll. Cambridge; Research Asst. Dept. of Anatomy and Embryology, Univ. Coll. London 1963–66, Asst. lecturer 1966–69, lecturer 1969–78; Univ. lecturer, Dept. of Genetics, Univ. of Cambridge 1978–91, Reader in Mammalian Genetics 1991, Prof. of Mammalian Genetics 1994–. *Publications:* 75 scientific publs. *Address:* Wellcome/CRC Institute, Tennis Court Road, Cambridge, CB2 1QR, England. *Telephone:* (01223) 334132. *Fax:* (01223) 334132.

EVANS, Matthew, C.B.E., B.SC.(ECONS.); British publishing executive; b. 7 Aug. 1941; s. of George Ewart and Florence E. Evans; m. 1st Elizabeth A. (née Mead) Evans 1966 (divorced 1991); two s.; m. 2nd Caroline Michel 1991; two s. one d.; ed. Friends' School, Saffron Walden and London School of Econs.; bookselling 1963–64; with Faber & Faber 1964–, Man. Dir. 1972–93, Chair. 1981–; Chair. Nat. Book League 1982–84, English Stage Co. 1984–90; mem. Council, Publishers' Asscn. 1978–84, Franco-British Soc. 1981–; Gov. B.F.I. 1982–97, Vice-Chair. 1996–97; Chair. Library and Information Comm. 1995–97; Dir. Which? Ltd. 1997–; mem. Arts Council Nat. Lottery Advisory Panel 1997–, Univ. for Industry Advisory Group 1997–, Royal Opera House Working Group 1997–. *Leisure interest:* cricket. *Address:* c/o Faber & Faber, 3 Queen Square, London, WC1N 3AU, England.

EVANS, Mostyn (Moss); British trade unionist; b. 13 July 1925; m. Laura Bigglestone 1947; three s. (one deceased) three d.; ed. Church Road Secondary Modern School, Birmingham; Union Official, Transport and Gen. Workers' Union: District Officer, Chemical and Eng. Industries, Birmingham 1956; Regional Officer, Midlands 1960, Nat. Officer, Eng. 1966; Nat. Sec. Chemical, Rubber and Oil Industries 1969, Eng. Industries 1969, Automotive Section 1969–73; Nat. Organizer T.G.W.U. 1973–78, Gen. Sec. T.G.W.U. 1978–85; Vice-Pres. Int. Chemical Workers Fed. (ICEF) 1980–82, Pres. ICEF 1982–; mem. TUC Gen. Council 1977–85, Int. Cttee. of TUC 1978–82, Chair. 1982–85; British Overseas Trade Bd. 1978–79; mem., Royal Inst. of Int. Affairs 1978–, of Council A.C.A.S. 1982–; Dir. Unity Trust 1984–; Councillor, Borough of King's Lynn and West Norfolk 1991–, Mayor 1996–97. *Address:* Cheney House, Cheney Hill, Heacham, King's Lynn, Norfolk, PE31 7BX, England. *Telephone:* (01485) 70477.

EVANS, Richard John, M.A., D.PHIL., LITT.D., F.R.HIST.SOC., F.B.A.; British historian; b. 29 Sept. 1947, Woodford, Essex; s. of late Ieuan Trefor Evans and of Evelyn Evans (née Jones); m. Elín Hjaltadóttir 1976 (divorced 1993); partner Christine L. Corton, two s.; ed. Forest School, London, Jesus Coll., Oxford, St. Antony's Coll., Oxford; lecturer in History, Stirling Univ. 1972–76; lecturer in European History, Univ. of E. Anglia 1976–83, Prof. 1983–89; Prof. of History, Birkbeck Coll., Univ. of London 1989–98; Vice-Master Birkbeck Coll. Univ. of London 1993–98, Acting Master 1997; Prof. of Modern History, Cambridge Univ. 1998–; Visiting Assoc. Prof. of European History, Col. Univ., New York 1980; Fellow Alexander von Humboldt Foundation, Free Univ. of Berlin 1981; Fellow Humanities Research Centre, A.N.U., Canberra, Australia 1986; Fellow Gonville and Caius Coll., Cambridge 1998; Hon. Fellow Jesus Coll., Oxford 1998; Stanhope Historical Essay Prize 1969, Wolfson Literary Award for History 1988, William H. Welch Medal, American Asscn. for the History of Medicine 1989, Hamburg Civic Medal for Arts and Sciences 1993, Fraenkel Prize in Contemporary History 1994. *Publications:* The Feminist Movement in Germany 1894–1933 1976, The Feminists 1977, Society and Politics in Wilhelmine Germany (Ed.) 1978, Death in Hamburg 1987, Comrades and Sisters 1987, Rethinking German History 1987, In Hitler's Shadow 1989, Kneipengespräche im Kaiserreich 1989, Proletarians and Politics 1990, Rituals of Retribution 1996, Rereading German History 1997, In Defence of History 1997, Tales from the German Underworld 1998. *Leisure interests:* gardening, music (playing the piano), reading, travelling. *Address:* Gonville and Caius College, Cambridge, CB2 1TA, England.

EVANS, Sir Richard Mark, K.C.M.G., K.C.V.O., M.A.; British diplomatist (retd.); b. 15 April 1928, British Honduras (now Belize); s. of late Edward Walter Evans and Anna Margaret Kirkpatrick Evans; m. 1st Margaret Elizabeth Sessinger 1960 (divorced 1970); m. 2nd Rosemary Grania Glen Birkett 1973; two s.; ed. Dragon School, Oxford, Repton School, and Magdalen Coll., Oxford; Third Sec., Peking 1955–57, Second Sec., London 1958–62, First Sec., Peking 1962–64, First Sec. (Commercial), Berne 1964–68, First Sec., London 1968–70, Head of Nr. Eastern Dept., FCO 1970–72 and Far Eastern Dept. 1972–74, Counsellor (Commercial), Stockholm 1975–77, Minister (Econ.), Paris 1977–79, Asst., then Deputy Under-Sec., FCO 1979–83, Amb. to People's Repub. of China 1984–88; Dir. Asia Opportunities Fund; Emer. Fellow, Wolfson Coll., Oxford 1995–. *Publication:* Deng Xiaoping and the Making of Modern China 1993. *Leisure interests:* music, reading, travel. *Address:* Sevenhampton House, Sevenhampton, Highworth, Wilts., SN6 7QA, England.

EVANS, Sir Robert, Kt., C.B.E., F.ENG., F.I.MECH.E., F.INST.E.; British engineer; b. 28 May 1927, Liverpool; s. of Gwilym Evans and Florence May Evans; m. Lilian Ward 1950; one s. one d.; ed. Old Swan Coll., Liverpool, City Tech. Coll., Liverpool, Blackburn Tech. Coll.; with North Western Gas Bd. 1950–56; Burmah Oil Co. 1956–62; Dir. of Eng., Southern Gas 1962–72; Deputy Dir. (Operations), Gas Council 1972; Dir. (Operations), British Gas Council 1972–75; Deputy Chair. North Thames Gas 1975–77; Chair. East Midlands Gas 1977–82; Man. Dir. for Supplies, British Gas PLC 1982–83, Chief Exec. 1983–92, Chair. 1989–93; Chair. Nat. Council for Hospice and Specialist Palliative Care Services; Hon. Fellow Inst. Gas Eng., City and Guilds of London Inst.; Companion Inst. of Man.; Freeman City of London 1974. *Leisure interest:* golf.

EVANS, Robert; American actor and film producer; b. 29 June 1930, Harlem, New York; s. of Josh Evans; m. 1st Ali McGraw (divorced); one s.; m. 2nd Phyllis George 1978 (divorced); child radio actor in more than 300 radio productions; partner women's clothing firm Evan-Picone 1952–67; ind. producer at 20th Century-Fox 1966–76; Vice-Pres. (Production) Paramount Pictures Corpn. 1966–69, Vice-Pres. (Worldwide Production) 1969–71, Exec. Vice-Pres. 1971–76; resigned to be ind. producer. *Films (as actor) include:* The Man of 1000 Faces 1957, The Sun Also Rises 1957, The Fiend Who Walked the West 1958, The Best of Everything 1959; *(as producer) include:* Chinatown 1974, Marathon Man 1976, Black Sunday 1977, Players 1979, Popeye 1980, Urban Cowboy 1980, Cotton Club 1984, The Two Jakes 1989, Sliver 1993, Jade, The Phantom, The Saint. *Publication:* The Kid Stays in the Picture 1994. *Address:* 242 North Beverly Drive, Beverly Hills, CA 90210, U.S.A.

EVANS, Robert John Weston, PH.D., F.B.A.; British historian; b. 7 Oct. 1943, Leicester; s. of T. F. Evans and M. Evans; m. Kati Robert 1969; one s. one d.; ed. Dean Close School, Cheltenham and Jesus Coll., Cambridge; Research Fellow, Brasenose Coll. Oxford 1968–97; Univ. Lecturer in Modern History of East-Central Europe, Oxford 1969–90, Reader 1990–92, Prof. of European History 1992–97, Regius Prof. of Modern History 1997–; ed. English Historical Review 1985–95; Fellow Austrian Acad. of Sciences 1997; Hon. Fellow Hungarian Acad. of Sciences 1995; Wolfson Literary Award for History 1980, Anton Gindely-Preis 1986 (Austria), František Palacký Medal 1991 (Czechoslovakia). *Publications:* Rudolf II and his World 1973; The Making of the Habsburg Monarchy 1979. *Address:* Oriel College, Oxford, OX1 4EW; 83 Norreys Road, Cumnor, Oxon., England (Home). *Telephone:* (01865) 277265 (Coll.).

EVANS, Sir (William) Vincent (John), G.C.M.G., M.B.E., Q.C., M.A., B.C.L.; British barrister-at-law; b. 20 Oct. 1915, London; s. of late Charles Evans and Elizabeth Jenkins; m. Joan Symons 1947; one s. two d.; ed. Merchant Taylors' School, Northwood, and Wadham Coll. Oxford; mil. service 1939–46, legal adviser, British Mil. Admin. Cyrenaica, rank of Lieut.-Col. 1945–46; Asst. Legal Adviser, Foreign Office 1947–54; Legal Counsellor, Perm. Mission of U.K. at UN, New York 1954–59; Deputy Legal Adviser, Foreign Office 1960–68; Legal Adviser, FCO 1968–75; U.K. Rep. on European Cttee. on Legal Cooperation, Council of Europe 1965–75, Chair. 1969–71; U.K. Rep. on Council of Europe Steering Cttee. on Human Rights 1976–80, Chair. 1979–80; mem. Human Rights Cttee. (Int. Covenant on Civil and Political Rights) 1977–84; Judge, European Court of Human Rights 1980–91; mem. Perm. Court of Arbitration 1987–97; Dir. (Chair.) Bryant Symons & Co. Ltd. 1964–85; mem. Council of Man., British Inst. of Int. and Comparative Law; Vice-Pres. Bd. of Govs. British Inst. of Human Rights; Vice-Pres. Hon. Soc. of Cymmrodorion; Hon. Fellow, Wadham Coll. Oxford; Hon. Bencher, Lincoln's Inn; Dr. h.c. (Essex) 1986. *Address:* 4 Bedford Road, Moor Park, Northwood, Middx., HA6 2BB, England. *Telephone:* (01923) 824085.

EVATT, Elizabeth Andreas, A.C., LL.M.; Australian lawyer; b. 11 Nov. 1933, Sydney; d. of Clive R. Evatt and Marjorie M. Evatt (née Andreas); m. Robert Southan 1960; one d.; ed. Univ. of Sydney and Harvard Univ.; called to Bar, Inner Temple; Chief Judge Family Court of Australia 1976–88; Deputy

Pres. Conciliation and Arbitration Comm. 1973–89, Australian Industrial Relations Comm. 1989–94; Pres. Australian Law Reform Comm. 1988–93, mem. 1993–94; mem. UN Nat. Cttee. on Elimination of Discrimination Against Women 1984–92, Chair. 1989–91; Chancellor, Univ. of Newcastle 1988–94; reviewed Aboriginal and Torres Strait Islander Heritage Protection Act 1984; Hearing Commr. (part-time), Human Rights and Equal Opportunity Comm.; mem. UN Human Rights Cttee. 1993–, Human Rights and Equal Opportunities Comm. 1995–; Australian Human Rights Medal 1995. *Address:* 13 Glenview Street, Paddington, N.S.W. 2021, Australia.

EVE, Trevor John; British actor; b. 1 July 1951; s. of Stewart Frederick Eve and Elsie Eve (née Hamer); m. Sharon Patricia Maughan 1980; two s. one d.; ed. Bromsgrove School, Kingston Art Coll., RADA; mem. Cttee. British Deaf Assen. *Theatre includes:* Children of a Lesser God 1981, The Genius 1983, High Society 1986, Man Beast and Virtue 1989, The Winter's Tale 1991, Inadmissible Evidence 1993, Uncle Vanya 1996 (Olivier Award for Best Supporting Actor 1997). *Television includes:* Shoestring 1980, Jamaica Inn, A Sense of Guilt 1990, Parnell and the Englishwoman 1991, A Doll's House 1991, The Politician's Wife 1995, Black Easter 1995, Under the Sun 1997. *Films include:* Hindle Wakes, Dracula, A Wreath of Roses, The Corsican Brothers, Aspen Extreme, Psychotherapy, The Knight's Tale, The Tribe. *Leisure interests:* polo, golf, tennis. *Address:* c/o ICM Ltd., Oxford House, 76 Oxford Street, London, W1N 0AX, England. *Telephone:* 0171-636 6565. *Fax:* 0171-323 0101.

EVENO, Bertrand; French publishing executive; b. 26 July 1944, Egletons; s. of Jean-Jacques Eveno and Suzanne Gavoille; m. 2nd Brigitte Pery 1984; five d. (three d. from previous m.); ed. Lycée Condorcet and Law Faculty, Paris; Treasury Inspector 1973–77; Tech. Consultant to Health Minister 1977–78; Cabinet Dir. for Minister of Culture and Communication 1978–81; mem. Atomic Energy Comm. Control Bd. 1981–83; Deputy Gen. Man. André Shoe Co. 1984–86; Chair. Editions Fernand Nathan 1987–; Pres. Conseil d'administration, Fondation nationale de la photographie 1981–95, Gens d'Image 1986–; Chair. Larousse-Nathan Int. 1988–90, Le Robert dictionaries 1989–, Editions Masson 1995–98; Dir.-Gen. Groupe de la Cité 1988–, Presses de la Cité 1991–95; Pres., Dir.-Gen. Larousse-Bordas 1996–; Zellidja Scholarship 1961. *Publication:* monograph on Willy Ronis in Les grands photographes 1983. *Address:* Editions Fernand Nathan, 9 rue Méchain, 75014 Paris (Office); 80 rue de Rennes, 75006 Paris, France (Home).

EVENSEN, Jens, LL.D.; Norwegian diplomatist, lawyer and politician; b. 5 Nov. 1917, Oslo; s. of Jens Evensen and Victoria Bjerkaas; m. Sylvei Brun Lie 1943; two s.; ed. law schools and Harvard Univ., U.S.A.; Jr. partner, law firm 1942–45; Legal Counsel to Solicitor-Gen. 1948–49; Advocate, Supreme Court 1951; Rockefeller Fellowship 1952–53; Dir.-Gen. Legal Dept., Ministry of Foreign Affairs 1961–73; Chair. Norwegian Petroleum Council 1965–75, Fishery Limits Comm. 1967–69, many other cttees.; Amb. for negotiating Trade Agreement with European Communities 1972; Minister of Commerce 1973–74, of Law of the Sea 1974–79; Chair. Norwegian Del. to Third UN Law of the Sea Conf. 1973, Vice Pres. UN Conf. on the Law of the Sea; Amb., Int. Law Adviser, Ministry of Foreign Affairs 1979–; Ad hoc Judge, Int. Court of Justice 1980–82, Judge 1985–94; Assoc. mem. Inst. de Droit International 1971; mem. Perm. Court of Arbitration 1978, Int. Law Comm. 1979. *Leisure interests:* sailing, skiing. *Address:* Linlandvn. 15, 1390 Vollen Asker, Oslo, Norway (Home). *Telephone:* Oslo 798515 (Home).

EVERED, David Charles, M.D., F.R.C.P., F.I.BIOL.; British scientific administrator and physician; b. 21 Jan. 1940, Beaconsfield; s. of Thomas C. Evered and Enid C. Evered; m. Anne Lings 1964 (deceased 1998); one s. two d.; ed. Cranleigh School, Surrey and Middlesex Hosp. Medical School; jr. hospital appts. London and Leeds 1964–70; First Asst. in Medicine, Wellcome Sr. Research Fellow and Consultant Physician, Univ. of Newcastle-upon-Tyne and Royal Vic. Infirmary 1970–78; Dir. The Ciba Foundation, London 1978–88; Second Sec., MRC, London 1988–96; mem. Council Int. Agency for Research into Cancer 1988–96, Royal Postgrad. Medical School 1994–96, Bd. Hammersmith Hosps. Nat. Health Service Trust 1995–96, numerous cttees., socs. and other professional bodies. *Publications:* Diseases of the Thyroid 1976, Atlas of Endocrinology (with R. Hall and R. Greene) 1979 1990, Collaboration in Medical Research in Europe (with M. O'Connor) 1981; numerous papers in professional journals. *Leisure interests:* reading, history, tennis, sailing. *Address:* Whitehall Cottage, Whitehall Lane, Checkendon, Oxon, RG8 0TR, England.

EVERETT, Douglas Hugh, D.SC., F.R.S., F.R.S.E., F.R.S.C., M.B.E.; British academic; b. 26 Dec. 1916, Hampton; s. of Charles and Jessie Everett; m. Frances Elizabeth Jessop 1942; two d.; ed. Hampton Grammar School, Univs. of Reading and Oxford; Research Asst. Univ. Coll., Dundee 1938–39; Ramsay Fellow, Balliol Coll., Oxford 1939–41; Maj., Special Duties, War Office 1942–45; ICI Fellow, Oxford Univ. 1945–47; Fellow and Lecturer, Exeter Coll., Oxford 1947–48; Prof. of Chemistry Univ. Coll. Dundee, St. Andrews Univ. 1948–54; Unilever Prof. of Physical Chemistry, Univ. of Bristol 1954–82, Prof. Emer. 1982–, Dean of Faculty of Science 1966–68; Pro-Vice-Chancellor 1973–76; Vice-Pres. and Gen. Sec. B.A.A.S. 1983–88; Pres. Int. Assen. of Colloid and Interface Scientists 1988–90; Tilden Lecturer, Chemical Soc., London, Award in Surface and Colloid Chemistry. *Publications:* Introduction to the Study of Chemical Thermodynamics 1959, Surface Tension and Adsorption (with others) 1965, Basic Principles of Celloid Science 1988, Adsorption of Gases on Heterogeneous Surfaces (with W. Rudinski) 1991, and many scientific papers. *Leisure interests:* walking, painting. *Address:* School of Chemistry, University of Bristol, Cantock's Close, Bristol, BS8 1TS (Office); 35 Downleaze, Bristol, BS9 1LX, England (Home). *Telephone:* (0117) 9682990 (Home).

EVERETT, Rupert; British actor; b. 1960, Norfolk; ed. Ampleforth School and Cen. School for Speech and Drama, London; apprenticed with Glasgow Citizen's Theatre 1979–82; has modelled for Versace, Milan; sometime image of Opium perfume for Yves Saint Laurent. *Stage appearances include:* Another Country 1982, The Vortex 1989, Private Lives, The Milk Train Doesn't Stop Here Anymore, The Picture of Dorian Gray, The Importance of Being Earnest. *Films include:* Another Country 1984, Dance with a Stranger 1985, The Right Hand Man 1985, Duet for One, Chronicle of Death Foretold 1987, Hearts of Fire 1987, Haunted Summer 1988, The Comfort of Strangers 1989, Inside Monkey Zetterland, Pret à Porter 1995, The Madness of King George 1995, Dunstan Checks In, My Best Friend's Wedding 1997, A Midsummer Night's Dream 1998, B. Monkey 1998, An Ideal Husband 1999. *TV includes:* Arthur the King, The Far Pavilions 1982, Princess Daisy 1983. *Publications:* Hello Darling, Are You Working? 1992, The Hairdressers of San Tropez 1995. *Address:* c/o ICM, 8942 Wilshire Boulevard, Beverly Hills, CA 90211, U.S.A.

EVERITT, Anthony Michael, B.A.; British academic, writer and fmr. administrative official; b. 31 Jan. 1940; s. of late Michael Everitt and Simone de Vergriette; ed. Cheltenham Coll. and Corpus Christi Coll. Cambridge; lecturer, Nat. Univ. of Iran, S.E. London Coll. of Further Educ., Birmingham Coll. of Art, Trent Polytechnic 1963–72; art critic, The Birmingham Post 1970–75, drama critic 1974–79, features ed. 1976–79; Dir. Midland Group Arts Centre, Nottingham 1979–80, E. Midlands Arts Assen. 1980–85; Chair. Ikon Gallery, Birmingham 1976–79, Birmingham Arts Lab. 1977–79; Vice-Chair. Council of Regional Arts Assens. 1984–85; mem. Drama Panel, Arts Council of G.B. 1974–78, Regional Cttee. 1979–80; mem. Cttee. for Arts and Humanities, Council for Nat. Academic Awards 1986–87, Performing Arts Cttee. 1987–; mem. Gen. Advisory Council, IBA 1987–90; Deputy Sec.-Gen. Arts Council of G.B. 1985–90, Sec.-Gen. 1990–94; Visiting Prof. in Visual and Performing Arts, Nottingham Trent Univ.; Hon. Fellow Dartington Coll. of Arts. *Publications:* Abstract Expressionism 1974, In from the Margins 1997, Joining In 1997; contribs. to newspapers and journals. *Address:* Westerlies, Anchor Hill, Wivenhoe, Essex, CO7 9BL, England.

EVERLING, Ulrich, DR.JUR.; German judge; b. 2 June 1925, Berlin; s. of Emil Everling; m. Lore Schwerdtfeger 1953; two s. two d.; ed. Zehlendorfer Gymnasium, Berlin and Univ. of Göttingen; lawyer, Fed. Ministry of Econs. 1953–80, Head of Dept. of European Policy 1970–80; Lecturer, Hon. Prof. of European Law, Univ. of Münster 1971–80, Univ. of Bonn 1981–; Judge, Court of Justice of the European Communities 1980–88. *Publications:* Die europäische Wirtschaftsgemeinschaft: Kommentar zum Vertrag (co-author) 1960, Das Niederlassungsrecht im Gemeinsamen Markt 1964, Das europäische Gemeinschaftrecht im Sparenvagsfeld von Politik und Wirtschaft, Ausgewählte Aufsätze 1964–1984 1986; numerous articles on European law and policy. *Address:* Dahlienweg 5, 53343 Wachtberg, Germany. *Telephone:* (0228) 324177. *Fax:* (0228) 314898.

EVERT, Chris(tine) Marie: American lawn tennis player (retd.); b. 21 Dec. 1954, Fort Lauderdale, Fla.; d. of James Evert; m. 1st John Lloyd 1979 (divorced 1987); m. 2nd Andy Mill 1988, three s.; ed. St. Thomas Aquinas High School, Fort Lauderdale; amateur player 1970–72; professional since 1972; Wimbledon Singles Champion 1974, 1976, 1981; French Champion 1974, 1975, 1979, 1980, 1983, 1985, 1986; U.S. Open Champion 1975, 1976, 1977, 1978, 1980, 1982; Italian Champion 1974, 1975, 1980; South African Champion 1973; Colgate Series Champion 1977, 1978; World Champion 1979; played Wightman Cup for U.S.A. 1971–73, 1975–82 had record in singles with 157 titles; won 1000th singles victory Australian Open Dec. 1984; played Federation Cup for U.S.A. 1977–82; Pres. Women's Tennis Assen. 1975–76, 1983–91; est. Chris Evert Charities for needy and drug-abusive mothers and their children 1989; owner Evert Enterprises/IMG, Boca Raton, Fla. 1989–; Dir. Pres.'s Council on Physical Fitness and Sports 1991–; involved in Chris Evert Pro-Celebrity Tennis Classic for charity 1989–. *Publication:* Lloyd on Lloyd (with John Lloyd) 1985. *Address:* Evert Enterprises/IMG, 7200 W Camino Real, #310, Boca Raton, FL 33433, U.S.A.

EVERT, Militiades; Greek politician; b. 1939, Athens; m. Lisa Evert (née Vanderpool); two d.; ed. Econ. Univ. of Athens; M.P. 1974–; Mayor of Athens 1986–90; Minister of Health and Welfare 1989–90, to the Prime Minister 1990–91; Leader New Democracy Party 1993–. *Address:* New Democracy Party, Odos Rigillis 18, 10674 Athens, Greece.

EVIN, Claude; French politician; b. 29 June 1949, Le Cellier, Loire-Atlantique; m. Françoise Guillet 1971; three d.; Sec. Saint-Nazaire Section, Parti Socialiste 1975–77, mem. Loire-Atlantique Fed. Cttee. of Socialist Party 1975–, mem. Nat. Cttee. 1991–; Mun. Councillor and Deputy Mayor of Saint-Nazaire 1977–; Deputy to Nat. Ass. 1978–88, 97–; M.P. Ass. of Council of Europe; Chair. Nat. Ass. Cultural, Family and Social Affairs Cttee. 1981–86; mem. Social Security Audit Comm. 1985; Vice-Pres. Nat. Ass. 1986–88; Minister-Del. attached to Minister of Social Affairs and Employment with responsibility for Social Protection May–June 1988; Minister of Solidarity, Health and Social Protection 1988–91; Conseiller régional Pays de la Loire 1992–; mem. Econ. and Social Council 1994–97. *Address:* 30 rue du Bois

Savary, 44600 Saint-Nazaire, France. *Telephone:* 0251101051. *Fax:* 0251101050.

EVISON, Frank Foster, O.B.E., PH.D., F.R.S.N.Z.; New Zealand professor of geophysics; b. 20 March 1922, Christchurch; s. of Sidney Roger Evison and Beatrice Maud Evison; m. Edith Joan Hutton 1949 (died 1990); one s. two d.; ed. Christchurch West High School, Wellington Coll., Vic. Univ. of Wellington, Imperial Coll. of Science and Tech., London; R.N.Z.A.F. 1942–45; physicist/geophysicist, N.Z. D.S.I.R. 1945–60, superintendent Seismological Observatory 1960–64, Dir. Geophysics Div. 1964–67; Prof. of Geophysics, Vic. Univ. of Wellington 1967–88, Chair. Inst. of Geophysics 1971–88, Prof. Emer. and Hon. Fellow 1988–; discovered the "Evison Wave" 1955; Chair. Int. symposium on Earthquake Prediction, UNESCO, Paris 1979; Sec. Int. Comm. on Earthquake Prediction 1979–83; Co-Chair. Int. Comm. on Earthquake Hazards 1983–87; Nuffield Fellow 1957–58, Japan S.P.S. Research Fellow 1980. *Publications:* 66 scientific papers on seismology, earthquake hazard, tectonophysics, applied geophysics. *Leisure interests:* hill- and bush-walking, skiing. *Address:* Institute of Geophysics, Victoria University of Wellington, P.O. Box 600, Wellington (Office); 1 Glen Road, Kelburn, Wellington, New Zealand (Home). *Telephone:* 04-4721000 (Office); 04-4759231 (Home). *Fax:* 04-4955186 (Office).

EVREN, Gen. Kenan; Turkish army officer; b. 1918; m.; three c.; ed. Military Acad., War Coll.; Artillery Officer 1938; served in Korea; Chief of Staff of the Land Forces, then Deputy Chief of Staff of the Armed Forces; Commdr. Fourth Army (Aegean Army), Izmir 1976; rank of Gen. 1974; Chief of the Land Forces 1977; Chief of Staff of the Armed Forces 1978; led coup deposing civilian govt. Sept. 1980; Head of State and Chair. Nat. Security Council 1980–89, Pres. of Turkey 1982–89; Head, Turkish mil. del. to U.S.S.R. 1975; numerous decorations. *Address:* Beyaz Ev Sokak 21, Armutalan, Marmaris, Turkey.

EWEN, Paterson; Canadian artist and teacher of fine art; b. 7 April 1925, Montreal, Quebec; four s.; ed. Montreal Museum of Fine Arts, School of Art and Design, McGill Univ., Montreal; solo exhbns. in Toronto 1969–; exhbns. in New Brunswick 1975, New Jersey, U.S.A. 1975, Calgary 1980, Basel, Switzerland 1978, Denmark 1980–81, Fed. Repub. of Germany 1981, Luxembourg 1981, Belgium 1981, Japan 1981, Venice, Italy 1982, London 1982, Vancouver 1992, 1995, New York 1993, 1994; group exhbns. New York 1993, Vancouver 1994; Assoc. Prof. Univ. of W. Ont. 1972–87, Prof. Emer. 1987–; Hon. D.Litt. (Western Ont.) 1989, Hon. D. Laws (Concordia Univ., Montreal) 1989; Nat. Award, Banff Centre School of Fine Arts 1987, Toronto Arts Award 1988, Chalmers Award for Visual Arts 1995. *Publications:* (catalogues) Carmen Lamanna at the Owens Art Gallery 1975, Paterson Ewen: Recent Works 1977, Paterson Ewen Phenomena, paintings, 1971–1987 1987, Paterson Ewen: the Montreal Years 1987, Paterson Ewen 1993. *Address:* 1015 Wellington Street, London, Ont., N6A 3T5, Canada (Home).

EWING, Maria Louise; American opera singer; b. 27 March 1950, Detroit; d. of Norman I. Ewing and Hermina M. Veraar; m. Sir Peter Hall (q.v.) 1982 (divorced 1989); one d.; ed. Cleveland Inst. of Music; début at Metropolitan Opera, New York singing Cherubino in The Marriage of Figaro 1976, closely followed by débuts with major U.S. orchestras including New York Philharmonic and at La Scala Milan; performs regularly at Glyndebourne including the Barber of Seville, L'Incoronazione di Poppea and Carmen; repertoire also includes Pelléas et Mélisande, The Dialogues of the Carmelites, Così fan Tutte, La Perichole, La Cenerentola, Marriage of Figaro (Susanna); Salome, Covent Garden 1988; Carmen, Earl's Court, London 1989; Tosca, Los Angeles 1989; Salome, Washington 1990; Madame Butterfly, Los Angeles, Tosca, Seville, Salome, Covent Garden 1992; Tosca, Los Angeles, Chicago, Salome, San Francisco, The Trojans, Metropolitan New York 1993, Madame Butterfly, Tosca, Vienna, The Trojans, Metropolitan, New York 1993/94; also appears as concert and recital singer; début Promenade Concerts, London 1987, Lady Macbeth of Mtzensk with Metropolitan Opera 1994. *Leisure interests:* home and family. *Address:* c/o Joel E. Bloch Artists Management, Herbert H Breslin Inc., 12 Cornelia Street, Suite 5C, New York, NY 10014; c/o Harold Holt Ltd., 31 Sinclair Road, London, W14 0NS, England.

EWING, Winifred Margaret, M.A., LL.B., F.R.A.S.; Scottish politician and solicitor; b. 10 July 1929, Glasgow; d. of George Woodburn and Christina B. Anderson; m. Stewart Martin Ewing 1956; two s. one d.; ed. Queen's Park School, Univ. of Glasgow, Peace Palace, The Hague; practising solicitor 1956–; mem. Parl. for Hamilton 1967–70, for Moray and Nairn 1974–79; mem. European Parl. 1975–, for the Highlands and Islands of Scotland 1979–; Pres. Scottish Nat. Party, European Free Alliance 1991–; Vice-Pres. European Democratic Alliance 1984, Animal Welfare Intergroup (European Parl.) 1989–; Chair. Cttee. on Youth, Culture, Educ., Information and Sport, European Parl. 1984–; Sec. Glasgow Bar Asscn. 1961–67, Pres 1970–71; mem. Exec. Cttee. Scottish Co. for Devt. and Industry 1972–; Dr. h.c. (Open Univ.) 1993; Hon. LL.D. (Glasgow) 1995. *Leisure interests:* hill walking, collecting paintings. *Address:* Goodwill, Milton Duff, Elgin, Moray IV30 3TL, Scotland. *Telephone:* (01343) 541144. *Fax:* (01343) 540011.

EXARCHOS, Antonios; Greek diplomatist; b. 1932, Athens; m.; three c.; ed. Univ. of Athens; joined Ministry of Foreign Affairs 1961; served at Consulate-Gen., Alexandria, Egypt 1964–67, Embassy, Belgrade 1967–70; Consul-Gen., Toronto 1970–71; mem. Greek del. to various int. orgs. Geneva 1974–75; Deputy Rep., Perm. Del. of Greece to EEC 1977–81; with Ministry of Foreign Affairs, Athens 1982–84, 1988–89; Amb. to Iraq 1984–86; Dir.-Co-ordinator Political Affairs, Athens 1989–90; Perm. Rep. to UN 1990–94. *Address:* c/o Ministry of Foreign Affairs, Odos Akademias 1, Athens, Greece.

EXON, J(ohn) James; American politician; b. 9 Aug. 1921, Geddes, S. Dakota; s. of John J. and Luella (Johns) Exon; m. Patricia Pros 1943; one s. two d.; ed. Univ. of Omaha; Vice-Chair., Neb. State Democratic Cen. Cttee. 1964–68; mem. Neb. Democratic Party Exec. Cttee. 1964–; Neb. Democratic Nat. Cttee. Man 1968–70; Gov. of Nebraska 1971–79; Senator from Nebraska 1979–97; mem. American Legion, Veterans of Foreign Wars. *Address:* 1615 Brent Boulevard, Lincoln, NE 68506, U.S.A.

EYADÉMA, Gen. (Etienne) Gnassingbe; Togolese politician and army officer; b. 26 Dec. 1937, Pya, Lama Kara District; served with French Army 1953–61 in Indo-China, Dahomey, Niger and Algeria; commissioned 1963; Army Chief of Staff 1965–; led army coup Jan. 1967; Pres. of Togo April 1967–, and Minister of Defence 1967, 1981–91; f. Rassemblement du Peuple Togolais, Paris 1969, Pres. 1969, mem. Political Bureau; Chair. ECOWAS 1980–81; Grand Officier, Ordre National de Mono, Mil. Cross, Chevalier, Légion d'honneur (France). *Leisure interest:* hunting. *Address:* Palais Présidentiel, avenue de la Marina, Lomé, Togo. *Telephone:* 21-27-01.

EYCKMANS, Luc A.F., M.D., PH.D.; Belgian professor of medicine; b. 23 Feb. 1930, Antwerp; s. of Robert Eyckmans and Alice van Genechten; m. Godelieve Cornelissen 1957; four s. three d.; ed. Univ. of Leuven; Fellowship in Tropical Medicine, Antwerp 1956–57; Hospital Physician, Kisantu (fmr. Belgian Congo) 1957–60; Fellowship in Infectious Diseases, Dallas and Cornell, New York 1961–64, in Tropical Medicine, Bahia, Brazil 1964; Lector in Infectious Diseases and Physician, Univ. of Leuven 1965–72; Prof. of Medicine (Infectious Diseases), Univ. of Antwerp 1973–76, Dir. Inst. of Tropical Medicine "Prince Leopold" 1976–95; Visiting Prof. Univ. of Antwerp 1977–95, Univ. of Leuven 1989–95; Exec. Dir. and mem. Bd. Franqui Foundation; mem. Royal Acad. of Overseas Sciences (Belgium), Acad. Europaea; Dr. h.c. (Lille). *Publications:* 130 contributions to professional journals. *Leisure interest:* hiking. *Address:* Wildenhoge 26, B 3020 Winksele, Belgium (Home).

EYKHOFF, Pieter, M.SC., PH.D.; Netherlands professor of electrical engineering (control engineering); b. 9 April 1929, The Hague; s. of Hendrik Eykhoff and Henderika Strating; m. Johanna N. F. Pabon 1955; two s.; ed. Delft Univ. of Tech. and Univ. of Calif. Berkeley; (Chief) Scientific Officer, Delft Univ. of Tech. 1956–64; Visiting Research Fellow (N.A.S.) at Univ. of Calif. Berkeley 1958–60; Prof. of Electrical Eng., Eindhoven Univ. of Tech. 1964–94, Emer. Prof. 1994–, Dean, Council Chair., Man. Electrical Eng. Dept. 1977–80; various functions in Int. Fed. of Automatic Control (IFAC) 1972–; Ed. Control Eng. Practice 1992–; Hon. Prof. Xi'an Jiaotong Univ., P.R. of China 1986; Chair. Netherlands-China Friendship Soc. 1984–91, Hon. Chair. 1991–; mem. Royal Netherlands Acad. of Arts and Sciences 1988–; Fellow I.E.E.E. 1979; Dr. h.c. (Free Univ. Brussels) 1990; IFAC Outstanding Service Award 1990; Kt., Order of Lion of The Netherlands 1991. *Publications:* System Identification; Parameter and State Estimation 1974, Trends and Progress in System Identification (Ed.) 1980 and numerous others including two "Citation Classics". *Leisure interests:* classical music, photography, Far Eastern cultures, wine. *Address:* Eindhoven University of Technology, EE Department, P.O. Box 513, NL-5600 MB Eindhoven (Office); Vermeerstraat 11, NL-5691 ED Son, The Netherlands (Home). *Telephone:* (40) 247 33 00 (Office); (499) 47 20 60 (Home). *Fax:* (40) 243 45 82 (Office); (499) 47 20 60 (Home).

EYRAUD, Francis-Charles, L. EN D., D.E.S.; French business executive; b. 16 Aug. 1931, Saint-Bonnet, Hautes Alpes; s. of Charles Eyraud and Francine Villaron; m. Simone Desmé 1967; two s. one d.; ed. Coll. du Rondeau Montfleury, Grenoble, Faculté de Droit, Lettres, I.E.P., Paris; E.N.A. promotion, Alexis de Tocqueville 1958; civil admin. of finance 1960; Prof. Centre de Formation des Finances 1961; in charge of practical studies, Faculté de Droit 1962; special mission to U.S.A. 1965; Chef de Bureau 1967; civil admin. 1968; Deputy Dir. 1973; judicial agent of Treasury 1979; Prés.-Dir. Gén. Société Nationale d'Exploitation Industrielle des Tabacs et Allumettes (SEITA) 1981–87; Man. Dir. CORESTA 1982, Vice-Pres. 1984–86, Pres. 1986; Paymaster of Seine-Maritime and of Haute-Normandie 1988–96, of Yvelines 1996–98; Officier Légion d'honneur, Commdr. Ordre Nationale du Mérite, Officier des Palmes académiques; Commdr. des Arts et des Lettres, and other decorations. *Publications:* Cours de Législation Financière 1965. *Address:* 33 rue Saint-Augustin, 75002 Paris, France (Home). *Telephone:* 47.42.50.67 (Home).

EYRE, Ivan; Canadian artist and professor emeritus; b. 15 April 1935, Tullymet, Sask.; s. of Thomas and Kay Eyre; m. Brenda Fenske 1957; two s.; mem. Faculty, Univ. of Manitoba, Winnipeg 1959–93, Head, Drawing Dept. 1974–78, Prof. of Drawing and Painting 1975–93, Prof. Emer. 1994–; one-man shows at Nat. Gallery of Canada, Ottawa, many other Canadian galleries, Frankfurter Kunstkabinett, W. Germany, Canada House, London, Canadian Cultural Centre, Paris, France, Talbot-Rice Galleries, Edinburgh, Scotland 1982, 49th Parallel Gallery, New York 1988; has participated in group shows in Colombia, Spain, U.S.A., Hong Kong Art Fair 1993, Taejon, S. Korea, Expo '93, and all the major cities of Canada; works represented in permanent collections at Winnipeg Art Gallery, Nat. Gallery, Ottawa, Edmonton Art Gallery, Montreal Museum of Fine Arts, Assiniboine Park Pavilion Gallery, Winnipeg, Man. etc.; Canada Council Sr. Fellow 1966–77; f. mem. Winnipeg Art Gallery 1996; mem. Royal Canadian Acad. of Arts;

Queen's Jubilee Medal 1977, Academic of Italy with Gold Medal 1980, Jubilee Award, Univ. of Manitoba Alumni Asscn. 1982, Molson Prize nominee 1996. *Address:* 1098 Des Trappistes Street, Winnipeg, Manitoba R3V 1B8, Canada. *Telephone:* (204) 261-8171.

EYRE, Sir Richard, Kt. D.LIT., C.B.E.; British theatre, film and television director; b. 28 March 1943; m. Sue Birtwistle 1973; one d.; ed. Sherborne School and Cambridge Univ.; Assoc. Dir. Royal Lyceum, Edinburgh 1967–70; Artistic Dir. Nottingham Playhouse 1973–78; Producer-dir. Play for Today for BBC 1978–80; Assoc. Dir. Nat. Theatre (now called Royal Nat. Theatre) 1980–86, Artistic Dir. 1988–97; Cameron Mackintosh Visiting Professorship, St. Catherine's Coll. Oxford 1997; BBC Gov. 1995–; Hon. Fellow Goldsmiths Coll. 1993, King's Coll. London 1994; Hon. mem. Guildhall 1996; Hon. D.Litt. (Nottingham) 1992, (S. Bank) 1994; Patricia Rothermere Award 1995. *Plays directed include:* Hamlet (Royal Court) 1980, Guys and Dolls, The Beggar's Opera, Schweyk in the Second World War (Nat. Theatre) 1982, The Government Inspector (Nat. Theatre) 1985, Futurists (Nat. Theatre) 1986, Kafka's Dick (Royal Court) 1986, High Society (W. End) 1987, The Changeling 1988, Bartholomew Fair 1988, Hamlet 1989, The Voysey Inheritance 1989, Racing Demon 1990, Richard III 1990, Napoli Milionaria 1991, Murmuring Judges 1991, White Chameleon 1991, The Night of the Iguana 1992, Macbeth 1993, The David Hare Trilogy—Racing Demon, Murmuring Judges, The Absence of War 1993 (Racing Demon, New York 1995), Johnny on a Spot 1994, Sweet Bird of Youth 1994, Skylight 1995, 1996 (New York 1996), La Grande Magia 1995, The Prince's Play 1996, John Gabriel Borkman 1996, Guys and Dolls 1996, 1997, King Lear 1997, Amy's View 1997, The Invention of Love 1997, The Judas Kiss 1998. *Films:* The Ploughman's Lunch (Evening Standard Award for Best Film) 1983, Laughterhouse (Venice TV Prize) 1984. *Television:* The Imitation Game 1980, Pasmore 1981, The Cherry Orchard, Country 1982, Past Caring, The Insurance Man (Tokyo Prize) 1986, Tumbledown 1987, Suddenly Last Summer 1992, The Absence of War 1995, King Lear 1998. *Opera:* La Traviata, Covent Garden 1994; STV Award for Best Dir. 1968, 1969, 1970, Evening Standard Award for Best Dir. 1982, SWET Award for Best Dir. 1982, Time Out Award Best Dir. 1986, Vittorio de Sica Award 1986, Special Award, Evening Standard Awards for Drama 1988, for Best Dir. 1997, Special Award for running Nat. Theatre 1997, RAI Prize 1988 (Tumbledown), Laurence Olivier Award for Outstanding Achievement 1997, South Bank Show Award for Outstanding Achievement 1997, Director's Guild Award for Outstanding Achievement 1997. *Publication:* Utopia and Other Places (memoirs) 1992. *Address:* c/o Judy Daish, 2 St. Charles Place, London, W10 6EG, England. *Telephone:* 0181-964 8811.

EYSKENS, Mark; Belgian politician; b. 29 April 1933, Louvain; m. Ann Rutsaert 1962; two s. three d.; ed. Catholic Univ. of Louvain; Econ. Adviser, Ministry of Finance 1962–65; Minister of Finance 1980–81; Prime Minister 1981; Minister for Econ. Affairs 1981–85, for Finance 1985–88, of Foreign Affairs 1988–92; mem. Royal Acad. of Sciences; Pres. Centre for European Culture. *Publications include:* Algemene economie 1970, Economie van nu en straks 1975, Une planète livrée à deux mondes 1980, La source et l'horizon, Le redressement de la société européenne 1985, Economie voor iedereen 1987, Vie et mort du Professeur Mortal 1989, Affaires etrangères 1992. *Leisure interests:* painting, writing, music. *Address:* Graaf de Grunnelaan, 3001 Heverlee, Belgium (Office).

EYSYMONTT, Jerzy, PH.D.; Polish politician, economist and computer scientist; b. 26 June 1937, Łuck; m. Elżbieta Eysymontt; ed. Warsaw Univ.; employee Planning Comm., then Planning Inst., Warsaw 1963–80; Polish Acad. of Sciences; recently with Statistics and Econometrics Faculty of Econ. Dept. Warsaw Univ.; worked on econ. programme in Balcerowicz's group 1980; mem. Centre Alliance 1990–92; Minister, head Cen. Planning Office 1991–92; deputy to Sejm (Parl.) 1991–97; Chair. Econ. Cttee. of Govt. and mem. Presidium of Govt. 1991–92; Deputy Minister of Econ. 1998–. *Leisure interests:* skiing, Airedale terriers. *Address:* Ministerstwo Gospodarki, pl. Trzech Krzyży 5, 00-507 Warsaw, Poland. *Telephone:* (22) 628 03 89, (22) 693 58 63. *Fax:* (22) 693 50 09.

EYTAN, Walter; M.A.; Israeli political consultant; b. 24 July 1910, Munich, Germany; s. of Dr. Maurice Leon Ettinghausen and Hedwig Kahn; m. Beatrice Levison; two s. one d.; ed. St. Paul's School, London, and Queen's Coll., Oxford; Lecturer in German, Queen's Coll., Oxford 1934–46; Prin., Public Service Coll., Jerusalem 1946–48; Dir.-Gen. Ministry Foreign Affairs, Israel 1948–59; Amb. to France 1960–70; Political Adviser to Foreign Minister 1970–72; Chair. Israel Broadcasting Authority 1972–78; mem. Bd. of Govs., Haifa Univ.; Hon. Fellow, Hebrew Union Coll. 1983; Hon. D.H.L. (Hebrew Union Coll.) 1995; Commdr., Légion d'honneur 1976. *Publication:* The First Ten Years 1958. *Address:* 18 Rehov Balfour, Jerusalem, Israel. *Telephone:* (02) 563-1268. *Fax:* (02) 561-0126.

EYTON, Anthony John Plowden, R.A., R.W.S., R.W.A.; British artist; b. 17 May 1923, Teddington, Middx.; s. of Capt. John S. Eyton and Phyllis A. Tyser; m. Frances M. Capell 1960 (divorced); three d.; ed. Twyford School, Canford School and Camberwell School of Art; part-time teacher, Camberwell Art School 1955–86, Royal Acad. Schools 1963–; one-man exhbns. St. George's Gallery 1955, New Art Centre 1959, 1961, 1968, New Grafton Gallery 1973, William Darby Gallery 1975, Browse & Darby 1978, 1981, 1985, 1987, 1990, 1993, 1996, South London Art Gallery (retrospective) 1980, Imperial War Museum 1983, Austin/Desmond Fine Art 1990, A. T. Kearney 1997, Prince of Wales Inst. of Architecture 1998; mem. Royal Cambrian Acad.; Hon. mem. Pastel Soc.; Hon. R.O.I.; several awards and prizes. *Leisure interest:* gardening. *Address:* 166 Brixton Road, London, SW9 6AU, England. *Telephone:* 0171-735 9859.

EZRA, Baron (Life Peer), cr. 1983, of Horsham in the County of West Sussex; **Derek Ezra,** Kt., M.B.E.; British business executive; b. 23 Feb. 1919; s. of David and Lillie Ezra; m. Julia Elizabeth Wilkins 1950; ed. Monmouth School and Magdalene Coll., Cambridge; mil. service 1939–47; rep. of Nat. Coal Bd. at Cttees. of OEEC and ECE 1948–52; mem. U.K. Del. to High Authority of European Coal and Steel Community 1952–56; Regional Sales Man. Nat. Bd. 1958–60, Dir.-Gen. of Marketing 1960–65; mem. Nat. Coal Bd. 1965, Deputy Chair. 1965–71, Chair. 1971–82; Chair. British Inst. of Man. 1976–78, Vice-Chair. 1978; Chair. British Coal Int.; Chair. British Nationalised Industries Chairmen's Group 1980–81, Pres. Nat. Materials Handling Centre 1978; Pres. Coal Industry Soc. 1981–86, British Standards Inst. 1983–86, Econ. Research Council 1985–, Inst. of Trading Standards Admin. 1987–92; Dir. Redland PLC 1982–89; Chair. Associated Heat Services PLC 1966–, British Iron and Steel Consumers Council 1983–86, Petrolex PLC 1982–85, Sheffield Heat and Power Ltd 1985–, Associated Gas Supplies Ltd. 1987–95, Energy and Tech. Services Group 1990–; Industrial Adviser to Morgan Grenfell 1982–88; Chair. Throgmorton Trust 1984–90; mem. British Overseas Trade Bd. 1972–82, Bd., Solvay, Belgium; Hon. Fellow Inst. of Civil Engineers 1986; Hon. LL.D. (Leeds) 1982; Order of Merit, Italy, Commdr. Order of Merit, Luxembourg, Officier, Légion d'honneur. *Publications:* Coal and Energy 1978, The Energy Debate 1983. *Address:* House of Lords, Westminster, London, SW1A 0PW, England. *Telephone:* 0171-219 3180.

F

FABBRI, Fabio; Italian politician, lawyer and journalist; b. 15 Oct. 1933, Ciano d'Enza, Reggio Emilia; s. of Nello Fabbri and Gisella Brechi; m. Minnie Manzini 1959; one s. one d.; ed. Univ. of Parma; fmr. journalist with Il Mondo and contrib. to Nord e Sud, Itinerari, Mondo Operario; now contrib. to L'Avanti and other political and cultural magazines; Chair. Parma Provincial Transport Authority 1968–70; Socialist Senator for Borgotaro Salsomaggiore, Emilia Romagna 1976; fmr. Under-Sec., Ministry of Agric. and Forestry; Minister for Regional Affairs 1982–83, for EEC Affairs 1986–87, of Defence 1993–94; Chair. of Socialist Parl. Group; Pres. Istituto per il dialogo e la cooperazione internazionale. *Leisure interests:* reading, trekking, skiing. *Address:* Piazza Garibaldi 17, 431000 Parma, Italy.

FABIANI, Simonetta (see Simonetta).

FABIUS, Laurent; French politician; b. 20 Aug. 1946, Paris; s. of André Fabius and Louise Mortimer; m. Françoise Castro 1981; two s.; ed. Lycées Janson-de-Sailly and Louis-le-Grand, Paris, Ecole normale supérieure, Ecole Nat. d'Admin.; Auditor, Council of State 1973; First Deputy Mayor of Grand-Quevilly 1977–, Mayor 1995–; Deputy (Seine-Maritime) to Nat. Assembly 1978–81, 1986–, Pres. 1988–92, 1997–99; Nat. Sec. Parti Socialiste, in charge of press 1979–81, 1991–92, First Sec. 1992–93, Pres. Groupe Socialiste in Nat. Ass. 1995–97; Minister-Del. for the Budget, attached to Minister of Econ. and Finance 1981–83; Minister of Industry and Research March 1983–84, Prime Minister 1984–86; Pres. Regional Council, Haute Normandie 1981–82; Pres. Syndicat intercommunal à vocations multiples (Sivom) 1989–; Grand Croix de l'ordre nat. du Mérite. *Publications:* La France inégale 1975, Le coeur du futur 1985, C'est en allant vers la mer 1990, Les Blessures de la Vérité 1995 (Prize for Best Political Book 1996). *Address:* Mairie 76120 Le Grand-Quevilly; Assemblée Nationale, 75355 Paris, France. *Telephone:* 40.63.60.00 (Office).

FABREGA, Jorge, M.L.; Panamanian professor of law and attorney; b. 19 April 1922, Santiago; m. Gloria de Fábrega 1960; two s. two d.; ed. Univ. of Southern California, Univ. of Pennsylvania, Univ. of Panama; Alt. Justice Court of Appeals 1960–68, Supreme Court of Panama 1970–80, 1989; Prof. of Law, Univ. of Panama 1967; Pres. Govt. Comm. drafting Labour Code 1969–71, Constitutional Comm. 1983, Panamanian Bar Asscn. 1983–85; mem. Govt. Comm. drafting new Judicial Code 1970–74; Hon. mem. Spanish Bar, Brazilian Labour Judicial Order. *Publications:* Enriquecimiento sin causa 1960, Institutes of Civil Procedure 1972, Casación 1978, Estudios Procesales 1984, Código de Trabajo Anotado 1970, 1971, 1986, Estudios Procesales 1988. *Leisure interests:* reading, travel. *Address:* Torre Swiss Bank, Primer Piso, Calle 53 Este, Urbanización, Marbella, Panamá, Republic of Panama.

FABRICIUS, Fritz, DR. JUR.; German professor of law; b. 18 May 1919, Fedderwardergroden; s. of Martin Fabricius and Helene (née Ehmen) Fabricius; m. Gisela Nagel 1948; one s.; ed. Münster Univ.; naval officer 1940–45; Asst. Münster Univ. 1956–61, lecturer 1961–64; Full Prof. of Commercial, Company and Labour Law Bochum Univ. 1964–84, Prof. Emer. 1984–; Man. Dir. Verwaltungs- und Wirtschaftsakademie Industriebezirk 1967–84; mem. Cttee. of Ind. Experts for the European Social Charter with the European Council, Strasbourg 1976–82, 1982–88, 1988–94; Grosses Verdienstkreuz des Verdienst-ordens der BRD. *Publications:* Relativität der Rechtsfähigkeit 1963, Mitbestimmung in der Wirtschaft 1970, Marktwirtschaft und Mitbestimmung 1978, Unternehmensrechtsreform und Mitbestimmung in einer sozialen Marktwirtschaft 1982, Rechtsprobleme gespaltener Arbeitsverhältnisse im Konzern 1982, Streik und Aussperrung im Internationalen Recht 1988, Human Rights and European Politics 1992, Kommentar zum Betriebsverfassungsgesetz (6th edn.) 1998. *Leisure interest:* music. *Address:* Dahlhauserstrasse 71, 45529 Hattingen, Germany. *Telephone:* 02324-829 83.

FABRIZI, Pier Luigi, B.ECON.; Italian banker and professor of finance; b. 23 April 1948, Siena; s. of Francesco Fabrizi and Bianca Corradeschi; m. Patrizia Vaselli; two c.; ed. Siena Univ.; Asst. Prof. of Banking Parma Univ. 1974–82, Assoc. Prof. of Banking 1982–87, Prof. of Financial Insts. 1987–93, Dean Faculty of Econs. 1990–97; Prof. of Financial Markets Bocconi Univ., Milan 1993–; Chair. Banca Monte dei Paschi di Siena SpA 1998–; mem. Bd. dirs. S. Paolo IMI, Turin 1998–; Grande Ufficiale, Ordine al Merito. *Publications:* L'attività in titoli con clientela nelle banche di deposito 1986, La gestione dei flussi finanziari nelle aziende di credito 1990, La gestione integrata dell'attivo e del passivo nelle aziende di credito 1991, Nuovi modelli di gestione dei flussi finanziari nelle banche 1995, Le banche nell' intermediazione mobiliare e nell'asset management 1996, La formazione nelle banche e nelle assicurazioni-bancaria (ed.) 1998. *Address:* Via Adelaide Coari 11, 20141 Milan, Italy. *Telephone:* (39 2) 55210884.

FADDEYEV, Ludvig Dmitriyevich; Russian mathematician and physicist; b. 23 March 1934, Leningrad; m.; two d.; ed. Leningrad Univ.; Sr. Research Fellow, Leningrad Branch, Inst. of Math., U.S.S.R. (now Russian) Acad. of Sciences 1965–, Deputy Dir. 1976–; mem. staff, Leningrad State Univ. 1967–, Prof. at Mathematical-Mechanical Faculty 1969–; Pres. Int. Mathematical Union 1986–; specialist in quantum mechanics; mem. U.S.S.R. (now Russian) Acad. of Sciences 1976, Acad.-Sec. Dept. of Mathematics; mem. American Acad. of Arts and Sciences, Boston 1979; D. Heinemann Prize, American Physical Soc. 1975, U.S.S.R. State Prize 1971, Max Planck Gold Medal 1995. *Address:* St. Petersburg Branch of V.A. Steklov Mathematical Institute, Nab. Fontanki 27, D-11, St. Petersburg, Russia. *Telephone:* 312-40-58 (Office); 553-58-53 (Home).

FADEYECHEV, Nikolay Borisovich; Russian ballet dancer; b. 27 Jan. 1933; m. 1st Nina Fetisova; m. 2nd Irina Kholina; two s.; ed. Bolshoi Theatre Ballet School; Bolshoi Theatre Ballet Co., 1952–76, coach Bolshoi Theatre 1971–; People's Artist of U.S.S.R. 1976. *Chief roles:* Siegfried (Swan Lake), Albert (Giselle), Jean de Brien (Raimonde), Harmodius (Spartacus), Frondoso (Laurensia), Danila (Stone Flower), Romeo (Romeo and Juliet), Prince Desire (Sleeping Beauty), José (Carmen Suite), Karenin (Anna Karenina), Prince (Nutcracker). *Address:* State Academic Bolshoi Theatre, Teatralnaya Ploshchad 1, Moscow, Russia. *Telephone:* 157-33-22 (Home).

FADUL, Francisco; Guinea-Bissau politician; fmr. adviser to Gen. Ansumane Mane; Prime Minister of Guinea-Bissau 1998–(99). *Address:* Office of the Prime Minister, Bissau, Guinea-Bissau.

FAECKE, Peter; German journalist and author; b. 3 Nov. 1940, Grunwald; awards include stipend of Villa Massimo, Rome and literature prizes of Lower Saxony, North-Rhine-Westphalia and City of Cologne. *Publications:* Die Brandstifter (novel) 1962, Der Rote Milan (novel) 1965, Postversand (novel) (with Wolf Vostell) 1970, Gemeinsam gegen Abriss: Ein Lesebuch aus Arbeitersiedlungen 1974, Das Unaufhaltsame Glück der Kowalskis 1982, Flug ins Leben 1988, Der Mann mit den besonderen Eigenschaften (novel) 1993, Grabstein für Fritz (documentary film) 1993, Als Elizabeth Arden Neunzehn war (novel) 1994, Eine Liebe zum Land (film script) 1994, Der Viehhändler, der Narr und der Schriftsteller (novel) 1996. *Address:* Mevissenstrasse 16, 50668 Cologne, Germany. *Telephone:* 0221-726207. *Fax:* 0221-723259.

FAGIN, Claire Mintzer, PH.D.; American professor of nursing; b. 25 Nov. 1926, New York; d. of Harry Fagin and Mae (Slatin) Mintzer; m. Samuel Fagin 1952; two s.; ed. Wagner Coll., Teachers' Coll., Columbia Univ. and New York Univ.; Staff Nurse, Sea View Hosp., Staten Island, New York 1947, Clinical Instructor 1947–48; Bellevue Hosp., New York 1948–50; Psychiatric Mental Health Nursing Consultant, Nat. League for Nursing 1951–52; Asst. Chief, Psychiatric Nursing Service Clinical Center, Nat. Inst. of Health 1953–54, Supt. 1955; Research Project Co-ordinator, Children's Hosp., Dept. of Psychiatry, Washington, D.C. 1956; Instructor in Psychiatric-Mental Health Nursing, New York Univ. 1956–58, Asst. Prof. 1964–67, Dir. Graduate Programs in Psychiatric-Mental Health Nursing 1965–69, Assoc. Prof. 1967–69; Prof. and Chair. Nursing Dept., Herbert H. Lehman Coll. 1969–77; Dir. Health Professions Inst., Montefiore Hosp. and Medical Center 1975–77; Dean, School of Nursing, Univ. of Pa., Philadelphia 1977–92, Prof. 1992–96, interim Pres. 1993–94, Dean Emer., Prof. Emer. 1996–; mem. Task Force Jt. Cttee. on Mental Health of Children 1966–69, Gov.'s Cttee. on Children, New York 1971–75, Inst. of Medicine, N.A.S. (Governing Council 1981–83), Comm. on Human Rights 1991–94, American Acad. of Nursing (Governing Council 1976–78), Expert Advisory Panel on Nursing, WHO 1974–, Nat. Advisory Mental Health Council, Nat. Inst. of Mental Health 1983–87, Bd. of Health Promotion and Disease Prevention 1990–94; Pres. American Orthopsychiatric Asscn. 1985; Dir. Salomon Inc. 1994–97; Pres. Nat. League for Nursing 1991–93; Consultant to many foundations, public and pvt. univs., health care agencies; speaker on radio and TV; Hon. D.Sc. (Lycoming Coll., Cedar Crest Coll., Univ. of Rochester, Medical Coll. of Pa., Univ. of Md., Loyola Univ., Wagner Coll.); Hon. LL.D. (Pa.); Hon. D.Hum.Litt. (Hunter Coll., Rush Univ.); numerous awards and distinctions. *Publications:* numerous books including Nursing Leadership: Global Strategies (Ed.) 1990 and over 75 articles on nursing and health policy. *Address:* Nursing Education Building, University of Pennsylvania, 354 NEB, Philadelphia, PA 19104; 420 Guardian Drive, Philadelphia, PA 19104, U.S.A. (Home).

FAHD IBN ABDUL AZIZ; King of Saudi Arabia; b. 1923, Riyadh; s. of King Abdul Aziz ibn Saud; Minister of Educ. 1953, of the Interior 1962–75; Second Deputy Prime Minister 1967–75, First Deputy Prime Minister 1975–82, Prime Minister June 1982–; became Crown Prince 1975; succeeded to the throne on the death of his brother 13 June 1982; assumed title "Servant of the Two Shrines" 1986. *Address:* Royal Diwan, Riyadh, Saudi Arabia.

FAHEY, John Joseph; Australian politician and lawyer; b. 10 Jan. 1945, New Zealand; s. of Stephen Fahey and Annie Fahey; m. Colleen McGurran 1968; one s. two d.; ed. St. Anthony's Convent, Picton, and Chevalier Coll. Bowral; mem. Parl. of N.S.W. 1984–95; Minister for Industrial Relations and Employment and Minister Assisting Premier of N.S.W. 1988–90; Minister for Industrial Relations, Further Educ., Training and Employment, N.S.W. 1990–92; Premier and Treas. of N.S.W. 1992; Premier and Minister for Econ. Devt. of N.S.W. 1993–95; Fed. mem. for Macarthur and Minister for Finance 1996–, for Admin. 1997–; Chair. Sydney 2000 Olympic Bid Co. 1992–93. *Leisure interest:* keen sports follower. *Address:* Department of Finance and Administration, Newlands Street, Parkes, A.C.T. 2600, Australia. *Telephone:* (2) 6263-2222. *Fax:* (2) 6273-3021.

FAHRNI, Fritz, PH.D.; Swiss business executive; b. 7 Sept. 1942; two d.; ed. Swiss Fed. Inst. of Tech. (ETH), Zürich, Ill. Inst. of Tech. Chicago and Harvard Business School; research worker, Ill. Inst. of Tech., NASA 1967–70; research and devt. eng. production, CIBA-GEIGY 1971–76; Head, Research and Devt. Gas Turbine Dept. Sulzer Bros. 1976–80, Head, Gas Turbine Dept. 1980–82, Head, Weaving Machine Group 1982–88; Pres. and C.E.O. Sulzer Corpn. 1988–. *Leisure interests:* sport, reading, music, garden. *Address:* Sulzer Corporation AG, Postfach, CH-8401 Winterthur, Switzerland.

FAILLARD, Hans, DR. PHIL; German professor of biochemistry; b. 2 April 1924, Cologne; s. of Hermann and Elisabeth (née Kühn) Faillard; m. 1st Maria Scholl 1952 (died 1989); one s.; m. 2nd Gisela Gaertner 1993; ed. Univ. of Cologne; Ordinary Prof. of Physiological Chem., Ruhr Univ., Bochum 1964–73, Rector 1969–72; Vice-Pres. West German Rectors' Conf. 1970–76; Ordinary Prof. of Biochem., Univ. of the Saarland, Saarbrücken 1973–, Pres. of Univ. 1973–79; Chair. Cttee. for Int. Contacts of the Alexander von Humboldt Foundation 1973–92; mem. Cen. Cttee. German Conf. of Ministers for Cultural Affairs 1978–92; mem. Cttee. for Research, German Rectors' Conf. 1980–92, Chair. Advisory Body 1994–96; Hochhaus Award, Univ. of Cologne; medals from Hebrew Univ., Israel, and Seoul Nat. Univ., Korea. *Publications:* more than 80 publs. in the field of glycoproteins and more than 30 papers on educational topics. *Address:* Universität des Saarlandes, D-66123 Saarbrücken (Office); Richard-Wagner Strasse 87, D-66125 Saarbrücken, 35 An der Wallburg, D-51427 Bensberg-Refrath, Germany (Home). *Telephone:* (0681) 3022440 (Office); (06897) 761660; (02204) 63437. *Fax:* (02204) 63437.

FAINSILBER, Adrien, D.P.L.G.; French architect and urban designer; b. 15 June 1932, Le Nouvion, France; s. of Fanny Moscovici and Sigismond Fainsilber; m. Julia Berg 1961; two s. one d.; ed. Ecole Nationale Supérieure des Beaux Arts; architect Univ. of Villetaneuse 1969–70, Univ. of Tech. of Compiegne 1973, Evry Hosp. 1980, La Géode, Parc de la Villette, Paris 1984, Cité of Science and Industry, Paris 1985, Water Treatment Plant, Valenton 1987, Museum of Beaux Arts, Clermont-Ferrand 1992, Town Hall, La Flèche 1994, HQ Unedic, Paris 1994, master plan and housing for Zac Richter, Port Marianne, Montpellier 1995, Montsouris Mutual Inst. psychiatric centre for adolescents, Paris 1996, Museum of Modern and Contemporary Art, Strasbourg 1997, Children's Hosp., Purpan, Toulouse 1998; mem. Int. Acad. of Architecture; Bronze Medal Soc. d'Encouragement à l'Art et à l'Industrie 1973, Silver Medal Acad. of Architecture 1986, Chevalier, Légion d'honneur 1987, U.I.A. Prix Auguste Perret 1990, Officier, Ordre des Arts et des Lettres 1997. *Leisure interests:* swimming, windsurfing, travel. *Address:* 7 rue Salvador Allende, 92000 Nanterre (Office); 9 cité de l'Alma, 75007 Paris, France (Home). *Telephone:* (1) 47 21 64 38. *Fax:* (1) 47 21 58 08.

FAIRBAIRN, John Sydney, M.A., F.C.A.; British business executive and charity administrator; b. 15 Jan. 1934, Steventon; s. of S.G. Fairbairn, M.C. and Angela Fairbairn (née Fane); m. Camilla Fry (née Grinling) 1968; one s. two d., two step-s. two step-d.; ed. Eton Coll., Trinity Coll. Cambridge; nat. service in 17th/21st Lancers 1952–54; articles to Monkhouse Stoneham & Co., Chartered Accountants 1957–60; joined M&G Group PLC 1961, Dir. 1974, Deputy Chair. 1980–89, Non-Exec. Dir. 1989–; Chair. Unit Trust Asscn. 1989–91; Chair. Esmée Fairbairn Charitable Trust 1988– (Trustee 1966–); Chair. Cen. European Growth Fund PLC 1994–; Hon. Fellow King's Coll. London; Hon. D.Univ. (Buckingham); D.L. West Sussex 1996–. *Leisure interests:* music, history, country pursuits. *Address:* Child & Co., 1 Fleet Street, London, EC4Y 1BD, England. *Telephone:* (01444) 412200.

FAIRBANKS, Douglas Elton, Jr.; American actor, writer and producer; b. 9 Dec. 1909, New York; s. of late Douglas Elton and Anna Beth (Sully) Fairbanks; m. 1st Joan Crawford 1929 (divorced 1933); m. 2nd Mary Lee Epling 1939 (died 1988); three d.; m. 3rd Vera Shelton 1991; ed. Pasadena Polytechnic, Harvard Mil. School, Los Angeles, Collegiate Mil. School, New York, tutored London and Paris; began film career 1923, stage career 1927; acted in more than 75 films and 20 plays in U.S. and U.K. (produced or co-produced 15); produced 160 one-act TV plays 1953–58; organized own production co., Criterion Films Corp. (U.K.) 1934; fmr. Chair. Dougfair Corp. and subsidiaries; Chair. The Fairbanks Co. (Calif.) 1946, Douglas Fairbanks Ltd. (U.K.) and associated cos. 1952–58; Pres. Fairtel Corp. (N.Y.) 1969; Dir./Consultant various int. cos. 1950–75; Gov. Ditchley Foundation; Trustee Edwina Mountbatten Trust; mem. Council on Foreign Relations, New York; mem. Mountbatten Memorial Trust (U.S.A.); mem. Bd. of Govs., Exec. Cttee. Royal Shakespeare Theatre, Stratford-on-Avon, Bd. Dirs. Shakespeare Globe Theatre; Nat. Vice-Chair. Cttee. Defend America by Aiding Allies 1940–41, Vice-Pres. Franco-British War Relief Asscn. 1939–41, Presidential Envoy, Special Mission to Latin America 1940–41; Chair. Share Through C.A.R.E. Comm. 1946–50, American Relief for Korea 1951–55; rank of Capt., U.S.N. Reserve 1954; Nat. Vice-Pres., American Asscn. for UN 1946–55; Sr. Churchill Fellow (Westminster Coll.); Visiting Fellow, St. Cross Coll., Oxford, Hon. D.F.A. (Westminster Coll.), Hon. LL.D. (Denver Univ.), Hon. M.A. (Oxford Univ.); also professional awards from U.S.A., Germany and Italy. U.S. Navy's Distinguished Public Service Award 1995, Shakespeare Globe Award 1995; Hon. K.B.E., D.S.C., K.St.J.; Officier Légion d'honneur, Croix de guerre avec palmes (France), U.S. Silver Star, Legion of Merit with Valor attachment, other military and diplomatic honours from Italy, West Germany, Belgium, Greece, Netherlands, Brazil, Chile, South Korea etc. *Films include:* Stella Dallas 1926, The Dawn Patrol 1930, Outward Bound 1930, Little Caesar 1930, Morning Glory 1933, Catherine the Great 1934, The Amateur Gentlemen, The Prisoner of Zenda 1937, The Young in Heart 1938, Gunga Din 1939, Angels over Broadway 1940, The Corsican Brothers 1941, The Exile 1946, Sinbad the Sailor 1946, Lady in Ermine 1947, The Fighting O'Flynn 1948, State Secret 1950, Ghost Story 1981. *Plays include:* Young Woodley, Moonlight is Silver, My Fair Lady, The Pleasure of His Company, The Secretary Bird, Present Laughter, Out on a Limb, Sleuth, etc. *Publications:* The Fairbanks Album (with Richard Shickel) 1975, Salad Days (autobiog. part I) 1988, A Hell of a War (autobiog. part II) 1993. *Leisure interests:* swimming, tennis, golf, travel, writing. *Address:* The Beekman, 575 Park Avenue, New York, NY 10021, U.S.A. *Telephone:* (212) 838-4900. *Fax:* (212) 688-2164.

FAIRCLOUGH, Anthony John, C.M.G., M.A., F.R.S.A.; British environmental consultant; b. 30 Aug. 1924, Birmingham; s. of Wilfrid Fairclough and Lillian Anne Fairclough (née Townshend); m. Patricia Monks 1957; two s.; ed. St. Philip's Grammar School, Birmingham and St. Catharine's Coll., Cambridge; Ministry of Aircraft Production and Ministry of Supply 1944–48; Colonial Office 1948–64; Sec. Nyasaland Comm. of Inquiry 1959; Private Sec. to Minister of State for Commonwealth Relations and for the Colonies 1963–64; Head, Pacific and Indian Ocean Dept. Commonwealth Office 1964–68; Head, W. Indian Dept. FCO 1968–70; Head, New Towns 1 Div. Dept. of Environment 1970–72, Head of Planning, Minerals and Countryside Directorate 1973–74; Dir. Cen. Unit on Environmental Pollution 1974–78; Dir. Int. Transport, Dept. of Transport 1978–81; Dir. for the Environment, Comm. of the EC 1981–85; Acting Dir.-Gen. for the Environment, Consumer Protection and Nuclear Safety, Comm. of the European Communities 1985–86, Deputy Dir.-Gen. for Devt., 1986–89, Special Adviser 1989–94, Hon. Dir.-Gen. European Comm. 1989–; Capacity 21, Adviser UNDP 1994–; Dir. Environmental Resources Management 1989–97. *Leisure interests:* travel, gardening, reading, photography. *Address:* Apt. 12, Résidence Balderic, 32 Quai aux Briques, 1000 Brussels, Belgium; 6 Cumberland Road, Kew, Richmond, Surrey, TW9 3HQ, England. *Telephone:* 0181-940 6999 (England). *Fax:* 0181-940 3758 (England).

FAIRCLOUGH, Sir John Whitaker, Kt., B.SC., F.I.E.E., F.ENG., F.R.S.A.; British engineer; b. 23 Aug. 1930, Thirsk; s. of Harold Whitaker and Elsinora Fairclough; m. Margaret A. Harvey 1954 (died 1996); two s. one d.; ed. Thirsk Grammar School and Manchester Univ.; Ferranti Ltd., U.K. and Ferranti Electric, U.S.A. 1954–57; Project Eng. IBM Poughkeepsie 1957–59; Project Man. IBM UK Labs. Ltd. 1959–64, Lab. Dir. 1964–68; Dir. of Data Processing for Marketing and Service, IBM UK 1968–70, Lucas Industries; Lab. Dir. IBM Lab. Raleigh, N.C. 1970–72; Vice-Pres. Communications Systems, IBM Corpn. 1972–74; Chair. IBM UK Labs. Ltd. 1974–82; Dir. Mfg. & Devt. and Chair. IBM UK Labs. Ltd. 1982–86; Chief Scientific Adviser, Cabinet Office 1986–89; Deputy Chair. Council Southampton Univ. 1996–; Dir. (non-exec.) Oxford Instruments Group PLC 1990–98, N. M. Rothschild & Sons Ltd. 1990–98, Infolink 1991–93, DSC (Europe) 1992–98, Lucas Industries 1992–96, Psion PLC 1995–, Southampton Innovation Ltd. 1996–; Chair. Centre for the Exploration of Science and Tech. 1990–95, Rothschild Ventures Ltd. 1990–, Eng. Council 1990–96; mem. Advisory Council on Science and Tech.; 1989–; Fellow, British Computer Soc., Nat. Acad. of Eng.; Gold Medal, Inst. of Production Engs. 1989; Hon. D.Sc. (Southampton) 1983, (Cranfield) 1987, (Manchester) 1988, (Aston) 1990, (Cen. London Polytechnic) 1991, (City Univ.) 1992; Hon. D.Tech. (Loughborough) 1990; Hon. Fellow Portsmouth Polytechnic; Hon. F.I.Mech.E 1996; Gold Medal Award of Merit, Co. of Carmen 1995. *Leisure interests:* woodwork, gardening. *Address:* The Old Blue Boar, St John's Street, Winchester, Hants., SO23 8HF; Flat 3, 57 Millbank, London, S.W.1, England. *Telephone:* (01962) 866308 (Winchester); 0171-630 9449 (London).

FAIRWEATHER, Sir Patrick (Stanislaus), K.C.M.G.; British diplomatist; b. 17 June 1936; s. of John Fairweather and Dorothy Boanus; m. Maria Merica 1962; two d.; ed. Ottershaw School, Surrey and Trinity Coll. Cambridge; entered FCO 1965; served Rome 1966–69, Paris 1970–73, Vientiane 1975–76, First Sec., UK Representation to EEC, Brussels 1976–78; Amb. to Angola 1985–87; Asst. Under-Sec. of State, FCO 1987–90, Deputy Under-Sec. of State 1990–92; Amb. to Italy (also accred. to Albania) 1992–96; Sr. Adviser, Schroders 1996–; Dir. Butrint Foundation 1997–. *Leisure interests:* travel, gardening, photography, sailing. *Address:* c/o Foreign & Commonwealth Office, London, SW1A 2AH, England.

FAITH, Adam (pseudonym of Terence Nelhams); British singer and actor; b. 23 June 1940, London; worked in cutting rooms, Pinewood Studios 1956; Asst. Editor, Beaconsfield Studios 1958; fmr. columnist Mail on Sunday; fmr. Dir. Savoy Hotel; TV début as singer in Oh Boy 1959. *Television appearances include:* Drumbeat, The Adam Faith Show, Boy Meets Girl, Budgie, Just Another Little Blues Song, Alfie, Minder on the Orient Express, Love Hurts; London stage appearances include: Night Must Fall, Alfie, Billy Liar, City Sugar, Budgie 1989. *Films include:* Beat Girl, Never Let Go, What A Whopper!, Stardust, McVicar, Foxes. *Play:* Now You Know 1995.

FAITHFULL, Marianne; British popular singer; b. 29 Dec. 1947, Ormskirk, Lancs.; d. of Glynn and Eva Faithfull; m. 1st John Dunbar; one s.; m. 2nd Ben Brierley; m. 3rd Giorgio della Terza; made first recording (As Tears Go By) aged 17; numerous albums include Broken English 1979, Strange Weather 1987, 20th Century Blues (Kurt Weill songs) 1996; performed in The Threepenny Opera, Gate Theatre, Dublin 1992. *Publication:* Faithfull (autobiography). *Address:* c/o The Coalition Group Ltd., 12 Barley Mow

Passage, London, W4 4PH, England. *Telephone:* 0181-987 0123. *Fax:* 0181-987 0345.

FAIVRE d'ARCIER, Bernard, L. ÈS L.; French civil servant; b. 12 July 1944, Abertville; s. of Guy Faivre d'Arcier and Geneviève Teilhard de Chazelles; m. 1st Sylvie Dumont 1966; one s.; m. 2nd Madeleine Levy 1991; ed. Hautes études commerciales and Inst. d'études politiques; Civil Admin. Ministry of Culture 1972–79; Dir. Festival d'Avignon 1979–84, Artistic Dir. 1992–; Tech. Adviser to the Prime Minister's Cabinet 1984–86; Pres. la SEPT (TV Channel) 1986; Consultant, UNESCO 1987–88; Adviser to the Pres. of the Nat. Ass. 1988–; Head of Dept. of Theatre, Ministry of Educ. and Culture 1992–; Dir. Nat. Centre for Theatre 1992–; Commdr. des Arts et des Lettres, Chevalier, Ordre du Mérite, Chevalier, Légion d'honneur. *Leisure interests:* art, theatre. *Address:* 6 rue Saint-Bon, 75004 Paris; Festival d'Avignon, 8 bis rue de Mons, 84000 Avignon, France. *Telephone:* (1) 42.72.84.38 (Paris); (4) 90 27 66 50 (Avignon). *Fax:* (4) 90 27 66 83 (Avignon).

FAKHFAKH, Mokhtar, B.S.; Tunisian banker; b. 10 Aug. 1930, Sfax; s. of Ahmed B. Abdessalem Fakhfakh and Fatouma Hamouda; m. Samira Fakhfakh; one s. one d.; ed. law studies; Pres. and Gen. Man. Soc. Hotelière et Touristique de Tunisie 1961–67; Dir. of Commerce, Ministry of Finance and Commerce 1967–69; Pres. and Gen. Man. Banque du Sud 1969–71; Gen. Man. Banque de Développement Economique de Tunisie 1971–78; Pres. and Gen. Man. Cie. Financière Immobilière et Touristique de Tunisie 1978–80, Banque Int. Arabe de Tunisie 1980, now Pres.; African Banker of Year 1994; Commdr. Ordre de la République. *Address:* Banque International Arabe de Tunisie, 70–72 Avenue Habib Bourguiba, B.P. 520, 1080 Tunis, Tunisia. *Telephone:* 340-733. *Fax:* 340-680.

FAKHR, Maj.-Gen. Ahmed Ismail, M.A., M.B.A.; Egyptian national security expert and strategic analyst; b. 5 April 1931, Cairo; m. Bahiga Bahgat Helmy 1956; two s.; ed. Nat. Defence Coll. Cairo, air defence studies in Moscow, Royal Coll. of Defence Studies, London and Nat. Defence Univ. Washington, D.C.; Dir. Nat. Defence Coll. Cairo 1980–82, Nasser Higher Mil. Acad. Cairo 1982–84; Ed.-in-Chief, Defence Magazine, Al-Ahram Asscn. Cairo 1985; Adviser on Foreign Aid to Prime Minister 1986–89; Rep. of UNIMEG (pvt. business consortium), Moscow 1990; now Dir. Nat. Center for Middle East Studies and elected Chair. of local people's council, Cairo Governate; mem. Egyptian del. to Madrid Peace Conf. 1992; other government appts.; Mil. Medal and other decorations. *Publications:* Defence of Egypt (classified) 1981, Arms Control Series 1992, Egypt and the 21st Century 1994, Conflict: Prevention and Resolution 1994, The Future of the Military in Egypt 1995, U.S.-Egyptian Relations 1995, The Middle East: Technological Edge 1995. *Leisure interests:* reading on int. affairs and nat. security, classical music, ballet. *Address:* National Center for Middle East Studies, 1 Kasr El Nil Street, 2nd Floor, Cairo; 27 Dr. Khalil Abdel Khalek Street, Heliopolis, Cairo, Egypt. *Telephone:* 771125; 770041; 770042 (Office); 2454551 (Home). *Fax:* 770063.

FALCON, Michael Gascoigne, C.B.E., J.P., D.L.; British insurance executive; b. 28 Jan. 1928; s. of late Michael Falcon and Kathleen Gascoigne; m. April Daphne Lambert 1954; two s. one d.; ed. Stowe School and Heriot Watt Coll. Edin.; Head Brewer and Jt. Man. Dir. E. Lacon & Co. Ltd., Great Yarmouth 1952–68; Exec. Dir. Edgar Watts (willow merchants) 1968–73; Dir. Norwich Union Insurance Group 1963–94, Vice-Chair. 1979–81, Chair. 1981–94; Chair. Norwich Winterthur Holdings Ltd. 1984–94, Norwich Health Authority 1988–94, Norfolk and Norwich Health Care Trust 1994–97; Chair. Nat. Seed Devt. Org. Ltd. 1972–82, Pauls & White PLC 1976–85, Eastern Counties Regional Bd. Lloyds Bank PLC 1979–91; Dir. Greene King & Sons PLC 1988–96, British Railways (Anglia) Bd. 1988–92. *Leisure interests:* country pursuits. *Address:* Keswick Old Hall, Norwich, Norfolk, NR4 6TZ; Kirkgate, Loweswater, Cockermouth, Cumbria, England. *Telephone:* (01603) 454348.

FALCONER, Douglas Scott, SC.D., F.R.S., F.R.S.E.; British geneticist; b. 10 March 1913, Aberdeenshire, Scotland; s. of Gerald S. Falconer and Lillias Douglas; m. Margaret Duke 1942; two s.; ed. Edinburgh Acad. and St. Andrews Univ.; joined Scientific Staff of Agric. Research Council 1947, Prof. of Genetics and Dir. of the Council's Unit of Animal Genetics, Dept. of Genetics, Univ. of Edin. 1968–80. *Publications:* Introduction to Quantitative Genetics 1960, 1981, 1989, 1996; research papers, mainly on mouse genetics and quantitative genetics. *Address:* 21 Mansionhouse Road, Edinburgh, EH9 ITZ, Scotland.

FALCONER OF THOROTON, Baron (Life Peer) cr. 1997, of Thoroton in the County of Nottinghamshire, **Charles Leslie Falconer,** Q.C.; British lawyer and politician; b. 19 Nov. 1951; s. of John Falconer and the late Anne Falconer; m. Marianna Hildyard 1985; three s. one d.; ed. Trinity Coll., Glenalmond, Queen's Coll., Cambridge; called to the Bar 1974, took silk 1991; Solicitor-Gen. May 1997–; Minister with responsibility for Millennium Dome 1998–; Labour. *Address:* 9 Buckingham Gate, London, SW1E 6JP, England.

FALDO, Nick; British golfer; b. 18 July 1957, Welwyn Garden City; m. 1st Melanie Faldo; m. 2nd Gill Faldo 1986; one s. two d.; won England Boys' Int. 1974, England Youth Int. 1975, Herts. Co. Championship, Berkshire Trophy, Scrutton Jug, S. African Golf Union Special Stroke Championship, was Co. Champion of Champions, mem. G.B. Commonwealth team, Sr. England Int. 1975; became professional 1976; won Skol Lager Int., Rookie of the Year (best British newcomer) 1977, Colgate PGA Championship 1978, 1980, 1981, five titles on PGA European tour, Golf Writers' Asscn. Trophy and Harry Vardon Trophy 1983, Open Championship, Muirfield 1987, French Open and Volvo Masters, Valderrama 1988, Masters, Augusta, Ga., U.S.A. 1989, French Open 1989, U.S. Masters 1989, 1990, 1996, Open Championship, St. Andrews 1990, Irish Open 1991, 1992, 1993, Open Championship, Muirfield 1992, Toyota World Match Play Championship 1992, Scandinavian Masters 1992, European Open 1992, Johnnie Walker World Championship 1992, (7 tournament victories 1992), Alfred Dunhill Belgian Open 1994, Doral Ryder Open, U.S.A. 1995; World No. 1 (Sony Ranking) 1992–94, Johnnie Walker Asian Classic 1993. *Publications:* In Search of Perfection (with Bruce Critchley) 1995, Faldo – A Swing for Life 1995. *Address:* c/o John Simpson Associates, Woodcock House, Gibbard Mews, High Street, London, SW19 5BY, England.

FALIK, Yuri Aleksandrovich; Russian composer and conductor; b. 30 July 1936, Odessa; s. of Aleksander Yefimovich Falik and Yevgeniya Mikhailovna Bochko; m. Valentina Alexandrovna Papkova; one s. one d.; ed. Odessa Specialised School, Leningrad State Conservatory as cellist (teachers A. Shtrimer and M. Rostropovich), as composer (B. Arapov); teacher Leningrad (now St. Petersburg) Conservatory 1965–88, Prof. of Composition and Instrumentation 1988–; toured as conductor with orchestras in Russia and U.S.A.; First Prize Int. Cellists Competition Helsinki 1962; Merited Worker of Arts of Russia 1981. *Compositions:* for musical theatre Orestea (choreographic tragedy) 1968, Scapin Antics (opera) 1981; for symphony orchestra: Symphony No. 1 1963, No. 2 (Kaddish) 1993, Light Symphony 1971, Concertos 1967, 1977, Mass over Igor Stravinsky 1975, Symphonietta for strings 1984; for instruments with orchestra: Concertino for oboe 1961, Violin Concerto 1971, Chamber Concerto for three flutes 1983, Concertino for bassoon 1987, Concerto della Passione for Cello 1988; vocal-symphony works: Five Poems by Anna Akhmatova for soprano and chamber orchestra 1978, Ringaday for mezzo-soprano and orchestra 1986, Polly and Dinosaurs (musical fairy-tale over Geraldine Freund) 1989, Mass 1996; works for choir a cappella, including Liturgy Chants 1992; chamber ensembles, including 7 Quartets 1955–93; romances, instrumental pieces. *Address:* Finlyandsky prospekt 1, Apt. 54, 194044 St. Petersburg, Russia. *Telephone:* (812) 542-63-06 (Home).

FALISE, Michel, D. EN D., D. ÈS SC. ECON.; French economist and university professor; b. 11 March 1931, Marcinelle; s. of A. Falise and L. Falise; m. Marie-Françoise de Gheldere 1957; three s. three d.; ed. Facultés Universitaires de Namur, Univ. Catholique de Louvain, Harvard Univ., U.S.A.; Econ. Adviser, Banque de Bruxelles 1958–60; Prof., Univ. Catholique de Lille 1960, Dean., Faculty of Social Sciences 1965–79, Pres.-Rector 1979–91, Pres. Conseil Supérieur 1991–95; Deputy Mayor of Lille 1995–; Consultant to OECD, WHO, EC and French Govt. offices; Pres. Int. Fed. of Catholic Univs. 1980–91, Féd. des Universités Catholiques Européennes 1991–97, Habitat et Humanisme 1994–; mem. Bd. Centre national des oeuvres universitaires 1987–, Asscn. Int. des Universités 1990–; Dr. h.c. (Leuven, Belgium), (Sacred Heart, U.S.A.); Prix Asscn. Française des Sciences Econs., Grand Prix de la Société Industrielle (Lille); Chevalier, Légion d'honneur; Commdr. Ordre de la Couronne (Belgium). *Publications:* La demande de monnaie 1960, L'équilibre macro-économique 1976, Une pratique chrétienne de l'Economie 1985, Repères pour une éthique d'entreprise 1992, Economie et Foi 1993. *Address:* 60 boulevard Vauban, P.O. Box 109, 59016 Lille cedex (Office); 9 allée Raoul Dufy, 59510 Hem, France. *Telephone:* 20-75-65-17.

FALL, Sir Brian James Proetel, G.C.V.O., K.C.M.G.; British diplomatist (retd.); b. 13 Dec. 1937; s. of John William Fall and Edith Juliette Fall (née Proetel); m. Delmar Alexandra Roos 1962; three d.; ed. St. Paul's School, Magdalen Coll. Oxford, Univ. of Michigan Law School, U.S.A.; joined H.M. Foreign (now Diplomatic) Service 1962, UN Dept., Foreign Office 1963, Moscow 1965, Geneva 1968, Civil Service Coll. 1970, Eastern European and Soviet Dept. and Western Orgs. Dept., Foreign Office 1971, New York 1975, Harvard Univ. Centre for Int. Affairs 1976, Counsellor Moscow 1977–79, Head of Energy, Science and Space Dept., FCO 1979–80, Head of Eastern European and Soviet Dept., FCO 1980–81, Prin. Pvt. Sec. to Sec. of State for Foreign and Commonwealth Affairs 1981–84, Dir. Cabinet Sec.-Gen. of NATO 1984–86, Asst. Under-Sec. of State (Defence), FCO 1986–88, Minister, Washington 1988–89, High Commr. in Canada 1989–92; Amb. to Russia (also accred. to several mems. of CIS) 1992–95; Prin. Lady Margaret Hall, Oxford 1995–. *Leisure interests:* reading, walking, travel. *Address:* Lady Margaret Hall, Oxford, OX2 6QA, England.

FALL, Cheikh Ibrahima, M.SC.ECON., M.B.A.; Senegalese international civil servant and banker; b. 1 Oct. 1947, Louga; m. Marième Diouma Faye 1972; two s. one d.; financial analyst, Operations Dept. Banque ouest-africaine de développement (BOAD) 1978–79, Rural Devt. and Infrastructural Operations Dept. 1979–81, Officer-in-Charge of Dept. 1981. Dir. of Dept. 1981–85, Dir. Loans and Equity Dept. 1985–86; Dir. Office of Pres. of African Devt. Bank (ADB) 1986–92, Dir. Co. Programmes, S. Region Dept. 1992–95, Officer-in-Charge of Admin. and Gen. Services and ADB restructuring exercise 1995–96, Sec.-Gen. ADB 1996–. *Leisure interests:* music, golf, reading. *Address:* African Development Bank, B.P. V 316, Abidjan, Côte d'Ivoire. *Telephone:* 204054. *Fax:* 204927.

FALL, Ibrahima; Senegalese politician and educator; b. 1942, Tivaouane, Thies; s. of Momar Khoudia Fall and Seynabou (Diakhate) Fall; m. Déguène Fall; four c.; ed. Univ. of Dakar, Inst. of Political Science, Paris, Faculty of

Law, Univ. of Paris; Prof. of Int. Law and Int. Relations, Dean of Faculty of Law, Univ. of Dakar 1975–81; Minister of Higher Educ. 1983–84, of Foreign Affairs 1984–89; Adviser, Supreme Court of Senegal; Asst. Gen. Sec. UN Dept. of Political Affairs; Consultant, UNESCO; mem. African Council for Higher Educ. *Publications:* articles in professional journals. *Address:* United Nations, United Nations Plaza, New York, NY 10017, U.S.A.; Sicap Fenêtre Mermoz, Dakar, Senegal (Home).

FALLACI, Oriana; Italian writer and journalist; b. 29 June 1930, Florence; d. of Edoardo and Tosca (Cantini) Fallaci; ed. Liceo Classico 'Galileo Galilei', Florence, and medical school; entered journalism 1946, special corresp. 1950, war corresp. since 1967 (Viet Nam, Indo-Pakistan war, Middle East, insurrections in South America); Hon. D.Litt. (Columbia Coll., Chicago); St. Vincent Prize for Journalism (twice), Bancarella Prize for Best Seller 1991, Hemingway Prize for Literature, numerous other prizes. *Publications:* The Useless Sex 1960, The Egotists 1965, If the Sun Dies 1968, Interview with History 1974; novels: Penelope at War 1963, Nothing and So Be It 1969, Letter to a Child Never Born 1975, A Man 1979 (Premio Viareggio 1979), Inshallah (novel) 1990; numerous articles in Life, Look, New York Times Magazine, Washington Post, New Republic, etc., and in Europe, Asia and South America. *Address:* c/o Rizzoli Corporation, 31 West 57th Street, New York, NY 10019, U.S.A. *Telephone:* (212) 308-2000.

FÄLLDIN, (Nils Olof) Thorbjörn; Swedish politician and farmer; b. 24 April 1926, Högsjö; s. of N. J. and Hulda (Olsson) Fälldin; m. Solveig Oberg 1956; two s. one d.; ed. secondary school; mem., Second Chamber of Parl. 1958–64, First Chamber 1967–70; mem. Riksdag (Parl.) 1971–85; Chair. Centre Party 1971–85; Prime Minister 1976–78, 1979–82; Chair. Bd. Nordic Museum 1986–96, Swedish Telecommunications Admin. 1987–93, Telia AB 1993–95, Föreningsbanken AB 1992–96. *Leisure interests:* fishing, athletics. *Address:* Ås, 870 16 Ramvik, Sweden (Home). *Telephone:* 0612/43097 (Home).

FALLON, Ivan Gregory, F.R.S.A.; Irish journalist; b. 26 June 1944; s. of Padraic Fallon and Dorothea Maher; m. 1st Susan Mary Lurring 1967 (dissolved 1997); one s. two d.; m. 2nd Elizabeth Rees-Jones 1997; ed. St. Peter's Coll. Wexford, Trinity Coll. Dublin; on staff of Irish Times 1964–66, Thomson Prov. Newspapers 1966–67, Daily Mirror 1967–68, Sunday Telegraph 1968–70; Deputy City Ed., Sunday Express 1970–71, Sunday Telegraph 1971–84, City Ed. 1979–84; Deputy Ed. Sunday Times 1984–94; Group Chief Editorial Adviser, Argus Group South Africa 1994–; Chief Exec. Ind. Newspapers Holdings Ltd., South Africa 1997–; mem. Council, Univ. of Buckingham 1982–, Council of Govs., United Medical and Dental Schools of Guy's and St. Thomas's Hosps. 1985–94; Trustee Project Trust 1984–94, Generation Trust, Guy's Hosp. 1985–; Dir. N. Brown Holdings 1994–. *Publications:* DeLorean: the rise and fall of a dream-maker (with James L. Srodes) 1983, Takeovers 1987, The Brothers: the rise of Saatchi and Saatchi 1988, Billionaire: the life and times of Sir James Goldsmith 1991, The Player: the life of Tony O'Reilly 1994. *Leisure interests:* tennis, walking. *Address:* Prospect House, Klein Constantia Road, Constantia, Cape Town, South Africa. *Telephone:* (21) 488-4015. *Fax:* (11) 633-2115.

FALLOON, John H.; New Zealand politician and farmer; Nat. Party M.P. for Pahiatua 1977–; fmr. Assoc. Minister of Finance and Minister of Inland Revenue and Statistics; Postmaster-Gen. 1981–82; Minister of Agric. 1984–96, of Forestry 1990–96, and of Racing. *Address:* Parliament Buildings, Wellington, New Zealand.

FALOTTI, Pier Carlo; business executive; fmrly. head of European, Middle East and African operations, Digital Equipment; fmrly. head of non-U.S.A. operations A.T.&T.; Sr. Vice-Pres. Oracle 1996–.

FÄLTHAMMAR, Carl-Gunne, PH.D.; Swedish professor of physics; b. 4 Dec. 1931, Markaryd; s. of Oskar Fälthammar and Ingeborg Fälthammar; m. Ann-Marie Sjunnesson 1957; one s. one d.; ed. Royal Inst. of Tech. (KTH), Stockholm; Asst. Prof. KTH 1966–69, Assoc. Prof. 1969–75, Chair. Dept. of Plasma Physics 1967–97, Prof. of Plasma Physics 1975–; mem. Swedish Nat. Cttee. for Radio Science 1970–96, Swedish Nat. Cttee. for Geodesy and Geophysics 1973–96; Chair. Swedish Geophysical Soc. 1978–80; mem. Royal Swedish Acad. of Sciences, Int. Acad. of Astronautics, Acad. Europaea; other professional affiliations; Ph.d. h.c. (Oulu) 1989; Basic Sciences Award, Int. Acad. of Astronautics 1996, Golden Badge Award, European Geophysical Union 1996, Hannes Alfvén Medal, European Geophysical Soc. 1998. *Publications:* Cosmical Electrodynamics (with H. Alfvén) 1963, Magnetospheric Physics (with B. Hultqvist) 1990; papers in plasma physics and space physics. *Address:* Division of Plasma Physics, Alfvén Laboratory, The Royal Institute of Technology, 10044 Stockholm, Sweden. *Telephone:* (08) 790 76 85. *Fax:* (08) 24 54 31.

FALWELL, Jerry L., B.A.; American ecclesiastic; b. 11 Aug. 1933, Lynchburg, Va.; s. of Cary H. Falwell and Helen V. Beasley; m. Macel Pate 1958; two s. and one d.; ed. Baptist Bible Coll., Springfield, Missouri; ordained American Baptist minister; founder and pastor Thomas Road Baptist Church, Lynchburg 1956–, now sr. pastor; founder and Pres. Moral Majority Inc. (now Liberty Fed.) 1979–89, Liberty Broadcasting Network 1985–; host TV show Old Time Gospel Hour (nat. syndication); public lecturer; founder Liberty Univ., Lynchburg 1971; Hon. D.D. (Tennessee Temple Theological Seminary); Hon. D.Litt. (California Grad. School of Theology); Hon. LL.D. (Central Univ., Seoul, Korea); Clergyman of the Year Award (Religious Heritage) 1979, Jabotinsky Centennial Medal, Israel 1980, and numerous other awards. *Publications:* Church Aflame (co-author) 1971, Capturing a Town for Christ (co-author) 1973, Listen, America! 1980, The Fundamentalist Phenomenon 1981, Finding Inner Peace and Strength 1982, When It Hurts Too Much to Cry 1984, Wisdom for Living 1984, Stepping Out on Faith 1984, If I Should Die Before I Wake 1986, Strength For the Journey (autobiog.) 1987, The New American Family 1992. *Address:* Liberty University, 1971 University Boulevard, Lynchburg, VA 24502, U.S.A.

FALZON, Michael, B.ARCH., A. & C.E.; Maltese politician and architect; b. 17 Aug. 1945, Gzira; m. Mary Anne Aquilina; one s.; ed. the Lyceum and Univ. of Malta; fmrly. in practice as architect; mem. Nat. Exec. Nationalist Party 1975; Sec. of Information of the Party; Ed. The Democrat (weekly paper) 1975; M.P. 1976–96; Shadow Minister for Information and Broadcasting 1976–81; for Industry 1981–87; Minister for Devt. of Infrastructure 1987–92, for Environment 1992–94, for Educ. and Human Resources 1994–96; Ed. The People and People on Sunday newspapers 1997–98; Chair. Water Services Corpn. 1998–. *Address:* Water Services Corporation, Qormi Road, Luga, LQA 05, Malta. *Telephone:* 249851. *Fax:* 223016.

FAN JINGYI; Chinese journalist; fmr. Dir. Foreign Languages Publ. and Distribution Bureau; Ed.-in-Chief Econ. Daily 1986–94, People's Daily 1994–98; Vice-Chair. Economy Cttee. of 8th CPPCC Nat. Cttee., Educ, Science, Culture and Public Health Cttee. of 9th NPC 1998–; Hon. Pres. Photo-Journalism Soc. 1994–. *Address:* c/o Standing Committee of the National People's Congress, Beijing, People's Republic of China.

FAN ZHILUN, Maj-Gen.; Chinese army official; b. 1935, Fushun Co., Sichuan Prov.; s. of Fan Ximing and Fan Zhougshi; m. Ding Xin 1966; one s. one d.; Deputy Commdr. and Chief of Staff Chinese People's Armed Police Force 1985–; Deputy Pres. Mil. Educ. Coll. and Mil. Staff Coll. 1991–; Deputy Chief of Staff, Beijing Mil. Region of PLA 1993–. *Leisure interests:* climbing, swimming, music, calligraphy. *Address:* Headquarters of the Beijing Military Region, No. Jia 1, Badachu, Western Hill, Beijing, People's Republic of China.

FANFANI, Amintore; Italian politician and economist; b. 6 Feb. 1908, Pieve S. Stefano; m. Maria Pia Tavazzani 1975; two s. five d.; Fellow, Catholic Univ. of Milan 1930, Titular Prof. in Econ. History 1936, later Prof. Univ. of Rome 1954; mem. Constituent Assembly for XVI Dist. 1946, M.P. for same dist. 1948–68; Minister of Labour and Social Security in 4th, 5th and 6th De Gasperi Cabinets 1947–50; Minister of Agric. and Forestry, 8th De Gasperi Cabinet July 1951, Minister of the Interior 1953, 1987–88, of Budget 1988–89, and Prime Minister Jan. 1954; Sec. Christian Democrat Party 1954–59, 1973–75, Chair. April-Oct. 1976; Prime Minister 1958–59, 1960–63, 1982–83; Minister of Foreign Affairs 1965, 1966–68; Pres. of Senate 1968–73, 1976–82, 1985; Life Senator 1972–; Pres. Senate Standing Cttee. for Foreign Affairs 1992–94; Pres. UN Gen. Assembly 1965–66; numerous hon. degrees. *Publications:* Le origini dello spirito capitalistico 1932, Cattolicesimo e protestantesimo nella formazione storica del capitalismo 1934, Storia delle dottrine economiche 1938–71, Indagini sulla rivoluzione dei prezzi 1939, Storia economica 1940–71, Storia del lavoro 1943, Colloqui sui poveri 1941, Persona, beni, società 1945, Le tre città 1946, Poemi Omerici ed Economia Antica 1960, Una Pieve in Italia 1964, Strategia della Sopravvivenza 1975, ONU 1965–66, 1976, Capitalismo, Socialità, Partecipazione 1976. *Address:* Senato della Repubblica, Piazza Madama, 00100 Rome, Italy.

FANG LIZHI; Chinese astrophysicist; b. 12 Feb. 1936, Hangzhou; s. of Cheng Pu and Peiji (née Shi) Fang; m. Li Shuxian 1961; two s.; ed. Univ. of Peking; Asst. teacher Univ. of Science and Tech. of China 1958–63, Lecturer 1963–78, Prof. of Physics 1978–87, Vice-Pres. of Univ. 1984–87; Prof. and Head Theoretical Astrophysics Group, Beijing Astronomical Observatory, Chinese Acad. of Sciences 1987–; Sr. Visiting Fellow Inst. of Astronomy, Cambridge Univ. 1979–80; Visiting Prof. Research Inst. of Fundamental Physics, Kyoto Univ. 1981–82, Physics Dept. Univ. of Rome 1983; mem. Inst. for Advanced Study, Princeton 1986; Assoc. mem. Int. Centre for Theoretical Physics, Trieste 1984–89; lived in asylum in U.S. Embassy, Beijing 1989–90, to London, then to U.S.A. 1990–; Prof. of Physics and Astronomy, Univ. of Ariz., Tucson 1991–; mem. Chinese Acad. of Sciences 1981–89, N.Y. Acad. of Sciences 1986–; mem. of Council Chinese Soc. of Physics 1982–87, Chinese Soc. of Astronomy 1982–85, Asscn. pro Centro Int. de Fisica 1983–87, Int. Centre for Theoretical Physics 1984–89, Int. Centre for Relativistic Astrophysics 1985–89, Chinese Soc. of History of Science and Tech. 1987–89; Pres. Chinese Soc. of Gravitation and Relativistic Astrophysics 1983–89; Vice-Pres. Chinese Soc. of Astronomy 1985–89; mem. various IAU and IUPAP comms., etc.; Ed. Scientia Sinica 1978–89, Acta Physica Sinica 1979–89, Acta Astronomica Sinica 1980–83, Acta Astrophysica Sinica 1982–83, Journal of Modern Physics, etc.; Dr. h.c. (Rome Univ.) 1990; Nat. Award for Science and Tech. 1978, Chinese Acad. of Sciences Award 1982, New York Acad. of Sciences Award 1988, Robert F. Kennedy Human Rights Award 1989 etc. *Publications:* Modern Cosmology Review (ed.) 1978, Astrophysics Today (ed.) 1980, Basic Concepts in Relativistic Astrophysics (with R. Ruffini) 1981, English ed. 1987, Cosmology of the Early Universe (ed. with R. Ruffini) 1984, Galaxies, Quasars and Cosmology (ed. with R. Ruffini) 1985, Advances in Science of China: Physics (ed. with others) 1986, Introduction to Mechanics (with S.X. Li) 1986, Observational Cosmology (ed. with others) 1987, Creation of the Universe (with S.X. Li) 1987, Quantum Cosmology (ed. with R. Ruffini) 1987, Collection of History of Sciences (ed.) 1987, Philosophy as a Tool of Physics 1988, Origin, Structure and Evolution of Galaxies (ed.) 1988. *Leisure interest:* swimming. *Address:* Department of Physics, University of Arizona, Tucson, AZ 85721, U.S.A.

FANG SHOUXIAN; Chinese nuclear physicist; b. 27 Oct. 1932, Shanghai City; m. 1st Run Moyin (died 1965); m. 2nd Yao Mayli 1968, two d.; ed. Shanghai Fudan Univ.; Prof. Research, Nuclear Physics Inst., Academia Sinica 1982–; Project Dir., Beijing Electron Positron Collider (BEPC) 1986; Dir. Inst. of High Energy Physics 1988; Dir. BEPC Nat. Lab. 1992–; mem. Chinese Acad. of Sciences 1992; Hon. Nat. Natural Science Award 1990. *Address:* c/o P.O. Box 918, Beijing 100039, People's Republic of China. *Telephone:* 8219574. *Fax:* 8213374.

FANG WEIZHONG; Chinese state official; b. 11 March 1928, Dongfeng Co., Jilin Prov.; three s.; ed. Dongbei Univ.; joined CCP 1950; Vice-Chair, State Planning Comm. 1977, Chair. Econ. Cttee. CPPCC 1995; alt. mem. 12th CCP Cen. Cttee. 1982–87; mem. 13th CCP Cen. Cttee. 1987–92; alt. mem. 14th CCP Cen. Cttee. 1992–; mem. CPPCC 8th Nat. Cttee. 1995–98, 9th Nat. Cttee. 1998–; Chair. Economy Cttee. 1995–; Pres. Chinese Macroeconomics Soc. 1995–; mem. Council of People's Bank of China 1974–. *Leisure interest:* calligraphy. *Address:* c/o National Committee of the Chinese People's Political Consultative Conference, 23 Taipingqiao Street, Beijing, People's Republic of China.

FANG ZUQI, Gen.; Chinese army officer; fmr. Dir. Political Dept., PLA Shenyang and Beijing Mil. Area Command; Political Commissar, Nanjing Mil. Region 1994–; rank of Lieut.-Gen., Gen. 1998; mem. 15th CCP Cen. Cttee. 1997–. *Address:* Political Commissar's Office, Nanjing Military Region, Jiangsu Province, People's Republic of China.

FANJUL, Oscar, PH.D.; Spanish economist; b. 1949, Santiago, Chile; ed. Univ. Complutense de Madrid; Visiting Scholar, Harvard Univ. and M.I.T.; served as Sec.-Gen. and Under-Sec. Dept. of Industry and Energy; mem. team which negotiated Spain's entry to EC; has also served in Instituto Nacional de Industria (INI) and at Confederación Española de Cajas de Ahorros; Chair. Instituto Nacional di Hidrocarburos (INH) 1985–, Repsol S.A. 1987–; mem. Bd. Argentaria (Corporación Bancaria Española) 1991–, Teneo 1992–; mem. Trilateral Comm. 1991–; Orden de Isabel la Católica, Order of Belgian Crown. *Publications:* several articles and books on industrial and financial matters. *Address:* P° de la Castellana, 278–280, 28046 Madrid, Spain. *Telephone:* 34-1-348-81.00/348.80.00. *Fax:* 34-1-314.28. 21/348.94.94.

FANO, Ugo, PH.D.; American physicist; b. 28 July 1912, Turin, Italy; s. of Gino Fano and Rosa Cassin; m. Camilla Lattes 1939; two d.; ed. Univ. of Turin; asst. lecturer Univ. of Rome 1938; Research Assoc. Washington Biophysical Inst. 1939–40; Fellow, Research Assoc., resident investigator Dept. of Genetics, Carnegie Inst. of Washington 1940–46; consultant and ballistician U.S. Army Ballistics Reserves 1944–45; physicist, chief of radiation theory, Sr. Research Fellow U.S. Nat. Bureau of Standards 1946–66; Prof. Dept. of Physics and J. Franck Inst., Univ. of Chicago 1966–82, Emer. Prof. 1982–, Chair. Dept. of Physics 1972–74; Int. Fellowship of Italian Ministry of Educ. 1936; Hon. Sc.D. (Queen's, Belfast) 1978, Dr. h.c. (Univ. Pierre & Marie Curie, Paris) 1979; Rockefeller Public Service Award 1956, Stratton Award of Nat. Bureau of Standards 1963, U.S. Dept. of Commerce Performance Award 1968, Davisson-Germer Award 1976, E. Fermi Award 1995; Gold Medal of Dept. of Commerce for Exceptional Service 1957. *Publications include:* (with L. Fano): Basic Physics of Atoms and Molecules 1959, Physics of Atoms and Molecules 1972, (with A.R.P. Rau): Symmetries in Quantum Physics 1966, Atomic Collisions and Spectra 1986. *Address:* 5640 S. Ellis Avenue, Chicago, IL 60637 (Office); 5801 S. Dorchester Avenue, Chicago, IL 60637, U.S.A. (Home). *Telephone:* (773) 702 7010 (Office); (773) 643 8487 (Home).

FARAH, fmr. Empress of Iran (see Pahlavi).

FARAH, Nuruddin; Somali novelist; b. 24 Nov. 1945, Baidoa; s. of Hassan Farah and Aleli Fatuma; m. Amina Mama 1992; one s. one d.; ed. Panjab Univ., Chandigarh, India, Univs. of London and Essex; lecturer Nat. Univ. of Somalia, Mogadishu 1971–74; Assoc. Prof. Univ. of Jos, Nigeria 1981–83; Writer-in-Residence Univ. of Minn. 1989, Brown Univ. 1991; Prof. Makerere Univ., Kampala 1990; Rhodes Scholar St. Antony's Coll., Oxford 1996; Visiting Prof. Univ. of Texas at Austin 1997; now full-time novelist; English-speaking Union Literary Prize 1980, Neustadt Int. Literary Prize 1998. *Publications:* From a Crooked Rib 1970, Sweet and Sour Milk 1979, Sardines 1981, Close Sesame 1983, Maps 1986, Gifts 1992, Secrets 1998. *Address:* c/o Deborah Rogers, Rogers, Coleridge & White, 20 Powis Mews, London, W11 1JN, England.

FAREED, Abdul Sabur; Afghanistan politician; Prime Minister in Interim Govt. 1992–93; mem. Hizb-i Islami. *Address:* c/o Office of the Prime Minister, Kabul, Afghanistan.

FARELL CUBILLAS, Arsenio, PH.D.; Mexican politician; b. June 1921, Mexico City; ed. Nat. Univ of Mexico; lecturer in Civil Law and Gen. Theory of Process, Nat. Univ. of Mexico and in Civil Law, Iberoamerican Univ., Mexico City; Pres. Nat. Chamber of Sugar and Alcohol Industries 1973; Dir.-Gen. Fed. Electricity Comm. 1973–76; Dir.-Gen. Social Security Inst. 1976–82; Sec. of State for Employment 1982–85, for Labour and Social Welfare 1985–95. *Publications:* essays and articles on legal matters. *Address:* c/o Secretaría del Trabajo y Previsión Social, Edificio A, 4°, Periférico Sur 4271, Coronel Fuentes del Pedregal, 14140 México, D.F., Mexico.

FAREMO, Grete, LL.B.; Norwegian politician; b. 16 June 1955, Byglandsfjord, Setesdal; with Ministry of Finance, Norwegian Agency for Devt. Co-operation; Head of Div. Ministry of Devt. Co-operation 1984, Minister 1991–93; Chief Negotiating Officer Aker Eiendom 1986; Dir. (of Cultural Affairs) Aker Brygge (business and leisure complex), Norsk Arbeiderpresse; Minister of Justice and Police 1994–97; mem. bd. Labour Party Forum for Art and Culture. *Address:* c/o Norwegian Labour Party, Youngstorget 2, P.O. Box 8743, Oslo, Norway.

FARHI, Nicole; French fashion designer; b. 25 July 1946; d. of Ephraim Farhi and Marcelle Farhi (née Babani); m. David Hare (q.v.) 1992; one d. by Stephen Marks; ed. Lycée Calmette, Nice, Cours Berçot Art School, Paris; designer for Pierre d'Albi 1968; founded French Connection with Stephen Marks 1973; fmr. designer Stephen Marks; founder and designer Nicole Farhi 1983–, Nicole Farhi For Men 1989–; opened Nicole's Restaurant 1994; British Fashion Award for Best Contemporary Designer 1995, 1996, 1997. *Leisure interest:* sculpture. *Address:* 16 Foubert's Place, London, W1V 1HH, England. *Telephone:* 0171-287-8787.

FARKAS, Ferenc; Hungarian composer; b. 15 Dec. 1905, Nagykanizsa; s. of Aladár Farkas and Blanka Saly; m. Margit Kummer 1939 (died 1992); one s.; ed. Budapest Music Acad. and Accademia Santa Cecilia, Rome, with Ottorino Respighi; film music composer and conductor in Vienna and Copenhagen 1932–36; Teacher of Composition, Metropolitan Higher Music School, Budapest 1936; State Conservatory of Kolozsvar 1941, Dir. 1943–44; Asst. Dir. of Choir, Hungarian State Opera 1945–46; Dir. State Conservatory of Székesfehérvár 1946–48; Prof. of Composition, Budapest Music Acad. 1949–75; Kossuth Prize 1950, 1992, Erkel Prize 1960, Eminent Artist title 1970, Herder Prize 1979; Order of Hungarian Standard (with Laurel Wreath) 1980; Cavaliere dell'Ordine della Repubblica Italiana 1984. *Works include:* Bűvös szekrény (Magic Cupboard), opera 1938–42, Furfangos diákok (Sly Students), ballet 1949, Csinom Palkó, musical play 1950, Vidróczki, opera 1964, Panegyricus, dance play 1972; cantatas: Szent János kutja (Cantata Lyrica) 1945, Cantus Pannonicus 1958, Tavaszvárás (Waiting for Spring) 1967, Bontott zászlók (Flying Flags) 1973, Kőröshegyi Betlehemes (Jeu de Crèches) 1970, Aspirationes Principis (Rákóczi Cantata) 1975, Vita Poetae 1976; Laudatio Szigethiana (oratorio); Psaumes de Fête 1975–77, Egy úr Velencéből (A Gentleman from Venice, two act opera) 1980, Vivit Dominus 1981, Omaggio a Pessoa 1985, Virgilii Georgica (cantatas) 1988, Proprium Tergestinum (choir and organ) 1988, Requiem pro memoria M 1992, 4 Masses, Magnificat 1994; various works for orchestra and choir; chamber music, song cycles, incidental film and stage music. *Leisure interests:* literature, visual arts. *Address:* Nagyajtai-utca 12, 1026 Budapest, Hungary. *Telephone:* 156-46-43.

FARLEY, Carole, MUS.B.; American soprano opera singer; b. 29 Nov. 1946, Le Mars, Ia.; d. of Melvin and Irene (Reid) Farley; m. José Serebrier 1969; one d.; ed. Indiana Univ. and Hochschule für Musik, Munich (Fulbright Scholar); operatic début in U.S.A. in title role of La Belle Hélène, New York City Opera 1969; début at Metropolitan Opera as Lulu 1977; now appears regularly in leading opera houses of the world and in concert performances with major orchestras in U.S.A. and Europe; roles include Monteverdi's Poppea, Massenet's Manon, Mozart's Idomeneo, Verdi's La Traviata, Offenbach's Tales of Hoffmann and Strauss's Salome; Metropolitan Opera première of Shostakovich's Lady Macbeth of Mitzensk (Katerina Ismailova); Wozzeck (Marie), Toulouse Opera; *recordings include:* Le Pré aux Clercs, Behold the Sun, French songs by Chausson, Duparc, Satie and Fauré, Prokofiev songs, Poulenc's The Human Voice, Menotti's The Telephone, Britten's Les Illuminations, Prokofiev's The Ugly Duckling, Kurt Weill songs, Milhaud songs (with John Constable), Tchaikovsky opera arias, Delius songs with orchestra; *videos:* Poulenc's La Voix Humaine, Menotti's The Telephone, Strauss's Four Last Songs and Songs with orchestra; mem. American Guild of Musical Artists; several awards and prizes including Grand Prix du Disque 1995, for Les Soldats Morts (by A. Lemeland) and Diapason d'Or (France) 1997. *Leisure interests:* skiing, jogging, swimming, dancing, cooking, entertaining, reading. *Address:* 270 Riverside Drive, New York, NY 10025, U.S.A.; 20 Queen's Gate Gardens, London, SW7 5LZ, England.

FARLEY, Francis James Macdonald, M.A., PH.D., F.INST.P., F.R.S.; British physicist; b. 13 Oct. 1920, Lucknow, India; s. of Brig. E. L. Farley and Helen C. Pemberton; m. 1st Josephine M. Hayden 1945; m. 2nd Margaret A. Slee 1977; three s. one d.; ed. Clifton Coll. and Univ. of Cambridge; radar research, Ministry of Supply 1941–45; Chalk River Labs., Canada 1945–46; research student, Cambridge 1946–49; Sr. Lecturer, Auckland Univ. 1950–57; muon (g-2) experiment, CERN, Geneva 1957–67; Dean, Royal Mil. Coll. of Science, Shrivenham 1967–82, now Prof. Emer.; Visiting Prof., Dept. of Eng., Univ. of Reading 1982–86; Hon. Fellow, Trinity Coll., Dublin; Visiting Research Physicist, Yale Univ. 1984–92; Visiting Research Prof. Boston Univ. 1989; mem. Court, Cranfield Inst. of Tech. 1989–93; Consultant, Centre Antoine Lacassagne, Nice 1986–91; Hughes Medal, Royal Soc. 1980. *Publications:* Elements of Pulse Circuits 1955; scientific papers on nuclear physics, cosmic rays, relativity, precise measurement of the gyromagnetic ratio of the muon, ocean wave energy, cancer therapy, etc. *Leisure interests:* skiing, gliding, windsurfing, travel. *Address:* Le Masage, chemin de Saint Pierre, 06620 Le Bar sur Loup, France. *Telephone:* (4) 93.42.45.12. *Fax:* (4) 93.42.94.07.

FARMER, James Leonard, Jr; American civil rights leader; b. 12 Jan. 1920, Marshall, Texas; s. of late James Leonard Farmer, PH.D. and late Pearl Marion Houston Farmer; m. Lula A. Peterson 1949 (died 1977); two d.; ed. Wiley Coll. and Howard Univ.; fmr. Program Dir., Nat. Assoc. for the

Advancement of Colored People (NAACP); fmr. Int. Rep. State, County and Municipal Employees Union; Dir. Congress of Racial Equality 1961–66; Pres. Center for Community Action Educ. 1965–66; Prof. of Social Welfare, Lincoln Univ. 1966–68; Adjunct Prof. New York Univ. 1968; Asst. Sec. for Admin., U.S. Dept. of Health, Educ. and Welfare 1969–70; Pres. Council on Minority Planning and Strategy 1973–76; Exec. Dir. Coalition of American Public Employees 1977–82; Virginia Commonwealth Prof., Mary Washington Coll., Fredericksburg, Va. 1985–87, Distinguished Visitng Prof. 1987–94, Distinguished Coll. Prof. 1994–; Visiting Prof., Antioch Univ., Philadelphia, Pa. 1984–86; Chair. Bd. Fund for an Open Society. *Publication:* Freedom—When? 1965, Lay Bare the Heart (autobiog.) 1985. *Leisure interests:* detective stories, fishing. *Address:* Mary Washington College, Monroe Hall, 1301 College Avenue, Fredericksburg, VA 22401 (Office); 3805 Guinea Station Road, Fredericksburg, VA 22408, U.S.A. (Home). *Telephone:* (540) 654-2118 (Office); (540) 898-2917 (Home). *Fax:* (540) 654-1074.

FARMER, Richard Gilbert, M.S., M.D., M.A.C.P.; American physician; b. 29 Sept. 1931, Kokomo, Ind.; s. of Oscar I. Farmer and Elizabeth J. Gilbert Farmer; m. Janice M. Schrank 1958; one s. one d.; ed. Indiana Univ., Univ. of Maryland, Milwaukee County Hosp. (Marquette Univ.), Mayo Foundation, Rochester, Minn. and Univ. of Minnesota; mil. service 1960–62; staff, Cleveland Clinic Foundation and Cleveland Clinic Hosp. 1962–91, Chair. Dept. of Gastroenterology 1972–82, Chair. Div. of Medicine 1975–91; Asst. and Assoc. Clinical Prof., Case Western Reserve Univ. School of Medicine 1972–91; Sr. Medical Adviser, Bureau for Europe, U.S. Agency for Int. Devt. 1992–94; consultant in health care, Eastern Europe and Soviet Union 1994–; Clinical Prof. of Medicine, Georgetown Univ. Medical Center 1992–; Medical Dir. Quality Health Int. 1997–, Eurasian Medical Educ. Program 1998–; medical consultant Scandinavian Care Consultants, Stockholm 1998–; mem. Inst. of Medicine, Nat. Advisory Bd., Nat. Foundation for Ileitis and Colitis, Nat. Comm. on Digestive Diseases 1977–79; Gov. for Ohio, American Coll. of Physicians 1980–84, Regent 1985–91; Chair. Health and Public Policy Comm. 1986–88; Pres. American Coll. of Gastroenterology 1978–79, Asscn. of Program Dirs. in Internal Medicine 1977–79; Interstate Postgraduate Medical Asscn. 1983–84; mem. Council to assess quality of care in the Medicare program, Gen. Accounting Office, U.S. House of Reps. 1986–89; Special Citation, American Coll. of Physicians 1984, Mastership American Coll. of Gastroenterology 1991, American Coll. of Physicians 1993, Founder's Award, Asscn. of Program Dirs. in Internal Medicine 1993, mem. Int. Org. for Study of Inflammatory Bowel Disease (Deputy Chair. 1982–86). *Publications:* author or co-author of 260 publs. in the medical literature, primarily relating to digestive diseases with a specific interest in inflammatory bowel disease and health care in Eastern Europe and the fmr. Soviet Union; ed. of six books and contrib. to others. *Leisure interests:* squash, tennis, running and reading (history and current events). *Address:* 9126 Town Gate Lane, Bethesda, MD 20817, U.S.A. (Home).

FARNDALE, Gen. Sir Martin Baker, K.C.B.; British army officer (retd.); b. 6 Jan. 1929, Trochu, Alberta, Canada; s. of the late Alfred Farndale and Margaret Louise Farndale (née Baker); m. Margaret Anne Buckingham 1955; one s.; ed. Yorebridge School, Yorks., R.M.A. Sandhurst and Staff Coll. Camberley; 1st Regt. Royal Horse Artillery, Egypt, Germany 1949–54; HQ 7 Armoured Div., Germany 1954–56, 22 Light Air Defence Regt., U.K. 1957–58; Staff Coll., U.K. 1959; HQ 17 Gurkha Div., Malaya 1960–62; War Office, Mil. Operations, London 1962–64; 1st Regt. Royal Horse Artillery, Command of The Chestnut Troop, Germany and Aden 1964–66; Staff Coll. Instructor 1966–69; 1st Regt. Royal Horse Artillery, in Command 1969–71; Ministry of Defence, Policy Staff, London 1971–73; Command 7th Armoured Brigade, Germany 1973–75; Dir. Public Relations, Ministry of Defence, London 1976–78, Dir. Mil. Operations 1978–80; Command 2nd Armoured Div., Germany 1980–83, Command 1st British Corps 1983–85, Command Northern Army Group/C.-in-C. British Army of the Rhine 1985–87; Master Gunner St. James's Park 1988–96; Col. Commdt. Royal Horse Artillery 1988–, Royal Artillery 1982–, Army Air Corps 1980–88; Hon. Col. 1st Regt. Royal Horse Artillery 1983–90, 3rd Battalion The Yorkshire Volunteers 1983–90; Pres. R.A. Council of N.I. 1988–; Chair. Royal United Services Inst. 1989–93; Vice-Pres. Royal Patriotic Fund Corpn. 1989–92; Dir. and Sr. Defence Adviser Short Bros. 1988–97; Defence Adviser Touche Ross (now Deloitte Touche) 1988–; Chair. English Heritage Battlefields of England Panel 1993–, R.A. Museums Ltd. 1996–; Pres. 2nd Div. Dinner Club 1982–, Cen. Volunteers Dinner Club 1985–, 7th Armoured Div. Dinner Club 1994–; Patron Air Observation Post Office Asscn. 1990–; Freeman, City of London and Liveryman, Wheelwrights Co. 1996–; Hon. D.Litt. (Greenwich) 1995. *Publications:* History of the Royal Artillery 1914–1918 in France and Flanders, History of the Royal Artillery 1914–18, Forgotten Fronts, and the Home Base 1914–18 1989, History of the Royal Artillery, The Years of Defeat 1939–41 1996, The War in the Far East 1939–46 1997. *Leisure interests:* military history and gardening. *Address:* c/o Lloyds Bank, Cox's and King's Branch, 7 Pall Mall, London, SW1Y 5NA, England.

FARNELL-WATSON, Peter; British business executive; b. 8 Feb. 1947, Royston, Herts.; m. Bunny Farnell-Watson; one s. one d.; ed. schools in S. Africa, U.K. and New Zealand, Colchester School of Art and Cen. School of Art, London; industrial designer, Unimark Int. 1970; Corp. Identity Man. Rennies Consolidated, S. Africa 1972, Dir. of Corp. Communications 1974; seconded to Jardine Matheson, Hong Kong 1977; Account Dir. Corp. Identity, Landor Assocs. San Francisco 1984, Vice-Pres. responsible for consulting and account. man., corp. and product branding 1986, Group Dir. responsible for corp. and retail branding operations in San Francisco 1988, Man. Dir. San Francisco office and mem. Bd. Dirs. Landor Assocs. 1990, Exec. Dir. Worldwide Accounts 1991, Co-Man. Dir. Landor Assocs. Europe 1992–96, Man. Dir. 1996–. *Address:* Landor Associates, 18 Clerkenwell Green, London, EC1R 0DP, England. *Telephone:* 0171-880 8360, 0171-880 8460.

FARNHAM, John Peter, A.O.; Australian (b. British) singer and entertainer; b. 1 July 1949, Essex, U.K.; m. 1973; two s.; ed. Lyndale High School; settled in Australia 1959; apprenticed as plumber; lead singer for Strings Unlimited 1965; began recording 1967; television appearances including nature series Survival with Johnny Farnham for ABC; f. John Farnham Band 1978; lead singer for Little River Band 1982–85. *Recordings include:* Sadie the Cleaning Lady 1967 (3 Gold Records), Friday Kind of Monday 1968, Rose Coloured Glasses 1968, One 1969, Raindrops Keep Falling on My Head 1969, Comic Conversation 1970, Rock Me Baby 1972, Don't You Know It's Magic 1973, Everything is Out of Season 1973, Uncovered 1980, The Net 1982, Playing to Win 1984, Whispering Jack 1986, Chain Reaction 1990, Full House 1991, Jesus Christ Superstar: The Album 1992, Then Again 1992, Romeo's Heart 1996, Anthology Series I, II and III 1997; 12 Gold Record awards; Australian of the Year, Bicentennial 1998. *Address:* c/o TalentWORKS, Suite 1, 663 Victoria Street, Abbottsford, Vic. 3067, Australia. *Telephone:* (03) 9429 6933. *Fax:* (03) 9428 7433.

FARQUHAR, John William, A.B., M.D.; American/Canadian physician and professor of medicine; b. 13 June 1927, Winnipeg, Canada; s. of John Giles Farquhar and Marjorie Victoria Roberts; m. Christine Louise Johnson 1968; one s. one d. (and two s. from previous m.); ed. Univ. of California, Berkeley and San Francisco; intern. Univ. of Calif. Hosp., San Francisco 1952–53, Resident 1953–54, 1957–58; Postdoctoral Fellow 1955–57; Resident Univ. of Minn. 1954–55; Research Assoc. Rockefeller Univ., New York 1958–62; Asst. Prof. of Medicine Stanford Univ. 1962–66, Assoc. Prof 1966–73, Prof. 1973–, C. F. Rehnborg Prof. in Disease Prevention 1989–; Dir. Stanford Centre for Research in Disease Prevention 1973–; Dir. Collaborating Centre for Chronic Disease Prevention WHO 1985–; assoc. chief of staff for health promotion, Stanford Univ. Hosp. 1994–; Pres. Soc. of Behavioral Medicine 1990–92; mem. N.A.S. Inst. of Medicine, American Soc. of Clinical Investigation, Acad. of Behavioral Medicine; James D. Bruce Award 1983; Myrdal Prize 1986, Charles A. Dana Foundation Award for Pioneering Achievements in Health 1990, Nat. Cholesterol Award for Public Educ. 1991, Research Achievement Award American Heart Asscn. 1992. *Publications:* The American Way of Life Need Not Be Hazardous to Your Health 1978, The Last Puff (with Gene Spiller) 1990, The Victoria Declaration for Heart Health 1992, The Catalonia Declaration: Investing in Heart Health 1996; contribs. to professional journals. *Address:* School of Medicine, Stanford University, Center for Research in Disease Prevention, 730 Welch Road, Palo Alto, CA 94304, U.S.A.

FARQUHAR, Robin Hugh, PH.D.; Canadian professor of public administration and fmr. university president and vice-chancellor; b. 1 Dec. 1938, Victoria, B.C.; s. of Hugh E. Farquhar and Jean MacIntosh; m. Frances Caswell 1963; three d.; ed. Vic. High School, Vic. Coll., Univ. of British Columbia, Univ. of Chicago, U.S.A.; teacher, Counsellor and Coach, Edward Milne Secondary School, Sooke, B.C. 1962–64; Assoc. Dir. and Deputy Dir. Univ. Council for Educational Admin. 1966–71; Chair. Dept. of Educational Admin., and Asst. Dir. Ont. Inst. for Studies in Educ., and Assoc. Prof., then Prof., School of Grad. Studies, Univ. of Toronto 1971–76; Dean of Educ. and Prof. Univ. of Sask., Saskatoon 1976–81; Pres., Vice-Chancellor and Prof., Univ. of Winnipeg 1981–89; Pres. Vice-Chancellor and Prof., Carleton Univ., Ottawa 1989–96; Fellow, Commonwealth Council for Educational Admin.; Hon. Diploma in Adult Educ.; Hon. Citizen City of Winnipeg; Hon. Scout. *Publications:* numerous books and articles on educational admin. *Leisure interests:* jogging, golf, cross-country skiing. *Address:* School of Public Administration, Carleton University, 1125 Colonel By Drive, Ottawa, K1S 5B6 (Office); 64 Queen Elizabeth Drive, Ottawa, K2P 1E3, Canada (Home). *Telephone:* (613) 230-4735 (Home). *Fax:* (613) 230-1094 (Home).

FARR, Dennis Larry Ashwell, C.B.E., M.A., F.R.S.A., F.M.A.; British art historian and museum director; b. 3 April 1929, Luton, Beds.; s. of Arthur W. Farr and Helen E. Farr; m. Diana Pullein-Thompson 1959; one s. one d.; ed. Luton Grammar School, and Courtauld Inst. of Art, Univ. of London; Asst. Witt Librarian, Courtauld Inst. 1952–54; Asst. Keeper, Tate Gallery, London 1954–64; Curator, Paul Mellon Collection, Washington, D.C. 1965–66; Sr. lecturer and Deputy Keeper Univ. Art Collections, Univ. of Glasgow 1967–69; Dir. City Museums and Art Gallery, Birmingham 1969–80; Dir. Courtauld Inst. Galleries 1980–93; Gen. Ed. Clarendon Studies in the History of Art, Oxford Univ. Press 1985–; Pres. Museums Asscn. 1979–80; Chair. Asscn. of Art Historians 1983–86; mem. Comité Int. d'Histoire de l'Art 1983–94, hon. mem. 1994–; mem. Registration Cttee., Museums and Galleries Comm. 1993–; Hon. D. Litt. (Birmingham) 1981. *Publications:* William Etty 1958, Tate Gallery Modern British School Catalogue (co-author) 1964, English Art 1870–1940 1978, Lynn Chadwick: Sculptor. A Complete Catalogue 1947–88 (with Eva Chadwick) 1990, Thomas Gambier Parry (1816–1888) as Artist and Collector (Ed. and contrib.) 1993, Francis Bacon: A Retrospective Exhibition (co-author) 1999. *Leisure interests:* avoiding academics, riding. *Address:* Orchard Hill, Swan Barn Road, Haslemere, Surrey, GU27 2HY, England. *Telephone:* (01428) 641880.

FARRAKHAN, Louis (b. Louis Eugene Wolcott); American religious leader; b. 11 May 1933, New York City; m. Betsy Wolcott; nine c.; ed. Winston-

Salem Teachers Coll.; fmrly. leader Nation of Islam mosque, Harlem, Nat. Spokesman; founder reorganized org. Nation of Islam 1977; organizer "Million Man March" 1995, Wash. DC. *Address:* Nation of Islam, 734 W. 79th Street, Chicago, IL 60620, U.S.A.

FARRELL, Patrick M.; Irish politician; b. 30 Aug. 1957, Leitrim; s. of Bill Farrell and Mamie Casey; m. Margaret Logan 1988; one s. one d.; ed. Man. College, Carrick-on-Shannon, Inst. of Public Admin.; Hosp. Admin. Sligo 1981–86; C.E.O. Galvia Hosp., Galway 1986–91; Gen. Sec. Fianna Fáil 1991–98; fmr. Chair. Irish Council of the European Movt.; mem. of Senate 1992; mem. Bd. of Friends of Fianna Fáil Inc., U.S.A. *Leisure interests:* current affairs, reading, writing. *Address:* c/o Aras De Valera, 13 Upper Mount Street, Dublin 2, Ireland. *Telephone:* 01-676 1551. *Fax:* 01-678 5960.

FARRELL, Suzanne; American ballerina; b. 1945; m. Paul Mejia (divorced 1997); ed. School of American Ballet; fmr. principal dancer with New York City Ballet until 1989; also danced with Béjart Ballet, Brussels; appeared in numerous Balanchine ballets choreographed for her including Mozartiana, Chaconne, Meditation, Vienna Waltzes; staged seven Balanchine ballets at John F. Kennedy Center for Performing Arts, Washington, D.C. 1995 and many other stagings of Balanchine's works; repetiteur for Balanchine Trust, including Kirov Ballet, Royal Danish Ballet and Paris Opéra Ballet; mem. Advisory Panel Princess Grace Foundation, Sr. Advisory Bd. of Arthritis Foundation; trains ballet dancers in camp The Adirondacks. *Publication:* Holding On To Air (autobiog.) 1990. *Address:* Kennedy Center for the Performing Arts, Washington DC 20566, U.S.A.

FARRELL, Terence (Terry Farrell), C.B.E., M.C.P., M.ARCH., M.R.T.P.I., R.I.B.A., F.C.S.D.; British architect; b. 12 May 1938; s. of Thomas Farrell and Molly Farrell (née Maguire); m. 1st Angela Rosemarie Mallam 1960; two d.; m. 2nd Susan Hilary Aplin 1973; two s. one d.; ed. St. Cuthbert's Grammar School, Newcastle upon Tyne, Newcastle Univ., Univ. of Pennsylvania, U.S.A.; Harkness Fellow, Commonwealth Fund, U.S.A. 1962–64; Partner, Farrell Grimshaw Partnership 1965–80, Terry Farrell Partnership 1980–87; Chair. Terry Farrell and Partners 1987–. *Major projects include:* Vauxhall Cross, London, The Peak, Kowloon, Charing Cross Station Redevt., Edinburgh Int. Conf. Centre, British Consulate and British Council Bldgs., Hong Kong. Hon. F.R.I.A.S. *Publications:* Architectural Monograph 1985, Urban Design Monograph 1993, The Master Architect Series: Terry Farrell 1994, Sketchbook 1998; articles in numerous journals. *Leisure interests:* walking, swimming. *Address:* 7 Hatton Street, London, NW8 8PL, England. *Telephone:* 0171-258 3433. *Fax:* 0171-723 7059.

FARRINGTON, David Philip, M.A., PH.D., F.B.A.; British professor of psychological criminology; b. 7 March 1944, Ormskirk, Lancs.; s. of William Farrington and Gladys Holden Farrington; m. Sally Chamberlain 1966; three d.; ed. Univ. of Cambridge; mem. staff, Inst. of Criminology, Univ. of Cambridge 1969–, Prof. of Psychological Criminology 1992–; Pres. European Assen. of Psychology and Law 1997–; Visiting Fellow, U.S. Nat. Inst. of Justice 1981; Chair. Div. of Criminological and Legal Psychology, British Psychological Soc. 1983–85; mem. Parole Bd. for England and Wales 1984–87; Vice-Chair. U.S. Nat. Acad. of Sciences Panel on Violence 1989–92; Visiting Fellow U.S. Bureau of Justice Statistics 1995–98; Co-Chair. U.S. Office of Juvenile Justice and Delinquency Prevention Study Group on Serious and Violent Juvenile Offenders 1995–97; Pres. British Soc. of Criminology 1990–93, Pres. American Soc. of Criminology 1998–99; Sellin-Glueck Award, American Soc. of Criminology 1984. *Publications:* 21 books and over 240 articles on criminology and psychology. *Address:* Institute of Criminology, University of Cambridge, 7 West Road, Cambridge, CB3 9DT (Office); 7 The Meadows, Haslingfield, Cambridge, CB3 7JD, England (Home). *Telephone:* (01223) 335384 (Office); (01223) 872555 (Home). *Fax:* (01223) 335356.

FARROW, Mia Villiers; American actress; b. 9 Feb. 1945, Calif.; d. of John Villiers Farrow and Maureen O'Sullivan; m. 1st Frank Sinatra (q.v.) 1966 (divorced 1968); m. 2nd André Previn (q.v.) 1970 (divorced 1979); fourteen c.; Stage début in The Importance of Being Earnest, New York 1963; French Acad. Award for best actress 1969, David Donatello Award (Italy) 1969, Rio de Janeiro Film Festival Award 1969, San Sebastian Award. *Stage appearances in London:* Mary Rose, The Three Sisters, House of Bernarda Alba 1972–73, The Marrying of Ann Leete (R.S.C.) 1975, The Zykovs 1976, Ivanov (R.S.C.) 1976; appeared in Romantic Comedy (Broadway) 1979. *Films include:* Guns at Batasi 1964, Rosemary's Baby 1968, Secret Ceremony 1969, John and Mary 1969, See No Evil 1970, The Great Gatsby 1973, Full Circle 1978, A Wedding 1978, Death on the Nile 1978, The Hurricane 1979, A Midsummer Night's Sex Comedy 1982, Zelig 1983, Broadway Danny Rose 1984, Purple Rose of Cairo 1985, Hannah and her Sisters 1986, Radio Days 1987, September 1988, Another Woman 1988, Oedipus Wrecks 1989, Crimes and Misdemeanours, Alice 1990, Shadows and Fog 1992, Husbands and Wives 1992, Widow's Peak 1994, Miami Rhapsody 1995, Private Parts 1997. *TV appearances:* Peyton Place 1964–66; Johnny Belinda 1965, Peter Pan 1975, Goodbye Raggedy Ann (TV film). *Leisure interests:* reading, mind wandering, listening to music and certain people. *Publication:* What Falls Away (autobiog.) 1996. *Address:* International Creative Management, c/o Sam Cohn, 40 West 57th Street, New York, NY 10019, U.S.A.

FARSON, Daniel Negley, B.A.; British writer and broadcaster; b. 8 Jan. 1927, London; s. of Negley Farson and Eve Farson; Lobby and Parl. Corresp., House of Commons; enlisted U.S.A.A.F.; photographer for Picture Post; journalist; TV interviewer with own series 1956–66; Arts Corresp. The Mail on Sunday 1991; art critic for Night and Day 1993–95. *Publications:* 22 books including Jack the Ripper, Swansdowne, Soho in the 50's, Gallery (based on his TV Art Quiz) 1990, Gilbert and George in Moscow 1991, Limehouse Days 1991, Guide to Turkey (revised edn.) 1991, The Gilded Gutter Life of Francis Bacon 1993, A Dry Ship to the Mountains: Down the Volga and Across the Caucasus in My Father's Footsteps 1994, Never a Normal Man (autobiog.) 1997. *Address:* 129 Irsha Street, Appledore, North Devon, England. *Telephone:* (01237) 479099.

FARULLI, Piero; Italian professor of viola; b. 13 Jan. 1920, Florence; s. of Lioniero and Maria (née Innocenti) Farulli; m. Antonia Parisi 1945; ed. Conservatorio Statale Luigi Cherubini, Florence (under Gioacchino Maglioni); Prof. of Viola 1957–77; for thirty years a mem. of Quartetto Italiano; has also collaborated with Amadeus and Berg Quartets; appeared with Trio di Trieste 1978; has lectured at Accad. Chigiana di Siena and at Salzburg Mozarteum; mem. of judging panel at several int. competitions and is active in many aspects of musical life and education in Italy, notably at the Scuola di Musica di Fiesole, which he founded in 1974; Medaglia della Cultura e dell'Arte. *Address:* Via G. d'Annunzio 153, Florence, Italy. *Telephone:* (55) 608007.

FASE, Martin M. G., PH.D.; Netherlands banker and economist; b. 28 Dec. 1937, Boskoop; s. of A. P. Fase and J. G. M. de Groot; m. Lida E. M. Franse 1965; two s.; ed. Univ. of Amsterdam; Research Assoc. Inst. of Actuarial Sciences and Econometrics, Amsterdam 1965–69; Ford Foundation Fellow, Dept. of Econs., Univ. of Wis., Madison, U.S.A. 1969–71; with De Nederlandsche Bank 1971–, Deputy Dir. 1985–; Extraordinary Prof. of Business Statistics, Erasmus Univ., Rotterdam 1978–86; Extraordinary Prof. of Monetary Econs., Univ. of Amsterdam 1986–; Fellow Royal Netherlands Acad. of Arts and Sciences, Hollandsche Maatschappij der Wetenschappen. *Publications:* An Econometric Model of Age-Income Profiles: a Statistical Analysis of Dutch Income Data 1970, The Monetary Sector of the Netherlands in 50 Equations: a Quarterly Monetary Model for the Netherlands 1970–79, in Analysing the Structure of Econometric Models (ed. J. P. Ancot) 1984, Seasonal Adjustment as a Practical Problem 1991; articles in European Economic Review, Journal of International Economics and other journals; several monographs. *Leisure interests:* Dutch literature, hiking. *Address:* De Nederlandsche Bank NV, Postbus 98, 1000 AB Amsterdam (Office); Ruysdaelweg 3b, 2051 EM Overveen, Netherlands (Home). *Fax:* 20-524 2529.

FASELLA, Paolo Maria, PH.D.; Italian scientific research director; b. 16 Dec. 1930, Rome; s. of Felice Fasella and Margherita Parazzoli; m. Sheila Hauck Dionisi 1957; four d.; ed. Univ. of Rome; Asst. Prof., Assoc. Prof. of Biological Chem. Univ. of Rome 1959–65; Research Assoc. M.I.T. 1961–62, Visiting Scientist (part-time) 1963–64; Assoc. Prof. then Prof. of Biochem. Univ. of Parma 1965–71; Visiting Prof. Cornell Univ. 1966; Prof. of Biological Chem. Univ. of Rome 1971–81; Dir.-Gen. of Directorate-Gen. for Science, Research and Devt. and Jt. Research Centre, Comm. of European Communities 1981–, represents European Comm., EUREKA; mem. Acad. Europaea (London), European Molecular Biology Org. (EMBO), Int. Foundation for Artificial Intelligence (Tokyo), Accad. Nazionale delle Scienze - detta dei XL, New York Acad. of Sciences, European Acad. of Science and Arts 1994; Hon. Fellow, Inst. of Biology, (Cambridge) 1990, Belgian Royal Acad. of Medicine; Hon. D.Sc. (Nat. Univ. Dublin) 1990; "Europe and Medicine" Prize (Inst. des Sciences de la Santé, Paris) 1993. *Publications:* more than 200 scientific papers on protein structure and functions, biological catalysis, biotech.; articles on scientific research policy and bioethics. *Address:* Directorate-General for Science, Research and Development, sq. de Meeûs 8, bur. 01/104, B-1040, Brussels (Office); drève Pittoresque 60, B-1640 Rhode-St.-Genèse, Belgium (Home). *Telephone:* (2) 2953570.

FASQUELLE, Jean-Claude; French publisher; b. 29 Nov. 1930, Paris; s. of Charles Fasquelle and Odette Cyprien-Fabre; m. 1st Solange de la Rochefoucauld; one d.; m. 2nd Nicla Jegher 1966; ed. Ecole des Roches, Verneuil-sur-Avre and Faculté de Droit, Paris; Pres.-Dir.-Gen. Société des editions Fasquelle 1953–67, Editions du Sagittaire 1958–; Admin.-Dir.-Gen. Editions Grasset et Fasquelle 1967, Pres.-Dir.-Gen. 1980–; Dir. Le Magazine littéraire (monthly) 1970–. *Address:* Éditions Grasset et Fasquelle, 61 rue des Saintes-Pères, 75006 Paris (Office); 13 Square Vergennes, 75015 Paris, France (Home).

FASSBAENDER, Brigitte; German mezzo-soprano; b. 3 July 1939, Berlin; d. of the late Willi Domgraf-Fassbaender and Sabine Peters; ed. Nuremberg Conservatoire and studied with father; début Bavarian State Opera, Munich 1961; has appeared at La Scala Milan, Vienna State Opera, Covent Garden London, Metropolitan New York, San Francisco and Salzburg; Teacher of Solo Vocal Music Musikhochschule, Munich; soloist, Dir. of opera, Braunschweig; Fellow Royal Northern Coll. of Music (U.K.) 1991–. *Address:* Am Theatre, 38100 Braunschweig, Germany.

FASSI-FIHRI, Ahmed, L. EN D.; Moroccan civil servant and diplomatist; b. 6 Aug. 1936, Oujda; m. Touria El Ouazzani; two s. two d.; private sec. of Minister of Interior 1956; Head of Office, Dept. of Minerals and Geology 1958; Head, Office of Minister of Foreign Affairs 1959; Chargé d'affaires, Moroccan Embassy, Berne 1960; Pres. Melnes Municipality 1963; founder and Dir. Nat. Documentation Centre 1967–, Information Science School 1974, Multimedia Centre 1993; Order of Ridha. *Publications:* articles in field of information science in Arabic and French. *Leisure interests:* listening to Arabic and classical music; reading of the Arabic intellectual literary productions. *Address:* Centre National de Documentation, BP 826, Rabat, Morocco. *Telephone:* (2127) 77 49 44; 77 31 39. *Fax:* (2127) 77 31 34.

FASSINO, Piero Franco Rodolfo, B.SC.; Italian politician; b. 7 Oct. 1949, Avigliana; m.; local councillor Turin 1975-80, 1985-90, Prov. Councillor 1980–85; various posts within Turin Fed. of Partito Comunista Italiano (P.C.I.) 1971–83, Prov. Sec. 1983–87, elected to P.C.I. Exec. 1983, Coordinator Nat. Secr. 1987, then Head of party org. during transition to P.D.S., mem. Nat. Secr. and Int. Sec. P.D.S. 1991–96, P.D.S. Rep. to Socialist Int. 1992; Pres. Cen. and W. Europe Cttee. Socialist Int. 1993; fmr. Vice-Pres. Socialist Group, Council of Europe; mem. Chamber of Deputies from Liguria (P.D.S.) 1994–96, from Piedmont 1996–; Under-Sec. Ministry for Foreign Trade 1996–98; Minister for Foreign Trade 1998–; mem. Parl. Asscn. for Cen. Europe Initiative; Vice-Pres. Italian–Israeli Parl. Friendship Asscn. 1995. *Address:* Ministero del Commercio Estero, Viale Boston 25, 00144 Rome, Italy. *Telephone:* (06) 59647465. *Fax:* (06) 59932168.

FAST, Howard; American writer; b. 11 Nov. 1914, New York; s. of Barney and Ida (née Miller) Fast; m. Bette Cohen 1937; one s. one d.; ed. Nat. Acad. of Design; began writing 1931; translated into 82 languages; film has been made of Spartacus; columnist N.Y. Observer 1989–92, Greenwich Time 1992–; Bread Loaf Literary Award 1934, Schomburg Award for Race Relations 1944, Newspaper Guild Award 1947, Peace Prize U.S.S.R. 1954, Screenwriters Award 1960, Secondary School Book Award 1962, Emmy Award (for The Ambassador) 1974. *Publications include:* Novels: The Children 1935, Place in the City 1937, Conceived in Liberty 1939, The Last Frontier 1941, The Unvanquished 1942, Citizen Tom Paine 1943, Freedom Road 1944, Clarkton 1947, My Glorious Brothers 1948, The Proud and the Free 1950, Spartacus 1951, Silas Timberman 1954, Moses, Prince of Egypt 1958, The Winston Affair 1959, April Morning 1961, Power 1962, Agrippa's Daughter 1964, Torquemada 1966, The Hunter and the Trap 1967, The Hessian 1972, A Touch of Infinity 1973, Time and the Riddle 1975, The Immigrants 1977, The Second Generation 1978, The Establishment 1979, The Legacy 1981, Max 1982, The Outsider 1984, The Immigrant's Daughter 1985, The Dinner Party, The Pledge 1988, The Confession of Joe Cullen 1989, The Trial of Abigail Goodman 1993, Seven Days in June 1994, The Bridge Builder's Story 1995; autobiog: Being Red 1990; Short stories: Patrick Henry and the Frigate's Keel, Departure and Other Stories, The Last Supper; History: Romance of a People, Peekshill: U.S.A., The American (Biography) 1946, The Passion of Sacco and Vanzetti 1953, The Naked God, The Jews 1969, The Crossing 1970; Plays: The Crossing, The Hill, The Ambassador (for TV) 1974, Citizen Tom Paine 1985, The Novelist 1986; Screenplays: Spartacus 1959, The Hill 1963, Martian Shop 1964, Torquemada 1966, The Hunter and the Trap 1967, The General Zapped an Angel 1970; numerous other novels and plays. *Leisure interests:* gardening, working about my country place. *Address:* c/o Sterling Lord, 65 Bleeker Street, New York, NY 10012, U.S.A.

FATAYI-WILLIAMS, Atanda, M.A., LL.M., F.R.S.A.; Nigerian judge (retd.); b. 22 Oct. 1918, Lagos; s. of late Alhaji Issa Williams and Alhaja S. Ashakun Williams; m. Irene Violet Lofts 1948; three s.; ed. Methodist Boys' School, Lagos, Trinity Hall, Cambridge, Middle Temple, London; Private practice, Lagos 1948–50; Crown Counsel, Lagos 1950–55; Deputy Commr. for Law Revision, W. Nigeria 1955–58; Chief Registrar, High Court of W. Nigeria 1958–60, High Court Judge 1960–67; Justice of Appeal, W. State 1967–69; Justice, Supreme Court of Nigeria 1969–79, Chief Justice 1979–83; Chair. Ports Arbitration Bd. 1971, All Nigeria Law Reports Cttee. 1972–75, Bd. of Trustees, Van Leer Nigerian Educ. Trust 1973–85, Body of Benchers 1979–80, Fed. Judicial Service Comm. 1979–83, Legal Practitioners Privileges Cttee. 1979–83, Judiciary Consultative Cttee. 1979–83, Council of Legal Educ. 1984–86; Hon. Fellow, Trinity Hall, Cambridge Univ. 1983–; Fellow Nigerian Inst. of Advanced Legal Studies 1983–; Chair. UBA Trustees Ltd. 1986–91, IDDO Investments Ltd. 1984–91, Presidential Cttee. on Medical Doctors' Remunerations 1990–; mem. Nigerian Inst. of Int. Affairs 1972–, Int. Comm. of Jurists, World Council of Judges, Nat. Council of State 1990–; Commdr. of the Fed. Repub. 1980, Grand Commdr. Order of the Niger 1983; Presidential Award for Outstanding Service to the Judiciary 1992. *Publications:* Revised Laws of Western Nigeria (with Sir John Verity) 1959, Ed. Western Nigeria Law Reports 1955–1958, Sentencing Processes, Practices and Attitudes, as seen by an Appeal Court Judge 1970, Faces, Cases and Places (autobiog.) 1983. *Leisure interests:* swimming, walking, reading. *Address:* 8 Adetokunbo Ademola Street, Victoria Island, Lagos, Nigeria. *Telephone:* 611315.

FATIN, Wendy, B.SC.; Australian politician; b. 10 April 1941, Harvey, W.A.; one s. one d.; ed. West Australian Inst. of Tech.; trained as registered nurse; Adviser to Minister for Repatriation and Compensation and Minister for Social Security 1974–75; Political Research Asst. 1975–77, 1981–83; mem. House of Reps. for Canning, W.A. 1983, for Brand, W.A. 1984–96; Minister for Local Govt., Minister Assisting Prime Minister for Status of Women 1990–93, Minister for Arts and Territories 1991–93; mem. Govt. Econ. Cttee. 1983–87; mem. House of Reps. Standing Cttee. on Community Affairs 1987–96, on Employment, Educ. and Training 1987–96; Fellow Coll. of Nursing, Australia; Founder mem. Women's Electoral Lobby; Labor Party. *Address:* Lot 46, Soldiers Road, Roleystone, W.A. 6111, Australia.

FATT, Paul, F.R.S.; British professor of biophysics; Reader in Biophysics, University Coll., London 1956–76, Prof. 1976–89, Prof. Emer. 1989–, Fellow 1973. *Publications:* papers in various journals. *Address:* 25 Tanza Road, London, NW3 2UA, England. *Telephone:* 0171-435 9802.

FAUCI, Anthony Stephen, M.D.; American medical researcher; b. 24 Dec. 1940, Brooklyn, New York; s. of Eugenia Fauci and Stephen Fauci; m. Christine Grady 1985; three d.; ed. Coll. of the Holy Cross, Cornell Univ. Medical Coll.; instructor in Medicine, Cornell Medical Coll. 1971–72; Medical Dir. U.S. Public Health Service 1968–70, 1972; Clinical Assoc. Lab. of Clinical Investigation, Nat. Inst. of Allergy and Infectious Diseases (NIAID) 1968–71; Sr. Staff Fellow, Lab. of Clinical Investigation 1970–71, Sr. Investigator 1972–74, Head Physiology Section 1974–80, Deputy Clinical Dir. Nat. Inst. of Allergy and Infectious Diseases 1977–84, Dir. 1984–; Chief Resident in Medicine, NY Hosp., Cornell Univ. Medical Center 1971–72; Chief Lab. of Immunoregulation 1980–; Dir. Office of AIDS Research and Assoc. Dir. Nat. Inst. of Health for AIDS Research 1988–94; consultant Naval Medical Center, Bethesda 1972–; ed. numerous learned journals on immunology. *Leisure interests:* jogging, tennis. *Address:* NIAID/NIH, 31 Center Drive MSC, Bethesda, MD 20892 (Office); 3012 43rd Street, N.W., Washington, DC 20016, U.S.A. (Home). *Telephone:* (301) 496 2263 (Office).

FAUCON, Bernard; French photographer; b. 12 Sept. 1950, Apt; ed. Lycée d'Apt, Université d'Aix en Provence, Sorbonne, Paris. *Exhibitions include:* Agathe Gaillard, Paris 1979, 1984, 1986, 1988, 1990; Castelli, New York 1979, 1981, 1983, 1986, 1989, 1991; Musée Georges Pompidou, Paris 1982; Musée de la Vieille Charité, Marseille 1986; Guggenheim Museum, New York, 1986; Walker Art Center, Minneapolis 1987; PARCO Gallery, Tokyo 1987, 1991; Espace photo de la ville de Paris 1988; Yvon Lambert, Paris 1991, 1993, 1995; Grand Prix Nat. de la photographie 1989. *Publications:* Les grandes vacances 1980, Summer Camp 1980, Les Papiers qui volent 1986, Les Chambres d'amour 1987, Tables d'amis 1991, Les Idoles et les sacrifices 1991, Les Ecritures 1993, Jours d'images 1995, La Fin de l'Image 1997, La peur du voyage 1999. *Leisure interest:* cookery. *Address:* 6 rue Barbanègre, 75019 Paris, France. *Telephone:* (01) 40-05-99-70.

FAUL, Mgr. Denis O'Beirne, B.A. (HONS.), S.T.L.; Irish ecclesiastic; b. 14 Aug. 1932, Dundalk, Co. Louth; s. of Dr. Joseph Faul and Anne F. O'Beirne; ed. Louth Nat. School, St. Mary's Coll. Dundalk, St. Patrick's Coll. Armagh, St. Patrick's Coll., Maynooth and Gregorian Univ., Rome; ordained priest 1956; teacher, St. Patrick's Acad. Dungannon, Co. Tyrone 1958–83, Prin. 1983–; cr. Mgr. 1995. *Publications:* 15 books and 20 leaflets on N. Ireland problems; papers on Patristics and history of Irish Catholic church. *Leisure interests:* books, modern languages. *Address:* St. Patrick's Boys' Academy, Dungannon, Co. Tyrone, Northern Ireland. *Telephone:* (018687) 22165, 22668. *Fax:* (01868) 722745.

FAULKS, Sebastian, B.A., F.R.S.L.; British author and journalist; b. 20 April 1953, Newbury, Berks.; s. of Peter Faulks and Pamela Lawless; m. Veronica Youlten 1989; two s. one d.; ed. Wellington Coll. and Emmanuel Coll., Cambridge; reporter Daily Telegraph newspaper 1979–83, feature writer Sunday Telegraph 1983–86; Literary Ed. The Independent 1986–89, Deputy Ed. The Independent on Sunday 1989–90, Assoc. Ed. 1990–91; columnist The Guardian 1992–, Evening Standard 1997–. *Leisure interests:* wine, sport. *Publications:* The Girl at the Lion d'Or 1989, A Fool's Alphabet 1992, Birdsong 1993, The Fatal Englishman 1996, Charlotte Gray 1998. *Address:* c/o Aitken and Stone, 29 Fernshaw Road, London, SW10 0TG, England. *Telephone:* 0171-351 7561. *Fax:* 0171-376 3594.

FAURE, Maurice Henri, D. EN D.; French politician; b. 2 Jan. 1922, Azerat (Dordogne); s. of René Faure and Irène Joudinaud; m. Andrée Guillemain 1945; two s.; ed. Lycée de Périgueux, Faculty of Law and Letters, Bordeaux and Toulouse Univs.; Deputy for Lot (Radical-Socialist) 1951 (re-elected to Nat. Assembly 1958, 1962, 1967, 1968, 1973, 1978, 1981); Sec. of State for Foreign Affairs (Mollet Cabinet) 1956–57, (Bourgès-Manoury Cabinet) June-Nov. 1957, (Gaillard Cabinet) 1957–58; Minister for European Insts. May-June 1958, for Justice May-June 1981; Minister of State for Equipment and Housing 1988–89; mem. Conseil Constitutionnel 1989–98; Pres. French del. Common Market and Euratom Conf., Brussels 1956; mem. del. 11th Session UN Gen. Assembly, New York 1956; Special Asst. Minister for Foreign Affairs on Morocco and Tunisia 1956–57; fmr. mem. European Coal and Steel Community Ass.; mem. European Parl. 1959–67, 1973–81; Senator of Lot 1983–88; fmr. Mayor of Prayssac (Lot), Mayor of Cahors 1965–90; Conseiller Général, Salviac canton (Lot) 1957–58, Montcuq canton 1963; Pres. Departmental Asscn. of Mayors of Lot, Mouvement européen; Pres. Entente démocratique of the Nat. Assembly 1960–62; Pres., later Leader, Parti republicain radical et radical-socialiste 1961–65, 1969–71; fmr. Pres. Rassemblement démocratique Group, Nat. Assembly; Pres. Econ. Devt. Comm. for Midi-Pyrénées 1964–70; Pres. Conseil général du Lot 1970–94, Hon. Pres. 1994–; resigned from Rassemblement pour la République May 1977; Vice-Pres. Conseil de la région Midi-Pyrénées 1974–; Commdr. Mérite civil and other awards. *Address:* 28 boulevard Raspail, 75007 Paris, France (Home).

FAURE, Roland; French journalist; b. 10 Oct. 1926, Montelimar; s. of Edmond Faure-Geors and Jeanne Gallet; m. Véra Hitzbleck 1956; three s.; ed. Enclos Saint-François, Montpellier and Faculté de Droit, Aix-en-Provence; journalist, Méridional-la France, Marseilles 1947; del. in America, Asscn. de la presse latine d'Europe et d'Amerique 1951, Sec.-Gen. 1954–; founder and Ed.-in-Chief, Journal français du Brésil, Rio de Janeiro 1952–53; Diplomatic Ed. L'Aurore 1954, Head of Diplomatic Service 1959, Ed.-in-Chief

1962, Dir. and Ed.-in-Chief 1968–78; attached to Cabinet of Minister of Public Works 1957–58; Dir. Toutes les nouvelles de Versailles 1954–86; mem. Admin. Bd. Antenne 2 1975–79; Dir. of Information, Radio-France 1979–81; founder and Dir. radio CVS 1982; Pres. Dir.-Gen. Société Nat. de programme Radio France 1986–89, Société Nat. de Radiodifffusion; Pres. Université radiophonique et télévisuelle int. (URTI) 1987–97, Communauté des radios publiques de langue française (CRPLF) 1987; Pres. Admin. Council Fondations Marguerite Long-Jacques Thibaud 1991–; Pres. Club DAB 1991–; mem. Conseil Supérieur de l'Audiovisuel (CSA) 1989–97, mem. numerous professional asscns. etc.; Officier, Légion d'honneur; Officier, Ordre Nat. du Mérite. *Publications:* Brésil dernière heure 1954; articles in newspapers and journals. *Address:* France Radio Numérique, 19 Rue Cognacq-Jay, 75007 Paris (Office); 94 boulevard de la Tour Maubourg, Paris 7e, France (Home). *Telephone:* (1) 49 55 01 15 (Office).

FAUROUX, Roger, L. ÈS L.; French business executive; b. 21 Nov. 1926, Montpellier (Hérault); s. of Théo and Rose (née Ségu) Fauroux; m. Marie Le Roy Ladurie 1953; three s. three d.; ed. Lycée de Besançon, Lycée Henri IV, Paris, Ecole normale supérieure, Ecole nationale d'admin.; Asst. Insp. of Finance 1956, Insp. 1958; Office of Minister of Educ. May–Nov. 1960; Admin. Dir. Cie. Pont-à-Mousson 1961, Finance Dir. 1964–69; Finance Dir. Cie. de Saint-Gobain-Pont-à-Mousson 1970, Asst. Dir.-Gen. 1972–75, Admin. Dir.-Gen. 1978–80, Pres. Dir.-Gen. 1980–86; Dir. Ecole nat. d'administration 1986–88; Pres. Soc. des investisseurs du Monde (newspaper) 1986–88; Minister of Industry, also of Territorial Devt., then of Regional Planning 1988–91; Mayor of Saint-Girons 1989–95; Pres. Cerf Editions 1987, 1992–97; Dir. Certain Teed Products, Fabbrica Pisana (Italy), Cristalería Española (Spain), Cie. Générale des Eaux, Banque Nationale de Paris, Institut Pasteur, Petrofina (Belgique); mem. Admin. Council Eurotunnel 1991–92, Commercial Union 1992–97, MK2 1993–; mem. Supervisory Bd. Vereinigte Glaswerke Siemens 1993–97, Commercial Union France 1994, Usinor 1995–; Officier, Légion d'honneur, Officier, Ordre Nat. du Mérite. *Address:* c/o Compagnie de Saint-Gobain, Les Miroirs, 92096 Paris-la-Défense Cedex, France.

FAUVET, Jacques, L. EN D.; French newspaper editor and author; b. 9 June 1914, Paris; s. of Pierre and Andrée (née Meunier-Pouthot) Fauvet; m. Claude Decroix 1939; five c.; ed. Lycée St. Louis, Paris, and Faculté de Droit, Univ. de Paris; an Ed., l'Est républicain, Nancy 1937–39; joined Le Monde 1945, Head of Domestic Politics Dept. 1948–58, Asst. Ed.-in-Chief 1958–63, Ed.-in-Chief 1963–83, Gen. Ed. 1968, Dir.-Gen. 1969–82; Chair. Nat. Comm. on Data Protection; Grand Officier, Légion d'honneur, Grand Croix Ordre Mérite, Croix de guerre (1939–45). *Publications:* Les partis politiques dans la France actuelle 1947, Les forces politiques en France 1951, La France déchirée 1957, La politique et les paysans 1958, La IVe République 1959, La fronde des généraux 1961, Histoire du parti communiste français, Vol. I 1964, Vol. II 1965, combined edn. 1977. *Address:* 5 rue Louis-Boilly, 75016 Paris, France. *Telephone:* (01) 45-20-14-57.

FAVIER, Jean, D. ÈS L.; French historian; b. 2 April 1932, Paris; m. Lucie Calisti 1956; four s.; ed. Faculté des Lettres, Paris, and Ecole nationale des chartes; mem. Ecole française de Rome 1956–58; Master of Confs., Faculté des lettres, Rennes 1964, Rouen 1966–69; Dir. of Studies, Ecole pratique des hautes études 1965–; Prof. of Medieval Econ. History, Univ. of Paris-Sorbonne 1969–; Dir. Inst. of History, Sorbonne 1971–75; Dir. Revue Historique 1973–; Dir.-Gen. Archives de France 1975–94; Head Bibliothèque Nationale de France 1996–97; Pres. Conseil d'admin., Ecole normale supérieure 1988–; Pres. Nat. Library of France 1994–96, Asscn. des lauréats du concours général, French Comm. for UNESCO 1997–; mem. Acads. of Lyon, Reims and Rouen; hon. mem. Luxembourg Acad.; several prizes including Prix des Ambassadeurs 1978 and Grand Prix Gobert (Acad. française) 1981; Chevalier Légion d'honneur; Officier, Ordre Nat. du Mérite; Commdr. des Arts et des Lettres; Chevalier des Palmes académiques and decorations from Belgium, Luxembourg and Poland. *Publications:* Un conseiller de Philippe-le-Bel: Enguerran de Marigny 1963, Les Finances pontificales à l'époque du grand schisme d'Occident 1966, De Marco Polo à Christophe Colomb 1968, Les contribuables parisiens à la fin de la guerre de cent ans 1970, Finance et fiscalité au bas moyen age 1971, Paris au XVe siècle 1974, Le trafic fluvial dans la région parisienne au XVe siècle 1975, Philippe-le-Bel 1978, La guerre de cent ans 1980, François Villon 1982, Le Temps des principautés 1984, Chronicle of the French Revolution 1788–1789 (co-ed.) 1988, L'univers de Chartres 1988, les Grandes découvertes, d'Alexandre à Magellan 1991, les Archives de la France (ed.) 1992, Dictionnaire de la France médiévale 1993, Paris, deux mille ans d'histoire 1997. *Leisure interests:* organ, photography. *Address:* Institut de France, 23 quai de Conti, 75006 Paris (Office); 9 rue Reiter, 94100 Saint-Maur-des-Fossés, France (Home).

FAVORSKY, Oleg Nikolayevich; Russian expert on thermal technology; b. 27 Jan. 1929; m.; two d.; ed. Moscow Aviation Inst.; engineer, sr. engineer, leading engineer, sr. researcher, First Deputy Dir. of Div. Cen. Inst. of Aviation Engine 1953–73, Deputy Dir. 1987–95; Dir.-Gen. and Chief Constructor "Sojuz" Scientific-Production Unit U.S.S.R. Ministry of Aviation Industry 1973–87; Acad.-Sec. Dept. of Physical-Tech. Problems of Energy Consumption 1995–; author of scientific works and practical devt. in the field of aviation gas-turbine engines, on thermal exchange in space and in high temperature devices, problems of space ecology; Corresp. mem. U.S.S.R. (now Russian) Acad. of Sciences 1982, mem. 1990; Lenin Prize. *Leisure interests:* tennis, stamp-collecting. *Address:* Russian Academy of Sciences, 32a Leninsky Prospekt, 117334 Moscow, Russia. *Telephone:* (095) 938 1400 (Office). *Fax:* (095) 938 1354 (Office).

FAVRE, Alexandre Jean Auguste; French scientist; b. 23 Feb. 1911, Toulon; s. of Auguste Favre and Annie Mercure; m. Luce Palombe 1939; one s. two d.; ed. Univs. Aix-Marseille and Paris; Asst. Lecturer, Faculty of Science, Univ. of Marseilles 1932–38, Lecturer 1938–41, Asst. Prof. 1941–45, Assoc. Prof. 1945–51, Prof. 1951–; Dir. Inst. of Mechanical Statistics of Turbulence 1960–80, Hon. Dir. 1981; Emer. Prof. Univ. of Aix-Marseille 1981; Scientific Asst. Ministry of Air 1932; Scientific Counsellor, Nat. Office of Aerospatial Studies and Research 1947, Atomic Energy Commissariat 1958; mem. Nat. Cttee. for Scientific Research 1963, Nat. Cttee. for Univs. 1972–75, Mathematical Soc. of France, Physical Soc. of France, American Physical Soc., mem. Acad. des Sciences 1977; Pres. Fédération universitaire de Mécanique; Hon. mem. Nat. Acad. for Air and Space 1983; Officier Légion d'honneur, Officier Ordre national du Mérite, Commdr. des Palmes académiques. *Major research includes:* hypersustentation 1934, hyperconvection 1951; inventor of centrifugal sub-trans-supersonic compressor 1940; inventor of apparatus for statistical measurement of time correlation 1942, and of appliance for detection of random noise 1952; research on turbulence of fluids and space-time correlations 1942–97, and on statistical equations of turbulent compressible gas 1948–97. *Publications:* la Turbulence en Mécanique des Fluides 1976, Chaos and Determinism (jtly.) 1995. *Leisure interest:* philosophy of sciences. *Address:* Le Chambord no. 1, 122 rue Cdt. Rolland, 13008 Marseille, France. *Telephone:* (04) 91-77-65-86.

FAVRHOLDT, David Cornaby, DR.PHIL.; Danish professor of philosophy; b. 24 April 1931, Oregon, U.S.A.; s. of Elias Favrholdt and Bertha Cornaby; m. 1st Nina Fønss 1961; m. 2nd Anne Birch 1968; ed. Copenhagen Univ.; Asst. Prof. in Philosophy, Copenhagen Univ. 1961–66; Prof. of Philosophy and Head of Dept., Odense Univ. 1966–; mem. Royal Danish Acad. of Science and Letters, Academia Europaea; mem. Danish Research Council for Humanities 1985–91; Aarhus Univ. Gold Medal 1958; Fyens Stiftstid. Research Prize 1972. *Publications:* An Interpretation and Critique of Wittgenstein's Tractatus 1964, Philosophy and Society 1968, Chinese Philosophy 1971, The List of Sins 1973, Lenin: His Philosophy and World View 1978, Niels Bohr's Philosophical Background 1992, Studies in Niels Bohr's Philosophy 1994; trans. of Wittgenstein and John Locke, articles on Niels Bohr. *Leisure interests:* piano, classical music. *Address:* Department of Philosophy, Odense University, Campusvej 55, 5230 Odense M (Office); Oehlenschlaegersvej 57, 5230 Odense M, Denmark (Home). *Telephone:* 66-158600. *Fax:* 65-93-23-75.

FAWCETT, Don Wayne, M.D.; American anatomist; b. 14 March 1917, Springdale, Iowa; s. of Carlos J. Fawcett and Mary Mable Kennedy; m. Dorothy Secrest 1941; two s. two d.; ed. Harvard Coll., Harvard Medical School; Capt., Medical Corps, U.S. Army 1943–46; Research Fellow in Anatomy, Harvard Medical School 1946, Instructor 1946–68, Assoc. 1948–51, Asst. Prof. 1951–55, Hersey Prof. of Anatomy and Head of Dept. 1959–85, Curator, Warren Anatomical Museum 1961–70, James Stillman Prof. of Comparative Anatomy 1962–85, Sr. Assoc. Dean for Preclinical Affairs 1975–77; scientist Int. Laboratory for Research on Animal Diseases, Kenya 1980–85; Prof. and Chair. Dept. of Anatomy, Cornell Medical Coll. 1955–59; Pres. American Asscn. of Anatomists 1965–66, American Soc. for Cell Biology 1961–62, Int. Fed. of Socs. for Electron Microscopy 1976–79; mem. N.A.S. and numerous socs.; numerous hon. degrees. *Publications:* Over 150 papers and two textbooks on histology, cell biology and reproductive biology. *Leisure interests:* photography of wild animals, shell collecting, zoological research. *Address:* 1224 Lincoln Road, Missoula, MT 59802, U.S.A. *Telephone:* (406) 549-1415.

FAYAT, Henri, D.LL.; Belgian politician and lawyer; b. 28 June 1908, Molenbeek-Sint-Jans; ed. Royal Athenaeum, Brussels and Univ. of Brussels; Advocate, Brussels 1935–73; Legal Attaché, Belgian Foreign Office, London 1942–43; Chief Asst. to the Belgian Ministry of the Interior, London 1943, and in Brussels 1944; Chief Asst. to Deputy Prime Minister 1944–45; mem. House of Reps. 1946–71; Prof. Faculty of Law, Univ. of Brussels (Vrije Univ.) 1948–78; mem. Consultative Ass. of the Council of Europe 1949–50, Common Ass. of the European Coal and Steel Community 1954–57; Minister of Foreign Trade 1957–58, 1968–71; Deputy Foreign Minister 1961–66; Sec. of State for Foreign Trade 1972–73, for Ports Policy 1973; Chair. Brussels Conf. on British application for membership of EEC 1963; Chair. Acad. Bd., Programme on Int. Legal Co-operation, Vrije Universiteit, Brussels 1974–88; Chair. Algemeen Nederlands Verbond 1978–87; in 1962 adapted Belgium's Foreign Service to country's bilingual character; successfully negotiated 1963 Treaty between Belgium and Netherlands on Scheldt-Rhine Canal. *Publications:* Op Zoek naar Vrede 1979, Memoirs (3 vols.): Niets is Voorbij 1983, In het teken van Artevelde 1985, Volharding 1988, Belgian Legislation in Exile 1993. *Address:* Kruisdagenlaan 87, 1200 Brussels, Belgium.

FAYE, Jean Pierre; French writer; b. 19 July 1925, Paris; m. Marie-Odile Demenge 1952; one s. one d.; ed. Univ. de Paris à la Sorbonne; teacher, Lycée de Reims 1951–54; Exchange Fellow Univ. of Chicago 1954–55; Asst. Prof. Univ. de Lille 1955–56, Univ. de Paris (Sorbonne) 1956–60; Research, Centre nat. de la Recherche scientifique 1960 (Dir. of Research 1983); Founder of the Collectif Change and Centre d'Analyse et de Sociologie des Langages (C.A.S.L.); Founder and Pres. High Council, Coll. Int. de Philosophie; f. and Pres. The European Philosophical Univ., now European

Univ. of Research, Paris 1985–90, 1993–, Inst. for Foundation of the European City of Culture 1997–; Ed. of the review Change 1968–85; Prix Renaudot 1964. *Publications:* Novels: Entre les rues 1958, La cassure 1961, Battement 1962, Analogues 1964, L'écluse 1964, Les troyens 1970, Inferno versions 1975, L'ovale 1975, Yumi, visage caméra 1983; Poems: Fleuve renversé 1959, Théâtre 1964 (produced at Odéon, Théâtre de France by Roger Blin 1965), Couleurs pliées 1965, Verres 1977, Syeeda 1984; Essays: Le récit hunique 1967, Langages totalitaires, Théorie du récit 1972, La critique du langage et son économie 1973, Migrations du récit sur le peuple juif 1974, Les Grandes Journées du Père Duchesne 1981, Dictionnaire Politique, essai de Philosophie Politique 1982, La raison narrative 1990, Le livre de Lioube 1992, La Grande Nap 1992, Ode Europe 1992, La déraison antisémite et son langage 1993, Le piège: La philosophie heideggerienne et le nationalsocialisme 1993, Didjla, le Tigre 1994, Nietzsche en vie 1995, Le langage meurtrier 1995, le Siècle des idéologies 1996, Qu'est-ce que la philosophie? 1997, Guerre trouvée 1997, Le Vrai Nietzsche 1998. *Address:* European University of Research, 1 rue Descartes, 75005 Paris, France.

FAYED, Mohamed al-; Egyptian business executive; b. 27 Jan. 1933, Alexandria; s. of Aly Aly Fayed; m. 1st Samira Khashoggi 1954 (divorced 1958); one s. (died 1997); m. 2nd Heini Wathen; four c.; f. co. in Alexandria 1956; involved in shipping, property, banking, oil and construction; Chair. and owner Ritz Hotel, Paris 1979–; owner Fulham Football Club 1997–; Chair. Harrods Ltd. 1985–, Harrods Holdings PLC 1994–; Hon. mem. Emmanuel Coll., Cambridge; Officier, Légion d'honneur 1993, La Grande Médaille de la ville de Paris 1985, Plaque de Paris 1989, Commdr. Order of Merit (Italy) 1990. *Address:* Harrods Ltd., Brompton Road, London, SW1X 7XL, England.

FAYEZ, Mohamad al-Ali al-; Saudi Arabian politician; b. 1937, Hail; Legal Adviser, Council of Ministers 1960–70; Gov., Chair. Bd. Dirs. Gen. Org. for Social Insurance; Deputy Minister of Labour and Social Affairs, Minister 1983–95. *Address:* c/o Ministry of Labour and Social Affairs, Omar bin al-Khatab Street, Riyadh 11157, Saudi Arabia.

FAZIO, Antonio; Italian central banker; b. 11 Oct. 1936, Alvito, Frosinone; s. of late Eugenio Fazio and Maria Giuseppa Persichetti; m. Maria Cristina Rosati; one s. four d.; ed. Univ. of Rome, Massachusetts Inst. of Tech., U.S.A.; Research Fellow, Research Dept., Banca d'Italia 1960, Consultant to Research Dept. 1961–66, Deputy Head, then Head Econometric Research Office 1966, Deputy Dir. Research Dept.'s Monetary Section 1972, Head Research Dept. 1973–79, Cen. Man. for Econ. Research 1980, Deputy Dir.-Gen. Banca d'Italia 1982–93, Gov. 1993–; Asst. Prof. of Demography, Univ. of Rome 1961–66; Paul Harris Fellow (Rotary Int.); Hon. D.Econ. (Bari), Hon. D.Litt. (Johns Hopkins); Kt. Grand Gross Order of Merit (Italy). *Publications:* texts dealing mainly with monetary theory, econ. policy and monetary policy issues. *Address:* Banca d'Italia, Via Nazionale 91, 00184 Rome, Italy. *Telephone:* (06) 47921. *Fax:* (06) 47923365.

FEARON, Douglas Thomas, B.A., M.D., F.R.C.P.; American professor of immunology; b. 16 Oct. 1942, Brooklyn, New York; s. of Henry Dana Fearon and Frances Fearon (née Eubanks); m. Clare M. Wheless 1977; one s. one d.; ed. Williams Coll., Johns Hopkins Univ. School of Medicine; residency Johns Hopkins Hosp. 1968–70; U.S. Army Medical Corps 1970–72; Postdoctoral Fellowship Harvard Medical School 1972–75, instructor Harvard Medical School 1975–76, Asst. Prof. of Medicine 1976–79, Assoc. Prof. 1979–84, Prof. of Medicine 1984–87; Prof. of Medicine, Johns Hopkins Univ. School of Medicine 1987–93; Wellcome Trust Prof. of Medicine, Cambridge Univ. 1993–; founding mem. Acad. of Medical Sciences; Fellow A.A.A.S.; Lee C. Howley Prize, Arthritis Foundation; Bronze Star (U.S. Army). *Publications:* over 100 articles in scientific journals. *Leisure interest:* golf. *Address:* Wellcome Trust Immunology Unit, MRC Centre, Hills Road, Cambridge, CB2 2SP, England.

FEAST, Michael William, D.SC., PH.D., F.R.A.S., F.R.S.S.A., A.R.C.S.; South African astronomer; b. 29 Dec. 1926, Deal, England; s. of Frederick Feast and Dorothy (née Knight) Feast; m. Elizabeth Constance Maskew 1962; one s. two d.; ed. Imperial Coll., London; Postdoctoral Fellow, Nat. Research Council of Canada 1949–51, astronomer Radcliffe Observatory 1952–74, South African Astronomical Observatory 1974–92, Dir. 1977–92; Royal Soc. Guest Fellow Inst. of Astronomy, Cambridge 1992–93; Pres. Int. Astronomical Union Comm. on Stellar Spectra 1967–70, on Variable Stars 1970–76; Vice-Pres. Int. Astronomical Union 1979–85; Pres. Astronomical Soc. of S.A. 1957–58, 1979–80; Founder mem. S. African Acad. of Science 1995–; Hon. Prof. of Astronomy, Univ. of Cape Town 1983–; Assoc. Royal Astronomical Soc.; Hon. D.Sc. (Cape Town) 1993; Gill Medal, Astronomical Soc. of S.A. 1983, de Beers' Gold Medal (S. African Inst. of Physics) 1992. *Publications:* over 300 astronomical and physics papers, mainly in Royal Astronomical Soc. notices. *Address:* Astronomy Department, University of Cape Town, Private Bag, Rondebosch 7700, South Africa. *Telephone:* (21) 650 2396. *Fax:* (21) 650 3342.

FEBRES CORDERO RIVADENEIRA, León; Ecuadorean businessman, engineer and politician; mem. Partido Social Cristiano (PSC); PSC cand. in elections 1978, 1979; Pres. of Ecuador 1984–88. *Address:* c/o Partido Social Cristiano, Carnón 548 y Reina Victoria, Casilla 9454, Quito, Ecuador.

FEDDEN, (Adye) Mary, R.A., O.B.E.; British painter; b. 14 Aug. 1915, Bristol; d. of H. V. Fedden and I. M. Prichard; m. Julian Trevelyan 1951 (deceased 1988); ed. Badminton School, Bristol, Slade School of Art, London; taught painting Royal Coll. of Art 1956–64, Yehudi Menuhin School 1964–74; exhbns. Redfern, Beaux Arts, Christopher Hull and New Grafton Galleries, London and various provincial galleries 1948–; works purchased by H.M. The Queen, Tate Gallery, Crown Prince of Jordan; Pres. Royal W. of England Acad. 1984–88; Hon. D.Litt. (Bath). *Leisure interests:* cycling, reading.

FEDERMAN, Raymond; American professor of literature and writer; b. 15 May 1928, Paris, France; m. Erica Hubscher 1960; one d.; ed. Univ. Calif. at Los Angeles and Columbia Univ.; Asst. Prof. Univ. of Calif. Santa Barbara 1959–64; Assoc. Prof. State Univ. of N.Y., Buffalo 1964–68, Prof. 1968–90, Distinguished Prof. of Literature 1990–, Melodia E. Jones Distinguished Prof. 1992–; Guggenheim Fellow 1966–67, N.E.A. Fellow 1986; American Book Award 1987. *Publications:* novels: Double or Nothing 1971, Take It or Leave It 1976, The Voice in the Closet 1979, The Twofold Vibration 1982, Smiles on Washington Square 1985, To Whom It May Concern 1990; essays: Journey to Chaos 1965, Surfiction 1976, Critifiction 1992, The Supreme Indecision of the Writer 1996, La Fourrure de Ma Tante Rachel 1996. *Leisure interests:* golf, tennis. *Address:* 46 Four Seasons W., Eggertsville, NY 14226, U.S.A. *Telephone:* (1) 716 835 9611. *Fax:* (1) 716 835 5210.

FEDERSPIEL, Thomas Holger; Danish lawyer; b. 25 Oct. 1935, Hellerup; s. of Per Torben and Elin (née Zahle) Federspiel; m. 1st Benedicte Buhl 1965 (divorced 1984); two s.; m. 2nd Bettina Hage 1997; ed. Krebs Skole, Rungsted Statsskole, Copenhagen Univ; joined Jonas Bruun 1961–66, Slaughter and May, Davis Polk & Wardwell 1966–67; partner Per Federspiel 1968, Gorrissen & Federspiel (now Gorrissen Federspiel Kierkegaard) 1989–; admitted to Court of Appeal 1964, Supreme Court 1969; F. Gorrissen & Federspiel 1989; Chair. Danish Bar Council Cttee. on pvt. int. law 1971–81; Pres. Int. Bar Asscn. 1980–82; mem. Int. Bar Asscn. 1971–84, Hon. mem. 1984; Hon. mem. American Bar Asscn. 1981; Hon. legal adviser to the British Embassy; mem. Bd. Queen Margrethe's and Prince Henrik's Foundation; Chair. and mem. Bd. various cos. and charitable foundations. *Leisure interests:* tennis, skiing, shooting. *Address:* 12 H.C. Andersens Boulevard, 1553 Copenhagen (Office); Rungsted Strandvej 22, 2950 Vedbaek, Denmark (Home). *Telephone:* 33.41.41.41 (Office); 45.86.13.42 (Home). *Fax:* 33.41.41.28.

FEDORENKO, Nikolay Prokofiyevich; Russian economist; b. 28 April 1917, Preobrazhenskoe Village, Zaporozhye Region; m. Nina Fedorenko; one d.; ed. Moscow M. V. Lomonosov Inst. of Fine Chemical Tech. and Higher Party School of CPSU Cen. Cttee.; Soviet Army 1942–45; Instructor, Head of Dept., Moscow M. V. Lomonosov Inst. of Fine Chemical Tech. 1946–62; Deputy Academician-Sec. Dept. of Econs., U.S.S.R. Acad. of Sciences 1962–63; Dir. Cen. Econ.-Mathematical Inst., U.S.S.R. Acad. of Sciences 1963–85, Adviser 1985–, Hon. Dir. 1987–; Corresp. mem. U.S.S.R. (now Russian) Acad. of Sciences 1962–64, mem. 1964; Academician-Sec. Dept. of Economy, 1972–85, mem. Presidium 1985–88, Adviser to Presidium 1988–; Hon. Dr. (Geneva); State Prize 1970, V.S. Nemchinov Prize 1984, G. M. Krzhizhanovsky Prize. *Publications:* numerous works on economics of chemical industry. *Leisure interests:* Russian and foreign painting. *Address:* Central Economics-Mathematical Institute, ul. Krasikova 22, 117418 Moscow, Russia. *Telephone:* 129-06-33.

FEDORENKO, Nikolay Trofimovich, D.PHIL.; Russian diplomatist and sinologist; b. 22 Nov. 1912, Pyatigorsk, Stavropol; s. of Matrena and Trofim Fedorenko; m. Lilia Fedorenko 1940; three d.; ed. Moscow Inst. of Oriental Studies; mem. CPSU 1943–91; Diplomatic service 1939–; Counsellor, Soviet Embassy, Chongqing 1946; Chargé d'Affaires, Nanjing 1948, Beijing 1952; Head, First Far East Dept. (China); mem. Policy Planning Bd., Ministry of Foreign Affairs 1950–55; Deputy Foreign Minister 1955–58; Amb. to Japan 1958–62; Perm. Rep. to UN 1963–68; Sr. Assoc. Inst. of Oriental Studies, Acad. of Sciences 1968–85, Adviser to Dir. 1985–; mem. CPSU Auditing Comm. 1966–71; Ed.-in-Chief Foreign Literature monthly 1970–88, Sec. Bd. of Writers' Union of U.S.S.R. 1970–85; Corresp. mem. U.S.S.R. (now Russian) Acad. of Sciences 1958–; mem. Accad. Fiorentina; Hon. mem. Inst. Sinologi, Tokyo. *Publications:* 35 books and over 250 articles on Chinese and Japanese literature and culture. *Address:* Institute of Oriental Studies, Rozhdestvenka str. 12, 103777 Moscow, Russia. *Telephone:* (095) 923-6120 (Office); 132-56-98 (Home).

FEDOROV, Boris Grigorievich, D.ECON.SC.; Russian politician and economist; b. 13 Feb. 1958, Moscow; s, of Grigory Fedorov and Nina Fedorov; m. 1983; one s. one d.; ed. Moscow Inst. of Finance; worked as economist, sr. economist, Head Currency and Econ. Dept. U.S.S.R. State Bank 1980–87; researcher Inst. of World Econ. and Int. Relations U.S.S.R. Acad. of Sciences 1987–90; consultant to Social-Econ. Dept. Cen. Cttee. CPSU 1980–90; Minister of Finance Govt. of Russian Fed. July–Dec. 1990, first minister who resigned in protest against denuniciation of Radical Reform Programme 500 Days; Counsellor of Pres. Boris Yeltsin on financial problems 1991; Sr. Banker, EBRD, London 1991–92; Exec. Dir., IBRD, Washington, D.C. Oct.–Dec. 1992; Deputy Chair. Govt. of Russia 1992–94; Minister of Finance 1993–94; mem. State Duma (Parl.) 1993–98; Leader Russia Forward! (political movt.) 1993–; f. and Pres. Liberal-Democratic Fund 1997; Head State Taxation Service 1998. *Leisure interest:* reading biographies, collecting coins. *Address:* Vpered Russiya!, Slavyanskaya pl. 4, Building 2, 103074 Moscow, Russia. *Telephone:* (095) 923-16-44.

FEDOROV, Nikolai Vasilievich, C.LAW; Russian/Chuvash politician and lawyer; b. 9 May 1958, Chuvash Autonomous Repub.; m.; one s. one d.; ed. Kazan State Univ.; worked in legal bodies since 1983; teacher Chuvash State Univ. 1980–82, 1985–89; U.S.S.R. People's Deputy 1989–91; Deputy Chair. Legis. Comm. Supreme Soviet 1989–90; Minister of Justice of R.S.F.S.R. (later Russia) 1990–93; Pres. Chuvash Repub. 1993–; mem. State Duma (Parl.) 1993–95; mem. Council of Fed. 1996–. *Address:* Office of the President, Cheboksary, Chuvash Republic; Council of Federation, Bolshaya Dmitrovka str. 26, 103031 Moscow, Russia. *Telephone:* (8352) 62-46-87 (Cheboksary); (095) 292-58-18 (Moscow).

FEDOROV, Svyatoslav Nikolaevich; Russian ophthalmologist; b. 8 Aug. 1927, Proskurov, Ukraine; s. of Nikolai Fedorov and Alexandra Danilovna Fedorova; m. Irene Efimovna; two d.; ed. Flying Acad., Rostov-on-Don, Rostov Medical Inst.; worked as eye-doctor in Veshenskaya, then in regional hosp.; head of faculty of Eye Inst., Cheboksary, and then Archangelsk, where he elaborated technique of lens-implant; Dir. Moscow Research Lab. of Experimental and Clinical Eye Surgery 1974; Dir. Moscow Research Inst. of Eye Microsurgery 1980–; Founder and Gen. Dir. Scientific-Tech. Complex Microsurgery of the Eye 1986–; People's Deputy of the U.S.S.R. 1989–91; co-f. and co-chair. Party of Econ. Freedom 1992–94; Founder and Chair. Working People's Self-Govt. Party 1995–; mem. State Duma (Parl.) 1995–; mem. Democratic Reform Movt.; Chair. Soviet Foundation for Charity and Health 1989; Corresp. mem. U.S.S.R. (now Russian) Acad. of Sciences 1987; mem. Acad. of Medical Science 1982; mem. numerous nat. and int. professional asscns.; Hero of Socialist Labour 1987. *Address:* Mikrokhirurgiya Glaza Co., Beskudnikovsky Boulevard 59a, 127486 Moscow (Office); 21 Korp. Apt. 32 Dostoevsky Lane, 103030 Moscow, Russia (Home). *Telephone:* 906-17-71 (Office), 281-33-07 (Home).

FEDOROV, Valentin Petrovich, DR.ECON.SC.; Russian politician and manager; b. 6 Sept. 1939, Zhatai, Yakutia; m.; two d.; ed. G. Plekhanov Moscow Inst. of Nat. Econ., Inst. of World Econ. and Int. Relations U.S.S.R. Acad. of Sciences; worked in State Planning Cttee. Yakutia 1964–78; jr. researcher, head of div., corresp. Journal of Inst. of World Econ. and Int. Relations in W. Germany 1978–84; Prorector on int. relations G. V. Plekhanov Moscow Inst. of Nat. Econ., 1987–90; Governor Sakhalin Region, acted as opponent to transfer of S. Kuril Islands to Japan 1990–93; People's Deputy of Russia 1990–93; Deputy Minister of Econ. 1993–94; Prime Minister of Sakhá (Yakutia) Repub. 1997–98; mem. Political Council Movt. for Democratic Reforms, Co-Chair. Duma of Russian Nat. Sobor; Vice-Pres. Russian Union of Industrialists and Entrepreneurs 1994–. *Publications:* several plays, collections of poems, monographs on econ. *Address:* Russian Union of Industrialists and Entrepreneurs, Staraya pl. 10/4, 103070 Moscow, Russia. *Telephone:* (095) 206-54-92.

FEDOROV, Volodymyr Grygorovych; Ukrainian diplomatist; b. 10 June 1939, Nikolskoye, Kursk Region; m.; one s. one d.; ed. Kharkiv Inst. of Mech. and Electrification of Agric., Higher CP School Cen. CPSU Cttee.; sr. engineer, head of workshop, chief engineer, Head Chernyakhovsk Dist. union Selkhoztekhnika Zhytomyr region 1962–67; Head Chernyakovsk Dist. Dept. of Agric. 1967–71; First Sec. Volodar-Volynsky Dist. Ukrainian CP Cttee. Zhytomyr Region 1970–73; First Sec. Novograd-Volynsky CP City Cttee. 1973–77; Sec. Zhytomyr Regional Cttee., Ukrainian CP 1977–84; Counsellor Council of Ministers of Ukraine 1984–85; Chair. Volynsky Regional Exec. Cttee. 1985–88; Sector Chief Cen. Cttee. of Ukrainian CP 1988–89; First Sec. Zhytomyr Regional Cttee. of Ukrainian CP and Chair. Zhytomyr Regional Council of People's Deputies 1989–91; Perm. Rep. Council of Ministers of Ukraine to Cabinet of Ministers of U.S.S.R. 1991–92; Minister-Counsellor Embassy of Ukraine to Russian Fed. 1992–94; Amb. to Russia 1995–. *Address:* Leontyevsky per. 18, 103009 Moscow, Russia (Office). *Telephone:* (095) 229 1079 (Office).

FEDOSEYEV, Vladimir Ivanovich; Russian conductor; b. 5 Aug. 1932, Leningrad; s. of Ivan Fedoseyev and Elena Fedoseyeva; m. Olga Dobrokhotova; two c.; ed. conductors' class of Moscow Musical Pedagogical Inst., Moscow Conservatoire; mem. CPSU 1963–91; Artistic Dir. and Chief Conductor Moscow Radio Symphony Orchestra of U.S.S.R. Radio Network (now Tchaikovsky Acad. Symphony Orchestra) 1974–; Music Dir. (elect) Vienna Symphony Orchestra 1997; first Perm. Guest Conductor Tokyo Philharmonic Orchestra 1996–; Perm. Guest Conductor Zürich Opera 1997–; works with Bolshoi and Mariinsky Theatres, opera productions and concerts abroad, including Italy, France, Austria, Germany, Japan, Switzerland, Spain, U.K., U.S.A.; People's Artist of U.S.S.R. 1980, R.S.F.S.R. State Prize 1989, Crystal Award of Asahi Broadcasting Corpn., Osaka 1989, Golden Orpheus, for recording of opera May Night with French Acad. of Music. *Address:* Moscow House of Recording and Broadcasting, Malaya Nikitskaya 24, 121069 Moscow, Russia. *Telephone:* 222-00-24 (Office); 229-83-23 (Home, Moscow); (1) 406-54-96 (Home, Vienna). *Fax:* 202-49-85

FEDOSOV, Yevgeny Aleksandrovich, DR. TECH. SC.; Russian automation and avionics specialist; b. 14 May 1929, Moscow; s. of Alexander Efimovitch Fedosov and Nadezhda Anempodistovna Smirnova; m. Lydia Petrovna Vasilyeva; one d.; ed. Bauman Tech. Inst.; post-graduate work at Inst. 1953–56; mem. CPSU 1959–91; research fellow, head of dept., Deputy Dir. of Inst. of Aviation Systems 1956–70, Dir. 1970–; simultaneously head of Dept. of Physico-Tech. Inst. 1970–; Prof. 1969; corresp. mem. U.S.S.R. Acad. of Sciences 1979, mem. 1984–; Lenin Prize 1976, Hero of Socialist Labour 1983, B.N. Petrov Gold Medal, Acad. of Sciences 1989, Honoured Scientist of Russian Fed. 1996. *Publications:* works on analysis and synthesis of complex multi-level operational systems. *Leisure interests:* tennis, gardening. *Address:* Institute of Aviation Systems, Viktorenko str. 7, 125319 Moscow, Russia. *Telephone:* 157-70-47. *Fax:* (095) 157-31-27.

FEDOTOV, Maxim Viktorovich; Russian violinist; b. 24 July 1961, Moscow; s. of Viktor Andreyevich Fedotov and Galina Nikolayevna Fedotova; m. Galina Yevgenyevna Petrova, pianist; one d.; ed. Specialized Music School for Gifted Children in Leningrad, Moscow State Conservatory (with D. Tsyganov and I. Bezrodny); concert tours since 1975; Prof. Moscow State Conservatory 1987–; prize winner All-Union Music Competition Riga 1981, N. Paganini Competition Genoa 1982, Vercelli 1984, P. Tchaikovsky (Moscow 1986), Tokyo 1986 (First Prize); as soloist plays with G. Petrova, regular recitals in Moscow and St. Petersburg; performed in Madrid, Berlin, Leipzig, Frankfurt, Cologne, Milan, Chicago and other cities; debut in London 1993 (Barbican Hall); took part in music festivals in Salzburg, Oakland, Bergen, Dresden, Klagenfurt; toured Australia, New Zealand, Korea, Turkey; Merited Artist of Russia. *Address:* Tolbukhin str. 8, korp. 1, Apt. 6, 121596 Moscow, Russia. *Telephone:* (095) 447 2560 (Home).

FEDOTOV, Mikhail Aleksandrovich, D.JUR; Russian politician and lawyer; b. 18 Sept. 1949, Moscow; m. 3rd Maria Fedotova; one s. one d; ed. Moscow State Univ., All-Union Inst. of Law; teacher of law All-Union Inst. of Law 1973–90; Deputy Minister of Press and Mass Information of Russia 1991–92, Minister 1992–93; rep. Pres. Yeltsin in Constitutional Court trial against CPSU 1992; Russian rep. at UNESCO, Paris 1993–97; Sec. Russian Union of Journalists 1998–; Dir.-Gen. Russian Agency of Intellectual Property (RAIS) Feb.–Dec. 1992. *Address:* Russian Union of Journalists, Lubovskiy blvd. 4, 119021 Moscow, Russia. *Telephone:* (095) 201-51-01.

FEDOTOV, Sergey Aleksandrovich; Russian geophysicist; b. 19 March 1931, Leningrad; m. Tamara Jacabovskaya 1957; two s.; ed. Moscow State Univ.; worked at O. Y. Schmidt Inst. of Earth Physics, U.S.S.R. (now Russian) Acad. of Sciences, Moscow 1957–71, led Pacific Seismological Expedition 1957–70; corresp. mem. Acad. of Sciences 1970–92, mem. 1992; Dir. Inst. of Vulcanology, Far Eastern Scientific Centre, Acad. of Sciences 1971–; Vice-Pres. Int. Asscn. of Vulcanology 1975, Pres. 1979; Ed.-in-Chief Vulcanologiya i seismologiya 1979–82. *Publications:* Active Volcanoes of Kamchatka (Ed.) 1992; numerous scientific works. *Address:* Institute of Vulcanology, Far Eastern Scientific Centre, Academy of Sciences, Piip blvd. 9, 683006 Petropavlovsk-Kamchatsky, Russia. *Telephone:* (41500) 5-06-03 (Office); 3-30-07 (Home).

FEHER, George, PH.D.; American professor of physics; b. 29 May 1924, Czechoslovakia; s. of Ferdinand Feher and Sylvia Feher (née Schwartz); m. Elsa Rosenvasser Feher 1961; three d.; ed. Univ. of California, Berkeley; Research Physicist Bell Telephone Labs., N.J. 1954–60; Visiting Assoc. Prof. Columbia Univ., N.Y. 1956–60; Prof. of Physics Univ. of Calif., San Diego Jan. 1960–; Visiting Prof. M.I.T. 1967–68; mem. American Physical Soc., Biophysical Soc. (Nat. Lecturer 1983), mem. Bd. of Dirs. Technion-Israel Inst. of Tech., Haifa, Israel 1968; mem. Bd. Govs. Weizmann Inst. of Science, Rehovot 1988; Fellow A.A.A., Int. EPR/ESR Soc. 1996; mem. N.A.S., American Acad. of Arts and Sciences; D.Phil. h.c. (Hebrew Univ. of Jerusalem) 1994; awards include American Physical Soc. Prize for origination and devt. of Electron Nuclear Double Resonance (ENDOR) technique and for applying it to solid state and nuclear research problems 1960, Biophysics Prize 1982, Oliver E. Buckley Solid State Physics Prize 1976, Inaugural Annual Award, Int. Electron Spin Resonance Soc. 1991, Bruker Lectureship, Oxford Univ., U.K. 1992, Rumford Medal, American Acad. of Arts and Sciences 1992, Zavoisky Award 1996. *Publications:* over 100 articles in numerous specialist scientific journals, reviews, symposia. *Leisure interests:* photography, sports. *Address:* Department of Physics 0319, University of California at San Diego, 9500 Gilman Drive, La Jolla, CA 92093-0319, U.S.A. *Telephone:* (619) 534-4389.

FEHRENBACH, Charles Max, D. ÈS SC.; French professor of astronomy; b. 29 April 1914, Strasbourg; s. of Charles Fehrenbach and Alma (née Holtkemper) Fehrenbach; m. Myriam Léonie Graff 1939 (deceased); two s. one d.; m. 2nd Reine Bonnaud 1989; ed. Lycée Fustel-de-Coulanges and Univ. of Strasbourg; Asst. Lecturer Univ. of Strasbourg 1934; Teacher Lycée Saint-Charles, Marseille 1939; Astronomer Strasbourg Observatory 1941; Asst. Dir. Haute Provence Observatory 1943, Dir. 1948–83; Prof. of Astronomy, Univ. of Marseilles 1948–83, Prof. Emer. 1983–; Dir. Marseille Observatory 1949–81; Pres. Comm. des instruments, Observatoire européen austral 1958–72, mem. Bd. 1965–72; mem. Bd. Canada France Hawaii Telescope 1975–79, Pres. 1979; mem. Int. Astronomical Union, Vice-Pres. 1973–79; mem. Bureau des Longitudes 1973, Pres. 1987; mem. Rotary Int., Hon. mem. S.A. Astronomical Soc. 1965; Assoc. mem. Royal Astronomical Soc., London 1961; mem. Acad. des Sciences Paris 1968, Int. Astronomical Acad. 1986, Acad. of New York 1991; Assoc. mem. Acad. Royale des Sciences de Belgique 1973, Acad. of Marseille 1979, Acad. of Athens 1980; Corresp. mem. Acad. of Coimbra 1953, Halle 1966, Vienna 1973, Royal Soc. Uppsala 1984; Dr. h.c. (Geneva) 1982; Croix de guerre, Commdr. Légion d'honneur, Palmes académiques, de Léopold II, Chevalier du Mérite agricole, Officier Ordre de Léopold de Belgique; Lauréat, Inst. de France, Acad. Royale de Belgique, Astron. Gesellschaft, Grand prix des sciences de la Ville de Paris 1976, Médaille d'or du C.N.R.S. 1978. *Publications:* Des hommes, des télescopes, des étoiles 1990; 280 publs. in int. reviews on astronomy and related topics. *Leisure interests:* gardening, fishing. *Address:* Les Magnanarelles, Lourmarin 84160, France. *Telephone:* (04) 90.68.00.28.

FEI XIAOTONG; Chinese social anthropologist; b. 2 Nov. 1910, Wujiang Dist., Jiangsu Prov.; s. of Fei Po-an and Yang Renglan; m. Meng Yin 1939; one d.; ed. Yanjing Univ., Beijing, Qinghua Univ., Beijing, London School of Econs.; Prof. of Social Anthropology, Nat. Yunnan Univ. 1939; Visiting Prof., Harvard Univ. (invited by State Dept.), later Inst. of Pacific Relations, New York 1943; Prof. of Anthropology, Qinghua Univ., Beijing 1945; Visiting Fellow, L.S.E. 1946; Deputy Dean, Qinghua Univ., Beijing 1949; Vice-Pres. Cen. Inst. of Nat. Minorities 1952; Vice-Chair. Nationalities Affairs Comm. (under State Council) 1957; Prof. of Anthropology, Cen. Inst. of Nat. Minorities 1957–1982; Pres. Sociology Soc. of China 1979; Prof. of Sociology, Beijing Univ. 1979; Dir. Inst. of Sociology, Chinese Acad. of Social Sciences 1980, Emer. 1983–; Hon. Pres. Western Returned Students' Asscn. 1986–, Minority Literature Foundation 1986–, Soc. of Social Devt. Science 1992–; Vice-Chair. Nat. Cttee. 6th CPPCC 1983–89; Vice-Chair. China Democratic League 1980–87, Chair. 1987–, Hon. Chair. 1997–; Vice-Chair. Standing Cttee. 7th NPC 1988–93, 8th NPC 1993–98; Vice-Pres. Asscn. for Int. Understanding of China 1988–; Hon. Chair. China Vocational Educ. Service 1994–; Huxley Lecturer, Royal Anthropological Inst. 1981; Hon. Fellow, L.S.E. 1982; Adviser Nationalities Affairs Comm. 1983; Malinowski Award 1980; Raymond Magsaysay Award 1994. *Publications include:* Peasant Life in China 1939, Earthbound China 1945, Systems of Child Rearing, Rural China 1947, Rural Reconstruction, Gentry Power and Imperial Power 1948, China's Gentry 1953, Toward a People's Anthropology 1981, Chinese Village Close-up 1983, Collections of Essays on Sociology 1985, Small Town in China 1986. *Leisure interests:* chess, jogging. *Address:* Institute of Sociology, Beijing University, Beijing, People's Republic of China.

FEIFFER, Jules; American cartoonist and writer; b. 26 Jan. 1929, New York; s. of David Feiffer and Rhoda Davis; m. 1st Judith Sheftel 1961; one d.; m. 2nd Jennifer Allen 1983; two c.; ed. Art Students League, Pratt Inst.; asst. to syndicated cartoonist Will Eisner 1946–51; cartoonist, author, syndicated Sunday page, Clifford, engaged in various art jobs 1953–56; contributing cartoonist Village Voice, New York City 1956–97; cartoons published weekly in The Observer (London) 1958–66, 1972–82, regularly in Playboy (magazine) 1959–; cartoons nationally syndicated in U.S. 1959–, New Yorker 1993–, New Statesman and Society 1994–; sponsor Sane; U.S. Army 1951–53; mem. Dramatists Guild Council 1970–; Hon. Fellow Inst. for Policy Studies 1987; Acad. Award for Animated Cartoon, Munro 1961; Special George Polk Memorial Award 1962; Best Foreign Play, English Press (for Little Murders) 1967, Outer Critics Circle Award (Obie) 1969, (The White House Murder Case) 1970, Pulitzer Prize, Editorial Cartooning 1986. *Publications:* books: Sick, Sick, Sick 1959, Passionella and other stories 1960, The Explainers 1961, Boy, Girl, Boy, Girl, 1962, Hold Me! 1962, Harry, The Rat With Women (novel) 1963, Feiffer's Album 1963, The Unexpurgated Memoirs of Bernard Mergendeiler 1965, The Great Comic Book Heroes 1967, Feiffer's Marriage Manual 1967, Pictures at a Prosecution 1971, Ackroyd (novel) 1978, Tantrum 1980, Jules Feiffer's America: From Eisenhower to Reagan 1982, Marriage is an Invasion of Privacy 1984, Feiffer's Children 1986, Ronald Reagan in Movie America 1988, Elliott Loves 1990 (book and play); plays: Crawling Arnold 1961, Little Murders 1966, God Bless 1968, The White House Murder Case 1970, Feiffer on Nixon: The Cartoon Presidency 1974, Knock Knock 1975, Grown Ups 1981, A Think Piece 1982; Carnal Knowledge 1988, Anthony Rose 1989; Feiffer The Collected Works Vol. 1, 2, 3 1990; children's stories: The Man in the Ceiling 1993, A Barrel of Laughs, a Vale of Tears 1995; screenplays: Little Murders 1971, Carnal Knowledge 1971, Popeye 1980, I Want to Go Home 1989. *Address:* c/o Universal Press Syndicate, 4520 Main Street, Kansas City, MO 64111, U.S.A.

FEILDEN, Sir Bernard Melchior, Kt., C.B.E., D.UNIV., A.A. DIPL. HONS., F.R.I.B.A., F.S.A., F.R.S.A.; British architect; b. 11 Sept. 1919, London; s. of Robert Humphrey Feilden, M.C., and Olive (née Binyon) Feilden; m. 1st Ruth Mildred Bainbridge 1949 (died 1994); two s. two d.; m. 2nd Christina Matilda Beatrice Murdoch 1995; ed. Bedford School, Univ. Coll., London, Architectural Asscn., London; qualified as architect 1949; Sr. Partner, Feilden and Mawson 1954–77, now Consultant; Architect, Norwich Cathedral 1963; Surveyor, York Minster 1965, St. Paul's Cathedral, London 1969; Consultant Architect Univ. of East Anglia 1969, Hyde Park Estate, London 1972; St. Giles Cathedral Project 1975, Conservation Plan for Chesterfield Town Centre 1976–81, R.I.B.A. Rep. on Ancient Monuments Bd. 1962–77, mem. R.I.B.A. Council 1975–77; Pres. Ecclesiastical Architects' and Surveyors' Asscn. 1976; Dir. Int. Centre for the Study and Preservation of Cultural Property, Rome (ICCROM) 1977–81, Dir. Emer. 1983; Pres. The Guild of Surveyors 1976; Chair. U.K. Cttee. of Int. Council on Monuments and Sites 1981; Architectural Conservation Consultant; mem. Cathedrals Advisory Comm. 1981–, Churches Conservation Cttee. 1981–; Trustee Intach U.K. Trust; Hon. mem. Icomos; Hon. F.A.I.A. 1987; Hon. Dr. (Göteborg) 1988; Hon. D.Lit. (Univ. East Anglia) 1989; Outstanding Conservation Award 1975, Aga Khan Award for Architecture 1986, three Civic Trust Awards and four Commendations. *Publications:* The Wonder of York Minster 1976, An Introduction to Conservation (for UNESCO) 1980, The Conservation of Historic Buildings 1982, Between Two Earthquakes 1987, Guidelines for Conservation 1989; Ed. Management Manual for World Cultural Heritage Sites (UNESCO). *Leisure interests:* painting, sailing, fishing, chess. *Address:* Stiffkey Old Hall, Stiffkey, Nr. Wells-on-Sea, Norfolk, NR23 1QJ, England. *Telephone:* (01328) 830585. *Fax:* (01328) 830585.

FEINBERG, Evgueniy Lvovich; Russian physicist; b. 27 June 1912, Baku; s. of Dr. Lev Borisovich Feinberg and Tatiana Abramovna Feinstein; m. Valentina Konen 1932 (died 1991); one d.; ed. Moscow Univ.; Postgraduate, Moscow Univ., 1935–38; Research Assoc., Lebedev Inst. of Physics U.S.S.R. (now Russian) Acad. of Sciences 1938–, Head of Sector 1952–88, Councillor to Acad. 1988–; lecturer, Asst. Prof. Moscow Power Inst. 1935–39; Prof. Gorky Univ. 1944–45; Prof. Moscow Eng. Physics Inst. 1946–54; Corresp. mem. U.S.S.R. (now Russian) Acad. of Sciences 1966–, Academician 1997–; U.S.S.R. State Prize 1983, L. I. Mandelshtam Prize, U.S.S.R. Acad. of Sciences 1950, S. I. Vavilov Gold Medal, Acad. of Sciences 1988. *Publications:* Propagation of Radiowaves along the Earth's Surface 1961, Art in the Science Dominated World 1987, Two Cultures. Intuition and Logic in Art and Science 1992, Epoch and Personality. Physicists. Essays and Recollections 1998; works on radiophysics, nuclear and neutron physics, cosmic rays, statistical acoustics, particle physics, philosophy of science and art. *Leisure interests:* chess. *Address:* P. N. Lebedev Institute of Physics, 53 Leninsky Prospekt, 117924 Moscow B-333 (Office); 52 Leninsky Prospekt, Apt. 452, 117333 Moscow B-333, Russia (Home). *Telephone:* 132-29-29 (Office); 137-03-10 (Home). *Fax:* (095) 135-85-33.

FEINBERG, Joel, PH.D.; American professor of philosophy; b. 19 Oct. 1926, Detroit, Mich.; s. of Abraham Feinberg and Marion Tahl Feinberg; m. Betty Grey Feinberg 1955; one s. one d.; ed. Univ. of Michigan; Asst. Prof. Brown Univ. 1955–62; Asst. Prof. Princeton Univ. 1962–64, Assoc. Prof. 1964–66; Prof. Univ. of Calif. Los Angeles 1966–67, Rockefeller Univ. 1967–77, Univ. of Arizona 1977, now Prof. Emer.; Guggenheim Fellowship and other awards. *Publications:* Doing and Deserving 1970, Social Philosophy 1973, Rights, Justice and the Bounds of Liberty 1980, Harm to Others 1984, Offence to Others 1985, Harm to Self 1986, Harmless Wrongdoing 1988, Freedom and Self-Fulfillment 1991. *Address:* Department of Philosophy, University of Arizona, Tucson, AZ 85721 (Office); 5322 N. Via Entrada, Tucson, AZ 85718, U.S.A. (Home). *Telephone:* (520) 621-3120 (Office); (520) 299-0164 (Home). *Fax:* (520) 621-9559 (Office).

FEINENDEGEN, Ludwig E., DR.MED.; German professor of nuclear medicine; b. 1 Jan. 1927, Garzweiler; s. of Ludwig Feinendegen and Rosa Klauth; m. Jeannine Gemuseus 1960; two s.; ed. Univ. of Cologne; Asst. Physician and Scientist, Medical Dept. Brookhaven Nat. Lab., Upton, U.S.A. 1958–63; Scientific Officer, Euratom, Brussels and Paris 1963–67; Dir. Inst. of Medicine Research Center Jülich G.m.b.H. and Prof. for Nuclear Medicine, Univ. Hospital, Düsseldorf 1967–93, Prof. Emer. 1993–; Scientist, Brookhaven Nat. Lab., U.S.A. 1993–98; Assignee, OBER Dept. of Energy, U.S.A. 1994–98; Fellow Inst. of Health, Bethesda 1998–; mem. Advisory Council, Fed. Ministries of Interior and Defence and other professional appts.; mem. Cttee. for meetings of Nobel Laureates 1978–; mem. Rhine Westfalian Acad. of Sciences (Vice-Pres. 1978–79); Dist. Gov. Rotary Int. 1992–93; numerous awards; Bundesverdienstorden. *Publications:* 600 publs. in nat. and int. scientific journals and books. *Address:* National Institute of Health, Department of Nuclear Medicine, Clinical Science Centre, Bethesda, MD 20892 (Office); 923 Beacon Square Court, 358, Gaithersburg, MD 20878, U.S.A. (Home). *Telephone:* (301) 216-0019 (Home).

FEINGOLD, Russell D., B.A., J.D.; American politician and lawyer; b. 2 March 1953, Janesville, Wis.; s. of Leon Feingold and Sylvia Binstock; m. 1st Susan Levine 1977; two d.; m. 2nd Mary Speerschneider 1991; two step-c.; ed. Univ. of Wisconsin, Madison, Magdalen Coll. Oxford, U.K., Harvard Univ. Law School; practised as attorney 1979–85; Democrat State Senator 1983–92, U.S. Senator from Wisconsin 1993–. *Address:* U.S. Senate, 716 Hart Senate Office Bldg., Washington, DC 20510; 8383 Greenway Boulevard, Middleton, WI 53562, U.S.A.

FEINSTEIN, Alvan Richard, M.D.; American professor of medicine and epidemiology; b. 4 Dec. 1925, Philadelphia, Pa.; ed. Univ. of Chicago; Intern, then Resident, Yale New Haven Hosp. 1952–54; Research Fellow, Rockefeller Inst. 1954–55; Resident, Columbia-Presbyterian Medical Center, New York 1955–56; Clinical Dir. Irvington House, Irvington-on-Hudson, New York 1956–62; Instructor then Asst. Prof., New York Univ. School of Medicine 1956–62; Chief, Clinical Pharmacology, West Haven Va. Hosp. 1962–64, Chief, Clinical Biostatistics 1964–74, Chief, Eastern Research Support Center 1967–74; mem. Faculty of School of Medicine, Yale Univ. 1962–, Prof. of Medicine and Epidemiology 1969–, Sterling Prof. 1991–, Dir. Clinical Scholar Program 1974–; Master A. C. P. 1996; Hon. Sc. D. (McGill) 1997; Francis Gilman Blake Award (Yale Univ.) 1969, Distinguished Service Award (Chicago Univ.) 1975, Ludwig Heilmeyer Soc. Gold Medal Award 1981, Richard and Hinda Rosenthal Foundation Award (American Coll. of Physicians) 1982, Charles V. Chapin Medal Award 1983, Yale Science and Eng. Asscn. Annual Award 1986, Robert J. Glaser Annual Award (Soc. for Gen. Internal Medicine) 1987, J. Allyn Taylor Int. Prize in Medicine 1987, Gairdner Foundation Int. Award 1993, Distinguished Teacher Award, American Coll. of Physicians 1997. *Publications:* Clinical Judgment 1967, Clinical Biostatistics 1977, Clinical Epidemiology 1985, Clinimetrics 1987, Muiltivariable Analysis 1996. *Leisure interests:* guitar, folk songs. *Address:* Yale University School of Medicine, 333 Cedar Street, P.O. Box 208025, New Haven, CT 06520; 18 Rockland Park, Branford, CT 06405, U.S.A. (Home). *Telephone:* (203) 785-4145 (University).

FEINSTEIN, Charles Hilliard, B.COM., M.A., PH.D., C.A. (S.A.), F.B.A.; British professor of economic history; b. 18 March 1932, Johannesburg, S. Africa; s. of Louis Feinstein and Rose Feinstein; m. 1st Ruth Loshak 1958; m. 2nd Anne Digby 1980; one s. three d.; ed. Parktown Boys' High School, Johannesburg, Univs. of Witwatersrand and Cambridge; Research Officer, Dept. of Applied Econs. Univ. of Cambridge 1958–63, Lecturer, Faculty of Econs. 1963–78; Fellow, Clare Coll., Cambridge 1963–78, Sr. Tutor 1969–78; Prof. of Econ. and Social History, Univ. of York 1978–87, Head, Dept. of Econs. and Related Studies 1981–86; Reader in Recent Social and Econ. History, Univ. of Oxford; Professorial Fellow, Nuffield Coll., Oxford 1987–89; Chichele Prof. of Econ. History, Univ. of Oxford 1989–; Fellow All Souls Coll., Oxford 1989–99; Man. Ed. Economic Journal 1980–86; mem. Council and Exec. Cttee. Royal Econ. Soc. 1980–90; mem. Council, Econ. History Soc. 1980–98; mem. Econ. Affairs Cttee., Econ. and Social Research Council 1982–86; mem. Council British Acad. 1990–93 (Vice-Pres. 1991–93); Visiting Scholar, Dept. of Econs., Harvard Univ. 1986–87; Visiting Prof. Div. of the Humanities and Social Sciences, Calif. Inst. of Tech. 1997. *Publications:* Domestic Capital Formation in the United Kingdom 1920–38 1965, Socialism, Capitalism and Economic Growth (essays, ed.) 1972, National Income, Expenditure and Output of the United Kingdom, 1855–1965, 1972, York 1831–1981 (ed.) 1981, British Economic Growth (with R.C.O. Matthews and J. Odling-Smee) 1982, The Managed Economy, Essays in British Economic Policy and Performance since 1929 (ed.) 1983, Studies in Capital Formation in the United Kingdom, 1750–1920 (with S. Pollard) 1988, Banking, Currency, and Finance in Europe between the Wars (ed.) 1995, The European Economy Between the Wars (with P. Temin and G. Toniolo) 1997, Chinese Technology Transfer in the 1990s (ed., with C. Howe) 1997. *Leisure interests:* reading, theatre, collecting secondhand books. *Address:* Treetops, Harberton Mead, Headington, Oxford, OX3 0DB, England. *Telephone:* (01865) 763993.

FEINSTEIN, Dianne; American politician; b. 22 June 1933, San Francisco, Calif.; d. of Leon and Betty (Rosenburg) Goldman; m. 1st Bertram Feinstein 1962 (deceased); one d.; m. 2nd Richard C. Blum 1980; ed. Stanford Univ., Calif.; Intern in Public Affairs, Coro Foundation, San Francisco 1955–56; Asst. to Calif. Industrial Welfare Comm., Los Angeles, also San Francisco 1956–57; Vice-Chair. Calif. Women's Bd. Terms and Parole 1962–66; Chair. San Francisco City and County Advisory Comm. for Adult Detention 1967–69; Supervisor City and County of San Francisco 1970–78; Mayor of San Francisco 1978–88; Senator from California 1993–; mem. numerous other public bodies etc.; Democrat. *Address:* U.S. Senate, 331 Senate Hart Office Building, Washington, DC 20510, U.S.A.

FELBER, René; Swiss politician; b. 14 March 1933, Biel; m.; three c.; teacher, Boudevilliers 1953–55, Le Locle 1955–64; joined Social Democratic Party 1958; Mayor of Gen. Council, Le Locle 1960; Mayor of Le Locle 1964–80; mem. of Parl., Neuchâtel 1965–76; Nat. Councillor 1967–81; mem. Govt. of Repub. and Canton of Neuchâtel; Head of Cantonal Dept. of Finances 1981–87; Pres. Govt. of Neuchâtel 1984; mem. Fed. Council 1988; Head Fed. Dept. of Foreign Affairs 1988; Vice-Pres. Jan.–Dec. 1991, Pres. of Switzerland Jan.–Dec. 1992. *Address:* c/o Social Democratic Party, Spitalgasse 34, 3001 Bern, Switzerland.

FELCH, William Campbell, M.D.; American physician; b. 14 Nov. 1920, Lakewood, Ohio; s. of Don H. W. Felch and Beth Campbell; m. Nancy Cook Dean 1945; two s. one d.; ed. Phillips Exeter Acad., Princeton Univ. and Columbia Coll. of Physicians and Surgeons; served U.S. Army 1942–48; in private practice, internal medicine 1951–88; Chief of Staff, United Hosp., Port Chester, New York 1975–77; Ed. The Internist 1975–86; Medical Dir. Osborn Home, Rye 1979–88; Exec. Vice-Pres. Alliance for Continuing Medical Educ. 1979–91 (Distinguished Service Award 1991); mem. Inst. of Medicine, N.A.S.; Fellow American Coll. of Physicians; Ed. ACME Almanac 1978–90, Journal of Continuing Educ. in the Health Professions 1992–94; Award of Merit, New York State Soc. of Internal Medicine 1976; Internist of Distinction, Soc. of Internal Medicine of New York 1973. *Publications:* Aspiration and Achievement 1981, Primer, Continuing Medical Education (Co.-Ed.) 1986, Decade of Decisions 1989, Vision of the Future 1991, The Secrets of Good Patient Care 1996, Alliance for Continuing Medical Education: The First 20 years 1996. *Leisure interest:* travel. *Address:* 26337 Carmelo Street, Carmel, CA 93923, U.S.A. *Telephone:* (831) 625-6593.

FELD, Eliot; American dancer and choreographer; b. 5 July 1942, Brooklyn, New York; s. of Benjamin Feld and Alice Posner; ed. High School of Performing Arts, New York; debut as Child Prince in Nutcracker, New York City Ballet 1954; mem. cast, West Side Story, Broadway 1958 (also appeared in film), I Can Get It For You Wholesale, Broadway 1962 and Fiddler on the Roof, Broadway; dancer and choreographer, American Ballet Theater 1963–68; founder, prin. dancer and choreographer, American Ballet Co. 1968–71; freelance choreographer, N. America and Europe 1971–73; founder, artistic dir. and choreographer, Feld Ballets, N.Y.; founder, The New Ballet School 1977, The Joyce Theater 1982, Ballet Tech 1996; co-founder, Lawrence A. Wien Center for Dance & Theater 1986; has choreographed 93 ballets since 1967; Guggenheim Fellow; Dance Magazine Award 1990; Dr h.c. (Juilliard) 1991. *Address:* c/o Ballet Tech., 890 Broadway, 8th Floor, New York, NY 10003, U.S.A. *Telephone:* (212) 777-7710. *Fax:* (212) 353-0936.

FELDBAEK, Ole, M.A., DR.PHIL.; Danish professor of economic history; b. 22 July 1936, Copenhagen; s. of Commdr. Henri Feldbaek and Kathy Feldbaek; m. Inge Kjaergaard 1976; one s. one d.; ed. Univ. of Copenhagen; Lecturer in Econ. History, Univ. of Copenhagen 1968, Prof. 1981–; Fellow, Royal Danish and Royal Norwegian Acads. *Publications:* books and articles on 18th century European and Asian history (econ., political and mil.). *Address:* 15 Efteraarsvej, 2920 Charlottenlund, Denmark.

FELDMAN, Jerome Myron, M.D.; American physician and medical scientist; b. 27 July 1935, Chicago, Ill.; s. of Louis Feldman and Marian (Swichkow) Feldman; m. Carol B. Feldman; one s. two d.; ed. Northwestern Univ., Michael Reese, Chicago, and Duke Univ.; Chief, Endocrinology and Metabolism, Durham Veteran's Admin. Hospital 1971–; Assoc. Prof. of Medicine, Duke Univ. 1972–98, Prof. of Medicine 1998–, Dir. Clinical Research Unit Core Lab. 1984–; mem. Duke Comprehensive Cancer Center 1982–; Ed. Journal of Clinical Endocrinology and Metabolism 1983–89. *Publications:* 218 research articles, book chapters and reviews dealing with hormone-secreting tumours, endocrinology and metabolism. *Leisure interests:* music, art. *Address:* Duke University Medical Center, Box 2963, Durham, NC 27710, U.S.A. *Telephone:* (919) 286-0411 Ext. 7329.

FELDMAN, Michael, PH.D.; Israeli biologist; b. 21 Jan. 1926, Tel Aviv; m. Lea Noyfeld 1946; one s. one d.; ed. Herzlia High School, Tel Aviv, Hebrew Univ., Jerusalem; British Council Scholar, Inst. of Animal Genetics, Edin., Scotland 1953–55; joined Weizmann Inst. of Science, Rehovot 1955; Dept. of Virology, Univ. of Calif., Berkeley, U.S.A. 1960–61; Visiting Scientist, Nat. Cancer Inst., N.I.H., Bethesda, Md., U.S.A. 1961; fmr. Head, Dept. of Cell Biology, Weizmann Inst. 1961, Chair. Scientific Council 1962–64, Dean, Feinberg Graduate School 1966–72, Faculty of Biology 1983–85; Visiting Prof., Stanford Medical School, Stanford, Calif., U.S.A. 1976–77; Scholar-in-Residence, John F. Fogarty Int. Center, N.I.H., Bethesda 1978–79; research activities include cancer research (in particular, control of tumour metastasis), cellular immunology and developmental biology; mem. Israel Acad. of Sciences and Humanities 1980–; Dr. h.c. (Ben-Gurion Univ.); Griffuel Prize, Paris 1984, Rothschild Prize, Jerusalem 1986. *Publications:* numerous publs. on cancer research immunology and developmental biology, in Scientific American, Ciba Symposium, Cancer Surveys and other int. journals. *Leisure interests:* the arts, art history. *Address:* c/o The Weizmann Institute of Science, P.O. Box 26, Rehovot 76300, Israel.

FELDMAN, Myer, B.S. (ECON.), LL.B.; American politician and lawyer; b. 22 June 1917, Philadelphia, Pa.; s. of Israel and Bella Kurland Feldman; m. 1st Silva Moskovitz 1941; m. 2nd Adrienne Arsht 1980; one s. one d.; ed. Univ. of Pennsylvania; Gowen Fellow, Univ. of Pennsylvania 1938–39, Prof. of Law 1940–42; Served U.S.A.A.F. 1942–46; Special Counsel, SEC, Exec. Asst. to Chair., SEC 1949–53; Counsel, Senate Banking and Currency Cttee. 1955–57; Prof. of Law, American Univ. 1956–59; Legislative Asst., Senator John F. Kennedy 1958–61; Dir. of Research, Democratic Nat. Cttee. 1960; Deputy Special Counsel to Pres. of the U.S. 1961–64, Counsel 1964–65; Gov. Weizmann Inst., Israel 1962–84; Overseer Coll. of the Virgin Islands 1963–; Trustee, Eleanor Roosevelt Foundation 1963–76, United Jewish Appeal 1965–, Jewish Publication Soc. 1965–78; Chair. Bd. Speer Publs., Capital Gazette Press Ind., Bay Publs. 1968–77; Contributor to The Saturday Review 1965–71; partner Ginsburg, Feldman and Bress 1965–; Dir. Flying Tiger Line 1966–82, Flame of Hope, Inc. 1967–; Del. to Democratic Nat. Convention 1968; Chair. Bd. of Dirs. of WWBA Inc., WLLH Inc. and WADK Inc., Financial Satellite Corpn. 1984–; Chair., Pres, and C.E.O. Totalbank Corpn. of Fla. 1987–; Pres. Ardman Broadcasting Corpn. 1987–; Vice-Chair. Congressional Leadership for the Future 1970; Pres. New York Int. Art Festival 1973–77; Pres. McGovern for Pres. Cttee. 1972; Chair. and Treas. Birch Bayh for Pres. Cttee. 1975–76; Dir. Special Olympics Inc. 1983–, Henry M. Jackson Found. 1984–; John F. Kennedy Library 1983–; Pres. Radio Assoc. Inc. 1959–81; Democrat. *Publications:* Standard Pennsylvania Practice (4 vols.). *Leisure interests:* tennis, swimming. *Address:* 1250 Connecticut Avenue, N.W., Washington, DC 20036, U.S.A. *Telephone:* (202) 637-9025.

FELDSTEIN, Martin Stuart, M.A., D.PHIL.; American economist; b. 25 Nov. 1939, New York; s. of Meyer and Esther (Gevarter) Feldstein; m. Kathleen Foley 1965; two d.; ed. Harvard and Oxford Univs.; Research Fellow, Nuffield Coll., Oxford 1964–65, Official Fellow 1965–67, Lecturer in Public Finance 1965–67; Asst. Prof. of Econs., Harvard Univ. 1967–68, Assoc. Prof. 1968–69, Prof. 1969–, George F. Baker Prof. 1984–; Pres. Nat. Bureau of Econ. Research 1977–82, 1984–; Chair. Pres.'s Council of Econ. Advisers 1982–84; Dir. American Int. Group, J. P. Morgan, TRW Inc.; Econ. Adviser, Prudential Securities; columnist, Wall Street Journal; Fellow, American Philosophical Soc., American Acad. of Arts and Sciences, Econometric Soc., Nat. Asscn. of Business Economists; mem. American Econ. Asscn. (John Bates Clark Medal 1977), Vice-Pres. 1988; mem. Inst. Medicine, N.A.S., Council on Foreign Relations, Trilateral Comm.; Foreign mem. Austrian Acad. of Sciences; Hon. Dr. of Laws (Univ. of Rochester) 1984, (Marquette) 1985. *Address:* National Bureau of Economic Research, 1050 Massachusetts Avenue, Cambridge, MA 02138 (Office); 147 Clifton Street, Belmont, MA 02178, U.S.A. (Home).

FELDT, Kjell-Olof, PH.D.; Swedish politician; b. 18 Aug. 1931, Holmsund; m. Birgitta von Otter; three c.; ed. Univs. of Uppsala and Lund; Budget Sec., Ministry of Finance 1962–64, Budget Dir. 1965, Under-Sec. 1967–70; Minister of Trade 1970–75, of Finance 1983–90; Minister without Portfolio 1975–76; M.P. 1971–90; mem. Exec. Cttee. Social Democratic Party 1978–90; Chair. Bank of Sweden 1967–70, 1994–, Swedish Road Fed. 1992–, Vin & Sprit AB 1991–93; mem. Bd. Dirs. Nordbanken 1991–94, Sandrew Theatre Co. 1990–. *Publication:* Memoirs 1991. *Address:* Sveriges Riksbank, 103 37 Stockholm, Sweden.

FELICI, H.E. Cardinal Angelo; Italian ecclesiastic; b. 26 July 1919, Segni; ordained Catholic priest 1942, elected Archbishop of Cesariana, Numidia 1967, consecrated Bishop 1967; cr. Cardinal 1988; Apostolic Nuncio in France; Prefect for the Congregation of the Causes of the Saints 1988; Pres. Pontifical Comm. Ecclesia Deo 1995–. *Address:* Piazza della Città Leonina 9, 00193 Rome, Italy.

FELL, Sir David, K.C.B., B.SC.; British business executive, banker and government official; b. 20 Jan. 1943, Belfast; s. of Ernest Fell and Jesse McCready; m. Sandra J. Moore 1967; one s. one d.; ed. Royal Belfast Academical Inst. and Queen's Univ. Belfast; Sales Man. Rank Hovis McDougall Ltd. 1965–66; teacher 1966–67; Research Assoc. 1967–69; Dept. of Agric. 1969–72, Asst. Sec. 1971–81; Dept. of Commerce 1972–82, Under-Sec. 1981–82; Deputy Chief Exec. Industrial Devt. Bd. 1982–84; Perm. Sec. Dept. of Econ. Devt. 1984–91; Second Perm. Under-Sec. N. Ireland Office and Head, N. Ireland Civil Service 1991–97; Chair. Northern Bank, Ulster (subsidiary of Nat. Australia Bank) 1998–, Boxmore Int. PLC 1998–; Dir. Nat. Australia Group Europe Ltd. 1998–, Dunloe Ewart PLC 1998–, Fred Olsen Energy ASA 1999–; Chair. Prince's Trust Volunteers, N.I. 1998–; Fellow Inst. of Bankers, Ireland. *Leisure interests:* music, reading, golf, rugby. *Address:* Northern Bank Ltd., Head Office, P.O. Box 183, Donegal Square, Belfast, BT1 6JS, Northern Ireland.

FELL, Robert, C.B., C.B.E., F.R.S.A.; British trade official; b. 6 May 1921; s. of Robert Fell and Mary Ann Fell; m. Eileen Wicks 1946; two s. one d.; ed. Whitehaven Grammar School; War Office 1939; mil. service 1940–46; Bd. of Trade 1947; Trade Commr., Queensland, Australia 1954–59; Asst. Sec., Tariff Div., Bd. of Trade 1961; Commercial Counsellor, Delhi 1961–66; Under-Sec. in charge of Export Promotion 1967–71; Sec. Export Credits Guarantee Dept. 1971–74; Chief Exec. The Stock Exchange 1975–82; Commr. for Securities and Commodities Trading, Hong Kong 1981–84, for Banking and Deposit-taxing Cos. 1984–87; mem. British Overseas Trade Bd. 1972–75; Pres., City Branch, B.I.M. 1976–82; Commr. of Banking, Hong Kong 1984–87. *Leisure interests:* Rugby football (watching) and gardening. *Address:* 60 The Drive, Craigweil, Aldwick, Bognor Regis, PO21 4DT, England.

FELLGETT, Peter Berners, PH.D., F.R.S.; British professor of cybernetics; b. 11 April 1922, Ipswich; s. of Frank Ernest Fellgett and Rowena Wagstaff; m. Janet Mary Briggs 1947; one s. two d.; ed. The Leys School, Cambridge and Cambridge Univ.; Sr. Observer, the Observatories, Cambridge Univ. 1952–59; Prin. Scientific Officer, Royal Observatories, Edin. 1959–65; Prof. of Cybernetics, Reading Univ. 1965–87, Prof. Emer. 1987–; R. W. Wood Prize (Optical Soc. of America) 1977. *Leisure interests:* beekeeping, natural dyestuffs, musical instruments, high-quality audio, classical literature, astronomy. *Address:* Little Brighter, St. Kew Highway, Bodmin, Cornwall PL30 3DU (Home). *Telephone:* (01208) 850337. *Fax:* (01208) 850416.

FELLNER, Fritz, PH.D. F.R.S.E.; Austrian professor of modern history; b. 25 Dec. 1922, Vienna; s. of Peter Fellner and Marie Obenaus; m. Liselotte Lamberg 1950; two s.; ed. Realgymnasium, Matura, Univ. of Vienna and Inst. für österreichische Geschichtsforschung; Research Fellow, Österreichisches Kulturinstitut, Rome 1951–52; Asst. lecturer, Univ. of Vienna 1954–64, Dozent 1960; Prof. of Modern History, Univ. of Salzburg 1964. *Publications:* Schicksalsjahre österreichs. Das pol. Tagebuch Josef Redlichs 1908 bis 1919 1953/54, Der Dreibund 1960, St. Germain im Sommer 1919 1977, Dichter und Gelehrter. Hermann Bahr und Josef Redlich in ihren Briefen 1896–1934 1980. *Address:* Ignaz-Rieder-Kai 19/3, 5020 Salzburg, Austria.

FELLS, Ian, M.A., PH.D., F.R.S.E., F.ENG., F.INST.E., F.R.S.C., F.I.CHEM.E., C.CHEM.; British professor of energy conversion; b. 5 Sept. 1932, Sheffield; s. of Dr. H. Alexander Fells, and Clarice Fells; m. Hazel Denton Scott 1957; four s.; ed. King Edward VII School, Sheffield and Trinity Coll. Cambridge; lecturer and Dir. of Studies, Dept. of Fuel Tech. and Chemical Eng. Univ. of Sheffield 1958–62; Reader in Fuel Science, King's Coll. Univ. of Durham 1962; Prof. of Energy Conversion, Univ. of Newcastle upon Tyne 1975–; mem. Science Consultative Group, BBC 1976–81, Electricity Supply Research Council 1979–90; Exec. David Davies Inst. of Int. Affairs 1975–; Pres. Inst. of Energy 1978–79; Scientific Adviser World Energy Council 1990–; Adviser to House of Commons and House of Lords Select Cttees.; other professional appts.; television series: Young Scientist of the Year, The Great Egg Race, Men of Science, Earth Year 2050, Take Nobody's Word For It, etc.; extensive radio contribs.; Hatfield Memorial Prize 1974, Beilby Memorial Medal and Prize 1976, Royal Soc. Faraday Medal and Prize 1993, Melchett Medal 1999. *Publications:* UK Energy Policy Post-Privatization 1991, Energy for the Future 1995, World Energy, 1923–1998 and Beyond. *Leisure interests:* cross country skiing, sailing, swimming. *Address:* 29 Rectory Terrace, Newcastle upon Tyne, NE3 1YB, England. *Telephone:* (0191) 285 5343. *Fax:* (0191) 285 5343.

FELTS, William Robert Jr., M.D.; American professor of medicine; b. 24 April 1923, Judsonia, Ark.; s. of Wylie R. Felts and Willie E. Lewis; m. 1st Jeanne E. Kennedy 1954 (divorced 1971); m. 2nd Lila Mitchell Dudley 1987 (died 1993); three s. one d.; ed. Univ. of Arkansas; Asst. Chief, Arthritis Research Unit, Veteran's Admin. Hosp., Washington, D.C. 1953–54, Adjutant Asst. Chief 1954–58, Chief 1958–62; Consultant in Rheumatology, U.S. Naval Hosp., Bethesda, Md. 1957–70; mem. staff of Medicine, George Washington Univ. 1958–, Prof. 1980–93, Prof. Emer. 1993–; Dir. Div. of Rheumatology 1970–79; mem. numerous advisory bds., professional orgs. etc.; Pres. Nat. Acads. of Practice 1993–96; Master, American Coll. of Rheumatology 1992; American Medical Asscn.'s Distinguished Service Award 1996. *Publications:* over 100 articles on medical socioeconomics, rheumatology and internal medicine. *Leisure interests:* photography, fishing, travel. *Address:* 2150 Pennsylvania Avenue, N.W., Washington, DC 20037 (Office); 1492 Hampton Hill Circle, McLean, VA 22101, U.S.A. (Home). *Telephone:* (202) 994-4377 (Office); (703) 356-6233 (Home). *Fax:* (703) 442-8550.

FELTUS, Alan E., M.F.A.; American artist and educator; b. 1 May 1943, Washington, D.C.; s. of Randolph Feltus and Anne Winter; m. Lani H. Irwin 1974; two s.; ed. Tyler School of Fine Arts, Cooper Union for Advancement of Art and Science, N.Y., Yale Univ., Conn.; instructor School of Dayton Art Inst., Ohio 1968–70; Asst. Prof. American Univ., Washington, D.C. 1972–84; full-time artist 1984–, represented by Forum Gallery, New York 1973–; exhibits regularly in U.S.A.; occasional teaching workshops and lectures; resident in Italy since 1987; Rome Prize Fellowship, American Acad. in Rome 1970–72, Nat. Endowment for Arts Fellowship 1981; Louis Comfort Tiffany Foundation Grant in Painting 1980, Pollock-Krasner Foundation Grant in Painting 1992; Thomas B. Clarke Prize, Nat. Acad. of Design 1984, Benjamin Altman Prize 1990, Joseph S. Isidor Memorial Medal 1995. *Address:* Porziano 68, 06081 Assisi PG, Italy. *Telephone:* (075) 80-24-36. *Fax:* (075) 80-24-36.

FENBY, Jonathan; British journalist; b. 11 Nov. 1942, London; s. of Charles Fenby and June Head; m. Renée Wartski 1967; one s. one d.; ed. King Edward's School, Birmingham, Westminster School and New Coll. Oxford; corresp. and ed. Reuters World Service, Reuters Ltd. 1963–77; corresp. France and Germany, The Economist 1982–86; Home Ed. and Asst. Ed. The Independent 1986–88; Deputy Ed. The Guardian 1988–93; Ed. The Observer 1993–95; Dir. Guardian Newspapers 1990–95; Ed. South China Morning Post 1995–; Chevalier, Ordre du Mérite (France). *Publications:* The Fall of the House of Beaverbrook 1979, Piracy and the Public 1983, The International News Services 1986, On the Brink, The Trouble with France 1998. *Address:* GPO Box 47, Hong Kong Special Administrative Region, People's Republic of China.

FENCHEL, Tom Michael, D.PHIL.; Danish professor of marine biology; b. 19 March 1940, Copenhagen; s. of W. Fenchel and Käte (née Sperling); m. 1st Anne Thane 1964; m. 2nd Hilary Adler 1978 (divorced 1989); one s. one d.; ed. Univ. of Copenhagen; lecturer in marine biology, Univ. of Copenhagen 1964–70; Prof. of Ecology and Zoology, Univ. of Aarhus 1970–87; Prof. of Marine Biology, Univ. of Copenhagen 1987–; Gold Medal, Univ. of Copenhagen 1964, Ecology Prize 1987, Huntsmann Award for Oceanography 1987. *Publications:* Theories of Populations in Biological Communities (with F. B. Christiansen) 1977, Bacteria and Mineral Cycling (with T. H. Blackburn) 1979, Ecology of Protozoa 1987, Ecology and Evolution in Anoxic Worlds (with B. J. Finlay), Bacterial Biochemistry (jtly.). *Address:* Marine Biological Laboratory, University of Copenhagen, Strandpromenaden 5, 3000 Helsinger, Denmark. *Telephone:* 49-21-33-44. *Fax:* 49-26-11-65.

FENDALL, Neville Rex Edwards, M.D., D.P.H., M.R.C.S., L.R.C.P., F.F.PH.M.; British professor of public health and int. health consultant; b. 9 July 1917, Auckland, N.Z.; s. of late Francis Alan Fendall and Ruby Inez (née Matthews) Fendall; m. Margaret Doreen Beynon 1942; ed. Univ. Coll. and Hosp. London; joined Colonial Medical Services Nigeria, Malaya, Singapore, Kenya (Dir. Medical Services 1962–64) 1944–64, British Mil. Admin., Malaya 1945–47; Staff mem. Rockefeller Foundation 1964–66; Regional Dir., Population Council Inc., New York 1966–71; Middlemass Hunt Prof. Int. Community Health 1971–81; Visiting Lecturer Tropical Public Health, Harvard 1966; Visiting Prof. of Public Health, Boston Univ. 1982–; Adjunct Prof. Community Health Sciences, Univ. of Calgary 1983–; Prof. Emer. Univ. of Liverpool 1981–; mem. Panel of Experts WHO 1960–85; Consultant to numerous int. orgs., particularly on public health in developing countries 1958–; Pres. E. African branch, Soc. of Medical Officers of Health 1959–60; Patron Commonwealth Human Ecology Council; Corresp. mem. Acad. of Medical Sciences, Guatemala 1986; Langley Memorial Prize 1963, Mrigendra Gold Medal Nepal 1983, Distinguished Fellow Center for Int. Health, Boston Univ. *Publications:* Auxiliaries in Health Care 1972, Paramedicals for PHC in the Commonwealth (jt. author) 1979, Health Planning, Manpower, Epidemiology, Primary Health Care 1948–1990, Community Approach to Health Promotion and Disease Prevention (Commonwealth Health Ministers Meeting, Melbourne) 1989, Health and Population: Ecology of Health 1991, and numerous papers. *Leisure interests:* travel, gardening, reading, corresponding, consulting. *Address:* The Coach House, Mill Street, Ludlow, South Shropshire, SY8 1BB, England. *Telephone:* (01584) 877195.

FENDER, Brian Edward Frederick, C.M.G., PH.D.; British academic; b. 15 Sept. 1934, Barrow; s. of George Clements Fender and Emily Goodwin; m. 1st 1956; one s. three d.; m. 2nd Ann Linscott 1986; ed. Carlisle and Sale Grammar Schools, Imperial Coll., London; Research Instructor, Univ. of Washington, Seattle 1959–61; Sr. Research Fellow, Nat. Chemical Lab. Teddington 1961–63; Fellow, St. Catherine's Coll., Oxford 1963–84, lecturer in Inorganic Chemistry 1965–80; Asst. Dir. Inst. Laue-Langevin, Grenoble 1980–82, Dir. 1982–85; Vice-Chancellor, Keele Univ. 1985–95; Chief Exec. Higher Educ. Funding Council for England 1995–; mem. Science and Eng. Research Council 1985–90; Hon. Fellow, St. Catherine's Coll., Oxford 1986. *Publications:* scientific articles on neutron scattering and solid state chemistry. *Leisure interests:* modern art, cooking. *Address:* Higher Education

Funding Council for England, Northlawn House, Coldharbour Lane, Bristol, BS16 1QD, England.

FENECH-ADAMI, Edward, LL.D.; Maltese politician, lawyer and journalist; b. 7 Feb. 1934, Birkirkara; s. of Luigi Fenech Adami and Josephine Pace; m. Mary Sciberras 1965; four s. one d.; ed. St. Aloysius Coll., Univ. of Malta; entered legal practice 1959; Ed. Il-Poplu (weekly) 1962–69; mem. Nat. Exec. Nationalist Party 1961, Asst. Gen. Sec. 1962–75, Pres. Gen. and Admin. Councils 1975–77, Leader April 1977–; mem. Parl. 1969–; Leader of Opposition 1977–82, 1983–87, 1996–98; Prime Minister 1987–96, also fmr. Minister of Foreign Affairs; Vice-Pres. European Union of Christian Democrat Parties 1979–. *Address:* 176 Main Street, Birkirkara, Malta.

FENEUILLE, Serge Jean Georges, PH.D.; French academic and company director; b. 16 Nov. 1940, Rheims; s. of Georges Feneuille and Marguerite Lemoine; m. Jeannine Large 1960; ed. Coll. Moderne de Rheims, Ecoles Normales d'Instituteurs de Chalons-sur-Marne and Nancy, Ecole Normale Supérieure de Saint-Cloud; Maître-Asst. Univ. of Paris 1964–69; Maître de recherche C.N.R.S. 1969–74, Dir. of Research 1974–; Prof. Univ. Paris-Sud 1979–; Dir. of Research Lafarge Coppée 1981–85, Scientific Dir. and mem. Exec. Cttee. 1985–86, Asst. Dir.-Gen. 1988–89, Dir.-Gen. and Head of Research, Tech. and Strategy 1989–94, Special Adviser to Chair. and C.E.O. 1995–; Man. Dir. Centre Expérimental du Bâtiment et des Travaux Publics 1998–; Dir.-Gen. C.N.R.S. 1986–88; Pres. Admin. Council Ecole Normale Supérieure de Lyon 1986–94; Chair. Orsan (subsidiary of Lafarge Coppée) 1992–94, Innovation and Research Comm., Conseil Nat. du Patronat Français (CNPF) 1993–97; Prix Daniel Guinier de la Soc. Française de Physique, Bronze medal C.N.R.S., Prix Servant de l'Académie des Sciences, Prix Jaffé de l'Institut de France; Chevalier Ordre des Palmes Académiques, Officier Ordre nat. du Mérite, Chevalier Légion d'honneur, Officier Ordre des Palmes Académiques. *Publications:* numerous articles in scientific journals. *Leisure interests:* bonsais, painting, literature. *Address:* Lafarge, 61 rue des Belles Feuilles, 75116 Paris (Office); 2 allée du Moulin Aubert, 91190 Gif-sur-Yvette, France (Home). *Telephone:* (1) 44-34-11-09 (Office). *Fax:* (1) 44-34-11-50.

FENG DUAN; Chinese physicist; b. 27 April 1923, Suzhou City, Jiangsu Prov.; s. of Feng Zhou-bai and Yan Su-qing; m. Chen Lian-fang 1955; three d.; ed. Nat. Cen. Univ.; Dir. of Grad. School of Nanjing Univ. 1984–88; mem. Dept. of Math. and Physics, Academia Sinica 1981–; Pres. Chinese Physical Soc. 1991–95; Hon. State Prize of Science of China 1982. *Leisure interest:* literature. *Address:* Institute of Solid State Physics, Nanjing University, Nanjing, 210008, Jiangsu Province, People's Republic of China. *Telephone:* (025) 3592096 or 3321103 (Home). *Fax:* 3300535.

FENG GONG; Chinese actor; b. Dec. 1957, Tianjin; joined China Railway Art Work Troupe 1980; actor China Broadcasting Art Troupe 1984–; performs comic dialogues with Niu Qun; numerous prizes. *Address:* China Broadcasting Art Troupe, Beijing, People's Republic of China.

FENG HE; Chinese sculptor; b. 12 Nov. 1931, Peixian, Jiangsu Prov.; s. of Feng Zigu and Chen Jiechen; m. Zhou Ji 1965; one s.; ed. Cen. Inst. of Fine Arts; mem. Sculpture Research Studio Inst. of Fine Arts, Deputy Dir. 1981–84, Vice-Dir. 1988–; specialized in ceramics and animal sculpture; exhibited work China Art Gallery 1979, 1981, also in France and Burma; *works include:* Woman's Head 1958, The Master of the Land 1964, Doe 1964, Bellicose Goat 1978, Buffalo 1979, You are always in our hearts dear Premier Zhou 1979, Ah Bing the Blind Man 1979, Buffalo and the Leopard 1985, Moonlight 1985, Winter 1986, Monument of Juvenile Heroes, The Song of the Young Pioneer 1990, Dream 1990, 12 Animals, Young Pioneer Park 1991. *Leisure interest:* drama. *Address:* Central Institute of Fine Arts, East Beijing 100730, People's Republic of China. *Telephone:* 55-4731 (Ext. 391).

FENG JINWEN; Chinese jurist; b. 1924, Suzhou Co., Jiangsu Prov.; ed. Chinese People's Anti-Japanese Military and Political Coll., joined CCP 1941; Deputy Mayor Fuzhou Municipality 1964; Deputy Procurator-General 1982–; Head Chinese Procurator Del. to Japan 1986. *Address:* Supreme People's Procuratorate, 147 Beiheyan, Dong An Men, Beijing 100726, People's Republic of China.

FENG LANRUI; Chinese economist; b. 16 Sept. 1920, Guiyang, Guizhou Province; d. of Feng Shaotang and Xie Guangyu; m. Li Chang 1946; two s. two d.; Sr. Research Fellow, Inst. of Marxism-Leninism and Mao Zedong Thought, Chinese Acad. of Social Sciences 1980–, Deputy Dir. 1980–82, Adviser 1983–; mem. Editorial Cttee., Encyclopedia of People's Repub. of China, for vol. Scientific Socialism 1980–, A Comprehensive Dictionary of Economics, for vol. Population, Labour and Consumption 1983–, Sun Yefang Prize for econ. article of 1984; Sec.-Gen. China Council of Econ. Asscns. 1981–; mem. Standing Cttee. Chinese People's Friendship Asscn. 1986–. *Publications:* Labour: Payment and Employment (collected articles) 1982, Regarding the Principle—To Each According to his Work, Chinese Research on Employment Theory 1982, Urban Employment and Wages in China (co-author) 1982, On the Relationship between Employment and Economic Growth (co-author) 1983, The Worldwide New Industrialization and China's Socialist Modernization (co-author) 1984, On Letting Some People Get Rich Ahead of Others 1984, The Incomplete Form of Distribution according to Work at the Initial Stage of Socialism 1985, Overcome Egalitarianism and Let Some People Get Rich Ahead of Others 1985, More on Letting Some People Get Rich Ahead of Others 1986, The Double Hundred Policy Cannot be Separated from Democracy and Freedom 1986, The Double Hundred Policy and Science Associations 1986, Distribution According to Work, Wage and Employment 1988, Employment at the Initial Stage of Socialism (co-author) 1988, On the Ageing of the Chinese Population 1989, The Labour Market of China 1991, Social Security must be Unified 1994, Actively Foster the Labour Market 1995, Can Inflation be Reduced under 10% for the Current Year?, Unemployment in China: 21% by the year 2000? 1996, The Restructuring of China's Social Security System 1997 and numerous articles on the market economy. *Address:* 34 Dongzongbu Hutong, Beijing 100005, People's Republic of China.

FENG MENGBO; Chinese pop artist; ed. Print-Making Dept. Cen. Acad. of Fine Arts, Beijing; work consists of computer animations and paintings which resemble video-game screens; has exhibited at galleries in London, Sydney, Taipei and Hong Kong and at 45th Venice Biennale. *Leisure interests:* collecting industrial antiques.

FENG YING; Chinese ballet dancer; b. 28 Feb. 1963, Harbin; ed. Beijing Dance Acad.; m. James Y. Ho 1989; one d.; Paris Opera Ballet School 1982–83; prin. dancer, Cen. Ballet of China 1980–; leading role in many classical and Chinese ballets; guest artist, 2nd Paris Int. Ballet Competition 1986; toured U.S.A., U.K., Russia, Japan, Singapore, Hong Kong, Taiwan; mem. Chinese Dancers' Asscn. 1982, China Ballet Art Soc. 1992; First Prize Pas de Deux, Nat. Ballet Competition 1987; award at 5th Japan World Ballet Competition 1987; First Class Dancer of the State 1987. *Address:* Central Ballet of China, 3 Taiping Street, Beijing 100050, People's Republic of China.

FENN, Sir Nicholas M., G.C.M.G., M.A.; British diplomatist; b. 19 Feb. 1936, London; s. of Rev. Prof. J. E. Fenn and Kathleen Fenn (née Harrison); m. Susan Clare Russell 1959; two s. one d.; ed. Kingswood School, Bath and Peterhouse, Cambridge; Flying Officer, R.A.F. 1954–56; Third Sec. Mandalay, then Rangoon 1959–63, Asst. Pvt. Sec. to Sec. of State for Foreign Affairs 1963–67, First Sec. British Interests Section, Swiss Embassy, Algiers 1967–69, First Sec. and Spokesman, U.K. Mission to the UN, New York 1969–72, Deputy Head Energy Dept. FCO 1972–75, Counsellor British Embassy, Beijing 1975–77, Royal Coll. of Defence Studies 1978, Head of News Dept. and Foreign Office Spokesman 1979–82; Amb. to Burma 1982–86, to Ireland 1986–91; High Commr. in India 1991–96; Chief Exec. Marie Curie Cancer Care 1996–. *Leisure interest:* sailing. *Address:* Marie Curie Cancer Care, 28 Belgrave Square, London, SW1X 8QG, England. *Telephone:* 0171-235 3325. *Fax:* 0171-823 2380.

FENNER, Frank John, A.C., C.M.G., M.B.E., M.D., F.A.A., F.R.S., F.R.A.C.P., F.R.C.P.; Australian research biologist; b. 21 Dec. 1914, Ballarat, Vic.; s. of Dr. and Mrs. Charles Fenner; m. E. M. Roberts 1944 (deceased); one d.; ed. Thebarton Tech. High School, Adelaide High School, Adelaide Univ.; Medical Officer, Hospital Pathologist, Australian Forces 1940–43, Malariologist 1943–46; Francis Haley Research Fellow, Walter and Eliza Hall Inst. for Medical Research, Melbourne 1946–48; Travelling Fellow, Rockefeller Inst. for Medical Research 1948–49; Prof. of Microbiology, Australian Nat. Univ. 1949–73, Dir. John Curtin School of Medical Research 1967–73, Dir. Centre for Resource and Environmental Studies 1973–79; F.R.S. 1958; Foreign Assoc., U.S. Nat. Acad. of Sciences 1977; Chair. Global Comm. for the Certification of Smallpox Eradication, WHO 1977–80; Univ. Fellow, Australian Nat. Univ. 1980–82; Visiting Fellow, John Curtin School of Medical Research 1983–; Harvey Lecturer, Harvey Soc. of New York 1958; Overseas Fellow, Churchill Coll., Cambridge 1961–62; David Syme Prize, Melbourne Univ. 1949; Mueller Medal 1964; ANZAAS Medal 1980; Britannica Australia Award 1967; ANZAC Peace Prize 1980; Leeuwenhoek Lecture 1961; Flinders Lecture 1967, David Lecture 1973, Florey Lecture 1983, Burnet Lecture 1985; Stuart Mudd Award 1986, Japan Prize 1988, Advance Australia Award 1989, Copley Medal 1995. *Publications:* about 250 scientific papers, mainly on acidfast bacili, pox viruses, viral classification and environmental problems, The Production of Antibodies (with F. M. Burnet) 1949, Myxomatosis (with F. N. Ratcliffe) 1965, The Biology of Animal Viruses 1968, Medical Virology (with D. O. White) 1970, Classification and Nomenclature of Viruses, Second Report 1976, The Australian Academy of Science: the First Twenty-five Years (ed. with A. L. G. Rees) 1980, Veterinary Virology (with others) 1987, Smallpox and its Eradication (with others) 1988, Human Monkeypox (with Z. Jezek) 1988, The Orthopoxviruses (with others) 1988, Portraits of Viruses (ed. with A. Gibbs) 1988, History of Microbiology in Australia (Ed.) 1990, The Australian Academy of Science: The First Forty Years (ed.) 1995, Biological Control of Vertebrate Pests (with B. Fantine) 1999. *Leisure interests:* gardening, tennis. *Address:* 8 Monaro Crescent, Red Hill, Canberra, A.C.T. 2603, Australia. *Telephone:* (612) 6295-9176 (Home). *Fax:* (612) 6247-4823 (Office).

FENTON, Alexander, C.B.E., M.A., D.LITT.; British professor of Scottish ethnology; b. 26 June 1929, Shotts, Lanarkshire; s. of Alexander Fenton and Annie S. Stronach; m. Evelyn E. Hunter 1956; two d.; ed. Univs. of Aberdeen, Cambridge and Edinburgh; Sr. Asst. Ed. Scottish Nat. Dictionary 1955–59; Dir. Nat. Museum of Antiquities of Scotland 1978–85; Research Dir. Nat. Museums of Scotland 1985–89; Dir. European Ethnological Research Centre 1989–; Prof. of Scottish Ethnology and Dir. School of Scottish Studies, Univ. of Edin. 1990–94; Hon. Prof. of Antiquities, Royal Scottish Acad.; Hon. D.Litt. (Aberdeen) 1989. *Publications:* Scottish Country Life, The Northern Isles: Orkney & Shetland, Rural Architecture of Scotland, The Shape of the

Past (two vols.), Country Life in Scotland, Wirds An' Wark 'E Seasons Roon', The Turra Coo, The Island Blackhouse, Craiters—or Twenty Buchan Tales. *Leisure interest:* languages. *Address:* European Ethnological Research Centre, c/o National Museums of Scotland, Chambers Street, Edinburgh, EH2 1JD (Office); 132 Blackford Avenue, Edinburgh, EH1 1JF, Scotland (Home). *Telephone:* (0131) 225-7534; (0131) 667-5456.

FENTON, James (Martin), M.A., F.R.S.L.; British poet, author and journalist; b. 25 April 1949; s. of Rev. Canon J.C. Fenton and Mary Hamilton Ingoldby; ed. Durham Choristers School, Repton School, Magdalen Coll. Oxford; Asst. Literary Ed., New Statesman 1971, Editorial Asst. 1972, Political Columnist 1976–78; freelance corresp. in Indo-China 1973–75; German Corresp., The Guardian 1978–79; Theatre Critic, Sunday Times 1979–84; Chief Book Reviewer, The Times 1984–86; Far East Corresp. The Independent 1986–88, columnist 1993–95; Prof. of Poetry, Oxford Univ. 1994–99. *Publications include:* Our Western Furniture 1968, Terminal Moraine 1972, A Vacant Possession 1978, A German Requiem 1980, Dead Soldiers 1981, A Memory of War 1982, You Were Marvellous 1983, Children in Exile 1984, Poems 1968–83 1985, The Fall of Saigon (in Granta 15) 1985, The Snap Revolution (in Granta 18) 1986, Cambodian Witness: the autobiography of Someth May (Ed.) 1986, Partingtime Hall (poems; with John Fuller) 1987, All the Wrong Places: adrift in the politics of Asia 1989, Underground in Japan, by Rey Ventura (Ed.) 1992, Out of Danger (poems) 1993. *Address:* c/o Peters, Fraser & Dunlop, 5th Floor, The Chambers, Chelsea Harbour, Lots Road, London, SW10 0XF, England.

FERENCZY, Oto, PH.DR.; Slovak composer; b. 30 March 1921, Brezovica nad Torysou, Prešov Dist.; s. of Gejza and Irena Ferenczy; m. Viera Kotuliak 1957 (died 1980); one d.; ed. Faculty of Arts, Slovak Univ., Bratislava 1939–45; Head of Musical Dept., Library of Comenius Univ., Bratislava 1945–51; teacher, Coll. of Musical Arts, Bratislava 1951, Dean 1953–55, Docent 1953–66, Pro-Rector 1956–62, Rector 1962–66, Prof. 1966–90; cand. mem. Cen. Cttee., CP of Slovakia 1968–71, mem. 1971–89, retd. 1990; Pres., Union of Slovak Composers 1970–72, 1982–87; Laureate Bartók Competition, Budapest 1948; Klement Gottwald State Prize 1981, Order of Labour 1981, Nat. Artist 1983. *Works include:* Music for four String Instruments 1947, Concertino for Chamber Orchestra 1949, Serenade for Strings, Harp and Wind Instruments 1955, Finale 1958, Elegy 1958, Sonata for Violin and Piano 1962, Partita 1964, Sonnets from Shakespeare 1965, The Northern Star 1960, An Uncommon Humoresque 1966, Symphonic Prologue 1973, Concerto for Piano and Orchestra 1978. *Publications:* Experience and Apprehension of Music 1947 and numerous articles on music aesthetics, philosophy of music, music education. *Leisure interest:* history. *Address:* Matusova 27, 811–04 Bratislava, Slovakia. *Telephone:* 374192.

FERENSZTAJN, Bogumił, D.TECH.; Polish politician; b. 20 April 1934, Radom; m.; ed. Mining Faculty of Silesian Tech. Univ., Gliwice; worked at Mining Design Bureau, Gliwice 1956–69, then at Main Bureau of Mining Research and Design, Katowice 1969–76; Gen. Dir., Studies and Classification Bureau, Katowice 1976–82; mem. Polish United Workers' Party (PZPR) 1961–90; Sec. for Econ. Matters, PZPR Voivodship Cttee., Katowice 1982–83; First Sec. PZPR Voivodship Cttee., Katowice 1983–87; alt. mem. PZPR Cen. Cttee. 1985–86, mem. 1986–89, alt. mem. Political Bureau of PZPR Cen. Cttee. 1986–87; Minister of Regional Planning and Construction 1987–89; mem. Econ. Cttee. Council of Ministers KERM 1988–89; Deputy to Sejm (Parl.) 1985–89, fmr. mem. Sejm Comm. of Mining and Power Industry; Knight's and Officer's Cross, Order of Polonia Restituta and other awards and decorations. *Publications:* numerous scientific works on mining tech.

FERGANI, Yacine; Algerian politician; b. 19 Jan. 1946, Jijel; ed. Ecole des Mines, Paris and Stanford Univ., U.S.A.; Asst. Dir.-Gen. SNTR 1970–72; Asst. Pres. Dir.-Gen. SONATRACH 1976–78, Vice-Pres. 1978–83; Sec. Gen. Ministry of Post and Telecommunications 1983–86; Deputy Minister of Chemical and Petrochemical Industries Feb. 1986–88; Minister of Posts and Telecommunications 1988–89. *Address:* c/o 4 blvd Salah Bouakouir, Algiers, Algeria.

FERGUS-THOMPSON, Gordon; British pianist; b. 9 March 1952, Leeds; s. of late George Thompson and Constance Webb; ed. Temple Moor Grammar School, Leeds and Royal Manchester Coll. of Music; debut, Wigmore Hall 1976; has appeared as soloist with orchestras including Orchestra of the Hague, Gotenburg Symphony Orchestra, Royal Liverpool Philharmonic, The Philharmonia, City of Birmingham Symphony, Halle, BBC Symphony; extensive tours in Europe, N. America, Australia, Far East and S. Africa; Prof. of Piano, Royal Coll. of Music 1996–; recordings include Complete Works of Debussy, Bach transcriptions 1990, Complete Works of Scriabin 1990, Complete Works of Ravel 1992; Gulbenkian Foundation Fellowship 1978. *Leisure interests:* art, chess, cooking, tennis, humour. *Address:* c/o John Humphreys Camerata Artists, 4 Margaret Road, Birmingham, B17 0EU (Agent); 150 Audley Road, Hendon, London, NW4 3EG, England (Home). *Telephone:* (0121) 426 6208 (Agent); 0181-202 5861 (Home).

FERGUSON, Alexander (Alex) Chapman, C.B.E.; British professional football manager; b. 31 Dec. 1941; s. of the late Alexander Beaton Ferguson and Elizabeth Hardy; m. Catherine Russell 1966; three s.; ed. Govan High School; player with Queen's Park 1958–60, St. Johnstone 1960–64, Dunfermline Athletic 1964–67, Glasgow Rangers 1967–69, Falkirk 1969–73, Ayr United 1973–74 (two Scottish League caps); managed the following clubs: E. Stirling 1974, St. Mirren 1974–78 (First Div. Champions 1976–77), Aberdeen 1978–86 (winners European Cup Winners' Cup, Super Cup 1983, Premier Div. Champions 1980, 1982, 1984, winners Scottish FA Cup on four occasions, League Cup 1985), Scottish Nat. Team (Asst. Man.) 1985–86, Manchester United 1986– (winners FA Cup 1990, 1994, 1996, European Cup Winners' Cup, Super Cup 1991, FA Premier League Championship 1992/93, 1993/94, 1996/97, League and FA Cup double 1994 and 1996 (new record)); Man. of the Year Scotland 1983–85, Man. of the Year England 1993–94; Hon. M.A. (Salford) 1996. *Publications:* A Light in the North 1985, Alex Ferguson: Six Years at United 1992, Just Champion 1994, A Year in the Life 1995, A Will to Win (jtly.) 1997. *Leisure interests:* golf, snooker. *Address:* Manchester United FC, Old Trafford, Manchester, M16 0RA, England. *Telephone:* (0161) 872 1661. *Fax:* (0161) 873 7210.

FERGUSON, C. David; American business executive; ed. Marietta Coll.; joined Engine Parts Div. Gould Inc. 1963, Foil Div. 1967; subsequently Group Vice-Pres. (Materials and Components); Exec. Vice-Pres. (Materials and Components); Chair., Pres. and C.E.O. Gould Inc. 1988–; Pres. and Gen. Man. Foil Div., Gould Inc., Eastlake, O.; mem. Bd. Gould Foils Ltd., Nikko Gould Foil Co., Ltd., Gould Electronics (Canada) Ltd.

FERGUSON, Glenn Walker, B.A., M.B.A., J.D.; American diplomatist and educator; b. 28 Jan. 1929, Syracuse, N.Y.; s. of Forrest E. and Mabel W. Ferguson; m. Patricia Lou Head 1950; two s. one d.; ed. Cornell Univ., Univ. of Santo Tomas (Manila), Univ. of Chicago and Univ. of Pittsburgh; U.S. Air Force 1951–53; Staff Assoc. Governmental Affairs Inst., Washington, D.C. 1954–55; Asst. Ed. and Asst. Sec.-Treas., American Judicature Soc., Chicago 1955–56; successively Admin. Asst. to Chancellor, Asst. Dean and Asst. Prof. Graduate School of Public and Int. Affairs, Assoc. Dir., Co-ordinated Educ. Center, Univ. of Pittsburgh 1956–60; Man. Consultant, McKinsey and Co., Washington, D.C. 1960–61; Special Asst. to Dir., U.S. Peace Corps 1961, Peace Corps Dir. in Thailand 1961–63, Assoc. Dir. Peace Corps, Washington, DC 1963–64; Dir. Vista Volunteers, Office of Econ. Opportunity, Washington, D.C. 1964–66; Amb. to Kenya 1966–69; Chancellor Long Island Univ. 1969–70; Pres. Clark Univ. 1970–73, Univ. of Connecticut 1973–78, Radio Free Europe and Radio Liberty 1978–82, Lincoln Center 1983–84, Equity for Africa, Inc. 1985–92, American Univ. of Paris 1992–95; Visiting Prof. (Foreign Policy), Conn. Coll. and Univ. of R.I. 1990–91; lecturer on Foreign Affairs and Higher Educ. 1995–; Assoc. Fellow Yale Univ.; mem. Fed. Bar Asscn., Council on Foreign Relations, American Bar Asscn., Bd. of Trustees, Cornell Univ. 1972–76, Nat. Press Club, French-American Comm. for Educ. Exchange 1992–94, Dir. Council of American Ambs.; USIS Lecturer (India, Sudan, Uruguay, Argentina) 1984–92; Consultant, Int. Exec. Service Corps (Uruguay) 1992; fmr. Dir. Foreign Policy Asscn. and Private Export Funding Corpn., Conn. Nat. Bank, Equator Bank; several hon. degrees; Arthur Flemming Award 1968. *Address:* 84 Wagner Road, Shelter Harbor, RI 02891, U.S.A.

FERGUSON, James L.; American business executive; b. 16 March 1926, Evanston, Ill.; s. of J. Larnard Ferguson and Justine Dickson Ferguson; m. 2nd Esther Baskin 1981; two s. one d.; ed. Hamilton Coll. and Harvard Business School; served U.S. Army Corps of Engineers in Pacific Theater, World War II; Assoc. Advertising Man. Procter & Gamble Co.; joined Gen. Foods Corpn. 1963, Gen. Man. Bird's Eye Div. 1967, Vice-Pres. 1968, Group Vice-Pres. 1970, Exec. Vice-Pres. 1972, C.O.O. and Dir. 1972, Pres. 1972, C.E.O. 1973, Chair., Pres. and C.E.O. 1974, Chair. and C.E.O. 1977–86, now Chair. Exec. Cttee.; Vice-Chair. Philip Morris Inc. (after merger with Gen. Foods Corpn. 1985); Dir. Union Carbide Corpn., Chase Manhattan Bank, Sawyer-Ferguson-Walker Co., Trustee, Hamilton Coll. *Leisure interests:* sports, music. *Address:* c/o General Foods Corporation, 250 North Street, White Plains, NY 10625, U.S.A. (Office). *Telephone:* (914) 335-2500 (Office).

FERGUSON, Marnie H., B.A.; Canadian business executive; b. 10 April 1949, Lindsay, Ont.; d. of Noble William Eberts and Gladys Eileen (née Smith-Emsley) Eberts; m. Garry S. Ferguson 1969; three s.; ed. Ryerson Polytechnic Inst., Waterloo Lutheran Univ., Univ. of Waterloo; various human resources man. posts in consumer packaged-goods industries; Dir. Human Resources, Monsanto Canada Inc. 1989–91, Vice-Pres., People, Quality and EH&S 1991–95, People-Canada and Transformation and Change, Monsanto Worldwide 1995–, Gen. Man. Monsanto Incite Consulting Div. 1991–94, Dir. Continuous Improvement Monsanto Canada, Sr. Consultant Incite Div. of Monsanto; Chair. Council on Total Quality Man. Conf. Bd. of Canada; mem. Personnel Asscn. of Ont., American Man. Asscn. *Leisure interests:* gardening, music, travel. *Address:* Monsanto Canada Inc., 2330 Argentia Road, P.O. Box 787, Streetsville, Mississauga, Ont., L5M 2G4, Canada. *Telephone:* (905) 826-9222 (Office). *Fax:* (905) 826-8961.

FERGUSON, Paul; South African stockbroker; b. 23 August 1943, Johannesburg; s. of Ray and Joy Ferguson; trained as chartered accountant; Dir. Fergusson Bros., Hall Stewart & Co. Inc. 1973–, Chair. 1983–; Pres. Johannesburg Stock Exchange 1982–84, Cttee. mem. 1979–, Chair. 1988–89, Vice-Chair. 1993–; Dir. of various cos. *Leisure interest:* squash. *Address:* P.O. Box 691, Johannesburg 2000 (Office); 60 Kent Road, Dunkeld, Johannesburg 2196, South Africa (Home). *Telephone:* (011) 833 5740 (Office); (011) 788 2227.

FERGUSON-SMITH, Malcolm Andrew, M.A., M.B., CH.B., F.R.C.PATH., F.R.C.P. (GLASG.), F.R.C.O.G., F.R.S., F.R.S.E.; British professor of pathology; b. 5 Sept. 1931, Glasgow, Scotland; s. of John Ferguson-Smith and Ethel May Ferguson-Smith (née Thorne); m. Marie Eva Gzowska 1960; one s. three d.; ed. Stowe School, Univ. of Glasgow; Registrar in Lab. Medicine, Dept. of

Pathology, Western Infirmary, Glasgow 1958–59; Fellow in Medicine and Instructor, Johns Hopkins Univ. School of Medicine 1959–61; Lecturer, Sr. Lecturer, then Reader in Medical Genetics, Univ. of Glasgow 1961–73, Prof. 1973–87; Prof. of Pathology, Univ. of Cambridge 1987–98, professional research scientist, Dept. of Clinical Veterinary Medicine 1998–; Fellow Peterhouse Coll., Cambridge 1987–98; Dir. W. of Scotland Medical Genetics Service 1973–87, East Anglian Regional Clinical Genetics Service 1987–95; Hon. Consultant in Medical Paediatrics, Royal Hosp. for Sick Children, Glasgow 1966–73, in Clinical Genetics, Yorkhill and Assoc. Hosps. 1973–87, in Medical Genetics, Addenbrooke's Hosp., Cambridge 1987–98; Pres. Clinical Genetics Soc. 1979–81, European Soc. of Human Genetics 1997–98, Int. Soc. for Prenatal Diagnosis 1998–; Ed. Prenatal Diagnosis 1980–; mem. Johns Hopkins Univ. Soc. of Scholars; Foreign mem. Polish Acad. of Science 1988; Hon. D.Sc. (Strathclyde Univ.) 1992; Bronze Medal, Univ. of Helsinki 1968, Makdougall-Brisbane Prize of Royal Soc. of Edin. 1984–86, San Remo Int. Prize for Research in Genetics 1990, Mauro Baschirotto Award for achievements in human genetics 1996. *Publications:* Early Prenatal Diagnosis (Ed.) 1983, Essential Medical Genetics (Co-Author) 1984, Prenatal Diagnosis and Screening (Jt. Ed.) 1992; papers on cytogenetics, gene mapping, human genetics and prenatal diagnosis in medical journals. *Leisure interests:* swimming, sailing, fishing. *Address:* Department of Clinical Veterinary Medicine, Cambridge University, Madingley Road, Cambridge, CB3 0ES, England. *Telephone:* (01223) 766496.

FERGUSSON, Sir Ewen Alastair John, G.C.M.G., G.C.V.O., M.A.; British diplomatist (retd.); b. 28 Oct. 1932, Singapore; s. of late Sir Ewen MacGregor Field Fergusson and Lady (Winifred Evelyn) Fergusson; m. Sara Carolyn Montgomery Cuninghame, née Gordon Lennox 1959; one s. two d.; ed. Rugby and Oriel Coll., Oxford; 2nd Lieut. 60th Rifles (KRRC) 1954–56; Foreign (Diplomatic) Service 1956–92; Asst. Private Sec. to Minister of Defence 1957–59; British Embassy, Addis Ababa 1960; Foreign and Commonwealth Office 1963; British Trade Devt. Office, New York 1967; Counsellor and Head of Chancery, Office of U.K. Perm. Rep. to European Communities 1972–75; Private Sec. to Foreign and Commonwealth Sec. 1975–78, Asst. Under-Sec. of State 1978–82; Amb. to South Africa 1982–84, to France 1987–92; Deputy Under-Sec. of State 1984–87; Chair. (non-exec.) Coutts & Co. 1993–, Savoy Hotel Group 1995– (Dir. 1993–); Dir. (non-exec.) BT 1993–, Sun Alliance 1993–96; Chair. Rugby School 1995– (Gov. 1985–); King at Arms, Most Distinguished Order of St. Michael and St. George 1996–; Trustee Nat. Gallery 1995–; Hon. Fellow Oriel Coll. 1988; Hon. D.LL. (Aberdeen) 1995. *Address:* Coutts & Co., 440 The Strand, London, WC2R 0QS, England.

FERLINGHETTI, Lawrence, M.A., DR.UNIV.; American writer and painter; b. 24 March 1920, Yonkers, New York; s. of Charles Ferlinghetti and Clemence Mendes-Monsanto; m. 1951; one s. one d.; ed. Columbia Univ., Univ. of Paris; one-man exhbns. at Ethel Guttman Gallery, San Francisco 1985, Peter Lembcke Gallery, San Francisco 1991. *Publications include:* Pictures of the Gone World (poems), Selections from Paroles by Jacques Prévert, A Coney Island of the Mind (poems), Her (novel), Starting from San Francisco (poems), Unfair Arguments with Existence (7 plays), Routines (plays), The Secret Meaning of Things (poems), Tyrannus Nix? (poem), Back Roads to Far Places (poems), Open Eye, Open Heart (poems), The Mexican Night (travel journal), Who are We Now? 1976, Landscapes of Living and Dying (poems) 1979, Endless Life: Selected Poems 1981; Literary San Francisco: A Pictorial History from the Beginnings to the Present (with Nancy J. Peters) 1980, Leaves of Life: Drawings from the Model 1983, Over All the Obscene Boundaries (poems) 1984, Seven Days in Nicaragua Libre 1984, Love in the Days of Rage (novel) 1988, When I Look at Pictures (poems and paintings) 1990, These Are My Rivers; New and Selected Poems 1993, A Far Rockaway of the Heart 1997; Ed. City Lights Books; also translations, film-scripts and phonograph records. *Address:* c/o City Lights Bookstore, 261 Columbus Avenue, San Francisco, CA 94133, U.S.A. *Telephone:* (415) 362-1901.

FERM, Anders; Swedish diplomatist; b. 1938, Ockeldo; m.; one c.; ed. Stockholm School of Econs.; Special Political Asst. to Minister of Transport 1965–69, Prime Minister's Chef de Cabinet 1969–73; Exec. Sec. of Ind. Comm. of Disarmament and Security Issues, Vienna 1980–83; Perm. Rep. to UN, New York 1983–88; Amb. to Denmark 1988–90; Ed.-in-Chief Arbetet 1990; exec. man. publishing 1973–80, fmr. mem. numerous cttees. and bds. including PEN Club, Publrs. Asscn., Swedish Television Corpn. *Address:* c/o Arbetet, P.O. Box 125, 201 21 Malmö, Sweden.

FERMOR, Patrick Michael Leigh, D.S.O., O.B.E., C.LIT.; British author; b. 11 Feb. 1915, London; s. of late Sir Lewis Leigh Fermor and Muriel Eileen Ambler; m. Hon. Joan Eyres-Monsell 1968; ed. King's School, Canterbury; travelled for four years in Cen. Europe, Balkans and Greece in 1930s; enlisted in Irish Guards 1939; "I" Corps 1940; Lieut. British Mil. Mission, Greece 1940; Liaison Officer, Greek GHQ, Albania; with Cretan Resistance for two years in German-occupied Crete; team-commdr. Special Allied Airborne Reconnaissance Force, N. Germany 1945; Deputy Dir. British Inst. Athens till mid-1946; travelled in Caribbean and Cen. America 1947–48; corresp. mem. Athens Acad.; Municipality of Athens Gold Medal of Honour 1988; Hon. Citizen of Heraklion, Crete 1947, Gytheion, Laconia 1966, Kardamyli, Messenia 1967; Hon. D.Litt. (Kent, Warwick, American Coll., Athens); Int. PEN/Time Life Silver Pen Award 1986; Chevalier des Arts et des Lettres. *Publications:* The Traveller's Tree (Heinemann Foundation Prize for Literature 1950, Kemsley Prize 1951), Colette's Chance Acquaintances (trans.) 1952, A Time to Keep Silence 1953, The Violins of Saint Jacques 1953, The Cretan Runner (trans.) 1955, Mani 1958 (Duff Cooper Prize), Roumeli 1966, A Time of Gifts 1977 (W. H. Smith Award 1978), Between the Woods and the Water 1986 (Thomas Cook Award 1986), Three Letters from the Andes 1991. *Leisure interests:* travel and reading. *Address:* c/o John Murray, 50 Albemarle Street, London, W.1., England.

FERMOSO GARCIA, Julio, D. EN MED.; Spanish professor of internal medicine; b. 30 Oct. 1948, Medina del Campo; s. of Isidoro Fermoso and Lucía García; m. Carmen Laplana 1971; two c.; post-graduate training in La Timone Hospital, Marsella 1976–77, specializing in internal medicine and neurology; Head of Internal Medicine at the Clinical Hosp., Salamanca and Asst. Prof. of Pathology and Clinical Medicine, Valladolid 1978–80; Prof. of Pathology and Clinical Medicine, Univ. of Salamanca 1980, Rector 1986–95; mem. Real Academia de Valladolid; Misael Bañuelos and Farreras Valentí Prizes; decorations from Portugal and the Dominican Repub. *Publications:* numerous articles on internal medicine and neurology, especially alcoholism and epilepsy. *Leisure interest:* fishing. *Address:* Avenida Italia 14-20, portal 4, 3° B., 37006 Salamanca, Spain (Home).

FERNANDES, Most Rev. Angelo Innocent, D.D., S.T.L.; Indian ecclesiastic; b. 28 July 1913, Karachi; s. of John Ligorio Fernandes and Evelyn Sabina Fernandes; ed. St. Patrick's, Karachi, St. Joseph's Seminary, Mangalore, Papal Univ. of Kandy, Sri Lanka; Archbishop of Delhi 1967–91, Archbishop Emer. 1991–; Sec. Gen. Catholic Bishops' Conf. of India 1960–72, Chair. Justice, Devt. and Peace Comm. 1968–76, 1986–90; mem. Vatican Justice and Peace Acad. 1966–76; Exec. Pres. World Conf. on Religion and Peace, New York and Geneva 1970–84, Pres. Emer. 1984–; attended five World Synods of Catholic Bishops and mem. of Synod Secr. 1971–74, 1980–83; Chair. Office of Ecumenical and Inter-religious Affairs of Fed. of Asian Bishops' Confs. 1985–89; Pres. Int. Catholic Educ. Org., Brussels 1990–. *Publications:* Apostolic Endeavour 1962, Religion, Development and Peace 1971, Religion and the Quality of Life 1974, Religion and a New World Order 1976, Towards Peace with Justice 1981, God's Rule and Man's Role 1982, Summons to Dialogue 1983, The Christian Way Today 1987, As You Pray So You Live 1992, Building Bridges: The Missing Dimension in Education 1993, Experience of Dialogue 1994, Vatican Two Revisited 1996. *Address:* c/o Archbishop's House, 1 Ashok Place, New Delhi 110 001, India. *Telephone:* (011) 343593, 343457, 312058. *Fax:* (011) 3746575.

FERNANDES, George; Indian trade unionist and politician; b. 3 June 1930, Bangalore, Karnataka; s. of John Fernandes and Alice Fernandes; m. Leila Kabir 1971; one s.; ed. St. Peter's Seminary, Bangalore; joined Socialist Party of India 1949; Ed. Konkani Yuvak (Konkani Youth) monthly in Konkani language 1949, Raithavani weekly in Kannada language 1949, Dockman weekly in English 1952–53, also New Society; fmr. Chief Ed. Pratipaksha weekly in Hindi; trade union work in South Kanara 1949, 1950, in Bombay and Maharashtra 1950–58; founding Pres. All-India Radio Broadcasters and Telecasters Guild, Khadi Comm. Karmachari Union, All-India Univ. Employees' Confed.; Pres. All-India Railwaymen's Fed. 1973–77; organized nat. railways strike 1974; Treas. All-India Hind Mazdoor Sabha 1958; formed Hind Mazdoor Panchayat 1958, Gen. Sec. for over 10 years; Convenor, United Council of Trade Unions; fmr. mem. Gen. Council of Public Services Int. (PSI), Int. Transport Workers' Fed. (ITF); Founder Chair. New India Co-operative Bank Ltd. (fmrly. Bombay Labour Co-operative Bank Ltd.); mem. Nat. Cttee. of Socialist Party of India 1955–77, Treas. 1964, Chair. 1971–77; Gen. Sec. Samyukta Socialist Party of India 1969–70; mem. Bombay Municipal Corpn. 1961–68; mem. for Bombay City, Lok Sabha 1967–77; went underground on declaration of emergency 1975; mem. Janata Party 1977, Gen. Sec. 1985–86; mem. for Muzzafarpur, Bihar, Lok Sabha 1977–79, also elected to Lok Sabha 1980, 1989, 1991, 1996, 1998; Minister for Communications March–July 1977, for Industry 1977–79 (resigned from govt. 1979), for Railways 1989–90, for Kashmir Affairs 1990–91, for Defence 1998–; Deputy Leader Lok Dal 1980–; mem. Standing Parl. Cttee. on Finance 1993–96, also Consultative Cttee. on Home Affairs; Pres. Samata Party 1994–; mem. Standing Parl. Cttee. on External Affairs 1996–, also Consultative Cttee. on Human Resources Devt.; Chair. Ed. Bd. Pratipaksh (Hindi monthly); Ed. The Other Side (English-language monthly); Pres. Hind Mazdoor Kisan Panchayat; Chair. India Devt. Group, London 1979, Schumacher Foundation 1979; fmr. mem. Press Council of India; mem. Amnesty Int., People's Union for Civil Liberties; involved in anti-nuclear and environmental campaigns. *Publications:* What Ails the Socialists: The Kashmir Problem, The Railway Strike of 1974, George Fernandes Speaks. *Leisure interests:* music, reading. *Address:* 30 Leonard Road, Richmond Town, Bangalore, Karnataka 560025, India. *Telephone:* (080) 221-4143.

FERNANDEZ, Dominique, D. ÈS L.; French author; b. 25 Aug. 1929, Neuilly-sur-Seine; s. of Ramon Fernandez and Liliane Chomette; m. Diane Jacquin de Margerie (divorced); one s. one d.; ed. Lycée Buffon, Paris and Ecole Normale Supérieure; Prof. Inst. Français, Naples 1957–58; Prof. of Italian, Univ. de Haute-Bretagne 1966–89; literary critic, L'Express 1959–84, Le Nouvel Observateur 1985–; music critic, Compact 1959–, Opera International 1978; mem. reading cttee. Edns. Bernard Grasset 1959–; Chevalier, Légion d'honneur, Officier, Ordre Nat. du Mérite; Prix Médicis 1974; Prix Goncourt 1982, Grand Prix Charles Oulmont 1986, Prix Prince Pierre de Monaco 1986, Prix Méditerranée 1988, Prix Oscar Wilde 1988. *Publications:* Le roman italien et la crise de la conscience moderne 1958,

L'ecorce des pierres 1959, L'aube 1962, Mère Méditerranée 1965, Les Evénements de Palerme 1966, L'echec de Pavèse 1968, Lettre à Dora 1969, Les enfants de Gogol 1971, Il Mito dell'America 1969, L'arbre jusqu'aux racines 1972, Porporino 1974, Eisenstein 1975, La rose des Tudors 1976, Les Siciliens 1977, Amsterdam 1977, L'étoile rose 1978, Une fleur de jasmin à l'oreille 1980, Le promeneur amoureux 1980, Signor Giovanni 1981, Dans la main de l'ange 1982, Le volcan sous la ville 1983, Le banquet des anges 1984, L'amour 1986, La gloire du paria 1987, Le rapt de Perséphone (opera libretto) 1987, Le radeau de la Gorgone 1988, Le rapt de Ganymede 1989, L'Ecole du Sud 1991, Porfirio et Constance 1992, Séville 1992, L'Or des Tropiques 1993, Le Dernier des Médicis 1993, la Magie Blanche de Saint-Pétersbourg 1994, Prague et la Bohême (jtly.) 1995, la Perle et le croissant 1995, le Musée idéal de Stendhal 1995, Saint-Pétersbourg 1996, Tribunal d'honneur 1997, Le musée de Zola 1997, Le voyage d'Italie 1998, Rhapsodie roumaine 1998, Palerme et la Sicile 1998. *Leisure interest:* operatic music. *Address:* Editions Bernard Grasset, 61 rue des Saints-Pères, 75006 Paris (Office); 14 rue de Douai, 75009 Paris, France (Home).

FERNANDEZ, Mary Joe; American tennis player; b. 19 Aug. 1971, Dominican Republic; d. of José Fernandez and Sylvia Fernandez; ranked No. 1 in U.S.A. 1984; turned professional 1986; reached quarter-finals French Open 1986, quarter-finals Geneva 1987, semi-finals Eastbourne 1988, semi-finals French Open 1989; runner-up to Graf in singles and runner-up with Fendick in doubles, Australian Open 1990; reached semi-finals Wimbledon and Australian Open, Italian Open, 1991; runner-up Australian Open 1992; won Bronze Medal in singles and Gold in doubles with G. Fernandez, Olympic Games 1992; reached semi-finals U.S. Open 1992; reached semi-finals Italian Open, quarter-finals Australian Open 1993; won singles title Strasbourg 1994, winner (with Davenport) French Open Doubles 1996; winner doubles Hilton Head, Carolina 1997, Madrid 1997, won singles title German Open 1997; mem. U.S. Fed. Cup Team, Atlantic City, N.J. 1996.

FERNÁNDEZ MALDONADO SOLARI, Gen. Jorge; Peruvian politician and army officer; b. 29 May 1922, Ilo, Moquegua; s. of Arturo Fernández Maldonado Soto and Amelia Solari de Fernández Maldonado; m. Estela Castro Faucheux; two s. two d.; ed. Chorillos Mil. School; Head of Army Intelligence Service; Dir. of Army Intelligence School, also of Mariscal Ramon Castilla Mil. School, Trujillo; Mil. Attaché, Argentina; mem. Pres. Advisory Cttee. (COAP); Minister of Energy and Mines 1968–75; Army Chief of Staff 1975–76; Prime Minister, Minister of War, Commdr.-Gen. of Army Feb.–July 1976; Senator 1985–; Sec.-Gen. Intergovernmental Council of Copper Exporting Countries 1990–.

FERNÁNDEZ-MURO, José Antonio; Argentinian painter; b. 1 March 1920; Dir. Nat. School of Fine Arts, Buenos Aires 1957–58; travelled and studied in Europe and America on UNESCO Fellowship of Museology 1957–58; lives in New York 1962–; one-man exhbns. in Buenos Aires, Madrid, Washington, New York, Rome and Detroit; represented in numerous Group Shows including 50 ans de Peinture Abstraite, Paris and The Emergent Decade, Guggenheim Museum 1965; prizes include Gold Medal, Brussels World Fair 1958, Guggenheim Int. and Di Tella Int. awards. *Major works:* Superimposed circles 1958, In Reds, Di Tella Foundation, Buenos Aires 1959, Horizonte terroso, Museum of Modern Art, Caracas 1961, Círculo azogado, Museum of Modern Art, New York 1962, Lacerated Tablet, Rockefeller, New York 1963, Elemental Forms, M.I.T. 1964, Silver Field, Guggenheim Museum 1965, Summit, Bonino Gallery, New York.

FERNÁNDEZ RETAMAR, Roberto, DR. EN FIL.; Cuban writer; b. 9 June 1930, Havana; s. of José M. Fernández Roig and Obdulia Retamar; m. Adelaida de Juan 1952; two d.; ed. Univ. de la Habana, Univ. de Paris à la Sorbonne and Univ. of London; Prof. Univ. de la Habana 1955–; Visiting Prof. Yale Univ. 1957–58; Dir. Nueva Revista Cubana 1959–60; Cultural Counsellor of Cuba in France 1960; Sec. Union of Writers and Artists of Cuba 1961–65; Ed. Casa de las Américas 1965–, now Pres.; Visiting lecturer Columbia Univ. 1957, Univ. of Prague 1965; Nat. Prize for Poetry, Cuba 1952; Nat. Literary Award Cuban Book Inst. 1989. *Publications:* Poetry: Elegía como un Himno 1950, Patrias 1952, Alabanzas, Conversaciones 1955, Vuelta de la Antigua Esperanza 1959, Con las Mismas Manos 1962, Poesía Reunida 1948–1965 1966, Buena Suerte Viviendo 1967, Que veremos arder 1970, A quien pueda interesar 1970, Cuaderno paralelo 1973; studies: La poesía Contemporánea en Cuba 1954, Idea de la Estilística 1958, Papelería 1962, Ensayo de otro mundo 1967, Introducción a Cuba: la historia 1968, Caliban 1971, Lectura de Martí 1972, El son de Vuelo popular 1972. *Leisure interests:* reading, swimming. *Address:* 508 H Street, Vedado, Havana, Cuba.

FERNÁNDEZ REYNA, Leonel; Dominican Republic politician; Leader Partido de la Liberación Dominicana; Pres. of Dominican Republic Aug. 1996–. *Address:* Secretariat of State for the Presidency, Santo Domingo, DN, Dominican Republic.

FERNANDO, Most Rev. Nicholas Marcus; B.A., PH.L., S.T.D.; Sri Lankan ecclesiastic; b. 6 Dec. 1932; s. of W. Severinus Fernando and M. M. Lily Fernando; ordained priest 1959; Rector, St. Aloysius Minor Seminary 1965–73; Archbishop of Colombo May 1977–; mem. Sacred Congregation for the Evangelization of Peoples 1989; Pres. Catholic Bishops' Conf. of Sri Lanka 1989–95. *Address:* Archbishop's House, 976 Gnanartha Pradeepaya Mawatha, Colombo 8, Sri Lanka. *Telephone:* 695471-2-3. *Fax:* (1) 692009.

FERNEYHOUGH, Brian John Peter; British composer and professor of composition; b. 16 Jan. 1943, Coventry; s. of Frederick G. Ferneyhough and Emily M. (née Hopwood) Ferneyhough; m. 1st Barbara J. Pearson 1967; m. 2nd Elke Schaaf 1980; m. 3rd Carolyn Steinberg 1984, m. 4th Stephanie Jan Hurtik 1990; ed. Birmingham School of Music, Royal Acad. of Music, Sweelinck Conservatorium, Amsterdam and Basle Conservatorium; Composition teacher, Musikhochschule, Freiburg, Germany 1973–78, Prof. of Composition 1978–86; Prin. Composition Teacher, Royal Conservatory of The Hague 1986; Prof. of Music, Univ. of Calif. at San Diego 1987–; leader of Master Class in Composition, Civica Scuola di Musica, Milan 1985–; Visiting Artist, Berlin 1976–77; Guest Prof. Musikhögskolan, Stockholm 1980, 1981, 1982, 1985; Visiting Prof. Univ. of Chicago 1986; Lecturer in Composition, Darmstadt Int. Courses 1976–96; Guest Prof. of Poetics, Mozarteum, Salzburg 1995; mem. Akad. der Künste, Berlin 1996; Koussevitsky Prize 1979, Grand Prix du Disque 1978, 1984, Chevalier des Arts et des Lettres 1984, A.R.A.M. 1991, Fellow Birmingham Conservatoire 1996, and other awards and prizes. *Works include:* Sonatas for String Quartet 1967, Firecycle Beta 1969–71, Transit 1972–74, Time and Motion Study III 1974, La Terre Est Un Homme 1976–79, Second String Quartet 1979–80, Lemma-Icon-Epigram 1981, Carceri d' Invenzione 1981–86, 3rd String Quartet 1987, Kurze Schatten II 1988, La Chute d'Icare 1988, Fourth String Quartet 1989–90, Allgebrah 1991, Bone Alphabet 1991, Terrain 1992, Maisons Noires 1993, On Stellar Magnitudes 1994, String Trio 1995, Incipit 1995–96, Kranichtänze II 1996, Allgebrah 1996, Flurries 1997, Unsichtbare Farben 1997. *Publications:* Complete Writings on Music 1994, Collected Writings 1996; various articles published separately. *Leisure interests:* reading, cats, wife, wine (not in that order). *Address:* 7150-D Calabria Court, San Diego, CA 92122, U.S.A. *Telephone;* (619) 558-0276. *Fax:* (619) 558-0276.

FERNIOT, Jean; French journalist; b. 10 Oct. 1918, Paris; s. of Paul Ferniot and Jeanne (née Rabu) Ferniot; m. 1st Jeanne Martinod 1942 (divorced); one s. two d.; m. 2nd Christiane Servan-Schreiber 1959 (divorced); two s.; m. 3rd Béatrice Lemaître 1984; ed. Lycée Louis-le-Grand; Head, Political Dept., France-Tireur 1945–57; Political Columnist, L'Express 1957–58; Chief Political Correspondent France-Soir 1959–63; Ed. L'Express 1963–66; with Radio Luxembourg 1967–83; Political Commentator France-Soir 1967–70, Asst. Chief Ed. 1969–70; Dir. at éditions Grasset, in charge of Collection Humeurs 1978–83; Dir. then Adviser Cuisine et vins de France 1981; Pres. Fondation Communication Demain 1980–89, Terminology Comm., Nat. Council for Tourism 1991–97; Pres. (Supervisory Council) Evénement du Jeudi 1992; mem. jury, Prix interallié 1970–; Prix Interallié 1961; Commdr. des Arts et des Lettres; Croix de Guerre, Chevalier du Mérite Agricole, Commdr. du Mérite (Italy). *Publications:* Les ides de mai 1958, L'ombre porté 1961, Pour le pire 1962, Derrière la fenêtre 1964, De Gaulle et le 13 mai 1965, Mort d'une révolution 1968, Paris dans mon assiette 1969, Complainte contre X 1973, De de Gaulle à Pompidou 1972, Ça suffit! 1973, Pierrot et Aline 1973, La petite légume 1974, Les vaches maigres (with Michel Albert) 1975, Les honnêtes gens 1976, C'est ça la France 1977, Vous en avez vraiment assez d'être français 1979, Carnet de croûte 1980, le Pouvoir et la sainteté 1982, Le Chien-loup 1983, Saint Judas 1984, Un mois de juin comme on les aimait 1986, Soleil orange 1988, Miracle au village 1989, Je recommencerais bien 1991, L'Europe à Table 1993, La France des Terroirs Gourmands 1993, Jérusalem, nombril du monde 1994, la Mouffe 1995, Morte saison 1996. *Address:* 11 bis rue d'Orléans, 92200 Neuilly-sur-Seine, France.

FERRAGAMO, Ferruccio; Italian business executive; b. 9 Sept. 1945, Fiesole, Florence; m. Amanda Collingwood; five c.; began career working on production side of family business Salvatore Ferragamo Italia S.p.A., later involved in worldwide management of Ferragamo stores; finance and admin. from 1983; now C.E.O. Salvatore Ferragamo S.p.A.; Vice-Pres. Polimoda, Florence; mem. Bd. Società Gaetano Marzotto & Fratelli, La Fondaria Assicurazioni, Banca Mercantile, Florence, Centro di Firenze per la Moda Italiana. *Leisure interests:* golf, shooting, sailing, tennis. *Address:* c/o Salvatore Ferragamo Italia, S.p.A., Via di Tornabuoni 2, 50123 Florence, Italy. *Telephone:* (055) 33601.

FERRARA, Abel; American film director and actor; b. 1951, Bronx, N.Y.; m. Nancy Ferrara; two d.; began making short films while at school; has used pseudonym Jimmy Laine; television work includes episodes of Miami Vice and pilot for NBC's Crime Story. *Films include:* Driller Killer (also acted) 1979, Ms.45 (also acted) 1981, Fear City 1984, China Girl, Cat Chaser, The King of New York, Bad Lieutenant 1993, Body Snatchers, Dangerous Game 1994, The Addiction 1995, The Funeral 1996. *Address:* c/o William Morris Agency, 151 S. El Camino Drive, Beverly Hills, CA 90212, U.S.A.

FERRARI BRAVO, Luigi; Italian professor of law; b. 5 Aug. 1933; ed. Univ. of Naples; Asst. Prof. Univ. of Naples 1956–61; Prof. of Int. Org. Univ. of Bari 1961–65, of Int. Law 1965–68, Full Prof. of Int. Law and Dir. Inst. of Int. Law 1968–74; Prof. of Int. Law, Istituto Universitario Orientale, Naples 1962–68, Full Prof. of Int. Org. 1974–79, Dean, Dept. of Political Science 1975–76; Prof. of EC Law, High School of Public Admin. Rome 1965–79, Full Prof. 1975; Full Prof. of EC Law, Faculty of Political Science, Univ. of Rome 1979–82, Full Prof. of Public Int. Law 1982–91; Full Prof. of EC Law, Faculty of Law, Univ. of Rome 1991–; lecturer, Hague Acad. of Int. Law 1975, 1982 and many other univs. and scientific insts.; numerous professional appts.; mem. Italian Bar, Int. Law Assn., American Soc. of Int. Law, Soc. Française de Droit Int. etc. *Publications:* articles in professional journals. *Address:* Faculty of Law, University of Rome, Piazzale Aldo Moro 5, 00185 Rome, Italy.

FERRARO, Geraldine Anne, J.D.; American politician and lawyer; b. 26 Aug. 1935, Newburgh, N.Y.; d. of Dominick and Antonetta L. (Corrieri) Ferraro; m. John Zaccaro 1960; one s. two d.; ed. Marymount Manhattan Coll., Fordham Univ.; lawyer in New York Bar 1961, U.S. Supreme Court 1978; practised law in New York 1961–74, Asst. Dist. Attorney, Queens County, New York 1974–78; mem. House of Reps. 1979–84; first woman from a major party to be a cand. for U.S. Vice-Pres. in 1984 presidential election; man. partner Keck Mahin Cate & Koether, New York 1993–94; apptd. by Pres. Clinton as U.S. Amb. to UN Human Rights Comm. 1994, 1995, World Conf., Vienna 1993, 4th World Conf. on Women 1995; Fellow Harvard Univ., Kennedy School of Govt., 1988; Pres. Int. Inst. of Women Political Leaders; mem. Nat. Democratic Inst. for Int. Affairs; Democrat. *Publications:* My Story (with Linda Bird Francke) 1985, Changing History: Women, Power and Politics 1993. *Address:* 218 Lafayette Street, New York, NY 10012, U.S.A. (Office).

FERRÉ, Gianfranco; Italian couturier; b. 15 Aug. 1944, Legnano, Milan; ed. Politecnico di Milano; started designing jewelry and belts 1969; designed first collection of clothes for women, under Baila label 1974; first collection under own name 1978; first collection for men 1982; introduced own perfume 1984; Artistic Dir. at Christian Dior, Paris 1989–96; designer Oaks by Ferré, Milan 1978–, Studio 0.001 by Ferré, Milan 1987–, Ferré Jeans 1989–; Prof. Domus Acad. 1983–89; designs included in exhbns. at M.I.T., Boston, U.S.A. 1982, La Jolla Museum of Contemporary Art, Calif., U.S.A. and Daimaru Museum, Osaka and Museum of Fashion and Costume Acad., Tokyo; Modepreis, Munich 1958, Cutty Sark Men's Fashion Award, New York 1985, Gold Medal of Civic Merit, Milan 1985, De d'Or Prize, Paris (Best Couturier of the Season) 1989, L'Occhio d'Oro Award (Best Collection at Milan women's ready-to-wear shows) 1983, 1983/84, 1985, 1986/87 and 1987/88; Commendatore of Italian Order of Merit, Lorenzo il Magnifico Award 1990, Il Fiorino d'Oro 1991, Diva-Wollsiegel 1992, Pitti Immagine Uomo 1993. *Leisure interests:* reading, classical and folk music, cinema, collecting modern art. *Address:* Via della Spiga 19/A, 20121 Milan, Italy. *Telephone:* 7600 8888; 7600 3394.

FERRER SALAT, Carlos; Spanish banker and business executive; Chair. Banco de Europa, Ferrer Int. (pharmaceutical co.); founder and first Chair. Spanish Employers' Fed. (CEOE); Pres. European Employers' Union (UNICE), Brussels 1991–; mem. Bds. Volkswagen, IBM Europe and others.

FERRIER, Johan Henri Eliza; Suriname politician; b. 12 May 1910, Paramaribo; Mem. Suriname Parl. 1946–48; Dir. Dept. of Educ., Paramaribo 1951–55; Prime Minister, Minister of Gen. Affairs, of Home Affairs 1955–58; Counsellor, Ministry of Educ., Arts and Science, Netherlands 1959–65; Man. Dir. Billiton Mining Co., Suriname 1966–67; Gov. of Suriname 1968–75; Pres. Repub. of Suriname 1975–80.

FERRIS, Martin; Irish politician; b. Ardfert, Co. Kerry, Northern Ireland; convicted of IRA membership 1975, 1976, fined and given suspended sentence for assaulting a Garda officer 1977, became Head of Southern Command 1984, released from prison 1994 following a sentence for IRA activities; mem. Sinn Féin, fmrly. mem. of Nat. Exec., involved in negotiations over future of Northern Ireland. *Address:* Sinn Féin, 51–55 Falls Road, Belfast, BT12, Northern Ireland. *Telephone:* (01232) 323214. *Fax:* (01232) 231723.

FERRY, Bryan; British singer and songwriter; b. 26 Sept. 1945, Washington, Co. Durham; s. of Frederick Charles Ferry and Mary Ann Ferry (née Armstrong); m. Lucy Margaret Mary Helmore 1982; three s. two d.; ed. Univ. of Newcastle upon Tyne; formed Roxy Music 1971; official debut, Lincoln Festival 1972; first U.S. concerts 1972; first British and European tours 1973; albums with Roxy Music: Roxy Music 1972, For Your Pleasure 1973 (Grand Prix du Disque, Golden Rose Festival, Montreux 1973), Stranded 1973, Country Life 1974, Siren 1975, Viva Roxy Music 1976, Manifesto 1979, Flesh & Blood 1980, Avalon 1982, The Atlantic Years 1983, Street Life 1987; Bryan Ferry albums: These Foolish Things 1973, Another Time Another Place 1974, Let's Stick Together 1976, In Your Mind 1977, The Bride Stripped Bare 1978, Boys And Girls 1985, Bete Noire 1987, The Ultimate Collection 1988, Taxi 1993, Mamouna 1995, Bryan Ferry and Roxy Music Video Collection 1996; singles include: Virginia Plain 1972, Pyjamarama 1973, All I Want Is You 1974, Dance Away 1979, Angel Eyes 1979, Over You 1980, Oh Yeah 1980, Same Old Scene 1980, Jealous Guy (tribute to John Lennon) 1981, Slave To Love 1985, I Put A Spell On You 1993. *Address:* c/o Christopher Scott, Virgin Records Ltd., Kensal House, 553/579 Harrow Road, London, W10 4RH, England. *Telephone:* 0181-964 6071. *Fax:* 0181-964 6073.

FERRY, John Douglass, PH.D.; American professor of chemistry; b. 4 May 1912, Dawson, Canada (of U.S. parents); s. of Douglass Hewitt Ferry and Eudora Beaufort Bundy; m. Barbara Norton Mott 1944; one s. one d.; ed. Stanford Univ. and Univ. of London; Instructor, Harvard Univ. 1936–38, Soc. of Fellows, Harvard 1938–41, Research Assoc. 1942–45; Assoc. Chemist, Woods Hole Oceanographic Inst. 1941–45; Asst. Prof., Univ. of Wisconsin 1946, Assoc. Prof. 1946–47, Prof. 1947–82, Farrington Daniels Research Prof. 1973–82, Prof. Emer. 1982–, Chair. Dept. of Chem. 1959–67; Pres. Soc. of Rheology 1961–63; Chair. Int. Cttee. on Rheology 1963–68; mem. N.A.S., Nat. Acad. of Eng.; Fellow American Acad. of Arts and Sciences; Hon. mem. Groupe français de Rhéologie, Soc. of Rheology, Japan; Special Lecturer, Kyoto Univ., Japan 1968, Univ. de Grenoble (Ecole d'Eté) 1973; Eli Lilly Award, A.C.S. 1946, Bingham Medal, Soc. of Rheology 1953, Kendall Award, A.C.S. 1960, High Polymer Physics Prize, American Physical Soc. 1966, Colwyn Medal, Inst. of the Rubber Industry (London) 1971, Witco Award, A.C.S. 1974, Tech. Award, Int. Inst. of Synthetic Rubber Producers 1977, Goodyear Medal, Rubber Div. A.C.S. 1981, Div. of Polymer Chem. Award, A.C.S. 1984. *Publication:* Viscoelastic Properties of Polymers 1961, 1970, 1980. *Leisure interest:* travel. *Address:* Department of Chemistry, University of Wisconsin, Madison, WI 53706; 5015 Sheboygan Avenue, Madison, WI 53705, U.S.A. (Home). *Telephone:* (608) 262-1485 (Office); (608) 233-4936 (Home). *Fax:* (608) 262-0381.

FERRY, Luc; French philosopher; b. 3 Jan. 1951, Colombes; s. of Pierre Ferry and Monique Faucher; one d.; ed. Lycée Saint-Exupéry, Centre national de télé-enseignement, Sorbonne, Univ. of Heidelberg; lecturer Teacher Training Coll., Arras; Asst. Lecturer Univ. of Reims 1977–79; Asst. Lecturer univ. teacher training college, rue d'Ulm, Paris 1977–79, 1980–82; Research Attaché Nat. Centre of Scientific Research (C.N.R.S.); Asst. lecturer Univ. of Paris I-Panthéon Sorbonne and Paris X-Nanterre 1980–88; Prof. of Philosophy Univ. of Caen 1989–97; Asst. lecturer Paris I 1989; Prof. of Philosophy Univ. of Paris VII-Jussieu 1997–; founder-mem., Sec. Gen. College of Philosophy 1974–; responsible for Ideas section then Editorial Adviser, l'Express 1987–94; Pres. Nat. Curriculum Council (C.N.P.) 1993–; Dir. Grasset edns. collection of Coll. of Philosophy; mem. Saint-Simon Foundation; columnist for Point 1995–; awarded Prix des Nouveaux Droits de l'homme, Membre du Siècle. *Publications:* Philosophie politique (3 vols. 1984–85), la Pensée 68, le Nouvel ordre écologique: l'arbre, l'animal et l'homme (Prix Médicis, Prix Jean-Jacques Rousseau) 1992, l'Homme Dieu ou le sens de la vie 1996, La Sagesse des Modernes 1998, Le Sens du Beau 1998, numerous articles on philosophy. *Address:* C.N.P., 1 rue Descartes, 75005 Paris (Office); 6 avenue de Lowendal, 75007 Paris, France (Home).

FERSHT, Alan Roy, M.A., PH.D., F.R.S.; British professor of organic chemistry; b. 21 April 1943, London; s. of Philip and Betty Fersht; m. Marilyn Persell 1966; one s. one d.; ed. Sir George Monoux Grammar School, Walthamstow and Gonville and Caius Coll., Cambridge; Research Fellow, Brandeis Univ. Waltham, Mass. 1968–69; Fellow, Jesus Coll., Cambridge 1969–72; mem. scientific staff, MRC Lab. of Molecular Biology, Cambridge 1969–77; Eleanor Roosevelt Fellow, Stanford Univ., Calif. 1978–79; Wolfson Research Prof. of Royal Soc. 1978–89; Prof. of Biological Chem., Imperial Coll., London 1978–88; Herchel Smith Prof. of Organic Chem., Cambridge Univ. 1988–; Dir. Cambridge Interdisciplinary Research Centre for Protein Eng. 1989–; Dir MRC Unit for Protein Function and Design 1989–; Fellow Gonville and Caius Coll., Cambridge 1988–; Foreign Assoc. N.A.S. (U.S.A.) 1993; FEBS Anniversary Prize 1980, Novo Biotech. Award 1986, Charmian Medal, for Enzyme Chem., Royal Soc. of Chem. 1986, Gabor Medal, Royal Soc. 1991, Max Tishler Prize (Harvard Univ.) 1992, Harden Medal (Biochem. Soc.) 1993, Feldberg Foundation Prize 1996, Davy Medal (Royal Soc.) 1998. *Publications;* Enzyme Structure and Mechanism 1977, Structure and Mechanism in Protein Science 1999; papers in scientific journals. *Leisure interests:* chess, horology. *Address:* Cambridge Centre for Protein Engineering, Department of Chemistry, University of Cambridge, Lensfield Road, Cambridge CB2 1EW (Office); 2 Barrow Close, Cambridge, CB2 2AT, England (Home). *Telephone:* (01223) 336341 (Office); (01223) 352963 (Home). *Fax:* (01223) 336445.

FERY, John Bruce, M.B.A.; American business executive; b. 16 Feb. 1930, Bellingham, Wash.; s. of Carl S. and Margaret Fery; m. Delores L. Carlo 1953; three s.; ed. Univ. of Washington and Stanford Univ. Graduate School of Business; Asst. to Pres., Western Kraft Corpn. 1955–56, Production Man. 1956–57; Asst. to Pres., Boise Cascade Corpn. 1957–58, Gen. Man. Paper Div. 1958–60, Vice-Pres. 1960–67, Exec. Vice-Pres. and Dir. 1967–72, Pres. 1972–78, Chair, C.E.O. 1978–94, Chair. 1995–; numerous directorships; Hon. Dr. of Natural Resources (Idaho) 1983, Hon. LL.D. (Gonzaga) 1982; Stanford Univ. School of Business Ernest Arbuckle Award 1980. *Address:* Boise Cascade Corporation, One Jefferson Square, Boise, ID 83728 (Office); 609 Wyndemere Drive, Boise, ID 83702, U.S.A. (Home). *Telephone:* (208) 384-7560 (Office).

FESHBACH, Herman, PH.D.; American professor of physics; b. 2 Feb. 1917, New York, N.Y.; s. of David and Ida Feshbach; m. Sylvia Harris 1940; two s. one d.; ed. City Coll., New York, N.Y. and M.I.T.; Tutor in Physics, City Coll., New York 1937–38; Asst. Prof. M.I.T. 1945–47, Assoc. Prof. 1947–54, Prof. of Physics 1954–87, Cecil and Ida Green Prof. 1976–83, Inst. Prof. 1983-87, Inst. Prof. Emer. 1987–, Dir. Center for Theoretical Physics 1967–73, Head, Dept. of Physics 1973–83; Guggenheim Fellow 1954–55, Ford Foundation Fellow 1962–63; Vice-Pres. American Acad. of Arts and Science 1973–76, Pres. 1982–86; Ed. Annals of Physics 1977–, Contemporary Concepts in Physics; Chair. DOE/NSF (Nat. Science Foundation) Nuclear Science Advisory Cttee. 1979–82; Pres. American Physical Soc. 1980–81; mem. Nat. Acad. of Sciences; mem. Bd. of Govs. Weizmann Inst. of Science; Trustee, Associated Univs. Inc. 1974–87, 1990–96, Hon. Trustee 1996–; Chair. Elect. Section B (Physics), A.A.A.S. 1986–87; Navy Ordnance Award 1943; Bonner Prize, American Physical Soc. 1973, Humboldt Sr. U.S. Scientist Award 1982–83, Nat. Medal of Science 1986. *Publications:* Methods of Theoretical Physics (with Philip M. Morse) two vols. 1953, Theoretical Nuclear Physics (with Amos de Shalit) 1974, Reaction Dynamics (with F. S. Levin) 1973, Theoretical Nuclear Physics: Nuclear Reactions 1992. *Address:* 5 Sedgwick Road, Cambridge, MA 02138, U.S.A. (Home). *Telephone:* (617) 354-2721 (Home).

FETISOV, Vyacheslav Aleksandrovich; Russian hockey player; b. 20 April 1958, Moscow; played with Cen. Army Sports Club 1975–89; U.S.S.R. Champion 1975, 1979–89; seven times World Champion with U.S.S.R. teams 1977–91; Olympic Champion 1984, 1988; with New Jersey Devils 1983, later Detroit Red Wings 1995–; Pres. Cup 1996, Stanley Cup 1997. *Address:* c/o Detroit Red Wings, 600 Civic Center Drive, Detroit, MI 48226, U.S.A.

FETSCHER, Iring, DR. PHIL.; German political scientist; b. 4 March 1922, Marbach; s. of Prof. Rainer Fetscher; m. Elisabeth Götte 1957; two s. two d.; ed. König-George-Gymnasium, Dresden, Eberhard-Karls-Universität, Tübingen, Université de Paris, and Johann Wolfgang Goethe-Univ., Frankfurt; Ed. Marxismusstudien 1956–; radio commentator on political, philosophical and sociological questions; Prof. of Political Science, Johann Wolfgang Goethe-Univ., Frankfurt 1963–88; Theodor-Heuss Prof. New School for Social Research, New York 1968–69; Guest Prof. Tel-Aviv Univ. 1972; Fellow, Netherlands Inst. for Advanced Study in the Humanities and Social Sciences 1972–73; Inst. for Advanced Studies, Australian Nat. Univ., Canberra; Extraordinary Prof. for Social and Political Philosophy, Catholic Univ. of Nijmegen 1974–75; Goethe Plakette (Frankfurt) 1992; Bundesverdienstkreuz (First Class) 1993; Chevalier Ordre des Palmes Académiques 1993. *Publications include:* Von Marx zur Sowjetideologie 1956, Uber dialektischen und historischen Materialismus (Commentary of Stalin) 1956, 1962, Rousseaus politische Philosophie 1960, 1968, 1975, Der Marxismus, seine Geschichte in Dokumenten Vol. I 1962, Vol. II 1964, Vol. III 1965, 4th edn. in one vol. 1983, Marx-Engels Studienausgabe (4 vols.) 1966, Introduction to Hobbes' Leviathan 1966, Karl Marx und der Marxismus 1967, Der Rechtsradikalismus 1967, Der Sozialismus 1968, Der Kommunismus 1969, Hegel: Grösse und Grenzen 1971, Modelle der Friedenssicherung 1972, Wer hat Dornröschen wachgeküsst?—das Märchenverwirrbuch 1972, 1974, Marxistische Porträts Vol. I 1975, Herrschaft und Emanzipation 1976, Terrorismus und Reaktion 1981, Analysen zum Terrorismus, Ideologien und Strategien 1981, Vom Wohlfahrtsstaat zur neuen Lebensqualität, die Herausforderungen des demokratischen Sozialismus 1982, Der Nulltarif der Wichtelmänner, Märchen- und andere Verwirrspiele 1982, Arbeit und Spiel (essays) 1983, Handbuch der politischen Ideen (Co-ed. with H. Münkler), Vols. 1, 3, 4, 5 1985–93, Überlebensbedingungen der Menschheit zur Dialektik des Fortschritts 1986 (enlarged edn.) 1991, Die Wirksamkeit der Träume, literarische Skizzen eines Sozialwissenschaftlers 1987, Utopien, Illusionen, Hoffnungen-Plädoyer für eine politische Kultur in Deutschland 1990, Toleranz—von der Unentbehrlichkeit einer kleinen Tugend für die Demokratie 1990, Neugier und Furcht. Versuch, mein Leben (autobiog.) 1995. *Leisure interests:* collects autographed letters and manuscripts. *Address:* J. W. Goethe Universität, P.O. Box 111932, D-60054 Frankfurt-am-Main (Office); Ganghoferstrasse 20, D-60320 Frankfurt-am-Main, Germany (Home). *Telephone:* (69) 52-15-42 (Home). *Fax:* (69) 51-00-34.

FETTING, Rainer; German painter and sculptor; b. 31 Dec. 1949, Wilhelmshaven; ed. Hochschule der Künste; co-founder, Galerie am Moritzplatz ("vehement painting") 1977; DAAD scholarship, Columbia Univ. New York 1978; one-man shows include: Mary Boone, New York, Bruno Bischoff Berger, Zürich 1981, Museum Folkwang, Essen, Kunsthalle, Basle and Marlborough Gallery, New York 1986, Museo di Barcelona 1989, Nationalgalerie, Berlin 1990, Harenberg City Centre, Dortmund 1994; group shows include: A New Spirit in Painting, Royal Acad. London 1981, Zeitgeist, Martin Gropius Bau, Berlin 1982, Berlin Art, Museum of Modern Art, New York 1987, Refigured Painting, Guggenheim Museum, New York 1988. *Address:* Hasenheide 61, 1000 Berlin 61, Germany.

FETTWEIS, Alfred Leo Maria, D. ÈS SC.APPL.; German professor of communication engineering; b. 27 Nov. 1926, Eupen, Belgium; s. of Paul Fettweis and Helene (née Hermanns) Fettweis; m. Lois J. Piaskowski 1957; two s. three d.; ed. Catholic Univ. of Louvain, Columbia Univ., Polytechnic Inst. of Brooklyn; Devt. engineer with Int. Telephone and Telegraph Corpn. (ITT), Belgium 1951–54, 1956–63 and U.S.A. 1954–56; Prof. of Theoretical Electricity, Eindhoven Univ. of Tech. 1963–67; Prof. of Communication Eng. Ruhr-Univ. Bochum 1967–92, Prof. Emer. 1992–; Visiting Distinguished Prof., Univ. of Notre Dame 1994–96; mem. Rheinisch-Westfälische Akad. der Wissenschaften, Acad. Europaea, Acad. Scientiarum et Artium Europaea; Fellow I.E.E.E. 1975; Dr. h.c. (Linköping) 1986, (Mons) 1988, (Leuven) 1988, (Budapest) 1995; Prix Acta Technica Belgica 1963, Darlington Prize Paper Award 1980, Prix George Montefiore 1981, VDE-Ehrenring 1984, I.E.E.E. Centennial Medal 1984, Tech. Achievement Award of I.E.E.E Circuits and Systems Soc. 1987, Karl-Küpfmüller-Preis of Informationstechnische Gesellschaft 1988, Basic Research Award of Eduard Rhein Foundation 1993, and other prizes. *Publications:* two books, many tech. papers on circuits, systems, telecommunications, digital signal processing, numerical integration, and related areas, about 30 patents. *Leisure interests:* hiking, music. *Address:* Lehrstuhl für Nachrichtentechnik, Ruhr-Universität Bochum, Universitätsstrasse 150, D-44780 Bochum (Office); Im Königsbusch 18, D-44797 Bochum, Germany (Home). *Telephone:* 0234-700 2497/3063 (Office); 0234-797922 (Home). *Fax:* 0234-709 4100.

FETTWEIS, Günter Bernhard Leo, DR. ING.; Austrian mining engineer and university professor emeritus; b. 17 Nov. 1924, Düsseldorf, Germany; s. of Ewald I. Fettweis and Aninhas M. (née Leuschner-Fernandes) Fettweis; m. Alice Y. Fettweis 1949; one s. three d.; ed. Univ. of Freiburg and Technical Univ. of Aachen; Scientific Asst. Tech. Univ. of Aachen 1950–52; Jr. Mining Inspector Nordrhein-Westfalen 1953–54; Ruhr coal-mining industry, then Production Man. of the Osterfeld, Sterkrade and Hugo Haniel coal mines, B.A.G. Neue Hoffnung, Oberhausen/Ruhr 1955–59; Prof. and Head Dept. of Mining Eng. and Mineral Econs., Montan Univ. Leoben 1959–93, Rector (Vice-Chair.) 1968–70; Vice-Pres., later Pres. Mining Soc. of Austria 1963–93; Vice-Pres. Austrian Soc., of Rock Mechanics 1968–81, Int. Organizing Cttee. World Mining Congress 1976–; mem. Supervising Bd. ÖBAG (Austrian State Mining Industry) 1988–95; Chair. Bd. Inst. for Research about Mineral Resources 1983–87; Corresp. mem. Austrian Acad. of Sciences 1977, mem. 1983; Hon. mem. Hungarian Acad. of Sciences 1990; Foreign mem. Polish Acad. of Sciences 1991, European Acad. of Sciences, Salzburg 1990, Paris 1996, Russian Acad. of Natural Sciences 1997; Dr. h.c. (Aachen), (Miskolc, Hungary), (Petrosani, Romania), (Moscow); Austrian State Award of Energy Research; nat. and int. medals. *Publications:* World Coal Resources, Methods of Assessment and Results 1976–79, Atlas of Mining Methods (co-author) 1963–66, Mining in the Process of Change (Ed.) 1988, Bergwirtschaft (mineral economics; Co-author) 1990, Deponietechnik und Entsorgungsbergbau (waste disposal) (Ed.), and about 250 other publs. *Leisure interests:* history, philosophy, Africa, sailing. *Address:* Institut für Bergbaukunde der Montanuniversität Leoben, Franz-Josef-Strasse 18, A-8700 Leoben (Office); Gasteigergasse 5, A-8700 Leoben, Austria (Home). *Telephone:* (3842) 402/538 (Office); (3842) 21190 (Home). *Fax:* (3842) 402/530 (Office); (3842) 21190 (Home).

FEYDER, Jean, D.JUR.; Luxembourg diplomatist; b. 24 Nov. 1947; m.; two c.; joined Ministry of Foreign Affairs 1974, Head, UN Dept. 1974–76, Deputy Perm. Rep. to UN, New York July-Dec. 1975; assigned to Luxembourg mission to European Community, Brussels (with responsibility for accession negotiations) 1977; Deputy Perm. Rep. to EEC 1983; Perm. Rep. to UN, New York 1987–93. *Address:* c/o Ministry of Foreign Affairs, 5 rue Notre Dame, 2240 Luxembourg.

FEYIDE, Chief Meshach Otokiti, A.C.S.M., D.I.C., C.ENG., F.I.M.M., F.INST.PET.; Nigerian chartered engineer; b. 31 March 1926, Ipele, Ondo State; s. of Chief Samuel and Juliana Elebe (née Adeola) Otokiti; m. Christiana Oluremi 1954; one s. two d.; ed. Govt. Coll., Ibadan, Camborne School of Mines, U.K., Imperial Coll. of Science and Tech., London; Insp. of Mines 1954–59; Petroleum Engineer, Ministry of Mines and Power 1960, Chief Petroleum Engineer 1964, Dir. Petroleum Resources 1970; Sec.-Gen. OPEC 1975–76; Chief Exec. Petroleum Inspectorate, Nigerian Nat. Petroleum Corpn. 1977–78; Petroleum Consultant 1979–; Publr. and Man. Ed. Nigerian Petroleum News 1984–; Nigerian American Chamber of Commerce Award to Leading Businessmen 1983; Austrian Grand Decoration of Honour 1978; Officer Order of the Fed. Repub. (OFR) 1982. *Leisure interests:* music, reading. *Address:* P.O. Box 1790, Lagos, Nigeria. *Telephone:* (01) 2636999.

FEYZIOĞLU, Turhan, LL.D.; Turkish university professor and government official; b. 19 Jan. 1922, Kayseri; s. of Sait Azmi and Neyyire Feyzioğlu; m. Leyla Firdevs 1949; one s.; ed. Galatasaray Lycée, Istanbul Univ., and Ecole nationale d'Administration, Paris; Asst. Prof. Ankara Political Science School 1945–47, Assoc. Prof. 1947–54; Research, Nuffield Coll., Oxford 1954; Co-ed. Forum 1954–58; Prof. Ankara Univ. 1955; Dean, Political Science School, Ankara 1956; Participant Harvard Int. Seminar 1956; M.P. 1957, 1961, 1965–80; mem. Nat. Exec. Cttee. Republican People's Party 1957–61, Vice-Pres. 1965, 1966; Pres. Middle East Tech. Univ. 1960; mem. Constituent Ass. 1960; Minister of Educ. 1960; Minister of State 1961; Deputy Prime Minister 1962–63; mem. Turkish High Planning Council 1961–63, 1975–78; Turkish Rep. Consultative Assembly Council of Europe 1964–66, 1972; Leader Republican Reliance Party 1967; Deputy Prime Minister 1975–77, Deputy Prime Minister and Minister of State Jan.–Sept. 1978, mem. Ataturk Research Centre 1983; Dr. h.c. (Kayseri Univ.) 1985. *Publications;* Administrative Law 1947, Judicial Review of Unconstitutional Laws 1951, Les partis politiques en Turquie 1953, The Reforms of the French Higher Civil Service 1955, Democracy and Dictatorship 1957, Communist Threat 1969, In the Service of the Nation 1975, Kemal Ataturk, Leader de la Libération Nationale 1981, Ataturk's Way 1982, Chypre, Mythes et Réalités 1984, Ataturk and Nationalism 1986, The Crux of the Cyprus Problem 1987. *Leisure interest:* gardening. *Address:* Ataturk Research Center, Ataturk Bulvarı, 217 Ankara (Office); Çevre sokak, 54/9, Çankaya, Turkey (Home). *Telephone:* 1270619 (Home).

FFORDE, John Standish, M.A.; British banker; b. 16 Nov. 1921, Broadstone, Dorset; s. of late F. C. Fforde; m. Marya Retinger 1951; three s. one d.; ed. Rossall School and Christ Church, Oxford; Asst. Prime Minister's Statistical Branch 1951–53; Fellow in Econs., Nuffield Coll., Oxford 1953–56; Adviser Bank of England 1957–59, Deputy Chief Cen. Banking Information Dept. 1959–64, Adviser to Govs. 1964–66, 1982–84, Chief Cashier 1966–70, Dir. 1970–82, official historian 1984–92; Dir. Mercantile House Holdings 1984–87, Halifax Bldg. Soc. 1984–92; Dir. The Jt. Mission Hosp. Equipment Bd. Ltd. (now Echo Int. Health Services Ltd.) 1979–85, Chair. 1985–93; Dir. Crédit Lyonnais Capital Markets (fmrly. CL-Alexanders Laing and Cruikshank Ltd.) 1987–91. *Publications:* The Federal Reserve System 1945–49 1953, An International Trade in Managerial Skills 1957, The Bank of England and Public Policy 1945–1958 1992. *Leisure interests:* travel, walking.

FFOWCS WILLIAMS, John Eirwyn, M.A., SC.D. (CANTAB), PH.D., C.ENG., F.ENG., F.R.Ae.S., F.INST.P., F.I.M.A.; British professor of engineering; b. 25 May 1935; m. Anne Beatrice Mason 1959; two s. one d.; ed. Derby Tech. Coll.,

Univ. of Southampton; eng. apprentice, Rolls-Royce Ltd. 1951–55; Spitfire Mitchell Memorial Scholar to Southampton Univ. 1955–60 (Pres. Students' Union 1957–58); joined Aerodynamics Div., NPL 1960–62; with Bolt, Beranek & Newman, Inc. 1962–64; Reader in Applied Mathematics, Imperial Coll. of Science and Tech. 1964–69, Rolls-Royce Prof. of Theoretical Acoustics 1969–72; Rank Prof. of Eng., Cambridge Univ. 1972–; Master Emmanuel Coll., Cambridge 1996– (Professorial Fellow 1972); Chair. Concorde Noise Panel 1965–75, Noise Research Cttee. ARC 1969–76, Topexpress Ltd. 1979–89; Dir. VSEL Consortium PLC 1987–95; Honoured Prof. Beijing Inst. of Aeronautics and Astronautics 1992–, Foreign Hon. mem. American Acad. of Arts and Sciences 1989, Foreign Assoc. N.A.E. (U.S.A.) 1995; F.A.I.A.A., F.Inst.Acoust, F.R.S.A.; Fellow Acoustical Soc. of America; Aero-Acoustics Medal, A.I.A.A. 1977, Rayleigh Medal, Inst. of Acoustics 1984, Silver Medal, Soc. Française d'Acoustique 1989, Gold Medal, R.Ae.S. 1990, Per Bruel Gold Medal, A.S.M.E. 1997. *Publications:* Sound and Sources of Sound 1983 (with A. P. Dowling), numerous articles in professional journals; film on Aerodynamic Sound (jtly.). *Leisure interests:* friends and cigars. *Address:* Emmanuel College, Cambridge, CB2 3AP, England.

FFRENCH-DAVIS, Ricardo, PH.D.; Chilean economist; b. 27 June 1936; m. Marcela Yampaglia 1966; ed. Catholic Univ. of Chile, Univ. of Chicago; Researcher and Prof. of Econs., Econ Research Cen., Catholic Univ. 1962–64; Prof. of Econs., Univ. of Chile 1962–73; Deputy Man. Research Dept., Cen. Bank of Chile 1964–70; Research Dir. Cen. on Planning Studies, Catholic Univ. 1970–75; Vice-Pres. and Dir. Corpn. for Latin American Econ. Research (CIEPLAN), Santiago 1976–90; Research Dir. Cen. Bank of Chile 1990; mem. Acad. Council, Latin American Program, The Woodrow Wilson Centre, Washington, D.C. 1977–80; mem. UN Cttee. on Econ. Planning 1990–92; mem. Exec. Cttee. Latin American Studies Asscn. 1992–; Visiting Fellow, Univ. of Oxford 1974; Visiting Prof., Boston Univ. 1976; Pres. Acad. Circle, Acad. de Humanismo Cristiano, Chile 1978–81; Co-ordinator Working Group on Econ. Issues of Inter-American Dialogue 1985–86; mem. Editorial Bds. Latin American Research Review, El Trimestre Economico and Colección Estudios Cieplan. *Publications:* Políticas Económicas en Chile: 1952–70 1973, El cobre en el desarrollo nacional (co-ed.) 1974, Economía internacional: teorías y políticas para el desarrollo 1979, Latin America and a New International Economic Order (co-ed.) 1981, 1985, The Monetarist Experiment in Chile 1982, Relaciones financieras externas y la economía latinoamericana (ed.) 1983, Development and External Debt in Latin America (co-ed.) 1988, Debt-equity swaps in Chile 1990, Capital Formation and the Macro-economic Framework 1992; over 70 articles on int. econs., Latin-American econ. devt., and Chilean econ. policies.

FICHTENAU, Heinrich, PH.D.; Austrian professor of medieval history; b. 10 Dec. 1912, Linz; s. of Heinrich von Fichtenau and Maria von Fichtenau (née Schachermeyr); m. Anna Widl 1954; two d.; ed. Univ. of Vienna, Austrian Inst. for Historical Research; Research Asst. Univ. of Vienna 1936–50, Assoc. Prof. 1950–62, Prof. of Medieval History and Auxiliary Sciences 1962–83, Emer. Prof. 1983–; Dir. Austrian Inst. for Historical Research 1962–83; Corresp. Fellow British Acad.; Corresp. Fellow Medieval Acad. of America; Fellow Austrian Acad. of Sciences. *Publications:* Mensch u. Schrift im Mittelalter 1946, Babenberger-Urkundenbuch (with E. Zoellnor), (Vol. 1) 1950, (Vol. 2) 1955, (Vol. 3) 1968, Arenga 1957, Carolingian Empire 1957, Urkundenwesen in Österreich 1971, Beiträge zur Mediaevistik, (Vol. 1) 1975, (Vol. 2) 1977, (Vol. 3) 1986, Lebensordnungen des 10. Jahrhunderts (2 vols.) 1984, Living in the Tenth Century 1991, Ketzer und Professoren 1992, Heretics and Scholars in the High Middle Ages, 1000–1200 1998. *Leisure interest:* bookworm. *Address:* 1A Mariahilfer Strasse, Vienna 1060, Austria.

FIEDLER, Leslie A., PH.D.; American professor of English and literary critic; b. 8 March 1917, Newark, N.J.; s. of Jacob Fiedler and Lillian Rosenstrauch; m. 1st Margaret Shipley 1939 (divorced 1972); three s. three d.; m. 2nd Sally Andersen 1973; two step-s.; ed. Harvard Univ., Univ. of Wisconsin and New York Univ. (Heights); mem. of Staff, Montana State Univ. 1941–63, Chair. Dept. of English 1954–56; Prof. of English, State Univ. of New York at Buffalo 1965–, Chair. Dept. of English 1974–77; Assoc. Fellow, Calhoun Coll., Yale Univ.; Samuel Clemens Prof., SUNY Distinguished Prof.; teaches at vacation courses at univs. in many parts of Europe and U.S.A.; Rockefeller Fellow 1946–47, Fulbright Fellow 1951–53, 1961–62; Kenyon Review Fellowship in Criticism and Christian Gauss Fellowship, Princeton Univ. 1956; Guggenheim Fellowship 1970–71; mem. American Acad. and Inst. of Arts and Letters 1988; Furioso Poetry Prize 1957, Award of Nat. Inst. of Arts and Letters 1957. *Publications include:* An End to Innocence: Essays on Culture and Politics 1955, The Art of the Essay 1958, Love and Death in the American Novel 1960, 1966, 1993, No! In Thunder: Essays on Myth and Literature 1960, Pull Down Vanity and Other Stories 1962, The Second Stone: A Love Story 1963, Waiting for the End 1964, Back to China 1965, The Last Jew in America 1966, The Return of the Vanishing American 1968, Nude Croquet and Other Stories 1969, Being Busted 1970, Collected Essays 1971, The Stranger in Shakespeare 1972; The Messengers Will Come No More 1974, In Dreams Awake 1975, Freaks 1977, 1993, Reader 1977, The Inadvertent Epic 1979, Olaf Stapledon 1982, What Was Literature? 1982, Fiedler on the Roof, Collected Essays 1991, Tyranny of the Normal 1996. *Leisure interests:* swimming and/or meditation. *Address:* Department of English, Clemens Hall, Amherst Campus, Buffalo, NY 14260; 154 Morris Avenue, Buffalo, NY 14214, U.S.A. (Home). *Telephone:* (716) 645-2573 (Office); (716) 838-4105 (Home).

FIELD, Helen; British singer; b. 14 May 1951, Wrexham, Clwyd, Wales; ed. Royal Northern Coll. of Music, Manchester and Royal Coll. of Music, London; studied Fed. Repub. of Germany; won triennial Young Welsh Singers' Competition 1976; roles with Welsh Nat. Opera include Musetta, Poppea, Kristina, Gilda, Marzelline, Mimi, Tatyana, Jenůfa, the Vixen, Marenka and Desdemona; has also appeared with Opera North and Scottish Opera; début at Royal Opera House, Covent Garden as Emma in Khovanschina 1982; début with English Nat. Opera, as Gilda 1982, at Metropolitan Opera, New York, as Gilda; has also appeared with Netherlands, Cologne and Brussels opera cos.; concert performances with several leading orchestras and regular radio and TV appearances; recordings include Rigoletto, A Village Romeo and Juliet and Osud. *Address:* c/o Lies Askonas Ltd., 186 Drury Lane, London, WC2B 5RY, England.

FIELD, Sir Malcolm David; British company director; b. 25 Aug. 1937, London; m. (divorced 1982); one d.; ed. Highgate School; joined W. H. Smith 1963, Wholesale Dir. 1970–78, Man. Dir. Retail Group 1978–82, Man. Dir. 1982–93; Group Chief Exec. 1994–96; Chair. C.A.A. 1996–; mem. Bd. of Man. NAAFI 1973–93, Chair. 1986–93; Dir. (non-exec.) MEPC 1989–, Scottish & Newcastle PLC 1993–98, Phoenix Group 1994–97, The Stationery Office 1996–, Walker Greenbank PLC 1997–, Sofa Workshop Ltd. 1998–. *Leisure interests:* cricket, tennis, ballet, art (watercolours), reading biographies. *Address:* 15 Eaton Square, London, SW1W 9DD, England. *Telephone:* 0171-245 0735.

FIELDHOUSE, David Kenneth, M.A., D.LITT. F.B.A.; British academic; b. 7 June 1925, India; s. of Rev E. Fieldhouse and C. H. B. Fieldhouse (née Cork); m. Sheila Elizabeth Lyon 1952; one s. two d.; ed. Dean Close School, Cheltenham, Queen's Coll. Oxford; war service as Sub.Lieut., R.N.V.R. 1943–47; Sr. History Master, Haileybury Coll. 1950–52; lecturer in History, Canterbury Univ., N.Z. 1953–57; Beit Lecturer in Commonwealth History, Oxford Univ. 1958–81; Vere Harmsworth Prof. of Imperial and Naval History, Cambridge Univ. 1981–92; Fellow Nuffield Coll. Oxford 1966–81, Jesus Coll. Cambridge 1981–92, Emer. 1992–. *Publications:* The Colonial Empires 1966, The Theory of Capitalist Imperialism 1967, Economics and Empire 1830–1914 1973, Unilever Overseas 1978, Black Africa 1945–1980 1986, Merchant Capital and Economic Decolonization 1994, The West and the Third World 1999. *Leisure interests:* golf, sailing, music. *Address:* Jesus College, Cambridge, CB5 8BL, England. *Telephone:* (01223) 339339.

FIELDING, Sir Leslie, K.C.M.G., F.R.S.A., F.R.G.S., LL.D.; British former diplomatist and university vice-chancellor; b. 29 July 1932, London; s. of Percy Archer Fielding and Margaret Calder Horry; m. Sally Harvey 1978; one s. one d.; ed. Emmanuel Coll., Cambridge, S.O.A.S., London, St. Antony's Coll., Oxford; with H. M. Diplomatic Service (served Teheran, Singapore, Phnom Penh, Paris and London) 1956–73; Dir. External Relations Directorate-Gen., European Comm., Brussels 1973–77; Visiting Fellow, St. Antony's Coll., Oxford 1977–78; Head European Community Del., Tokyo 1978–82; Dir.-Gen. for External Relations, Brussels 1982–87; Vice-Chancellor Univ. of Sussex 1987–92; mem. Japan-EC Asscn. 1988–, UK-Japan 2000 Group 1993–; mem. House of Laity of Gen. Synod of Church of England 1990–92; Hon. Pres. Univ. Asscn. for Contemporary European Studies 1990–; Hon. Fellow Sussex European Inst. 1993–; White Rose of Finland; Silver Order of Merit (Austria) 1989; Grand Officer's Star of Order of St. Agatha of San Marino. *Leisure interests:* country life, theology. *Address:* 5 St. Julian's Avenue, Ludlow, Shropshire, SY8 1ET, England.

FIELDSEND, Sir John Charles Rowell, K.B.E., B.A., LL.B.; British judge; b. 13 Sept. 1921, Lincoln; s. of Charles and Phyllis Fieldsend; m. Muriel Gedling 1945; one s. one d.; ed. Michaelhouse, Natal, Rhodes Univ. Coll., Grahamstown, S.A.; served Royal Artillery 1943–45; called to the Bar, S. Rhodesia 1947, Q.C. 1959; Advocate in private practice 1947–63; Pres. Special Income Tax Court for Fed. of Rhodesia and Nyasaland 1958–63; High Court Judge, S. Rhodesia 1963–68 (resigned); Asst. Solicitor, Law Comm. for England and Wales 1968–78; Sec. Law Comm. 1978–80; Chief Justice of Zimbabwe 1980–83; Chief Justice, Turks and Caicos Islands 1985–87; Judge, Court of Appeal, Falkland Islands and British Antarctic Territory 1985–96, Court of Appeal, Gibraltar 1985–97 (Pres. 1990); Prin. Legal Adviser, British Indian Ocean Territory 1984–87, Chief Justice 1987–. *Leisure interest:* travel. *Address:* Great Dewes, Ardingly, Sussex, RH17 6UP, England.

FIENNES, Ralph Nathanial; British actor; b. 22 Dec. 1962; s. of Mark Fiennes and Jini Lash; ed. St. Kieran's Coll., Kilkenny, Ireland, Bishop Wordsworth's School, Salisbury, Chelsea School of Art, Royal Acad. of Dramatic Art, London. *Plays include:* Twelfth Night, A Midsummer Night's Dream, Ring Round the Moon, Romeo and Juliet, Six Characters in Search of an Author, Fathers and Sons, Ting Tang Mine 1987, Hamlet 1995, Ivanov 1997; RSC plays include Much Ado About Nothing, King John, title role of Henry VI, in The Plantagenets 1988, The Man Who Came to Dinner, Playing with Trains 1989, Troilus and Cressida, King Lear, Love's Labour's Lost 1991. *Films include:* A Dangerous Man: Lawrence after Arabia (TV), Wuthering Heights, The Baby of Macon, The Cormorant (TV), Schindler's List, Quiz Show, Strange Days, The English Patient, Oscar and Lucinda, The Avengers, Eugene Onegin, The Taste of Sunshine. *Leisure interests:*

swimming, reading, music. *Address:* c/o Larry Dalzell Associates, 91 Regent Street, London, W1R 7TB, England.

FIENNES, Sir Ranulph Twisleton-Wykeham-, 3rd Bt., O.B.E., cr. 1916; British travel writer, lecturer and explorer; b. 7 March 1944, Windsor; s. of Lieut.-Col. Sir Ranulph Twisleton-Wykeham-Fiennes, D.S.O., 2nd Bt., and Audrey Newson; m. Virginia Pepper 1970; ed. Eton; Lieut. Royal Scots Greys 1966, Capt. 1968, retd. 1970; attached 22 SAS Regt. 1966, Sultan of Muscat's Armed Forces 1968; Leader, British Expdns. to White Nile 1969, Jostedalsbre Glacier 1970, Headless Valley, B.C. 1971, (Towards) North Pole 1977; Leader, Transglobe Expdn. (1st polar circumnavigation of world on its polar axis) 1979–82; led first unsupported crossing of Antarctic continent and longest unsupported polar journey in history Nov. 1992–Feb. 1993; Exec. Consultant to Chair. of Occidental Petroleum Corpn. Sept. 1984–; Hon. D.Sc. (Loughborough Coll.) 1986; Hon. D.Univ. (Univ. of Cen. England in Birmingham) 1995; Dhofar Campaign Medal 1969, Sultan's Bravery Medal 1970, Livingstone Medal, Royal Scottish Geographical Soc., Gold Medal of Explorers Club of N.Y. 1983, Founders Medal Royal Geographical Soc. 1984, Polar Medal for Arctic and Antarctic, with Bars 1985, with clasp 1995, ITN Award for Int. Exploit of the Decade 1989. *Publications:* A Talent for Trouble 1970, Ice Fall in Norway 1972, The Headless Valley 1973, Where Soldiers Fear to Tread 1975, Hell on Ice 1979, To the Ends of the Earth 1983, Bothie—The Polar Dog (with Virginia Twisleton-Wykeham-Fiennes) 1984, Living Dangerously 1987, The Feather Men 1991, Atlantis of the Sands 1992, Mind over Matter 1993, The Sett 1996, Fit for Life 1998. *Leisure interests:* langlauf, photography. *Address:* Greenlands, Exford, Minehead, West Somerset, TA24 7NU, England. *Telephone:* (01643) 831350.

FIERSTEIN, Harvey; American actor and screenwriter; b. 6 June 1954, Brooklyn, New York; ed. Pratt Univ.; began acting career as founding mem. The Gallery Players, Brooklyn; professional acting debut in Pork 1971; over sixty stage roles; wrote, and acted in, Torch Song Trilogy 1981 (Tony Award, Theatre World Award, Drama Desk Award for Best Actor; Tony and Drama Desk awards for Best Playwright); wrote, and acted in, Safe Sex 1987; *films include:* Annie Hall, Dog Day Afternoon, Mrs. Doubtfire, White Lies, Bullets Over Broadway, Dr Jekyll & Mrs Hyde, The Celluloid Closet 1995, Independence Day 1996, Everything Relative 1996, Krull the Conqueror 1997, Safe Men 1998, Legend of Mulan 1998; *TV appearances include:* The Demon Murder Case, Apology, Cheers 1992, Murder She Wrote 1992, Swellegant Elegance 1993; narrated The Life and Times of Harvey Milk, La Cage Aux Folles, Legs Diamond. *Address:* c/o AGF Inc., 30 W. 21st Street, Fl. 7, New York, NY 10010, U.S.A.

FIGES, Eva, B.A.; British writer; b. 15 April 1932, Berlin; d. of Emil Figes and Irma Unger; m. John Figes 1954 (divorced 1963); one s. one d.; ed. Kingsbury Co. School, Queen Mary Coll., Univ. of London; awarded Guardian Fiction Prize. *Publications include:* Patriarchal Attitudes 1970, Waking 1981, Light 1983, The Knot 1995. *Leisure interests:* music, films, theatre, visual arts. *Address:* 24 Fitzjohn's Avenue, London, NW3 5NB, England.

FIGGIS, Brian Norman, PH.D., D.SC., F.A.A.; Australian professor of inorganic chemistry; b. 27 March 1930, Sydney; s. of John N. E. Figgis and Dorice B. M. (née Hughes) Figgis; m. Jane S. Frank 1968; one s. one d.; ed. Univ. of Sydney, Univ. of New South Wales; Research Fellow, then Lecturer, Univ. Coll. London 1957–62, Visiting Prof. Univ. of Texas 1961, Reader Univ. of W. Australia 1963–69, Prof. 1969–, Visiting Prof. Univ. of Ariz. 1968, Univs. of Florence and Sussex 1975, Visiting Scientist Institut Laue-Langevin, Brookhaven Nat. Lab. and Argonne Nat. Lab. 1984, 1991; Burrows Award Royal Australian Chemical Inst. 1985, Walter Burfitt Prize, Royal Soc. of N.S.W. 1986; H. G. Smith Medal, Royal Australian Chemical Inst. 1989. *Publications:* Introduction to Ligand Fields 1966; 200 articles, Ed. Transition Metal Chemistry, Vols. 8 & 9, 1984–85. *Leisure interest:* building construction. *Address:* Department of Chemistry, University of Western Australia, Nedlands, W.A. 6907 (Office); 9 Hamersley Street, Cottesloe, W.A. 6011, Australia (Home). *Telephone:* 9 3803157 (Office); 9 3843032 (Home). *Fax:* 9 3801005.

FIGGIS, Mike; British film director, writer and musician; b. 1949, Kenya; came to England 1957; studied music, performing in band Gas Boad; musician in experimental theatre group The People Show in early 1970s; made ind. films including Redheugh, Slow Fade, Animals of the City; made film The House for Channel 4. *Films include:* Stormy Monday (debut, also screenplay and music) 1988, Internal Affairs (also music) 1990, Liebestraum (also screenplay and music) 1991, Mr. Jones 1993, The Browning Version 1994, Leaving Las Vegas (also screenplay and music) 1995; IFP Ind. Spirit Award 1996, Nat. Soc. of Film Critics Award. *Address:* c/o ICM, 8942 Wilshire Boulevard, Beverly Hills, CA 90211, U.S.A.

FIGUEIREDO, Elisio de; Angolan diplomatist; b. 13 June 1940; ed. studies in political science and int. affairs; mem. People's Movement for the Liberation of Angola (MPLA), active in independence campaign; worked at UN Secr., later spokesman of MPLA in various countries; MPL 89; rep. in U.S.A. 1974–76; Perm. Rep. to UN 1976–88; Amb. to U.K. 1988–89, to France 1989–94. *Address:* c/o Ministry of Foreign Affairs, Luanda, Angola.

FIGUEIREDO, Gen. João Baptista de; Brazilian politician and army officer; b. 15 Jan. 1918, Rio de Janeiro; s. of Euclydes and Valentina de Oliveira Figueiredo; m. Dulce Maria Guimarães de Castro 1942; two s.; ed. Mil. Acad., Advanced Training School for Officers, and Army Staff Coll.; became instructor at these establishments; with Brazilian Mil. Mission, Paraguay 1955–57; mem. Armed Forces Gen. Staff; Head Fed. Intelligence and Counter-Intelligence Service; Commdr. Public Security Force of State of São Paulo 1966–67, Horse Guards Regt. 1967–69; promoted to Brig.-Gen. 1969; Head of the Mil. Household 1969–74, of Nat. Information Service; Maj.-Gen. 1974, Gen. 1978; Pres. of Brazil 1979–85; Aliança Renovadora Nacional. *Address:* Av. Prefeito Mendes de Morães 1400/802, S. Conrado, Rio de Janeiro, Brazil.

FIGUERES OLSEN, José María; Costa Rican politician; s. of José Figueres Ferrer (fmr. Pres. of Costa Rica); mem. Partido de Liberación Nacional (PLN); fmr. Minister of Agric.; Pres. of Costa Rica 1994–98. *Address:* c/o Partido de Liberación Nacional, Sabana Oeste, San José, Costa Rica.

FIGUEROA, Adolfo, PH.D.; Peruvian economist, university professor and international consultant; b. 14 April 1941, Carhuaz; s. of Jose Manuel and Modesta Figueroa; m. Yolanda Vásquez 1965; one s. one d.; ed. Colegio Guadalupe (High School), Lima, San Marcos Univ., Lima, Vanderbilt Univ., Nashville, Tenn., U.S.A; Prof. of Econs., Catholic Univ. of Lima 1970–, Head Dept. of Econs. 1976–79, 1987–90, 1996–98; Dir. Research Project on Productivity and Educ. in Agric. in Latin America, ECIEL Program 1983-85; Consultant to ILO, FAO, Inter-American Foundation, Ford Foundation, IFAD, Inter-American Devt. Bank, World Bank; Visiting Prof. Univ. of Pernambuco, Brazil 1973, St. Antony's Coll., Oxford 1976, Univ. of Ill., U.S.A. 1980, Econs. Dept., Univ. of Nicaragua 1985, Univ. of Notre Dame, U.S.A. 1992, Univ. of Tex., Austin 1997; mem. Exec. Council Latin American Studies Asscn. (LASA) 1988–91, Editorial Advisory Bd., Journal of Int. Devt. 1988–92, World Devt. 1997–; Int. Network for Econ. Method, European Econ. Asscn., New York Acad. of Sciences. *Publications:* Estructura del Consumo y Distribución de Ingresos en Lima 1968–1969 1974, Distribución del Ingreso en el Perú 1975, La Economía Campesina de la Sierra del Perú 1981, Capitalist Development and the Peasant Economy in Peru 1984, Educación y Productividad en la Agricultura Campesina de América Latina 1986, Teorías Económicas del Capitalismo 1992, Crisis Distributiva en el Perú 1993, Social Exclusion and Inequality in Peru; articles in econ. journals. *Address:* Departamento de Economía, Universidad Católica del Perú, Apartado 1761, Lima 1 (Office); Robert Kennedy 129, Lima 21, Peru (Home). *Telephone:* (1) 4602870 (Office); (1) 4622286 (Home). *Fax:* (1) 460-1126; (1) 261-6241.

FIGUEROA SERRANO, Carlos; Chilean politician and lawyer; b. 28 Nov. 1930, Angol; s. of Carlos Figueroa and Isabel Serrano; m. Sara Guzmán 1953; seven c.; ed. Colegio de los Sagrados Corazones, School of Law, Universidad de Chile; practising lawyer 1957–, served at Appeals Court, Santiago 1971–72; Prof. of Procedural Law, Catholic Univ. of Chile 1960–76; joined Partido Demócrata Cristiano (PDC) 1957; Under-Sec. for Agric. 1967–69; Minister of Economy 1969–70; Acting Minister of Foreign Relations and of Finance, various occasions 1967–70; Pres. PDC Political Cttee. 1980; Del. for Providencia to Prov. Bd. of Eastern Santiago 1984–87; Head Communications and Publicity, Patricio Aylwin's Presidential Campaign 1989; Amb. to Argentina 1990–93; Dir. Communications and Publicity, Eduardo Frei's Presidential Campaign 1993; Minister for Foreign Affairs March–Sept. 1994, for Interior Sept. 1994–; Dir. CIC S.A. 1971–, Financiera Condell 1986–90, Pesquera Guafo S.A. 1987–89; Gen. Man. VEEP S.A. (bldg. contractors) 1980–86; Pres. Asociación Radiodifusoras de Chile 1972–78; Counsellor Asociación Iberamericana de Radiodifusión 1973–79, Sec. Bd. of Dirs. 1975–77. *Address:* Ministro del Interior, Palacio de la Moneda, Santiago, Chile.

FIIL, Niels Peter, PH.D.; Danish business executive; b. 8 Feb. 1941; s. of Svend Rasmussen and Gerda Fiil Rasmussen; m. Berthe M. Willumsen 1978; one d.; ed. Univ. of Copenhagen; Assoc. and Asst. Prof. Univ. of Copenhagen 1970–81; Visiting Prof. Harvard Medical School 1978–79; Man. Molecular Biology R&D, Novo Industri A/S 1980–86, Vice-Pres. 1987–, Vice-Pres., Pharmaceutical Biotechnology, Novo Nordisk A/S 1989–; mem. European Molecular Biology Org. 1979, Royal Danish Acad. of Science and Letters 1982, Royal Swedish Acad. of Eng. Science 1988. *Publications:* scientific papers in the field of microbial genetics and biotechnology. *Address:* Novo Nordisk A/S, Healthcare Chemistry, Novo Nordisk Park, 2760 Maalov (Office); Fuglebakkevej 5, 2000 Frederiksberg, Denmark (Home). *Telephone:* (45) 4444 8888 (Office).

FIKENTSCHER, Wolfgang, D.JUR.; German professor of law; b. 17 May 1928, Nuremberg; s. of Erich Fikentscher and Elfriede (née Albers) Fikentscher; m. Irmgard van den Berge 1956; three s. one d.; ed. Univs. of Erlangen, Munich and Ann Arbor, Mich.; teacher of Labour Law, Trade Union Schools 1952–56; Prof. of Law, Univ. of Münster 1958–65, Univ. of Tübingen 1965–71, Univ. of Munich 1971–; legal adviser Wacker-Chemie GmbH 1951–52; Fellow Netherlands Inst. for Advanced Study in the Social Sciences 1971–72, Santa Fe Inst. 1991–92, 1995–96, Gruter Inst. for Law and Behavioural Research 1992–. *Publications:* Methoden des Rechts in vergleichender Darstellung, (5 vols.) 1975–77, Wirtschaftsrecht (2 vols.) 1983, Modes of Thought 1995, Schuldrecht[9] 1997, numerous books and articles on civil and commercial law, antitrust law, int. law. *Leisure interest:* anthropology. *Address:* Institut für internationales Recht der Universität München, Ludwigstr. 29/II, 80539 Munich (Univ.); Mathildenstr. 8a, 82319 Starnberg, Germany (Home). *Telephone:* (089) 2180-2939 (Univ.); (08151) 13454 (Home).

FIKRE-SELASSIE, Wogderess; Ethiopian politician; mem. Shengo; fmr. Deputy Chair. Provisional Mil. Admin. Council, now mem.; Prime Minister of Ethiopia 1987–89.

FILALI, Abdellatif; Moroccan politician and diplomatist; b. 26 Jan. 1928, Fez; m.; ed. Univ. of Paris; joined Ministry of Foreign Affairs, rank of Amb. 1957; Perm. Rep. to the UN 1958–59; Chief of Royal Cabinet 1959–61; Chargé d'affaires, Embassy to France 1961–62; Amb. to Belgium, the Netherlands and Luxembourg 1962–63, to People's Repub. of China 1965–67, to Algeria 1967–68, to Spain 1970–71 and 1972–78; Minister of Higher Educ. 1968–70, of Foreign Affairs 1971–72; Perm. Rep. to the UN 1978–80; Amb. to U.K. 1980–81; Minister of Foreign Affairs, Co-operation and Information 1985–86, of Foreign Affairs and Co-operation 1986–98, Prime Minister of Morocco 1994–98; Perm. Sec. Acad. of Kingdom of Morocco 1981. *Address:* c/o Office of the Prime Minister, Rabat, Morocco.

FILARDO, Leonor, M.S.; Venezuelan banker and finance official; b. 1944; d. of Jesus Filardo and Carmen Vargas de Filardo; m. (divorced); three d.; ed. Caracas Catholic Univ., Surrey Univ.; worked for Cen. Bank of Venezuela 1970–75, Sr. Vice-Pres. Int. Operations 1979–84; Sr. Vice-Pres. of Int. Finance, Venezuelan Investment Fund 1975–79; Exec. Dir., World Bank Exec. Bd. 1984–86; Alt. Exec. Dir. IMF 1986–88, Exec. Dir. Nov. 1988–90; Vice-Pres. Cen. Bank of Venezuela, Rep. Office, Washington, D.C. 1990; fmr. Adviser to Cen. American and Venezuelan govts. on stabilization and structural adjustment programmes, participant in negotiations with IMF for External Fund Facility for Venezuela; Francisco de Miranda Medal, (1st Class) Venezuala 1990. *Leisure interests:* art, music, opera, travel, workout.

FILARET (see Philaret).

FILATOV, Sergey Alexandrovich, C.TECH.SC.; Russian politician; b. 10 July 1936, Moscow; s. of Alexander Filatov and Maria Filatova; m.; two d.; ed. Moscow Energy Inst.; constructor, head of project dept. "Serp i Molot" metallurgical plant 1957–66, engineer in Cuba 1966–68, chief engineer of project, leading constructor, Head of lab., Head of dept. Tselikov All-Union Research Inst. of Metallurgic Machine Construction 1969–90; People's Deputy of Russia 1990–93; mem. Supreme Soviet 1990–91, Sec. Presidium of Supreme Soviet 1991, First Vice-Chair. Supreme Soviet of Russia 1991–93; Head of Staff of Russian Pres. 1993–96; Chair. Comm. of Pres. of Russian Fed. for State Prizes in Literature and Art 1993–; f. Union of Progressive Forces 1997; State Prize of U.S.S.R. *Publication:* On the Way to Democracy 1995. *Address:* c/o Administration of the President, Staraya pl. 4, 103132 Moscow, Russia.

FILATOVA, Ludmila Pavlovna; Russian opera singer (mezzo-soprano); b. 6 Oct. 1935, Orenburg; d. of Pavel Filatov and Valentina Semoylova; m. Rudakov Igor 1971; ed. Faculty of Mathematics, Leningrad Univ.; mem. CPSU 1969–91; began singing in choir; mem. of Kirov Opera choir 1958–60; soloist with Kirov (now Mariinsky) Opera 1962–; teacher of singing, Leningrad Conservatoire 1973–; gives chamber concerts: Shostakovich, Tchaikovsky, Rachmaninov, Glinka etc.; Glinka Prize 1960; People's Artist of U.S.S.R. 1983. *Major roles include:* Lyubasha in A Bride for the Tsar, Marfa in Khovanshchina, Carmen, Marta-Ekaterina in Petrov's Peter I, Countess in The Queen of Spades. *Address:* Mariinsky Theatre, Teatralnaya pl. 1, St. Petersburg, Russia.

FILBINGER, Hans Karl, D. IUR.; German politician and lawyer; b. 15 Sept. 1913, Mannheim; s. of Johann Filbinger and Luise Filbinger; m. Ingeborg Breuer 1950; one s. four d.; ed. Albert-Ludwigs-Univ., Freiburg im Breisgau, Ludwig-Maximilians-Univ., Munich, and Univ. de Paris; teacher, Univ. of Freiburg 1937–40; war service and P.O.W. 1940–46; lawyer, Freiburg 1946–60; mem. Landtag of Baden-Württemberg 1960; Minister of Interior, Baden-Württemberg 1960–66; Minister-Pres. of Baden-Württemberg 1966–78; Pres. Bundesrat (Upper House) 1973–74; mem. Comm. on Decartelization Questions 1947; Founder mem. German-French Soc., Freiburg, Soc. for Supra-national Co-operation; mem. NATO Parl. Conf.; Chair. Baden-Württemberg Democrat (CDU) Fed.; Pres. Studienzentrum Weikersheim e.V.; Dr.rer.nat. h.c.; Grosskreuz des Bundesverdienstkreuzes, Officier Légion d'honneur and other awards. *Publications:* Die Schranken der Mehrheitsherrschaft im Aktienrecht und Konzernrecht 1942, Entscheidung zur Freiheit 1972, Hans Filbinger—der Fall und die Fakten 1980, Hans Filbinger—ein Mann in unserer Zeit 1983, Hans Filbinger-die geschmähte Generation 1987, Festschrift für Hans Filbinger. Deutschland als Kulturstaat 1993, Filbinger: Die Wahrheit aus den Stasi-Akten 1994. *Leisure interests:* mountain climbing, skiing. *Address:* Riedbergstrasse 29, 79100 Freiburg, Germany. *Telephone:* (0761) 290661. *Fax:* (0761) 290663.

FILIMON, Valeria; Romanian journalist; b. 29 May 1949, Butimanu; d. of Ion Dumitrescu and Maria Dumitrescu; m. Vasile Filimon 1984; ed. Univ. of Bucharest; freelance journalist for various Romanian dailies and literary magazines 1967–90; Assoc. Prof. 1970–90; journalist 1990–93; Ed.-in-Chief, The Modern Woman (magazine) 1993–98; Ed.-in-Chief Regala 1998–; Project Co-ordinator in Romania, Int. Fed. of Journalists 1996–; Vice-Pres. Journalists' Soc. of Romania; Romanian Writers' Union Prize. *Publications:* co-author of critical edition of Romanian novelist Liviu Rebreanu 1968–75; Lyceum (collection of literary criticism in two vols.) 1974. *Address:* Bd. Pache Protopopescu No. 11, Sector 2, 70311 Bucharest, Romania. *Telephone:* (00401) 315 24 82. *Fax:* (00401) 313 06 75.

FILIPACCHI, Daniel; French journalist; b. 12 Jan. 1928, Paris; s. of Henri Filipacchi and Edith Besnard; typographer, Paris-Match 1944, photographer 1948, head of information and dir. of photographic service 1953; fashion photographer, Marie-Claire 1957; producer of radio transmissions, Europe no 1, 1955, 1960; owner and dir. Jazz Magazine 1955, Cahiers du cinéma 1961–70; founder and dir. Salut les copains (became Salut 1976) 1961, Lui, Mlle Age tendre (became OK Age tendre 1976), Pariscope 1965, Photo 1967, Le monde des Grands Musées 1968, Ski 1969, Union 1972, Playboy France 1973–84, Girls 1982; editorial adviser to Newlook 1982, Penthouse 1984; Pres.-Dir.-Gen. WEA Filipacchi Music S.A. 1971–84, Cogedipresse; Owner and fmr. Dir. Paris-Match 1976–; mem. editorial cttee. Elle 1981–; Vice-Pres. Hachette 1981–93, Pres.-Dir.-Gen. Hachette Magazines Inc. (U.S.A.) 1990–; Pres.-Dir.-Gen. Filipacchi Médias SA 1993–97; Jt. Man. Cogédipresse 1994–97; Admin. and Hon. Pres. 1997 Hachette Filipacchi Médias 1997–. *Address:* Hachette Filipacchi Médias, Immeuble Europa, 149–151 rue Anatole-France, 92534 Levallois-Peret cedex, France.

FILIPOV, Grisha; Bulgarian politician (retd.); b. 13 July 1919, Kadiyevka, Ukraine; ed. Moscow Univ., USSR; returned to Bulgaria 1936; joined Bulgarian CP 1940; arrested for political activities and sentenced to 15 years' imprisonment 1941; released after coup 1944; various posts in party, including Head of Inspectorate in Ministry of Industry 1947; Counsellor, Deputy Head and Deputy Chair. of Cttee. on Planning 1951–58; Deputy Head of a Dept., Cen. Cttee. of Bulgarian CP 1958; cand. mem. Cen. Cttee. of Bulgarian CP 1962–66, mem. 1966–89, Sec. Cen. Cttee. 1971–82, 1986–89; Deputy Chair. State Planning Comm. 1962–66; mem. Politburo 1974–89; mem. State Council 1986–89; Chair. Council of Ministers 1981–86; fmr. mem. Nat. Assembly; arrested on corruption charges July 1992.

FILIPPENKO, Aleksander Georgyevich; Russian actor; b. 2 Sept. 1944, Moscow; m. 2nd Marina Ishimbayeva; one d.; ed. Moscow Inst. of Physics and Tech., Moscow, Shchukin Higher School of Theatre; sr. engineer Inst. of Geochemistry, U.S.S.R. Acad. of Sciences 1967–69; actor Amateur Theatre Nash Dom 1967–69, Taganka Theatre 1969–75, Vakhtangov Theatre 1975–94; f. and actor Experimental One-Man Theatre 1995–; staged Train to Chatanooga, Dead Souls, Fanbala. *Films include:* Star and Death of Joakin Murietta, My Friend Ivan Lapshin, Master and Marguerita; leads TV programme If 1997–98; Merited Artist of Russia. *Address:* Spiridonyevsky per. 8, Apt. 17, 103104 Moscow, Russia (Home). *Telephone:* (095) 202 77 15 (Home).

FILIPPOV, Vladimir Mikhailovich, DR. PHYSICS-MATH.; Russian politician and mathematician; b. 1951; m.; two c.; ed. Patrice Lumumba Univ. of Friendship of Peoples, Steklov Math. Inst. U.S.S.R. Acad of Sciences; asst., Chair of Higher Math., Chair. Council of Young Scientists, Head Dept. of Science, Lumumba Univ. of Friendship of Peoples 1973–85; Prof., Head, Chair of Math. Analysis, Dean, Faculty of Physics, Math. and Natural Sciences, Lumumba Univ. 1985–93, Rector 1993–98; Minister of Gen. and Professional Educ. of Russian Fed. Sept. 1998–. *Publications:* over 80 scientific works. *Address:* Ministry of General and Professional Education, Lyusinovskaya str. 51, 113833 Moscow, Russia. *Telephone:* (095) 928 4584 (Office).

FILLIOUD, Georges, L. EN D.; French politician and journalist; b. 7 July 1929, Lyon; s. of Marius Fillioud and Camille Metifiot; m. 1st Aimée Dieunet 1949; one s. one d.; m. 2nd Danielle Evennou 1996; ed. Ecole nationale professionnelle de Lyon, Univs. of Paris and Lyon; Journalist, Chief Reporter, then Sr. Ed., Europe No.1 radio station 1956–66; Deputy (Drôme) to Nat. Assembly 1967–68, 1973–81; Asst. Sec.-Gen. Convention des institutions républicaines 1970; Councillor, Romans 1970–77, Mayor 1977–81; Press Sec. Parti socialiste 1971–; Sec.-Gen. Féd. des élus socialistes et républicains 1972–; mem. Parl. Del. for French broadcasting 1974; Vice-Pres. Nat. Ass. Socialist Group 1978–79; Minister of Communication 1981–83, Sec. of State 1983–86; Conseiller d'État 1986; Admin., Pres. Institut national de l'audiovisuel (Ina) 1990–94. *Publications:* Le dossier du Vercors 1965, L'affaire Lindemans 1966, la Mort d'un chien 1988. *Address:* Ina, 4 av. de l'Europe, 94366 Bry-sur-Marne cedex (Office); 139 boulevard du Général Koening, 92200 Neuilly-sur-Seine, France (Home).

FILLON, François-Charles Amand; French politician; b. 4 March 1954, Mans; s. of Michel Fillon and Annie Soulet; m. Penelope Clarke 1980; three s. one d.; ed. Univ. of Maine, Univ. René-Descartes, Paris and Fondation Nationale des Sciences Politiques; Parl. Asst. to Joël Le Theule 1976–77; served in Office of Minister of Transport 1978–80, Office of Minister of Defence 1980–81; Head of Legis. and Parl. Work, Ministry of Industry 1981; Town Councillor, Sablé-sur-Sarthe, Mayor 1983–; Pres. Conseil Général, Sarthe 1992–98; RPR Deputy to Nat. Ass. 1981–93; Pres. Comm. for Nat. Defence and Armed Forces 1986–88; Minister for Higher Educ. and Research 1993–95; Minister of Information Tech. and Posts May–Nov. 1995, Minister del. Nov. 1995–97; spokesman Exec. Comm. RPR 1998–; Chair. Conseil régional des Pays de la Loire 1998–. *Address:* Mairie, 72300 Sablé-sur-Sarthe; Conseil régional des Pays de la Loire, 1 rue de la Loire, 44066 Nantes cedex 02 (Offices); Beaucé, 72300 Solesmes, France (Home).

FILMON, Gary Albert, M.SC.; Canadian politician; b. 24 Aug. 1942, Winnipeg, Man.; s. of Albert Filmon and Anastasia (Dosckocz) Filmon; m. Janice Wainwright 1963; two s. two d.; ed. Sisler High School, Univ. of Manitoba; consulting engineer, Underwood McLellan Ltd. 1964–69; Pres. Success/Angus Commercial Coll. 1969–80; Winnipeg City Councillor 1975–79; mem. Legis. Ass. for River Heights 1979–81, for Tuxedo 1981–; Minister of Consumer and Corp. Affairs and Environment, and Minister Reponsible for Man. Housing and Renewal Corpn. 1981; Leader Man. Progressive Conservative Party 1983–; Premier of Man., Pres. Exec. Council, Minister of Fed. Prov. Relations 1988–. *Address:* Office of the Premier, Legislative Building, Winnipeg, Man., R3C 0V8, Canada. *Telephone:* (204) 945-3714 (Office).

FILO, David; American computer executive; b. Moss Bluff, La.; ed. Stanford Univ. Calif.; co-f., Chief Exec. Yahoo! Inc. 1994–. *Address:* Yahoo! Incorporated, 3400 Central Expressway, 2nd Floor, Santa Clara, CA 95051, U.S.A.

FILOSA, Renato, PH.D.; Italian banker and economist; ed. Univ. of Rome, M.I.T.; joined Research Dept., Banca d'Italia 1967, Dir., Int. Div. 1984–86; Prof. of Political Econ., Univ. of Rome 1981–83; fmr. Asst. to Pres. of Ente Nazionale Idrocarburi (E.N.I.) and Dir., Energy and Econs Research Dept.; Exec. Dir. IMF 1989–93. *Address:* c/o Ministry of Finance, Viale America 242, 00144 Rome, Italy.

FINCH, Jon Nicholas; British actor, writer and director; b. 2 March 1943, Caterham, Surrey; s. of Arthur Leonard Finch and Nancy Karen Houghton; m. Catriona MacColl 1981 (divorced 1989); one d.; ed. Caterham School; served 21 Special Air Service (SAS) Regt. (Artists) Reserve 1960–63; theatre technician and dir. etc. 1963–67, actor in TV 1967–70; Hon. Dr. of Metaphysics; Most Promising Artiste, Variety Club of G.B. 1972. *Feature films since 1970 include:* lead role in Roman Polanski's Macbeth, Alfred Hitchcock's Frenzy, Lady Caroline Lamb, The Final Programme, El hombre de la cruz verde, Die estandarte, La sabina, Gary Cooper que estas en los cielos, La amenaza, La piú bella del reame, Une femme fidèle, Death on the Nile, Breaking Glass, Girocity, Doktor Faustus, Riviera, Paradiso, Plaza Real, Streets of Yesterday, The Voice, Beautiful in the Kingdom, Mirror, Mirror, Lurking Fear (U.S.A.), Darklands (U.K.), Lucan, Essex Boys. *TV films:* The Rainbow, Unexplained Laughter, A Love Renewed, Beautiful Lies, Maigret, Sherlock Holmes: The Mazarin Stone, Merlin's Crystal Cave, Dangerous Curves (U.S.A.), The Acts of Peter and Paul (U.S.A.), White Men are Cracking Up. *TV appearances:* Counterstrike (series), Steve, Ben Hall (series), Richard II, Henry IV parts I and II, Much Ado About Nothing, Make or Break, The Odd Job Man (series), Mary Queen of Scots, Casualty. *Theatre:* Les Liaisons Dangereuses, King Lear, The Importance of Being Earnest, Music to Murder By, The Invisible Man. *Leisure interests:* reading, collecting hip flasks. *Address:* 135 New King's Road, London, SW6 4SL, England. *Telephone:* 0171-736 6556.

FINCHAM, John Robert Stanley, PH.D., F.R.S.; British professor of genetics; b. 11 Aug. 1926, Southgate, Middx.; s. of Robert Fincham and Winifred Western; m. Ann Katherine Emerson 1950; one s. three d.; ed. Peterhouse and Botany School, Univ. of Cambridge; Lecturer in Botany, Univ. Coll. Leicester 1950–54, Reader in Genetics, Univ. of Leicester 1954–60; Head, Dept. of Genetics, John Innes Inst. 1960–66; Prof. and Head, Dept. of Genetics, Univ. of Leeds 1966–76, Univ. of Edinburgh 1976–84, Hon. Fellow Div. of Biology 1992–; Arthur Balfour Prof. of Genetics Univ. of Cambridge 1984–91, now Emer.; Professorial Fellow, Peterhouse, Cambridge 1984–91, now Emer.; Emil Christian Hansen Medal (Copenhagen) 1977. *Publications:* Fungal Genetics (with P. R. Day, later edns. also with A. Radford) 1963, Microbial and Molecular Genetics 1965, Genetic Complementation 1966, Genetics 1983, Genetically Engineered Organisms 1991, Genetic Analysis 1994, numerous articles in professional journals. *Address:* 20 Greenbank Road, Edinburgh, EH10 5RY, Scotland.

FINCK, August von; German business executive; b. 11 March 1930; owner, Bankhaus Merck, Finck & Co., Munich, Deutsche Spar- & Kreditbank AG, Munich, Carlton Holdings (controller of Mövenpick restaurant chain); majority shareholder, Löwenbräu AG, Munich, Würzburger Hofbräu AG. *Address:* Pacellistrasse 4, 80333 Munich, Germany.

FINDLAY, Ian Herbert Fyfe; British insurance broker; b. 5 Feb. 1918, Aberystwyth, Wales; s. of Prof. Alexander Findlay and Alice Mary (de Rougemont) Findlay; m. Alison Mary Ashby 1950; two s. one d.; ed. Fettes Coll., Edinburgh; served as Capt., R.A. 1939–45; Dir. Price, Forbes & Co. Ltd. 1953, Chair. 1967–72; Deputy Chair. Sedgwick Forbes (Holdings) Ltd. 1972–74, Chair. 1974–77; Chair. Lloyds Insurance Brokers Asscn. 1969–70, Cttee. of Lloyds 1971–74, 1976–79, Deputy Chair. Lloyds 1977, Chair. 1978–79; Chair. British Insurance Brokers' Asscn. 1980–82, Chair. Guide Dogs for the Blind Asscn. 1981–87, Vice-Pres. 1987–; Trustee, St. George's English School, Rome 1980–91; Gov. Brighton Coll. 1980–88; Pres. Sr. Golfers' Soc. 1990–93. *Leisure interests:* golf, postal history. *Address:* West Cottage, 1 The Close, Eliot Vale, London, SE3 0UR, England. *Telephone:* 0181-318 4644.

FINDLAY, Paul Hudson Douglas, B.A.; British opera director; b. 26 Sept. 1943; s. of the late John Niemeyer Findlay and Aileen May (née Davidson) Findlay; ed. Univ. Coll. School, London, Balliol Coll., Oxford, London Opera Centre; m. Françoise Christiane 1966; one s. one d.; Production and Technical Man. New Opera Co. 1967; Dir. London Sinfonietta 1967–; Stage Man. Glyndebourne Touring Opera and English Opera Group 1968; Asst. Press Officer Royal Opera House, Covent Garden 1968–72, Personal Asst. to Gen. Dir. 1972–76, Asst. Dir. 1976–87, Opera Dir. 1987–93; Man. Dir. Royal Philharmonic Orchestra 1993–95; Planning Dir. European Opera Centre 1997–; currently Arts Man. Kirov Ballet; Chair. Opera 80 1987; Cavaliere Ufficiale del Ordine al Merito della Repubblica Italiana; Chevalier des Arts et des Lettres 1991. *Leisure interests:* tennis, gardening, walking. *Address:* The London Sinfonietta, 4 Maguire Street, London, S.E.1., England.

FINE, Kit, PH.D.; British professor of philosophy; b. 26 March 1946, Farnborough; s. of Maurice Fine and Joyce Cicely Woolf; two d.; ed. Cheltenham Grammar School for Boys, Balliol Coll. Oxford; Prof., Univ. of Mich., Ann Arbor, U.S.A. 1978–88, Univ. of Calif., L.A. 1988–97, New York Univ. 1997–; Ed. Journal of Symbolic Logic 1978–87, Notre Dame Journal of Formal Logic 1984–87, Studies in Logic 1989–93; Guggenheim Fellow 1978–79; Fellow American Council of Learned Socs. 1981–82. *Publications:* Worlds, Times and Selves (with A. N. Prior) 1977, Reasoning with Arbitrary Objects 1985. *Leisure interests:* music, gardening, cooking. *Address:* Philosophy Department, 503 Main Building, New York University, New York, NY 10003, U.S.A.

FINETTE, Jean Regis, L. ÈS L.; Mauritian politician; b. 8 July 1934; m.; three c.; ed. Coll. Royal Curepipe and Port Louis, Univ. of Mauritius; Lecturer in Co-operative Studies, Univ. of Mauritius for 17 years; Deputy to Legis. Ass. 1982–; Minister for Local Govt. 1988–93, of Health 1993–96; Officier des Palmes Académiques. *Address:* Lothar Koenig Street, Cité Rosray, Beau Bassin, Mauritius.

FINI, Gianfranco; Italian politician; b. Bologna; mem. Movimento Sociale Italiano-Destra Nazionale (MSI) (now Alleanza Nazionale), Sec.-Gen. 1987–; fmr. journalist. *Address:* Alleanza Nazionale, Via della Scrofa 39, 00186 Rome, Italy. *Telephone:* (6) 68803014. *Fax:* (6) 6548256.

FINK, Gerald R., PH.D.; American professor of genetics; b. 1 July 1940, Brooklyn, New York; s. of Rebecca Fink and Benjamin Fink; m. Rosalie Lewis 1961; two d.; ed. Amherst Coll., Yale Univ.; Postdoctoral Fellow, Nat. Insts. of Health 1965–66, 1966–67; Instructor, Nat. Insts. of Health Graduate Program 1966; Instructor, Cold Spring Harbor Summer Program 1970–; Asst. Prof. of Genetics Cornell Univ. 1967–71, Assoc. Prof. 1971–76, Prof. 1976–79, Prof. of Biochemistry 1979–82; Prof. of Molecular Genetics, M.I.T. 1982–; American Cancer Soc. Prof. of Genetics 1979–; mem. Whitehead Inst. for Biomedical Research 1982–, Dir. 1990–; Sec. Genetics Soc. of America 1977–80, Vice-Pres. 1986–87, Pres. 1988–89; mem. N.A.S., American Acad. of Arts and Sciences; Hon. D.Sc. (Amherst Coll.) 1982; N.A.S.—U.S. Steel Prize in Molecular Biology 1981, Genetics Soc. of America Medal 1982, Yale Science and Eng. Award 1984, Emil Christian Hansen Foundation Award for Microbiological Research 1986. *Publications:* numerous scientific publs. *Address:* Whitehead Institute for Biomedical Research, 9 Cambridge Center, Cambridge, MA 02142, U.S.A.

FINLAY, Frank, C.B.E.; British actor; b. 6 Aug. 1926, Lancs.; s. of Josiah Finlay and Margaret Finlay; m. Doreen Joan Shepherd 1954; two s. one d.; ed. St. Gregory the Great, Farnworth, Royal Acad. of Dramatic Art, London; repertory 1950–52, 1954–57; Hon. Fellow (Bolton Inst.) 1992; Clarence Derwent Best Actor Award (for Chips with Everything) 1962, Best Actor Award, San Sebastian (for Othello) 1966, Soc. of Film and TV Arts Awards (for The Lie and Don Quixote), Best Actor Award (for Bouquet of Barbed Wire). *Stage appearances include:* Belgrade, Epitaph for George Dillon 1958, Sugar in the Morning, Sergeant Musgrave's Dance, Chicken Soup with Barley, Roots, I'm Talking About Jerusalem, The Happy Haven, Platonov, Chips with Everything 1958–62 (all at Royal Court), St. Joan, The Workhouse Donkey, Hobson's Choice 1963, Othello, The Dutch Courtesan 1964, The Crucible, Much Ado About Nothing, Mother Courage 1965, Juno and the Paycock, The Storm 1966 (all at Nat. Theatre), After Haggerty (Aldwych, Criterion), Son of Man (Leicester Theatre, Round House) 1970, Saturday Sunday Monday, The Party 1973, Plunder, Watch It Come Down, Weapons of Happiness 1976, Amadeus 1982 (all at Nat. Theatre), Kings and Clowns (Phoenix), Filumena (Lyric) 1978, The Girl in Melanie Klein 1980, The Cherry Orchard 1983, Mutiny (Piccadilly) 1985, Beyond Reasonable Doubt 1987, Black Angel 1990, A Slight Hangover 1991, The Heiress 1992, The Woman in Black 1993–94, Capt. Hook/Mr Darling in Peter Pan 1994, Gaslight 1995, The Handyman 1996. *Film appearances include:* The Longest Day, Private Potter, The Informers, A Life for Ruth, Loneliness of the Long Distance Runner, Hot Enough for June, The Comedy Man, The Sandwich Man, A Study in Terror, Othello, The Jokers, I'll Never Forget What's 'Is Name, The Shoes of the Fisherman, Deadly Bees, Robbery, Inspector Clouseau, Twisted Nerve, Cromwell, The Molly Maguires, Assault, Victory for Danny Jones, Gumshoe, Shaft in Africa, Van Der Walk and the Girl, Van Der Walk and the Rich, Van Der Walk and the Dead, The Three Musketeers, The Ring of Darkness, The Wild Geese, The Four Musketeers, The Thief of Baghdad, Sherlock Holmes—Murder by Decree, Enigma, Return of the Soldier, The Ploughman's Lunch, A Christmas Carol, The Key, Life Force, Sakharov, The Return of the Musketeers, King of the Wind, Cthulhu Mansion, Charlemagne, The Sparrow. *TV appearances include:* Julius Caesar, Les Misérables, This Happy Breed, The Lie, Casanova, The Death of Adolf Hitler, Don Quixote, Candide, Voltaire, Merchant of Venice, Bouquet of Barbed Wire, 84 Charing Cross Road, Saturday Sunday Monday, Count Dracula, The Last Campaign, Napoleon in Betzi, Dear Brutus, Tales of the Unexpected, Tales from 1001 Nights, Aspects of Love—Mona, Arc de Triomphe, In the Secret State, Verdict on Erebus, Mountain of Diamonds, Encounters, The Other Side, Stalin, Charlemagne, Exchange of Fire, Heartbeat, Dalgliesh, Sherlock Holmes. *Leisure interests:* reading, walking, the countryside. *Address:* c/o Ken McReady Ltd., 91 Regent Street, London, W1R 7TB, England. *Telephone:* 0171-439 1456. *Fax:* 0171-734 6530.

FINLAY, Ian Hamilton; Scottish artist and poet; b. 28 Oct. 1925, Nassau, Bahamas; s. of James Hamilton Finlay and Annie Whitelaw Finlay; one s. one d.; ed. Larchfield School, Helensborough, Dollar Acad.; served in army 1944–47; fmrly. shepherd, road labourer, author, gardener. *Solo exhibitions:*

'Inter Artes et Naturam', Musée d'Art Moderne, Paris 1987, 'Ideologische Ausserungen', Frankfurter Kunstverein 1991, Phila. Museum of Art 1991, 'Wildwachsende Blumen', Lenbachhaus, Munich 1993, 'Works, Pure and Political', Deichtorhallen, Hamburg 1995; also represented in various group exhbns. *Publications include:* Ian Hamilton Finlay—A Visual Primer 1992, Werke in Europa 1995, IHF, Prints 1963–97 1997. *Leisure interests:* model boats, model aeroplanes, fishing. *Address:* Stonypath, Little Sparta, Dunsyre, Lanark, ML11 8NG, Scotland. *Telephone:* (0189) 981-0252. *Fax:* (0189) 981-0252

FINLAY, Thomas Aloysius, B.A.; Irish lawyer; b. 17 Sept. 1922; s. of Thomas A. Finlay and Eva Finlay; m. Alice Blayney 1948; two s. three d.; ed. Xavier School, Dublin, Clongowes Wood Coll., University Coll.; called to the Bar, Dublin, King's Inn 1944; mem. Dail Eireann 1954–57; Sr. Counsel 1961; Bencher 1972; Judge of the High Court 1972, Pres. 1974; Chief Justice 1985–94; Hon. Bencher (Inn of Court, N. Ireland) 1985, (Middle Temple) 1986; Hon. LL.D. (Dublin, Nat. Univ. of Ireland) 1992. *Leisure interests:* fishing, shooting, conversation. *Address:* 22 Ailesbury Drive, Dublin 4, Ireland. *Telephone:* 2693395.

FINLEY, Gerald Hunter, M.A.; Canadian baritone; b. 30 Jan. 1960, Montreal; s. of Eric Gault Finley and Catherine Rae Hunter; m. Louise Winter 1990; two s.; ed. Glebe Collegiate Inst., Ottawa, Univ. of Ottawa, Royal Coll. of Music, London, U.K., Nat. Opera Studio, London, King's Coll. Cambridge; chorister St. Matthew's Church, Ottawa 1969–78; mem. Ottawa Choral Soc., Cantata Singers, Ont. Youth Choir 1977–78, Glyndebourne Festival Chorus, U.K. 1986–89; debut as opera soloist, Papageno in The Magic Flute, London 1989; roles at Glyndebourne: Sid (Albert Herring) 1989, Papageno, Guglielmo, Count Dominik (Arabella), Kuligin (Katya Kabanova) 1990–93, Figaro (Marriage of Figaro) at opening of new opera house 1994; Owen Wingrave, Olivier (Capriccio); debut Canadian Opera Co., Sid (Albert Herring) 1991; has sung Figaro at Covent Garden London and many other opera houses worldwide 1992–; other roles at Covent Garden include Pilgrim (Pilgrim's Progress), Achilla (Giulio Cesare); roles at Opéra de Paris include Valentin, Sharpless, Papageno, Figaro; debut Metropolitan Opera, New York, Papageno (Magic Flute) 1998; role of Mr. Fox in Fantastic Mr. Fox, L.A. Opera 1998; concert soloist and lieder singer. *Recordings:* Papageno, Guglielmo, Sid, Masetto, Haydn's The Creation, Brahms' Requiem, Pilgrim's Progress, Dido and Aeneas; John Christie Award, Glyndebourne 1989, A.R.C.M. 1980. *Leisure interests:* roller blading, interior/exterior design. *Address:* c/o IMG Artists Europe, 3 Burlington Lane, London, W4 2TH, England; c/o IMG Artists, 420 West 45th Street, New York, NY 10036, U.S.A. *Telephone:* 0181-233 5800 (London); (212) 541-5640 (U.S.A.). *Fax:* 0181-742 8758 (London); (212) 265-5483 (New York).

FINN, Victor Konstantinovich; DR.SC.; Russian philosopher, logician and computer scientist; b. 15 July 1933, Moscow; m. Irina Yevgenyevna Yavchunovskaya-Belova; one d.; ed. Moscow State Univ.; researcher, Head of sector, Lab. of Electromodelling, U.S.S.R. Acad. of Sciences 1957–59; Head of lab. All-Union Inst. for Scientific and Tech. Information (VINITI) 1959–; lecturer Moscow State Univ. 1967–68; Prof., Head Dept. of Artificial Intelligence Moscow State Inst. of History and Archives (now Russian Humanitarian Univ.) 1979–; mem. Acad. of Natural Sciences; mem. bd. int. journals Studia Logica, Foundation of Science; mem. Council Russian Asscn. of Artificial Intelligence. *Publications:* over 100 scientific papers and books Logical Problems of Information Search 1976, Epistemological and Logical Problems of History (with K. Khvostova) 1995. *Address:* 1st Miusskaya str. 20, Apt. 19, 125047 Moscow, Russia (Home). *Telephone:* (095) 251 0899 (Home).

FINNBOGADÓTTIR, Vigdís; Icelandic politician and teacher; b. 15 April 1930, Reykjavík; d. of Finnbogi Rutur Thorvaldsson and Sigridur Eiriksdóttir; m. (divorced); one adopted d.; ed. Junior Coll., Menntaskólinn i Reykjavík, Univs. of Grenoble and Sorbonne, France, Univ. of Iceland; taught French, Junior Colls., Menntaskólinn i Reykjavík, Menntaskólinn vid Hamrahlid; Iceland Tourist Bureau, Head Guide Training; Dir. Reykjavík Theatre Co. 1972–80; taught French drama, Univ. of Iceland; worked for Icelandic State TV; fmr. Chair. Alliance Française; mem. Advisory Cttee. on Cultural Affairs in Nordic Countries 1976–80, Chair. 1978–80; Pres. of Iceland 1980–96; Hon. Dr. (Grenoble) 1985, (Bordeaux) 1987, (Smith Coll., U.S.A.) 1988, (Luther Coll., U.S.A.) 1989, (Manitoba) 1989, Hon. LL.D. (Nottingham) 1990; Hon. G.C.M.G. 1982. *Leisure interest:* theatre.

FINNEY, Albert; British actor; b. 9 May 1936; m. 1st Jane Wenham (dissolved); one s.; m. 2nd Anouk Aimée 1970 (divorced 1978); ed. Salford Grammar School and Royal Acad. of Dramatic Art; Birmingham Repertory Co. 1956–58; Shakespeare Memorial Theatre Co. 1959; Nat. Theatre 1965, 1975; formed Memorial Enterprises 1966; Assoc. Artistic Dir. English Stage Co. 1972–75; Dir. United British Artists 1983–86; Hon. Litt.D. (Sussex) 1966; Lawrence Olivier Award 1986; London Standard Drama Award for Best Actor 1986, Dilys Powell Award, London Film Critics Circle 1999. *Plays include:* Julius Caesar, Macbeth, Henry V, The Beaux' Stratagem, The Alchemist, The Lizard on the Rock, The Party 1958, King Lear, Othello 1959, A Midsummer Night's Dream, The Lily-White Boys 1960, Billy Liar 1960, Luther 1961, 1963, Much Ado About Nothing, Armstrong's Last Goodnight 1965, Miss Julie 1965, Black Comedy 1965, Love for Love 1965, A Flea in her Ear 1966, A Day in the Death of Joe Egg 1968, Alpha Beta 1972, Krapp's Last Tape 1973, Cromwell 1973, Chez Nous 1974, Loot (Dir.) 1975, Hamlet 1976, Tamburlaine the Great 1976, Uncle Vanya 1977, Present Laughter 1977, The Country Wife 1977–78, The Cherry Orchard 1978, Macbeth 1978, Has "Washington" Legs? 1978, The Biko Inquest (Dir.) 1984, Sergeant Musgrave's Dance (Dir.) 1984, Orphans 1986, J. J. Farr 1987, Another Time 1989, Reflected Glory 1992, Art 1996. *Films acted in include:* The Entertainer 1959, Saturday Night and Sunday Morning 1960, Tom Jones 1963, Night Must Fall 1963, Two for the Road 1967, Scrooge 1970, Gumshoe 1971, Murder on the Orient Express 1974, Wolfen 1979, Loophole 1980, Looker 1980, Shoot the Moon 1981, Annie 1982, Life of John Paul II 1983, The Dresser 1983, Under the Volcano 1983, Miller's Crossing 1989, The Image 1989; Directed and acted in Charlie Bubbles 1968, Orphans 1987, The Playboys 1992, Rich in Love 1992, The Browning Version 1993, The Run of the Country 1995, Washington Square, Breakfast of Champions 1998. *TV appearances include:* The Endless Game 1989, The Green Man (mini-series) 1990, Karaoke 1995. *Address:* c/o Michael Simkins, 45/51 Whitfield Street, London, W1P 6AA, England. *Telephone:* 0171-631 1050.

FINNEY, David John, C.B.E., M.A., SC.D., F.R.S., F.R.S.E.; British professor of statistics and consultant biometrician; b. 3 Jan. 1917, Latchford, Warrington; s. of Robert George Stringer Finney and Bessie Evelyn Finney (née Whitlow); m. Mary Elizabeth Connolly 1950; one s. two d.; ed. Univs. of Cambridge and London; statistician, Rothamsted Experimental Station 1939–45; Lecturer in the Design and Analysis of Scientific Experiment, Univ. of Oxford 1945–54; Reader in Statistics, Univ. of Aberdeen 1954–64, Prof. of Statistics 1964–66; Prof. of Statistics, Univ. of Edin. 1966–84; Dir. Agricultural Research Council's Unit of Statistics 1954–84; Dir. Research Centre, Int. Statistical Inst., Netherlands 1987–88; Pres. Biometric Soc. 1964–65; Chair. Computer Bd. for Univs. 1970–74; Pres. Royal Statistical Soc. 1973–74; Visiting Scientist Int. Rice Research Inst. 1984–85; FAO "Key Consultant" to Indian Agricultural Statistics Research Inst. 1983–91; Hon. D. ès Sciences agronomiques (Gembloux), D.Sc. (City Univ., Heriot-Watt Univ.); Hon. Dr. Math. (Waterloo, Ont.) 1989. *Publications:* Probit Analysis 1947, 1952, 1971, Biological Standardization (with J.H. Burn and L.G. Goodwin) 1950, Statistical Method in Biological Assay 1952, 1964, 1978, Introduction to Statistical Science in Agriculture 1953, 1962, 1972, Experimental Design and its Statistical Basis 1955, Técnica y Teoría en el Diseño de Experimentos 1957, Introduction to the Theory of Experimental Design 1960, Statistics for Mathematicians 1968, Statistics for Biologists 1980; about 290 papers. *Leisure interests:* music, travel, statistics. *Address:* 13 Oswald Court, South Oswald Road, Edinburgh, EH9 2HY, Scotland. *Telephone:* (0131) 667-0135. *Fax:* (0131) 667-0135.

FINNEY, Joan Marie McInroy, B.A.; American politician; b. 12 Feb. 1925, Topeka; d. of Leonard McInroy and Mary M. Sands; m. Spencer W. Finney Jr. 1957; one s. two d.; ed. Washburn Univ.; mem. staff of Senator Frank Carlson 1953–69; Commr. of elections, Shawnee County, Kan. 1970–72; admin. asst. to Mayor of Topeka 1973–74; Treas. State of Kansas 1974–91; Gov. of Kansas 1991–95; mem. Bd. Dirs. Hayden High School, St. Francis Hosp., Fed. Democrat Women's Club and other bodies; Democrat. *Address:* c/o Governor's Mansion, State Capitol, Topeka, KS 67730, U.S.A.

FINNEY, Sir Tom, Kt., C.B.E.; British football official; b. 5 April 1922, Preston; joined Preston North End Football Club 1940, retd. 1960, now Pres.; played 433 league games for Preston, scored 187 goals; 76 England caps, scored 30 goals; Footballer of the Year 1954, 1957. *Publication:* Football Around the World 1953. *Address:* Preston North End Football Club, Deepdale, Sir Tom Finney Way, Preston, PR1 6RU, England. *Telephone:* (01772) 902020.

FINNIE, Linda Agnes; British singer; b. 9 May 1952, Paisley, Scotland; d. of William Finnie and Agnes Finnie; ed. John Neilson Institution, Paisley, Carrick Acad., Maybole, Royal Scottish Acad. of Music and Drama; concert performances in many European countries, Australasia, the Far East and U.S.A., and regular radio broadcasts; has sung with all the major British orchestras and with Chiacago, Boston, Pittsburgh and San Francisco Symphony orchestras, Hong Kong Philharmonic, Orchestre de Paris, Orchestre Philharmonique de Radio France, RAI Orchestra (Turin) and Danish Radio Orchestra, under many leading conductors, including Claudio Abbado, Lorin Maazel, Daniel Barenboim, André Previn, Michael Tilson-Thomas, Jeffrey Tate, Sir John Pritchard, Sir Colin Davis, Simon Rattle, Andrew Davis, Esa Pekka Salonen, Neemi Jarvi and Richard Hickox; opera roles with English Nat. Opera include Amneris, Eboli, Brangäne and Ulrica, with Royal Opera House, Waltraute, Mme. Larina, Second Norn; has also sung at Geneva, Nice, Bayreuth and Frankfurt; recordings include Alexander Nevsky, Elijah, Beethoven's 9th Symphony, Songs of the British Isles, Armide, La Rondine and l'Enfant et les Sortilèges; Kathleen Ferrier Memorial Award; Kathleen Ferrier Prize, 's Hertogenbosch Concours, John Noble Bursary, Countess of Munster Scholarship, Sir James Scholarship. *Leisure interests:* reading, driving, sewing, going to concerts and opera. *Address:* 16 Golf Course, Girvan, Ayrshire, KA26 9HW, Scotland.

FINNIS, John Mitchell, LL.B., D.PHIL., F.B.A.; Australian university teacher and barrister; b. 28 July 1940, Adelaide; s. of late Maurice M. S. Finnis and of Margaret McKellar Stewart; m. Marie Carmel McNally 1964; three s. three d.; ed. St. Peter's Coll., Adelaide, Univ. of Adelaide, Oxford Univ.; Fellow and Praelector in Jurisprudence, Univ. Coll., Oxford 1966–; Stowell Civil Law Fellow 1973–; Lecturer in Law, Oxford Univ. 1966–72, Rhodes Reader in the Laws of the British Commonwealth and the United States 1972–89, Prof. of Law and Legal Philosophy 1989–, mem. Philosophy Sub-

Faculty 1984–, Chair. Bd. of Faculty of Law 1987–89; Prof. and Head of Dept. of Law, Univ. of Malawi 1976–78; Biolchini Prof. of Law, Univ. of Notre Dame, Ind., U.S.A. 1995–; Barrister, Gray's Inn 1970–; Gov., Plater Coll., Oxford 1972–92; Consultor, Pontificia Commissio Iustitia et Pax 1977–89, mem. 1990–95; Special Adviser, Foreign Affairs Cttee., House of Commons, on role of U.K. Parl. in Canadian Constitution 1980–82; mem. Catholic Bishops' Jt. Cttee. on Bio-ethical Issues 1981–89, Int. Theological Comm. (Vatican) 1986–92; Gov., Linacre Centre for Medical Ethics 1981–96, 1998– (Vice-Chair. 1987–96); Distinguished Visiting Prof., Boston Coll. Law School 1993–94. *Publications:* Halsbury's Laws of England, 4th edn., vol. 6 (Commonwealth and Dependencies) 1974, Natural Law and Natural Rights 1980, Fundamentals of Ethics 1983, Nuclear Deterrence, Morality and Realism (with Joseph Boyle and Germain Grisez) 1987, Moral Absolutes 1991, Aquinas: Moral, Political and Legal Theory 1998; articles on constitutional law, legal philosophy, ethics and moral theology. *Address:* University College, Oxford, OX1 4BH; 12 Staverton Road, Oxford, OX2 6XJ, England (Home); Notre Dame Law School, Indiana, IN 46556, U.S.A. (Sept.–Dec.). *Telephone:* (01865) 276641 (Univ. Coll.); (01865) 558660 (Home); (219) 631-5989 (U.S.A.).

FINO, Bashkim Muhamet; Albanian politician and economist; b. 12 Oct. 1962, Gjirokaster; m.; two c.; ed. Tirana Univ.; economist Economic Data Inst., Gjirokaster Dist. 1986–89, Dir. 1989–92; Mayor of Gjirokaster (Socialist Party of Albania) 1992–96; Prime Minister of Albania March-July 1997; Deputy Prime Minister 1997–98. *Address:* c/o Council of Ministers, Këshilli i Ministrave, Tirana, Albania.

FIOLET, Herman Antonius, D.THEOL.; Netherlands ecclesiastic and writer; b. 15 Aug. 1920, Amsterdam; ed. High School, Katwijk and R. C. Univ., Nijmegen; ordained Priest 1946; Dir. Inst. for Lay Educ. 1953–59; Prof. of Dogmatical and Ecumenical Theol. 1959–73; Gen. Sec. Council of Churches in the Netherlands 1970–85; mem. Bd. of Ecumenical Devt. Co-operative Soc. 1974–83; many nat. and int. study comms.; Coebergh Prize for best ecumenical book in Netherlands (1960–68) 1968. *Publications:* 15 books including: Een kerk in onrust om haar belijdenis dissertation 1953, Verdeelde christenen in gesprek 1960, Onvermoed perspectief op de oecumene 1964, Dilemma doorbroken 1965, Vreemde Verleiding 1968, Tweede Reformatie 1969, De Kerk op de kruispunten van de geschiedenis (1882), Een vlinder kan niet terug in zijn cocon 1988, Als de graankorel niet sterft 1991, De zon verdwijnt niet, als zij ondergaat achter onze horizon 1994; and many articles in nat. and int. theological periodicals. *Leisure interests:* music, chess and skiing. *Address:* 's-Gravelandseweg 86 A 21, 1217 EW Hilversum, Netherlands. *Telephone:* 035-6212530.

FIONDA, Andrew, M.A.; British fashion designer; ed. Nottingham Trent Univ., Royal Coll. of art; designer for fashion houses in U.K. and for John McIntyre, Hong Kong; launched Pearce Fionda collection with Reynold Pearce (q.v.) 1994; exhbns. include Design of the Times, R.C.A. 1996, The Cutting Edge of British Fashion 1997; with Reynold Pearce received British Apparel Export Award for Best New Designer 1994, New Generation Award Lloyds Bank British Fashion Award 1995, Int. Apparel Fed. World Young Designers Award 1996. *Address:* Pearce Fionda, Studio S, 27 Horsell Road, London, N5 1XL, England. *Telephone:* 0171-609 6470. *Fax:* 0171-609 6470.

FIORENTINO, Linda; American actress; b. 1958, Philadelphia, Pa.; ed. Rosemont Coll., Circle in the Square Theatre School; mem. Circle in the Square Performing Workshops. *Films:* Vision Quest 1985, Gotcha! 1985, After Hours 1985, The Moderns 1988, Queens Logic 1991, Shout 1991, Wildfire 1992, Chain of Desire 1993, The Desperate Trail 1994, The Last Seduction 1994, Bodily Harm 1995, Jade 1995, Unforgettable 1997, The Split 1997, Men in Black 1997, Kicked in the Head 1997, Dogma 1998. *Films for TV include:* The Neon Empire 1989, The Last Game 1992, Acting on Impulse 1993, Beyond the Law 1994, The Desperate Trail. *Address:* c/o United Talent Agency, 9560 Wilshire Boulevard, Floor 5, Beverly Hills, CA 90212, U.S.A.

FIORI, Publio; Italian politician and lawyer; b. 1938; elected Christian Democrat mem. Rome City Council 1971, Lazio Regional Council 1975; Christian Democrat Deputy 1979–94, Alleanza Nazionale Deputy March 1994–; fmr. mem. Parl. Comm. on Finance, Under-Sec. for Posts and Telecommunications, for Health; Minister of Transport 1994–95. *Address:* c/o Alleanza Nazionale,Via della Scrofa 39, 00186 Rome, Italy.

FIRTH, Colin; British actor; b. 10 Sept. 1960; s. of David Firth and Shirley Firth; ed. Montgomery of Alamein School, Winchester and Drama Centre, London. *Theatre includes:* Another Country 1983, Doctor's Dilemma 1984, The Lonely Road 1985, Desire under the Elms 1987, The Caretaker 1991, Chatsky 1993. *Television appearances:* Dutch Girls 1984, Lost Empires (series) 1985–86, Robert Lawrence in Tumbledown 1987, Out of the Blue 1990, Hostages 1992, Master of the Moor 1993, The Deep Blue Sea 1994, Mr Darcy in Pride and Prejudice 1994. *Radio:* Richard II in Two Planks and a Passion 1986, Rupert Brooke in The One Before The Last 1987. *Films:* Another Country 1983, Camille 1984, A Month in the Country 1986, Apartment Zero 1988, Valmont (title role) 1988, Wings of Fame 1989, Femme Fatale 1990, The Hour of the Pig 1992, Good Girls 1994, Circle of Friends 1995, The English Patient 1996, Fever Pitch 1996, Shakespeare in Love 1998. Radio Times Best Actor award for Tumbledown, 1996 Best Actor award of Broadcasting Press Guild for Pride and Prejudice. *Address:* c/o ICM Ltd., Oxford House, 76 Oxford Street, London, W1N 0AX, England. *Telephone:* 0171-636 6565. *Fax:* 0171-323 0101.

FIRTH, Peter; British actor; b. 27 Oct. 1953, Bradford; s. of Eric Firth and Mavis Firth; m. Lindsey Readman 1990; one s. one d.; has appeared with Nat. Theatre in Equus, Romeo and Juliet, Spring Awakening; Broadway appearances include role of Mozart in Amadeus; has appeared in several TV films, plays and series. *Films include:* Brother Sun and Sister Moon, Daniel and Maria, Diamonds on Wheels, Aces High, Joseph Andrews, Equus, When You Coming Back Red Ryder?, Tess, Lifeforce, Letter to Brezhnev, A Tree of Hands, Prisoner of Rio, Burndown, The Pleasure Principle, The Perfect Husband, White Angel, Shadowlands, Brighton Boy, An Awfully Big Adventure, Brother Son and Sister Moon, Amistad, Mighty Joe Young; *Plays:* Equus, Romeo and Juliet, Spring Awakening; *TV appearances include:* The Flaxon Boys, Home and Away, Black Beauty, The Picture of Dorian Gray, Northanger Abbey, A Murder in Eden, The Laughter of God, Children Crossing, Anna Lee, The Man at the Top. *Address:* Susan Smith Associates, 121 North San Vicente Boulevard, Beverly Hills, CA 90211, U.S.A.

FIRTH, Sir Raymond William, Kt., M.A., PH.D., F.B.A.; British social anthropologist; b. 25 March 1901, Auckland, N.Z.; s. of Wesley Hugh Bourne Firth and Marie Elizabeth Jane Firth (née Cartmill); m. Rosemary Upcott 1936; one s.; ed. Auckland Univ. Coll. and London School of Econs.; field research in anthropology, Tikopia, Solomon Islands 1928–29; Lecturer in Anthropology, Univ. of Sydney 1930–31, Acting Prof. 1931–32; Lecturer in Anthropology, London School of Econs. (L.S.E.) 1932–35, Reader 1935–44, Prof. 1944–68; Emer. Prof. Univ. of London 1968–; Prof. Pacific Anthropology, Hawaii Univ. 1968–69; Visiting Prof. Univ. of British Columbia 1969, Cornell Univ. 1970, Univ. of Chicago 1955, 1970–71, Grad. Center City Univ. of New York 1971–72, Australia Nat. Univ., Canberra 1972–73, Univ. of Calif., Davis 1974, Berkeley 1977, Univ. of Auckland 1978; Hon. Sec. Royal Anthropological Inst. 1936–39, Pres. 1953–55; research in peasant econs. and anthropology in Malaya as Leverhulme Research Fellow 1939–40; served with Naval Intelligence Div. Admiralty 1941–44; Sec. of Colonial Social Science Research Council, Colonial Office 1944–45; research surveys in W. Africa 1945, Malaya 1947, New Guinea 1951; field research in Tikopia 1952, 1966, in Tikopia settlements 1973; Life Pres. Asscn. of Social Anthropologists of the Commonwealth; Hon. Life mem. N.Z. Asscn. of Social Anthropologists; Fellow, Center for Advanced Study in the Behavioral Sciences, Stanford, Calif. 1959; Hon. Fellow, L.S.E. and S.O.A.S., London Univ.; Foreign Hon. mem. American Acad. of Arts and Sciences, American Philosophical Soc., Royal Soc. of N.S.W., Royal Soc. of N.Z., Royal Danish Acad. of Sciences and Letters; Hon. Ph.D. (Oslo) 1965, (Jagiellonian Univ., Cracow) 1984, Hon. LL.D. (Michigan) 1967, Hon. D.Litt. (East Anglia) 1968, (Australian Nat. Univ.) 1969, (Exeter) 1972, (Auckland) 1978, Hon. D.Hum. Letters (Chicago) 1968, Hon. D.Sc. (British Columbia) 1970, Hon. D.Sc. Econ. (London) 1984; Viking Fund Medal 1959, Huxley Memorial Medal 1959. *Publications:* The Kauri Gum Industry 1924, Primitive Economics of the New Zealand Maori 1929, Art and Life in New Guinea 1936, We, The Tikopia: A Sociological Study of Kinship in Primitive Polynesia 1936, Human Types 1938, Primitive Polynesian Economy 1939, The Work of the Gods in Tikopia 1940, Malay Fishermen: Their Peasant Economy 1946, Elements of Social Organization 1951; Ed. Two Studies of Kinship in London 1956, Ed. Man and Culture: An Evaluation of the Work of Malinowski 1957, Social Change in Tikopia 1959, History and Traditions of Tikopia 1961, Essays on Social Organization and Values 1964, Ed. Themes in Economic Anthropology 1967, Tikopia Ritual and Belief 1967, Rank and Religion in Tikopia 1970, Families and their Relatives (with Jane Hubert and Anthony Forge) 1970, The Sceptical Anthropologist, Social Anthropology and Marxist Views of Society 1972, Symbols Public and Private 1973, Tikopia-English Dictionary 1985, Tikopia Songs (with Mervyn McLean) 1990, Religion: A Humanist Interpretation 1996. *Leisure interests:* Romanesque art, 15th-18th century music. *Address:* 33 Southwood Avenue, London, N.6, England. *Telephone:* 0181-348 0768.

FISCHER, Adam; Austrian conductor; b. 9 Sept. 1949, Budapest, Hungary; m. Doris Fischer 1979; one s. one d.; ed. Budapest School of Music; conducting and composition studies in Budapest and Vienna with Swarowsky; won jt. first prize Milan Cantelli Competition 1973; held posts at Graz Opera, Karlsruhe; Gen. Music Dir. Freiburg; work with Bavarian State Opera; regular conductor with Vienna State Opera 1973–, recently with Zurich Opera; major debuts Paris Opera 1984, La Scala 1986, Royal Opera House 1989, ENO 1991, San Francisco Opera 1991, Chicago Lyric Opera 1991, Metropolitan Opera, New York 1994; has conducted many world-class orchestras, particularly Helsinki Philharmonic and Vienna Chamber Orchestra; concert tours to Japan and U.S.A.; Music Dir. Kassel Opera 1987–92, f. and Artistic Dir. first Gustav Mahler Festival, Kassel 1989; f. Austro-Hungarian Haydn Festival and Orchestra, Eisenstadt, Austria 1987, now Music Dir. AHHO. *Address:* c/o Askonas Holt Ltd., Lonsdale Chambers, 27 Chancery Lane, London, WC2A 1PF, England. *Telephone:* 0171-400 1700. *Fax:* 0171-400 1799.

FISCHER, Andrea; German politician; b. 14 Jan. 1960, Arnsberg; ed. Freie Univ. Berlin 1985–90; trained as offset printer 1978–81; printer and corrector in Hamburg and Berlin 1981–85, also mem. Print and Paper TU, German TU Fed.; joined Greens Party 1985; worked as journalist 1985–90; research asst. for labour market and social affairs European Parl. 1990–91; researcher Berlin Science Centre 1991–94; mem. Bundestag 1994–; spokesperson of Alliance 90/Greens Parl. Group 1994–; Fed. Minister of Health 1998–.

Address: Ministry of Health, Am Proptshof 78A, 53121 Bonn, Germany. *Telephone:* (228) 9410. *Fax:* (228) 941-49-00.

FISCHER, Edmond H., D. ÈS SC.; American professor of biochemistry; b. April 1920, Shanghai, China; s. of Oscar Fischer and Renee C. (née Tapernoux) Fischer; m. Beverley B. Bullock; two s.; ed. Faculty of Sciences, Univ. of Geneva, Asst. Labs. of Organic Chem. Univ. of Geneva 1946–47; Fellow, Swiss Nat. Foundation 1948–50; Research Fellow, Rockefeller Foundation 1950–53; Privat-dozent, Univ. of Geneva 1950; Research Assoc. Div. of Biology, Calif. Inst. of Tech. 1953; Asst. Prof. Univ. of Washington 1953–56, Assoc. Prof. 1956–61, Prof. of Biochem. 1961–90, Prof. Emer. 1990–; mem. numerous cttees., professional orgs. etc.; mem. N.A.S., A.A.A.S., American Acad. of Arts and Sciences, Swiss Chem. Soc., British Biochem. Soc.; shared Nobel Prize for Medicine 1992, several other awards and honours; Dr. h.c. (Montpellier) 1985, (Basel) 1988. *Leisure interests:* classical piano, flying (private pilot). *Address:* 5540 N.E. Windermere Road, Seattle, WA, U.S.A. (Home). *Telephone:* 206-523-7372 (Home).

FISCHER, Erik, M.A.; Danish art historian; b. 8 Oct. 1920, Copenhagen; s. of Adolf Fischer and Ellen Henius; ed. Univ. of Copenhagen; Asst. Keeper of Prints and Drawings, Royal Museum of Fine Arts, Copenhagen 1948–57, Keeper of Prints and Drawings 1957–90; Asst. Prof. of Art History, Univ. of Copenhagen 1964–90; Chair. Danish State Art Foundation 1965–67, Bd., Queen Margrethe and Prince Henrik Foundation 1970–; Pres. Int. Advisory Cttee. of Keepers of Public Collections of Graphic Art 1971–76; Hon. mem. Germanisches Nationalmuseum, Nuremberg 1977; mem. Bd. Politiken Foundation 1990–; Fellow, Royal Danish Acad.; Assoc. Ateneo Veneto; D. Phil. h.c. (Copenhagen) 1991; Klein Prize 1973; Amalienborg Medal 1983, N.L. Høyen Medal, Royal Danish Acad. of Fine Arts 1989, Danish Literary Acad. Prize 1989, Ingenio et Arti Medal 1990; Kt., Order of Dannebrog, Order of Nordstjernen. *Publications:* Moderne dansk Grafik 1957, Melchior Lorck Drawings 1962, Tegninger af C.W. Eckersberg 1983, Von Abildgaard bis Marstrand 1985, Billedtekster (anthology) 1988, C. W. Eckersberg—His Mind and Times 1993. *Leisure interests:* nursing my arboretum, playing my piano. *Address:* Agergårdsvej 5, Ammendrup, DK-3200 Helsinge, Denmark. *Telephone:* 48-79 44 04. *Fax:* 48-79-44-04.

FISCHER, Ernst Otto, DR.RER.NAT., DIPL.CHEM.; German professor of chemistry, b. 10 Nov. 1918, München-Solln; s. of late Prof. Dr. Karl Tobias Fischer and Valentine Danzer; ed. Theresiengymnasium and Tech. High School, Munich; Lecturer in Chem. 1954–57, Prof. of Inorganic Chem. 1964; Prof. of Inorganic Chem., Munich Univ. 1957–64, Univ. of Marburg 1960, 1964; Firestone Lecturer, Univ. of Wis. 1969; Visiting Prof., Univ. of Fla. 1971; Inorganic Chem. Pacific West Coast Lecturer, U.S.A., Canada 1971; Arthur D. Little Visiting Prof., M.I.T. 1973; Visiting Distinguished Lecturer, Univ. of Rochester 1973; mem. Bayerische Akad. der Wissenschaften 1964, Deutsche Akad. der Naturforscher Leopoldina 1969; corresp. mem. Austrian Acad. of Sciences 1976, Acad. of Sciences Göttingen 1977; foreign mem. Accad. Naz. dei Lincei 1976; foreign hon. mem. American Acad. of Arts and Sciences 1977; Hon. Dr.rer.nat. (Univs. of Munich 1972, Erlangen, Nuremberg 1977, Veszprém 1983), Hon. D.Sc. (Strathclyde) 1975; American Chem. Soc. Centennial Fellow 1976; Göttinger Acad. Prize for Chem. 1957, Alfred-Stock-Gedächtnis Prize 1959, Nobel Prize for Chem. 1973. *Publications:* 500 scientific publs., $Fe(C_5H_5)_2$ Structure 1952, $Cr(C_6H_6)_2$ 1955, Übergangsmetall-Carben-Komplexe 1964, Übergangsmetall-Carbin-Komplexe 1973, Metal-Complexes Vol. I (with H. Werner) 1966. *Leisure interests:* history, arts, mountaineering. *Address:* Sohnckestrasse 16, 81479 Munich 71, Germany. *Telephone:* 794623.

FISCHER, Ivan; Hungarian/Dutch conductor; b. 20 Jan. 1951, Budapest; s. of Sándor Fischer and Éva Boschán; two d.; ed. B. Bartók Music Conservatory, Budapest and Wiener Hochschule für Musik under Hans Swarowsky, Mozarteum, Salzburg under Nikolaus Harnoncourt; Jt. Music Dir. Northern Sinfonia of England, Newcastle 1979–82; Music Dir. Kent Opera 1984–; Prin. Guest Conductor Cincinnati Symphony Orchestra 1989–96; founder and Music Dir. Budapest Festival Orchestra 1983; debut in London with Royal Philharmonic Orchestra 1976; concert tours with London Symphony Orchestra to Spain 1981, U.S.A. 1982, world tour 1983; concerts with Berlin Philharmonic Orchestra, Concertgebouw Orchestra etc.; main performances in U.S.A.: Los Angeles Philharmonic, Cleveland, Philadelphia, San Francisco Symphony and Chicago Symphony Orchestras; Operas: Idomeneo, Don Giovanni, Julius Caesar, La Bohème, La Clemenza di Tito, Marriage of Figaro, Magic Flute, in London, Paris, Vienna; Premio Firenze 1974, Rupert Foundation Award, BBC, London 1976, Gramophone Award for Best Orchestral Recording of the Year (for The Miraculous Mandarin), Philips 1998. *Address:* 1061 Budapest, 1 Andrássy út 27, Hungary. *Telephone:* (1) 342-6061.

FISCHER, Joschka; German politician; b. 12 April 1948, Gerabronn; mem. Greens Party 1982–, currently Leader; mem. German Bundestag 1983–85; Minister for Environment and Energy, Hessian Land 1985–87, for Environment, Energy and Fed. Affairs 1991–94; deputy mem. Bundesrat 1985–; Chair. Green Parl. Group Hessian Parl. 1987–91; Deputy Minister-Pres. of Hesse 1991–98; Vice-Chancellor and Minister of Foreign Affairs, Fed. Govt. Oct. 1998–; Speaker Parl. Group Alliance 90/Greens, Bundestag 1994–. *Address:* Bundeshaus, 53113 Bonn, Germany.

FISCHER, Karl Ingmar Roman; Austrian diplomatist; b. 1922; m. Eva Saga Paulsson 1979; ed. Volkschule, Realgymnasium, univ.; Fed. Ministry of Foreign Affairs 1949–53; Second Sec., Lisbon 1953–55, First Sec., Washington, D.C. 1955–59; Counsellor Ministry of Foreign Affairs 1954–63; Embassy, Paris 1963–70; in charge of Bilateral Econ. Relations, Ministry of Foreign Affairs 1970–74; Amb. to Sweden 1974–79; Chef de Cabinet, Deputy Sec.-Gen. for Foreign Affairs, Fed. Ministry of Foreign Affairs 1979–82; Amb. to Principality of Liechtenstein (resident in Vienna) 1981–84; Perm. Rep. of Austria to UN 1982–88; Vice-Pres. Austrian Cttee. of UNICEF 1989–. *Address:* Margaretenstrasse 6/14, A-1040 Vienna, Austria.

FISCHER, Paul Henning, D.IUR.; Danish diplomatist; b. 24 March 1919, Copenhagen; s. of Ernst Fischer and Ellen Dahl; m. Jytte Kalckar 1945; one s.; ed. Lyceum Alpinum, Zuoz, Switzerland and Univ. of Copenhagen; Foreign Service 1944–89, Stockholm, The Hague, Ministry of Foreign Affairs 1944–60; Asst. Prof. Univ. of Copenhagen 1948–52; Del. Gen. Ass., UN 1959, 1961; Amb. to Poland 1960–61; Perm. Under-Sec. of State for Foreign Affairs 1961–71; Amb. to France 1971–80, to Fed. Repub. of Germany 1980–89; mem. UN register for fact-finding experts in internal disputes; mem. Perm. Court of Arbitration, The Hague 1982; Judge ad hoc Int. Court of Justice, The Hague 1988; mem. CSCE Dispute Settlement Mechanism; Treasurer of the Royal Orders; Chamberlain of H.M. Queen Margrethe; Grand Cross Order of Dannebrog and foreign decorations. *Publications:* European Coal and Steel Community, International Law Studies on International Co-operation; numerous articles. *Leisure interests:* literature, music. *Address:* Straedet 8, Borsholm, DK-3100 Hornbaek, Denmark.

FISCHER, Robert James (Bobby); American chess player; b. 9 March 1943, Chicago, Ill.; s. of Gerard and Regina (Wender) Fischer; started to play chess aged 6; mem. Manhattan Chess Club 1955; U.S. Junior Chess Champion 1956, 1957; winner, U.S. Open Championship 1957, 1959, 1960, 1962, 1963; participated in Interzonal Tournament, Portoroz, Yugoslavia 1958; named Int. Grand Master (the youngest ever) 1958; has participated in numerous int. chess tournaments 1958–; defeated Boris Spassky (q.v.) to become World Chess Champion 1972–75, 1992; City of New York Gold Medal 1972. *Publications:* Games of Chess 1959, My Sixty Memorable Games 1969, Bobby Fischer Teaches Chess 1972. *Address:* c/o United States Chess Federation, 186 Route 9W, New Windsor, NY 12550, U.S.A.

FISCHER, Stanley, M.SC., PH.D.; American economist; b. 15 Oct. 1943, Lusaka, Zambia; s. of Philip Fischer and Ann Kopelowitz; m. Rhoda Keet 1965; three s.; ed. Univ. of London and M.I.T.; Postdoctoral Fellow Univ. of Chicago 1969–70, Asst. Prof. of Econs. 1970–73; Assoc. Prof. M.I.T. 1973–77, Prof. 1977–88, 1990, Killian Prof. 1992–94, Head of Dept. 1993; Vice-Pres. and Chief Economist World Bank, Washington D.C. 1988–90; Visiting Sr. Lecturer Hebrew Univ., Jerusalem 1972, Fellow Inst. for Advanced Studies 1976–77, Visiting Prof. 1984; Visiting Scholar Hoover Inst. Stanford Univ. 1981–82; Consultant on Israeli Economy Dept. of State 1984–87, 1991–94; First Deputy Man. Dir. IMF Sept. 1994–; Fellow Econometric Soc., American Acad. of Arts and Sciences. *Publications:* Rational Expectations and Economic Policy (Ed.) 1980, Indexing, Inflation, and Economic Policy 1986, Macroeconomics and Finance: Essays in Honor of Franco Modigliani (Ed.) 1987, Economics (with Dornbusch and Schmalensee) 1988, Lectures in Macroeconomics (jtly.) 1989, Macroeconomics (with Dornbusch) 1994, Ed. NBER Macroeconomics Annual and work on int. economic and macroeconomic issues. *Address:* Room 12, 300F, IMF, 700 19th Street, N.W., Washington, DC 20431; 15 Gralynn Road, Newton, MA 02159, U.S.A. (Home). *Telephone:* (617) 964-2494 (Home).

FISCHER, Timothy Andrew; Australian politician; b. 3 May 1946, Lockhart, N.S.W.; s. of J. R. Fischer; m. 1992; one s.; ed. Boree Creek School, Xavier Coll., Melbourne; joined Army 1966, officer with First Bn., Royal Australian Regt., Australia and Vietnam 1966–69; farmer. Boree Creek, N.S.W.; mem. N.S.W. Legis. Ass. 1970–84; M.P. for Farrer, N.S.W. 1984–; Shadow Minister for Veterans' Affairs 1985–89, and Deputy Man. of Opposition Business 1989–90; Leader Nat. Party of Australia 1990–; Shadow Minister for Energy and Resources 1990–93, for Trade 1993–96; Deputy Prime Minister and Minister for Trade March 1996–. *Leisure interests:* chess, tennis, skiing, water skiing, bush-walking, mountaineering. *Address:* Department of Foreign Affairs and Trade, Locked Bag 40, QVT, Canberra, A.C.T. 2600; P.O. Box 10, Boree Creek, N.S.W. 2652, Australia.

FISCHER-APPELT, Peter, DR.THEOL.; German university administrator; b. 28 Oct. 1932, Berlin; s. of Hans Fischer-Appelt and Margret Appelt; m. Hildegard Zeller 1959; two s. one d.; ed. Schubart-Oberschule, Aalen and Univs. of Tübingen, Heidelberg and Bonn; Scientific Asst., Protestant Theology Faculty, Univ. of Bonn 1961–70; Pastor, Köln-Mülheim 1964–65; co-founder and Chair. Bundesassistentenkonferenz, Bonn 1968–69; Pres. Univ. of Hamburg 1970–91, teaching assignment in Systematic Theology 1972–; Pres. 'Cyril and Methodius' Int. Foundation, Sofia 1992–96; mem. Exec. Cttee. Inter-Univ. Centre for Postgrad. Studies, Dubrovnik 1974–81, Chair. of Council 1981–98; mem. Standing Conf. on Univ. Problems, Council of Europe 1987–94, Deputy Chair. 1987–88, Chair. 1989–90; Chair. Steering Group, Higher Educ. Legislation Reform Programme for Cen. and Eastern Europe 1992–; mem. and Chair. Bd. of Trustees UNESCO Inst. for Educ., Hamburg 1992–96; mem. German Comm. UNESCO 1991–; mem. Bd. of Trustees, Deutscher Akad. Austauschdienst and various other comms., etc.; numerous hon. degrees; Gold Medal, Bulgarian Acad. of Sciences, Pro Cultura Hungarica Medal. *Publications:* Metaphysik im Horizont der Theologie Wilhelm Herrmanns 1965, Albrecht Ritschl und Wilhelm Herrmann 1968, Rechtfertigung 1968, Wissenschaft und Politik 1971, Zum Verständnis des Glaubens in der liberaten und dialektischen Theologie 1973, Zum Gedenken an Ernst Cassirer 1975, Integration of Young Scientists into the University 1975, Wilhelm Herrmann 1978, Hiob oder die Unveräusserlichkeit der Erde 1981, The Future of the University as a Research Institution 1982, Was darf ich hoffen? Erwartungen an das Musiktheater 1982, Die Oper als Denk- und Spielmodell 1983, Die Kunst der Fuge: Ein deutsches Forschungsnetz im Aufbau 1984, Dialogue and Co-operation for World Peace Today 1985, Die Universität zwischen Staatseinfluss und Autonomie 1986, Die Universität im Prozess der Humanisierung der Gesellschaft 1987, The University in the 21st Century 1988, Die Ostpolitik der Universitäten 1992, Wer hat Angst vor den Wandlungen der Universität 1994, Die Erhellung des Mythos durch die Sprache der Musik 1995, The University. Past, Present, and Future 1996, Concepts of the University 1997, Die Buchstaben und Europa 1997. *Leisure interests:* chess, skiing, music, opera, theatre. *Address:* Waldweg 22, D-25451 Quickborn-Heide, Germany. *Telephone:* (4106) 71212 (Home). *Fax:* (4106) 78637.

FISCHER-DIESKAU, Dietrich; German baritone; b. 28 May 1925, Berlin; s. of Dr. Albert Fischer-Dieskau and Dora Klingelhöffer; m. 1st Irmgard Poppen 1949 (died 1963); three s.; m. 2nd Ruth Leuwerik 1965 (divorced 1967); m. 3rd Kristina Pugell 1968; m. 4th Julia Varady 1978; ed. high school in Berlin, singing studies with Prof. Georg Walter and Prof. Hermann Weissenborn; mil. service 1943–45; P.O.W. in Italy until 1947; First Lyric and Character Baritone, Berlin State Opera 1948–; mem. Vienna State Opera Co. 1957–; Prof. of Singing Musikhochschule Berlin 1981; numerous concert tours in Europe, U.S.A. and Asia; has appeared at a number of festivals: Bayreuth, Salzburg, Lucerne, Montreux, Edinburgh, Vienna, Holland, Munich, Berlin, Coventry, etc.; best-known roles in Falstaff, Don Giovanni, The Marriage of Figaro, etc.; first performances of contemporary composers Britten, Henze, Tippett, etc.; mem. Akad. der Künste, Bayerische Akademie der Schönen Künste, Munich, Int. Mahler-Gesellschaft (Vienna) and German Section, Int. Music Council; Hon. mem. Wiener Konzerthausgesellschaft 1963, Royal Acad. of Music (London), Royal Acad. (Stockholm), Deutschen Oper, Berlin 1978, Royal Philharmonic Soc.; Hon. D.Univ. (Oxford) 1978, Hon. D.Mus. (Paris-Sorbonne) 1980, (Yale) 1980; Int. Recording Prizes almost every year since 1955; Berlin Kunstpreis 1950, Mantua Golden Orpheus Prize 1955; Bundesverdienstkreuz, 1st Class 1958; Edison Prize 1960, 1962, 1964, 1965, 1967, 1970; President's Prize, Charles Gros Acad., Paris 1980, Förderungspreis der Ernst-von-Siemens-Stiftung 1980; Mozart Medal 1962, Golden Orpheus 1967; Grosses Verdienstkreuz des Verdienstordens der Bundesrepublik Deutschland 1974; Grammy Award (more than once); Prix Mondial Montreux (more than once), etc.; Chevalier Légion d'honneur 1990; Ernst-Reuter-Plak 1993. *Publications:* Texte deutscher Lieder 1968, Auf den Spuren der Schubert-Lieder 1971, Wagner und Nietzsche, der Mystagoge und sein Abtrünniger 1974, Franz Schubert, ein Portrait 1976, Robert Schumann-Wort und Musik 1981, Töne sprechen, Worte klingen-Zur Geschichte und Interpretation des Gesanges 1985, Nachklang 1987, Wenn Musik der Liebe Nahrung ist: Künstlerschicksale im 19. Jahrhundert 1990, Johann Friedrich Reichardt: Kapellmeister dreier Preussenkönige 1992. *Leisure interest:* painting.

FISCHL, Eric, B.F.A.; American artist; b. 9 March 1948; ed. Phoenix Junior Coll., Ariz., Arizona State Univ., Tempe; California Inst. of the Arts; taught painting Nova Scotia Coll. of Art and Design, Halifax 1974–78; first one-man exhbn. Dalhousie Art Gallery, Halifax 1976; subsequent exhbns. at Mary Boone Gallery, New York, Whitney Museum, Mendel Art Gallery, Saskatoon, Sask., Edward Thorp Gallery, New York, Mario Diacono Gallery, Rome, Italy, Museum of Contemporary Art, Chicago, Sidney Janis Gallery, New York, 1984 Venice Biennale, 13th Biennale de Paris, 1985 Carnegie Int., Pittsburgh, numerous other exhbns.; works in Museum of Contemporary Art, L.A., Whitney Museum etc. and in pvt. collections, including Saatchi Collection, London, U.K.

FISCHLER, Franz; Austrian politician; b. 23 Sept. 1946, Absam, Tyrol; m.; one s. two d.; ed. Franciscan secondary school, Tyrol and Agricultural Univ., Vienna; Asst. Univ. of Vienna Dept. of Agricultural Man. 1973–79; Dept. Head Tyrolean Provincial Chamber of Agric. 1979, Sec. 1982, Dir. 1985–89; Minister of Agric. and Forestry 1989–94; EC Commr. for Agric. and Rural Devt. Jan. 1995–. *Address:* European Commission, av. d'Auderghem 45, B-1040, Brussels, Belgium. *Telephone:* (2) 299-1111.

FISHBURNE, Laurence; American actor; b. 30 July 1961, Augusta, Ga.; m. Hanja Moss 1985 (divorced); one s. one d. *Stage appearances include:* Short Eyes, Two Trains Running, Riff Raff (also writer and dir.). *Television appearances include:* One Life to Live (series, debut aged 11), Pee-wee's Playhouse, Tribeca (Emmy award 1993), A Rumour of War, I Take These Men, Father Clements Story, Decoration Day, The Tuskegee Airmen. *Film appearances include:* Cornbread Earl and Me 1975, Fast Break, Apocalypse Now, Willie and Phil, Death Wish II, Rumble Fish, The Cotton Club, The Color Purple, Quicksilver, Band of the Hand, A Nightmare on Elm Street 3: Dream Warriors, Gardens of Stone, School Daze, Red Heat, King of New York, Cadence, Class Action, Boyz N the Hood, Deep Cover, What's Love Got to Do With It? Searching for Bobby Fischer, Higher Learning, Bad Company, Just Cause, Othello, Fled, Hoodlums (also exec. producer), Event Horizon. *Address:* c/o Paradigm, 10100 Santa Monica Boulevard, 25th Floor, Los Angeles, CA 90067, U.S.A.

FISHER, Carrie; American actress and author; b. 21 Oct. 1956; d. of Eddie Fisher and Debbie Reynolds; m. Paul Simon 1983 (divorced 1984); one d.; ed. Beverly Hills High School and Cen. School of Speech and Drama, London; appeared with her mother in nightclub act aged 13; appeared in chorus of Broadway production of Irene, starring Debbie Reynolds, aged 15; Broadway stage appearances in Censored Scenes from King Kong, Agnes of God; several TV credits; film debut in Shampoo (Photoplay Award as Best Newcomer of the Year) 1974; PEN award for first novel Postcards From the Edge (also wrote screenplay). *Films include:* Star Wars, The Empire Strikes Back, Return of the Jedi, The Blues Brothers, Under the Rainbow, Garbo Talks, The Man With One Red Shoe, When Harry Met Sally . . ., Hannah and Her Sisters, The 'Burbs, Loverboy, Sibling Rivalry, Drop Dead Fred, Soapdish, This is My Life, Austin Powers. *Publications:* Postcards From the Edge 1987, Surrender the Pink 1990, Delusions of Grandma 1994 (novels); short stories. *Address:* Creative Artists Agency, 9830 Wilshire Boulevard, Beverly Hills, CA 90212, U.S.A.

FISHER, George, M.S., PH.D.; American business executive; b. 30 Nov. 1940, Anna, Illinois; m. Patricia Ann Wallace 1965; three c.; ed. Illinois Univ., Brown Univ.; joined research and devt. dept. Bell Telephone Labs. 1966; joined communications products div. Motorola Inc. 1976, Corp. Vice-Pres. 1983, Pres., C.E.O. 1988, Chair. 1990–93; Chair., Pres., C.E.O. Eastman Kodak 1993–; U.S. Council on Competitiveness. *Address:* Office of the Chairman, Eastman Kodak, 343 State Street, Rochester, NY 14650; P.O. Box 546, Pittsford, NY 14534, U.S.A.

FISHER, Hon. Sir Henry Arthur Pears, Kt., M.A.; British business executive, lawyer and college principal; b. 20 Jan. 1918, Repton, Derbyshire; s. of late Lord Fisher of Lambeth (Archbishop of Canterbury, 1945–61) and of Lady Fisher of Lambeth; m. Felicity Sutton 1948; one s. three d.; ed. Marlborough Coll., Christ Church, Oxford; served in Leics. Regt. (rank of Hon. Lieut.-Col.) 1940–46; Barrister-at-law 1947–68, Q.C. 1960, Judge of the High Court 1968–70; Dir. J. Henry Schroder Wagg and Co. Ltd. 1970–75, Thomas Tilling Ltd. 1970–83, Equity and Law Life Assurance Soc. Ltd. 1975–88; conducted inquiry into the Confait Case 1976–77; Chair. Bd. of Govs. Imperial Coll. 1975–88, of Council, Marlborough Coll. 1977–82, Cttee. of Inquiry into self-regulation at Lloyd's 1979–80, Appeal Cttee. of City Takeover Panel 1981–87, Investment Man. Regulatory Org. 1986–89; Pres. Wolfson Coll., Oxford 1975–85, Hon. Fellow 1985; Trustee, Pilgrim Trust 1965–92, Chair. 1979–83, 1989–92; Fellow, All Souls Coll., Oxford 1946–73, 1991–, Emer. 1976–91; Hon. mem. Lloyd's 1983; Hon. Fellow, Darwin Coll., Cambridge 1984; Hon. LL.D. (Hull) 1979. *Leisure interest:* music. *Address:* Garden End, Cross Lane, Marlborough, Wilts, SN8 1LA, England.

FISHER, Joel, B.A.; American sculptor; b. 6 June 1947, Ohio; s. of James R. and Marye (née Giffin) Fisher; m. Pamela Robertson-Pearce 1977 (separated); one s.; ed. Kenyon Coll. Ohio; over 30 one-person exhbns. and many group exhbns. in U.S.A. and Europe 1961–; works in many public collections; Kress Foundation Art History Award 1967, Gast der Berliner Kunstler Program des DAAD 1973–74, George A. and Eliza Gardner Howard Foundation Fellow 1987, Guggenheim Fellow 1993, Pollock-Krassner Foundation Award 1993. *Address:* 99 Commercial Street, Brooklyn, NY 11222 (Studio); P.O. Box 349, River Road, North Troy, VT 05859, U.S.A. (Home). *Telephone:* (718) 383-3704 (Studio); (802) 988-2870 (Home). *Fax:* (718) 389-6441.

FISHER, Michael Ellis, PH.D., F.R.S.; British professor of chemistry, physics and mathematics; b. 3 Sept. 1931, Trinidad, West Indies; s. of Harold Wolf Fisher and Jeanne Marie Fisher (née Halter); m. Sorrel Castillejo 1954; three s. one d.; ed. King's Coll., London; London Univ. Postgraduate Studentship 1953–56; DSIR Sr. Research Fellow 1956–58; Lecturer in Theoretical Physics, King's Coll., London 1958–62, Reader in Physics 1962–64, Prof. 1965–66; Prof. of Chem. and Math., Cornell Univ., U.S.A. 1966–73, Horace White Prof. of Chem., Physics and Math. 1973–89, Chair. Dept. of Chem. 1975–78; Wilson H. Elkins Prof., Inst. for Science and Tech., Univ. of Md. 1987–93, Distinguished Univ. Prof. and Regent's Prof. 1993–; Guest Investigator, Rockefeller Inst., New York 1963–64; Visiting Prof. of Applied Physics, Stanford Univ., U.S.A. 1970–71; Walter Ames Prof., Univ. of Wash. 1977; Visiting Prof. of Physics, M.I.T. 1979; Visiting Prof. of Theoretical Physics, Oxford 1985; Lorentz Prof., Univ. of Leiden 1993; Visiting Prof., Nat. Inst. of Standards and Tech., Gaithersburg, Md. 1993; George Fisher Baker Lecturer, Cornell Univ. 1997; John Simon Guggenheim Memorial Fellow 1970–71, 1978–79; mem. American Philosophical Soc.; Fellow A.A.A.S., American Acad. of Arts and Sciences; Foreign Assoc., N.A.S.; Foreign mem. Brazilian Acad. of Sciences; Festschrift and Conf. in honour of 60th Birthday: Current Problems in Statistical Mechanics 1991; Hon. F.R.S.E.; Hon. D.Sc. (Yale) 1987; D.Phil. h.c. (Tel Aviv) 1992; Jr. Collectors Silver Cup, British Philatelic Exhbn. 1946, Irving Langmuir Prize in Chemical Physics, American Physical Soc. 1970, Award in Physical and Math. Sciences, New York Acad. of Sciences 1978, Guthrie Medal, Inst. of Physics 1980, Wolf Prize in Physics, Israel 1980, Michelson-Morely Award, Case-Western Reserve Univ. 1982, James Murray Luck Award, N.A.S. U.S.A. 1983, Boltzmann Medal, Int. Union of Pure and Applied Physics 1983, Lars Onsager Medal, Norwegian Inst. of Tech. 1993, Joel H. Hildebrand Award for Chem. of Liquids 1995, Hirschfelder Prize in Theoretical Chem., Univ. of Wis. 1995, First Lars Onsager Memorial Prize, American Physical Soc. 1995, G. N. Lewis Memorial Lecture Award, Univ. of Calif. 1995. *Publications:* Analogue Computing at Ultra-High Speed (with D. M. MacKay) 1962, The Nature of Critical Points 1964; contribs. to scientific journals. *Leisure interests:* Flamenco guitar, travel. *Address:* Institute for Physical Science and Technology,

University of Maryland, College Park, MD 20742, U.S.A. *Telephone:* (301) 405-4819 (Office). *Fax:* (301) 314-9404.

FISHLOW, Albert, PH.D.; American professor of economics; b. 21 Nov. 1935, Philadelphia; m. Harriet Fishlow 1957; one s. two d.; ed. Univ. of Pennsylvania, Harvard Univ.; Acting Asst. Prof., Assoc. Prof., then Prof., Univ. of Calif. at Berkeley 1961–77, Prof. of Econs. 1983–, Chair. Dept. of Econs. 1973–75, 1985–89, Dean Int. and Area Studies 1990, Dir. Int. House 1990–, mem. Berkeley Foundation Trustees Int. Cttee. 1990–; Prof. of Econs., Yale Univ. 1978–83; Visiting Fellow, All Souls Coll. Oxford 1972–73 (Guggenheim Fellow); Co-Ed. Journal of Devt. Econs. 1986–; Dir.-at-large, Bd. of Social Science Research Council 1990–; Deputy Asst. Sec. of State for Inter-American Affairs 1975–76; mem. Council on Foreign Relations 1975–; Consultant to Rockefeller, Ford and other foundations, fmr. Consultant to World Bank, Inter-American Devt. Bank, UNDP; David Wells Prize, Harvard 1963, Arthur H. Cole Prize, Econ. History Asscn. 1966, Joseph Schumpeter Prize, Harvard 1971, Outstanding Service Award, Dept. of State 1976. *Publications include:* American Railroads and the Transformation of the Ante Bellum Economy 1965, International Trade, Investment, Macro Policies and History: Essays in Memory of Carlos F. Diaz-Alejandro (Co-Ed.) 1987; numerous articles. *Address:* Department of Economics, University of California, Berkeley, CA 94720, U.S.A. *Telephone:* (510) 642-4827. *Fax:* (510) 642-6615.

FISIAK, Jacek, O.B.E., PH.D., D.LITT.; Polish philologist and linguist; b. 10 May 1936, Konstantynów Łódzki; s. of Czesław Fisiak and Jadwiga Fisiak; ed. Warsaw Univ.; staff mem. Łódź Univ. 1959–67, Asst. Prof. 1962–67; staff mem. Adam Mickiewicz Univ., Poznań 1965–, Head English Philology Dept. 1965–69, Dir. English Philology Inst. 1969–, Extraordinary Prof. 1971–77, Prof. 1977–, Rector 1985–88; Chair. Comm. on Modern Languages and Literature, Ministry of Higher Educ. 1974–88; Minister of Educ. 1988–89; participant Round Table debates 1989; Visiting Prof. Univ. of Calif., L.A. 1963–64, Univ. of Kan. 1970, Univ. of Fla. 1974, State Univ. of New York 1975, American Univ., Washington, D.C. 1979–80, 1991–92, Univ. of Kiel 1979–80, Vienna Univ. 1983, 1988–89, 1990–91, Univ of Zürich 1984, 1994, Univ. of Tromsø 1986, Univ. of Jyväskylä 1987, Univ. of Saarbrücken 1990, 1993, Univ. of Bamberg 1994; Ed. Studia Anglica Posnaniensia 1967–, Papers and Studies in Contrastive Linguistics 1972–, Ed.-in-Chief Folia Linguistic Historia 1978–; Chair. Neophilological Cttee., Polish Acad. of Sciences 1981–93; mem. Finnish Acad. of Sciences and Humanities 1990, Academia Europaea 1990, Norwegian Acad. of Sciences 1996, New York Acad. of Sciences 1996; ; Pres. Polish-British Friendship Soc. 1989–(2000); mem. editorial bds. of numerous foreign and int. philological journals, numerous scientific socs.; Dr. h.c. (Jyväskylä) 1982; Commdr.'s Cross of Polonia Restituta Order with Star, Nat. Educ. Comm. Medal, Commdr.'s Cross of Lion of Finland Order, Officier, Ordre des Palmes académiques and numerous other decorations. *Publications:* 153 publs., 33 books including Morphemic Structure of Chaucer's English 1965, A Short Grammar of Middle English 1968, Recent Developments in Historical Phonology 1978 (ed.), Historical Syntax (ed.) 1983, A Bibliography of Writings for the History of English 1987, Historical Dialectology (ed.) 1990, An Outline History of English 1993, Medieval Dialectology 1995, Linguistic Change Under Contact Conditions 1995. *Leisure interests:* history, sport. *Address:* ul. Sniadeckich 30 m. 8, 60 774 Poznań, Poland. *Telephone:* (61) 865-97-64.

FISICHELLA, Domenico: Italian politician and university professor; b. 15 Sept. 1935, Messina, Sicily; Prof. of Political Science, Università La Sapienza and Libera Università Internazionale degli Studi Sociali (LUISS), Rome; co-f. Alleanza Nazionale Party 1992, elected Senator March 1994; Minister of Culture 1994–95. *Publications:* numerous books on political subjects; articles in national dailies. *Address:* c/o Ministero per i beni culturali e Ambientali, Via del Collegio Romano 27, 00186 Rome, Italy.

FISK, David John, SC.D.; British government scientist; b. 9 Jan. 1947; s. of late John Fisk and Rebecca Haynes; m. Anne Thoday 1972; one s. one d.; ed. Stationers' Co. School, Hornsey, St. John's Coll. Cambridge and Univ. of Manchester; joined Bldg. Research Establishment, Sr. Prin. Scientific Officer, Head, Mechanical and Electrical Eng. Div. 1978–84; Asst. Sec. Dept. of Environment, Cen. Directorate of Environmental Protection 1984–87; Under-Sec. Dept. of Environment 1987–, Chief Scientist 1988–97, Dir. Air Climate and Toxic Substances 1990–95, Environmental Protection and Int. Directorate 1995–; Visiting Prof. Univ. of Liverpool 1988–. *Publications:* Thermal Control of Buildings; numerous papers on bldg. science, systems theory and econs. *Leisure interests:* theatre, music. *Address:* c/o Department of the Environment, Transport and the Regions, Ashdown House, 123 Victoria Street, London, SW1E 6DE, England.

FISMER, Christiaan Loedolff; South African politician; b. 1956, Pretoria; s. of William Fismer and Elizabeth Fismer; m. Linda Mills; twin d.; ed. Univ. of Pretoria; mil. service; admitted to Pretoria Bar 1986; practised as advocate 1986–87; fmr. Chair. Student Rep. Council, Univ. of Pretoria, Pres. Afrikaanse Studentebond (ASB – umbrella org. for univ. governing bodies); mem. Nat. Party; co-f. Nat. Party Youth Action; M.P. for Rissik 1987, Sr. Transvaal Whip of Nat. Party 1989; apptd. party rep. to Conf. for a Democratic S. Africa (CODESA) working group on implementation of decisions 1991; Prov. leader Nat. Party in Eastern Transvaal 1994; fmr. Deputy Minister in Office of State Pres. F.W. de Klerk; Deputy Minister of Justice 1994–95; Minister of Gen. Services 1995–96, of Provincial and Constitutional Affairs March–May 1996; pvt. law practice 1996–; Univ. of Pretoria Gold Medal. *Address:* c/o National Party, Private Bag X402, Pretoria 0001, South Africa. *Telephone:* (12) 348-3100. *Fax:* (12) 348-5645.

FISZEL, Roland Henri Léon; French engineer; b. 16 July 1948, Paris; s. of Jean Fiszel and Marie Eber; m. Nadine Kohn 1974; one s. two d.; ed. Lycée Pasteur, Neuilly-sur-Seine, Ecole polytechnique, Massachusetts Inst. of Tech., U.S.A.; Head of Housing Dept., Ministry of Construction 1974–77; Head of Studies and Planning Group, Infrastructure Div., Hauts-de-Seine department 1977–81; Deputy Sec.-Gen. Codis-Cidise, in charge of Treasury 1981–82; Tech. Adviser, Office of Minister of Social Affairs and Nat. Solidarity 1983–84, then of Minister of the Economy and Finance 1984–86; Dir. Nat. Printing Office 1986–92; Adviser to Chair. of Euris 1996–; Ingénieur en chef des ponts et chaussées; Dir. representing State, Agence Havas 1986–87; Dir. Antenne 2 1988–92; fmr. Sec.-Gen. Caisse nationale du Crédit agricole. *Leisure interests:* skiing, tennis. *Address:* Euris, 83 rue du Faubourg Saint-Honoré, 75008 Paris (Office); 4 rue Jobbé Duval, 75015 Paris, France (Home).

FITCH, Val Logsdon, B.ENG., PH.D.; American physicist; b. 10 March 1923, U.S.A.); s. of Fred B. and Frances M. (née Logsdon) Fitch; m. 1st Elise Cunningham 1949 (died 1972); two s. (one deceased); m. 2nd Daisy Harper Sharp 1976; ed. McGill and Columbia Univs.; U.S. Army 1943–46; Instructor, Columbia Univ. 1953–54, Princeton Univ. 1954, Prof., Princeton Univ. 1960–, Chair. Dept. of Physics 1976, Cyrus Fogg Brackett Prof. of Physics 1976–84; James S. McDonnel Distinguished Univ. Prof. of Physics 1984–; Sloan Fellow 1960–64; mem. N.A.S., American Acad. of Arts and Sciences, President's Science Advisory Cttee. 1970–73; Research Corpn. Award 1968; Ernest Orlando Laurence Award 1968, John Witherill Medal, Franklin Inst. 1976; Nobel Prize for Physics jointly with J. W. Cronin (q.v.) for work on elementary particles 1980, Minister of Provincial Affairs and of Constitutional Devt. 1994–96. *Publications:* Major publs. in area of elementary particles. *Leisure interest:* conservation. *Address:* P.O. Box 708, Princeton University, Department of Physics, Princeton, NJ 08544, U.S.A. *Telephone:* (609) 452-4374.

FITCHEW, Geoffrey Edward, C.M.G., M.A., M.SC.; British international civil servant; b. 22 Dec. 1939, Manchester; s. of Stanley Edward Fitchew and Elizabeth Scott; m. Mary Theresa Spillane 1966; two s.; ed. Uppingham School, Magdalen Coll., Oxford and London School of Econs.; Pvt. Sec. to Perm. Sec., Dept. of Econ. Affairs, 1966–67, Pvt. Sec. to Minister of State, H.M. Treasury 1967–68; Financial Counsellor, U.K. Perm. Rep. to EEC 1978–80; Under-Sec. European Communities Group 1983–85, Under-Sec. External Finance Group 1985–86, Dir. Gen., Banking, Financial Insts. and Co. Law, Comm. of the European Communities 1986–93; Deputy Sec. Cabinet Office 1993–94; Chair., First Commr. Bldg. Socs. Comm., Chief Registrar of Friendly Socs. 1994–; mem. Bd. of Dirs., European Investment Bank 1983–85; Gwilym Gibbon Research Fellow, Nuffield Coll., Oxford 1973–74; Oxford Univ. Ancient History Prize 1962. *Leisure interests:* golf, tennis, squash, reading. *Address:* Building Societies Commission, Victory House, 30-34 Kingsway, London, WC2B 6ES, England.

FITERMAN, Charles; French politician; b. 28 Dec. 1933, Saint-Etienne; s. of Moszek Fiterman and Laja Rozenblum; m. Jeannine Poinas 1953; Departmental Sec. Jeunesse Communiste 1952; Sec. CGT, Saint-Etienne S.F.A.C. 1958–62; Dir. Cen. School, Parti communiste français (PCF) 1963–65; elected to PCF Cen. Cttee. 1972, to Political Bureau and Cen. Cttee. Sec. 1976; Gen. Councillor, Head, econ. section and PCF Rep. to liaison cttee. of signatory parties to Common Programme of the Left 1977; Deputy (Val-de-Marne) to Nat. Assembly 1978–81; Minister of State, Minister of Transport 1981–84; Deputy for Rhône 1986–88; Mayor of Tavernes 1989–; f. Refondations movt. 1990, Convention pour une alternative progressiste 1994; Pres. Forum Alternatives Européennes. *Address:* Forum Alternatives Européennes, 1 bis rue de Paradis, 75010 Paris, France. *Telephone:* (01) 44.83.93.40.

FITOUSSI, Jean-Paul Samuel, D. ÈS SC. ECON.; French economist; b. 19 Aug. 1942, La Goulette; s. of Joseph Fitoussi and Mathilde Cohen; m. Anne Krief 1964; one s. one d.; ed. Acad. Commerciale, Paris and Univs. of Paris and Strasbourg; Asst. lecturer 1968–71; Dir. of Studies 1971–73; Maître de conférence agrégé 1974–75; Prof. 1975–78; Titular Prof. 1978–82; Dean. Faculty of Econ. Science and Dir. Dept. of Econ. Science, Strasbourg 1980–81; Prof. in charge of research prog. on foundation of macroeconomic policy, Inst.universitaire européen, Florence 1979–83; Prof. Inst. d'Etudes Politiques, Paris 1982–; Dir. Dept. of Studies Observatoire Français des Conjonctures Economiques (OFCE) 1982–89, Pres. 1990–; Chair. Scientific Council of Inst. d'Etudes Politiques, Paris 1997–; Sec.-Gen. Int. Econ. Asscn. 1984–; consultant to EC Comm. 1978–; mem. Bd. Ecole Normale Supérieure, Paris 1998–; External Prof. Univ. européenne, Florence 1984–93; Prize of Asscn. Française de Sciences Economiques, Prize of Acad. des Sciences Morales et Politiques; Chevalier Ordre nat. du Mérite. *Publications:* Inflation, équilibre et chômage 1973, Le fondement macroeconomique de la théorie Keynesienne 1974, Modern Macroeconomic Theory 1983, Monetary Theory and Economic Institutions (with N. de Cecco) 1985, The Slump in Europe (with E. Phelps) 1988, Competitive Disinflation (with others) 1993, Pour l'emploi et la cohésion sociale 1994, Le débat interdit: monnaie, Europe, pauvreté 1995, Economic Growth, Capital and Labour Markets 1995, Le nouvel âge des inégalités (with Pierre Rosanvallon) 1996; contrib. to collected publs. *Leisure interests:* travel, cinema, guitar, scuba-diving. *Address:* Observatoire Français des Conjonctures Economiques, 69 quai d'Orsay, 75340 Paris Cedex 07, France. *Telephone:* (01) 44.18.54.01. *Fax:* (01) 44.18.54.71.

FITT, Baron (Life Peer), cr. 1983, of Bell's Hill in the County of Down, **Gerard Fitt;** British politician; b. 9 April 1926, Belfast; s. of George Patrick Fitt and Mary Ann Fitt; m. Susan Doherty 1947 (died 1996); five d. (and one d. deceased); entered local politics in Belfast 1955; mem. Northern Ireland Parl., Stormont, for Dock Constituency 1962–72; mem. U.K. Parl., Westminster, for Belfast West 1966–83 (Republican Labour 1966–70, SDLP 1970–79, Socialist 1979–83); Deputy Chief Exec., N. Ireland Assembly 1974–1975; Leader, Social Democratic and Labour Party (SDLP), resigned Nov. 1979. *Address:* House of Lords, London, SW1A 0PW, England.

FITTIPALDI, Emerson; Brazilian racing driver; b. 12 Dec. 1946, São Paulo; s. of Wilson and Juze Fittipaldi; m. 1st Maria Helena Dowding 1970; one s. two d.; m. 2nd Teresa Hotte 1995; ed. scientific studies; Brazilian Champion Formula V and Go-Kart 1967; Formula 3 Lombard Championship 1969; World Champion 1972, 1974; Second in World Championship 1973, 1975. *Leisure interests:* tennis, radio control aeroplanes and all kinds of sports.

FITZGERALD, Edmund B., B.S.E.; American business executive; b. 5 Feb. 1926, Milwaukee; s. of Edmund and Elizabeth Bacon Fitzgerald; m. Elisabeth McKee Christensen 1947; two s. two d.; ed. Univ. of Michigan; fmr. Chair. and C.E.O. Cutler-Hammer Inc., Milwaukee; then Vice-Chair. and C.O.O., Industrial Products, Eaton Corpn. (following merger with Cutler-Hammer); Pres. Northern Telecom Inc., U.S.A. (subsidiary of Northern Telecom Ltd.) 1980–82; C.E.O. Northern Telecom Ltd. 1984–89, Chair. 1985–90; Adjunct Prof. of Man. Vanderbilt Univ., Nashville 1990–; Man. Dir. Woodmont Assocs., Nashville 1990–; Dir. Ashland Oil Inc., Becton Dickinson and Co., GTI; mem. Pres. Reagan's Nat. Telecommunications Security Advisory Council; Trustee, Cttee. for Econ. Devt., Washington, D.C.; fmr. Pres. Nat. Electrical Mfrs. Asscn.; fmr. Vice-Chair. Industry Advisory Council, Dept. of Defense. *Address:* Woodmont Associates, 3434 Woodmont Blvd., Nashville, TN 37215, U.S.A.

FITZGERALD, Frances; American author; b. 1940; d. of Desmond Fitzgerald and Marietta Peabody Fitzgerald Tree; ed. Radcliffe Coll.; author of series of profiles for Herald Tribune magazine; freelance author of series of profiles, Vietnam 1966; Overseas Press Club Award 1967; Nat. Inst. of Arts and Letters Award 1973; Pulitzer Prize 1973; Nat. Book Award 1973; Sydney Hillman Award 1973; George Polk Award 1973; Bancroft Award for History 1973. *Publications:* Fire in the Lake: The Vietnamese and the Americans in Vietnam 1972, America Revised 1979; articles in magazines. *Address:* c/o Simon and Schuster Inc., 1230 Avenue of the Americas, New York, NY 10020, U.S.A.

FITZGERALD, Garret; Irish politician and economist; b. 9 Feb. 1926, Dublin s. of late Desmond Fitzgerald and Mabel McConnell; m. Joan O'Farrell 1947; two s. one d.; ed. Belvedere Coll., Univ. Coll. and King's Inns, Dublin; called to the Bar 1946; Research and Schedules Man. Aer Lingus 1947–58; Rockefeller Research Asst., Trinity Coll., Dublin 1958–59; Lecturer in Political Econ. Univ. Coll., Dublin 1959–73; fmr. Chair. and Hon. Sec. Irish Br., Inst. of Transport; mem. Seanad Éireann 1965–69; mem. Dáil Éireann for Dublin South-East 1969–92; Leader and Pres. Fine Gael 1977–87; Minister for Foreign Affairs 1973–77; Taoiseach (Prime Minister) of Repub. of Ireland 1981–82, 1982–87; Pres. Council of Ministers of EEC Jan.–June 1975, European Council July–Dec. 1984, fmr. Pres. Irish Council of European Movt.; fmr. Vice-Pres. European People's Party, European Parl.; mem. Senate Nat. Univ. of Ireland 1973–; fmr. Man. Dir. Economist Intelligence Unit of Ireland; mem. Trilateral Comm. 1987–95; Dir. GPA Group 1987–93, Int. Inst. for Econ. Devt., London 1987–, Trade Devt. Inst. 1987–, Comer Int. 1989–94, Point Systems Int. 1996–; mem. Radio Telefís Éireann Authority; fmr. Irish Corresp. BBC, Financial Times, Economist, Columnist Irish Times; Hon. LL.D. (New York, St. Louis, Keele, Boston Coll., Westfield Coll., Mass., Nat. Univ. of Ireland); Hon. D.C.L. (St. Mary's Univ., Halifax, Nova Scotia) 1985, (Oxford) 1987, Order of Christ (Portugal) 1986, Order of Merit (Germany) 1987, Grand Cordon, Order of the Rising Sun (Japan) 1989, Commdr. Légion d'honneur 1995. *Publications:* State-sponsored Bodies 1959, Planning in Ireland 1968, Towards a New Ireland 1972, Unequal Partners (UNCTAD) 1979, Estimates for Baronies of Minimum Level of Irish Speaking Amongst Successive Decennial Cohorts 1771–1781 to 1861–1871 1984, The Israeli/Palestinian Issue 1990, All in a Life (autobiog.) 1991. *Address:* 30 Palmerston Road, Dublin 6, Ireland. *Telephone:* 496-2600. *Fax:* 496-2126.

FITZGERALD, Penelope Mary, B.A.; British writer and teacher; b. 17 Dec. 1916, Lincoln; d. of E. V. Knox and Christina Hicks; m. Desmond Fitzgerald 1942; one s. two d.; ed. Somerville Coll., Oxford; English Tutor, Westminster Tutors, London 1965–; Booker McConnell Prize for Fiction 1979, Rose Mary Crawshay Prize for Charlotte Mew and her Friends 1984, Heywood Hill Award for Literary Achievement 1996. *Publications:* (biography) Edmund Burne-Jones 1975, The Knox Brothers 1977; (novels) The Golden Child 1978, The Bookshop 1978, Offshore 1979, Human Voices 1980, At Freddies 1982, Charlotte Mew and her Friends 1984, Innocence 1986, The Beginning of Spring 1988, The Gate of Angels 1990, The Blue Flower 1995; ed. William Morris's Unpublished Novel on Blue Paper 1982. *Leisure interests:* her nine grandchildren. *Address:* c/o HarperCollins, 77–85 Fulham Palace Road, Hammersmith, London, W6 8JB, England.

FITZGERALD, Peter Gosselin, A.B., J.D.; American politician; b. 20 Oct. 1960, Elgin, Ill.; s. of Gerald Francis Fitzgerald and Marjorie (née Gosselin) Fitzgerald; m. C. Nina Kerstiens 1987; one s.; ed. Dartmouth Coll., Univ. of Michigan; called to Bar Ill. 1986; with U.S. Dist. Court Ill. 1986; Assoc. Isham, Lincoln & Beale 1986–88; partner Riordan, Larson, Bruckert & Moore 1988–92; counsel Harris Bankmont Inc. 1992–96; mem. Ill. Senate 1993–99, Chair. State Govt. Operations Cttee. 1997–99, Senator from Illinois Jan. 1999–; mem. various bds. and asscns.; Republican. *Address:* 117 West Slade Street, Palatine, IL 60067, U.S.A.

FITZGERALD, Peter Hanley, PH.D., D.SC., F.R.C.PATH., F.R.S.N.Z.; New Zealand director of cancer research (retd.); b. 10 Oct. 1929, Gore; s. of John J. Fitzgerald and Nora Eileen (née Hanley) Fitzgerald; m. Kathleen O'Connell 1955 (divorced 1988); three s. two d.; ed. St. Bede's Coll., Christchurch, Univ. of Canterbury, Univ. of New Zealand and Univ. of Adelaide; Dir. Cancer Soc. of N.Z. Cytogenetic and Molecular Oncology Unit, Christchurch School of Medicine 1967–95; Pres. N.Z. Genetics Soc. 1978, N.Z. Soc. for Oncology 1973–74; mem. Nat. Scientific Cttee. Cancer Soc. of N.Z. 1981–85, Int. Scientific Advisory Bd. Cancer Congress, Seattle 1982, Canterbury Museum Trust Bd. 1985–, Royal Soc. of N.Z. Council 1986–89; Hon Cytogeneticist Canterbury Area Health Bd. 1967–95; Hon. Lecturer in Botany and Zoology Univ. of Canterbury 1971–95, in Pathology 1979–90, Prof. (Research Fellow), Christchurch School of Medicine, Univ. of Otago 1990–95; Sir George Grey Scholarship 1952; N.Z. Nat. Research Fellowship 1955–57; Human Genetics Soc. of Australia Orator 1994 (Pres. N.Z. Branch 1990); Hon. Life mem. Cancer Soc. N.Z. 1995, N.Z. Soc. for Oncology 1995. *Publications:* over 140 publs. on cancer-related topics. *Leisure interests:* gardening, walking, music, literature. *Address:* Cytogenetic and Molecular Oncology Unit, Christchurch Hospital, Christchurch (Office); 115 Gardiners Road, Christchurch 5, New Zealand (Home). *Telephone:* (64)3 3640881 (Office); (64)3 3594244 (Home). *Fax:* (64)3 3640750 (Office); (64) 3 3594104 (Home).

FITZGERALD, Stephen Arthur, A.O., B.A., PH.D.; Australian scholar and diplomatist; b. 18 Sept. 1938, Hobart, Tasmania; s. of F. G. FitzGerald; m. Helen Overton; one s. two d.; ed. Tasmania Univ., Australian Nat. Univ.; Dept. of Foreign Affairs 1961–66; Research Scholar, Australian Nat. Univ. 1966–69, Research Fellow 1969–71, Fellow 1972–73, Professorial Fellow 1977–,Head Dept. of Far Eastern History 1977–79, Head Contemporary China Centre, Research School of Pacific Studies 1977–79; Amb. to People's Repub. of China (also accred. to Democratic People's Repub. of Korea) 1973–76; Ed. Australian Journal of Chinese Affairs; Deputy Chair. Australia-China Council 1979–86; mem. Australian Acad. of Science Sub-Cttee. on Relations with China; Trustee, Australian Cancer Foundation 1985–; Chair. Asian Studies Council 1986–91; Chair. and Man. Dir. Stephen Fitzgerald and Co. Ltd.; Chair. Asia-Australia Inst., also Prof. Univ. of New South Wales 1990–; Co-Chair. Jt. Policy Cttee. on Relations between Northern Territory and Indonesia; mem. council Musica Viva Australia. *Publications:* China and the Overseas Chinese 1972, Talking with China 1972, China and the World 1977, Immigration A Commitment to Australia (jtly.) 1988, A National Strategy for the Study of Asia in Australia (jtly.) 1988, Asia in Australian Education (jtly.) 1989, Australia's China (jtly.) 1989, Ethical Dimension to Australia's Engagement with Asia 1993, Is Australia an Asian Country? 1997. *Address:* P.O. Box 620, Woollahra, N.S.W. 2025, Australia. *Telephone:* (02) 9665-7603. *Fax:* (02) 9665-9108.

FITZGERALD, Tara; British actress; b. 1969; stage debut in Our Song, London; appeared in London as Ophelia in Hamlet 1995; TV appearances include The Black Candle, The Camomile Lawn, Anglo-Saxon Attitudes, Six Characters in Search of an Author, Fall from Grace, The Tenant of Wildfell Hall, The Student Prince, Woman in White, Frenchman's Creek. Theatre: Our Song (London), Hamlet (New York). *Films:* Sirens 1994, The Englishman who went up a hill but came down a mountain 1995, Brassed Off 1996, Childhood 1997, Conquest 1998, New World Disorder 1998. *Address* c/o Caroline Dawson Associates, 19 Sydney Mews, London, SW3 6HL, England.

FITZGERALD, William Henry Gerald, B.S.; American diplomatist and banker; b. 23 Dec. 1909, Boston; s. of William FitzGerald and Mary Smith; m. Annelise Petschek 1943; one s. one d.; ed. U.S. Naval Acad. and Harvard Law School; with Borden Co., New York 1936–41; personal business interests in Mexico 1946–47; with Metallurgical Research and Devt. Co. Washington, D.C. 1947, Vice-Pres. and Treas. 1947–56, Pres. 1956–58, Chair. 1960–82; with FitzGerald Corpn. 1959, Pres. 1980–; Chair. and Dir. numerous business and public appts.; Amb. to Ireland 1992–93; mem. Bretton Woods Comm. 1992–, Council of American Ambs. 1992–; decorations from Peru, Malta etc.; Hon. D.Sc. (Adelphi Univ.) 1962, Hon. LL.D. (Catholic Univ. of America) 1990. *Leisure interests:* tennis, skiing, sailing. *Address:* Suite 1105, 1730 Rhode Island Avenue, N.W., Washington, DC 20036 (Office); 2305 Bancroft Place, N.W., Washington DC 20008, U.S.A. (Home). *Telephone:* (202) 659-8850.

FITZWATER, Marlin, B.A.; American government official; b. 24 Nov. 1942, Salina, Kan.; s. of Max Fitzwater and Phyllis Seaton; m.; two c.; ed. Univ. of Kansas; Sec. and speechwriter Dept. of Transport, Washington 1970–72; with press relations dept. Environmental Protection Agency 1972–74, Dir. Press Office 1974–81; Deputy Asst. Sec. for Public Affairs, Dept. of Treasury

1981–83; Deputy Press Sec. to Pres. 1983–85, Press Sec. to Vice-Pres. 1985–87; Prin. Deputy Press Sec. to Pres. 1987–89; Press Sec. to Pres. 1989–93; Advertising Pres. Fitzwater & Tutweiler, Inc. 1993–; served with U.S.A.F. 1968–70; Presidential Merit Award 1982. *Publication:* Call the Briefing 1995.

FIVE, Kaci Kullmann; Norwegian politician; b. 13 April 1951, Oslo; m.; two c.; Deputy mem. Storting 1977–81, mem. 1981–; Deputy Chair. Conservative Party 1982–88; Vice-Chair. Conservative Party Parly. Group 1985–89; mem. Baerum Municipal Council 1975–81; Deputy mem. Nat. Council on Youth Affairs 1979–81; Exec. Officer, Norwegian Employers' Fed. 1980–81; Minister of Trade and Shipping 1989–90; mem. Storting 1981–; Leader Conservative Party 1991–94; Conservative Party Spokesperson for Foreign Affairs and EU 1994.

FIXMAN, Marshall, PH.D.; American chemist and teacher; b. 21 Sept. 1930, St. Louis, Mo.; s. of Benjamin Fixman and Dorothy Finkel; m. 1st Marian Beatman 1959 (died 1969); one s. two d.; 2nd Branka Ladanyi 1974; ed. Univ. City High School, Mo., Washington Univ., Mo. and M.I.T.; Postdoctoral Fellow, Yale Univ. 1953–54; served U.S. Army 1954–56; Instructor in Chem., Harvard Univ. 1956–59; Sr. Fellow, Mellon Inst., Pa. 1959–61; Dir. Inst. of Theoretical Science, Univ. of Ore. 1961–64, Prof. of Chem. 1961–65; Sloan Visiting Prof. of Chem., Harvard Univ. 1965; Prof. of Chem., Yale Univ. 1965–79; Prof. of Chem. and Physics, Colo. State Univ. 1979–, Distinguished Prof. 1986–; Fellow American Acad. of Arts and Sciences, American Physical Soc.; mem. N.A.S.; Alfred P. Sloan Fellowship 1962–64; Assoc. Ed. Journal of Chemical Physics 1994–; mem. Editorial Bd. Macromolecules, Journal of Physical Chem., Accounts of Chemical Research, Journal of Polymer Science; American Chemical Soc. Award in Pure Chem. 1964, American Physical Soc. High Polymer Physics Prize 1980, American Chemical Soc. Polymer Chem. Award 1991. *Leisure interests:* hiking and photography. *Address:* Department of Chemistry, Colorado State University, Fort Collins, CO 80523, U.S.A. *Telephone:* (970) 491-6037. *Fax:* (970) 491-3361.

FJÆRVOLL, Dag Jostein; Norwegian politician; b. 20 Jan. 1947, Hadsel; s. of Edmund Fjaervoll; m.; two c.; fmr. teacher; Head Teacher Melbu School 1984; mem. Hadsel Municipal Council 1975, mem. Exec. Bd. 1980–, Mayor 1980–85; mem. Storting Nordland Co. 1985–87; mem. Standing Cttee. on Local Govt. and the Environment 1985–89, on Shipping and Fisheries 1989–93, on Scrutiny and the Constitution 1993–97; Vice-Pres. Lagting 1989–93, Odelsting 1993–97; Minister of Defence Oct. 1997–; Christian Democratic Party. *Address:* Ministry of Defence, Myntgt. 1, P.O. Box 8126 Dep., 0030 Oslo, Norway. *Telephone:* 22-40-20-01.

FLAMMARION, Charles-Henri, L. ÈS SC., L. ÈS LET., M.B.A.; French publishing executive; b. 27 July 1946, Boulogne-Billancourt; s. of the late Henri Flammarion and of Pierrette Chenelot; m. Marie-Françoise Mariani 1968; one s. two d.; ed. Lycée de Sèvres, Sorbonne, Paris, Institut d'Etudes Politiques, Paris and Columbia Univ., U.S.A.; Asst. Man. Edns. Flammarion 1972–81, Gen. Man. 1981–85, Pres. Flammarion SA 1985–; Pres. Edns. J'ai Lu 1982–, Audie-Fluide Glacial 1990–; mem. Bureau du Syndicat Nat. de l'Édition 1979–88, 1996–; Vice-Pres. Cercle de la librairie 1988–94, Pres. 1994–. *Leisure interests:* cooking, travel, skiing, walking. *Address:* Flammarion SA, 26 rue Racine, 75006 Paris (Office); 5 avenue Franco-Russe, 75007 Paris, France (Home).

FLANAGAN, Barry, O.B.E., R.A.; British sculptor; b. 11 Jan. 1941, Prestatyn, N. Wales; ed. Mayfield Coll., Sussex, Birmingham Coll. of Arts and Crafts and St. Martin's School of Art, London; one-man exhbns. at Rowan Gallery, London (several, 1966–74), Waddington Galleries, London (several, 1980–85, 1990–94), Serpentine and Whitechapel Art Galleries, London, Centre Georges Pompidou, Paris, Museum of Modern Art, New York and many others in Europe, U.S.A., Argentina and Japan; works in public collections including Art Inst., Chicago, Kunsthaus, Zurich, Museum of Modern Art, New York, Nagaoka Museum, Tokyo, Nat. Gallery of Canada, Ottawa, Stedelijk Museum, Amsterdam, Tate Gallery and Victoria and Albert Museum, London and Walker Art Gallery, Liverpool; outdoor sculpture commissioned by City of Ghent and by Camden Borough Council, London for Lincoln's Inn Fields, London, Equitable Life Tower West, N.Y., Stockley Park, Uxbridge, Kawakyo Co., Osaka; mem. Zoological Soc. of London. *Address:* c/o Waddington Galleries, 11 Cork Street, London, W1X 1PD, England.

FLANNERY, Joseph Patrick, B.S., M.B.A.; American business executive; b. 20 March 1932, Lowell, Mass.; s. of Mary Agnes Egan Flannery; m. Margaret Barrows 1957; three s. three d.; ed. Lowell Tech. Inst., Harvard Grad. School of Business Admin.; Pres. Uniroyal Chemical Co. 1975–77; Exec. Vice-Pres. Uniroyal Inc., Middlebury, Conn. 1977; Pres. of parent co. and mem. Bd. of Dirs. and Exec. Cttee. 1977–, C.E.O. Feb. 1980–; Chair. Uniroyal Inc. Feb. 1982–; Chair., Pres. and C.E.O. Uniroyal Holding, Inc. 1986–; fmr. Partner Clayton & Dubilier, Inc.; Dir. Newmont Mining Corpn., K Mart Corpn., Ingersoll-Rand Co., O.M. Scott & Sons, The Kendall Co., APS Inc., Newmont Gold Co., Arvin Industries. *Address:* Uniroyal Holding Inc., 70 Great Hill Road, Naugatuck, CT 06770, U.S.A.

FLAVELL, Richard Anthony, PH.D., F.R.S.; British professor of immunobiology; b. 23 Aug. 1945, Chelmsford; s. of John Trevor Flavell and Iris (née Hancock) Flavell; m. Madlyn (née Nathanson) Flavell 1987; one d.; two s. from fmr. marriage; ed. Univ. of Hull, Univ. of Amsterdam, and Univ. of Zurich, Wetenschappelijk Medewerker, Univ. of Amsterdam, The Netherlands 1974–79; Head Lab. of Gene Structure and Expression, Nat. Inst. for Medical Research, Mill Hill, London 1979–82; Pres. and Chief Scientific Officer Biogen N.V. 1982–88; Prof. and Chair. of Immunobiology, Yale Univ. School of Medicine and Investigator, Howard Hughes Medical Inst., Conn., U.S.A. 1988–; FEBS Anniversary Prize 1980, Colworth Medal 1980. *Publications:* approx. 388 scientific articles. *Address:* Section of Immunobiology, Yale University School of Medicine, 310 Cedar Street, 412 FMB, New Haven, CT 06520, U.S.A.

FLECKENSTEIN, Günther; German theatre director; b. 13 Jan. 1925, Mainz; m. Heike Kaase 1965; two d.; ed. Realgymnasium, Mainz, and Univ. Mainz; producer of plays and operas; Dir. Deutsches Theater, Göttingen 1966–86, honorary member 1990–; freelance producer 1986–; Guest Dir. for theatres in Berlin, Hamburg, Stuttgart and Moscow; Guest Dir. TV in Munich, Stuttgart and Berlin; Dir. Hersfelde Festspiele 1976–81; has dramatized for stage and TV Der Grosstyrann und das Gericht (Bergengruen); stage production in German of Les jeux sont faits (Sartre), Im Räderwerk (Sartre); productions for children's and young people's theatre; Zückmayer Medal for services to the German language 1979, Hon. Plaque, Bad Hersfeld 1982, Hon. Plaque, Göttingen 1984, Polish Medal for Cultural Service 1986, Niedersachsen Verdienstkreuz 1990. *Address:* Sandstrasse 14, 82110 Germering, Germany.

FLEISCHER, Ezra; Israeli poet and professor; b. 7 Aug. 1928, Romania; m. Anat Rappaport 1955; one s. one d.; ed. Univ. of Bucharest and Hebrew Univ., Jerusalem; political prisoner in Romania 1952–55; emigrated to Israel 1960; Dir. Geniza Research Inst. for Hebrew Poetry, Israel Nat. Acad. of Sciences and Humanities 1967–; Prof. of Medieval Hebrew Poetry, Hebrew Univ., Jerusalem 1973–; mem. Israel Acad. of Sciences and Humanities 1984; Corresp. Fellow, American Acad. for Jewish Research; Pres. World Union of Jewish Studies 1989; Hon. D.H.L. (H.U.C., Jerusalem, J.T.S., New York); Israel Prize for Poetry 1959, Bialik Prize for Judaic Studies 1986, Rothschild Prize for Jewish Studies 1992. *Publications:* Poetry: Fables 1957, The Burden of Gog 1959, At Midnight 1961; research: The Poems of Shelomo Ha-Bavli 1973, The Pizmonim of Anonymus 1974, Hebrew Liturgical Poetry in the Middle Ages 1975, The Yozer, its Emergence and Development 1984, Eretz Israel Prayer and Prayer Rituals as Portrayed in the Geniza Documents 1988, The Proverbs of Sa'id Ben Bābshād 1990, The History of Hebrew Poetry in Muslim Spain (jtly.) 1995, The History of Hebrew Poetry in Christian Spain and Southern France (jtly.) 1997, numerous articles in periodicals. *Address:* Hebrew University of Jerusalem, Mount Scopus, 91905 Jerusalem; 5 Radak Street, Jerusalem 92301, Israel.

FLEISCHER, Richard O., M.F.A.; American film director; b. 8 Dec. 1916, Brooklyn, New York; ed. Brown Univ., Yale Univ.; joined RKO Pathe 1942. *Films:* Flicker Flashbacks (writer, producer), This is America (dir., writer), Design for Death (co-producer), Child of Divorce, Banjo, So This is New York, Bodyguard, Follow Me Quietly, The Clay Pigeon, Narrow Margin, The Happy Time, Arena, 20,000 Leagues Under the Sea, Violent Saturday, Girl in the Red Velvet Swing, Bandido, Between Heaven and Hell, The Vikings, These Thousand Hills, Compulsion, Crack in the Mirror, The Big Gamble, Barabbas, Fantastic Voyage, Doctor Dolittle, Boston Strangler, Tora! Tora! Tora!, Ten Rillington Place, The Last Run, See No Evil, The New Centurions, Soylent Green, The Don is Dead, The Spikes Gang, Mister Majestyk, Mandingo, The Incredible Sarah, Crossed Swords, Ashanti, The Jazz Singer, Tough Enough, Amityville 3-D, Conan the Destroyer, Red Sonja, Million Dollar Mystery, Call From Space. *Publication:* Just Tell Me When To Cry. *Address:* The Gersh Agency, 232 N. Canon Drive, Beverly Hills, CA 90210, U.S.A.

FLEISCHHAUER, Carl-August, DR.JUR.; German lawyer; b. 9 Dec. 1930, Düsseldorf; s. of Kurt and Leonie (née Schneider-Neuenburg) Fleischhauer; m. Liliane Sarolea 1957; two d.; ed. Univs. of Heidelberg, Grenoble, Paris and Chicago; Research Fellow, Max-Planck Inst. for Comparative Foreign Public Law and Int. Law, Heidelberg 1960–62; with Foreign Service of Fed. Repub. of Germany 1962–83, Legal Adviser to Fed. Foreign Office 1975, Legal Adviser and Dir.-Gen. Legal Dept. 1976; Under-Sec.-Gen. for Legal Affairs, Legal Counsel, UN 1983–94; Judge, Int. Court of Justice 1994–; mem. numerous orgs.; Bundesverdienstkreuz and foreign decorations. *Publications:* various legal publications. *Leisure interests:* modern history, literature. *Address:* c/o International Court of Justice, Peace Palace, KJ 2517, The Hague, The Netherlands.

FLEISCHMANN, Martin, PH.D., F.R.S., F.R.S.C.; British professor of chemistry; b. 29 March 1927, Carlsbad, Czechoslovakia; s. of Hans Fleischmann and Margarethe Srb; m. Sheila Flinn 1950; one s. two d.; ed. Worthing High School, and Imperial Coll. London; ICI Fellow, Univ. of Durham 1952–57; lecturer, then Reader, Univ. of Newcastle-upon-Tyne 1957–67; Electricity Council Faraday Prof. of Electrochem. Univ. of Southampton 1967–77; Sr. Fellowship, Science and Eng. Research Council 1977–82; Pres. Int. Soc. of Electrochemistry 1970–72; Research Prof. Dept. of Chem. Univ. of Southampton 1983–, Univ. of Utah 1988–. *Publications:* numerous papers and book chapters. *Leisure interests:* skiing, walking, music, cooking. *Address:* Bury Lodge, Duck Street, Tisbury, Wilts., SP3 6LJ, England. *Telephone:* (01747) 870384.

FLEISCHMANN, Peter; German film director and producer; b. 26 July 1937, Zweibrücken; s. of Alexander Fleischmann and Pascal Fleischmann;

two c.; ed. IDHEC Film School, Paris; fmrly. asst. to dir. of short feature films, documentaries and animations; co-founder Hallelujah Film with Volker Schlondorff; now produces and directs feature and documentary films; Consultant to Studio Babelsberg; Pres. Fédération Européene des Réalisateurs Audiovisuels; Chair. European Audiovisual Centre, Babelsberg; mem. EC Expert Council for reform of audiovisual politics. *Films include:* Alexander und das Auto ohne linken Scheinwerfer 1965 (animation), Herbst der Gammler 1967 (documentary), Jagdszenen aus Niederbayern (feature) 1968, Der Dritte Grad 1971 (feature), Hamburger Krankheit 1979 (feature), Frevel 1983 (feature), Al Capone von der Pfalz 1984 (documentary), Es ist nicht leicht ein Gott zu sein 1988 (feature), Deutschland, Deutschland 1991 (documentary), Mein Onkel, der Winzer 1993 (documentary). *Address:* Europäisches Filmzentrum Babelsberg, August-Bebel-Strasse 26-53, 14482 Potsdam, Germany. *Telephone:* (331) 721-20-59. *Fax:* (331) 721-20-70.

FLEMING, Graham Richard, PH.D., F.R.S.; British professor of chemistry; b. 3 Dec. 1949, Barrow; s. of Maurice N.H. Fleming and Lovima E. Winter; m. Jean McKenzie 1977; one s.; ed. Univs. of London and Bristol; Research Fellow Calif. Inst. of Tech., U.S.A. 1974–75; Univ. Research Fellow Univ. of Melbourne, Australia 1975, ARGC Research Asst. 1976; Leverhulme Fellow, Royal Inst. 1977–79; Asst. Prof., Univ. of Chicago, U.S.A. 1979–83, Assoc. Prof. 1983–85, Prof. 1985–87, Arthur Holly Compton Distinguished Service Prof. 1987–97; Prof. of Chem. Univ. of Calif. Berkeley 1997–, Dir. Physical Biosciences Div., Lawrence Berkeley Nat. Lab. 1997–; Fellow American Acad. of Arts and Sciences; Marlow Medal, Royal Soc. of Chem., A.P. Sloan Foundation Fellow, Coblentz Award, Guggenheim Fellowship, Tilden Medal, Nobel Laureate Signature Award for Grad. Educ. in Chemistry (American Chemical Soc.), Peter Debye Award in Physical Chem., American Chemical Soc. *Leisure interest:* climbing mountains. *Address:* Department of Chemistry, 884 Hildebrand #1460, University of California at Berkeley, Berkeley, CA 94720, U.S.A. *Telephone:* (510) 643-2735. *Fax:* (510) 642-6340.

FLEMING, Renée, M.MUS.; American opera singer and vocalist; b. 14 Feb. 1959, Indiana, Pa.; d. of Edwin Davis Fleming and Patricia (Seymour) Alexander; m. Richard Lee Ross 1989; two d.; ed. Potsdam State Univ., Eastman School of Music of Univ. of Rochester, Juilliard School American Opera Center; debuts Houston Grand Opera (Marriage of Figaro) 1988, Spoleto Festival, Charleston and Italy 1986–90, New York City Opera (La Bohème) 1989, San Francisco Opera, Metropolitan Opera, Paris Opera at Bastille, Teatro Colon, Buenos Aires (all Marriage of Figaro) 1991, Glyndebourne (Cosí fan tutte) 1992, La Scala Milan (Don Giovanni) 1993, Vienna State Opera (Marriage of Figaro) 1993, Lyric Opera of Chicago (Susannah) 1993, San Diego Opera (Eugene Onegin) 1994, Paris Opera 1996; Fulbright Scholar to Germany 1984–85; George London Prize 1988, Richard Tucker Award 1990, Solti Prize, Acad. du Disque Lyrique 1996, Vocalist of the Year, (Musical America) 1977, Prize Acad. du Disque Lyrique 1998. *Address:* c/o M. L. Falcone Public Relations, 155 West 68th Street, Apt. 1114, New York, NY 10023, U.S.A. *Telephone:* (212) 580-4302. *Fax:* (212) 787-9638.

FLEMMING, John Stanton, M.A., F.B.A.; British economist; b. 6 Feb. 1941, Reading, Berks.; s. of Sir Gilbert Nicolson Flemming and Virginia Flemming (née Coit); m. Jean Briggs 1963; three s. one d.; ed. Rugby School and Trinity and Nuffield Colls., Oxford; Lecturer and Fellow in Econs. Oriel Coll., Oxford 1963–65; Official Fellow in Econs. Nuffield Coll., Oxford 1965–80, Bursar 1970, Fellow Emer. 1980–; Ed. Economic Journal 1976–80; Chair. Econ. Affairs Cttee. Social Science Research Council 1980–84; Chief Adviser and Head of Econs. Div. Bank of England 1980–84, Econ. Adviser to Gov. 1984–88, Exec. Dir. 1988–91; Chief Economist EBRD London 1991–93; Warden Wadham Coll., Oxford 1993–; mem. Royal Comm. on Environmental Pollution 1995–; mem. Council, Royal Econs. Soc. 1976–98, Inst. for Fiscal Studies, Advisory Bd. on Research Councils (U.K.) 1986–91, Council European Econ. Asscn. 1985–88, British Acad. 1993– (Hon. Treas. 1995–); Chair. Man. Cttee. Nat. Inst. for Econ. and Social Research 1996–; Harkness Fellow, Harvard Univ. 1968–69. *Publications:* Inflation 1976; articles in academic journals. *Address:* The Lodgings, Wadham College, Oxford, OX1 3PN, England. *Telephone:* (01865) 277903. *Fax:* (01865) 277937.

FLETCHER, Hugh Alasdair, M.COM., M.B.A.; New Zealand business executive; b. 28 Nov. 1947, Auckland; s. of Sir James Muir Cameron Fletcher (q.v.) and Margery V. (née Gunthorp) Fletcher; m. Sian Seerpoohi Elias 1970; two s.; ed. Auckland Univ. and Stanford Univ.; C.E.O. Fletcher Holdings Ltd. 1980, Man. Dir. Fletcher Challenge Ltd. 1981, C.E.O. Oct. 1987–97; Chair. Air New Zealand 1985–89; mem. Prime Minister's Enterprise Council 1992–, Asia-Pacific Advisory Cttee. N.Y. Stock Exchange 1995–; Harkness Fellowship 1970–72. *Leisure interest:* horse riding/hunting. *Address:* P.O. Box 11468, Penrose, Auckland (Office); 79 Penrose Road, Auckland, New Zealand (Home). *Telephone:* 0649 5794.226 (Home).

FLETCHER, Sir James Muir Cameron, Kt., O.N.Z., F.C.A.; New Zealand business executive; b. 25 Dec. 1914, Dunedin; s. of Sir James Fletcher; m. Margery V. Gunthorp 1942; three s.; ed. Waitaki Boys' High School and Auckland Grammar School; South British Insurance Co. 1931–37; Fletcher Construction Co. and Fletcher Holdings; Pres. Fletcher Challenge Ltd., Auckland –1990. *Address:* Fletcher Challenge Ltd., Private Bag, Auckland (Office); 119 St. Stephens Avenue, Parnell, Auckland, New Zealand (Home).

FLETCHER, Sir Leslie, Kt., F.C.A.; British business executive; b. 14 Oct. 1922; s. of Ernest Fletcher and Lily Fletcher; m. Audrey Jackson 1947; one s. one d.; ed. Nether Edge Secondary School, Sheffield; Helbert Wagg & Co. Ltd. (later J. Henry Schroder Wagg & Co. Ltd.) 1955–71, Dir. 1966–71; Chair. Glynwed Int. 1971–86; Deputy Chair. Standard Chartered PLC 1983–89; Dir. RMC Group 1983–96, Deputy Chair. 1991–96; Jt. Deputy Chair. Westland Group PLC 1988–89, Chair. 1989–94; Dir. Rank Org. 1984–95, Chair. 1992–95. *Leisure interests:* gardening, golf, photography. *Address:* Hafod, The Green, Sherfield-on-Loddon, Hook, Hants., RG27 0EN, England.

FLETCHER, Neville Horner, A.M., PH.D., D.SC., F.A.A., F.T.S.E.; Australian physicist; b. 14 July 1930, Armidale, N.S.W.; s. of Alleine Horner Fletcher and Florence Mabel Glass; m. Eunice M. Sciffer 1953; one s. two d.; ed. Armidale High School, New England Univ. Coll., Univ. of Sydney, Harvard Univ.; Research Engineer, Clevite Transistor Products, U.S.A. 1953–55; Researcher, CSIRO Radiophysics Lab. 1956–59, Dir. Inst. of Physical Sciences 1983–88; Chief Research Scientist 1988–95; at Univ. of New England 1960–83, Sr. Lecturer in Physics 1960–63, Prof. of Physics 1963–83, Dean, Faculty of Science 1963–65, mem. Univ. Council 1968–72, Chair. Professorial Bd. 1970–72, Pro Vice-Chancellor 1969–72, Prof. Emer. 1983–; Adjunct Prof., Australian Nat. Univ. 1990–95, Visiting Fellow 1996–; Chair. Antarctic Science Advisory Cttee. 1990–96; mem. Australian Research Grants Cttee. 1974–78, 1995–98; Sec. for Physical Sciences, Australian Acad. of Science 1980–84; Pres. Inst. of Physics 1981–83; mem. Govt. Meteorology Policy Cttee. 1981–84, Int. Comm. on Acoustics 1985–90; Edgeworth David Medal (Royal Soc. of N.S.W.) 1963, Lyle Medal (Australian Acad. of Science) 1993, Dist. Alumni Award (Univ. of New England) 1994, Silver Medal in Musical Acoustics (Acoustical Soc. of America) 1998. *Publications:* The Physics of Rainclouds 1962, The Chemical Physics of Ice 1970, Physics and Music 1976, The Physics of Musical Instruments 1990, Acoustic Systems in Biology 1992, Principles of Vibration and Sound 1995; over 140 papers in scientific journals. *Leisure interests:* music (flute, bassoon and organ). *Address:* Department of Electronic Materials Engineering, Research School of Physical Sciences and Engineering, Australian National University, Canberra, A.C.T. 0200 (Office), 30 Rosebery Street, Fisher, A.C.T. 2611, Australia (Home). *Telephone:* (02) 6249-4406 (Office); (02) 6288-8988 (Home). *Fax:* (02) 6249-0511.

FLETT, Kathryn Alexandra; British journalist; b. 1 April 1964, Herts.; d. of Douglas J. Flett and Patricia Jenkins; ed. Notting Hill & Ealing High School and Hammersmith & West London Coll.; staff writer, I-D magazine 1985–87; Fashion Ed., Features Ed. The Face magazine 1987–89; freelance contrib. to many int. publs. including The Times, The Sunday Times, The Observer, The Guardian, The Face, Arena, Elle, Harpers Bazaar, etc. 1989–92; Contributing Ed. Arena Magazine 1991–92, Ed. 1992–; Ed. Arena Homme Plus 1992–; columnist, The Observer 1994–. *Address:* Arena Magazine, 3rd Floor Block A, Exmouth House, Pine Street, London E.C.1, England. *Telephone:* 0171-837 7270. *Fax:* 0171-837 3906.

FLEURY, Gen. Jean André; French air force officer; b. 1 Dec. 1934, Brest; s. of René Fleury and Blanche-Marie Marsille; Commdt. Saint Dizier Air Base 1977–78; Head, Office of Supply, Air Force Gen. Staff 1978–81; Deputy Chief of Planning, Armed Forces Gen. Staff 1983–85; Commdt. Strategic Air Forces 1985–87; Chief of Staff to Pres. of Repub. 1987–89; Chief of Staff of Army and Air Force 1989–91; mem. Supreme Council of Army and Air Forces 1989; Pres. Aéroports de Paris 1992–, Int. Council World Asscn. of Airports 1998–; Grand Croix, Légion d'honneur, Commdr. Ordre nat. du Mérite, Croix de la Valeur militaire. *Address:* Aéroports de Paris, 291 boulevard Raspail, 75675 Paris, Cedex 14, France.

FLEXNER, James Thomas; American author; b. 13 Jan. 1908, New York; s. of Simon Flexner and Helen Thomas Flexner; m. Beatrice Hudson 1950; one d.; ed. Lincoln School of Teachers Coll. and Harvard Univ.; Reporter, New York Herald Tribune 1929–31; Exec. Sec. Noise Abatement Comm. of New York City Bd. of Health 1931–33; Pres. American Center PEN 1954–55, Soc. of American Historians 1975–77; mem. American Acad. and Inst. of Arts and Letters; Goiz Medal for eminence in biography, 1988; Parkman Prize 1962, Pulitzer Prize 1972, Nat. Book Award 1972. *Publications:* Doctors on Horseback 1937, America's Old Masters 1938, Steamboats Come True 1944, History of American Painting, (3 vols.) 1947, 1954, 1962, The Traitor and the Spy 1953, George Washington, (4 vols.) 1965, 1967, 1970, 1972, Washington, The Indispensable Man 1974, The Young Hamilton 1978, An American Saga: The Story of Helen Thomas and Simon Flexner 1983, Poems from the 1920s, 1991, On Desperate Seas: A Biography of Gilbert Stuart 1995, Maverick Progress: An Autobiography 1996, Random Harvest 1997. *Address:* 530 East 86th Street, New York, NY 10028; Fordham University Press, University Box L, Bronx, New York, NY 10458, U.S.A.

FLIMM, Jürgen; German theatre director; b. 17 July 1941, Giessen; s. of Werner Flimm and Ellen Flimm; m. Susanne Ottersbach 1990; early work at the Munich Kammerspiele; Dir. Nationaltheater, Mannheim 1972–73; Prin. Dir. Thalia Theater, Hamburg 1973–74; directed plays in Munich, Hamburg, Bochum, Frankfurt 1974–79 and in Zürich, Amsterdam, Salzburg, Vienna, Milan; Dir. Cologne Theatre 1979–85, Thalia Theatre, Hamburg 1985–. *Address:* Alstertor, 20095 Hamburg, Germany. *Telephone:* (004940) 328140. *Fax:* (004940) 32814102.

FLINDT, Flemming Ole; Danish ballet dancer and choreographer; b. 30 Sept. 1936; m. Vivi Gelker 1967; three d.; ed. Royal Danish Ballet School; ballet dancer 1955–; solo dancer Royal Theatre, Copenhagen 1957–60; Danseur Etoile Théâtre Nat. de l'Opéra, Paris 1960–65; Artist Dir. Royal Danish

Ballet 1966–78, Dallas Ballet 1981–; guest artist Royal Ballet Covent Garden 1963; guest choreographer Metropolitan Opera House, New York and la Scala, Milan 1965; Grand Prix Italia (La Leçon) 1963. *Choreography:* La leçon, (Ionesco) 1963, Jeune homme à marier, (Ionesco) 1964, The Three Musketeers 1966, The Miraculous Mandarin 1966, The Triumph of Death, Dreamland 1974, Caroline Mathilde 1990; choreography and libretto: Felix Luna 1973.

FLISOWSKI, Zdobysław; Polish politician and electrical engineer; b. 22 Sept. 1931, Brzešć on the Bug; m.; one s. one d.; ed. Warsaw Univ. of Tech.; scientific worker, Inst. of Grand Power and High Voltages, Electrical Faculty of Warsaw Univ. of Tech. 1952–, Prof. 1987–, Vice-Rector 1988–92; assoc. several foreign univs.; Chair. Polish Cttee. for Lighting Protection; mem. Warsaw Scientific Soc., Electrical Eng. Cttee. of Polish Acad. of Sciences; Councillor, Mokotów Dist. Council and mem. Council of Warsaw 1990–92; non-party; mem. Solidarity Ind. Self-Governing Trade Union 1980–; Minister of Nat. Educ. 1992–93; Kt.'s Cross Order of Polonia Restituta, Gold Cross of Merit and other decorations. *Publications:* more than 120 scientific works on electrical eng. and lightning protection. *Address:* Instytut Wielkich Napięć i Wysokich Mocy PW, ul. Koszykowa 75, 00-662 Warsaw, Poland.

FLOOD, Philip James, A.O., B.ECONS.; Australian diplomatist; b. 2 July 1935, Sydney; s. of Thomas C. Flood and Maxine S. Flood; m. 2nd Carole Henderson 1990; two s. one d. from previous m.; ed. North Sydney High School, Univ. of Sydney; joined Australian Public Service 1958, mem. staff Mission to EC and Embassy, Brussels 1959–62, Rep. to OECD Devt. Assistance Cttee., Paris 1966–69, Asst. Sec. Dept. of Foreign Affairs 1971–73, High Commr. in Bangladesh 1974–76, Minister, Embassy, Washington D.C. 1976–77, C.E.O. Dept. Special Trade Representations 1977–80; First Asst. Sec. Dept. of Trade 1980–84, Deputy Sec. Dept. of Foreign Affairs 1985–89, Amb. to Indonesia 1989–93, Dir.-Gen. Australian Int. Devt. Assistance Bureau (AIDAB) 1993–95, Dir.-Gen. Office of Nat. Assessments 1995–96, Sec. Dept. of Foreign Affairs and Trade 1996–98; High Commr. in London 1998–; Fellow Royal Australian Inst. Public Admin. *Leisure interests:* reading, music, golf, swimming. *Address:* Australian High Commission, Australia House, The Strand, London, WC2B 4LA, England (Office), 96 Jervois Street, Deakin, A.C.T. 2600, Australia (Home). *Telephone:* 0171-379 4334 (Office). *Fax:* 0171-240 5333 (Office).

FLOR, Claus Peter; German conductor; b. 16 March 1953, Leipzig; adopted s. of Richard Flor and Sigrid Langer; m. Sabine Winni 1985; one s.; ed. Music School, Weimar and High School of Music, Weimar/Leipzig; studied under Rolf Reuter, Rafael Kubelik and Kurt Sanderling; learnt violin and clarinet before commencing conducting studies; Chief Conductor, Suhl Philharmonic 1981–84; Chief Conductor, Music Dir. Berliner Sinfonie Orchester 1984–92; Prin. Conductor, Artistic Adviser, Zürich Tonhalle Orchestra 1991–; Prin. Guest Conductor, Philharmonia Orchestra, London 1991–; U.S. debut with Los Angeles Philharmonic 1985; debut with Berlin Philharmonic 1988; Prin. Guest Conductor Dallas Symphony Orchestra; regular appearances with Vienna Symphony, Orchestre de Paris, Royal Concertgebouw, Rotterdam Philharmonic and maj. German orchestras; frequent guest engagements with leading orchestras in U.K., U.S.A., Canada etc.; conductor of opera at many German opera houses including Berlin Staatsoper and Deutsche Oper, Berlin. *Leisure interests:* collecting red wines, history and genealogy of European nobility. *Address:* c/o Intermusica Artists' Management Ltd., 16 Duncan Terrace, London, N1 8BZ, England. *Telephone:* 0171-278 5455. *Fax:* 0171-278 8434.

FLORAKIS, Charilaos Ioannou; Greek politician; b. 20 July 1914, Rahoula; ed. Coll. of Telegraph, Telephone, Post Office and Public Utility, law school; fmr. Sec. Exec. Cttee., Fed. of Telegraphists; joined CP of Greece (KKE) during war; partisan during occupation; Commdr. unit of First Div. of Democratic Army of Greece during civil war; mem. Cen. Cttee. KKE 1949, First Sec. 1973, Gen. Sec. 1978–89, Pres. 1989; M.P. for Athens 1974, 1977, 1981; Friendship of the People Award (U.S.S.R.), Karl Marx Decoration (G.D.R.), Dimitrov Decoration (Bulgaria), Elas Decoration, Decoration of Military Valour, (Democratic Army of Greece), Order of Lenin 1984. *Address:* 6 Pythias Street, 152 33 Halandri, Greece. *Telephone:* 01-2592111 *Fax:* 01-2592 286.

FLORENTZ, Jean-Louis; French composer; b. 19 Dec. 1947, Asnières; s. of Jean-Paul Florentz and Reine Mathieu; m. 2nd Anne Le Forestier; ed. Collège Mariste, St. Chamond (Loire), Conservatoire de Paris, Ecole Pratique des Hautes Etudes; studied ethno-musicology, Arab and Ethiopian literature, natural science, and music with Olivier Messiaen and Pierre Schaeffer; student at Acad. de France, Rome (Villa Médicis) 1979–81, Casa de Velázquez, Madrid and Palma de Mallorca 1983–85; numerous study trips to North Africa and the Sahara, Niger, Côte d'Ivoire, Egypt, Kenya, Antilles, Polynesia and Israel 1971–; Visiting Prof., Kenyatta Univ. Coll., Nairobi; teaches ethno-musicology and comparative musical analysis, CNSM, Lyon; mem. Acad. des Beaux-Arts Inst. de France; Prix de Rome, Prix de Madrid, Prix de la Fondation Prince Pierre de Monaco, Prix de la Ville de Paris, Prix de l'Institut de France, Prix de la SACEM, Grand Prix de la Musique symphonique, SACEM 1991, Prix R. Daumesnil, Académie des Beaux Arts 1993, and several other prizes; Officier des Arts et des Lettres, Chevalier des Palmes Académiques. *Compositions:* Ténéré: Incantation sur un verset coranique, for orchestra 1979, Magnificat: Antiphone pour la visitation, for tenor, mixed choir and orchestra 1980, Les Marches du soleil, for orchestra 1984, Les Laudes, for organ 1985, Chant de Nyandarua, for four cellos 1986, Requiem de la Vierge, for soprano, tenor, baritone, children's choir, mixed choir and orchestra 1988, Debout sur le Soleil, for organ 1991, Asmarâ, for mixed choir 1992, Le Songe de Lluc Alcari, for cello and orchestra 1994, L'Ange du Tamaris, for cello 1995, Second Chant de Nyandarua, for 12 Cellos 1996, Les Jardins d'Amĕnta, for orchestra 1997, L'Anneau de Salomon, for orchestra 1999. *Publications:* contribs. to L'Orgue, Journal de Psychologie and other publs. *Leisure interests:* flying, ornithology. *Address:* c/o Ed. Alphonse Leduc, 175 rue St. Honoré, 75040 Paris Cedex 01, France. *Telephone:* (01) 42.96.89.11.

FLORES FACUSSE, Carlos Roberto, B.ENG., M.INT.ECON., PH.D.; Honduran politician; b. 1 March 1950, Tegucigalpa; s. of Oscar A. Flores and Margarita Facusse de Flores; m. Mary Carol Flake; one s. one d.; ed. American School, Tegucigalpa and Louisiana State Univ.; Rep. for Francisco Morazan to Liberal Convention, Pres. Departmental Liberal Council, Francisco Morazan; Finance Sec. Nat. Directorate Movimiento Liberal Rodista; Congressman Nat. Ass. for Francisco Morazan 1980–97; Presidential Sec. 1982–83; Gen. Co-ordinator Movimiento Liberal Florista; Pres. Cen. Exec. Council Partido Liberal de Honduras; Pres. of Honduras Jan. 1998–; co-owner, Man. and mem. editorial Bd. La Tribuna, co-owner and Man. Lithopress Industrial; fmr. Man. CONPACASA; fmr. Prof. School of Business Admin., Nat. Univ. of Honduras (UNAH), Cen. American Higher School of Banking; fmr. mem. Bd. of Dirs. Honduran Inst. of Social Security, Cen. Bank of Honduras, Inst. Nacional de Formación Profesional (INFOP); mem. Industrial Eng. Asscn. of Honduras, Nat. Asscn. of Industries (ANDI), Consejo Hondureño de la Empresa Privada (COHEP), Honduran Inst. of Inter-American Culture. *Publication:* Forjemos Unidos el Destino de Honduras. *Address:* Oficina del Presidente, Palacio José Cecilio del Valle, Boulevard Juan Pablo II, Tegucigalpa, Honduras. *Telephone:* 32-62-82. *Fax:* 31-00-97.

FLORES TORRES, Gen. Jorge; Peruvian government minister and army officer; minister; b. 11 April 1929, Tacna; began mil. career as soldier in Cavalry School 1947; cadet at Chorrillos Mil. School 1948–52; fmr. Instructor at School of Equitation, Dir. of Cavalry School, Chief of Nat. Defence Secr., Maj.-Gen. First Mil. Region, Piura; rank of Gen. 1984; Minister of Defence (Army) 1985. *Address:* c/o Ministry of Defence (Army), Lima, Peru.

FLOWERS, Baron (Life Peer) cr. 1979, of Queen's Gate in the City of Westminster; **Brian Hilton Flowers;** M.A., D.SC., F.INST.P., F.R.S.; British physicist; b. 13 Sept. 1924, Blackburn, Lancs.; s. of late Rev. Harold J. Flowers and Marion V. (née Hilton) Flowers; m. Mary Frances Behrens 1951; two step s.; ed. Bishop Gore Grammar School, Swansea, Gonville and Caius Coll., Cambridge, and Univ. of Birmingham; Anglo-Canadian Atomic Energy Mission (Tube Alloys) at Montreal and Chalk River, Canada 1944; joined staff Atomic Energy Research Establishment, Harwell 1946, Head of Theoretical Physics Div. 1952–58; Prof. of Theoretical Physics, Manchester Univ. 1958–61, Langworthy Prof. of Physics 1961–72, Chancellor 1994–; Chair. Science Research Council 1967–73; Rector Imperial Coll. of Science and Tech., London 1973–85; Vice-Chancellor Univ. of London 1985–90; Chair. Computer Bd. for Univs. and Research Councils 1966–70; Pres. Inst. of Physics 1972–74, European Science Foundation 1974–80, Nat. Soc. for Clean Air 1977–79; Chair. Royal Comm. on Environmental Pollution 1973–76, Standing Comm. on Energy and the Environment 1978–81, Univ. of London Working Party on future of medicine and dentistry teaching resources 1979–80, Cttee. of Vice-Chancellors and Prins. of the Univs. of the U.K. 1983–85; Founder-mem. Academia Europaea 1988; Vice-Chair. Asscn. of Commonwealth Univs. 1987–90; Chair. House of Lords Select Cttee. on Science and Tech. 1989–93, Nuffield Foundation 1987–98, Cttee. on Org. of the Academic Year 1992–93; Pres. Asscn. for Colleges 1993–; Fellow Physical Soc. 1956, Inst. of Physics 1961; mem. Royal Irish Acad. 1976; Corresp. mem. Swiss Acad. of Eng. Sciences 1986; Sr. Fellow, Royal Coll. of Art 1983; Hon. Fellow (Imperial Coll.) 1972, (Gonville and Caius Coll., Cambridge) 1974, (Univ. of Manchester Inst. of Science and Tech.) 1985; Hon. F.I.E.E. 1975, Hon. F.R.C.P. 1992; Hon. D.Sc. (Sussex) 1968, (Wales) 1972, (Leicester) 1973, (Manchester) 1973, (Liverpool) 1974, (Bristol) 1982, (Oxford) 1985, (Univ. of Ireland) 1990, (Reading) 1996, (London) 1997; Hon. Sc.D. (Dublin) 1984; Hon. LL.D. (Dundee) 1985, (Glasgow) 1987; Hon. D.Eng. (Nova Scotia) 1983; Chevalier Légion d'honneur 1975, Officier 1981; Rutherford Medal and Prize (Inst. of Physics and the Physical Soc.) 1968, Chalmers Medal (Sweden) 1980, Glazebrook Medal (Inst. of Physics) 1987. *Publications:* Properties of Matter (with E. Mendoza) 1970; numerous scientific papers in the journals of learned societies on nuclear reactions and the structure of atomic nuclei, on science policy and on energy and the environment. *Leisure interests:* music, walking, computing, painting, gardening *Address:* 53 Athenaeum Road, London, N20 9AL, England. *Telephone:* 0181-446 5993.

FLYNN, Padraig; Irish politician; b. 9 May 1939, Castlebar; m. Dorothy Tynan; one s. three d.; ed. St. Patrick's Teacher Training Coll., Dublin; fmr. school teacher and publican; mem. Mayo County Council 1967–86; mem. Dáil. 1977–92; Minister of State, Dept. of Transport and Power 1980–81; Minister for the Gaeltacht March-Oct. 1982; Minister for Trade, Commerce and Tourism Oct.–Dec. 1982; Minister for Environment 1987–91, Minister for Justice Feb.–Dec. 1992, for Industry and Commerce Nov.–Dec. 1992; EU Commr. for Employment and Social Affairs, and for Relations with the Econ.

and Social Cttee. 1993–; Fianna Fáil. *Address:* European Commission, 45 avenue d'Auderghem, 1040 Brussels, Belgium. *Telephone:* 295 2111.

FO, Dario; Italian playright, clown and actor; b. 24 March 1926; m. Franca Rame 1954; one c.; Comedian teatro di rivista; Jt. Founder theatre group La Comune; Hon. D. Litt. (Westminster) 1997; Nobel Prize for Literature 1997. *Plays include:* Accidental Death of an Anarchist, Can't Pay? Won't Pay!, Manuale et minimo dell attore 1987, Mistero Buffo 1977, Coming Home, History of Masks, Archangels Don't Play Pinball, Hooters, Trumpets and Raspberries, The Tricks of the Trade 1991, The Pope and the Witch 1989, L'Eroina-Grassa e'Bello 1991, Johan Padan a la Descoverta de le Americhe 1991, Dario Fo Recita Ruzzante 1993, Il Diavolo con le Zinne 1997. *Address:* CTFR Srl, Viale Piave 11, 20129 Milan, Italy.

FOALE, Marion Ann; British designer; b. 13 March 1939, London; d. of S. D. Foale; one s. one d.; ed. S. W. Essex Tech and School of Art, R.C.A.; career fashion designer; f. partner (with Sally Tuffin) Foale and Tuffin Ltd. 1961–72; signed with Puritan Fashion Corps, N.Y. 1965–70; designed clothes for films; Susannah York (q.v.) in Kaleidoscope 1966, Audrey Hepburn in Two for the Road 1966; f. own label Marion Foale–Knitwear Designer 1982. *Publication:* Marion Foale's Classic Knitwear 1987. *Leisure interest:* studying fine art. *Address:* Foale Ltd., Church Farm, Orton on the Hill, Nr. Atherstone, Warwicks., CV9 3NG, England. *Telephone:* (01827) 880348. *Fax:* (01827) 880807.

FOBES, John Edwin; American diplomatist and international official; b. 16 March 1918, Chicago, Ill.; s. of Wilfred Franklin Fobes and Mabel Skogsberg; m. Hazel Ward Weaver 1941; one s. one d.; ed. Northwestern Univ., Fletcher School of Law and Diplomacy and School for Advanced Int. Studies, Johns Hopkins Univ.; U.S.A.A.F. 1942–45; UN Secr., London and New York 1945–46; Admin. Analyst, U.S. Bureau of the Budget 1947–48; Asst. Dir. Tech. Assistance, U.S. Marshall Plan, Washington 1948–51; Deputy Dir. Org. and Planning, Mutual Security Agency, Washington 1951–52; Adviser, U.S. Del. to NATO and European Regional Orgs., Paris 1952–55; Dir. Office of Int. Admin., Dept. of State 1955–59; (elected) mem. UN Advisory Cttee. on Admin. and Budgetary Questions 1955–60; Sr. Adviser, U.S. Del. to the 10th-14th sessions of UN Gen. Ass.; Special Adviser to Asst. Sec. of State, Washington 1959–60; Program Officer and Deputy Dir. U.S. Agency for Int. Devt. Mission to India 1960–64; Asst. Dir.-Gen. (Admin.), UNESCO, Paris 1964–70, Deputy Dir.-Gen. 1971–77, Chair. U.S. Nat. Comm. for UNESCO 1980–81, Vice-Chair. 1982–83; Pres. Americans for Universality of UNESCO 1984–; Chair. U.S. Asscn. for the Club of Rome 1982–87; mem. Club of Rome 1983–; Pres. American Library in Paris 1968–70, Western N. Carolina UNA 1991–93, N.C. Div. UNA 1993–96; Visiting Scholar Indiana and Harvard Univs. 1970, D. H. Bucknell Univ. 1973; Visiting Scholar and Adviser on Int. Studies Duke Univ. 1978–82, Univ. of North Carolina, Adjunct Prof. of Political Science Western Carolina Univ. 1982–95; Lecturer, Univ. of North Carolina/Asheville. *Leisure interests:* community service, walking, reading, writing. *Address:* 28 Beaverbrook Road, Asheville, NC 28804, U.S.A. *Telephone:* (828) 253-5383.

FOCKE, Katharina, DR.PHIL.; German politician and journalist; b. 8 Oct. 1922, Bonn; d. of Ernst Friedlaender and Dr. Franziska (née Schulz) Friedlaender; m. Dr. Ernst Günter Focke 1954 (died 1961); ed. Hamburg Univ.; journalist 1946–54; joined Social Democratic Party 1964; mem. North Rhine Westphalia Diet 1966; mem. Bundestag 1969–80; Parl. State Sec. of Fed. Chancellor 1969–72; Fed. Minister for Youth, Family Affairs and Health 1972–76; mem. Cttee. for Devt. of Deutscher Bundestag 1976–79, European Parl. 1979–89, Cttee. for Devt. and Cooperation of European Parl. 1979; Social Democrat. *Publications:* Europa über den Nationen 1962, Europäer in Frankreich 1965. *Address:* Droste-Hülshoffstr. 21, 50968 Cologne, Germany. *Telephone:* 0221/385236.

FODOR, Gábor, D. JUR.; Hungarian politician and lawyer; b. 27 Sept. 1962, Gyöngyös; s. of Árpád Fodor and Klára Révfalvi; m. Barbara Czeizel; one s.; ed. János Nagy Berze Secondary School and Loránd Eötvös Univ. of Sciences, Budapest; teacher, István Bibó Special Coll. 1988–89; Research Fellow, Cen. European Research Group 1989–90; asst. lecturer, Faculty of Philosophy, Eötvös Loránd Univ. of Sciences; co-founder, Alliance of Young Democrats (FIDESZ), Vice-Pres. April-Nov. 1993; mem. Nat. Security Cttee. 1990–92; mem. Parl. 1993–; Minister of Culture and Educ. 1994–95; Pres. Standing Cttee. on Human Rights, Ethnic Minorities and Religious Affairs of Parl. Nov. 1993; mem. Council of Europe Cttee. on Human Rights 1992, Constitutional and Legis. Cttee. 1996–, Human Rights Minorities and Religious Affairs Cttee. 1998, Environmental Cttee. 1998; Leadership of Alliance of Free Democrats (SZDSZ) 1996–. *Leisure interest:* reading. *Address:* Képviselöi Irodaház, 1358 Budapest, Széchenyi rkp. 19, Hungary. *Telephone:* (1) 268 58 30. *Fax:* (1) 268 59 52.

FOGEL, Robert William, PH.D.; American historian, university professor and economist; b. 1 July 1926, New York; s. of Harry Gregory and Elizabeth (Mitnik) Fogel; m. Enid Cassandra Morgan 1949; two s.; ed. Cornell, Columbia, Cambridge, Harvard and Johns Hopkins Univs.; Instructor, Johns Hopkins Univ. 1958–59; Asst. Prof., Univ. of Rochester 1960–64; Assoc. Prof., Univ. of Chicago 1964–65, Prof. 1965–75; Prof., Harvard Univ. 1975–81; Charles R. Walgreen Distinguished Service Prof. of American Insts., Univ. of Chicago 1981–, Dir. Center for Population Econs. 1981–; Chair. History Advisory Cttee. of the Math. Social Science Bd. 1965–72; Pres. Econ. History Asscn. 1977–78; Social Science History Asscn. 1980–81; Nat. Bureau of Econ. Research Assoc.; Fellow Econ. Soc., American Acad. of Arts and Sciences, N.A.S., Royal Historical Soc., A.A.A.S.; Arthur H. Cole Prize 1968, Schumpeter Prize 1971, Bancroft Prize in American History 1975, shared Nobel Prize in Econs. 1993. *Publications:* The Union Pacific Railroad 1960, Railroads and American Economic Growth 1972, Time on the Cross 1974, Ten Lectures on the New Economic History 1977, Which Road to the Past?: Two Views of History 1983, Without Consent or Contract: The Rise and Fall of American Slavery (Vol I) 1989, (Vols. II–IV) 1992. *Leisure interests:* carpentry, photography. *Address:* Center for Population Economics, University of Chicago, Graduate School of Business, 1101 East 58th Street, RO 118, Chicago, IL 60637 (Office); 5321 S. University Avenue, Chicago, IL 60615, U.S.A. (Home). *Telephone:* (312) 702-7709 (Office). *Fax:* (312) 702-2901.

FOGELBERG, Graeme, M.COM., M.B.A., PH.D.; New Zealand university administrator; b. 10 Dec. 1939, Wellington; s. of the late Frederick Edward Fogelberg and Evelyn Fogelberg (née Greenwell); m. (divorced); three s. two d.; ed. Wellington Coll., Victoria Univ. of Wellington and Univ. of W. Ontario; Prof. of Business Admin. Victoria Univ. of Wellington 1970, Dean Faculty of Commerce Admin. 1977–82, Deputy Vice-Chancellor 1986–92; professorial appts. at Univ. of W. Ont. 1975–76, 1986–87 and Pa. State Univ. 1992–93; Vice-Chancellor Univ. of Otago, Dunedin 1994–; Fellow N.Z. Soc. of Accountants, N.Z. Inst. of Dirs. *Publications:* New Zealand Case Studies of Marketing 1972 and articles in accounting, business, man. and econs. journals. *Leisure interests:* tennis, skiing and fine New Zealand wines. *Address:* University of Otago, Union Street, P.O. Box 56, Dunedin, New Zealand. *Telephone:* (64) 3 479 8253. *Fax:* (64) 3 479 8544.

FOGELHOLM, Markus, M.A.; Finnish banker; b. 11 March 1946, Helsinki; s. of Eila Fogelholm and Georg Fogelholm; m. Saara R.I. Suokas 1969; one s. one d.; ed. Univ. of Helsinki; joined Bank of Finland 1972, Head Foreign Financing Dept. 1984–87, Market Operations Dept. 1992–; special asst. to Exec. Dir. of UN Centre on Transnational Corpns. 1978–81; Alt. Exec. Dir. IMF 1987–89, Exec. Dir. 1989–91; Bd. mem. Forex Finland. *Leisure interests:* wine, music, tennis, swimming. *Address:* Bank of Finland, Snellmanninaukio, P.O. Box 160, SF-00101 Helsinki, Finland.

FOGG, Gordon Elliott, C.B.E., B.SC., PH.D., SC.D., LL.D., F.I.BIOL., F.R.S.; British botanist; b. 26 April 1919, Langar, Notts.; s. of Rev. Leslie Charles Fogg and Doris Mary Fogg (née Elliott); m. Elizabeth Beryl Llechid Jones 1945 (died 1997); one s. one d.; ed. Dulwich Coll., Queen Mary Coll., Univ. of London, and St. John's Coll., Cambridge; Asst. for Seaweed Survey of Britain, Marine Biological Asscn. 1942; Plant Physiologist, Pest Control Ltd. 1943–45; Asst. Lecturer, Dept. of Botany, Univ. Coll. London 1945–47, Lecturer 1947–53, Reader 1953–60; Prof. of Botany in Univ. of London at Westfield Coll. 1960–71; Prof. of Marine Biology, Univ. Coll. of N. Wales 1971–85, Prof. Emer., Univ. of Wales 1985–; Rockefeller Fellow 1954; Hon. Sec. Inst. of Biology 1953–56, Vice-Pres. 1961–62, Pres. 1976–77; Botanical Sec., Soc. for Experimental Biology 1957–60; Pres. British Phycological Soc. 1962–63, Int. Phycological Soc. 1964; Jt. Hon. Sec. Xth Int. Botanical Congress, Edinburgh 1964; Visiting Research Worker, British Antarctic Survey 1966, 1974, 1979; Gen. Sec. British Asscn. 1967–72; Royal Soc./Leverhulme Visiting Prof. Univ. of Kerala 1970; Chair. of Council, Freshwater Biol. Asscn. 1974–85; Trustee, British Museum (Natural History) 1976–85, Royal Botanic Gardens, Kew 1983–89; mem. Royal Comm. on Environmental Pollution 1979–85, Natural Environment Research Council 1981–82; Leverhulme Emer. Fellowship 1986–88. *Publications:* The Metabolism of Algae 1953, The Growth of Plants 1963, Algal Cultures and Phytoplankton Ecology (with B. A. Thake) 1987, Photosynthesis 1968, The Blue-Green Algae (with W. D. P. Stewart, P. Fay and A. E. Walsby) 1973, The Explorations of Antarctica (with D. Smith) 1990, A History of Antarctic Science 1992, The Biology of Polar Habitats 1998. *Leisure interests:* watercolour painting, walking, listening to music, photography. *Address:* Marine Science Laboratories, Menai Bridge, Isle of Anglesey, LL59 5EY, Wales. *Telephone:* (01248) 351 151. *Fax:* (01248) 716 367.

FOIGHEL, Isi, D.LL.; Danish politician and professor of jurisprudence; b. 21 Dec. 1927, Chemnitz, Germany; s. of Hania Foighel; one s. one d.; emigrated to Denmark in early 1930s; Prof. of Jurisprudence, Univ. of Copenhagen 1964–80, Prof. of Tax Law 1980–; Judge European Court of Human Rights 1988–; Chair. U.S.A./U.K. Arbitration on Heathrow Airport User Charges 1989–93; mem. UN Cttee. for Elimination of Racial Discrimination 1988–91; Pres. Bd. of Govs. Danish Broadcasting Corpn. 1991–95; Chair. Comm. for Home Rule for Greenland; M.P. 1984–87, Minister for Fiscal Affairs 1982–87; Conservative. *Publications:* Nationalization and Compensation 1968; books on int. law and taxation law. *Address:* Nyhavn 35, DK-1051, Copenhagen K, Denmark. *Telephone:* 33 14 14 07. *Fax:* 33 14 14 07.

FOKIN, Vitold Pavlovych; Ukrainian politician; b. 1932; fmr. mem. C.P.; engineer 1954–71; Deputy Chair. Council of Ministers of Ukraine 1987–90; Chair. State Cttee. for Econs. Aug.–Nov. 1990; Chair. Council of Ministers (Prime Minister) of Ukraine 1990–92. *Address:* c/o Cabinet of Ministers, Kiev, Ukraine.

FOKIN, Yuri Yevgenyevich; Russian diplomatist; b. 2 Sept. 1936, Gorky (now Nizhny Novgorod); m.; one s.; ed. Moscow Inst. of Int. Relations; on staff U.S.S.R. Ministry of Foreign Affairs 1960–; with U.S.S.R. Mission in UN 1960–65, Secr. of Minister of Foreign Affairs 1966–73, sr. advisor Dept.

of Planning of Int. Events 1973–76; Deputy Perm. Rep. of U.S.S.R. to UN 1976–79; Deputy Dir.-Gen. Ministry of Foreign Affairs 1979–80, Dir.-Gen. 1980–86; Amb. to Cyprus 1986–90, to Norway 1995–97, to U.K. 1997– (recalled Dec. 1998); Head Second European Dept. Ministry of Foreign Affairs 1990–92, Dir. Second European Dept. Russian Ministry of Foreign Affairs 1991–95. *Address:* Russian Embassy, 13 Kensington Palace Gardens, London, W8 4QZ, England. *Telephone:* 0171-229 2666 (Office).

FOLEY, Thomas Stephen, B.A., LL.B.; American politician; b. 6 March 1929, Spokane, Wash.; s. of Ralph E. Foley and Helen Marie Higgins; m. Heather Strachan 1968; ed. Washington Univ.; Partner Higgins and Foley 1957–58; Deputy Prosecuting Attorney, Spokane Co. 1958–60; Instructor of Law, Gonzaga Univ. 1958–60; Asst. Attorney Gen., Wash. State 1960–61; Interior and Insular Affairs Cttee., U.S. Senate, Washington 1961–64; mem. 89th–100th Congresses from 5th Dist. Wash. 1965–94, Chair. Agric. Cttee. 1975–81, Vice-Chair. 1981–86; Chair. House Democratic Caucus 1976–80, House Majority Whip 1981–87, Majority Leader 1987–89, Speaker House of Reps. 1989–95; Partner Akin, Gump, Strauss, Hauer & Feld, Washington, D.C. 1995–98; Amb. to Japan 1998–; Democrat. *Publication:* Measuring Lives (novel) 1996. *Address:* American Embassy, 1-10-5, Akasata, Minato-ku, Tokyo 107, Japan.

FØLLESDAL, Dagfinn, PH.D.; Norwegian professor of philosophy; b. 22 June 1932, Askim; s. of Trygve Føllesdal and Margit Teigen; m. Vera Heyerdahl 1957; five s. one d.; ed. Univs. of Oslo and Göttingen and Harvard Univ.; Research Asst. in Ionospheric Physics, Norwegian Research Council 1955–57; Instructor and Asst. Prof. of Philosophy, Harvard Univ. 1961–64; Prof. of Philosophy, Univ. of Oslo 1967–; Prof. of Philosophy, Stanford Univ. 1968–76, C.I. Lewis Prof. of Philosophy 1976–; Visiting Prof. Coll. de France 1977; Guggenheim Fellow 1978–79; Fellow, Center for Advanced Study in Behavioral Sciences 1981–82, American Council of Learned Socs. 1983–84, Inst. for Advanced Study, Princeton 1985–86, Wissenschaftskolleg, Berlin 1989–90, Centre for Advanced Study, Oslo 1995–96; mem. American Acad. of Arts and Sciences, Acad. Europaea and scientific acads. in Norway, Denmark, Sweden and Finland; Pres. Norwegian Acad. of Science 1993, 1995, 1997; Alexander von Humboldt Research Award 1997. *Publications:* Husserl und Frege 1958, Referential Opacity and Modal Logic 1966, Argumentasjonsteori språk og vitenskapsfilosofi (with L. Walløe and J. Elster) 1977; ed. Journal of Symbolic Logic 1970–82; numerous articles on philosophy of language, phenomenology, existentialism, action theory, educational and ethical issues. *Address:* Department of Philosophy, Stanford University, Stanford, CA 94305, U.S.A. (Office); Staverhagan 7, 1312 Slependen, Norway (Home). *Telephone:* (415)-723-2547 (Office); (47) 67 55 00 01 (Home). *Fax:* (47) 67 55 00 02 (Home).

FOLLETT, Ken, B.A.; British author; b. 5 June 1949, Cardiff, Wales; s. of Martin D. Follett and Veenie. Evans; m. 1st Mary Elson 1968 (divorced 1985); one s. one d.; m. 2nd Barbara Broer 1985; one step-s. two step-d.; ed. Univ. Coll. London; trainee reporter, South Wales Echo, Cardiff 1970–73; reporter, London Evening News 1973–74; Editorial Dir. Everest Books, London 1974–76, Deputy Man. Dir. 1976–77; full-time writer 1977–; Edgar Award of Mystery Writers of America, Best Novel category, for Eye of the Needle 1979; Fellow Univ. Coll. London. *Publications:* Eye of the Needle 1978, Triple 1979, The Key to Rebecca 1980, The Man from St. Petersburg 1982, On Wings of Eagles 1983, Lie Down with Lions 1986, The Pillars of the Earth 1989, Night Over Water 1991, A Dangerous Fortune 1993, A Place Called Freedom 1995, The Third Twin 1996, The Hammer of Eden 1998. *Leisure interest:* left-wing politics. *Address:* 1 Bowling Green, Stevenage, Herts., SG1 3BH, England.

FOLTINEK, Herbert, DR. PHIL.; Austrian literary historian; b. 29 April 1930, Vienna; s. of Helmut Foltinek and Elisabeth Foltinek (née Jaeschke); m. Elisabeth Sengstschmid 1964; ed. Univ. of Vienna and Univ. of London; lecturer in German, Univ. of Cambridge 1957–59; Asst., English Dept., Univ. of Vienna 1959–66, Docent 1966, Prof. of English and American Language and Literature 1966; mem. Austrian Acad. of Sciences. *Publications:* Arthur Schnitzler: Grosse Szene (Ed.) 1959, Vorstufen zum Viktorianischen Realismus: Der englische Roman von Jane Austen bis Charles Dickens 1968, Susan Ferrier: Marriage (Ed.) 1971, Fielding's Tom Jones und das österreichische Drama 1976, George Eliot 1982, Dramatische Ansätze in der englischen Romanliteratur des achtzehnten Jahrhunderts 1983, Charles Dickens und der Zwang des Systems 1987. *Address:* Ferrogasse 48/7, A-1180 Vienna, Austria (Home).

FOLZ, Jean-Martin; French motor executive; b. 11 Jan. 1947, Strasbourg; s. of Robert Folz and Marianne Bock; m. Marie-Claire Picardet 1968; two d.; ed. Lycée Carnot, Dijon, Ecole Sainte-Geneviève à Versailles and Ecole Polytechnique; Maison Franco-Japonaise, Tokyo 1970-71; mining engineer, Rouen 1972–74; Adviser, Office of Minister of Commerce and Crafts 1974–76; Asst. Dir. Office of Minister for Quality of Life 1976–77; Dir. Office of Sec. of State at Ministry of Industry, Commerce and Crafts 1977–78; Factory Man. Rhône-Poulenc Polymères, Saint Fons 1979–80; Deputy Gen. Man. Rhône-Poulenc Special Chemicals 1981–84; Deputy Gen. Man. then Man. Dir. Jeumont-Schneider 1984–87; Gen. Man. Péchiney 1987–91; Pres. Carbone Lorraine 1987–91; Gen. Man. Eridania Béghin-Say 1991–95; Man. Automobile Div. PSA Peugeot-Citroën 1996–97, Chair. Directorate PSA 1997–, Chair Bd. of Dirs. Automobiles Citroën 1997–; Automobiles Peugeot 1997–; Chevalier, Ordre nat. du Mérite, Chevalier du Mérite agricole. *Address:* Peugeot SA, 75 avenue de la Grande Armée, 75116 Paris (Office); 3 allée des Drocourtes, 78290 Croissy-sur-Seine, France (Home). *Telephone:* 01 40 66 55 11 (Office).

FOMENKO, Anatoly Timofeyevich; Russian mathematician; b. 13 March 1945; m.; ed. Moscow State Univ.; asst., sr. researcher, Prof. Moscow State Univ.; corresp. mem. U.S.S.R. (now Russian) Acad. of Sciences 1990, mem. 1994; research in theory of minimal surfaces, topology of multidimensional multiples, simplectic geometry and theory of topological classifications of integrable differential equations; Chair. Moscow Math. Soc. *Publications include:* Simplectic Geometry: Methods and Applications 1988, The Plateau Problem 1990. *Leisure interests:* statistical analysis of historical texts, painting. *Address:* Moscow State University, Vorobyevy gory, 119899 Moscow, Russia. *Telephone:* (095) 939 3940 (Office).

FOMENKO, Piotr Naumovich; Russian stage director; b. 13 July 1932, Moscow; m. Maya Andreyevna Tushkova; one s.; ed. Ippolitov-Ivanov Higher School of Music, V. Lenin Pedagogical Inst., State Inst. of Theatre Art; stage dir. in amateur clubs and studios of Moscow 1953–61; guest dir. in Moscow theatres including Taganka, Na Maloy Bronnoy, Cen. Children's, Mayakovsky, Cen. Theatre of Soviet Army, Satire and others 1961–84; among productions Death of Tarelkin (M. Saltykov-Shchedrin), Fruit of Education (L. Tolstoy), New Mysteria-Buff (after V. Mayakovsky), Interrogation (P. Weiss), As You Like It (W. Shakespeare); stage dir. Theatre of Comedy in Leningrad 1972–78, Chief Stage Dir. 1978–82; staged over 20 productions, some of them were banned; dir. Vakhtangov Theatre in Moscow 1985–; among productions Guilty Without Guilt (A. Ostrovsky) and The Queen of Spades (A. Pushkin); f. Little Stage (Under the Roof) Mossoviet Theatre, produced Caligula by A. Camus; f. Theatre-Workshop of P. Fomenko 1991, toured in Europe; directed films and TV productions 1965–; TV productions: Childhood, Boyhood and Youth (trilogy by L. Tolstoy), Belkin's Stories by A. Pushkin, To the Rest of the Lifetime (4 series); films: Almost Funny Story, About a Ride by Old Car; lecturer State Inst. of Theatre Art 1982, Prof. 1989; master classes in Paris Conservatory, Cen. Reimschad (Germany); People's Artist of Russia; Crystal Turandot Prize, K. Stanislavsky Prize and others. *Address:* Pobedy pl. 1, korp. A, Apt. 75, 121293 Moscow, Russia. *Telephone:* (095) 148 0773 (Home).

FONCHA, John Ngu; Cameroonian politician; b. 21 June 1916, Nkwen, N.W. Prov.; s. of Foncha and Magdalene Ngebi; m. Anna Atang 1945; four s. three d.; ed. Bamenda Govt. School, St. Michael's School, Delta Pastoral Church, Buguma, St. Charles' Coll. Onitsha, Agric. Coll., Moore Plantation, Ibadan; Probationary teacher and teacher 1934–56; Co-founder Kamerun United Nat. Congress (KUNC) 1952; mem. Eastern Regional Ass., Nigeria 1951–53; mem. S. Cameroons Quasi-Regional Ass. 1954-65; Founder-Pres. Kamerun Nat. Democratic Party (KNDP) 1955–66; Prime Minister and Minister of Local Govt., Southern Cameroons 1959–61, Prime Minister W. Cameroon 1961–65; Vice-Pres. Fed. Repub. of Cameroon 1961–70; Co-founder and Vice-Pres. Cameroon Nat. Union (CNU) 1966; Vice-Pres. Political Bureau 1970–75, Cen. Cttee. 1975; Grand Chancellor of Cameroon Nat. Orders 1979. *Publication:* Farewell to Prime Minister and People of West Cameroon. *Leisure interest:* gardening. *Address:* P.O. Box 157, Bamenda, N.W. Province, United Republic of Cameroon.

FONDA, Bridget; American actress; b. 27 Jan. 1964, Los Angeles, Calif.; d. of Peter Fonda (q.v.) and Susan Fonda; ed. New York Univ. theater programme; studied acting at Lee Strasberg Inst. and with Harold Guskin; workshop stage performances include Confession and Pastels. *Films:* Aria (Tristan and Isolde sequence) (debut) 1987, You Can't Hurry Love 1988, Shag 1988, Scandal 1989, Strapless 1989, Frankenstein Unbound 1990, The Godfather: Part III 1990, Doc Hollywood 1991, Out of the Rain 1991, Single White Female 1992, Singles 1992, Bodies Rest and Motion 1993, Point of No Return 1993, Little Buddha 1994, It Could Happen To You 1994, Camilla 1994, The Road to Welville 1994, Rough Magic 1995, Balto (voice) 1995, Grace of My Heart 1996, City Hall 1996, Drop Dead Fred, Light Years (voice), Iron Maze, Army of Darkness, Little Buddha, Touch. *TV:* (series) 21 Jump Street, Jacob Have I Loved, WonderWorks (episode) 1989, The Edge (The Professional Man); (film) Leather Jackets 1991, In the Gloaming 1997. *Address:* c/o IFA, 8730 West Sunset Boulevard, Suite 490, Los Angeles, CA 90069, U.S.A.

FONDA, Jane; American actress; b. 21 Dec. 1937; d. of the late Henry Fonda and of Frances Seymour; m. 1st Roger Vadim (q.v.) 1967 (dissolved 1973); one d.; m. 2nd Tom Hayden 1973 (dissolved 1989); one s.; m. 3rd Ted Turner 1991; ed. Vassar Coll. *Films include:* Tall Story 1960, A Walk on the Wild Side 1962, Period of Adjustment 1962, Sunday in New York 1963, The Love Cage 1963, La Ronde 1964, Histoires extraordinaires 1967, Barbarella 1968, They Shoot Horses Don't They? 1969, Klute 1970, Steelyard Blues 1972, Tout va bien 1972, A Doll's House 1973, The Blue Bird 1975, Fun with Dick and Jane 1976, Julia 1977, Coming Home 1978, California Suite 1978, The Electric Horseman 1979, The China Syndrome 1979, Nine to Five 1980, On Golden Pond 1981, Roll-Over 1981, Agnes of God 1985, The Morning After 1986, The Old Gringo 1988, Stanley and Iris 1990; producer Lakota Woman 1994. *Plays include:* There Was a Little Girl, Invitation to a March, The Fun Couple, Strange Interlude. *TV:* The Dollmaker (ABC-TV) 1984 (Emmy Award); Acad. Award for Best Actress 1972, 1979; Golden Globe Award 1978. *Publications:* Jane Fonda's Workout Book 1982, Women Coming of Age 1984, Jane Fonda's new Workout and Weight Loss Program

1986, Jane Fonda's New Pregnancy Workout and Total Birth Program 1989, Jane Fonda Workout Video, Jane Fonda Cooking for Healthy Living 1996. *Address:* c/o CAA, 9830 Wilshire Boulevard, Beverly Hills, CA 90212, U.S.A.

FONDA, Peter; American film actor, director and producer; b. 23 Feb. 1940, New York; s. of the late Henry Fonda and of Frances Seymour; m. Susan Brewer (divorced 1974); two c.; ed. Univ. of Omaha. *Films include:* Tammy and the Doctor 1963, The Victors 1963, Lilith 1964, The Young Lovers 1964, The Wild Angels 1966, The Trip 1967, Easy Rider (also co-screenplay writer, co-producer) 1969, The Last Movie 1971, The Hired Hand (also dir.) 1971, Two People (also dir.) 1973, Dirty Mary, Crazy Harry 1974, Race with the Devil 1975, 92 in the Shade 1975, Killer Force 1975, Fighting Mad 1976, Futureworld 1976, Outlaw Blues 1977, High Ballin' 1978, Wanda Nevada (also dir.) 1979, Open Season, Smokey and the Bandit II 1980, Split Image 1982, Certain Fury 1985, Dead Fall 1993, Nadja 1994, Love and a 45 1994, Painted Hero 1996, Escape from L.A. 1996, Idaho Transfer (also dir.), Ulee's Gold 1997, Spasm, Fatal Mission, Reckless, Cannonball Run (cameo), Dance of the Dwarfs, Mercenary Fighters, Jungle Heat, Diajobu My Friend, Peppermint Frieden, The Rose Garden, Family Spirit, South Beach, Bodies Rest and Motion, Deadfall, Molly and Gina. *TV films:* The Hostage Tower 1980, Don't Look Back 1996, A Reason to Live, A Time of Indifference, Sound, Certain Honorable Men, Montana. *Address:* IFA Talent Agency, 8730 West Sunset Boulevard, Suite 490, Los Angeles, CA 90069, U.S.A.

FONG WONG KUT MAN, Nellie; Chinese government official and accountant; b. 7 Feb. 1949, Hong Kong; m. Eddie C. Fong; one c.; practices as chartered accountant; mem. Hong Kong Urban Council 1983–89, Legis. Council 1988–91, People's Repub. of China Hong Kong Special Admin. Region Preliminary and Preparatory Cttees. 1993–97 (Leader Econ. Sub-Group), Exec. Council of Hong Kong Special Admin. Region July 1997–; Chair. Employees' Compensation Insurance Levies Man. Bd. 1990–93, Exec. Cttee. The Better Hong Kong Foundation 1995–; mem. Standing Comm. on Civil Service Salaries and Conditions of Service 1989–93, Hong Kong Baptist Univ. Council 1990–92, numerous other cttees. and bds. *Address:* Executive Council Secretariat, 1st Floor, Main Wing, Central Government Offices, Central, Hong Kong Special Administrative Region, People's Republic of China.

FONSECA PIMENTEL, A(ntônio); Brazilian author and fmr. government official; b. 3 July 1916, Ouro Fino, Minas Gerais; s. of Antônio Pimentel Jr. and Maria Ignacia Pimentel; m. Irma (née Machado) de Mello 1945; three s. three d.; ed. Ginasio Culto à Ciência, Campinas, São Paulo, Colegio Brasil, Ouro Fino, and American Univ. Washington, D.C.; Adviser, Brazilian School of Public Admin. 1953–55; joined Dept. of Civil Service 1955, Dir.-Gen. 1961–63; Regional Adviser UN Cen. America Tech. Assistance Bd. 1963–65; Asst. Dir. Personnel and Man., FAO 1966–69; Asst. Head, Civil Staff of Presidency of Repub. 1969–71; Special Adviser Getúlio Vargas Foundation, Brasília 1971–94; mem. UN Int. Civil Service Comm. 1975–98; mem. Acaddemia Brasiliense de Letras and other acads.; several medals including Medal Baron Rio Branco and Medal Estácio de Sá. *Publications:* A Apuração do Merecimento 1945, O Teatro de Nelson Rodrigues 1951, Alguns Aspectos do Treinamento 1954, Machado de Assis e Outros Estudos 1962, A Paz e o Pão (Desafio às Nações Unidas) 1970, A Presença Alemã na Obra de Machado de Assis 1974, Introdução à Administração Internacional de Recursos Humanos 1975, Democratic World Government and the United Nations 1979, Can a Third World War (Nuclear) be Avoided? 1983; memoirs: Memorial dos Setenta 1989, Retoques e Acréscimos ao Memorial dos Setenta 1990, Reflexões 1992, Padre Germano e o Terceiro Milênio (Uma Visão do Apocalipse) 1998. *Leisure interests:* classical music, farming. *Address:* SQS 208: Bloco F - Apt. 101, 70254-060 Brasília DF, Brazil. *Telephone:* (061) 242-2523. *Fax:* (061) 224-6314.

FONTAINE, André; French journalist; b. 30 March 1921, Paris; s. of Georges Fontaine and Blanche Rochon-Duvigneaud; m. Isabelle Cavaillé 1943; two s. one d.; ed. Coll. Ste. Marie de Monceau, Paris, Sorbonne and Faculty of Law, Paris Univ.; journalist 1946–, joined Le Monde 1947, Foreign Ed. 1951–69, Chief Ed. 1969–85, Ed.-in-Chief and Dir. 1985–91, Consultant to Dir. 1991–; mem. Bd. French Inst. of Int. Relations –1992, Bank Indosuez 1983–85; Chair. Group on Int. Strategy for the Ninth French Plan 1982; Atlas international Ed. of the Year 1976. *Publications:* L'alliance atlantique à l'heure du dégel 1960, History of the Cold War (two vols.) 1965, 1967, La guerre civile froide 1969, Le dernier quart du siècle 1976, La France au bois dormant 1978, Un seul lit pour deux rêves 1981, Sortir de l'hexagonie (with others) 1984, L'un sans l'autre 1991, Après eux le déluge 1995. *Address:* Le Monde, 21 bis rue Claude-Bernard, 75262 Paris Cédex 05, France. *Telephone:* (01) 40.65.25.21.

FONTAINE, Maurice Alfred, D. ÈS SC.; French physiologist; b. 28 Oct. 1904, Savigny-sur-Orge; s. of Emile Fontaine and Lea Vadier; m. Yvonne Broca 1928; one s.; ed. Lycée Henri IV, Paris, and Faculty of Sciences and Faculty of Pharmacy, Univ. of Paris; various posts at Faculty of Sciences, Paris and Faculty of Pharmacy, Paris; Dir. Lab. at Ecole pratique des hautes études 1946; Dir. Inst. Océanographique, Paris 1957–68, 1975; Pres. Soc. Européenne d'Endocrinologie comparée 1969; Dir. of Museum Nat. d'Histoire naturelle, Paris 1966–71; lectures on comparative and ecological physiology, particularly of marine animals; specializes in comparative endocrinology and fish migration; Dir. of Research in these fields and also the study of ectocrine substances in sea water and marine pollution; fmr. Pres. Acad. des Sciences; mem. Acad. nat. de Médecine, Acad. d'Agric., New York Acad. of Sciences; hon. mem. Romanian Acad. 1991; Commdr. Légion d'honneur, Commdr. Ordre de Sahametrei (Cambodia), Commdr. Ordre de St. Charles (Monaco). *Publication:* Physiologie (collection La Pléïade) 1969. *Leisure interests:* the sea, especially migrations of fish, thalasso-éthique. *Address:* 25 rue Pierre Nicole, 75005 Paris, France (Home).

FONTANA, Carlo; Italian opera house director; b. 15 March 1947, Milan; s. of Ciro Fontana; m. Roberta Cavallini; ed. Univ. Statale di Milano; journalist 1968–77; responsible for youth activities, Piccolo Teatro di Milano 1968–71; Asst. to Gen. Man. Teatro all Scala, Milan 1977–79, mem. Admin. Council 1980–84; Deputy Admin. Fonit Cetra 1979–84; Pres. AS.LI.CO. 1980–83; Dir. Music Section, Venice Biennale 1983–86; Dir. Ente Autonomo Teatro Comunale di Bologna 1984–90; Pres. Associazione Nazionale Enti Lirici e Sinfonici 1986–; mem. Commissione Centrale Musica, Consiglio Nazionale dello Spettacolo; Gen. Man. Teatro alla Scala, Milan 1990–; Prof. Univ. of Pavia. *Address:* Teatro alla Scala, Via Filodrammatici 2, 20121 Milan, Italy. *Telephone:* 88791. *Fax:* 8879388.

FOOT, Michael David Kenneth Willoughby, M.A.; British banker; b. 16 Dec. 1946; s. of Kenneth Willoughby Foot and Ruth Joan Foot (née Cornah); m. Michele Annette Cynthia Macdonald 1972; one s. two d.; ed. Pembroke Coll., Cambridge and Yale Univ.; joined Bank of England 1969, Man. 1978, Sr. Man. 1985; seconded to IMF, Washington as U.K. Alt. Exec. Dir. 1985–87; Head Foreign Exchange Div., Bank of England 1988–90, European Div. 1990–93, Banking Supervision Div. 1993–94, Deputy Dir. Supervision and Surveillance 1994–96, Exec. Dir. 1996–98; Man. Dir. and Head of Financial Supervision, Financial Services Authority 1998–. *Publications:* essays on monetary econs. in various books and professional journals. *Leisure interests:* choral singing, voluntary youth work. *Address:* Financial Services Authority, 25 North Colonnade, Canary Wharf, London, E14 5HS, England.

FOOT, Rt. Hon. Michael Mackintosh, P.C., M.P.; British politician and journalist; b. 23 July 1913; s. of the late Isaac Foot; (brother of the late Lord Caradon); m. Jill Craigie 1949; ed. Forres School, Swanage, Leighton Park School, Reading, and Wadham Coll., Oxford; Pres. Oxford Union 1933; contested Monmouth 1935; Asst. Ed. Tribune 1937–38, Jt. Ed. 1948–52, Ed. 1952–59, Man. Dir. 1952–74; mem. staff Evening Standard 1938, Acting Ed. 1942–44; political columnist Daily Herald 1944–64; M.P. for Plymouth, Devonport 1945–55, for Ebbw Vale 1960–83, for Blaenau Gwent 1983–92; fmr. Opposition spokesman on European Policy; Sec. of State for Employment 1974–76; Lord Pres. of Council, Leader of House of Commons 1976–79, Shadow Leader 1979–80; Deputy Leader of Labour Party 1976–80, Leader 1980–83; Hon. Fellow, Wadham Coll., Oxford 1969; Hon. mem. N.U.J. 1985; Hon. D.Litt. (Univ. of Wales) 1985, (Nottingham) 1990, (Plymouth) 1993; Hon. LL.D. (Exeter) 1990; Spanish Republican Order of Liberation 1973; Labour. *Publications:* Armistice 1918–1939 1940, Trial of Mussolini 1943, Brendan and Beverley 1944, part author Guilty Men 1940 and Who Are the Patriots? 1949, Still At Large 1950, Full Speed Ahead 1950, The Pen and the Sword 1957, Parliament in Danger 1959, Aneurin Bevan Vol. I 1962, Vol. II 1973, Harold Wilson: A Pictorial Biography 1964, Debts of Honour 1980, Another Heart and Other Pulses 1984, Loyalists and Loners 1986, The Politics of Paradise 1988, H.G.: The History of Mr. Wells 1995, Aneurin Bevan 1897–1960 1997, Dr. Strangelove I Presume 1999. *Address:* 308 Gray's Inn Road, London, WC1X 8DY; 66 Pilgrims Road, London, N.W.3, England.

FOOT, Paul Mackintosh; British writer and journalist; b. 8 Nov. 1937; m.; three s. one d.; Pres. Oxford Union 1961; Ed. Isis 1961; TUC del. from Nat. Union of Journalists 1967, 1971; Ed. Socialist Worker 1974–75; with The Daily Mirror 1979–93, Private Eye 1993–; Socialist Workers' Party parl. cand. Birmingham, Stechford 1977; Journalist of the Year, What The Papers Say Awards 1972, 1989, Campaigning Journalist of the Year, British Press Awards 1980, George Orwell Prize for Journalism (jtly. with Tim Laxton) 1994. *Publications:* Immigration and Race in British Politics 1965, The Politics of Harold Wilson 1968, The Rise of Enoch Powell 1969, Who Killed Hanratty? 1971, Why You Should Be a Socialist 1977, Red Shelley 1981, The Helen Smith Story 1983, Murder at the Farm: who killed Carl Bridgewater? 1986, Who Framed Colin Wallace? 1989, Words as Weapons 1990. *Address:* c/o Private Eye, 6 Carlisle Street, London W1V 5RG, England.

FOOT, Philippa Ruth, M.A., F.B.A.; British university professor; b. 3 Oct. 1920, Owston Ferry, Lincs.; d. of W. S. B. and Esther Cleveland Bosanquet; m. M. R. D. Foot 1945 (dissolved 1960); ed. Somerville Coll. Oxford; Lecturer in Philosophy, Somerville Coll. Oxford 1947–50, Fellow and Tutor 1950–69, Vice-Prin. 1967–69, Sr. Research Fellow 1970–88, Hon. Fellow 1988–; Prof. of Philosophy, Univ. of Calif. Los Angeles 1974–91, Griffin Prof. 1988–91, Prof. Emer. 1991–; fmr. Visiting Prof. Cornell Univ., M.I.T., Univ. of Calif. Berkeley, Princeton Univ., City Univ. of New York; Pres. Pacific Div. American Philosophical Asscn. 1983–84; mem. American Acad. of Arts and Sciences. *Publications:* Theories of Ethics (ed.) 1967, Virtues and Vices 1978; articles and reviews in professional journals. *Leisure interests:* reading, walking, gardening. *Address:* 15 Walton Street, Oxford, OX1 2HG, England. *Telephone:* (01865) 557130.

FORAY, Cyril; Sierra Leonean historian, diplomatist and fmr. politician; b. March 1934, Baiama, Bo Dist.; s. of Michael Keman Foray and Mary Bridget Foray; ed. St. Edward's Catholic Secondary School, Freetown, Fourah Bay Coll., Durham Univ., U.K.; teacher, St. Edward's School; Sales Man. BP 1962–64; lecturer, Faculty of Educ., Univ., of Njala; lecturer Univ.

of Calif. at L.A.; entered politics as APC candidate in gen. elections 1967; following mil. coup, imprisoned briefly 1967; temporary lecturer, Fourah Bay Coll. 1968; elected M.P. for Bo 1969, Minister for Foreign Affairs 1969–71, for Health 1971; withdrew from Parl. 1973; imprisoned briefly 1974; Sr. Lecturer and Head Dept. of History, Fourah Bay Coll. 1977–81, Assoc. Prof. 1981–85, Prof. and Prin. 1985–93; Public Orator, Univ., of Sierra Leone 1976–85, Dean Faculty of Arts 1978–82; High Commr. in U.K. 1993–95, 1996–. *Publications:* numerous books including Historical Dictionary of Sierra Leone 1977, The Road to the One Party—the Sierra Leone Experience 1988. *Address:* Sierra Leone High Commission, 33 Portland Place, London, W1N 3AG, England.

FORBES, Bryan; British film executive, director and screenwriter; b. 22 July 1926, Stratford, London; m. Nanette Newman (q.v.) 1958; two d.; ed. West Ham Secondary School; studied at Royal Acad. Dramatic Art, first stage appearance 1942; served in Intelligence Corps 1944–48; entered films as actor 1948; wrote and co-produced The Angry Silence 1959; Dir. Whistle Down the Wind 1961; Writer and Dir. The L-Shaped Room 1962, Seance on a Wet Afternoon 1963, King Rat 1964; Writer Only Two Can Play 1962; Producer and Dir. The Wrong Box 1965; Writer, Producer and Dir. The Whisperers 1966, Deadfall 1967, The Madwoman of Chaillot 1968, The Raging Moon (Long Ago Tomorrow in U.S.A.) 1970; Dir. Macbeth 1980, Killing Jessica 1986, Star Quality 1986, The Living Room 1987; Writer, Producer and Dir. filmed biography of Dame Edith Evans for Yorkshire TV 1973; filmed documentary on life style of Elton John for ATV 1974; wrote and dir. The Slipper and the Rose 1975, Ménage à trois (Better Late than Never in U.S.A.) 1981, The Endless Game 1989 (for Channel 4 TV); Dir. British segment of The Sunday Lovers 1980; Dir. The King in Yellow (for LWT Television) 1982, The Naked Face 1983; produced, wrote and dir. International Velvet 1977; Head of Production, Assoc. British Picture Corpn. 1969–71, subsequently became EMI Film Productions Ltd.; mem. Gen. Advisory Council of BBC 1966–69, Experimental Film Bd. of British Film Acad.; Govt. Nominee BBC Schools Broadcasting Council 1972; Pres. Beatrix Potter Soc. 1982–, Nat. Youth Theatre 1984–, Writers Guild of G.B. 1988–91; Dir. Capital Radio Ltd.; Hon. D.Litt. (Council for Nat. Academic Awards) 1987; British Film Acad. Award for The Angry Silence; Best Screenplay Awards for Only Two Can Play, Seance on a Wet Afternoon; UN Award for The L-Shaped Room; many Film Festival prizes. *Publications:* Truth Lies Sleeping (short stories) 1951, The Distant Laughter (novel) 1972, Notes for a Life (autobiog.) 1974, The Slipper and the Rose 1976, Ned's Girl (biography of Dame Edith Evans) 1977, International Velvet (novel) 1978, Familiar Strangers (novel, U.S. title Stranger) 1979, That Despicable Race—a History of the British Acting Tradition 1980, The Rewrite Man (novel) 1983, The Endless Game (novel) 1986, A Song at Twilight (novel) 1989, A Divided Life (autobiog.) 1992, The Twisted Playground (novel) 1993, Partly Cloudy (novel) 1995, Quicksand (novel) 1996, The Memory of All That 1999. *Leisure interests:* collecting books, running a bookshop, landscape gardening, collecting Napoleonic relics, avoiding bores. *Fax:* (01344) 845174.

FORBES, Malcolm Stevenson, Jr., L.H.D.; American publishing executive; b. 18 July 1947, Morristown, N.J.; s. of Malcolm Forbes and Roberta Laidlaw; m. Sabina Beekman 1971; ed. Princeton Univ. and Lycoming Coll. Jacksonville Univ.; with Forbes Inc., New York 1970–, Pres. and C.O.O. 1980–90, Deputy Ed.-in-Chief 1982–90, Ed.-in-Chief, Pres. and C.E.O. 1990–; Chair. Forbes Newspapers 1989–; mem. Bd. for Int. Broadcasting 1983–93, Chair. 1985–93; mem. Advisory Council, Dept. of Econs. Princeton Univ. 1985–; several hon. degrees. *Author:* Some Call It Greed (film script) 1977. *Publication:* Fact and Comment (ed.) 1974. *Address:* Forbes Inc., 60 Fifth Avenue, New York, NY 10011, U.S.A.

FORCHHAMMER, Jes, D.SC., M.D.; Danish cancer research scientist; b. 5 April 1934, Aarhus; s. of Nels B. Forchhammer and Margrethe Høgstrøm; m. Anne Jette Edinger (née Balle); two s. one d.; ed. Copenhagen Univ.; Research Fellow, Dept. of Antibiotics, State Serum Inst. 1961–63; lecturer, Dept. of Microbiology, Copenhagen Univ. 1963–73; Visiting Asst. Prof. Dept. of Biochem. Pittsburgh Univ. Medical School 1969–70; EMBO Sr. Research Fellow, Dept. of Biological Sciences, Stanford Univ. 1970–71; Dept. of Molecular Oncology, The Fibiger Inst. Danish Cancer Soc. 1973–; Head Inst. of Cancer Biology 1994–, of Cancer Epidemiology 1996–; mem. Royal Danish Acad. *Publications:* co-author: Cancer and Chemicals 1981–85, Viral Carcinogenesis 1987. *Leisure interests:* hockey, tennis, skiing, music. *Address:* Institute of Cancer Biology, Danish Cancer Society, Strandboulevarden 49, 2100 Copenhagen Ø, Denmark. *Telephone:* 35 25 73 11. *Fax:* 35 25 77 21.

FORD, Anna, B.A.; British broadcaster; b. 2 Oct. 1943; d. of John Ford and Jean Beattie Winstanley; m. 1st Alan Holland Bittles (dissolved 1976); m. 2nd Charles Mark Edward Boxer (died 1988); two d.; ed. Minehead Grammar School, White House Grammar School, Brampton and Manchester Univ.; work for students' interests, Manchester Univ. 1966–69; lecturer Rupert Stanley Coll. of Further Educ., Belfast 1970–72; staff tutor, Social Sciences, Northern Ireland Region, Open Univ. 1972–74; presenter and reporter Granada TV 1974–76, Man Alive BBC 1976–77, Tomorrow's World BBC 1977–78; newscaster ITN 1978–80; with TV am 1980–82; freelance broadcasting and writing 1982–86; BBC news and current affairs 1989–; Trustee Royal Botanic Gardens, Kew; Hon. LL.D. (Manchester) 1998. *Publication:* Men: A Documentary 1985. *Leisure interests:* talking, writing, drawing. *Address:* BBC Television Centre, Wood Lane, London, W12 7RJ, England. *Telephone:* 0181-624 9996.

FORD, David Frank, M.A., PH.D., S.T.M.; Irish professor of divinity; b. 23 Jan. 1948, Dublin; s. of George Ford and Phyllis Woodman; m. Deborah Hardy 1982; one s. two d. (one d. deceased); ed. High School, Dublin, Trinity Coll., Dublin, St. John's Coll., Cambridge and Yale Univ.; lecturer in Theology, Univ. of Birmingham 1976–90, sr. lecturer 1990–91; Regius Prof. of Divinity, Univ. of Cambridge 1991–, Chair. Faculty Bd. of Divinity 1993–95; Fellow, Selwyn Coll. Cambridge 1991–; Foundation mem. Trinity Coll. Cambridge 1991–; Chair. Council, Westcott House Theological Coll. 1991–97; mem. Archbishop of Canterbury's Urban Theology Working Group 1991–; Fellow, Center of Theological Inquiry, Princeton Univ. 1993–; mem. Syndicate Cambridge Univ. Press 1993–; Chair. Man. Cttee. of Centre for Advanced Religious and Theological Studies, Univ. of Cambridge 1995–; Pres. Soc. for the Study of Theology 1997–(99). *Publications:* Barth and God's Story 1981, Jubilate: Theology in Praise (with D. W. Hardy) 1984, Meaning and Truth in 2 Corinthians (with F. M. Young) 1987, The Modern Theologians, The Shape of Living 1997. *Leisure interests:* literature, walking, ball games, gardening, family and friends. *Address:* Faculty of Divinity, St. John's Street, Cambridge, CB2 1TW, England. *Telephone:* (01223) 332592. *Fax:* (01223) 332582.

FORD, Sir David Robert, K.B.E., L.V.O.; British government official (retd.); b. 22 Feb. 1935; s. of William E. Ford and Edna Ford; m. 1st Elspeth A. Muckart 1958 (divorced 1987); two s. two d.; m. 2nd Gillian Petersen (née Monsarrat) 1987; ed. Tauntons School; officer, R.A. 1955–72 retd. from army, rank of Maj.; seconded to Hong Kong Govt. 1967; Deputy Dir. Hong Kong Govt. Information Service 1972–74, Dir. 1974–76; Deputy Sec. Hong Kong Govt. Secr. 1976; Under-Sec. Northern Ireland Office 1977–79; Sec. for Information, Hong Kong Govt. 1979–80; Hong Kong Commr. in London 1980–81, 1994–96; Royal Coll. of Defence Studies 1982; Dir. of Housing, Hong Kong Govt. 1983–84, Sec. for Housing 1985, for the Civil Service 1985–86; Chief Sec., Hong Kong 1986–93, Hong Kong Commr. in London 1994–97; retd. from public service June 1997; Chair. Council for Protection of Rural England 1998–. *Address:* Culverwell, Branscombe, Devon, EX12 3DA, England.

FORD, Gerald Rudolph, Jr.; American politician and lawyer; b. 14 July 1913, Omaha, Neb.; s. of Gerald R. Ford, Sr. and Dorothy Gardner Ford; m. Elizabeth (Betty) Bloomer 1948; three s. one d.; ed. Univ. of Michigan and Yale Univ. Law School; partner, law firm Ford and Buchen 1941–42; U.S.N. service 1942–46; mem. law firm Butterfield, Keeney and Amberg 1947–49; mem. U.S. House of Reps. 1949–73; House Minority Leader 1965–73; Vice-Pres. of U.S.A. 1973–74, Pres. of U.S.A. 1974–77; Visiting Prof. in Govt., Univ. of Mich.; Chair. Bd. of Acad. for Educational Devt. 1977; mem. Interparl. Union, Warsaw 1959, Brussels 1961, Belgrade 1963; mem. U.S.-Canadian Interparl. Group, Chair. House of Repub. Conf. 1963; Advisor American Express Co. 1981, Texas Commerce Bancshares, Inc.; mem. Warren Comm., American Enterprise Inst.; Bd. mem. The Traveler's Inc., Alexander & Alexander; numerous hon. degrees and awards; Republican. *Publications:* Portrait of the Assassin (with John R. Stiles), A Time to Heal (memoirs) 1979, The Humor and the Presidency 1987. *Address:* P.O. Box 927, Rancho Mirage, CA 92270, U.S.A.

FORD, Harrison; American actor; b. 1942, Chicago; m. 1st Mary Ford; two s.; m. 2nd Melissa Ford; one s. one d.; ed. Ripon Coll.; numerous TV appearances. *Films include:* Dead Heat on a Merry-Go-Round 1966, Luv 1967, The Long Ride Home 1967, Getting Straight 1970, Zabriskie Point 1970, The Conversation 1974, American Graffiti 1974, Star Wars 1977, Heroes 1977, Force 10 from Navarone 1978, Hanover Street 1979, Frisco Kid 1979, The Empire Strikes Back 1980, Raiders of the Lost Ark 1981, Blade Runner, Return of the Jedi 1983, Indiana Jones and the Temple of Doom, Witness, The Mosquito Coast 1986, Working Girl 1988, Frantic 1988, Indiana Jones and the Last Crusade 1989, Presumed Innocent 1990, Regarding Henry 1991, The Fugitive 1992, Patriot Games 1992, Clear and Present Danger 1994, Sabrina 1995, Air Force One 1996, Six Days and Seven Nights 1998. *Address:* 10279 Century Woods Drive, Los Angeles, CA 90067, U.S.A.

FORD, Sir Hugh, Kt., F.R.S., PH.D., D.SC., F.ENG.; British professor and engineering consultant; b. 16 July 1913, Thornby, Northants.; s. of Arthur Ford and Constance Mary Ford; m. 1st Wynyard Scholfield 1942 (died 1991); two d.; m. 2nd Thelma Alys Jensen (née Morgan) 1993; ed. Northampton School and Imperial Coll., Univ. of London; served apprenticeship Great Western Railway 1931–36; Research engineer Imperial Coll. 1936–39, Imperial Chemical Industries 1939–42; Chief Tech. Officer British Iron and Steel Fed. 1942–47; Tech. Dir. Paterson Eng. 1947–48; Reader, then Prof. Imperial Coll. 1948–65, Prof. of Mechanical Eng. and Head of Dept. 1969–80, Pro-Rector 1978–80, Prof. Emer. 1980–; Dir. Davy Ashmore, Alfred Herbert Ltd., etc. 1965–78; Chair. Ford and Dain Partners 1972–82 (Dir. 1972–93), Sir Hugh Ford and Assocs. 1982–; Pres. Inst. of Mechanical Engineers 1976–77, The Welding Inst. 1983–85, Inst. of Metals 1985–87; Dr. h.c. (Belfast, Sheffield, Aston, etc.); Hawkesley Gold Medal 1948, Sir James Ewing Medal, James Watt Int. Gold Medal, *Publications:* Advanced Mechanics of Materials 1962, 100 scientific papers. *Leisure interests:* music, gardening, model engineering. *Address:* 18 Shrewsbury House, Cheyne Walk, London, SW3 5LN; Shamley Cottage, Stroud Lane, Shamley Green, Surrey, GU5 0ST, England (Home). *Telephone:* 0171-352 4948 (London); (01483) 898012 (Surrey). *Fax:* 0171-352 5320.

FORD, Richard; American writer; b. 16 Feb. 1944, Jackson, Miss.; m. Kristina Hensley Ford 1968; lecturer, William Coll. 1979–80, Princeton Univ. 1980–81, Harvard Univ. 1994–; American Acad. and Inst. of Arts and Letters Award for Literature 1989. *Publications:* (novels) A Piece of my Heart 1976, The Ultimate Good Luck 1981, The Sportswriter 1986, Wildlife 1990, Independence Day 1995; (stories) Rocksprings 1987, screenplay Bright Angel 1991. *Address:* c/o Amanda Urban, ICM, 40 West 57th Street, New York, NY 10019. *Telephone:* (212) 5565764.

FORD, Richard John, B.A., DIP. ARCH.; British business executive; b. 10 April 1949; s. of late Arthur Ford and of Violet Banbury; m. Janet K. Ford; one s.; ed. Portsmouth Polytechnic and Polytechnic of London; Exec. Creative Dir. responsible for all creative product for Landor Assocs. 1984–; commissions include identity and environmental design for British Airways 1984, Chase Manhattan Bank Europe 1985, Royal Jordanian Airlines and Alfred Dunhill 1986, BAe and Abbey National 1987, Cespa Petroleum Spain, Depasco Convenience Stores Spain and Ballantyne Cashmere 1988, Emlak Bank, Turkey 1989, Deutsche Shell 1990, Egnatia Bank Greece 1991, Seville Expo and Neste Petroleum Finland 1992, Lincoln Mercury U.S.A., Telia (Swedish Telecom) and Cathay Pacific Airline 1993, Royal Mail and Delta Air Lines U.S.A. 1994, Montell (Worldwide) and KF (Swedish Co-op) 1995, R.I.B.A. 1993, Adtranz (Worldwide) and Air 2000 (U.K.) 1996, Credit Lyonnais 1997. *Address:* Landor Associates, Klamath House, 18 Clerkenwell Green, London, EC1R 0DP, England. *Telephone:* 0171-880 8000.

FORD, Robert Arthur Douglass, C.C., M.A., D.LITT.; Canadian diplomatist; b. 8 Jan. 1915, Ottawa; s. of Arthur Rutherford Ford and May Lavinia Scott; m. Maria Thereza Gomes 1946 (died 1983); ed. Univ. of Western Ontario and Cornell Univ.; Instructor, History Dept., Cornell Univ. 1939–40; Dept. of External Affairs 1940, served Rio de Janeiro, Moscow, London 1940–51; Chargé d'Affaires, Moscow 1951–54; Head of European Div., Dept. of External Affairs 1954–57; Amb. to Colombia 1957–58, to Yugoslavia 1959–61, to U.A.R. 1961–63, to U.S.S.R. 1964–80; Special Adviser on East-West Relations 1980; Founder mem. Int. Inst. of Geopolitics; mem. Palme Comm. on Disarmament and Security Issues; Hon. Pres. Asscn. France-Canada du Bourbonnais; Hon. D.Litt. (Western Ontario) 1965; Hon. LL.D. (Toronto) 1987; Gov.-Gen.'s Award for Poetry 1956, Award of Merit, Univ. of Western Ont. 1988, Gold Medal of Professional Inst. of Public Service of Canada 1971. *Publications:* Poetry: A Window on the North 1956, The Solitary City 1969, Holes in Space 1979, Needle in the Eye 1983, Doors, Words and Silence 1985, Dostoyevsky and Other Poems 1988, Coming from Afar: Selected Poems 1990; Russian Poetry: A Personal Anthology 1984, A Diplomat's Reflections on The Soviet Union 1989, Diplomate et Poète à Moscou 1990, A Moscow Literary Notebook, Among the Great Artists of Russia from 1946 to 1980, 1991, and articles on foreign affairs. *Leisure interests:* travel, poetry, translations (Russian, Portuguese). *Address:* La Poivrière, St. Sylvestre-Pragoulin, 63310 Randan, France. *Telephone:* 70-59-01-47.

FORD, Tom; American fashion designer; b. 1962, Texas; ed. New York Univ., Parsons School of Design; fmrly. acted in TV commercials, asst. to designer Cathy Hardwick, with Perry Ellis Co.; joined Gucci 1990, head of advertising 1994, Creative Dir. 1995–; involved in fund-raising in U.S. and Europe. *Address:* c/o Gucci, 685 Fifth Avenue, New York, NY 10022, U.S.A.

FORD, Wendell Hampton; American politician; b. 8 Sept. 1924, Owensboro, Ky.; s. of E. M. and Irene (Schenk) Ford; m. Jean Neel 1943; one s. one d.; ed. Daviess County High School, Univ. of Kentucky, Maryland School of Insurance; served U.S. Army, Ky. 1944–46, Nat. Guard 1949–62; Chief Asst. to Gov. of Kentucky 1959–61; mem. Ky. Senate 1966–67; Lieut.-Gov. Kentucky 1967–71, Gov. 1971–74; U.S. Senator from Kentucky 1974–97; Asst. Minority Leader 1995–97; fmr. mem. Senate Energy and Natural Resources Cttee., Commerce, Science, Transportation Cttee. (Chair. Consumer Sub-Cttee.); mem. Democratic Steering Cttee., Chair. Democratic Nat. Campaign Cttee. 1976, Head of Democratic Senatorial Campaign Cttee.; Majority Whip 1991–97; Chair. Senate Rules Cttee., Jt. Cttee. on Printing; Chair. Nat. Democratic Govs. 1973–74; Chair. Jt. Congressional Cttee. on Inaugural Ceremonies; fmr. mem. Nat. Democratic Party Advisory Council; fmr. Chair. common law enforcement, justice and public safety, Southern Govs.' Conf.; mem. U.S. Chamber of Commerce, Pres. 1956–57; Int. Vice-Pres. Jaycees. *Leisure interests:* fishing, hunting. *Address:* 2017 Fieldcrest Drive, Owensboro, KY 42301, U.S.A. (Home).

FORD, William Clay, B.S.(ECON.); American businessman; b. 14 March 1925, Detroit; s. of Edsel Ford and Eleanor Clay Ford; brother of Henry Ford II (q.v.); m. Martha Firestone 1947; one s. three d.; ed. Yale Univ.; Dir. Ford Motor Co. 1948–; mem. of Sales and Advertising Staff 1948 and of the Industrial Relations Staff 1949; quality control Man. Lincoln-Mercury Div. Jet Engine Defence Project 1951; Man. Special Product Operations 1952; Vice-Pres. Ford Motor Co. and Gen. Man. Continental Div. 1953, Group Dir. Continental Div. 1955, Vice-Pres. Product Design 1956–80, Chair. Exec. Cttee. 1978–, Vice-Chair. of Bd. 1980–89, mem. Company Finance Cttee. 1987–; Pres./Owner Detroit Lions Professional Football Team; Chair. Emer. Edison Inst.; Trustee Eisenhower Medical Center, Thomas A. Edison Foundation; mem. Bd. of Dirs. Nat. Tennis Hall of Fame, Boys Club of America. *Address:* Ford Motor Company Design Center, P.O. Box 6012, Dearborn, MI 48121, U.S.A.

FORD, William Clay, Jr.; American motor company executive; b. 1957; s. of William Clay Ford and Martha Firestone; ed. Princeton Univ., Massachusetts Inst. of Tech.; Pres. Detroit Lions Football Team 1980–95, Vice-Chair. 1995–; with Ford Motor Co. 1979–, fmrly. Gen. Man. Climate Control Div., Vice-Pres. Commercial Truck Vehicle Centre, Chair. Finance Cttee. 1995–, currently Chair.; mem. World Econ. Forum's Global Leaders for Tomorrow; Vice-Chair., Dir. Greater Downtown Partnership Inc.; Trustee Edison Inst. *Address:* c/o Ford Motor Company Ltd., World Headquarters, 2000 The American Road, Dearborn, MI 48121, U.S.A.

FORDE, Sir Henry deBoulay, Kt., P.C., LL.M., Q.C.; Barbadian politician and lawyer; b. 20 March 1933, Christ Church, Barbados; adopted s. of late Courtley Ifill and of Elise Ifill; m. Cheryl Wendy Roach; four s.; ed. Harrison Coll., Barbados, Christ's Coll., Cambridge, Middle Temple, London; Research Asst., Dept. of Criminology, Univ. of Cambridge 1958, Research Student, Int. Law, worked on British Digest of Int. Law, Univ. of Cambridge 1958–59, Supervisor and Tutor in Int. Law, Emmanuel Coll., Cambridge 1958–59; called to English Bar 1959, to Barbadian Bar 1959; Lecturer, Extra-Mural Programme, Univ. of West Indies 1961–68, Part-time Lecturer, Caribbean Studies, 1964–69; mem. House of Ass. for Christ Church West 1971–; Minister of External Affairs and Attorney-Gen. 1976–81; Minister of State 1993; Leader of the Opposition 1986–89, 1991–93; mem. Privy Council 1976–92, 1996–; Chair. and Political Leader, Barbados Labour Party 1986–93; Chair. Commonwealth Observer Group to the Seychelles 1991; mem. Commonwealth Cttee. on Vulnerability of Small States 1985, Commonwealth Parl. Asscn., Editorial Bds. of The Round Table, Int. Comm. of Jurists 1987–92, Barbados Bar Asscn., Hon. Soc. of Middle Temple, Int. Tax Planning Asscn., Interparl. Human Rights Network, Barbados Nat. Trust, Int. Acad. of Estate and Trust Law, Int. Inst. for Democracy and Electoral Assistance, Inter-American Comm. on Human Rights. *Leisure interests:* reading, walking, gardening. *Address:* Juris Chambers, Suite 205, Kays House, 13–14 Roebuck Street, Bridgetown (Office); Codrington Court, Society, St. John, Barbados, West Indies (Home). *Telephone:* (246) 429-5320, 429-2208 (Office); (246) 423-3881 (Home). *Fax:* (246) 429-2206.

FORDICE, Kirk, Jr. (Daniel Kirkwood Fordice), M.SC.; American politician and business executive; b. 10 Feb. 1934, Memphis, Tenn.; s. of Daniel Kirkwood Fordice and Clara Augustine; m. Patricia Louise Owens 1955; three s. one d.; ed. Purdue Univ.; worked as engineer in Miss. and La.; with Exxon, Baton Rouge 1956–62; partner Fordice Construction Co., Vicksburg, Mo. 1962–76, Pres. and C.E.O. 1976–; Gov. of Missouri 1992; Sec. Mo. Repub. Party 1981–88; Vice-Chair. Southern Govs' Asscn. 1992–, Chair. 1994–; mem. American Construction Industry Forum (Pres. 1991), Confed. Int. Contractor's Asscns. (Vice-Pres. 1990–); Fellow A.S.C.E; numerous awards for contribs. in construction eng. field; Republican. *Address:* Fordice Construction Company, 4111 Warrenton Road, Vicksburg, MO 39180, U.S.A.

FORERO DE SAADE, María Teresa, D. MED.; Colombian politician and doctor; b. 28 Feb. 1939, Vergara, Cundinamarca; m. Rafael Saade Abdala; three s.; ed. Instituto Pedagógico Nacional, Colegio Departamental de la Merced, Bogotá and Pontificia Universidad Javeriana; qualified as doctor 1966; specialist in pediatrics; Prof. of Pediatrics at Univ. of Rosario 1968–69; Prof. of Pediatrics at Faculty of Nursing, Nat. Red Cross 1971–72; Gen.-Dir. of Colsubsidio Clinic for Children 1974–82; Deputy Senator 1978–82; Vice-Minister of Health 1982; Minister at the Ministry of Health 1982; Minister of Labour and Social Security 1989–90.

FORGEARD, Noël, L.N. ÈS. SC.ECON.; French business executive and mining engineer; b. 8 Dec. 1946, Ferté-Gaucher; s. of Henri Forgeard and Laurence Duprat; m. Marie-Cécile de Place 1972; one s. three d.; ed. Lycée Louis-le-Grand, Ecole Polytechnique, Paris; qualified as mining engineer; entered mining industry in Clermont-Ferrand, industry rep. to Auvergne prefecture 1972–73; Asst. Sec.-Gen. Dept. of Mining, Ministry for Industry 1973–76, Sec.-Gen. 1976–78; Tech. Adviser to Minister of Transport 1978–80, of Defence 1980; Head of Industrial Affairs and Armaments, Ministry of Defence 1980–81; Deputy Pres., Asst. Gen. Man. Compagnie française des aciers spéciaux (CFAS) 1982–84, Prés., Dir.-Gen. 1984–86; Man. Dir. then Prés., Dir.-Gen. Ascometal 1985–86; Chair. Asfor Steel Products 1986–87; Tech Adviser and Head of Industrial Affairs, Office of the Prime Minister 1986–87; Man. Defence and Space Divs. Matra 1987, Prés., Dir.-Gen. Matra-défense espace finance co. (Sofimades), Matra Hautes technologies, Matra Bac Dynamics, mem. Exec. and Strategy Cttee. and Gen. Man. Lagardère SCA 1993–98; Man. Dir. Airbus Industrie 1998–; Dir. Matra systèmes et information, Snecma, Matra-Marconi Space NV; Vice-Pres. Groupement des industries de l'aéronautique et de l'espace (Gifas); Public Enterprise Foundation Award 1971; Chevalier, Légion d'honneur, Ordre nat. du Mérite. *Leisure interests:* modern art, swimming. *Address:* Airbus Industrie, Ronde Point Maurice Bellonte 1, 31700 Blagnac (Office); 85 av. de Wagram, 75017 Paris (Home); Le Roc, 35800 Saint-Briac-sur-Mer, France (Home).

FORGEOT, Jean; French business executive; b. 10 Oct. 1915, Paris; s. of P. E. Forgeot and Aydée Lefebvre; m. Sylviane Busck 1948; one d.; ed. Faculté de Droit, Paris; Insp., Ministry of Finance 1942–55; Adviser to the Cabinet of Vincent Auriol; Sec.-Gen. to Pres. of Repub. 1947–54; fmr. Pres. Dir.-Gen. Schneider S.A., Hon. Pres. 1970–; Vice-Pres. Chrysler-France (fmrly. Soc. des Automobiles Simca) 1955; Pres. Dir.-Gen. Cie. Financière de l'Union européenne 1971, Dir. 1976; Dir. Esso-Standard, Cie. Maritime des Chargeurs réunis, Imprimerie Georges Lang; Pres. Dir.-Gen. Creusot-

Loire 1971; Hon. Pres., Admin. Groupement des industries mécaniques (Gimeca) 1989–; Officier Légion d'honneur, Croix de guerre (1939–45), Officier du Mérite maritime. *Leisure interests:* tennis, golf. *Address:* 20 boulevard Suchet, 75116 Paris, France.

FORLANI, Arnaldo; Italian politician; b. 8 Dec. 1925, Pesaro; s. of Luigi and Caterina Forlani; m. Alma Ioni 1956; three s.; ed. Univ. of Urbino; mem. Chamber of Deputies 1958; Deputy Sec. of Christian Democrat Party 1962–69, Political Sec. (Leader) 1969–73, 1989; Minister of State Enterprises 1969–70, of Defence 1974–76, of Foreign Affairs 1976–79; Prime Minister 1980–81, Deputy Prime Minister 1983–87; Pres. Christian Democratic Party 1986–89, Sec. Gen. 1989–92. *Leisure interest:* journalism. *Address:* Piazzale Schumann 15, Rome, Italy. *Telephone:* 6784109.

FORMAN, Sir Denis, Kt., O.B.E.; British business executive; b. 13 Oct. 1917, Beattock, Scotland; s. of the late Rev. Adam Forman and of Flora (née Smith) Forman; m. 1st Helen de Mouilpied 1948 (died 1987); two s.; m. 2nd Moni Cameron 1990; one step-s. one step-d.; ed. Loretto and Pembroke Coll., Cambridge; war service with Argyll and Sutherland Highlanders 1940–45 (Commdt. Orkney and Shetland Defences Battle School 1942, wounded, Cassino 1944); Chief Production Officer, Cen. Office of Information Films 1947; Dir. British Film Inst. 1948–55, Chair. Bd. of Govs. 1971–73; Jt. Man. Dir., Granada TV Ltd. 1965–81, Chair. 1974–87; Dir. Granada Group 1964–, Deputy Chair. 1984–90, Consultant 1990–96; Chair. Novello & Co. 1971–78, Chair. Scottish Film Production Dept. 1990–; Dir. Royal Opera House, Covent Garden 1981–, Deputy Chair. 1983–92, Fellow, B.F.I. 1993; Dir. Harold Holt Ltd. 1992–; mem. Council Royal Northern Coll. of Music (RNCM) 1975–84, Hon. mem. 1981; several hon. degrees; Fellow, British Acad. of Film and TV Arts 1977–; Ufficiale dell' ordine al Merito della Repubblica Italiana. *Publications:* Mozart's Piano Concertos 1971, Son of Adam 1990, To Reason Why 1991. *Leisure interests:* music, shooting. *Address:* The Mill House, Howe Street, Chelmsford, Essex, CM3 1BG, England.

FORMAN, Miloš; American film director; b. 18 Feb. 1932, Čáslav; ed. Film Faculty, Acad. of Music and Dramatic Art, Prague; Dir. Film Presentations, Czechoslovak TV 1954–56; of Laterna Magika, Prague 1958–62; mem. Artistic Cttee., Šebor-Bor Film Producing Group; Czechoslovak Film Critics' Award for Peter and Pavla 1963, Grand Prix 17th Int. Film Festival, Locarno, for Peter and Pavla 1964, Prize Venice Festival 1965, Grand Prix of French Film Acad. for A Blonde in Love 1966, Klement Gottwald State Prize 1967, Acad. Award (Best Dir.) for One Flew Over the Cuckoo's Nest 1976, Acad. Award, also César Award for Amadeus 1985. *Films include:* Talent Competition, Peter and Pavla 1964, The Knave of Spades, A Blonde in Love 1965, Episode in Zruč, Like a House on Fire (A Fireman's Ball) 1968, Taking Off 1971; Co-Dir. Visions of Eight 1973, One Flew Over the Cuckoo's Nest 1975, Hair 1979, Ragtime 1980, Amadeus 1983, Valmont 1988, The People Vs. Larry Flynt 1995; appeared in New Year's Day 1989. *Publication:* Turnaround: A Memoir (with Jan Novak) 1993. *Address:* c/o Robert Lantz, 888 7th Avenue, New York, NY 10106, U.S.A.

FORMICA, Salvatore; Italian politician; b. 1 March 1927, Bari; Senator, Milan VI 1979–83; Socialist (P.S.I.) M.P. for Bari 1983; Minister of Transport in second Cossiga Govt. and Forlani Govt.; fmr. Minister of Finance; Minister for Foreign Trade 1986–87, for Labour 1987–88, April 1988–89, of Finance 1989–90; mem. Parl. Comm. of Inquiry into Masonic Lodge P2.

FORMIGONI, Roberto; Italian politician; b. 30 March 1947, Lecco; s. of Emilio Formigoni and Doralice Formigoni; Leader Movimento Popolare (political arm of Catholic movt. Comunione e Liberazione); mem. Christian Democratic Party governing directorate; fmr. Vice-Pres. European Parl. *Address:* Movimento Popolare, Via Copernico 7, 20125 Milan, Italy. *Telephone:* (02) 606641.

FORREST, Sir (Andrew) Patrick (McEwen), Kt., M.D., F.R.C.S., F.R.S.E.; British surgeon; b. 25 March 1923, Mount Vernon, Scotland; s. of Andrew J. Forrest and Isabella Pearson; m. 1st Margaret B. Hall 1955 (died 1961); m. 2nd Margaret A. Steward 1964; one s. two d.; ed. Dundee High School and St. Andrews Univ.; Mayo Foundation Fellow, Rochester, Minn. 1952–53; lecturer and sr. lecturer, Univ. of Glasgow 1954–62; Prof. of Surgery, Welsh Nat. School of Medicine 1962–71; Regius Prof. of Clinical Surgery, Univ. of Edin. 1970–88, Prof. Emer. 1989–, Hon. Fellow, Faculty of Medicine 1989–95; Visiting Scientist, Nat. Insts. of Health 1989–90; Assoc. Dean (Clinical Studies) Int. Medical Coll., Kuala Lumpur 1993–96; mem. Medical Research Council 1975–79; Chief Scientist, Scottish Home and Health Dept. (part-time) 1981–87; mem. Advisory Bd. for Research Councils 1982–85; Lister Medal 1987; Gold Medal, Netherlands Surgical Assn. 1988; Hon. F.A.C.S.; Hon. F.R.A.C.S.; Hon. F.R.C.S. (Canada); Hon. F.R.C.R.; Hon. D.Sc. (Wales, Chinese Univ. of Hong Kong), Hon. LL.D. (Dundee). *Publications:* Prognostic Factors in Breast Cancer (jt. ed.) 1968, Principles and Practice of Surgery (jtly.) 1985, Breast Cancer: The Decision to Screen 1990; over 250 publs. in scientific and medical journals. *Leisure interests:* golf, sailing. *Address:* 19 St. Thomas Road, Edinburgh, EH9 2LR, Scotland (Home). *Telephone:* 0131-667 3203 (Home).

FORSÉN, K. Sture, M.SC., D.TECH.; Swedish professor of physical chemistry; b. 12 July 1932, Piteå; s. of Helmer Forsén and Signe Forsén; m. Dr. Gunilla Isaksson 1973 (divorced 1986); ed. Royal Inst. of Tech. Stockholm; Assoc. Prof. of Chemical Physics, Royal Inst. of Tech. 1963–67, Prof. of Physical Chem., Univ. of Lund 1966; mem. Bd. of Dirs. Swedish Natural Science Research Council 1983–86, Perstorp AB 1986–, Swedish Nat. Chemicals Inspectorate 1989–; Fairchild Scholar, CalTech. 1986–87, Fogarty Scholar, N.I.H., U.S.A. 1987–94, Visiting Investigator Scripps Research Inst., La Jolla 1990–; mem. Scientific Advisory Council of Volvo Research Foundation 1987–; mem. Royal Swedish Acad. of Sciences 1973–, Nobel Cttee. for Chem. 1982–; mem. Royal Swedish Acad. of Eng. Sciences 1986–; Celsius Gold Medal, Royal Soc. of Uppsala 1979. *Publications:* co-author of two books on NMR spectroscopy 1972, 1976; over 300 scientific articles, at present mainly concerning biophysical studies of calcium-binding proteins, in int. journals. *Leisure interests:* music from Frescobaldi to Keith Jarrett, renovating old farmhouses. *Address:* St Laurentiigatan 8 IV, S-222 21 Lund, Sweden (Home). *Telephone:* 46144803 (Home). *Fax:* 41451457.

FORSTER, Margaret, B.A.; British writer; b. 25 May 1938, Carlisle; d. of Lilian Hind and Arthur Gordon Forster; m. Edward Hunter Davies 1960; one s. two d.; ed. Carlisle County High School and Somerville Coll., Oxford. *Publications:* numerous novels since 1964; The Rash Adventurer: the rise and fall of Charles Edward Stuart 1973, work on Thackeray, and Significant Sisters: History of Active Feminism 1839–1940 1984, Elizabeth Barrett Browning: A Life 1988, Elizabeth Barrett Browning, selected poems (ed.) 1988, Daphne du Maurier: The Authorised Biography 1993, Hidden Lives: A Family Memoir 1995, Rich Desserts and the Captain is Thin: A Family and Their Times 1831–1931 1997, Precious Lives 1998. *Leisure interests:* fell walking and reading contemporary fiction. *Address:* 11 Boscastle Road, London, NW5 1EE; Grasmoor House, Loweswater, near Cockermouth, Cumbria, CA13 0RU, England. *Telephone:* 0171-485 3785 (London); (01900) 85303 (Cumbria).

FORSTER, Sir Oliver Grantham, K.C.M.G., L.V.O.; British diplomatist; b. 2 Sept. 1925, London; s. of Norman and Olive Forster; m. Beryl Evans 1953; two d.; ed. Hurstpierpoint and King's Coll., Cambridge; H.M. Forces 1944–48; Commonwealth Relations Office (CRO) 1951; Pvt. Sec. to Parl. Under-Sec. of State 1953; Second Sec., Karachi 1954; First Sec. CRO 1956–59, Madras 1959–62, Washington 1962–65; Pvt. Sec. to Sec. of State for Commonwealth Affairs 1965–67; Counsellor and Head of Chancery, Manila 1967–70; Counsellor (Commercial/Economic) later Minister (March 1975), New Delhi 1970; Asst. Under-Sec. of State and Deputy Chief Clerk, FCO 1975–79; Amb. to Pakistan 1979–84; Chair. Royal Commonwealth Soc. and Commonwealth Trust 1992–96; HQA (Pakistan) 1984. *Address:* 71 Raglan Road, Reigate, Surrey, RH2 0HP, England.

FORSYTH, Bill; British film-maker; b. 1947, Glasgow; one s. one d.; ed. Nat. Film School, Beaconsfield; Hon. D.Litt. (Glasgow) 1984, Hon. Ph.D. (Stirling) 1989; BAFTA Award best screenplay 1982, best dir. 1983. *Films:* That Sinking Feeling 1979, Gregory's Girl 1980, Local Hero 1982, Comfort and Joy 1984, Housekeeping 1987, Breaking In 1988, Being Human 1994. *Address:* c/o A.D. Peters, The Chambers, Chelsea Harbour, Lots Road, London, SW10 0XF, England.

FORSYTH, Elliott Christopher, B.A., DIP.ED., D. UNIV.; Australian professor of French; b. 1 Feb. 1924, Mount Gambier; s. of Samuel Forsyth and Ida Muriel (née Brummitt) Forsyth; m. Rona Lynette Williams 1967; two d.; ed. Prince Alfred Coll., Adelaide, Univ. of Adelaide and Univ. of Paris; teacher Friends' School, Hobart, Tasmania 1947–49; Lecturer, Sr. Lecturer in French Univ. of Adelaide 1955–66; Visiting Lecturer Univ. of Wisconsin, Madison 1963–65; Foundation Prof. of French La Trobe Univ., Melbourne 1966–87, Emer. Prof. 1988–; Visiting Prof., Univ. of Melbourne 1992, Sr. Assoc. 1993–; Fellow Australian Acad. of Humanities 1973, Australian Coll. of Educ. 1977; Commdr. Ordre des Palmes Académiques. *Publications:* La Tragédie française de Jodelle à Corneille (1553–1640): le thème de la vengeance 1962, 1994, Saül le furieux/La Famine (tragédies de Jean de la Taille) (ed.) 1968, Concordance des 'Tragiques' d'Agrippa d'Aubigné 1984, Baudin in Australian Waters (ed. with J. Bonnemains and B. Smith) 1988. *Leisure interests:* music, photography, bushwalking and church activities. *Address:* 25 Jacka Street, N. Balwyn, Vic. 3104, Australia. *Telephone:* (03) 9857 4050.

FORSYTH, Frederick, C.B.E.; British author; narrated Soldiers (TV) 1985. *Publications:* The Biafra Story 1969, The Day of the Jackal 1971, The Odessa File 1972, The Dogs of War 1974, The Shepherd 1975, The Devil's Alternative 1979, No Comebacks 1982, The Fourth Protocol 1984, The Negotiator 1988, The Deceiver 1991, Great Flying Stories (ed.) 1991, The Fist of God 1993, Icon 1996; Frederick Forsyth Presents (TV) 1989. *Leisure interests:* sea angling, reading. *Address:* c/o Bantam Books, 62/63 Uxbridge Road, London, W5 5SA, England.

FORSYTH, Murray Greensmith, M.A., F.R.HIST.S.; British university professor; b. 30 Oct. 1936, Hong Kong; s. of Maj. H. R. Forsyth and M. E. Forsyth; m. Marie Edelin de la Praudière; one s. two d.; ed. Wellington Coll., Balliol Coll., Oxford, Coll. of Europe. Bruges, Belgium; Research Officer, Political and Econ. Planning (PEP) 1960–64; lecturer in Politics, Univ. of Leicester 1964–70, Reader in Int. Politics 1971–90, Dir. Centre for Fed. Studies 1988–94, Prof. of Politics 1990–94, Emer. Prof. 1994–; Prof. of Govt. and Political Science, Hong Kong Baptist Univ. 1995–97; Robert Schuman Prof., Fudan Univ., Shanghai 1998; Visiting Prof., Coll. of Europe 1993–94; Pres. European Consortium for Regional and Fed. Studies 1993–94. *Publications:* Unions of States: The Theory and Practice of Confederation 1981, Reason and Revolution: The Political Theory of the Abbé Sieyes 1987, The Political Classics (3 vols.; Co-Ed.) 1988–96. *Leisure interests:* collecting prints and watercolours. *Address:* Blackmore House, Blackmore Park Road, Malvern, Worcs., WR14 3LF, England. *Telephone:* (01684) 560901. *Fax:* (01684) 565268.

FORSYTHE, William; American choreographer; b. 1949, New York; ed. Jacksonville Univ., Fla., Joffrey Ballet School, N.Y.; joined Stuttgart Ballet 1973, dancer, then choreographer; choreographed works commissioned by cos. including Basle and Munich Ballets, Deutsche Opera Ballet, Berlin, and Nederlands Dans Theater; Dir. Ballet Frankfurt 1984–. *Ballets include:* Urlicht 1976, Gänge 1983, Artifact 1984, Impressing the Czar 1988, Limb's Theorem 1991, The Loss of Small Detail 1991, Eidos: Telos 1995. *Address:* Ballet Frankfurt, Untermainanlage 11, 60311 Frankfurt, Germany.

FORT, Dame Maeve Geraldine, D.C.M.G.; British diplomatist; b. 19 Nov. 1940; ed. Trinity Coll., Dublin, Sorbonne; joined Foreign Service 1963; Perm. Mission to UN, New York 1964–65, Alt. Perm. Rep. Security Council, mem. Contact Group on Namibia 1978–82; Commonwealth Relations Office 1965–66; seconded to SEATO, Bangkok 1966–68; Embassy, Bonn 1968–71; Second Sec., Chancery, High Comm., Lagos 1971–73; Second Sec., First Sec., FCO 1973–78, Counsellor with special responsibility for Namibia 1982–83, Head of W. African Dept. 1986–89; with Royal Coll. of Defence Studies 1983; Counsellor, Head of Chancery, Consul-Gen., Santiago 1984–86; Amb. to Chad 1987–89, to Mozambique 1989–92, to Lebanon 1992–96; High Commr. in S. Africa 1996–. *Address:* Greystoke, 255 Hill Street, Pretoria 0083, South Africa.

FORT-BRESCIA, Bernardo, B.A., M.ARCH., F.A.I.A.; American architect; b. 19 Nov. 1951, Lima, Peru; s. of Paul Fort and Rosa Brescia; m. Laurinda Spear 1976; five s. one d.; ed. Princeton Univ., Harvard Univ.; co-f. (with Laurinda Spear (q.v.)) Arquitectonica Int. Corpn. 1977–; projects in U.S.A., Europe, S. America, Cen. America, Asia and Caribbean; designs include: corp. HQs, office blocks, banks, hotels, condominium apartments, symphony halls, public bldgs., retail complexes; Prof. Univ. of Miami 1975–77; numerous A.I.A. Awards and Honors for Design Excellence, Architectural Digest AD100. *Publications:* Arquitectonica 1991, numerous articles in specialist and non-specialist journals. *Address:* Arquitectonica, 550 Brickell Avenue, Miami, FL 33131, U.S.A. *Telephone:* (305) 372-1812. *Fax:* (305) 372-1175.

FORTE, Baron (Life Peer), cr. 1982, of Ripley in the County of Surrey; **Charles Forte,** Kt.; British hotelier and caterer; b. 26 Nov. 1908, Monforte Casalattico, Frosinone, Italy; s. of Rocco and Maria Luigia Forte; m. Irene Mary Chierico 1943; one s. five d.; ed. Alloa Acad., Dumfries Coll., and Mamiani, Rome; came to London and opened first milk bar 1935; acquired Criterion Restaurant 1953, Monico Restaurant, Café Royal, Slater and Bodega chain 1954, Hungaria Restaurant 1956, Waldorf Hotel 1958, Fuller's Ltd. 1959; Chair. Forte's (Holdings) Ltd., Les Grands Hôtels Associés Ltd., Paris, Hôtel George V, Paris; Deputy Chair. Trust House Forte Ltd. (now Forte PLC) 1970–78, C.E.O. 1971–75, Joint Chief Exec. 1975–78, Chair. 1982–92, Pres. 1992–96; Chair. Snamprogetti 1978–80; Dir. TraveLodge Int. Inc., TraveLodge Australia; Dir. Forte's and Co. Ltd., Nat. Sporting Club, Theatre Restaurants Ltd., etc.; Hon. Consul-Gen. of San Marino in London; Pres. Italian Chamber of Commerce for G.B. 1952–78, Pres. Westminster Chamber of Commerce 1983–86; mem. British Inst. of Florence, Italy; Bd. mem. British Travel Asscn.; Hon. Ph.D. (Stirling) 1983; Free Enterprise Award from Aims of Industry 1981; Grand Officer of the Order of the Italian Repub., Cavaliere di Gran Croce della Repubblica Italiana; Knight of Magistral Grace of Sovereign and Mil. Order of Malta; Grande Médaille de Vermeil de la Ville de Paris 1979. *Publications:* Forte (autobiography) 1986, articles for catering trade journals. *Leisure interests:* literature, music, fishing, golf. *Address:* c/o House of Lords, London, SW1A 0PW, England.

FORTE, Hon. Sir Rocco (John Vincent), Kt., M.A., F.C.A.; British business executive; b. 18 Jan. 1945; s. of Lord Forte (q.v.); m. Aliai Ricci 1986; one s. two d.; ed. Downside and Pembroke Coll. Oxford; Dir. of Personnel, Trusthouse Forte 1973–78, Deputy Chief Exec. 1978–82, Jt. Chief Exec. 1982–83; Chief Exec. Trusthouse Forte PLC 1983–92; Chair. Forte PLC 1992–96; Chair. RF Hotels Ltd. 1996–; mem. Chair's Cttee. Savoy Group 1994–96; fmr. Vice-Pres. Commonwealth Games Council for England. *Address:* Savannah House, 11 Charles II Street, London, SW1Y 4QU, England (Office).

FORTIER, Most Rev. Jean-Marie; Canadian ecclesiastic; b. 1 July 1920, Quebec; s. of Joseph Fortier and Alberta Jobin; ed. Petit Séminaire de Québec, Laval Univ., Univ. of Louvain, Belgium, Gregorian Univ., Rome; History Teacher, Grand Séminaire de Québec 1950–60; Auxiliary Bishop of Ste.-Anne-de-la-Pocatière 1960; Bishop of Gaspé 1965; Archbishop of Sherbrooke 1968–96, now Emer.; mem. Vatican's Sacred Congregation of Sacraments and Divine Worship 1975–84; Vice-Pres. of A.E.Q. 1981–85, Pres. 1985–89; mem. Comité du Laïcat 1985–90; mem. Cttee. of Ministers 1991–. *Address:* 2 rue Port-Dauphin, Que. G1R 5K5, Canada. *Telephone:* (418) 692-3935.

FORTIER, L. Yves, C.C., Q.C., B.C.L., B.LITT.; Canadian diplomatist and lawyer; b. 11 Sept. 1935, Quebec City; s. of François and Louise (Turgeon) Fortier; m. Cynthia Carol Eaton 1959; one s. two d.; ed. Univ. of Montreal, McGill Univ. and Univ. of Oxford; called to Bar of Quebec 1960; Chair. and Sr. partner, Ogilvy, Renault (law firm), Montreal; Pres. Jr. Bar Asscn. Montreal 1965–66, Jr. Bar Section, Canadian Bar Asscn. 1966–67; mem. Gen. Council, Bar of Quebec 1966–67; Councillor, Bar of Montreal 1966–67; Pres. London Court of Int. Arbitration; mem. Council, Canadian Section, 1st Comm. of Jurists 1967–87; mem. Canadian Bar Asscn. (Pres. Quebec br. 1975–76, Nat. Pres. 1982–83); Founding Dir. Canadian Bar Asscn. Law for the Future Fund; mem. Perm. Court of Arbitration, The Hague, American Arbitration Asscn. Panel of Arbitrators and other arbitration insts.; Fellow American Coll. of Trial Lawyers (Regent 1992–); Hon. mem. American Bar Asscn.; Dir. Canadian Inst. of Advanced Legal Studies, Canadian Law Inst. of the Pacific Rim 1986–88; mem. Int. Trade Advisory Council (ITAC) Canada; Amb. and Perm. Rep. to UN, New York 1988, Pres. UN Security Council 1989, Vice-Pres. UN Gen. Ass. 1990; Dir. Dupont Canada Inc., Hudson's Bay Co. (also Gov.), Northern Telecom Ltd., Royal Bank of Canada, Nova Chemicals, Southam Inc. and other cos.; Gov. McGill Univ. 1970–85; Rhodes Scholar, Oxford Univ. 1958–60, Dir. Canadian Asscn. of Rhodes Scholars (Pres. 1975–77). *Leisure interests:* skiing, tennis, golf, squash, reading. *Address:* Suite 1100, 1981 McGill College Avenue, Montreal, Quebec, H3A 3C1 (Office); 19 Rosemount Avenue, Westmount, Quebec, H3Y 3G6, Canada (Home). *Telephone:* (514) 847-4747. *Fax:* (514) 286-5474.

FORTOV, Vladimir Yevgenyevich; Russian physicist; b. 23 Jan. 1946, Noginsk, Moscow Region; m.; one d.; ed. Moscow Inst. of Physics and Tech.; researcher, head of lab. Inst. of Chemical Physics U.S.S.R. Acad. of Sciences 1975–86; head div. Inst. of High Temperature Physics U.S.S.R. (now Russian) Acad. of Sciences 1986–93; Dir. Research Cen. of Thermal Physics of Pulse Influences, Inst. of High Temperature Physics Acad. of Sciences 1992–93, 1998–; Chair. Russian Foundation of Fundamental Research 1993–97; Deputy Chair., then Chair. State Cttee. on (now Ministry of) Science and Tech. of Russian Fed. 1996–98; Corresp. mem. U.S.S.R. (now Russian) Acad. of Sciences 1987, mem. 1992, Vice-Pres. 1996–; Prof. All-Union Polytech. Inst. by corresp. 1977; Corresp. mem. Int. Asscn. on Physics and Tech. of High-Pressures, mem. scientific councils Russian Acad. of Sciences; U.S.S.R. State Prize. *Publications:* numerous works on thermophysics of extremely high temperatures and pressures, physics of gasdynamics and physics of strong shock waves. *Address:* Presidium of the Russian Academy of Sciences, Leninski prospekt 32A, 117993 Moscow; Institute of High Temperature Physics, Izhozskaya str. 13/19, 127412 Moscow, Russia.

FOSS, Lukas; American composer, conductor, pianist and professor of music; b. 15 Aug. 1922, Berlin, Germany; s. of Martin Fuchs and Hilda Schindler; m. Cornelia B. Brendel 1950; one s. one d.; ed. Lycée Pasteur, Paris, Curtis Inst. of Music, Yale Univ. Music School; Prof. of Conducting and Composition, Univ. of Calif. at Los Angeles 1951–62; Founder Dir. Center for Creative and Performing Arts, Buffalo Univ. 1963–; Musical Dir. Conductor Buffalo Philharmonic Orchestra 1962–70; Musical Dir. Conductor Brooklyn Philharmonic Orchestra 1971–90 (conductor laureate 1990–), Jerusalem Symphony Orchestra 1972–76, Milwaukee Symphony Orchestra 1981–87; Dir., Conductor Ojai Festival, Calif. 1955, 1956, 1957, Festival of the Arts Today, Buffalo 1960–67, Franco-U.S. Festival (New York Philharmonic Orchestra) 1964, Stravinsky Festival (New York Philharmonic Orchestra) 1965; Visiting Prof. Harvard Univ. 1969–70, Manhattan School of Music 1972–73, Carnegie Mellon Univ. 1987–90; Prof. of Composition, Boston Univ. 1991–; Visiting Prof. of Composition, Tanglewood 1989, 1990, Yale Univ. 1991; mem. Nat. Acad. of Arts and Letters; nine hon. degrees; New York Music Critics' Circle Awards; Prix de Rome; Guggenheim Fellowship; Ditson Award 1973. *Compositions include:* Time Cycle, Echoi, Baroque Variations, Paradigm, Geod, three operas, Orpheus, Map, Percussion Concerto, String Quartets, American Cantata, Night Music for John Lennon, Thirteen Ways of Looking at a Blackbird, Solo Observed, Flute concerto, Clarinet concerto, Guitar concerto, Symphony No. 3 (Symphony of Sorrows). *Leisure interest:* literature. *Address:* 1140 Fifth Avenue, New York, NY 10128, U.S.A. *Telephone:* (212) 722-8003.

FOSSIER, Robert, D. ÈS L.; French professor of history; b. 4 Sept. 1927, Le Vésinet; s. of late René Fossier and Marcelle Brillot; m. Lucie Dupont 1949; three s. two d.; ed. Ecole des Chartes; Librarian of City of Paris 1949–53; Prof. Lycée de Fontainebleau and Lycée Carnot, Paris 1953–57; Asst. Sorbonne 1957–62; Dir. of Studies, then Prof. Univ. of Nancy 1962–71; Prof. of Medieval History, Sorbonne, Paris 1971–93, Prof. Emer. 1993–; Officier des Palmes Académiques. *Publications:* La terre et les hommes en Picardie jusqu'à la fin du XIIIe siècle 1968, Histoire sociale de l'occident médiéval 1971, Chartes de coutume en Picardie 1975, Polyptyques et censiers 1978, Le village et la maison au moyen age 1980, La Picardie au moyen age 1981, Enfance de l'Europe (Xe-XIIe) 1982, Le moyen age 1984, Cartulaire: Chronique de S. Georges d'Hesdin, Paysans d'occident (Xe-XIVe) 1984, La Société mediévale 1992, Villages et villageois au moyen âge 1995. *Leisure interests:* gardening, mountain-walking. *Address:* Université de Paris 1, 17 rue de la Sorbonne, 75005 Paris (Office); 2 rue du Bel Air, 92190 Meudon; Le Serre, 84240 La Tour-d'Aigues, France (Homes).

FOSTER, Brendan, M.B.E., B.SC.; British athlete; b. 12 Jan. 1948, Hebburn, Co. Durham; s. of Francis and Margaret Foster; m. Susan Margaret Foster 1972; one s. one d.; ed. Sussex Univ., Carnegie Coll., Leeds; competed Olympic Games, Munich 1972, 5th in 1,500 m.; Montreal 1976, won bronze medal in 10,000 m., 5th in 5,000 m., Moscow 1980, 11th in 10,000 m.; competed Commonwealth Games, Edinburgh 1970, won bronze medal at 1,500 m.; Christchurch 1974, won silver medal at 5,000 m.; Edmonton 1978, won gold medal at 10,000 m. and bronze medal 5,000 m; European champion at 5,000 m. 1974 and bronze medallist at 1,500 m. 1971; has held World record at 3,000 m. and 2 miles; European record holder at 10,000 m., Olympic record holder at 5,000 m.; Dir. Recreation, Gateshead March 1982; Man. Dir. Nike Int. 1982–86, Vice-Pres. Marketing (Worldwide) and Vice-Pres. (Europe) 1986–87; Chair. and Man. Dir. Nova Int.; BBC TV Commentator 1980–; Hon. Master of Educ. (Newcastle Univ.); Hon. Fellow (Sunderland Polytechnic); Hon. D.Litt. (Sussex Univ.) 1982; BBC Sports Personality of the Year 1974. *Publication:* Brendan Foster with Cliff Temple 1978. *Leisure interests:* sport and running every day. *Address:* Whitegates, 31 Meadowfield Road, Stocksfield, Northumberland, England. *Telephone:* (01661) 843143.

FOSTER, Sir Christopher David, Kt., M.A.; British economist; b. 30 Oct. 1930, London; s. of George C. Foster; m. Kay S. Bullock 1958; two s. three d.; ed. Merchant Taylors School and King's Coll. Cambridge; Fellow and Tutor, Jesus Coll. Cambridge 1964–66; Dir.-Gen. of Econ. Planning, Ministry of Transport 1966–70; Head, Unit for Research in Urban Econs., L.S.E. 1970–76, Prof. of Urban Studies and Econs. 1976–78, Visiting Prof. 1978–86; Gov. Centre for Environmental Studies 1967–70, Dir. 1976–78; Visiting Prof. of Econs. M.I.T. 1970; Head of Econ. and Public Policy Div. Coopers & Lybrand (fmrly. Coopers & Lybrand Assocs., then Coopers & Lybrand Deloitte) 1978–84, Public Sector Practice Leader and Econ. Adviser 1984–86, Dir. and Head Econs. Practice Div. 1988–, partner 1988–94, mem. Man. Cttee. 1988–90, Adviser to Chair. 1990–92, 1994–; Special Adviser to Sec. of Transport on Privatization of British Rail 1992–94; mem. bd. Railtrack 1994–; Commercial Adviser to Bd. of British Telecommunications PLC 1986–88; Hon. Fellow Jesus Coll. 1992. *Publications:* The Transport Problem 1963, Politics, Finance and the Role of Economics: The Control of Public Enterprise (jtly.) 1972, Local Government Finance 1980, Privatization, Public Ownership and the Regulation of Natural Monopoly 1992, The State Under Stress 1996; papers in various econ. and other journals. *Leisure interests:* theatre, reading. *Address:* 6 Holland Park Avenue, London, W11 3QU, England. *Telephone:* 0171-727 4757. *Fax:* 0171-213 4405 (Office).

FOSTER, David Manning, PH.D.; Australian writer; b. 15 May 1944, Katoomba; m. 1st Robin Bowers 1964; one s. two d.; m 2nd Gerda Busch 1975; one s. two d.; ed. Univ. of Sydney, Australian Nat. Univ., Univ. of Pennsylvania; professional fiction writer 1973–; numerous awards including Miles Franklin Award 1997. *Publications include:* Moonlite 1981, Plumbum 1983, Mates of Mars 1991, The Glade within the Grove 1996, In the New Country 1999. *Leisure interests:* tae kwondo (black belt, second dan), gardening, bush-walking, fire-fighting, motorcycling. *Address:* P.O. Box 57, Bundanoon, N.S.W. 2578, Australia.

FOSTER, Joanna Katharine; British administrator; b. 5 May 1939, Canterbury, Kent; d. of Michael Mead and Lesley Mead; m. Jerome Foster 1961; one s. one d.; ed. Benenden School, Kent, Grenoble Univ., France; fmr. mem. staff Vogue magazine London, New York and San Francisco Chronicle; Man. Adviser The Industrial Soc. 1967–71, Head Pepperell Unit. 1981–88; Press. Attaché, Ed. INSEAD Business School, Fontainebleau, France 1971–79; Dir. of Corp. Educ. Pittsburgh Univ., U.S.A. 1979–81; Chair. Equal Opportunities Comm. 1988–93; Pres. European Comm.'s Advisory Cttee. on Equal Opportunities Jan.–Dec. 1992, Vice-Pres. Jan.–April 1993; Chair. U.K. Council of U.N. Int. Year of the Family 1994, Nat. Work-Life Forum; Pres. Relate 1993–96; Deputy Chair. Lloyds TSB Foundation for England and Wales; Deputy Chair. of Govs. Oxford Brookes Univ. 1993–; Gov. Birkbeck Coll., Univ. of London 1996–; Dir. The BT Forum 1995, 1995–97, Chair. 1997–; Trustee Employment Policy Inst.; mem. advisory group ERA; mem. Industrial Soc., European Women's Foundation; Hon. Fellow (St. Hilda's Coll. Oxford) 1988; Hon. D.Litt. (Kingston) 1993, (Salford) 1994; Hon. D.Univ. (Essex) 1993; Hon. LL.D. (Oxford Brookes) 1993, (Univ. of West of England) 1993, (Strathclyde) 1994, (Bristol) 1996. *Leisure interests:* family, friends, food. *Address:* Confessor's Gate, Islip, Oxford, OX5 2SN, England.

FOSTER, Jodie (Alicia Christian), B.A.; American actress and film director and producer; b. 19 Nov. 1962, Los Angeles; d. of Lucius Foster and Evelyn (née Almond) Foster; ed. Yale Univ.; acting début in TV programme Mayberry 1969; Hon. D.F.A. (Yale) 1997. *Films include:* Napoleon and Samantha 1972, Kansas City Bomber 1972, Menace of the Mountain, One Little Indian 1973, Tom Sawyer 1973, Alice Doesn't Live Here Any More 1975, Taxi Driver 1976, Echoes of a Summer 1976, Bugsy Malone 1976, Freaky Friday 1976, The Little Girl Who Lives Down the Lane 1977, Candleshoe 1977, Foxes 1980, Carny 1980, Hotel New Hampshire 1984, The Blood of Others 1984, Siesta 1986, Five Corners 1986, The Accused 1988 (Acad. Award for Best Actress 1989), Stealing Home 1988, Catchfire 1990, The Silence of the Lambs (Acad. Award for Best Actress 1992) 1990, Little Man Tate (also dir.) 1991, Shadows and Fog 1992, Sommersby 1993, Maverick 1994, Nell 1994, Home for the Holidays (dir., co-producer only) 1996, Contact 1997, The Baby Dance (exec. producer only) 1997, Waking the Dead (exec. producer only) 1998, Contact 1998. *Address:* E.G.G. Pictures Production Co., 7920 Sunset Boulevard, Suite 200, Los Angeles, CA 90046, U.S.A.

FOSTER, Lawrence; American conductor; b. 23 Oct. 1941, Los Angeles; m. Angela Foster 1972; one d.; studied with Fritz Zweig and Karl Böhm and at Bayreuth Festival Master Classes; Music Dir. Young Musicians Foundation, Los Angeles 1960–64; Conductor San Francisco Ballet 1960–64; Asst. Conductor L.A. Philharmonic Orchestra 1965–68; Chief Guest Conductor Royal Philharmonic Orchestra, London 1969–74; Music Dir. Houston Symphony Orchestra 1971–78; Music Dir. Orchestre Philharmonique, Monte Carlo 1978–96; Music Dir. Duisburg Orchestra, Fed. Repub. of Germany 1982–86; Music Dir. Chamber Orchestra of Lausanne 1985; conductor Jerusalem Symphony Orchestra 1990; music Dir. Aspen Music Festival and School 1990–96; Music Dir. Orquestra Ciutat de Barcelona 1995–; Koussevitsky Memorial Conducting Prize, Tanglewood 1966. *Leisure interests:* reading history and biographies, films. *Address:* c/o ICM, 8942 Wilshire Boulevard, Los Angeles, CA 90211, U.S.A.; c/o Harrison Parrott Ltd., 12 Penzance Place, London, W.11, England.

FOSTER, Murphy J., Jr. (Mike Foster), B.SC.; American business executive and politician; b. Shreveport, La.; m.; ed. Louisiana State Univ.; sugar cane farmer, La.; founder Bayou Sale, La.; Pres. Sterling Sugars Inc.; Senator St. Mary/Assumption Parish Dist., La. State Senate 1987, Chair. Commerce Cttee. 1991; now Gov. of Louisiana. *Leisure interests:* hunting, fishing, tennis. *Address:* Office of the Governor, P.O. Box 94004, Baton Rouge, LA 70804, U.S.A.

FOSTER, Sir Norman Robert, Kt., O.M., DIP.ARCH., M.ARCH., R.A., R.W.A., R.I.B.A.; British architect; b. 1 June 1935, Manchester; s. of Lilian Foster and Robert Foster; m. 3rd Elena Ochoa 1996; ed. Manchester Univ. School of Architecture and Dept. of Town and Country Planning, Yale Univ. School of Architecture; Urban Renewal and City Planning Consultants work 1962–63; pvt. practice, as "Team 4 Architects" (with Wendy Cheesman, Georgie Wolton, Richard Rogers q.v.) London 1963–67, Foster Associates (now Foster and Partners), offices Berlin, Glasgow, Hong Kong, Singapore 1967–; collaboration with Buckminster Fuller 1968–83; Consultant Architect to Univ. of E. Anglia 1978–87; fmr. External Examiner R.I.B.A. Visiting Bd. of Educ.; fmr. mem. Architectural Asscn. Council (Vice-Pres. 1974); fmr. teacher Univ. of Pa., Architectural Asscn., London, London Polytechnic, Bath Acad. of Arts; F.C.S.D. 1975; IBM Fellow, Aspen Design Conf. 1980; Council mem. R.C.A. 1981–; mem. I.A.A., European Acad. of Sciences and Arts, American Acad. of Arts and Sciences; Hon. F.A.I.A. 1980; Royal West of England Academician; Hon. Fellow Royal Acad., Inst. of Structural Engineers, Royal Coll. of Eng., Kent Inst. of Art and Design; mem. Order of French Architects, Akademie der Kunst, Royal Acad. of Fine Arts, Sweden; Hon. mem. BDA, RDI; Assoc. Acad. Royale de Belgique; Hon. Litt.D. (Univ. of E. Anglia) 1980; Hon. D.Sc. (Bath) 1986, (Humberside) 1992, (Valencia) 1992, (Manchester) 1993, Dr h.c. (Royal Coll. of Art) 1991, (Tech. Univ. Eindhoven) 1996; Hon. D. Litt. (Oxford) 1996, (London) 1997; Architectural Design Projects Awards 1964, 1965, 1966, 1969, Financial Times Industrial Architecture Awards 1967, 1974, 1984, citations 1970, 1971, 1981, 1993, R.I.B.A. Awards 1969, 1972, 1977, 1978, 1992, 1993, 1997, commendation 1981; R.S.A. Business and Industry Award 1976, 1991, Int. Design Awards (Brussels) 1976, 1980, R. S. Reynolds Int. Memorial Awards (U.S.A.) 1976, 1979, 1986, Structural Steel Awards 1972, 1978, 1984, 1986, 1992, citation 1980, Ambrose Congreve Award 1980, Royal Gold Medal for Architecture 1983, Civic Trust Award 1984, 1992, 1995, Constructa-European Award Program for Industrial Architecture 1986, Premio Compasso d'Oro Award 1987, Japan Design Foundation Award 1987, PA Innovations Award 1988, Annual Interiors Award (U.S.A.) 1988, 1992, 1993, 1994, Kunstpreis Award, Berlin 1989, BCI Award 1989, 1991, 1992, 1993, 1997; Pritzker Prize for Architecture 1999; Mies van der Rohe Award, Barcelona 1991, Gold Medal, French Acad. 1991, Concrete Soc. Award 1992, 1993, American Inst. of Architects Gold Medal 1994, Queen's Award for Export Achievement 1995, AIA Award 1995, 1997, "Mipim" Man of the Year 1996, "Building" Construction Personality of the Year, Silver Medal of Chartered Soc. of Designers 1997, and winner of numerous competitions; Officier Ordre des Arts et des Lettres (France), Order of N. Rhine Westphalia. *Major works include:* Pilot Head Office for IBM, Hampshire 1970, Tech. Park for IBM, Greenford 1975, Faber and Dumas, Ipswich 1975, Sainsbury Centre for Visual Arts, Norwich 1977, Head Office for Willis, Centre for Renault Car Co. U.K. 1983, Hong Kong Bank HQ 1986, Third London Airport Terminal Stansted 1991, Century Tower Tokyo 1991, Barcelona Telecommunications Tower 1992, Sackler Galleries, Royal Acad. 1991, Cranfield Univ. Library 1992, Arts Centre, Nimes 1993, Lycée, Fréjus 1993, Microelectronics Park, Duisburg 1993, Bilbao Metro System 1995, Univ. of Cambridge Faculty of Law 1996, American Air Museum, Duxford 1997, Commerzbank HQ Frankfurt 1997, Chek Lap Kok Airport, Hong Kong 1998, new German Parl. bldg. (in progress), contract to design new Greater London Authority Bldg., London; work exhibited in France, Germany, Spain, Japan, The Netherlands, London, U.S.A. and Switzerland; work in perm. collection of Museum of Modern Art, New York, and Centre Georges Pompidou, Paris. *Publications:* Norman Foster: Buildings and Projects Vols. 1, 2, 3, 4, and numerous contributions to the architectural and tech. press. *Leisure interests:* flying, skiing, running. *Address:* Foster and Partners, Riverside Three, 22 Hester Road, London, SW11 4AN, England; Foster and Partners Hong Kong, F/31 Fook Lee Commercial Centre, Town Place, 33 Lockhart Road, Wanchai, Hong Kong. *Telephone:* 0171-738 0455 (London). *Fax:* 0171-738 1107 (London).

FOTTRELL, Patrick, D.SC., M.R.I.A.; Irish university administrator; b. 26 Sept. 1933, Youghal, Co. Cork; s. of Matthew Fottrell and Mary (née O'Sullivan) Fottrell; m. Esther Kennedy 1963; two s. two d.; ed. C.B.S. Youghal and North Mon schools, Univ. Coll., Cork, Univ. of Glasgow, Scotland, Univ. Coll., Galway; Sr. Research Officer, Agric. Inst., Johnstown Castle, Wexford 1963–65; lecturer, later Assoc. Prof., Prof. of Biochem., Univ. Coll., Galway 1965–; Visiting Prof., Harvard Univ., U.S.A. 1972, 1982; Beit Memorial Fellow; mem. Royal Irish Acad. EEC Science Writers Award. *Publications include:* Perspectives on Coeliac Disease (jt.-author); over 100 scientific publs. in int. journals on biochem. *Leisure interests:* walking, music, soccer. *Address:* University College, Galway (Office); Bunowen, Taylorshill, Galway, Ireland (Home). *Telephone:* (091) 24411 (Office); (091) 21022 (Home).

FOU TS'ONG (FU CONG); Chinese pianist; b. 10 March 1934; s. of late Fu Lei; m. 1st Zamira Menuhin 1960 (dissolved 1970); one s.; m. 2nd Hijong Hyun 1973 (dissolved 1978); m. 3rd Patsy Toh 1987; one s.; ed. Shanghai and Warsaw; first performance, Shanghai 1953, concerts in Eastern Europe and U.S.S.R. 1953–58; London debut 1959, concerts in Europe, N. and S. America, Australia and Far East. *Leisure interests:* bridge, sport, oriental art. *Address:* 62 Aberdeen Park, London, N5 2BL, England. *Telephone:* 0171-226 9589. *Fax:* 0171-704 8896.

FOULKES, Sir Nigel Gordon, Kt., M.A., C.B.I.M., F.R.S.A.; British business executive; b. 29 Aug. 1919, London; s. of Louis Augustine and Winifred Foulkes; m. Elisabeth Walker 1948; ed. Gresham's School and Balliol Coll., Oxford; Production Man., H. P. Bulmer & Co., Ltd. 1947–51; Man. Consultant, P.E. Consulting Group Ltd. 1951–56; Sr. Personnel Officer, Birfield Ltd. 1957–58; Dir. Greaves and Thomas Ltd. 1959–61; Exec. Asst. to Chair., Int. Nickel Ltd. 1961–64; Man. Dir. Rank Xerox Ltd. 1964–70; Chair. F.O.B.A.S. Ltd. 1970–76, British Airports Authority 1972–77, Civil Aviation Authority 1977–82, Equity Capital for Industry 1983–86, Equity Capital Trustee Ltd. 1983–90; Chair. ECI Man. (Jersey) Ltd. 1986–91, ECI Int. Man. Ltd. 1987–91; Dir. Imagic Holdings 1971–77, Charterhouse Group 1972–85, Bekaert Group (Belgium) 1973–85, Council, British Inst. of Man. 1972–77, Stone-Platt Industries 1975–82. *Address:* Westway House, West Adderbury, Banbury, Oxon., OX17 3EU, England.

FOURCADE, Jean-Pierre; French politician; b. 18 Oct. 1929, Marmande; s. of Raymond and Germaine (née Raynal) Fourcade; m. Odile Mion 1958; one s. two d.; ed. Coll. de Sorèze, Bordeaux Univ. Faculté de Droit, Inst. des Etudes politiques; student, Ecole Nat. d'Admin. 1952–54; Insp. des Finances 1954–73; Chargé de Mission to Sec. of State for Finance (later Minister of Finance) 1959–61, Conseiller technique 1962, Dir. adjoint du Cabinet 1964–66; Asst. Head of Service, Inspection gén. des Finances 1962; Head of Trade Div., Directorate-Gen. of Internal Trade and Prices 1965, Dir.-Gen. 1968–70; Asst. Dir.-Gen. Crédit industriel et commercial 1970, Dir.-Gen. 1972–74, Admin. 1973–74; Admin., later Pres. and Dir.-Gen. Soc. d'Epargne mobilière 1972–74; Admin. Banque transatlantique 1971–74, Soc. commerciale d'Affrètement et de Combustibles 1972–74; Minister of Econ. and Finance 1974–76, of Supply 1976–77, of Supply and Regional Devt. 1977; Mayor of Saint-Cloud 1971–92, of Boulogne-Billancourt 1995–; Conseiller-Gén., canton of Saint-Cloud 1973–89; Conseiller Régional, Ile de France 1976, Vice-Pres. 1982–86, First Vice-Pres. 1986–; Senator, Hauts de Seine 1977; Pres. Comité des Finances Locales 1980–, Comm. des Affaires Sociales du Sénat 1983–; Pres. Clubs Perspectives et Réalités 1975–82; Vice-Pres. Union pour la Démocratie française (U.D.F.) 1978–86, mem. 1978–; mem. Admin. Council of RATP 1984–93, Epad 1985–95, SNCF 1993–98; Officier, Ordre national du Mérite. *Publications:* Et si nous parlions de demain 1979, la Tentation social-démocrate 1985, Remèdes pour l'assurance maladie 1989. *Address:* Mairie, 26 Ave. André Morizet, 92100 Boulogne-Billancourt; Sénat, Palais du Luxembourg, 75291 Paris, cedex 06; 8 Parc de Béarn, 92210 Saint-Cloud, France (Home).

FOURNIER, Jacques, L. EN D.; French lawyer; b. 5 May 1929, Épinal; s. of Léon Fournier and Ida Rudmann; m. 1st Jacqueline Tazerout (deceased); three s.; m. 2nd Michèle Dubez 1980 (divorced); m. 3rd Noëlle Fréaud-Lenoir 1989; ed. Inst. for Political Studies, Paris and Nat. School of Admin.; Civil Servant, French State Council 1953, Master of Petitions 1960, State Councillor 1978; Legal Adviser, Embassy in Morocco 1961–64; Head of Dept. of Social Affairs, Gen. Planning Office 1969–72; Asst. Sec.-Gen. to Pres. of France 1981–82; Sec.-Gen. of the Govt. 1982–86; Pres. of Admin. Council of Gaz de France 1986–88; Pres. S.N.C.F. 1988–94, Centre européen des entreprises publiques 1988–94, Sceta 1989–94, Ciriec-France 1994–; Chair. Carrefour 1992–98; fmr. mem. Council of State, renewed mem. 1994–; Chevalier, Ordre Nat. du Mérite; Officier, Légion d'honneur. *Publications:* Politique de l'Education 1971, Traité du social, situations, luttes politiques, institutions 1976, Le Pouvoir du social 1979, Le travail gouvernemental 1987, le Train, l'Europe et le service public 1993. *Address:* Conseil d'Etat, 75100 Paris RP (Office); 19 rue Montorgueil, 75001 Paris, France (Home). *Telephone:* 47 54 22 24 (Office).

FOWDEN, Sir Leslie, Kt., PH.D., F.R.S.; British plant chemist; b. 13 Oct. 1925, Rochdale, Lancs.; s. of Herbert Fowden and Amy D. Fowden; m. Margaret Oakes 1949; one s. one d.; ed. Univ. Coll., London; mem. Scientific Staff, Human Nutrition Research Unit, Medical Research Council 1947–50; Lecturer in Plant Chem., Univ. Coll., London 1950–55, Reader 1956–64, Prof. of Plant Chem. 1964–73 and Dean of Faculty of Science 1970–73; Dir. Rothamsted Experimental Station 1973–86; Dir of Arable Crops Research, Agricultural and Food Research Council 1986–88; mem. Council of Royal Soc. 1970–72; Scientific Advisory Panel Botanical Gardens, Kew 1977–83 (Trustee 1983–93); Consultant Dir. Commonwealth Bureau of Soils 1973–88; Chair. Agricultural and Veterinary Advisory Cttee., British Council 1987–95; Hon. D.Sc. *Leisure interests:* opera, walking. *Address:* 31 Southdown Road, Harpenden, Herts., AL5 1PF, England. *Telephone:* (01582) 764628.

FOWKE, Philip Francis, F.R.A.M.; British concert pianist; b. 28 June 1950, Gerrards Cross; s. of Francis H. V. Fowke and Florence L. (née Clutton) Fowke; ed. Downside Abbey School; began piano studies with Marjorie Withers; awarded Royal Acad. of Music Scholarship to Study with Gordon Green 1967; Wigmore Hall début 1974; U.K. concerto début with Royal Liverpool Philharmonic 1975; Royal Festival Hall début 1977; BBC Promenade Concert début 1979; U.S. début 1982; débuts in Denmark, Bulgaria, France, Switzerland, Hong Kong, Belgium and Italy 1983; Austrian début at Salzburg Mozart week 1984; German début 1985; now appears regularly with all the leading orchestras in U.K. and gives regular recitals and concerto performances for BBC Radio; Prof. Royal Acad. of Music 1984–91, Welsh Coll. of Music and Drama 1994; Dir. of Keyboard Studies, Trinity Coll. of Music, London 1995–; recordings of Bliss, Chopin, Delius, Finzi, Rachmaninoff, Tchaikovsky and Hoddinott piano concertos; presenter and contrib. to music programmes on BBC Radio; Countess of Munster Musical Trust Award 1972, Nat. Fed. of Music Socs. Award 1973, BBC Piano Competition 1974, Winston Churchill Fellowship 1976, and numerous other awards and prizes. *Publications:* reviews and obituaries in nat. press. *Leisure interests:* architecture, monasticism. *Address:* c/o Patrick Garvey Management, 59 Lansdowne Place, Hove, E. Sussex, BN3 1FL, England.

FOWLER, Sir (Edward) Michael (Coulson), Kt., M.ARCH., F.N.Z.I.A., A.R.I.B.A.; New Zealand architect; b. 19 Dec. 1929, Marton; s. of William Coulson and Faith Agnes Fowler (née Netherclift); m. Barbara Hamilton Hall 1953; two s. one d.; ed. Christ's Coll., Christchurch, Auckland Univ.; with Ove Arup & Partners, London 1954–55; Partner, Gray Young, Morton Calder & Fowler, Wellington 1959; Sr. Partner, Calder, Fowler & Styles 1960–; travelled abroad to study cen. banking systems security methods; work includes Overseas Terminal, Wellington, Reserve Bank, Wellington, Dalmuir House, Wellington Club, office bldgs., factories, houses, churches; mem. Wellington City Council 1968–74; Chair. NZIA Educ. Cttee. 1967–73; Mayor of Wellington 1974–83; Chair. Queen Elizabeth II Arts Council of N.Z. 1983–86; Pres. N.Z. Youth Hostel Assen. 1983–86. *Publications:* Country Houses of New Zealand 1972, Wellington Sketches: Folios I, II 1973, The Architecture and Planning of Moscow 1980, Eating Houses in Wellington 1980, Wellington-Wellington 1981, Eating Houses of Canterbury 1982, Wellington Celebration 1983, The New Zealand House 1983, Buildings of New Zealanders 1984, Michael Fowler's Wellington 1993, Michael Fowler's University of Auckland 1993. *Leisure interests:* sketching, writing, boating, fruit-growing. *Address:* Branches, Giffords Road, R.D.3, Blenheim, New Zealand (Home). *Telephone:* 3 572-8987 (Home).

FOWLER, Henry Hamill, A.B., LL.B., J.S.D.; American government official, lawyer and investment banker; b. 5 Sept. 1908, Roanoke, Va.; s. of Mack Johnson Fowler and Bertha (née Browning) Fowler; m. Trudye Pamela Hathcote 1938; one s. (deceased) two d.; ed. Roanoke Coll. and Yale Univ. Law School; admitted to Va. Bar 1933, D.C. Bar 1946; Counsel Tenn. Valley Authority 1934–38, Asst. Gen. Counsel 1939; Asst. Gen. Counsel Office of Production Man. 1941, War Production Bd. 1942–44; Econ. Adviser, U.S. Mission Econ. Affairs, London 1944; served Foreign Econ. Admin. 1945; Admin. Nat. Production Authority 1951–52; Admin. Defense Production Admin.; Dir. Office of Defense Mobilization and mem. Nat. Security Council 1952–53; sr. mem. law firm, Fowler, Leva, Hawes and Symington, Washington D.C., 1946–51, 1953–61, 1964–65; Under-Sec. U.S. Treasury 1961–64, Sec. 1965–68; Gen. Partner Goldman, Sachs, New York 1969–81, Ltd. Partner 1981–; Chair. Goldman Sachs Int. Corpn. 1969–84, U.S. Treasury Advisory Comm. on Int. Monetary Affairs 1974–84; Chair. Atlantic Council of the U.S. 1972–77, Vice-Chair. 1978–; Co-Chair. Cttee. on Present Danger 1976–88, Bretton Woods Cttee. 1985–89, Citizens' Network for Foreign Affairs 1987–; Trustee, Lyndon B. Johnson Foundation; Councillor, Conf. Bd., Roanoke Coll.; mem. Council, Miller Center of Public Affairs, Univ. of Va. 1980–91; Democrat. *Leisure interests:* tennis, bridge, books. *Address:* c/o Goldman, Sachs & Co., 85 Broad Street, New York, NY 10004 (Office); 209 South Fairfax Street, Alexandria, VA 22314; 200 East 66th Street, New York, NY 10021, U.S.A.

FOWLER, Rt. Hon. Sir (Peter) Norman, Kt., P.C., M.A.; British politician; b. 2 Feb. 1938; s. of the late N. F. Fowler and Katherine Fowler; m. Fiona Poole 1979; two d.; ed. King Edward VI School, Chelmsford, Trinity Hall, Cambridge; Nat. Service Comm., Essex Regt. 1956–58; joined The Times 1961, Special Corresp. 1962–66, Home Affairs Corresp. 1966–70; mem. Council, Bow Group 1967–69, Editorial Bd., Crossbow 1962–69; Vice-Chair. N. Kensington Conservative Assen. 1967–68; Chair. E. Midlands Area, Conservative Political Centre 1970–73; M.P. for Nottingham South 1970–74, for Sutton Coldfield Feb. 1974–; mem. Parl. Select Cttee. on Race Relations and Immigration 1970–74; Jt. Sec. Conservative Parl. Home Affairs Cttee. 1971–72, Vice-Chair. 1974; Parl. Pvt. Sec. N. Ireland Office 1972–74; Opposition Spokesman on Home Affairs 1974–75; Chief Opposition Spokesman on Social Services 1975–76, on Transport 1976–79; Minister of Transport 1979–81, Sec. of State for Transport 1981, for Social Services 1981–87, for Employment 1987–90; Chair. Conservative Party 1992–94; Opposition front bench Spokesman on Environment, Transport and the Regions 1997–98, on Home Affairs 1998–; mem. Lloyds 1989–; Chair. Nat. House Bldg. Council 1992–98, Midland Independent Newspapers 1992–; mem. Bd. Group 4 Security 1990–93; Dir. NFC 1990–. *Publications:* The Cost of Crime 1973, The Right Track 1977, After the Riots: the Police in Europe, Ministers Decide: a memoir of the Thatcher years 1991. *Address:* The House of Commons, London, SW1A 0AA, England.

FOWLES, John; British author; b. 31 March 1926, Essex; s. of Robert J. Fowles and Gladys M. Richards; m. 1st Elizabeth Whitton 1954 (died 1990); m. 2nd Sarah Smith 1998; ed. Bedford School and Univ. of Oxford; PEN Silver Pen Award 1969, W. H. Smith Literary Award (for The French Lieutenant's Woman) 1969; Hon. D.Litt. (Exeter) 1983; Hon. Litt. D. (E. Anglia) 1997.

Publications: The Collector 1963, The Aristos 1964, The Magus 1965, The French Lieutenant's Woman 1969, Poems 1973, Shipwreck 1974, The Ebony Tower 1974, Daniel Martin 1977, Islands (with Fay Godwin) 1978, The Tree 1979, The Enigma of Stonehenge 1980, Mantissa 1982, Thomas Hardy's England 1984, Land 1985, A Maggot 1985, The Tree 1991, Wormholes 1998. *Leisure interests:* local and natural history. *Address:* c/o Sheil Land Associates, 43 Doughty Street, London, WC1N 2LF, England.

FOX, Edward; British actor; b. 13 April 1937; s. of Robin and Angela Fox; brother of James Fox (q.v.); m. 1st Tracy Pelissier 1958 (divorced 1961); one d.; one s. one d. by Joanna David; ed. Ashfold School, Harrow School and Royal Acad. of Dramatic Art; actor since 1957; started in provincial repertory theatre 1958 and has since worked widely in films, stage plays and television; recipient of several awards for television performance as Edward VIII in Edward and Mrs Simpson 1978; *stage appearances include:* Knuckle 1973, The Family Reunion 1979, Anyone for Denis 1981, Quartermaine's Terms 1981, Hamlet 1982, The Dance of Death 1983, Interpreters 1986, The Admirable Crichton 1988, Another Love Story 1990, The Philanthropist 1991, My Fair Lady, Father 1995, A Letter of Resignation 1997. *Films include:* The Go-Between 1971, The Day of the Jackal, A Doll's House 1973, Galileo 1976, A Bridge Too Far, The Duellists, The Cat and the Canary 1977, Force Ten from Navarone 1978, The Mirror Crack'd 1980, Gandhi 1982, Never Say Never Again 1983, Wild Geese, The Bounty 1984, The Shooting Party, Return from the River Kwai 1989, Circles of Deceit (TV) 1989, Prince of Thieves 1990, They Never Slept 1991, A Month by the Lake 1996. *Leisure interest:* playing the piano.

FOX, Frederick Donald; milliner; b. 2 April 1931; s. of the late Lesley James Fox and Ruby Mansfield (née Elliott); ed. St. Joseph's Convent School, Jerilderie, New South Wales, Australia; started millinery business 1962; currently designer for the Royal Family, granted Royal Warrant to H.M. The Queen 1974; Pres. Millinery Trades Benevolent Asscn.; Freeman City of London 1989, Liveryman Worshipful Co. of Feltmakers 1989. *Leisure interests:* gardening, photography. *Address:* Model Hats, 87–91 Bond Street, London, W1Y 9LA, England. *Telephone:* 0171-629 5705/6. *Fax:* 0171-629 3048.

FOX, Sir (Henry) Murray, G.B.E., M.A., D.LITT., F.R.I.C.S.; British chartered surveyor; b. 7 June 1912; s. of the late Sir Sidney Fox; m. Helen Isabella Margaret Crichton 1941 (died 1986); one s. two d.; ed. Malvern and Emmanuel Coll., Cambridge; Chair. Trehaven Trust Group 1962–; Pres. City and Metropolitan Bldg. Soc. 1985–91, Chair. 1976–85; Dir. Toye, Kenning and Spencer Ltd. 1976–91, City of London Sinfonia 1979, Chair. 1983–91; Man. Trustee, Municipal Mutual Insurance Ltd. 1977–91; Sheriff, City of London 1971–72; Lord Mayor of London 1974–75; Trustee, Morden Coll. 1976–. *Leisure interests:* golf, walking, reading. *Address:* 5 Audley Court, 32-34 Hill Street, London, W1X 7FT, England.

FOX, James; British actor; b. 19 May 1939, London; s. of Robin Fox and Angela (née Worthington) Fox; brother of Edward Fox (q.v.); m. Mary Elizabeth Fox 1973; four s. one d.; ed. Ashfold Prep. School and Harrow School. *Films include:* Mrs Miniver 1952, The Servant 1963, King Rat 1965, Those Magnificent Men in Their Flying Machines 1965, Thoroughly Modern Millie 1966, Isadora 1967, Performance 1969, Passage to India 1984, Runners 1984, Farewell to the King 1987, Finding Mawbee (video film as the Mighty Quinn) 1988, She's Been Away 1989, The Russia House 1990, Afraid of the Dark 1991, Patriot Games 1991, As You Like It 1992, The Remains of the Day 1993, The Old Curiosity Shop 1994, Gulliver's Travels 1995, Elgar's Tenth Muse 1995, Uncle Vanya 1995, Anna Karenina 1997. *Publication:* Comeback: An Actor's Direction 1983. *Leisure interests:* windsurfing, tennis. *Address:* c/o Michael Whitehall, 125 Gloucester Road, London, SW7 4TE, England.

FOX, Sir (John) Marcus, Kt., M.B.E.; British politician; b. 11 June 1927; s. of late Alfred H. Fox; m. Ann Tindall 1954; one s. one d.; ed. Wheelwright Grammar School, Dewsbury; mem. Dewsbury Co. Borough Council 1957–65; mem. Parl. for Shipley 1970–97; Asst. Govt. Whip 1972–73; a Lord Commr. of H.M. Treasury 1973–74; Opposition Spokesman on Transport 1975–76; Vice-Chair. Conservative Party Org. 1976–79; Parl. Under-Sec. of State, Dept. of Environment 1979–81; Vice-Chair. Conservative 1922 Cttee. 1983–92, Chair. 1992–97. *Leisure interests:* reading, tennis, walking. *Address:* 10 Woodvale Crescent, Oakwood Park, Bingley, W. Yorks., BD16 4AL, England.

FOX, Kerry; New Zealand actress; m. Jaime Robertson; ed. New Zealand Drama School; fmr. lighting designer. *Television appearances include:* Mr Wroe's Virgins, A Village Affair, Saigon Baby, The Affair. *Films include:* Country Life, An Angel at My Table (Elvira Notari Best Performance award), The Last Days of Chez Nous, Friends, Shallow Grave.

FOX, Liam, M.B., CH.B.; British politician and physician; b. 22 Sept. 1961; s. of William Fox and Catherine Young; ed. St. Bride's High School, E. Kilbride, Univ. of Glasgow; civilian army medical officer Royal Army Educ. Corps 1981–91; gen. practitioner, Beaconsfield 1987–91; Div. Surgeon St. John's Ambulance 1987–91; contested Roxburgh and Berwickshire 1987; M.P. for Woodspring 1992–; Parl. Pvt. Sec. to Home Sec. Michael Howard 1993–94, Asst. Govt. Whip 1994–95, Lord Commr. H.M. Treasury (Sr. Govt. Whip) 1995–96, Parl. Under-Sec. of State FCO 1996–97, Opposition Front Bench Spokesman on Constitutional Affairs 1997–98, Shadow Sec. of State for Constitutional Affairs 1998–; mem. Scottish Select Cttee. 1992–93; Sec. Conservative Backbench Health Cttee. 1992–93; Pres. Glasgow Univ. Conservative Club 1982–83; Nat. Vice-Chair. Scottish Young Conservatives 1983–84; mem. Conservative Political Centre; Sec. Conservative West Country Mems. Group. 1992–93. *Publications include:* Making Unionism Positive 1988, Bearing the Standard (contrib.) 1991, contrib. to House of Commons Magazine. *Leisure interests:* tennis, swimming, cinema, theatre. *Address:* House of Commons, London, SW1A 0AA, England. *Telephone:* 0171-219 4086.

FOX, Maurice Sanford, PH.D.; American professor of molecular biology; b. 11 Oct. 1924; s. of Albert Fox and Ray Fox; m. Sally Cherniavsky 1955; three s.; ed. Stuyvesant High School, Univ. of Chicago; Instructor, Univ. of Chicago 1951–53; Asst., Rockefeller Univ. 1953–55, Asst. Prof. 1955–58, Assoc. Prof. 1958–62; Assoc. Prof., M.I.T. 1962–66, Prof. 1966–79, Lester Wolfe Prof. of Molecular Biology 1979–96, Head, Dept. of Biology 1985–89; mem. Bd. Council for a Liveable World 1962–; Breast Cancer Task Force 1977–80; mem. Inst. of Medicine, N.A.S., American Acad. of Arts and Sciences, Radiation Effects Research Unit, Hiroshima, Int. Bioethics Cttee., UNESCO; Fellow A.A.A.S., Nuffield Research Fellow 1957. *Publications:* numerous learned papers. *Leisure interest:* ancient history. *Address:* Department of Biology, Massachussets Institute of Technology, 77 Massachusetts Avenue, Cambridge, MA 02139 (Office); 983 Memorial Drive, Cambridge, MA 02138, U.S.A. (Home). *Telephone:* 617-253 4728 (Office).

FOX, Michael J.; American actor; b. 9 June 1961, Vancouver, B.C., Canada; s. of Bill Fox and Phyllis Fox; m. Tracy Pollan 1988; one s. *TV appearances include:* Leo and Me 1976, Palmerstown U.S.A. 1980, Family Ties 1982–89 (Emmy Awards 1987, 1988), Spin City 1996. *TV films include:* Letters from Frank 1979, Poison Ivy 1985, High School U.S.A. 1985. *Film appearances include:* Midnight Madness 1980, Class of '84 1981, Back to the Future 1985, Teen Wolf 1985, Light of Day 1986, The Secret of my Success 1987, Bright Lights, Big City 1988, Back to the Future II 1989, Back to the Future III 1989, The Hard Way 1991, Doc Hollywood 1991, The Concierge 1993, Give Me a Break 1994, Greedy 1994, The American President 1995, Mars Attacks! 1996, The Frighteners 1996. *Address:* c/o CAA, 9830 Wilshire Blvd., Beverly Hills, CA 90212, U.S.A.

FOX, Sir Paul Leonard, Kt., C.B.E.; British business executive; b. 27 Oct. 1925; m. Betty R. Nathan 1948; two s.; ed. Bournemouth Grammar School; Parachute Regt. 1943; reporter, Kentish Times 1946, The People 1947; scriptwriter, Pathe News 1947; BBC TV scriptwriter 1950; Ed. Sportsview 1953, Panorama 1961; Head, BBC TV Public Affairs Dept. 1963, Current Affairs Group 1965; Controller, BBC 1 1967–73; Dir. of Programmes, Yorkshire TV 1973–74, Man. Dir. Yorkshire TV 1977–89, Dir. of Programmes 1973–84; Dir. Independent Television News 1977–86, Chair. 1986–89; Man. Dir. BBC TV 1988–91; Chair. BBC Enterprises 1988–91, Stepgrades Consultants 1991–; Chair. ITV Network Programme Cttee. 1978–80, Council, Independent Television Cos. Asscn. Ltd. 1982–84; mem. Royal Comm. on Criminal Procedure 1978–80; Pres. Royal TV Soc. 1985–92; Dir. Channel Four 1985–88, World TV News 1986–88, Thames TV Ltd. 1991–95; Chair. Racecourse Asscn. Ltd. 1993–97, Racecourse Tech. Services 1994–, Disasters Emergency Cttee. 1996–; Dir. British Horse Racing Bd. 1993–97, Horserace Betting Levy Bd. 1993–97, Barnes TV Trust Ltd. 1997–; consultant Oflot 1994–; mem. Cttee. Nat. Museum of Photography, Film and TV 1985–95, Cinema and TV Benevolent Fund 1986–92, Pres. 1992–95; Hon. LL.D. (Leeds) 1984; Hon. D.Litt. (Bradford) 1991. *Leisure interests:* television, attending race meetings. *Address:* c/o Stepgrades Consultants, 10 Charterhouse Square, London, EC1M 6LQ, England.

FOX, Peter Kendrew, M.A.; British university librarian; b. 23 March 1949, Beverley, Yorks.; s. of Thomas Kendrew Fox and Dorothy Wildbore; m. Isobel McConnell 1983; two d.; ed. Baines Grammar School, Poulton-le-Fylde, Lancs., King's Coll. London and Univ. of Sheffield; Asst. Library Officer, Cambridge Univ. Library 1973–77, Asst. Under-Librarian 1977–78, Under-Librarian 1978–79; Deputy Librarian, Trinity Coll. Dublin 1979–84, Librarian 1984–94; Univ. Librarian, Univ. of Cambridge 1994–; Fellow, Selwyn Coll., Univ. of Cambridge 1994–; mem. British Library Project on Teaching and Learning Skills for Librarians 1978–79, SCONUL Advisory Cttee. on Information Services 1979–91 (Chair. 1987–91), An Chomhairle Leabharlanna 1982–94, Cttee. on Library Co-operation in Ireland 1983–94 (Chair. 1990–91), Nat. Preservation Advisory Cttee. (British Library) 1984–95, Wellcome Trust Library Advisory Cttee. 1996–, Consortium of Univ. Research Libraries (Chair. of Bd. 1997–); Jt. Ed. An Leabharlann: The Irish Library 1982–87; Assoc. King's College, Library Asscn. *Publications:* Reader Instruction Methods in Academic Libraries 1974, User Education in the Humanities in US Academic Libraries 1979, Trinity College Library Dublin 1982; Ed.: Library User Education—Are New Approaches Needed? 1980, Second (and Third) Int. Conf. on Library User Educ. Proc. 1982 (and 1984), Treasures of the Library—Trinity College Dublin 1986, Commentary Volume: Book of Kells Facsimile 1990, Cambridge University Library: The Great Collections 1998; contribs. to books and journals. *Address:* University Library, West Road, Cambridge, CB3 9DR, England. *Telephone:* (01223) 333045. *Fax:* (01223) 339973.

FOX, William F., Jr., J.D., LL.M.; American professor of law; b. 20 Nov. 1942, Lamar, Colo.; m. 1970; ed. George Washington Univ., The Catholic Univ. of America, Harvard Law School; Instructor in Law, Boston Univ., Boston, Mass. 1973–74; Asst. Prof. of Law, Indiana Univ., Indianapolis, Ind. 1974–75; Prof. of Law and Dir. of Comparative and Int. Law Program, The Catholic Univ. of America, Washington, D.C. 1975–; Sr. Assoc. mem. St. Antony's Coll., Oxford Univ., Visiting Scholar, L.S.E. 1983–84. *Publications:* Federal Regulation of Energy 1983, Understanding Administrative Law 1987, International Commercial Agreements: A Primer on Drafting, Negotiating and Resolving Disputes 1988. *Address:* School of Law, The Catholic University of America, Washington, DC 20064, U.S.A. *Telephone:* (202) 635-5140.

FOX BASSETT, Nigel; British lawyer; b. 1 Nov. 1929; m. Patricia Anne Lambourne 1961; one s. one d.; ed. Trinity Coll. Cambridge; joined Coward Chance (solicitors) after graduation; firm merged with Clifford Turner to form Clifford Chance (Europe's largest law firm) 1987; Sr. Partner, Clifford Chance 1990–93; Commr. Building Socs. Comm. 1993–; Dir. London First Centre 1993–98, Dir. Council London First 1998–; mem. Council 1977–; Chair. Council and Exec. Cttee. British Inst. of Int. and Comparative Law 1986–95; Council mem. London Chamber of Commerce and Industry 1993–; mem. numerous legal councils, cttees. and socs. *Address:* Building Societies Commission, c/o U.K. Deposit Takers Department, The Financial Services Authority, 14th Floor, 25 North Colonnade, Canary Wharf, London, E14 5HS; c/o Clifford Chance, 200 Aldersgate, London, EC1A 4JJ, England. *Telephone:* 0171-676 0684 (Building Socs. Comm.). *Fax:* 0171-600 5555.

FOXLEY RIOSECO, Alejandro, M.SC., PH.D.; Chilean politician and economist; b. 26 May 1939, Viña del Mar; s. of Harold Foxley (Chapman) and Carmen Rioseco; m. Gisela Tapia 1963; two c.; ed. Univ. of Wisconsin, Harvard Univ. and Catholic Univ., Valparaíso; Dir. Global Planning Div., Nat. Planning Office, Govt. of Chile 1967–70; Dir. Center for Nat. Planning Studies, Catholic Univ. of Chile 1970–76; mem. Exec. Council, Latin-American Social Science Council (CLACSO) 1975–81; mem. Joint Cttee. Latin-American Studies, Social Science Research Council, New York 1975–78; Pres. Corpn. for Latin-American Econ. Research (CIEPLAN), Santiago 1976–90; Minister of Finance 1990–94; Pres. Christian Democratic Party (PDC) 1994; Helen Kellogg Prof. of Econs. (part-time) and Int. Devt., Univ. of Notre Dame 1982–; Assoc. Ed. Journal of Development Economics 1977–; Visiting Fellow, Univ. of Sussex 1973, Oxford 1975, M.I.T. 1978; Ford Int. Fellow 1963–64, Daugherty Foundation Fellow 1965–66; Ford Foundation Fellow 1970; mem. Exec. Cttee. Inter-american Dialogue, Wash., Int. Advisory Bd. Journal Latin American Studies. *Publications:* Redistributive Effects of Government Programmes, Income Distribution in Latin-America, Estrategia de Desarrollo y Modelos de Planificación, Legados del Monetarismo: Argentina y Chile, Para una Democracia Estable 1985, Chile y su futuro: un país posible 1989, Chile puede más 1989, numerous articles and working papers. *Address:* c/o Partido Demócrata Cristiano (PDC), Carmen 8, 6°, Santiago; Golfo de Darién 10236, Santiago (Las Condes), Chile (Home). *Telephone:* 20 79 24 (Home).

FOYLE, Christina Agnes Lilian; British bookseller; b. 1911; d. of the late William Foyle; m. Ronald Batty 1938 (died 1994); ed. Parliament Hill School and Aux Villas Unspunnen, Switzerland; entered book trade 1928; began Foyle's Literary Luncheons 1930; Man. Dir. W. & G. Foyle Ltd.; Hon. D.Univ. (Essex) 1975. *Publication:* So Much Wisdom (Ed.) 1984. *Address:* c/o W. & G. Foyle Ltd., 119 Charing Cross Road, London, WC2H 0EB; Beeleigh Abbey, Maldon, Essex, CM3 4AD, England.

FRADKOV, Mikhail Yefimovich; Russian politician; b. 1 Sept. 1950, Moscow; m.; two c.; ed. Moscow Inst. of Machines and Tools, U.S.S.R. Acad. of Foreign Trade; on staff office of Counsellor on econ. problems U.S.S.R. Embassy to India 1973–75; on staff Foreign Trade Agency Tyazhpromexport, U.S.S.R. State Cttee. on Econ. Relations 1975–84; Deputy, First Deputy Dir. of Dept. U.S.S.R. State Cttee. on Econ. Relations 1985–91; sr. adviser Perm. Mission of Russian Fed. to UN; Deputy, First Deputy Minister of External Econ. Relations Russian Fed. 1992; Interim Acting Minister of External Econ. Relations 1997; Minister of External Econ. Relations and Trade Russian Fed. 1997–98; Chair. Bd. of Dirs. Ingosstrakh 1998–. *Address:* Ingosstrakh, Pyatnitskaya str. 12, 113805 Moscow, Russia. *Telephone:* (095) 231-1677.

FRAENKEL-CONRAT, Heinz, M.D., PH.D.; American professor of molecular biology; b. 29 July 1910, Breslau, Germany (now Wrocław, Poland); s. of Prof. Ludwig Fraenkel and Lili Conrat; m. 1st Jane Opermann 1939 (divorced 1964); two s.; m. 2nd Beatrice Singer 1964; ed. Breslau, Vienna, Munich, Geneva and Univ. of Edinburgh; Rockefeller Inst. 1936–37; Instituto Butantan, São Paulo 1937–38; Inst. of Experimental Biology, Univ. of Calif. (Berkeley) 1938–42; Western Regional Lab., Albany, Calif. 1942–49; Rockefeller Fellow working with Linderstrøm-Lang (Copenhagen), F. Sanger (Cambridge), R. R. Porter (London) 1950; Dept. of Virology, Dept. of Molecular Biology, Univ. of Calif. (Berkeley) 1951–, Prof. 1955–81, Prof. Emer. 1981–; Visiting Prof. Postgraduate Medical Coll., Univ. of London 1986; mem. N.A.S., American Acad. of Arts and Sciences; Lasker Award 1958; Humboldt Award 1985, and other distinctions. *Publications:* five books and 310 articles in scientific journals; Ed. (with R.R. Wagner) Comprehensive Virology (19 vols.) and The Viruses (30 vols.). *Leisure interests:* reading, hiking, swimming, bridge. *Address:* 870 Grizzly Peak Blvd., Berkeley, CA 94708, U.S.A. (Home).

FRAGA IRIBARNE, Manuel: Spanish politician, writer and diplomatist; b. 23 Nov. 1922, Villalba, Lugo; m. María del Carmen Estévez 1948 (died 1996); two s. three d.; ed. Santiago and Madrid Univs.; Prof. of Political Law, Valencia Univ. 1945; Diplomatic Service 1945–; Prof. Theory of State and Constitutional Law, Madrid Univ. 1948; Gen. Sec. Inst. of Hispanic Culture 1951; Gen. Sec. Nat. Educ. Ministry 1955; Dir. Inst. of Political Studies 1961; Minister of Information and Tourism 1962–69; also Sec.-Gen. of Cabinet 1967–69; Amb. to U.K. 1973–75; Minister of the Interior and Deputy Premier for Internal Affairs 1975–76; f. Alianza Popular (now Partido Popular) 1976, Leader 1979–86, 1989–90; mem. European Parl. 1987–89; Pres. Govt. of Galicia Feb. 1990–; mem. Cttee. for Defence of Christian Civilization, Union of Family Orgs. *Publications:* 75 books on political, constitutional and social subjects. *Leisure interests:* hunting, fishing. *Address:* Xunta de Galicia, Edificio San Caetano, No. 1 Santiago de Compostela; Palacio de Rajoy, Plaza del Obradeiro, Santiago de Compostela, Spain. *Telephone:* (81) 54.12.15 (San Caetano); (81) 54.49.15 (Palacio de Rajoy). *Fax:* (81) 54.12.19.

FRAHM, Sheila, B.S.; American politician; b. 22 March 1945, Colby, Kan.; m. Kenneth Frahm; three d.; ed. Fort Hays State Univ.; mem. Kan. Senate, Topeka 1988–94, Senate Majority Leader 1993–94, Lieut.-Gov. Kan. 1995–96; Republican Senator from Kansas 1996–; mem. Shakespeare Fed., Kan. Corn Growers, Kan. Livestock Asscn; Republican. *Address:* Suite 401, 700 South West Jackson, Topeka, KS 66603 (Office); 6005 South West 39th Street, Topeka, KS 66610, U.S.A. (Home).

FRAME, Frank Riddell, M.A., LL.B.; British lawyer; b. 15 Feb. 1930, Scotland; m. Maureen Milligan 1958; one s. one d.; ed. Univ. of Glasgow; North of Scotland Hydro-Electric Bd. 1955–60; UKAEA 1960–68; The Weir Group PLC 1968–76; joined The Hongkong and Shanghai Banking Corpn. Ltd. as Group Legal Adviser 1977, Exec. Dir. 1985, retd. as Deputy Chair. 1990, Adviser to the Bd. HSBC Holdings PLC 1990–98; Chair. South China Morning Post Ltd. 1981–87, Far Eastern Economic Review Ltd. 1981–87, Wallem Group Ltd. 1992–; Dir. The British Bank of the Middle East 1986–90, Marine Midland Banks Inc. 1986–90, Swire Pacific Ltd. 1986–90, Securities and Futures Comm., Hong Kong 1989–90, Baxter Int. Inc. 1992–, Edinburgh Dragon Trust PLC 1994–. *Publication:* The Law relating to Nuclear Energy (with Prof. Harry Street) 1966. *Address:* 43 Shrewsbury House, Cheyne Walk, London, SW3 5LW, England. *Telephone:* 0171-352 3968.

FRAME, Janet, C.B.E.; New Zealand writer; b. 1924, Dunedin; ed. Oamaru North School, Waitaki Girls' High School, Dunedin Training Coll. and Otago Univ.; Hubert Church Award for N.Z. Prose; N.Z. Scholarship in Letters 1964, Burns Fellow, Otago Univ., Dunedin. *Publications:* Lagoon 1951, Owls do Cry 1957, Faces in the Water 1961, The Edge of the Alphabet 1962, Scented Gardens for the Blind 1963, The Reservoir (stories), Snowman, Snowman (fables), The Adaptable Man 1965, A State of Siege 1967, The Pocket Mirror (poetry), Yellow Flowers in the Antipodean Room 1968, Mona Minim and the Smell of the Sun (children's book) 1969, Intensive Care (novel) 1971, Daughter Buffalo (novel) 1972, Living in the Maniototo (novel) 1979, The Carpathians 1988, An Autobiography 1990.

FRAME, Ronald William Sutherland, M.A., M.LITT.; British author; b. 23 May 1953, Glasgow, Scotland; s. of Alexander D. Frame and Isobel D. Frame (née Sutherland); ed. The High School of Glasgow, Univ. of Glasgow, Jesus Coll. Oxford; full-time author 1981–; Betty Trask Prize (jtly.) (first recipient) 1984, Samuel Beckett Prize 1986; TV Industries' Panel's "Most Promising Writer New to Television" Award 1986. *Publications: books:* Winter Journey 1984, Watching Mrs. Gordon 1985, A Long Weekend with Marcel Proust 1986, Sandmouth People 1987, Paris (TV play) 1987, A Woman of Judah 1987, Penelope's Hat 1989, Bluette 1990, Underwood and After 1991, Walking My Mistress in Deauville 1992, The Sun on the Wall 1994, The Lantern Bearers 1999. *TV screenplays:* Paris 1985, Out of Time 1987, Ghost City 1994, A Modern Man 1996, M. R. James 1999. *Radio scripts include:* Winter Journey 1985, Cara 1989, The Lantern Bearers 1997, The Hydro (serial) 1997–99, Havisham 1998, Maestro 1999, The Cuckoo Storm 1999. *Leisure interests:* swimming, walking, classical music. *Address:* c/o Curtis Brown Ltd., 28/29 Haymarket, London, SW1Y 4SP, England. *Telephone:* 0171-396 6600. *Fax:* 0171-396 0110/1.

FRANÇA, José-Augusto, D. ÈS L., D.HIST.; Portuguese writer and art historian; b. 16 Nov. 1922, Tomar; s. of José M. França and Carmen R. França; m. 2nd Marie-Thérèse Mandroux; one d. (by previous m.); ed. Lisbon Univ., Ecole des Hautes Etudes and Univ. of Paris; travels in Africa, Europe, Americas and Asia 1945–; Ed. Lisbon literary review Unicornio 1951–56, Co-ed. Cadernos de Poesia 1951–53; Founder-Dir. Galeria de Marco, Lisbon 1952–54; art critic 1946–; film critic 1948–; lexicographical publr. 1948–58; lived in Paris 1959–63; Ed. Pintura & Näo 1969–70; Ed. Colóquio Artes 1970–96; Prof. Cultural History and History of Art, Dir. Dept. of Art History, New Univ. of Lisbon 1974–92, Prof. Emer. 1992–, Dir. elect Faculty of Social Sciences 1982; Dir. Fondation C. Gulbenkian, Centre Culturel Portugais, Paris 1983–89; Visiting Prof. Univ. of Paris III 1985–89; Vice-Pres. Int. Asscn. of Art Critics 1970–73, Pres. 1985–87, Pres. of Honour 1987–; Vice-Pres. Acad. Européenne de Sciences, Arts et Lettres Paris 1985–; City Councillor, Lisbon 1974–75; mem. of City Ass. Lisbon 1990–93; Pres. Inst. Cultura Portuguesa 1976–80; mem. Int. Asscn. of Art Critics, Int. Cttee. of Art History, PEN Club, Soc. Européenne de Culture, Soc. de l'Histoire de l'Art français, Acad. Nacional de Belas Artes (Pres. 1977–80), Acad. das Ciencias de Lisboa, Acad. Européenne de Sciences, Arts et Lettres, World Acad. of Arts and Science, Acad. Nat. Sciences, Arts et Lettres de Bordeaux, Ateneo Veneto, Real Acad. Bellas Artes San Fernando (Spain); Officier Ordre national du Mérite; Chevalier Ordre des Arts et Lettres (France); Commdr. Ordem Rio Branco (Brazil); Grand Cross Order of Public Instruction; Grand Officer Ordem Infante Dom Henrique; Officer Ordem Santiago; Medal of Honour (Lisbon). *Publications:* Natureza Morta (novel) 1949, Azazel (play) 1957, Despedida Breve (short stories) 1958; Essays: Charles Chaplin—the Self-Made Myth 1952, Amadeo de Souza-Cardoso 1957, Situação da Pintura Ocidental 1959, Da Pintura Portuguesa 1960, Dez Anos de Cinema 1960, Une ville des lumières: La Lisbonne de Pombal 1963, A Arte em Portugal no Século XIX 1967, Oito Ensaios sobre Arte Contemporânea 1967, Le romantisme au Portugal 1972, Almada, o Português sem Mestre 1972, A Arte na Sociedade Portuguesa no Século XX 1972, Antonio Carneiro 1973, A

Arte em Portugal no século XX 1974, Zé Povinho 1975, Manolo Millares 1977, Lisboa: Urbanismo e Arquitectura, O Retrato na Arte Portuguesa, Rafael Bordalo Pinheiro, o Português tal e qual 1980, Malhoa & Columbano, Historia da Arte Occidental 1780–1980 1987, Os Anos 20 em Portugal 1992, Bosch ou le visionnaire intégral, Thomar revisited 1994, Lisboa 1898, (In) definições de Cultura 1997. *Leisure interests:* travel and detective stories. *Address:* Mailing address: Rua Escola Politécnica 49/4 1250 Lisbon; 9 Villa Virginie, 75014 Paris; "Le Pavillon", 49140 Jarzé, France. *Telephone:* 3462028 (Lisbon); (01) 45.40.49.19 (Paris); (02) 41.95.40.04 (Jarzé).

FRANCHET, Yves Georges; French international public servant; b. 4 March 1939, Paris; m. Marie Bernard Robillard; two s.; ed. Ecole polytechnique, Paris, Université Paris I; Dir. Statistics Office, UDEAC, Brazzaville, Congo 1964–68; mem. govt. econ. planning staff 1968–69; economist, World Bank, Washington, D.C. 1969–74; Head of Planning, Co-operation Div., INSEE 1974–77; Dir. ENSAE 1977–80; Deputy Dir. European Office of World Bank, Paris 1980–83; Vice-Pres. IDB, Washington, D.C. 1983–87; Dir.-Gen. Statistical Office of the European Communities (Eurostat) 1987–; Chevalier Légion d'honneur. *Address:* Statistical Office of the European Communities (Eurostat), Bâtiment Jean Monnet, Rue Alcide de Gasperi, 2920 Luxembourg (Office); 7 Rue J. P. Brasseur, 1258 Luxembourg (Home). *Telephone:* 4301-33107 (Office). *Fax:* 4301–33015 (Office).

FRANCIS, Dick (see Francis, Richard Stanley).

FRANCIS, Freddie; British film director, producer and cinematographer; b. 1917, London; joined Gaumont British Studios as apprentice to stills photographer; fmr. clapper boy B.I.P. Studios, Elstree; fmr. camera asst. British Dominion; fmr. cameraman Shepperton Studios. *Films:* dir.: Two and Two Make Six (A Change of Heart/ The Girl Swappers 1962), Paranoiac, Vengeance, The Evil of Frankenstein, Nightmare, Traitor's Gate, Hysteria, Dr. Terror's House of Horrors, The Skull, The Psychopath, The Deadly Bees, They Came from Beyond Space, Torture Garden, Dracula Has Risen from the Grave, Mumsy Nanny Sonny and Girly, Trog, Tales from the Crypt, The Creeping Flesh, Tales That Witness Madness, Son of Dracula, Craze, The Ghoul, Legend of the Werewolf, The Doctor and the Devils, Dark Tower; cinematographer: Moby Dick, A Hill in Korea (Hell in Korea), Time Without Pity, Room at the Top, The Battle of the Sexes, Saturday Night and Sunday Morning, Sons and Lovers (Acad. Award 1960), The Innocents, Night Must Fall, The Elephant Man, The French Lieutenant's Woman, Dune, Memed My Hawk, Clara's Heart, Her Alibi, Brenda Starr, Glory (Acad. Award 1989), Man in the Moon, Cape Fear, School Ties, Princess Caraboo, A Life in the Theatre (TV movie). *Address:* CAA Personal Management Ltd., 4 Court Lodge, 48 Sloane Square, London, SW1W 8AT (Office); 12 Ashley Drive, Twickenham, Middx. TW7 5QA, England (Home).

FRANCIS, Richard (Dick) Stanley, O.B.E.; British author; b. 31 Oct. 1920, Tenby, S. Wales; s. of George V. and Catherine M. Francis; m. Mary M. Brenchley 1947; two s.; fighter and bomber pilot, R.A.F. 1940–46; amateur steeplechase jockey (Nat. Hunt racing) 1946–48; professional steeplechase jockey 1948–57; champion steeplechase jockey 1953–54; racing columnist, Sunday Express 1957–73; author and novelist 1957–; Hon. D. Hum. Litt. (Tufts Univ., Mass., U.S.A.) 1991; Edgar Allan Poe Awards (for Forfeit, Whip Hand, Come to Grief), Crime Writers' Asscn. Silver Dagger Award (for For Kicks), Gold Dagger Award (for Whip Hand), Cartier Diamond Dagger Award for life's work 1990, named Grand Master by Mystery Writers of America 1996. *Publications include:* The Sport of Queens (autobiog.) 1957, Dead Cert (novel) 1962, For Kicks 1965, Forfeit 1968, Whip Hand 1979, Lester (biog. of Lester Piggott) 1986, Straight, The Edge, Longshot 1990, Comeback 1991, Driving Force 1992, Decider 1993, Wild Horses 1994, Come to Grief 1995, To The Hilt 1996, 10lb Penalty 1997, Field of 13 1998, and many novels of adventure and risk. *Leisure interests:* attending race meetings worldwide, travel, boating, living in the W. Indies. *Address:* c/o John Johnson (Author's Agent) Ltd., 45/47 Clerkenwell Green, London, EC1R 0HT, England.

FRANCISCI DI BASCHI, Marco, D.IUR.; Italian diplomatist b. 3 Feb. 1920, Angleur, Belgium; s. of Francesco Francisci and Berthe Berlemont; m. Franca Angelini 1974; three c.; ed. Rome Univ.; entered diplomatic service 1948; Sec., Washington Embassy 1950–51; mem. Perm. Del. to UN, New York 1951–55; Consul, Klagenfurt, Austria 1955–58; Dir. Int. Orgs. Branch, Gen. Econ. Affairs Directorate, Foreign Ministry 1958–75; Amb. to People's Repub. of China 1975–80; Amb. and Perm. Rep. to OECD, Paris 1980–83, Amb. and Perm. Rep. to FAO, Rome 1983–85; Pres. Italy-China Asscn.1985; mem. and Counsellor ISMEO (Inst. for the Middle and Far East) 1985–. *Address:* Via Cesalpino 10, 00161 Rome, Italy. *Telephone:* (06) 44231857.

FRANCK, Edouard; Central African Republic politician; fmrly. Minister in charge of Cabinet Secr.; Prime Minister of the Cen. African Repub. 1991–93; Pres. Supreme Court 1995–. *Address:* Cour Suprême, BP 926, Bangui, Central African Republic. *Telephone:* 61-41-33.

FRANCO, Itamar Augusto Cantiero; Brazilian politician; b. 28 June 1931, Juiz de Fora, Minas Gerais; s. of Augusto Cesar Stiebler Franco and Itália Cautiero Franco; two d.; ed. univ. studies in civil and electronic eng., Minas Gerais; Mayor of Juiz de Fora, Minas Gerais 1967–71, 1973–74; Senator of the Repub. 1974, 1982; Pres. Parl. Tech. Cttees. on Econ. and Finance 1983–84; Vice-Pres. of Brazil 1989–92; Acting Pres. of Brazil Oct.–Dec. 1992, Pres. Dec. 1992–94; Amb. to Portugal 1995. *Publications:* books on anthropology, history, nuclear energy and political issues. *Address:* c/o Ministry of Foreign Affairs, Palácio do Hamaraty, Esplanada dos Ministérios, 70170 Brasília, Brazil.

FRANCO ESTADELLA, Antonio; Spanish journalist; b. 21 Jan. 1947, Barcelona; s. of Alfonso Franco and Lolita Estadella; m. Marie-Hélène Bigata; one s. one d.; Ed. Sports Section Diario Barcelona 1970, Ed.-in-Chief 1973, Asst. Dir. 1975; Dir. Siete Días (TV programme) 1977; f. El Periódico de Catalunya 1977, Ed. 1987–; Jt. Ed. El País 1982. *Leisure interests:* literature, music, sports. *Address:* El Periódico de Catalunya, Consell de Cent 425–427, 08009 Barcelona, Spain. *Telephone:* (3) 2655353. *Fax:* (3) 4846512.

FRANÇOIS-PONCET, Jean André, PH.D.; French diplomatist; b. 8 Dec. 1928, Paris; s. of André François-Poncet and Jacqueline Dilais; m. Marie-Thérèse de Mitry 1959; two s. one d.; ed. Wesleyan Univ., Fletcher School of Law and Diplomacy at Tufts Univ., Paris Law School, Nat. School of Public Admin., Paris and Stanford Univ. Graduate School of Business; joined Ministry of Foreign Affairs 1955; worked in office of Sec. of State 1956–58; Sec.-Gen. of Del. to Negotiations for Treaties for EEC and EURATOM 1956–57; Head of European Institutions section in Ministry 1958–61; Prof., Institut d'études politiques de Paris 1960–; Head of Assistance and Co-operation Mission in Morocco 1961–63; in charge of African Affairs in Ministry 1963–68; Counsellor, Embassy in Iran 1968–70; Chair. of Bd., Pres. and C.E.O., Etablissements J. J. Carnaud & Forges 1971–75; Sec. of State for Foreign Affairs Jan.-July 1976; Sec.-Gen. to Presidency of French Repub. 1976–78; Minister of Foreign Affairs 1978–81; mem. Conseil Général, Lot-et-Garonne 1967–, Pres. 1978–94, 1998–; Senator for Lot-et-Garonne 1983–; Dir. FMC Corpn. 1982–; Reporter, Figaro 1984–; Chair. Cttee. Senate; Chevalier Légion d'honneur; Ordre nationale du Mérite. *Publication:* The Economic Policy of Western Germany 1970. *Address:* Senate, Palais du Luxembourg, 75291 Paris cedex 06; Conseil général du Lot-et-Garonne, cité Saint-Jacques, 47922 Agen cedex 09 (Offices); 6 boulevard Suchet, 75116 Paris, France (Home). *Telephone:* 504-13-37 (Home).

FRÄNGSMYR, Tore, D.PHIL.; Swedish professor of history of science; b. 8 July 1938, Skelleftea; s. of Johan Frängsmyr and Linnea (née Lindberg) Frängsmyr; m. Birgitta Thunholm 1970; two s. two d.; ed. Uppsala Univ.; Assoc. Prof., Uppsala Univ. 1969, Prof. of History of Science 1982–; Prof. of Tech. and Social Change, Linkoping Univ. 1981–82; Dir. Center for History of Science, Royal Swedish Acad. of Sciences, Stockholm 1988–; Ed. Les Prix Nobel 1988–; Sec.-Gen. Int. Union of History of Science 1989–93; Fellow Royal Swedish Acad. of Sciences, Royal Acad. of Eng. Sciences, Academia Europaea. *Publications include:* Linnaeus, the Man and His Work 1984, Science in Sweden; The Royal Swedish Acad. of Sciences 1739–1989 1989, The Quantifying Spirit in the Eighteenth Century (co-ed.) 1990, Solomon's House Revisited: The Organization and Institutionalization of Science 1990, Enlightenment Science in the Romantic Era: The Chemistry of Berzelius and its Cultural Setting (co-ed.) 1992. *Address:* Uppsala University, Box 256, 751 05, Uppsala, Sweden.

FRANK, Charles Raphael, Jr., PH.D.; American banker and economist; b. 15 May 1937, Pittsburgh., Pa.; s. of Charles Raphael Frank and Lucille Frank (née Briscoe); m. 1st Susan Patricia Buckman (divorced 1976); one s. one d.; m. 2nd Eleanor Sebastian 1976; two s.; one step s. one step d.; ed. Rensselaer Polytechnic Inst. and Princeton Univ.; Sr. Research Fellow East African Inst. for Social Research, Makerere Univ. Coll., Kampala 1963–65; Asst. Prof. Econs. Yale Univ. 1965–67; Assoc. Prof. Econs. and Int. Affairs Princeton Univ. 1967–70, Prof. 1970–74; Assoc Dir. Research Programme on Econ. Devt., Woodrow Wilson School 1967–70, Dir. 1970–74; Sr. Fellow Brookings Inst. 1972–74; mem. Policy Planning staff, U.S. Dept. of State 1974–77, Deputy Asst. Sec. of State for Econ. and Social Affairs and Chief Economist 1977–78; Vice-Pres. Salomon Bros., Inc. 1978–87; Pres. Frank & Co., Inc. 1987–88; Vice-Pres. for Business Devt. GE Capital Corpn., Stamford, Conn. 1988–97; First Vice-Pres. EBRD 1997–; Consultant to various American and foreign insts. including IBRD 1964–75; mem. Council on Foreign Relations. *Publications:* The Sugar Industry in East Africa 1965, Production Theory and Indivisible Commodities 1969, Economic Accounting and Development Planning (with Brian Van Arkadie) 1969, Debt and the Terms of Aid 1970, Statistics and Econometrics 1971, American Jobs and Trade with the Developing Countries 1973, Foreign Exchange Regimes and Economic Development: The Case of South Korea 1975, Foreign Trade and Domestic Adjustment 1976, Income Distribution and Economic Growth in the Less Developed Countries (jtly.) 1977. *Address:* European Bank for Reconstruction and Development, 1 Exchange Square, London, E.C.2 (Office); 175 Bishopsgate, London, EC2A 2EH, England; 25 East 86th Street, Apt. 10A, New York, NY 10028, U.S.A. (Home). *Telephone:* 0171-338 6000. *Fax:* 0171-338 6100.

FRANK, Sergey Ottovich; Russian politician; b. 13 Aug. 1960, Novosibirsk; m.; one s.; ed. Far E. Higher Marine School of Eng., Far E. State Univ., Higher School of Commerce, Ministry of Foreign Econ. Relations of Russian Fed.; Sec., Comsomol Cttee., later Deputy Head, Far E. Higher Marine School; on staff Far E. Marine Navigation Agency 1989–93, Deputy Dir.-Gen. 1993–95; Deputy Head, Dept. of Marine Transport, Ministry of Transport of Russian Fed. 1995–96; First Deputy Minister of Transport of Russian Fed. 1997–98, Minister March 1998–. *Address:* Ministry of Transport, Sadovaya-Samotechnaya str. 10, 101433 Moscow, Russia. *Telephone:* (095) 200 0803 (Office).

FRANKEL, Max, M.A.; American journalist; b. 3 April 1930, Gera, Germany; s. of Jacob A. Frankel and Mary (Katz) Frankel; m. 1st. Tobia Brown 1956 (deceased 1987); two s. one d.; m. 2nd Joyce Purnick 1988; ed. Columbia Univ., New York; mem. staff, The New York Times 1952, Chief Washington Corresp. 1968–72, Sunday Ed. 1973–76, Editorial Pages Ed. 1977–86, Exec. Ed. 1986–, also columnist New York Times magazine; Pulitzer Prize for Int. Reporting 1973. *Publication:* The Time of My Life and My Life with the Times 1999. *Address:* The New York Times Co., 229 West 43rd Street, New York, NY 10036, U.S.A.

FRANKEN, Hendrik, PH.D.; Netherlands professor of jurisprudence and information law; b. 17 Sept. 1936, Haarlem; s. of Albert J. Franken and Catherine G. Weijland; m. 1st Boudewine D. M. Bonebakker 1966 (divorced 1993); two s. one d.; m. 2nd Ingrid L. E. Sanders 1995; ed. Univ. of Leiden, Sorbonne, Paris, Univ. of Amsterdam; Sec., Mil. Tribunal 1960; Asst. Prosecutor, Dist. Court, Rotterdam 1964; mem. Rotterdam Bar 1967; Judge 1969; Prof. of Jurisprudence, Erasmus Univ., Rotterdam 1974, of Jurisprudence, Univ. of Leiden 1977–, of Information Law 1987–; Prof. of Information Law, Univ. of Groningen; mem. State Council 1982–87, Court of Appeal, The Hague 1977–; Chair. Nat. Cttee. of Information Tech. and Law; mem. Social Econ. Council, Royal Acad. of Arts and Sciences; Modderman Prijs 1973, Wolffert van Borselenpenning 1982; Kt. of Netherlands Lion. *Publications:* Vervolgingsbeleid: the Policy of Public Prosecutors 1973, Maat en Regel: Jurimetrics and the Rule of Law 1975, The New Law and Economics 1982, Models of Contracts in Information Law 1992, Introduction to the Law (7th edn.) 1995, A Sense of Direction 1995, Trusted Third Parties 1996, Law and Computer (2nd edn.) 1997. *Address:* Juridisch Studiecentrum, Hugo de Groot, P.O. Box 9520, 2300 RA Leiden (Office); Weipoortseweg 95A, 2381 NJ Zoeterwoude, Netherlands (Home). *Telephone:* 71-5277548 (Office); 71-5804764 (Home). *Fax:* 71-5277600.

FRANKENHAEUSER, Marianne, PH.D.; Swedish professor of psychology; b. 30 Sept. 1925, Helsinki, Finland; d. of Tor von Wright and Ragni Alfthan; m. Bernhard Frankenhaeuser 1946; one d.; ed. Oxford Univ., U.K., Univs. of Helsinki, Finland and Stockholm and Uppsala, Sweden; Asst. Prof. of Psychology, Univ. of Stockholm 1960–63; Research Fellow, Swedish Council for Social Science Research 1963–65; Assoc. Prof. of Experimental Psychology, Swedish Medical Research Council 1965–69, Prof. 1969–80; Prof. of Psychology, Karolinska Institutet 1980–92, Chair. Dept. of Psychology 1980–82, Head Psychology Div., Dept. of Psychiatry and Psychology 1980–92; Research Dir. Swedish Inst. for Man. and Work 1990–95; Resident Scholar, Rockefeller Foundation Study and Conf. Centre, Bellagio, Como, Italy 1980; Gildersleeve Prof., Barnard Coll., Columbia Univ., U.S.A. 1981; Fellow Centre for Advanced Study in the Behavioural Sciences, Stanford, U.S.A. 1995–96; Visiting Scholar Inst. for Research on Women and Gender, Stanford Univ. 1997–98; Chair. Scientific Council of Swedish Psychological Asscn. 1970–73; Pres. European Brain and Behaviour Soc. 1974–76; Foreign mem. N.A.S. (U.S.A.), Finnish Soc. of Sciences and Letters 1994; Corresp. mem. Académie Internationale de Philosophie des Sciences; mem. Academia Europaea; D. Pol.Sc. h.c. (Turku, Finland) 1990; Royal Award: The King of Sweden's Medal 1985, Swedish Nat. Award for Zealous and Devoted Service 1986 and other awards. *Publications:* Estimation of Time 1959, Stress (with Maj Ödman) 1983, Women, Work and Health (with Ulf Lundberg and Margaret Chesney) 1991, Stress and Gender 1993, and articles on psychology in various journals. *Leisure interests:* reading, writing and outdoor life in clean nature. *Address:* Department of Psychology, University of Stockholm, S-106 91 Stockholm (Office); Skeppargatan 32, S-114 52 Stockholm, Sweden.

FRANKENHEIMER, John Michael, B.A.; American film and stage director; b. 19 Feb. 1930, New York; s. of Walter Martin and Helen Mary (Sheedy) Frankenheimer; m. 1st Carolyn Diane Miller 1954 (divorced 1961); two d.; m. 2nd Evan Evans 1964; ed. LaSalle Mil. Acad., Williams Coll.; actor 1950–51. *TV programmes directed:* You Are There, Danger, Climax (Emmy Award 1956), Studio One, Playhouse 904 1954–59 (Emmy Awards 1957, 1958, 1959), For Whom the Bell Tolls, The Comedian (Acapulco Film Festival award 1962), The Days of Wine and Roses, Old Man, The Browning Version, The Turn of the Screw, The Rainmaker, The Burning Season 1995. *Films include:* The Young Stranger 1956, The Young Savages 1961, The Birdman of Alcatraz 1962, All Fall Down 1962, The Manchurian Candidate 1962, Seven Days in May 1963, The Train 1964, Seconds 1965, Grand Prix 1966, The Fixer 1968, Gypsy Moths 1969, I Walk the Line 1970, The Horsemen 1971, Impossible Object 1972, The Iceman Cometh 1973, Dead 1974, French Connection II 1975, Black Sunday 1977, Prophecy 1979, Challenge 1982, The Holcroft Covenant 1984, 52-Pick-up 1986, Year of the Gun 1991, Against the Wall (TV) 1994, The Island of Dr. Moreau 1996, Ronin 1998; Christopher Award 1954; Grand Prize for best film dir., Locarno Film Festival 1955; Critics' Award for Best Direction 1956–59. *Address:* William Morris Agency, c/o Johnny Levin, 151 S. El Camino Drive, Beverly Hills, CA 90212, U.S.A.

FRANKENTHALER, Helen, B.A.; American artist; b. 1928, New York; m. 1st Robert Motherwell 1958 (divorced 1971); m. 2nd Stephen M. DuBrul, Jr. 1994; ed. Bennington Coll., Vt.; Trustee Bennington Coll. 1967; Fellow Calhoun Coll., Yale Univ. 1968; solo exhbns. throughout U.S.A. and Europe, particularly at André Emmerich Gallery 1959–, Whitney Museum of American Art, and Metropolitan Museum of Art, New York 1951–73, Guggenheim Museum, New York 1975, retrospective 1985 (exhbn. travelled U.S.A., Canada 1986), Corcoran Gallery, Washington, D.C. 1975, Museum of Fine Arts, Houston 1976, Modern Art Museum, Fort Worth, 1989 (painting retrospective, travelled U.S.A.), Nat. Gallery of Art, Washington, D.C. 1993 (graphic retrospective, travelled U.S.A., Japan), U.S.I.A. (United States Information Agency) exhbn., Janie C. Lee Gallery, Dallas 1973, 1975, 1976, 1978, 1980, Knoedler Gallery, London 1978, 1981, 1983, 1985, Sterling & Francine Clark Art Inst., Williamstown, Mass. 1980, Knoedler and Co., New York 1992, 1994; mem. American Acad. and Inst. of Arts and Letters 1974, NEA Council on the Arts 1985–92, Corpn. of Yaddo 1973–78; Trustee Bennington Coll. 1967–82; Fellow, Calhoun Coll., Yale Univ. 1968; mem. American Acad. of Arts and Sciences 1991; travelled to Far East, Australia, Latin America 1978–79; numerous hon. degrees; First Prize, Paris Biennale 1959; Joseph E. Temple Gold Medal Award, Pennsylvania Acad. of Fine Arts 1968, Spirit of Achievement Award, Albert Einstein Coll. of Medicine 1970, Gold Medal of the Commune of Catania, Florence 1972, Garrett Award, Art Inst. of Chicago 1972, Creative Arts Award, American Jewish Congress 1974, Art and Humanities Award, Yale Women's Forum 1976, Extraordinary Woman of Achievement Award, Nat. Conf. of Christians and Jews 1978; Mayor's Award of Honor for Art and Culture, New York City 1986, Conn. Arts Award 1989, Lifetime Achievement Award, Coll. Art Asscn. 1994. *Address:* c/o M. Knoedler and Co. Inc., 19 East 70th Street, New York, NY 10021, U.S.A.

FRANKEVICH, Yevgeniy Leonidovich, DR. PHYS.-MATH. SC.; Russian scientist; b. 19 Feb. 1930, Samara; s. of V. Eseleva and L. V. Frankevich; m. Irene Lenchenko 1957; one s. one d.; ed. Polytechnic Inst., Leningrad (now St. Petersburg); postgrad. jr. then sr. researcher 1957–71; mem. CPSU 1961–91; head of lab. U.S.S.R. Acad. of Sciences Inst. of Chemical Physics 1971–88; Prof. Moscow Inst. of Physics and Tech. 1972–; Head of Lab., U.S.S.R. (now Russian) Acad. of Sciences Inst. of Energy Problems of Chemical Physics 1988–; Inst. for Molecular Science, Okazaki, Japan 1992–93, 1994; mem. Russian Acad. of Natural Science 1990–; Lenin Prize for Science 1986; two diplomas for scientific discoveries. *Publications include:* Chemical Generation and Reception of Radio- and Microwaves 1994, and 250 papers in the field of radiation and photo physics, organic semiconductors, and magnetic spin effects. *Leisure interests:* gardening, jogging. *Address:* Institute of Energy Problems of Chemical Physics, Leninsky Prosp. 38, Moscow 334, Russia. *Telephone:* (095) 939-7993 (Office); 336-11-84 (Home). *Fax:* (095) 137-3479.

FRANKL, Peter; British concert pianist; b. 2 Oct. 1935, Budapest, Hungary; s. of Tibor and Laura Frankl; m. Annie Feiner 1958; one s. one d.; ed. High School, Franz Liszt Music Acad., Budapest; began career in late 1950s, won first prize in several int. competitions; London début 1962, New York début 1967; has performed with world's maj. orchestras, including Berlin Philharmonic, Amsteram Concertgebouw, Israel Philharmonic, Leipzig Gewandhaus, and all the London and the maj. American orchestras, under conductors including Abbado, Boulez, Colin Davis, Haitink, Maazel, Masur, Muti, Solti. *Recordings include:* complete works for piano by Schumann and Debussy, a solo Bartók and Chopin album, a Hungarian Anthology, Mozart concerti with mems. of English Chamber Orchestra, the complete 4-hand works by Mozart with Tamás Vásáry, and Brahms, Schumann, Dvořák and Martinů quintets with the Lindsay Quartet. *Leisure interests:* football, opera, theatre. *Address:* 5 Gresham Gardens, London, NW11 8NX, England. *Telephone:* 0181-455 5228.

FRANKLIN, Aretha; American singer; b. 25 March 1942, Memphis; d. of Rev. C. L. Franklin; m. 1st Ted White (divorced); m. 2nd Glynn Turman 1978; made first recordings at father's Baptist church, Detroit; toured as gospel singer; moved to New York, signed contract with Columbia Records 1960, with Atlantic 1966, with Arista 1980; recipient numerous Grammy Awards 1967–87; American Music Award 1984, John F. Kennedy Center Award 1994; Rock and Roll Hall of Fame 1987. *Recordings include:* Aretha 1961, The Electrifying Aretha Franklin 1962, Laughing on the Outside, The Tender, the Moving, the Swinging Aretha Franklin 1963, Running out of Fools, The Gospel Sound of Aretha Franklin 1964, Soul Sister 1966, I Never Loved a Man the Way I Love You 1967, Lady Soul, Aretha Now, Aretha in Paris 1968, Aretha's Gold 1969, This Girl's in Love with You, Spirit in the Dark 1970, Live at Fillmore West 1971, Young, Gifted and Black, Amazing Grace 1972, Hey Now Hey, The Best of Aretha Franklin, The First Twelve Sides 1973, Let Me in Your Life, With Everything I Feel in Me 1974, You 1975, Sparkle, Ten Years of Gold 1976, Sweet Passion 1977, Almighty Fire 1978, La Diva 1979, Aretha 1980, Love All the Hurt Away 1981, Jump to It 1982, Get It Right 1983, One Lord, One Faith 1988, Through the Storm 1989, What You See Is What You Sweat 1991, Jazz to Soul 1992, Aretha After Hours, Chain of Fools 1993, Unforgettable: A Tribute to Dinah Washington 1995, Love Songs 1997. *Address:* 8450 Linwood Street, Detroit, MI 48206; c/o William Morris Agency, 151 S. El Camino Drive, Beverly Hills, CA 90212, U.S.A.

FRANKLIN, Barbara Hackman, B.A., M.B.A.; American business executive and fmr. government official; b. 19 March 1940, Lancaster, Pa.; d. of Arthur A. Hackman and Mayme M. Hackman (née Haller); m. 2nd Wallace Barnes 1986; ed. Pennsylvania State Univ., Harvard Business School; with Singer Co., New York 1964–68; Asst. Vice-Pres. Citibank, New York 1969–71; Asst. on White House Staff for Recruiting Women to Govt., Washington, D.C. 1971–73; Commr. and Vice-Chair. U.S. Consumer Product Safety Comm., Washington, D.C. 1973–79; Sr. Fellow and Dir. Govt. and Business Program, Wharton School, Univ. of Pa. 1979–88; Pres. and C.E.O. Franklin Assocs.,

Washington, D.C. 1984–92, Barbara Franklin Enterprises 1995–; U.S. Sec. of Commerce, Dept. of Commerce, Washington, D.C. 1992–93; mem. Pres.'s Advisory Cttee. Trade Policy and Negotiations 1982–86, 1989–92, Chair. task force on tax reform 1985–86; mem. Services Policy Advisory Cttee. of U.S. Trade Reps. 1986–89; Alt. Rep. and Public Del. to 44th Session of UN Gen. Ass. 1989–90; Adviser to Comptroller-Gen. of U.S.A. 1984–92, 1995–; mem. Bd. of Dirs. Aetna Inc. 1979–92, 1993–, Dow Chemical Co. 1980–92, 1993–, AMP Inc. 1993–, NASDAQ Stock Market 1995–, MedImmune Inc. 1995–, Cincinnati Milacron 1996–; fmr. Dir. Black & Decker Corpn., Nordstrom, Westinghouse Electric Corpn. and other cos.; mem. Council on Foreign Relations 1991–, Bd. Dirs. Atlantic Council 1995–, Bretton Woods Cttee., U.S.-China Business Council; Fellow Nat. Asscn. of Corp. Dirs.; Founder mem. Int. Women's Forum; several hon. degrees and numerous awards for business and social achievement. *Leisure interests:* exercise, skiing, sailing, reading. *Address:* 2600 Virginia Avenue, NW, Suite 506, Washington, DC 20037 (Office); 1875 Perkins Street, Bristol, CT 06010, U.S.A. *Telephone:* (202) 337-9100 (Office); (860) 582-2500 (Bristol).

FRANKLIN, John Hope, A.M., PH.D.; American writer and university professor; b. 2 Jan. 1915, Bentiesville, Okla.; s. of Buck Colbert and Mollie (née Parker) Franklin; m. Aurelia E. Whittington 1940; one s.; ed. Fisk Univ., Harvard Univ.; Instructor in History Fisk Univ. 1936–38; Prof. of History St. Augustine's Coll. 1939–43, N.C. Coll., Durham 1943–47, Howard Univ. 1947–56; Chair. Dept. of History Brooklyn Coll. 1956–64; Prof. of American History Univ. of Chicago 1964–82, Chair. Dept. of History 1967–70, John Matthews Manly Distinguished Service Prof. 1969–82; James B. Duke Prof. of History Duke Univ. 1982–85, Emer. 1985–; Prof. of Legal History, Duke Law School 1985–92; Pitt Prof. of American History and Institutions Cambridge Univ. 1962–63; Visiting Prof. Harvard, Wis., Cornell, Hawaii, Calif. and Cambridge Univs., and Salzburg Seminar; Chair. Bd. of Foreign Scholarships 1966–69, Nat. Council on Humanities 1976–79; Dir. Ill. Bell Telephone Co. 1972–80; Edward Austin Fellow 1937–38, Rosenwald Fellow 1937–39, Guggenheim Fellow 1950–51, 1973–74; Pres.'s Fellow, Brown Univ. 1952–53, Center for Advanced Study in Behavioral Science 1973–74; Sr. Mellon Fellow, Nat. Humanities Center 1980–82; Fulbright Prof., Australia 1960; Jefferson Lecturer in Humanities 1976; mem. Bd. of Dirs. Salzburg Seminar, Museum of Science and Industry 1968–80; mem. American Historical Asscn. (Pres. 1978–79), Southern Historical Asscn. (Pres. 1970–71), Org. of American Historians (Pres. 1970–75), Asscn. for Study of Negro Life and History, American Studies Asscn., American Philosophical Soc., American Asscn. of Univ. Profs.; numerous hon. degrees; Jefferson Medal (American Philosophical Soc.) 1993, Presidential Medal of Freedom 1995. *Publications:* Free Negro in North Carolina 1943, From Slavery to Freedom: A History of Negro Americans 1947, 6e. 1987, Militant South 1956, Reconstruction After the Civil War 1961, The Emancipation Proclamation 1963, Land of the Free (with others) 1966, Illustrated History of Black Americans 1970, A Southern Odyssey 1976, Racial Equality in America 1976, George Washington Williams: A Biography 1985, Race and History: Selected Essays 1938–88 1990, The Color Line: Legacy for the 21st Century 1993; Ed. Civil War Diary of James T. Ayers 1947, A Fool's Errand (by Albion Tourgee) 1961, Army Life in a Black Regiment (by Thomas Higginson) 1962, Color and Race 1968, Reminiscences of an Active Life (by John R. Lynch) 1970. *Leisure interests:* cultivating orchids, fly fishing, classical music. *Address:* 208 Pineview Road, Durham, NC 27707, U.S.A. (Home).

FRANKLIN, Raoul Norman, C.B.E., D.SC., F.ENG.; British scientist and university administrator; b. 3 June 1935, Hamilton, N.Z.; s. of N. G. Franklin and T. B. (née Davis) Franklin; m. Faith Ivens 1961; two s.; ed. Auckland Grammar School, Auckland Univ., Oxford Univ.; Sr. Research Fellow, Royal Mil. Coll. of Science 1961–63; Tutorial Fellow, Keble Coll., Oxford 1963–78, Univ. Lecturer, Eng. Science, Oxford Univ. 1967–78; Consultant, UKAEA Culham Lab. 1968–; Vice-Chancellor, City Univ. 1978–98, Prof. Plasma Physics and Tech. 1986–98; Visiting Prof. Open Univ., Oxford Research Unit; Chair. City Tech. Ltd. 1978–93; Chair. Assoc. Examining Bd. 1994–98, Assessment and Qualifications Alliance (AQA) 1998–; Vice-Chair. Gen. Bd. of the Faculties, Oxford Univ. 1971–74; mem. of Hebdomadal Council, Oxford Univ. 1971–74, 1976–78, of Science Bd., Science and Eng. Research Council 1982–85, of London Pensions Fund Authority 1989–95, of Bd. Arab-British Chamber of Commerce 1995–; mem. Council Gresham Coll. 1980; mem. Int. Cttee. of ESCAMPIG 1993–96; Gov. Ashridge Man. Coll. 1986–, Council City & Guilds 1996–; Hon. Fellow, Keble Coll., Coll. of Preceptors; Freeman, City of London. *Publications:* Plasma Phenomena in Gas Discharges 1976, Physical Kinetics, vol. XII (ed.) 1981, Interaction of Intense Electromagnetic Fields with Plasmas (ed.) 1981. *Leisure interests:* walking, tennis, gardening. *Address:* Open University Oxford Research Unit, Foxcombe Hall, Boars Hill, Oxford, OX1 5HR (Office); 12 Moreton Road, Oxford, OX2 7AX, England (Home). *Telephone:* (01865) 558311 (Home). *Fax:* (01865) 326322 (Office).

FRANKS, Lynne; British public relations executive; b. 16 April 1948; d. of Leslie Samuel Franks and Angela Franks (née Herman); m. Paul Howie (separated 1992); one s. one d.; ed. Minchenden Grammar School, London; Sec. Petticoat Magazine 1965–67; est. Lynne Franks Ltd. public relations consultants 1971, left full-time employment 1992; clients have included Katherine Hamnett, Ruby Wax, Lenny Henry, Gerald Ratner, Jasper Conran, Neil Kinnock, Brylcreem, Swatch, Harvey Nichols, Next, Littlewoods, Comic Relief, Greenpeace, Amnesty Int. *Publication:* Absolutely Now!: A Futurist's Journey to Her Inner Truth 1997. *Leisure interests:* New Age spirituality, healing, the environment. *Address:* 327–329 Harrow Road, London, W9 3RB, England. *Telephone:* 0171-724 6777. *Fax:* 0171-724 8484.

FRANTZ, Justus; pianist; b. Hohensalza; ed. under Prof. Eliza Hansen in Hamburg and Wilhelm Kempf in Positano; prizewinner, Int. Music Competition, Munich 1967; since 1969 has appeared at all maj. European concert venues and toured U.S.A., Far East and Japan; has made many tours and recordings in piano duo with Christoph Eschenbach and received Edison Int. Award for their recording of Schubert marches 1983; co-founder and dir. Schleswig-Holstein Music Festival; Prof. Hamburg Musikhochschule; recordings include works by Scarlatti, Beethoven, Mozart and concertos for two, three and four pianos by J. S. Bach.

FRANTZ, Rodolphe Charles Henri; French airline executive; b. 14 Jan. 1941, Colmar, Haut Rhin; s. of Paul Frantz and Maria Hoerdt; m. Kazuyo Shinaki 1968; one s.; ed. Lycée Kléber, Strasbourg, Ecole des Hautes Etudes Commerciales, Paris and Berlin Tech. Univ.; Sales Man. for W. Germany, Air France, Frankfurt-am-Main 1969–72, Regional Man. for N. Japan, Tokyo 1972–77, Gen. Man. for Iran and Afghanistan, Tehran 1977–80, Gen. Man. for W. Germany, Frankfurt-am-Main 1980–82; Pres. Air Charter, Paris 1982–87, Chair. 1991–93; Chair. and C.E.O. Méridien, Paris 1987–93; Chair. Aéromaritime, Paris 1991–93; Pres. and C.E.O. Air France 1993–95; Chevalier, Ordre Nat. du Mérite, Légion d'honneur. *Address:* 7 Parc de Béarn, 92210 Saint Cloud, France (Home).

FRANZEN, Ulrich J., B.F.A., M.ARCH., L.H.D., F.A.I.A.; American architect; b. 15 Jan. 1921, Rhineland, Germany; s. of Erik Franzen and Elizabeth (Hellersberg) Franzen; m. 1st Joan Cummings 1942 (divorced 1962); two s. one d.; m. 2nd Josephine Laura Hughes 1980; ed. Williams Coll., and Harvard Univ.; Designer, I. M. Pei & Partners, New York 1950–55; Head of Ulrich Franzen and Assocs., New York 1955–; Visiting Critic, Prof., Washington, St. Louis, Yale, Harvard and Columbia Univs., various occasions 1960–84; Chair. Architectural Bd. of Review, Rye, N.Y. 1960–62; mem. Cincinnati Architectural Bd. Review Bd. 1964–65; mem. Architectural League New York (Pres. 1968–70, memm. Bd. of Dirs. 1962–); Commr. New York City Landmarks Preservation Comm., Century Asscn.; numerous awards including Brunner Memorial Prize, Nat. Inst. of Arts and Letters 1962, Thomas Jefferson Award, A.I.A. 1970, Gold Medal, A.I.A.; decorated Bronze Star, Croix de Guerre avec Palme (Belgium). *Principal works include:* Alley Theatre 1968 (A.I.A. Honor 1970), Agronomy Bldg. 1970 (A.I.A. Honor 1971), Christensen Hall 1970 (A.I.A. Honor 1972), Harlem School of Arts 1982, Hunter Coll. New York 1984, Philip Morris World HQ 1984, Whitney Museum Br. 1984, Champion Int. World HQ with Whitney Museum Br. 1985. *Address:* Ulrich Franzen Architect, 168 East 74th Street, New York, NY 10021, U.S.A. *Telephone:* (212) 535-3631. *Fax:* (212) 535-6509.

FRASER, Lady Antonia, M.A., F.R.S.L.; British author; b. 27 August 1932, London; d. of the Earl and Countess of Longford (q.v.); m. 1st Hugh Fraser 1956 (divorced 1977, died 1984); three s. three d.; m. 2nd Harold Pinter (q.v.) 1980; ed. Dragon School, Oxford, St. Mary's Convent, Ascot and Lady Margaret Hall, Oxford; mem. Cttee. English PEN 1979– (Pres. 1988–89, Vice-Pres. 1990–), Crimewriters Asscn. 1980–86; Hon. D.Litt. (Hull) 1986, (Sussex) 1990, (St. Andrews) 1994. *Publications:* King Arthur 1954, Robin Hood 1955, Dolls 1963, History of Toys 1966, Mary, Queen of Scots 1969 (James Tait Black Memorial Prize), Cromwell: Our Chief of Men 1973, King James VI and I 1974, Scottish Love Poems, A Personal Anthology 1974, Kings and Queens of England (Ed.) 1975, Love Letters (anthology) 1976, Quiet as a Nun 1977, The Wild Island 1978, King Charles II 1979, Heroes and Heroines (Ed.) 1980, A Splash of Red 1981, Cool Repentance 1982, Oxford In Verse (Ed.) 1982, The Weaker Vessel 1984 (Wolfson History Prize), Oxford Blood 1985, Your Royal Hostage 1987, Boadicea's Chariot: The Warrior Queens 1988, The Cavalier Case 1990, Jemima Shore at the Sunny Grove 1991, The Wives of Henry VIII 1992, Charles II: His Life and Times 1993, Political Death: A Jemima Shore Mystery 1994, The Gunpowder Plot (St. Louis Literary Award 1996, CWA Non Fiction Gold Dagger 1996) 1996, The Lives of the Kings and Queens of England 1998; ed. The Pleasure of Reading 1992; television adaptations of Quiet as a Nun 1978, Jemima Shore Investigates 1983. *TV plays:* Charades 1977, Mister Clay 1985. *Address:* c/o Curtis Brown, Haymarket House, 28/29 Haymarket, London SW1Y 4SP, England.

FRASER, Bernard William, B.A.; Australian bank governor; b. 26 Feb. 1941, Junee, N.S.W.; s. of K. Fraser; m. Edna Gallogly 1965 (dissolved); one s. two d.; ed. Junee High School, N.S.W., Univ. of New England, Armidale, N.S.W., Australian Nat. Univ., A.C.T.; joined Dept. of Nat. Devt. 1961; joined Dept. of Treasury 1963, Treasury Rep., London, U.K. 1969–72, First Asst. Sec. 1979, Sec. Dept. 1984–89; with Dept. of Finance 1976; Dir. Nat. Energy Office 1981–83; Chair. and Gov. Reserve Bank of Australia 1989–96; Trustee Construction and Bldg. Unions Superannuation Trust (C+BUS) 1996–, Superannuation Trust of Australia 1996–, Australian Retirement Fund 1996–. *Leisure interest:* farming. *Address:* Construction and Building Unions Superannuation Trust, Level 12, 313 La Trobe Street, Melbourne, Vic. 3000, Australia.

FRASER, Sir Campbell (see Fraser, Sir (James) Campbell).

FRASER, Donald Hamilton, R.A.; British artist; b. 30 July 1929, London; s. of Donald Fraser and Dorothy Lang; m. Judith Wentworth Sheilds 1954; one d.; ed. Maidenhead Grammar School, St. Martin's School of Art, London and in Paris (French Govt. Scholarship); has held more than 70 one-man exhbns. in Europe, N. America and Japan; work represented in public, corp. and pvt. collections throughout the world; taught at Royal Coll. of Art 1958–83, Fellow 1970; mem. Royal Fine Art Comm. 1986–; Hon. Curator, Royal Acad. 1992–, Trustee 1993–. *Publications:* Gauguin's 'Vision After the Sermon' 1969, Dancers 1989. *Address:* c/o Royal Academy of Arts, Burlington House, Piccadilly, London, W1V 0DS, England.

FRASER, George MacDonald, F.R.S.L.; British author; b. 2 April 1925, Carlisle; s. of William Fraser and Anne Struth Donaldson; m. Kathleen Margarette Hetherington 1949; two s. one d.; ed. Carlisle Grammar School, Glasgow Acad.; joined Army 1943, served as infantryman XIVth Army, Burma, later Lieut. Gordon Highlanders; journalist in England, Canada, Scotland 1947–65; Deputy Ed. Glasgow Herald 1965–69; author 1969–. *Publications include:* Flashman series of historical novels, The Pyrates, Mr American, Black Ajax, The General Danced at Dawn, The Steel Bonnets, The Candlemass Road 1993, Black Ajax 1997; screenplays: The Three Musketeers 1973, The Four Musketeers 1974, The Prince and the Pauper 1977, Octopussy 1981, Red Sonja 1985, Casanova 1987, The Return of the Musketeers 1989. *Leisure interests:* reading, writing. *Address:* c/o Curtis Brown, 28/29 Haymarket, London, SW1Y 4SP, England; Baldrine, Isle of Man.

FRASER, Honor; British model; b. 18 Dec. 1974, Beaufort Castle, Inverness; d. of the late Hon. Simon Augustine Fraser, Master of Lovat and of Virginia Fraser (née Grose); granddaughter of the late 17th Lord Lovat; first catwalk appearance in Milan at 19; with Storm Model Man., then with Select Model Man. 1997–; campaign for Givenchy 1997; appeared in campaigns for Ungaro and Nina Ricci; columnist Scotland on Sunday 1998–. *Address:* Select Model Management, Thomas Archer House, 43 King Street, London, WC2E 8RJ, England. *Telephone:* 0171-470 5200. *Fax:* 0171-470 5233.

FRASER, Sir (James) Campbell, Kt., B.COM., F.R.S.E., C.B.I.M.; British business executive; b. 2 May 1923, Dunblane, Scotland; s. of Alexander Ross and Annie McGregor Fraser; m. Maria Harvey (née McLaren) 1950 (died 1975); two d.; ed. Glasgow Univ. and Dundee School of Econs; served in R.A.F. 1941–45; Raw Cotton Comm. 1950–52; Economist Intelligence Unit 1952–57; with Dunlop Rubber Co. Ltd. 1957–83; Exec. Dir. Dunlop Holdings Ltd. 1969, Man. Dir. 1972–78, Chair. 1978–83, Pres. 1983–84; Chair. Scottish TV 1975–91; fmr. Pres. Soc. of Business Economists; Dir. Tandem Computers Inc., Chair. Tandem Computers Ltd.—1997; Dir. British Petroleum PLC 1978–91, BAT Industries PLC 1980–93, Bridgewater Paper Co. 1984–, Proudfoot PLC 1987–95; Chair. Advisory Bd. Wells Fargo 1989–95; Chair. Riversoft Ltd.; Deputy Pres. CBI 1981–82, Pres. 1982–84; mem. Council Confed. of British Industry, Council of SMMT; Dir. (non-exec.) Arlen PLC 1991–95 (Chair. 1993–95), Barkers Communications Scotland Ltd. 1992–95 (Chair. 1994–95); fmrly. Visiting Prof. Univ. of Stirling and Univ. of Strathclyde; Trustee, The Economist; Hon. Dr. Univ. (Stirling), Hon. LL.D. (Strathclyde) 1979, Hon. D.C.L. (Bishops Univ.) 1990. *Leisure interests:* athletics, reading, cinema, walking. *Address:* Silver Birches, 4 Silver Lane, Purley, Surrey, England.

FRASER, John Allen, P.C., Q.C., M.P., LL.B.; Canadian politician; b. 15 Dec. 1931, Yokohoma, Japan; m. Catherine Findlay; three d.; ed. Univ. of British Columbia; called to Bar, B.C. 1955–; mem. House of Commons 1972–; Minister of the Environment and Postmaster Gen. 1979; Minister of Fisheries and Oceans 1984–85 (resgnd.), Speaker of the House of Commons 1986–93; Amb. for the Environment 1994–; fmr. Caucus Spokesperson for Post Office, Labour and Environment; fmr. mem. Parl. Special Cttee. on acid rain; fmr. Chair. of Progressive Conservative Party Cttee. on Pollution, Environment and Fisheries; fmr. Chair. Environmental Law Subsection of Canadian Bar Asscn. *Address:* Lester B. Pearson Building, 125 Sussex Drive, Ottawa, Ont., K1A 0G2; Suite 2000, 300 West Georgia Street, Vancouver, B.C., V6B 6E1, Canada. *Telephone:* (613) 944-0886 (Ottawa); (604) 666-5423 (Vancouver). *Fax:* (613) 944-0892 (Ottawa); (604) 666-7981 (Vancouver).

FRASER, Rt. Hon. (John) Malcolm, A.C., C.H., P.C., M.A.; Australian politician; b. 21 May 1930, Melbourne; s. of the late J. Neville Fraser and of Una Fraser; m. Tamara Beggs 1956; two s. two d.; ed. Melbourne Grammar School and Oxford Univ.; mem. Parl. for Wannon 1955–83; mem. Jt. Parl. Cttee. of Foreign Affairs 1962–66; Chair. Govt. Mems.' Defence Cttee.; Sec. Wool Cttee.; mem. Council of Australian Nat. Univ., Canberra 1964–66; Minister for the Army 1966–68, for Educ. and Science 1968–69, for Defence 1969–71, for Educ. and Science 1971–72; Parl. Leader of Liberal Party 1975–83; Prime Minister 1975–83; Co-Chair. Commonwealth Eminent Persons Group (EPG) 1985–86; Hon. Fellow Magdalen Coll., Oxford 1982; Hon. Vice-Pres. Oxford Soc. 1983; Sr. Adjunct Fellow, Center for Strategic and Int. Studies 1983; Fellow for Int. Council of Assocs. at Claremont Univ. 1985; Chair. UN Cttee. on African Commodity Problems 1989–90; mem. InterAction Council for Fmr. Heads of Govt. 1983– (Chair. 1997–), ANZ Int. Bd. of Advice 1987–93, Chair. 1997–; Chair. CARE Australia 1987–; Pres. CARE Int. 1990–95, Vice-Pres. 1995–; Bd. mem. Jnt-Crisis Group 1995–; Hon. LL.D. (S. Carolina) 1981, Hon. D.Litt (Deakin Univ.) 1989; B'nai B'rith Gold Medal 1980. *Leisure interests:* fishing, photography, vintage cars, motorcycles. *Address:* 44th Floor, ANZ Tower, 55 Collins Street, Melbourne, Vic. 3000, Australia. *Telephone:* (03) 9654 1822. *Fax:* (03) 9654 1301.

FRASER, Peter Marshall, M.C., M.A., F.B.A.; British classical scholar; b. 6 April 1918; s. of Archibald Fraser; m. 1st Catharine Heaton-Renshaw 1940 (marriage dissolved); one s. three d.; m. 2nd Ruth Elsbeth Renfer 1955; two s.; m. 3rd Barbara Ann Norbury 1973; ed. City of London School and Brasenose Coll. Oxford; served Seaforth Highlanders 1941–45, Mil. Mission to Greece 1943–45; Sr. Scholar, Christ Church Oxford 1946–47; Lecturer in Hellenistic History, Oxford Univ. 1948–64, Reader 1964–85; Fellow of All Souls Coll. Oxford 1954–87, Domestic Bursar 1962–65, Sub-Warden 1980–82, Acting Warden 1985–87, Emer. Fellow 1987–; Jr. Proctor, Oxford Univ. 1960–61; Dir. British School at Athens 1968–71; Chair. Man. Cttee., Soc. of Afghan Studies 1972–82; Ordinary mem. German Archaeological Inst.; Hon. Vice-Pres. Archaeological Soc. of Athens; Gen. Ed., British Acad. Cttee., Lexicon of Greek Personal Names 1973– (Chair. 1973–95); Chair. Man. Cttee. of Afghan Studies 1972–82; Hon. D.Phil. (Trier) 1984; Hon. D.Litt (La Trobe) 1996. *Publications:* The Rhodian Peraea and Islands (with G. E. Bean) 1954, Boeotian and West Greek Tombstones (with T. Rönne) 1957, Samothrace, The Inscriptions (Vol. I, Excavations of Samothrace) 1960, The Wares of Autolycus; Selected Literary Essays of Alice Meynell (Ed.) 1965, Ptolemaic Alexandria 1972, Rhodian Funerary Monuments 1977, A Lexicon of Greek Personal Names (Vol. I, with E. Matthews) 1987, (Vol. III, with E. Matthews) 1997, Memorial Addresses of All Souls College (ed.) 1989, Cities of Alexander 1996. *Address:* All Souls College, Oxford, OX1 4AL, England.

FRASER, Sir William Kerr, G.C.B., M.A., LL.D., F.R.S.E.; British civil servant and administrator; b. 18 March 1929, Glasgow; s. of late Alexander M. Fraser and Rachel Fraser; m. Marion Anne Forbes (Lady Marion Fraser) 1956; three s. one d.; ed. Eastwood School, Clarkston and Univ. of Glasgow; Flying Officer R.A.F. 1952–55; joined Scottish Office, Edin. 1955, Perm. Under-Sec. of State 1978–88; Prin. and Vice-Chancellor Univ. of Glasgow 1988–95, Chancellor 1996–, Chair. Royal Comm. on the Ancient and Historical Monuments of Scotland 1995–; Hon. F.R.C.P. (Glas.) 1992; Hon. F.R.S.A.M.D. 1995; Hon. LL.D. (Glasgow) 1982, (Strathclyde) 1991, (Aberdeen) 1993; Dr. h.c. (Edin.) 1995. *Leisure interests:* reading, doing nothing. *Address:* Broadwood, Edinburgh Road, Gifford, East Lothian, EH41 4JE, Scotland. *Telephone:* (01620) 810 319. *Fax:* (01620) 810 319.

FRASER OF CARMYLLIE, Baron (Life Peer), cr. 1989 in the District of Angus; **Peter Lovat Fraser,** B.A., LL.B., Q.C., M.P.; British politician and lawyer; b. 29 May 1945; s. of Rev. George Robson Fraser and Helen Jean Meiklejohn; m. Fiona Macdonald Mair 1969; one s. two d.; ed. St. Andrew's Prep. School, Grahamstown, S.A., Loretto School, Musselburgh, Gonville and Caius Coll., Cambridge, Edinburgh Univ.; called to Scottish Bar 1969; Lecturer in Constitutional Law, Heriot-Watt Univ. 1972–74; Standing Jr. Counsel in Scotland to FCO 1979; Chair. Scottish Conservative Lawyers Law Reform Group 1976; Conservative M.P. for S. Angus 1979–83, for Angus East 1983–87; Parl. Pvt. Sec. to Sec. of State for Scotland 1981–82; Solicitor Gen. for Scotland 1982–89, Lord Advocate 1989–92; Minister of State, Scottish Office 1992–95, Dept. of Trade and Industry 1995–97; Deputy Leader of Opposition, House of Lords 1997–; Dir. Int. Petroleum Exchange 1997–. *Leisure interests:* skiing, golf, wind-surfing. *Address:* Slade House, Carmyllie, by Arbroath, Angus, DD11 2RE, Scotland. *Telephone:* 0124 16 215.

FRASER-MOLEKETI, Geraldine J.; South African politician; b. 24 Aug. 1960, Cape Town; m. Jabulani Moleketi; three c.; fmrly. worked in Admin. and Communications, World Lutheran Fed.; fmr. Personal Asst. to Gen. Sec. of S.A. CP; fmr. Office Man. and Nat. Admin. Union of Democratic Univ. Staff; exiled from S.A. 1980–90; fmr. mem. Man. Cttee. and Convention for a Democratic S.A.; Nat. Deputy Elections Coordinator, ANC 1993–94; M.P. 1994; Deputy Minister of Welfare and Population Devt. 1995–96, Minister 1996–; fmr. mem. Patriotic Health Forum, Nat. Health Forum; co-founder and fmr. Trustee Jabulile Ndlovu Educare Trust; observer of nat. elections, Pakistan 1993; mem. Nelson Mandela Children's Fund. *Address:* Ministry of Welfare and Population Development, Hallmark Bldg., Vermeulen Street, Pretoria 0002; Private Bag X885, Pretoria 0001, South Africa (Office). *Telephone:* 12-328-4600 (Office). *Fax:* 12-325-7071 (Office).

FRASYNIUK, Władysław; Polish politician and union leader; b. 25 Nov. 1954, Wrocław; s. of Stanisław Frasyniuk and Zofia Frasyniuk; m. 1978; three d.; driver, mechanic Municipal Transport, Wrocław, organizer of strike in bus depot, Wrocław Aug. 1980; press spokesman Founding Cttee. of Ind. Self-Governing Trade Union; Chair. Solidarity Trade Union, Lower Silesia 1981–90 (resgnd.); mem. Nat. Consultative Comm. of Solidarity; active underground under martial law, jt. founder Provisional Exec. Cttee. of Solidarity; arrested 1982, amnestied 1984; arrested again Feb. 1985, sentenced to over 4 years, amnestied 1986; mem. Provisional Council of Solidarity 1986–87, Nat. Exec. Comm. of Solidarity Nov. 1987–90; mem. Citizens' Cttee. of Solidarity Chair. 1988–90; took part in Round Table talks, Comm. for Trade Union Pluralism Feb.–April 1989; one of f. and leaders Citizens' Movt. for Democratic Action (ROAD) 1990–91; mem. Social-Liberal faction of Democratic Union 1991–94; Vice-Chair. Democratic Union 1991–94; mem. Freedom Union 1994–; Deputy to Sejm (Parl.) 1991–. *Leisure interests:* music, dogs, individual sports. *Address:* Sejm R.P., ul.Wiejska 4/6/8, 00-902 Warsaw, Poland. *Telephone:* (22) 694 20 97, 694 21 35. *Fax:* (22) 694 24 33.

FRATINI, Georgina Carolin; British fashion designer; b. 22 Sept. 1931, Kobe, Japan; d. of The Hon. Somerset Butler, C.I.E. and Mrs. Somerset Butler; m. 2nd Renato Fratini 1961; m. 3rd Jimmy Logan 1967 (divorced 1985); ed. in Toronto, Simla, Rangoon, Hathrop Castle, Glos. and Royal Coll. of Art; Asst. Costume and Set. Designer, Katherine Dunham Dance Group

1951–53; freelance designer 1953–63; founder, Designer and Dir. Gina Fratini Ltd. 1964–. *Leisure interests:* gardening, horse-racing.

FRAYN, Michael; British playwright and author; b. 8 Sept. 1933; s. of late Thomas A. Frayn and Violet A. Lawson; m. 1st Gillian Palmer 1960 (divorced 1989); three d.; m. 2nd Claire Tomalin (q.v.) 1993; ed. Kingston Grammar School and Emmanuel Coll., Cambridge; reporter, The Guardian 1957–59, columnist 1959–62; columnist, The Observer 1962–68; recipient of numerous drama awards; *stage plays:* The Two of Us 1970, The Sandboy 1971, Alphabetical Order 1975, Donkeys' Years 1976, Clouds 1976, Balmoral 1978, Liberty Hall (new version of Balmoral) 1980, Make and Break 1980, Noises Off 1982, Benefactors 1984, Look Look 1990, Here 1993, Now You Know 1995, Copenhagen 1998, Alarms and Excursions 1998; *plays and documentaries for TV include:* Jamie, on a Flying Visit (BBC) 1968, Birthday (BBC) 1969 (plays); Second City Reports (with John Bird—Granada) 1964, Beyond a Joke (with John Bird and Eleanor Bron—BBC) 1972, Making Faces (BBC) 1975 (series); One Pair of Eyes 1968, Laurence Sterne Lived Here 1973, Imagine a City Called Berlin 1975, Vienna: The Mask of Gold 1977, Three Streets in the Country 1979, The Long Straight (Great Railway Journeys of the World) 1980, Jerusalem 1984, Magic Lantern, Prague 1993, Budapest: Written in Water 1996 (all BBC documentaries); *cinema:* Clockwise 1986, Remember Me? 1997; *trans. plays, including:* The Cherry Orchard, Three Sisters, The Seagull, Uncle Vanya, Wild Honey, The Sneeze (Chekhov), The Fruits of Enlightenment (Tolstoy), Exchange (Trifonov), Number One (Anouilh). *Publications:* novels: The Tin Men 1965, The Russian Interpreter 1966, Towards the End of the Morning 1967, A Very Private Life 1968, Sweet Dreams 1973, The Trick of It 1989, A Landing on the Sun 1991 (Sunday Express Book of the Year), Now You Know 1992; non-fiction: Constructions (philosophy) 1974, Speak after the Beep 1995; several vols. of collections of columns, plays and translations; *films:* Clockwise 1985, First and Last 1989. *Address:* c/o Greene & Heaton Ltd., 37A Goldhawk Road, London, W12 8QQ, England.

FRAYSSE, Jean-Pierre; French banker; b. 18 Nov. 1930, Casablanca, Morocco; m. (divorced); one s. one d.; started banking career with Société Générale 1954–62; with Int. Div. of Banque Louis Dreyfus 1962–71; Exec. Dir. Lloyds Bank Int. Ltd. 1971–76; Exec. Deputy Chair. Guinness Mahon & Co. Ltd., London 1976. *Leisure interests:* swimming, reading, tennis. *Address:* Guinness Mahon & Co. Ltd., 32 St. Mary at Hill, London, E.C.3, England (Office).

FRAZEE, Rowland C., C.C., B.COMM.; Canadian banker; b. 12 May 1921, Halifax, N.S.; s. of Rowland Hill and Callie Jean (née Cardwell) Frazee; m. Marie Eileen Tait 1949; one s. one d.; ed. King's Coll. and Dalhousie Univ., Halifax; served with Carleton and York Regt., Second World War; joined Royal Bank of Canada 1939, Asst. Gen. Man., Montreal 1964–65, Dist. Gen. Man., Winnipeg 1965–68, Gen. Man. Canadian Dists. 1968–70, Vice-Pres., Toronto 1970–72, Vice-Pres. and Chief Gen. Man., Montreal 1972–73, Dir., Exec. Vice-Pres. and Chief Gen. Man. 1973–77, Pres. 1977–80, C.E.O. 1979–86, Chair. 1980–86; Chair. Ganong Bros. Ltd. 1994–96; Dir. Int. Minerals & Chemical Corpn. (Canada) Ltd., Ganong Bros. Ltd., Newfoundland Capital Corpn. Ltd., Continental Airlines Inc., Huntsman Marine Science Centre, Montreal Children's Hosp. Foundation; Chair. Roosevelt Int. Park Comm.; several honorary degrees. *Leisure interests:* golf, swimming, reading. *Address:* c/o Royal Bank of Canada, 1 Place Ville Marie, P.O. Box 6001, Montreal, Que. H3C 3A9, Canada.

FRCKOVSKY, Lubomir; Macedonian politician; b. 2 Dec. 1957; ed. Skopje Univ., Ljubljana Univ.; mem. Inst. Francais des Relations Int., Paris; mem. Int. Law Assen. Skopje, Forum for Human Rights Macedonia; Prof. of Int. Law and Theory of Int. Relations Skopje Univ.; co-author of new Constitution of Repub. of Macedonia 1991; Minister without Portfolio 1990; Minister of Interior 1994; Minister of Foreign Relations 1996–97; Prof., Skopje Univ. 1996–98; Fellow Schloss Leopoldskron, Salzburg; Fellow 21st Century Trust, London. *Address:* c/o Ministry of Foreign Relations, Dame Grueva 66, 91000 Skopje, Macedonia. *Telephone:* (91) 236 311 (Office).

FREARS, Stephen Arthur; British film director; b. 20 June 1941, Leicester; s. of Dr. Russell E. Frears and Ruth M. Frears; m. Mary K. Wilmers 1968 (dissolved 1974); two s.; partner Anne Rothenstein; one s. one d.; ed. Gresham's School, Holt, Trinity Coll., Cambridge; Asst. Dir. Morgan, a Suitable Case for Treatment 1966, Charlie Bubbles 1967, If. . . 1968; worked for TV for 13 years, including several TV films and plays in collaboration with Alan Bennett (q.v.); Officier Ordre des Arts et des Lettres. *Films include:* Gumshoe 1971, Bloody Kids 1980, Going Gently 1981, Walter 1982, Saigon 1983, The Hit 1984, My Beautiful Laundrette 1985, Prick Up Your Ears 1986, Sammy and Rosie Get Laid 1987, Dangerous Liaisons 1989, The Grifters 1990, Hero 1992, The Snapper 1992, Mary Reilly 1996, The Van 1996. *Address:* c/o Casarotto Ramsay, National House, 60 Wardour Street, London, W1V 3TE, England.

FRECCIA, Massimo; American conductor; b. 19 Sept. 1906; ed. Cherubini Royal Conservatoire, Florence; guest conductor New York Philharmonic Orchestra 1938, 1939, 1940; Musical Dir. and Conductor, Havana Philharmonic Orchestra 1939–43, New Orleans Symphony Orchestra 1944–52, Baltimore Symphony Orchestra 1952–59; Chief Conductor Rome (R.A.I.) Orchestra 1959–; frequent appearances as guest conductor of famous orchestras in Europe and U.S.; tours in Australia 1963, Japan 1967, South Africa 1969; appeared at various int. festivals, including Vienna, Prague, Berlin, Lisbon, Montreux; Hon. D.Mus. Tulane Univ., New Orleans; Order of the Star of Italian Solidarity. *Address:* 25 Eaton Square, London, S.W.1, England (Home).

FRÉCHETTE, Louise; Canadian international official and politician; with Dept. of External Affairs, Govt. of Canada early 1970s–, envoy to Argentina 1985; Asst. Deputy Minister for Latin America and the Caribbean, Ministry of Foreign Affairs, for Int. Econ. and Trade Policy 1990–92; Amb. to UN 1992–94; Assoc. Deputy Minister, Dept. of Finance 1994–95, Dept. of Defence 1995–98; Deputy Sec.-Gen. UN Jan. 1998–. *Address:* United Nations Secretariat, United Nations Plaza, New York, NY 10017, U.S.A. *Telephone:* (212) 963-1234. *Fax:* (212) 963-4879.

FREDERICK, Robert Rice, A.B.; American business executive; b. 12 Jan. 1926, Elkhart, Ind.; s. of Vard W. Frederick and Beryl C. Rice; m. Carolyn N. Smith 1949; two d.; ed. DePauw Univ.; with General Electric Co. 1948–82, Sr. Vice-Pres. Corporate Strategic Planning 1977–79, Exec. Vice-Pres. Int. Sector 1979–82; Pres. and C.O.O. RCA Corpn. 1982, C.E.O. 1985–87.

FREEDMAN, Eugene M., M.S.; American business executive; b. 1932; ed. Columbia Univ. and Univ. of Pennsylvania; joined Coopers & Lybrand 1954, Deputy Chair., Vice-Chair. N.E. region, mem. Int. Exec. Comm., Chair. 1991–93, Chair. C.E.O. Coopers and Lybrand Int., New York 1993–. *Address:* Coopers & Lybrand, 1301 Avenue of the Americas, New York, N.Y. 10019, U.S.A.

FREEDMAN, Lawrence David, C.B.E., D.PHIL.; British university professor; b. 7 Dec. 1948, Tynemouth; s. of late Lieut.-Commdr. Julius Freedman and Myra Robinson; m. Judith Hill 1974; one s. one d.; ed. Whitley Bay Grammar School and Univs. of Manchester, Oxford and York; Research Assoc. Int. Inst. for Strategic Studies 1975–76; Research Fellow, Royal Inst. of Int. Affairs 1976–78, Head of Policy Studies 1978–82; Head Dept. of War Studies, King's Coll. London 1978–, Prof. 1982–; mem. Council, Int. Inst. for Strategic Studies 1984–92, 1993–, School of Slavonic and E. European Studies 1993–97; Chair. Cttee. on Int. Peace and Security, Social Science Research Council (U.S.A.) 1993–; columnist, The Independent 1987–93, The Times 1993–; Hon. Dir. Centre for Defence Studies 1990–; Fellow, British Acad. 1995. *Publications:* U.S. Intelligence and Soviet Strategic Threat 1978, Britain and Nuclear Weapons 1980, The Evolution of Nuclear Strategy 1981, 1989, The Atlas of Global Strategy 1985, The Price of Peace 1986, Britain and the Falklands War 1988, Signals of War (with V. Gamba) 1989, The Gulf Conflict 1990–91 (with E. Karsh) 1993, War: a Reader 1994; (ed.) Military Intervention in Europe 1994, (ed.) Strategic Coercion 1998, The Politics of British Defence Policy 1979–1998 1999; articles etc. *Leisure interests:* tennis, political cartoons. *Address:* c/o Department of War Studies, King's College, The Strand, London, WC2R 2LS, England. *Telephone:* 0171-873 2025. *Fax:* 0171-873 2026.

FREEDMAN, Ronald, PH.D.; American sociologist-demographer; b. 8 Aug. 1917, Winnipeg, Canada; s. of Ada Freedman and Issadore Freedman; m. Deborah Selin 1941; one s. one d.; ed. Univs. of Michigan and Chicago, U.S.A.; Instructor to Prof. of Sociology, Univ. of Michigan 1946–79, Roderick D. McKenzie Distinguished Prof. of Sociology 1979–87, Prof. Emer. 1987–; Founder and Dir. Population Studies Center 1962–71, Assoc. Dir. 1971; Study Dir. Nat. Survey on Growth of American Families 1954–55; Co-Dir. Taiwan Population Studies Center 1962–64; Tech. Adviser and Consultant World Fertility Survey 1972–84; Pres. Population Assen. of America 1964–65; mem. President's Cttee. on Population and Family Planning 1968; Chair. Tech. Advisory Cttee., Demographic Health Surveys 1985–95; Consultant Leading Group on Birth Planning, People's Repub. of China, Taiwan Prov. Inst. of Family Planning, World Bank, Rockefeller Foundation, Ford Foundation, WHO, Hewlett Foundation, Population Council, East-West Population Inst. and nat. family planning programmes in Malaysia, Korea, India, Indonesia, Hong Kong; Guggenheim Fellow and Fulbright Fellow 1957–58; mem. N.A.S.; Fellow Center for Advanced Study in Behavioral Sciences; awards include Taeuber Award 1981. *Publications:* Recent Migration to Chicago 1950, Principles of Sociology (with others) 1952, Family Planning, Sterility and Population Growth (with others) 1959, World Population: The Vital Revolution (Ed.) 1964, The Sociology of Human Fertility: An Annotated Bibliography 1975, The Contribution of Social Science to Population Policy 1987, Local Area Variations in Reproductive Behaviour in the People's Republic of China 1973–1982 (with others) 1988, The Rise of Female Education in Chinese National and Regional Patterns (with others) 1990, and many others. *Address:* 2125 Nature Cove Road, Apt. 2068, Ann Arbor, MI 48104, U.S.A. (Home). *Telephone:* (313) 975-9361 (Home).

FREEH, Louis; American intelligence officer and judge; ed. Rutgers Law School; agent F.B.I. 1974–80, Dir. July 1993–; asst. attorney New York 1980–90, Fed. Judge 1990–92; Adjunct. Assoc. Prof. of Law Fordham Law School 1988–. *Address:* U.S. Department of Justice, Federal Bureau of Investigation, J. Edgar Hoover Building, 950 Pennsylvania Avenue, N.W., Washington, DC 20530, U.S.A.

FREELING, Nicolas; writer; b. 1927; m. Cornelia Termes 1954; four s. one d.; primary and secondary educ.; worked as cook in hotel restaurants all over Europe 1945–60; novelist 1960–. *Publications:* Love in Amsterdam 1961, Because of the Cats 1962, Gun before Butter 1962, Valparaiso 1963, Double Barrel 1963, Criminal Conversation 1964, King of the Rainy Country 1965, Dresden Green 1966, Strike Out Where Not Applicable 1967, This is the Castle 1968, Tsing-Boum 1969, Kitchen Book 1970, Over the High Side 1971, Cook Book 1971, A Long Silence 1972, Dressing of Diamond 1974, What Are the Bugles Blowing For? 1975, Lake Isle 1976, Gadget 1977, The Night Lords 1978, The Widow 1979, Castang's City 1980, One Damn Thing After Another 1981, Wolfnight 1982, Back of the North Wind 1983, No Part in Your Death 1984, A City Solitary 1985, Cold Iron 1986, Lady Macbeth 1987, Not as Far as Velma 1989, Sandcastles 1989, Those in Peril 1990, The Pretty How Town 1992, You Who Know 1993, Criminal Convictions 1994, The Seacoast of Bohemia 1994, A Dwarf Kingdom 1996, One More River 1997. *Address:* Grandfontaine, 67130 Schirmeck, France.

FREEMAN, Alan Leslie, M.B.E.; Australian radio and television presenter; b. 6 July 1927; s. of the late Edward Ernest Freeman and Annie Leer (née Bowers); radio announcer with 7LA Launceston Tasmania 1952–53, 3KZ Melbourne 1953–57, Radio Luxembourg 1958–68; joined BBC Radio Light Programme 1960, presented Pick of the Pops 1961, Saturday Rock Show 1973–78; with Capital Radio 1978–89; joined BBC Radio 1 as presenter Pick of the Pops 1989–92, Saturday Rock Show 1989–94; rejoined Capital Radio 1994 as presenter Pick of the Pops Take 3 Saturdays and Pick of the Pops Take 3 Special Sundays. *TV includes:* Top of the Pops, All Systems Freeman. *Film appearances include:* Absolute Beginners, Just for Fun, Dr Terror's House of Horrors; Best Radio Show (for Pick of the Pops) 1971, Top Radio Show (for The Saturday Rock Show 1974–78), Radio Personality of the Year, Sony Award 1987, Outstanding Contrib. to Music Radio, Radio Acad. Award 1988. *Leisure interests:* opera, tennis. *Address:* Capital Radio PLC, 30 Leicester Square, London, WC2H 7LA, England.

FREEMAN, Cathy; Australian athlete; b. 16 Feb. 1973, Mackay; works as public relations adviser; winner Australian 200m. 1990–91, 1994, 1996, Australian 100m. 1996, Amateur Athletics Fed. 400m. 1992, 200m. 1993; Gold Medallist 4x100m. Commonwealth Games 1990; Gold Medallist 200m., 400m., Silver Medallist 4x100m. Commonwealth Games 1994; Silver Medallist 400m., Olympic Games, Atlanta 1996; winner World Championships 400m., Athens 1997 (first Aboriginal winner at World Championships); set 2 Australian 200m. records, 5 Australian 400m. records 1994–96; Media and Communications Officer, Australia Post; numerous nat. awards. *Address:* c/o Melbourne International Track Club, 43 Fletcher Street, Essendon, Vic. 3040, Australia.

FREEMAN, Charles (Chas.) Wellman, Jr., B.A., J.D.; American diplomatist; b. 2 March 1943, Washington, D.C.; s. of Charles W. Freeman and Carla Park; m. 1st Patricia Trenery 1962 (divorced 1993); three s. (one deceased) one d.; m. 2nd Margaret Van Wagenen Carpenter 1993; ed. Milton Acad., Milton, Mass., Nat. Autonomous Univ. of Mexico, México, Yale Univ., Harvard Law School, Harvard Univ., Foreign Service Inst. School of Chinese Language and Area Studies; entered U.S. Foreign Service 1965, Vice-Consul, Madras, India 1966–68, Taiwan 1969–71, State Dept., China Desk 1971–74, Visiting Fellow, E. Asian Legal Research, Harvard Univ. 1974–75, Deputy Dir., Taiwan Affairs, Dept. of State 1975–76, Dir. Public Programs, Dept. of State 1976–77, Plans and Man. 1977–78, Dir. U.S. Information Agency programs 1978–79, Acting U.S. Co-ordinator for Refugee Programs 1991–, Dir., Chinese Affairs, Dept. of State 1979–81, Minister, U.S. Embassy, Beijing 1981–84, U.S. Embassy, Bangkok 1984–86, Prin. Deputy Asst. Sec. of State for African Affairs 1986–89, Amb. to Saudi Arabia 1989–92; Asst. Sec. of Defense (Int. Security Affairs) 1993–94; Chair. Bd. Project Int. Assocs. 1995–; Vice-Chair. Atlantic Council of U.S.A. 1996; Co-Chair. U.S.-China Policy Foundation 1996; Pres. Middle East Policy Council 1997; Distinguished Fellow, Inst. for Nat. Strategic Studies, Nat. Defense Univ. 1992–93; U.S. Inst. of Peace, Wash. 1994–95; Forrest Prize, Yale Univ., Superior Honor Awards 1978, 1982, Presidential Meritorious Service Awards 1984, 1987, 1989, Group Distinguished Honor Award 1988, Sec. of Defense Award for Meritorious Civilian Service 1991, Distinguished Honor Award 1991; Order of King 'Abd Al-Aziz (First Class) 1992. *Leisure interests:* swimming, sailing, tennis, reading, computers, cookery. *Address:* Project International Inc., 1800 K Street, N.W., Suite 1018, Washington, D.C. 20006, U.S.A.

FREEMAN, Rt. Hon. John, P.C., M.B.E.; British diplomatist and journalist, businessman (retd.); b. 19 Feb. 1915; s. of Horace Freeman; m. 1st Elizabeth Johnston 1938 (divorced 1948); m. 2nd Margaret Kerr 1948 (died 1957); m. 3rd Catherine Dove 1962 (divorced 1976); m. 4th Judith Mitchell 1976; two s. three d. and one adopted d.; ed. Westminster School and Brasenose Coll., Oxford; Advertising Consultant 1937–40; active service in North Africa, Italy and North-West Europe 1940–45; M.P. (Lab.) Watford 1945–55; Financial Sec. to the War Office 1946–47; Under-Sec. of State for War 1947–48; Parl. Sec. to the Ministry of Supply 1948–51 (resgnd.); retd. from politics 1955; Deputy Ed. New Statesman 1958–61, Ed. 1961–65; British High Commr. in India 1965–68; Amb. to U.S.A. 1969–71; Chair. London Weekend Television 1971–84, C.E.O. 1971–76; Chair. and C.E.O. LWT (Holdings) 1977–84; Visiting Prof. of Int. Relations, Univ. of Calif. (Davis) 1985–90; mem. Bd., ITN (Ind. Television News) 1971–76, Chair. 1976–81; mem. Bd., Ind. Television Publs. 1971–76; Chair. Bd. of Govs., British Film Inst. 1976–77; Vice-Pres. Royal Television Soc. 1975–84; Chair. Communications and Marketing Foundation 1977–79; Chair. Page and Moy (Holdings) Ltd. 1979–84; mem. (fmr. Chair.) Hutchinson Ltd. 1978–84; Trustee Reuters 1984–88; Gold Medal (Royal Television Soc.) 1981.

FREEMAN, Michael Alexander Reykers, B.A., M.B., B.CH., M.D., F.R.C.S.; British orthopaedic surgeon; b. 17 Nov. 1931, Surrey; s. of Donald G. Freeman and Florence J. Elms; m. 3rd Patricia Gill 1968; one s. (deceased) one d.; two s. two d. by previous marriages; ed. Corpus Christi Coll. Cambridge and London Hosp. Medical Coll.; Intern, London Hosp.; resident in Orthopaedic Surgery, Westminster Hosp. and Middx. Hosp. 1962–68; Consultant, London Hosp. 1968–96; Hon. Consultant Royal Hosps. NHS Trust 1996–; European Ed.-in-Chief Journal of Arthroplasty 1996–; co-founder/Dir. Biomechanics Unit, Imperial Coll. London 1956–75; fmr. mem. Bd. MRC; inventor prostheses and surgical procedures for replacement of hip, knee, ankle and joints of the foot; Past-Pres. British Hip Soc.; Past-Pres. British Orthopaedic Soc.; Pres. European Fed. of Nat. Asscns. of Orthopaedics and Traumatology (EFORT) 1994–95; mem. numerous professional socs. etc.; awards include Robert Jones Medal (British Orthopaedic Asscn.) 1964. *Publications:* The Scientific Basis of Joint Replacement 1977, Arthritis of the Knee 1980; 200 papers on hip and knee surgery; Ed. Adult Articular Cartilage 1973–79. *Leisure interests:* gardening, reading. *Address:* 79 Albert Street, London, NW1 7LX, England (Home). *Telephone:* 0171-387 0817 (Home).

FREEMAN, Morgan; American actor and director; b. 1937, Memphis, Tenn.; s. of Grafton Freeman and Mayme Revere; m. 1st Jeanette Bradshaw 1967 (divorced 1979); m. 2nd Myrna Colley-Lee 1984; four c.; ed. Los Angeles City Coll.; stage debut in Niggerlover 1967; other stage appearances include: Hello Dolly, Broadway 1967, Jungle of Cities 1969, The Recruiting Officer 1969, Purlie, ANTA Theatre, New York 1970, Black Visions 1972, Mighty Gents 1978 (Clarence Derwent Award, Drama Desk Award) 1978, White Pelicans 1978, Coriolanus, New York Shakespeare Festival 1979, Mother Courage and Her Children 1980, Othello Dallas Shakespeare Festival, 1982, Medea and the Doll 1984, The Gospel at Colonus (Obie Award), Driving Miss Daisy 1987, The Taming of the Shrew; appearances in TV shows and films. *Films include:* Who Says I Can't Ride a Rainbow? 1971, Brubaker 1980, Eyewitness 1980, Harry and Son 1983, Teachers 1984, Street Smart 1987, Clean and Sober 1988, Lean On Me 1989, Johnny Handsome 1989, Driving Miss Daisy (Golden Globe Award) 1989, Glory 1989, Robin Hood 1991, Unforgiven 1992, The Power of Ore 1992, Chain Reaction 1997, The Shawshank Redemption 1994, Outbreak 1995, Seven 1996, Moll Flanders, Amistad (NAACP Image Award) 1997, Kiss the Girls 1998; Dir. Bopha 1993, Long Walk to Freedom 1999. *Address:* c/o William Morris Agency, 151 S. El Camino Drive, Beverly Hills, CA 90212; 2472 Broadway, #227, New York, NY 10025, U.S.A.

FREEMAN, Orville Lothrop, LL.B.; American politician and lawyer; b. 9 May 1918, Minneapolis, Minn.; s. of Orville E. Freeman and the late Frances (née Schroeder) Freeman; m. Jane C. Shield 1942; one s. one d.; ed. Cen. High School, Minneapolis, Minnesota Univ. Law School; Chair., Civil Service Comm., Minn. 1946–48; admitted to Minn. Bar 1947; partner in law firm 1947–55; Gov. State of Minn. 1955–61; nominated John F. Kennedy at Democratic Nat. Convention, Los Angeles 1960; U.S. Sec. of Agric. 1961–69; Pres. EDP Tech. Int. Inc. 1969–70; Pres. Business Int. Corpn. 1970–81, C.E.O. 1971–81, Chair. 1981–86; Sr. Partner int. law firm, Popham, Haik, Schnobrich, Kaufman and Doty Ltd., Washington 1985–95; Visiting Scholar Hubert Humphrey Inst., Univ. of Minn., Minneapolis 1995–; Chair. U.S. Group, India-U.S. Business Council, U.S. Group, U.S.-Nigerian Joint Agric. Consultative Comm., Bd. of Govs. UN Asscn. of U.S.A., Sime-Derby Int. Plant Research Inst. 1982–; Chair. World Watch Inst. 1990–96, Chair. Emer. 1997–; mem. Exec. Cttee. Advisory Council on Japan-U.S. Econ. Relations; mem. Bd. of Dirs. Cttee. for the Future, Natomas Corpn., Franklin Mint, UNA of U.S.A., Multinational Agribusiness Systems Inc.; mem. Council on Foreign Relations; Faculty mem. Salzburg Seminar 1974, 1977; Hon. mem. Soil Conservation Soc. of America; Hon. Ph.D. (Univ. Seoul, American Univ., Washington, D.C., Fairleigh Dickinson Univ., Rutherford, N.J., St. Joseph's Coll., Philadelphia, Pa.). *Publications:* World Without Hunger and many articles. *Leisure interests:* reading, hiking, fishing. *Address:* Walker Place #802, 3701 Bryant Avenue S., Minneapolis, MN 55409, U.S.A.

FREEMAN, Raymond, M.A., D.PHIL., D.SC., F.R.S.; British research scientist; b. 6 Jan. 1932; s. of late Albert and Hilda F. Freeman; m. Anne-Marie Périnet-Marquet 1958; two s. three d.; ed. Nottingham High School and Lincoln Coll., Oxford; Engineer, French Atomic Energy Comm., Centre d'Etudes Nucléaires de Saclay 1957–59; Sr. Scientific Officer, Nat. Physical Lab. 1959–63; Man. NMR Research, Instrument Div., Varian Assocs., Palo Alto, Calif. 1963–73; Univ. Lecturer in Physical Chem. and Fellow, Magdalen Coll., Oxford 1973–87, Aldrichian Praelector in Chem. 1982–87; John Humphrey Plummer Prof. of Magnetic Resonance, Univ. of Cambridge 1987–, Fellow Jesus Coll., Cambridge; Hon. D.Sc. (Durham) 1998. *Publications:* A Handbook of Nuclear Magnetic Resonance 1987, Spin Choreography: Basic Steps in High Resolution NMR 1997; several scientific papers on nuclear magnetic resonance spectroscopy in various journals. *Leisure interests:* swimming, traditional jazz. *Address:* Department of Chemistry, Lensfield Road, Cambridge, CB2 1EW (Office); Jesus College, Cambridge, CB5 8BL; 29 Bentley Road, Cambridge, CB2 2AW, England (Home). *Telephone:* (01223) 336450 (Office); (01223) 323958 (Home).

FREETH, Peter, R.A.; British artist; b. 15 April 1938, Birmingham; s. of Alfred William Freeth and Olive Freeth (née Walker); m. Mariolina Meliadó 1967; two s.; ed. King Edward's Grammar School, Aston, Birmingham, Slade School, London, British School, Rome; exhbns. include: Christopher Mendez Gallery 1987–89, City Lights, Royal Acad. 1991; works in British Museum, Victoria & Albert Museum, Arts Council of England, Fitzwilliam Museum, Cambridge, Ashmolean Museum, Oxford, Nat. Gallery, Washington, D.C., U.S.A., Metropolitan Museum, New York; Prix de Rome (engraving) 1960,

Best Print, Royal Acad. 1986. *Leisure interests:* books, music. *Address:* c/o Royal Academy of Arts, Burlington House, Piccadilly, London, W1V 0DS, England. *Telephone:* 0171-439 7438.

FREI, Ephraim Heinrich, D.PHIL.; Israeli professor of electronics; b. 2 March 1912, Vienna, Austria; s. of the late Dr. Siegmund Frei and Franziska (Wiener) Frei (both killed in Nazi concentration camp); m. 1st Yael Fanny Rosenfeld 1948 (deceased); two c.; m. 2nd Malli Stolberg (née Kunstatt); ed. Vienna and Hebrew Univs.; Broadcasting Engineer, British Army; attached to British Embassy, Athens 1944–46; mem. staff Scientific Dept., Ministry of Defence 1948–50; Prof. and Head Dept. of Electronics, Weizmann Inst. of Science 1960–77, Prof. Emer. Medical Physics, Dept. of Electronics 1977–; Visiting Prof. Hebrew Univ., Jerusalem 1982–; mem. Inst. for Advanced Study, Princeton, N.J. 1952; Int. Research Fellow, Stanford Research Inst. Calif. 1960; mem. Bd. of Dirs. Yeda 1963–82, Chair. 1975–79; mem. Editorial Bd., Journal of Cardiovascular Tech.; Chair. XII Int. Conf. Medical and Biological Eng., and V Int. Conf. Medical Physics; Del., Int. Union of Radio Science (URSI), Chair. Israel Cttee. on Bio-Effects 1985–; Fellow, I.E.E.E. 1967, Life mem. 1982; Hon. Life mem. Magnetics Soc. 1979; Hon. Fellow, Israel Soc. Medical and Biological Eng. 1981; mem. N.Y. Acad. of Science 1995; Jubilee Dr. Phil. (Vienna) 1986; Computer Pioneer NCC 1975; Weizmann Prize 1957. *Publications:* scientific papers on electronics, physics and biomedical engineering. *Leisure interests:* hiking, archeology. *Address:* Weizmann Institute, P.O. Box 26, Rehovot, Israel. *Fax:* 8-9344109.

FREI RUIZ-TAGLE, Eduardo; Chilean politician; s. of late Eduardo Frei Montalva (fmr. Pres. of Chile); joined Christian Democrat (CD) Party 1958, fmr. Pres.; CD presidential cand. Dec. 1993, Pres. of Chile March 1994–; C.-in-C. of Armed Forces 1998–; elected to Senate 1990. *Address:* Office of the President, Palacio de la Moneda, Santiago; Christian Democrat Party, Carmen 8, 6°, Santiago, Chile. *Telephone:* (2) 33-8535.

FREIVALDS, Laila, LL.B.; Swedish lawyer; b. 22 June 1942, Riga, Latvia; m. Johan Hedström; one d.; ed. Uppsala Univ.; service in dist. court 1970–72, Svea Court of Appeal 1973–74; Reporting Clerk, Court of Appeal 1974; Counsel, Västerås rent tribunal 1974–75; served in Riksdag Information Office 1975–76; Sr. Admin. Officer, Head. of Div. Nat. Bd. for Consumer Policies 1976–79, Dir.-Gen. and Consumer Ombudsman 1983–88; Minister for Justice 1988–91, Oct. 1994–; Legal consultant, Baltic states 1991–94. *Address:* Ministry of Justice, Rosenbad 4, 10333 Stockholm; Riksdagen, 10012 Stockholm, Sweden.

FRÉMAUX, Louis Joseph Félix; French orchestral conductor; b. 13 Aug. 1921, Air-sur-Lys; ed. Conservatoire National Supérieur de Musique, Paris; Musical Dir. and Perm. Conductor of Orchestre Nat. de l'Opéra de Monte-Carlo, Monaco 1955–66; Prin. Conductor, Rhônes-Alpes Philharmonic Orchestra, Lyons 1968–71; Prin. Conductor and Musical Dir., City of Birmingham Symphony Orchestra 1969–78; Chief Conductor, Sydney Symphony Orchestra 1979–81, Prin. Guest Conductor 1982–85; 8 Grand Prix du Disque Awards; Koussevitsky Award; Chevalier Légion d'honneur; Croix de Guerre (twice). *Address:* c/o Tennant Artists, Unit 2, 39 Tadema Road, London, SW10 0PY, England. *Telephone:* 0171-376 3758.

FRENCH, Charles Stacy, S.B., M.A., PH.D.; American scientist; b. 13 Dec. 1907, Lowell, Mass.; s. of Charles Ephraim French and Helena Stacy French; m. 1st Margaret Wendell Coolidge 1938 (died 1992); one s. one d.; m. 2nd Lee Penland 1993; ed. Loomis School and Harvard Univ.; Research Fellow, Biology, Calif. Inst. of Tech.; Pasadena, Calif. 1934–35; Guest Worker, Kaiser Wilhelm Inst. Berlin-Dahlem 1935–36; Austin Teaching Fellow, Biochem., Harvard Medical School, Boston 1936–38; Instructor (Research), Chem., Univ. of Chicago 1938–41; Asst., Assoc. Prof. Botany, Univ. of Minn. 1941–47; Dir. Dept. of Plant Biology, Carnegie Inst. 1947–73, Dir. Emer. 1973–; Prof. (by courtesy) Biology, Stanford Univ.; Chair. Western Section, American Soc. Plant Physiologists 1954 (Charles Ried Barnes Life Membership Award 1971); mem. Nat. Acad. of Sciences, American Acad. of Arts and Sciences, Deutsche Akad. der Naturforscher Leopoldina, Soc. Gen. Physiologists (Pres. 1955–56), Harvard Club of the Peninsula (Pres. 1973–75), Botanical Soc. of America (Award of Merit 1973); Hon. Ph.D. (Göteborg) 1974. *Publications:* Numerous articles and reviews in tech. journals on photosynthesis and the spectroscopy and functions of plant pigments; annual reports in Carnegie Inst. of Washington Year Book 1948–. *Leisure interests:* mountaineering, conservation of natural areas, development of instruments for plane table plotting for maps. *Address:* Carnegie Institution, Stanford, CA 94305 (Office); 11970 Rhus Ridge Drive, Los Altos, CA 94022, U.S.A. (Home). *Telephone:* (415) 325-1521 (Office); (415) 948-8318 (Home).

FRENCH, Dawn; British actress and comedienne; m. Lenny Henry (q.v.); one d. (adopted); ed. Manchester Univ; stage shows and TV series with Jennifer Saunders (q.v.). *Stage appearances include:* Silly Cow, When We are Married 1996. *TV appearances include:* The Comic Strip (Strike, Consuela, Five Go Mad in Dorset, Supergrass, Ken, The Yob, Suzy), French and Saunders, The Vicar of Dibley. *Address:* c/o BBC, Broadcasting House, London, W1A 1AA, England.

FRENCH, Marilyn, M.A., PH.D.; American author and critic; b. 21 Nov. 1929, New York; d. of E. C. Edwards and Isabel Hazz; m. Robert M. French, Jr. 1950 (divorced 1967); one s. one d.; ed. Hofstra Coll. and Harvard Univ.; secretarial and clerical work 1946–53; Lecturer, Hofstra Coll. 1964–68; Asst. Prof. Holy Cross Coll. Worcester, Mass. 1972–76; Mellon Fellow, Harvard Univ. 1976–77. *Publications:* The Book as World—James Joyce's Ulysses 1976, The Women's Room (novel) 1977, The Bleeding Heart (novel) 1981, Shakespeare's Division of Experience 1981, Beyond Power: On Women, Men and Morals 1985, Her Mother's Daughter 1987, The War Against Women 1992, Our Father (novel) 1994, My Summer with George (novel) 1996, A Season in Hell (memoir) 1998. *Address:* c/o Charlotte Sheedy Literary Agency, 65 Bleecker Street, New York, NY 10012, U.S.A.

FREND, Rev. William Hugh Clifford, T.D., D.PHIL., D.D., F.R.S.E., F.B.A., F.S.A.; British professor of ecclesiastical history and clergyman; b. 11 Jan. 1916, Shotterhill, Surrey; s. of Edwin George Clifford Frend and Edith Frend (née Bacon); m. Mary Grace Crook 1951; one s. one d.; ed. Haileybury Coll., Keble Coll. Oxford, Sorbonne, Paris and Berlin Univs.; served in War Office and War Cabinet Offices, and as Intelligence Officer, Political Warfare Exec. 1940–47; full-time mem. Editorial Bd., German Foreign Ministry Documents 1947–51; Research Fellow, Nottingham Univ. 1951–52; S. A. Cook Bye-Fellow, Gonville and Caius Coll. Cambridge 1952–54, 1997–98; Asst. Lecturer, then Lecturer in Church History and Doctrine, Cambridge Univ. 1953–69, Fellow of Gonville and Caius Coll. 1956–69, Dir. of Studies in Archaeology and Anthropology 1961–69; Prof. of Ecclesiastical History, Glasgow Univ. 1969–84, Prof. Emer. 1984–; Priest in Charge of Barnwell and Thurning with Luddington 1984–90; T.A., rank of Capt. 1947–67; ordained Church of England 1982; Pres. Comité Int. d'Histoire Ecclésiastique Comparée 1980–83; Vice-Pres. Asscn. Int. d'Etudes Patristiques 1983–87; Hon. D.D. (Edin.) 1974. *Publications:* The Donatist Church 1952, Martyrdom and Persecution in the Early Church 1965, The Early Church 1965, The Rise of the Monophysite Movement (2nd edn.) 1979, The Rise of Christianity 1984, Saints and Sinners in the Early Church 1985, History and Archaeology in the Study of Early Christianity 1988, The Archaeology of Early Christianity: A History 1996. *Leisure interests:* Romano-British archaeology, collecting old stamps and coins, gardening. *Address:* The Clerks Cottage, Little Wilbraham, Cambridge, CB1 5LB, England. *Telephone:* (01223) 811731.

FRENDO, Michael, LL.D., LL.M.; Maltese politician and lawyer; b. 29 July, 1955; s. of the late Joseph Frendo and of Josephine (née Felice) Frendo; m. Irene Brincat 1984; one s. one d.; ed. Univs. of Malta and Exeter; admitted to the Bar 1977; lecturer, Faculty of Law, Univ. of Malta 1987–; Nat. Chair. for Malta, World Jurist Ass. 1975–; Dir. press and media relations and Editorial Dir. (newspapers) of Nationalist Party (Christian Democrat) 1982–85; M.P. 1987–; mem. of Parl. Ass., Council of Europe 1987–92; mem. Malta Parl. Del. to European Parl. 1987–90, 1996– (Chair. 1990–92); Parl. Sec. for Youth, Culture and Consumer Protection 1990–92; Minister for Youth and the Arts 1992–94, for Transport, Communications and Tech. 1994–96; lawyer in pvt. practice 1996–; Nationalist Party. *Publications:* books and articles in local and int. magazines and insts. *Address:* Mrammiti, Lourdes Lane, St Julian's, STJ 02, Malta. *Telephone:* 341835. *Fax:* 341835.

FRENI, Mirella; Italian opera singer; b. 27 Feb. 1935, Modena; d. of Ennio Freni and Gianna (née Arcelli) Freni; m. Leone Magiera 1955; one d.; debut 1955, debut at La Scala, Milan 1962, Glyndebourne Festival 1961, Royal Opera House, Covent Garden 1961, Metropolitan Opera, N.Y. 1965; has sung at Vienna State Opera and at Salzburg Festival and leading opera houses throughout the world. *Major roles include:* Nanetta in Falstaff, Mimi in La Bohème, Zerlina in Don Giovanni, Susanna, Adina in L'elisir d'amore, Violetta in La Traviata, Desdemona in Otello. *Address:* c/o John Coast Opera Management, 31 Sinclair Road, London, W14 0NS, England.

FRENKEL, Jacob A., PH.D.; Israeli economist; b. 8 Feb. 1943, Tel-Aviv; m. Niza Frenkel 1968; two d.; ed. Univ. of Chicago, Hebrew Univ.; on staff Chicago Univ. 1973–87, various positions including Ed. Journal of Political Economy, David Rockefeller Prof. of Int. Econs.; Econ. Counsellor, Dir. of Research IMF 1987–91; joined Tel-Aviv Univ. 1991, Weisfeld Prof. of Econs. of Peace and Int. Relations 1994–; Gov. Bank of Israel 1991–; Co-Chair. of Israeli del. to multilateral peace talks on Regional Econ. Devts. 1991; Chair. Bd. Govs. Inter-American Devt. Bank 1995–96; Research Assoc. Nat. Bureau of Econ. Research; distinguished mem. Advisory Cttee. Inst. for Global Econs., Korea; mem. G-7 Council, Advisory Cttee. for Int. Econs., G-30, Exec. Cttee. Int. Econs. Asscn.; Foreign hon. mem. American Acad. of Arts and Science, Japan Soc. of Monetary Econs.; Fellow Econometric Soc.; Karel Englis Prize in Econs. (Czech Repub.); Gran Cruz, Orden de Mayo al Mérito (Argentina). *Publications:* numerous books and articles on int. econs. and macro-econs. *Address:* Bank of Israel, P.O. Box 780, Jerusalem 91007, Israel. *Telephone:* (2) 652-2701. *Fax:* (2) 652-8419.

FRENZEL, Michael; German business executive; b. 2 March 1947, Leipzig; mem. Bd. Preussag AG 1988–92, Vice-Chair. 1992–93, Chair. 1994–; Chair. Bd. Amalgamated Metal Corpn. PLC, London; Chair. Supervisory Bd. Howaldtswerke-Deutsche Werft AG, Kiel, Preussag Stahl AG, Salzgitter; Vice-Chair. Supervisory Bd. Algeco S.A., Paris/Macon; mem. Supervisory Bd. VTG Vereinigte Tanklager und Transportmittel GmbH, Hamburg, Linke-Hofmann-Busch Waggon-Fahrzeug-Maschinen GmbH, Salzgitter, Creditanstalt-Bankverein AG, Vienna, PreussenElektra AG, Hannover, IVG Industrieverwaltungs AG, Bonn, Lufthansa Commercial Holding GmbH, Cologne, Thyssen Aufzüge GmbH, Neuhausen a.d.F.; mem. Consultative Bd. Hannoversche Lebensversicherung AG, Hannover, Landesbank Rheinland-Pfalz, Mainz, Allianz AG, Hannover. *Address:* Preussag AG, Karl-Wiechert-Allee 4, 30625 Hannover; Postfach 610209, 30602 Hannover, Germany. *Telephone:* 0511/566-00. *Fax:* 0511/566-1901.

FRÈRE, Jean; Belgian diplomatist and banker; b. 15 November 1919, Chatou, Seine-et-Oise, France; s. of Maurice Frère and Germaine Schimp; m. Marie-Rose Vanlangenhove 1949; one s. three d.; ed. Germany, Austria, Brussels Univs.; with Solvay & Cie. (Chemical Industries), Brussels 1941–46; entered diplomatic service 1946, Attaché (Commercial and Econ.), Belgian Legation, Prague 1948–51; Political Div., Ministry of Foreign Affairs 1951–52; First Sec. (Econ.), Belgian Embassy, Rome 1952–58; Gen. Sec. EIB 1958–; mem. Belgian Del. Conf. between EEC mem. countries and Britain 1962; Conseiller Banque Lambert 1962–, Man. Partner 1967–; Conseiller Général Banque Bruxelles Lambert S.A. 1975–81, Conseiller Général Honoraire 1981–; fmr. Chair. BBL-Australia; fmr. mem. of Bd. and Exec. Cttee Banco di Roma; many Belgian and foreign decorations. *Leisure interests:* violin, painting, photography, electronics. *Address:* 3315 San Marco, 30124 Venice, Italy. *Telephone:* (041) 5222647. *Fax:* (041) 522647.

FRERE, Sheppard Sunderland, C.B.E., D.LITT., F.B.A.; British professor of the archaeology of the Roman Empire; b. 23 Aug. 1916, Graffham, Sussex; s. of Noel Gray Frere and Barbara Sunderland; m. Janet Cecily Hoare 1961; one s. one d.; ed. Lancing Coll. and Magdalene Coll. Cambridge; Asst. Master, Epsom Coll. 1938–40; Nat. Fire Service 1941–46; Asst. Master, Lancing Coll. 1946–54; Lecturer in Archaeology, Manchester Univ. 1954–55; Reader in the Archaeology of the Roman Provs., London Univ. 1955–61, Prof. 1961–66; Prof. of the Archaeology of the Roman Empire, Oxford Univ. 1966–83, Emer. Prof. 1983–, Fellow of All Souls, now Emer. Fellow; Pres. Royal Archaeological Inst. 1978–80, Soc. for the Promotion of Roman Studies 1983–86; Ed. Britannia 1970–79, Britannia Monograph Series 1980–89. *Publications:* Britannia, A History of Roman Britain 1967, Verulamium Excavations (Vol. I) 1972, (Vol. II) 1983, (Vol. III) 1984, Roman Britain From the Air (with J. K. St. Joseph) 1983, Trajan's Column (with F. A. Lepper) 1988, Strageath: Excavations within the Roman Fort (with J. J. Wilkes) 1989, The Roman Inscriptions of Britain, Vol. II, Fascicules 1 1990, 2 1991, 3 1991, 4 1992, 5 1993, 6 1994, 7, 8 and Epigraphic Indexes 1995. *Address:* Netherfield House, Marcham, Abingdon, Oxon., OX13 6NP, England. *Telephone:* (01865) 391486.

FRESCO, Paolo; Italian business executive; fmr. Vice-Chair. Gen. Electric; fmr. mem. Bd. Fiat, Chair. June 1998–. *Address:* Fiat S.p.A., Corso Marconi 10, 10125 Turin, Italy. *Telephone:* (11) 686-1111. *Fax:* (11) 686-3704.

FRESNO LARRAIN, H.E. Cardinal Juan Francisco; Chilean ecclesiastic; b. 26 July 1914; ordained 1937; consecrated Bishop of Copiapó 1958; Archbishop of La Serena 1967, of Santiago de Chile 1983; Chancellor Univ. Católica de Chile 1983; created Cardinal 1985. *Address:* Erasmo Escala 1822, Santiago 30-D, Chile.

FRESTON, Thomas E., B.A., M.B.A.; American media executive; b. 22 Nov. 1945, New York; s. of Thomas E. Freston and Winifred Geng; m. Margaret Badali 1980; one s.; Dir. of Marketing MTV, MTV Networks, New York 1980–81; Dir. of Marketing, The Movie Channel 1982–83; Vice-Pres. Marketing MTV, MTV Networks 1983–84, Vice-Pres. Marketing 1984–85, Sr. Vice-Pres. and Gen. Man. Affiliate Sales, Marketing 1985, Sr. Vice-Pres. and Gen. Man. MTV, VH-1 1985–86, Pres. Entertainment 1986–87, Pres. and C.E.O. 1987–; now Chair. and C.E.O. MTV Networks; mem. Bd. Dirs. Cable Advertising Bureau 1987–, MTV Europe, London 1986–, Rock and Roll Hall of Fame 1986–; mem. Smithsonian Comm. Music in America 1987–, Cable TV Admin. and Marketing Asscn., Nat. Acad. of Cable Programming. *Leisure interests:* photography, travel, antique rugs. *Address:* MTV Networks, 1212 Broadway, New York, NY 10004, U.S.A.

FRETWELL, Sir John Emsley, G.C.M.G., M.A.; British diplomatist (retd.); b. 15 June 1930, Chesterfield; s. of F. T. Fretwell; m. Mary Ellen Eugenie Dubois 1959; one s. one d.; ed. Chesterfield Grammar School, Lausanne Univ., King's Coll., Cambridge; H.M. Forces 1948–50; entered diplomatic service 1953, Third Sec., Hong Kong 1954–55, Second Sec., Embassy in Beijing 1955–57, Foreign Office 1957–59, 1962–67, First Sec., Moscow 1959–62, First Sec. (Commercial), Washington 1967–70, Commercial Counsellor, Warsaw 1971–73, Head of European Integration Dept. (Internal), FCO 1973–76, Asst. Under-Sec. of State 1976–79, Minister, Washington 1980–81; Amb. to France 1982–87; Political Dir. and Deputy to Perm. Under-Sec. of State, FCO 1987–90; mem. Council of Lloyd's 1991–92; Specialist Adviser, House of Lords 1992–93; Chair. Franco-British Soc. 1995–. *Leisure interests:* skiing, walking. *Address:* c/o Brooks's, St. James's Street, London, SW1A 1LN, England.

FREUD, Bella; British fashion designer; b. 1961, London; d. of Lucian Freud (q.v.) and Bernardine Coverley; ed. Accademia di Costuma e di Moda, Rome and Institutto Mariotti, Rome; asst. to Vivienne Westwood (q.v.) on her designer collections 1986–89; launched her own label presenting autumn/winter collection of tailored knitwear and accessories 1990; exhibited at London Designer Show Oct. 1991, London Fashion Week 1993; winner Innovative Design—The New Generation Category (British Fashion Awards) 1991. *Address:* 48 Rawstorne Street, London, EC1V 7ND, England. *Telephone:* 0171-713 6466.

FREUD, Lucian, O.M., C.H.; British painter; b. 8 Dec. 1922; s. of the late Ernst Freud and Lucie Freud; m. 1st Kathleen Epstein 1948 (divorced 1952); two d.; m. 2nd Lady Caroline Maureen Blackwood 1953 (divorced 1957, died 1996); ed. Cen. School of Art, E. Anglian School of Painting and Drawing; Teacher at Slade School of Art, London 1948–58; first one-man exhbn. 1944, subsequently 1946, 1950, 1952, 1958, 1963, 1968, 1972, 1978, 1979, 1982, 1983, 1988, 1990–96; retrospectives: Hayward Gallery 1974, 1988, 1989, Tate Gallery, Liverpool 1992; works included in public collections: Tate Gallery, Nat. Portrait Gallery, Victoria and Albert Museum, Arts Council of Great Britain, British Council, British Museum, Fitzwilliam Museum, Cambridge, Nat. Museum of Wales, Cardiff, Scottish Nat. Gallery of Modern Art, Edinburgh, Walker Art Gallery, Liverpool, Ashmolean Museum of Art, Oxford, etc.; in Australia at Brisbane, Adelaide, Perth; in France at Musée Nat. d'Art Moderne, Centre Georges Pompidou, Paris; in U.S.A. at The Art Inst. of Chicago, Museum of Modern Art, New York, Cleveland Museum of Art, Ohio, Museum of Art, Carnegie Inst., Pittsburgh, Achenbaach Foundation for Graphic Arts and Fine Arts, San Francisco, The St. Louis Art Museum, Hirshhorn Museum and Sculpture Garden, Smithsonian Inst., Washington; Rubenspreis, City of Siegen 1997. *Address:* c/o Diana Rawstron, Goodman Derrick, 90 Fetter Lane, London, EC4A 1EQ, England.

FREUND-ROSENTHAL, Miriam Kottler (Mrs. Harry Rosenthal), M.A., PH.D.; American Zionist leader; b. 17 Feb. 1906, New York; d. of Harry Kottler and Rebecca Zindler; m. 1st Milton Freund 1927 (died 1968); two s.; m. 2nd Harry Rosenthal 1974; ed. Hunter Coll., New York Univ.; Teacher public high schools, New York to 1943; mem. Nat. Bd. Hadassah (Women's Zionist Org.) 1940–, Chair. Youth Activities 1943–48, Vocational Educ. 1948–53, Nat. Youth Aliyah 1953–56; Vice-Pres. Hadassah 1953–56, Pres. 1956–60; Ed. Hadassah Magazine 1966–71; Del. to American Jewish Conf. 1943, to 21st Orientalist Congress, Moscow 1960; Co-chair. American Zionist Youth Comm. 1944–49; Founding charter mem. Brandeis Youth Foundation 1944; mem. Actions Cttee., World Zionist Org. 1956–; mem. Presidium, World Zionist Congress 1960–64; Chair. Exec. Cttee., American Zionist Council 1960–65; mem. Nat. Board, Jewish Nat. Fund, Vice-Pres. 1960–; mem. Bd. United Israel Appeal (UIA) 1960–; mem. Exec., World Council Synagogues 1966–; mem. Nat. Council, Nat. Planning Asscn. 1970; mem. Assembly, Jewish Agency June 1971–; Vice-Pres. American Zionist Fed. 1970–72, Women's Cttee., Brandeis Univ.; Chair. Israel Seminars Foundation, Nat. Liaison with Yaal; Nat. Vice-Pres. Mercaz 1978–83; mem. Cabinet, State of Israel Bonds, Chair. Women's Div., State of Israel Bonds 1983–; mem. American Asscn. Univ. Women, American Jewish Hist. Soc., Bd. of Trustees, American Friends of the Hebrew Univ. 1978; Henrietta Szold Centennial Lectures for Hebrew Univ. and American Jewish Hist. Soc.; recipient citation of Jewish Book Council, America 1954; Hunter Coll. Hall of Fame 1972. *Publications:* Jewish Merchants in Colonial America 1936, Jewels for a Crown 1963; Israel's Services to Arab Citizens 1982 (Ed.); articles in various journals. *Leisure interests:* travel, painting, writing. *Address:* 50 West 58th Street, New York, NY 10019, U.S.A. (Office). *Telephone:* (212) 355-7900 (Office).

FREY, Bruno S.; Swiss professor of economics; b. 4 May 1941, Basel; s. of Leo Frey and Julie Frey (née Bach); ed. Univs. of Basel and Cambridge; Assoc. Prof. Univ. of Basel 1969–; Prof. of Econs. Univ. of Konstanz 1970–77, Univ. of Zurich 1977–; Visiting Fellow All Souls Coll., Oxford 1983; Fellow Coll. of Science, Berlin 1984–85; Visiting Research Prof. Univ. of Chicago, Ill. 1990; Visiting Prof. Univ. of Rome 1996–97, Gothenburg Univ. 1998; Hon. D.Univ. (St. Gallen) 1998, (Gothenburg) 1998. *Publications include:* International Political Economics 1984, Muses and Markets 1989, Economics as a Science of Human Behaviour 1992, Not Just for the Money 1997, A New Federation for Europe 1999. *Leisure interest:* travel. *Address:* Institute for Empirical Economic Research, University of Zurich, Bluemlisalpstrasse 10, CH-8006 Zurich, Switzerland. *Telephone:* (1) 634-3730. *Fax:* (1) 634-4907.

FREYNDLIKH, Alisa Brunovna; Russian actress; b. 8 Dec. 1934; d. of Bruno Arturovich Freyndlikh; ed. Leningrad Theatre Inst.; worked with Komissarzhevskaya Theatre, Leningrad 1957–61; then with Lensoviet Theatre, Leningrad 1961–83, Gorky Theatre 1983–; worked in films 1958–; R.S.F.S.R. State Prize 1976, U.S.S.R. People's Artist 1981, State Prize 1995. *Films include:* Family Happiness 1970, My Life 1973, The Princess and the Pea 1977, An Everyday Novel 1977, Always With Me 1977, The Business Love Affair 1977, Stalker 1980, An Old-Fashioned Comedy 1980, Agony 1981, The Canary Cage 1984, Success 1985, The Nights near Moscow, The Hunt. *Stage roles include:* Lady Milford in Schiller's Perfidy and Love 1990, Autumn Violins 1997, and many others. *Address:* Rubinstein str. 11, Apt. 7, 191002 St. Petersburg, Russia. *Telephone:* (812) 314-88-40.

FRICK, Mario, DR.IUR.; Liechtenstein politician and civil servant; b. 8 May 1965, Balzers; s. of Kuno and Melita Frick-Kaufmann; m. Andrea Haberlander 1992; one s. one d.; ed. St. Gall University, Switzerland; State Admin. Legal Service 1991–93; mem. Municipal Council of Balzers 1991–93; Deputy Head of Govt. May–Dec. 1993, Head of Govt. Dec. 1993–, also Minister of Finance and Construction. *Leisure interests:* football, tennis, biking. *Address:* Office of Prime Minister, Government Building, FL-9490 Vaduz, Liechtenstein. *Telephone:* 236 61 11. *Fax:* 236 66 22.

FRICKE, Manfred; German professor and university administrator; b. 24 June 1936, Hainichen; m. Edith (née Feldhahn) Fricke; two s.; ed. Tech. Univ. Berlin; univ. lecturer, Tech. Univ. Berlin 1970, Dean Faculty of Transport and Communications 1970–75, Prof. 1978–, Vice-Pres. 1978–82, Pres. 1985–93; Bundesverdienstkrenz (1st Class) 1994. *Leisure interests:* surfing, tennis, cycling. *Address:* Temmeweg 6a, 14089 Berlin, Germany.

FRIDAY, William Clyde, B.S., LL.B., LL.D., D.C.L.; American educator; b. 13 July 1920, Raphine, Va.; s. of David Latham and Mary Elizabeth Rowan

Friday; m. Ida Willa Howell 1942; three d.; ed. Wake Forest Coll., N. Carolina State Coll. and Univ. of N. Carolina Law School; Asst. Dean of Students, Univ. of N. Carolina at Chapel Hill 1948–51, Acting Dean of Students 1950–51, Admin. Asst. to Pres. 1951–54, Sec. of Univ. 1954–55, Acting Pres. 1956, Pres. 1956–86; Pres. The William R. Kenan, Jr. Fund 1986–; Chair. Center for Creative Leadership 1981–96, Regional Literacy Center Comm. 1989–90, Southern Growth Policies Bd. 1989–; Hon. LL.D. (Wake Forest Coll., Belmont Abbey, Duke Univ., Princeton Univ., Elon Coll., Davidson Coll. Kentucky and Mercer Univs.), Hon. D.C.L. (Univ. of the South) 1976, (St. Augustine's Coll.) 1986, Hon. D.P.S. (Univ. of N.C. at Charlotte) 1986, Hon. D.F.A. (N. Carolina School of Arts) 1987, Hon. L.H.D. (Univ. of North Carolina at Greensboro) 1988; Nat. Humanities Medal 1997. *Leisure interests:* gardening, golf, reading. *Address:* The William R. Kenan, Jr. Fund, University of North Carolina, P.O. Box 3858, Bowles Drive, Chapel Hill, NC 27515, U.S.A.

FRIDERICHS, Hans, DR.RER.POL.; German politician and banker; b. 16 Oct. 1931, Wittlich; m. Erika Wilhelm; two d.; Man., Rhineland-Hesse Chamber of Industry and Trade 1959–63; Deputy Business Man. FDP 1963–64, Business Man. 1964–69; mem. Bundestag 1965–69, 1976–77; Sec. of State, Ministry of Agric., Viniculture and Protection of the Environment for Rhineland Palatinate 1969–72; Fed. Minister of Econs. 1972–77; Dir. Dresdner Bank 1977–85, Chair. Bd. Man. Dirs. 1978–85; Deputy Chair. FDP 1974–77; mem. Supervisory Bd. AEG Telefunken Dec. 1979, Chair. 1980–84, now Pres., Int. adviser Goldman Sachs Int., London. *Leisure interests:* art, sport. *Address:* Kappelhofgasse 2, 55116 Mainz, Germany.

FRIDH, Åke Josefsson, M.A., PH.D.; Swedish professor of Latin; b. 25 July 1918, Sollefteå; s. of Josef H. Fridh and Anna Burström; m. Britt Marie Fridh-Haneson 1975; ed. Göteborgs Högre Latinläroverk and Univ. of Göteborg; served in Swedish Army 1939–44; Sr. Asst. Master, Arvika 1951–53, Varberg 1953–58, Göteborg 1958–63; lecturer, Asst. Prof. Univ. of Göteborg 1963–72, Prof. of Latin 1972–83, Prof. Emer. 1983–; mem. Royal Acad. of Letters, History and Antiquities and Göteborg Royal Soc.; Ahrenberg Prize 1956, För nit och redlighet i rikets tjänst 1981. *Publications:* Etudes critiques et syntaxiques sur les Variae de Cassiodore 1951, Terminologie et formules dans le Variae de Cassiodore 1956, Le problème de la Passion des saintes Perpétue et Félicité 1968, Contributions à la critique et à l'interprétation des Variae de Cassiodore 1968, Der sogennante prospektive Konjunktiv im Lateinischen 1971, Cassiodorus Variae 1972, L'emploi causal de la conjonction ut en latin tardif 1977; several articles on classical philology and ancient history. *Address:* Utlandagatan 8 C, 41261, Göteborg, Sweden. *Telephone:* (031) 18 58 90. *Fax:* (031) 18 58 90.

FRIDJONSSON, Thordur, M.A. ECON.; Icelandic economist; b. 2 Jan. 1952, Reykjavik; s. of Fridjon Thordarson and Kristin Sigurdardottir; m. Thrudur Haraldsdottir 1971; two s. two d.; ed. Univ. of Iceland and Queen's Univ., Ont., Canada; Chief Economist, Fed. of Icelandic Industries 1978–80; Econ. Adviser to Prime Minister of Iceland 1980–86; part-time lecturer Dept. of Econs., Univ. of Iceland 1979–87; Man. Dir. Nat. Econ. Inst. 1987–98; Sec.-Gen. Ministry of Industry and Commerce 1998–; mem. Bd. Dirs. Nordic Project Fund 1982–; Chair. Asscn. of Icelandic Economists 1982–85, Icelandic Man. Asscn. 1986–87, Econ. Research. Inst. for Agric. 1991–, Co-ordinating Cttee. Iceland-Norsk Hydro 1998; alt. gov. EBRD 1998–, IMF 1998–; rep. for Iceland EDRC and OECD 1987–; mem. Econ. Policy Cttee. OECD 1987–; John Hicks Fellowship. *Publications:* Icelandic Economy 1984; numerous papers in journals and books. *Leisure interests:* outdoor activities and sport. *Address:* Engjasel 9, 109 Reykjavik, Iceland. *Telephone:* 569 9500. *Fax:* 562 6540.

FRIDLYANDER, Yosif Naumovich; Russian physicist; b. 28 Sept. 1913, Andizhan, Uzbekistan; s. of Naum Abramovich Fridlyander and Cherna Osipovna Fridlyander; m. Tamara Pheodorovna Satarova 1963; two d.; ed. Moscow Higher Technical School; sr. technician, engineer, leading engineer All-Union Inst. of Aviation Industry; head of lab. Research Inst. of Aviation Materials; corresp. mem. U.S.S.R. (now Russian) Acad. of Sciences 1976, mem. 1984; research in creation and processing of aluminium and beryllium alloys and metallic composite materials; Deputy Chair. Scientific Council Construction. Materials for New Technologies; Lenin Prize, U.S.S.R. State Prize. *Publications include:* Aluminium Alloys 1984, Aluminium Deformable Construction Alloys 1979, Metal Matrix Composites 1994, Non-Ferrous Metals and Alloys 1998; 36 patents. *Leisure interests:* swimming, skiing, theatre, travelling. *Address:* Research Institute of Aviation Materials (VIAM), Radio str. 17, 107005 Moscow, Russia. *Telephone:* (095) 263-8831. *Fax:* (095) 938 2140.

FRIDOVICH, Irwin, PH.D.; American biochemist; b. 2 Aug. 1929, New York; s. of Louis Fridovich and Sylvia Applebaum Fridovich; m. Mollie D. Finkel 1951; two d.; ed. City Coll. of New York, Duke Univ. Medical Center, Durham; Instructor in Biochem., Duke Univ. 1956–58, Assoc. in Biochem. 1958–62, Asst. Prof. of Biochem. 1961–66, Assoc. Prof. of Biochem. 1966–71, Prof. 1971–76, James B. Duke Prof. 1976–, Prof. Emer. 1996–; Visiting Research Assoc., Harvard Univ. 1961–62; mem. N.A.S., American Cancer Soc., Editorial Bd. Journal of Biological Chemistry, American Soc. of Biological Chemists (Pres. 1982), N.C. Acad. Sciences, Soc. for Free Radical Research (Pres. 1992); Herty Award, Georgia Section of American Chem. Soc. 1980; Founders' Award for Outstanding Research in Toxicology 1980; Cressy A. Morrison Award, New York Acad. of Sciences; North Carolina Award in Science 1986; Sr. Passano Foundation Laureate 1987; Hon. D.Sc. (Paris) 1980; Townsend Harris Medal 1990, Cresson Medal, Franklin Inst. 1997. *Publications:* approximately 360 articles in major scientific journals. *Leisure interests:* hiking, canoeing, gardening. *Address:* Duke University Medical Center, P.O. Box 3711, Durham, NC 27710; 3517 Courtland Drive, Durham, NC 27707, U.S.A. (Office).

FRIDRIKSSON, Fridrik Thor; Icelandic film director; b. 12 May 1954; s. of Fridrik Gudmundson and Gudridur Hjaltested; m. (divorced); one s. one d.; founder Reykjavík Film Festival; est. Icelandic Film Corp. 1984. *Films:* Eldsmiðurinn (The Blacksmith) 1981, Rokk í Reykjavík (Rock in Reykjavik) 1982, Kúreakr norðursins (Icelandic Cowboys) 1984, Hringurinn (The Circle) 1985, Skytturnar (White Whales) 1987, Flugprá (Sky Without Limit) 1989, Englakroppar (Pretty Angels) 1990, Börn náttúrunnar (Children of Nature) 1991, Bíódagar (Movie Days) 1994, Á köldum klaka (Cold Fever) 1995, Djöflaeyjan (Devil's Island) 1996. *Address:* Icelandic Film Corporation, Hverfisgata 46, 101 Reykjavík (Office); Bjarkargata 8, 101 Reykjavík, Iceland (Home). *Telephone:* 551-2260 (Office); 552-8566 (Home). *Fax:* 552-5154 (Office).

FRIED, Charles, M.A., LL.B.; American lawyer; b. 15 April 1935, Prague, Czechoslovakia; s. of Anthony Fried and Marta (Wintersteinova) Fried; m. Anne Sumerscale 1959; one s. one d.; ed. Princeton, Oxford and Columbia Univs.; law clerk to Assoc. Justice John M. Harlan, U.S. Supreme Court 1960; mem. Faculty, Harvard Law School 1961–, Prof. of Law 1965–85, Carter Prof. of Gen. Jurisprudence 1981–85, 1989–95, Prof. Emer., Distinguished Lecturer 1995–; Deputy Solicitor-Gen. and Counsellor to Solicitor-Gen. 1985, Solicitor-Gen. of U.S.A. 1985–89; Carter Prof. Emer., Distinguished Lecturer Harvard Law School 1995–; Assoc. Justice Supreme Judiciary Court of Mass., Boston 1995–. *Publications:* An Anatomy of Values 1970, Medical Experimentation: Personal Integrity and Social Policy 1974, Right and Wrong 1978, Contract as Promise: A Theory of Contractual Obligation 1981, Order and Law: Arguing the Reagan Revolution 1991; contributions to legal and philosophical journals. *Address:* Supreme Judiciary Court, Boston, MA 02108, U.S.A.

FRIED, Josef, PH.D.; American organic chemist; b. 21 July 1914, Przemysl, Poland; s. of Abraham and Frieda Fried; m. Erna M. Werner 1939 (died 1986); one d.; ed. Univs. of Leipzig, Zürich and Columbia; Research Assoc., Squibb Inst. for Medical Research, New Brunswick, N.J. 1944–47, Head of Dept. 1947–49, Dir. Div. of Organic Chem. 1959–63, Prof. Depts. of Chem., Biochem., and Ben May Laboratory for Cancer Research, Univ. of Chicago 1963–, Louis Block Prof. 1973–, Chair. Dept. Chem. 1977–80; mem. N.A.S., American Acad. of Arts and Sciences, A.C.S., American Soc. Biol. Chemists, British and Swiss Chem. Socs.; Fellow, A.A.A.S., New York Acad. of Sciences; Hon. D.Sc. (Cambridge) 1995; A.C.S. Award in Medical Chem. 1974, Gregory Pincus Medal 1994, numerous other awards and prizes. *Publications:* concerning chemistry and bio-chemistry of steroids, prostaglandins, carcinogenic hydrocarbons. *Leisure interests:* violin (chamber music), skiing, sailing, growing orchids. *Address:* 5715 South Kenwood Avenue, Chicago, IL 60637, U.S.A. (Home). *Telephone:* (312) 702-7264.

FRIEDAN, Betty; American feminist leader; b. 4 Feb. 1921, Peoria, Illinois; d. of Harry and Miriam (Horwitz) Goldstein; m. Carl Friedan 1947 (divorced 1969); two s. one d.; ed. Smith Coll.; f. Nat. Org. for Women 1966, first Pres. 1966–70, Chair. 1970–72; Organizer Nat. Women's Political Caucus 1971, Int. Feminist Congress 1973, First Women's Bank & Trust Co. 1973; Visiting Prof. of Sociology, Temple Univ. 1972, Yale Univ. 1974, Queen's Coll. 1975; Contributing Ed., McCalls Magazine 1971–74; Jt. Chair. Nat. Comm. for Women's Equality; numerous lectures in U.S.A. and Europe; Distinguished Visiting Prof. George Mason Univ. 1995, Mount Vernon Coll. 1996; Dr. h.c. (Columbia) 1994; mem. PEN; American Humanist Award 1975. *Publications:* The Feminine Mystique 1963, It Changed My Life: Writings on the Women's Movement 1976, The Second Stage 1982, The Fountain of Age 1993, Through the Prison of Gender 1998; articles in McCall's, Harper's, etc. *Address:* 2022 Columbia Road, N.W., Washington, DC 20009, U.S.A.

FRIEDEL, Jacques; French physicist; b. 11 Feb. 1921, Paris; s. of Edmond Friedel and Jeanne Friedel (née Bersier); m. Mary Winifred Horder 1952; two s.; ed. Ecole Polytechnique, Ecole des Mines de Paris, Bristol Univ.; Mining engineer, Ecole des Mines de Paris 1948–56; Maître de Conférences, Univ. de Paris 1956–59; Prof. of Solid State Physics, Univ. de Paris (later Paris Sud) 1959–89, Dir. Third Cycle: Exact and Nat. Sciences 1974–77; Pres. Section 21, Consultative Cttee. on Univs. 1975–80; Pres. Consultative Comm. of Scientific and Tech. Research 1978–80; mem. Acad. of Sciences 1977–, Vice-Pres. 1991–92, Pres. 1992–94; Pres. Observatoire nat. de la lecture 1994–; Hon. mem. Royal Soc., London, N.A.S., American Acad. of Sciences and Letters, Swedish Acad. of Sciences, Leopoldina, Belgian Royal Acad. of Sciences, Brazilian Acad. of Sciences, American Physical Soc., Inst. of Physics, Nat. Acad. of Sciences; Hon. D.Sc. (Bristol) 1977, (Lausanne) 1979, (Geneva) 1992, (Cambridge) 1995, (Zagreb) 1995; Grand Officier, Légion d'honneur, Commdr. Ordre du Mérite. *Publications:* Dislocations 1956, Graine de Mandarin 1994. *Leisure interest:* gardening. *Address:* 2 rue Jean-François Gerbillon, 75006 Paris, France. *Telephone:* (01) 42-22-25-85.

FRIEDKIN, William; American film director; b. 29 Aug. 1939; s. of Louis Friedkin and Rae Green; m. 1st Lesley-Anne Down (divorced); one s.; m. 2nd Sherry Lansing (q.v.). *Films directed include:* Good Times 1967, The Night They Raided Minsky's 1968, The Birthday Party 1968, The Boys in the Band 1970, The French Connection 1971 (Acad. Award for Best Picture, 1971), The Exorcist 1973, Sorcerer 1977, The Brinks Job 1979, Cruising 1980, Deal of the Century 1983, To Live and Die in L.A. 1985, C.A.T. Squad 1986, The Guardian 1990, Rampage 1992, Blue Chip 1993, Jade 1995, Twelve Angry Men 1997; several TV films. *Address:* c/o ICM, 8942 Wilshire Blvd., Los Angeles, CA 90211, U.S.A.

FRIEDLANDER, Frederick Gerard, PH.D., F.R.S.; British university teacher of mathematics; b. 25 Dec. 1917, Vienna; ed. Univ. of Cambridge; Fellow, Trinity Coll. Cambridge 1940–42, 1945–46; temporary Experimental Officer, Admiralty 1943–45; Faculty Asst. Lecturer, Univ. of Cambridge 1945–46, lecturer 1954–79, Reader in Partial Differential Equations 1979–82, Reader Emer. 1982–; Lecturer, Univ. of Manchester 1946–54; Hon. Research Fellow, Univ. Coll. London 1984–. *Publications:* Sound Pulses 1958, The Wave Equation on a Curved Space-Time 1975, Introduction to the Theory of Distributions 1982; papers in mathematical journals. *Address:* Department of Pure Mathematics and Mathematical Statistics, University of Cambridge, 16 Mill Lane, Cambridge, CB2 1SB; 28 Greenlands, Cambridge, CB2 2QY, England (Home). *Telephone:* (01223) 243119 (Home).

FRIEDMAN, Jane; American publishing executive; joined Random House 1968; fmr. Pres. Random House Audio; fmr. Exec. Vice-Pres. Knopf Publishing Group, Random House Inc.; fmr. Publr. Vintage Books; fmr. mem. Random House Exec. Cttee.; Pres., C.E.O. HarperCollins 1997–. *Address:* c/o HarperCollins, 10 East 53rd Street, New York, NY 10022, U.S.A.

FRIEDMAN, Jerome Isaac, PH.D.; American professor of physics; b. 28 March 1930, Chicago; s. of Selig Friedman and Lillian Warsaw; m. 1st 1956; two s. two d.; m. 2nd Tania Baranovsky 1972; ed. Univ. of Chicago; Research Assoc. Univ. of Chicago 1956–57, Stanford Univ. 1957–60; Asst. Prof., Assoc. Prof. Mass. Inst. of Tech. 1960–67, Prof. of Physics 1967–, Dir. Lab. of Nuclear Science 1980–83, Head, Dept. of Physics 1983–88, William A. Coolidge Prof. 1988–, Inst. Prof. 1990–; mem. N.A.S.; Fellow, American Acad. of Arts and Sciences, American Physical Soc.; Hon. D.Sc. (Trinity College) co-recipient, W.K.H. Panofsky Prize (American Physical Soc.) 1989, co-recipient, Nobel Prize in Physics 1990. *Leisure interests:* painting, Asian ceramics, African Art. *Address:* Department of Physics, Room 24-502, Massachusetts Institute of Technology, Cambridge, MA 02139 (Office); 75 Greenough Street, Brookline, MA 02146, U.S.A. (Home). *Telephone:* (617) 253-7585 (Office). *Fax:* (617) 253-1755 (Office).

FRIEDMAN, Michael A., B.A., M.D.; American administrator; ed. Univs. of Tulane, Texas, Stanford; Assoc. Prof. Dept. of Medicine San Francisco Medical Center, Univ. of Calif. 1975–83, also Dir. Clinical Affairs, Interim Dir. Cancer Research Inst.; with Chief Clinical Investigation Br. Div. of Cancer Treatment, Nat. Cancer Inst. 1988–95; Deputy Commr. for Operations Food and Drugs Admin. 1995–97, Lead Deputy Commr. Operations 1997–. *Publications:* articles in professional journals. *Address:* Food and Drugs Administration, 5600 Fishers Lane, Rockville, MD 20857, U.S.A.

FRIEDMAN, Milton, PH.D.; American economist; b. 31 July 1912, New York; s. of Jeno Saul and Sarah Esther Friedman; m. Rose Director 1938; one s. one d.; ed. Rutgers Univ., Chicago and Columbia Univs.; Assoc. Economist, Nat. Resources Cttee. 1935–37, Nat. Bureau of Econ. Research 1937–45 (on leave 1940–45), 1948–81; Prin. Economist, Div. of Tax Research, U.S. Treasury Dept. 1941–43; Assoc. Dir. Statistical Research Group, Div. of War Research, Columbia Univ., New York 1943–45; Prof. of Econs., Univ. of Chicago 1948–83, Prof. Emer. 1983–; Sr. Research Fellow, Hoover Inst. of Stanford Univ., Calif. 1976–; Bd. of Eds. Econometrica; mem. Advisory Bd., Journal of Money, Credit and Banking 1968–94; Pres. American Econ. Asscn. 1967; mem. President's Comm. on All-Volunteer Armed Force 1969–70, on White House Fellows 1971–73, President's Econ. Policy Advisory Bd. 1981–88; Pres. Mont Pelerin Soc. 1970–72, Western Econ. Asscn. 1984–85; mem. N.A.S. 1973–; numerous hon. degrees; Nobel Prize for Econ. Science 1976; Inst. for World Capitalism Prize on Moral-Cultural Affairs 1993; Grand Cordon First Class Order of the Sacred Treasure (Japan) 1986; Nat. Medal of Science (U.S.) 1988; Presidential Medal of Freedom (U.S.) 1988. *Publications:* Income from Independent Professional Practice (with Simon Kuznets) 1946, Sampling Inspection (with others) 1948, Essays in Positive Economics 1953, A Theory of the Consumption Function 1957, A Program for Monetary Stability 1960, Capitalism and Freedom 1962, Price Theory; a provisional text 1962, A Monetary History of the United States 1867–1960 (with Anna J. Schwartz) 1963, Inflation: Causes and Consequences 1963, The Balance of Payments: Free Versus Flexible Exchange Rates (with Robert V. Roosa) 1967, Dollars and Deficits 1968, Optimum Quantity of Money and Other Essays 1969, Monetary Statistics of the United States (with Anna J. Schwartz) 1970, A Theoretical Framework for Monetary Analysis 1972, Social Security: Universal or Selective (with Wilbur J. Cohen) 1972, An Economist's Protest 1972, Money and Economic Development 1973, Milton Friedman's Monetary Framework (with others) 1974, Price Theory 1976, Tax Limitation, Inflation and the Role of Government 1978, Free to Choose (with Rose D. Friedman) 1980, Monetary Trends in the United States and the United Kingdom (with Anna J. Schwartz) 1982, Bright Promises, Dismal Performance: An Economist's Protest (with William R. Allen) 1983, Tyranny of the Status Quo (with Rose D. Friedman) 1984, The Essence of Friedman 1987, Money Mischief 1992, Friedman and Szasz on Liberty and Drugs (with Thomas S. Szasz) 1992, Two Lucky People: Memoirs (with Rose D. Friedman) 1998. *Leisure interests:* tennis, carpentry, talk. *Address:* Hoover Institution, Stanford University, Stanford, CA 94305, U.S.A.

FRIEL, Brian, F.R.S.L.; Irish writer; b. 9 Jan. 1929, Omagh, Co. Tyrone; s. of Patrick Friel and Christina MacLoone; m. Anne Morrison 1954; one s. four d.; ed. St. Columb's Coll., Derry, St. Patrick's Coll., Maynooth, St. Joseph's Training Coll., Belfast; taught in various schools 1950–60; full-time writer 1960–; mem. Irish Acad. of Letters, Aosdana 1983–, American Acad. of Arts and Letters; Hon. Fellow Univ. Coll. Dublin; Hon. D.Litt. (Nat. Univ. of Ireland) 1983, (Queen's Univ., Belfast) 1992. *Publications:* The Last of the Name (ed.) 1988; collected stories: The Saucer of Larks 1962, The Gold in the Sea 1966; *plays:* Philadelphia, Here I Come! 1965, The Loves of Cass McGuire 1967, Lovers 1968, The Mundy Scheme 1969, Crystal and Fox 1970, The Gentle Island 1971, The Freedom of the City 1973, Volunteers 1975, Living Quarters 1976, Aristocrats 1979, Faith Healer 1979, Translations 1981 (Ewart-Biggs Memorial Prize, British Theatre Asscn. Award), Three Sisters (trans.) 1981, The Communication Cord 1983, Fathers and Sons 1987, Making History (Best Foreign Play, New York Drama Critics Circle 1989) 1988, A Month in the Country 1990, Dancing at Lughnasa 1990, The London Vertigo 1991, Wonderful Tennessee 1993, Selected Stones 1994, Molly Sweeney 1995, Give Me Your Answer, Do! 1997. *Leisure interests:* reading, trout-fishing, slow tennis. *Address:* Drumaweir House, Greencastle, County Donegal, Ireland.

FRIEND, Lionel; British orchestral conductor; b. 13 March 1945, London; s. of Norman A. C. Friend and Moya L. Dicks; m. Jane Hyland 1969; one s. two d.; ed. Royal Grammar School, High Wycombe, Royal Coll. of Music, London, London Opera Centre; with Welsh Nat. Opera 1969–72, Glyndebourne Festival/Touring Opera 1969–72; 2nd Kapellmeister, Staatstheater, Kassel, Fed. Repub. of Germany 1972–75; Conductor English Nat. Opera 1976–89; Musical Dir. New Sussex Opera 1989–96, Nash Ensemble; Guest Conductor BBC Symphony, Philharmonia, Scottish Chamber, Royal Ballet, and in Denmark, France, Hungary, Norway, Spain, Germany, Netherlands, Belgium, Sweden, U.S.A. *Leisure interests:* reading, theatre, cooking. *Address:* 136 Rosendale Road, London, SE21 8LG, England. *Telephone:* 0181-761 7845.

FRIGGEBO, Birgit; Swedish politician; b. 25 Dec. 1941, Falköping; m. 1st Lennart Rydberg 1968, one s.; m. 2nd Bo Södersten 1997; accountant in estate agency 1960; chief negotiator Swedish Asscn. of Municipal Housing Cos. (SABO) 1969–76, rep. at Rents and Tenancies Court of Appeal 1975–76; Chair. Liberal Youth Stockholm 1963–64, mem. Exec. Cttee. Liberal Party Nat. Youth League 1964–69; mem. Nat. Bd. Liberal Party 1972–93, First Vice-Chair. and mem. Exec. Cttee. 1983–93, Sec. 1983–85, Leader Parl. Liberal Party Group Council 1990–91; mem. Stockholm Social Welfare Bd. 1967–70, Comm. on Housing for Young Persons 1968–70, Stockholm County Council 1971–76; M.P. 1979–82, 1985–97; Minister of Housing and Physical Planning 1976–82, of Cultural Affairs and Immigration 1991–94; mem. Parl. Standing Cttee. on the Constitution 1985–91 (Chair. 1994–), mem. Bd. Parl.'s Cen. Services Office 1986–91, Cttee. on Child Pornography 1995–97, Cttee. on local Pvt. Radio 1996–97; mem. Nat. Debt Office, Data and Access to Information Comm., Cttee. on Swedish Security 1985–88; Co-Gov. Jönköping 1998–. *Address:* County Administrative Board, S-551 86 Jönköping, Sweden. *Telephone:* (36) 157001.

FRIMPONG-ANSAH, Jonathan Herbert, PH.D.; Ghanaian banker; b. 22 Oct. 1930, Mampong, Ashanti; s. of Hammond Owusu-Ansah and Elizabeth Achiaa; m. Selina Agyemang 1954; three s. one d.; ed. Univ. of Ghana, London School of Economics and Univ. of Salford, U.K.; Statistician, Ghana Govt. 1954–59; Bank of Ghana, Dir. of Research 1961–65, Deputy Gov. 1965–68, Gov. 1968–73; Chair. Ghana Diamond Marketing Bd. 1969–72; Dir. Volta River Authority 1972–; Chair. Ashanti Goldfields Corpn. Ltd. 1973–96; Vice-Chair. Deputies of the Cttee. of the Bd. of Govs. on Reform of the Int. Monetary System and Related Issues, IMF, Wash. 1973–74; Consultant World Bank 1975; Chair. Standard Bank Ghana, Ltd., Accra 1975–81, Akosombo Textiles Ltd. 1975–; Chair. UN Experts Group on Establishment of African-Caribbean-Pacific Investment and Trade Bank 1978–79 Dir. SIFIDA, Geneva 1981; Fellow Center for Int. Affairs, Harvard 1978–, Ghana Acad. of Arts and Sciences 1979–; Hon. Prof. of Finance, Univ. of Ghana 1979–. *Publications:* Trade and Development in Africa, 1991, Saving for Africa's Economic Recovery 1991, The Vampire State in Africa—Political Economy of Decline in Ghana 1991; articles in Economic Bulletin (Ghana), Bulletin of the Inter Credit Bank (Geneva), Univ. of Ghana journals; contribs. in International Monetary Reform—Documents of the Committee of Twenty 1974. *Leisure interest:* art. *Address:* 3 Eleventh Road, Ridge, P.O. Box C1582, Accra, Ghana. *Telephone:* 21-227711.

FRISCHENSCHLAGER, Friedhelm, DR.JUR.; Austrian politician; b. 6 Oct. 1943, Salzburg; m.; two c.; ed. schools in Salzburg and Univ. of Vienna; reader, Univ. of Vienna; municipal councillor and mem. Salzburg City Bd. 1972; mem. Nationalrat 1977–; Fed. Minister for Nat. Defence 1983–86; mem. Austrian Freedom Party (FPÖ) and leader of its Parl. Group. *Leisure interests:* sport, literature. *Address:* c/o Freedom Party of Austria, 28 Kärntnerstr., 1010 Vienna 1, Austria.

FRISINGER, Haakan H. J., M.ENG.; Swedish business executive; b. 8 Dec. 1928, Skoevde; s. of Anna and Anders Johansson; m. Annakarin Lindholm 1953; two s. one d.; ed. Chalmers Univ. of Tech., Gothenburg and Harvard Business School; Head, Man. Unit Product and Production Co-ordination,

AB Volvo 1966; Head, Volvo Köping Plant 1971; Head of Volvo Car Production and mem. Corporate Exec. AB Volvo 1975; Head, Volvo Car Industry Div. and Exec. Vice-Pres. AB Volvo 1977; Pres. Volvo Car Corpn. 1978; Pres. and C.O.O., AB Volvo 1983–87, Dir. 1994–, Chair. 1997–. *Leisure interests:* music, art, golf, sport, hunting. *Address:* AB Volvo, S-405 08 Gothenburg, Sweden. *Telephone:* (31) 59 00 90.

FRISO, Enzo; Italian international trade union official; b. 23 Dec. 1927, Padua; apprenticed as metal turner in Padua where he was active trade unionist; one of founders of Confederazione Italiana Sindicati Lavoratori (CISL) in which he held various positions during 1950s; Dir. ICFTU Office, Beirut 1962; Rep. of ICFTU in Indonesia 1968; moved to ICFTU HQ, Brussels 1970, Asst. Gen. Sec. 1984, Gen. Sec. 1992–94. *Address:* c/o International Confederation of Free Trade Unions, 155 boulevard Emile Jacqmain, 1210 Brussels, Belgium. *Telephone:* 224 02 11. *Fax:* 201 58 15.

FRIST, Bill, M.D.; American politician and transplant surgeon; b. 22 Feb. 1952, Nashville, Tenn.; m. Karyn McLaughlin; three s.; f., transplant surgeon, Vanderbilt Transplant Medical Center 1986–; Senator from Tennessee Jan. 1995–; Republican. *Address:* United States Senate, 567 Dirksen Senate Office Bldg., Washington, DC 20510, U.S.A.

FRITSCHE, Claudia; Liechtenstein diplomatist; b. 26 July 1952; m. Manfred Fritsche 1980; ed. business and language schools in Schaan and St. Gall; personal secretary to Head of Govt. 1970–74; joined Office for Foreign Affairs 1978; Diplomatic Collaborator 1980–87; Sec. to Liechtenstein Parl. del. to Council of Europe and EFTA; First Sec., Liechtenstein Embassy, Berne 1987–90, Vienna (concurrently) 1989–90; Perm. Rep. of Liechtenstein to UN 1990–. *Address:* Permanent Mission of Liechtenstein to the United Nations, 405 Lexington Avenue, 43rd Floor, New York, NY 10174, U.S.A. *Telephone:* (212) 599-0220. *Fax:* (212) 599-0064.

FRITZ, Johann P.; Austrian press and broadcasting executive; b. 15 April 1940, Ober-Eggendorf; s. of Johann Fritz and Amalia Piringer; m. Brigitte Weick 1964; one d.; ed. Univ. of Vienna, Western Reserve Univ., Cleveland, Ohio and Hochschule für Welthandel, Vienna; Sec.-Gen. Österreichische Jungarbeiterbewegung 1964–67, Exec. Vice-Pres. 1967–70; Ed. Der Jungarbeiter 1964–70, MC Report 1970–75; Deputy Sec.-Gen. Österreichischer Wirtschaftsbund 1970–75; Man. Dir. Die Presse 1975–91; Man. Dir. Kabel TV Wien 1975–83; founder and Co-Man. Radio Adria 1977–84, consultant 1984–90; co-founder and Sec. Gen. Man.-Club 1970–75; founder and Chair., Cable TV Asscn., Austrian Chamber of Commerce 1980–90; mem. Supervisory Bd. Telekabel Wien GmbH 1983–98, Bd. Austrian Press Agency (APA) 1982–91; Dir. Int. Press Inst. (IPI) April 1992–; mem. numerous professional asscns. etc.; life-time Kommerzialrat award 1991. *Leisure interests:* skiing, ice-skating, jazz, art deco, jugendstil. *Address:* Hasenauerstrasse 37, 1180 Vienna, Austria. *Telephone:* (1) 512 9011. *Fax:* (1) 512 9014.

FRITZ, Walter Helmut; German writer; b. 26 Aug. 1929, Karlsruhe; s. of Karl T. Fritz and Hedwig Fritz; ed. Univ. of Heidelberg; poetry teacher, Univ. of Mainz; has lectured in Europe, America and Africa; mem. Akad. der Wissenschaften und der Literatur, Mainz, Bayerische Akad. der Schönen Künste, Munich, Deutschen Akad. für Sprache und Dichtung, Darmstadt, PEN; Stuttgarter Literaturpreis, Villa Massimo-Stipendium, Georg-Trakl-Preis. *Publications:* poetry and prose, including: Gesammelte Gedichte 1979, Wunschtraum Alptraum (poems) 1981, Werkzeuge der Freiheit (poems) 1983, Cornelias Traum, Aufzeichnungen 1985, Immer einfacher immer schwieriger (poems) 1987, Zeit des Sehens (prose) 1989, Mit einer Feder aus den Flügen des Ikarus, Ausgewählte Gedichte, Mit einem Nachwort von Harald Hartung 1989, Die Schlüssel sind vertauscht (poems) 1992, Gesammelte Gedichte 1979–1994 1994, Das offene Fenster 1997. *Address:* Kolbergerstrasse 2A, 76139 Karlsruhe, Germany. *Telephone:* 0721-683346.

FRODSHAM, John David, M.A., PH.D., F.A.H.A.; British/Australian university professor and consultant; b. 5 Jan. 1930, Cheshire, U.K.; s. of J. K. Frodsham and W. E. Frodsham; m. Tan Beng-choo 1964; three s. two d.; ed. Emmanuel Coll., Cambridge, Australian Nat. Univ.; lecturer in English Univ. of Baghdad 1956–58, in Oriental Studies Univ. of Sydney 1960–61, in Far Eastern History Univ. of Malaya 1961–65, Sr. Lecturer in Far Eastern History Univ. of Adelaide 1965–67; Reader in Chinese Australian Nat. Univ. 1967–71; Prof. of Comparative Literature Univ. of Dar es Salaam 1971–73, Foundation Prof. English and Comparative Literature Murdoch Univ. 1973–; Visiting Prof. Cornell 1965, Hawaii 1968, American Coll. of Greece 1985, Tamkang Univ. of Taiwan 1985; Visiting Fellow, Inst. of E. Asian Philosophies, Univ. of Singapore 1989; Sr. Teaching Fellow, NTU, Singapore 1990–92; Consultant Ausean Int. Ltd. 1987–89; Fellow and Pres. Professors' World Peace Acad. 1983; Pres. Australasian Soc. of Physical Research 1979–; mem. Australia-China Council 1979–83; Current Affairs Commentator for ABC 1958–. *Publications:* An Anthology of Chinese Verse, Vol. 1 1967, The Murmuring Stream (2 vols.) 1967, The Poems of Li Ho 1970, New Perspectives in Chinese Literature 1971, The First Chinese Embassy to the West 1973, Foundations of Modernism: Modern Poetry 1980, Goddesses, Ghosts and Demons: The Collected Poems of Li He 1983, Classicism & Romanticism: A Comparative Period Study (4 vols.) 1986, Turning Point 1988, Education for What? 1990, The Crisis of the Modern World and Traditional Wisdom 1990, The Decline of Sensate Culture 1990. *Leisure interests:* psychical research, sailing, swimming. *Address:* School of Arts, Murdoch University, Murdoch, Western Australia 6150 (Office); 52 Fleming Avenue, Wilson, Western Australia 6107 (Home). *Telephone:* (08) 936 06203 (Office); (08) 935 80945 (Home).

FROGGATT, Sir Leslie (Trevor), Kt; Australian business executive; b. 8 April 1920; s. of Leslie Froggatt and Mary H. Brassey; m. Elizabeth Grant 1945; three s.; ed. Birkenhead Park School, Cheshire; joined Asiatic Petroleum Co., Ltd. 1937; Shell Singapore, Shell Thailand, Shell Malaya 1947–54, Shell Egypt 1955–56; Dir. of Finance, Gen. Man. Kalimantan, Borneo and Deputy Chief Rep. PT Shell Indonesia 1958–62; Area Co-ordinator, S. Asia and Australasia, Shell Int. Petroleum Co., Ltd. 1962–63, various assignments in Europe 1964–66; Shell Oil Co. Atlanta, Ga. 1967–69; Chair. and C.E.O. Shell Group Australia 1969–80; Chair. Ashton Mining Ltd. 1981–94, BRL Hardy Ltd. 1992–95, Tandem Computers Pty. Ltd. 1992–98, Cooperative Research Centre for Cochlear Implant, Speech and Hearing Inst. 1993–; Dir. Pacific Dunlop Ltd. 1978–, Chair. 1986–90; Dir. Australian Industry Devt. Corpn. 1978–90; Dir. Australian Inst. of Petroleum Ltd. 1976–80, 1982–84, Chair. 1977–79; mem. Australian Nat. Airlines Comm. 1981–87, Vice-Chair. 1984–87. *Leisure interests:* reading, music, racing, golf. *Address:* 20 Albany Road, Toorak, Vic. 3142, Australia. *Telephone:* (03) 9666-5200/1 (Office); (03) 9822-1357 (Home). *Fax:* (03) 9666 5449.

FRÖHLICH, Albrecht, PH.D., F.R.S.; British professor of pure mathematics; b. 22 May 1916; s. of Julius Fröhlich and Frida Fröhlich; m. Dr. Evelyn Ruth Brooks 1950; one s. one d.; ed. Realgymnasium, Munich, Germany and Bristol Univ.; Asst. Lecturer in Math., Univ. Coll., Leicester 1950–52; Lecturer in Math., Univ. Coll. of N. Staffs. 1952–55; Reader in Pure Math., King's Coll., Univ. of London 1955–62, Prof. 1962–81, Emer. Prof. 1982–, Head Dept. of Math. 1971–81; Sr. Research Fellow, Imperial Coll., Univ. of London 1982–96; Fellow Robinson Coll., Cambridge 1982–84, Emer. Fellow 1984–; Visiting Royal Soc.-Israeli Acad. Research Prof. 1978; George A. Miller Prof., Univ. of Ill., U.S.A. 1981–82; Gauss Prof., Göttingen Acad. of Sciences, Fed. Repub. of Germany 1983; Corresp. mem. Heidelberg Acad. of Sciences 1982; Fellow King's Coll. 1977; Hon. D.Sc. (Bordeaux), (Bristol) 1998; Sr. Berwick Prize, London Math. Soc. 1976, Humboldt Foundation Research Prize 1992, De Morgan Medal, London Math. Soc. 1992. *Publications:* Formal Groups 1968, Galoi's Module Structure of Algebraic Integers 1983, Class Groups and Hermitian Modules 1984, Algebraic Number Theory (jtly.) 1991; papers in mathematical journals. *Leisure interests:* cooking, eating, walking, music. *Address:* Robinson College, Cambridge, CB3 9AN, England. *Telephone:* (01223) 311431.

FROHNMAYER, John Edward, M.A., J.D.; American civil servant, lawyer and author; b. 1 June 1942, Medford, Ore.; s. of Otto Frohnmayer and Marabel Frohnmayer; m. Leah Thorpe 1967; two s.; ed. Stanford Univ., Univs. of Chicago and Oregon; partner Tonkon, Torp, Galen, Marmaduke & Booth 1975–89; Chair. Ore. Arts Comm. 1980–84; mem. art selection cttee. Ore. State Capitol Bldg.; Chair. Nat. Endowment for the Arts 1989–92; Visiting Professional Scholar, The Freedom Forum, 1st Amendment Center, Vanderbilt Univ. 1993; trial lawyer in pvt. practice, Bozeman, Mont. 1995–; People for the American Way, 1st Amendment Award 1992, Oregon Gov.'s Award for the Arts 1993; Republican. *Publication:* Leaving Town Alive 1993, Out of Tune: Listening to the First Amendment 1994. *Leisure interests:* skiing, rowing, reading, music. *Address:* 14080 Lone Bean Road, Bozeman, MT 59715, U.S.A. *Telephone:* (406) 585-5910. *Fax:* (406) 582-4997.

FROLOV, Ivan Timofeyevich, DR.PHIL.SC.; Russian philosopher; b. 1 Sept. 1929, Dobroye, Lipetsk region; m. Galina Leonidovna; two d.; ed. Moscow Univ.; head of section, chief sec. of journal Voprosy filosofii 1956–62, Ed.-in-Chief 1968–77; mem. CPSU 1960–91; consultant ed. deputy chief sec. of journal Problems of Peace and Socialism 1962–65; asst. to sec. of CPSU Cen. Cttee. 1965–68; Chief Sec. Problems of Peace and Socialism 1977–79; Deputy Dir. of All-Union Inst. of Systems Analysis 1979–80; Pres. of Council of Philosophy with Acad. of Sciences Presidium 1980–86; Ed.-in-chief Kommunist 1986–88, Pravda 1989–91; Corresp. mem. U.S.S.R. (now Russian) Acad. of Sciences 1976–87, mem. 1987–; mem. of CPSU Cen. Cttee. 1986–91, Asst. to Gen. Sec. of CPSU Cen. Cttee. 1987–89, Sec. 1989–91; mem. CPSU Politburo 1990–91; Deputy to U.S.S.R. Supreme Soviet 1987–89, U.S.S.R. People's Deputy 1989–91; Pres. U.S.S.R. (now Russian) Philosophical Soc. 1987–; Head Interdepartmental Inst. for Human Studies 1992–; Hon. mem. Int. Acad. of Science History 1989; UNEP Prize 1991. *Publications:* Man, Science, Humanism: A new Synthesis 1991, numerous other books and articles. *Address:* Institute for Human Studies, Volkhonka str. 14, 119842 Moscow, Russia (Office). *Telephone:* (095) 203-9067 (Office); (095) 209-2508 (Home).

FROLOV, Konstantin Vasilyevich, D.TECH.SCI.; Russian machine construction specialist; b. 22 July 1932; m.; one s.; ed. Bryansk Inst. of Transport and Machine Construction; (Prof. 1971–); engineer at Leningrad Metallurgical Plant 1956–58; research work U.S.S.R. (now Russian) Acad. of Sciences Inst. of Machine Construction 1961–63, Head of Lab. 1963–75, Dir. 1975–; Vice-Pres. U.S.S.R. (now Russian) Acad. of Sciences, Acad. Sec. of Mechanics Section 1985–; mem. U.S.S.R. (now Russian) Acad. of Sciences 1984–, Vice-Pres. 1985–; mem. CPSU 1965–91, cand. mem. CPSU Cen. Cttee. 1986–89, mem. 1990–91; U.S.S.R. People's Deputy 1989–91; mem. Supreme Soviet 1989–91; concurrently Prof. at Moscow Univ. 1960–62, Moscow Inst. of Technology 1962–75, Moscow Bauman Tech. College 1975–; Dir. Inst. of Eng. Science 1991–; Chair. Bd. Int. Soc. "Znanie" 1991–; Scientific Dir. Russian-American Centre for Devt. of Tech. 1992–; mem. Agricultural Acad.

1985–; Hon. mem. Slovak Scientific Soc. of Eng. 1982–, Madrid Polytechnical Univ. 1990–; Foreign mem. Swedish Royal Eng. Acad. 1989, Nat. Acad. of Eng., U.S.A. 1990; Silver Medal, Czechoslovak Acad. of Science 1982, U.S.S.R. State Prize 1986, Lenin Prize 1988. *Address:* Institut Mashinovedeniya, Malyi Khazitonyevski per. str. 4, Moscow, Russia. *Telephone:* (095) 928-87-30.

FROMENT-MEURICE, Henri, L. ÈS L.; French diplomatist; b. 5 June 1923, Paris; m. Gabrielle Drouilh 1948 (deceased); three s. one d.; ed. Ecole libre des Sciences Politiques, Ecole Nat. d'Admin.; Sec., Ministry of Foreign Affairs 1950–52, Sec. for Far East, Tokyo 1952–53, Chief of Diplomatic Staff, Commissariat Gén. de France en Indochine 1953–54, Asst. Pvt. Sec. to Sec. of State for Foreign Affairs 1954–56, First Sec. Embassy, Moscow 1956–59, with Cen. Admin. (Europe) 1959–63, Chargé d'Affaires, Embassy, United Arab Repub. (now Egypt) 1963–64, First Counsellor, Cairo Embassy, 1964–65, Chief of Cultural Exchange Service, Cen. Admin. 1965–68, Minister Plenipotentiary 1968, Advisory Minister, Moscow 1968–69, Dir. Cen. Admin., Asia and Pacific Ocean 1969–75, Econ. Affairs 1975–79, Amb. to U.S.S.R. 1979–81, to Fed. Repub. of Germany 1982–83; Ambassadeur de France 1984; Adviser to Chair. Banque Paribas 1985–91; Adviser Jeantet et Associés 1991–; Dir. Phillips France 1984–96, Robert Bosch (France) 1984–97; Commandeur Légion d'honneur, Officier Ordre national du Mérite. *Publications:* Une puissance nommée Europe 1984 (Adolphe Bentinck Prize), Une éducation politique 1987, Europe 1992 1988; several articles in Preuves, Commentaire and Revue des Deux Mondes. *Leisure interests:* music, piano. *Address:* Jeantet et Associés, 87–89 avenue Kléber, 75016 Paris (Office); 8 avenue Perronet, 92200 Neuilly-sur-Seine, France (Home).

FROMM, Hans Walther Herbert, DR.PHIL.; Finnish/German professor of philology; b. 26 May 1919, Berlin; s. of Rudolf Fromm and Luise (née Hennig) Fromm; m. 1st Lore Sprenger 1950 (divorced 1974); one d.; m. 2nd Beatrice Müller-Hansen 1974; ed. Berlin Univ.; lecturer and Prof. of Germanic Philology, Univ. of Turku 1952–58; Prof. of German Philology and Finno-Ugric Languages, Univ. of Munich 1960–87, Prof. Emer. 1987–; mem. Bayerische Akad. der Wissenschaften 1971, Finnish Acad. of Sciences 1979, Acad. of Finland 1990–, Akad. der Wissenschaften, Göttingen 1992; Chair. Scientific Reviewers' Cttee., Deutsche Forschungsgemeinschaft, Bonn 1972–76, Comm. for Medieval German Literature, Bayerische Akad., Munich 1978–; Dr. phil. h.c. (Turku) 1969, Bundesverdienstkreuz (1st Class), Commdr. Order of Kts. of the Finnish Lion (1st Class) 1985, Brüder-Grimm-Preis 1987. *Publications:* Bibliographie deutscher Übersetzungen aus dem Französischen (6 vols.) 1950–53, Germanistische Bibliographie seit 1945, Theorie u. Kritik 1960, Der deutsche Minnesang (2 vols.) 1961, 1985, Kalevala (2 vols.) 1967, Konrad von Fussesbrunnen (Ed.) 1973, Finnische Grammatik (1982), Esseitä Kalevalasta 1987, Arbeiten z. deutschen Literatur d. Mittelalters 1989, Heinrich von Veldeke 1992. *Leisure interest:* chess. *Address:* Roseggerstrasse 35a, 85521 Ottobrunn, Germany. *Telephone:* (089) 605882.

FROMME, Friedrich Karl, DR.PHIL.; German journalist; b. 10 June 1930, Dresden; s. of Prof. Dr. med. Albert and Dr. med. Lenka Fromme; m. 1st Traute Kirsten 1961 (died 1992); m. 2nd Brigitte Bürkert 1997; ed. studies in science, politics and public law; teaching asst., Univ. of Tübingen 1957–62; Ed. Süddeutscher Rundfunk 1962–64, Frankfurter Allgemeine Zeitung (FAZ) 1964–68; Bonn corresp. FAZ 1968–73; Ed. responsible for internal politics and co-ordination, FAZ 1974–97. *Publications:* Von der Weimarer Verfassung zum Bonner Grundgesetz 1962, Der Parlamentarier — ein Freier Beruf? 1978, Gesetzgebung im Widerstreit 1980. *Address:* Mohrengarten 60, 40822 Metlmann, Germany. *Telephone:* (02104) 958768.

FROMSTEIN, Mitchell S.; American business executive; b. 1928; ed. Univ. of Wis.; Krueger Homes Inc. 1948–49; Account Exec. Maultner Advertising Agency 1949–53; former Pres. TV Parts Inc.; Partner, Fromstein Assocs.; Pres., C.E.O. and Dir. The Parker Pen Co., Janesville, Wis. 1985–86; Chair., Pres. and C.E.O. Manpower Inc., Milwaukee 1976–; C.E.O. Blue Arrow PLC 1989–, also Dir. *Address:* Manpower Inc., P.O. Box 2053, 5301 North Ironwood Road, Milwaukee, WI 53217, U.S.A.

FROST, Sir David Paradine, Kt., O.B.E., M.A.; British television personality and writer; b. 7 April 1939, Tenterden, Kent; s. of Rev. W. J. Paradine Frost; m. 1st Lynne Frederick 1981 (divorced 1982); m. 2nd Lady Carina Fitzalan Howard 1983; three s.; ed. Gillingham and Wellingborough Grammar Schools, Gonville and Caius Coll., Cambridge; appeared in BBC TV satire series That Was The Week That Was 1962; other programmes with BBC included A Degree of Frost 1963, 1973, Not So Much A Programme More A Way of Life 1964–65, The Frost Report 1966–67, Frost Over England 1967; appeared in The Frost Programme, ITA 1966–67, 1967–68, 1972; Chair. and C.E.O. David Paradine Ltd. 1966–; Jt. Founder London Weekend Television 1967; Joint Deputy Chair. Equity Enterprises 1973–76 (Chair. 1972–73); Jt. Founder and Dir. TV-am 1981–93, host of numerous programmes including Frost On Friday, Frost On Saturday, Frost On Sunday etc., David Frost Show (U.S.A.) 1969–72, David Frost Revue (U.S.A.) 1971–73, Frost over Australia 1972–77, Frost over New Zealand 1973–74, That Was The Year That Was (U.S.A.) 1973, The Frost Interview 1974, We British 1975, The Sir Harold Wilson Interviews 1967–77, The Nixon Interviews 1976–77, The Crossroads of Civilisation 1977–78; David Frost Presents the Int. Guinness Book of World Records 1981–86, Frost over Canada 1982–83, The Spectacular World of Guinness Records 1987–88, Talking with David Frost 1991–; Presenter Sunday Breakfast with Frost Jan. 1993–; The Frost Programme 1993–; Pres. Lord's Taverners 1985, 1986; Companion TV and Radio Industries Club 1992; Hon. Prof. Thames Valley Univ. 1994; Golden Rose, Montreux (for Frost over England) 1967, Royal TV Soc's. Award 1967, Richard Dimbleby Award 1967, Emmy Award 1970, 1971, Religious Heritage of America Award 1970, Albert Einstein Award (Communication Arts) 1971. *Films produced:* The Rise and Rise of Michael Rimmer 1970, Charley One-Eye 1972, Leadbelly 1974, The Slipper and the Rose 1975, Dynasty 1975, The Ordeal of Patty Hearst 1978, The Remarkable Mrs Sanger 1979. *Publications include:* That Was The Week That Was 1963, How to Live Under Labour 1964, Talking With Frost 1967, To England With Love (with Antony Jay) 1967, The Americans 1970, Whitlam and Frost 1974, I Gave Them a Sword 1978, I Could Have Kicked Myself 1982, Who wants to be a Millionaire? 1983, The Mid-Atlantic Companion (jtly.) 1986, The Rich Tide (jtly.) 1986, The World's Shortest Books 1987, David Frost An Autobiography: Part One 1993. *Address:* David Paradine Ltd., 5 St Mary Abbots Place, Kensington, London, W8 6LS, England. *Telephone:* 0171-371 1111. *Fax:* 0171-602 0411.

FROST, Sir Terence Ernest Manitou, Kt.; British artist; b. 13 Oct. 1915, Leamington; five s. one d.; ed. Campion Central School, Camberwell Coll. of Arts and Crafts; Prof. of Painting Univ. of Reading 1977–81, Prof. Emer. 1981; numerous exhbns. including Waddington Galleries 1958–, Adelson Gallery, New York 1992–94, Belgrave Gallery, London 1997; represented in public collections in U.K., Canada, U.S.A., Germany, Australia; Hon. LL.D. (Council for Nat. Academic Awards). *Address:* Gernick Field Studio, Tredavoe Lane, Newlyn, Penzance, Cornwall, TR18 5DL, England. *Telephone:* (01736) 365902.

FROST, Thomas Pearson, F.C.I.B., F.R.S.A.; British banker (retd.); b. 1 July 1933; s. of James Watterson Frost and Enid E. C. Pearson; m. Elizabeth Morton 1958; one s. two d.; ed. Ormskirk Grammar School; joined Westminster Bank 1950; C.E.O. and Vice-Chair. NBNA (now Nat. Westminster Bank U.S.A.) 1980; Gen. Man. Business Devt. Div. Nat. Westminster Bank 1982, Dir. Nat Westminster Bank 1984–93, Group Chief Exec. 1987–92, jt. Deputy Chair. (part time) 1992–93; Chair. ICCH Ltd. 1993–, London Clearing House Ltd. 1993–96; Dir. Five Oaks Investments PLC 1993–95 (Chair. 1995–98), Fenchurch PLC 1993–97; mem. British Overseas Trade Bd. 1986–93, UK Advisory Bd., British-American Chamber of Commerce 1987–93; Chair. CBI Business and Urban Regeneration Task Force 1987–88; Gov. Royal Ballet School 1988–98; Fellow World Scout Foundation, Freeman, City of London 1978. *Leisure interests:* golf, greenhouse, theatre. *Address:* Five Oaks Investment PLC, 130 Jermyn Street, London, SW1Y 4UJ, England.

FROWEIN, Jochen Abraham, DR.JUR., M.C.L.; German professor of law; b. 8 June 1934, Berlin; s. of Dr. jur. Abraham Frowein and Hilde Frowein (née Matthis); m. Lore Flume 1962; one s. two d.; ed. Univs. of Kiel, Berlin, Bonn and Univ. of Michigan Law School, Ann Arbor; research fellow, Max-Planck-Inst. for comparative public and int. law 1962–66; Prof. Univ. of Bochum 1967–69, Univ. of Bielefeld 1969–81; Dir. Max-Planck-Inst. and Prof. Univ. of Heidelberg 1981; mem. European Comm. of Human Rights 1973–93, Vice-Pres. 1981–93; Vice-Pres. German Research Foundation 1977–80; Dr. Iur. h.c. (Seville) 1984, (Louvain) 1997. *Publications:* Das de facto-Regime im Völkerrecht 1968, EMRK-Kommentar (with W. Peukert) 1985 and many articles and contributions. *Address:* Max-Planck-Institut für ausländisches öffentliches Recht und Völkerrecht, Jan Neuenleimer Feld 535, 69120 Heidelberg, Germany. *Telephone:* (6221) 48-22-58.

FRUGOLI, Amadeo; Argentine politician and lawyer; b. 26 Feb. 1932, Mendoza; ed. San José Coll., and Univ. of Buenos Aires; Prof., various colls. under Nat. Univ., Cuyo; taught history and civic instruction; Juridical Adviser, Mendoza Prov. Govt. 1965, later Sec.-Gen.; Minister of Govt., Mendoza Prov. 1970; Minister of Social Welfare, Nat. Govt. 1971; Senator and mem. Inst. of Int. Relations 1973–76; Minister of Justice 1981, of Defence Jan.–July 1982.

FRÜH, Eugen; Swiss painter and illustrator; b. 22 Jan. 1914, St. Gallen; s. of Huldreich and Teresa Früh; m. Erna Yoshida Blenk (artist) 1934; ed. Zürich School of Art and in Paris and Rome; C. F. Meyer Foundation Fine Arts Prize 1943, Fine Arts Prize, Kanton Zürich 1967. *Works include:* Die kleine Stadt 1941, Pastorale d'été 1946, La comédie et la musique 1947, Capricci 1948, Spanisches Gespräch 1951, Notturno 1957, Château d'artiste 1962, Gartenfest 1964, Bambuswald 1972, Lotus 1973–74; also murals and book illustrations. *Leisure interests:* literature, music, travel. *Address:* Römergasse 9, 8001 Zürich, Switzerland. *Telephone:* 01-478863.

FRÜHBECK DE BURGOS, Rafael; Spanish conductor; b. 15 Sept. 1933, Burgos; s. of Wilhelm and Stephanie (née Ochs) Frühbeck; m. María Carmen Martínez 1959; one s. one d.; ed. music acads. in Bilbao, Madrid, and Munich, and Univ. of Madrid; Chief Conductor, Municipal Orchestra, Bilbao 1958–62; Music Dir. and Chief Conductor, Spanish Nat. Orchestra, Madrid 1962–78; Music Dir. of Düsseldorf and Chief Conductor Düsseldorf Symphoniker 1966–71; Music Dir. Montreal Symphony Orchestra 1974–76; Prin. Conductor Yomiuri Nippon Symphony Orchestra 1980–90, Hon. Conductor 1991–; Prin. Guest Conductor Nat. Symphony Orchestra, Washington, D.C. 1980–90; Music Dir. Vienna Symphony Orchestra 1991–96; Gen. Music Dir. Deutsche Oper Berlin 1992–97; Gen. Musik Dir. Rundfunk Symphony Orchestra, Berlin 1994–; Hon. Conductor Spanish Nat. Orchestra 1998; mem. Real Academia de Bellas Artes, Madrid 1975–; Dr. h.c. (Univ. of

Navarra) 1994, (Univ. of Burgos) 1998; Prize for Musical Interpretation, Larios Foundation CEOE, Madrid 1992, Fundación Guliero Prize for Spanish Music, Madrid 1996, Gold Medal Int. Gustav Mahler Soc., Vienna 1996; Gran Cruz al Mérito Civil Orden de Alfonso X 1966, Orden de Isabel la Católica 1966, Gold Medal City of Vienna 1995, Medal of Civil Merit Austrian Repub. 1996. *Address:* 28007 Madrid, Avenida del Mediterráneo 21, Spain (Home). *Telephone:* (341) 5016933 (Home).

FRUMKIN, Allan, PH.B.; American art dealer; b. 5 July 1926, Chicago, Ill.; s. of Joseph Frumkin and Libbie Frumkin; m. Jean Martin 1960; two s.; ed. Univ. of Chicago, Cornell Univ. and New School for Social Research; started Frumkin Gallery in Chicago 1952; opened New York Gallery 1959; partnership with George Adams in Frumkin/Adams Gallery, New York 1990–95, currently dealing privately; Distinguished Alumni Award, Univ. of Chicago 1981. *Leisure interests:* reading, music, travel. *Address:* 1185 Park Avenue, New York, NY 10128, U.S.A. *Telephone:* (212) 427-1664. *Fax:* (212) 860-3660.

FRUTON, Joseph Stewart, PH.D.; American biochemist; b. 14 May 1912, Czestochowa, Poland; s. of Charles Fruton and Ella Eisenstadt; m. Sofia Simmonds 1936; ed. Columbia Univ.; Assoc., Rockefeller Inst. for Medical Research 1934–45; Assoc. Prof. of Physiological Chem., Yale Univ. 1945–50, Prof. of Biochem. 1950–57, Chair. Dept. of Biochem. 1951–67, Eugene Higgins Prof. of Biochem. 1957–82, Emer. 1982–, Dir. Div. of Science 1959–62, Prof. History of Medicine 1980–82, Emer. 1982–; Exec. Sec. Yale Corpn. Presidential Search Cttee. 1985–86; Assoc. Ed. Journal of Biological Chemistry and Journal of Biochemistry; Harvey Lecturer 1955, Dakin Lecturer 1962; Visiting Prof. Rockefeller Univ. 1968–69; Sarton Lecturer 1976; Xerox Lecturer 1977; Benjamin Franklin Fellow, Royal Soc. of Arts; mem. American Philosophical Soc., N.A.S., American Acad. of Arts and Sciences, Harvey Soc., American Chemical Soc., American Soc. of Biological Chemists, Biochemical Soc., History of Science Soc.; Fellow, Guggenheim Foundation 1983–84; Hon. Sc.D. (Rockefeller Univ.) 1976; Eli Lilly Award in Biological Chem. 1944, Pfizer Award in History of Science 1973, John Frederick Lewis Award (American Philosophical Soc.) 1990, Dexter Award in History of Chem. 1993. *Publications:* General Biochemistry (with S. Simmonds) 1953, Molecules and Life 1972, Selected Bibliography of Biographical Data for the History of Biochemistry since 1800 1974, a Bio-bibliography for the History of the Biochemical Sciences since 1800 1982, Contrasts in Scientific Style 1990, A Skeptical Biochemist 1992, Eighty Years 1994, Proteins, Enzymes, Genes 1999; numerous scientific articles in Journal of Biological Chemistry, Biochemistry, Journal of American Chemical Soc., Proceedings of N.A.S., and other journals. *Leisure interests:* history of science, music. *Address:* 123 York Street, New Haven, CT 06511, U.S.A. *Telephone:* (203) 624-3735. *Fax:* (203) 737-4130.

FRY, Christopher, F.R.S.L.; British dramatist; b. 18 Dec. 1907, Bristol; s. of Emma Marguerite Hammond and Charles John Harris; m. Phyllis Marjorie Hart 1936; one s.; ed. Bedford Modern School; Actor, Citizen House, Bath 1927; teacher, Hazelwood Preparatory School 1928–31; Dir. Tunbridge Wells Repertory Players 1932–35; Dir. Oxford Repertory Players 1940 and 1944–46; at Arts Theatre, London 1945; Hon. Fellow, Manchester Polytechnic (now Manchester Metropolitan Univ.) 1988; Hon. Dip. Arts (Manchester) 1962, D.Litt. (Lambeth) 1988, Hon. D.Litt. (Sussex, De Montfort) 1994; Queen's Gold Medal for Poetry 1962. *Publications:* The Boy with the Cart 1939, The Firstborn 1946, A Phoenix too Frequent 1946, The Lady's Not for Burning 1949, Thor, with Angels 1949, Venus Observed 1950, A Sleep of Prisoners 1951, The Dark is Light Enough 1954, Curtmantle (R. S. L. Heinemann Award) 1962, A Yard of Sun 1970, The Brontës of Haworth (four plays for television) 1973, Can You Find Me 1978; Trans. Ring Round the Moon 1950, The Lark (Anouilh) 1954, Tiger at the Gates 1955, Duel of Angels 1958, Judith (Giraudoux) 1962, Peer Gynt 1970, Cyrano de Bergerac 1975, The Best of Enemies (play for television) 1976, Sister Dora (three-part play for television) 1977, introduction and text Charlie Hammond's Sketchbook 1980, Selected Plays 1985, One Thing More, or Caedmon Construed 1986, Genius, Talent and Failure 1987, Looking for a Language 1992, foreword and ed. A Sprinkle of Nutmeg 1994. *Film Scripts:* The Beggar's Opera. The Queen is Crowned, Ben Hur, Barabbas, The Bible. *Leisure interest:* gardening. *Address:* The Toft, East Dean, nr. Chichester, Sussex, England.

FRY, Hedy; Canadian politician and physician; b. 1941, Trinidad; three s.; ed. Coll. of Physicians and Surgeons, Dublin, Ireland; fmr. family physician, Vancouver Centre, B.C.; elected M.P. for Vancouver Centre 1993; Parl. Sec. to Minister of Health 1993; Sec. of State (Multiculturalism, Status of Women) 1996–; fmr. Pres. B.C. Medical Assn.; Liberal. *Address:* House of Commons, Ottawa, Ont., Canada.

FRY, Jonathan Michael, M.A.; British business executive; b. 9 Aug. 1937, Jerusalem; s. of Stephen Fry and Gladys Yvonne Blunt; m. Caroline Mary Dunkerly 1970 (divorced 1997); four d.; ed. Repton School, Trinity College, Oxford; Account Exec., Pritchard Wood Ltd. 1961–65; Account Supervisor, Norman Craig & Kummel Inc. 1965–66; Consultant, McKinsey & Co. 1966–73; Devt./Marketing Dir. Unigate Foods Div. 1973, Man. Dir. 1973, Chair. 1976–78; Group Planning Dir. Burmah Oil Trading Ltd. 1978–81, Chief Exec. Burmah Speciality Chemicals Ltd. 1981–87; Chair. Burmah Castrol PLC 1998 (Man. Dir. 1990–93, Chief Exec. 1993–98); Chief Exec. Burmah Castrol Trading Ltd. 1993–98, Chair. 1998– (Man. Dir. 1990–93); Chair. Castrol Int. (fmrly. Castrol Ltd.) 1993– (Chief Exec. 1987–93); Deputy Chair. Northern Foods PLC 1996– (non-exec. Dir. 1991–); Chair. Christian Salvesen PLC 1997– (non-exec. Dir. 1995–); Chair. Elementis PLC (fmrly. Harrisons & Crosfield PLC) 1997–. *Leisure interests:* cricket, skiing, archaeology. *Address:* Burmah Castrol PLC, Burmah Castrol House, Pipers Way, Swindon, Wilts., SN3 1RE (Office); Beechingstoke Manor, Pewsey, Wilts., SN9 6HQ, England (Home). *Telephone:* (01793) 511521 (Office); (0167285) 1669 (Home). *Fax:* (01793) 513419 (Office).

FRY, Marion Golda, M.A., B.LITT; Canadian university president (retd.); b. 16 April 1932, Halifax, N.S.: d. of George Fry and Marion Fry; ed. Univ. of King's Coll. Halifax, Dalhousie and Oxford Univs.; Asst. Prof. of Philosophy and Asst. Dean. of Women, Bishop's Univ. Lennoxville, Québec 1958–64; Prin. Catharine Parr Traill Coll., Trent Univ. 1964–69, Assoc. Prof. of Philosophy, Trent Univ. 1964–86, Vice-Pres. 1975–79; Pres. and Vice-Chancellor, Univ. of King's Coll. Halifax 1987–93; Adjunct Prof. Dept. of Philosophy, Dalhousie Univ. 1988–93; Hon. D.C.L (King's) 1985; Hon. D.Litt. (Trent) 1989. *Leisure interests:* travel, classical music, walking. *Address:* 652 Walkerfield Avenue, Peterborough, Ont. K9J 4W2, Canada.

FRY, Stephen John, M.A.; British actor and writer; b. 24 Aug. 1957; s. of Alan John Fry and Marianne Eve Fry (née Newman); ed. Uppingham School, Queens' Coll. Cambridge; Columnist The Listener 1988–89, Daily Telegraph 1990–; appeared with Cambridge Footlights in revue The Cellar Tapes, Edin. Festival 1981; *plays:* Latin, Edin. Festival 1980, Lyric Hammersmith 1983, Forty Years On, Chichester Festival and London 1984, The Common Pursuit, London 1988 (TV 1992); *TV series:* Alfresco 1982–84, The Young Ones 1983, Happy Families 1984, Saturday Night Live 1986–87, A Bit of Fry and Laurie 1989–95, Blackadder's Christmas Carol 1988, Blackadder Goes Forth 1989, Jeeves and Wooster 1990–92, Stalag Luft 1993, Laughter and Loathing 1995; radio: Loose Ends 1986–87, Whose Line Is It Anyway? 1987, Saturday Night Fry 1987; re-wrote script Me and My Girl, London, Broadway, Sydney 1984; Patron Studio 3 (arts for young people), Freeze (nuclear disarmament charity); *films:* The Good Father, A Fish Called Wanda, A Handful of Dust, Peter's Friends 1992, IQ 1995, Wind in the Willows, Wilde 1997, A Civil Action, Cold Comfort Farm 1997, A Civil Action 1997; mem. Amnesty Int., Comic Relief; Hon. LL.D. (Dundee) 1995. *Publications:* Paperweight (collected essays) 1992, The Liar (novel), The Hippopotamus 1994, Fry and Laurie 4 (with Hugh Laurie) 1994, Paperweight 1995, Making History 1996, Moab is my Washpot 1997 (autobiog.). *Leisure interests:* smoking, drinking, swearing, pressing wild flowers. *Address:* c/o Hamilton Asper Management, Ground Floor, 24 Hanway Street, London, W1P 9DD, England. *Telephone:* 0171-636 1221. *Fax:* 0171-636 1226.

FRYE, Richard Nelson, PH.D.; American orientalist; b. 10 Jan. 1920, Birmingham, Ala.; s. of Nels Frye and Lillie Hagman; m. 1st Barbara York 1948 (divorced 1973); two s. one d.; m. 2nd Eden Naby 1975; one s.; ed. Univ. of Illinois, Harvard Univ., and School of Oriental and African Studies, London; Jr. Fellow, Harvard 1946–49; Visiting Scholar, Univ. of Teheran 1951–52; Aga Khan Prof. of Iranian Studies, Harvard 1957–; Visiting Prof., Oriental Seminary, Frankfurt Univ. 1958–59; Visiting Prof., Hamburg Univ. 1968–69; Dir. Asia Inst., Pahlavi Univ., Shiraz 1969–74; Assoc. Ed. Cen. Asian Journal, Bulletin of the Asia Inst.; Corresp. Fellow, German Archaeological Inst. 1966–; Hon. D. Litt. (Oxford) 1987. *Publications:* Notes on the Early Coinage of Transoxiana 1949, History of the Nation of the Archers 1952, Narshakhi, The History of Bukhara 1954, Iran 1956, Heritage of Persia 1962, Bukhara, The Medieval Achievement 1965, The Histories of Nishapur 1965, Persia 1968, Inscriptions from Dura Europos 1969, Excavations at Qasr-i-Abu-Nasr 1973, The Golden Age of Persia 1975; Ed. Vol. 4 Cambridge History of Iran 1975, The Ancient History of Iran 1983, The Heritage of Central Asia 1996. *Address:* Harvard University, 6 Divinity Avenue, Cambridge, MA 02138 (Office); Tower Hill Road, Brimfield, MA 01010, U.S.A. (Home).

FRYER, Geoffrey, D.SC., PH.D., F.R.S.; British biologist; b. 6 Aug. 1927; s. of W. Fryer and M. Fryer; m. Vivien G. Hodgson 1953; one s. one d.; ed. Huddersfield Coll. and Univ. of London; colonial research student 1952–53; H.M. Overseas Research Service, Malawi 1953–55, Zambia 1955–57, Uganda 1957–60; Sr., then Prin., then Sr. Prin. Scientific Officer, Freshwater Biological Assn. 1960–81; Deputy Chief Scientific Officer, Windermere Lab., Freshwater Biological Assn. 1981–88; Hon. Prof., Univ. of Lancaster 1988–; H. R. Macmillan Lecturer, Univ. of B.C. 1963; Distinguished Visiting Scholar, Univ. of Adelaide 1985; Distinguished Lecturer Dept. of Fisheries and Oceans, Canada 1987; Frink Medal, Zoological Soc. of London 1983, Linnean Medal for Zoology, Linnean Soc. of London 1987, Elsdon-Dew Medal, Parasitological Soc. of S.A. 1998. *Publications:* The Cichlid Fishes of the Great Lakes of Africa: their biology and evolution (with T. D. Iles) 1972, A Natural History of the Lakes, Tarns and Streams of the English Lake District 1991, The Freshwater Crustacea of Yorkshire: A faunistic and ecological survey 1993; numerous articles in scientific journals. *Leisure interests:* natural history, walking, church architecture, photography. *Address:* Elleray Cottage, Windermere, Cumbria, LA23 1AW, England.

FU HAO; Chinese diplomatist; b. April 1916, Li Quan County, Xian Yang City, Shanxi Prov.; m. Jiao Ling 1945; two s., one d.; ed. N.W. China Teachers Coll.; served in PLA during the civil war; CPC rep. (Col.) Group of Beiping Exec. HQ of CPC, Kuomintang and U.S.A. in Dezhou, Shandong Prov. 1946; Counsellor, Embassy in Mongolia 1950–53; Deputy Dir. Asian Affairs Dept., Ministry of Foreign Affairs 1952–55; Counsellor, frequently Chargé d'Affaires, Embassy in India 1955–62; Dir. Personnel Dept, Ministry of Foreign Affairs 1963–69; Dir. Gen. Office, Ministry of Foreign Affairs 1969–72; Rep. to 26th Session UN Gen. Ass. 1971; Vice-Minister of Foreign Affairs 1972–74; Amb. to Democratic Repub. of Viet Nam 1974–77, to Japan 1977–82; Vice Minister, Adviser on Foreign Affairs 1982; Deputy 6th NPC, mem. Standing Cttee., Vice-Chair. Foreign Affairs Cttee. 1983–88; Chinese mem. 21st Century Cttee. for Sino-Japanese Friendship 1984–95, Chair. 1996–; Chair. NPC China-Japan Friendship Group 1985–93; Deputy 7th NPC, mem. Standing Cttee., Vice-Chair. Foreign Affairs Cttee. 1988–; mem. Exec. Cttee. IPU 1989–91; Pres. China-Vietnamese Friendship Asscn. 1992–96; Chair. Asscn. of Fmr. Diplomats of China, Inst. for Diplomatic History of People's Repub. of China 1994, Editor's Cttee. of The China Classical Stratagems 1995–; Grand Cordon of the Sacred Treasure (Japan). *Publication:* Tian Nan Di Bei (poems) 1992. *Leisure interests:* poems and literature. *Address:* 69 Bao Fang Lane, East District, Beijing 100010, People's Republic of China. *Telephone:* 65252010.

FU KUIQING, Lieut.-Gen.; Chinese army officer; b. 1920, Yingshan Co., Anhui Prov.; Sec. CCP Prov. Cttee., Heilongjiang 1971–74; Vice-Gov., Heilongjiang 1972–74; Deputy Political Commissar, Shenyang Mil. Region, PLA 1977; Political Commissar, Fuzhou Mil. Region, PLA 1981–85; mem. 12th CCP Cen. Cttee. 1982–87; Political Commissar Nanjing Mil. Region, PLA 1985–90, rank of Lieut.-Gen. PLA 1988; mem. Standing Cttee. of 7th NPC; (3rd class) order of Independence and Freedom, 2nd Class Order of Liberation. *Address:* Nanjing Military Region Headquarters, Nanjing, Jiangsu, People's Republic of China.

FU MINGXIA; Chinese diver; b. Aug. 1978, Wuhan, Hubei Prov.; ten-metre platform diving world champion at the age of 13; ten-metre platform diving Gold Medallist at 25th Olympics, Barcelona and 26th Olympics, Atlanta. *Address:* c/o State General Bureau for Physical Culture and Sports, 9 Tiyuguan Road, Chongwen District, Beijing, People's Republic of China.

FU QIFENG; Chinese historian of magic and acrobatics; b. 15 March 1941, Chengdu, Sichuan; d. of Fu Tianzheng and Ceng Qingpu; m. Xu Zhuang 1961; one s. one d.; performer, acrobatics troupe, Beijing 1960–70; Founder and Deputy Chief Ed. Acrobatics and Magic (journal); mem. Research Dept., Asscn. of Chinese Acrobats 1987–, Council mem. 1991–; mem. Editorial Cttee. Acrobatics, in series Contemporary China 1991–; mem. China Magic Cttee. 1993–. *Publications:* Chinese Acrobatics Through the Ages 1986, The Art of Chinese Acrobatics 1988; (with brother) Acrobatics in China 1983, History of Chinese Acrobatics 1989, History of Chinese Artistic Skills (in Japanese) 1993; (co-author) Literature and Art volume of China Concise Encyclopedia 1994, Secret of Spiritualist Activities 1995, Illusions and Superstitions 1997. *Address:* 5-2-501 Hongmiao Beili, Jintai Road, Beijing 100025, People's Republic of China. *Telephone:* 65002547.

FU QUANYOU, Gen.; Chinese army officer; b. 1930, Yuanping Co., Shanxi Prov.; joined Red Army 1946, CCP 1947; Army Chief of Staff 1981–83; Army Commdr. 1983–85; Commdr. Chengdu Mil. Region, PLA 1985–90; mem. 12th CCP Cen. Cttee. 1985, 13th CCP Cen. Cttee. 1987–92; mem. 14th CCP Cen. Cttee. 1992–97; mem. 15th CCP Cen. Cttee. 1997–; mem. Cen. Mil. Comm. of CCP 1992–, Gen. 1993–; Deputy Sec. CCP Cttee., Commdr. Lanzhou Mil. Region 1990–92; Dir. Gen. Logistics Dept. 1992–95; Chief of Gen. Staff Oct. 1995–. *Address:* c/o Chinese Communist Party Central Committee, Zhongnanhai, Beijing, People's Republic of China.

FU TIANLIN; Chinese poet; b. 24 Jan. 1946, Zizhong Co., Sichuan Prov.; ed. Chongqing Middle School, Electronic Tech. School; worked in orchard Chongqing 1962–79; clerk, Beibei Cultural Centre 1980–82; Ed. Chongqing Publishing House 1982–; First Prize of Chinese Poetry 1983. *Publications:* Green Musical Notes 1981, Between Children and the World 1983, Island of Music 1985, Red Strawberry 1986, Selected Poems of Seven Chinese Poets 1993. *Address:* Chongqing Publishing House, 205 Changjiang 2 Road, 630050, Chongqing City, Sichuan, People's Republic of China.

FU TIESHAN; Chinese ecclesiastic; b. 1931, Qingyuan Co., Hebei Prov.; ed. Major Seminar in Beijing; Bishop of Beijing Diocese 1979–; Vice-Chair. China Patriotic Catholic Asscn. 1980; Sec.-Gen. Chinese Catholic Bishops College; Deputy Dir. Chinese Catholic Bishops' Coll. 1985, Nat. Admin. Comm. of the Chinese Catholic Church 1986; mem. of Standing Cttee. 7th CPPCC 1988; mem. 8th NPC 1993–, Educ. Science, Culture and Public Health Cttee.; NPC Deputy Beijing Municipality.

FU XISHOU; Chinese government official and engineer; b. 1931, Beijing; ed. Dept. of Civil Engineering, Qinghua Univ.; joined CCP 1959; Deputy Sec. Anhui Prov. CP Cttee. 1987–; Deputy Gov. of Anhui Prov. 1988–90, Gov. 1991–95; mem. 14th CCP Cen. Cttee. 1992–; NPC Deputy to Anhui Prov.; Deputy Sec. CPC 5th Anhui Provincial Cttee. 1988–; Gov. Anhui Provincial People's Govt. 1989–94; Chair. People's Armament Cttee. 1991–. *Address:* c/o Office of Provincial Governor, Hefei City, Anhui Province, People's Republic of China.

FU ZHIHUAN; Chinese politician; b. March 1938, Haicheng Co., Liaoning Prov.; ed. Moscow Railways Inst., U.S.S.R.; joined CCP 1966; chief engineer, Science and Tech. Bureau, Ministry of Railways 1984; Dir. Science and Tech. Bureau, Ministry of Railways 1985; Dir. Harbin Railway Bureau 1989; Vice-Minister of Railways 1991–98, Minister 1998–; mem. CCP Cen. Comm. for Inspecting Discipline 1992–; mem. 15th CCP Cen. Cttee. 1997–. *Address:* Ministry of Railways, 10 Fuxing Lu, Haidan Qu, Beijing 100844, People's Republic of China.

FUÀ, Giorgio; Italian professor of economics; b. 19 May 1919, Ancona; s. of Riccardo Fuà and Elena Segre; m. Erika Rosenthal 1943; three s.; ed. Scuola Normale Superiore, Pisa, Univ. of Pisa, Univ. of Lausanne, Switzerland, Graduate Inst. of Int. Studies, Geneva; Jr. Econ. Adviser to Pres. Adriano Olivetti, Olivetti S.p.A. 1941–45; with Istituto Mobiliare Italiano (finance corpn.), Rome 1946–47; Assoc. Prof. of Econ. Statistics, Univ. of Pisa 1947–50; Econ. Affairs Officer, UN Econ. Comm. for Europe, Geneva 1950-54; Chief Econ. Adviser to Pres. Enrico Mattei, Ente Nazionale Idrocarburi (state oil and gas corpn.), Rome 1954–60; Prof. of Econs., Faculty of Econs., Ancona 1960–; Pres. ISTAO (managerial education), Ancona 1967–, Società Italiana degli Economisti, Genoa 1983–1986; mem. Accademia Nazionale dei Lincei 1986–. *Publications:* Reddito nazionale e politica economica 1957, Idee per la programmazione economica 1963, Lo Stato e il risparmio privato 1970, Occupazione e capacità produttiva 1976, Lo sviluppo economico in Italia: Lavoro e reddito 1981, Problems of Lagged Development in OECD Europe 1980, Industrializzazione senza fratture 1983, Troppe Tasse sui Redditi 1985, Small-scale Industry in Rural Areas: the Italian Experience 1988, Conseguenze economiche della evoluzione demografica 1986, Orientamenti per la politica del territorio 1991, Crescita economica (Le insidie delle cifre) 1993. *Address:* ISTAO, Via Zuccarini 15, 60020 Candia di Ancona; Via Monte d'Ago 75, 60131 Ancona, Italy (Home). *Telephone:* 071-2901080 (ISTAO); 071-894629 (Home). *Fax:* 071-2900953 (ISTAO).

FUCHS, Anke, LL.M.; German politician and lawyer; b. 5 July 1937, Hamburg; m.; two c.; ed. Hamburg, Innsbruck and School of Public Admin., Speyer; mem. Regional Exec., Young Socialist Org. 1954; joined Social Democratic Party (SPD) 1956; trainee, regional org. of German Fed. of Trade Unions, Nordmark (Hamburg) 1964–68; Regional Sec. Metal Workers' Union (IG Metall), mem. Reform Comm. on Training for Legal Profession, mem. SPD Regional Exec., mem. Hamburg Judge Selection Cttee. 1968–70; mem. SPD Party Council 1970–, former Deputy Chair., Party Man. 1987–91; mem. Bundestag 1980–; mem. Hamburg Citizens' Assembly 1970–77; Exec. Sec. IG Metall 1971–77; State Sec. Fed. Ministry of Labour and Social Affairs 1977–80, Parl. State Sec. 1980–82; Chair. SPD Party Council 1993–; Pres. des deutschen Mieterbundes 1995–; Fed. Minister for Youth, Family Affairs and Health April-Oct. 1982. *Address:* Bundeshaus, 53113 Bonn, Germany.

FUCHS, Victor Robert, M.A., PH.D.; American professor of economics; b. 31 Jan. 1924, New York; s. of Alfred Fuchs and Frances S. (Scheiber) Fuchs; m. Beverly Beck 1948; two s. two d.; ed. New York and Columbia Univs.; Assoc. Prof. of Econs. New York Univ. 1959–60; Program Assoc. Econs. Ford Foundation 1960–62; Research Assoc. Nat. Bureau of Econ. Research 1962–; Prof. of Community Medicine, Mount Sinai School of Medicine 1968–74; Prof. of Econs. City Univ. of New York Graduate Center 1968–74; Prof. of Econs. (in Depts. of Econs. and Health Research and Policy) Stanford Univ. 1974–95, Henry J. Kaiser Jr. Prof. 1988–95, Emer. Prof. 1995–; Pres. American Econ. Asscn. 1995; mem. Inst. of Medicine; Fellow, American Acad. of Arts and Sciences; mem. American Philosophical Soc.; Madden Memorial Award 1982, Distinguished Fellow, American Econ. Asscn. 1990, and other awards. *Publications:* The Economics of the Fur Industry 1957, Changes in the Location of Manufacturing in the U.S. since 1929 1962, The Service Economy 1968, Production and Productivity in the Service Industries 1969, Who Shall Live? Health, Economics and Social Choice 1975, Economic Aspects of Health (ed.) 1982, How We Live 1983, The Health Economy 1986, Women's Quest for Economic Equality 1988, The Future of Health Policy 1993, Individual and Social Responsibility: Child Care, Education, Medical Care, and Long Term Care in America (ed.) 1996. *Address:* National Bureau of Economic Research, 204 Alta Road, Stanford, CA 94305; 796 Cedro Way, Stanford, CA 94305, U.S.A. (Home). *Telephone:* (650) 326-7639 (Office). *Fax:* (650) 328-4163.

FUCHS, Sir Vivian Ernest, PH.D., F.R.S.; British geologist and explorer; b. 11 Feb. 1908, Freshwater, Isle of Wight; s. of Ernest and Violet Anne Fuchs (née Watson); m. 1st Joyce Connell 1933 (died 1990); one s. one d. (one d. deceased); m. 2nd Eleanor Honnywill 1991; ed. St. John's Coll., Cambridge; with Cambridge East Greenland Expedition 1929, Cambridge Expedition to East African Lakes 1930–32; Leader, Lake Rudolf Rift Valley Expedition 1933–34; Leader, Lake Rukwa Expedition 1937–38; served Second World War; Commdr. Falkland Islands Dependencies Survey (Antarctica) 1947–50; Dir. Falkland Islands Dependencies Scientific Bureau 1951–60; Leader, Trans-Antarctic Expedition 1955–58; Dir. British Antarctic Survey 1960–73; Pres. Int. Glaciological Soc. 1961–63, British Assoc. for Advancement of Science 1972, Royal Geog. Soc. 1982–84; Hon. Fellow, Wolfson Coll., Cambridge 1970, St. John's Coll., Cambridge 1983; Hon. mem. Chilean Soc. of History and Geography 1982–; Hon. LL.D. (Edinburgh, Birmingham), Hon. D.Sc. (Durham) 1958, (Cambridge) 1959, (Wales) 1971, (Leicester) 1972; Founder's Gold Medal (Royal Geog. Soc.) 1951, Polar Medal 1953, and Clasp, Special Gold Medal (Royal Geog. Soc.), 1958, Silver Medal (R.S.A.), Gold Medal (Royal Scottish Geog. Soc.), Richthofen Gold Medal (Berlin Geog. Soc.), Kirchenpauer Gold Medal (Hamburg Geog. Soc.), Gold Medal (Paris Geog. Soc.) 1958, Hubbard Gold Medal (American Nat. Geog. Soc.), Gold Medal (Royal Netherlands Geog. Soc.) 1959, Hans Egede Medal (Royal Danish Geog. Soc.) 1961, Prestwich Medal (Geological Soc., London) 1960, Medal of Chilean Soc. of History and Geography 1982. *Publications:* The Crossing of Antarctica (with Sir Edmund Hillary) 1958, Antarctic Adventure

1959, Of Ice and Men 1982, A Time to Speak 1990 (autobiog.); Ed. Great Explorers, The Forces of Nature 1976, The Physical World 1985; various geological and geographical papers. *Leisure interest:* gardening. *Address:* 106 Barton Road, Cambridge, CB3 9LH, England. *Telephone:* (01223) 359238.

FUENTES, Carlos; Mexican author and diplomatist; b. 11 Nov. 1928, Mexico City; s. of Rafael Fuentes Boettiger and Berta Macías Rivas; m. 1st Rita Macedo 1957; one d.; m. 2nd Sylvia Lemus 1973; one s. one d.; ed. Univ. of Mexico, Inst. des Hautes Etudes Internationales, Geneva; mem. Mexican Del. to ILO, Geneva 1950–51; Asst. Head, Press Section, Ministry of Foreign Affairs, Mexico 1954; Asst. Dir. Cultural Dissemination, Univ. de Mexico 1955–56; Head Dept. of Cultural Relations, Ministry of Foreign Affairs 1957–59; Ed. Revista Mexicana de Literatura 1954–58, Co-Ed. El Espectador 1959–61, Ed. Siempre and Politica 1960–; Amb. to France 1974–77; fmr. Prof. of Spanish and Comparative Literature, Columbia Univ., New York; Prof. of Comparative Literature, Harvard Univ. 1984–86, Robert F. Kennedy Prof. of Latin American Studies 1987–; Prof.-at-Large Brown Univ. 1995–; Pres. Modern Humanities Research Assen. 1989–; fmr. Adjunct Prof. of English and Romance Languages, Univ. of Pennsylvania, Pa.; Fellow, Woodrow Wilson Int. Center for Scholars, Washington, D.C. 1974; Fellow of the Humanities, Princeton Univ.; Virginia Gildersleeve Visiting Prof., Barnard Coll., New York; Edward Leroc Visiting Prof., School of Int. Affairs, Columbia Univ., New York; Norman Maccoll Lecturer, Univ. of Cambridge, England; mem. Mexican Nat. Comm. on Human Rights 1989–; The Biblioteca Breve Prize (for A Change of Skin) 1967, The Javier Villaurrutia Prize (for Terra Nostra) 1975, Rómulo Gallegos Prize (for Terra Nostra) 1977, Mexican Nat. Award for Literature 1984, Miguel de Cervantes Prize (for Cristobal Nonato) 1987, Ruben Dario Prize 1988, IUA Prize (for The Old Gringo) 1989, and numerous other awards; Hon. Dr. (Harvard, Wesleyan, Essex, Cambridge); Order of Merit, Chile 1992, Légion d'honneur 1992; Hon. Citizen of Santiago de Chile 1993, Buenos Aires 1993, Veracruz 1993. *Publications:* Los días enmascarados 1954, La región más transparente 1958, Las buenas conciencias 1959, Aura 1962, La muerte de Artemio Cruz 1962, Cantar de ciegos 1965, Zona sagrada 1967, Cambio de piel (Biblioteca Breve Prize 1967), Paris, La Revolución de Mayo 1968, La Nueva Novela Hispanoamericana 1969, Cumpleaños 1969, Le Borgne est Roi 1970, Casa con Dos Puertas 1970, Todos los gatos son pardos 1970, Tiempo Mexicano 1971, Don Quixote or the Critique of Reading 1974, Terra Nostra 1975, La Cabeza de la Hidra 1978, Orchids in the Moonlight (play) 1982, The Old Gringo 1985, The Good Conscience 1987, Cristóbal Nonato (novel) 1987, Myself With Others (Essays) 1988, Christopher Unborn 1989, Constancia and Stories for Virgins 1991, The Campaign (novel) 1991, The Buried Mirror (essays, also TV series) 1992, Geography of the Novel (essays) 1993, El Naranjo (novellas) 1993, Diana: The Goddess Who Hunts Alone 1995, The Crystal Frontier 1995, A New Time for Mexico 1997, Por un Progreso Incluyente 1997. *Address:* c/o Brandt & Brandt, 1501 Broadway, New York, NY 10036; 401 Boylston Hall, Harvard Univ., Cambridge, MA 02138, U.S.A. *Telephone:* (617) 495-2543.

FUGARD, Athol; South African actor and playwright; b. 11 June 1932; s. of Harold David Fugard and Elizabeth Magdelene Potgiefer; m. Sheila Fugard 1956; one d.; leading role in Meetings with Remarkable Men (film) 1977, The Guest (BBC production) 1977; acted in and wrote script for Marigolds in August (film); winner Silver Bear Award, Berlin Film Festival 1980, New York Critics Award for A Lesson From Aloes 1981, London Evening Standard Award for Master Harold and the Boys 1983, Commonwealth Award for Contribution to American Theatre 1984; Hon. D.Lit. (Natal and Rhodes Univs.), Dr. h.c. (Univ. of Cape Town, Georgetown Univ., Washington, D.C.). *Plays:* The Blood Knot, Hello and Goodbye, People are Living Here, Boesman and Lena 1970, Sizwe Banzi is Dead 1973, The Island 1973, Statements after an Arrest under the Immorality Act 1974, No Good Friday 1974, Nongogo 1974, Dimetos 1976, The Road to Mecca 1984, My Children, My Africa; The Guest (film script) 1977, A Lesson from Aloes 1979 (author and dir. Broadway production 1980), Master Harold and the Boys 1981, A Place with the Pigs (acted and dir.) 1988, Playland 1992, Sign of Hope 1992, Valley Song (actor and dir.) 1996, The Captain's Tiger 1999; *film:* Marigolds in August 1981, The Guest 1984; acted in films Gandhi 1982, Road to Mecca 1991 (also Co-dir.); Hon. D.F.A. (Yale Univ.) 1973, Dr. h.c. (New York, Pennsylvania, City Univ. of New York). *Publications:* Notebooks 1960–77, Playland 1992; novel: Tsotsi 1980; plays: Road to Mecca 1985, A Place with the Pigs 1988, Cousins: A Memoir 1994. *Address:* P.O. Box 5090, Walmer, Port Elizabeth 6065, South Africa.

FUHRMAN, Robert Alexander, M.S.E., F.R.AE.S.; American business executive and aerospace engineer b. 23 Feb. 1925, Detroit, Mich.; s. of Alexander A. Fuhrman and Elva Brown Fuhrman; m. 1st Nan E. McCormick 1949 (died 1988); two s. one d.; m. 2nd Nancy Ferguson Richards 1989; ed. Univs. of Michigan and Maryland, Stanford Univ. Grad. School of Business; Vice-Pres. and Gen. Man. Missiles Systems Div., Lockheed Corpn. 1966–70, Pres. Georgia Co. 1970–71, Pres. California Co. 1971–74, Pres. Missiles & Space Co. 1976–83, Group Pres. Missiles Space & Electronics 1983–85, Pres. and C.O.O. Lockheed Corpn. 1985–88, Vice-Chair. and C.O.O. 1988–90, Sr. Adviser 1990–; Chair. Bd. Bank of the West 1990–, U.S. Air Force Science and Tech. Bd. 1996–; mem. Bd. Charles Stark Draper Lab. 1986–, Burdeshaw Assoc. Ltd. 1994–; mem. Defense Science Bd.; mem. Nat. Acad. of Eng.; Hon. Fellow A.I.A.A., Pres. 1992–93; Mich. Aviation Hall of Fame 1991. *Publications:* The Fleet Ballistic Weapon System: Polaris to Trident (A.I.A.A. Von Karman Lecture) 1976, Defense Science Bd. Task Force Report: The Defense Industrial Base (Chair.) 1988, The C-17 Review (Chair.) 1993. *Leisure interest:* golf. *Address:* P.O. Box 9, 1543 Riata Road, Pebble Beach, CA 93953, U.S.A. *Telephone:* (408) 625-2125. *Fax:* (408) 625-2393.

FUHRMANN, Horst, D.PHIL.; German historian; b. 22 June 1926, Kreuzburg; s. of Karl and Susanna Fuhrmann; m. Dr. Ingrid Winkler-Lippoldt 1954; one s. one d.; collaborator, Monumenta Germaniae Historica 1954–56; Asst., Rome 1957; Asst. and lecturer 1957–62; Prof. Univ. of Tübingen 1962–71; Pres. Monumenta Germaniae Historica, Munich and Prof. Univ. of Regensburg 1971–94; Pres. Bavarian Acad. of Humanities and Science 1992–; Dr.Iur. h.c. (Tübingen); D.Phil. h.c. (Bologna, Columbia, New York); Premio Spoleto 1962, Cultore di Roma 1981, Upper Silesian Culture Prize 1989, Premio Ascoli Piceno 1990; Orden Pour le mérite; Grosses Bundesverdienstkreuz mit Stern, Bayerischer Verdienstorden. *Publications:* The Donation of Constantine 1968, Influence and Circulation of the Pseudoisidorian Forgeries (3 vols.) 1972–74, Germany in the High Middle Ages 1978, From Petrus to John Paul II: The Papacy 1980, Invitation to the Middle Ages 1987, Far from Cultured People: An Upper Silesian Town around 1870 1989, Pour le Mérite: On Making Merit Visible 1992, Scholarly Lives 1996, Überall ist Mittelalter 1996. *Address:* Bayerische Akademie der Wissenschaften, Marstallplatz 8, 80539 Munich (Office); Sonnenwinkel 10, 82237 Wörthsee, Germany (Home). *Telephone:* 089/23 031-135 (Office). *Fax:* 089/ 23 031 100.

FUJII, Hirohisa; Japanese politician; mem. House of Reps., Chair. Finance Cttee.; fmr. mem. House of Councillors, Chair. Finance Cttee.; Parl. Vice-Minister of Finance; Minister of Finance 1993–94; mem. Japan Renewal Party (Shinseito) (JRP). *Address:* House of Representatives, Tokyo, Japan.

FUJIMORI, Alberto Kenyo; Peruvian politician and academic; b. 1939, Lima; s. of late Nagochi Minami and Matsue Inomoto; m. Susana Higushi (divorced 1996); two s. two d.; ed. Nat. School of Agric.; fmr. Rector, Nat. Agrarian Univ.; Pres. Nat. Ass. of Rectors 1984–89; founder-mem. Cambio '90 (political party); Pres. of Peru 1990–. *Address:* Office of the President, Lima, Peru.

FUJIMORI, Masamichi; Japanese executive; b. 22 Dec. 1921, Osaka; s. of Tatsumaro Fujimori and Kimiko Ono; m. Yoko Sato 1951; two d.; ed. Tokyo Imperial Univ.; lecturer, First Faculty of Tech., Tokyo Univ. 1948; joined Sumitomo Metal Mining Co. Ltd. 1950, Gen. Man. Metallurgy Dept. 1971, Dir. 1972, Man. Dir. 1977, Sr. Man. Dir. 1979, Exec. Vice-Pres. 1981, Pres. 1983–88, Chair. 1988–92, Adviser 1992–; Pres. Japan Mining Industry Assen. 1987–88; Exec. Dir. Fed. of Econ. Orgs. 1988–92; Hon. Fellow Inst. of Mining and Metallurgy 1985; Blue Ribbon Medal 1982; Order of the Sacred Treasure (First Class) 1995. *Leisure interest:* bonsai. *Address:* Sumitomo Metal Mining Co. Ltd., 5-11-3, Shimbashi, Minato-ku, Tokyo, Japan (Office). *Telephone:* 03-3436-7744 (Office).

FUJIMOTO, Takao; Japanese politician; b. 1931, Kagawa Pref.; m.; one s.; ed. Faculty of Law, Tokyo Univ.; joined Nomura Securities Co. Ltd. 1944; joined Nippon Telegraph and Telephone Public Corpn. 1957; elected House of Reps. for 1st constituency Kagawa Pref. 1963; Parl. Vice-Minister of Science and Tech. Agency 1970; Chair. Liberal Democratic Party (LDP) Science and Tech. Sub-Cttee. of the Policy Research Cttee. 1972; Parl. Vice-Minister of the Environment Agency 1973; Chair. Standing Cttee. on Foreign Affairs 1976, LDP Standing Cttee. on Public Information 1983; Minister of State, Dir.-Gen. Okinawa Devt. Agency 1985; Deputy Sec.-Gen. LDP 1985–86; Minister of Health and Welfare 1987–88, of Agric., Forestry and Fisheries 1996–98. *Leisure interests:* sports (baseball), reading, golf, karaoke singing. *Address:* c/o Liberal-Democratic Party, 1-11-23 Nagata-cho, Chiyoda-ku, Tokyo 100, Japan.

FUJINAMI, Takao; Japanese politician; b. 3 Dec. 1932; ed. Waseda Univ.; mem. House of Reps. 1967–94, (mem. Cttee. on Audit 1990–93); Parl. Vice-Minister for Science and Tech. 1972, for Educ. 1973; Minister of Labour 1979–80; Chair. Educational Affairs Div. 1975 and Vice-Chair. Policy Affairs Research Council 1978; Minister of State and Chief Cabinet Sec. 1983–85; mem. Liberal Democratic Party. *Address:* c/o Liberal-Democratic Party, 1-11-23, Nagata-cho, Chiyoda-ku, Tokyo 100, Japan.

FUJIOKA, Masao; Japanese banker; b. 31 Oct. 1924, Tokyo; m.; two s. one d.; ed. Tokyo Univ. and Univ. of Chicago; Economist, IMF 1960–64; Dir. of Short-Term Capital Div. of Int. Finance Bureau, Ministry of Finance 1964–66; took part in preparatory work at ECAFE to establish Asian Devt. Bank (ADB) 1966; Dir. Admin. Dept., ADB 1966–69; Dir. Co-ordination Dept., Overseas Econ. Co-operation Fund 1969; Deputy Dir.-Gen. Int. Finance Bureau, Ministry of Finance 1970–75, Dir.-Gen. 1975–77; Exec. Dir., Export-Import Bank of Japan 1977–81; Adviser to Minister of Finance 1981; Chair. and Pres. Asian Devt. Bank ADB 1981–89; founder Asian Pacific Bankers' Club 1980. *Publications:* Government Loans and Investment 1957, Income Doubling Plan of Japan 1963, Evolving International Finance 1975, New IMF (ed.) 1976, Growing International Finance 1977, Japan's International Finance—Today and Tomorrow 1979; numerous articles and reports on int. finance and econ. co-operation.

FUJITA, Akira; Japanese financial executive; b. 9 Dec. 1929; ed. Tokyo Univ.; fmr. Man. Dir. The Daiwa Bank Ltd., fmr. Pres.; now Counsellor. *Leisure interests:* reading, sport. *Address:* Daiwa Bank Ltd., 21 Bingomachi 2-chome, Higashi-ku, Osaka 541, Japan.

FUJITA, Hiroyuki, M.E., PH.D.; Japanese university professor; b. 13 Dec. 1952, Tokyo; s. of Shigeru Fujita and Tokiko Fujita; m. Yumiko Kato 1982; ed. Univ. of Tokyo; lecturer, Inst. of Industrial Science, Univ. of Tokyo 1980–81, Assoc. Prof. 1981–93, Prof. 1993–; Visiting Scientist, Francis Bitter Nat. Magnet Lab. Mass. Inst. of Tech. (MIT) 1983–85; M. Hetényi Award for Experimental Mechanics 1987. *Publications:* contribs. to books and numerous scientific papers in professional journals. *Leisure interests:* reading, skiing, tennis. *Address:* Institute of Industrial Science, 7-22-1 Roppongi, Minato-ku, Tokyo 106; 1-9-14 Senkawa, Toshima-ku, Tokyo 171, Japan (Home). *Telephone:* 81-3-3402-6231 ext. 2353 (Office).

FUJITA, Yoshio, DR.SC.; Japanese astronomer; b. 28 Sept. 1908, Fukui City; s. of Teizo Fujita; m. Kazuko Nezu 1941; two s. one d.; ed. Tokyo Univ.; Asst. Prof. Univ. of Tokyo 1931, Prof. 1951–69, Emer. Prof. 1969–; Visiting Prof. Pa. State Univ. 1971; Guest Investigator Dominion Astrophysical Observatory 1960, Mount Wilson and Palomar Observatories 1972, 1974; mem. Japan Acad. 1965–, Pres. 1994–; Foreign mem. Royal Soc. of Sciences, Liège 1969–; Imperial Prize, Japan Acad. 1955, Cultural Merit Award, Fukui City 1971, Hon. Citizen, Fukui City 1979, Cultural Merit Award 1996. *Publication:* Interpretation of Spectra and Atmospheric Structure in Cool Stars 1970. *Address:* 6-21-7 Renkoji, Tama-shi 206, Japan. *Telephone:* (0423) 74-4186.

FUKAYA, Takashi; Japanese politician; fmr. Minister of Posts and Telecommunications; fmr. Parl. Vice-Minister of Labour; mem. House of Reps., fmr. Chair. Cttee. on Communications; Minister of Home Affairs 1995–96. *Address:* c/o Ministry of Home Affairs, 2-1-2, Kasumigaseki, Chiyoda-ku, Tokyo 100, Japan.

FUKUKAWA, Shinji; Japanese business executive; b. 8 March 1932, Tokyo; s. of Tokushiro Fukukawa and Maki Fukukawa; m. Yoriko Kawada 1961; two d.; ed. Univ. of Tokyo; served at Ministry of Int. Trade and Industry (MITI) 1955–88, Deputy Vice-Minister 1983–84, Dir.-Gen. Industrial Policy Bureau 1984–86, Vice-Minister 1986–88; Pvt. Sec. to fmr. Prime Minister Ohira 1978–80; Sr. Adviser to MITI 1988–90, to Japan Industrial Policy Research Inst. 1988–90, to Global Industrial and Social Progress Research Inst. 1988–, to Nomura Research Inst. 1989–90; Exec. Vice-Pres. Kobe Steel Ltd. 1990–94; Chair. and C.E.O., Dentsu Inst. for Human Studies 1994–. *Publication:* Japan's Role in the 21st Century: Three Newisms 1990. *Leisure interests:* tennis, golf, classical music, reading. *Address:* Dentsu Isntitute for Human Studies, 7-4-17, Ginza, Chuo-ku, Tokyo 104 (Office); 7-11, Okusawa 8-chome, Setagaya-ku, Tokyo 158, Japan (Home). *Telephone:* (03) 3575-1711 (Office); (03) 3701-4956 (Home).

FUKUYAMA, Francis, PH.D.; American writer and social scientist; b. New York; ed. Cornell and Harvard Univs.; fmrly. a sr. social scientist, RAND Corpn., Washington, D.C. and Deputy Dir. State Dept.'s Policy Planning Staff; Hirst Prof. of Public Policy, George Mason Univ., Fairfax, Va. *Publications:* The End of History and the Last Man 1992, Trust: The Social Virtues And the Creation of Prosperity 1996. *Address:* George Mason University, Fairfax, VA 22030, U.S.A.

FULCI, Francesco Paolo, LL.D., M.C.L.; Italian diplomatist; b. 19 March 1931, Messina; s. of Sebastiano Fulci and Enza Sciascia; m. Claris Glathar 1965; three c.; ed. Messina Univ., Columbia Univ., New York, Coll. of Europe, Bruges, and Acad. Int. Law, The Hague; entered Italian Foreign Service 1956; First Vice-Consul of Italy, New York 1958–61; Second Sec. Italian Embassy, Moscow 1961–63; Foreign Ministry, Rome 1963–68; Counsellor Italian Embassy, Paris 1968–74, Minister Italian Embassy, Tokyo 1974–76; Chief of Cabinet Pres. of Senate, Rome 1976–80; Amb. to Canada 1980–85; Amb. and Perm. Rep. to NATO, Brussels 1985–91; Sec.-Gen. Exec. Comm. of Information and Security Services, Rome 1991–93; Amb. and Perm. Rep. to UN, New York 1993–; Hon. LL.D. (Windsor Univ., Ont.); Cross of Merit (Fed. Repub. of Germany); Officier, Légion d'honneur (France); Commdr. Imperial Order of the Sun (Japan); Great Cross, Order of Merit (Italy); Kt. Order of Malta. *Leisure interest:* swimming. *Address:* 2 United Nations Plaza, 24th Floor, New York, NY 10017, U.S.A.

FULLER, Arthur Orpen, PH.D., F.R.S.S.A.; South African geologist; b. 28 Aug. 1926, Cape Town; s. of Thomas Arthur Fuller and Doris Erpingham Orpen; m. Anne Jane Low 1954; two d.; ed. Univ. of Cape Town and Princeton Univ.; geologist Union Corpn. Ltd. 1949–53; Assoc. Prof., Univ. of Cape Town 1957–88, Head of Geology and Mineralogy Dept. 1983–89, Emer. Assoc. Prof. 1989; N.S.F. Sr. Fellowship, Mich. Tech. Univ. 1970–71; NASA Consultant 1980; Pres. Geological Soc. of S.A. 1985. *Publications:* numerous articles in int. journals, including Nature and Econ. Geology. *Leisure interests:* music, golf, rock angling. *Address:* c/o Department of Mineralogy and Geology, University of Cape Town, Rondebosch C.P. 7700, South Africa.

FULLER, Lawrence Robert, B.J.; American newspaper publisher; b. 9 Sept. 1941, Toledo; s. of Kenneth Fuller and Marjory Rairdon; m. Suzanne Hovik 1967; one s. one d.; ed. Univ. of Missouri; reporter, Globe Gazette, Mason City, Ia. 1963–67; reporter, later city ed. Minneapolis Star 1967–75; Exec. Ed. Messenger-Inquirer, Owensborough, Ky. 1975–77; Exec. Ed. Argus Leader, Sioux Falls, S.D. 1977–78, Pres., Publr. 1974–84, 1986–; Pres. Gannett News Media, Washington 1984–85; Dir. Corp. Communications, Gannett Co. Inc. Washington 1985–86; Vice-Pres. Gannett/West Regional Newspaper Group 1986–, The Honolulu Advertisers 1986–; several directorships; mem. American Newspaper Publishers' Asscn., American Soc. of Newspaper Eds. etc. *Address:* 605 Kapiolani Boulevard, Honolulu, HI 96813, U.S.A.

FULLERTON, R. Donald, B.A.; Canadian banker; b. 7 June 1931, Vancouver, B.C.; s. of late C. G. and late Muriel E. Fullerton; m.; ed. Univ. of Toronto; joined Canadian Bank of Commerce (now CIBC), Vancouver 1953; Agent, New York 1964; Regional Gen. Man., Regina 1966; Regional Gen. Man., Int. 1967; Deputy Chief Gen. Man. 1971; Exec. Vice-Pres. and Chief Gen. Man. 1973; Dir. CIBC 1974–, Pres. and Chief Operating Officer 1976–80, Vice-Chair. and Pres. 1980–84, Pres. and C.E.O. 1984–85, Chair. and C.E.O. 1985–92, Chair. Exec. Cttee. 1992–; Dir. Asiasat, CIBC, Geo. Westons Ltd., Hollinger Inc., Honeywell Inc., Orange PLC, Westcoast Energy Inc.; mem. advisory bd. IBM (Canada) Ltd.; mem. Bd. of Govs. Corpn. of Massey Hall and Roy Thomson Hall; Hon. Gov. Nat. Ballet Co. of Canada. *Address:* c/o CIBC, Head Office, Commerce Court W., Toronto, Ont., M5L 1A2, Canada.

FULLERTON, William Hugh, C.M.G., M.A.; British diplomatist; b. 11 Feb. 1939, Wolverhampton; s. of late Major A.H.T.F. Fullerton and of M. Fullerton (née Parker); m. Arlene Jacobowitz 1968; one d.; ed. Cheltenham Coll. and Queens' Coll., Cambridge; Shell Int. Petroleum Co. Uganda 1963–65; Foreign Office 1965; MECAS, Shemlan, Lebanon 1965–66; Information Officer, Jeddah 1966–67; U.K. Perm. Mission to UN, New York 1967; FCO 1968–70; Head of Chancery, High Comm., Jamaica (also accred. to Haiti) 1970–73, Embassy, Ankara 1973–77; FCO 1977–80; Counsellor, Islamabad 1980–83; Head of Chancery, Consul Gen. 1981–83; Amb. to Somalia 1983–87; on loan to Ministry of Defence 1987–88; Gov. Falkland Islands, Commr. for S. Georgia and S. Sandwich Islands 1988–92, concurrently High Commr., British Antarctic Territory 1988–89; Amb. to Kuwait 1992–96, to Morocco and Mauritania 1996–99; Kuwait Medallion (First Class) 1995. *Leisure interests:* travelling in remote places, reading, sailing, music. *Address:* c/o Foreign and Commonwealth Office, Heads of Mission Section, King Charles Street, London, SW1A 2AH, England.

FUMAROLI, Marc; French professor of rhetoric; b. 10 June 1932, Marseilles; Prof. Sorbonne, Paris; Ed.-in-Chief Commentaire 1978–; Titular Prof. Chair. of Rhetoric and European Soc. of 16th and 17th Centuries, Collège de France 1986–; Prof. Univ. of Chicago 1996–; Ed.-in-Chief Commentaire 1978–; Dir. XVIIe siècle (journal) 1981–88; mem. Advisory Council, Bibliothèque Nationale 1988–92; fmr. Pres. Soc. Int. d'Histoire de la Rhétorique; Pres. Soc. of Friends of the Louvre 1996; mem. Acad. Française 1995–; other appointments; Chevalier Légion d'honneur, des Palmes académiques, Officier Ordre nat. du Mérite, Cmmdr. des Arts et des Lettres. *Publications include:* L'Age de l'éloquence 1980, La Diplomatie de l'esprit 1994, L'école du silence 1994, Trois institutions Littéraires 1994, la Période 1600–1630 1994, Fables de Jean de la Fontaine (Ed., Vol I 1985, Vol. II 1995), Le Poète et le roi, Jean de La Fontaine et son siècle 1997, numerous articles in professional journals; numerous pamphlets, essays and articles. *Address:* Collège de France, 52 rue du Cardinal Lemoine, 75231 Paris cedex 05 (Office); 11 rue de l'Université, 75007 Paris, France (Home).

FUNADA, Hajime; Japanese politician; b. 22 Nov. 1953, Utsunomiya City, Tochigi Pref.; s. of Yuzuru Funada and Masako Funada; m. Rumi Funada 1978; one s. two d.; ed. Keio Univ.; mem. House of Reps. from Tochigi 1979–; Head, Youth Section of Nat. Organizing Cttee., LDP 1985–86; State Sec. for Man. and Co-ordination Agency 1986–87, for Ministry of Educ. 1987–88; Dir. Educ. Div. of Policy Research Council, LDP 1988–89; Dir. Foreign Affairs Div. 1990–92; Chair. Sub-Cttee. of Counselling Japan Overseas Co-operation Volunteers 1989–90; Minister of State for Econ. Planning 1992–93; co-founder of Japan Renewal Party (Shinseito) 1993, Deputy Sec. Gen. for Organizational Affairs 1993–94, Deputy Sec. Gen. for Political Affairs 1994; Vice-Chair. Diet Man. Cttee., 'Reform' In-House Grouping (Kaikaku) 1994; co-founder New Frontier Party (Shinshinto) 1994, Vice-Chair. Org. Cttee. 1994–95, Deputy Sec. Gen. 1995, Assoc. Chair. Gen. Council 1995–96, resgnd. from Party 1996; Head of '21st Century' In-House Grouping (21seiki) 1996; rejoined Liberal Democratic Party Jan. 1997, Chair. Sub-Cttee. on Asia and the Pacific, mem. Policy Deliberation Comm., mem. Gen. Council 1997–; mem. Ruling Parties Consultative Cttee. on Guidelines for Japan—U.S. Defence Co-operation 1997–; Dir. Cttee. on Health and Welfare, House of Reps. 1998–. *Leisure interests:* astronomy, driving. *Address:* Shugiin Daini Giinkaikan, Room 412, 2-1-2 Nagata-cho, Chiyoda-ku, Tokyo 100, Japan. *Telephone:* (3) 3508-7412. *Fax:* (3) 3500-5612.

FUNAHASHI, Masao; Japanese business executive; b. 3 May 1913, Aichi Pref.; s. of Azuma and Suzu Funahashi; m. Keiko Matsubara 1946; one s. one d.; ed. Tokyo Univ.; Man. Purchasing Dept., Furukawa Electric Co. Ltd. 1959, of Finance and Accounting Dept. 1961, Man. Dir. 1968, Exec. Dir. 1971, Vice-Pres. 1973, Pres. 1974–83, Chair. 1983–89; Chair. Japan-Jordan Friendship Asscn. 1981–, Japan-Somalia Friendship Asscn. 1983–. *Leisure interest:* golf. *Address:* c/o Furukawa Electric Co. Ltd., 6-1, Marunouchi 2-chome, Chiyoda-ku, Tokyo, Japan.

FUNCKE, Liselotte; German politician; b. 20 July 1918, Hagen; d. of Oscar Funcke and Bertha (née Osthaus) Funcke; ed. commercial studies in Berlin; fmrly. in industry and commerce, Hagen and Wuppertal; mem. Diet of North Rhine-Westphalia 1950–61; mem. Bundestag 1961–79, Vice-Pres. Bundestag 1969–79; Chair. Bundestag Finance Cttee. 1972–79; mem. Presidium, FDP 1968–82, Deputy Chair. FDP 1977–82; Minister of Economy and Transport, North Rhine-Westphalia 1979–80; Govt. Rep. responsible for integration of overseas workers and their families 1981–91; Bundesverdienstkreuz (1973) and other medals. *Address:* Ruhr-Str. 15, 58097 Hagen, Germany (Home). *Telephone:* (02331) 182034.

FUNG, Victor K.; Chinese businessman; Chair., C.E.O. Prudential Asia Investments Ltd.; Chair. Hong Kong Trade Devt. Council Sept. 1991–. *Address:* Hong Kong Trade Development Council, 39th Floor, Office Tower, Convention Plaza, 38F, 1 Harbour Road, Wanchai, Hong Kong Special Administrative Region, People's Republic of China.

FUNKE, Karl-Heinz; German politician; b. 29 April 1946, Dangast; m. Petra Timm 1982; three c.; ed. Hamburg Univ.; apprenticeship in admin. 1960–63; joined Social Democratic Party of Germany (SPD) 1966; mil. service 1966–68; dist. councillor Friesland 1972–, also city councillor Varel; worked at Varel vocational school and on family farm 1974, took over family farm 1983; mem. Lower Saxony Landtag 1978–; Mayor of Varel 1981–96; Minister of Food, Agric. and Forestry Lower Saxony 1990–98; Fed. Minister of Food, Agric. and Forestry 1998–. *Leisure interests:* literature, history, hunting. *Address:* Ministry of Food, Agriculture and Forestry, Rochusstrasse 1, 53123 Bonn; Calenberger Strasse 2, 30169 Hannover, Germany. *Telephone:* (228) 5290 (Bonn). *Fax:* (228) 529-42-62 (Bonn).

FURCHGOTT, Robert Francis, PH.D.; American professor of pharmacology b. 4 June 1916, Charleston, S.C.; m. 1941; three c.; ed. Univ. of N. Carolina, Northwestern Univ.; Research Fellow in Medicine, Medical Coll., Cornell Univ. 1940–43, Research Assoc. 1943–47, instructor in Physiology 1943–48, Asst. Prof. of Medical Biochemistry 1947–49; Asst. Prof., later Assoc. Prof. of Pharmacology, Medical School, Wash. Univ. 1949–56; Chair. of Dept., S.U.N.Y. Health Sciences Center, Brooklyn 1956–83; Prof. of Health Sciences Center, Brooklyn State Univ. 1956–88, Univ. Distinguished Prof. 1988–, Emer. Prof. of Pharmacology 1990–; Visiting Prof. Univ. of Geneva 1962–63, Univ of Calif., San Diego 1971–72, Medical Univ. of S.C. 1980, Univ. of Calif. 1980; Adjunct Prof. of Pharmacology, School of Medicine, Univ. of Miami 1989–; Hon. D.M. (Madrid) 1984, (Lund) 1984; Hon. D.Sc. (N.C.) 1989, (Ghent) 1995; mem. A.A.A.S., N.A.S., American Chem. Soc., American Soc. Biochemistry, American Soc. Pharmacology and Experimental Therapeutics (Pres. 1971–72); Goodman and Gilman Award 1984, Research Achievement Award, American Heart Asscn. 1990, Bristol-Myers Squibb Award for achievement in cardiovascular research 1991, Gairdner Fund Int. Award 1991, Roussel Uclaf Prize for research in cell communication and signalling 1994, ASPET Award for Experimental Therapeutics 1996, jt. winner Nobel Prize for Medicine 1998; Medal of N.Y. Acad. of Medicine 1992, Wellcome Gold Medal, British Pharmacology Soc. 1995. *Address:* State University of New York Health Sciences Center, Brooklyn, NY 11203, U.S.A.

FÜRER, Arthur Carl Othmar, D.IUR., D.ECON.; Swiss business executive and lawyer; b. 18 Dec. 1920, Gossau; s. of Carl and Clara Fürer (née Staub); m. Bea Hofer 1951; one s.; ed. Gymnasium Feldkirch, Austria, Univs. of Fribourg, Berne and St.-Gall; practised as attorney in St.-Gall 1944–46; joined Société pour le Développement de l'Economie Suisse, Zürich 1946–47; Legal Adviser and Man. Sec. to Georg Fischer AG, Schaffhausen 1947–54; with Nestlé Alimentana S.A. (now Nestlé S.A.), Vevey 1954–84, Gen. Man. 1969, Man. Dir. 1975–82, Chair. 1982–84; Chair. Bank Leu AG, Zürich 1984–88; Dr. h.c. (Universidad Autónoma de Guadalajara, Mexico). *Address:* Chemin des Roches, 1803 Chardonne, Switzerland (Home). *Telephone:* (021) 921-47-94 (Home).

FURGLER, Kurt, DR.IUR.; Swiss politician and lawyer; b. 24 June 1924, St.-Gall; m. Ursula Stauffenegger; two s. four d.; ed. Univs. of Fribourg, Zürich, Geneva, Grad. Inst. for Int. Studies, Geneva; Lawyer, St.-Gall 1950–71; mem. Nat. Council 1955–71; Leader of Christian Dem. Party Group in Fed. Council; mem. Fed. Council Jan. 1972–, Vice-Pres. Jan.–Dec. 1976, Jan.–Dec. 1980, Jan.–Dec. 1984, Pres. of the Swiss Fed. Jan.–Dec. 1977, Jan.–Dec. 1981, Jan.–Dec. 1985; Head of Fed. Dept. of Justice and Police 1972–83, of Dept. of Public Economy 1983–86; Hon. D.Jur. (Boston Univ.) 1985. *Leisure interests:* sport, music, literature. *Address:* Dufourstr. 34, 9000 St.-Gall, Switzerland.

FURLAUD, Richard Mortimer, LL.B.; American finance executive; b. 15 April 1923, New York; s. of Maxime Furlaud and Eleanor Mortimer; m. Isabel Phelps Furlaud; one s. two d. from fmr. marriage; ed. Inst. Sillig, Villars, Switzerland and Princeton and Harvard Univs.; admitted New York Bar 1949; Assoc. Root, Ballantine, Harlan, Bushby & Palmers 1947–51; legal dept. Olin Mathieson Chem. Corpn. 1955–56, Asst. to Exec. Vice-Pres. for Finance 1956–57, Asst. Pres. 1957–59, Vice-Pres. 1959–64, Gen. Counsel 1957–60, Gen. Man., Vice-Pres. Int. Div. 1960–64, Exec. Vice-Pres. 1964–66, Dir. 1964–94; Pres., Dir. E.R. Squibb & Sons Inc. 1966–68; Pres., Chief Exec., Dir. Squibb Beech-Nut Inc. (renamed Squibb Corpn. 1971), Princeton, NJ 1968–74; Chair., Chief Exec., Dir. Squibb Corpn. (merged with Bristol-Myers Co.), New York 1974–89; Pres. Bristol-Myers Co. (renamed Bristol-Myers Squibb Co.) New York 1989–93, also mem. Bd. of Dirs. 1989–91; other directorships and professional appts. *Address:* 35 E. Dune Lane, Box 478, East Hampton, NY 11937, U.S.A. (Home).

FURNO, H. E. Cardinal Carlo, PH.D.; Italian ecclesiastic; b. 2 Dec. 1921, Bairo Canavese; Sec. to Nunciature to Colombia 1953–57, to Ecuador 1957–60; Sec. Apostolic Del. to Jerusalem 1960–62; Sec. of State 1962–73; Apostolic Nuncio to Peru 1973–78, to Lebanon 1978–82, to Brazil 1982–92, to Italy 1992–94; Grand Master Equestrian Order of the Sacred Sepulchre of Jerusalem 1995–; Papal Del. to Basilica of St. Francis of Assisi 1996–. *Address:* Piazza Della Citta Leonina, 1-00193 Rome, Italy. *Telephone:* 6988-2053. *Fax:* 6980-2298.

FURSENKO, Aleksander Aleksandrovich; Russian historian; b. 11 Nov. 1927; s. of Alexander Vasilievich Fursenko and Vanda Vladislavovna Fursenko (née Rokitskaya); m. Natalia L'vovna Fursenko (Gol'dina) 1948; two s.; ed. Leningrad State Univ.; researcher Leningrad br. of Inst. of History U.S.S.R. Acad. of Sciences; fmr. First Deputy Chair. Presidium Scientific Cen. Acad. of Sciences; corresp. mem. U.S.S.R. (now Russian) Acad. of Sciences 1987, mem. 1990, Acad.-Sec. Dept. of History 1996–; with St. Petersburg Inst. of History; research in history of U.S.A., econ. history, int. relations. *Publications include:* Struggle for the Partition of China and the American Open Doors Doctrine 1956, Oil Trusts and World Politics 1880–1918 1965, Rockefellers' Dynasty 1970, American Revolution and Formation of U.S.A. 1978, The Battle for Oil: The Economics and Politics of International Corporate Conflict over Petroleum 1990, One Hell of a Gamble: Khrushchev, Kennedy and Castro 1958–64 (with Timothy Naftali) 1997. *Leisure interests:* mountain skiing. *Address:* 32a Leninskiy prospekt, Presidium of Academy of Sciences, Department of History, 117993 Moscow; 7 Petrozavodskaya ul., Institute of History, 197110 St. Petersburg, Russia. *Telephone:* (095) 938-1763 (Moscow); (812) 230-6850, (812) 235-4198 (St. Petersburg). *Fax:* (095) 938-1844 (Moscow); (812) 235-6485 (St. Petersburg).

FÜRST, Janos Kalman; British orchestral conductor; b. 8 Aug. 1935, Budapest, Hungary; s. of Lajos Fürst and Borbala Spitz; m. 1st Antoinette Reynolds 1962 (divorced 1977); two s.; m. 2nd Ingeborg Nordenfelt; ed. Franz Liszt Acad. of Music, Budapest and Brussels Conservatory; Dir. Irish Chamber Orchestra 1963–66; Resident Conductor Ulster Orchestra 1967–71; Chief Conductor Malmö Symphony Orchestra 1974–78; Music Dir. Marseilles Opera 1981–; Music Dir. Aalborg Symphony Orchestra 1980–83; Dir. Marseilles Philharmonic Orchestra 1985–; Chief Conductor Irish Radio and TV Symphony Orchestra 1987–; Swedish Gramophone Prize 1980. *Leisure interests:* reading and history.

FURTH, Harold Paul, PH.D.; American physicist; b. 13 Jan. 1930, Vienna, Austria; s. of Otto Furth and Gertrude (Harteck) Furth; m. Alice M. Lander 1959 (divorced 1977); one s.; ed. Hill School, Harvard and Cornell Univs.; physicist, Univ. of Calif. Lawrence Radiation Lab., Livermore 1956–65, Group Leader 1965–67; Prof. of Astrophysical Sciences, Princeton Univ. 1967–, Co-Head, Experimental Div., Plasma Physics Lab. 1967–78, Assoc. Dir. and Head, Research Dept. Plasma Physics Lab. 1978–80, Program Dir. Plasma Physics Lab. 1980–81, Dir. Plasma Physics Lab. 1981–90; mem. N.A.S.; Delmer S. Fahrney Medal (Franklin Inst.) 1992, and several awards. *Address:* Princeton Plasma Physics Laboratory, P.O. Box 451, Princeton, NJ 08543 (Office); 36 Lake Lane, Princeton, NJ 08540, U.S.A. (Home). *Telephone:* (609) 283-3555 (Office).

FURTH, Warren Wolfgang, A.B., J.D.; American international official, consultant and fmr. lawyer; b. 1 Aug. 1928, Vienna, Austria; s. of John W. Furth and Hedwig von Ferstel; m. Margaretha F. de la Court 1959; one s. one d.; ed. Harvard Coll., and Harvard Law School; Law Clerk, Palmer, Dodge, Gardner, Bickford & Bradford, Boston, Mass. 1951; admitted to New York Bar 1952; Law Clerk to Hon. H.M. Stephens, Chief Judge, U.S. Court of Appeals, Dist. of Columbia Circuit 1952–53; U.S. Army 1953–57; Assoc. Cravath, Swaine & Moore (law firm) 1957–58; with ILO, Geneva 1959–70, Exec. Asst. to Dir.-Gen. 1964–66, Chief of Tech. Co-operation Branch and Deputy Chief, Field Dept. 1966–68, Deputy Chief, later Chief, Personnel and Admin. Services Dept. 1968–70; Asst. Dir.-Gen. WHO (Admin. Services; Co-ordinator, Special Programme for Research & Training in Tropical Diseases and responsibility for Special Programme for Research, Devt. and Research Training in Human Reproduction) 1971–89; int. health consultant to U.S. Govt., EBRD and pharmaceutical industry 1989–94; Assoc. Exec. Dir. American Citizens Abroad 1994–. *Address:* 13 route de Presinge, 1241 Puplinge (Geneva), Switzerland (Home). *Telephone:* (022) 3497267.

FUSSELL, Paul, M.A., PH.D.; American author and university professor; b. 22 March 1924, Pasadena, Calif.; s. of Paul Fussell and Wilhma Wilson Sill; m. 1st Betty Harper 1949 (divorced 1987); one s. one d.; m. 2nd Harriette Behringer 1987; ed. Pomona Coll., Harvard Univ.; Instructor in English, Conn. Coll. 1951–54; Asst. Prof. then Prof. of English, Rutgers Univ. 1955–76, John DeWitt Prof. of English Literature 1976–83; Donald T. Regan Prof. of English Literature, Univ. of Pa. 1983–94; Hon. Litt.D. (Pomona Coll.) 1980, (Monmouth Coll., N.J.) 1985; Nat. Book Award; Nat. Book Critics Circle Award; Emerson Award. *Publications:* Theory of Prosody in 18th Century England 1954, Poetic Meter and Poetic Form 1965, The Rhetorical World of Augustan Humanism 1965, Samuel Johnson and the Life of Writing 1971, The Great War and Modern Memory 1975, Abroad: British Literary Travelling between the Wars 1980, The Boy Scout Handbook and Other Observations 1982, Class: A Guide through the American Status System 1983, Sassoon's Long Journey (ed.) 1983, The Norton Book of Travel (ed.) 1987, Thank God for the Atom Bomb and Other Essays 1988, Wartime: Understanding and Behaviour in the Second World War 1989, Killing in Verse and Prose and other essays 1990, The Norton Book of Modern War (ed.) 1991, BAD: or, The Dumbing of America 1991, The Bloody Game: An Anthology of Modern War 1992, The Anti-Egotist: Kingsley Amis, Man of Letters 1994, Doing Battle: The Making of a Skeptic 1996. *Leisure interest:* reading. *Address:* Apt. 4-H, 2020 Walnut Street, Philadelphia, PA 19103, U.S.A. *Telephone:* (215) 557-0144.

FYFE, William Sefton, C.C., PH.D., F.R.S., F.R.S.C.; Canadian professor of geochemistry; b. 4 June 1927, N.Z.; s. of Colin and Isabella Fyfe; m. Patricia Walker 1981; two s. one d.; ed. Univ. of Otago, N.Z.; Lecturer in Chemistry, Otago Univ. 1955–58; Prof. of Geology, Univ. of Calif., Berkeley 1958–66; Royal Soc. Prof. Manchester Univ. 1966–72; Chair. Dept. of Geology, Univ. of Western Ont. 1972–84, Prof. of Geology 1984–92, Prof. Emer. 1992–, Dean Faculty of Science 1986–90; Pres. Int. Union of Geological Sciences 1992–96; Hon. mem. Brazilian, Russian and Indian Acad. of Sciences; Hon. D.Sc. (Memorial Univ.) 1989, (Lisbon) 1990, (Lakehead) 1990, (Guelph) 1992, (St. Mary's) 1994, (Otago) 1995, (Univ. of Western Ont.) 1995; awards include Guggenheim Fellowships, Logan Medal, Holmes Medal, European Union of Geosciences 1989, Day Medal, Geological Soc. of America 1990, N.Z. Commemorative Medal 1991, Canada Gold Medal 1992, Roebling Medal 1995, Nat. Order of Scientific Merit, Brazil 1996. *Publications:* 5 books, 600 scientific papers. *Leisure interests:* wildlife, swimming, travel. *Address:* 1197 Richmond Street, London, Ont., N6A 3L3, Canada (Home).

G

GABLENTZ, Otto von der; German diplomatist; b. 9 Oct. 1930, Berlin; s. of Prof. Otto Heinrich von der Gablentz and Hilda (née Zietlow); m. Christa Gerke 1965; one s. four d.; ed. Univs. of Berlin and Freiburg, Coll. of Europe, Bruges, St. Anthony's Coll. Oxford, and Harvard Univ.; joined foreign service of Fed. Repub. of Germany 1959; served in Australia 1961–64, worked in Bonn on Berlin and Germany 1964–67, German Embassy, London 1967–72, Dept. of European Political Co-operation 1973–78, seconded to Chancellor's Office 1978, Head of Section, Foreign and Defence Policy 1981; Amb. to Netherlands 1983–90; Amb. to Israel 1990–93; Amb. to Russia 1993–95; Rector Coll. of Europe, Bruges 1996–. *Address:* Konstantinstrasse 22, D53179 Bonn, Germany; College of Europe, Dijver II, 8000 Bruges, Belgium. *Telephone:* 228-355654 (Germany); 50-449911 (Belgium). *Fax:* 228-357234 (Germany); 50-449900 (Belgium).

GABRE-SELLASSIE, Zewde, PH.D.; Ethiopian diplomatist; b. 12 Oct. 1926, Metcha, Shoa; ed. Haile Sellassie I Secondary School, Coll. des Frères and St. George School, Jerusalem, Coll. des Frères and American Mission, Cairo, Univ. of Exeter, Oxford Univ. and Lincoln's Inn, London; Econ. Attaché, later Head of Press, Information and Admin. Div., Ministry of Foreign Affairs 1951–53; Dir.-Gen. Maritime Affairs 1953–55; Deputy Minister, Ministry of Public Works, Transport and Civil Aviation 1955–57; Mayor and Gov. of Addis Ababa 1957–59; Amb. to Somalia 1959–60; Minister of Justice 1961–63; Senior mem. St. Antony's Coll., Oxford 1963–71; Perm. Rep. to the UN 1972–74; Minister of Interior March-May 1974, of Foreign Affairs May-Dec. 1974; Deputy Prime Minister July-Sept. 1974; Visiting lecturer, Univ. of Calif., U.S.A. 1965; Vice-Pres. ECOSOC 1974; Officer of Menelik II, Grand Cross of Phoenix (Greece), of Istiqlal (Jordan), Grand Officer Flag of Yugoslavia, Order of Merit (Fed. Repub. of Germany).

GABRIADZE, Revaz (Rezo) Levanovich; Georgian scriptwriter, film director, sculptor and artist; b. 29 June 1936, Kutaisi; m. 2nd Yelena Zakharyevna Dzhaparidze; one s. one d.; ed. Tbilisi State Univ., Higher Courses of Scriptwriters and Film Directors in Moscow; worked as corresp. Molodezh Gruzii; works for Gruzia Film Studio 1970–; wrote scripts for over 35 films including Unusual Show 1970, Do not Grieve 1969; Serenade (after M. Zoshchenko) 1969, Jug (after L. Pirandello) 1970, Cranks 1974, White Stone 1973, Road, Mimino 1978, Kin-dza-dza; f. and Artistic Dir. Tbilisi Puppets Theatre 1981, wrote and produced plays Traviata, Diamond of Marshal Fantier, Fall of Our Spring (U.S.S.R. State Prize), Daughter of the Emperor of Trapezund; puppets productions in Switzerland and France 1991–94 including Ree Triste la Fine de Allee (Lausanne), Kutaisi (Rennes); Artistic Dir. Cen. Puppets Theatre in Moscow 1994–95; Dir. St. Petersburg Satire Theatre 1996; among productions Song about Volga 1996; author of numerous monumental and miniature sculptures including Chizhik-Pyzhik, Nose (after N. Gogol) in St. Petersburg, Rabinovich (Odessa); graphic and painting shows in Moscow, St. Petersburg, Paris, Rennes, Berlin, Lausanne; author china on show in Dijon and St. Petersburg; illustrations works of A. Pushkin. *Address:* Pyryeva str. 26. korp. 1, Apt. 14, 119285 Moscow, Russia. *Telephone:* (095) 147 4594 (Home).

GABRIEL, Michal; Czech sculptor; b. 25 Feb. 1960, Prague; s. of František Gabriel and Jarmila Gabrielová; m. Milada Dočekalová 1987; two s. one d.; ed. Secondary School of Applied Arts, Prague, Acad. of Fine Arts, Prague; apprenticed in timber industry; worked as skilled joiner 1975–78; graduated as woodcarver 1982, as sculptor 1987; Founding mem. creative group Tvrdohlavi ("The Stubborn" group) 1987; First Prize for statue Pegasus, Prague 1988 (work subsequently completed), for gates for Nat. Gallery Bldg. 1989 (completed 1992); Angel Sculpture (bronze), Bank in Opava 1995, "The Winged Leopard", gilded bronze sculpture, entrance Pres.'s Office, Prague Castle 1996; group exhbns. Graz, Austria 1989, Hořicev Podkrkonoší 1990, Jindřich Chalupecký Prize 1994. *Address:* Dlouhá 32, 110 00 Prague 1, Czech Republic (Home). *Telephone:* (02) 231 46 44.

GABRIEL, Peter; British rock singer and songwriter; b. 13 Feb. 1950, Woking; ed. Charterhouse school; co-f. Genesis rock band 1966; left group to start career as soloist 1975; numerous solo albums; founded World of Music, Arts and Dance (WOMAD) featuring music from around the world 1982; f. Real World Group to develop interactive projects in arts and tech. 1985, Real World Studios 1986, Real World Records (world music record label) 1989, Real World Multimedia 1994; launched "Witness" Human Rights Programme 1992; Dr. h.c. (City Univ.) 1991, Hon. M.A. (Univ. Coll., Salford) 1994; Hon. D. Mus. (Bath) 1996. *Songs include:* Solsbury Hill, Games Without Frontiers, Shock the Monkey, Big Time, Sledgehammer, Don't Give Up, Biko, In Your Eyes. *Solo albums:* PG I-IV, PG Plays Live 1983, So 1986, Shaking the Tree (compilation) 1990, Us 1992. *Soundtrack albums:* Birdy, Passion (Last Temptation of Christ). *Address:* Real World, Box Mill, Box, Wilts. SN14 9PL, England.

GABRIELIDES, Andreas, M.SC.; Cypriot politician; b. 1949, Amiantos; m.; three c.; ed. Higher Commercial Lyceum, Nicosia, Prague Univ., Czechoslovakia, Univ. of Aberdeen, Scotland; served Nat. Guard 1966–67; Agronomist, Dept. of Agric. 1967–70, 1972–81; Gen. Man. Cyprus Dairy Industry Org. 1981–88; Minister of Agric. and Natural Resources 1988–90; Fellow Inst. of Econ. Devt., World Bank. *Address:* c/o Ministry of Agriculture and Natural Resources, Nicosia, Cyprus.

GABUNIA, Georgy Vasilyevich; Russian politician; b. 6 Sept. 1952, Moscow; ed. Moscow Inst. of Int. Relations; on staff UN Conference on Trade and Dev. 1974–90; adviser, U.S.S.R. Ministry of Foreign Affairs 1990; head of dept., Ministry of Foreign Econ. Relations of Russian Fed. 1991; Deputy Minister, First Deputy Minister of Foreign Econ. Relations and Trade 1992–97; Acting Minister of Industry and Trade May–July 1998; Minister of Trade Sept. 1998–. *Address:* Ministry of Trade, Ovchinnikovskaya nab. 18/1, 113324 Moscow, Russia. *Telephone:* (095) 950 1918 (Office).

GADAMER, Hans-Georg, DR.PHIL.; German professor of philosophy; b. 11 Feb. 1900, Marburg; two d.; ed. Univ. of Marburg; Prof. of Philosophy, Univ. of Leipzig 1939, Rector 1946–47; Prof. Univ. of Frankfurt/Main 1947, Univ. of Heidelberg 1949, Prof. Emer. 1968; mem. Sächsische Akad. der Wissenschaften, Leipzig and Acads. of Heidelberg, Darmstadt, Athens, Budapest and Turin; mem. Acad. Nazionale dei Lincei, Rome; Hon. mem. American Acad. of Arts and Sciences, British Acad.; Dr.phil. h.c. (Ottawa) 1977, (Washington) 1979; Orden pour le mérite Grosses Bundesverdienstkreuz mit Stern; Reuchlin Prize (Pforzheim) 1971; Hegel Prize (Stuttgart) 1979, Jaspers Preis Univ. Heidelberg 1986, Martin Schleyer Preis 1987. *Publications:* Platos dialektische Ethik 1968, Wahrheit und Methode. Grundzüge einer philosophischen Hermaneutik 1975; essays, studies and articles on philosophy. *Address:* Am Büchsenackerhang 53, 69118 Heidelberg, Germany.

GADDA CONTI, Piero, LL.D.; Italian writer; b. 13 Feb. 1902, Milan; s. of Giuseppe and Matilde Gadda Conti; m. Anna Maria Castellini 1939; one s.; ed. Pavia Univ.; Novelist and journalist; Italian Literary Prizewinner 1930, Bagutta Prize for Literature for La Paura 1971. *Publications:* L'Entusiastica Estate 1924, Liuba 1926, Verdemare 1927, Mozzo 1930, A Gonfie Vele 1931, Gagliarda 1932, Orchidea 1934, Festa da Ballo 1937, Nuvola 1938, Moti del Cuore 1940, Vocazione Mediterranea 1940, Incomparabile Italia 1947, Beati Regni 1954, Vita e melodie di Giacomo Puccini 1955, Adamira 1956, Vanterie Adolescenti 1960, Cinema e civiltà 1960, Cinema e Giustizia 1961, Cinema e Sesso 1962, Cinema e Libertà 1963, La Milano dei Navigli 1965, Cinema e Società 1965, La Brianza 1966, La Paura 1970, Confessioni di Carlo Emilio Gadda 1974, Concerto d'Autunno 1976; plays: La Veste d'Oro 1924, Dulcinea 1927. *Address:* Piazza Castello 20, Milan, Italy. *Telephone:* 873-771, 80-33-58.

GADDAFI, Col. Mu'ammar Muhammad al-; Libyan political leader and army officer; b. 1942, Serte; s. of Mohamed Abdulsalam Abuminiar and Aisha Ben Niran; m. 1970; four s. one d.; ed. Univ. of Libya, Benghazi; served with Libyan Army 1965–; Chair. Revolutionary Command Council 1969– (Head of State); C.-in-C. of Armed Forces Sept. 1969; Prime Minister 1970–72; Minister of Defence 1970–72; Sec.-Gen. of Gen. Secr. of Gen. People's Congress 1977–79; Chair. OAU 1982–83; mem. Pres. Council, Fed. of Arab Republics 1972; rank of Maj.-Gen. Jan. 1976, retaining title of Col. *Publications:* The Green Book (3 vols.), Military Strategy and Mobilization, The Story of the Revolution. *Address:* Office of the President, Tripoli, Libya.

GADDAFI, Wanis; Libyan politician; Head of Exec. Council in Cyrenaican Prov. Govt. 1952–62; Fed. Minister of Foreign Affairs 1962–63, of Interior 1963–64, of Labour 1964; Amb. to Fed. Repub. of Germany 1964–65; Minister of Planning and Devt. 1966–68, of Foreign Affairs 1968; Prime Minister 1968–69; imprisoned for two years 1971–73.

GADDAM, Encik Kasitah bin, B.A.; Malaysian politician; b. 18 Oct. 1947, Ranau, Sabah; m. Puan Rosnie bte Ambuting; four c.; ed. Sabah Coll., Kota Kinabalu and Univ. of Malaya; Admin. Officer, Chief Minister's Dept. Kota Kinabalu, Sabah 1971; Asst. Dir. of Immigration, Sabah 1971–76; Regional Man. K.P.D. for Kundasang, Ranau and Tambunan, Admin. Officer/Purchasing Man. K.P.D. Headquarters, Kota Kinabalu 1977–80; Dir. of Personnel for East Malaysia and Brunei, Inchcape Malaysia Holding Bhd. 1980–83; Chair. Sabah Devt. Bank, Sabah Finance Bd., Soilogen (Sabah) Sdn. Bhd. 1985; mem. Parl. 1986–; Minister, Prime Minister's Dept. 1986–89, Minister of Land and Regional Devt. 1989–90; Vice-Pres. Parti Bersatu Sabah 1984. *Address:* c/o Parti Bersatu Sabah, Kota Kinabalu, Sabah, Malaysia.

GADDUM, Johann Wilhelm; German banker; b. 18 June 1930, Berlin; s. of Paul Gaddum and Dorothea Gaddum; m. Ursula Horneff-Gaddum; two s. two d.; with family business 1954–71; Minister of Finance and Fed. Affairs Parl. of Rhineland-Palatinate 1971–85; Pres. Land Cen. Bank, Rhineland-Palatinate 1985–86; Vice-Pres. Deutsche Bundesbank 1993– (mem. bd. 1986–); mem. Bundesrat 1971–85. *Publications:* Wirtschafts- und Finanzpolitik im Bundesstaat 1980, Steuerreform: Einfach und gerecht 1986, numerous econ. and political articles. *Leisure interests:* history, rowing. *Address:* Deutsche Bundesbank, Wilhelm-Epstein-Strasse 14, 60431 Frankfurt am Main, Germany. *Telephone:* (069) 9566-1.

GADGIL, Vithal Narhar, M.P., B.SC.; Indian politician; b. 22 Sept. 1928, Pune; s. of Narhar Vishnu Gadgil and Anandi Gadgil; m. Janhavi Gadgil 1955; one s. one d.; ed. L.S.E.; Prof. of Econ., Ruparel Coll., Bombay 1955–60;

Prof. of Constitutional Law, New Law Coll., Bombay 1960–66; mem. Rajya Sabha 1971; Minister for Defence Production 1975–77, of Communications 1983–84, of Information and Broadcasting 1985–86; Advocate Supreme Court; Consulting Ed. Marathi Encyclopaedia; Gen. Sec. Congress Party; mem. Exec. Cttee. of Maritha Sahitya Parishad. *Leisure interests:* reading, classical music, theatre. *Address:* 419 Shanwar Peth, Pune 411030, India (Home). *Telephone:* 451697.

GADSDEN, Sir Peter Drury Haggerston, G.B.E., M.A., D.SC., F.ENG., F.I.M.M., F.INST.M., F.R.S.H., F.R.C.A.; British business executive; b. 28 June 1929, Mannville, Alta., Canada; s. of late Rev. Basil C. and Mabel F. (née Drury) Gadsden; m. Belinda Ann de Marie Haggerston 1955; four d.; ed. Rockport, Belfast, The Elms, Colwall, Wrekin Coll., Wellington and Jesus Coll., Cambridge; dir. of cos. since 1952; marketing economist (mineral sands), UNIDO 1969; Dir. City of London (Arizona) Corpn. 1970–88 (Chair. 1985–88), Clothworkers' Foundation 1978–; Chair. Pvt. Patients Plan 1984–96, Pres. 1996–98; Chair. PPP Healthcare Medical Trust Ltd. 1996–; Deputy Chair. W. Canning PLC 1990– (Dir. 1989–); Dir. William Jacks PLC 1984–; Sheriff of London 1970–71; Alderman of the City of London 1971–, Lord Mayor of London 1979–80; Pres. Metropolitan Soc. for the Blind 1979–, Ironbridge Gorge Museum Devt. Trust, Australian-N.Z. Chamber of Commerce 1997–; Hon. Pres. Australian Heritage Soc. 1986–; Vice-Pres. Sir Robert Menzies Memorial Trust, Blackwood Little Theatre 1986–; Chancellor, The City Univ. 1979–80; Chair. Britain-Australia Bicentennial Cttee. 1984–88, Chair. Britain-Australia Bicentennial Trust 1984–88; Vice-Pres. Britain-Australia Soc. 1992–; Chair. Royal Commonwealth Soc. 1984–88; Chair. City of London (Arizona) Corpn. 1985–88; Hon. mem. London Metal Exchange, Inst. of Royal Engineers 1986; mem. Crown Agents 1981–87; Gov. The Hon. The Irish Soc. 1984–87; Patron Guild of Rahere 1986–, numerous other orgs.; Vice-Patron Museum of Empire and Commonwealth Trust 1986–; Trustee Chichester Festival Theatre 1986–, Chair. Govs. The Elms School 1993–; Fellow Royal Acad. of Eng. 1980–, Royal Soc. of Health 1993, Royal Coll. of Anaesthetists 1994; Liveryman, Clothworkers' Co. (Master 1989–90), Master Worshipful Co. of Engineers 1983–85; Hon. Liveryman, Plaisterers' Co., Marketors' Co., Actuaries' Co.; Officier Etoile Equatoriale (Gabon) 1970; H.M.'s Comm. of Lieutenancy for the City of London 1979–; Hon. A.C.; K. St. J; Christ Church-Midnite Award, Perth, W.A. 1997. *Publications:* articles on minerals and the minerals industry in professional journals. *Leisure interests:* sailing, walking, forestry, farming, photography. *Address:* 13 Cavendish Square, London, W1M 9DA, England. *Telephone:* 0171-307 2545. *Fax:* 0171-307 2442.

GAEBLER, (Gerhard Otto) Rainer, DR. ING.; German church leader and engineer; b. 30 March 1938, Leipzig; s. of Otto Gaebler and Charlotte Fischer; m. Uta Neef 1964; one d.; gas tech. engineer 1959–94; work in admin. law and professional rehabilitation 1994–96; Leader, Saxony Authority for rehabilitation from injustice in fmr. G.D.R. 1997–; Pres. Länd Synod of Evangelical-Lutheran Church in Saxony 1983-84, Vice-Pres. 1984–96; Pres. Synod of Union of Evangelical Churches in G.D.R. 1986–90; mem. Conf. of Evangelical Church Leaders and Bd. of Union of Evangelical Churches in G.D.R. 1986–90; mem. Synod of Evangelical Churches in Germany 1990–97. *Publication:* Gut gedacht ist halb gelöst. *Address:* Schwantesstrasse 67, 04347 Leipzig, Germany. *Telephone:* (0341) 2 31 41 53.

GAEHTGENS, Thomas Wolfgang, DR. PHIL.; German art historian; b. 24 June 1940, Leipzig; m. Barbara Feiler 1969; two s.; ed. Univs. of Bonn, Freiburg and Paris; teacher Univ. of Göttingen 1973, Prof. of Art History 1974–79, Technische Hochschule, Aachen 1979, Freie Univ. Berlin 1979–; awarded bursary for the J. Paul Getty Center for the History of Art and the Humanities, Santa Monica, Calif. 1985–86; mem. Akademie der Wissenschaften, Göttingen. *Publications:* Napoleon's Arc de Triomphe 1974, Versailles als Nationaldenkmal 1984, Joseph-Marie Vien 1988, Anton von Werner 1990, Die Berliner Museuminsel im Deutschen Kaiserreich 1992. *Address:* Peter-Lenne-Strasse 20, 14195 Berlin, Germany.

GAFT, Valentin Iosifovich; Russian actor; b. 2 Sept. 1935, Moscow; m.; ed. Studio-School of Moscow Art Theatre; worked in Mossoviet Theatre, Na Maloy Bronnoy, Lenkom, Satire Theatre 1959–69; leading actor Sovremennik Theatre 1969–; dozens of roles in classical and contemporary plays; in cinema since 1956; regularly acts on TV; People's Artist of Russia 1984. *Theatre roles include* Glumov (Balalaikin and Co.), Lopatin (From the Notes of Lopatin), George (Who's Afraid of Virginia Woolf?), Governor (Inspector), Vershinin (Three Sisters), Bridegroom (Something Like a Comedy). *Film roles include* Murder on Dante Street 1956, First Courier 1968, Crazy Gold 1977, Centaurs 1979, Parade 1980, Fuette 1986, Thieves by Law 1988, Blessed Heavens 1991, roles in TV productions and TV films including Buddenbrooks, The Mystery of Edwin Drood, Archipelago Lenoire, Kings and Cabbage. *Leisure interests:* writing verses and epigrams. *Address:* T. Shchevchenko nab. 1/2, Apt. 62, 121059 Moscow, Russia. *Telephone:* (095) 243 7667 (Home).

GAGE, Peter William, M.B., CH.B., PH.D., D.SC.; Australian professor of physiology; b. 21 Oct. 1937, Auckland, New Zealand; s. of John and Kathleen (née Burke) Gage; m. Jillian Shewan 1960 (divorced 1991); two s. two d.; ed. Univ. of Otago; house surgeon, Auckland Hosp. 1961; research asst. Green Lane Hosp., Auckland 1962; research scholar, A.N.U., Canberra 1963–65; N.I.H. Int. Postdoctoral Fellow, Dept. of Physiology and Pharmacology, Duke Univ., Durham, N.C. 1965–67, Asst. Prof. 1967–68; Sr. Lecturer, School of Physiology and Pharmacology, Univ. of N.S.W. 1968–70, Assoc. Prof. 1971–76, Prof. 1976–84, Dir. Nerve-Muscle Research Centre 1982–84; Prof. of Physiology, John Curtin School of Medical Research, A.N.U. 1984–; Fellow, Australian Acad. of Science. *Leisure interests:* horse-riding, agriculture. *Address:* c/o JCSMR, G.P.O. Box 334, Canberra, A.C.T. 2601; RMB 22, Powell Drive, Greenacres Estate, Queanbeyan, N.S.W. 2620, Australia.

GAGNON, H.E. Cardinal Edouard, P.S.S.; Canadian ecclesiastic; b. 15 Jan. 1918, Port-Daniel, Gaspé; ordained 1940; consecrated Bishop of Saint Paul in Alberta 1969, renounced position 1972; Archbishop (Titular See of Iustiniana prima) 1983; cr. Cardinal 1985; Pres. Pontifical Council for the Family 1985–90, of Pontifical Cttee. for Int. Eucharistic Congresses 1991–. *Address:* Piazza San Calisto 16, 00153 Rome, Italy.

GAGNON, Jean-Marie, PH.D., M.B.A., F.R.S.C.; Canadian professor of finance; b. 7 July 1933, Fabre; s. of Pierre Gagnon and Yvette Langlois; m. Rachel Bonin 1959; three s.; ed. Univ. of Chicago and Univ. Laval; chartered accountant, Clarkson, Gordon, Cie. 1957–59; Prof. of Finance, Univ. Laval 1959–; Visiting Prof. Faculté Universitaire Catholique à Mons, Belgium 1972–74, Univ. of Nankai, People's Repub. of China 1985; mem. Bd. of Dirs. SSQ-Vie; commr. Comm. des Valeurs Mobilières du Québec. *Publications:* Income Smoothing Hypothesis 1970, Belgian Experience with Mergers 1982, Taux de rendement et risque 1982, Traité de gestion financière (with N. Khoury) 1987, Taxes and Financial Decisions 1988, Taxes and Dividends 1991, Corporate Governance Mechanisms and Board Composition 1995, Distribution of Voting Rights and Takeover Resistance 1995. *Address:* 1340 Corrigan, Sainte Foy, G1W 3E9, Canada. *Telephone:* (418) 656-5535. *Fax:* (418) 656-2782.

GAHMBERG, Carl G., M.D.; Finnish professor of biochemistry; b. 1 Dec. 1942, Helsinki; s. of Gustaf-Adolf Gahmberg and Marie-Louise Gahmberg; one s. one d.; Post-doctoral Fellow, Univ. of Washington 1972–74; Docent of cell biology, Univ. of Helsinki 1974; Prof. of Biochem. Åbo Akad. 1979–81, Univ. of Helsinki 1981–; Research Prof. Acad. of Finland 1986–91; Visiting Prof. La Jolla Cancer Research Fed. 1988–89; Vice-Chair. Finnish Medical Assen. 1998–99; mem. Finnish Acad. of Science, Finnish Soc. of Sciences and Letters (Perm. Sec.), European Molecular Biology Org., Academia Europea, World Cultural Council; Komppa Prize 1971, Scandinavian Jahre Prize 1981, 150th anniversary Prize, Finnish Medical Assen. 1985, Prof. of the Year in Finland 1995, The Finnish Äyräpää Prize for Medicine 1997. *Publications:* 210 int. publs. on cell membrane, glycoproteins, cell adhesion, cancer research. *Leisure interests:* nature, classical music. *Address:* Department of Biosciences, Division of Biochemistry, P.O. Box 56, Viikinkaari 5, 00014 University of Helsinki, Finland. *Telephone:* 358-0-70859028. *Fax:* 358-0-70859068.

GAIDAR, Yegor (see Gaydar, Yegor).

GAILIS, Maris; Latvian politician and business executive; b. 1951, Riga, Latvia; ed. Riga Polytech. Inst., Latvian State Univ.; started work in furniture factory, worked in trade unions, co-operatives, author of book Furniture for Young People, f. Riga Videocentre and Cinema Forum Arsenal, responsible for problems of foreign econ. relations in various state insts. 1990–; State Sec. Ministry of Foreign Affairs 1992–93; elected to Saeima (Parl.) 1993; Minister for State Reforms, Deputy Prime Minister 1993–94; Prime Minister 1994–95; business exec. 1995–.

GAINUTDIN, Ravil ibn Ismail; Tatar religious leader; b. 25 Aug. 1959, Tatarstan; m.; two d.; ed. Islam Medrese Mir-Arab Bukhara; First Imam-Khatyb Kazan Mosque Nur Islam; Exec. Sec. Ecclesiastical Dept. of Moslems European Section of U.S.S.R and Siberia, Ufa 1985–87; Imam-Khatyb Moscow Mosque 1987–88; Chief Imam-Khatyb 1988–; Pres. Islam Cen. of Moscow and Moscow Region 1991–; Chair. Council of Muftis of Russia, Prof. Moscow Higher Islam Coll.; mem. Int. Acad. of Sciences of Eurasia; Int. Slavic Acad., Int. Acad. of Information; mem. Council on Co-operation with Religious Unions, Russian Presidency. *Publications include:* books on Moslem dogma and rituals. *Address:* Moslem Centre of European Region of Russia, Vypolzov per. 7, 129090 Moscow, Russia (Office). *Telephone:* (095) 281 4904 (Office).

GAJDUSEK, Daniel Carleton, M.D.; American medical research scientist; b. 9 Sept. 1923, Yonkers, N.Y.; s. of Karl Gajdusek and Ottilia Dobroczki; 65 adopted s. and d. from Melanesia and Micronesia; ed. Boyce Thompson Inst. of Plant Research, Yonkers, N.Y., Marine Biological Laboratory, Woods Hole, Mass., Univ. of Rochester, Harvard Medical School, Calif. Inst. of Tech.; served in Medical Corps; Babies Hosp. of Columbia Presbyterian Medical Center, N.Y. 1946–47; Cincinnati Children's Hosp. 1947–48; Medical Mission in Germany 1948; Sr. Fellow, Nat. Research Council, Calif. Inst. of Tech. 1948–49; Children's Hosp., Boston, Mass. 1949–51; Research Fellow, Harvard Univ. and Senior Fellow, Nat. Foundation for Infantile Paralysis 1949–52; Walter Reed Army Medical Center 1952–53; Institut Pasteur, Teheran, Iran and Univ. of Md. 1954–55; Visiting Investigator at Walter and Eliza Hall Inst., Australia 1955–57; Lab. Chief Nat. Inst. of Neurological Disorders and Stroke, N.I.H., Bethesda, Md. 1958–97, Chief of Study of Child Growth and Devt. and Disease Patterns in Primitive Cultures, and of Laboratory of Slow, Latent and Temporate Virus Infections 1958–97; Chief of Cen. Nervous System Studies Lab. 1970–97; Prof., Inst. of Human Virology, Univ. of Md. 1996–; Silliman Prof., Yale Univ. 1981; Hitchcock Prof., Univ. of Calif. Berkeley 1982; Merrian Prof., Univ. of N.C. 1984; Hon.

Curator Melanesian Ethnology, Peabody Museum, Salem, Mass.; Hon. Prof. of Virology Hupei Medical Coll., People's Repub. of China 1986, Beijing Medical Univ. 1987; mem. Soc. for Paediatric Research, American Paediatric Soc., N.A.S., American Acad. of Arts and Sciences, American Philosophical Soc., Deutsche Akademie der Naturforscher Leopoldina, Third World Acad. of Science, American Acad. of Neurology, Russian Acad. of Medicine, Sakha (Iakut) Siberian Acad. of Science br. Russian Acad. of Science; Hon. mem. Australian Acad. of Science, Czech Acad. of Science and Mexican, Colombia and Belgian Acads. of Medicine; Meade Johnson Award, American Acad. of Pediatrics 1961, Dautrebande Prize 1976, shared Nobel Prize in Physiology or Medicine for discoveries concerning new mechanisms for the origin and dissemination of infectious diseases 1976, Cotzias Prize 1978, Huxley Medal, Royal Anthropological Inst. of G.B. and Ireland 1988, Stuart Mudd Prize 1989, award of 3rd Int. Congress on Alzheimer's Disease 1992, award of 3rd Pacific Rim Biotech. Conf. 1992, Gold Medal, Slovak Acad. of Science 1996; several hon. degrees. *Publications:* Hemorrhagic Fevers and Mycotoxicoses 1959, Slow, Latent and Temperate Virus Infections 1965, Correspondence on the Discovery of Kuru 1976, Kuru (with Judith Farquhar) 1980, Research, Travel and Field Expedition Journals (51 vols.) 1954–96, Vilinisk Encephalomyelitis 1996; and over 1,000 papers on microbiology, immunology, pediatrics, neurology, cognitive and psychosexual devt. and genetics. *Leisure interests:* linguistics, mountaineering. *Address:* c/o Institute of Human Virology, Room N460, 725 West Lombard Street, Baltimore, MD 21201, U.S.A.

GÁL, Zoltán, D. JUR.; Hungarian politician and lawyer; m. Krisztina Pölz; one s.; ed. Eötvös Loránd Univ.; with Trade Union HQ 1964–74; worked at Exec. and Admin. Dept. of Cen. Cttee. of Hungarian Socialist Workers Party (HSWP) 1974–86; lecturer, Political Coll. 1987–89; Deputy Minister of Interior, then State Sec. and Minister of Interior 1987–90; mem. Parl. 1990–94; leader faction of Hungarian Socialist Party 1990–94; mem. Cttee. on Constitution, Legislation and Justice 1990–94; Chair. Cttee. for Constitutional Reform 1994–; Speaker of Nat. Ass. 1994–. *Leisure interests:* tennis, swimming and reading. *Address:* H-1357 Budapest, Kossuth Lajos tér 1–3, Hungary.

GALA, Antonio; Spanish author; b. 2 Oct. 1936, Córdoba; s. of Luis Gala and Adoración Velasco; ed. Univs. of Seville and Madrid; Nat. Prize for Literature, Hidalgo Prize, Planeta Prize; many other literary and theatre awards; Dr. h.c. (Córdoba). *Publications:* plays: Los Verdes Campos del Edén, Los Buenos Días Perdidos, Anillos Para Una Dama, La Vieja Señorita del Paraíso, El Cementerio de los Pájaros, Petra Regalada, El Hotelito, Carmen Carmen, Los Bellos Durmientes; novels: El Manuscrito Carmesí, La Pasión Turca, Más Allá del Jardín 1995, La Regla de Tres 1996; poetry: Enemigo Intimo, Sonetos de la Zubia, Testamento Andaluz; essays: Charlas con Troyo, La Soledad Sonora. *Address:* Calle Macarena No. 16, 28016 Madrid, Spain. *Telephone:* 359.20.37.

GALADARI, Abdel-Wahab; United Arab Emirates business executive; b. 1938, Dubai; ed. American Univ., Beirut; Clerk with British Bank of the Middle East, then admin. post with Dubai Electrical Co.; founded re-export business with brothers Abdel-Rahim and Abdel-Latif 1960, real estate co. *c.* 1962; Dir. Nat. Bank of Dubai 1965–69; left family business 1976; formed Union Bank of the Middle East 1977, Chair. –1983; Chair. A. W. Galadari Holdings and over 20 associated cos.; Propr. Hyatt Regency and Galadari Galleria hotels; sponsored 1980 Dubai Grand Prix motor race. *Address:* A. W. Galadari Group of Companies, P.O. Box 22, Dubai, United Arab Emirates.

GALAL, Mohamed Noman, PH.D.; Egyptian diplomatist; b. 10 April 1943, Assiut; m. Kawther Elsherif 1969; two s.; ed. Univ. of Cairo; joined Ministry of Foreign Affairs 1965; Third Sec. Jordan 1969–72; Vice-Consul, Kuwait 1972; Consul, Abu Dhabi 1972–73; Second Sec. Oslo 1975–79; lecturer, Diplomatic Inst. 1979–80; First Sec. New Delhi 1980, Counsellor 1981–85; Counsellor, Cabinet of Deputy Prime Minister and Minister of Foreign Affairs 1985–87; Counsellor, Egyptian Mission at UN 1987–90, Minister and Deputy Perm. Rep. 1990–92; Perm. Rep. to League of Arab States, Cairo 1992–95; Amb. to Pakistan 1995–; Visiting lecturer, Farleigh Dickinson Univ. 1989–91, Univ. of Cairo 1994–95; Nat. Medal for Merit, St. Olav Medal (Norway). *Publications:* more than 40 publs. in Arabic and English on Arab and int. affairs, foreign policy, human rights, etc. *Address:* Egyptian Embassy, 37 6th Avenue, P.O. Box 2088, Ramna 6/4, Islamabad, Pakistan.

GALANOS, James; American fashion designer; b. 20 Sept. 1924, Philadelphia, Pa.; s. of Gregory Galanos and Helen (née Gorgoliatos) Galanos; ed. Traphagen School of Fashion, New York 1943; began career selling sketches to N.Y. clothing mfrs.; worked for Hattie Carnegie 1944; asst. to Jean Louis, head designer, Columbia Studios, Hollywood 1946–47; apprentice, Robert Piguet, Paris 1947–48; designer, Davidow, New York 1949–50; est. own business, Galanos Originals, Beverly Hills, Calif. 1951–63, Los Angeles 1963–; produced collection of couture-quality furs in collaboration with Neustadter Furs 1968; designed costumes for Rosalind Russell in films Never Wave at a WAC, 1952, and Oh Dad, Poor Dad, Mama's Hung You in the Closet and I'm Feeling So Sad 1967; retrospective exhbns. Los Angeles Co. Museum of Art 1974, 1997, Inst. of Technology, New York 1976, Western Reserve Historical Soc. 1996, L.A. Co. Museum of Art 1997; designed Inaugural Gown worn by Nancy Reagan 1981; work represented in perm. collections including Metropolitan Museum of Art, New York, Smithsonian Inst. Washington and Art Inst. of Chicago; Council of Fashion Designers of America Lifetime Achievement Award 1985, and numerous fashion awards. *Leisure interests:* collecting art books, music, reading, architecture. *Address:* 2254 South Sepulveda Blvd., Los Angeles, CA 90064, U.S.A. *Telephone:* (213) 272-1445. *Fax:* (310) 473-6725.

GALASSI, Jonathan White, M.A.; American publishing executive; b. 4 Nov. 1949, Seattle; s. of Gerard Goodwin and Dorothea Johnston Goodwin (née White); m. Susan Grace Galassi 1975; two d.; ed. Harvard and Cambridge Univs.; Ed. Houghton Mifflin Co., Boston, New York 1973–81; Sr. Ed. Random House, Inc., New York 1981–86; Exec. Ed. and Vice-Pres. Farrar, Strauss & Giroux Inc., New York 1986–87, Ed.-in-Chief and Sr. Vice-Pres. 1988–93, Exec. Vice-Pres. 1993–; Poetry Ed. Paris Review 1978–88; Roger Klein Award for Editing, PEN 1984, Guggenheim Fellow 1989; mem. Acad. of American Poets (Dir. 1990–, Pres. 1994–). *Publications:* Morning Run (poetry) 1988, The Second Life of Art: Selected Essays of Eugenio Montale (ed., trans.) 1982, Otherwise: Last and First Poems of Eugenio Montale (ed., trans.) 1986, Eugenio Montale, Collected Poems 1916–56 (ed., trans.) 1998. *Address:* Farrar, Strauss & Giroux Inc., 19 Union Square W., New York, NY 10003 (Office); 239 Sackett Street, Brooklyn, NY 11231, U.S.A. (Home).

GALATERI DI GENOLA, Count Gabriele, D.IUR., M.B.A.; Italian business executive; b. 11 Jan. 1947, Rome; s. of Gen. Angelo Galateri di Genola and Carla Fontana; m. Evelina Christillin; one d.; ed. Liceo Ennio Quirino Visconti, Rome, Univ. of Rome, Columbia Univ., New York, U.S.A.; Asst. Lecturer in Econ. Science, Univ. of Rome 1969–70; Head Financial Analysis Dept., later Int. Financing Dept., Banco di Roma 1971–74; Financial Dir. Saint Gobain, Italy, then Asst. to Financial Group Dir., Paris 1974–77; Head Foreign Finance Div., Fiat S.p.A. 1977–83, Financial Dir. 1983–86, Man. Dir. and Gen. Man. IFI S.p.A. 1993–, Man. Dir. IFIL S.p.A. 1986–; Gen. Partner Giovanni Agnelli e C., C. Sapaz; mem. Bd. Fiat, Accor, Arjo Wiggins Appleton, La Rinascente, Toro Assicurazioni, Peroni, Alpitour, Banca Brignone, Piaggio, Galbani, Worms. *Leisure interests:* arts, music, tennis, skiing, gym. *Address:* IFI Sp.A., Corso Matteotti 26, 10121 Turin, Italy. *Telephone:* (11) 6620.266. *Fax:* (11) 673.915.

GALAZOV, Akhsarbek Khadzhimurzayevich; Russian/Ossetian politician; b. 15 Oct. 1929, Khoumalag, N. Ossetia; two s. one d.; ed. N. Ossetian Pedagogical Inst.; mem. CPSU 1959–91; worked as school teacher 1952–58; Dir. Inst. of Teachers' Training, Ministry of Educ., N. Ossetia –1960; instructor N. Ossetian Regional CPSU Cttee. 1960–61; Minister of Educ. N. Ossetian Autonomous Repub. 1961–75; Deputy Chair. Council of Ministers 1975–76; Rector N. Ossetian Univ. 1976–90; First Sec. N. Ossetian Republican CPSU Cttee. 1990–91; mem. CPSU Cen. Cttee. 1990–91; Chair. Supreme Soviet N. Ossetia 1990–93; People's Deputy of Russia 1990–93; mem. Council of Fed. of Russia 1993–98; elected Pres. of N. Ossetia 1994–98, concurrently Prime Minister 1994–95.

GALBRAITH, J. Kenneth, PH.D.; American economist, diplomatist and writer; b. 15 Oct. 1908, Iona Station, Ont., Canada; m. Catherine Merriam Atwater 1937; three s.; ed. Toronto, California and Cambridge (England) Univs.; Research Fellow, Calif. Univ. 1931–34; Instructor, Harvard Univ. 1934–39, Lecturer 1948–49, Prof. of Econs. 1949–75, Emer. Prof. 1975–; Asst. Prof. Princeton Univ. 1939–42; Asst. then Deputy Admin. Office of Price Admin. 1941–43; mem. Bd. of Editors Fortune Magazine 1943–48; Amb. to India 1961–63; Dir. Office of Econ. Security Policy, State Dept. 1946; BBC Reith Lecturer 1966; American Econ. Asscn. (Pres. 1971), American Farm Econs. Asscn., Americans for Dem. Action (Chair. 1967–68); Fellow American Acad. of Arts and Sciences (Pres. Bd. Dirs. 1984–87); mem. American Acad., Inst. of Arts and Letters 1984–; Commdr. Légion d'honneur; numerous hon. degrees; Freedom Medal 1946. *Publications include:* Theory of Price Control, American Capitalism 1952, The Great Crash, Economics and the Art of Controversy 1955, The Affluent Society 1958, Journey to Poland and Yugoslavia 1959, The Liberal Hour 1960, Made to Last 1964, The New Industrial State 1967, The Triumph (novel) 1968, Ambassador's Journal 1969, Indian Painting (co-author) 1969, A Contemporary Guide to Economics, Peace and Laughter 1971, A China Passage 1973, Economics and the Public Purpose 1974, Money: Whence It Came, Where It Went 1975, The Age of Uncertainty 1976, The Galbraith Reader 1978, Almost Everyone's Guide to Economics 1979, The Nature of Mass Poverty 1979, Annals of an Abiding Liberal 1980, A Life in Our Times (autobiog.) 1981, The Anatomy of Power 1984, A View from the Stands: Of People, Military Power and the Arts 1986, Economics in Perspective: A Critical History 1987, History of Economics: The Past as the Present 1987, Capitalism, Communism and Coexistence (with S. Menshikov, novel) 1988, A Tenured Professor (novel) 1990, A Short History of Financial Euphoria 1990, The Culture of Contentment 1992, A Journey through Economic Time 1994, The World Economy Since the War: A Personal View, The Good Society: The Humane Agenda 1996. *TV series:* The Age of Uncertainty (BBC) 1977. *Address:* 30 Francis Avenue, Cambridge, MA 02138, U.S.A.

GALBRAITH, Nicol Spence, C.B.E., M.B., F.R.C.P., F.F.C.M., D.P.H.; British medical epidemiologist; b. 17 March 1927, Southborough, Kent; s. of Dr. S. N. Galbraith and May Gledhill; m. Zina-Mary Flood 1952; three d.; ed. Rose Hill School, Tunbridge Wells, Tonbridge School, and Guy's Hosp. Medical School, Univ. of London; House Officer, Guy's and Lewisham Hosps. 1950–51; army medical officer 1952–53; Sr. House Officer, Brook Gen. Hosp. 1954–55; Medical Registrar, Lewisham Hosp. 1955–58; Epidemiologist, Research Lab. of Public Health Lab. Service 1958–63; Deputy Medical Officer of Health, later Medical Officer of Health, London Borough of Newham 1963–73; Area Medical Officer, City and East London Area Health Authority 1973–77; Sr. Lecturer in Community Medicine, London School of Hygiene and Tropical Medicine 1973–; Lecturer in Community Medicine, St. Bartholomew's Hosp. 1975–80; Dir. Communicable Disease Surveillance Centre, Public Health Lab. Service 1977–88; mem. Govt. Cttee. on Microbiological Safety of Food; fmr. mem. Dept. of Health Aids Cttee., Joint Cttee. on Immunisation and Vaccination; Past Pres. Section of Epidemiology and Community Medicine, Royal Soc. of Medicine; Past Pres. Infection Control Nurses' Asscn.; Past-Pres. British Soc. for the Study of Infection; Neech Prize (Soc. Medical Officers of Health) 1969, Stewart Prize, British Medical Asscn. 1984, Harben Medal (Royal Inst. of Public Health and Hygiene) 1988, Alwyn Smith Medal (Faculty of Community Medicine) 1988, Jenner Medal, Royal Soc. of Medicine 1990. *Publications:* co-author of a book on infection, chapters in books and papers on the epidemiology of communicable disease; papers on the org. of public health and epidemiological services, training in communicable disease control, port health services, changing pattern of infection in England and Wales, The Early Life of Dr. John Snow (1813–1858). *Address:* 22 Fen Road, Chesterton, Cambridge, CB4 1TX, England. *Telephone:* (01223) 424956. *Fax:* (01223) 424956.

GALE, Ernest Frederick, PH.D., SC.D., F.R.S.; British professor of chemical microbiology; b. 15 July 1914, Luton, Beds.; s. of Ernest Francis Edward Gale and Nellie Annie Gale; m. Eiry Mair Jones 1937; one s.; ed. Weston-super-Mare Grammar School and St. John's Coll., Cambridge; research in chemical microbiology, Cambridge 1937–83; Sr. Student, Royal Comm. for Exhbn. of 1851 1939–41; Beit Memorial Fellow 1941–43; mem. Staff, Medical Research Council 1943–60, Dir. MRC Unit for Chemical Microbiology 1948–60; Prof. of Chemical Microbiology, Univ. of Cambridge 1960–81, Prof. Emer. 1981–; Fellow, St. John's Coll., Cambridge 1949–88; Meetings Sec. Soc. for Gen. Microbiology 1952–58, Int. Rep. 1963–67, Pres. 1967–69, Hon. mem. 1978; Herter Lecturer, Baltimore 1948; Hanna Lecturer, Western Reserve Univ. 1951; Harvey Lecturer, N.Y. 1955; Leeuwenhoek Lecturer, Royal Soc. 1956; Malcolm Lecturer, Syracuse Univ. 1967; Linacre Lecturer, St. John's Coll., Cambridge Univ. 1973; Squibb Lecturer, Nottingham Univ. 1986; Fellow of Royal Soc. 1953–. *Publications:* Chemical Activities of Bacteria 1947, Organisation and Synthesis in Bacteria 1959, Promotion and Prevention of Synthesis in Bacteria 1968, The Molecular Basis of Antibiotic Action 1972, 1981; scientific papers and reviews in journals of biochemistry and microbiology. *Leisure interests:* photography, wood carving. *Address:* 7 Hazeldene, Sandhills Road, Salcombe, Devon, TQ8 8JP, England. *Telephone:* (01548) 843426 (Home).

GALE, Gwendoline Fay, A.O., PH.D.; Australian university vice-chancellor and geographer; b. 13 June 1932, Balaklava, S. Australia; d. of George Jasper Gilding and Kathleen Gertrude Pengelley; one s. one d.; ed. Methodist Ladies' Coll., Univ. of Adelaide, S. Australia; lecturer, then Sr. Lecturer, Univ. of Adelaide 1966–74, Reader 1975–77, Prof. of Geography 1978–89, Pro-Vice-Chancellor 1988–89, Prof. Emer. 1989–; Australian Heritage Commr. 1989–95; Vice-Chancellor Univ. of Western Australia 1990–97; Pres. Inst. of Australian Geographers 1989–90; Chair. Social Justice Advisory Cttee. 1989; Pres. Australian Vice-Chancellors Cttee. 1996–97; Pres. Acad. of Social Sciences of Australia 1998–; mem. Humanities and Social Science Panel, Australian Research Council 1987–89, Chair. 1989; Exec. mem. Acad. of the Social Sciences in Australia 1980–82, 1988–89; Elin Wagner Fellowship 1971, Catherine Helen Spence Fellowship 1972, British Council Award 1972, Fellow Acad. of Social Sciences of Australia 1978. *Publications:* Women's Role in Aboriginal Society (Ed.) 1970, Urban Aborigines 1972, Race Relations in Australia: the Aboriginal situation 1975, Poverty Among Aboriginal Families in Adelaide 1975, We are Bosses Ourselves: the Status and Role of Aboriginal Women Today (Ed.) 1983, Tourists and the National Estate: Procedures to protect Australia's Heritage 1987, Aboriginal Youth and the Criminal Justice System: the Injustice of Justice 1990, Inventing Places: Studies in Cultural Geography 1991, Changing Australia 1991, Boyer Lectures 1991, Juvenile Justice: Debating the Issues 1993, Tourism and the Protection of Aboriginal Sites 1994. *Leisure interests:* hiking, camping, music, theatre. *Address:* c/o Office of the Vice-Chancellor, The University of Western Australia, Nedlands, Perth, W.A. 6009, Australia. *Telephone:* (09) 380 2801.

GALE, Michael Denis, PH.D., F.R.S.; British plant research scientist; b. 25 Aug. 1943; s. of Sydney Ralph Gale and Helen Mary Gale (née Johnston); m. Susan Heathcote Rosbotham 1979; two d.; ed. West Buckland School, Barnstaple, Birmingham Univ., Univ. Coll. Wales, Aberystwyth; Researcher, Plant Breeding Inst. (subsequently Agric. and Ford Research Council Inst. of Plant Science Research), Cambridge 1968–86, Head Cereals Research Dept. and Individual Merit Sr. Prin. Scientific Officer, Cambridge Lab. 1986–92, Head Cambridge Lab., Norwich 1992–94; Research Dir. John Innes Centre, Norwich 1994–98, Acting Dir. Sept.–Dec. 1998, Dir. 1999–; Farrer Memorial Bicentennial Fellow, N.S.W. Dept. of Agric. 1989; Hon. Research Prof. Inst. of Crop Germplasm Resources, Academia Sinica 1992; Adviser Inst. of Genetics, Beijing 1992; Research Medal, Royal Agric. Soc. of England 1994, Rank Prize for Nutrition 1997, Darwin Medal 1998. *Publications:* 200 scientific papers and articles on plant genetics and cytogenetics, especially dwarfism, quality and genome research in wheat. *Leisure interests:* golf, tennis. *Address:* John Innes Centre, Norwich Research Park, Colney, Norwich, NR4 7UH, England. *Telephone:* (01603) 452571. *Fax:* (01603) 456844.

GALEA, Censu, B.E., B.A.; Maltese politician and architect; b. 28 Aug. 1956; s. of Joseph Galea; m. Grace Sammut; two s. two d.; ed. Univ. of Malta; practising architect 1982; Sec.-Gen. then Pres. of Nationalist Party Youth Section 1978–81; M.P. Nationalist Party 1987–; Parl. Sec. Ministry for Social Security 1992–94; Minister for Food, Agric. and Fisheries 1994–96, for Transport and Communications 1998–; Shadow Minister and Opposition Spokesman for Transport and Ports 1996–98, Sec. and Whip Nationalist Party Parl. Group 1997–98. *Address:* Ministry for Transport and Communications, House of Four Winds, Hastings Gardens, Valletta, CMR 02, Malta. *Telephone:* 225200. *Fax:* 248937.

GALEA, Louis, LL.D., M.P.; Maltese politician and lawyer; b. 2 Jan. 1948, Mqabba; s. of Joseph Galea and Joan (née Farrugia) Galea; m. Vincienne Zammit 1977; one s. three d.; mem. Gen. Council and Exec. Cttee. Nationalist Party 1972–, Gen. Sec. 1977–87; mem. Parl. 1972–; Minister for Social Policy including Health 1987–92, for Home Affairs and Social Development including Health 1992–95, Minister for Social Devt. 1995–96; Shadow Minister for Educ. 1996–98; Minister of Educ. 1998–; Nationalist Party. *Leisure interests:* reading, music, tennis. *Address:* Ministry of Education, Floriana CMR02, Malta. *Telephone:* 231374, 231375. *Fax:* 221634.

GALEYEV, Albert Abubakirovich, DR.PHY.MATH.SC.; Russian physicist; b. 19 Oct. 1940; m.; two c.; ed. Univ. of Novosibirsk; worked at U.S.S.R. Acad. of Sciences Inst. of Nuclear Physics 1961–70; sr. researcher at Acad. of Sciences Inst. of High Temperatures 1970–73; mem. CPSU 1976–91; Corresp. mem. U.S.S.R. (now Russian) Acad. of Sciences 1987–92, mem. 1992; Head of Section at Acad. of Sciences Inst. of Space Research 1973–88, Dir. 1988–; Ed.-in-Chief Earth Research from Space; Lenin Prize 1984. *Publications:* works on physics of plasma and cosmic physics. *Address:* Institute of Space Research, Profsoyuznaya 84/32, 117810 Moscow, Russia. *Telephone:* (095) 333-25-88 (Office); (095) 438-22-89 (Home).

GALIMOV, Erik Mikhailovich, PH.D., D.SC.; Russian geochemist; b. 29 July 1936, Vladivostok; s. of Zeya Galimova and Mikhail Piskunov; m. 1st; one d.; m. 2nd Galina Andriukhina; two d.; ed. Moscow Inst. of Oil and Gas; operational engineer 1959–60; head of geophysics expeditions 1960–63; sr. researcher 1965–73; Dir. V. I. Vernadsky Inst. of Geochem. and Analytical Chem. 1992– (head of lab. 1973–92); Prof. Moscow State Univ.; Chair. Geochem. Council of Russian Acad. of Sciences, Int. Lunar Exploration Working Group; Vice-Pres. Int. Asscn. of Geochem. Cosmochemistry; mem. Ed. Bd. Geochem., Chemical Geology; Corresp. mem. U.S.S.R. (now Russian) Acad. of Sciences 1991, mem. 1994; foreign mem. German Acad. of Sciences and Literature 1998; Geochemical Fellow 1998; Vernadsky Prize 1984; research in geochem. of stable isotopes, organic geochem. and geochem. of oil and gas. *Publications include:* Geochemistry of Stable Carbon Isotopes 1968, Carbon Isotopes in Oil and Gas Geology 1973, Biological Isotope Fractionation 1985, Sources and Mechanism Formation of Natural Gases 1988, Kimberlite Magmatism and Diamond Formation 1991, Evolution of the Biosphere 1995, Origin of the Moon 1996. *Address:* V. I. Vernadsky Institute of Geochemistry and Analytical Chemistry, Kosygin Street 19, Moscow 117975 (Office); Nikitski Blvd. 5–5, Moscow 121019, Russia (Home). *Telephone:* (095) 137-4127 (Office); (095) 291-4860 (Home). *Fax:* (095) 938-2054.

GALIN, Aleksandr (pseudonym of Aleksandr Mikhailovich Pourer); Russian playwright; b. 10 Sept. 1947; s. of Mikhail Pourer and Lubov Pourer; m. Galina Alekseyevna Pourer 1970; one s.; factory worker, later actor in puppet theatre; freelance writer 1978–. *Plays include:* The Wall 1971, Here Fly the Birds 1974, The Hole 1975, The Roof 1976, Retro 1979, The Eastern Tribute 1980, Stars in the Morning Sky 1982, The Toastmaster 1983, Jeanne 1986, Sorry 1990, The Title 1991, The Czech Photo 1993, The Clown and the Bandit 1996, The Anomaly 1996, Sirena and Victoria 1997, The Competition 1998; plays translated into several languages including Stars in the Morning Sky (selected plays translated into English) 1989. *Film:* (scriptwriter and dir.) Casanova's Coat (The Delegation); Amb. of the Arts, Fla. *Publication:* Selected Plays 1989. *Address:* Pokrovka str. 34, Apt. 3, 103062 Moscow, Russia. *Telephone:* (095) 916-26-57.

GALJAARD, Hans, M.D., PH.D.; Netherlands professor of cell biology; b. 8 April 1935, Leiden; m. Henriette H. van Boven 1960; two s. one d.; ed. State Univ. Leiden; radiobiology training at Medical Biology Lab. Nat. Defense Org. Rijswijk 1962–65 and Atomic Energy Research Establishment, Harwell, England 1965; Prof. of Cell Biology, Erasmus Univ. Rotterdam 1966–; Chair. Dept. of Clinical Genetics, Univ. Hosp. 1980–; Dir. Rotterdam Foundation of Clinical Genetics 1980–; mem. Nat. Health Council, Nat. Council for Science Policy, Advisory Council on Tech.; consultant for WHO and UNFPA; mem. Royal Dutch Acad. of Sciences 1984–, Acad. Europaea; Hon. mem. Dutch Soc. for Human Genetics, Indian Soc. for Prenatal Diagnosis and Therapy; Carter Memorial Medal, British Clincial Genetics Soc. *Publications:* The Life of the Dutchman 1981; some 400 articles in scientific journals, book chapters and monographs. *Leisure interests:* writing, filming, sailing. *Address:* Department of Cell Biology and Genetics, Erasmus University, P.O. Box 1738, 3000 DR Rotterdam, Netherlands. *Telephone:* (0) 10-408732.

GALL, Hugues; French opera house director; b. 1940, Honfleur; ed. Inst. des Sciences Politiques; fmr. official, Ministries of Agric., Educ. and Culture; Sec.-Gen. Réunion des Théâtres Lyriques 1969–73; Deputy Dir.-Gen. Paris Opéra 1973–80; Dir.-Gen. Grand Theatre, Geneva 1980–95; Dir.-Gen. Paris Opéra July 1995–; Dir. Ecole du Louvre 1998–; Prix Montaigne 1996;

Chevalier Legion d'honneur, des Palmes académiques, du Mérite agricole; Commdr. des Arts et des Lettres; Officier ordre national du Mérite. *Address:* Opéra National de Paris, 120 rue de Lyon, 75012 Paris, France.

GALL, Joseph Grafton, PH.D.; American professor of biology; b. 14 April 1928, Washington, D.C.; s. of late John C. and Elsie (Rosenberger) Gall; m. 1st Dolores M. Hogge 1955; one s. one d.; m. 2nd Diane M. Dwyer 1982; ed. Yale Univ.; Instructor, Asst. Prof., Assoc. Prof., Prof., Dept. of Zoology, Univ. of Minnesota 1952–64; Prof. of Biology and Molecular Biophysics and Biochem., Yale Univ. 1964–83; mem. staff Dept. of Embryology, Carnegie Inst. 1983–, American Cancer Soc. Prof. of Developmental Genetics 1984–98; mem. Cell Biology Study Section, N.I.H. 1963–67, Chair. 1972–74; Pres. American Soc. for Cell Biology 1968, Soc. for Developmental Biology 1984–85; mem. Bd. of Scientific Counsellors, Nat. Inst. of Child Health and Human Devt., N.I.H. 1986–90; mem. Bd. of Scientific Advisers, Jane Coffin Childs Memorial Fund for Medical Research 1986–94; Visiting Prof. St. Andrews Univ. 1960, 1968, Univ. of Leicester 1971; Visiting Scientist Max Planck Inst., Tübingen 1960; mem. N.A.S., A.A.A.S., American Acad. of Arts and Sciences, American Philosophical Soc., Acad. Naz. dei Lincei (Rome) 1988; Fellow, Yale Corpn. 1989–95; E. B. Wilson Medal, American Soc. for Cell Biology 1983, Wilbur Cross Medal of Yale Univ. 1988, A.A.A.S. Mentor Award for Lifetime Achievement 1996. *Publications:* scientific articles on chromosome structure, nucleic acid biochemistry, cell fine structure, organelles of the cell. *Leisure interest:* collecting books on the history of biology. *Address:* c/o Department of Embryology, Carnegie Institution, 115 West University Parkway, Baltimore, MD 21210 (Office); 107 Bellemore Road, Baltimore, MD 21210, U.S.A. (Home). *Fax:* (410) 243-6311

GALLAGHER, Liam; British singer; s. of Peggy Gallagher; brother of Noel Gallagher (q.v.); m. Patsy Kensit 1997; singer with Oasis 1991–; tours in Britain and America; Brit Award, four platinum discs for Definitely Maybe in U.K., eight platinum discs for (What's The Story) Morning Glory? in the U.K. (May 1996), three Brit Awards 1996. *Singles include:* Supersonic (debut) 1994, Shakermaker, Live Forever, Cigarettes and Alcohol, Some Might Say, Wonderwall, Cast No Shadow, Don't Look Back in Anger, D'You Know What I Mean, All Around the World. *Albums:* Definitely Maybe (debut) 1994, (What's The Story) Morning Glory? 1995, Be Here Now 1997. *Address:* c/o Creation Records Limited, 109x Regents Park Road, London, NW1 8UR, England. *Telephone:* 0171-722 8866. *Fax:* 0171-722 3443.

GALLAGHER, Noel; British songwriter, musician and singer; s. of Peggy Gallagher; brother of Liam Gallagher (q.v.); m. Meg Matthews 1997; fmrly. worked with Inspiral Carpets; songwriter, guitarist and singer with Oasis 1991–; tours in Britain and America; four platinum discs for Definitely Maybe in U.K., eight platinum discs for (What's The Story) Morning Glory? in the U.K. (May 1996), three Brit Awards 1996. *Singles include:* Supersonic (debut) 1994, Shakermaker, Live Forever, Cigarettes and Alcohol, Some Might Say, Wonderwall, Cast No Shadow, Don't Look Back in Anger, D'You Know What I Mean, All Around the World. *Albums:* Definitely Maybe (debut) 1994, (What's The Story) Morning Glory? 1995, Be Here Now 1997. *Address:* c/o Creation Records Limited, 109x Regents Park Road, London, NW1 8UR, England. *Telephone:* 0171-722 8866. *Fax:* 0171-722 3443.

GALLAIS, Fernand Georges, DR. ÈS SC., DR. EN PHARMACIE; French professor of chemistry; b. 3 May 1908, Paris; m. Françoise Hine 1941; one s. two d.; ed. Faculté des Sciences, Sorbonne, Faculté de Pharmacie, Paris; research asst. 1934; lecturer Science Faculty, Univ. of Toulouse 1943–50, Prof. 1950; Dir. Ecole Nat. Supérieure de Chimie 1950–65; Vice-Dir. C.N.R.S. 1965–66, Scientific Dir. 1967–73, Dir. Co-ordination Chemistry Lab. C.N.R.S. 1973–78, now Hon. Dir.; Prof. Toulouse Univ. 1973–78, now Prof. Emer.; Corresp. mem. Acad. of Science 1966, mem. 1973–; Officier, Légion d'honneur, Commdr. Palmes Académiques. *Publications:* more than 150 scientific papers in chemistry, textbooks on gen. and inorganic chemistry 1958–62. *Leisure interests:* yachting, skiing. *Address:* 2 rue de l'Aubisque, 31500 Toulouse, France (Home). *Telephone:* 05161-20-52-63 (Home).

GALLAND, Yves; French politician; b. 8 March 1941; m. Anne Marie Chauvin 1967; one s. two d.; Pres. of publishing and publicity cos. 1969; mem. European Parl. 1979–, Vice-Pres. 1989–91; Deputy Mayor of Paris in charge of housing 1983–95, of architecture 1995–; Minister of Local Affairs and Decentralization 1986–88, of Industry 1995, of Finance and Foreign Trade 1995–97; Pres. Valoise Radical Party 1988–94; mem. nat. council Union pour la démocratie française, delegate to Paris 1979, mem. nat. political bureau 1984–, Pres. Liberal Group, European Parl. 1991–94. *Address:* Hôtel de Ville, 75196 Paris RP; 6 rue des Haudriettes, 75003 Paris, France.

GALLEY, Robert; French politician and engineer; b. 11 Jan. 1921, Paris; s. of Léon and André (neé Habrial) Galley; m. Jeanne Leclerc de Hauteclocque 1960; two s.; ed. Lycée Louis-le-Grand, Paris, Lycée Hoche, Versailles, Ecole centrale des arts et manufactures and Ecole Nat. Supérieure du pétrole et des moteurs; Engineer, Société chérifienne des pétroles 1950–54; in Commissariat à l'Energie atomique 1955–66; Adviser on information tech. to Prime Minister 1966–68; Pres. Institut de recherche d'informatique (IRIA) 1967; mem. Nat. Ass. (representing L'Aube) 1968–78, 1981, R.P.R. Deputy to Nat. Ass. for L'Aube 1981–; Treasurer R.P.R. 1984–90; fmr. Minister holding various portfolios, including Infrastructure and Housing, Scientific Research, Posts and Telecommunications, Transport, the Armed Forces and Devt. Co-operation; Mayor of Troyes 1972–95; Chair. Comité de bassin Seine-Normandie 1987–; Pres. Parl. Office for Scientific and Tech. Evaluation 1996–; Bd. Dir. Caisse Nationale de l'Industrie 1988–; mem. Comm. de la production et des échanges; mem. French del. to Council of Europe Consultative Ass. 1988; Commdr., Légion d'honneur, Compagnon de la Libération, Croix de guerre (1939–45). *Address:* Assemblée nationale, 75355 Paris; 18 boulevard Victor Hugo, 10000 Troyes, France.

GALLI, Paolo; Italian diplomatist; b. 10 Aug. 1934, Belgrade, Yugoslavia; s. of Carlo Galli and Bianca Metral-Lambert; m. Maria Calioni 1959; two d.; ed. Univ. of Padua; entered diplomatic service 1958; Vice-Consul, Cardiff 1961–63; Second Sec. Washington, D.C. 1963–65; Ministry of Foreign Affairs 1965–68; First Sec., later Counsellor and First Counsellor, London 1968–72; First Counsellor, Warsaw 1972–75; Ministry of Foreign Affairs 1975–79; Minister-Counsellor, Deputy Perm. Rep. to EEC, Brussels 1980–85; Minister 1985; Amb. to Poland 1986–88; Ministry of Foreign Affairs 1988–89; Amb. to Japan 1992–95, to U.K. 1995–; Cavaliere di Gran Croce, Ordine al Merito della Repubblica Italiana 1981. *Leisure interests:* classical music, the arts, fencing. *Address:* Italian Embassy, 14 Three Kings Yard, London, W1Y 2EH, England. *Telephone:* 0171-312 2200.

GALLIANO, John Charles; British fashion designer; b. 28 Nov. 1960, London; s. of John J. Galliano and Anita Guillen; ed. Wilsons Grammar School and St. Martin's School of Art; presenter of designer collections 1985–; worked on Courtelle project 1985; first British designer ever to show collection in Paris at the Louvre during Paris Fashion Week 1990; introduced Galliano's Girl 1991; designer of costumes for Ballet Rambert 1990, Kylie Minogue's U.K. tour 1991; Chief Designer Givenchy 1995–96, Christian Dior 1996–; Designer of Year Award (British Council) 1987, 1994, 1995, 1997 (jt. winner), Int. Womenswear Designer of the Year, CFDA 1997, VH1 Womenswear Designer of the Year 1997, Int. Designer Award, Council of Fashion Designers of America 1998 and other awards. *Address:* 60 rue d'Avron, 75020 Paris, France. *Telephone:* 015525 11 11. *Fax:* 015525 11 12.

GALLINER, Peter; British publisher; b. 19 Sept. 1920, Berlin, Germany; s. of Dr. Moritz Galliner and Hedwig Isaac; m. 1st Edith Marguerite Goldschmidt 1948; one d.; m. 2nd Helga Stenschke 1990; ed. in Berlin and London; worked for Reuters, London 1942–45; Foreign Man. Financial Times, London 1945–61; Chair. of Bd. and Man. Dir. Ullstein Publishing Group, Berlin 1961–64; Vice-Chair. and Man. Dir. British Printing Corpn. Publishing Group, London 1967–70; Int. Publishing Consultant 1965–67, 1970–75; Chair. Peter Galliner Assocs. 1970–; Dir. Int. Press. Inst. 1975–93; Dir. Emer., Int. Press Inst., Zürich 1993–; Chair. Int. Encounters London/Zürich 1995–; Fed. Cross of Merit, First Class (Fed. Repub. of Germany), Encomienda, Orden de Isabel la Católica (Spain), Kt. Commdr.'s Cross (Badge and Star) of Order of Merit (Fed. Repub. of Germany). *Leisure interests:* reading, music. *Address:* 27 Walsingham, St. John's Wood Park, London, NW8 6RH, England; Untere Zäune 9, 8001 Zürich, Switzerland. *Telephone:* 071-722 5502 (London); 251 8664 (Zürich).

GALLO, Max Louis, D. EN H., D. ÈS L.; French politician, writer and university teacher; b. 7 Jan. 1932, Nice; s. of Joseph Gallo and Mafalda Galeotti; ed. Univ. de Paris and Inst. d'Etudes Politiques; teacher lycée de Nice 1960–65; sr. lecturer Univ. of Nice 1965–70; Gen. Ed. book series Ce Jour-là, l'Histoire que nous vivons, la Vie selon . . ., le Temps des révélations; contrib. to various newspapers; devised TV programme Destins du Siècle 1973; Deputy (Socialist) for Alpes-Maritimes 1981–83; jr. minister and govt. spokesman 1983–84; Ed. Matin de Paris newspaper 1985–86; M.E.P. 1984–94; Nat. Sec. (Culture) Parti Socialiste 1988–90. *Publications:* L'Italie de Mussolini 1964, La Grande Peur de 1989 (as Max Laugham) 1966, L'Affaire d'Ethiopie 1967, Maximilien Robespierre, Histoire d'une solitude 1968, Gauchisme, réformisme et révolution 1968, Histoire de l'Espagne franquiste 1969, Cinquième Colonne 1930–1940 1970, la Nuit des longs couteaux 1970, Tombeau pour la Commune, Histoire de l'Espagne franquiste 1971, Le Cortège des vainqueurs 1972, La Mafia, un pas vers la mer 1973, L'Affiche, miroir de l'Histoire (illustrated) 1973, L'Oiseau des origines 1974: La Baie des anges (Vol. I) 1975, Le Palais des fêtes (Vol. II) 1976, La Promenade des Anglais (Vol. III) 1976, Le Pouvoir à vif, Despotisme, démocratie et révolution, Que sont les siècles pour la mer 1977, Les hommes naissent tous le même jour: Aurore (Vol. I) 1978, Crépuscule (Vol. II) 1979, Une affaire intime 1979, L'Homme Robespierre: histoire d'une solitude 1978, Un crime très ordinaire 1982, Garibaldi 1982, La Demeure des puissants 1983, La Troisième alliance, pour un nouvel individualisme, Le Grand Jaurès 1984, Le Beau Rivage 1985, Lettre ouverte à Maximilien Robespierre sur les nouveaux Muscadins, Belle Epoque 1986, Que passe la justice du roi, la Route Napoléon 1987, Jules Vallès 1988, Une Affaire publique 1989, Les Clés de l'histoire contemporaine 1989, Manifeste pour une fin de siècle obscure 1989, La Gauche est morte, vive la gauche! 1990, Le Regard des femmes 1991, La Fontaine des innocents (Prix Carlton 1992), Une femme rebelle: Vie et mort de Rosa Luxembourg 1992, L'Amour au temps des solitudes 1993, Les Rois sans visage 1994, Le Condottiere 1994, Le Fils de Klara H. 1995, L'Ambitieuse 1995, La Part de Dieu 1996, Le Faiseur d'or 1996, La Femme derrière le miroir, Napoléon, Le chant du départ (biog., Vol. I). *Address:* Editions Robert Laffont, 24 avenue Marceau, 75008 Paris, France.

GALLO, Robert, M.D.; American biomedical scientist; b. 23 March 1937, Waterbury, Conn.; m. Mary J. Hayes 1961; two s.; ed. Providence Coll., Jefferson Medical Univ., Philadelphia and Yale Univ.; Intern and Resident in Medicine, Univ. of Chicago 1963–65; Clinical Assoc. Nat. Cancer Inst. Bethesda, Md. 1965–68, Sr. Investigator 1968–69, Head, Section on Cellular Control Mechanisms 1969–72, Chief, Lab. of Tumor Cell Biology, Div. of Cancer Etiology 1972–93; head Dept. of Human Virology, Univ. of Md. Baltimore 1993–; Rep. World Conf. Int. Comparative Leukemia and Lymphoma Asscn. 1981–; Hon. Prof. Johns Hopkins Univ. 1985–; mem. Bd. of Govs. Franco American AIDS Foundation, World AIDS Foundation 1987; jt. discoverer of AIDS virus and first human retroviruses; Lasker Award for Basic Biomedical Research 1982; Gen. Motors Cancer Research Award 1984; Armand Hammer Cancer Research Award 1985; Lasker Award for Clinical Research 1986, Gairdner Foundation Award and other awards for cancer research; 1st Dale McFarlin Award for Research, Int. Soc. of Human Retrovirology 1994, Pomesa Award 1996, Nomura Prize for AIDS and Cancer Research, Japan 1998, Warren Alpert Prize, Harvard Univ. 1998; 11 hon. degrees. *Publications:* over 700 scientific publs. *Leisure interests:* swimming, reading historical novels, tennis, theatre. *Address:* University of Maryland Baltimore, 3300 Metzerott Road, Adelphi, MD 20783, U.S.A.

GALLOIS, Louis; French business executive; b. 26 Jan. 1944, Montauban, Tarn-et-Garonne; s. of Jean Gallois and Marie Prax; m. Marie-Edmée Amaudric du Chaffaut 1974; one s. two d.; ed. Ecole Nat. d'Admin.; Head of Bureau, Treasury 1972; Dir. of Cabinet of M. Chevènement, Ministry of Research and Tech. 1981–82, Ministry of Research and Industry 1982; Dir.-Gen. for Industry, Ministry of Research and Industry 1983; Civil Admin. Ministry of Econ. and Finance 1986; Dir. of Civil and Mil. Cabinet, Minister of Defence 1988–89; Pres.-Dir.-Gen. Soc. Nationale d'Etude et de Construction de Moteurs d'Aviation (SNECMA) 1989–92; Pres. (Econ. Interest Group) Avion de Combat européen-Rafale 1989; Pres., Dir.-Gen. of Aérospatiale 1992–96; Pres. SNCF 1996–; Pres. Société Gestion de Participations Aéronautiques (SOGEPA) 1993–96; Vice-Pres. Supervisory Council Airbus-Industrie 1992–96; mem. Dassault aviation 1992–; Chevalier, Ordre nat. du Mérite. *Address:* SNCF, 88 rue Saint-Lazare, 75436 Paris cedex 09, France.

GALMOT, Yves; French judge; b. 5 Jan. 1931, Paris; s. of Jean-Jacques Galmot and Marie Germaine Lengauer; m. Katrine-Marie Nicholson 1958; two s.; ed. Lycée Louis le Grand, Paris, Inst. d'Etudes Politiques de Paris, Ecole Nat. d'Administration; auditor, Council of State 1956; Tech. Adviser, Office of High Commr. for Youth and Sport 1958; Maître des Requêtes, Council of State 1962–; Govt. Commr. Legal Section, Council of State 1964–68; Sec.-Gen. Entreprise Minière et Chimique 1970–74; Councillor of State 1981–94; Judge, Court of Justice of European Communities 1982–88; Chair. Financial Section, Council of State 1994–96; mem. Court of Budget and Finance 1994–; Chair. Comm. Interministérielle des Installations Nucléaires de Base 1995–. *Leisure interest:* golf. *Address:* Conseil d'Etat, 75100 Paris RP (Office); 95 rue de la Santé, 75013 Paris, France (Home).

GALPIN, Rodney D., C.B.I.M.; British business executive and banker; b. 5 Feb. 1932; s. of Sir Albert Galpin, K.C.V.O.; m. Sylvia Craven 1956; one s. one d.; ed. Haileybury and Imperial Service Coll.; joined Bank of England 1952; Sec. to Gov. 1962–66, Deputy Prin. Discount Office 1970–74, Deputy Chief Cashier Banking and Money Markets Supervision 1974–78, Chief Establishments 1978–80, Chief Corp. Services 1980–82, Assoc. Dir. 1982–84, Dir. 1984–88; Chair. and Group C.E.O. Standard Chartered PLC 1988–93, Standard Chartered Bank 1988–93; Chair. Alpha Airports Group 1994–, Code of Banking Practice Review Cttee. 1994–; Dir. (non-exec.) Cater Allen Holdings 1993–97, Capital Shopping Centres PLC 1994–, Ascot Holdings PLC 1995–, P.O. 1996–, Abbey National Treasury Services PLC 1997–; Life Gov. and Council mem. Haileybury 1973–; mem. Council Scout Asscn. 1972–, mem. Council Foundation for Man. Educ. 1984–86; Chair. Look Ahead Housing Asscn. 1994–; Freeman City of London Award 1981; Order of St. John. *Leisure interests:* tennis, gardening, music. *Address:* Alderman's Cottage, Lutmans Haven, Knowl Hill, Reading, Berks., RG10 9YN, England.

GALSWORTHY, Anthony Charles, C.M.G., M.A.; British diplomatist; b. 20 Dec. 1944, London; s. of Sir Arthur Galsworthy and Lady Galsworthy; m. Jan Dawson-Grove 1970; one s. one d.; ed. St. Paul's School, Corpus Christi Coll. Cambridge; Foreign Office, London 1966, Third Sec., Hong Kong 1967, Third, later Second Sec., Beijing 1970, Second, later First Sec., FCO, London 1972, First Sec., Rome 1977, First Sec., later Counsellor, Beijing 1981, Counsellor and Head Hong Kong Dept., FCO 1984, Prin. Pvt. Sec. to Sec. of State for Foreign and Commonwealth Affairs 1986, with Royal Inst. of Int. Affairs, London 1988, British Sr. Rep., Jt. Liaison Group, Hong Kong 1989, Cabinet Office 1993, Deputy Under-Sec. of State, FCO 1995, Amb. to People's Repub. of China 1997–. *Leisure interests:* wildlife, entomology. *Address:* British Embassy, 11 Guang Hua Lu, Jian Guo Men Wai, Beijing, People's Republic of China. *Telephone:* 6532 1961. *Fax:* 6532 1937.

GALTIERI, Lieut.-Gen. Leopoldo Fortunato; Argentinian politician and army officer; b. 15 July 1926, Caseros (Prov. of Buenos Aires); m. Lucia Noemi Gentili 1949; one s. two d.; ed. Buenos Aires, Nat. Mil. Coll.; Sub-Lieut., Engineers 1945, Lieut. 1947, First Lieut. 1949, Capt. 1952; joined Batallón 4 de Zapadores (Sappers), 1952–54; became Major 1957, Infantry Div. Commdr. 1962, Lieut.-Col. 1967; Prof. at Escuela Superior de Guerra 1962; Sub.-Dir. Engineers' Training School 1964–67; promoted Col. 1967, Brig.-Gen. commanding 9th Infantry Brigade 1972–73, 7th Brigade 1974–75; Major-Gen. 1975; Deputy Chief of Staff 1975; Commdr. 2nd Army Corps 1976, 1st Army Corps Jan.–Dec. 1979; Lieut.-Gen. Dec. 1979, C.-in-C. of the Army 1979–82; also mem. ruling military junta 1979–82; Pres. of Argentina 1981–82; seized Falkland Is. April 1982; court-martialled for conduct during Falklands War (on trial for violations of human rights 1983, acquitted Dec. 1985); sentenced to 12 years in prison for negligence for starting and losing the Falklands conflict 1986, released and pensioned Oct. 1989; numerous military decorations.

GALTUNG, Johan, PH.D.; Norwegian professor of peace studies; b. 24 Oct. 1930, Oslo; s. of August Galtung and Helga Holmboe; m. 1st Ingrid Eide 1956 (divorced 1968); two s.; m. 2nd Fumiko Nishimura; one s. one d.; ed. Univ. of Oslo; Prof. of Sociology, Columbia Univ., N.Y. 1957–60; f. and Dir. Int. Peace Research Inst., Oslo 1959–69; Prof. of Peace Research, Univ. of Oslo 1969–77; Prof., Princeton Univ. 1985–89; Prof. of Peace Studies, Univ. of Hawaii 1985–; Prof. of Peace and Co-operation Studies, Univ. Witten-Herdecke, Germany; Olof Palme Prof. of Peace, Stockholm, Sweden 1990–91; Dir. Transcend (peace and devt. network); Hon. Prof. Berlin, Alicante, Sichuan; Dr. h.c. (Finland, Romania, Uppsala, Tokyo, Sichuan, Witten/Herdecke, Osnabrück, Turin); Alternative Nobel Peace Prize (Right Livelihood Award), Bajaj Int. Gandhi Prize. *Publications include:* Theory and Methods of Social Research 1967, There are Alternatives 1983, Hitlerism, Stalinism, Reaganism 1984; Essays in Peace Research Vols. I-VI 1974–88, Human Rights in Another Key, Peace Studies: Peace, Conflict, Development, Civilization. *Leisure interests:* travel, writing. *Address:* Skogbrynet 15F, Oslo 2, Norway; Casa 227, Urb. Escandinavia, ALFAZ Del Pi, Alicante, Spain; 2047 Nuuanu Avenue, Suite No. 1601, Honolulu, HI 96817, U.S.A.; 51 Bois Chatton, 01210 Versonnex, France. *Telephone:* 450.42.73.06 (France); (808) 523-5029 (Honolulu). *Fax:* 450.42.75.06 (France); (808) 523-5029 (Honolulu).

GALUN, Esra, PH.D.; Israeli university professor; b. 7 April 1927, Leipzig, Germany; s. of David Mendel Galun and Erna Esther Markus; m. Margalith Katz 1953; two s.; ed. Hebrew Univ. Jerusalem, California Inst. of Tech., U.S.A.; Sr. Scientist, Plant Genetics, Weizmann Inst. of Science 1963–67, Assoc. Prof. of Plant Genetics 1968–72, Head Dept. of Plant Genetics 1970–88, Prof. of Biology 1972–, Dean Feinberg Grad. School 1974–75, Dean Faculty of Biology 1988–91; Maria Moors Cabot Research Fellow Biological Labs., Harvard Univ., U.S.A. 1967–68; Chair. Israeli Nat. Council for Research and Devt. 1982–84; Distinguished Visiting Scientist The Roche Inst. of Molecular Biology, Nutley, NY 1985; Armando Kaminitz Award for Achievements in Agric. Research. *Publications:* Pollination Mechanisms, Reproduction and Plant Breeding (jtly.) 1977, Transgenic Plants (with Adina Breiman) 1997, over 180 publs. in learned journals. *Leisure interests:* music, archaeology, philosophy. *Address:* Department of Plant Sciences, The Weizmann Institute of Science, Rehovot 76100, Israel. *Telephone:* 89-9343585. *Fax:* 8-9344181.

GALUŠKA, Vladimír, J.D.; Czech diplomatist and lawyer; b. 2 Oct. 1952, Prague; s. of Miroslav Galuška and Milena Galušková (née Králová); m. Marcela Wintrová 1975; two s.; ed. Charles Univ., Prague; corp. lawyer Škoda Co., Prague 1975–90; Consul, Deputy Chief of Mission, Czech Embassy, Washington, D.C. 1990–94; Dir. Personnel Dept., Ministry of Foreign Affairs 1994–97; Perm. Rep. of Czech Repub. to UN 1997–. *Address:* Permanent Mission of the Czech Republic to the United Nations, 1109 Madison Avenue, New York, NY 10028, U.S.A. *Telephone:* (212) 772-0314. *Fax:* (212) 772-0586.

GALVAO FILHO, Orlando, M.A.; Brazilian business executive; b. 14 July 1940, Itabuna, Bahia; s. of Orlando Galvão and Myrthes Galvão; two s.; ed. Navy Acad. and Catholic Univ. of Rio de Janeiro; fmr. lecturer in Industrial Econs. and Org.; joined Petrobrás 1974, Head Finance Dept. 1981–88, Chair. and C.E.O. 1989, mem. Bd. of Dirs. 1993, C.E.O. Petrobrás Distribuidora—BR 1993; Chair. Ogefi Financial Consulting 1989–93; mem. Brazilian Asscn. of Professional Economists. *Address:* c/o Petrobrás, Av. República do Chile 65, Suite 2301, Rio de Janeiro, 20035-900, Brazil. *Telephone:* (021) 534.2040, 534.2041. *Fax:* (021) 262.1152.

GALVÊAS, Ernane; Brazilian politician, economist and banker; b. 1 Oct. 1922, Cachoeiro do Itapemirim; s. of José Galvêas and Maria de Oliveira; m. Odaléa dos Santos 1948; one s. one d.; ed. Coll. of Economics and Finance, Rio de Janeiro Univ., Centro de Estudios Monetarios Latino-Americanos, Mexico and Yale Univ.; fmrly. Prof. of Banking and Finance, Coll. of Econs. and Finance, Rio de Janeiro, subsequently Prof. of Int. Trade, of Monetary Policy and of Int. Monetary Policy; Assoc. Chief, Econs. Dept., Supervisory Council for Finance and Credit (SUMOC) 1953–61; Econ. Consultant to Minister of Finance 1961–63; Financial Dir. Merchant Marine Comm. 1963–65; Dir. Foreign Trade Dept., Banco do Brasil 1966–68; Pres. Banco Central do Brasil 1968–74, 1979; Minister of Finance 1980–84; Exec. Vice-Pres. Aracruz Celulose S.A. 1974–79, Gen. Man. GB-Repres. Negócios Ltda. 1987–; Econ. Consultant Nat. Conf. on Commerce 1987–; Pres. APEC Asscn. to Promote Econ. Studies 1985–; Dir. Lorentzen Empreendimentos, Cia. Paraibuna de Metais, Quimio Ind. Farmacêutica, Banco Santista, SANBRA S.A.; mem. Acad. of Int. Law and Econs. (São Paulo). *Publications:* Brazil—Frontier of Development 1974, Development and Inflation 1976, Brazil—Open or Closed Economy? 1978, Apprentice of Entrepreneur 1983, Financial System and Capital Market 1985, The Saga of the Crisis 1985, The Oil Crisis 1985, The Two Faces of Cruzado 1987, Inflation, Deficit and Monetary Policy 1995; numerous articles on economic and financial topics. *Address:* Avenida Atlântica, 2492 Apt. 301, Rio de Janeiro, RJ Brazil. *Fax:* 21-2406920.

GALVIN, Gen. John Rogers; American army officer; b. 13 May 1929, Melrose, Mass.; s. of John James Galvin and Mary Josephine Logan; m. Virginia Lee Brennan 1961; four d.; ed. U.S. Military Acad., Columbia Univ.,

Univ. of Pennsylvania, Command and Gen. Staff Coll. and Fletcher School of Law and Diplomacy; commissioned 2nd Lieut. U.S. Army 1954; Military Asst. and ADC to Sec. of U.S. Army 1968–69; Commdr. 1st Bn. 8th Cavalry 1970; Mil. Asst. to Supreme Allied Commdr., Europe (SACEUR) 1974–75; Commdr. Div. Support Command 3rd Infantry Div. 1975–77, Chief of Staff 1977–78; Commanding Gen. 24th Infantry Div. 1981–83; VII (U.S.) Corps 1983–85; Commdr.-in-Chief U.S. Southern Command 1985–87; Supreme Allied Commdr. Europe and C.-in-C. U.S. European Command 1987–92; Olin Distinguished Prof. of Nat. Security, U.S. Military Acad., West Point 1992–93; Distinguished Visiting Policy Analyst Mershon Center, Ohio State Univ. 1994–95; Dean Fletcher School of Law and Diplomacy, Tufts Univ., Boston 1995–; Defense Distinguished Service Medal, Army Distinguished Service Medal, Silver Star, Legion of Merit (with 2 oak leaf clusters), Soldier's Medal, Bronze Star with 2 oak leaf clusters, Combat Infantryman Badge, Ranger Tab and 20 foreign decorations. *Publications:* The Minute Men 1967, Air Assault 1969, Three Men of Boston 1974 and 80 articles on leadership, tactics and training. *Leisure interests:* reading, writing and walking. *Address:* 114 South Street, Medford, MA 02155, U.S.A. *Telephone:* (617) 627-3050. *Fax:* (617) 627-3508.

GALVIN, Robert W.; American executive; b. 9 Oct. 1922, Marshfield, Wis.; m. Mary Barnes 1944; two s. two d.; ed. Univs. of Notre Dame and Chicago; Motorola Inc. Chicago 1940–, Pres. 1956, Chair. of Bd. 1964–90, C.E.O. 1984–86, Chair. Exec. Cttee. 1990; Dir. Harris Trust and Savings Bank, Chicago; Trustee Illinois Inst. of Tech.; Fellow, Univ. of Notre Dame; Dir. Junior Achievement of Chicago; mem. Pres.'s Comm. on Int. Trade and Investment; Electronic Industries Asscn. Medal of Honour 1970. *Leisure interests:* skiing, water-skiing, tennis, horse-riding. *Address:* c/o Motorola Inc., 1303 East Algonquin Road, Schaumburg, IL 60196, U.S.A. (Office).

GALWAY, James, O.B.E., F.R.C.M.; British flautist; b. 8 Dec. 1939, Belfast; s. of James and Ethel Stewart (née Clarke) Galway; m. 1st 1965; one s.; m. 2nd 1972; one s. two d. (twins); m. 3rd Jeanne Cinnante 1984; ed. Mountcollyer Secondary School, Royal Coll. of Music, Guildhall School of Music, Conservatoire National Supérieur de Musique, Paris; first post in Wind Band of Royal Shakespeare Theatre, Stratford-on-Avon; later worked with Sadler's Wells Orchestra, Royal Opera House Orchestra, BBC Symphony Orchestra; Prin. Flute, London Symphony Orchestra and Royal Philharmonic Orchestra; Prin. Solo Flute, Berlin Philharmonic Orchestra 1969–75; int. soloist 1975–; soloist/conductor 1984–; has made numerous recordings; Hon. M.A. (Open Univ.) 1979, Hon. D.Mus. (Queen's Univ., Belfast) 1979, Hon. D.Mus. (New England Conservatory of Music) 1980; Grand Prix du Disque 1976, 1989; Officier des Arts et des Lettres 1987. *Publications:* James Galway: An Autobiography 1978, Flute (Menuhin Music Guide) 1982, James Galway's Music in Time 1983. *Leisure interests:* music, walking, swimming, films, theatre, TV, computing, chess, backgammon, talking to people. *Address:* c/o Kathryn Enticott, IMG Artists (Europe), Media House, 3 Burlington Lane, London, W4 2TH, England.

GAMA, Jaime; Portuguese politician; b. 1947, Azores; Minister of Home Affairs 1978, Minister of Foreign Affairs 1983–85, 1995–; unsuccessful cand. in contest for leadership of Socialist Party 1986, 1988. *Address:* Ministry of Foreign Affairs, Largo do Rilvas, 1354 Lisbon, Portugal. *Telephone:* (1) 3928340. *Fax:* (1) 3909708.

GAMASSI, Gen. Mohamed Abdul Ghani al–; Egyptian government official and army officer; b. 9 Sept 1921, el-Batanoun, Menoufia Governorate; ed. Mil. Acad., Staff Coll., Nasser Higher Mil. Acad.; Asst. Dir. of Mobilization Dept. 1954–55; Commdr. 5th Reconnaissance Regt. 1955–57; Staff Officer, Armoured Corps 1957–59; Commdr. 2nd Armoured Brigade 1959–61; Commdr. Armour School 1961–66; Chief, Army Operational Branch 1966–67; Chief of Staff, Eastern Mil. Zone 1967–68; Deputy Dir. Reconnaissance and Intelligence Dept. 1968–70; Commdr. Operational Group, Syrian Front 1970–71; Chief, Armed Forces Training Dept. 1971–72; Chief of Operations Dept. and Deputy Chief of Staff of Armed Forces 1972–73; Chief of Staff of Armed Forces 1973–74; Minister of War and C.-in-C. of Armed Forces 1974–78, also a Deputy Prime Minister 1975–78; Mil. Adviser to Pres. 1978; Order of Liberation 1952, Memorial Order of Founding of U.A.R. 1958, Star of Honour 1973, Star of Honour (PLO) 1974, Kt. Order of Mil. Honour (Syria) 1974, Order of Courage (Libya) 1974, Order of the Two Niles, First Class (Sudan) 1974, Order of King Abdel Aziz, First Class (Saudi Arabia) 1974, Order of Homayoun, First Class (Iran) 1975; numerous ribbons and medals. *Address:* Office of the President, Abdeen, Cairo, Egypt.

GAMBARI, Ibrahim Agboola; Nigerian diplomatist and academic; b. 24 Nov. 1944, Ilorin, Kwara State; m. Fatima Oniyangi 1969; one s. one d.; ed. Kings Coll., Lagos, L.S.E., Columbia Univ.; lecturer, Queen's Coll. 1969–74; Asst. Prof., State Univ. of New York (Albany) 1974–77; Sr. Lecturer, Ahmadu Bello Univ., Zaria 1977–80, Assoc. Prof. 1980–83, Prof. 1983–89; Dir.-Gen. Nigerian Inst. of Int. Affairs 1983–84; Minister for Foreign Affairs 1984–85; Visiting Prof., Johns Hopkins Univ. School of Advanced Int. Studies, Howard Univ., Georgetown Univ. and Brookings Inst. 1986–89; Resident Scholar, Rockefeller Foundation Bellagio Study and Conf. Centre, Italy Nov.–Dec. 1989; Perm. Rep. to UN 1990–; Hon. Prof. Chugsan Univ., Guangzhou, People's Repub. of China 1985; fmr. Guest Scholar, Wilson Center for Int. Scholars, Smithsonian Inst., U.S.A.; Chair. Nat. Seminar to Commemorate 25th Anniversary of OAU, Lagos 1988. *Publications:* Party Politics and Foreign Policy in Nigeria During the First Republic 1981, Theory and Reality in Foreign Policy Making: Nigeria After the Second Republic 1989, Political and Comparative Dimensions of Regional Integration: the Case of ECOWAS 1991. *Address:* Permanent Mission of Nigeria to the United Nations, 828 Second Avenue, New York, NY 10017, U.S.A. *Telephone:* (212) 953-9130. *Fax:* (212) 697-1970.

GAMBAROV, Isa Yunis ogly; Russian-Azerbaijani politician and historian; b. Feb. 1957, Baku, Azerbaijan; s. of Yunis Gambarov and Tahira Gambarov; m. 1986; two s.; ed. Baku State Univ.; researcher Inst. of Oriental Studies Azerbaijan Acad. of Sciences; active participant in democratic movt. in late 1980s, Head of organizational div. of Popular Front 1990–, Deputy Chair. 1991–; mem. Azerbaijan Supreme Soviet 1990–95, mem. Milli-Medzhlis and Chair. Comm. on Foreign Affairs; Chair. Azerbaijan Supreme Soviet 1992–93; Chair. Musavat (Muslim Democratic Party) 1992–. *Address:* Azerbaijan Prospekti 37, Baku 370000, Azerbaijan. *Telephone:* 611500. *Fax:* 983166, 982088.

GAMBIER, Dominique, D. ÈS SC.ECON.; French university teacher; b. 14 Aug. 1947, Rouen; s. of Michel and Yvette Morel; two d.; ed. Lycée Corneille, Rouen and Ecole Centrale de Paris; Asst. Univ. of Rouen 1972–81; Prof. Ecole Centrale de Paris 1981–83; special assignment, Commissariat Général au Plan 1983–84; Maître de conférences, and Dir. Inst. of Research and Documentation in Social Sciences (I.R.E.D.), Univ. of Rouen 1984–87; expert adviser, EEC, Brussels 1980–81; scientific adviser, Observatoire français des conjonctures économiques (OFCE) 1981–83; Regional Councillor, Haute-Normandie 1986–, Vice-Pres. of Regional Council 1998–; Pres. Univ. of Rouen 1987–88; Deputy for Seine Maritime 1988–93; Mayor of Déville-les-Rouen 1995–. *Publications:* Analyse conjoncturelle du chômage, Théorie de la politique économique en situation d'incertitude 1980, Le marché du travail 1991, L'emploi en France 1997; numerous articles on economy of work and labour etc. *Leisure interests:* football, tennis, skiing. *Address:* Mairie de Déville, 1 Place François Mitterrand, 76250 Déville; 5 allée du Houssel, 76130 Mont-St-Aignan, France (Home). *Telephone:* 35.76.88.18. *Fax:* 35.74.30.73.

GAMBLE, Christine Elizabeth, PH.D.; British cultural administrator; b. 1 March 1950, Rotherham; d. of Albert Edward Gamble and Kathleen Laura Wallis; m. Edward Barry Antony Craxton; ed. Royal Holloway Coll., Univ. of London; worked in Anglo-French cultural org. 1974–75; Office of the Cultural Attaché, British Embassy, Moscow 1975–76; joined British Council, New Delhi 1977, returned to U.K. (Stratford-upon-Avon) 1979, posted to Harare 1980–82, Regional Officer for the Soviet Union and Mongolia 1982–85, Deputy Dir. Athens 1985–87, with Corp. Planning Dept. 1988–90, Head Project Pursuit Dept. and Dir. Chancellor's Financial Sector Scheme 1990–92, Dir. Visitor's Dept. 1992–93, Gen. Man. Country Services Group and Head European Services 1993–96, Dir. French Section 1996–98; Dir. Royal Inst. of Int. Affairs, London 1998–. *Leisure interests:* literature, art, music, theatre. *Address:* The Royal Institute of International Affairs, Chatham House, 10 St. James's Square, London, SW1Y 4LE, England. *Telephone:* 0171-957 5700. *Fax:* 0171-957 5710.

GAMBLING, William Alexander, PH.D., D.SC., F.ENG., F.R.S.; British opto-electronics researcher and industrial consultant; b. 11 Oct. 1926, Port Talbot, Glamorgan; s. of George Alexander and Muriel Clara Gambling; m. 1st Margaret Pooley 1952 (separated 1987); one s. two d.; m. 2nd Barbara Colleen O'Neil 1994; ed. Univs. of Bristol and Liverpool; Lecturer in Electric Power Eng., Univ. of Liverpool 1950–55; Fellow, Nat. Research Council, Univ. of B.C. 1955–57; Lecturer, Sr. Lecturer and Reader, Univ. of Southampton 1957–64, Prof. of Electronics 1964–80, Dean of Eng. and Applied Science 1972–75, Head of Dept. 1974–79, British Telecom Prof. of Optical Communication 1980–95, Dir. Opto-electronics Research Centre 1989–95; Royal Soc. Visiting Prof. and Dir., Opto-electronics Research Centre, City Univ. of Hong Kong 1996–; Visiting Prof., Univ. of Colo. 1966–67, Bhabha Atomic Research Centre, India 1970, Osaka Univ., Japan 1977; Hon. Prof. Huazhong Univ. of Science and Tech., Wuhan, 1986–, Beijing Univ. of Posts and Telecommunications, Shanghai Univ. of Science and Tech. 1991–; Hon. Dir. Beijing Optical Fibres Lab., People's Repub. of China 1987–; Pres. I.E.R.E. 1977–78; Chair. Comm.D, Int. Union of Radio Science 1981–84, Eng. Council 1983–88; mem. Bd., Council of Eng. Insts. 1974–79, Electronics Research Council 1977–80, Nat. Electronics Council 1977–78 and 1984–; Dir. York Ltd. 1980–97; mem. British Nat. Cttee. for Radio Science 1978–87, Educational Advisory Council, IBA 1980–82, Eng. Industries Training Bd. 1985–88; mem. Council, Royal Acad. of Eng. 1989–92; Hon. Fellow I.E.E.; Selby Fellow, Australian Acad. of Science 1982; Foreign mem. Polish Acad. of Sciences 1985; Freeman, City of London 1988, Liveryman, Worshipful Co. of Engineers 1988; Dr. h.c. (Madrid) 1994, (Aston) 1995; Academic Enterprise Award 1982, J. J. Thomson Medal, IEE 1982, Faraday Medal, IEE 1983, Churchill Medal, Soc. of Engineers 1985, Simms Medal, Soc. of Engineers 1988, Micro-optics Award (Japan) 1989, Dennis Gabor Award (U.S.A.) 1990, Rank Prize for Optoelectronics 1991, C & C Medal (Japan) 1993, Mountbatten Medal 1993. *Publications:* papers on electronics and optical fibre communications. *Address:* Opto-electronics Research Centre, City University of Hong Kong, Tat Chee Avenue, Kowloon, Hong Kong. *Telephone:* (852) 2788 7828.

GAMBON, Sir Michael John, Kt., C.B.E.; British actor; b. 19 Oct. 1940, Dublin; s. of Edward Gambon and Mary Gambon; m. Anne Miller 1962; one s.; ed. St. Aloysius School for Boys, London; fmr. Mechanical Engineer; first stage appearance with Edwards/Mácliammoir Co., Dublin 1962; Nat.

Theatre, Old Vic 1963–67; Birmingham Repertory and other provincial theatres 1967–69, title roles including Othello, Macbeth, Coriolanus; R.S.C. Aldwych 1970–71; The Norman Conquests 1974, Otherwise Engaged 1976, Just Between Ourselves 1977, Alice's Boys 1978; with Nat. Theatre 1980, appearing in Galileo (London Theatre Critics' Award for Best Actor), Betrayal, Tales from Hollywood; with R.S.C., Stratford and London 1982–83, title roles in King Lear, Antony and Cleopatra, Old Times 1985, A Chorus of Disapproval, Nat. Theatre 1985 (Olivier Award for Best Comedy Performance), A Small Family Business 1987, Uncle Vanya 1988, Mountain Language 1988, Othello 1990, Taking Steps 1990, Skylight (play) 1995, Volpone (Evening Standard Drama Award) 1995, Tom and Clem 1997, The Unexpected Man 1998. *TV:* numerous appearances including: Ghosts, Oscar Wilde, The Holy Experiment, Absurd Person Singular, The Borderers, The Singing Detective, The Heat of the Day, Maigret 1992, The Entertainer, Truth. *Films:* The Beast Must Die 1975, Turtle Diary 1985, Paris by Night 1988, The Cook, the thief, his wife and her lover, A Dry White Season 1989, The Rachel Papers 1989, State of Grace 1989, The Heat of the Day 1989, Mobsters 1992, Toys 1992, Clean Slate 1993, Indian Warrior 1993, The Browning Version 1993, Mary Reilly 1994, Two Deaths 1994, Midnight in Moscow 1994, A Man of No Importance 1995, The Innocent Sleep 1995, All our Fault 1995, Two Deaths 1996, Nothing Personal 1996, The Gambler 1996, Dancing at Lughnasa 1997, Plunket and McClean 1997, the Last September 1998, Sleepy Hollow 1998; Trustee Royal Armouries 1995–. *Leisure interests:* flying, gun collecting, clock making. *Address:* c/o ICM, Oxford House, Oxford Street, London, W1N 0AX, England.

GAMES, David Edgar, PH.D., C.CHEM., F.R.S.C.; British university professor; b. 7 April 1938, Ynysddu; s. of Alfred William Games and Frances Elizabeth Bell Games (née Evans); m. Marguerite Patricia Lee 1961; two s.; ed. Lewis School, Pengam, King's Coll., Univ. of London; lecturer, Sr. Lecturer, Reader and Personal Chair. Univ. Coll., Cardiff 1965–89; Prof. of Mass Spectrometry and Dir. of Mass Spectrometry Research Unit, Univ. of Wales at Swansea 1989–, Head Dept. of Chem. 1996–; Royal Soc. of Chem. Award in Analytical Separation Methods 1987, The Chromatographic Soc. Martin Medal 1991, Royal Soc. of Chem. SAC Gold Medal 1993, J. J. Thomson Gold Medal, Int. Mass Spectrometry Cttee. 1997. *Leisure interests:* swimming, walking. *Address:* Mass Spectrometry Research Unit, University of Wales Swansea, Singleton Park, Swansea, SA2 8PP (Office); 9 Heneage Drive, West Cross, Swansea, SA3 5BR, Wales (Home). *Telephone:* (01792) 295298 (Office); (01792) 405192 (Home). *Fax:* (01792) 295717 (Office).

GAMKRELIDZE, Thomas V.; Georgian linguist; b. 23 Oct. 1929, Kutaisi, Georgia; s. of Valerian and Olimpiada Gamkrelidze; m. Nino Djavakhishvili 1968; one s. one d.; ed. Tbilisi Univ.; post-grad. work 1952–55; Lecturer, Georgian Acad. of Sciences Inst. of Linguistics 1956–60; Head of Dept. 1960–73, Dir., The Oriental Inst. 1973–; Head of Dept. Tbilisi State Univ. 1966–72; main work in area of theoretical linguistics, Kartvelian, Semitic and Indo-European linguistics and semiology; People's Deputy of the U.S.S.R. 1989–91; mem. Parl. Repub. of Georgia 1992–(99); Ed.-in-Chief Voprosy Jazykoznanija (Russian Acad. of Sciences) 1988–94; mem. Georgian Acad. of Sciences 1974; mem. U.S.S.R. (now Russian) Acad. of Sciences 1984; Foreign Hon. mem. American Acad. of Arts and Sciences; Corresp. F.B.A.; mem. Austrian Acad. of Sciences; Foreign mem. Sächsische Akad. der Wissenschaften, Hon. mem. Indogermanische Gesellschaft, Linguistic Soc. of America, Societas Linguistica Europaea (Pres. 1986); Dr. h.c. (Bonn, Chicago); Lenin Prize 1988, Humboldt Prize (Fed. Repub. of Germany) 1989, Djavakhishvili Prize (Tbilisi Univ.) 1992. *Publications:* Indo-European and the Indo-Europeans (2 vols.) (with V. V. Ivanov) 1984, Alphabetic Writing and the Old Georgian Script. Typology and Provenance of alphabetic writing systems 1989. *Leisure interests:* music, tennis. *Address:* The Oriental Institute, Georgian Academy of Sciences, Acad. Tsereteli Street 3, 380062 Tbilisi, Georgia. *Telephone:* (32) 23-38-85 (Office); (32) 22-64-92 (Home). *Fax:* (32) 99-88-23; (32) 23-38-85.

GAMZATOV, Rasul Gamzatovich; Avar poet; b. 8 Sept. 1923, Tsadasa, Daghestan autonomous republic; s. of G. Tsadasa (nat. poet); ed. Moscow A. M. Gorky Literary Inst.; mem. CPSU 1944–91; worked on newspaper Bolshevik Gor 1941–51; radio ed. of programmes in Avar language, Daghestan; mem. staff, Maxim Gorky Inst., Moscow 1945–50; Chair. Bd. Union of Daghestan Writers 1951–; Deputy of Supreme Soviet of U.S.S.R. 1962–66; People's Deputy of U.S.S.R. 1989–91; mem. Presidium; mem. Soviet Cttee. of solidarity with countries of Asia and Africa –1991; State Prize 1952, Lenin Prize 1963, Hero of Socialist Labour. *Publications:* Hot Love and Burning Hate 1943, My Country 1947, Our Mountains 1947, The Homeland of a Miner 1950, Verse 1950, Tales of my Elder Brother 1952, Poems 1954, Spring in Daghestan 1955, My Heart is in the Mountains 1959, Stars on High 1962, Mountains and Valleys 1963, Zarema 1963, And Star Speaks with Star 1964, Selected Lyrics 1965, Mutlaka 1966, Sick Teeth (poetry) 1967, My Daghestan 1968, The Last Price 1978 (Firdausi Prize), Look After Mothers 1978, Collected Works (5 vols.) 1980–82, Island of Women 1983, The Wheel of Life 1987, The Dawn of Hope 1988, The Moment and the Eternity 1989, The Bowl of Life 1992, Collected Works (3 vols.) 1993. *Address:* M. Gorky str. 15, 367000 Makhachkala, Russia. *Telephone:* (87200) 77282.

GAN ZHIJIAN; Chinese government official and senior engineer; b. 1927, Shanghai; ed. Zhijang Univ. and in U.S.S.R.; joined CCP 1950; mem. State Planning Comm. 1982–85; Vice-Minister for State Planning 1985–88, for Construction 1988; mem. Financial and Econ. Cttee.; NPC Deputy for Shanghai Prov. *Address:* State Planning Commission, 38 Yuetan Nanjie Street, Sanlihe, Beijing 100824, People's Republic of China.

GAN ZIYU; Chinese government official and senior engineer; b. 15 Oct. 1929, Canton; two s.; ed. Zhongshan Univ.; joined CCP 1953; Vice-Chair. of State Planning Comm. 1978–, of Admin. Comm. on Import and Export Affairs 1981–82, of State Foreign Investment Comm. 1981–82; Vice-Chair. Drafting Cttee. for Nat. Defence Law of PRC 1993–; Deputy Chair. Nat. Leading Group for Work Concerning Foreign Capital 1994–; mem. Preliminary Working Cttee. of the Preparatory Cttee. of the Hong Kong Special Admin. Region 1993–97; Chair. Overseas Chinese Affairs Cttee., 9th NPC 1998–. *Address:* c/o Standing Committee of the National People's Congress, Beijing, People's Republic of China.

GANBAATAR, Adyagiin; Mongolian politician and academic; b. 8 Feb. 1959, Ulan Bator; s. of Adiya Ganbaatar and Ichinthorlo Ganbaatar; m.; three d.; lecturer, Mongolian State Univ. 1983–90; Chair. Democratic Socialist Movt. 1990; mem. State Great Hural (Parl.) 1993–, Chair. Standing Cttee. on the Budget 1997–; Vice-Chair. Cen. Asia Devt. Foundation 1992–; Pres. Mongolian Tennis Assc. 1997–. *Leisure interests:* chess, tennis. *Address:* Parliament, State House, Ulan Bator 12, Mongolia. *Telephone:* (1) 372980. *Fax:* (1) 372980.

GANBOLD, Davaadorjiin, M.SC.ECON., PH.D.; Mongolian politician; b. 26 June 1957, Ulan Bator; s. of Tsedevsuren Davaadorj and Lodongiin Oyun; m. M. Tserengav Oyun; two d.; ed. Moscow State Univ., U.S.S.R.; Asst. to Prof. of Political Econ., Mongolian State Univ. 1979–84; Prof. of Political Econ., State and Social Studies Acad. 1988–90; Founder-mem. Nat. Progress Party, Chair. Party Council; First Deputy Prime Minister 1990; mem. Great Hural (legislature) July 1992–; Chair. Standing Cttee. on Budget, Finance and Econs.; Chair. Mongolian Nat. Democratic Party (merger of four opposition parties) 1992–96, Deputy Leader 1998. *Leisure interests:* fishing, cycling, collecting stamps and model cars. *Address:* Room 221, Government House, Ulan Bator, Mongolia. *Telephone:* 320879 (Office); 322669 (Home). *Fax:* 328172.

GANDHI, Maneka Anand; Indian politician; b. 26 Aug. 1956, New Delhi; d. of the late Col. T. S. Anand and of Amteshwar Anand; m. Sanjay Gandhi 1974 (died 1980); one s.; ed. Jawaharlal Univ., New Delhi; Ed. Surya (Sun) magazine 1977–80; founder and leader of political party Rashtriya Sanjay Manch (merged with Janata Party 1988) 1983; Minister of State for the Environment and Forests 1989–91; M.P. 1996–; Chair. People for Animals Trust, Cttee. on Control and Supervision of Experiments on Animals, Soc. for Prevention of Cruelty to Animals; Founder Greenline Trees; Special Adviser to Voice (consumer action forum); cr. environmental film series New Horizons; writer and anchorwoman nat. TV programmes on animals Heads and Tails, Maneka's Ark; Pres. Ruth Cowell Trust, Sanjay Gandhi Animal Care Centre; Lord Erskine Award (R.S.P.C.A.) 1991, Vegetarian of the Year (Vegetarian Soc.) 1995, Prani Mitra Award (Nat. Animal Welfare Bd.) 1997, Marchig Prize (Marchig Animal Welfare Trust, G.B.) 1997. *Publications:* Sanjay Gandhi 1980, Mythology of Indian Plants, Animal Quiz, Penguin Book of Hindu Names, The Complete Book of Muslim and Parsi Names, First Aid for Animals, Animal Laws of India. *Leisure interests:* reading, working with animals. *Address:* A-4 Maharani Bagh, New Delhi 110065, India. *Telephone:* 684 7576. *Fax:* 682 3144.

GANDHI, Sonia; Indian (b. Italian) politician; b. 9 Dec. 1946, Italy; m. Rajiv Gandhi 1968 (fmr. Prime Minister of India) (deceased); ed. Univ. of Cambridge, Nat. Gallery of Modern Art, Delhi; Pres. Rajiv Gandhi Foundation; mem. All India Congress Cttee (I), leader March 1998–. *Address:* Rajiv Gandhi Foundation, Jawahar Bhawan, Dr. Rajendra Prasad Road, New Delhi 110001; All India Congress Committee (I), 24 Akbar Road, New Delhi 110011, India. *Telephone:* 3755117 (Rajiv Ghandi Foundation); 3019080 (All India Congress Cttee. (I)).

GANDOIS, Jean Guy Alphonse; French company executive; b. 7 May 1930, Nieul; s. of Eugène and Marguerite (née Teillet) Gandois; m. Monique Testard 1953; two s.; ed. École Polytechnique, Paris; Civil Engineer, Ministry of Public Works, French Guinea 1954–58; mem. of tech. co-operation missions to Brazil and Peru 1959–60; Asst. to Commercial Dir. Wendel & Cie 1961, Econ. Dir. 1966; Econ. and Commercial Dir. Wendel-Sidelor 1968; Gen. Man. Sacilor 1973; Pres., Dir.-Gen. Sollac 1975; Dir.-Gen. Rhône-Poulenc SA 1976, Vice-Pres. 1977–79, Chair. and C.E.O. 1979–82 (resigned); Chair. and C.E.O. Pechiney 1986–94; Chair. Cockerill-Sambre (Belgium); Pres. CNPF (Nat. Council of French Employers) 1994, now Hon. Pres.; mem. Bd. of Dirs. Danone (fmrly. BSN), Compagnie Financière de Paribas, Lyonnaise des Eaux, Vallourec, Banque Nationale de Paris (all in France), Société Générale de Belgique (Belgium), Siemens (Germany); mem. Supervisory Council Akzo (Netherlands); Commdr., Légion d'honneur; Grand Croix, Ordre de la Couronne (Belgium); Grand Officier, Ordre du Chêne (Luxembourg). *Address:* 4 rue Quentin Bauchart, 75008 Paris (Office); 23 Quai Voltaire, 75007 Paris, France (Home).

GANELIUS, Tord Hjalmar, D.PHIL; Swedish mathematician; b. 23 May 1925, Stockholm; s. of Hjalmar Ganelius and Ebba Bejbom; m. Aggie Hemberg 1951; three s. one d.; ed. Stockholm Univ.; Asst. Prof. Lund Univ. 1953–57; Prof. of Math., Univ. of Göteborg 1957–80, Dean, Faculty of Science 1963–65, 1977–80; Scientific Sec.-Gen. Swedish Royal Acad. of Sciences

1981–91; mem. Bd. of Dirs., Nobel Foundation 1981–89, V. and E. Hasselblad Foundation 1983–95; Guest Prof. Univ. of Washington, Seattle 1962, Cornell Univ. 1967–68, Madras Inst. of Math. Sciences 1969, Univ. of Calif., San Diego 1972–73; Fellow, Swedish Royal Acad., Finnish Acad., Royal Soc. of Göteborg, European Acad. of Arts and Sciences. *Publications:* Tauberian Remainder Theorems 1971, Lectures on Approximation, etc. 1982. *Address:* Bergianska trädgården, 104 05 Stockholm, Sweden (Home). *Telephone:* (0) 8-158548.

GANELLIN, Charon Robin, B.SC., PH.D., D.SC., F.R.S., F.R.S.C.; British professor in medicinal chemistry; b. 25 Jan. 1934, London; s. of Leon Ganellin and Beila Cluer; m. Tamara Greene 1956; one s. one d.; ed. Harrow County Grammar School for Boys and Queen Mary Coll., Univ. of London; Research Assoc. M.I.T. 1960; Research Chemist in Medicinal Chem., Smith Kline and French Labs. Ltd. (U.K.) 1958–59, Head of Dept. 1961–75, Dir. of Histamine Research, Smith Kline and French Research Ltd. 1975–80, Vice-Pres. Research 1980–84, Vice-Pres. Chemical Research 1984–86; Hon. Lecturer, Dept. of Pharmacology, Univ. Coll., London 1975–86, Smith Kline and French Prof. of Medicinal Chem. 1986–; Hon. Prof. of Medicinal Chem., Univ. of Kent 1979–; Fellow Queen Mary and Westfield Coll., Univ. of London 1992; Hon. mem. Sociedad Española de Química Terapéutica 1982–; Hon. D.Sc. (Aston) 1995; U.K. Chemical Soc. Medallion in Medicinal Chemistry 1977, Prix Charles Mentzer, Soc. de Chimie Thérapeutique (France) 1978, American Chemical Soc., Div. of Medicinal Chem. Award 1980, Royal Soc. of Chem. Tilden Medal 1982, Soc. for Chemical Industry Messel Medal 1988, Soc. for Drug Research Award 1989, Nat. Inventors Hall of Fame (U.S.A.) 1990, Royal Soc. of Chemistry Adrien Albert Medal 1999. *Publications:* Pharmacology of Histamine Receptors 1982, Frontiers in Histamine Research 1985, Dictionary of Drugs 1990, Medicinal Chemistry 1993, Dictionary of Pharmacological Agents 1997; research papers and reviews in various journals. *Address:* Department of Chemistry, University College London, 20 Gordon Street, London, WC1H 0AJ, England. *Telephone:* 0171-387 7050.

GANEV, Stoyan; Bulgarian politician and lawyer; b. 1955; specialises in constitutional law; Minister of Foreign Affairs 1991–92; a Deputy Prime Minister of Bulgaria 1991–92; mem. Union of Democratic Forces (UDF). *Address:* c/o Union of Democratic Forces, Boulevard Rakovski 134, 1000 Sofia, Bulgaria.

GANIĆ, Ejup, D.SC.; Bosnia and Herzegovina politician and scientist; b. 3 March 1946, Novi Pazar; ed. Belgrade Univ., Massachusetts Inst. of Tech.; researcher, consultant, Prof. of Mechanical Eng., Univ. of Ill. Chicago 1975–82; returned to Bosnia and Herzegovina 1982; worked as Exec. Dir. UNIS Co.; Prof. Sarajevo Univ.; advisor to Govt. of Bosnia and Herzegovina on tech. and devt.; mem. Presidency of Bosnia and Herzegovina 1990–96, Vice-Pres. 1992–96; Vice-Pres. Fed. of Bosnia and Herzegovina 1994–96, Co-Pres. 1996–98. *Address:* c/o Presidency of the Federation of Bosnia and Herzegovina, 71000 Sarajevo, Bosnia and Herzegovina.

GANIEV, Rivner Fazilovich; Russian mechanical engineer; b. 1 April 1937, Bashkiriya; m. Galina Mikhailovna Antonovskaya; two s.; ed. Ufa Aviation Inst.; engineer constructor, jr., sr. researcher, head of dept. Inst. of Mechanics Ukrainian Acad. of Sciences 1959–78; head of lab. Research Inst. of Machine Devt. 1978–89, Deputy Dir. 1989–95; Dir. of Non-linear Wave Mechanics and Tech. Centre, Russian Acad. of Sciences 1995–; corresp. mem. U.S.S.R. (now Russian) Acad. of Sciences 1987, mem. 1994; research in theory of resonance phenomena at nonlinear spatial oscillations of solid and deformable matter, theory of nonlinear oscillations of multiphase systems, vibration and wave processes and tech.; mem. Scientific Council on Problem Reliability of Machines. *Publications include:* Dynamics of Particles under Influence of Vibrations 1975, Solid Matter Oscillations 1976, Oscillatory Phenomena in Multiphase Media and their Applications to Technology 1980, numerous articles in scientific journals. *Leisure interests:* sport, skiing. *Address:* Wave Mechanics and Technology Centre, Russian Academy of Sciences, 4 Bardin Street, 117334 Moscow, Russia. *Telephone:* (095) 135 5593 (Office). *Fax:* (095) 135 6126.

GANSER, Gérard Robert Gaston; French civil servant; b. 6 Jan. 1949, Montreuil-Sous-Bois; s. of Pierre Ganser and Simone Braillon; m. Aimée Fontaine (divorced); one s.; ed. Lycées Paul Valéry and Louis le Grand, Nat. School of Admin.; auditor Court of Revenue 1976–80, public auditor 1980, chief adviser 1993–98, Sec.-Gen. 1998–; with Interministerial Mission of the Sea 1979–80; commercial adviser Mexico 1981–82; with Ministry of Agric. 1983, Jt. Dir. Ministry of Trade and Tourism 1983–84, with Ministry of Industrial Redeployment and Trade 1984, Ministry for Communications 1988, Dir. 1989–91; Jt. Dir.-Gen. Commercial Affairs Télédiffusion de France 1984–86; reporter to Constitutional Council 1987–88; Pres., Dir.-Gen. Soc. financière de radiodiffusion (Sofirad) 1991–94; Vice-Pres. Radio Monte Carlo 1991–94; auditor European Examinations Office 1995; auditor Inst. des hautes études de la défense nat. 1996; Chevalier Ordre nat. du Mérite. *Address:* Cour des Comptes, 13 rue Cambon, 75001 Paris (Office); 11 rue de Verneuil, 75007 Paris, France (Home).

GANSHOF VAN DER MEERSCH, Viscount Walter, LL.D.; Belgian jurist; b. 1900, Bruges; m. Elizabeth Orts 1923; one s. one d.; ed. King's Coll., Wimbledon, England, Royal Athenaeum, Bruges, and Univs. of Paris and Brussels; Prof. of Constitutional Law 1938, European Law 1958, Comparative Law 1960, Univ. of Brussels; Pres. Inst. of European Studies, Brussels, and Inter-Univ. Centre of Public Law; Pres. Inter-Univ. Centre of Comparative Law; Judge Advocate-Gen. 1940; served in Belgian Army in both World Wars; Lieut.-Gen.; High Commr. for Security of the Realm 1943; mem. Supreme Court of Justice 1947–; Minister of Gen. Affairs in Africa 1960; Judge ad hoc, Int. Court of Justice, The Hague 1960–68; Attorney-Gen. 1968; Vice-Pres. European Court of Human Rights, Strasbourg 1973; lecturer, Hague Acad. of Int. Law 1975; Francqui Chair., Univ. Louvain 1975; Hon. Bencher Gray's Inn, London; mem. Acad. Int. de Droit comparé, Acad. Royale des Sciences d'Outremer, Acad. Royale des Lettres et des Sciences de Belgique (Pres.); Dr. h.c. (Strasbourg); Hon. C.B. (U.K.), Grand Cross Order of Crown (Belgium), Grand Cross Order of Léopold (Belgium), Commdr. Legion of Merit (U.S.A.), Commdr. Légion d'honneur, Grand Officier Order Crown of Oak (Luxembourg), Belgian and French Croix de guerre and other war medals. *Publications:* Pouvoir de fait et règle de droit dans le fonctionnement des institutions politiques 1956, Fin de la souveraineté belge au Congo 1963, Le droit des organisations européennes 1964, Le droit des communautés européennes 1969.

GANTIN, H.E. Cardinal Bernardin; Benin ecclesiastic; b. 8 May 1922, Toffo; ordained priest 1951; elected to titular Church of Tipasa, Mauritania 1956, consecrated 1957; apptd. to Cotonou, Benin 1960; cr. Cardinal 1977; Prefect, Sacred Congregation of Bishops 1984–; Dean, Coll. of Cardinals 1993–; Titular Bishop of Suburbicarian Church, Ostia Antica 1993–; fmrly. Pres. Pontifical Cttee. for Justice and Peace, now Pres. Pontifical Comm. for Latin America; Deacon of the Sacred Heart of Christ the King; Pres. Papal Council "Cor unum"; Cardinalizia di Vigilanza, Inst. per le Opere di Religione. *Address:* Congregation for the Bishops, Palazzo delle Congregazioni, Piazza Pio XII 10, 00193 Rome, Italy.

GANTNER, Carrillo Baillieu, M.F.A.; Australian theatre manager, director and actor; b. 17 June 1944, San Francisco, Calif.; s. of Vallejo Gantner and Neilma Gantner; m.; four s. one d. (deceased); ed. Melbourne Grammar School and Melbourne, Stanford and Harvard Univs.; Fellow, Stanford Univ. 1968–69; Asst., Admin. Adelaide Festival of Arts 1969–70; Drama Officer, Australian Council for the Arts 1970–73; Gen. Man. Melbourne Theatre Co. 1973–75; Exec. Dir. Playbox Theatre Co. Ltd. 1976–84, The CUB Malthouse; Cultural Counsellor, Australian Embassy, Beijing 1985–87; Artistic Dir. Playbox Theatre Centre 1988–93, Chair. Playbox Malthouse Ltd. 1994–96; Councillor, City of Melbourne 1996–99 (Chair. Planning and Devt. Cttee. 1996–98, Docklands Cttee. 1998–99, Deputy Chair. Finance and Service Cttee. and Audit Cttee. 1998–99); Chair. Performing Arts Bd. Australia Council 1990–93, Nat. Circus Summit 1990, Nat. Dance Summit 1991, Nat. Advisory Council, Musica Viva 1993–, Melbourne Int. Comedy Festival 1995–; Pres. Melbourne Chapter of URASENKE 1995–; Dir. Myer Foundation 1984–92 (Vice-Pres. 1992–), Asialink 1990–92 (Chair. 1992–), Mayfair Hanoi Ltd. (Hong Kong) 1996–98, Deputy Chair. 1999–; mem. Australia–China Council 1989–94, Australia Abroad Council 1991–95, Exec. Cttee. Asia Pacific Philanthropy Consortium 1994–, Nat. Advisory Council, Adelaide Festival 1996–; Corresp. mem. The Hague Club 1994–; Trustee Sidney Myer Fund 1991–; Gov. Fed. for Asian Cultural Promotion 1994–; Japan Foundation Visitors Program 1991; mem. Working Group to establish an Asian Business Council for the Arts 1997–98; Chair. Arts Man. Course Advisory Cttee., Victorian Coll. of the Arts 1996–98; other professional appts.; Chair. Barclay Investment Pty. Ltd., Myer Investment Pty. Ltd. 1998–. *Publications:* articles in professional journals. *Leisure interests:* viticulture, tennis. *Address:* Level 45, 55 Collins Street, Melbourne, Vic. 3000, Australia. *Telephone:* (03) 9207 3050. *Fax:* (03) 9207 3061.

GANZURI, Kamal Ahmad Al-, M.A., PH.D.; Egyptian politician; b. 1933; ed. Cairo Univ. and Michigan Univ.; Gov. of Beni Suef and Under-Sec. Ministry of Planning 1975; fmr. consultant for planning and devt. at UN; fmr. Head, Nat. Planning Inst., Minister of Planning 1982–85; Deputy Prime Minister and Minister of Planning 1985–96, Int. Co-operation 1985–87; Prime Minister of Egypt Jan. 1996–; Minister of Planning and Int. Co-operation 1997–. *Address:* Office of the Prime Minister, Cairo, Egypt.

GAO CHANGLI; Chinese politician; b. July 1937, Yutai, Shandong Prov.; ed. Chinese People's Univ.; joined CCP 1956; cadre Yutai Co. People's Govt., cadre Office of CCP Jining Pref. Cttee.; Vice-Sec. CCP Yishui Co. Cttee., Sec. CCP Rizhao Co. Cttee., Vice-Chief Sec. then Chief Sec. CCP Shandong Prov. Cttee.; Vice-Gov. of Shandong Prov. and Sec. Political and Legal Cttee. of CCP Shandong Prov. Cttee.; mem. Trial Cttee. of Supreme People's Court; Vice-Chair. Supreme People's Court 1993–98; Minister of Justice 1998–; alt. mem. CCP 15th Cen. Cttee. 1997. *Address:* Ministry of Justice, 11 Xiaguangli, Sanyuanqiao, Chao Yang Qu, Beijing 100016, People's Republic of China.

GAO DEZHAN; Chinese state official and senior engineer; b. 6 Aug. 1932; joined CCP 1950; worked in chemical, petrochemical and light industries; alt. mem. 12th CCP Cen. Cttee.; Dir. Jilin Prov. Econ. Comm. Vice-Gov., Jilin 1983–85, Gov. 1985–87; Deputy Sec. CCP Prov. Cttee., Jilin 1985; Minister of Forestry 1987–93; Vice-Chair. All-China Greening Cttee. 1988–93; a Deputy Head State Leading Group for Comprehensive Agricultural Devt. 1990–; Deputy Head Cen. Forest Fire Prevention 1988–93; alt. mem. 13th CCP Cen. Cttee. 1987–92; mem. 14th CCP Cen. Cttee. 1992–97; Sec. Tianjin City CCP Cttee. 1993–; Chair. Agric. and Rural Affairs Cttee. 9th NPC 1998–. *Address:* c/o Standing Committee of the National People's Congress, Beijing, People's Republic of China.

GAO JINGDE, D.TECH.SCI.; Chinese professor of electrical engineering; b. 5 Feb. 1922, Shaanxi; s. of Gao Jirong and Miao Ning; m. Jiang Huiru 1939; two s. one d.; ed. Northwestern Inst. of Tech., Leningrad Inst. of Tech.; Prof. of Electrical Eng., Tsinghua Univ., Beijing 1956–, Pres. of Univ. 1983–88; Vice-Chair. Univ. Council 1989–; mem. Chinese Acad. of Sciences 1980–, Ed. and Cultural Cttee. 7th CPPCC 1988–, Nat. Academic Degrees Cttee. 1988–; Vice-Pres. Chinese Electrical Eng. Soc. 1980; Pres. Chinese Electro-technical Soc. 1981–90; mem. CPPCC 8th Nat. Cttee. 1993–; Fellow, I.E.E.E. (U.S.A.) 1986–; Excellent Textbook Award for Higher Educ. 1988. *Publications:* Transients of the AC Machines and Analysis of their Performance, Basic Theory and Analysing Methods of Electric Machine Transients. *Address:* Office of the President, Tsinghua University, Beijing 100084, People's Republic of China. *Telephone:* 2560922. *Fax:* 2568116.

GAO SHANGQUAN; Chinese government official and professor of economics; b. 1929, Jia Ding County, Shanghai; s. of Gao Ruyu and Xiang Shi; m. Cha Peijun 1958; one s.; ed. St. John's Univ., Shanghai; worked as researcher, Deputy Div. Chief, Div. Chief, Bureau for Machine-Bldg. Industry of Ministry of Industry of local North-Eastern People's Govt.; Policy Research Dept., First Ministry of Machine-Bldg. Industry; Research Dept., Ministry of Agricultural Machine-Bldg. Industry; Office of Agricultural Mechanization, State Council; Policy Research Dept., State Comm. of Machine-Bldg. Industry; Research Fellow, Research Centre for Agricultural Devt., and Sr. Economist, State Comm. of Machine-Bldg. Industry; State Comm. for Restructuring Econ. System 1982, then Deputy Dir. and Head, Research Inst. of Restructuring the Econ. System; Vice-Minister in charge of State Comm. for Restructuring the Econ. System 1985–93; mem. Nat. Cttee. of CPPCC, preliminary working cttee. of preparatory cttee. of the Hong Kong S.A.R. and Head of Econ. Panel 1993–97; mem. Sino-Japanese Econ. Exchange Comm.; Vice-Group-Leader, Leading Group for Restructuring Housing System, under State Council; Vice-Pres. China Research Soc. for Restructuring the Econ. Systems; Pres. China Soc. of Enterprise Reform and Devt.; Pres. China Reform & Devt. Inst., China Soc. of Urban Housing System Reform, Asscn. of Future Market of China; Vice-Pres. Asscn. of China's Urban Economy, Asscn. of China's Industrial Economy, Asscn. for Study of China's Specific Condition, Asscn. of Social and Economics Publs.; Chair. Research Group for Rural and Urban Housing Reform 1995–; mem. UN Cttee. for Devt. Planning; Doctorate Supervisor, Prof., Beijing Univ. and Shanghai Jiaotong Univ.; Prof. Nankai Univ., Chinese People's Univ., Shanghai Univ. of Finance and Econs.; MBA programme adviser of Nat. Univ. of Australia; Outstanding Scholar Award Hong Kong Polytechnic. *Publications:* Enterprises Should Enjoy Certain Autonomy 1956, Follow A Road of Our Own In Agricultural Modernization 1982, Nine Years of Reform in China's Economic System 1987, A Road To Success 1987, Selected Works of Gao Shangquan 1989, China: A Decade of Economic Reform 1989, China's Economic Reform 1991, Lead to a Powerful Country 1991, On Planning and Market in China 1992, From Planned Economy to the Socialist Market Economy 1993, An Introduction to Socialist Market Economy 1994, China: The Second Revolution 1995; also ed. of numerous publications. *Address:* State Commission for Restructuring the Economic System, 22 Xianmen Street, Beijing 100017, People's Republic of China. *Telephone:* 63096649. *Fax:* 66014562.

GAO TIANZHENG, Maj.-Gen.; Chinese army officer and party official; b. 1931, Tongxian Co., Hebei Prov.; joined PLA 1948, CCP 1949; Deputy Political Commissar PLA Guangzhou Mil. Area Command 1988–96; mem. 14th CCP Cen. Cttee. 1992–. *Address:* Political Department of Guangzhou Military Area Command, Guangzhou City, Guangdong Province, People's Republic of China.

GAO YAN; Chinese government official and engineer; b. 1942, Yushu Co., Jilin Prov.; joined CCP 1965; Vice-Gov. of Jilin Prov. 1988–92; Gov. 1992–95; Sec. CCP Cttee., Yunan Prov. 1995–97; Dir. Political Dept., Chinese People's Armed Police Force; Sec. CPC 6th Yunnan Prov. Cttee; mem. 14th CCP Cen. Cttee. 1992–97, 15th CCP Cen. Cttee. 1997–; Gen. Man. State Electrical Power Corpn. 1998–. *Address:* c/o State Council, Beijing, People's Republic of China.

GAO YING; Chinese author; b. 25 Dec. 1929, Jiaozuo, Henan; s. of Gao Weiya and Sha Peifen; m. Duan Chuanchen 1954; one s. two d.; Vice-Chair. Sichuan Br., and mem. Council, Chinese Writers' Asscn.; Deputy Dir. Ed. Bd., Sichuan Prov. Broadcasting Station 1983–; mem. Sichuan Political Consultative Conf. *Publications*: The Song of Ding Youjun, Lamplights around the Three Gorges, High Mountains and Distant Rivers, Cloudy Cliff (long novel), Da Ji and her Fathers (novel and film script), The Orchid (novel), Loving-Kindness of the Bamboo Storey (collection of prose), Mother in my Heart (autobiographical novel), Songs of Da Liang Mountains (collection of poems), Frozen Snowflakes (collection of poems), Reminiscences, Xue Ma (novel), Gao Ying short novel collection. *Leisure interests:* painting, music. *Address*: Sichuan Branch of Chinese Association of Literary and Art Workers, Bu-hou-jie Street, Chengdu, Sichuan, People's Republic of China. *Telephone:* 667828-36.

GAO YISHENG, PH.D.; Chinese scientist; ed. Oxford Univ.; fmr. Dir. Shanghai Inst. of Materia Medica; won Nat. Prize of Science 1990. *Address:* Shanghai Institute of Materia Medica, 294 Tai-Yuan Road, Shanghai 20031, People's Republic of China.

GAO YOUXI; Chinese physicist; b. 1920; Dir. Plateau Atmospheric Physics Inst. 1981–; mem. Dept. of Earth Sciences, Academia Sinica, 1985–; Nat. Science Award 1989. *Address:* Plateau Atmospheric Physics Institute, Lanzhou, People's Republic of China.

GAO ZHANXIANG; Chinese party official; b. 1935, Tongxian Co., Hebei Prov., joined CCP 1953; mem. Communist Youth League Cen. Cttee. 1964, Sec. 1978–82; alt. mem. 12th CCP Cen. Cttee. 1982–87; mem. 8th CCP Nat. Cttee. 1993–; Sec. CCP Cttee., Hebei Prov. 1983–86; Vice-Minister of Culture 1986–96; Pres. Soc. of Mass Culture 1990–93; Vice-Pres. 1993–, Chinese Asscn. for Promotion of Population Culture; Pres. China Children's Culture and Art Promotion Soc. 1993–; Chair. Soc. of Photographic Arts 1994; Sec. Party Group China Fed. of Literary and Art Circles, Vice-Chair. 1996; Dir., Ed.-in-Chief Chinese Arts. *Address:* c/o Ministry of Culture, A83 Beiheyan, Dongamen, Beijing 100722, People's Republic of China.

GAPONOV-GREKHOV, Andrey Viktorovich; Russian physicist; b. 7 June 1926, Moscow; m.; one d.; ed. Gorky State Univ.; Instructor, Gorky Polytech. Inst. 1952–55; Sr. Scientific Assoc., Head of Dept. of Radio Physics, Applied Physics Inst., Gorky (now Nizhni Novgorod) State Univ. 1955–, Dir. 1984–; Corresp. mem. U.S.S.R. (now Russian) Acad. of Sciences 1964–68, mem. 1968–; U.S.S.R. People's Deputy 1989–91; Hero of Socialist Labour 1986; State Prize 1967, 1983. *Publications:* numerous theoretical and experimental works in field of inducted cyclotronic radiation, which led to development of a new class of electronic instruments—masers with cyclotronic resonance. *Address:* Institute of Applied Physics, Ulyanova str. 46, Nizhni Novgorod GSP-120, Russia. *Telephone:* (8312) 36-66-69 (Office); (8312) 36-36-67 (Home).

GAPRINDASHVILI, Nona; Georgian chess player; b. 3 May 1941, Zugdidi, Georgia; one s.; ed. Tbilisi State Univ.; 5 times World Champion 1962–78; 11 times Olympic Champion, Gold Medals bearer; twice won European Cup of Champions, First Chess Oscar Prize for the best achievements of the year 1980; winner of numerous int. chess tournaments; First Chair. Nat. Olympic Cttee. of Georgia 1985–96. *Leisure interests:* snooker, football. *Address:* Georgian Chess Federation, Tbilisi, Georgia.

GARABEDIAN, Paul R., PH.D.; American professor of mathematics; b. 2 Aug. 1927, Cincinnati, Ohio; s. of Carl A. Garabedian and Margaret R. Garabedian; m. 1st Gladys Rappaport 1949 (divorced 1963); m. 2nd Lynnel Marg 1966; two d.; ed. Brown and Harvard Univs.; Nat. Research Council Fellow 1948–49; Asst. Prof. of Math., Univ. of Calif. 1949–50; Asst. Prof. of Math., Stanford Univ. 1950–52, Assoc. Prof. 1952–56, Prof. 1956–59; Scientific Liaison Officer, ONR-London 1957–58; Prof., Courant Inst. of Math. Sciences, New York Univ. 1959–, Dir. Courant Math. and Computing Lab. of U.S. Dept. of Energy. 1972–73, Dir. Div. of Computational Fluid Dynamics 1978–; Sloan Foundation Fellowship 1961–63; Guggenheim Fellowship 1966, 1981–82; Fairchild Distinguished Scholar, Calif. Inst. of Tech. 1975; mem. N.A.S., American Acad. of Arts & Sciences, American Math. Soc., American Physical Soc., American Inst. of Aeronautics and Astronautics, Soc. Industrial and Applied Math. Ed. Bd. Applicable Analysis, Complex Variables and Applications; NASA Public Service Group Achievement Award 1976; NASA Certificate of Recognition 1980; Boris Pregal Award, New York Acad. of Sciences 1980; Birkhoff Prize in Applied Math. 1983; von Karman Prize, S.I.A.M. 1989; Applied Mathematics and Numerical Analysis Prize, N.A.S. 1998. *Publications:* numerous papers in learned journals. *Leisure interest:* piano. *Address:* Courant Institute of Mathematical Sciences, New York University, 251 Mercer Street, New York, NY 10012; 110 Bleecker Street, New York, NY 10012, U.S.A. (Home).

GARAIKOETXEA URRIZA, Carlos; Spanish (Basque) politician, lawyer and economist; b. 2 June 1939, Pamplona; s. of Juan Garaikoetxea and Dolores Urriza; m. Sagrario Mina Apat 1966; three s.; mem. Inst. Príncipe de Viana, org. to protect and promote Basque culture, Navarra Dist. Council 1971; Dist. Councillor, Navarra 1971; Chair. Navarra Chamber of Commerce and Industry 1971; mem. Regional Council of Partido Nacionalista Vasco (Basque Nationalist Party—PNV) 1974, Chair. Nat. Council PNV 1977, re-elected 1978; mem. Navarra Dist. Parl. 1979; Pres. Gen. Council of the Basque Country 1979; elected to Basque Parl. as PNV cand. for Guipúzcoa March 1980; Pres. of Basque Govt. 1980–86; Hon. Pres. and gold medals from many orgs. and asscns. *Leisure interests:* music (especially classical), skiing, Basque pelota, reading (especially political essays and history). *Address:* Palacio de Ajuria-Enea, Vitoria-Gasteiz, Spain. *Telephone:* (945) 23 16 16.

GARANG, Col. John, PH.D.; Sudanese guerrilla leader; b. 1943, Jonglei; ed. Cornell Univ., Iowa State Univ.; Sudanese Army 1969–70; trained as Co. Commdr., Fort Benning, U.S.A., later Lieut.-Col. Mil. Research Center, Khartoum; f. and fmr. Leader Sudan People's Liberation Movt., f. and Leader Sudan People's Liberation Army 1983– (SPLA).

GARAS, Klára, PH.D.; Hungarian art historian; b. 19 June 1919, Rákosszentmihály; d. of Pál Garas and Irén Strasser; ed. Budapest Univ. of Sciences; joined staff Budapest Museum of Fine Arts 1945, subsequent posts to Gen. Dir. 1964–84; Ordinary mem. Hungarian Acad. of Sciences 1972, mem. 1985–; Labour Order of Merit (golden degree) 1974, 1979. *Leisure interests:* 15th to 18th-century European and Hungarian painting. *Publications:* Magyarországi festészet a XVII. században (Hungarian Painting in the 17th century) 1953, Magyarországi festészet a XVIII. században (Hungarian

Painting in the 18th century) 1955, Franz Anton Maulbertsch 1724–1796, with preface by Oskar Kokoschka 1960, Olasz reneszánsz portrék a Szépművészeti Muzeumban (Italian Renaissance Portraits in the Museum of Fine Arts) 1965, 1973, Carlo Innocenzo Carloni (co-author) Milano 1966, Franz Anton Maulbertsch. Leben und Werk 1974, A velencei settecento festészete (Venetian Paintings of the 18th Century) 1977, A 17. század német és osztrák rajzmüvészete (Deutsche und Österreichische Zeichnungen des 18. Jahrhunderts) 1980; several publs. on the Budapest Museum of Fine Arts. *Address:* 1126 Budapest, Kiss János altábornagy utca 48/c, Hungary.

GARAUDY, Roger Jean Charles, D. ÈS L., D.ÈS.SC.; French author and university professor; b. 17 July 1913, Marseilles; s. of Charles Garaudy and Marie Garaudy; m. 1st Henriette Vialatte 1937 (divorced) 1937; m. 2nd Paulette Gayraud; two s. one d.; ed. Sorbonne, Paris; prisoner-of-war 1940–43; Deputy to Nat. Ass. 1945–58, Vice-Pres. 1956–58; Senator 1959–62; Dir. Inst. Int. pour le Dialogue des Cultures, Geneva 1974–; Prof. of Philosophy, Univ. of Paris (Sorbonne); f. Univ. des Mutants, Dakar, Senegal; f. Fondation Roger Garaudy, Cordoba, Spain; f. of only museum in Spain devoted to Islamic art; Croix de Guerre; Prix Méditerranée; Prix Faycal; Prix Brennam (Barcelona); Dr. h.c. (Konya, Turkey). *Publications:* 53 books translated into 29 languages including: Hegel 1962, Karl Marx 1965, De l'anathème au dialogue 1965, Appel aux vivants 1979, A contre-Nuit (poem) 1987, Mon Tour du siècle en solitaire (memoirs) 1989, Vers une guerre de religion 1995, les Etats-Unis, avant-garde de la décadence 1996, l'Avenir, Mode d'emploi 1997, The Founding Myths of Israeli Politics 1998. *Address:* 69 rue de Sucy, 94430 Chennevières-sur-Marne, France. *Telephone:* 331.45.76.90.38. *Fax:* 331.49.62.77.94.

GARBA, Maj.-Gen. Joseph Nanven, M.P.A.; Nigerian diplomatist, fmr. army officer and politician; b. 17 July 1943, Langtang; m. Evelyn Okon Edem; one s. five d.; ed. Sacred Heart School, Shendam, Nigerian Mil. School, Zairia, Mons Officer Cadet School, Aldershot, Staff Coll., Camberley, England, Harvard Univ.; Platoon Command, 4th Bn. 1963, Co. Command 1963–64, Mortar Platoon Command 1964; Second in Command Fed. Guards 1964–65; Gen. Staff Officer, 3 HQ, Second Brigade 1965; UN Officer, India and Pakistan 1965–66; Officer Commdg. Fed. Guards 1966–68; Commdr. Brigade of Guards 1968–75; mem. Supreme Mil. Council 1975–79; Commr. for External Affairs 1975–78; Commdt. Nigerian Defence Acad. 1978–79; Amb. and Perm. Rep. to UN 1984–89; Pres. UN Gen. Ass. 1989–90; Fellow Inst. of Politics and Cen. for Int. Affairs Harvard Univ. 1980–83. *Leisure interests:* basketball, photography. *Address:* c/o Ministry of External Affairs, 23 Marina, PMB 12600, Lagos, Nigeria.

GARBERS, Christoph Friedrich, D.PHIL.; South African scientist; b. 21 Aug. 1929, Piet Retief, Transvaal.; s. of Andris Wilhelm Friedrich and Lucy Sophia Carolina (née Wolhuter) Garbers; m. Barbara Z. G. Viljoen 1957; three s. one d.; ed. Pretoria Univ., Zürich Univ.; Research Officer Klipfontein Organic Products 1951; student Zürich Univ. 1951–54; Research Officer Council for Scientific and Industrial Research (CSIR) 1954–58; Sr. lecturer, Stellenbosch Univ. 1958–65, Prof. Organic Chem. 1966–78; Vice-Pres. CSIR 1979, Deputy Pres. 1980, Pres. 1980–90; Chair. S. African Acad. for Science and Arts 1983–85; Chair. S. African Inventions Devt. Corpn. 1980–90; Dir. Tech. Finance Corpn. (Pty) Ltd. 1988–90; Chair. Certification Bd. for Technikons 1989–95; Chancellor Univ. of S.A. 1990–; Chair. Foundation for Research Devt. 1990–91; mem. Scientific Advisory Council 1980–87 (Chair. 1991–94), Water Research Comm. 1980–89, Advisory Council for Tech. 1987–89; Council mem. Univ. of S.A. 1980–90; Trustee Hans Merensky Foundation 1980–97 (Vice-Pres. 1992–97), Trust for Health Systems Planning and Devt. 1992–95; Dir. (non-exec.) Allied Technologies Ltd. 1991–96, Power Technologies Ltd. 1992–96; mem. Nat. Comm. for Higher Educ. 1995–96, IUPAC/UNESCO Int. Council for Chemistry; Rep. at ICSU 1980–90; Hon. D.Sc. (UNISA) 1989, (Cape Town) 1990, (Stellenbosch) 1991, (Pretoria) 1994; Havenga Prize for Chem. 1977, Gold Medal, S.A. Chem. Inst. 1980, State Pres. Order for Meritorious Service (Gold) 1989, M.T. Steyn Gold Medal 1990, S.A. Medal (Gold) 1990, H. J. van Eck Medal 1991. *Address:* P.O. Box 36716, Menlo Park 0102; 5 Domein, 443 Sussex Street, Lynnwood, Pretoria, South Africa. *Telephone:* 473574. *Fax:* 475114.

GARCIA, Andy; Cuban film actor; b. 12 April 1956, Havana; m. Marivi García; moved to U.S.A. 1961; ed. Florida Int. Univ.; several years acting with regional theatres Florida; *Films include:* The Mean Season 1985, 8 Million Ways to Die, The Untouchables, Black Rain, Internal Affairs, The Godfather III, A Show of Force, Stand and Deliver, American Roulette, The Sixth Family, Dead Again, When A Man Loves A Woman, Steal Big Steal Little, Things to Do in Denver When You're Dead 1996, Night Falls on Manhattan 1996, Lorca 1997, Hoods 1997, Desperate Measures 1997, The Scalper (also producer) 1998; dir., producer: Cachao, Like His Rhythm There Is No Other; music producer Cachao Master Sessions Vol. I 1994 (Grammy Award), Vol. II 1995; *TV work includes:* Hill Street Blues, Brothers, Foley Square, Clinton and Nadine. *Address:* Paradigm, 25th Fl., 10100 Santa Monica Boulevard, Los Angeles, CA 90067, U.S.A.

GARCÍA MÁRQUEZ, Gabriel (Gabo); Colombian writer; b. 1928, Aracataca; m. Mercedes García Márquez; two s.; ed. secondary school and Univ. of Bogotá, Univ. of Cartagena; began writing books 1946; lived in Baranquilla; Corresp. Espectador in Rome, Paris; first novel published while living in Caracas, Venezuela 1957; est. bureau of Prensa Latina (Cuban press agency) in Bogotá; worked for Prensa Latina in Havana, Cuba, then as Deputy Head of New York Office 1961; lived in Spain, contributing to magazines, Mundo Nuevo, Casa de las Américas; went to Mexico; invited back to Colombia by Pres. July 1982; Rómulo Gallegos Prize 1972; Nobel Prize for Literature 1982. *Publications include:* La hojarasca (Leaf Storm) 1955, El coronel no tiene quien le escriba (No One Writes to the Colonel) 1961, La mala hora (In Evil Hour) 1962, Los funerales de la Mamá Grande (Big Mama's Funeral) 1962, Cien años de soledad (One Hundred Years of Solitude) 1967, La increíble y triste historia de la cándida Eréndira (Innocent Erendira and other stories) 1972, El otoño del patriarca (The Autumn of the Patriarch) 1975, Crónica de una muerte anunciada (Chronicle of a Death Foretold) 1981, El Olor de la Guayaba (Fragrance of Guava) 1982, El amor en los tiempos del cólera (Love in the Time of Cholera) 1984, Relato de un náufrago (The Story of a Shipwrecked Sailor) 1986, Miguel Littín's Adventure: undercover in Chile 1986, The General in His Labyrinth (translated from Spanish edn. of 1989) 1991, Amores Difíciles 1989, I Rent Myself Out to Dream 1989, Collected Stories 1991, Strange Pilgrims: Twelve Stories 1993, Of Love and Other Demons 1995, News of a Kidnapping 1997. *Address:* c/o Agencia Literaria Carmen Balcelos, Diagonal 580, Barcelona, Spain.

GARCÍA PELÁEZ, Raúl, LL.D.; Cuban politician, diplomatist and lawyer; b. 15 Jan. 1922; ed. Univ. of Havana; fmr. mem. July 26th Revolutionary Cttee.; later Prosecutor at Camagüey Court of Appeal, then Chair. Camagüey Municipal Council for Co-ordination and Inspection; then Gen. Treas. Revolutionary Forces in Camagüey Prov., Rep. of Nat. Inst. of Agrarian Reform in Nuevitas, and Gen. Sec. Matanzas Prov. Cttee. of United Party of Cuban Socialist Revolution; mem. Cen. Cttee. of Cuban CP 1965–80, Head of Revolutionary Orientation Comm. of Cent. Cttee. of Cuban CP until 1967; Amb. to U.S.S.R. 1967–74. *Address:* c/o Partido Comunista, Plaza de la Revolución, Havana, Cuba.

GARCÍA PÉREZ, Alan; Peruvian politician; b. 23 May 1949, Lima; s. of Carlos García Ronceros and Nyta Pérez de García; m. Pilar Norse; four d.; ed. José María Eguren Nat. Coll., Universidad Católica, Lima, Universidad Nacional Mayor de San Marcos (graduated as lawyer), Universidad Complutense, Madrid, Spain, Sorbonne and Inst. of Higher Latin American Studies, Paris, France; mem. of Partido Aprista Peruano since his teens; returned to Peru and elected mem. of Constituent Ass. 1978; subsequently apptd. Org. Sec. and Chair. Ideology of Aprista Party (now Alianza Popular Revolucionaria Americana), Parl. Deputy 1980–85, Sec.-Gen. of Party 1982, later Pres.; Senator for Life 1990–; nominated Presidential Candidate 1984; obtained largest number of votes, Nat. Presidential Elections April 1985; on withdrawal of Izquierda Unida candidate, Alfonso Barrantes Lingán, proclaimed Pres.-elect June 1985, assuming powers 1985–89; granted political asylum in Colombia June 1992.

GARCÍA RAMÍREZ, Sergio, PH.D.; Mexican politician and lawyer; b. 1938, Guadalajara; ed. Nat. Univ. of Mexico; Research Fellow and teacher of penal law, Inst. of Juridical Research, Nat. Univ. of Mexico 1966–76; Dir. Correction Centre, State of Mexico and Judge, Juvenile Courts; Asst. Dir. of Govt. Ministry of Interior; Attorney-Gen. of Fed. Dist.; Under-Sec. Ministries of Nat. Resources, Interior, Education, Industrial Devt.; Dir. Prevention Centre of Mexico City; fmr. Minister of Labour; Attorney-Gen. 1982–88; mem. Mexican Acad. of Penal Sciences, Mexican Inst. of Penal Law, Nat. Inst. of Public Admin., Ibero-American Inst. of Penal Law etc. *Publications include:* Teseo Alucinado 1966, Asistencia a Reos Liberados 1966, El Artículo 18 Constitucional 1967, La Imputabilidad en el Derecho Penal Mexicano, El Código Tutelar para Menores del Estado Michoacán 1969, La Ciudadanía de la Juventud 1970, La Prisión 1975, Los Derechos Humanos y el Derecho Penal 1976, Legislación Penitenciaria y Correccional Comentada 1978, Otros Minotauros 1979, Cuestiones Criminológicas y Penales Contemporáneas 1981, Justicia Penal 1982. *Address:* c/o Oficina del Procurador General, México, D.F., Mexico.

GARCIA VARGAS, Julián; Spanish politician; b. 1946, Chamberri, Madrid; m.; two s.; economist; fmrly on staff of fmr. Office of Provision and Transport; fmr. Financial Tax Inspector, Ministry of Trade, Deputy Dir.-Gen., Directorate-General of Financial Policy, Man. Consortium of Urban Contrib. of Madrid; Pres. Instituto de Crédito Oficial 1982–86; Minister for Health and Consumer Affairs 1986–95, for Defence 1991–95; mem. Movt. of Civil Servants of the Admin. *Address:* c/o PSOE, Ferraz 68 y 70, 28008 Madrid, Spain.

GARCÍA-VALDECASAS Y FERNÁNDEZ, Rafael, D.JUR.; Spanish judge; b. 9 Jan. 1946, Granada; m. Rosario Castaño Parraga 1975; ed. Univ. of Granada; lawyer, Office of Attorney-Gen. 1976; mem. Office of Attorney-Gen. Tax and Judicial Affairs Office, Jaén 1976–85; mem. Office of Attorney-Gen. Econ. and Admin. Court of Jaén 1979–85; mem. Jaén Bar 1979–89, Granada Bar 1981–89; mem. Office of Attorney-Gen. Econ. and Admin. Court of Córdoba 1983–85, Tax and Judicial Affairs Office of Granada 1986–87; Head, Spanish State Legal Service for cases before EC Court of Justice (Ministry of Foreign Affairs) 1987–89; Judge, Court of First Instance of European Communities 1989–. *Publications:* Comentarios al Tratado de Adhesión de España a la C.E.: La Agricultura 1985, El 'acquis' comunitario 1986, El medio ambiente: conservación de espacios protegidos en la legislación de la C.E. 1992, La Jurisprudencia del Tribunal de Justicia C.E. sobre la libertad de establecimiento y libre prestación de servicios por los abogados 1993, El Tribunal de Primera Instancia de las Comunidades Europeas 1993; also papers in books and learned journals. *Leisure interests:* swimming, cycling, fishing. *Address:* European Court of First Instance of the European Communities, Bâtiment C, Bureau 4051, blvd Konrad Adenauer, 2925 Luxembourg.

GARDAM, Jane Mary, B.A., F.R.S.L.; British novelist; b. 11 July 1928, Coatham; d. of William Pearson and Kathleen Pearson (née Helm); m. David Hill Gardam 1954; two s. one d.; ed. Saltburn High School for Girls, Bedford Coll. for Women, London Univ.; Co-ordinator UK Hosp. Libraries British Red Cross 1951–53; Literary Ed. Time and Tide 1952–54; Prix Baudelaire (for God on the Rocks), Whitbread Literary Award (for The Hollow Land), Whitbread Novel Award (for The Queen of the Tambourine), David Highams Award, Winifred Holtby Award (for Black Faces, White Faces); Katherine Mansfield Award (for The Pangs of Love) 1984. *Publications:* novels: A Long Way From Verona 1971, The Summer After the Funeral 1973, Bilgewater 1977, God on the Rocks 1978, The Hollow Land 1981, Bridget and William 1981, Horse 1982, Kit 1983, Crusoe's Daughter 1985, Kit in Boots 1986, Swan 1987, Through the Doll's House Door 1987, The Queen of the Tambourine 1991, Faith Fox 1996, Tufty Bear 1996; short stories: A Few Fair Days 1971, Black Faces, White Faces 1975, The Sidmouth Letters 1980, The Pangs of Love 1983, Going into a Dark House 1994, Missing the Midnight 1997; non-fiction: The Iron Coast 1994. *Leisure interests:* agriculture. *Address:* Haven House, Sandwich, Kent; Throstlenest Farm, Crackpot, N. Yorks; 34 Denmark Road, London, S.W.19, England.

GARDEL, Louis; French publishing editor, novelist and screenplay-writer; b. 8 Sept. 1939, Algiers, Algeria; s. of Jacques Gardel and Janine Blasselle; m. 1st Béatrice Herr (deceased) 1963; m. 2nd Hélène Millerand 1990; two s. two d.; ed. Lycée Bugeaud, Algiers, Lycée Louis-le-Grand, Paris and Institut d'Etudes Politiques, Paris; Head of Dept. Inst. des Hautes Etudes d'Outre-Mer 1962–64; Man. Soc. Rhône-Progil 1964–74; Head of Dept. Conseil Nat. du Patronat 1974–80; Literary Consultant Editions du Seuil 1980, Literary Ed. 1980–; mem. juries Prix Renaudot, Prix Albert Camus. *Publications:* L'Eté Fracassé 1973, Couteau de chaleur 1976, Fort Saganne 1980 (Grand Prix du Roman de l'Académie Française), Notre Homme 1986, Le Beau Rôle 1989, Darbaroud 1993. L'Aurore des Bien-Aimés 1997. *Film screenplays:* Fort Saganne, Nocturne Indien, Indochine, La Marche de Radetzky etc. *Leisure interest:* horses. *Address:* Editions du Seuil, 27 rue Jacob, 75004 Paris (Office); 25 rue de la Cerisaie, 75004, Paris, France (Home). *Telephone:* 40 46 50 50.

GARDEN, Sir Timothy, K.C.B., M.A., M.PHIL., F.R.Ae.S.; British research institute director; b. 23 April 1944, Worcester; s. of Joseph Garden and Winifred Mayes; m. Susan Button 1965; two d.; ed. King's School, Worcester, St. Catherine's Coll. Oxford, Magdalene Coll. Cambridge and Army Staff Coll. Camberley; R.A.F. pilot and flying instr. 1965–75; Staff Officer to Air Mem. for Personnel, Ministry of Defence 1977–79; Squadron Commdr. No. 50 Squadron (Vulcan bombers) 1979–81; Dir. of Defence Studies for R.A.F. 1982–85; Station Commdr. R.A.F. Odiham (Support Helicopters) 1985–87; Dir. of Air Force Staff Duties, Ministry of Defence 1988–90; Asst. Chief of Air Staff 1991–92; Asst. Chief of Defence Staff (programmes) 1992–94; Commdt. Royal Coll. of Defence Studies (Air Marshal) 1994–95; retd. from R.A.F. 1996; Dir. Royal Inst. of Int. Affairs, Chatham House 1997–98; mem. advisory bd. NATO Defense Coll., Rome 1996–, Int. Studies Centre, Cambridge Univ. 1996–, Centre for Strategic Studies, Univ. of Hull 1996– ; Dir. UK-Japan 2000 Group 1997–; Trustee World Humanity Action Trust 1996–; Hon. Fellow, St. Catherine's Coll. Oxford 1994; Fellow, Royal United Services Inst. 1996. *Publications:* Can Deterrence Last? 1984, The Technology Trap 1989. *Leisure interests:* computing, writing, dining-out, bridge.

GÄRDENFORS, Peter, PH.D.; Swedish professor of cognitive science; b. 21 Sept. 1949, Degeberga; s. of Torsten Gärdenfors and Ingemor Gärdenfors (née Jonsson); m. Annette Wald 1975; two s. one d.; ed. Lund Univ.; lecturer in Philosophy, Lund Univ. 1974–80, Reader in Philosophy of Science 1975–77, Reader in Philosophy 1980–88; Prof. of Cognitive Science, Lund Univ. 1988–; Visiting Fellow, Princeton Univ., U.S.A. 1973–74, Australian Nat. Univ. 1986–87; Visiting Scholar, Stanford Univ., U.S.A. 1983–84; Visiting Prof., Univ. of Buenos Aires 1990; Ed. Theoria 1978–86, Journal of Logic, Language and Information 1991–. *Publications:* Generalized Quantifiers (Ed.) 1986, Knowledge in Flux 1988, Decision, Probability and Utility (with N.-E. Sahlin) 1988, Belief Revision (ed.) 1992, Blotta Tanken 1992. *Leisure interests:* botany, walking, judo, windsurfing. *Address:* Department of Philosophy, Kungshuset, Lundagard, 222 22 Lund, Sweden. *Telephone:* (46) 2224817. *Fax:* (46) 2224817.

GARDENT, Paul; French mining executive; b. 10 July 1921, Grenoble; s. of Louis and Edith (née Rocher) Gardent; m. Janine Robert 1958; one s.; ed. Ecole Polytechnique; Mining Engineer, Valenciennes 1944–48; Asst. Chief Mining Engineer, Lille 1948–49, Chief Mining Engineer 1950; Tech. Adviser to J. M. Louvel (Minister of Industry and Commerce) 1950–52; Dir. of Gen. Studies, Charbonnages de France 1952–58; Dir. of Gen. Studies and Financial Services, Houillères du bassin de Lorraine 1958–63; Asst. Dir., then Dir.-Gen. Houillères du bassin du Nord et du Pas-de-Calais 1963–68; Dir.-Gen. Charbonnages de France 1968–80; Conseiller d'Etat 1980–86; Pres. Coll. de la Prévention des Risques Technologiques 1989–91; Pres. Comm. Interministérielle des Radioéléments artificiels 1981–, Comm. d'Aide aux Riverains des Aéroports 1985–97; Commdr. Légion d'honneur, Commdr. Ordre national du Mérite. *Address:* 5 rue de la Chaise, Paris 75007, France (Home). *Telephone:* (01) 45-44-03-43.

GARDINER, Sir John Eliot, Kt., C.B.E., M.A., F.R.S.A.; British conductor; b. 20 April 1943; s. of late Rolf Gardiner and of Marabel (Hodgkin) Gardiner; m. Elizabeth S. Wilcock 1981 (divorced 1997); three d.; ed. Bryanston School, King's Coll., Cambridge, King's Coll., London and in Paris and Fontainebleau with Nadia Boulanger; f. Monteverdi Choir, 1964, Monteverdi Orchestra 1968, English Baroque Soloists 1978, Orchestre Révolutionnaire et Romantique 1990; concert début Wigmore Hall, London 1966; operatic début Sadler's Wells, London 1969; Prin. Conductor CBC Vancouver Orchestra 1980–83; Musical Dir. Lyon Opera 1982–88, Chef fondateur 1988–; Artistic Dir. Göttingen Handel Festival 1981–90, Veneto Music Festival 1986; Prin. Conductor NDR Symphony Orchestra 1991–94; residency at the Châtelet, Paris Oct. 1999–; regular guest conductor with maj.orchestras in Europe; over 200 recordings; Hon. Fellow King's Coll., London 1992, Royal Acad. of Music 1992; Dr. h.c. (Univ. Lumière de Lyon) 1987; Commdr. Ordre des Arts et des Lettres 1997 (Officier 1988); 15 Gramophone awards including Record of the Year 1991, Artist of the Year 1994; many other awards including 7 Edison awards, 2 Arturo Toscanini Music Critics awards, 3 Deutscher Schallplattenpreis. *Publications:* Claude le Jeune Hélas, Mon Dieu (ed.) 1971, contrib. Gluck's Orfeo 1980. *Leisure interests:* forestry, organic farming. *Address:* c/o IMG Artists Europe, Media House, 3 Burlington Lane, London, W4 2TH; Gore Farm, Ashmore, Salisbury, Wilts., SP5 5AR, England (Home). *Telephone:* 0181-233 5800 (Agent). *Fax:* 0181-233 5801 (Agent).

GARDNER, David Pierpont, M.A., PH.D.; American university president and professor of education; b. 24 March 1933, Berkeley, Calif.; s. of Reed S. Gardner and Margaret Pierpont Gardner; m. Elizabeth Fuhriman 1958 (died 1991); four d.; ed. Brigham Young Univ. and Univ. of Calif. Berkeley; Admin. Asst., Personnel Man. and Prin. Asst. to Chief Admin. Officer, Calif. Farm Bureau Fed. Berkeley 1958–60; Field and Scholarship Dir. Calif. Alumni Asscn., Univ. of Calif. Berkeley 1960–62, Dir. Calif. Alumni Foundation 1962–64; Asst. to Chancellor and Asst. Prof. of Higher Educ., Univ. of Calif. Santa Barbara 1964–67, Asst. Chancellor and Asst. Prof. of Higher Educ. 1967–69, Vice-Chancellor, Exec. Asst. and Assoc. Prof. of Higher Educ. 1969–70; Vice-Pres. Univ. of Calif. and Prof. of Higher Educ. (on leave from Univ. of Calif. Santa Barbara) 1971–73; Pres. Univ. of Utah and Prof. of Higher Educ. 1973–83, Pres. Emer. 1985; Pres. Univ. of Calif. 1983–92, Prof. of Higher Educ., Univ. of Calif. Berkeley 1983–92; Pres. William and Flora Hewlett Foundation, Menlo Park Calif. 1993–; Visiting Fellow, Clare Hall, Cambridge Univ. 1979, Life mem. 1979–; numerous professional appts., directorships, trusteeships etc.; Fellow, American Acad. of Arts and Sciences, Nat. Acad. of Public Admin.; mem. Nat. Acad. of Educ., American Philosophical Soc.; Assoc. Clare Hall, Cambridge; Fulbright Fellow, Japan 1987; Légion d'honneur (France); ten hon. degrees and many other awards and distinctions. *Publications:* The California Oath Controversy 1967; numerous articles in professional journals. *Address:* William and Flora Hewlett Foundation, 525 Middlefield Road, Suite 200, Menlo Park, CA 94025; 70 Rincon Road, Kensington, CA 94707, U.S.A. (Home).

GARDNER, John William, PH.D., LL.D.; American writer and consultant; b. 8 Oct. 1912, Los Angeles; s. of William and Marie Flora Gardner; m. Aida Marroquin 1934; two d.; ed. Stanford Univ., and Univ. of Calif.; Teaching Asst. in Psychology, Univ. of Calif. 1936–38; Instructor in Psychology, Conn. Coll. 1938–40; Asst. Prof. Mount Holyoke Coll. 1940–42; Head Latin-American Section, Foreign Broadcasting Intelligence Service, Fed. Communications Comm. 1942–43; served U.S. Marine Corps 1943–46; staff mem. Carnegie Corpn. of New York 1946–47, Exec. Assoc. 1947–49, Vice-Pres. 1949–55, Pres. 1955–65, Consultant 1968–77; Pres. Carnegie Foundation 1955–65; U.S. Secretary of Health, Educ. and Welfare 1965–68; Head of Urban Coalition (Campaign to transform cities of America) 1968–70; Dir. New York Telephone Co. 1961–65, Shell Oil Co. 1962–65, Time Inc. 1968–72, American Airlines 1968–71; founder Common Cause (Citizen's Lobby), Founding Chair. Independent Sector 1980–83; Chair. Nat. Civic League 1993–96; Miriam and Peter Haas Prof. Stanford Univ. 1989–96, Consulting Prof. 1996–; Chair. Soc. Sciences Panel, Scientific Advisory Bd., U.S.A.F. 1951–55; Dir. New York School of Social Work 1949–55, Metropolitan Museum of Art 1957–65, Stanford Univ. 1968–82, Rockefeller Brothers Fund 1968–77, New York Foundation 1970–76, Sr. Exec. Council, Conf. Bd. 1970–75; mem. Pres. Kennedy's Task Force on Educ. 1960; Chair. U.S. Advisory Comm. on Int. Educ. and Cultural Affairs 1962–64, Pres. Johnson's Task Force on Educ. 1964, White House Conf. on Educ. 1965, Pres.'s Comm. on White House Fellowships 1977–81; mem. Pres.'s Comm. on Agenda for the 1980's, Pres.'s Task Force on Private Sector Initiative 1981–82; Fellow, American Acad. of Arts and Sciences; hon. degrees from numerous American colls. and univs.; U.S.A.F. Exceptional Service Award 1956, Presidential Medal of Freedom 1964, Nat. Acad. of Sciences Public Welfare Medal 1966, UAW Social Justice Award 1968, AFL-CIO Murray Green Medal 1970. *Publications:* Excellence 1961 (revised edn. 1984), Self-Renewal 1963 (revised edn. 1981), No Easy Victories 1968, The Recovery of Confidence 1970, In Common Cause 1972, Know or Listen to Those Who Know (with Francesca Gardner Reese) 1975, Ed. To Turn the Tide (by John F. Kennedy), Morale 1978, Quotations of Wit and Wisdom 1980, On Leadership 1990. *Address:* School of Education, Stanford University, Stanford, CA 94305-3084 (Office); 836 Lathrop Drive, Stanford, CA 94305, U.S.A. (Home).

GARDNER, Richard Lavenham, PH.D., F.R.S.; British scientist; b. 10 June 1943, Dorking; s. of the late Allan Constant and Eileen May Gardner; m.

Wendy Joy Cresswell 1968; one s.; ed. St. John's School, Leatherhead, N.E. Surrey Coll. of Tech., St. Catharine's Coll. Cambridge; Research Asst. Physiological Lab., Cambridge 1970–73; lecturer in Devt. and Reproductive Biology Dept. of Zoology, Oxford 1973–77, Research Student Christ Church 1974–77, Ordinary Students 1978–, Royal Soc. Henry Dale Research Prof. 1978–; Hon. Dir. Imperial Cancer Research Fund Developmental Biology Unit 1986–96; independent mem. Advisory Bd. for the Research Councils 1990–93; Scientific Medal, Zoological Soc. 1977. *Publications:* various scientific papers. *Leisure interests:* ornithology, music, sailing, gardening, painting. *Address:* Christ Church, Oxford, OX1 1DP, England.

GARDNER, Richard Newton, D.PHIL.; American diplomatist; b. 9 July 1927, New York; s. of Samuel I. and Ethel E. Gardner; m. Danielle Almeida Luzzatto 1956; one s. one d.; ed. Harvard Univ., Yale Law School, Oxford Univ.; Rhodes Scholar to Oxford Univ. 1951–54; Prof. of Law and Int. Org., Columbia Univ. 1957–61, 1965–76, 1981–; Deputy Asst. Sec. of State for Int. Org. Affairs, U.S. State Dept. 1961–65; U.S. Amb. to Italy 1977–81; Lawyer, Coudert Bros. 1981–93; Consultant to Sec.-Gen., UN Conf. on Environment and Devt. 1992; Amb. to Spain 1993–97; counsel Morgan, Lewis and Bockius 1997–; mem. U.S. Advisory Cttee. on Law of the Sea 1971–76, Pres.'s advisory cttee. for Foreign Trade Policy on Negotiations 1998–; Arthur S. Flemming Award 1963. *Publications:* Sterling-Dollar Diplomacy 1956, In Pursuit of World Order 1964, Blueprint for Peace 1966, The Global Partnership: International Agencies and Economic Development 1968, Negotiating Survival: Four Priorities after Rio 1992. *Leisure interests:* tennis, classical music, reading. *Address:* Columbia University School of Law, 435 West 116th Street, New York, NY 10027, U.S.A.

GARDNER, Roy Alan, F.C.C.A.; British business executive; b. 20 Aug. 1945, Chiswick, London; s. of Thomas Gardner and Iris Gardner; m. Carol Gardner 1969; one s. two d.; ed. Strodes School, Egham; Finance Dir., The Marconi Co. Ltd. 1984–85; Finance Dir. STC PLC, Man. Dir. STC Communications Ltd. 1986–89, mem. Bd. Dirs. STC PLC 1989–91; C.O.O. Northern Telecom Europe Ltd. 1991–92; Man. Dir. GEC-Marconi Ltd. 1992–94; Dir. GEC PLC 1994; Finance Dir. British Gas PLC 1994–95, Exec. Dir. 1995–96; Chief Exec. Centrica PLC 1997–; Dir. (non-exec.) Laporte PLC. *Leisure interests:* golf, running family. *Address:* Centrica PLC, Charter Court, 50 Windsor Road, Slough, Berks., SL1 2HA, England. *Telephone:* (01753) 758000. *Fax:* (01753) 758011.

GARDNER, W. Booth, M.B.A.; American state governor; b. 21 Aug. 1936, Tacoma; m. Jean Gardner; one s. one d.; ed. Univ. of Washington and Harvard Univ.; Asst. to Dean, School of Business Admin. Harvard Univ. 1966; Dir. School of Business & Econs. Univ. of Puget Sound, Tacoma 1967–72; Pres. Laird Norton Co. 1972–80; mem. Washington Senate 1970–73; County Exec. Pierce Co., Tacoma 1981–84; Gov. State of Washington 1985–93; Democrat. *Address:* c/o Legislative Building, AS-13, Olympia, WA 98504, U.S.A.

GAREGIN I (SARKISYAN, Nshan), Catholicos of All Armenians; Armenian ecclesiastic; b. 27 Aug. 1932, Kesab, Syria; ed. Theological Seminary of Kiliki Catholicosat, Oxford Univ.; ordained monk and named Garegin 1952, inspector of theological seminary 1956–57, 1960–64; Bishop 1964, Archbishop 1973, elected Vicar of Irano-Indian Eparchy 1971, leader of separate E. Eparchy of U.S.A. 1973, elected Catholicos-co-ruler 1973–77, Catholicos of the Great House of Kilikiya 1983, elected Catholicos of all Armenians April 1995; mem. Bd. of Trustees fund Alastan. *Publications:* theological work, including Divinity of Armenian Church in Armenian songs, Khalkidyas Council and Armenian church, other books and essays written in Armenian, English and French. *Address:* Residence of the Catholicos of Armenians, Echmiadzin, Armenia. *Telephone:* (2) 151-198. *Fax:* (2) 151-077.

GARFUNKEL, Art, M.A.; American singer and actor; b. 13 Oct. 1941, Forest Hills, New York; m. Kim Cermak 1988; one s.; ed. Columbia Univ.; fmrly. mem. singing duo Simon (Paul Simon, q.v.) and Garfunkel 1964–71, now solo performer; *songs with Simon include:* The Sounds of Silence, Dangling Conversation, Homeward Bound, I Am a Rock, At the Zoo, 7 O'Clock News, Silent Night, 59th Street Bridge Song, Scarborough Fair, Parsley, Sage, Rosemary and Thyme, Mrs. Robinson, The Boxer, Bridge Over Troubled Water; *albums with Simon:* Wednesday Morning 3 a.m. 1964, Sounds of Silence 1966, Parsley, Sage, Rosemary and Thyme 1966, The Graduate 1968, Bookends 1968, Bridge Over Troubled Water 1970; *solo albums include:* Angel Clare 1973, Breakaway 1975, Watermark 1978, Fate for Breakfast (Doubt for Dessert) 1979, Art Garfunkel 1979, Scissors Cut 1981, Simon & Garfunkel: The Concert in Central Park 1982, The Animals' Christmas 1986, Garfunkel 1989, Up Till Now 1993; *films include:* Catch-22 1970, Carnal Knowledge 1971, Bad Timing . . . A Sensual Obsession 1980, Good to Go 1986, Lefty 1988, Boxing Helena; recipient two Grammy Awards for song Mrs. Robinson 1969, six Grammy Awards for album Bridge Over Troubled Water 1970, Grammy Award for film soundtrack of The Graduate; mem. Rock and Roll Hall of Fame 1990.

GARLAND, George David, PH.D., F.R.S.C.; Canadian geophysicist; b. 29 June 1926, Toronto, Ont.; s. of N. L. Garland and Jean McPherson; m. Elizabeth MacMillan 1949; two s. one d.; ed. Univ. of Toronto and St. Louis Univ.; Geophysicist, Dominion Observatory, Ottawa 1950–54; Prof. of Geophysics, Univ. of Alberta, Edmonton 1954–63; Prof. of Geophysics, Univ. of Toronto 1963; Deputy Gen. Sec. Int. Union of Geodesy and Geophysics 1960–63, Gen. Sec. 1963–73, Pres. 1979–; Vice-Pres. Acad. of Science, Royal Soc. of Canada 1980–. *Publications:* The Earth's Shape and Gravity 1965, and papers in scientific journals dealing with gravity, terrestrial magnetism, structure of the earth's crust, electrical conductivity of the crust, heat flow from the earth. *Leisure interests:* canoeing, history of Canadian exploration, early maps. *Address:* 5 Mawhiney Court, Huntsville, Ont., P0A 1K0, Canada.

GARLAND, Patrick, M.A.; British theatre and television director and writer; b. 10 April 1935, London; s. of the late Ewart Garland and Rosalind Fell; m. Alexandra Bastedo 1980; ed. St. Mary's Coll., Southampton, St. Edmund Hall, Oxford; actor, Bristol Old Vic 1959, Age of Kings, BBC TV 1961; lived Paris 1961–62; wrote two plays for ITV 1962; Research Asst., Monitor, BBC TV 1963; Dir. and Producer, BBC Arts Dept. 1962–74; Hon. Fellow St. Edmund Hall, Oxford 1997; Hon. D.Litt. (Southampton) 1994. *Plays directed:* Forty Years On 1968, 1984, Brief Lives 1968, Getting On 1970, Cyrano 1971, Hair (Israel) 1972, The Doll's House (New York and London) 1975, Under the Greenwood Tree 1978, Look After Lulu 1978, Beecham 1980, York Mystery Plays 1980, My Fair Lady (U.S.A.) 1980, Kipling (London and New York) 1984, Canaries Sometimes Sing 1987, The Secret of Sherlock Holmes 1988, Victory 1989, A Room of One's Own 1989, Song in the Night 1989, The Dressmaker 1990, Tovarich 1991, Pickwick! 1993–96, The Tempest 1996, The Importance of Being Oscar 1997, Talking Heads 1998, Chimes at Midnight (Chichester Festival) 1998, Ages of Man 1999; wrote and directed Brief Lives (on tour and West End) 1998; Co-Author of Underneath the Arches 1982–83; Artistic Dir. Chichester Festival Theatre (The Cherry Orchard, The Mitford Girls, On the Rocks, Cavell, Goodbye, Mr Chips, As You Like It, Forty Years On, Merchant of Venice) 1980–84, 1991–94. *Films:* The Snow Goose 1974, The Doll's House 1976; produced: Fanfare for Elizabeth (Queen's 60th birthday gala) 1986, Celebration of a Broadcaster (for Richard Dimbleby Cancer Fund) 1986; writer and creative consultant Christmas Glory from St. Paul's. *Publications:* Brief Lives 1967, The Wings of the Morning 1989, Oswald the Owl 1990, Angels in the Sussex Air: an Anthology of Sussex Poets 1995, The Incomparable Rex 1996; poetry in London Magazine, New Poems, Poetry West, Encounter; short stories in Transatlantic Review; England Erzählt, Gemini, Light Blue Dark Blue. *Leisure interests:* Victorian novels, walking in Corsica. *Address:* Poplars Farm House, Almodington, Chichester, W. Sussex, PO20 7LD, England.

GARLAND, Sir Victor, K.B.E., B.A., F.C.A.; Australian fmr. politician and diplomatist; b. 5 May 1934, Perth; s. of Idris Victor Garland and Doris Garland; m. Lynette May Jamieson 1960; two s. one d.; ed. Hale School and Univ. of W. Australia; in practice as chartered accountant 1958–70; mem. Fed. House of Reps. 1969–81; Fed. Exec. Councillor 1971–; Minister for Supply 1971–72; Minister assisting the Treas. 1972, 1975–76; Chief Opposition Whip 1974–75; Chair. House of Reps. Expenditure Cttee. 1976–77; Minister for Special Trade Representations (GATT trade negotiations in Europe, the U.S.A., Canada and Japan) 1977–79, for Business and Consumer Affairs 1979–80; represented Australian Govt. at numerous int. conferences 1973–79; Chair. Commonwealth Dels. to UNCTAD V, Manila May 1979; High Commr. in the U.K. 1981–83; Chair. Glenchewton PLC 1993–; Dir. U.K. cos. including Prudential Corpn. PLC 1984–93, Throgmorton Trust PLC 1985–, Henderson Far East Income Trust PLC 1984– (Chair. 1990–), Dunedin Berkeley Fund Ltd. 1986–, Nelson Hurst 1993–, Govett Funds Inc. 1991– (Pres. 1997–), Fidelity Asian Values 1996–; Vice-Chair. South Bank Bd. 1985–; Freeman City of London 1982. *Leisure interests:* music, reading, skiing, sports. *Address:* Wilton Place, Knightsbridge, London, SW1X 8RL, England.

GARN, Edwin Jacob (Jake), B.S.; American politician; b. 12 Oct. 1932, Richfield, Utah; s. of Jacob E. Garn and Fern Christensen; m. 1st Hazel R. Thompson 1957 (died 1976); two s. two d.; m. 2nd Kathleen Brewerton 1977; two s. one d.; ed. Univ. of Utah; Special Agent, John Hancock Mutual Life Insurance Co., Salt Lake City 1960–61; Asst. Man. Home Life Insurance Co. New York, Salt Lake City 1961–66; Gen. Agent, Mutual Trust Life Insurance Co., Salt Lake City 1966–68; City Commr. Salt Lake City 1968–72, Mayor 1972–74; Dir. Met. Water Dist. 1968–72; Senator from Utah 1974–93; Vice-Chair. Huntsman Chemical Corpn., Salt Lake City 1993–; Republican. *Publication:* Night Launch 1989. *Address:* Huntsman Chemical Corporation, 500 Huntsman Way, Salt Lake City, UT 84108, U.S.A.

GARN, Stanley Marion, PH.D.; American physical anthropologist and educator; b. 27 Oct. 1922, New London, Conn.; s. of Harry Garn and Sadie Edith (Cohen); m. Priscilla Crozier 1950; one s. one d.; ed. Harvard Coll. and Harvard Univ.; Research Assoc., Chemical Eng., Chemical Warfare Service Devt. Lab., M.I.T. 1942–44; Tech. Ed., Polaroid Co. 1944–46, Consultant in Applied Anthropology 1946–47; Research Fellow, Cardiology, Mass. Gen. Hosp., Boston 1946–52; Instructor in Anthropology, Harvard Univ. 1948–52; Anthropologist, Forsyth Dental Infirmary, Boston 1947–52; Dir. Forsyth Face Size Project, Army Chemical Corps 1950–52; Chair. Dept. of Growth and Genetics, Fels Research Inst., Yellow Springs, Ohio 1952–68; Fellow Center for Human Growth and Devt., Univ. of Mich., Ann Arbor 1968–, Prof. of Nutrition 1968–92, Prof. of Anthropology 1972–92, Prof. Emer. 1993–; Harvey White Lecturer, Children's Hosp., Chicago; Walker-Ames Visiting Prof., Univ. of Washington; Raymond Pearl Memorial Lecturer, Human Biology Council; Neuhauser Lecturer, Soc. for Pediatric Radiology; Fellow, American Acad. of Arts and Sciences, American Inst. of Nutrition; Hon. Fellow American Acad. of Pediatrics; mem. N.A.S.; Distinguished Faculty Award, Univ. of Mich. *Publications:* Races 1950, Readings on Race 1960, Human Races 1961, Culture and the Direction of Human Evolution 1964, The Earlier Gain and Later Loss of Cortical Bone 1970, Writing the Biomedical Research Paper 1970. *Leisure interests:* photomicrography and culture of succulents. *Address:* Center for Human Growth and Development, 300 North Ingalls Street, Ann Arbor, MI 48109; 2410 Londonderry Road, Ann Arbor, MI 48109, U.S.A. (Home). *Telephone:* (734) 764-2443 (Office); (734) 665-5235 (Home).

GARNAUT, Ross Gregory, A.O., B.A., PH.D.; Australian economist and diplomatist; b. 28 July 1946, Perth, W.A.; s. of late L. Garnaut and P. W. Garnaut; m. Jayne Potter 1974; two s.; ed. Perth Modern School, W.A. and Australian Nat. Univ., Canberra; Research Fellow, Sr. Research Fellow and Sr. Fellow Econs. Dept. Research School of Pacific Studies A.N.U. 1972–75, 1977–83; First Asst. Sec.-Gen. Financial and Econ. Policy, Papua New Guinea Dept. of Finance 1975, 1976; Research Dir. ASEAN-Australia Econ. Relations Research Project 1980–83; Sr. Econ. Adviser to Prime Minister Bob Hawke (q.v.) 1983–85; Amb. to People's Repub. of China 1985–88; Prof. of Econs., Head of Dept., Research School of Pacific Studies, A.N.U. 1989–; Chair. Bd. of Dirs. Aluminium Smelters of Victoria 1988, 1989, Rural and Industries Bank of Western Australia 1988–95, Primary Industry Bank of Australia 1988–94, Lihir Gold 1995–, Australian Centre for Int. Agric. Research 1994–. *Publications:* Irian Jaya: The Transformation of a Melanesian Economy 1974, ASEAN in a Changing Pacific and World Economy 1980, Indonesia: Australian Perspectives 1980, Taxation and Mineral Rents 1983, Exchange Range and Macro-Economic Policy in Independent Papua New Guinea 1984, The Political Economy of Manufacturing Protection: Experiences of ASEAN and Australia 1986, Australian Protectionism: Extent, Causes and Effects 1987, Australia and the Northeast Asian Ascendancy (report to Prime Minister) 1989, Economic Reform and Internationalization 1992, Grain in China 1992, Structuring for Global Realities (report on Wool Industry to Commonwealth Governments) 1993, The Third Revolution in the Chinese Countryside 1996, Open Regionalism: An Asian Pacific Contribution to the World Trading System 1996. *Leisure interests:* cricket, tennis, watching Australian football, and the history of humanity. *Address:* Department of Economics, Research School of Pacific and Asian Studies, Australian National University, Canberra A.C.T. 0200, Australia. *Telephone:* (02) 6249 3100. *Fax:* (02) 6249 8057.

GARNER, Alan; British author; b. 17 Oct. 1934; s. of Colin Garner and Marjorie Garner (née Greenwood Stuart); m. 1st Ann Cook 1956; one s. two d.; m. 2nd Griselda Greaves 1972; one s. one d.; ed. Manchester Grammar School, Magdalen Coll. Oxford; mil. service with rank of Lieut., R.A.; mem. Ed. Bd. Detskaya Literatura Publrs., Moscow. *Publications: books:* The Weirdstone of Brisingamen 1960, The Moon of Gomrath 1963, Elidor 1965, Holly from the Bongs 1966, The Old Man of Mow 1967, The Owl Service 1967 (Library Asscn. Carnegie Medal 1967, Guardian Award 1968), The Hamish Hamilton Book of Goblins 1969, Red Shift 1973, The Breadhorse 1975, The Guizer 1975, The Stone Book 1976, (Phoenix Award, Children's Book Asscn. of U.S. 1996), Tom Fobble's Day 1977, Granny Reardun 1977, The Aimer Gate 1978, Fairy Tales of Gold 1979, The Lad of the Gad 1980, A Book of British Fairy Tales 1984, A Bag of Moonshine 1986, Jack and the Beanstalk 1992, Once Upon a Time 1993, Strandloper 1996, The Little Red Hen 1997, The Voice That Thunders 1997, The Well of the Wind 1998. *Plays:* Holly from the Bongs 1965, Lamaload 1978, Lurga Lom 1980, To Kill a King 1980, Sally Water 1982, The Keeper 1983, Pentecost 1997. *Dance drama:* The Green Mist 1970; *libretti:* The Bellybag 1971, Potter Thompson 1972, Lord Flame 1996. *Screenplays:* The Owl Service 1969, Red Shift 1978, Places and Things 1978, Images 1981 (First Prize, Chicago Int. Film Festival), Strandloper 1992. *Leisure interest:* work. *Address:* Blackden, Holmes Chapel, Cheshire, CW4 8BY, England.

GARNER, James (James Baumgardner); American actor; b. 7 April 1928, Norman, Okla.; m. Lois Clarke 1956; one s. two d.; ed. New York Berghof School; worked as travelling salesman, oil field worker, carpet layer, bathing suit model; toured with road cos. *TV appearances include:* Cheyenne, Maverick 1957–62, Nichols 1971–72, The Rockford Files 1974–79, Space 1985, The New Maverick, The Long Summer of George Adams, The Glitter Dome, Heartsounds, Promise (also exec. producer), Obsessive Love, My Name is Bill (also exec. producer), Decoration Day, Barbarians at the Gate, The Rockford Files; A Blessing in Disguise. *Films include:* Toward the Unknown, Shoot-out at Medicine Bend 1957, Darby's Rangers 1958, Sayonara, Up Periscope 1959, The Americanization of Emily 1964, 36 Hours 1964, The Art of Love 1965, A Man Could Get Killed 1966, Duel at Diablo 1966, Mister Buddwing 1966, Grand Prix 1966, Hour of the Gun 1967, Marlowe 1969, Support Your Local Sheriff 1971, Support Your Local Gunfighter 1971, Skin Game 1971, They Only Kill Their Masters 1972, One Little Indian 1973, Health 1979, The Fan 1980, Victor/Victoria 1982, Murphy's Romance 1985, Promise (made for TV) 1986, Sunset 1987, Decoration Day (TV film) 1990, Fire in the Sky 1993, Maverick (TV) 1994, My Fellow Americans 1996; Emmy Award; Purple Heart. *Address:* c/o Charles Stern Agency, 11755 Wilshire Boulevard, Building 2320, Los Angeles, CA 90025-1530, U.S.A.

GARNER, Wendell Richard, PH.D.; American psychologist and university professor; b. 21 Jan. 1921, Buffalo, N.Y.; s. of Richard Charles and Lena Cole Garner; m. Barbara Chipman Ward 1944; one s. two d.; ed. Franklin and Marshall Coll. and Harvard Univ.; Instructor, rising to Prof., Johns Hopkins Univ. 1946–67, Chair. Dept. of Psychology 1954–64; James Rowland Angell Prof. of Psychology, Yale Univ. 1967–89, Prof. Emer. 1989–, Dir. of Social Sciences 1972–73, 1981–88, Chair. Dept. of Psychology 1974–77, Dean of the Graduate School 1978–79; mem. Nat. Acad. of Sciences; Hon. D.Sc. (Franklin and Marshall Coll.) 1979, D.Hum.Litt. (Johns Hopkins Univ.) 1983; Distinguished Scientific Contribution Award, American Psychological Asscn. 1964, Warren Medal, Soc. of Experimental Psychologists 1976. *Publications:* Applied Experimental Psychology (with A. Chapanis and C. T. Morgan) 1949, Uncertainty and Structure as Psychological Concepts 1962, The Processing of Information and Structure 1974, Ability Testing (ed. with A. Wigdor) 1982. *Leisure interests:* gardening, hiking. *Address:* P.O. Box 650, Branford, CT 06405, U.S.A. (Home). *Telephone:* (203) 481-0007 (Home).

GAROFANO, Giuseppe; Italian engineer; b. 25 Jan. 1944, Nereto, Teramo; ed. Milan Polytechnic Inst., Bocconi Univ. Business School; Man. Dir. Cotonificio Cantoni 1981–84; Vice-Chair. and Man. Dir. Iniziativa ME.T.A. S.p.A. 1984–88, Chair. and C.E.O. 1988; Man. Dir. Ferruzzi Finanziaria S.p.A. 1988–92, Vice-Chair. 1989–; Vice-Chair. Milano Assicurazioni S.p.A. 1987–, Fondiaria S.p.A. 1989–, La Previdente Assicurazioni S.p.A. 1991–; Vice-Chair. Montedison S.p.A. 1989–90, Chair. 1990–92.

GAROUSTE, Gérard; French painter and sculptor; b. 10 March 1946, Paris; s. of Henri Garouste and Edmée Sauvagnac; m. Elizabeth Rochline 1970; two s.; ed. Académie Charpentier, Beaux-Arts de Paris; first exhbn. Galerie Zunini, Paris 1969; other exhbns. include Paris 1978, 1980, 1988 (Centre Pompidou), Milan 1980, Noto 1981, New York 1982, 1983, 1985, 1988, Venice Biennale 1982, Düsseldorf 1982 (Kunsthalle), 1984, 1989 (Kunsthalle), Rome 1984, Charleroi 1984, Dublin 1986, Munich 1986, Budapest 1986, Tokyo 1986 (Museum of Modern Art), 1990, Montreal 1986 (Musée d'art contemporain), Seoul 1987, Bordeaux 1987, Bienale de São Paulo 1987, Yugoslavia 1988, 1990, Amsterdam 1989 (Stedelikmuseum); created Le classique et l'Indien show 1977; sets, Théâtre de la ville 1978, Palace et Privilège, Théâtre du Chatelet, Paris 1990; fresco, Elysée Palace 1983; subject of several monographs and catalogues; Chevalier des Arts et des Lettres. *Address:* La Mésangère, 27810 Marcilly-sur-Eure, France. *Telephone:* 37.48.47.18.

GARRARD, Rose, DIP.A.D.; British sculptor and mixed media artist; b. 21 Sept. 1946, Bewdley, Worcs.; d. of Col. W. V. Garrard. and Germaine Garrard; m. (divorced); no c.; ed. Stourbridge, Birmingham and Chelsea Colls. of Art and Acad. des Beaux Arts, Paris; freelance designer, model and prop-maker to magazines, theatres, advertisers and TV 1969–83; arts consultant to architects advising on public works projects including Liverpool Shopping Precinct and Elephant & Castle Shopping Centre 1971–74; Artist in Schools Residency, Cen. Foundation School for Girls, Bow, E. London 1982; Artist-in-Residence, Birmingham City Art Gallery 1983; Sr. Lecturer, half full-time, Art and Social Context, Dartington Coll. of Arts; has held various other part-time teaching and lecturing appts. throughout U.K.; solo exhbns. in Worcester 1967, London 1977, 1983, Cambridge 1983, Birmingham, Liverpool, Bristol, Nottingham and Rochdale 1984, Inst. of Contemporary Art (ICA), London 1984; has participated in numerous group exhbns. in U.K., Europe, U.S.A., Canada, and Australia since 1967; works in many public and pvt. collections including Victoria & Albert Museum, Contemporary Art Soc. and Arts Council of G.B.; mem. numerous selection panels etc.; Int. Multiples Prize Award by Paolozzi 1969; Prix d'honneur de Paris for Sculpture 1971; Arts Council of G.B. Purchase Award 1979; Greater London Arts Asscn. Major Award 1980. *Address:* Studio 21, 105 Carpenters Road, London, E.18, England. *Telephone:* 0181-519 6321.

GARRATT, Sheryl, B.A.; British journalist; b. 29 March 1961, Birmingham; d. of Frank Garratt and June (née Fray) Garratt; m. Mark McGuire 1994; one s.; ed. Barr Beacon Comprehensive, Univ. Coll., London; various freelance and staff positions including contribs. to New Musical Express, Honey, Looks, News on Sunday, The Observer, The Sunday Telegraph; Music Ed. City Limits; joined The Face 1988, Ed. 1990–95; freelance journalist 1995–98; ed. The Observer Magazine 1998–. *Leisure interests:* clubbing, drinking, sitting up all night talking afterwards. *Publications:* Signed, Sealed and Delivered 1984, Adventures in Wonderland – a Decade of Club Culture 1998. *Address:* 56C St Thomas's Road, London, N4 2QW, England. *Telephone:* 0171-266 8836. *Fax:* 0171-503 6748.

GARRETT, Lesley, F.R.A.M.; British opera singer; b. 10 April 1955; d. of Derek Arthur Garrett and Margaret Wall; m. 1991; one s. one d.; ed. Thorne Grammar School, Royal Acad. of Music, Nat. Opera Studio; winner Kathleen Ferrier Memorial Competition 1979; performed with Welsh Nat. Opera, Opera North, at Wexford and Buxton Festivals and at Glyndebourne; joined E.N.O. (Prin. Soprano) 1984. *Major roles include:* Susanna in The Marriage of Figaro, Despina in Così Fan Tutte, Musetta in La Bohème, Jenny in The Rise and Fall of The City of Mahaggony, Atalanta in Xerxes, Zerlinda in Don Giovanni, Yum-Yum in The Mikado, Adèle in Die Fledermaus, Oscar in A Masked Ball, Dalinda in Ariodante, Rose in Street Scene, Bella in A Midsummer Marriage, Eurydice in Orpheus and Eurydice and title roles in The Cunning Little Vixen and La Belle Vivette; numerous concert hall performances in U.K. and abroad (including Last Night of the Proms); TV and radio appearances; Hon. D.Arts (Plymouth) 1995; Best Selling Classical Artist, Gramophone Award 1996. *Leisure interest:* watching cricket. *Address:* PV Productions, Park Offices, 121 Dora Road, London, SW19 7JT, England. *Telephone:* 0181-946 8848. *Fax:* 0181-944 1317.

GARRISON-JACKSON, Zina; American tennis player (retd.); b. 16 Nov. 1963, Houston, Tex.; m. Willard Jackson Jr. 1989; winner WTA Championships 1985; Singles semi-finalist, Wimbledon Championships 1985, finalist 1990 (lost to Martina Navratilova q.v.); semi-finalist U.S. Open 1988, 1989; Gold Medal winner, Ladies Doubles (with P. Shriver), Seoul Olympic Games 1988; winner Mixed Doubles (with S. Stewart), Australian Open 1987, Wimbledon Championships 1988; winner U.S. Open, Ladies Doubles (with Mary Joe Fernandez q.v.) 1993. *Address:* c/o USTA, 70 W. Red Oak Lane, White Plains, NY 10604; c/o Advantage International, 1751 Pinnacle Drive, Suite 1500, McLean, VA 22102, U.S.A.

GARTON, George Alan, PH.D., D.SC., F.R.S.E., F.R.S.; British biochemist; b. 4 June 1922, Scarborough, Yorks.; s. of late William E. and Frances M. E. Garton; m. Gladys F. Davison 1951; two d.; ed. Scarborough High School for Boys and Univ. of Liverpool; experimental asst., Ministry of Supply 1942–45; Johnston Research and Teaching Fellow, Univ. of Liverpool 1949–50; Rowett Research Inst., Aberdeen 1950–83, Head, Lipid Biochem. Dept. 1963, Deputy Dir. 1968, Hon. Research Assoc. 1983–90, Hon. Professorial Fellow 1991–; Visiting Prof. of Biochem. Univ. of N. Carolina 1967; Chair. British Nat. Cttee. for Nutritional and Food Sciences 1982–87; mem. Council, British Nutrition Foundation 1982–, Inst. of Brain Biochem. and Human Nutrition 1990–; Hon. Research Fellow, Univ. of Aberdeen 1987–; Pres. Int. Confs. on Biochemistry of Lipids 1982–89; Advisory mem. Steering Cttee. Int. Confs. on Biochemistry of Lipids 1990–; a Dir. of Mother and Child Foundation 1994–; Serving Brother, Most Venerable Order of the Hosp. of St. John of Jerusalem. *Publications:* many papers, reviews and chapters in books on the subjects of lipid biochemistry and nutrition. *Leisure interests:* golf, gardening, philately, foreign travel. *Address:* Ellerburn, 1 St. Devenick Crescent, Cults, Aberdeen, AB15 9LL, Scotland. *Telephone:* (01224) 867012.

GARWIN, Richard L., M.S., PH.D.; American physicist; b. 19 April 1928, Cleveland, Ohio; s. of Robert and Leona S. Garwin; m. Lois E. Levy 1947; two s. one d.; ed. public schools in Cleveland, Case Western Reserve Univ. and Univ. of Chicago; Instructor and Asst. Prof. of Physics, Univ. of Chicago 1949–52; mem. staff, IBM Watson Lab., Columbia Univ. 1952–65, 1966–70; Adjunct Prof. of Physics, Columbia Univ. 1957–; Dir. of Applied Research, IBM T. J. Watson Research Center 1965–66, IBM Fellow 1967–93, Fellow Emer. 1993–; mem. Defense Science Bd. 1966–69; mem. President's Science Advisory Cttee. 1962–66, 1969–72; mem. IBM Corporate Tech. Cttee. 1970–71; Adjunct Prof. Col. Univ. 1957; Prof. of Public Policy, Kennedy School of Govt., Harvard 1979–81, Adjunct Research Fellow 1982–; Andrew D. White Prof.-at-Large, Cornell Univ. 1982–87; mem. Council on Foreign Relations; mem. N.A.S. 1966–, Inst. of Medicine 1975–81, Nat. Acad. of Eng. 1978–, American Philosophical Soc. 1979–; Consultant to Los Alamos 1950–93, to Sandia Nat. Lab. 1994–; Fellow, American Physical Soc. American Acad. of Arts and Sciences; Ford Foundation Fellow, CERN, Geneva 1959–60; Hon Dr. (Case Western Reserve Univ.) 1966, (Rensselaer Polytechnic Inst.), (State Univ. of New York); R. V. Jones Intelligence Award (Nat. Foreign Intelligence Community) 1996, Enrico Fermi Award 1997. *Publications:* Co-Author: Nuclear Power Issues and Choices 1977, Nuclear Weapons and World Politics 1977, Energy, the Next Twenty Years (co-author) 1979, The Dangers of Nuclear Wars 1979, Unresolved Issues in Arms Control 1988, A Nuclear-Weapon-Free World: Desirable? Feasible? 1993, Managing the Plutonium Surplus: Applications and Technical Options 1994, U.S. Intervention Policy for the Post-Cold War World: New Challenges and New Responses 1994, Feux Follets et Champignons Nucléaires (with G. Charpak) 1997; about 200 published papers and 42 U.S. patents. *Leisure interests:* skiing, military technology, arms control, social use of technology. *Address:* c/o T. J. Watson Research Center, P.O. Box 218, Yorktown Heights, New York, NY 10598, U.S.A.

GASCOIGNE, Paul John; British professional footballer; b. 27 May 1967, Gateshead; s. of John Gascoigne and Carol Gascoigne (née Harold); m. Sheryl Failes 1996 (divorced 1998); ed. Heathfield Sr. School; played for Newcastle United 1985–88; transferred to Tottenham Hotspur 1988 (FA Cup winners' medal 1991); transferred to Lazio, Italy 1992–95; transferred to Rangers 1995–98; transferred to Middlesbrough 1998–; played for England, 13 under-21 caps, over 20 full caps, World Cup Italy 1990. *Leisure interests:* football, fishing, tennis, swimming. *Address:* c/o Arram Berlyn Gardner, Holborn Hall, 100 Grays Inn Road, London, WC1X 8BY, England. *Telephone:* 0171-753 5511. *Fax:* 0171-404 0109.

GASH, Norman, C.B.E., M.LITT., F.R.S.E., F.B.A., F.R.HIST.S., F.R.S.L.; British historian; b. 16 Jan. 1912, Meerut, India; s. of Frederick Gash and Kate Gash née Hunt; m. 1st Ivy Dorothy Whitehorn 1935 (died 1995); two d.; m. 2nd Ruth Frances Jackson 1997; ed. Reading School and St. John's Coll. Oxford; Lecturer in History, Univ. Coll. London 1936–40; war service in army 1940–46; Lecturer in History, St. Salvator's Coll., St. Andrews 1946–53; Prof. of Modern History, Univ. of Leeds 1953–55; Prof. of History, St. Andrews Univ. 1955–80, now Prof. Emer., Vice-Prin. 1967–71, Dean of Faculty of Arts 1978–80; Hinkley Visiting Prof., Johns Hopkins Univ., U.S.A. 1962; Ford's Lecturer in English History, Oxford Univ. 1963–64; Sir John Neale Lecturer, Univ. Coll. London 1981; Wellington Lecturer, Southampton Univ. 1992; Hon. Fellow St. John's Coll., Oxford 1987; Hon. D.Litt. (Strathclyde) 1984, (St. Andrews) 1985, (Southampton) 1988. *Publications:* Politics in the Age of Peel 1953, Mr Secretary Peel 1961, Reaction and Reconstruction in English Politics 1832–52 1965, Sir Robert Peel 1973, Aristocracy and People: Britain 1815–65 1979, Lord Liverpool 1984, Pillars of Government 1986, Robert Surtees and Early Victorian Society 1993. *Leisure interests:* gardening, swimming. *Address:* Old Gatehouse, Portway, Langport, Somerset, TA10 0NQ, England. *Telephone:* (01458) 250334.

GASKILL, William; British theatre and opera director; b. 24 June 1930; ed. Salt High School, Shipley, and Hertford Coll., Oxford; Dir., Granada Television 1956–57; Asst. Artistic Dir. Royal Court Theatre, London 1958–60; Dir. Royal Shakespeare Co. 1961–62; Assoc. Dir. Nat. Theatre, London 1963–65, 1979; Artistic Dir. English Stage Co., Royal Court Theatre 1965–72; Dir. Joint Stock Theatre Group 1974–83. Stage productions include: (Royal Court Theatre) Epitaph for George Dillon, One Way Pendulum, Saved, Early Morning, Man is Man, Lear, Big Wolf, The Sea, The Gorky Brigade; (National Theatre) The Recruiting Officer, Mother Courage, Philoctetes, Armstrong's Last Goodnight, The Beaux Stratagem, The Madras House, A Fair Quarrel, Man, Beast and Virtue, Black Snow; (Royal Shakespeare Co.) The Caucasian Chalk Circle, Richard III, Cymbeline; (Joint Stock) The Speakers, Fanshen, Yesterday's News, A Mad World, My Masters, The Ragged Trousered Philanthropists; other productions include The Way of the World; Opera productions include: The Barber of Seville, La Bohème and Lucia di Lammermoor (Welsh Nat. Opera). *Publication:* A Sense of Direction: life at the Royal Court (autobiog.) 1988. *Address:* 124A Leighton Road, London, NW5 2RG, England.

GASPAROV, Mikhail Leonovich, D.LITT.; Russian literary scholar; b. 13 April 1935, Moscow; m.; two c.; ed. Moscow State Univ.; jr., sr. researcher, head of div., chief researcher Inst. of World Literature 1957–90; chief researcher Inst. of Russian Language U.S.S.R. Acad. of Sciences 1990–99; corresp. mem. U.S.S.R. (now Russian) Acad. of Sciences 1990, mem. 1992; research in Latin poetics, Russian poetry, study of versification. *Publications include:* Classical Literary Fable 1971, Contemporary Russian Verse 1974, Survey of History of Russian Verse 1984, History of European Versification 1989. *Leisure interests:* reading, translation of classics and poetry. *Address:* Institute of Russian Language, Russian Academy of Sciences, Volkhonka str. 18/2, 121019 Moscow, Russia. *Telephone:* (095) 202-65-10.

GAŠPAROVIČ, Ivan, LL.D.; Slovak politician and lawyer; b. 27 March 1941, Poltár Lučenec Dist.; s. of Vladimír Gašparovič and Elena Gašparovič; m. Silvia Gašparovičová 1964; one s. one d.; ed. Komenský Univ., Bratislava; clerk, Prosecutor's Office, Martin Trenčín 1965–66; Mun. Public Prosecutor, Bratislava 1966–68; teacher, Faculty of Law, Komenský Univ., Bratislava 1968–90, Vice-Rector 1990–; Gen. Prosecutor of C.S.F.R. 1990–92; mem. Movt. for Democratic Slovakia 1992–; deputy to Slovak Nat. Council, mem. of Presidium; Chair. of Slovak Nat. Council 1992–98; Chair. Special Body of Nat. Council of Slovakia for Control of Slovak Intelligence Services 1993–98. *Publications:* author and co-author of many univ. textbooks, numerous articles and reviews on criminal law. *Leisure interests:* tennis, hockey, motoring. *Address:* Mudroňova 1, 812 80 Bratislava, Slovakia. *Telephone:* (7) 534 1111 (Office).

GASSIYEV, Nikolai Tengizovich; Russian tenor; b. 2 Feb. 1952, Tskhinvali, Ga.; ed. Leningrad State Conservatory; soloist Mariinsky Opera and Ballet Theatre 1990–; debut in Metropolitan Opera as Yurodivy (Boris Godunov) and Agrippina (Fairy Angel) 1992, Dresdner Staatsoper 1993, Brooklyn School of Music 1995, Edin. Festival 1995, Albert Hall 1995, La Scala 1996; Prize of Union of Theatre Workers Best Actor of the Year 1994. *Address:* Mariinsky Theatre, Teatralnaya pl. 1, St. Petersburg, Russia (Office). *Telephone:* (812) 315 5724 (Office).

GASSMAN, Vittorio; Italian actor and director; b. 1 Sept. 1922; ed. Law Univ. of Rome and Dramatic Acad. of Rome. *Plays acted in include:* Hamlet, Othello, As You Like It, Troilus and Cressida, Oedipus Rex, Prometheus Bound, Ghosts, Peer Gynt, Orestes, Rosencrantz and Guildenstern are Dead, Richard III, etc.; has directed his own group since 1951. *Films acted in include:* Bitter Rice, Anna, Rhapsody, War and Peace, the Miracle, I Soliti Ignoti, The Family, I Picari, A Wedding, The Nude Bomb, Immortal Bachelor, The Hateful Dead, The Long Winter, Sleepers, etc.; Dir. Kean 1956 and The Great War, Venice Festival winner; Dir. musical- play Irma la Douce; four awards for the best Italian theatre actor of the year, four for the best film actor; created Teatro Popolare Italiano (mobile theatre, 3,000 seats); dir. and played Agamemnon in production of Aeschylus' Oresteia, Syracuse 1960.

GAT, Joel R., M.SC., PH.D.; Israeli professor of isotope research; b. 17 Feb. 1926, Munich, Germany; m.; two c.; ed. Hebrew Univ., Jerusalem; Asst. Dept. of Physical Chem., Hebrew Univ. 1949–50; Research Officer Ministry of Defence Labs., Jerusalem 1950–52; Israel Atomic Energy Comm., Rehovot 1952–59; at Isotope Dept. (renamed Dept. of Environmental Sciences and Energy Research 1990), Weizmann Inst. of Science, Rehovot 1959–, Acting Prof. 1967–71, Prof. 1971–, Head of Dept. 1975–86, Dean, Faculty of Chem., Weizmann Inst. 1986–89; Visiting Prof. Enrico Fermi Inst. for Nuclear Science, Univ. of Chicago 1955–56, Scripps Inst. of Oceanography, Univ. of Calif. 1964–65, Nat. Centre for Atmospheric Research, Boulder, Colo. 1972–73, Univ. of Wis. 1988–89; mem. editorial bd. Isotope Geosciences, Earth and Planetary Science Letters; undertook IAEA-sponsored projects in Brazil, Iran, Mexico and Turkey; mem. Bd. of Govs. Inter-Univ. Inst. for Marine Research, Eilat. *Address:* Department of Environmental Sciences and Energy Research, The Weizmann Institute of Science, P.O. Box 26, Rehovot, Israel.

GATES, Henry Louis, Jr., M.A., PH.D.; American professor of Afro-American studies, author and editor; b. 16 Sept. 1950, Piedmont, W. Va.; s. of Henry-

Louis Gates and Pauline Augusta Gates (née Coleman); m. Sharon Lynn Adams 1979; two d.; ed. Yale Univ. and Clare Coll. Cambridge; fmr. European corresp. for Time magazine; lecturer in English, Yale Univ. 1976–79, Asst. Prof. English and Afro-American Studies 1979–84, Assoc. Prof. 1984–85; Prof. of English, Comparative Literature and Africana Studies, Cornell Univ. 1985–90; John Spencer Bassett Prof. of English, Duke Univ. 1990–91; Prof., Chair. Dept. of Afro-American Studies, Harvard Univ. 1991–; also Dir. W. E. B. DuBois Inst. for Afro-American Research (Prof. of Literature 1988–90, of Humanities 1991), Harvard Univ. 1991–; Pres. Afro-American Acad. 1984–; ed. African American Women's Writings (Macmillan reprint series), Encyclopedia Africana; columnist, New Yorker, New York Times; American Book Award for The Signifying Monkey; McArthur Foundation Award; numerous hon. degrees. *Publications include:* Figures in Black (literary criticism) 1987, The Signifying Monkey 1988, Loose Canons (literary criticism) 1992, Colored People (short stories) 1994, The Future of the Race (with Cornel West) 1996, Thirteen Ways of Looking at a Black Man. *Address:* Department of Afro-American Studies, Barker Center, 12 Quincy Street, Cambridge, MA 02138, U.S.A. *Telephone:* (617) 496-5468. *Fax:* (617) 495-9490.

GATES, Marshall De Motte, Jr.; American professor of chemistry; b. 25 Sept. 1915, Boyne City, Mich.; s. of Marshall D. Gates and Virginia Orton Gates; m. Martha L. Meyer 1941; two s. two d.; ed. Rice and Harvard Univs.; Asst. Prof. of Chem., Bryn Mawr Coll. 1941–46, Assoc. Prof. 1947–49; Tech. Aide, Nat. Defense Research Council 1943–46; Lecturer in Chem., Univ. of Rochester 1949–52, part-time Prof. 1952–60, Prof. 1960–68, Charles Houghton Prof. of Chem. 1968–81, Prof. Emer. 1981–; first synthesis of morphine 1952; Visiting Prof. Dartmouth 1982, 1984, 1985; mem. Cttee. on Drugs Addiction and Narcotics, Div. of Medical Sciences, Nat. Research Council 1956–69; Charter Fellow Coll. of Problems of Drug Dependence 1992–; mem. N.A.S., American Chem. Soc.; Fellow, American Acad. of Arts and Sciences, New York Acad. of Sciences; Asst. Ed. Journal of American Chemical Society 1949–62, Ed. 1963–69; Max Tishler Lecturer, Harvard 1953, Welch Foundation Lecturer 1960; mem. President's Cttee. on Nat. Medal of Science 1968–70, Advisory Bd., Chem. Abstract Services 1974–76; E. P. Curtis Award 1967, Distinguished Alumnus Award, Rice Univ. 1987. *Leisure interests:* skiing, sailing. *Address:* 41 West Brook Road, Pittsford, New York, U.S.A. (Home).

GATES, Robert M., PH.D.; American intelligence officer; b. 25 Sept. 1943, Wichita, Kansas; m. Becky Gates; two c.; ed. Coll. of William and Mary, Indiana Univ., Georgetown Univ.; service with U.S.A.F. 1966–68; career training program CIA 1968, intelligence analyst 1969–72, staff of Special Asst. to the Dir. of Central Intelligence for Strategic Arms Limitations 1972–73, Asst. Nat. Intelligence Officer for Strategic Programs 1973–74, staff Nat. Security Council The White House 1974–76, staff Center for Policy Support 1976–77, Special Asst. to Asst. to the Pres. for Nat. Security Affairs 1977–79, Dir. Strategic Evaluation Center 1979–80, Exec. Asst. to Dir. of Cen. Intelligence and Dir. of the Exec. Staff, Dir. of Office of Policy and Planning and Nat. Intelligence Officer for the Soviet Union and Eastern Europe 1980, Deputy Dir. for Intelligence 1981–82, Chair. Nat. Intelligence Council 1982–86, Acting Dir. of Central Intelligence 1986–87, Deputy Dir. of Central Intelligence 1986–89, Asst. to the Pres. and Deputy for Nat. Security Affairs The White House 1989–91, Dir. C.I.A. 1991–93; Nat. Intelligence Distinguished Service Medal, Distinguished Intelligence Medal (twice), Intelligence Medal of Merit, Arthur S. Fleming Award. *Publication:* From the Shadows 1996. *Address:* c/o Central Intelligence Agency, Washington, DC 20505, U.S.A.

GATES, William Henry (Bill) III; American computer software executive; b. 28 Oct. 1955, Seattle; s. of William Gates and Mary Maxwell; m. Melinda French 1994; one d.; ed. Lakeside School, Harvard Univ.; joined MITS 1975; Programmer for Honeywell 1975; Founder, Chair. Bd. Microsoft Corpn. (disk operating system, windows system) 1976–, now C.E.O.; Howard Vollum Award, Reed Coll. Portland, Ore. 1984; named CEO of Year Chief Executive Magazine. *Publications:* The Future 1994, The Road Ahead 1996. *Leisure interest:* tennis. *Address:* Microsoft Corporation, 1 Microsoft Way, Redmond, WA 98052, U.S.A.

GATT, Lawrence, B.ARCH., M.P.; Maltese politician; b. 12 May 1941, Rabat, Malta; s. of Joseph Gatt and Rose Sammut; m. Agnes Sciberras 1967; two s. one d.; ed. the Lyceum and Univ. of Malta; practising architect and civil engineer 1967; M.P. 1971–96; Asst. Whip. 1971–76, mem. Exec. Council and mem. Gen. Council, Nationalist Party 1971–; Shadow Minister of Tourism then Party Spokesman on Agric. and Fisheries 1976–87; Minister of Productive Devt. 1987–90; Minister of Agric. and Fisheries 1990–92; Minister for Food, Agric. and Fisheries 1992–94; Nationalist Party. *Leisure interests:* writing poems and short stories, soccer and athletics. *Address:* Villa Gatt, Hope Street, Mosta, Malta.

GATTAZ, Yvon; French business executive; b. 17 June 1925, Bourgoin; s. of Marceau Gattaz and Gabrielle Brotel; m. Geneviève Beurley 1954; two s. one d.; ed. Coll. of Bourgoin, Lycée du Parc, Lyon, Ecole Centrale des Arts et Manufactures, Paris; with Aciéries du Nord 1948–50; Automobiles Citroën 1950–54; founder Soc. Radiall 1952, Chair. 1952–93, Pres. Supervisory Council 1994–; Chair. group of commercial and industrial cos., Rosny-sous-Bois 1967–81; Admin. Centre for External Trade 1979–82, Nat. Council for Scientific Research 1979–81; founder Mouvement des entreprises à taille humaine industrielles et commerciales (ETHIC) 1976, Pres. 1976–81, Hon. Pres. 1981–; founder Les Quatre Vérités 1974, Co-Ed. 1974–81; mem. Conseil economique et social 1979–89; Pres. Conseil National du Patronat Français 1981–86, Hon. Pres. 1986; Pres. admin. council Fondation jeunesse et entreprise 1986–; Pres. Comité d'expansion de Seine-Saint-Denis 1987 (Hon. Pres. 1998–), association Entreprises Télévision Educ. Formation (ETEF) 1994, ASMEP (Association des moyennes entreprises patrimoniales) 1995–; mem. Institut de France (Acad. des Sciences morales et politiques) 1989; Commdr. Légion d'honneur; Commdr., Ordre nat. du Mérite. *Publications:* Les hommes en gris 1970, La fin des patrons 1980, Les patrons reviennent 1988, Le modèle français 1993 (prix du Livre de l'entreprise 1995). *Address:* 4 rue Léo-Delibes, 75116 Paris, France (Office).

GATTI, Daniele; Italian conductor; b. 6 Nov. 1961, Milan; m. Silvia Chiesa 1990; ed. Milan Conservatory; founded Stradivari Chamber Orchestra 1986; début at La Scala, Milan with Rossini's L'occasione fa il Ladro 1987–88 season; US début with American Symphony Orchestra, Carnegie Hall, New York 1990; Covent Garden début with I Puritani 1992; Music Dir. Accad. di Santa Cecilia, Rome 1992–; Prin. Guest Conductor, Royal Opera House, Covent Garden 1994–; début at Metropolitan Opera, New York with Madam Butterfly 1994–95 season; début with Royal Philharmonic 1994, Music Dir. 1996–; Music Dir. Teatro Communale, Bologna 1997–; début with New York Philharmonic 1995; has conducted many leading orchestras in Europe and U.S.A. and at many of the world's leading opera houses. *Address:* c/o Royal Philharmonic Orchestra, 16 Clerkenwell Green, London, EC1R 0DP, England.

GATTING, Michael William, O.B.E.; British cricketer; b. 6 June 1957, Kingsbury, Middx.; m. Elaine Gatting; two s.; ed. John Kelly High School; right-hand batsman and right-arm medium bowler; played for Middx. 1975–98 (Capt. 1983–97); 79 Tests for England 1977–95 (23 as Capt.), scoring 4,409 runs (average 35.5) including 10 hundreds; scored 36,549 first-class runs (94 hundreds); toured Australia 1986–87 (Capt.), 1987–95; Capt. rebel cricket tour to S.A. 1989–90; 92 limited-overs ints., 37 as Capt.; mem. England Selection Cttee. 1997–. *Publications:* Limited Overs 1986, Triumph in Australia 1987, Leading from the Front (autobiog) 1988. *Leisure interests:* golf, soccer and sport. *Address:* c/o Middlesex County Cricket Club, Lord's Cricket Ground, St. John's Wood Road, London, NW8 8QN, England. *Telephone:* 0171-289 1300.

GAUDRY, Roger, C.C., D.SC.; Canadian chemist and university administrator; b. 1913, Quebec City; s. of Joseph-Marc Gaudry and Marie-Ange Frenette; m. Madeleine Vallée 1941; two s. three d.; ed. Laval Univ.; Rhodes Scholar, Oxford Univ. 1937–39; Lecturer in Organic Chem., Faculty of Medicine, Laval Univ. 1940, Assoc. Prof. 1945–50, Prof. 1950–54; Guest Speaker at La Sorbonne under the auspices of the Inst. Scientifique Franco-Canadien; Asst. Dir. of Research, Research Labs., Ayerst McKenna and Harrison Ltd. 1954, Dir. of Research 1957–65 (and of Ayerst Labs., N.Y.), Vice-Pres. 1963–65; Rector, Univ. de Montréal 1965–75; Vice-Chair. Science Council of Canada 1966–72, Chair. 1972–75; Chair. Council, UN Univ. 1974–76, mem. bd. 1974–80; Fellow, Royal Soc. of Canada 1954; Pres. Chemical Inst. of Canada 1955–56, Canadian Asscn. of Rhodes Scholars 1960–61; mem. Bd. Société de Chimie Industrielle de France 1960–, Bd. of Govs. and Exec. Cttee. Univ. de Montréal 1961–65, Defence Research Bd. of Canada 1962–66, Bd. Nat. Research Council of Canada 1963–68, Nat. Cancer Inst. of Canada 1963–, Bd. Asscn. des Universités partiellement ou entièrement de langue française 1965–75 (Vice-Pres. 1972–75); mem. Acad. du Monde latin 1967, Inst. de la Vie, Paris 1968–; Pres. Asscn. of Univs. and Colls. of Canada 1969–71; mem. Bd. Int. Asscn. of Univs. 1970–, Pres. 1975–80; Gen. Trust of Canada 1970–75; mem. Econ. Council of Canada 1970–73; Pres. Conf. of Rectors and Principals of Quebec Univs. 1970–72; Hon. Life mem. Corpn. of Professional Chemists of Quebec 1964, Asscn. professionnelle des pharmaciens d'industrie du Québec 1972; Hon. mem. Royal Coll. of Physicians and Surgeons of Canada 1971; and mem. admin. Bd. of many commercial and philanthropic socs.; Pres. Jules & Paul-Emile Léger Foundation 1983–95, Science Tech. and Industry Centre 1988–90; Chair. Nordic Labs. Inc. 1976–91, Network for Neural Regeneration and Recovery 1990–94; Hon. LL.D. (Toronto) 1966, D.Sc. (Royal Mil. Coll. of Kingston) 1966, D.Sc. (Univ. of B.C.) 1967, LL.D. (McGill) 1967, Doctorate (Univ. de Clermont-Ferrand, France) 1967, LL.D. (St. Thomas Univ., Fredericton, N.B.) 1968, LL.D. (Brock Univ., St. Catherines, Ont.) 1969, LL.D. (Bishop's Univ.) 1969, LL.D. (Concordia Univ., Montreal) 1980, D.Sc. (Sask., Regina) 1970, (Western Ont.) 1976; Prov. of Quebec Science Award (three times), Pariseau Medal, Asscn. canadienne-française pour l'avancement des sciences 1958, Kt. of Malta 1976, Grand Officier, Ordre du Québec 1992, World Award of Educ. (World Cultural Council, Mexico) 1996. *Publications:* numerous scientific papers on organic and biological chemistry. *Address:* Université de Montréal, 2910 boulevard Edouard-Montpetit, app. 6, CP 6128, Montreal H3C 3J7, Quebec, Canada.

GAULTIER, Jean-Paul; French fashion designer; b. 24 April 1952, Arcueil, Paris; launched first collection with his Japanese partner 1978; since then known on int. scale for his men's and women's collections; first jr. collection 1988; costume designs for film The Cook, The Thief, His Wife and Her Lover 1989, for ballet le Défilé de Régine Chopinot 1985, Madonna's World Tour 1990; released record How to Do That (in collaboration with Tony Mansfield) 1989; launched own perfume 1993; designed costumes for Victoria Abril (q.v.) in Pedro Almodóvar's (q.v.) film Kika 1994, film la Cité des Enfants

Perdus 1995, The Fifth Element 1996; launched perfume brands Jean-Paul Gaultier (1993), Le Mâle (1995); Fashion Oscar 1987, Progetto Leonardo Award for How to Do That 1989; Chevalier des Arts et des Lettres. *Address:* Jean-Paul Gaultier S.A., 30 rue du Faubourg-Saint-Antoine, 75012 Paris, France.

GAUS, Günter; German journalist, diplomatist and politician; b. 23 Nov. 1929, Braunschweig (Brunswick); s. of Willi and Hedwig Gaus; m. Erika Butzengeiger 1955; one d.; ed. Oberrealschule Braunschweig and Munich Univ.; journalist with various daily and weekly newspapers, and Second German TV 1953–65; Programme Dir. Südwestfunk 1965–69; Chief Ed. Der Spiegel 1969–73; State Sec., Chancellery of Fed. Repub. of Germany, Bonn 1973; Head of Perm. Representation of Fed. Repub. of Germany, Berlin (G.D.R.) 1974–81; Senator (Minister) for Science and Research, West Berlin Jan.–June 1981; Adolf Grimme Prize, Bronze 1964, Silver 1965; Fr.-Ebert-Stiftung Das Politische Buch des Jahres 1987; Adolf Grimme Prize: Besondere Ehrung 1988, Kritikerpreis 1990. *Publications:* Zur Person (two vols.), Bonn ohne Regierung 1965, Gespräche mit Herbert Wehner 1966, Zur Wahl gestellt 1969, Wo Deutschland liegt 1983, Deutschland und die NATO 1984, Die Welt der Westdeutschen 1986, Deutschland im Juni 1988, Wendewut 1990, Zur Person 1990, Porträts in Frage und Antwort (4 vols.) 1991–93, Zur Person (3 vols.) 1997–98, Kein einig Vaterland 1998. *Address:* Bahnsenallee 74, 21465 Reinbek, Germany.

GAVA, Antonio; Italian politician; b. 30 July 1930, Castellamare di Stabia; Chair. Union of Provs. of Italy 1968, Naples Prov. Sec. 1969, Chair. of First Regional Ass. of Campania, Chair. of Christian Democrat (C.D.) Group in Campania; M.P. for Naples-Caserta 1972–; Minister of Posts and Telecommunications 1986–87, of Finance 1987–88, of the Interior 1988–90. *Address:* c/o Ministry of the Interior, Piazza Viminale, Palazzo Viminale, Via Depretis, 00184 Rome, Italy.

GAVASKAR, Sunil Manohar, B.A.; Indian cricketer and business executive; b. 10 July 1949, Bombay; m. Marshniel Mehrotra 1974; one s.; ed. St. Xavier's High School, Bombay, and St. Xavier's College, Bombay Univ.; right-hand opening batsman; played for Bombay 1967–87, Somerset 1980; 125 Tests for India 1970–97 (47 as capt.), scoring 10,122 runs (average 51.1) with 34 hundreds (world record) and holding 108 catches; toured England 1971, 1974, 1975 (World Cup), 1979, 1982, 1983 (World Cup); scored 25,834 first-class runs with 81 hundreds; highest score (236 v. Australia Dec. 1983) by Indian in Test match; Arjuna Award 1975, Padma Bhushan 1980, both Govt. of India; first player to score more than 10,000 Test runs 1987; first player to score over 2,000 runs against three countries 1987; only man to play in a hundred successive Tests; nominated to Rajya Sabha 1992. *Publications:* Sunny Days—An Autobiography 1976, Idols (autobiog.) 1982, Runs 'n Ruins 1984. *Address:* Nirlon Synthetic Fibres and Chemicals Ltd., Nirlon House, 254-B, Dr. Annie Besant Road, Worli, Bombay-18, India (Office).

GAVIN, John, B.A.; American actor and diplomatist; b. 8 April 1932, Los Angeles; s. of Herald Ray Gavin and Delia Diana Pablos; m. Constance Mary Towers; one s. three d.; ed. Stanford Univ.; actor in feature films 1956–80; *films include:* A Time to Live, A Time to Die, Psycho, Midnight Lace, Backstreet, Spartacus, Thoroughly Modern Millie, Mad Woman of Chaillot, Jennifer, History of the World Part I, Seesaw (musical); Special Adviser to Sec.-Gen. OAS 1961–74; Vice-Pres. Atlantic Richfield Co. (to head Fed. & Int. Relations Unit) 1986–87; Pres. Univisa Satellite Communications 1987–90; Pres. Gamma Services Corpn. 1968–; spokesman Bank of America 1973–80; Amb. to Mexico 1981–86; Chair. the Century Council 1990–; partner Gavin, Dailey & Co. L.A. 1990–; consultant to Dept. of State; mem. Screen Actors' Guild (Pres. 1971–73).

GAVIRIA TRUJILLO, César; Colombian politician; m. Milena Gaviria; mem. town council of Pereira; mem. Chamber of Deputies and Dir. Comm. for Econ. Affairs 1972; Vice-Minister for Devt.; Minister of Finance and Public Credit 1986, of the Interior 1988; Pres. of Colombia 1990–94; Sec.-Gen. OAS March 1994–. *Address:* Organization of American States, 1889 F Street, NW, Washington, DC 20006, U.S.A.

GAVISH, Yeshayahu; Israeli business executive; b. 1925, Tel Aviv; m.; two c.; ed. Staff Coll., France; various commands in Israeli Defence Force 1948–62; Officer Commanding, Southern Command 1962–69; Gen. Man. Koor Metals Ltd. 1969; fmr. Gen. Man. Koor Industries and Head, Koor Metals Steel Group. *Address:* Neve Relim 23, Neveh Magen, Israel. *Telephone:* 03-471644.

GAVRILOV, Andrei Vladimirovich; Russian pianist; b. 21 Sept. 1955, Moscow; ed. Moscow Conservatory; performs regularly throughout Europe, America and Japan, including recitals at Salzburg, Roque d'Antheron, Schleswig-Holstein, Istanbul and Chichester Festivals; has performed in England with the Philharmonia, London Philharmonic, Royal Philharmonic, BBC Symphony and London Symphony Orchestras, in America with the Baltimore Symphony, Detroit Symphony, New York Philharmonic, and the Philadelphia Orchestra; disc awards include the French suites of J. S. Bach and the Etudes of Chopin; winner of the Tchaikovsky Competition in Moscow 1974; several int. prizes; lives in Germany. *Address:* c/o Konzertdirektion Schlote, Danreitergasse 4, A-5020 Salzburg, Austria.

GAY, Peter, PH.D.; American professor of history; b. 20 June 1923, Berlin, Germany; s. of Morris Fröhlich and Helga Fröhlich; m. Ruth Slotkin 1959; three step-d.; ed. Univ. of Denver and Columbia Univ.; left Germany 1939; Dept. of Public Law and Govt., Columbia Univ. 1947–56, Dept. of History 1956–69, Prof. of History 1962–69, William R. Shepherd Prof. 1967–69; Prof. of Comparative European Intellectual History, Yale Univ. 1969–, Durfee Prof. of History 1970–84, Sterling Prof. of History 1984–93, Sterling Prof. Emer. 1993–; Guggenheim Fellow 1967–68; Overseas Fellow, Churchill Coll., Cambridge, England 1970–71; Visiting Fellow, Inst. for Advanced Study, Berlin 1984; Dir. Center for Scholars and Writers, New York Public Library 1997–; mem. American Historical Assen., French Historical Soc.; Hon. D.Hum. Litt. (Denver) 1970, (Md.) 1979, (Hebrew Univ. Coll., Cincinnati) 1983, (Clark Univ., Worcester) 1985; Nat. Book Award 1967, Melcher Book Award 1967. *Publications:* The Dilemma of Democratic Socialism: Eduard Bernstein's Challenge to Marx 1951, Voltaire's Politics: The Poet as Realist 1959, Philosophical Dictionary 1962, The Party of Humanity: Essays in the French Enlightenment 1964, The Loss of Mastery: Puritan Historians in Colonial America 1966, The Enlightenment: An Interpretation, Vols. I, II 1966, 1969, Weimar Culture: The Outsider as Insider 1969, The Bridge of Criticism: Dialogues on the Enlightenment 1970, The Question of Jean-Jacques Rousseau 1974, Modern Europe (with R. K. Webb) 1973, Style in History 1974, Art and Act: On Causes in History—Manet, Gropius, Mondrian 1976, Freud, Jews and Other Germans: Masters and Victims in Modernist Culture 1978, The Bourgeois Experience: Victoria to Freud, Vols. I, II, III 1984, 1986, 1993, Freud for Historians 1985, Freud: A Life for Our Time 1988, A Freud Reader 1989, Reading Freud: Explorations and Entertainments 1990, The Cultivation of Hatred 1993, The Naked Heart 1995, Pleasure Wars 1998; also translations and anthologies. *Leisure interests:* reading, listening to music. *Address:* 105 Blue Trail, Hamden, CT 06518, U.S.A. (Home). *Telephone:* (203) 228-6752 (Home).

GAYDAR, Yegor Timurovich, D.SC.ECONS.; Russian politician; b. 19 Mar. 1956, Moscow; s. of Timur Gaydar and Ariadna (Bajova) Gaydar; m. 2nd Maria Strugatskaya 1986; three s.; ed. Moscow State Univ.; journalist Kommunist and Pravda 1987–90; Dir. Inst. of Econ. Policy of U.S.S.R. (now Russian) Acad. of Sciences 1990–91; Deputy Chair. Russian Govt. (and co-ordinator of the 13 ministries responsible for econ. affairs) 1991–92; Acting Chair. Russian Govt. June–Dec. 1992; Dir. Inst. for the Economy in Transition 1992–93, 94–; Adviser to Pres.Yeltsin on Econ. Reform 1992–93; First Deputy Chair. Russian Govt. 1993–94, Minister of Econ. 1993–94; Head Political bloc, Russian Choice (Vibor Rossii) 1993–94; f. and leader Democratic Choice of Russia party 1994–; mem. State Duma (Parl.) 1993–95; joined right-wing coalition 1998. *Publications:* State and Evolution 1994, Anomalies of Economic Growth 1995, Days of Defeats and Victories 1996; articles in scientific journals and newspapers. *Address:* Gazetny per. 5, 111024 Moscow, Russia (Institute). *Telephone:* (095) 229-64-13. *Fax:* (095) 229-64-48.

GAYDON, Alfred Gordon, D.SC., F.R.S.; British physicist; b. 26 Sept. 1911; s. of Alfred Bert Gaydon and Rosetta Juliet Gordon; m. Phyllis Maude Gaze 1940 (died 1981); one s. one d.; ed. Kingston Grammar School, Kingston-on-Thames, Imperial Coll., London; Warren Research Fellow of Royal Soc. 1945–74; Prof. of Molecular Spectroscopy, Imperial Coll. of Science and Tech., London 1961–73, Prof. Emer. 1973–, Fellow 1980; worked on molecular spectra and on measurement of high temperatures, on spectra and structure of flames, and shock waves; Dr. h.c. (Dijon) 1957; Rumford Medal, Royal Soc. 1960, Bernard Lewis Gold Medal, Combustion Inst. 1960. *Publications:* Identification of Molecular Spectra (with R. W. B. Pearse) 1941, Spectroscopy and Combustion Theory 1942, Dissociation Energies and Spectra of Diatomic Molecules 1947, Flames, their Structure, Radiation and Temperature (with H. G. Wolfhard) 1953, The Spectroscopy of Flames 1957, The Shock Tube in High-temperature Chemical Physics (with I. Hurle) 1963. *Leisure interests:* wildlife photography and fmrly. rowing. *Address:* Dale Cottage, Shellbridge Road, Slindon Common, Near Arundel, West Sussex, BN18 0LT, England. *Telephone:* (01243) 814277.

GAYER, Yevdokiya Alexandrovna, CAND. HIST. SC.; Russian/Nanai ethnographer and politician; b. 8 March 1934, Podali, Khabarovsk Territory; m. (deceased); two s.; ed. in Vladivostok; researcher Inst. of History, Archaeology and Ethnography Far E. br. of U.S.S.R. Acad. of Sciences in Vladivostok 1969–89; U.S.S.R. People's Deputy, mem. Soviet of Nationalities, mem. Comm. on Problems of Int. Relations and Nat. Policy 1989–92; adviser to Pres. 1992–; Deputy Chair. State Cttee. on Social-Econ. Devt. of the North 1993–; mem. Council of Fed. of Russia 1993–96; Deputy Chair. Comm. of the North and Indigenous Peoples 1996–; Sec.-Gen. Int. League of Small Nations and Ethnic Groups 1996–. *Address:* Rublyovskoye Sh. 3, korp. 2, Apt. 388, 121609 Moscow, Russia. *Telephone:* (095) 413-76-95.

GAYOOM, Maumoon Abdul, M.A.; Maldivian politician; b. 29 Dec. 1937; m. Nasreena Ibrahim 1969; two s. two d.; ed. Al-Azhar Univ., Cairo; Research Asst. in Islamic History, American Univ. of Cairo 1967–69; Lecturer in Islamic Studies and Philosophy, Abdullahi Bayero Coll., Ahmadu Bello Univ., Nigeria 1969–71; Teacher, Aminiya School 1971–72; Man. Govt. Shipping Dept. 1972–73; Writer and Trans. Press Office 1972–73, 1974; Under-Sec. Telecommunications Dept. 1974; Dir. Telephone Dept. 1974; Special Under-Sec. Office of the Prime Minister 1974–75; Deputy High Commr. to Sri Lanka 1975–76; Under-Sec. Dept. of External Affairs 1976; Perm. Rep. to UN 1976–77; Deputy Minister of Transport 1976, Minister 1977–78; Pres. of Repub. of Maldives and C.-in-C. of the Armed Forces 1978–; Gov. Maldives Monetary Authority 1981–; Minister of Defence and

Nat. Security 1982–; Minister of Finance 1989–93; Minister of Finance and Treasury 1993–; mem. Constituent Council of Rabitat Al-Alam Al-Islami; Hon. D.Litt. (Aligarh Muslim Univ. of India) 1983, Hon. Ph.D. (Int. Univ. Foundation, U.S.A.) 1988, Hon. Dr. Lit. (Jamia Millia Islamia Univ., India) 1990; Hon. D.Lit. (Pondicherry) 1994; Global 500 Honour Roll (UN Environment Progamme) 1988; Man of the Sea Award (Lega Navale Italiana) 1991; Hon. G.C.M.G. 1997; WHO Health-for-All Gold Medal 1998. *Leisure interests:* astronomy, calligraphy, photography, badminton, cricket. *Address:* The President's Office, Boduthakurufaanu Magu, Malé (Office); The Presidential Palace (Theemuge), Orchid Magu, Malé, 20-02, Maldives (Official Residence). *Telephone:* 323701. *Fax:* 325500.

GAYSSOT, Jean-Claude; French politician and trade unionist; b. 6 Sept. 1944, Béziers (Hérault); m. Jacqueline Guiter 1963; three c.; ed. Lycée technique, Béziers; worked as technician, SNCF (French state railways); official in Railworkers' Union, then in Conféd. générale du travail (CGT) 1976–79; mem. Parti Communiste Français 1963–, mem. Nat. Secr. 1985–, head dept. for relations with other political parties and trade union and community movt. 1994–; elected municipal councillor, Bobigny (Seine-Saint-Denis) 1977; Nat. Ass. Deputy for 5th Seine-Saint-Denis Constituency 1986–97; Minister for Public Works, Transport and Housing 1997–; Mayor of Drancy 1997–. *Address:* Ministry for Public Works, Transport and Housing, 246 boulevard Saint-Germain, 75007 Paris, France.

GAZE, Raymond Michael, D.PHIL., F.R.S.E., F.R.S.; British biologist; b. 22 June 1927; s. of William Mercer Gaze and Kathleen Grace (née Bowhill) Gaze; m. Robinetta Mary Armfelt 1957; one s. two d.; ed. School of Medicine of the Royal Colls., Edinburgh, Oxford Univ.; House Physician, Chelmsford and Essex Hosp. 1949; Nat. Service Medical Officer in R.A.M.C. 1953–55; Lecturer in Physiology, Univ. of Edin. 1955–62; Alan Johnston, Lawrence and Moseley Research Fellow of Royal Soc. 1962–66; Reader in Physiology, Univ. of Edinburgh 1966–70; Head, Div. of Developmental Biology, Nat. Inst. for Medical Research, London 1970–83; Head, MRC Neural Devt. and Regeneration Group, Zoology Dept., Edinburgh Univ. 1984–92. *Publications:* The Formation of Nerve Connections 1970, numerous articles on developmental neurobiology in learned journals. *Leisure interests:* music, drawing and hill-walking. *Address:* 37 Sciennes Road, Edin., EH9 1NS, Scotland (Home). *Telephone:* 0131-667 6915 (Home).

GAZENKO, Oleg Georgievich, PH.D., M.D.; Russian physiologist; b. 12 Dec. 1918, Nikolayevka, Stavropol territory; m.; one s. one d.; ed. Moscow Medical Inst; service in the Army 1941–46; Research Assoc. Kirov Mil. Medical Acad. 1946–47; U.S.S.R. Acad. of Sciences Inst. of Experimental Medicine 1947–69, Dir. Inst. of Medical and Biological Problems 1969–88; Consultant 1988–; mem. CPSU 1953–91; Corresp. mem. U.S.S.R. (now Russian) Acad. of Sciences 1966, mem. 1976–; mem. Int. Acad. of Astronautics, Aerospace Medical Asscn.; Corresp. mem. American Physiological Soc. 1979–; Pres. U.S.S.R. (now Russian) Nat. Physiological Soc. 1983–91; People's Deputy of the U.S.S.R. 1989; Ed.-in-Chief Space Biology and Medicine; mem. New York Acad. of Sciences; Order of Lenin, Daniel and Florence Guggenheim Int. Astronautics Award 1975. *Publications:* works on experimental physiology and space medicine; co-author Mankind and Outer Space 1990; Co-ed. Foundations of Space Biology and Medicine (U.S.A.-U.S.S.R. joint publ.). *Leisure interests:* mountaineering, canoeing. *Address:* Institute of Medical and Biological Problems, Khroshevskoye sh. 76A, 123007 Moscow, Russia. *Telephone:* (095) 195-23-63.

GAZIT, Maj.-Gen. Shlomo; Israeli army officer and administrator; b. 1926, Turkey; s. of Efrayim and Zippora Gazit; m. Avigayil-Gala Gazit; one s. two d.; ed. Tel Aviv Univ.; joined Palmach 1944, Co. Commdr. Harel Brigade 1948; Dir. Office of Chief of Staff 1953; Liaison Officer with French Army Del., Sinai Campaign 1956; Instructor Israel Defence Forces Staff and Command Coll. 1958–59; Gen. Staff 1960–61; Deputy Commdr. Golani Brigade 1961–62; Instructor Nat. Defence Coll. 1962–64; Head IDF Intelligence assessment div. 1964–67; Co-ordinator of Govt. Activities in Administered Territories, Ministry of Defence 1967–74; rank of Maj.-Gen. 1973; Head of Mil. Intelligence 1974–79; Fellow at Center for Int. Affairs, Harvard Univ. 1979–80; Pres. Ben Gurion Univ. of the Negev 1981–85; Dir.-Gen. Jewish Agency, Jerusalem 1985–88; Sr. Research Fellow Jaffee Centre for Strategic Studies, Tel Aviv Univ. 1988–94; Fellow Woodrow Wilson Center, Washington, DC 1989–90; Distinguished Fellow U.S. Inst. of Peace, Washington, DC 1994–95; Adviser to Israeli Prime Minister on Palestinian Peace Process 1995–96. *Publications:* Estimates and Fortune-Telling in Intelligence Work 1980, Early Attempts at Establishing West Bank Autonomy 1980, Insurgency, Terrorism and Intelligence 1980, On Hostages' Rescue Operations 1981, The Carrot and the Stick—Israel's Military Govt. in Judea and Samaria 1985, The Third Way—The Way of No Solution 1987, Policies in the Administered Territories 1988, Intelligence Estimates and the Decision Maker 1988, (ed.) The Middle East Military Balance 1988–89, 1990–91, 1993–94. *Address:* 20 Tarpad Street, Ramat Hasharon 47250, Israel (Home). *Telephone:* (03) 5492077 (Home). *Fax:* (03) 5497731.

GAZIZULLIN, Farid Rafikovich, D.SC.; Russian Tatar politician; b. 20 Sept. 1946, Zelenodolsk, Tatar A.S.S.R.; m.; one s.; ed. Gorky (now Nizhny Novgorod) Inst. of Water Transport Eng.; engineer Zelenodolsk 1965–67; Comsomol and CP work 1967–87; Head of Dept., First Deputy Chair., State Planning Cttee. Tatar Autonomous Repub. 1987–95; Vice-Prime Minister of Tatarstan, Chair. State Cttee. on Property 1995–96; First Deputy Chair., Cttee. on State Property of Russian Fed. 1996–97; Deputy Chair., Govt. of Russian Fed. 1997–98; Minister of State Property 1997–; Chair. Gazprom June 1998–. *Address:* Ministry of State Property, Nikolsky per. 9, 102132 Moscow, Russia. *Telephone:* (095) 206 1525 (Office).

GAZZAR, Abdel Hadi el; Egyptian artist; b. 1925; ed. Cairo and Rome Acad. of Fine Arts; Prof. of Painting, Cairo Faculty of Fine Arts; rep. at numerous exhbns., including the 28th and 30th Venice Biennale, Brussels Int. Exhbn. 1958 and São Paulo Bienal 1961; exhbns. in Cairo, Alexandria and Rome; First Prize "10 Years of the Revolution" Exhbn. 1962. *Address:* Faculty of Fine Arts, Cairo University, Cairo, Egypt.

GBEZERA-BRIA, Michel, B.L.; Central African Republic politician and diplomatist; b. 1946, Bossongoa, Cen. African Repub.; m.; five c.; ed. Brazzaville School of Law, Caen School of Econs. and Int. Inst. of Public Admin.; with civil service 1973–, Vice-Minister Sec.-in-charge of diplomatic missions 1975; Deputy Minister of Foreign Affairs 1976; Minister of Public Works, Labour and Social Security 1976–77, of Foreign Affairs 1977–78, of Public Works and Social Security 1978–79; State Comptroller 1979–80, Perm. Rep. to UN, Geneva 1980–83, New York 1983–89; Minister of Justice 1987–88, of Foreign Affairs 1988–90; Prime Minister of Cen. African Repub. Jan. 1997–; Dir. Econ. Man. Project 1991–. *Address:* Office of the Prime Minister, Bangui, Central African Republic.

GDLYAN, Telman Khorenovich; Russian/Armenian prosecutor and politician; b. 20 Dec. 1940, Samsar, Georgia; m. Susanna Aramovna Gdlyan; one s. one d.; ed. Saratov Inst. of Law; mem. CPSU 1962–90, when expelled; investigator Ulyanovsk Dist. 1968–83, investigator for important cases, Office of Public Prosecutor of U.S.S.R. 1983–90; successfully prosecuted mems. of political establishment of Uzbekistan for corruption; U.S.S.R. People's Deputy 1989–91; mem. Armenian Supreme Soviet 1990–; f. and Chair. People's Party of Russia 1990; expelled from Prosecutor's Office 1990, reinstated 1991; f. All-Russian Fund of Progress, Defence of Human Rights and Charity; mem. State Duma (Parl.) Dec. 1995–. *Publications:* Piramide, Mafia in Times of Lawlessness. *Address:* People's Party, Novy Arbat 15, 121012, Moscow, Russia. *Telephone:* (095) 202-01-09.

GE HONGSHENG; Chinese government official; b. 1931, Ju'nan Co., Shandong Prov.; joined CCP 1948; section chief CCP Taizhou Prefectural Cttee. 1949–56; Dir. of Propaganda Dept. Xin'anjiang Electric Power Eng. Bureau –1960; Deputy Dir. and Deputy Sec. No.9 Eng. Bureau Ministry of Electric Power 1963–74; Gen. Dir. and Sec. CCP Zhejiang Banshan Power Plant GHQ 1974–77; Dir. Electric Power Bureau Zhejiang Prov. –1983; Vice-Chair. Zhejiang Prov. Econ. Comm. –1983; Sec. CCP Ningbo Municipal Cttee. 1983–88; Standing Cttee. mem. CCP Zhejiang Prov. Cttee. 1986–88; Deputy Sec. CCP Zhejiang Prov. Cttee. 1988–93; mem. CCP 14th Cen. Cttee. 1992–97; Gov. Zhejiang Prov. 1991–93; Deputy Dir. Special Econ. Zones Office 1994–96, Dir. 1996–98; Vice-Chair. Finance and Econ. Cttee. 9th NPC 1998. *Address:* c/o Standing Committee of National People's Congress, Beijing, People's Republic of China.

GE WUJUE; Chinese writer; b. 12 Sept. 1937, Wenzhou, Zhejiang; s. of Ge Luyan and Zhang Wencang; m. Zhao Baoqing 1962 (divorced); one s.; ed. Beijing Univ.; worked as journalist for over 20 years; published first book 1961; in political disgrace 1963–77; some works translated into English, French and Japanese; Vice-Chair. Fed. of Art and Literature, Ningxia and Ningxia Branch of Union of Chinese Writers. *Publications:* The Wedding, A Journalist and Her Story, An Experience in the Summer, She and her Girl Friend, The Golden Deer, A View of an Ancient Ferry (short stories), Meditate on the Past (novel), Years and Man (novel), Going to the Ancient Ferry on Today (TV Drama), Four Days in All of Life 1988 (short stories), The Earth. The Moon (novel), The Passport on the Earth, Zhang Daqian in Dunhuan (TV drama) 1991, Quality of Life (reportage) 1995, Tango. Rumba (screenplay) 1996. *Leisure interests:* sports, music, drawing, calligraphy. *Address:* 268-9 Bailidong Road, Wenzhou, Zhejiang, People's Republic of China. *Telephone:* (577) 8282374 (Office); (577) 8525866 (Home).

GE YOU; Chinese actor; b. 1957; Beijing, joined All-China Fed. of Trade Unions Art Troupe 1979. *Films include:* Farewell My Concubine; Best Actor Award for To Live (Cannes). *Address:* All-China Federation of Trade Unions Art Troupe, Beijing, People's Republic of China.

GE ZIPING; Chinese businessman; b. Sept. 1927, Raoyang Co., Hebei Prov.; Man., Tianjin Chemicals Import and Export 1958–65; Gen. Man., Zhongyi Hong Kong Ltd. Co. 1965–; Chair. of Bd. of Dirs. and Gen. Man., Lida Group Corpn. 1993–; mem. 8th CPPCC 1993–. *Address:* Lida Group Corporation, Tianjin City, People's Republic of China.

GEACH, Peter (Thomas), M.A., F.B.A.; British professor of logic; b. 29 March 1916, London; s. of George Hender Geach and Eleonora Frederyka Adolfina Sgonina; m. Gertrude Elizabeth Margaret Anscombe 1941; three s. four d.; ed. Balliol Coll. Oxford; Gladstone Research Student, St. Deiniol's Library 1938–39; Postgrad. studies Cambridge Univ. with Profs. Wittgenstein and Von Wright; Asst. Lecturer, Lecturer, Sr. Lecturer, then Reader in Logic, Univ. of Birmingham 1951–65; Prof. of Logic, Univ. of Leeds 1965–81, Emer. Prof. 1981–; Foreign mem. American Acad. of Arts and Sciences 1987; Alexander von Humboldt Prize 1984. *Publications:* Mental Acts 1957, Reference and Generality 1962, God and the Soul 1969, Providence and Evil 1977, The Virtues 1977, Truth, Love and Immortality 1979, Logic Matters. *Leisure interests:* reading thrillers, reading and marginally annotating bad old logic books. *Address:* 3 Richmond Road, Cambridge, CB4 3PP, England. *Telephone:* (01223) 353950.

GEBRSELASSIE, Haile; Ethiopian athlete; b. 18 April 1973, Arssi; set 14 world records or best times indoors and outdoors 1994–98, including world 5,000m. and 10,000m. records 1997, 1998; Silver Medal World Jr. Cross Country Championships 1992; Gold Medals World Jr. Championships 5,000m. and 10,000m. 1992; Gold Medal World Championships 10,000m. 1995, 1997; Silver Medal World Championships 5,000m. 1993; Gold Medal Olympic Games 10,000m. 1996; Gold Medal World Indoor Championships 3,000m. 1997.

GEDDA, Nicolai; Swedish operatic tenor; b. 11 July 1925, Stockholm; s. of Michael Ustinov and Olga (née Gedda) Ustinov; m. Anastasia Caraviotis 1965; one s. one d.; ed. Musical Acad., Stockholm; Debut, Stockholm 1952; Concert appearances Rome 1952, Paris 1953, 1955, Vienna 1955, Aix-en-Provence 1954, 1955; first operatic performances in Munich, Lucerne, Milan and Rome 1953, Paris, London and Vienna 1954; Salzburg Festival 1957–59, Edinburgh Festival 1958–59; with Metropolitan Opera, N.Y. 1957–, Tokyo Opera 1975–; world-wide appearances in opera, concerts and recitals; numerous recordings. *Address:* c/o Lies Askonas Ltd., 6 Henrietta Street, London WC2E 8LA, England. *Telephone:* 0171-405 1708.

GEE, Maggie, PH.D., F.R.S.L.; British author and journalist; b. 2 Nov. 1948, Poole; d. of V. V. Gee and Aileen Gee (née Church); m. Nicholas Rankin 1983; one d.; ed. Horsham High School, Somerville Coll., Oxford; Writing Fellow Univ. of E. Anglia 1982; Visiting Fellow Sussex Univ. 1986–, Teaching Fellow 1996–; Writer-in-Residence Northern Arts 1996; regular reviews in Daily Telegraph, Times Literary Supplement, Sunday Times; judge Booker Prize 1989; mem. Man. Cttee. Soc. of Authors 1991–94; Hawthornden Fellow 1989; Best of Young British Novelists 1982. *Publications:* (novels) Dying in Other Words 1981, The Burning Book 1983, Light Years 1985, Grace 1988, Where are the Snows 1991, Lost Children 1994, The Ice People 1998. *Leisure interests:* visual arts, swimming, walking, film, theatre. *Address:* c/o Society of Authors, 84 Drayton Gardens, London, SW10 9SB, England. *Telephone:* 0181-969 8832. *Fax:* 0181-969 8832.

GEE, Maurice Gough, M.A.; New Zealand novelist; b. 22 Aug. 1931, Whakatane; m. Margaretha Garden 1970; one s. two d.; ed. Avondale Coll., Auckland, Auckland Univ.; school teacher, librarian, other casual employment 1954–75; Robert Burns Fellow Univ. of Otago 1964; Writing Fellow Vic. Univ. of Wellington 1989; Katherine Mansfield Memorial Fellow, Menton, France 1992; N.Z. Fiction Award 1976, 1979, 1982, 1991; N.Z. Book of the Year Award (Wattie Award) 1979, 1993; James Tait Black Memorial Prize 1979; N.Z. Children's Book of the Year Award 1986, 1995; Hon. D.Litt. (Vic.) 1987. *Publications include:* The Plumb Trilogy 1978–84, Prowlers 1987, The Burning Boy 1990, Going West 1992, Crime Story 1994, Loving Ways 1996, Live Bodies 1998, Collected Stories 1986; for children: Under the Mountain 1979, The O Trilogy 1982–85, The Fat Man 1994; also scripts for film and TV. *Address:* 41 Chelmsford Street, Ngaio, Wellington, New Zealand.

GEENS, André, M.B.A.; Belgian politician; b. 26 May 1941, Boortmeerbeek; s. of Jan Geens and Bertha Peeters; m. 2nd Jo Nachtergaele 1985; three s. two d.; ed. Hoger Inst. De Nayer, Malines, Tech. Hogeschool Delft and Centre Postuniversitaire Limbourg; Tech. salesman, OCP-Bruxelles 1966–74; Sales Man., ECOPUR SA Bruxelles 1974–76; Admin. Conhag Hydrochemie SA Bruxelles 1976–82; Dir. Vlaams Nat. Studiecentrum 1982–88; Adviser, Ministry of Finances and the Budget 1982–85; Adviser, Zottegem Council 1977–; Deputy Mayor, Finance and Personnel, Zottegem 1983–88; Senator for Audenaerde-Alost 1985–; Minister of Co-operation and Devt. 1988–91.

GEENS, Gaston, M.ECON.SCI., DR.JUR.; Belgian politician; b. 10 June 1931, Kersbeek-Miskom, Brabant; m. Maria Thielman 1959; three s. one d.; ed. Catholic Univ. at Louvain, Johann Wolfgang Goethe Univ., Frankfurt-am-Main, Fed. Repub. of Germany; Demonstrator at Catholic Univ. at Louvain and Sec. of Centre for Econ. Studies 1955–61; Asst. Dir. CEPESS 1961–72, Dir. 1973–; Senator and Sec. of State for Budget and Science Policy 1974–76, Minister of Budget and Science Policy 1976–77, of Finance 1977–80, of the Budget May–Oct. 1980, for Flemish Community Affairs 1980–81, Econs. and Employment 1981–85, 1985–88, Finance and Budget 1988–92; Pres. of the Govt. of Flanders 1981–92; Flemish Community Minister of Econs. 1988, Finance and the Budget 1988–; Senator 1992–95, Hon. Senator 1995–; Minister of State; Pres. Adnetex Co. 1995–; Pres. Inno.Com. 1998; mem. Stichting Flanders Tech. 1992–. *Publications:* Het arrondissement Leuven—een regionaal economisch onderzoek 1959, Basisgegevens voor sociale politiek 1963, De Wet op de universitaire expansie 1965, De Staatshervorming 1971, De Europese begroting 1976; co-author Perspectieven voor de landbouw in de Euromarkt 1958, Op eigen kracht 1987. *Leisure interests:* reading, classical music, gardening. *Address:* Predikherenberg 32, 3020 Herent, Belgium. *Telephone:* (16) 23-78-67. *Fax:* (16) 23-78-67.

GEERTZ, Clifford, PH.D.; American anthropologist; b. 23 Aug. 1926, San Francisco; s. of Clifford James and Lois (née Brieger) Geertz; m. 1st Hildred Storey 1948 (divorced 1981); m. 2nd Karen Blu; one s. one d.; ed. Antioch Coll., Harvard Univ.; Asst. Prof. of Anthropology, Univ. of Calif. 1958–60; Asst. Prof., then Prof. Dept. of Anthropology, Univ. of Chicago 1960–70, mem. Cttee. for Comparative Study of New Nations 1962–70; Prof. of Social Science, Inst. for Advanced Study 1970–, Harold F. Linder Prof. of Social Science 1982–; field work in Java 1952–54, 1986, Bali 1957–58, Morocco 1965–66, 1985–86; Fellow N.A.S., American Philosophical Soc., American Acad. of Arts and Sciences; Corresp. F.B.A. *Publications:* The Religion of Java 1960, Person, Time and Conduct in Bali 1966, Local Knowledge 1983, Works and Lives 1988 (Nat. Book Critics Circle Award for Criticism), After the Fact 1995 and others. *Address:* Institute for Advanced Study, Princeton, NJ 08540, U.S.A. *Telephone:* (609) 734-8000.

GEFFEN, David; American film, recording and theatre executive; b. 21 Feb. 1943, Brooklyn, New York; s. of Abraham Geffen and Batya (Volovskaya) Geffen; ed. New Utrecht High School, Brooklyn; joined William Morris talent agency as mail clerk 1964, promoted to jr. agent; launching new film studio with Steven Spielberg (q.v.) and Jeffrey Katzenberg (q.v.); f. music publishing co. Tunafish Music, with Laura Nyro; joined Ashley Famous Agency, then apptd. Exec. Vice-Pres. Creative Man. (now Int. Creative Man.) 1968; f. Asylum Records and Geffen-Roberts Man. Co. with Elliot Roberts 1970; sold Asylum to Warner Communications, but remained Pres. 1971, merged it with Elektra, signed up Bob Dylan and Joni Mitchell, Vice-Chair. Warner Brothers Pictures 1975–76; f. Geffen Records, Pres. 1980–, signed up Elton John, John Lennon and Yoko Ono, and many others, sold label to Music Corpn. of America Inc. 1990; f. Geffen Film Co., produced Little Shop of Horrors, Beetlejuice 1988, Men Don't Leave, Defending Your Life; Co-producer musical Dreamgirls 1981–85, Little Shop of Horrors, Cats 1982, M. Butterfly 1986, Social Security, Chess 1990, Miss Saigon; f. DGC record label, co-f. Dreamworks SKG 1995–. *Address:* Dreamworks SKG, 100 Universal Plaza, Building 477, Universal City, CA 91608, U.S.A.

GEGHMAN, Yahya Hamoud; Yemeni diplomatist; b. 24 Sept. 1934, Jahanah; s. of Hamoud Geghman and Ezziya Geghman; m. Cathya Geghman 1971; one s. one d.; ed. Law Schools, Cairo, Paris, Damascus and Boston and Columbia Univs.; Teacher of Arabic Language and Literature, Kuwait 1957–59; Dir.-Gen. Yemen Broadcasting System 1962–63; Gov. Yemen Bank for Reconstruction and Devt. 1962–63; Sec.-Gen. Supreme Council for Tribal Affairs 1962–63; Special Adviser, Ministry of Foreign Affairs 1962–63; Deputy Perm. Rep. to UN 1963–66, 1967–68; Minister Plenipotentiary, Yemen Arab Repub. (Y.A.R.) Embassy to U.S.A. 1963–67; Minister of Foreign Affairs 1968–69; Minister of State, Personal Rep. of the Pres. 1969; Deputy Prime Minister, Pres. Supreme Council for Youth Welfare and Sport 1969–71; Perm. Rep. to UN 1971–73; Amb. to U.S.A. 1972–74; Minister for Foreign Affairs 1974–75; Deputy Prime Minister for Econ. and Foreign Affairs 1975–76; Personal Rep. of Pres. of the Repub. 1977–85; Chief, Bureau of South Yemen Affairs and Chair. Yemen Reunification Comms. 1980–83; Amb. to Switzerland and Perm. Rep. to UN in Vienna and UNIDO 1985–90; Perm. Rep. to UN European HQ and Int. Orgs., Geneva, 1985–; Gov. and Exec. Dir. UN Common Fund for Commodities, Amsterdam 1989–; mem. Governing Council, UN Compensation Comm. 1991; Pres. Diplomatic Cttee. on Host Country Relations 1991. *Publications:* articles on politics, economics and literature, poems. *Leisure interests:* reading, horseback riding, swimming, writing, chess, music. *Address:* Permanent Mission of the Republic of Yemen, 19 chemin du Jonc, 1216 Cointrin, Geneva, Switzerland. *Telephone:* 798-53-33.

GEH, Hans-Peter, DR.PHIL.; German librarian; b. 11 Feb. 1934, Frankfurt-am-Main; ed. Univs. of Frankfurt and Bristol and Library School, Cologne; Dir. Württembergische Landesbibliothek Stuttgart 1970–97; Pres. Int. Fed. of Library Asscns. and Insts. (IFLA) 1985–91; Pres. European Foundation for Library Cooperation (EFLC) 1991–95. *Publication:* Tudor Policy in England before the Tudors. *Leisure interest:* travel. *Address:* Hebbergstr. 7611, 70794 Filderstadt, Germany (Home). *Telephone:* 0711-777 331. *Fax:* 0711-7777-331.

GEHRING, Gillian Anne, D.PHIL., M.A., F.INST.P.; British professor of physics; b. 19 May 1941, Nottingham; d. of H.L. (Max) Murray and F. Joan Murray; m. Karl A. Gehring 1968; two d.; ed. Univs. of Manchester and Oxford; Leverhulme Postdoctoral Research Fellowship, St. Hugh's Coll. Oxford 1965–67; NATO Fellowship, Univ. of Calif. (Berkeley) 1967–68; Fellow and Tutor in Physics, St. Hugh's Coll. Oxford 1968–70; CUF lecturer in Theoretical Physics, Univ. of Oxford 1970–89; Prof. of Solid State Physics, Univ. of Sheffield 1989–. *Publications:* research papers on theoretical condensed matter physics. *Leisure interests:* family activities. *Address:* Department of Physics, University of Sheffield, Sheffield, S10 2TN (Office); 27 Lawson Road, Broomhill, Sheffield, S10 5BU, England (Home). *Telephone:* (0114) 276 8555 Ext. 4299 (Office); (0114) 268 2238 (Home).

GEHRING, Walter Jakob, PH.D.; Swiss professor of genetics and developmental biology; b. 20 March 1939, Zurich; s. of late Jakob Gehring and of Marcelle Gehring-Rebmann; m. Elisabeth Lott 1964; two s.; ed. Realgymnasium, Zürich, Univ. of Zürich and Yale Univ., U.S.A.; Assoc. Prof., Depts. of Anatomy and Molecular Biophysics, Yale Univ. 1969–72; Prof. of Genetics and Developmental Biology, Dept. of Cell Biology, Univ. of Basel 1972–; Foreign mem. Royal Soc. 1997; Otto Naegeli Prize, Prix Charles-Leopold, Warren Triennial Prize, Prix Louis Jeantet de médecine, Gairdner Int. Award. *Publications:* Zoologie (with R. Wehner) 1990; over 160 publs. *Leisure interests:* bird watching, photography. *Address:* Biozentrum, University of Basel, Department of Cell Biology, Klingelbergstrasse 70, 4056 Basel (Office); Hochfeldstrasse 32, 4106 Therwil, Switzerland (Home). *Telephone:* (061) 2672051 (Office); (061) 7213593 (Home). *Fax:* (061) 2672078.

GEHRY, Frank Owen; American architect; b. 29 Feb. 1929, Toronto, Canada; s. of Irving Gehry and Thelma Caplan; m. Berta Aguilera 1975;

two s.; two d. (from previous m.); ed. Univ. of S. Calif. and Harvard Univ.; designer, Victor Gruen Asscn. Los Angeles 1953–54, planning, design and project dir. 1958–61; project designer, planner, Pereira & Luckman, L.A. 1957–58; Prin. Frank O. Gehry & Assocs., Santa Monica, Calif. 1962–; architect for Temporary Contemporary Museum 1983, Calif. Aerospace Museum 1984, Loyola Law School 1981–84, Frances Howard Goldwyn Regional Br. Library 1986, Information and Computer Science Eng. Research Facility, Univ. of Calif. Irvine 1986, Vitra Furniture Mfg. Facility and Design Museum, Germany 1989, Chiat/Day HQ, Venice, Calif. 1991, American Center, Paris 1992–94, Weisman Art Museum, Minneapolis 1993, Disney Ice, Anaheim 1995, EMR Communication & Tech. Centre, Bad Oeynhausen, Germany 1995, Team Disneyland Admin., Anaheim 1996, ING Office Bldg., Prague 1996, Guggenheim Museum, Bilbao 1997; Fellow, American Inst. of Architects; Charlotte Davenport Chair. Yale Univ. 1982, 1985; Eliot Noyes Design Chair. Harvard 1984; Arnold W. Brunner Memorial Architecture Prize 1983, Pritzter Architecture Prize 1989, shared Wolf Prize 1992, Imperial Prize (Japan) 1992; Lillian Gish Award 1994, Gold Medal of Inst. of Architects 1999. *Publications:* Individual Imagination and Cultural Conservatism 1995. *Address:* Frank O. Gehry & Associates, 1520-B Cloverfield Boulevard, Santa Monica, CA 90404, U.S.A. *Telephone:* (310) 828-6088.

GEIDUSCHEK, E(rnest) Peter, PH.D.; American scientist and professor of biology; b. 11 April 1928, Vienna, Austria; s. of Sigmund Geiduschek and Frieda Tauber; m. Joyce B. Brous 1955; two s.; ed. Columbia and Harvard Univs.; Instructor in Chem. Yale Univ. 1952–53, 1955–57; Asst. Prof. of Chem., Univ. of Mich. 1957–59; Asst. Prof. of Biophysics and Research Assoc. in Biochemistry, Univ. of Chicago 1959–62, Assoc. Prof. of Biophysics and Research Assoc. in Biochemistry 1962–64, Prof. of Biophysics and Research Assoc. in Biochemistry 1964–70; Prof. of Biology, Univ. of Calif., San Diego 1970–94, Chair. 1981–83, (acting) 1994, Research Prof. of Biology 1994–; EMBO Lecturer 1977, Hilleman Lecturer, Univ. of Chicago 1978, Paul Doty Lecturer, Harvard Univ. 1993, Adriano Buzzati-Traverso Lecture, Rome 1996; Lalor Foundation Faculty Fellow, Yale 1957, Guggenheim Fellow, Inst. de Biologie Moléculaire, Geneva 1964–65; Fellow A.A.A.S., Acad. of Microbiology (U.S.A.); mem. N.A.S., American Acad. of Arts and Sciences; Grande Ufficiale, Ordine al Merito della Repubblica Italiana. *Publications:* numerous articles on molecular biology, biochemistry and virology. *Address:* University of California, San Diego, Department of Biology, Center for Molecular Genetics (0634), 9500 Gilman Drive, La Jolla, CA 92093-0634, U.S.A. *Telephone:* (619) 534-3029. *Fax:* (619) 534-7073.

GEIGER, Helmut; German banker and lawyer; b. 12 June 1928, Nuremberg; m.; one s. one d.; ed. Univs. of Erlangen and Berlin; legal asst. Deutsche Bundestag and asst. lawyer, Bonn 1957–59; lawyer in Bonn and man. of office of Öffentliche Bausparkassen 1959–66; Man. Dir. Deutsche Sparkassen-und Giroverband 1966–72, Pres. 1972–93; Pres. Int. Inst. der Sparkassen (Int. Savings Bank Inst.), Geneva 1978–84; Pres. EEC Savings Banks Group, Brussels 1985–; Chair. Sparkassenstiftung für Internale Kooperation 1992–; mem. Bundestag 1965; mem. Admin. Bd. Deutsche Girozentrale Int., Luxembourg, Kreditanstalt für Wiederaufbau, Frankfurt, Landwirtschaftliche Rentenbank, Frankfurt, Rhineland-Westphalian Inst. of Econ. Research, Essen; mem. Cen. Cttee., German Group, ICC; mem. Presidium, German Red Cross; Chair. and mem. of various charitable and professional bodies; Dr. h.c. (Cologne); Grand Fed. Cross of Merit. *Publications:* Herausforderungen für Stabilität und Fortschritt 1974, Bankpolitik 1975, Gespräche über Geld 1986, Die deutsche Sparkassen-organisation 1992 and numerous publications on banking matters. *Address:* Königswinterer Strasse 550, 53227 Bonn, Germany. *Telephone:* 0228-97-03-6-10.

GEINGOB, Hage Gottfried, M.A.; Namibian politician; b. 3 Aug. 1941, Grootfontein Dist.; m. Loine Kandume 1993; one s. three d. from previous marriage; ed. Augustineum Coll. Okahandja and studies in int. relations in U.S.A.; joined South-West Africa People's Org. (SWAPO) 1962; teacher, Tsumeb 1962; exiled for political activities Dec. 1962; became SWAPO Asst. Rep. Botswana 1963–64; subsequently moved to U.S.A., studied at Fordham Univ. and New School for Social Research, New York, and became SWAPO Rep. at UN –1971; mem. SWAPO Politburo 1975; Dir. UN Inst. for Namibia, Lusaka, Zambia 1975–89; returned to Namibia as Election Dir. 1989; Chair. Constituent Ass. and Namibia Independence Celebrations Cttee. 1989; Prime Minister of Namibia March 1990–; Hon. LL.D. (Col. Coll., Chicago) 1994; Officier Palmes Académiques 1980, Ongulumbashe Medal for bravery and long service 1987. *Leisure interests:* playing tennis, reading, watching soccer and rugby. *Address:* Office of the Prime Minister, Robert Mugabe Avenue, Private Bag 13338, Windhoek, Namibia. *Telephone:* (061) 2879111. *Fax:* (061) 226189.

GEISS, Johannes, DR.RER.NAT.; Swiss professor of physics; b. 4 Sept. 1926, Stolp, Pomerania (Poland); s. of Hans Geiss and Irene Wilke; m. Carmen Bach 1955; one d.; ed. Univ. of Göttingen; Research Assoc., Enrico Fermi Inst., Univ. of Chicago 1955–56; Assoc. Prof., Marine Lab., Univ. of Miami 1958–59; Assoc. Prof., Univ. of Berne 1960, Prof. of Physics 1964, Dir. Inst. of Physics 1966–90; Visiting Scientist, NASA Goddard Inst. for Space Studies, New York 1965, NASA Manned Spacecraft Center, Houston 1968–69; Chair. Launching Programme Advisory Cttee., European Space Agency, Paris 1970–72; Visiting Prof. Univ. of Toulouse 1975; Chair. Space Science Cttee., European Science Foundation 1979–86; Rector, Univ. of Berne 1982–83; Hon. Dr. (Univ. of Chicago); Fellow of the American Geophysical Union; Foreign mem. American Acad. of Arts and Sciences, N.A.S., Max-Planck-Inst. für Aeronomie, Int. Acad. of Astronautics, Max-Planck-Inst. für Kernphysik, Austrian Acad. of Sciences; mem. Academia Europaea; NASA Medal for Exceptional Scientific Achievement. *Publications:* over 300 publications on nucleosynthesis, cosmology, the origin of the solar system, geochronology, climatic history of the earth, the age of meteorites and lunar rocks, comets, solar wind, solar terrestrial relations. *Address:* c/o Physics Institute, University of Berne, Sidlerstrasse 5, 3012 Berne, Switzerland. *Telephone:* (031) 9012310.

GEISSLER, Heiner, DR.JUR.; German politician; b. 3 March 1930, Oberndorff; m. Susanne Thunack 1962; three s.; ed. Univs. of Tübingen and Munich; Dir. Office of Minister of Labour and Social Welfare, Baden-Wurttemberg; mem. Bundestag 1965–67, 1980–; Minister for Social Welfare, Health and Sport, Rheinland-Pfalz 1967–77; mem. Parl. of Rheinland-Pfalz 1971–79; Gen. Sec. CDU 1977–89, Deputy Chair. 1989–90, mem. Presiding Bd. 1990–; Deputy Chair. CDU/CSU Parl. group 1991–; mem. CDU Parl. Cttee. 1994–; mem. Television Council, Second German Television 1970–82, 1987–92; Fed. Minister for Youth, Family and Health 1982–85; Bundesverdienstkreuz 1970, Bergverlagspreis Deutsches Alpenverein 1983. *Publications:* Die neue soziale Frage 1976, Der Weg in die Gewalt 1978, Sicherheit für unsere Freiheit 1978, Verwaltete Bürger-Gesellschaft in Fesseln 1978, Grundwerte in der Politik 1979, Zukunftschancen der Jugend 1979, Sport—Geschäft ohne Illusionen? 1980, Mut zur Alternative 1981, Zugluft-Politik in stürmischer Zeit 1990, Heiner Geissler im Gespräch mit Gunter Hofmann und Werner A. Perger 1993, Gefährlicher Sieg 1995, Der Irrweg der Nationalismus 1995, Bergsteigen 1997, Das nicht gehaltene Versprechen 1997. *Leisure interest:* mountaineering. *Address:* Bundeshaus, 53113 Bonn, Germany. *Telephone:* (0228) 161.

GEITONAS, Costas I.; Greek politician; b. Lagadia, Arcadia; ed. Nat. Tech. Univ. of Athens; Gen. Sec. Ministry of Public Works 1981–85; Deputy Minister of Environment, Land Use and Public Works 1985–86, Alt. Gen. Dir. Pvt. Political Office of Prime Minister 1986–89; an M.P. for Athens 1989–; Deputy Minister of Public Order 1993–94; Alt. Minister of Environment, Land Use and Public Works 1994–96, Minister of Public Order 1996, Minister of Health and Welfare 1996–; mem. Cen. Cttee. PASOK (Panhellenic Socialist Movt.). *Address:* Ministry of Health and Welfare, Odos Aristotelous 17, 104 33 Athens, Greece. *Telephone:* (01) 5232820. *Fax:* (01) 5231707.

GELBARD, Robert Sidney, M.P.A.; American diplomatist; b. 6 March 1944, New York; s. of Charles Gelbard and Ruth Fisher Gelbard; m. Alene Marie Hanola 1968; one d.; ed. Colby Coll., Harvard Univ.; volunteer Peace Corps, Bolivia 1964–66, Assoc. Dir., Philippines 1968–70; joined Foreign Service 1967, Staff Asst. Sr. Seminar in Foreign Policy 1967–68; Vice-Consul Porto Alegre, Brazil 1970–71, Prin. Officer 1971–72; int. economist Office of Devt. Finance 1973–75, Office of Regional Political and Econ. affairs 1976–78; First Sec. Embassy, Paris 1978–82; Deputy Dir. Office of W. European Affairs, Washington, D.C. 1982–84; Dir. Office of S. African Affairs, Washington, D.C. 1984–85; Deputy Asst. Sec. Bureau of Inter-American Affairs, Washington, D.C. 1985–88; Amb. to Bolivia 1988–91; Prin. Deputy Asst. Sec. of State for Bureau of Inter-American Affairs 1991–93, Asst. Sec. of State for Int. Narcotics and Law Enforcement Affairs 1993–97; Special Rep. for Implementation of the Dayton Peace Accords April 1997–; mem. Museum of American Folk Art int. advisory council, N.Y., American Foreign Service Asscn. *Address:* Department of State, 2201 C Street, Washington, D.C. 20520, U.S.A. *Telephone:* (202) 647-6575. *Fax:* (202) 647-6738.

GELBART, Larry; American playwright and scriptwriter; b. 25 Feb. 1928, Chicago, Ill.; s. of Harry Gelbart and Frieda Gelbart; m. Pat Marshall 1956; three s. two d.; prin. writer, sometime dir. and co-producer (first four seasons) M*A*S*H*; other television shows including Caesar's Hour, United States, The Bob Hope Show, The Danny Kaye Show; scriptwriter for various radio shows; Dir. A Funny Thing Happened on the Way to the Forum, Chichester Festival Theatre, U.K. 1986; mem. Writers Guild of America, Authors League, Motion Picture Acad. of Arts and Sciences, Directors Guild of America, PEN Int. etc.; Tony Award for co-authoring A Funny Thing Happened on the Way to the Forum; Writers Guild of America Awards for Oh, God, Movie Movie, Tootsie, 3 M*A*S*H* episodes; Peabody Awards for M*A*S*H*, The Danny Kaye Show; Emmy Awards for M*A*S*H* and V.I.P.; Edgar Allan Poe Award for Oh, God; Los Angeles Film Critics, New York Film Critics and Nat. Soc. of Film Critics Awards for Best Screenplay for Tootsie; Golden Rose, Montreux for writing/producing The Marty Feldman Comedy Machine; Hon. D.Litt. (Union Coll.) 1986; other awards and distinctions. *Plays:* My L.A. (revue), The Conquering Hero (musical), A Funny Thing Happened on the Way to the Forum (musical), Jump, Mastergate, Sly Fox, City of Angels (musical), Power Failure. *Films:* Notorious Landlady 1962, The Thrill of it All 1963, The Wrong Box 1966, Oh, God 1977, Movie Movie 1978, Neighbors 1981, Tootsie 1982, Blame it on Rio 1984, Barbarians at the Gate 1994, Weapons of Mass Distraction 1997. *Publication:* Laughing Matters 1998. *Leisure interest:* travel. *Address:* 807 North Alpine Drive, Beverly Hills, CA 90210, U.S.A.

GELDOF, Bob; Irish rock singer and charity promoter; b. 5 Oct. 1954, Dublin; m. Paula Yates 1986 (divorced 1996); three d.; ed. Black Rock Coll.; many casual jobs, lorry-driving, busking, teaching English, working in factory, etc., then journalist on pop music paper, Georgia Strait, Vancouver, Canada; returned Dublin and f. rock group, Boomtown Rats; brought group to London 1977, recorded for Ensign Records, then Phonogram; organized recording of Do They Know It's Christmas? by Band Aid, raising £8 million for African famine relief Nov. 1984, f. Band-Aid Trust to distribute proceeds 1985, Chair.; organized Live Aid concerts Wembley, London and Philadelphia, U.S.A. with int. TV link-up by satellite, raising £48 million July 1985; f. Live Aid Foundation, U.S.A.; organized publ. of Live Aid book The Greatest Show on Earth 1985; *film appearances include:* Number One, Pink Floyd—The Wall; Hon. K.B.E. 1986; Third World Prize 1986; Dr. h.c. (Ghent) 1986; Hon. D.Lit. (London) 1987; Freeman of Ypres 1986; Elder of the Repub. of Tanzania. *Publication:* Is That It? (autobiog.) 1986. *Address:* Davington Priory, Kent, England.

GELFAND, Israel Moiseyevich, D.SC.; Russian mathematician and biologist; b. 2 Sept. 1913, Krasnye Okny, Ukraine; s. of Moshe Gelfand and Perl Gelfand; m. 1st Zorya Yakovlevna Shapiro 1942 (divorced); m. 2nd Tanya Alekseevskaya 1979; two s. one d.; ed. Moscow State Univ.; Asst. Professor, Dept. of Mathematics, Moscow State Univ. 1935–40, Prof. 1940–91; Corresp. mem. U.S.S.R. (now Russian) Acad. of Sciences 1953, mem. 1984; Head of Laboratory of Mathematical Methods in Biology, Moscow State Univ.; f. and ed. Funktsionalny analiz i yego prilozheniya 1967–91; Prof. Rutgers Univ. 1991–; Head of Dept., Inst. of Applied Maths., Acad. of Sciences 1953–91; Prof. Foreign mem. Royal Soc., N.A.S., Acad. des Sciences (France), Royal Swedish Acad. of Sciences, Royal Irish Soc., American Acad. of Arts and Sciences; Hon. mem. Moscow Mathematical Soc., London Mathematical Soc.; Dr. h.c. (Univs. of Oxford, Harvard, Uppsala, Milan, Pisa, Paris); State Prize 1951, 1953, Lenin Prize 1961, Wolf Prize in Mathematics 1978, Kyoto Prize 1989; McArthur Fellowship 1994. *Publications:* numerous works including Unitary Representations of Classical Groups 1950, Generalized Functions Vols. I-VI 1958–66, Normed Rings 1960, Automorphic Functions and the Theory of Representations 1962, Cohomology of Infinite Dimensional Lie Algebras and Some Questions of Integral Homology 1970, Representations of the Group SL 2R, Where R is a Ring of Functions 1973, Mechanisms of Morphogenesis in Cell Structures 1977, Collected Papers (Vols. 1–3) 1986–89, Discriminants, Resultants and Multidimensional Determinants 1994. *Leisure interest:* classical music. *Address:* 118 North 5 Avenue, Highland Park, NJ 08904, U.S.A. *Telephone:* (908) 819-8440 (Home).

GÉLIN, Daniel Yves; French actor; b. 19 May 1921, Anger; s. of Alfred and Yvonne (née Le Méner) Gélin; m. 1st Danièle Girard 1946 (divorced); one s.; m. 2nd Sylvie Hirsch 1954 (divorced); two s. (one deceased) one d.; m. 3rd Lydie Zaks 1973; one d.; ed. Lycée de St. Malo, Paris Conservatoire; mem. Théâtre Nat. Populaire Co. 1960–; Chevalier, Légion d'honneur, Officier des Arts et des Lettres. *Films and plays include:* La ronde, Dieu a besoin des hommes 1950, Les mains sales, Paris-Canaille, Les amants du Tage 1955, En effeuillant la Marguerite, Mort en fraude, Charmants garçons 1957, Suivez-moi jeune homme, Ce corps tant désiré, Austerlitz, Monsieur Masure, La morte saison des amours, La proie pour l'ombre, Le Testament d'Orphée 1960, Carthage en flammes, Peur panique, Le jour le plus long, Règlements de compte, La bonne soupe 1963, Vacances portugaises, Le soleil noir 1966, Duel à la vodka 1967, Le mois le plus beau 1968, Slogan, Hallucinations sadiques, Détruite dit-elle 1969, La servante 1970, Le souffle au coeur 1970, Un linceul n'a pas de poches 1975, Dialogue d'exilés 1975, La police au service du citoyen 1975, Nous irons tous au paradis 1977, l'honorable société 1978, Qu'il est joli garçon, l'assassin de Papa, L'oeil du maître 1979, Huis-clos 1981, La nuit de Varennes 1982, Les enfants 1985, Georges Dandin 1988, La vie est un long fleuve tranquille 1988, Securité publique 1988, Itinéraire d'un enfant gâté 1988, Mister Frost 1990, Mauvaise fille 1991, les Eaux dormantes 1992, Coup de Jeune 1993, les Petites Femmes de Maupassant 1993, Les Marmottes 1993 (play and film), Des Feux Mal Eteints 1993; has also appeared on TV. *Publications:* poetry: Fatras 1950, Dérives 1965, Poèmes à dire 1970, Deux ou trois vies qui sont les miennes 1977, Mon jardin et moi 1984, Cent poètes côté jardin (poetic anthology) 1990, Mon Père 1995, le Sang de mes songes 1996. *Address:* 42 rue Victor Basch, 92120 Montrouge, France.

GÉLINAS, Gratien, O.C., F.R.S.C.; Canadian actor, playwright and producer; b. 8 Dec. 1909, St.-Tite-de-Champlain, Quebec; s. of Mathias Gélinas and Genève Davidson; m. 1st Simone Lalonde 1935 (died 1967); five s. one d.; m. 2nd Huguette Oligny 1973; ed. Coll. de Montréal, School of Higher Commercial Studies, Montreal; after 2 months in first job with Dupuis Frères (Dept. Store), Montreal, joined La Sauvegarde Insurance Co. as accountant 1929–37; casual radio and stage performances, including creation of character of 'Fridolin' in series of monologues at cabaret Mon Paris, Montreal, culminating in appearance in Télévise-moi-ça, St. Denis Theatre, Montreal 1936; radio debut with 'Fridolin' in Carrousel de la gaîté (later Le train de plaisir) 1937, Fridolinons Revue 1938; left radio for theatre 1941; directed, produced and starred in annual reviews, Montreal and Quebec City 1940–46; leading part in St. Lazare's Pharmacy, Chicago 1945, wrote and starred in TV serial Les quat' fers en l'air 1954–55; Fridolinades (revue), Orpheum Theatre, Montreal 1956; appeared as Charles VI (Henry V), and Dr. Caius (Merry Wives of Windsor), with Stratford Shakespearean Festival Co., Stratford (Ontario) and Edinburgh Festival 1956; films: La Dame aux Camélias 1942, Tit-Coq 1952, Bonheur d'occasion 1982, Agnes of God 1984, Les Tisserands du Pouvoir 1987; dir. first production L'alouette 1958, played Charles VII in English adaptation The Lark; wrote Bousille et les justes, appearing in title-role at Montreal premiere 1959, then on tour in Canada including Vancouver Int. Festival 1962, Seattle World Fair 1962; wrote, produced, and acted in Le diable à quatre (satirical review) 1964, author and dir. Hier les enfants dansaient, Montreal premiere 1966, appeared in English adaptation Yesterday the Children were Dancing, Charlottetown Summer Festival 1967; wrote and played title role in La Passion de Narcisse Mondoux, Le Théâtre du Petit Bonheur, Toronto 1986, Le Théâtre du Rideau Vert, Montreal 1987; f. La Comédie-Canadienne, Montreal, after taking over Gaiety Theatre 1957, Gen. Dir. 1957–72; mem. Bd. of Govs., Nat. Film Bd. of Canada 1950–52; Vice-Pres. Asscn. Canadienne du Théâtre Amateur 1950–61; Pres. Canada Theatre Inst. 1959–60; founding mem. Nat. Theatre School of Canada 1960; mem. Royal Soc. of Canada 1958–; Chair. Canada Film Devt. Corpn. 1969–78; Hon. D.Litt. (Montreal) 1949, (Toronto) 1951, Hon. LL.D. (Sask) 1966, (McGill) 1968, (New Brunswick) 1969, (Trent) 1970, (Mount Allinson) 1973; Grand Prix (Dramatists Soc.) for Tit-Coq 1949, Film of Year Award for Tit-Coq 1953, Victor Morin Prize for 1967 (St. Jean Baptiste Soc.) 1967. *Publications:* series of ten topical revues starring 'Fridolin', Tit-Coq (play) 1949, Les quat' fers en l'air (TV serial) 1954–55, Fridolinades (revue) 1956, Bousille et les justes 1959, Le diable à quatre (satirical revue) 1964, Hier les enfants dansaient 1966; films: La Dame aux Camélias 1942, Tit-Coq. *Leisure interests:* classical music, boating, tennis, skating, travel. *Address:* 316 Girouard Street, Box 207, Oka, Quebec J0N 1E0, Canada (Home).

GELL-MANN, Murray, PH.D.; American physicist; b. 15 Sept. 1929, New York City; s. of the late Arthur and Pauline (Reichstein) Gell-Mann; m. 1st J. Margaret Dow 1955 (died 1981); one s. one d.; m. 2nd Marcia Southwick 1992; one step-s.; ed. Yale Univ. of Massachusetts Inst. of Tech.; mem. Inst. for Advanced Study, Princeton 1951, 1955; Instructor, Asst. Prof., and Assoc. Prof., Univ. of Chicago 1952–55; Assoc. Prof., Calif. Inst. of Tech. 1955–56, Prof. 1956–66, R. A. Millikan Prof. of Theoretical Physics 1967–93; Research Assoc. Univ. of Illinois 1951, 1953; Visiting Assoc. Prof. Columbia Univ. 1954; Visiting Prof. Collège de France and Univ. of Paris 1959–60, Mass. Inst. of Tech. 1963; Consultant, Inst. for Defense Analyses, Arlington, Va. 1961–70, Rand Corpn., Santa Monica, Calif. 1956; mem. N.A.S.A. Physics Panel 1964, President's Science Advisory Cttee. 1969–72, Council on Foreign Relations 1975; Consultant to Los Alamos Scientific Laboratory, Los Alamos, N.M. 1956; Citizen Regent, Smithsonian Inst. 1975–88; Chair. Western Center, American Acad. of Arts and Sciences 1970–76; Chair. of Bd. Aspen Center for Physics 1973–79; Co-Chair. Science Bd. 1985–; Founding Trustee Santa Fe Inst. 1982; Chair. Bd. of Trustees 1982–85; Dir. Physics, Santa Fe Inst. 1993–; mem. Bd. Calif. Nature Conservancy 1984; Dir. J. D. and C. T. MacArthur Foundation 1979–; mem. Science and Grants Cttee., Leakey Foundation 1977–, mem. N.A.S., American Physical Soc., American Acad. of Arts and Sciences, Pres. Advisory Cttee. on Science and Tech. 1994–; Foreign mem. Royal Soc. 1978–; Hon. Sc.D. (Yale) 1959, (Chicago) 1967, (Illinois) 1968, (Wesleyan) 1968, (Utah) 1970, (Columbia) 1977, Dr. h.c. (Turin, Italy) 1969, (Oxford) 1992, Hon. Sc.D. (Cambridge Univ.) 1980; Dannie Heineman Prize, American Physical Soc. 1959; Ernest O. Lawrence Award 1966, Franklin Medal 1967, John J. Carty Medal (Nat. Acad. of Sciences) 1968, Nobel Prize in Physics 1969, U.N. Environmental Program Roll of Honour for Environmental Achievement 1988. *Major works:* Developed strangeness theory, theory of neutral K mesons, eightfold way theory of approximate symmetry; current algebra, quark scheme; contributed to theory of dispersion relations, theory of weak interaction and formulation of quantum chromodynamics. *Publications:* (with Yuval Ne'eman q.v.) The Eightfold Way 1964, The Quark and the Jaguar 1994. *Leisure interests:* historical linguistics, wilderness trips. *Address:* c/o Santa Fe Institute, 1399 Hyde Park Road, Santa Fe, NM 87501, U.S.A. *Telephone:* (505) 984-8800. *Fax:* (505) 982-0565.

GELMAN, Aleksandr Isaakovich; Russian playwright and scenarist; b. 25 Oct. 1933, Moldavia; m. Tatyana Pavlovna Kaletskaya; one s.; ed. Kishinev Univ; mem. CPSU 1956–90; worked in factories 1956–67; corresp. for daily papers 1967–71; wrote scripts for series of documentary films 1971–74; People's Deputy of the U.S.S.R. 1989–91; U.S.S.R. State Prize 1976. *Film scripts include:* Night Shift 1971, Consider me Grown Up 1974, Xenia, Fyodor's Favourite Wife (all with T. Kaletskaya) 1974, First Prize 1975, Clumsy Man 1979, We, The Undersigned 1981, Zinulya 1984, Misha's Party (with R. Nelson) 1993. *Theatre work includes:* A Man with Connections, The Bonus. *Address:* Tverskoy blvd. 3, Apt. 12, 103104 Moscow, Russia. *Telephone:* (095) 202-68-59.

GELOVANI, Victor Archilovich; Georgian scientist; b. 8 Oct. 1944, Nikolaev; m. Nana Gelovani (née Andjaparidze); one s.; ed. Moscow Inst. of Physics and Tech.; jr. researcher Inst. of Applied Math., U.S.S.R. Acad. of Sciences 1971–74; sr. researcher Inst. of Man., U.S.S.R. Acad. of Sciences 1974–76; Head of Lab., Head of Div. All-Union Inst. of System Research 1976–; Corresp. mem. U.S.S.R. (now Russian) Acad. of Sciences 1987; Dir.-Gen. Int. Centre for Scientific Culture, World Lab., Moscow br. 1990, research in the field of applied math., system analysis, computation tech., expert systems. *Publications include:* Man-Machine System of Modelling Global Development 1980, Interactive Modelling System as a Tool for Analyzing Complex Gnocioeconomic Problems 1984, Problems of Computer Modelling 1990. *Leisure interest:* mountain skiing. *Address:* Prechistenka 30, apt. 56, 119034 Moscow, Russia. *Telephone:* (095) 202-3262.

GEMAYEL, Amin; Lebanese politician; b. 1942, Bikfayya; s. of Pierre Gemayel; ed. St. Joseph Univ., Beirut; M.P. 1970–; Pres. of Lebanon 1982–88; f. The House of the Future, The Amin Gemayel Educational Foundation, Le

Reveil newspaper; mem. Al-Katae'b Party (Phalanges Libanaises). *Address:* c/o Al-Katae'b Party, P.O. Box 992, place Charles Hélou, Beirut, Lebanon.

GEMS, Iris Pamela (Pam); British playwright; b. Bransgrove, Dorset; d. of the late Jim Price and Elsie Mabel Annetts; m. Keith Leopold Gems 1949; two s. two d.; ed. Brockenhurst Grammar School, Univ. of Manchester; career playwright; mem. Theatre Writers' Union, Dramatists' Guild (U.S.A.), Writers' Guild. *Plays:* Dusa, Fish, Stas and Vi 1976, Queen Cristina 1977, Piaf 1978, Franz into April 1978, The Treat 1979, Pasionaria 1981, Camille 1985, The Danton Affair 1986, The Blue Angel 1991, Deborah's Daughter 1994, Stanley 1995 (Best Play, Evening Standard Awards 1996, Best Play, Olivier Awards 1997), Marlene 1996, The Snow Palace 1998. *Novels:* Mrs Frampton 1989, Bon Voyage, Mrs Frampton 1990. *Leisure interest:* gardening. *Address:* c/o Jenny Casarotto, National House, 60–66 Wardour Street, London W1V 4ND, England. *Telephone:* 0171-287 4450. *Fax:* 0171-287 9128.

GENDREAU-MASSALOUX, Michèle; French public servant; b. 28 July 1944, Limoges; d. of François Massaloux and Marie-Adrienne Delalais; m. Pascal Gendreau 1970; ed. Ecole Normale Supérieure de Jeunes Filles, Sèvres, Inst. d'Etudes Politiques, Paris; univ. teacher, Sorbonne, Villetaneuse (Paris XIII), then Univ. of Limoges (fmr. Vice-Pres.); Rector Acad. d'Orléans-Tours 1981–84; Tech. Adviser to Secr.-Gen. for Nat. Educ. and Univs., Presidency of the Repub., then to Secr.-Gen. for Admin. Reform and Improvement of Relations between Public Services and their Users, Deputy Sec.-Gen. 1985–88, Spokesperson 1986–88, Head of Mission May 1988; Rector, Acad. de Paris 1989–98; Conseiller d'Etat 1998; mem. Comm. Nat. de la Communication et des Libertés 1988–89, French Comm. for UNESCO 1991, Conseil orientation Ecole du Louvre 1991, Council, Coll. Univ. Français de Moscou 1991, Council, Coll. Univ. Français de Saint-Petersbourg 1992, Conseil Scientifique de la Cinquième 1996; Chevalier, Légion d'honneur, Officier, Ordre Nat. du Mérite, Chevalier, Ordre des Palmes Académiques. *Publication:* Recherche sur l'Humanisme de Francisco de Quevedo 1977, works and translations concerning the Spanish Golden Age. *Leisure interest:* music. *Address:* Conseil d'Etat, 75100 Paris 01 SP (Office); 38 avenue Charles Floquet, 75007 Paris, France (Home).

GENERALOV, Sergey Vladimirovich; Russian politician; b. 7 Sept. 1963, Simferopol; ed. Moscow Inst. of Energy, Higher School of Man. at State Acad. of Man.; Commercial Dir. TET 1991–92; Deputy Chair. NIPEBANK 1992–93; Head of Div., Head of Dept., Promradtechbank 1993; with UYKOS Oil Co., 1993–97, Vice-Pres. 1994–; Sr. Vice-Pres. ROSPROM; Deputy Chair. MENATEP 1997–98; Minister of Fuel and Power Eng. of Russian Fed. May 1998–. *Address:* Ministry of Fuel and Power Engineering, Kitayskiy proyezd 7, 103074 Moscow, Russia. *Telephone:* (095) 220 8080 (Office).

GENILLARD, Robert Louis, M.A. (ECON.); Swiss financier; b. 15 June 1929, Lausanne; Vice-Chair. TBG Holdings N.V., Netherlands; Chair. Clariden Bank, Switzerland, Chair. TBG Management s.a.m., Monaco; Dir. Crédit Suisse, Switzerland, CS Holding, Switzerland, Sandoz A.G., Switzerland, Soc. des Bains de Mer, Monaco, CS First Boston Inc., New York; Adviser to Bd. American Express Co., New York; Dir. Emer. Corning Inc., New York. *Publications:* articles in professional journals. *Address:* 29 Princesse Charlotte, 98007 Monaco; 1 quai du Mont-Blanc, 1211 Geneva 1, Switzerland (Offices).

GENIYEVA, Yekaterina Yuryevna; Russian librarian; b. 1 April 1946, Moscow; one d.; ed. Moscow State Univ.; nurse Moscow hosp. 1962–63; sr. ed., Deputy Dir. All-Union State Library of Foreign Literature 1971–93, Dir. 1993–; Chair. Exec. Bd. Inst. Open Soc. (Soros Foundation) 1995; mem. Council on Culture, Russian Presidency 1996–; Vice Pres. Russian Library Asscn. 1997–; mem. Russian Comm. on Problems of UNESCO 1997–; mem. Ed. Bds. journals Biblioteka, Libri, Inostrannaya Literatura, Znamya, Detskaya Literatura, Mir Bibliotek. *Publications include:* monographs, trans. of English authors, numerous articles. *Leisure interests:* books, travelling. *Address:* VGBIL, Nikoloyamskaya str. 1, 109189 Moscow, Russia (Office). *Telephone:* (095) 915 3636 (Office). *Fax:* (095) 915 3637 (Office).

GENNES, Pierre-Gilles de, PH.D.; French physicist; b. 24 Oct. 1932, Paris; ed. Ecole Normale Supérieure; Research Scientist, Centre d'Etudes Nucléaires de Saclay 1955–59; Prof. of Solid State Physics, Univ. of Paris, Orsay 1961–71; Prof. Coll. de France 1971–, also Dir. Ecole de Physique et Chimie, Paris 1976–; mem. Académie des Sciences, Dutch Acad. of Sciences, Royal Soc., American Acad. of Arts and Sciences, N.A.S.; Hollweck Prize 1968, Prix Cognac-Jay 1970, Prix Ampère 1977, Gold Medal (C.N.R.S.) 1981, Matteuci Medal 1987, Harvey Prize 1988, Wolf Prize 1990, Nobel Prize 1991, Heyrovsky Medal 1993, Onsager Medal 1996. *Publications:* Superconductivity of Metals and Alloys 1965, The Physics of Liquid Crystals 1973, Scaling Concepts in Polymer Physics 1979, Simple views on condensed matter 1992, Les Objets Fragiles (jtly.) 1994. *Leisure interests:* skiing, drawing, windsurfing. *Address:* 11 place Marcelin-Berthelot, 75005 Paris (Office); 10 rue Vauquelin, 75005 Paris, France (Home).

GENOVÉS, Juan; Spanish artist; b. 1930, Valencia; ed. Escuela Superior de Bellas Artes, Valencia; has taken part in numerous group exhbns.; one-man exhbns. in Spain, Portugal, U.S.A., Italy, Germany, Netherlands, Japan, U.K. and S. America 1956–; took part in Paris Biennale 1961, Venice Biennale 1962, 1966, São Paulo Biennale 1965, etc.; Gold Medal, San Marino Biennale 1967, Premio Marzotto 1968. *Address:* c/o Marlborough Fine Art, 6 Albemarle Street, London, W.1, England.

GENSCHER, Hans-Dietrich; German politician; b. 21 March 1927, Reideburg, Saale; s. of Kurt Genscher and Hilda Kreime; m. 1st Luise Schweitzer 1958; m. 2nd Barbara Schmidt 1969; one d.; ed. Leipzig and Hamburg Univs.; Scientific Asst., Parl. Free Democratic Party (FDP) 1956, later Sec., Hon. Chair. 1992–; Fed. Party Man. 1962–64, Vice-Chair. 1968–74, Chair. 1974–85; Deputy in Bundestag 1965–; Fed. Minister of the Interior 1969–74; Vice-Chancellor, Minister of Foreign Affairs 1974–92; Chair. Bd. of Trustees Franckesche Stiftungen 1992–, Asscn. Friends and Patrons State Opera, Berlin; Hon. Citizen of Costa Rica 1988; Hon. Dr. (Madras) 1977, (Salamanca) 1987, (Athens) 1988, (Seoul) 1988, (Budapest) 1988; Hon. D.C.L. (Durham) 1992; Onassis Foundation Award 1991; Bundesverdienstkreuz 1973 and other medals; Freeman of Halle 1993, of Berlin 1997. *Publications:* Bundestagsreden 1972, Deutsche Aussenpolitik, Reden und Aufsätze aus 10 Jahren, 1974–84, Nach vorn gedacht ... Perspektiven deutscher Aussenpolitik 1986, Erinnerungen (memoirs) 1995. *Leisure interest:* reading. *Address:* c/o Bundeshaus, 53113 Bonn, Germany.

GENZMER, Harald; German composer; b. 9 Feb. 1909, Blumenthal; s. of Felix and Helen Genzmer; m. Gisela Klein 1949; ed. Hochschule für Musik, Berlin; co-repetiteur and dir. of studies, Breslau 1934–37; conservatory and Volkshochschule, Berlin 1938–45; Prof. Musikhochschule, Freiburg im Breisgau 1946–57, Munich 1957–75; Hon. mem. Senate, Musikhochschule, Munich; Music Prize of Bavarian Acad. of Arts; Bundesverdienstkreuz; Maximilians Orden; works include: chamber music, organ works, choral music, orchestral pieces and electronic works. *Leisure interests:* philosophy, graphics and astronomy. *Address:* Eisensteinstrasse 10, 81679 Munich, Germany. *Telephone:* 980484.

GEOGHEGAN-QUINN, Máire; Irish business consultant and fmr. politician; b. 5 Sept. 1950, Carna, Co. Galway; d. of the late John Geoghegan and of Barbara Folan; m. John V. Quinn 1973; two s.; ed. Carysfort Teacher Training Coll. Blackrock, Co. Dublin; fmr. primary school teacher; mem. Galway City Council 1985–; mem. Dáil 1975–97; Parl. Sec. to Minister of Industry, Commerce and Energy 1977–78; Minister of State with responsibility for Consumer Affairs, Ministry of Industry, Commerce and Energy 1977–78; Minister for the Gaeltacht 1979–81; Minister of State with responsibility for Youth and Sport, Dept. of Educ. March–Dec. 1982; Minister of State, Dept. of Taoiseach 1987, 1989; Minister for Tourism, Transport and Communications 1992, of Justice 1993; columnist Irish Times 1997–; consultant to several cos.; Chair. Wanting Older Women Well; Chair. The Saffron Initiative; Chair. Fianna Fáil; Non-Exec. Dir. The Ryan Hotel Group; TV broadcaster. *Publication:* The Green Diamond (novel) 1996. *Leisure interests:* reading, writing and travel. *Address:* Tearmann, 5 Woodfield, Cappagh Road, Barna, Galway, Ireland. *Fax:* 91 591375.

GEORGE, Donald William, A.O., PH.D., F.T.S., F.I.E.E., F.I.MECH.E., F.I.E.AUST., F.A.I.P.; Australian professor of engineering; b. 22 Nov. 1926, Adelaide; s. of late H. W. George; m. Lorna M. Davey 1950; one s. one d.; ed. Canberra High School, Univ. of Sydney; Senior Lecturer, Electrical Eng., Univ. of Sydney 1960–66, Assoc. Prof. 1967–69, P. N. Russell Prof. of Mech. Eng. 1969–74; Prof. Emer. of Eng.; Vice-Chancellor and Principal, Univ. of Newcastle, N.S.W. 1975–86; Chair. Australian Atomic Energy Comm. 1976–83; Dir. Australian-American Educ. Foundation 1976–84, Chair. 1977–84; Chair. Australian Vice-Chancellors' Cttee. 1980–81; mem. Bd. of Trustees, Asian Inst. of Tech., Bangkok 1978–98 (Deputy Chair. 1982–98); Chair. Cen. Coast Area Health Service 1993–. *Publications:* various scientific and tech. papers. *Address:* "Shamley Green", Glenning Road, Glenning Valley, N.S.W. 2261, Australia (Home).

GEORGE, Edward Alan John, M.A.; British banker; b. 11 Sept. 1938; s. of Alan George and Olive Elizabeth George; m. Clarice Vanessa Williams 1962; one s. two d.; ed. Dulwich Coll., Emmanuel Coll., Cambridge; joined Bank of England 1962, seconded to BIS 1966–69, to IMF as asst. to Chair. of Deputies of Cttee. of Twenty on Int. Monetary Reform 1972–74, Adviser on Int. Monetary Questions 1974–77, Deputy Chief Cashier 1977–80, Asst. Dir. Gilt-Edged Div. 1980–82, Exec. Dir. 1982–90, Deputy Gov. 1990–93, Gov. June 1993–; Hon. D.Sc. (Econ.) (Hull) 1993, D.Litt. (Loughborough) 1994, D.Sc. (City) 1995, (Cranfield) 1997; Hon. Ph.D. (London Guildhall) 1996. Dr. h.c. (Glasgow) 1997, Hon. LL.D. (Exeter) 1997. *Leisure interests:* family, sailing, bridge. *Address:* Bank of England, Threadneedle Street, London, EC2R 8AH, England. *Telephone:* 0171-601 4444.

GEORGE, H.E. Cardinal Francis Eugene, O.M.I.; American ecclesiastic; b. 16 Jan. 1937, Chicago, Ill.; ordained priest 1963; Bishop of Yakima 1990, of Portland in Oregon 1996–97; Archbishop of Chicago 1997–; cr. Cardinal Feb. 1998. *Address:* Archdiocese of Chicago Pastoral Center, P.O. Box 1979, Chicago, IL 60690, U.S.A.

GEORGE, Jennie, B.A.; Australian trade unionist; b. 20 Aug. 1947, Italy; ed. Sydney Univ.; Gen. Sec. N.S.W. Teachers Fed. 1980–82, Pres. 1986–89; mem. Exec. Australian Council of Trade Unions (ACTU) 1983, Vice-Pres. 1987, Asst. Sec. 1991–95, Pres. 1996; Asst. Nat. Dir. Trade Union Training Authority 1989–91. *Address:* ACTU, North Wing, Trades Hall, 54 Victoria Street, Carlton South, Vic. 3053, Australia.

GEORGE, Kenneth Montague, LL.M.; Guyanese judge; b. 12 March 1930; s. of Stephen N. George and Etheline George; m. Hazel Ester McLean 1965; two s. two d.; ed. London and Harvard Univs. and Gray's Inn, London; Registrar of Supreme Court 1964–66, Judge 1967–76; Justice of Appeal

1976–81; Chief Justice 1981–88; Chancellor of the Judiciary and Pres. Court of Appeal 1988; Cacique's Crown of Honour, Order of Roraima. *Leisure interest:* reading. *Address:* c/o Court of Appeal, 60 High Street, Kingston, Georgetown (Office); 43 Arakaka Place, Bel Air Park, Georgetown, Guyana (Home). *Telephone:* 02-65906 (Home).

GEORGE, Richard Lee, B.S., J.D.; Canadian businessman; b. 16 May 1950, Colorado; s. of Albert H. George and Betty Lou McDill; m. Julie G. White 1972; two s. one d.; ed. Harvard Business School, Univ. of Houston, Colorado State Univ.; Deputy Man. Dir. Sun Oil Britain, London 1982–86, District Man., Aberdeen 1986–87; Vice-Pres. Sun Exploration and Production, Dallas 1987–88; Man. Dir. Sun Int. Exploration and Production, London, U.K. 1988–91, Pres. and C.O.O. Suncor Inc. Ontario, Canada Feb.–Oct. 1991, Pres. and C.E.O. 1991–93, Pres., C.E.O. Jan. 1993– (fmr. Chair.); Dir. IPL Energy Inc., Dofasco Inc. *Leisure interests:* skiing, golf, fitness. *Address:* Suncor Energy Inc., 112 4th Ave, S.W., P.O. Box 38, Calgary, Alberta, T2P 2V5, Canada. *Telephone:* (403) 269-8100. *Fax:* (403) 269-6221.

GEORGE, Susan; British actress; b. 26 July 1950; m. Simon MacCorkindale 1984; began acting career 1954. *Films include:* Cup Fever, Davey Jones' Locker, Billion Dollar Brain, Twinky 1969, Spring and Port Wine 1970, Eyewitness 1970, Straw Dogs 1971, Dirty Mary and Crazy Larry 1974, Mandingo 1975, Out of Season 1975, A Small Town in Texas 1977, Tomorrow Never Comes 1978, Venom 1980, A Texas Legend 1981, The House Where Evil Dwells 1982, The Jigsaw Man 1984, Czechmate 1985, Lightning, The White Stallion 1986, Stealing Heaven (producer) 1987, That Summer of White Roses (producer) 1988, The House That Mary Bought (also producer) 1994. *TV appearances include:* Swallows and Amazons, Human Jungle, The Right Attitude 1968, Dr. Jekyll and Mr. Hyde 1973, Lamb to the Slaughter 1979, Royal Jelly 1979, The Bob Hope Special 1979, Pajama Tops 1982, Masquerade 1983, Hotel 1985, Blacke's Magic 1986, Jack the Ripper 1988, Castle of Adventure 1990, Cluedo 1992, Stay Lucky 1992. *Theatre:* The Sound of Music 1962, The Country Girl 1984, Rough Crossing 1987; partner Amy Int. Productions, London. *Publication:* illustrated book of poetry 1987. *Address:* c/o MacCorkindale & Holton, P.O. Box 2398, 1-2 Langham Place, London, W1A 3DD, England. *Telephone:* 0171-636 1888.

GEORGEL, Pierre, D. EN LETT.; French museum director; b. 14 Jan. 1943, Safi, Morocco; s. of Lucien Georgel and Santia Maria Georgel (née Santini); m. Chantal Martinet 1985; ed. Univs. of Montpellier, Paris and Lille, Ecole du Louvre, Paris; Asst., Musée du Louvre 1966–70; seconded to C.N.R.S., Paris 1970–74; Curator of Graphic Art, Musée National d'Art Moderne 1974–79; Dir. Musée des Beaux-Arts, Dijon 1980–86; Dir. Musée Picasso, Paris 1986–89; Chief Curator of French Museums (based at Musée Picasso) 1989–93; Dir. Musée nat. de l'Orangerie des Tuileries 1993; Prof. Ecole du Louvre 1980–85, 1995–96. *Publications include:* Dessins de Victor Hugo 1971, La Gloire de Victor Hugo 1985, La Peinture dans la peinture 1987, Courbet: le Poème de la nature 1995. *Address:* Musée de l'Orangerie, Jardin des Tuileries, 75041 Paris, Cedex 01 (Office); 24 rue Richer, 75009 Paris, France (Home). *Telephone:* 42-97-48-16. *Fax:* 42-61-30-82.

GEORGES, Rt. Hon. Philip Telford, B.A.; Trinidad and Tobago judge; b. 5 Jan. 1923, Dominica; s. of John H. D. Georges and Milutine C. Cox; m. 1st Grace E. Georges 1954; m. 2nd Joyce L. Georges 1981; two s. two d.; ed. Univ. of Toronto and Middle Temple, London; pvt. practice as barrister-at-law 1949–62; Judge, High Court of Trinidad & Tobago 1962–65, 1971–74; Chief Justice of Tanzania 1965–71; Prof. of Law, Univ. of W. Indies 1974–81; Judge, Supreme Court of Zimbabwe 1981–84, Chief Justice June–Dec. 1984, of The Bahamas 1984–89; Judge, Court of Appeal, Cayman Islands 1984–, Bermuda 1990–94; Judge Court of Appeal, Belize 1992–97, mem. 1993–; mem. Juridical Cttee., OAS 1992–95; Law Reform Commr. The Bahamas 1989–; Judge, Admin. Tribunal, IADB 1993; Hon. LL.D. (Toronto, Dar es Salaam, West Indies, Dalhousie); Order of the Caribbean Community, Award of Dominica. *Leisure interests:* walking, swimming. *Address:* Kilimani, 5A The Mount, St. George, Barbados. *Telephone:* 435-1185. *Fax:* 429-0223.

GEORGESCU, Florin, PH.D.; Romanian politician and economist; ; b. 25 Nov. 1953, Bucharest; ed. Acad. of Econ. Studies, Bucharest; Fulbright Scholar 1991–92; author of more than 200 studies and papers; worked at Finance Ministry, Prof. at Acad. of Econ. Studies; State Sec. of the Economy and Finance Ministry 1992, Minister of Finance and Deputy Prime Minister 1992–96; M.P. Dec. 1996–. *Address:* Chamber of Deputies, 76 117 Bucharest, Parliament Buildings, September 13 Avenue 1, Sector 5, Romania.

GEORGESCU, Peter Andrew, M.B.A.; American advertising executive; b. 9 March 1939, Bucharest, Romania; s. of V.C. Rica Georgescu and Lygia Bocu; m. Barbara A. Armstrong 1965; one s.; ed. Princeton and Stanford Univs.; joined Young & Rubicam Inc., New York 1963–, Dir. of Marketing 1977–79; Exec. Vice-Pres. and Dir. Cen. Region, Young & Rubicam Inc., Chicago 1979–82; Pres. Young & Rubicam Int. New York 1982–86, Young & Rubicam Advertising, New York 1986–, Young & Rubicam Inc. 1990– (C.E.O. 1994–); mem. Bd. of Dirs. Briggs & Stratton Inc.; mem. Council on Foreign Relations. *Address:* Young & Rubicam Inc., 285 Madison Avenue, New York, NY 10017, U.S.A.

GEORGIEVSKI, Ljubiša (Ljupčo); Macedonian politician and philologist; b. 1966, Stip; ed. Skopje Univ.; active in movt. for autonomous and independent Macedonia 1990–; Vice-Pres. Repub. of Macedonia 1991–92; f. and Pres. Democratic Party for Macedonian Nat. Unity VMRO-DPMNE 1993–; Prime Minister of Macedonia 1998–. *Publications:* books of poetry Apocalypse 1988, City 1991, Direct Investments and Short Stories (essays) 1994, numerous articles. *Address:* Office of the Prime Minister, Dame Grueva 6, 91000 Skopje, Macedonia. *Telephone:* (3891) 20 12 11 (Office).

GEORGIYEV, Georgy Pavlovich; Russian biologist; b. 4 Feb. 1933; m.; one s. one d.; ed. First Moscow Medical Inst.; researcher A. Severtsev Inst. of Morphology of Animals U.S.S.R. Acad. of Sciences 1956-61; head of lab. V. Engelgart Inst. of Molecular Biology U.S.S.R. Acad., of Sciences 1963–88; Prof. Moscow Univ. 1986–; Dir. Inst. of Gen. Genetics 1988–91; Founder and Dir. Inst. of Biology of Genes U.S.S.R. Acad. of Sciences 1991–; corresp. mem. U.S.S.R. (now Russian) Acad. of Sciences 1970, mem. 1987; research in molecular biology and genetics; author of discoveries of pro-m RNA and study of nuclear RNP particles, containing pro-m RNA and investigation of a new type of nucleoprotein complex structure; first description of nuclear skeleton components and elucidation of the nature of DNA; discovery of mobile elements in animals; typical studies of chromosome structure and transcription-active chromatin; mem. European Acad., Royal Acad. of Spain, German Acad. Leopoldina; Lenin Prize, U.S.S.R. State Prize. *Publications include:* Genes of Higher Organisms and their Expression 1989, over 300 scientific articles. *Leisure interest:* mountain climbing. *Address:* Institute of Biology of Gene, Russian Academy of Sciences, Vavilov str. 34/5, 117894 Moscow, Russia. *Telephone:* (095) 135 6089 (Office).

GEPHARDT, Richard Andrew, B.S., J.D.; American politician; b. 31 Jan. 1941, St. Louis; s. of Louis Andrew Gephardt and Loreen Estelle Cassell; m. Jane Ann Byrnes 1966; one s. two d.; ed. Northwestern Univ. and Univ. of Michigan; mem. Mo. Bar 1965; Partner firm Thompson and Mitchell, St. Louis 1965–76; Alderman 14th Ward, St. Louis 1971–76, Democratic Committeeman 1968–71; mem. 95th to 105th Congress from Third Missouri Dist. 1979–; Cand. for Democratic nomination to U.S. Presidency 1988; Majority Leader 1989–94; Democratic Leader 1995–; Pres. Children's Hematology Research Asscn., St. Louis Children's Hosp. 1973–76; mem. Bar Asscn., St. Louis, Mo., American Legion, Young Lawyers' Soc. (Chair. 1972–73). *Address:* U.S. House of Representatives, 1226 Longworth House Office Building, Washington, DC 20515, U.S.A.

GEPPAART, Chris P. A., D.JUR.; Netherlands professor of law; b. 2 Dec. 1931, Breda; m. Louise Pauline Heÿkoop 1959; one s. two d.; Inspector of Taxes 1959; clerk Netherlands Supreme Court 1960–66; Prof. of Law, Univ. of Tilburg 1966–96, Dean of Law Faculty 1984–92, Pro-Rector of Univ. 1986–92; mem. Royal Netherlands Acad. of Science 1978. *Publications:* Fiscale Rechtsvinding 1965, Vermogensbelasting, (Vol. 1) 1972, (Vol. 4) 1995, Fiscale Rechtsvinding in het Kader van de Europese Unie 1996. *Address:* Arthur Van Schendelpark 39, 5044 LG Tilburg, Netherlands. *Telephone:* 013-4672694.

GERASHCHENKO, Victor Vladimirovich; Russian banker; b. 21 Dec. 1937, Leningrad; s. of Vladimir Geraschenko and Anastasia Klinova; m. Nina Drozdkova 1960; one s. one d.; ed. Moscow Financial Inst.; Man. Div. of Foreign Exchange Dept., U.S.S.R. Bank for Foreign Trade (BFT) 1960–65, Man. Dir. of Dept. 1972–74, Man. Dir. Foreign Exchange Dept. 1982–83, Deputy Chair. 1983–89; Dir. Moscow Narodny Bank (MNB), Ltd., London 1965–67; Gov. Beirut br., MNB Ltd. 1967–71, Singapore br. 1977–81; Chair. Bd. Ost-West Handelsbank, Frankfurt-am-Main 1975–76; Chair. Bd. State Bank of U.S.S.R. 1989–91, Head of Dept. Fund Reforma 1991–92; Chair. Cen. Bank of Russian Fed. 1992–94, 1998–, Adviser 1994–98; Chair. Bd. Moscow Int. Bank (MIB) 1996–98. *Leisure interest:* literature. *Address:* Central Bank of Russian Federation, Neglinnaya str. 12, Moscow, Russia. *Telephone:* (095) 928-32-01.

GERE, Richard; American actor; b. 31 Aug. 1949; m. Cindy Crawford (q.v.) 1991 (divorced); ed. Univ. of Massachusetts; fmrly. played trumpet, piano, guitar and bass and composed music with various groups; stage performances with Provincetown Playhouse and off-Broadway; appeared in London and Broadway productions of The Taming of the Shrew, A Midsummer Night's Dream and Broadway productions of Habeas Corpus and Bent; film debut 1975; founding Chair. and Pres. Tibet House, New York; Hon. D.Lit (Leicester) 1992. *Films include:* Report to the Commissioner 1975, Baby Blue Marine 1976, Looking for Mr Goodbar 1977, Days of Heaven 1978, Blood Brothers 1978, Yanks 1979, American Gigolo 1980, An Officer and a Gentleman 1982, Breathless 1983, Beyond the Limit 1983, The Cotton Club 1984, King David 1985, Power 1986, No Mercy 1986, Miles From Home 1989, 3000 1989, Internal Affairs 1990, Pretty Woman 1990, Rhapsody in August 1991, Final Analysis 1991, Sommersby (co-exec. producer) 1993, Mr. Jones (co-exec. producer) 1994, Intersection 1994, First Knight 1995, Primal Fear. 1996, Red Corner 1997, Burn Hollywood Burn 1998, Runaway Bride 1999. *Publication:* Pilgrim Photo Collection 1998. *Address:* c/o Andrea Jaffe Inc., 9229 Sunset Boulevard, Los Angeles, CA 90069, U.S.A.

GEREMEK, Bronisław; Polish politician and historian; b. 6 March 1932, Warsaw; s. of Stefan Geremek and Maria Geremek; m. Hanna Geremek 1952; two s.; ed. Warsaw Univ., Ecole Pratique des Hautes Etudes, Paris; scientific worker History Inst., Polish Acad. of Sciences, Warsaw 1954–60; lecturer, Sorbonne, Paris 1962–65; staff mem. History Inst. of Polish Acad. of Sciences, Warsaw 1965–85, Asst. Prof. 1972, Head Research Unit of History of Medieval Culture 1965–80, Prof. 1989–; mem. Polish United Workers' Party (PZPR) 1950–68; co-f. and lecturer Scientific Courses Soc. 1978–81; adviser to Interfactory Strike Cttee., Gdańsk Shipyard Aug. 1980, subsequently to Interfactory Founding Cttee. of Solidarity Ind. Self-governing Trade Union, Gdańsk and to Nat. Understanding Comm. of Solidarity Trade Union 1980; Chair. Programme Council of Social and Labour Study Centre attached to Nat. Comm. of Solidarity 1980–81; Chair. Programme Comm., First Nat. Congress of Solidarity Trade Union, Gdańsk 1981; interned 1981–82; adviser to Provisional Co-ordinating Comm. of Solidarity Trade Union and to Lech Wałęsa (q.v.) 1983–87; arrested May 1983, released under amnesty July 1983; adviser to Nat. Exec. Comm. of Solidarity Trade Union 1987–90; mem. Civic Cttee. attached to Lech Wałęsa, Chair. of Solidarity Trade Union 1988–91; participant Round Table debates, mem. and Co-Chair. group for political reforms Feb.–April 1989; Deputy to Sejm (Parl.) 1989–; Chair. Civic Parliamentary Club 1989–90; Chair. Constitutional Comm., Chair. Sejm Cttee. of Foreign Affairs 1991–97; Chair. Parl. Club 'Democratic Union' 1991–94; Prof. Collège de France 1992–; Chair. Parl. Club 'Freedom Union' 1994–97; Minister of Foreign Affairs 1997–; mem. Polish Historical Soc., PEN Club, Soc. Européenne de Culture, Asscn. of Authors of Scientific Works, Academia Europaea, European Medieval Acad., Académie Universelle des Cultures; Dr. h.c. (Tours) 1982, (Utrecht) 1986, (Columbia Univ.) 1989, (Bologna) 1989, (Oberlin Coll., U.S.A., Univ. of Paris—Sorbonne) 1990, (Univ. Libre, Brussels) 1991, (Leicester) 1992, (Brown Univ., Providence) 1994; Alfred Jurzykowski Foundation Award, New York 1986, Prix Louise Weiss 1989, Herder Foundation Award, Vienna 1990, Société Européenne de Culture Prize 1993; Officier, Légion d'honneur. *Publications:* numerous works on medieval history of Europe (mainly France) and on medieval history of Polish culture, including Najemna siła robocza w rzemiośle Paryża XIII–XV w., Ludzie, towary, pieniądze (co-author) 1968, Ludzie marginesu w średniowiecznym Paryżu XIV-XVw. 1971 (Acad. française award 1976), Życie codzienne w Paryżu Franciszka Villona 1972, Inutiles au monde. Vagabonds et marginaux en Europe aux XIV–XVI siècles 1980, Dzieje kultury średniowiecznej Polski (co-author) 1985, Litość i szubienica 1989, Świat Opery żebraczej. Obraz włóczęgów i nędzarzy w literaturach europejskich XV-XVII wieku 1989, La Democrazia in Europa (co-author) 1993, Passions communes (co-author) 1993. *Address:* Ministerstwo Spraw Zagranicznych, al. J.Ch. Szucha 23, 00-580 Warsaw, Poland (Office). *Telephone:* (22) 623 90 80. *Fax:* (22) 629 05 00.

GERGEN, David Richmond, J.D.; American government official; b. 9 May 1942, Durham, N.C.; ed. Yale and Harvard Univs.; Staff Asst. Nixon Admin. Washington, D.C. 1971–72; special asst. to Pres. and chief, White House writing/research team 1973–74; special counsel to Pres. Ford and Dir. White House Office Communications 1975–77; Research Fellow, American Enterprise Inst.; Man. Ed. American Enterprise Inst. Public Opinion magazine 1977–81; Asst. to Pres. Reagan, Staff Dir. White House 1981; Asst. to Pres. Reagan for Communications 1981–83; Research Fellow, Inst. of Politics, John F. Kennedy School of Govt. Cambridge, Mass. 1983–85; Man. Ed. U.S. News & World Report, Washington, D.C. 1985–86, Ed. 1986, later Ed.-at-Large; Advisor to Pres. Clinton 1993–, for Foreign Policy 1994–95, to Sec. of State 1994; Visiting Prof. Duke Univ. N. Carolina 1995–; Sr Fellow Aspen Inst. *Address:* 2700 S. Quincy Street; 240, Arlington, VA 22206, U.S.A.

GERGIEV, Valery Abesalovich; Russian conductor; b. 1953, Moscow; ed. Leningrad Conservatory; prize winner at All-Union Conductors' Competition, Moscow (while still a student), and at Karajan Competition, Berlin; Chief Conductor of Armenian State Orchestra 1981–84; Asst. Conductor (to Yuriy Temirkanov q.v.) of Kirov Opera, Leningrad; Music Dir. Kirov (now Mariinsky) Opera Theatre 1988– (Artistic Man. 1996–); Prin. Guest Conductor of Rotterdam Philharmonic 1989–92, Prin. Conductor 1992–; Prin. Guest Conductor New York Metropolitan Opera 1998–; tours extensively in Europe and the U.S.A.; has guest-conducted Berlin Philharmonic, Dresden Philharmonic, Bayerischer Rundfunk, Royal Concertgebouw, London Philharmonic, City of Birmingham Symphony, Royal Philharmonic, London Symphony, Orchestra of Santa Cecilia, Japan Philharmonic; orchestras of Boston, Chicago, Cleveland, New York, San Francisco and Toronto; operas at Covent Garden, Metropolitan and San Francisco; State Prize of Russia 1993, Classical Music Awards 1994, Musician of the Year (Musical Life Magazine) 1992, 1993, Conductor of the Year (Musical America Yearbook) 1996. *Address:* c/o Columbia Artists, 165 West 57th Street, New York, NY 10019, U.S.A.; Mariinsky Theatre, Teatralnaya pl. 1, St. Petersburg, Russia. *Telephone:* (212) 841-9506 (New York). *Fax:* (212) 841-9599 (New York).

GERHARDT, Wolfgang; German politician; b. 31 Dec. 1943, Ulrichstein-Helpershain; two c.; Hessian Minister for Science and Art 1970; Party Whip Freie Demokratische Partei (FDP) (Free Democratic Party), State Parl., Hesse 1983–87, 1991–94, Rep. and Deputy Prime Minister 1987–91; Chair. FDP June 1995–. *Address:* Freie Demokratische Partei, 53113 Bonn, Thomas-Dehler-Haus, Adenauerallee 266; 65191 Wiesbaden, Liebenaustrasse 8B, Germany. *Telephone:* (0228) 547400 (Bonn). *Fax:* (0228) 547298 (Bonn).

GERINGER, James E. (Jim); American politician; b. 24 April 1944, Wheatland, Wyo.; m. Sherri Geringer; five c.; farmer and substitute teacher; fmr. Wyo. State Rep. Platte Co.; mem. Wyo. State Senate for Platt County, Dist. 3 until 1995; Gov. of Wyoming Jan. 1995–; Republican. *Address:* Office of the Governor, Capitol Building, 200 West 24th Street, Cheyenne, WY 82002, U.S.A. *Telephone:* (307) 777-7434. *Fax:* (307) 632-3909.

GERKAN, Meinhard von; German architect; b. 3 Jan. 1935, Riga, U.S.S.R. (now Latvia); freelance architect in collaboration with Volkwin Marg 1965– (four other partners 1974–); with Freie Akad. der Künste Hamburg 1972–74; Prof. Inst. für Baugestaltung A, Technische Univ. Brunswick 1974–; with Kuratorium Jürgen-Ponto-Stiftung Frankfurt 1982; Guest Prof. Nihon Univ. Tokyo 1988, Univ. of Pretoria 1993; mem. Akad. der Künste; Hon. Fellow A.I.A. 1995, Inst. of Mexican Architects 1995; work includes airport bldgs., railway stations, hotels, offices, public bldgs. and housing throughout Germany and in Saudi Arabia, Italy, Latvia, China and Algeria; recipient of more than 320 prizes at nat. and int. competitions. *Publications:* Architektur 1966–1978 1978, Die Verantwortung des Architekten 1982, Architektur 1978–1983 1983, Alltagsarchitektur, Gestalt und Ungestalt 1987, Architektur 1983–1988 1988, Architektur 1988–1991 1992, von Gerkan, Marg and Partners 1993, Idea and Model: 30 years of architectural models 1994, Architektur im Dialog 1994, Culture Bridge 1995, Architektur 1991–1995 1995, Architecture for Transportation 1997, Architecture 1995–97 1998, Möbel Furniture 1998. *Address:* Elbchaussee 139, 22763 Hamburg, Germany (Office). *Telephone:* (040) 88 15 1-0 (Office).

GERMAIN, Paul, D. ÈS SC.; French professor of theoretical mechanics; b. 28 Aug. 1920, Saint-Malo; s. of Paul Germain and Elisabeth Frangeul; m. Marie-Antoinette Gardent 1942; one s. one d.; ed. Ecole Normale Supérieure de Paris and Univ. of Paris; Research Engineer, Office Nat. d'Etudes et de Recherches Aérospatiales (O.N.E.R.A.) 1946–49, Dir. 1962–68; Assoc. Prof. Univ. of Poitiers 1949–54; Prof. Univ. of Lille 1954–58; Prof. of Theoretical Mechanics Univ. of Paris 1958–77, Ecole Polytechnique 1977–85, Univ. Pierre and Marie Curie 1985–87; Visiting Prof., Brown Univ. 1953–54, Stanford Univ. 1969–70; mem. Acad. des Sciences 1970–, Perm. Sec. 1975–96, Hon. Perm. Sec. 1996–; mem. Int. Acad. of Astronautics, Pontifical Acad. of Sciences; Foreign mem. Accad. Nazionale dei Lincei, Rome 1976, Polish Acad. of Sciences 1978; Foreign Assoc. Nat. Acad. of Eng., Washington 1979; Hon. Fellow, A.I.A.A. 1981; Foreign Assoc. Acad.-Royale Belgique des Lettres, des Sciences et des Arts 1984, Acad. of Sciences (U.S.S.R.) 1988; Commdr. Légion d'honneur, Grand-Croix Ordre nat. du Mérite, Medaille de l'aéronautique, Commdr. des Palmes académiques; Dr. h.c. (Louvain) 1961, (Strathclyde) 1975, (Madrid Univ.) 1980, (Brussels) 1984. *Publications:* Mécanique des milieux continus 1962, Cours de mécanique des milieux continus 1973, Mécanique 1986 and more than 100 papers on theoretical aerodynamics, magnetohydrodynamics, shock wave theory and mechanics of continua. *Leisure interests:* hiking, swimming, skiing. *Address:* Académie des Sciences, 23 quai de Conti 75006, Paris (Office); 3 Avenue de Champaubert, 75015 Paris, France (Home). *Telephone:* 01-44-41-43-52 (Office); 01-43-06-35-53 (Home).

GERMAN, Aleksey Georgievich; Russian film director; b. 20 July 1938, Leningrad; s. of Yuri Pavlovich German and Tatyana Rittenberg; m. Svetlana Karmalina; one s.; ed. Leningrad State Inst. of Theatre, Music and Cinema; Dir. theatres in Leningrad and Smolensk; works with Lenfilm Studios 1964–; Head, St. Petersburg experimental film studio; U.S.S.R. State Prize 1988, State Prize of Russia, Triumph Prize 1998. *Films include:* The Seventh Traveller 1968, Twenty Days Without War 1977, My Friend Ivan Lapshin 1984, Trial on the Road 1986, Khrustalev, My Car! 1997. *Address:* Marsovo Pole 7, Apt. 37, 191041 St. Petersburg, Russia. *Telephone:* (812) 315-17-06.

GERMANI, Fernando; Italian musician; b. 5 April 1906; ed. Rome Conservatoire and Pontifical Inst. of Sacred Music; Prof. of Organ Music at the Rome Conservatoire, Chigiana Music Acad. (Siena), Curtis Inst. (Philadelphia); recitals in the Americas, Australasia, South Africa, Europe; Commdr. Order of St. Gregory the Great, Commdr. Order of St. Sylvester, Kt. Crown of Italy. *Publications:* Revision of works of Girolamo Frescobaldi 1936, A Method of Organ Playing 1942. *Address:* Via delle Terme Deciane 11, Rome, Italy.

GERMANOVA, Yevdokiya Alekseyevna; Russian actress; b. 8 Nov. 1959, Moscow; ed. State Inst. of Theatre Art; with Oleg Tabakov Theatre Studio 1983–; roles in productions including Mystery by J. B. Priestley (production in Austria), Trust, Love, Hope by O. Horvat (dir. M. Schell); roles in numerous films including Moslem (dir. V. Khotinenko), Close Circle (A. Konchalovsky), Kix (S. Livnev), Crazy (S. Garazov), Here is Freedom (A. Waida), Niagara (A. Vizir), We Cannot Guess (O. Narutskaya); numerous prizes for best women's roles at int. and nat. festivals in Kiev, Karlovy Vary, Nizhny Novgorod, Ange, Moscow. *Address:* Chaplygina Str., 1A, Oleg Tabakov Theatre Studio, Moscow, Russia. *Telephone:* (095) 916 2121 (Office).

GERSHEVITCH, Ilya, PH.D., F.B.A.; British academic; b. 24 Oct. 1914, Zürich, Switzerland; s. of Arkadi Gershevitch and Mila Gershevitch; m. Lisbeth Syfrig 1951; one d.; ed. Univs. of Rome and London; monitored foreign broadcasts, London 1942–47; lecturer in Iranian Studies, Cambridge Univ. 1948–65, Reader 1965–82, now Emer., Fellow of Jesus Coll. 1962–; Visiting Prof. Columbia Univ., New York, U.S.A. 1960–61, 1965–66; Univ. Exchange Visitor, U.S.S.R. 1965; Ratanbai Katrak Lecturer, Oxford Univ. 1968; mem. Danish Acad. 1982; Foreign Fellow, Accademia dei Lincei 1987; Pres. Philological Soc. 1980–84; Hon. Ph.D. (Berne). *Publications:* A Grammar of Manichean Sogdian 1954, The Avestan Hymn to Mithra 1959, Philologia Iranica 1985; articles in specialist journals, encyclopaedias and collective books. *Leisure interest:* music. *Address:* Jesus College, Cambridge CB5 8BL; 54 Owlstone Road, Cambridge, CB3 9JH, England (Home). *Telephone:* (01223) 314552 (Coll.); (01223) 357996.

GERSON, Mark, F.B.I.P.P.; British photographer; b. 3 Oct. 1921, London; s. of Bernard Gerson and Esther Gerson; m. Renée Cohen 1949; two d.; ed.

Cen. Foundation School for Boys, London and Regent Polytechnic, London; served in R.A.F. 1941–46; taught photography under E.V.T. scheme while serving in R.A.F. in Paris 1946; specialist portrait photographer concentrating on literary personalities and industrialists; ran photographic studio 1947–87; now freelance photographer; major exhbns. Fox Talbot Museum, Lacock, Wilts. 1981, Shaw Theatre, London 1983, Writers Observed, Nat. Theatre, London 1984, The Poetry Library, Royal Festival Hall 1991, Literati, Nat. Portrait Gallery, London 1996. *Leisure interests:* cinema, theatre. *Address:* 3 Regal Lane, Regent's Park, London, NW1 7TH, England. *Telephone:* 0171-286 5894; 0171-267 9246. *Fax:* 0171-267 9246.

GERSTNER, Louis Vincent, Jr., M.B.A.; American business executive; b. 1 March 1942, New York; s. of Louis Vincent Gerstner and Marjorie Rutan; m. Elizabeth Robins Link 1968; one s. one d.; ed. Dartmouth Coll. and Harvard Univ.; Dir. McKinsey & Co., New York 1965–78; Exec. Vice-Pres. American Express Co., New York 1978–81, Vice-Chair. 1981–85, Pres. 1985–89, Vice-Pres. 1989; Chair., C.E.O. RJR Nabisco 1989–93; Chair., C.E.O. IBM 1993–; Vice-Chair. New American Schools Devt. Corp; Dir. The New York Times Co., Bristol-Myers Squibb Co., Japan Soc., RJR Nabisco Inc., The New American Schools Devt. Corpn.; mem. Exec. Cttee., Bd. of Trustees Joint Council on Econ. Educ. 1975–87, Chair. 1983–85; Bd. of Mans. Memorial Sloan Kettering Hospital 1978–89; mem. Policy Cttee., Business Roundtable; mem. Bd., Lincoln Center for the Performing Arts; mem. Bd. of Overseers Annenberg Inst. for School Reform, Brown Univ.; mem. Business Council, American China Soc., Council on Foreign Relations, Nat. Security Telecommunications Advisory Cttee., Advisory Cttee. for Trade Policy and Negotiations; Trustee N.Y. Public Library 1991–; Hon. D.B.A. (Boston Coll.) 1994; Hon. LL.D. (Wake Forest, Brown) 1997; numerous awards for work in educ. *Publication:* Reinventing Education (co-author.) 1994. *Address:* IBM Corporation, New Orchard Road, Armonk, NY 10504, U.S.A.

GERTH, Donald R., PH.D.; American university president; b. 4 Dec. 1928, Chicago, Ill.; s. of late George C. Gerth and Madeleine A. Canavan; m. Beverly J. Hollman 1955; two d.; ed. Univ. of Chicago; U.S.A.F. 1952–56; lecturer in History, Univ. of Philippines 1953–54; Admissions Counsellor, Univ. of Chicago 1956–58; Assoc. Dean of Students, Admissions and Records and mem. Dept. of Govt., San Francisco State Univ. 1958–63; Assoc. Dean of Institutional Relations and Student Affairs, Calif. State Univ., Chico 1963–64, Dean of Students 1964–68, Prof. of Political Science 1964–76, Co-Dir. Danforth Foundation Research Project 1968–69, Coordinator, Inst. for Local Govt. and Public Service and of Public Admin. 1968–70, Assoc. Vice-Pres. for Acad. Affairs and Dir. Int. Programs (Dir. of Center at Univ. of Skopje, Yugoslavia) 1969–70, Vice-Pres. for Acad. Affairs 1970–76; Pres. and Prof. of Political Science and Public Admin., Calif. State Univ., Dominguez Hills 1976–84; Pres. and Prof. of Govt. and Public Admin. Calif. State Univ., Sacramento 1984–; Pres. Int. Asscn. of Univ. Presidents 1996–; numerous other appts. *Leisure interest:* international affairs. *Address:* California State University, 6000 J Street, # 206, Sacramento, CA 95819; 417 Webster's Court, Roseville, CA 95747, U.S.A. (Home). *Telephone:* (916) 278-7737 (Office); (916) 771-3412 (Home). *Fax:* (916) 278-6959 (Office.)

GERWEL, Gert Johannes (Jakes), D.LITT., D.PHIL.; South African university vice-chancellor; b. 18 Jan. 1947, Somerset East; s. of John Gerwel and Sarah Becket; m. Phoebe Abrahams 1970; one s. one d.; ed. Paterson High School, Port Elizabeth and Univs. of W. Cape and Brussels; Educ. adviser, S.A. Students' Org. Durban 1972–73; lecturer, Sr. lecturer, Prof., Dean, Univ. of W. Cape, Rector and Vice-Chancellor 1987–94; Dir.-Gen. Office of Pres. and Sec. to Parl. 1994–; Chair. Careers Research and Information Centre, Cape Town, Equal Opportunity Foundation, Johannesburg, Community Agency for Social Enquiry, Johannesburg. *Publication:* Literatuur en Apartheid 1983. *Leisure interest:* cricket. *Address:* Private Bag X1000, Cape Town 8000, South Africa.

GESANG DOJE; Chinese party official; b. Feb. 1936, Qinghai Prov.; s. of Giamucuo and Sangdang Shiji; m. Zenen Namu 1956; one s. three d.; ed. Nat. Middle School, Sining, Qinghai and in Beijing; returned to Sining as a corresp. 1955; Vice-Chair. Qinghai Provincial People's Congress Standing Cttee. 1991–; started writing poetry 1956. *Publications include:* Legend of Hot Spring, The Childbirth of a New Town at Daybreak, The Name of Maji Snow Mountain, You are an Infant of Daylight, Raindrops from the Clouds 1992. *Leisure interests:* riding, hunting, painting.

GETTY, Donald; Canadian politician; b. 30 Aug. 1933, Westmount, Quebec; m. Margaret Mitchell; four s.; ed. Univ. of Western Ont.; joined Imperial Oil Ltd. Edmonton 1955; Lands and Contracts Man. Midwestern Industrial Gas Ltd. 1961; Pres. and Man. Dir. Baldonnel Oil and Gas Ltd. 1964–67; Partner, Doherty, Roadhouse & McCuaig Ltd. (investment firm) 1967; mem. Alberta Legis. 1967–79, 1985–; Minister of Fed. and Intergovernmental Affairs, Prov. of Alberta 1971–75, of Energy and Natural Resources 1975–79; Pres. D. Getty Investments Ltd. 1979; Chair. of Bd. Ipsco 1981–85; Pres., C.E.O. Sunnybank Investments Ltd. 1985–93; served as dir. of numerous cos.; Leader Progressive Conservative Party, Alberta 1985–93; Premier of Alberta 1985–92. *Leisure interests:* golf, horse-racing, hunting. *Address:* 3145 Manulife Place, 10180-101 Street, Edmonton, Alberta, T5J 3S4; Box 300, Erskine, Alberta T0C 1G0, Canada.

GETTY, Sir J(ohn) Paul, Kt.; British philanthropist; b. 7 Sept. 1932; s. of J. Paul Getty and Ann Rork; m. 1st Gail Harris 1956 (divorced); two s. two d.; m. 2nd Talitha Pol 1966 (died 1971); one s.; m. 3rd Victoria Holdsworth 1994; with Getty Oil Italia 1959–70; donations include £40 million to Nat. Gallery, London 1985; provides charitable trust to help the homeless, community projects for young offenders, the preservation of old churches, programmes to rehabilitate prison inmates; Hon. K.B.E. *Leisure interests:* watching cricket and old movies, bibliography. *Address:* P.O. Box 8799, London SW1A 1ZD, England.

GHAFAR BABA, Abdul; Malaysian politician and business executive; b. 1925; Chief Minister for Melaka 1959–67; Deputy Prime Minister, Minister of Nat. and Rural Devt. 1986; Vice-Pres. United Malay Nat. Org. (UMNO) May 1987; fmr. Sec.-Gen. Nat. Front; Chair. PEGI, Batang Berjuntai; Dir. (non-exec.) Dunlop Holdings Ltd. 1983.

GHAFFARI, Abolghassem, D.SC., PH.D.; Iranian mathematician; b. 1909, Teheran; s. of Hossein Ghaffari and Massoumeh Shahpouri; m. Mitra Meshkati 1966; two d.; ed. Darolfonoun School, Teheran, and Univs. of Nancy, Paris, London and Oxford; Assoc. Prof. Teheran Univ. 1937–42, Prof. of Math. 1942–72; Temp. Sr. Lecturer in Math. King's Coll. London 1946–48; Sr. Research Fellow and Research Assoc. in Mathematics, Harvard 1950–51; Visiting Fellow Princeton Univ. 1951–52; mem. Inst. for Advanced Study, Princeton 1951–52; Senior mathematician, Nat. Bureau of Standards, Washington, D.C. 1956–57; Aeronautical research scientist 1957–64; Aerospace scientist NASA, Goddard Space Flight Center, Greenbelt, Md. 1964–72; Professorial Lecturer in Mathematics and Statistics, American Univ. Washington, D.C. 1958–60, and other American Univs.; Prof. Emer. of Mathematics (Teheran Univ.) 1972; mem. American, French (1935–70) and London Mathematical Socs., American Astronomical Soc., Philosophical Soc. of Washington (1958–80); Fellow, New York Acad. of Sciences 1961, Washington Acad. of Sciences 1963, A.A.A.S. 1965; Chair. Washington Acad. of Science Awards Cttee. for Math., Statistics and Computer Science 1975–90; Orders of Homayoun, Danesh (1st class) and Sepass (1st class), U.S. Special Apollo Achievement Award, Apollo 11 Commemorative Certificate. *Publications:* Sur l'équation fonctionnelle de Chapman-Kolmogoroff 1936, The Hodograph Method in Gas Dynamics 1950, about 60 research articles on Differential Equations in the Large, Brownian Motion, Transonic and Supersonic Aerodynamics, Lunar Flight Optimization and Orbit Determination, Astrodynamics, General Relativity and Relativistic Cosmology. *Address:* 7532 Royal Dominion Drive, Bethesda, MD 20817-4659, U.S.A. *Telephone:* (301) 469-7372. *Fax:* (301) 469-7372.

GHAI, Dharam Pal, PH.D.; Kenyan international civil servant and economist; b. 29 June 1936, Nairobi; s. of Basti Ghai and Widya Wati; m. Neela Korde 1963; one s. two d.; ed. Queen's Coll. Oxford, Yale Univ.; lecturer in Econs., Makerere Univ., Uganda 1961–65; Visiting Fellow Econ. Growth Centre, Yale Univ. 1966–67; Research Prof. and Dir. of Econs. Research, Inst. of Devt. Studies, Univ. of Nairobi 1967–71, Dir. Inst. of Devt. Studies 1971–74; Sr. Economist, Comm. on Int. Devt. (Pearson Comm.), Washington, DC 1968–69; Chief, World Employment Programme Research Br., Employment and Devt. Dept., ILO, Geneva 1973–74, Chief, Tech. Secr., World Employment Conf. 1975–76, Chief, Rural Employment Policies Br., Employment and Devt. Dept. 1977–87; Dir. UNRISD 1987–; Fellow African Acad. of Sciences. *Publications:* Taxation for Development: A Case Study of Uganda 1966, Collective Agriculture and Rural Development in Soviet Central Asia (with A.R. Khan) 1979, Planning for Basic Needs in Kenya (co-author) 1979, Agricultural Prices, Policy and Equity in Sub-Saharan Africa (with Lawrence Smith) 1987, Labour and Development in Rural Cuba (co-author) 1987; ed., co-ed. and contrib. several other books. *Leisure interests:* photography, gardening, swimming. *Address:* United Nations Research Institute for Social Development, Palais des Nations, 1211 Geneva 10 (Office); 32 chemin des Voirons, 1296 Coppet, Vaud, Switzerland (Home). *Telephone:* (022) 7988400 (Office); (022) 7765281 (Home).

GHAIDAN, Gen. Saadoun; Iraqi politician and army officer; b. 1930; m.; five c.; ed. secondary educ. in Aana and Military Coll.; commissioned 2nd Lieut. 1953; Commdr. Repub. Body-Guard Forces 1968; Gen. commanding Baghdad Forces 1969; mem. Revolutionary Command Council 1968; Minister of the Interior 1970–74, of Communications 1974–82; Deputy Prime Minister 1979–82.

GHANEM, Mohamed Hafez, PH.D.; Egyptian government official and lawyer; b. 28 Sept. 1925; m. Jouman M. Gaafar 1956; two s. one d.; ed. Cairo Univ. and Univ. de Paris; Lecturer, Faculty of Law, Alexandria Univ. 1949; Prof. of Public Int. Law and Vice-Dean, Faculty of Law, Ain Shams Univ. 1960–68; Minister of Tourism 1968–69, of Educ. 1969–71; Sec.-Gen. Arab Socialist Union 1973–75; Deputy Prime Minister 1975–78, Minister of Higher Educ. 1975–76, for Social Devt. and Services, Presidency Affairs and the Sudan 1976–78; Head of Ministerial Cttee. for Local Govt. 1976; Attorney, Legal and Econ. Consultant 1978–; Prof. of Public Int. Law, Ain Shams Univ. 1978–; fmr. Pres. Egyptian Soc. of Int. Law; mem. Arbitration, Conciliation and Mediation Comm. of Org. of African Unity 1966–71; mem. Legal Consultative Comm. for Afro-Asian Countries 1958–65; State Prize for best publ. in field of Int. Law and Political Science 1960. *Publications:* Public International Law (Arabic) 1964, International Organization 1967, International Responsibility 1972. *Leisure interests:* fishing, reading. *Address:* 3 Sharia El Bergass, Garden City, Cairo, Egypt (Home). *Telephone:* 970431, 976572, 972501 (Office); 980987, 988030 (Home).

GHANIM, Faraj Said bin; Yemeni politician; Prime Minister of Yemen 1997–98; independent. *Address:* c/o Office of the Prime Minister, San'a, Yemen.

GHARBI, El Mostafa, LL.B.; Moroccan international postal official; b. 9 Feb. 1935, El Jadida; m. Lalla Hafida Regragui 1962; three d.; ed. Ecole Nat. Supérieure des Postes, Télégraphes et Téléphones, Paris; various positions, Ministry of Posts, Telegraphs and Telephones, Rabat 1956–65, Dir. of Postal and Financial Services 1965–71; Counsellor, Universal Postal Union (UPU), Berne 1971–78, Sr. Counsellor 1978–81, Asst. Dir.-Gen. in charge of postal services and studies 1981–90, in charge of legal and admin. questions 1990–; Médaille de Chevalier. *Publications include:* The UPU: Present Situation—Main Policies 1990; other books on postal services and strategies. *Leisure interests:* reading, sport. *Address:* Merzenacker 29, 3006 Berne, Switzerland. *Telephone:* 31/941 00 46. *Fax:* 31/350 31 10.

GHASIMI, Mohammad Reza, PH.D.; Iranian banker; b. 5 June 1947, Teheran; s. of Reza Ghasimi and Akhtar Ghasimi; m. Shahrbanoco Nawabi 1980; one d.; ed. Univ. of Cambridge, L.S.E., Univ. of Lancaster; Deputy Dir. Econ. Research Dept., Cen. Bank of Iran 1976–78, Dir. 1979–86; Dir.-Gen. Econ. Policy Dept., Ministry of Econ. Affairs and Finance 1978–79; Asst. to Exec. Dir., World Bank 1986–88, Advisor to Exec. Dir. 1988; Exec. Dir. IMF 1988–90. *Publications:* Boosting Non-Oil Exports 1975, A Marketing Strategy for Exports 1975, An Investigation of the Instruments of Monetary Policy 1985, A Textbook on Macroeconomics 1986, numerous articles. *Leisure interests:* reading, tennis. *Address:* c/o Ministry of Finance, Teheran, Iran.

GHAZALA, Lieut.-Gen. Mohamed Abdel Halim Abu- (see Abdel Halim Abu-Ghazala, Marshal Mohamed).

GHEORGHIU, Angela; Romanian soprano; b. 1965, Adjud; m. 1st Andrei Gheorghiu 1988; m. 2nd Roberto Alagna (q.v.); ed. Bucharest Acad.; début Nat. Opera, Cluj 1990; first appearance at Royal Opera House Covent Garden, London 1992, Vienna State Opera 1992, New York Metropolitan Opera 1993. *Operas:* Don Giovanni, La Bohème, Turandot, Carmen, Cherubin, La Traviata, L'Elisir d'Amore, Falstaff. *Recordings include:* La Traviata (as Violetta) 1995, selection of arias; Belvedere Prize, Vienna, Schatzgraber-Preis, Hamburg State Opera, Gulbenkian Prize. *Address:* c/o Royal Opera House, Covent Garden, London, W.C.2, England.

GHEORGHIU, Ion (Alin), Romanian painter and sculptor; b. 29 Sept. 1929, Bucharest; s. of Emil Gheorghiu and Chiriachița Gheorghiu; m. Anamaria Smigelschi 1970; ed. N. Grigorescu Fine Arts Coll.; mem. Fine Arts Union, Sec. 1978–; creator of extensive cycles: "Suspended Gardens" (paintings), "Around Archimboldo" (drawings, paintings, sculpture), "Chimeras" (sculpture); has held exhbns. in Romania, Helsinki, Moscow, London, Paris, Warsaw, Rome, Philadelphia, Washington, Glasgow, Tokyo, Venice, Szczecin, Mannheim, Lisbon, Geneva, Prague, Tel Aviv, Tunis, Athens, Madrid, Mexico, Oslo, New York, etc.; Corresp. mem. Romanian Acad. 1993–, Hon. mem. Fine Arts Union of Bulgaria; Romanian Acad. Award 1966, Yomiuri Shimbun Award, Tokyo 1971, Great Award of the Fine Arts Union 1972, Italian Acad. Award and Gold Medal 1980, Trionfo '81 Prize 1981, Homage to Picasso Prize 1981, Homage to Raphael Prize 1993, Sofia Biennial Great Prize 1985, Ministry of Culture Prize (Chișinău, Moldova) 1996, Bucharest Municipality First Prize for Painting 1996. *Leisure interests:* hunting and fishing. *Address:* 27–29 Emil Pangratti Street, Bucharest (Studio); 6 Aviator Petre Crețu Street, Bucharest, Romania (Home). *Telephone:* 6.33.55.60 (Studio).

GHEORGHIU, Mihnea, PH.D., D.LITT.; Romanian university professor and writer; b. 5 May 1919, Bucharest; m. Anda Boldur 1953; one d.; ed. Univ. of Bucharest and studies in France, Italy and U.K.; Chief Ed. Scînteia Tineretului (newspaper) 1944–45; Ed. and Founder, Secolul 20 (monthly int. literary review) 1960–64; Ed.-in-Chief Romanian–American Review; Chair. of Bd. Social Future (sociology and political sciences bi-monthly), Studies in the History of Art 1975–; Univ. Prof. 1946–72; Pres. Council of Cinematography 1962–65; Deputy Minister of Culture and Arts 1965–67; Pres. Inst. for Cultural Rels. 1967–72, Acad. of Social and Political Sciences 1972–88, Romanian Filmmakers' Union 1990; corresp. mem. Romanian Acad. 1974, mem. 1993; Adviser UNESCO European Centre for Higher Educ.; Nat. State Prize; Special Prize, Int. Film Festivals 1964, 1966; Ordre des Arts et des Lettres (France); Italian Order of Merit; Grosse Verdienstkreuz mit Stern (Fed. Repub. of Germany); Order of Orange-Nassau (Netherlands); Acad. Award 1972; mem. Club of Rome, Société Européenne de Culture, Académie Mondiale de Prospective Sociale (Geneva), New York Acad. of Sciences. *Publications:* Orientations in World Literature 1957, Scenes of Shakespeare's Life 1958, Dionysos 1969, Letters from Neighbourhood 1971, Scenes of Public Life 1972, The Last Landscape (poems) 1974, Five Worlds as Spectacle (collection of plays) 1980, Tobacco Flowers (essays) 1984, Enigma in Fleet Street (novel) 1988, The Two Roses (collection of tales) 1991; translations from Shakespeare, Walt Whitman, Burns, Gabriel García Márquez, etc. *Address:* Dionisie Lupu 74, Bucharest, Romania (Home). *Telephone:* 6504969 (Home); 6505741 (Office). *Fax:* 3111246 (Office).

GHERSON, Adolph Randolph Albert, M.S.M., B.SC.ECON.; Canadian diplomatist (retd.); b. 9 Jan. 1928, Cairo, Egypt; m. Joan Evelyn Slater 1951; one s. one d.; ed. London School of Econs. and Acad. of Int. Law, The Hague; Research Asst. The Economist Intelligence Unit, London 1949–50; Econ. Research Div., Econ. Co-operation Admin. (Marshall Plan) 1950–52; Economist and Asst. to Chair. Int. Wheat Council, London 1952–58; joined Dept. of Trade and Commerce, Ottawa 1958; Head Commodity Trade Policy Div. 1963–64; Gen. Relations and Int. Orgs. Div. 1964–66, U.S. Div. 1966–68; Deputy Head of Mission to EEC, Brussels 1968–72, Acting Head 1970–71; Minister-Counsellor (Econ.), Washington, D.C. 1972–76; Dir.-Gen. Western Hemisphere Bureau, Dept. of Industry, Trade and Commerce 1976–80; Amb. and Perm. Rep. to OECD, Paris 1980–83; Dir.-Gen. European Summit Countries and European Community Bureau, Dept. of External Affairs, Ottawa 1983–86; Chief Air Negotiator, Dept. of External Affairs, Ottawa 1986–91, Amb. for Fisheries Conservation, Dept. of Foreign Affairs and Int. Trade, Ottawa 1991–94; Govt. of Canada Merit Award 1994, 125th Anniversary of Confed. of Canada (1867–1992) Medal 1994, Meritorious Service Medal 1994. *Leisure interests:* bird watching, 17th and 18th century maps and engravings.

GHIAUROV, Nicolai; Bulgarian singer; b. 13 Sept. 1929, Velingrad; m. Zlatina Ghiaurov; two c.; ed. Sofia Music Acad., Moscow Conservatoire; played violin, piano and clarinet from an early age; debut at Sofia Opera House as Don Basilio in Barber of Seville 1955, debut in Bologna 1958, debut at La Scala, Milan as Varlaam in Boris Godunov 1959; regular appearances at La Scala, Metropolitan Opera, New York, Vienna State Opera; major roles include title role in Boris Godunov, Mephistopheles in Faust.

GHIUSELEV, Nicola; Bulgarian bass opera singer; b. 17 Aug. 1936, Pavlikeni; s. of Nicolai Ghiuselev and Elisaveta Ghiuseleva; ed. Acad. of Art, Sofia and singing studies under Christo Brumbarov; m. 1st Roumiana Ghiuseleva 1960, 2nd Annamaria Petrova-Ghiuseleva 1984; two s. one d.; joined State Opera Co., Sofia; debut as Timur in Puccini's Turandot, State Opera, Sofia 1961; has since appeared at most of the maj. opera houses of the world and is noted for Russian roles such as Boris Godunov, Dositheus, Prince Igor, Ivan the Terrible and the bass repertoire of Verdi, Rossini, Bellini, Donizetti, Mozart, Berlioz, Cherubini, Ponchielli, etc. *Address:* Villa Elpida, 1616 Sofia, Bulgaria; Via della Pisana 370/B2, 00163 Rome, Italy. *Telephone and fax:* (2) 562929 (Sofia); (6) 66162834 (Rome).

GHIZ, Joseph Atallah, B.COM., LL.B., LL.M., M.L.A., Q.C.; Canadian fmr. politician and judge; b. 27 Jan. 1945, Charlottetown, P.E.I.; s. of Atallah J. Ghiz and Marguerite F. (McKarris) Ghiz; m. Rose Ellen McGowan 1972; one s. one d.; ed. Prince of Wales Coll. and Dalhousie and Harvard Univs.; Sr. Partner, Scales, Ghiz, Jenkins & McQuaid 1970–81; Crown Prosecutor, Queens County 1970–72; Fed. Narcotics Drug Prosecutor 1970–79; pvt. law practice 1981–86; Leader Liberal Party of P.E.I. 1981; mem. Legis. Ass. 1982–95; Leader of Opposition 1982–86; Premier of P.E.I. 1986–93; Dean Faculty of Law Dalhousie Univ. 1993–95; Justice Supreme Court, P.E.I. 1995–; mem. Bd. Dirs. Canada's Nat. History Soc. 1994–; trustee McGill Inst. for the Study of Canada 1993–; Hon. LL.D. (Univ. of Prince Edward Island) 1987. *Publications:* Towards a New Canada (co-author) 1978, final chapter of thesis, Constitutional Impasse over Oil and Gas, in Univ. of N.B. Law Journals 1982. *Address:* Judges Chambers, Supreme Court, of P.E.I., Sir Louis Henry Davies Law Courts, 42 Water Street, P.O. Box 2000, Charlottetown, P.E.I., C1A 7N8, Canada. *Telephone:* (902) 368-6596. *Fax:* (902) 368-6123.

GHIZIKIS, Gen. Phaidon; Greek army officer; b. 16 June 1917, Volos; widower; one s.; ed. Mil. Acad., War Coll. and Nat. Defence Coll.; Lieut.-Col. 1957, Col. 1966, Brig.-Gen. 1968, Maj.-Gen. 1969, Lieut.-Gen. 1971, Gen. 1973, Commdr. of Raiding Force, Dept. of Hellenic Army Command 1970; Deputy Commdr. of Hellenic Army Command 1971; Commdr. C Corps 1972; Commdr. of First Army 1973; Pres. of Repub. of Greece 1973–74; Kt. Commdr. Royal Order of George I, Grand Cross of the Redeemer. *Address:* 25 Kountouriotou, 151 21 Pefki, Greece. *Telephone:* 01-8021-530.

GHOSH, Gautam; Indian film director; b. 24 July 1950, Calcutta; s. of Prof. Himangshu Ghosh and Santana Ghosh; m. Neelanjana Ghosh 1978; one s. one d.; ed. Cathedral Mission School, Calcutta, City Coll., Calcutta and Calcutta Univ.; mem. Int. Jury (Oberhausen) 1979; official del., Cannes and London Film Festivals 1982, Venice and Tokyo Film Festivals 1984; mem. Nat. Jury 1985; Exec. Dir. Nat. Film Inst. 1987; Dir. Nat. Film Devt. Corpn., West Bengal Film Devt. Corpn.; Pres. Award (five times), Human Rights Award (France), Silver Medal and UNESCO Award, Grand Prix Award (U.S.S.R.) *Films include:* Hungry Autumn 1974, Ma Bhoomi 1980, Paar 1984, Antarjali Yatra 1988, Dakhal 1982, Padma Nadir Majhi 1992, Patang 1994. *Publications:* numerous articles on the cinema. *Leisure interests:* music, reading, travel. *Address:* Block 5, Flat 50, 28/1A Gariahat Road, Calcutta 700029, India.

GHOZALI, Sid Ahmed; Algerian politician and petroleum executive; b. 31 March 1937, Marnia; ed. Ecole des Ponts et Chaussées, Paris; fmr. Dir. of Energy, Ministry of Industry and Energy; Adviser, Ministry of the Economy 1964; Under-Sec., Ministry of Public Works 1964–65; Pres., Dir.-Gen. Société nationale pour la recherche, la production, le transport, la transformation et la commercialisation des hydrocarbures (SONATRACH) 1966–84, Chair., Man. Dir.; Minister of Hydraulics March–Oct. 1979, of Foreign Affairs 1989–91; Prime Minister of Algeria 1991–92; Amb. to Belgium 1987–89, to France 1992–93; mem. Cen. Cttee. Front de Libération National; mem. Org. technique de mise en valeur des richesses du sous-sol saharien 1962. *Address:* c/o Ministry of Foreign Affairs, Algiers, Algeria.

GIACCONI, Riccardo, PH.D.; American astrophysicist; b. 6 Oct. 1931, Genoa, Italy; s. of Antonio Giacconi and Elsa Giacconi Canni; m. Mirella Manaira 1957; one s. two d.; ed. Univ. of Milan; Asst. Prof. of Physics, Univ. of Milan 1954–56; Research Assoc. Indiana Univ. 1956–58, Princeton Univ., 1958–59; joined American Science & Eng. Inc. 1959–73, mem. Bd. of Dirs. 1966, Exec. Vice-Pres. 1969–73; Assoc. Harvard Coll. Observatory 1970–72; Assoc. Dir. Center for Astrophysics 1973–81; Prof. of Astrophysics, Harvard Univ. 1973–81; Prof. of Astrophysics, Johns Hopkins Univ. 1981–; Dir. Space Telescope Science Inst., Baltimore 1981–92; Prof. of Astrophysics, Milano Univ., Germany 1991–; Dir.-Gen. European Southern Observatory, Garching, Germany 1992–; Chair. Task Group on Directions in Space Science 1995–; mem. NASA Space Science Advisory Cttee. 1978–79, NASA Advisory Council's Informal Ad Hoc Advisory Subcommittee for the Innovation Study 1979–; mem. N.A.S. (mem. Space Science Bd. and High Energy Astrophysics Panel of the Astronomy Survey Cttee. 1979–), American Acad. of Arts and Sciences, A.A.A.S., American Astronomical Soc., American Physical Soc. (Fellow 1976), Italian Physical Soc., Int. Astronomical Union; Vice-Chair. COSPAR, I.S.C.E.-1 1980; Astronomy Rep. to Int. Astronomical Union 1979–81; mem. High Energy Astrophysics Division, American Astronomical Soc., Chair. 1976–77, Fachbeirat, Max-Planck Institut für Physik und Astrophysik, Comitato Scientifico del Centro Internazionale di Storia dello Spazio e del Tempo; Foreign mem. Accademia Nazionale dei Lincei; Laurea Honoris Causa in Astronomy, Univ. of Padua, 1984; Fulbright Fellow 1956–58; Hon. D.Sc. (Chicago) 1983; Space Science Award, A.I.A.A. 1976, NASA Medal for Exceptional Scientific Achievement 1980, Gold Medal, Royal Astronomical Soc. 1982, A. Cressy Morrison Award in Natural Sciences, New York Acad. of Sciences 1982, Wolf Prize 1987 and numerous other awards. *Publications:* X-ray Astronomy (co-editor) 1974, Physics and Astrophysics of Neutron Stars and Black Holes (co-editor) 1978, A Face of Extremes: The X-ray Universe (co-ed.) 1985, also numerous articles in professional journals. *Leisure interest:* painting. *Address:* European Southern Observatory, Karl-Schwarzschild-Str. 2, 85748 Garching; Frauenstrasse 6, 80469 Munich, Germany (Home). *Telephone:* (089) 32006227 (Office); (089) 2605333 (Home). *Fax:* (089) 32006366 (Office); (089) 2605336.

GIACOMELLI, Giorgio, M.A.; Italian international civil servant and diplomatist; b. 25 Jan. 1930, Milan; s. of Gino Giacomelli and Maria Van der Kellen; one s. one d.; ed. Padua Univ., Cambridge Univ., England and Geneva Inst. of Higher Int. Studies, Switzerland; joined diplomatic service 1956, Second Sec., Madrid 1958, Second Sec., NATO Del. 1961, First Sec. 1962, Chargé d'affaires, Léopoldville (now Kinshasa) 1964, Counsellor, New Delhi 1966, Ministry of Foreign Affairs, Rome: Personnel 1969, Cultural Dept. 1971, Head of Service for Tech. Co-operation 1972, Amb. to Somalia 1973, to Syria 1976; Deputy Dir.-Gen., Emigration Dept., with Ministry of Foreign Affairs, Rome 1980, Dir.-Gen. 1981, Dir.-Gen. Devt. Co-operation Dept. 1981; Commr.-Gen. UNRWA 1985–90; Under-Sec. Gen. UN Vienna Office 1992–97; Exec. Dir. UN Int. Drug Control Program; Dir. Gen. UN Office, Vienna; Silver Medal for Civil Bravery (Italy); Légion d'honneur (France); Kt. Order of Merit (Italy). *Leisure interests:* music, literature, mountaineering, hunting and riding. *Address:* c/o United Nations, Vienna International Centre, P.O. Box 500, 1400 Vienna, Austria.

GIAEVER, Ivar, PH.D.; American physicist; b. 5 April 1929, Bergen, Norway; s. of John A. Giaever and Gudrun M. Skaarud; m. Inger Skramstad 1952; one s. three d.; ed. Norwegian Inst. of Tech., Rensselaer Polytechnical Inst., N.Y.; Norwegian Army 1952–53; Patent Examiner, Norwegian Patent Office 1953–54; Mechanical Engineer, Canadian Gen. Electric Co. 1954–56; Applied Mathematician, Gen. Electric Co. 1956–58; Physicist, Gen. Electric Research and Devt. Center 1958–88; Inst. Prof., Physics Dept., Rensselaer Polytechnic, N.Y. 1988–; Prof. Univ. of Oslo 1988; mem. N.A.S. 1974–; Oliver E. Buckley Prize 1965, Guggenheim Fellowship 1970, Nobel Prize for Physics 1973. *Publications in Physics Review Letters:* Energy Gap in Superconductors Measured by Electron Tunneling 1960, Study of Superconductors by Electron Tunneling 1961, Detection of the AC Josephson Effect 1965, Magnetic Coupling Between Two Adjacent Superconductors 1965, The Antibody-Antigen Reaction: A Visual Observation 1973. *Leisure interests:* skiing, sailing, tennis, hiking, camping. *Address:* Physics Department, Rensselaer Polytechnic Institute, Troy, NY 12180 (Office); 2080 Van Antwerp Road, Schenectady, NY 12309, U.S.A. (Home). *Telephone:* 518-FR4-9708 (Home).

GIANVITI, François Paul Frédéric, D. EN D.; French professor of law; b. 2 Aug. 1938, Paris; s. of Dominique Gianviti and Suzanne Fournier; m. Barbara Zawadsky 1965; one s. two d.; ed. Lycées Henri IV and Louis-le-Grand, Paris, Faculté des Lettres et de Droit, Paris and New York Univ. School of Law; Asst. Faculté de Droit, Paris 1963–67; Dir. of Studies, Faculté de Droit, Nancy 1967–68, Caen 1968–69; Maître de conférences, Faculté de Droit, Besançon, on secondment to IMF 1970–74; Maître de conferences, Univ. of Paris XII 1974–75, Prof. of Law 1975–, Dean 1979–85; Dir. of Legal Affairs, IMF 1986–; Chevalier, Ordre Nat. du Mérite; Chevalier des palmes académiques. *Publication:* Les Biens 1984. *Address:* International Monetary Fund, Legal Department, Washington, DC 20431, U.S.A.; Faculté de Droit, Université de Paris XII, 38 Avenue Didier, 94210 La Varenne-Saint-Hilaire, France (Offices); 11402 Dorchester Lane, Rockville, MD 20852, U.S.A. (Home).

GIAP, Gen. Vo Nguyen (see Vo Nguyen Giap, Gen.).

GIBARA, Samir G.; M.B.A.; French business executive; b. 23 April 1939, Cairo, Egypt; s. of late Selim Gibara and Renée Bokhazi; m. Salma Tagher 1968; ed. Harvard Business School; Adviser, Inst. for Int. Trade, Paris 1967–70; Pres. and Man. Dir. Goodyear France 1983; Pres. and C.E.O. Goodyear Canada 1989; Vice-Pres. and Gen. Man. Goodyear Europe 1990; Vice-Pres. Strategic Planning and Acting Chief Financial Officer, Goodyear Tire & Rubber Co. 1992, Exec. Vice-Pres. N. American Operations 1994, Pres. and C.O.O. 1995–96, Chair., Pres. and C.E.O. Jan. 1996–, Chair. (elect) and C.E.O. (elect) July 1996–; Chevalier, Ordre Nat. du Mérite; Chevalier du Tastevin. *Publications:* articles in Le Monde and business journals. *Leisure interests:* theatre, music, reading, tennis, swimming. *Address:* The Goodyear Tire & Rubber Co., 1144 East Market Street, Akron, OH 44316, U.S.A.; Goodyear France, 101 avenue de la Chataigneraie, B.P. 310, 92506 Reuil-Malmaison, France. *Telephone:* (216) 796-3840 (Office). *Fax:* (216) 796-2108 (Office).

GIBB, Barry; British singer and songwriter; b. 1 Sept. 1947, Isle of Man; s. of late Hughie Gibb; m. Linda Gray; four c.; emigrated to Australia 1958, returned to U.K. 1967; formed Bee Gees with brothers Maurice Gibb (q.v.) and Robin Gibb (q.v.), and late Andy Gibb; started singing in nightclubs, Australia; first single Spikes and Specks 1966 numerous best-selling singles and albums; albums include: Bee Gees 1st, Odessa, Main Course, Children of the World, Saturday Night Fever (has sold over 40 million copies, more than any other soundtrack), Spirits Having Flown, High Civilisation, Size Isn't Everything, Still Waters; singles include: N.Y. Mining Disaster 1941, Massachusetts, To Love Somebody, Holiday, I've Gotta Get a Message to You, I Started a Joke, Lonely Days, How Can You Mend a Broken Heart, Jive Talkin', Staying Alive, Night Fever, How Deep Is Your Love, Too Much Heaven, Tragedy, Love You Inside Out, One, You Win Again, First of May; writer or co-writer of numerous songs for other artists including: Elvis Presley (Words), Sarah Vaughn (Run to Me), Al Green, Janis Joplin, Barbra Streisand (Guilty album), Diana Ross (Chain Reaction), Dionne Warwick (Heartbreaker), Dolly Parton and Kenny Rogers (Islands in the Stream), Ntrance (Staying Alive), Take That (How Deep is Your Love), Boyzone (Words), Yvonne Elliman (If I Can't Have You); 7 Grammy awards; elected to Rock and Roll Hall of Fame 1996 (inducted 1997), Int. Achievement Award American Music Awards 1997, Brit Award for Outstanding Contribution to Music 1997, World Music Award for Lifetime Achievement 1997; the Bee Gees are 5th most successful recording artists ever, have sold over 100 million records world-wide. *Address:* c/o Polygram Music, Worldwide Plaza, 825 8th Avenue, New York, NY 10019, U.S.A.

GIBB, Sir Francis (Frank) Ross, Kt., C.B.E., F.ENG., F.I.C.E.,; British engineer; b. 29 June 1927, London; s. of Robert Gibb and Violet M. Gibb; m. Wendy M. Fowler 1950 (died 1997); one s. two d.; ed. Loughborough Coll.; Joint Man. Dir. Taylor Woodrow PLC 1979–85, Jt. Deputy Chair. 1983–85, Chair. and Chief Exec. 1985–89; Man. Dir. Taylor Woodrow Construction Ltd. 1970–78, Chair. 1978–85, Pres. 1985–; Dir. Taylor Woodrow Int. Ltd. 1969–85; Chair. Taywood Santa Fe Ltd. 1975–85; Jt. Deputy Chair. Seaforth Maritime Ltd. 1986–89; Dir. Seaforth Maritime Holdings 1978–89, Eurotunnel PLC 1986–87, Babcock Int. Group PLC 1989–97, Nuclear Electric PLC 1990–94, Steetley PLC 1990–92, Energy Saving Trust Ltd. 1992– (Chair. 1995–), H. R. Wallingford 1995–; Chair. Nat. Nuclear Corpn. Ltd. 1981–88; mem. Group of Eight 1979–81; mem. Bd. British Nuclear Associates 1980–88; Chair. Agrément Bd. 1980–82; Chair. Fed. of Civil Eng. Contractors 1979–80, Pres. 1984–87; Vice-Pres. Inst. of Civil Engineers 1988–90; Dir. (non-exec.) A.M.C.O. Ltd. 1995–; Hon. F.C.G.I.; Hon. FINucE; Dr. h.c. (Loughborough) 1989; Hon. D.Tech. *Leisure interests:* ornithology, gardening, walking, music. *Address:* Ross Gibb Consultants, 18 Latchmoor Avenue, Gerrards Cross, Bucks., SL9 8LJ, England.

GIBB, Maurice; British singer and songwriter; b. 22 Dec. 1949, Isle of Man; s. of late Hughie Gibb; m. Yvonne Gibb; one s. one d.; emigrated to Australia 1958, returned to U.K. 1967; formed Bee Gees with brothers Barry Gibb (q.v.) and Robin Gibb (q.v.), and late Andy Gibb; started singing in nightclubs, Australia; first single Spikes and Specks 1966 (no. 1, Australia); numerous best-selling singles and albums; albums include: Bee Gees 1st, Odessa, Main Course, Children of the World, Saturday Night Fever (has sold over 40 million copies, more than any other soundtrack), Spirits Having Flown, High Civilisation, Size Isn't Everything, Still Waters; singles include: N.Y. Mining Disaster 1941, Massachusetts, To Love Somebody, Holiday, I've Gotta Get a Message to You, I Started a Joke, Lonely Days, How Can You Mend a Broken Heart, Jive Talkin', Staying Alive, Night Fever, How Deep Is Your Love, Too Much Heaven, Tragedy, Love You Inside Out, One, You Win Again, First of May; writer or co-writer of numerous songs for other artists including: Elvis Presley (Words), Sarah Vaughn (Run to Me), Al Green, Janis Joplin, Ntrance (Staying Alive), Take That (How Deep is Your Love), Boyzone (Words), Yvonne Elliman (If I Can't Have You); 7 Grammy awards; elected to Rock and Roll Hall of Fame 1996 (inducted 1997), Int. Achievement Award American Music Awards 1997, Brit Award for Outstanding Contribution to Music 1997, World Music Award for Lifetime Achievement 1997; the Bee Gees are 5th most successful recording artists ever, have sold over 100 million records world-wide. *Address:* Polygram Music, Worldwide Plaza, 825 8th Avenue, New York, NY 10019, U.S.A.

GIBB, Robin; British singer and songwriter; b. 22 Dec. 1949, Isle of Man; s. of late Hughie Gibb; m. Divina Murphy; one s.; emigrated to Australia 1958, returned to U.K. 1967; formed Bee Gees with brothers Barry Gibb (q.v.) and Maurice Gibb (q.v.), and late Andy Gibb; started singing in nightclubs, Australia; first single Spikes and Specks 1966 (no. 1, Australia);

numerous best-selling singles and albums; albums include: Bee Gees 1st, Odessa, Main Course, Children of the World, Saturday Night Fever (has sold over 40 million copies, more than any other soundtrack), Spirits Having Flown, High Civilisation, Size Isn't Everything, Still Waters; singles include: N.Y. Mining Disaster 1941, Massachusetts, To Love Somebody, Holiday, I've Gotta Get a Message to You, I Started a Joke, Lonely Days, How Can You Mend a Broken Heart, Jive Talkin', Staying Alive, Night Fever, How Deep Is Your Love, Too Much Heaven, Tragedy, Love You Inside Out, One, You Win Again, First of May; writer or co-writer of numerous songs for other artists including: Elvis Presley (Words), Sarah Vaughn (Run to Me), Al Green, Janis Joplin, Ntrance (Staying Alive), Take That (How Deep is Your Love), Boyzone (Words), Yvonne Elliman (If I Can't Have You); 7 Grammy awards; elected to Rock and Roll Hall of Fame 1996, Int. Achievement Award American Music Awards 1997, Brit Award for Outstanding Contribution to Music 1997, World Music Award for Lifetime Achievement 1997; mem. Songwriters' Hall of Fame 1994, Rock 'n' Roll Hall of Fame 1997; the Bee Gees are 5th most successful recording artists ever, have sold over 100 million records world-wide. *Address:* Middle Ear, 1801 Bay Road, Miami, FL 33139, U.S.A.

GIBBARD, Allan Fletcher, PH.D.; American professor of philosophy; b. 7 April, 1942, Providence, R.I.; s. of Harold A. Gibbard and Eleanor Reid Gibbard; m. 1st Mary Craig 1972 (died 1990); m. 2nd Beth Genné 1991; two s.; ed. Swarthmore Coll., Harvard Univ.; teacher of math. and physics with U.S. Peace Corps, Achimota School, Ghana 1963–65; Asst. Prof. then Assoc. Prof. of Philosophy, Univ. of Chicago 1969–74; Assoc. Prof. of Philosophy, Univ. of Pittsburgh 1974–77; Prof. of Philosophy, Univ. of Mich., Ann Arbor 1977–, Richard B. Brandt Prof. 1992–; Fellow Econometric Soc. 1984, American Acad. of Arts and Sciences 1990. *Publications:* Wise Choices, Apt Feelings: A Theory of Normative Judgement 1990; articles in journals. *Address:* Department of Philosophy, University of Michigan, Ann Arbor, MI 48109, U.S.A. *Telephone:* (313) 764-6285 (Office); (313) 769-2628 (Home). *Fax:* (313) 763-8071.

GIBBONS, Ian Read, PH.D., F.R.S.; British professor of biophysics; b. 30 Oct. 1931, Hastings, Sussex; s. of Arthur A. Gibbons and Hilda R. Cake; m. Barbara R. Hollingworth 1961; one s. one d.; ed. Faversham Grammar School and King's Coll., Cambridge; Research Fellow, Univ. of Pa. 1957, Harvard Univ. 1958; Asst. Prof. of Biology, Harvard Univ. 1963; Assoc. Prof. of Biophysics, Univ. of Hawaii 1967, Prof. 1969–97; Research Cell Biologist, Univ. of Calif. at Berkeley 1997–; Visiting Prof., Univ. of Siena 1981–82; Guggenheim Fellowship 1973. *Publications:* numerous articles in learned journals related to cell motility, especially that of cilia, flagella and other microtubule organelles. *Leisure interests:* gardening, music, computer programming. *Address:* Department of Molecular and Cell Biology, University of California, 335 LSA-3200, Berkeley, CA 94720, U.S.A. *Telephone:* (510) 642-2439.

GIBBONS, Hon. Sir John David, K.B.E., B.A., J.P., C.B.I.M.; British politician; s. of the late Edmund G. Gibbons and Winifred G. Gibbons; m. Lully Lorentzen 1958; three s.; one d. by fmr. marriage; ed. Saltus Grammar School, Bermuda, Hotchkiss School, Lakeville, Conn., U.S.A., Harvard Univ., U.S.A.; Government service in Bermuda with Social Welfare Bd. 1948–58, Bd. of Civil Aviation 1958–60, Bd. of Educ. 1956–59, Chair. 1973–74; mem. Governing Body and later Chair. Bermuda Tech. Inst. 1956–70; Trade Devt. Bd. 1960–74; M.P. 1972–84; Minister of Health and Welfare 1974–75, of Finance 1975–84; Prime Minister 1977–82; Chair. Bermuda Monetary Authority 1984–86, Bank of N. T. Butterfield & Son Ltd. 1986–97, Econ. Council 1984–87, Global Asset Man. Ltd. 1986–, Colonial Insurance Co. 1986–; mem. Law Reform Cttee. 1966–72. *Leisure interests:* tennis, golf, skiing, swimming. *Address:* Edmund Gibbons Ltd., 21 Reid Street, Hamilton, HM 11 (Office); Leeward, 5 Leeside Drive, Pembroke, HM 05, Bermuda (Home). *Telephone:* (441) 295-2396 (Home).

GIBBONS, John H., PH.D.; American physicist; b. 15 Jan. 1929, Harrisonburg, Va.; s. of Howard Gibbons and Jesse Conrad; m. Mary Hobart 1955; three c.; ed. Randolph-Macon Coll. Va. and Duke Univ. N.C.; Group leader (nuclear geophysics), Oak Ridge Nat. Lab. 1954–69, Environmental Programme Dir. 1969–73; Dir. of Energy, Environmental and Resources Center and Prof. of Physics, Univ. of Tennessee 1973–79; Dir. Office of Energy Conservation, Fed. Energy Admin. 1974; Dir. Office of Tech. Assessment 1979–92; Asst. to Pres. Clinton for Science and Tech. and Dir. Office of Science and Tech. Policy 1993–98; Fellow, American Asscn. for Advancement of Science, American Physical Soc., Nat. Acad. of Eng.; numerous professional appts. and affiliations; Commdr. Ordre des Palmes Académiques (France); Bundesverdienstkreuz (Germany); Hon. Ph.D. (Mount Sinai Medical School) 1995; Hon. Sc.D. (Duke) 1997, (Maryland) 1997; NASA Distinguished Service Medal 1998; many other awards and distinctions. *Publications:* This Gifted Age: Science and Technology at the Millennium 1997; numerous books and articles in areas of energy and environmental policy, etc. *Address:* P.O. Box 497, The Plains, VA 20198, U.S.A.

GIBBS, Anthony Matthews, M.A., B.LITT., F.A.H.A.; Australian professor of English; b. 21 Jan. 1933, Victoria; s. of J. F. L. Gibbs and S. T. Gibbs; m. 1st Jillian Irving Holden 1960; m. 2nd Donna Patricia Lucy 1983; two s. one step d.; ed. Ballarat Church of England Grammar School, Univ. of Melbourne and Oxford Univ.; lecturer in English, Univ. of Adelaide 1960–66, Univ. of Leeds 1966–69; Prof. of English, Univ. of Newcastle, N.S.W. 1969–75, Macquarie Univ. 1975–; mem. Exec. Cttee. Int. Asscn. for the Study of Anglo-Irish Literature 1973–78, Exec. Cttee. English Asscn. (Sydney Br.) 1975–91; Rhodes Scholarship 1956; Vice-Pres. Australian Acad. of Humanities 1988–89; Ed. 1989–93. *Publications:* Shaw 1969, Sir William Davenant 1972, The Art and Mind of Shaw 1983, Shaw: Interviews and Recollections 1990, Bernard Shaw: Man and Superman and Saint Joan 1992, "Heartbreak House": Preludes of Apocalypse 1994. *Leisure interests:* theatre, cooking. *Address:* School of English and Linguistics, Macquarie University, N.S.W. 2109 (Univ.); 4 Acacia Close, S. Turramurra, N.S.W. 2074, Australia (Home).

GIBBS, Rt. Hon. Sir Harry (Talbot), P.C., G.C.M.G., A.C., K.B.E., B.A., LL.M.; Australian lawyer; b. 7 Feb. 1917, Sydney; s. of Harry Victor Gibbs and Flora MacDonald Gibbs; m. Muriel Ruth Dunn 1944; one s. three d.; ed. Ipswich Grammar School, Queensland and Univ. of Queensland; admitted to Queensland Bar 1939; war service 1939–45 (despatches); Judge, Supreme Court, Queensland 1961, Fed. Court of Bankruptcy and Supreme Court of Australian Capital Territory 1967–70; Justice, High Court, Australia 1970–81; Chief Justice of Australia 1981–87; Chair. Court of Appeal of Kiribati 1988–, Australian Tax Research Foundation 1990–; Hon. LL.D.; Hon. D.Univ.; Hon. Bencher, Lincoln's Inn. *Leisure interests:* reading, tennis, swimming. *Address:* 30 Lodge Road, Cremorne, N.S.W. 2090, Australia (Home).

GIBBS, Lancelot Richard; Guyanese cricketer and sports organizer; b. 29 Sept. 1934, Georgetown, British Guiana (now Guyana); s. of Ebenezer and Marjorie Gretna (Archer) Gibbs; m. Joy Roslyn Margarete Rogers 1963; one s. one d.; ed. St. Ambrose Anglican Primary School and Day Commercial Standard High School; right-arm off-spin bowler; played for British Guiana/Guyana 1953–54 to 1974–75, Warwickshire 1967 to 1973, S. Australia 1969–70; played in 79 Tests for West Indies 1957–58 to 1975–76, taking then world record 309 wickets (average 29); only bowler to take 100 or more wickets against both England and Australia; toured England 1963, 1966, 1969, 1973, 1975 (World Cup); took 1,024 first-class wickets; Man. 1991 West Indies tour of England; now a sports organizer based in U.S.A., which he represented against Canada 1983; several decorations. *Leisure interests:* reading, all sport. *Address:* 276 Republic Park, Peter's Hall, E.B.D., Guyana.

GIBBS, Sir Roger Geoffrey, Kt.; British business executive and administrator; b. 13 Oct. 1934, Herts.; s. of Sir Geoffrey Gibbs, K.C.M.G. and Lady Gibbs; ed. Eton Coll. and Millfield School; with Jessel Toynbee & Co. Ltd. 1954–64, Dir. 1960, de Zoete & Gorton (later de Zoete & Bevan) stockbrokers 1964–71; Gov. The Wellcome Trust 1983– (Chair. 1989–); Chair. London Discount Market Asscn. 1984–86; Dir. Arsenal Football Club 1980–, Gerrard & Nat. Holdings PLC 1989–94 (Chair. 1975–89), Howard De Walden Estates Ltd. 1989– (Chair. 1993–98), The Colville Estate Ltd. 1989–; Chair. Arundel Castle Cricket Foundation 1986–95, Council for Royal Nat. Pension Fund for Nurses 1975–, Court of Advisers, St. Paul's Cathedral 1989–; mem. cttee. Marylebone Cricket Club 1991–94; Freeman, City of London; Liveryman, Merchant Taylor's Co. *Leisure interests:* sport, travel. *Address:* The Wellcome Trust, 183 Euston Road, London, NW1 2BE, England. *Telephone:* 0171-611 8888. *Fax:* 0171-611 8545.

GIBBS, Field-Marshal Sir Roland Christopher, G.C.B., C.B.E., D.S.O., M.C., J.P.; British army officer; b. 22 June 1921, Barrow Gurney; s. of Guy Melvil Gibbs and Margaret Olivia St. John; m. Davina Jean Merry 1955; two s. one d.; ed. Eton Coll. and Royal Mil. Coll., Sandhurst; commissioned into 60th Rifles 1940; served in N. Africa, Italy, N.W. Europe 1939–45; commanded Parachute Bn. 1960–62; British Army Staff, Washington, D.C. 1962–63; commanded Parachute Brigade 1963–66; Chief of Staff, HQ Middle East 1966–67; Commdr. British Forces, Gulf 1969–71, British First Corps 1972–74; C.-in-C. U.K. Land Forces 1974–76; Chief of Gen. Staff 1976–79; Regional Dir. Lloyds Bank 1979–91; Constable of H.M. Tower of London 1985–90; Lord-Lieut. for Wilts. 1989–96. *Leisure interests:* pictures, country pursuits. *Address:* Patney Rectory, Devizes, Wilts. SN10 3QZ, England. *Telephone:* (01380) 840 733.

GIBBS, Stephen, C.B.E.; British business executive; b. 12 Feb. 1920, Birmingham; s. of Arthur Edwin Gibbs and Anne Gibbs; m. Louie Pattison 1941; one s. one d.; ed. Oldbury Grammar School and Univ. of Birmingham; Dir. British Industrial Plastics Ltd. and Chair. subsidiary cos. 1956–68; Dir. Turner and Newall Ltd. 1968–82, Man. Dir. 1972–76, Deputy Chair. 1976–79, Chair. 1979–82; Chair. Gibbs Assocs. Ltd. 1984–95; Dir. Whitford Hall & Dodderhill 1990–95; Fellow, Inst. Materials. *Leisure interests:* gardening, photography. *Address:* Corner House, 11 Dodderhill Road, Droitwich, Worcs., WR9 8ON, England. *Telephone:* (0121) 456 1466 (Office).

GIBSON, Baron (Life Peer), cr. 1975, of Penn's Rocks in the County of East Sussex; **Richard Patrick Tallentyre Gibson;** British company director; b. 5 Feb. 1916, London; s. of Thornely Carbutt Gibson and Elizabeth Anne Augusta Wetzlar-Coit; m. Elisabeth Dione Pearson 1945; four s.; ed. Eton Coll., Magdalen Coll., Oxford; Vice-Chair. Westminster Press Ltd. 1953–76; Chair. Pearson Longman Ltd. 1967–79; Deputy Chair. S. Pearson & Son Ltd. 1969–75, Exec. Deputy Chair. 1975–77, Chair. 1978–83; Chair. Arts Council of Great Britain 1972–77, Financial Times Ltd. 1975–78, Nat. Trust 1977–86 (mem. Exec. Cttee. and Council 1966–86). *Leisure interests:* music, architecture, gardening. *Address:* Penn's Rocks, Groombridge, Tunbridge Wells, TN3 9PA, England. *Telephone:* (01892) 864244.

GIBSON, Eleanor Jack, M.A., PH.D.; American psychologist (retd.); b. 7 Dec. 1910, Peoria, Ill.; d. of William and Isabel Grier Jack; m. James Gibson

1932; one s. one d.; ed. Smith Coll. and Yale Univ.; Instructor, Smith Coll., Northampton, Mass. 1933–40, Asst. Prof. 1940–49; Research Assoc. in Psychology, Cornell Univ. 1949–65, Prof. of Psychology 1972; Visiting Prof. M.I.T. 1973, Univ. of Pa. 1984, Univ. of S.C. 1987, Emory Univ. 1988–90, Univ. of Conn. 1988; Montgomery Fellow, Dartmouth Coll. 1985; Pres. Eastern Psychology Asscn. 1968, Experimental Div., American Psychological Asscn. 1977; Chair. Division J, American Asscn. for the Advancement of Science 1982–83; mem. N.A.S., American Acad. of Arts and Sciences; Hon. D.Sc. (Smith Coll., Mass.) 1972, (Rutgers) 1973, (Trinity Coll.) 1982, (Bates Coll., Maine) 1985, (S.C.) 1987, (Emony Univ.) 1990, (Middlebury Coll., Vt.) 1993; D.Hum.Litt. (Albany) 1984, (Miami) 1989, (Oxford, Ohio) 1989; Distinguished Scientist Award, American Psychological Asscn. 1968, G. Stanley Hall Medal, American Psychological Asscn. 1971, Guggenheim Fellow 1972–73, Wilbur Cross Medal, Yale 1973, Howard Crosby Warren Medal 1977, Distinguished Scientific Contribution Award (S.R.C.D.) 1981, Gold Medal, American Psychological Foundation 1986; Pres.'s Nat. Medal of Science 1992; Hon. D.S.M. (Columbia Univ.) 1983. *Publications:* Principles of Perceptual Learning and Development 1969, Psychology of Reading (with Harry Levin) 1975, An Odyssey in Learning and Perception 1991; articles in all psychological journals. *Address:* RR1 Box 265A, Middlebury, VT 05753, U.S.A. (Home). *Telephone:* (802) 388-6340 (Home).

GIBSON, Frank William Ernest, D.PHIL., D.SC., F.A.A., F.R.S.; Australian professor of biochemistry; b. 22 July 1923, Melbourne; s. of John William and Alice Ruby (née Hancock) Gibson; m. 1st Margaret Burvill 1949 (divorced 1979); two d.; m. 2nd Robin Barker (née Rollason) Gibson 1980; one s.; ed. Collingwood Tech. Coll., Univs. of Queensland, Melbourne and Oxford; Research Asst. Melbourne and Queensland Univs. 1938–47, Sr. Demonstrator Melbourne Univ. 1948–49, Sr. Lecturer 1953–58, Reader in Chemical Microbiology 1959–65, Prof. 1965–66; Australian Nat. Univ. Scholar, Oxford 1950–52; Research Assoc. Stanford Univ. 1959; Dir. of John Curtin School and Howard Florey Prof. of Medical Research Australian Nat. Univ. 1977–80, Prof. of Biochemistry 1967–88, Prof. Emer. 1989–; Visiting Prof. and Fellow Lincoln Coll., Oxford 1982–83; Fellow A.N.U. 1989–; Pres. Australian Biochemical Soc. 1978–79; Gowland Hopkins Medallist, Biochemical Soc. 1982, Burnet Medallist, Australian Acad. of Sciences 1991. *Publications:* many scientific papers and reviews on biochemistry and microbial metabolism. *Leisure interests:* tennis, skiing, music. *Address:* John Curtin School of Medical Research, P.O. Box 334, Canberra, A.C.T. 2601 (Office); 7 Waller Crescent, Campbell, A.C.T., 2601, Australia (Home). *Telephone:* (02) 62495056 (Office); (02) 62470760 (Home).

GIBSON, Mel, A.O.; Australian actor and producer; b. 1956, Peekskill, N.Y., U.S.A.; s. of Hutton Gibson and Anne Gibson; m. Robyn Moore; five s. one d.; ed. Nat. Inst. for Dramatic Art, Sydney; f. ICONS productions; Commdr. Ordre des Arts et des Lettres. *Films include:* Summer City, Mad Max 1979, Tim 1979, Attack Force Z, Gallipoli 1981, The Road Warrior (Mad Max II) 1982, The Year of Living Dangerously 1983, The Bounty 1984, The River 1984, Mrs. Soffel 1984, Mad Max Beyond Thunderdome 1985, Lethal Weapon, Tequila Sunrise, Lethal Weapon II, Bird on a Wire 1989, Hamlet 1990, Air America 1990, Lethal Weapon III 1991, Man Without a Face (also dir.) 1992, Maverick 1994, Braveheart (also dir., co-producer, Acad. Award for Best Picture 1996) 1995, Ransom 1996, Conspiracy Theory 1997, Lethal Weapon 4 1998, Playback 1997, The Million Dollar Hotel 1999. *Plays include:* Romeo and Juliet, Waiting for Godot, No Names No Pack Drill, Death of a Salesman. *Address:* c/o ICONS Productions, 4000 Warner Boulevard, Room, 17, Burbank, CA 91522, U.S.A.; c/o Shanahan Management, P.O. Box 478, Kings Cross, N.S.W. 2011, Australia.

GIBSON, Rt. Hon. Sir Peter (Leslie), Kt., **Rt. Hon. Lord Justice Peter Gibson;** British judge; b. 10 June 1934; s. of Harold Leslie Gibson and Martha Lucy Diercking; m. Katharine Mary Beatrice Hadow 1968; two s. one d.; ed. Malvern Coll., Worcester Coll., Oxford; nat. service R.A. 1953–55; called to Bar, Inner Temple 1960; Bencher, Lincoln's Inn 1975; Second Jr. Counsel to Inland Revenue (Chancery) 1970–72; Jr. Counsel to the Treasury (Chancery) 1972–81; Judge of the High Court of Justice, Chancery Div. 1981–93; Chair. Law Comm. for England and Wales 1990–92; a Judge of the Employment Appeal Tribunal 1984–86; Lord Justice of Appeal 1993–; Hon. Fellow Worcester Coll., Oxford 1993; Treasurer Lincoln's Inn 1996. *Address:* Royal Courts of Justice, Strand, London, WC2A 2LL, England.

GIBSON, Rex; South African journalist; b. 11 Aug. 1931, Salisbury; s. of Arthur David Gibson and Mildred Joyce Adam; three d.; ed. King Edward VII School, Johannesburg; articled clerk 1948–52; entered journalism 1952, joined Rand Daily Mail 1959, Chief Sub-Ed. 1962, Arts Ed. 1969, Asst. Ed. then Chief Asst. Ed. 1969–72, Deputy Ed. 1973–76, Ed. 1982–85; Founding Ed. Mining News 1967; Ed. The Northern Reporter (first local suburban newspaper) 1968–69; Ed. The Sunday Express 1976–82; Deputy Ed. The Star, Johannesburg 1985–93; Deputy Man. Dir. Sussens Mann Communications 1993–; Bursar Imperial Relations Trust 1960; Atlas World Review Joint Int. Ed. of the Year Award 1979, Pringle Award for Journalism 1979. *Leisure interests:* reading, tennis, golf. *Address:* P.O. Box 1014, Johannesburg 2000, South Africa.

GIBSON, Robert Dennis, M.SC., PH.D., D.SC., F.T.S., F.A.I.M.; Australian university vice-chancellor; b. 13 April 1942, Newcastle, England; s. of Edward Gibson and Euphemia Gibson; m. 1st. 1964; one s. two d.; m. 2nd Catherin Bull 1994; ed. Hull and Newcastle Univs.; Prof. and Head, School of Math. and Computing, Newcastle Polytechnic 1977–82; Deputy Dir. Queensland Inst. of Tech. 1982–83, Dir. 1983–88; Vice-Chancellor Queensland Univ. of Tech. 1989–; mem. Australian Research Council; Hon. D.Sc. (C.N.A.A.) 1984. *Publications:* over 80 publs. in mathematical modelling. *Leisure interests:* cricket, running. *Address:* Queensland University of Technology, 2 George Street, Brisbane, Queensland 4000, Australia.

GIBSON, Roy; British space administrator; b. 4 July 1924, Manchester; m. Inga Elgerus 1971; one s. one d. (by previous marriage); ed. Chorlton Grammar School, Wadham Coll., Oxford, London School of Econs. Colonial Admin. Service, Malaya 1948–58; U.K. Atomic Energy Authority, London 1959–67; Deputy Dir. Technical Centre, European Space Research Org. (ESRO) 1967–71, Dir. of Admin. ESRO 1971–74, Acting Dir.-Gen. 1974–75; Dir.-Gen., European Space Agency 1975–81, Aerospace Consultant 1980–; Dir.-Gen. British Nat. Space Centre 1985–87; Special Adviser to Dir.-Gen., Int. Maritime Satellite Org. 1987–. *Publications:* Space 1992; numerous articles in aerospace technical journals. *Leisure interests:* music, languages, bridge, walking. *Address:* Résidence Les Hespérides, 51 Allée J. de Beins, 34000 Montpellier, France. *Telephone:* (4) 67-64-81-81. *Fax:* (4) 67-22-34-02.

GIBSON-BARBOZA, Mário, G.C.M.G.; Brazilian diplomatist; b. 13 March 1918, Olinda, Pernambuco; s. of Oscar Bartholomeu Alves Barboza and Evangelina Gibson Barboza; m. Julia Blacker Baldessarri Gibson-Barboza 1975; ed. Faculdade de Direito de Recife, Superior War Coll. 1951; joined diplomatic service 1940; Vice-Consul, Houston; Sec., Washington, Brussels; Minister-Counsellor, Buenos Aires 1956–59; Deputy Perm. Rep. to UN 1959–60; Amb. to Austria 1962–66, to Paraguay 1967–68; Sec.-Gen. for Foreign Affairs 1968–69; Amb. to U.S.A. 1969; Minister of Foreign Affairs 1969–74; Amb. to Greece 1974–77, to Italy 1977–82, to U.K. 1982–86; recipient of Grand Cross of Order of Brazil and other decorations. *Leisure interests:* riding, reading, theatre. *Address:* c/o Ministério dos Asuntos Exteriores, Palácio do Hamaraty, Esplanada dos Ministérios, 70.170 Brasília, DF, Brazil.

GIDADA, Negaso, PH.D.; Ethiopian politician; fmr. Minister of Health; Pres. of Ethiopia Aug. 1995–. *Address:* Office of the President, Addis Ababa, Ethiopia.

GIDASPOV, Boris Veniaminovich, D.SC.; Russian scientist; b. 16 April 1933, Kuibyshev; s. of Veniamin Aleksandrovich Gidaspov and Maria Aleksandrovna Smirnova; m. Zinaida Ivanovna Kuznetsova 1961; one s.; ed. Kuibyshev Industrial Inst.; mem. CPSU 1962–91; research, Kuibyshev Chemical Inst. 1955–59 and Leningrad Tech. Inst. 1959–77; Dir. State Inst. of Applied Chem. 1977–89; Consultant Russian Scientific Center 'Applied Chemistry' 1989–; Dir. Technoferm Eng. (representation in St. Petersburg) 1993–; founder mem. of Tekhnokhim (a commercial asscn. for research), Leningrad 1985–88, Chair. Tekhnokhim Corpn. 1991–; corresp. mem. U.S.S.R. (now Russian) Acad. of Sciences 1981–; U.S.S.R. People's Deputy 1989–91; First Sec. Leningrad CPSU City Cttee. 1989–91; mem. and Sec. CPSU Cen. Cttee. 1990–91; mem. Russian Eng. Acad. of Science 1994–; Lenin Prize 1976; U.S.S.R. State Prize 1981. *Leisure interests:* Russian history, sport. *Address:* 'Tekhnokhim', Angliyskaya nab. 10, St. Petersburg 190000, Russia. *Telephone:* (812) 311-60-01 (Office); 316-72-31 (Home). *Fax:* (812) 311-47-69.

GIDDENS, Anthony, PH.D.; British university administrator and sociologist; b. 18 Jan. 1938; s. of T. G. Giddens; m. Jane M. Ellwood 1963; ed. Hull Univ., L.S.E., Cambridge Univ.; lecturer, later Reader in Sociology, Univ. of Cambridge 1969–85, Prof. of Sociology 1985–97, Fellow King's Coll. 1969–96; Dir. L.S.E. Jan. 1997–; Hon. D.Litt. (S. Bank) 1997. *Publications:* Capitalism and Modern Social Theory 1971, ed. Sociology of Suicide 1972, Politics and Sociology in the Thought of Max Weber 1972, ed. and trans. Emile Durkheim: Selected Writings 1972, ed. Positivism and Sociology 1974, New Rules of Sociological Method 1976, Studies in Social and Political Theory 1976, Central Problems in Social Theory 1979, Class Structure of the Advanced Societies (2nd edn.) 1981, Contemporary Critique of Historical Materialism: (Vol. 1), Power, Property and State 1981, (Vol. 2), Nation, State and Violence 1985, jtly. Classes, Power and Conflict 1982, Profiles and Critiques in Social Theory 1983, jt. ed. Social Class and the Division of Labour 1983, Constitution of Society 1984, Durkheim 1985, Sociology: a brief but critical introduction 1986, Social Theory and Modern Sociology 1987, jt. ed. Social Theory Today 1987, Sociology 1989, The Consequences of Modernity 1990, Modernity and Self-Identity 1991, The Transformation of Intimacy 1992, Beyond Left and Right 1994, In Defence of Sociology 1996, Third Way 1998. *Address:* London School of Economics, Houghton Street, London, WC2A 2AE, England. *Telephone:* 0171-405 7686.

GIELEN, Michael Andreas; Austrian conductor and composer; b. 20 July 1927, Dresden, Germany; m. Helga Augsten 1957; one s. one d.; ed. Univ. of Buenos Aires; studied composition under E. Leuchter and J. Polnauer; Pianist in Buenos Aires; on music staff of Teatro Colón 1947–51; with Vienna State Opera 1951–60, Perm. Conductor 1954–60; First Conductor, Royal Swedish Opera, Stockholm 1960–65; conductor and composer in Cologne 1965–69; Musical Dir. Nat. Orchestra of Belgium 1969–73; Chief Conductor Netherlands Opera 1973–75; Music Dir. and Gen. Man. Frankfurt Opera House Sept. 1977–87; Music Dir. Cincinnati Symphony 1980–86; Prin. Conductor SWF Radio Orchestra, Baden-Baden 1986–; Prof. of Conducting, Mozarteum, Salzburg 1987–95, Emer. 1995–; Chief Guest Conductor, BBC

Symphony Orchestra 1979–82, Frankfurt Music Prize 1999. *Address:* Sudermannstrasse 8/12, 79114 Freiburg, Germany.

GIELGUD, Sir (Arthur) John, Kt., O.M., C.H., D.LITT. (brother of the late Val Gielgud); British actor and theatrical producer; b. 14 April 1904, London; s. of Frank Gielgud and Kate Lewis; ed. Westminster; first stage appearance at Old Vic 1921; Pres. Shakespeare Reading Soc. 1958–, RADA 1977–89, Hon. Fellow 1989; Fellow B.A.F.T.A. 1992; New Standard Special Award 1982; Dr. h.c. (Brandeis); Chevalier, Légion d'honneur 1960; Shakespeare Globe Trust Award 1993; awarded Praemium Imperiale 1994. *Plays acted in include:* Shakespeare's plays, Restoration comedies, The Constant Nymph, The Good Companions, Richard of Bordeaux, The Potting Shed, Ivanov, Forty Years On, The Battle of Shrivings, Home, Caesar and Cleopatra, Veterans, Bingo, No Man's Land, Half-Life 1977, The Best of Friends 1988. *Productions include:* Shakespeare, Restoration drama, The Importance of Being Earnest, The School for Scandal, The Three Sisters, Dear Brutus, The Circle, The Heiress, The Lady's not for Burning, Ivanov. *Plays directed include:* A Day by the Sea, The Chalk Garden, Nude with Violin, Five Finger Exercise, The Last Joke, Big Fish, Little Fish, School for Scandal, Halfway Up the Tree, Private Lives, The Constant Wife. *Films played in include:* The Barretts of Wimpole Street, St. Joan, Julius Caesar, Richard III, Becket, The Loved One, Chimes at Midnight, Mister Sebastian, The Charge of the Light Brigade, The Tempest, Eagle in a Cage, Lost Horizon, 11 Harrowhouse, Murder on the Orient Express, Providence, Joseph Andrews, Caligula, Portrait of the Artist as a Young Man, Aces High 1976, Romeo and Juliet (TV) 1978, Richard II (TV) 1978, Le Chef d'orchestre 1980, The Formula 1980, Brideshead Revisited (TV) 1980, Arthur 1981, Priest of Love 1981, Sphinx 1981, Richard Wagner 1982, Inside the Third Reich 1982, The Shooting Party 1984, Plenty 1985, The Whistle Blower 1985, Appointment with Death 1987, Arthur 2: On the Rocks 1988, Loser Takes All, Summer's Lease (TV), Getting It Right 1989, Prospero's Books, Shining Through, The Power of One 1991, Swan Song 1993, Portrait of a Lady 1996, Shine, Hamlet. *Operas directed:* The Trojans (Berlioz), A Midsummer Night's Dream (Britten); Shakespeare recital: Ages of Man in Europe, America and Australasia; Hon. LL.D. (St. Andrews) 1950; Hon. D.Litt. (Oxford) 1953, (London) 1977; Best Supporting Actor (Arthur) 1981, Soc. of Film and TV Arts 1974, Companion, Légion d'honneur. *Publications:* Early Stages 1938, Stage Directions 1963, 1964, Distinguished Company 1972, An Actor and his Time (with John Miller and John Powell) (autobiog.) 1979, Backward Glances (essays) 1989, Shakespeare—Hit or Miss 1991, Notes from the Gods 1994. *Leisure interests:* reading, music. *Address:* South Pavilion, Wotton Underwood, Aylesbury HP18 0SB, England.

GIELGUD, Maina Julia Goroon; British ballet director; b. 14 Jan. 1945, London; d. of late Lewis Gielgud and of Elisabeth Grussner; with Cuevas Co. and Roland Petit Co. until 1963; Grande Ballet Classique de France 1963–67; Béjart Co. 1967–71; Berlin 1971; London Festival Ballet 1972–76; ballerina, Sadler's Wells Royal Ballet 1976–78; freelance ballerina and guest artist 1978–82; rehearsal dir. London City Ballet 1982; Artistic Dir. The Australian Ballet 1983–96; Ballet Dir. Royal Danish Ballet 1997–; Hon. A.O. 1991. *Address:* Royal Danish Ballet, The Royal Theatre, P.O. Box 2185, 1017 Copenhagen K, Denmark; Stirling Court, 3 Marshall Street, London, W1V 1LQ, England. *Telephone:* 33-69-65-60 (Denmark); 0171-734 6612 (England). *Fax:* 33-69-65-75 (Denmark).

GIENOW, Herbert Hans Walter, DR.JUR.; German business executive; b. 13 March 1926, Hamburg; s. of Günther and Margarethe Gienow; m. Imina Brons 1954; one s. one d.; ed. Hamburg Univ.; Head Clerk Deutsche Warentreuhand AG, mem. Bd. of Man. 1959; mem. Hamburg Bar; chartered accountant 1961; mem. Bd. of Man. Klöckner-Werke AG 1962, Chair. Exec. Bd. 1974–91; Pres. ALSTOM Germany 1991–98; Chair. Supervisory Bd. ALSTOM GmbH, Maschinenfabrik Niehoff GmbH; Chair. Consultative Cttee. Deutsche Bank AG, Essen; mem. Supervisory Bd. ALSTOM LBH GmbH, ASL Aircraft Services Lemwerder. *Leisure interests;* books, sailing, model soldiers. *Address:* GEC ALSTHOM N.V., Bottroper Str. 398, 45356 Essen (Office); Am Adels 7, 40883 Ratingen, Germany (Home). *Telephone:* (0201) 8667-631 (Office).

GIEREK, Edward; Polish politician; b. 6 Jan. 1913, Porąbka, Będzin district; m. Stanisława Gierek; two s.; ed. Acad. of Mining and Metallurgy, Cracow; lived in France 1923–34 and in Belgium 1937–48; one of the organizers and leaders of Belgian resistance movement during German occupation in World War II; after the war Chair. Nat. Council of Poles in Belgium and one of the organizers of the PPR and Union of Polish Patriots in Belgium; returned to Poland 1948; mem. Polish United Workers' Party (PZPR) 1948–81, Sec. Voivodship Cttee. Katowice 1949–54, First Sec. 1957–70; mem. Cen. Cttee. 1954–80, Head Dept. of Heavy Industry, Cen. Cttee. 1954–56, mem. Politburo Cen. Cttee. 1956–80, Sec. Cen. Cttee. 1956–64, First Sec. Cen. Cttee. 1970–80; Deputy to Sejm (Parl.) 1952–80; mem. Presidium All-Polish Cttee. of Nat. Unity Front 1971–80; mem. Council of State 1976–80; internee Dec. 1981, released Dec. 1982; Order of Banner of Labour First Class, Order of Builders of People's Poland, Order of Lenin 1973, Order of Great Yugoslav Star 1973, Frédéric Joliot-Curie Gold Medal 1974, José Marti Nat. Order (Cuba) 1975, Great Ribbon of Leopold's Order with Swords (Belgium) 1977, Great Cross of Order Polonia Restituta 1978, Order of October Revolution (U.S.S.R.) 1978, Order of Old Planina with Ribbon (Bulgaria) 1979, Grand Croix Légion d'honneur, and other decorations. *Publications:* Przerwana dekada 1990, Replika 1990. *Leisure interests:* poetry, football. *Address:* Ustronie Śląskie, Poland.

GIEROWSKI, Stefan; Polish painter; b. 21 May 1925, Częstochowa; s. of Józef Gierowski and Stefania (Wasilewska) Gierowska; m. Anna Golka 1951; one s. one d.; ed. Acad. of Fine Arts, Cracow; Docent, Acad. of Fine Arts, Warsaw, Dean of Painting Dept. 1975–80, Extraordinary Prof. 1976–; mem. Polish Asscn. of Plastic Artists, Sec.-Gen. 1957–59, Pres. of Painting Section 1959–61, 1963–66; Knight's and Officer's Cross, Order of Polonia Restituta; Silver Medal, Third Festival of Fine Arts, Warsaw 1978, Prize of Chair. Council of Ministers (1st class) 1979, Jan Cybis Prize 1980. *One-man shows:* Warsaw 1955, 1957, 1960, 1967, 1972, 1974, 1978, 1986, 1992, K. Pułaski Museum, Warka 1973, Galerie la Cloche, Paris 1961, 1965, Auverrier Galerie Numaga, Neuchâtel 1967, 1976, 1987, Galerie Simone Von Dormoel, Brussels 1977, Teatr Studio, Warsaw 1983, Cracow 1991; exhibited in group shows: Contemporary Art Exhbn., Warsaw 1957, Carnegie Inst., Pittsburgh 1964, 1967, Biennale Int. d'arte, San Marino 1965, 34th Biennale, Venice 1968, Triennale of India, New Delhi 1968, Mexico 1975, Lisbon 1976, Madrid 1977, Naples 1986, Kleinjassen 1987, Apeldoorn 1989, Vienna 1992, Berlin 1992. *Address:* ul. Gagarina 15 m. 97, 00-753 Warsaw, Poland. *Telephone:* 41 16 33.

GIERSCH, Herbert, DR.RER.POL.; German economist; b. 11 May 1921, Reichenbach; s. of Hermann and Helene (née Kleinert) Giersch; m. Dr. Friederike Koppelmann 1949; two s. one d.; ed. Univs. of Breslau, Kiel and Münster; Asst. to Prof. Walther Hoffmann, Univ. of Münster 1947–48; British Council Fellow, London School of Econs. 1948–49; Admin., Econs. Directorate, OEEC 1950–51; Lecturer Univ. of Münster 1951–55; Counsellor and Head of Div., Trade and Finance Directorate, OEEC 1953–54; Prof. of Econs. Saar Univ., Saarbrücken 1955–69; Visiting Prof. of Econs., Yale Univ. 1962–63, Dean Acheson Visiting Prof. at Yale Univ. 1977–78; Prof. of Econs., Univ. of Kiel, and Pres. Inst. of World Econs., Kiel 1969–89; Chair. Asscn. of German Econ. Research Insts. 1970–82; Pres. Assoc. of European Business Cycle Research Insts. 1974–78; mem Advisory Council, Fed. Ministry of Econs. 1960–; founding mem. German Council of Econ. Advisers 1964–70, Council and Exec. Comm. Int. Econ. Asscn. 1970–82, Treas. 1974–83, Hon. Pres. 1983–; Hon. mem. American Econ. Asscn.; Hon. Fellow, London School of Econs.; Corresp. Fellow, British Acad. 1983; Foreign mem. Royal Swedish Acad. of Eng. Sciences, Stockholm 1987; Dr. h.c. (Erlangen-Nürnberg) 1977, (Basle) 1984, (Saarbrücken) 1993; Grosses Bundesverdienstkreuz, mit Stern und Schulterband 1995, mem. Order of Merit for Sciences and Arts; Ludwig Erhard Award; Paolo Baffi Int. Prize for Econs. 1989; Orden pour le Mérite für Wissenschaften und Künste; Prognos Preis (Basle) 1993. *Publications:* Allgemeine Wirtschaftspolitik, Vol. I Grundlagen 1960, Vol. II Konjunktur- und Wachstumspolitik 1977, Kontroverse Fragen der Wirtschaftspolitik 1971, Economic Policy for the European Community (co-author) 1974, Im Brennpunkt: Wirtschaftspolitik. Kritische Beiträge von 1967–77, 1978, Perspectives on the World Economy 1986, Gegen Europessimismus. Kritische Beiträge von 1977–85 1986, Offener Rat. Kolumnen aus der Wirtschaftswoche 1986, The World Economy in Perspective: Essays on International Trade and European Integration 1991, The Fading Miracle: Four Decades of Market Economy in Germany (co-author) 1992, Openness for Prosperity, Essays in World Economics 1993, Marktwirtschaftliche Perspektiven für Europa. Das Licht im Tunnel 1993. *Address:* Preusserstrasse 17–19, 24105 Kiel, Germany (Home). *Telephone:* 0431/561872 (Home). *Fax:* 0431/8814-500.

GIESBERT, Franz-Olivier; French journalist and author; b. 18 Jan. 1949, Wilmington, Del., U.S.A.; s. of Frederick Giesbert and Marie Allain; m. Christine Fontaine 1974; two s. one d.; journalist at Le Nouvel Observateur 1971, sr. corresp. in Washington 1980, Political Ed. 1981, Ed.-in-Chief 1985–88; Ed.-in-Chief Le Figaro 1988–, Figaro Magazine 1997–, mem. Editorial Bd. Le Figaro 1993–, Figaro Magazine 1997–; presenter 'le Gai savoir' TV programme, Paris Première cable channel 1997–; mem. jury Prix Théophraste Renaudot 1998–; Aujourd'hui Best Essay Prize 1975, Prix Gutenberg 1987, Prix Pierre de Monaco 1997. *Publications:* François Mitterrand ou la tentation de l'Histoire (essay) 1977, Monsieur Adrien (novel) 1982, Jacques Chirac (biography) 1987, le Président 1990, l'Affreux 1992 (Grand Prix du Roman de l'Académie Française 1992), la Fin d'une Époque 1993, la Souille (William the Conqueror and Interallie Prize), le Vieil homme et la Mort 1996, François Mitterrand, une vie 1996, Le Sieur Dieu 1998. *Address:* Le Figaro, 37 rue du Louvre, 75002 Paris, France. *Telephone:* (1) 42-21-62-00.

GIESKE, Friedhelm, D.JUR.; German business executive; b. 12 Jan. 1928, Schwege/Osnabrück; began career with RWE AG 1953, Deputy mem. Man. Bd. 1968, mem. Man. Bd. (Finance) 1972, Bd. Spokesman 1988, Chair. Man. Bd. 1989–94; mem. Supervisory Bd. ALLIANZ AG, Munich, Dresdner Bank AG, Frankfurt, Karstadt AG, Essen, MAN AG, Munich, National-Bank, Essen, RWEAG, Essen, Thyssen AG, Duisburg.

GIEYSZTOR, Aleksander; Polish historian; b. 17 July 1916, Moscow; s. of Alexander and Barbara (Popiel) Gieysztor; m. Irena Czarnecka 1938; one s. (died 1989) one d.; ed. Warsaw Univ.; lecturer, Asst. Prof. Warsaw Univ. 1945–49, Prof. 1949–86, Prof. Emer. 1986–, Dir. of Research into origins of Polish State 1949–53, Pro-Rector 1956–59, Dir. Historical Inst. 1955–75; Dir. Royal Castle Warsaw 1980–91, Chair. Scientific Council 1991–; host and leader, Round Table debates; mem. Bureau Int. Cttee. of Historical Sciences 1965– (Vice-Pres. 1975–80, Pres. 1980–85); Assoc. Prof. Coll. de France 1968; Corresp. Fellow, Medieval Acad. of America 1968–; Assoc.

Royal Historical Soc. 1981–; Visiting Fellow, All Souls Coll., Oxford 1968–69; Visiting Prof., Harvard Univ. 1977–78; Chair. Scientific Council of Historical Inst., Polish Acad. of Sciences (P.A.N.) 1972–80, Nat. Cttee. ICOM 1981–89; mem. Comité Int. de Paléographie; mem. Polish Acad. of Sciences 1972– (Pres. 1980–83, 1990–92), Warsaw Learned Soc. 1952– (Pres. 1986–89), Koninklijke Akad. voor Wetenschappen, Brussels 1972, Acad. Royale de Belgique 1976, Acad. Belles Lettres 1981, Royal Swedish Acad. 1982, British Acad. 1985, Hungarian Acad. 1989, Academia Europaea, Ukrainian Acad. 1991; Dr. h.c. (Aix-Marseille, Bordeaux, Paris IV-Sorbonne, Budapest, Moscow, Oxford, Poznań, Cracow, Lublin Catholic Univs.); State Prize (1st class) 1953, 1988; Silver Cross Virtuti Militari, Kt. Commdr's. Cross, Order of Polonia Restituta, Officier, Légion d'honneur, Commdr. Ordre de Mérite, Commdr., Ordine al Merito della Repubblica Italiana 1975, Kt. White Eagle Order 1994, Nicolaus Copernicus Medal, Grosses Verdienstkreuz (F.R.G.) 1988. *Publications include:* Władza Karola Wielkiego (Rule of Charles the Great) 1938, Genesis of the Crusades 1950, History of Poland (co-author) 1968, Zarys dziejów pisma łacińskiego (Outline of the History of the Latin Alphabet) 1973, Thousand Years of Poland (with S. Herbst and B. Leśnodorski) 1976, Mitologia Słowiańska (Slav Mythology) 1982, numerous articles on medieval history. *Address:* ul. Wilcza 8 m. 20, 00-532 Warsaw, Poland. *Telephone:* (22) 628 41 38. *Fax:* (22) 635 04 98.

GIFFEN, John A., M.B.A.; Canadian business executive; b. 17 Dec. 1938, Ingersoll, Ont.; s. of John Giffen and Kathleen Marion (née McQuinn) Giffen; m. Joan E. Rothwell 1962; one s. two d.; ed. Univ. of Windsor; plant foreman, Hiram Walker 1962, Project Engineer 1965, Div. Supt. 1972, Inventory Man. 1973, N. American Distribution Man. 1977, Asst. to Pres. 1979, Vice Pres. Worldwide Production 1980; Chair. Corby Distilleries Ltd. 1992– (Dir. 1980–); Regional Chair.—The Americas, Allied-Lyons 1992–93; Chair., C.E.O. The Hiram Walker Group 1991–92; Man. Dir. Hiram Walker-Allied Vintners 1989–91; Pres. HW-G & W Ltd. 1989–92; Deputy Chair. 1992–93; Chair., C.E.O. Hiram Walker-Allied Vintners (Canada) Ltd. 1988–89; Pres. Hiram Walker & Sons Ltd. 1987–88; Allied-Lyons PLC 1988–93, HW-G & W Ltd. 1982–86, 1988–93; Dir. Hallmark Technologies Inc. 1995–; mem. of Windsor Advisory Bd. Royal Trustco, of Canadian-U.K. Cttee., Canadian Chamber of Commerce 1983–91; Dir. and Vice-Pres., Windsor Chamber of Commerce 1979–83; Gov. Metropolitan Gen. Hosp., Windsor 1979–85; Dir. Inst. of Canadian-American Studies 1983–86. *Leisure interests:* golf, curling. *Address:* Walkerville, P.O. Box 2518, Ont., Canada.

GIFFORD, Charles Henry, M.A., F.B.A.; British professor of English; b. 17 June 1913, Blackheath, London; s. of Walter Stanley Gifford and Constance Lena Gifford (née Henry); m. Mary Rosamond van Ingen 1938; one s. one d.; ed. Harrow School and Christ Church, Oxford; war service in R.A.C. (Palestine and N.W. Europe) 1940–46; on teaching staff, English Dept., Univ. of Bristol 1946–76, Prof. of Modern English Literature 1963, Winterstoke Prof. of English 1967, Prof. of English and Comparative Literature 1975, Emer. Prof. 1976–; Ed. Cambridge Studies in Russian Literature 1980–85; Clark Lecturer, Trinity Coll. Cambridge 1985. *Publications:* The Novel in Russia 1964, Comparative Literature 1969, Pasternak: A Critical Study 1977, Tolstoy (Past Masters) 1982, Poetry in a Divided World (1985 Clark Lectures) 1986. *Address:* 10 Hyland Grove, Bristol, BS9 3NR, England.

GIFFORD, Michael Brian, B.SC. (ECON.); British business executive; b. 9 Jan. 1936; s. of Kenneth Gifford and Maude Palmer; m. 2nd Asa M. Lundin; one s. one d. (and one s. one d. by previous m.); m. 3rd Nancy Baytos; ed. London School of Econs.; joined Leo Computers (later part of ICL) 1960; Man. Dir. ICL (Pacific) 1973–75; Chief Exec. Cadbury Schweppes Australia 1975–78; Finance Dir. Cadbury Schweppes PLC 1978–83; Man. Dir. and Chief Exec. Rank Org. 1983–96; Dir. Fuji Xerox 1984–96, English China Clays PLC 1992–, The Gillette Co. 1993–. *Address:* 11216 Tamiami Trail N., Suite 334, Naples, FL 33410, U.S.A.

GILBERT, Kenneth Albert, O.C., D.MUS.; Canadian harpsichordist; b. 16 Dec. 1931, Montreal; s. of Albert George Gilbert and Reta M. (Welch); ed. Conservatoire de Musique, Montreal and Conservatoire de Paris; Prof. Conservatoire de Musique, Montreal 1965–72; Assoc. Prof. Laval Univ. 1970–76; Guest Prof. Royal Antwerp Conservatory 1971–73; Dir. Early Music Dept. Conservatoire de Strasbourg 1981–85; Prof. Staatliche Hochschule für Musik, Stuttgart 1981–89, Hochschule Mozarteum, Salzburg 1984–, Paris Conservatoire 1988–96; Instructor at other music acads., summer schools etc.; Fellow, Canada Council 1968, 1974, Calouste Gulbenkian Foundation 1971; has recorded complete harpsichord works of Couperin, Scarlatti and Rameau, suites and partitas of J. S. Bach, Well-tempered clavier of Bach and concertos for 2, 3, 4 harpsichords by Bach; Officier Ordre des Arts et des Lettres; *Publications:* editions of complete harpsichord works of Couperin, Scarlatti and Rameau and Bach's Goldberg Variations.

GILBERT, Lewis, C.B.E.; British film director; b. 6 March 1920, London; m. Hylda Henrietta Tafler; two s.; entered films as child actor; joined R.A.F. and became Asst. Dir. to William Keighley on Target for Today, etc. 1939; joined G.B. Instructional (G.B.I.) 1944, for whom wrote and dir. The Ten Year Plan, Sailors Do Care, Arctic Harvest, etc. 1946–47; wrote and dir. The Little Ballerina 1947–48, worked on series of documentaries for G.B.I.; Producer/ Dir. Int. Realist 1948; numerous awards including Special Evening Standard Film Award 1996. *Films directed include:* The Little Ballerina 1947, Once a Sinner 1950, Scarlet Thread 1951, There is Another Sun 1951, Time Gentlemen Please 1952, Emergency Call 1952, Cosh Boy, Johnny on the Run 1953, Albert R.N. 1953, The Good Die Young 1954, The Sea Shall Not Have Them 1954, Cast a Dark Shadow 1955, Reach for the Sky 1956, The Admirable Crichton 1957, Carve Her Name With Pride 1957, A Cry From the Streets 1958, Ferry to Hong Kong 1959, Sink the Bismarck 1960, Light Up The Sky 1960, The Greengage Summer 1961, H.M.S. Defiant 1962, The Seventh Dawn 1964, Alfie 1966, You Only Live Twice 1967, Paul and Michelle (also producer) 1973, Seven Men at Daybreak 1975, Seven Nights in Japan 1976, The Spy Who Loved Me 1977, Moonraker 1978, Dubai (also producer), Educating Rita 1982, Shirley Valentine (also producer) 1989, Stepping Out 1991, Haunted; co-produced Spare The Rod 1959–60. *Address:* 19 blvd. de Suisse, Monaco.

GILBERT, Sir Martin (John), Kt., C.B.E., M.A., F.R.S.L.; British historian; b. 25 Oct. 1936; s. of Peter and Miriam Gilbert; m. 1st Helen Robinson 1963; one d.; m. 2nd Susan Sacher; two s.; ed. Highgate School and Magdalen Coll., Oxford; Sr. Research Fellow, St. Antony's Coll., Oxford 1960–62, Fellow, Merton Coll., Oxford 1962–; Visiting Prof. Univ. of S. Carolina 1965, Tel-Aviv 1979, Hebrew Univ. of Jerusalem 1980–; official biographer of Sir Winston Churchill 1968–; Gov., Hebrew Univ. of Jerusalem 1978–; Non-Governmental Rep. UN Commn. on Human Rights, Geneva 1987, 1988; mem. Prime Minister's del. to Israel, Gaza and Jordan 1995, to U.S.A. 1995; has lectured on historical subjects throughout Europe and U.S.A.; adviser to BBC and ITV for various documentaries; script designer and co-author, Genocide (Acad. Award for best documentary feature film) 1981; presenter History Channel 1996–; Recent History Corresp. Sunday Times 1967; Hon. D.Litt. (Westminster Coll., Fulton, Mo.) 1981. *Publications:* The Appeasers (with R. Gott) 1963, Britain and Germany between the Wars 1964, The European Powers 1900–1945 1965, Plough My Own Furrow: The Life of Lord Allen of Hurtwood 1965, Servant of India: A Study of Imperial Rule 1905–1910 1966, The Roots of Appeasement 1966, Recent History Atlas 1860–1960 1966, Winston Churchill 1966, British History Atlas 1968, American History Atlas 1968, Jewish History Atlas 1969, First World War Atlas 1970, Winston S. Churchill, Vol. III, 1914–16 1971, companion vol. 1973, Russian History Atlas 1972, Sir Horace Rumbold: Portrait of a Diplomat 1973, Churchill: a photographic portrait 1974, The Arab-Israeli Conflict: its history in maps 1974, Winston S. Churchill, Vol. IV, 1917–22 1975, companion vol. 1977, The Jews in Arab Lands: their history in maps 1975, Winston S. Churchill, Vol. V, 1922–39, 1976, companion vols. 1980, 1981, 1982, The Jews of Russia: Illustrated History Atlas 1976, Jerusalem Illustrated History Atlas 1977, Exile and Return: The Emergence of Jewish Statehood 1978, Children's Illustrated Bible Atlas 1979, Final Journey, the Fate of the Jews of Nazi Europe 1979, Auschwitz and the Allies 1981, Atlas of the Holocaust 1982, Winston S. Churchill, Vol. VI, 1939–41 1983, The Jews of Hope: A study of the Crisis of Soviet Jewry 1984, Jerusalem: Rebirth of a City 1985, Shcharansky: Hero of our Time 1986, Winston S. Churchill, Vol. VII, 1941–45 1986, The Holocaust, The Jewish Tragedy 1986, Winston Churchill, Vol. VIII 1945–65 1988, Second World War 1989, Churchill, A Life 1991, The Churchill War Papers: At the Admiralty (ed.), Atlas of British Charities 1993, In Search of Churchill; A Historian's Journey 1994, The First World War: A Complete History 1994, The Churchill War Papers: 'Never Surrender' (ed.) 1995, The Day the War Ended 1995, Jerusalem in the 20th Century 1996, The Boys, Triumph over Adversity 1996, A History of the World in the Twentieth Century (Vol. I 1900–1933) 1997, (Vol. II 1933–51) 1998, Holocaust Journey: Travelling in Search of the Past 1997, Israel, A History 1998, Winston Churchill and Emery Reeves; Correspondence 1998. *Leisure interest:* travel. *Address:* Merton College, Oxford, England.

GILBERT, Michael Francis, C.B.E., LL.B.; British writer and fmr. solicitor; b. 17 July 1912, Billinghay, Lincs.; s. of Bernard Gilbert and Berwyn Mina Cuthbert; m. Roberta Mary Marsden 1947; two s. five d.; ed. Blundells School, Univ. Coll., London; Asst. Master Salisbury Cathedral School 1931–38; with Royal Horse Artillery 1938–46; partner Trowers & Hamline 1950–82; legal adviser to Govt. of Bahrain 1960; f. mem. Crime Writers' Asscn.; mem. Arts Council Cttee. on Public Lending Right 1968, Royal Literary Fund 1969, Council of Society of Authors 1975; Grand Master Mystery Writers of America 1987; Crime Writers' Asscn. Diamond Dagger 1994. *Publications:* novels: Close Quarters 1947, They Never Looked Inside 1948, The Doors Open 1949, Smallbone Deceased 1950, Death has Deep Roots 1951, Death in Captivity 1952, Fear to Tread 1953, Sky High 1955, Be Shot for Sixpence 1956, The Tichborne Claimant 1957, Blood and Judgement 1958, After the Fine Weather 1963, The Crack in the Tea Cup 1965, The Dust and the Heat 1967, The Etruscan Net 1969, The Body of a Girl 1972, The Ninety Second Tiger 1973, Flast Point 1974, The Night of the Twelfth 1976, The Empty House 1978, Death of a Favourite Girl 1980, The Final Throw 1983, The Black Seraphim 1983, The Long Journey Home 1985, Trouble 1987, Paint Gold and Blood 1989, The Queen against Karl Mullen 1991, Roller Coaster 1993, Ring of Terror 1995, Into Battle 1997, Over and Out 1999; plays: A Clean Kill, The Bargain, Windfall, The Shot in Question; short stories: Game Without Rules 1967, Stay of Execution 1971, Petrella at Q 1977, Mr Calder and Mr Behrens 1982, Young Petrella 1988, Anything for a Quiet Life 1990; Crime in Good Company 1959 (ed.), The Oxford Book of Legal Anecdotes 1986 (ed.), The Fraudsters 1988 (ed.), Prep School 1991 (ed.), also radio and TV plays. *Leisure interests:* bridge, walking. *Address:* The Old Rectory, Luddesdown, Gravesend, Kent, DA13 0XE, England.

GILBERT, Stephen; British painter and sculptor; b. 15 Jan. 1910, Fife, Scotland; s. of F. G. W. and Cicely (née Kellett) Gilbert; m. Jocelyn Chewett

1935 (died 1979); one s. one d.; ed. Univ. Coll. School and Slade School of Art, London; Group Cobra 1948–51; one-man exhbns. in London, Dublin, Paris, Amsterdam, Copenhagen, Sheffield, Hull, Cardiff and The Hague 1938–90; has participated in many group exhbns. in Paris and elsewhere; work exhibited in Tate Gallery, London, and museums in Denmark, Holland, U.S.A., Venezuela; public works for London Co. Council 1965, Chappell of Bond St. 1966, British Steel, London 1971; Gulbenkian Foundation Award 1962; Tokyo Biennale First Award 1962; Welsh Arts Council Award for Sculpture 1966. *Address:* 13 rue Rambuteau, 75004 Paris; 7 Impasse du Rouet, 75014 Paris, France. *Telephone:* (1) 48-87-99-39; (1) 45-42-69-42.

GILBERT, Walter, PH.D.; American molecular biologist; b. 21 March 1932, Boston, Mass.; s. of Richard V. Gilbert and Emma (née Cohen) Gilbert; m. Celia Stone 1953; one s. one d.; ed. Harvard and Cambridge Univs.; Nat. Science Foundation Postdoctoral Fellow, Harvard 1957–58, lecturer in physics 1958–59, Asst. Prof. of Physics 1959–64, Assoc. Prof. of Biophysics 1964–68, Prof. of Biochemistry 1968–72; American Cancer Soc. Prof. of Molecular Biology 1972–81, Prof. of Biology 1985–86; H. H. Timken Prof. of Science 1986–87; Carl M. Loeb Univ. Prof. 1987–, Chair. Dept. of Cellular and Developmental Biology 1987–93; Chair. Scientific Bd., Biogen NV 1978–83, Co-Chair. Supervisory Bd. 1979–81, Chair. Supervisory Bd. and C.E.O. 1981–84; Vice-Chair. Bd. of Dirs., Myriad Genetics, Inc. 1992–; Chair. Bd. of Dirs., NetGenics Inc. 1996–; Foreign mem. Royal Soc.; mem. N.A.S., American Physical Soc., American Soc. of Biological Chemists, American Acad. of Arts and Sciences; Guggenheim Fellowship, Paris 1968–69; V. D. Mattia Lectureship, Roche Inst. of Molecular Biology 1976; Smith, Kline and French Lecturer, Univ. of Calif. at Berkeley 1977; Hon. D.Sc. (Univ. of Chicago, Columbia Univ.) 1978, (Univ. of Rochester) 1979, (Yeshiva Univ.) 1981; U.S. Steel Foundation Award in Molecular Biology (N.A.S.) 1968; Ledlie Prize, Harvard Univ. (with M. Ptashne) 1969; Warren Triennial Prize, Mass. Gen. Hosp. (with S. Benzer, q.v.) 1977; Louis and Bert Freedman Award, New York Acad. of Sciences 1977; Prix Charles-Léopold Mayer, Acad. des Sciences, Inst. de France (with M. Ptashne and E. Witkin) 1977; Harrison Howe Award of the Rochester br. of the American Chem. Soc. 1978; Louisa Gross Horwitz Prize, Columbia Univ. (with F. Sanger, q.v.) 1979; Gairdner Foundation Annual Award 1979; Albert Lasker Basic Medical Research Award (with F. Sanger) 1979; Prize for Biochemical Analysis, German Soc. for Clinical Chem. (with A. M. Maxam, F. Sanger and A. R. Coulsen) 1980; Sober Award, American Soc. of Biological Chemists 1980; Nobel Prize for Chemistry 1980 with F. Sanger (q.v.) and P. Berg (q.v.) for work on deoxyribonucleic acid (DNA). *Address:* Biological Laboratories, 16 Divinity Avenue, Cambridge, MA 02138, U.S.A. *Telephone:* 617-495-0760 (Office). *Fax:* (617) 496-4313.

GILDRED, Theodore Edmonds, B.A.; American diplomatist; b. 18 Oct. 1935, Mexico City; s. of Theodore Gildred and Maxine Edmonds; m. 1st Suzanne Gail Green (divorced 1975); three s. one d.; m. 2nd Stephanie Ann Moscini 1978 (divorced 1992); one s. one d.; ed. Stanford Univ., Univ. of Paris (Sorbonne), France and Univ. of Heidelberg, Fed. Repub. of Germany; served with US Army 1955–57, US Air Force 1957–69; Project Supervisor, Investors Marine, Inc., Newport Beach, Calif. 1961; owner, Pres. and C.E.O. Costa Pacifica, Inc., Newport Beach, Calif. 1961–65; Admin. Grupo Lindavista, S.A., Mexico City 1965–68; owner, Pres. and C.E.O. The Lomas Santa Fe Group, Solana Beach, Calif. 1968–86; Chair. Bd. of Dirs., Torrey Pines Bank, Solana Beach 1979–86, Inst. of Americas, La Jolla, Calif. 1984–86; Amb. to Argentina 1986–89; mem. Univ. of Calif. at San Diego Center for US-Mexican Studies; f. Chair. Bd. of Govs., Inst. of Americas; trustee and Pres. Gildred Foundation; mem. Bd. Dirs. Security Pacific Nat. Bank, Int. Advisory Bd., N. American Airlines, numerous other orgs.; numerous awards. *Address:* The Lomas Santa Fe Group, 265 Santa Helena, Suite 200, Solana Beach, CA 92075 (Office); 16056 El Camino Real Rancho, Santa Fe, CA 92067, U.S.A. (Home)

GILES, Alan James, M.A., M.S.; British business executive; b. 4 June 1954, Dorchester, Dorset; m. Gillian Rosser 1978; two d.; ed. Blandford School, Dorset, Merton Coll. Oxford, Stanford Univ., U.S.A.; buyer, Boots the Chemists 1975–78, Promotions Man. 1978–80, Asst. Merchandise Controller 1980–82; Retail Devt. Man., W.H. Smith 1982–85, Merchandise Controller (Books) 1985–88, Operations & Devt. Dir., Do It All 1988–92; Man. Dir. Waterstone's Booksellers 1992–; Jt. Chief Exec. HMV Media Group PLC 1998–. *Address:* Waterstone's, Capital Court, Capital Interchange Way, Brentford, Middx., TW8 0EX, England. *Telephone:* 0181-742 3800. *Fax:* 0181-742 0216.

GILIOMEE, Hermann Buhr, M.A., D.PHIL.; South African university professor; b. 4 April 1938, Sterkstroom; s. of Gerhardus Adriaan Giliomee and Catherine Geza Giliomee; m. Annette van Coller 1965; two d.; ed. Porterville High School and Univ. of Stellenbosch; lecturer in History, Univ. of Stellenbosch 1967–83; Prof. of Political Studies Univ. of Cape Town 1983–98; recipient of Fellowships to Yale Univ. 1977–78, Cambridge Univ. 1982–83, Woodrow Wilson Center for Int. Scholars, Washington, DC 1992–93; Pres. South African Inst. of Race Relations 1995–97; political columnist. *Publications:* The Shaping of South African Society 1652–1820 1979, Ethnic Power Mobilized: Can South Africa Change? 1979, Afrikaner Political Thought 1750–1850 1983, Up Against the Fences: Poverty, Passes and Privilege 1985, From Apartheid to Nation-building 1990, The Bold Experiment: South Africa's New Democracy, The Awkward Embrace: Dominant-Party Rule and Democracy in Semi-Industrialized Countries 1998. *Leisure interest:* tennis. *Address:* 5 Dennerand, Stellenbosch 7600, South Africa. *Telephone:* 021-8832964. *Fax:* 021-8878026.

GILL, Sir Anthony (Keith), Kt., F.ENG., B.SC.(ENG.), F.C.G.I., F.I.MECH.E.; British business executive; b. 1 April 1930, Colchester; s. of Frederick W. Gill and Ellen Gill; m. Phyllis Cook 1953; one s. two d.; ed. Colchester High School and Imperial Coll. London; Nat. Service REME 1954–56; Production Engineer, Bryce Berger Ltd. 1956, Dir. 1960, Gen. Man. 1965; Dir. Lucas CAV Ltd. 1967; Gen. Man. Fuel Injection Equipment 1972, Gen. Man. 1974; Dir. Joseph Lucas Ltd. 1974, Div. Man. Dir. 1978; Dir. Lucas Industries PLC 1978, Jt. Group Man. Dir. 1980, Group Man. Dir. 1984–87, Deputy Chair. 1986–87, Chair. 1987–94 and C.E.O. 1987–94; Pres. Inst. of Production Eng. 1985–86; Chair. London Docklands Light Railway 1994–99; mem. Council I. Mech. E. 1986–91, Advisory Council on Science and Tech. 1985–91; Chair. Educ. and Training Comm. 1988–91, Tarmac PLC 1992–; Non-Exec. Dir. Post Office 1989–91, Nat. Power PLC 1990–98; mem. Eng. Council (Deputy Chair. 1994–96); Chair. Teaching Co. Scheme 1990–96; Pro-Chancellor Cranfield Univ. 1991–; mem. Nat. Training Task Force 1991–94; Vice-Pres. Inst. of Man. 1992 (Chair. Council 1996–99), Pres. 1998–99; Hon. F.I.E.E.; Hon. D.Eng. (Univ. of Birmingham) 1990; Hon. D.Sc. (Cranfield Univ.) 1991, (Southampton Univ.) 1992, (Warwick Univ.) 1992, Hon. D.Tech. (Coventry Univ.) 1992; Dr. h.c. (Sheffield Hallam Univ.) 1993. *Leisure interests:* music, boating. *Address:* The Point House, Astra Court, Hythe Marina Village, Hythe, Hants., SO45 6DZ, England. *Telephone:* (01703) 840165. *Fax:* (01703) 840175.

GILLAM, Sir Patrick, Kt., B.A.; British business executive; b. 15 April 1933, London; s. of the late Cyril B. Gillam and of Mary J. Gillam; m. Diana Echlin 1963; one s. one d.; ed. L.S.E.; Foreign Office 1956–57; joined British Petroleum (BP) 1957; Vice-Pres. BP North America Inc. 1971–74; Gen. Man. Supply Dept. 1974–78; Dir. BP Int. Ltd. 1978–82; Chair. BP Shipping Ltd. 1981–88, BP Minerals Int. Ltd. 1981–88; Man. Dir. BP Co. 1981–91, Chair. BP Africa Ltd. 1982–88, BP Coal Inc. 1988–90, BP Nutrition 1989–91, BP America 1989–91, BP Oil 1990–91; Chair. Booker Tate Ltd. 1991–93, Asda Group PLC 1991–96, Royal and Sun Alliance March 1997–; Deputy Chair. Standard Chartered Bank Africa PLC 1988–89, Standard Chartered Overseas Holdings Ltd. 1988–89, Standard Chartered Bank Aug.–Nov. 1988, Standard Chartered PLC 1991–92, Chair. Jan. 1993– (Dir. 1988–); Non-exec. Dir. Commercial Union PLC 1991–96; Chair. ICC (UK) 1989–98; mem. of Court of Govs., L.S.E. 1989–. *Leisure interest:* gardening. *Address:* Standard Chartered PLC, 1 Aldermanbury Square, London, EC2V 7SB, England. *Telephone:* 0171-280 7500.

GILLARD, Francis (Frank) George, C.B.E., B.SC., F.R.S.A.; British broadcasting and communications consultant; b. 1 Dec. 1908, Tiverton, Devon; s. of Francis Henry and Emily Jane Gillard; ed. St. Luke's Coll., Exeter; Schoolmaster 1931–41; BBC War Corresp. 1941–45; BBC W. Region Programme Dir. 1945–55; Chief Asst. Dir. of Sound Broadcasting 1955–56; Controller W. Region 1956–63; Dir. (later Man. Dir.) BBC Radio, also Dir. of Regions 1963–70; Gov. Wellington School, Somerset 1960–91, Chair. 1974–80; mem. Council, Educational Foundation for Visual Aids 1964–87, Chair. 1977–86; mem. Finance Cttee., Univ. of Exeter 1966–86; Consultant EMI Ltd. 1970–80, Corpn. for Public Broadcasting, U.S.A. 1970–80, Cttee. of Enquiry into ABC Australia 1979–81; Fellow Radio Acad. of G.B. 1996; Hon. LL.D. (Exeter); Hon. Citizen Creully, Normandy 1995. *Leisure interests:* country life, reading, travel. *Address:* Trevor House, Poole, Wellington, Somerset, TA21 9HN, England. *Telephone:* (01823) 662890.

GILLÈS, Daniel; Belgian writer; b. 1917, Bruges; m. Simone Lambinon 1948; one d.; ed. law studies; Prix Rossel (Belgium); Grand Prix de la critique littéraire (France) 1967, Prix Triennal du Roman. *Publications include:* Jetons de présence, Le coupon 1944, Les brouillards de Bruges, L'état de grâce, La termitière, Mort-la-douce, La rouille (stories), Le festival de Salzbourg, Nés pour mourir, La tache de sang, Le spectateur Brandebourgeois; biographies: Tolstoi, D. H. Lawrence ou le puritain scandaleux, Tchékhov. *Leisure interests:* travel, tennis, painting.

GILLES, Herbert Michael Joseph, K.ST.J., D.MED.SC., D.SC., M.D., F.R.C.P., F.F.P.H.M., D.T.M. & H.; British professor of tropical medicine; b. 10 Sept. 1921, Port Said, Egypt; s. of Joseph Gilles; m. 1st Wilhelmina Caruana 1955 (died 1972); three s. one d.; m. 2nd Mejra Kacic-Dimitri 1979; ed. St. Edward's Coll., Malta, Royal Univ. of Malta, Univ. of Oxford; mem. Scientific Staff MRC 1954–58; Sr. lecturer in Tropical Medicine Univ. of Ibadan, Nigeria 1959–61, Prof. 1962–65; Sr. lecturer in Tropical Medicine Univ. of Liverpool, England 1965–70, Prof. 1970–86, Emer. Prof. 1986–; Dean Liverpool School of Tropical Medicine 1978–83, Vice-Pres. 1991–; Visiting Prof. of Public Health, Univ. of Malta 1989–; Visiting Prof. of Int. Health, Royal Coll. of Surgeons in Ireland 1994–, of Tropical Medicine, Mahidol Univ. Bangkok 1994–; Pres. Royal Soc. of Tropical Medicine and Hygiene 1985–87; Consultant in Malariology, British Army 1972–86, in Tropical Medicine, R.A.F. and D.H.S.S. 1972–86; Rhodes Scholar (Malta) 1943; WHO Darling Foundation Medal and Prize 1989, Mary Kingsley Medal 1995. *Publications:* Management and Treatment of Tropical Diseases 1971, Pathology in the Tropics 1976, Tropical Medicine for Nurses 1979, Recent Advances in Tropical Medicine 1984, Human Antiparasitic Drugs 1985, Epidemiology and Control of Tropical Diseases 1986, Preventive Medicine for the Tropics 1990, Hookworm Infections 1991, Management of Severe and Complicated Malaria 1991, Essential Malariology 1993, Atlas of Tropical Medicine and Parasitology 1994. *Leisure interests:* swimming, music. *Address:* 3 Conyers Avenue, Birkdale, Southport, PR8 4SZ, Merseyside, England.

GILLESPIE, Charles Anthony, Jr., B.A.; American diplomatist and consultant; b. 22 March 1935, Long Beach, Calif.; s. of Charles A. Gillespie and Ann H. Gillespie; m. Vivian Havens 1958; one s. one d.; ed. Univ. of Calif. at Los Angeles, Maxwell School of Public Affairs (Syracuse Univ.) and Nat. War Coll. Washington, D.C.; entered foreign service 1965; served at embassies in Manila, Djakarta, Brussels, Mexico City and Managua, at U.S. Mission to NATO and at State Dept.; Amb. and Chief of Mission in Grenada, concurrently serving as Deputy Asst. Sec. of State for the Caribbean and Deputy for Operations, Bureau of Inter-American Affairs, State Dept. 1983–85; Amb. to Colombia 1985–88, to Chile 1988–91; Special Asst. to the Pres. and Sr. Dir., Latin America and the Caribbean, Nat. Security Council 1992–93; Dir. N. American Free Trade Agreement Task Force, State Dept. 1993–94; Sr. Co-ordinator, Summit of the Americas 1994, State Dept.; Sr. Assoc. The Forum for Int. Policy 1995–; mem. The Scowcroft Group 1995–. *Address:* 900 17th Street, N.W., Suite 500, Washington, DC 20006, U.S.A. *Telephone:* (202) 296-9312. *Fax:* (202) 296-9395.

GILLESPIE, Iain E., M.D., M.SC., F.R.C.S.; British professor of surgery; b. 4 Sept. 1931, Glasgow; s. of John Gillespie and Flora MacQuarie; m. Muriel McIntyre 1957; one s. one d.; ed. Hillhead High School, Glasgow and Univ. of Glasgow; various appts. Univs. of Glasgow and Sheffield 1953–70; nat. service R.A.M.C. 1954–56; U.S.P.H.S. Postdoctoral Fellow 1961; Prof. of Surgery, Univ. of Manchester and Hon. Consultant in Surgery to Manchester Royal Infirmary 1970–92; Dean, Manchester Medical School 1983–86; mem. Univ. Grants Cttee., Medical Subcttee. 1975–86; mem. Univs. and Polytechnics Grants Cttee., Medical Subcttee., Hong Kong 1984–89; Pres. Manchester Medical Soc. 1993–94; Rorer Prize for Gastroenterology 1962. *Publications:* articles in professional journals. *Leisure interests:* golf, reading, music. *Address:* 27 Athol Road, Bramhall, Cheshire, SK7 1BR, England (Home). *Telephone:* (0161) 439-2811 (Home).

GILLESPIE, Rhondda, B.MUS.; British concert pianist; b. 3 Aug. 1941, Sydney, Australia; d. of David Gillespie and Marie Gillespie; m. Denby Richards 1972; ed. N.S.W. Conservatorium with Alexander Sverjensky and in London with Louis Kentner and Denis Matthews; debut on Australian radio aged 8 1949; first public recital 1953; winner N.S.W. Concerto Competition, Sydney 1959; European debut in London with Tchaikovsky Piano Concerto 2 1960; since then has played with major orchestras throughout U.K., Netherlands, Germany, Scandinavia, Far East and U.S.A. and made many festival appearances. *Leisure interests:* golf, languages, exotic cooking. *Address:* 2 Princes Road, St. Leonards-on-Sea, East Sussex, TN37 6EL, England. *Telephone:* (01424) 715167. *Fax:* (01424) 712214.

GILLESPIE, Ronald James, PH.D., D.SC., F.R.S., F.R.S.C., F.R.S.C. (U.K.), F.C.I.C.; Canadian/British professor of chemistry; b. 21 Aug. 1924, London; s. of James A. Gillespie and Miriam Gillespie (née Kirk); m. Madge Ena Garner 1950; two d.; ed. London Univ.; Asst. Lecturer, Dept. of Chem., Univ. Coll. London 1948–50, Lecturer 1950–58; Commonwealth Fund Fellow, Brown Univ., R.I., U.S.A. 1953–54; Assoc. Prof., Dept. of Chem., McMaster Univ., Hamilton, Ont., Canada 1958–60, Prof. 1960–88, Prof. Emer. 1988–, Chair. Dept. of Chem. 1962–65; Professeur Associé, Univ. des Sciences et Techniques de Languedoc, Montpellier, France 1972–73; Visiting Prof. Univ. of Geneva, Switzerland 1976, of Göttingen, Fed. Rep. of Germany 1978; mem. Chem. Soc., American Chem. Soc.; Hon. LL.D. (Concordia) 1988, (Dalhousie) 1988, Dr. h.c. (Montpellier) 1991; Hon. D.Sc. (McMaster Univ.) 1993; numerous medals and awards. *Publications:* Molecular Geometry 1972, Chemistry (jtly.) 1986, 1989, The VSEPR Model of Molecular Geometry (with I. Hargittai) 1991, Atoms, Molecules and Reactions: An Introduction to Chemistry (jtly.) 1994; papers in scientific journals. *Leisure interests:* skiing, sailing. *Address:* Department of Chemistry, McMaster University, Hamilton, Ont., L8S 4M1; 150 Wilson Street West, Ancaster, Ont. L9G 4E7, Canada (Home). *Telephone:* (905) 525-9140, ext. 23307 (Office); (905) 648-8895 (Home). *Fax:* (905) 522-2509.

GILLETT, Sir Robin Danvers Penrose, Bt., G.B.E.; British company executive; b. 9 Nov. 1925, London; s. of Sir (Sydney) Harold Gillett, Bt., M.C. (Lord Mayor of London 1958–59), and Audrey Isobel Penrose Gillett (née Wardlaw); m. Elizabeth Marion Grace Findlay 1950 (died 1997); two s.; ed. Nautical Coll., Pangbourne; served Canadian Pacific Steamships 1943–60, Master Mariner 1951, Staff Commdr. 1957; Consultant, Sedwick Ltd.; Underwriting Mem. of Lloyd's; Common Councilman for Ward of Bassishaw, City of London 1965–69, Alderman 1969–96, Sheriff 1973–74, Lord Mayor of London 1976–77; Chancellor of The City Univ. 1976–77; Liveryman and past Master of the Hon. Co. of Master Mariners; Chair. of local Civil Defence Cttee. 1967–68; Pres. Nat. Waterways Transport Asscn. 1978–83; U.K. Pres. Royal Life Saving Soc. 1978–82, Deputy Commonwealth Pres. 1982–96 (Vice-Pres. 1996–); Vice Pres. City of London Centre, St. John Ambulance Asscn.; Vice-Chair. Port of London Authority 1979–84; Vice-Pres. City of London District Red Cross; Chair of Govs. Pangbourne Coll. 1979–92; Chair. St Katharine Haven 1990–93; Chair. Council Maritime Volunteer Service 1998–; Founder mem. and Fellow, Nautical Inst.; Fellow, Inst. of Admin. Man., Pres. 1980–84 (Inst.'s Medal 1982); R.N.R. Decoration (RD) 1965, Hon. Commdr. R.N.R. 1971; H.M. Lieut. for City of London 1975; Elder Brother of Trinity House; Trustee, Nat. Maritime Museum 1982–92; Gentleman Usher of the Purple Rod 1985–; Fellow Royal Coll. of Music 1991; Hon. D.Sc. (City Univ.) 1976; K. St. J.; Officer, Order of the Leopard (Zaire), Commdr., Royal Order of Dannebrog (Denmark), Order of Johan Sedia Makhota (Malaysia), Grand Cross of Municipal Merit (Lima, Peru) 1977, Admin. Management Soc. Gold Medal (U.S.A.) 1983. *Leisure interest:* sailing. *Address:* 4 Fairholt Street, Knightsbridge, London, SW7 1EQ, England. *Telephone:* 0171-589 9860. *Fax:* 0802-174734.

GILLIAM, Terry Vance, B.A.; American animator, film director, actor, illustrator, writer; b. 22 Nov. 1940, Minn.; s. of James Hall and Beatrice (Vance) Gilliam; m. Margaret Weston 1973; one s. two d.; ed. Occidental Coll.; Assoc. Ed. HELP! magazine 1962–64; freelance illustrator 1964–65, advertising copywriter/art dir. 1966–67; with Monty Python's Flying Circus (U.K.) 1969–76; animator, And Now For Something Completely Different (film); co-dir. and actor, Monty Python and the Holy Grail; dir. Jabberwocky; designer, actor, animator, Monty Python's Life of Brian; co-author, producer, dir. Time Bandits; actor and dir. Monty Python Live at the Hollywood Bowl 1982; co-writer Monty Python's Meaning of Life (film) 1983; co-writer and dir. Brazil 1985, The Adventures of Baron Munchhausen 1988; dir. The Fisher King (film) 1991, Twelve Monkeys 1996; Presenter (TV Series) The Last Machine 1995; exec. producer Monty Python's Complete Waste of Time 1995, 1995; Hon. Dr. of Arts (Occidental Coll.); Hon. D.F.A. (Royal Coll. of Art, London) 1989. *Publications:* Monty Python's Big Red Book, Monty Python's Papperbok 1977, Monty Python's Scrapbook 1979, Animations of Mortality 1979, Monty Python's The Meaning of Life, Monty Python's Flying Circus—Just the Words (co-ed.) 1989, The Adventures of Baron Munchhausen 1989. *Address:* The Old Hall, South Grove, Highgate, London, N6 6BP, England. *Telephone:* 0181-341 5203.

GILMAN, Alfred Goodman, M.D., PH.D.; American professor of pharmacology; b. 1 July 1941, New Haven, Conn.; s. of Alfred Gilman and Mabel Schmidt; m. Kathryn Hedlund 1963; one s. two d.; ed. Yale and Case Western Reserve Univs.; Research Assoc. Nat. Insts. of Health, Bethesda, Md. 1969–71; Asst. Prof., Assoc. Prof. of Pharmacology, Univ. of Va., Charlottesville 1971–77, Prof. 1977–81; Prof. of Pharmacology and Chair. Dept. of Pharmacology Univ. of Texas Southwestern Medical Center, Dallas 1981–, Raymond and Ellen Willie Distinguished Chair. of Molecular Neuropharmacology 1987–, Regental Prof. 1994–; Dir. Regeneron Pharmaceutics 1989–, Eli Lilly and Co. 1995–; mem. numerous scientific, advisory and editorial bds.; mem. N.A.S., Inst. of Medicine of N.A.S., American Soc. of Biological Chemists etc.; Fellow, A.A.A.S., American Acad. of Arts and Sciences; Gairdner Foundation Int. Award 1984; Albert Lasker Basic Medical Research Award 1989; Nobel Prize for Medicine (with Martin Rodbell) 1994; many other awards and distinctions. *Address:* Department of Pharmacology, University of Texas Southwestern Medical Center, 5323 Harry Hines Boulevard, Dallas, TX 75235, U.S.A.

GILMARTIN, Raymond V., M.B.A.; American business executive; b. 6 March 1941, Washington, D.C.; m. Gladys Higham 1965; one s. two d.; ed. Union Coll. and Harvard Univ.; Devt. Engineer Eastman Kodak 1963–67; various exec. positions, Becton Dickinson & Co. 1976–92, Chair., Pres. and C.E.O. 1992–94; Chair., Pres. and C.E.O. Merck & Co., Inc. 1994–. *Address:* Merck and Co., 1 Merck Drive, Whitehouse Station, NJ 08889, U.S.A.

GILMORE, James Stuart, III, J.D.; American politician and lawyer; b. 6 Nov. 1949, Richmond, Va; s. of James Stuart Gilmore, Jr. and Margaret Kandle Gilmore; ed. Univ. of Virginia; U.S. army 1971–74; practising attorney 1977–80, 1984–87; fmrly. Commonwealth's Attorney, Henrico Co., Va; fmr. Attorney Gen. State of Va; Gov. of Virginia Nov. 1997–; Alt. Del. Repub. Nat. Convention 1976; Chair. Henrico Co. Repub. Cttee. 1982–85, now Vice-Chair.; Republican. *Address:* Office of the Governor, Capitol Building, Third Floor, P.O. Box 1475, Richmond, VA 23219, U.S.A.

GILMORE, Rosalind E.J., C.B., M.A., F.R.S.A., C.I.M.; British business executive; b. 23 March 1937, London; d. of Sir Robert Fraser and Lady (Betty) Fraser; m. Brian Terence Gilmore 1962; ed. King Alfred School, N. London, Univ. Coll. London and Newnham Coll. Cambridge; entered H.M. Treasury 1960; Exec. Asst. to Econs. Dir. IBRD 1966–67; Cabinet Office 1974; Asst. Sec. H.M. Treasury 1975, Head Financial Insts. Div. 1977–80; Press Sec. to Chancellor of Exchequer 1980–82; Gen. Man. Corp. Planning, Dunlop Ltd. 1982–83; Dir. of Marketing, Nat. Girobank 1983–86; Directing Fellow, St. George's House, Windsor Castle 1986–89; Dir. Mercantile Group PLC 1986–89, Mercantile Credit Co., Ltd. 1986–89, London and Manchester Group PLC 1986–89; Marketing Consultant, FI Group PLC (Software) 1986–89; mem. Financial Services Act Tribunal 1986–89; Deputy Chair. and Commr. Bldg. Socs. Comm. 1989–91, Chair. 1991–94; Chief Registrar of Friendly Socs. and Industrial Insurance Commr. 1991–94; Chair. Homeowners Friendly Society Ltd. 1996–98, Arrow Broadcasting 1996–98; Dir. Moorfields Eye Hosp. Trust, B.A.T. Industries PLC 1996–98, Zurich Financial Services AG (Zurich) 1998–, Allied Zurich PLC 1998–; mem. Securities and Investment Bd. 1993–96; Vice-Pres. for Leadership, Int. Women's Forum 1997–; Dir. Leadership Foundation 1997–; mem. Court, Cranfield Univ. 1992–; mem. bd. Opera North 1993–; mem. Lloyd's Regulatory Bd. 1994– (Dir. Regulatory Services, Lloyds 1994–95); Hon. Fellow, Newnham Coll. Cambridge 1986; Fellow, Univ. Coll. London 1988. *Publication:* Mutuality for the Twenty-first Century 1998. *Leisure interests:* music, reading, house in Greece. *Address:* 3 Clarendon Mews, London, W2 2NR, England. *Telephone:* 0171-262 4459.

GILMOUR OF CRAIGMILLAR, Baron (Life Peer) of Cragmillar in the District of the City of Edinburgh; **Ian (Hedworth John Little) Gilmour,** Bt., P.C., M.P.; British politician; b. 8 July 1926; s. of Lieut.-Col. Sir John Little Gilmour and Hon. Victoria Laura; m. Lady Caroline Margaret Montagu-Douglas-Scott 1951; four s. one d.; ed. Eton Coll., Balliol Coll., Oxford; served with Grenadier Guards 1944–47, rank of Second Lieut. 1945; called to the Bar, Inner Temple 1952; Ed. The Spectator 1954–59; M.P. for Norfolk Central 1962–74, for Chesham and Amersham 1974–92; Parl. Under-Sec., Ministry of Defence 1970–71, Minister of State for Defence Procurement 1971–72, for Defence 1972–74, Sec. of State for Defence 1974; Lord Privy Seal 1979–81; Chair. Conservative Research Dept. 1974–75; Pres. Medical Aid for Palestinians 1992–96. *Publications:* The Body Politic 1969, Inside Right, A Study of Conservatism 1977, Britain Can Work 1983, Riot, Risings and Revolution 1992, Dancing with Dogma 1992, Whatever Happened to the Tories? 1997. *Address:* The Ferry House, Old Isleworth, Middx., TW7 6BD, England.

GILRUTH, Robert Rowe, M.S.; American engineer; b. 8 Oct. 1913, Nashwauk, Minn.; s. of Henry A. Gilruth and Frances M. (Rowe) Gilruth; m. 1st Esther Jean Barnhill 1937 (died 1972); one d.; m. 2nd Georgene Hubbard Evans 1973; one s.; ed. Univ. of Minnesota; with Nat. Advisory Cttee. for Aeronautics (later NASA) 1937–, Dir. Space Task Group (project Mercury) 1958; Dir. NASA Manned Spacecraft Center (Projects Mercury, Gemini and Apollo) 1961–72; Dir. Key Personnel Devt. NASA 1972–73, retd. 1973; Consultant to NASA Administrator 1974–; Fellow, American Rocket Soc., Inst. of Aerospace Sciences, American Astronautical Soc.; Gov. Nat. Rocket Club; Sylvanus Albert Reed Award 1950, Outstanding Achievement Award (Univ. of Minn.) 1954, Louis W. Hill Space Transportation Award 1962, NASA Distinguished Service Medal 1962, U.S. Chamber of Commerce Great Living American Award 1962, Dr. Robert J. Goddard Memorial Award of American Rocket Soc. 1962; Hon. Fellow, Inst. of Aerospace Sciences 1963; Spirit of St. Louis Medal by American Soc. of Mechanical Engineers 1965; Americanism Award by China-Burma-India Veterans Asscn. 1965; mem. Int. Acad. of Astronautics 1965–; mem. Houston Philosophical Soc. 1966–; Daniel Florence Guggenheim Award, Int. Acad. of Astronautics Soc.; mem. Nat. Acad. of Eng. 1968, Nat. Acad. of Sciences 1974, Int. Space Hall of Fame 1976; four hon. degrees; NASA Distinguished Service Medal 1969; Rockefeller Public Service Award 1969; Hon. Fellow, Royal Aeronautical Soc.; U.S. Nat. Space Hall of Fame Award 1969, American Soc. of Mech. Engineers Medal 1970, Inst. of Mechanical Engineers James Watt Int. Medal 1971, Nat. Aviation Club Award for Achievement 1971, Robert J. Collier Trophy (Nat. Aeronautic Asscn. and Nat. Aviation Club) 1972, Nat. Air and Space Museum Trophy for Outstanding Achievement in Aerospace Tech. 1985, named to Nat. Aviation Hall of Fame, Dayton, Ohio 1994–. *Leisure interests:* boating and boat building. *Address:* 2600 Barracks Road, # 38 Charlottesville, VA 22901, U.S.A.

GIMFERRER, Pere; Spanish writer and literary manager; b. 22 June 1945, Barcelona; s. of Pere Gimferrer and Carmen Torrens; m. María Rosa Caminals 1971; no c.; ed. Univ. of Barcelona; Head Literary Dept. Editorial Seix Barral 1970, Literary Consultant 1973, Literary Man. 1981–; Academician Real Acad. Española 1985–; Nat. Prize for Poetry 1966, 1989, Critic's Prize 1983, 1989. *Publications:* Arde el Mar 1966, L'Espai Desert 1977, Dietari 1981, Fortuny 1983, El Vendaval 1988, La Llum 1991, The Roots of Miró 1993, Complete Catalan Work, Vol. I 1995, Vol. II 1995, Vol. III 1996, Vol. IV 1996, Vol. V 1997, Masquerade (poem) 1996, L'Agent Provocador 1998. *Leisure interests:* cinema, travel. *Address:* Editorial Seix Barral, Córcega 270, Barcelona 08008 (Office); Rambla de Catalunya 113, Barcelona 08008, Spain (Home). *Telephone:* 2186400 (Office). *Fax:* 2184773.

GINER, Salvador, PH.D.; Spanish sociologist and university professor; b. 10 Feb. 1934, Barcelona; m. Montserrat Sariola 1966; one s. one d.; ed. Int. School Barcelona, Univs. of Barcelona, Cologne, Germany and Chicago, U.S.A.; Visiting Prof., Univ. of Puerto Rico 1962–63; lecturer, Univ. of Reading, U.K. 1965–70; Sr. Lecturer, Univ. of Lancaster, U.K. 1970–76; Reader, then Prof. and Head Dept. of Sociology and Social Anthropology, Brunel Univ., West London, U.K. 1976–87; Prof. and Head Dept. of Sociology, Univ. of Barcelona 1987–90; Dir. Inst. of Advanced Social Studies, Higher Council for Scientific Research 1988–97; Pres. Spanish Sociological Asscn. 1986–91; Ed. Revista Internacional de Sociología 1992–; Asst. Ed. European Journal of Social Theory 1988–; mem. Scientific Cttee. European Prize for Social Science (Amalfi Prize) 1989–. *Publications:* Contemporary Europe (Vol. I) 1971, (Vol. II) 1978, Mass Society 1976, Ensayos Civiles 1985, El Destino de la Libertad 1988, España: Sociedad y Política 1990, La Gobernabilidad 1992, Historia del Pensamiento Social (revised edn.) 1994, Sociology (revised edn.) 1996; Religión y Sociedad en España 1994, Carta sobre la democracia 1996, Buen Gobierno y Política Social 1997, La Societat Catalana 1998, Diccionario de Sociología (ed.) 1998. *Address:* Department of Sociology, University of Barcelona, Diagonal 690, 08034 Barcelona, Spain. *Telephone:* (3) 403 5553. *Fax:* (3) 402 1894.

GINGRICH, Newt (Newton Leroy), PH.D., A.A.A.S.; American politician; b. 17 June 1943, Harrisburg, Pa.; s. of Robert Bruce Gingrich and Kathleen (née Daugherty) Gingrich; m. 2nd Marianne Ginther 1981; two d. by previous marriage; ed. Emory and Tulane Univs.; mem. faculty, W. Ga. Coll., Carrollton 1970–78, Prof. of History –1978; mem. 96–103rd Congresses from 6th Dist. of Ga. 1979–92; Chair. GOPAC, now Chair. Emer.; House Republican Whip 1989; Speaker House of Reps. 1994–98; Adjunct Prof. Reinhardt Coll., Waleska, Ga. 1994–95; co-f. Congressional Mil. Reform Caucus, Congressional Space Caucus; mem. A.A.A.S. *Publications:* Window of Opportunity, 1945 1995, To Renew America 1995. *Address:* c/o U.S. House of Representatives, 2428 Rayburn House Office Building, Washington, D.C. 20515, U.S.A.

GINOLA, David; French professional footballer and sportsman; b. 25 Jan. 1967, Gassin, Var; s. of René Ginola and Mireille Collet; m. Coraline Delphin 1990; two d.; ed. Lycée du Parc Impérial, Nice; with the following clubs: first div. Toulon clubs 1986–87, Matraracing, Paris 1987–88, Racing Paris 1 1988–89, Brest-Armorique 1989–90, Paris-Saint-Germain 1991–95 (French nat. champions 1993–94, winners Coupe de France 1993, 1995, winners Coupe de la ligue 1995); with Newcastle United, England, 1995–97, Tottenham Hotspur 1997–; elected Top Player in France by sports journalists and fellow players 1993–94; anti-landmine campaigner for Red Cross 1998–. *Leisure interests:* golf, tennis, skiing, car racing. *Address:* Tottenham Hotspur Football & Athletic Co. Ltd.; 748 High Street, London N17, England.

GINSBURG, Ruth Bader, LL.B.; American judge; b. 15 March 1933, Brooklyn; d. of Nathan Bader and Celia Amster; m. Martin Ginsburg 1954; one s. one d.; ed. Cornell Univ. and Harvard and Columbia Law Schools; admitted New York Bar 1959, D.C. Bar 1975, U.S. Supreme Court Bar 1967; Law Sec. to Judge, U.S. Dist. Court (southern dist.) New York 1959–61; Research Assoc. Columbia Law School, New York 1961–62, Assoc. Dir. project on int. procedure 1962–63; Asst. Prof. Rutgers Univ. Law School, Newark 1963–66, Assoc. Prof. 1966–69, Prof. 1969–72; Prof. Columbia Univ. School of Law, New York 1972–80; Fellow, Center for Advanced Study in Behavioral Sciences, Stanford, Calif. 1977–78; U.S. Circuit Judge, U.S. Court of Appeals, D.C. Circuit, Washington, D.C. 1980–93; Judge, U.S. Supreme Court 1993–; mem. American Bar Asscn., A.A.A.S., American Law Inst., Council on Foreign Relations; numerous hon. degrees. *Publications include:* Civil Procedure in Sweden (with A. Bruzelius) 1965, Swedish Code of Judicial Procedure 1968, Sex-Based Discrimination (with others); articles in legal journals. *Address:* United States Supreme Court, 1 First Street, N.E., Washington, DC 20543, U.S.A.

GINZBERG, Eli, PH.D.; American economist; b. 30 April 1911, New York; s. of Louis Ginzberg and Adele Katzenstein; m. Ruth Szold 1946 (died 1995); one s. two d.; ed. Columbia Univ.; Faculty, School of Business 1935–, Prof. of Econs. 1967–79, now Special Lecturer; Dir. conservation of human resources project 1950–90, Eisenhower Center for the Conservation of Human Resources 1990–; Chair. Nat. Manpower Advisory Cttee. 1962–73; Chair. Nat. Comm. for Employment Policy 1974–81; Consultant to various govt. depts.; Special Lecturer, Barnard Coll., Columbia Univ. 1981–88, Special Lecturer, Health and Society, School of Public Health 1989–; Chair. Bd. Manpower Demonstration Research Corpn. 1974–82, Chair. Bd. Emer. 1982–97; Chair. Academic Advisory Council to O.R.T. 1991–; Dir. Revson Fellows Program on Future of the City of N.Y. 1979–; mem. bd. dirs. Foundation for Biomedical Research 1988–; mem. N.A.S. Inst. of Medicine; Fellow A.A.A.S.; Hon. D.Litt. (Jewish Theological Seminary of America) 1966, (Columbia) 1982; Hon. LL.D. (Loyola) 1969, (Philadelphia Coll. for Osteopathic Medicine) 1994; Hon. L.H.D. (Rush) 1985, (Kirksville Coll. for Osteopathic Medicine) 1993, (State Coll. of Optometry, State Univ. of N.Y.) 1995; Hon. Sc.D. (N.Y. Coll. of Osteopathic Medicine) 1996; Medal, Int. Univ. of Social Studies, Rome 1957. *Publications include:* The House of Adam Smith 1934, The Unemployed 1943, Occupational Choice 1951, The Ineffective Soldier: Lessons for Management and the Nation (3 vols.) 1959, The Troublesome Presence: American Democracy and the Negro 1964, Men, Money and Medicine 1969, The Human Economy 1976, American Medicine: The Power Shift 1985, Beyond Human Scale: The Large Corporation at Risk 1985, Understanding Human Resources: Perspectives, People and Policy 1985, From Physician Shortage to Patient Shortage: The Uncertain Future of Medical Practice 1986, Technology and Employment: Concepts and Clarifications 1986, Medicine and Society: Changing Relations 1950–2000 1987, The Skeptical Economist 1987, Executive Talent: Developing and Holding Leaders 1988, The Financing of Biomedical Research 1989, My Brother's Keeper 1989, Does Job Training Work—The Clients Speak Out 1989, The Medical Triangle 1990, Health Services Research, Key to Health Policy 1991, Changing Health Care in Four Metros 1993, The Eye of Illusion 1993, The Economics of Medical Education 1993, The Road to Reform: The Future of Health Care in America 1994, Medical Gridlock and Health Reform 1994, The Changing US Labor Market 1994, Critical Issues in US Health Care Reform 1994, The Financing of Medical Schools in an Era of Health Reform 1995, Tomorrow's Hospital: A Look to the 21st Century 1996, Improving the Health Care of New York City's Poor: Lessons for Policy 1997, Urban Medical Centers: Balancing Academic and Patient Care Functions 1996, New Deal Days 1933–34 1997. *Leisure interests:* walking, swimming. *Address:* Eisenhower Center, Columbia University, 475 Riverside Drive, Suite 248, New York, NY 10115; 845 West End Avenue, New York, NY 10025, U.S.A. (Home). *Telephone:* (212) 854-3410; (212) 864-1857 (Home).

GINZBURG, Aleksandr Ilyich (b. Chizov); French journalist; b. 1936, Moscow; s. of L. I. Ginzburg; m. I. S. Zholkovskaya 1969; two c.; studied journalism, Moscow Univ. 1956–60 and at Moscow Historical Archive Inst. 1966–67; numerous jobs; ed. 3 issues of samizdat poetry for "Sintaksis" 1959–60; expelled from univ. 1960 and sentenced to 2 years' imprisonment in camps 1960–62; participated in dissident demonstrations; wrote The White Book (English translation On Trial. The Case of Sinyavsky and

Daniel) 1966; sentenced to 5 years' imprisonment 1968, released 1972; founded (with Solzhenitsyn (q.v.)) aid-scheme for families of dissidents 1974; exchanged with E. Kuznetsov and others for two Soviet spies 1979.

GINZBURG, Vitaly Lazarevich, DR.SC.; Russian physicist; b. 4 Oct. 1916, Moscow; s. of Lazar and Augusta Ginzburg; m. Nina Ginzburg 1946; one d.; ed. Moscow Univ.; at P. N. Lebedev Physical Inst., U.S.S.R. (now Russian) Acad. of Sciences 1940–; Prof. Gorky Univ. 1945–68, Moscow Inst. of Physics 1968–, Adviser to Dir. 1987–; Corresp. mem. U.S.S.R. (now Russian) Acad. of Sciences 1953–66, mem. 1966–; U.S.S.R. People's Deputy 1989–91; mem. Int. Acad. of Astronautics 1969; Assoc. Royal Astronomical Soc., London 1970; Foreign Hon. mem. American Acad. of Art and Science 1971; Foreign mem. Royal Danish Acad. of Sciences and Letters 1977; Hon. Fellow, Indian Acad. of Science 1977; Foreign Fellow, Indian Nat. Science Acad. 1981; Foreign Assoc., N.A.S., U.S.A. 1981; Foreign mem. Royal Soc., London 1987; mem. Academia Europaea 1990; Hon. D.Sc. (Sussex) 1970; Mandelstam Prize 1947, Lomonosov Prize 1962, U.S.S.R. State Prize 1953, Lenin Prize 1966, Gold Medal, Royal Astronomical Soc. 1991, Bardeen Prize 1991, Wolf Prize 1994, 1995, Vavilov Gold Medal (Russian Acad. of Sciences) 1995, Lomonosov Gold Medal (Russian Acad. of Sciences) 1995, Order of Lenin, etc. *Publications:* works on theoretical physics (superconductivity, etc.), astrophysics and radiophysics. *Address:* P. N. Lebedev Physical Inst., Russian Academy of Sciences, Leninsky Prospect 53, 117924 GSP, Moscow B-333, Russia. *Telephone:* (095) 135-85-70 (Office); (095) 135-10-96 (Home). *Fax:* (095) 938-22-51, (095) 135-85-33.

GIORDANO, H.E. Cardinal Michele; Italian ecclesiastic; b. 26 Sept. 1930, S. Arcangelo (Pz); ordained 1953, elected to the titular Church of Lari Castello 1971, consecrated bishop 1972, prefect at Matera e Irsina 1974, transferred to Naples 1987; cr. Cardinal 1988. *Address:* Arcivescovado di Napoli, Largo Donnaregina 23, 80138 Naples, Italy. *Telephone:* (081) 44.91.18. *Fax:* (081) 29.24.87.

GIORDANO, Richard Vincent, B.A., LL.B., PH.D.; American business executive; b. 24 March 1934, New York; s. of Vincent and Cynthia (née Cardetta) Giordano; m. Barbara Claire Beckett 1956 (divorced); one s. two d.; ed. Stuyvesant School, New York, Harvard Univ. and Columbia Univ. Law School; admitted New York Bar 1961; Assoc. Shearman and Sterling (law firm), New York 1969–63; Asst. Sec. Air Reduction Co. Inc., New York 1963–64, Vice-Pres. Distribution of Products Div. 1964–65, Exec. Vice-Pres. 1965–67, Group Vice-Pres. 1967–71, Pres. and C.O.O. 1971–74, C.E.O. 1977–79; Dir. BOCI 1974; Man. Dir. and C.E.O. BOC Group 1979–84, Chair. 1985–92, C.E.O. 1985–91, Chair. (non-exec.) 1994–96; Dir. (non-exec.) Reuters 1991–94; Chair. British Gas PLC (renamed BG PLC 1997) 1994–; Dir. (non-exec.) Cen. Electricity Generating Bd. 1982–89, Georgia Pacific Corpn. 1984–, Grand Metropolitan 1985–97 (Deputy Chair. (non-exec) 1991–97), RTZ (non-exec.) 1992–, Lucas Industries (non-exec.) 1993–94; Hon. K.B.E.; Hon. D.C.S. (St. John's Univ., U.S.A.). *Address:* c/o BG PLC, Eagle House, 108-110 Jermyn Street, London, SW1Y 6RH, England.

GIOVANNI, Nikki, B.A.; American poet; b. 7 June 1943, Knoxville, Tenn.; d. of Jones Giovanni and Yolande Watson; one s.; ed. Fisk Univ. and Univ. of Pennsylvania; Asst. Prof. of Black Studies, City Coll. of New York 1968; Assoc. Prof. of English, Rutgers Univ. 1968–72; Prof. of Creative Writing, Coll. Mt. St. Joseph on the Ohio 1985; Prof. Va. Polytechnic Inst. and State Univ. Blacksburg 1987–; founder, Nixtom Ltd. 1970; Visiting Prof. Ohio State Univ. 1984; recordings and TV appearances; recipient of numerous awards and hon. degrees. *Publications include:* Black Feeling, Black Talk 1968, Black Judgement 1968, Re: Creation 1970, Poem of Angela Yvonne Davis 1970, Spin A Soft Black Song 1971, Gemini 1971, My House 1972, A Dialogue: James Baldwin and Nikki Giovanni 1973, Ego Tripping and Other Poems for Young Readers 1973, A Poetic Equation: Conversations Between Nikki Giovanni and Margaret Walker 1974, The Women and the Men 1975, Cotton Candy on a Rainy Day 1978, Vacationtime 1980, Those Who Ride the Night Winds 1983, Sacred Cows . . . and other Edibles 1988, Conversations with Nikki Giovanni 1992, Racism 101 1994, Grand Mothers 1994. *Address:* Department of English, P.O. Box 0112, Virginia Polytechnic Institute and State University, Blacksburg, VA 24063, U.S.A.

GIRARD, René Noël, PH.D.; French/American professor and author; b. 25 Dec. 1923, Avignon; s. of Joseph Girard and Thérèse Fabre; m. Martha Virginia McCullough 1951; two s. one d.; ed. Lycée d'Avignon, Ecole des Chartes and Indiana Univ.; Instructor of French, Indiana Univ. 1947–51, Duke Univ. 1952–53; Asst. Prof. Bryn Mawr Coll. 1953–57; Assoc. Prof. The Johns Hopkins Univ. 1957–61, Prof. 1961–68, Chair. Romance Languages 1965–68, James M. Beall Prof. of French and Humanities 1976–80; Prof. Inst. d'études françaises Bryn Mawr, Avignon 1961–68, Dir. 1969; Distinguished Faculty Prof. of Arts and Letters, State Univ. of New York at Buffalo 1971–76; Andrew B. Hammond Prof. of French Language, Literature and Civilization, Stanford Univ. 1981–95, Courtesy Prof. of Religious Studies and Comparative Literature 1986–95, Dir. Program of Interdisciplinary Research, Dept. of French and Italian 1987–95, Prof. Emer. 1995–; mem. Center for Int. Security and Arms Control, 1990–95; mem. Emer. 1995–; Chevalier, Ordre Nat. de la Légion d'honneur 1984, Officier, Ordre des Arts et Lettres 1984; Fellow American Acad. of Arts and Sciences 1979–, Guggenheim Fellow 1960, 1967; Hon. D.Lit. (Vrije Univ.) 1985, Hon. D.Theol. (Innsbruck) 1988; Acad. Française Prize 1973, Grand Prix de Philosophie 1996; Prix Médicis-Essai 1990. *Publications include:* Mensonge romantique et vérité romanesque 1961, Dostoïevski: du double à l'unité 1963, La violence et le sacré 1972, Des choses cachées depuis la fondation du monde 1978, Le bouc émissaire 1982, La route antique des hommes pervers 1985, Violence et vérité: autour de René Girard (ed. by Paul Dumouchel) 1985, Shakespeare: Les feux de l'envie 1990, A Theatre of Envy. William Shakespeare 1991, Quand ces choses commenceront 1994, The Girard Reader (ed. by James Williams) 1996. *Address:* 705 Frenchman's Road, Stanford, CA 94305, U.S.A.

GIRARDOT, Annie Suzanne; French film actress; b. 25 Oct. 1931, Paris; m. Renato Salvatori 1962 (deceased); one d.; ed. Centre d'art dramatique, Paris, Conservatoire nat. d'art dramatique; with Comédie-Française 1954–57; Suzanne-Bianchetti Prize 1956, Prize for Best Actress, Venice Film Festival (for Trois chambres à Manhattan) 1965, Courteline Prize (for Déclics et des claques) 1965, Prize for Best Actress, Mar del Plata Festival (for Vivre pour vivre) 1968, Best Actress of the Year (for Docteur Françoise Gailland) 1976; Commdr. des Arts et des Lettres. *Plays acted in:* La tour Eiffel qui tue, la Paix chez soi, le Jeu de l'amour et du hasard, la Machine à écrire, les Amants magnifiques, Aux innocents les mains pleines, Une femme trop honnête, Deux sur une balançoire, l'Idiote, Après la chute 1965, le Jour de la tortue 1965, Seule dans le noir 1966, Persephone (speaking part, La Scala, Milan) 1966, Madame Marguerite (1974–75), Marguerite et les autres 1983, L'avare 1986, Première jeunesse 1987, Le roi se meurt 1988, Helden platz 1991, Les Chutes du Zambèze 1995. *Films include:* Treize à table 1955, l'Homme aux clefs d'or 1956, Le rouge est mis, Maigret tend un piège, le Désert de Pigalle 1957, La Corde raide, Recours en grâce 1959, la Française et l'Amour, la Proie pour l'ombre, Rocco et ses frères 1960, le Rendez-vous, les Amours célèbres, le Bateau d'Emile 1961, le Vice et la Vertu 1962, l'Autre Femme 1963, Déclics et des claques, Trois Chambres à Manhattan, l'Or du duc 1965, Vivre pour vivre 1967, Les gauloises bleues, la Bande à Bonnot 1968, Il pleut dans mon village, Erotissimo, Un homme qui me plaît 1969, Dillinger est mort, l'Histoire d'une femme, Elle boit pas, elle fume pas, elle drague pas, mais . . . elle cause, Disons un soir à dîner, les Novices, le Clair de terre 1970, Mourir d'aimer, la Vieille Fille, la Mandarine 1971, les Feux de la chandeleur, Elle cause plus . . . elle flingue 1972, Traitement de choc, Jessua 1973, Il n'y a pas de fumée sans feu 1972, Ursule et Grelu 1973, Juliette et Juliette, la Gifle 1974, Il faut vivre dangereusement, le Gitan, Il pleut sur Santiago 1975, Docteur Françoise Gailland, le Soupçon, D'amour et d'eau fraîche, Cours après moi . . . que je t'attrape 1976, A chacun son enfer 1977, le Dernier Baiser, jambon d'Ardenne, le Point de mire 1977, la Zizanie, la Clé sur la porte, l'Amour en question 1978, Vas-y maman 1978, Cause toujours . . . tu m'intéresses 1979, Bobo, Jacco, le Grand embouteillage 1979, la Vie continue, une Robe noire pour un tueur, la Revanche 1981, Partir, Revenir 1985, Adieu Blaireau 1985, Prisonnières 1988, Cinq jours en juin 1989, Comédie d'Amour 1989, Il y a des jours . . . et des lunes 1990, Merci la Vie 1991, Les Misérables 1995 (César award for Best Supporting Actress). *Television appearances:* le Pain de ménage 1966, Bobo, Jaco, Florence ou la vie de château 1987, le Vent des moissons 1989, Un Pull Par-Dessus l'Autre 1993, Jeanne 1994. *Publication:* Vivre d'aimer 1989. *Address:* c/o Artmédia, 10 avenue George V, 75008 Paris, France.

GIRAUD, Michel; French politician and business executive; b. 14 July 1929, Pontoise, Val d'Oise; s. of Jean Giraud; m. Simonne Wietzel 1952; two s. (one deceased) one d.; ed. secondary school at Saint-Martin de France-Pontoise, Lycée Louis le Grand and Univ. de Paris; Deputy Dir. Société Centrale des Bois 1951–57; Dir. Société A. Charles & Fils 1960–72; Pres. Dir.-Gen. SONIBAT 1972–93; Pres. Dir.-Gen. Société d'Economie Mixte d'Aménagement et de Gestion du Marché d'Intérêt Nat. de Paris-Rungis 1975–77; Senator for Val-de-Marne 1977–88; Conseiller-Gén. Val de Marne 1967–85; Administrator, Conseil d'Admin. Parisian Regional Dist. 1968–, Sec. 1969–72, Pres. 1972–73; Pres. Conseil Régional, Ile-de-France 1976–88, 1992–98; R.P.R. Deputy for Val-de-Marne 1988–93, 1995–; Mayor of Perreux-sur-Marne 1971–92 (Municipal Councillor 1971–); Pres. Nat. Fed. of Local Councillors 1977–83, Asscn. of Mayors of France 1983–92; Founder, Pres. World Asscn. of Major Metropolises—Metropolis 1985–; Minister of Labour, Employment and Professional Training 1993–95; Chevalier, Légion d'honneur, Ordre Nat. du Mérite, des Palmes Académiques, Médaille d'Argent de la Jeunesse et des Sports. *Publications:* Nous tous la France 1983, Raconte-moi Marianne 1984, Notre Ile-de-France Région Capitale 1985, Le Perreux, 100 ans d'histoire 1987, le Temps des Métropoles 1987, Histoire de l'Ile de France 1996, Histoires de Communes 1996, Citadins de l'an 2000 1997. *Leisure interests:* sport, history, music. *Address:* Assemblée nationale, 75355 Paris (Office); 4 Grande rue, 91250 Morsang-sur-Seine, France (Home).

GIRAY, I. Safa: Turkish politician; b. 5 March 1931, Izmir; s. of Nuri Giray and Nimet Giray; m. 1st Sema Babaç 1955; m. 2nd Misler Ünlüyol 1972; two s. one d.; ed. Istanbul Tech. Univ.; planning engineer at Gen. Directorate of Electricity Works Study Dept. 1968; worked on project studies of Keban and Oymapinar Dams; adviser at Gen. Directorate of Electrical Works; Man. Black Sea Copper Enterprises 1969–74; Gen. Man. Akkardan Co. 1974–80; Gen. Man. Anadolu Machine Co. 1980–83; Deputy for Istanbul 1983–; Minister of Public Works and Housing 1983–89, of Defence 1989–90, of Foreign Affairs 1991, M.P. 1991–. *Leisure interests:* music, games. *Address:* Abidin Daver Sk. No. 20/7, Çankaya-Ankara, Turkey. *Telephone:* 0312-442 3496.

GIRI, Tulsi; Nepalese politician; b. Sept. 1926; Deputy Minister of Foreign Affairs 1959; Minister of Village Devt. 1960; Minister without Portfolio 1960;

Minister of Foreign Affairs, the Interior, Public Works and Communications 1961; Vice-Chair. Council of Ministers and Minister of Palace Affairs 1962; Chair. Council of Ministers and Minister of Foreign Affairs 1962–65; mem. Royal Advisory Cttee. 1969–74; Adviser to the King 1974–; Prime Minister, Minister of Palace Affairs and Defence 1975–77. *Address:* Jawakpurdham, District Dhanuka, Nepal.

GIROLAMI, Sir Paul, Kt., B.COM., F.C.A.; British business executive and chartered accountant; b. 25 Jan. 1926, Fanna, Italy; m. Christabel Mary Gwynne Lewis 1952; two s. one d.; ed. London School of Economics; with Chantrey and Button (Chartered Accountants) 1950–54, Coopers and Lybrand, 1954–65; joined Glaxo as Financial Controller 1965, mem. of Bd. and Finance Dir. 1968, Chief Exec. 1980–86, Deputy Chair. April-Dec. 1985; Chair. Glaxo Holdings 1985–94; Pres. Glaxo Finanziaria SpA Italy; Dir. Nippon Glaxo Ltd., Japan, Glaxo-Sankyo Ltd., Credito Italiano Int. 1990–93, Forte plc 1992–96, UIS France 1994–; mem. CBI Council 1986–93; Chair. Senate for Chartered Accountants in Business 1990–; Chair. Council Goldsmith's Coll., Univ. of London 1994–; Dir. American Chamber of Commerce (U.K.) 1983; Hon. mem. Emmanuel Coll., Cambridge 1994–; mem. Appeal Cttee. of Inst. of Chartered Accountants 1987, Stock Exchange Listed Cos. Advisory Cttee. 1987–92, Open Univ. Visiting Cttee. 1987–89, Court of Assts. of The Worshipful Company of Goldsmiths 1986; Chair. Senate of the Bd. for Chartered Accountants in Business 1989; Dr. h.c. (Aston) 1991, (Trieste) 1991, Hon. D.Sc. (Sunderland) 1991, (Bradford) 1993; Hon. LL.D. (Singapore) 1993, (Warwick) 1996; Grande Ufficiale, Ordine al Merito della Repubblica Italiana 1987; City and Guilds Insignia Award in Tech. (h.c.) 1988; Freeman, City of London Liveryman 1980; Hon. Fellow, L.S.E. 1989; Insignia of the Order of the Rising Sun; Cavaliere del Lavoro 1991. *Leisure interest:* reading. *Address:* 11 Curzon Street, London, W1Y 7FJ, England.

GIROUD, Françoise; French politician and journalist; b. 21 Sept. 1916, Geneva, Switzerland; d. of Salih Gourdji and Elda Faragi; one s. (deceased), one d.; ed. Lycée Molière, Coll. de Groslay; began in cinema as script-girl 1932, Asst. Dir. 1937; Ed. Elle 1945–52; Co-founder L'Express 1953, Ed. 1953–71, Dir. 1971–74; Pres. Express-Union 1970–74; mem. Gov. Bd. of Express Group 1971–74; Sec. of State for Women's Affairs 1974–76, for Culture 1976–77; Vice-Pres. Parti Radical 1975–76, Union pour la Démocratie française 1978–; Pres. Action Int. contre la Faim 1984–88, Hon. Pres. 1988–; Pres. Comm. to improve cinema ticket sales 1989–91; Chief Columnist on Le Nouvel Observateur 1983–; literary critic Le Journal du Dimanche 1990–94, Le Figaro 1994–; mem. Prix Femina Jury 1992–; Hon. Dr. (Ann Arbour Univ.) 1976, (Goucher Coll.) 1977; Officier Légion d'honneur 1983. *Publications:* Le tout Paris 1952, Nouveaux portraits 1953, La nouvelle vague: portrait de la jeunesse 1958, Si je mens 1972, Une poignée d'eau 1973, La comédie du pouvoir 1977, Ce que je crois 1978, Une femme honorable 1981, Le Bon Plaisir 1983, Alma Mahler ou l'art d'être aimée 1988, Leçons particulières 1990, Jenny Marx ou la femme du diable 1992, Les hommes et les femmes (co-author) 1993, Journal d'une parisienne 1993, Mon très cher amour 1994, Cœur de tigre 1995, Chienne d'année 1996, Cosima la sublime 1996, Gais-Z et contents 1997, Arthur ou le bonheur de vivre 1997, Deux et deux font trois 1998. *Films:* Antoine et Antoinette 1947, La belle que voilà 1950, L'amour, madame 1951, Julietta 1953, Le bon plaisir 1984, Le quatrième pouvoir 1985, Marie Curie (Nymphe d'or, Int. TV Festival of Monte Carlo) 1991. *Address:* Editions Fayard, 75 rue des Saints Pères, 75006 Paris, France. *Fax:* (1) 45-55-65-80.

GISCARD D'ESTAING, François, L. EN D.; French civil servant; b. 17 Sept. 1926; ed. Ecole Nat. d'Admin., Inst. d'Etudes Politiques; Deputy Insp. of Finance 1952, Insp. 1954; Technical Adviser to Minister of Agriculture 1955–56, 1958–59, to Sec. of State for the Budget 1956–57; Head of Cen. Admin. Ministry of Agriculture 1957; Dir. Banque Cen. des Etats d'Afrique Equatoriale et du Cameroun 1959–68; Dir. Banque Française du Commerce Extérieur 1970, Dir.-Gen. 1974, Chair. 1977–82; Inspecteur-Gén. des Finances 1976; Chair. American Express Bank (France) S.A. 1985–88, 1991–92; Mayor of Saint-Amant-Tallende 1965–71; mem. man. industrial and commercial bank of Marais 1989–, of Vernes 1989–92; Dir. Tandem France and Tandem Europe 1992–96, Proudfoot PLC 1996–97; Vice-Prin. Lycée Jean Lefebvre 1996–; Croix de guerre, Officier, Légion d'honneur, Officier, Ordre nat. du Mérite. *Publications:* Financement et garantie du commerce international 1977, Notre-Dame de Paris—les rois retrouvés (with Michel Fleury and Alain Erlande-Brandenburg). *Leisure interests:* big-game hunting, archaeology. *Address:* 3 rue Louis Boilly, 75016 Paris, France (Home). *Telephone:* 45-20-50-94 (Home).

GISCARD D'ESTAING, Valéry, K.C.B.; French politician and civil servant; b. 2 Feb. 1926, Koblenz, Germany; s. of the late Edmond Giscard d'Estaing and May Bardoux; m. Anne-Aymone de Brantes 1952; two s. two d.; ed. Ecole Polytechnique, Ecole Nat. d'Admin.; Official, Inspection des Finances 1952, Insp. 1954; Deputy Dir. du Cabinet of Prés. du Conseil June-Dec. 1954; Deputy for Puy de Dôme 1956–58, re-elected for Clermont 1958, for Puy du Dôme 1962, 1967, 1984, 1986, 1988, resgnd. 1989. Sec. of State for Finance 1959, Minister for Finance and Econ. Affairs 1962–66, 1969–74; Pres. Comm. des Finances, de l'Economie général et du plan 1967–68; Pres. Cttee. des Affaires Etrangères 1987–89; Pres. of the French Repub. 1974–81; Founder-Pres. Fed. Nat. des Républicains, Indépendants (from May 1977 Parti Républicain) 1965; Del. to UN Gen. Assembly 1956, 1957, 1958; Chair. OECD Ministerial Council 1960; mem. Conseil Constitutionnel 1981–; Conseiller gen., Puy-de-Dome 1982–88; Pres. Regional Council of Auvergne 1986–; Pres. U.D.F. 1988–96; Deputy to European Parl. 1989–93; Pres. European Movt. Int. 1989–97; Pres. Council of European Municipalities and Regions 1997–; Deputy for Puy-de-Dôme 1993–; Pres. Comm. of Foreign Affairs, Nat. Ass. 1993–97; Grand Croix, Ordre de la Légion d'honneur, Grand Croix, Ordre national du Mérite, Croix de guerre, Chevalier, Ordre de Malte, Grand Cross, Order of Isabel la Católica, Nansen Medal 1979, etc. *Publications:* Démocratie française 1976, Deux français sur trois 1984, Le pouvoir et la vie, (Vol. I) 1988, (Vol. II, l'Affrontement) 1991, Le Passage 1994, Dans cinq ans, l'an 2000 (essay) 1995. *Leisure interests:* shooting, skiing. *Address:* Conseil régional d'Auvergne, 13–15 Avenue de Fontmaure, P.O. Box 60, 63402 Chamalières cedex; 199 blvd. Saint-Germain, 75007 Paris, France. *Telephone:* (1) 45.44.30.30. *Fax:* (1) 45.49.11.16.

GISLASON, Gylfi Th., DR. RER. POL.; Icelandic politician and economist; b. 7 Feb. 1917, Reykjavík; s. of Thorsteinn Gislason and Thórunn Pálsdóttir; m. Gudrún Vilmundardóttir 1939; three s.; ed. Reykjavík Coll., Univs. of Frankfurt am Main and Vienna; Lecturer of Econs., Univ. of Iceland 1941–46, Prof. 1946–56; mem. of Parl. 1946–78; Minister of Educ. and Industries 1956–58, of Educ. and Commerce 1958–71; Prof. of Econs. 1972–87; mem. Cen. Cttee. Social-Democratic Party 1942, Sec. 1946–65, Vice-Chair. 1965–68, Chair. 1968–74; Chair. Social-Democratic Parl. Group 1974–78; Pres. of Parl. 1974; Gov. for Iceland, IMF 1956–65, IBRD 1965–71; mem. Bd. of Govs. Iceland Bank of Devt. 1953–66, Devt. Fund of Iceland 1966–71, Nat. Theatre 1954–87; Chair. State Research Council 1965–71; mem. Icelandic Science Soc.; mem. Nordic Council 1971–78, Chair. Cultural Cttee. 1971–78; Dr. Oecon. h.c. *Publications:* General Business Theory 1941, Book-keeping 1942, Finance of Private Business Enterprises 1945, Management of Industrial Enterprises 1953, Accountancy 1955, The Marshall Plan 1948, Socialism 1949, Capitalism, Socialism and the Co-operative Movement 1950, The Foreign Policy of Iceland 1953, The Problem of Being an Icelander 1973, Enterprise and Society 1974, Fishery Economics 1975, Essays on Business Administration 1975, Book-keeping 1976, Book-keeping and Balance Sheets 1976, Essays on Commercial Law 1976, Social Democracy 1977, Economics 1981, Business Administration Vol. I 1986, Vols. II, III 1987, Fishery Economics 1990, The Challenge of Being an Icelander 1990, The Years of Reconstruction 1993, The Privilege and Challenge of Being an Icelander 1994; 20 songs arranged by Jon Thorarinsson 1985. *Leisure interest:* music; has composed songs for four LP records. *Address:* University of Iceland, 101 Reykjavík (Office); Aragata 11, 101 Reykjavík, Iceland (Home). *Telephone:* 525 4500 (Office); 551 5804 (Home).

GITARI, Most Rev. David Mukuba, B.A., B.D.; Kenyan ecclesiastic; b. 16 Sept. 1937; s. of Samuel Mukuba Gituku and Jessie Wanjiku; m. Grace Wanjiro Gajembo 1966; three c.; ed. Kangaru School, Embu, Royal Coll., Nairobi, Tyndale Coll. Bristol; Gen. Sec. Pan-African Evangelical Fellowship 1966–68, Bible Soc. of Kenya 1971–75; Anglican Bishop of Diocese of Mt. Kenya E. 1975–90, of Diocese of Kirinyaga 1990–96; Archbishop of Anglican Church of Kenya and Bishop of Diocese of Nairobi 1976–; Dir. Oxford Centre for Mission Studies 1983–; Chair. Kenya Students Christian Fellowship (KSCF) 1971–74, Kenya Peace 1978–, World Evangelical Fellowship Theological Comm. 1978–88, Nat. Council of Churches of Kenya (NCCK) 1978–80, 1981–83; Deputy Chair. WCC Comm. on Evangelism 1983–91; First Chair. Int. Fellowship of Mission Theologians 1981–94; Hon. D.D. (Ashland Seminars, Ohio, U.S.A.) 1983, (Univ. of Canterbury) 1993. *Publications:* Let the Bishop Speak, In Season and Out of Season. *Leisure interests:* driving, farming (keeping pigs and cows and growing mangoes). *Address:* Anglican Church of Kenya, Provincial Office, P.O. Box 40502, Nairobi, Kenya. *Telephone:* (02) 714755 (Office); (0161) 30832 (Home). *Fax:* (02) 718442 (Office); (0161) 30824 (Home).

GITELSON, Yosif Isayevich; Russian biophysicist; b. 6 July 1928; m.; four d.; ed. Krasnoyarsk Inst. of Medicine; worked as practitioner Krasnoyarsk Blood Transfusion Station 1952–53; docent Krasnoyarsk Inst. of Agric. 1953–57; sr. researcher, Head of lab. Inst. of Physics, Siberian br. of U.S.S.R. Acad. of Sciences 1957–82; head of lab. Inst. of Biophysics Siberian br. of U.S.S.R. Acad. of Sciences 1982–86, Dir. 1986–96, Adviser 1996–; corresp. mem. U.S.S.R. Acad. of Sciences 1979, mem. 1990–; Adviser to Russian Acad. of Sciences 1996–. *Publications include:* Experimental Ecological Systems Including Man, Problems of Space Biology 1975, Light from the Sea 1986, Distant Studies of Siberia 1988, numerous articles in scientific journals. *Address:* Institute of Biophysics, Akademgorodok, 660036 Krasnoyarsk, Russia (Office). *Telephone:* (3912) 43 46 23 (Office), 22 11 59 (Home), (095) 433 6357 (Home).

GIULIANI, Rudolph W., B.A., J.D.; American politician and lawyer; b. 28 May 1944, New York City; m. Donna Hanover; one s. one d.; ed. Manhattan Coll., New York Univ.; law clerk; Judge U.S. Dist. Court, New York City 1968–70; Asst. U.S. Attorney Southern Dist., New York; U.S. Attorney 1983–89; with Patterson, Belknap, Webb and Tyler 1977–81; with White & Case 1989–90; with Anderson Kill Olick & Oshinsky 1990–93; Mayor of New York 1993–. *Address:* Office of the Mayor, City Hall, New York, NY 10007, U.S.A.

GIULINI, Carlo Maria; Italian conductor; b. 9 May 1914; m.; three s.; ed. Accad. S. Cecilia, Rome; debut as conductor, Rome 1944; f. Orchestra of Milan Radio 1950; Prin. Conductor La Scala, Milan 1953–55; debut in U.K., Verdi's Falstaff, Edin. Festival 1955; closely associated with Philharmonia Orchestra 1955–; debut Covent Garden, Verdi's Don Carlos 1958; Prin. Prin.

Guest Conductor Chicago Symphony Orchestra 1969–78; Music Dir. Vienna Symphony Orchestra 1973–76, Los Angeles Philharmonic Orchestra 1978–84; Hon. mem. Gesellschaft der Musikfreunde, Vienna 1978; Hon. D.Hum.Litt. (DePaul Univ., Chicago) 1979; Gold Medal, Bruckner Soc. 1978, Gold Medal of Honour, Vienna, Légion d'honneur. *Publication:* Una vita nella musica. *Leisure interest:* sailing. *Address:* c/o Francesco Giulini, Via Bonnet 7, 20121 Milan, Italy. *Telephone:* (02) 6575021. *Fax:* (02) 6575021.

GIURANNA, Bruno; Italian viola player and conductor; b. 6 April 1933, Milan; ed. Coll. S. Giuseppe and Conservatorio di Musica Santa Cecilia, Rome, and Conservatorio di Musica S. Pietro a Maiella, Naples; Founder mem. I Musici 1951–61; Prof. Conservatorio G. Verdi, Milan 1961–65, Conservatorio S. Cecilia, Rome 1965–78, Prof. Acad. Chigiana, Siena 1966–83; Prof. Nordwest-deutsche Musikakademie, Detmold, Germany 1969–83; Prof. Hochschule der Künste, Berlin 1981–98; Prof. W. Stauffer Foundation 1985–; Prof. Royal Music Acad., London 1994–96; Prof. Acad. S. Cecilia, Rome 1995–97; mem. Int. Music Competition jury, Munich 1961–62, 1967, 1969, Geneva 1968, Budapest 1975; soloist at concerts in festivals including Edinburgh Festival, Holland Festival and with orchestras including Berlin Philharmonic Orchestra, Amsterdam Concertgebouw Orchestra and Teatro alla Scala, Milan; Artistic Dir. of Orchestra de Camera di Padova 1983–92; Academician of Santa Cecilia 1974. *Address:* Via Bembo 96, 31011 Asolo TV, Italy. *Telephone:* 423.55734. *Fax:* 423.520115.

GIURESCU, Dinu C., PH.D.; Romanian historian; b. 15 Feb. 1927; s. of Constantin C. Giurescu and Maria S. Giurescu; m. Anca Elena Dinu 1960; two d.; ed. Univ. Bucharest; curator Bucharest Art Museum 1956–64; with Ministry of Foreign Affairs 1964–68; Prof. of European Civilization, Acad. of Fine Arts, Bucharest 1968–87; lecturer in Switzerland, France, Bulgaria, Hungary, Fed. Repub. of Germany, U.S.A.—Dallas 1977, Washington 1980, Univs. of Columbia, Ind., Ill., Ariz., Calif. (Berkeley), Kan., Colo., Ore., Neb., Ohio, Rochester and Huntington Coll. 1982–85; Prof. Faculty of History, Univ. of Bucharest 1990–; Visiting Prof., William Paterson Coll., N.J., U.S.A. 1988–89, Texas A. and M. Univ., U.S.A. 1989–90, Cen. European Univ., Hungary 1993; Corresp. mem. Romanian Acad. 1990; Prize of the Romanian Acad. *Publications:* Ion Vodă cel Viteaz 1966, Istoria românilor din cele mai vechi timpuri pînă astăzi (History of the Romanians from Ancient Times Until Today) 1971 (with C. C. Giurescu); Ţara Românească în secolele XIV-XV (Wallachia in the 14th–15th Centuries) 1971; Istoria Romănilor I-II, Din cele mai vechi timpuri pînă la finele sec. XVI (History of the Romanians I-II. From Ancient Times to the end of the XVI century) 1974–76 (with C. C. Giurescu); Illustrated History of the Romanian People (in Romanian, English, French, German, Russian, Spanish) 1981–82, The Razing of Romania's Past 1989, The Communist Takeover in Romania, I 1994, The Radescu Government (in Romanian) 1996. *Leisure interests:* walking, visiting sites and museums, jazz music. *Address:* 30–33 32nd Street, apt. 3i, Astoria, NY 11102, U.S.A.; P.O. Box 284, Post Office 12, Bucharest, Romania. *Telephone:* (718) 545-7269 (New York); (1) 6594940 (Bucharest).

GIVENCHY, Hubert de; French fashion designer; b. 21 Feb. 1927, Beauvais; s. of Lucien Taffin de Givenchy and Béatrice Badin; ed. Coll. Félix-Fauré, Beauvais, Ecole Nat. Supérieure des Beaux-Arts, Paris and Faculté de Droit, Univ. de Paris; apprentice, Paris fashion houses of Lucien Lelong 1945–46, Robert Piguet 1946–48, Jacques Fath 1948–49, Elsa Schiaparelli 1949–51; est. own fashion house in Parc Monceau, Paris 1952–56, in Avenue George V 1956; Pres.-Dir.-Gen. Soc. Givenchy-Couture and Soc. des Parfums Givenchy, Paris 1954; Hon. Pres. Admin. Council Givenchy SA 1988–; Pres. Christie's France 1997–; work included in Fashion: An Anthology, Victoria and Albert Museum, London 1971; costume designer for films Breakfast at Tiffany's 1961, Charade 1963, The VIPs 1963, Paris When It Sizzles 1964, How to Steal a Million 1966; Chevalier, Légion d'honneur. *Address:* 3 Avenue George V, 75008 Paris, France.

GJERDE, Bjartmar; Norwegian politician; b. 6 Nov. 1931, Sande Sunnmøre; s. of Astrid Gjerde and Hjalmar Gjerde; m. Anna Karin Hoel 1954; three s.; Journalist Sunnmøre Arbeideravis 1948–53; Ed. Fritt Slag 1953–58; Chair. Labour League of Youth 1958–61; mem. State Youth Council; Sec. Labour Parl. Group 1961–62; Chief. Sec. Workers' Educ. League 1962–71; mem. Council on Broadcasting 1963–74, UNESCO Comm. 1964–66, Norwegian Cultural Council 1965–85, Council on Adult Educ. 1966–71; Minister of Church and Educ. 1971–72, 1973–76, for Industries 1976–78, for Petroleum and Energy 1978–80; mem. Labour Party Nat. Exec. 1973–81; Dir.-Gen. Norwegian Broadcasting Corpn. (NRK) 1981–89, Dir. Gen. Directorate of Labour 1989–94. *Address:* Mariboesgt. 8, 0032 Oslo, Norway.

GJESTEBY, Kari; Norwegian politician; b. 16 May 1947, Oslo; m. Mikael Klingberg; ed. Norwegian School of Econs. and Business Admin.; State Sec. Ministry of Church and Educ. 1976–86, Ministry of Finance 1979–81; Minister of Trade and Shipping; First Deputy Gen. Sec. Nordic Council of Ministers Sec. in Oslo 1983–86; State Sec. Ministry of Foreign Affairs 1986–88; Minister of Justice 1990–92; Dir. Norges Bank 1989; fmr. mem. Nat. Wages Arbitration Bd.

GJØNNES, Jon Kjell, DR.PHIL.; Norwegian professor of physics; b. 26 Jan. 1931, Brevik; s. of Knut Gjønnes and Ulrikka Gjønnes; m. Joy Angell-Baustad 1955; two d.; ed. Univ. of Oslo; Research Fellow, Royal Norwegian Council for Science and Humanities 1958–59; Research Fellow in Chemical Physics, CSIRO, Melbourne 1960–61; Univ. Fellow, Univ. of Oslo 1961–63; Sr. Research Fellow, Univ. of Melbourne 1964; Sr. lecturer in physics, Univ. of Oslo 1965–81, Prof. of Physics 1982; Visiting Prof. Tohoku Univ. Sendai, Japan 1974, 1994; Political Adviser, Ministry of Labour and Local Govt. 1980–81; Visiting Prof. Arizona State Univ. 1986; Chair. Norwegian Council for Information Tech. Policies 1988–90. *Publications:* numerous scientific articles on crystallography, materials research, solid state physics; chapters in several books on electron diffraction and electron microscopy. *Address:* Maridalsvn. 238, 0467 Oslo, Norway (Home). *Telephone:* 22 18 40 56 (Home). *Fax:* 22 95 87 49.

GJØNNES, Kåre; Norwegian politician; b. 30 Jan. 1942, Orkdal; m.; two c.; farmer 1967–; mem. Orkdal Municipal Council 1972–85, mem. Exec. Bd. 1976–; Mayor of Orkdal 1980–83; mem. Storting for Sør-Trøndelag Co. 1985–93; Deputy Chair. Standing Cttee. on Agric. 1985–89; Sec. Standing Cttee. on Foreign Affairs and the Constitution 1989–93; Co. Gov., Sør-Trøndelag 1993; Minister of Agric. Oct. 1997–; Christian Democratic Party. *Address:* Ministry of Agriculture, Akersgt. 42, P.O. Box 8001 Dep., 0030 Oslo, Norway. *Telephone:* 22-24-91-00.

GLADILIN, Anatoliy Tikhonovich; Russian writer; b. 21 Aug. 1935, Moscow; s. of Tikhon Illarionovich Gladilin and Polina Moïseevna Dreizer; m. Maria Gladilina 1955; two d.; ed. Gorky Literary Inst., Moscow; fmr. mem. of U.S.S.R. Writers' Union; literary activity started 1956; one of main contributors (with V. Aksyonov, q.v.) to Katayev's journal Youth 1960–65; one of founders of "Youth Prose" movement in early 1960s; signed letter of 80 writers in support of Solzhenitsyn's letter on abolition of censorship 1967; left U.S.S.R., expelled from Union of Writers 1976; settled in France. *Publications include:* Chronicle of the Times of Viktor Podgursky 1956, The Gospel from Robespierre 1970, Prognosis for Tomorrow 1972, The Dreams of Shlisselburg Fortress 1974, The Making and Unmaking of a Soviet Writer 1979, The Paris Fair 1980, A Big Race Day 1983, F.S.S.R. The French Soviet Socialist Republic Story 1985, As I Was Then: Tales 1986, The Beast Pell Killed Me 1991. *Address:* 11 Château Gaillard, Maisons Alfort, 94700 Paris, France. *Telephone:* (1) 43.96.21.99.

GLADSTONE, Sir (Erskine) William, Bt., J.P., M.A.; British scout and former schoolmaster; b. 29 Oct. 1925, Eton; s. of Charles A. and Isla M. (née Crum) Gladstone; m. Rosamund A. Hambro 1962; two s. one d.; ed. Eton and Christ Church, Oxford; Royal Navy 1943–46; Asst. Master, Shrewsbury School 1949–50, Eton Coll. 1951–61; Headmaster, Lancing Coll. 1961–69; Deputy Lieut. of Flintshire 1969, Clwyd 1974, Lord-Lieut. 1985; Chief Scout, U.K. and Overseas branches 1972–82; Chair. World Cttee. of the Scout Movt. 1979–81; Chair. Council of Glenalmond Coll. 1981–86; Lord Lieut. of Clwyd 1985–; Chair. Rep. Body, Church in Wales 1977–92; Hon. LL.D. (Liverpool) 1998. *Leisure interests:* reading history, gardening, shooting, watercolours. *Address:* Hawarden Castle, Flintshire, Wales (Home). *Telephone:* (01244) 520210.

GLAMANN, Kristof, O.B.E.; Danish business executive, professor of history and author; b. 26 Aug. 1926, Kerteminde; s. of Kai Kristof Glamann and Ebba H. K. Glamann (née Madsen); m. Kirsten Jantzen 1954; two s.; ed. Univ. of Copenhagen; Assoc. Prof. of History, Univ. of Copenhagen 1948–60, Prof. of Econ. History 1961–80; Visiting Prof., Univ. of Pa. 1960, Univ. of Wisconsin 1961, Visiting Northern Scholar, London School of Econs. 1966, Visiting Overseas Fellow, Churchill Coll., Cambridge Univ. 1971–72, 1993, Visiting Fellow, Toho Gakkai, Tokyo 1977; Master, 4th May and Hassager Coll., Copenhagen; mem. and Chair. Danish Research Council on Humanities 1968–70; mem. Bd. of Dirs., Carlsberg Foundation 1969–93, Pres. 1976–93; mem. Bd. of Dirs., Carlsberg Ltd. 1970–94, Deputy Chair. 1975–77, Chair. 1977–93; mem. Bd. of Dirs., Carlsberg Brewery Ltd. 1978–94, Royal Copenhagen Ltd. 1978–93, Fredericia Brewery 1979–94, Politiken Foundation 1990; Chair. Council, Investor and Reinvest Ltd.; Deputy Chair. The Scandinavia-Japan Sasakawa Foundation 1985–; mem. Royal Danish Acad. of Science and Letters 1969, Royal Danish History Soc. 1961, Swedish Acad., Lund 1963, History Soc. of Calcutta 1962, Corresp. mem. French History Soc. 1972; Hon. Pres. Int. Econ. History Assn. 1974; Hon. F.B.A. 1985; Corresp. Fellow Royal Belgian Acad. 1989; Hon. Dr. Soc. Sci. (Univ. of Gothenburg) 1974; Commdr. Order of Dannebrog (First Class); Commdr. Falcon of Iceland 1987, Das Grosse Verdienstkreuz (Germany) 1989, Order of Gorkha Dakshina Bahu (3rd Class) 1989. *Publications:* History of Tobacco Industry in Denmark 1875–1950 1950, Prices and Wages 1500–1800 1958, Dutch-Asiatic Trade 1620–1740 1958, Brewing 1962, European Trade 1500–1750 1971, Carlsberg Foundation 1976, Contributed to the Cambridge Economic History of Europe (Vol. V) 1977, Mercantilism 1982, Festschrift 1983, J. C. Jacobsen of Carlsberg: A biography 1990, Beer and Marble: A biography of Carl Jacobsen 1995, The Carlsberg Group Since 1970 1997; Ed.-in-Chief Scandinavian Econ. History Review 1961–80. *Leisure interests:* walking and drawing. *Address:* Bjerregaardsvej 6, 2500 Valby, Denmark. *Telephone:* 36 16 13 47. *Fax:* 36 45 44 30.

GLANVILLE, Brian Lester; British author and journalist; b. 24 Sept. 1931, London; s. of James A. Glanville and Florence Manches; m. Elizabeth De Boer 1959; two s. two d.; ed. Charterhouse; sports columnist and football corresp. Sunday Times 1958–92; sports columnist, The People 1992–96, The Times 1996–; literary adviser, Bodley Head 1958–62; Silver Bear Award, Berlin Film Festival, for European Centre Forward (BBC TV documentary) 1963. *Publications:* novels: Along the Arno 1956, The Bankrupts 1958, Diamond 1962, A Roman Marriage 1966, The Olympian 1969, A Cry of

Crickets 1970, The Comic 1974, The Catacomb 1988, Champions of Europe 1991, Story of the World Cup 1993; short stories: A Bad Streak 1961, The Things He Loves 1973; plays: A Visit to the Villa 1981, Underneath the Arches (musical) (co-author) 1981, The Diary (radio play) 1986. *Leisure interest:* playing football. *Address:* 160 Holland Park Avenue, London, W11 4UH, England. *Telephone:* 0171-603 6908.

GLASER, Donald Arthur, PH.D.; American physicist; b. 21 Sept. 1926, Cleveland, Ohio; s. of William Joseph and Lena Glaser; one s. one d.; ed. Case Inst. of Technology, California Inst. of Technology; Univ. of Mich. 1949–59; Univ. of Calif. 1960–; Nat. Science Foundation Fellow 1961; Guggenheim Fellow 1961–62; Biophysicist, Univ. of Calif., Berkeley 1962–64; Prof. of Physics, Neurobiology, and Molecular and Cell Biology, Univ. of Calif. 1964–; mem. N.A.S.; Hon. Sc.D.; Henry Russell Award 1955, Charles Vernon Boys Prize (The Physical Soc.) 1958, Nobel Prize 1960; several awards. *Publications:* Some Effects of Ionizing Radiation on the Formation of Bubbles in Liquids 1952, A Possible Bubble Chamber for the Study of Ionizing Events 1953, Bubble Chamber Tracks of Penetrating Cosmic-Ray Particles 1953, Progress Report on the Development of Bubble Chambers 1955, Strange Particle Production by Fast Pions in Propane Bubble Chamber 1957, Weak Interactions: Other Modes, Experimental Results 1958, The Bubble Chamber 1958, Development of Bubble Chamber and Some Recent Bubble Chamber Results in Elementary Particle Physics 1958, Decays of Strange Particles, 1959, Computer Identification of Bacteria by Colony Morphology 1972, Effect of Nalidixic Acid on DNA Replication by Toluene-treated E. coli 1973, The Isolation and Partial Characterization of Mutants of E. coli and Cold-sensitive Synthesis of DNA 1974, Rates of Chain Elongation of Ribosomal RNA Molecules in E. Coli 1974, Chromosomal Sites of DNA-membrane Attachment in E. coli 1974, Effect of Growth Conditions in DNA-membrane Attachment in E. coli 1975, Characteristics of Cold-sensitive Mutants of E. coli K12 Defective in Deoxyribonucleic Acid Replication 1975, A New Anisotrophy in Apparent Motion 1986, Differences betweeen Vertical and Horizontal Apparent Motion 1987, Speed Discrimination using Simple Sampled-Motion Stimuli 1987, Motion Interference in Speed Discrimination 1989, Influence of Remote Objects on Local Depth Perception 1991, Shape Analysis and Stereopsis for Human Depth Perception 1992, Depth Discrimination of a Line is Improved by Adding Other Nearby Lines 1992, Temporal Aspects of Depth Contrast 1993, Comparison of Human Performance with Algorithms for Estimating Fractal Dimension of Fractional Brownian Statistics 1993, Depth Discrimination of a Crowded Line Is Better When It Is More Luminant than the Lines Crowding It 1995, Stereopsis Due to Luminance Difference in the Two Eyes 1995, Multiple Matching of Features in Simple Stereograms 1996; many papers written jointly with other physicists. *Leisure interests:* skiing, sailing, skin diving, music. *Address:* Department of Molecular and Cell Biology, 229 Stanley Hall, University of California at Berkeley, CA 94720, U.S.A. *Telephone:* (510) 642-7231.

GLASER, Robert Joy, S.B., M.D., F.R.C.P. (U.K.); American foundation executive and physician; b. 11 Sept. 1918, St. Louis, Mo.; s. of Joseph and Regina Glaser; m. Helen H. Hofsommer 1949; two s. one d.; ed. Harvard Coll. and Medical School; appointments Instructor to Assoc. Prof., Washington Univ. School of Medicine 1949–57, Assoc. Dean 1955–57; Dean and Prof. of Medicine, Univ. of Colo. School of Medicine 1957–63, Vice-Pres. for Medical Affairs 1959–63; Prof. of Social Medicine, Harvard Univ. 1963–65; Vice-Pres. for Medical Affairs, Dean of the School of Medicine, Prof. of Medicine, Stanford Univ. 1965–70, Acting Pres. 1968, Visiting Prof. of Medicine 1972–73, Consulting Prof. 1972–; Clinical Prof. of Medicine, Columbia Univ. Coll. of Physicians and Surgeons 1971–72; Vice-Pres. The Commonwealth Fund 1970–72; Pres. and C.E.O. The Henry J. Kaiser Family Foundation 1972–83; Dir. First Boston Inc. 1982–88; Dir. Hewlett-Packard Co. 1971–91, Calif. Water Service Co. 1973–93, The Equitable Life Assurance Soc. of the U.S. 1979–86; mem. Bd. of Dirs. Alza Corpn., DCI, Pharmagenesis, Hanger Orthopedic Group; charter mem., Inst. of Medicine, Nat. Acad. of Science; mem., Bd. of Trustees, Washington Univ., St. Louis, Mo.; Lucille P. Markey Charitable Trust Dir. for Medical Science 1984–97, Trustee 1989–97; Trustee, Albert and Mary Lasker Foundation 1997–; Trustee, David and Lucile Packard Foundation 1985–97; Fellow, American Acad. of Arts and Sciences 1964–; eight hon. degrees; Centennial Award for Distinguished Service, Univ. of Colo. 1983; Medal for Distinguished Service, Univ. of Calif., San Francisco 1983; Abraham Flexner Award, Asscn. of American Medical Colls. 1984; Hubert H. Humphrey Cancer Research Center Award 1985. *Publications:* 126 papers on experimental streptococcal infections, antibiotics and other topics concerning medicine and medical educ.; numerous chapters in medical books. *Leisure interests:* travel, swimming, reading and music. *Address:* 1 Elm Place, Atherton, CA 94027, U.S.A. *Telephone:* (650) 328-5869.

GLASHOW, Sheldon Lee, PH.D.; American physicist; b. 5 Dec. 1932, New York; s. of Lewis Glashow and Bella Rubin; m. Joan Shirley Alexander 1972; three s. one d.; ed. Bronx High School of Science, Cornell and Harvard Univs.; Nat. Science Foundation Post-Doctoral Fellow, Univ. of Copenhagen 1958–60; Research Fellow, Calif. Inst. of Tech. 1960–61; Asst. Prof., Stanford Univ. 1961–62; Assoc. Prof., Univ. of Calif. (Berkeley) 1962–66; Prof. of Physics, Harvard 1967–, Higgins Prof. 1979–; Mellon Prof. of Sciences 1988–; Alfred P. Sloan Foundation Fellowship 1962–66; Visiting Scientist, C.E.R.N. 1968; Visiting Prof., Univ. of Marseille 1970, M.I.T. 1974, 1980–81, Boston Univ. 1983–84; Consultant, Brookhaven Lab. 1966–73, 1975–; Affil. Sr. Scientist, Univ. of Houston 1983–; Univ. Scholar, Texas A & M Univ. 1983–86, Distinguished Visiting Scientist, Boston Univ. 1984–; Fellow, American Physical Soc., A.A.A.S.; Pres. Int. Sakharov Cttee. 1980–85; mem. American Acad. of Arts and Sciences, N.A.S.; Sponsor, Fed. of American Scientists (F.A.S.) and Bulletin of the Atomic Scientists; mem. Advisory Council American Acad. of Achievement 1979–, Science Policy Cttee., C.E.R.N. 1979–; founding Ed. Quantum (magazine) 1989–; Dr. h.c., Univ. of Aix-Marseille 1982; Oppenheimer Memorial Medal 1977; George Ledlie Award 1978; Hon. D.Sc. (Yeshiva Univ.) 1978, (Bar Ilan Univ., Gustavus Adolphus Coll., Adelphi Univ.) 1989; shared Nobel Prize for Physics with Abdus Salam and Steven Weinberg (qq.v.) for work on elementary particles 1979. *Publications:* Interactions (with Ben Bova) 1989, Charm of Physics 1990, From Alchemy to Quarks 1994; over 200 articles on elementary particle physics. *Address:* 30 Prescott Street, Brookline, MA 02146, U.S.A. (Home). *Telephone:* 617-495-2904.

GLASS, David D., American business executive; b. 1935; m.; Gen. Man. Crank Drug Co. 1957–67; Vice-Pres. Consumers Markets Inc. 1967–76; Exec. Vice-Pres. Wal-Mart Stores Inc. –1976, Chief Financial Officer 1976–84, Pres. 1984–, C.O.O. 1984–88, C.E.O. 1988–, also Dir.; C.E.O. and Chair. Bd. Dirs. Kansas City Royals 1993–. *Address:* Wal-Mart Stores Inc., 702 SW 8th Street, Bentonville, AR 72716; Kansas City Royals, P.O. Box 419969, Kansas City, MO 64141, U.S.A.

GLASS, Philip; American composer; b. 31 Jan. 1937, Baltimore; s. of Benjamin Glass and Ida (Gouline) Glass; m. 1st JoAnne Akalaitis; m. 2nd Luba Burtyk (divorced); one s. one d.; m. 3rd Candy Jernigan (died 1991); ed. Univ. of Chicago and Juilliard School of Music; Composer-in-Residence, Pittsburgh Public Schools 1962–64; studied with Nadia Boulanger, Paris 1964–66; f. Philip Glass Ensemble 1968, concert tours U.S.A. and Europe 1968–; f. record co. Chatham Square Productions, New York 1972; *Compositions include:* (operas, theatre and film scores) Orphée, The Voyage, The Juniper Tree, The Palace of the Arabian Nights, The Fall of the House of Usher, Einstein on the Beach 1976, Satyagraha 1980, The Photographer 1982, The Civil Wars 1982–84, Akhnaten 1984, The Making of the Representative for Planet 8 1988, Mattogrosso 1989, 1,000 Airplanes on the Roof (with David Henry Hwang) 1989, Hydrogen Jukebox (with Allen Ginsberg) 1990; (film scores) North Star 1977, Koyaannisqatsi 1983, Mishima 1985, Powaqqatsi 1987, The Thin Blue Line 1988, Hamburger Hill 1989, Mindwalk 1990, A Brief History of Time 1991, Anima Mundi 1991, Candyman 1992, The Voyage 1992, Orphee 1993, Candyman II: Farewell to the Flesh 1994, Monsters of Grace 1998, Bent 1998, Kundun 1998; (instrumental works) String Quartets (1–4), Violin Concerto, Low Symphony and numerous other works; Broadcast Music Industry Award 1960, Lado Prize 1961, Benjamin Award 1961, 1962, Young Composer's Award, Ford Foundation 1964–66, Fulbright award 1966–67, New York Dance and Performance Award 1995 and other awards. *Publication:* Opera on the Beach 1988. *Address:* c/o IPA, 584 Broadway, Room 1008, New York, NY 10012, U.S.A.

GLASSPOLE, Sir Florizel Augustus, G.C.M.G., G.C.V.O.; Jamaican politician; b. 25 Sept. 1909, Kingston; s. of Rev. Theophilus A. Glasspole and Florence Glasspole (née Baxter); m. Ina Josephine Kinlocke 1934; one d.; ed. Wolmer's Boys' School, Ruskin Coll., Oxford; Accountant 1932-44; Gen. Sec. Jamaica United Clerks Asscn. 1937–48, Jamaica Trades Union Congress 1939–52, Water Comm. and Manual Workers Asscn. 1941–48, Municipal and Parochial Gen. Workers Union 1945–47, Nat. Workers Union 1952–55; Pres. Jamaica Printers and Allied Workers Union 1942–48; Gen. Hospital and Allied Workers Union 1944–47, Mental Hospital Workers Union 1944–47, Machado Employees Union 1945–52; Dir. City Printery Ltd. 1944–50; mem. House of Reps. 1944–73, Leader 1955–62, 1972–73; Minister of Labour 1955–57, of Educ. 1957–62, 1972–73; Vice-Pres. PNP; Sec. PNP Parl. Group 1944–73; Gov.-Gen. of Jamaica 1973–91; mem. Standing Cttee on West Indian Fed. 1953–58, House of Reps. Cttee. preparing Jamaica's independence constitution, mem. Del. finalizing constitution with British Govt. 1962; workers' rep. on several Govt. Bds. 1942–53; mem. Bd. of Govs. Inst. of Jamaica 1944–57, Kingston School Bd.; ex officio mem. K.S.A.C. 1944–55; Hon. LL.D. (Univ. of West Indies) 1982; two Jamaican decorations and Order of Andrés Bello (1st Class) (Venezuela) 1973. *Leisure interests:* sports, gardening. *Address:* c/o Kings House, Hope Road, Kingston 10, Jamaica.

GLATZ, Ferenc, PH.D.; Hungarian historian; b. 2 April 1941; Research Fellow Inst. of History of Hungarian Acad. of Sciences 1968–, Scientific Deputy Dir. 1986–88, Dir. of Inst. 1988–; Corresp. mem. Hungarian Acad. of Sciences 1993–, Pres. 1996–; Prof. Eötvös Loránd Univ., Budapest 1974–; Minister for Culture and Educ. 1989–90; organizer and Dir. Europa Inst., Budapest 1990–. *Publications:* numerous studies and books on 19th and 20th century history of Hungarian and European culture and historiography. *Address:* Magyar Tudományos Akadémia, 1051 Budapest, Roosevelt tér. 9, Hungary. *Telephone:* 332-7176. *Fax:* 332-8943.

GLAVIN, William F., M.B.A.; American business executive; b. 29 March 1932, Albany, New York; s. of John Glavin; m. Cecily McClatchy 1955; three s. four d.; ed. Coll. of the Holy Cross, Worcester and Wharton Graduate School of the Univ. of Pennsylvania; fmr. Exec. Int. Business Machines and Vice-Pres. Operations, Service Bureau Corpn. (an IBM subsidiary); Exec. Vice-Pres. Xerox Data Systems 1970, Group Vice-Pres. 1972, Man. Dir. and C.O.O. 1974, Exec. Vice-Pres. Xerox 1980, and Exec. Vice-Pres. for Reprographics and Operations 1982, Pres. Business Equipment Group

1983–89, Vice-Chair. Xerox Corpn. 1985–89; mem. Bd. of Dirs. Xerox, Fuji Xerox and Rank Xerox, also the Xerox Foundation; Pres. Babson Coll., Wellesley, Mass. 1989–; mem. Bd. of Dirs. Gould Inc., State Street Boston Corpn., Norton Co.; mem. Bd. of Trustees and Pres.'s Council Coll. of the Holy Cross. *Leisure interests:* golf, reading, art, music. *Address:* Office of the President, Babson College, Babson Park, MA 02157, U.S.A.

GLAZER, Nathan, PH.D.; American educationist; b. 25 Feb. 1923, New York; s. of Louis Glazer and Tillie (Zacharevich) Glazer; m. 1st Ruth Slotkin 1943 (divorced 1958); three d.; m. 2nd Sulochana Raghavan 1962; ed. City Coll. of New York, Univ. of Pennsylvania and Columbia Univ; mem. of staff, Commentary Magazine 1944–53; Ed. and Editorial Adviser, Doubleday Anchor Books 1954–57; Visiting Lecturer, Univ. of Calif., Berkeley 1957–58; Instructor, Bennington Coll., Vermont 1958–59; Visiting Lecturer, Smith Coll. 1959–60; Prof. of Sociology, Univ. of Calif., Berkeley 1963–69; Prof. of Educ. and Social Structure, Harvard Univ. 1969–93; Fellow, Center for Advanced Study in the Behavioural Sciences, Stanford, Calif. 1971–72; co-ed. The Public Interest Magazine 1973–; mem. American Acad. of Arts and Sciences, Library of Congress Council of Scholars; Guggenheim Fellow 1954, 1966; Hon.LL.D. (Franklin and Marshall Coll.) 1971, LL.D. (Colby Coll.) 1972, D.H.L. (Long Island Univ.) 1978, (Hebrew Union Coll.) 1986. *Publications:* American Judaism 1957, 1972, The Social Basis of American Communism 1961, Remembering the Answers 1970, Affirmative Discrimination 1976, Ethnic Dilemmas 1964–1982 1983, The Limits of Social Policy 1989; co-author: The Lonely Crowd 1950, Faces in the Crowd 1952, Studies in Housing and Minority Groups 1960, Beyond the Melting Pot 1963, Conflicting Images, India and the United States 1990, We Are All Multiculturalists Now 1997; co-editor: The Public Interest 1973–. *Address:* 12 Scott Street, Cambridge, MA 02138, U.S.A. *Telephone:* (617) 868-5459. *Fax:* (617) 496-3095.

GLAZ'IEV, Sergey Yurievich, DR.EC.SC.; Russian economist; b. 1 Jan. 1961, Zaporozhye; m.; three c.; ed. Moscow State Univ.; Head of Lab., Cen. Econ. Math. Inst. 1986–91; First Deputy Chair. Cttee. on External Econ. Relations Ministry of Foreign Affairs 1991–92; First Deputy Minister of External Econ. Relations of Russia 1992, Minister 1992–93; mem. State Duma (Parl.) 1993–95; Chair. Cttee. for Econ. Policy of State Duma 1994–95; Chair. Nat. Cttee. of Democratic Party of Russia 1994–96; Head of Econ. Dept., Security Council 1996; Head, Information-Analytical Bd., Council of Fed. (Parl.) 1996–. *Publications:* Economic Theory of Technical Development 1993, Economy and Politics 1994, One and a Half Years in the Duma 1995, Under the Critical Level 1996, Genocide 1997 1998. *Address:* Council of the Federation, Federal Assembly of the Russian Federation, Bolshaya Dmitrovka str. 26, 103426 Moscow, Russia. *Telephone:* (095) 203-78-58. *Fax:* (095) 203-96-23.

GLAZUNOV, Ilya Sergeyevich; Russian painter; b. 10 June 1930, Leningrad; s. of S. F. Glazunov and O. K. Glazunova (née Flug); m. M. Vinogradova-Benua; one s. one d.; ed. Repin Arts Inst. (pupil of B. Ioganson); First Prize Int. Art Exhbn., Prague 1956; first one-man show, Moscow 1957; teacher of drawing in Izhevsk, then Ivanovo; returned to Moscow 1960; Prof., Surikov Inst., Moscow 1978–; exhibited in art exhbns. in Warsaw, Rome, Copenhagen, Vietnam, Laos, Paris, Leningrad, Santiago, Stockholm, Berlin (East and West), Leipzig, Fed. Germany 1960–77, London (Barbican) 1987; participated in restoration of Cathedral of the Saviour, Moscow 1994–; f. and Pres. All-Russian Acad. of Painting, Sculpture and Architecture 1991–; People's Artist of the U.S.S.R. 1980; Order (First Class) for Services to the Motherland 1996; Russian State Prize 1997; Order of Sergei Radonezsky 1998. *Publications:* The Road to You 1965, Russia Crucified 1996. *Leisure interests:* philosophy, history, classical music. *Address:* RAZHVIZ Academy, Kamergersky per. 2, 103009 Moscow, Russia (Office). *Telephone:* (095) 292-33-74 (Office).

GLEDHILL, David Anthony, C.B.E., J.P.; British business executive; b. 16 Oct. 1934, Karachi, Pakistan; s. of Arnold C. Gledhill and Marjorie Y. Johnson; m. Kyoko Takeuchi 1968; ed. Ellesmere Coll. Shropshire and Sidney Sussex Coll. Cambridge; joined John Swire & Sons (H.K.) 1958–92; served Hong Kong, Osaka, Yokohama, Tokyo; The China Navigation Co., Ltd. Hong Kong 1963–65; Shipping Man. John Swire & Sons (Japan) 1966–73; Dir. John Swire & Sons (H.K.) 1973–84, Deputy Chair. 1984–88, Chair. 1988–92; Chair. Swire Shipping (Agencies) 1973–88; Dir. Swire Pacific 1973–88, Deputy Chair. 1984–88, Chair. 1988–92; Chair. Swire Properties 1973–92; Chair. Swire Pacific Offshore Services 1975–88, Swire Pacific Ltd. 1976–88, Modern Terminals 1981–94 (Dir. 1973–81), Cathay Pacific Airways 1988–92; Dir. Hongkong & Shanghai Banking Corpn. 1988–92, Swire Pacific Offshore Holdings Ltd. 1988–92, Lee Garden Int. Hotels 1988–92, Community Chest of Hong Kong 1988, Mass Transit Railway Corpn. 1990–98, Hysan Devt. Co. 1990–98, China Investment & Devt. Fund Ltd. 1992–98, Peregrine Int. Holdings Ltd. 1993–98, IBM Hong Kong/China Bd. 1993–99 (now IBM Greater China Advisory Bd), IBM World Trade Asia Pacific Bd. 1989–93, KLM Royal Dutch Airlines 1995–99, Fleming Chinese Investment Trust PLC 1996–99; Chair. Employers' Fed. of Hong Kong 1989–91, Hong Kong Sports Devt. Bd. 1992–96; Dir. Securities and Futures Comm. 1990–93; mem. Council, Hong Kong Gen. Chamber of Commerce 1988–92; mem. Aviation Advisory Bd., Consultative Cttee. for Basic Law 1988–92; mem. Provision Airport Authority (now Airport Authority Hong Kong) 1990–; mem. Business and Professionals Fed. Bd. of Trustees 1990–; mem. PA Man. Consultants Advisory Bd. 1993–98; mem. Textron Int. Advisory Bd. 1996–98; mem. Univ. of Hong Kong. *Leisure interests:* swimming, sailing, fishing. *Address:* c/o Modern Terminals Ltd., Berth One, Kwai Chung, Hong Kong Special Administrative Region, People's Republic of China; 29 The Little Boltons, London, S.W.10, England. *Telephone:* (852) 2115 3530 (Hong Kong). *Fax:* (852) 2481 6794 (Hong Kong).

GLEICH, Walter A.; German business executive and consultant; b. 4 Nov. 1924, Hamburg; s. of Walter H. and Ferdinande (née von Gossler) Gleich; m. Inta Köhn; four d.; ed. High School, Hamburg; joined Norddeutsche Affinerie AG 1942, mem. Man. Bd. 1961–86, Pres. 1976–86; various Bd. memberships. *Leisure interests:* sailing, tennis. *Address:* Golfstrasse 3, 22605 Hamburg, Germany. *Telephone:* (40) 82-06-71. *Fax:* (40) 822-60-89.

GLEMP, H.E. Cardinal Józef, DR.IUR.UTR.; Polish ecclesiastic; b. 18 Dec. 1929, Inowrocław; s. of Kazimierz and Salomea (née Kośmicka) Glemp; ed. Primatial Spiritual Seminary, Gniezno and Poznań, and Pontifical Lateran Univ., Rome; ordained priest, Gniezno 1956; educational and catechistic work 1956–58; studied in Rome 1958–64; various posts, Curia, Tribunal, and Lecturer, Primatial Spiritual Seminary, Gniezno 1964–67; with Secr., Primate of Poland 1967–79; Roman Law Lecturer, Acad. of Catholic Theology, Warsaw 1967–79; mem. Episcopal Comm. for Revision of Canon Law and Sec. Comm. for Polish Insts. Rome 1975–79; Hon. Chaplain to His Holiness the Pope 1972; Gremial Canon of the Primatial Capitular, Gniezno 1976; Bishop and Ordinary, Diocese of Warmia, Olsztyn 1979–81; Archbishop-Metropolitan of Gniezno and Warsaw and Primate of Poland 1981–92, Archbishop-Metropolitan of Warsaw and Primate of Poland 1992–; cr. Cardinal 1983; Co.-Chair. Working Group for Legis. Affairs, Joint Comm. of Govt. and Episcopate Jan.–July 1981; Chair. Chief Council of Polish Episcopate, Chair. Conf. of Polish Episcopate 1981; Pres. Bishop's Cttee. for Pastoral Care of Poles Abroad; Pres. Bishop's Cttee. for Catholic Univ. of Lublin 1981; Ordinary for the Armenian-rite Communities in Poland 1981–92, for the Greek-Catholic Communities in Poland 1981–89, for believers of Oriental rites 1992; mem. Congregation for the Oriental Churches 1983, Pontifical Council for Justice and Peace, Pontifical Council of Culture 1993; High Chancellor Acad. of Catholic Theology and Pontifical Dept. of Theology, Warsaw; Dr. h.c. (Acad. of Catholic Theology, Warsaw) 1982, (Villanova Univ., U.S.A.) 1985, (Lublin Catholic Univ.) 1985, (St. Thomas Univ., Manila) 1988, (Univ. of Bari) 1990, (Seton Hall Univ., N.J.) 1991, (Loyola Univ. of Chicago) (Pontifical Dept. of Theology and Main School of Farming (S.O.G.W.) Warsaw) 1992. *Publications:* De conceptu fictionis iuris apud Romanos 1974, Lexiculum iuris romani 1974, Solidarietà. La Polonia che sogniamo 1991, Przez sprawiedliwość ku miłości 1982, Człowiek wielkiej wiary 1983, Kościół na drogach Ojczyzny 1985, Chcemy z tego sprawdzianu wyjść prawdomówni i wiarygodni 1985, Kościół i Polonia 1986, Umocnieni nadzieją 1987, W tęczy Franków orzeł i krzyż 1987, O Eucharystii 1987, Nauczanie pasterskie (4 vols.) 1981–88, A wołanie moje niech do Ciebie przyjdzie 1988, Boże, coś Polskę posłał nad Tamizę 1988, Nauczanie społeczne 1981–1986, 1989, Na dwóch wybrzeżach 1990, U przyjaciół Belgów 1990, I uwierzyli uczniowie 1990, Zamyślenia Maryjne 1990, Słowo Boże nad Łyną 1991, Tysiąclecie wiary Świętego Włodzimierza 1991, Gniezno ciągła odnowa 1991, Służyć Ewangelii słowem 1991, Na Skałce—na opoce 1991, Niebo ściągają na ziemię 1991, Między Ewangelią a konstytucją 1992, Na wyspie Świętego Patryka 1992, Idźmy do Betlejem 1992, Wartości chrześcijańskie nabywane pod Kalwarią 1993, W blaskach Zmartwychwstania 1994, Być znakiem miłości 1994, Rodzina drogą Kościoła 1995, Boskie i cesarskie 1995, Idzie, idzie Bóg prawdziwy 1995, Les chemins des pèlerins 1996, Od Kalwarii na drogi Europy 1997, Święci idą przez Warszawę 1997, Poles—Now We Enter the Twenty-First Century 1998. *Address:* Rezydencja Prymasa Polski, ul. Miodowa 17/19, 00-246 Warsaw, Poland. *Telephone:* (22) 831 21 57. *Fax:* (22) 635 87 45.

GLEMSER, Oskar Max, DR.-ING.; German chemist; b. 12 Nov. 1911, Stuttgart; s. of Karl Glemser and Amalie Gogel; m. Ida-Maria Greiner 1938; one s. one d.; ed. Gymnasium Bad-Canstatt and Technische Hochschule, Stuttgart; Sr. Engineer, Inst. for Inorganic Chemistry and Electro Chemistry, Technische Hochschule, Aachen 1939–41, Dozent 1941–48, Extra-Mural Prof. 1948–52; Prof. and Dir. of the Inst. of Inorganic Chemistry Univ. of Göttingen 1952–80; Pres. of Acad. of Sciences, Göttingen 1962–70; mem. Bureau IUPAC 1973–77; Pres. German Chemical Soc. 1976–77; mem. Leopoldina German Acad. for Scientific Research, Halle, Austrian Acad. of Sciences, New York Acad. of Sciences, American Assn. for the Advancement of Science; Hon. mem. German Chemical Soc. 1988–; Dr. Ing. e.h., Dr. rer. nat. h.c., Dr. h.c.; Liebig Medal of German Chemical Soc. 1970; Silver Medal of Univ. of Helsinki 1972; Medal of Jozef Stefan Inst., Ljubljana, Henri Moissan Medal of Société Française de Chimie 1986, ACS Award for Creative Work in Fluorine Chemistry 1994. *Leisure interests:* archaeology, literature, skiing, swimming. *Address:* Tammannstrasse 4, 37077 Göttingen (Office); Hannoversche Str. 152, Apt. 28, 37077 Göttingen, Germany (Home). *Telephone:* 0551-393067 (Office); 0551-57814 (Home). *Fax:* 0551-392582.

GLEN, Sir Alexander Richard, K.B.E., D.S.C.; British business executive; b. 18 April 1912; s. of the late R. Bartlett Glen; m. 1st Nina Nixon (divorced 1945); one s.; m. 2nd Baroness Zora de Collaert 1947; ed. Fettes Coll., and Balliol Coll., Oxford; Organizer and Leader, Oxford Univ. Arctic Expedition 1933, 1935–36; Banking, New York and London 1936–39; R.N.V.R. 1939–59; Chair. H. Clarkson & Co. Ltd. 1962–72; Deputy Chair. Export Council for Europe 1960–64, Chair. 1964–66; mem. Council Royal Geographical Soc. 1945–47, 1954–57, 1961–62; mem. Council, Mount Everest Foundation

1955–57; Chair. British Tourist Authority 1969–77; Group Chair. Anglo World Travel 1978–81; Deputy Chair. British Transport Hotels 1978–83; Dir. Gleneagles Hotels 1980–83; mem. Historic Bldgs. Council for England 1976–80, Horse-race Totalisator Bd. 1976–84, Advisory Council, Victoria and Albert Museum 1976–, Chair. 1978–84; Pres. British Air Line Pilots' Asscn. 1982–94, Vice-Pres. 1994–; numerous medals and decorations. *Publications:* Young Men in the Arctic 1935, Under the Pole Star 1937, Footholds Against a Whirlwind (autobiog.) 1975. *Leisure interests:* travel, skiing, sailing. *Address:* The Dower House, Stanton, Broadway, Worcs., WR12 7NE, England.

GLENAMARA, Baron (Life Peer), cr. 1977; **Edward Watson Short,** P.C., C.H.; British politician; b. 17 Dec. 1912; m. Jennie Sewell 1941; one s. one d.; ed. Bede Coll., Durham; served Second World War and became Capt. in Durham Light Infantry; Headmaster, Princess Louise County Secondary School, Blyth, Northumberland 1947; Leader Labour Group, Newcastle City Council 1950; M.P. for Newcastle upon Tyne Central 1951–76; Opposition Whip (N. Area) 1955–62; Deputy Chief Opposition Whip 1962–64; Parl. Sec. to Treasury and Govt. Chief Whip 1964–66; Postmaster-Gen. 1966–68; Sec. of State for Educ. and Science 1968–70; Deputy Leader of Labour Party 1972–76; Lord Pres. of Council, Leader of House of Commons 1974–76; Chair. Cable and Wireless Co. 1976–80; Pres. Finchdale Abbey Training Coll. for the Disabled, Durham; Chancellor Univ. of Northumbria (fmrly. Polytechnic of Newcastle upon Tyne) 1984–; Hon. D.C.L. (Durham), D.Univ. (Open Univ.) 1989; D.Litt. (C.N.A.A.) 1990. *Publications:* The Story of the Durham Light Infantry 1944, The Infantry Instructor 1946, Education in a Changing World 1971, Birth to Five 1974, I Knew My Place 1983, Whip to Wilson: The Crucial Years of Labour Government 1989. *Address:* House of Lords, London S.W.1; 21 Priory Gardens, Corbridge, Northumberland, NE45 5HZ, England.

GLENCROSS, David, C.B.E., B.A.; British broadcasting executive; b. 3 March 1936, Salford; s. of John William Glencross and Elsie May Glencross; m. Elizabeth Louise Richardson 1965; one d.; ed. Salford Grammar School, Trinity Coll., Cambridge; BBC Gen. Trainee 1958–59, Producer 1959–68, Exec. (North Region) 1968–70; Sr. Programme Officer, Independent TV Authority 1970–76, Head of Programme Services 1976–77, Deputy Dir. of TV 1977–83, Dir. of TV 1983–90; Chief Exec. Ind. TV Comm. 1990–96; Chair. British Screen Advisory Council 1996–97; Dir. Ind. Media Support Ltd. 1996–; Trustee Sandford St. Martin Trust 1998–; Fellow Royal TV Soc. 1981; Hon. M.A. (Salford) 1993. *Publications:* various articles in European newspapers and magazines. *Leisure interests:* music, walking, travel, theatre, cinema. *Address:* Independent Media Support Limited, 21 Soho Square, London, W1V 5FD, England. *Telephone:* 0171-440 5400.

GLENDENING, Parris Nelson, M.A., PH.D.; American state governor; b. 11 June 1942, Bronx, N.Y.; m. Frances A. Hughes 1976; one s.; ed. Florida State Univ. Fort Lauderdale and Tallahassee; Asst. Prof. Univ. of Md., College Park 1967–72, Assoc. Prof. 1972–95; Co. Exec. Prince George's Co. Council, Upper Marlboro, Md. 1982–95; various public appts. at co. level; Dir. World Trade Center 1990–97; Gov. of Maryland Jan. 1995–; mem. A.A.A.S., American Political Science Asscn. etc.; Democrat. *Publications:* Controversies of State and Local Political Systems (with M. M. Reeves) 1972, Pragmatic Federalism 1977; articles in professional publications. *Address:* Office of the Governor, State House, Annapolis, MD 21401, U.S.A. *Telephone:* (410) 974-3901. *Fax:* (410) 974-3278.

GLENDINNING, Hon. Victoria, C.B.E., M.A., F.R.S.L.; British author and journalist; b. 23 April 1937, Sheffield; d. of Baron Seebohm of Hertford and Lady Seebohm (née Hurst); m. 1st O. N. V. Glendinning 1959 (divorced 1981); four s.; m. 2nd Terence de Vere White 1981 (died 1994); m. 3rd Kevin O'Sullivan 1996; ed. St. Mary's School, Wantage, Millfield School, Somerville Coll., Oxford and Univ. of Southampton; part-time teaching 1960–69; part-time psychiatric social work 1970–73; Editorial Asst. Times Literary Supplement 1974–78; Hon. D. Litt. (Southampton Univ.) 1994, Dr h.c. (Ulster) 1995, Litt.D. (Dublin Univ.) 1995. *Publications:* A Suppressed Cry 1969, Elizabeth Bowen: portrait of a writer 1977, Edith Sitwell: a unicorn among lions 1981, Vita: a biography of V. Sackville-West 1983, Rebecca West: a life 1987, The Grown-Ups (novel) 1989, Hertfordshire 1989, Trollope 1992, Electricity (novel) 1995, Sons and Mothers (co-ed.) 1996, Jonathan Swift 1998; articles in newspapers and journals. *Address:* c/o David Higham Associates, 5-8 Lower John Street, Golden Square, London, W1R 4HA, England.

GLENN, Sir Archibald (see Glenn, Sir Joseph Robert Archibald).

GLENN, Lt.-Col. John Herschel, Jr.; American astronaut, politician and aviator; b. 18 July 1921, Cambridge, Ohio; s. of John H. Glenn and Clare Sproat; m. Anna Margaret Castor 1943; one s. one d.; ed. Muskingum Coll., Univ. of Maryland; naval aviation cadet 1942; commissioned Marine Corps 1943; Marine Fighter Squadron 155 in Marshall Islands 1944 (59 combat missions); mem. Fighter Squadron 218 North China Patrol; Instructor Corpus Christi, Texas 1948–50; Marine Fighter Squadron Korea (63 missions); Fighter Design Branch, Navy Bureau of Aeronautics, Washington 1956; speed record Los Angeles—New York (3 hr. 23 min.) 1957; training for space flight 1960–61; completed 3 orbits of the earth in Spaceship Friendship VII, 20th Feb. 1962; resigned from U.S. Marine Corps 1965; Dir. Royal Crown Cola Co. 1965–74; Consultant to NASA; U.S. Senator from Ohio 1975–99; announced return as astronaut Oct. 1997, on board Discovery shuttle 1998; D.F.C. (8 times) and Air Medal with 18 clusters; NASA Distinguished Service Medal 1962; U.S. Nat. Space Hall of Fame Award 1969; Democrat. *Publications:* (co-author) We Seven 1962, P.S., I Listened to Your Heart Beat. *Address:* c/o U.S. Senate, 503 Hart Senate Office Building, Washington, DC 20510, U.S.A.

GLENN, Sir (Joseph Robert) Archibald, Kt, O.B.E., B.C.E. F.I.E. (AUST.), F.I.CHEM.E.; Australian chemicals executive and engineer; b. 24 May 1911, Sale, Victoria; s. of Joseph Robert Glenn; m. 1st Elizabeth M. M. Balderstone 1939 (died 1988); one s. three d.; m. 2nd Suzanne Debenham (née Hennessey) 1992; ed. Scotch Coll., Melbourne, Melbourne and Harvard Univs.; Chief Engineer ICI Australia Ltd. 1947–49, Gen. Man. 1949–53, Man. Dir. 1953–73, Chair. 1963–73; Dir. ICI Ltd. 1970–75; Chair. Fibremakers Ltd. 1963–73; Dir. Bank of New South Wales (now called Westpac Banking Corpn.) 1967–84; Chair. IMI Australia Ltd. 1970–78, Collins Wales Pty. Ltd. 1973–84, Tioxide Australia Ltd. 1973–86, IC Insurance Australia Ltd. 1974–86; Dir. Alcoa Australia Ltd. 1973–86, Hill Samuel Australia Ltd. 1973–83, Westralian Sands Ltd. 1977–86, Newmont Pty. Ltd. (now Newcrest Australia Ltd.) 1976–88; Gov. Atlantic Inst. of Int. Affairs; Chair. Council, Scotch Coll. 1953–82, Ormond Coll. Council 1976–81, Pacific Inst. Council 1976–96; Chancellor, La Trobe Univ., Melbourne 1966–72; mem. Red Cross Nat. Finance Cttee. 1980–98; Hon. D.Univ. (La Trobe) 1981. *Publication:* Things to be Remembered. *Leisure interests:* reading, travel, farming. *Address:* 8 Freemans Road, Mt. Eliza, Vic. 3930, Australia. *Telephone:* (03) 9787-5850. *Fax:* (03) 9787-0309.

GLENNIE, Evelyn Elizabeth Ann, O.B.E., G.R.S.M., F.R.A.M., F.R.C.M.; British musician; b. 19 July 1965, Aberdeen; d. of Isobel Glennie and Herbert Arthur Glennie; m. Gregorio Malcangi 1993; ed. Ellon Acad., Aberdeenshire, Royal Acad. of Music, London; studied in Japan 1986; solo debut at Wigmore Hall, London, 1986; concerto, chamber and solo percussion performances worldwide; gave Promenade concerts' first-ever percussion recital 1989; numerous TV appearances, including three documentaries on her life; many works written for her by composers, including Bennett, Bourgeois, Heath, Macmillan, McLeod, Muldowney and Musgrave; f. Evelyn Glennie Percussion Composition Award; Hon. Fellow Welsh Coll. of Music and Drama; Hon. D.Mus. (Aberdeen) 1991, (Bristol, Portsmouth) 1995, (Leicester) 1997; Hon. D.Litt. (Warwick) 1993, (Loughborough) 1995; Hon.D.Mus. (Queen's, Belfast) 1998; many prizes and awards, including Queen's Commendation Prize at R.A.M., Shell/LSO Music Gold Medal 1984, Munster Trust Scholarship 1986, Charles Heidsieck Soloist of the Year, Royal Philharmonic Soc. 1991, Personality of the Year, Int. Classical Music Awards 1993. *Recordings include:* Rhythm Song, Dancin', Light in Darkness, Rebounds, Veni Veni Emmanuel, Wind in the Bamboo Grove, Drumming, Her Greatest Hits, The Music of Joseph Schwantner, Sonata for Two Pianos and Percussion (Bartók), Last Night of the Proms—100th Season, Street Songs, Reflected in Brass. *Publication:* Good Vibrations (autobiography) 1990. *Leisure interests:* reading, walking, cycling. *Address:* P.O. Box 6, Sawtry, Huntingdon, Cambs., PE17 5WE, England. *Telephone:* (01480) 891772. *Fax:* (01480) 893910.

GLESKE, Leonhard, DR.RER.POL.; German banker; b. 18 Sept. 1921; s. of Gustav Gleske and Lydia Gohl; m. Christa Reimann 1956; one s. three d.; fmr. mem. of the Bd. and mem. Central Bank Council, Deutsche Bundesbank; Deputy Chair. Bd. of Dirs. Bank of Tokyo (Deutschland) AG; mem. Advisory Bd. J. P. Morgan GmbH; Dr. h.c. (Univ. of Münster) 1985; Hon. Prof. (Mannheim) 1986. *Address:* Kaiser-Friedrich Promenade 151, 61352 Bad Homburg, Germany.

GLICKMAN, Daniel Robert, J.D.; American politician; b. 24 Nov. 1944, Wichita, Kan.; s. of Milton Glickman and Gladys A. Kopelman; m. Rhoda J. Yura 1966; one s. one d.; ed. Univ. of Michigan, Ann Arbor and George Washington Univ.; mem. Kansas Bar 1969, Mich. Bar 1970; trial attorney, Securities & Exchange Comm. 1969–70; Assoc. then partner, Sargent, Klenda & Glickman, Wichita 1971–76; mem. 95th–103rd Congresses from 4th Kansas Dist. 1977–95; Sec. of Agric. 1995–; Democrat. *Address:* Department of Agriculture, Suite 200A, 1400 Independence Avenue, SW, Washington, DC 20250, U.S.A. *Telephone:* (202) 447-2791. *Fax:* (202) 447-5340.

GLIDEWELL, Rt. Hon. Sir Iain (Derek Laing), Kt., P.C.; British judge; b. 8 June 1924; s. of Charles Norman Glidewell and Nora Glidewell; m. Hilary Winant 1950; one s. two d.; ed. Bromsgrove School, Worcester Coll., Oxford; served R.A.F.V.R. 1942–46; called to Bar, Gray's Inn 1949, Bencher 1977, Treas. 1995; Q.C. 1969; a Recorder of the Crown Court 1976–80; a Judge of Appeal, Isle of Man 1979–80; a Judge of the High Court of Justice, Queen's Bench Div. 1980–85; Presiding Judge, N.E. Circuit 1982–85; a Lord Justice of Appeal 1985–95; conducted review of Crown Prosecution Service 1997–98; a Judge of Court of Appeal, Gibraltar 1998–; mem. Senate of Inns of Court and the Bar 1976–79, Supreme Court Rule Cttee. 1980–84; Chair. Judicial Studies Bd. 1989–92, Panels for Examination of Structure Plans: Worcs. 1974, W. Midlands 1975; conducted Heathrow Fourth Terminal Inquiry 1978; Hon. Fellow Worcester Coll., Oxford 1986. *Leisure interests:* walking, theatre. *Address:* Rough Heys Farm, Macclesfield, Cheshire, SK11 9PF, England.

GLIGOROV, Kiro; Macedonian politician; b. 3 May 1917, Štip; s. of Blagoje and Katarina Gligorov; m. Nada Gligorov; one s. two d.; ed. Faculty of Law, Univ. of Belgrade; mem. Presidium of Antifascist Assembly of People's Liberation of Macedonia, and Antifascist Council People's Liberation of Yugoslavia during Second World War; Deputy Sec.-Gen. to Govt. of Yugoslavia 1946–47; Asst. Minister of Finance 1947–52; Prof. of Econs. Belgrade Univ. 1948–49; Deputy Dir. Exec. Council for Gen. Econ. Affairs 1955–62; Fed. Sec. for Finance 1962–67; Vice-Pres. Fed. Exec. Council 1967–69; mem. League of Communists of Yugoslavia (mem. Exec. Bureau 1969–74); mem. Presidency, Socialist Fed. Repub. of Yugoslavia 1971–72; Pres. Parl. 1974–78; Pres. of Macedonia Jan. 1991–; holder of many Yugoslav and foreign honours. *Publications:* many articles and studies in finance and economics. *Leisure interests:* tennis, hunting. *Address:* Office of the President, 91000 Skopje, Dame Grueva 6, Macedonia.

GLISTRUP, Mogens; Danish politician and lawyer; b. 28 May 1926, Rønne; s. of Lektor Lars Glistrup; m. Lene Borup Svendsen 1950; one s. three d.; ed. Rønne, Copenhagen Univ.; training in American law Univ. of Calif., Berkeley 1951–52; teacher in income tax law Univ. of Copenhagen 1956–63; law practice 1950–81, own firm 1956–82; founded Progress Party 1972 expelled Nov. 1990; mem. Parl. 1973–83, re-elected 1984, returned to prison Feb. 1984; on trial for alleged tax evasion and fraud since 1974, convicted June 1983 and sentenced to three years in gaol for infringing tax laws, released March 1985; mem. Parl. 1987–. *Publications:* Skatteret 1957, Income Tax—Enemy Number One of Society 1979, Glistrup on Glistrup Case 1983, Tax Reform 1986, Salvation of Denmark 1989. *Leisure interests:* chess, bicycling, bridge, football. *Address:* c/o Progress Party, Folketinget, Christiansborg, 1240 Copenhagen K, Denmark.

GLITMAN, Maynard Wayne, M.A.; American diplomatist; b. 8 Dec. 1933, Chicago; s. of Ben and Reada (née Kutok Klass) Glitman; m. G. Christine Amundsen 1956; three s. two d.; ed. Univ. of Illinois, Fletcher School of Law and Diplomacy, Univ. of California; with U.S. army 1957; with Foreign Service Dept. of State 1956, 1966–67, Dir. Office of Int. Trade 1973–74, Deputy Asst. Sec. of State for Internal Trade policy 1974–76; economist 1956–59; Vice-Consul Bahamas 1959–61; Econ. Officer Embassy, Ottawa 1961–65; mem. Del. to UN Gen. Ass. 1967, Nat. Security Council Staff 1968; Political Officer, First Sec. Embassy in Paris 1968–73; Deputy Asst. Sec. of Defense for Europe and NATO 1976–77, Deputy Perm. Rep. to NATO 1977–81; Amb. and Deputy Chief U.S. Del. to Intermediate Nuclear Forces Negotiations, Arms Control and Disarmament Agency, Switzerland 1981–84; Amb. and U.S. Rep. Mutual and Balanced Forces Negotiation, Vienna 1985; Amb. and Chief U.S. Negotiator Intermediate Nuclear Forces Negotiation, Geneva 1985–88; Amb. to Belgium 1988–91; Diplomat in Residence, Univ. of Vt. 1991–94; Adjunct Prof. of Political Science, Univ. of Vt. 1994–; Consultant, U.S. Arms Control and Disarmament Agency 1994–; Public Service Medal (U.S.A. Dept. of Defense) 1981, Presidential Distinguished Service Award 1989. *Address:* P.O. Box 438, Jeffersonville, VT 05464-0438, U.S.A. (Home).

GLOAG, Ann Heron; British business executive; b. 10 Dec. 1942; d. of Iain Souter and Catherine Souter; m. 1st Robin N. Gloag 1965; one s. one d.; m. 2nd David McCleary 1990; ed. Perth High School; trainee nurse Bridge of Earn Hosp., Perth 1960–65, Theatre Sister 1969–80; ward sister Devonshire Royal Hosp., Buxton 1965–69; founding partner Gloagtrotter (re-named Stagecoach Express Services) 1980–83, Co-Dir. Stagecoach Ltd. 1983–86, Exec. Dir. Stagecoach Holdings PLC 1986–; Scottish Marketing Woman of the Year, Scottish Univs. 1989; U.K. Businesswoman of the Year, Veuve Clicquot and Inst. of Dirs. 1989–90. *Leisure interests:* family, travel, charity support. *Address:* Stagecoach Holdings PLC, Charlotte House, 20 Charlotte Street, Perth PH1 5LL, Scotland. *Telephone:* (01738) 442111.

GLOBUS, Yoram; Israeli film producer; b. 7 Sept. 1943; f. Noah Films with Menahem Golan (q.v.) 1963; bought Cannon Films (U.S.A.) with Menahem Golan 1979 and has since produced over 100 motion pictures, including Over the Top, Barfly, Dancers, Missing in Action I, II & III, Death Wish IV, The Assault (winner of 1986 Acad. Award for Best Foreign Language Film), Surrender, Runaway Train, Hanna's War, Masters of the Universe, King Lear, Tough Guys Don't Dance, Shy People, A Cry In The Dark; Chair., C.E.O. Cannon Entertainments 1989; Officer Cannon Group Inc. 1989; Co-Pres. Pathé Communications Corpn., Chair., C.E.O. Pathé Int. until 1991.

GLOCK, Sir William Frederick, Kt., C.B.E.; British musician; b. 3 May 1908, London; s. of William G. Glock and Gertrude Maltby; m. Anne Geoffroy-Dechaume 1952; ed. Christ's Hospital, West Horsham, Gonville and Caius Coll., Cambridge and under Artur Schnabel, Berlin; Music critic, Daily Telegraph 1934, The Observer 1934–45, New Statesman 1958–59; served with R.A.F. 1941–46; Dir. Summer School of Music, Bryanston 1948–52, Dartington Hall, Devon 1953–79; Founder and Ed. The Score 1949–61; Chair. British Section, Int. Soc. of Contemporary Music 1954–58; Controller of Music, BBC 1959–72; mem. Bd. of Dirs. Royal Opera House, Covent Garden 1968–73; Artistic Dir. Bath Festival 1975–84; Chair. London Orchestral Concert Bd. 1975–86; mem. South Bank Bd. 1986–90; Pres. Bath Festival Soc. 1990; Ed. Eulenburg books on music 1974–86; Hon. mem. Royal Philharmonic Soc. 1971; mem. Arts Council of G.B. 1972–75; Hon. D.Univ. (York); Hon. D.Mus (Nottingham, Plymouth); Hon. Fellowship Royal Northern Coll. of Music 1981, Hon. D.Litt. (Bath); Gold Medal of R.S.A. 1971. *Publication:* Notes In Advance 1991. *Address:* Vine House, Brightwell-cum-Sotwell, Wallingford, Oxon., OX10 0RT, England. *Telephone:* (01491) 837144.

GLOSSOP, Peter; British opera singer (baritone); b. 6 July 1928, Sheffield; s. of Cyril Glossop and Violet Elizabeth Wright; m. 1st Joyce Blackham 1955 (divorced 1976); m. 2nd Michele Yvonne Amos 1977 (divorced 1987); two d.; ed. High Storrs Grammar School, Sheffield; joined Sadler's Wells Opera 1952; with Covent Garden Opera Co. 1962–66; freelance singer 1966–; First Prize Bulgarian First Competition for Young Opera Singers 1961; debut at La Scala, Milan as Rigoletto 1965; Hon. D.Mus. (Sheffield) 1970; 'Amici di Verdi' Gold Medal 1995; *films:* Pagliacci, Otello. *Leisure interest:* golf. *Address:* End Cottage, 7 Gate Close, Hawkchurch, near Axminster, Devon, England. *Telephone:* (01297) 678266.

GLOUCESTER, H.R.H. The Duke of; Prince Richard Alexander Walter George, K.G., G.C.V.O., the Earl of Ulster and the Baron Culloden; b. 26 Aug. 1944; s. of the late Duke of Gloucester (third s. of H.M. King George V) and The Lady Alice Montagu-Douglas-Scott (d. of the 7th Duke of Buccleuch); m. Birgitte van Deurs 1972; one s. (Alexander, Earl of Ulster) two d. (Lady Davina Windsor and Lady Rose Windsor); ed. Wellesley House, Broadstairs, Eton Coll. and Magdalene Coll., Cambridge; Corporate mem. R.I.B.A. 1972; Commdr.-in-Chief St. John Ambulance Brigade 1972–74; Col.-in-Chief Gloucestershire Regt. 1974–94, Deputy Col.-in-Chief Royal Gloucestershire, Berks. and Wilts. Regt. 1994–; Deputy Col.-in-Chief The Royal Logistic Corps 1993–; Hon. Col. Royal Monmouthshire Royal Engineers (Militia) 1977–; Hon. Air Cdre. R.A.F. Odiham 1993–; Grand Prior Order of St. John 1975–; Royal Trustee, British Museum 1973–; Pres. Inst. of Advanced Motorists 1971, Cancer Research Campaign 1973, Nat. Asscn. of Boys' Clubs 1974, Christ's Hosp. 1975, St. Bartholomew's Hosp. 1975, Royal Smithfield 1975, British Consultants Bureau 1978; Patron of Heritage of London Trust 1982; Commr. Historic Buildings and Monuments Comm. for England 1983; Sr. Fellow Royal Coll. of Art 1984; as Rep. of H.M. The Queen visited Australia 1963, wedding of Crown Prince of Nepal 1963, seventieth birthday celebrations of King Olav V of Norway 1973, Mexico 1973, Nepal 1975, Saudi Arabia and the Philippines 1975, independence celebrations of Seychelles 1976 and of Solomon Islands 1978, Australia and Hawaii 1979, independence celebrations of Vanuatu 1980, Philippines, Indonesia and Burma 1981, India, Cyprus and Belgium 1982, France, Repub. of Korea, Canada, Jordan and U.A.E. 1983, U.S.A., Thailand, Brunei, Bahrain, Kuwait and Qatar 1984, New Zealand, Canary Islands, Egypt, Algeria and Tunis 1985, U.S.S.R., Fed. Repub. of Germany, Berlin and Italy 1986, Spain, Sweden, Saudi Arabia, Indonesia, Bangladesh and Hong Kong 1987, U.S.A., Gibraltar, Turkey, Pakistan, Kenya, Bahrain and Qatar 1988, Netherlands, Denmark and Portugal 1989, Canada, U.S.A., France, Laos, Malaysia and Singapore 1990, Poland, Dubai, France, Luxembourg, Germany, Hungary and Czechoslovakia 1991, Egypt, Spain, Belgium and U.S.A. 1992, Ukraine 1993, U.S.A., Singapore, Japan and Portugal 1994, France, India, Malaysia and Mexico 1995, U.S.A., Vietnam, Philippines, Indonesia and South Africa 1996, Repub. of Korea, Luxembourg, Yemen, Bahrain, Qatar and U.A.E. 1997; K.St.J. *Publications:* On Public View, The Face of London, Oxford and Cambridge. *Address:* Kensington Palace, London, W8 4PU, England.

GLOVER, Danny; American actor; b. 22 July 1947, Georgia; m. Asake Bomani; one d.; ed. San Francisco State Univ.; researcher, Office of Mayor, San Francisco 1971–75; mem. American Conservatory Theatre's Black Actor Workshop; Broadway debut, Master Harold . . . and the Boys 1982; other stage appearances include: The Blood Knot 1982, The Island, Sizwe Banzi is Dead, Macbeth, Suicide in B Flat, Nevis Mountain Dew, Jukebox; appearances in TV movies and series; with his wife f. Bomani Gallery, San Francisco. *Films:* Escape from Alcatraz 1979, Chu Chu and the Philly Flash 1981, Out 1982, Iceman 1984, Places in the Heart 1984, Birdy 1984, The Color Purple 1984, Silverado 1985, Witness 1985, Lethal Weapon 1987, Bat 21 1988, Lethal Weapon II 1989, To Sleep with Anger 1990, Predator 2 1990, Flight of the Intruder 1991, A Rage in Harlem 1991, Pure Luck 1991, Grand Canyon 1992, Lethal Weapon III 1992, The Saint of Fort Washington 1993, Bopha 1993, Angels in the Outfield 1994, Operation Dumbo Drop 1995, America's Dream 1996, The Rainmaker 1997, Wings Against the Wind 1998, Beloved 1998, Lethal Weapon IV 1998, Prince of Egypt (voice) 1998. *Address:* William Morris Agency, 151 El Camino Blvd., Beverly Hills, CA 90212, U.S.A.

GLOVER, Gen. Sir James (Malcolm), K.C.B., M.B.E.; British fmr. army officer and business executive; b. 25 March 1929; s. of Maj.-Gen. Malcolm Glover; m. Janet Diones De Pree 1958; one s. one d.; ed. Wellington Coll., R.M.A., Sandhurst; R.A. 1949; Royal Horse Artillery 1950–54; Instructor, R.M.A., Sandhurst 1955–56; transferred to Rifle Brigade 1956; Brigade Maj., 48 Gurkha Brigade 1960–62; Directing Staff, Staff Coll. 1966–68; C.O., 3rd Bn. Royal Green Jackets 1970–71; Col. Gen. Staff, Ministry of Defence 1972–73; Commdr. 19 Airportable Brigade 1974–75; Brig. Gen. Staff (Intelligence), Ministry of Defence 1977–78; Commdr. Land Forces Northern Ireland 1979–80; Deputy Chief of Defence Staff (Intelligence) 1981–83; Vice-Chief of Gen. Staff, and mem. Army Bd. 1983–85; C.-in-C., U.K. Land Forces 1985–87; has served in Fed. Repub. of Germany, Malaya, Singapore, Hong Kong, Cyprus and Northern Ireland; Dir. British Petroleum PLC 1987–; Chair. Royal Armouries Int. PLC 1993–, Merlin Communications (Int.) 1997–; D.L. Hants. 1997. *Leisure interests:* travel, gardening, shooting, mountain walking. *Address:* c/o Lloyds Bank, Cox's & King's Branch, 7 Pall Mall, London, SW1Y 5NA, England.

GLOVER, Jane Alison, M.A., D.PHIL.; British conductor; b. 13 May 1949; d. of Robert Finlay Glover and Jean Muir; ed. Monmouth School for Girls and St. Hugh's Coll., Oxford; Jr. Research Fellow St. Hugh's Coll. 1973–75, Lecturer in Music 1976–84, Sr. Research Fellow 1982–84; Lecturer St. Anne's Coll., Oxford 1976–80, Pembroke Coll. 1979–84; mem. Oxford Univ.

Faculty of Music 1979–; professional conducting debut at Wexford Festival 1975; operas and concerts for BBC, Glyndebourne, Royal Opera House, Covent Garden, English Nat. Opera, London Symphony Orchestra, London Philharmonic Orchestra, Royal Philharmonic Orchestra, Philharmonia, Royal Scottish Orchestra, English Chamber Orchestra, Royal Danish Opera, Glimmerglass Opera, New York, Australian Opera and many orchestras in Europe and U.S.A.; Prin. Conductor London Choral Soc. 1983–; Artistic Dir. London Mozart Players 1984–91; Prin. Conductor Huddersfield Choral Soc. 1989–96; mem. BBC Cen. Music Advisory Cttee. 1981–85, Music Advisory Cttee. Arts Council 1986–88; Gov. R.A.M. 1985–90, BBC 1990–95; Hon. D.Mus. (Exeter) 1986, (C.N.A.A.) 1991, (London) 1992, (City Univ.) 1995, (Glasgow) 1996; Hon. D.Litt. (Loughborough) 1988, (Bradford) 1992; Hon. Dr. (Open Univ.) 1988. *TV:* documentaries and series, and presentation, especially Orchestra 1983, Mozart 1985. *Publications:* Cavalli 1978; contribs. to The New Monteverdi Companion 1986, Monteverdi 'Orfeo' Handbook 1986; articles in numerous journals. *Leisure interests:* The Times crossword puzzle and theatre. *Address:* c/o Lies Askonas Ltd., 6 Henrietta Street, London, WC2E 8LA, England.

GLOVER, Michael James Kevin; Mauritian politician; b. 11 July 1940; m.; one c.; ed. Univ. of London; fmr. Dean, Saint Esprit Coll. Junior School; fmr. nat. football player; fmr. Pres. Mauritius Nat. Football Asscn., Mauritius Handball Asscn.; mem. Legis. Ass. 1983–; Minister of Youth and Sport (now of Sports and Leisure) 1983–95, of Tourism and Craft 1988–91. *Address:* c/o Ministry of Youth and Sport, Emmanuel Anquetil Building, Sir Seewoosagur Ramgoolan Street, Port Louis, Mauritius.

GŁOWACKI, Janusz; Polish writer and playwright; b. 13 Sept. 1938, Poznań; m.; one d.; ed. Warsaw Univ.; columnist in Kultura weekly 1964–81; lecturer in many colls. and univs. in U.S.A. including Bemington, Yale, Cornell, Columbia; playwright in residence New York Shakespeare Festival 1984 and Mark Taper Forum, Los Angeles 1989; Fellow in Writing Univ. of Iowa 1977, 1982; Guggenheim Fellowship 1988, Nat. Endowment for the Arts Fellowship 1988, Master of Arts Atlantic Center for the Arts 1991. *Short stories:* Nowy taniec La-ba-da 1970, Paradis 1973, Polowanie na muchy 1974, My Sweet Raskolnikov 1977, Opowiadania wybrane 1978, Skrzek. Coraz trudniej kochać 1980; novel: Moc truchleje 1981; film scripts: Rejs 1970, Psychodrama (with Marek Piwowski) 1971, Polowanie na muchy 1971, Trzeba zabić tę miłość 1974; plays: Cudzołóstwo ukarane 1971, Mecz 1977, Obciach 1977, Kopciuch 1981 (Premio Moliere, Argentina 1986), Fortinbras Gets Drunk 1986, Hunting Cockroaches 1986 (1st Prize, American Theatre Critics Asscn.); Joseph Kesserling Award 1987, Drama League of New York Playwrighting Award 1987, Antigone in New York 1993. *Address:* ul. Bednarska 7 m. 4, 00-310 Warsaw, Poland; 845 West End Avenue Apt. 4B, New York, NY 10025, U.S.A.

GLUSHCHENKO, Fedor Ivanovich; Russian conductor; b. 29 March 1944, Rostov Region; m. 1st; one s. one d.; m. 2nd Galina Baryshnikova; one d.; ed. Leningrad State Conservatory, Vienna Acad. of Music, studied under Herbert von Karajan; Chief Conductor, Karelian Radio and TV Symphony Orchestra, Petrozavodsk 1971–73; Chief Conductor and Artistic Dir., Ukrainian State Symphony Orchestra, Kiev 1973–87; Conductor, Istanbul Opera 1990–91; Chief Conductor and Artistic Dir., J. S. Bach Chamber Orchestra, Yekaterinburg 1996–; Prin. Guest Conductor, Moscow Philharmonic Orchestra. *Address:* 1st Pryadilnaya str. 11, apt. 5, 105037 Moscow, Russia. *Telephone:* (095) 165 4946 (Home).

GLUSHENKO, Yevgeniya Konstatinovna; Russian actress; b. 4 Sept. 1952; m. Aleksandr Kalyagin (q.v.); ed. Shchepkin Theatre School; worked with Maly Theatre 1974–. *Films include:* Unfinished Play for Mechanical Piano 1977, Profile and Front-View 1979, Oblomov 1980, First-Time Married 1980, In Love of One's Own Accord 1982, (Moscow and West Berlin Film Festival Prizes 1983), Zina-Zinulya 1985. *Stage roles:* Liza in Misfortune from Sense 1975, Cordelia in King Lear 1979, Masha in The Savage 1990, Yefrosinya in Infanticide 1991, Matrena in The Hot Heart 1992, Susanna in A Criminal Mother or the Second Tartuffe 1993, Glafira in The Feast of Victors 1995, Madeleine in Queen Margo 1996. *Address:* 1905 Goda str. 3, Apt. 91, 123100 Moscow, Russia. *Telephone:* (095) 205-26-54.

GLYNN, Ian Michael, M.D., PH.D., F.R.C.P., F.R.S.; British professor of physiology; b. 3 June 1928, London; s. of Hyman and Charlotte Glynn; m. Jenifer Muriel Franklin 1958; one s. two d.; ed. City of London School, Trinity Coll. Cambridge, Univ. Coll. Hosp. London; House Physician Cen. Middlesex Hosp. 1952–53; Nat. Service R.A.F. Medical Branch 1956–57; MRC Scholar Physiological Lab. Cambridge 1956, Fellow Trinity Coll. 1955–, demonstrator in Physiology 1958–63, Lecturer 1963–70, Reader 1970–75, Prof. of Membrane Physiology 1975–86, Prof. of Physiology 1986–95, Prof. Emer. 1995–, Vice-Master Trinity Coll. 1980–86; Visiting Prof. Yale Univ. 1969; mem. British MRC 1976–80, Council of Royal Soc. 1979–81, 1991–92, Agric. Research Council 1981–86; Chair. Editorial Bd. Journal of Physiology 1968–70; Hon. foreign mem. American Acad. of Arts and Sciences 1984, American Physiological Soc.; Hon. M.D. (Univ. of Aarhus) 1988. *Publications:* The Sodium Pump (with J. C. Ellory) 1985 and papers in scientific journals. *Address:* Trinity College, Cambridge, CB2 1TQ; Daylesford, Conduit Head Road, Cambridge, CB3 0EY, England. *Telephone:* (01223) 338415 (Trinity Coll.); (01223) 353079.

GNANAM, A., PH.D.; Indian scientist; b. 5 Oct. 1932, C. Veeracholagan, Tamil Nadu; m. 1953; one s. three d.; ed. Cornell Univ., U.S.A.; Asst. Prof. of Plant Sciences, Cornell Univ. 1967–68; Lecturer, Annamalai Univ. 1968–69; reader, Madurai Kamaraj Univ. 1969–73, Prof. 1973–85, Dir. Centre for Plant Molecular Biology 1990–91; Vice-Chancellor Pondicherry Univ. 1991–; Vice-Chancellor, Bharathidasan Univ., Trichy 1985–88, Univ. of Madras 1988–90; elected Founder Fellow Tamil Nadu Acad. of Sciences 1976; Nat. Fellow Univ. Grants Comm. 1978, Nat. Lecturer in Botany 1980; Fellow Indian Nat. Science Acad., New Delhi 1984, Nat. Acad. of Sciences, Allahabad 1985; Rafi Ahmed Kidwai Award for best contrib. in plant genetics; Best Teacher Award, Govt. of Tamil Nadu. *Publications:* numerous scientific papers. *Leisure interests:* photography, music, pets. *Address:* Office of the Vice-Chancellor, University of Pondicherry, R. Venkataraman Nagar, Kalapet, Pondicherry 605014, India.

GNEDOVSKY, Yuri Petrovich; Russian architect; b. 3 July 1930, Sverdlovsk; m. Yelena Andreyevna Borisova; one s. one d.; ed. Moscow Inst. of Architecture, Acad. of Architecture; sr. researcher Research Inst. of Public Construction Acad. of Architecture 1957–63; Head of div., Deputy Dir. Cen. Research Inst. of Public Bldg. Design 1964–82; Sec. Bd. U.S.S.R. Union of Architects 1982–91; Pres. Russian Union of Architects 1992–; mem. Council of Int. Union of Architects 1996–; author of projects of numerous bldgs. including Taganka Theatre, Meyerhold Cen., Cultural Cen. Riverside Towers in Moscow. *Publications include:* Architecture of Soviet Theatre, Architecture of Public Buildings, over 60 articles. *Address:* Russian Union of Architects, Granatny per. 22, 103001 Moscow, Russia (Office). *Telephone:* (095) 291 5578 (Office).

GNEHM, Edward W., Jr., M.A.; American diplomatist; b. 10 Nov. 1944, Ga.; s. of Edward W. Gnehm, Sr. and Beverly Thomasson; m. Margaret Scott 1970; one s. one d.; ed. George Washington Univ. and American Univ. Cairo; Head, Liaison Office, Riyadh 1976–78; Deputy Chief of Mission, Embassy, Sanaa 1978–81; Dir. Jr. Officer Div. Personnel, Washington, D.C. 1982–83, Dir. Secr. Staff 1983–84; Deputy Chief of Mission, Amman 1984–87; Deputy Asst. Sec. of Defense for Near East and S. Asia 1987–89; Deputy Asst. Sec. of State, Bureau of Near East and S. Asian Affairs 1989–90; Amb. to Kuwait 1990–94; Deputy Perm. Rep. to UN 1994–97; Dir.-Gen. of Foreign Service, Dir. of Personnel U.S. Dept. of State, Washington D.C. 1997–. *Leisure interests:* history, foreign policy, jogging, stamps. *Address:* M/DgP, Room 6218, Department of State, 2201 C Street, Washington, DC 20520, U.S.A.

GNEUSS, Helmut Walter Georg, DR. PHIL.; German professor of English; b. 29 Oct. 1927, Berlin; s. of Kurt Gneuss and Margarete (née Grimm) Gneuss; m. Mechthild Gretsch 1974; ed. Freie Universität Berlin, St. John's Coll., Cambridge; lecturer German Dept., Durham Univ. 1955–56, Dept. of English, Freie Univ. Berlin 1956–62, Heidelberg Univ. 1962–65; Prof., English Univ. of Munich 1965–; Visiting Professorial Fellow Emmanuel Coll., Cambridge 1970, Visiting Prof. Univ. of N.C., Chapel Hill 1974; mem. Bayerische Akad. der Wissenschaften, British Acad., Österreichische Akad. der Wissenschaften, Medieval Acad. of America; Vice-Pres. Henry Bradshaw Soc. *Publications:* Lehnbildungen und Lehnbedeutungen im Altenglischen 1955, Hymnar und Hymnen im englischen Mittelalter 1968, English Language Scholarship 1996, Language and History in Early England 1996, Books and Libraries in Early England 1996. *Address:* Institut für Englische Philologie, Universität München, Schellingstrasse 3, 80799 Munich, Germany. *Telephone:* 89-2180-2369. *Fax:* 89-2180-3399.

GNUTTI, Vito; Italian politician, chemical engineer and industrialist; b. 14 Sept. 1939, Lumezzate, Brescia; s. of Basilio Gnutti and Leoni Cenzina; m. Nerina Codini 1965; two d.; Chair. Lombardy Regional Group, Young Industrialists 1975–78, mem. Nat. Council, Confindustria (nat. employers' org.) –1993; mem. Chamber of Deputies 1992–, re-elected as Lega Nord Deputy 1994, elected as Lega Nord Senator April 1996; Minister of Industry 1994–95. *Address:* Via Leno 4, 25010 Isorella, Italy. *Telephone:* (030) 9958130. *Fax:* (030) 9958244.

GOBURDHUN, Jagdishwar; Mauritian politician; b. 1 Jan. 1946; m. 1981; one s. one d.; ed. diplomas in cooperative and industrial man.; f. and Sec. Mauritius Planters' Asscn.; Sec. Mauritius Planters' and By-Products Cooperative Credit Soc.; mem. Legislative Ass. 1976–; Minister of Health 1983–90, Minister of Co-operatives and Handicraft 1990–96. *Address:* c/o Ministry of Co-operatives, Life Insurance Corporation of India Building, 3rd Floor, John Kennedy Street, Port Louis, Mauritius.

GODAL, Bjørn Tore; Norwegian politician; b. 20 Jan. 1945, Skien; s. of Kari Godal and Aksel Godal; m. Gro Balas 1988; one c.; ed. Oslo Univ.; office clerk, Skien 1964–65; Pres. Labour League of Youth 1971–73 (sec. for org. 1970–71), Fritt Forum (Labour Party's Student Org.) 1967–68; research officer Labour Party 1973–80, Sec.-Gen. Oslo Labour Party 1980–82, Leader 1982–90 (mem. Cen. Cttee. Labour Party 1983–90); Pres. Council of European Nat. Youth Cttees. (CENYC) 1973–75; Head of Secr. Labour Party Group of the Oslo Municipal Council 1986; Deputy Rep. Storting (Parl.) then elected Rep.; Minister of Trade and Shipping 1991–94, of Foreign Affairs 1994–97; mem. council for the study of power distribution in Norway 1972–80, Standing Cttee. on Finance 1986–89, on Foreign and Constitutional Affairs 1989–91, on Defence 1997–, Storting; mem. North Atlantic Ass. 1997–. *Address:* Norwegian Parliament, 0159 Oslo, Norway.

GODARD, Jean-Luc; French film director; b. 3 Dec. 1930, Paris; s. of Paul Godard and Odile Monad; m. 1st Anna Karina 1961 (divorced); m. 2nd Anne

Wiazemsky 1967; ed. Lycée Buffon and Faculté des lettres, Paris; journalist and film critic; film director 1958–; mem. Conseil supérieur de la langue française 1989–; Prix Jean Vigo for A bout de souffle 1960, Jury's Special Prize and Prix Pasinetti, Venice Festival 1962, Diploma of Merit, Edinburgh Film Festival 1968 for Weekend, Grand Prix National 1982; Chevalier, Ordre nat. du Mérite. *Films:* Opération Béton 1954, Une femme coquette 1955, Tous les garçons s'appellent Patrick 1957, Charlotte et son Jules 1958, Une histoire d'eau 1958, A bout de souffle 1959, Le petit soldat 1960, Une femme est une femme 1961, Les sept péchés capitaux 1961, Vivre sa vie 1962, RoGoPaG 1962, Les carabiniers 1963, Le mépris 1963, Les plus belles escroqueries du monde 1963, Paris vu par ... 1963, Bande à part 1964, Une femme mariée 1964, Alphaville 1965, Pierrot le fou 1965, Masculin-féminin 1966, Made in U.S.A. 1966, Deux ou trois choses que je sais d'elle 1966, La chinoise 1967, Loin du Vietnam 1967, Weekend 1967, Le plus vieux métier du monde 1967, Vangelo '70 1967, Le gai savoir (TV) 1968, Un film comme les autres 1968, One Plus One 1968, One American Movie-1 a.m. 1969, British Sounds 1969, Le vent d'est 1969, Lotte in Italia 1970, Vladimir et Rosa 1971, Tout va bien 1972, Numéro deux 1975, Ici et ailleurs 1976, Bugsy 1979, Sauve qui peut 1980, Passion 1982, Prénom Carmen 1983, Detective 1984, Je vous salue, Marie 1985, King Lear 1987, Soigne ta droite 1987, Aria (segment) 1987, Nouvelle Vague 1989, Allemagne Neuf Zero 1991, Hélas Pour Moi 1993, JLG/JLG 1995, Forever Mozart 1996. *Publication:* Introduction à une véritable histoire du cinéma 1980. *Address:* 26 ave Pierre 1er de Serbie, 75116 Paris, France; 15 rue du Nord, 1180 Roulle, Switzerland.

GODDARD, Leonard, M.A., B.PHIL., F.A.H.A.; British professor of philosophy; b. 13 Feb. 1925, Nottingham; s. of Bertram Goddard and Frances Goddard; m. 1st Phyllis Dunsdon 1945 (divorced 1981); m. 2nd Patricia Johnson 1988 (divorced 1997); two d.; ed. Univ. of St. Andrews, Univ. of Cambridge; R.A.F. 1943–47; Asst. Lecturer, Univ. of St. Andrews 1952–55; lecturer and then Sr. Lecturer Univ. of New England, Australia 1956–61, Prof. of Philosophy, Univ. of New England 1961–66, Dean of Arts 1964–66; Prof. of Logic and Metaphysics, Univ. of St. Andrews 1966–77, Dean of Arts 1972–74; Boyce Gibson Prof. of Philosophy, Univ. of Melbourne 1977–90, Prof. Emer. 1990–; Visiting Fellow Australian Nat. Univ. 1974–76. *Publications:* (with R. Routley) The Logic of Significance and Context, Vol. 1 1973, Philosophical Problems 1977, (with B. Judge) The Metaphysics of Wittgenstein's Tractatus 1982. *Leisure interests:* golf, boating. *Address:* Department of Philosophy, University of Melbourne, Parkville, Vic., Australia 3052. *Telephone:* 03-9344 5142.

GODEAUX, Baron Jean, D. EN D., LIC.ECON.; Belgian banker; b. 3 July 1922, Jemeppe sur Meuse; s. of Léon Godeaux and Claire de Barsy; m. Thérèse Ceron 1950; two s. three d.; ed. Univ. Catholique de Louvain; Bar of Namur 1944–47; Asst., Inst. for Econ. and Social Research 1947; Nat. Bank of Belgium 1947–49; Technical Asst., IMF 1949–50, Alt. Exec. Dir. 1950–54, Exec. Dir. 1954, Adviser 1992–; Man. Banque Lambert 1955–59, Man. Partner 1960–72, Pres. 1973–74; Pres. Banking Comm. 1974–82; Gov. Nat. Bank of Belgium 1982–89; Pres. and Chair. BIS 1985–87; Hon. Dir. Société Générale de Belgique 1990–; Grand officier de l'Ordre de Léopold, Officier, Légion d'honneur, Commdr., Ordre de St. Grégoire le grand, Grand Croix, ordre du mérite (Luxembourg), (Austria), Grand Croix, Order of Orange-Nassau (Netherlands), Grand Cordon, Order of Sacred Treasure (Japan), Grand Cordon, Order of Infante Enrique (Portugal). *Leisure interests:* skiing, tennis. *Address:* rue de De Jonghe 53, Boîte 7, 1150 Brussels, Belgium (Home). *Telephone:* (2) 779.33.20. *Fax:* (2) 779.33.19.

GODFREY, Malcolm Paul Weston, M.B., B.S., F.R.C.P.; British medical practitioner; b. 11 Aug. 1926, London; s. of Harry Godfrey and Rose Godfrey; m. Barbara Goldstein 1955; one s. two d. (one deceased); ed. Hertford Grammar School, King's Coll. London and King's Coll. Hosp. Medical School; various appts. in Nat. Health Service 1950–60; Fellow in Medicine and Asst. Physician, Johns Hopkins Hosp. Baltimore, Md. 1957–58; H.Q. staff, Medical Research Council (MRC) 1960–74; Dean, Royal Postgrad. Medical School, Hammersmith Hosp. 1974–83; Second Sec. MRC 1983–88; Chair. Public Health Lab. Service Bd. 1989–96, United Medical and Dental Schools of Guys and St. Thomas' Hosps. 1996–98. *Publications:* articles on cardiorespiratory disorders in medical and scientific journals. *Leisure interests:* theatre, reading, current affairs. *Address:* 17 Clifton Hill, St. John's Wood, London, NW8 0QE, England. *Telephone:* 0171-624 6335. *Fax:* 0171-328 9474.

GODINE, David R., M.A., ED.M.; American publisher; b. 4 Sept. 1944, Cambridge, Mass.; s. of Morton R. Godine and Bernice Beckwith; m. Sara Sangree Eisenman 1988; one s. one d.; ed. Dartmouth Coll., Harvard Univ.; f. David R. Godine, Publisher and Pres. 1969–; mem. Bds. Massachusetts Historical Soc., Massachusetts Horticultural Soc.; Fellow Pierpoint Morgan Library; Dwiggins Award 1984. *Publication:* Renaissance Books of Science 1970. *Leisure interests:* sailing, skiing. *Address:* David R. Godine Publishers Inc., 9 Hamilton Place, Boston, MA 02108, USA. (Office).

GODLEY, Georgina, M.A.; British fashion designer; b. 11 April 1955, London; d. of Michael Godley and Heather Godley; m. Sebastian Conran 1988; two s.; ed. Putney High School, Thames Valley Grammar School, London, Wimbledon School of Art, Brighton Polytechnic and Chelsea School of Art; designer, Browns, London and Paris 1979–80; partner and designer, Crolla, London 1980–85; Dir. and sole designer Georgina Godley Ltd. (produces own label collections) 1986–; mem. British Fashion Council Designer Cttee.; Visiting lecturer at various fashion and art colls. in London and elsewhere in U.K.; work included in perm. exhbn. at Victoria & Albert Museum, London and Bath Costume Museum; ICA Young Contemporaries award 1978. *Address:* 42 Bassett Road, London, W10 6UL, England (Home). *Telephone:* 0171-912 0713. *Fax:* 0171-460 0299.

GODLEY, Wynne Alexander Hugh; British economist; b. 2 Sept. 1926; s. of Hugh John, 2nd Baron Kilbracken and Elizabeth Helen Monteith; m. Kathleen Eleonora Epstein 1955; one d.; ed. Rugby School, New Coll., Oxford, Conservatoire de Musique, Paris; professional oboist 1950; joined econ. section, HM Treasury 1956, Deputy Dir. 1967–70, Econ. Consultant 1975; Dir. Investing in Success Ltd. 1970–85, Royal Opera House, Covent Garden 1976–87; Dir. Applied Econs. Dept., Cambridge Univ. 1970–85, Prof. 1980–93, Dir. (a.i.) 1985–87; Official Adviser Select Cttee. on Public Expenditure 1971–73; Visiting Prof., Aalborg Univ. 1987–88; Distinguished Scholar, Jerome Levy Econs. Inst., Annandale-on-Hudson, New York 1991–92, 1993–95, 1996–; Fellow of King's Coll., Cambridge 1970–98; Dir. Kent Opera 1993–; mem. Panel of Economists to advise the Chancellor of the Exchequer 1992–95. *Publications include:* Pricing in the Trade Cycle (jtly.) 1978, Macroeconomics (jtly.) 1983; numerous articles in magazines and journals. *Address:* Jasmine House, The Green, Cavendish, Suffolk, England. *Telephone:* (01787) 281166.

GODMANIS, Ivars; Latvian politician and scientist; b. 27 Nov. 1951, Riga; s. of Teodors Godmanis and Ingride Godmanis; m. Ramora Godmanė 1978; two s. one d.; ed. Latvian State Univ.; scientific work since 1973, staff-mem. of the Physical Inst. of Latvian Acad. of Sciences 1973–86; teacher in Latvian Univ. 1986–90; active involvement in the Movt. for Independence of Latvia, Deputy Chair. of the People's Front; Chair. Council of Ministers of the Latvian Republic 1990–93; with commercial co. SWH (Software House) 1994–95; Vice-Chair. Asscn. of Commercial Banks of Latvia 1995–96; Pres. Latvia Savings Bank (jt. stock co.) 1996–. *Leisure interest:* tennis. *Address:* Palasta Street 1, 1954 Riga, Latvia. *Telephone:* (371) 722 2871. *Fax:* (371) 721 0807.

GODREJ, Adi Burjor, M.S.; Indian business executive; b. 3 April 1942; s. of Dr Burjori Pirojsha Godrej and Jai Burjor Godrej; m. Parmeshwar Mader 1966; one s. two d.; ed. St. Xavier's High School & Coll., Bombay and Massachusetts Inst. of Technology; Chair. Godrej Foods Ltd., Godrej Agrovet Ltd., Godrej & Kis Ltd., Godrej Hl Care Ltd., Godrej Properties & Investments Ltd., Godrej Pillsbury Ltd., Godrej Oil Palm Konkan Pvt. Ltd.; Man. Dir. Godrej Soaps Ltd.; Dir. Godrej & Boyce Mfg. Co. Ltd., Swadeshi Detergents Ltd., Vora Soaps Ltd., Godrej Investments Ltd., Godrej-GE Appliances Ltd., Godrej Capital Ltd., Godrej Pacific Technology Ltd., Godrej Telecom Ltd., Ensemble Holdings & Finance Pvt. Ltd., Godrej Int. Ltd.; Chair. Bd. of Trustees of Dadabhai Naoroji; mem. Nat. Council, Confed. of Indian Ind.; fmr. Chair. or Pres. Indian Soap & Toiletries Makers' Asscn., Cen. Org. for Oil Industry and Trade, Solvent Extractors' Asscn. of India, Indo-American Soc., Compound Livestock Feeds, Mfrs. Asscn. *Leisure interests:* sailing and motor boating, water-skiing, horse riding, squash, bridge, reading. *Address:* Godrej Soaps Ltd., Eastern Express Highway, Vikhroli, Bombay 400079 (Office); Godrej House, 2 Military Road, Juhu, Bombay 400049, India (Home). *Telephone:* 584461 (Office); 6200489/6200795 (Home).

GODSELL, Robert Michael, M.A.; South African business executive; b. 14 Sept. 1952, Johannesburg; s. of Cyril H. Godsell and Winnefred (née Stephens) Godsell; m. Gillian Hall 1975; three d.; Deputy Provincial Leader Progressive Party, Natal 1969–70, Nat. Youth Chair. 1975–76; Dir. Industrial Relations and Public Affairs Anglo-American Corpn. 1974–95, C.E.O. Gold Div. 1995–, Deputy Chair. 1995–96, Chair. 1996–, Exec. Dir. 1991–; C.E.O. Anglo Gold Dur.; Pres. Chamber of Mines 1992, 1997–98; mem. Nat. Econ. Forum 1994–. *Publications:* A Future South Africa: Visions, Strategies and Relations 1988 (co-ed.); ed. of econ. report. *Leisure interest:* squash. *Address:* P.O. Box 61587, Marshalltown 2107, South Africa. *Telephone:* (011) 638-3167.

GODSOE, Peter C., B.SC., M.B.A., F.C.A.; Canadian banker; b. 2 May 1938, Toronto; s. of Joseph Gerald Godsoe and Margaret Graham Cowperthwaite; m. Shelagh Cathleen Reburn 1963; three c.; ed. Univ. of Toronto, Harvard Univ.; fmr. Deputy Chair. Bd., Pres., C.E.O. and Dir. Bank of Nova Scotia, Chair. C.E.O. Jan. 1995–, also Chair. Bd. Dirs. Bank of Nova Scotia Int. 1995–; Chair. and Dir. Scotia Centre Ltd., Scotia Futures Ltd., Scotia Mortgage Corpn.; Vice-Chair. and Dir. Bank of Nova Scotia Properties Inc., Scotia Properties Quebec Inc., Scotia Realty Ltd.; Dir. various Bank of Nova Scotia subsidiary cos., Alexander & Alexander Services Inc., Reed Stenhouse Cos. Ltd., Nova Scotia Corpn., Scotiabank Jamaica Trust and Merchant Bank Ltd., West India Co. of Merchant Bankers Ltd., etc.; fmr. Chair. Canadian Bankers' Asscn. *Address:* Bank of Nova Scotia, Scotia Plaza, 44 King Street W., Toronto, Ont., M5H 1H1, Canada.

GODUNOV, Sergey Konstantinovich; Russian mathematician; b. 17 July 1929; m.; two c.; ed. Moscow State Univ.; jr., sr. researcher, head of div. Inst. of Math. U.S.S.R. Acad. of Sciences 1951–66; head of div. Inst. of Applied Math. U.S.S.R. Acad. of Sciences 1966–69; head of div. Computer's Cen. Siberian br. U.S.S.R. Acad. of Sciences 1969–80; head of lab., Deputy Dir., Exec. Dir. Inst. of Math. Siberian br. U.S.S.R. Acad. of Sciences 1980–86; head of dept., S. Sobolev Inst. of Math. Siberian br. Acad. of Sciences; corresp. mem. U.S.S.R. (now Russian) Acad. of Sciences 1976, mem. 1994; research in computational math., differential equations, mathematical physics, mem. Scientific Council Math. Modelling; mem. Ed. Board Siberian Math. Journal; Lenin Prize, A. Krylov Prize. *Publications:* On Minkowsky Problem 1948, On the Idea of Generalized Solution 1960, Numerical Solution of Multidimensional Problems of Gas Dynamics 1976 and others. *Address:* Institute of Mathematics, Siberian Branch of Russian Academy of Sciences, Universitetskyi pr. 4, 630090 Novosibirsk, Russia. *Telephone:* (3832) 35-06-53 (Office); 35-60-84 (Home).

GODWIN, Fay S.; British photographer; b. 17 Feb. 1931, Berlin, Germany; d. of British father and American mother; m. Tony Godwin; two s.; ed. many schools all over the world; had no photographic training; started photographing her young children 1966; touring exhbns. relating to publ. of The Oldest Road 1975; commissioned by Nat. Trust to photograph the Trust's historic properties and sites in Wessex 1982; British Council's overseas tour of Fay Godwin's Landscape Photographs started 1984; major retrospective landscape exhbn., Serpentine Gallery, London 1985; Land exhbn. at Yale Center for British Art, U.S.A.; Our Forbidden Land exhbn., Royal Photographic Soc. Gallery and nat. tour; joined Network Photographers Picture Agency 1991; teaches at photographic schools and workshops; Pres. Ramblers Asscn. 1987–90, Life Vice-Pres. 1990–; major award from Arts Council of G.B. to continue landscape work in British Isles 1978; Bradford Fellowship 1986/87; Fellow Nat. Museum of Photography, Bradford 1987; Hon. Fellow Royal Photographic Soc. 1991, Royal Inst. of Scottish Architects 1992. *Publications:* The Oldest Road: An Exploration of the Ridgeway (with J. R. L. Anderson) 1975, The Oil Rush (with Mervyn Jones) 1976, The Drovers' Roads of Wales (with Shirley Toulson) 1977, Islands (with John Fowles) 1978, Remains of Elmet: A Pennine Sequence (with poems by Ted Hughes) 1979, Romney Marsh and the Royal Military Canal (with Richard Ingrams) 1980, Tess: The Story of a Guide Dog (with Peter Purves) 1981, The Whisky Roads of Scotland (with Derek Cooper) 1982, Bison at Chalk Farm 1982, The Saxon Shore Way from Gravesend to Rye (with Alan Sillitoe) 1983, The National Trust Book of Wessex 1985, Land (with an essay by John Fowles) 1985, The Secret Forest of Dean 1986, Our Forbidden Land 1990, The Edge of the Land 1995. *Leisure interests:* walking, photography and reading. *Address:* c/o Fay Godwin Network, 3–4 Kirby Street, London, E4N 8TS, England. *Telephone:* 0171-831 3633.

GODWIN, Gail Kathleen, PH.D.; American author; b. 18 June 1937, Birmingham, Ala.; d. of Mose Godwin and Kathleen Krahenbuhl; m. 1st Douglas Kennedy 1960 (divorced 1961); m. 2nd Ian Marshall 1965 (divorced 1966); ed. Peace Jr. Coll. Raleigh, N.C. and Univs. of N.C. and Iowa; news reporter, Miami Herald 1959–60; reporter, consultant, U.S. Travel Service, London 1961–65; Editorial Asst. Saturday Evening Post 1966; Fellow, Center for Advanced Study, Univ. of Ill. Urbana 1971–72; lecturer, Iowa Writers' Workshop 1972–73, Vassar Coll. 1977, Columbia Univ. Writing Program 1978, 1981; American specialist, USIS 1976; Guggenheim Fellow 1975–76; librettist for various productions; mem. PEN, Authors' Guild, Authors' League, Nat. Book Critics' Circle; American Acad. and Inst. of Arts and Letters Literature Award 1981; other awards and distinctions. *Publications:* novels including: The Perfectionists 1970, Glass People 1972, The Odd Woman 1974, Violet Clay 1978, A Mother and Two Daughters 1982, The Finishing School 1985, A Southern Family 1987, Father Melancholy's Daughter 1991, The Good Husband 1994, Evensong 1998; short stories and librettos. *Address:* P.O. Box 946, Woodstock, NY 12498, U.S.A.

GOEHR, Alexander, M.A.; British composer; b. 10 Aug. 1932, Berlin; s. of Walter Goehr; m. 1st Audrey Baker 1954; m. 2nd Anthea Felicity Staunton 1972; m. 3rd Amira Katz; one s. three d.; ed. Berkhamstead School, Royal Manchester Coll. of Music, Paris Conservatoire (with Oliver Messiaen), and privately with Yvonne Loriod; composer, teacher, conductor 1956–; held classes at Morley Coll., London; part-time post with BBC, being responsible for production of orchestral concerts 1960–; works performed and broadcast worldwide; Hon. Fellow Royal Manchester Coll. of Music; awarded Churchill Fellowship 1968; Composer-in-Residence, New England Conservatory, Boston, Mass. 1968–69; Assoc. Prof. of Music, Yale Univ. 1969–70; Prof. West Riding Chair of Music Univ. of Leeds 1971–76; Prof. of Music, Univ. of Cambridge 1976–99, Fellow of Trinity Hall, Cambridge 1976–; Reith Lecturer 1987; Hon. D.Mus. (Southampton) 1973, (Manchester), (Nottingham) 1994); Hon. A.R.C.M. 1976, Hon. F.R.N.C.M. 1980, Hon. F.R.C.M. 1981; Hon. mem. American Acad. and Inst. of Arts and Letters. *Works include:* Songs of Babel 1951, Sonata 1952, Fantasias 1954, String Quartet 1956–57, Capriccio 1957, The Deluge 1957–58, La belle dame sans merci 1958, Variations 1959, Four Songs from the Japanese 1959, Sutter's Gold 1959–60, Suite 1961, Hecuba's Lament 1959–61, A Little Cantata of Proverbs 1962, Concerto for Violin and Orchestra 1961–62, Two Choruses 1962, Virtutes 1963, Little Symphony 1963, Little Music for Strings 1963, Five Poems and an Epigram of William Blake 1964, Three Pieces for Piano 1964, Pastorals 1965, Piano Trio 1966, Arden muss sterben (Arden Must Die—opera) 1966, Warngedichte 1967, String Quartet 1967, Romanza 1968, Naboth's Vineyard 1968, Konzertstück 1969, Nonomiya 1969, Paraphrase 1969, Symphony in One Movement 1970, Shadowplay 1970, Sonata about Jerusalem 1970, Concerto for eleven instruments 1970, Piano Concerto 1972, Chaconne for wind 1974, Lyric Pieces 1974, Metamorphosis/Dance 1974, String Quartet No. 3 1976, Psalm IV 1976, Fugue on the notes of the Fourth Psalm 1976, Romanza on the notes of the Fourth Psalm 1977, Prelude and Fugue for Three Clarinets 1978, Chaconne for Organ 1979, Das Gesetz der Quadrille 1979, Babylon the Great is Fallen 1979, Sinfonia 1980, Cello Sonata 1984, Behold the Sun 1984, Two Imitations of Baudelaire 1985, Symphony with Chaconne 1986, Eve Dreams in Paradise 1987, Carol for St. Steven 1989, . . . in real time 1989, Sing, Ariel 1989, String Quartet No. 4 1990, Still Lands 1990, Bach Variations 1990, The Death of Moses 1991, The Mouse Metamorphosed into a Maid 1991, Colossus or Panic 1992, I Said, I Will Take Heed 1993, Cambridge Hocket 1993, Arianna (opera) 1995. *Address:* Trinity Hall, Cambridge, CB3 9DP; University Music School, 11 West Road, Cambridge CB3 9DP (until Sept. 1999); c/o Schott and Co. Ltd., 48 Great Marlborough Street, London, W1V 2BN, England.

GOENKA, Harsh Vardhan, M.B.A.; Indian industrialist; b. 10 Dec. 1957, Calcutta; s. of Rama Prasad Goenka and Sushila Goenka; m. Mala Sanghi 1977; one s. one d.; ed. St. Xavier's Coll., Calcutta, Int. Man. Inst., Geneva; joined family business RPG Enterprises, became Dir.-in-Charge Aryodaya Ginning Mills, Agarpara Jute Mills; Vice-Chair. Ceat Ltd.; Chair. RPG Enterprises 1988–, Searle (India) Ltd., KEC International Ltd., RPG Cables, etc.; Dir. numerous cos. *Leisure interests:* sports, theatre. *Address:* RPG Enterprises Ltd., CEAT Mahal, 463 Dr. Annie Besant Road, Bombay 400 025, India. *Telephone:* (22) 493 0621 (Office); 828 0872 (Home). *Fax:* (22) 493 8933.

GOES, Albrecht; German writer; b. 22 March 1908; s. of Eberhard Goes and Elisabeth (née Panzerbieter); m. Elisabeth Schneiter 1933; three d.; ed. Tübingen Univ; Evangelical pastor, Württemberg 1930–52; writer 1953–; mem. Berliner Akad. für Künste, Deutsche Akad. für Sprache und Dichtung; Dr. h.c. Theology (Mainz) 1974; Lessing Prize, Hamburg 1953, Buber-Rosenzweig Medal 1978, Literaturförderpreis, Stuttgart 1995. *Publications:* Unruhige Nacht, Von Mensch zu Mensch 1949, Gedichte 1950, Das Brandopfer 1953, Freude am Gedicht 1954, Vertrauen in das Wort 1955, Ruf und Echo 1956, Genesis 1957, Hagar am Brunnen 1958, Rede auf Goethes Mutter 1958, Ravenna 1959, Aber im Winde das Wort 1963, Das Löffelchen 1965, Im Weitergehen 1966, Der Knecht macht keinen Lärm 1968, Die guten Gefährten 1969, Kanzelholz 1971, Tagwerk, Prosa und Verse 1976, Lichtschutten Du (poems) 1979. *Address:* Im Langen Hau 5, 70565 Stuttgart-Rohr, Germany. *Telephone:* 749103.

GOETZ, Hannes, PH.D.; Swiss airline executive; b. 27 March 1934, Schaffhausen; m.; one s.; ed. Fed. Inst. of Tech. Zürich; Sika AG, Zürich 1961–62; Sika U.S.A. 1962–66; Sika Int. 1966–71; C.E.O. Sika Finance AG 1971–79; mem. Bd. and Pres. Sika Finanz AG 1979–83, Georg Fischer AG, Schaffhausen 1981–83; mem. Bd. and C.E.O. Georg Fischer AG 1983–92; Chair. Bd. SAirGroup 1992–. *Address:* SAirGroup, P.O. Box, CH-8058 Zürich-Airport, Switzerland. *Telephone:* 0041-1-812 12 12. *Fax:* 0041-1-812 80 46.

GOFF, Philip Bruce, M.A., M.P.; New Zealand politician; b. 22 June 1953, Auckland; s. of Bruce Charles Goff and Elaine Loyola Goff; m. Mary Ellen Moriarty 1979; two s. one d.; ed. Papatoetoe High School; Lecturer in political science at Auckland Univ.; field officer in Insurance Workers' Union; fmr. Chair. Labour Youth Council; M.P. for Roskill 1981–90, 1993–96; M.P. for New Lynn 1996–; Minister of Housing, for the Environment, responsible for Government Life Insurance Corpn., responsible for State Insurance Office, in charge of the Public Trust Office 1986–87, of Employment, of Youth Affairs and Assoc. Minister of Educ. 1987–89, Minister of Educ. 1989–90, of Tourism 1987–88; currently Opposition front bench Spokesman on Justice; British Council Scholarship to Nuffield Coll. 1992; Labour. *Leisure interests:* sports, gardening, squash. *Address:* Parliament Buildings, Wellington (Office); Creightons Road RD 2, Papakura, Auckland, New Zealand (Home). *Telephone:* (04) 4719108 (Office); (09) 2928377 (Home). *Fax:* (04) 4722015.

GOFF OF CHIEVELEY, Baron (Life Peer), cr. 1986, of Chieveley in the Royal County of Berkshire; **Robert (Lionel Archibald) Goff,** Kt., P.C., D.C.L., F.B.A.; **Rt. Hon. Lord Goff of Chieveley;** British lawyer; b. 12 Nov. 1926; s. of L. T. Goff; m. Sarah Cousins 1953; two s. (one deceased) two d.; ed. Eton Coll., New Coll., Oxford; served in Scots Guards 1945–48 (Commissioned 1945); called to the Bar, Inner Temple 1951; Bencher 1975; Q.C. 1967; Fellow and Tutor, Lincoln Coll., Oxford 1951–55; in practice at the Bar 1956–75; a Recorder 1974–75; Judge of the High Court, Queen's Bench Div. 1975–82; Judge in charge of Commercial List, and Chair. Commercial Court Cttee. 1979–81; Chair. Council of Legal Educ. 1976–82, Vice-Chair. 1972–76, Chair. Bd. of Studies 1970–76; Chair. Common Professional Examination Bd. 1976–78; Chair. British Inst. of Int. and Comparative Law 1986–, Court of Univ. of London 1986–91, Sub-Cttee. E (Law) of House of Lords Select Cttee. on European Communities 1986–88; Chair. Pegasus Scholarship Trust 1987–; Pres. Bentham Club 1986, Chartered Inst. of Arbitrators 1986–91, Holdsworth Club 1988; Hon. Prof. of Legal Ethics, Univ. of Birmingham 1980–81; Maccabean Lecturer 1983; Lionel Cohen Lecturer (Jerusalem) 1987; Cassel Lecturer (Stockholm) 1993; mem. Gen. Council of the Bar 1971–74; mem. Senate of Inns and Court and Bar 1974–82; Chair. Law Reform and Procedure Cttee. 1974–76; Lord Justice of Appeal 1982–86; Lord of Appeal in Ordinary 1986–98; Sr. Law Lord 1996–98; High Steward Oxford Univ. 1990–; Hon. Fellow, Lincoln Coll., Oxford, New Coll., Oxford; Hon. Fellow, American Coll. of Trial Lawyers 1997; Hon. D.Litt. (City) 1977, (Buckingham) 1989; Hon. LL.D. (Reading, London) 1990, (Bristol) 1996. *Publications:* The Law of Restitution (with Prof. Gareth Jones) 1966. *Address:* House of Lords, Westminster, London, S.W.1, England.

GOGOBERIDZE, Lana, D.LITT.; Georgian politician, film director and translator; b. 13 Oct. 1928, Tbilisi; d. of Levan Gogoberidze and Ninio

Gogoberidze; m. Lado Aleksi-Meskhishvili 1958 (died 1978); two d.; ed. Tbilisi State Univ., State Univ. of Cinematography (VGIK), Moscow; mem. CPSU 1965–89; Dir. of studio at Rustaveli Theatre School 1975–; Dir. Kartuli Filmi (Georgian Film) 1988–; Chair. Liberal Democratic Faction 1992–95; mem. Georgian Parl. 1994–, Leader of Majority 1995–, Head, Georgia-France Friendship Group 1997–; mem. Citizens' Union party 1997–; Head, Perm. Nat. Del. to Council of Europe 1997–; Pres. Int. Asscn. of Women Film-Makers; mem. Bd. of Union of Georgian Film-Makers; San Remo Film Festival Prize (Grand Prix) 1979, U.S.S.R. State Prize 1980, Tokyo Film Festival Prize (Best Dir.) 1986, Venice Film Festival Prize 1992, Berlin Film Festival Prize 1993; People's Artist of Georgian S.S.R. 1979, Culture Diploma of Honor, American Biographical Inst. 1995, Ordre Nat. du Mérite (France) 1997. *Films include:* documentary: Gelathi 1957, Tbilisi—1500 1958, Letters to the Children 1981; fiction: Under the Same Sky 1961, I See the Sun 1965, Boundaries 1970, When the Almond Blossomed 1973, Turmoil 1974, Interviews on Personal Problems 1979, A Day Longer than Night 1985, Turnover 1986, Waltz on the Pechora River 1986 (five prizes). *Publications:* Walt Whitman 1955, Walt Whitman: Leaves of Grass (trans.) 1956, Rabindranath Tagore (trans.) 1957, Foreign Poetry in Georgian (trans.) 1995. *Leisure interests:* tennis, skiing, painting. *Address:* Parliament of Georgia, Rustaveli Avenue 8, Tbilisi (Office); Kazbegi Str. 17, Apt. 26, Tbilisi, Georgia (Home). *Telephone:* 93-19-92 (Office); 22-76-79 (Home). *Fax:* 99-58-53 (Office).

GOH CHOK TONG, M.A.; Singaporean politician; b. 20 May 1941, Singapore; s. of Goh Kah Khoon (deceased) and Quah Kwee Hwa; m. Tan Choo Leng 1965; one s. one d. (twins); ed. Raffles Inst., Univ. of Singapore and Williams Coll., U.S.A.; with Singapore Admin. Service 1964–69, Neptune Orient Lines Ltd. 1969–77; M.P. 1976–; First Org. Sec. Peoples' Action Party 1979, Second Asst. Sec.-Gen. 1979–84, Asst. Sec.-Gen. 1984–89, First Asst. Sec.-Gen. 1989–92, Sec.-Gen. 1992; Sr. Minister of State, Ministry of Finance 1977–79, Minister for Trade and Industry 1979–81, Minister for Health and Second Minister for Defence 1981–82, Minister for Defence and Deputy Minister for Health 1982–85; First Deputy Prime Minister and Minister for Defence 1985–90; Prime Minister of Singapore 1990–; Chair. Singapore Labour Foundation, Bd. of Dirs. Nat. Trades Union Congress (NTUC) Fairprice and NTUC Income; mem. Econs. Soc., Singapore; Medal of Honour, NTUC Congress 1987. *Leisure interests:* tennis, golf. *Address:* Prime Minister's Office, Annexe, Istana, Singapore 238823.

GOH KENG SWEE, PH.D.; Singaporean politician; b. 6 Oct. 1918, Malacca; s. of Goh Leng Inn and Tan Swee; m. Alice Woon 1942; one s.; ed. Anglo-Chinese School, Singapore, and Raffles Coll., London Univ; fmrly. Vice-Chair. People's Action Party; fmr. mem. Legis. Assembly from Kreta Ayer Div. and Minister for Finance 1959–65; initiated Singapore's industrialization plan, the establishment of Econ. Devt. Board; Minister of Defence 1965–67, of Finance 1967–70, of Educ. 1979–81, 1981–84, of Defence 1970–79, concurrently Deputy Prime Minister 1973–80, First Deputy Prime Minister 1980–84 and with responsibility for the Monetary Authority of Singapore 1980–81 (Deputy Chair. –1992); Econ. Adviser to Chinese Govt. July 1985–; mem. Governing Council, Asian Inst. for Econ. Devt. and Planning, Bangkok 1963–66; Ramon Magsaysay Award for Govt. Service 1972. *Publications:* Urban Incomes and Housing; a Report on the Social Survey of Singapore, 1953–54 1958, Economics of Modernization and Other Essays 1972, The Practice of Economic Growth 1977. *Address:* c/o Ministry of Foreign Affairs, 2nd Floor, City Hall, St. Andrews Road, Singapore 0617.

GOHEEN, Robert Francis, PH.D.; American diplomatist, educator and public servant; b. 15 Aug. 1919, Vengurla, India; s. of Robert H. H. and Anne (Ewing) Goheen; m. Margaret M. Skelly 1941; two s. four d.; ed. Lawrenceville School and Princeton Univ.; Instructor, Princeton Univ. 1948–50, Asst. Prof. 1950–57, Prof. 1957–72, Pres. 1957–72, Pres. Emer. 1972–; Senior Fellow in Classics, American Acad. in Rome 1952–53; Dir. Nat. Woodrow Wilson Fellowship Programme 1953–56; Sr. Fellow Woodrow Wilson School 1981–; Dir. Mellon Fellowships in the Humanities 1981–92; mem. Bd. Asia Soc., Bharatiya Vidya Bhavan (U.S.A.), Carnegie Endowment for Int. Peace, Inst. for Int. Educ., Fund for New Jersey, United Bd. for Christian Higher Educ. in Asia, Midlantic Banks Inc., Thomson Newspapers Inc.; mem. Int. Advisory Bd. Chemical Bank and Advisory Panel, Bureau of Oceans and Int. Scientific and Environmental Affairs, U.S. Dept. of State; Chair. Council on Foundations, Inc. 1972–77; Pres. Edna McConnell Clark Foundation 1977; Amb. to India 1977–80; fmr. Gov. Reza Shah Kabir Univ. (Iran); fmr. Regent, Smithsonian Inst.; fmr. Co-Chair. Indo-U.S. Sub-comm. on Educ. and Culture; fmr. Dir. Equitable Life Assurance Soc. of U.S., Dreyfus Third Century Fund; fmr. mem. Bd. American Acad. in Rome, Rockefeller Foundation, Carnegie Foundation for Advancement of Teaching; mem. Council on Foreign Relations, American Acad. of Arts and Sciences; Hon. LL.D., Litt.D., L.C.D., L.H.D., degrees from 26 univs. and colls. including Harvard, Yale, Madras, North Carolina, Notre Dame. *Publications:* The Imagery of Sophocles' Antigone 1951, The Human Nature of a University 1969. *Leisure interests:* golf, tennis, reading. *Address:* 1 Orchard Circle, Princeton, NJ 08540, U.S.A.

GOIPORIA, Maneck Nadirshaw, B.COMM., A.C.A.; Indian banker; b. 8 July 1932; Chair. and Man. Dir. Dena Bank 1978–85, Bank of Baroda Feb.–April 1985, Cen. Bank of India 1985–90; fmr. Chair. State Bank of India, State Banks of Bikaner and Jaipur, Hyderabad, Indore, Mysore, Patiala, Saurashtra, Travancore, SBI Capital Markets Ltd., SBI (Calif.), Los Angeles, SBI (Canada) Toronto; Chair. and ex-officio Dir. S.B. India Hong Kong Finance Ltd.; Dir. Agricultural Finance Corpn. Ltd., Industrial Devt. Bank, Discount & Finance House of India Ltd., Nat. Bank for Agric. and Rural Devt., Export Credit & Guarantee Corpn., Gen. Insurance Corpn. of India, Industrial Finance Corpn. of India, Export and Import Bank of India; Chair. Indian Banks Asscn., Vice-Pres. Indian Inst. of Bankers; Trustee Unit Trust of India; mem. Governing Bd. Nat. Inst. of Bank Man., Governing Body India Investment Centre, New Delhi, Governing Council Nat. Inst. for Entrepreneurship and Small Business Devt.; Chair. Nat. Asscn. for the Blind, and Cttee. on Rehabilitation, Training and Employment. *Address:* State Bank of India, Central Office, New Administrative Building, Madame Cama Road, Bombay 400 021 (Office); Dunedin, 5 J.M. Mehta Road, Bombay 400 006, India (Home).

GOLAN, Menahem; Israeli film director and producer; b. 31 May 1929, Tiberius; ed. Old Vic., London; f. Noah Films with Yoram Globus (q.v.) 1963; Sr. Vice-Pres. Cannon Group Inc. 1979–89; f. and Chair., C.E.O. 21st Century Production Corpn. Feb. 1989–; *directed films include:* Over the Top, Delta Force, Over the Brooklyn Bridge, Enter the Ninja, The Magician of Lublin; films include: Barfly, Surrender, Death Wish IV, Superman IV, Street Smart, Dancers, 52 Pickup, Otello, The Assault, Hanoi Hilton, Cannon Movie Tales, Masters of the Universe, Duet for One, Tough Guys Don't Dance, Shy People, Hanna's War, The Rose Garden; all have Golan and Globus as exec. producers.

GOLANI, Rivka; Canadian viola soloist; b. 22 March 1946, Israel; d. of Jacob Golani and Lisa Gulnik; m. Jeremy Fox 1993; one s.; ed. Univ. of Tel Aviv; studied with Oedon Partos; concerts as soloist worldwide; has inspired many new works including viola concerti by Holloway, Hummel, Fontajn, Colgrass, Vagn Holmboe, Yuasa, and Turner, solo works by Holliger, Holmboe and others. *Publication:* Birds of Another Feather (book of drawings). *Leisure interest:* painting. *Address:* c/o Margaret Barkman, Fox Jones & Associates, 2nd Floor, 243 College Street, Toronto, Ont., M5T 1R5, Canada. *Telephone:* (416) 586-1302. *Fax:* (416) 586-0287.

GOLANT, Victor Yevgenyevich; DR. PHYS.-MATH. SC.; Russian physicist; b. 14 Jan. 1928; m.; one s. two d.; ed. Leningrad Polytech Inst.; engineer, head of lab. factories in Leningrad; sr. researcher, head of lab, head of div. Inst. of Physics and Eng.; Prof., Head of Chair Leningrad Tech. Univ.; Dir. Ioffe Inst. of Physics and Tech.; corresp. mem. U.S.S.R. Acad of Sciences 1984, mem. 1990–; research in physics of plasma and thermonuclear synthesis; U.S.S.R. State Prize 1991. *Publications include:* Fundamentals of Plasma Physics 1977, Super High-Frequency Method of Plasma Diagnostics 1985. *Address:* Ioffe Institute of Physics and Technology, Polytekhnicheskaya 26, St. Petersburg 194021, Russia (Office). *Telephone:* (812) 247 4150 (Office); 552-59-08 (Home).

GÖLCÜKLÜ, Ahmet Feyyaz; Turkish judge and academic; b. 4 Oct. 1926, Ula; s. of Zeki and Ruhiye Gölcüklü; m. (divorced 1975); two s.; ed. Univ. of Istanbul and Univ. of Neuchâtel; became Asst. Prof. at Faculty of Political Sciences Univ. of Ankara 1954, Assoc. Prof. 1958, Prof. 1965, Dir. School of Journalism and Broadcasting 1969 and 1972, Dean, Faculty of Political Sciences 1973–76, now Prof. Emer.; Judge, European Court of Human Rights 1977–98; mem. Turkish Consultative Assembly (Constituent Assembly) 1981–82; Dir. of Human Rights Research and Implementation Centre, Ankara Univ. 1988–. *Publications:* Examination of the Accused Person in Penal Matters 1952, Personal Liberty of the Accused in Criminal Procedure 1958, A Research on Juvenile Delinquency in Turkey 1963, Turkish Penal System 1965, Mass Communication Law 1973, The European Convention on Human Rights and its Implementation 1994. *Address:* Pilot Sokak 8/4, Çankaya, 06690 Ankara, Turkey. *Telephone:* 4393008.

GOLD, Jack, B.SC.(ECONS.), LL.B., F.R.S.A.; British film director; b. 28 June 1930; m. Denyse Macpherson 1957; two s. one d.; ed. London Univ.; Asst. Studio Man., BBC radio 1954–55; Ed. Film Dept., BBC 1955–60; Dir. TV and film documentaries and fiction 1960–. *TV films include:* Tonight, Death in the Morning (British Acad. of Film and TV Arts Award) 1964, Modern Millionairess, Famine, Dowager in Hot Pants, World of Coppard (B.A.F.T.A. Award 1967), Mad Jack (Grand Prix, Monte Carlo) 1971, The Resistable Rise of Arturo Ui, Stockers Copper (B.A.F.T.A. Award 1972), Catholics (Peabody Award) 1974, The Naked Civil Servant (Italia Prize, Int. Emmy and Critics Award) 1976, (Desmond Davies Award 1976), Thank You Comrades, A Walk in the Forest, Merchant of Venice, Praying Mantis, Macbeth, L'Elégance 1982, The Red Monarch 1983, The Tenth Man 1988, The Rose and the Jackal 1989, Ball Trap on Côte Sauvage 1989, The Shlemiel, The Shlemazi and The Doppess 1990, The War that Never Ends 1991, She Stood Alone 1991, The Last Romantics 1992, Spring Awakening 1995, Kavanagh Q.C. 1995, Heavy Weather 1996, Mute of Malice 1997, Blood Money 1997, Into the Blue 1997, Care in the Community 1998, Goodnight Mr. Tom 1998. *Theatre:* Council of Love, Devils Disciple, Danger Memory, This Story of Yours. *Films include:* The Bofors Gun 1968, The National Health 1973, (Evening News Best Comedy Film 1973), Who? 1974, Aces High (Evening News Best Film Award) 1976, The Medusa Touch 1977, The Sailor's Return (Monte Carlo Catholic Award, Monte Carlo Critics Award) 1978, Little Lord Fauntleroy (Christopher Award) 1981, A Lot of Happiness (Int. Emmy Award) 1983, Sakharov 1984, (Ace Award), Me and the Girls 1985, Murrow (Ace Award) 1986, Escape from Sobibor 1987, (Golden Globe Award), Stones for Ibarra 1988, The Lucona Affair 1993. *Film/TV:* Return of the Native 1994. *Leisure interests:* music, reading. *Address:* 24 Wood Vale, London, N10 3DP, England. *Telephone:* 0181-883 3491. *Fax:* 0181-444 3406.

GOLD, Sir Joseph, Kt., LL.M., S.J.D.; British lawyer; b. 12 July 1912, London; m. Ruth Schechter 1939; one s. two d.; ed. London and Harvard Univs; Lecturer in Law, London Univ. 1937–39; mem. British Govt. Mission to Washington 1942–46; with IMF 1946–79, Gen. Counsel, Dir. Legal Dept. 1960–79, Sr. Consultant 1979–; Hon. LL.D; Columbia Univ. Medal; A.B.A. Prize in Int. Law. *Publications:* Fund Agreement in the Courts (vol. I) 1962, (vol. II) 1982, (vol. III) 1986, (vol. IV) 1989, The Stand-By Arrangements of the IMF 1970, Voting and Decisions in the IMF 1972, Membership and Nonmembership in the IMF 1974, Aspectos Legales de la Reforma Monetaria 1979, Legal and Institutional Aspects of the International Monetary System: Selected Essays, Vol. 1 1979, Vol. 2 1984, Exchange Rates in International Law and Organization 1988, Legal Effects of Fluctuating Exchange Rates 1990, Interpretation: the IMF and International Law 1996, and contributions to various IMF publs. and to professional journals in various countries. *Address:* International Monetary Fund, 700 19th Street, N.W., Washington, DC 20431 (Office); 7020 Braeburn Place, Bethesda, MD 20817, U.S.A. (Home). *Telephone:* (301) 229-3278 (Home).

GOLD, Phil, C.C., O.Q., M.D.C.M., PH.D., F.R.C.P.(C), M.A.C.P.; Canadian professor of medicine; b. 17 Sept. 1936, Montreal; m. Evelyn Katz; three c.; ed. McGill Univ.; postgraduate training and research, The McGill Univ. Medical Clinic of The Montreal Gen. Hosp.; Medical Research Council of Canada Centennial Fellow 1967–68, Assoc. and Career Scientist 1969–80; Lecturer, Teaching Fellow, Asst. and Assoc. Prof., Dept. of Physiology and Dept. of Medicine, McGill Univ. 1965–73, Prof. of Medicine and Clinical Medicine, 1973–, of Physiology 1974–, of Oncology 1989–; Chair. Dept. of Medicine 1985–90, Douglas G. Cameron Prof. of Medicine 1987–; Dir. McGill Cancer Centre 1978–80; Dir. McGill Univ. Medical Clinic (now Centre), The Montreal Gen. Hosp. 1980–, Dir. Clinical Research Centre 1995–; Sr. Physician, The Montreal Gen. Hosp. 1973–, Physician-in-Chief 1980–95, Sr. Investigator Hosp. Research Inst.; Hon. Consultant, Royal Victoria Hosp., Montreal 1981–; mem. numerous professional socs., scientific research bds. and orgs. etc.; numerous honours and awards. *Publications:* 146 articles in professional journals (1988). *Address:* Room D13-173, Clinical Research Center, The Montreal General Hospital, 1650 Cedar Avenue, Montreal, Que. H3G 1A4, Canada (Office).

GOLD, Thomas, F.R.S., SC.D.; American astronomer; b. 22 May 1920, Vienna, Austria; s. of Max Gold and Josefine Gold; m. 1st Merle Eleanor Tuberg 1947; m. 2nd Carvel Lee Beyer 1972; four d.; ed. Zuoz Coll., Switzerland, and Trinity Coll., Cambridge; Experimental Officer, British Admiralty (radar research) 1943–46; Fellow, Trinity Coll., Cambridge 1947; Chief Asst. to Astronomer Royal, Royal Greenwich Observatory 1952–56; Prof. of Astronomy, Harvard Univ. 1957–59; Prof. of Astronomy, Cornell Univ. 1971–86, Prof. Emer. 1987–; Dir. Cornell Univ. Center for Radiophysics and Space Research 1959–81; Hon. Fellow, Trinity Coll. Cambridge 1986–; Fellow, Royal Soc., London; mem. N.A.S., American Philosophical Soc; Fellow American Acad. of Arts and Sciences; Gold Medal, Royal Astronomical Soc. 1985. *Publications:* The Steady State Theory of the Expanding Universe 1948, The Alignment of Galactic Dust 1952, The Field of a Uniformly Accelerated Charge 1954, Instability of the Earth's Axis of Rotation 1955, The Lunar Surface 1956, Cosmic Rays from the Sun 1957, Plasma and Magnetic Fields in the Solar System 1959, The Origin of Solar Flares 1960, The Nature of Time 1967, Rotating Neutron Stars as the Origin of the Pulsating Radio Source 1968, Rotating Neutron Stars and the Nature of Pulsars 1969, Apollo 12 Seismic Signal: Indication of a Deep Layer of Powder 1970, Terrestrial Sources of Carbon and Earthquake Outgassing 1978, Power from the Earth 1987, The Deep, Hot Biosphere 1992, The Origin of Methane in the Crust of the Earth 1993. *Leisure interests:* skiing, water skiing. *Address:* 7 Pleasant Grove Lane, Ithaca, NY 14850, U.S.A. *Telephone:* (607) 257-6696. *Fax:* (607) 257-7969.

GOLDANSKII, Vitalii Iosifovich; Russian physicist and chemist; b. 18 June 1923, Vitebsk; s. of Iosif Efimovich Goldanskii and Yudif Iosifovna Melamed; m. Lyudmila Nikolayevna Semenova 1947; two s.; ed. Moscow Univ.; mem. of staff of U.S.S.R. (now Russian) Inst. of Chemical Physics 1942–52, 1961–, sr. positions 1961–, Dir. 1988–94; Gen. Dir. Jt. Inst. of Chemical Physics, Russian Acad. of Sciences 1994–; mem. of staff of U.S.S.R. Acad. of Sciences Inst. of Physics 1952–61; Asst. Prof. of Moscow Physical-Tech. Inst. 1947–51, with Inst. of Physical Engineering, Moscow 1951– (posts of Asst. Prof., Prof.); People's Deputy of the U.S.S.R. 1989–91; mem. Cttee. of Int. Affairs, U.S.S.R. Supreme Soviet, Presidium U.S.S.R. Parl. Group 1989–91; Chair. U.S.S.R. (now Russian) Pugwash Cttee., mem. Pugwash Council and Exec. Cttee. 1987–; Ed.-in-Chief High Energy Chemistry journal 1967–87; Chem. Physics (Soviet) journal 1988–; mem. U.S.S.R. (now Russian) Acad. of Sciences 1981 (Corresp. mem. 1962–81); main work on chemical physics, radiation and nuclear chem., nuclear physics, biophysics; discoveries in radioactivity 1960, 1980; mem. Royal Danish Acad. of Sciences and Letters 1977, Deutsche Akad. Naturforsch. Leopoldina 1976, Brazilian Acad. of Sciences 1977, American Acad. of Arts and Sciences 1987, Acad. of Sciences of the D.D.R. 1987, American Philosophical Soc. 1989, Academia Europaea 1990, Finnish Acad. of Sciences 1991, Royal Swedish Acad. of Sciences 1992, World Acad. of Arts and Sciences 1993; Foreign Assoc. Nat. Acad. of Sciences of the U.S.A. 1995; Hon. Life mem. New York Acad. of Sciences 1975; Foreign mem. Georgian Acad. of Sciences 1996; Centennial Foreign Fellow American Chemical Soc. 1976; Fellow American Physics Soc.; Hon. mem. Hungarian Physics Soc. 1974; Lenin Prize 1980, Karpinskii Prize, City of Hamburg FVS Foundation 1983; Golden Mendeleev Medal 1975, Boris Pregel Award, N.Y. Acad. of Sciences 1990, Alexander von Humboldt Award (Germany) 1992, Golden Semenov Medal 1996; numerous orders and other decorations. *Publications:* Kinematics of Nuclear Reactions 1959, Counting Statistics of Nuclear Particles 1959, Mössbauer effect and its applications in chemistry 1963, Physical chemistry of positron and positronium 1968, Tunnelling phenomena in chemical physics 1986, Kinematical methods in high energy physics 1987; books, reviews, articles. *Leisure interests:* aphorisms, humour, movies, records. *Address:* N. N. Semenov Institute of Chemical Physics, Russian Academy of Sciences, Ul. Kosygina 4, Moscow 117334, Russia. *Telephone:* 137-35-45 (Office); 135-11-36 (Home). *Fax:* (095) 938-21-56.

GOLDBERG, Sir Abraham, Kt., M.D., D.SC., F.R.C.P., F.R.S.E.; British professor of medicine (retd.); b. 7 Dec. 1923, Edinburgh; s. of the late Julius Goldberg and Rachel Goldberg; m. Clarice Cussin 1957; two s. one d.; ed. George Heriots School, Edin. and Univs. of Edinburgh and Glasgow; Nuffield Research Fellow, Univ. Coll. Hosp., London 1952–54; Eli Lilly Travelling Fellow in Medicine, Univ. of Utah 1954–56; Regius Prof. of Materia Medica, Univ. of Glasgow 1970–78, Regius Prof. of Practice of Medicine 1978–89; Chair. Cttee. on Safety of Medicines 1980–86; mem. other medical research cttees. etc.; Founder Pres. of Faculty of Pharmaceutical Medicine of Royal Colls. of Physicians (U.K.) 1989–91; Hon. Professorial Research Fellow Dept. of Modern History, Univ. of Glasgow 1991–; Sydney Watson Smith Lectureship, Royal Coll. of Physicians (Edinburgh) 1964; Henry Cohen Lectureship, Hebrew Univ. 1973; Alex Fleck Award (Univ. of Glasgow) 1967, Fitzpatrick Lecture, Royal Coll. of Physicians (London) 1988, Arch. Goodall Lecturer, Royal Coll. of Physicians and Surgeons (Glasgow) 1989; City of Glasgow Lord Provost's Award for Public Service 1988. *Publications:* Diseases of Porphyrin Metabolism (jtly.) 1962, Recent Advances in Haematology (Jt. Ed.) 1971, Clinics in Haematology "The Porphyrias" (jtly.) 1980, Disorders of Porphyrin Metabolism (jtly.) 1987, Pharmaceutical Medicine and the Law (Jt. Ed.) 1991. *Leisure interests:* medical history, literature, writing, walking, swimming. *Address:* 16 Birnam Crescent, Bearsden, Glasgow, G61 2AU, Scotland (Home).

GOLDBERG, Edward David, PH.D.; American professor of chemistry; b. 2 Aug. 1921, Sacramento, Calif.; s. of Edward Davidow Goldberg and Lillian Rothholz Goldberg; one s. three d.; ed. Univ. of California (Berkeley) and Univ. of Chicago; practising marine chemist specialising in marine pollution and wastes of soc.; Prof. of Chem., Scripps Inst. of Oceanography 1960–; served as consultant to many nat. and int. bodies (including UNESCO and FAO); has given over 200 scientific papers; mem. N.A.S.; Guggenheim Fellow 1960; NATO Fellow 1970; B. H. Ketchum Award 1984, Tyler Prize for Environmental Achievement 1989, John H. Martin Medal of Excellence in Marine Science 1996. *Publications:* The Health of the Oceans 1976, Black Carbon in the Environment 1985, Coastal Zone Space 1994. *Address:* Scripps Institution of Oceanography, La Jolla, CA 92093; 750 Val Sereno Drive, Encinitas, CA 92024, U.S.A. (Home). *Telephone:* (619) 534-2407 (Office).

GOLDBERG, Whoopi; American actress; m. 2nd Dave Claessen 1986 (divorced 1988); one d.; m. 3rd Lyle Trachtenberg 1994 (divorced 1995); first stage appearance, aged 8, Hudson Guild Theatre, New York; worked with Helena Rubinstein Children's Theatre; moved to San Diego 1974; co-f. San Diego Repertory Theatre, appeared in Mother Courage (Brecht) and Getting Out (Marsha Norman); moved to San Francisco, became mem. Blake St. Hawkeyes Theatre; toured U.S.A. in The Spook Show; co-wrote and appeared in Moms (one-woman show); Broadway debut, Lyceum Theatre 1984; films: The Color Purple (Acad. Award nomination as Best Actress, Image Award from NAACP, Golden Globe Award, Hollywood Foreign Press Asscn.), Sarah's Heart, Jumpin' Jack Flash, Burglar, The Telephone, Fatal Beauty, Ghost 1990, Sarafina 1992, Sister Act, Made in America 1992, Alice 1993, Sister Act II 1993, Corrina Corrina 1993, Boys on the Side 1994, Star Trek Generation 5, Moonlight and Valentino, Bogus, Eddie, The Associate 1996, The Ghost of Mississippi 1996, How Stella Got Her Groove Back 1998; TV appearances in comedy series Moonlighting 1985–86 (Emmy nomination), own TV show 1992–93; Grammy Award for Best Comedy Album 1985, Hans Christian Andersen Award for Outstanding Achievement by a Dyslexic.

GOLDBERGER, Marvin Leonard, PH.D.; American professor of physics; b. 22 Oct. 1922, Chicago, Ill.; s. of Joseph and Mildred Sedwitz Goldberger; m. Mildred C. Ginsburg 1945; two s.; ed. Carnegie Inst. of Technology and Univ. of Chicago; Research Assoc. Radiation Lab., Univ. of Calif. (Berkeley) 1948–49, M.I.T. 1949–50; Asst. Prof., Prof., Univ. of Chicago 1950–57; Eugene Higgins Prof. of Physics, Princeton Univ. 1957–77, Chair. Physics Dept. 1970–76, Joseph Henry Prof. of Physics 1977–78; Pres. Calif. Inst. of Tech. 1978–87; Dir. Inst. for Advanced Study 1987–91; Prof. of Physics, Univ. of Calif. L.A. 1991–93, Univ. of Calif., San Diego 1993– (Dean Div. of Natural Sciences 1994–); Chair. Fed. of American Scientists 1971–72; mem. N.A.S., American Acad. of Arts and Sciences; Dannie Heineman Prize for Mathematical Physics 1961; Hon. Sc.D. (Carnegie-Mellon Univ. 1979, Univ. of Notre Dame 1979, Brandeis Univ. 1991); Hon. LL.D. (Occidental Coll. 1980); Hon. D.H.L. (Hebrew Union Coll. 1980, Univ. of Judaism 1982). *Publication:* Collision Theory (with K. M. Watson) 1964. *Leisure interests:* running, tennis, cooking.

GOLDBLUM, Jeff; American actor; b. 22 Oct. 1952, Pittsburgh; m. 2nd Geena Davis (q.v.) (divorced); studied at New York Neighborhood Playhouse.

Films include: California Split 1974, Death Wish 1974, Nashville 1975, Next Stop Greenwich Village 1976, Annie Hall 1977, Between the Lines 1977, The Sentinel 1977, Invasion of the Bodysnatchers 1978, Remember My Name 1978, Thank God it's Friday 1978, Escape from Athena 1979, The Big Chill 1983, The Right Stuff 1983, Threshold 1983, The Adventures of Buckaroo Banzai 1984, Silverado 1985, Into the Night 1985, Transylvania 6-5000 1985, The Fly 1986, Beyond Therapy 1987, The Tall Guy 1989, Earth Girls are Easy 1989, First Born (TV) 1989, The Mad Monkey 1990, Mister Frost 1991, Deep Cover 1992, The Favour, the Watch and the Very Big Fish 1992, Father and Sons 1993, Jurassic Park 1993, Lushlife (TV) 1994, Future Quest (TV) 1994, Hideaway 1995, Nine Months 1995, Independence Day 1996, The Lost World 1997; producer Little Surprises 1995, Holy Man 1999. *Address:* c/o Peter Lemie, William Morris Agency, 151 El Camino Drive, Beverly Hills, CA 90212, U.S.A.

GOLDENBERG SCHREIBER, Efrain; Peruvian politician and businessman; b. 28 Dec. 1929, Lima; s. of Aron Goldenberg and Charna Schreiber; m. Irene Pravatiner 1952; one s. four d.; ed. San Andrés (fmrly. Anglo-Peruvian) School, Universidad Nacional Mayor de San Marcos; pvt. entrepreneur 1951–; fmr. Dir. FOPEX, Sociedad Nacional de Pesquería and other cos.; Minister of Foreign Affairs 1993–94, Pres. Council of Ministers (Prime Minister) and Minister of Foreign Affairs 1994–95; working in pvt. sector 1995–. *Address:* P.O. Box 293, Lima 100, Peru. Telephone: (1) 421-2264. *Fax:* (1) 221-6458.

GOLDHABER, Maurice, PH.D.; American physicist; b. 18 April 1911, Lemberg, Austria; s. of Charles Goldhaber and Ethel Frisch Goldhaber; m. Gertrude Scharff 1939 (died 1998); two s.; ed. Berlin Univ. and Cambridge Univ., U.K.; Prof. of Physics, Univ. of Ill. 1938–50; Senior scientist, Brookhaven Nat. Lab. 1950–60, Chair. Dept. of Physics 1960–61, Dir. 1961–73; Adjunct Prof. of Physics, New York State Univ. 1965–; mem. N.A.S., American Philosophical Soc.; Fellow, American Acad. of Arts and Sciences, A.A.A.S., Chair. Section B, Physics 1981, American Physical Soc., Pres. 1982; Tom W. Bonner Prize in Nuclear Physics of American Physical Soc. 1971, Associated Univs. Inc. Distinguished Scientist 1973–; U.S. Atomic Energy Comm. Citation for Meritorious Contributions 1973, J. Robert Oppenheimer Memorial Prize 1982, Wolf Foundation Prize 1991; Rabi Scholar Lecturer 1995; Hon. Ph.D. (Tel-Aviv) 1974, Hon. Dr. h.c. (Univ. of Louvain-La-Neuve) 1982. *Publications:* numerous articles in professional scientific journals on neutron physics, radioactivity, nuclear isomers, nuclear photo-electric effect, nuclear models, fundamental particles. *Leisure interests:* tennis, hiking. *Address:* Brookhaven National Laboratory Building, 510 Upton, NY 11973, U.S.A.

GOLDIN, Daniel S., B.SC.; American space research administrative official; b. 23 July 1940, New York; m. Judith Kramer; two d.; ed. City Coll. of New York; research scientist, NASA Lewis Research Center, Cleveland 1962–67; joined TRW Space & Tech. Group, Redondo, Calif. 1967, Vice-Pres. and Gen. Man. until 1992; Admin., National Aeronautics and Space Administration (NASA) April 1992–. *Address:* Office of the Administrator, National Aeronautics and Space Administration HQ, 300 East Street, S.W., Washington, DC 20546, U.S.A. *Telephone:* (202) 453-8400.

GOLDMAN, John Michael, D.M., F.R.C.P., F.R.C.PATH.; British physician; b. 30 Nov. 1938, London; s. of Carl Heinz Goldman and Bertha (née Brandt) Goldman; m. Jeannine Fuller 1967; one s. two d.; ed. Westminister School, Magdalen Coll., Oxford, St. Bartholomew's Hosp., London; MRC perm. mem. of staff Leukaemia Unit, Hammersmith Hosp., 1976–93, Dir. Leukaemia Research Fund Unit 1988–; Prof. of Leukaemia Biology Royal Postgrad. Medical School, London 1987–, Chair. Dept. of Haematology 1994–; Pres. European Haematology Asscn. 1996–, British Soc. for Blood and Marrow Transplantation 1996–; fmr. Pres. Int. Soc. for Experimental Hematology 1983, European Group for Bone Marrow Transplantation 1990–94; Sec. World Marrow Donor Asscn.; Medical Dir. Anthony Nolan Bone Marrow Trust 1988–; Hon. M.D. (Louvain, Poitiers). *Leisure interests:* reading, riding, skiing. *Publications:* books, chapters and papers on leukaemia, oncogenes, bone marrow transplantation. *Address:* Department of Haematology, Hammersmith Hospital/Imperial College School of Medicine, Du Cane Road, London, W12 0NN; 33 Northumberland Place, London, W2 5AS, England. *Telephone:* 0181-740 3238; 0171-727 6092. *Fax:* 0181-740 9679.

GOLDMAN, Sir Samuel, K.C.B.; British civil servant and fmr. banker; b. 10 March 1912, London; s. of late Philip and Sarah Goldman; m. Patricia Rosemary Hodges 1943 (died 1990); one s.; ed. Davenant Foundation School, Raines Foundation School and London School of Econs.; Moody's Economist Services 1934–38; Sebag and Co. 1938–39; Bank of England 1940–47; joined Civil Service as statistician, Central Statistical Office Jan. 1947, transferred to Treasury 1947, Chief Statistician 1948, Asst. Sec. 1952, Under-Sec. 1960, Third Sec. 1962; Second Perm. Sec., Treasury 1968–72; fmr. Man. Dir. Orion Bank Ltd.; fmr. Chair. Henry Ansbacher Holdings Ltd.; fmr. Chair. Covent Garden Market Authority. *Leisure interests:* gardening, music. *Address:* 3 Little Tangley, Wonersh, Guildford, Surrey, England. *Telephone:* (01483) 568913.

GOLDMAN, William, M.A.; American author; b. 12 Aug. 1931, Chicago, Ill.; s. of M. Clarence Goldman and Marion Weil; m. Ilene Jones 1961; two d.; ed. Oberlin Coll. and Columbia Univ.; Acad. Award for best original screenplay for Butch Cassidy and the Sundance Kid 1970; Acad. Award for best screenplay adaptation 1977. *Publications:* novels: The Temple of Gold 1957, Your Turn to Curtsy, My Turn to Bow 1958, Soldier in the Rain 1960, Boys and Girls Together 1964, The Thing of It Is 1967, No Way to Treat a Lady (under pseudonym Harry Longbaugh), Father's Day 1971, Marathon Man 1974, Wigger 1974, Magic 1976, Tinsel 1979, Control 1982, The Silent Gondoliers 1983, The Color of Light 1984; play: Blood Sweat and Stanley Poole 1961 (with James Goldman); musical comedy: A Family Affair (with James Goldman and John Kander) 1962; non-fiction: Adventures in the Screen Trade 1983, Hype and Glory 1990; Four Screenplays 1995, Five Screenplays 1997; screenplays: Harper 1966, Butch Cassidy and the Sundance Kid 1969, The Princess Bride 1973, Marathon Man 1976, All the President's Men 1976, A Bridge Too Far 1977, Magic 1978, Heat 1985, Brothers 1987, Year of the Comet 1992, Memoirs of an Invisible Man 1992, Chaplin 1992, Indecent Proposal 1993, Maverick 1994, Ghost and the Darkness 1996, Absolute Power 1997. *Address:* c/o CAA, 9830 Wilshire Boulevard, Beverly Hills, CA 90212, U.S.A.

GOLDMARK, Peter Carl, Jr., B.A.; American newspaper executive; b. 2 Dec. 1940, New York; s. of Peter Carl Goldmark and Frances Charlotte Trainer; m. Aliette Marie Misson 1964; three d.; ed. Harvard Univ.; worked for U.S. Office of Econ. Opportunity, Washington; fmr. teacher of history Putney School, Vt.; employed in Budget Office, City of New York for four years, later Asst. Budget Dir. Program Planning and Analysis then Exec. Asst. to the Mayor 1971; Sec. Human Services, Commonwealth of Mass. 1972–75; Dir. of Budget, N.Y. State 1975–77; Exec. Dir. Port Authority of N.Y. and N.J. 1977–85; joined Times Mirror Co., Los Angeles 1985, fmr. Sr. Vice-Pres. Eastern Newspapers Div.; Pres. Rockefeller Foundation 1988–97; Chair. and C.E.O. Int. Herald Tribune March 1998–; mem. Bd. dirs. Financial Accounting Foundation. *Address:* International Herald Tribune, 181 Avenue Charles de Gaulle, 92521 Neuilly Cédex, France. *Telephone:* (1) 41-43-93-01. *Fax:* (1) 41-43-92-20.

GOLDREICH, Peter, PH.D.; American professor of planetary science and astronomy; b. 14 July 1939, New York, N.Y.; s. of Paul Goldreich and Edith Rosenfield Goldreich; m. Susan Kroll 1960; two s.; ed. Cornell Univ; Post-Doctoral Fellow Cambridge Univ. 1963–64; Asst. Prof. Astronomy and Physics, Univ. of Calif. (Los Angeles Campus) 1964–66, Assoc. Prof. 1966; Assoc. Prof. Planetary Science and Astronomy Calif. Inst. Tech. 1966–69, Prof. 1969–, Lee Du Bridge Prof. of Astrophysics and Planetary Physics 1981–; mem. N.A.S. 1972–; Chapman Medal, Royal Astronomical Soc. 1985, Dirk Brouwer Award, American Astronomical Soc. 1986. *Publications:* on planetary dynamics, pulsar theory, radio emission from Jupiter, galactic stability and interstellar masers. *Leisure interests:* competitive athletics. *Address:* California Institute of Technology, 1201 East California Boulevard, Pasadena, CA 91109 (Office); 471 S. Catalina Avenue, Pasadena, CA 91106, U.S.A. (Home).

GOLDSCHMIDT, Neil Edward, A.B., LL.B.; American politician and lawyer; b. 16 June 1940, Eugene, Ore.; s. of Lester H. and Annette G. (Levin) Goldschmidt; m. Margaret Wood 1965; one s. one d.; ed. Univs. of Oregon and California; Civil Rights Worker, Miss. 1964; Attorney with Legal Aid Service, Portland, Ore. 1967–70; City Commr., Portland 1971–72; Mayor of Portland 1973–79; U.S. Sec. of Transportation 1979–81; Vice-Pres. Int. Marketing NIKE/BRS Inc., Beaverton, Ore. 1981–; Chair. Standing Cttee. on Housing and Community Devt. 1976–79, Ad Hoc Housing Task Force 1977–79, Energy Task Force of the Nat. League of Cities 1977–79; Trustee, U.S. Conf. of Mayors 1978–79; Gov. of Oregon 1987–91; fmrly. mem. Advisory Cttee. on State and Local Govt. Affairs, Harvard's John F. Kennedy School of Govt.; mem. Bd. of Kaiser Health and Hospital Plan, Oakland, Calif. 1981–, Bd. of Nat. Semiconductor, Santa Clara, Calif., Bd. of Gelco Corpn., Eden Prairie, Minn. *Leisure interests:* reading, swimming, all spectator sports.

GOLDSMITH, Harvey, C.B.E.; British impresario; b. 1946, London; m. Diana Goldsmith 1971; one s.; ed. Christ's College and Brighton Coll. of Tech.; joined Big O Posters, Kensington Market 1966; organized open-air free concerts, Parl. Hill Fields 1968; in partnership with Michael Alfandary opened Round House, London 1968; organized 13 Garden Party concerts at Crystal Palace, London 1969; merged with John Smith Entertainment 1970–75; formed Harvey Goldsmith Entertainment promoting rock tours by Elton John, Rolling Stones etc.; in partnership with Ed Simons, rescued Hotel Television Network 1983; formed Allied Entertainment Group as public co. 1984–86, returned to private ownership 1986; subsidiary Harvey Goldsmith Entertainment promotes some 250 concerts per year; formed Classical Productions with Mark McCormack, promoting shows at Earls Court including Pavarotti concert and lavish productions of Aida 1988, Carmen 1989, Tosca 1991; produced Bob Dylan Celebration, New York 1992, Mastercard Masters of Music (Hyde Park), The Eagles (Wembley), Three Tenors (Wembley), Lord of the Dance (world tour) 1996, Music for Montserrat (Royal Albert Hall), Boyzone (tour), Paul Weller (tour), Pavarotti (Manchester), Cirque du Soleil (Royal Albert Hall) 1997, Alegria (Royal Albert Hall), The Bee Gees (Wembley), Ozzfest (Milton Keynes Bowl), Paul Weller (Victoria Park) 1998; Chair. Nat. Music Day; Vice-Chair. Prince's Trust Bd.; Vice-Pres. React; Trustee Gret, Band Aid, Live Aid Foundation; Dir. Pres.'s Club, London First, London Tourist Bd.; mem. Advisory Group Red Cross. *Address:* Harvey Goldsmith Entertainments Ltd., Greenland Place, 115–123 Bayham Street, London, NW1 0AG, England. *Telephone:* 0171-482 5522. *Fax:* 0171-428 0504.

GOLDSMITH, Jerry, MUS.D.; American film music composer; b. 10 Feb. 1929, Los Angeles; m. Carol Sheinkopf; ed. Los Angeles City Coll., Berklee Coll. of Music; studied with Jakob Gimpel, Mario Castelnuovo-Tedesco. *Radio scores:* Romance, Suspense, CBS Radio. *TV scores:* Twilight Zone, General Electric Theatre, Doctor Kildare, Gunsmoke, Climax, Playhouse 90, Studio One, Star Trek: Voyager (Emmy Award 1995). *Film scores include:* Black Patch 1956, Lonely Are The Brave 1961, Freud 1962, The Stripper 1962, Lilies of the Field 1963, The Prize 1963, Seven Days in May 1963, In Harm's Way 1964, The Man from UNCLE 1965, Von Ryan's Express 1965, A Patch of Blue 1965, The Blue Max 1965, Our Man Flint 1965, Seconds 1965, Stagecoach 1965, The Sand Pebbles 1966, In Like Flint 1967, Planet of the Apes 1968, The Ballad of Cable Hogue 1969, Tora! Tora! Tora! 1970, Patton 1970, Wild Rovers 1971, The Other 1972, The Red Pony (Emmy Award) 1972, Papillon 1973, QB VII (Emmy Award) 1974, Chinatown 1974, The Reincarnation of Peter Proud 1974, Logan's Run 1975, The Wind and the Lion 1976, The Omen (Acad. Award) 1976, Islands in the Stream 1976, MacArthur 1977, Coma 1977, The Boys from Brazil 1978, Damien – Omen II 1978, Alien 1979, Babe (Emmy Award), Masada (Emmy Award) 1981, Star Trek: The Motion Picture 1979, The Final Conflict 1981, Outland 1981, Raggedy Man 1981, Mrs. Brisby: The Secret of NIMH 1982, Poltergeist (Edgar Allan Poe Award) 1982, First Blood 1982, Twilight Zone: The Movie 1983, Psycho II 1983, Under Fire 1983, Gremlins (Saturn Award) 1984, Legend (European version) 1985, Explorers 1985, Rambo: First Blood II 1985, Poltergeist II: The Other Side 1986, Hoosiers 1986, Innerspace 1987, Extreme Prejudice 1987, Rambo III 1988, Criminal Law 1989, The 'Burbs 1989, Leviathan 1989, Star Trek V: The Final Frontier 1989, Total Recall 1990, Gremlins 2: The New Batch 1990, The Russia House 1990, Not Without My Daughter 1991, Sleeping With the Enemy 1991, Medicine Man 1991, Love Field 1992, Mom and Dad Save the World 1992, Basic Instinct 1992, Mr. Baseball 1992, Forever Young 1992, Matinee 1992, The Vanishing 1993, Dennis the Menace 1993, Malice 1993, Rudy 1993, Six Degrees of Separation 1993, Angie 1994, Bad Girls 1994, The Shadow 1994, I.Q. 1994, The River Wild 1994, First Knight 1995, Congo 1995, Powder 1995, City Hall 1995, Executive Decision 1996, Chain Reaction 1996, The Ghost and the Darkness 1996, Star Trek: First Contact 1996, Fierce Creatures 1996, L.A. Confidential 1997, Air Force One 1997, The Edge 1997, Deep Rising 1997; guest conductor with many American and European symphony orchestras. *Ballet scores include:* A Patch of Blue 1970, Othello 1971, Capricorn One 1989; Max Steiner Award, Nat. Film Soc. 1982, first annual Richard Kirk Award, BMI 1987, Golden Score Award, American Soc. of Music Arrangers 1990, Career Achievement Award, Soc. for Preservation of Film Music 1993, first American Music Legend Award, Variety 1995. *Address:* c/o Savitsky & Co., Suite 1450, 1901 Ave. of Stars, Los Angeles, CA 90067, U.S.A.

GOLDSMITH, Stephen, A.B., J.D.; American state governor; b. 12 Dec. 1946, Indianapolis; s. of Joseph Goldsmith and Marjorie Holmes; m. Margaret McDaniel 1988; four c.; ed. Wabash Coll. and Univ. of Michigan; called to bar, Ind. 1972, U.S. Dist. Court (So. Dist.), Ind. 1972, U.S. Court of Appeal (7th circuit) 1974, U.S. Supreme Court 1977; Deputy corp. counsel, City of Indianapolis 1974–75, Chief, Trial Dept. 1976–78; Assoc. Barnes, Hickman, Pantzer & Boyd, Indianapolis 1971–78; Prosecuting attorney, Marion County, Indianapolis 1979–90; with Dann, Pecar, Newman, Talesnick & Klieman 1990–91; Asst. Prof. Indiana Univ. 1989–; many other professional and public appts.; Mayor of Indianapolis 1991–97; Gov. of Indiana 1997; Republican. *Address:* c/o Office of the Governor, State Capitol, Indianapolis, Indiana, U.S.A.

GOLDSTEIN, Abraham S., M.A.; American professor of law; b. 27 July 1925, New York, N.Y.; s. of Isidore and Yetta (Crystal) Goldstein; m. 1st Ruth Tessler 1947 (died 1989); one s. one d.; m. 2nd Sarah Feidelson 1995; ed. City Coll. N.Y. and Yale Law School; Assoc., Cook and Berger, Washington, D.C. 1949; Law Clerk to Circuit Judge David Bazelon (q.v.), U.S. Court of Appeals 1949–51; Partner, Donohue and Kaufman 1951–56; Assoc. Prof., Yale Law School 1956–61, Prof. 1961–, Dean 1970–75, Sterling Prof. of Law 1975–; Visiting Prof. of Law, Stanford Law School 1963; Visiting Fellow, Inst. of Criminology, Cambridge Univ. 1964–65; mem. Faculty, Salzburg Seminar in American Studies 1969; Visiting Prof. Hebrew Univ. Jerusalem 1976, UN Asia and Far East Inst. for Prevention of Crime, Tokyo 1983, Tel Aviv Univ. 1986; mem. Comm. to Revise Criminal Statutes of Conn. 1966–70; Consultant, President's Comm. on the Admin. of Criminal Justice 1966–67; mem. Gov.'s Planning Comm. of Criminal Admin. 1967–71, Conn. Bd. of Parole 1967–69; Vice-Pres. Conn. Bar Foundation 1976–79; Sr. Vice-Pres. American Jewish Congress 1977–84, mem. Gov. Council 1977–94; mem. American Acad. of Arts and Sciences 1975–; Hon. M.A. (Cambridge, Yale), Hon. LL.D. (New York Law School, Depaul Univ.). *Publications:* The Insanity Defence 1967, Crime, Law and Society (with J. Goldstein) 1971, Criminal Procedure (with L. Orland) 1974, The Passive Judiciary 1981; articles and book reviews in professional journals. *Address:* Yale Law School, New Haven, CT 06520, U.S.A. (Office).

GOLDSTEIN, Avram, M.D.; American professor of pharmacology and neurobiologist; b. 3 July 1919, New York; s. of Israel Goldstein and Bertha Markowitz; m. Dora Benedict 1947; three s. one d.; ed. Harvard Coll. and Harvard Medical School; Instructor, then Asst. Prof. in Pharmacology, Harvard 1948–55; Prof. and Chair., Pharmacology, Stanford Univ. 1955–70, Prof. 1970–89, Prof. Emer. 1989–; Dir. Addiction Research Foundation, Palo Alto, Calif. 1974–87; mem. N.A.S.; Franklin Medal, Sollmann Award, Nathan Eddy Award. *Publications:* Biostatistics 1964, Principles of Drug Action 1968, Addiction: From Biology to Drug Policy 1994; over 300 articles in the primary scientific journals. *Leisure interests:* aviation and aviation writing. *Address:* 735 Dolores Street, Palo Alto, CA 94305, U.S.A. (Home).

GOLDSTEIN, Joseph Leonard, M.D.; American genetics educator and physician; b. 18 April 1940, Sumter, S.C.; s. of Isadore E. Goldstein and Fannie A. Goldstein; ed. Washington and Lee Univ., Lexington, Va., Univ. of Texas Southwestern Medical Center; Intern, then Resident in Medicine, Mass. Gen. Hosp., Boston 1966–68; Clinical Assoc., Nat. Insts. of Health 1968–70; Postdoctoral Fellow, Univ. of Washington, Seattle 1970–72; mem. Faculty, Univ. of Texas Southwestern Medical Center, Dallas 1972–, Paul J. Thomas Prof. of Medicine, Chair. Dept. of Molecular Genetics 1977–, Harvey Soc. Lecturer 1977, Regental Prof. 1985–; Chair. Albert Lasker Medical Research Awards Jury 1996–; mem. Advisory Bd. Howard Hughes Medical Inst. 1985–90; non-resident Fellow, The Salk Inst. 1983–93; mem. Scientific Advisory Bd. Welch Foundation 1986–, Bd. Dirs. Passano Foundation 1985–, Rockefeller Foundation 1994–, Bd. of Scientific Govs., Scripps Research Inst. 1996–; mem. Editorial Bd. Cell, Arteriosclerosis and Science; mem. N.A.S. (mem. Council 1991–94), American Acad. of Arts and Sciences, American Philosophical Soc., Inst. of Medicine, Asscn. of American Physicians, American Soc. of Clinical Investigation (Pres. 1985–86), American Soc. of Human Genetics, American Soc. of Biological Chemists, American Fed. of Clinical Research; Foreign mem. Royal Soc., London; Hon. D.Sc. (Univ. of Chicago, Rensselaer Polytech. Inst., Washington and Lee Univ., Univ. of Paris-Sud, Univ. of Buenos Aires, Southern Methodist Univ., Univ. of Miami); Heinrich-Wieland Prize 1974, Pfizer Award in Enzyme Chem., American Chemical Soc. 1976, Passano Award, Johns Hopkins Univ. 1978, Gairdner Foundation Award 1981, Award in Biological and Medical Sciences, New York Acad. of Sciences 1981, Lita Annenberg Hazen Award 1982, Research Achievement Award, American Heart Asscn. 1984, Louisa Gross Horwitz Award 1984, 3M Life Sciences Award 1984, Albert Lasker Award in Basic Medical Research 1985, Nobel Prize in Physiology or Medicine 1985, Trustees' Medal, Mass. Gen. Hosp. 1986, U.S. Nat. Medal of Science 1988. *Publication:* The Metabolic Basis of Inherited Disease (Co-author) 1983. *Address:* Department of Molecular Genetics, University of Texas Southwestern Medical Center at Dallas, 5323 Harry Hines Boulevard, Dallas, TX 75235; 3831 Turtle Creek Boulevard, Apt. 22-B, Dallas, TX 75219, U.S.A. (Home).

GOLDSTINE, Herman Heine, M.S., PH.D.; American mathematician; b. 13 Sept. 1913, Chicago, Ill.; s. of Isaac O. Goldstine and Bess (Lipsey) Goldstine; m. 1st Adele Katz 1941 (died 1964); m. 2nd Ellen Watson 1966; one s. one d.; ed. Univ. of Chicago; research asst. Univ. of Chicago 1936–37, Instructor 1937–39; in charge of ENIAC Project for U.S. Army 1942–46; Instructor Univ. of Mich. 1939–42, Asst. Prof. 1942–50; Assoc. Project Dir. Electronic Computer Project, Inst. for Advanced Study, Princeton 1946–55, Acting Project Dir. 1954–57; Perm. mem. Inst. for Advanced Study, Princeton 1952–; Dir. Math. Sciences Dept. IBM Research; Dir. Scientific Devt. IBM Data Processing H.Q., White Plains, New York; Consultant to Dir. of Research, IBM, now IBM Fellow; consultant to various govt. and mil. agencies; mem. N.A.S., American Philosophical Soc., American Acad. of Arts and Sciences, American Math. Soc., Academic Cttee., Annenberg Research Inst. 1987–91, Bd. Nat. Constitution Center 1987–90; Exec. Officer, American Philosophical Soc. 1984–; Hon. Ph.D. (Lund) 1974; Hon. D.Sc. (Adelphi) 1978, (Amherst) 1978, (Rutgers) 1994; Nat. Medal of Science, (Dept. of Army) Distinguished Service Medal 1996, Distinguished Civilian Service Medal 1996 and other honours. *Publications include:* The Computer from Pascal to von Neumann 1972, A History of Numerical Analysis from the 16th to the 19th Century 1977, A History of the Calculus of Variations from the 17th Century through the 19th Century 1980; Ed. Mathematical Papers of John I and James I Bernoulli 1988. *Address:* 56 Pasture Lane, Bryn Mawr, PA 19010, U.S.A.

GOLDSTONE, David Joseph, LL.B.; British property executive; b. 21 Feb. 1929; s. of Solomon Goldstone and Rebecca Goldstone (née Degotts); m. Cynthia Easton 1957; one s. two d.; ed. Dynevor Secondary School, Swansea and London School of Econs.; admitted Solicitor 1955; legal practice 1955–66; Chief Exec. Regalian Properties PLC 1970–, Chair. 1990–; Dir. Swansea Sound Commercial Radio 1974–95, London Welsh Rugby Football Club 1997–, Wales Millennium Centre 1998–; mem. Court of Govs. L.S.E. 1985–; mem. Council Football Asscn. of Wales 1970–72, Atlantic Coll. 1987–, Welsh Nat. Orchestra 1984–89, Inst. of Jewish Affairs 1990–, London Univ. 1994–; Hon. Fellow, L.S.E. 1995. *Leisure interests:* family, reading, sport. *Address:* 44 Grosvenor Hill, London, W1A 4NR, England. *Telephone:* 0171-493 9613.

GOLDSTONE, Jeffrey, M.A., PH.D., F.R.S.; British physicist; b. 3 Sept. 1933, Manchester; s. of Hyman and Sophia Goldstone; m. Roberta Gordon 1980; one s.; ed. Manchester Grammar School and Trinity Coll., Cambridge; Research Fellow, Trinity Coll., Cambridge 1956–60, Staff Fellow 1962–82; Univ. lecturer, Applied Math. and Theoretical Physics, Cambridge 1961–76, Reader in Mathematical Physics 1976; Prof. of Physics, M.I.T. 1977–83, Dir. Center for Theoretical Physics 1983–89, Cecil and Ida Green Prof. of Physics 1983–; Fellow, American Acad. of Arts and Sciences, American Physical Soc.; Heineman Prize, American Physical Soc. 1981; Guthrie Medal, Inst. of Physics 1983, Dirac Medal, Int. Centre for Theoretical Physics 1991. *Publications:* articles in scientific journals. *Address:* Department of Physics, 6-313, Massachusetts Institute of Technology, Cambridge, MA 02139

(Office); 18 Orchard Road, Brookline, MA 02146, U.S.A. (Home). *Telephone:* 617-253-6263 (Office); (617) 277-5932 (Home).

GOLDSTONE, Richard J., LL.B.; South African judge; b. 26 Oct. 1938, Boksburg; m. Noleen Behrman 1962; two d.; ed. King Edward VII School, Johannesburg and Univ. of Witwatersrand; admitted to Johannesburg Bar 1963, Sr. Counsel 1976; Judge, Transvaal Supreme Court 1980–89; Judge, Appellate Div. Supreme Court of S.A. 1989–94; Justice, S. African Constitutional Court 1994–; Chair. Comm. of Inquiry regarding Public Violence and Intimidation 1991–94; Prosecutor, Int. Criminal Tribunal for the frmr. Yugoslavia and Int. Criminal Tribunal for Rwanda 1994–96; Nat. Pres. Nat. Inst. for Crime Prevention and Rehabilitation of Offenders 1982–; mem. Council, Univ. of Witwatersrand (1988–94), Chancellor 1996–; mem. Standing Advisory Cttee. on Co. Law (Chair. 1991–), Exec. Cttee. World ORT Union (Pres. 1997–); Chair. Bd. Human Rights Inst. of S.A.; Gov. Hebrew Univ. of Jerusalem 1982–; Chair. Bradlow Foundation 1989–; other professional appts.; Faculty mem. Salzburg Seminar 1996, 1998; Fellow Centre for Int. Affairs, Harvard Univ. 1989; Hon. Bencher Inner Temple, London; Hon. Fellow, St. John's Coll. Cambridge; Hon. LL.D. (Cape Town) 1993, (Natal, Hebrew Univ. of Jerusalem, Witwatersrand) 1994, (Wilfred Laurier Univ., Waterloo, Canada) 1995; several awards including Toastmasters Int. Communication and Leadership Award 1994, Int. Human Rights Award (American Bar Asscn.) 1994. *Leisure interests:* reading, walking, wine. *Address:* Constitutional Court, Pvt. Bag X32, Braamfontein 2017, South Africa. *Telephone:* (011) 359 7407. *Fax:* (011) 403 9131.

GOLDSTÜCKER, Eduard, PH.D.; British university professor; b. 30 May 1913, Podbiel; s. of Jozef Goldstücker and Terezie Altmann; m. Marta Borčová 1937; two d.; ed. Charles Univ., Prague, and Oxford Univ., England; Sec. of League for Human Rights, Prague 1936–38; secondary school teacher 1938–39; in U.K. 1939–45, worked at Czechoslovak Ministry of Foreign Affairs in London 1943–44; Ambassadorial Sec., Paris 1944–45; Deputy Amb. in London 1947–49; Envoy to Tel-Aviv 1950–51; political imprisonment 1951–55; Dept. of German Literature, Faculty of Philosophy, Charles Univ., Prague 1956–69, Prof. 1963–69, Pro-Rector of Charles Univ. 1966–69; Chair. Union of Czechoslovak Writers 1968–69; Deputy to Czech Nat. Council 1968–69; Visiting Prof. of Comparative Literature, Sussex Univ. 1969–71, Prof. 1971–78, now Emer.; Visiting Fellow, Center Study of Democratic Insts., Santa Barbara, Calif. 1972–73; Corresp. mem. Deutsche Akad. für Sprache und Dichtung 1976–; Hon. Ph.D. (Univ. of Constance) 1986; several awards including Goethe Gold Medal of Goethe Inst., Munich 1967, Klement Gottwald Award 1968, Lessing Award (Saxony) 1999; Litteris et Artibus Order (Austria) 1993, Grosses Verdienstkreuz (Germany) 1994; deprived of state citizenship of Czechoslovak Socialist Repub. 1974, citizenship returned 1990. *Publications:* History of German literature, especially German literature in Prague; Rainer Maria Rilke und Franz Werfel 1960, Franz Kafka 1964 (Prize of Publishing House of Czechoslovak Writers), Libertà e Socialismo 1968, The Czech National Revival, the Germans and the Jews 1972, Da Praga a Danzica 1981, Prozesse (Memoirs) 1989. *Address:* Lohniskeho 902, 152 00 Prague 5, Czech Republic. *Telephone:* (2) 5813534.

GOLDSWORTHY, Andrew Charles, B.A.; British sculptor; b. 25 July 1956, Cheshire; s. of Allin Goldsworthy and Muriel Goldsworthy (née Stanger); m. Judith Elizabeth Gregson 1982; two s. two d.; ed. Bradford and Lancaster Art Colls.; has exhibited internationally in U.S.A., France, Australia, Germany and Japan; numerous public and pvt. comms. 1984– including pieces for Grizedale Forest, Cumbria 1984, 1985, 1991, 'Enclosure', Royal Botanic Gardens, Edin. 1990, 'Seven Holes', Greenpeace, London 1991, 'Steel Cone', Gateshead 1991, 'Black Spring', Botanical Gardens, Adelaide 1992, 'Fieldgate', Poundridge, N.Y. 1993, Laumeier Sculpture Park 1994, two pieces for Nat. Museum of Scotland, Edin. 1998; works represented in collections at Michael Hue-Williams Fine Arts Ltd., London, Galerie Lelong, New York and Paris, Haines Gallery, San Francisco, Galerij S65, Belgium; residency Yorks. Sculpture Park 1988; featured on Royal Mail Spring issue stamps 1995; collaborated in Regine Chopinot's ballet Vegetal 1995; sr. lecturer in Fine Art and Craft Univ. of Herts. 1996; collaborated with Cirque du Soleil, Montreal 1998; Hon. Fellow Univ. of Cen. Lancs. 1995; Hon. B.A. (Bradford) 1993; North West Arts Award 1979, Yorks. Arts Award 1980, Northern Arts Award 1981, 1995, Scottish Arts Council Award 1988. *Film:* Two Autumns (for Channel 4) 1991. *Publications include:* A Collaboration With Nature 1989, Hand to Earth 1991, Touching North 1994, Stone 1994, Wood 1996. *Leisure interests:* fishing, reading, listening to music. *Address:* c/o Michael Hue-Williams Fine Art Ltd., 21 Cork Street, London, W1X 1HB, England. *Telephone:* 0171-434 1318. *Fax:* 0171-434 1321.

GOLDTHORPE, John Harry, M.A., F.B.A.; British sociologist and academic; b. 27 May 1935, Barnsley; s. of Harry and Lilian Eliza Goldthorpe; m. Rhiannon Esyllt Harry 1963; one s. one d.; ed. Wath-upon-Dearne Grammar School, Univ. Coll. London, London School of Econs.; Asst. Lecturer Dept. of Sociology, Univ. of Leicester 1957–60; Fellow, King's Coll. Cambridge 1960–69; Asst. Lecturer then Lecturer in Faculty of Econs. and Politics, Univ. of Cambridge 1962–69; Official Fellow, Nuffield Coll., Oxford 1969–; mem. British Econ. and Social Research Council 1988–91, Academia Europaea 1989; Hon. D.Phil. (Stockholm Univ.) 1990; Helsinki Univ. Medal. *Publications:* The Affluent Worker series (3 vols.) (with David Lockwood et al.) 1968–69, The Social Grading of Occupations (with Keith Hope) 1974, The Political Economy of Inflation (with Fred Hirsch, eds.) 1978, Social Mobility and Class Structure 1980, Order and Conflict in Contemporary Capitalism (ed. and contrib.) 1984, Die Analyse soziales Ungleichheit: Kontinuitat, Erneuerung, Innovation (with Hermann Strasser, ed. and contrib.) 1985, The Constant Flux: a Study of Class Mobility in Industrial Societies (with Robert Erikson) 1992, The Development of Industrial Society in Ireland (with Christopher T. Whelan, ed. and contrib.) 1992. *Leisure interests:* lawn tennis, bird watching, computer chess. *Address:* Nuffield College, Oxford, OX1 1NF; 32 Leckford Road, Oxford, OX2 6HX, England. *Telephone:* (01865) 278516 (Office); (01865) 556602 (Home). *Fax:* (01865) 278621.

GOLEMBIOVSKY, Igor Nestorovich; Russian journalist; b. 7 Sept. 1935, Samtradia (Georgia); m.; one s.; ed. Tbilisi State Univ.; journalist activities since 1958; with Izvestia 1966–, deputy-editor of div., special corresp., deputy-exec. sec., exec. sec., First Deputy-Ed.-in-Chief 1988–91, Ed.-in-Chief 1991–97; f. and Ed. Noviye Izvestia 1997. *Publications:* author of articles on key problems of social and political life. *Leisure interests:* tennis, football. *Address:* Dolgorukovskaya str. 19/8, 103006 Moscow, Russia. *Telephone:* 795-31-57. *Fax:* 795-31-38.

GÖLHAN, Mehmet; Turkish politician and engineer; b. 1929, Adapazari; m.; two c.; ed. Istanbul Tech. Univ.; Chief Industrial Dept., Ministry of Industry 1974; Dir.-Gen. Road, Water and Electricity Authority (YSE), Turkish Petroleum Corpn. (TPA); Under-Sec. Ministry of Industry and Tech. –1980; a founding mem. Grand Turkey Party and Doğru Yol Partisi (DYP), fmr. Acting Chair.; parl. deputy (DYP) 1987; Minister of Nat. Defence 1993–96. *Address:* c/o Doğru Yol Partisi, Selanik Cad. 40, Kızılay, Ankara, Turkey.

GOLITSYN, Georgy Sergeyevich; Russian physicist; b. 23 Jan. 1935, Moscow; s. of Sergei Golitsyn and Claudia Golitsyna; m. Ludmila Lisitskaya; two d.; ed. Moscow State Univ.; Head of Lab., Head of Div., Dir. Inst. of Physics of Atmosphere, U.S.S.R. (now Russian) Acad. of Sciences 1958–; Corresp. mem. U.S.S.R. (now Russian) Acad. of Sciences 1979, mem. 1987, mem. Presidium 1988; Chair. Council, Int. Inst. of Applied Systems Analysis 1992–97; main research on geophysical fluid dynamics, climate theory; Demidov Prize, A. Friedmann Prize. *Publications include:* Introduction to Dynamics of Planet Atmospheres 1973, Study of Convection with Geophysical Applications and Analogies 1980, Global Climate Catastrophes 1986, Convection of Rotating Fluids 1995. *Leisure interests:* history, art, literature. *Address:* A. M. Obukhov Institute of Atmospheric Physics, Russian Academy of Sciences, Pyzh'yevsky per. 3, 109017 Moscow, Russia (Office). *Telephone:* (095) 951 5565 (Office); 331-32-69 (Home). *Fax:* (095) 953 1652.

GÖLLNER, Theodor, PH.D.; German professor of musicology; b. 25 Nov. 1929, Bielefeld; s. of Friedrich Göllner and Paula Brinkmann; m. Marie Louise Martinez 1959; one s. one d.; ed. Univs. of Heidelberg and Munich; lecturer, Univ. of Munich 1958–62, Asst. Prof., Assoc. Prof. 1962–67; Assoc. Prof., then Prof. Univ. of Calif. Santa Barbara 1967–73; Prof., Chair. Inst. of Musicology, Univ. of Munich 1973–; mem., Dir. Comm. of Music History, Bavarian Acad. of Sciences 1982–. *Publications:* Formen früher Mehrstimmigkeit 1961, Die mehrstimmigen liturgischen Lesungen 1969, Die Sieben Worte am Kreuz 1986; (ed.) Münchner Veröffentlichungen zur Musikgeschichte 1977–, Münchner Editionen zur Musikgeschichte 1979–. *Address:* Institute of Musicology, University of Munich, Geschwister-Scholl-Platz 1, 80539 Munich (Office); Bahnweg 9, 82229 Seefeld, Germany (Home). *Telephone:* 089-2180-2364 (Office).

GOLOVNEV, Gen.-Lieut. Anatoly Andreyevich; Russian army officer; b. 1942, Medvedovka, Smolensk Region; ed. Moscow Higher Gen. Army Command School, Frunze Mil. Acad., U.S.S.R. Gen. Staff Mil. Acad.; high command positions in Far East, Ukraine, Western group of troops 1963–89; First Deputy Commdr. Moscow mil. command 1989–92; Deputy C.-in-C. Land Forces of Russia 1992–. *Address:* Ministry of Defence, ul. Myasnitskaya 37, 103175 Moscow, Russia.

GOLU, Mihai, M.A., PH.D.; Romanian politician and scientist; b. 4 March 1934, Bumbeşti-Pitic, Gorj County; s. of Ion Golu and Gheorghita Golu; m. Elena Filip 1957; two s.; ed. Psychology Coll., Bucharest and Lomonosov Univs.; worked as psychologist, Prof., Bucharest Univ.; research at Carnegie-Mellon Univ. (U.S.A.) 1973–74; deputy (independent cand.) 1990–92, Party of Social Democracy 1992–96; Minister of Educ. and Science 1991–92, of Culture 1992–93; Deputy, Parl. Ass. of Council of Europe 1993–96; Pres. Romanian Asscn. of Psychologists 1990–, Nat. Soc. for Educ. 1993–; Nat. Comm. for UNESCO 1990–95; mem. Acad. of Scientists 1998–; mem. N.Y. Acad. of Science; Romanian Acad. Prize, Pablo Picasso Medal, UNESCO. *Publications:* numerous books, scientific papers and articles. *Leisure interests:* reading biographies of famous people, classical music. *Address:* Bulevardul Libertatii 22, Bloc 102, Scara 5, Apt. 89, Bucharest, Romania. *Telephone:* 336-66-62.

GOLUB, Harvey, B.S.; American finance executive; b. 16 April 1939, New York; s. of Irving Golub and Pearl Fader; m. Roberta Glunts 1980; one s. and two s. one d. by previous m.; jr. partner, McKinsey & Co. Inc. New York 1967–74, Sr. partner 1977–83; Pres. Shulman Air Freight, New York 1974–77; sr. officer, American Express Co. New York 1983–84, Vice-Chair. 1990–93, C.E.O., Chair. Jan. 1993–; Chair., C.E.O. IDS Financial Services (now American Express Financial Advisors) Minneapolis 1984–. *Address:* American Express Co., American Express Tower C, 3 World Financial Center, 200 Vesey Street, New York, NY 10285, U.S.A.

GOLUB, Leon, M.F.A.; American artist; b. 23 Jan. 1922, Chicago, Illinois; m. Nancy Spero 1951; three s.; ed. School of the Art Inst. of Chicago, Univ.

of Chicago; solo exhbns. include: Pasadena Museum of Art, Calif. 1956, I.C.A., London 1957, Hayden Gallery, MA 1970, Nat. Gallery of Vic., Australia 1971, Musée de L'Abbaye Saint Croix, France 1973, San Francisco Art Inst. 1976, Honolulu Acad. of Arts, Hawaii (Leon Golub: Mercenaries, Interrogations and Other Works) 1983, Stanford Univ. Museum of Art (Prints) 1985, Kunstmuseum, Luzern, Switzerland 1987, The Saatchi Collection, London 1988, Cranbrook Acad. of Art Museum, MI 1989, Spertus Museum of Judaica, Chicago IL 1990, The Brooklyn Museum, NY (Worldwide) 1991, Inst. Contemporary Art, Philadelphia 1992, Musée d'Art Contemporain de Montréal, Quebec 1992, Kunstverein, Munich 1993, List Visual Arts Center, Cambridge, Mass. 1994, Burnett Miller Gallery, La. 1994, Vancouver Art Gallery 1995, Ronald Fezoman Fine Art, NY 1996, Darthea Speyer Gallery, Paris 1996, Hiroshima City Museum of Contemporary Art 1996; numerous group exhibitions; work in public and pvt. collections include: Art Inst. of Chicago, Eli Broad Family Foundation, L.A., Jewish Museum, New York, Musée des Beaux Arts, Montreal, Nat. Museum of American Art, Smithsonian Inst. Washington, DC, Nat. Gallery of Vic., Australia, Museum of Modern Art, New York, Tate Gallery, London; John C. Van Dyck Prof. of Visual Arts, Rutgers Univ. 1984–; Ford Foundation Grant 1960, Cassandra Foundation Grant 1967, Guggenheim Grant 1968; Hon. D.F.A. (Swarthmore Coll.) 1985, School of the Art Inst. of Chicago 1982; mem. American Acad. of Arts and Letters, Nat. Inst. of Arts and Letters 1973. *Address:* 530 La Guardia Place, New York, NY 10012, U.S.A. (Studio).

GOMA, Col. Louis Sylvain; Republic of the Congo politician and army officer; b. 1941; ed. Versailles and Saint-Cyr; Asst. Dir. of Mil. Engineers until 1968; Chief of Staff of Congolese People's Nat. Army 1968, promoted Capt. 1968; mem. Parti Congolais du Travail (PCT) 1969, Cen. Cttee. 1970, Special Gen. Staff of Revolution 1974, Political Bureau; Sec. of State for Defence 1969–70; Minister of Public Works and Transport 1970–74; promoted Maj. 1973; Chief of Gen. Staff of Armed Forces 1974; Prime Minister 1975–84, 1991, responsible for Plan 1975–79; mem. Council of State 1975–77; mem. PCT Mil Cttee. (Second Vice-Pres.) 1977–79. *Address:* c/o Office du Premier Ministre, Brazzaville, Republic of the Congo.

GOMARD, Bernhard, D.JUR.; Danish professor of law; b. 9 Jan. 1926, Karise; s. of C. J. Gomard and Karen (née Magle) Gomard; m. 1st 1974; one s.; m. 2nd Marianne Rosen 1994; ed. Univ. of Copenhagen; Legal Adviser Danish Dept. of Justice 1950–58, Danish Atomic Comm. 1956–76, Danish Insurance Cos. 1958–; Prof. of Law, Univ. of Copenhagen 1958–96; Prof. of Law, Copenhagen Business School 1996–; mem. Bd. of Dirs. Den Danske Bank –1996; mem. and Chair. numerous govt. cttees.; Hon. Prof. Univ. of Freiburg; mem. Danish Acad. of Sciences 1975, Academia Europae 1989, Inst. of Int. Business Law and Practice; Nordic Jurists Prize 1987; Oersted Medal 1995. *Publications:* articles and treatises on contract co. law, civil procedure, with particular emphasis on Danish law. *Leisure interests:* opera, French art and literature. *Address:* Law Dept., Copenhagen Business School, Nansengade 19, 1366 Copenhagen K (Office); 3 Hammerensgade, 1267 Copenhagen K, Denmark (Home). *Telephone:* 38-15-26-26 (Office); 33-22-80-20 (Home). *Fax:* 38-15-26-10 (Office).

GOMBOSUREN, Tserenpiliin; Mongolian politician; b. 5 Jan. 1943, Hujirt Dist., Oborkhangai Prov.; s. of T. Tserenpil and O. Handjav; m. Dembereliin Surenhorlo 1970; three s.; ed. Printing Inst. of U.S.S.R., Higher Party School of CPSU Cen. Cttee., U.S.S.R.; engineer, State Printing Factory 1967–74; Head of Dept., Deputy Minister of Foreign Affairs 1976–84; Minister-Counsellor, Embassy in Moscow 1984–87; Deputy Head External Relations, Mongolian People's Revolutionary Party (MPRP) Cen. Cttee. 1987–88; Minister of Foreign Affairs 1988–90, of External Relations 1990–96; mem. Political Bureau of MPRP Cen. Cttee. March–April 1990, mem. Presidium April–Nov. 1990; mem. State Great Hural 1992–96; Chair. Mongolian Nat. Security Printing Co. 1997–. *Leisure interest:* translating from Russian. *Address:* Mongolian National Security Printing Company, Khudaldaany Gudamj 6, Chingeltey Duure 6, Ulan Bator 13, Mongolia.

GOMBRICH, Sir Ernst (Hans Josef), Kt., O.M., C.B.E., PH.D., F.B.A., F.S.A., F.R.S.L.; British art historian; b. 30 March 1909, Vienna, Austria; s. of Dr. Karl Gombrich and Prof. Leonie Gombrich (née Hock); m. Ilse Heller 1936; one s.; ed. Theresianum, Vienna, and Vienna Univ.; Research Asst., Warburg Inst., Univ. of London 1936–39; BBC Monitoring Service, Second World War; Senior Research Fellow, Warburg Inst. 1946–48, Lecturer 1948–54, Reader 1954–56, Special Lecturer 1956–59, Dir. 1959–76; Prof. of History of the Classical Tradition, Univ. of London 1959–76, Prof. Emer. 1976–; Slade Prof. of Fine Art, Univ. of Oxford 1950–53; Durning-Lawrence Prof. of History of Art, Univ. Coll., London 1956–59; Visiting Prof. Harvard Univ. 1959; Slade Prof. of Fine Art, Univ. of Cambridge 1961–63; Hon. Fellow, Jesus Coll., Cambridge 1963; Prof. at Large, Cornell Univ. 1970–76; Trustee, British Museum 1974–79; mem. Standing Comm. on Museums and Galleries (now Museums and Galleries Comm.) 1976–83; Sr. Fellow, Royal Coll. of Art 1984; Corresp. mem. Turin, Uppsala, Netherlands, Bavarian, Belgian and Swedish Acads.; Hon. mem. Austrian Acad., American Acad. of Arts and Sciences, German Acad. of Language and Literature 1988, Accademia Virgiliana of Mantua; Foreign mem. American Philosophical Soc., American Acad. and Inst. of Arts and Letters; Hon. Fellow, R.I.B.A., The Warburg Inst., Royal Acad., London, Göttingen Acad.; Hon. D.Lit. (Queen's Univ., Belfast, Univ. of New York), (American Univ. in London) 1993; Hon. LL.D. (St. Andrews); Hon. D.Litt. (Leeds, Oxford); Hon. Litt.D. (Cambridge, Manchester); Hon. D.Hum.Litt. (Chicago Univ.) 1975, (Pa. Univ.) 1977, (Emory Univ., Atlanta, Ga.) 1991; Hon. D.Litt. (Harvard, London) 1976, D.Univ. (Essex) 1977; Hon. L.H.D. (Brandeis Univ.) 1981, (Urbino) 1992; Dr. h.c. (Universidad Complutense de Madrid) 1992; W. H. Smith and Son Annual Literary Award 1964, Medal of N.Y. Univ. 1970, Erasmus Prize 1975, Hegel Prize from City of Stuttgart 1977, Balzan Preis 1985, Preis der Stadt Wien 1986, Ludwig Wittgenstein Preis 1988, Britannica Award 1989, Goethe Medaille 1989, Pergameno d'onore, Faenza 1991, Goethepreis 1994, Gold Medal (Vienna) 1994, Mongan Prize, I Tatti, Florence 1996; Austrian Cross of Honour 1st class 1975, Pour le Mérite 1977, Hon. Citizen Mantova 1998; Österreichisches Ehrenzeichen. *Publications:* Caricature (with E. Kris) 1940, The Story of Art 1950, (16 editions), Art and Illusion 1959, Meditations on a Hobby Horse 1963, Norm and Form 1966, In Search of Cultural History 1969, Aby Warburg 1970, Symbolic Images 1972, Illusion in Nature and Art (ed. with R. L. Gregory) 1973, Art History and the Social Sciences 1974, The Heritage of Apelles 1976, The Sense of Order 1978, Ideals and Idols 1979, The Image and the Eye 1982, Tributes 1984, New Light on Old Masters 1986, Reflections on the History of Art (Ed. R. Woodfield) 1987, Topics of our Time 1991, Ce que nous dit l'image (with D. Eribon) 1991, Gastspiele: zur Deutschen Sprache *v* Germanistik 1992, Künstler, Kenner, Kunden (Wiener Vorlesungen im Rathaus) 1993, Das Forschende Auge 1994, Shadows 1995, The Visual Arts in Vienna, *c.* 1900 1997, Speis der Malerknaben 1997, The Uses of Images 1998. *Leisure interest:* music. *Address:* 19 Briardale Gardens, London, NW3 7PN, England. *Telephone:* 0171-435 6639.

GOMER, Robert, PH.D.; American professor of chemistry; b. 24 March 1924, Vienna, Austria; s. of Richard Gomer and Mary Gomer; m. Anne Olah 1955; one s. one d.; ed. Pomona Coll. and Univ. of Rochester; Instructor, then Assoc. Prof., James Franck Inst. and Dept. of Chem., Univ. of Chicago 1950–58, Prof. 1958–96, Dir. James Franck Inst. 1977–83, Carl William Eisendrath Distinguished Service Prof. of Chem. 1984–96, Prof. Emer. 1996–; Assoc. Ed. Journal of Chemical Physics 1957–59, Review of Scientific Instruments 1963–65; mem. Editorial Bd. Surface Science 1964–70; Consultant, Pres.'s Science Advisory Bd. 1961–65; Chair. Editorial Bd. Bulletin of the Atomic Scientists 1965–70, mem. Bd. of Dirs. 1960–84; Assoc. Ed. Applied Physics 1974–89; Co-Ed. Springer Series in Chemical Physics 1978–; mem. N.A.S., American Acad. of Arts and Sciences and Leopoldina Akademie der Naturforscher; Bourke Lecturer, Faraday Soc. 1959; Kendall Award in Colloid or Surface Science, American Chemical Soc. 1975; Davisson-Germer Prize, American Physical Soc. 1981, M. W. Welch Award, American Vacuum Soc. 1989, A. Adamson Award, American Chemical Soc. 1996. *Publications:* about 235 scientific articles; Field Emission and Field Ionization 1961. *Leisure interests:* skiing, music and literature. *Address:* The University of Chicago, The James Franck Institute, 5640 South Ellis Avenue, Chicago, IL 60637; 4824 South Kimbark, Chicago, IL 60615, U.S.A. (Home). *Telephone:* (773) 702-7191 (Univ.). *Fax:* (773) 702-5863.

GOMES, Marshal Francisco da Costa; Portuguese army officer; b. 30 June 1914, Chaves; s. of António José Gomes and Idalina Júlia Monteiro da Costa Gomes; m. Maria Estela née Furtado de Antas Varejão 1952; one s.; ed. Military Coll., Cavalry School, Univs. of Coimbra and Oporto and Inst. de Altos Estudos Militares; Chief of Staff, Military Command, Macau 1949–51; mem. H.Q. staff, NATO, Norfolk, U.K., 1954–56; Under-Sec. of Army Staff 1959–61; 2nd-in-Command Mil. Forces, Mozambique 1965–68; C.-in-C. Mil. Forces, Mozambique 1968–69; C.-in-C. Mil. Forces, Angola 1970–72; Chief of Staff, Armed Forces of Portugal 1972–74, 1974–76; mem. Junta de Salvação Nacional 1974–75; Pres. of Portugal 1974–76; mem. Supreme Revolutionary Council of Armed Forces Movt. 1975–76; Grand Officer Ordem Nacional do Cruzeiro do Sul do Brasil, Medalha de Mérito Militar 1st Class, Campaign Medals Mozambique, Angola, and numerous other awards. *Leisure interests:* riding, swimming. *Address:* Av dos EUA 121-9°C, Lisbon, Portugal. *Telephone:* 7969170.

GOMEZ, Alain Michel, LIC. EN DROIT; French businessman; b. 18 Oct. 1938, Paris; s. of Francis Gomez and Simone Blet; m. 1st Francine le Foyer 1967 (divorced); m. 2nd Clémentine Gustin 1986; two d.; ed. Univ. of Paris, Ecole nat. d'administration; Inspecteur des Finances 1965–69; Asst. Dir. of Finance, Saint-Gobain S.A. 1970–71, Financial Dir. 1971–72, Pres. and Dir.-Gen. 1977–; joined Société Générale pour l'Emballage 1972, Dir.-Gen. 1972, Pres. 1977–; Pres. and Dir.-Gen. Saint-Gobain Desjonquères 1973–, Saint-Gobain Emballage 1974–, Dir. Duralex branch, Saint-Gobain 1978–, Dir. Saint-Gobain Pont à Mousson 1977–; Pres. Thomson SA and Thomson-CSF 1982–; Chair. and C.E.O. Thomson CSF 1982–96; Vice-Pres., Dir.-Gen. Sefimeg 1996–; Counsellor to Bank Wasserstein Perella 1997–; mem. Exec. Cttee. Fimalac 1996–; Chevalier, Légion d'honneur. *Publications:* (co-author under name Jacques Mandrin) L'Enarchie 1967, Socialisme ou Social-médiocratie 1968. *Address:* Fimalac, 97 rue de Lille, 75007 Paris, France.

GOMEZ, Jill, F.R.A.M.; British opera and concert singer; b. 21 Sept. 1942, New Amsterdam, British Guiana; ed. Royal Acad. of Music, Guildhall School of Music; operatic début as Adina in L'Elisir d'Amore with Glyndebourne Touring Opera 1968 and has since sung leading roles with Glyndebourne Festival Opera incl. Mélisande, Calisto and Ann Truelove in The Rake's Progress; has appeared with The Royal Opera, English Nat. Opera and Scottish Opera in roles incl. Pamina, Ilia, Fiordiligi, the Countess in Figaro, Elizabeth in Elegy for Young Lovers, Tytania, Lauretta in Gianni Schicchi, and the Governess in The Turn of the Screw; cr. the role of Flora in Tippett's The Knot Garden, at Covent Garden 1970 and of the Countess in Thea Musgrave's Voice of Ariadne, Aldeburgh 1974; sang title role in Massenet's

Thaïs, Wexford 1974 and Jenifer in The Midsummer Marriage with Welsh Nat. Opera 1976; cr. title role in William Alwyn's Miss Julie for radio 1977, Tatiana in Eugene Onegin with Kent Opera 1977; Donna Elvira in Don Giovanni, Ludwigsburg Festival 1978; cr. title role in BBC world premiere of Prokofiev's Maddalena 1979; Fiordiligi in Così fan tutte, Bordeaux 1979; sang in première of the Eighth Book of Madrigals in Zürich Monteverdi Festival 1979; Violetta in Kent Opera's production of La Traviata, Edinburgh Festival 1979; Cinna in Lucio Silla, Zurich 1981; The Governess in The Turn of the Screw, Geneva 1981; Cleopatra in Giulio Cesare, Frankfurt 1981; Teresa in Benvenuto Cellini, Berlioz Festival, Lyon 1982, Leila in Les Pêcheurs de Perles, Scottish Opera 1982–83; Governess in The Turn of the Screw, English Nat. Opera 1984; Helena in Glyndebourne's production of Britten's A Midsummer Night's Dream; Donna Anna in Don Giovanni, Frankfurt Opera 1985 and with Kent Opera 1988; Rosario in Goyescas by Granados 1988, Helena in Midsummer Night's Dream, London Opera 1990; cr. role of Duchess of Argyll in Thomas Adès's Powder Her Face, Cheltenham Int. Music Festival and London 1995; regular engagements including recitals in France, Austria, Belgium, Netherlands, Germany, Scandinavia, Switzerland, Italy, Spain and the U.S.A.; Festival appearances include Aix-en-Provence, Spoleto, Bergen, Versailles, Flanders, Netherlands, Prague, Edinburgh and BBC Promenade concerts; masterclasses Pears-Britten School, Aldeburgh, Trinity Coll. of Music, London, Dartington Summer Festival, Meridian TV; numerous recordings, including Vespro della Beata Vergine 1610 (Monteverdi), Acis and Galatea (Handel), The Knot Garden (Tippett), three recital discs of French, Spanish and Mozart songs, Quatre Chansons Françaises (Britten), Trois Poèmes de Mallarmé (Ravel), Chants d'Auvergne (Canteloube), Les Illuminations (Britten), Bachianas Brasileiras No. 5 (Villa Lobos), Cabaret Classics with John Constable, Knoxville-Summer of 1915 (Barber), South of the Border (Down Mexico Way . . .) arranged by Christopher Palmer for Jill Gomez, Britten's Blues (songs by Britten and Cole Porter); première recordings of Cantiga—The Song of Inês de Castro commissioned by her from David Matthews, Seven Early Songs (Mahler), A Spanish Songbook (with John Constable), Powder Her Face, The Knot Garden, Miss Julie. *Address:* 16 Milton Park, London, N6 5QA, England.

GÓMEZ, Luis María; Argentinian international civil servant; ed. Buenos Aires Nat. Univ.; joined UNDP 1966, served in various posts including Area and Programme Officer, Regional Bureau for Latin America and as UNDP Deputy Resident Rep., Ecuador and Acting Resident Rep., Colombia, Resident Rep., Uruguay 1973–76, Chief, Country Programmes Div., Regional Bureau for Latin America 1976–78, then Dir. Integrated Systems Improvement Project, Office of Admin. 1978–80, Dir. Programming and Implementation Div., Dept. of Tech. Co-operation for Devt. 1980–83, Dir. Nat. Resources and Energy Div. 1983–84, Assoc. Admin. UNDP 1990–96; UN Asst. Sec.-Gen. for Programme Planning and Co-ordination, Dept. of Int. Econ. and Social Affairs 1984–87, UN Asst. Sec.-Gen. and Controller for Programme Planning, Budgeting, Monitoring and Evaluation 1987–90. *Address:* United Nations Development Programme, 1 United Nations Plaza, New York, NY 10017, U.S.A.

GOMORY, Ralph Edward, PH.D.; American foundation executive, mathematician and business executive; b. 7 May 1929, Brooklyn Heights, N.Y.; s. of Andrew L. Gomory and Marian Schellenberg; m. Laura Secretan Dumper 1954 (divorced 1968); two s. one d.; ed. Williams Coll., King's Coll., Cambridge, and Princeton Univ.; Lieut., U.S. Navy 1954–57; Higgins Lecturer and Asst. Prof., Princeton Univ. 1957–59; joined IBM 1959, Fellow 1964, filled various managerial positions including Dir. Mathematical Science Dept., Dir. of Research 1970–86, Vice-Pres. 1973–84, Sr. Vice-Pres. 1985–89, mem. Corporate Man. Bd. 1983–89, Sr. Vice-Pres. for Science and Tech. 1986–89; Andrew D. White Prof.-at-Large, Cornell Univ. 1970–76; Pres. Alfred P. Sloan Foundation, New York 1989–; Dir. Bank of New York 1986–88, Industrial Research Inst. 1986–91; mem. N.A.S., Nat. Acad. of Eng., American Acad. of Arts and Sciences, Council on Foreign Relations, White House Science Council (1986–89); Fellow, Econometric Soc., American Acad. of Arts and Sciences 1973; Trustee, Hampshire Coll. 1977–86, Princeton Univ. 1985–89; Hon. D.Sc. (Williams Coll.) 1973, (Polytechnic Univ.) 1987, (Syracuse Univ.) 1989, (Carnegie Mellon Univ.) 1989; Hon. L.H.D. (Pace Univ.) 1986; Lanchester Prize, Operations Research Soc. of America 1964, John von Neumann Theory Prize 1984, Harry Goode Memorial Award 1984, I.R.I. Medal 1985, IEEE Eng. Leadership Recognition Award 1988, Nat. Medal of Science 1988, Presidential Award (New York Acad. of Sciences) 1992, Arthur M. Bueche Award (N.A.E.) 1993. *Address:* Alfred P. Sloan Foundation, 630 Fifth Avenue, New York, NY 10111 (Office); 260 Douglas Road, Chappaqua, NY 10514, U.S.A. (Home).

GOMRINGER, Eugen; Swiss professor of aesthetics; b. 20 Jan. 1925, Cachuela Esperanza, Bolivia; m. 1st Klara Stöckli 1950; m. 2nd Nortrud Ottenhausen; five s. one d.; ed. Kantonsschule, Zürich, and Univ. of Berne; Sec. and Docent, Hochschule für Gestaltung, Ulm 1954–58; Art Dir. Swiss Industrial Abrasives 1959–67; Man. Dir. Schweizer Werkbund, Zürich 1961–67; Man. of Cultural Relations, Rosenthal AG, Germany 1967–; Prof. of Aesthetics, Düsseldorf Art School 1976–90; Man. Int. Forum for Design, Ulm 1988–; Hon. Prof. Univ. of Zwickau; mem. Akad. der Künste, Berlin. *Publications:* several books of poetry and monographs in the art field. *Leisure interests:* mountaineering, art collecting, farming, dogs. *Address:* Wurlitz 22, 95111 Rehau, Germany (Home). *Telephone:* 09283-1324 (Home). *Fax:* 09283-4441 (Home).

GONÇALVES, Gen. Vasco dos Santos; Portuguese army officer; b. 3 May 1921, Lisbon; s. of Victor Candido Gonçalves and Alda Romana dos Santos; m. Aida Rocha Afonso 1950; one s. one d.; ed. Army School; joined Portuguese Army 1942; mem. teaching staff, Bridges and Roads Section, Army School; promoted to rank of Lieut. 1946, Capt. 1954, Maj. 1963, Lieut.-Col. 1967, Brig. 1974, Gen. 1975; various commissions in Eng. Branch of Army, later mem. Directorate, Eng. Branch; mem. Armed Forces Movt. 1974–75, Supreme Revolutionary Council March-Sept. 1975; Prime Minister 1974–75; several awards and decorations. *Leisure interests:* political economy, philosophy, history, natural history. *Address:* Avenida Estados Unidos da América, 86, 5° esq., 1700 Lisbon, Portugal.

GONCHAR, Nikolai Nikolayevich, C.ECON.SC.; Russian politician; b. 16 Oct. 1946, Murmansk; m.; one d.; ed. Moscow Energy Inst.; engineer, then head of div. Moscow City Council on research activities of students 1972–75; Head of Div. Research Inst. of Complex Devt. of Nat. Econs. of Moscow 1976–82; Deputy, then First Deputy Chair. Exec. Cttee. of Deputies, Soviet of Bauman Region of Moscow 1987–89, Chair. 1990–91; Sec. Regional CPSU Cttee. 1989–90; Deputy Chair. Moscow City Soviet of People's Deputies 1990–91, Chair. 1991–93; mem. Council of Fed. 1993–95, Deputy Chair. Cttee. on Budget and Financial Regulations 1994–95; mem. State Duma 1995–. *Address:* State Duma, Okhotny Ryad 1, 103265 Moscow, Russia (Office). *Telephone:* 292 7508 (Office).

GONCHIGDORJ, Radnaasumbereliin, PH.D., D.SC.; Mongolian politician and mathematician; b. 1954, Tsakhir Dist., Arkhangai Prov.; s. of Radnaasumberel Gonchigdorj and Namjaa Gonchigdorj; m. Damdinsurengiin Hishigt 1977; two s. two d.; ed. Mongolian State Univ.; Lecturer in Math., Mongolian State Univ. 1975–88; Dir. Inst. of Math., Mongolian Acad. of Sciences 1988–90; Chair. Exec. Cttee. Mongolian Social-Democratic Movt. 1990; Chair. Mongolian Social-Democratic Party 1994–; Deputy to Great People's Hural 1990–92; Vice-Pres. of Mongolia and Chair. State Little Hural 1990–92; mem. State Great Hural 1992–96, Chair. 1996–. *Address:* c/o State Great Hural, Government House, Ulan Bator 12, Mongolian People's Republic. *Telephone:* (1) 326877. *Fax:* (1) 322866.

GÖNCZ, Árpád, LL.D.; Hungarian politician and writer; b. 10 February 1922, Budapest; s. of Lajos Göncz and Ilona Heimann; m. Mária Zsuzsanna Göntér 1946; two s. two d.; ed. Pázmány Péter University of Budapest; employed as banking clerk with Land Credit Inst.; joined Ind. Smallholders, Landworkers and Bourgeois Party; leading positions in Ind. Youth Org. Ed.-in-Chief Generation (weekly); sentenced in 1957 to life imprisonment as defendant in political Bibó trial; released under amnesty 1963; then freelance writer and literary translator, especially of English works; Wheatland Prize, Attila József Prize; Pres. Hungarian Writers Federation 1989–90; founding mem. Free Initiatives Network, Free Democratic Fed., Historic Justice Cttee.; mem. of Parliament 1990; Acting Pres. of Hungary May–Aug. 1990, Pres. of Hungary 1990–; Hon. K.C.M.G. 1991. *Leisure interests:* reading, walking. *Address:* Office of the President, 1357 Budapest, Kossuth tér 1–3, Hungary. *Telephone:* (361) 269-0367. *Fax:* (361) 268-4863.

GONG BENYAN; Chinese state official; b. Jan. 1927, Wendeng Co., Shandong Prov.; s. of Gong Yunliang and Shao Yuehua; m. Lin Lezhi 1949; two s. one d.; joined Communist Youth League 1943, Party 1944; Dir. Qiqihar No. 1 Machine Tools Plant 1967, jailed by followers of 'Gang of Four' 1966–71, reinstated 1972; Dir. Fulaerji No. 1 Heavy-duty Machinery Plant 1978; mem. CCP Standing Cttee., Heilongjiang Prov. 1981; Dir. Industry and Communications Office, and Chair. Prov. Econ. Comm., Heilongjiang 1981; alt. mem. 12th CCP Cen. Cttee. 1983–87; Vice-Gov., Heilongjiang 1983–85; Mayor of Harbin 1985; Consultant to CPC Harbin Cttee. *Leisure interest:* reading works of literature. *Address:* 22 Majia Street, Nangang Dist., Harbin, Heilongjiang; Heilongjiang Provincial People's Government, Harbin, Heilongjiang, People's Republic of China. *Telephone:* 417262, 410730 (Office); 347066 (Home). *Fax:* 86 451 417845.

GONG LI; Chinese actress; m. Ooi Hoe-Seong 1996. *Films include:* Red Sorghum 1987, Raise the Red Lantern, Farewell My Concubine, To Live, Shanghai Triad.

GONG PUSHENG; Chinese diplomatist (retd.); b. 6 Sept. 1913, Shanghai; m. Chang Hanfu (deceased); two d.; Deputy Dir. Int. Orgs. and Confs. Dept., Ministry of Foreign Affairs 1949–58, Dir. 1958–67; mem. 1st-4th Exec. Cttee., All-China Democratic Women's Fed. 1949–84; Vice-Pres. Red Cross Soc. of China 1979–85; Amb. to Ireland 1980–83; mem. of Nat. Cttee., Chinese People's Political Consultative Conf. 1983–93, Council, Chinese People's Inst. of Foreign Affairs 1985–; Vice-Pres. China UN Asscn. 1985–; Vice-Chair. Yenching Grad. Inst. 1993–; Prof. Foreign Affairs Coll., Beijing 1985–; mem. Foreign Affairs Cttee. of Nat. Cttee. CPCC 1988–93; Hon. Pres. Beijing Society for Comparative Int. Studies 1991–. *Address:* c/o Ministry of Foreign Affairs, Chaoyangmennei Street, Dongsi, Beijing, China.

GONG YUZHI; Chinese politician; b. 1929, Xiangtan, Hunan Prov.; ed. Qinghua Univ.; researcher, CCP Cen. Cttee. Propaganda Dept. 1952–66; Deputy Office Dir. Cttee. for Editing and Publishing Works of Mao Zedong 1977–80; Deputy Dir. CCP Cen. Cttee. Party Documents Research Office 1982; Deputy Dir. CCP Cen. Cttee. Propaganda Dept. 1988; mem. 5th to 8th CPPCC Nat. Cttee.; Vice-Pres. CCP Cen. Cttee. Party School 1994–96, Soc. of Research on History of CCP; Dir. Research Centre for Theory of Building Socialism with Chinese Characteristics; Exec. Deputy Dir. Cen.

Party History Research Centre; fmr. mem. Academic Council, Inst. of Philosophy, Chinese Acad. of Social Sciences; fmr. part-time Prof. Beijing and Qinghua Univs. *Publications include:* Some Questions on the Law of Development for Natural Sciences, On Science, Philosophy and Society, From New Democracy to Primary Stage of Socialism. *Address:* c/o Central Committee of the Chinese Communist Party, Beijing, People's Republic of China.

GONZALES POSADA, Luis; Peruvian politician and lawyer; b. 30 July 1945, Pisco; fmr. Legal Adviser, Banco Industrial, Corporación Financiera de Desarrollo, Electricidad del Perú and of Social Security Dept.; mem. of Bd. of Dirs., Seguro Social Obrero, Seguro Social del Empleado, Empresa Nacional de Turismo del Perú, La Crónica, Futura and Visión Peruana publishing cos.; Dir. and Founder of the daily Hoy and the weekly Visión; has been on staff of La Tribuna, La Prensa, Correo and La Crónica; mem. Colegio de Abogados de Lima and of Colegio de Periodistas de Lima; Minister of Justice 1985–86. *Address:* c/o Ministry of Justice, Palacio de Gobierno, Pescadería, Lima, Peru.

GONZÁLEZ, Ángel; Spanish poet; b. 1925, Oviedo; Prof. Univ. of New Mexico, Albuquerque 1972–90; mem. Spanish Royal Acad. 1996–; winner of several literary prizes including Premio Príncipe de Asturias 1985. *Publications include:* Áspero mundo (Harsh World), Prosemas y menos, Palabra sobre palabra (Word over Word). *Address:* c/o Spanish Royal Academy, Calle Felipe IV 4, 28014 Madrid, Spain.

GONZALEZ, Antonio Erman; Argentinian politician; b. 16 May 1935, La Rioja Prov.; ed. Nat. Univ. of Córdoba; fmr. Prof. of Accountancy, La Rioja Univ.; econ., accountancy and taxation adviser to various firms in La Rioja; accountant, Inst. for Social Security and Welfare (IPSAS), La Rioja Prov. 1961–64; Sec. for Finance, Buenos Aires Municipality 1963–64, Econ. Adviser ad honorem 1964–66; Gen. Man. IPSAS 1964–65; auditor, Bank of La Rioja Prov. 1966; Under-Sec. of Finance, Prov. of La Rioja 1967; mem. Bd. IPSAS 1967–69; mem. State Exchequer of La Rioja 1971–72, 1974–75; Pres. Bank of La Rioja 1972–74, 1985, econ. consultant 1981–82, Dir. 1984, adviser 1987; Minister of Finance and Public Works 1985–87, 1988–89, of Health and Social Welfare 1989, of Economy 1989–92; dist. deputation 1987–88; elected Deputy 1989–; Vice-Pres. Argentine Cen. Bank 1989. *Publications:* numerous tech. papers.

GONZÁLEZ CASANOVA, Pablo; Mexican researcher and professor; b. 11 Feb. 1922, Toluca; s. of Pablo González Casanova and Concepción del Valle; m. Natalia Henríquez Ureña 1947; three s.; ed. El Colegio de México, Escuela Nacional de Antropología, Univ. Nacional Autónoma de México and Univ. de Paris; Asst. Researcher, Inst. de Investigaciones Sociales, Univ. Nacional Autónoma de México (UNAM) 1944–50, Researcher 1950–52, Full-time Researcher 1973–78; Researcher, El Colegio de México 1950–54; Sec. Gen. Asscn. of Univs. 1953–54; Titular Prof. of Mexican Sociology, Escuela Nacional de Ciencias Políticas y Sociales, UNAM 1952–66, of Gen. Sociology 1954–58; Dir. Escuela Nacional de Ciencias Políticas y Sociales 1957–65, Full-time Titular Prof. 1964–65, Titular Prof. of Research Planning 1967–; Dir. Inst. Investigaciones Sociales, UNAM 1966–70; Rector, UNAM 1970–72; Visiting Prof. Cambridge Univ. 1981–82; Pres. Admin. Cttee. Facultad Latinoamericana de Ciencias Sociales, Santiago and Centro Latinoamericano de Investigaciones Sociales, Rio de Janeiro, UNESCO 1959–65; Consultant UN Univ. 1983–87; Dir. Centro de Investigaciones Interdisciplinarias en Humanidades Univ. Nacional Autónoma de Mexico 1986–; mem. Asscn. Int. de Sociologues de Langue Française, Comité Int. pour la Documentation des Sciences Sociales, Acad. de la Investigación Científica; Pres. Asociación Latinoamericana de Sociología 1969–72. *Publications include:* El Poder al Pueblo 1985, El misoneísmo y la modernidad cristiana 1948, Satira del Siglo XVIII (with José Miranda) 1953, Una utopia de América 1953, La literatura perseguida en la crisis de la Colonia 1958, La ideología norteamericana sobre inversiones extranjeras 1955, Estudio de la técnica social 1958, La Democracia en México 1965, Las categorías del desarrollo económico y la investigación en ciencias sociales 1967, Sociología de la explotación 1969, América Latina: Historia de Medio Siglo 1925–1975 (2 vols., Editor) 1977, Historia del Movimiento Obrero en América Latina, Siglo XX 1981, El Estado y los Partidos Políticos en México 1981, América Latina, Hoy 1990, El Estado y la Política en el Sur del Mundo 1994. *Address:* Peña Pobre 28, Tlalpan, México, D.F. 14050, Mexico. *Telephone:* 5506702.

GONZÁLEZ DEL VALLE, Jorge; Guatemalan international official and economist; ed. Univ. of San Carlos, Guatemala, Columbia Univ., New York, Yale Univ., New Haven, Conn.; worked in Bank of Guatemala and Cen. American Bank for Econ. Integration; Exec. Dir. IMF for four years; Exec. Sec. Cen. American Monetary Council for nine years; Head Centre for Latin American Monetary Studies (CEMLA) 1978–90.

GONZÁLEZ MÁRQUEZ, Felipe; Spanish politician and lawyer; b. 5 March 1942, Seville; m. Carmen Romero; two s. one d.; ed. lower and high school, school of law, continued studies at Catholic Univ. of Louvain, Belgium; on graduating from law school, opened first labour law office to deal with workers' problems in Seville 1966; mem. Spanish Socialist Youth 1962; mem. Spanish Socialist Party (Partido Socialista Obrero Español P.S.O.E.) 1964–, mem. Seville Provincial Cttee. 1965–69, Nat. Cttee. 1969–70, mem. Exec. Bd. 1970, First Sec. 1974–79, resigned; re-elected Sept. 1979, then Sec.-Gen. –1997; mem. for Madrid, Congress of Deputies 1977–; Prime Minister of Spain and Pres. Council of Ministers Dec. 1982–96; Chair. Socialist Parl. Group; mem. Japanese Bonsai Asscn.; Grand Cross of the Order of Mil. Merit 1984, Order of Isabel the Catholic 1996. *Publications:* What is Socialism? 1976, P.S.O.E. 1977. *Leisure interests:* reading, bonsai plants. *Address:* c/o Fundación Socialismo XXI, Gobelas 31, 28023 Madrid, Spain.

GONZÁLEZ MARTÍN, H.E. Cardinal Marcelo; Spanish ecclesiastic; b. 16 Jan. 1918, Villanubla, Valladolid; ordained 1941; consecrated Bishop of Astorga 1961; titular Archbishop of Case Mediane 1966; auxiliary Archbishop of Barcelona 1967; Archbishop of Toledo and Primate of Spain 1971–95; created Cardinal by Pope Paul VI 1973. *Address:* Arco de Palacio 3, 45002 Toledo, Spain. *Telephone:* 224 100.

GONZALEZ PANTALEON, Rafael; Dominican diplomatist and doctor; b. 1937, Yayabo; m., seven c.; ed. Faculty of Medicine, St. Thomas Aquinas Univ. (now Autonomous Univ. of San Domingo), Massillon State Hosp., O. and Mount Vernon Hosp., N.Y.; Resident Physician, St. Vincent de Paul Hosp.; Medical Dir. Social Security Clinic, Yayabo 1964; Gen. Practitioner Salvador B. Gautier Hosp. and Prof. of Anatomy, Autonomous Univ. 1965–68; Medical Dir., Pocahontas Memorial Hosp., W. Va. 1974; Gen. Dir. Dominican Social Security Inst., 1986; Medical and Social Security Adviser to Exec. Branch of Govt. of Dominican Repub.; Perm. Rep. to the UN 1989–91; f. Enriquillo Cultural Soc. 1977; Doctor of the Year, Mount Vernon Hosp. 1971. *Address:* c/o Ministry of Foreign Affairs, Roseau, Dominica.

GONZI, Lawrence, LL.D.; Maltese politician and lawyer; b. 1 July 1953; s. of Louis Gonzi and Inez Gonzi (née Galea); m. Catherine Gonzi (née Callus); two s. one d.; ed. Malta Univ.; practised law 1975–88; Speaker House of Reps. 1988–96; M.P. Nationalist Party 1996–; Shadow Minister and Opposition Spokesman for Social Policy 1996–98, Sec. and Whip Nationalist Party Parl. Group 1996–97; Minister for Social Policy 1998–, Leader of the House 1998–; Chair., then Pres. Nat. Comm. for Persons with Disabilities 1987–96; Sec. Gen. of Nationalist Party 1997–; Gen. Pres. Malta Catholic Action 1976–86; Chair. Pharmacy Bd. 1987–88, Nat. Comm. for Persons with Disabilities 1987–94 (Pres. 1994–96), Nat. Comm. for Mental Health Reform, Electoral System (Revision) Comm. 1994–95, Mizzi Org. Bd. of Dirs. 1989–97; mem. Prisons Bd. 1987–88. *Address:* Ministry for Social Policy, Palazzo Ferreria, Republic Street, Valletta, CMR 02, Malta. *Telephone:* 246811; 249449. *Fax:* 243166-9.

GOOCH, Graham Alan, O.B.E.; British cricketer; b. 23 July 1953, Leytonstone; s. of late Alfred and Rose Gooch; m. Brenda Daniels 1976; three d.; ed. Norlington Junior High School, Leytonstone; right-hand opening batsman, right-arm medium bowler; played for Essex 1973–97 (capt. 1986–87 and 1989–94), Western Province 1982–83 and 1983–84; played in 118 Tests for England 1975 to 1994–95, 34 as capt., scoring 8,900 runs (England record) (average 42.5) including 20 hundreds (highest score 333 and record Test match aggregate of 456 v. India, Lord's 1990, becoming only batsman to score a triple century and a century in a first-class match) and holding 103 catches; scored 44,841 runs (128 hundreds) and held 555 catches in first-class cricket; toured Australia 1978–79, 1979–80, 1990–91 (captain) and 1994–95; 125 limited-overs internationals, including 50 as captain (both England records); mem. England Selection Cttee. 1996–; Man. England Tour to Australia 1998–99. *Publications include:* Testing Times 1991, Gooch: My Autobiography 1995. *Leisure interests:* squash, golf, football. *Address:* c/o Essex County Cricket Club, The County Ground, New Writtle Street, Chelmsford, Essex, CM2 0PG, England.

GOOD, Anthony Bruton Meyrick, F.I.P.R.; British public relations executive; b. 18 April 1933, Sutton, Surrey; s. of Meyrick G. B. Good and Amy M. Trussell; m. (divorced); two d.; ed. Felsted School, Essex; man. trainee, Distillers Group; Editorial Asst. Temple Press 1952–55; Public Relations Officer, Silver City Airways; Public Relations and Marketing Man., Air Holdings Group 1955–60; f. and Chair. Good Relations Ltd. (later Good Relations Group PLC) 1961–89; Dir. Cox and Kings Travel Ltd. 1971–, Chair. 1975–; Chair. Good Relations (India) Ltd. 1988–, Cox and Kings (India) Ltd. 1988–, Good Consultancy Ltd. 1989–, Millbank Public Relations 1997–; non-exec. dir. IM Group Ltd., Matrix Partnership. *Leisure interest:* travel. *Address:* Clench Lodge, Wootton Rivers, Marlborough, Wilts., SN8 4NT, England (Home). *Telephone:* (01672) 810126 (Office). *Fax:* (01672) 810869 (Office).

GOODALL, Sir (Arthur) David (Saunders), G.C.M.G., M.A.; British diplomatist (retd.); b. 9 Oct. 1931, Blackpool; s. of Arthur William Goodall and Maisie Josephine Byers; m. Morwenna Peecock 1962; two s. one d.; ed. Ampleforth Coll., Trinity Coll., Oxford; army service in Kenya, Aden, Cyprus 1954–56; joined Foreign (now Diplomatic) Service 1956, served at Nicosia, Jakarta, Bonn, Nairobi, Vienna 1956–75, Head Western European Dept., FCO 1975–79, Minister, Bonn 1979–82, Deputy Sec., Cabinet Office 1982–84, Deputy Under-Sec. of State, FCO 1984–87, High Commr. in India 1987–92; Joint Chair. Anglo-Irish Encounter 1992–; Chair. Leonard Cheshire Foundation 1995– (Chair. Int. Cttee. 1992–95); Vice-Chair. British-Irish Asscn. 1994–97, Chair. 1997–; Dir. (non-exec.) Govett India Fund Ltd. 1993–, Oryx (India) Fund Ltd. 1994–; Visiting Prof. in Irish Studies, Univ. of Liverpool 1996–; mem. Council Univ. of Durham 1992– (Vice-Chair. 1997–); Hon. Fellow Trinity Coll., Oxford; Hon. LL.D. (Hull) 1994. *Publications:* Remembering India 1997, contribs. on theological and historical subjects to The Tablet, The Ampleforth Journal, The Past, The Irish Genealogist. *Leisure interests:* painting in watercolours, reading. *Address:* Leonard Cheshire Foundation, 30 Millbank, London, SW1P 4QD, England.

GOODALL, Jane, C.B.E., PH.D.; British ethologist; b. 3 April 1934, London; d. of Mortimer Herbert Morris-Goodall and Vanne Morris-Goodall (née Joseph); m. 1st Hugo Van Lawick 1964 (divorced 1974); one s.; m. 2nd M. Derek Bryceson 1975 (died 1980); ed. Uplands School, Univ. of Cambridge; Sec. Oxford Univ.; Asst. Ed. Documentary Film Studio; waitress; Asst Sec. to Louis Leakey, worked in Olduvai Gorge, then moved to Gombe Stream Game Reserve (now Gombe Nat. Park), camp became Gombe Stream Research Centre 1964; Scientific Dir. Gombe Wildlife Research Inst. 1967–; Founder Cttee. for Conservation and Care of Chimpanzees 1986; Hon. Visiting Prof. in Zoology Dar es Salaam Univ. 1973–; A. D. White Prof.-at-Large Cornell Univ. 1996–; Visiting lecturer numerous univs. including Yale Univ., U.S.A.; speaker on conservation issues, appearing on numerous TV shows including: 20/20, Nightline, Good Morning America; contrib. to New York Times; Hon. Foreign mem. American Acad. for Advancement of Sciences; Conservation Award (New York Zoological Soc.) Franklin Burr Award (twice, Nat. Geographic Soc.), Nat. Geographic Soc. Centennial Award, Hubbard Medal 1995, Medal of Mt. Kilimanjaro 1996, Public Service Award, Nat. Scientific Bd. 1998, John Hay Award, Orion Soc. 1998. *Publications:* Shadow of Man, Chimpanzees of Gombe 1986, Through a Window 1990, The Chimpanzee: The Living Link Between "Man" and "Beast" 1992, Visions of Caliban 1993, Jane Goodall: with love 1994. *Address:* c/o The Jane Goodall Institute for Wildlife Research, Education and Conservation, P.O. Box 14890, Silver Spring, MD 20911, U.S.A. *Telephone:* (301) 565-0086. *Fax:* (301) 565-3188.

GOODE, Anthony William, B.S., M.D., F.R.C.S.; British surgeon; b. 3 Aug. 1945, Newcastle-upon-Tyne; s. of William Henry Goode and Eileen Veronica Goode; m. Patricia Josephine Flynn 1987; ed. Corby School and Univ. of Newcastle-upon-Tyne; clinical surgical posts in Newcastle Hosps. Group 1968–76; Univ. of London Teaching Hosps. 1976–; Prof. of Endocrine and Metabolic Surgery, Univ. of London, Consultant Surgeon Royal London Hosp., Whitechapel, and St. Bartholomew's Hosp., Hon. Prof. Centre for Biological and Medical Systems, Imperial Coll. 1982–; Clinical Dir. Helicopter Emergency Medical Service, London 1998–; Ed.-in-Chief Medicine, Science and the Law 1996–; Asst. Sec. Gen. British Acad. of Forensic Science 1982–87; Hon. Sec. British Asscn. of Endocrine Surgeons 1983–96; Fellow Royal Soc. of Medicine 1971–; mem. Int. Soc. of Surgery 1984–, Int. Soc. of Endocrine Surgeons 1984–, New York Acad. of Sciences 1986–, MCC 1982–; Trustee Smith and Nephew Foundation 1990–; Liveryman, Worshipful Soc. of Apothecaries of London; Freeman City of London 1992. *Publications:* numerous papers and articles on nutrition in surgical patients, endocrine diseases, metabolic changes in manned spaceflight and related topics. *Leisure interests:* cricket, music (especially opera). *Address:* The Surgical Unit, The Royal London Hospital, Whitechapel, London, E1 1BB, England.

GOODE, Richard; American pianist; b. 1 June 1943, New York; m. Marcia Weinberg; ed. Mannes Coll. of Music, Curtis Inst.; studied with Nadia Reisenberg and Rudolf Serkin; has played with Baltimore, Boston, Chicago, Cleveland, New York, Philadelphia, Berlin Radio, Finnish Radio and Bamberg Symphony Orchestras; mem. Piano Faculty, Mannes Coll. of Music 1969–; concerts and recitals in U.S.A., Europe, Japan; Carnegie Hall recital début 1990; prizes include Young Concert Artists Award, 1st Prize Clara Haskil Competition, Avery Fischer Prize, Grammy Award (with clarinettist Richard Stoltzman). *Address:* c/o Frank Salomon Associates, 201 W. 54th Street, Apt. 1C, New York, NY 10019, U.S.A.

GOODE, Royston Miles, C.B.E., Q.C., LL.D., F.B.A., F.R.S.A.; British professor of law; b. 6 April 1933, London; s. of Samuel Goode and Bloom Goode; m. Catherine A. Rueff 1964; one d.; ed. Highgate School and Univ. of London; admitted solicitor 1955; partner, Victor Mishcon & Co. (solicitors) 1966–67; called to Bar, Inner Temple 1988, Hon. Bencher 1992–; Prof. of Law, Queen Mary Coll. London 1971–73, Crowther Prof. of Credit and Commercial Law 1973–89, Head of Dept. and Dean of Faculty of Laws 1976–80, Dir. and founder, Centre for Commercial Law Studies 1980–89; Norton Rose Prof. of English Law, Univ. of Oxford 1990–98, Prof. Emer. 1998–; Fellow, Queen Mary & Westfield Coll. London 1991, St. John's Coll. Oxford 1990–98 (Emer. Fellow 1998–); mem. Monopolies and Mergers Comm. 1981–86, Council of the Banking Ombudsman 1989–92; Chair. Pension Law Review Cttee. 1992–93; mem. Council and Chair. Exec. Cttee. JUSTICE 1994–96; Hon. Pres. Centre for Commercial Law Studies 1990–, Oxford Inst. of Legal Practice 1994–; Hon. D.Sc. (London) 1997. *Publications include:* Consumer Credit 1978, Commercial Law 1982, Legal Problems of Credit and Security 1982, Payment Obligations in Commercial and Financial Transactions 1983, Proprietary Rights and Insolvency in Sales Transactions 1985, Principles of Corporate Insolvency Law 1990, Consumer Credit Legislation (looseleaf); books on hire purchase; contribs. to Halsbury's Laws of England (4th edn.). *Leisure interests:* chess, reading, walking, browsing in bookshops. *Address:* c/o St. John's College, Oxford, OX1 3JP, England.

GOODENOUGH, Ward Hunt, PH.D.; American anthropologist; b. 30 May 1919, Cambridge, Mass.; s. of Erwin R. Goodenough and Helen M. Lewis; m. Ruth A. Gallagher 1941; two s. two d.; ed. Groton School, Cornell and Yale Univs.; Instructor in Anthropology, Univ. of Wis. 1948–49; Asst. Prof. of Anthropology, Univ. of Pa. 1949–54, Assoc. Prof. 1954–62, Chair. of Dept. 1976–82, Prof. and Curator of Oceanian Ethnology 1962–80, Univ. Prof. 1980–89, Prof. Emer. 1989–; Visiting Prof. of Anthropology, Cornell Univ. 1961–62, Univ. of Hawaii 1982–83; Fulbright Lecturer, St. Patrick's College, Maynooth, Ireland 1987; Bd. Chair., Human Relations Area Files Inc. 1971–81; mem. Bd. of Dirs. A.A.A.S. 1972–75, E. Rock Inst. 1986–98 (Sec. 1995–98); Pres. American Ethnological Soc. 1963, Soc. for Applied Anthropology 1964; mem. American Philosophical Soc., American Acad. of Arts and Sciences, Nat. Acad. of Sciences; Ed. American Anthropologist 1966–70. *Publications:* Property, Kin and Community on Truk 1951, Co-operation in Change 1963, Explorations in Cultural Anthropology 1964, Description and Comparison in Cultural Anthropology 1970, Culture, Language and Society 1971, Trukese-English Dictionary 1980, Supplementary vol. 1990. *Leisure interests:* music, stamp collecting. *Address:* c/o University Museum, University of Pennsylvania, Philadelphia, PA 19104; 3300 Darby Road, Apt. 5306, Haverford, PA 19041, U.S.A. *Telephone:* (215) 898-7461 (Office).

GOODES, Melvin Russell, B.COMM., M.B.A.; Canadian business executive; b. 11 April 1935, Hamilton, Ont.; s. of late Cedric P. Goodes and of Mary M. (Lewis) Goodes; m. Arlene M. Bourne 1963; one s. two d.; ed. Queen's Univ., Kingston, Ont. and Univ. of Chicago; Research Assoc. Canadian Econ. Research Assocs. Toronto 1957–58; Market Planning Coordinator, Ford Motor Co. of Canada 1960–64; Asst. to Vice-Pres. O'Keefe Breweries, Toronto 1964–65; joined Warner-Lambert Co. 1965, Pres. Warner-Lambert Mexico 1970–76, Pres. Pan-Am Zone 1976–77, Pres. Pan-Am (Asia Zone) 1977–79, Pres. Consumer Products Div. 1979–80, Sr. Vice-Pres. then Pres. Consumer Products Group 1981–83, Exec. Vice-Pres. then Pres. U.S. Operations 1984–85, Pres. and C.O.O. 1985–91, Chair. C.E.O. 1991–; Ford Foundation Fellow 1958; Sears, Roebuck Foundation Fellow 1959; Trustee Queen's Univ. 1988–. *Leisure interests:* golf, tennis, racquetball, bridge. *Address:* Warner-Lambert Company, 201 Tabor Road, Morris Plains, NJ 07950, U.S.A. *Telephone:* (201) 540-3636.

GOODHART, Charles Albert Eric, C.B.E., PH.D., F.B.A.; British economist; b. 1936, London; s. of Sir A. L. Goodhart; m. Margaret (Miffy) Smith 1960; one s. three d.; ed. Eton Coll., Trinity Coll., Cambridge, Harvard Univ.; asst. lecturer Dept. of Econs. Cambridge Univ. and Prize Fellow, Trinity Coll., economist Dept. of Econ. Affairs, London 1965–66; lecturer L.S.E. 1966–68, Norman Sosnow Prof. of Banking and Finance 1985–; Adviser on Monetary Affairs Bank of England 1968–85, external mem. Monetary Policy Cttee. 1997–; mem. Exchange Fund Advisory Council, Hong Kong 1988–97. *Publications:* Money, Information and Uncertainty 1989, The Evolution of Central Banks 1985, The Central Bank and the Financial System 1995, The Emerging Framework of Financial Regulation (ed.) 1998. *Leisure interest:* sheep farming. *Address:* Financial Markets Group, London School of Economics, Houghton Street, London, WC2A 2AE (Office); 27 Abbotsbury Road, London, W14 8EL, England (Home). *Telephone:* 0171-955 7555 (Office); 0171-242 1006 (Home).

GOODING, Cuba, Jr.; American actor; b. 2 Sept. 1968, Bronx, N.Y.; s. of Cuba Gooding Sr. and Shirley Gooding; two N.A.A.C.P. Awards; Acad. Award, Best Supporting Actor (for Jerry Maguire) 1997; Chicago Film Critics Award; Screen Actor Guild Award. *Television appearances include:* Kill or Be Killed 1990, Murder with Motive: The Edmund Perry Story 1992, Daybreak 1993, The Tuskegee Airmen. *Film appearances include:* Coming to America 1988, Sing 1989, Boyz N the Hood 1991, Gladiator 1992, A Few Good Men 1992, Hitz 1992, Judgement Night 1993, Lightning Jack 1994, Losing Isaiah 1995, Outbreak 1995, Jerry Maguire 1996, The Audition 1996, Old Friends 1997, As Good As It Gets 1997, What Dreams May Come 1998. *Address:* c/o Rogers and Cowan, 1888 Century Park East, Suite 500, Los Angeles, CA 90067, U.S.A.

GOODISON, Sir Nicholas Proctor, Kt., PH.D., F.S.A., F.R.S.A.; British banker; b. 16 May 1934, Radlett; s. of Edmund Harold Goodison and Eileen Mary Carrington Proctor; m. Judith Abel Smith 1960; one s. two d.; ed. Marlborough Coll. and King's Coll., Cambridge; joined H. E. Goodison & Co. (now named Quilter & Co. Ltd.) 1958–88, partner 1962, Chair. 1975–88; mem. Council of The Stock Exchange 1968–88, Chair. 1976–88; Pres. British Bankers Asscn. 1991–96; Pres. Int. Fed. of Stock Exchanges 1985–86; Chair. TSB Group plc 1989–95; Chair. TSB Bank PLC 1989–; Deputy Chair. Lloyds TSB Group PLC 1995–; Dir. (non-exec.) British Steel 1989– (Deputy Chair. 1993–); Dir. Gen. Accident 1987–95; Trustee, Nat. Heritage Memorial Fund 1988–97; Vice-Chair. Bd. of English Nat. Opera 1980–98 (Dir. 1977–98); Chair. Nat. Art-Collections Fund, Courtauld Inst., Crafts Council, Bd. Burlington Magazine Publs.; Hon. Keeper of Furniture, Fitzwilliam Museum, Cambridge; Pres. Furniture History Soc.; Gov. Marlborough Coll. 1981–97; Sr. Fellow Royal Coll. of Art 1991; Hon. F.R.I.B.A. 1992; Hon. D.Litt. (City Univ.); Hon. LL.D. (Exeter); Hon. D.Sc. (Aston Univ.) 1994; Légion d'honneur 1990. *Publications:* English Barometers 1680–1860 1968, Ormolu: the Work of Matthew Boulton 1974; many papers and articles on the history of furniture, clocks and barometers. *Leisure interest:* history of furniture and decorative arts. *Address:* Lloyds TSB Group PLC, 71 Lombard Street, London, EC3P 3BS, England. *Telephone:* 0171-356 2074. *Fax:* 0171-356 2050.

GOODLAD, John I., PH.D.; American university teacher; b. 19 Aug. 1920, N. Vancouver, B.C., Canada; s. of William Goodlad and Mary Inkster; m. Evalene M. Pearson 1945; one s. one d.; ed. Univs. of British Columbia and Chicago; fmr. school teacher, school prin. and dir. of educ. in B.C.; consultant in curriculum, Atlanta (Ga.) Area Teacher Educ. Service 1947–49; Assoc. Prof. Emory Univ. and Agnes Scott Coll. 1949–50; Prof. and Dir. Div. of Teacher Educ. Emory Univ. and Dir. Agnes Scott Coll.—Emory Univ., Teacher Educ. Program 1950–56; Prof. and Dir. Center for Teacher Educ. Univ. of Chicago 1956–60; Dir. Corinne A. Seeds Univ. Elementary School,

Univ. of Calif., Los Angeles 1960–84; Prof. Graduate School of Educ., Univ. of Calif. (L.A.) 1960–85, Dean 1967–83; Dir. of Research, Inst. for Devt. of Educ. Activities Inc. 1966–82; Prof., Dir. of Center for Educ. Renewal, Coll. of Educ. Univ. of Washington 1985–; Pres. Inst. for Educ. Inquiry 1992–; 18 hon. degrees and other awards. *Publications:* numerous books and articles in educ. journals. *Leisure interests:* boating, fishing, walking. *Address:* University of Washington, College of Education, 313 Miller Hall, Box 353600, Seattle, WA 98195-3600, U.S.A. *Telephone:* 206-543-6230; 206-543-6162, U.S.A.

GOODMAN, Elinor Mary; British political broadcaster and journalist; b. 11 Oct. 1946; d. of Edward Weston Goodman and Pamela Longbottom; m. Derek John Scott 1985; ed. pvt. schools and secretarial coll.; Consumer Affairs Corresp. Financial Times newspaper 1971–78, Political Corresp. 1978–82; Political Corresp. Channel Four News (TV) 1982–88, Political Ed. 1988–. *Address:* Martinscote, Oare, Marlborough, Wilts., SN8 4JA, England.

GOODMAN, John, B.F.A.; American film actor; b. 20 June 1952, St. Louis; m. Annabeth Hartzog 1989; one d.; ed. Meramac Community Coll. and S.W. Missouri State Univ.; Broadway appearances in Loose Ends 1979, Big River 1985; appearances on TV include: The Mystery of Moro Castle, The Face of Rage, Heart of Steel, Moonlighting, Chiefs (mini-series), The Paper Chase, Murder Ordained, The Equalizer, Roseanne (series). *Films include:* The Survivors 1983, Eddie Macon's Run 1983, Revenge of the Nerds 1984, C.H.U.D. 1984, Maria's Lovers 1985, Sweet Dreams 1985, True Stories 1986, The Big Easy 1987, Burglar 1987, Raising Arizona 1987, The Wrong Guys 1988, Everybody's All-American 1988, Punchline 1988, Sea of Love 1989, Always 1989, Stella 1990, Arachnophobia 1990, King Ralph 1990, Barton Fink 1991, The Babe 1992, Born Yesterday 1993, The Flintstones 1994, Kingfish: A Story of Huey P. Long 1995, Pie in the Sky, Mother Night 1996, Fallen 1997, Combat! 1997, The Borrowers 1997, The Big Lebowski 1998, Blues Brothers 2000 1998. *Address:* c/o Fred Spektor, CAA, 9830 Wilshire Boulevard, Beverly Hills, CA 90212, U.S.A.

GOODMAN, Raymond John; British international civil servant; b. 26 Oct. 1916, London; s. of J. S. Goodman and Helena Taylor; m. Dorothy Bruchholz 1953; two s. two d.; ed. London School of Econs. and Univs. of Copenhagen and Oslo; War Service, R.N.V.R. 1940–46; Dir. Political and Econ. Planning (P.E.P.), London 1946–53; Asst. to Chair. of Marks and Spencer Ltd. 1953–56; joined World Bank Staff 1956, Asst. Dir. of Admin. 1962–65, Deputy Dir. Far East (later Asia) Dept. 1965–68, Dir. E. Asia and Pacific Dept. 1968–74, Dir. Financial Policy 1975–77, Asst. to Sr. Vice-Pres. (Operations) 1977–80; Consultant to World Bank 1982–; Adviser to Fed. Gov. of Nigeria 1984; Team Leader, Ind. Review of Papua New Guinea economy 1985 (published by Australian Nat. Univ. 1985); Chief of Mission to review Netherlands Antilles and Aruba Economies 1986; Team Leader, Special Study on Indonesia 1989; Team Leader, Review of Nat. Devt. Studies Centre, Australian Nat. Univ. 1989; Hon. Vice-Pres. Consumers Asscn. of G.B. 1957–; Pres. Group Health Asscn. of Washington, DC 1962–63, American Friends of L.S.E. 1993–95. *Address:* 2946 Macomb Street, N.W., Washington, DC 20008, U.S.A. (Home). *Telephone:* (202) 362-2946 (Home). *Fax:* (202) 363-7499.

GOODPASTER, Gen. Andrew Jackson, M.S.E., PH.D.; American army officer (retd.); b. 12 Feb. 1915, Granite City, Ill.; s. of Andrew Jackson Goodpaster and Teresa Mary (Mrovka) Goodpaster; m. Dorothy Anderson 1939; two d.; ed. McKendree Coll., Lebanon, Ill., U.S. Mil. Acad., Command and Gen. Staff School, Fort Leavenworth, Kan., and Princeton Univ.; C.O. 48th Engineer Battalion, Italy 1943; Staff Officer, War Dept. 1944–47; Graduate study, Princeton Univ. 1947–50; Special Asst. to Chief to Staff, Supreme HQ Allied Powers Europe (SHAPE) 1950–54; District Engineer, San Francisco 1954; Staff Sec. to Pres. of U.S.A. 1954–61; Asst. Div. Commdr. 3rd Infantry Div. 1961; Commdg. Gen. 8th Infantry Div., Europe 1961–62; Asst. to Chair. Joint Chiefs of Staff 1962–66; Dir. Joint Staff, Org. of Joint Chiefs of Staff 1966–67; Commandant, Nat. War Coll., Washington, D.C., with added duty as U.S. Army Rep., UN Mil. Staff Cttee. 1967–68; mem. U.S. Del. to Paris talks on Viet Nam April–June 1968; Deputy Commdr. U.S. Mil. Assistance Command, Viet Nam 1968–69; C.-in-C. U.S. European Command 1969–74; Supreme Allied Commdr. Europe (NATO) 1969–74; Fellow, Woodrow Wilson Int. Center for Scholars, Washington, D.C. 1975–76; Prof., Govt. and Int. Studies, The Citadel, Charleston, S.C. 1976–77; Supt. U.S. Mil. Acad., West Point 1977–81; Chair. American Battle Monuments Comm. 1985–90, Atlantic Council of the U.S. 1985–; Chair. George C. Marshall Foundation 1992–; U.S. Medal of Freedom 1984; Distinguished Service Cross, Defense D.S.M. with Oak Leaf Cluster, Army D.S.M. with Three Oak Leaf Clusters, Navy D.S.M.; Air Force D.S.M., Silver Star, Legion of Merit with Oak Leaf Cluster, Purple Heart with Oak Leaf Cluster, numerous other U.S. and foreign decorations from Italy, Repub. of Korea, Netherlands, Belgium, Luxembourg, Fed. Repub. of Germany, Turkey and Portugal. *Publication:* For the Common Defense 1977. *Address:* c/o Eisenhower Institute, 1620 I Street N.W., Washington, DC 20006, U.S.A. *Telephone:* (202) 778-4940 (Office). *Fax:* (202) 463-7241.

GOODWIN, John Forrest, M.D., F.R.C.P., F.A.C.C.; British professor of clinical cardiology; b. 1 Dec. 1918, Ealing; s. of Col. W. R. P. Goodwin and Myrtle Dale Goodwin; m. Barbara Cameron Robertson 1943; one s. one d.; ed. Cheltenham Coll., St. Mary's Hosp. Medical School, Univ. of London; Lecturer, Sr. Lecturer and Prof. of Clinical Cardiology, Royal Postgraduate Medical School, London 1949–84, Prof. Emer. 1984–; Pres. British Cardiac Soc. 1972–76, Int. Soc. and Fed. of Cardiology 1978–80; Second Vice-Pres. Royal Coll. of Physicians of London 1979–80; mem. of Council British Heart Foundation 1975–85, Expert Cttee. on Cardiovascular Disease WHO; Chair. Coronary Prevention Group, U.K. 1985–88, Nat. Forum for Coronary Heart Disease Prevention 1987–93; Pres. Hypertrophic Cardiomyopathy Asscn. 1991; mem. Acad. of Experts 1996–; Hon. Consulting Cardiologist St. George's Hosp., London 1986; Star of Pakistan, Commdr. of the Icelandic Falcon; Dr. h.c. (Lisbon); Hon. F.A.C.P. *Publications:* Cardiomyopathies (Jt. Ed.) 1993 and numerous scientific papers to medical journals. *Leisure interests:* history, photography, travel. *Address:* Cromwell Hospital, Cromwell Road, London, SW5 0TU (Office); 2 Pine Grove, Lake Road, Wimbledon, London, SW19 7HE, England (Home). *Telephone:* 0171-370 4233 (Office); 0181-947 4851 (Home). *Fax:* 0181-947 5578.

GOODWIN, Leonard George, C.M.G., B.SC., M.B., B.S., F.R.C.P., F.R.S.; British medical scientist; b. 11 July 1915; s. of Harry George Goodwin and Lois Goodwin; m. Marie Evelyn Coates 1940; ed. William Ellis School, London, Univ. Coll. London, Univ. Coll. Hosp.; Demonstrator, School of Pharmacy, London 1935–39; Protozoologist, Wellcome Labs. of Tropical Medicine 1939–63, Head of Labs. 1958–63; Dir. Nuffield Labs. of Comparative Medicine, Inst. of Zoology, The Zoological Soc. of London 1964–80, Dir. of Science, Zoological Soc. of London 1966–80; Consultant, Wellcome Trust 1984–; Jt. Hon. Sec. Royal Soc. of Tropical Medicine and Hygiene 1968–74, Pres. 1979–81; Chair. Trypanosomiasis Panel, Overseas Devt. Ministry 1974–77, Filariasis Steering Cttee., WHO Special Programme 1978–82; Chair. Editorial Bd. Parasitology 1980–, Royal Soc./U.F.A.W. Steering Group on Guidelines on Care of Lab. Animals 1985; Hon. Dir. Wellcome Museum for Medical Science 1984–85, Wellcome Trust Film Unit 1986; Fellow Univ. Coll. London 1981; Hon. D.Sc. (Brunel) 1986; Soc. of Apothecaries Gold Medal 1974, Harrison Memorial Medal 1978, Schofield Medal, Guelph Univ. 1979, Silver Medal, Zoological Soc. 1980, Manson Medal (Royal Soc. of Tropical Medicine and Hygiene) 1992. *Publications:* Biological Standardization (Jt. Author) 1950, Biochemistry and Physiology of Protozoa (Contrib.) 1955, A New Tropical Hygiene (Jt. Author) 1960, Recent Advances in Pharmacology (contrib.) 1962; many contribs. to scientific journals, mainly on pharmacology and chemotherapy of tropical diseases, especially malaria, trypansomiasis and helminth infections. *Leisure interests:* dabbling in arts and crafts, especially pottery (slipware), gardening and passive participation in music and opera. *Address:* Shepperlands Farm, Park Lane, Finchampstead, Berks., RG40 4QF, England. *Telephone:* (0118) 973-2153.

GOODY, Joan Edelman, M.A., M.ARCH.; American architect; b. 1 Dec. 1935, New York; d. of Sylvia Feldman Edelman and Beril Edelman; m. 1st Marvin E. Goody 1960 (died 1980); m. 2nd Peter H. Davison 1984; ed. Harvard Univ. Grad. School of Design, Cornell Univ.; Prin. Goody, Clancy & Assocs. Inc., Architects 1961–; Design Critic and Asst. Prof. Harvard Univ. Grad. School of Design 1973–80, Eliot Noyes Visiting Critic 1985; Faculty for Mayors Inst. for City Design 1989–; Chair. Boston Civic Design Comm. 1992–; Dir. Historic Boston, WGBH-TV; Honor Award for Design (A.I.A.) 1980, Citation for Excellence in Urban Design (A.I.A.) 1988, F.A.I.A. 1991. *Address:* Goody, Clancy & Associates, Inc., 334 Boylston Street, Boston, MA 02116, U.S.A. *Telephone:* 617 262-2760.

GOONETILLEKE, Albert, M.D., F.R.C.P.A., F.R.C. PATH.; Sri Lankan pathologist; b. 4 Feb. 1936, Colombo; s. of late Arlis Goonetilleke; m. Sunanaseele Wijesinghe 1958; one s. one d.; medical officer Sri Lanka Health Dept. 1962–68; lecturer Univ. of Edin. 1968–70, Univ. of Leeds 1970–71; with Charing Cross Medical School, London 1972–80; Consultant Pathologist, Charing Cross & Westminster Medical School 1980–88; Chief Pathologist, King Faisal Hosp., Saudi Arabia 1988–94; Chief Pathologist, Royal Comm. Hosp.; Saudi Arabia 1994–96; Consultant Pathologist, Princess Margaret Hosp., Swindon 1996–; Ananda Coll. Gold Medal Sri Lanka 1954; mem. British Asscn. for Forensic Medicine C. H. Milburn Award (B.M.A.). *Publications:* Injuries Caused By Falls from Heights, Safety at Work, Safety in the Home, various articles in forensic medicine and pathology. *Leisure interests:* still and video filming, water colour painting. *Address:* 4 Ascott Avenue, Ealing, London, W5 5QB, England (Office). *Telephone:* 0181-579 7308.

GOOS, Bernd, M.B.A., PH.D.; German international finance official; fmrly served in int. dept. of Deutsche Bundesbank; Asst. to German Exec. Dir. at IMF 1974–77; Alt. Exec. Dir. for Germany, IMF 1984–90, Exec. Dir. 1990–93. *Address:* c/o Ministry of Economics, Villemombler Strasse 76, P.O. Box 140260, 53113 Bonn, Germany.

GOPAL, Sarvepalli, M.A., D.PHIL., D.LITT.; Indian professor of history; b. 23 April 1923, Madras; s. of late Sir Sarvepalli Radhakrishnan (fmr. Pres. of India); ed. Univs. of Madras and Oxford; lecturer and reader in history, Andhra Univ., Waltair, 1948–52; Asst. Dir. Nat. Archives, New Delhi, 1952–54; Dir. Historical Div., Ministry of External Affairs, New Delhi, 1954–66; reader in S. Asian history, Oxford 1966–71; Fellow, St. Antony's Coll., Oxford 1966–95, Hon. Fellow 1995–; Prof. of Contemporary History, Jawaharlal Nehru Univ., New Delhi, 1971–83, Prof. Emer. 1983–; Chair. Nat. Book Trust of India 1973–76, Indian Inst. of Advanced Study 1992–, Madras Inst. of Devt. Studies 1995–97, Indian Inst. of Social Studies 1995–98; mem. Exec. Bd. of UNESCO 1976–80; Hon. D.Litt. (Andhra Univ.) 1975, (Sri Venkateswara Univ., Tirupati) 1979, (Banaras Univ.) 1984, (Hyderabad Univ.) 1993; Sahitya Akademi Award 1976; Corresp. Fellow, Royal

Historical Soc. 1980. *Publications include:* The Viceroyalty of Lord Ripon 1953, The Viceroyalty of Lord Irwin 1957, British Policy in India 1965, Jawaharlal Nehru (Vols. I, II and III), Radhakrishnan: A biography 1989. *Address:* 'Girija', 97 Radhakrishna Salai, Mylapore, Madras 600004, India (Home). *Telephone:* 044-842230.

GOPPEL, Michael; German European Union official; b. 3 Aug. 1936, Kaiserslautern; m. Isolde Hock 1963; three d.; ed. Univs. of Frankfurt and Munich; official, Comm. of EU 1965–; First Sec. Del. of EU, Washington, D.C. 1975–80; Deputy Head of Del. of EU to OECD, Paris 1980–82; Head, Del. of EU to Int. Orgs. Vienna 1982–88; Amb. and Head of Del. of EU in Austria 1988; Dir.-Gen. Euratom Supply Agency, Comm. of EU 1989–. *Leisure interests:* music, theatre, photography, hiking. *Address:* Commission of the European Communities, 200 rue de la Loi, MDB7/13, 1049 Brussels, Belgium. *Telephone:* (32-2) 295.55.86. *Fax:* (32-2) 295.05.27.

GORAI, Rt. Rev. Dinesh Chandra, B.A., B.D., D.D.; Indian ecclesiastic; b. 15 Jan. 1934, West Bengal; s. of Joyram and Sushila Gorai; m. Binapani Gorai 1962; two s.; ed. Calcutta Univ. and Serampore Coll.; ordained Priest as Methodist 1962; consecrated as Church of N. India Bishop 1970; Bishop of Barrackpore 1970–82, of Calcutta 1982; Moderator Church of North India 1983–86; social worker and rural devt. expert, ecumenical leader. *Address:* c/o Bishop's House, 51 Chowringhee Road, Calcutta 700 071, India.

GÖRANSSON, Bengt; Swedish politician; b. 25 July 1932, Stockholm; ed. Univ. of Stockholm; courier, Reso Ltd. (travel org.) 1960–71; Chair. Manilla School for the Deaf 1970–78; Head, Community Centre Asscn. 1971; Chair. of Bd. Nat. Theatre Centre 1974–82; mem. various official cttees.; Chair. of Bd. Fed. of Workers' Educational Asscns. 1980–82; Minister for Cultural Affairs 1982–89, Minister of Educ. and Cultural Affairs 1989–91; Chair. Ansvar Insurance Co. 1991–97, Int. Inst. of Alcohol Policy 1996–, Center for Biotechnology 1996–, Parl. Cttee. on Democracy 1997–. *Address:* ABF, P.O. Box 1305, 11183 Stockholm, Sweden.

GORBACHEV, Mikhail Sergeyevich; Russian politician; b. 2 March 1931, Privolnoye, Krasnogvardeisky Dist., Stavropol Territory; s. of Sergei Andreevich Gorbachev and Maria Panteleimonovna Gorbachev (née Gopcalo); m. Raisa Titarenko (now Gorbachev) 1953; one d.; ed. Faculty of Law, Moscow State Univ. and Stavropol Agricultural Inst.; began work as machine operator 1946; joined CPSU 1952; Deputy Head, Dept. of Propaganda, Stavropol Komsomol Territorial Cttee. 1955–56, Second, then First Sec. 1958–62; First Sec. Stavropol Komsomol City Cttee. 1956–58; Del. to CPSU Congress 1961, 1971, 1976, 1981, 1986, 1990; Party Organizer, Stavropol Territorial Production Bd. of Collective and State farms 1962; Head, Dept. of party bodies of CPSU Territorial Cttee. 1963–66; First Sec. Stavropol City Party Cttee. 1966–68; Second Sec. Stavropol Territorial CPSU Cttee. 1968–70, First Sec. 1970–78; mem. CPSU Cen. Cttee. 1971–91, Sec. for Agric. 1978–85, alt. mem. Political Bureau CPSU, Cen. Cttee. 1979–80, mem. 1980–91, Gen. Sec. CPSU Cen. Cttee. 1985–91; Deputy Supreme Soviet of U.S.S.R. 1970–89 (Chair. Foreign Affairs Comm., Soviet of the Union 1984–85), mem. Presidium 1985–88, Chair. 1988–89, Supreme Soviet of R.S.F.S.R. 1980–90, elected to Congress of People's Deputies of U.S.S.R. 1989, Chair. 1989–90; Pres. of U.S.S.R. 1990–91; Head Int. Foundation for Socio-Economic and Political Studies (Gorbachev Fund) 1992–; Head Int. Green Cross/Green Crescent 1993–; syndicated columnist for numerous leading newspapers worldwide 1992–; Nobel Peace Prize 1990; Jt. recipient Albert Schweitzer Leadership Award, Ronald Reagan Freedom Award 1992, Hon. Citizen of Berlin 1992; Freeman of Aberdeen 1993; Urania-Medaille (Berlin) 1996; Order of Lenin (three times), Orders of Red Banner of Labour, Badge of Honour and other medals. *Publications:* A Time for Peace 1985, The Coming Century of Peace 1986, Speeches and Writings 1986–90, Peace has no Alternative 1986, Moratorium 1986, Perestroika: New Thinking for Our Country and the World 1987, The August Coup (Its Cause and Results) 1991, December 1991: My Stand 1992, The Years of Hard Decisions 1993, Life and Reforms 1995. *Leisure interests:* literature, theatre, music, walking. *Address:* International Foundation for Socio-Economic and Political Studies, Leningradsky prosp. 49, 125468 Moscow, Russia. *Telephone:* (095) 943-99-90. *Fax:* (095) 943-95-94.

GORBUNOVS, Anatolijs; Latvian politician; b. 1942, Ludza Dist.; s. of Valerians Gorbunovs and Aleksandra Gorbunova (née Mekša); m. Lidija Klavina; one. s.; ed. Riga Polytech. Inst., Moscow Acad. of Social Sciences; constructor on a state farm; sr. Mechanic Riga Polytech. Inst. 1959–62; served Red Army 1962–65; various posts in the structure of the Latvian CP 1974–88; Chair. Supreme Council of Latvia 1988–93; Chair. of Saeima (Parl.) 1993–95; MP for Latvia's Way party; Chair. Saeima Cttee. on European Affairs Feb.–Aug. 1996; Minister of Environmental Protection and Regional Devt., Deputy Prime Minister 1996–; Chair. Latvian-Russian Intergovernmental Comm. 1996–. *Leisure interests:* hunting, gardening. *Address:* Ministry of Environmental Protection and Regional Development, 25 Peldu Street, 1494 Riga, Latvia (Office). *Telephone:* 702 6400 (Office). *Fax:* 782 0442 (Office).

GORCHAKOVA, Galina Vladimirovna; Russian opera singer (soprano); b. 28 Dec. 1963, Novokuznetsk; m. Nikolai Petrovich Mikhalsky; one s.; ed. Novosibirsk State Conservatory; soloist Sverdlovsk (now Yekaterinburg) Theatre of Opera and Ballet 1987–91, Kirov (now Mariinsky) Theatre 1991–96; leading roles in opera productions Madam Butterfly, Prince Igor, The Invisible City of Kitezh, Queen of Spades, Aida, Don Carlos, Tosca, Cavalleria Rusticana; regularly performs in European and American opera theatre including Covent Garden (debut Renata, The Fiery Angel by Prokofiev 1991), La Scala, Metropolitan Opera, Opera Bastille, also in Tokyo; Merited Artist of Russia. *Leisure interest:* travelling by car. *Address:* c/o Askonas Holt, Lonsdale Chambers, 27 Chancery Lane, London, WC2A 1PF, England. *Telephone:* 0171-400 1700.

GORCHAKOVSKY, Pavel Leonidovich; Russian biologist; b. 3 Jan. 1920; m.; one s.; ed. Siberian Inst. of Wood Tech.; Chair. Urals Inst. of Wood Tech. 1945–58; head of Lab. Inst. of Ecology of Plants and Animals Urals branch, U.S.S.R. Acad. of Sciences 1958–88; chief researcher; corresp. mem. U.S.S.R. (now Russian) Acad. of Sciences 1990, mem. 1994; research in ecology and geography of plants, genesis of flora, protection of environment; Merited Worker of Science. *Publications include:* Main problems of Historical Phytogeography of Urals 1969, Flora of High-mountain Urals 1975, numerous articles in scientific journals. Leisure interests: fiction, travel. *Address:* Institute of Ecology of Plants and Animals, Urals Branch of Russian Academy of Sciences, 8 March str. 202, 620219 Yekaterinburg, Russia. *Telephone:* (3432) 29-40-92 (Office); 55-23-85 (Home).

GORDEYEV, Vyacheslav Mikhailovich; Russian ballet dancer and choreographer; b. 3 Aug. 1948, Moscow; s. of Mikhail Gordeyev and L'ubov Gordeyeva; m. Maya Saidova 1987; one s. one d.; ed. Moscow State Univ., State Inst. of Theatrical Arts; leading dancer of Bolshoi Theatre 1968–87; mem. CPSU 1977–90; Founder and Dir. Russian State Ballet Theatre of Moscow 1990–95; Head, Ballet co. of Bolshoi Theatre 1995–97; First Prize Moscow Int. Ballet Competition 1973, U.S.S.R. People's Artist 1984. *Roles include:* Prince, Désiré (Tchaikovsky's Nutcracker, Sleeping Beauty), Romeo (Prokofiev's Romeo and Juliet), Spartacus, Ferhat (Melnikov's Legend of Love), Albert (Giselle), Basile (Minkus's Don Quixote). *Choreographic works:* Revived Pictures, Memory, Surprise Manoeuvres, or Wedding with the General, and more than 30 choreographic compositions; own versions of classical ballets Paquita, Don Quixote and Walpurghisnacht, Nutcracker 1993, Last Tango (Bolshoi Theatre) 1996. *Leisure interests:* classical music, athletics, tennis. *Address:* Tverskaya str. 9, Apt. 78, Moscow 103009, Russia. *Telephone:* (095) 229-13-36.

GORDIMER, Nadine, F.R.S.L.; South African writer; b. 20 Nov. 1923, South Africa; d. of Isidore Gordimer and Nan Myers; m. 2nd Reinhold Cassirer 1954; one s. one d.; ed. convent school; Hon. mem. American Acad. and Inst. of Arts and Letters, American Acad. of Arts and Sciences; Vice-Pres. Int. PEN, Officier Ordre des Arts et des Lettres 1987; mem. A.N.C. 1990–; Charles Eliot Norton Lecturer in Literature, Harvard Univ. 1994; Dr. h.c. (Cambridge) 1992, (Oxford) 1994; W. H. Smith Literary Award 1961, Thomas Pringle Award (English Acad. of S.A.) 1969, James Tait Black Memorial Prize 1971, Booker Prize (co-winner) 1974, Grand Aigle d'Or Prize (France) 1975, CNA Literary Award (S. Africa) 1974, 1979, 1981, 1991, Scottish Arts Council Neil M. Gunn Fellowship 1981, Modern Language Asscn. Award (U.S.A.) 1981, Premio Malaparte (Italy) 1985, Nelly Sachs Prize (Germany) 1985, Officier, Ordre des Arts et des Lettres 1986, Bennett Award (U.S.A.) 1987, Benson Medal (Royal Soc. of Literature) 1990, Nobel Prize for Literature 1991. *Publications:* The Soft Voice of the Serpent (stories), The Lying Days (novel) 1953, Six Feet of the Country (stories) 1956, A World of Strangers (novel) 1958, Friday's Footprint (stories) 1960, Occasion for Loving (novel) 1963, Not For Publication (stories) 1965, The Late Bourgeois World (novel) 1966, A Guest of Honour (novel) 1970, Livingstone's Companions (stories) 1972, The Black Interpreters (literary criticism) 1973, The Conservationist (novel) 1974, Selected Stories 1975, Some Monday for Sure (stories) 1976, Burger's Daughter 1979, A Soldier's Embrace (stories) 1980, July's People (novel) 1981, Something Out There (novella) 1984, Six Feet of Country (short stories) 1986, A Sport of Nature (novel) 1987, The Essential Gesture (essays) 1988, My Son's Story (novel) 1990, Jump (short stories) 1991, Crimes of Conscience (short stories) 1991, None to Accompany Me (novel) 1994, Writing and Being (lectures) 1995, The House Gun 1997; co-editor South African Writing Today 1967. *Address:* c/o A. P. Watt, 20 John Street, London, WC1N 2DR, England.

GORDON, Donald; South African business executive; b. 24 June 1930, Johannesburg; s. of Nathan Gordon and Sheila Gordon; m. Peggy Cowan 1958; two s. one d.; ed. King Edward VII School, Johannesburg; C.A. and auditor Kessel Feinstein 1955–57, now partner; founder Liberty Life Asscn. of Africa Ltd., Chair. and C.E.O. 1957–; Chair. Liberty Holdings Ltd. 1968–, Liberty Investors Ltd. 1971–, First Int. Trust Ltd. 1977–, Guardian Nat. Insurance Co. Ltd. 1980–, TransAtlantic Holdings PLC (UK) 1981–, Capital & Counties plc (UK) 1982–, The Continental & Industrial Trust PLC (UK) 1986–; Deputy Chair. Standard Bank Investment Corp. Ltd. 1979–, Premier Group Holdings Ltd. 1983–; Dir. Guardbank Man. Corpn. Ltd. 1969–, Guardian Royal Exchange Assurance PLC (UK) 1971–94, The South African Breweries Ltd. 1982–, Charter Life Insurance Co. Ltd. 1985–, Beverage & Consumer Industry Holdings Ltd. 1989–, GFSA Holdings Ltd. 1990–94, Sun Life Corpn. PLC (UK) 1992–; Hon. D.Econ.Sc. (Witwatersrand) 1991; Financial Mail Businessman of the Year 1965; Sunday Times Man of the Year 1969; Business Statesman Award (Harvard Business School). *Leisure interest:* tennis. *Address:* Liberty Life Association of Africa Ltd., P.O. Box 10499, Johannesburg, South Africa 2000. *Telephone:* 011-408-2100. *Fax:* 011-403-3171.

GORDON, Douglas, M.A.; British artist; b. 20 Sept. 1966, Glasgow; s. of James Gordon and Mary Clements Gordon (née McDougall); ed. Glasgow

School of Art, Slade School of Art; works in painting, installation and film; works include List of Names, Something Between My Mouth and Your Ear, 24 Hour Psycho, Hysterical, The Confessions of a Justified Sinner; contrib. to The British Art Show and Spellbound 1996; Turner Prize 1996. *Address:* c/o Lisson Gallery, 67 Lisson Street, London, NW1 5DA, England.

GORDON, Pamela; Bermudan politician; d. of E. F. Gordon; fmr. Minister of the Environment; Leader United Bermuda Party; Prime Minister of Bermuda 1997–98. *Address:* c/o United Bermuda Party, Central Office, 87 John F. Burrows Building, Chancery Lane, P.O. Box HM 715, Hamilton, HM CX, Bermuda.

GORDON, William Edwin, PH.D.; American radio physicist; b. 8 Jan. 1918, Paterson, N.J.; s. of William and Mary Scott Gordon; m. Elva Freile 1941; one s. one d.; ed. Montclair State Coll., N.J. and New York and Cornell Univs.; Assoc. Prof. Cornell Univ. 1953–59, Prof. 1959–65, Walter R. Read Prof. of Eng. 1965–66; Dir. Arecibo Ionospheric Observatory, Puerto Rico 1960–66 (conceived and directed construction of world's largest antenna reflector); Prof. of Electrical Eng. and Space Physics and Astronomy, Rice Univ. 1966–86, Dean of Eng. and Science 1966–75, Vice-Pres. 1969–72, Dean, School of Natural Sciences 1975–80, Provost and Vice-Pres. 1980–86, Distinguished Prof. Emer. 1986–; Foreign Sec., N.A.S. 1986–90; Chair. Bd. of Trustees, Upper Atmosphere Research Corpn. 1971–72, 1973–78; Pres. Taping for the Blind, Houston 1993–97; Vice-Pres. Int. Union of Radio Science 1975–78, Senior Vice-Pres. 1978–81, Pres. 1981–85, Hon. Pres. 1990–; Bd. of Trustees and Exec. Cttee. Univ. Corpn. for Atmospheric Research 1975–81, Vice-Chair. Bd. of Trustees 1977–78, Chair. 1978–81, Trustee 1975–81, 1986–89, 1991–92; Bd. of Trustees, Cornell Univ. 1976–80; mem. Arecibo Observatory Advisory Bd. 1977–80, 1990–93; mem. N.A.S., A.A.A.S., Nat. Acad. of Eng., Foreign Assoc. Acad. of Eng. Japan; mem. Int. Council of Scientific Unions 1981, Vice-Pres. 1988–93; Councillor American Meteorological Soc.; Fellow, American Geophysical Union, Inst. of Electrical and Electronic Engineers, Guggenheim Fellow 1972–73; Hon. D.S. (Austin Coll.) 1978; Balth Van der Pol Gold Medal for distinguished research in radio sciences 1966, 50th Anniversary Medal of American Meteorological Soc. 1970, Arktowski Medal 1984, U.S.S.R. Medal Geophysics 1985. *Publications:* numerous articles in learned journals. *Leisure interests:* sailing, swimming, music. *Address:* c/o Department of Space Physics, Rice University, P.O. Box 1892, Houston, TX 77251, U.S.A. *Telephone:* (713) 527-6020.

GORE, Albert, Jr.; American politician; b. 31 March 1948; s. of the late Albert and Pauline (LaFon) Gore; m. Mary E. Aitcheson 1970; one s. three d.; ed. Harvard and Vanderbilt Univs.; investigative reporter, editorial writer, The Tennessean 1971–76; home-builder and land developer, Tanglewood Home Builders Co. 1971–76; livestock and tobacco farmer 1973–; Head Community Enterprise Bd. 1993–; mem. House of Reps. 1977–79; Senator from Tennessee 1985–93; Vice-Pres. of U.S.A. Jan. 1993–; Dr. h.c. (Harvard) 1994, (New York) 1998; Democrat. *Publication:* Earth in the Balance 1992. *Address:* Office of the Vice-President, The White House, Old Executive Office Building, N.W., Washington, DC 20501, U.S.A.

GORE, Frederick John Pym, C.B.E., R.A.; British painter; b. 8 Nov. 1913; s. of Spencer Frederick Gore and Mary Joanna (née Kerr) Gore; ed. Lancing Coll. and Trinity Coll., Oxford, Ruskin, Westminster and Slade Schools of Art; war service 1939–45; taught at Westminster School of Art 1937, Chelsea and Epsom 1947, St. Martin's 1946–79, Head of Painting Dept. 1951–79, Vice-Prin. 1961–79; one-man exhbns. at Galerie Borghèse, Paris 1938, Redfern Gallery 1937, 1949, 1950, 1953, 1956, 1962, Mayor Gallery 1958, 1960, Juster Gallery, New York 1963, Royal Acad., Retrospective 1989; Chair. R.A. exhbns. cttee. 1976-87; Trustee Imperial War Museum 1967–84. *Publications:* Abstract Art 1956, Painting, Some Principles 1965, Piero della Francesca's 'The Baptism' 1969. *Leisure interest:* Russian folk dancing. *Address:* Flat 3, 35 Elm Park Gardens, London, SW10 9QF, England. *Telephone:* 0171-352 4940.

GÓRECKI, Henryk Mikołaj; Polish composer; b. 6 Dec. 1933, Czernica, near Rybnik; s. of Otylia Górecka and Roman Górecki; m. Jadwiga Górecka 1959; one s. one d.; studied composition at State Higher School of Music, Katowice, under B. Szabelski; Docent, Faculty of Composition, State Higher School of Music, Katowice, Rector 1975–79, Extraordinary Prof. 1977–79; Symphony No. 3 (threnodies for soprano and orchestra) 1976 (more than 700,000 records sold); Dr. h.c. (Acad. of Catholic Theology, Warsaw) 1993, (Warsaw Univ.) 1994, (American Catholic Univ., Washington, D.C.) 1995, (Ann Arbor Univ., Mich.) 1996, (Concordia Univ., Montreal) 1998; First Prize, Young Composers' Competition, Warsaw, for Monologhi 1960, Paris Youth Biennale, for 1st Symphony 1961; Prize, UNESCO Int. Tribune for Composers for Refrain 1967, for Ad Matrem 1973; First Prize, Composers' Competition, Szczecin, for Kantata 1968; Prize of Union of Polish Composers 1970, of Cttee. for Polish Radio and TV 1974, of Minister of Culture and Arts 1965, 1969, 1973; State Prize 1st class for Ad Matrem and Nicolaus Copernicus Symphony 1976. *Address:* ul. H. A. Górnika 4 m.1, 40-133 Katowice, Poland. *Telephone:* (32) 58 17 58.

GORENSHTEIN, Fridrikh Naumovich; Russian writer; b. 18 March 1932; scriptwriter for Solaris (by A. Tarkovsky) 1972; most of works were not published in U.S.S.R.; emigrated to W. Germany 1980; wrote for émigré magazines; since late 1980s most of stories and novels published in Russia. *Publications:* Redemption (novel), 1984; Psalom (novel 1986; Doleful Novel 1993, Stories of Chok-chok, Old Woman, Last Summer on the Volga, Winter of 1953, Spark, The Day Left over the Abyss and others; plays Infanticide, Arguments about Dostoyevsky; Collected Works (3 vols.) 1991. *Address:* Sachsische Str. 73, 10707 Berlin, Germany. *Telephone:* (30) 861 6999.

GORENSTEIN, Mark Borisovich; Russian conductor; b. 16 Sept. 1946, Odessa, Ukraine; m. 2nd; one s.; ed. Chişinău State Conservatory as violinist, Novosibirsk State Conservatory as conductor; violinist with Bolshoi Theatre Orchestra 1973–75; State Academic Symphony Orchestra 1975–84; Chief Conductor and Artistic Dir., MAV Orchestra, Budapest, Hungary 1985–88; Chief Conductor, Pusan City Symphony Orchestra, South Korea 1989–91; f., Chief Conductor and Artistic Dir. Russian State Symphony Orchestra (RSSO) Young Russia 1992–. *Address:* Rublevskoye shosse 28, apt. 25, 121609 Moscow, Russia (Home). *Telephone:* (095) 414 5203 (Home). *Fax:* (095) 414 5023 (Home).

GORETTA, Claude; Swiss film director; b. 23 June 1929, Geneva. *Films include:* Le fou 1970, Le jour des noces 1971, L'invitation 1973, The Wonderful Crook 1976, The Lacemaker 1977, Bonheur toi-même 1980, The Girl from Lorraine 1981, The Death of Mario Ricci 1983, Orpheus 1985, Si le soleil ne revenait pas 1987. *Address:* 10 Tour de Boël, 1204 Geneva, Switzerland.

GORIN, Grigory Izraylevich; Russian playwright; b. 12 March 1940, Moscow; s. of Israel and Frida Ofstein; m. Lyubov Pavlovna Kereselidze 1966; ed. First Moscow Inst. of Medicine; worked as ambulance physician 1963–69; concurrently wrote short stories, topical satire, plays; freelance, mem. Union of Writers 1968–; author of 13 plays; Merited Worker of Arts of Russia; Golden Ostap Prize. *Plays include:* To Forget Herostratus 1970, That Munchhausen 1974, Goodbye, compere 1975, Funeral Pray 1989, Kin IY 1991, Royal Games 1995; many plays were first staged by M. Zakharov in theatre and TV (Formula of Love, The House That Swift Built), by E. Ryazanov (Say a Word about the Poor Hussar), by A. Gabrilovich (Andrei). *Publications:* I Want Kharcho (short stories) 1966, Comic Fantasy 1986, Formula of Love 1992, The House That Swift Built 1996, Plague on Both Your Houses 1997, Schastlivtsev and Neschastlivtsev 1998, Balakirev the Fool 1999, Collected Works (2 vols.) 1999. *Leisure interest:* fishing. *Address:* Leningradsky prospekt 60A, Apt. 43, 125167 Moscow, Russia. *Telephone:* (095) 151 4433 (Home). *Fax:* (095) 151 4433.

GOR'KOV, Lev Petrovich, PH.D., D.PHYS.SC.; Russian physicist; b. 14 June 1929, Moscow; s. of Petr Ivanovich Gorkov and Antonina Grigor'evna Gorkova; m. Donara Chernikova 1965; two s. (one d. from 1st marriage); ed. Moscow Inst. of Mechanics; jr. then sr. researcher Inst. of Physical Problems 1953–64; Head of Sector Inst. of Chemical Physics 1964–65; Head of Sector L. D. Landau Inst. of Theoretical Physics 1965–88, Deputy Dir. 1988–91; Prof. and Dept. Head, Inst. for Physics and Tech. 1965–92; Theory Program Dir. and Prof., Nat. High Magnetic Field Lab., Fla. State Univ. 1992–; main research on concept of order parameter in microscopic theory of superconductivity, phenomenon of gapless superconductivity, microscopic derivation of Ginzburg-Landau equations for superconductors and superconducting alloys, thermodynamic diagrammatic technique, electron localization by disorder in one and two dimensions, theory of organic conductors; Fellow Russian Acad. of Sciences, American Physical Soc.; Foreign Hon. mem. American Acad. of Art and Science; Dr. h.c. (N.Y. City Univ., Univ. of Illinois); Lenin's Prize, L. D. Landau Prize, Bardeen Prize in Superconductivity. *Publications:* Methods of Quantum Field Theory in Statistical Physics 1962, Superconducting Properties and Structural Transitions in Compounds with A-15 Lattice 1976, Physical Phenomena in New Organic Superconductors 1984, Phase Stratification of Liquid in New Superconductors 1987, Superconductivity in Heavy Fermion Systems 1987, articles in scientific journals. *Address:* National High-Magnetic Field Laboratory, Florida State University, 1800 E. Paul Dirac Drive, Tallahassee, FL 32310, U.S.A. *Telephone:* (850) 644-4187 (Office); (095) 137-32-44 (Moscow). *Fax:* (850) 644-5038.

GORMAN, Joseph Tolle, B.A., LL.B.; American business executive; b. 1937, Rising Sun, Ind.; m. Bettyann Gorman; ed. Kent State Univ. and Yale Univ.; Assoc. Baker, Hostetler & Patterson, Cleveland 1962–67; Legal Dept. TRW Inc., Cleveland 1968–69, Asst. Sec. 1969–70, Sec. 1970–72, Vice-Pres. Sr. Counsel, Automotive Worldwide Operations 1972–73, Vice-Pres. Asst. Gen. Counsel 1973–76, Vice-Pres. Gen. Counsel 1976–80, Exec. Vice-Pres. Industrial and Energy Sector 1980–84, Exec. Vice-Pres., Asst. Pres. 1984–85, Chair., Pres. and C.O.O. 1985–91, Chair., C.E.O. 1991–; mem. Bd. of Dirs. Soc. Corpn., Soc. Nat. Bank, Cleveland, Standard Oil Co.; mem. Council on Foreign Relations and other public appts.; Japan Prime Minister's Trade Award 1994. *Address:* TRW Inc., 1900 Richmond Road, Cleveland, OH 44124, U.S.A. *Fax:* (212) 334-2463.

GORMAN, William Moore, B.A., F.B.A.; British professor of economics; b. 17 June 1923, Kesh, Co. Fermanagh, Northern Ireland; s. of the late Richard Gorman and Sarah Crawford Gorman (née Moore); m. Dorinda Maud Scott 1950; ed. Mount Temple School, Dublin, Foyle Coll., Derry and Trinity Coll. Dublin; Rating, then Petty Officer, R.N. 1943–46; Asst. Lecturer, Lecturer then Sr. Lecturer in charge, Dept. of Econometrics and Social Statistics, Birmingham Univ. 1949–61; Prof. of Econs., Oxford Univ. and Prof. Fellow of Nuffield Coll. 1962–67; Prof. of Econs., L.S.E. 1967–79; Official Fellow, Nuffield Coll., Oxford 1979–84, Sr. Research Fellow 1984–90, Emer. Fellow 1990–; Visiting Prof. at various U.S. univs. between 1956 and 1980; Hon. D.Soc.Sc. (Birmingham) 1973, Hon. D.Sc. (Southampton) 1974, Hon.

D.Econ.Sc. (Nat. Univ. of Ireland) 1986; Fellow Econometric Soc. (Pres. 1972); Hon. Foreign mem. American Acad. of Arts and Sciences 1986; Hon. Foreign mem. American Econ. Asscn. 1987; mem. Acad. Europaea 1990; Hon. Fellow Trinity Coll. Dublin 1990, London School of Econs. 1993. *Publications:* Collected Papers, Vol. I 1995, articles in various econ. periodicals. *Leisure interests:* talking and reading. *Address:* c/o Nuffield College, Oxford, OX1 1NF, England (Office); Moorfield, Fountainstown, Myrtleville, Co. Cork, Republic of Ireland (Home). *Telephone:* (01865) 278605 (Office); (021) 831174 (Myrtleville).

GORMLEY, Antony, O.B.E., M.A., D.F.A.; British sculptor; b. 30 Aug. 1950, London; s. of Arthur J. C. Gormley and Elsbeth Brauninger; m. Vicken Parsons 1980; two s. one d.; ed. Ampleforth Coll., Trinity Coll., Cambridge, Cen. School of Arts and Crafts, London, Goldsmiths' Coll., Univ. of London and Slade School of Fine Arts, London; one-man exhbns. Whitechapel Art Gallery, London 1981, Coracle Press Gallery London 1983, Salvatore Ala, New York, Riverside Studios, London, Salvatore Ala Gallery, Milan and Chapter Gallery, Cardiff 1984; Salvatore Ala, New York, Frankfurt Kunstverein, Regensburg Städtisches Museum, Salvatore Ala, Milan 1985, Victoria Miro, London 1986, Serpentine Gallery, London, Salvatore Ala, New York, Seibu Contemporary Arts, Tokyo, Le Criée, Rennes 1987, Burnett Miller, L.A. 1988, Contemporary Sculpture Centre, Tokyo 1988, Leeds City Art Gallery 1988, Louisiana Museum, Denmark 1989, Salvatore Ala, N.Y. 1989, Scottish Nat. Gallery of Modern Art, Edin. 1989, Art Gallery of N.S.W., Australia 1989; Galerie Isy et Christine Brachot, Brussels, Galerie Nordenhake, Stockholm, Modern Art Museum, Fort Worth, Tex. 1991, Centro Cultural Arte Contemporáneo, Mexico City, San Diego Museum of Contemporary Art, La Jolla, Calif., Burnett Miller, L.A., Contemporary Sculpture Centre, Tokyo, Learning to Think, British School, Rome 1992, Field, Corcoran Gallery, Washington and Montreal Museum of Fine Arts, Oktagon, Stuttgart, Galerie Thaddeus Ropac, Paris and Salzburg, Konsthall Malmo, Tate Gallery, Liverpool, Galerie Nordenhake, Stockholm 1993, Irish Museum of Modern Art, Moderna Galerija, Ljubljana, White Cube, London, Muzej Suvremene Umjetnosti, Zagreb, Ludwig Museum, Budapest, Oriel Mostyn, Llandudno, Galeria Pedro Oliveira, Porto 1994, Prague Castle, Prague, Sala Ronda, Bucharest, Orchard Gallery, Derry, Ikon Gallery, Birmingham, Nat. Gallery of Wales, Cardiff, Kohji Ogura Gallery, Nagoya, Pace Roberts Foundation for Contemporary Art, San Antonio, StadtRaum Remise, Vienna 1995, Obala Art Centar, Sarajevo, Galerie Xavier Hufkens, Brussels, Arts 04, St. Rémy de Provence, Hayward Gallery, London, Museum of Modern Art, Kamakura 1996 (then touring Japan 1996–97), Koelnischer Kunstverein, Cologne, Kunsthalle, Kiel, Galerie Nordenhake, Stockholm, Cuxhaven, Germany, Herning Museum, Denmark 1997, Jablonka Galerie, Cologne, Royal Acad., London, Stavanger, Norway, Rupertinum, Salzburg 1998; has participated in numerous group exhbns. in Europe, N. America, Japan, Brazil, Russia, Australia and N.Z.; works in collections of Tate Gallery, London, Scottish Nat. Galley of Modern Art, Moderna Museet, Stockholm, Neue Museum, Kassel, Victoria and Albert Museum, London, British Council, Arts Council of G.B., Art Gallery of N.S.W., Sydney, Leeds City Art Galleries, Modern Art Museum of Fort Worth, Louisiana Museum of Modern Art, Humblebaek, Denmark, Irish Museum of Modern Art, Dublin, Sapporo Sculpture Park, Japan; sculpture in public places: Out of the Dark, Martinsplatz, Kassel 1987, Open Space, Place Jean Monnet, Rennes 1993, Iron: Man, Vic. Square, Birmingham 1994, Havmann, Mo I Rana, Norway 1995, Angel of the North, Gateshead 1998; Hon. Fellow Goldsmith's Coll., Univ. of London 1998; Dr. h.c. (Univ. of Cen. England, Birmingham) 1998; Turner Prize 1994. *Leisure interests:* walking, talking. *Address:* 153A Bellenden Road, London, SE15 4DH (Studio); 13 South Villas, London, NW1 9BS, England (Home). *Telephone:* 0171-639 1303 (Studio); 0171-482-7383 (Home). *Fax:* 0171-639 2674 (Studio); 0171-267 8336 (Home).

GORMLY, Allan Graham, C.B.E.; British business executive and accountant; b. 18 Dec. 1937, Paisley, Scotland; s. of William Gormly and Christina Swinton Flockhart; m. Vera Margaret Grant 1962; one s. one d.; ed. Paisley Grammar School; with Peat Marwick Mitchell & Co. 1956–61, Rootes Group 1961–65; joined John Brown PLC, apptd. Chief Exec. 1983, Dir. Trafalgar House PLC (when it acquired John Brown PLC) 1986–95, C.E.O. 1992–94; Deputy Chair. Royal Insurance Holdings PLC 1992–93, Chair. 1994–96 (mem. Bd. 1990–96), Deputy Chair. Royal and Sun Alliance Insurance Group PLC 1996–98; Chair. BPB PLC 1997– (Dir. 1995–); Chair. Overseas Projects Bd. 1989–91; Deputy Chair. Export Guarantees Advisory Council 1990–92; Dir. Brixton Estate PLC 1994–, European Capital Co. 1996–, Bank of Scotland 1997–; Dir. (non-exec.) Nat. Grid. Co. 1994–95; mem. British Overseas Trade Bd. 1989–91, Top Salaries Review Body 1990–92. *Leisure interest:* golf. *Address:* 56 North Park, Gerrards Cross, Bucks., SL9 8JR, England (Home). *Telephone:* (01753) 885079 (Home).

GORTON, Rt. Hon. Sir John Grey, P.C., G.C.M.G., A.C., C.H., M.A.; Australian politician (retd.); b. 9 Sept. 1911, Melbourne; s. of J. R. Gorton; m. 1st Bettina Brown 1935 (died 1983); two s. one d.; m. 2nd Nancy Home 1993; ed. Geelong Grammar School and Brasenose Coll., Oxford; served R.A.A.F. during Second World War; Councillor Kerang Shire 1947–52, and Pres. of Shire; Senator for State of Victoria 1949–68, Govt. Leader in Senate 1967–68; Minister for Navy 1958–63; Minister Assisting Minister for External Affairs 1960–63; Minister-in-Charge CSIRO 1962–68; Minister for Works and under-Prime Minister, Minister-in-Charge of Commonwealth Activities in Educ. and Research 1963–66; Minister for Interior 1963–64, for Works 1966–67; Minister for Educ. and Science 1966–68; Prime Minister of Australia 1968–71; Minister of Defence and Deputy Leader of Liberal Party March–Aug. 1971; mem. Parl. Liberal Party Exec.; Spokesman on Environment and Conservation, Urban & Regional Devt.; Deputy Chair. of Jt. Parl. Cttee. on Prices 1973–74; mem. House of Reps. 1968–75; fmrly. Liberal; Independent May-Nov. 1975. *Leisure interests:* reading, gardening. *Address:* 32 Parsley Road, Vaucluse, N.S.W. 2030, Australia.

GORTON, Slade; American politician and lawyer; b. 8 Jan. 1928, Chicago, Ill.; m. Sally Clark 1958; one s. two d.; ed. Evanston High School, Ill., Dartmouth Columbia Univ. Law School; U.S Army 1945–46, U.S.A.F. 1953–56, presently Col. U.S.A.F. Reserve; admitted to Bar, Wash. State 1953; mem. Wash. State House of Reps. 1958–68, Majority Leader 1967–68; Wash. State Attorney-Gen. 1968–80; Senator from Washington State 1981–87, 1989–; Partner Davis, Wright and Jones, Seattle 1987–89; mem. Wash. State Law and Justice Comm. 1969–80 (Chair. 1969–70), State Criminal Justice Training Comm. 1969–80 (Chair. 1969–76), Pres.'s Consumer Advisory Council 1975–77, Nat. Asscn. of Attorneys-Gen. 1969–80 (Pres. 1976–77); Wyman Award 1980; Republican. *Address:* US Senate, 730 Hart Senate Building, Washington, DC 20510, U.S.A.

GORYSZEWSKI, Henryk Józef, LL.D.; Polish politician and lawyer; b. 20 Jan. 1941, Drążewo; m.; two d.; ed. Warsaw Univ.; scientific worker, Faculty of Law, Warsaw Univ.; expert on transport org., worked in various research insts. and state offices; Dir. Legal Dept. of Ministry of Transport 1989–91; mem. and co-founder, Christian Nat. Union (ZChN) 1989–, Deputy Pres. ZChN Gen. Bd. 1990–96; Deputy to Sejm (Parl.) 1991–93, 1997–; Chair. Parl. Comm. for Econ. Policy, Budget and Finance 1991–93, for Public Finance 1997–; Deputy Chair. of Council of Ministers (responsible for econ. matters) 1992–93; Sec. of State in Chancellery of Pres., Sec. Cttee. of Nat. Security; Chair. of Nat. Security Office 1994–95. *Address:* Sejm RP, ul. Wiejska 4/6/8, 00-902 Warsaw, Poland. *Telephone:* (22) 694-10-42; 694-14-21. *Fax:* (22) 694-19-40.

GOSLING, Sir Donald, Kt.; British business executive; b. 2 March 1929; m. Elizabeth Shauna Ingram 1959 (divorced 1988); three s.; joined R.N. 1944, served on H.M.S. Leander; Jt. Chair. Nat. Car Parks Ltd. 1950–; Chair. Palmer & Harvey 1967–; Chair. Council of Man. White Ensign Asscn. Ltd. 1978–83, Vice-Pres. 1983–93, Pres. 1993– (mem. 1970–); mem. Exec. Cttee. Imperial Soc. of Kts. Bachelor 1977–; Chair. Berkeley Square Ball Trust 1982–, Mountbatten Memorial Hall Appeals Cttee. 1980; Vice-Pres. King George's Fund for Sailors 1993–; Hon. Capt. R.N.R. 1993–; Trustee Fleet Air Arm Museum, Yeovilton 1974–, Royal Yachting Asscn. Seamanship Foundation 1981–; Patron Submarine Memorial Appeal 1978–, H.M.S. Ark Royal Welfare Trust 1986–. *Leisure interests:* swimming, sailing, shooting. *Address:* National Car Parks Limited, P.O. Box 4N1, 21 Bryanston Street, London, W1A 4NH, England. *Telephone:* 0171-499 7050.

GOSLING, Justin Cyril Bertrand, B.PHIL., M.A.; British philosopher; b. 26 April 1930, Wolverhampton; s. of Vincent Gosling and Dorothy Gosling; m. Margaret Clayton 1958; two s. two d.; ed. Ampleforth Coll. and Wadham Coll. Oxford; Fereday Fellow, St. John's Coll., Oxford 1955–58; Lecturer in Philosophy, Pembroke and Wadham Colls., Oxford 1958–60; Fellow in Philosophy, St. Edmund Hall, Oxford 1960–82, Prin. 1982–96; Sr. Proctor, Oxford Univ. 1977–78; Barclay Acheson Prof. Macalester Coll., Minn., U.S.A. 1964; Visiting Research Fellow, Australian Nat. Univ., Canberra 1970. *Publications:* Pleasure and Desire 1969, Plato 1973, Plato, Philebus 1975, The Greeks on Pleasure (with C. C. W. Taylor) 1982, Weakness of the Will 1990. *Address:* Joymount, Northcourt Lane, Abingdon, OX14 1QA, England. *Telephone:* (01235) 523310.

GOSS, Richard John; South African chartered accountant; b. 8 July 1928, Cape Town; s. of John Archer Goss; m. Myrtle Atherstone 1955; one s. two d.; ed. Rondebosch Boys' High School; joined S.A. Breweries as Man. Accountant, Head Office, Johannesburg 1952, Chief Accountant 1954–57, Asst. Admin. Man. 1957–60, Group Commercial Man. 1960–64; attended Harvard Business School, U.S.A. 1964; Gen. Man., Beer Div., S.A. Breweries 1965–67, Group Man. Dir. 1967–83; Chair. Kersaf Investments Ltd. 1983–89; Deputy Chair. Nedcor 1996–, Old Mutual 1997–; Dir. Safren. *Leisure interests:* game conservation, tennis. *Address:* P.O. Box 163, Constantia 7848, South Africa. *Telephone:* (021) 794 2225.

GOTCHEV, Dimitar; Bulgarian judge; b. 27 Feb. 1936, Sofia; s. of Maj.-Gen. Boncho Gotchev and Zdravka Gotchev; m. Jova Gotcheva-Cholakova 1976; one d.; ed. Univ. of Sofia St. Kliment Ochridsky; legal adviser 1959–66; Arbiter, State Court of Arbitration 1966–89; Judge, Supreme Court 1990, Judge, Head of Commercial Div. 1990–, Deputy Chief Justice, Supreme Court 1993–; Judge, Constitutional Court 1994–; Judge, European Court of Human Rights, Strasbourg 1992–98. *Address:* Constitutional Court of Republic of Bulgaria, Bul. Dondoukov 1, 1202 Sofia (Office); Koslodui Str. N34, 1202 Sofia, Bulgaria (Home). *Telephone:* 87.91.49 (Office); 31.54.25 (Home).

GÖTHE, (Lars) Staffan; Swedish playwright, actor and director; b. 20 Dec. 1944, Luleå; s. of late Thorsten Göthe and of Margit Grape-Göthe; m. Kristin Byström 1969; one s.; ed. Acad. of Performing Arts, Gothenburg; actor and playwright, regional theatre of Växjö 1971, Folkteatern, Gothenburg 1974; Headmaster Acad. of Performing Arts, Malmö 1976; actor, Folkteatern, Gävleborg 1983; Dir. The RTC Co. 1986–95; actor and playwright, Royal

Dramatic Theatre, Stockholm 1995–. *Publications:* En natt i februari 1972, Den gråtande polisen 1980, La strada dell'amore 1986, En uppstoppad hund 1986, Den perfekta Kyssen 1990, Arma Irma 1991, Boogie Woogie 1992, Blått Hus Med Röda Kinder 1995, Ruben Pottas Eländiga Salonger 1996. *Address:* Vindragarvägen 8, 117 50 Stockholm, Sweden. *Telephone:* 08/668 38 18 (Stockholm).

GOTLIEB, Allan Ezra, C.C., B.C.L., M.A., LL.B.; Canadian diplomatist; b. 28 Feb. 1928, Winnipeg; s. of David Phillip and Sarah (née Schiller) Gotlieb; m. Sondra Kaufman 1955; one s. two d.; ed. Univ. of Calif., Univ. of Oxford, Harvard Univ.; joined Dept. of External Affairs 1957; Asst. Under-Sec. of State for External Affairs and Legal Adviser 1967–68; Deputy Minister of Communications 1968–73, of Manpower and Immigration 1973–76; Chair. Employment and Immigration Comm. 1976–77; Under-Sec. of State for External Affairs 1977–81; Amb. to U.S.A. 1981–89; Visiting Prof. of Canadian Studies, Harvard Univ. 1989; Chair. Canada Council 1989–94, Donner Canadian Foundation 1996–; Claude Bissell Visiting Prof., Univ. of Toronto 1989–90; Co-Chair. of Bd. and Hon. Co-Publr. Saturday Night Magazine 1989–; Chair. Ont. Heritage Foundation 1998–; Dir. numerous cos.; Addison-Browne Prize in Private Int. Law, Harvard Law School 1954; Deak Prize, American Soc. of Int. Law 1974, Elise and Walter A. Haas Int. Award 1985. *Publications:* Disarmament and International Law 1965, Canadian Treaty-Making 1968, Human Rights, Federalism and Minorities 1970, Impact of Technology on International Law 1982, I'll Be With You in a Minute, Mr Ambassador 1990. *Address:* Suite 5300, Commerce Court West, Toronto, Ont., M5L 1B9, Canada. *Telephone:* (416) 869-5664. *Fax:* (416) 947-0866.

GOTODA, Masaharu; Japanese politician; b. 9 Aug. 1914; ed. Tokyo Univ.; mem. House of Reps. 1976–; with Ministry of Home Affairs 1939; Chief Sec., Home Affairs Ministry, 1959, Dir., Local Tax Bureau 1959–62; Sec.-Gen. Nat. Police Agency 1962–63, Dir. of Security Bureau 1963–65, Dir.-Gen. 1969–72; Deputy Chief Cabinet Sec. 1972–73; Minister of Home Affairs 1979–80; Chief Cabinet Sec. 1982–83, 1985–87; Dir.-Gen. Nat. Public Safety Comm. 1979–80, Hokkaido Devt. Agency 1979–80, Admin. Man. Agency 1983–84, Man. Co-ordination Agency 1984–85; Minister of Justice 1992–93; Deputy Prime Minister Aug.–April 1993.

GOTT, Karel; Czech singer; b. 14 July 1939, Plzeň; two d.; ed. Prague Conservatory (studied under Prof. Karenin); mem. Semafor Theatre, Prague 1963–65; mem. Apollo Theatre, Prague, 1965–67; freelance artist 1967–; numerous foreign tours; charity concerts with Eva Urbanová 1998; f. and Chair. Interpo Foundation 1993–96; Golden Nightingale trophy (annual pop singer poll 1963–66, 1968–81, 1983, 1989–90, 1996–97), MIDEM Prize, Cannes 1967, MIDEM Gold Record 1969, Polydor Gold Record 1970, Supraphon Gold Record 1972, 1973, 1979, 1980, 1996, Music Week "star of the year 1974" (UK) 1975, Artist of Merit 1982, "Gold Aerial 1983", radio station BRT (Belgium) 1984, Nat. Artist 1985, Polydor Golden Pin (Germany) 1986, Czech Nightingale Trophy 1996, 1997, Czech TV Prize 1997, Platinum Record (for duets with Lucia Bílá) 1998 and many other awards. *Address:* Nad Bertramkou 18, 150 00 Prague 5, Czech Republic (Home).

GÖTTE, Klaus, DR.JUR.; German business executive; b. 22 April 1932, Diepholz; s. of Heinrich and Anneliese (née Engel) Götte; m. Grazia Michaela Elsaesser 1958; one s. two d.; ed. Göttingen; Man. Bankhaus C.G. Trinkhaus, Düsseldorf 1955–68, Fried. Krupp GmbH, Essen 1968–72; mem. Bd. of Man., Allianz Versicherungs-AG, Munich, and Allianz Lebensversicherungs-AG, Stuttgart 1972–80; Man. Partner, Friedrich Flick Industrieverwaltung KGaA, Düsseldorf 1980–82; Chair. Bd. Man. Dirs. MAN Aktiengesellschaft (fmrly. Gutehoffnungshütte Aktienverein), Munich 1983–96, Chair. Supervisory Bd. 1996–; Chair. Sup. Bd. P.W.A. 1995–. *Address:* Ungererstrasse 69, 80805 Munich, Germany. *Telephone:* 089-360980.

GOTTLIEB, Paul, B.A.; American publishing company executive; b. 16 Jan. 1935, New York; s. of Vitaly Matthew and Liza (Rabinowitz) Gottlieb; m. 1st Linda Ellen Salzman 1960 (divorced 1989); two s.; m. 2nd Elisabeth Lohman Scharlatt 1990; one step-s.; ed. Swarthmore Coll.; literary agent with William Morris Agency, New York 1956–57, 1959–60; Asst. to Pres. Omni Products Corpn., New York 1960–62; with American Heritage Publishing Co. Inc., New York 1962–75, Pres. 1970–75; Pres. Paul Gottlieb Assocs. Inc. 1975–, Thames and Hudson Inc. 1977–79; Pres., Publr., Ed.-in-Chief Harry N. Abrams Inc., New York 1980–, Pres. and C.E.O.; Dir. Tanya Corpn.; Publishing Consultant 1967; Guide at U.S. exhbns., Moscow 1959, 1961; Trustee Museum of Modern Art, Dalton School; mem. Bd. of Dirs. Nat. Foundation for Depressive Illness, Acad. of American Poets; mem. Asscn. of American Publishers; Chevalier des Arts et des Lettres. *Address:* Harry N. Abrams Inc., 100 Fifth Avenue, New York, NY 10011 (Office); 1 Fifth Avenue, New York, NY 10003, U.S.A. (Home).

GOTTLIEB, Robert Adams, B.A.; American editor; b. 29 April 1931, New York; s. of Charles Gottlieb and Martha (née Kean) Gottlieb; m. 1st Muriel Higgins 1952; m. 2nd Maria Tucci 1969; two s. one d.; ed. Columbia Coll. and Cambridge Univ.; employee Simon and Schuster 1955–65, Ed.-in-Chief 1965–68; Ed.-in-Chief Alfred A. Knopf 1968–87, Pres. 1973–87; Ed.-in-Chief The New Yorker 1987–92. *Publication:* Reading Jazz 1996. *Leisure interests:* ballet, movies, reading. *Address:* 237 East 48th Street, New York, NY 10017, U.S.A.

GOTTSCHALK, Gerhard, PH.D.; German professor of microbiology; b. 27 March 1935, Schwedt/Oder; s. of Gerhard Gottschalk and Irmgard Gottschalk (née Ploetz); m. Ellen-Marie Hrabowski 1960; two s. one d.; ed. Univs. of Berlin and Göttingen; Research Assoc. Dept. of Biochem., Univ. of Calif. Berkeley 1964–66; Dozent, Univ. of Göttingen 1967–70, Prof. of Microbiology 1970–, Rector 1975–76, Vice-Pres. 1979–81; Vice-Pres. Acad. of Science, Göttingen 1996, Pres. 1998–; Philip Morris Prize 1992. *Publications:* Bacterial Metabolism 1986, Biotechnologie 1986. *Address:* Institute of Microbiology, University of Göttingen, Grisebachstrasse 8, 37077 Göttingen, Germany. *Telephone:* 0551/393781.

GÖTZE, Heinz, DR. PHIL.; German publisher; b. 8 Aug. 1912, Dresden; ed. Univs. of Leipzig, Munich and Naples; Partner (Co-Proprietor) Springer-Verlag, Berlin, Heidelberg, New York, London, Paris, Tokyo, Hong Kong, Barcelona, Budapest 1957–, Lange & Springer, Scientific Bookshop, Berlin 1957–; Hon. F.R.C. Path.; Dr. med. h.c. (Heidelberg, Erlangen) 1972. *Address:* Ludolf Krehl-Strasse 41, 69120 Heidelberg, Germany (Home). *Telephone:* 06221-470717 (Home).

GOUDEV, Vladimir Victorovich; Russian diplomatist; b. 17 Sept. 1940, Moscow; s. of Victor Goudev; m. Valentina Goudeva 1960; one d.; ed. Moscow Inst. of Int. Relations; sr. posts in Ministry of Foreign Affairs at home and abroad 1963–75; Embassy First Sec. in Iraq 1975–79; Chief of Section, Deputy Chief of Near East Dept. of Ministry of Foreign Affairs 1979–86; Deputy Dir., Chief of Dept. in Directorate of Near East and North Africa 1986–87; Amb. to Iran 1987–93; Head of Africa and Near East Dept., Russian Ministry of Foreign Affairs 1993–95; Amb. to Egypt 1995–. *Address:* Russian Embassy, 95 Sharia Giza, Cairo, Egypt. *Telephone:* (02) 348-93-53; 348-93-54. *Fax:* (02) 360-90-74.

GOUGH, Barry Morton, M.A., PH.D., D.LIT.; Canadian professor of history and consultant; b. 17 Sept. 1938, Victoria, B.C.; s. of John Gough and Dorothy Mouncy Morton Gough; m. 1st B. Louise Kerr 1964 (divorced 1977); one s. one d.; m. 2nd Marilyn J. Morris 1981; two s.; ed. Vic. public schools, Univs. of B.C. and Montana and King's Coll., London; Prof. of History, Western Washington Univ. and Wilfrid Laurier Univ. 1972–; Adjunct Prof. of War Studies, Royal Mil. Coll. of Canada 1994–; founding mem. Asscn. for Canadian Studies in U.S. and Co-Dir. and archivist, Center for Pacific Northwest Studies, Western Washington Univ. Bellingham, Wash. 1968–72; founding mem. Asscn. of Canadian Studies; mem. Canadian Historical Asscn., Canadian Nautical Research Soc., Visiting Prof., Duke Univ., Univ. of B.C., Otago Univ. etc.; Archives Fellow, Churchill Coll. Cambridge; Pres. North American Soc. for Oceanic History, Canadian Nautical Research Soc.; Vice-Pres. Social Sciences Fed. of Canada; Ed. American Neptune: Maritime History and Arts 1995–; Roderick Haig-Brown and other book prizes. *Publications:* Royal Navy and the Northwest Coast 1971, Distant Dominion 1980, Gunboat Frontier 1984, Journal of Alexander Henry the Younger 1988, The Northwest Coast 1992, Falkland Islands/Malvinas 1992, First Across The Continent: Sir Alexander Mackenzie 1997; numerous reviews and articles. *Leisure interests:* golfing, flute, collecting benefactions. *Address:* 37 Ahrens Street, W., Kitchener, Ont. N2H 4B6, Canada; 107 Pall Mall, London, SW1Y 5ER, England.

GOUGH, Douglas Owen, M.A., PH.D., F.R.S.; British astrophysicist; b. 8 Feb. 1941, Stourport; s. of Owen Albert John Gough and Doris May (Camera) Gough; m. Rosanne Penelope Shaw 1965; two s. two d.; ed. Hackney Downs School, London, St. John's Coll. Cambridge; Research Assoc., JILA, Univ. of Colo., U.S.A. 1966–67; Nat. Acad. of Sciences Sr. Postdoctoral Research Assoc., New York 1967–69; mem. Grad. Staff, Inst. of Theoretical Astronomy, Cambridge 1969–73, lecturer in Astronomy and Applied Math., Inst. of Astronomy and Dept. of Applied Math. and Theoretical Physics, Cambridge Univ. 1973–85, Reader in Astrophysics, Inst. of Astronomy 1985–93, Prof. of Theoretical Astrophysics, Cambridge Univ. 1993–, Deputy Dir. Inst. of Astronomy 1993–99, Dir. 1999–; Fellow Churchill Coll. Cambridge 1972; Foreign mem. Royal Danish Acad. of Sciences and Letters 1998; James Arthur Prize, Harvard Univ., U.S.A. 1982, William Hopkins Prize, Cambridge Philosophical Soc. 1984, George Ellery Hale Prize, American Astronomical Soc. 1994. *Publications:* Problems in Solar and Stellar Oscillations (Ed.) 1983, Seismology of the Sun and the Distant Stars (Ed.) 1986, Challenges to Theories of the Structure of Moderate-Mass Stars (Ed. with J. Toomre) 1991. *Leisure interest:* cooking. *Address:* Institute of Astronomy, Madingley Road, Cambridge, CB3 0HA, England. *Telephone:* (01223) 337518. *Fax:* (01223) 337523.

GOUGH, Michael; British actor; b. 23 Nov. 1917, Malaya; numerous film and TV appearances. *Films include:* Women in Love, Velvet House, Julius Caesar, Trog, The Go Between, Henry VIII and his Six Wives, Horror Hospital, Boys from Brazil, Memed, Out of Africa, Wittgenstein, Caravaggio, Machenka, Batman, Blackeyes, Batman Returns, The Age of Innocence, The Life of Galileo, Uncovered, Batman Forever.

GOULD, Bryan Charles, LL.M. (N.Z.), M.A., B.C.L. (OXON); British politician; b. 11 Sept. 1939, Hawera, N.Z.; s. of Charles T. and Elsie M. (née Driller) Gould; m. Gillian A. Harrigan 1967; one s. one d.; ed. Victoria and Auckland Univs., N.Z. and Balliol Coll., Oxford; in diplomatic service, British Embassy Brussels 1964–68; Fellow and Tutor in Law, Worcester Coll., Oxford 1968–74; M.P. for Southampton Test 1974–79, Dagenham 1983–94; presenter and reporter Thames TV 1977–83; Opposition Spokesman on Trade 1983–86, on Trade and Industry 1987–89, on the Environment 1989–92; mem. of Shadow Cabinet, Labour's Campaign Co-ordinator 1986–89; Shadow Heritage Secretary 1992, resgnd. 1992; Vice-Chancellor Waikato Univ. 1994–. *Publica-*

tions: Monetarism or Prosperity? 1981, Socialism and Freedom 1985, A Future for Socialism 1989, Goodbye to All That (memoirs) 1995. *Leisure interests:* food, wine, gardening. *Address:* University of Waikato, Private Bag 3105, Hamilton, New Zealand.

GOULD, Elliott; American actor; b. 29 Aug. 1938, Brooklyn, New York; s. of Bernard and Lucille (née Gross) Goldstein; m. 1st Barbra Streisand (q.v.) 1963 (divorced 1971); one s; m. 2nd Jenny Bogart 1973 (divorced 1975, remarried 1978); one s. one d.; made Broadway début in Rumple 1957; other appearances include Say Darling 1958, Irma La Douce 1960, I Can Get It For You Wholesale 1962, Drat! The Cat 1965, Alfred in Little Murders 1967; toured in The Fantastiks with Liza Minnelli; nat. tour Deathtrap. *Films include:* The Confession 1966, The Night They Raided Minsky's 1968, Bob and Carol and Ted and Alice 1969, Getting Straight 1970, M*A*S*H 1970, The Touch 1971, Little Murders 1971, The Long Good-Bye 1972, Nashville 1974, I Will . . . I Will . . . For Now 1976, Harry and Walter Go to New York 1976, A Bridge Too Far 1977, The Silent Partner 1979, The Lady Vanishes 1979, Escape to Athens 1979, The Muppet Movie 1979, Falling in Love Again 1980, The Devil and Max Devlin 1981, Over the Brooklyn Bridge 1984, The Naked Face 1984, Act of Betrayal 1988, Dead Men Don't Die 1989, Secret Scandal 1990, Strawanser, The Player, Exchange Lifeguards, Wet and Wild Summer, Naked Gun 33⅓: The Final Insult (cameo), White Man's Burden, The Glass Shield, Kicking and Screaming, A Boy Called Hate, Johns, The Big Hit, American History, X, Bugsy, Hoffman's Hunger, Capricorn One; numerous TV appearances, including Doggin' Around (BBC TV). *Address:* c/o Ottigan Productions Inc., 915 Flower Avenue, CA 90291, U.S.A.

GOULD, Stephen Jay, PH.D., F.R.S.E.; American professor of geology; b. 10 Sept. 1941, New York; s. of the late Leonard and of Eleanor (née Rosenberg) Gould; m. Deborah Lee Gould 1965; two s.; ed. Antioch Coll., Columbia Univ.; Asst. Prof. of Geology and Asst. Curator of Invertebrate Paleontology, Harvard Univ. 1967–71, Assoc. Prof. and Assoc. Curator 1971–73, Prof. of Geology and Curator 1973–, Alexander Agassiz Prof. of Zoology 1982–; mem. Cttee. of Profs. Dept. of Biology, Adjunct mem. Dept. of History of Science; Pres. Paleontological Soc. 1985–86, Soc. for the Study of Evolution 1990–91; mem. Advisory Bd. NOVA 1980–92, Bd. of Eds. Science Magazine 1986, Council, Nat. Portrait Gallery 1989–, Space Exploration Council, NASA 1989–91, Int. Bd. of Advisers Galerie de l'Evolution, Muséum d'Histoire Naturelle, Paris 1989–, Bd. SIPI 1991–, Bd. British Museum (Natural History) Int. Foundation 1992–; Trustee Bermuda Biological Station 1988–; Nat. Science Foundation Fellow, Hon. Woodrow Wilson Fellow, Hon. Columbia Univ. Fellow 1963–67, Prin. Investigator, various NSF grants 1969–; many lectureships including Tanner Lectures, Cambridge Univ. 1984, Terry Lectures, Yale Univ. 1986, Tanner Lectures, Stanford Univ. 1989, Mike Mansfield Lecture, Tokyo 1989, first Isaiah Berlin Annual Lecture, Wolfson Coll., Oxford Univ. 1991; Associé du Muséum Nat. d'Histoire Naturelle, Paris; Fellow, A.A.A.S., (mem. Council 1974–76), American Acad. of Arts and Sciences, Royal Soc. of Edin.; Foreign mem. Linnaean Soc. of London; Hon. Foreign Fellow European Union of Geosciences; mem. N.A.S.; over 30 hon. degrees; numerous medals and awards, including Nat. Book Award, Science (for The Panda's Thumb) 1981, Scientist of the Year, Discover Magazine 1981, Silver Medal, Zoological Soc. of London 1984, Distinguished Service Award, American Geological Inst. 1986, Sue T. Friedman Medal, Geological Soc. of London 1989, Rhône-Poulenc Prize (for Wonderful Life) 1991, Gold Medal, Linnaean Soc. of London 1992. *Publications:* Ontogeny and Phylogeny 1977, Ever Since Darwin 1977, The Panda's Thumb 1980, The Mismeasure of Man (Nat. Book Critics Circle Award 1982) 1981, Hen's Teeth and Horse's Toes 1983, The Flamingo's Smile 1985, Time's Arrow, Time's Cycle 1987, An Urchin in the Storm 1987, Wonderful Life 1989, Bully for Brontosaurus 1991, Finders, Keepers 1992, Eight Little Piggies 1993, Dinosaur in a Haystack 1996, Life's Grandeur 1996, Questioning the Millennium 1997 and numerous articles. *Leisure interests:* baseball, choral singing. *Address:* Museum of Comparative Zoology, Harvard University, Department of Earth Sciences, Cambridge, MA 02138, U.S.A. *Telephone:* (617) 495 2470.

GOULDEN, Sir (Peter) John, Kt., B.A., K.C.M.G.; British diplomatist and civil servant; b. 21 Feb. 1941; s. of George H. Goulden and Doris Goulden; m. Diana Waite 1962; one s. one d.; ed. Queen's Coll., Oxford; joined FCO 1962, Ankara 1963–67, Manila 1969–70, Dublin 1976–79, Head Personnel Services Dept. 1980–82, News Dept. 1982–84, Asst. Under-Sec. of State 1988–92; Counsellor, Head Chancery Office of U.K. Perm. Rep. to EC 1984–87; Amb. to Turkey 1992–95; Amb., Perm. Rep. North Atlantic Council and Western European Union 1995–. *Leisure interests:* bookbinding, early music, skiing. *Address:* NATO, 1110 Brussels, Belgium. *Telephone:* 2-728-41-11. *Fax:* 2-728-41-17.

GOULDING, Sir Marrack Irvine, K.C.M.G.; British diplomatist, international civil servant and university college warden; b. 2 Sept. 1936, Plymouth; s. of Sir Irvine Goulding and Gladys Goulding; m. 1st Susan Rhoda D'Albiac 1961 (divorced 1996); two s. one d.; m. 2nd Catherine Pawlow 1996; ed. St. Paul's School and Magdalen Coll. Oxford; joined H.M. Foreign (later Diplomatic) Service 1959; with Middle East Centre for Arab Studies 1959–61; Kuwait 1961–64; Foreign Office 1964–68; Tripoli, Libya 1968–70; Cairo 1970–72; Private Sec. Minister of State for Foreign and Commonwealth Affairs 1972–75; seconded to Cabinet Office 1975–77; Counsellor, Lisbon 1977–79; Counsellor and Head of Chancery, U.K. Mission to UN, New York 1979–83; Amb. to Angola and concurrently to São Tomé and Príncipe 1983–85; UN Under-Sec.-Gen. for Special Political Affairs, 1986–91, for Peace-keeping Operations 1992–93, for Political Affairs 1993–97; Warden St. Antony's Coll., Oxford 1997–. *Leisure interests:* travel and birdwatching. *Address:* St. Antony's Coll., Oxford, OX2 6JF, England.

GOULED APTIDON, Hassan; Djibouti politician; b. 1916, Djibouti; Rep. of French Somaliland (now Repub. of Djibouti) to French Govt. 1952–58; Vice-Pres. Territorial Ass. 1958–59; Deputy to French Nat. Ass. 1959–62; Minister of Educ. 1963–67; mem. (later Pres.) Ligue Populaire Africaine pour l'Indépendance—LPAI (fmrly. Ligue Populaire Africaine) 1967–79; Pres. Council of Govt., responsible for Co-operation May-June 1977; Chair. Rassemblement Populaire pour le Progrès (RPP) March 1979–; Pres. Repub. of Djibouti, C.-in-C. of the Armed Forces June 1977–. *Address:* Présidence de la République, Djibouti, Republic of Djibouti.

GOULIAN, Mehran, A.B., M.D.; American physician; b. 31 Dec. 1929, Weehawken, N.J.; s. of Dicran Goulian and Shamiram Mzrakjian; m. Susan Hook 1961; three s.; ed. Columbia Coll. and Columbia Coll. of Physicians and Surgeons; Medical Internship, Barnes Hosp. 1954–55; Medical Residency, Mass. Gen. Hosp. 1958–59, 1960; Fellow in Medicine (Hematology), Yale Univ. School of Medicine 1959–60; Research Fellow in Medicine (Hematology), Harvard Univ. July–Dec. 1960, 1962–63, Instructor in Medicine 1963–65; Clinical and Research Fellow in Medicine (Hematology), Mass. Gen. Hosp. July–Dec. 1960, 1962–63, Asst. in Medicine, 1963–65; Fellow in Biochem., Stanford Univ. School of Medicine 1965–67; Research Assoc. in Biochem., Univ. of Chicago and Argonne Cancer Research Hospital 1967–69, Assoc. Prof. of Medicine 1967–70, Assoc. Prof. of Biochem. 1969–70; Prof. of Medicine, Univ. of Calif., San Diego 1970–. *Leisure interest:* music. *Address:* Department of Medicine, University of California, San Diego, La Jolla, CA 92093-0613, U.S.A. *Telephone:* (619) 534-3946.

GOULLI, Salah Eddine el, D.IUR.; Tunisian fmr. diplomatist and business executive; b. 22 June 1919, Sousse; m. M. J. Zeineb Larre 1958; one d.; ed. Univ. of Paris (Sorbonne); Consul Gen., Marseilles 1956–57; Minister, Embassy, Washington, D.C. 1958–61; Amb. to Belgium (also accred. to Netherlands, Luxembourg, EEC) 1962–69, to UN 1969, to U.S.A. (also accred. to Venezuela and Mexico) 1970–73, to Netherlands 1976–78; Adviser to Minister of Foreign Affairs 1973–75, 1979–81; Pres. Philips Electronics Tunisia 1981–90, World Trade Centre, Tunis 1990–; Grand Cordon of the Repub., Gold Cross of Leopold and Grand Cross Crown of Belgium; Grand Cross Chêne and Grand Cross Nassau, Luxembourg. *Publications:* lectures on political and econ. matters in U.S.A., Europe and Middle East; numerous articles in European press. *Leisure interests:* golf, reading, swimming. *Address:* 2 rue des Roses, 2070 Lamarsa, Tunisia. *Telephone:* (1) 774 307. *Fax:* (1) 807 955.

GOUMBA, Abel, D. EN MED.; Central African Republic politician and professor of medicine; b. 18 Sept. 1926, Grimari; m.; 15 children; ed. Univ. of Bordeaux; doctor in People's Repub. of Congo 1950–56; Vice-Pres. Gov. Council of Oubangui-Chari, Minister of Finance and Planning and Deputy to Regional Ass. 1957–58, Pres. Gov. Council July–Nov. 1958; Minister of Finance and Econ. Affairs, Central African Repub. 1958–59; Minister of State April–Oct. 1959; Deputy to Nat. Ass. 1959; Senator 1960; under house arrest 1960; political prisoner 1964; in exile abroad 1964–81; lecturer, Ecole Nat. de la Santé Publique, Rennes 1971–73; Prof. of Public Health, Faculty of Medicine Butaré-Rwanda 1973–77; Prof. of Public Health, Centre Régional de Développement Sanitaire, Cotonou, Benin 1977–81; Prof. of Public Health, Univ. of Bangui 1981–82, 1988–, mem. of Nat. Assembly 1988; Rector Jan.–Aug. 1982; presidential cand. 1981; political prisoner 1982–83, 1983–84; unemployed 1985–88; fmr. leader of Consultative Group of Democratic Forces (CFD), alliance of 14 opposition groups; presidential cand. Sept. 1993; now Leader Front patriotique pour le progrès (FPP). *Address:* Front patriotique pour le progrès, B.P. 259, Bangui, Central African Republic. *Telephone:* 61-37-91. *Fax:* 61-52-23.

GOUNARIS, Elias, LL.M.; Greek diplomatist; b. 7 Sept. 1941, Athens; s. of Panayotis Gounaris and Christine Gounaris; m. Irene Hadjilias 1970; ed. Univ. of Athens; Consul, New York 1969; Ministry of Foreign Affairs 1973; Sec. Perm. Mission of Greece to int. orgs. Geneva 1975; Counsellor 1976; Embassy, Belgrade 1979; Ministry of Foreign Affairs 1983; Minister-Counsellor, then Minister, Embassy, Bonn 1987, Minister Plenipotentiary 1988; Amb. to U.S.S.R. (also accred. to Mongolia) 1989; Amb. to U.K. 1993–96; with Ministry of Foreign Affairs 1996–, Dir. Gen. for Political Affairs 1997–; decorations from Austria, Finland, Germany, Ukraine and the Russian Orthodox Church. *Address:* Akadimias Street 1, 106 71 Athens, Greece. *Telephone:* (1) 360.87.36, 360.87.67. *Fax:* (1) 36.24.081.

GOUNELLE DE PONTANEL, Hugues; French professor of medicine; b. 27 Feb. 1903, Chateauroux; m. Jeanne Gamas 1940; one s. two d.; ed. Lycée de Chateauroux; Intern and Chef de Clinic, Faculté de Médecine, Strasbourg 1925–32; Prof. Agrégé, Val de Grâce, Paris 1938; founder, Foch Research Centre for Human Nutrition 1940; Pres. Acad. Nat. de Médecine 1983; Commandeur Légion d'honneur; Commdr. Ordre nat. du Mérite, du Mérite agricole, Croix de Guerre, etc. *Publications:* 400 scientific publications. *Address:* 5 rue Auguste Maquet, 75016 Paris, France (Home).

GOURAD HAMADOU, Barkad; Djibouti politician; fmr. mem. of French Senate; fmr. Minister of Health; Prime Minister of Djibouti Sept. 1978–, Minister of Ports 1978–87, Minister of Planning and Land Devt. 1987; now

Prime Minister, Minister of Nat. and Regional Devt.; mem. Rassemblement Populaire pour le Progrès (RPP). *Address:* Office du Premier Ministre, P.O. Box 2086, Djibouti, Republic of Djibouti. *Fax:* 355049.

GOURISSE, Daniel, D. ÈS SC.; French administrator and professor of chemical engineering; b. 13 March 1939, Charleville; s. of Robert Gourisse and Marie-Marguerite Lalle; m. Michèle Maës 1961; three s.; ed. Ecole Centrale de Paris; Laboratory head, Commissariat à l'Energie Atomique (Atomic Energy Comm.) 1964–73, Tech. adviser to the Gen. Admin. 1973–76, Head, Chem. Eng. Dept. 1976–84; Prof. of Chem. Eng., Ecole Centrale de Paris (now Ecole centrale des arts et manufactures) 1969–76, of Gen. and Ind. Sciences 1977–78, Dir. Ecole Centrale 1978–; Pres. Conf. des Grandes Ecoles 1985–93 (now Hon. Pres.), Office de robotique et de productique du Commissariat à l'énergie atomique 1985–89; Scientific Adviser to Dir. du Cycle du Combustible 1990–; Officier, Ordre nat. du Mérite, Commdr., Palmes académiques, Chevalier, Légion d'honneur. *Publications:* many articles in international journals. *Address:* Ecole centrale des arts et manufactures, Grande Voie des Vignes, 92295 Chatenay-Malabry Cedex; 12 avenue de la Cure d'Air, 91400 Orsay, France (Home). *Telephone:* 01.41.13.12.54 (Ecole Centrale).

GOUTARD, Noel; French business executive; b. 22 Dec. 1931, Casablanca, Morocco; s. of F. Antoine Goutard and M. Edmée (née Lespinasse) Goutard; m. Dominique Jung 1964; one s. one d.; ed. Lycée Louis le Grand, Paris, Univ. of Bordeaux and Pace Coll., New York; Vice-Pres. Frenville Co., New York 1954–60; Finance Exec. Warner Lambert Int., Morris Plains, N.J. 1960–62; African Area Man. Pfizer Inc., New York 1962–66; Exec. Vice-Pres. Gevelot S.A. Paris 1966–71; Pres. and C.O.O. Compteurs Schlumberger S.A., Paris 1971–76; Exec. Vice-Pres. and mem. Bd. of Dirs. Chargeurs S.A., Paris 1976–83; Exec. Vice-Pres. and C.O.O. Thomson S.A., Paris 1983–84, Dir.-Gen. 1983–86; Pres.-Dir. Gen. Valéo SA 1987–; mem. Bd. Thomson CSF, Banque Thomson, Thomson-Brandt Armements, Imétal 1996–, Alcatel-Alsthom 1997–, etc.; Officier, Légion d'honneur. *Leisure interests:* tennis, travel. *Address:* Valéo SA, 43 rue Bayen, 75848 Paris cedex 17, France.

GOUYON, H.E. Cardinal Paul; French ecclesiastic (retd.); b. 24 Oct. 1910, Bordeaux; s. of Louis Gouyon and Jeanne Chassaing; ed. Inst. Catholique de Paris, Gregorian Univ., Rome; ordained priest 1937; consecrated Bishop 1957; Bishop of Bayonne 1957; Titular Archbishop of Pessinonte 1963; Archbishop of Rennes 1964–85; cr. Cardinal 1969; Nat. Pres. Pax Christi 1966–82; mem. Secretariat for non-believers; Lauréat de l'Acad. française; Officier, Légion d'honneur, Commdr., ordre nat. du Mérite, Croix de guerre 1939–45. *Publications:* Introduction de la reforme disciplinaire tridentine dans la diocèse de Bordeaux 1582–1624 1957, Commentoire de la Declaration conciliare sur l'education chretienne 1966, L'intercommunion—est-elle possible? 1976, Marcel Callo, témoin d'une génération 1981. *Address:* Ma Maison, 181 rue Judaïque, 33000 Bordeaux Cedex, France.

GOUYOU BEAUCHAMPS, Xavier; French television executive; b. 25 April 1937, Paris; m. 2nd Geneviève Decugis 1986; two s. (from previous marriage); ed. Ecole Saint Joseph à Sarlat, Inst. d'études politiques and Ecole nat. d'admin.; Dir. of Staff Loiret Pref. 1964–66; Asst. Head of Staff, Minister of Agric. 1966–68, Minister of Educ. 1968–69; Official Staff Rep., Minister of Econ. and Finance 1969–74; Press Sec. to the Pres. 1974–76; Prefect of Ardèche 1976–77; Pres. and Dir.-Gen. SOFIRAD 1977–81; Pres. Télédiffusion de France 1986–92, Pres. Asscn. des organismes français de radiodiffusion et de télévision (OFRT) 1990–92; Pres. French broadcasters' group (GRF) of European Union of Radio and TV (UER) 1990–, Vice-Pres. UER 1990–; Pres. Admin. Council Nat. Park of Port Cros, Sofipost 1992–94; Dir.-Gen. France 3 1994–96; Pres., Dir.-Gen. France 2 and France 3 cos. 1996–; Chevalier, Légion d'honneur, Officier, ordre nat. du Mérite, Chevalier du Mérite agricole, Croix de la Valeur militaire. *Publication:* Le ministère de l'économie et des Finances, un Etat dans l'Etat? 1976. *Address:* France-Télévision, 42 avenue d'Iéna, 75016 Paris; 38 rue Lacépède, 75005 Paris, France.

GOVORUKHIN, Stanislav Sergeyevich; Russian politician, film director and actor; b. 29 March 1936, Berezniki, Sverdlovsk Region; m.; one s.; ed. All-Union Inst. of Cinematography; with Odessa Film Studio 1967–89; Mosfilm Studio 1989–. *Films include:* Vertical 1967, The Day of the Angel 1969, White Explosion 1970, The Life and Wonderful Adventures of Robinson Crusoe 1973, Smuggle 1975, A Wind of Hope 1978, The Place of Meeting Cannot be Changed (TV) 1979, Adventures of Tom Sawyer 1981, In Search of Captain Grant, Drops of Champagne; act in Assa, On first breath; documentaries: It is impossible to live so 1990 (Nica Prize), The Russia we have lost 1992, Aleksander Solzhenitsyn 1992, Great Criminal Revolution 1994; active participant opposition movt. since early 1990s; mem. State Duma 1993–, mem. Cttee. on security 1994–95, Chair. Cttee. on Culture 1996–; one of leaders Democratic Party of Russia, Chair. Deputies of Democratic Party of Russia in State Duma 1995; leader Block of Stanislav Govorukhin in elections to Duma 1995. *Publications:* Pirates of the 20th Century, Secrets of Madame Vong, Great Criminal Revolution, articles in periodicals. *Address:* State Duma, Okhotny Ryad 1, 103265 Moscow, Russia. *Telephone:* (095) 292 8401 (Office).

GOW, Gen. Sir (James) Michael, G.C.B.; British army officer (retd.); b. 3 June 1924, Sheffield, Yorks.; s. of late J. C. Gow and late Mrs. Alastair Sanderson; m. Jane Emily Scott 1946; one s. four d.; ed. Winchester Coll.; commissioned Scots Guards 1943; served N.W. Europe 1944–45; Malayan Emergency 1949; Equerry to H.R.H. Duke of Gloucester 1952–53; graduated Staff Coll. 1954; Brigade Maj. 1955–57; Regimental Adjt. Scots Guards 1957–60; Instructor Army Staff Coll. 1962–64; commanded 2nd Bn. Scots Guards, Kenya and England 1964–66; G.S.O.1 HQ, London Dist. 1966–67; Commdr. 4th Guards Brigade 1968–70; at Imperial Defence Coll. 1970; Brig.-Gen. Staff (Int.) HQ, British Army of the Rhine (BAOR), and Asst. Chief of Staff G2 HQ, Northag 1971–73; G.O.C. 4th Armoured Div., BAOR 1973–75; Col. Commandant Intelligence Corps 1973–86; Dir. Army Training 1975–78; G.O.C. Scotland 1979–80; Gov. Edinburgh Castle 1979–80; Commdr. Northern Army Group and C.-in-C. BAOR, 1980–83; Commandant, Royal Coll. of Defence Studies 1984–86; A.D.C. Gen. to H.M. The Queen 1981–83; Commr. British Scouts W. Europe 1980–83; Ensign, Queen's Bodyguard for Scotland (Royal Co. of Archers); Vice-Pres. Royal Caledonian Schools, Bushey 1980–96, Royal Patriotic Fund Corpn. 1983–88; Pres. Royal British Legion Scotland and Earl Haig Fund Scotland 1986–96; Sec.-Gen. The Prince's Youth Business Trust 1986; Chair. Scottish Ex-Service Charitable Orgs. (SESCO) 1989–96, Scots at War Trust 1994–; Pres. Nat. Asscn. of Supported Employment 1993–; Vice-Pres. Scottish Nat. Inst. for War Blinded 1995–; Patron Disablement Income Group Scotland 1993–; Freeman City of London, Freeman and Liveryman Painters and Stainers Co. F.S.A. (Scotland). *Publications:* Trooping The Colour—A History of the Sovereign's Birthday Parade 1980, Jottings in a General's Notebook 1989, General Reflections: A Military Man at Large 1991; articles in military and historical journals. *Leisure interests:* sailing, music, travel, reading. *Address:* 18 Ann Street, Edinburgh, EH4 1PJ, Scotland. *Telephone:* (0131) 332-4752.

GOWAN, James, F.R.C.A.; British architect; b. 18 Oct. 1925, Glasgow; s. of James Gowan and Isabella G. MacKenzie; m. Marguerite A. Barry 1947; two d.; ed. Hyndland School, Glasgow, Glasgow School of Art and Kingston School of Art; pvt. practice 1956–, in partnership with James Stirling (q.v.) 1956–63, design of new hosp., Milan 1991, Techint Int. co. HQ offices, Milan 1999; tutor, Architectural Asscn. London 1958–60, 1970–72; Visiting Prof. Princeton Univ. 1965, Simón Bolívar Univ. Venezuela 1982, Heriot Watt Univ. Edin. 1990; Banister Fletcher Prof. Univ. Coll. London 1975; Sr. tutor, Royal Coll. of Art 1983–86; Dr. h.c. of Design (Kingston Univ.) 1996; Reynolds Memorial Award (with James Stirling) 1965; exhbn. of drawings at R.I.B.A. Heinz Gallery 1994, at Scottish Nat. Gallery of Modern Art 1994. *Publications:* Projects: Architectural Association 1946–71, 1972, A Continuing Experiment 1975, James Gowan (monograph) 1978, Style and Configuration 1994. *Leisure interests:* drawing, reading. *Address:* 2 Linden Gardens, London, W2 4ES, England. *Telephone:* 0171-229 0642. *Fax:* 0171-792 9771.

GOWANS, Sir James Learmonth, Kt., C.B.E., M.D., D.PHIL., F.R.C.P., F.R.S., F.R.S.A.; British medical scientist and administrator; b. 7 May 1924, Sheffield; s. of John Gowans and Selma Josefina Ljung; m. Moyra Leatham 1956; one s. two d.; ed. Trinity School, Croydon, King's Coll. Hospital Medical School, Oxford Univ.; Fellow, St. Catherine's Coll., Oxford Univ. 1961–; Sec. Gen. Human Frontiers Science Programme, Strasbourg 1989–93; Consultant, WHO Global Programme on AIDS 1987–88; Henry Dale Research Prof. of Royal Soc. 1962–77; Dir. MRC Cellular Immunology Unit 1963–77, mem. MRC 1965–69, Sec. and Deputy Chair. 1977–87, Chair. MRC Biological Research Bd. 1967–69; mem. Advisory Bd. for the Research Councils 1977–87; mem. Council and a Vice-Pres. Royal Soc. 1973–75; Dir. Celltech PLC 1980–87; Chair. European Medical Research Councils 1985–87; mem. Council of Man. St. Christopher's Hospice; mem. Acad. Europaea 1991; Foreign Assoc. N.A.S. (U.S.A.); Hon. Sc.D. (Yale) 1966, Hon. D.Sc. (Chicago) 1971, (Birmingham) 1978, (Rochester, N.Y.) 1987, Hon. M.D. (Edin.) 1979, Hon. LL.D. (Glasgow) 1988; Hon. D.M. (Southampton) 1987; Gairdner Award, Ehrlich Prize, Feldberg Award, Royal Medal of Royal Soc., Wolf Prize, Medawar Prize, Galen Medal. *Publications:* articles in scientific journals. *Address:* 75 Cumnor Hill, Oxford, OX2 9HX, England. *Telephone:* (01865) 862304. *Fax:* (01865) 865548.

GOWER, David Ivon, O.B.E.; British cricketer; b. 1 April 1957, Tunbridge Wells, Kent; s. of Richard Hallam Gower and Sylvia Mary Gower; m. Thorunn Ruth Nash 1992; two d.; ed. King's School, Canterbury and Univ. Coll. London; left-hand batsman; played for Leicestershire 1975 to 1989 (Capt. 1984–86), Hampshire 1990 to 1993; played in 117 Tests for England 1978 to 1992, 32 as captain, scoring then England record 8,231 runs (average 44.2) with 18 hundreds; toured Australia 1978–79, 1979–80, 1982–83, 1986–87 and 1990–91; scored 26,339 first-class runs with 53 hundreds; 114 limited-overs internationals; Sunday Express Cricket Correspondent 1993–95; Public Relations Consultant for cricket sponsorship Nat. Westminster Bank 1993–; commentator, Sky TV 1993–; commentator and presenter, BBC TV 1994–; columnist, Sunday Telegraph 1995–. *Publications:* The Autobiography 1992; articles in Wisden Cricket Monthly. *Leisure interests:* Cresta run, skiing, tennis, photography. *Address:* c/o David Gower Promotions Ltd., 6 George Street, Nottingham, NG1 3BE, England. *Telephone:* (0115) 948 3206.

GOWERS, (William) Timothy, PH.D.; British mathematician; b. 20 Nov. 1963, Marlborough; s. of (William) Patrick Gowers and Caroline (Molesworth) Maurice; m. Emily Joanna Thomas 1988; two s. one d.; ed. Eton Coll., Trinity Coll., Cambridge; lecturer Univ. Coll. London 1991–94, Reader 1994–95; Fellow Trinity Coll., Cambridge 1989–93, 1995–; lecturer Univ. of Cambridge 1995–98, Rouse Ball Prof. of Mathematics 1998–; Jr. Whitehead Prize, London Mathematical Soc. 1995, European Mathematical Soc. Prize 1996; Fields Medal 1998. *Publications:* mathematical papers in various journals. *Leisure interest:* playing jazz piano. *Address:* Department of Pure Mathematics and Mathematical Statistics, 16 Mill Lane, Cambridge, CB2 1SB; Trinity College, Cambridge, CB2 1TQ, England. *Telephone:* (01223) 337999 (Department); (01223) 338400 (Trinity Coll.) *Fax:* (01223) 337920 (Department); (01223) 338564 (Trinity Coll.)

GOWON, Gen. Yakubu, B.A., PH.D; Nigerian army officer; b. 19 Oct. 1934, Garam, Pankshin Div., Plateau State; s. of Yohanna and Saraya Gowon; m. Victoria Hansatu Zakari 1969; one s. two d.; ed. St. Bartholomew's School, Wusasa, Zaria, Govt. Coll. (Barewa), Zaria, Royal Military Acad., Sandhurst, Staff Coll., Camberley and Jt. Services Staff Coll., Latimer, England; Adjutant, Nigerian Army March 1960; with UN peacekeeping force, Congo 1960–61, Jan.-June 1963; promoted Lieut.-Col. and apptd. Adjutant-Gen. Nigerian Army June 1963; Chief of Staff 1966; Maj.-Gen. June 1967; promoted Gen. Oct. 1971; Head of Fed. Mil. Govt. and C.-in-C. of Armed Forces of Fed. Repub. of Nigeria 1966–75 (deposed in coup); studying at Warwick Univ. 1975–83, Postgraduate 1978–82; Chair. Assembly of Heads of State, OAU 1973–74; Chair. Nigerian Nat. Oil and Chemical Marketing Co. 1996–; Chair. Trustees, Commonwealth Human Ecology Foundation 1986–; Hon. LL.D., Hon. D.Sc., Hon. D.Litt. *Leisure interests:* squash, tennis, photography, pen-drawings. *Publication:* Faith in Unity 1970. *Address:* National Oil and Chemical Marketing Co., 38–39 Marina, P.M.B. 2052, Lagos, Nigeria.

GOWRIE, Rt. Hon. The Earl of, Alexander Patrick Greysteil Hore-Ruthven, P.C., B.A., A.M.; British/Irish politician and company director; b. 26 Nov. 1939, Dublin, Eire; s. of The Hon. A. H. P. Hore-Ruthven and Pamela Margaret Fletcher; m. 1st Xandra Bingley 1962 (divorced 1973); one s.; m. 2nd Adelheid Gräfin von den Schulenburg 1974; ed. Eton Coll., Balliol Coll. Oxford and Harvard Univ., U.S.A.; Fellow and Tutor, Lowell House, Harvard Univ. 1965–68; Asst. Prof., Emerson Coll., Boston 1967–68; Lecturer in English and American Literature, Univ. Coll. London 1969–72; a U.K. del. to UN 1971; a Lord-in-Waiting to H.M. the Queen 1972–74; Govt. Whip, House of Lords 1972–74; Consultant, Thomas Gibson Fine Art 1974–79; Opposition Spokesman on Econ. Affairs and Adviser to Margaret Thatcher 1977–79; Minister of State, Dept. of Employment 1979–81; Minister of State and Deputy to the Sec. of State, Northern Ireland Office 1981–83; Minister of State, Privy Council Office and Minister for the Arts 1983–84; mem. of Cabinet as Chancellor of the Duchy of Lancaster (retaining portfolio as Minister for the Arts) 1984–85; Chair. The Really Useful Group 1985–90, Sotheby's Europe 1985–86, Arts Council 1994–98 (Chair. Literature Panel 1995–); Dir. Sotheby's Holdings Inc. 1985–, Chair. 1987–94; Provost R.C.A. 1986–95; Chair. Devt. Securities 1995–; Dir. (non-exec.) Ladbrooke and Guinness. *Publications:* A Postcard from Don Giovanni (poems) 1972, The Genius of British Painting: The Twentieth Century 1975, Derek Hill: An Appreciation 1987. *Leisure interests:* reading, writing, looking at pictures, music. *Address:* Development Securities, Portland House, Stag Place, London, SW1E 5DS, England. *Telephone:* 0171-828 4777.

GOYER, Hon. Jean-Pierre, P.C., Q.C., B.A., LL.B.; Canadian fmr. politician, lawyer and business executive; b. 17 Jan. 1932, St. Laurent, Quebec; s. of Gilbert and Marie-Ange Goyer; m. 1960; three d.; ed. Univ. of Montreal; Called to the Bar of Quebec and Ont.; M.P. for Montreal-Dollard 1965, re-elected 1968, 1972, 1974; Parl. Sec. to Sec. of State for External Affairs 1968–70; mem. Cabinet and Solicitor-Gen. of Canada 1970–72; Minister of Supply and Services and Receiver Gen. of Canada 1972–78; practises law in Montreal; partner, Clarkson, Tétrault, Montreal 1979–82; Chair. Bd. and Dir. Technocap Inc., Roger Pilon & Assocs.; Dir. Bombardier Inc.; mem. Bd. of Trustees, J. Armand Bombardier Foundation; mem. Bd. Orford Arts Center; fmr. Pres. Arts Council of Montreal Urban Community; Liberal. *Leisure interests:* tennis, skiing, golf. *Address:* Apt. 518, Habitat 67, Montreal, Quebec H3C 3R6, Canada (Home).

GOYTISOLO, Juan; Spanish author; b. 5 Jan. 1931, Barcelona; ed. Univs. of Barcelona and Madrid; emigrated to France 1957; reporter, Cuba 1965; assoc. with Gallimard Publishing Co.; Visiting Prof. at various univs. in U.S.A.; Premio Europalia 1985; numerous awards for novel Juegos de manos. *Publications:* novels: Juegos de manos 1954, Duelo en el paraíso 1955, El circo 1957, Fiestas 1958, La resaca 1958, La isla 1961, Señas de identidad 1966, Reivindicación del Conde don Julián 1970, Juan sin tierra 1975, Makbara 1980, Paisajes después de la batalla 1982; autobiography: Coto vedado 1985, En los reinos de taifa 1986; The Marx Family Saga 1996; short stories, travel narratives, literary criticism, essays etc.

GRAAFF, Sir de Villiers, Bt., M.B.E., M.A.; South African fmr. politician; b. 8 Dec. 1913; s. of Sir D. P. de Villiers Graaff; m. Helena le Roux Voigt 1939; two s. one d.; ed. Univs. of Cape Town, Oxford and Leiden (Netherlands); served Second World War; M.P. 1948–58, 1958–77; Chair. United Party, Cape Province 1956–58; Leader of the Opposition (United S. African Nat. Party) 1956–77; participated in formation of New Repub. Party, Interim Leader 1977; Hon. LL.D. (Rhodes Univ.); Hon. D.Lit. et H. (Univ. of S.A.) 1989; Decoration for Meritorious Service (S.A.) 1979. *Address:* De Grendel, Private Bag, GPO, Cape Town, South Africa.

GRABER, Pierre; Swiss politician; b. 6 Dec. 1908, La Chaux-de-Fonds; s. of Paul and Blanche (née Vuilleumier) Graber; ed. Gymnasiums in Neuchâtel and Berne and Univs. of Neuchâtel and Vienna; Lawyer, Lausanne 1933–46; mem. Lausanne Legis. Council 1933–46; mem. Great Council of Vaud 1937–46; Mayor of Lausanne 1946–49; mem. Lausanne City Council and Dir. Dept. of Finance, Lausanne 1949–62; mem. Council Canton Vaud, Dir. Dept. of Finance 1962–70, Pres. 1968; mem. Nat. Council 1942–69, Pres. 1966; Leader of Socialist Group in Fed. Ass. 1967–69; mem. Fed. Council 1970–77, Head of Fed. Political (Foreign Affairs) Dept. 1970–77; Vice-Pres. Fed. Council Jan.–Dec. 1974; Pres. of Swiss Confed. Jan.–Dec. 1975; Social Democrat. *Address:* CH 1073, Savigny, Switzerland.

GRABINER, Anthony Stephen, Q.C., LL.M.; British barrister; b. 21 March 1945, London; s. of late Ralph Grabiner and Freda Grabiner (née Cohen); m. Jane Aviva Portnoy 1983; three s. one d.; ed. Cen. Foundation Boys' Grammar School, L.S.E.; called to the Bar (Lincoln's Inn) 1968; Droop Scholar, Lincoln's Inn 1968; Jr. Counsel to Dept. of Trade 1976–81; Q.C. 1981; Bencher 1989–; Recorder 1990–; now Deputy High Court Judge; Vice-Chair. Court of Govs. L.S.E. 1993–98, Chair. 1998–; Head of Chambers One Essex Court 1994–. *Publication:* Sutton and Shannon on Contracts. *Leisure interests:* golf, theatre. *Address:* 1 Essex Court, Temple, London, EC4Y 9AR, England. *Telephone:* 0171-583 2000. *Fax:* 0171-583 0118.

GRACH, Eduard Davidovich; Russian violinist; b. 19 Dec. 1930, Odessa; s. of David Grach and Evelina Grach; m. 2nd Valentina Vasilenko 1990; one s. one d.; ed. P. Stolyarsky Odessa School of Music, Moscow State Conservatory (pupil of A. Yampolsky); winner of int. competitions in Budapest 1949 (1st prize), J. Thibaud in Paris 1955, P. Tchaikovsky in Moscow 1962; solo performances since 1953 in most countries of Europe; performer of classical and contemporary concertos and sonatas for violin; participant in the Trio with pianist Y. Malinin and cellist N. Shakhovskaya 1960–70; first performer of a number of works by Russian composers dedicated to him, including concertos by A. Eshpai; Head Violin Dept., Moscow State Conservatory; f. and Artistic Dir. Moskovia Chamber Orchestra 1994–; gives master classes in several countries; People's Artist of U.S.S.R. 1987, 1990. *Leisure interest:* football. *Address:* Moscow State Conservatory, Bolshaya Nikitskaya str. 13, 103871 Moscow (Office); 1st Smolensky per. 9, kv. 98, 121099 Moscow, Russia (Home). *Telephone and fax:* 241-21-57 (Home).

GRACHEV, Army Gen. Pavel Sergeevich; Russian army officer; b. 1 Jan. 1948, Revy, Tula Region; m.; two s.; ed. Ryazan Air Landing Force School, Military Acad., Gen. Staff Acad.; mem. CPSU 1968–91; commdr. parachute landing platoon, Kaunas, co. commdr., Ryazan, commdr. of bn., Lithuania 1969–81; Deputy Commdr., Commdr. 354 Parachute landing regt., Afghanistan 1981–83, Head of Staff 7th Army, Lithuania 1983–85, Div. Commdr., Afghanistan 1985–88; First Deputy Commdr. U.S.S.R. Air Landing Forces 1990–91, Commdr. Jan.–Aug. 1991; First Deputy Minister of Defence of U.S.S.R. (later C.I.S.) 1991–92, Minister of Defence of Russia 1992–96; took part in neutralization of revolt Oct. 1993; Adviser, Deputy Dir.-Gen. Rosvooruzheniye 1997–; Hero of Soviet Union and other decorations. *Address:* Ovchinnikovskaya nab. 18/1, 113324 Moscow, Russia. *Telephone:* (095) 220-17-52.

GRACHEVA, Nadezhda Aleksandrovna; Russian ballet dancer; b. 21 Dec. 1969, Semipalatinsk; d. of Aleksander Aleksandrovich Grachev and Vera Petrovna Gracheva; m. Aleksei Yuryevich Seregin; ed. Moscow School of Choreography; with Bolshoi Theatre 1987–; leading parts in Bayadera, Swan Lake, Nutcracker, Sleeping Beauty, Les Sylphides, Stone Flower, Romeo and Juliet and others; toured in many European and American countries, Japan, Israel, New Zealand; Benoît Prize 1991; prizes at int. competitions Varna 1984, 1986, Moscow 1987, Osaka 1995; State Prize of Russia 1996; People's Artist of Russia 1996. *Leisure interests:* cooking. *Address:* Bolshoi Theatre, Teatralnaya pl. 1, 103009 Moscow; 1st Truzhennikov per. 17, Apt. 49, 119121 Moscow, Russia (Home). *Telephone:* (095) 248 2753 (Home).

GRACQ, Julien; French writer and professor; b. 27 July 1910, St. Florent le Vieil, Maine et Loire; ed. Ecole Normale Supérieure and Ecole des Sciences Politiques, Paris (Prof. agrégé d'histoire); Prof. d'histoire 1935–47; Prof. d'histoire Lycée Claude Bernard, Paris 1947–70; retd. *Publications:* Au château d'Argol 1939, Un beau ténébreux 1945, Le roi pêcheur 1947, Liberté grande 1947, André Breton 1947, La littérature à l'estomac 1950, Le rivage des Syrtes 1951, Un balcon en forêt 1958, Préférences 1961, Lettrines 1967, La presqu'île 1970, Lettrines 2 1974, Les eaux étroites 1976, En lisant, En écrivant 1981, La forme d'une ville 1985, Autour des Sept Collines 1988, Carnets du Grand Chemin 1992. *Leisure interest:* chess. *Address:* 3 rue du Grenier à Sel, 49410 St. Florent le Vieil, France.

GRADE, Michael Ian, C.B.E., F.R.T.S.; British broadcasting executive; b. 8 March 1943, London; s. of Leslie Grade; m. 1st Penelope Jane Levinson 1967 (divorced 1981); one s. one d.; m. 2nd Hon. Sarah Lawson 1982 (divorced 1991); m. 3rd Francesca Mary Leahy 1998; ed. St. Dunstan's Coll., London; trainee journalist Daily Mirror 1960, Sports Columnist 1964–66; Theatrical Agent Grade Org. 1966; Jt. Man. Dir. London Man. and Representation 1969–73; Deputy Controller of Programmes (Entertainment) London Weekend TV 1973–77, Dir. of Programmes and mem. Bd. 1977–81; Pres. Embassy TV 1981–84; Controller BBC 1 1984–86, Dir. of Programmes BBC TV 1986–87; C.E.O. Channel Four 1988–97; Chair. VCI PLC 1995–; Chair. First Leisure Corpn. 1997– (Dir. 1991–, non-exec. Chair. 1995–97); Chair. Ind. Inquiry into Fear of Crime 1989, Devt. Council, Royal Nat. Theatre 1997–; Deputy Chair. Soc. of Stars 1995–; Pres. TV and Radio Industries Club 1987–88, Newspaper Press Fund 1988–89, Entertainment Charities Fund 1994–, Royal TV Soc. 1995–97; Vice-Pres. Children's Film Unit 1993–; Dir. ITN 1989–93, Open Coll. 1989–97, Delfont Macintosh Theatres Ltd. 1994–, Charlton Athletic Football Club 1997–, Jewish Film Foundation 1997–, New Millennium Experience Co. 1997–; mem. Int. Council. Nat. Acad. of TV Arts and Sciences 1991–97; mem.

Council, London Acad. of Music and Dramatic Art 1981–93, B.A.F.T.A. 1981–82, 1986–88 (Fellow 1994), Gate Theatre, Dublin 1990–, Cities in Schools 1991–95, Cinema and TV Benevolent Fund 1993–, Royal Acad. of Dramatic Art 1996–, Royal Albert Hall 1997–; mem. 300 Group, Milton Cttee., British Screen Advisory Council 1986–97, Nat. Comm. of Inquiry into Prevention of Child Abuse 1994–96; mem. Bd. of Govs. BANFF TV Festival 1997–; Hon. Prof. Thames Valley Univ. 1994; Hon. Treas. Stars Org. for Spastics 1986–92; Trustee Band Aid, Nat. Film and TV School, Virgin Health Care Foundation; Hon. LL.D. (Nottingham) 1997. *Leisure interest:* entertainment. *Address:* First Leisure Corporation PLC, 7 Soho Street, London, W1V 5FA, England. *Telephone:* 0171-437 9727.

GRADIN, Anita; Swedish politician; b. 12 Aug. 1933, Hörnefors, Västerbotten Co.; m. Lieut.-Col. Bertil Kersfelt; one d.; ed. Coll. of Social Work and Public Admin., Stockholm and in U.S.A.; journalist 1950, 1956–58, 1960–63; with Swedish Union of Forest Workers and Log Drivers 1952; with Social Welfare Planning Cttee. and Municipal Exec. Bd. Cttee. on Women's Issues, Stockholm 1963–67; mem. Exec. Cttee., Nat. Fed. of Social Democratic Women 1964–93, Vice-Chair. 1975–93; mem. Stockholm City Council 1966–68; First Sec. Cabinet Office 1967–82; mem. SDP Exec. Cttee. of Stockholm 1968–82; mem. Parl. 1968–92; Chair. Dist. Br., Fed. of Social Democratic Women, Stockholm 1968–82; Chair. Swedish Union of Social Workers and Public Admin. 1970–81; Chair. Nat. Bd. for Intercountry Adoptions 1973–80; del. Council of Europe 1973–82, Chair. Cttee. on Migration, Refugees and Democracy 1978–82; Minister with responsibility for Migration and Equality Affairs 1982–86; Vice-Chair. Socialist Int. Women's Council 1983–86, Chair. Socialist Int. Women 1986–92, Vice-Chair. Socialist Int. 1986–92; Minister with responsibility for Foreign Trade and European Affairs 1986–91; Amb. to Austria, Slovenia and to UN insts. including IAEA, UNIDO and UNRWA 1992–94; EC Commr. for Migration, Home and Judicial Affairs 1995–; Chair. of Stockholm Conf. on Vietnam 1974–76, of Swedish Cttee. for Vietnam, Laos and Cambodia 1977–82; mem. Exec. Cttee. of RFSU (Nat. Asscn. for Sexual Enlightenment) and Otterfonden 1969–92; mem. EFTA del. 1991–92; Pro Merito Medal, Council of Europe 1992; Cavalieri di Gran Croce (Italy) 1991, Order of Merit (Australia) 1995. *Address:* Commission of the European Communities, 200 rue de la Loi, 1049 Brussels, Belgium.

GRAF, Hans, DR.ING.; German business executive; b. 5 Oct. 1931, Bad Marienberg; consultant, fmr. mem. Exec. Bd. Krupp Stahl AG. *Address:* Baumgartenstrasse 1, 44869 Bochum, Germany (Home). *Telephone:* (02327) 79477.

GRAF, Steffi; German tennis player; b. 14 June 1969, Bruehl; d. of Peter Graf; coached by her father; won Orange Bowl 12s 1981, European 14-and under and European Circuit Masters 1982, Olympic demonstration event, L.A.; winner German Open 1986, French Open 1987, 1988, 1993, 1995, 1996; Australian Open 1988, 1989, 1990, 1994; Wimbledon 1988, 1989, 1991, 1992, 1993, 1995, 1996, US Open 1988 1989, 1993, 1995, 1996, won ATP Tour World Championship 1996, German Open 1989, numerous Women's Doubles Championships with Gabriela Sabatini (q.v.), Federation Cup 1992; Olympic Champion 1988; ranked No. 1 Aug. 1987; named Official World Champion 1988; Grand Slam winner 1988, 1989; youngest player to win 500 Singles victories as a professional Oct. 1991; 100 tournament wins, 21 Grand Slam titles (July 1996).

GRAFFMAN, Gary; American pianist; b. 14 Oct. 1928; s. of Vladimir and Nadia (Margdin) Graffman; m. Naomi Helfman 1952; ed. Curtis Inst. of Music, Philadelphia under Mme. Isabelle Vengerova; Professional début with Philadelphia Orchestra 1947; concert tours all over the world; appears annually in America with major orchestras; Dir. Curtis Inst. 1986–, Pres. 1995–; year offstage to correct finger injury 1980–81; gramophone recordings for Columbia Masterworks and RCA Victor including concertos of Tchaikovsky, Rachmaninoff, Brahms, Beethoven, Chopin and Prokofiev; Leventritt Award 1949; several hon. degrees. *Publication:* I Really Should be Practising (autobiog.) 1981. *Address:* Office of the Director, Curtis Institute of Music, 1726 Locust Street, Philadelphia, PA 19103, U.S.A.

GRAHAM, Sir Alexander Michael, G.B.E., J.P., D.C.L., C.B.I.M., F.C.I.I., F.C.I.S., F.R.S.A.; British insurance broker; b. 27 Sept. 1938, London; s. of Dr. Walter Graham and Suzanne Simon; m. Carolyn Stansfeld 1964; three d.; ed. St. Paul's School; nat. service with Gordon Highlanders 1957–59; broker, Frizzell Group Ltd. 1957–67, Dir. 1967–73, Man. Dir. 1973–90, Deputy Chair. 1990–92; Alderman, City of London 1979–, Sheriff 1986–87, Lord Mayor 1990–91; Chair. Nat. Employers Liaison Cttee. for T.A. and Reserve Forces 1992–97; Chair. First City Insurance Brokers Ltd. 1993–98; Chair. Council, Order of St. John, Herts. 1993–; Chair. Bd. of Trustees, Morden Coll. 1995–; Chair. Folgate Insurance Co. Ltd., Employment Conditions Abroad Ltd., Euclidian PLC, United Response; Pres. British Insurance Law Asscn. 1994–96; Underwriting mem. of Lloyd's; Fellow Chartered Insurance Inst.; Liveryman Mercers' Co.; K.St.J.; Grand Cross Order of Merit (Chile); Order of Wissam Alouite Class 3 (Morocco). *Leisure interests:* golf, shooting, tennis, swimming, wine, music. *Address:* 13–15 Folgate Street, London, E1 6BX (Office); Walden Abbotts, Whitwell, Hitchin, Herts., SG4 8AJ, England (Home). *Telephone:* 0171-247 6595 (Office); (01438) 871223 (Home).

GRAHAM, Andrew Winston Mawdsley, M.A.; British economist; b. 20 June 1942; s. of Winston Mawdsley Graham; m. Peggotty Fawssett 1970; ed. Charterhouse, St. Edmund Hall, Oxford; Econ. Asst. Nat. Econ. Devt. Office 1964, with Dept. of Econ. Affairs 1964–66, Asst. to Econ. Adviser to Cabinet 1966–68, Econ. Adviser to Prime Minister 1968–69; Fellow, and Tutor in Econs. Balliol Coll. Oxford 1969–97, Estates Bursar 1978, Investment Bursar 1979–83, Vice Master 1988, 1992–94, Acting Master 1997–; Policy Adviser to Prime Minister (leave of absence from Balliol) 1974–75; Econ. Adviser to Shadow Chancellor of Exchequer 1988–92, to Leader of Opposition 1992–94; Tutor Oxford Univ. Business Summer School 1971, 1972, 1973, 1976; Visiting Scholar M.I.T., Visiting Fellow Center for European Studies, Harvard Univ., U.S.A. 1994; Chair. St. James Group (Econ. Forecasting) 1982–84, 1985–92; Consultant BBC 1989–92; Bd. mem. Channel 4 TV 1998–; mem. Media Advisory Cttee., Inst. for Public Policy Research 1994–, Council of Man. Templeton Coll. Oxford 1990–96; Founder mem. Editorial Bd. Library of Political Economy 1982–94; Trustee Foundation for Information Policy Research 1998–. *Publications:* Government and Economies in the Postwar Period (Ed.) 1990; contribs. to books on econs. and philosophy. *Leisure interest:* windsurfing. *Address:* Balliol College, Oxford, OX1 3BJ, England. *Telephone:* (01865) 277777.

GRAHAM, Billy (see Graham, William Franklin).

GRAHAM, Christopher Forbes, D.PHIL., F.R.S.; British biologist; b. 23 Sept. 1940; ed. Oxford Univ.; fmrly. Jr. Beit Memorial Fellow in Medical Research, Sir William Dunn School of Pathology; Lecturer, Dept. of Zoology, Univ. of Oxford 1970–85, Prof. of Animal Devt. 1985–; Professorial Fellow St. Catherine's Coll., Oxford 1985–; mem. British Soc. for Cell Biology, British Society for Developmental Biology, Soc. for Experimental Biology, Genetical Soc. *Publication:* Developmental Control in Plants and Animals 1984. *Address:* Department of Zoology, University of Oxford, South Parks Road, Oxford, OX1 3PS, England.

GRAHAM, Daniel Robert (Bob), B.A., LL.D.; American politician and farmer; b. 9 Nov. 1936, Coral Gables, Fla.; s. of Ernest R. Graham and Hilda Simmons; m. Adele Khoury 1959; four d.; ed. Univ. of Florida and Harvard Univ.; Vice-Pres. Sengra Devt. Corpn. 1963–79; Florida State Rep. from Coral Gables 1966–70; Florida State Senator from Coral Gables 1970–78; Gov. of Florida 1979–87, Senator 1987–; Audubon Soc. Conservation Award 1974; Democrat. *Leisure interests:* golf, tennis and reading. *Address:* U.S. Senate, 524 Hart Senate Building, Washington, DC 20510, U.S.A.

GRAHAM, Donald Edward, B.A.; American newspaper publisher; b. 22 April 1945, Baltimore, Md.; s. of late Philip L. Graham and of Katharine Meyer Graham (q.v.); m. Mary L. Wissler 1967; one s. three d.; ed. Harvard Univ.; joined the Washington Post 1971, Asst. Man. Ed./Sports 1974–75, Asst. Gen. Man. 1975–76, Exec. Vice-Pres. and Gen. Man. 1976–79, Publr. 1979–; Pres., C.E.O. Washington Post Co. 1991–93, Chair, C.E.O. 1993–; fmrly. reporter and writer for Newsweek. *Address:* The Washington Post, 1150 15th Street, N.W., Washington, DC 20071, U.S.A. *Telephone:* (202) 334 7138.

GRAHAM, Douglas (Doug) Arthur Montrose, P.C., LL.B.; New Zealand politician; b. 12 Jan. 1942, Auckland; m. Beverley V. Graham 1966; two s. one d.; ed. Southwell School, Auckland Grammar School and Univ. of Auckland; practising lawyer since 1965; est. own practice 1968; barrister and solicitor of High Court of N.Z.; lecturer in Legal Ethics, Univ. of Auckland 1973–83; mem. Parl. 1984–; Minister of Justice, and of Courts, also in charge of Treaty of Waitangi Negotiations 1990–; Attorney Gen. 1997–; fmr. Minister of Disarmament and Arms Control and Cultural Affairs; fmr. Min. of National Party. *Publication:* Trick or Treaty? 1997. *Leisure interests:* golf, music, rugby football. *Address:* Ministry of Justice, P.O. Box 180, Wellington; Elderslie, Manuwai Lane, RD2 Drury, South Auckland, New Zealand.

GRAHAM, Katharine Meyer; American newspaper executive; b. 16 June 1917, New York; d. of Eugene and Agnes Meyer; m. Philip L. Graham 1940 (died 1963); three s. (incl. Donald E. Graham, q.v.) one d.; ed. Madeira School, Vassar Coll., and Univ. of Chicago; Reporter San Francisco News 1938–39; various depts. The Washington Post 1939–45; Pres. The Washington Post Co. (owns The Washington Post, Washington, Newsweek magazine, several TV stations and over 50 cable TV systems) 1963–73, Chair. of Bd. and C.E.O. 1973–91, Chair. 1991–93, Chair. Exec. Cttee. 1993–; Publr., The Washington Post 1969–79; Co-Chair. of Bd. of Int. Herald Tribune 1983; Trustee, The Conf. Bd., The Urban Inst., Fed. City Council, Univ. of Chicago, Reuters; mem. Ind. Comm. on Int. Devt. Issues (Brandt Comm.) Conf. Bd. 1982, Reuters 1989; Hon. Trustee George Wash. Univ.; Vice-Chair. Urban Inst.; mem. Council on Foreign Relations, Overseas Devt. Council, Cttee. on Public Educ.; Co-Chair. Circle of Nat. Gallery of Art, mem. Collectors' Cttee.; mem. Bd. Newspaper Advertising Bureau, Inc., American Newspaper Publrs. Asscn. (Past Chair. and Pres.); fmr. mem. Bd., Assoc. Press; mem. American Soc. of Newspaper Eds.; Fellow American Acad. of Arts and Sciences; John Peter Zenger Award 1973, Vermiel Medal (City of Paris) 1992; Pulitzer Prize 1998. *Publication:* Personal History (autobiog.) 1996. *Address:* Washington Post Co., 1150 15th Street, N.W., Washington, DC 20071 (Office); 2920 R Street, N.W., Washington, DC 20007, U.S.A. (Home). *Telephone:* (202) 334-6642 (Office).

GRAHAM, Patricia Albjerg, PH.D.; American educator; b. 9 Feb. 1935, Lafayette, Ind.; d. of Victor L. Graham and Marguerite Hall Albjerg; m. Loren R. Graham 1955; one d.; ed. Purdue and Columbia Univs.; Teacher Deep Creek and Maury High Schools, Norfolk, Va. 1955–58; Chair. History Dept., St. Hilda's and St. Hugh's School, New York 1958–60, Part-time Coll. Adviser 1961–63, 1965–67; Lecturer, Ind. Univ., School of Educ., Bloomington 1964–65; Asst. Prof., Barnard Coll. and Columbia Teacher's Coll., New York 1965–68, Assoc. Prof. 1968–72, Prof. 1972–74; Prof., Harvard Univ. Graduate School of Educ., Cambridge, Mass. 1974–79, Warren Prof. 1979–, Dean Graduate School of Educ. 1982–91; Dean Radcliffe Inst. and Vice-Pres. for Institutional Planning, Radcliffe Coll., Cambridge, Mass. 1974–76, Dean Radcliffe Inst. and Vice-Pres. Radcliffe Coll. 1976–77; Dir. Nat. Inst. of Educ. 1977–79; Vice-Pres. for Teaching, American Historical Asscn. 1985–89; Pres. Nat. Acad. of Educ. 1985–89; Dir. Spencer Foundation 1983–, Pres. Chicago Br. 1991–; Dir. Johnson Foundation 1983–; several hon. degrees. *Publications:* Progressive Education: From Arcady to Academe, A History of the Progressive Education Association 1967, Community and Class in American Education, 1865–1918 1974, Women in Higher Education (co-ed. with Todd Furniss) 1974, S.O.S. Sustain Our Schools 1992. *Address:* Harvard University Graduate School of Education, Longfellow Hall, Appian Way, Cambridge, MA 02135; The Spencer Foundation, 900 North Michigan Avenue, Suite 2800, Chicago, IL 60611, U.S.A.

GRAHAM, Sir Peter Alfred, Kt., O.B.E., D.SC., F.I.B., C.B.I.M.; British banker; b. 25 May 1922, London; s. of Alfred Graham and Margaret Graham; m. Luned Mary Kenealy-Jones 1953; two s. two d.; ed. St. Joseph's Coll.; war service in Fleet Air Arm; joined Chartered Bank of India, Australia and China 1947, serving throughout Far East 1947–62, Chief Man., Hong Kong 1962–70, Gen. Man., London 1970–75, Deputy Man. Dir. of Standard Chartered Bank PLC (now Standard Chartered PLC) 1975–77, Group Man. Dir. 1977–83, Sr. Deputy Chair. 1983–87, Chair. and Chief Exec. 1987–88; Chair. Standard Chartered Merchant Bank PLC 1977–82, Mocatta and Goldsmid Ltd. 1983–87, Crown Agents for Oversea Govts and Admins. 1983–90; Deputy Chair. Council Inst. of Bankers 1980–81, Chartered Trust PLC 1983–85, ICC United Kingdom 1985–91; Chair. of Council, City Univ. Business School 1985–92; Dir. Employment Conditions Abroad Ltd. 1988–94, Singapore Land Ltd. 1989–90; Chair. Equatorial Bank PLC 1989–93; Pres. Inst. of Bankers 1981–83; Dir. Dolphin Man. Services 1993–; mem. Court, City Univ. 1997–; Freeman City of London 1982; Hon. D.Sc. (City Univ.) 1985. *Leisure interests:* golf, tennis, skiing. *Address:* Heron Lea, Hobbs Lane, Beckley, nr. Rye, Sussex, TN31 6TT, England.

GRAHAM, William B., B.S., J.D.; American business executive and lawyer; b. 14 July 1911, Chicago, Ill.; s. of William Graham and Elizabeth Burden Graham; m. 1st Edna Kanaley 1940 (died 1981); two s. two d.; m. 2nd Catherine Van Duzer Gaubin 1984; ed. Univ. of Chicago; Patent Lawyer 1936–39; Partner Dawson and Oooms 1940–45; Vice-Pres. and Gen. Man. Baxter Int. Inc., Deerfield 1945–53, Pres., C.E.O. 1953–71, Chair., C.E.O. 1971–80, Chair. 1980–85, Sr. Chair. 1985–95, Chair. Emer., Hon. Dir. 1995–; Dir. First Nat. Bank of Chicago, Northwest Industries, Deere and Co.; Pres., Dir. Lyric Opera of Chicago, Dir. Nat. Park Foundation, Washington, D.C., Botanic Garden Skokie, Ill.; Trustee Univ. of Chicago, Evanston Hosp. and Orchestral Asscn.; Ill. St. Andrew Award 1974; Weizman Inst. Professional Chair. 1978; several hon. degrees; HIMA Pioneering Award, Nat. Kidney Foundation First Award, Achievement Award, Medical Technical Services 1983, Chicago Civil Award, De Paul Univ. 1986, Making History Award, Chicago Historical Soc. 1996. *Address:* 40 Devonshire Lane, Kenilworth, IL 60043, U.S.A. (Home).

GRAHAM, William Franklin (Billy), A.B., B.TH.; American evangelist; b. 7 Nov. 1918, Charlotte, N.C.; s. of William Franklin and Morrow Graham; m. Ruth M. Bell 1943; two s. three d.; ed. Florida Bible Inst., Tampa and Wheaton Coll.; ordained to Baptist Ministry 1939; Minister First Baptist Church, Western Springs, Ill. 1943–45; First Vice-Pres. Youth for Christ Int. 1945–50; Pres. Northwestern Schools, Minneapolis 1947–52; founder World Wide Pictures, Burbank, Calif.; worldwide evangelistic campaigns 1949–; speaker weekly Hour of Decision radio programme 1950–; also periodic crusade telecasts; founder, Billy Graham Evangelistic Asscn.; Hon. Chair. Lausanne Congress on World Evangelization 1974; Hon. Dr. (Hungarian Calvinist Church) (Christian Acad. of Theol.) 1981; numerous awards including Bernard Baruch Award 1955, Humane Order of African Redemption 1960, Gold Award, George Washington Memorial Inst. 1963, Horatio Alger Award 1965, Int. Brotherhood Award Nat. Conf. of Christians and Jews 1971, Sylvanus Thayer Award, Asscn. of Graduates of U.S. Mil. Acad. 1972, Franciscan Int. Award 1972; Man of South Award 1974, Liberty Bell Award 1975, Templeton Prize 1982, Pres. Medal of Freedom 1983, William Booth Award 1989, Congressional Gold Medal 1996. *Publications:* Peace with God 1953 (revised edn. 1984), The Secret of Happiness 1955, My Answer 1960, World Aflame 1965, The Challenge 1969, The Jesus Generation 1971, Angels—God's Secret Agents 1975, How to be Born Again 1977, The Holy Spirit 1978, Till Armageddon 1981, Approaching Hoofbeats: The Four Horsemen of the Apocalypse 1983, A Biblical Standard for Evangelists 1984, Unto The Hills 1986, Facing Death and the Life After 1987, Answers to Life's Problems 1988, Hope for the Troubled Heart 1991, Storm Warning 1992, Just As I Am (autobiog.) 1997. *Address:* P.O. Box 9313, Minneapolis, MN 55440-9313, U.S.A. (Office). *Telephone:* (612) 338-0500 (Office). *Fax:* (612) 335-1289.

GRAHAM-DIXON, Anthony Philip, Q.C., M.A.; British barrister (retd.); b. 5 Nov. 1929, London; s. of Leslie C. Graham Dixon, Q.C. and Dorothy Rivett; m. Suzanne Villar 1956; one s. one d.; ed. Westminster School and Christ Church, Oxford; served, R.N.V.R. 1953–55; called to Bar, Inner Temple 1956; Q.C. 1973; Bencher, Inner Temple 1982; retd. from practice at Bar 1986; Chair. London Concertino Ltd. 1982–90; Trustee, Soc. for Promotion of New Music 1988–97 (Chair. Trustees 1994–97); Deputy Chair. Public Health Lab. Service Bd. 1988–96; Gov. Bedales School 1988–96. *Leisure interests:* music, gardening, tennis, pictures. *Address:* Masketts Manor, Nutley, Uckfield, E. Sussex, England. *Telephone:* (01825) 712010.

GRAHAM-SMITH, Sir Francis, Kt., PH.D., F.R.S., F.R.A.S.; British professor of radio astronomy; b. 25 April 1923, Roehampton, Surrey; m. Elizabeth Palmer 1946; three s. one d.; ed. Rossall School, Epsom Coll., Downing Coll., Cambridge; with Telecommunications Research Establishment 1943–46; Cavendish Lab. 1947–64; 1851 Exhbn. 1951–52; Warren Research Fellow, Royal Soc. 1959–64; Prof. of Radio Astronomy, Univ. of Manchester 1964–74, 1981–87, Pro-Vice-Chancellor 1987, Dir. Nuffield Radio Astronomy Labs. 1981–88, Langworthy Prof. of Physics 1987–90, Prof. Emer.; Deputy Dir. Royal Greenwich Observatory 1974–75, Dir. 1976–81; Astronomer Royal 1982–90; Visiting Prof. of Astronomy, Univ. of Sussex 1975–81; Sec. Royal Astronomical Soc. 1964–71, Pres. 1975–77; Sec., Vice-Pres. Royal Soc. 1988–94; Fellow Downing Coll. 1953–64, Hon. Fellow 1970; Chair. of Govs., Manchester Grammar School 1987–98; Hon. D.Sc. (Queens Univ., Belfast) 1986, (Keele) 1987, (Birmingham) 1989, (Nottingham) 1990, (Trinity Coll. Dublin) 1990, (Manchester) 1993; Royal Medal, Royal Soc. 1987, Glazebrook Medal, Inst. of Physics 1991. *Publications:* Radio Astronomy 1960, Optics (with J. H. Thomson) 1971, Pulsars 1977, Pathways to the Universe (with Sir Bernard Lovell) 1988, Introduction to Radioastronomy (with B. F. Burke) 1997, Pulsar Astronomy (with A. G. Lyne) 1998. *Leisure interest:* gardening. *Address:* Old School House, Henbury, Macclesfield, Cheshire, SK11 9PH, England. *Telephone:* (01625) 612657.

GRAINVILLE, Patrick; French novelist; b. 1 June 1947, Villers-sur-mer; s. of Jacques and Suzanne (née Laquerre) Grainville; m. Françoise Lutgen 1971; ed. Lycée Deauville, Sorbonne; teacher, Lycée de Sartrouville 1975–96; mem. C.N.R.S. literature section 1975; Prix Goncourt for Les flamboyants 1976; Officier, Ordre nat. du Mérite, Ordre des Arts et des lettres. *Publications:* La toison 1972, La lisière 1973, L'abîme 1974, Les flamboyants 1976, La Diane rousse 1978, Le dernier viking 1980, Les fortresses noires 1982, La caverne céleste 1984, Le paradis des orages 1986, L'Atelier du peintre 1988, L'Orgie, La Neige 1990, Colère 1992, Mathieu (jtly.) 1993, les Anges et les Faucons 1994, Le Lien 1996, Le tyran éternal 1998. *Address:* c/o Editions du Seuil, 27 rue Jacob, 75261 Paris cedex 06, France.

GRAMM, (William) Philip, PH.D.; American politician; b. 8 July 1942, Fort Benning, Ga.; s. of Kenneth M. and Florence (Scroggins) Gramm; m. Wendy Lee 1970; two s.; ed. Univ. of Georgia; mem. Faculty, Dept. of Econs. Tex. A. and M.U. Coll. Station 1967–78, Prof. 1973–78; Partner, Gramm & Assocs. 1971–78; mem. House of Reps. 1979–85; Senator from Texas Jan. 1985–; Chair. Senate Steering Cttee; fmr. Democrat; Republican. *Publications:* articles in professional journals. *Address:* United States Senate, 370 Senate Russell Building, Washington, DC 20510, U.S.A.

GRAMS, Rod; American politician, construction executive and television producer; b. 1948; m. Laurel Grams; one s. three d.; ed. Univ. of Minnesota, Brown Inst. Minneapolis and Carroll Coll. Helena, Mont.; eng. consultant, Orr-Schelen Mayeron & Assoc. Minneapolis; anchor, producer KFBB-TV, Great Falls, Mont., WSAU-TV, Wausau, Wis., WIFR-TV, Rockford, Ill., KMSP-TV, Minneapolis; Pres. and C.E.O. Sun Ridge Builders; mem. 103rd Congress from 3rd Minn. Dist. 1993–95; Senator from Minnesota Jan. 1995–; Republican. *Address:* United States Senate, 257 Dirksen Senate Office Bldg., Washington, DC 20510, U.S.A.

GRANBERG, Aleksandr Grigorevich, DR.ECON.SC.; Russian economist; b. 25 June 1936, Moscow; m. Tatyana Baranova 1962; one s.; ed. Moscow Econ. Inst.; Prof. Univ. of Novosibirsk 1965–91; Dir. Inst. of Econ. and Org. of Production, Siberian Dept., U.S.S.R. (now Russian) Acad. of Sciences (IEOPP) 1985–91; corresp. mem. of Acad. of Sciences 1984, mem. 1990; People's Deputy of Russia 1990–93; Chair. Cttee. of the Supreme Soviet for Interrepublican Relations and Regional Policy 1990–92; Counsellor to Russian Pres. 1992–93; Chair. Council for Location of Productive Forces and Econ. Co-operation 1992–; Chair. Nat. Cttee. on Pacific Econ. Co-operation; Prof. Acad. of Nat. Econ. 1993–; mem. New York Acad. of Sciences 1993; V. S. Nemchinov Prize 1990. *Publications:* studies on cooperation in industry and in methodology of modelling of economic processes; Russian Social Economy, Analytical Profile 1992, Coalition Analysis of Multi-regional Systems: U.S.S.R. on the Eve of Collapse 1993. *Address:* Council for Location of Productive Forces, Vavilov St. 7, Moscow 117822, Russia. *Telephone:* 135-61-08 (Office); 135-10-18 (Home).

GRANDMONT, Jean-Michel, L. ÈS SC., PH.D.; French economist and researcher; b. 22 Dec. 1939, Toulouse; s. of Jancu Wladimir Grunberg and Paule Cassou; m. 1st Annick Duriez 1967 (divorced 1978); m. 2nd Josselyne Bitan 1979; two d.; ed. Ecole Polytechnique, Paris, Ecole Nationale des Ponts et Chaussées, Paris, Université de Paris, Univ. of California at Berkeley, U.S.A.; Research Assoc., Centre Nat. de la Recherche Scientifique (CNRS), Centre d'Etudes Prospectives d'Economie Mathématique Appliquées à la Planification (CEPREMAP) 1970–75, then Dir. various research units, Dir. of Research, CNRS and CEPREMAP 1987–96, Dir. Research Unit CNRS 928, "Recherches Fondamentales en Economie Mathématiques" 1991–96, Dir. of Research, CNRS and CREST 1996–; Assoc. Prof., Ecole Polytechnique, Palaiseau 1977–92, Prof. 1992–, Chair. Dept. of Econs. 1997–; Prof. (part-time), Yale Univ., U.S.A. 1987, 1989–91, 1994; Pres. Econometric Soc. 1990; Hon. mem. American Econ. Asscn.; mem. Academia Europaea 1989–; Dr. h.c. (Lausanne) 1990; Foreign Hon. mem. American Acad. of Arts and Sciences 1992–. *Publications:* Money and Value 1983, Nonlinear Economic Dynamics (Ed.) 1987, Temporary Equilibrium (Ed.) 1988; articles in scientific econ. journals. *Leisure interests:* skiing, swimming. *Address:* CREST, 15 blvd. Gabriel Péri, 92245 Malakoff Cedex (Office); 55 boulevard de Charonne, Les Doukas 23, 75011 Paris, France (Home). *Telephone:* 01.41.17.78.04 (Office); 01.43.70.37.28 (Home). *Fax:* 01.41.17.60.46.

GRANDY, Marshal of the R.A.F. Sir John, G.C.B., G.C.V.O., K.B.E., D.S.O.; British air force officer; b. 8 Feb. 1913, Northwood, Middx.; s. of late Francis Grandy and Nell Grandy (née Lines); m. Cecile Elizabeth Florence Rankin 1937 (died 1993); two s.; ed. Univ. Coll. School, London; Pilot Officer 1931; served Second World War; Deputy Dir. Operational Training, Air Ministry 1946–49; Air Attaché, Brussels 1949–50; Commdr. Northern Sector Fighter Command 1950; Air Staff H.Q. Fighter Command 1952–54; Commdt. Cen. Fighter Establishment 1954–57; Imperial Defence Coll. 1957; Commdr. Task Force Grapple 1957–58; Asst. Chief of Air Staff 1958–61; C.-in-C. R.A.F. Germany, Commdr. 2nd Allied Tactical Air Force 1961–63; A.O.C.-in-C. Bomber Command 1963–65; C.-in-C. British Forces Far East and U.K. Mil. Rep. to SEATO 1965–67; Air Commodore 1956; Air Vice-Marshal 1958; Air Marshal 1961; Air Chief Marshal 1965; Marshal of the R.A.F. 1971; Chief of Air Staff 1967–71; Gov. and Commdr.-in-Chief of Gibraltar 1973–78; Constable and Gov. Windsor Castle 1978–88; Dir. Brixton Estate Ltd. 1971–73, 1978–83; Sr. Pres. The Officers Asscn. 1980–82, Disablement in the City, Berkshire Branch BLESMA; Deputy Chair. Council R.A.F. Benevolent Fund 1980–95; Patron Polish Air Force Asscn., G.B. 1979–; Chair. Trustees Imperial War Museum 1978–79; Trustee R.A.F. Church St. Clement Danes 1971–97, Shuttleworth Remembrance Trust 1978–88, RAF Trustee, Burma Star Asscn., 1979–96, The Prince Philip Trust Fund 1982–92; Pres. The Air League 1984–87; a Vice-Pres. Nat. Asscn. of Boys Clubs; mem. Cttee. Royal Humane Soc. 1978–95, Life Vice-Pres. RNLI 1988–; Hon. Panglima Mangku Negara; Hon. Liveryman of the Haberdashers' Co.; Freeman of City of London; Kt.St.J. *Address:* c/o Whites', St. James's Street, London SW1, England.

GRANE, Leif, DR. THEOL.; Danish professor of church history; b. 11 Jan. 1928, Lyngby; s. of Jens Grane and Emma (née Christensen) Grane; m. Vreni Welti 1968; two s. one d.; ed. Univ. of Copenhagen, studies at Univs. of Lund and Tübingen; church minister, Brønshøj 1954–56; Prof. of Religion and History, Teachers' Training School 1956–60; Sr. Scholar Univ. of Copenhagen 1960–64, Prof. of Church History 1964–98; Head Coll. Domus Regiae, Copenhagen 1979–97; Chair. Steering Cttee. Int. Congresses for Lutheran Research 1975–83; Dean and mem. Steering Bd. Univ. of Copenhagen 1967–72, 1978–83; mem. Royal Acad. of Sciences and Letters 1981–, Academia Europaea 1989; corresp. mem. Akademie der Wissenschaften, Göttingen; Dr. Theol. h.c. (Munich) 1980, (Oslo) 1986, (Helsinki) 1990, (Reykjavik) 1997. *Publications:* Confessio Augustana 1959, Contra Gabrielem 1962, Peter Abelard 1964 (German and English), Protest og Konsekvens 1968 (Finnish), Modus loquendi theologicus: Luthers Kampf um die Erneuerung der Theologie 1975, Det teologiske Fakultet 1830–1979, 1980, Kirken i det 19. århundrede 1982 (German), Evangeliet for folket: Drøm og virkelighed i Martin Luthers liv 1983, Den Uberegnelige Luther 1993, Martinus noster Luther in The German Reform Movement 1518–1521 1994, Kristendommen i historien 1998. *Leisure interests:* friendships and carpentry. *Address:* Brobergsgade 3 st. th., DK-1427, Copenhagen K. (Home); Institute of Church History, Købmagergade 44-46, DK-1150, Copenhagen K., Denmark (Office). *Telephone:* 35 32 36 11 (Office); 32 96 76 15 (Home).

GRANELLI, Luigi; Italian politician; b. 1 March 1929, Lovere, Milan; Christian Democrat (D.C.) M.P. for Milan-Pavia 1968–79; Senator for Cantù 1979–1983, for Vimercate 1983–; Minister without Portfolio for Scientific and Tech. Research 1986–87. *Address:* Camera del Deputati, Rome, Italy.

GRANGE, Kenneth Henry, C.B.E., R.D.I., F.C.S.D.; British industrial designer; b. 17 July 1929; s. of Harry Alfred Grange and Hilda Gladys Grange (née Long); ed. London; Tech. Illustrator Royal Soc. of Painter-Printmakers (fmrly. of Painter-Etchers and Engravers) 1948–50; Design Asst. Arcon Chartered Architects 1948; Bronek Katz & Vaughn 1950–51; Gordon Bowyer & Partners 1951–54; Jack Howe & Partners 1954–58; industrial designer in pvt. practice 1958–; f. partner Pentagram Design 1972–; Pres. Chartered Soc. of Designers 1987–88; Master of Faculty R.D.I. 1985–87; Royal Designer for Industry 1969. Hon. Prof. Heriot-Watt Univ. 1987; Dr. h.c. R.C.A. 1985, D.Univ. Heriot-Watt 1986. ten Design Council Awards, Duke of Edin. Award for Elegant Design. *Leisure interests:* tennis, skiing. *Address:* Pentagram, 11 Needham Road, London, W11 2RP, England.

GRANIC, Mate, DR.SC.; Croatian politician and physician; b. 19 Sept. 1947, Baska Voda; m. Jadranka Granic; one s. two d.; ed. Zagreb Univ.; physician, Vuk Vrhovac Inst. for Diabetes Endocrinology and Metabolic Diseases, School of Medicine, Zagreb Univ. 1975–79; Head of Clinical Dept. Vuk Vrhovac Inst. 1979–85; Prof., Depty Dir. 1985–89; Vice-Dean, Faculty of Medicine, Zagreb Univ. 1989, Dean 1990–; mem., Vice-Pres. Croatian Democratic Union; Deputy Prime Minister 1991–; concurrently Minister of Foreign Affairs 1993–. *Publications:* papers and articles on diabetes. *Address:* Office of Deputy Prime Minister, Murkovtrg 2, 41000 Zagreb, Croatia. *Telephone:* 41/469-205.

GRANIN, Daniil Aleksandrovich; Russian writer; b. 1 Jan. 1919, Volya, Kursk; ed. Leningrad Polytechnic Inst.; mem. CPSU 1942–90; engineer 1940–50; first publs. 1949; U.S.S.R. People's Deputy 1989–91; Hero of Socialist Labour 1989. *Publications:* Second Variant 1949, Those Who Seek 1955, The House on Fontanka 1958, After the Wedding 1958, I Challenge the Storm 1962, Selected Works 1978, The Picture 1980, The Blockade Book (with A. Adamovich), 1981, The Leningrad Catalogue 1984, Buffalo 1987, The Clemency 1988, Collected Works (5 vols.) 1989, Our Dear Roman Avdeyevich 1991, The Destroyed Clemency 1993. *Address:* Brat'yev Vasilyevich Str. 8, Apt. 14, 197046 St. Petersburg, Russia (Home). *Telephone:* (812) 232-85-53.

GRANN, Phyllis, B.A.; American publisher and editor; b. 2 Sept. 1937, London, U.K.; d. of Solomon Grann and Louisa (Bois-Smith) Eitingon; m. Victor Grann 1962; two s. one d.; ed. Barnard Coll.; Sec., Doubleday Publrs., New York 1958–60; Ed., William Morrow Inc., New York 1960–62, David McKay Co., New York 1962–70, Simon & Schuster Inc., New York 1970; Vice-Pres. Simon & Schuster Inc. 1976; Pres., Publr. G. P. Putnam's & Sons, New York 1976–86; Pres. Putnam Publishing Group Inc. (now Penguin Putnam Inc.), New York 1986–96, C.E.O. 1987–96, Chair. 1997–. *Address:* Penguin Putnam Inc., 200 Madison Avenue, New York, NY 10016, U.S.A.

GRANÖ, Olavi Johannes, PH.D.; Finnish professor of geography; b. 27 May 1925, Helsinki; s. of Prof. Dr. J. Gabriel Granö and Hilma Ekholm; m. Eeva Kaleva 1953; two d.; ed. Turku, Helsinki and Copenhagen Univs.; Asst. Prof. of Geography, Helsinki Univ. and Helsinki School of Econs. 1948–57; Assoc. Prof. of Geography, Turku Univ. 1958–61, Prof. 1962–88, Chancellor 1984–94; Pres. Archipelago Research Inst. 1965–84; Pres. Finnish Nat. Research Council for Sciences 1964–69; Pres. Cen. Bd. of Research Councils (Acad. of Finland) 1970–73; mem. Science Policy Council 1964–74; Pres. Advisory Cttee. for Research of Nordic Council of Ministers 1976–82; Acad. of Finland 1980; mem. Finnish Acad. of Science and Letters 1970; (Chair. 1993–95); Visiting Fellow, Clare Hall, Cambridge Univ. 1982 Hon. Corresp. mem. Royal Geographical Soc. (London) 1980; Hon. mem. Geographical Soc. of S. Sweden 1981, mem. Royal Swedish Acad. of Sciences 1985, Academia Europaea 1989; Dr. h.c. (Toruń, Poland) 1980, (Tartu, Estonia) 1989, (Åbo Academy, Turku) 1993; Finnish Geographical Soc. Fennia Medal 1988. *Publications:* scientific publications on geography, geology, history of science and science policy. *Address:* Department of Geography, Turku University, 20014 Turku (Office); Sirppitie 1A, 20540 Turku, Finland (Home). *Telephone:* (2) 333 5595 (Office); (2) 237 0640. *Fax:* (2) 333 5896.

GRANT, Allan Kerr, A.O., M.B., B.S., F.R.A.C.P., F.R.C.P., F.R.C.P. (E); Australian gastroenterologist; b. 29 Oct. 1924, Adelaide; s. of Sir Kerr Grant and Kate Moffatt; m. Mary Raymond Hone 1949; three s. one d.; ed. St. Peter's Coll., Adelaide, Univ. of Adelaide; Consultant Gastroenterological, Repatriation Gen. Hosp., S. Australia 1954–78; Sr. Dir. Gastroenterology Univ., Queen Elizabeth Hosp. 1964–84, Consultant 1984–; Hon. Assoc. Physician, Adelaide Children's Hosp. 1965–84; Physician, S. Vietnam 1969; Hon. Clinical Lecturer, Univ. of Adelaide 1966–78, Clinical Reader 1982–84, Assoc. Dean Postgrad. Studies in Medicine 1985–89; Army Officer (Col.), Consultant Physician 1978–84; Sr. Visiting Physician Flinders Medical Centre 1984–; Clinical Assoc. Prof., Dept. of Medicine, Assoc. Dean, Flinders Univ. of S. Australia 1984–94; Pres. R.A.C.P. 1980–82, mem. Exec. 1973–82; mem. Medical Bd. of S. Australia 1983–98, American Gastroenterological Asscn.; Hon. mem. British Soc. of Gastroenterology 1996; Hon. M.D. (Flinders Univ. of S. Australia) 1996; D. Univ. (Adelaide); R.F.D.; E.D. *Publication:* Clinical Diagnosis of Gastrointestinal Disease (with A. P. Skyring) 1981. *Leisure interests:* ornithology, bird photography, nature conservation, opera, ballet, fishing. *Address:* 7 Duncraig Lane, Stirling, S.A. 5152, Australia (Home). *Telephone:* 8339 7319.

GRANT, Bruce Alexander, B.A.; Australian writer; b. 4 April 1925, Perth; s. of Leslie John Grant and Myrtle Rapson Williams; m. 3rd Ratih Hardjono 1997; three s. two d. from previous marriages; ed. Perth Modern School, Univ. of Melbourne, Harvard Univ., served Royal Australian Navy 1943–45; with The Age 1950–65, Film, Theatre Critic and Literary Ed. 1950–53, Foreign Corresp., Europe 1954–57, Asia 1959–63, Wash. 1964–65; Fellow in Political Science Univ. of Melbourne 1965–68, Visiting Fellow 1976; columnist 1968–72; High Comm. to India (also accred. to Nepal) 1973–76; Research Assoc. Int. Inst. for Strategic Studies., London 1977; Dir. Inst. Political Science 1979–; Dir. then Chair. Australian Dance Theatre 1979–82; Writer-in-Residence Monash Univ. 1981; Adviser on Arts Policy State Govt. of Victoria 1982–86; Visiting Fellow, Australian Nat. Univ., Canberra 1983; Pres. Melbourne Spoleto Festival of Three Worlds 1984–87; Chair. Victorian Premier's Literary Awards 1984–86, Victorian Australian Bicentennial Authority 1985–86; Consultant to Minister for Foreign Affairs and Trade 1988–91; Chair. Australia-Indonesia Inst. 1989–92; Prof. of Diplomacy and Statecraft, Dept. of Man., Monash Univ. 1994–. *Publications:* Indonesia 1964, The Crisis of Loyalty 1972, Arthur and Eric 1977, The Boat People 1979, Cherry Bloom 1980, Gods and Politicians 1982, The Australian Dilemma 1983, What Kind of Country? 1988, Australia's Foreign Relations (with Gareth Evans) 1991, The Budd Family 1995, A Furious Hunger: America in the 21st Century 1999; numerous short-stories, articles and chapters in books on int. affairs. *Leisure interests:* films, theatre, Asian literature, swimming. *Address:* c/o Curtis Brown (Australia) Pty. Ltd., 19 Union Street, Sydney, N.S.W. 2021, Australia.

GRANT, Hugh John Mungo, B.A.; British actor; b. 9 September 1960, London; s. of James Murray Grant and Fynvola Susan Grant (née Maclean); ed. Latymer Upper School, Hammersmith, New College, Oxford; acting in theatre, TV and films, and producer for Simian Films; began career in theatre performing Jockeys of Norfolk (written with Chris Lang and Andy Taylor); Best Actor, Venice Film Festival (jtly. with James Wilby q.v.) 1987; Golden Globe Award 1995, B.A.F.T.A. Award for Best Actor in Four Weddings and a Funeral 1995. *Principal films:* White Mischief 1987, Maurice 1987, Lair of the White Worm 1988, La Nuit Bengali 1988, Impromptu 1989, Bitter Moon 1992, Remains of the Day 1993, Four Weddings and a Funeral 1994, Sirens 1994, The Englishman who went up a hill but came down a mountain 1995, Nine Months 1995, An Awfully Big Adventure 1995, Sense and Sensibility 1995, Restoration 1996, Extreme Measures (for Simian Films) 1996, Mickey Blue

Eyes (for Simian Films) 1998, Notting Hill 1998. *Leisure interests:* soccer, singing. *Address:* c/o Simian Films, 3 Cromwell Place, London, SW7 2JE, England. *Telephone:* 0171-589 6822. *Fax:* 0171-589 9405.

GRANT, Keith Frederick, A.R.C.A., F.R.G.S.; British landscape painter, muralist and lecturer; b. 10 Aug. 1930, Liverpool; s. of Charles Grant and Gladys Emma Grant; m. Gisèle Barka Djouadi 1964; one s. (deceased) one d.; one d. by Hilde Ellingsen; ed. Bootle Grammar School, Willesden School of Art and R.C.A., London; State Scholarship to Norway 1960; Head of Fine Art Dept., Maidstone Coll. of Art, Kent 1968–71; Gulbenkian Award Artist-in-Residence, Bosworth Coll., Leics. 1973–75; mem. Fine Art Bd. Council for Nat. Academic Awards 1978–81; Head of Painting Dept., Newcastle Polytechnic 1979–81; Head of Dept. of Art, The Roehampton Inst., London 1981–90, Artist-in-Residence 1990–95; Expedition Artist to Guyana 1991; Art Dir. Operation Raleigh 1991–; one-man shows in London 1960–, and shows in Iceland, Norway, France, Italy and Luxembourg; recorded volcanic eruption, Iceland 1973; painted launch of Ariane Rocket 1982; visited Soviet Union for Anglo-Soviet cultural exchange programme of the British Council 1979; other British Council tours to Cyprus 1976, Hungary, Cuba 1985 and Norway 1987; visited Sarawak 1984 and 1985; designed prints for use in Earthlife Foundation's Rainforest Campaign; designed book covers for 6 Peter Mattheissen works 1988–89; visited Greenland to study icebergs at Ilulissat (Jakobshavn); Guest Artist, Ben Gurion Univ. of the Negev and British Israel Art Foundation 1988; works in many public collections including Arts Council of G.B., Nat. Gallery of N.Z., Nat. Gallery of S. Australia, Hamilton Art Gallery, Ontario, Trondheim Art Gallery, Norway, Contemporary Art Soc., Fitzwilliam Museum, Cambridge, Abbot Hall Gallery, Kendal, British Council, All Souls Coll. Oxford, Univ. of Bradford, Imperial Coll. London, Victoria and Albert Museum, Richmond College, London; mural/mosaics, Charing Cross Hosp., London, Gateshead Metro Station; painting, Guildhall School of Music and Drama, London; sculpture, Shaw Theatre, London; elected mem. Telemark Artists' Asscn., Norway 1996; Silver Medal for Mural Painting, R.C.A. 1958. *Leisure interests:* walking, music, travel and writing. *Address:* Arnes Brygge, 3810 Gvarv, Telemark, Norway (Studio). *Telephone:* 35959795 (Studio).

GRANT, Sir (Matthew) Alistair, Kt.; British business executive; b. 6 March 1937; s. of John Grant and Jessie Grant; m. Judith Mary Grant (née Dent); two s. one d.; ed. Woodhouse Grove School, Yorks.; nat. service 1955–57; joined Unilever 1958; founder and Dir. Safeway PLC (fmrly. Argyll Group PLC) 1977–96, Deputy Chair. and Chief Exec. 1986–88, Chair. and Chief Exec. 1988–93, Chair. 1993–96; Gov. Bank of Scotland PLC 1998– (non-exec. Dir. 1992–); Chair., Scottish & Newcastle PLC 1997– (non-exec. Dir. 1994–); Chair. Biotech. and Biological Sciences Research Council 1991–98; Vice-Pres. Chartered Inst. of Marketing; Pres. Inst. of Grocery Distribution 1991–94, Royal Agric. Soc. of England 1993–94; Visiting Prof. Univ. of Strathclyde; Trustee Nat. Museums of Scotland, Trustee regent, Royal Coll. of Surgeons, Edin.; Hon. D.B.A. (Strathclyde) 1992, (Napier, Edin.) 1994, Hon. D.Sc. (Cranfield Inst. of Tech.) 1993, Hon. D. Univ. (Edin.) 1993. *Leisure interests:* hunting, fishing, painting, reading, music. *Address:* Bank of Scotland, P.O. Box 5, The Mound, Edinburgh, EH1 1YZ, Scotland. *Telephone:* (0131) 442 7777. *Fax:* (0131) 243 5566.

GRANT, Peter James; British business executive; b. 5 Dec. 1929; s. of late Lieut-Col. P. C. H. Grant and Mrs. Grant (née Gooch); m. 1st Ann Pleydell-Bouverie; one s. one d.; m. 2nd Paula Eugster; one s. two d.; ed. Winchester Coll. and Magdalen Coll. Oxford; Lieut. Queens Own Cameron Highlanders; joined Edward de Stein & Co. 1952, merged with Lazard Brothers & Co., Ltd. 1960; Dir. Standard Industrial Group 1966–72, Charrington, Gardner, Lockett & Co., Ltd. 1970–74, Walter Runciman PLC 1973–90; Dir. Sun Life Assurance Soc. PLC 1973–, Vice-Chair. 1976, Chair. 1983–95; Chair. PaineWebber Int. (U.K.) Ltd. 1988–90, Highlands & Islands Airports Ltd. 1993–; Deputy Chair. LEP Group PLC 1988; Dir. London Merchant Securities 1985– (Deputy Chair. 1994–), Scottish Hydro-Electric PLC 1990–94; mem. Industrial Devt. Bd. 1985–92, Council and Policy Exec. Cttee., Inst. of Dirs. 1989–, Civil Aviation Authority 1993–, Cromarty Firth Port Authority 1994–95. *Leisure interests:* shooting, golf, gardening. *Address:* 14 Eaton Row, London, SW1W 0JA, England; Mountgerald, nr. Dingwall, Ross-shire, IV15 9TT, Scotland. *Telephone:* (01349) 62244 (Dingwall).

GRANT, Peter Raymond, B.A., PH.D., F.R.S.; British professor of biology; b. 26 Oct. 1936, London; s. of Frederick Thomas Charles Grant and Mavis Irene Grant; m. Barbara Rosemary Matchett 1962; two d.; ed. Cambridge Univ. and Univ. of British Columbia; Postdoctoral Fellowship Yale Univ. 1964–65; Asst. Prof. of Biology McGill Univ., Canada 1965–68, Assoc. Prof. 1968–73, Prof. 1973–78; Prof. Univ. of Michigan 1978–85; Prof. of Biology Princeton Univ. 1985–89, Class of 1877 Prof. of Zoology 1989–; F.L.S.; Fellow American Asscn. for Advancement of Science, American Acad. of Arts and Science; mem. American Philosophical Soc. 1991; Hon. Ph.D. (Uppsala) 1986. *Publications:* Ecology and Evolution of Darwin's Finches 1986, Evolutionary Dynamics of a Natural Population: The Large Cactus Finch of the Galápagos (with B. Rosemary Grant) 1989, Evolution on Islands (ed.) 1998. *Leisure interests:* camping, hiking, music and reading. *Address:* Department of Ecology and Evolutionary Biology, Princeton University, Princeton, NJ 08544-1003, U.S.A. *Telephone:* (609) 258 5156.

GRANT, Richard E.; actor; b. 1957; s. of late Hendrick Grant and of Leonie Grant; m. Joan Washington; one d.; ed. S. Africa; grew up in Swaziland; stage appearances include: Man of Mode 1988, The Importance of Being Earnest 1993, A Midsummer Night's Dream 1994; TV appearances include: Honest, Decent, Legal and True 1986, Here is the News 1989, Suddenly Last Summer 1992, Hard Times 1993, Karaoke 1996. *Films:* Withnail and I 1986, How to Get Ahead in Advertising 1989, Warlock 1989, Henry and June 1990, Mountains of the Moon 1990, LA Story 1991, Hudson Hawk 1991, Bram Stoker's Dracula 1992, The Player 1993, The Age of Innocence 1993, Prêt à Porter 1995, Jack and Sarah 1995, Portrait of a Lady 1995, Twelfth Night 1995, The Serpent's Kiss 1996, Food of Love 1996, All For Love 1997, Spice World—The Movie 1997, The Scarlet Pimpernel (TV) 1998, The Match 1998. *Publications:* With Nails: The Film Diaries of Richard E. Grant 1995, Twelfth Night 1996, By Design—a Hollywood Novel. *Address:* c/o ICM, Oxford House, 76 Oxford Street, London, W1N 0AX, England.

GRANT, Verne E., PH.D.; American biologist; b. 17 Oct. 1917, San Francisco, Calif.; s. of Edwin E. and Bessie C. (Swallow) Grant; m. 1st Alva Day 1946 (divorced 1959); one s. two d.; m. 2nd Karen S. Alt 1960; ed. Univ. of California (Berkeley); Visiting Investigator, Carnegie Inst. of Washington, Stanford, Calif. 1949–50; Geneticist and experimental taxonomist, Rancho Santa Ana Botanic Garden, Claremont, Calif. 1950–67; Prof. of Biology, Inst. of Life Science, Texas A. & M. Univ. 1967–68; Prof. of Biological Sciences, Univ. of Ariz. 1968–70; Dir. Boyce Thompson Arboretum, Ariz. 1968–70; Prof. of Botany, Univ. of Tex. 1970–87, Prof. Emer. 1987–; Nat. Research Council Fellowship 1949–50; Phi Beta Kappa Award in Science 1964; Certificate of Merit, Botanical Soc. of America 1971; mem. N.A.S.; Fellow American Acad. of Arts and Sciences. *Publications:* Natural History of the Phlox Family 1959, The Origin of Adaptations 1963, The Architecture of the Germplasm 1964, Flower Pollination in the Phlox Family (with Karen Grant) 1965, Hummingbirds and Their Flowers (with Karen Grant) 1968, Plant Speciation 1971, 1981, Genetics of Flowering Plants 1975, Organismic Evolution 1977, The Evolutionary Process 1985, The Edward Grant Family and Related Families in Massachusetts, Rhode Island, Pennsylvania, and California 1997; numerous papers on plant genetics, plant evolution and gen. evolution. *Leisure interests:* railroading, classical music. *Address:* Department of Botany, University of Texas at Austin, Austin, TX 78712 (Office); 2811 W. Fresco Drive, Austin, TX 78731, U.S.A. (Home).

GRASS, Günter; German writer and artist; b. 16 Oct. 1927, Danzig (now Gdańsk, Poland); m. 1st Anna Schwarz 1954; three s. one d.; m. 2nd Utte Grunert 1979; ed. art school; mem. Akademie der Künste, Berlin (Pres. 1983–86), American Acad. of Arts and Sciences; mem. Social Democratic Party (resgnd. Dec. 1992); Dr.h.c. (Kenyon Coll.) 1965, (Harvard) 1976; Lyric Prize, Süddeutscher Rundfunk 1955, Group 47 Prize 1959, Literary Prize, Asscn. of German Critics 1960, Georg-Büchner Prize 1965, Theodor-Heuss Prize 1969, Int. Feltrinelli Prize 1982, Karel Čapek Prize 1994, Sonning Arts Prize (Denmark) 1996, Thomas Mann Prize 1996; Hermann Kestan Medal 1995. *Publications:* Die Vorzüge der Windhühner (poems and drawings) 1955, Die Blechtrommel 1959 (film The Tin Drum 1979), Gleisdreieck (poems and drawings) 1960, Katz und Maus 1961 (film 1967), Hundejahre 1963, Ausgefragt (poems) 1967, Über das Selbstverständliche 1968, Örtlich betäubt 1969, Aus dem Tagebuch einer Schnecke 1972, Dokumente zur politischen Wirkung 1972, Die Bürger und seine Stimme 1974, Der Butt 1976, Denkzettel 1978, Das Treffen in Telgte 1979, Kopfgeburten 1980, Aufsätze zur Literatur 1980, Zeichnen und Schreiben Band I 1982, Widerstand lernen-Politische Gegenreden 1980–83 1984, Band II 1984, On Writing and Politics 1967–83 1985, Die Ratte 1987, Zünge Zeigen 1988, Werkansgabe, 10 vols. 1988, Two States—One Nation? 1990, Vier Jahrzehnte 1992, Der Ruf der Kröte (novel) 1992, Ein Weitas Feld 1995, Fundsachen für Nichtleser (poems) 1997; plays: Hochwasser 1956, Noch 10 Minuten bis Buffalo 1958, Onkel, Onkel 1958, Die bösen Köche 1961, Die Plebejer proben den Aufstand 1965, Davor 1968. *Leisure interest:* cooking. *Address:* Glockengiesserstr. 21, 23552 Lübeck, Germany.

GRASSLEY, Charles E., M.A.; American politician, farmer and teacher; b. 17 Sept. 1933, New Hartford, Ia.; m. Barbara Ann Speicher; five c.; ed. Univs. of Northern Iowa and Iowa; farmer; Instructor Political Science, Drake Community Coll. 1962, Charles City Coll. 1967–68; mem. Ia. House of Reps. 1959–75; mem. House of Reps. 1975–81 from 3rd Dist., Ia.; Senator from Iowa 1981–; Republican; mem. Nat. Farm Bureau. *Address:* U.S. Senate, 135 Hart Senate Office Building, Washington, DC 20510, U.S.A.

GRASSO, Richard A., B.S.; American stock exchange executive; ed. Pace and Harvard Univs.; New York Stock Exchange 1968–, Dir. Listing and Marketing 1973–77, Vice-Pres. Corp. Services 1977–81, Sr. Vice-Pres. Corp. Services 1981–83, Exec. Vice-Pres. Marketing Group 1983–86, Exec. Vice-Pres. Capital Markets 1986–88, Pres., C.O.O. 1988–93, Exec. Vice-Chair., Pres. 1993–95, Chair. C.E.O. 1995–. *Address:* New York Stock Exchange, 11 Wall Street, New York, NY 10005, U.S.A.

GRATZ, Leopold; Austrian politician; b. 4 Nov. 1929, Vienna; m.; ed. Faculty of Law, Univ. of Vienna; served in Fed. Ministry for Social Admin. 1952–53; mem. Secr. Socialist Parl. Party 1953, Sec. 1957; Sec. Socialist Party Exec. 1963; mem. Bundesrat 1963–66, Nationalrat 1966–; Chair. Educational Policy Comm. of Exec. of Socialist Party 1968; Minister of Educ. 1970–71; Mayor of Vienna 1973–84; Minister of Foreign Affairs 1984–86; Pres. Nat. Council 1986–89. *Address:* c/o Social Democratic Party of Austria, Löwelstrasse 18, 1014 Vienna, Austria.

GRAUERT, Johannes (Hans), D.RER.NAT.; German professor of mathematics; b. 8 Feb. 1930, Haren/Ems; s. of Clemens Grauert; m. Marie-Luise Meyer 1956; one s. one d.; ed. Univs. of Mainz and Münster and ETH, Zürich; Inst.

for Advanced Study, Princeton 1957–59; Inst. des Hautes Etudes, Paris 1959 (mem. Supervisory Bd. 1976–82); Prof. Univ. of Göttingen 1959–; mem. acads of Göttingen, Mainz, Catania, Leopoldina and Acad. Europaea, Acad. of Bayern (von Staudt Prize 1991); Dr.rer.nat. h.c. (Bayreuth, Bochum, Bonn). *Publications:* seven books and numerous papers in leading journals. *Leisure interests:* pure mathematics, philosophy. *Address:* Ewaldstrasse 67, 37075 Göttingen, Germany. *Telephone:* 4-15-80.

GRAVE, Walter Wyatt, C.M.G., PH.D.; British educationist; b. 16 Oct. 1901, King's Lynn; s. of the late Walter and Annie Grave; m. Kathleen Margaret Macpherson 1932; two d.; ed. Emmanuel Coll., Cambridge; Fellow of Emmanuel Coll., Cambridge 1926–66, 1972–, Tutor 1936–40; Lecturer in Spanish, Cambridge Univ. 1936–40, Sr. Proctor 1938–39; Admin. Officer Ministry of Labour and Nat. Service 1940–43; Univ. Registrary, Cambridge 1943–52; Prin. Univ. Coll. of West Indies 1953–58; Censor Fitzwilliam House, Cambridge, 1959–66; Master Fitzwilliam Coll., Cambridge 1966–71, Hon. Fellow 1971–; Hon. LL.D. (Cambridge and McMaster Univs.). *Publication:* Fitzwilliam College, Cambridge 1869–1969 1983. *Address:* 125A Long Road, Cambridge, CB2 2HE, England. *Telephone:* (01223) 845310.

GRAVEL, Mike; American politician; b. 13 May 1930, Springfield, Mass.; s. of Alphonse and Maria Gravel; m. Rita Martin 1959; one s. one d.; ed. Columbia Univ.; Real estate developer; mem. Alaska House of Reps. 1962–66; Speaker, Alaska House of Reps. 1965; U.S. Senator from Alaska 1969–81; f. Mike Gravel Resource Analysts, Anchorage, Alaska 1981–; Democrat. *Publications:* Jobs and More Jobs, Citizen Power, The Pentagon Papers (editor). *Address:* 512 1/2 G Street, S.E., Washington, DC 20022, U.S.A.

GRAVES, William Preston; American politician; b. 9 Jan. 1953, Salina, Kan.; s. of William Graves and Helen Mayo; ed. Kansas Wesleyan Univ. Salina and Univ. of Kansas; Deputy Asst. Sec. of State, Kan. 1980–85, Asst. Sec. of State 1985–87, Sec. of State 1987–95; Gov. of Kansas Jan. 1995–; Trustee Kansas Wesleyan Univ. 1987–; Republican. *Leisure interests:* running, reading, travel. *Address:* Office of the Governor, State Capitol, 2nd Floor, Topeka, KS 66612, U.S.A. *Telephone:* (913) 296-3232. *Fax:* (913) 296-5669.

GRAY, Alasdair James; British writer and painter; b. 28 Dec. 1934, Glasgow; s. of Alexander Gray and Amy Fleming; m. 1st Inge Sørensen (divorced); one s.; m. 2nd Morag McAlpine 1991; art teacher, Glasgow and Lanarkshire 1958–62; scene painter, Pavilion and Citizens' theatres 1962–63; freelance writer and painter 1963–76; artist recorder, People's Palace Local History Museum, Glasgow 1976–77; Writer-in-Residence, Glasgow Univ. 1977–79; freelance writer and painter 1979–; works in collections of People's Palace Local History Museum, Glasgow, Collin's Gallery, Strathclyde Univ.; mural paintings in Palace Rigg Nature Reserve Exhibition Centre, New Cumbernauld, Abbot's House Local History Museum, Dunfermline. *Publications include:* The Comedy of the White Dog (short story) 1979, Lanark: A Life in Four Books (novel) 1981, Unlikely Stories 1982, Janine (novel) 1984, The Fall of Kelvin Walker (novel) 1985, Lean Tales (co-writer) 1985, Five Scottish Artists (catalogue) 1986, Saltire Self-Portrait 4 (autobiographical sketch) 1988, Old Negatives (four verse sequences) 1989, Something Leather (novel) 1990, McGrotty and Ludmilla (novel) 1990, Poor Things (novel) 1992, Why Scots Should Rule Scotland (polemic) 1992, Ten Tales Tall and True (Short Stories) 1993, A History Maker (novel) 1994, Mavis Belfrage (novel) 1996, Songs of Scotland 1997, Working Legs (play) 1997, The Anthology of Prefaces 1999. *Leisure interests:* reading, walking. *Address:* 2 Marchmont Terrace, Glasgow, G12 9LT, Scotland. *Telephone:* (0141) 339-0093.

GRAY, Douglas, M.A., F.B.A.; British/New Zealand professor of English Literature and Language; b. 17 Feb. 1930, Melbourne; s. of Emmerson Gray and Daisy Gray; m. Judith Claire Campbell, 1959; one s.; ed. Wellington Coll. N.Z., Victoria Univ. of Wellington, Merton Coll., Oxford; asst. lecturer Vic. Univ. of Wellington 1952–54, lecturer in English, Pembroke and Lincoln Colls. Oxford 1956–61, Fellow in English, Pembroke Coll. 1961–80, J.R.R. Tolkien Prof. of English Literature and Language and Fellow of Lady Margaret Hall, Oxford 1980–97, Emer. Prof. 1997–, Hon. Fellow 1997–; Hon. Lit.D. (Victoria Univ. of Wellington) 1995. *Publications:* Themes and Images in the Medieval English Lyric 1972, A Selection of Religious Lyrics 1974, Robert Henryson 1979, Oxford Book of Late Medieval Verse and Prose 1985 (Ed.), J. A. W. Bennett, Middle English Literature 1986 (Ed.); From Anglo-Saxon to Early Middle English 1994 (jt. Ed.). *Leisure interests:* travel, walking. *Address:* 31 Nethercote Road, Tackley, Oxford, OX5 3AW, England (Home). *Telephone:* (01865) 983319 (Home).

GRAY, Dulcie Winifred Catherine, C.B.E., F.R.S.A.; British actress, playwright and author; b. 20 Nov. 1920; d. of the late Arnold Savage Bailey and Kate Edith Clulow Gray; m. Michael Denison (deceased) 1939; ed. England and Malaya; has worked in theatre since 1939; repertory includes Aberdeen, Edin., Glasgow, Harrogate; debut as Sorrel in Hay Fever 1939; in BBC serial Front Line Family 1941. *Theatre includes:* The Little Foxes, Midsummer Night's Dream 1942, Brighton Rock, Landslide 1943, Lady from Edinburgh 1945, Dear Ruth, Wind is 90 1946, Queen Elizabeth Slept Here 1949, Sweet Peril 1952, We Must Kill Toni, The Diary of a Nobody 1954, Love Affair (also writer) 1956, Double Cross 1958, Let Them Eat Cake 1959, Candida 1960, Heartbreak House 1961, Where Angels Fear to Tread 1963, An Ideal Husband 1965, Happy Family 1967, Number 10 1967, Out of the Question 1968, Three 1970, The Wild Duck 1970, Ghosts 1972, At the End of the Day 1973, Time and the Conways (tour) 1977, A Murder is Announced 1977, Lloyd George Knew my Father (tour) 1980, A Coat of Varnish 1982, School for Scandal (British Council 50th Anniversary European Tour) 1983, The Living Room 1987, The Best of Friends (tour) 1990, 1991, The Importance of Being Earnest (tour) 1991, Tartuffe 1991–92, Two of a Kind (tour) 1995. *Films include:* They Were Sisters 1944, Wanted for Murder 1945, A Man about the House 1946, Mine Own Executioner 1947, There Was a Young Lady 1953, A Man Could Get Killed 1965, The Black Crow 1994. *TV:* Howard's Way (series) 1985–90, several plays; Fellow Linnean Soc. 1984, Queen's Silver Jubilee Medal 1977. *Publications:* Murder on the Stairs, Murder in Melbourne, Baby Face, Epitaph for a Dead Actor, Murder on a Saturday, Murder in Mind, The Devil Wore Scarlet, No Quarter for a Star, The Murder of Love, Died in the Red, The Actor and His World (with Michael Denison), Death in Denims, Butterflies on my Mind (Times Educational Supplement Sr. Information Book Prize 1978), Dark Calypso, The Glanville Women, Anna Starr, Mirror Image, Looking Forward, Looking Back (autobiog.). *Leisure interests:* swimming, butterflies. *Address:* c/o Barry Burnett PLC, 42 Grafton House, 2 Golden Square, London, W1X 6JD; Shardeloes, Amersham, Bucks., HP7 0RL, England.

GRAY, George William, C.B.E., PH.D., C.CHEM., F.R.S.C., F.R.S.E., F.R.S.; British professor of chemistry; b. 4 Sept. 1926, Edinburgh; s. of John William Gray and Jessie Colville (née Hunter); m. Marjorie Mary Canavan; three d.; ed. Univs. of Glasgow and London; mem. staff, Dept. of Chem., Univ. of Hull 1946–, Sr. Lecturer 1960, Reader 1964, Prof. of Organic Chem. 1978–84, G. F. Grant Prof. of Chem. 1984–90; Research Co-ordinator E. Merck Ltd. 1990–93, Consultant 1993–; Emer. Prof. Univ. of Hull, Visiting Prof. Univ. of Southampton 1990–; Ed. Liquid Crystals; Foreign mem. Japanese Acad. of Eng. 1996; Hon. D.Sc. (Hull) 1991, (Nottingham Trent Univ.) 1994, (Univ. of Southampton) 1996, (Univ. of E. Anglia) 1997; Queen's Award for Technological Achievement 1979, 1992; Rank Prize for Optoelectronics 1980; Leverhulme Medal of Royal Soc. 1987; Royal Soc. of Chemistry Fine Chemicals Award 1992; Kyoto Prize Laureate in Advanced Tech. 1995; Karl Ferdinand Braun Medal of Soc. for Information Display 1996; Freedericksz Medal of Russian Liquid Crystal Soc. 1997. *Publications:* Molecular Structure and the Properties of Liquid Crystals 1962, Liquid Crystals and Plastic Crystals (Ed. and jtly. with P. A. Winsor) 1974, The Molecular Physics of Liquid Crystals (Ed. and jtly. with G. R. Luckhurst) 1979, Smectic Liquid Crystals—Textures and Structures (with J. W. Goodby) 1984; Thermotropic Liquid Crystals (Ed.) 1987, Handbook of Liquid Crystals (four vols.) (Jt. Ed.) 1998; 350 papers on liquid crystals in scientific journals. *Leisure interests:* gardening, philately. *Address:* P.O. Box 3307, Wimborne, Dorset, BH21 4YD (Office); Juniper House, Furzehill, Wimborne, Dorset, BH21 4HD, England (Home). *Telephone:* (01202) 880164 (Office and Home). *Fax:* (01202) 840702 (Home).

GRAY, Harry Barkus, PH.D; American chemist; b. 14 Nov. 1935, Kentucky; m. Shirley Barnes 1957; two s. one d.; ed. Northwestern Univ. and Univ. of Copenhagen; Asst. Prof. of Chem., Columbia Univ. 1961–63, Assoc. Prof. 1963–65, Prof. 1965–66; Prof. of Chem. Calif. Inst. of Tech. 1966–, now Arnold O. Beckman Prof.; mem. N.A.S., American Acad. of Arts and Sciences; Foreign mem. Royal Danish Soc. of Science and Letters; Franklin Award 1967, Fresenius Award 1970, American Chem. Soc. Award in Pure Chem. 1970, Harrison Howe Award 1972, MCA Award 1972, Guggenheim Fellow 1972–73, American Chem. Soc. Award in Inorganic Chem. 1978, Remsen Award 1979, Tolman Award 1979, Centenary Medal 1985, Nat. Medal of Science 1986, Pauling Medal 1986, Calif. Scientist of the Year 1988, Alfred Bader Award 1990, Gold Medal American Inst. of Chemists 1990, Waterford Prize 1991, Priestley Medal 1991, Gibbs Medal 1992, Linderstrøm-Lang Prize 1992. *Publications:* Electrons and Chemical Bonding 1965, Molecular Orbital Theory 1965, Ligand Substitution Processes 1966, Basic Principles of Chemistry 1967, Chemical Dynamics 1968, Chemical Principles 1970, Models in Chemical Science 1971, Chemical Bonds 1973, Electronic Structure and Bonding 1981, Molecular Electronic Structures 1980. *Leisure interests:* tennis, music. *Address:* Noyes Laboratory of Chemical Physics, California Institute of Technology, 127-72 1201 East California Blvd, Pasadena, CA 91125 (Office); 1415 East California Boulevard, Pasadena, CA 91106, U.S.A. (Home). *Telephone:* (626) 395-6500 (Office); (626) 793-1978 (Home).

GRAY, Herb E.; Canadian politician; b. 25 May 1931, Windsor, Ont.; s. of late Harry and of Fannie Gray; m. Sharon Sholzberg 1967; one s. one d.; ed. Victoria Public School, Kennedy Coll. Inst. Windsor, McGill Univ., Montréal and Osgoode Hall Law School, Toronto; M.P. 1962–; Chair. of House of Commons Standing Cttee. on Finance, Trade and Econ. Affairs 1966–68; Parl. Sec. to Minister of Finance 1968–69; Minister without Portfolio (Finance) 1969–70, Minister of Nat. Revenue 1970–72, of Consumer and Corporate Affairs 1972–74, of Industry, Trade and Commerce 1980–82, of Regional Economic Expansion Jan.–Oct. 1982; Pres. of Treasury Bd. 1982–84; Opposition House Leader 1984–90, Deputy Opposition Leader 1989–90, Leader of the Opposition 1990, Opposition Finance Critic 1991–93; Solicitor Gen. and Leader of the Govt. in House of Commons 1993–97; Deputy Prime Minister 1997–; responsible for co-ordinating Govt. of Canada's activities to mark new Millennium 1997–; Govt. Observer Inter-American Conf. of Ministers of Labour, Bogotá 1963; Vice-Chair. Del. to NATO Parl. Conf., Paris 1963; mem. Del. to Canada-France Interparl. Conf. 1966; mem. Canadian Del. to IMF and IBRD meeting 1967, Canada-U.S. Interparl. Conf. 1967–68; Liberal.

Address: House of Commons, Ottawa, Ont. K1A 0A6 (Office); 1504–75 Riverside Drive East, Windsor, Ont., N9A 7C4, Canada (Home).

GRAY, Sir John Archibald Browne, M.A., M.B., B.CHIR., SC.D., F.R.C.P., F.R.S.; British administrator (retd.) and physiologist; b. 30 March 1918, London; s. of Sir Archibald Gray, K.C.V.O., C.B.E.; and Elsie Cooper; m. Vera K. Mares 1946; one s. and d.; ed. Cheltenham Coll., Clare Coll., Cambridge and Univ. Coll. Hospital London; Service Research for MRC 1943–45; Surgeon Lieut., R.N.V.R. 1945–46; MRC Scientific Staff, Nat. Inst. for Medical Research 1946–52; Reader in Physiology, Univ. Coll. London 1952–58, Prof. of Physiology 1958–66; Dean, Faculty of Science, Univ. of London 1960–65; Second Sec. MRC 1966–68, Sec. 1968–77; Chair. of Council, Int. Agency for Cancer Research 1972–74, of EU Cttee. for Medical Research 1973–75; mem. Scientific Staff MRC 1977–83; Hon. Fellow Clare Coll., Cambridge 1976; Pres. Freshwater Biological Asscn. 1983–88, Vice-Pres. 1988–; mem. Council, Marine Biological Asscn. 1969–88, Vice-Pres. 1989–; Hon. D.Sc. (Exeter) 1985. *Publications:* numerous papers on sensory receptors and sensory nervous system. *Leisure interest:* painting. *Address:* Seaways, Kingsway, Kingsand, Nr. Torpoint, Cornwall, PL10 1NG 1960–65; England. *Telephone:* (01752) 822745.

GRAY, John Malcolm; British banker; b. 1934, Hong Kong; m. Ursula Siong Koon 1984; three d.; ed. Sydney, Australia and Strathallan School, Scotland; served R.A.F.; joined Hong Kong Bank 1952, Chief Accountant 1979, Asst. Gen. Man. Finance 1981, Gen. Man. Group Finances 1985, Exec. Dir. Finance 1986–90; Deputy Chair. The Hongkong and Shanghai Banking Corpn. Ltd. 1990–93, Chair. 1993–96, C.E.O. 1993–96; Deputy Chair. HSBC Holdings PLC 1991–93, Exec. Dir. 1993–96; Chair. Hong Kong Port Devt. Bd.; mem. Council, Univ. of Hong Kong; mem. Hong Kong Exec. Council 1993–96; Deputy Chair. Harvey Nichols Group 1996–. *Address:* Harvey Nichols Group, 67 Brompton Road, London, S.W.3., England.

GRAY, Sir John (Walton David), K.B.E., C.M.G.; British diplomatist (retd.) and consultant; b. 1 Oct. 1936, Burry Port; s. of Myrddin Gray and Elsie Gray (née Jones); m. Anthoula Yerasimou 1957; one s. two d.; ed. Blundell's School, Devon, Christ's Coll. Cambridge, Oxford Univ. Middle East Centre and American Univ. Cairo; nat. service, R.A.S.C. 1954–56; joined Foreign Office 1962; served Beirut, Bahrain, FCO, Geneva, Sofia 1962–77; Counsellor, Jeddah 1978–81; Head of Dept. FCO 1982–85; Amb. to Lebanon 1985–88; Perm. Rep. to OECD, Paris 1988–92; Amb. to Belgium 1992–96; Chair. Consultancy Bd., Spadel UK 1997–, Deffrainc Ltd. 1998–; Adviser to Chief Exec., Hyder plc 1996–, Generale Bank 1998–; Vice-Pres. Welsh Centre for Int. Affairs 1994–96, Chair. 1996–; Pres. Wales Council, European Movt. 1997–; Trustee Nat. Botanic Garden of Wales 1998–; *Leisure interests:* rugby football, history, light walking, things Welsh. *Address:* 10 Marine Parade, Penarth, Vale of Glamorgan, CF64 3BG, Wales.

GRAY, Paul Edward, M.S.; American academic; b. 7 Feb. 1932, Newark, N.J.; s. of Kenneth F. Gray and Florence Gilleo; m. Priscilla W. King 1955; one s. three d.; ed. Grover Cleveland High School, Caldwell, N.J. and Mass. Inst. of Tech.; faculty mem. in electrical eng. M.I.T. 1960–71, 1990–, Dean, School of Eng. 1970–71; Chancellor, M.I.T. 1971–80, Pres. 1980–90, Chair. of Corpn. 1990–, Dir. 1990–97, Pres. Emer. 1997–; Dir. The New England, Boston, Arthur D. Little Inc., Cambridge, Mass., Shawmut Nat. Corpn., The Boeing Co., Seattle, Eastman Kodak Co., Rochester; Trustee Kennedy Memorial Trust, U.K.; Dir. Nat. Action Council for Minorities in Eng. Inc., N.Y.; Corporator, Woods Hole Oceanographic Inst.; Fellow, American Acad. of Arts and Sciences, A.A.A.S., I.E.E.E., Nat. Acad. of Eng. (Treasurer 1994–); corresp. mem. Nat. Acad. of Eng. in Mexico; various trusteeships and other professional appts. *Publications:* The Dynamic Behavior of Thermoelectric Devices 1960, Introduction to Electronics 1967; co-author of six other books. *Address:* Massachusetts Institute of Technology, 77 Massachusetts Avenue, Cambridge, MA 02139; 100 Memorial Drive, Apartment 11-4A, Cambridge, MA 02142, U.S.A.

GRAY, Peter, M.A., SC.D., F.R.S.; British professor of physical chemistry; b. 25 Aug. 1926, Newport, Monmouthshire; s. of the late Ivor Hicks Gray and Rose Ethel Gray; m. 1st Barbara Joan Hume 1952 (died 1992); two s. two d.; m. 2nd Rachel Katherine (née Buxton) Herzig 1996; ed. Newport High School, Gonville and Caius Coll., Cambridge; Univ. Demonstrator in Chemical Eng., Univ. of Cambridge 1951–55; Lecturer, Physical Chem. Dept., Univ. of Leeds 1955–59, Reader 1959–62, Prof. 1962–88; Master Gonville and Caius Coll., Cambridge 1988–96, Life Fellow 1996; Visiting Prof., Univ. of B.C. 1958–59, Univ. of W. Ont. 1969, Univ. of Göttingen 1979, Macquarie Univ. 1980, Beijing Inst. of Tech. 1984, Univ. of Paris VI 1986, Univ. of Gottingen 1986, Univ. of Calabria 1988; Assoc. Ed., Royal Soc. 1983–97; Pres. Faraday Soc. 1983–85, Cambridge Philosophical Soc. 1990–93; Larmor Lecture 1995; Hon. D.Sc. (Univ. of Leeds) 1997; Meldola Medal, Royal Inst. of Chem. 1956, Marlow Medal, Faraday Soc. 1959, Lewis Medal 1978, Award for Combustion, Royal Soc. of Chemistry 1986, Italgas Prize for Chemistry 1988, Bruylants Award, Louvain-la-Neuve 1994. *Publications:* Chemical Oscillations and Instabilities 1990; numerous papers in scientific journals. *Leisure interest:* hill-walking. *Address:* Gonville and Caius College, Cambridge, CB2 1TA; 13A Causeway, Horsham, RH12 1HE, England. *Telephone:* (01223) 332478.

GRAY, Robert Keith, M.B.A.; American business executive; b. 2 Sept. 1923, Hastings, Neb.; s. of Garold Gray and Marie Burchess; ed. Carleton Coll. and Harvard Univ.; Assoc. Prof. of Finance, Hastings Coll. Neb. 1950–51; Prof. Univ. of S. Calif. Los Angeles 1952; Special Asst. to Sec. of Navy 1954; Special Asst. to Pres. Eisenhower, White House, Washington, D.C. 1955–57, Appts. Sec. 1958; Sec. Eisenhower Cabinet, Washington, D.C. 1959–60; Vice-Pres. Hill & Knowlton Inc., Washington, D.C. 1961–64, Sr. Vice-Pres. 1965–70, Exec. Vice-Pres. 1971–76, Vice-Chair. 1977–81, C.E.O., Chair. 1991–; Founder, Chair. Gray & Co. Public Communications Int. (merger Hill & Knowlton Inc.), Washington 1981–86; Chair. and C.E.O. Hill & Knowlton Public Affairs Worldwide 1986–91; Chair. and Pres. Gray & Co. II 1988–; Chair. Gray Investment Properties Inc., 1988–; Pres., C.E.O. mem. Services Co., Washington 1988–; Chair. and C.E.O. Powerhouse Leasing Corpn. 1988–; Dir. First America Bank; Chair. Hill & Knowlton, U.S.A.; mem. numerous bds., advisory cttees. etc. *Publications:* Casebook on Organization and Operation of a Small Business Enterprise 1950, Eighteen Acres Under Glass 1962. *Address:* Gray & Co., 4731 Pine Tree Drive, Miami, FL 33133 (Office); 4953 Rock Spring Road, Arlington, VA 22207, U.S.A. (Home).

GRAY, Robin Trevor, D.D.A.; Australian politician; b. 1 March 1940, Victoria; s. of Rev. W. J. Gray; m. Judith F. Boyd 1965; two s. one d.; ed. Box Hill High School, Dookie Agric. Coll. and Univ. of Melbourne; teacher, Victoria Educ. Dept. 1961, Middx. County Council, U.K. 1964; agric. consultant Colac, Victoria 1965, Launceston, Tasmania 1965–76; part-time lecturer in Agric. Econs. Univ of Tasmania 1970–76; Deputy Leader of Opposition, Tasmania 1979–81, Leader of Opposition 1981–82, 1989–91, Premier 1982–89, Minister for Racing and Gaming 1982–84, for Energy 1982–88, for Forests 1984–86, for State Devt. 1984–89, for Primary Industry and Sea Fisheries 1992, for Energy 1992, for TT-Line 1993; Chair. R. T. Gray and Assocs. Pty. Ltd. 1995–; partner Evers Gray 1996–; Liberal. *Leisure interests:* cricket, golf, reading. *Address:* 11 Beech Road, Launceston, Tasmania 7250, Australia.

GRAY, Simon James Holliday,M.A.; British writer and teacher; b. 21 Oct. 1936; s. of Dr. James Davidson Gray and Barbara Cecelia Mary Holliday; m. Beryl Mary Kevern 1965; one s. one d.; ed. Westminster School, Dalhousie Univ., Halifax, N.S., Univ. of Cambridge; Supervisor in English, Univ. of B.C. 1960–63, Sr. Instructor 1963–64; lecturer in English, Queen Mary Coll., Univ. of London 1965–84; Hon. Fellow, Q.M.C., Univ. of London. *Publications:* Novels: Colmain 1963, Simple People 1965, Little Portia 1967, A Comeback for Stark 1968, non-fiction: An Unnatural Pursuit and Other Pieces 1985, How's That for Telling 'Em, Fat Lady (memoirs) 1988, Fat Chance 1995; Plays: Wise Child 1968, Sleeping Dog 1968, Dutch Uncle 1969, The Idiot 1971, Spoiled 1971, Butley 1971 (Evening Standard Award), Otherwise Engaged 1975 (Best Play, New York Drama Critics' Circle, Evening Standard Award), Plaintiffs and Defendants 1975, Two Sundays 1975, Dog Days 1976, Molly 1977, The Rear Column 1978, Close of Play 1979, Quartermaine's Terms 1981, Tartuffe 1982, Chapter 17 1982, Common Pursuit 1984, Melon 1987, The Holy Terror and Tartuffe 1990, Hidden Laughter 1990, Cell Mates 1994, Simply Disconnected 1996, Life Support 1997, Just the Three of Us 1997, The Late Middle Classes 1999. *Television:* After Pilkington 1987, Old Flames 1990, They Never Slept 1991, Running Late 1992, Unnatural Pursuits 1992 (Emmy Award, New York 1993), Femme Fatale 1993. Film: A Month in the Country 1987. *Leisure interests:* squash, watching cricket and football, tennis, swimming. *Address:* c/o Judy Daish Associates, 2 St. Charles Place, London, W10 6EG, England.

GRAYDON, Air Chief Marshal Sir Michael (James), G.C.B., C.B.E., F.R.AE.S., F.R.S.A.; British air force officer; b. 24 Oct. 1938, Kew, London; s. of James Graydon and Rita Alkan; m. Margaret Clark 1963; ed. Wycliffe Coll. and R.A.F. Coll. Cranwell; qualified flying instr. No. 1, Flight Training School, Linton-on-Ouse 1960–62; No. 56 Squadron 1962–64; No. 226 Operational Conversion Unit (Queen's Commendation) 1965–67; Flight Command, No. 56 Squadron 1967–69; R.A.F. Staff Coll. Bracknell 1970; Personal Staff Officer to Deputy C.-in-C. Allied Forces Cen. Europe, Brunssum 1971–73; Operations, Jt. Warfare, Ministry of Defence 1973–75; Nat. Defence Coll. Latimer 1976; Officer Commdg. No. 11 Squadron, Binbrook 1977–79; Mil. Asst. to Chief of Defence Staff 1979–81; Officer Commdg. R.A.F. Leuchars 1981–83, R.A.F. Stanley, Falkland Islands 1983; Royal Coll. of Defence Studies 1984; Sr. Air Staff Officer, 11 Group, Bentley Priory 1985–86; Asst. Chief of Staff, Policy, SHAPE 1986–89; Air Officer Commdg.-in-Chief, R.A.F. Support Command 1989–91, H.Q. Strike Command 1991–92; Chief of Air Staff 1992–97; Air A.D.C. to H.M. The Queen 1992–97; Gov. Wycliffe Coll. 1986–; Freeman City of London 1995. *Publications:* contribs. to professional journals. *Leisure interests:* golf, birdwatching, reading. *Address:* c/o Lloyds Bank, Cox & King's Branch, P.O. Box 1190, 7 Pall Mall, London, SW1Y 5NA, England.

GRAZER, Brian; Amerian film company executive; Co-Chair. Imagine Films Entertainment. *Films produced include:* Night Shift 1982, Splash 1984, Real Genius 1985, Spies Like Us (jtly.) 1985, Armed and Dangerous (jtly.) 1986, Like Father, Like Son (jtly.) 1987, Parenthood 1989, Cry Baby (jtly.) 1990, Kindergarten Cop 1990, Closet Land (jtly.) 1991, The Doors (jtly.) 1991, Backdraft (jtly.) 1991, My Girl 1991, Far and Away (jtly.) 1992, Housesitter 1992, Boomerang 1992, CB4 (jtly.) 1993, For Love Or Money 1993, The Paper (jtly.) 1994, My Girl 2 1994, Greedy 1994, The Cowboy Way 1994, Apollo 13 (jtly.) 1995, Sergeant Bilko 1996, Ransom 1996. *Address:* Imagine Films Entertainment, 1925 Century Park East, Suite 2300, Los Angeles, CA 90067, U.S.A.

GREAVES, Derrick, A.R.C.A.; British artist; b. 5 June 1927, Sheffield; s. of Harry Greaves and Mabel Greaves; m. Mary Margaret Johnson 1951; two

s. one d.; ed. R.C.A., London and British School at Rome; part-time teacher St. Martins School of Art 1954–64, Maidstone Coll. of Art and Royal Acad. Schools 1960; Head of Printmaking, Norwich Coll. of Art 1983–; first one-man exhbn., Beaux Arts Gallery 1953; subsequent one-man exhbns. at Zwemmer Gallery 1958, 1960, 1962, 1963, Inst. of Contemporary Arts (ICA), London 1969, 1971, Bear Lane Gallery, Oxford 1970, 1973, Belfast 1972, Dublin 1972, Whitechapel Gallery 1973, Monika Kinley 1973–, City Gallery, Milton Keynes 1975–, Cranfield Inst. of Tech. 1978, Exposicion Int. de la Plastica, Chile 1978; group exhbns. include Contemporary Arts Soc. 1956, Venice Biennale 1956, Pushkin Museum, Moscow 1957, Whitechapel Gallery 1963, Carnegie Int. Exhbn., Pa. 1964, Haymarket Gallery 1974, Royal Acad. 1977, Graves Art Gallery, Sheffield 1980, Fischer Fine Art 1980, Mall Galleries, London 1981, Mappin Art Gallery 1986, Leeds Art Gallery 1986, Philadelphia Museum of Art 1986, Walker Art Gallery; Prize John Moore's Exhbn. 1957, Belfast Open Painting Exhbn. purchase prize 1962. *Publications:* Derrick Greaves. Paintings 1958–80, numerous catalogues.

GREBENÍČEK, Miroslav, PH.D.; Czech politician; b. 21 March 1947, Staré Město, Uherské Hradiště Dist.; m.; one s. two d.; ed. Masaryk Univ., Brno; worked as teacher at several schools; specialist with Regional Museum, Mikulov 1973–75; mem. CP of Czechoslovakia 1975; lecturer 1975–86, Reader 1986–89, Teaching-Training Coll., Masaryk Univ., Brno; Deputy to House of Nations, Fed. Ass. of Č.S.F.R. 1990–92; First Vice-Pres. Aug.–Nov. 1991, Pres. 1991–92, Council of the Fed. of CP of Czechlands and Moravia and Party of the Democratic Left; mem. Presidium, Fed. Ass. of Č.S.F.R. 1992; Chair. CP of Czechlands and Moravia 1992–; M.P. 1996–, of Organisational Cttee. of Parl. 1996–98, of Parl. Cttee. for Petitions 1996–98, for Culture, Youth and Physical Training 1998–. *Publications:* monographs, articles and reviews focusing on the history of 19th and 20th Centuries. *Address:* Komunistická strana Čech a Moravy, Politických vězňů 9, Prague 1, (Office); Zlámalova 9, 692 01 Mikulov, Czech Republic. (Home) *Telephone:* 24 21 01 72 (Office).

GREBENSHCHIKOV, Boris Borisovich; Russian rock musician and popular musician; b. 27 Nov. 1953, Leningrad; s. of Boris A. Grebenshchikov and Ludmila Grebenshchikova; m.; one s. one d.; ed. Leningrad Univ.; worked as a computer programmer 1977–80; lead singer and guitarist of rock group Akvarium 1975–; recordings include Akvarium (U.S.S.R.) 1987, Radio Africa 1987, Equinox 1988, Radio Silence 1989; sound track albums include Assa 1988, Black Rose 1990, St. Petersburg Sands 1993, The Snow Lion 1996; tours and recordings in U.S.A., Canada, Great Britain, all-Russia tour 1991 (110 concerts in 68 cities); as a painter has taken part in various art exhbns. throughout fmr. U.S.S.R. *Publications:* Ivan and Danilo 1989, various poems. *Leisure interests:* music, painting, writing, religions. *Address:* 2 Marata Street, Apt. 3, 191025 St. Petersburg, Russia. *Telephone:* 311-04-58.

GRECH, Joe Debono; Maltese politician; b. 17 Sept. 1941, B'Kara; s. of Carmelo Debono and Giovanna Grech; m. Edith Vella; two c.; ed. St. Aloysius Coll.; mem. Gen. Workers, Union Rep. for Gozo 1971; Sec. Petrol and Chemicals Section 1973–76; fmr. Pres. Nat. Exec. Socialist Youth Movt., Gen. Sec. 1967–76; fmr. mem. Nat. Exec. Labour Party, Propaganda Sec. 1971–88; Man. Nat. Cargo Handling Co., Interprint; M.P. 1976–; Minister of Parastatal and People's Investments May–Sept. 1983, of Agric. and Fisheries 1983–87, for Transport and Ports 1996–; Deputy Leader Labour Party 1988. *Leisure interests:* reading, farming. *Address:* Ministry for Transport and Ports, Lascaris, Valletta, Malta CMR 02. *Telephone:* 243880. *Fax:* 243758.

GREEN, Albert Edward, PH.D., SC.D., F.R.S.; British professor of natural philosophy; m. Gwendoline May Rudston 1939; ed. Jesus Coll., Cambridge; Fellow, Jesus Coll., Cambridge 1936–39; Lecturer in Math., Durham Colls., Univ. of Durham 1939–48; Prof. of Applied Math., Univ. of Newcastle upon Tyne 1948–68; Sedleian Prof. of Natural Philosophy, Univ. of Oxford 1968–77, Prof. Emer. 1977–; Fellow, The Queen's Coll., Oxford 1968–77, Supernumerary Fellow 1977–; Hon. D.Sc. (Durham) 1969, (Nat. Univ. of Ireland) 1977; Hon. LL.D. (Glasgow) 1975; Timoshenko Medal, A.S.M.E. 1974; Theodore von Karmen Medal, American Soc. of Civil Engineers 1983. *Address:* 25 Ritchie Court, 380 Banbury Road, Oxford, OX2 7PW, England. *Telephone:* (01865) 552116.

GREEN, Anthony Eric Sandall, DIP. FINE ART, R.A.; British artist; b. 30 Sept. 1939, Luton; s. of Frederick Sandall and Marie Madeleine (née Dupont) Green; m. Mary Louise Cozens-Walker 1961; two d.; ed. Highgate School, Slade School of Fine Art, Univ. Coll. London; Asst. Art Master, Highgate School 1961–67; Harkness Fellowship U.S.A. 1967–69; Fellow, Univ. Coll. London; held over 50 one-man exhbns.; works in public and private collections worldwide; French Govt. Scholarship, Paris 1960, Exhibit of the Year R.A. Summer Exhbn. 1977. *Publication:* A Green Part of the World (with Martin Bailey) 1984. *Leisure interests:* family, travel. *Address:* Mole End, 40 High Street, Little Eversden, Cambridge, CB3 7HE, England. *Telephone:* (01223) 262292.

GREEN, Rev. Bernard, M.A., B.D.; British ecclesiastic; b. 11 Nov. 1925, Walgrave, Northants.; s. of George Samuel Green and Laura Agnes Annie (née Holliday) Green; m. Joan Viccars 1952; two s. one d.; ed. Wellingborough School, Bristol Univ., Bristol Baptist Coll., St. Catherine's Coll., Oxford and Regent's Park Coll., Oxford; nat. service in coal mines 1944–47; ordained 1952; Minister Yardley Baptist Church, Birmingham 1952–61; Mansfield Road Baptist Church, Nottingham 1961–76, Horfield Baptist Church, Bristol 1976–82; Baptist Chaplain Nottingham Univ. 1961–66; Gen. Sec. Baptist Union of G.B. 1982–91; Moderator Free Church Fed. Council 1988–89; frequent broadcaster and mem. religious advisory panels BBC Radio Nottingham and Bristol 1970–82; Chair. Mansfield Road Baptist Housing Asscn. 1968–76, Horfield Housing Asscn. 1976–82; Vice-Pres. Churches' Council for Health and Healing 1987–; Dir. Baptist Times Ltd. 1982–91, Baptist Holiday Fellowship Ltd. 1982–91, Baptist Union Corpn. Ltd. 1982–91, Baptist Insurance PLC 1982–93, London Baptist Property Bd. 1982–91, Baptist House Ltd. 1989–91. *Publications:* Patterns and Prayers for Christian Worship (co-author) 1991, Baptist Praise and Worship (mem. ed. cttee.) 1991, Tomorrow's Man: A Biography of James Henry Rushbrooke 1997, Crossing the Boundaries: A History of the European Baptist Federation 1999. *Leisure interests:* reading, music, gardening, walking. *Address:* 34 Mill Road, Abingdon, Oxon., OX14 5NS, England.

GREEN, Dan, B.A.; American book publishing executive; b. 28 Sept. 1935, Passaic, N.J.; s. of Harold Green and Bessie Roslow; m. Jane Oliphant 1959; two s.; ed. Syracuse Univ., N.Y.; Publicity Dir. Dover Press 1957–58; Station WNAC-TV 1958–59; Bobbs-Merrill Co. 1959–62; Simon & Schuster Inc. 1962–85, Assoc. Publr. 1976–80, Vice-Pres., Publr. 1980–84; Pres. Trade Publishing Group 1984–85; Founder, Publr., Kenan Press 1979–80; C.E.O. Grove Press and Weidenfeld & Nicolson, New York 1985–89; Pres. Kenan Books, New York 1989–, Pom Literary Agency 1989. *Address:* Pom Inc., 611 Broadway, New York, NY 10012; Kenan Books, 15 W 26th Street, New York, NY 10010, U.S.A. *Telephone:* (212) 673-3835. *Fax:* (212) 673-4653.

GREEN, The Hon. Sir Guy Stephen Montague, A.C., K.B.E., LL.B.; Australian administrator and judge; b. 26 July 1937, Launceston, Tasmania; s. of the late Clement Francis Montague and Beryl Margaret Jenour (née Williams) Green; m. Rosslyn Marshall 1963; two s. two d.; ed. Launceston Church Grammar School and Univ. of Tasmania; admitted to Bar 1960; Partner Ritchie & Parker Alfred Green & Co. 1963–71; Pres. Tasmanian Bar Asscn. 1968–70; Magistrate 1971–73; Chief Justice of Tasmania 1973–95; Lieut.-Gov. of Tasmania 1982–95; Gov. of Tasmania 1995–; mem. Faculty of Law Univ. of Tasmania 1974–85; Chair. Council of Law Reporting 1978–85; Chair. Tasmanian Cttee., Duke of Edin.'s Award in Australia 1975–80; Dir. Winston Churchill Memorial Trust 1975–85, Deputy Nat. Chair. 1980–85; Chancellor, Univ. of Tasmania 1985–95; Deputy Chair. Australian Inst. of Judicial Admin. 1986–88; Pres. St. John Council 1984–92; Priory Exec. Officer, Order of St. John in Australia 1984–91, Chancellor 1991–95; Deputy Prior St. John Ambulance Australia 1995–; Hon. LL.D. (Univ. of Tasmania) 1996; Kt. of Grace, Most Venerable Order of the Hosp. of St. John of Jerusalem. *Address:* Government House, Domain Road, Hobart, Tasmania 7000, Australia. *Telephone:* (03) 6234 2611. *Fax:* (03) 6234 2556.

GREEN, Hamilton; Guyanese politician; b. 9 Nov. 1934, Georgetown; s. of Wilfred Amelius Green and Edith Ophelia Dorothy Green; m. 1st Shirley Field-Ridley 1970 (died 1982); five s. three d.; m. 2nd Dr. Jennifer Veronica Basdeo 1990; two d.; ed. Queen's Coll.; fmrly. Gen. Sec., People's Nat. Congress, Minister of Works, Hydraulics and Supply, of Public Affairs, of Co-operatives and Nat. Mobilization, of Health, Housing and Labour; fmrly. Vice-Pres. with responsibility for Public Welfare, Vice-Pres. with responsibility for Production; Vice-Pres. and Prime Minister of Guyana 1985–92; expelled from People's Nat. Congress 1992; f. environmental group A Good And Green Guyana; Mayor of Georgetown 1994. *Publication:* From Pain to Peace—Guyana 1953–1964 (series of lectures at Cyril Potter Coll. of Educ. 1986). *Leisure interest:* reading (history and philosophy), table tennis, boxing and fitness training. *Address:* c/o City Hall, Regent Street, Georgetown (Office); Plot 'D' Lodge, Georgetown, Guyana (Home). *Telephone:* 02-57870 (Office). *Fax:* 02-57871.

GREEN, Howard, M.D., M.SC.; American medical school professor and scientist; b. 10 Sept. 1925, Toronto, Canada; s. of Benjamin Green and Rose M. Green; m. Rosine Kauffmann; ed. Univ. of Toronto and Northwestern Univ., U.S.A.; Research Asst., Dept. of Physiology, Northwestern Univ. 1948–50; Research Assoc. (Instructor), Dept. of Biochemistry, Univ. of Chicago 1951–53; Instructor, Dept. of Pharmacology, New York Univ. School of Medicine 1954; Capt., M.C., U.S. Army Reserve, Immunology Div., Walter Reed Army Inst. of Research 1955–56; Dept. of Pathology, New York Univ. School of Medicine 1956–68, Prof. and Chair., Dept. of Cell Biology 1968–70; Prof. of Cell Biology, M.I.T. 1970–80; Higgins Prof. of Cellular Physiology and Chair. Dept. of Physiology and Biophysics, Harvard Medical School 1980–86, George Higginson Prof. of Physiology 1986–, Chair. Dept. of Cellular and Molecular Physiology 1988–93, Higgins Prof. of Cell Biology 1993–; Mr and Mrs J. N. Taub Int. Memorial Award for Psoriasis Research 1977; Selman A. Waksman Award in Microbiology 1978; Lewis S. Rosenstiel Award in Basic Medical Research 1980, Lila Gruber Research Award, American Acad. of Dermatology 1980, The Passano Award 1985. *Publications:* numerous articles on cell biology, genetics, growth and differentiation. *Address:* Department of Cell Biology, Harvard Medical School, 240 Longwood Avenue, Boston, MA 02115 (Office); 82 Williston Road, Brookline, MA 02146, U.S.A. (Home).

GREEN, Michael Boris, PH.D., F.R.S.; British professor of physics; b. 22 May 1946, London; s. of Genia Green and Absalom Green; ed. William Ellis School, London, Cambridge Univ.; Post-doctoral Fellowship Inst. for Advanced Study, Princeton, N.J., U.S.A. 1970–72, Cambridge Univ. 1972–77; SERC Advanced Fellowship, Oxford Univ. 1977–79; lecturer, Queen Mary and Westfield Coll., London 1979–85, Prof. of Physics 1985–93; John Humphrey Plummer Prof. of Theoretical Physics, Cambridge Univ. July 1993–; SERC Sr. Fellowship 1986–91; numerous fellowships at U.S. and European Insts. including Distinguished Fairchild Fellowship, Calif. Inst. of Tech. 1990; Maxwell Medal, Inst. of Physics 1987, William Hopkins Prize, Cambridge Philosophical Soc. 1987, Dirac Medal, Int. Center for Theoretical Physics 1989. *Publications:* Superstring Theory (2 vols.; with J.H. Schwarz and E. Witten) 1987; numerous publs. in scientific journals. *Leisure interests:* pottery, music. *Address:* Department of Applied Mathematics and Theoretical Physics, University of Cambridge, Cambridge, CB2 1TN, England. *Telephone:* (01223) 330884.

GREEN, Michael Philip; British business executive; b. 2 Dec. 1947; s. of Cyril Green and Irene Green; m. 1st Hon. Janet F. Wolfson 1972 (divorced 1989); two d.; m. 2nd Theresa Buckmaster 1990; two s.; ed. Haberdashers' Aske's School; Dir. and co-founder, Tangent Industries 1968; Chief Exec. Carlton Communications PLC 1983–91, Chair. 1983–; Chair. Carlton TV Ltd. 1991–94; Chair. ITN 1993–; Chair. British Digital Broadcasting PLC 1997–; Chair. The Open Coll. 1986–; founder Tangent Charitable Trust 1984; Dir. GMTV Ltd. 1992–, Reuters Holdings PLC 1992–, Getty Communications PLC 1997–98; Chair. The Media Trust 1997–; Gov. Theale Green School 1992–. *Leisure interests:* reading, bridge, television. *Address:* Carlton Communications PLC, 25 Knightsbridge, London, SW1X 7RZ, England. *Telephone:* 0171-663 6363.

GREEN, Norman Michael, PH.D., F.R.S.; British biochemist; b. 6 April 1926; s. of Ernest Green and Hilda Margaret Carter; m. Iro Paulina Moschouti 1953; two s. one d.; ed. Dragon School, Oxford, Clifton Coll., Bristol, Magdalen Coll., Oxford, and Univ. Coll. Hosp. Medical School, London; Research Student, Univ. of Wash., Seattle 1951–53; Lecturer in Biochemistry, Univ. of Sheffield 1953–55; Research Fellow and Lecturer in Chem. Pathology, St. Mary's Hosp. Medical School, London 1956–62; Visiting Scientist, N.I.H., Md. 1962–64; Research Staff, Div. of Biochem., Nat. Inst. for Medical Research 1964–91, affiliated to Dept. of Mathematical Biology 1992–. *Publications:* research papers in scientific journals on the structure of proteins and of membranes. *Leisure interests:* mountain climbing, pyrotechnics. *Address:* 57 Hale Lane, Mill Hill, London, NW7 3PS, England.

GREEN, Sir Owen (Whitley), Kt., F.C.A.; British business executive; b. 14 May 1925, Stockton-on-Tees; m. Doreen M. Spark 1948; one s. two d.; served R.N.V.R. 1942–46; with Charles Wakeling & Co. (accountants) 1947–56; joined BTR 1956, Asst. Man. Dir. 1956, Man. Dir. 1967–86, Chair. BTR PLC 1984–93; Dir. The Spectator 1988–93; Businessman of the Year 1982; British Inst. of Management Gold Medal 1984; Founding Socs. Centenary Award, I.C.A. 1985. *Leisure interest:* golf. *Address:* Edgehill, Succombs Hill, Warlingham, Surrey, CR6 9JG, England.

GREEN, Pauline, B.A., M.SC.; British politician; b. 8 Dec. 1948; d. of late Bertram Wiltshire and of Lucy Wiltshire; m. Paul Adam Green 1971; one s. one d.; ed. John Kelly Secondary Modern School for Girls, Brent, London, Kilburn Polytechnic, Open Univ., London School of Econs.; fmr. policewoman with Metropolitan Police; Sec. Chipping Barnet Labour Party 1981, Chair. 1983; Political Consultant on European Affairs to Co-operative Movt. 1986–89; M.E.P. for London N. 1989–, Leader European Parl. Labour Party 1993–94; Leader Parl. Group of Party of European Socialists, European Parl. 1994–; mem. Nat. Exec. Cttee. Labour Prty 1998–; Vice-Pres. Socialist Int.; Hon. D.Univ. (Middx.) 1988. *Leisure interests:* music, swimming. *Address:* European Parliament, 97–113 rue Belliard, 1047 Brussels, Belgium; Broad House, 205 Fore Street, London, N18 2TZ, England (Office).

GREEN, Roger Curtis, PH.D., F.R.S.N.Z.; American/New Zealand professor of prehistory; b. 15 March 1932, Ridgewood, N.J.; s. of Robert J. Green and Eleanor Richards; m. 1st Kaye Chandler Smith 1959; m. 2nd Valerie J. Sallen 1984; two c.; ed. Univ. of New Mexico and Harvard Univ.; Research Assoc. American Museum of Natural History 1959; Sr. Lecturer in Prehistory, Univ. of Auckland 1961–66, Assoc. Prof. 1966–67, Prof. in Prehistory 1973–92, Prof. Emer. 1992–, Head, Dept. of Anthropology 1980–84; Anthropologist, B.P. Bishop Museum 1967–73, Research Assoc. 1973–; R.S.N.Z. Capt. James Cook Fellowship 1970–73; Assoc. Prof. in Anthropology, Univ. of Hawaii 1967–70, James Cook Visiting Prof. 1981–82; Visiting Prof. Miller Inst. for Research in Basic Science, Univ. of Calif., Berkeley; mem. Bd. Foundation for Research Science and Tech. 1993–95; mem. N.A.S. (U.S.A.) and numerous other learned socs.; Fulbright Scholar 1958–59; Elsdon Best Medal, Polynesian Soc. 1973; Maharaia Winiata Memorial Prize 1974; Hector Memorial Medal, Royal Soc. of N.Z. 1992. *Publications:* numerous articles in historical, anthropological, archaeological journals etc. *Leisure interests:* music, travel, walking. *Address:* Department of Anthropology, University of Auckland, Private Bag 92019, Auckland; P.O. Box 60-054 Titirangi, Auckland 1230, New Zealand. *Telephone:* (9) 373-7599 (Ext. 8567); (9) 817-7608 (Home). *Fax:* (9) 373-7441.

GREENAWAY, Peter; British film director, writer and painter; b. 1942, Wales; m.; two d.; ed. Forest School and Walthamstow Coll. of Art; trained as painter and first exhibited pictures at Lord's Gallery 1964; film ed. Cen. Office of Information 1965–76; began making own films in 1966, numerous curatorial exhbns., one-man shows and group shows in Europe, U.S.A., Australia and Japan 1988–; Officier Ordre des Arts et des Lettres. *Films include:* Train, Tree 1966, Revolution, Five Postcards from Capital Cities 1967, Intervals 1969, Erosion 1971, H is for House 1973, Windows, Water, Water Wrackets 1975, Goole by Numbers 1976, Dear Phone 1977, 1–100, A Walk Through H (Hugo Award, Chicago), Vertical Features Remake 1978, Zandra Rhodes (Hugo Award, Chicago 1981) 1979, The Falls (BFI Award, L'Age d'Or Brussels) 1980, Act of God (Melbourne Short Film Prize, Sydney Short Film Prize) 1981, The Draughtsman's Contract 1982, Four American Composers 1983, Making a Splash 1984, Inside Rooms: 26 Bathrooms 1985, A Zed & Two Noughts 1986, The Belly of An Architect (Best Actor Prize, Chicago) 1987, Drowning by Numbers (Best Artistic Contribution Prize), Fear of Drowning, Death in the Seine 1988, A TV Dante Cantos 1–8, Hubert Bals Handshake 1989, The Cook, The Thief, His Wife and Her Lover 1989, Prospero's Books, M is for Man, Music, Mozart 1991, Rosa (Dance Screen Prize), Darwin 1992, The Baby of Macon 1993, The Stairs, Geneva 1994, The Pillow Book (Le Distinction Gervais, Cannes, Best Film and Best Cinematographer, Sitges, Spain) 1995, Flying over Water 1997, 8½ Women. *Opera:* Rosa, a Horse Drama 1994. *Publications:* Zed and Two Noughts 1986, Belly of an Architect 1987, Drowning By Numbers, Fear of Drowning 1988, The Cook, The Thief, His Wife and Her Lover 1989, Papers 1990, Prospero's Books 1991, Prospero's Subjects (picture book) 1992, Rosa, The Falls, The Baby of Macon 1993, The Draughtsman's Contract 1994, The Pillow Book 1996. *Address:* c/o The Vue, 387b King Street, London, W6 9NJ, England.

GREENBERG, Bernard, PH.D.; American professor of biological sciences; b. 24 April 1922, New York; s. of Isidore Greenberg and Rose Gordon; m. Barbara Muriel Dickler 1949; two s. two d.; ed. Brooklyn Coll. and Univ. of Kansas; Prof. of Biological Sciences, Univ. of Ill. at Chicago 1966–90, Prof. Emer. 1990–; Visiting Scientist, Istituto Superiore di Sanità, Rome, Italy 1960–61, 1967–68, Inst. de Salubridad y Enfermedades Tropicales, Mexico 1962, 1963; Fulbright-Hays Sr. Research Scholar, Rome 1967–68; Consultant and Expert Witness in Forensic Entomology; Scientific Gov. Chicago Acad. of Sciences; Fellow A.A.A.S.; numerous research grants and contracts from Nat. Science Foundation, Nat. Insts. of Health and other bodies. *Publications:* over 100 scientific publs. including Flies and Disease (2 vols.) 1971, 1973. *Leisure interests:* antiquities, art, archaeology and travel. *Address:* 1463 East 55th Place, Chicago, IL 60637, U.S.A. *Telephone:* (312) 996-3103 (Univ.); (773) 667-5380 (Home). *Fax:* (312) 413-2435.

GREENBERG, Jack, B.SC., J.D., C.P.A.; American business executive; b.1942; s. of Edith S. Scher; m. Donna Greenberg; one s. two d.; ed. DePaul Univ., Chicago; with Arthur Young & Co. 1964–82; Chief Finance Officer and Exec. Vice-Pres. McDonald's Corpn. 1982–, Vice-Chair. 1992–, also Dir.; Dir. Arthur J. Gallagher & Co., DePaul Univ.; mem. American Inst. of Certified Public Accountants. *Address:* McDonald's Corporation, 1 McDonald's Plaza, Oak Brook, IL 60521, U.S.A.

GREENBERG, Jeffrey; American business executive; fmrly. with Marsh & McLennan; fmr. head property/casualty American Int. Group; joined Marsh & McLennan Risk Capital 1996.

GREENBERG, Joseph Harold, PH.D.; American professor of anthropology; b. 28 May 1915, Brooklyn, N.Y.; s. of Jacob Greenberg and Florence Pilzer Greenberg; m. Selma Berkowitz 1940; ed. Columbia Coll. and Northwestern Univ.; Army service in Signal Intelligence Corps 1940–45; Instructor and Asst. Prof. Univ. of Minn. 1946–48; Asst., Assoc., then Prof., Columbia Univ. 1948–62; Dir. West African Languages Survey 1959–66; Prof. of Anthropology, Stanford Univ. 1962–85, Ray Lyman Wilbur Distinguished Prof. of Social Sciences 1971; Collitz Prof. Summer Linguistic Inst., Stanford 1987; First Distinguished Lecturer, American Anthropological Asscn. 1970; mem. N.A.S., American Acad. of Arts and Sciences 1972–, American Philosophical Soc. 1975; Pres. Linguistic Soc. of America 1977; Guggenheim Fellow 1955, 1982; Fellow Stanford Humanities Center 1982; Hon. D.Sc. (Northwestern Univ.) 1982; Haile Selassie I Prize for African Research 1967, N.Y. Acad. of Sciences Award for Behavioral Sciences 1980, Distinguished Africanist Award 1987, Talcot Parsons Prize for Social Science 1997. *Publications:* The Languages of Africa 1963, Universals of Language (Ed.) 1963, Anthropological Linguistics: An Introduction 1968, Language Universals—A Research Frontier (in Science) 1969, The Indo-Pacific Hypothesis (in Current Trends in Linguistics Vol. 8, Ed. Thomas Sebeok) 1970, Language, Culture and Communication 1971, New Invitation to Linguistics 1977, Universals of Human Language (4 vols.) 1978, Language in the Americas 1987, On Language: The Selected Writings of Joseph H. Greenberg 1990. *Leisure interest:* playing the piano. *Address:* 860 Mayfield Avenue, Stanford, CA 94305, U.S.A. (Home). *Telephone:* (415) 857-0147 (Home).

GREENBLATT, Stephen J., PH.D.; American academic; b. 7 Nov. 1943, Cambridge, Mass.; s. of Harry Greenblatt and Mollie Brown; m. Ellen J. Schmidt 1969; two s.; ed. Yale Univ., Univ. of Cambridge (Fulbright Scholar); Prof. of English Univ. of Calif., Berkeley 1969–97; Prof. of English Harvard Univ. 1997–; numerous visiting professorships; Fellow American Acad. of Arts and Sciences; Porter Prize 1969, British Council Prize 1982; Guggenheim Fellow 1975. *Publications:* Three Modern Satirists: Waugh, Orwell and Huxley 1965, Sir Walter Raleigh 1970, Renaissance Self-Fashioning 1980, Shakespearean Negotiations 1988, Learning to Curse 1990, Marvelous Possessions 1991; Ed. Allegory and Representation 1981, Power of Forms 1982, Representing the English Renaissance 1988, Redrawing the Boundaries of Literary Study in English 1992, New World Encounters 1992, The Norton Shakespeare 1997. *Address:* Department of English, Harvard University, Cambridge, MA 02138, U.S.A.

GREENBURY, Sir Richard, Kt.; British business executive; b. July 1936; m. 1st Sian Eames Hughes (dissolved); two s. two d.; m. 2nd Gabrielle Mary McManus 1985 (divorced 1996); remarried Sian Eames Hughes 1996; ed. Ealing Co. Grammar School; jr. man. trainee, Marks and Spencer 1953, Alt. Dir. 1970, Dir. 1972, Jt. Man. Dir. responsible for Clothing Depts. 1978, responsible for Food Div., Homeware, Footwear, Gifts and Export 1983–85, responsible for all U.K. service depts. 1985–86; C.O.O. Marks and Spencer PLC 1986, C.E.O. March 1988–, Chair. 1991–; part-time mem. British Gas Corpn. 1976–87; Dir. (non-exec.) Metal Box PLC 1985–89, ICI 1992–96, Lloyds Bank (now Lloyds TSB Group) 1992–97, Zeneca 1993–; mem. Supervisory Bd., Philips Electronics NV 1998–; mem. UK Advisory Bd., British American Chamber of Commerce 1989–; Trustee R.A. 1992–. *Leisure interest:* tennis. *Address:* Marks and Spencer PLC, Michael House, 57 Baker Street, London, W1A 1DN, England. *Telephone:* 0171-935 4422 (Office).

GREENE, Graham Carleton, C.B.E., M.A.; British publisher; b. 10 June 1936, Berlin, Germany; s. of Sir Hugh Carleton Greene and Helga Mary Connolly; m. 1st Judith Margaret Gordon-Walker 1957 (divorced); m. 2nd Sally Georgina Horton 1976; one s.; also one step-s. one step-d.; ed. Eton and Univ. Coll., Oxford; Dir. Jonathan Cape Ltd. 1962–90, Man. Dir. 1966–88; Dir. Chatto, Virago, Bodley Head and Cape Ltd. 1969–88, Chair. 1970–88; Dir. Book Reps (N.Z.) Ltd. 1971–88, CVBC Services 1972–88, Australasian Publishing Co. Ltd. (Chair. 1978–88) 1969–88, Guinness Peat Group 1973–87, Triad Paperbacks 1975–88, Greene, King PLC 1979–, Statesman and Nation Publishing Co. (Chair. 1981–85) 1980–85, Statesman Publishing Co. Ltd. (Chair. 1981–85) 1980–85, Random House Inc. 1987–88, Jupiter Int. Investment Trust PLC 1989–, Henry Sotheran Ltd. 1990–, Ed Victor Ltd. 1991–, Rosemary Sandberg Ltd. 1991–, Libra KFT (Budapest) 1991–, London Merchant Securities PLC 1996–; Chair. Random House UK Ltd. 1988–90, British Museum Devt. Trust 1986–93 (Vice-Chair. 1993–), British Museum Publications (now British Museum Company) Ltd. 1988–96, Museums and Galleries Comm. 1991–96, Bd. of Trustees, British Museum 1996–; Chair. Nation Pty. Co. Ltd. 1981–86, New Society 1984–86, Great Britain–China Centre 1986–; Dir. Garsington Opera Ltd. 1996–; mem. Bd. of British Council 1977–88, mem. Council of Publishers Asscn. (Pres. 1977–79) 1969–88; Trustee, British Museum 1978–, Open Coll. of the Arts 1990–; Int. Cttee. of Int. Publishers Asscn. 1977–88, Groupe des Editeurs de Livres de la CEE (Pres. 1984–86) 1977–86; Chevalier, Ordre des Arts et des Lettres. *Address:* 6 Bayley Street, Bedford Square, London WC1B 3HB, England. *Telephone:* 0171-304 4101.

GREENE, Jack Phillip, PH.D.; American professor of history; b. 12 Aug. 1931, Lafayette, Ind.; s. of Ralph B. Greene and Nellie A. (Miller) Greene; m. 1st Sue L. Neuenswander 1953 (divorced 1990); one s. one d.; m. 2nd Amy Turner Bushnell 1990; ed. Univ. of N.C., Indiana Univ. and Duke Univ., Durham, N.C.; History Instructor Mich. State Univ., E. Lansing 1956–59; Asst. Prof. of History Western Reserve Univ., Cleveland, Ohio 1959–62, Assoc. Prof. 1962–65; Visiting Assoc. Prof. and Visiting Ed. William and Mary Quarterly Coll. of William and Mary in Va., Williamsburg 1961–62; Assoc. Prof. of History Univ. of Mich., Ann Arbor 1965–66; Visiting Assoc. Prof. of History Johns Hopkins Univ., Baltimore, Md. 1964–65, Prof. 1966–75, Chair. Dept. of History 1970–72, Andrew W. Mellon Prof. in Humanities 1975–, Distinguished Prof., Univ. of Calif., Irvine 1990–92; Harmsworth Prof. of American History Oxford Univ. 1975–76; Visiting Prof. Hebrew Univ. of Jerusalem 1979, Ecole des Hautes Etudes en Science Sociale 1986–87; Freeman Prof., Univ. of Richmond, Va., 1996; Sweet Prof., Mich. State Univ. 1997; mem. Inst. for Advanced Study 1970–71, 1985–86; Fellow, Woodrow Wilson Int. Center for Scholars 1974–75, Center for Advanced Study in Behavioral Sciences 1979–80, Churchill Coll., Cambridge 1986–, Nat. Humanities Center 1987–88, Guggenheim Fellow 1964–65; Freeman Prof. Univ. of Richmond 1996. *Publications:* twenty-nine books, including Quest for Power 1963, Diary of Colonel Landon Carter of Sabine Hall (2 vols.) 1965, Settlements to Society 1966, Colonies to Nation 1967, Reinterpretation of American Revolution 1968, All Men are Created Equal 1976, Colonial British America 1983, Encyclopedia of American Political History 1984, Peripheries and Center 1986, Political Life in Eighteenth Century Virginia 1986, Intellectual Heritage of the Constitutional Era 1986, Magna Carta for America 1986, American Revolution 1987, Pursuits of Happiness 1988, Selling the New World 1988, Encyclopedia of the American Revolution (co-ed.) 1991, Imperatives, Behaviors and Identities 1992, Intellectual Construction of America 1993, Negotiated Authorities 1994, Understanding the American Revolution 1995, Interpreting Early America 1996. *Leisure interest:* travel. *Address:* 1606 Highfield House, 4000 N. Charles Street, Baltimore, MD 21218, U.S.A.

GREENE, Maurice; American athlete; b. 23 July 1974, Kansas City, Mo.; world record-holder indoor 60m. 1998 (6.39 seconds); coached by John Smith Sept. 1996–; Silver Medal U.S. Championships 60m. 1995; Gold Medal U.S. Indoor Championships 60m. 1997; Gold Medal U.S. Championships 100m. 1997; Gold Medal World Championships 100m. 1997.

GREENE OF HARROW WEALD, Baron (Life Peer), cr. 1974, of Harrow in Greater London; **Sidney Francis Greene,** Kt., C.B.E.; British trade unionist; b. 12 Feb. 1910, London; s. of Frank J. Greene and Alice Kerrod; m. Masel E. Carter 1936; three d.; ed. in London; Gen. Sec. Nat. Union of Railwaymen 1957–74; mem. Gen. Council, TUC 1957–75, Chair 1969–70; Chair. TUC Econ. Cttee. 1968–75; mem. N.E.D.C. 1962–75; mem. Advisory Council, Export Credits Guarantee Dept. 1967–70; Dir. Bank of England 1970–78, Times Newspapers Holdings Ltd. (fmrly. Times Newspapers Ltd.) 1974–82, Rio Tinto Zinc Corpn. 1975–80, Nat. Freight Corpn. 1973–77, Southern Electricity Bd. 1964–77, Industry and Parl. Trust Ltd. 1977, Trades Union Unit Trust 1970–80. *Leisure interests:* cricket, gardening. *Address:* 26 Kynaston Wood, Boxtree Road, Harrow Weald, Middx., HA3 6UA, England.

GREENER, Anthony Armitage, F.C.M.A.; British business executive; b. 26 May 1940; s. of William Greener and Diana Greener; m. Min Ogilvie 1974; one s. one d.; ed. Marlborough Coll.; Marketing Man. Thames Board Mills 1969; Retail Controller, Alfred Dunhill Ltd. (later Dunhill Holdings PLC) 1972, Dir. 1974, Man. Dir. 1975; Man. Dir. United Distillers 1987–92; Dir. Guinness PLC 1986–97, Jt. Man. Dir. 1989–91, Chief Exec. 1992–97, Chair. 1993–97; Co-Chair. Diageo (after merger with Grand Metropolitan PLC) PLC 1997–98, Chair. 1998–; Dir. Louis Vuitton Moet Hennessy 1989–97, Reed Int. 1990–, Reed Elsevier 1993–. *Leisure interests:* skiing, sailing. *Address:* Diageo, 8 Henrietta Place, London, W1M 9AG, England. *Telephone:* 0171-927 5200.

GREENFIELD, Susan Adele, D.PHIL.; British pharmacologist; b. 1 Oct. 1950; d. of Reginald Myer Greenfield and Doris Margaret Winifred Greenfield; m. Peter William Atkins 1991; ed. Godolphin and Latymer School for Girls, St. Hilda's Coll., Oxford; MRC Training Fellow Univ. Lab. of Physiology, Oxford 1977–81; fmrly. with Coll. de France, Paris; MRC-INSERM French Exchange Fellow 1979–80; Jr. Research Fellow Green Coll., Oxford 1981–84, lecturer in Synaptic Pharmacology 1985–96, Prof. in Synaptic Pharmacology 1996–, Gresham Prof. of Physic Gresham Coll. 1995–; Dir. Royal Inst. 1998–; Visiting Fellow Inst. of Neuroscience La Jolla, U.S.A. 1995; Visiting Distinguished Scholar Queen's Univ., Belfast 1996; Hon. D.Sc. (Oxford Brookes) 1997. *Publications include:* Mindwaves (ed. with C. B. Blakemore) 1987, Journey to the Centres of the Brain (with G. Ferry) 1994, Journey to the Centres of the Mind 1995, The Human Mind Explained (ed.) 1996, The Human Brain: A Guided Tour 1997, numerous articles in learned journals. *Leisure interests:* aerobics, travel. *Address:* Lincoln College, Oxford, OX1 3DR, England. *Telephone:* (01865) 271628.

GREENHILL OF HARROW, Baron (Life Peer), cr. 1974, of the Royal Borough of Kensington and Chelsea; **Denis Arthur Greenhill,** G.C.M.G., O.B.E. (MIL.); British diplomatist; b. 7 Nov. 1913, Woodford, Essex; s. of James and Susie Greenhill; m. Angela McCulloch 1941; two s. (one s. deceased); ed. Bishop's Stortford Coll. and Christ Church, Oxford; served in Second World War in Egypt, N. Africa, Italy, India and S.E. Asia, demobilized with rank of Col.; in British Foreign Service 1946–73, in Sofia 1947–49, Washington, D.C. 1949–52; at Foreign Office 1952–54; at Imperial Defence Coll. 1954; U.K. Del. to NATO, Paris 1955–57, to Singapore 1957–59; Counsellor, Washington, D.C. 1959–62, Minister 1962–64; Asst. Under-Sec. of State, Foreign Office 1964–66; Deputy Under-Sec. of State 1966–69; Perm. Under-Sec. of State for Foreign and Commonwealth Affairs 1969–73; Gov. BBC 1973–78; led British mission to Rhodesia Feb. 1976; Dir. S. G. Warburg and Co. 1974–87 (Adviser 1987–95), Clerical, Medical and Gen. Assurance, Wellcome Foundation 1974–85, BAT Industries Ltd. 1974–83, Hawker Siddeley Group 1974–84, British Petroleum 1973–78, BL Int. 1977–82; Gov. BUPA 1978–83, S.O.A.S. 1978–85; Chair. King's Coll. Hosp. Medical School 1977–83; Trustee Rayne Foundation 1974–; mem. Security Comm. 1977–82, Int. Advisory Cttee., First Nat. Bank of Chicago 1976–81; Fellow King's Coll., London 1984; Hon. Student Christ Church Oxford; Grand Cross Lion of Finland 1984. *Publication:* More By Accident (memoir) 1992. *Address:* 25 Hamilton House, Vicarage Gate, London, W8 4HL, England (Home). *Telephone:* 0171-937 8362 (Home).

GREENLAND, Dennis James, D.PHIL., F.R.S.; British university professor; b. 13 June 1930, Portsmouth; s. of James John Greenland and Lily Gardener; m. Edith Mary Johnston 1955; one s. two d.; ed. Portsmouth Grammar School, Christ Church, Oxford; lecturer Univ. of Ghana 1955–59; lecturer Waite Inst., Univ. of Adelaide, Australia 1960–63, Reader and Head of Soil Science 1963–70, Hanniford Lecturer 1978; Prof. and Head of Dept. of Soil Science, Univ. of Reading 1970–79, Visiting Prof. 1988–; Chair. Scientific Advisory Panel, Commonwealth Devt. Corpn. 1991–96; Research Dir. Int. Inst. of Tropical Agric. (seconded from Univ. of Reading) 1974–76; Deputy Dir. Gen. (Research) Int. Rice Research Inst., Philippines 1979–87; Dir. Scientific Services, CAB Int., U.K. 1987–92; Blackman Lecturer, Univ. of Oxford 1988; Hon. mem. American Soc. of Agronomy, American Soc. of Soil Science 1993. *Publications:* The Soil Under Shifting Cultivation (jtly.) 1960, The Sustainability of Rice Farming 1997; numerous scientific articles in learned journals. *Leisure interests:* golf, walking, watching cricket. *Address:* Low Wood, The Street, South Stoke, Oxon., RG8 0JS, England.

GREENSPAN, Alan, M.A., PH.D.; American economist; b. 6 March 1926, N.Y.; s. of Herbert Greenspan and Rose Goldsmith; m. Andrea Mitchell 1997; ed. New York and Columbia Univs.; Pres., C.E.O. Townsend-Greenspan & Co. Inc. 1954–74, 1977–87; mem. Nixon for Pres. Cttee. 1968–69; mem. Task Force for Econ. Growth 1969, Comm. on an All-Volunteer Armed Force 1969–70, Comm. on Financial Structure and Regulation 1970–71; Consultant to Council of Econ. Advisers 1970–74, to U.S. Treasury 1971–74, to Fed. Reserve Bd. 1971–74; Chair. Council of Econ. Advisers 1974–77, Nat. Comm. on Social Security Reform 1981–83; Chair. Bd. of Govs. Fed. Reserve System 1987–; Dir. Council on Foreign Relations; mem. Sec. of Commerce's Econ. Comm.'s Cen. Market System Cttee. 1972, G.N.P. Review Cttee. of Office of

Man. and Budget, Time Magazine's Bd. of Economists 1971–74, 1977–87, President's Econ. Policy Advisory Bd. 1981–87, President's Foreign Intelligence Advisory Bd. 1983–85, Exec. Cttee. Trilateral Comm.; Sr. Adviser Brookings Inst. Panel on Econ. Activity 1970–74, 1977–87; Adjunct Prof. Graduate School of Business Man., New York 1977–87; Past Pres., Fellow, Nat. Asscn. of Business Economists; Dir. Trans World Financial Co. 1962–74, Dreyfus Fund 1970–74, Gen. Cable Corpn. 1973–74, 1977–78, Sun Chemical Corpn. 1973–74, Gen. Foods Corpn. 1977–86, J. P. Morgan & Co. 1977–87, Mobil Corpn. 1977–87, Aluminum Co. of America (ALCOA) 1978–87; Jefferson Award 1976; William Butler Memorial Award 1977. *Leisure interest:* golf. *Address:* Office of the Chairman, Federal Reserve System, 20th and C Streets, N.W., Washington, DC 20551, U.S.A.

GREENSTOCK, Jeremy Quentin, C.M.G., M.A.; British diplomatist; b. 27 July 1943; s. of the late John Wilfrid Greenstock and Ruth Margaret Logan; m. Anne Derryn Ashford Hodges 1969; one s. two d.; ed. Harrow School and Worcester Coll., Oxford; asst. master Eton Coll. 1966–69; entered diplomatic service 1969, with MECAS 1970–72, served in Dubai 1972–74, Pvt. Sec. to Amb., Washington 1974–78, with FCO (Planning, Personnel Operations Dept., N. East and N. African Dept.) 1978–83, Commercial Counsellor, Jeddah 1983–85, Riyadh 1985–86, Head of Chancery, British Embassy, Paris 1987–90, Asst. Under-Sec. of State, FCO 1990–93, Minister, British Embassy, Washington 1994–95, Deputy Under-Sec. of State FCO 1995, Political Dir. FCO 1996–98, Perm. Rep. to UN 1998–. *Leisure interests:* travel, photography, golf, skiing. *Address:* Permanent Mission of the United Kingdom to the United Nations, 1 Dag Hammarskjöld Plaza, 885 2nd Avenue, New York, NY 10017, U.S.A.

GREENWALD, Gerald, M.A.; American business executive; b. 11 Sept. 1935, St. Louis, Mo.; s. of Frank and Bertha Greenwald; m. Glenda Lee Gerstein 1958; three s. one d.; ed. Princeton Univ., Wayne State Univ., Detroit; U.S.A.F. 1957–60; with Ford Motor Co. 1957–79, Pres. Ford Venezuela, Dir. Non-Automative Operations, Europe; Vice-Chair. Chrysler Corpn., Highland Park, Mich. 1979–85; Chair. Chrysler Motors 1985–88; Vice-Chair. Chrysler Corpn. 1988–90; Pres., Man. Dir. Dillon, Read and Co. Inc. 1991–92; Pres., Deputy C.E.O. Olympia and York 1992–94; Chair., C.E.O. United Airlines 1994–; Chair. Tafra. *Address:* United Airlines, P.O. Box 66100, Elk Grove Village, IL 60007, U.S.A.

GREENWALT, Tibor Jack, M.D.; American medical director; b. 23 Jan. 1914, Budapest, Hungary; s. of late Bela Greenwalt and Irene Greenwalt; m. 1st Margaret Hirschfeld (died 1948); m. 2nd Shirley Johnson (died 1970); m. 3rd Pia Glas 1971 (died 1996); one s.; ed. New York Univ. Coll. of Medicine; various hosp. appointments 1937–41; Maj., U.S. Army Medical Corps. 1942–46; Asst. Chief of Medicine, Station Hosp., Ft. Leavenworth, Kan. 1942–44; Chief of Lab. Services, 181st Gen. Hospital, Karachi 1944–46; Medical Dir. Milwaukee Blood Center 1947–66; Medical Dir. (Dir. 1976), Blood Program, American Nat. Red Cross 1967–78; Dir. Hoxworth Blood Center 1979–87, Dir. of research 1987–; Prof. of Medicine, Univ. of Cinn. Medical Center 1979–84, Deputy Dir. for Research 1987–; Emer. Prof. of Medicine 1984–; Sr. mem. Inst. of Medicine; mem. Ohio Science and Eng. Roundtable. *Publications:* several books and numerous articles in scientific journals. *Leisure interests:* literature, music, Mesopotamian Archaeology. *Address:* Hoxworth Blood Center, 3130 Highland Avenue, Cincinnati, OH 45267-0055 (Office); 2444 Madison Road # 1501, Cincinnati, OH 45208-1228, U.S.A. (Home). *Telephone:* (513) 558-1520 (Office); (513) 533-4534 (Home). *Fax:* (513) 558-1522.

GREENWOOD, Duncan Joseph, C.B.E., D.SC., F.R.S.; British agronomist; b. 16 Oct. 1932, New Barnet, Herts; s. of Herbert James Greenwood and Alison Fairgrieve Greenwood; ed. Hutton Grammar School, Liverpool Univ. and Aberdeen Univ.; Research Fellow, Aberdeen Univ. 1957–59; Research Leader, Nat. Vegetable Research Station 1959–66; Head of Soil Science, Horticulture Research Int. (fmrly. Nat. Vegetable Research Station) 1966–92, Emer. Fellow 1992–; Visiting Prof. of Plant Sciences, Leeds Univ. 1985–93; Hon. Prof. of Agricultural Chem., Birmingham Univ. 1986–93; Pres. Int. Cttee. Plant Nutrition 1978–82; Pres. British Soc. of Soil Science 1990–92; Sir Gilbert Morgan Medal, Soc. of Chemical Industry 1962, Research Medal of the Royal Agricultural Soc. of England 1979. *Publications:* over 160 publs. in scientific journals, mostly on soils and plant nutrition. *Address:* Horticulture Research International, Wellesbourne, Warwick, CV35 9EF, England. *Telephone:* (01789) 470382. *Fax:* (01789) 470552.

GREENWOOD, Norman Neill, PH.D., D.SC., SC.D., C.CHEM., F.R.I.C., F.R.S.; British professor of inorganic and structural chemistry; b. 19 Jan. 1925, Melbourne, Australia; s. of late Prof. J. Neill Greenwood and late Gladys Uhland; m. Kirsten M. Rydland; three d.; ed. Univs. of Melbourne and Cambridge; Resident Tutor and Lecturer, Trinity Coll., Univ. of Melbourne 1946–48; Sr. Harwell Research Fellow, A.E.R.E. 1951–53; Lecturer, then Sr. Lecturer in Inorganic Chem. Univ. of Nottingham 1953–61; Prof. and Head, Dept. of Inorganic Chem. Univ. of Newcastle upon Tyne 1961–71; Prof. and Head, Dept. of Inorganic and Structural Chem. Univ. of Leeds 1971–90, Emer. Prof. 1990–; Visiting Prof. at univs. in Australia, U.S.A., Canada, China, Japan and Denmark since 1966; Pres. British Asscn. for the Advancement of Science, Section B (Chemistry) 1990–91; Foreign Assoc. Académie des Sciences, Institut de France 1992; D. de l'Univ. h.c. (Nancy) 1977; Tilden Lectureship and Medal (Chem. Soc.) 1966; R.S.C. Medal for Main Group. Element Chem. 1974; Gold Medal of City of Nancy (France) 1977; A. W. von Hofmann Lectureship (Gesellshaft Deutscher Chemiker) 1983; Liversidge Lectureship and Medal (R.S.C.) 1984; Egon Wiberg Lectureship (Univ. of Munich) 1989; Ludwig Mond Lectureship and Medal 1991; Medal for Tertiary Educ. 1993; and other awards and distinctions. *Publications:* several books and over 450 original research papers in journals. *Leisure interests:* music, skiing. *Address:* School of Chemistry, University of Leeds, Leeds, LS2 9JT, England. *Telephone:* (0113) 2336406. *Fax:* (0113) 2336565.

GREER, David Steven, M.D.; American medical specialist; b. 12 Oct. 1925, Brooklyn, New York; s. of Jacob Greer and Mary (Zaslawsky) Greer; m. Marion Clarich 1950; one s. one d.; ed. Univs. of Notre Dame and Chicago; Intern, Yale-New Haven Medical Center 1953–54; Resident in Medicine, Univ. of Chicago Clinics 1954–57; specialist in internal medicine, Fall River, Mass. 1957–74; Chief of Staff, Dept. of Medicine, Fall River Gen. Hosp. 1959–62; Medical Dir. Earle E. Hussey Hosp., Fall River 1962–72; Chief of Staff, Dept. of Medicine, Truesdale Clinic and Truesdale Hosp., Fall River 1971–74; Faculty mem. Tufts Univ. Coll. of Medicine, Boston, Mass. 1969–78; Faculty mem. Brown Univ. Program in Medicine 1973–75, Prof. of Community Health 1975–, Assoc. Dean 1974–81, Dean 1981–92, Acting Dir. Generalist Physician Programs, AAMC 1993–94; mem. N.A.S. Inst. of Medicine; various public appts.; Cutting Foundation Medal for Service to Religion and Medicine 1976 and other awards. *Publications:* numerous articles on chronic disease, geriatrics, long-term care and health-care evaluation. *Leisure interest:* squash. *Address:* Brown University, Box G, Providence, RI 02912, U.S.A. *Telephone:* (401) 863-3822.

GREER, Germaine, PH.D.; Australian feminist and author; b. 29 Jan. 1939, Melbourne; d. of Eric Reginald Greer and Margaret May (Lafrank) Greer; ed. Melbourne and Sydney Univs. and Cambridge Univ., England; Sr. Tutor in English, Sydney Univ. 1963–64; Asst. Lecturer then Lecturer in English, Warwick Univ. 1967–72; lecturer throughout N. America with American Program Bureau 1973–78, to raise funds for Tulsa Bursary and Fellowship Scheme 1980–83; Visiting Prof., Grad. Faculty of Modern Letters, Univ. of Tulsa 1979, Prof. of Modern Letters 1980–83, Founder-Dir. of Tulsa Centre for the Study of Women's Literature, Founder-Ed. Tulsa Studies in Women's Literature 1981; Prof. of English, Warwick Univ. 1998–; Dir. Stump Cross Books 1988–; Special Lecturer and Unofficial Fellow, Newnham Coll., Cambridge 1989–; broadcaster/journalist 1972–79; Jr. Govt. Scholarship 1952, Diocesan Scholarship 1956, Sr. Govt. Scholarship 1956, Teacher's Coll. Studentship 1956, Commonwealth Scholarship 1964; numerous television appearances and public talks including discussion with Norman Mailer (q.v.) in The Theatre of Ideas, New York. *Publications:* The Female Eunuch 1969, The Obstacle Race: The Fortunes of Women Painters and Their Work 1979, Sex and Destiny: The Politics of Human Fertility 1984, Shakespeare (Co-Ed.) 1986, The Madwoman's Underclothes (selected journalism) 1986, Kissing the Rod: An Anthology of 17th Century Women's Verse 1988, Daddy, We Hardly Knew You 1989 (J. R. Ackerly Prize and Premio Internazionale Mondello), The Uncollected Verse of Aphra Behn (Ed.) 1989, The Change: Women, Ageing and the Menopause 1991, Shakespeare and Cultural Traditions: The Selected Proceedings of The Int. Shakespeare Asscn. World Congress 1991, Slip-Shod Sibyls 1995, The Whole Woman 1999; articles for Listener, Spectator, Esquire, Harper's Magazine, Playboy, Private Eye and other journals. *Leisure interest:* gardening. *Address:* c/o Aitken and Stone, 29 Fernshaw Road, London, SW10 0TG, England.

GREET, Rev. Dr. Kenneth Gerald; British minister of religion; b. 17 Nov. 1918, Bristol; s. of Walter and Renée Greet; m. Mary Eileen Edbrooke 1947; one s. two d.; ed. Cotham Grammar School, Bristol, Handsworth Coll., Birmingham; Cwm and Kingstone Methodist Church 1940–42; Ogmore Vale Methodist Church 1942–45; Tonypandy Cen. Hall 1947–54; Sec. Dept. of Christian Citizenship of Methodist Church and Social Responsibility Div. 1954–71; Sec., Methodist Conf. 1971–84, Pres. 1980–81; mem. British Council of Churches 1955–84 (Chair. Exec. 1977–80), World Methodist Council 1957– (Chair. Exec. Cttee. 1976–81); Chair. Exec. Temperance Council of Christian Churches 1961–71; Moderator, Free Church Fed. Council 1982–83; Co-Chair. World Disarmament Campaign 1982–86, Pres. 1989–94, Vice-Pres. 1994–; Rep. to Cen. Cttee., WCC, Addis Ababa 1971, Nairobi 1975; Beckly Lecturer 1962, Willson Lecturer, Kansas City 1966, Cato Lecturer, Sydney 1975; Chair. of Govs., Southlands Coll. 1986–; Hon. D.D. (Ohio) 1997; Hon. D. Univ. (Surrey). *Publications:* The Mutual Society 1962, Man and Wife Together 1962, Large Petitions 1962, Guide to Loving 1965, The Debate About Drink 1969, The Sunday Question 1969, The Art of Moral Judgement 1970, When the Spirit Moves 1975, A Lion from a Thicket 1978, The Big Sin: Christianity and the Arms Race 1982, Under the Rainbow Arch 1984, What Shall I Cry 1986, Jabez Bunting: a biography 1995, Fully Connected 1997. *Leisure interest:* photography. *Address:* 89 Broadmark Lane, Rustington, Sussex, BN16 2JA, England. *Telephone:* (01903) 773326.

GREEVY, Bernadette; Irish mezzo-soprano concert singer; b. 1940, Dublin; d. of Patrick J. Greevy and Josephine F. Miller; m. Peter A. Tattan 1965 (died 1983); one s.; ed. Convent of the Holy Faith, Clontarf, Dublin; London début, Wigmore Hall 1964; has since appeared on maj. concert platforms in Europe, U.S.A., Canada and Far East; recordings of works by Brahms, Handel, Haydn, Bach, Berlioz, Britten, Elgar and Mahler; mem. Bd. Nat. Concert Hall 1981–86, 1991–; Harriet Cohen Int. Music Award; Hon. D.Mus. (Univ. Coll., Dublin), (Trinity Coll., Dublin);Order of Merit (Order of Malta);

Dame of the Holy Sepulchre; Pro Ecclesia et Pontifice (Vatican). *Leisure interests:* gardening, cooking, painting. *Address:* Melrose, 672 Howth Road, Dublin 5, Ireland.

GREGER, Janet L., M.S., PH.D.; American professor of nutritional sciences; b. 18 Feb. 1948, Illinois; d. of Harold Greger and Marjorie Greger; ed. Univ. of Ill. and Cornell Univ.; Asst. Prof. Purdue Univ. 1973–78; Asst. Prof., Assoc. Prof. Univ. of Wis.-Madison 1978–83, Prof. of Nutritional Sciences 1983–, Assoc. Dean, Grad. School 1990–96, Assoc. Dean, Medical School 1996–98; A.A.A.S. Congressional Sciences Eng. Fellow 1984–85; mem. Bd. of Man. COGR 1993–99; mem. Bd. of Dirs. AAALAC 1992–99. *Publications:* Nutrition for Living 1994; over 160 papers in scientific journals. *Leisure interests:* travel, reading. *Address:* Department of Nutritional Sciences, 1415 Linden Drive, University of Wisconsin, Madison, WI 53706, U.S.A. *Telephone:* (608) 262-9972; (608) 262-6375. *Fax:* (608) 262-5860.

GREGG, Judd, J.D., LL.M.; American politician; b. 14 Feb. 1947, Nashua, N.H.; m. Kathleen MacLellan 1973; one s. two d.; ed. Columbia and Boston Univs.; admitted N.H. Bar 1972; law practice, Nashua, N.H.; mem. 97th–100th Congresses from 2nd N.H. Dist. 1981–89; mem. N.H. Gov.'s Exec. Council 1978–80; Gov. of New Hampshire 1989–93; Senator from New Hampshire Jan. 1993–; Republican. *Address:* U.S. Senate, 393 Russell Senate Building, Washington, DC 20510, U.S.A.

GREGORIAN, Vartan, M.A., PH.D.; American professor of history; b. 8 April 1934, Tabriz, Iran; s. of Samuel B. Gregorian and Shushanik G. (née Mirzaian) Gregorian; m. Clare Russell 1960; three c.; ed. Coll. Armenien, Stanford Univ.; Instructor, Asst. Prof., Assoc. Prof. of History San Francisco State Coll. 1962–68; Assoc. Prof. of History Univ. of Calif., L.A. 1968, Univ. of Texas, Austin 1968–72, Dir. Special Programs 1970–72; Tarzian Prof. Armenian and Caucasian History Univ. of Pa. 1972–80, Dean 1974–79, Provost 1978–80; Prof. of History and Near Eastern Studies, New York City 1984–89; Prof. New School for Social Research, New York 1984–89; Pres. New York Public Library 1981–89; Pres. Brown Univ. 1989–97, mem. Nat. Humanities Faculty 1970–; Pres. Carnegie Corpn. of New York 1997–; mem. Acad. of Arts and Letters 1989–, Historical Asscn., Asscn. for Advancement of Slavic Studies, American Philosophical Soc.; John Simon Guggenheim Fellow 1971–72; Silver Cultural Medal Italian Ministry of Foreign Affairs 1977, Gold Medal of Honour City and Province of Vienna 1976, Ellis Island Medal of Honor 1986. *Publications:* The Emergence of Modern Afghanistan 1880–1946 1969, numerous articles for professional journals. *Address:* Office of the President, Carnegie Corporation of New York, 437 Madison Avenue, New York, NY 10022, U.S.A. *Telephone:* (212) 371-3200.

GREGORIOS, Metropolitan Paulos, M.DIV., S.T.M., D.TH., F.I.I.C.S. (formerly **Verghese, Rev. Thadikkal Paul**); Indian ecclesiastic, educationist and writer; b. 9 Aug. 1922, Tripunithura, India; s. of T. P. Piely and Aley Piely; ed. Goshen Coll., Oklahoma and Yale Univs., Princeton Theological Seminary, Keble Coll., Oxford, Serampore Univ.; journalist 1937–42; with Indian Posts and Telegraphs Union 1942–47; taught in govt. schools in Ethiopia 1947–50; Assoc. Sec. Indian Posts and Telegraphs Union of India for Travancore and Cochin 1945–47; studied in U.S.A. 1950–54; Gen. Sec. Orthodox Christian Student Movement of India 1955–57; Hon. lecturer in Religion, Union Christian Coll., Alwaye 1954–56; Special Staff Asst. H.I.M. Haile Sellassie I 1956–59; Chief Adviser Haile Sellassie Foundation 1959; Assoc. Gen. Sec. and Dir. of the Div. of Ecumenical Action, WCC, Geneva 1962–67; Prin., Syrian Orthodox Theological Seminary, Kottayam, Kerala 1967–; consecrated as Bishop 1975; Chair. Church and Soc. Working Group, WCC, Kerala Study Group, Oriental Orthodox Curriculum Cttee.; Metropolitan of Delhi 1976–; Gen. Pres. Indian Philosophical Congress 1991; Pres. Inter-Religious Fed. for World Peace; Vice-Chair. Kerala Philosophers' Congress; Vice-Pres. M.O.C.M.M. Hospital, Kolencheri, Christian Peace Conf., Prague; mem. various WCC and Christian Peace Conf. comms. and cttees.; mem. Presidium WCC 1983–91; mem. Comparative Education Soc. in Europe, London, Societas Liturgica (Int.), Gregory of Nyssa Soc. (Int.), Indian Philosophical Congress, Int. Soc. of Metaphysics, Asscn. of Humanist Psychologists (Int.), Asscn. of Christian Philosophers of India; Chief Ed. Star of the East (quarterly, Kottayam); Ed. New Frontiers in Higher Education (quarterly, Delhi); fmr. leader WCC del. to UNESCO; mem. Senate Kerala Univ. 1972–76, Serampore Univ. 1970–74; Fellow, Int. Inst. of Community Service, Int. Biographical Asscn.; Hon. TH.D. Leningrad Theological Acad., Lutheran Theological Acad., Budapest; Order of St. Vladimir (U.S.S.R.), and numerous other awards. *Publications:* Joy of Freedom 1967, The Gospel of the Kingdom 1968, The Freedom of Man 1970, Be Still and Know 1971, Koptisches Christentum 1973, Die Syrischen Christen in Indien 1974, Freedom and Authority 1974, The Quest for Certainty 1975, The Human Presence 1978, Truth without Tradition? 1978, Cosmic Man 1980, Science for Sane Societies 1980, The Indian Orthodox Church 1982, The Meaning of Diakonia 1988, Enlightenment: East and West 1989, A Light too Bright 1991, A Human God 1992. *Leisure interests:* boating, mountain hikes. *Address:* Orthodox Seminary, P.O. Box 98, Kottayam, Kerala 686001; Delhi Orthodox Centre, 2 Tughlakabad Inst. Area, New Delhi 110062, India. *Telephone:* (011) 643-6417 (Office); 647-4975 (Home).

GREGSON, Sir Peter Lewis, G.C.B., M.A.; British civil servant; b. 28 June 1936, Yorkshire; s. of late Walter Henry Gregson and Lillian Margaret Gregson; ed. Nottingham High School, Balliol Coll., Oxford and London Business School; Nat. Service 1959–61; official Bd. of Trade 1961–68; Pvt. Sec. to the Prime Minister 1968–72; Asst. Sec., Dept. of Trade and Industry, also Sec. Industry, Industrial Devt. Bd. 1972–74; Under Sec., Dept. of Industry, also Sec., Nat. Enterprise Bd. 1975–77; Under Sec., Dept. of Trade 1977–80, Deputy Sec. 1980–81; Deputy Sec., Cabinet Office 1981–85; Perm. Under-Sec. of State, Dept. of Energy 1985–89; Perm. Sec., Dept. of Trade and Industry 1989–96; Dir. Scottish Power PLC 1996–, Woolwich PLC 1998–. *Leisure interests:* gardening, listening to music. *Address:* Scottish Power PLC, 1 Atlantic Quay, Glasgow, G2 8SP, Scotland. *Telephone:* 0141-636 4513. *Fax:* 0141-636 4577.

GREGURIĆ, Franjo, D.SC.; Croatian politician; b. 12 Oct. 1939, Lobor, Zlata Bistrica; m. Jozefina Gregurić (née Abramović); one s. one d.; ed. Univ. of Zagreb; worked in chemical factories; tech. dir. Radonia at Sisak; Dir.-Gen. Chromos factory, Zagreb; rep. of Foreign Trade Co. Astra in Moscow, Gen. Dir. Astra-Int. Trade, Zagreb –1990; Vice-Dir., then Dir. Chamber of Econs., Zagreb; mem. Christian Democratic Union (CDU); Deputy Premier of Croatia 1990; Prime Minister 1991–92; mem. of Croatian Parl. for Sabor 1990–; Adviser to Pres. of Croatia 1992–; Dir. INA Co., Zagreb 1992–; numerous nat. and int. awards for econs. *Leisure interests:* oenology, pomology. *Address:* Ilica 49, 41000 Zagreb, Croatia. *Telephone:* (41) 517-230 (Office). *Fax:* 650-110.

GREIG, Sir (Henry Louis) Carron, K.C.V.O., C.B.E., D.L.; British businessman; b. 21 Feb. 1925, London; s. of Sir Louis and Lady Greig; m. Monica Stourton 1955; three s. one d.; ed. Eton Coll. and Royal Military Coll., Sandhurst; Scots Guards 1943–47, attained rank of Capt.; joined Horace Clarkson and Co. Ltd. 1948, Dir. 1954, Man. Dir. 1962, Chair. 1973–85; Chair. Horace Clarkson Holdings PLC 1976–93; Dir. James Purdey and Sons Ltd. 1972–, Baltic Exchange Ltd. 1978–82, Vice-Chair. 1982, Chair. 1983–85; Dir. Williams and Glyn's Bank 1983–85, Royal Bank of Scotland 1985–95; Gentleman Usher to H.M. the Queen 1961–95. *Address:* Brook House, Fleet, Hants., England; Binsness, Forres, Moray, Scotland. *Telephone:* (01252) 617596; (01309) 672334.

GREILSAMER, Laurent, L. ÈS L.; French journalist; b. 2 Feb. 1953, Neuilly; s. of Marcel Greilsamer and Alice Greilsamer; m. Claire Méheut 1979; three s.; ed. Ecole Supérieure de Journalisme, Lille; teacher, Lycée Henri IV 1970–73; ed. Le Figaro 1974–76, Quotidien de Paris 1976; ed. Le Monde 1977–84, Sr. reporter 1984–94, Ed.-in-Chief 1994. *Publications:* Interpol, le siège de soupçon 1986, Un certain Monsieur Paul, l'affaire Touvier 1989, Hubert Beuve-Méry 1990, Enquête sur l'affaire du sang contaminé 1990, Les juges parlent 1992, Interpol, Policiers sans frontières 1997. *Leisure interests:* painting, reading. *Address:* c/o Le Monde, 21 bis, rue Claude Bernard, 75005 Paris, France.

GREINER, Walter Albin Erhard, M.SC., PH.D., F.R.S.A.; German physicist; b. 29 Oct. 1935, Neuenbau/Thür; s. of Albin and Elsa (Fischer) Greiner; m. Bärbel Chun 1960; two s.; ed. Univs. of Darmstadt and Freiburg; Research Asst., Univ. of Freiburg 1961–62; Asst. Prof., Univ. of Md., U.S.A. 1962–64; Prof. and Dir. Inst. of Theoretical Physics, Univ. of Frankfurt am Main 1965–; Guest Prof., numerous univs. worldwide; Adjunct Prof., Vanderbilt Univ., Nashville, Tenn., U.S.A., and Oak Ridge Nat. Lab., Tenn. 1978, 1979, 1981; Perm. Consultant, Gesellschaft für Schwerionenforschung, Darmstadt 1976–97; European Ed. Int. Journal of Modern Physics 1991–; Hon. D.Sc. (Witwatersrand) 1982, (Tel Aviv, Louis Pasteur, Strasbourg, Bucharest) 1991, (Debrecen) 1997; Max Born Prize, Inst. of Physics, U.K. 1974; Otto Hahn Prize, Frankfurt 1982; Hon. mem. Lorand Eötvös Soc. (Budapest) 1989, Romanian Acad. of Science 1992; Dr. h.c. (Tel Aviv) 1991, (Louis Pasteur Univ., Strasbourg) 1991, (Bucharest) 1992, (Lajos Kossuth Univ., Hungary) 1997; Alex von Humboldt Medal 1998. *Publications:* Nuclear Theory (with Eisenberg) (3 vols.) 1972, Lectures on Theoretical Physics (12 vols.), Dynamics of Heavy-Ion Collisions (with Cindro and Ricci), Quantum Electrodynamics of Strong Fields (jtly.) 1985; over 500 papers in nat. and int. journals. *Leisure interests:* music, mycology, fishing, walking. *Address:* Institut für Theoretische Physik, Johann Wolfgang Goethe Universität, Robert Mayer Strasse 8–10, 60054 Frankfurt am Main, Germany.

GREKOVA, Irina Nikolaevna (pseud. of Elena Sergeevna Venttsel); Russian author; b. 21 March 1907, Reval (Tallinn); ed. Moscow Univ. Prof. of Cybernetics, Moscow Air Force Acad. 1955–67; published first story 1957. *Publications include:* Beyond the Entryway 1962, The Lady's Hairdresser 1963, Under the Streetlight 1966, During the Tests 1967, Little Garnsov 1970, The Landlady 1976, Life at the Department: Tales 1981, The Rapids (novel) 1984, A Legendary Figure 1987, The Break 1987, Though Fresh Is Its Renown (novel) 1995. *Address:* Leningradsky Prosp. 44, Apt. 29, 125167 Moscow, Russia. *Telephone:* 212-32-69.

GRENFELL, 3rd Baron, cr. 1902, of Kilvey; **Julian Pascoe Francis St. Leger Grenfell;** British politician; b. 23 May 1935, London; s. of late 2nd Baron Grenfell of Kilvey; m. 1st Loretta Reali 1961 (dissolved 1970; one d.; m. 2nd Gabrielle Raab 1970; two d.; m. 3rd Elizabeth Porter Scott 1987 (dissolved 1992); m. 4th Dagmar Langbehn Debreil 1993; ed. Eton Coll., King's Coll., Cambridge; Second Lieut., Kings Royal Rifle Corps 1954–56; Pres. Cambridge Union 1959; Capt. Queen's Royal Rifles (Territorial Army) 1963; television journalist 1960–64; with World Bank 1965–95, Chief of Information and Public Affairs in Europe 1969–72, Deputy Dir. European Office 1973–74, Special Rep. to the UN Orgs. 1974–81, Adviser HQ 1983–90, Head External Affairs, European Office 1990–95; mem. U.K. del. to Council of Europe 1997–; Chair. House of Lords Sub-Cttee. on Econ. and Financial

Affairs 1998–, mem. Select Cttee. on EU 1998–; Labour. *Publication:* Margot (novel) 1984. *Leisure interest:* writing fiction. *Address:* c/o House of Lords, London, SW1A 0PW, England. *Telephone:* 0171-219 3210. *Fax:* 0171-219 4931.

GRENIER, Jean-Marie René, LIC. EN DROIT; French business executive; b. 27 June 1926, Paris; s. of Henri Grenier and Germaine Pissavy; m. Marie-Alix Bonnet de Paillerets 1958; three s. one d.; ed. Lycée Fustel-de-Coulanges, Strasbourg, Ecole Bossuet, Lycée Louis-le-Grand, Faculté de Droit, Paris and Ecoles des Hautes Etudes Commerciales, Paris; Deputy Dir. Soc. des Usines Chimiques Rhône-Poulenc 1962, Dir. 1970, Commercial Dir. 1971; Dir. Rhône-Poulenc S.A. 1977–82; Pres. Syndicat de l'industrie chimique organique de synthèse et biochimie 1975–84, Hon. Pres. 1984–; Adviser Foreign Trade 1975–; Chevalier ordre nat. du Mérite, Croix de la valeur militaire. *Leisure interest:* tennis. *Address:* Le Moulin Pocancy (Marne), 51130 Vertus; 74 rue Claude Bernard, 75005 Paris, France (Home). *Telephone:* (3) 26.70.93.15; (1) 47.07.79.82 (Home).

GRENS, Elmar; Latvian molecular biologist; b. 9 Oct. 1935, Riga; s. of Janis Grens and Melita Grenė; m. Eva Stankevich 1957; one s. one d.; ed. Latvian State Univ.; researcher, Head of Lab., Research Dir. Inst. of Organic Synthesis Latvian Acad. of Sciences 1958–90, Dir. Inst. of Molecular Biology, Latvian Acad. of Sciences 1991–93; Dir. Biomedical Research and Study Centre, Univ. of Latvia 1993–; mem. Latvian Acad. of Sciences, Academia Europaea; main research in molecular biology of viruses, fine biotech., genetic eng. *Publications include:* RNA Bacteriophages 1957; more than 180 scientific articles. *Leisure interest:* downhill skiing. *Address:* Biomedical Research and Study Centre, University of Latvia, Ratsupites 1, Riga 1067, Latvia. *Telephone:* (2) 427117. *Fax:* (2) 427521.

GRETZKY, Wayne; American ice hockey player; b. 26 Jan. 1961, Brantford, Canada; s. of Walter Gretzky and Phyllis Gretzky; m. Janet Jones 1988; two s. one d.; fmr. player with Edmonton; played with Los Angeles Kings 1988–96, with St. Louis Blues 1996, with N.Y. Rangers 1996–; most prolific scorer in Nat. Hockey League history; Most Valuable Player (nine times); winner Stanley Cup with Edmonton (four times). *Address:* New York Rangers, Madison Square Garden, 2 Pennsylvania Plaza, New York, NY 10121, U.S.A.

GREVISSE, Fernand; French judge and public servant; b. 28 July 1924, Boulogne-Billancourt; m. Suzanne Seux 1958; two d.; ed. Ecole Nationale d'Administration; apptd. Auditeur, Conseil d'Etat 1949, Maître des Requêtes 1956; apptd. Head of Office of Minister of Justice 1959; Dir.-Gen., Water Resources and Forests, Ministry of Agric. 1964–65, Rural Areas 1965–66; Deputy-Chair. Nat. Forestry Office; Head of Office of Minister of State in charge of civil service April–July 1967; Dir.-Gen., Admin. and Civil Service Dept., Govt. Secr.-Gen. 1967–71; mem. Conseil d'Etat 1973–, Chair. Public Works Section 1984–88, Hon. Chair. 1988, mem. Consultative Comm.; Prof., Institut d'études politiques de Paris 1977–80; Chair. Centre d'études supérieures du management public 1977–79; Judge, EC Court of Justice 1981–82, 1988–89, 1989–94; Commdr. Légion d'honneur, Médaille militaire, Commdr. Ordre nat. du Mérite, Croix de guerre. *Address:* 28 rue Desaix, 75015 Paris, France (Home).

GREY, Dame Beryl Elizabeth, D.B.E.; British prima ballerina; b. 11 June 1927, London; d. of Arthur Ernest and Annie Elizabeth Groom; m. Dr. Sven Gustav Svenson 1950; one s.; ed. Dame Alice Owens School, London, Madeline Sharp School, Royal Ballet School, and de Vos School of Dance; début Sadler's Wells Co. 1941; Prima Ballerina with Royal Ballet until 1957; freelance int. prima ballerina since 1957; first full-length ballet Swan Lake on 15th birthday; has appeared since in leading roles of classical and numerous modern ballets including Giselle, Sleeping Beauty, Sylvia, Casse Noisette, Les Sylphides, Checkmate, Donald of the Burthens, Dante Sonata, Three Cornered Hat, Ballet Imperial, Lady and the Fool, Les Rendezvous; American, Continental, African, Far Eastern tours with Royal Ballet since 1945; guest artist European Opera Houses in Norway, Finland, Sweden, Denmark, Belgium, Romania, Germany, Italy, etc.; guest artist South and Central America, Middle East, Union of South Africa, Rhodesia, Australasia; first foreign guest artist ever to dance with the Bolshoi Ballet in Russia 1957–58 (Moscow, Leningrad, Kiev, Tiflis) and first to dance with Peking Ballet and Shanghai Ballet 1964; Dir.-Gen. of Arts Educational Trust, London 1966–68; Artistic Dir. of London Festival Ballet 1968–79; produced and staged Giselle, Perth, Australia 1984, 1986, Sleeping Beauty, Royal Swedish Ballet, Stockholm 1985; Pres. Dance Council for Wales 1982–, Keep-fit Soc. 1992–93; Vice-Pres. Royal Acad. of Dancing 1981–; Chair. Imperial Soc. Teachers of Dancing 1982–91, Pres. 1991–; Gov. Royal Ballet 1993– (Vice-Chair. 1995–); Trustee of Royal Ballet Benevolent Fund (Chair. 1992–), Dance Teachers' Benevolent Fund (Vice-Chair. 1987–), Discs 1994–; Vice-Pres. Fed. of Music Festivals, The Music Therapy Charity 1980–; Patron Dancers Resettlement Trust, Benesh Inst., Language of Dance Centre, Lisa Ullman Travelling Scholarship Fund 1986–, Friends of Sadler's Wells 1991–, Furlong Hip Replacement 1993–, Osteopathic Centre for Children 1994–; Theatre Design Trust for Dance 1995–; Fellow Imperial Soc. of Teachers of Dancing 1966–; Hon. D.Mus. (Leicester) 1970, (London) 1996; Hon. D.Lit. (City of London) 1974, (Buckingham) 1993; Hon. D.Ed. (CNAA), 1989; Queen Elizabeth II Coronation Award, Royal Acad. of Dancing. *Publications:* Red Curtain Up 1958, Through the Bamboo Curtain 1965; edited My Favourite Ballet Stories 1981. *Leisure interests:* piano playing, painting, swimming. *Address:* Fernhill, Priory Road, Forest Row, East Sussex, RH18 5JE, England. *Telephone:* (0134282) 2539.

GREY, Linda; American publisher; fmr. Vice-Pres. and Editorial Dir. (adult fiction and non-fiction), Bantam Books Inc., New York, Vice-Pres. and Ed.-in-Chief –1992; Pres. Linda Grey Books 1992–. *Address:* Ballantine/Del Rey/Fawcett/Ivy Books, 201 E. 50th Street, New York, NY 10022, U.S.A.

GREY OF NAUNTON, Baron (Life Peer), cr. 1968; **Ralph Francis Alnwick Grey,** G.C.M.G., G.C.V.O., O.B.E., LL.B.; British civil servant (retd.); b. 15 April 1910, Wellington, New Zealand; s. of Francis A. Grey and Mary W. Spence; m. Esmé Burcher 1944 (died 1996); two s. one d.; ed. Scots Coll., Wellington Coll., Auckland Univ. Coll., Pembroke Coll., Cambridge; Barrister and Solicitor, Supreme Court of N.Z. 1932, Judge's Assoc. N.Z. 1932–36; Cadet, Colonial Admin. Service, Nigeria 1937, Asst. Financial Sec. 1948, Admin. Officer (First Class) 1951, Devt. Sec. 1952, Sec. to the Gov.-Gen. and Council of Ministers 1954; Chief Sec. Fed. of Nigeria 1955–57, Deputy Gov.-Gen. 1957–59; mem. Council of Ministers, Fed. of Nigeria 1955–57, and mem. Council of Ibadan Univ. Coll.; Gov. and C.-in-C. British Guiana 1959–64; Gov. and C.-in-C. Bahamas 1964–68, also Gov. Turks and Caicos Islands 1965–68; Gov. of N. Ireland 1968–73; Deputy Chair. Commonwealth Devt. Corpn. 1973–79, Chair. 1979–80; Bristol Regional Bd., Lloyds Bank Ltd. 1973–81; Chair. Royal Overseas League 1976–81, Pres. 1981–93, Grand Pres. 1993; mem. Council, Cheltenham Ladies' Coll. 1975–87; Pres. Scout Council, Northern Ireland 1969–94, Britain-Nigeria Asscn. 1983–89, Overseas Service Pensioners Asscn. 1983–97; Chancellor, New Univ. of Ulster 1980–84; Chancellor Univ. of Ulster 1984–93; Hon. LL.D. (Queen's Univ., Belfast, Nat. Univ. of Ireland); Hon. D.Litt. (New Univ. of Ulster); Hon. D.Sc. (Univ. of Ulster); Hon. Bencher, Inn of Court Northern Ireland, Gray's Inn London; Bailiff of Egle, Order of St. John 1975–87, Chancellor 1987–88, Lord Prior 1988–91; Grand Cross Order of St. John 1975, Gran Crose dell'Ordine al Merito Melitense 1989; Hon. Freeman, City of Belfast, Borough of Lisburn; Freeman, City of London. *Leisure interests:* golf, reading. *Address:* Overbrook, Naunton, Glos., GL54 3AX, England. *Telephone:* (01451) 850263.

GRIER, Pam; American actress, writer and singer; b. 1949, Winston-Salem, N.C.; d. of Clarence Ransom Grier and Gwendolyn (Sylvia) Samuels; mem. Acad. of Motion Picture Arts and Sciences. *Films:* The Big Doll House 1971, Women in Cages 1971, Big Bird Cage 1972, Black Mama, White Mama 1972, Cool Breeze 1972, Hit Man 1972, Twilight People 1972, Coffy 1973, Scream, Blacula, Scream! 1973, The Arena 1973, Foxy Brown 1974, Bucktown 1975, Friday Foster 1975, Sheba Baby 1975, Drum 1976, Greased Lightning 1977, Fort Apache: The Bronx 1981, Something Wicked This Way Comes 1983, Stand Alone 1985, The Vindicator 1986, On the Edge 1986, The Allnighter 1987, Above The Law 1988, The Package 1989, Class of 1999 1991, Bill and Ted's Bogus Journey 1991, Tough Enough, Posse 1993, Serial Killer 1995, Original Gangstas 1996, Escape from L.A. 1996, Mars Attacks! 1996, Strip Search 1997, Fakin' Da Funk 1997, Jackie Brown 1997, Holy Smoke 1999. *TV:* (mini-series) Roots: The Next Generations 1979; (films) Badge of the Assassin 1985, A Mother's Right: The Elizabeth Morgan Story 1992. *Stage appearances:* Fool for Love, Frankie and Johnnie, In the Claire De Lune; Best Actress NAACP 1986. *Leisure interests:* skiing, scuba diving, western and English horseback riding, tennis.

GRIERSON, Philip, M.A., LITT.D., F.B.A., F.S.A.; British historian; b. 15 Nov. 1910, Dublin; s. of Philip Henry Grierson and Roberta Ellen Jane Pope; ed. Marlborough Coll., Gonville and Caius Coll., Cambridge; Univ. Lecturer in History, Cambridge 1945–59; Reader in Medieval Numismatics, Cambridge 1959–71; Prof. of Numismatics, Univ. of Cambridge 1971–78, Emer. Prof. 1978–; Prof. of Numismatics and History of Coinage, Univ. of Brussels 1948–81; Ford's Lecturer in History, Univ. of Oxford 1956–57; Fellow, Gonville and Caius Coll., Cambridge 1935–, Librarian 1944–69, Pres. 1966–76; Literary Dir. Royal Historical Soc. 1945–55; Hon. Keeper of the Coins, Fitzwilliam Museum, Cambridge 1949–; Adviser in Byzantine Numismatics to Dumbarton Oaks Library and Collection, Harvard Univ., Washington, D.C., U.S.A. 1955–98; Pres. Royal Numismatic Soc. 1961–66; Corresp. mem. Koninklijke Vlaamse Acad. 1955; Assoc. mem. Acad. Royale de Belgique 1968; Corresp. Fellow, Medieval Acad. of America 1972; Hon. Litt.D. (Ghent) 1958, (Leeds) 1978; Hon. LL.D. (Cambridge) 1993. *Publications:* Les Annales de Saint-Pierre de Gand 1937, Books on Soviet Russia 1917–42 1943, Sylloge of Coins of the British Isles, Vol. I (Fitzwilliam Museum: Early British and Anglo-Saxon Coins) 1958, Bibliographie numismatique 1966, English Linear Measures: a study in origins 1973, Catalogue of the Byzantine Coins in the Dumbarton Oaks Collection and in the Whittemore Collection, Vols. I, II and III (with A. R. Bellinger) 1966–73, Vol. V 1999, Numismatics 1975, Monnaies du Moyen Age 1976, The Origins of Money 1977, Les monnaies 1977, Dark Age Numismatics 1979, Later Medieval Numismatics 1979, Byzantine Coins 1982, Medieval European Coinage, 1: The Early Middle Ages (5th-10th Centuries) (with M. Blackburn) 1986, 14: Italy (III) (with Lucia Travaini) 1998, Coins of Medieval Europe 1991, Catalogue of the Late Roman Coins in the Dumbarton Oaks Collection and in the Whittemore Collection (with M. Mays) 1992; Ed.: C. W. Previté-Orton, The Shorter Cambridge Medieval History 1952; H. E. Ives, The Venetian Gold Ducat and its Imitations 1954, Studies in Italian History presented to Miss E. M. Jamison 1956, O. Mørkholm, Early Hellenistic Coinage (with U. Westermark) 1991; trans. Feudalism (F. L. Ganshof) 1952. *Leisure interest:*

science fiction. *Address:* Gonville and Caius College, Cambridge, CB2 1TA, England. *Telephone:* (01223) 332450.

GRIERSON, Sir Ronald Hugh, Kt., M.A.; British/German banker; b. 6 Aug. 1921, Nuremberg, Germany; s. of Ernest Grierson and Gerda Grierson; m. Elizabeth Heather, Viscountess Bearsted 1966 (died 1993); one s.; ed. Realgymnasium, Nuremberg, Lycée Pasteur, Paris, Highgate School, London and Balliol Coll. Oxford; Dir. S.G. Warburg & Co. Ltd. 1948–86; Deputy Chair. and Chief Exec. Industrial Reorganization Corpn. 1966–68; Chair. Orion Bank 1970–73; Dir.-Gen. for Industry and Tech., Comm. of the European Communities 1973–74; Dir. Chrysler Corpn., W. R. Grace, Inc. 1987; Dir. General Electric Co. PLC 1968–91, Vice-Chair. 1983–91; Chair. GEC Inc. 1984–, Bain & Co. Int. 1988–, Advisory Bd. Blackstone Group 1989–, GEC Int. 1992–, Daily Mail & Gen. Trust 1993–; Exec. Chair. South Bank Centre 1985–90; Dir. W. R. Grace & Co. 1987–94; Hon. D.C.L. (Grove City Coll., Pa.) 1986; Commdr.'s Cross, Order of Merit (Germany) 1993; Officier, Légion d'honneur 1994. *Address:* 7 Hertford Street, London, W1Y 8LP, England.

GRIFFEY, George Kenneth (Ken), Jr.; American baseball player; b. 21 Nov. 1969, Donora, Pa.; ed. high school, Cincinnati; Outfielder Seattle Mariners 1987–; Golden Glove Award 1990–96; on numerous All Star teams 1990–96. *Address:* Seattle Mariners, P.O. Box 4100, 83 King Street, Seattle, WA 98104, U.S.A.

GRIFFIN, Jasper, M.A., F.B.A.; British classical scholar; b. 29 May 1937, London; s. of Frederick William Griffin and Constance Irene Cordwell; m. Miriam Tamara Dressler 1960; three d.; ed. Balliol Coll., Oxford; Jackson Fellow, Harvard Univ. 1960–61; Dyson Research Fellow, Balliol Coll., Oxford 1961–63, Fellow and Tutor in Classics 1963–, Univ. Reader 1989–, Prof. of Classical Literature 1992–, Public Orator 1992–; T. S. Eliot Memorial Lectures, Univ. of Kent 1984. *Publications:* Homer on Life and Death 1980, Snobs 1982, Latin Poets and Roman Life 1985, The Mirror of Myth 1985, Virgil 1986; Ed. The Oxford History of the Classical World 1986, Homer: The Odyssey 1987, The Iliad: Book Nine 1995. *Leisure interests:* music, wine. *Address:* Balliol College, Oxford, England. *Telephone:* (01865) 277782.

GRIFFIN, Very Rev. Victor Gilbert Benjamin, M.A., D.THEOL.; Irish ecclesiastic; b. 24 May 1924, Carnew, Co. Wicklow; s. of Gilbert Benjamin Griffin and Martha Violet Crowe; m. Daphne Elizabeth Mitchell 1958; two s.; ed. Mountjoy School, Dublin, Kilkenny Coll., and Trinity Coll., Dublin; Curate St. Augustine's, Londonderry 1947–50; Christchurch, Londonderry 1950–57, Rector 1957–69; Dean St. Patrick's Cathedral, Dublin 1969–91; Lecturer in Philosophy, Magee Univ. Coll., Londonderry 1950–69; Hon. D.D. (Trinity Coll. Dublin) 1992; Scholar and Prizeman Trinity Coll.; Irish People of the Year Award 1979. *Publications:* Trends in Theology (1870–1970) 1970, Anglican and Irish 1976, Pluralism and Ecumenism 1983, Mark of Protest (autobiog.) 1993, The Vision of Jonathan Swift 1995, The Great Dean of St. Patrick's, Swift's Message to Ireland Today 1995, Religion and Madness 1996, The Irish Churches and Sectarianism 1996, Wolf Tone and Our "Common Irishness" 1997. *Leisure interests:* golf, walking and music. *Address:* 7 Tyler Road, Limavady, BT49 0DW, Northern Ireland. *Telephone:* 62093.

GRIFFITH, Alan Richard, M.B.A.; American banker; b. 17 Dec. 1941, Mineola, N.Y.; s. of Charles E. Griffith and Amalia Guenther; m. Elizabeth Ferguson 1964; one s. one d.; ed. Lafayette Coll. and City Univ. of New York; Asst. credit officer, The Bank of New York 1968–72, Asst. Vice-Pres. 1972–74, Vice-Pres. 1974–82, Sr. Vice-Pres. 1982–85, Exec. Vice-Pres. 1985–88, Sr. Exec. Vice-Pres. 1988–90, Pres. 1990–94, Vice-Chair. 1994–. *Address:* The Bank of New York, 48 Wall Street, New York, NY 10286, U.S.A.

GRIFFITH, Gavan, A.O., Q.C., LL.M., D.PHIL.; Australian lawyer; b. 11 Oct. 1941, Melbourne; m. Vanessa Fitts 1968; one s. three d.; ed. Melbourne Univ. and Magdalen Coll. Oxford; barrister 1963; Q.C. 1981; Solicitor-Gen. of Australia 1984–97; del. to UN Int. Trade Law Comm. (UNCITRAL) 1984–97, Vice-Chair. 1987–88, 1994–95; Agent and counsel for Australia at Int. Court of Justice 1989–95; mem. Perm. Court of Arbitration, The Hague 1987–; mem. Intelsat Panel of Legal Experts 1988–97, Chair. 1993–94; del. Hague Conf. of Pvt. Int. Law 1992–; Arbitrator, Int. Comm. for Settlement of Int. Disputes (ISCID) 1994–; Consultant, Office of Legal Counsel, UN, New York 1994–95; Dir. Australian Centre for Int. Commercial Arbitration 1997–; mem. Council, Nat. Gallery of Australia 1986–92; Visiting Fellow, Magdalen Coll. Oxford 1973–74, 1976, 1980, 1995. *Address:* Owen Dixon Chambers, West 205 William Street, Melbourne, Vic. 3000, Australia.

GRIFFITH, Kenneth; Welsh actor, director and writer; b. 12 Oct. 1921, Tenby; grandson of Ernest Griffiths and Emily Griffiths; m. three times, divorced three times; three s. two d.; ed. Tenby Council School and Tenby Grammar School; began acting at Festival Theatre, Cambridge 1938; Old Vic (under Tyrone Guthrie) 1942 and 1944; Royal Air Force 1942–44; has acted in approx. 100 films; researched, wrote and made over 25 factual films, and films for TV, including lives of Cecil Rhodes, Michael Collins, Clive of India, Edmund Kean, Thomas Paine, David Ben Gurion, Roger Casement, Napoleon, Dr. Ambedkar, Alfred Dreyfus. etc. *Publications:* Thank God We Kept the Flag Flying 1974, Curious Journey 1982, The Discovery of Nehru 1989, The Fool's Pardon (autobiog.) 1994. *Leisure interest:* postal history of the second British/Boer war (1899–1902). *Address:* Michael Collins House, 110 Englefield Road, Islington, London, N1 3LQ, England. *Telephone:* 0171-226 9013.

GRIFFITH, Melanie; American actress; b. 9 Aug. 1957, New York; d. of Tippi Hedren and Peter Griffith; m. 1st Don Johnson 1975 (divorced 1976, remarried 1989, divorced 1993); one d.; m. 2nd Steven Bauer (divorced); m. 3rd Antonio Banderas 1996; one d.; ed. Hollywood Professional School; moved to Los Angeles aged four. *Films:* Night Moves 1975, Smile 1975, The Drowning Pool 1975, One on One 1977, Underground Aces 1979, Roar, Fear City, Body Double 1984, Something Wild 1986, Stormy Monday 1987, The Milagro Beaufield War 1988, Working Girl 1988, Pacific Heights, Bonfire of the Vanities, Shining Through, Paradise 1991, A Stranger Amongst Us 1992, Close to Eden 1993, Born Yesterday 1993, Milk Money 1994, Nobody's Fool 1994, Now and Then, Two Much, Mulholland Falls 1996, Lolita 1996, Celebrity, Crazy in Alabama. *Television:* Once an Eagle (mini-series), Carter Country (series), Coast to Coast, Steel Cowboy, Golden Gate, She's in the Army Now, Starmaker. *Address:* c/o Creative Artists Agency, 9830 Wilshire Boulevard, Beverly Hills, CA 90212, U.S.A.

GRIFFITH, Nanci; American singer, songwriter and guitarist; b. 6 July 1953, Seguin, Tex.; d. of Griff Griffith and Ruelene Griffith; fmr. schoolteacher; albums include: There's A Light Beyond These Woods 1977, Once In A Very Blue Moon 1984, The Last Of The True Believers 1985, Poet In My Window 1986, Lone Star State of Mind 1987, Little Love Affairs 1988, One Fair Summer Evening 1988, Storms 1989, Late Night Grand Hotel 1991, The MCA Years—A Retrospective 1993, Other Voices, Other Rooms 1993 (Grammy Award—Best Folk Album), Flyer 1994; appeared in Nanci Griffith on Broadway 1994. *Publications:* novels and short stories including Two Of A Kind Heart 1988, Love Wore A Halo Back Before The War. *Address:* c/o Gold Mountain Entertainment, 1111 16th Avenue, S. Suite 302, Nashville, TN 37212, U.S.A.

GRIFFITHS, Baron (Life Peer), cr. 1985, of Govilon in the county of Gwent; **William Hugh Griffiths,** Kt., M.C., P.C.; British judge; b. 26 Sept. 1923; s. of late Sir Hugh Griffiths, C.B.E.; m. Evelyn Krefting 1949; one s. three d.; ed. Charterhouse and St. John's Coll. Cambridge; called to Bar, Inner Temple 1949, Q.C. 1964; Treas. Bar Council 1968–69; Recorder of Margate 1962–64, Cambridge 1964–70; Judge, Queen's Bench Div., High Court of Justice 1971–80; a Lord Justice of Appeal 1980–85; a Lord of Appeal in Ordinary 1985–93; Chair. Security Comm. 1985–92; Chair. Advisory Cttee. on Legal Educ. and Conduct 1991–93; Judge, Nat. Industrial Relations Court 1973–74; mem. Advisory Council on Penal Reform 1967–70; Vice-Chair. Parole Bd. 1976–77; Capt. Royal and Ancient Golf Club, St. Andrews; mem. Chancellor's Law Reform Cttee. 1976–93; Hon. mem. Canadian Bar Asscn. 1981; Hon. Fellow American Inst. of Judicial Admin. 1985, American Coll. of Trial Lawyers 1988; Hon. LL.D. (Wales) 1987, (De Montfort) 1993. *Leisure interests:* golf, fishing. *Address:* c/o House of Lords, London, SW1A 0PW, England.

GRIFFITHS, Alan Gordon, B.ECONS., LL.B; Australian politician; b. 4 Sept. 1952, Melbourne; s. of Alan and Joy Griffiths; m. Shirley Griffiths 1970; two d.; ed. Traralgon High School, Vic., Monash Univ.; with firm of solicitors, specializing in trade union affairs 1979–82; industrial officer, Federated Rubber and Allied Workers' Union of Australia 1982; Labor mem. House of Reps. for Maribymong, Vic. 1983–96; Minister for Resources and Energy 1990–93, for Tourism 1991–93, for Industry, Tech. and Regional Devt. 1993–94; Chair. Griffiths Group Int. Pty. Ltd. 1996–. *Leisure interests:* the arts, sport, politics, travel. *Address:* Level 11, 533 Little Lonsdale Street, Melbourne, Vic. 3000, Australia.

GRIFFITHS, Phillip A., PH.D.; American professor of mathematics; b. 18 Oct. 1938, Raleigh, N.C.; s. of Phillip Griffiths and Jeanette (Field) Griffiths; m. 1st Anne Lane Crittenden 1958 (divorced 1967); one s. one d.; m. 2nd Marian Jones; two d.; Miller Fellow, Univ. of Calif. (Berkeley) 1962–64, 1975–76, Faculty mem. 1964–67: Visiting Prof. Princeton Univ. 1967–68, Prof. 1968–72; Prof. Harvard Univ. 1972–83, Dwight Parker Robinson Prof. of Math. 1983; Provost and James B. Duke Prof. of Math. Duke Univ. 1983–91; Guest Prof. Univ. of Beijing 1983; Dir. Inst. for Advanced Study, Princeton 1991–; mem. Bd. of Dirs., Bankers Trust, N.Y.; mem. N.A.S.; hon. degrees from Wake Forest, Angers and Beijing Univs.; Guggenheim Fellow 1980–82; other awards and distinctions. *Publications:* some 90 articles in professional journals. *Leisure interest:* sailing. *Address:* Office of the Director, Institute for Advanced Study, Olden Lane, Princeton, NJ 08540, U.S.A. *Telephone:* (609) 734-8200. *Fax:* (609) 683-7605.

GRIFFITHS, Terry; British snooker player; b. 16 Oct. 1947, Llanelli, Wales; s. of Martin Griffiths and late Ivy Griffiths; m. Annette Jones 1968; two s.; turned professional snooker player 1978; Embassy World Champion 1979, Coral UIT Champion 1982, Benson & Hedges Masters Champion 1980, Benson & Hedges Irish Masters Champion 1981 (twice), 1982, Welsh Champion three times. *Publications:* Championship Snooker, Complete Snooker, Griff. *Leisure interests:* golf, music, playing snooker. *Address:* West-Side, Ar-y-Bryn, Pembrey, Llanelli, Dyfed, SA16 0AX, Wales.

GRIFFITHS, Trevor, B.A.; British playwright; b. 4 April 1935; s. of Ernest Griffiths and Anne Connor; m. 1st Janice Elaine Stansfield 1961 (died 1977); one s. two d.; m. 2nd Gillian Cliff 1992; ed. Manchester Univ.; taught English language and literature 1957–65; Educ. Officer, BBC 1965–72; Dir. Saint Oscar 1990, The Gulf Between Us 1992, Who Shall be Happy . . .? 1995, Food for Ravens 1997; Writer's Award, British Acad. of Film and TV Artists 1981, W.G.A. Award for Reds 1981. *Publications:* Occupations 1972, Sam Sam 1972, The Party 1974, Comedians 1976, All Good Men, and Absolute

Beginners 1977, Through the Night, and Such Impossibilities 1977, Thermidor and Apricots 1977, Deeds (Jt. Author) 1978, The Cherry Orchard (trans.) 1978, Country 1981, Oi for England 1982, Sons and Lovers (TV version) 1982, Judgement Over the Dead 1986, Fatherland 1987, Real Dreams 1987, Collected Plays for TV 1988, Piano 1990, The Gulf Between Us 1992, Hope in the Year Two 1994, Thatcher's Children 1994, Plays One (Collected Stage Plays) 1996, Food for Ravens 1998. *Address:* c/o Peters Fraser & Dunlop, 503/4, The Chambers, Chelsea Harbour, Lots Road, London, SW10 0XF, England.

GRIFFITHS OF FFORESTFACH, Baron (Life Peer), cr. 1991 of Fforestfach in the County of West Glamorgan; **Brian Griffiths,** M.SC.; British professor of banking and international finance; b. 27 Dec. 1941; s. of Ivor Winston Griffiths and Phyllis Mary Griffiths (née Morgan); m. Rachel Jane Jones 1965; one s. two d.; ed. Dynevor Grammar School and L.S.E.; Asst. Lecturer in Econs., L.S.E. 1965–68, Lecturer 1968–76; Dir. Centre for Banking and Int. Finance, City Univ., London 1977–82, Prof. of Banking and Int. Finance 1977–85, Dean, City Univ. Business School 1982–85; Dir. Bank of England 1984–86, mem. Panel of Acad. Consultants 1977–86; Head of Prime Minister's Policy Unit 1985–90; Chair. Centre for Policy Studies 1991–; Head School Examinations and Assessment Council 1991–93; Vice-Chair. Goldman Sachs (Europe) 1991–; Dir. Thorn-EMI 1991–96, Hermann Miller 1991–, HTV 1991–93, Times Newspapers Ltd 1991–, Servicemaster 1992–, Telewest 1994–, English, Welsh and Scottish Railway 1996–. *Publications:* Is Revolution Change? (Ed. and Contrib.) 1972, Mexican Monetary Policy and Economic Development 1972, Invisible Barriers to Invisible Trade 1975, Inflation: The Price of Prosperity 1976, Monetary Targets (Ed. with G. E. Wood) 1980, The Creation of Wealth 1984, Monetarism in the United Kingdom (Ed. with G. E. Wood) 1984, Morality and the Market Place 1989. *Leisure interests:* the family and reading. *Address:* c/o House of Lords, London, SW1A 0PW, England.

GRIGNASCHI, Giancarlo, B.ENG.; Italian industrial executive; b. 30 Oct. 1926, Acqui Terme, Alessandria; s. of Giuseppe Grignaschi and Ninetta Caffa di Cortemilia; m. Ada Rapetti 1957; one s. two d.; ed. Genoa Univ.; with Esso Standard Italiana 1956–67, Vice-Man. Augusta Refinery, Sicily 1967–68, Man. Econ. Studies Office 1968, then Man. Programming and Control for refining sector, Man. Augusta refinery 1970–71, Gen. Man. logistic operations for Italy, Esso Italiana 1971–72, Div. Man. Programming logistic operations for Europe, London 1972, then Man. of operations and logistic programming for Exxon's European affiliates; headed commercial operation of Esso Italiana 1975–76, responsible for logistic operations 1977; Founding partner ENECO S.p.A. specializing in ecological energy 1978; mem. Supervisory Cttee. for extraordinary admin. procedure Liquigas group cos.; Vice-Pres. Ente Nazionale Idrocarburi (ENI) Nov. 1982; Grande Ufficiale of Republic of Italy. *Leisure interests:* piano playing, twentieth-century poetry.

GRIGORESCU, Dan, M.A., PH.D.; Romanian historian of culture and critic; b. 13 May 1931, Bucharest; s. of Vasile Grigorescu and Tomescu (Grigorescu) Ecaterina; m. Petrovan Valentina; one s. one d.; ed. Bucharest Univ.; ed. State Publishing House for Art and Literature 1954–58; museographer Nat. Museum of Art, Bucharest 1958–63; chief ed. Meridiane Publishing House 1963–68; Dir. Fine Arts Dept., State Cttee. for Culture and Arts 1968; Dir. Romanian Library New York 1971–74; Prof. in Comparative Literature Bucharest Univ. 1963–; Dir. Inst. of Literary History and Theory, Romanian Acad.; Visiting Prof. Univ. of Wash., Seattle 1970–71, UCLA 1970; Vice-Pres. Int. Soc. for the History of Culture 1973–85; Prize of the Romanian Acad.; R. W. Emerson Award; mem. Romanian Acad., Romanian Fine Arts Union, Romanian Writers' Union, Int. Asscn. of Art Criticism, Int. Asscn. of Comparative Literature, Int. Asscn. for the History of Culture. *Works include:* Shelley, a monograph 1962; Three Romanian Painters in the 1848 Revolution 1965, Expressionism 1969, Cubism 1971, Pop Art 1972, American Art—a History 1974, Tendencies in 20th Century Poetry 1975, Shakespeare and the Romanian Modern Culture 1975, A Chronological Dictionary of American Literature 1977, The Buffalo's Song, an anthology of Indian American verse and prose 1978, The Adventures of the Image 1979, History of a Lost Generation—The Expressionists 1980, Brancusi 1982, Reality, Myth, Symbol: A Portrait of James Joyce 1984, North of Rio Grande 1986, Primitive and Modern Art 1988, A History of English Art 1989, Sentiment and Idea: Trends in Contemporary Romanian Art 1991, History of Culture and its Anxieties, The Twilight of Postmodernism 1992, Mr. Rubens and His Voyages 1994, Columbus and the Flying Islands 1996, Introduction to Comparative Literature 1997. *Address:* 7 Edgar Quinet, Bucharest 70118 (Office); 3-5 Vasile Conta, Bucharest 70138, Romania (Home).

GRIGORIEV, Anatoly Ivanovich; Russian physiologist; b. 23 March 1943, Jitomir Region, Ukraine; m.; two s.; ed. Moscow Medical Inst.; researcher, Dir. Inst. of Biomedical Problems; Co.-Dir. Space Biomedical Centre for Research and Training, Moscow Univ.; mem. Russian Acad. of Sciences 1997, Acad. of Medical Sciences 1993; Vice-Pres. Inst. Acad. of Astronautics; Dr. h.c. Bernard Univ. (France); U.S.S.R. State Prizes, Struggold Prize, American Space Aviation Asscn., Korolev Medal, Gagarin Medal and other decorations. *Leisure interest:* reading of memoirs. *Address:* Institute of Biomedical Problems, Khoroshevskoye shosse 76a, 123007 Moscow, Russia. *Telephone:* (095) 195-23-63. *Fax:* (095) 195-22-53.

GRIGOROVICH, Yuriy Nikolayevich; Russian ballet-master; b. 2 Jan. 1927, Leningrad; s. of K. A. Grigorovich-Rozay and N. E. Grigorovich; m. Natalya Igorevna Bessmertnova (q.v.); ed. Leningrad Choreographic School and Lunarcharski Inst. of Theatrical Art, Moscow; soloist, Kirov (now Mariinsky) Theatre 1946–64, Ballet-Master 1962–64; Chief Ballet Master, Bolshoi Theatre, Moscow 1964–95; Chief Choreographer, Artistic Dir. Kremlin Palace of Congresses Ballet 1998–; now works in various theatres in Russia and abroad; Ed.-in-Chief Soviet Ballet Encyclopaedia 1981; f. Bolshoi Ballet Grigorovich Co. (now Grigorovich-Ballet) 1990–; Lenin Prize 1970; People's Artist of U.S.S.R. 1973, U.S.S.R. State Prize 1985; Hero of Socialist Labour 1986. *Ballets include:* Stone Flower (Kirov-Mariinsky) 1957, Spartaacus 1968, Legend of Love (Kirov-Mariinsky) 1960, Sleeping Beauty (Bolshoi) 1963, Nutcracker (Bolshoi) 1966, Spartacus 1968, Swan Lake 1969, Ivan the Terrible 1975, Angara 1976, Romeo and Juliet (Paris) 1978, Giselle 1979, Golden Age (Bolshoi) 1982, Raymonda 1984, Bayaderka 1991, Elektra (Grigorovich Ballet co-produced with Melanin and Bobrov) 1992, La Fille Mal Gardée (Grigorovich Ballet) 1993, Le Corsaire (Bolshoi) 1994. *Address:* Sretenskii blvd. 6/1, Apt. 9, Moscow, Russia. *Telephone:* (095) 925-6431 (Home).

GRIGORYANTS, Sergey Ivanovich; Russian human rights activist and journalist; b. 12 May 1941, Kiev; s. of Ivan Arkadievich Grigoriants and Vera Sergeevna Shenberg; m. Tamara Vsevolodovna Grigoryants; one s. (died 1995) one d.; studied Moscow Univ., was expelled by KGB 1968; f. and ed. Information Bulletin on violation of human rights in U.S.S.R. 1982–83; imprisonment for political activities 1975–80, 1983–87; Founder, Ed. and Publr. Glasnost magazine 1987–91, Glasnost Information Agency 1991–; Founder, Chair. Public Fund Glasnost 1990–; organized regular Conf. KGB Yesterday, Today, Tomorrow; Head Centre on Information and Analysis, Russian Special Service 1993, Initiator of Int. Non-Governmental Tribunal on the War Crimes and Crimes Against Humanity, Chechnya; Co-Chair. Coalition for Support for Int. Criminal Court. *Leisure interests:* collecting paintings, antiques, early medieval artefacts. *Address:* 1st Naprudnaya Str. 3, Apt. 121, 129346 Moscow, Russia. *Telephone:* 474-45-90 (Home).

GRIGULL, Ulrich, DR. ING.; German professor, editor and consultant; b. 12 March 1912, Gallingen; s. of Wilhelm Grigull and Anna Wormit; m. Lydia Freiheit 1937; two d.; ed. Technische Hochschule, Danzig and Brunswick; Air Transport Research Establishment, Brunswick 1937–45; Farbenfabriken Bayer, Leverkusen 1952–60; Prof. Technische Univ. Munich 1960–80, Prof. Emer. 1980–, Rector, later Pres. 1972–80; Pres. Asscn. of Int. Heat Transfer Confs. 1970–74, 1982–86, Int. Asscn. for Properties of Steam 1977–79, 1986–88 (Hon. Fellow 1988–), Int. Centre for Heat and Mass Transfer 1982–86; mem. Bayerische Akad. der Wissenschaften, Braunschweig Wissenschaftliche Gesellschaft; Dr. Ing. h.c. (Stuttgart) 1982; Max Jakob Award 1973, Arnold Eucken Medaille 1979, C. F. Gauss Medal 1982, A.V. Luikov Medal 1982, Bayerischer Maximiliansorden 1984, Dechema Medal 1985. *Publications:* several textbooks and 130 scientific papers. *Leisure interest:* mountaineering. *Address:* Heinrich-Vogl-Strasse 1, D-81479 Munich, Germany. *Telephone:* (089) 79 65 57 (Home); (089) 289 16228 (Institute). *Fax:* (089) 289 16218.

GRILICHES, Zvi, PH.D.; American economist and educator; b. 12 Sept. 1930, Kaunas, Lithuania; m. Diane Asseo 1952; one s. one d.; ed. Hebrew Univ., Jerusalem and Univs. of California (Berkeley) and Chicago; served with Israeli Army 1948–49; naturalized U.S. citizen 1960; Asst. Prof. of Econs. Univ. of Chicago 1956–59, Assoc. Prof. 1960–64, Prof. 1964–69; Prof., Harvard Univ. 1969–78, Nathaniel Ropes Prof. of Political Economy 1979–87, Paul M. Warburg Prof. of Econs. 1987–; Chair. Dept. of Econs. 1980–83; Research Assoc. Nat. Bureau of Econ. Research 1959–60, 1978–, Dir. Programme on Productivity 1978–; numerous visiting professorships; Consultant Rand Corpn., Brookings Inst.; consultant to Bd. of Govs. Fed. Reserve System; mem. Advisory Comm. to U.S. Senate on the CPI 1995–96; mem. int. advisory cttee. Patinkin School of Econs., Hebrew Univ. 1996–, Econ. Educ. and Research Consortium on Russia 1996–; mem. Bd. of Govs., Ford Foundation; mem. American Econ. Asscn. (Vice-Pres. 1984, Pres. 1993); Fellow, A.A.A.S., N.A.S., American Statistical Asscn., Econometric Soc. (Pres. 1975), American Statistical Asscn., American Agricultural Econ. Asscn. *Publications:* Price Indexes and Quality Change 1971, Economies of Scale and the Form of the Production Function 1971, Handbook of Econometrics (Ed.) 1984, R & D, Patents and Productivity (Ed.) 1984, Technology, Education and Productivity 1988, Output Measurement in the Service Sectors (Ed.) 1992, R & D and Productivity: The Econometric Evidence 1998, Practicing Econometrics: Essays in Method and Application 1998, articles in professional journals. *Address:* Department of Economics, Harvard University, Cambridge, MA 02138; 62 Shepard Street, Cambridge, MA 02138, U.S.A.

GRILLI, Enzo, PH.D.; Italian banker and economist; b. 7 Oct. 1943, Casarza Ligure; s. of Agostino Grilli and Dominica Giambruno Grilli; m. Mary A. Jacobs; two d.; ed. Univ. of Genoa and Johns Hopkins Univ. U.S.A.; Dir. Econ. Research, Confed. of Italian Industries, Rome 1978–80; Dir.-Gen. Ministry of Budget and Planning 1982–84; Dir. Econ. Advisory Staff, IBRD, Washington, D.C. 1989–92; Exec. Dir. for Italy, Greece, Portugal, Albania and Malta, IBRD 1993–95; Exec. Dir. for Italy, Greece, Portugal, Albania, Malta and San Marino, IMF, Washington, D.C. 1995–98; Fulbright Fellow; St. Vincent Prize for Econs. 1995; Grand Officer of Italian Repub. *Publications:* The European Community and the Developing Countries 1993, Interdipenze Macroeconomiche Nord–Sud 1995, Regionalism and Multilateralism after the Uruguay Round (ed.) 1997. *Leisure interests:* reading, book collection, tennis. *Address:* Bologna Center, Johns Hopkins University, 40126 Bologna, Italy.

GRIMES, Don, A.O., M.B., B.S.; Australian politician and doctor; b. 4 Oct. 1937, Albury, N.S.W.; s. of Walter John Grimes and Annie Mildred Grimes; m. 1st Margaret Schofield 1962; m. 2nd Helen Knight 1984; m. 3rd Esther Timmermans 1991; two s. two d.; ed. N.S.W. High Schools, Univ. of Sydney; Medical Practitioner 1962–74; Senator for Tasmania 1974–87, Opposition Spokesman for Social Security 1976–83, for Repatriation and Compensation 1976–77, for Veterans' Affairs and Compensation 1977, 1980–83, Deputy Leader of the Opposition 1980–83; Deputy Chair. Asia-Pacific Socialist Org. 1981; Minister for Social Security 1983–84, and Deputy Leader of Govt. in Senate 1983–87; Minister for Community Services 1984–87; Amb. to the Netherlands 1987–91; Sr. mem. Admin. Appeals Tribunal 1991–96; Bd. mem. Australian Inst. of Family Studies 1991–96; Chair. Australian Nat. Council on AIDS 1992–96; Chair. Bd. S. Eastern Sydney Area Health Service 1995–, AusHealth Int. 1997–. *Leisure interests:* jazz, reading. *Address:* P.O. Box 73, Surry Hills, N.S.W. 2010, Australia.

GRIMLEY EVANS, Sir John, Kt., M.A., M.D., F.R.C.P., F.F.P.H.M.; British physician and academic; b. 17 Sept. 1936, Birmingham; s. of Harry Walter Grimley Evans and Violet Prenter Walker; m. Corinne Jane Cavender 1966; two s. one d.; ed. King Edward's School, Birmingham, St. John's Coll., Cambridge, Balliol Coll., Oxford; visiting scientist Univ. of Mich. 1966–67; Research Fellow, Wellington, New Zealand 1967–70; lecturer Univ. of London 1970–71; Prof. of Medicine Univ. of Newcastle-upon-Tyne 1973–84; Prof. of Clinical Geratology, Univ. of Oxford 1985–, Fellow Green Coll., Oxford 1985–; Consultant Physician, Oxford Hospitals 1985–; mem. MRC 1993–95, Chair. Health Services Research Bd. 1990–95; Vice-Pres. Royal Coll. of Physicians 1993–95; Ed. Age and Ageing 1988–95, Oxford Textbook of Geriatric Medicine; Harveian Orator Royal Coll. of Physicians 1997. *Publications:* papers on epidemiology and gerontology. *Address:* Department of Clinical Geratology, Radcliffe Infirmary, Oxford, OX2 6HE, England. *Telephone:* (01865) 224475. *Fax:* (01865) 224815.

GRIMMEISS, Hermann Georg, DR.RER.NAT.; Swedish physicist; b. 19 Aug. 1930, Hamburg, Germany; s. of Georg Grimmeiss and Franziska März; m. Hildegard Weizmann 1956; one s. one d.; ed. Oberschule Nördlingen and Univ. of Munich; Prof. of Solid State Physics, Head of Dept. Univ. of Lund 1965–96, Prof. Emer. 1996–, Dean for Research 1993–96; Chair. Nobel Symposium, Sweden 1996; mem. Programme Cttee. for Physics-Math. Swedish Natural Science Research Council 1971–80; mem. Bd. Swedish Nat. Cttee. for Physics 1971–72, 1981–; Prof. of Physics, Dir., Univ. of Frankfurt-am-Main 1973–74; mem. Cttee. for Electronics, Swedish Bd. for Tech. Devt. 1978–80; mem. Bd. Swedish-German Research Asscn. 1980–; mem. f. cttee. Univ. Frankfurt/Oder (Germany) 1991–93; mem. Cttee. for Science and Research, Brandenburg (Germany) 1993–95; Vice-Pres. RIFA (mem. Ericsson Group) 1981–83; Visiting Prof. Univ. of Calif. Berkeley 1990; Dir. Inst. of Semiconductor Physics, Frankfurt (Oder), Germany 1991–93; mem. Bd. Einstein Forum, Potsdam, Germany 1993–; mem. several other bds.; ed. and co-ed. several int. journals; mem. Royal Physiographic Soc. Lund, Royal Swedish Acad. of Eng. Sciences, Royal Swedish Acad. of Sciences, Societas Scintarum Sennica, New York Acad. of Sciences; Fellow, American Physical Soc.; Hon. mem. Ioffe Inst., St. Petersburg, Russia 1998; Order of North Star 1969, Bundesverdienstkreuz 1 Klasse 1993, King's Medal of 8th Dimension with Blue Ribbon, Stockholm 1998. *Publications:* more than 250 scientific publs. in int. journals and books. *Leisure interests:* tennis, music. *Address:* Department of Solid State Physics, University of Lund, Box 118, 221 00 Lund (Office); Målsmansvägen 5, 22467 Lund, Sweden (Home). *Telephone:* 46-2227675 (Office); 46-140980 (Home). *Fax:* 46-2223403.

GRIMSHAW, Nicholas Thomas, C.B.E., R.A., F.C.S.D., R.I.B.A.; British architect; b. 9 Oct. 1939, Hove; s. of Thomas Cecil Grimshaw and Hannah Joan Dearsley; m. Lavinia Russell 1972; two d.; ed. Wellington Coll., Edin. Coll. of Art, Architectural Asscn. School, London; Chair. Nicholas Grimshaw & Partners Ltd. 1980–; maj. projects include: Channel Tunnel Terminal, Waterloo, London; British Pavilion for Expo '92, Seville; Berlin Stock Exchange and Communications Centre; British Airways Combined Operations Centre, Heathrow Airport, London; Financial Times Printing Plant; HQ for Igus GmbH, Cologne, Germany; head office and printing press for Western Morning News, Plymouth; BMW HQ, Bracknell; new satellite and piers, Heathrow Airport; Western Region HQ for RAC; Herman Miller Factory, Bath; Oxford Ice Rink; Gillingham Business Park; Research Centre for Rank Xerox; J. Sainsbury Superstore, Camden, London; Redevt. of Terminal One, Manchester Airport; New Teaching and Research Bldg., Univ. of Surrey; Regional HQ for Orange Telecommunications, Darlington; Railway Terminus, Pusan, Korea; Redevt. Zurich Airport, Restoration Paddington Station 1996; Restoration of Spa, new bldg., Bath & E. Somerset Council 1997; Caixa Gallicia Foundation, Coruna, Spain; mem. Council, Architectural Asscn., Council of Royal Acad.; Assessor for British Construction Industry Awards, R.I.B.A., Dept. of Environment, British Gas; Hon. F.A.I.A.; Hon. D.Litt.; awards and commendations include: 13 R.I.B.A. awards 1975–96; 7 Financial Times Awards for Industrial Architecture 1977–97; 9 Structural Steel Design Awards 1969–95; 8 Civic Trust Awards 1978–96; 6 British Construction Industry Awards 1988–95; 3 Royal Fine Art Comm./Sunday Times Bldg. of the Year Award 1989–94; Constructa Preis for Industrial Architecture in Europe 1990; European Award for Steel Structures 1981; Quaternario Foundation Int. Awards for Innovative Tech. in Architecture; Gold Award 1993; Mies Van der Rohe Pavilion Award for European Architecture 1994; R.I.B.A. Bldg. of the Year Award 1994; Design Innovation Award 1996; British Council for Offices Award 1996; Int. Brunel Award 1996. *Publications:* articles for RSA Journal. *Leisure interests:* sailing, tennis. *Address:* 1 Conway Street, Fitzroy Square, London, W1P 6LR, England. *Telephone:* 0171-631 0869.

GRÍMSSON, Ólafur Ragnar, PH.D.; Icelandic politician; b. 14 May 1943, Isafjördur; s. of Grimur Kristgeirsson and Svanhildur Ólafsdóttir; m. Guðrún Katrín Þorbergsdóttir 1974; two d. (twins); ed. Reykjavík Higher Secondary Grammar School, Univ. of Manchester; fmr. lecturer in political science Univ. of Iceland, Prof. 1973; involved in production of political TV and radio programmes 1966–70; mem. Bd. Progressive Party Youth Fed. 1966–73, Exec. Bd. Progressive Party 1971-73, alt. mem. Althing representing East Iceland (Liberal and Left Alliance) 1974–75; Chair. Exec. Bd. Liberal and Left Alliance 1974–75; mem. Althing for Reykjavík 1978–83, for Reykjanes 1991– (People's Alliance); Leader People's Alliance 1987–95; Minister of Finance 1988–91; Pres. of Iceland 1996–; Chair. cttee on relocation of public insts. 1972–75, Icelandic Social Sciences Asscn. 1975, Organising Cttee. Parl. Conf. of Council of Europe: 'North-South: Europe's Role' 1982-84, Parliamentarians for Global Action 1984–90 (also fmr. Pres., mem. Bd. 1990–); Vice-Chair. Icelandic Security Comm. 1979–90; mem. Bd. Icelandic Broadcasting Service 1971–75, Nat. Power Co. 1983–88; mem. Parl. Ass. Council of Europe 1980–84, 1995–; fmr. adviser to several Icelandic cos. *Address:* Office of the President, Reykjavík, Iceland.

GRIMWADE, Sir Andrew (Sheppard), Kt., C.B.E., M.A., F.A.I.M.; Australian industrialist; b. 26 Nov. 1930, Melbourne; s. of Frederick Grimwade and Gwendolen Grimwade; m. Barbara Gaerloch Kater 1959 (died 1990); one s.; ed. Melbourne Grammar School, Trinity Coll., Melbourne Univ., Oriel Coll. Oxford, England; Dir. Commonwealth Industrial Gases Ltd. 1960–90, Nat. Australia Bank Ltd 1965–85, IBM Australia 1975–82, Sony (Australia) 1975–82, Turoa Holdings Ltd. 1975–82; Chair. Australian Consolidated Industries Ltd. 1977–82; Vice-Chair. Nat. Mutual Life 1988– (Dir. 1970–); mem. Australian Govt. Remuneration Tribunal 1976–82; mem. First Australian Govt. Trade Mission to China 1973; Pres. Walter and Eliza Hall Inst. of Medical Research 1978– (Bd. mem. 1963–); Deputy Pres. Australiana Fund 1978–82; Trustee Nat. Gallery of Vic., Trustee Emer. 1990–, Pres. 1976–90, mem. Felton Bequests Cttee. 1973–; Trustee Victorian Arts Centre 1980–90; mem. Council for Order of Australia 1975–82. *Publication:* Involvement: The Portraits of Clifton Pugh and Mark Strizic 1969. *Leisure interests:* skiing, Santa Gertrudis cattle breeding, Australian art. *Address:* P.O. Box 134, East Melbourne, Victoria 3002, Australia. *Telephone:* (03) 822 5990.

GRINDENKO, Tatyana Tikhonovna; Russian violinist; b. 29 March 1946, Kharkov, Ukraine; m. 1st Gidon Kremer; m. 2nd Vladimir Martynov; ed. Moscow State Conservatory; Prize, World Int. Youth Competition in Bulgaria 1968, Wieniawski Competition in Poland 1972; repertoire includes baroque, avant-garde, jazz, rock, experimental music; co-f. (with A. Lyubimov) Moscow Acad. of Ancient Music. *Address:* Moscow State Philharmonia, Tverskaya str. 31, 103050 Moscow, Russia. *Telephone:* (095) 253 7425 (Home).

GRINDROD, Most Rev. John Basil Rowland, K.B.E., M.A.; Australian ecclesiastic; b. 14 Dec. 1919, Aughton; s. of Edward B. Grindrod and Dorothy G. (née Hunt) Grindrod; m. 1st Ailsa W. Newman 1949 (died 1981); two d.; m. 2nd Dell Judith Cornish 1983; ed. Repton School, Univ. of Oxford and Lincoln Theological Coll.; ordained priest, Manchester; Rector All Souls, Ancoats 1956–60; Archdeacon of Rockhampton, Queensland 1960–65; Vicar of Christ Church, S. Yarra, Melbourne 1965–66; Bishop of Riverina, N.S.W. 1966–71; Bishop of Rockhampton 1971–80; Archbishop of Brisbane 1980–89, Primate of Anglican Church of Australia 1982–89. *Address:* 14B Thomas Street, Murwillumbah, N.S.W. 2484, Australia. *Telephone:* (02) 6672 6640.

GRINEVSKY, Oleg Alekseyevich; Russian diplomatist (retd.); b. 3 June 1930, Moscow; m.; three c.; ed. Moscow Inst. of Int. Relations; diplomatic service 1957–; Sec., Counsellor, Deputy Head Dept. of Int. Orgs. 1957–74; participated negotiations on PTBT 1963, NPT 1968, SALT 1 and ABM Treaty 1972; Deputy Chief Dept. of Near East Countries 1974–79, Chief 1979–83; Special Envoy, Head of U.S.S.R. dels. to conf. for strengthening trust and security in Europe, Stockholm 1983–86, Vienna 1989–91; Russian Amb. to Sweden 1991–97; Dr. h.c. (Southampton Univ.). *Publications:* Före Poltava 1993, Töväder och kalt krig 1995; numerous articles on int. affairs and Russian history. *Address:* c/o Ministry of Foreign Affairs, Smolenskaya-Sennaya 32/34, Moscow, Russia.

GRININ, Vladimir Mikhailovich; Russian diplomatist; b. 15 Nov. 1947; m.; one d.; ed. Moscow State Inst. of Int. Relations, Diplomatic Acad., U.S.S.R. Ministry of Foreign Affairs; Russian Amb. to Austria 1996–. *Address:* Russian Embassy, Reisnerstrasse 45–47, 1030 Vienna, Austria. *Telephone:* (1) 713 1215; (1) 712 1229 (Office). *Fax:* (1) 712 3388 (Office).

GRINSTEAD, Sir Stanley (Gordon), Kt., F.C.A., C.B.I.M.; British business executive; b. 17 June 1924; s. of Ephraim Grinstead and Lucy Taylor; m. Joyce Preston 1955; two d.; ed. Strodes, Egham; served R.N. 1943–46; Franklin, Wild & Co. (chartered accountants) 1946–56; Hotel York Ltd. 1957; Grand Metropolitan Ltd. 1957–62; Union Properties (London) Ltd. 1958–66; Grand Metropolitan Ltd. 1964–87, Deputy Chair. and Group Man. Dir. 1980–82, Group Chief Exec. 1982–86, Chair. 1982–87; Dir. Reed Int. PLC 1981–90, Chair. 1988–89; Chair. and Dir. Harmony Leisure Group 1989–92. *Leisure interest:* gardening.

GRINSTEIN, Gerald, LL.B.; American business executive; b. 1932; m.; ed. Yale and Harvard Univs.; Counsel to merchant marine and transport subcttees., Chief Counsel, U.S. Senate Commerce Cttee. 1958–67; Admin. Asst. to U.S. Senator Warren Magnuson 1967–69; partner, Preston, Thorgrimson, Ellis & Holman 1969–73; Chair. Bd. Western Air Lines Inc. L.A. 1983–84, Pres. and C.O.O. 1984–85, C.E.O. 1985–86, Chair. and C.E.O. 1986–87; Vice-Chair. Burlington Northern Inc. Fort Worth 1987–88, Pres., C.E.O. 1989–90, Chair. 1990–96, C.E.O. 1990–95; Pres., C.E.O. Burlington Northern R.R. Co. 1989–90, Chair. 1990–96, C.E.O. 1990–95; Chair. Delta Airlines Inc. 1997–; mem. Bd. Dirs. Burlington Northern Inc., Seattle First Nat. Bank, Browning Ferris Industries Inc., Sundstrand Corpn. *Address:* 1000 2nd Avenue, Suite 3700, Seattle, WA 98104, U.S.A.

GRISEZ, Germain, M.A., PH.L., PH.D.; American professor of Christian ethics; b. 30 Sept. 1929, University Heights, Ohio; m. Jeannette Selby 1951; four c.; ed. John Carroll Univ., Univ. Heights, Ohio, Dominican Coll. of St. Thomas Aquinas, River Forest, Ill. and Univ. of Chicago; Asst. Prof. to Prof. Georgetown Univ. Washington, D.C. 1957–72; part-time Lecturer in Medieval Philosophy, Univ. of Va., Charlottesville 1961–62; Special Asst. to Cardinal O'Boyle, Archbishop of Washington 1968–69; consultant (part-time) Archdiocese of Washington 1969–72; Prof. of Philosophy, Campion Coll. Univ. of Regina, Canada 1972–79; Most Rev. Harry J. Flynn Prof. of Christian Ethics, Mount Saint Mary's Coll. Emmitsburg, Md. 1979–; mem. Catholic Theol. Soc. of America, American Catholic Philosophical Assen., Fellowship of Catholic Scholars; Pro ecclesia et pontifice medal 1972; Cardinal Wright Award for service to the Church 1983 and other awards. *Publications:* The Way of the Lord Jesus, Vol. I, Christian Moral Principles (with others) 1983, Vol. II, Living a Christian Life (with others) 1993, Vol. III, Difficult Moral Questions (with others) 1997, Nuclear Deterrence, Morality and Realism (with J. Finnis and Joseph M. Boyle) 1987, Beyond the New Morality: The Responsibilities of Freedom (with R. Shaw) 3rd edn. 1988; numerous articles in learned journals. *Address:* Mount Saint Mary's College, Emmitsburg, MD 21727-7799, U.S.A. *Telephone:* 301-447-5771. *Fax:* (301) 447-5755.

GRISHAM, John; American author and lawyer; b. 8 Feb. 1955, Jonesboro, Ark.; m. Renée Grisham; one s. one d.; ed. law school; ran one-man criminal defence practice in Southhaven, Miss. 1981–90. *Publications:* The Pelican Brief, A Time to Kill, Stand in Line at a Super Crown, The Firm, The Client, The Chamber, The Rainmaker, The Runaway Jury, The Partner, The Street Lawyer, The Testament 1999. *Address:* Doubleday & Co. Inc., 1540 Broadway # Bdd, New York, NY 10036, U.S.A.

GRITSAI, Alexei Michailovich; Russian painter; b. 7 March 1914, Leningrad; s. of Michail A. Gritsai and Nadezhda A. Gritsai; m. Valentina S. Gritsai 1940; one s.; ed. All-Russian Acad. of Arts (now I. E. Repin Art Inst. Leningrad) 1932–39; teacher at Moscow Surikov Inst. of Art 1948–, Prof. 1966–; corresp. mem. U.S.S.R. (now Russian) Acad. of Arts 1954, mem. 1964; People's Artist of U.S.S.R. 1974; awarded U.S.S.R. and R.S.F.S.R. State Prizes 1951, 1952, 1978; Bronze Medal of Int. Exhbn. Brussels 1958. *Leisure interest:* music. *Address:* Verkhnaya Maslovka Str. 3, Apt. 11, 125083 Moscow, Russia. *Telephone:* 212-63-67.

GROENING, Matthew, B.A.; American writer and cartoonist; b. 15 Feb. 1954, Portland, Ore.; s. of Homer Philip Groening and Margaret Ruth Wiggum; m. Deborah Lee Caplan; two c.; ed. Evergreen State Coll.; cartoonist Life in Hell syndicated weekly comic strip, Sheridan, Ore. 1980–; Pres. Matt Groening Productions, Inc., L.A. 1988–, Bongo Entertainment, Inc., L.A. 1993–; creator The Simpsons interludes The Tracey Ullman Show 1987–89; creator and Exec. Producer The Simpsons TV show 1989–; founder and publr. Bongo Comics Group; founder and publr. Zongo Comics (including Jimbo 1995, Fleener 1996). *Publications:* Love Is Hell 1985, Work Is Hell 1986, School Is Hell 1987, Childhood Is Hell 1988, Akbar and Jeff's Guide to Life 1989, Greetings from Hell 1989, The Postcards That Ate My Brain 1990, The Big Book of Hell 1990, The Simpsons Xmas Book 1990, Greetings from The Simpsons 1990, With Love from Hell 1991, The Simpsons Rainy Day Fun Book 1991, The Simpsons Uncensored Family Album 1991, The Simpsons Student Diary 1991, How to Go to Hell 1991, Maggie Simpson's Alphabet Book 1991, Maggie Simpson's Counting Book 1991, Maggie Simpson's Book of Colors and Shapes 1991, Maggie Simpson's Book of Animals 1991, The Road to Hell 1992, The Simpsons Fun in the Sun Book 1992, Making Faces with the Simpsons 1992, Bart Simpson's Guide to Life 1993, The Simpsons Ultra-Jumbo Rain-Or-Shine Fun Book 1993, Cartooning with the Simpsons 1993, Bongo Comics Group Spectacular 1993, Binky's Guide to Love 1994, Love Is Hell 10th Anniversary Edition 1994, Simpsons Comics Extravaganza 1994, Simpsons Comics Spectacular 1994, Bartman: The Best of the Best 1994, Simpsons Comics Simps-O-Rama 1995, Simpsons Comics Strike Back 1995, Simpsons Comics Wing Ding 1997, The Huge Book of Hell 1997; Bongo Comics.

GRÖER, H.E. Cardinal Hans Hermann, O.S.B.; Austrian ecclesiastic (retd.); b. 13 Oct. 1919, Vienna; ordained 1942, elected bishop of Vienna 1986, consecrated 1986; Archbishop of Vienna 1987–95; cr. Cardinal 1988; fmr. Pres. Bishop's Conf. (Austria); Ordinand for the faithful in the Byzantine Rite resident in Austria; mem. Congregation for Catholic Educ., Congregation for Divine Worship and the Discipline of the Sacraments, Insts. of Consecrated Life and for Socs. of Apostolic Life; sent into monastic seclusion abroad 1998.

GROMOV, Aleksey Alekseyevich; Russian politician; b. 1960; m.; two c.; ed. Moscow State Univ.; on staff U.S.S.R. Ministry of Foreign Affairs 1985; fmr. Counsellor Gen. Consulate in Karlovy Vary, U.S.S.R. Embassy in Czechoslovakia; Counsellor Russian Embassy to Slovakia 1992–96; Head Press Service of Russian President 1996–. *Address:* The Kremlin, korp. 14a, Moscow, Russia (Office). *Telephone:* (095) 910 0738 (Office).

GROMOV, Col.-Gen. Boris Vsevolodovich; Russian army officer; b. 7 Nov. 1943, Saratov; m. 2nd Faina Gromov; two s. two adopted d.; ed. Leningrad Gen. Troops School, Frunze Mil. Acad., Gen. Staff Acad.; mem. CPSU 1966–91; commdr. of platoon, co., bn., regt., div. 1965–87, Commdr. 40 Army in Afghanistan 1987–89, Commdr. of troops Kiev Command 1989–90, First Deputy Minister of Internal Affairs of U.S.S.R. 1990–91, First Deputy Commdr. of Armed Forces of C.I.S. 1991–92, First Deputy Minister of Defence of Russia 1992–95; Chief Mil. Expert and Deputy Minister of Foreign Affairs 1995–; mem. State Duma 1996–, Chair. Sub-Cttee. on Arms Control and Int. Security; f. war veterans' movt., Fighting Fraternity 1997–; Hero of Soviet Union and other decorations. *Publication:* Memoirs of the Afghan War 1994. *Leisure interests:* tennis, bicycling. *Address:* Ministry of Foreign Affairs, Smolenskaya-Sennaya 32/34, 121200 Moscow, Russia. *Telephone:* (095) 2900703.

GROMOV, Adm. Felix Nikolaevich; Russian naval officer (retd); b. 29 Aug. 1937, Vladivostok; m.; two c.; ed. Pacific Higher Mil. Navigation School, Mil. Navigation Acad.; commdr. of battery, sr. asst.-commdr.; commdr. of torpedo boat destroyer, cruiser, Head of Staff, Head of Formation in the Pacific Ocean –1976, First Deputy Commdr. of North Navy 1984–88, Commdr. 1988–92; First Deputy C.-in-C. of C.I.S. Mil. Navy, C.-in-C. of Russian Navy 1992–97. *Address:* c/o Ministry of Defence, Novy Arbat 4, K-160 Moscow, Russia. *Telephone:* 204 22 77 (Office).

GROMOV, Mikhael, PH.D.; Soviet-born (now stateless) mathematician; b. 23 Dec. 1943, Boksitogorsk, U.S.S.R.; s. of Lea Rabinovitz and Leonid Gromov; m. Margarita Gromov 1967; ed. Univ. of Leningrad; Asst. Prof., Univ. of Leningrad 1967–74; Prof., Univ. of New York, Stony Brook, U.S.A. 1974–81; Prof., Univ. of Paris VI, France 1981–82; Perm. Fellow, Dept. of Math., Institut des Hautes Etudes Scientifiques 1982–; Foreign Assoc. mem. N.A.S. (U.S.A.); Foreign mem. American Acad. of Art and Science; Foreign Assoc., Académie des Sciences, Institut de France, mem. 1997–; Moscow Math. Soc. Prize 1971, Oswald Veblen Prize for Geometry, American Math. Soc. 1981, Prix Elie Cartan, Académie des Sciences, Paris 1984, Prix Union des Assurances de Paris 1989. *Publications:* Structures métriques pour les variétés riemanniennes 1981, Partial Differential Equations 1986. *Address:* Institut des Hautes Etudes Scientifiques, 35 route de Chartres, 91440 Bures-sur-Yvette (Office); 91 rue de la Santé, 75013 Paris, France (Home). *Telephone:* (33 1) 69.07.48.53 (Office); (33 1) 45.88.14.42 (Home).

GROMOV, Vassily Petrovich; Russian diplomatist; b. 1 Oct. 1936, Navesnoye, Orlov Region; m.; two d.; ed. Timiryazev Acad. of Agric., All-Union Acad. of External Trade; economist on Cuba 1961–68; on staff U.S.S.R. Embassies in Chile, Mexico, Ecuador, Nicaragua; Div. of Latin America U.S.S.R. Ministry of Foreign Affairs 1971–92; Russian Amb. to Chile 1992–96; Dir. Latin American Dept. Ministry of Foreign Affairs 1996–. *Address:* Ministry of Foreign Affairs, Smolenskaya-Sennaya 32/34, 121200 Moscow, Russia (Office). *Telephone:* (095) 244 3295 (Office).

GROMYKO, Anatoly Andreyevich, DR.HIST.SC.; Russian political scientist; b. 15 April 1932, Borisov; s. of Andrey Gromyko and Lidia Dmitrievna Gromyko; m.; two s. one d.; ed. Moscow Inst. of Int. Rels.; mem. CPSU 1956–91; First Sec., U.S.S.R. Embassy in London 1961–65; Head of Int. Rels. section, Africa Inst. of U.S.S.R. Acad. of Sciences 1966–68; Head of Section for U.S. Foreign Policy, Inst. of the United States and Canada (U.S.S.R. Acad. of Sciences) 1968–73; Minister Plenipotentiary Wash. Embassy 1973–74, Berlin 1974–76; Dir. Africa Inst. (U.S.S.R., now Russian, Acad. of Sciences) 1976–92; Pres. of Centre for Global and Strategic Studies (RAS), Africa Inst. 1992–94; living in Cyprus 1994–; Corresp. mem. of Acad. of Sciences 1981–; U.S.S.R. State Prize 1980. *Publications:* U.S. Congress: Elections, Organization, Powers 1957, The 1,036 Days of President Kennedy 1968, The Foreign Policy of the U.S.A.: Lessons and Reality the 60's and 70's 1978, The Conflict in the South of Africa: international aspects 1979, Africa: Progress, Problems, Prospects 1981, Masks and Sculpture of Sub-Saharan Africa 1984, New Thinking in the Nuclear Age 1984, Kennedy Brothers 1985, Breakthrough (Ed.) 1986, Will We Survive? (with others) 1989. *Leisure interest:* lawn tennis. *Address:* c/o Africa Institute, Russian Academy of Sciences, 30/1 Alexey Tolstoy Str., Moscow 103001, Russia. *Telephone:* 290-63-85 (Office); (2) 4588814 (Cyprus).

GRONCHI, Divo, PH.D.; Italian banker; b. 21 Jan. 1939, Pisa; m. Anna Maria Alocchi; two c.; ed. Univ. of Florence; employed at Banca Toscana 1958; joined Monte dei Paschi di Siena as Deputy Cen. Man. (Balance Sheets and Planning) 1988, Deputy Man. Dir. 1993–96, Man. Dir. and C.E.O. 1996–; Chair. Credito Commerziale S.p.A. 1990–91; mem. Bd. Dirs. and C.E.O. Monte Paschi Finanza Sim S.p.A. 1988–95, Monte Paschi Mercato Sim S.p.A. 1989–93, Mediocredito Toscano S.p.A. 1992–93; Chair. Monte Paschi Vita S.p.A., Ticino Assicurazioni S.p.A., Ticino Vita S.p.A. 1993; mem. Bd. Dirs. and Exec. Cttee. A.B.I. (Italian Banking Assen.) 1995–, Istituto Bancario S. Paolo di Torino–IMI S.p.A. (following merger with Istituto Mobiliare Italiano) 1998–; mem. Bd. Cassa di Risparmio di Trento e Rovereto S.p.A. 1995–96; Grand Officer, Order of Merit of Italian Repub. *Leisure interest:*

reading. *Address:* Banca Monte dei Paschi di Siena S.p.A., Piazza Salimbeni 3, 53100 Siena, Italy. *Telephone:* (39) 577 294111.

GRØNDAHL, Kirsti Kolle; Norwegian politician. b. 1 Sept. 1943, Røyken; m. Svein Erik Groendahl 1967; two c.; mem. Røyken Municipal Council and Municipal Exec. Bd. 1972–77, Chair. Røyken Labour Party 1980–82, Spikkestad Labour Party 1990–, mem. Labour Party's Cttee. for Environment 1983–; mem Storting 1977–; mem. Standing Cttee. on Church and Educ. 1977–85, on Foreign and Constitutional Affairs 1989–, Minister of Church and Educ. 1986–88, of Devt. Co-operation 1988–89, Vice-Pres. Storting 1990–93, Pres. 1993–; mem. Norwegian del. to Parl. Ass. of Council of Europe 1989–90; Leader del. to CSCE Parl. Ass. 1991–; mem. Nordic Council and of Council's Presidium 1990–93, Leader Norwegian del. to Nordic Council 1992–93. *Address:* Stortinget, Karl Johansgt. 22, 0026 Oslo, Norway.

GRONKIEWICZ-WALTZ, Hanna, LL.D.; Polish banker and lawyer; b. 4 Nov. 1952, Warsaw; m.; one d.; ed. Warsaw Univ.; academic researcher Div. of Admin. Comparative Law and State Econ. Man. Inst. of Legal Admin. Sciences 1975–; expert on public and econ. law. Polish Parl. 1989; mem. of academic staff, Acad. of Catholic Theology 1990–92; Pres. Nat. Bank of Poland 1992–; charter mem. Solidarity 1980; Chair. faculty Solidarity branch 1989–92; ind. cand. in presidential election 1995; Global Finance magazine award for Best Chair. of a Cen. Bank 1994, 1997, The Central European Award 1995, Życie Gospodarne Award 1995, The Warsaw Voice Award 1995. *Publications:* Central Bank from Centrally Controlled Economy to Market Oriented Economy: Legal Aspects 1993, Economic Law (co-author) 1996; over 40 works and articles in econ. and financial journals. *Address:* National Bank of Poland, ul. Świętokrzyska 21, 00 919 Warsaw, Poland. *Telephone:* 653 10 00.

GROOT, Per Søltoft, D.IUR.; Danish diplomatist; b. 21 Nov. 1924, Copenhagen; s. of Henrik and Caroline Groot; m. Inger Sorensen 1974; one s. one d.; ed. Univ. of Copenhagen; entered Danish Foreign Service 1949, seconded to NATO Int. Staff, Paris 1954–57, Prin. in Foreign Ministry 1957–61; Deputy Perm. Rep., Danish NATO Del., Paris 1962–64; Head of Dept., Political Affairs, Foreign Ministry 1964–67; Deputy Under-Sec. of State, Econ. Affairs, Foreign Ministry 1967–73; Amb. to German Democratic Repub. 1973–76, to Japan 1976–84; Govt. Adviser on Arms Control and Disarmament 1984–86; Amb. to Netherlands 1986–92; Del. to UN Gen. Ass. 1966, 1974, 1975, 1980, 1984, 1985; Chair. OECD Drafting Group (New Treaty) 1960; Head of Del. to UN Habitat Conf., Vancouver 1976, Non-Proliferation Treaty Review Conf., Geneva 1985; Pres. Danish Lawyers and Economists Asscn. 1970–73; Commdr. (First Class) Order of Dannebrog, Commdr. Italian Order of Merit, First Class Order of Rising Sun (Japan), Netherlands Order of Orange-Nassau (First Class). *Leisure interests:* golf, international security studies. *Address:* Bakkedraget 76, 3480 Fredensborg, Denmark. *Telephone:* 48.48.43.77.

GROOTHAERT, Jacques, M.A.; Belgian fmr. diplomatist; b. 25 Nov. 1922, Heist; m. Madeleine Williot 1945; two s.; ed. Univs. of Brussels and Ghent; served in Prague, Moscow, Paris and San Francisco (Consul-Gen.) 1961–64; Minister, London 1964–67, Amb. to Mexico 1967–72, to People's Repub. of China 1972–76; Dir.-Gen. Foreign Econ. Relations, Ministry of Foreign Affairs 1976–80; Chair. Bd. of Dirs. Générale Bank, Brussels 1980–91, S.A.B.C.A. 1980–; Chair. European Bd. America-European Community Asscn.; Hon. Chair. Générale de Banque 1992–; mem. Trilateral Commission, and many other public appts.; Grand Officier de l'Ordre de Léopold II; Commdr. Ordre de la Couronne; decorations from Mexico, Spain, Denmark, Iceland and France. *Publications:* Le Passage du Témoin, L'Europe aux miroirs 1996, and several other publs. and articles. *Address:* c/o Generale Bank, Warandeberg, 1000 Brussels, Belgium.

GROS, André; French judge; b. 19 May 1908, Douai; s. of Maurice Gros and Adèle Berr; m. Dulce Simões-Corrêa 1940; two s.; ed. Univs. of Lyon and Paris; Asst., Law Faculty Paris 1931, Asst. Prof. Univ. Nancy 1935, Toulouse 1937, Univ. Prof. Public Law 1938–63; seconded to Ministry of Foreign Affairs 1939; Prof. Political Science Rio de Janeiro Univ. 1939, 1941–42; served France 1940; legal Counsellor to French Embassy in London; French Rep. on War Crimes Comm., London 1943; legal adviser to French Del. Council of Foreign Ministers and Peace Conf. Paris 1946; Legal Adviser Ministry of Foreign Affairs 1947; mem. Perm. Court of Arbitration, The Hague 1950; del. to Comm. for the Rhine 1950; Agent to Int. Court of Justice 1950–60; Conseiller d'Etat 1954; Judge, Int. Court of Justice, The Hague 1964; mem. Chamber of Court for delimitation maritime boundary Canada–U.S.A. 1982; mem. Inst. of Int. Law 1959, Vice-Pres. 1977–79; mem. UN Int. Law Comm. 1961; mem. Court of Arbitration in Beagle Channel case between Argentina and Chile 1977; mem. Court of Arbitration between France and U.K. (continental shelf delimitation) 1977; mem. Court of Arbitration between Senegal and Guinea-Bissau (delimitation of maritime boundary) 1986. Hon. Master of the Bench (Inner Temple) 1972; Commdr., Légion d'honneur, Croix de guerre (1939–45). *Publications:* Survivance de la raison d'état 1932, Problèmes politiques de l'Europe 1942–44 (Spanish trans. 1943), La Convention de Genève sur les pêcheries 1959, Traités et documents diplomatiques (with Paul Reuter) 1960, La protection diplomatique (in Encyclopédie française) 1964. *Leisure interests:* reading, golf. *Address:* Hôtel Beau-Rivage, Lausanne, 6 Ouchy, CH-1000, Switzerland (Home).

GROS, Francisco Roberto André, B.A.; Brazilian banker and economist and banker; b. 21 April 1942, Rio de Janeiro; s. of André Paul Adolphe Gros (q.v.) and Dulce Simões Corrêa Gros; m. 1st Sandra Mattmann 1968; m. 2nd Isabel Teixeira Mendes; two s. one d.; ed. Woodrow Wilson School of Public and Int. Affairs, Princeton Univ., U.S.A.; Founding mem. Brazilian Securities and Exchange Comm. 1977–81; Exec. Dir. in charge of investment banking activities, Unibanco—Banco de Investimento do Brasil 1981–85; Exec. Dir. Nat. Devt. Bank (BNDES) 1985–87; Pres. Cen. Bank of Brazil Feb.–May 1987, 1991–92; Pres. and C.E.O. Aracruz S.A. (eucalyptus pulp exporter) 1987–89; Founding Partner and C.E.O. BFC Banco S.A., Rio de Janeiro 1989–91, 1993; Man. Dir. Morgan, Stanley and Co., New York 1994–; several Brazilian decorations; Officier Légion d'honneur. *Leisure interests:* travel, tennis, fishing. *Address:* 238 East 62nd Street, New York, NY 10021, U.S.A. *Telephone:* (212) 688-1311.

GROS, François; French biochemist; b. 24 April 1925, Paris; s. of Alexandre Gros and Yvonne Haguenauer; m. 1st Françoise Chasseigne (divorced 1963); m. 2nd Danièle Charpentier 1964; three s.; ed. Lycée Pasteur, Neuilly, Univs. of Toulouse and Paris, Rockefeller Inst., Univ. of Illinois, U.S.A.; joined C.N.R.S. 1947, Researcher, Lab. Prof. J. Monod 1955, Head of Research 1959–62, Scientific Dir. 1962–; Head of Dept. Inst. de Biologie Physico-chimique 1963–69; Prof., Faculté des Sciences de Paris 1968, Inst. Pasteur 1972, Collège de France (Chair in Cellular Biochemistry) 1973–; Dir. Inst. Pasteur 1976–81, Dir. of Biochemistry Unit 1981; Adviser to Prime Minister 1981–85; mem. EC's CODEST 1984–90; Pres. Asscn. Franco-Israélienne pour la recherche scientifique et tech. 1983, Scientific Council of Asscn. Française de lutte contre la myopathie 1987–; Scientific Council of Nat. Agency for Research into AIDS 1989–; Chief Ed. Bulletin de la Société de chimie biologique 1964; Perm. Sec. Science Acad. (France) 1991–; mem. Nat. Consultative Cttee. on the Ethics of Life and Health Sciences 1990–94; mem. EU Ass. on Science and Tech. 1994–97; mem. Institut Français, Acad. des Sciences, N.A.S., Acad. of Athens, Indian Nat. Acad. Sciences 1990; Assoc. mem. Acad. Royale de Belgique; Dr. h.c. (Weizmann Inst., Israel); Gold Medal, Pontifical Acad. of Sciences 1964, Fondation Lacassagne Prize 1968, Charles Léopold Mayer Prize, Acad. des Sciences 1969, Alexander von Humboldt Prize 1990; Officier Légion d'honneur; Commdr. ordre nat. du Mérite; several foreign decorations. *Publications:* Initiation à la Biochimie (with others); Sciences de la Vie et Société (with others) 1979, Les Secrets du Gène 1986, La civilisation du gène 1989, L'Ingénierie du vivant 1990, Regard sur la biologie contemporaine 1992. *Leisure interests:* music, drawing. *Address:* 102 rue de la Tour, 75116 Paris, France. *Telephone:* 45.04.80.63.

GROSS, Johannes; German journalist and author; b. 6 May 1932, Neunkhausen; s. of Albert and Martha Gross; m. Elisabeth Gotthardt 1961; one d.; ed. Univs. of Marburg and Bonn; Bonn corresp. Deutsche Zeitung 1959, Political Ed. 1961; Head, Political Dept. Deutschlandfunk, Cologne 1962; Dir. of Programmes and Dep. Dir.-Gen. Deutsche Welle 1968; Ed. Capital 1974; Editorial Dir. Capital and Impulse 1980; Dir. Gruner und Jahr AG & Co. 1983–94; Commentator and host of political talk-show, Second German Nat. Television (ZDF); Columnist, Frankfurter Allgemeine Zeitung. *Publications:* Lauter Nachworte 1965, Absagen an die Zukunft, Festschrift für Ludwig Erhard (ed. and co-author) 1972, Unsere letzten Jahre 1980, Notizbuch 1985, Phoenix in Asche 1989, Das neue Notizbuch 1990, Über die Deutschen 1992, Für- und Gegenwitz 1993, Begründung der Berliner Republik 1995, Tacheles gesprochen 1996. *Address:* 70 Eupener Strasse, 50933 Cologne, Germany. *Telephone:* 0221-4908216. *Fax:* 0221-4908106.

GROSS, John Jacob, M.A.; British author, editor and publisher; b. 12 March 1935, London; s. of late Abraham and Muriel Gross; m. Miriam May 1965 (divorced 1988); one s. one d.; ed. City of London School, Wadham Coll., Oxford; Ed. with Victor Gollancz Ltd. 1956–58; lecturer, Queen Mary Coll., Univ. of London 1959–62, Hon. Fellow 1988; Fellow of King's Coll., Cambridge 1962–65; Asst. Ed. Encounter 1963–65; Literary Ed. New Statesman 1972–73; Ed. Times Literary Supplement 1974–81; Literary Ed. Spectator 1983; journalist, New York Times 1983–88; theatre critic Sunday Telegraph 1989–; Dir. Times Newspapers Holdings Ltd. (fmrly. Times Newspapers Ltd.) 1982; editorial consultant The Weidenfeld Publishing Group 1982; a Trustee Nat. Portrait Gallery 1977–84; Fellow Queen Mary Coll. 1987; Duff Cooper Memorial Prize 1969. *Publications:* The Rise and Fall of the Man of Letters 1969, James Joyce 1971, Shylock; Ed. The Oxford Book of Aphorisms 1983, The Oxford Book of Essays 1991, The Modern Movement 1992, The Oxford Book of Comic Verse (ed.) 1994, The New Oxford Book of English Prose (ed.) 1998. *Address:* 74 Princess Court, Queensway, London, W2 4RE, England.

GROSS, Ludwik, M.D.; American research professor of medicine; b. 11 Sept. 1904, Cracow, Poland; s. of Dr. Adolf and Augusta Gross; m. Dorothy L. Nelson 1943; one d.; ed. Jagellon Univ., Cracow; Intern and Resident St. Lazar Hosp., Cracow 1929–32; clinical training, Salpêtrière Hosp., Univ. de Paris à la Sorbonne 1932–39; cancer research, Pasteur Inst., Paris 1932–39, Christ Hosp., Cincinnati, Ohio, U.S.A. 1941–43; Capt. to Major, Medical Corps, U.S. Army 1943–46; Chief, Cancer Research Unit, Veterans Admin. Hosp., New York 1946–; Consultant, Sloan-Kettering Inst. 1953–56, Assoc. Scientist 1957–60; Research Prof., Mount Sinai School of Medicine, City Univ. of New York 1971–73, Emer. 1973–; Dir. American Asscn. for Cancer Research 1973–76; Distinguished Physician of the Veterans Administration 1977–82; mem. N.A.S., American Medical Asscn., American Soc. of Haematology and other socs.; F.A.C.P., New York Acad. of Sciences, A.A.A.S., Int. Soc. of Haematology; Diplomate, American Bd. of Internal Medicine; Hon. D.Sc. (Mt. Sinai School of Medicine) 1983; awards include Prix Chevillon, Acad. Médecine, Paris 1937, R. R. de Villiers Int. Award for Leukaemia Research 1953, Walker Prize, Royal Coll. Surgeons, England 1962, Pasteur Silver Medal, Pasteur Inst., Paris 1962, L. W. James Award, James Ewing Soc., New York 1962, WHO UN Prize 1962, Bertner Foundation Award, Univ. of Texas 1963, Albert Einstein Centennial Medal, Philadelphia 1965, Albion O. Bernstein M.D. Award, N.Y. State Med. Soc. 1971, Special Virus Cancer Program Award, Nat. Cancer Inst. 1972, William S. Middleton Award, Veterans Admin. 1974, Albert Lasker Basic Medical Research Award, New York 1974; Award for Cancer Immunology, Cancer Research Inst., New York 1975, Prin. Paul Ehrlich-Ludwig Darmstaedter Prize, Frankfurt 1978, Prix Griffuel (Paris) 1978, Katherine Berken Judd Award, Memorial Sloan-Kettering Cancer Center, New York 1985, Alfred Jurzykowski Foundation Award, New York 1985; Légion d'honneur. *Publications:* Oncogenic Viruses 1961, 1970, 1983 and over 200 papers on experimental cancer and leukaemia. *Leisure interests:* music, piano. *Address:* Veterans Administration Medical Center, 130 West Kingsbridge Road, Bronx, NY 10468, U.S.A. *Telephone:* (718) 579-1601. *Fax:* (718) 562-9120.

GROSS, Nahum David; Israeli journalist; b. 22 May 1923, London, England; s. of Rabbi Samuel Gross and Millie Gross; m. Ruth Korner 1957; three s. one d.; ed. Central Foundation Boys' School, London, Queen Mary Coll., London Univ., London School of Econs.; emigrated to Israel 1949; joined editorial staff Jerusalem Post 1950; served with Israeli Defence Forces 1951–53; various editorial posts, Jerusalem Post 1953– (author Caleb's Column –1989), Ed.-in-Chief 1990–92. *Leisure interests:* gardening, resting, classical music. *Address:* 24 Beit Zeit, 90815 Judean Hills, Israel. *Telephone:* (02) 346034.

GROSSART, Sir Angus McFarlane McLeod, Kt., C.B.E., M.A., LL.B., F.R.S.E.; British merchant banker and company director; b. 6 April 1937; s. of William John White Grossart and Mary Hay Gardiner; m. Gay Thomson 1978; one d.; ed. Glasgow Acad. and Gasgow Univ.; mem. Faculty of Advocates 1963; practised at Scottish Bar 1963–69; Man. Dir. Noble Grossart Ltd. Merchant Bankers, Edin. 1969–, Chair. 1990–; Chair. Scottish Investment Trust PLC 1975–; Dir. of numerous cos. including Royal Bank of Scotland PLC 1982– (Vice-Chair. 1996–), Edin. Fund Mans. PLC 1991– (Chair. 1983–91, Deputy Chair. 1991–), Mirror Group PLC 1998–; Chair. Bd. of Trustees Nat. Galleries of Scotland 1988–97; Vice-Pres. Scottish Opera 1986–93; Dir. Edin. Int. Film Festival 1994–96; mem. Scottish Industrial Devt. Advisory Bd.; Hon. LL.D. (Glasgow) 1985, Hon. D.L. (Edin.) 1996, Hon. D.B.A. (Strathclyde) 1998; Livingstone Captain of Industry Award 1990, Lord Provost of Glasgow Award for public service 1994. *Leisure interests:* golf (captained Scottish Youth int. team 1956 and 1957), the applied and decorative arts, Scottish castle restoration. *Address:* 48 Queen Street, Edin., EH2 3NR, Scotland. *Telephone:* (0131) 226 7011.

GROSSER, Alfred, D. ÈS L.; French professor, author and journalist; b. 1 Feb. 1925, Frankfurt; s. of the late Paul Grosser and Lily (née Rosenthal) Grosser; m. Anne-Marie Jourcin 1959; four s.; ed. Univs. of Aix en Provence and Paris; Asst. Dir. UNESCO Office in Germany 1950–51; Asst. Prof. Univ. of Paris 1951–55; lecturer, later Prof. Inst. d'études politiques 1954, Prof. Emer. 1992; Dir. Studies and Research, Fondation nat. des Sciences politiques 1956–92; with Ecole des hautes études commerciales 1961–66, 1986–88, with Ecole Polytechnique 1974–95; Political Columnist La Croix 1955–65, 1984–, Le Monde 1965–94, Ouest-France 1973–, L'Expansion 1979–89; Pres. Centre d'information et de recherche sur l'Allemagne contemporaine 1982–, Eurocréation 1986–92 (Hon. Pres. 1992–); Dir. L'Express 1998–; Peace Prize, Union of German Publrs. 1975; Commdr. Légion d'honneur. *Publications:* L'Allemagne de l'Occident 1953, La Démocratie de Bonn 1958, Hitler, la presse et la naissance d'une dictature 1959, La Quatrième Republique et sa politique extérieure 1961, La Politique extérieure de la Ve Republique 1965, Au nom de quoi? Fondements d'une morale politique 1969, L'Allemagne de notre temps 1970, L'Explication politique 1972, Les Occidentaux: Les pays d'Europe et les Etats Unis depuis la guerre 1978, Le Sel de la Terre. Pour l'engagement moral 1981, Affaires extérieures: La politique de la France 1944–84, 1984 (updated 1989), L'Allemagne en Occident 1985, Mit Deutschen streiten 1987, Vernunft und Gewalt. Die französische Revolution und das deutsche Grundgesetz heute 1989, Le crime et la mémoire 1989 (revised 1991), Mein Deutschland 1993, Allemagne (jtly.) 1994, Was ich denke 1995, Les Identités difficiles 1996, Une Vie de français (memoirs) 1997, Deutschland in Europe 1998. *Leisure interest:* music. *Address:* 8 rue Dupleix, 75015 Paris, France (Home). *Telephone:* 43 06 41 82 (Home).

GROTENFELT, Georg Erik Jan; Finnish architect; b. 7 June 1951, Helsinki; s. of Nils Grotenfelt and Antonia Marsman; m. Hannele Grönlund 1992; one d.; ed. Helsinki Polytechnic Univ.; Sr. tutor and lecturer, Dept. of Architecture, Helsinki Polytechnic 1984–96, Helsinki Univ. of Art and Design 1990–95; guest ed.-in-chief, Arkkitehti (architectural journal); projects include wooden saunas, leisure bldgs. and family homes. *Leisure interests:* nature, film, photography, tennis, books. *Address:* Huvilakatu 4, 00150 Helsinki (Office); Kapteeninkatu 20D, 00140 Helsinki, Finland (Home). *Telephone:* 625034 (Office); 625184 (Home).

GROTTANELLI DE' SANTI, Giovanni, LL.D.; Italian lawyer; b. 1928, Livorno; m. Felicity Bennett 1962; three c.; ed. Ginnasio Liceo E.S. Piccolomini, Siena, Univ. of Siena, Yale Law School and Coll. of Europe, Bruges; admitted to bar 1952; Univ. Asst. 1955; law clerk, Constitutional Court, Rome 1956–62; Asst. in Constitutional Law, Univ. of Rome 1956–62; libero docente (constitutional law), Univ. of Siena 1962; also taught at Univ. of Florence; Visiting Fellow, Wolfson Coll. Cambridge 1981–82; Visiting Fellow Commoner, Trinity Coll. Cambridge 1985; Visiting lecturer, Tulane Law School, Univ. of Ga. Law School, Dean Rusk Center of Int. and Comparative Law, Athens, Ga. 1991; Chair. Monte dei Paschi di Siena 1992–98, Italian Int. Bank 1993–, Accad. Chigiana di Siena 1993–; Deputy Chair. Monte Paschi Banque 1993–; mem. Bd. British Inst. of Florence 1993–, Fondo Interbancario Tutela dei Depositi 1993–, Associazione Bancaria Italiana 1993–, Consorzio Siena Ricerche 1993–, IMI S.p.A. 1995–, IMI Int. 1996–. *Publications:* books, articles and reviews on constitutional and comparative law.

GROUÈS, Henri (called **Abbé Pierre**); French ecclesiastic and philanthropist; b. 5 Aug. 1912, Lyons; s. of Antoine Grouès and Eulalie Perra; ed. Collège des Jésuites and Univ. of Lyons; entered Capuchin Order 1930; left for health reasons 1938; ordained priest 1938; almoner at the hosp. of La Mure and in charge of the Groupements de Jeunesse and the Orphanage of the Côte Ste. André 1940, vicar of Grenoble Cathedral 1941; f. an escape org. through the Alps and the Pyrenees, f. the cttee. against forced labour; joined Free French Forces in Algiers as Almoner to the Fleet 1944; Deputy for Meurthe-et-Moselle 1946–51; organized help for the destitute and the homeless in France and abroad, and cr. the Centre d'Emmaüs through an appeal to public opinion; f. the revue Faims et Soifs 1954; Grand Officier, Légion d'honneur 1981, Croix de guerre (2 citations avec palmes), Médaille de la Résistance, Médaille des Evadés, Médaille des Combattants Volontaires, Médaille des Maquisards Belges, Médaille Albert Schweitzer 1975. *Publications:* 23 mois de vie clandestine, Vers l'homme, Feuilles éparses (poems), L'Abbé Pierre vous parle, Emmaüs 1959, Pleine vie, Le scandale de la faim interpelle l'église, Abbé Pierre Emmaüs ou Venger l'homme 1979, Revue 'Faims et Soifs' des hommes, Le Mystère de la joie 1985, Dieu et les hommes 1993, Testament 1994, Mémoire d'un croyant 1997. *Address:* La Halte d'Emmaüs, 76690 Esteville, France.

GROUSSARD, Serge, L. ÈS L.; French writer and journalist; b. 18 Jan. 1921, Niort; s. of Col. Georges Groussard and Vera Bernstein; m. 3rd Monique Berlioux 1956; two d. (from previous marriages); ed. Lycée La Rochelle and Lycée Gouraud, Rabat, École Nat. d'Administration, Ecole Libre des Sciences Politiques, and Univ. de Paris; Chief Reporter Le Figaro 1954–62, L'Aurore 1962–69; Special Contrib. Le Figaro 1969–75; Chevalier des Arts et des Lettres, Officier, Légion d'honneur, Croix de guerre, Médaille de la Résistance, Croix de la Valeur Militaire; Prix Claude Blanchard 1948, Prix International du Grand Reportage 1948, Prix du Roman populiste 1949, Prix Fémina 1950, Grand Prix de la Nouvelle 1957. *Publications:* Crépuscule des vivants 1946, Pogrom 1948, Solitude espagnole 1948, Des gens sans importance 1949, La femme sans passé 1950, Talya 1951, La ville de joie 1952, Un officier de tradition 1954, Une chic fille 1956, La belle espérance 1958, Quartier chinois 1958, La passion du Maure 1959, Jeunesse sauvage 1960, Une espionne doit mourir 1962, Les chacals 1964, Mektoub 1968, Tu es soleil 1970, Taxi de nuit 1971, l'Algérie des adieux 1972, La médaille de sang 1973, La guerre oubliée 1974, les Cobras 1981 and others. *Leisure interests:* sport, painting. *Address:* 38 avenue Marceau, 75008 Paris, France. *Telephone:* 48-25-17-43.

GROVE, Andrew S, PH.D.; American business executive; b. 1936, Budapest, Hungary; m.; two c.; ed. City Coll. of New York and Univ. of Calif. Berkeley; Fairchild Instrument & Camera Co. 1963–67; Pres. and C.O.O. Intel Corpn., Santa Clara, Calif. 1967–87, Pres. 1987–, C.E.O. 1987–98, Chair. May 1997–; also mem. Bd. Dirs.; mem. Nat. Acad. of Eng.; Heinz Family Foundation Award for Tech. and Economy 1995; Hon. D.Sc. (City Coll. of N.Y.) 1985; Hon. D. Eng. (Worcester Polytechnic Inst.) 1989; other awards and distinctions. *Publication:* Only the Paranoid Survive 1996. *Address:* Intel Corporation, P.O. Box 58119, 2200 Mission College Boulevard, Santa Clara, CA 95052, U.S.A.

GRUENBERG, Erich, O.B.E., F.R.C.M., F.G.S.M.; British violinist and music teacher; b. 12 Oct. 1924, Vienna, Austria; s. of Herman and Kathrine Gruenberg; m. Korshed Madan 1956; two d.; ed. in Vienna, Jerusalem and London; Leader, Philomusica of London 1954–56, Stockholm Philharmonic Orchestra 1956–58, London Symphony Orchestra 1962–65, Royal Philharmonic Orchestra 1972–76; leader of London String Quartet and mem. Rubbra-Gruenberg-Pleeth Piano Trio in 'fifties; now appears as soloist with leading orchestras in Britain and abroad; taught at Royal Coll. of Music 1960–65; fmr. Prof. Guildhall School of Music and Drama 1981; Prof. Royal Acad. of Music; winner, Carl Flesch Int. Violin Competition. *Leisure interests:* family, garden, sport. *Address:* c/o Intermusica Artists' Management, 16 Duncan Terrace, London, N1 8BZ; 80 Northway, Hampstead Garden Suburb, London, NW11 6PA, England. *Telephone:* 0171-278 5455; 0181-455 4360. *Fax:* 0171-278 8434.

GRUMBACH, Melvin Malcolm, M.D.; American physician and university professor; b. 21 Dec. 1925, New York; s. of Emanuel Grumbach and Adele (Weil) Grumbach; m. Madeleine F. Butt 1951; three s.; ed. Columbia Coll. and Columbia Univ. Coll. of Physicians and Surgeons; Resident in Pediatrics, Babies' Hosp., Presbyterian Hosp., New York, 1949–51; Visiting Fellow, Oak Ridge Inst. of Nuclear Studies 1952; Post-doctoral Fellow, Asst. in Pediatrics,

Johns Hopkins School of Medicine 1953–55; mem. Faculty, Columbia Univ. Coll. of Physicians and Surgeons 1955–65; Asst. Attending Pediatrician, subsequently Assoc. Prof. of Pediatrics, Head of Pediatric Endocrine Div. and Postdoctoral Training Programme in Pediatric Endocrinology, Babies' Hosp. and Vanderbilt Clinic, Columbia-Presbyterian Medical Center 1955–65; Prof. of Pediatrics, Chair. Dept., Univ. of Calif. School of Medicine, San Francisco 1966–86, Edward B. Shaw Prof. of Pediatrics 1983–, Acting Dir. Lab. of Molecular Endocrinology 1987–89; Dir. Pediatric Service Univ. of Calif. Hosps. 1966–86; Pres. Asscn. of Pediatric Dept. Chairmen 1973–75, Lawson Wilkins Pediatric Endocrine Soc. 1975–76, Western Soc. for Pediatric Research 1978–79, Endocrine Soc. 1981–82, American Pediatric Soc. 1989–90; Exec. Cttee. Int. Soc. of Endocrinology 1984–92; mem. N.A.S., Inst. of Medicine of N.A.S.; Hon. mem. Royal Soc. of Medicine, London, etc.; Fellow A.A.A.S., American Acad. of Arts and Sciences; Dr. h.c. (Geneva) 1991; Joseph M. Smith Prize, Columbia Univ. 1962, Career Scientist Award, Health Research Council, New York 1961–66, Silver Medal, Bicentenary Columbia Coll. of Physicians and Surgeons 1967, Borden Award, American Acad. of Pediatrics 1971, Robert H. Williams Distinguished Leadership Award, Endocrine Soc. 1980, Alumni Gold Medal, Columbia Coll. of Physicians and Surgeons 1988, Fred Conrad Koch Award, Endocrine Soc. 1992, Lifetime Achievement Award: Medical Educ., American Acad. of Pediatrics 1996, John Howland Award, American Pediatric Soc. 1997, and many others. *Publications:* numerous scientific and clinical papers and monographs. *Leisure interests:* tennis, gardening, literature. *Address:* University of California San Francisco School of Medicine, San Francisco, CA 94143-0434, U.S.A. *Telephone:* (415) 476-2244. *Fax:* (415) 476-4009.

GRUNBERG-MANAGO, Marianne, PH.D.; French biochemist; b. 6 Jan. 1921, Leningrad, U.S.S.R. (now St. Petersburg, Russia); d. of Vladimir Grunberg and Catherine Riasanoff; m. Armand Manago 1948 (deceased); one s. one d.; ed. Univ. of Paris; Research Asst., subsequently Researcher then Sr. Researcher, Nat. Centre for Scientific Research, (CNRS) 1946–61, Head Dept. of Biochemistry, Inst. of Physico-Chemical Biology 1959, Dir. of Research, CNRS 1961, Head Biochemistry Div. 1967–; Assoc. Prof., Univ. of Paris VII 1972–; Ed.-in-Chief Biochimie; Pres.-elect Int. Union of Biochemistry 1983, Pres. 1985–88; Vice-Pres. Comm. for Sciences and Tech., UNESCO 1985; Pres. Acad. des Sciences 1995– (Vice-Pres. 1994, mem. 1982–); mem. Soc. de Chimie Biologique, American Soc. of Biological Chemists, Int. Council of Scientific Unions Gen. Cttee., Acad. des Sciences; Foreign mem. American Acad. of Arts and Sciences, New York Acad. of Sciences, Acad. of Sciences of Russia (Ukraine), American Philosophical Soc.; Foreign Hon. mem. N.A.S. (U.S.A.); Charles-Léopold Mayer Prize 1955, 1966; Fogarty Fellow 1977–82; Officier Légion d'honneur, Commdr., ordre nat. du Mérite. *Publications:* Polynucleotide phosphorylase, in Journal of American Chemical Soc. (with S. Ochoa) 1955, Biosynthèse des acides nucléïques (with F. Gros) 1974, :threonine tRNA ligase gene in *Escherichia coli,* in P.N.A.S. (with others) 1986, Escherichia coli and Salmonella typhimurium 1987; more than 300 scientific articles. *Leisure interest:* paintings. *Address:* Institut de Biologie Physico-chimique, 13 rue Pierre-et-Marie Curie, 75005 Paris; 80 Boulevard Pasteur, 75015 Paris, France. *Telephone:* (1) 43.25.26.09.

GRUNFELD, Henry; British (b. German) banker; b. 1 June 1904; m. Berta Lotte Oliven 1931 (died 1993); one s.; Chair. S. G. Warburg & Co. Ltd. 1969–74, Pres. 1974–87, Pres. S. G. Warburg Group PLC 1987–95, Sr. Adviser Warburg Dillon Read 1995–. *Address:* 1 Finsbury Avenue, London, EC2M 2PP, England. *Telephone:* 0171-568 2478. *Fax:* 0171-568 0050.

GRUNWALD, Henry Anatole, L.H.D.; American editor, diplomatist and author; b. 3 Dec. 1922, Vienna; s. of Alfred Grunwald and Mila Loewenstein; m. 1st Beverly Suser 1953 (died 1981); one s. two d.; m. 2nd Louise Melhado 1987; ed. New York Univ.; mem. editorial staff, Time Magazine 1945–87, Asst. Man. Ed. 1966–68, Man. Ed. 1968–77; Corp. Ed., Time Inc. 1977–79, Ed.-in-Chief 1979–87; Amb. to Austria 1988–90; Trustee New York Univ., American-Austrian Foundation; Dir. Metropolitan Opera Guild, Center for Communication, Int. Media Fund; Vice-Chair. World Press Freedom Cttee.; mem. Council on Foreign Relations; mem. Bd. of Dirs. Int. Rescue Cttee. 1997–; Sr. Fellow, Salzburg Seminar; Fellow R.S.A.; mem. Century Asscn.; Hon. LL.D. (Iona Coll.) 1981, (Webster Univ., Vienna) 1989; Hon. L.H.D. (Bennett Coll.) 1983. *Publications:* Salinger, a Critical and Personal Portrait 1962, Churchill, The Life Triumphant 1965, The Age of Elegance 1966, One Man's America: A Journalist's Search for the Heart of His Country 1997 (memoirs); contrib. to various journals, newspapers and magazines. *Address:* 654 Madison Avenue, Suite 1605, New York, NY 10021, U.S.A.

GRYAZNOVA, Alla Georgiyevna, DR. ECON.; Russian professor of economics; b. 27 Nov. 1937, Moscow; m.; one c.; ed. Moscow Inst. of Finance; asst., lecturer, sr. lecturer, docent, Prof., Moscow Inst. of Finance (now Acad. of Finance of Russian Govt.) 1964–74, Pro-rector on int. relations and research 1976–85, Rector 1985–; organizer various int. symposia and confs. on banking problems; Ed.-in-Chief Banking System in Russia; Merited Worker of Science of Russian Fed.; mem. New Way Movt. 1995; First Vice-Pres., Guild of Financiers; Vice-Pres., Acad. of Man. and Market; Pres., Moscow Int. School of Finance and Banking. *Publications:* over 200 articles on econ. problems 1994. *Leisure interests:* tennis, ballet, volleyball, poetry. *Address:* Academy of Finance, Leningradsky prosp. 49, 125468 Moscow, Russia. *Telephone:* (095) 943 9855 (Office).

GRZEŚKOWIAK, Alicja, PH.D.; Polish politician; b. 10 June 1941, Świrz, Lvov Prov, Ukraine; m. (husband deceased); one d.; ed. Nicolaus Copernicus Univ., Toruń; research worker Faculty of Law and Admin. of Nicolaus Copernicus Univ., Toruń 1966–96, Prof. 1990; Catholic Univ. of Lublin (KUL) 1990, Prof. 1991, mem. Scientific Council of John Paul II Inst.; lecturer in Religious Law Higher Ecclesiastic Seminary, Toruń; mem. Solidarity Trade Union 1980; Senator 1989–, Vice-Marshal of Senate 1991–93, Marshal 1997–, del. Parl. Ass. of the Council of Europe 1989–91, mem. 1991–, Chair. Group of Christian Democrats 1992–; mem. Admin. Council of John Paul II Foundation, Vatican 1992; consultor of Pontifical Council for the Family 1993; Dame of the Holy Sepulchre Friars, Jerusalem; founder Foundation of Assistance to Single Mothers, Toruń; hon. mem. Ass. of Catholic Families; Dr. h.c. (Acad. of Catholic Theology, Warsaw); Pro Ecclesia et Pontyfice medal 1992. *Publications:* numerous scientific publs. on penal law, human rights and family rights. *Leisure interests:* reading, listening to music. *Address:* Kancelaria Senatu R.P., ul. Wiejska 6, 00-902 Warsaw, Poland. *Telephone:* (22) 694 14 39.

GU CHAOHAO; Chinese mathematician; b. 15 May 1926; ed. Fudan Univ. and U.S.S.R.; Prof. Dept. of Math. at Fudan Univ., Shanghai 1960; Deputy, 3rd NPC 1964–66; mem. Scientific Council of Academia Sinica 1981; Deputy, 6th NPC 1983–88; Vice-Pres. Fudan Univ. 1984–88; mem. Dept. of Math. and Physics, Academia Sinica 1985; Vice-Chair. China–Brazil Friendship Group of NPC 1986; Pres. Science and Tech. Univ. Hefei Feb. 1988; Dir. Mathematical Research Centre, Shanghai Communications Univ. 1988; Standing Cttee. mem. CPPCC 8th Nat. Cttee. 1993–. *Address:* c/o Science and Technology University, 59 Tunxi Road, Hefei, Anhui Province 230009, People's Republic of China. *Telephone:* 74711.

GU GENGYU; Chinese business executive; b. 1920, Chongqing City, Sichuan Prov.; Vice-Chair. of Exec. Cttee. Fed. of Industrialists and Businessmen 1987; Dir., China Int. Trust and Investment Corpn. 1993; Hon. Vice-Chair. All-China Fed. of Industry and Commerce. *Address:* China International Trust and Investment Corporation, 19 Jianwai Dajie Street, Beijing 100020, People's Republic of China.

GU GONGXU, M.SC.; Chinese geophysicist; b. 5 July 1908, Jiashan Co., Zhejiang Prov.; ed. Shanghai Datong Univ., Colorado School of Mines U.S.A.; researcher, Calif. Inst. of Tech. 1936–38; researcher, Inst. of Physics, Peiping (now Beijing) 1938–49; Deputy Dir., Inst. of Geophysics, Academia Sinica 1950–79; Deputy, First NPC 1954–58, 2nd NPC 1958–64, 3rd NPC 1964–66, 5th NPC 1978–83, 6th NPC 1983–88, 7th NPC 1988–92; mem. Standing Cttee. Dept. of Earth sciences, Pres. Geophysics Soc. 1958–88; Head, Chinese geophysical study group visiting Iran 1976; mem. UNESCO Int. Advisory Cttee. on Earthquake Risks 1977; Pres. Soc. of Seismology 1979–84; Dir. Geophysics Inst. 1980; mem. Dept. of Earth Sciences, Academia Sinica 1985–. *Address:* Room 212, Bldg. 15, Academia Sinica, Zhong Guan Cun, Beijing 100080, People's Republic of China.

GU HUA (born Luo Hongyu); Chinese novelist; b. 20 June 1942, Jiahe County, Hunan; ed. Chenzhou Agricultural School, Coll. for Young Writers; research worker, Chenzhou Agricultural Research Inst. 1961–75; mem. writing staff, Chenzhou Song and Dance Ensemble 1975–79; mem. Writers' Asscn. of Hunan Prov. 1981–87; Hon. Fellow Univ. of Iowa, Int. Writing Program 1987–. *Publications include:* A Log Cabin Overgrown with Creepers, A Small Town Called Hibiscus, The Prison for the Scholars, Virgin Widows, Pagoda Ridge. *Leisure interest:* travel. *Address:* Chenzhou Association of Literary and Art Workers, Chenzhou, People's Republic of China.

GU JINCHI; Chinese party and government official; b. 1932, Xiong Co., Hebei Prov.; joined CCP 1949; Vice-Gov. Sichuan Prov. 1982–86; mem. 13th CCP Cen. Cttee. 1987–92; mem. 14th CCP Cen. Cttee. 1992–97; Deputy Sec. Sichuan Provincial Cttee. 1988–90; Sec. Gansu Provincial Cttee. 1990–93, Sec. CCP Liaoning Prov. Cttee. 1993–97; Vice-Chair Internal Affairs and Judicial Cttee. of 9th NPC 1998–. *Address:* c/o Standing Committee of National People's Congress, Beijing, People's Republic of China.

GU MU; Chinese politician (retd.); b. 1914, Roncheng City, Shandong Prov.; joined CP 1932; Mayor of Jinan 1950–52; Deputy Sec. CCP Shanghai 1953–54; Vice-Chair. State Construction Comm. 1954–56, State Econ. Comm. 1956–65; Chair. State Capital Construction Comm. 1965–67; criticized and removed from office during Cultural Revolution 1967; Minister of State Capital Construction Comm. 1973–81, of Foreign Investment Comm. 1979–82, of Import-Export Comm. 1979–82; Political Commissar, PLA Capital Construction Engineering Corps 1979–; Vice-Premier, State Council 1975–82; mem. 11th Cen. Cttee. CCP 1977, Deputy for Shandong, 5th NPC 1978, mem. Secr. 1980–82, 1982–85, State Councillor, State Council 1982–88; mem. 12th Cen. Cttee. CCP 1982–87, Exec. Chair. 1988–92; Head Co-ordination Group for Tourist Industry 1986–, for Econ. Devt. of Ningbo 1985–; Most Hon. Pres. Asscn. of Enterprises with Foreign Investment; Hon. Pres. Soc. for Study of Econs. of Capital Construction 1980–, Confucius Foundation 1986–, China Asscn. for Promotion of Int. Science and Tech. 1988–, China Asscn. for Advancement of Int. Friendship; Pres. China Econ. Law Research Soc. 1984–92, China Strategy and Admin. Research Soc.; Hon. Chair. China Tourism Asscn. 1986–; Vice Chair. of the Nat. Cttee. of 7th CPPCC 1988–92; Chair. Econ. Cttee. 7th CPPCC 1988–92; Pres. China Population Welfare Foundation 1994–; Hon. Adviser "Happiness Project" Organisation Cttee.; mem. Presidium of 14th CCP Nat. Congress Oct. 1992. *Address:* Chinese People's Political Consultative Conference, Taiping Qiao Road, Beijing, People's Republic of China.

GU XIULIAN; Chinese party and government official; b. 1935, Jiangsu Prov.; cadre, State Council 1970; Vice-Minister State Planning Comm., State Council 1973–83; alt. mem., Cen. Cttee., CCP 1977; Vice-Chair. Cen. Patriotic Sanitation Campaign Cttee., Cen. Cttee. 1981–89; mem. 12th Cen. Cttee., CCP 1982–87; mem. 13th Cen. Cttee. CCP 1987–92; mem. 14th Cen. Cttee. CCP 1992–97; Deputy Sec. CCP Prov. Cttee., Jiangsu 1982–89; Gov. of Jiangsu 1983–89; Minister of Chemical Industry 1989–93, 1993–98 (also Party Cttee. Sec. at the Ministry); mem. 15th Cen. Cttee. CCP 1997–; fmr. Standing mem. Nat. Fed. of Women. *Address:* c/o Ministry of Chemical Industry, Hepingli Street, Anding Menwai, Beijing 100723, People's Republic of China.

GU YINGQI; Chinese politician; b. 19 1930, Xinmin, Liaoning; m.; two s. one d.; joined PLA 1948, CCP 1950; Vice-Minister of Public Health 1984–95; Chief Physician; mem. Standing Cttee. 8th Nat. Cttee. 1993–; Co-ordinator State Co-ordination of Control of Narcotics and Against Drugs 1987–90; Head of del. to UN Int. Conf. on Drug Abuse and Illicit Trafficking 1987, to Signing of Sino-U.S. Memorandum of Understanding on Co-operation and Control of Narcotic Drugs, Washington 1987, to UN Conf. for Adoption of a Convention Against Illicit Traffic in Narcotic Drugs and Psychotropic Substances 1988, to 17th Special Session of UN Gen. Ass. on Int. Co-operation against Drugs 1990, to 44th Gen. Ass. of WHO 1991, to Int. Conf. for Protection of War Victims, Geneva 1993, to 9th Session of Gen. Ass. of Int. Fed. of Red Cross and Red Crescent Socs., Birmingham, U.K. 1993; Conf. Chair. 15th Meeting of Nat. Drug Law Enforcement Agencies for Asia and Pacific 1990, 4th Asia and Pacific Red Cross and Red Crescent Conf., Beijing 1993; Head of Chinese Red Cross del. to 26th Int. Conf. of Red Cross and Red Crescent, Geneva 1995; Pres. China Rural Hygiene Asscn. 1986–, Chinese Asscn. of Rehabilitation Medicine 1985–, Chinese Asscn. of Hosp. Man.; Exec. Vice-Pres. Red Cross Soc. of China 1990–; Vice-Pres. Int. Fed. of Red Cross and Red Crescent Socs. 1991–93. *Address:* c/o Red Cross Society of China, 53 Ganmian Hutong, Beijing 100010, People's Republic of China. *Telephone:* (10) 513-5838. *Fax:* (10) 512-4169.

GU YUNFEI; Chinese government official; b. 1930, Wujiang; mem. 13th and 14th CCP Cen. Disciplinary Cttee.; Sec. Working Cttee. of depts. directly under CCP Cen. Cttee. *Address:* Chinese Communist Party Central Committee, Beijing, People's Republic of China.

GUAN GUANGFU; Chinese politician and banker; b. 1931, Muling Co., Heilongjiang Prov.; joined CCP 1948; Vice-Pres. Hubei Br. People's Bank of China 1971–78, Pres., Hubei Br. 1978–82; Sec. Hubei Prov. CCP Cttee. 1983–94; First Political Commissar, First Party Sec. Hubei Prov. Mil. Dist. 1983–; Chair. Hubei Prov. 8th People's Congress 1993–; mem. 12th Cen. Cttee. 1985, 13th Cen. Cttee. 1987, 14th Cen. Cttee. 1992; mem. Presidium, 13th and 14th Nat. Congresses CCP. *Address:* Shui Guo Hu, Wuhan, Hubei Province, People's Republic of China.

GUAN SHANYUE; Chinese artist; b. 1912, Huangdong Prov.; exponent of Lingnan School of painting; studied with Gao Jinafu, Chun Shui Art School; followed Gao Jianfu to Macau 1938; mem. Progressive People's Art Soc., Hong Kong 1948; Vice-Chair. Chinese Artists' Asscn. 1979–; exhbn. in Tokyo 1982; mem. Presidium 5th NPC 1978–82, 6th NPC 1983–87, 7th NPC 1988–; Hon. mem. China Fed. of Literary and Art Circles 1996.

GUAN WEIYAN; Chinese physicist; b. 18 Aug. 1928, Rudong Co., Jiangsu Prov.; s. of Guan Deyi and Han Quanzheng; m. Zheng Zongshuang 1960; one s. one d.; ed. Harbin Polytechnical Inst., Tsinghua, Beijing, Leningrad, Tbilisi and Moscow Univs.; researcher, Inst. of Physics, U.S.S.R. Acad. of Sciences 1957–60; researcher, Inst. of Physics, Chinese Acad. of Sciences, Beijing 1960–, Deputy Dir. 1978–81, Dir. 1981–85, mem. Dept. of Math. and Physics; Visiting Scholar, Low-temperature Research Centre, Grenoble, France 1980; Pres. Univ. of Science and Tech. of China, Hefei 1984–87, Asscn. of Science and Tech., Anhui Prov. 1986; Vice-Pres. Chinese Physics Soc. 1987–; Visiting Prof. Univ. Giesson 1987, KFK Karlsruhe, Germany 1988, Univ. of Notre Dame (U.S.A.) 1989, Univ. of Houston 1989–90, KFA, Julich, Germany 1990–91, National Tsing Hua Univ. (Taiwan) 1991–, Dan Jiang Univ. (Taiwan) 1995–; mem. ed. bd. of various Chinese and int. journals; mem. Int. Cttee., Int. Conf. on Low Temperature Physics 1981–. *Address:* Room 1201, Bldg. 812, Zhong Guan Cun, Beijing 100080, People's Republic of China. *Telephone:* 6255-4965.

GUBAIDULINA, Sofia Asgatovna; Russian (b. Tatar) composer; b. 24 Oct. 1931, Chistopol; d. of Asgat Gubaidulin and Fedossia Gubaidulina; m. Peter Meschaninov; one d.; ed. Kazan and Moscow Conservatories, composition class Nikolai Peiko and Vissarion Shebalin, piano Grigori Kogan; first noticed abroad Paris 1979; British debut 1987 (Symphony in 12 Movements); lives in Germany 1991–. *Compositions include:* (orchestral pieces) The Steps 1971, The Hour of Soul 1976, Offertorium 1980, Stimmen... verstummen (symphony) 1986, Zeitgestalten (symphony) 1994; 2nd cello concerto 1994, Viola concerto 1998; concertos for solo instruments with chamber orchestra; (cantatas) The Night in Memphis 1968, Rubaiyat 1969, Perception 1983, Dedication to Marina Tsvetayeva 1984; instrumental music for non-traditional groups. *Address:* 2d Pugachevskaya 8, Korp. 5, Apt. 130, 107061 Moscow, Russia; Ziegeleiweg 12, 25482 Appen, Germany. *Telephone:* (095) 161-80-61 (Moscow).

GUBBAY, Hon. Mr. Justice Anthony Roy, M.A., L.L.M.; Zimbabwean judge; b. 26 April 1932, Manchester, England; m. Wilma Sanger 1962; two s.; ed. Univ. of Witwatersrand, S. Africa, Univ. of Cambridge; admitted to practice 1957; advocate Bulawayo, S. Rhodesia 1958, Sr. Counsel 1974; Pres. Matabeleland and Midlands Valuations Boards; Nat. Pres. Special Court for Income Tax Appeals, Fiscal Court and Patents Tribunal; Vice-Chair. Bar Asscn.; Judge of the High Court, Bulawayo 1977–83, Judge of the Supreme Court 1983; Chair. Legal Practitioners' Disciplinary Tribunal 1981–87, Law Devt. Comm., Judicial Service Comm.; Chief Justice of Zimbabwe 1990–; mem. Perm. Court of Arbitration; Pres. Oxford and Cambridge Soc. of Zimbabwe; Patron Commonwealth Magistrates and Judges Asscn.; mem. Advisory Bd. of Commonwealth Judicial Educ. Inst., Commonwealth Reference Group on the Promotion of the Human Rights of Women and the Girl Child through the Judiciary; Hon. Fellow Jesus Coll. Cambridge; Hon. Bencher of Lincoln's Inn (U.K.); Dr. h.c. (Univ. of Essex) 1994. *Address:* Chief Justice's Chambers, CY 870, Causeway, Zimbabwe. *Fax:* 4-731867.

GUBBAY, Raymond; British music promoter; b. 2 April 1946, London; s. of the late David Gubbay and Ida Gubbay; m. Johanna Quirke 1972 (divorced 1988); two d.; ed. Univ. Coll. School, Hampstead; concert promoter 1966–; f. and Man. Dir. Raymond Gubbay Ltd. 1966–; presents regular series of concerts at maj. London and regional concert halls including Royal Albert Hall, Royal Festival Hall, Barbican Centre, Symphony Hall Birmingham, Bridgewater Hall Manchester, Royal Concert Hall Glasgow and in Ireland, Belgium and Scandinavia; has presented productions of: (operas and operettas) The Ratepayer's Iolanthe 1984, Turandot 1991–92, La Bohème (centenary production) 1996, Carmen 1997, Madame Butterfly 1998, The Pirates of Penzance 1998–99, Tosca 1999; (ballets) Swan Lake 1997, 1999, Romeo and Juliet 1998; Hon. F.R.A.M. 1989. *Leisure interest:* living in Paris. *Address:* Raymond Gubbay Limited, Knight House, 29/31 East Barnet Road, New Barnet, Herts., EN4 8RN, England. *Telephone:* 0181-216 3000. *Fax:* 0181-216 3001.

GUBBINS, David, B.A., PH.D., F.R.S., F.INST.P.; British professor of geophysics; b. 31 May 1947, Southampton; s. of Albert Edmund Gubbins and Joyce Lucy Gubbins (née Rayner); m. Margaret Stella McCloy 1972; one s. two d.; ed. King Edward VI Grammar School, Trinity Coll., Cambridge; Visiting Research Fellow Univ. of Colorado 1972–73; instructor M.I.T. 1973–74; Asst. Prof. Univ. of Calif. at L.A. 1974–76; Asst. Dir. of Research Dept. of Geodesy & Geophysics, Univ. of Cambridge 1976–89; Fellow Churchill Coll., Cambridge 1978–90; Ed. Geophysical Journal of the Royal Astronomical Soc. 1982–90, Physics of the Earth and Planetary Interior 1990–; Head of Geophysics Univ. of Leeds 1989–; Fellow American Geophysical Union 1985; Murchison Medal of Geological Soc. of London 1998. *Publications:* Seismology and Plate Tectonics 1990; over 100 articles in scientific journals. *Leisure interests:* sailing, walking. *Address:* School of Earth Sciences, University of Leeds, Leeds, LS2 9JT, England. *Telephone:* (0113) 233 5255. *Fax:* (0113) 233 5259.

GUBENKO, Nikolai Nikolayevich; Russian actor and theatrical director; b. 17 Aug. 1941, Odessa; m. Jeanna Bolotova; ed. All-Union Inst. of Cinema; mem. CPSU 1987–91, Cen. Cttee. 1990–91, CP of Russian Fed. 1992–; actor at Taganka Theatre, Moscow 1964–, Artistic Dir. 1987–89; Founder and Head of Concord of Taganka actors 1993–; Dir. several films including The Orphans (Soviet entry Cannes Film Festival 1977), The Life of Holiday-makers (based on story by Ivan Bunin), Life . . . Tears . . . Love, Restricted Area 1988; stage appearances include Boris Godunov; U.S.S.R. Minister of Culture 1989–91; CP mem. State Duma (Parl.) 1995–; Deputy Chair. Cttee. for Culture 1997–; Pres. Int. Asscn. of Help for Culture 1992–; R.S.F.S.R. People's Artist 1985. *Address:* Franzenskaya nab. 46, Apt. 65, 110270 Moscow, Russia. *Telephone:* (095) 292-90-36 (Duma); 242-65-58 (Home).

GUCCIONE, Robert Charles Joseph Edward Sabatini; American publisher; b. 17 Dec. 1930, Brooklyn; m. Kathy Keeton 1988; five c. from previous m.; artist 1948–55, 1992–; fmr. cartoonist and greetings card designer; Man. ed. London American; founder/publr. Penthouse Magazine, U.K. 1965–; also publr. Forum, Variations, Penthouse Letters, Omni, Saturday Review, Four Wheeler, Longevity, Girls of Penthouse, Compute, Open Wheel, Stock Car Racing, Superstock and Drag, Hot Talk; Chair. Gen. Media Int. Inc. 1988–; producer of film Caligula 1979; exec. producer, TV show Omni: The New Frontier, Omni: Visions of Tomorrow. *Address:* General Media International, 1965 Broadway, New York, NY 10023, U.S.A.

GUÐMUNDSSON, Finnbogi, DR.PHIL.; Icelandic teacher and librarian; b. 8 Jan. 1924, Reykjavík; s. of Dr. Guðmundur Finnbogason and Laufey Vilhjálmsdóttir; m. Kristjana P. Helgadóttir 1955 (deceased); one d.; ed. Univ. of Iceland; Assoc. Prof. of Icelandic Language and Literature, Univ. of Manitoba, Canada 1951–56; lecturer in Icelandic, Univs. of Oslo and Bergen 1957–58; teacher, Reykjavík Gymnasium 1959–64; Docent, Univ. of Iceland 1962–64; Nat. Librarian 1964–94; Chair. Asscn. of Icelandic Studies 1962–64, Div. of Icelandic Research Librarians 1966–73, Icelandic Patriotic Soc. 1967–84; Hon. mem. Icelandic Nat. League, Winnipeg, Canada, The Icelandic Library Asscn. *Publications:* Hómersthýðingar Sveinbjarnar Egilssonar (S. Egilsson's Translations of Homer) 1960, Að vestan og heiman (collection of speeches and articles) 1967, Stephan G. Stephansson in Retrospect 1982, collections of articles 1983, 1989, Gamansemi Snorra Sturlusonar (The Humour of Snorri Sturluson) 1991; ed. of several vols. including Nat. Library Yearbook, Andvari, Orkneyinga Saga, Selected Letters to Stephan G. Stephansson (3 vols.) 1971–75, Poets' Letters to Guðmundur Finnbogason 1987, A New Selection from Andvökur 1998; transl. The Ulysses Voyage 1996. *Leisure interest:* writing. *Address:* Keilugrande 6, 107 Reykjavík, Iceland (Home). *Telephone:* 5550928 (Home).

GUEGUINOU, Jean; G.C.V.O.; French diplomatist; b. 17 Oct. 1941; ed. Ecole Nat. d'Admin.; Press and Information Dept. Ministry of Foreign Affairs 1967–69; Second Sec. London 1969–71; Head of Mission, Ministry of State/ Ministry of Defence 1971–73; Head of Cabinet and Counsellor 1973–76; Dir. of Cabinet of Sec. of State reporting to Prime Minister 1976–77; Asst. Dir. for Southern Africa and Indian Ocean 1977–82; Consul-Gen. Jerusalem 1982–86; Dir. Press and Information Service 1986–90; Amb. to Czechoslovakia 1990–92, to Czech Repub. 1993; Amb. to U.K. 1993–98, to Holy See 1998–; mem. Admin Council, Agence France-Presse 1986–90; Chevalier, Légion d'honneur, Ordre Nat. Du Mérite; Commdr. Order of St. Gregory the Great. *Address:* French Embassy, Via Piave 23, 00187 Rome, Italy. *Telephone:* (6) 4883841.

GUEILER TEJADA, Lidia; Bolivian politician and diplomatist; b. Cochabamba; active role in revolution of 1952; became Pvt. Sec. to Pres. Paz Estenssoro 1952; mem. Chamber of Deputies 1956; left Movimiento Nacional Revolucionario and joined Partido Revolucionario de la Izquierda Nacional (PRIN) 1964; f. PRIN-Gueiler as part of Alianza Democrática de la Revolución Nacional 1979; Pres. Chamber of Deputies July–Nov. 1979; Pres. Congress Aug.–Nov. 1979; interim Pres. of Bolivia 1979–80 (overthrown in coup); in exile in Paris, France 1980–82; Amb. to Colombia 1983–86, to Venezuela 1992–. *Address:* Bolivian Embassy, Avda Luis Roche Con 6a Transversal, Altamira, Caracas, Venezuela; Ministry of Foreign Affairs, Cancellería de la República de Bolivia, Plaza Murillo esq. Ingarí, La Paz, Bolivia.

GUELAR, Diego Ramiro; Argentinian diplomatist and lawyer; b. 24 Feb. 1950; m. Magdalena D. Custodio; three c.; Prof. Sociology of Law, Univ. of Buenos Aires 1971; outlawed by military for political activities (nat. leader, Peronist Youth) 1972–73; attorney, Justicialist Party of Buenos Aires Province 1973–76; Prof. Faculties of Architecture and Law, Univ. of Buenos Aires 1973–76; outlawed for political activities 1976–78; nat. adviser of coordinator for Justicialist activities 1978–83; Vice-Pres. Comm. for Budget and Finance, Nat. Chamber of Deputies 1984; Sec.-Gen. bloc of Nat. Justicialist Deputies 1985; Ed. and Dir. La Razón (newspaper) 1987; Head, Foundation for Growth Arrangement (FUNCRE); Amb. to EC (now EU) 1989–96. *Publications include:* Chronicles of Transition (collection), political and econ. works etc. *Address:* c/o Embassy of Argentina, 1600 New Hampshire Avenue, N.W., Washington, DC 20009, U.S.A.; Callao, 1433–1024 Buenos Aires, Argentina (Office).

GUÉNA, Yves René Henri; French politician; b. 6 July 1922, Brest; m. Oriane de la Bourdonnaye 1945; five s. two d.; ed. Ecole Nat. d'Administration; mem. Free French Forces 1940–45; Official in Morocco 1947, Maître des Requêtes, Conseil d'Etat 1957, Dir. de Cabinet to M. Debré (Minister of Justice) 1958–59, Deputy Dir. de Cabinet to M. Debré (Prime Minister) Jan.–July 1959; High Commr. Ivory Coast 1959–60, Envoy Extraordinary (Dean of Diplomatic Corps) 1960–61; elected Deputy for Dordogne, Nat. Ass. 1962, 1967, 1968, 1973, 1974, 1978, lost seat 1981, re-elected 1986, lost seat 1988; elected Senator for Dordogne 1989; Vice-Pres. of Senate 1992–95, 1995–97; mem. Constitutional Council 1997–; Minister of Posts and Telecommunications 1967–68, 1968–69, of Information May-July 1968, of Transport 1973–74, of Industrial and Scientific Devt., March-May 1974; Deputy Sec.-Gen. UDR 1974, Sec.-Gen. 1976; Political Adviser and Nat. Treasurer, Rassemblement pour la République 1977–79; Mayor of Périgueux (Dordogne) 1971, re-elected 1977, 1983, 1989, 1995–97 (resgnd.); Conseiller d'Etat 1972; Commdr., Légion d'honneur, Croix de guerre, Médaille de la Résistance. *Publications:* Historique de la communauté 1962, Maintenir l'état 1970, L'enjeu (in collaboration) 1975, Le temps des certitudes 1940–69 1982, Catilina ou la gloire dérobée 1984, Les cent premiers jours (co-author) 1985, Ecrits et Discours (25 années de vie publique) 1987, Moi duc de Lauzun, citoyen Biron 1997. *Address:* Conseil constitutionnel, 2 rue Montpensier, 75001 Paris; 13 rue René Bazin, 75016 Paris, France (Home).

GUENÉE, Bernard Marie Albert, D. ÈS L.; French university teacher; b. 6 Feb. 1927, Rennes; s. of Ernest Guenée and Antoinette (née Caisso) Guenée; m. Simonne Lucas 1955; ed. Ecole Normale Supérieure, Paris, Fondation Thiers; Prof. Univ. de Strasbourg 1958–65, Sorbonne 1965–95 (Prof. Emer. 1995–); Dir. of Studies Ecole Pratique des Hautes Etudes 1980–; mem. of Institut de France (Académie des Inscriptions et Belles-Lettres) 1981. *Publications:* Tribunaux et Gens de Justice dans le bailliage de Senlis à la fin du Moyen Age (vers 1380-vers 1550) 1963, Les Entrées royales françaises de 1328 à 1515, 1968, L'Occident aux XIVe et XVe siècles: Les Etats 1971, Histoire et Culture historique dans l'Occident médiéval 1980, Politique et Histoire au Moyen Age: Recueil d'articles sur l'histoire politique et l'historiographie médiévales (1956–81) 1981, Entre l'Eglise et l'Etat: Quatre vies de prélats français à la fin du Moyen Age 1987, Un meurtre, une société: l'assassinat du duc d'Orléans, 23 novembre 1407 1992. *Address:* 8 rue Huysmans, 75006 Paris, France. *Telephone:* (1) 45.48.44.40.

GUENIN, Marcel André, PH.D.; Swiss university professor and company director; b. 17 July 1937, Geneva; s. of Léandré André and Isabelle Guenin-Bontempo; m. Ingrid Marina Selbach 1962; three s.; ed. Edgenössische Technische Hochschule Zürich, Univ. of Geneva and Harvard Univ., U.S.A.; Asst. and Master Asst., Univ. of Geneva 1960–64; Research Assoc., Princeton Univ. 1964–66; Lecturer, Grad. Programme, Univs. of Lausanne, Neuchâtel and Geneva 1966–68; Asst. Prof., Univ. of Geneva 1968–70, Professeur extraordinaire 1970–73, Professeur ordinaire 1973–, Dir. Dept. of Theoretical Physics 1974–77, Dir. Group of Applied Physics (GAP) 1993–, Vice-Rector Univ. of Geneva 1980–83, Rector 1983–87; Pres. PBG Pvt. Bank, Geneva 1987–89; Chair. Bd. COGITAS 1988–94; mem. Bd. BBC Brown Boveri Ltd. 1987–96, Brunet 1990–93, Lasarray 1990–93, Soc. d'Instruments de physique (SIP) 1998–; Sec.-Gen. European Physical Soc. 1974–79, Fellow 1980; Sec. Swiss Physical Soc. 1975–79; mem. Bd. Soc. Financière de Genève 1988–89; Founding mem. Int. Asscn. of Math. Physicists; mem. American Physical Soc. *Publications:* three books and about 40 scientific publs. *Leisure interests:* skiing, sailing, music. *Address:* 2B chemin des Manons, 1218 Grand-Saconnex (GE), Switzerland (Home).

GUÉRARD, Michel Etienne; French chef, restaurateur and hotelier; b. 27 March 1933, Vetheuil; s. of Maurice Guérard and Georgine Guérard; m. Christine Barthelemy 1974; two d.; ed. Lycée Corneille, Rouen; apprentice patissier, Mantes la Jolie; head patissier, Hotel Crillon, Paris; chef to brothers Clérico, Lido, Paris; created restaurant le Pot au Feu, Asnières (two Michelin stars); undertook complex renovation of hotel and thermal treatment centre Les Prés d'Eugénie, Eugénie les Bains; consultant to Nestlé; opened first Comptoir Gourmand Michel Guérard; restored Chai de Bachen and produced a white Tursan, Baron de Bachen; Chevalier, Légion d'honneur 1990; Officier, ordre nat. du mérite; Chevalier, Ordre nat. du mérite agricole; Officier des arts et des lettres. *Publications:* La Grande Cuisine Minceur 1976, La Cuisine Gourmande 1978, Mes Recettes à la TV 1982, Minceur Exquise 1989, Le Sud-Ouest Gourmand de Relais en Châteaux 1993, La Cuisine Gourmande des Juniors 1997. *Leisure interests:* antiques, painting, sketchbooks, food and wine. *Address:* Les Prés d'Eugénie, 40320 Eugénie les Bains, Geaune, France. *Telephone:* (05) 58 05 06 07. *Fax:* (05) 58 51 10 10.

GUERRAOUI, Abdellatif; Moroccan government minister; b. 10 July 1939, Safi; s. of Abdeslam Guerraoui and Oumhani Benazzouz; m. Laila Laoufir 1968; one s. two d.; ed. ENSEEIHT, Toulouse, France; Chief of Staff, Computer Systems, Cherifien Office of Phosphates (O.C.P.) 1964–70, Chief of Personnel Admin. Div. 1970–71, Sec.-Gen. of O.C.P. 1971–90, mem. Bd. of Dirs.; Man. Dir. Moroccan-Saudi Investment Soc. (ASMA-INVEST) 1991–96; Minister of Energy and Mines 1993–97, of Social Affairs, Health, Youth and Sports, Nat. Mutual Aid 1997–98; Admin. Del. Sud Actif Groupe Finance (SAGFI) 1998–; mem. Bd. of Dirs. many pvt. cos. 1998–; consultant (econ. adviser); Chair. bd. of dirs. of many public insts. 1993–97; Throne Award from King of Morocco 1985. *Leisure interests:* classical literature, history, management, economy, futurology. *Address:* 45 rue Ksar El Badii, Hay El Hana, Préfecture Ain Chock—Hay Hassani, Casablanca 20200, Morocco. *Telephone:* (2) 39.60.09; (2) 94.52.52. *Fax:* (2) 35.38.97.

GUESNERIE, Roger Sylvain Maxime Auguste, D. ÈS SC. ECON.; French economist; b. 17 Feb. 1943, Ste Gemmes Le Rt.; s. of Sylvain Guesnerie and Marie Chapelière; ed. Lycée de Rennes, Ecole Polytechnique and Ecole Nat. des Ponts et Chaussées; Research Assoc. CNRS 1976, Research Dir. 1978–; Dir. of Studies, Ecole des Hautes Etudes en Sciences Sociales (EHESS) 1978; Dir. Asscn. pour le Développement de la Recherche en Economie et Statistique (ADRES) 1989–94; Dir. Delta (mixed research unit. of CNRS-EHESS-ENS) 1988–; various part-time appts.; Vice-Pres. European Econ. Asscn. 1992, Pres. 1994; Fellow, Econometric Soc., Pres. 1996; Hon. Foreign mem. American Econ. Asscn. 1997; Silver Medal, C.N.R.S. 1994; Chevalier, Ordre du Mérite. *Publications:* La Documentation Française, 2 vols. (co-author), Modèles de l'Economie Publique 1980, A Contribution to the Pure Theory of Taxation 1995, l'Economie de marché 1996, about 80 articles in econ. journals. *Leisure interests:* cycling, jogging, walking. *Address:* DELTA, ENS, 48 boulevard Jourdan, 75014 Paris, France. *Telephone:* 01.43.13.63.15 (Office).

GUEST, George Howell, C.B.E., M.A., MUS.D., F.R.C.O., F.R.S.C.M.; Welsh musician; b. 9 Feb. 1924, Bangor; s. of Ernest Joseph and Gwendolen Guest; m. Nancy Mary Talbot 1959; one s. one d.; ed. Friars' School, Bangor, King's School, Chester, St. John's Coll., Cambridge; Chorister, Bangor Cathedral 1933–35, Chester Cathedral 1935–39; served R.A.F. 1942–46; Organ Student, St. John's Coll., Cambridge 1947–51, Organist 1951–91, Fellow 1956–, Univ. Lecturer in Music 1956–82; Prof. of Harmony and Counterpoint, R.A.M. 1960–61; conducting and adjudicating tours in U.S.A., Canada, Japan, Brazil, Australia, the Philippines, S. Africa, Argentina, Greece and most Western European countries; Pres. Royal Coll. of Organists 1978-80, Cathedral Organists' Asscn. 1979–81, Inc. Asscn. of Organists 1987–89, Friends of Cathedral Music; Hon. mem. of Gorsedd of Nat. Eisteddfod of Wales; Hon. R.A.M.; Hon. Fellow, Univ. Coll. of N. Wales, Welsh Coll. of Music and Drama; Fellow Royal Canadian Coll. of Organists; Hon. D.Mus. (Wales); Hon. Mus.D. (Cantuar); John Edwards Memorial Award 1986. *Publications:* A Guest at Cambridge; various articles in musical journals. *Leisure interest:* Yr iaith Gymraeg. *Address:* St. John's College, Cambridge; 9 Gurney Way, Cambridge, England (Home). *Telephone:* (01223) 338683 (College); (01223) 354932 (Home).

GUEST, John Rodney, D.PHIL., F.R.S.; British professor of microbiology; b. 27 Dec. 1935, Leeds; s. of Sidney R. Guest and Kathleen (Walker) Guest; m. Barbara Dearsley 1962; one s. two d.; ed. Campbell Coll., Leeds Univ. and Trinity Coll. Oxford; Guinness Research Fellow, Oxford Univ. 1960–65; Research Assoc. and Fulbright Scholar, Stanford Univ. 1963, 1964; Lecturer in Microbiology, Univ. of Sheffield 1965–68, Sr. Lecturer and Reader 1968–81, Prof. of Microbiology 1981–; Science and Eng. Research Council Sr. Fellowship 1981–86; Royal Soc. Leeuwenhoek Lecturer 1995. *Publications:*

research papers in scientific journals. *Leisure interests:* hill walking, squash, beekeeping. *Address:* Department of Molecular Biology and Biotechnology, University of Sheffield, Western Bank, Sheffield, S10 2TN, England. *Telephone:* (0114) 222 4406, 222 4403.

GUI, Luigi; Italian politician; b. 26 Sept. 1914, Padua; s. of Corinto Gui and Angelina Pinzan; m. Alessandra Volpi 1947; three s.; war service, Italy and Russia 1941–43; Christian Democrat underground movement 1943–45; elected to Constituent Ass. 1946, re-elected 1948, 1953, 1958, 1963, 1968, 1972, 1976, 1979; fmr. Sec. of the Parl. Comm. on Agric. and Under-Sec. Ministry of Agric. and Forestry; Minister of Labour 1957–58; of Educ. 1962–68, of Defence 1968–70, of Health 1973–74, of Civil Service Reform March-Nov. 1974, of Interior 1974–76; Pres. Christian Democrat Deputies Parl. Group 1958–62; Senate 1976–79, Chamber of Deputies 1979–83, Pres. 1st Comm. on Constitutional affairs; mem. European People's Party, Paduan Acad. of Sciences, Letters and Arts, Council of European Soc. of Culture; Pres. Nat. Petrarch Soc., Casa di Dante, Rome; Hon. Pres. Associazione Nazionale Combattenti Reduci. *Publications:* works on history of philosophy, political history, education and travel. *Address:* Via S. Rosa 38, 35141 Padua, Italy. *Telephone:* 049/656607.

GUI SHIYONG; Chinese politician; b. Feb. 1935, Huzhou City, Zhejiang Prov.; ed. Chinese People's Univ.; joined CCP 1956; Dir. Econs. Inst. of Chinese Acad. of Sciences; Deputy Ed.-in-Chief Renmin Ribao (People's Daily); alt. mem. 13th CCP Cen. Cttee. 1987; mem. State Planning Comm. and Vice-Dir. Research Office of the State Council 1988; Vice-Chair. State Planning Comm. and Dir. Econs. Research Centre 1989; alt. mem. 14th CCP Cen. Cttee. 1992; Vice-Pres. State Admin. Inst. 1994–; mem. 15th CCP Cen. Cttee. 1997–. *Address:* Office of the President, State Administrative Institute, Beijing, People's Republic of China.

GUICHARD, Baron Olivier Marie Maurice; French politician; b. 27 July 1920, Néac; s. of Baron Louis Guichard and Madeleine Brisson; m. 1st Suzanne Vincent 1944 (deceased); three d.; m. 2nd Daisy de Galard 1990; ed. Univ. de Paris and Ecole libre des sciences politiques; mem. Rassemblement du peuple français, and Prin. Sec. to Gen. de Gaulle 1947–54; Press Officer Atomic Energy Commissariat 1955–58; Asst. Dir. Office of Gen. de Gaulle 1958, Tech. Adviser to the Pres. 1959–60; Del. Gen. of Org. des régions sahariennes 1960–62; Gen. Asst. Office of the Prime Minister 1962–67; Del. for Regional and Territorial Affairs 1963–67; elected Deputy for Loire-Atlantique, Nat. Ass. 1967–97; Minister of Industry 1967–68, of Econ. Planning 1968–69, of Educ. 1969–72, of Supply 1972–73, of Supply, Housing, Tourism and Territorial Devt. 1973–74, of Transport March–May 1974; Minister of State, Keeper of the Seals, and Minister of Justice 1976–77; Mayor of La Baule 1971–95; Pres. Conseil régional des Pays de la Loire 1974–98; Conseiller d'Etat 1978–87; Dir. Cie. nat. du Rhône 1966–67; mem. Council of Admin. Radiodiffusion-Télévision française 1964–67; Pres. Mouvement pour l'indépendance de l'Europe 1975; Pres. Admin. Council Conservatoire de l'espace littoral et des rivages lacustres 1986–89; Pres. Syndicat de conception et d'animation de la métropole de Nantes 1987–; Pres. Centre culturel de l'Ouest, Fontevraud 1998–; Médaille militaire; Officier, Légion d'honneur, Croix de guerre. *Publications:* Aménager la France 1965, Education nouvelle 1971, Un chemin tranquille 1975, Mon Général 1980 (Prix des Ambassadeurs). *Address:* SCE, Baronne Guichard, Château Siourac, 33500 Néac (Office); 30 rue Washington, 75008 Paris, France (Home).

GUIG, Mohamed Lemine Ould; Mauritanian politician; fmr. Dir. of Higher Educ.; Prime Minister of Mauritania 1997–98. *Address:* c/o Office of the Prime Minister, Nouakchott, Mauritania.

GUIGNABODET, Liliane, L. ÈS L.; French author; b. 26 March 1939, Paris; d. of Moïse and Olympia N. Graciani; m. Jean Guignabodet 1961; one s. two d.; ed. primary school in Sofia (Bulgaria), Lycée Jules Ferry, Paris, Sorbonne and Univ. of London; Prof. of French, San José, U.S.A. 1961–62; Prof. of Arts and Culture, Ecole Technique d'IBM France 1966–69; author 1977–; mem. PEN Club Français, Asscn. des Ecrivains Croyants, Société des Gens de Lettres, Acad. Européenne des Sciences, des Arts et des Lettres; Prix George Sand 1977, Grand Prix du Roman, Acad. Française 1983, Grand prix du Roman, Ville de Cannes 1991. *Publications:* L'écume du silence 1977, Le bracelet indien 1980, Natalia 1983, Le livre du vent 1984, Dessislava 1986, Car les hommes sont meilleurs que leur vie 1991, Un sentiment inconnu 1998. *Leisure interests:* piano, travel, decorating, skiing. *Address:* 55 rue Caulaincourt, 75018 Paris; 16 chemin du Clos d'Agasse, 06650 Le Rouret, France.

GUIGOU, Elisabeth Alexandrine Marie, L. ÈS L.; French politician; b. 6 Aug. 1946, Marrakesh, Morocco; d. of Georges Vallier and Jeanne Flecchia; m. Jean-Louis Guigou 1966; one s.; ed. Lycée Victor Hugo, Marrakesh, Lycée Descartes, Rabat, Facultés des Lettres, Rabat and Montpellier, Faculté des Sciences Economiques, Montpellier and Ecole Nat. d'Admin.; civil servant, Ministry of Finance 1974, Office of the Treasury 1974–75, Office of Banks 1976–78, Office of Financial Markets 1978–79; Deputy Chair. Finance Cttee. VIIth Plan 1975–78; Maître de Conférences, Inst. d'Etudes Politiques, Paris 1976; Financial Attaché, Embassy, London 1979–81; Head, Office for Europe, America and Asia, Treasury 1981; Tech. Counsellor, Office of Minister of Economy and Finance 1982; Tech. Counsellor 1982–88; Office of Pres. of Repub. 1988–90; Sec.-Gen. Interministerial Cttee. on European Econ. Cooperation 1985–90; Minister Delegate of European Affairs 1990–93; mem. Regional Council of Provence Alpes Côte-d'Azur 1992–, European Parl. 1994–97; elected Deputy to Nat. Ass. for Vaucluse (Socialist Party) 1997; Minister of Justice 1997–. *Publications:* Pour Les Européens 1994, Etre Femme en politique 1997. *Address:* Ministère de la Justice, 13 place Vendôme, 75042 Paris; Conseil Régional de Provence Alpes Côte d'Azur, 27 place Jules Guesde, 13481 Marseille cedex, France.

GUILFOYLE, Dame Margaret Georgina Constance, D.B.E., LL.B.; Australian politician and accountant; b. 15 May 1926, Belfast, Northern Ireland; d. of William McCartney and Elizabeth Jane Ellis; m. Stanley Martin Leslie Guilfoyle 1952; one s. two d.; chartered sec. and accountant 1947–; Liberal mem. Senate for Victoria 1971–87; Minister for Educ. Nov.–Dec. 1975, for Social Security 1975–80, for Finance 1980–83; Deputy Chair. Mental Health Research Inst. 1988–, Infertility Treatment Authority 1996–; Chair. Judicial Remuneration Tribunal 1995–, Ministerial Advisory Cttee. on Women's Health 1996–, Australian Political Exchange Council 1996–; Dir. Australian Children's TV Foundation 1989–; mem. Nat. Inquiry Concerning Human Rights of People with Mental Illness 1990–93; Fellow, Australian Soc. of Accountants; Fellow, Chartered Inst. of Secs. and Administrators. *Leisure interests:* reading, opera. *Address:* 21 Howard Street, Kew, Victoria 3101, Australia (Home).

GUILLAUD, Jean Louis; French news agency executive; b. 5 March 1929, Caen; m. 2nd Catherine Chichet 1978; one d.; one s. one d. from previous relationships; ed. Inst. d'Etudes Politiques, Paris; political journalist, Soc. Générale de Presse 1953–58, Paris-Jour 1958–60, France-Soir and Nouveau Candide 1961–63; Ed.-in-Chief, ORTF 1963, Dir. of TV news 1968–69; special assignment at Secr.-Gen. of Presidency of Repub. 1970–72; Dir. of Regional Stations and Third Channel, ORTF 1972–74; Dir.-Gen. TFI 1975–78, Pres. Dir.-Gen. 1978–81 ; later TV Dir. Hachette Group; Pres. Dir.-Gen. Agence France Presse (AFP) 1987–90; Pres. Polycom SA 1988–90; Pres., Dir.-Gen. HDSA 1990–95, Media Campus 1990–95; Pres. TV France Int. 1994–; mem. (Admin. Council) Revue de Défense Nationale 1991–; Officier, Légion d'honneur, Officier, ordre nat. du Mérite, Chevalier des Arts et des Lettres. *Address:* Office of the President, TV France International, 64 rue des Mathurins, 75008 Paris (Office); 12 rue des Nonnains d'Hyères, 75004 Paris, France (Home).

GUILLAUME, Gilbert, L. EN D.; French judge; b. 4 Dec. 1930, Bois-Colombes; s. of Pierre Guillaume and Berthe Guillaume; m. Marie-Anne Hidden 1961; one s. two d.; ed. Univ. of Paris, Paris Inst. of Political Studies and Ecole Nat. d'Administration; mem. Council of State 1957; Legal Adviser, State Secr. for Civil Aviation 1968–79; French Rep. Legal Cttee. of ICAO 1968–69, Chair. of Cttee. 1971–75; Chair. Conciliation Comm. OECD 1973–78; Dir. of Legal Affairs, OECD 1979; mem. European Space Agency Appeals Bd. 1975–78; French Rep. Central Comm. for Navigation of the Rhine 1979–87, Chair. 1981–82; Dir. of Legal Affairs, Ministry of Foreign Affairs 1979–87; Conseiller d'Etat 1981–96; Prof. Inst. d'études politiques de Paris 1983–95; Counsel/agent for France in int. arbitration proceedings, numerous cases before European Courts etc.; mem. Perm. Court of Arbitration 1980–; del. to numerous int. legal and diplomatic confs.; Prof. Inst. of Political Studies, Univ. of Paris and other lecturing appts.; mem. various legal asscns., insts. etc.; Judge, Int. Court of Justice 1987–; Officier, Légion d'honneur, Chevalier, ordre nat. du Mérite, du Mérite agricole, du Mérite maritime, Commdr. des arts et des lettres. *Publications:* numerous books and articles on administrative and international law. *Address:* International Court of Justice, Peace Palace, Carnegieplein 2, 2517 KJ The Hague, The Netherlands (Office); 36 rue Perronet, 92200 Neuilly-sur-Seine, France (Home). *Telephone:* (70) 302.2.323 (Office).

GUILLAUMONT, Antoine Jean-Baptiste, D. ÈS L.; French professor; b. 13 Jan. 1915, L'Arbresle (Rhône); s. of Pierre Guillaumont and Cécile (née Gallon) Guillaumont; m. Claire Boussac 1948; three c.; ed. Faculté des Lettres, Montpellier, Ecole pratique des Hautes Etudes, Paris; teacher at the Lycée de Monaco 1943–45; Researcher C.N.R.S. 1946–51; Dir. of Studies, Ecole pratique des Hautes Etudes, Hebrew and Aramaic 1952–74, Oriental Christianity 1957–81; Prof. in Oriental Christian Studies, Collège de France 1977–86, Prof. Emer. 1986–; mem. Institut de France, Acad. des Inscriptions et Belles lettres 1983–; Dr. h.c. Uppsala, Louvain and Liège; Croix de guerre, Palmes académiques. *Publications:* L'Asceticon copte de l'abbé Isaïe 1956, Les Six Centuries des 'Képhalaia Gnostica' d'Evagre le Pontique 1958, Les 'Kephalaia Gnostica' d'Evagre le Pontique et l'histoire de l'origénisme chez les Grecs et chez les Syriens 1962, Evagre le Pontique, Traité pratique (co-ed.) 1971, Aux origines du monachisme chrétien, Abbaye de Bellefontaine 1979, Le Gnostique (co-ed.) 1989, Etudes sur la spiritualité de l'Orient Chrétien 1996. *Address:* 164 rue de Vaugirard, 75015 Paris, France. *Telephone:* (01) 47.34.38.73.

GUILLEM, Sylvie; French ballet dancer; b. 23 Feb. 1965, Le Blanc Mesnil; joins Ecole de Danse, Paris Opera 1976; Ballet de l'Opéra as Quadrille 1981, promoted to Coryphée 1982, to Sujet 1983, Première Danseuse, later Etoile 1984; with Royal Ballet, London 1989–; Chevalier, Légion d'honneur, Commdr. des Arts et Lettres 1988. *Leading roles in:* Romeo and Juliet, Don Quixote, Raymonda, Swan Lake, Giselle, Notre Dame de Paris, Manon. *Created roles include:* Cendrillon, In the Middle, somewhat elevated, Magnificat, Le Martyre de Saint-Sébastien; *created and produced:* Evidentia (TV) 1995; Prize for Excellence and Gold Medal, Varna Int. Dance Competition 1983, Prix Carpeau 1984, Hans Christian Andersen Award 1988, Arpège Prize (Lanvin perfumes) 1989. *Address:* c/o Royal Ballet, Royal Opera House, London, WC2E 9DD, England.

GUILLEMIN, Roger Charles Louis, M.D., PH.D.; American professor of medicine; b. 11 Jan. 1924, Dijon, France; s. of Raymond and Blanche Guillemin; m. Lucienne Jeanne Billard 1951; one s. five d.; ed. Univs. of Dijon, Lyons, Montreal; Prosector of Anatomy, Univ. of Dijon Medical School 1946–47; Research Asst., Inst. of Experimental Medicine and Surgery, Univ. of Montreal 1949–51, Assoc. Dir. and Asst. Prof. of Experimental Medicine 1951–53; Asst. Prof. of Physiology, Coll. of Medicine, Baylor Univ., Houston, Tex. 1953, Assoc. Prof. 1957, Prof. of Physiology and Dir. Laboratories for Neuroendocrinology 1963–70, Adjunct Prof. of Physiology 1970–; Consultant in Physiology, Veterans' Admin. Hosp., Houston 1954–60, 1967–70; Lecturer in Experimental Endocrinology, Dept. of Biology, W. M. Rice Univ., Houston 1958–60; Assoc. Dir., Dept. of Experimental Endocrinology, Coll. de France, Paris, as jt. appointment with Coll. of Medicine, Baylor Univ. 1960–63; Resident Fellow and Research Prof., The Salk Inst. for Biological Studies, San Diego, Calif. 1970–89, Dean 1972–73, 1976–77, Distinguished Prof. 1997–; Distinguished Scientist, Whittier Inst. for Diabetes and Endocrinology, La Jolla 1989–93, Medical and Scientific Dir., Dir. 1993–94, 1995–97; Adjunct Prof. of Medicine Univ. of Calif., San Diego 1995–97; mem. N.A.S. 1974–, American Acad. of Arts and Sciences, American Physiological Soc., Soc. for Experimental Biology and Medicine, Int. Brain Research Org., Int. Soc. for Research in Biology and Reproduction, Swedish Soc. of Medical Sciences, Acad. Nat. de Médecine, France, Acad. des Sciences, France, Acad. Royale de Médecine de Belgique, Belgium; Pres. The Endocrine Soc. 1986; Hon. degrees (Univ. of Rochester, N.Y.) 1976, (Univ. of Chicago, Ill.) 1977, (Baylor Coll. of Medicine, Houston, Tex.) 1978, (Univ. of Ulm) 1978, (Univ. of Dijon) 1978, (Univ. Libre de Bruxelles) 1979, (Univ. de Montréal) 1979, (Univ. of Manitoba) 1984, (Univ. of Turin) 1985, (Kung Hee Univ., Seoul) 1986, (Paris VII) 1986, (Autónoma, Madrid) 1988, (McGill) 1988; Bonneau and La Caze Awards in Physiology (Acad. des Sciences) 1957, 1960, Gairdner Award (Toronto) 1974, Officier, Légion d'honneur, Lasker Foundation Award 1975, co-recipient of Nobel Prize in Physiology or Medicine with Andrew V. Schally (q.v.) for discoveries relating to peptide hormones 1977, Nat. Medal of Science 1977, Barren Gold Medal 1979, Dale Medallist, U.K. Soc. for Endocrinology 1980; numerous int. awards and lectureships. *Address:* The Salk Institute, 10010 North Torrey Pines Road, La Jolla, CA 92037, U.S.A.

GUILLERMIN, John; British film director; b. 11 Nov. 1925, London. *Films include:* Torment 1949, Smart Alec 1951, Two on the Tiles 1951, Four Days 1951, Bachelor in Paris 1952, Miss Robin Hood 1952, Operation Diplomat 1953, Adventure in the Hopfields 1954, The Crowded Day 1954, Dust and Gold 1955, Thunderstorm 1955, Town on Trial 1957, The Whole Truth 1958, I Was Monty's Double 1958, Tarzan's Greatest Adventure 1959, The Day they Robbed the Bank of England 1960, Never Let Go 1960, Waltz of the Toreadors 1962, Tarzan Goes to India 1962, Guns at Batasi 1964, Rapture 1965, The Blue Max 1966, P.J. 1968, House of Cards 1969, The Bridge at Remagen 1969, El Condor 1970, Skyjacked 1972, Shaft in Africa 1973, The Towering Inferno 1974, King Kong 1976, Death on the Nile 1978, Mr Patman 1980, Sheena 1984, King Kong Lives 1986, The Favourite.

GUILLERY, Rainer W., PH.D., F.R.S.; British university teacher, anatomist and neurobiologist; b. 28 Aug. 1929, Greifswald, Germany; s. of Eva Hackel and Hermann Guillery; m. Margot Cunningham Pepper 1954; three s. one d.; ed. Univ. Coll. London; Asst. Lecturer, Anatomy Dept., Univ. Coll. London 1953–56, Lecturer 1956–63, Reader 1963–64; Assoc. Prof., Dept. of Anatomy, Univ. of Wis., Madison, U.S.A. 1964–68, Prof. 1968–77, Visiting Prof. 1996–; Prof., Dept. of Pharmacological and Physiological Sciences and Chair. Cttee. on Neurobiology, Univ. of Chicago, U.S.A. 1977–84; Dr. Lee's Prof. of Anatomy, Oxford Univ., England 1984–96; Pres. Anatomical Soc. of Great Britain and Ireland 1994–96; Ed.-in-Chief European Journal of Neuroscience 1988–92; Fellow, Hertford Coll., Oxford 1984–96, Univ. Coll. London 1987. *Publications:* contribs. to Journal of Comparative Neurology, Journal of Neuroscience, Neuroscience, Brain Research, etc. *Address:* c/o Department of Anatomy, University of Wisconsin, 1300 University Avenue, Madison, WI 53706, U.S.A. *Telephone:* (608) 263-4763.

GUINIER, André Jean, D. ÈS SC.; French professor of physics; b. 1 Aug. 1911, Nancy; s. of Philibert and Lucie (née Le Monnier) Guinier; m. Claire Chasse 1934; one d.; ed. Lycée de Nancy, Ecole Normale Supérieure, Paris; Prof. of Physics, Univ. of Paris 1949–77; Visiting Prof., Harvard Univ. and Univ. of Ill., U.S.A. 1952–53, American Univ., Cairo 1965; Dir. Lab. of Solid State Physics, Paris 1960–71; Pres. Soc. française de minéralogie et cristallographie 1960, Soc. française de physique 1962, Teaching Comm., Int. Union of crystallography 1966–69, mineral and crystallography section of Nat. Cttee., C.N.R.S. 1966–70, Pres. Int. Union of crystallography 1969–72; mem. Acad. des Sciences; Chevalier, Légion d'honneur, Officier, Ordre nat. du Mérite; Dr h.c. Eth (Zurich); several awards and prizes for physics. *Publications:* Radiocristallographie 1945, Théorie et Technique de la radiocristallographie 1956, X-Ray Diffraction 1963, La Structure de la Matière 1980, Les Rayons X 1984, La Matière à l'état solide 1987. *Address:* 87 rue Denfert-Rochereau, 75014 Paris, France. *Telephone:* (01) 46.33.38.05.

GUINNESS, Sir Alec, Kt., C.H., C.B.E.; British actor; b. 2 April 1914, London; m. Merula Salaman 1938; one s.; ed. Pembroke Lodge, Southbourne and Roborough, Eastbourne; entered Advertising Agency as Copywriter 1933; Scholarship to Fay Compton Studio of Dramatic Art 1934; First Stage appearance April 1934; played in seasons for John Gielgud and Old Vic Theatre Co.; Hamlet in modern dress 1938; served R.N.V.R. 1940–44; began film career 1945; Acad. Award for services to film 1980; Hon. Dr. Fine Arts (Boston Coll), Hon. D.Litt. (Oxford) 1977; Hon. Litt.D. (Cambridge) 1991; BAFTA Award 1980, 1983, Shakespeare Prize 1985, Soc. of West End Theatres Special Award 1989, BAFTA Fellowship 1989, BFI Life Achievement Award 1991, Evening Standard Film Award for Lifetime Achievement 1995. *Films include:* Great Expectations 1946, Oliver Twist 1947, Kind Hearts and Coronets 1948, The Lavender Hill Mob 1951, The Man in the White Suit 1951, The Bridge on the River Kwai 1957, (Oscar 1958), The Horse's Mouth 1958, Our Man in Havana 1959, Tunes of Glory 1960, Lawrence of Arabia 1962, Dr. Zhivago 1966, The Comedians 1967, Cromwell 1969, Murder by Death 1975, Star Wars 1976, Little Lord Fauntleroy 1980, Lovesick 1982, A Passage to India 1984, Little Dorrit 1986, A Handful of Dust 1987, Kafka 1991. *Plays include:* The Prisoner 1954, Hotel Paradiso 1956, Ross 1957, Exit the King, Dylan 1963, Macbeth 1965, Wise Child 1967, 1968, A Voyage Round My Father 1971, Habeas Corpus 1973, A Family and a Fortune 1975, Yahoo 1976, The Old Country 1977, The Merchant of Venice 1984, A Walk in the Woods 1988. *TV includes:* Tinker, Tailor, Soldier, Spy 1979, Smiley's People 1981, Edwin 1983, Monsignor Quixote 1985, Tales from Hollywood 1991, A Foreign Field 1992, Eskimo Day 1995. *Publications:* Blessings in Disguise 1985, My Name Escapes Me 1996, A Positively Final Appearance 1999. *Address:* c/o McReddie, 91 Regent Street, London, W1R 7TB, England.

GUITTON, Jean Marie Pierre; French university professor; b. 18 Aug. 1901; s. of Auguste Guitton and Gabrielle Bertrand; m. Marie-Louise Bonnet (deceased); ed. Ecole Normale Supérieure; fmr. teacher in schools at Troyes, Moulins, Lyon, and Univs. of Montpellier and Dijon; Prof. of Phil. and History of Phil., Univ. of Paris 1955–68; mem. Programmes Cttee. Radiodiffusion et Télévision Française (ORTF) 1965; Observer at 2nd Vatican Council 1963; mem. Acad. Française 1961, Acad. des Science Morales et Politiques 1987; Foreign mem. Acad. of Athens 1986–, Sofia Acad. of Sciences 1986–; Commdr., Légion d'honneur, Commdr. Ordre national du Mérite, Ordre des Arts et des Lettres, Grand-Croix de St. Grégoire-le-Grand; Grand Prix de Littérature, Acad. Française 1954, Grand Médaille, Bordeaux Acad. of Arts, Sciences and Belles-Lettres 1969, Prix Osiris, Inst. de France 1972. *Publications:* Le temps et l'éternité chez Plotin et Saint Augustin, La philosophie de Newman, L'existence temporelle, Essai sur l'amour humain, Le problème de Jésus, Le nouvel art de penser, Le travail intellectuel, Portrait de Monsieur Pouget, Jésus, Apprendre à vivre et à penser, Le Cardinal Saliège, La vocation de Bergson, L'Eglise et l'évangile, Problème et mystère de Jeanne d'Arc, Journal oecuménique, Le clair et l'obscur vers l'unité, Dialogues avec Paul VI, Profiles paralleles, Histoire et destinée, Oeuvres completes (6 vols.), Ce que je crois, la famille et l'amour, Paul VI secret, le temps d'une vie 1980, Crise dans l'Eglise: le Christ écartelé 1981, Portrait de Marthe Robin, Silence sur l'Essential 1986, Le Nouveau Testament: une nouvelle lecture 1987, Un siècle, une vie 1988 (Prix Pierre-Lafue 1989), Portraits et circonstances 1989, L'Impur 1991, Portrait du Père Lagrange celui que a réconcilié la science et la foi 1992, Les pouvoirs mystérieux de la foi 1993, Lettres Ouvertes 1993, Celui qui croyait au ciel et celui qui n'y croyait pas (conversation with Jacques Lanzmann) 1994, le Siècle qui s'annonce 1997. *Leisure interest:* painting. *Address:* 1 rue de Fleurus, 75006 Paris; La Pensée, Champagnat, 23190 Bellegarde-en-Marche, France.

GUJRAL, Inder Kumar, M.A.; Indian politician; b. 4 Dec. 1919, Jhelum (now in Pakistan); s. of late Avtar Narain Gujral and Pushpa Gujral; m. Sheila Gujral 1944; two s.; ed. Forman Christian Coll. and Hailey Coll. of Commerce in Lahore, Punjab Univ.; jailed for participation in freedom movt. 1930–31 (and again during Quit India movt. 1942); Pres. Lahore Students' Union; Gen.-Sec. Punjab Students' Fed.; migrated to India 1947; helped nat. effort for rehabilitation of displaced persons; Vice-Pres. New Delhi Municipal Cttee. 1959–64; M.P. 1964–76, 1989–91, 1992–98, mem. Lok Sabha Punjab 1998–; Leader Rajya Sabha June–Nov. 1996, 1997–98; mem. Council of Ministers, Govt. of India 1967–76 holding portfolios for Communications and Parl. Affairs, Information, Broadcasting and Communications, Works, Housing and Urban Devt., Information and Broadcasting, and Planning 1975–76; Minister of External Affairs 1989–90, 1996–97; Prime Minister of India 1997–98; Chair. Parl. Cttee. on External Affairs 1998–; Amb. to U.S.S.R. (with ministerial rank) 1976–80; Vice-Pres. New Delhi Municipal Cttee. 1959–64; helped organize Citizens Cttee, for Civil Defence; leader several Indian dels. to UNESCO 1970–77, to UN Special Session on Econ. Devt. 1990, to UN Gen. Ass. 1990, 1996, to UN Session on Human Rights, Geneva 1995, and leader or mem. numerous Indian dels. to other int. orgs.; mem. UN Panel of Eminent Persons to study and report on situation in Algeria 1998; Pres. Inst. of Defence Studies and Analysis; Chair. Indian Council of S. Asian Co-operation; Founder-Pres. Delhi Arts Theatre; Treas. Fed. of Film Socs. of India; Chancellor Vishva Bharati Univ., Shanti Niketan. *Leisure interests:* theatre, poetry, painting, ecological problems. *Address:* 5, Janpath, New Delhi 110011, India. *Telephone:* 379-4433; 301-4300. *Fax:* 379-4444.

GULBINOWICZ, H.E. Cardinal Henryk Roman, D.THEOL.; Polish ecclesiastic; b. 17 Oct. 1928, Szukiszki (now in Lithuania); s. of Antoni Gulbinowicz and Waleria Gajewska; ed. Metropolitan Higher Ecclesiastic Seminary, Vilnius and Białystok, Catholic Univ. of Lublin (KUL); ordained priest 1950; Titular Bishop, Apostolic Admin. Archdiocese of Białystok 1970–76, Archbishop Metropolitan of Wrocław 1975–; mem. Congregation for Eastern Churches, Congregation Clergy Affairs; mem. Main Council Polish Episcopate and several episcopate cttees.; High Chancellor Pontifical Theology

Dept., Wrocław; cr. Cardinal 1985. *Publications:* more than 240 works on moral theology, ethics, ecumenism and history of the Polish Eastern Territories. *Address:* ul. Katedralna 11, 50-328 Wrocław, Poland. *Telephone:* (71) 22 42 14.

GULDBERG, Ove; Danish politician, civil engineer and lawyer; b. 2 Dec. 1918, Nysted; s. of Frede and Else Guldberg (née Richter); m. Else Christiansen 1942; three s.; employed by Vejle City Admin. 1942; with Civil Eng. Contractor, K. Hindhede 1943; Copenhagen City Engineer's Office 1944; at Research Lab., Ministry of Fisheries 1946–47; mem. Cen. Cttee., Inst. of Danish Engineers 1946–48, Sec. 1948, Dir. 1952–65; Sec. Asscn. of Consultant Engineers 1956, Dir. 1965; Man. of the bldg. of the Inst. of Danish Engineers 1957; mem. Folketing (Parl.) 1964–77; Minister for Transport and Communications 1968–71; mem. European Parl. 1973–77, Vice-Pres. 1975–77; Minister for Foreign Affairs 1973–75; Sec. Conf. of Reps. from Eng. Socs. of W. Europe and U.S.A. (EUSEC) 1955–58; Pres. Civil Defence Union 1962–65; mem. Civil Defence Council 1962–68; Pres. Danish Cttee. for a European Union (EU) 1986–87; f. and spokesman for Civil Rights Cttee. of 5 June 1994–; Commdr., Order of Dannebrog (First Class), Knight Grand Cross St. Michael and St. George, Grand Cross (Fed. Repub. of Germany), Grand Cross St. Olav (Norway), Grand Cross of the Yugoslav Flag, Encomienda de Número, Orden del Mérito Civil (Spain); Liberal Party. *Address:* Paseo de Venezuela 233, Elviria, Marbella, Spain. *Telephone:* (952) 83.63.99.

GULEGHINA, Maria (née Muradyan); Belarus/Armenian soprano; b. 1959, Odessa; m. Mark Gulegin; ed. Odessa Conservatory (pupil of A. Dzhamagorzyan, studied with Yevgeni Ivanov); soloist Minsk Opera Theatre 1983–90; First Prize All-Union Glinka Competition 1984; taught in Minsk Conservatory 1986–90; lives in Hamburg 1990–; regular appearances in La Scala (since 1986), Wiener Staatsoper, other major European theatres; opera parts in Tosca, Manon Lescaut (Puccini), Due Foscari, Il Trovatore, Un Ballo in Maschera, Ernani, Aida, Otello, Nabucco (Verdi), La Gioconda (Ponchielli), Cavalleria Rusticana (Mascagni), Andrea Chenier, Fedora (Giordano), Yolanta, Eugene Onegin, Queen of Spades (Tchaikovsky); performs in concert performances of Verdi's Requiem, Janáček's Glagolitic Mass; solo recitals in Germany, Italy, Switzerland, Austria, France, Hungary. *Address:* c/o Askonas Holt, Lonsdale Chambers, 27 Chancery Lane, London, WC2A 1PF, England. *Telephone:* 0171-400 1700. *Fax:* 0171-400 1799.

GULIEV, Rasul Bairam ogly; Azerbaijani politician; b. 1947; m.; three c.; Head of div., Deputy Chief Engineer, Dir. Baku Oil processing factory –1992; Vice-Pres. Azerbaijan State Oil Co. 1992–93; Vice-Prime Minister of Azerbaijan May–Nov. 1993; Chair. Nat. Ass. (Milli Majlis) of Azerbaijan Repub. 1993–96; mem. Ass. of the Black Sea Econ. Co-operation (PABSEC). *Address:* Parliament House, Baku, Azerbaijan.

GULIYEV, Fuat Khalil-ogly; Azerbaijani politician; b. 6 July 1941, Baku; m.; two c.; ed. Azerbaijani Inst. of Oil Chem.; worked in Belorussia in oil chemical industry; chief eng. later Dir. Air Conditioners Factory, Baku; First Deputy Prime Minister of Azerbaijan 1994–95; Prime Minister of Azerbaijan 1995–96; mem. Milli Majlis (Nat. Ass.) 1991–; mem. New Azerbaijan Party. *Address:* House of Government, Azizbekova Prospecti 1, 370001 Baku, Azerbaijan.

GULLICHSEN, Johan Erik, M.SC.; Finnish professor of pulping technology and engineer; b. 28 June 1936, Pihlava; s. of Harry Gullichsen and Maire Ahlström; m. Anna Ramsay 1958; one s. two d.; ed. Abo Akademi, Helsinki Univ. of Tech.; Research Asst., FPPRI 1962–64; project engineer, EKONO 1964–70; Pres. and partner, Arhippainen, Gullichsen & Co. 1970–; Prof. of Pulping Tech., Helsinki Univ. of Tech. 1989–; fmrly. Chair. Bd. of Dirs. A. Ahlström Oy; Dir. Kymmene Oy; D. Tech. h.c. (Abo Akademi) 1988; Engineer of the Year in Finland 1984, The Marcus Wallenberg Prize 1986. *Publications:* tech. and scientific papers on pulping tech., econs. and environmental control. *Leisure interest:* yachting. *Address:* Teknillinen Korkeakoulu, Otakaaril, 02150 Espoo; Arhippainen, Gullichsen & Co., Tekniikantie 12, 02150 Espoo, Finland. *Telephone:* 09-4354 2505.

GULLIT, Ruud; Netherlands footballer; b. 1 Sept. 1962, Suriname; played for Haarlem, Netherlands 1979–82, Feyenoord 1982–84, PSV Eindhoven 1984–86, AC Milan, Italy 1986–93, 1994–95, Sampdoria 1993–94, Chelsea, U.K. 1995–98; Player/Man., Chelsea 1996–98; Man. Newcastle United 1998–; won 65 caps and scored 16 goals for Netherlands team, including one in European Championship final victory over Russia 1988; European and World Player of the Year 1987.

GULYAEV, Yury Vasilievich, D.PHYSICAL-MATH.SC.; Russian physicist; b. 18 Sept. 1935; m.; two c.; ed. Moscow Inst. of Physics and Tech.; jr. researcher, sr. researcher, Head of Lab., Vice-Dir. Inst. of Radioelectronics and Electrotech., U.S.S.R. Acad. of Sciences 1960–87, Dir. 1988–; Corresp. mem. U.S.S.R. (now Russian) Acad. of Sciences 1979, mem. 1984–, mem. Presidium 1992–; Chair. Saratov br., Russian Acad. of Sciences 1981–; mem. Russian Acad. of Natural Sciences; U.S.S.R. People's Deputy 1989–91; U.S.S.R. State Prize, Prize of European Hewlett-Packard Physical Soc.; mem. Polish Acad. of Sciences; Vice-Pres. World Fed. of Eng. Orgs. (WFEO). *Publications:* more than a hundred articles mainly on acoustic electronics, acoustic optics and spin-wave electronics. *Address:* Institute of Radiotechnology and Electronics, Mokhovaya ul. 11, 103907 Moscow, Russia. *Telephone:* 200-5258. *Fax:* 203-8414.

GULYÁS, Dénes; Hungarian opera singer; b. 31 March 1954; s. of Dénes Gulyás and Mária Szitár; m. Judit Szekeres; two s. one d.; ed. Liszt Ferenc Acad. of Music, Budapest; joined State Opera, Budapest 1978; debut as Rinuccio in Gianni Schicchi; debut in USA, Carnegie Hall and Avery Fisher Hall, New York: concert performances; numerous tours in the USA. *Repertoire includes:* Faust, des Grieux (Manon), Werther, Hoffman, Titus (La Clemenza di Tito), Percy (Anne Boleyn), Ernesto (Don Pasquale), Duke of Mantua (Rigoletto), Fenton (Falstaff), Ferrando (Così fan tutte), Don Ottavio, Tamino, Alfredo (La Traviata), Edgardo (Lucia di Lammermoor), Nemorino, Rodolfo (La Bohème), Tom Rakewell (The Rake's Progress); 1st prize Parma 1979, won Luciano Pavarotti singing competition, Philadelphia 1981; Holder of Liszt Prize, titled Merited Artist. *Leisure interests:* riding, sailing, viticulture. *Address:* Hungarian State Opera, Budapest 1062, Andrássy ut 22, Hungary. *Telephone:* 36/1/131-2550.

GUMBEL, Bryant Charles; American broadcaster; b. 29 Sept. 1948, New Orleans; s. of Richard Gumbel and Rhea LeCesne; m. June C. Baranco 1973; one s. one d.; ed. Bates Coll.; writer, Black Sports (magazine), New York 1971, Ed. 1972; sportscaster, KNBC-TV, Burbank, Calif. 1972–76, Sports Dir. 1976–81; sports host, NBC Sports 1975–82; co-host, Today Show, NBC 1982–97; recipient of two Emmy Awards and two Golden Mike Awards (Los Angeles Press Club); Edward R. Murrow Award (Overseas Press Club) 1988. *Address:* c/o NBC Today, 30 Rockefeller Plaza, Ste 1508, New York, NY 10112, U.S.A.

GUMEDE, Archiebald Jacob; South African politician and attorney; b. 1 March 1914, New Scotland, Natal; s. of Josiah Tshangana Gumede and Lilian Mggoggoza; m. Edith Mona 1949; five s. two d.; ed. Lovedale Missionary Inst., Alice and S.A. Native Coll., Fort Hare; Health Asst., Sanitary Inspector 1936–40; Legal Clerk 1947–56; Articled Clerk 1958–; admitted as attorney 1967; own legal practice, Pinetown 1970; joined African National Congress (ANC) 1944; arrested Dec. 1956, charged with treason, charges dropped 1957; active in all major ANC campaigns 1957–60; banned under Suppression of Communism Act. Oct. 1963; detained under 90-day legislation 1963–64; active in Educ. Action Comm. 1976; participated in formation of United Democratic Front (UDF) and elected Pres. 1983, Jt. Pres. –1991; fmr. Pres. Natal Regional Exec., UDF; Chair. Release Mandela Campaign 1979–90; charged and tried for treason 1985–86, charges dismissed Nov. 1986, restricted 1988; mem. del. on Talks about Talks with S.A. Govt. 1990; ANC mem. parl. for Govt. of Nat. Unity 1994–. *Address:* House of Assembly, Cape Town, South Africa.

GUMMER, Rt. Hon. John Selwyn, M.A., M.P.; British politician, b. 26 Nov. 1939, Stockport; s. of the late Canon Selwyn Gummer and Sybille Gummer (née Mason); brother of Peter Selwyn Gummer, now Lord Chadlington (q.v.); m. Penelope J. Gardner 1977; two s. two d.; ed. King's School, Rochester and Selwyn Coll., Cambridge; Ed., Business Publs. 1962–64; Ed.-in-Chief, Max Parrish and Oldbourne Press 1964–66; Special Asst. to Chair. BPC Publishing 1967; Dir. Shandwick Publishing Co. 1966–81; Dir. Siemssen Hunter Ltd. 1973–80, Chair. 1979–80; Man. Dir. EP Group of Cos. 1975–81; Chair. Selwyn Sancroft Int. 1976–81; M.P. for Lewisham W. 1970–74, Eye, Suffolk (now Suffolk Coastal) 1979–; Parl. Pvt. Sec. to Minister of Agric. 1972; Vice-Chair. Conservative Party 1972–74, Chair. 1983–85; Asst. Govt. Whip 1981, Lord Commr. Treasury (Whip) 1982; Under-Sec. of State for Employment Jan.–Oct. 1983, Minister of State for Employment 1983–84, Paymaster-Gen. 1984–85; Minister of State at Ministry of Agric., Fisheries and Food 1985–88; Minister for Local Govt., Dept. of Environment 1988–89; Minister of Agric. 1989–93; Sec. of State for the Environment 1993–97; Chair. Conservative Group for Europe 1997–, Marine Stewardship Council 1998–; mem. Gen. Synod of Church of England 1979–92 (resgnd.); joined Roman Catholic Church 1994. *Publications:* When the Coloured People Come 1966, To Church with Enthusiasm 1969, The Permissive Society 1970, The Christian Calendar (with L. W. Cowie) 1971, Faith in Politics (with Alan Beith and Eric Heffer) 1987, Christianity and Conservatism 1990. *Leisure interests:* gardening, Victorian buildings. *Address:* House of Commons, London, SW1A 0AA, England (Office).

GUNA-KASEM, Pracha, PH.D.; Thai diplomatist; b. 29 Dec. 1934, Bangkok; s. of Jote and Rabieb Guna-Kesem; m. Sumanee Chongcharoen 1962; one s.; ed. Dhebsirinda School, Bangkok, Marlborough Coll., Hertford Coll., Oxford and Yale Univ.; joined Ministry of Foreign Affairs 1959, Chief of Section, Political Div. of Dept. of Int. Org. 1960–61, Second Sec. SEATO Div. 1962–63, Alt. Mem. for Thailand, SEATO Perm. Working Group 1962–63, Embassy in Egypt 1964–65, Chief of Foreign News Analysis Div. of Information Dept. and concurrently in charge of Press Affairs 1966–69, Chief of Press Div. 1970–71, Consul-Gen. in Hong Kong 1971–73, Dir.-Gen. of Information Dept. 1973–75; Perm. Rep. to UN 1975–80, UN (Geneva) 1980–82; Dir.-Gen. ASEAN-Thailand 1982; Dir-Gen. Dept. of Econ. Affairs, Foreign Ministry 1984–85; Amb. to France and Algeria 1985–87; Perm. Del. to UNESCO 1985; Dir.-Gen. Dept. of Econ. Affairs, Bangkok 1988; Perm. Sec. Ministry of Foreign Affairs 1992–; Special Lecturer, Thammasat Univ., Thai Nat. Defence Coll.; mem. del. to UN Gen. Ass. 1962, 1968, 1970, 1974, to 2nd Afro-Asian Conf., Algeria 1965, to SEATO Council 1966; Kt. Grand Cordon of Order of White Elephant, Grand Cordon (Highest Class) of the Order of the Crown of Thailand, Commdr. Order of Chula Chomklao. *Leisure interests:* golf, bridge, tennis, swimming. *Address:* Department of Economic Affairs, Ministry of Foreign Affairs, Bangkok, Thailand. *Telephone:* 245 5442.

GUNDAREVA, Natalya Georgiyevna; Russian actress; b. 28 Aug. 1948, Moscow; m. Mikhail Filippov; ed. B. Shchukin Theatre School; with

Mayakovsky Theatre since 1971; cinema debut in 1973. *Films include:* Hello and Goodbye 1973, Autumn 1975, Sweet Woman 1977, Autumn Marathon 1979, Once Twenty years Later 1981, The Term of Prescription 1983, Dogs' Feast 1990, The Promised Heaven 1991, Chicken 1991, The Petersburg Secrets 1997, and many others; mem. State Duma (Parl.) (rep. of Political Movt. Women of Russia) 1993–96; U.S.S.R. People's Actress, U.S.S.R. State Prize 1984, State Prize of Russia 1981. *Address:* Mayakovsky Theatre, Bolshaya Nikitskaya str. 19, Moscow, Russia (Office), Tverskaya 42, Apt. 14, 125047 Moscow, Russia (Home). *Telephone:* 250 4355 (Home).

GUNGAADORJ, Sharavyn; Mongolian politician; b. 2 May 1935, Ikh Khet soum, Dornogobi Aimak (Prov.); ed. Acad. of Agriculture, U.S.S.R.; Chief Agronomist, "Amgalan" State farm; agronomist, Dept. of State Farms 1959–67; Instructor at the Mongolian People's Revolutionary Party (MPRP) Cen. Cttee. 1967–68; Deputy Minister for Agric.; Head of fodder farm in Zabhan Aimak (Prov.); Head of group, Ministry of Agric. 1968–80; First Deputy Minister for State Farms 1980–81; First Sec. Party Cttee. of Selenge Aimak (Prov.) 1981–86; Minister for Agric. 1986–90; Deputy Chair. Council of Ministers 1987–90; Alt. mem. MPRP Cen. Cttee. 1981–86, mem. 1986–; Deputy to Great People's Hural (Assembly) 1981–89, Chair. Council of Ministers April–Sept. 1990, Counsellor to the Pres., Chair. of the Civic Council attached to the Pres. 1990–91; Amb. to Democratic People's Repub. of Korea and Kazakhstan 1991–96; Pres. Co-operatives Asscn. 1997–. *Address:* c/o Ministry of External Relations, Ulan Bator, Mongolia. *Telephone:* 321870. *Telex:* 245.

GUNGAH, Dwarkanath, B.ED., M.SC.; Mauritian politician; b. 22 Jan. 1940, New Grove, Grand Port-Savanne Dist.; m.; three d.; ed. Univ. of Delhi and Punjab; worked at Coll. du St. Esprit, Quatre Bornes 1970–83; mem. Legis. Ass. 1976–; Minister of Housing, Lands and the Environment 1983–86, of Econ. Planning and Devt. 1986–87, of Trade and Shipping 1987–91, 1994–95, of Works 1991–94. *Address:* c/o Ministry of Trade and Shipping, 4th Floor, New Government Centre, Port Louis, Mauritius.

GUNN, (Alan) Richard, C.B.E.; Saint Vincent and the Grenadines diplomatist; b. 19 Jan. 1936; s. of Alan L. Gunn and Violet A. Hazell; m. Flora B. Richardson 1962; one s. two d.; ed. Boys' Grammar School, St. Vincent, W.I., Southern Coll. of Art, Portsmouth and Regent Street Polytechnic, London; Dir. Hazells 1964–74, Vincentian Newspapers Ltd. 1970–; Chair. and C.E.O., Property Investments Ltd. 1974–87; Pres. St. Vincent Chamber of Industry and Commerce 1984–86; Dir. Caribbean Asscn. of Industry and Commerce 1984–87; High Commr. for E. Caribbean States in U.K. 1987–94 (also Amb. accred. to Germany, France and EC 1990–94). *Leisure interest:* sailing. *Address:* Fairhall, P.O. Box 126, Saint Vincent and the Grenadines.

GUNN, John Charles, C.B.E., M.D., F.R.C.PSYCH.; British psychiatrist; b. 6 June 1937; m. Celia Willis 1959 (divorced 1986, died 1989); one s. one d.; m. 2nd Pamela Taylor 1989; ed. Brighton, Hove and Sussex Grammar School, Reigate Grammar School, Birmingham Univ. Medical School; Consultant Psychiatrist, Bethlem Maudsley Hosp. 1971–; Dir. Special Hosps. Research Unit 1975–78; Prof. of Forensic Psychiatry, Inst. of Psychiatry, Univ. of London 1978–; Chair. Research Cttee., Royal Coll. of Psychiatrists 1976–80; Chair. Academic Bd., Inst. of Psychiatry 1980–85; Chair. Forensic Specialist Cttee., Jt. Cttee. on Higher Psychiatric Training 1982–85; consultant European Cttee. for Prevention of Torture 1993–; Ed. Criminal Behaviour and Mental Health 1991–; mem. Ont. Govt. Enquiry in Oakridge, Ont., Canada 1984–85, Home Sec.'s Advisory Bd. on Restricted Patients 1982–91, Bethlem Maudsley Special Health Authority 1986–90, Royal Comm. on Criminal Justice 1991–93, Council, Royal Coll. of Psychiatrists 1997–; RMPA Bronze Medal 1970, H. B. Williams Travelling Professorship to Australasia 1985. *Publications:* Violence 1973, Epileptics in Prison 1977, Psychiatric Aspects of Imprisonment 1978, Current Research in Forensic Psychiatry and Psychology (Vols 1–3) 1982–85, Forensic Psychiatry: Clinical, Legal and Ethical Issues 1993. *Leisure interests:* theatre, cinema, opera, walking, photography. *Address:* Department of Forensic Psychiatry, Institute of Psychiatry, De Crespigny Park, Denmark Hill, London, SE5 8AF, England (Office). *Telephone:* 0171-701 7063.

GUNN, Sir Robert Norman, Kt., M.A., C.B.I.M.; British business executive; b. 16 Dec. 1925, Edinburgh; s. of Donald M. and Margaret (née Pallister) Gunn; m. Joan Parry 1956; one d.; ed. Royal High School, Edinburgh, Worcester Coll., Oxford; joined The Boots Co. 1951, Merchandise Buyer 1962–70, Head of Warehousing and Distribution 1971–73, Dir. of Property 1973–78, Dir. Industrial Div. 1979–83 (Man. Dir. 1980–83), Vice-Chair, and Chief Exec. The Boots Co. PLC 1983–85, Chair. and C.E.O. 1985–87, Chair. 1987–90; Dir. Foseco PLC 1984–91, East Midlands Electricity 1989–95, Nottingham Bldg. Soc. 1990–97; Chair. Further Educ. Funding Council for England 1992–97; mem. Council, CBI 1985–90, Business in the Community 1985–88, Scottish Business in the Community 1985–89, Polytechnics and Colls. Funding Council 1989–93, Higher Educ. Funding Council for England 1992–94; Deputy Lieut. (Notts.) 1995; Hon. LL.D. (Nottingham) 1993. *Leisure interests:* gardening, theatre. *Address:* Tor House, Pinfold Lane, Elston, Nr. Newark, Notts., England.

GUNN, Thomson William (Thom Gunn); British poet; b. 29 Aug. 1929; s. of Herbert Gunn and Ann Thomson; ed. Univ. Coll. School, Hampstead and Trinity Coll. Cambridge; moved to Calif. 1954; lecturer, later Assoc. Prof. Dept. of English, Univ. of Calif. (Berkeley) 1958–66, Visiting Lecturer 1975–90, Sr. Lecturer 1990–99; Forward Prize 1992, MacArthur Fellowship 1993. *Publications:* Poetry from Cambridge 1953, Fighting Terms 1954, The Sense of Movement 1957, My Sad Captains 1961, Selected Poems (with Ted Hughes) 1962, Five American Poets (ed. with Ted Hughes) 1962, Positives (with Ander Gunn) 1966, Touch 1967, Poems 1950–66: a selection 1969, Moly 1971, Jack Straw's Castle and other poems 1976, Selected Poems 1979, The Passages of Joy 1982, The Occasions of Poetry (ed. Clive Wilmer) 1982, The Man with Night Sweats 1992, Collected Poems 1993, Shelf Life 1994. *Leisure interests:* cheap thrills. *Address:* 1216 Cole Street, San Francisco, CA 94117, U.S.A.

GUNN, Sir William Archer, A.C., K.B.E., C.M.G.; Australian company director and grazier; b. 1 Feb. 1914, Goondiwindi, Queensland; s. of the late Walter Gunn and Doris Isabel Gunn; m. Mary Phillipa Haydon 1939; one s. two d.; ed. The King's School, Parramatta, New South Wales; Chair. Australian Wool Bd. 1963–72, Int. Wool Secr. Bd. 1961–73, Queensland Advisory Bd., Devt. Finance Corpn. 1962–72; Chair. Gunn Devt. Pty. Ltd., Eagle Corpn. Ltd., Cattle Investments Ltd., Livestock Man. Pty. Ltd., Moline Pastoral Co. Pty. Ltd., Roper Valley Pty. Ltd., Coolibah Pastoral Co. Pty. Ltd., Mataranka Pty. Ltd., Unibeef Australia Pty. Ltd.; Dir. Rothmans of Pall Mall (Australia) Ltd., Grazcos Co-operative Ltd., Clausen Steamship Co. (Australia) Pty. Ltd., Walter Reid & Co. Ltd., Gunn Rural Man. Pty. Ltd.; mem. Commonwealth Bank Bd. 1952–59, Faculty of Veterinary Science, Univ. of Queensland 1953–, Reserve Bank Bd. 1959–, Australian Meat Bd. 1953–66, Australian Wool Bureau 1951–63 (Chair. 1958–63), Australian Woolgrowers Council 1947–60 (Chair. 1955–58), Graziers Fed. Council of Australia 1950–60 (Pres. 1951–54), Australian Woolgrowers and Graziers Council 1960–65, Export Devt. Council 1962–65, Exec. Council, United Graziers Asscn. of Queensland 1944–69 (Vice-Pres. 1947–51, Pres. 1951–59), Australian Wool Testing Authority 1958–63, C.S.I.R.O. State Cttee. 51-68, Australian Wool Corpn. 1973; Chair. The Wool Bureau Inc. New York 1962–69, etc.; Trustee Queensland Cancer Fund; Golden Fleece Achievement Award (Nat. Asscn. of Wool Manufacturers of America) 1962; Award of the Golden Ram (Nat. Wool Growers' Asscn. of S. Africa) 1973.

GUNNARSSON, Birgir Ísleifur; Icelandic politician, lawyer and banker; b. 19 July 1936, Reykjavík; s. of Gunnar Espólín Benediktsson and Jorunn Ísleifsdóttir; m. Sonja Backman 1956; ed. Univ. of Iceland; Advocate to lower courts 1962, Supreme Court 1967; Leader Heimdallur Youth Soc. 1959–62; Sec.-Gen. Youth Fed. of Independence Party 1959–62; mem. Reykjavík City Council 1962–82; Mayor of Reykjavík 1972–78; M.P. for Reykjavík 1979–91; Second Deputy Speaker of Althing 1983–87; Minister for Culture and Educ. 1987–88; Chair. Cttee. on Heavy Industry 1983–87; mem. Bd. Nat. Power Co. 1965–91, Civil Aviation Bd. 1984–87; Gov. Cen. Bank of Iceland 1991–. *Leisure interests:* music, outdoor life. *Address:* Central Bank of Iceland, Kalkofnsvegur 1, 150 Reykjavík, Iceland.

GUNNELL, Sally, O.B.E.; British athlete (retd.); b. 29 July 1966, Chigwell, Essex; m. Jon Bigg 1992; one d.; specializes in hurdles; coached by Bruce Longdon; mem. Essex Ladies Athletic Club; competed 400-metre hurdles Olympic Games, Seoul 1988, Gold Medal, Barcelona 1992; second 400-metre hurdles World Championship, Tokyo 1991; Bronze Medal 400-metre relay, Olympic Games, Barcelona 1992; Women's Team Captain Olympic Games, Barcelona 1992; Gold Medal, 400-metre hurdle, World Championships 1993 (world record); Gold Medal 400-metre hurdles European Championships, Helsinki 1994; Gold Medal 400-metre hurdles Commonwealth Games, Canada 1994, retd. 1997; now works as TV presenter. *Publication:* Running Tall (with Christopher Priest) 1994. *Address:* 18 Shepherd's Croft, Brighton, E. Sussex, England.

GUNSON, Ameral Blanche Tregurtha; British classical singer; b. 25 Oct. 1948, London; d. of Charles Cumbria and Auriol Cornwall; m. 1st Maurice Powell 1969 (divorced 1974); m. 2nd Philip Kay 1979; two s.; ed. Convent of Jesus and Mary, London, and Guildhall School of Music and Drama; freelance singing career 1972–74, with BBC Singers 1976–80; solo singing career in Britain and abroad, Proms Seasons 1979, 1985, 1988, 1989, 1990; Assoc. Guildhall School of Music and Drama; Gramophone Award for recording of Peter Grimes 1997; Lubslith Asscn. (Finland) Award for vocal teaching 1997. *Leisure interests:* gardening, reading, walking, Russian music, relaxation. *Address:* 40 Brooklands Way, Redhill, Surrey, RH1 2BW, England. *Telephone:* (01737) 762726.

GUNTHER, Gerald, M.A., LL.B.; American professor of law and writer; b. 26 May 1927, Usingen im Taunus, Germany; s. of Otto Gutenstein and Minna Gutenstein; m. Barbara Kelsky 1949; two s.; ed. Brooklyn Coll., Columbia Univ. New York, Harvard Law School; law clerk to Learned Hand, U.S. Court of Appeals for Second Circuit 1953–54, to Chief Justice Earl Warren, U.S. Supreme Court 1954–55; Prof. of Law, Columbia Law School 1956–62; Prof. of Law, Stanford Univ. Law School 1962–; William Nelson Cromwell Prof. of Law 1972–95, Prof. Emer. 1995–; many visiting professorships and lectures; specializes in constitutional law and legal history; Fellow Center for Advanced Study in Behavioral Sciences 1969–70; Consultant, Ford Foundation 1974–80; mem. American Law Inst., American Philosophical Soc.; Fellow American Acad. of Arts and Sciences; Guggenheim Fellow 1962–63; 5 hon. degrees. *Publications:* Learned Hand: The Man and the Judge 1994, Individual Rights in Constitutional Law (5th edn.) 1992, Constitutional Law (13th edn., with K. M. Sullivan) 1997; ed. and contrib. several other works; many articles in legal and other publs. *Leisure interests:* reading, arts. *Address:* Stanford Law School, Stanford University, Stanford, CA 94305, U.S.A. *Telephone:* (650) 723-4447. *Fax:* (650) 725-0253.

GUO BOXIONG, Lieut.-Gen.; Chinese army officer; b. 1942, Liquan Co., Shaanxi Prov.; joined PLA 1961; joined CCP 1963; Divisional Chief-of-Staff; Army Chief-of-Staff; Deputy Chief-of-Staff Lanzhou Mil. Area Command; Army Group Commdr. 1990; Vice-Commdr. Beijing Mil. Area Command; mem. 15th CCP Cen. Cttee. 1997–. *Address:* Beijing Military Area Command Headquarters, Beijing, People's Republic of China.

GUO CHAOREN; Chinese party official and journalist; b. 1934, Guangji Co., Hubei Prov.; ed. Dept. of Chinese Language and Literature, Beijing Univ.; joined CCP 1980; Deputy Dir.-Gen. Xinhua News Agency 1984–92, (Dir.-Gen. 1997–), Party Group Sec. 1992–; Vice-Chair. All-China Journalists' Asscn.; mem. 14th CCP Cen. Cttee. 1992–97, Cen. Leading Group for Propaganda and Thought; mem. 15th Cen. Cttee. CCP 1997–. *Address:* Xinhua News Agency, 57 Xuanwumen Xidajie, Beijing 100803, People's Republic of China.

GUO DONGPO; Chinese politician; b. Aug. 1937, Jiangdu Co., Jiangsu Prov.; ed. Beijing Foreign Trade Inst.; joined CCP 1960; Vice-Chair. China Council for the Promotion of Int. Trade 1982; Dir. Macau Br. of Xinhua News Agency 1990; Vice-Dir. Drafting Cttee. of the Basic Law of Macau Special Admin. Zone 1990; mem. CPPCC 1991; alt. mem. 14th CCP Cen. Cttee. 1992; Dir. Office of Overseas Chinese Affairs of the State Council 1997–; mem. 15th CCP Cen. Cttee. 1997–. *Address:* Office of Overseas Chinese Affairs, State Council, Beijing, People's Republic of China.

GUO FENGMIN; Chinese diplomatist; b. 1930, Shantou City, Guangdong Prov.; ed. Tongji Univ., Shanghai; attaché Berne Embassy 1950–60; forced to work on a tea farm during Cultural Revolution 1966–73; Deputy Dir., Inst. of Foreign Affairs 1973–83; Dir. Dept. for West European Affairs 1983–85; Amb. to Fed. Repub. of Germany 1986–93; mem. Preliminary Working Cttee. of the Preparatory Cttee. of the Hong Kong Special Admin. Region 1994–. *Address:* c/o Ministry of Foreign Affairs, 225 Chaoyangmennei Daije, Dongsi, Beijing 100701, People's Republic of China.

GUO LIWEN; Chinese politician; b. 1920, Weixian, Hebei; joined CCP 1938; counsellor Chinese Embassies in Hungary, Guinea, Italy, France 1964–80; Sec. Chinese Women's Fed. 1980–82, First Sec. 1982–; Adviser All-China Fed. of Women Lawyers 1993–; mem. 12th CCP Cen. Cttee. 1982–87; Deputy Hubei Prov., mem. Law Cttee., Credentials Cttee., Standing Cttee. 7th NPC 1988–, Adviser Law Cttee. *Address:* Chinese Women's Federation, Beijing, People's Republic of China.

GUO MUSUN (Mooson Kwauk); Chinese academic; b. 9 May 1920, Hangyang; s. of Zung-Ung Kwauk and Za-Nan Chow; m. Huichun Kwei Kwauk 1950; two s. one d.; ed. Univ. of Shanghai, Princeton Univ., U.S.A.; Prof. Inst. of Chemical Metallurgy, Chinese Acad. of Sciences 1956, Dir. 1982–86, Emer. Dir. 1986–; Visiting Prof. Ohio State Univ. 1989; Vice-Pres. Chemical Industry and Eng. Soc. of China 1978–; Davis-Swindin Memorial Lecturer, Loughborough Univ., England 1985; Visiting Prof. Virginia Polytechnic Inst. and State Univ. 1986–87; mem. Chinese Acad. of Sciences 1981–; Pres. Chinese Soc. of Particuology 1986–; Corresp. mem. Swiss Acad. of Eng. Sciences 1997–; Distinguished Scholar, CSCPRC Program, U.S. Nat. Acad. of Science 1984; Danckwerts Memorial Lecturer, Inst. of Dirs., London 1989; Int. Fluidization Award 1989. *Publications:* Fluidization: Idealized and Bubbleless, with Applications 1992, Fast Fluidization 1994, Geometric Mobiles 1998. *Leisure interests:* kites, mobiles. *Address:* Institute of Chemical Metallurgy, Chinese Academy of Sciences, Beijing, 100080, People's Republic of China. *Telephone:* 10-6255-4241 (Office); 10-6255-4050 (Home). *Fax:* 10-6255-8065 (Office).

GUO PINGTAN; Chinese politician; b. 1933, Taiwan; ed. Waseda Univ., Tokyo; staff mem. of China Travel Service 1983–; Vice-Pres., Fed. of Taiwan Compatriots (now Fed. for Reunification of the Motherland) 1985–, All-China Fed. of Taiwan 1985–. *Address:* China Travel Service, Changan Dejie, Beijing, People's Republic of China.

GUO XIEXIAN; Chinese chemist; b. 9 Feb. 1925, Hangzhou City, Zhejiang Prov.; m. Liang Yuan 1950; two s. one d.; Deputy Dir., Chemical Physics Inst. 1982–; mem. Dept. of Chemistry Academia Sinica 1985–; Hon. State Prize of Science of China 1986. *Address:* Chemical Physics Institute, Dalian City, Liaoning Province, People's Republic of China. *Telephone:* 0411-3631730. *Fax:* 0411-3632426.

GUO ZHENQIAN; Chinese party and government official; b. Feb. 1933, Loning Co., Henan Prov.; ed. Trade Dept. People's Univ. of China; joined CCP 1949; Vice-Gov. Hubei Prov. 1983–84, Acting Gov. Jan. 1986, Gov. May–Oct. 1986; Dir. Hubei Branch People's Construction Bank of China 1983–84; Deputy Sec. Hubei Prov. CCP Cttee. 1985–; Gov. Hubei Provincial People's Govt. 1986–90; First Vice-Pres. People's Bank of China 1990–93; First Deputy Auditor-Gen. of People's Repub. of China 1993–94, Auditor-Gen. 1994–98; Sr. Economist, concurrently Prof., People's Univ. of China; Pres. Securities Asscn. of China 1991–; mem. 13th and 14th CCP Cen. Cttee. 1985–98. *Leisure interests:* reading, swimming, tennis, table tennis. *Address:* National Audit Office of the People's Republic of China, 1 Beiluyuan, Zhanlan Road, Xicheng District, People's Republic of China. *Telephone:* (10) 8301214, 8301216. *Fax:* (10) 8330958.

GUPTA, Sunil Kumar; Bangladeshi politician; b. 13 Oct. 1928, Sihipasha; s. of late Akhya Kumar Gupta; m. Kamala Gupta 1958; four s. two d.; ed. Brajo Mohan Coll., Barisal; mem. East Pakistan Democratic Party 1950, Vice-Pres. Barisal Dist. Cttee.; mem. Nat. Awami Party, then Vice-Pres. Barisal Dist. Cttee. 1957–73, Vice-Pres. Cen. Cttee. 1973; fmr. mem. Cen. Cttee. Bangladesh Nationalist Party; Minister of State for Petroleum and Mineral Resources 1979, 1985, for Ministry of Communications 1985–86, Minister of Textiles 1986–88, of Youth and Sports March–Dec. 1988, of Fisheries and Livestock 1989–90. *Leisure interests:* reading, gardening and music. *Address:* c/o Ministry of Fisheries and Livestock, Dhaka, Bangladesh.

GUPTE, Shridhar, PH.D.; Indian university vice-chancellor and professor of geography; b. 4 Feb. 1933, Bombay; s. of Shri Chandrashekhar Trimbak Gupte; m. 1961; two s.; lecturer in Geography, Univ. of Poona, Maharashtra 1959–77, Reader 1977–79, Prof. 1979–, Vice-Chancellor 1989–95; Best Teacher's Award (Poona Municipal Corpn.) 1982. *Leisure interests:* music and reading. *Address:* Department of Geography, University of Poona, Ganeshkhind, Pune-411 007 (Maharashtra), India. *Telephone:* 330765 (Home).

GURCHENKO, Ludmila Markovna; Russian actress; b. 12 Nov. 1935, Kharkov; ed. Moscow All-Union Inst. of Cinema; has worked in films since 1956; People's Artist of U.S.S.R. 1983. *Major roles include:* Lena in Carnival Night, Sonya in Baltic Sky, Anna Georgevna in Old Walls, Tamara Vasilevna in Five Evenings, Rita in Mechanic Gavrilov's Favourite Woman (Best Actress Award, Manila Film Festival), Vera in Station for Two (Best Actress Award, 16th All-Union Cinema Festival Leningrad 1983), Mrs Chirley in Ideal Husband, Raisa in Love and Doves, Larisa in Dreams and Waking Flights, Marty in Secret of Her Youth; *appeared in films:* Applause, Applause, Forgive Us, Stepmother Russia, White Clothes, The Sex Tale, The Pretender, The Burn, Listen, Fellini, and others; concert appearances as a singer. *Publications:* My Grown-up Childhood 1980, Applause, Applause. *Address:* Trekhprudny per. 5/15, Apt. 22, 103001 Moscow, Russia. *Telephone:* 209-68-37.

GURDON, Sir John Bertrand, Kt., D.PHIL., F.R.S.; British cell biologist; b. 2 Oct. 1933, Hampshire; s. of W. N. and E. M. Gurdon (née Byass); m. Jean Elizabeth Margaret Curtis 1964; one s. one d.; ed. Edgeborough School, Eton Coll., Univ. of Oxford; Beit Memorial Fellow 1958–61; Gosney Research Fellow, Calif. Inst. of Tech., U.S.A. 1961–62; Research Fellow, Univ. of Oxford 1962–72, Departmental Demonstrator 1963–64, Lecturer, Dept. of Zoology 1966–72; Visiting Research Fellow, Carnegie Inst., Baltimore, Md., U.S.A. 1965; mem. Scientific Staff, Medical Research Council, Molecular Biology Lab., Univ. of Cambridge 1973–83, Head of Cell Biology Div. 1979–83, John Humphrey Plummer Prof. of Cell Biology 1983–; Master, Magdalene Coll. Cambridge 1995–; Fellow of Churchill Coll., Cambridge 1973–95; Croonian Lecturer, Royal Soc. 1976; Dunham Lecturer, Harvard Medical School 1974; Carter-Wallace Lecturer, Princeton Univ. 1978; Fellow Eton Coll. 1978–93; Hon. Student, Christ Church, Oxford 1985; Fullerian Prof. of Physiology and Comparative Anatomy, Royal Inst. 1985–91; Pres. Int. Soc. for Developmental Biology 1990–94; Hon. Foreign mem. American Acad. of Arts and Sciences 1978; Foreign Assoc., N.A.S., U.S.A. 1980, Belgian Royal Acad. of Science, Letters and Fine Arts 1984, French Acad. of Sciences 1990; Foreign mem. American Philosophical Soc. 1983; Gov. The Wellcome Trust 1995–; Hon. D.Sc. (Chicago) 1978, (Oxford) 1988, (Hull) 1998; Hon. Dr. (Paris) 1982; Albert Brachet Prize (Belgian Royal Acad.) 1968, Scientific Medal of Zoological Soc. 1968, Feldberg Foundation Award 1975, Paul Ehrlich Award 1977, Nessim Habif Prize (Univ. of Geneva) 1979, CIBA Medal, Biochem. Soc. 1981, Comfort Crookshank Award for Cancer Research 1983, William Bate Hardy Triennial Prize (Cambridge Philosophy Soc.) 1983, Charles Léopold Mayer Prize (Acad. des Sciences, France) 1984, Ross Harrison Prize (Int. Soc. for Devt. Biology) 1985, Royal Medal (Royal Soc.) 1985, Emperor Hirohito Int. Biology Prize 1987, Wolf Prize for Medicine (jtly. with Edward B. Lewis, q.v.) 1989. *Publications:* Control of Gene Expression in Animal Development 1974. *Leisure interests:* skiing, horticulture, lepidoptera. *Address:* The Master's Lodge, Magdalene College, Cambridge, CB3 0AG, England. *Telephone:* (01223) 32100.

GURFINKEL, Viktor Semenovich; Russian physiologist; b. 2 April 1922; ed. Kyrgyz State Medical Inst.; during World War II head. div. of blood transfusion 19th Army 1941–45, chief dr. hospital 1946–48; sr. researcher, head of lab. Inst. of Orthopaedics 1949–58; head of lab. Inst. of Experimental Biology and Medical Siberian br. U.S.S.R. Acad. of Sciences 1949–58; head of lab. Inst. of Biophysics U.S.S.R. Acad. of Sciences 1960–67; head of lab. Inst. for Information Transmission Problems, Russian Acad. of Sciences; corresp. mem. U.S.S.R. (now Russian) Acad. of Sciences 1987, mem. 1994; research in physiology of movts., space physiology and medicine; author of 3 books and numerous articles in scientific journals; U.S.S.R. State Prize, R. Dow Prize (USA), Humboldt Foundation Award. *Leisure interests:* fishing. *Address:* Institute for Information Transmission Problems, Russian Academy of Sciences, Bolshoi Karetny per. 19, 101447 Moscow, Russia. *Telephone:* (095) 208 2895 (Office); 159-91-90 (Home). *Fax:* (095) 209 0579.

GURGULINO de SOUZA, Heitor, B.SC., LIC.; Brazilian educator and scientist; b. 1 Aug. 1928, São Lourenço, Minas Gerais; s. of Arthur Gurgulino de Souza and Catarina Sachser de Souza; m. Lilian Maria Quilici; ed. Univ. of Mackenzie, São Paulo, Aeronautics Inst. of Tech., Univ. of Kansas, U.S.A., Univ. of São Paulo; Program Specialist, Interamerican Science Program, Pan American Union, Wash. D.C. 1962–64; Head, Unit of Educ. and Research, Dept. of Scientific Affairs, OAS, Wash. D.C. 1964–69; Rector, Fed. Univ. of São Carlos, State of São Paulo 1970–74; Dir., Dept. of Univ.

Affairs (DAU), Ministry of Educ. and Culture, Brasilia 1972–74; Chair. Interamerican Cttee. on Science and Tech. (CICYT) of the Council for Educ., Culture, OAS, Wash. D.C. 1974–77; Dir. CNPq (Nat. Council for Scientific and Tech. Devt.), Brasilia 1975–78, Special Adviser to Pres. 1979–80; Vice Pres., Int. Asscn. Univ. Pres. (IAUP) 1985–87; Pres., Grupo Universitario Latinoamericano (GULERPE), Caracas 1985–87; Rector, UN Univ., Tokyo 1987–97; Special Adviser to Dir.-Gen. for Higher Education, UNESCO, Paris 1997–; Vice-Pres. Fed. Council of Educ. of Brazil (CFE), mem. 1982–88; mem. Order of Educational Merit, MEC, Brasilia 1973, Order of Rio Branco, MRE, Brasilia 1974. *Publications:* Gamma-rays from the proton bombardment of Natural Silicon 1957, Computers and Higher Education in Brazil 1984 (articles); (co-ed.) Science Policy 1974; author of chapter on Brazil in International Encyclopedia of Higher Education 1978. *Leisure interests:* sailing, swimming, music. *Address:* c/o Director-General for Higher Education, UNESCO, 7 place de Fontenoy, 75352 Paris, France (Office); S.Q.S. 116 Bloco B, Apto. 501, Edificio Cap Ferrat, Brasilia, D.F., CEP 70386-020, Brazil (Home). *Telephone:* (61) 3461414 (Home). *Fax:* (61) 3460938 (Home).

GURLEY BROWN, Helen; American author and editor; b. 18 Feb. 1922, Green Forest, Ark.; d. of Ira M. and Cleo (Sisco) Gurley; m. David Brown 1959; ed. Texas State Coll. for Women, Woodbury Coll.; Exec. Sec. Music Corpn. of America 1942–45, William Morris Agency 1945–47; Copywriter Foote, Cone & Belding advertising agency, Los Angeles 1948–58; advertisement writer and account exec. Kenyon & Eckhard advertising agency, Hollywood 1958–62; Ed.-in-Chief Cosmopolitan magazine 1965–97, Editorial Dir. Cosmopolitan Int. Edns. 1972–, Ed.-in-Chief 1997–; mem. Authors League of America, American Soc. of Magazine Eds., AFTRA; Hon. LL.D. (Woodbury) 1987; Hon. D.Litt. (Long Island) 1993; Francis Holm Achievement Award 1956–59, Univ. of S. Calif. School of Journalism 1971, Special Award for Editorial Leadership of American Newspaper Woman's Club 1972, Distinguished Achievement Award in Journalism, Stanford Univ. 1977, New York Women in Communications Inc. Award 1985, Publrs.' Hall of Fame 1988, Henry Johnson Fisher Award, Magazine Publrs. of America 1995; establishment of Helen Gurley Brown Research Professorship at Northwestern Univ. 1986. *Publications:* Sex and the Single Girl 1962, Sex and the Office 1965, Outrageous Opinions 1967, Helen Gurley Brown's Single Girl's Cook Book 1969, Sex and the New Single Girl 1970, Having It All 1982, The Late Show: A Semiwild but Practical Survival Guide for Women over 50 1993, The Writer's Rules: The Power of Positive Prose 1998. *Address:* Cosmopolitan, 959 8th Avenue, New York, NY 10019 (Office); 1 West 81st Street, New York, NY 10024, U.S.A. (Home).

GURNEY, Albert R., M.F.A.; American playwright; b. 1 Nov. 1930, Buffalo, N.Y.; s. of Albert R. Gurney and Marion (née Spaulding) Gurney; m. Mary F. Goodyear 1957; two s. two d.; joined M.I.T., Faculty of Humanities 1960–96, Prof. 1970–96. *Publications include:* plays: The Dining Room, The Cocktail Hour, Love Letters, Later Life, A Cheever Evening, Sylvia, Overtime; Let's Do It!, The Guest Lecturer, Labor Day; novels: The Gospel According to Joe, Entertaining Strangers, The Snow Ball. *Address:* 40 Wellers Bridge Road, Roxbury, CT 06783, U.S.A. *Telephone:* (203) 354-3692. *Fax:* (203) 354-3692.

GURRÍA TREVIÑO, José Angel, B.ECON., M.FIN.; Mexican politician; b. 8 May 1950, Tampico, Tamaulipas State; s. of Francisco José Lacroix Gurria and Carmen Humana Treviño; m. Lulu Ululani Quintana Pali 1973; one s. two d.; Dir. Gen. for Public Credit, Ministry of Finance 1983–88, Under Sec. for Int. Financial Affairs 1989–92; Pres. and C.E.O. Nat. Bank for Foreign Trade (Bancomext) 1993, Nac. Financiera 1993–94; Sec. for Foreign Affairs Nat. Exec. Cttee. Institutional Revolutionary Party (PRI) April–Nov. 1994; Minister of Foreign Affairs 1994; decorations from several countries. *Publications:* The Politics of External Debt 1994 and articles on Mexican economy. *Leisure interests:* tennis, reading, swimming. *Address:* c/o Secretariat of State for Foreign Affairs, Avda. Ricardo Flores Magón 2, 4°, Col. Nonoalco Tlatelolco, 09600 Mexico City, Mexico.

GUSAROV, Yevgeny Petrovich; Russian diplomatist; b. 30 July 1950, Moscow; m.; one s.; ed. Moscow State Inst. of Int. Relations; on staff Ministry of Foreign Affairs 1972–; advisor U.S.S.R. Gen. Consulate, Montreal 1972–77; attaché, Third, Second Sec. Second European Dept. Ministry of Foreign Affairs 1977–81; Second, First Sec., Counsellor U.S.S.R. Embassy to Canada 1981–86; Head of sector, Deputy Head Second European Dept. 1986–88; Deputy Head Div. (then Dept.) of U.S.A. and Canada 1988–90, Deputy Head Dept. of Security and Co-operation in Europe U.S.S.R. Ministry of Foreign Affairs 1990–92; Head Dept. of Europe Russian Ministry of Foreign Affairs 1992; Amb. to Repub. of S. Africa (also accred. to Lesotho) 1992–98; Dir. Dept. of All-European Co-operation, Ministry of Foreign Affairs 1998–. *Address:* Ministry of Foreign Affairs, Smolenskaya-Sennaya 32/34, Moscow, Russia.

GUSEV, Pavel Nikolayevich; Russian journalist; b. 1949; ed. Moscow Inst. of Geological Survey, Maxim Gorky Inst. of Literature; Komsomol work 1976–; First Sec. Komsomol Cttee. of Krasnaya Presnya Region of Moscow 1976–80; Exec. Cen. Komsomol Cttee. 1980–83; Ed.-in-Chief. Moskovsky Komsomolets (newspaper) 1983–; Minister Govt. of Moscow, Head Dept. of Information and Mass Media Jan.–Oct. 1992; press adviser to Mayor of Moscow 1992–95. *Address:* Moskovsky Komsomolets, 1905 Goda Str. 7, 123848 Moscow, Russia. *Telephone:* 259-50-36.

GUSINSKY, Vladimir Aleksandrovich; Russian banker; b. 6 Oct. 1952, Moscow; m. Yelena Gusinskaya; two s.; ed. Gubkin Moscow Inst. of Oil and Chem., A. Lunacharsky State Inst. of Theatre Art; Dir. cultural programme Moscow Festival of Youth and Students 1982–85; Dir. cultural programme Goodwill Games in Moscow 1985–86; f. co-operative Infex, later transformed into Holding Most, now comprising over 40 enterprises in the field of construction, construction materials production, real estate and trade operations, also Most-Bank est. 1991; owner maj. non-state TV company NTV, Segodnya (newspaper) 1992, radio station Ekho Moskvy, Obscheye Delo weekly, weekly TV programme 7 Days; Dir.-Gen. Holding Group Most 1989–97, concurrently Pres. Most-Bank 1992–97, Gen. Dir. Media-Most co. 1997–; Vice Pres. Asscn. of Russian Banks, Chair. Council of Authorized Banks of the Govt. of Moscow; Pres. Jewish Congress of Russia 1995. *Address:* Mostbank, Novy Arbat str. 36, 121205 Moscow, Russia. *Telephone:* (095) 202 9239, 290 7172 (Office). *Fax:* (095) 203 2976.

GUSTAFSSON, Lars Erik Einar, D.PHIL.; Swedish author, philosopher and educator; b. 17 May 1936, Västerås; s. of Einar Gustafsson and Margaretha Carlsson; m. Dena Alexandra Chasnoff 1982; two s. two d.; ed. Uppsala Univ.; Editor-in-Chief, Bonniers Litterära Magasin 1966–72; Research Fellow, Bielefeld Inst. of Advanced Studies 1980–81; Adjunct Prof. Univ. of Texas at Austin 1983–, Jamail Distinguished Prof. 1998–; Aby Warburg Foundation Prof., Hamburg 1997; mem. Akademie der Wissenschaften und der Literatur, Mainz, Akademie der Künste, Berlin, Royal Swedish Acad. of Eng.; Prix Charles Veillon, Heinrich Steffen Preis, Övralidspriset, Bellman Prize of Swedish Acad.; John Simon Guggenheim Memorial Fellow of Poetry 1993; Officier des Arts et des Lettres; Kommendör des Bundesverdienstzeichens. *Publications:* The Death of a Beekeeper 1978, Language and Lie 1978, Stories of Happy People 1981, Bernard Foy's Third Castle 1986, The Silence of the World before Bach (poems) 1988, Fyra Poeter 1988, Problemformuleringsprivilegiet 1989, Det sällsamma djuret från norr 1989, The Afternoon of a Tiler 1991, Historien med Hunden 1993, The Case with the Dog 1997. *Leisure interests:* painting, boating. *Address:* 2312 Tower Drive, Austin, TX 78203, U.S.A. *Telephone:* (512) 477-6859. *Fax:* (512) 472-6722.

GUSTAFSSON, Leif Axel, M.SC.; Swedish business executive; b. 2 Jan. 1940, Hofors; s. of Axel Gustafsson and Brita Brandström; m. Monica Stellan 1965; one s. one d.; ed. Royal Inst. of Tech.; operation engineer rolling mill, Hagfors (Uddeholm) 1966–69; rolling and steel mill man. SKF Steel, Hofors 1969–77; Man. Dir. Smedjebacken AB 1978–82; Man. Dir. Smedjebacken-Boxholm Stål AB 1982–87; Pres. and C.E.O. SSAB Swedish Steel AB 1987–. *Leisure interests:* hunting, sports. *Address:* SSAB Svensk Stål AB, P.O. Box 26 208, S-100 40 Stockholm, Sweden. *Telephone:* (8) 45 45 700.

GUSTOV, Vadim Anatolyevich; Russian politician; b. 26 Dec. 1948, Kalinino, Vladimir Region; m.; two c.; ed. Moscow State Inst. of Geological Prospecting, Leningrad Inst. of Politology; Head of uranium mines Navoi Metallurgy Factory, Uzbekistan 1971–77; Head of mine, Phosphorite Kingisepp, Leningrad Region 1977–78; instructor, Head of Div., Kingisepp City CP Cttee. 1978–86; First Deputy Chair. Kingisepp City Exec. Cttee. 1986–87; Second Sec. Kingisepp City CP Cttee. 1987–90; Chair. Kingisepp City Soviet 1990–91; Chair. Soviet of People's Deputies Leningrad Region 1991–93; mem. Council of Feds. of Russia, Chair. Cttee. on C.I.S. Cos. 1993–98; Gov. Leningrad Region 1996–98; First Deputy Chair., Govt. of Russian Fed. Sept. 1998–. *Leisure interests:* hunting, fiction, sports. *Address:* Parliament Buildings, Krasnopresnenskaya nab. 2, 103274 Moscow, Russia. *Telephone:* (095) 205 4203 (Office).

GUT, Rainer Emil; Swiss banker; b. 24 Sept. 1932, Baar; s. of Emil Anton and Rosa (Müller) Gut; m. Josephine Lorenz 1957; two s. two d.; ed. Cantonal School of Zug.; undertook professional training periods, France and England; N. American Rep. Union Bank of Switzerland, N.Y. 1963; Gen. Partner Lazard Frères & Co., N.Y. 1968; Chair. and C.E.O., Swiss American Corpn. (Crédit Suisse's U.S. investment banking affiliate) 1971; Deputy Gen. Man., Head Office Crédit Suisse, Zürich 1973, mem. Exec. Bd. Crédit Suisse 1957, Speaker of Exec. Bd. 1977, Pres. 1982, Chair. Bd. of Dirs. of Crédit Suisse 1983–, now Crédit Suisse Group 1996–; Pres., Chair. Bd. of Dirs. CS Holding Zürich 1986; Vice-Chair. Bd. of Dirs. Nestlé S.A., Vevey, Suisse Re, Zürich; mem. Bd. of Dirs. Ciba-Geigy, Basel, Daimler-Benz Holding, Zürich, Sofina S.A., Brussels, Union Carbide Corpn., Danbury, Conn., U.S.A.; Ordre des Arts et des Lettres 1986, Commdr. Verdienstkreuz (Germany) 1988. *Address:* Crédit Suisse, 8070 Zürich, Switzerland. *Telephone:* 01-333-11-11.

GUTERRES, António Manuel de Oliveira; Portuguese politician; b. 30 April 1949, Lisbon; m. (wife deceased); one s. one d.; ed. Inst. Superior Técnico; trained as electrical engineer; joined Socialist Party 1974; Chief of Staff to Sec. of State for Industry 1974–75; fmr. asst. to several cabinet ministers; Pres. Municipal Ass. of Fundão 1979–95; Deputy to Ass. of the Repub. 1976–83, 1985–, Pres. several Parl. Comms., Pres. Socialist Parl. Group 1988–91; Strategic Devt. Dir. I.P.E. (State Investment and Participation Agency) 1984–85; mem. Council of State 1991–; Leader of Socialist Party Feb. 1992–; Vice-Pres. Socialist Int. Sept. 1992–; Prime Minister of Portugal 1995–; Co-ordinator Tech. Electoral Comm. 1980–87; f., Vice-Pres. Portuguese Asscn. for the Defence of the Consumer 1973–74; mem. Asscn. for Econ. and Social Devt. 1970–96. *Publications:* various articles for newspapers and magazines. *Leisure interests:* travel, history (especially Middle Ages), cinema, opera. *Address:* Office of the Prime Minister, Presidencia do Conselho de Ministros, Rua da Imprensa à Estrela 2, 1200 Lisbon, Portugal. *Fax:* (1) 3951616.

GUTERSON, David, B.A., M.F.A.; American author; b. 4 May 1956, Seattle; s. of Murray Guterson and Shirley (Zak) Guterson; m. Robin Ann Radwick 1979; three s. one d.; ed. Univ. of Washington, Brown Univ.; fmr. high school English teacher; sometime Contributing Ed. Harper's; PEN/Faulkner Award, Barnes & Noble Discovery Award, Pacific N.W. Booksellers Award (all for Snow Falling on Cedars 1995). *Publications:* The Country Ahead of Us, The Country Behind (short stories) 1989, Family Matters: Why Home Schooling Makes Sense 1992, Snow Falling on Cedars 1995. *Address:* c/o Georges Borchardt Inc., 136 East 57th Street, New York, NY 10020, U.S.A.

GUTFREUND, Herbert, PH.D., F.R.S.; British academic; b. 21 Oct. 1921, Vienna, Austria; s. of Paul and Clara (née Pisko) Gutfreund; m. Mary Kathelen Davies 1958; two s. one d.; ed. Vienna and Cambridge Univs.; Research Fellow, Univ. of Cambridge 1947–57; with Agricultural Research Council, Univ. of Reading 1957–64; Visiting Prof., Univ. of Calif. 1965, Max Planck Inst., Germany 1966, Dir. Molecular Enzymology Lab. and Prof. of Physical Biochem., Univ. of Bristol 1967–86, Prof. Emer. 1986–; part-time Scholar in Residence, Nat. Insts. of Health, Bethesda, U.S.A. 1986–89; Scientific mem. (external) Max Planck Inst. for Medical Research 1987–; Fogarty Scholar, Nat. Insts. of Health, Washington 1987. *Publications:* An Introduction to the Study of Enzymes 1966, Enzymes: Physical Principles 1972, Molecular Evolution 1981, Biothermodynamics 1983, Kinetics for the Life Sciences: Receptors, Transmitters and Catalysts 1995. *Leisure interests:* hill walking, reading. *Address:* 12A The Avenue, Bristol, BS9 1PA, England.

GUTH, Alan Harvey, PH.D.; American physicist; b. 27 Feb. 1947, New Brunswick, N.J.; s. of Hyman Guth and Elaine Cheiten; m. Susan Tisch 1971; one s. one d.; ed. Mass. Inst. of Tech.; Instructor Princeton Univ. 1971–74; Research Assoc. Columbia Univ. New York 1974–77, Cornell Univ. 1977–79, Stanford Linear Accelerator Center, Calif. 1979–80; Assoc. Prof. of Physics, M.I.T. 1980–86, Prof. 1986–89, Jerrold Zacharias Prof. of Physics 1989–91; Victor F. Weisskopf Prof. of Physics 1992–; Physicist, Harvard-Smithsonian Center for Astrophysics 1984–89, Visiting Scientist 1990–91; Alfred P. Sloan Fellow 1981; Fellow, American Physics Soc. (Chair. Astrophysics Div. 1989–90), AAAS, American Acad. of Arts and Sciences; mem. N.A.S., American Astronomical Soc., Rennie Taylor Award of the American Tentative Soc. 1991, Julius E. Lilienfeld Prize of the American Physical Soc. 1992. *Address:* Center for Theoretical Physics, Massachusetts Institute of Technology, 77 Massachussets Ave, Cambridge, MA 02139, U.S.A. *Telephone:* (617) 253-6265.

GUTH, Wilfried, DR.RER.POL.; German banker; b. 8 July 1919, Erlangen; mem. Supervisory Bd., Deutsche Bank AG, Shareholders' Cttee. of Robert Bosch Industrietreuhand KG; Deputy Chair. Supervisory Bd. (DEG), German Investment and Devt. Co. *Address:* Deutsche Bank AG, 60262 Frankfurt/Main, Germany.

GUTHARDT, Helmut; German banking executive; b. 8 June 1934, Breuna; s. of Wilhelm and Sophie (née Schmale) Guthardt; m. 1st Margret Weymann 1956; one s. two d.; m. 2nd Marga Ackermann 1984; studied Frankfurt Banking Acad. 1958–60; Man. Dir. Raiffeisen-Rechenzentrum GmbH, Kassel 1963–70, Raiffeisenbank Kurhessen eG, Kassel 1964–65, Raiffeisen-Zentralbank Kurhessen AG, Kassel 1965–70; Man. Dir. Deutsche Genossenschaftsbank 1970–73, Vice-Chair. Bd. of Man. Dirs. 1973–81, Chair. 1981; Dir. several other cos.

GUTHRIE, Gen. Sir Charles (Ronald Llewelyn), G.C.B., L.V.O., O.B.E., ADC(GEN.); British army officer; b. 17 Nov. 1938, London; s. of late Ronald Guthrie and Nina Llewelyn; m. Catherine Worrall 1971; two s.; ed. Harrow School and Royal Mil. Acad. Sandhurst; commissioned Welsh Guards 1959; served BAOR, Aden; 22 SAS Regt. 1965–69; Staff Coll. 1972; Mil. Asst. (GSO2) to Chief of Gen. Staff, Ministry of Defence 1973–74; Brigade Maj. Household Div. 1976–77; Commdg. Officer, 1st Bn. Welsh Guards, Berlin and N. Ireland 1977–80; Col. Gen. Staff, Mil. Operations, Ministry of Defence 1980–82; Commdr. British Forces New Hebrides 1980; 4th Armoured Brigade 1982–84; Chief of Staff 1st (British) Corps 1984–86; Gen. Officer Commdg. N.E. Dist. and Commdr. 2nd Infantry Div. 1986–87; Asst. Chief of Gen. Staff, Ministry of Defence 1987–89; Commdr., 1st (British) Corps 1989–91; Commdr., Northern Army Group 1992–93 and C.-in-C. British Army of the Rhine 1992–94; Col. Commdt. Intelligence Corps 1986–96; A.D.C. Gen. to H.M. the Queen 1993–; Chief of Gen. Staff 1994–97, of the Defence Staff 1997–; Freeman of City of London. *Leisure interests:* tennis, skiing, travel. *Address:* Ministry of Defence, Whitehall, London, SW1A 2HB, England.

GUTHRIE, Roy David (Gus), A.M., D.SC.; Australian fmr. vice-chancellor and consultant; b. 29 March 1934, England; s. of David Ephraim Guthrie and Ethel (née Kimmins) Guthrie; m. 2nd Lyn Fielding 1982; three s. from first m.; ed. King's Coll., London Univ.; Research Officer, Shirley Inst. 1958–60; Asst Lecturer then Lecturer, Univ. of Leicester 1963–73; Lecturer then Reader, Univ. of Sussex 1963–73; Foundation Prof. Griffith Univ., Australia 1973–81, Pro-Vice-Chancellor 1980–81, Emer. Prof. 1981–; Vice-Chancellor, Univ. of Tech., Sydney 1986–96; Provost Insearch Educ. 1996–97; Prin. Consultant, Gus Guthrie Consulting Pty. Ltd.; Sec.-Gen. Royal Soc. of Chem. 1982–85. *Publications:* Introduction to Carbohydrate Chemistry (with J. Honeyman), over 130 research papers in learned chemical journals. *Leisure interests:* gardening, theatre, croquet, Tai Chi. *Address:* P.O. Box 403, Pymble, N.S.W. 2073, Australia.

GUTIÉRREZ, Gustavo, D.THEOL.; Peruvian ecclesiastic; b. 8 June 1928, Lima; ed. Univ. Nacional Mayor de San Marcos, Lima, Univ. Catholique de Louvain, Univ. de Lyon, Univ. Gregoriana and Inst. Catholique de Paris; ordained priest 1959; Adviser, Nat. Union of Catholic Students 1960–; Prof. Catholic Univ. of Lima 1960–; mem. Pastoral-Theological team, Latin American Conf. of Catholic Bishops (CELAM) 1967–68; Bd. Dir. Inst. Bartolomé Las Casas-Rímac 1974–; Assoc. Vicar, Rímac, Lima 1980–; Visiting Prof. and lecturer at univs., colls. and seminaries in U.S.A. and elsewhere; mem. EATWOT (Ecumenical Asscn. of Third World Theologians); Dr. h.c. (Nijmegen) 1979, (Tübingen) 1985, (King's Coll., U.S.A.) 1989, (Haverford Coll., U.S.A.) 1990, (Fribourg, Germany) 1990, (San Marcos, Lima) 1991, (Montreal) 1993, (Universidad Nacional de Ingeniería, Peru) 1993. *Publications:* A Theology of Liberation 1971, The Power of the Poor in History 1980, El Dios de la Vida 1982, We Drink from Our Own Wells: the Spiritual Journey of a People 1983, On Job, God-talk and the Suffering of the Innocent 1986, La Verdad los hará libres 1986, Dios o el Oro en las Indias 1989, El Dios de la Vida 1989, Entre las Calandrias 1990, En Busca de los Pobres de Jesucristo 1992. *Leisure interests:* swimming, literature. *Address:* Instituto Bartolomé Las Casas-Rímac, Apartado 3090, Lima 100, Peru. *Telephone:* 820028; 709088; 723410. *Fax:* 820028.

GUTMAN, Natalia Grigorievna; Russian cellist; b. 14 Nov. 1942; m. Oleg Kagan (deceased); three c.; ed. Gnessin Music School, Moscow (under R. Shposhnikov), Moscow Conservatory (under Prof. Kozolupova and Mstislav Rostropovich); tours include: visits to Europe, U.S.A. and Japan, appearing with Berlin Philharmonic orchestra, the Vienna Philharmonic orchestra, the London Symphony orchestra, the Orchestre Nat. de France, and the Orchestre de Paris; played chamber music in U.S.S.R. and Europe with Eliso Virsaladze and Oleg Kagan 1982–; played sonatas, trios and quartets with Sviatoslav Richter; plays sonata and concerto written for her by Alfred Schnittke; Solo tours include: the U.S.A. with U.S.S.R. State Symphony Orchestra and Yevgeny Svetlanov, Italy with BBC Symphony and Yuri Temirkanov, U.S.S.R. with Sir John Pritchard; performed with Royal Philharmonic Orchestra under Yuri Temirkanov, Royal Festival Hall, London, the Concertgebouw, the London Philharmonic, the Munich Philharmonic, the Berlin Philharmonic, the Orchestre Nat. de France, the L.A. Philharmonic under André Previn, the Chicago Symphony under Claudio Abbado 1988–89; teacher at Moscow Conservatory 1967–77; Prof. Stuttgart Conservatory 1997–; prizes at the Vienna Student Festival Competition, the Tchaikovsky Competition, the Munich Chamber Music Competition and the Dvořák Competition, Prague. *Address:* Askonas Holt, Lonsdale Chambers, 27 Chancery Lane, London, WC2A 1PF, England. *Telephone:* 0171-400 1700.

GUTMANN, Francis Louis Alphonse Myrtil; French government official; b. 4 Oct. 1930, Paris; s. of Robert and Denise (née Coulom) Gutmann; m. Chantal de Gaulle 1964; two s. one d.; ed. Lycée Pasteur, Neuilly-sur-Seine; Head of dept., Ministry of Foreign Affairs 1951–57; Asst. Head Office of Sec. of State for Econ. Affairs 1955, mem. French del. to Econ. and Social Council and to UN Gen. Ass. 1952–55, to Common Market Conf., Brussels 1956–57; Adviser Pechiney Co. 1957–59, Sec.-Gen. 1963, Dir. 1970–71; Sec.-Gen. Fria 1960–62; Pres. Alucam 1968–72; Dir. (chemical div.) Pechiney-Ugine-Kuhlmann group; Pres.-Dir.-Gen. Ugine-Kuhlmann 1971–76, mem. governing bd. Pechiney-Ugine-Kuhlmann group in charge of social affairs 1975–78; Pres. Frialco and Vice-Pres. Friguia 1977–81; Dir.-Gen. French Red Cross 1980–81; Sec.-Gen. Ministry for External Relations 1981–85; Admin. representing the State, Parisbas 1982–84, Gaz de France 1984–85, St. Gobain 1982–85; Amb. to Spain 1985–88; Pres. Admin. Council Gaz de France 1988–93, Hon. Pres. 1993–; Pres. Fondation Méditerranéenne d'Etudes Stratégiques 1989–, Assoc. Eurogas-Union 1990–94, (Admin. Council) Institut Français du Pétrole (IFP) 1993–96; Vice-Pres. Mémoire et espoirs de la Résistance 1994–; attached to Ministry of Foreign Affairs 1996–; Pres. Scientific Council for Defence, Ministry of Defence 1998–; Dir. French Red Cross 1992–; Chevalier, Légion d'honneur; Officier, Ordre nat. du Mérite; Grand croix de l'ordre du Merité (Spain). *Publications:* Les chemins de l'effort 1975, le Nouveau Décor International 1994. *Address:* c/o Institut Français du Pétrole, 1–4 ave. de Bois-Préau, BP 311, 92506 Rueil-Malmaison cedex, France (Office).

GUTOWSKY, Herbert Sander, PH.D.; American physical chemist; b. 8 Nov. 1919, Bridgman, Mich.; s. of Otto Gutowsky and Hattie Meyer; m. 1st Barbara Joan Stuart 1949 (divorced 1981); three s. (one deceased); m. 2nd Virginia Annette Warner 1982; ed. Indiana and Harvard Univs. and Univ. of Calif. (Berkeley); served in U.S. Army 1941–45; Instructor, Univ. of Ill. 1948, Asst. Prof. 1951–55, Assoc. Prof. 1955–56, Prof. of Chem. 1956–83, Head, Div. of Physical Chem. 1956–62, Head, Dept. of Chem. and Chemical Eng. 1967–70, Dir. School of Chemical Sciences, Head, Dept. of Chem. 1970–83, Assoc. mem. Center for Advanced Study, Univ. of Ill. 1962–63; Prof. Center for Advanced Study and Research Prof. of Chemistry, Univ of Ill. 1983–; Guggenheim Fellow 1954–55; Walker Ames Visiting Prof. at Univ. of Wash. 1957; mem. N.A.S., American Acad. of Arts and Sciences, American Philosophical Soc.; Hon. D.Sc. (Indiana Univ.) 1983; A.C.S. awards: Irving Langmuir Award in Chemical Physics 1966, Mid-west Award of St. Louis Section 1973, Peter Debye Award in Physical Chem. 1975; Award of the Int. Soc. of Magnetic Resonance 1974, G. N. Lewis Memorial Lecturer, Univ. of Calif. (Berkeley) 1976, G. B. Kistiakowsky Lecturer, Harvard Univ.

1980, Nat. Medal of Science 1977, Wolf Foundation Prize 1983/84, Chemical Pioneer Award of the American Inst. of Chemists 1991, Pittsburgh Spectroscopy Award of the Spectroscopy Soc. of Pittsburgh 1992, Kuebler Award 1996. *Publications:* Scientific articles, mainly in Journal of American Chemical Soc., Journal of Chemical Physics, Physical Review, Discussions of Faraday Soc., Journal of Physical Chemistry. *Leisure interests:* rose gardening. *Address:* Department of Chemistry, University of Illinois, 117 Noyes Laboratory, 505 South Mathews Street, Urbana, IL 61801; 202 W. Delaware Ave, Urbana, IL 61801, U.S.A. (Home). *Telephone:* 217-333-7621.

GUTTON, André Henry Georges; French architect and town planner; b. 8 Jan. 1904, Fontenay-sous-Bois; s. of Henry B. Gutton and Amelia Hoesli; m. Elisabeth Lafargue 1927; two s. one d.; ed. Ecole nationale supérieure des beaux arts and Inst. d'Urbanisme de l'Univ. de Paris; Architect for pvt. bldgs. and nat. palaces 1936–; Prof. Inst. of Town Planning 1946–63; Prof. of Theory of Architecture, Nat. School of Fine Arts 1949–58, of Town Planning 1958–74; Tech. Counsellor, Govt. of Syria 1951; mem. Exec. Cttee. Int. Union of Architects 1949–57, Pres. Town Planning Comm. 1951–58; Consultant Town-Planner Canton of Geneva 1960–70, Bilbao 1962, Brasilia 1967, Bratislava 1967, Belgrade 1986; mem. (rapporteur) Planning Cttee. for the Parisian Region 1965–73; Hon. Pres. Order of Architects 1960–66; Vice-Pres. Congress of Architects 1965; mem. Acad. of Architecture, Royal Acad. of Belgium; Hon. Fellow A.I.A.; Int. Prize for Anvers (I.M.A.L.S.O.) 1933; first Int. Prize for plan for Place des Nations, Geneva 1958; Officier, Légion d'honneur, Polar Star (Sweden), Kt., Order of Orange-Nassau, of Dannebrog, Officier des Palmes académiques, Officier des Arts et des Lettres. *Major works:* Chief Architect of Institut de France 1936–70, Post Office Buildings, Paris 1945, The Opera 1950–54, Post Office Buildings at Paris, Versailles, Nancy, Besançon, Chateauroux, Roanne, Neuilly-sur-Marne, Lyon, Chambéry and schools and offices in France, Town Planning: Plans for Nancy 1938, Dakar (Senegal), Boulogne, Issy 1945, Aleppo (Syria) 1952, Sihanoukville (Cambodia) 1960. *Publications:* Charte de l'urbanisme 1941, Conversations sur l'architecture: (L'édifice dans la cité, La maison des hommes, Les églises et les temples, Les écoles, lycées, universités, L'urbanisme au service de l'homme) 1952–62, De la nuit à l'aurore 1985, Urbanisme et urbanité 1993. *Leisure interests:* painting, writing. *Address:* 3 avenue Vavin, 75006 Paris, France (Home). *Telephone:* (1) 46-33-72-76.

GUTZWILLER, Peter Max, DR.IUR., LL.M.; Swiss lawyer; b. 30 April 1941, Basle; s. of Max and Helly Gutzwiller; m. 1st Vreny Lüscher 1971 (divorced); one s.; m. 2nd Barbara Menzel; ed. Univs. of Basle and Geneva and Harvard Law School; Assoc. Staehelin Hafter & Partners 1970–76, Partner 1977–; mem. Bd. of Int. Law Asscn. (Swiss Branch) 1975–; Sec. Swiss Asscn. of Int. Law 1976; Major, Swiss Army 1979. *Publications:* Swiss International Divorce Law 1968, Von Ziel und Methode des IPR 1968, Arbeitsbewilligungen für Ausländer 1975, 1976, Grundriss des schweizerischen Privat- und Steuerrechtes (co-author) 1976. *Leisure interests:* art collection (cartoons), music, travel. *Address:* Bleicherweg 58, 8027 Zurich (Office); Sonnenrain 15, 8700 Küsnacht, Switzerland (Home). *Telephone:* 201 45 40 (Office); 910-9988 (Home).

GUZE, Samuel Barry, M.D.; American psychiatrist, educator and university official; b. 18 Oct. 1923, New York; s. of Jacob Guze and Jenny (Berry) Guze; m. Joy Lawrence Campbell 1946; one s. one d.; ed. Washington Univ., St. Louis, Mo.; Intern in Medicine, Barnes Hosp. 1945–46, Fellow in Medicine, Barnes Hosp. and Washington Univ. School of Medicine 1946 and 1948–49, Fellow in Psychiatry 1950–53; Resident in Medicine, Newington Veterans' Admin. Hosp., Conn. 1949–50; Instructor in Medicine, Washington Univ. School of Medicine, St. Louis, Mo. 1951–53, Asst. Prof. 1953–55, Lecturer in Social Work, George Warren Brown School of Social Work 1954–60, Asst. Prof. of Psychiatry and Asst. Prof. of Medicine 1955–59, Assoc. Prof. of Psychiatry and Asst. Prof. of Medicine 1959–64, Prof. of Psychiatry and Assoc. Prof. of Medicine 1964–, Asst. to Dean 1965–71, Vice-Chancellor for Medical Affairs 1971–89, Co-Head, Dept. of Psychiatry 1974–75, Spencer T. Olin Prof. of Psychiatry 1974–, Head of Dept. of Psychiatry 1975–89, Head 1993–97, Pres. Washington Univ. Medical Center 1971–89; Asst. Physician, Barnes Hosp. 1951–; Consulting Psychiatrist, Jewish Hosp. of St. Louis 1975–; Psychiatrist-in-Chief, Barnes, Renard and St. Louis Children's Hosps. 1975–89, Psychiatrist 1989–93, Psychiatrist-in-Chief 1993–97; Samuel Hamilton Medal of the American Psychopathological Asscn. 1982 and the Paul Hoch Medal 1986, Achievement Award, American Acad. of Clinical Psychiatrists 1987, Distinguished Public Service Award, Dept. of Health and Human Services 1987, Sarnat Prize, Inst. of Medicine, N.A.S. 1995. *Publications:* Psychiatric Diagnosis (with others) 1974 (several trans.), Criminality and Psychiatric Disorders 1976, Childhood Psychopathology and Development (Ed. with others) 1983, Schizophrenia, Affective Disorders, and Organic Mental Disorders (Ed. with others) in Psychiatry (Ed. Cavenar) 1985, Why Psychiatry is a Branch of Medicine 1992, Washington University Adult Psychiatry (Ed.) 1997. *Address:* Department of Psychiatry, Washington University School of Medicine, 4940 Children's Place, St. Louis, MO 63110 (Office); Apartment 14A, 710 South Hanley Road, St. Louis, MO 63105, U.S.A. (Home). *Telephone:* (314) 362-7772 (Office). *Fax:* (314) 362-6501 (Office).

GVISHIANI, Jermen Mikhailovich, D.PHIL.; Georgian politician and sociologist; b. 24 Dec. 1928, Akhaltsikhe, Georgia; s. of Mikhail Maksimovich and Irma Khristophorovna Gvishiani; m. Lyudmila Alekseyevna Kosygina (d. of the late Aleksey Kosygin, Chair. of U.S.S.R. Council of Ministers 1964–80) (died 1990); one s. one d.; ed. Moscow State Inst. of Int. Relations, Moscow State Univ., Inst. of Philosophy, U.S.S.R. Acad. of Science; navy service 1951–55; with State Cttee. for Science and Tech., Int. Relations Dept. 1955–65, Deputy Chair. 1965–85; Prof. of Philosophy, Moscow State Univ. 1960–71; Deputy Chair. State Planning Cttee. 1985–86; Chair. Cttee. for Systems Analysis, Presidium of Acad. of Sciences 1971–86, Chair. Council Int. Inst. for Applied Systems Analysis 1972–81, Int. Research Inst. for Man. Problems 1977–85, Int. Council for New Initiatives in East-West Co-operation (Int. Vienna Council) 1979–85, Deputy Chair. 1985–93, Hon. Chair. 1993–; mem. UN Advisory Cttee. on Applications of Science and Tech. (ACAST), Bd. of Trustees of UNITAR 1962–71; Co-Chair. U.S.A.-U.S.S.R. Trade and Econ. Council, Sub-cttee. for Science and Tech. 1974–91; Dir. Inst. for Systems Studies/Inst. for Systems Analysis 1976–92, Hon. Dir. and Head of Dept. 1992–; Vice-Chair. Jt. Perm. U.S.S.R.-France Comm. 1967, Soviet Div., U.S.S.R.-Fed. Repub. of Germany Comm. for Econ. and Tech. Co-operation 1972; mem. Presidium, Soviet Sociologists' Asscn. 1972–86; mem. U.S.S.R. (now Russian) Acad. of Sciences 1979, Int. Man. Acad., Sweden Royal Acad. of Eng. Sciences, American Man. Asscn., American Man. Acad., Foreign mem. Finnish Acad. Tech. Sciences; mem. The Club of Rome; Dr h.c. (Prague High Econ. School); R.S.F.S.R. State Prize 1979, Gold Mercury Int. Award, and various medals; Grosse Goldene Ehrenzeichen mit Stern (Austria). *Publications:* Sociology of Business, Organization and Management, Social Function of Science and Science Policy, Scientific and Technological Revolution and Social Progress, etc. *Leisure interests:* music, sport. *Address:* Institute for Systems Studies, 60 Years of October prosp. 9, 117312 Moscow 312, Russia (Office). *Telephone:* 135-75-75 (Office); 137-25-44 (Home).

GWATHMEY, Charles, M.ARCH.; American architect; b. 19 June 1938, Charlotte, N.C.; m. Bette A. Damson 1974; ed. Music and Art High School, New York, Univ. of Pa. School of Arch. and Yale Univ. School of Arch.; William Wirt Winchester Travelling Fellowship 1962; Fulbright Fellow in France 1962–63; pvt. practice in New York 1964–66; partner, Gwathmey-Henderson, New York 1966–70, Gwathmey-Henderson-Siegel 1970–71; partner, with Robert Siegel, Gwathmey Siegel & Assocs. New York 1971–; Prof. of Architectural Design, Pratt Inst. Brooklyn, New York 1964–66, Yale Univ. 1966, Princeton Univ. 1966–69, 1975–76, Harvard Univ. 1970–72, Cooper Union, New York 1971–72, Univ. of Calif. at Los Angeles 1973–74, Columbia Univ. 1976–77; Eliot Noyes Prof. of Arch. Harvard Univ. 1985; works include single houses, housing projects, school and coll. bldgs., libraries, offices, public bldgs., interiors etc. throughout U.S. and addition to Solomon Guggenheim Museum, New York 1995; mem. American Acad., American Inst. of Arts and Letters; Fellow, American Inst. of Architects; numerous awards and distinctions including Distinguished Architecture Award 1982, 1984, Medal of Honor 1983, Nat. Honor Award 1968, 1976, 1984 and Nat. Firm Award, American Inst. of Architects 1982. *Address:* Gwathmey, Siegel and Associates, Architects, 475 Tenth Avenue, New York, NY 10018 (Office); 1115 5th Ave, New York, NY 10128, U.S.A.

GWYNN-JONES, Peter Llewellyn, C.V.O., M.A., F.S.A.; British public official; b. 12 March 1940; s. of late Maj. Jack Llewellyn Gwynn-Jones and Mary Muriel Harrison, and step-s. of late Lieut.-Col. Gavin David Young; ed. Wellington Coll., Trinity Coll. Cambridge; Asst. to Garter King of Arms 1970; Bluemantle Pursuivant of Arms 1973; House Comptroller Coll. of Arms 1982; Lancaster Herald of Arms 1982–95; Garter Prin. King of Arms 1995–; Genealogist Order of the Bath, O.St.J.; Insp. of Regimental Colours, of R.A.F. Badges; Hon. Genealogist Order of St Michael and St George; Sec. Harleian Soc. 1981–94; K.St.J. *Publications:* Heraldry 1993, The Art of Heraldry 1998. *Leisure interests:* tropical forests, wildlife conservation, fishing. *Address:* College of Arms, Queen Victoria Street, London, EC4V 4BT (Office); 79 Harcourt Terrace, London, S.W.10, England (Home).

GYIBUG PUNCOG CEDAIN; Chinese politician; b. 1930, Tibet; Vice-Chair. of People's Govt. of Tibet Autonomous Region, 1983–; deputy for Tibet to 7th NPC 1988. *Address:* People's Government of Tibet Autonomous Region, Lhasa, People's Republic of China.

GYLL, John Sören; Swedish company executive; b. 26 Dec. 1940, Skorped; s. of Josef and Gertrud Gyll; m. Lilly Margareta Hellman 1974; two s. one d.; Marketing Dir. and Vice-Pres. Rank Xerox 1963–77; Pres. Uddeholm Sweden AB 1977–79, Exec. Vice-Pres. Uddeholms AB 1979–81, Pres. and C.E.O. 1981–84; Pres. and C.E.O. Procordia AB 1984–92; Pres. and C.E.O. AB Volvo 1992–97, also Dir. *Leisure interests:* hunting, skiing. *Address:* c/o AB Volvo, S-405 08 Gothenburg, Sweden.

GYLLENHAMMAR, Pehr Gustaf, B.LL.; Swedish business executive; b. 28 April 1935, Gothenburg; s. of Pehr Gustaf Victor Gyllenhammar and Aina Dagny Kaplan; m. Eva Christina Engellau 1959; one s. three d.; ed. Univ. of Lund, studied int. law in England, vocational studies in maritime law, U.S.A., Cen. d'Etudes Industrielles, Geneva; employed by Mannheimer & Zetterlöf (Solicitors), Gothenburg 1959, Haight, Gardner, Poor & Havens (Admiralty Lawyers), New York 1960, Amphion Insurance Co., Gothenburg 1961–64; Asst. Admin. Man. Skandia Insurance Co., Stockholm 1965–66, Vice-Pres. Corporate Planning 1966–68, Exec. Vice-Pres. 1968, Pres. and C.E.O. 1970; joined AB Volvo, Gothenburg 1970, Man. Dir. and C.E.O. 1971–83, Chair. of Bd. and C.E.O. 1983–90, Exec. Chair. Bd. of Dirs. 1990–93; Chair. Bd. MC European Capital SA 1994–96; Chair. Bd. of Dirs. Swedish Ships' Mortage Bank 1976–, Procordia AB 1990–92; Sr. Adviser Lazard Frères & Co. 1996–; Chair. Cofinec N.V. 1996–, CGU PLC 1998–; mem. Bd.

of Dirs., Skandinaviska Enskilda Banken 1979–94, United Technologies Corpn. 1981–, Kissinger Assocs., Inc. 1982–, Pearson PLC 1983–97, Reuters Holdings PLC 1984–97, Philips Electronics NV 1990–96, Renault SA 1990–93, and numerous other cos. and orgs.; Trustee Reuters Founder Share Co. Ltd. 1997–; mem. Royal Swedish Acad. of Eng. Sciences 1974; Dr. Med. h.c. (Gothenburg Univ.) 1981, Hon. D.Tech. (Brunel) 1987, Hon. D.Eng. (Nova Scotia) 1988, Hon. D. Soc. Sc. (Helsinki) 1990, Hon. LL.D. (Vermont) 1993; Officer (1st Class) Royal Order of Vasa 1973, Commdr. Order of the Lion of Finland 1977, Commdr. Ordre nat. du Mérite 1980, Golden Award, City of Gothenburg 1981, King's Medal (12th Size) with ribbon of Order of the Seraphim 1981, Commdr. St. Olav's Order 1984, Commdr. Order of the Lion of Finland (1st Class) 1986, Commdr. Légion d'honneur 1987, Kt. Grand Officer, Order of Merit (Italy) 1987, Commdr. Order of Leopold 1989. *Publications:* Mot sekelskiftet på måfå (Towards the Turn of the Century at Random) 1970, Jag tror på Sverige (I Believe in Sweden) 1973, People at Work 1977, En industripolitik för människan (Industrial Policy for Human Beings) 1979. *Leisure interests:* tennis, sailing, skiing, riding. *Address:* CGU PLC, St. Helen's, 1 Undershaft, London, EC3P 3DQ, England. *Telephone:* 0171-662 2926. *Fax:* 0171-283 0067.

GYLLENSTEN, Lars Johan Wictor, M.D.; Swedish writer and physician; b. 12 Nov. 1921, Stockholm; s. of Carl Gyllensten and Ingrid Gyllensten (née Rangström); m. Inga-Lisa Hultén 1946; one d.; Prof. of Histology Karolinska Inst. 1969–73; mem. Swedish Acad. 1966–89; mem. Nobel Cttee. for Literature 1967–87, Chair. 1981–87, Bd. mem. Nobel Foundation 1979–93; mem. Royal Swedish Acad. of Sciences 1975; Hon. mem. Royal Swedish Acad. of History, Arts and Antiquities 1979; Hon. D.Tech. 1993; Hon. D.Theol. 1998; 20 literary prizes. *Publications:* Senilia 1956, Juvenilia 1965, Palatset i parken 1970, Grottan i öknen 1973, I skuggan av Don Juan 1975, Skuggans återkomst 1985, Det himmelska gästabudet 1991, Anteckningar från en vindskupa 1993, Ljuset ur skuggornas värld 1995, Kistbrev 1998. *Address:* c/o Albert Bonniers Forlag AB, Box 3159, S10363 Stockholm, Sweden.

GYLYS, Povilas, D.SC. (ECON.); Lithuanian politician; b. 14 Feb. 1948, Didziokai, Moletai Region; m. Nijole Rezaitė 1969; two s.; ed. Vilnius Univ.; lecturer, Prof. of Econs. 1969–92; Head of Dept. of Int. Econ. Relations, Vilnius Univ. 1992; mem. Parl. (Seimas), Minister of Foreign Affairs 1992–96; mem. of Parl. (Seimás) 1996–. *Address:* Seimás of Lithuania, Gediminas prosp. 53, 2026 Vilnius, Lithuania. *Telephone:* (2) 621-632.

GYNGELL, Bruce; Australian broadcasting executive; b. 8 July 1929, Melbourne; m. 1st Ann Barr; one s. two d.; m. 2nd Kathy Rowan; two s.; ed. Sydney Grammar School, Sydney Univ. and Columbia Univ., New York; trainee, Australian Broadcasting Corpn. 1950; joined Channel Nine TV 1956, first person to appear on Australian TV 16 Sept. 1956, Programme Dir. 1956–66, Man. Dir. 1966–69; Deputy Man. Dir. ATV, England 1972–76; Deputy Man. Dir. ITC Entertainment 1972–75; Chair. Network Planning Cttee. 1974–76; Chair. Australian Broadcasting Tribunal 1977–80; Chief Exec. Special Broadcasting Service (TV Service for ethnic minorities) 1980; Man. Dir. TV-am 1984–92, Chair. 1990–92; Exec. Chair. Nine Network Australia Ltd. 1993–94; Man. Dir. Yorkshire-Tyne Tees TV 1995–97; Chair. British Independent TV Enterprises (BRITE) 1995–. *Leisure interests:* surfing, skiing, jogging, yoga. *Address:* c/o Yorkshire Television, The Television Centre, Leeds, LS3 1JS, England.

GYOHTEN, Toyoo; Japanese banker; b. 1931, Yokohama; m.; one s. one d.; ed. Univ. of Tokyo, Princeton Univ., U.S.A.; joined Ministry of Finance 1955; Japan Desk, Asian Dept. IMF 1964–66; Special Asst. to Pres. of Asian Devt. Bank, Manila, Philippines 1966–69; Dir.-Gen. Int. Finance Bureau 1984–86, Vice-Minister of Finance for Int. Affairs 1986–89; Visiting Prof., Business School, Harvard Univ., U.S.A. 1990, Woodrow Wilson School, Princeton Univ. 1990–91, Univ. of St. Gallen, Switzerland 1991; joined Bank of Tokyo Ltd. (merged with Mitsubishi Bank Ltd 1996) 1991, Chair. Bd. 1992–96, Sr. Adviser The Bank of Tokyo-Mitsubishi Ltd., Pres. Inst. for Int. Monetary Affairs 1996–; Chair. Working Party III, OECD, Paris 1988–90, Inst. of Int. Finance Inc., U.S.A. 1994–97; mem. Bd. of Trustees, Princeton in Asia, U.S.A. 1989–, Advisory Panel, E. African Devt. Bank, Kampala, Uganda 1990–, Asia Pacific Advisory Cttee., New York Stock Exchange 1990–, Int. Council, The Asia Soc., New York 1991–, Exec. Cttee. of Trilateral Comm., New York, Paris and Tokyo 1991–, Bd. of Trustees, The Aspen Inst., Colo., U.S.A. 1992–, Group of Thirty, Washington, D.C. 1992–, Council of Inst. Aspen France, The Aspen Inst. Japan Council, Int. Advisory Bd. MATIF S.A., France, Int. Advisory Panel, Monetary Authority of Singapore, Banking Advisory Group of IFC, Washington, D.C.; Founding mem. Int. Advisory Bd. of Council on Foreign Relations, New York; Pres. Princeton Club of Japan; Fulbright Scholar 1956–58. *Publication:* Changing Fortunes (with Paul Volcker) 1992. *Address:* 2-2, Nihombashi Hongokucho 1-chome, Chuo-ku, Tokyo 103-0021, Japan.

GYSI, Gregor; German politician and lawyer; m. 1st (divorced); two s.; m. 2nd; one d.; defence lawyer; elected leader Communist Party (CP) Nov. 1989, name changed to Partei des Demokratischen Sozialismus (PDS) (Party of Democratic Socialism), now parl. leader; mem. Bundestag 1990–. *Address:* Partei des Demokratischen Sozialismus, Kleine Alexanderstr. 28, 10178 Berlin, Germany.

H

HA VAN LAU; Vietnamese diplomatist; b. 9 Dec. 1918, Thua Thien; m.; three c.; served with Viet Nam People's Army 1945–54; a del. of Democratic Repub. of Viet Nam to Geneva Conf. on Indochina 1954, Paris Conf. on Viet Nam 1968; Asst. Minister of Foreign Affairs 1973; Amb. to Cuba 1974–78; Perm. Rep. to UN 1978–82, Deputy Minister for Foreign Affairs 1982–84; Amb. to France (also accred. to Belgium, The Netherlands and Luxembourg) 1984–89.

HAACKE, Hans Christoph Carl, M.F.A.; German artist and professor of art; b. 12 Aug. 1936, Cologne; s. of Dr. Carl Haacke and Antonie Haacke; m. Linda Snyder 1965; two s.; ed. State Art Acad., Kassel; Asst. Prof. Cooper Union, New York 1971–75, Assoc. Prof. 1975–79, Prof. 1979–; Guest Prof. Hochschule für Bildende Künste, Hamburg 1973, 1994, Gesamthochschule, Essen 1979. *solo exhbns. include:* Galerie Schmela, Düsseldorf 1965, Howard Wise Gallery, New York 1966, 1968, 1969, Galerie Paul Maenz, Cologne 1971, 1974, 1981, Museum Haus Lange, Krefeld 1972, John Weber Gallery, New York, 1973, 1975, 1977, 1979, 1981, 1983, 1985, 1988, 1990, 1992, 1994, Kunstverein, Frankfurt 1976, Lisson Gallery, London 1976, Galerie Durand-Dessert, Paris 1977, 1978, Museum of Modern Art, Oxford 1978, Stedelijk van Abbemuseum, Eindhoven 1979, Tate Gallery, London 1984, Neue Gesellschaft für Bildende Kunst, Berlin 1984, Kunsthalle, Berne 1985, Le Consortium, Dijon 1986, The New Museum of Contemporary Art, New York 1986, Victoria Miro Gallery, London 1987, Centre Georges Pompidou, Paris 1989, Venice Biennale, German Pavilion 1993, Fundació Tàpies, Barcelona 1995, Boijmans Van Beuningen Museum, Rotterdam 1996; participant in numerous group exhbns. 1962–; *stage set:* Volksbühne, Berlin 1994; numerous awards and honours including Hon. D.F.A. (Oberlin Coll.) 1991; Dr. h.c. (Bauhaus-Universität, Weimar) 1998. *Publications:* Werkmonographie (with Edward F. Fry) 1972, Framing and Being Framed (jtly.) 1975, Nach allen Regeln der Kunst 1984, Unfinished Business (with others) 1987, Artfairismes 1989, Bodenlos (with others) 1993, Libre-Echange (with Pierre Bourdieu) 1994, Obra Social 1995, Ansichtssachen (Viewing Matters) 1999; numerous articles and interviews in int. art magazines. *Address:* c/o Cooper Union for the Advancement of Science and Art, Cooper Square, New York, NY 10003, U.S.A.

HAAG, Rudolf, DR.RER.NAT.; German professor of theoretical physics; b. 17 Aug. 1922, Tubingen; s. of Albert Haag and Anna (née Schaich) Haag; m. 1st Kaethe Fues 1948 (died 1991); three s. one d.; m. 2nd Barbara Klie 1992; ed. Tech. Univ., Stuttgart and Univ. of Munich; Prof. of Physics, Univ. of Ill., U.S.A 1960–66; Prof. of Theoretical Physics, Hamburg Univ. 1966–87, Prof. Emer. 1987–; Dr. h.c. (Aix-Marseille) 1979; Max-Planck-Medal 1970. *Publications:* Local Quantum Physics 1992, and over 100 articles on fundamental physical theory. *Address:* Waldschmidt Strasse 4b, 83727 Schliersee-Neuhaus, Germany. *Telephone:* 08026-7444.

HAAKONSEN, Bent, LL.B.; Danish diplomatist; b. 10 Jan. 1936; m. Kirsten Haakonsen; one d.; joined Ministry of Foreign Affairs 1961; served Bonn 1964–67, Perm. Representation to EEC, Brussels 1972–74; Amb. to Czechoslovakia 1978–79; Head, Danish del. to CSCE, Madrid 1980–81; Under-Sec. for Trade Relations 1983–86; Perm. Under-Sec. of State 1986–91; Perm. Rep. to UN 1991–95; Amb. to Germany 1995–. *Address:* Royal Danish Embassy, Pfälzer Strasse 14, 53111 Bonn, Germany.

HAAN, Pieter de, M.A.; Netherlands academic; b. 4 Nov. 1927, Augustinusga; s. of Aan de Haan and Klaaske de Beer; m. F. A. Zijlstra 1956; two c.; ed. Univ. of Groningen; Asst. Sec. Landbouwschap, The Hague 1956; Scientific Asst. Univ. of Agriculture Wageningen 1956–61; Prof. of Land Law, Delft Univ. of Tech. 1961–88; Prof. of Admin. Law and Land Law, Free Univ. Amsterdam 1974–88; Pres. Inst. of Construction Law 1972–97, Scientific Council Inst. of Agrarian Law 1993, Visiting Cttee. Faculties of Law 1990–91; mem. Advisory Council for Physical Planning 1976–90, Royal Netherlands Acad. of Sciences 1979–; Dr. h.c. (Amsterdam) 1990. *Publications:* Land Law, 7 Vols. 1969, 1973, 1983, 1984, 1988, 1992, 1996, Administrative law, (7 vols.) 1978, 1981, 1986, 1996, 1998. *Leisure interests:* travelling, gardening, fishing. *Address:* Fabriciuslaan 74, 9203 LH Drachten, Netherlands (Home). *Telephone:* 0512-510376 (Home).

HAAS, Peter E., M.B.A.; American business executive; b. 20 Dec. 1918, San Francisco; s. of Walter A. Haas and Elise Stern; m. 1st Josephine Baum 1945, 2nd Mimi Lurie 1981; two s. one d.; ed. Deerfield Acad., Univ. of Calif. and Harvard Univ.; joined Levi Strauss & Co., San Francisco 1945, Exec. Vice-Pres. 1958–70, Pres. 1970–81, C.E.O. 1976–81, Chair. 1981–89, Chair. Exec. Cttee. 1989–; Dir. AT&T 1966, now Dir. Emer.; fmr. Pres. Jewish Welfare Fed.; various public and charitable appts. *Address:* Levi Strauss & Co., P.O. Box 7215, San Francisco, CA 94120, U.S.A.

HAAS, Richard John, B.S., M.F.A.; American artist; b. 29 Aug. 1936, Spring Green, Wis.; s. of Joseph F. Haas and Marie Nachreiner Haas; m. 1st Cynthia Dickman 1963 (divorced 1970), 2nd Katherine Sokolnikoff 1980; one s.; ed. Univ. of Wisconsin-Milwaukee and Univ. of Minnesota; Instr. of Art, Univ. of Minn. 1963–64; Asst. Prof. of Art, Mich. State Univ. 1964–68; Instr. in Printmaking, Bennington Coll. 1968–80; Fine Arts Faculty, School of Visual Arts 1977–81; mem. New York City Art Comm. 1976–79; mem. Bd. Public Art Fund 1980–84, N.Y. State Preservation League 1983–90; Gov. Skowhegan School of Painting and Sculpture 1980–; mem. Bd. of Trustees, Hudson River Museum 1989–; numerous one-man exhbns. including San Francisco Museum of Modern Art 1980, Young-Hoffman Gallery, Chicago 1981, 1982, Rhone Hoffman Gallery, Chicago 1983, Univ. of Tennessee 1984, Aspen Art Museum, Colo. 1985, Williams Coll. Museum of Art, Mass. 1987, Brooke Alexander, New York 1989, Richard Haas: Architectural Projects 1983–89 and Architectural Facades 1976–86, Rhona Hoffman, Chicago 1990, The Century Asscn., N.Y. 1996, Huntington Museum of Art 1997; participant in numerous group exhbns. since 1962; more than 120 commissioned outdoor and indoor murals, including The Fontainebleau Hotel, Miami Beach, New York Public Library Periodical Room 1975–; A.I.A. Medal of Honor 1977; Municipal Art Soc. Award 1977; Nat. Endowment for the Arts Fellowship 1978; Guggenheim Fellowship 1983; Doris C. Freedman Award 1989. *Publication:* Richard Haas: An Architecture of Illusion. *Leisure interest:* tennis. *Address:* 361 West 36th Street, New York, NY 10018, U.S.A. *Telephone:* (212) 947-9868.

HAAS, Robert Douglas, M.B.A.; American business executive; b. 3 April 1942, San Francisco; s. of late Walter Haas and of Evelyn Danzig; m. Colleen Gershon 1974; one d.; ed. Univ. of Calif. (Berkeley) and Harvard Univ.; with Peace Corps, Ivory Coast 1964–66; with Levi Strauss & Co., San Francisco 1973–, Sr. Vice-Pres. (corp. planning and policy) 1978–80, Pres. New Business Group 1980, Pres. Operating Groups 1980–81, Exec. Vice-Pres. and C.O.O. 1981–84, Pres. and C.E.O. 1984–89, C.E.O., Chair. Bd. 1989–; Hon. Dir. San Francisco AIDS Foundation; Trustee Ford Foundation; mem. Bd. of Dirs. Levi Strauss Foundation. *Address:* Levi Strauss & Co., 1155 Battery Street, San Francisco, CA 94111, U.S.A.

HAAVELMO, Trygve; Norwegian economist; b. 13 Dec. 1911; one of founders of modern econometrics (quantitative branch of econs.); renowned for contribs. to Econometria, (journal of Econometric Soc.) 1943–44; Research Asst. Cowles Comm. Univ. of Chicago 1945–56; Prof. Econs. Univ. Oslo 1948; mem. American Econ. Asscn., American Acad. of Arts and Letters; Nobel Prize for Econs. 1989. *Publications include:* Study in the Theory of Economic Evolution 1954, Investment Decision 1960. *Address:* Department of Economics, University of Oslo, POB 1095, Blindern, 0317 Oslo 3, Norway.

HAAVIKKO, Paavo Juhani; Finnish writer and publisher; b. 25 Jan. 1931, Helsinki; s. of Heikki Adrian Haavikko and Rauha Pyykönen; m. 1st Marja-Liisa Vartio (née Sairanen) 1955 (died 1966); one s. one d.; m. 2nd Ritva Rainio (née Hanhineva) 1971; worked in real estate concurrently with career as writer 1951–67; mem Bd., Finnish Writers' Asscn. 1962–66; mem. State Cttee. for Literature 1966–67; mem. Bd. of Yhtyneet Kuvalehdet magazine co. and Suuri Suomalainen Kirjakerho (Great Finnish Book Club) 1969; Literary Dir. Otava Publishing Co. 1967–83; Publr. Arthouse Publishing Group 1983–; Academician h.c.; six state prizes for literature; Neustadt Int. Prize for Literature 1984, Nordic Prize of Swedish Acad.; Pro Finlandia Medal. *Publications:* Tiet etäisyyksiin 1951, Tuuliöinä 1953, Synnyinmaa 1955, Lehdet lehtiä 1958, Talvipalatsi 1959, Runot 1962, Puut, kaikki heidän vihreytensä 1966, Neljätoista hallitsijaa 1970, Puhua vastata opettaa 1972, Runoja matkalta salmen ylitse 1973, Kaksikymmentä ja yksi 1974, Kaksiky m mentä ja yksi 1974, Runot 1949–1974 1975, Runoelmat 1975, Viiniä, Kirjoitusta 1976, Toukokuu, ikuinen 1988 (poems); Poésie 1965, Jahre 1967, Gechichte 1967, Selected Poems 1968, The Superintendent 1973, Le palais d'hiver 1976 (translations); Münchhausen, Nuket 1960, Ylilääkäri 1968, Sulka 1973, Harald Pitkäikäinen 1974 (plays); Ratsumies 1974 (libretto); Yksityisiä Asioita 1960, Toinen taivas ja maa 1961, Vuodet 1962, Lasi Claudius Civiliksen salaliittolaisten pöydällä 1964 (prose), Kansakuninan linja 1977, Yritys omaksikuvaksi 1987, Vuosien aurinkoiset varjot (memoirs), Prospero (memoirs) 1967–1995. *Address:* Art House Oy, Bulevardi 19C, 00120 Helsinki, Finland. *Telephone:* (90) 6932727. *Fax:* (90) 6949028.

HAAVISTO, Heikki Johannes, M.SC., LL.M.; Finnish politician; b. 20 Aug. 1935, Turku; s. of Johan Haavisto and Alli Svensson; m. Maija Rihko 1964; three s.; Head of Dept. Oy Vehnä Ab 1963–66; Sec.-Gen. Cen. Union of Agricultural Producers and Forest Owners in Finland (MTK) 1966–75, Pres. 1976–94; Vice-Pres. Int. Fed. of Agricultural Producers (IFAP) 1977–80, 1986–90, mem. Bd. of Dirs. 1984–86; mem. Cen. Council of Nordic Farmer Orgs. (NBC), Pres. 1977, 1985–87; Chair. Del. of Finn Cooperative Pellervo (Confed. of Finnish Cooperatives) 1979–; mem. Admin. Council, Osuuskunta Metsäliitto, Vice-Chair. 1976–82, Pres. 1982–93; Vice-Chair. Admin. Council, OKO (Cen. Union of Cooperative Credit Banks) 1985–93; mem. Bd. Dirs. Metsä-Serla Oy 1986–93; mem. Int. Policy Council on Agric. and Trade 1988–; Minister for Foreign Affairs 1993–95, for Devt. Co-operation 1994–95; three hon. doctorates. *Address:* Hintsantie 2, 21200 Raisio, Finland. *Telephone:* 02-4383020. *Fax:* 02-4383499.

HABAKKUK, Sir Hrothgar John, Kt., M.A., F.B.A.; British economic historian; b. 13 May 1915, Barry, Glam.; s. of Evan Guest Habakkuk and Anne Bowen; m. Mary Richards 1948; one s. three d.; ed. Barry County School, Univ. Coll., Cardiff, St. John's Coll., Cambridge; Fellow, Pembroke Coll.,

Cambridge 1938–50, Dir. of Studies in History 1946–50; Lecturer, Faculty of Econs., Cambridge 1946–50; Chichele Prof. of Econ. History, Fellow, All Souls Coll., Oxford 1950–67; Prin. Jesus Coll., Oxford 1968–84; Vice-Chancellor Univ. of Oxford 1973–77; Pres. Univ. Coll. of Swansea 1975–84; Pres. Royal Historical Soc. 1976–80; Chair. Cttee. of Vice-Chancellors and Prins. 1976–77, Advisory Group on London Health Services 1979–80, Oxon. Health Authority 1982–84; mem. Royal Comm. on Historical Manuscripts 1978–90; Fellow, All Souls Coll. 1988–; Rhodes Trustee 1977–85; Hon. Fellow, St. John's and Pembroke Colls., Cambridge, Jesus Coll., Oxford, University Coll., Swansea; Foreign mem. American Acad. of Arts and Sciences, American Philosophical Soc.; Hon. D.Litt. (Cambridge, Wales, Pa., Kent, Ulster). *Publications:* American and British Technology in the Nineteenth Century 1962, Population Growth and Economic Development since 1750 1971, Editor, Cambridge Economic History of Europe Vol. VI, Marriage, Debt and the Estates System 1994. *Address:* 28 Cunliffe Close, Oxford, OX2 7BL, England. *Telephone:* (01865) 556583.

HABASH, George, M.D.; Palestinian nationalist leader; b. 1925, Lydda, Palestine; ed. American Univ. of Beirut; mem. Youth of Avengeance 1948 and Arab Nationalists' Movement early 1950s; practised as doctor 1950s; leader of Popular Front for the Liberation of Palestine Nov. 1967– (introduced Marxist-Leninist thought to the Palestinian cause); leader Arab Nationalists' Movt. *Address:* Popular Front for the Liberation of Palestine, Box 12144, Damascus, Syria.

HABBEL, Wolfgang R., DR.JUR.; German business executive and lawyer; b. 25 March 1924, Dillenburg; s. of Werner and Dorothea Habbel; m. Susan Roedter 1951; two s.; Asst. to Bd. of Man., Auto Union GmbH 1951–59; Personnel Man., European Labour Relations Co-ordinator, Ford of Europe 1960–69; mem. Man. Bd., Boehringer, Ingelheim 1970–71, Audi NSU 1971–78; Chair. Man. Bd., Audi NSU (Audi AG from Jan. 1985) 1979–87; mem. Man. Bd., Volkswagen 1979–, des Landesverbandes der Bayerischen Ind.; mem. Bd. of Dirs., Gerresheimer Glas AG, Triumph Adler Werke AG, Digital Equipment GmbH, Maynard, Deutsche Sport-Marketing; Pres. Gesellschaft für Sicherheitswissenschaft; Manager Junge Industriemagazin 1984; dir. numerous cos. and other appointments, State Medal for Services to the Bavarian Economy 1984; Hon. Senator Univ. of Bayreuth 1987. *Leisure interest:* golf. *Address:* Höhenstrasse 5, 85276 Pfaffenhofen, Germany. *Telephone:* 08441/22 33.

HABERER, Jean-Yves; French government official; b. 17 Dec. 1932, Mazagan, Morocco; m. Anne du Crest 1959; two c.; ed. Inst. d'Etudes politiques, Ecole Nat. d'Admin.; Insp. des Finances 1959, Insp. Gen. 1980; Tech. Adviser to Finance Ministry 1966–68; an Asst. Dir. of Treasury 1967–69, in charge of Intervention Service, Treasury 1969, of Financial Activities 1970, of Int. Business 1973; Dir. of Treasury 1978–82; Head of Office of Minister of Foreign Affairs 1968, of Minister of Defence 1969, of Minister of Econ. and Finance 1976; Prof. Inst. d'Etudes politiques 1970–82; Chair. Monetary Cttee. of the EEC 1980–82; Pres. and Dir.-Gen. Bank Paribas and Cie. Financière de Paribas 1982–86, Chair. of Supervisory Bd. Compagnie Bancaire 1982–88; Chair. Crédit Lyonnais 1988–93, Crédit Nat. 1993–94; Dir. Cie. Bancaire, Pallas Invest, Fondation Recherche Médicale, Institut Vaisseaux et Sang; Officier Ordre nat. du Mérite 1981, Officier, Légion d'honneur 1988. *Address:* 82 avenue Marceau, 75008 Paris (Office); 10 rue Rémusat, 75016 Paris, France (Home). *Telephone:* (01) 53.57.93.12 (Office). *Fax:* (01) 53.57.93.16.

HABERMAS, Jürgen, D.PHIL.; German professor of philosophy; b. 18 June 1929, Düsseldorf; m. Ute Habermas-Wesselhoeft 1955; one s. two d.; ed. Univs. of Bonn and Göttingen; Research Asst., Inst. für Sozial Forschung, Frankfurt 1956; Prof. of Philosophy, Univ. of Heidelberg 1961, of Philosophy and Sociology, Univ. of Frankfurt 1964; Dir. Max Planck Inst., Starnberg, Munich 1971; Prof. of Philosophy, Univ. of Frankfurt 1983–94, Prof. Emer. 1994–; Hon. D.D. (New School for Social Research) 1984, hon. degrees from Hebrew Univ. (Jerusalem), Univs. of Hamburg, Buenos Aires, Evanston (Northwestern), Utrecht, Athens, Bologna, Paris, Tel Aviv; Foreign mem. American Acad. of Arts and Sciences 1984, British Acad. of Science 1994; Hegel Prize 1972, Sigmund Freud Prize 1976, Adorno Prize 1980, Geschwister Scholl Prize 1985, Leibniz Prize 1986, Sonning Prize 1987. *Publications:* Strukturwandel der Öffentlichkeit 1962, Theorie und Praxis 1963, Erkenntnis und Interesse 1968, Legitimationsprobleme im Spätkapitalismus 1973, Theorie des kommunikativen Handelns 1981, Moralbewüsstsein und Kommunikatives Handeln 1983, Der Philosophische Diskurs ober Moderne 1985, Eine Art Schadensabwicklüng 1987, Nachmetaphysisches Denken 1988, Nachholende Revolution 1990, Texte und Kontexte 1991, Erläuterungen zur Diskursetnik 1991, Faktizität und Geltung 1992, Vergangenheit als Zukunft 1993, Die Normalität einer Berliner Republik 1995, Die Einbeziehung des Anderen 1996, Vom sinnlichen Eindruck zum symbolischen Ausdruck 1997, Die postnationale Konstellation 1998, Wahrheit und Recht Fertigung 1999. *Address:* Department of Philosophy, University of Frankfurt, Dantestrasse 4–6, 60325 Frankfurt am Main; Ringstrasse 8B, 82319 Starnberg, Germany.

HABGOOD, Baron (Life Peer) cr. 1995, of Calverton in the County of Buckinghamshire; **Rt. Rev. and Rt. Hon. Dr. John Stapylton Habgood,** P.C., D.D., M.A., PH.D.; British ecclesiastic; b. 23 June 1927, Stony Stratford; s. of Arthur Henry Habgood and Vera Chetwynd-Stapylton; m. Rosalie Mary Anne Boston 1961; two s. two d.; ed. Eton Coll., King's Coll. Cambridge Univ. and Cuddesdon Coll. Oxford; Demonstrator in Pharmacology, Cambridge Univ. 1950–53; Fellow, King's Coll. Cambridge Univ. 1952–55; Curate, St. Mary Abbott's Church, Kensington 1954–56; Vice-Prin. Westcott House, Cambridge 1956–62; Rector, St. John's Church, Jedburgh, Scotland 1962–67; Prin. Queen's Coll., Birmingham 1967–73; Bishop of Durham 1973–83; Archbishop of York 1983–95; Pres. (U.K.) Council on Christian Approaches to Defence and Disarmament 1976–95; Chair. World Council of Churches' Int. Hearing on Nuclear Weapons 1981; mem. Council for Science and Society 1975–90, Council for Arms Control 1981–95; Moderator of Church and Soc. Sub-Unit, World Council of Churches 1983–90; Chair. U.K. Xenotransplantation Interim Regulatory Authority 1997–; Hon. D.D. (Durham) 1975, (Cambridge) 1984, (Aberdeen) 1988, (Huron) 1990, (Hull) 1991, (Oxford) 1996, (Manchester) 1996; Hon. D. Univ. (York) 1996; Hon. Fellow King's Coll., Cambridge 1984. *Publications:* Religion and Science 1964, A Working Faith 1980, Church and Nation in a Secular Age 1983, Confessions of a Conservative Liberal 1988, Making Sense 1993, Faith and Uncertainty 1997, Being a Person 1998. *Leisure interests:* carpentry, painting. *Address:* 18 The Mount, Malton, North Yorks., YO17 0ND, England.

HABIB, Randa, M.A.; Jordanian/French journalist; b. 16 Jan. 1952, Beirut, Lebanon; s. of Farid Habib; m. Adnan Gharaybeh 1973; one s. one d.; ed. French Lycée, Rio de Janeiro and Univ. of Beirut; corresp. Agence France Presse (AFP) 1980, Dir. and Head AFP Office, Amman 1987–; corresp. Radio Monte Carlo 1988–, also for several int. publs. and TV. *Publications:* articles in Politique Internationale. *Leisure interests:* reading, swimming, painting. *Address:* Agence France Presse, Jebel Amman, 2nd Circle, P.O. Box 3340, Amman, Jordan. *Telephone:* 4642976, 4644978. *Fax:* 4654680.

HABIB-DELONCLE, Michel, L. ÈS L., L. EN D.; French politician, lawyer and international consultant; b. 26 Nov. 1921, Neuilly-sur-Seine; s. of Louis Habib and Jeanne Deloncle; m. Colette Sueur 1944; three s. (one deceased) two d.; ed. Ecole libre des Sciences Politiques, Paris and Faculties of Law and Letters (Sorbonne), Univ. of Paris; Resistance Movement 1941–45; Journalist, France Catholique 1945–53; Sec.-Gen. Parl. Group Rassemblement du Peuple Français 1948–54; barrister, Cour d'Appel, Paris 1955–89, hon. barrister, 1990–; Deputy, Nat. Assembly 1958–63, 1967–73; Sec. of State to the Ministry of Foreign Affairs 1962–66, to the Ministry of Educ. 1966–67; mem. European Parl. 1967–73, Vice-Pres. 1972; mem. del. UN Gen. Assembly 1967–72; Int. Relations Del., Exec. Cttee. Union des Démocrates pour la République (UDR) 1968–74; Deputy Sec.-Gen. UDR 1971; mem. Cen. Cttee. RPR 1977–, mem. Nat. Council 1990–, Exec. Council 1995–; Political Ed. La Nation 1968–74; Pres. Chambre de Commerce Franco-arabe 1970–; Chair. Soc. Marseillaise de Credit SA 1995–; Vice-Pres. Union Paneuropéenne Int. 1989–; First Vice-Pres. French Cttee. for Paneuropean Union 1993–; Dir. Unistrat Assurances 1994–, int. consultant 1995–; Officier Légion d'honneur; Croix de guerre. *Publication:* La Ve République: un chef d'oeuvre en péril 1988. *Leisure interest:* music. *Address:* 124 rue de Tocqueville, 75017 Paris, France. *Telephone:* (1) 44.93.39.15 (Office). *Fax:* (1) 47.66.70.25.

HABIBI, Hassan Ebrahim; Iranian politician; ed. in France; with the late Ayatollah Ruholla Khomeini, Paris 1978–79; apptd. mem. Revolutionary Council 1979, Minister of Justice 1984, First Vice-Pres. 1989–. *Address:* Office of the Vice-President, Teheran, Iran.

HABICHT, Werner, DR. PHIL.; German professor of English; b. 29 Jan. 1930, Schweinfurt; s. of Wilhelm Habicht and Magda (née Müller) Habicht; ed. Univ. of Munich, Johns Hopkins Univ., Univ. of Paris; Asst. Freie Universität, Berlin 1957–60, Univ. of Munich 1960–65; Prof. of English, Univ. of Heidelberg 1966–70, Univ. of Bonn 1970–78, Univ. of Würzburg 1978–; Visiting Prof. Univ. of Texas at Austin 1981, Univ. of Colorado, Boulder 1987, Ohio State Univ., Columbus 1988, Univ. of Cyprus 1995–96; mem. Akademie der Wissenschaften und der Literatur, Mainz, Bayerische Akademie der Wissenschaften; Pres. Deutsche Shakespeare-Gesellschaft West 1976–88, Vice-Pres. 1988–93. *Publications:* Die Gebärde in englischen Dichtungen des Mittelalters 1959, Studien zur Dramenform vor Shakespeare 1968, Shakespeare and the German Imagination 1994; Ed. English and American Studies in German 1968–82; Ed. Jahrbuch, Deutsche Shakespeare-Gesellschaft West 1982–95; Co-ed. Literatur Brockhaus, 3 vols. 1988; numerous articles on English literature and drama. *Address:* Institut für Englische Philologie, Universität Würzburg, Am Hubland, 97074 Würzburg, Germany. *Telephone:* (0931) 8885658. *Fax:* (0931) 8885674.

HABRAKEN, Nicolaas John; Netherlands architect; b. 29 Oct. 1928, Bandung, Indonesia; s. of late J.W.L. Habraken and of J.L.S. Heyting; m. E. Marleen van Hall 1958; one s. one d.; ed. Delft Tech. Univ.; architect, Lucas & Niemeyer (architects), Voorburg 1961–65; Dir. Stichting Architecten Research (SAR), Voorburg 1965–66, Eindhoven 1966–75; Prof. and First Chair. Dept. of Architecture, Eindhoven Tech. Univ. 1966–70, Prof. of Architecture 1966–75; Head, Dept. of Architecture, M.I.T. 1975–81, Prof. of Architecture 1975–89, Prof. Emer. 1989–; partner, Infill Systems BV, Delft 1986–; David Roell Prize 1979, ACSA Creative Achievement Award 1989, Hon. mem. Architectural Inst. of Japan 1994, B.K.V.B. Nat. Architecture Award 1996. *Publications:* Supports: An Alternative to Mass Housing 1962, Transformations of the Site 1983, The Appearance of the Form 1985, The Structure of the Ordinary 1998; research reports and numerous articles. *Address:* 63 Wildernislaan, 7313 BD Apeldoorn, The Netherlands. *Telephone:* (55) 355 6354. *Fax:* (55) 355 4765.

HABRÉ, Hissène; Chadian politician; formerly one of the leaders of the Front de Libération Nationale du Tchad (FROLINAT); head of Northern Armed Forces Command Council -1977; held the French archaeologists M. and Mme Claustre captive 1974–77; Leader of Forces Armées du Nord 1977; negotiated with Govt. of Brig.-Gen. Félix Malloum 1978; Prime Minister Aug. 1978–March 1979; resigned after Kano peace agreement with FROLINAT forces led by Goukouni Oueddei March 1979; Minister of State for Defence and War Veterans in Provisional Govt. April–May 1979; Minister of Defence 1979 (in conflict with Goukouni Oueddei in civil war, reported in exile 1980); Minister of Nat. Defence, Veterans and War Victims 1986–90; Pres. of Chad (desig.) June–Oct. 1982, Pres. 1982–90 (ousted in coup); living in Cameroon 1990.

HABSBURG-LOTHRINGEN, Georg von; Hungarian business executive and diplomatist; b. 16 Dec. 1964, Starnberg, Bavaria, Germany; s. of Otto von Habsburg-Lothringen (q.v.) and Regina, Princess of Sachsen-Meiningen; m. Eilika Habsburg Lothringen, Duchess of Oldenburg 1997; ed. Univ. of Munich; settled in Hungary 1993; Vice-Pres. MTM TV2; Dir. MTM Communications; Amb.-at-large of Hungary 1996–. *Address:* Prime Minister's Office, 4 Kossuth Square, 1055 Budapest; MTM-SBS Hungary, Rona u 174, 1145 Budapest, Hungary. *Telephone:* (1) 268 3393; (1) 167 6419. *Fax:* (1) 268 3392; (1) 220 5921.

HABSBURG-LOTHRINGEN, Otto von, DR.POL.SC.; Austrian/German/Hungarian politician and author; b. 20 Nov. 1912, Reichenau, Austria; s. of late Archduke Charles, later Emperor of Austria and King of Hungary, and Zita, Princess of Bourbon-Parma; m. Regina, Princess of Sachsen-Meiningen 1951; two s. five d.; ed. Univ. of Louvain, Belgium; mem. Pan-European Union 1936–, rep. in Washington 1940–46, Vice-Pres. 1957, Pres. 1973–; M.E.P. for Bavaria (on list of Christian Social Union) 1979–; lectures throughout the world on int. affairs and is author of weekly column appearing in 21 daily papers in 5 languages since 1953; mem. Acad. des Sciences Morales et Politiques, Inst. de France, Paris, Real Acad. de Ciencias Morales y Políticas, Madrid, Acad. da Cultura Portuguesa, Acad. Mejicana de Derecho Internacional, Acad. of Morocco, etc.; Dr. h.c. (Univs. of Nancy, Tampa, Cincinnati, Ferrara, Pécs, Budapest, Turku, Veszprém); numerous awards and decorations, including Bayerischer Verdienstorden, Order of Gregory the Great (Vatican), etc.; Robert Schuman Gold Medal 1977, Gold Medal of City of Paris, Medal of Europe of Free State of Bavaria 1991; Konrad Adenauer Prize 1977. *Publications:* 40 books in seven languages on history, politics, world affairs and especially European politics. *Address:* Hindenburgstrasse 15, 82343 Pöcking-Starnberg, Germany. *Telephone:* 08157-7015.

HACHETTE, Jean-Louis, L. EN D.; French publisher; b. 30 June 1925, Paris; s. of Louis and Blanche (née Darbou) Hachette; m. Y. de Bouillé 1954; one s. two d.; ed. Collège Stanislas, Paris, and Faculté de Droit, Paris; joined Librairie Hachette (founded by great-grandfather in 1826) 1946 (now Hachette Livre); entire career spent with Librairie Hachette, Admin. Dir. 1971–; Pres. Librairie Gén. Française 1954–. *Leisure interests:* polo, golf, skiing. *Address:* c/o Hachette Livre, 83 avenue Marceau, 75116 Paris, France.

HACKING, Ian MacDougall, PH.D., F.R.S.C., F.B.A.; Canadian professor of philosophy; b. 18 Feb. 1936, Vancouver; s. of Harold Eldridge Hacking and Margaret Elinore MacDougall; m. 1st Laura Anne Leach 1962, 2nd Judith Polsky 1983; one s. two d.; ed. Univ. of British Columbia, Cambridge Univ.; Asst. then Assoc. Prof., Univ. of B.C. 1964–69; Univ. Lecturer in Philosophy, Cambridge and Fellow of Peterhouse 1969–74; Prof., then Henry Waldgrave Stuart Prof. of Philosophy, Stanford Univ. 1975–82; Prof., Univ. of Toronto 1983–, Univ. Prof. 1991–; Fellow American Acad. of Arts and Sciences 1991. *Publications:* Logic of Statistical Inference 1965, Why Does Language Matter to Philosophy? 1975, The Emergence of Probability 1975, Representing and Intervening 1983, The Taming of Chance 1991, Le Plus pur nominalisme 1993, Rewriting the Soul: Multiple Personality and the Sciences of Memory 1995, Mad Travelers 1998, The Social Construction of What? 1999. *Leisure interests:* walking, canoeing. *Address:* 215 Huron Street, Toronto, Ont., M5S 1A1 (Office); 391 Markham Street, Toronto, Ont., M6G 2K8, Canada (Home). *Telephone:* (416) 978 4951. *Fax:* (416) 978 8703.

HACKMAN, Gene; American actor; b. 30 Jan. 1930, San Bernardino, Calif.; s. of Eugene Ezra Hackman; m. Fay Maltese 1956 (divorced 1985); one s. two d.; studied acting at the Pasadena Playhouse. *Films include:* Lilith 1964, Hawaii 1966, Banning 1967, Bonnie and Clyde 1967, The Split 1968, Downhill Racer 1969, I Never Sang For My Father 1969, The Gypsy Moths 1969, Marooned 1970, The Hunting Party 1971, The French Connection 1971, The Poseidon Adventure 1972, The Conversation 1973, Scarecrow 1973, Zandy's Bride 1974, Young Frankenstein 1974, The French Connection II 1975, Lucky Lady 1975, Night Moves 1976, Domino Principle 1977, Superman 1978, Superman II 1980, All Night Long 1980, Target 1985, Twice in a Lifetime 1985, Power 1985, Bat 21, Superman IV 1987, No Way Out 1987, Another Woman 1988, Mississippi Burning 1988, The Package 1989, The Von Metz Incident 1989, Loose Connections 1989, Full Moon in Blue Water 1989, Postcards from the Edge 1989, Class Action 1989, Loose Canons 1990, Narrow Margin 1990, Necessary Roughness 1991, Company Business 1991, The William Munny Killings 1991, The Unforgiven 1992, The Firm 1992, Geronimo, Wyatt Earp 1994, Crimson Tide, The Quick and the Dead 1995, Get Shorty, Birds of a Feather, Extreme Measures 1996, The Chamber 1996, Absolute Power 1996, Twilight 1998, Enemy of the State 1998; television includes many guest appearances on US series; also My Father, My Mother, CBS Playhouse 1968, and Shadow on the Land 1971; *Stage plays include:* Children From Their Games 1963, Cass Henderson in Any Wednesday 1964, Poor Richard, 1964, Death and the Maiden 1992; Academy Award for Best Actor, New York Film Critics' Award, Golden Globe Award, British Acad. Award, The French Connection, British Acad. Award, The Poseidon Adventure, Cannes Film Festival Award, Scarecrow, Nat. Review Bd. Award, Mississippi Burning 1988, Berlin Film Award 1989, Acad. Award, The Unforgiven 1993. *Address:* c/o Barry Haldeman, 1900 Avenue of the Stars, Suite 2000, Los Angeles, CA 90067; c/o Fred Spektor, Creative Artists Agency, 9830 Wilshire Boulevard, Beverly Hills, CA 90212, U.S.A.

HACKNEY, Francis Sheldon, PH.D.; American historian; b. 5 Dec. 1933, Birmingham, Ala.; s. of Cecil Hackney and Elizabeth Morris; m. Lucy Durr 1957; one s. two d.; ed. Vanderbilt and Yale Univs.; mem. faculty, Princeton Univ. 1965–75; Assoc. Prof. of History 1969–72, Prof. and Provost 1972–75; Pres. Tulane Univ. New Orleans 1975–80; Prof of History Univ. of Pa. 1981–93, Pres. 1981–93; mem. Bd. Dirs. Carnegie Foundation for Advancement of Teaching 1976–84, 1986–93; Chair. Nat. Endowment for the Humanities 1993–97; mem. American Philosophical Soc., American History Asscn. *Publications:* Populism to Progressivism in Alabama 1969, Populism: The Critical Issues (ed.), Understanding the American Experience (with others) 1973. *Address:* c/o Department of History, University of Pennsylvania, 100 College Hall, Philadelphia, PA 19104, U.S.A.

HACKNEY, Roderick Peter, PH.D., P.P.R.I.B.A.; British architect and developer; b. 3 March 1942, Liverpool; s. of William Hackney and Rose (Morris) Hackney; m. Christine Thornton 1964; one s.; ed. John Bright's Grammar School, Llandudno, School of Architecture, Manchester Univ.; Job Architect, Expo '67, Montreal, for monorail stations 1967; Housing Architect for Libyan Govt., Tripoli 1967–68; Asst. to Arne Jacobsen, working on Kuwait Cen. Bank, Copenhagen 1968–71; est. practice of Rod Hackney Architect, Macclesfield 1972, architectural practices in Birmingham, Leicester, Belfast, Cleator Moor, Workington, Carlisle, Millom, Clitheroe, Manchester, Stirling, Burnley, Chesterfield and Stoke on Trent 1975–88; Council mem. R.I.B.A., including Vice-Pres. for Public Affairs and Vice-Pres. for Overseas Affairs 1978–84, Pres. 1987–89, mem. of Council 1991–, Vice-Pres. Int. Affairs 1992–94, Hon. Librarian 1998–; Council mem. Int. Union of Architects 1981–85, 1991–, Pres. 1987–90; Hon. Fellow American Inst. of Architects, Fed. de Colegios de Arquitectos de la Repúb. Mexicana, United Architects of the Philippines, Royal Arch. Inst. of Canada, Indian Inst. of Architects; Patron Llandudno Museum and Art Gallery 1988–; Pres. Snowdonia Nat. Park Soc. 1987–; Pres. North Wales Centre of The Nat. Trust 1990–; mem. Editorial Bd., UIA Journal of Architectural Theory and Criticism; Jury mem. Cembureau Award for Low Rise Housing in France 1982, for Prix Int. d'Architecture de l'Institut Nat. du Logement 1983; Chair. Jury for Herouville Town Centre Competition, France 1982–83; Pres. Young Architects Forum, Sofia 1985, Building Communities (Int. Community Architecture Conf.), London 1986; presentation of case for Int. Year of Shelter for the Homeless to all 4 party confs. 1986; Chair. Times/R.I.B.A. Community Enterprise Scheme 1985–89, Trustees of Inner City Trust 1986–97; Special Prof. in Architecture, Univ. of Nottingham 1987–91; Int. Adviser Univ. of Manchester School of Architecture Centre for Int. Architectural Studies 1992–; Adviser on regeneration and inner city problems in Sweden, Italy and the U.S.A. 1990–; consultant, World Architecture Review Agency 1992–; Adviser, Centre for Human Settlements Int. 1994–, Habitat Centre News Journal, India 1996; Consultant to Chapman Clarke Films' Forever England, Central TV 1995; TV features: Build Yourself a House 1974, Community Architecture 1977, BBC Omnibus 1987; musical Good Golly Miss Molly; mem. Chartered Inst. of Building 1987–, Asscn. of Planning Supervisors 1996–; attained registration for BSI ISO9001 1996; Hon. D. Litt. (Keele) 1989; Dept. of Environment Good Design in Housing Award 1975, 1980, First Prize, for St Ann's Hospice, Manchester 1976, Prix Int. d'Architecture de l'Institut Nat. du Logement 1979–80, RICS/Times Conservation Award 1980, Civic Trust Award of Commendation 1980, 1981, 1984, Sir Robert Matthews Award (Honourable Mention) 1981, Manchester Soc. of Architects Pres.'s Award 1982, Otis Award 1982, Gold Medal, Bulgarian Inst. of Architects 1983, Gold Medal, Young Architect of the Year, Sofia 1983, Grand Medal of Federación de Colegios de Arquitectos (Mexico) 1986, Commendation, Business Enterprise Award for Housing 1993, Millennium Expo Competition Greenwich (short-listed), Citation for World Habitat Awards 1996, Stone Award 1996. *Publications:* Highfield Hall, A Community Project 1982, The Good, the Bad and the Ugly 1990, Good Golly Miss Molly 1991 (musical play). *Leisure interests:* outdoor pursuits, walking, Butterfly Society, fossils, geology, travelling, ballooning, looking at buildings, talking at conferences. *Address:* St. Peter's House, Windmill Street, Macclesfield, Cheshire, SK11 7HS, England. *Telephone:* (01625) 431792.

HADDAD, Sulaiman Ahmed el; Kuwaiti politician and banker; b. 1930; ed. Kuwait Aazamieh Secondary School, and Cairo Univ.; Sec. of Educ. Council of Kuwait; fmr. Financial Asst., Ministry of Educ. and mem. Constituent Assembly for formation of Kuwaiti Constitution; mem. Nat. Ass. 1963; fmr. Chair. and Man. Dir. Arab African Bank; Chair. ARTOC Bank Ltd., Int. Resources and Finance Bank, Arab Investment Co. in Asia and Kuwait; mem. Bd. Arab African Bank, Cairo; Deputy Chair. and Man. Dir. ARTOC (S.A.K.). *Address:* ARTOC, El Sour Street, Arab Gulf Building, P.O. Box 23074, Safat, Kuwait.

HADDADIN, Muwaffaq, PH.D.; Jordanian pharmacist and administrator; b. 1942, Ma'in, Jordan; m.; two s.; ed. American Univ. of Beirut, Lebanon, Univs. of Washington and Kansas, U.S.A.; Asst. and Assoc. Prof Coll. of Medicine, Univ. of Jordan 1972–80; Prof., Dean of Pharmacy School, Yarmouk Univ. 1980–83; Chair. Bd. Société Arabe des Industries Pharmacéutiques (SAIPH), Tunis; mem. Bd. Arab Co. for Antibiotics Industry in Baghdad, Iraq; Dir. Arab Co. for Drug Industries and Medical Appliances (ACDIMA) 1983–; mem. Jordanian Pharmacist Soc.; two medals of honour, Yarmouk Univ. *Publications:* several articles in scientific journals. *Leisure interests:* swimming, chess and classical music. *Address:* Arab Company for Drug Industries and Medical Appliances, P.O. Box 925161, Amman (Office); University of Jordan Street, P.O. Box 1076, Jubaiha 11941, Jordan.

HADDIDI, Helmi El-; Egyptian politician; b. Oct. 1925; Prof. of Bone Diseases, Faculty of Medicine, Univ. of Cairo; Asst. Sec.-Gen. Cttee. for Social Affairs, Nat. Democratic Party; fmr. mem. People's Ass.; mem. Shoura Council 1984–; Minister of Health 1985–86. *Address:* c/o Ministry of Health, Sharia Magles El Shaab, Cairo, Egypt.

HADDON-CAVE, Sir (Charles) Philip, K.B.E., C.M.G., M.A.; British overseas administrator; b. 6 July 1925, Hobart, Tasmania; m. Elizabeth Alice Simpson 1948; two s. one d.; ed. Univ. of Tasmania, King's Coll., Cambridge; entered Colonial Admin. Service 1952; successively posted in Kenya, Seychelles and Hong Kong; Financial Sec. Hong Kong 1971–81, Chief Sec. 1981–85; Chair. Fleming Overseas Investment Trust 1988–95 (Dir. 1986–95); Dir. Kleinwort Benson Group 1986–95. *Publication:* Air Transport in Australia (with D. M. Hocking) 1951. *Leisure interest:* golf. *Address:* The Old Farmhouse, Nethercote Road, Tackley, Oxon., England.

HADID, Zaha; Iraqi architect; b. 31 Oct. 1950, Baghdad; ed. American Univ. Beirut, Architectural Asscn. London; won competition for The Peak leisure complex, Hong Kong 1982 (project later cancelled); designed restaurant interior, Sapporo 1991 (first completed work), fire station, Vitra Furniture Co., Germany 1991, block of flats, Berlin; won competition for Cardiff Bay Opera House, Wales 1994 (design subsequently rejected by financing body, the Millennium Comm.); commissioned to design Contemporary Arts Center, Cinn. 1998; Kenzo Tange Prof., Columbia Univ. 1994; Sullivan Prof., Univ. of Ill. 1997; guest Prof. Hochschüle fur Bildende Kunst, Hamburg 1997; numerous exhbns. worldwide. *Address:* Studio 9, 10 Bowling Green Lane, London, EC1R 0BD, England. *Telephone:* 0171-253 4147. *Fax:* 0171-251 8322.

HADLEE, Sir Richard John, Kt., M.B.E.; New Zealand cricketer; b. 3 July 1951, Christchurch; s. of W. A. Hadlee (New Zealand cricketer); m. Karen Hadlee; ed. Christchurch Boys High School; middle-order left-hand batsman, right-arm fast-medium bowler; played for Canterbury 1971–72 to 1988–89, Nottinghamshire 1978 to 1987, Tasmania 1979–80; played in 86 Tests 1972–73 to 1990, scoring 3,124 runs (average 27.1) and taking then world record 431 wickets (average 22.9); first to take 400 Test wickets (at Christchurch in Feb. 1990 in his 79th Test); took 5 or more wickets in an innings a record 36 times in Tests; highest test score 151 v Sri Lanka, Colombo 1987; best test bowling performance 9–52 v Australia, Brisbane 1985–86; toured England 1973, 1978, 1983, 1986, 1990; scored 12,052 first-class runs (14 hundreds) and took 1,490 wickets, including 5 or more in an innings 102 times; achieved Double (1,179 runs and 117 wickets) 1984. *Publication:* Rhythm and Swing (autobiography) 1989. *Address:* Box 29186, Christchurch, New Zealand. *Fax:* (64 3) 3594452.

HAEBLER, Ingrid; Austrian pianist; b. 20 June 1926, Vienna; ed. Vienna, Salzburg and Geneva; won 1st Prize, Int. Competition Munich 1954; specializes in Haydn, Mozart, Schubert and Schumann; mem. Faculty, Salzburg Mozarteum 1969–; Mozart Medal, Vienna 1971.

HAENDEL, Ida, C.B.E.; Polish-born British violinist; b. 15 Dec. 1928, Chelm, Poland; ed. Warsaw Conservatoire, pvt. tuition in Paris and London; studied with Carl Flesch and Georges Enesco; first public appearance in G.B., Queen's Hall, London 1938; performances throughout world with many noted conductors including tour with London Philharmonic Orchestra to first Hong Kong Festival of Arts, and China and three tours of U.S.S.R.; participated in centenary anniversary Festival of Bronislav Huberman, Tel-Aviv 1982; celebrated 50th anniversary of debut at Promenade Concerts, London 1987; numerous recordings; Hon. mem. R.A.M. 1982–; Sibelius Medal (Finland) 1982. *Publication:* Woman with Violin (autobiog.) 1970. *Leisure interests:* drawing, reading. *Address:* c/o Harold Holt Ltd., 31 Sinclair Road, London, W14 0NS, England. *Telephone:* 0171-603 4600. *Fax:* 0171-603 0019.

HAFEZ, Maj.-Gen. Amin El; Syrian politician and army officer; b. 1911; fmr. Mil. Attaché in Argentina; took part in the revolution of March 1963; Deputy Prime Minister, Mil. Gov. of Syria and Minister of Interior March–Aug. 1963; Minister of Defence and Army Chief of Staff July–Aug. 1963; Pres. of Revolutionary Council and C.-in-C. of Armed Forces 1963–64; Prime Minister Nov. 1963–May 1964, Oct. 1964–Sept. 1965; Chair. of Presidency Council 1965–66; sentenced to death in absentia Aug. 1971; living in exile.

HAFTMANN, Werner, DR. PHIL.; German art historian and writer; b. 28 April 1912, Glowno; m. Evelyn Gutbrod 1987; ed. Univs. of Berlin and Göttingen; First Asst. Inst. of History of Art, Florence 1935–40; Dozent in Art History, State High School for Fine Arts, Hamburg 1951–55; Freelance writer 1956–66; Dir. Nat. Gallery, Berlin 1967–74; Lessing Prize, City of Hamburg 1962; Goethe-Plakette (Hesse) 1964; Reuter-Plakette (Berlin) 1974, Wilhelm-Heinse-Medaille der Akademie der Wissenschaften und Literatur zu Mainz 1986, Bayerischer Maximilians orden für Wissenschaft und Kunst 1991. *Publications:* Das italienische Säulenmonument 1939, Paul Klee: Wege bildnerischen Denkens 1950, 1961, Malerei im XX. Jahrhundert (2 vols.) 1954, Emil Nolde 1958, E. W. Nay 1960, Skizzenbuch: Zur Kultur der Gegenwart 1961, Nolde-Ungemalte Bilder 1963, Wols-Aufzeichnungen 1963, Guttuso, Autobiographische Bilder 1970, Marc Chagall 1972, Jorge Castillo 1975, Marc Chagall, Gouachen, Zeichnungen, Aquarelle 1975, Hans Uhlmann 1975, Klaus Fussmann 1976, Baumeister, Gilgamesch 1976, Der Bildhauer Ludwig Kasper 1978, Der Mensch und seine Bilder 1980, Horst Antes: 25 Votive 1984, Verfemte Kunst 1986, Der Bildhauer Martin Mayer 1988, E.W. Nay 1991, Baumeister, Saul 1996. *Address:* Schaftlacherstrasse 21, 83666 Waakirchen, Germany. *Telephone:* 08021 8562.

HAGEDORN, Jürgen, DR. RER. NAT.; German professor of geography; b. 10 March 1933, Hankensbüttel; s.of Ernst Hagedorn and Dorothea Schulze; m. Ingeborg A. Carl 1965; one d.; ed. Hermann-Billung-Gymnasium, Celle, Tech. Hochschule Hannover and Univ. of Göttingen; Asst. Lecturer Univ. of Göttingen 1962–69, Dozent 1969–70, Prof. 1970–72, Prof. of Geography and Dir. Inst. of Geography 1972–; mem. Göttingen Acad., Akad. Leopoldina. *Publications:* Geomorphologie des Uelzener Beckens 1964, Geomorphologie griechischer Hochgebirge 1969, Late Quaternary and Present-Day Fluvial Processes in Central Europe 1995. *Address:* Jupiterweg 1, 37077 Göttingen, Germany. *Telephone:* 0551/21323.

HAGEL, Charles; American politician; b. 4 Oct. 1946, North Platte, Neb.; m. Lilibet Ziller; two s.; ed. Brown Inst. of Radio & Television, Minn., Univ. of Nebraska; with U.S. Army 1967–68; Deputy Admin. Va. 1981–82; Pres., C.E.O. World U.S.O. 1987–90; Pres. McCarthy & Co. 1991–96; Senator from Nebraska 1996–; f., Dir. Vanguard Cellular Systems Inc.; mem. numerous U.S. Senate cttees.; mem. American Legion for Veterans of Foreign Wars; active in numerous charitable orgs.; Trustee Omaha Chamber of Commerce. *Address:* 346 Russell Senate Office, Washington, DC 20510, U.S.A.

HAGEN, Carl I.; Norwegian politician; b. 6 May 1944, Oslo; s. of Ragnar Hagen and Gerd Gamborg Hagen; m. 1st Nina Aamodt 1970; m. 2nd Eli Engum Hagen 1983; one s. one d.; ed. Inst. of Marketing, London; M.P. 1974–77, 1981–; Leader of Progress Party and Parl. Group 1978–. *Publication:* Aerlighet Varer Lengst (biog.). *Leisure interests:* tennis, family. *Address:* Fremskrittspartiet, P.O. Box 8903, Youngstorget, 0028 Oslo; Stortinget, Karl Johansgt. 22, 0026 Oslo, Norway. *Telephone:* 22-31-30-50. *Fax:* 22-31-38-28.

HAGEN, Uta Thyra; American actress; b. 12 June 1919, Göttingen, Germany; d. of Oskar F. L. Hagen and Thyra Leisner; m. 1st José V. Ferrer 1938, 2nd Herbert Berghof 1957 (died 1990); one d.; ed. Univ. of Wisconsin High School, Royal Acad. of Dramatic Art, London, and Univ. of Wisconsin; début as Ophelia in Hamlet, Dennis, Mass. 1937; Teacher (and Co-Founder) Herbert Berghof Studio (School of Acting) 1947–; Hon. D.F.A. (Smith Coll.) 1978, Hon. Dr. (De Paul Univ., Chicago) 1980, Hon. D.Hum.Litt. (Worcester Coll.) 1982; Critics Award 1951, 1963, Tony Award 1951, 1963, Donaldion Award 1951, London Critics Award 1964, New York City Mayor's Liberty Medal 1986, Lucille Lortell, Drama League, Boston Critics Lifetime Achievement Awards 1996. *Plays acted in include:* The Seagull, Arms and the Man, The Latitude of Love, The Happiest Days, Key Largo, Othello, The Master Builder, Angel Street, A Streetcar Named Desire, The Country Girl, Saint Joan, Tovarich, In Any Language, The Lady's not for Burning, The Deep Blue Sea, Cyprienne, A Month in the Country, The Good Woman of Setzuan, The Affairs of Anatol, The Queen and the Rebels, Who's Afraid of Virginia Woolf?, The Cherry Orchard, Charlotte 1980, Mrs. Warren's Profession (with Roundabout Theatre, New York) 1985, You Never Can Tell, Circle in the Square (Broadway) 1986, Mrs. Klein (off Broadway) 1995–96, (nat. tour) 1996–97. *Films:* The Other 1972, The Boys from Brazil 1978, Reversal of Fortune 1990. *Television appearances:* numerous guest star appearances 1950–. *Publications:* Respect for Acting 1973, Love for Cooking 1976, Sources (memoirs) 1983, A Challenge for the Actor 1991. *Leisure interests:* gardening, cooking, needlework. *Address:* Herbert Berghof Studio, 120 Bank Street, New York City, NY 10014, U.S.A.

HAGLER, Marvelous Marvin; American boxer (retd.) and actor; b. 23 May 1954, Newark; s. of Robert James Sims Hagler and Ida Mae Lang; m. Bertha Joann Dixon 1980; five c.; undisputed World Middleweight Champion 1980–87; won Championship from Alan Minter and defended it successfully 11 times before losing WBC version to Sugar Ray Leonard (q.v.) April 1987; stripped of other versions of title for agreeing to fight unranked Leonard March 1987; 63 professional fights, 57 wins, 2 draws, 4 defeats; now acts in action films.

HAGUE, Rt. Hon. William Jefferson, M.P., M.A., M.B.A.; British politician; b 26 March 1961; s. of Timothy N. Hague and Stella Hague; m. Ffion Jenkins 1997; ed. Wath-upon-Dearne Comprehensive School, Magdalen Coll. Oxford and Insead; Pres. Oxford Union 1981; man. consultant, McKinsey & Co. 1983–88; political adviser, H.M. Treasury 1983; mem. Parl. for Richmond, Yorks. 1989–; Parl. Pvt. Sec. to Chancellor of Exchequer 1990–93; Parl. Under-Sec. of State, Dept. of Social Security 1993–94; Minister for Social Security and Disabled People, Dept. of Social Security 1994–95; Sec. of State for Wales 1995–97; Leader of Conservative Party June 1997–. *Address:* House of Commons, London, SW1A 0AA, England.

HAHN, Carl Horst, DR.RER.POL.; German business executive; b. 1 July 1926, Chemnitz; m. Marisa Traina 1960; three s. one d.; Chair. of Bd., Continental Gummi-Werke AG 1973–81; Chair. Man. Bd., Volkswagen AG 1981–92; Chair. Supervisory Bd., Gerling-Konzern Speziale Kreditversicherungs-AG, Cologne; mem. Supervisory Bd. HAWESKO, Hamburg, Sachsenring AG, Zwickau; mem. Int. Advisory Bd. Textron Inc., Providence, Timken Co. Colmar; Vice-Chair. Bd. BATA COMPASS, Bermuda; mem. Int. Advisory Cttee., Salk Inst., Calif.; Chair. CR (German Chamber of Commerce, Kunstmuseum Wolfsburg. *Address:* Porschestrasse 53, 38440 Wolfsburg, Germany. *Telephone:* 5361-26680. *Fax:* 2668-15.

HAHN, Erwin Louis, PH.D.; American professor of physics; b. 9 June 1921, Sharon, Pa.; s. of Israel and Mary Hahn; m. 1st Marian Ethel Failing 1944 (deceased); one s. two d.; m. 2nd Natalie Woodford Hodgson 1980; ed. Juniata Coll. and Univ. of Illinois; Asst., Purdue Univ. 1943–44; Research Asst., Univ. of Illinois 1950; Nat. Research Council Fellow, Stanford Univ. 1950–51, Instructor 1951–52; Research Physicist Watson IBM Lab., New York 1952–55; Assoc. Columbia Univ. 1952–55, Calif. Univ., Berkely 1955–; Asst. Prof. 1955–56, Assoc. Prof. 1956–61, Assoc. Prof. Miller Inst. for Basic Research 1958–59, Prof. of Physics 1961–91, Prof. Emer. 1991–; Visiting Fellow, Brasenose Coll., Oxford 1960–61, 1981–82 (Hon. Fellow 1982–); Eastman (Visiting) Prof., Balliol Coll., Oxford 1988–89; mem. N.A.S.; Fellow American Acad. of Arts and Sciences, American Physical Soc., Int. Soc. of Electron Paramagnetic Spin Resonance; Assoc. mem. Slovenian Acad. of Sciences; Foreign Assoc. mem. Acad. des Sciences (France); Miller Prof. Univ. of Calif. 1985–86; Guggenheim Fellow, 1961, 1970; Hon. D.Sc. (Juniata Coll.) 1966, (Purdue Univ., Indiana) 1975; Buckley Prize 1971, Int. Soc. of Magnetic Resonance Prize 1971, Alexander Humboldt Foundation Award (Fed. Repub. of Germany) 1976–77, co-winner Wolf Foundation Prize 1983/84, Calif. Inventors Hall of Fame 1984, The Berkeley Citation 1991, Comstock Prize (co-recipient), N.A.S. (for research in radiation and electromagnetism) 1993, and other prizes and awards. *Publication:* Nuclear Quadrupole Resonance Spectroscopy (with T.P. Das) 1958. *Leisure interests:* violin, chamber music. *Address:* Department of Physics, University of California, Berkeley, CA 94720, U.S.A. *Telephone:* (510) 642-2305.

HAHN, Frank, PH.D., F.B.A.; British university professor; b. 26 April 1925, Berlin, Germany; s. of Arnold and Maria Hahn; m. Dorothy Salter 1946; ed. Bournemouth Grammar School, London School of Econs.; Lecturer, then Reader in Mathematical Econs., Univ. of Birmingham 1948–60; Lecturer in Econs., Univ. of Cambridge 1960–67; Prof. of Econs., L.S.E. 1967–72; Prof. of Econs., Univ. of Cambridge 1972–92, Prof. Emer. 1992–; Professore Ordinario, Univ. of Siena, Italy 1989–; Frank W. Taussig Resident Prof., Harvard Univ. 1974; Visiting Prof., M.I.T. 1956–57, 1971–72, 1982, Univ. of Calif., Berkeley 1959–60; Pres. Econometric Soc. 1968–69; Man.-Ed. Review of Economic Studies 1963–66; Pres. Royal Econ. Soc. 1986–89; Pres. Section F., British Asscn. 1990; Fellow of Churchill Coll., Cambridge 1960–; Fellow of British Acad., American Acad. of Arts and Sciences; Hon. mem. American Econ. Asscn. 1986; Foreign Assoc. N.A.S. 1988; Hon. Fellow L.S.E. 1989; mem. Academia Europaea 1989; Hon. D.Soc.Sc. (Univ. of Birmingham) 1981; Hon. D.Litt. (Univ. of East Anglia) 1984; Dr. h.c. (Univ. Louis Pasteur, Strasbourg) 1984; Hon. D.Sc. (Econ.) (London) 1985, Hon. Dr. (Univ. of York) 1991; Hon. D.Litt. (Leicester) 1993; Hon. Ph.D. (Athens) 1993; Palacky Gold Medal of Czechoslovak Acad. of Sciences 1991. *Publications:* General Competitive Analysis (with K. J. Arrow, q.v.) 1971, The Share of Wages in National Income 1972, Money and Inflation 1982, Equilibrium and Macroeconomics 1984, Money, Growth and Stability 1985, The Economics of Missing Markets, Information, and Games 1989 (Ed.), Handbook of Monetary Economics 1990 (Jt. Ed.), A Critical Essay on Modern Macroeconomic Theory (with Robert Solow) 1995, New Theories in Growth and Development (Jt. Ed.) 1998; also more than 80 articles in learned journals. *Leisure interests:* reading, gardening. *Address:* 16 Adams Road, Cambridge, CB3 9AD, England. *Telephone:* (01223) 352560.

HAHN, Heinz W., D.ENG.; German engineering executive; b. 13 Feb. 1929, Rüsselsheim; m. Lisel Hummel 1955; one d.; ed. Tech. Univ. Darmstadt, Tech. Univ. Karlsruhe; diesel engine engineer Motoren-Werke, Mannheim 1958–61; Chief Eng. Hanomag-Henschel, Hanover 1961–69; Dir. and mem. Bd. Klöckner-Humboldt-Deutz AG, Cologne 1970–74; Pres. and C.E.O. Magirus-Deutsch AG, Ulm 1975–81; Exec. Vice-Pres. and Deputy Chair. IVECO, Ulm 1981–85; Vice-Pres. IVECO, Turin 1985–89, Deputy Chair. 1989–. *Address:* Ginsterweg 31, 89233 Neu-Ulm, Germany (Home).

HAÏDALLA, Lieut.-Col. Mohamed Khouna Ould; Mauritanian politician and army officer; Chief of Staff of Mauritanian Army 1978–79; Minister of Defence April–May 1979, 1980, Prime Minister 1979–80, Pres. of Mauritania 1980–84 (overthrown in coup); Chair. Mil. Cttee. for Nat. Recovery (now Cttee. for Nat. Salvation) 1978–84.

HAIDER, Jörg; Austrian politician; b. 26 Jan. 1950, Carinthia; m.; two d.; ed. Vienna Univ.; joined Liberal Youth Movt. 1964, Freedom Party 1971; worked in pvt. industry 1976–77; mem. Parl. 1979–83, 1986–; Leader Freedom Party 1986–; fmr. Gov. Carinthia (resgnd. 1991), re-elected Gov. 1999. *Address:* Freedom Party of Austria, Kärntnerstr. 28, 1010 Vienna, Austria. *Telephone:* (1) 512-35-35. *Fax:* (1) (1) 513-88-58.

HAIG, Gen. Alexander Meigs, Jr.; American army officer and politician; b. 2 Dec. 1924, Philadelphia, Pa.; s. of Alexander M. and Regina Murphy Haig; m. Patricia Fox 1950; two s. one d.; ed. U.S. Mil. Acad., Naval War Coll. and Georgetown Univ.; joined U.S. Army 1947, rising to Brig.-Gen. 1969, Maj.-Gen. 1972, Gen. 1973; Deputy Special Asst. to Sec. and Deputy Sec. of Defence 1964–65; Battalion and Brigade Commdr. 1st Infantry Div., Repub. of Viet Nam 1966–67; Regimental Commdr. and Deputy Commdt. U.S. Mil. Acad. 1967–69; Sr. Mil. Advisor to Asst. to Pres. for Nat. Security Affairs, the White House 1969–70; Deputy Asst. to Pres. for Nat. Security Affairs 1970–73; Vice-Chief of Staff, U.S. Army Jan.–July 1973; special emissary to Viet Nam Jan. 1973; retd. from U.S. Army Aug. 1973; Asst. to Pres. and White House Chief of Staff Aug. 1973–Oct. 1974; recalled to active duty, U.S. Army Oct. 1974; C.-in-C., U.S. European Command 1974–79; Supreme Allied Commdr. Europe, NATO 1974–79; Pres., C.O.O. and Dir. United Technologies Corpn. 1980–81; Sec. of State 1981–82; Chair. Atlantic and Pacific Advisory Councils of United Technologies 1982; Dir. Commodore Int. Ltd. 1984, Quantum Computer Services 1989, Interneuron Pharmaceuticals Inc. 1990, MGM Grand Inc. 1990; mem. Presidential Comm. on Strategic Forces 1983–84; Sr. Fellow, Hudson Inst. for Policy Research 1982–84; Pres. Worldwide Associates Inc. 1984–; Hon. LL.D. (Utah and Niagara); Gold Medal Nat. Inst. of Social Sciences 1980; numerous medals and awards. *Leisure interests:* golf, tennis, squash, horse-riding. *Publications:* Caveat: Realism, Reagan and Foreign Policy 1984, Inner Circles: How America changed the World, A Memoir 1992. *Address:* Suite 800, 1155 15th Street, N.W., Washington, DC 20005, U.S.A.

HAILEY, Arthur; British/Canadian author; b. 5 April 1920, Luton, Beds., England; s. of George and Elsie Hailey (née Wright); m. 1st Joan Fishwick (dissolved 1950); three s., m. 2nd Sheila Dunlop 1951; one s. two d.; served as pilot/Flight-Lieut. R.A.F. 1939–47 (Air Efficiency award); mem. Writers Guild of America; Life mem. Authors League of America; Hon. Life mem. Alliance of Canadian Cinema, TV and Radio Artists. *Publications:* Runway Zero Eight (with John Castle) 1958, The Final Diagnosis 1959, In High Places 1962, Hotel 1965, Airport 1968, Wheels 1971, The Moneychangers 1975, Overload 1979, Strong Medicine 1984, The Evening News 1990, Detective 1997; novels published in 39 languages; collected plays: Close-Up 1960. *Films include:* Zero Hour, Time Lock, The Young Doctors, Hotel, Airport, The Moneychangers, Wheels 1978, Overload 1983, Strong Medicine 1986. *Poem:* A Last Request. *Leisure interests:* reading, music, wine. *Address:* Nancy Stauffer Associates, 17 Cliff Avenue, Darien, CT 06820, U.S.A. (Office); Lyford Cay, P.O. Box N-7776, Nassau, Bahamas (Home). *Fax:* (242) 362-4411 (Home).

HAILSHAM OF ST. MARYLEBONE, Baron (Life Peer), cr. 1970, of Herstmonceux in the County of Sussex; **Quintin McGarel Hogg,** K.G., P.C., C.H., F.R.S., D.C.L., LL.D.; British politician; b. 9 Oct. 1907, London; s. of the late Douglas McGarel Hogg, 1st Viscount Hailsham, and Elizabeth Brown; m. 2nd Mary Evelyn Martin 1944 (died 1978); two s. three d.; m. 3rd Deirdre Shannon 1986 (died 1998); ed. Eton Coll. and Christ Church, Oxford; Fellow, All Souls Coll., Oxford 1931–38, 1961–; Barrister, Lincoln's Inn 1932, Bencher 1956, Treas. 1975; Q.C. 1953; M.P. 1938–50, 1963–70; mem. House of Lords 1950–63, 1970–; served Second World War 1939–45; Parl. Under-Sec. to Air Ministry 1945; First Lord of Admiralty 1956–57; Minister of Educ. 1957; Lord Pres. of Council 1957–59, 1960–64; Chair. Conservative Party 1957–59; Lord Privy Seal 1959–60; Minister for Science and Tech. 1959–64; Leader of House of Lords 1960–63; Sec. of State for Educ. and Science April–Oct. 1964; Lord Chancellor 1970–74, 1979–87; Minister responsible for dealing with unemployment in the North East 1963–64; succeeded his father as 2nd Viscount Hailsham 1950, disclaimed title 1963; Rector, Glasgow Univ. 1959–62; Chancellor, Univ. of Buckingham 1983–92; Dr. h.c. (Buckingham) 1992; Hon. LL.D. (Leeds) 1982, (Cambridge), (Polytechnic of Cen. London) 1989; Hon. D.C.L. (Oxford) 1974, (Newcastle, Ulster, Sussex, C.N.A.A., Delhi, St. Andrews, Greenwich). *Publications:* The Law of Arbitration 1935, One Year's Work 1944, The Law and Employer's Liability 1944, The Times We Live In 1944, Making Peace 1945, The Left was never right 1945, The Purpose of Parliament 1946, The Case for Conservatism 1947, The Law Relating to Monopolies, Restrictive Trade Practices and Resale Price Maintenance 1956, The Conservative Case 1959, Interdependence 1961, Science and Politics 1963, The Devil's Own Song 1968, The Door Wherein I Went 1975, Elective Dictatorship 1976, The Dilemma of Democracy: Diagnosis and Prescription 1978, Law, Ethics and Authority 1979, Hamlyn Revisited—The British Legal System 1983, A Sparrow's Flight: The Memoirs of Lord Hailsham 1990, On the Constitution 1992, Values: Collapse and Cure 1994; Ed. Halsbury's Laws of England, 4th Edn. 1972–98. *Address:* House of Lords, London, SW1A 0PW; The Corner House, Heathview Gardens, London, SW15 3SZ, England (Home). *Telephone:* 0181-788 2256.

HAIRIKYAN, Paruir Arshavirovich; Armenian nationalist leader; b. 1949; ed. Yerevan Univ.; leading role in Nat. United Party of Armenia 1968–; sentenced to imprisonment for various kinds of nationalist activity 1969–73, 1974–87; 1988–; latest arrest after mass demonstrations in Yerevan in 1988; deprived of Soviet citizenship 1989, deported from U.S.S.R.; citizenship restored 1990; elected to Parl. 1990; cand. for Presidency of Armenia Oct. 1991; Chair. Union of Nat. Self-determination (UNS) 1991–96; Adviser to Pres. of Armenia 1998–. *Address:* Union of Self-Determination, Demirchan str. 25, 375002 Yerevan, Armenia.

HAITHEM, Muhammad Ali; Yemeni politician; b. 1940, Dathina, Southern Arabia; fmr. school teacher; Minister of Interior 1967; mem. Presidential Council of S. Yemen 1969–71; Chair. Council of Ministers 1969–70; mem. Nat. Front Gen. Command. Living in Cairo, Egypt.

HAITINK, Bernard; Netherlands conductor; b. 4 March 1929, Amsterdam; Conductor Netherlands Radio Philharmonic Orchestra 1955–61; appeared regularly as Guest Conductor for Concertgebouw Orchestra, Amsterdam 1956–61, Joint Conductor 1961–64, Chief. Conductor and Musical Dir. 1964–88; Prin. Conductor London Philharmonic Orchestra 1967–79, Artistic Dir. 1970–78, Pres. 1990–; Musical Dir. Glyndebourne Festival Opera 1978–88, Royal Opera House, Covent Garden 1987–99, European Union Youth Orchestra 1994–; Prin. Guest Conductor Boston Symphony Orchestra 1995–; tours with Concertgebouw in Europe, N. and S. America, Japan, with London Philharmonic in Europe, Japan, U.S.A.; Guest Conductor Los Angeles Philharmonic, Boston Symphony, Cleveland, Chicago Symphony, New York Philharmonic, Berlin Philharmonic, Vienna Philharmonic, Dresden Staatskapelle, Concertgebouw and other orchestras; records for Philips, Decca and EMI; Hon. mem. R.A.M., London 1973, Int. Gustav Mahler Soc.; Hon. D. Mus. (Oxford) 1988, (Leeds) 1988; Medal of Honour, Bruckner Soc. of America 1970, Gold Medal of Int. Gustav Mahler Soc. 1971, Erasmus Prize 1991; Royal Order of Orange-Nassau, Chevalier, Ordre des Arts et des Lettres, Officer, Order of the Crown (Belgium). *Address:* c/o Harold Holt Ltd., 31 Sinclair Road, London, W14 0NS, England. *Telephone:* 0171-603 4600. *Fax:* 0171-603 0019.

HAJNAL, John, M.A., F.B.A.; British university teacher of statistics; b. 26 Nov. 1924, Darmstadt, Germany; s. of Kalman and Eva Hajnal-Konyi; m. Nina Lande 1950; one s. three d.; ed. Univ. Coll. School, Hampstead, London, England and Balliol Coll. Oxford; Research Asst., Royal Comm. on Population, London 1944–48; Statistician, UN, New York 1948–51; Research Worker, Princeton Univ., N.J., U.S.A. 1951–53; Simon Research Fellow, Univ. of Manchester, England 1953–54, lecturer in Medical Statistics 1954–57; successively Lecturer and Reader in Demography, Reader in and Prof. of Statistics, L.S.E., London Univ. 1957–86. *Publications:* The Student Trap 1972; articles in learned journals on demography, statistics, math., etc. *Address:* 95 Hodford Road, Golders Green, London, NW11 8EH, England.

HÄKKÄNEN, Matti Klaus Juhani, LL.M.; Finnish diplomatist; b. 21 July 1936, Helsinki; s. of Klaus Häkkänen and Kaiju Broms; m. Pirkko Hentola 1962; two s.; ed. Univ. of Helsinki; served in Finnish Foreign Service Helsinki, Paris, New York, Moscow and Peking 1960–76; Amb. to Romania (concurrently to Albania) 1976–80; Under-Sec. of State 1980–83; Amb. to Netherlands (also accred. to Ireland) 1983–87, to Argentina (also accred. to Chile and Uruguay) 1987–88, to France 1988–93, to Italy (also accred. to Malta and San Marino 1993–97, to Portugal (also accred. to Morocco) 1997–; Kt. Commdr., Order of Lion of Finland, Grand Cross, Orange Nassau of the Netherlands, Officer, Black Star of France, Grand Cross, Nat. Merit of Italy, Kt. Commdr., Ordre nat. du mérite; Mil. Medal of Finland. *Leisure interests:* cycling, practical map studies. *Address:* Rua Miguel Lupi 12, 1200 Lisbon, Portugal. *Telephone:* (1) 3907551. *Fax:* (1) 3904758.

HAKKINEN, Mika; Finnish racing driver; b. 28 Sept. 1968, Helsinki; m. Erja Honkanen; fmrly. go-kart driver, Formula Ford 1600 driver, Finnish, Swedish and Nordic Champion 1987; Formula 3 driver, British Champion with West Surrey Racing 1990; Formula 1 driver Lotus 1991–93, McLaren 1993–; Grand Prix wins: European 1997, Australia 1998, Brazil 1998, 1999, Spain 1998, Monaco 1998, Austria 1998, Germany 1998, Luxembourg 1998, Japan 1998; Formula One Driver's Championship Winner 1998.

HAKOPIAN, Vilen Paruirovich; Armenian university rector and neuropharmacologist; b. 1 May 1938, Garnahovit, Talin; s. of Paruir Hakopian and Inthizar Hakopian; m. Rosa Hovhannes Gasparian; one s. one d.; ed. Yerevan Medical Inst.; jr. research worker, Biochem. Inst., Nat. Acad. of Sciences of Armenia 1961–65; sr. research worker and asst., Dept. of Pharmacology, Yerevan State Medical Univ. (YSMU) 1965–80, Prof. 1980–94, Dean of Foreign Students 1972–79, Dean of Medical Faculty 1979–83, Vice-Rector of Educational Affairs 1986–87, Rector of YSMU 1987–, Head Dept. of Pharmacology 1994–; mem. Nat. Acad. of Sciences of Armenia, N.A.S. (U.S.A.), Int. Union of Pharmacology (Belgium), Int. Pharmaceutical Fed. (Netherlands), Int. Information Acad., Moscow, Int. Higher Educ. Acad. of Sciences, Moscow, Int. Acad. of Ecology and Life Protection Sciences, St. Petersburg, Fellow Scientific Council of Int. Coll. of Angiology, New York; Ed.-in-Chief Medical Science of Armenia; mem. Editorial Bd. Experimental and Clinical Pharmacology (Moscow) 1993–, Int. Asscn. of Pathophysiology (Moscow) 1991–, and many other scientific bodies. *Publications:* nearly 200 works, including 9 monographs. *Leisure interests:* chess, reading, geology, apiculture. *Address:* Department of Pharmacology, Yerevan State Medical University, 2 Korjun Street, 375025 Yerevan (Office); Apt. 33, 28 Orbelli Street, Yerevan 375012, Armenia (Home). *Telephone:* (2) 521711 (Office); (2) 22575 (Home). *Fax:* (2) 151812.

HAKSAR, Parmeshwar Narain, M.SC.; Indian government official and former diplomatist; b. 4 Sept. 1913, Gujranwala, Punjab; s. of late Jagdish Narain Haksar and Dhanraj Haksar; m. Urmila Sapru (deceased) 1952; two d.; ed. Univ. of Allahabad, Univ. Coll., London, London School of Econs., Lincoln's Inn; Joint Sec. in charge of Admin., Ministry of External Affairs 1959–60; served as Amb. and High Commr. in various countries 1960–67; Prin. Sec. to Prime Minister 1967–73; Chief Negotiator, India-Pakistan-Bangladesh 1972–73; Deputy Chair. Planning Comm. with Cabinet rank 1975–77; Chair. Giri Inst. 1976–, Indian Statistical Inst., Zaheer Science Foundation, Nat. Cttee. on Science and Tech. 1975–77, Nat. Inst. of Public Finance and Policy 1972–75, Centre for Research in Rural and Industrial Devt., Chandigarh 1982–; Vice-Pres. Council of Science and Tech. 1975–77; Co-Chair. Indo-Soviet Jt. Comm. 1975–77; fmr. Chair. Nat. Labour Inst.; Co-signatory Global Initiative for Restoration of Morality, Tolerance and Humanism in 21st Century, Seoul 1995; Ed. Man and Development; Dir. Press Trust of India; Vice-Pres. Krishna Menon Memorial Soc.; Chair. Soc. Tech. and Nat. Devt., New Delhi, High Powered Cttee. to review Sahitya, Sangeet, Natak and Lakit Akademis and the Nat. School of Drama; Chair. Centre for Area Devt. and Action Research Studies, New Delhi; elected to Diplomatic Conf. for Revision of Red Cross Conventions 1949; mem. Neutral Nations Repatriation Comm. 1953–54, UN Cttee. of Experts on UN Public Information 1958, UN Int. Civil Service Comm. 1975–80, mem. Atomic Energy Comm. of India, Space Comm. UGC Standing Advisory Cttee. on Area Studies Programme, Nehru Foundation, Nat. Integration Council; Convenor, Sub-Group Nat. Integration Council, Hony; fmr. Chancellor Jawaharlal Nehru Univ., New Delhi; Hon. LL.D. (Patiala, Utkal and Kashmir Univs.), Hon. D.Lit. Andhra Pradesh Open Univ.; Kasturi Ranga Nat. Award 1981, Soviet Land Nehru Award 1987, Indian Science Congress Award 1989, Indira Gandhi Nat. Award for Nat. Integration 1989, Nat. Kakasaheb Gadgil Award 1995. *Publications:* Premonitions 1979, Reflections of our Times 1982, Problems of Foreign Policy, One More Life (autobiography). *Leisure interests:* cooking, photography, reading. *Address:* 4/9 Shanti Niketan, New Delhi 110021, India. *Telephone:* 6886149; 4673545.

HALE, Sir John Rigby, Kt., M.A., D.LITT., F.B.A., F.S.A., F.R.HIST.S.; British historian; b. 17 Sept. 1923, Ashford, Kent; s. of Dr. E. R. S. Hale and Hilda Birks; m. 1st Rosalind Williams 1953; one s. two d.; m. 2nd Sheila Haynes MacIvor 1965; one s.; ed. Jesus Coll., Oxford, Johns Hopkins and Harvard Univs.; Fellow and Tutor in Modern History, Jesus Coll., Oxford 1949–64; Visiting Prof. Cornell Univ. 1959; Prof. of History, Univ. of Warwick 1964–69; Prof. of Italian History, Univ. Coll., London 1970–88, of Italian 1985–88, Prof. Emer.; Visiting Prof. Univ. of Calif., Berkeley 1969–70, U.C.L.A. 1990; Chair. British Soc. for Renaissance Studies 1973–78, Trustees of the Nat. Gallery, London 1975–81 (Trustee 1973–80); mem. Royal Mint Advisory Cttee. 1979–92; Public Orator, Univ. of London 1980–83; Trustee, Victoria and Albert Museum 1983–86, British Museum 1985–93; Commr. Museums and Galleries Comm. 1983–93; Pres. British Asscn. of Friends of Museums; mem. Princeton Inst. for Advanced Study 1983–84; Chair. Advisory Cttee. Govt. Art Collection 1984–93; Hon. Fellow, Regent's Coll. 1988; Foreign mem. Accad. Arcadia (Rome) 1972 Academicus ex classe (bronze award), Acad. Medicea (Florence) 1980, Ateneo Veneto 1987, Bolla Prize (Services to Venice) 1982, Serena Medal for Italian Studies 1987, Time-Life Silver Pen Award 1993, Royal Soc. of Literature Award 1993; Commendatore, Ordine al Merito della Repubblica Italiana. *Publications:* England and the Italian Renaissance 1954, 1996, The Italian Journal of Samuel Rogers 1956, Machiavelli and Renaissance Italy 1961, The Literary Works of Machiavelli 1961, The Evolution of British Historiography 1964, Ed. Certain Discourses Military by Sir John Smyth 1964, Renaissance Europe 1480-1520 1971, Ed. Renaissance Venice 1973, Italian Renaissance Painting 1977, Florence and the Medici: the Pattern of Control 1977, Renaissance Fortification: Art or Engineering? 1977, The Italian Journal of Antonio de Beatis 1979, Renaissance War Studies 1983, Venice: The Military Organization of a Renaissance State (with M. E. Mallet) 1983, War and Society in Renaissance Europe 1984, Artists and Warfare in the Renaissance 1990, The Civilization of Europe in the Renaissance 1993. *Leisure interest:* Venice. *Address:* 26 Montpelier Row, Twickenham, Middlesex, TW1 2NQ, England. *Telephone:* 0181-892 9636.

HALEFOĞLU, Vahit M., K.C.V.O., M.A.; Turkish diplomatist; b. 19 Nov. 1919, Antakya; s. of Mesrur and Samiye Halefoğlu; m. Zehra Bereket 1951; one s. one d.; ed. Antakya Coll. and Univ. of Ankara; Turkish Foreign Service 1943–, served Vienna, Moscow, Ministry of Foreign Affairs, London 1946–59; Dir.-Gen., First Political Dept., Ministry of Foreign Affairs 1959–62; Amb. to Lebanon 1962–65, concurrently accred. to Kuwait 1964–65, Amb. to U.S.S.R. 1965–66, to Netherlands 1966–70; Deputy Sec.-Gen. of Political Affairs, Ministry of Foreign Affairs 1970–72; Amb. to Fed. Repub. of Germany 1972–82, to U.S.S.R. 1982–83; Minister of Foreign Affairs 1983–87; M.P. 1986; Dr. h.c.; Légion d'honneur, and other French, Finnish, British, Lebanese, Saudi and Italian decorations. *Leisure interests:* classical literature, history, international relations, music, walking, swimming. *Address:* c/o Ministry of Foreign Affairs, Dişişleri Bakanlığı, Yeni Hizmet Binası, 06520 Balgat, Ankara, Turkey.

HALES, Antony John, B.SC.; British business executive; b. 25 May 1948, Blackpool; s. of S. A. Hales and M. J. Hales; m. Linda Churchlow 1975; three s. one d.; ed. Repton School and Bristol Univ.; Marketing Man. Cadbury Schweppes 1969–79; joined Allied Domecq 1979, Marketing Dir. Joshua Tetley 1979–83, Man. Dir. Hall's Oxford S.W. 1983–85, Man. Dir. Taylor Walker 1985–87, Man. Dir. Ansells 1987–89, Dir. Allied Breweries, Chair. C.E.O. Allied Domecq Spirits and Wine (fmrly. Hiram Walker Group) 1995–; C.E.O. J. Lyons 1989–91, Dir. Allied Domecq (fmrly. Allied-Lyons) PLC 1989–, C.E.O. 1991–; Dir. Hyder PLC 1994–97, Midland Bank PLC, Aston Villa PLC. *Address:* Allied Domecq PLC, 24 Portland Place, London, W1N 4BB, England.

HALEY, John C., B.A., M.S., LL.D.; American banker; b. 24 July 1929, Akron, Ohio; s. of Arthur Reed Haley and Kathryn Moore; m. Rheba Hopkins 1951; two s. two d.; ed. Miami and Columbia Univs.; Asst. Treas., Chase Manhattan Bank N.A. 1959, Second Vice-Pres. 1962, Vice-Pres. 1964, Sr. Vice-Pres. 1971; Chief Exec. Orion Banking Group 1970–73; Sr. Vice-Pres. Chase Manhattan Overseas Corpn. 1970–73; Exec. Vice-Pres. Corporate and Institutional Relations, Chase Manhattan Bank N.A. 1973–84, mem. Policy Advisory Cttee.; Deputy Chair. Kissinger Associates 1984–85; Chair. and C.E.O. Business Int. Corpn. 1986–87; Dir. Armco Steel Corpn. 1975–, Chair. Bd. of Dirs. 1995–96; Trustee, Siemens Foundation; Chair. Emer. Pace Univ. *Address:* 8 Deer Run Path, Mendon, VT 05701, U.S.A.

HALÍK, Tomáš, TH.D., PH.D.; Czech philosopher, academic and priest; b. 1 June 1948, Prague; s. of Miroslav and Marie Halík; ed. Charles Univ., Prague, Pontifical Lateran Univ., Rome; psychologist, Inst. of Ministry of Industry 1972–89; clandestinely ordained priest, Erfurt 1978; psychotherapist U apolináře hospital, Prague 1984–90; involved in "underground" R.C. Church as close co-worker with Cardinal Tomášek; Gen. Sec. Czech Bishops' Conf. 1990–93; Prof., Head Dept. of Philosophy of Religion, Faculty of Philosophy, Charles Univ., Rector Univ. church; lectures in univs. around the world; Pres. Czech Christian Acad.; mem. European Acad. of Sciences and Arts and various bds. and socs. in Czech Repub. and abroad. *Publications:* over 200 works (some distributed secretly in Czechoslovakia before 1989). *Address:* Czech Christian Academy, Vyšehradská 49, Prague 2 120 00, Czech Republic. *Telephone:* (02) 24 91 72 10. *Fax:* (02) 24 91 62 37.

HALIMI, Gisèle Zoïza, LIC. EN DROIT ET PHIL.; French writer and lawyer; b. 27 July 1927, Ga Joulette, Tunisia; d. of the late Edouard Taïeb and Fortunée Metoudi; m. Claude Faux; three s.; Counsel, Paris Courts 1956–; Deputy to Nat. Ass. 1981–84; Amb. of France to UNESCO and Pres. Human Rights Cttee. 1985–87; f. and Pres. feminist movt. Choisir la Cause des Femmes 1972; lecturer; Chevalier Légion d'honneur, Grand Officier Ordre de la République (Tunisia), Medal of Achievement of the Greek People. *Publications:* Djamila Boupacha 1962, Le lait de l'oranger 1988, Resistance Against Tyranny 1966, Le procès de Burgos 1971, La cause des femmes 1974, Le programme commun des femmes 1978, La nouvelle cause des femmes 1997; for Choisir: Avortement: une loi en procès. L'affaire de Bobigny 1973, Viol: le procès d'Aix-en-Provence 1978, Choisir de donner la vie 1979, Quel Président pour les femmes? 1981, Fini le féminisme 1984, Femmes: moitié de la terre, moitié du pouvoir 1994, Une embellie perdue 1996. *Leisure interest:* classical music. *Address:* 102 rue Saint Dominique, 75007 Paris, France (Office). *Telephone:* 47 05 21 48.

HALL, Aleksander, M.A.; Polish politician, historian and publicist; b. 20 May 1953, Gdańsk; ed. Gdańsk Univ.; history teacher, Secondary School No 6, Gdańsk 1977; active in Acad. Pastoral Cure, Gdańsk in early 1970s; mem. Movt. for Defence of Human and Civic Rights (ROPCIO) 1977–79; Ed. Bratniak 1977–81; co-f. and leader, Young Poland's Movt. 1979; mem. Solidarity Trade Union 1980–; co-f. Cttee. for Defence of Persons Imprisoned because of their Opinions, attached to Solidarity Trade Union 1980; mem. Regional Co-ordinative Comm. of Solidarity Trade Union, Gdańsk 1981–84; publicist, Przegląd Katolicki (Catholic Revue) 1984–89, Polityka Polska (Polish Politics) 1982–89; mem. Primatial Social Council 1986–; mem. Civic Cttee. attached to Lech Wałęsa, Chair. Solidarity Trade Union 1988–90, Vice-Pres., Dziekania Political Thought Club 1988–89; participant Round Table debates, mem. group for political reforms Feb.–April 1989; Minister-mem. Council of Ministers (for co-operation with political orgs. and asscns.) 1989–90; Deputy to Sejm (Parl.) 1991–93, 1997–; Vice-Chair. Solidarity Election Action Parl. Club; leader Democratic Right Forum 1990–92; Co-f. and leader Conservative Party 1992–96; mem. Conservative Peasant Party (SKL) 1996–, mem. Bd. and Political Council. *Publications:* Refleksje i polemiki, Wybor publicystyki politycznej 1989, numerous articles in Polish periodicals. *Leisure interests:* reading, history, politics, political thought and history of ideas, culture and history of France. *Address:* Sejm RP, ul. Wiejska 4/6/8, 00-902 Warsaw, Poland. *Telephone:* (22) 694 18 59; 694 19 34. *Fax:* (22) 694 19 36.

HALL, Alfred Rupert, M.A., PH.D., LITT.D., F.B.A.; British science historian; b. 26 July 1920, Stoke-on-Trent; s. of Alfred Dawson Hall and Margaret Catherine Ritchie; m. 1st Annie Shore Hughes, 2nd Marie Boas; two d.; ed. Alderman Newton's School, Leicester, Christ's Coll., Cambridge; served Royal Corps of Signals 1940–45; Fellow, Christ's Coll., Cambridge 1949–59, Univ. Lecturer, Cambridge 1950–59; posts at Univs. of Calif. and Indiana 1959–63; Prof. History of Science and Tech., Imperial Coll., London 1963–80, Prof. Emer. 1980–; Consultant, Wellcome Trust 1980–85; Pres. Int. Acad. of the History of Science 1977–81; Allen Scholar, Cambridge 1948, Sarton Medal, Royal Soc. Wilkins Lecturer 1973, Leeuwenhoek Lecturer 1988. *Publications:* various books and articles on history of science and tech. including Philosophers at War 1980, The Revolution in Science 1500–1750 1983, Physic and Philanthropy: a history of the Wellcome Trust 1986, Henry More: Magic, Religion and Experiment 1990, Isaac Newton: Adventurer in Thought 1992, Newton, His Friends and His Foes 1993, All Was Light: an Introduction to Newton's Opticks 1993, Science and Society (essays) 1994, Isaac Newton: Eighteenth Century Perspectives 1998. *Leisure interests:* walking, gardening. *Address:* 14 Ball Lane, Tackley, Oxford, OX5 3AG, England. *Telephone:* (0186) 9331257.

HALL, Anthony Vincent, PH.D., F.L.S., F.R.S.S.A.; British professor of botany, systematist and conservationist; b. 22 April 1936, Bedford; s. of Alfred Smith Hall and Lucy Vincentia Wynniatt; m. Grizelda Purdie (née Gray); three s.; ed. Univ. of Cape Town; Research Asst. (Limnology), Rhodes Univ. 1956; Lecturer in Botany, Asst. Curator Bolus Herbarium, Univ. of Cape Town 1963–85, Sr. lecturer 1970–82, Assoc. Prof. 1982–96, Keeper Bolus Herbarium 1988–96, Assoc. Prof. Emer. 1997–, Hon. Research Assoc. 1997–; Gen. Sec. Royal Soc. of S.A. 1968–85; Chair. Co-ordinating Council for Nature Conservation in the Cape 1970–85, Cape Peninsula Conservation Trust 1980–85; Pres. The Athenaeum Trust 1985–87; Fellow Explorers Club New York; Hon. Life Forest Officer; Merit Award, S. African Council for Conservation and Anti-Pollution 1976; Cape Times Centenary Medal 1986, Hon. Certificate Royal Soc. of S.A. 1990. *Publications:* over 90 scientific publs., including Studies of the South African Species of Eulophia 1965, Threatened Plants of Southern Africa 1980, Revision of the Southern African Species of Satyrium 1982, South African Red Data Book: Plants—Fynbos and Karoo Biomes 1985, A Unifying Theory for Methods of Systematic Analysis 1991. *Leisure interests:* photography, dinghy sailing, travel, restoration of classic cars. *Address:* Bolus Herbarium, University of Cape Town, Rondebosch 7700 (Office); 29 Barmbeck Avenue, Newlands 7700, South Africa (Home). *Telephone:* (021) 650-3773 (Office); (021) 64-4637 (Home). *Fax:* (021) 64-1356.

HALL, Anthony William (Tony), M.A.; British broadcasting executive; b. 3 March 1951, Birkenhead; s. of D. Hall and H. Hall; m. Cynthia Hall; one s. one d.; ed. Keble Coll., Oxford; joined BBC 1973, News Ed. 1987–90, Dir. News and Current Affairs 1990–93, Man. Dir. News and Current Affairs 1993–96, Chief Exec. BBC News 1996–; Fellow, Vice-Chair. Royal TV Soc. (Chair. 1998–). *Publications:* King Coal: A History of the Miners 1981, Nuclear Politics 1984, articles in various periodicals. *Leisure interests:* reading, writing, church architecture, opera, walking in Dorset. *Address:* BBC, Room 3006, Television Centre, Wood Lane, London, W12 7RJ, England. *Telephone:* 0181-576 7312. *Fax:* 0181-576 7120.

HALL, Sir Arnold Alexander, Kt., M.A., F.R.S., D.ENG., F.ENG.; British administrator and aviation and electrical engineer; b. 23 April 1915, Liverpool; s. of Robert Alexander Hall and Ellen Elizabeth Hall; m. 1st Moira Constance Dione Sykes 1947 (deceased); three d.; m. 2nd Iola Mary Hall 1986; ed. Alsop High School, Liverpool and Clare Coll., Cambridge; Research Fellow in Aeronautics of Co. of Armourers and Braziers 1936–38; Royal Aircraft Establishment, Farnborough 1938–45; Zaharoff Prof. of Aviation, Univ. of London 1945–51; Dir. Royal Aircraft Establishment, Farnborough 1951–55; Dir. Hawker Siddeley Group Ltd. 1955–86, Lloyds Bank PLC 1966–85, Lloyds Bank U.K. Man. Ltd. 1979–84, Rolls-Royce Ltd. 1983–88; Man. Dir. Bristol Siddeley Engines Ltd. 1958–63; Vice-Chair. and Man. Dir. Hawker Siddeley Group Ltd. 1963–67, Chair. and Man. Dir. 1967–81, Chair. Hawker Siddeley Group PLC 1967–86; Pro-Chancellor, Univ. of Warwick 1964–70; mem. Advisory Council on Tech. (Ministry of Tech.) 1964, Electricity Supply Research Council 1963–71; Pres. British Electrical and Allied Mfrs. Asscn. March 1967–68; Dir. Phoenix Assurance PLC 1969–85, ICI PLC 1970–85, Onan Corpn. 1976–80; Chair. Industrial Policy Group 1972–74; Vice-Pres. Soc. British Aerospace Cos. Ltd. 1971–72, Pres. 1972–73; Chair. Fasco Industries Inc. 1980–81; Dir. Royal Ordnance PLC 1984–87; Vice-Pres. Eng. Employers' Fed. 1984–87; Chancellor Univ. of Loughborough 1980–89; Chair. Trustees of the Science Museum 1983–85; Fellow, Imperial Coll. of Science and Tech., Hon. Fellow Clare Coll., Cambridge; Hon. F.R.Ae.S., Hon. F.A.I.A.A., Hon. A.C.G.I., Hon. F.I.Mech.E., Hon. F.I.E.E., Hon. D.Tech. Foreign Assoc. of U.S. Nat. Acad. of Eng., Hon. mem. A.S.M.E.; Hon. Sc.D. (Cambridge) 1986; British Inst. of Man. Gold Medal 1981, Albert Medal, R.S.A. 1983, Gold Medal Royal Aeronautical Soc. 1962, Von Brumhauer Medal, Royal Netherlands Aero Club 1959; Freeman, City of London. *Leisure interest:* sailing. *Address:* Wakehams, Boveney Road, Dorney, Windsor, Berks., SL4 6QD, England. *Telephone:* (01753) 864916.

HALL, David Oakley, PH.D.; British professor of biology; b. 14 Nov. 1935; s. of Charles Hall and Ethel Oakley; m. Peta Smyth 1981; two d.; ed. Kearsney Coll. S. Africa, Univ. of Natal and Univ. of Calif. Berkeley; Fellow, Johns Hopkins Medical School, Baltimore 1963–64; lecturer, King's Coll. London 1964–68, Reader 1968–74, Prof. of Biology 1974–93, Research Prof. 1993–; Visiting Sr. Research Scientist, Princeton Univ. 1990–91; Chair. UK SCOPE Cttee. Royal Soc. 1994–; mem. numerous scientific cttees. etc.; consultant to govts., int. orgs. and industry. *Publications:* Photosynthesis 1972, Plants as Solar Collectors 1983, Bioproductivity of Plants in a Changing Environment 1993, Biomass, Energy and Environment 1996; more than 400 articles in professional journals etc. *Address:* King's College London, Campden Hill Road, London, W8 7AH, England. *Telephone:* 0171-333 4317. *Fax:* 0171-333 4500.

HALL, Donald, L.H.D., D.LITT.; American writer; b. 20 Sept. 1928, New Haven; s. of Donald A. Hall and Lucy (née Wells) Hall; m. 1st Kirby Thompson 1952 (divorced 1969); one s. one d.; m. 2nd Jane Kenyon 1972 (died 1995); ed. Harvard Univ., Oxford Univ., Stanford Univ.; Jr. Fellow Harvard Univ. 1954–57; Asst. Prof. Univ. of Michigan 1957–61, Assoc. Prof. 1961–66, Prof. 1966–77; Poetry Ed. Paris Review 1953–61; Consultant Harper & Row 1964–81; Newdigate Prize for Poetry from Oxford Univ. 1952, Lamont Poetry Selection, Acad. of American Poets 1955, Leonore Marshal Award 1987, New England Booksellers Asscn. Award 1993, Ruth Lilly Prize 1994, and other awards; Guggenheim Fellow 1963, 1972; mem. Authors Guild. *Publications: poems:* Exiles and Marriages 1955, The Dark Houses 1958, A Roof of Tiger Lilies 1963, The Alligator Bride 1969, The Yellow Room 1971, The Town of Hill 1975, A Blue Wing Tilts at the Edge of the

Sea 1975, Kicking the Leaves 1978, The Toy Bone 1979, The One Day (Nat. Book Circle Critic's Award 1989) 1988, Old and New Poems 1990, The Museum of Clear Ideas 1993, Lucy's Christmas 1994, I Am the Dog, I Am the Cat 1994, Lucy's Summer 1995; numerous essays and plays; as Ed.: Harvard Advanced Anthology (with L. Simpson and R. Pack) 1950, The New Poets of England and America (with R. Pack) 1957, Second Selection 1962, A Poetry Sampler 1962, Contemporary American Poetry (with W. Taylor) 1962, Poetry in English (with S. Spender) 1963, A Concise Encyclopaedia of English and American Poets and Poetry 1963, Faber Book of Modern Verse 1966, The Modern Stylists 1968, A Choice of Whitman's Verse 1968, Man and Boy 1968, Anthology of American Poetry 1969, Pleasures of Poetry (with D. Emblen) 1971, A Writer's Reader 1976, To Read Literature 1981, To Read Poetry 1982, Oxford Book of American Literary Anecdotes 1981, Claims for Poetry 1982, Oxford Book of Children's Verse in America 1985, To Read Fiction 1987, Anecdotes of Modern Art 1990, Their Ancient Glittering Eyes 1992.

HALL, Henry Edgar, PH.D., F.R.S.; British professor of physics; b. 1928; s. of John A. Hall; m. Patricia A. Broadbent 1962; two s. one d.; ed. Latymer Upper School, Hammersmith and Emmanuel Coll. Cambridge; Royal Soc. Mond Lab. Cambridge 1952–58; Sr. Student, Royal Comm. for Exhbn. of 1851, 1955–57; Research Fellow, Emmanuel Coll. Cambridge 1955–58; Lecturer in Physics, Univ. of Manchester 1958–61, Prof. 1961–95, Emer. Prof. 1995–; has held visiting professorships in Australia, U.S.A. and Japan; Simon Memorial Prize (with W. F. Vinen) 1963. *Publications:* Solid State Physics 1974; papers in scientific journals. *Leisure interest:* mountain walking. *Address:* The Schuster Laboratory, The University, Manchester, M13 9PL, England.

HALL, Jerry; American model and actress; b. 2 July 1956, Texas; m. Mick Jagger (q.v.) 1990; two s. two d.; began modelling career in Paris in 1970s; numerous television appearances including David Letterman Show, U.S.A.; stage debut in William Inge's Bus Stop, Lyric Theatre, London 1990. *Films:* Batman, Princess Caraboo 1994, Diana and Me 1996, RPM 1996. *Address:* c/o ICM Ltd., Oxford House, 76 Oxford Street, London, W1N 0AX, England.

HALL, John R., B.S.CHEM.ENG.; American business executive; b. 30 Nov. 1932, Dallas, Texas; m. Donna Stauffer 1980; one s.; ed. Vanderbilt Univ., Nashville, Tenn.; with Ashland Oil Inc. 1963–; Co-ordinator, United Carbon Div. 1963; Dir. 1968, Admin. Vice-Pres. 1968–70, Sr. Vice-Pres. 1970–71, Pres. Ashland Chemical Co. (div. of Ashland Oil) 1971–74; Exec. Vice-Pres. Ashland Oil Co. 1974–76, Group Operating Officer 1976–78, C.E.O. for Company petroleum and chemical operations 1978–79, Vice-Chair. and C.O.O. 1979–81, Chair. and C.E.O. Sept. 1981–; fmr. Chair. Nat. Petroleum Refiners' Asscn.; dir. several cos.; Trustee Vanderbilt Univ. Nashville. *Leisure interest:* golf. *Address:* Ashland Oil Inc., P.O. Box 391, Ashland, KY 41114 (Office); 99 Stoneybrook Drive, Ashland, KY 41101, U.S.A. (Home).

HALL, Nigel John, M.A. (R.C.A.); British sculptor; b. 30 Aug. 1943, Bristol; s. of Herbert John Hall and Gwendoline Mary (née Olsen) Hall; m. Manijeh Yadegar 1986; ed. Bristol Grammar School, West of England Coll. of Art, R.C.A., London; Harkness Fellowship to U.S.A. 1967–69; first one-man exhbn., Galerie Givaudan, Paris 1967; solo exhbns. include: Robert Elkon Gallery, New York 1974, 1977, 1979, 1983, Annely Juda Gallery, London 1978, 1981, 1985, 1987, 1991, 1996, Galerie Maeght, Paris 1981, 1983, Staatliche Kunsthalle, Baden-Baden 1982, Nishimura Gallery, Tokyo 1980, 1984, 1988, Garry Anderson Gallery, Sydney 1987, 1990, Hans Mayer Gallery, Düsseldorf 1989, 1999, Fondation Veranneman, Kruisthoutem, Belgium 1987, 1995, 1997, Galerie Ziegler, Zürich 1986, 1988, 1995, Park Gallery, Seoul 1997; group shows include: Documenta VI, Kassel 1977, British Sculpture in the Twentieth Century, Whitechapel Gallery, London 1981, Aspects of British Art Today, Tokyo Metropolitan Museum 1982, Britannica: Thirty Years of Sculpture, Le Havre Museum of Fine Art 1988, Drawings in Black and White, Museum of Modern Art, New York 1993, Prints of Darkness, Fogg Art Museum, Harvard Univ. 1994, British Sculpture, Schloss Ambras, Innsbruck 1998; represented in the following collections: Tate Gallery, London, Musée Nat. d'Art Moderne, Paris, Nat. Galerie, Berlin, Museum of Modern Art, New York, Australian Nat. Gallery, Canberra, Art Inst. of Chicago, Kunsthaus, Zurich, Tokyo Metropolitan Museum, Musée d'Art Moderne, Brussels, Louisiana Museum, Denmark, Nat. Museum of Art, Osaka, Museum of Contemporary Art, Sydney, and numerous others; sculpture commissioned for Thameslink Tunnel, London 1993. *Address:* 11 Kensington Park Gardens, London, W11 3HD, England. *Telephone:* 0181-675 5945; 0171-727 3162.

HALL, Sir Peter Geoffrey, Kt.; M.A., PH.D., F.B.A.; British professor of geography and planning; b. 19 March 1932, London; s. of Arthur Vickers and Bertha (née Keefe) Hall; m. 1st Carla M. Wartenberg 1962 (dissolved 1967), 2nd Magdalena Mróz 1967; ed. Blackpool Grammar School and St. Catharine's Coll., Cambridge; Asst. Lecturer, Birkbeck Coll., Univ. of London 1956–60, Lecturer 1960–65; Reader in Geography with special reference to planning, L.S.E. 1966–67; Prof. of Geography, Univ. of Reading 1968–89, Prof. Emer. 1989–; Prof. of City and Regional Planning, Univ. of Calif. (Berkeley) 1980–92, Prof. Emer. 1993–, Dir. Inst. of Urban and Regional Devt. 1989–92; Special Adviser to Sec. of State for the Environment 1991–94; Prof. of Planning, Bartlett School of Planning, Univ. College, London 1992–; mem. South East Econ. Planning Council 1966–79, Social Science Research Council 1974–80; Gill Memorial Prize, Royal Geographical Soc. 1968, Adolphe Bentinck Prize 1979, Founder's Medal, Royal Geographical Soc. 1988. *Publications:* London 2000 1963, The World Cities 1966, The Containment of Urban England 1973, Urban and Regional Planning 1974, Europe 2000 1977, Growth Centres in the European System 1980, Great Planning Disasters 1980, The Inner City in Context 1981, Silicon Landscapes 1985, Can Rail Save the City? 1985, High-Tech America 1986, Western Sunrise 1987, Cities of Tomorrow 1988, The Carrier Wave 1988, London 2001 1989, The Rise of the Gunbelt 1992, Technopoles of the World 1993, Cities in Civilization 1998. *Leisure interests:* reading, talking. *Address:* University College, 22 Gordon Street, London, WC1H 0QB (Office); 12 Queens, London, W5 2SA, England (Home). *Telephone:* 0171-380 7456 (Office); 0181-997 3717 (Home). *Fax:* 0171-380 7502 (Office).

HALL, Peter George, B.SC.; British oil industry executive; b. 10 Dec. 1924; s. of Charles Hall and Rosina Hall; m. Margaret Gladys Adams 1949; two s. two d.; ed. Sandown Grammar School, Isle of Wight, Southampton Univ.; Anglo-Iranian Oil Co. 1946–51; various posts at Fawley Refinery, Esso Petroleum Co. Ltd. 1951–63, Man. Milford Haven Refinery 1963–66, Employee Relations Man. 1966–70; Vice.-Pres., Gen. Sekiyu Seisei, Tokyo 1971–74; Asst. Gen. Man., Refining, Imperial Oil Ltd., Toronto 1974–76; Refining Man., Exxon Corpn., New York 1976–77; Dir., Esso Petroleum Co. Ltd., London 1977–78, Vice-Pres., Esso Europe Inc., London 1979–81, Man. Dir. Esso Petroleum Co. 1982–84, Pres. Esso Norge 1984–87; Chair. Snamprogetti Ltd. 1988–97. *Leisure interests:* opera, classical music, walking, gardening. *Address:* Oakley, Mill Lane, Burley, Ringwood, Hants., BH24 4HP, England. *Telephone:* (01425) 402482.

HALL, Sir Peter Reginald Frederick, Kt., C.B.E., M.A.; British theatre, opera and film director; b. 22 Nov. 1930, Bury St. Edmunds, Suffolk; s. of Reginald and Grace Hall; m. 1st Leslie Caron 1956 (dissolved 1965); one s. one d.; m. 2nd Jacqueline Taylor 1965 (dissolved 1981); one s. one d.; m. 3rd Maria Ewing (q.v.) 1982 (divorced 1989); one d.; m. 4th Nicola Frei 1990; one d.; ed. Perse School and St. Catharine's Coll., Cambridge; Produced and acted in over 20 plays at Cambridge; first professional production Windsor 1953; produced in repertory at Windsor, Worthing and Oxford Playhouse; two Shakespearean productions for Arts Council; Artistic Dir. Elizabethan Theatre Co. 1953; Asst. Dir. London Arts Theatre 1954, Dir. 1955–56; formed own producing co., Int. Playwright's Theatre 1957; Man. Dir. Royal Shakespeare Theatre, Stratford-on-Avon and Aldwych Theatre, London 1960–68; mem. Arts Council 1969–72; Co-Dir., Nat. Theatre (now Royal Nat. Theatre) with Lord Olivier April-Nov. 1973, Dir. 1973–88; f. Peter Hall Co. 1988; Artistic Dir. Glyndebourne 1983–90; Artistic Dir. The Old Vic 1995–; Assoc. Prof. of Drama, Warwick Univ. 1966–; mem. Bd. Playhouse Theatre 1990–91; Dr. h.c. (York) 1966, (Reading) 1973, (Liverpool) 1974, (Leicester) 1977; Hon. D. Soc. Sc. (Birmingham) 1989; London Theatre Critics' Award for Best Dir. for The Wars of the Roses 1963, The Homecoming and Hamlet 1965; Antoinette Perry Award for Best Dir. for The Homecoming 1966, Amadeus 1981; Hamburg Univ. Shakespeare Prize 1967; Chevalier, Ordre des Arts et Lettres 1965. *Productions:* Blood Wedding, Immoralist, The Lesson, South, Mourning Becomes Electra, Waiting for Godot, Burnt Flowerbed, Waltz of the Toreadors, Camino Real, Gigi, Wrong Side of the Park, Love's Labours Lost, Cymbeline, Twelfth Night, A Midsummer Night's Dream, Coriolanus, Two Gentlemen of Verona, Troilus and Cressida, Ondine, Romeo and Juliet, Becket, The Collection, Cat on a Hot Tin Roof, The Rope Dancers (on Broadway), The Moon and Sixpence (opera, Sadlers Wells), Henry VI (parts 1, 2 and 3), Richard III, Richard II, Henry IV (parts 1 and 2), Henry V, Eh?, The Homecoming, Moses and Aaron (opera, Covent Garden), Hamlet, The Government Inspector, The Magic Flute (opera), Staircase, Work is a Four Letter Word (film), Macbeth, Midsummer Night's Dream (film), Three into Two Won't Go (film), A Delicate Balance, Dutch Uncle, Landscape and Silence, Perfect Friday (film), The Battle of Shrivings, La Calisto (opera, Glyndebourne Festival 1970), The Knot Garden (opera, Covent Garden) 1970, Eugene Onegin (opera, Covent Garden) 1971, Old Times 1971, Tristan and Isolde (opera, Covent Garden) 1971, All Over 1972, Il Ritorno di Ulysses (opera, Glyndebourne Festival) 1972, Alte Zeiten (Burgtheater, Vienna) 1972, Via Galactica (musical, Broadway) 1972, The Homecoming (film) 1973, Marriage of Figaro (Glyndebourne) 1973, The Tempest 1974, Landscape (film) 1974, Akenfield (film) 1974, No Man's Land 1975, Happy Days 1975, John Gabriel Borkman 1975, Judgement 1975, Hamlet 1975, Tamburlaine the Great 1976, Volpone 1977, Bedroom Farce 1977, The Country Wife 1977, The Cherry Orchard 1978, Macbeth (Nat. Theatre) 1978, Betrayal (Nat. Theatre) 1978, Cosi Fan Tutte (opera, Glyndebourne) 1978, Fidelio (opera, Glyndebourne) 1979, Amadeus (Nat. Theatre) 1979, Betrayal (New York) 1980, Othello (Nat. Theatre) 1980, Amadeus (New York) 1980, Family Voices (Nat. Theatre) 1981, The Oresteia (Nat. Theatre) 1981, A Midsummer Night's Dream (opera, Glyndebourne) 1981, The Importance of Being Earnest (Nat. Theatre) 1982, Other Places (Nat. Theatre) 1982, The Ring (operas, Bayreuth Festival) 1983, Jean Seberg (Nat. Theatre) 1983, L'Incoronazione di Poppea (opera, Glyndebourne) 1984, Animal Farm (Nat. Theatre) 1984, Coriolanus (Nat. Theatre) 1984, Yonadab (Nat. Theatre) 1985, Carmen (opera, Glyndebourne) 1985, and (Metropolitan Opera) 1986, Albert Herring (opera, Glyndebourne) 1985, The Petition (New York and Nat. Theatre) 1986, Simon Boccanegra (Glyndebourne) 1986, Salome (Los Angeles) 1986, Coming in to Land (Nat. Theatre) 1986, Antony and Cleopatra (Nat. Theatre) 1987, Entertaining Strangers (Nat. Theatre) 1987, La Traviata (Glyndebourne) 1987, Falstaff (Glyndebourne) 1988, Salome (Covent Garden) 1988, Cymbeline (Nat. Theatre) 1988, The Winter's

Tale (Nat. Theatre) 1988, The Tempest 1988, Orpheus Descending 1988, Salome (opera, Chicago) 1988, Albert Herring 1989, Merchant of Venice 1989, She's Been Away (TV) 1989, New Year (opera, Houston and Glyndebourne) 1989, The Wild Duck 1990, Born Again 1990, The Homecoming 1990, Orpheus Descending (film) 1990, Twelfth Night 1991, The Rose Tattoo 1991, Tartuffe 1991, The Magic Flute 1992, The Camomile Lawn (TV) 1992, Four Baboons Adoring the Sun (New York) 1992, Sienna Red 1992, All's Well That Ends Well (R.S.C.) 1992, The Gift of the Gorgon (R.S.C.) 1992, The Magic Flute (L.A.) 1993, Separate Tables 1993, Lysistrata 1993, She Stoops to Conquer 1993, Piaf 1993, An Absolute Turkey (Le Dindon) 1993, On Approval 1994, Hamlet 1994, Jacob (TV) 1994, Never Talk to Strangers (film) 1995, Julius Caesar (R.S.C.) 1995, The Master Builder 1995, The Final Passage (TV) 1995, Mind Millie for Me 1996, The Oedipus Plays (Nat. Theatre at Epidaurus and Nat. Theatre) 1995, A School for Wives 1995, A Streetcar Named Desire 1997, The Seagull 1997, Kafka's Dick 1998, The Visitor 1999; acted in The Pedestrian (film) 1973. *Publications:* The War of the Roses 1970, Shakespeare's three Henry VI plays and Richard III (adapted with John Barton), John Gabriel Borkman (English version with Inga-Stina Ewbank), Peter Hall's Diaries: The Story of a Dramatic Battle 1983, Animal Farm: a stage adaptation 1986, The Wild Duck 1990, Making an Exhibition of Myself (autobiog.) 1993, An Absolute Turkey (new trans. of Feydeau's Le Dindon, with Nicki Frei) 1993, The Master Builder (with Inga-Stina Ewbank) 1995, Mind Millie for Me (new trans. of Feydeau's T'occupe-toi d'Amélie, with Nicki Frei). *Leisure interest:* music. *Address:* c/o Piccadilly Theatre, Denman Street, Piccadilly, SW1, London.

HALL, Philip David; British journalist; b. 8 Jan. 1955; s. of Norman Philip Hall and Olive Jean Hall; m. Marina Thomson 1997; ed. Beal Grammar School, Ilford; reporter Dagenham Post 1974–77, Ilford Recorder 1977–80; Sub-Ed. Newham Recorder 1980–84, Weekend Magazine 1984–85; reporter The People 1985–86, Chief Reporter 1986–89, News Ed. 1989–92; News Ed. Sunday Express 1992–93; Asst. Ed. (Features) News of the World 1993–94, Deputy Ed. 1994–95, Ed. 1995–. *Leisure interests:* golf, cinema, theatre. *Address:* News of the World, 1 Virginia Street, London, E1 9XR, England. *Telephone:* 0171-782 4406.

HALL, Rodney, A.M.; Australian writer, musician and actor; b. 18 Nov. 1935; s. of D.E. Hall; m. Maureen McPhail 1962; three d.; ed. City of Bath School for Boys, U.K., Brisbane Boy's Coll., Univ. of Queensland; leader Baroque Music Group; published over 500 poems in Australia, U.K., U.S.A., U.S.S.R., Philippines, France, India, several published books of poetry and novels; Creative Arts Fellow A.N.U. 1968, Literary Bd. Fellow 1974–80, tutor New England Univ. Summer School of Music 1967–71, 1977–80; lecturer Dept. of Foreign Affairs; Recorder Canberra School of Music 1979–83; Chair. Australia Council 1991–94; Miles Franklin Award 1994. *Publications include:* Selected Poems 1975, Just Relations 1982, Kisses of the Enemy 1987, Captivity Captive 1988, The Second Bridegroom 1991, The Grisly Wife 1994, The Island in the Mind 1996. *Address:* P.O. Box 788, Strawberry Hills, N.S.W. 2012, Australia.

HALL, Wesley Winfield; Barbadian cricketer and politician; b. 12 Sept. 1937; m. (divorced); four c.; ed. Combermere School and Industrial Soc. London (personnel man.); played amateur and professional cricket in England, Australia, N.Z., India, Sri Lanka and throughout W. Indies including 48 Test Matches in which he took 192 wickets and first hat-trick by a West Indian 1961–69; Man. W.I. Cricket Team throughout W.I. and abroad 1983–85; trainee telegraphist, Cable and Wireless, Barbados 1955–60; Public Relations Consultant, Esso, Queensland, Australia 1960–63, British American Tobacco Co. Ltd. (Trinidad and Tobago) 1968–78; Personnel and Public Relations Man. Banks Barbados Breweries Ltd. 1975–85; Independent Senator, Barbados Senate 1971–76, Opposition Senator 1981–86; Minister of Employment, Labour Relations and Community Devt. 1986; Minister of Employment, Labour Relations and Community Devt. 1986–88, of Tourism and Sports 1988–93, of Industrial Relations Community Devt. and Sports 1993–94; Life mem. MCC, Hon. Life mem. Barbados Football Asscn.; Humming Bird Gold Medal 1987. *Publications:* Secrets of Cricket 1962, Pace Like Fire 1965. *Address:* c/o Ministry of Tourism and Sports, Harbour Road, St. Michael, Barbados.

HALL, William K., B.S.E., M.B.A., PH.D.; American business executive; b. 8 Oct. 1943, Adrian, Mich.; s. of Daniel S. Hall and Jeanne (Isley) Hall; m. Valerie Worth Smith 1964; three s. one d.; ed. Adrian High School, Adrian, Mich. and Univ. of Mich.; Prof. of Business Admin. Univ. of Mich., Harvard Business School, European Inst. of Business Admin., France 1970–81; Man. Consultant to AT&T, Chrysler Corpn., Eastman Kodak, Ford Motor Co., Gen. Electric Co., Gen. Motors, Mobil Oil Co., Union Carbide Corpn. and other cos.; Exec. Vice-Pres. Cummins Engine Co., Inc. 1981–84; Dir. Cummins Engine Foundation; Pres. and C.O.O. Farley Industries 1984–87; Pres. and C.O.O. Eagle Industries, Chicago 1987–, now Chair. and C.E.O. Falcon Building Products (fmrly. Eagle Industries); Pres. and C.O.O. Jepson Corpn. 1987; Dir. several cos. *Address:* Falcon Building Products, 233 South Wacker Drive, # 3500, Chicago, IL 60606 (Office); 855 Lamson Drive, Winnetka, IL 60093, U.S.A. (Home). *Telephone:* (312) 906-8700 (Office).

HALLBERG, Paul Thure, FIL.LIC.; Swedish library director; b. 10 Dec. 1931, Gothenburg; s. of late Severin Hallberg and Eva Hallberg (née Theorell); m. Elisabeth Löfgren 1958; one s.; ed. Gothenburg Univ. and Yale Univ., U.S.A.; Asst. Teacher, Dept. of English Language and Literature, Gothenburg Univ. 1958–59; Librarian, Gothenburg Univ. Library 1960–68, Head of Dept. 1968–77, Dir. 1977–96; Sec. Main Cttee. for Scandia Plan 1964–65; Sec. Scandinavian Fed. of Research Librarians 1966–69, mem. Bd. 1979–84; mem. and Librarian, Royal Soc. of Arts and Sciences in Gothenburg 1977–; mem. Nat. Bibliographic Council 1983–96; Chair. Swedish Cataloguing Cttee. 1979–85; Chair. Steering Group of Swedish LIBRIS system 1992–96; mem. of Bd. NORDINFO (Nordic Council for Scientific Information and Research Libraries) 1986–88; mem. Standing Cttee., Int. Fed. of Library Asscns. and Insts., Section on Acquisition and Exchange 1977–85, mem. Standing Cttee., Section of Univ. Libraries and other Gen. Research Libraries 1985–93, Sec. 1985–89; Fil. Dr. h.c. (Gothenburg Univ.) 1997. *Publications:* A Passage to China: Colin Campbell's Diary of the First Swedish East India Company Expedition to Canton 1732–33 (ed. with C. Koninckx) 1996; author and ed. of numerous books and articles on bibliography and librarianship. *Leisure interests:* music and country cottage. *Address:* Orangerigatan 34, SE-412 66 Gothenburg, Sweden. *Telephone:* (031) 40 23 18.

HALLDÉN, Lars Harry, M.S., PH.D.; Swedish business executive; b. 12 Aug. 1935, Eskilstuna; s. of Harry Halldén and Margareta Norbäck; m. Berit von Grothusen; three s. one d.; joined Alfa-Laval 1963, Group Vice-Pres. responsible for operations in Lund 1971–78, Exec. Vice-Pres. 1978, fmr. Pres. and C.E.O. Tetra Alfa-Laval Group; Légion d'honneur. *Leisure interest:* golf.

HALLIER, Hans-Joachim, D.IUR.; German diplomatist; b. 25 April 1930, Offenbach; s. of Christian L. Hallier and Sophie Heberer; m. Almuth H. Frantz 1966; two s.; ed. Lessing Gymnasium, Frankfurt and Univs. of Frankfurt and Heidelberg; attaché, German NATO Del. Paris 1960–61; Second Sec. Djakarta 1962–66; First Sec. Tokyo 1966–69; Dir. Cabinet of Foreign Minister, Bonn 1970–74; Amb. to Malaysia 1974–76, to Indonesia 1980–83, to Japan 1986–90, to Holy See 1990–95; Dir.-Gen. Foreign Office, Bonn 1983–86. *Publications:* books and research papers on int. law.

HALLIWELL, Geri; British singer; mem. (with Victoria Adams, Melanie Brown, Emma Bunton and Melanie Chisholm) The Spice Girls 1993–98; UN Goodwill Amb. 1998–; Best Single (for Wannabe) Brit Awards 1997, Best Video for Say You'll Be There 1997; two Ivor Novello songwriting awards 1997; Best British Band Smash Hits Show 1997; three American Music Awards 1998; Special Award for Int. Sales Brit Awards 1998. *Albums include:* Spice Girls 1996, Spiceworld 1997. *Singles include:* Wannabe 1996, Say You'll Be There 1996, 2 Become 1 1996, Mama/Who Do You Think You Are 1997, Spice Up Your Life 1997, Too Much 1997, Stop 1998, Viva Forever 1998, Look at Me (solo) 1999. *Film:* Spiceworld the Movie 1997. *Address:* c/o Chrysalis Records, 43 Brook Green, London, W6 7EF, England. *Telephone:* 0171-605 5000.

HALLMAN, Viola; German business executive; b. 8 Dec. 1944, Hagen, North Rhine Westphalia; d. of Werner and Helga Flachmeier; m. Olof J. Hallman 1971; one d.; ed. Univs. of Hamburg, Marburg and Padua; Chief Exec. Theis Group; Chief Exec. Friedrich Gustav Theis Kaltwalzwerke GmbH 1972, Friedrich Gustav Theis GmbH & Co. Flachdraht- und Profilwerk Hagen-Hohenlimburg 1972, Theis Verpackungssysteme GmbH, Packbandwerk Gelsenkirchen 1975, Alte & Schröder GmbH & Co., Stahl- und NE-Veredlungswerke Halver und Hagen-Halden 1979; Chair. and C.E.O. Theis Group; mem. Fed. Cttee. of Business Econs. (BBW) of the RKW, Eschborn, VvU Asscn. of Women Entrepreneurs, Cologne, ASU Working Asscn. of Independent Business Entrepreneurs, Bonn; Manager of the Year 1979. *Publication:* Entrepreneur—Profession Without Future? *Leisure interests:* riding, swimming, literature, history. *Address:* Bandstahlstrasse 14-18, 58093 Hagen-Halden, Germany. *Telephone:* 02331/693-0.

HALLSTRÖM, Lasse; Swedish film director; b. 1946; m. Lena Olin; directed: A Lover and his Lass 1975, Abba—The Movie 1977, Father-to-be 1979, The Rooster 1981, Happy We 1983, My Life as a Dog 1985 (Film of the Year 1985, Oscar nomination for Best Director), The Children of Bullerby Village 1986, More about the Children of Bullerby Village 1987, Once Around 1991, What's Eating Gilbert Grape (also co-exec. producer), Something to Talk About.

HALLYDAY, Johnny (b. Jean-Philippe Smet); French popular singer; b. 15 June 1943, Paris; m. Sylvie Vartan; m. Laetitia Boudou 1996; appeared on stage aged 5; music hall tours with his cousin and her husband, American dancer Lee Halliday; several film; albums include Hamlet-Halliday 1976; numerous concerts; 60 Gold Discs. *Film:* Detective 1985.

HALONEN TARJA, Kaarina; Finnish politician and lawyer; b. 24 Dec. 1943; lawyer, Lainvalvonta Oy 1967–68; social welfare officer, organizing Sec. Nat. Union of Finnish Students 1969–70; lawyer, Cen. Org. of Finnish Trade Unions 1970–; Parl. Sec. to Prime Minister Sorsa 1974–75; mem. Parl. 1979–; Second Minister, Ministry of Social Affairs and Health 1987–90; Minister of Justice 1990–91, of Foreign Affairs 1995–; Social Democratic Party. *Address:* Ministry of Foreign Affairs, Merikasarmi, P.O. Box 176, 00161 Helsinki, Finland.

HALPERIN, Bertrand Israel, PH.D.; American professor of physics; b. 6 Dec. 1941, Brooklyn, New York; s. of Morris Halperin and Eva Teplitsky Halperin; m. Helena Stacy French 1962; one s. one d.; ed. George Wingate High School, Brooklyn, Harvard Coll. and Univ. of California Berkeley; NSF Postdoctoral Fellow Ecole Normale Supérieure, Paris 1965–66; mem. tech. staff Bell Labs. 1966–76; Prof. of Physics Harvard Univ. 1976–, Chair. Dept.

of Physics 1988–91, Hollis Prof. of Math. and Natural Philosophy 1992–; Assoc. Ed. Reviews of Modern Physics 1974–80; mem. N.A.S., American Acad. of Arts and Sciences, American Philosophical Soc.; Fellow American Physical Soc.; Oliver Buckley Prize for Condensed Matter Physics 1982. *Publications:* about 150 articles in scientific journals. *Address:* Lyman Laboratory of Physics, Harvard University, Cambridge, MA 02138, U.S.A. *Telephone:* (617) 495-4294.

HALPERIN, Tulio, D.PHIL.; Argentinian historian; b. 27 Oct. 1926; ed. Univ. de Buenos Aires, Ecole Pratique des Hautes Etudes, Paris; Prof., Univ. Nac. del Litoral (Rosario, Argentina) 1955–61; Prof. Univ. de Buenos Aires 1959–66, Univ. of Oxford 1970–71, Univ. of Calif. (Berkeley) 1971–; Lecturer, History Dept., Harvard Univ. 1967–. *Publications:* El Pensamiento de Echeverría 1951, Un Conflicto Nacional: Moriscos y Cristianos Viejos en Valencia 1955, El Río de la Plata al Comenzar el Siglo XIX 1960, Tradición Política Española e Ideología Revolucionaria de Mayo 1961, Historia de la Universidad de Buenos Aires 1962, Argentina en el Callejón 1964, Historia contemporánea de América Latina 1969, Hispanoamérica después de la Independencia 1972 (in English The Aftermath of Revolution in Latin America 1973), Revolución y guerra 1972 (in English Politics, Economics and Society in Argentina in the Revolutionary Period 1975). *Address:* History Department, University of California, Berkeley, CA 94720, U.S.A.

HALPERN, Daniel, M.F.A.; American editor and author; b. 11 Sept. 1945, Syracuse, N.Y.; s. of Irving Halpern and Rosemary Halpern; m. Jean Carter 1982; ed. California State Univ. and Columbia Univ.; Editor-in-Chief, The Ecco Press (Antaeus) 1970–; Adjunct Prof. Columbia Univ. 1975–; Dir. Nat. Poetry Series 1978–; Visiting Prof. Princeton Univ. 1975–76, 1987–88; Nat. Endowment for the Arts Fellowship 1974, 1975, 1987; Robert Frost Fellowship, CAPS; Guggenheim Fellow 1988; Carey Thomas Award for Creative Publishing, etc. *Publications include:* poetry: Travelling on Credit 1972, Street Fire 1975, Life Among Others 1978, Seasonal Rights 1982, Tango 1987, Halpern's Guide to the Essential Restaurants of Italy 1990, Foreign Neon 1991, Selected Poems 1994, Antaeus 1970 1996, Something Shining 1998; ed. several anthologies. *Leisure interest:* cooking. *Address:* 100 West Broad Street, Hopewell, NJ 08525, U.S.A. *Telephone:* (609) 466-4748 (Office).

HALPERN, Jack, PH.D., F.R.S.; American university professor; b. 19 Jan. 1925, Poland; s. of Philip Halpern and Anna Sass; m. Helen Peritz 1949; two d.; ed. McGill Univ., Montreal; NRC Postdoctoral Overseas Fellow, Univ. of Manchester 1949–50; Prof. of Chem., Univ. of B.C., Canada 1950–62; Nuffield Fellow, Univ. of Cambridge 1959–60; Louis Block Distinguished Service Prof., Univ. of Chicago 1962–; External Scientific Mem. Max Planck Inst. für Kohlenforschung, Mulheim 1983–; Visiting Prof. at various univs. in U.S.A. and Copenhagen; mem. Council N.A.S. 1990– (Chair. Chemistry Section 1991–, Vice-Pres. 1993–); Chair. German-American Council 1993–; numerous other lectureships, professional and editorial appointments; Hon. Fellow Royal Soc. of Chem. 1987; Fellow American Acad. of Arts and Sciences; Hon. D.Sc. (Univ. of B.C.) 1986, (McGill) 1997; American Chemical Soc. Award in Inorganic Chem. 1968, Royal Soc. of Chem. Award in Catalysis 1977, Humboldt Award 1977, Richard Kokes Award 1978, American Chemical Soc. Award for Distinguished Service in the Advancement of Inorganic Chem. 1985, Willard Gibbs Medal 1986, Bailar Medal 1986, German Chemical Soc. August Wilhelm von Hoffman Medal 1988, American Inst. of Chemists Chemical Pioneer Award 1991, Swiss Chemical Soc. Paracelsus Prize 1992, Basolo Medal 1993, Robert A. Welch Award 1994, American Chemical Soc. Award in Organo-metallic Chem. 1995, Int. Precious Metals Inst. Henry Alberts Award 1995; Cross of Merit (Germany) 1996. *Publications:* more than 250 scientific articles in various scientific journals. *Leisure interests:* art, music, theatre. *Address:* Department of Chemistry, University of Chicago, Chicago, IL 60637 (Office); 5630 S. Dorchester Avenue, Chicago, IL 60637, U.S.A. *Telephone:* (773) 702-7095 (Office); (773) 643-6837 (Home).

HALPERN, Sir Ralph (Mark), Kt., C.B.I.M.; British business executive; b. 1938; s. of Bernard Halpern and Olga Halpern; m. Joan Halpern; one d.; ed. St. Christopher School, Letchworth; former trainee Selfridges; joined Burton Group PLC 1961, Chief Exec. and Man. Dir. 1978–90, Chair. 1981–90; co-founder, Top Shop 1970; Chair. CBI Marketing and Common Affairs Cttee. 1984; mem. CBI City-Industry Task Force 1986; mem. Pres.'s Cttee., Chair. British Fashion Council 1990–94; mem. advisory council Prince's Youth Business Trust 1991–. *Address:* c/o The Reform Club, Pall Mall, London, W.1, England.

HALSBURY, 3rd Earl of; **John Anthony Hardinge Giffard,** B.SC., F.R.I.C., F.INST.P., C.ENG., F.I.PROD.E., F.ENG., F.R.S.; British scientific consultant; b. 4 June 1908; s. of 2nd Earl of Halsbury and the late Esme Stewart; m. 1st Ismay C. Crichton-Stuart 1930; one s.; m. 2nd Elizabeth A. Faith (née Godley) 1936 (died 1983); two d.; ed. Eton Coll.; Lever Bros. 1935–42; Brown-Firth Research Labs. 1942–47; Dir. of Research, Decca Record Co. 1947–49; Man. Dir. Nat. Research Devt. Corpn. 1949–59; Consultant and Dir. Joseph Lucas Industries 1959–74, Distillers Co. Ltd. 1959–78, Head-Wrightson Ltd. 1959–78; Chancellor, Brunel Univ. 1966–97; mem. numerous advisory cttees. etc.; Hon. F.I.C.E.; Hon. A.R.C.V.S.; Hon. F.R.S.C.; Hon. D.Tech. (Brunel) 1966; Hon. D. Univ. (Essex.) 1968. *Address:* 4 Campden House, 29 Sheffield Terrace, London, W8 7NE, England. *Telephone:* 0171-727 3125.

HALSE, Bengt Gösta, DR.ENG.; Swedish business executive; b. 2 Feb. 1943, Gothenburg; ed. Chalmers Inst. of Tech., Gothenburg; with Ericsson Group 1974–95; Pres., C.E.O. Saab AB 1995–. *Address:* Saab AB, SE-581 88, Linköping, Sweden. *Telephone:* (13) 180000. *Fax:* (13) 187111.

HALSEY, Albert Henry, M.A., PH.D.; British university professor; b. 13 April 1923, London; s. of William T. Halsey and Ada Draper; m. Gertrude M. Littler 1949; three s. two d.; ed. London School of Econs.; research worker, Univ. of Liverpool 1952–54; Lecturer, Univ. of Birmingham 1954–62; Fellow, Centre for Advanced Study of Behavioural Sciences, Palo Alto, Calif. 1956–57; Prof. of Sociology, Univ. of Chicago 1959–60; Dir. Barnett House and Fellow, Nuffield Coll., Oxford 1962–90; Prof. of Social and Admin. Studies, Univ. of Oxford 1978–90, Prof. Emer. 1990–; Sr. Fellow British Acad. 1995; mem. Acad. Europaea 1992; Foreign mem. American Acad. of Arts and Sciences 1988; Hon. Fellow Goldsmiths Coll. London 1992, L.S.E. 1993; Hon. D.Sc. (Birmingham) 1987; Hon. Dr. (Open Univ.) 1989. *Publications:* Origins and Destinations 1980, Change in British Society 1986, English Ethical Socialism (with Norman Dennis) 1988, The Decline of Donnish Dominion 1992, No Discouragement: an Autobiography of A. H. Halsey 1996, Education, Culture, Economy and Society 1997. *Leisure interest:* gardening. *Address:* Nuffield College, Oxford, OX1 1NF (Office); 28 Upland Park Road, Oxford, OX2 7RU, England (Home). *Telephone:* (01865) 278521 (Office); (01865) 558625 (Home).

HALSTEAD, Sir Ronald, Kt., C.B.E., M.A., C.B.I.M., F.R.S.C., F.R.S.A.; British business executive; b. 17 May 1927, Lancaster; s. of Richard and Bessie Harrison Halstead; m. Yvonne Cecile de Monchaux 1968 (deceased); two s.; ed. Queens' Coll., Cambridge; Research Chemist H.P. Bulmer & Co. 1948–53; Mfg. Man. Macleans Ltd. 1954–55; Factory Man. Beecham Products Inc. (U.S.A.) 1955–60, Asst. Man. Dir. Beecham Research Lab. Ltd. 1960–62, Pres. Beecham Research Labs., Inc. (U.S.A.) 1962–64, Vice-Pres. Marketing, Beecham Products, Inc. (U.S.A.) 1962–64, Chair. Food and Drink Div. Beecham Group 1964–67; Chair. Beecham Products 1967–84, Man. Dir. (consumer products) Beecham Group 1973–84, Chair. and Chief Exec. Beecham Group PLC 1984–85; Dir. The Otis Elevator Co. Ltd. 1978–83, Burmah Oil 1983–89; Dir. (Non-exec.) American Cyanamid Co. 1986–94, Davy Corpn. PLC 1986–91, Gestetner Holdings PLC 1986–95; Dir. Laurentian Financial Group PLC 1991–95; Chair. CAB Int. 1995–; Deputy Chair. Tech. Colls. Trust 1993–; Vice-Chair. Proprietary Asscn. of G.B. 1968–77; Pres. Nat. Advertising Benevolent Soc. 1978–80; Vice-Pres. Inst. of Packaging 1979–81, Pres. 1981–83; Non-Exec. Dir. British Steel Corpn. 1979–86, Deputy Chair. 1986–94; Gov. Ashridge Man. Coll. 1970–, Vice-Chair. 1977–; Pres. Inc. Soc. of British Advertisers 1971–73; Chair. British Nutrition Foundation 1970–73, Council mem. 1967–79; Vice-Chair. Advertising Asscn. 1973–81; Vice-Chair. Food & Drink Industries Council 1973–76; Pres. Food Mfrs. Fed. 1974–76; Fellow, Inst. of Marketing 1975–, Vice-Pres. 1980–; mem. Council, Food Mfrs Fed. Inc. 1966–85; mem. CBI 1970–86, B.I.M. 1972–77, Cambridge Univ. Appointments Bd. 1969–73, Agric. Research Council 1978–84; Dir. Nat. Coll. of Food Tech. 1977–78, Chair. of Bd. 1978–83; Chair. Knitting Sector Working Group, NEDO 1978–90, Textile and Garment Working Group, 1991–93; Fellow, Inst. of Grocery Distribution 1979–, Marketing Soc. 1981–; Trustee, Inst. of Econ. Affairs 1980–93; mem. Monopolies and Mergers Comm. Newspaper Panel 1980–92; mem. Industrial Devt. Advisory Bd. Dept. of Trade and Industry 1983–93, Chair. 1984–93; Hon. Treas. and Dir., Centre for Policy Studies 1984–93; mem. Priorities Bd. for Research and Devt. in Agric. and Food, Ministry of Agric. Fish and Food 1984–87; Chair. Bd. of Food Studies Univ. of Reading 1983–86; Pres. Eng. Industries Asscn. 1991–; mem. Monopolies and Mergers Comm. 1993–; Council mem. European Policy Forum 1993–; Council mem. Univ. of Buckingham 1973–95, Univ. of Reading 1978–98; Council and Exec. Cttee. mem., Imperial Soc. of Kts. Bachelor 1985–; Chair. Conservative Foreign and Commonwealth Council 1995–; Hon. Fellow Inst. of Food Science and Tech., Inst. of Marketing; Hon. Fellow, Queens' Coll. Cambridge 1985; Gov. De Montfort Univ. (fmrly. Leicester Polytechnic) 1989–97; Hon. D.Sc. (Reading) 1982, (Univ. of Lancaster) 1987. *Leisure interests:* sailing, squash racquets, skiing. *Address:* 37 Edwardes Square, London, W8 6HH, England. *Telephone:* 0171-603 9010.

HAMAD, Abdul-Latif Yousef al-, B.A.; Kuwaiti international official, banker and politician; b. 1936; m.; four c.; ed. Claremont Coll., Calif., Harvard Univ.; mem. del. to UN 1962; Dir.-Gen. Kuwait Fund for Arab Econ. Devt. 1963–81; Dir., then Man. Dir. Kuwait Investment Co. 1963–71; Man. Dir. Kuwait Investment Co. 1965–74; Chair. Kuwait Prefabricated Bldg. Co. 1965–78, United Bank of Kuwait Ltd., London 1966–84; Exec. Dir. Arab Fund for Econ. and Social Devt. 1972–81, Dir.-Gen. and Chair. Bd. of Dirs. 1985–; Chair. Compagnie Arabe et Internationale d'Investissements, Luxembourg 1973–81; mem. Bd. of Trustees, Corporate Property Investors, New York 1975–, mem. Governing Body Inst. of Devt. Studies, Sussex, U.K. 1975–87; mem. Ind. Comm. on Int. Devt. Issues (Brandt Comm.) 1976–79; mem. Bd. Int. Inst. for Environment and Devt., London 1976–80; Minister of Finance and Planning 1981–83; Gov. for Kuwait, World Bank and IMF 1981–83; mem. UN Cttee. for Devt. Planning 1982–91, Chair. 1987; mem. IFC Banking Advisory Bd. Group 1987–, Advisory Group on Financial Flows for Africa (UN) 1987–88, South Comm. 1987–89, Group of Ten (African Devt. Bank) 1987–, World Bank's Pvt. Sector Devt. Review Group 1988–, UN Panel for Public Hearings on Activities of Transnat. Corpns. in S. Africa and Namibia 1989–92, Bd. Trustees of Stockholm Environment Inst. 1989–92, Comm. on Global Governance 1992–. *Address:* Arab Fund for Economic and Social Development, P.O. Box 21923, Safat 13080, Kuwait.

HAMAMOTO, Manso; Japanese politician; Chair. Social Democratic Party of Japan (SDPJ) Diet Affairs Cttee. for House of Councillors; Chair. of SDPJ mems. in House of Councillors; Minister of Labour 1994–96. *Address:* c/o Social Democratic Party of Japan, 1-8-1, Nagata-cho, Chiyoda-ku, Tokyo 100-0014, Japan.

HAMARI, Julia; Hungarian mezzo-soprano; b. 21 Nov. 1942, Budapest; d. of Sándor Hamari and Erzsébet Dokupil; m. Lajos Petö; ed. Franz Liszt Music Acad. of Budapest; performed in festivals of Edinburgh, Glyndebourne, Florence (Maggio Musicale); specialises in Rossini, Mozart, Bellini; lieder recitalist and oratorio performer; Prof. Staatliche Hochschule für Musik, Stuttgart 1989–; Kodály Prize 1987. *Address:* Stuttgart 40, Max Brodweg 14, Germany.

HAMARNEH, Sami K., PH.D.; American medical historian and university professor; b. 2 Feb. 1925, Madaba, Jordan; s. of Khalaf Odeh Hamarneh and Nora Zumot Hamarneh; m. Nazha T. Ajaj 1948; one s.; ed. Syrian Univ., Damascus, Syria, North Dakota State Univ., Fargo and Wisconsin Univ., Madison, Wis.; Curator, Div. of Medical Sciences, Smithsonian Inst. 1977–, U.S. Nat. Museum, Washington, D.C. 1959–78; Prof. of History of Medical Sciences, Aleppo Univ., Syria 1978–79, King Abdulaziz Univ., Saudi Arabia 1982–83; Prof. and Researcher, Yarmouk Univ., Jordan 1984–87, Prof. and Researcher (History of Medicine, Nursing and Pharmacy), Univ. of Jordan 1987–90; Prof. of Islamic Medicine, Int. Inst. of Islamic Thought and Civilization (ISTAC), Kuala Lumpur, Malaysia 1993–; Hon. D. Litt. (Hamdard Univ., Karachi) 1998; Ed. Kremers Award (U.S.A.), Citation of Merit, Univ. of Wis. 1997; Star of Jordan Medal. *Publications:* Customs and Civilization in Bible Lands 1960, Bibliography on Medicine and Pharmacy in Medieval Islam 1964, Origins of Pharmacy and Therapy in the Near East 1973, The Physician, Therapist and Surgeon, Ibn al-Quff 1974, Catalogue on Medicine and Pharmacy at the British Library 1975, Directory of Historians of Arab-Islamic Science 1980, Health Sciences in Early Islam; collected papers 1983–85, Promises, Heritage and Peace 1986, History of Arabic Medicine and Allied Health Sciences 1986, Introduction to al-Biruni's Book on Precious Stones and Minerals 1988, Ibn al-Quff al-Karaki's Book on the Preservation of Health 1989, Ibn al-Quff al-Karaki's Book on Surgery 1994, Directory of Historians of Islamic Medicine and the Allied Sciences 1995, Arabic-Islamic Medicine and Pharmacy During the Golden Age 1997. *Leisure interests:* reading, jogging, travel. *Address:* 4631 Massachusetts Avenue, N.W., Washington, DC 20016-2361, U.S.A.; International Institute of Islamic Thought and Civilization (ISTAC), P.O. Box 11961, Kuala Lumpur, 50762, Malaysia. *Telephone:* (202) 966-7196 (U.S.A.); 254-4444 (Malaysia). *Fax:* 254-8343 (Malaysia).

HAMBIDGE, Most Rev. Douglas Walter, D.D.; British ecclesiastic (retd.); b. 6 March 1927, London; s. of late Douglas Hambidge and late Florence Driscoll; m. Denise Colvill 1956; two s. one d.; ed. Univ. of London, London Coll. of Divinity and Anglican Theological Coll.; ordained priest 1954; St. Mark & St. Bartholomew, U.K. 1953–56; Cassiar, B.C., Canada 1956–58; Smithers, B.C. 1958–64; Fort St. John, B.C. 1964–69; Rural Dean, Tweedsmuir 1960–64; Canon, St. Andrew's Cathedral 1965; Rural Dean of Peace River 1965–69; Bishop of Caledonia 1969; Metropolitan of Ecclesiastical Province of B.C. and Archbishop of New Westminster 1981–93; Prin. St. Mark's Theological Coll., Dar es Salaam, Tanzania 1993–95; Asst. Bishop of Dar es Salaam 1993–95. *Address:* 520 Pym Street, Parksville, B.C., V9P 1B6, Canada.

HAMBLING, Maggi, O.B.E.; British artist; b. 23 Oct. 1945, Sudbury, Suffolk; d. of Harry Leonard Hambling and Marjorie Rose Hambling; ed. Hadleigh Hall School and Amberfield School, Suffolk, Ipswich School of Art, Camberwell School of Art, London, Slade School of Fine Art, London; studied painting with Lett Haines and Cedric Morris 1960–; first solo exhbn. at Hadleigh Gallery, Suffolk 1967; further solo exhbns. in London 1973, 1977; at Nat. Gallery 1981, Nat. Portrait Gallery 1983, 1997, Serpentine Gallery 1987, Richard Demarco Gallery, Edin. 1988, Arnolfini Gallery, Bristol 1988, Bernard Jacobson Gallery 1990, Yale Center for British Art, U.S.A. 1991, Northern Centre for Contemporary Art, Sunderland, Cornerhouse, Manchester, Angel Row, Nottingham, Christchurch Mansions, Ipswich, Barbican, London, Harris Museum, Preston 1993–94, Marlborough Fine Arts, London 1996, Yorkshire Sculpture Park 1997, Hugh Lane Gallery, Dublin 1997; Oscar Wilde memorial Adelaide St., London 1998; tutor Morley Coll.; Boise Travel Award 1969, Arts Council Award 1977, First Artist in Residence, Nat. Gallery, London 1980–81, shared Jerwood Prize 1995. *Public collections:* include Arts Council, Ashmolean Museum, Oxford, British Council, British Museum, Chelmsford and Essex Museum, Contemporary Art Soc., European Parl. Collection, Imperial War Museum, Ipswich Museum, Leicestershire Ed. Cttee., Minories Colchester, Nat. Gallery, Nat. Portrait Gallery, Royal Army Medical Coll., Rugby Museum, Southampton Art Gallery, Tate Gallery, William Morris School, Birmingham City Art Gallery, Morley Coll. London, Clare Coll. Cambridge, Whitworth Art Gallery, Gulbenkian Foundation, Preston Art Gallery, HTV Bristol, Scottish Nat. Gallery of Modern Art, Scottish Nat. Portrait Gallery, St. Thomas' Hosp., London, Univ. Coll., London, Wakefield Art Gallery, Swindon Museum, Art Gallery, All Souls Coll., Oxford, Nat. Gallery of Australia, Yale Center for British Art, New Hall, Cambridge, Victoria & Albert Museum, London, Norwich Castle Museum, Templeton Coll., Oxford, Jesus Coll. Cambridge, The Prudential, Barclays Bank, Govt. Art Collection, Usher Gallery, Lincoln. *Address:* Morley College, Westminster Bridge Road, London, SE1 7HT, England.

HAMBRO, (Baron) Life Peer, cr. 1994, of Dixton and Dumbleton in the County of Gloucestershire; **Charles Eric Alexander Hambro**; British banker; b. 24 July 1930; s. of late Sir Charles Hambro and Pamela Cobbold; m. 1st Rose E. Cotterell 1954 (dissolved 1976); two s. one d.; m. 2nd Cherry Twiss 1976; ed. Eton Coll.; in Coldstream Guards 1949–52; joined Hambros Bank Ltd. 1952, Man. Dir. 1957–65, Deputy Chair. 1965–72, Chair. 1972–83; Chair. Hambros PLC 1983–97; Deputy Chair. Guardian Royal Exchange Assurance Co. 1974–88, Chair. 1988–; Dir. Taylor Woodrow Ltd. 1962–97, P & OSN Co. 1987–; Chair. Royal Nat. Pension Fund for Nurses 1968; Chair. Sovereign Oil and Gas 1980–; Sr. Hon. Treas. Conservative Party Feb. 1993–; Dir. General Oriental 1984–, P & OSN 1987–; Trustee British Museum 1984–94. *Leisure interests:* shooting, racing, flying. *Address:* Dixton Manor, Gotherington, Cheltenham, Glos., GL52 4RB, England. *Telephone:* (0124 267) 2011.

HAMBRO, Rupert Nicholas; British banker; b. 27 June 1943, London; s. of late Jocelyn Olaf Hambro and Ann Silvia Muir; m. Mary Robinson Boyer 1970; one s. one d.; ed. Eton Coll., Aix-en-Provence; joined Hambros Bank 1964, Dir. 1969, Chair. 1983–86; Group Man. Dir. J. O. Hambro & Co. 1986–94, Chair. 1994–; Chair Wilton's (St. James's) Ltd. 1987–, Mayflower Corpn. PLC 1988–, Int. Advisory Bd. Montana AG, Vienna 1988–, CTR Group 1990–97, Fenchurch PLC 1993–97, Longshot Ltd. 1996–, Woburn Golf & Country Club Ltd., Asscn. of Int. Bond Dealers 1979–82; Dir. Telegraph Group Ltd. 1983–, Anglo-American Corpn. of S.A. Ltd. 1981–97, Pioneer Concrete Holdings PLC 1982–; mem. Int. Council U.S. Information Agency 1988–; Chair. of Trustees, Boys' Club Trust, Silver Trust, Fairground Heritage Trust; Patron Royal Soc. of British Sculptors; Treas. Nat. Art Collections Fund; Deputy Pres. Anglo-Danish Soc. 1987–; Chair. of Govs. Museum of London 1996–; Liveryman Fishmongers' Co., Goldsmiths' Co.; mem. Court of Worshipful Co. of Goldsmiths; Kt. of the Falcon (Iceland). *Leisure interests:* racing, shooting. *Address:* 10 Park Place, London, SW1A 1LP, England. *Telephone:* 0171-222 2020. *Fax:* 0171-222 1993.

HAMBURGER, Michael Peter Leopold, O.B.E., M.A.; poet; b. 22 March 1924, Berlin; s. of late Richard Hamburger and L. (née Hamburg) Hamburger; m. Anne Ellen File 1951; one s. two d.; ed. Westminster School and Christ Church, Oxford; army service 1943–47; freelance writer 1948–52; Asst. Lecturer in German Univ. Coll., London 1952–55; lecturer, then Reader Univ. of Reading 1955–64; Florence Purington Lecturer Mount Holyoke Coll., Mass. 1966–67; Visiting Prof. State Univ. of N.Y., Buffalo 1969, Stony Brook 1971; Visiting Fellow Center for Humanities Wesleyan Univ., Conn. 1970; Visiting Prof. Univ. of S.C. 1973; Regent's Lecturer Univ. of Calif., San Diego 1973; Visiting Prof. Boston Univ. 1975–77; Prof. (part-time) Univ. of Essex 1978; Bollingen Foundation Fellow 1959–61, 1965–66; F.R.S.L. 1972–86; Corresp. mem. Deutsche Akademie für Sprache und Dichtung, Darmstadt 1973, Akademie der Künste, Berlin, Akademie der Schönen Künste, Munich; D. Litt. h.c. (Univ. of East Anglia) 1988; D.Phil. h.c. (Technische Universität, Berlin) 1995; prizes for translation: Deutsche Akademie für Sprache und Dichtung 1964, Arts Council 1969, Arts Prize, Inter Nationes, Bonn 1976, Medal, Inst. of Linguists 1977, Schlegel-Tieck Prize, London 1978, 1981, Wilhelm-Heinse Prize (medallion), Mainz 1978, Goethe Medal 1986; European Translation Prize 1990, Hölderlin Prize, Tübingen 1991, Petrarca Prize, Modena 1992. *Publications: poetry:* Flowering Cactus 1950, Poems 1950–51 1952, The Dual Site 1958, Weather and Season 1963, Feeding the Chickadees 1968, Penguin Modern Poems (with A. Brownjohn and C. Tomlinson) 1969, Travelling 1969, Travelling I-V 1973, Ownerless Earth 1973, Travelling VI 1975, Real Estate 1977, Moralities 1977, Variations 1981, Collected Poems 1984, Trees 1988, Selected Poems 1988, Roots in the Air 1991, Collected Poems 1941–1994 1995, Late (Variations III) 1997; *translations:* Poems of Hölderlin 1943, C. Baudelaire, Twenty Prose Poems 1946, L. van Beethoven, Letters, Journals and Conversations 1951, J. C. F. Hölderlin, Selected Verse 1961, G. Trakl, Decline 1952, A. Goes, The Burnt Offering 1956, H. von Hofmannsthal, Poems and Verse Plays (with others) 1961, B. Brecht, Tales from the Calendar 1961, Modern German Poetry 1910–1960 (with C. Middleton) 1962, H. von Hofmannsthal, Selected Plays and Libretti (with others) 1964, G. Büchner, Lenz 1966, H. M. Enzensberger, Poems 1966, G. Grass, Selected Poems (with C. Middleton) 1966, J. C. F. Hölderlin, Poems and Fragments 1967, enlarged edns. 1980, 1994, H. M. Enzensberger, The Poems of Hans Magnus Enzensberger (with J. Rothenberg and the author) 1968, H. M. Enzensberger, Poems for People Who Don't Read Poems 1968, Selected Poems 1994, G. Grass, Poems (with C. Middleton) 1969, P. Bichsel, And Really Frau Blum Would Very Much Like to Meet the Milkman 1968, G. Eich, Journeys 1968, N. Sachs, Selected Poems 1968, Peter Bichsel, Stories for Children 1971, Paul Celan, Selected Poems 1972, East German Poetry (Ed.) 1972, Peter Huchel, Selected Poems 1974, German Poetry 1910–1975 1977, Helmut Heissenbüttel, Texts 1977, Franco Fortini, Poems 1978, An Unofficial Rilke 1981, Peter Huchel, The Garden of Theophrastus 1983, Goethe, Poems and Epigrams 1983, Poems of Paul Celan 1988, Pigeons and Moles: Selected Writing of Günter Eich 1991, 1995, Hölderlin: Poems and Fragments 1994 Dingfest/Thingsure: Selected Poems by Ernst Jandl 1997, Paul Celan: Wolf's-Bean 1997, H. M. Enzenberger: Kiosk 1997; *criticism:* Reason and Energy 1957, From Prophecy to Exorcism 1965, The Truth of Poetry 1969, 1982, 1996, Hugo von Hofmannsthal 1973, Art as Second Nature 1975, A Proliferation of Prophets 1983, After the Second Flood: essays in modern German Literature 1986, Testimonies 1989; *autobiography:* A Mug's Game 1973, String of Beginnings

1991. *Leisure interest:* gardening. *Address:* c/o John Johnson Ltd., Clerkenwell House, 45/47 Clerkenwell Green, London, EC1R 0HT, England.

HAMDANI, Smail; Algerian politician; m.; one c.; fmrly. Govt. Sec.-Gen., adviser to Presidency, Amb. to Scandinavia, Spain, France, to UNESCO, Sec.-Gen. at Foreign Ministry; mem. Council of the Nation; Pres. of Algeria Dec. 1998–; fmr. lecturer École Nat. d'Admin.; consultant and mem. Nat. Inst. for Strategic Studies; Chair. Algerian Asscn. for Int. Relations. *Address:* Office of the President, el-Mouradia, Algiers, Algeria. *Telephone:* (2) 69-15-15. *Fax:* (2) 69-15-95.

HAMDOON, Nizar, B.ARCH.; Iraqi diplomatist; b. 18 May 1944, Baghdad; m. Sahar Hamdoon; two d.; ed. Baghdad Coll. and Univ. of Baghdad; Iraqi Air Force 1968–70; worked at Arab Ba'ath Party Nat. Command 1970–81; Under-Sec. Ministry of Culture and Information 1981–83; joined Ministry of Foreign Affairs 1983; Head, Iraqi Interests Section, Washington, D.C. 1983; Amb. to U.S.A. 1984–87; Under-Sec. Ministry of Foreign Affairs 1987–92; Amb. and Perm. Rep. of Iraq to UN 1992–; founder and Chair. Soc. of Iraqi Architects 1990. *Address:* Permanent Mission to Iraq at the United Nations, 14 East 79th Street, New York, NY 10021, U.S.A. *Telephone:* (212) 737-4434. *Fax:* (212) 772-1794.

HAMEED, A. C. S.; Sri Lankan politician; b. 10 April 1929; M.P. for Harispattuwa 1960–; Minister of Foreign Affairs 1977–89, of Educ., Science and Tech. 1989–90, of Justice 1990–93, of Foreign Affairs 1993–94; first to hold separate portfolio of foreign affairs; Chair. United Nat. Party (UNP) 1995. *Publications:* In Pursuit of Peace 1983, Owl and the Lotus 1986, Disarmament—a multi-lateral approach 1988, Foreign Policy Perspectives of Sri Lanka 1988. *Address:* c/o United National Party, 400 Kotte Road, Pita-kotte, Sri Lanka.

HAMELIN, Louis-Edmond, O.C., M.A., PH.D., D. ÈS L., F.R.S.C.; Canadian researcher and consultant in polar affairs; b. 21 March 1923, St. Didace; m. Colette Lafay 1951; one s. one d.; ed. Laval Univ., Canada and Univs. of Grenoble and Paris, France; Prof. Laval Univ. 1951–78, Dir. Inst. of Geography 1955–61, Founding-Dir. Centre of Northern Studies 1962–72; mem. Legis Ass., Yellowknife, Northwest Territories, Canada 1971–75; Rector Université de Québec, Trois-Rivières 1978–83; Gov. Int. Devt. Research Centre, Ottawa 1984–88; Corresp., Inst. de France, Paris 1989; Dr. h.c. (McGill, Ottawa, Waterloo, Sherbrooke, Montreal, Trois-Rivières); Gov.-Gen. Award 1976, Grand Prix Geography (Paris) 1977, Molson Foundation Prize (Canada) 1982, Human Sciences Prize (Québec) 1987; Grand Officier Québec. *Publications:* Illustrated Glossary of Periglacial Phenomena 1967, Atlas du Monde 1967, Canada: A Geographical Perspective 1973, Canadian Nordicity 1979, The Canadian North 1988, Obiou 1990, Le rang d'habitat 1993, Écho des pays froids 1996. *Leisure interests:* travel, mountaineering, photography. *Address:* 1244 Albert-Lozeau, Sillery, Québec, G1T 1H4, Canada. *Telephone:* (418) 6830386.

HAMER, Hon. Sir Rupert James, A.C., K.C.M.G., E.D., LL.M., F.A.I.M.; Australian politician and solicitor; b. 29 July 1916, Melbourne; m. April Mackintosh 1944; two s. two d.; ed. Melbourne and Geelong Grammar Schools, Univ. of Melbourne; joined Australian Imperial Forces 1940, served 5½ years N. Africa, New Guinea, N.W. Europe; C.O. Vic. Scottish Regt., Citizen Mil. Forces 1954–58; mem. Vic. Legis. Council for E. Yarra 1958–71; Minister for Immigration, Vic. 1962–64, for Local Govt., Vic. 1964–71; mem. Vic. Legis. Assembly for Kew 1971–81; Chief Sec., Deputy Premier, Vic. 1971–72, Premier 1972–81, Treas. and Minister of the Arts 1972–79, Minister of State Devt., Decentralization and Tourism 1979–81; Chair. Bd. Advanced Data Connection 1993–; Pres. Victorian Coll. of Arts 1982–; Nat. Pres. Save the Children Fund Australia, Friends of Royal Botanic Gardens Melbourne, Friend of Australian Broadcasting Comm.; Chair. Vic. State Opera 1981–95, Pres. 1995–; Pres. Greenhouse Action Australia 1989–, Consultative Council on Cancer and Heart Disease 1994–, Nat. Heritage Foundation 1995–; Fellow Trinity Coll. Melbourne Univ.; Trustee Melbourne Cricket Ground, Yarra Bend Nat. Park 1975–; Hon. LL.D. (Melbourne). *Leisure interests:* tennis, sailing, football, reading, music. *Address:* 35 Heather Grove, Kew, Vic. 3101, Australia. *Telephone:* (03) 9817-2272. *Fax:* (03) 9817-2893.

HAMILTON, James Dundas, C.B.E.; British company director and writer; b. 11 June 1919, Woking, Surrey; s. of Arthur Douglas Hamilton and Jean Scott Hamilton (née Brown); m. Linda Jean Ditcham 1954; two d.; ed. Rugby School and Clare Coll., Cambridge; war service (Lieut.-Col. R. A.) 1939–46; mem. Stock Exchange, London 1948–93; partner, Fielding Newson-Smith & Co., Stockbrokers 1951–86 (Sr. Partner 1977–85); Dir. (and Vice-Chair.) Richard Clay PLC 1971–84, LWT Holdings PLC 1981–91, United Dominions Trust 1984–89 (Chair. 1985–89), Datastream Holdings PLC 1982–86, TSB Group PLC 1985–90, WIB Publs. Ltd. 1987–98 (Chair. 1992–96), Camp Hopson and Co. Ltd. 1990–; Chair. Wates City of London Properties PLC 1984–94, LWT Pension Trustees Ltd. 1992–94; mem. Council of The Stock Exchange 1972–78, Deputy Chair. 1973–76; Deputy Chair. British Invisible Exports Council 1976–86; Chair. City and Industrial Liaison Council 1970–73, 1991–95, mem. 1987–98; Gov. Pasold Research Fund 1976–90 (Chair. 1978–86). *Publications:* The Erl King (radio play) 1949, Lorenzo Smiles on Fortune (novel) 1953, Three on a Honeymoon (TV series) 1956, Six Months' Grace (play jtly. with Robert Morley) 1957, Stockbroking Today 1968, Stockbroking Tomorrow 1986, 21 Years to Christmas 1994. *Leisure interests:* writing, golf, swimming, watching tennis, photography. *Address:* 45 Melbury Court, Kensington, London, W8 6NH, England. *Telephone:* 0171-602 3157. *Fax:* 0171-602 6956.

HAMILTON, Linda; American actress; b. 26 Sept. 1956, Salisbury, Md.; m. 1st Bruce Abbott (divorced); m. 2nd James Cameron (q.v.) 1996; one d. *Stage appearances:* Looice 1975, Richard III 1977. *Films include:* T.A.G.: The Assassination Game 1982, Children of the Corn 1984, The Stone Boy 1984, The Terminator 1984, Black Moon Rising 1986, King Kong Lives! 1986, Mr Destiny 1990, Terminator 2: Judgment Day 1991, Silent Fall 1994, The Shadow Conspiracy 1997, Dante's Peak 1997. *TV series include:* The Secrets of Midland Heights 1980–81, King's Crossing 1982, Beauty and the Beast 1987–90. *TV films include:* Reunion 1980, Rape and Marriage—The Rideout Case 1980, Country Gold 1982, Secrets of a Mother and Daughter 1983, Secret Weapons 1985, Club Med 1986, Go Toward the Light 1988. *Address:* c/o International Creative Management, 8942 Wilshire Blvd., Beverly Hills, CA 90211, U.S.A.

HAMILTON, Richard; British artist; b. 24 Feb. 1922; s. of Peter and Constance Hamilton; m. 1st Terry O'Reilly 1947 (died 1962); one s. one d.; m. 2nd Rita Donagh 1991; ed. elementary school, evening classes, St. Martin's School of Art, Royal Academy Schools and Slade School of Art; jig and tool draughtsman, Design Unit 1941–42, Electrical & Musical Industries (EMI) 1942–45; exhbn. of Reaper engravings, Gimpel Fils 1950; devised Growth and Form exhbn., Inst. of Contemporary Arts (ICA) 1951; teacher of design, Cen. School of Arts and Crafts 1952–53; mem. Independent Group, ICA 1952–55; Lecturer, Fine Art Dept., King's Coll., Univ. of Durham (later Univ. of Newcastle upon Tyne) 1953–66; teacher of Interior Design R.C.A. 1957–61; exhbns. of paintings 1951–55 and 1956–64, Hanover Gallery 1955 and 1964; organized exhbn. of works by Marcel Duchamp, Tate Gallery 1966; exhbn. of Guggenheim reliefs and studies, London 1966; exhbns. in Kassel 1967, New York 1967, Studio Marconi, Milan 1968, Hamburg 1969; exhbn. of Swinging London 1967 and beach scene paintings, London 1969; exhbn. of Cosmetic Studies, Milan 1969, Berlin 1970; other solo exhbns. Edin. 1988, Stockholm 1989, Hanover 1990, Valencia 1991, London 1991, 1995, San Francisco 1996; retrospective exhbns., Tate Gallery 1970, (seen in Switzerland, Netherlands Eindhoven and Bern), also 1992, Guggenheim Museum, New York 1973, Nationalgalerie, Berlin 1974, Paintings, Pastels, Prints, London 1975, Amsterdam 1976, Musée Grenoble 1977, Drawings retrospective, Bielefeld 1978, Prints retrospective, Vancouver 1978, Interfaces exhbn., Denmark 1979, Interiors exhbn., London, New York 1980, Paris 1981, Image and Process exhbn., London 1983, Dublin 1992; Venice Biennale 1993 (awarded Golden Lion); William and Noma Copley Foundation award for painting 1960, Joint First Prize, John Moores Liverpool Exhbn. 1969, Talens Prize, Amsterdam 1970, World Print Award 1983, Nord/LB Prize 1996, Arnold Bode Prize 1997. *Publications:* Polaroid Portraits (Vol. I) 1972, (Vol. II) 1977, (Vol. III) 1983, Collected Words 1982, Image and Process 1983, Prints 1939–83 1984. *Address:* Northend Farm, Northend, Oxon., RG9 6LQ; c/o Tate Gallery, Millbank, London, SW1P 4RG, England.

HAMILTON, William Donald, PH.D., F.R.S.; British zoologist; b. 1 Aug. 1936, Cairo, Egypt; s. of Archibald M. Hamilton and Bettina M. (Collier) Hamilton; m. Christine A. Friess 1967; three d.; ed. Tonbridge School and Univs. of Cambridge and London; Lecturer in Genetics, Imperial Coll. London 1964–77; Prof. of Evolutionary Biology, Museum of Zoology and Div. of Biological Sciences, Univ. of Mich. 1978–84; Royal Soc. Research Prof. Dept. of Zoology and Fellow, New Coll. Oxford, 1984–; Foreign mem. American Acad. of Arts and Sciences, Royal Soc. of Sciences of Uppsala, Brazilian Acad. of Sciences, Acad. of Finland; Darwin Medal, Royal Soc. 1988, Linnean Medal for Zoology 1989, Frink Medal, Zoological Soc. 1991, Wander Prize 1992, Crafoord Prize 1993, Kyoto Prize 1993, Fyssen Prize 1996. *Publications:* Narrow Roads of Gene Land (Vol. 1) 1996; articles in scientific journals. *Address:* Department of Zoology, South Parks Road, Oxford, OX1 3PS, England.

HAMLISCH, Marvin, B.A.; American composer; b. 2 June 1944, New York; s. of Max and Lilly (née Schachter) Hamlisch; m. Terre Blair 1989; ed. Queen's Coll., New York; on tour with Groucho Marx 1974–75; made his debut as pianist with Minn. Orchestra 1975; conductor of orchestras throughout U.S.A.; Musical Dir. and Conductor Barbra Streisand (q.v.) Tour 1994 (Emmy Award 1995); Prin. Pops Conductor Pittsburgh Symphony Orchestra 1995–, Baltimore Symphony Orchestra 1996–. *Compositions include:* Film scores: The Swimmer 1968, Take the Money and Run 1969, Bananas 1971, The Way We Were 1974, The Sting 1974, Same Time Next Year 1979, Starting Over 1979, Ordinary People 1980, Seems Like Old Times 1980, Sophie's Choice 1982, D.A.R.Y.L. 1985, Frankie and Johnny 1991, Switched at Birth 1991; popular songs: Sunshine, Lollipops and Rainbows 1960, Good Morning America 1975, Nobody Does It Better 1977; theme songs for The January Man 1988, Three Men and a Baby, Little Nikita, The Experts, composed symphonic work in one movement Anatomy of Peace 1991, composed music for global anthem One Song (lyrics by Alan and Marilyn Bergman): int. debut at Barcelona Olympics 1992; Broadway musicals: A Chorus Line 1975, They're Playing Our Song 1979, The Goodbye Girl 1993. *Publication:* The Way I Was 1992. *Address:* c/o Nancy Shear Arts Services, 180 West End Avenue, # 28N, New York, NY 10023, U.S.A.

HAMLYN, Baron (Life Peer) cr. 1998, of Edgeworth in the County of Gloucestershire; **Paul Bertrand Hamlyn,** C.B.E.; British publisher; b. 12 Feb. 1926, Berlin, Germany; s. of late Prof. Richard and Mrs. L. (née

Hamburg) Hamburger; m. 1st Eileen Margaret Watson 1952 (dissolved 1969); m. 2nd Helen Guest 1970; one s. one d.; ed. St. Christopher's School, Letchworth, Herts.; f. Hamlyn Publishing Group; formed Books for Pleasure 1949, Prints for Pleasure 1960, Records for Pleasure (marketing long-playing classical records), Golden Pleasure Books 1961, Music for Pleasure (EMI) 1965; Paul Hamlyn Group acquired by IPC 1964; joined IPC Bd. with special responsibility for all book publishing activities; acquired Butterworth and Co. 1968; Dir. IPC 1965–70, Chair. IPC Books, controlling Hamlyn Publishing Group (fmrly. Chair. Paul Hamlyn Holdings Ltd. and assoc. cos.) 1965–70; Joint Man. Dir. News Int. Ltd. 1970–71; Co-founder and Dir. Sundial Publs. 1973–86, Octopus Books Int. BV (Holland) 1973–86, Co-founder (with Sir Terence Conran), Co-founder, Co-chair. Conran Octopus 1983–97; Founder and Chair. Octopus Publishing Group (London, New York and Sydney) 1971–97 (part of Reed Int. PLC 1987–97), Mandarin Offset Ltd. (fmrly Mandarin Publrs.), Hong Kong 1971–97, Chair Heinemann Publrs., Oxford 1971–97, Hamlyn Publishing Group 1986 (co. sold 1965, re-purchased 1986), Book Club Assocs. 1993–97, Brandchart Ltd., Château de Bagnols Ltd., Bibendum Restaurant Ltd., Michelin House Investment Co. Ltd., Michelin House Devt. Ltd; f. The Paul Hamlyn Foundation to fund projects in arts, educ., and book publishing in UK and Continental Europe, with a number of projects in Third World, mainly Indian sub-continent 1972; Chancellor Thames Valley Univ. 1993–; Dir. Center for Int. Health and Co-operation, New York; mem. Int. Council, Irish Museum of Modern Art, ublin; Hon. Fellow Royal Coll. of Surgeons in Ireland 1993; Hon. D. Litt. (Keele) 1988, (Warwick) 1991; Royal Soc. of Arts Albert Medal 1993. *Address:* 18 Queen Anne's Gate, London, SW1H 9AA, England (Office).

HAMMADI, Sadoon; Iraqi politician and economist; b. 22 June 1930, Karbala; m. Lamia Hammadi 1961; five s.; ed. in Beirut, Lebanon and U.S.A.; Prof. of Econs., Univ. of Baghdad 1957; Deputy Head of Econ. Research, Nat. Bank of Libya, Tripoli 1961–62; Minister of Agrarian Reform 1963; Econ. Adviser to Presidential Council, Govt. of Syria 1964; Econ. Expert, UN Planning Inst., Syria 1965–68; Pres. Iraq Nat. Oil Co. (INOC) 1968; Minister of Oil and Minerals 1969–74, of Foreign Affairs 1974–83; Deputy Prime Minister 1991; Prime Minister of Iraq March–Sept. 1991; Speaker of Nat. Ass. 1984–88, 1996–; Adviser to Pres.; mem. Revolutionary Command Council; mem. Iraqi Acad. *Publications:* Towards a Socialistic Agrarian Reform in Iraq 1964, Views about Arab Revolution 1969, Memoirs and Views on Oil Issues 1980, About Nationalism and Arab Unity 1993. *Leisure interests:* swimming, walking, coin collection, reading novels. *Address:* National Assembly, Hamorabi Building, Baghdad, Iraq.

HAMMARSKJÖLD, Knut Olof Hjalmar Akesson, PH.M.; Swedish diplomatist; nephew of the late Dag Hammarskjöld, Sec.-Gen. of the UN; b. 16 Jan. 1922, Geneva, Switzerland; s. of Åke Hammarskjöld and the late Britte Hammmarskjöld; four s.; ed. Stockholm Univ.; entered Foreign Service 1946, served Paris, Vienna, Moscow, Bucharest, Kabul, Sofia 1947–55; First Sec. Foreign Office 1955–57; Head of Foreign Relations Dept., Royal Bd. of Civil Aviation, Stockholm 1957–59; Deputy Head, Swedish Del. to OEEC, Paris 1959–60; Deputy Sec.-Gen. European Free Trade Asscn. (EFTA) 1960–66; Minister Plenipotentiary 1966–; Dir.-Gen. of Int. Air Transport Asscn. (IATA), Montreal, Geneva 1966–84, Chair. Exec. Cttee. 1981–84; Dir. Inst. of Air Transport, Paris 1974–, Dir. Gen. 1985–; Chair, C.E.O. Atwater Inst., Montreal 1985–; Special Adviser to Dir.-Gen. UNESCO; mem. Inst. of Transport, London; mem. Alexander S. Onassis Public Benefit Foundation Int. Cttee. for Award of Athens and Olympia Prizes 1977–83; Gov. Atlantic Inst. for Int. Affairs 1983–87; Chair. Corporate Bd. Sydvenska Dagbladet AB, Newspaper Conglomerate, Malmö 1987–94, (Dir. 1948–), now Emer. Chair.; Hon. Fellow, Canadian Aeronautics and Space Inst.; Commdr. Order of the Lion (Finland), Order of the Falcon (1st Class) (Iceland), Commdr. Order of Orange-Nassau (Netherlands), Légion d'honneur and Order of the Black Star (France), Grand Officer, Order Al-Istiqlal (Jordan); Commdr. (1st Class) Order of the North Star (Sweden), NOR (Sweden), Grand Cross of the Order of Civil Merit (Spain). *Publications:* articles on political, economic and aviation topics. *Address:* Rue St. Germain 11, Geneva, Switzerland.

HAMMEL, Eugene Alfred, PH.D.; American professor of anthropology and demography; b. 18 March 1930, New York; s. of William Hammel and Violet Brookes; m. Joan Marie Swingle 1951; ed. Univ. of Calif., Berkeley; field work in archaeology and linguistics, Calif. 1947–51, in ethnography, Peru 1957–58, in archaeology and ethnography in New Mexico 1959–61, in ethnography in Mexico 1963, in Yugoslavia and Greece 1963, 1965–66; Asst. Prof. Univ. of New Mexico 1959–61; Asst. Prof. Univ. of Calif. (Berkeley) 1961–63, Assoc. Prof. 1963–66, Prof. 1966–88, Prof. Emer. 1988–, Prof. of Anthropology and Demography 1978–, Dir. Quantitative Anthropology Lab. 1974, Chair. Demography 1978–88, now Chair. Demography Grad. Group; Adjunct Prof. Physiology and Biophysics, Univ. of Ind. Bloomington 1989–; Foreign Sciences mem. Max Planck Inst. for Physiology and Clinical Research 1978–; archival research in Yugoslavia, Hungary, Austria 1983–; mem. N.A.S. *Publications:* Wealth, Authority and Prestige in the Ica Valley, Peru 1962, Ritual Relations and Alternative Social Structures in the Balkans 1968, The Pink Yoyo: Occupational Mobility in Belgrade c. 1915–65 1969, Statistical Studies of Historical Social Structure (with Wachter and Laslett) 1978; approximately 100 articles. *Leisure interests:* hiking, guitar, carpentry, photography. *Address:* Department of Demography, University of California, Berkeley, 2232 Piedmont Avenue, CA 94720, U.S.A. *Telephone:* 415-642-3391.

HAMMERSLEY, John Michael, D.SC., F.R.S.; British mathematician; b. 21 March 1920, Helensburgh, Scotland; s. of Guy Hugh and Marguerite (née Whitehead) Hammersley; m. Shirley Gwendolene Bakewell 1951; two s.; ed. Sedbergh School, Emmanuel Coll., Cambridge; Maj. R.A. 1940–46; Prin. Scientific Officer Theoretical Physics Div., A.E.R.E., Harwell 1955–59; Graduate Asst. Design and Analysis of Scientific Experiments, Oxford 1948–55, Sr. Research Fellow Trinity Coll. 1960–69, Sr. Research Officer, Inst. of Econ. 1960–69, Reader in Math. Statistics 1969–87, Emer. Reader 1987–, Professorial Fellow 1969–87, Emer. Fellow 1987–; numerous short appointments in U.S.A. 1952–84; Rouse Ball Lecturer, Cambridge 1980; Fulbright Fellow 1955, Erskine Fellow 1978; Polya Prize 1997; Von Neumann Medal (Brussels) 1966, IMA Gold Medal 1984. *Publications:* Monte Carlo Methods (with D. C. Handscomb) 1964. *Address:* Trinity College, Oxford, OX1 3BH (Office); 11 Eynsham Road, Oxford, OX2 9BS, England (Home). *Telephone:* (01865) 862181 (Home).

HAMMES, Gordon G., PH.D.; American university vice-chancellor and professor of chemistry; b. 10 Aug. 1934, Fond du Lac, Wis.; s. of Jacob Hammes and Betty (Sadoff) Hammes; m. Judith Ellen Frank 1959; one s. two d.; ed. Princeton Univ. and Univ. of Wisconsin; Postdoctoral Fellow Max Planck Inst. für physikalische Chemie Göttingen, Fed. Repub. of Germany 1959–60; instructor, subsequently Assoc. Prof. M.I.T., Cambridge, Mass. 1960–65; Prof., Cornell Univ. 1965–88, Chair. Dept. of Chem. 1970–75, Horace White Prof. of Chem. and Biochemistry 1975–88, Dir. Biotech. Program 1983–88; Prof., Univ. of Calif., Santa Barbara 1988–91, Vice-Chancellor for Academic Affairs 1988–91; Prof. Duke Univ., Durham, N.C. 1991–, Vice-Chancellor Duke Univ. Medical Center 1991–, Univ. Distinguished Service Prof. of Biochemistry 1996–; mem. Physiological Chem. Study Section, Physical Biochemistry Study Section, Training Grant Cttee., Nat. Insts. of Health; mem. Bd. of Counsellors, Nat. Cancer Inst. 1976–80, Advisory Council, Chem. Dept., Princeton 1970–75, Polytechnic Inst., New York 1977–78, Boston Univ. 1977–85; mem. Nat. Research Council, U.S. Nat. Comm. for biochemistry 1989–; mem. American Chem. Soc., American Soc. of Biochemistry and Molecular Biology, N.A.S., American Acad. of Arts and Sciences; ed. Biochemistry 1992–. *Publications:* Principles of Chemical Kinetics, Enzyme Catalysis and Regulation, Chemical Kinetics: Principles and Selected Topics (with I. Amdur); articles. *Address:* 11 Staley Place, Durham, NC 27705, U.S.A.

HAMMES, Michael Noel, M.B.A.; American business executive; b. 25 Dec. 1941, Evanston, Ill.; s. of Ferdinand Hammes and Winifred Hammes; m. Lenore Lynn Forbes 1964; three s. two d.; ed. Georgetown Univ., New York Univ.; Asst. Controller, Ford Motor Assembly Div. 1974, Plant Man., Ford Wixom Assembly Plant 1975, Man. Program Planning, Ford Automotive Ass. Div. 1976, Dir. Int. Business Planning, Int. Operations, Ford 1977, Man. Dir. and Pres., Ford Motor Co. of Mexico 1979, Vice-Pres. Truck Operations, Ford of Europe 1983–; Vice-Pres., Int. Operations, Chrysler Motors Corpn. 1986–. *Leisure interests:* skiing, tennis, golf, antique cars. *Address:* Chrysler Motors Corporation, 12000 Chrysler Drive, Highland Park, MO 48288, U.S.A.

HAMMOND, Nicholas Geoffrey Lempriere, C.B.E., D.S.O., F.B.A.; British professor of Greek; b. 15 Nov. 1907, Ayr, Scotland; s. of James Vavasor Hammond and Dorothy Hammond; m. Margaret Campbell Townley 1938; two s. three d.; ed. Fettes Coll., Edinburgh, Gonville and Caius Coll., Cambridge, British School of Archaeology, Athens; Fellow of Clare Coll., Cambridge 1930–54, Tutor 1947–54; Headmaster, Clifton Coll., Bristol 1954–62; Prof. of Greek, Univ. of Bristol 1962–73, Prof. Emer. 1973–; Visiting Prof. Reed Coll., St. Olaf Coll., Univ. of Wis. Haverford Coll., Swarthmore Coll., Univ. of Pa., Trinity Coll., Hartford, Univ. of Adelaide, Univ. of Auckland, Univ. of Ioannina, Univ. of Newcastle, N.S.W.; Fellow, Inst. of Advanced Study, Princeton, The Inst. for Research in the Humanities, Madison, The Nat. Humanities Center, The Nat. Hellenic Research Foundation, Carleton Coll., Minn., Univ. of Washington; Foreign mem. Acad. of Athens; mem. American Acad. of Arts and Sciences; Hon. Fellow Clare Coll. 1973–; Hon. D. Litt. (Univ. of Wis., St. Olaf Coll., Carleton Coll.), Hon. Dr. (Univ. of Ioannina); Officer of the Royal Hellenic Order of the Phoenix; Companion of the Friends of the Greek People 1992. *Publications:* John Edwin Sandys 1932, History of Greece to 322 B.C. 1959, Epirus 1967, Studies in Greek History 1973, History of Macedonia I 1972, II 1980, III 1988, The Classical Age of Greece 1975, Migrations and Invasions of Greece 1976, Alexander the Great 1980, Atlas of the Greek and Roman World 1981, Venture into Greece: with the Guerrillas 1943–44 1983, Three Historians of Alexander 1983, The Macedonian State 1989, The Miracle that was Macedonia 1991, Sources for Alexander the Great 1993, The Allied Military Mission and the Resistance in West Macedonia 1943–44 1993, Collected Studies I 1993, II 1994, III 1994, IV 1998, Philip of Macedon 1994, The Genius of Alexander The Great 1996. *Leisure interests:* gardening, walking. *Address:* 4 Barrington House, Southacre Park, Chaucer Road, Cambridge, CB2 2TY, England. *Telephone:* (01223) 357151.

HAMMOND, Norman David Curle, PH.D., F.S.A., F.B.A.; British archaeologist; b. 10 July 1944, Brighton; s. of William Hammond and Kathleen Jessie Howes; m. Jean Wilson 1972; one s. one d.; ed. Varndean Grammar School, Peterhouse, Cambridge; Research Fellow, Centre of Latin American Studies, Cambridge 1967–71, Leverhulme Research Fellow 1972–75; Research Fellow, Fitzwilliam Coll., Cambridge 1973–75; Sr. Lecturer, Univ. of Bradford 1975–77; Visiting Prof., Univ. of Calif. (Berkeley) 1977, Rutgers Univ.,

U.S.A. 1977–78, Assoc. Prof. 1978–84, Prof. of Archaeology 1984–88; Prof. of Archaeology, Boston Univ. and Assoc. in Maya Archaeology, Peabody Museum, Harvard Univ. 1988–; Archaeology Corresp. The Times 1967–; Ed. South Asian Archaeology 1970–73, Afghan Studies 1976–79; Consulting Ed. Library of Congress, U.S.A. 1977–89; Archaeological Consultant Scientific American 1979–95; Curl Lecturer, Royal Anthropological Inst. 1985; Bushnell Lecturer, Cambridge Univ. 1997, Stone Lecturer, Archaeological Inst. of America 1998; Acad. Trustee Archaeological Inst. of America 1990–93; mem. Council, Soc. of Antiquaries of London 1996–; excavations and surveys in Libya and Tunisia 1964, Afghanistan 1966, Belize 1970–98, Ecuador 1972–84; Fellow Dumbarton Oaks, Washington, D.C.; Visiting Fellow, Worcester Coll., Oxford, Peterhouse, Cambridge; Hon. D.Sc. (Bradford) 1999. *Publications include:* South Asian Archaeology (Ed.) 1973, Mesoamerican Archaeology (Ed.) 1974, Lubaantun: a Classic Maya realm 1975, Social Process in Maya Prehistory (Ed.) 1977, The Archaeology of Afghanistan (Ed. with F. R. Allchin) 1978, Ancient Maya Civilisation 1982, Nohmul: excavations 1973–83, 1985, Cuello: an early Maya community in Belize 1991; Archaeology Procs. 44th Congress of Americanists (Gen. Ed.) 1982–84; contribs. to learned and other journals. *Leisure interests:* heraldry, hetairi. *Address:* Wholeway, Harlton, Cambridge, CB3 7ET, England; 83 Ivy Street, Apt. 32, Brookline, MA 02446, U.S.A. *Telephone:* (01223) 262376 (U.K.); (617) 739-9077 (U.S.A.).

HAMNETT, Katharine; British designer; b. 16 Aug. 1948; two s.; ed. Cheltenham Ladies' Coll. and St. Martin's School of Art; Tuttabankem 1969–74; designed freelance in New York, Paris, Rome and London 1974–76; f. Katharine Hamnett Ltd. 1979; launched Choose Life T-Shirt collection 1983; involved in Fashion Aid 1985; opening of first Katharine Hamnett shop, London 1986, followed by two more shops in 1988; production moved to Italy 1989; Visiting Prof. London Inst. 1997–; Int. Inst. of Cotton Designer of the Year 1982, British Fashion Industry Designer of the Year 1984, Bath Costume Museum Menswear Designer of the Year Award 1984, British Knitting and Clothing Export Council Award for Export 1988. *Publications:* various publs. in major fashion magazines and newspapers. *Address:* Katharine Hamnett Ltd., 202 New North Road, London N1 7BJ, England. *Telephone:* 0171-354 4400. *Fax:* 0171-354 5246.

HAMPE, Michael, D.PHIL.; German theatre, opera and television director and actor; b. 3 June 1935, Heidelberg; s. of Hermann and Annemarie Hampe; m. Sibylle Hauck 1971; one d.; ed. Falckenberg Schule, Munich, Univs. of Vienna and Munich and Syracuse Univ., U.S.A.; Deputy Dir. Schauspielhaus, Zürich 1965–70; Dir. Nat. Theatre, Mannheim 1972–75, Cologne Opera 1975–95, Dresden Music Festival; directs opera at La Scala, Milan, Covent Garden, London, Paris Opera, Salzburg and Edinburgh Festivals, Munich, Stockholm, Cologne, Geneva, Brussels, Zürich, San Francisco, Sydney, Los Angeles, Tokyo; directs drama at Bavarian State Theatre, Munich Schauspielhaus, Zürich, etc.; directs and acts in film and TV; Prof. State Music Acad., Cologne and Cologne Univ.; mem. bd. European Acad. of Music, Bayern; theatre-bldg. consultant; Bundesverdienstkreuz, Commendatore Ordine al Merito (Italy), Goldenes Ehrenabzeichen des Landes Salzburg. *Address:* Tiergartenstrasse 36, 01219 Dresden, Germany.

HAMPEL, Sir Ronald Claus, Kt., M.A.; British businessman; b. 31 May 1932, Shrewsbury; s. of Karl Victor Hugo Hampel and Rutgard Emil Klothilde Hauck; m. Jane Bristed Hewson 1957; three s. one d.; ed. Canford School, Wimborne, Dorset, Corpus Christi Coll., Cambridge; nat. service 2nd Lieut. Royal Horse Artillery 1950–51; joined ICI 1955; Vice-Pres. ICI Agrochemicals U.S.A. 1973–75, ICI Latin America 1975–77; ICI Gen. Man. Commercial 1977–80; Chair. ICI Paints 1980–83, ICI Agrochemicals 1983–85; Dir. ICI 1985–99, C.O.O. ICI 1991–93, C.E.O. ICI 1993–95, Chair. 1995–99; Dir. (non-exec.) Powell Duffryn 1983–88, Commercial Union 1987–95, British Aerospace 1989–, ALCOA 1995–; Dir. American Chamber of Commerce 1985–90; mem. Exec. Cttee. British North America Cttee. 1989–96, Listed Companies Advisory Cttee., London Stock Exchange 1996–, Nomination Cttee., N.Y. Stock Exchange 1996–; mem. European Round Table 1995–, U.K. Advisory Bd. INSEAD 1994–, Exec. Cttee. All England Lawn Tennis Club 1994–; Chair. Cttee. on Corp. Governance 1995–. *Leisure interests:* tennis, golf, skiing. *Address:* c/o ICI, ICI Group Headquarters, 9 Millbank, London, SW1 3JF, England. *Telephone:* 0171-834 4444.

HAMPSHIRE, Sir Stuart, Kt., F.B.A.; British university professor; b. 1 Oct. 1914, Healing, Lincs.; s. of George N. Hampshire and Marie West; m. 1st Renée Orde-Lees 1961 (died 1980); m. 2nd Nancy Cartwright 1985; two d.; ed. Repton School and Balliol Coll., Oxford; Fellow, All Souls Coll., Oxford 1936–45; service in army and Foreign Office 1940–46; lecturer in Philosophy Univ. Coll., London 1947–50; Fellow, New Coll., Oxford 1950–55; Research Fellow, All Souls Coll., Oxford 1955–60; Prof. of Philosophy, Univ. Coll., London 1960–63; Prof. and Chair. Dept. of Philosophy, Princeton Univ. 1963–70; Warden of Wadham Coll., Oxford 1970–84; Prof. Stanford Univ. 1985–91; Fellow, British Acad., American Acad. of Arts and Sciences; Hon. D.Litt (Glasgow) 1973. *Publications:* Spinoza 1951, Thought and Action 1959, Freedom of the Individual 1965, Modern Writers and Other Essays 1969, Freedom of Mind and Other Essays 1971, Morality and Pessimism 1972, The Socialist Idea (joint ed.) 1975, Two Theories of Morality 1977, Public and Private Morality (ed.) 1978, Morality and Conflict 1983, Innocence and Experience 1989. *Address:* 7 Beaumont Road, The Quarry, Headington, Oxford, England. *Telephone:* (01865) 761688.

HAMPSHIRE, Susan, O.B.E.; British actress; b. 12 May 1937; d. of George Kenneth Hampshire and June Hampshire; m. 1st Pierre Granier-Deferre 1967 (dissolved 1974); one s. (one d. deceased); m. 2nd Sir Eddie Kulukundis (q.v.) 1981; ed. Hampshire School, Knightsbridge; Hon. D.Litt. (City Univ., London 1984, (St. Andrews) 1986, Dr. h.c. (Kingston) 1994, Hon.D.Arts (Pine Manor Coll., Boston, U.S.A.) 1994. *Stage roles include:* Expresso Bongo 1958, Follow that Girl 1960, Fairy Tales of New York 1961, Marion Dangerfield in Ginger Man 1963, Kate Hardcastle in She Stoops to Conquer 1966, On Approval 1966, Mary in The Sleeping Prince 1968, Nora in A Doll's House 1972, Katharina in The Taming of the Shrew 1974, Peter in Peter Pan 1974, Jeannette in Romeo and Jeannette 1975, Rosalind in As You Like It 1975, Miss Julie 1975, Elizabeth in The Circle 1976, Ann Whitefield in Man and Superman 1977, Siri Von Essen in Tribades 1978, Victorine in An Audience Called Edouard 1978, Irene in The Crucifer of Blood 1979, Ruth Carson in Night and Day 1979, Elizabeth in The Revolt 1980, Stella Drury in House Guest 1981, Elvira in Blithe Spirit 1986, Marie Stopes in Married Love, The Countess in A Little Night Music 1989, Mrs Anna in The King and I 1990, Gertie in Noel and Gertie 1991, The Countess of Marshwood in Relative Values 1993, Suzanna Andler, Alicia Christie in Black Chiffon 1995–96. *TV roles:* Andromeda, Fleur Forsyte in The Forsyte Saga (Emmy Award for Best Actress 1970), Becky Sharp in Vanity Fair (Emmy Award for Best Actress 1973), Sarah Churchill, Duchess of Marlborough, in The First Churchills (Emmy Award for Best Actress 1971), Glencora Palliser in The Pallisers, Lady Melford in Dick Turpin 1980, Madeline Neroni in The Barchester Chronicles 1982, Martha in Leaving 1984, Martha in Leaving II 1985, Going to Pot 1985, Don't Tell Father, Esme Harkness in The Grand 1996–98, Miss Catto in Coming Home 1998–99. *Films include:* During One Night 1961, The Three Lives of Thomasina 1963, Night Must Fall 1964, Wonderful Life 1964, Paris in August, The Fighting Prince of Donegal 1966, Monte Carlo or Bust 1969, Rogan, David Copperfield, Living Free 1972, A Time for Loving 1972, Malpertius (E. Poe Prizes du Film Fantastique, Best Actress) 1972, Neither the Sea Nor the Sand, Roses and Green Peppers, Bang. *Publications:* Susan's Story (autobiographical account of dyslexia) 1981, The Maternal Instinct, Lucy Jane at the Ballet 1985, Lucy Jane on Television 1989, Trouble Free Gardening 1989, Every Letter Counts 1990, Lucy Jane and the Dancing Competition 1991, Easy Gardening 1991, Lucy Jane and the Russian Ballet 1993, Rosie's First Ballet Lesson 1997. *Leisure interests:* gardening, music, studying antique furniture. *Address:* c/o Chatto & Linnit Ltd., 123A King's Road, London, SW3 4PL, England. *Telephone:* 0171-352 7722.

HAMPSON, Christopher, C.B.E., B.ENG.; Canadian/British business executive; b. 6 Sept. 1931, Montreal; s. of Harold Ralph Hampson and Geraldine Mary Hampson (née Smith); m. Joan Margaret Cassils Evans 1954; two s. three d.; ed. Ashbury Coll. School, Ottawa, McGill Univ.; joined Canadian Industries Ltd. (subsidiary of ICI) 1956, Vice-Pres., Dir. 1973; seconded to ICI PLC as Gen. Man. Planning 1978, Sr. Vice-Pres. Canadian Industries Ltd. 1982, fmr. C.E.O., Dir. ICI Australia Ltd., Exec. Dir., mem. Bd. ICI 1987–94; Chair. Yorks. Electricity Group 1995–97, R.M.C. Group 1996–, British Biotech PLC 1998–; Dir. BG PLC, TransAlfa Corp.; mem. Bd. U.K. Environment Agency. *Leisure interests:* gardening, tennis, skiing. *Address:* 77 Kensington Court, London, W8 5DT, England. *Telephone:* 0171-937 0325. *Fax:* 0171-376 1906.

HAMPSON, Norman, M.A.; British academic; b. 8 April 1922, Leyland, Lancs.; s. of Frank Hampson and Elizabeth Jane Hampson (née Fazackerley); m. Jacqueline Gardin 1948; two d.; ed. Manchester Grammar School and Univ. Coll. Oxford; war service in R.N. and Free French Navy 1941–45; Lecturer and Sr. Lecturer in French History, Univ. of Manchester 1948–67; Prof. of Modern History, Univ. of Newcastle upon Tyne 1967–74; Prof. of History, Univ. of York 1974–89; D. de l'Univ. (Paris); Hon. D. Litt. (Edin.) 1989. *Publications:* La Marine de l'An II 1959, A Social History of the French Revolution 1963, The Enlightenment 1968, The Life and Opinions of Maximilien Robespierre 1974, Danton 1978, Will and Circumstance: Montesquieu, Rousseau and the French Revolution 1983, Prelude to Terror 1988, Saint-Just 1991, The Perfidy of Albion 1998. *Leisure interest:* gardening. *Address:* 305 Hull Road, York, YO1 3LB, England. *Telephone:* (01904) 412661.

HAMPSON, Stuart, M.A.; British business executive; b. 7 Jan. 1947; s. of Kenneth Hampson and Mary Hampson; m. Angela McLaren 1973; one s. one d.; ed. Royal Masonic School, Bushey, St. John's Coll., Oxford; with Board of Trade 1969–72; FCO Mission to U.N., Geneva 1972–74; Dept. of Prices and Consumer Protection 1974–79; Dept. of Trade 1979–82; with John Lewis Partnership 1982–, Dir. of Research and Expansion 1986, Deputy Chair. 1989–93, Chair. 1993–. *Address:* John Lewis Partnership, 171 Victoria Street, London, SW1E 5NN, England. *Telephone:* 0171-828 1000.

HAMPTON, Christopher James, M.A., F.R.S.L. British playwright; b. 26 Jan. 1946, Fayal, the Azores, Portugal; s. of Bernard Patrick and Dorothy Patience (née Herrington) Hampton; m. Laura Margaret de Holesch 1971; two d.; ed. Lancing Coll., New Coll., Oxford; wrote first play When Did You Last See My Mother? 1964; Resident Dramatist, Royal Court Theatre 1968–70; freelance writer 1970–; Evening Standard Award for best comedy 1970, 1983 and for best play 1986; Plays and Players London Critics' Award for best play 1970, 1973, 1985; Los Angeles Drama Critics Circle Award 1974; Laurence Olivier Award for Best Play 1986; New York Drama Critics' Circle Award for Best Foreign Play 1987, Prix Italia 1988, Writers Guild of

America Screenplay Award 1989, Oscar for Best Adapted Screenplay 1989; BAFTA for best screenplay 1990, Special Jury Award, Cannes Film Festival 1995, Tony Awards for Best Original Score (lyrics) and Best Book of a Musical 1995, Scott Moncrieff Prize 1997. *Publications:* When Did You Last See My Mother? 1967, Total Eclipse 1969 (film 1995), The Philanthropist 1970, Savages 1973, Treats 1976, Able's Will (TV) 1978, The History Man (TV adaptation of novel by Malcolm Bradbury, q.v.) 1981, The Portage to San Cristobal of A.H. (play adaptation of novel by George Steiner) 1983, Tales from Hollywood 1983; The Honorary Consul (film adaptation of a novel by Graham Greene) 1983, Les Liaisons Dangereuses (adaptation of a novel by Laclos) 1985, Hotel du Lac (TV adaptation of a novel by Anita Brookner, q.v.) 1986, The Good Father (film adaptation of a novel by Peter Prince) 1986, Wolf at the Door (film) 1986, Dangerous Liaisons (film) 1988, The Ginger Tree (adaptation of novel by Oswald Wynd, TV) 1989, White Chameleon 1991, Sunset Boulevard (book and lyrics with Don Black) 1993, Alice's Adventures Underground (with Martha Clarke) 1994, Carrington (film) 1995, Mary Reilly (film) 1996, The Secret Agent (film) 1996, Nostromo (screenplay) 1997; Dir. Carrington 1995, The Secret Agent 1996. *Translations include:* Marya (Babel) 1967, Uncle Vanya, Hedda Gabler 1970, A Doll's House 1971 (film 1974), Don Juan 1972, Tales from the Vienna Woods 1977 (film 1979), Don Juan Comes Back from the War 1978, The Wild Duck 1980, Ghosts 1983, Tartuffe 1984, Faith, Hope and Charity 1989, Art 1996, An Enemy of the People 1997, The Unexpected Man 1998. *Leisure interests:* travel, cinema. *Address:* 2 Kensington Park Gardens, London, W.11, England. *Telephone:* 0171-229 2188.

HAMZA, Ahmed Amin, PH.D.; Egyptian professor of experimental physics; b. 8 March 1941, Giza; s. of late Amin Hamza and Hanim Abdel Meguid; m. Sahar Khalil 1968; three d.; ed. Saaidiya Secondary School, Giza and Ain Shams Univ. Cairo; Head, Printing Dept. Cairo Dyeing & Finishing Co. 1962–72; Lecturer in Physics, Univ. of Mansoura 1972–76, Asst. Prof. 1976–81, Prof. of Experimental Physics 1981–, Head, Dept. of Physics 1984–86, Vice-Dean, Faculty of Science 1986–92, Vice-Pres. Univ. for Community and Environmental Devt. 1992–94; Pres. Univ. of Mansoura 1994; mem. Cttee. for Promoting Asst. Profs. of Physics 1985–; mem. Cttee. (affiliated to Egyptian Acad. of Science and Tech.) for Researches in Textile Industries 1989–; Fellow, Royal Microscopical Soc. (Oxford), Inst. of Physics (London); mem. Int. Soc. for Optical Eng.; Egyptian Nat. Award in Physics 1987; Senior Academic Prize and Certificate Distinction of the Univ. of Mansoura in Basic Sciences 1992; First-Class Medal for Distinction 1995. *Publications:* Interferometry of Fibrous Materials (co-author) 1990; numerous publs. in fields of interferometry, fibre optics, colour measurement and polymer physics. *Leisure interest:* playing football. *Address:* University of Mansoura, El-Gomhoria Street, Mansoura (Office); 6 Korash Street, 6th District, Nasr City, Cairo, Egypt (Home). *Telephone:* (050) 347800 (Office); (02) 2708999 (Home). *Fax:* (050) 347900.

HAMZAH, Tengku Tan Sri Datuk Razaleigh (see Razaleigh).

HAMŽÍK, Pavol, LL.D.; Slovak politician and university lecturer; b. 20 Aug. 1954, Trenčín; s. of Pavol Hamžík and Júlia Hamžíková; m. Dagmar Hamžíková (née Kiššová) 1976; two d.; lawyer 1978–84; joined Czechoslovak Foreign Ministry 1984; Consul in Copenhagen 1985; studied at Diplomatic Acad., Moscow 1989–91; Vice-Chair. del. to int. disarmament negotiations, Vienna 1991; mem. del. to CSCE 1991, Pres. CSCE Man. Group on crisis in Yugoslavia 1992, head Slovak del. to CSCE 1993, head Slovak Perm. Mission to CSCE 1993; Slovak Amb. to Germany 1994–96; Foreign Minister 1996–97; f. Party of Civic Understanding Feb. 1998, elected M.P. Sept. 1998, Vice Prime Minister Oct. 1998–; lecturer, mem. of Scientific Bd. Faculty of Political Sciences and Int. Relations, Matej Bell Univ. 1997–. *Leisure interests:* skiing, literature, tennis. *Address:* Úrad vlády SR, nám Slobody 1, 813 70 Bratislava, Slovakia. *Telephone:* (7) 534 1111 (Office).

HAN HUAIZHI, Lieut.-Gen.; Chinese army official; b. 1922, Pingshan Co., Hebei Prov.; Asst. to the Chief of the PLA Gen. Staff 1980–85; Deputy, 6th NPC 1983–87, 7th NPC 1988–; Dir. of the Mil. Training Dept. under the PLA Gen. Staff 1984–85; Deputy Chief of the PLA Gen. Staff 1985; Lieut.-Gen. PLA 1985–; Chair. Sports Comm. 1990—; mem. Nat. Degrees Cttee. Oct. 1988–. *Address:* Chinese People's Liberation Army General Staff, Beijing, People's Republic of China.

HAN SHAO GONG; Chinese writer; b. 1 Jan. 1953, Chang Sha; s. of Han Ke Xian and Zhang Jing Xing; m. Liang Yu Li 1980; one d.; ed. Hunan Teacher's Univ.; Council mem. Chinese Writer's Asscn. 1984; Vice-Chair. Hunan Youth Union 1985; Chief Ed. of Hainan Review 1988; Pres. Hainan Literature Correspondence Coll. 1988; mem. Standing Cttee. CPCC Hainan Prov. 1988; Prize for Best Chinese Stories 1980, 1981. *Publications:* Biography of Ren Bi Shi 1979; (collections of short stories): Yue Nan 1981, Flying Across the Blue Sky 1983, New Stories 1986, Fondness for Shoes 1994, Red Apple is an Exception 1994; To Face the Mystical and Wide World (selection of articles) 1985, The Other Shore (selection of prose pieces) 1988, The Murder 1990, Pa Pa Pa and Seduction and Femme Femme Femme 1990–91, Homecoming 1992, The Play and Holy War 1993, Raving of a Pedestrian in the Night 1994, The Thought of the Sea 1994, Dictionary of Ma-Bridge (novel) 1995; trans: The Unbearable Lightness of Being (Kundra) 1987; also film script, Deaf Mute and His Suona 1984. *Leisure interest:* Chinese calligraphy. *Address:* Room 2-602, Hainan Teachers' University, Hai Kou 571158, Hainan, People's Republic of China. *Telephone:* (898) 5882748.

HAN SUNG-JOO; Korean politician; b. 1940; ed. Seoul Nat. Univ. and Univ. of Calif. Berkeley; Prof. of Political Science, Korea Univ.; Vice-Chair. Int. Political Science Asscn.; columnist, Newsweek; Minister of Foreign Affairs 1993–95; Pres. Int. Relations Inst. Korea Univ., Seoul. *Address:* Korea University 1-5-gu, Anam-dong, Sungbuk, Seoul, Republic of Korea.

HAN SUYIN, M.B., B.S., L.R.C.P., M.R.C.S.; British author and medical practitioner; b. 12 Sept. 1916, Xinyang, China; d. of Y. T. Chow (Zhou) and M. Denis; m. 1st Gen. P. H. Tang 1938 (died 1947); m. 2nd L. F. Comber 1952 (divorced 1968); m. 3rd Col. Vincent Ruthnaswamy 1971; two adopted d.; ed. Yenching Univ., Peking, Univ. of Brussels, Belgium, Royal Free Hospital, London Univ.; in London 1945–49; employed Queen Mary Hospital, Hong Kong 1948–52, Johore Bahru Hospital, Malaya 1952–55; pvt. medical practice 1955–64; Lecturer in Contemporary Asian Literature, Nanyang Univ., Singapore 1958–60; Hon. Prof. Univ. of Alberta and six Chinese Univs. *Publications:* Destination Chungking 1942, A Many-Splendoured Thing 1952, . . . And the Rain My Drink 1956, The Mountain is Young 1958, Cast but One Shadow 1962, Winter Love 1962, The Four Faces 1963, The Crippled Tree 1965, A Mortal Flower 1966, China in the Year 2001 1967, Birdless Summer 1968, Morning Deluge—Mao Tse-tung and the Chinese Revolution 1972, Wind in the Tower 1976, Lhasa, the Open City 1977, My House has Two Doors 1980, Phoenix Harvest 1980, Till Morning Comes 1982, The Enchantress (novel) 1985, A Share of Loving 1987, Tigers and Butterflies 1990, Fleur de Soleil, Les Yeux de Demain, La Peinture Chinoise, Chine Insolite, Wind in My Sleeve (autobiog.) 1992, Eldest Son: Zhou Enlai and the making of Modern China (1898–1976) 1994; three photography books. *Leisure interests:* economics, travel, lecturing. *Address:* 37 Montoie, Lausanne 1007, Switzerland.

HAN WAN-SANG; Korean politician and professor of sociology; b. 18 March 1936; s. of Han Young-Jik; m. 1966; three d.; ed. in U.S.A.; Prof. of Sociology, Seoul Nat. Univ. 1970–; adviser to Kim Young Sam; Deputy Prime Minister and National Unification Bd. Minister 1993; Chair. Korea Cable Communication Comm. 1994–; Pres. Korea Nat. Open Univ. 1994–. *Leisure interest:* tennis. *Address:* 169 Dong Sung-Dong, Chong Ro-ku, Seoul, Republic of Korea. *Telephone:* 762-3606. *Fax:* 747-9878.

HAN XIDUN, Maj.-Gen.; Chinese army official; fmr. Vice-Pres. Mil. Acad. of Econ., PLA, Pres. July 1993–. *Address:* c/o Ministry of National Defence, Jingshanqianjie, Beijing, People's Republic of China.

HAN ZHUBIN; Chinese politician; b. Feb. 1932, Harbin, Heilongjiang Prov.; ed. Beijing Econs. Corresp. Univ.; joined CCP 1950; fmr. railway worker; fmr. Vice-Sec., then Sec. Communist Youth League, Liuzhou Railway Bureau Cttee., Dir. 1975–83; Dir. and Party Sec. Shanghai Railway Bureau 1983–90; Vice-Sec. CCP Group and Sec. CCP Cttee. for Discipline Inspection, Ministry of Railways 1990–92; Minister of Railways 1993–98; Deputy Head Leading Group for Beijing-Kowloon Railway Construction 1993–; Deputy Sec. Cen. Comm. for Discipline Inspection 1997–; Chair. Supreme People's Procuratorate 1998; mem. 14th and 15th Cen. Cttee. CCP 1992–. *Address:* Supreme People's Procuratorate, Beijing, People's Republic of China.

HANAFUSA, Hidesaburo, PH.D.; Japanese biochemist; b. 12 Jan. 1929, Nishinomiya; m. Teruko Inoue 1958; one d.; ed. Univ. of Osaka; Research Assoc. Research Inst. for Microbial Diseases, Univ. of Osaka 1958–61; Postdoctoral Fellow, Virus Lab. Univ. of Calif. Berkeley 1961–64; Visiting Scientist, Coll. de France, Paris 1964–66; Assoc. mem., Chief, Dept. of Viral Oncology, Public Health Research Inst. of N.Y. 1966–68, mem. 1968–73; Prof. Rockefeller Univ. 1973–, Leon Hess Prof. 1986–; Foreign Assoc. N.A.S.; mem. editorial bd. Journal of Virology 1975–, Molecular Cell Biology 1984–; Harvey Lecturer 1980; H. T. Ricketts Award 1981; Albert Lasker Basic Medical Research Award 1982; Clowes Memorial Award 1986; Japan Culture Merit Award 1991; Alfred Sloan Prize 1993, Order of Culture 1995. *Publications:* contribs. on retroviruses and oncogenes to professional journals. *Address:* Department of Biochemistry, Rockefeller University, 1230 York Avenue, New York, NY 10021 (Office); 500 East 63rd Street, New York, NY 10021, U.S.A. (Home). *Telephone:* (212) 327-8803 (Office). *Fax:* (212) 327-7943 (Office).

HANAWA, Yoshikazu; Japanese business executive; ed. Tokyo Univ.; joined Nissan 1957, Pres. Nissan N. America 1989, various marketing and planning positions, Exec. Vice-Pres. 1991–96, Pres. 1996–. *Address:* Nissan Motor Co., 17-1 Ginza 6-chome, Chuo-ku, Tokyo 104-23, Japan (Office). *Telephone:* 3-3543-5523.

HANCOCK, Herbert Jeffrey (Herbie Hancock); American jazz pianist and composer; b. 12 April 1940, Chicago, Ill.; s. of Wayman Edward Hancock and Winnie Griffin; m. Gudrun Meixner 1968; ed. Roosevelt Univ., Chicago, Manhattan School of Music and New School for Social Research; owner and publr. Hancock Music Co. 1962–; founder Hancock and Joe Productions 1989–; Pres. Harlem Jazz Music Center, Inc.; performed with Chicago Symphony Orchestra 1952, Coleman Hawkins, Chicago 1960, Donald Byrd 1960–63, Miles Davis Quintet 1963–68; recorded with Chick Corea; composed film music for: Blow Up 1966, The Spook Who Sat by the Door 1973, Death Wish 1974, A Soldier's Story 1984, Jo Jo Dancer, Your Life is Calling 1986, Action Jackson 1988, Colors 1988, Harlem Nights 1989, Livin' Large 1991; wrote score and appeared in film Round Midnight 1986 (Acad. Award Best Original Score 1986). *Albums include:* Takin' Off 1963, Succotash 1964, Speak Like a Child 1968, Fat Albert Rotunda 1969, Mwandishi 1971, Crossings 1972, Sextant 1972, Headhunters 1973, Thrust 1974, The Best of Herbie Hancock 1974, Man-Child 1975, The Quintet 1977, V.S.O.P. 1977, Sunlight 1978, An Evening with Herbie Hancock and Chick Corea In Concert 1979, Feets Don't Fail Me Now 1979, Monster 1980, Greatest Hits 1980, Lite Me Up 1982, Future Shock 1983, Perfect Machine 1988, Jamming 1992, Cantaloupe Island 1994, Tribute to Miles 1994, Dis Is Da Drum 1995; numerous awards including Citation of Achievement, Broadcast Music, Inc. 1963, Jay Award, Jazz Magazine 1964, Grammy Award for Best Rhythm and Blues Instrumental Performance 1983, 1984, for Best Jazz Instrumental Composition (co-composer) 1987, Best Jazz Instrumental Performance 1995. mem. Nat. Acad. of Recording Arts and Sciences, Jazz Musicians Asscn., Nat. Acad. of TV Arts and Sciences, Broadcast Music. *Address:* Hancock Music, 1250 N. Doheny Drive, Los Angeles, CA 90069, U.S.A.

HANDLEY, Eric Walter, C.B.E., M.A., F.B.A.; British professor of Greek; b. 12 Nov. 1926, Birmingham; s. of Alfred Walter Handley and A. Doris Cox; m. Carol Margaret Taylor 1952; ed. King Edward's School, Birmingham and Trinity Coll. Cambridge; Asst. Lecturer in Greek and Latin, Univ. Coll., London 1946, Lecturer 1949, Reader 1961, Prof. 1967, Prof. of Greek and Head of Greek Dept. 1968–84; Dir. of Inst. of Classical Studies, Univ. of London 1967–84; Regius Prof. of Greek, Cambridge Univ. 1984–94, Fellow of Trinity Coll. 1984–; Prof. of Ancient Literature, Royal Acad. of Arts 1990–; Foreign Sec. British Acad. 1979–88; Pres. Classical Asscn. 1984–85, Soc. for the Promotion of Hellenic Studies 1993–96; Hon. Fellow, Univ. Coll., London 1989; Hon. R.A.; Cromer Greek Prize (jtly.) 1958. *Publications:* The Telephus of Euripides (with John Rea) 1958, The Dyskolos of Menander 1965, Relire Ménandre (with A. Hurst) 1990, Aristophane (with J.-M. Bremer) 1993, Images of the Greek Theatre (with Richard Green) 1995; edns. of Greek literary papyri, papers in classical journals. *Leisure interests:* walking and travel. *Address:* Trinity College, Cambridge, CB2 1TQ, England. *Telephone:* (01223) 338400. *Fax:* (01223) 338564.

HANDLEY, Vernon George, B.A., F.R.C.M.; British conductor; b. 11 Nov. 1930, Enfield; s. of Vernon Douglas and Claudia Lillian Handley; m. 1st Barbara Black 1954 (divorced); one s. one d. (one s. deceased); m. 2nd Victoria Parry-Jones (divorced); one s. one d.; m. 3rd Catherine Newby 1987; one s.; ed. Enfield School, Balliol Coll., Oxford, Guildhall School of Music; Conductor, Oxford Univ. Musical Club and Union 1953–54, Oxford Univ. Dramatic Soc. 1953–54, Tonbridge Philharmonic Soc. 1958–61, Hatfield School of Music and Drama 1959–61, Proteus Choir 1962–81; Musical Dir. and Conductor, Guildford Corpn., and Conductor, Guildford Philharmonic Orchestra and Choir 1962–83; Assoc. Conductor, London Philharmonic Orchestra 1983–86 (Guest Conductor 1961–83); Prof. for Orchestra and Conducting, Royal Coll. of Music 1966–72, for Choral Class 1969–72; Prin. Conductor, Ulster Orchestra 1985–89, Malmö Symphony Orchestra 1985–89; Prin. Guest Conductor Royal Liverpool Philharmonic Orchestra 1989–95 (Conductor Laureate 1995–) Melbourne Symphony Orchestra 1992–95; Chief Conductor W. Australian Symphony Orchestra 1993–; Assoc. Conductor Royal Philharmonic Orchestra 1994– (Guest Conductor 1961–94); Bournemouth Symphony Orchestra, B.B.C. Welsh Orchestra, B.B.C. Northern Symphony (now B.B.C. Philharmonic) Orchestra, Ulster Orchestra, B.B.C. Scottish Symphony Orchestra, New Philharmonia (now Philharmonia) Orchestra; conducted London Symphony Orchestra in int. series, London 1971; Fellow Goldsmiths' Coll., London 1987; tours of Germany 1966, 1980, S. Africa 1974, Holland 1980, Sweden 1980, 1981, Germany, Sweden, Holland and France 1982–83, Australia 1986, Japan 1988, Australia 1989, 1991, 1992; Hon. R.C.M. 1970; Hon. mem. Royal Philharmonic Soc. 1989; Hon. D.Univ. (Surrey) 1980; Hon. D.Mus. (Liverpool) 1992; Hon. D.Litt. (Bradford) 1998; Arnold Bax Memorial Medal for Conducting 1962; Conductor of the Year, British Composer's Guild 1974; Hi-Fi News Audio Award 1982; Gramophone Record of the Year 1986, 1989; British Phonographic Industry Award 1988. *Leisure interests:* bird photography, building furniture. *Address:* Cwm Cottage, Bettws, Abergavenny, Monmouthshire, NP7 7LG, Wales. *Telephone:* (01873) 890135.

HANDLIN, Oscar, PH.D., LL.D., L.H.D., D.H.L., LITT.D.; American academic; b. 29 Sept. 1915, Brooklyn; s. of Joseph and Ida (née Yanowitz) Handlin; m. 1st Mary Flug 1937; one s. two d.; m. 2nd Lilian Bombach 1977; ed. Univs. of Harvard, Michigan, Seton Hall, Lowell and Cincinatti; History instructor, Brooklyn Coll. 1936–38, Harvard Univ. 1939–44; Asst. Prof., Harvard Univ. 1944–48, Assoc. Prof. 1948–54, Prof. of History 1954–, Dir. Cen. for Study of Liberty in America 1958–66, Winthrop Prof. of History 1962–65, Charles Warren Prof. of History 1965–72, Dir. Charles Warren Cen. for Studies in American History 1965–72, Carl H. Pforzheimer Univ. Prof. 1972–84, Dir. Univ. Library 1979–83, Carl M. Loeb Prof. 1984–86; Harmsworth Prof., Oxford Univ. 1972–73; Vice-Chair. U.S. Bd. Foreign Scholarships 1962–65, Chair. 1965–66; Trustee New York Public Library 1973–; Guggenheim Fellow 1954, Brandeis Univ. Fellow 1965–; Fellow American Acad. of Arts and Sciences 1983; History Prize, Union League Club 1934, J.H. Dunning Prize, American History Asscn. 1941, Award of Honour, Brooklyn Coll., 1945, Pulitzer Prize for History 1952, Christopher Award 1958, Robert H. Lord Award 1972. *Publications:* Boston's Immigrants 1941, Commonwealth 1947, This was America 1949, The Uprooted, The American People in the Twentieth Century 1954, Adventure in Freedom 1954, Chance or Destiny 1955, Race and Nationality in American Life 1956, Readings in American History, Al Smith and his America 1958, Immigration as a Factor in American History 1959, The Newcomers – Negroes and Puerto Ricans in a Changing Metropolis 1959, American Principles and Issues 1961, The Dimensions of Liberty 1961, The Americans 1963, Fire-Bell in the Night 1964, Children of the Uprooted 1966, Popular Sources of Political Authority 1967, History of the United States 1967, America, a History 1968, The American College and American Culture 1970, Statue of Liberty 1971, Facing Life–Youth and the Family in American History 1971, A Pictorial History of Immigration 1972, The Wealth of the American People 1975, Truth in History 1979, Abraham Lincoln and the Union 1980, The Distortion of America 1981, Liberty and Power 1986, Liberty in Expansion 1989, Liberty in Peril 1991, Liberty and Equality 1994, From the Outer World 1997; ed. several publs. *Address:* 18 Agassiz Street, Cambridge, MA 02140, U.S.A.

HANDS, Terence David (Terry) B.A.; British theatre director; b. 9 Jan. 1941, Aldershot; s. of Joseph Ronald and Luise Bertha (Köhler) Hands; m. 1st Josephine Barstow 1964 (dissolved 1967); m. 2nd Ludmila Mikael (dissolved 1980); one d.; m. 3rd Julia Lintott; two s.; ed. Woking Grammar School, Birmingham Univ., RADA; Founder-Dir. Everyman Theatre, Liverpool 1964–66; Artistic Dir. Theatregoround, R.S.C. 1966; Assoc. Dir. R.S.C. 1967–77, Jt. Artistic Dir. 1978–86, Artistic Dir. and Chief Exec. 1986–91, Dir. Emer. 1991; Dir. Clwyd Theatr Cymru 1997–; Consultant Dir. Comédie Française 1975–80; Hon. Fellow Shakespeare Inst. 1990; Hon. D.Lit. (Birmingham) 1988; Meilleure Spectacle de l'Année for Richard III 1972, for Twelfth Night 1976; Plays and Players Award for Henry VI 1977, Society of West End Theatre Award 1978 and 1984; Pragnell Shakespeare Award 1991; Evening Standard Best Dir. Award 1993; Chevalier, Ordre des Arts et des Lettres; Hon. LL.D. (Middx.) 1997. *Productions:* over 40 plays with R.S.C., 5 with Comédie Française, 2 with Burgtheater, Vienna, one opera at Paris Opera House, one at Covent Garden, London, one at Bremen, five at Theatre Clwyd; Women Beware Women, Teatro Stabile di Genova, Italy; Arden of Faversham, Schauspielhaus, Zürich; Hamlet, Paris 1994, Merry Wives of Windsor, Oslo 1995, Kongsemnerne 1996, The Seagull 1998; recording: Murder in the Cathedral 1976; transl. (with Barbara Wright), The Balcony (Genet) 1971, Pleasure and Repentance 1976, Henry V (ed. Sally Beauman) 1976, Cyrano de Bergerac (TV). *Translation:* Hamlet, into French. *Address:* Clwyd Theatr Cymru, Mold, Flintshire, N. Wales. *Telephone:* (01352) 756331.

HANEGBI, Tzachi, B.A.; Israeli politician; b. 1957, Jerusalem; m.; three c.; ed. Herbrew Univ. of Jerusalem; served in an Israeli Defence Forces paratroopers unit 1974–77; Pres. Hebrew Univ. Student Union 1979–80, Nat. Union of Israeli Students 1980–82; Adviser to Minister of Foreign Affairs 1984–86; Bureau Dir., Prime Minister's Office 1986–88; mem. Knesset (Parl.) 1988–, mem. Knesset Foreign Affairs and Defence Cttee.; Cttee. on Constitution, Law and Justice, Knesset House Cttee., Cttee. on Labour and Social Welfare, Cttee. on Educ. and Culture 1988–92; Head (in rotation) Econ. Affairs Cttee. mem. Cttee. on Constitution, Law and Justice 1992–96; Minister of Health 1996–97, Minister of Justice 1997–; mem. Likud-Tzomet-Gesher political group. *Address:* Ministry of Justice, 29 Rehov Salahadin, Jerusalem 91010, Israel. *Telephone:* 2-6708511. *Fax:* 2-6708714.

HANEKOM, Derek; South African politician; b. 1953; Chair. Man. Cttee. Nat. Rural Devt. Forum; mem. ANC; fmr. ANC Co-ordinator of Land and Agricultural Devt.; Minister of Land Affairs 1994–, of Agric. 1996–; arrested 1977 for protesting against detentions, imprisoned for ANC activities 1983–86; in exile in Zimbabwe 1987–90. *Address:* Ministry of Agriculture and Land Affairs, Private Bag X844, Pretoria 0001, South Africa. *Telephone:* (12) 3235212. *Fax:* (12) 3211244.

HANFT, Ruth, PH.D.; American health policy consultant; b. 12 July 1929; d. of Ethel Schechter and Max Samuels; m. Herbert Hanft 1951; one s. one d.; ed. School of Industrial and Labor Relations, Cornell Univ. and Hunter Coll.; Social Science Analyst, Social Security Admin. 1964–66; Program Analyst, Office of Econ. Opportunity 1966–68, Dept. of Health, Educ. and Welfare 1968–72; Snr. Research Assoc., Inst. of Medicine, N.A.S. 1972–76; Deputy Asst. Sec., U.S. Dept. of Health and Human Services 1977–81; Health Policy Consultant 1981–88; Visiting Prof., Dartmouth Medical School 1976–; Consultant, Research Prof. Dept. of Health Services and Admin., George Washington Univ. 1988–91, Prof. 1991–95, consultant 1995–; mem. Inst. of Medicine, N.A.S.; Fellow, Hastings Inst.; Walter Patenge Medal of Public Service. *Publications:* Hospital Cost Containment (with M. Zubkoff and I. Raskin) 1978, Improving Health Care Management in the Workplace (with J. Rossow and R. Zager) 1985, Physicians and Hospitals: Changing Dynamics, in The Health Policy Agenda (Ed. M. Lewin) 1985; Human in Vitro Fertilization; Political, Legal and Ethical Issues, in Gynecology and Obstetrics Vol. 5 Chapter 98 1984; articles in professional journals. *Leisure interests:* gardening, needlepoint, travel. *Address:* 3609 Cameron Mills Road, Alexandria, VA 22305, U.S.A. (Home). *Telephone:* (703) 836-3945 (Home).

HANHAM, Harold John, PH.D., F.R.HIST.S., F.A.A.A.S.; British university vice-chancellor; b. 16 June 1928, Auckland, New Zealand; s. of John N. Hanham and Ellie Malone; m. Ruth S. Arnon 1973; ed. Mount Albert Grammar School, Auckland Univ. Coll., Univ. of N.Z. and Selwyn Coll. Cambridge; Asst. lecturer to Sr. lecturer in Govt. Univ. of Manchester 1954–63; Prof. and Head, Dept. of Politics, Univ. of Edin. 1963–68; Prof. of History and Fellow of Lowell House, Harvard Univ. 1970–73; Prof. of History and Political Science, M.I.T. 1972–85, Dean School of Humanities and Social Sciences 1973–84; Vice-Chancellor Univ. of Lancaster 1985–95, Hon. Prof. of History 1985–; Guggenheim Fellow 1972–73; Hon. A.M. (Harvard) 1968. *Publications:* Elections and Party Management 1969, The Nineteenth Century Constitution 1969, Scottish Nationalism 1969, Bibliography of British

History 1851–1914 1976. *Leisure interests:* discovering Canada, squash. *Address:* Long Barn, Cross Howe Lane, Clapham, Lancaster, LA2 8DL, England.

HANIN, Roger (pseudonym of Roger Paul Levy); French actor and director; b. 20 Oct. 1925, Algiers; s. of Joseph Levy and Victorine Hanin; m. 2nd Christine Gouze-Renal 1959; one d.; ed. Faculté Mixte de Médecine et de Pharmacie, Algiers; Dir. Pau Festival; producer, Lucrèce Borgia 1979 (play); author and producer, Argent mon bel amour (play) 1983; numerous stage and TV appearances, including Shakespearean roles; Chevalier, Ordre nat. du Mérite. *Films include:* Le Protecteur (also dir.) 1973, Big Guns 1974, L'Intrépide 1975, Le Faux Cul (also dir.) 1975, Le coup de Sirocco, Le Sucre 1978, Le Grand Pardon 1981, La Baraka 1982, L'Etincelle 1984, La Galette du Roi 1985, Train d'enfer (also dir.) 1985, Dernier été à Tanger 1986, La Rumba (also dir.) 1987, L'Orchestre Rouge 1989, Jean Galmot, aventurier 1990, Le Grand Pardon II 1992. *Publications:* plays: Ciel, où sont passées les dattes de tes oasis? 1968, Virgule 1974; books: L'Ours en lambeaux 1981, Le Voyage d'Arsène 1985, Les Gants Blancs 1994. *Address:* 9 rue du Boccador, 75008 Paris, France.

HANKEL, Wilhelm; German economist and professor; b. 10 Jan. 1929, Danzig; s. of Oskar and Jenny (née Schoffmann) Hankel; m. Uta Wömpner; three d.; ed. Univs. of Mainz and Amsterdam; worked in Cen. Planning Bureau of Netherlands Govt. 1951; subsequently joined Deutsche Bundesbank; served in Ministry of Econ. Co-operation and later in Foreign Ministry 1954–57; with Berliner Bank, Berlin and Kreditanstalt für Wiederaufbau, Frankfurt-am-Main 1957–68; Dir. Money and Credit Dept., Fed. Ministry of the Economy and Finance 1968–72; Pres. Hessische Landesbank, Girozentrale, Frankfurt-am-Main 1972–74; lecturer, Univ. of Frankfurt 1966–70, Hon. Prof. 1971–; Monetary Adviser EEC, Brussels 1974–76; Visiting Prof., Harvard, Georgetown and Johns Hopkins Univs., U.S.A. and Wissenschaftszentrum, Berlin. *Publications:* Die zweite Kapitalverteilung 1961, Währungspolitik 1971, Heldensagen der Wirtschaft oder schöne heile Wirtschaftswelt 1975, Der Ausweg aus der Krise 1976, Weltwirtschaft 1977, Caesar 1978, Gegenkurs, von der Schuldenkrise zur Vollbeschaftigung 1984, Keynes, Die Entschlüsselung des Kapitalismus 1986, Vorsicht, unser Geld 1989, Eine Mark für Deutschland 1990, Dollar und Ecu, Leitwährungen im Wettstreit 1992, Die sieben Todsünden der deutschen Vereinigung 1993; various articles, lectures, etc. *Leisure interests:* literature, music. *Address:* Berghausenerstrasse 190, 53639 Königswinter 21, Germany. *Telephone:* (02244) 7447.

HANKES-DRIELSMA, Claude Dunbar; British banker; b. 8 March 1949; Manufacturers Hanover 1968–72; Robert Fleming & Co., Ltd. 1972–77, Dir. 1974–77; Chair. Man. Cttee. Price Waterhouse and Partners 1983–89, Action Resource Centre 1986–91; Adviser to the Bd. of Corange (Boehringer Mannheim) 1988–94; mem. Gov. Council, Business in the Community 1986–91, Pres.'s Cttee. 1988–91; Deputy Chair. Leutwiler and Partners Ltd. 1992–96; assisted Dr. Fritz Leutwiler (q.v.) in his role as independent mediator between S.A. Govt. and foreign banks 1985; Nobel Independent Report 1991; Chair. Advisory Cttee. to Jordan on Strategic Econ. Policy Matters 1993–94; Dir. Shaw & Bradley 1993–; Trustee Windsor Leadership Trust 1998–; Hon. Fellow Corpus Christi Coll. Oxford. *Publication:* The Dangers of the Banking System: Funding Country Deficits 1975. *Leisure interests:* gardening, walking, skiing, reading, ancient art. *Address:* Stanford Place, Faringdon, Oxon., SN7 8EX, England. *Telephone:* (01367) 240547. *Fax:* (01367) 242853.

HANKS, Tom; American actor; b. Oakland, Calif.; m. 1st Samantha Lewes 1978 (divorced 1985); two c.; m. 2nd Rita Wilson 1988; two s.; began acting career with Great Lakes Shakespeare Festival; appeared in Bosom Buddies, ABC Television 1980, Acad. Award for Best Actor for Philadelphia 1994, for Forrest Gump 1995. *Films include:* Splash, Bachelor Party, The Man with One Red Shoe, Volunteers, The Money Pit, Dragnet, Big, Punch Line, The Burbs, Nothing in Common, Every Time We Say Goodbye, Joe Versus the Volcano 1990, The Bonfire of the Vanities 1990, A League of Their Own 1991, Sleepless in Seattle, Philadelphia 1993, Forrest Gump 1994, Apollo 13 1995, That Thing You Do (also dir.), Turner & Hooch 1997, Saving Private Ryan 1998, You've Got Mail 1998, Cast Away 1999. *Address:* c/o CAA, 9830 Wilshire Boulevard, Beverly Hills, CA 90212, U.S.A.

HANLEY, Rt. Hon. Sir Jeremy James, K.C.M.G., F.C.A., F.C.C.A., F.C.I.S.; British politician and chartered accountant; b. 17 Nov. 1945; s. of late Jimmy Hanley and of Dinah Sheridan; m. Verna, Viscountess Villiers (née Stott) 1973; two s. one d.; ed. Rugby School; with Peat Marwick Mitchell & Co. 1963–66; Dir. Anderson Thomas Frankel (ATF) 1969, Man. Dir. ATF (Jersey and Ireland) 1970–73; Deputy Chair. The Financial Training Co. Ltd. 1973–90; Sec. Park Place PLC 1977–83; Chair. Fraser Green Ltd. 1986–90; Parl. Adviser to ICA 1986–90; Conservative M.P. for Richmond and Barnes 1983–97; Parl. Under-Sec. of State, Northern Ireland Office 1990–93; Minister for Health, Social Security and Agric. 1990–92, for Political Devt., Community Relations and Educ. 1992–93; Minister of State for the Armed Forces, Ministry of Defence 1993–94; Cabinet Minister without Portfolio 1995; Chair. Conservative Party 1994–95; Foreign Office Minister of State for the Middle East and Hong Kong 1995–97; Chair. AdVal Group PLC, Int. Trade and Investment Ltd. 1998–; Dir. ITE Group PLC, Fields Aerospace, Inc., Brass Tacks Publishing Group Ltd. 1998–; mem. British-American Parl. Group 1983–97, Anglo-French Parl. Group 1983–97, CPA 1983–97, IPU 1983–97, British-Irish Interparl. Body 1990; Vice-Chair. Nat. Anglo-West Indian Conservative Soc. 1982–83; Chair. Conservative Candidates Asscn. 1982–83; mem. Bow Group 1974–, European Movt. 1974–, Mensa 1968–; Freeman City of London 1989; mem. Court of Assts. Worshipful Co. of Chartered Accountants.. *Leisure interests:* cookery, chess, cricket, languages, theatre, cinema, music, golf. *Address:* 6 Butts Mead, Northwood, Middx., HA6 2TL, England. *Telephone:* (01923) 826675.

HANNAH, Daryl; American actress; b. 1960, Chicago, Ill.; ed. Univ. of Calif. at Los Angeles; studied with Stella Adler; studied ballet with Marjorie Tallchief (q.v.); appeared on TV in Paper Dolls. *Films:* The Fury 1978, The Final Terror, Hard Country, Blade Runner, Summer Lovers, Splash, The Pope of Greenwich Village, Reckless, Clan of the Cave Bear, Legal Eagles, Roxanne, Wall Street, High Spirits, Steel Magnolias, Crazy People, At Play in the Fields of the Lord, Memoirs of an Invisible Man, Grumpy Old Men, Attack of the 50 ft Woman, The Tie That Binds, Grumpier Old Men 1995, Two Much 1996, The Last Days of Frankie the Fly 1996; dir. The Last Supper 1994, A Hundred and One Nights 1995. *Address:* c/o ICM, 8942 Wilshire Blvd., Beverly Hills, CA 90211, U.S.A.

HANNAH, John; British actor; b. Glasgow; s. of John Hannah and Susan Hannah; m. Joanna Roth; ed. Royal Scottish Acad. of Music and Drama; fmrly. electrician; fmrly. with Workers' Theatre Co. *Television appearances include:* McCallum (series), Joan, Faith. *Film appearances include:* Four Weddings and a Funeral, Sliding Doors, The James Gang, The Mummy.

HANNAY, Sir David Hugh Alexander, G.C.M.G., B.A.; British diplomatist; b. 28 Sept. 1935, London; s. of Julian Hannay and Eileen Hannay; m. Gillian Rosemary Rex 1961; four s.; ed. Craigflower School, Torryburn, Fife, Scotland, Winchester Coll. and New Coll. Oxford; Second Lieut., King's Royal Irish Hussars 1954–56; Persian language student, Foreign Office and British Embassy, Tehran 1959–61; Oriental Sec., British Embassy, Kabul 1961–63; Second Sec., Eastern Dept., Foreign Office, London 1963–65; Second, then First Sec., U.K. Del. to European Community, Brussels 1965–70, First Sec. U.K. Negotiating Team 1970–72, Chef de Cabinet to Sir Christopher Soames, Vice-Pres. of the European Community Comm. 1973–77; Counsellor, Head of Energy, Science and Space Dept., FCO, London 1977–79, Counsellor, Head of Middle East Dept. 1979, Asst. Under-Sec. of State (E.E.C.) 1979–84; Minister, British Embassy, Washington, D.C. 1984–85; U.K. Perm. Rep. to E.C. 1985–90, to UN 1990–95; British Govt. and EU Presidency Special Rep. for Cyprus 1996–; British Prime Minister's Personal Envoy to Turkey 1998; mem. Court and Council, Univ. of Birmingham 1998–. *Leisure interests:* gardening, travel, photography. *Address:* 3 The Orchard, London, W4 1JZ, England. *Telephone:* 0181-987 9012. *Fax:* 0181-987 9012.

HANNIBALSSON, Jón Baldvin, M.A.; Icelandic politician and diplomatist; b. 21 Feb. 1939, Ísafjörður; s. of Hannibal Valdimarsson and Sólveig Ólafsdóttir; m. Bryndís Schram 1959; one s. three d.; ed. Menntaskólinn í Reykjavík, Univ. of Edinburgh, Nationalökonomiska Inst., Stockholm, Univ. of Iceland and Harvard Univ.; teacher secondary school, Reykjavík 1964–70; journalist Frjáls thjód, Reykjavík 1964–68; Headmaster Menntaskólinn á Isafirdi, Ísafjörður 1970–79; Chief Ed. Althýdubladid, Reykjavík 1979–82; M.P. 1982–98; Minister of Finance 1987–88, for Foreign Affairs and Foreign Trade 1988–95; Chair. SDP 1984–96; Chair. Council of Ministers, EFTA 1989, 1992, 1994; Amb. to U.S.A. 1998–. *Leisure interests:* reading, swimming. *Address:* Embassy of Iceland, 1156 15th Street, N.W., Washington, DC 20005, U.S.A. *Telephone:* (202) 265-6653. *Fax:* (202) 265-6656.

HANNOVER, Georg Wilhelm, Prinz von, DR.IUR.; German educationist; b. 25 March 1915, Brunswick; s. of the Duke and Duchess of Brunswick; m. Princess Sophie of Greece and Denmark (sister of H.R.H. the Duke of Edinburgh q.v.) 1946; eight c.; ed. Hamelin/Weser High School, Marlborough Coll., Schule Schloss Salem, Univs. of Vienna and Göttingen; Head, Salemer Schulen 1948–59, now mem. Bd. of Dirs.; Chair. Outward Bound Mountain School (Austria), King Edward VII Foundation (German side); mem. Inst. for Town Planning; Pres. Riding Acad. Munich 1959–62; Hon. Vice-Pres. World Asscn. of Building Socs. and Saving for Bldg. Banks; mem. German Soc. for European Educ.; Pres. Int. Olympic Acad. 1966–70; mem. IOC 1966–71; Nat. Olympic Cttee. for Germany 1966–, Organizing Cttee. for Munich Olympic Games 1966–72; Pres. Modern Pentathlon Asscn., Bavaria 1972–; Hon. Vice-Pres. Int. Union of Bldg. Socs. and Savings Banks 1985–. *Address:* Georgi-Haus, 83727 Schliersee, Upper Bavaria, Germany. *Telephone:* Schliersee 72 65.

HANS-ADAM II, Reigning Prince of Liechtenstein; b. 14 Feb. 1945; s. of late Prince Franz Josef II and late Princess Gina; m. Countess Marie Aglaë Kinsky von Wchinitz und Tettau 1967; three s. one d.; ed. Schottengymnasium, Vienna, School of Econs. and Social Sciences, St. Gallen, Switzerland; Chief Exec. of Prince of Liechtenstein Foundation 1970–84; took over exec. authority of Liechtenstein Aug. 1984. *Address:* Schloss Vaduz, FL-9490 Vaduz, Principality of Liechtenstein.

HANSEID, Einar; Norwegian journalist; b. 19 Nov. 1943, Sandefjord; m. Mari Onsrud 1977; two s.; reporter, Sandefjords Blad 1965; News Ed. Dagbladet 1974; Chief Ed. Hjem & Fritid 1982; Man. Ed. Verdens Gang 1984, Chief Ed. 1987–93; Chief Ed. Aftenposten 1994–. *Address:* Aftenposten, Akersgt. 51, P.O. Box 1178 Sentrum, 0107 Oslo, Norway.

HANSEN, Barbara C., PH.D.; American scientist and university administrator; b. 24 Nov. 1941, Boston, Mass.; d. of Reynold Caleen and Dorothy

Richarson Caleen; m. Kenneth D. Hansen 1976; one s.; ed. Univ. of Calif., Los Angeles and Univ. of Washington, Seattle; Research Fellow, Univ. of Pa. Inst. of Neurosciences 1966–68; Asst. and Assoc. Prof. Univ. of Washington 1971–76; Prof. and Assoc. Dean Univ. of Michigan, Ann Arbor 1977–83; Assoc. Vice.-Pres. of Academic Affairs and Research and Dean of Grad. School, Southern Ill. Univ., Carbondale 1983–85; Vice-Pres. for Grad. Studies and Research, Univ. of Md., Baltimore 1986–90, Prof. of Physiology Univ. of Md. 1990–, Dir. Obesity and Diabetes Research Center 1990–; Pres. Int. Asscn. for Study of Obesity 1987–90, N. American Asscn. for Study of Obesity 1984–85, American Soc. of Clinical Nutrition 1995–96; mem. several advisory cttees. etc.; mem. N.A.S. Inst. of Medicine. *Publications:* Controversies in Obesity (Ed.) 1983, The Commonsense Guide to Weight Loss for People with Diabetes 1998, book chapters and articles in learned journals. *Leisure interests:* sailing, scuba diving, golf, reading. *Address:* Obesity and Diabetes Research Center, University of Maryland School of Medicine, MSTF600, 10 S. Pine Street, Baltimore, MD 21201, U.S.A. *Telephone:* (410) 706-3168. *Fax:* (410) 706-7540.

HANSEN, Bent, FIL. DR.; Swedish economist; b. 1 Aug. 1920, Ildved, Denmark; s. of Henrik Poulsen and Anna Louise (Pedersen) Hansen; m. Soad Ibrahim Refaat 1962; two s. four d.; ed. Univs. of Copenhagen and Uppsala; civil servant, State Dept., Copenhagen 1946; Lecturer Uppsala Univ. 1947–48 and 1950–51, Gothenburg 1948–50; Reader, Uppsala 1951–55; Prof. and Head of Konjunkturinst. (Nat. Inst. of Econ. Research), Stockholm 1955–64, Consultant, Inst. of Nat. Planning, Cairo 1962–65; Special Consultant for OECD, Paris 1965–67; Prof. of Political Economy, Stockholm Univ. 1967–68; Prof. of Econs. Univ. of Calif., Berkeley 1967–87, Prof. Emer. 1987–, Chair. Dept. of Econs. 1977–85; Consultant ECAFE Bangkok 1970–73, IMF 1973, U.S. Treasury 1974, Morocco 1976–77, Bogadizi Univ., Istanbul 1978, World Bank 1985–89 (Consultant Emer. 1987–); Chief ILO Employment Mission to Egypt 1980–81. *Publications:* A Study in the Theory of Inflation 1951, The Economic Theory of Fiscal Policy 1958, Foreign Trade Credits and Exchange Reserves 1961, Development and Economic Policy in the UAR (Egypt) 1965, Lectures in Economic Theory, I and II 1967, Long and Short Term Planning 1967, Fiscal Policy in Seven Countries, OECD, 1969, A Survey of General Equilibrium Systems 1970, Exchange Controls and Development: Egypt 1975, Employment Opportunities and Equity: Egypt in the 1980s, 1982, Political Economy of Poverty, Equity and Growth, Egypt and Turkey 1990. *Address:* 8336 Terrace Drive, El Cerrito, CA 94530, U.S.A. (Home). *Telephone:* 415-525-0704 (Home).

HANSEN, Clifford Peter, B.S.; American politician and rancher; b. 16 Oct. 1912, Zenith, Wyo.; s. of Peter and Sylvia (Wood) Hansen; m. Martha Elizabeth Close 1934; one s. one d.; ed. Univ. of Wyoming; Vice-Pres. Jackson State Bank 1953–74; Trustee Univ. of Wyo. 1946–63, Pres. Bd. 1956–63; fmr. Chair. Advisory Cttee. on Livestock Research and Marketing to Sec. of Agriculture; Gov. of Wyoming 1963–66; Senator from Wyoming 1967–79; Sec. Republican Conf. 1977; mem. Bd. Pacificorp 1979–83, Wyo. Bancorp. 1979–83; mem. Wyo. Stock Growers' Asscn., Pres. 1953–55; mem. American Nat. Cattlemen's Asscn., Second Vice-Pres. 1956–57; mem. Exec. Cttee. Nat. Govs. Conf. and Western Govs. Conf. 1963–67; mem. Bd. Trustees Buffalo Bill Historical Soc., Univ. of Wyo. Foundation, Pres. Reagan's Cttee. on Federalism, Political Economy Research Center, Gottsche Foundation 1979–; Emer. Dir. Mountain States Legal Foundation; Hon. LL.D. (Wyo.) 1965; Medallion Service Award, Univ. of Wyo. 1983, Nat. Cowboy Hall of Fame 1995, Stockman of the Century (Wyo.), Univ. of Wyo. Dedicated Life award 1995, named Citizen of the West 1996; Republican. *Leisure interests:* hiking, riding. *Address:* P.O.B. 448, Jackson, WY 83001, U.S.A. (Home). *Telephone:* (307) 733 3423. *Fax:* (307) 733-7590.

HANSEN, Kai Aaen, M.SC.; Danish central banker and international civil servant; b. 26 Nov. 1942, Hadsten; s. of Hans Helge Hansen and Kathrine Elisabeth Hansen; m. Ann Marie Skovløv 1970; ed. Univ. of Aarhus; economist, Danmarks Nat. Bank 1972–77, Asst. Head of Dept. 1980–82, Head of Dept. 1985–91, Dir. 1992–97; economist, OECD, Paris 1977–80; Econ. Adviser, IMF, Washington, D.C. 1983–85, Exec. Dir. 1998–; Deputy Chair. Nordic Comm. on Money Transmission 1981–83; mem. UN Informal Group on Money Transmission 1981–83, Govt. Comm. on Money Transmission 1982–83, Econ. Ministry Cttee. on Econ. Policies 1987–91, on Econ. and Monetary Union Issues 1996–97; alt. mem. EU Comm. of Cen. Bank Govs. 1991–94, European Monetary Comm. 1987–93; alt. Council mem. European Monetary Inst. 1994–97; part-time Asst. Prof., Copenhagen School of Econs. 1974–77, 1980–83; Kt. Order of Dannebrog. *Publications:* The International Monetary System, an Essay to Interpretation (with Erik Hoffmeyer) 1991, Pengepolitiske Problemstillinger 1993. *Address:* International Monetary Fund, Room 11-204, 700 19th Street, N.W., Washington, DC 20431, U.S.A. *Telephone:* (202) 623-4571. *Fax:* (202) 623-5385.

HANSEN, Kurt, DR.ING.; German businessman and chemist; b. 11 Jan. 1910, Yokohama, Japan; m. Irmi Strähuber 1937; one s. one d.; ed. Technische Hochschule, Munich; with I. G. Farbenindustrie AG/Farbenfabriken Bayer AG, Leverkusen 1936–74, Man. Uerdingen Factory, Farbenfabriken Bayer Jan. 1955, Wuppertal-Elberfeld Factory 1956–57, mem. Bd. of Man. Bayer AG (fmrly. Farbenfabriken Bayer) 1957–61, Chair. 1961–74, Chair. Supervisory Bd. 1974–84, Hon. Chair. Supervisory Bd. 1984–; Hon. mem. Presidential Bd. Fed. of German Industries, Cologne. *Address:* Sürderstrasse 14, 51375 Leverkusen, Germany. *Telephone:* (214) 51850.

HANSEN, Mogens Herman, D.PHIL.; Danish reader in classical philology; b. 20 Aug. 1940, Copenhagen; s. of Herman Hansen and Gudrun Maria (née Heslet) Hansen; m. Birgitte Holt Larsen; one s.; ed. Univ. of Copenhagen; Research Fellow, Inst. of Classics, Univ. of Copenhagen 1967–69, lecturer in Classical Philology 1969–88, Reader 1988–; Dir. The Copenhagen Polis Centre 1993–; Visiting Fellow, Wolfson College, Cambridge 1974; Visiting Prof., Melbourne Univ. 1988; mem. Inst. for Advanced Study, Princeton 1983; Fellow Royal Danish Acad. of Sciences and Letters; Corresp. mem. British Acad., Deutsches Archaeologisches Institute. *Publications include:* The Sovereignty of the People's Court in 4th Century Athens 1974, Aspects of Athenian Society 1975, Apagoge, Endeixis and Ephegesis 1976, The Athenian Ecclesia I 1983, II 1989, Demography and Democracy 1985, The Athenian Assembly 1987, The Athenian Democracy in the Age of Demosthenes 1991, Acts of the Copenhagen Polis Centre I 1993, II 1995, III 1996, IV 1997, V 1998, and over 100 articles in int. journals on Athenian democracy and ancient Greek constitutional history. *Leisure interests:* playing the flute, writing poetry, book binding. *Address:* Wilhelm Marstrandsgade 15, 2100 Copenhagen Ø, Denmark. *Telephone:* (35) 32 91 03 (Univ.); (35) 26 15 88 (Home). *Fax:* 32 54 89 54.

HANSEN, P. Gregers, M.SC., D.PHIL.; Danish physicist; b. 11 Jan. 1933, Frederiksberg; m. Bitten Bisbjerg 1957; two s.; ed. Tech. Univ. of Denmark, Copenhagen; Research Scientist, Group. Leader, Atomic Energy Research Inst. 1956–66; Prof. of Physics at the Univ. of Aarhus 1966–95; John A. Hannah Prof. Mich. State Univ. 1995–; Sr. Research Physicist and Group. Leader, C.E.R.N. Geneva 1969–79; mem. numerous scientific advisory bds., primarily in Germany, France and at C.E.R.N.; mem. Danish Royal Acad. of Sciences and Letters. *Publications:* many research papers and review articles on subjects in nuclear and atomic physics. *Leisure interests:* skiing, mountaineering, hiking, literature. *Address:* NSCL-Cyclotron, Michigan State University, East Lansing, MI 48824 (Office); 1127 Farwood Drive, East Lansing, MI 48823, U.S.A. (Home). *Telephone:* (517) 333-6433 (Office); (517) 337-2587 (Home).

HANSENNE, Michel, D. EN D.; Belgian politician; b. 23 March 1940, Rotheux-Rimiere; M.P. 1974–89; Minister of French Culture 1979–81, of Employment and Labour 1981–88, for Civil Service 1988–89; Dir.-Gen. Int. Labour Org., Geneva 1989–98. *Publication:* Emploi, les scenarios du possible. *Address:* c/o International Labour Organization, 4 route des Morillons, 1211 Geneva 22, Switzerland.

HANSON, Baron (Life Peer), cr. 1983, of Edgerton in the County of West Yorkshire; **James Edward Hanson,** Kt., F.R.S.A., C.B.I.M.; British business executive; b. 20 Jan. 1922; s. of late Robert Hanson, C.B.E. and Louisa A. (Cis) Rodgers; m. Geraldine Kaelin 1959; two s. one step-d.; Chair. Hanson PLC 1965–97, Chair. Emer. 1998–, Chair. Hanson Transport Group, Ltd. 1965–96; Fellow Cancer Research Campaign; mem. Court of Patrons, Royal Coll. of Surgeons of England 1991–; Trustee Hanson Fellowship of Surgery; Hon. Fellow St. Peter's Coll. Oxford 1996, Royal Coll. of Radiologists 1998; Hon. LL.D. (Leeds) 1984, Hon. D.B.A. (Huddersfield) 1991; Freeman of London; Hon. Liveryman, Worshipful Co. of Saddlers. *Address:* 1 Grosvenor Place, London, SW1X 7JH, England. *Telephone:* 0171-245 6996.

HANSON, Curtis; American film director and screenplay writer; b. 24 March 1945, Los Angeles, Calif.; Ed. Cinema magazine; began film career as screenplay writer. *Films directed:* The Arousers 1970, Sweet Kill (also screenplay) 1972, Little Dragons (also co-producer) 1977, Losin' It 1983, The Bedroom Window (also screenplay) 1988, Bad Influence 1990, The Hand that Rocks the Cradle 1992, The River Wild 1994, L.A. Confidential 1998, The Children of Times Square (TV film). *Screenplays:* The Dunwich Horror 1970, The Silent Partner 1978, White Dog 1982, Never Cry Wolf 1983. *Address:* United Talent Agency, 9560 Wilshire Boulevard, Floor 5, Beverly Hills, CA 90212, U.S.A.

HANSON, Sir John Gilbert, K.C.M.G., C.B.E., M.A., F.R.S.A.; British fmr. government official and university college warden; b. 16 Nov. 1938, Sheffield; s. of Gilbert F. Hanson and Gladys Kay; m. Margaret Clark 1962; three s.; ed. Manchester Grammar School and Wadham Coll. Oxford; War Office 1961–63; British Council, Madras, India 1963–66; Middle East Centre for Arab Studies, Lebanon 1966–68; British Council, Bahrain 1968–72, London H.Q. 1972–75, Dir. British Council, Iran and Cultural Counsellor, British Embassy, Tehran 1975–79, Controller (Finance), British Council, London 1979–82; Royal Coll. of Defence Studies 1983; Dir. British Council, India and Minister (Cultural), British High Comm. New Delhi 1984–88; Deputy Dir.-Gen. British Council 1988–92, Dir.-Gen. 1992–98; Warden Green Coll., Oxford 1998–; Chair. Trustees, British Skin Foundation 1997–; mem. Gov. Council, S.O.A.S. 1991–, London Univ. 1996–; Hon. Fellow Wadham Coll., Oxford 1997; Hon. D.Litt. (Oxford Brookes) 1995, (Lincolnshire & Humberside) 1996, (Greenwich) 1996; Patron GAP 1989–98. *Leisure interests:* books, music, sport, travel. *Address:* Warden's Lodgings, Green College, Woodstock Road, Oxford, OX2 6HG, England. *Telephone:* (01865) 274770. *Fax:* (01865) 274796.

HANUSZKIEWICZ, Adam; Polish actor and theatre director; b. 16 June 1924, Lvov, Ukraine; s. of Włodzimierz Hanuszkiewicz and Stanisława Szydłowska; m. 1st Zofia Ryś; one s. two d.; m. 2nd Zofia Kucówna; m. 3rd Magdalena Cwenówna; ed. State High School of Drama, Łódź, and State Higher School of Drama, Warsaw; début as actor 1945, acted in Cracow, Poznań and Warsaw; début as dir. 1953, directed in Poznań and Warsaw;

Artistic Dir. Theatre of Polish TV 1956–63; Dir. and Producer, Teatr Powszechny (Popular Theatre), Warsaw 1963–68, visited, with theatre company, Prague 1964, 1966, Moscow 1965, London, Paris 1966, Helsinki 1967, Bucharest 1968, Stockholm, Oslo 1969; Gen. Man. and Artistic Dir. Teatr Narodowy, Warsaw 1968–82, visited Helsinki, Leningrad, Moscow 1973, Berlin 1975, Bremen, Budapest, Moscow 1976; Gen. Man. and Artistic Dir. Teatr Nowy, Warsaw 1989–; visited Wilno 1989; acted in 50 major roles in theatre; directed 30 plays in theatre, 100 television plays; State Prize (First Class) for TV work, City of Warsaw Award for theatre work, Theatre Critics' Prize 1964, Order of Banner of Labour, 1st Class 1974, Ekran Gold Screen TV Award 1978, Prize of Minister of Foreign Affairs 1979. *Principal roles include:* Hamlet (Hamlet) 1951–59, Tytus (Bérénice) 1962, Prospero (The Tempest) 1963, Raskolnikov (Crime and Punishment) 1964, Don Juan (Don Juan) 1965, Fantazy (Fantazy) 1967, Count Henryk (Un-divine Comedy) 1969, Duncan (Macbeth) 1972, Créon (Antigone) 1973. *Plays directed include:* Wesele (The Wedding, Wyspiański), Crime and Punishment, Coriolanus, Don Juan, The Columbus Boys (Bratny), Kordian (Słowacki), St. Joan 1969, Hamlet 1970, Norwid 1970, Beniowski (Słowacki) 1971, Three Sisters 1971, 1983, 1988, Twelfth Night 1971, Macbeth 1973, Antigone 1973, The Inspector General 1973, Balladyna (Słowacki) 1974, A Month in the Country 1974, Wacława dzieje (Garczyński) 1974, Kartoteka (Różewicz) 1974, Don Juan 1975, Wesele (Wyspiański) 1976, Mickiewicz 1976, Mąż i żona (Fredro) 1977, Phèdre 1977, Peace 1977, Sen srebrny Salomei (Słowacki) 1977, Wyszedł z domu (Różewicz) 1978, Dziady (Mickiewicz) 1978, Białe małżeństwo (Różewicz) 1978, Treny (Kochanowski) 1979, The Brothers Karamazov, The Decameron 1980, As You Like It, Platonov 1962, 1980, School of Wires, Leśmian 1982, Śpiewnik domowy 1982, 1984, 1989, Wilno, Cyd 1984, 1991, Così fan tutte 1985, Figaro's Wedding 1987, Komedia pasterska 1991, Gombrowicz 1992, Panna Isabela (Prus) 1993, Lilla Weneda (Słowacki) 1995, Dulska-musical (Zapolska), Balladyna 1996, Romeo i Julia 1997. *Opera:* Don Giovanni 1997, The Dance of Death 1998, Six Figures 1998. *Television:* Fuga 1994, Nim przyjdzie wiosna (Jwaszkiewicz) 1994, Panienka z poczty 1994. *Publication:* Psy, hondy i drabina 1991. *Address:* ul. Drzymały 1c, 02-495 Warsaw, Poland.

HAO BAILIN; Chinese physicist; b. 26 June 1934, Beijing; s. of Hao Kingsheng and Zhao Weimei; m. Zhang Shuyu 1959; one s. one d.; mem. Chinese Acad. of Sciences 1980–; Dir. Inst. of Theoretical Physics 1989; Science and Tech. Progress Award. *Publications:* 7 books, including Elementary Symbolic Dynamics and Chaos in Dissipative Systems 1989; 110 scientific papers on theoretical physics, computational physics, nonlinear science. *Leisure interests:* reading classical Chinese poems. *Address:* c/o Institute of Theoretical Physics, P.O. Box 2735, Beijing 100080, People's Republic of China.

HAO JIANXIU; Chinese politician; b. 1935, Qingdao; worker, State Operated Cotton Factory No. 6, Qingdao; originated Hao Jianxiu Work Method; mem. Exec. Council, Women's Fed. 1953; mem. Cen. Cttee., Communist Democratic Youth League 1953; joined CCP 1954; Deputy Dir. Cotton Factory No. 6, Qingdao 1964; mem. Cen. Cttee. Communist Youth League 1964–Cultural Revolution; mem. Qingdao Municipality Revolutionary Cttee. 1967; mem. Standing Cttee., Cotton Factory No. 6 Revolutionary Cttee. 1968; Vice-Chair. Qingdao Municipality Revolutionary Cttee. 1971, Trade Union, Shandong 1975; Chair. Women's Fed., Shandong 1975; mem. Standing Cttee., Shandong Prov. CCP Cttee. 1977; mem. 11th CCP Cen. Cttee. 1977–82; Vice-Minister of Textile Industry 1978–81, Minister 1981–83; Vice-Minister State Planning Cttee. 1987–; mem. Politburo 13th Cen. Cttee. CCP 1985; Vice-Chair. Women's Fed. 1978; Vice-Chair. State Tourism Cttee. 1988; Nat. Model Worker in Industry 1951, mem. 12th Cen. Cttee. CCP 1982–87, 13th Cen. Cttee. CCP 1987–92; mem. 14th Cen. Cttee. CCP 1992–97; mem. 15th Cen. Cttee. CCP 1997–; Alt. Sec. Secr. 1982, Sec. 1985; mem. Financial and Econ. Leading Group, CCP Cen. Cttee. 1986; Hon. Pres. Factory Dirs'. Study Soc., Acad. of Social Sciences 1985; Deputy Dir. Leading Group for the Placement of Demobilized Army Officers 1993–; Vice-Chair. Cttee. for Women and Children's Work 1987–. *Address:* Zhonggong Zhongyang, A8, Taipingjie Street, Beijing 100050, People's Republic of China.

HARAD, George Jay, B.A., M.B.A.; American business executive; b. 24 April 1944, Newark, N.J.; s. of Sidney Harad and Irma Harad; m. Beverly Marcia Harad 1966; one s. one d.; ed. Franklin & Marshall Coll., Harvard Business School; Admin. Asst. to Sr. Vice-Pres. Housing Group, Boise Cascade Corpn. 1971–72, Finance Man. Boise Cascade Realty Group 1972–76; Man. Corp. Devt., Boise Cascade Corpn. 1976–80, Dir. Retirement Funds 1980–82, Vice-Pres. Controller 1982–84, Sr. Vice-Pres., Chief Financial Officer 1984–89, Exec. Vice-Pres., Chief Financial Officer 1989–90, Exec. Vice-Pres. Paper 1990–91, Pres., C.O.O. 1991–94, Pres., C.E.O. 1994–95, Chair. Bd. and C.E.O. 1995–, Chair. 1995–; George F. Baker Scholar. *Leisure interest:* golf. *Address:* Boise Cascade Corporation, 1111 West Jefferson Street, P.O. Box 50, Boise, ID 83728 (Office); 224 East Braemere Road, Boise, ID 83702, U.S.A. *Telephone:* (208) 384-7557 (Office); (208) 345-0808 (Home).

HARALD V; King of Norway; b. 21 Feb. 1937, Skaugum; s. of the late King Olav V and Crown Princess Märtha; m. Sonja Haraldsen 1968; one s. one d.; ed. Oslo Katedralskole, Cavalry Officers' Cand. School, Mil. Acad. and Balliol Coll. Oxford; lived in Washington, D.C. 1940–45; has participated in many int. sailing competitions representing Norway at Olympic Games several times; undertook frequent official visits abroad while Crown Prince; succeeded his father, King Olav V, Jan. 1991. *Address:* Royal Palace, Oslo, Norway. *Telephone:* 22 04 87 00.

HARBISON, Peter, M.A., DR.PHIL., M.R.I.A., F.S.A.; Irish archaeologist, art historian and editor; b. 14 Jan. 1939, Dublin; s. of Dr James Austin Harbison and Sheelagh Harbison (née McSherry); m. Edelgard Soergel 1969; three s.; ed. St. Gerard's School, Bray, Glenstal, Univ. Coll. Dublin and Univs. of Marburg, Kiel and Freiburg; awarded travelling scholarship by German Archaeological Inst. 1965; archaeological officer, Irish Tourist Bd. 1966–84, editorial publicity officer 1984–86, Ed. Ireland of the Welcomes (magazine) 1986–95; Sec. Friends of the Nat. Collections of Ireland 1971–76; mem. Council, Royal Irish Acad. 1981–84, 1993–, Vice-Pres. 1992–93, Hon. Academic Ed. 1995–; Prof. of Archaeology, Royal Hibernian Acad. of Arts; Chair. Nat. Monuments Advisory Council 1986–90; corresp. mem. German Archaeological Inst. *Publications:* Guide to National Monuments of Ireland 1970, The Archaeology of Ireland 1976, Irish Art and Architecture (co-author) 1978, Pre-Christian Ireland (Archaeological Book of the Year Award 1988) 1988, Pilgrimage in Ireland 1991, Beranger's Views of Ireland 1991, The High Crosses of Ireland 1992, Irish High Crosses 1994, Ancient Ireland (with Jacqueline O'Brien) 1996, Ancient Irish Monuments 1997, Beranger's Antique Buildings of Ireland, L'Art Médiéval en Irlande 1998, Spectacular Ireland 1999; articles in books and journals. *Leisure interests:* music, travel, wining, dining, cruising. *Address:* 5 St. Damian's, Loughshinny, Skerries, Co. Dublin, Republic of Ireland. *Telephone:* (01) 8490940.

HARCOURT, Geoffrey Colin, A.O., PH.D., LITT.D., F.A.S.S.A.; Australian economist; b. 27 June 1931, Melbourne; s. of Kenneth and Marjorie (née Gans) Harcourt; m. Joan Bartrop 1955; two s. two d.; ed. Univs. of Melbourne and Cambridge; lecturer in econs., Univ. of Adelaide 1958–62, Sr. lecturer 1963–65, Reader 1965–67, Prof. (Personal Chair) 1967–85, Prof. Emer. 1988; lecturer in econs. and politics, Univ. of Cambridge 1964–66, 1982–90, Reader in the History of Econ. Theory 1990–98, Emer. Reader 1998–, Dir. of Studies in Economics and Fellow of Trinity Hall, Cambridge 1964–66, Fellow and Lecturer in Econs., Jesus Coll., Cambridge 1982–98, Emer. Fellow 1998–, Pres. 1988–92; Visiting Fellow, Clare Hall, Cambridge 1972–73; Visiting Prof., Univ. of Toronto, Canada 1977, 1980; Hon. Prof., Univ. of N.S.W. 1997; Visiting Fellow, Australian Nat. Univ. 1997; Fellow, Acad. of the Social Sciences in Australia 1971–; Pres. Economic Soc. of Australia and New Zealand 1974–77; Wellington Burnham Lecturer, Tufts Univ., Medford, Mass. 1975, Edward Shann Memorial Lecturer, Univ. of Western Australia 1975, Newcastle Lecturer in Political Economy, Univ. of Newcastle 1977, Acad. Lecturer, Acad. of the Social Sciences in Australia 1978, G. L. Wood Memorial Lecturer, Univ. of Melbourne 1982, John Curtin Memorial Lecturer, A.N.U. 1982, special lecturer in econs., Univ. of Manchester 1984, Lecturer Nobel Conf. XXII, Gustavus Adolphus Coll., Minn. 1986, Laws Lecturer, Univ. of Tennessee at Knoxville 1991, Donald Horne Lecturer 1992, Sir Halford Cook Lecturer, Queen's Coll., Univ. of Melbourne, Kingsley Martin Memorial Lecturer, Cambridge 1996, Colin Clark Memorial Lecturer, Brisbane 1997; mem. Council Royal Econ. Soc. 1990–95, Life mem. 1998–; Distinguished Fellow, Econ. Soc. of Australia 1996; Hon. Litt.D. (De Montfort Univ.) 1997. *Publications:* Economic Activity (with P. H. Karmel and R. H. Wallace) 1967, Readings in the Concept and Measurement of Income (ed., with R. H. Parker) 1969, 2nd edn. (with R. H. Parker and G. Whittington) 1986, Capital and Growth, Selected Readings (ed., with N. F. Laing) 1971, Some Cambridge Controversies in the Theory of Capital 1972, The Microeconomic Foundations of Macroeconomics (ed.) 1977, The Social Science Imperialists, Selected Essays (edited by Prue Kerr) 1982, Keynes and his Contemporaries (ed.) 1985, Controversies in Political Economy, Selected Essays of G. C. Harcourt (edited by Omar Hamouda) 1986, Int. Monetary Problems and Supply-Side Economics: Essays in Honour of Lorie Tarshis (edited with Jon S. Cohen) 1986, On Political Economists and Modern Political Economy, Selected Essays of G. C. Harcourt (ed. by Claudio Sardoni) 1992, Post-Keynesian Essays in Biography: Portraits of Twentieth Century Political Economists 1993, The Dynamics of the Wealth of Nations. Growth, Distribution and Structural Change: Essays in Honour of Luigi Pasinetti (edited with Mauro Baranzini) 1993, Income and Employment in Theory and Practice. Essays in Memory of Athanasios Asimakopoulos (Ed. with Alessandro Roncaglia and Robin Rowley) 1994, Capitalism, Socialism and Post-Keynesianism. Selected Essays of G. C. Harcourt 1995, A 'Second Edition' of The General Theory, 2 vols. (ed. with P. A. Riach) 1997, and articles in journals. *Leisure interests:* running (not jogging), bike riding, cricket, reading. *Address:* Jesus College, Cambridge, CB5 8BL; 43 New Square, Cambridge, CB1 1EZ, England (Home). *Telephone:* (01223) 339 436 (Jesus College); (01223) 360833 (Home).

HARDCASTLE, Jack Donald, M.A., M.CHIR., F.R.C.S., F.R.C.P.; British professor of surgery; b. 3 April 1933, Yorks.; s. of Albert Hardcastle and Bertha Hardcastle (née Ellison); m. Rosemary Hay-Shunker 1965; two c.; ed. Emmanuel Coll. Cambridge; House Physician, London Hosp. 1959–60; House Surgeon, Hammersmith Hosp., London 1961–62; Research Asst. London Hosp. 1962, lecturer in Surgery 1963, Registrar in Surgery 1964, Registrar in Surgery, Thoracic Unit 1965, Sr. Registrar 1965, Sr. Lecturer 1968; Sr. Registrar St. Mark's Hosp., London 1968; Prof. of Surgery Univ. of Nottingham 1970–; Sir Arthur Sims Commonwealth Travelling Prof., Royal Coll. of Surgeons 1985; Mayne Visiting Prof. Univ. of Brisbane, Australia 1987; Dir. of Educ. Royal Coll. of Surgeons 1993, mem. Council 1995–, Vice-Pres. 1995–97, Dir. of Overseas Office 1996–; Hon. Fellow Royal

Coll. of Physicians and Surgeons (Glasgow). *Publications:* Isolated Organ Perfusion (with H.D. Ritchie) 1973; articles in professional journals. *Leisure interest:* golf, gardening. *Address:* Department of Surgery, Faculty of Medicine, Queen's Medical Centre, University of Nottingham, Nottingham, NG7 2UH (Office); Goverton Heights, Goverton, Bleasby, Notts., NG14 7FN, England (Home). *Telephone:* 0115-970 9245 (Office). *Fax:* 0115-970 9428.

HARDER, Manfred, DR.IUR; German professor of law; b. 15 Nov. 1937, Frankfurt/Main; s. of Karl and Erna (née Kopf) Harder; m. Judis Kalinowski 1966; one s. one d.; ed. Freie Univ., Berlin; part-time asst. Frei Univ., Berlin 1960–63, teaching asst. 1964–70, Asst. Prof. 1970–71, Prof. 1971; Prof. of Roman and Civil Law, Univ. of Mainz 1972–, Pres. of Univ. 1980–84; Justice of the Palatine Supreme Court, Zweibrücken 1987–93. *Publications:* Zuwendungen unter Lebenden auf den Todesfall 1968, Die Leistung an Erfüllungs Statt 1976, Grundzüge des Erbrechts 1983, articles in learned journals and contributions to legal books. *Address:* Johannes-Gutenberg-Universität, Jakob-Welder-Weg 9, 55099 Mainz; Alfred Mumbächer-Strasse 36, 55128 Mainz, Germany (Home). *Telephone:* 06131/39-2777 (Office); 06131/35924 (Home).

HARDIE, (Charles) Jeremy (Mawdesley), C.B.E., B.PHIL.ECONS., A.C.A.; British business executive; b. 9 June 1938; s. of Sir Charles Hardie; m. 1st Susan Chamberlain 1962 (divorced 1976); two s. two d.; m. 2nd Xandra, Countess of Gowrie 1978 (divorced 1994); one d.; m. 3rd Kirsteen Margaret Tait 1994; ed. Winchester Coll. and New Coll. Oxford; Nuffield Coll. Oxford 1966–67; Jr. Research Fellow, Trinity Coll. Oxford 1967–68; Fellow and Tutor in Econs. Keble Coll. Oxford 1968–75; partner, Dixon Wilson & Co. 1975–82; Dir. John Swire and Sons Ltd. 1982–; Dir. W. H. Smith Group 1988– (Deputy Chair. 1992–94, Chair. Jan. 1994–); Chair. Nat. Provident Inst. 1980–89, Alexander Syndicate Man. Ltd. 1982–95, Radio Broadland Ltd. 1983–85, David Mann Underwriting Agency Ltd. 1983–, Dir. Alexanders Discount Co. Ltd. 1978–87, Alexanders Laing & Cruickshank Gilts Ltd. 1986–87; Dir. Northdor Holdings 1989–93; Chair. Centre for Econ. Policy Research 1984–89; other business and public appts.; parl. cand. (SDP), Norwich South 1983, (SDP/Alliance) 1987. *Leisure interests:* sailing, skiing. *Address:* 13 Ainger Road, London, NW3 3AR, England *Telephone:* (0171) 722 6916.

HARDIE BOYS, Sir Michael, G.N.Z.M., G.C.M.G.; New Zealand Governor-General and fmr. judge; b. 6 Oct, 1931, Wellington; s. of Justice Reginald Hardie Boys and Edith May (née Bennett) Hardie Boys; m. Edith Mary Zohrab 1957; two s. two d.; ed. Wellington Coll., Victoria Univ. of Wellington; barrister, solicitor with pvt. practice 1950–80; Councillor then Pres. Wellington Dist. Law Soc. 1974–79; Judge High Court 1980–89, Court of Appeal 1989–95; Gov.-Gen. of N.Z. 1996–; mem. Legal Aid Bd. (Chair.); Hon. Bencher of Gray's Inn; Hon. Fellow Wolfson Coll., Cambridge; Hon. LL.D. (Victoria Univ., Wellington) 1997. *Leisure interest:* the outdoors. *Address:* Government House, Private Bag, Wellington, New Zealand. *Telephone:* (4) 389-8055. *Fax:* (4) 389-5536.

HARDIN, Clifford Morris, B.S., M.S., DR. AGRIC. ECON.; American consultant; b. 1915, Knightstown, Ind.; s. of J. Alvin and Mabel (Macy) Hardin; m. Martha Love Wood 1939; two s. three d.; ed. Purdue Univ.; Asst. Prof. of Agricultural Econs., Univ. of Wis. 1942–44; Assoc. Prof., Prof. and Chair. Agricultural Econs. Dept., Mich. State Univ. 1946–48, Dir. Agricultural Experimental Station 1948–53, Dean of Agric. 1953–54; Chancellor, Univ. of Neb. 1954–69; U.S. Sec. of Agriculture 1969–71; Vice-Chair. Ralston Purina Co. 1971–80; Dir. and Scholar-in-Residence, Center for Study of American Business, Washington Univ., St. Louis 1981–85; mem. Exec. Cttee. Council of Higher Educ. of the American Repubs. 1963–69; Consultant and Dir. Stifel, Nicolaus & Co., St. Louis 1980–87; Trustee, Rockefeller Foundation 1961–69, 1972–81, Farm Foundation 1973–83, Gallup Inc. 1983–, Halifax Corpn. 1983–; mem. Bd. Nat. Science Foundation 1966–70; Trustee Univ. of Neb. Foundation 1975–. *Address:* 10 Roan Lane, St. Louis, MO 63124, U.S.A. (Home).

HARDING, Marshal of the Royal Air Force Sir Peter Robin, G.C.B., D.SC., F.R.AE.S., C.B.I.M.; British air force officer (retd.); b. 2 Dec. 1933; s. of Peter Harding and Elizabeth Kezia Clear; m. Sheila Rosemary May 1955; three s. one d.; ed. Chingford High School; joined R.A.F. 1952; Pilot, numerous appts. in fighter, light bomber, strike/attack, reconnaissance and helicopters; Air Officer Commanding Number 11 Group 1981–82; Vice-Chief Air Staff 1982–84, of Defence Staff 1985; Air Officer Commanding-in-Chief, RAF Strike Command, and C.-in-C. U.K. Air Forces (NATO) 1985–88; Chief of Air Staff 1988–92, Chief of Defence Staff 1993–94; ADC to H.M. the Queen 1975, Air ADC to H.M. the Queen 1988–92; Deputy Chair. Marconi Ltd. 1995–; Dir. Double Sky Co. Ltd. 1995–; Council mem. Winston Churchill Memorial Trust 1990–; Gov. Sutton's Hosp. in Charterhouse 1990–; Hon. mem. and Vice-Patron Portland Coll. 1993–; Vice-Pres. The Guild of Aviation Artists 1994–; Liveryman Guild of Air Pilots and Navigators; Fellow and Hon. Companion Royal Aeronautical Soc. 1989; mem. Pilgrims Soc. of G.B.; Hon. D.Sc. (Cranfield Inst. of Tech.) 1990. *Publications:* articles for professional journals and magazines. *Leisure interests:* five grandchildren, tennis, piano, bridge, birdwatching and shooting (normally separately).

HARDWICK, Elizabeth, M.A.; American author; b. 27 July 1916, Lexington, Ky.; d. of Eugene Allen Hardwick and Mary (née Ramsey) Hardwick; m. Robert Lowell 1949 (divorced 1972); one d.; ed. Kentucky Univ., Columbia Univ.; Assoc. Prof. Barnard Coll.; Guggenheim Fellow 1947; recipient George Jean Nathan award 1966; mem. American Acad., Inst. of Arts and Letters (Gold Medal for Criticism 1993). *Publications: novels:* The Ghostly Lover 1945, The Simple Truth 1955, Sleepless Nights 1979; *essays:* A View of My Own 1962, Seduction and Betrayal 1974, Bartleby in Manhattan 1983, Sight Readings 1998; Ed. The Selected Letters of William James 1960; contribs. to New Yorker. *Address:* 15 W. 67th Street, New York, NY 10023, U.S.A.

HARDY, Sir David William, Kt., C.B.I.M.; British business executive; b. 14 July 1930; s. of late Brig. John H. Hardy; m. Rosemary Collins 1957; one s. one d.; ed. Wellington Coll. and Harvard Business School; chartered accountant; with Funch Edye Inc. and Imperial Tobacco, U.S.A. 1954–70; H.M. Govt. Coordinator of Industrial Advisers 1970–72; Group Finance Dir. Tate & Lyle Ltd. 1972–77; Dir. Ocean Transport & Trading PLC 1977–83; Dir. Globe Investment Trust PLC 1976–90, Exec. Chair. 1983–90; Chair. Ocean Inchcape 1980–83, London Park Hotels 1983–87, Docklands Light Railway 1984–87, Swan Hunter 1986–88, MGM Assurance 1986–, London Docklands Devt. Corpn. 1988–92, Europa Minerals 1991–94, Bankers Trust Investment Man. Ltd. 1992–94, Burmine 1992–96, James Fisher 1992–, Y. J. Lovell 1994–, Imperial Tobacco Group 1996–, Milner Estates 1996, Sons of Gwalia 1996–98; Non-exec. Dir. Hanson 1991–, Ciba Geigy 1991–96, J. Devenish 1991–93; numerous other directorships, professional appts. etc.; Chair. of Trustees Nat. Maritme Museum 1995–, Transport Research Lab. 1996–. *Address:* National Maritime Museum, Greenwich, London, SE10 9NF, England. *Telephone:* 0181-312 6630. *Fax:* 0181-312 6648.

HARDY, Françoise; French singer, author and astrologer; b. 17 Jan. 1944, Paris; m. Jacques Dutronc 1981; one s.; first record, Tous les garçons et les filles 1962; last record, Décalages 1988; now writes lyrics for musicians including Diane Tell, Julien Clerc, Khalil Chahine, Guesch Patti and composer-arranger Alain Lubrano; presents Horoscope RTL; several awards and prizes. *Publications:* Le grand livre de la Vierge (with B. Guenin), Entre les lignes entre les signes (with Anne-Marie Simond) 1986, Notes Secrètes (with E. Dumont) 1991; contribs. to Françoise Hardy présente l'Astrologie Universelle 1986, Entre les lignes, entre les signes 1986. *Leisure interest:* reading, especially books dealing with spirituality. *Address:* 13 rue Hallé, Paris 75014, France.

HARDY, John Philips, M.A., D.PHIL., F.A.H.A.; Australian professor of English; b. 1 Jan. 1933, Brisbane; s. of late E. A. Hardy and N. A. (née Philips) Hardy; m. 1st 1961 (divorced); three s. one d.; m. 2nd 1992; ed. Church of England Grammar School, Brisbane, Univ. of Queensland and Univ. of Oxford; Fellow Magdalen Coll., Oxford 1962–65; Asst. Prof. Univ. of Toronto, Canada 1965–66; Prof. of English Univ. of New England 1966–72, Australian Nat. Univ. 1972–87; Foundation Prof. of Humanities and Social Sciences, Bond Univ. 1988–94; Queensland Rhodes Scholar 1957; Sec. Australian Acad. of the Humanities 1981–88; Harold White Hon. Fellow, Nat. Library of Australia 1992. *Publications:* Reinterpretations: Essays on Poems by Milton, Pope and Johnson 1971, Samuel Johnson 1979, Jane Austen's Heroines 1984, Stories of Australian Migration (Ed.) 1988, Terra Australis to Australia (Ed. with Alan Frost) 1989, European Voyaging towards Australia (Ed. with Alan Frost) 1990. *Leisure interests:* swimming, fishing. *Address:* 26 Rawson Street, Deakin, Canberra, A.C.T. 2600, Australia.

HARDY, Robert, C.B.E.; British actor and author; b. 29 Oct. 1925; s. of late Major Henry Harrison Hardy and Edith Jocelyn Dugdale; m. 1st Elizabeth Fox 1952 (divorced); one s.; m. 2nd Sally Pearson 1961 (divorced 1986); two d.; theatre appearances include four seasons of Shakespeare at Stratford-on-Avon, two at Old Vic; world tours include Henry V and Hamlet, U.S.A.; numerous appearances London and Broadway theatres 1952–; Trustee, Royal Armouries 1984–; Consultant, Mary Rose Trust 1979–, Trustee 1991–; Master of Worshipful Co. of Bowyers 1988–90; Hon. D.Litt (Reading) 1990; writer and/or presenter of numerous TV programmes including The Picardy Affair, The History of the Longbow, Heritage, Horses in our Blood, Gordon of Khartoum etc.; other TV appearances have included Prince Hal and Henry V in Age of Kings, Prince Albert in Edward VII, Malcolm Campbell in Speed King, Winston Churchill in the Wilderness Years, Siegfried Farnon in All Creatures Great and Small, Twiggy Rathbone and Russell Spam in Hot Metal, the Commandant in The Far Pavilions, Sherlock Holmes, Inspector Morse, Middlemarch, Castle Ghosts, Gulliver's Travels. *Films include:* How I Won the War, Yellow Dog, Dark Places, Young Winston, Ten Rillington Place, Le Silencieux, Gawain and the Green Knight, The Spy Who Came In From The Cold, La Gifle, Robin Hood, The Shooting Party, Paris by Night, War and Remembrance, Mary Shelley's Frankenstein, Sense and Sensibility, Mrs. Dalloway, The Tichborne Claimant 1998. *Publication:* Longbow 1976. *Leisure interests:* making and shooting longbows, riding, most country pursuits. *Address:* c/o Chatto and Linnit, 123A King's Road, London, SW3 4PL, England. *Telephone:* 0171-352 7722.

HARE, Sir David, Kt., M.A., F.R.S.L.; British playwright; b. 5 June 1947, Hastings, Sussex; s. of Clifford Theodore Rippon Hare and Agnes Cockburn Gilmour; m. 1st Margaret Matheson 1970 (dissolved 1980); two s. one d.; m. 2nd Nicole Farhi (q.v.) 1992; ed. Lancing Coll., Jesus Coll., Cambridge; Literary Man. and Resident Dramatist, Royal Court 1969–71; Resident Dramatist, Nottingham Playhouse 1973; f. Joint Stock Theatre Group 1975, Greenpoint Films 1983; Assoc. Dir. Nat. Theatre 1984–88, 1989–; Evening Standard Drama Award 1970, John Llewelyn Rhys Prize 1974, BAFTA Best Play of the Year 1978, U.K./U.S. Bicentennial Fellowship 1978, New York Critics' Circle Award 1983, Golden Bear Award for Best Film 1985, Evening

Standard Drama Award for Best Play 1985, Plays and Players Best Play 1985, City Limits Best Play 1985, Drama Magazine Awards Best Play 1988, Plays and Players Best Play Award 1988 and 1990, Critics Circle Award for Best Play 1990, Laurence Olivier Best Play of the Year 1990, Time Out Award 1990, Dramalogue Award 1992, Laurence Olivier Best Play of the Year 1996, New York Critics Circle Award 1997, Time Out Award for Outstanding Theatrical Achievement 1998; Officier, Ordre des Arts et des Lettres 1997. *Plays:* Slag, Hampstead 1970, The Great Exhibition, Hampstead 1972, Knuckle, Comedy Theatre 1974, Brassneck, Nottingham Playhouse 1973, Fanshen, Jt. Stock Theatre Group 1975, Teeth 'n' Smiles, Royal Court 1975, Plenty, National Theatre 1978, Broadway 1983, A Map of the World, Adelaide Festival 1982, Nat. Theatre 1983, Pravda, Nat. Theatre 1985, The Bay at Nice and Wrecked Eggs, Nat. Theatre 1986, The Secret Rapture, Nat. Theatre 1988, Broadway 1989, Racing Demon, Nat. Theatre 1990, Broadway 1995, Murmuring Judges, Nat. Theatre 1991, The Absence of War, Nat. Theatre 1993, Skylight, Nat. Theatre and Vaudeville 1995, Wyndhams and Broadway 1996, Amy's View Nat. Theatre 1997, Aldwych 1998, The Judas Kiss, Playhouse and Broadway 1998, The Blue Room, Donmar Warehouse and Broadway 1998, Via Dolorosa, Royal Court 1998; adapted: The Rules of the Game 1992, The Life of Galileo 1994, Mother Courage 1995, Ivanov 1996. *Films for TV:* Licking Hitler 1978, Dreams of Leaving 1980, Saigon: Year of the Cat 1983, Heading Home 1991, The Absence of War 1995. *Films:* Wetherby 1984, Plenty 1985, Paris by Night 1988, Strapless 1989, Damage 1992, The Secret Rapture 1993, The Designated Mourner (dir. only) 1996. *Opera:* The Knife, New York Shakespeare Festival 1987. *Publications:* Writing Lefthanded 1991, Asking Around 1993. *Address:* c/o Casarotto Ramsay Ltd., 60–66 Wardour Street, London, W1V 3HP, England.

HARE, (Frederick) Kenneth, C.C., PH.D., F.R.S.C.; Canadian professor of geography; b. 5 Feb. 1919, Wylye, Wilts., England; s. of Frederick E. Hare and Irene Smith; m. 1st Suzanne A. Bates 1941 (dissolved 1952); m. 2nd Helen N. Morrill 1953; two s. one d.; ed. Univs. of London and Montreal; Asst., Assoc. and Full Prof. of Geography, McGill Univ. 1945–62, Chair. Geography Dept. 1950–62, Dean of Arts and Science 1962–64; Prof. of Geography King's Coll., London 1964–66; Master of Birkbeck Coll., Univ. of London 1966–68; Pres. Univ. of British Columbia 1968–69; Prof. of Geography and Physics, Univ. of Toronto 1969–84, Univ. Prof. Emer. 1984–; Dir. Inst. for Environmental Studies 1974–79, Provost of Trinity Coll. 1979–86; Chancellor Trent Univ. 1988–95; Chair. Royal Soc. of Canada Comm. on Lead in the Environment 1984–86; Commr. Ont. Nuclear Safety Review 1986–88; Chair. Tech. Advisory Panel on Nuclear Safety, Ont. Hydro 1991–94; numerous hon. degrees, medals and awards. *Publications:* author and co-author of books and articles on climate, environment, nuclear safety, etc. *Leisure interests:* music, gardening. *Address:* 301 Lakeshore Road West, Oakville, Ont. L6K 1G2, Canada.

HARE, Richard Mervyn, M.A., F.B.A.; British philosopher; b. 21 March 1919, Backwell, Avon; s. of Charles F. A. Hare and Louise K. Simonds; m. Catherine Verney 1947; one s. three d.; ed. Rugby School and Balliol Coll., Oxford; Fellow and Tutor, Balliol Coll., Oxford 1947–66; White's Prof. of Moral Philosophy and Fellow, Corpus Christi Coll., Oxford 1966–83; Grad. Research Prof. of Philosophy, Univ. of Fla. 1983–94; Hon. Fellow, Balliol and Corpus Christi Colls.; Foreign Hon. mem. American Acad. of Arts and Sciences; Tanner Award (Utah); Hon. Ph.D. (Lund) 1991. *Publications:* The Language of Morals 1952, Freedom and Reason 1963, Practical Inferences 1971, Essays on Philosophical Method 1971, Essays on the Moral Concepts 1972, Applications of Moral Philosophy 1972, Moral Thinking 1981, Plato 1982, Hare and Critics 1988, Essays in Ethical Theory 1989, Essays on Political Morality 1989, Essays on Religion and Education 1992, Essays on Bioethics 1993, Zum moralischen Denken 1994, Sorting Out Ethics 1997, Objective Prescriptions and Other Essays 1999. *Leisure interests:* music, gardening. *Address:* Bywater, The Street, Ewelme, Nr. Wallingford, Oxon., OX10 6HQ, England. *Telephone:* (01491) 839239.

HARE DUKE, Rt. Rev. Michael Geoffrey, M.A.; British ecclesiastic; b. 28 Nov. 1925, Calcutta, India; s. of A. R. A. Hare Duke and Dorothy Holmes; m. Grace Lydia Frances McKean Dodd 1949; one s. three d.; ed. Bradfield Coll., Berks., Trinity Coll., Oxford, Westcott House, Cambridge; Sub-Lieut. R.N.V.R. 1944–46; ordained Deacon 1952, Priest 1953; Curate St. John's Wood, London 1952–56; Vicar St. Mark's, Bury 1956–62; Pastoral Dir. Clinical Theology Asscn. 1962–64; Vicar St. Paul's, Daybrook 1964–69; Bishop of St. Andrews, Dunkeld and Dunblane 1969–94; Chair. Age Concern Scotland 1994–; Hon. D.D. (St. Andrews). *Publications:* Understanding the Adolescent 1969, The Break of Glory 1970, Freud 1972, Good News 1976, Stories, Signs and Sacraments in the Emerging Church 1982, Praying for Peace: Reflections on the Gulf Crisis 1991, Hearing the Stranger: Reflections, Poems and Hymns 1994. *Leisure interests:* writing and broadcasting. *Address:* 2 Balhousie Avenue, Perth, PH1 5HN, Scotland. *Telephone:* (01738) 622642. *Fax:* (01738) 622642.

HAREWOOD, 7th Earl of, cr. 1812; **George Henry Hubert Lascelles,** K.B.E.; British musical administrator; b. 7 Feb. 1923, London; s. of the late 6th Earl of Harewood and H.R.H. Princess Mary, The Princess Royal (d. of H.M. King George V); m. 1st Maria Donata Stein 1949 (dissolved 1967); three s. (she m. 1973 the Rt. Hon. Jeremy Thorpe, q.v.); m. 2nd Patricia Tuckwell 1967; one s.; ed. Eton Coll. and King's Coll., Cambridge; Capt. Grenadier Guards 1942–46; P.O.W. 1944–45; A.D.C. to Earl of Athlone, Gov.-Gen. of Canada 1945–46; Counsellor of State during absence of the Sovereign 1947, 1954 and 1956; mem. Bd. of Dirs. Royal Opera House, Covent Garden 1951–53, 1969–72, Admin. Exec. 1953–60; Dir.-Gen. Leeds Musical Festival 1958–74; Artistic Dir. Edinburgh Int. Festival 1961–65; Chair. British Council Music Advisory Cttee. 1956–66, Arts Council Music Panel 1966–72; Artistic Adviser New Philharmonia Orchestra, London 1966–76; Pres. English Football Asscn. 1964–71, Leeds United Football Club; Chancellor, York Univ. 1963–67; mem. Gen. Advisory Council of BBC 1969–77, Gov. of BBC 1985–87; Man. Dir. English Nat. Opera 1972–85, Chair. 1986–95; Pres. British Bd. of Film Classification 1985–97; Artistic Dir. Adelaide Festival for 1988; Artistic Adviser Buxton Festival 1993–98; Ed. Opera 1950–53, Kobbé's Complete Opera Book 1954, 1976, 1987, 1997; Austrian Great Silver Medal of Honour 1959, Lebanese Order of the Cedar 1970, Janáček Medal 1978. *Publication:* The Tongs and the Bones (autobiog.) 1981, Kobbé's Illustrated Opera Book 1989, Pocket Kobbé 1994. *Leisure interests:* looking at painting, sculpture, football, cricket. *Address:* Harewood House, Leeds, Yorkshire, LS17 9LG, England.

HARIRI, Rafik Bahaa Edine; Lebanese politician and business executive; b. 1944, Sidon, Lebanon; emigrated to Saudi Arabia 1965; teacher, then auditor with eng. co.; prin. Civil Construction Establishment (CICONEST) 1970–78; f. Saudi Oger (with Oger Enterprises) 1978; prin. Oger Co. 1979, Oger Liban, Saudi Oger Services U.K.; Prime Minister of Lebanon and Minister of Finance, 1992–98, also of Posts and Telecommunications; f. Hariri Foundation for Culture and Higher Educ. 1979; Chevalier, Légion d'honneur 1981, Kt. of the Italian Repub. 1982, Nat. Cedars Medal (Lebanon) 1983, Saint Butros and Saint Boulos Medal 1983, Save the Children 50th Anniversary Award 1983, King Faisal Medal 1983, Médaille de Paris 1983, Beirut Golden Key 1983. *Address:* Office of President of Council of Ministers, Grand Sérail, rue des Arts et Métiers, Sanayeh, Beirut, Lebanon. *Telephone:* (1) 862001. *Fax:* (1) 602020.

HARISH, Michael, B.A.; Israeli politician and economist; b. 28 Nov. 1936, Romania; s. of Joseph Harish and Esther Harish; m. Edith Normand 1963; three s. one d.; ed. studies in econs. and political science; Sec.-Gen. Labour Party's Student Org. 1961–63; Dir. and Chair. Int. Dept. Israel Labour Party 1967–82, Sec.-Gen. Israel Labour Party 1989–92; Minister of Industry and Trade 1992–96; mem. Knesset 1974–; Deputy Chair. Defence and Foreign Affairs Cttee. 1984–88; Chair. Finance Cttee. 1988–89; Co-Chair. Jt. Science and Tech. Cttee. (U.S.-Israel); mem. several ministerial cttees. including Econ. Affairs, Immigrants' Absorption, Devt. Areas, Jerusalem Affairs; mem. Cttee. for co-ordinating activities between Govt. and the Jewish Agency and the Zionist Org. *Leisure interests:* sport, music. *Address:* 1 Mishmar Hayarden Street, Givatayim, 53582 Israel (Home). *Telephone:* (03) 5715233 (Home).

HARKIANAKIS, Stylianos, D.D.; Australian ecclesiastic; b. 29 Dec. 1935, Rethymnon, Crete, Greece; ed. Theological School of Halki, Univ. of Athens; Deacon Constantinople (Istanbul) 1957; priest Rethymnon 1958; abbot Holy Patriarchal Monastery of Vlatadon, Thessaloniki 1966; Pres. Patriarchal Inst. of Patristic Studies; lecturer Univ. of Thessaloniki 1969–75, Univ. of Sydney 1975–85; Titular Bishop of Miletoupolis 1970; Exarch of Mount Athos 1970–75; Visiting Prof. Univ. of Regensberg 1973; Archbishop Greek Orthodox Church of Australia 1975, Primate 1975–; Co.-Chair. official theological dialogue between Roman Catholic and Orthodox churches 1980–; Dean St Andrew's Greek Orthodox Theological Coll. 1986–; mem. jt. official comm. of theological dialogue between Orthodox and Anglicans 1970; Gottfried von Herder Prize (Vienna) 1973, Award for Poetry (Acad. of Athens) 1980, Golden Cross of St Andrew (Constantinople), Golden Cross of Holy Sepulchre, Archdiocese of Thyateira); Dr h.c. (Univ. of Lublin) 1985; awarded Key to City of Adelaide 1995. *Publications include:* The Infallibility of the Church in Orthodox Theology 1965, The Constitution "De Ecclesia" of the Second Vatican Council 1969, Orthodoxy and Catholicism, 20 vols. of poetry, over 50 theological essays in periodicals. *Leisure interests:* poetry, reading, swimming, walking. *Address:* 242 Cleveland Street, Redfern, Sydney 2016, Australia. *Telephone:* (612) 9698-5066. *Fax:* (612) 9698-5368.

HARKIN, Thomas R., J.D.; American politician; b. 19 Nov. 1939, Cumming, Ia.; s. of Patrick and Frances Harkin; m. Ruth Raduenz 1968; two d.; ed. Iowa State Univ. and Catholic Univ. of America; mem. House of Reps. 1975–85; Senator from Iowa 1984–; mem. Small Business Cttee., various subcttees., Democratic Steering Cttee.; Democrat. *Publication:* Five Minutes to Midnight 1990. *Address:* United States Senate, 731 Hart Senate Office Bldg., Washington, DC 20510, U.S.A.

HARLAN, Jack Rodney, PH.D.; American professor of plant genetics; b. 7 June 1917, Washington, D.C.; s. of Harry Vaughn Harlan and Augusta Griffing Harlan; m. Jean Yocum 1939; two s. two d.; ed. George Washington Univ. and Univ. of California at Berkeley; Geneticist, U.S. Dept. of Agric. 1942–61; Prof. of Agronomy, Okla. State Univ. 1951–66; Prof. of Plant Genetics, Univ. of Ill. 1966–84, Prof. Emer. 1984–; Botanist, Dept. of Agric. (plant exploration and introduction) Turkey, Syria, Iraq 1948, Iran, Afghanistan, Pakistan, India, Ethiopia 1960; Sr. Staff mem. Iranian Prehistoric Project, Oriental Inst., Univ. of Chicago 1960, Turkish Prehistoric Project 1964; plant exploration and collection in 16 countries in Sub-Saharan Africa 1967–71; mem. int. bd. Plant Genetic Resources 1974–79, Nabta Playa Archaeological Project, Egypt 1994; mem. Dead Sea Archaeological Project 1977, 1979, 1983; Guggenheim Fellow 1960; mem. N.A.S., A.A.A.S., American Soc. of Agronomy, Crop Science Soc. of America (Pres. 1966); Fellow American Acad. of Arts and Sciences. *Publications:* Theory and Dynamics of Grassland Agriculture 1956, Origins of African Plant Domestication (Co.-Ed.) 1975, Crops and Man 1975; more than 200 articles in journals. *Leisure interests:* sailing, bird watching, nature conservation. *Address:* c/o University of Illinois, Department of Agronomy, AE-120, Turner Hall, Urbana, IL 61801 (Office); 1016 North Hagan Street, New Orleans, LA 70119, U.S.A. (Home).

HARLAND, Bryce, M.A.; New Zealand diplomatist; b. 11 Dec. 1931, Wellington; s. of Edward Harland and Annie McDonald (Gordon) Harland; m. 1st 1957; m. 2nd 1979; four c. (one deceased); ed. Victoria Univ., Wellington and Tufts Univ., U.S.A.; with Ministry of Foreign Affairs 1953–91, various missions in Singapore, Bangkok, New York 1956–62, Head S. Pacific and Antarctic Div. 1962–64, Counsellor, Washington, D.C. 1965–69, Head Research Div., then Head Asian Affairs Div. 1969–70; Amb. to China (also accred. to Viet Nam) 1973-76; Asst. Sec. 1976–81, also Dir. of External Aid Div. 1981–82; Perm. Rep. to UN 1982–85; High Commr. in U.K. (also accred. to Ireland) 1985–91; Dir. N.Z. Inst. of Int. Affairs 1997–; Visiting Fellow, All Souls Coll., Oxford 1991; Queen's Service Order 1992. *Publications:* On Our Own, Asia: What Next? 1992, Collision Course 1996. *Leisure interests:* walking, music. *Address:* 9 Tinakori Road, Wellington, New Zealand.

HARLIN, Renny; film director; b. 1958, Helsinki; m. Geena Davis (q.v.); ed. Univ. of Helsinki Film School; f. The Forge production co. with Geena Davis. *Films:* Born American (debut) 1986, Prison, A Nightmare on Elm Street IV: The Dream Master, Die Hard 2, The Adventures of Ford Fairlane, Rambling Rose (producer only), Cliffhanger, Speechless (co-producer only), Cutthroat Island (also producer), The Long Kiss Goodnight (also producer). *Address:* c/o ICM, 8992 Wilshire Boulevard, Beverly Hills, CA 90211, U.S.A.

HARMAN, Gilbert Helms, PH.D.; American professor of philosophy; b. 26 May 1938, E. Orange, N.J.; s. of William H. Harman, Jr. and Marguerite Page; m. Lucy Newman 1970; two d.; ed. Swarthmore Coll. and Harvard Univ.; mem. Dept. of Philosophy, Princeton Univ. 1963–, Prof. of Philosophy 1971–, Co. Dir. Cognitive Science Lab. 1986–, Chair. Cognitive Studies Programme 1992–97. *Publications:* Thought 1973, The Nature of Morality: An Introduction to Ethics 1977, Change in View: Principles of Reasoning 1986, Skepticism and the Definition of Knowledge 1990, Concepts of the Human Mind (Ed.) 1993, Moral Relativism and Moral Objectivity (with Judith Jarvis Thomson) 1996. *Address:* Department of Philosophy, Princeton University, Princeton, NJ 08544-1006, U.S.A. *Telephone:* (609) 258-4301. *Fax:* (609) 258-1502.

HARMAN, Rt. Hon. Harriet, P.C.; British politician; b. 30 July 1950; d. of John Harman and Anna Spicer; m. Jack Dromey 1982; two s. one d.; ed. St. Paul's Girls' School and Univ. of York; Brent Community Law Centre 1975–78; Legal Officer, Nat. Council for Civil Liberties 1978–82; M.P. for Peckham 1982–97, for Camberwell and Peckham 1997–; Shadow Chief Sec. to Treasury 1992–94; Shadow Spokesperson on Employment 1994–95, on Health 1995–96, on Social Security 1996–97; Sec. of State for Social Security 1997–98; Labour. *Publications:* Sex Discrimination in Schools 1977, Justice Deserted: the subversion of the jury 1979, The Century Gap 1993. *Address:* House of Commons, London, SW1A 0AA, England.

HARMEL, (Count) Pierre Charles José Marie, D. EN D.; Belgian politician and university professor; b. 16 March 1911, Uccle, Brussels; s. of Charles Harmel and Eusébie André; m. Marie-Claire van Gehuchten 1946; four s. two d.; Prof., Faculty of Law, Univ. of Liège 1947–81; Prof. Emer.; mem. Chamber of Reps. 1946–71; Minister of Public Instruction and Fine Arts 1950–54; Minister of Justice 1958; Minister of Cultural Affairs 1959–60; Minister of Admin. 1960–61; Prime Minister 1965–66; Minister of Foreign Affairs 1966–73; co-opted Senator 1971; Minister of State Feb. 1973; Pres. of Senate 1973–77; mem. Acad. Royale de Belgique 1977–; Croix de guerre avec palmes 1940. *Publications:* Principes non bis in idem et les droits d'enregistrement 1942, La famille et l'impôt en Belgique 1944, Culture et profession 1944, Les sources et la nature de la responsabilité civile des notaires, en droit Belge de 1830 à 1962 1964, Organisation et déontologie du notariat 1977, Droit commun de la Vente 1985, Grandes avenues du droit 1988. *Address:* 8 avenue de l'Horizon, 1150 Brussels, Belgium. *Telephone:* 02-762 4680.

HARMOKO, Haji; Indonesian politician and journalist; b. 7 Feb. 1939, Kertosono, E. Java; ed. Sr. High School, Kediri, E. Java and Inst. of Nat. Defence (LEMHANAS), Jakarta; journalist, Merdeka (magazine and daily) 1960–65; Ed., Api (daily); Man. Ed. Merdeka and Chief Ed. Merdiko 1966–68; Chief Ed. Mimbar Kita 1968–69; Gen. Man., Chief Ed. Pos Kota (daily); mem. Bd. of Film Censors 1974; mem. Press Council 1975; Chief Ed. Warna Sari 1976–83; mem. House of Reps. and People's Consultative Ass. and Head of Information and Mass Media Div. of Functional Group (GOLKAR) 1978, Chair. Golkar Party Oct. 1993–; Head of Advisory Bd. of Newspaper Publrs. Asscn. 1979–84; mem. Exec. Bd. Press and Graphics Asscn. 1980–84; Minister of Information 1983–97; Speaker People's Consultative Ass. and House of Reps. 1997–. *Address:* People's Consultative Assembly, Jalan Gatot Subroto 6, Jakarta, Indonesia.

HARMS, Hans Heinrich, DR.THEOL.; German ecclesiastic; b. 4 July 1914, Osterholz–Scharmbeck; s. of Wilhelm and Christine Harms; m. Marianne Kiel 1940; two d.; ed. Göttingen and Bonn Univs. and Princeton Theological Seminary, U.S.A.; Pastor, Duderstadt 1939, Roringen, Herberhausen 1943; Inspector of Studies, Göttingen 1949; Oberkirchenrat Foreign Office of Church 1950–52; Sec., then Assoc. Dir., Div. of Studies, World Council of Churches (WCC) 1952–60; Sr. Pastor in Hamburg 1960–67; mem. Cen. Cttee. WCC 1961–68, 1975–83, mem. Exec. Cttee. 1975–83; teaching assignment Univ. of Göttingen 1946, Univ. of Hamburg 1961; mem. Council, Evangelical Church in Germany 1973–85; Bishop of Evangelical-Lutheran Church in Oldenburg 1967–85; co-ed. Die Kirchen der Welt, Ökumenische Rundschau, Evangelische Missionszeitschrift, Das Wort in der Welt; Dr. h.c. (Göttingen); Winner of the Niedersachsen Landesmedaille 1985. *Address:* Beethovenstrasse 9, 26135 Oldenburg, Germany (Home). *Telephone:* (0441) 14384 (Home).

HARNICK, Sheldon Mayer; American lyricist; b. 30 April 1924, Chicago; s. of Harry M. and Esther (née Kanter) Harnick; m. 1st Mary Boatner 1950 (annulled 1957); m. 2nd Elaine May 1962 (divorced 1963); m. 3rd Margery Gray 1965; one s. one d.; ed. Northwestern Univ.; wrote songs for univ. musicals; contributor to revues: New Faces of 1952, Two's Company 1953, John Murray Anderson's Almanac 1954, The Shoestring Revue 1955, The Littlest Revue 1956, Shoestring '57 1957; with composer Jerry Bock (q.v.) wrote shows Body Beautiful 1958, Fiorello 1959 (Pulitzer Prize), Tenderloin 1960, Smiling the Boy Fell Dead (with David Baker) 1961, She Loves Me 1963, Fiddler on the Roof (Tony Award) 1964, The Apple Tree 1966, The Rothschilds 1970, Captain Jinks of the Horse Marines (opera, with Jack Beeson) 1975, Rex (with Richard Rodgers) 1976, Dr. Heidegger's Fountain of Youth (opera, with Jack Beeson) 1978, Gold (cantata, with Joe Raposo) 1980, translations: The Merry Widow 1977, The Umbrellas of Cherbourg 1979, Carmen 1981, A Christmas Carol 1981 (musical; book and lyrics), Songs of the Auvergne 1982, A Wonderful Life 1986, The Appeasement of Aeolus 1990, Cyrano 1994. *Address:* c/o Alvin Deutsch, Deutsch and Blasband, 800 3rd Avenue, New York, NY 10022, U.S.A.

HARNONCOURT, Nikolaus; Austrian musician and conductor; b. 6 Dec. 1929, Berlin, Germany; s. of Eberhard and Ladislaja (née Meran) Harnoncourt; m. Alice Hoffelner 1953; three s. one d.; ed. Matura Gymnasium, Graz, Acad. of Music, Vienna; mem. of Vienna Symphony Orchestra 1952–69; Prof., Mozarteum and Inst. of Musicology, Univ. of Salzburg 1972–; founder mem. of Concentus Musicus, Ensemble for Ancient Music 1954; Conductor, Zürich Opera and Amsterdam Concertgebouw Orkest; has given numerous concerts in Europe, Australia and the U.S.A.; shared Erasmus Prize 1980; H.G. Nägeli Medal, Zürich 1983; Hon. D.Mus. (Univ. of Edin.) 1987; numerous awards for recordings. *Publications:* Musik als Klangrede, Wege zu einem neuen Musikverstärdnis 1982, Der musikalische Dialog 1983. *Leisure interests:* cultural history, woodwork. *Address:* 38 Piaristengasse, 1080 Vienna, Austria.

HARNOY, Ofra, C.M.; Israeli/Canadian cellist; b. 31 Jan. 1965, Israel.; d. of Jacob Harnoy and Carmela Harnoy; m. Robert S. Cash; studied with her father in Israel, William Pleeth in London, Vladimir Orloff in Toronto and in master classes with Mstislav Rostropovich, Pierre Fournier and Jacqueline du Pré; professional début, aged 10, with Boyd Neel Orchestra, Toronto; solo appearances with many maj. orchestras in the U.S.A., Canada, Japan, Europe, Israel and Venezuela; TV appearances in Canada, the U.K. and other European countries, Japan and Australia; played world premiere performance Offenbach cello concerto, N. American premiere Bliss cello concerto, world premiere recording of several Vivaldi cello concertos; many solo recordings; prizes and awards include: JUNO Award for Best Classical Soloist (Canada) 1987/88, 1988/89, 1991, 1992, 1993; First Prize Montreal symphony competition 1978, Canadian Music Competition 1979, Concert Artists Guild, New York 1982; Young Musician of the Year, Musical America magazine, U.S.A. 1983; Grand Prix du Disque; Critics' Choice, Best Records of the Year, The Gramophone, U.K. 1986, 1988, 1990. *Address:* P.O. Box 23046, 437 Spadina Road, Toronto, Ont. M5P 2W0, Canada. *Telephone:* (416) 863-1060. *Fax:* (416) 861-0191.

HARPER, Charles Michel, M.B.A.; American business executive; b. 26 Sept. 1927, Lansing, Mich.; s. of Charles F. Harper and Alma Michel; m. Joan F. Bruggema 1950; one s. three d.; ed. Purdue Univ. and Univ. of Chicago; Gen. Motors Corpn., Detroit 1950–54; Pillsbury Co., Minneapolis 1954–74, Group Vice-Pres. Poultry, Food Service and Venture Businesses 1970–74; Exec. Vice-Pres., C.O.O., Dir. Conagra Inc., Omaha 1974–76, Chair., C.E.O. 1976–81, Chair. 1981–92; C.E.O. 1981–92, C.E.O. RJR Nabisco Holdings Inc. 1993–95, Chair. Bd. 1995–96; mem. Bd. of Dirs. Norwest Corpn., Valmont Industries, Inc., Peter Kiewit Sons Inc. and numerous other cos.; several hon. degrees. *Address:* One Central Park Plaza, North Tower, Suite 1500, Omaha, NE 68102, U.S.A.

HARPER, Edward James, B.A., B.MUS., A.R.C.M., L.R.A.M.; British composer; b. 17 March 1941, Taunton, Somerset; m. 1st Penelope Teece 1969 (divorced 1984); m. 2nd Dorothy C. Shanks 1984; one s. one d.; ed. King Edward VI Grammar School, Guildford, Royal Coll. of Music and Christ Church, Oxford; Lecturer in Music, Univ. of Edin. 1964, Sr. Lecturer 1972–90, Reader 1990–; Dir. New Music Group of Scotland 1973–91. *Compositions include:* Bartok Games 1972, Fanny Robin (chamber opera) 1975, Ricercari 1975, 7 Poems by E. E. Cummings 1977, Symphony 1979, Clarinet Concerto 1981, Hedda Gabler (opera) 1985, Qui creavit coelum (mass) 1986, The Mellstock Quire (opera) 1987, Homage to Thomas Hardy (orchestra, song cycle) 1990, The Lamb (soprano, chorus and orchestra) 1990, Overture for chamber orchestra 1992, And Winds, Austere and Pure (three songs for choir and piano duet)

1993, Chanson Minimale (for chamber orchestra) 1994, chamber opera based on William Golding's The Spire 1996, Psalm 150 (for unaccompanied choir) 1996, Scena (for solo cello) 1996, Trio (for clarinet, cello and piano) 1997, Souvenir for Two Pianos and Percussion 1998. *Address:* 7 Morningside Park, Edinburgh, EH10 5HD, Scotland.

HARPER, Heather, C.B.E., F.R.C.M.; British soprano; b. 8 May 1930, Belfast; d. of Hugh and Mary Eliza Harper; m. 2nd Eduardo J. Benarroch 1973; ed. Trinity Coll. of Music, London; created soprano role in Britten's War Requiem, Coventry Cathedral 1962; toured U.S.A. with BBC Symphony Orchestra 1965, U.S.S.R. 1967, soloist opening concerts at the Maltings, Snape 1967, Queen Elizabeth Hall 1967; annual concert and opera tours U.S.A. 1967–91 (retd.); prin. soloist BBC Symphony Orchestra on 1982 tour of Hong Kong and Australia; prin. soloist Royal Opera House U.S. visit 1984; also concerts in Asia, Middle East, Australia, European Music Festivals, S. America; principal roles at Covent Garden, Bayreuth Festival, La Scala (Milan), Teatro Colón (Buenos Aires), Edinburgh Festival, Glyndebourne, Sadler's Wells, Metropolitan Opera House (New York), San Francisco, Frankfurt, Deutsche Oper (Berlin), Japan (with Royal Opera House Covent Garden Co.), Netherlands Opera House, New York City Opera; renowned performances of Arabella, Ariadne, Chrysothemis, Kaiserin, Marschallin (Richard Strauss); TV roles include Ellen Orford (Peter Grimes), Mrs. Coyle (Owen Wingrave), Ilia (Idomeneo), Donna Elvira (Don Giovanni), La Traviata, La Bohème; recordings include Les Illuminations (Britten), Symphony No. 8 (Mahler), Don Giovanni (Mozart), Requiem (Verdi) and Missa Solemnis (Beethoven), Seven Early Songs (Berg), Marriage of Figaro, Peter Grimes, 4 Last Songs (Strauss), 14 Songs with Orchestra; 25 consecutive years as prin. soloist at the Promenade concerts; Dir. Singing Studies at the Britten-Pears School for Advanced Musical Studies, Aldeburgh, Suffolk 1986–; Prof. of Singing and Consultant Royal Coll. of Music, London 1985–93; First Visiting Lecturer in Residence, Royal Scottish Acad. of Music 1987; retd. from operatic stage 1986 (operatic farewell, Teatro Colón, Buenos Aires 1986); from concert stage 1991; mem. BBC Music Panel 1989, Royal Soc. of Arts 1989–; Hon. Fellow Trinity Coll. of Music; Hon. mem. R.A.M., Hon. D.Mus. (Queen's Univ.); Edison Award 1971, Grammy Award 1979, 1984, 1991. *Leisure interests:* gardening, painting, cooking, swimming, tennis.

HARPER, John Lander, C.B.E., M.A., D.PHIL., F.R.S.; British research biologist, consultant and author; b. 27 May 1925, Rugby, Warwicks.; s. of John H. and Harriet M. (née Archer) Harper; m. Borgny Lerø 1954; one s. two d.; ed. Magdalen Coll., Oxford; Demonstrator, Dept. of Agric., Univ. of Oxford 1951–52, lecturer 1953–59; Rockefeller Foundation Fellow, Univ. of Calif. (Davis) 1959–60; Prof., Dept. of Agric. Botany, Univ. Coll. of N. Wales, Bangor 1960–67, Prof. of Agric. Botany and Head, School of Plant Biology 1967–78, Prof. of Botany and Head, School of Plant Biology 1978–82, Prof. Emer. 1982–, Dir. of Unit. of Plant Population Biology 1982–90; mem. Jt. Nature Conservation Cttee. 1991–94; Ed. Proceedings of the Royal Soc., B. 1993–; Foreign Assoc. N.A.S. (1984), and other learned socs.; Hon. Dir. Univ. Nacional Autónoma de México 1997; Hon. D.Sc. (Sussex) 1984; Dr. h.c. (Nat. Autonomous Univ. of Mexico) 1996; Darwin Medal, Royal Soc. 1990. *Publications:* Population Biology of Plants 1977, Ecology: Individuals, Populations and Communities 1986, 1990, 1996; numerous papers in scientific journals. *Leisure interest:* gardening. *Address:* The Lodge, Chapel Road, Brampford Speke, Exeter, EX5 5HG, England. *Telephone:* (01392) 841929.

HARPER, Judson Morse, PH.D.; American professor, academic administrator and consultant; b. 25 Aug. 1936, Lincoln, Neb.; s. of Floyd Harper and Eda Harper; m. Patricia A. Kennedy 1958; three s.; with General Mills 1963–70, latterly Man. for New Business Ventures in Research Div.; Prof. of Chemical and Bioresource Eng. Colorado State Univ. 1970–82, Vice-Pres. for Research and Information Tech. 1982–, Interim Pres. 1989–90; Fulbright Scholar, Dept. of Food Eng. and Biotech. Technion, Haifa, Israel 1978–79; holder of six U.S. patents; several professional awards. *Publications include:* Extrusion of Foods 1981, Extrusion Cooking 1989. *Leisure interests:* running, skiing, gardening. *Address:* Office of the Vice-President for Research and Information Technology, Colorado State University, Fort Collins, CO 80523 (Office); 1818 Westview Road, Fort Collins, CO 80524, U.S.A. (Home). *Telephone:* (970) 491-7194. *Fax:* (970) 491-5541.

HARPPRECHT, Klaus Christoph; German author and television producer; b. 11 April 1927, Stuttgart; s. of Christoph and Dorothea (née Bronisch) Harpprecht; m. Renate Lasker 1961; ed. Evangelical Theological Seminary, Blaubeuren, Württemberg and Univs. of Tübingen, Munich and Stuttgart; junior ed. and Bonn corresp. Christ und Welt 1948–53; commentator and corresp., RIAS Berlin (Rundfunk im amerikanischen Sektor), Sender Freies Berlin and Westdeutscher Rundfunk, Cologne 1953–61; America corresp., Zweites Deutsche Fernsehen 1962–65; Publr., S. Fischer Verlag, and ed. Der Monat 1966–71; consultant and chief speech writer to Chancellor Willy Brandt 1972–74; ed. GEO magazine, Hamburg 1978–79; now ind. writer; Theodore Wolff and Drexel awards. *Publications:* The East German Rising 1954, Viele Grüse an die Freiheit 1964, Beshädigte Paradiese 1966, Willy Brandt: Portrait 1970, Deutsche Themen 1973, L'Evolution Allemande 1978, Der Fremde Freund Amerika: Eine Innere Geschichte 1982, Amerikaner: Freunde, Freunde, Ferne Nachbarn 1984, (with Thomas Hoepker) Amerika die Geschichte seiner Eroberung 1986, Georg Forster—oder die Liebe zur Welt 1987, Das Ende der Gemuetlichkeit 1987, Die Lust der Freiheit. Deutsche Revolutionaere in Paris 1989, (with Hans Hillmann) Die Leute von Port Madeleine-Dorfge-schichten aus der Provence 1989, Welt-Anschauung Reisebilder 1991, Thomas Mann. Eine Biographie 1995, Schreibspiele: Bemerkungen zur Literatur 1996. *Leisure interests:* music, literature, history. *Address:* 15 Boulevard des Palmeraies, 83420 La Croix-Valmer, France. *Telephone:* 94.79.60.76. *Fax:* 94.54.20.30.

HARRELL, Lynn; American 'cellist; b. 30 Jan. 1944, New York; s. of Mack Harrell and Marjorie Fulton; m. Linda Blandford 1976; one s. one d.; ed. Juilliard School of Music, New York, and Curtis Inst. of Music, Philadelphia; principal 'cellist, Cleveland Orch. (under George Szell) 1963–71; now appears as soloist with the world's major orchestras; Piatigorsky Prof. of Cello at Univ. of Southern Calif. 1987–93; Prof. Int. Cello Studies Royal Acad. of Music, London 1988–93, 1993–95; Artistic Dir. L.A. Philharmonic Inst. 1988; soloist Memorial Concert for Holocaust Victims, Vatican 1994; Music Adviser, San Diego Symphony Orchestra 1988–89; recording artist, Decca Records, London. *Leisure interests:* chess, fishing. *Address:* c/o IMG Europe, 3 Burlington Lane, Chiswick, London, W4 2TH, England; IMG New York, 420 W. 45th Street, New York, NY 10036, U.S.A.

HARRELSON, Woody, B.A.; American actor; b. 23 July 1961, Midland, Tex.; m. Laura Louie 1997; one c.; ed. Hanover Coll. *Theatre includes:* The Boys Next Door, 2 on 2 (author, producer, actor), The Zoo Story (author, actor), Brooklyn Laundry. *Television includes:* Cheers, Bay Coven, Killer Instinct. *Films include:* Wildcats, Cool Blue, L.A. Story, Doc Hollywood, Ted and Venus, White Men Can't Jump, Indecent Proposal, I'll Do Anything, The Cowboy Way, Natural Born Killers, Money Train, The Sunchaser, Kingpin, The People vs. Larry Flynt, Kingpin, Wag the Dog. *Leisure interests:* sports, juggling, writing, chess. *Address:* c/o Creative Artists Agency, 9830 Wilshire Boulevard, Beverly Hills, CA 90212, U.S.A.

HARRIES, Rt. Rev. Richard Douglas, D.D., F.K.C., F.R.S.L.; British ecclesiastic; b. 2 June 1936; s. of Brig. W. D. J. Harries and G. M. B. Harries; m. Josephine Bottomley 1963; one s. one d.; ed. Wellington Coll., Royal Mil. Acad, Sandhurst, Selwyn Coll, Cambridge, Cuddesdon Coll., Oxford; Lieut., Royal Corps of Signals 1955–58; Curate, Hampstead Parish Church 1963–69; Chaplain, Westfield Coll. 1966–69; Lecturer, Wells Theological Coll. 1969–72; Warden of Wells, Salisbury and Wells Theological Coll. 1971–72; Vicar, All Saints, Fulham, London 1972–81; Dean, King's Coll., London 1981–87; Bishop of Oxford 1987–; Vice-Chair. Council of Christian Action 1979–87, Council for Arms Control 1982–87; Chair. Southwark Ordination Course 1982–87, Shalom, End Loans to South Africa (ELSTA) 1982–87, Christian Evidence Soc.; Chair. Church of England Bd. of Social Responsibility 1996–; Consultant to the Archbishops on Jewish-Christian Relations 1986–92; mem. Home Office Advisory Cttee. for Reform of Law on Sexual Offences 1981–85; mem. Royal Comm. on Lords Reform 1999–; mem. bd. Christian Aid 1994–; Hon. D. D. (London) 1996; Sir Sigmund Steinberg Award 1989. *Publications:* Prayers of Hope 1975, Turning to Prayer 1978, Prayers of Grief and Glory 1979, Being a Christian 1981, Should Christians Support Guerrillas? 1982, The Authority of Divine Love 1983, Praying Round the Clock 1983, Seasons of the Spirit (Co-Ed.) 1984, Prayer and the Pursuit of Happiness 1985, Reinhold Niebuhr and the Issues of Our Time (Ed.) 1986, Morning has Broken 1985, Christianity and War in a Nuclear Age 1986, C. S. Lewis: the man and his God 1987, Christ is Risen 1988, Is There a Gospel for the Rich? 1992, Art and the Beauty of God 1993, The Value of Business and its Values (jtly.) 1993, The Real God 1994, Questioning Faith 1995, A Gallery of Reflections 1995; contrib. to several books; numerous articles. *Leisure interests:* theatre, literature, sport. *Address:* Diocesan Church House, North Hinksey, Oxford, OX2 0NB, England. *Telephone:* (01865) 208222. *Fax:* (01865) 790470.

HARRIS, Rt. Rev. Augustine; British ecclesiastic; b. 27 Oct. 1917, Liverpool; s. of Augustine Harris and Louisa Beatrice Rycroft; ed. St. Francis Xavier's Coll., Liverpool and Upholland Coll., Lancs.; ordained 1942; Curacies 1942–52; Prison Chaplain 1952–66; Prin. Roman Catholic Prison Chaplain 1958–66; Auxiliary Bishop of Liverpool 1966–78; Bishop of Middlesbrough 1978–92; Chair., Dept. for Social Responsibility, Bishops' Conf. of England and Wales 1984–92. *Publications:* articles for criminological publs. *Leisure interests:* golf and walking. *Address:* 17 Old Town Lane, Formby, Merseyside, L37 3HJ, England. *Telephone:* (01704) 875403.

HARRIS, Chauncy Dennison, PH.D., D.LITT.; American geographer; b. 31 Jan. 1914, Logan, Utah; s. of Franklin S. and Estella S. Harris; m. Edith Young 1940; one d.; ed. Brigham Young Univ., Oxford and Chicago Univs.; Prof. of Geography, Univ. of Chicago 1947–84, Samuel N. Harper Distinguished Service Prof. 1969–84, Prof. Emer. 1984–, Dean, Grad. Div. of Social Sciences 1954–60; Dir. Centre for Int. Studies 1966–84; Asst. to the Pres. 1973–75, Vice-Pres. for Academic Resources 1975–78; mem. Bd. of Dirs., Social Science Research Council 1959–70, Vice-Chair. 1963–65, mem. Cttee. on Programs and Policy 1959–67, Exec. Cttee. 1967–70; mem. Exec. Cttee., Nat. Research Council Div. of Behavioural Sciences 1967–70; mem. Int. Research and Exchanges Bd. 1968–71; mem. Exec. Cttee. ICSU 1969–72; Del. 17th Gen. Conf. UNESCO, Paris 1972; Vice-Pres. Int. Geographical Union 1956–64, Sec.-Gen. 1968–76; mem. Asscn. of American Geographers (Pres. 1957), American Asscn. for Advancement of Slavic Studies (AAASS) (Pres. 1962), American Geographical Soc. (Vice-Pres. 1969–74), Nat. Council for Soviet and East European Research (Bd. of Dirs. 1977–83); mem. Council of Scholars, Library of Congress 1980–83, Visiting Cttee. Univ. of Chicago Library (Life mem.); Conseil de la Bibliographie Géographique Internationale 1986–94; del. to numerous Int. Geographic Congresses 1949–; Foreign mem. Polish Acad. of Sciences, Hon. mem. Royal Geographical Soc. and geographical socs. of Paris, Berlin, Frankfurt, Rome, Florence, Warsaw, Belgrade and Japan; D.Econ. h.c. (Catholic Univ., Chile), Hon. LL.D. (Indiana Univ.); Hon. D.Sc. (Univ. of Bonn, Univ. of Wisconsin-Milwaukee); Honors Award, Asscn. of American Geographers 1976, Lauréat d'honneur, Int. Geographical Union 1976, Alexander Csoma de Körösi Memorial Medal, Hungarian Geographical Soc. 1971, Alexander von Humboldt Gold Medal, Gesellschaft für Erdkunde zu Berlin 1978, Award for Distinguished Contributions to Slavic Studies, AAASS 1978, Cullom Geographical Medal, American Geographical Soc. 1985, Master Teacher Award, Nat. Council for Geographic Educ. 1986, Victoria Medal, Royal Geographical Soc. 1987. *Publications:* Economic Geography of the U.S.S.R. 1949, International List of Geographical Serials 1980, Soviet Geography: Accomplishments and Tasks 1962, Cities of the Soviet Union 1970, Annotated World List of Selected Current Geographical Serials 1980, Guide to Geographical Bibliographies and Reference works in Russian or on the Soviet Union 1975, Bibliography of Geography Part I, Introduction to General Aids 1976, Part II, Regional (Vol. 1) United States of America 1984, A Geographical Bibliography for American Libraries 1985, Directory of Soviet Geographers 1946–1987 1988; contributor to Sources of Information in the Social Sciences 1973, 1986, Encyclopaedia Britannica 1989, Columbia Gazetteer of the World 1998; articles in professional journals. *Address:* Department of Geography, University of Chicago, 5828 University Avenue, Chicago, IL 60637, U.S.A.

HARRIS, Edward Allen (Ed), B.F.A.; American actor; b. 28 Nov. 1950, Englewood, N.J.; s. of Bob L. Harris and Margaret Harris; m. Amy Madigan; ed. Columbia Univ., Univ. of Oklahoma, Norman, Calif. Inst. of Arts. *Stage appearances include:* A Streetcar Named Desire, Sweet Bird of Youth, Julius Caesar, Hamlet, Camelot, Time of Your Life, Grapes of Wrath, Present Laughter, Fool for Love (Obie award 1983), Prairie Avenue (L.A. Drama Critics Circle award 1981), Scar 1985 (San Francisco Critics award), Precious Sons 1986 (Theater World award), Simpatico 1994. *Films include:* Come 1978, Borderline 1978, Knightriders 1980, Creepshow 1981, The Right Stuff 1982, Swing Shift 1982, Under Fire 1982, A Flash of Green 1983, Places in the Heart 1983, Alamo Bay 1984, Sweet Dreams 1985, Code Name: Emerald 1985, Walker 1987, To Kill a Priest 1988, Jacknife 1989, The Abyss 1989, State of Grace 1990, Paris Trout 1991, Glengarry Glen Ross 1992, Needful Things 1993, The Firm 1993, China Moon 1994, Milk Money 1994, Apollo 13 1995, Just Cause 1995, Eye for an Eye 1995, The Rock 1996, Riders of the Purple Sage 1996, Absolute Power 1997; *TV films include:* The Amazing Howard Hughes 1977, The Seekers 1979, The Aliens are Coming 1980, The Last Innocent Man 1987, Running Mates 1992, The Stand 1994. *Address:* 22031 Carbon Mesa Road, Malibu, CA 90265, U.S.A.

HARRIS, Sir Henry, Kt., F.R.C.P., F.R.C.PATH., F.R.S.; British cell biologist; b. 28 Jan. 1925; s. of Sam and Ann Harris; m. Alexandra Brodsky 1950; one s. two d.; ed. Sydney Boys High School, Univ. of Sydney, Lincoln Coll., Oxford; Dir. of Research, Cancer Research Campaign, Sir William Dunn School of Pathology, Oxford 1954–59; Visiting Scientist, Nat. Inst. of Health, U.S.A. 1959–60; Head Dept. of Cell Biology, John Innes Inst. 1960–63; Prof. of Pathology, Univ. of Oxford 1963–79, Regius Prof. of Medicine 1979–92; Head of the Sir William Dunn School of Pathology, Oxford 1963–94; Corresp. mem. Australian Acad. of Science; Foreign Hon. mem. American Acad. of Arts and Sciences; Foreign mem. Max Planck Soc.; Foreign Prof. Coll. de France; Hon. mem. American Asscn. of Pathologists, German Soc. of Cell Biology; Hon. Fellow, Cambridge Philosophical Soc.; Hon. F.R.C.Path. (Australia); Hon. D.Sc. (Edinburgh); Hon. M.D. (Geneva, Sydney); Feldberg Foundation Award; Ivison Macadam Memorial Prize; Prix de la Fondation Isabelle Decazes de Nöue for cancer research, Madonnina Prize for Medical Research; Katherine Burkan Judd Award of the Memorial-Sloan Kettering Cancer Center 1991; Medal of Honour, Univ. of Pavia, Royal Medal of the Royal Soc., Osler Medal of the Royal Coll. of Physicians. *Publications:* Nucleus and Cytoplasm 1968, Cell Fusion 1970, La fusion cellulaire 1974, The Balance of Improbabilities 1987, The Cells of the Body 1995, The Birth of the Cell 1998; papers on cellular physiology and biochemistry in various scientific books and journals, and some fiction. *Leisure interests:* history and literature. *Address:* Sir William Dunn School of Pathology, South Parks Road, Oxford, OX1 3RE. *Telephone:* (01865) 275503. *Fax:* (01865) 275501.

HARRIS, John Robert, F.R.I.B.A., F.R.S.A.; British architect; b. 5 June 1919; s. of Maj. Alfred Harris, C.B.E., D.S.O. and Rosa A. Alderson; m. Gillian Rowe 1950; one s. one d.; ed. Harrow School and Architectural Asscn. School of Architecture; Lieut. Royal Engineers, Hong Kong 1940–41, prisoner-of-war 1941–45; f. and Sr. Partner, John R. Harris Architects, London 1949– (also assoc. firms in Oman, Qatar, Dubai and Hong Kong); partner, Courbe Duboz et Harris, Paris 1978–; *Projects won in int. competition:* State Hosp. Qatar 1953, New Dubai Hosp. 1976, Corniche Devt. and Traffic Intersection, Dubai 1978, H.Q. for Ministry of Social Affairs and Labour, Oman 1979, Tuen Mun Hosp. Hong Kong 1981, Ruler's Office Devt. Dubai 1984, architects and planners for Zhuhai New Town, Econ. Zone, P.R. of China 1984, Q-Tel HQ Qatar 1991, Deira Sea Corniche masterplan Dubai 1993. *Major works in UK include:* Royal Northern Hosp., London 1973, Ealing Hosp. 1976, RAF Upper Heyford Hosp. 1982, Stoke Mandeville Hosp. 1983 and several dept. stores, redevt. of Dorchester Hotel 1989, Gloucester Park Devt., London, Redevt. Sheraton Grand Hotel, Edin. 1993; major works abroad include Dubai Int. Trade Centre (third tallest bldg. in Arab world), British Amb.'s Residence, Abu Dhabi, 3000-seat Conference Centre, Doha 1997 and numerous banks, hosps., shopping centres, particularly in Gulf States; Silver Jubilee Medal. *Publications:* John R. Harris Architects (jtly) 1984; contribs. to books and architectural and tech. journals. *Leisure interests:* architecture, sailing, travel. *Address:* 24 Devonshire Place, London, W1N 2BX, England. *Telephone:* 0171-935 9353.

HARRIS, Julie; American actress; b. 2 Dec. 1925, Mich.; d. of William Picket and Elsie (née Smith) Harris; m. 1st Jay I. Julien 1946 (divorced 1954); 2nd Manning Gurian 1954 (divorced 1967); one s.; 3rd Walter Erwin Carroll 1977 (divorced 1982); ed. Yale Drama School. *Theatre work includes:* Sundown Beach 1948, The Young and Fair 1948, Magnolia Alley 1949, Montserrat 1949, The Member of the Wedding 1950, Sally Bowles in I am a Camera 1951, The Lark 1956, A Shot in the Dark 1961, Marathon 33 1964, Ready When You Are, C.B. 1964, And Miss Reardon Drinks a Little 1971, Voices 1972, The Last of Mrs. Lincoln 1973, In Praise of Love 1974, The Belle of Amherst, New York 1976, London 1977, Break a Leg, New York 1979, Mixed Couples, New York 1980, Driving Miss Daisy 1988, Lucifer's Child 1991, Lettice and Lovage, The Fiery Furnace (off-Broadway debut) 1993, The Glass Menagerie 1996, The Gin Game 1997. *Films include:* East of Eden 1955 (Antoinette Perry Award), I Am a Camera 1956, Poacher's Daughter 1960, The Haunting, The Moving Target, Voyage of the Damned 1976, The Bell Jar 1979, Gorillas in the Mist, Housesitter, The Dark Half, Carried Away. *Television:* Little Moon of Alban (TV film) 1960, Knots Landing 1982, Scarlett, The Christmas Tree, Ellen Foster. New York Drama Critics' Award for I Am a Camera; numerous other awards. *Address:* c/o William Morris Agency, 1325 Avenue of the Americas, New York, NY 10019, U.S.A.

HARRIS, Kenneth, C.B.E., M.A.; British author, journalist and broadcaster; b. 11 Nov. 1919 Aberaman, Wales; s. of David Harris and Kathleen Powell; m. Doris Young-Smith 1949 (died 1970); m. 2nd Jocelyn Rymer 1987; two step-d.; ed. Trowbridge High School for Boys and Wadham Coll., Oxford; war service, R.A. 1940–45; Washington Corresp., The Observer 1950–53, Assoc. Ed. 1976–84, Dir. 1978–93; Chair. George Outram Ltd. 1981–92, Caledonian Newspapers 1992–93; radio and TV work (mainly for BBC) 1957–85. *Publications:* Travelling Tongues: Debating Across America 1949, About Britain 1967, Conversations 1968, Life of Attlee 1982, The Wildcatter 1987, David Owen Personally Speaking 1987, Thatcher 1988, The Queen 1994. *Leisure interests:* reading, walking, horse racing. *Address:* 45 Molyneux Street, London, W1H 5HW, England. *Telephone:* 0171-262 6172.

HARRIS, Lagumot; Nauruan politician; M.P. 1968–; Pres. of Nauru April–May 1978, 1995–96; fmr. Minister for Health and Educ. and Minister Assisting the Pres.; fmr. mem. Nauru Party, now independent. *Address:* c/o Office of the President, Yaren, Nauru.

HARRIS, Martin Best, C.B.E., PH.D.; British university vice-chancellor; b. 28 June 1944, Ruabon, Wales; s. of William Best Harris and Betty Evelyn Harris (née Martin); m. Barbara Mary Daniels 1966; two s.; ed. Devonport High School, Plymouth, Queens' Coll., Cambridge, School of Oriental and African Studies, London Univ.; lecturer in French Linguistics, Univ. of Leicester 1967–72; Sr. Lecturer in French Linguistics, Univ. of Salford 1972–76, Prof. of Romance Linguistics 1976–87, Pro-Vice-Chancellor 1981–87; Vice-Chancellor Univ. of Essex 1987–92; Vice-Chancellor Univ. of Manchester 1992–; Chair. Cttee. of Vice-Chancellors and Prins. 1997–(99); mem. Univ. Grants Cttee. 1984–87, Chair. Northern Ireland Sub-Cttee. 1985–87; Chair. Northern Ireland Cttee., Univs. Funding Council 1987–91, Nat. Curriculum Working Group on Modern Languages 1989–90, HEFCE/CVCP review of postgraduate educ. 1995–96; Chair. Clinical Standards Advisory Group 1996–; Chair. of Govs., Centre for Information on Language Teaching 1990–96; Crown Gov. S.O.A.S. 1990–93; Gov. Anglia Polytechnic Univ. 1989–93; mem. High Council, European Univ. Inst., Florence 1992–97; Hon. mem. Royal Northern Coll. of Music 1996; Hon. Fellow Queens' Coll., Cambridge 1992, Bolton Inst. 1996; Hon. LL.D. (Queen's Univ., Belfast) 1992, Hon. D.Univ. (Essex) 1993, Hon. D.Litt. (Salford) 1995; D.L. *Publications:* The Evolution of French Syntax 1978, The Romance Languages (with N. Vincent) 1988; numerous articles in anthologies and professional journals. *Leisure interests:* gardening, walking. *Address:* University of Manchester, Oxford Road, Manchester, M13 9PL, England. *Telephone:* (0161) 275-7399. *Fax:* (0161) 272 6313.

HARRIS, Richard R. St. Johns; Irish actor; b. 1 Oct. 1933, Limerick; s. of Ivan Harris; m. 1st Hon. (Joan) Elizabeth Rees-Williams 1957 (divorced 1969); three s.; m. 2nd Ann Turkel 1974; ed. L.A.M.D.A.; made professional theatre début as Micksee in The Quare Fellow, Theatre Royal, Stratford 1956; also appeared in A View From the Bridge 1956, Paulino in Man, Beast and Virtue 1958; toured U.S.S.R. and East Europe with Joan Littlewood's Theatre Workshop 1958; The Ginger Man 1959; Diary of a Madman, Royal Court 1963; Camelot 1981, Henry IV 1990. *Films include:* Alive and Kicking 1958, Shake Hands with the Devil 1959, The Wreck of the Mary Deare 1959, A Terrible Beauty 1960, All Night Long 1961, The Guns of Navarone 1961, Mutiny on the Bounty 1962, This Sporting Life, Major Dundee 1965, The Heroes of Telemark 1965, The Bible 1966, Hawaii 1966, Caprice 1966, Camelot 1967, The Molly Maguires 1969, A Man Called Horse 1969, Bloomfield 1970, Cromwell 1970, Man in The Wilderness 1971, The Deadly Trackers 1973, 99 and 44/100 Dead 1974, Juggernaut 1975, Robin and Marian 1975, The Return of a Man Called Horse 1976, Orca 1977, The Cassandra Crossing 1977, Golden Rendezvous 1977, The Wild Geese 1978,

The Sea Wolves 1979, Ravagers 1979, Tarzan and the Ape Man 1981, Triumphs of a Man Called Horse 1983, Highpoint 1984, Outlaws 1989, King of the Wind 1989, The Field 1990, Patriot Games, Unforgiven, Silent Tongue 1993, Wrestling Ernest Hemingway 1994, Cry the Beloved Country 1995, The Barber of Siberia 1997. *Recordings:* MacArthur Park and This Time, The Prophet, In the Membership of My Days. *Television appearances include:* The Iron Harp 1958, The Snow Goose 1971, Camelot, Maigret, The Return, The Bible; Cannes Film Festival Best Actor Award for This Sporting Life.

HARRIS, Richard Travis; British company director; b. 15 April 1919, Epsom, Surrey; s. of Douglas Harris and Rose Emmiline Mary Travis; m. 1st June Constance Rundle 1941; two d.; m. 2nd Margaret Sophia Nye (née Aron) 1953; one s. one d.; ed. Charterhouse, R.M.A. Woolwich; commissioned 2nd Lieut. Royal Signals 1939; served World War II 1939–45; twice mentioned in despatches; Lt.-Col. G.S.O.I. Sigs. BAOR 1946; Sudan Defence Force 1947–50; retd. with rank of Lt.-Col. 1950; Management Trainee Rediffusion 1950, Man. Dir. Rediffusion (Nigeria) Ltd. 1951–54, Deputy Gen. Man. Associated Rediffusion. 1954–57; Man. Dir. Coates & Co. (Plymouth) Ltd. 1957–63, Dollond & Aitchison Ltd. 1964–70; Chair. and Chief Exec. Dollond & Aitchison Group Ltd. 1970–78; Dir. Gallaher Ltd. 1970–87, Deputy Chair. 1978–84; Dir. Burton Group PLC 1984–92; Founder Chair. Devon & Cornwall Branch Inst. of Dirs.; mem. Council Inst. of Dirs. 1975–89, Chair. 1982–85, Vice-Pres. 1985–89; mem. of Policy and Executive Cttee. Inst. of Dirs. 1976–88; mem. Council Birmingham Univ. 1978–93; Gov. Royal Shakespeare Theatre 1980–94. *Leisure interest:* fly fishing. *Address:* Hunters Care Centre, Cherry Tree Lane, Cirencester, Glos., GL7 5DT, England. *Telephone:* (01285) 658649.

HARRIS, Robert Dennis, F.R.S.L.; British journalist and author; b. 7 March 1957, Nottingham; s. of Dennis Harris and Audrey Harris; m. Gill Hornby 1988; one s. two d.; ed. Univ. of Cambridge; Pres. Cambridge Union; dir. and reporter, BBC 1978–86; Political Ed. Observer 1987–89; columnist Sunday Times 1989–92, 1996–97. *Publications:* non-fiction: A Higher Form of Killing (with Jeremy Paxman, q.v.) 1982, Gotcha! 1983, The Making of Neil Kinnock 1984, Selling Hitler 1987; Good and Faithful Servant 1990; novels: Fatherland 1992, Enigma 1995, Archangel 1998. *Address:* Old Vicarage, Kintbury, Berkshire, RG17 9TR, England.

HARRIS, Rolf, O.B.E., A.M.; Australian entertainer; b. 30 March 1930, Perth; s. of C. G. Harris and A. M. Harris (née Robbins); m. Alwen Hughes 1958; one d.; ed. Perth Modern School, Univ. of Western Australia, Claremont Teachers' Coll.; appeared in "The Rolf Harris Show" (BBC TV) 1967–71; represented Australia at seven World Fairs 1969–85; host of BBC TV's "Animal Hospital" and "Rolf's Amazing Animals" 1997–; host and narrator of TV documentary series "Bligh of the Bounty—World Navigator" 1998–99. *Singles include:* Tie Me Kangaroo Down Sport 1960, Two Little Boys 1969. *Publications include:* Rolf Harris Picture Book of Cats 1978, Your Cartoon Time 1986, Win or Die 1989, Your Animation Time 1991. *Leisure interests:* painting and portraiture, photography, wood carving, lapidary. *Address:* c/o Billy Marsh and Associates, 174–178 North Gower Street, London, NW1 2NB, England. *Telephone:* 0171-388 6858. *Fax:* 0171-388 6848.

HARRIS, Stephen, M.S., PH.D.; American professor of electrical engineering and applied physics; b. 29 Nov. 1936, Brooklyn, New York; s. of Henry Harris and Anne Alpern Harris; m. Frances J. Greene 1959; one s. one d.; ed. Rensselaer Polytechnic, Troy, New York and Stanford Univ.; Prof. of Electrical Eng. Stanford Univ. 1963–79, of Electrical Eng. and Applied Physics 1979–, Dir. Edward L. Ginzton Lab. 1983–88, Kenneth and Barbara Oshman Prof. 1988–, Chair. Dept. of Applied Physics 1993–96; Guggenheim Fellowship 1976–77; mem. N.A.S., Nat. Acad. of Eng.; A. Noble Prize 1965, McGraw Research Award 1973, Sarnoff Award 1978, Davies Medal 1984, C. H. Townes Award 1985, Einstein Prize 1991, Quantum Electronics Award 1994. *Publications:* articles in professional journals. *Leisure interests:* skiing, jogging, hiking. *Address:* Edward L. Ginzton Laboratory, Stanford University, 450 Via Palou, Stanford, CA 94305, U.S.A. *Telephone:* (415) 497-0224.

HARRIS, Thomas; American writer; b. 1940, Jackson, Tenn.; s. of William Thomas Harris, Jr. and Polly Harris; m. (divorced); one d.; ed. Baylor Univ., Tex.; worked on newsdesk Waco News-Tribune; mem. staff Associated Press, New York. *Publications:* Black Sunday, Red Dragon (filmed as Manhunter), The Silence of the Lambs (filmed). *Address:* St. Martin's Press, 175 Fifth Avenue, New York, NY 10010, U.S.A.

HARRIS OF HIGH CROSS, Baron (Life Peer) cr. 1979, of Tottenham in Greater London; **Ralph Harris,** M.A.; British economist; b. 10 Dec. 1924; m. Jose Pauline Jeffery 1949; two s. (one deceased) one d.; ed. Tottenham Grammar School, Queens' Coll. Cambridge; lecturer in Political Economy, St. Andrews Univ. 1949–56; Gen. Dir. Inst. of Econ. Affairs 1957–87, Chair. 1987–89, Founder Pres. 1990–; Conservative parl. cand., Kirkcaldy 1951, Edin. Cen. 1955; Trustee and Hon. Treasurer Ross McWhirter Foundation; Chair. Bruges Group 1989–91, FOREST 1989–; Jt. Chair. Int. Centre for Research into Econ. Transformation, Moscow 1990–95; Dir. (Ind. Nat.) Times Newspapers Holdings Ltd. 1988–; Hon. D.Sc. (Buckingham) 1984. *Publications include:* Politics Without Prejudice (biography of R. A. Butler) 1956, Libraries: Free for All? (with A. P. Herbert) 1962, Welfare Without the State (with Arthur Seldon) 1987, Beyond the Welfare State 1988, and numerous others. *Leisure interests:* conjuring and devising spells against over-government. *Address:* 5 Cattley Close, Wood Street, Barnet, Herts., EN5 4SN, England.

HARRISON, Bryan Desmond, C.B.E., PH.D., F.R.S., F.R.S.E.; British plant virologist; b. 16 June 1931, Purley; s. of John William Harrison and Norah (née Webster) Harrison; m. Elizabeth Latham-Warde 1968; two s. one d.; ed. Whitgift School, Croydon and Univs. of Reading and London; ARC Postgrad. Studentship, Rothamsted Experimental Station, Harpenden 1952–54, Research Scientist 1957–66; Scottish Horticultural (later Crop) Research Inst., Dundee 1954–57, Head Virology Dept. 1966–91; Prof. of Plant Virology, Univ. of Dundee 1991–96, Prof. Emer. 1997–; Pres. Asscn. of Applied Biologists 1980–81; Hon. Prof. St. Andrew's Univ. 1987–; Hon. Visiting Prof. Dundee Univ. 1988–91; Foreign Assoc. Nat. Acad. of Sciences, U.S.A. 1998; Dr. h.c. (Helsinki). *Publications:* Plant Virology: the Principles (with A. J. Gibbs) 1976, and over 200 research papers and reviews on plant viruses and virus diseases. *Address:* Scottish Crop Research Institute, Invergowrie, Dundee, DD2 5DA, Scotland. *Telephone:* (01382) 562731. *Fax:* (01382) 562426.

HARRISON, Sir David, Kt., C.B.E., SC.D., F.ENG., F.R.S.C., F.I.CHEM.E., C.B.I.M., F.R.S.A.; British academic; b. 3 May 1930, Clacton-on-Sea; s. of Harold David Harrison and Lavinia Wilson; m. Sheila Rachel Debes 1962; one s. one d. (one s. deceased); ed. Bede School, Sunderland, Clacton County High School, Selwyn Coll., Cambridge Univ.; lecturer in Chemical Eng., Cambridge Univ. 1956–79, Sr. Tutor, Selwyn Coll. 1967–79; Vice-Chancellor Univ. of Keele 1979–84, Univ. of Exeter 1984–94; Master Selwyn Coll., Cambridge 1994–, Chair. Faculty of Eng. 1994–; mem. Council, Cambridge 1967–75, 1995–, Deputy Vice-Chancellor 1995–, Pro-Vice-Chancellor 1997; Visiting Prof. of Chemical Eng., Univ. of Delaware, U.S.A. 1967, Univ. of Sydney, Australia 1976; Chair. Faculty Bd. of Educ., Cambridge Univ. 1976–78; Hon. Ed. Transactions, Inst. of Chemical Engineers 1972–78; Chair., Bd. of Trustees, Homerton Coll., Cambridge 1979–, Univs. Cen. Council for Admissions 1984–91, Church & Associated Colls. Advisory Cttee. of the Polytechnics and Colls. Funding Council 1989–91, Cttee. of Vice-Chancellors & Prins. of U.K. 1991–93, Shrewsbury School 1989–, Advisory Cttee. on Safety of Nuclear Installations 1993–, Eastern Arts Bd. 1994–98, Arts Council of England 1996–98; Dir. Salters' Inst. of Industrial Chem. 1993–; Vice-Pres. Inst. of Chemical Engineers 1989; Pres. Inst. of Chemical Engineers 1991–92; Fellow Selwyn Coll., Cambridge 1957–; Hon. D.Univ. (Keele) 1992; Hon. D.Sc. (Exeter) 1995; Liveryman, Salters' Co. 1998. *Publications:* Fluidised Particles (with J. F. Davidson) 1963, Fluidization (with J. F. Davidson) 1971, Fluidization (with J. F. Davidson and R. Clift) 1985. *Leisure interests:* music, tennis, hill walking, good food. *Address:* The Master's Lodge, Selwyn College, Cambridge, CB3 9DQ, England. *Telephone:* (01223) 335889. *Fax:* (01223) 335888.

HARRISON, Sir Ernest Thomas, Kt., O.B.E., F.C.A.; British business executive; b. 11 May 1926, London; s. of Ernest Horace Harrison and Gertrude Rebecca Gibbons Harrison; m. Phyllis Brenda Knight 1960; three s. two d.; ed. Trinity Grammar School; Sec. and Chief Accountant, Racal Electronics Ltd. (now PLC) 1951, Dir. 1958, Deputy Man. Dir. 1961, Chair. 1966–, Chief Exec. 1966–92, Chair. Vodafone Group PLC (fmrly. Racal Telecom) 1988–98; Chair. Chubb Security PLC 1992–97; Dir. Camelot Group PLC 1993–; Chair. Ronald Raven Chair in Clinical Oncology Trust 1991–; active in Nat. Savings Movement 1964–76; Hon. F.C.G.I. 1991, F.Eng. 1997; Hon. D.Sc. (Cranfield) 1981, (City) 1982; Hon. D.Univ. (Surrey) 1981, (Edin.) 1983; Businessman of Year 1981, Founding Society's Centenary Award ICA 1990, Mountbatten Medal, Nat. Electronics Council 1992. *Leisure interests:* horse racing (owner), gardening and sport. *Address:* Racal Electronics PLC, Western Road, Bracknell, Berks. RG12 1RG, England.

HARRISON, George, M.B.E.; British musician and songwriter; b. 25 Feb. 1943, Wavertree, Liverpool; m. 1st Patricia (Patti) Anne Boyd 1966 (divorced 1977); m. 2nd Olivia Arias 1978; one s.; ed. Dovedale Primary School and Liverpool Inst.; had first guitar at age of 14, now plays guitar, organ and a variety of Indian instruments; ran guitar quintet The Rebels 1956–58; joined The Quarrymen 1958; appeared under various titles until formation of The Beatles 1960; appeared with The Beatles in Hamburg 1960, 1961, 1962, The Cavern, Liverpool 1960, 1961; toured Scotland, Sweden, U.K. 1963, Paris, Denmark, Hong Kong, Australia, New Zealand, U.S.A., Canada 1964, France, Italy, Spain, U.S.A. 1965, Germany, Spain, Philippines, U.S.A. 1966; attended transcendental meditation course at Maharishi's Acad., Rishikesh, India Feb.-April 1968; formed Apple Corpn. Ltd., parent org. of The Beatles Group of Cos. 1968; composed, arranged and recorded own music for film Wonderwall 1968; organized and performed at The Concert for Bangladesh 1971, concert, film and record proceeds for refugees to UNICEF; tour of U.S.A. and Canada 1974; Co-founder Hand Made Films (owner–1994); founder of Material World Charitable Foundation. *Recordings by the Beatles include:* Please Please Me, With the Beatles 1963, A Hard Day's Night 1964, Beatles for Sale 1965, Help! 1965, Rubber Soul 1966, Revolver 1966, Sergeant Pepper's Lonely Hearts Club Band 1967, Magical Mystery Tour 1967, The Beatles (White Album) 1968, Yellow Submarine 1969, Abbey Road 1969, Let It Be 1970, Anthology I 1995, Anthology II 1996. *Solo recordings include:* All Things Must Pass, Living in the Material World, Dark Horse, Extra Texture, 33+, Somewhere in England, Gone Tropo, Cloud Nine 1987. *Films by The Beatles:* A Hard Day's Night 1964, Help! 1965, Yellow Submarine (animated colour cartoon film) 1968, TV film Magical Mystery Tour 1967, Let It Be 1970; producer Little Malcolm and His Struggle against the Eunuchs 1973, Shanghai Surprise 1986; *Films produced include:* Life of Brian 1979, Time Bandits 1981, The Missionary 1982, Privates on Parade

1984, A Private Function 1985, Mona Lisa 1986, Withnail and I 1987; Raga (with Ravi Shankar (q.v.) and Yehudi Menuhin) 1974. *Publication:* I, Me, Mine 1980.

HARRISON, Sir Richard, Kt., M.D., D.SC., F.R.S.; British anatomist (retd.); b. 8 Oct. 1920, London; s. of the late Dr. G. A. Harrison; m. 2nd Barbara Jean Fuller (died 1988); m. 3rd Gianetta Drake 1990; two s. one d. from 1st marriage; ed. Oundle School, Gonville and Caius Coll., Cambridge, St. Bartholomew's Hosp., London; Prof. of Anatomy, London Hosp. Medical Coll., Univ. of London 1954–68: Prof. of Anatomy, Cambridge Univ. 1968–82, Prof. Emer. 1982–; Hon. Fellow Downing Coll., Cambridge 1982; Chair. Farm Animal Welfare Council 1979–88, Bd. of Trustees, British Museum (Natural History) 1978–88; Pres. Int. Fed. of Asscns. of Anatomists 1985–87; Hon. mem. British, American and European Anatomical Socs. *Publications:* Functional Anatomy of Marine Mammals 1972–77, Handbook of Marine Mammals 1981–98, Research on Dolphins 1986, Whales, Dolphins and Porpoises 1988. *Leisure interest:* gardening. *Address:* Milestone House, 58A High Street, Barkway, Royston, Herts., SG8 8EE, England.

HARRISON, Rowland John Hill, LL.M.; Australian/Canadian public servant, lawyer and professor of law; b. 25 Sept. 1943, Hobart, Tasmania; s. of Colin Darrell Hill Harrison and Beryl Mary Harrison (née Sibley); m. Charlene Alexandra Maria Baker 1972; two s.; ed. St. Virgil's Coll., Hobart, Univ. of Tasmania, Univ. of Alberta, Canada; Asst. Prof. of Law, Univ. of Alberta 1970–72; Asst. then Assoc. Prof. of Law, Dalhousie Univ. 1972–79; Prof. of Law, Univ. of Calgary 1979–81; Exec. Dir. Canadian Inst. of Resources Law 1979–81; Dir.-Gen. Land Man. Br., Canada Oil and Gas Lands Admin. 1981–84; Prof. of Law, Univ. of Ottawa 1984–89; Visiting Prof., World Maritime Univ., Malmö, Sweden 1986–92; Assoc., Messrs. Stikeman, Elliott 1987–91, partner 1991–97; mem. Nat. Energy Bd. of Canada 1997–; mem. Editorial Advisory Bd., Journal of Energy and Resources Law 1984–95; Council mem., Section on Energy and Resources Law, Int. Bar Asscn. 1986–94 (Sec. 1990–94). *Publications:* various publs. on energy regulation and constitutional law in scholarly periodicals. *Leisure interests:* sailing, music. *Address:* 97 Woodpath Terrace, S.W., Calgary, Alta., T2W 5Z6, Canada (Home).

HARRISON, Sir Terence, Kt., D.L., F.ENG., F.I.MECH.E., F.I.MAR.E.; British business executive; b. 7 April 1933; s. of late Roland Harrison and Doris Wardle; m. June Forster 1956; two s.; ed. A. J. Dawson Grammar School, Co. Durham, West Hartlepool and Sunderland Tech. Colls. and Univ. of Durham; marine eng. apprenticeship, Richardson's Westgarth, Hartlepool 1949–53; mil. service, Nigeria 1955–57; Clarke Chapman Ltd., Gateshead 1957–77, Man. Dir. 1976–77; Northern Eng. Industries 1977, Chief Exec. 1983–86, Exec. Chair. 1986–89; Dir. Rolls-Royce PLC 1989–96, Chief Exec. 1992–96; Chair. Alfred McAlpine PLC 1995–; Hon. D.Eng. (Newcastle) 1991; Hon. D. Tech. (Sunderland) 1995; Hon. D.Sc. (Durham) 1996. *Publications:* technical papers. *Leisure interests:* golf, fell walking. *Address:* 2 The Garden Houses, Whalton, Northumberland, NE61 3HB, England.

HARRISON, Tony, F.R.S.L.; British poet; b. 30 April 1937, Leeds; s. of Harry Ashton Harrison and Florence (née Wilkinson) Horner; m. 1st Rosemarie Crossfield 1960; one s. one d.; m. 2nd Teresa Stratas 1984; ed. Leeds Grammar School and Univ. of Leeds; Cholmondeley Award for Poetry, Geoffrey Faber Memorial Award, European Poetry Translation Prize, Whitbread Poetry Prize (for Gaze of the Gorgons) 1993, Mental Health Award 1994, Prix d'Italia 1994. *Television and film work includes:* The Big H 1984, 'V' 1987, Loving Memory 1987, Yan Tan Tethera 1987, The Blasphemers' Banquet 1989, The Gaze of the Gorgon 1992, Black Daisies for the Bride 1993, A Maybe Day in Kazakhstan 1994, The Shadow of Hiroshima 1995. *Theatre includes:* Aikin Mata 1965, The Misanthrope 1973, Phaedra Britannica 1975, The Passion 1977, Bow Down 1977, The Bartered Bride 1978, The Oresteia 1981, Yan Tan Tethera 1983, The Mysteries 1985, The Trackers of Oxyrhynchus 1988–90, The Common Chorus 1992; Square Rounds (Nat. Theatre) 1992, Poetry or Bust 1993, The Kaisers of Carnuntum 1995, The Labourers of Herakles 1995, The Prince's Play 1996. *Publications include (poetry):* Earthworks 1964, The Loiners 1970, Palladas: Poems 1975, The School of Eloquence and Other Poems 1978, Continuous 1981, A Kumquat for John Keats 1981, US Martial 1981, Selected Poems 1984, 'V' 1985, 'V' and other poems 1990, A Cold Coming: Gulf War Poems 1991, The Gaze of the Gorgon, and other poems 1992, The Shadow of Hiroshima and other film/poems 1995, Permanently Bard 1995, Plays 3 1996, The Prince's Play 1996. *Address:* c/o Gordon Dickerson, 2 Crescent Grove, London, SW4 7AH, England.

HARRISON, Wayne David, B.A.; Australian theatre director and arts administrator; b. 7 March 1953, Melbourne; s. of Lindsay Graham Harrison and Florence Rosina Cannell; ed. Christian Brothers' Coll., Melbourne, Univ. of Melbourne, Univ. of N.S.W.; Dramaturge, Sydney Theatre Co. 1981–86; Asst. Dir. Northside Theatre Co., N.S.W. 1987–89; Dir. Sydney Theatre Co. 1990–. *Address:* P.O. Box 34, Ashfield, N.S.W. 2131, Australia.

HARRISS, Gerald Leslie, M.A., D.PHIL., F.B.A.; British historian and university teacher; b. 22 May 1925, London; s. of W. L. Harriss and M. J. O. Harriss; m. Margaret Anne Sidaway 1959; two s. three d.; ed. Chigwell School, Essex, Magdalen Coll., Oxford; war service in R.N.V.R. 1944–46; Oxford Univ. 1946–53; Lecturer, Durham Univ. 1953–65, Reader 1965–67; Fellow and Tutor in History, Magdalen Coll., Oxford 1967–92, Emer. Fellow 1992–, Reader in Modern History, Univ. of Oxford 1990–92. *Publications:* King, Parliament and Public Finance in Medieval England 1975, Henry V: the Practice of Kingship (Ed.) 1985, Cardinal Beaufort 1988; (Ed.) K. B. McFarlane, Letters to Friends 1997. *Address:* Fairings, 2 Queen Street, Yetminster, Sherborne, Dorset, DT9 6LL, England.

HARRY, Deborah Ann; American singer; b. 11 July 1945, Miami, Fla.; d. of Richard Smith and Catherine (Peters) Harry; ed. Centenary Coll.; singer and songwriter, rock group Blondie 1975–83; awarded Gold, Silver and Platinum records. *Songs:* Heart of Glass, Call Me, Tide is High, Rapture. *Albums:* Blondie: The Hunter, Plastic Letters, Parallel Lines, Eat to the Beat, Autoamerican, Koo Koo (solo), Rockbird, Def, Dumb and Blond. *Film appearances:* Union City Blues, Videodrome, Roadie, Hairspray, Tales from the Darkside: The Movie. *TV appearances:* Saturday Night Live, The Muppet Show, Tales from the Darkside, Wiseguys. *Theatre:* Teaneck Tanzi, The Venus Flytrap.

HARRY, Ralph Lindsay, A.C., C.B.E.; Australian diplomatist (retd.); b. 10 March 1917, Geelong, Victoria; s. of the late A. H. Harry; m. Dorothy Sheppard 1944; one s. two d.; ed. Univ. of Tasmania and Lincoln Coll., Oxford; joined Dept. of External Affairs 1940; Pvt. Sec. to Minister of External Affairs; A.I.F. (Papua) 1942; Asst. Official Sec., Ottawa 1943–45; Second Sec., later First Sec., Washington, D.C. 1945–49 (at UN, New York 1947–48); Dept. of External Affairs, Canberra 1949–53; Consul-Gen. in Geneva 1953–56; Rep. in Singapore, Brunei, Sarawak and North Borneo 1956–57; Dir. Australian Secret Intelligence Service 1958–59; Asst. Sec. Dept. of External Affairs 1960–65; Amb. to Belgium and the EEC 1965–68, to Repub. of Viet Nam 1968–70, to Fed. Repub. of Germany 1971–75, to UN 1975–78; Dir. Australian Inst. of Int. Affairs 1979–81; Visiting Fellow, Univ. of Tasmania 1979; Hon. LL.D. 1990; Pres. Australian Esperanto Asscn. 1980–88; mem. Nat. Australia Day Cttee. 1980–84. *Publications:* The Diplomat who Laughed 1983, The North Was Always Near 1994, No Man Is a Hero 1998, Aventuroj en Esperantujo, Australian-Esperanto Dictionary. *Address:* V-319, Bayview Gardens, 36–42 Cabbage Tree Road, Bayview, N.S.W. 2104, Australia. *Telephone:* (02) 9999 4102.

HARRYHAUSEN, Ray; American film producer, writer and special effects creator; b. 29 June 1920, Los Angeles, Calif.; s. of Frederick W. Harryhausen and Martha Reske; m. Diana Livingstone 1962; one d.; ed. Los Angeles City Coll.; model animator for George Pal's Puppetoons in early 1940s; served U.S. Signal Corps; made series of filmed fairy tales with animated puppets for schools and churches; asst. to Willis O'Brien working on Mighty Joe Young 1946; designed and created special effects for The Beast from 20,000 Fathoms; evolved own model animation system Dynarama used for first time in conjunction with producer Charles H. Schneer in film It Came from Beneath the Sea; subsequently made many films in Dynarama with Schneer, Gordon E. Sawyer Award 1992. *Films include:* Twenty Million Miles to Earth, The Three Worlds of Gulliver, Jason and the Argonauts, The First Men in the Moon, One Million Years B.C., The Valley of the Gwangi, The Golden Voyage of Sinbad, Sinbad and the Eye of the Tiger, Clash of the Titans.

HARSANYI, John Charles, M.A., PH.D.; American professor of business administration; b. 29 May 1920, Budapest, Hungary; s. of Charles Harsanyi and Alice Harsanyi; m. Anne Klauber 1951; one s.; ed. Univs. of Budapest and Sydney and Stanford Univ.; Asst. Univ. of Budapest 1947–48; lecturer, Univ. of Queensland, Brisbane 1954–56; Visiting Asst. Prof. Stanford Univ. 1958; Sr. Fellow, Australian Nat. Univ. Canberra 1959–61; Prof. of Econs. Wayne State Univ. Detroit 1961–63; Prof. of Business Admin. Univ. of Calif. Berkeley 1964–90, Prof. Emer. 1990–; Fellow, Center for Advanced Study in Behavioral Sciences, Stanford, Calif. 1965–66; Fellow, Econometric Soc., American Acad. of Arts and Sciences; mem. N.A.S.; Distinguished Fellow American Econ. Asscn.; shared Nobel Prize in Econs. (with John Nash and Reinhard Selten) 1994; Hon. D.Sc. (Northwestern) 1989. *Publications:* Essays on Ethics, Social Behavior and Scientific Explanation 1976, Rational Behavior and Bargaining Equilibrium 1977, Papers in Game Theory 1982, A General Theory of Equilibrium Selection in Games (with R. Selten) 1988; numerous articles in professional publs. *Address:* University of California, Haas School of Business, Berkeley, CA 94720-1900, U.S.A.

HART, Garry Richard Rushby, LL.B.; British solicitor; b. 29 June 1940, London; s. of Dennis George Hart and Evelyn Mary Hart; m. 1st Paula Lesley Shepherd 1966 (dissolved 1986); two s. one d.; m. 2nd Valerie Elen Mary Davies 1986; two d.; ed. Northgate Grammar School, Ipswich, Univ. Coll. London; solicitor, Herbert Smith 1966–70, partner 1970–98, Head of Property Dept. 1988–97; Special Adviser to Lord Chancellor 1998–; Trustee Architecture Foundation 1997–; Chair. of Trustees Almeida Theatre 1997–. *Leisure interests:* travel, sheep farming in N. Wales, talking. *Address:* Lord Chancellor's Department, Selborne House, Victoria Street, London, S.W.1, England. *Telephone:* 0171-210 8500.

HART, Gary, LL.B.; American politician and lawyer; b. 28 Nov. 1936, Ottawa, Kan.; m. Lee Ludwig 1958; one s. one d.; ed. Bethany Coll., Okla., Yale Univ.; called to bar 1964; Attorney, U.S. Dept. of Justice, and Special Asst. to Sec., U.S. Dept. of Interior 1964–67; legal practice, Denver, Colo. 1967–70, 1972–74; Nat. Campaign Dir., George McGovern Democratic Presidential Campaign 1970–72; Senator for Colorado 1975–86; with Davis, Graham & Stubbs, Denver 1985–; assisted in John F. Kennedy Presidential Campaign 1960; voluntary organizer, Robert F. Kennedy Presidential Campaign 1968; fmr. mem. of commrs., Denver Urban Renewal Authority; fmr.

mem., Park Hill Action Cttee. *Publications:* Right From the Start, A New Democracy 1983, The Double Man (with W. S. Cohen, q.v.) 1985, America Can Win 1986, The Strategies of Zeus 1987, Russia Shakes the World 1991. *Address:* Davis, Graham & Stubbs, 370 17th Street, Denver, CO 80202, U.S.A.

HART, Michael, C.B.E., PH.D., F.INST.P., C.PHYS., F.R.S.; British professor of physics; b. 4 Nov. 1938; s. of Reuben H. V. Hart and Phyllis M. Hart (née White); m. Susan M. Powell 1963; three d.; ed. Cotham Grammar School, Bristol and Univ. of Bristol; Research Assoc. Dept. of Materials Science and Eng. Cornell Univ. 1963–65; Dept. of Physics, Univ. of Bristol 1965–67, Lecturer in Physics 1967–72, Reader 1972–76; Sr. Resident Research Assoc. Nat. Research Council, NASA Electronics Research Center, Boston, Mass. 1969–70; Special Adviser, Cen. Policy Review Staff 1975–77; Wheatstone Prof. of Physics, King's Coll. London 1976–84; Prof. of Physics, Univ. of Manchester 1984–93, Emer. Prof. of Physics 1993–; Visiting Prof. of Applied Physics, De Montfort Univ. 1993–, Hon. Prof. in Eng., Warwick Univ. 1993–; Science Programme Coordinator (part-time), Daresbury Lab. Science and Eng. Research Council 1985–88; Chair. Nat. Synchrotron Light Source, Brookhaven Nat. Lab., U.S.A 1995–. *Publications:* contributions to learned journals. *Leisure interests:* flying kites, cookery. *Address:* National Synchrotron Light Source, Bldg. 725B, Brookhaven National Laboratory, P.O. Box 5000, Upton, NY 11973, U.S.A.

HART, Oliver D'Arcy, PH.D.; British professor of economics; b. 9 Oct. 1948, London; s. of Philip D'Arcy Hart and Ruth Meyer; m. Rita B. Goldberg 1974; two s.; ed. Univs. of Cambridge and Warwick and Princeton Univ.; lecturer in Econs. Univ. of Essex 1974–75; Asst. lecturer, then lecturer in Econs. Univ. of Cambridge 1975–81; Prof. of Econs. L.S.E. 1981–85, BP Visiting Centennial Prof. 1992–93, 1997–; Prof. of Econs. M.I.T. 1984–93, Harvard Univ. 1993–97, Andrew E. Furer Prof. of Econs. 1997–; Fellow, American Acad. of Arts and Sciences; Dr. h.c. (Free Univ. of Brussels) 1992; Hon. Dr. Phil. (Basle) 1994. *Publications:* Firms, Contracts and Financial Structure 1995; numerous articles in professional journals. *Address:* Department of Economics, Harvard University, Littauer 200, Cambridge, MA 02138, U.S.A. *Telephone:* (617) 496-3461. *Fax:* (617) 495-7730.

HART, Stanley Robert, M.S., PH.D.; American professor of geology and geochemistry; b. 20 June 1935, Swampscott, Mass,; s. of Robert Hart and Ruth M. Hart; m. 1st Joanna Smith 1956 (divorced 1976); m. 2nd Pamela Shepherd 1980; one s. two d.; ed. Mass. Inst. of Technology, Calif. Inst. of Technology; Fellow, Carnegie Inst. of Washington 1960–61, mem. staff 1961–75; Visiting Prof. Univ. of Calif. San Diego 1967–68; Prof. of Geology and Geochem. M.I.T. 1975–89; mem. N.A.S.; Fellow, American Geophysical Union, Geological Soc. of America, European Asscn. of Geochemistry; Goldschmidt Medal (Geochem. Soc.) 1992, Hess Medal (American Geophysical Union) 1997, Columbus O'Donnell Iselin Chair for Excellence in Oceanography. *Publications:* more than 190 articles in scientific journals. *Leisure interests:* woodworking, fishing, running. *Address:* Woods Hole Oceanographic Institution, Woods Hole, MA 02543; 53 Quonset Road, Falmouth, MA 02540, U.S.A. (Home).

HARTARTO; Indonesian politician; b. 30 May 1932, Delanggu, Cen. Java; ed. Inst. of Technology, Bandung and Univ. of New South Wales; mem. Man. Bd. state-owned paper factories of Padalarang and Leces 1959; Tech. Dir. Leces paper factory 1961; Man. Dir. of Bd. dealing with paper industries, Dept. of Industry 1965; Dir. Silicate Industry Div., Directorate-Gen. of Basic Chem. Industries, Dept. of Industry 1974, Dir.-Gen. for Basic Chem. Industries 1979; Minister of Industry 1983–93, Co-ordinating Minister for Industrial and Trade Affairs 1993–96; Co-ordinating Minister for Production and Distribution 1996–98, for Devt. Supervision and State Admin. Reform 1998–. *Address:* Office of Co-ordinating Minister for Development Supervision and State Administrative Reform, Jalan Veteran III/2, Jakarta Pusat, Indonesia. *Telephone:* (21) 3847028. *Fax:* (21) 3847028.

HARTFORD, Huntington, B.A.; American art patron and financier; b. 18 April 1911, New York; s. of Edward and Henrietta (Guerard) Hartford; m. 1st Mary Lee Epling (dissolved 1939); m. 2nd Marjorie Steele 1949 (dissolved 1961); one s. and one d.; m. 3rd Diane Brown 1962 (dissolved 1970); one d.; m. 4th Elaine Kay 1974 (divorced 1981); ed. St. Paul's School, and Harvard Univ.; Co-Chair. Oil Shale Corpn. (New York) 1949; Founder Huntington Hartford Foundation Calif. 1949, Huntington Hartford Theatre Hollywood 1954, Gallery of Modern Art (New York) 1964 (now called New York Cultural Center in asscn. with Fairleigh Dickinson Univ.); fmr. Developer and owner Paradise Island (Nassau, Bahamas) 1959; Publr. Show Magazine; Adviser Cultural Affairs to Pres. of Borough of Manhattan 1967; Patron Lincoln Center for the Performing Arts; mem. Advisory Council of Columbia Univ. Dept. of Art History and Archaeology, Nat. Council of the Arts 1969, U.S. People's Fund for UN Inc.; Hon. Fellow, Nat. Sculpture Soc., Broadway Asscn. Man. of Year Award; OAS Award 1966. *Publications:* Jane Eyre (play) 1958, Art or Anarchy 1964, You Are What You Write 1973. *Address:* 295 Madison Ave, New York, NY 10017, U.S.A.

HARTINGTON, Marquess of; Peregrine Andrew Morny Cavendish, C.B.E.; British horse racing executive; b. 27 April 1944; s. of 11th Duke of Devonshire; m. Amanda Carmen Heywood-Lonsdale 1967; one s. two d.; ed. Eton, Exeter Coll., Oxford; Sr. Steward Jockey Club 1989–94; Chair. British Horseracing Bd. 1993–96; Dir. Sotheby's Holdings Inc. 1994–, Deputy Chair. 1996–; H.M.'s Rep. at Ascot 1997–. *Address:* Beamsley Hall, Skipton, N. Yorks., BD23 6HD, England.

HARTKAMP, Arthur Severijn; Netherlands lawyer; b. 10 Jan. 1945, Amsterdam; m. Ebeltje Jonxis 1972; two d.; ed. Univ. of Amsterdam; lecturer in Roman Law, Univ. of Amsterdam 1968–74; Civil Code Revision Office, Ministry of Justice 1974–89; lecturer (part-time) in Civil Law, Univ. of Leiden 1977–83; Judge (part-time), Court of Appeal, Amsterdam 1982–86; Advocate-Gen. Supreme Court of Netherlands 1986; Prof. of Pvt. Law (part-time), Utrecht Univ. 1991; mem. Governing Council UNIDROIT (Rome); mem. and Gen. Sec. Royal Acad. of Sciences, American Law Inst.; Assoc. mem. Int. Acad. of Comparative Law. *Publications:* several books and book chapters on legal topics. *Leisure interests:* literature, classical languages, music. *Address:* Faculty of Law, Heidelberglaan 8, P.O. Box 80125, 3508 TC Utrecht, Netherlands.

HARTLAND, Michael (see James, Michael Leonard).

HARTLEY, Brian Selby, PH.D., F.R.S.; British professor of biochemistry; b. 16 April 1926, Rawtenstall; s. of Norman and Hilda Hartley; m. Kathleen Maude Vaughan 1949; three s. one d.; ed. Queens' Coll. Cambridge, Univ. of Leeds; ICI Fellow, Cambridge 1952–58, Fellow and Lecturer in Biochemistry, Trinity Coll. Cambridge 1964–74; Helen Hay Whitney Fellow Univ. of Washington, Seattle 1958–60; mem. scientific staff MRC Lab. of Molecular Biology 1961–74; Prof. of Biochemistry 1974–91 and Dir. of Centre for Biotechnology, Imperial Coll., Univ. of London 1982–91, Prof. Emer. 1991; Chair. Agrol Ltd. 1993–; Hon. mem. American Soc. of Biological Chemists 1961–74, mem. Royal Soc. Council 1981–83; British Drug Houses Medal for Analytical Biochemistry 1969. *Publications:* papers and articles in scientific journals. *Leisure interests:* fishing, gardening. *Address:* Grove Cottage, 21 Smith Street, Elsworth, Cambridge, CB3 8HY, England. *Telephone:* (01954) 267271 (Home). *Fax:* (01954) 267028.

HARTLEY, Frank Robinson, D.SC., F.R.S.C., F.R.AE.S.; British chemist; b. 29 Jan. 1942, Epsom; s. of Sir Frank Hartley and Lydia May England; m. Valerie Peel 1964; three d.; ed. Kings Coll. School, Wimbledon, Magdalen Coll., Oxford; post-doctoral Fellow, Commonwealth Scientific and Industrial Research Org., Div. of Protein Chem., Melbourne, Australia 1966–69; ICI Research Fellow and Tutor in Physical Chem., Univ. Coll., London 1969–70; Lecturer in Inorganic Chem., Univ. of Southampton 1970–75; Prof. of Chem. and Head of Dept. of Chem. and Metallurgy, Royal Mil. Coll. of Science, Shrivenham 1975–82, Acting Dean 1982–84, Prin. and Dean 1984–89; Man. Dir. CIT Holdings Ltd. 1989–; Dir. (non-exec.) T & N PLC 1989–98, Nat. Westminster Bank Eastern Region Advisory Bd. 1990–92, Kalon PLC 1994–, Kenwood PLC 1995–; Asscn. of Commonwealth Univs. Sr. Travelling Fellow 1986; Special Adviser on Defence Systems to the Prime Minister 1988–90; Specialist Adviser to House of Lords Select Cttee. on Science and Tech. 1993–94; Chair. AWE Academic Council 1998–; mem. Int. Advisory Bd. Kanazawa Acad. of Science and Tech., Japan 1989–; Dir. Shuttleworth Trust 1994–97; Trustee Lorch Foundation 1994–. *Publications:* The Chemistry of Platinum and Palladium (Applied Science) 1973, Elements of Organometallic Chemistry (Chemical Soc.) 1974, Solution Equilibria (with C. Burgess and R. M. Alcock) 1980; The Chemistry of the Metal Carbon Bond (vol. 1–5) 1983–89, Supported Metal Complexes 1985, Brasseys New Battlefield Weapons Systems and Technology series 1988– (Ed.-in-Chief), The Chemistry of Organophosphorus Compounds Vols. 1–4 1990–96, Chemistry of the Platinum Group Metals 1991, papers in inorganic, co-ordination and organometallic chemistry in major English, American and Australian journals. *Leisure interests:* cliff walking, golf, swimming, squash, gardening. *Address:* Cayley Lodge, Cranfield University, Cranfield, Beds., MK43 0SX, England (Office). *Telephone:* (01234) 754013 (Office). *Fax:* (01234) 752583.

HARTLEY, Hal, (also known as Ned Rifle); American film director, producer and scriptwriter; b. 1960, Long Island, N.Y.; ed. State Univ. of New York-Purchase Film School. *Films:* Kid 1984, Home of The Brave 1986, The Cartographer's Girlfriend 1987, Dogs 1988, The Unbelievable Turn 1990, Trust 1991, Simple Men 1992, From a Motel 6 1993, Iris 1993, The Only Living Boy in New York 1993, Flirt 1993, Amateur 1994, Henry Fool. *TV films:* Surviving Desire 1989, Achievement 1991, Ambition 1991. *Address:* True Fiction Pictures, 12 W. 27th Street, New York, NY 10001, U.S.A.

HÄRTLING, Peter; German writer and journalist; b. 13 Nov. 1933, Chemnitz; s. of Rudolf and Erika (Häntzschel) Härtling; m. Mechthild Maier 1959; two s. two d.; ed. Gymnasium (Nürtingen/Neckar); childhood spent in Saxony, Czechoslovakia and Württemberg; journalist 1953–; Literary Ed. Deutsche Zeitung und Wirtschaftszeitung, Stuttgart and Cologne; Ed. of magazine Der Monat 1962–70, also Co-publisher; Ed. and Man. Dir. S. Fischer Verlag, Frankfurt 1968–74, Ed. Die Väter; mem. PEN, Akademie der Wissenschaften und der Literatur Mainz, Akademie der Künste Berlin, Deutsche Akademie für Sprache und Dichtung Darmstadt; Literaturpreis des Deutschen Kritikerverbandes 1964, Literaturpreis des Kulturkreises der Deutschen Industrie 1965, Literarischer Förderungspreis des Landes Niedersachsen 1965, Prix du meilleur livre étranger, Paris 1966, Gerhart Hauptmann Preis 1971, Deutscher Jugendbuchpreis 1976, Stadtschreiber von Bergen-Enkheim 1978–79, Hölderlin-Preis 1987, Lion-Feuchtwanger-Preis 1992, Stadtschreiber von Mainz 1995, Leuschner-Medaille des Landes Hessen 1996. *Publications:* Yamins Stationen (poetry) 1955, In Zeilen zuhaus (essays) 1957, Palmström grüsst Anna Blume (essays) 1961, Spielgeist-Spiegelgeist (poetry) 1962, Niembsch oder Der Stillstand (novel) 1964, Janek (novel)

1966, Das Familienfest (novel) 1969, Gilles (play) 1970, Ein Abend, Eine Nacht, Ein Morgen (novel) 1971, Zwettl—Nachprüfung einer Erinnerung (novel) 1973, Eine Frau (novel) 1974, Hölderlin (novel) 1976, Anreden (poetry) 1977, Hubert oder Die Rückkehr nach Casablanca (novel) 1978, Nachgetragene Liebe (novel) 1980, Die dreifache Maria 1982, Das Windrad (novel) 1983, Felix Guttmann (novel) 1985, Waiblingers Augen (novel) 1987, Der Wanderer (novel) 1988, Briefe von drinnen und draußen (poetry) 1989, Herzwand (novel) 1990, Schubert (novel) 1992, Božena (novel) 1994, Schumanns Schatten (novel) 1996. *Address:* Finkenweg 1, 64546 Mörfelden-Walldorf, Germany. *Telephone:* 06105-6109. *Fax:* 06105-74687.

HARTLING, Poul; Danish United Nations official (retd.); b. 14 Aug. 1914, Copenhagen; s. of late M. Hartling (fmr. Minister of Education) and late Mathilde Hartling; m. Dr. (medical) Elsebeth Kirkemann 1940; three s. one d.; Master of Divinity; Sec. to Student Christian Movt. 1934–35, to Denmark's Christian Movt. of Sr. Secondary Students 1939–43, Curate of Frederiksberg Church 1941–45; Chaplain of St. Luke Foundation 1945–50; Prin. of Zahle's Teachers' Training Coll. 1950–68; mem. Folketing 1957–60, 1964–77; Chair. Liberal Party Parl. Group 1965–68; mem. Nordic Council 1964–68, Pres. 1966–73, Vice-Pres. 1977; Minister of Foreign Affairs 1968–71; Prime Minister 1973–75; Chair. Liberal Party 1973–77; UN High Commr. for Refugees 1978–85; Dr. h.c. Valparaiso Univ., Ind. 1981; Grand Cross of Dannebrog and numerous other decorations. *Publications:* Sursum corda (History of Student Christian Movement); Ed. Church, School, Culture 1963, The Danish Church 1964, From 17 years in Danish Politics 1974, I dine haender 1977, Bladet i Bogen 1980, Politisk Udspil 1981, Godt vejr og dårligt vejr 1983, Otte år i FN's flygtningearbejde 1985, Erik Eriksen 1990. *Leisure interest:* music. *Address:* Emilievej 6E, 2920 Charlottenlund, Denmark. *Telephone:* 39 63 5312.

HARTMAN, Arthur A., A.B.; American diplomatist (retd.); b. 12 March 1926, New York; m. Donna Van Dyke Ford; three s. two d.; ed. Harvard Univ., Harvard Law School; served in U.S. Army Air Corps 1944–46; Econ. Officer, Econ. Co-operation Admin., Paris 1948–52; Econ. Officer of U.S. del. to European Army Conf., Paris 1952–54; Politico-Mil. officer, U.S. Mission to NATO, Paris 1954–55; Econ. officer, Joint U.S. Embassy/Agency for Int. Devt. Mission, Saigon, Repub. of Viet Nam 1956–58; Int. Affairs Officer, Bureau of European Affairs, Dept. of State 1958–61; Staff Asst. to Under-Sec. of State for Econ. Affairs 1961–62, Special Asst. 1962–63; Head of Econ. Section, U.S. Embassy, London 1963–67; Special Asst. to Under-Sec. of State 1967–69; Staff Dir. of Sr. Interdepartmental Group 1967–69; Deputy Dir. of Coordination to Under-Sec. of State 1969–72; Deputy Chief of Mission and Minister-Counsellor, U.S. Mission to European Communities, Brussels 1972–74; Asst. Sec. of State for European Affairs 1974–77; U.S. Amb. to France 1977–81, to U.S.S.R. 1981–87; Consultant APCO Consulting Group, Wash. 1989–; Chair. Barings' First NIS Regional Investment Fund; mem. Bd., ITT Hartford Insurance Group, Dreyfus Funds, Lawter Int. Ford Meter Box Co.; mem. Council on Foreign Relations; mem. Bd. French-American Foundation Fund for Devt. and Democracy; fmr. Pres. Harvard Univ. Bd. of Overseers; Hon. degrees (Wheaton Coll., American Coll. in Paris); Presidential Management Improvement Award 1970, Distinguished Honor Award 1972, Veterans of Foreign Wars Medal of Honor 1981, Sec. of State's Distinguished Service Award 1987, Dept. of State Wilbur J. Carr Award 1987, Annual Nat. Conf. on Soviet Jewry Award 1987. *Address:* APCO Consulting Group, 1615 L Street N.W., Washington, DC 20036 (Office); 2738 McKinley Street, N.W., Washington, DC 20015, U.S.A. (Home).

HARTMAN, George Eitel, M.F.A.; American architect; b. 7 May 1936, Fort Hancock, N.J.; s. of George E. Hartman and Evelyn Ritchie; m. Ann Burdick 1965; one s. one d.; ed. Princeton Univ.; with Keyes Lethbridge & Condon Architects 1960–64; own pvt. practice George E. Hartman 1964–65, Hartman-Cox Architects 1965–; mem. U.S. Comm. of Fine Arts 1990–(93), Architectural Advisory Bd., Foreign Bldg. Office, U.S. Dept. of State 1991–, American Inst. of Architects (AIA) Coll. of Fellows; Fellow American Acad. Rome; AIA Nat. Honor Awards 1970, 1971, 1981, 1988, 1989, and numerous other awards. *Buildings include:* U.S. Embassy, Kuala Lumpur 1979, 1001 Pennsylvania Avenue, Washington, DC 1979, HEB HQ, San Antonio, Tex. 1982, Chrysler Museum, Norfolk, N.J. 1984, Georgetown Univ. Law Library 1989, Market Square, Washington, DC 1990, 800 N Capital Street, Washington, DC 1990, 1200 K Street and 154 K Street, Washington, DC 1991. *Leisure interest:* sailing. *Address:* Hartman Cox Architects, 1074 Thomas Jefferson Street, Washington, DC 20007 (Office); 3525 Hamlet Place, Bethesda, MD 20815, U.S.A. (Home). *Telephone:* (202) 333-6446.

HARTMANN, Peter, D.PHIL.; German diplomatist; b. 9 Oct. 1935, Aachen; s. of Leonhard Hartmann and Gertrud Hartmann; m. Lonny Freiin von Blomberg 1968; two d.; ed. Gymnasium, Aachen; joined Foreign Service 1965, Consulate, Karachi, Pakistan 1968–71, EC Del. Brussels 1971–74, Foreign Ministry Bonn 1974–77, Embassy, Buenos Aires, Argentina 1977–80, Head of Office for Foreign Relations CDU, Bonn 1981–84, Chancellor's Office, Bonn 1984–93, Head European Policy 1987–91, Foreign and Security Policy 1991–93; Amb. to U.K. 1993–95; State Sec. and Minister of Foreign Affairs 1995; Hon. K.B.E. *Publication:* Interessenpluralismus und politische Entscheidung 1966. *Leisure interests:* tennis, literature. *Address:* c/o Christlich-Demokratische Union Deutschlands, Konrad-Adenauer-Haus, Friedrich-Ebert Allee 73–75, 53113 Bonn, Germany.

HARTMANN, Peter C., D. PHIL.; German professor of history; b. 28 March 1940, Munich; s. of Alfred Hartmann and Manfreda Knote; m. Beate Just 1972; two s. two d.; ed. Univs. of Munich and Paris; Research Assoc. Deutsches Historisches Institut, Paris 1970–81; Privatdozent, Munich 1979; Prof. Univ. of Passau 1982; Prof. of History, Univ. of Mainz 1988–; Hon. D. Univ. (Paris); Strasbourg Int. Prize. *Publications:* Pariser Archive, Bibl. u. Dok.zentren 1976, Geld als Instrument europäischer Machtpolitik im Zeitalter des Merkantilismus 1978, Das Steuersystem der europäischen Staaten am Ende der Ancien Regime 1979, Karl Albrecht-Karl VII: Glücklicher Kurfürst, Unglücklicher Kaiser 1985, Französische Geschichte 1914–1945, Französische Verf.geschichte der Neuzeit (1450–1980), Ein Überblick 1985, Bayerns Weg in die Gegenwart: Vom Stammesherzogtum bis zur Freistaat heute 1989, Der Jesuitenstaat in Südamerika 1609–1768 1994, Franz. Könige u. Kaiser der Neuzeit 1994, Regionen in der Frühen Neuzeit 1994, Der Mainzer Kurfürst als Reichserzkanzler 1996, Der Bayerische Reichskreis (1500–1803) 1997. *Address:* 55099 Mainz Histor. Sem., Saarstrasse 21, Germany.

HARTMANN, Ulrich; German business executive; b. 7 Aug. 1938, Berlin; m.; two c.; legal studies in Munich, Berlin and Bonn; Auditor, Treuarbeit AG, Düsseldorf 1967–71; Asst. to Man. Bd. Deutsche Leasing AG, Frankfurt 1971–72; Corp. Counsel, VEBA Kraftwerke Ruhr AG, Gelsenkirchen 1973–75; Head, Bd. Office and Public Relations, VEBA AG, Düsseldorf 1975–80; mem. Man. Bd. Nordwestdeutsche Kraftwerke AG, Hamburg 1980–85, PreussenElektra AG, Hanover 1985–89; mem. Man. Bd. VEBA AG 1989–, Chief Finance Officer 1990–, C.E.O. and Chair. 1993–; Chair. Supervisory Bd. of maj. group cos. and Münchener Rückversicherungs-Gesellschaft AG, Munich, RAG Aktiengesellschaft, Essen, Degussa AG 1998–; Consul-Gen. of Norway 1993–; Dir. (non-exec.) Cable and Wireless PLC, London; mem. Supervisory Bd. Daimler-Benz AG, Stuttgart, Deutsche Lufthansa AG, Cologne, Hochtief AG, Essen, IKB Deutsche Industriebank AG, Düsseldorf, Münchener Rückversicherungs-Gesellschaft AG, Munich. *Address:* VEBA AG, Bennigsenplatz 1, 40474 Düsseldorf, Germany. *Telephone:* (0211)-4579-1. *Fax:* (0211)-4579-501.

HARTOG, Harold Samuel Arnold, K.B.E.; Netherlands business executive; b. 21 Dec. 1910, Nijmegen; s. of Jacob and Suzanne Henriette (Elias) Hartog; m. Ingeborg Luise Michael; ed. Wiedemann Coll., Geneva; joined Unilever 1931; mem. Netherlands forces, Second World War; joined Unilever in France after Second World War, later in charge of Unilever cos. in Netherlands; mem. Bd. Unilever N.V. 1948–71; mem. Unilever Rotterdam Group Management responsible for Unilever activities in Germany, Austria and Belgium 1952–60; mem. Unilever Cttee. for Overseas Interests, London 1960–62; one of two World Coordinators, Unilever's food interests, London 1962–66; Chair. Unilever N.V. 1966–71 (retd.); Knight Order of Netherlands Lion. *Leisure interest:* collecting Chinese ceramics and porcelain. *Address:* Kösterbergstrasse 40b, 22587 Hamburg, Germany. *Telephone:* 40-862 725. *Fax:* 40-862 012

HARTOG, Jan de; Netherlands writer; b. 22 April 1914, Haarlem; s. of Arnold and Lucretia de Hartog-Meyjes; m. Marjorie Eleanor Mein; two s. four d.; Commdr. Orde van de Nederlandse Leeuw 1996. *Publications:* Het Huis met de Handen 1934, Ave Caesar 1936, Oompje Owadi 1938, Holland's Glory 1940, God's Geuzen Vol. I 1947, Vol. II 1948, Vol. III 1949, Stella 1950, Mary 1951, The Lost Sea 1951, Thalassa 1952, Captain Jan 1952, The Little Ark 1954, The Inspector 1961, Waters of the New World (travel) 1961, The Artist 1963, The Hospital 1965, The Captain 1967, The Children 1969, The Peaceable Kingdom 1972, The Lamb's War 1980, Herinneringen aan Amsterdam 1981, The Trail of the Serpent 1983, Star of Peace 1984, The Commodore 1986, The Centurion 1989, The Peculiar People 1992, The Outer Buoy 1994; *plays:* De Ondergang van de Vrijheid 1937 (Great Nat. Drama Prize 1939), Mist 1938, Skipper Next to God 1946, Death of a Rat 1946, The Fourposter 1946 (Tony Award 1952); detective stories under pseudonym of F. R. Eckmar: Een Linkerbeen gezocht 1935, Spoken te koop 1936, Ratten op de trap 1937, Drie Dode Dwergen 1937, De Maagd en de Moordenaar 1938. *Leisure interests:* travel, reading. *Address:* c/o Andrew Nurnberg Associates, Clerkenwell House, 45/47 Clerkenwell Green, London, EC1R 0HT, England.

HARTSHORN, Michael Philip, F.R.S.N.Z., D.PHIL.,; British/New Zealand university teacher; b. 10 Sept. 1936, Coventry, England; m. Jacqueline Joll 1963; four s.; ed. Imperial Coll. of Science and Tech., London, University Coll., Oxford; Lecturer in Chem., Univ. of Canterbury, N.Z. 1960–66, Sr. Lecturer 1966–68, Reader 1968–72, Prof. 1972–97, Prof. Emer. 1997–; Fulbright Visiting Prof., Cornell Univ., New York 1966–67; Guest Prof., Lund Univ., Sweden 1991–92, 1995, 1997; Fürth Visiting Lecturer, Royal Soc. of Edin. 1991; Wilsmore Fellow Melbourne Univ. June-July 1996; Fellowship N.Z. Inst. of Chem. 1969, Hector Medal, Royal Soc. of N.Z. 1973. *Publications:* approx. 255 scientific papers, Steroid Reaction Mechanisms (with D. N. Kirk) 1968. *Leisure interests:* reading, music, gardening. *Address:* 1 Repton Street, Christchurch 1, New Zealand. *Telephone:* (64-3) 3556-450. *Fax:* (64-3) 3558-357.

HARTUNG, Harald; German poet, professor and critic; b. 29 Oct. 1932, Herne; s. of Richard Hartung and Wanda Hartung; m. Freia Schnackenburg 1979; two s.; secondary school teacher 1960–66; Prof., Pädagogische Hochschule Berlin 1971–80, Tech. Univ. Berlin 1980–; mem. Akad. der Künste, Berlin, PEN; Kunstpreis Berlin, Drostepreis 1987. *Publications:* Experimentelle Literatur und Konkrete Poesie 1975, Das Gewöhnliche Licht 1976, Augenzeit 1978, Deutsche Lyrik seit 1965 1985, Traum im Deutschen

Museum 1986, Luftfracht 1991, Jahre mit Windrad 1996, Masken und Stimmen 1996. *Address:* Chausseestrasse 51, 14109 Berlin, Germany.

HARTWELL, Baron (Life Peer), cr. 1968, of Peterborough Court in the City of London; **(William) Michael Berry,** M.B.E., T.D.; British newspaper editor (retd.); b. 18 May 1911, Weybridge, Surrey; s. of the late 1st Viscount Camrose and Viscountess Camrose (née Mary Agnes Corns); m. Lady Pamela Smith 1936 (died 1982); two s. two d.; ed. Eton Coll. and Christ Church, Oxford; served 1939–45 war, Lieut-Col. R.A.; Ed. Sunday Mail, Glasgow 1934–35; Man. Ed. Financial Times 1937–39; fmr. Deputy Editor-in-Chief The Daily Telegraph, Chair. and Editor-in-Chief 1954–87, Dir. (non-exec.) –1996; Chair. and Editor-in-Chief The Sunday Telegraph 1961–87; Chair. Amalgamated Press Ltd. 1954–59; Dir. Reuters 1960–63, Trustee 1963–89. *Publications:* Party Choice 1948, William Camrose: Giant of Fleet Street 1992. *Address:* 18 Cowley Street, London, SW1P 3LZ (Home); Oving House, Whitchurch, nr. Aylesbury, Bucks, HP22 4HN, England (Home). *Telephone:* 0171-222 4673 (London); (01296) 641307 (Whitchurch).

HARTZENBERG, Ferdinand, D.SC.; South African politician; b. 8 Jan. 1936, Lichtenburg; s. of Ferdinand Hartzenberg; m. Magdalena Judith de Wet 1962; two s.; ed. Sannieshof, Hoër Volkskool, Potchefstroom and Univ. of Pretoria; mem. Parl. for Lichtenburg; Chair. Conservative Party 1993–; Deputy Minister of Devt. 1976; Minister of Educ. and Training 1979–82. *Address:* Conservative Party of South Africa, 203 Soutpansberg Road, Rietondale, Pretoria 0001, South Africa.

HARVEY, Anthony; British film director; b. 3 June 1931; s. of Geoffrey Harrison and Dorothy Leon; entered film industry, joining Crown Film Unit 1949; edited numerous films including Private Progress, Brothers-in-law, Carleton Brown of the Foreign Office, I'm Alright Jack, The Angry Silence, The Millionairess, Lolita, the L-Shaped Room, Dr. Strangelove, The Spy Who Came in from the Cold, the Whisperers; directed Dutchman 1968, The Lion in Winter 1969, They Might be Giants 1970, The Abdication 1973, The Glass Menagerie 1973, This Can't Be Love (CBS) 1974, The Disappearance of Aimee (TV) 1978, Eagle's Wing, Players 1979, Richard's Things 1980, The Patricia Neal Story 1981, Svengali (TV) 1982, Grace Quigley, This Can't Be Love (TV) 1994. *Leisure interest:* gardening. *Address:* c/o Arthur Greene, 101 Park Avenue, 43rd Floor, New York, NY 10178; c/o APA, Seventh Avenue, New York, NY, U.S.A.

HARVEY, Barbara Fitzgerald, C.B.E., M.A., B.LITT., F.R.HIST.S., F.S.A., F.B.A.; British academic; b. 21 Jan. 1928, Teignmouth, Devon; d. of Richard Henry Harvey and Anne Fitzgerald Harvey née Julian; ed. Teignmouth Grammar School, Bishop Blackall School, Exeter and Somerville Coll. Oxford; Asst., Univ. of Edin., Scotland 1951–52; Lecturer, Queen Mary Coll., Univ. of London 1952–55; Tutor, Somerville Coll. Oxford 1955–93, Fellow 1956–93, Emer. Fellow 1993–, Vice-Prin. 1976–79 and 1981–83; Ford's Lecturer, Univ. of Oxford 1989, Reader in Medieval History 1990–93; Vice-Pres. Royal Historical Soc. 1986–90; Gen. Ed. Oxford Medieval Texts 1987–; mem. Royal Comm. on Historical Manuscripts 1991–97; Jt. winner Wolfson Foundation Prize for History 1993. *Publications:* Westminster Abbey and its Estates in the Middle Ages 1977, The Westminster Chronicle, 1381–94 (Ed. with L. C. Hector) 1982, Living and Dying in England 1100–1540: The Monastic Experience 1993; articles in learned journals. *Address:* 66 Cranham Street, Oxford, OX2 6DD, England.

HARVEY, Cynthia Theresa; American ballet dancer and teacher; b. 17 May 1957, San Rafael, Calif.; d. of Gordon Harvey and Clara Harvey; m. Christopher D. Murphy 1990; ed. High School of Professional Children's School, New York; joined American Ballet Theater 1974, Prin. ballerina 1982–86, 1988–; with Royal Ballet, London 1986–88; guest appearances touring with Mikhail Baryshnikov, Rudolf Nureyev and Alexander Godunov; has performed with Stuttgart Ballet, Birmingham Royal Ballet and Northern Ballet Theatre; teacher of ballet at many leading schools in U.S.A. *Publication:* The Physics of Dance and the Pas de Deux (with Ken Laws) 1994. *Leisure interests:* motor racing, music, theatre, soccer, design. *Address:* c/o American Ballet Theater, 890 Broadway, 3rd Floor, New York, NY 10003, U.S.A. *Telephone:* (212) 477-3030.

HARVEY, Jonathan Dean, M.A., PH.D., D.MUS., F.R.C.M.; British composer and professor of music; b. 3 May 1939, Sutton Coldfield; s. of Gerald Harvey and Noelle Harvey; m. Rosaleen Marie Barry 1960; one s. one d.; ed. St. Michael's Coll., Tenbury, Repton, St. John's Coll., Cambridge, Glasgow Univ., Princeton Univ.; Lecturer, Southampton Univ. 1964–77; Reader, Sussex Univ. 1977–80, Prof. of Music 1980–; Prof. of Music, Stanford Univ. 1995–; mem. Arts Council of England's Music Advisory Panel 1995–, British Council's Music Advisory Panel 1993–95, Acad. Europaea 1989, Acad. Cttee. of Royal Coll. of Music 1990; Hon. D.Mus. (Southampton, Bristol). *Compositions:* Three Quartets 1977, 1989 and 1995, Mortuos plango, vivos voco (for tape) 1980, Passion and Resurrection 1981, Bhakti 1982, Gong Ring 1984, Song Offerings 1985, Madonna of Winter and Spring 1986, Lightness and Weight 1986, Tendril 1987, Time Pieces 1987, From Silence 1988, Valley of Aosta 1989, Ritual Melodies 1990, Cello Concerto 1990, Inquest of Love (opera) 1991, Serenade in Homage to Mozart 1991, Scena 1992, One Evening 1993, The Riot 1993, Missa Brevis 1995, Percussion Concerto 1996, Ashes Dance Back 1997, Wheel of Emptiness 1997, Death of Light/Light of Death 1998, Calling Across Time 1998, Tranquil Abiding 1998; about 20 works for choir. *Leisure interests:* tennis, meditation. *Address:* c/o Faber Music, 3 Queen Square, London, WC1N 3AU, England. *Telephone:* 0171-833 7911. *Fax:* 0171-833 7939.

HARVEY-JONES, Sir John (Henry), Kt., M.B.E.; British business executive; b. 16 April 1924, London; s. of Mervyn and Eileen Harvey-Jones; m. Mary Evelyn Bignell 1947; one d.; ed. Tormore School, Deal, Royal Naval Coll., Dartmouth; served with Royal Navy 1937–56, specialising in submarines, later working with Naval Intelligence; resgnd. with rank of Lieut. Commdr. 1956; joined ICI as Work Study Officer 1956, then held various commercial posts at Wilton and with Heavy Organic Chemicals Div. until appointed Techno-Commercial Dir. 1967; Deputy Chair. HOC Div. 1968; Chair., ICI Petrochemicals Div. 1970–73; appointed to Main Bd. ICI 1973, Deputy Chair 1978–82, Chair. 1982–87; Chancellor Bradford Univ. 1986–91; mem. Tees and Hartlepool Port Authority 1970–73; Chair. Phillips-Imperial Petroleum 1973–75; Non-Exec. Dir. Burns Anderson 1987–91 (Chair. 1987–90); Chair. Parallax Enterprises Ltd. 1987–97; Non-Exec. Chair. Business Int. Bd. Cttee. 1988–91; Non-Exec. Dir. Reed Int. PLC 1975–84, Carrington Viyella Ltd. 1974–79 (Dir. 1981–82), Grand Metropolitan PLC 1983–94, (Deputy Chair. 1987–91), The Economist 1987–94 (Chair. 1989–94), G.P.A. Ltd. 1987–93 (Deputy Chair. 1989–93), Trendroute Ltd. 1988–91; Pres. Conseil Européen des Fédérations de l'Industrie Chimique 1982–84; Vice-Pres. Hearing and Speech Trust 1985–, Heaton Woods Trust 1986, Book Trust Appeal Fund 1987–, Wider Share Ownership Council 1988–92; Chair. Council, Wildfowl Trust 1987–94; Vice-Chair. Policy Studies Inst. 1980–85, B.I.M. 1980–85 (mem. 1978–); Hon. Vice-Pres. Inst. of Marketing 1982–89; mem. Court of British Shippers' Council 1982–87, Police Foundation 1983–91 (Chair. Trustees 1984–88), Advisory Editorial Bd. of New European 1987–; mem. Council, Chemical Industries Asscn. Ltd. 1980–82, British-Malaysian Soc. 1983–87, Youth Enterprise Scheme 1984–86; mem. Foundation Bd., Int. Man. Inst., Geneva 1984–87; mem. Bd. Welsh Devt. Int. 1989–93; mem. Advisory Council, Prince's Youth Business Trust 1986–; mem. Int. Council, European Inst. of Business Admin. 1984–87; Trustee Science Museum 1983–87, Conf. Bd. 1984–86; Hon. mem. The City & Guilds of London Inst. 1988–; Patron Cambridge Univ. Young Entrepreneurs Soc. 1987–91, Manpower Services Comm. Nat. Training Awards 1987, Nat. Canine Defence League 1990–, Steer Org.; Vice-Patron British Polio Fellowship 1988–; Hon. Consultant, Royal United Services Inst. for Defence Studies 1987–; Gov. English Speaking Union 1987–91; Fellow Smallpiece Trust 1988–; mem. R.S.A., Soc. of Chemical Industry; Hon. Fellow, Royal Soc. of Chemistry 1985, The Inst. of Chemical Engineers 1985; Hon. LL.D. (Manchester) 1985, (Liverpool) 1986, (London) 1987, Cambridge (1987); D.Univ. (Surrey) 1985; Hon. D.Sc. (Bradford) 1986, (Leicester) 1986, (Keele, Exeter) 1989; Hon. D.C.L. (Newcastle) 1988; Hon. D.Tech. (Loughborough Univ. of Tech.) 1991; Jo Hambro British Businessman of the Year 1986; Int. Asscn. of Business Communicators Award of Excellence in Communication 1987; Radar Man of the Year 1987; City & Guilds Insignia Award in Tech. (h.c.) 1987; Commdr.'s Cross of Order of Merit (Fed. Repub. of Germany). *Publications:* Making it Happen, Reflections on Leadership 1987, Troubleshooter 1990, Getting it Together (memoirs) 1991, Troubleshooter 2 1992, Managing to Survive 1993, All Together Now 1994, Troubleshooter Returns 1995. *Leisure interests:* ocean sailing, swimming, the countryside, cooking, contemporary literature. *Address:* P.O. Box 18, Ross-on-Wye, Herefordshire, HR9 7PH, England. *Telephone:* (01989) 567171.

HARWOOD, Ronald, C.B.E., F.R.S.L.; British author and playwright; b. 9 Nov. 1934, Cape Town, South Africa; s. of the late Isaac Horwitz and Isobel Pepper; m. Natasha Riehle 1959; one s. two d.; ed. Sea Point Boys' High School, Cape Town and Royal Acad. of Dramatic Art; actor 1953–60; author 1960–; Artistic Dir. Cheltenham Festival of Literature 1975; presenter, Kaleidoscope, BBC Radio 1973, Read All About It, BBC TV 1978–79, All The World's A Stage, BBC TV; Chair. Writers' Guild of G.B. 1969; Visitor in theatre, Balliol Coll. Oxford 1986; Pres. PEN (England) 1989–93, Int. PEN 1993–97; Gov. Cen. School of Speech and Drama; Chevalier, Ordre Nat. des Arts et des Lettres; author of numerous TV plays and screenplays. *Plays include:* Country Matters 1969, The Good Companions (musical libretto) 1974, The Ordeal of Gilbert Pinfold 1977, A Family 1978, The Dresser, After the Lions 1982, Tramway Road 1984, The Deliberate Death of a Polish Priest 1985, Interpreters 1985, J.J. Farr 1987, Ivanov (from Chekhov) 1989, Another Time 1989, Reflected Glory 1992, Poison Pen 1994, Taking Sides 1995, The Handyman 1996, Equally Divided. *Publications include:* All the Same Shadows 1961, The Guilt Merchants 1963, The Girl in Melanie Klein 1969, Sir Donald Wolfit, CBE: His Life and Work in the Unfashionable Theatre (biography) 1971, Articles of Faith 1973, The Genoa Ferry 1976, César and Augusta 1978, Home 1993, The Faber Book of the Theatre (Ed.) 1994; vols. of essays and short stories. *Leisure interests:* cricket, tennis. *Address:* c/o Judy Daish Associates, 2 St. Charles Place, London, W10 6EG, England.

HASANI, Baqir Husain, B.SC., LL.B.; Iraqi/Italian diplomatist; b. 12 Feb. 1915, Baghdad; ed. Columbia Univ., New York and Law Coll. Baghdad Univ.; Dir. of Commerce and Registrar of Patents, Trade Marks and Companies, Ministry of Econs. Iraq 1947–51; Dir.-Gen. of Contracts and Econ. Research, Devt. Bd. 1951–54; Dir.-Gen. of Income Tax, Ministry of Finance 1954–55; Dir.-Gen. and Chair. Bd. of Dirs. Tobacco Monopoly Admin. 1955–59; Envoy Extraordinary and later Amb. to Austria 1959–63; Chair. Bd. of Govs. IAEA 1961–62; Special Adviser to Dir.-Gen. IAEA, Vienna 1963–66, 1970–76; Adviser to Saudi Arabian Mission in Vienna 1978–81; consultant on Middle

Eastern Affairs 1985–; mem. numerous govt. cttees. and del. to the UN and to int. confs., etc.; lecturer Coll. of Business Admin., Coll. of Pharmacy, Mil. Staff Coll.; Rafidain Decoration; Austrian Grand Golden Decoration. *Publications:* numerous articles in newspapers and magazines. *Leisure interests:* horse riding, swimming, collecting stamps and coins. *Address:* Via Civelli 9, 21100 Varese, Italy; 7 Ashenden Road, Guildford, Surrey, GU2 5UU, England. *Telephone:* (0332) 22 9633 (Italy); (01483) 838371 (England).

HASEEB, Khair El-Din, M.SC., PH.D.; Iraqi economist and statistician; b. 1 Aug. 1929; m. 1955; one s. two d.; ed. Univ. of Baghdad, London School of Econs. and Univ. of Cambridge; civil servant, Ministry of Interior 1947–54; Head of Research and Statistics Dept., Iraqi Oil Co. 1959–60; Full-time Lecturer, Univ. of Baghdad 1960–61, Part-time 1961–63; Dir.-Gen. Iraqi Fed. of Industries 1960–63; Pres. Gen. Org. for Banks 1964–65; Acting Pres. Econ. Org., Iraq 1964–65; Gov. and Chair. of Bd., Cen. Bank of Iraq 1963–65; Assoc. Prof., Dept. of Econs. Univ. of Baghdad 1965–71, Prof. of Econs. 1971–74; Chief, Programme and Co-ordination Unit, and Natural Resources, Science and Tech. Div. UN Econ. Comm. for Western Asia, then Lebanon and Iraq 1974–76 and 1976–83; Acting Dir.-Gen. Centre for Arab Unity Studies, Lebanon 1978–83, Dir.-Gen. 1983–; mem. Bd. of Dirs. Iraq Nat. Oil Co. 1967–68. *Publications:* The National Income of Iraq 1953–1961, 1964, Workers' Participation in Management in Arab Countries (in Arabic) 1971, Sources of Arab Economic Thought in Iraq 1900–71 (in Arabic) 1972, (Co-Ed.) Arab Monetary Integration 1982, (Ed.) Arabs and Africa 1985; numerous articles. *Address:* Centre for Arab Unity Studies, Sadat Tower Bldg., 9th Floor, Lyon Street, Hamra, P.O. Box 113-6001, Beirut, Lebanon. *Telephone:* (1) 801582. *Fax:* (1) 865548.

HASHIMOTO, Ryutaro; Japanese politician; b. 29 July 1937; s. of Ryogo Hashimto; m. Kumiko Hashimoto; two s. three d., ed. Keio Univ.; previous posts include: Chair. Cttee. on Social and Labour Problems, House of Reps.; Deputy Chair. Liberal Democratic Party (LDP) Policy Research Council; Chair. LDP Research Comm. on Public Admin. and Finances; Minister of Transport 1986–87, of Finance 1989–91, of Int. Trade and Industry 1994–96; Prime Minister of Japan 1996–98; Sec.-Gen. LDP July–Aug. 1989, Pres. 1995–98; Liberal Democratic Party. *Leisure interests:* Kendo (5th dan), mountaineering, photography. *Address:* c/o Liberal-Democratic Party, 1-11-23 Nagata-cho, Chiyoda-ku, Tokyo 100, Japan.

HASINA WAJED, Sheikh; Bangladeshi politician; b. 28 Sept. 1947, Tungipara, Gopalganj Dist., E. Pakistan (now Bangladesh); d. of late Sheikh Mujibur Rahman (fmr. Prime Minister of Bangladesh) and Begum Fazilatunnesa; m. M. A. Wazed Miah; one s. one d.; ed. Univ. of Dhaka; active in politics as a student; arrested during civil war 1971; assumed leadership of opposition Awami League (AL) from her father; lived in exile 1975–81; arrested and placed under house arrest on several occasions during 1980s; Prime Minister of Bangladesh June 1996–, also Minister of the Armed Forces Div., of the Cabinet Div., of Special Affairs, of Defence, of Power, Energy and Mineral Resources, and of the Establishment; shared Houphonet-Boigny Peace Prize 1999. *Publications:* several books and numerous articles. *Address:* Office of the Prime Minister, Dhaka, Bangladesh.

HASIOR, Władysław; Polish sculptor; b. 14 May 1928, Nowy Sącz; s. of Antoni and Waleria Hasior; m. Joanna Narkiewicz; one s.; ed. Acad. of Fine Arts, Warsaw; Teacher of sculpture, Coll. of Art Techniques, Zakopane 1957–70; scenographer State Dramatic Theatre, Wrocław 1964–70, Polish Theatre, Wrocław 1970–71; mem. Pres. Council for Culture 1992–; mem. Polish Fine Arts Assen. 1958–82, 1983–; numerous one-man exhbns. in Poland, Stockholm, Oslo, Paris, Brussels, Copenhagen, Helsinki, Venice, New York, São Paulo, Montevideo, Göteborg, Malmö, Vienna, Helsinki, London, Coventry, etc.; creator of many monuments commemorating victims of World War II; some works permanently in museums in Stockholm, Göteborg, Oslo, Amsterdam, Bochum, Rome, Milan and Duisburg; Władysław Hasior Gallery opened at The Tatra Museum, Zakopane 1995; prize of Ministry of Culture and Art 1971; Kt.'s Cross, Order of Polonia Restituta 1974. *Address:* ul. Jagiellońska 18B, "Borek", 34-500 Zakopane, Poland. *Telephone:* (018) 201 5191.

HASKELL, (Donald) Keith, C.M.G., C.V.O., M.A.; British diplomatist (retd.); b. 9 May 1939, Southsea; s. of Donald Eric Haskell and Beatrice Mary (neé Blair) Haskell; m. Maria Luisa Soeiro Tito de Morais; two s. two d.; ed. Portsmouth Grammar School, St. Catharine's Coll., Cambridge; joined FCO 1961, served in Baghdad 1962–66, Libya 1969–72; Chargé d'Affaires, Consul-Gen. Santiago, Chile 1975–78; Consul-Gen. Dubai, U.A.E. 1978–81; Head Nuclear Energy Dept. FCO 1981–83, Head Middle East Dept. 1983–84, on secondment to Industry 1988–89; Counsellor Bonn, Fed. Repub. of Germany 1985–88; Amb. to Peru 1990–95, to Brazil 1995–99; Grand Cross, Order of Rio Branco (Brazil). *Leisure interests:* rifle and pistol shooting, skiing, squash, tennis, wine and food. *Address:* Barn Cottage, Brightstone Lane, Farringdon, Alton, Hants., GU34 3DP, England. *Telephone:* (01420) 588485. *Fax:* (01420) 588485.

HASKELL, Francis, M.A., F.B.A.; British professor of history of art; b. 7 April 1928, London; s. of the late Arnold Haskell and Vera Haskell (née Saitzoff); m. Larissa Salmina 1965; ed. Eton Coll. and King's Coll. Cambridge; Jr. Library Clerk, House of Commons 1953–54; Fellow of King's Coll. Cambridge 1954–67; Librarian of Fine Arts Faculty, Cambridge Univ. 1962–67; Prof. of History of Art and Fellow, Trinity Coll., Oxford Univ. 1967–95, Prof. Emer. 1995; Foreign mem. American Philosophical Soc.; Foreign Hon. mem. American Acad. of Arts and Sciences; Corresp. mem. Accad. Pontaniana, Naples, Ateneo Veneto; Hon. mem. Academia Clementina of Bologna; Dr. h.c. Free Univ. of Berlin 1993; Hon. D.Litt. (Southampton Inst.) 1998; Mitchell Prize 1977, Serena Medal 1985, Prix Vasari; Officier Ordre des Arts et des Lettres 1990. *Publications:* Patrons and Painters 1963, Rediscoveries in Art 1976, L'Arte e il Linguaggio della Politica 1977, Taste and the Antique (with Nicholas Penny) 1981, Past and Present in Art and Taste 1987, The Painful Birth of the Art Book 1988, History and its Images: Art and the Representation of the Past 1993. *Leisure interest:* foreign travel. *Address:* Trinity College, Oxford, OX1 3BH, England.

HASKINS, Caryl Parker, PH.D.; American scientist; b. 12 Aug. 1908, Schenectady, N.Y.; s. of Caryl Davis and Frances Julia Parker; m. Edna Ferrell 1940; ed. Yale and Harvard Univs.; mem. of research staff Gen. Electric Co., Schenectady 1931–35; Research Assoc. M.I.T. 1935–44; Pres. and Research Dir. Haskins Laboratories, Inc. 1935–55, Dir. 1935–, Chair. 1969–; Research Prof. in Biophysics, Union Coll., Schenectady 1937–55; Liaison Officer 1940–43, Exec. Asst. to the Chair. 1943–44 and Deputy Exec. Officer 1944–45, Nat. Defence Research Cttee.; Scientific Adviser to the Policy Council 1947 and to the Research and Devt. Bd. of the Nat. Mil. Establishment 1948–51; Chair. Advisory Cttee. to the Sec. of Defense on special weapons 1948–49; Consultant to the Sec. of Defense 1948–60, to the Sec. of State 1950–60; mem. President's Science Advisory Cttee. 1955–58, Consultant 1959–70; Pres. Carnegie Inst. of Washington, D.C. 1956–71, Trustee 1949–; Dir. E. I. Du Pont de Nemours & Co. 1971–84; mem. sec. Navy Advisory Cttee. on Naval History 1971–84, Vice-Chair. 1975–84; Dir. Center for Advanced Study in Behavioural Sciences 1960–75, Thomas Jefferson Memorial Foundation 1972–79, Wildlife Preservation Trust Int. Inc. 1976–; Trustee Carnegie Corpn. of New York 1955–80, Hon. Trustee 1980–; Regent Smithsonian Inst. 1956–80, Regent Emer. 1980–; Trustee Rand Corpn. 1955–65, 1966–75 (Advisory Trustee 1988–), Council of Foreign Relations 1961–75, (Emer. Trustee 1975–), Woods Hole Oceanographic Inst. 1964–73 (mem. Council 1973–), Nat. Geographic Soc. 1964–84, American Museum of Natural History 1973–89 (mem. Bd. of Man. 1973–89), Nat. Humanities Center 1977–, Council on Library Resources 1965–; Successor Trustee Yale Univ. 1962–77; Fellow A.A.A.S., American Philosophical Soc. (mem. Council, Library Council); mem. R.S.A. (G.B.), N.A.S., New York Acad. of Sciences; Presidential Certificate of Merit and King's Medal for Service in the Cause of Freedom, Joseph Henry Medal, Smithsonian Inst., Centenary Medal (Harvard Univ.) 1992. *Publications:* Of Ants and Men 1939, The Amazon, The Life History of a Mighty River 1943, Of Societies and Men 1951, Scientific Revolution and World Politics 1964, The Search for Understanding 1967. *Leisure interests:* gardening. *Address:* Greenacres, 22 Green Acre Lane, Westport, CT 06880, U.S.A. (Home). *Telephone:* (203) 227 2428 (Home).

HASKINS, Sam (Samuel Joseph); British, South African; photographer and designer; b. 11 Nov. 1926, Kroonstad, s. of Benjamin G. Haskins and Anna E. Oelofse; m. Alida Elzabé van Heerden 1952; two s.; ed. Helpmekaar School and Witwatersrand Technical Coll., Johannesburg, Bolt Court School of Photography, London; freelance work, Johannesburg 1953–68, London 1968–; one-man exhbns. in Johannesburg 1953, 1960, Tokyo 1970, 1973, 1976, 1979, 1981, 1985, 1990, 1992, 1993, 1996, London 1972, 1976, 1978, 1980, 1997, Paris 1973, 1981, Amsterdam 1974, 1981, Geneva 1981, Zurich 1981, New York 1981, San Francisco 1982, Toronto 1982, 1986, Bologna 1984, Cologne 1990, Osaka 1990, 1992, 1993, 1997, Auckland 1991, Sydney 1991, Hong Kong 1991, Taipei 1991, Singapore 1991, Palermo 1993, Prague 1993, Glasgow 1997; Prix Nadar (France) for Cowboy Kate and Other Stories 1964, Israel Museum Award, Int. Art Book Contest Award, Gold Medal Award for Haskins Posters, New York 1974, Kodak Book Prize 1980 (for Photo Graphics). *Publications:* Five Girls 1962, Cowboy Kate and Other Stories 1964, African Image 1966, November Girl 1967, Haskins Posters 1972, Photo Graphics 1980, Sam Haskins à Bologna 1984, and portfolios in most major international photographic magazines. *Leisure interests:* vintage car rallying, books, music, horticulture. *Address:* 9A Calonne Road, London, SW19 5HH; P.O. Box 59, Wimbledon, London, S.W.19, England. *Telephone:* 0181-946 9660.

HASLAM, Baron (Life Peer) cr. 1990, of Bolton in the County of Greater Manchester, **Robert Haslam,** B.SC., F.I.M.E.; British business executive; b. 4 Feb. 1923, Bolton, Lancs. (now Greater Manchester); s. of Percy Haslam and Mary Haslam; m. 1st Joyce Quin 1947 (died 1995); two s.; m. 2nd Hon. Mrs. Elizabeth Sieff 1996; ed. Bolton School and Univ. of Birmingham; joined ICI Nobel Div. 1947, Personnel Dir. Nobel Div. 1960–63, Commercial Dir. ICI Plastics Div. 1963–66, Deputy Chair. Plastics Div. 1966–69, Deputy Chair. ICI Fibres Div. 1969–71, Chair. Fibres Div. 1971, Dir. ICI Ltd. 1974, Deputy Chair. 1980–83; Chair. Tate & Lyle 1983–86, British Steel Corpn. 1983–86, Wasserstein Perella & Co. Ltd. 1991–, Bechtel Ltd. 1991–94; mem. British Overseas Trade Bd. 1981–85; mem. Bd. Cable and Wireless 1982–83; mem. Nationalized Industries Chairmen's Group 1983–90, Chair. 1985–86; mem. NEDC 1985–89; Dir. Bank of England 1984–93; fmr. Non-Exec. Deputy Chair. British Coal 1985, Chair. 1986–90; Advisory Dir. Unilever PLC 1986–93; Chair. Manchester Business School 1985–90, Govs. of Bolton School 1990–97, British Occupational Health Research Foundation; mem. Council Royal Holloway and Bedford New Coll. 1992–96, London; Hon. D.Tech. (Brunel) 1987; Hon. D. Eng. (Birmingham) 1987. *Leisure interests:* golf, travel. *Address:* House of Lords, London, SW1A 0PW, England. *Telephone:* 0171-219 3000.

HASQUIN, Hervé; Belgian politician and professor of history; b. 31 Dec. 1942, Charleroi; s. of René-Pierre Hasquin and Andrée Jacquemart; m. Michèle Nahum 1986; one s.; Dean Faculty of Arts and Philosophy, Université Libre de Bruxelles 1979–82, Rector 1982–86, Chair. Bd. of Dirs. 1986–, Pres. Inst. for Religious and Secular Studies 1987–; Head French-speaking network Scientific Information and Technological Devt. 1986–87; Vice-Pres. Parti Réformateur Libéral (PRL) 1986–89, Gen. Sec. 1990–92, Head PRL Group, Council of Brussels, Capital Region 1991–; Senator 1988–; Regional Councillor, Brussels 1989–; Royal Acad. of Belgium Prize, Literary Prize of French-speaking Community Council 1981 and other prizes; Chevalier, Légion d'honneur. *Publications:* La Wallonie: Le Pays et les Hommes, Histoire de la Laïcité principalement en Belgique et en France; about 70 articles and papers in Belgian and foreign learned journals. *Address:* Université Libre de Bruxelles, Ave. F. Roosevelt 50, 1050 Brussels (Office); Ave du Prince Héritier 105, 1200 Brussels, Belgium (Home). *Telephone:* (2) 650-2315 (Office); (2) 736-6249 (Home). *Fax:* (2) 650-3594 (Office).

HASSAN II, King of Morocco; 17th Sovereign of the Alaouite Dynasty; b. 9 July 1929; ed. Bordeaux Univ.; son of Mohammed V; invested as Crown Prince Moulay Hassan 1957; C.-in-C. and Chief of Staff of Royal Moroccan Army 1957; Minister of Defence 1960–61; Vice-Premier 1960–61; succeeded to throne on death of his father, 26 Feb. 1961; Prime Minister 1961–63, 1965–67; Minister of Defence 1972–73, Commdr.-in-Chief of the Army 1972; Chair. OAU Assembly of Heads of State 1972, Al Quods Cttee. of Islamic Conf. *Publication:* The Challenge (memoirs) 1979, Le Mémoire d'un Roi 1993. *Address:* Royal Palace, Rabat, Morocco.

HASSAN IBN TALAL, H.R.H. G.C.V.O., M.A.; fmr. Crown Prince of Jordan; b. 20 March 1947, Amman; m. Sarrath Khujista Akhter Banu 1968; one s. three d.; ed. Harrow School, England, Christ Church, Oxford Univ.; brother of the late Hussein ibn Talal, King of Jordan, and heir to the throne until announcement by the late King Hussein Jan. 1999; fmrly. acted as Regent during absence of King Hussein; Ombudsman for Nat. Devt. 1971–; Founder of Royal Scientific Soc. of Jordan 1970, Royal Acad. for Islamic Civilization Research (Al AlBait) 1980, Arab Thought Forum 1981, Forum Humanum (now Arab Youth Forum) 1982; Co-Chair. Independent Comm. on Int. Humanitarian Issues; Co-Patron Islamic Acad. of Sciences; Pres. Higher Council for Science and Tech.; Hon. Gen. of Jordan Armed Forces; Hon. Ph.D. (Econ.) (Yarmouk) 1980; Hon. D.Sc. (Bogazici, Turkey) 1982; Hon. Dr. Arts and Sciences (Jordan) 1987; Hon. D.C.L. (Durham) 1990; Dr. h.c. (Ulster) 1996; Medal of Pres. of Italian Repub. 1982; Kt. of Grand Cross of Order of Merit (Italy) 1983. *Publications:* A Study on Jerusalem 1979, Palestinian Self-Determination 1981, Search for Peace 1984. *Leisure interests:* polo, squash, scuba diving, mountaineering, archaeology, Karate, Taekwondo, helicopter piloting, skiing. *Address:* The Royal Palace, Amman, Jordan.

HASSAN, Jean-Claude Gaston; French banker and public servant; b. 11 Nov. 1954, Tunis, Tunisia; s. of Charles Hassan and Yvonne Lellouche; m. Françoise Benhamou 1981; two s. one d.; ed. Lycée de Mutuelleville, Tunis, Lycée Louis-le-Grand, Paris, Ecole normale supérieure, Ecole nat. d'admin.; mem. Conseil d'Etat, Auditeur 1981, Counsel 1985; Tech. Adviser to Office of Minister of Social Affairs and Nat. Solidarity 1984–85; Deputy Dir.-Gen. Banque Stern 1986–89, Dir.-Gen. 1989–92; Dir-Gen. Banque Worms 1992–94; rejoined Conseil d'Etat 1994. *Address:* Conseil d'Etat, Palais-Royal, 75100 Paris RP, France.

HASSAN SHARQ, Mohammad; Afghanistan politician; b. 1925, Farah, Afghanistan; Deputy Prime Minister, 1974–77; Prime Minister of Afghanistan 1988–89. *Address:* c/o Office of the Prime Minister, Kabul, Afghanistan.

HASSANALI, Noor Mohamed; Trinidad and Tobago fmr. Head of State and fmr. judge; b. 13 Aug. 1918; m. Zalayhar Mohammed 1952; one s. one d.; ed. Naparima Coll. San Fernando and Univ. of Toronto; called to Bar, Gray's Inn, London 1948; pvt. practice as barrister-at-law in Trinidad and Tobago 1948–53; magistrate, Vic. Tobago 1953–60; sr. magistrate, Trinidad and Tobago 1960; Sr. Crown Counsel, Attorney-Gen.'s Chambers 1960; Asst. Solicitor-Gen. 1965; Judge, High Court 1966; Justice of Appeal, Supreme Court of Trinidad and Tobago 1978; retd. 1985; mem. Judicial and Legal Service Comm. 1985–, Trinidad and Tobago Defence Force Comms. Bd. 1985–; Pres. of Trinidad and Tobago 1987–97. *Address:* c/o President's House, St. Ann's, Trinidad and Tobago.

HASSANOV, Hassan Azizoglou; Azerbaijani politician; b. 20 Oct. 1940, Tbilisi; s. of Aziz Hassanov and Ruhsara Adjalova; m. 1964; one s. one d.; ed. Azerbaijan Polytech. Inst., Higher Party School; mem. CPSU 1962–91; various posts in youth, political, and public admin. orgs. of Azerbaijan and U.S.S.R. 1962–75; First Sec. Azerbaijani CP Dist. Cttee. of a cen. dist. of Baku, then City Cttees. of Sumgait and Gandja 1975–81; subsequently held sr. posts with responsibility for politics, culture, construction and transport, and economy; mem. Azerbaijani Supreme Soviet (now Milli Mejlis) 1977–96; People's Deputy of U.S.S.R. 1979–84; elected to first session of Milli Mejlis 1996; the first Prime Minister of Azerbaijan Repub. 1990–92; the first Amb. Extraordinary and Plenipotentiary of Azerbaijan Repub. 1992–; Perm. Rep. of Azerbaijan to UN, to CSCE Council of Ministers, Gen. Session of UNESCO, elected Deputy Chair. Preparatory Cttee. of 2nd World Conf. on Human Settlements (Habitat) 1992–93; Minister of Foreign Affairs 1993–98; mem. Constitutional Comm. *Publications:* more than 100 articles on Azerbaijani economy, policies, diplomacy and history. *Leisure interests:* art, music, history. *Address:* Gendjler Meydani 3, Baku, Azerbaijan. *Telephone:* 925606; 926856. *Fax:* 651038; 988480.

HASSELFELDT, Gerda; German politician; b. 7 July 1950, Straubing, Lower Bavaria; m. Volker Hasselfeldt 1974; one s. one d.; worked at Fed. Inst. of Labour, Nuremberg 1975–77; Head Section for Training Placement, Job Centre, Munich 1977–78; Careers Adviser to Abiturienten and Undergraduates, Deggendorf Job Centre 1978–85, Head, Careers Advice Dept. 1985–87; joined Junge Union 1968, Chair. Haibach asscn. 1968–74, mem. various exec. cttees. 1968–85; Dist. Chair. Women's Union 1975–; mem. Regen Dist. Council (Kreistag) 1978–; CSU Dist. Chair. Regen 1987–; mem. Deutscher Bundestag 1987–; Fed. Minister for Regional Planning, Bldg. and Urban Devt. 1989–91, of Health 1991–92. *Address:* Koblenzerstrasse 112, 5300 Bonn 2, Germany.

HASSELL, Michael Patrick, M.A., PH.D., F.R.S.; British professor of insect ecology; b. 2 Aug. 1942, Tel Aviv; s. of Albert Hassell and Ruth Hassell; m. 1st Glynis M. Everett 1966; m. 2nd Victoria A. Taylor 1982; three s. one d.; ed. Whitgift School, Croydon, Clare Coll., Cambridge and Oriel Coll., Oxford; Visiting Lecturer, Univ. of Calif., Berkeley 1967–68; NERC Research Fellowship, Hope Dept. of Entomology, Oxford 1968–70; Lecturer, Dept. of Zoology and Applied Entomology, Imperial Coll., London 1970–75, Reader 1975–79, Prof. of Insect Ecology, Dept. of Biology 1979–, Deputy Head, Dept. of Biology 1984–92, Head 1993–, Dir. Imperial Coll., Silwood Park 1988–; Storer Life Sciences Lecturer, Univ. of Calif., Davis 1985; Pres. British Ecological Soc. 1998–99; Fellow Acad. Europea 1998; Scientific Medal (Zoological Soc.) 1981, Gold Medal (British Ecological Soc.) 1994, Weldon Prize (Univ. of Oxford) 1995. *Publications:* Insect Population Ecology (with G. C. Varley and G. R. Gradwell) 1973, The Dynamics of Competition and Predation 1975, The Dynamics of Arthropod Predator-Prey Systems 1978; numerous publs. on population ecology. *Leisure interests:* walking, croquet. *Address:* Silwood Lodge, Silwood Park, Ascot, Berks., SL5 7PZ, England. *Telephone:* (01344) 294207. *Fax:* (01344) 874957.

HASSELMO, Nils, PH.D.; American university president; b. 2 July 1931, Köla, Sweden; s. of Wilner Hasselmo and Anna Backlund; m. Patricia Tillberg 1958; two s. one d.; ed. Uppsala Univ., Augustana Coll. Rock Island, Ill. and Harvard Univ.; Asst. Prof. of Swedish, Augustana Coll. 1958–59, 1961–63; Visiting Asst. Prof. in Scandinavian Studies, Univ. of Wis. 1964–65; Assoc. Prof. of Scandinavian Lang. and Literature, Univ. of Minn. 1965–70, Dir. Center for N.W. European Lang. and Area Studies 1970–73, Prof. of Scandinavian Language and Literature 1970–73, Assoc. Dean and Exec. Officer, Coll. of Liberal Arts 1973–78, Vice-Pres. for Admin. and Planning 1980–83; Prof. of English and Linguistics and Sr. Vice-Pres. for Academic Affairs and Provost, Univ. of Ariz. 1983–88; Pres. Univ. of Minn. 1988–97, Asscn. of American Univs. 1998–; mem. numerous professional orgs. etc.; Dr. h.c. (Uppsala) 1979, (North Park Univ., Chicago) 1992, (Augustana Coll., Ill.) 1995; recipient of many honours and awards including Royal Order of North Star (Sweden), King Carl XVI Gustaf Bicentennial Gold Medal. *Publications:* books and articles and reviews in learned journals. *Leisure interests:* reading, music, hiking, tennis, golf. *Address:* AAU, 1200 New York Ave., N.W., Suite 550, Washington, DC 20005, U.S.A. (Office). *Telephone:* (202) 408 7500. *Fax:* (202) 408 8184.

HASSON, Maurice; French/Venezuelan violinist; b. 6 July 1934, Berck-Plage; m. Jane Hoogesteijn, 1969; one s. three d.; ed. Conservatoire National Supérieure de Musique, Paris, further studies with Henryk Szeryng (q.v.); Prof. Royal Acad. of Music, London; concert artist in major concert halls throughout world, also in TV and radio performances; Hon. mem. Royal Acad. of Music, London: First Prize Violin, Prix d'honneur, and First Prize Chamber Music, Conservatoire National Supérieure de Musique, Paris 1950, Int. Prize Long Thibaut 1951, Int. Prize Youth Festival, Warsaw 1955, Grand Prix Music de Chambre 1957. *Recordings include:* Concerto No. 1 (Paganini), Concerto No. 2 (Prokofiev), Debussy Sonatas, Fauré Sonatas, Concerto No. 1, Scottish Fantasy (Bruch), Concerto for 2 and 4 violins (Vivaldi), Double Concerto (Bach), Concerto (Brahms), Brilliant Showpieces for the Violin, Tzigane (Ravel), Rondo Capriccioso (Saint Saëns), Poème (Chausson), Gypsy Airs (Sarasate), Violin Concerto (Castellanos-Yumar), Sonata (Franck), virtuoso pieces. *Leisure interests:* painting, sport, cars. *Address:* c/o Manygate Management, 13 Cotswold Mews, 30 Battersea Square, London, SW11 3RA; 18 West Heath Court, North End Road, London, NW11 7RE, England (Home). *Telephone:* 0171-223 7265 (Agent); 0181-458 3647 (Home). *Fax:* 0171-585 2830 (Agent); 0181-458 3647 (Home).

HASTERT, (J.) Dennis, B.A., M.S.; American politician; b. 2 Jan. 1942, Aurora, Ill.; m. Jean Kahl 1973; two s.; ed. Wheaton Coll., Ill., Northern Illinois Univ.; fmr. teacher Yorkville High School, Ill., also wrestling coach; mem. Ill. House of Reps., Springfield 1980–86; mem. 100th–105th Congresses from 14th Dist. Ill. 1987–, mem. Commerce Comm., Govt. Reform and Oversight Comm.; Speaker of House of Reps. 1999–; Republican. *Address:* United States House of Representatives, 2241 Rayburn House Office Building, Washington, DC 20515, U.S.A.

HASTINGS, Rev. Adrian Christopher, M.A., TH.D., D.D.; British Catholic priest and university professor; b. 23 June 1929, Kuala Lumpur, Malaysia; s. of William George Warren Hastings and Hazel Mary Hastings (née

Daunais); m. Elizabeth Ann Spence 1979; ed. Douai Abbey School, Worcester Coll., Oxford, Coll. of Propaganda Fide, Rome, Christ's Coll., Cambridge; ordained Catholic priest 1955; pastoral and educational work, Uganda 1958–66, Tanzania and Zambia 1966–70; Consultant to Anglican archbishops in Africa on marriage problems 1971–72; Research Officer, S.O.A.S., London 1973–76; Lecturer in Religious Studies, Univ. of Aberdeen, Scotland 1976–80, Reader 1980–82; Prof. of Religious Studies, Univ. of Zimbabwe, Harare 1982–85; Prof. of Theology, Univ. of Leeds 1985–94; Ed. Journal of Religion in Africa 1985–. *Publications:* Prophet and Witness in Jerusalem 1958, One and Apostolic 1963, Church and Mission in Modern Africa 1967, A Concise Guide to the Documents of the Second Vatican Council (2 vols.) 1968, Christian Marriage in Africa 1973, Wiriyamu 1974, The Faces of God 1975, In Filial Disobedience 1978, A History of African Christianity 1950–1975 1979, In the Hurricane 1986, A History of English Christianity 1920–1985 1986, African Catholicism 1989, The Theology of a Protestant Catholic 1990, Robert Runcie 1991, Church and State, the English Experience 1991, Ed. Modern Catholicism 1991, SOS Bosnia 1992, The Church in Africa, 1450–1950 1994, The Shaping of Prophecy: Passion, Perception and Practicality 1995, Elias of Dereham 1997, The Construction of Nationhood: Ethnicity, Religion and Nationalism 1997, (Ed.) A World History of Christianity 1998. *Leisure interests:* walking, visiting ancient buildings, cutting hedges on the Malvern Hills. *Address:* Department of Theology and Religious Studies, The University, Leeds, LS2 9JT (Office); 3 Hollin Hill House, 219 Oakwood Lane, Leeds, LS8 2PE, England (Home). *Telephone:* (0113) 233 3640 (Office); (0113) 240 0154 (Home).

HASTINGS, Max Macdonald, F.R.S.L.; British journalist; b. 28 Dec. 1945, London; s. of Macdonald Hastings and Anne Scott-James (Lady Lancaster); m. Patricia Edmondson 1972 (divorced 1994); two s. one d.; ed. Charterhouse and Univ. Coll., Oxford; reporter, London Evening Standard 1965–67, 1968–70; Fellow, U.S. World Press Inst. 1967–68; reporter, current affairs, BBC Television 1970–73; freelance journalist, broadcaster and author 1973–; columnist, Evening Standard 1979–85, Daily Express 1981–83, Sunday Times 1985–86; Ed., Daily Telegraph 1986–96, Dir. 1989–96, Ed.-in-Chief 1990–96; Ed. Evening Standard 1996–; Dir. Associated Newspapers PLC 1996–; Evening Standard Ltd. 1996–; mem. Press Complaints Comm. 1990–92; Trustee Nat. Portrait Gallery 1995–; Journalist of the Year 1982; Reporter of the Year 1982; Somerset Maugham Prize for Non-fiction 1979; Ed. of the Year 1988; Hon. D.Litt. (Leicester) 1992. *Publications:* America 1968: The Fire, The Time 1968, Ulster 1969 1970, Montrose: The King's Champion 1977, Yoni: Hero of Entebbe 1979, Bomber Command 1979, Das Reich 1981, Battle for the Falklands (with Simon Jenkins) 1983, Overlord 1984, Victory in Europe 1985, The Oxford Book of Military Anecdotes (Ed.) 1985, The Korean War 1987, Outside Days 1989. *Leisure interests:* shooting, fishing. *Address:* Northcliffe House, 2 Derry Street, Kensington, London, W8 5EE, England. *Telephone:* 0171-538 5000.

HATA, Tsutomu; Japanese politician; b. 24 Aug 1935, Tokyo; ed. Seijo Univ.; fmr. bus tour operator; elected to House of Reps. 1969; fmr. Parl. Vice-Minister of Posts and Telecommunications, Agric., Forestry and Fisheries; fmr. Minister of Agric., Forestry and Fisheries; Chair. Liberal-Democratic Party (LDP) Research Comm. on the Election System; Minister of Finance 1991–92; left LDP to f. Shinseito (New Life Party) Pres. 1993–94, Shinseito dissolved 1994 (merged with eight others to form New Frontier Party); leader Good Governance Party 1998–; Deputy Prime Minister and Minister of Foreign Affairs 1993–94; Prime Minister of Japan May–June 1994. *Address:* House of Representatives, Tokyo, Japan.

HATANAKA, Masakazu, M.D., PH.D.; Japanese virologist; b. 23 March 1933; s. of Kazuo Hatanaka and Yasue Sakai; m. Kazuko Fujimoto 1963; two s.; with Salk Inst., San Diego 1964–65, Nat. Insts. of Health, Bethesda, Md. 1965–97, Flow Labs., Rockville, Md. 1967–70; Expert, Section Head Nat. Cancer Inst., Bethesda 1971–75; Prof., Kyoto Univ. 1975–80; Dir. Inst. for Virus Research 1980–91, Shionogi Inst. of Medical Science 1991–; Fogarty Scholar-in-Residence, Nat. Insts. of Health 1995–; Exec. Vice-Pres. Shionogi & Co. Ltd. 1997–. *Address:* 5-13-3-1405 Nakano-cho, Miyakojima-ku, Osaka 534, Japan.

HATANO, Yoshio, B.A.; Japanese diplomatist; b. 3 Jan. 1932, Tokyo; s. of Keizo Hatano and Tatsuko Hatano; m. Sumiko Shimazu 1961; one s. one d.; ed. Tokyo Univ., Princeton Univ., U.S.A.; joined Foreign Ministry 1953, held various positions including Dir. Econ. Affairs, Asian Affairs and Treaties Bureaux, Personnel Div., Gen. Co-ordination Div.; First Sec., Embassy, London 1970; Counsellor, Embassy, Jakarta 1971; Minister, Embassy, Washington, D.C. 1979, Envoy Extraordinary and Minister Plenipotentiary 1981; Dir.-Gen. Middle Eastern and African Affairs Bureau, Dir.-Gen. for Public Information and Cultural Affairs, Ministry of Foreign Affairs 1982–87; Perm. Rep. to int. orgs. in Geneva 1987–90; Perm. Rep. to UN, New York 1990–94; Pres. Foreign Press Center 1994. *Leisure interests:* golf, opera. *Address:* 2-14-13 Hiroo, Shibuya-ku, Tokyo, Japan. *Telephone:* 03-3407-0463. *Fax:* 03-3501-3622.

HATCH, Henry Clifford, Jr.; Canadian business executive; b. 30 April 1916, Toronto, Ont.; s. of Harry C. Hatch and Elizabeth Carr; m. Joan Ferriss 1940; two s. two d.; ed. St. Michael's College School, Toronto; Salesman, T. G. Bright & Co., Ltd., Niagara Falls 1933–37; Merchandising Staff Hiram Walker Inc., Walkerville, Ont. 1937, Dir. 1938; Dir. Hiram Walker-Gooderham & Worts Ltd. 1946, Vice-Pres. 1955, Exec. Vice-Pres. 1961, Pres. 1964–78, Chair. and Chief Exec. Officer 1978–81; Chair. and Dir. Hiram Walker Resources Ltd. 1980–87, C.E.O. 1986–87; Dir. T. G. Bright & Co. Ltd., The Toronto-Dominion Bank, Bell Canada, London Life Insurance Co. Ltd., R. Angus Alberta Ltd. *Leisure interests:* sailing, curling, swimming, reading, golf. *Address:* 70 Rosehill Avenue, Suite 807, Toronto, Ont., M4T ZW7, Canada.

HATCH, Marshall Davidson, A.M., PH.D., F.A.A., F.R.S.; Australian research scientist; b. 24 Dec. 1932, Perth; s. of Lloyd D. Hatch and Alice Dalziel; m. 2nd Lyndall Langman 1983; two s.; ed. Newington Coll., Sydney, Sydney Univ. and Univ. of Calif.; research scientist, CSIRO 1955–59; post-doctoral fellow, Univ. of Calif. 1959–61; research scientist, Colonial Sugar Refining Co., Ltd. 1961–70; Chief Research Scientist, Div. of Plant Industry, CSIRO, Canberra 1970–, Foreign Assoc. N.A.S. 1990; Dr. h.c. (Göttingen) 1992; Clark Medal (Royal Soc. of N.S.W.) 1973, Lemberg Medal (Australian Biochem. Soc.) 1974, Charles Kettering Award for Photosynthesis (American Soc. of Plant Physiologists) 1980, Rank Award (Rank Foundation) 1981, Int. Prize for Biology (Japan Soc. for Promotion of Science) 1991. *Publications:* over 150 review articles, chapters in books and research papers. *Address:* Division of Plant Industry, CSIRO, P.O. Box 1600, Canberra (Office); 34 Dugdale Street, Cook, A.C.T. 2614, Australia (Home). *Telephone:* 062-465264 (Office); 062-515159 (Home).

HATCH, Orrin Grant, B.S., J.D.; American politician and lawyer; b. 22 March 1934, Homestead Park Pa.; s. of Jesse Hatch and Helen Kamm Hatch; m. Elaine Hansen 1957; three s. three d.; ed. Brigham Young Univ., Univ. of Pittsburgh; journeyman metal lather; Partner, Thomson, Rhodes & Grigsby 1962–69; Senior Vice-Pres. and Gen. Counsel, American Minerals Man. and American Minerals Fund Inc., Salt Lake City, Utah 1969–71; Partner, Hatch & Plumb, Salt Lake City 1976; Senator from Utah Jan. 1977–; Chair. Senate Labor and Human Resources Cttee. 1981, Senate Judiciary Cttee. 1995–, Jt. Cttee. on Taxation, Cttee. on Indian Affairs, Sub Cttee. on Taxation; mem. Senate Cttee. on Finance, Senate Cttee. on Intelligence; Dir. Holocaust Memorial Museum; Republican. *Publications:* ERA Myths and Realities 1983, Good Faith under the Uniform Commercial Code, articles in legal journals. *Address:* U.S. Senate, 135 Russell Senate Building, Washington, DC 20510, U.S.A.

HATFIELD, Mark O.; American politician; b. 12 July 1922, Dallas, Oregon; s. of Mr. and Mrs C. D. Hatfield; m. Antoinette Kuzmanich 1958; two s. two d.; ed. Willamette Univ. and Stanford Univ.; U.S. Navy Second World War; Instructor, Asst. Prof., Assoc. Prof. in Political Science, Willamette Univ. 1949–56, Dean of Students 1950–56; State Rep., Marion County 1951–55, State Senator, Marion County 1955–57; Sec. of State, Oregon 1957–59; Gov. of Oregon 1959–67; U.S. Senator from Oregon 1967–97; Chair. Senate Appropriations Cttee. 1981–97; fmr. mem. Energy and Natural Resources Cttee., and Senate Rules and Admin. Cttee.; numerous awards; Republican. *Publications:* Not Quite So Simple (autobiography), Conflict and Conscience (religious speeches), Between a Rock and a Hard Place 1976, The Causes of World Hunger (co-author) 1982, What About the Russians? 1984 (jtly.). *Leisure interests:* gardening, reading. *Address:* 4380 S.W. Macadam, Suite 460, P.O. Box 8639, Portland, OR 97201 (Office); 6036 S.W. Riverpoint Lane, Portland, OR 97201, U.S.A. (Home).

HATOYAMA, Kunio; Japanese politician; mem. House of Reps.; fmr. Parl. Vice-Minister for Educ., Dir. Liberal-Democratic Party (LDP) Educ. Div., Chair. Cttee. on Educ. House of Reps.; Minister of Educ. 1991–92, of Labour May–June 1994; mem. Renaissance Party 1993. *Address:* c/o Ministry of Education, 3-2 Kasumigaseki, Chiyoda-ku, Tokyo, Japan.

HATTERSLEY, Baron (Life Peer) cr. 1997, of Sparkbrook in the County of West Midlands; **Roy Sydney George Hattersley,** P.C., B.SC.(ECON.), M.P.; British politician; b. 28 Dec. 1932; s. of Frederick Roy and Enid Hattersley (née Brackenbury); m. Molly Loughran 1956; ed. Sheffield City Grammar School, Univ. of Hull; Journalist and Health Service exec. 1956–64; mem. Sheffield City Council 1957–65; M.P. for Sparkbrook Div. of Birmingham 1964–97; Parl. Private Sec. to Minister of Pensions and Nat. Insurance 1964–67; Dir. Campaign for European Political Community 1965; Joint Parl. Sec. Dept. of Employment and Productivity 1967–69; Minister of Defence for Admin. 1969–70; Opposition Spokesman for Defence 1970–72, Education 1972–74, for the Environment 1979–80, for Home Affairs 1980–83, on Treasury and Econ. Affairs 1983–87, on Home Affairs 1987–92; Deputy Leader of the Labour Party 1983–92; Minister of State for Foreign and Commonwealth Affairs 1974–76; Sec. of State for Prices and Consumer Protection 1976–79; Public Affairs Consultant IBM 1971, 1972; Columnist Punch, The Guardian, The Listener 1979–82; Visiting Fellow, Inst. of Politics, Univ. of Harvard 1971, 1972, Nuffield Coll., Oxford 1984–; Hon. LL.D. (Hull) 1985; Dr. h.c. (Aston) 1997; Labour. *Publications:* Nelson—A Biography 1974, Goodbye to Yorkshire—A Collection of Essays 1976, Politics Apart—A Collection of Essays 1982, Press Gang 1983, A Yorkshire Boyhood 1983, Choose Freedom: The Future for Democratic Socialism 1987, Economic Priorities for a Labour Government 1987, The Maker's Mark (novel) 1990, In That Quiet Earth 1991, Skylark's Song 1994, Between Ourselves 1994, Who Goes Home? 1995, Fifty Years On 1997, Buster's Diaries: As Told to Roy Hattersley 1998. *Address:* House of Lords, Westminster, London, SW1A 0PW, England.

HATTON, Stephen Paul, B. COMM.; Australian politician; b. 28 Jan. 1948, Sydney; s. of Stanley J. and Pauline (née Taylor) Hatton; m. 1st Deborah J.

Humphreys 1969 (divorced 1993), three s. one d.; m. 2nd Cathy Huyer 1995, one d.; ed. Univ. of New South Wales; Personnel Officer, James Hardie & Co. Pty. Ltd. 1965–70; Industrial Officer Nabalco Pty. Ltd. 1970–75; Exec. Dir. N.T. Confed. of Industries and Commerce Inc. 1975–83; elected N.T. Legislative Ass. (Nightcliff) 1983–, Minister for Lands, Conservation, Ports and Fisheries, Primary Production 1983–84, for Mines and Energy, Primary Production 1986, for Health and Community Services 1989, for Conservation 1989, for Industries and Devt. and for Trade Devt. Zone and Liquor Comm. 1990–91, for Lands, Housing and Local Govt. and Minister for Aboriginal Devt. 1992, for Constitutional Devt. 1994, Attorney-Gen., Minister for Educ., for Sport and Recreation, for Constitutional Devt. 1995, for Correctional Services, for Sport and Recreation, for Parks and Wildlife, for Ethnic Affairs 1996–97; Chief Minister for N.T. 1986–88. *Leisure interests:* sport. *Address:* Shop 4, Nightcliff Shopping Centre, Oleander Street, Nightcliff, N.T. 0810, Australia.

HAUER, Rutger; Netherlands actor; b. 23 Jan. 1944, Amsterdam; m. 2nd Ieneke Hauer 1985; commercials for Guinness 1989. *Films include:* Turkish Delight 1973, The Wilby Conspiracy 1975, Keetje Tippel 1975, Max Havelaar 1976, Mysteries 1978, Soldier of Orange 1978, Woman Between Dog and Wolf 1979, Spetters 1980, Nighthawks 1981, Chanel Solitaire 1981, Blade Runner 1982, Eureka 1982, Outsider in Amsterdam 1983, The Osterman Weekend 1983, A Breed Apart 1984, Ladyhawke 1984, Flesh and Blood 1985, The Hitcher 1986, Wanted Dead or Alive 1986, The Legend of the Holy Drinker 1989, Salute of the Juggler, Ocean Point, On a Moonlit Night, Split Second, Buffy the Vampire Slayer, Past Midnight, Nostradamus, Surviving the Game, The Beans of Egypt Maine, Angel of Death. *Address:* c/o William Morris Agency, 151 El Camino Drive, Beverly Hills, CA 90212, U.S.A.

HAUERWAS, Stanley, M.A., M.PHIL., PH.D.; American professor of theological ethics; b. 24 July 1940, Dallas, Texas; s. of Coffee Martin and Johanna Hauerwas; m. Paula E. Gilbert; one s.; ed. Southwestern Univ. and Yale Univ.; fmr. teacher, Augustana Coll. Rock Island, Ill.; mem. Faculty, Univ. of Notre Dame 1970–84; mem. Faculty, Duke Univ. 1984, Dir. of Grad. Studies 1985–91, now Gilbert T. Rowe Prof. of Theological Ethics; Dr. h.c. (DePaul) 1988, (Edin.) 1991. *Publications include:* Resident Aliens: Life in the Christian Colony 1989, Naming the Silences: God, Medicine, and the Problem of Suffering 1990, After Christendom 1991, Preaching to Strangers 1992, Unleashing the Scriptures 1993, Dispatches from the Front: Theolgical Engagements with the Secular 1994, In Good Company: The Church as Polis 1995. *Address:* The Divinity School, Duke University, Durham, NC 27708, U.S.A.

HAUFF, Volker, DR.RER.POL.; German politician; b. 9 Aug. 1940, Backnang; s. of Richard and Ilse (Dieter) Hauff; m. Ursula Irion 1967; two s.; ed. Free Univ. of Berlin; with IBM Deutschland, Stuttgart 1971–72; Sec. of State to Fed. Minister for Research and Tech. 1972–78; Fed. Minister for Research and Tech. 1978–80, of Transport 1980–82; mem. Bundestag 1969; mem. Social Democratic Party (SPD) 1959, Vice-Pres. of Parl. Group 1983; Mayor of Frankfurt 1989–91; Generalbevollmächtigbe KPMG Germany 1995–; mem. IG Metall; mem. UN World Comm. on Environment and Devt. *Publications:* Programmierfibes—Eine verständliche Einführung in das Programmieren digitaler Automaten 1969, Wörterbuch der Datenverarbeitung 1966, Für ein soziales Bodenrecht 1973, Modernisierung der Volkswirtschaft 1975, Politik als Zukunftsgestaltung 1976, Damit der Fortschritt nicht zum Risiko wird 1978, Sprachlose Politik 1979. *Leisure interests:* modern art, cooking. *Address:* Roesbergerstr. 7, 50968 Cologne, Germany (Office). *Telephone:* (0221) 382111. *Fax:* (0221) 375546.

HAUGHEY, Charles James; Irish politician; b. 16 Sept. 1925, Castlebar, Co. Mayo; s. of Commandant John Haughey and Sarah Ann McWilliams; m. Maureen Lemass 1951; three s. one d.; ed. Scoil Mhuire, Marino, Dublin, St. Joseph's Christian Brothers' School, Fairview, Dublin, Univ. Coll. Dublin and King's Inns, Dublin; commissioned Officer Reserve Defence Force 1947–57; Mem. Dublin City Council 1953–55; M.P. 1957–92; represented Dublin (North Central)); Parl. Sec. to Minister for Justice 1960–61, Minister for Justice 1961–64; Minister of Agric. 1964–66, Minister for Finance 1966–70, for Health and Social Welfare 1977–79; Taoiseach (Prime Minister) 1979–81, March–Dec. 1982, 1987–92, Minister for the Gaeltacht 1987–92; Leader of the Opposition 1981–82, 1982–87; Chair. Irish Parl. Joint Cttee. on the Secondary Legislation of the European Communities 1973–77; Pres. Fianna Fáil 1979–92; Pres. European Council 1990; mem. Bd. of Trustees Int. Green Cross; Fellow Inst. of Chartered Accountants; Hon. Ph.D. (Dublin City Univ.), Hon. LL.D. (Univ. Blaise-Pascal, France), (Univ. Notre Dame, U.S.A.). *Leisure interests:* reading, music, riding, swimming. *Address:* Abbeville, Kinsealy, Co. Dublin, Ireland. *Telephone:* 01 8450111.

HAUGHTON, Rosemary Elena Konradin; British/American writer, lecturer, social philosopher, theologian; b. 13 April 1927, London; d. of Peter Luling and Sylvia Luling (née Thompson); m. Algernon Haughton 1948; seven s. three d.; had no formal educ. after age of 15; has lectured internationally; Assoc. Dir. Wellspring House Inc., providing shelter for homeless families, educ., low-income housing and econ. devt. in Mass., U.S.A 1981–; 5 hon. degrees. *Publications:* 35 books including The Transformation of Man, The Drama of Salvation, Tales from Eternity, Elizabeth's Greeting, The Catholic Thing, The Passionate God, The Re-Creation of Eve, Song in a Strange Land, The Tower that Fell (illustrated), Images for Change: The Vision of Hospitality. *Leisure interests:* painting, embroidery, gardening, reading, country cottage. *Address:* Wellspring House Inc., 302 Essex Avenue, Gloucester, MA 01930, U.S.A.; 5 Draper Corner, Heptonstall, Hebden Bridge, W. Yorkshire, HX7 7EY, England. *Telephone:* (508) 281-3221 (U.S.A.).

HAUGLAND, Aage; Danish opera singer; m. Anette Munk-Andersen 1970; one s. one d.; ed. Univ. of Copenhagen; mem. Norwegian Opera 1968–70, Bremer Opera, Fed. Repub. of Germany 1970–73, Royal Danish Opera 1973–; guest appearances with all maj. opera cos. and orchestras, especially in Wagner, Strauss and Russian operas 1974–; recordings, TV and films; Kt. of Dannebrog; Kgl. Kammersanger. *Address:* Skovbrinken 7, 3450 Allerød, Denmark. *Telephone:* (45) 48175454; (45) 59919392.

HĂULICĂ, Dan; Romanian art critic; b. 7 Feb. 1932, Iaşi; s. of Neculai Hăulică and Lucreţia Hăulică; m. Cristina Isbăşescu 1971; one d.; ed. Coll. of Philology, Iaşi, N. Grigorescu Fine Arts Inst., Bucharest; reader Iaşi Coll. of Philology 1954–56; edited Literary Magazine, Bucharest 1956–58; researcher of the Inst. for Literary History and Theory of the Romanian Acad. 1958–63; Deputy Ed.-in-Chief Secolul 20 (journal) 1963–67, Ed.-in-Chief 1967; Prof. N. Grigorescu Coll. of Fine Arts, Bucharest 1965; Chair. Int. Asscn. of Arts Critics 1981–84, Hon. Chair. 1984; Chair. Conseil audiovisuel mondial pour l'édition et la recherche sur l'art (CAMERA) 1986; UNESCO consultant; Amb. to UNESCO 1990–; mem. European Soc. of Culture 1988, European Acad. of Sciences, Letters and Arts 1987; Chair. Int. Confs. on Arts, TV and problems of the image: Paris, UNESCO 1981, Biennale di Venezia 1982, Sophia Antipolis, Moscow-Tashkent 1982, Helsinki 1983, Caracas 1983, Delphi 1984, Lisbon, Gulbenkian 1984, Paris 1986, Prague 1987, Alger-Tipasa 1987; Chair. Int. Jury of the Arts Film Festivals Montreal 1984, Le Carnival et la Fête, Nice 1985, Politiques culturelles et Télévision, Paris 1986; mem. leading bds. Romanian Writers' Union, Romanian Fine Arts Union; Prize of the Romanian Fine Arts Union 1967, Prizes of the Romanian Writers' Union 1974, 1984; Prize of the Romanian Film Studio Al. Sahia, Great Prize of the Romanian Fine Arts Union 1975; Grand Prix Int. de la meilleure revue d'art (Festival Int. d'Art de Beaubourg) Paris 1987. *Works include:* Peintres roumains (UNESCO, vol. I 1963, vol. II 1965), Brancusi ou l'anonymat du génie 1967, Critică şi cultură (Criticism and Culture) 1967, Calder, Variations sur le thème Homo Faber 1971, Geografii spirituale (Spiritual Geographies) 1973, Nostalgia sintezei (The Nostalgia for Synthesis) 1984. *Address:* Str. Docenţilor 26, Bucharest 71311, Romania (Home).

HAUMER, Hans, LL.D.; Austrian banker; b. 29 Sept. 1940, Vienna; ed. Vienna Univ., Univ. of Tübingen, Fed. Repub. of Germany; lecturer in Social Sciences, Univ. of Puerto Rico 1963–64; Asst. to Man. Bd. Girozentrale Vienna 1964–66, in Int. Banking Div. 1970–74, Chair. and C.E.O. (now GiroCredit Bank) 1989; staff mem., working on stabilization policies in Latin America and Africa, IMF, Washington, D.C. 1966–69; apptd. mem. Man. Bd. Die Erste Österreichischen Spar-Casse 1974, Chair. Man. Bd. and C.E.O. of Bank 1977–96; Vice-Chair. Vienna Stock Exchange; Pres. Austrian Soc. for Foreign Policy and Int. Relations. *Publications:* Die Neuen Macher 1990. *Leisure interests:* music, sports.

HAUPTFUHRER, Robert, M.B.A.; American oil industry executive; b. 31 Dec. 1931, Philadelphia; s. of George J. Hauptfuhrer and Emilie M. Schoenhut; m. Barbara Dunlop 1963; two s. one d.; ed. Princeton and Harvard Univs.; joined Sun Company 1957, Vice-Pres. Sun Ventures 1973–75, Pres. Sun Enterprises 1975–79, Sr. Vice-Pres. Sun Co. 1981–83, Pres. Sun Exploration & Production Co. 1984–86, Pres. and C.O.O. Sun Co. 1987; Chair. and C.E.O. Oryx Energy Co. 1988–94; Trustee Princeton Univ. 1987–; Assoc. Trustee Univ. of Pa. 1987–; mem. Nat. Petroleum Council, Natural Gas Supply Asscn., Independent Producers Asscn. of America. *Leisure interests:* golf, skiing. *Address:* 602 Old Eagle School Road, Wayne, PA 19087, U.S.A.

HAUSER, Erich; German sculptor and professor; b. 15 Dec. 1930, Rietheim, Tübingen; s. of Ludwig and Berta Hauser; m. Gretl Kawaletz 1955; one s. one d.; ed. Volksschule, Rietheim, Oberschule, Spaichingen and evening classes at Freie Kunstschule, Stuttgart; studied engraving in Tuttlingen and drawing and modelling under Pater Ansgar, Kloster Beuron; independent sculptor, Schramberg 1952; Visiting Lecturer, Hochschule für bildende Künste, Hamburg 1964–65, Visiting Prof. 1984; Visiting Prof., Hochschule der Künste, Berlin 1984–85; has held many one-man exhbns. in galleries throughout Germany and in Austria and Switzerland since 1961; has participated in many group exhbns. in Europe, New Delhi, Cairo and the São Paulo Biennale 1969; has executed sculptures for many public buildings in Germany including Säulenwand for Univ. of Konstanz, a relief for theatre foyer, Bonn and a sculpture for the Düsseldorf Stock Exchange; mem. Akad. der Künste, Berlin; Kunstpreis der Stadt Wolfsburg für Plastik 1965, Burdapreis für Plastik 1966, Premio Itamaraty 1969, Grand Prix, São Paulo Biennale 1969, Verdienstkreuz am Bande des Verdienstordens der Bundesrepublik 1972, Biennale Preis für Kleinplastik, Budapest 1975, Verdienstkreuz, 1st Class 1979, Helmut-Kraft-Stiftung First Prize 1988, Oberschwäbischer Kunstpreis, Rottweil 1995, Gründung der Erich Hauserstiftung 1996. *Address:* Saline 36, 78628 Rottweil, Germany. *Telephone:* (0741) 280018-0. *Fax:* (0741) 280018-21.

HAUSPURG, Arthur, M.S.E.E., F.I.E.E.E.; American business executive; b. 27 Aug. 1925, New York; s. of Otto and Charlotte (Braul) Hauspurg; m. Catherine Dunning Mackay 1947; three s.; ed. Columbia Univ., New York; Asst. Vice-Pres. American Electric Power Corpn. 1968; Vice-Pres. Consolidated Edison Co. of New York Inc. 1969, Sr. Vice-Pres. 1973, Exec. Vice-Pres. 1975, C.O.O. 1975–81, Pres. 1975, C.E.O. 1981, Chair. 1982; mem. of numerous bodies including Nat. Acad. of Eng. *Publications:* numerous articles and papers on engineering. *Address:* 5 John Jay Place, Rye, NY 10580, U.S.A. (Home).

HAUSSMANN, Helmut, D.ECON., DR.RER.POL.; German politician; b. 18 May 1943, Tübingen; m. Margot Scheu 1980; business exec. 1968–71; Research and Academic Asst., Univ. of Erlangen-Nuremberg 1971–75; joined Free Democratic Party (FDP) 1969; mem. Bad Urach Town Council, FDP Dist. Chair., Reutlingen 1975–80; mem. Deutscher Bundestag 1976–; Econ. Cttee. 1977–88; mem. FDP Fed. Exec. Cttee. 1978–; Ombudsman FDP Econs. Cttee. 1980–; Econ. Spokesman, FDP Parl. Party 1980–84; Vice-Chair. FDP in Land Baden-Württemberg 1983–88, 1995–; Sec.-Gen. FDP 1984–88; Fed. Minister of Econ. Affairs 1988–91; mem. Foreign Affairs Cttee. and Spokesman on EC Policy 1991–. *Leisure interests:* tennis and golf. *Address:* Am Forst 1, 72574 Bad Urach, Germany. *Telephone:* (228) 1683325 (Office). *Fax:* (228) 1686223.

HAVEL, Richard Joseph, M.D.; American professor of medicine; b. 20 Feb. 1925, Seattle, Wash.; s. of Joseph Havel and Anna Fritz; m. Virginia J. Havel 1947; three s. one d.; ed. Reed Coll., Portland, Ore., Univ. of Ore. Medical School and Cornell Univ. Medical Coll.; Asst. in Biochem. Univ. of Ore. Medical School 1945–49; Asst. Resident in Medicine, New York Hospital 1950–51, Chief Resident in Medicine 1952–53; Instructor Cornell Univ. Medical Coll. 1952–53; Clinical Assoc. Nat. Heart Inst. 1953–54, Research Assoc. 1954–56; Asst. Prof. of Medicine, Univ. of Calif., San Francisco 1956–59, Assoc. Prof. 1959–64, Prof. of Medicine 1964–, Chief Metabolism Section 1967–97, Dir. Cardiovascular Research Inst. 1973–92; Dir. Arteriosclerosis Specialized Center of Research 1970–96; Chair. Food and Nutrition Bd., NRC 1987–90; Co-ed. Advanced Lipid Research 1991–; mem. Editorial Bd., Journal of Arteriosclerosis 1980–; mem. Food and Nutrition Bd., Nat. Research Council 1983, (Chair. 1987–90); mem. N.A.S., Inst. of Medicine, American Acad. of Arts and Sciences, American Soc. of Clinical Nutrition, Asscn. of American Physicians; T. Smith Award, A.A.A.S. 1960, Bristol-Myers Award for nutrition research 1989, McCollum Award 1993, Gold Medal Charles Univ. (Czech Repub.) 1996, Mayo Soley Award 1997. *Publications:* over 290 scientific articles and book chapters. *Address:* University of California, Cardiovascular Research Institute, San Francisco, CA 94143 (Office); P.O. Box 1791, Ross, CA 94957-1791, U.S.A. (Home).

HAVEL, Václav; Czech politician, playwright and writer; b. 5 Oct. 1936, Prague; s. of Václav M. Havel and Božena (Vavrečková) Havel; m. 1st Olga Šplíchalová 1964 (died 1996); m. 2nd Dagmar Veškrnová 1997; ed. Acad. of Arts, Drama Dept., Prague; worked as freelance ed.; fmr. spokesman for Charter 77 human rights movement, received a sentence of 14 months in 1977, suspended for 3 years, for "subversive" and "antistate" activities, under house arrest 1978–79; Cttee. for the Defence of the Unjustly Prosecuted (VONS), convicted and sentenced to 4½ years' imprisonment for sedition 1979, released March 1983, arrested Jan. 1989 and sentenced to 9 months imprisonment for incitement and obstruction Feb. 1989; sentence reduced to 8 months, and charge changed to misdemeanour March 1989; released May 1989; f. Civic Forum Nov. 1989; Pres. of Czechoslovakia 1989–92, Pres. of Czech Repub. Jan. 1993–; C.-in-C. of Armed Forces 1989–92; Chair. Prague Heritage Fund 1993–; mem. jury Int. Prize Awarding Body for Human Rights 1994–; mem. Acad. des Sciences Morales et Politiques; Hon. mem. Acad. of Sciences and Arts, Salzburg; numerous hon. degrees including Dr. h.c. (Bar Ilan Univ.) Israel, Kyjev Univ., Ukraine, Jordan Univ. 1997, Oxford 1997, Glasgow Univ. 1998; Austrian State Prize for European Literature 1968, Jan Palach Prize 1982, Erasmus Prize 1986, Olof Palme Prize 1989, German Book Trade Peace Prize 1989, Simón Bolívar Prize 1990, Malaparte Prize 1990, Sonning Cultural Prize 1991, Athinai Prize (Onassis Foundation) 1993, Indira Gandhi Prize 1994, European Cultural Soc. Award 1993, Philadelphia Liberty Medal 1994, Premi Internacional Catalunya 1995, TGM Prize (Canada) 1997, Medal of Danish Acad. 1997, European Statesman Prize (U.S.A.), 1997, Husajn bin Ali Distinction (Jordan) 1997, J.W. Fulbright Prize for Int. Understanding (U.S.A.) 1997, Le Prix Spécial Europe, European Theatre Council 1997, Cino del Duca Prize (France), Prince of Asturias Prize (Spain) 1997; Order of White Eagle, Poland 1993, Golden Hon. Order of Freedom, Slovenia 1993, Chain of Order of Isabel of Castille, Spain 1995; Charles Univ. Medal 1998; Hon. K.C.B., U.K. 1996. *Plays include:* Garden Party 1963, Memorandum 1965, The Increased Difficulty of Concentration 1968, The Conspirators 1971, The Beggar's Opera 1972, Audience 1975, Vernissage 1975, The Mountain Resort 1976, Protest 1978, The Mistake 1983, Largo Desolato 1984, Temptation 1985, Redevelopment 1987, Tomorrow! 1988. *Publications include:* Letters to Olga (Czech) 1983, Disturbing the Peace (in Czech, as Dálkový výslech) 1986, (English) 1990, Václav Havel or Living in Truth (essays, in English) 1986, Open Letters: Selected Writings 1965–1990 (in English) 1991, Selected Plays by Václav Havel (in English) 1992, Summer Meditations (Czech) 1991, (English) 1992, Plays (in Czech, as Hry) 1991, Toward a Civil Society 1994, The Art of the Impossible (speeches) 1997. *Address:* Kancelář prezidenta republiky, 119 08 Prague Hrad, Czech Republic. *Telephone:* (2) 2437 1111. *Fax:* (2) 2437 3300.

HAVELANGE, Jean Marie Faustin Godefroid (João); Brazilian lawyer; b. 8 May 1916, Rio de Janeiro; m.; practising lawyer 1936–; Head of Importation and Exportation, Cia. Siderúrgica Belgo-Mineira 1937–41; Dir.-Pres. Viação Cometa S.A., EMBRADATA, Orwec Química e Metalúrgica Ltda.; took part in Olympic Games as swimmer, Berlin 1936, as water-polo player, Helsinki 1952, Head of Brazilian Del., Sydney 1956; Pres. Fed. Paulista de Natação, São Paulo 1949–51, Fed. Metropolitana de Natação (GB) 1952–56; mem. Brazilian Olympic Cttee. 1955–73; Vice-Pres. Confed. Brasileira de Desportos 1956–58, Pres. 1958–73; Dir., mem. for South America Cttee. of Int. Cyclists Union 1958; mem. Int. Olympic Cttee. 1963; Pres. Indoor Football Int. Fed. (FIFUSA) 1971; Pres. Int. Fed. of Asscn. Football (FIFA) 1974–98; Portuguese and Brazilian decorations. *Leisure interests:* swimming and water-polo. *Address:* Av. Rio Branco 89-B, conj. 602 Centro, 20040-004 Rio de Janeiro, RJ, Brazil.

HAVIARAS, Stratis, M.F.A.; Greek author; b. 28 June 1935, Nea Kios, Argos; s. of Christos Haviaras and Georgia Hadzikyriakos; m. 1st Gail Flynn 1967 (divorced 1973); m. 2nd Heather Cole 1990; one d.; fmr. construction worker; lived in U.S.A. 1959–61; went to U.S.A. following colonels' coup in Greece 1967, obtaining position at Harvard Univ. Library; Curator, Poetry Room, Harvard Univ. Library 1974–; Founder and Ed. Harvard Review 1992–. *Publications:* four vols. of Greek verse 1963, 1965, 1967, 1972; Crossing the River Twice (poems in English) 1976; novels: When the Tree Sings 1979, The Heroic Age 1984; ed. Seamus Heaney, a Celebration 1996. *Leisure interest:* wood sculpture. *Address:* Poetry Room, Harvard University, Cambridge, MA 02138, U.S.A. *Telephone:* (617) 495-2454 (Office); (617) 354-4724 (Home). *Fax:* (617) 496-3692.

HAVIGHURST, Clark Canfield, J.D.; American professor of law; b. 25 May 1933, Evanston, Ill.; s. of Harold Canfield and Marion Clay (Perryman) Havighurst; m. Karen Waldron 1965; one s. one d.; ed. Princeton and Northwestern Univs.; Research Assoc. Duke Univ. School of Law 1960–61; Private Practice, Debevoise, Plimpton, Lyons & Gates, New York 1958, 1961–64; Assoc. Prof. of Law, Duke Univ. 1964–68, Prof. 1968–86, William Neal Reynolds Prof. 1986–; Prof. of Community Health Sciences, Duke Univ. Medical Center 1974–; numerous other professional appts.; mem. Inst. of Medicine, NAS. *Publications:* Deregulating the Health Care Industry 1982, Health Care Law and Policy 1988, Health Care Choices: Private Contracts as Instruments of Health Reform 1995; articles on regulation in the health services industry, the role of competition in the financing and delivery of health care and anti-trust issues arising in the health care field. *Address:* Duke University School of Law, Durham, NC 27708 (Office); 3610 Dover Road, Durham, NC 27707, U.S.A. (Home). *Telephone:* (919) 613-7061 (Office); (919) 489-4970 (Home). *Fax:* (919) 613-7231.

HAVILAND, Denis William Garstin Latimer, C.B., M.A., F.I.I.M.; British industrialist; b. 15 Aug. 1910, London; s. of late William Alexander Haviland and of Edyth Louise Latimer; ed. Rugby School and St. John's Coll., Cambridge; London Midland and Scottish Railway 1934–39; Army service 1940–46, rising to rank of Col.; Prin., Control Office for Germany and Austria 1946–47; Asst. Sec. Foreign Office, German Section 1947–50; Imperial Defence Coll. 1950; Ministry of Supply 1951–59, Under-Sec. 1953–59, Deputy Sec. 1959; Deputy Sec. Ministry of Aviation 1959–64; Chair. European Launcher Devt. Org. (ELDO) Preparatory Group 1962–64; Deputy Chair. Staveley Industries 1964–65, Chair. and Man. Dir. 1965–69; Dir. Wheelabrator Corpn. of Mishawaka 1967–72, Short Brothers and Harland Ltd. 1964–81, Organized Office Designs Ltd. 1971–92; mem. Council British Inst. of Management 1967–83 (Vice-Chair. 1973), Chair. Membership Cttee. 1969–75, Chair. Professional Standards Cttee. 1975–82; mem. Business and Man. Bd., Council for Nat. Academic Awards 1977–82, Business and Man. Cttee. and Academic Cttee. 1982–84, Post-graduate Studies Bd. 1980–84; mem. of court, Cranfield Inst. of Tech. Man. 1970–83; Vice-Pres. Inst. of Industrial Mans. 1979–89; Chair. Confed. of Healing Orgs. 1981, 1990, Consultant 1990–; Chair. Holistic Council for Cancer 1984–86; mem. Nat. Consultative Council for Alternative and Complementary Medicine 1990–; mem. Council, British Complementary Medicine Asscn.; Liveryman, Co. of Coachmakers; Verulam Gold Medal, B.I.M. 1983. *Leisure interests:* travel, bird watching, gardening. *Address:* 113 Hampstead Way, London, NW11 7JN, England (Office and Home). *Telephone:* 0181-455 2638.

HAWKE, Ethan; American actor; b. 6 Nov. 1970, Austin, Tex. co-f. Malaparte Theatre Co. *Theatre appearances include:* Casanova 1991, A Joke, The Seagull 1992, Sophistry. *Films include:* Explorers 1985, Dead Poets Society 1989, Dad 1989, White Fang 1991, Mystery Date 1991, A Midnight Clear 1992, Waterland 1992, Alive 1993, Rich in Love 1993, Straight to One 1993 (dir.), Reality Bites 1994, Quiz Show 1994, Floundering 1994, Before Sunrise 1995, Great Expectations, Gattaca, Joe the King 1999. *Address:* Creative Artists Agency, 9830 Wilshire Boulevard, Beverly Hills, CA 90212, U.S.A.

HAWKE, Gary Richard, D.PHIL., F.R.S.N.Z.; New Zealand economic historian; b. 1 Aug. 1942, Napier; s. of Vyvyan Nesbitt Hawke and Jean Avis Hawke (née Carver); m. Helena Joyce Pourie 1965; two s.; ed. Victoria Univ. of Wellington, Balliol and Nuffield Colls., Oxford; lecturer Victoria Univ. of Wellington 1968–70, Reader 1971–73, Prof. of Econ. History 1974–; Dir. Inst. of Policy Studies 1987–97; visiting appointments Stanford Univ. 1972–73, All Souls Coll., Oxford 1977–78, Japan Foundation 1993, Japan Soc. for Promoting Knowledge 1994; Chair. N.Z. Planning Council 1986–91. *Publications include:* Railways and Economic Growth 1970, Between Governments and Banks 1973, Economics for Historians 1980, The Making of New Zealand 1985, The Thoroughbred Among Banks 1997. *Leisure interests:* classical music, armchair criticism. *Address:* School of Economics and Finance, Victoria University of Wellington, P.O. Box 600, Wellington, New Zealand. *Telephone:* (4) 495-5233. *Fax:* (4) 495-5014.

HAWKE, Robert James Lee, A.C., B.A., LL.B., B.LITT.; Australian politician and fmr. trade unionist; b. 9 Dec. 1929, Bordertown, S. Australia; s. of A. C. Hawke; m. 1st Hazel Masterson 1956 (divorced 1995); one s. two d.; m. 2nd Blanche d'Apulget 1995; ed. Univs. of Western Australia and Oxford; Rhodes scholar 1953; Research Officer, Australian Council of Trade Unions 1958–70, Pres. 1970–80; Senior Vice-Pres. Australian Labor Party 1971–73, Pres. 1973–78, Leader 1983–91; Prime Minister 1983–91, mem. Nat. Exec. 1971–91; reporter 1992; Business Consultant 1992; Adjunct Prof. Research School of Pacific Studies and Social Sciences, A.N.U. 1992–95; Hon. Visiting Prof. in Industrial Relations Sydney Univ.; mem. Advisory Council of Inst. for Int. Studies, Stanford Univ., Calif.; Chair. Cttee. of Experts on mem. of Educ. Int. 1993–, Sydney City Mission Fundraising Task Force; Dir. Quantum Resources Ltd. 1996–; mem. Bd. Reserve Bank of Australia 1973–83, Governing Body ILO 1972–80; mem. Australian Council for Union Training, Australian Population and Immigration Council; mem. Australian Manufacturing Council 1977, Nat. Labour Consultative Council 1977–92, Australian Refugee Advisory Council; M.P. for Wills, Melbourne 1980–92; Hon. Fellow, Univ. Coll., Oxford 1984; Dr. h.c. (Nanjing) 1986; Hon. D.Phil. (Hebrew Univ. of Jerusalem) 1987; Hon. LL.D. (Univ. of N.S.W.) 1987; U.N. Media Peace Prize 1980. *Leisure interests:* tennis, golf, cricket, reading. *Publication:* The Hawke Memoirs 1994. *Address:* c/o GPO Box 36, Sydney, N.S.W. 2001, Australia.

HAWKER, Graham Alfred, F.C.C.A., F.R.S.A.; British business executive; b. 12 May 1947; s. of Alfred Hawker and Sarah Rebecca Bowen; m. Sandra Ann Evans 1967; one s. one d.; ed. Bedwelty Grammar School; trainee accountant Caerphilly Dist. Council 1964–66; accountant Abercarn Dist. Council 1966–67, Chief Accountant 1967–68, Deputy Treas. 1968–70; Chief Auditor Taf Fechan Water Bd. 1970–74; Audit Man. Welsh Water Authority 1974–78, Div. Finance Man. 1978–84, Chief Accountant 1984–86, Dir. Planning and Devt. 1986–87, Finance 1987–89; Dir. Finance Welsh Water PLC 1989–91, Group Man. Dir. 1991–93, Chief Exec. Hyder (fmrly. Welsh Water) PLC 1993–; Chair. Dwr Cymru Ltd. 1993–, Hyder Consulting (fmrly. Acer) 1993–, Swalec 1996–; Dir. Welsh Devt. Agency 1995–; Dir. (non-exec.) Bank of England; Chair. BITC (Wales) 1994–; mem. CBI Council, Wales 1995–; Companion Inst. of Man; Fellow Inst of Certified Accountants. *Leisure interests:* family, walking, wine, career. *Address:* Hyder PLC, Plas-y-Ffynnon, Cambrian Way, Brecon, Powys, LD3 7HP (Office); St. Teilo House, Llantilio Pertholey, Abergavenny, Gwent, NP7 6NY, Wales (Home). *Telephone:* (01874) 614424.

HAWKING, Stephen William, C.H., C.B.E., PH.D., F.R.S.; British professor of mathematics; b. 8 Jan. 1942; s. of Dr. F. and Mrs. E. I. Hawking; m. 1st Jane Wilde 1965; two s. one d.; m. 2nd Elaine Mason 1995; ed. St. Albans School, Univ. Coll., Oxford, Trinity Hall, Cambridge; Research Fellow, Gonville and Caius Coll., Cambridge 1965–69, Fellow for Distinction in Science 1969–; Research Asst., Inst. of Astronomy, Cambridge 1972–73; Research Asst., Dept. of Applied Math. and Theoretical Physics, Cambridge Univ. 1973–75, Reader in Gravitational Physics 1975–77, Prof. 1977–79, Lucasian Prof. of Math. 1979–; mem. Inst. of Theoretical Astronomy, Cambridge 1968–72; mem. Papal Acad. of Science 1986; Foreign mem. American Acad. Arts and Sciences 1984; several hon. degrees; William Hopkins Prize, Cambridge Philosophical Soc. 1976, Wolf Prize 1988, Maxwell Medal, Inst. of Physics 1976, Hughes Medal, Royal Soc. 1976, Albert Einstein Award 1978, Gold Medal Royal Astronomical Soc. 1985, Sunday Times Special Award for Literature 1989, Britannica Award 1989. *Publications:* The Large Scale Structure of Space-Time (with G. F. R. Ellis) 1973, General Relativity: an Einstein centenary survey 1979, Superspace and Supergravity (jt. Ed.) 1981, The Very Early Universe (jt. Ed.) 1983, 300 Years of Gravitation 1987, A Brief History of Time 1988, Black Holes and Baby Universes 1993, The Nature of Space and Time (with Roger Penrose) 1996, and other essays. *Address:* Department of Applied Mathematics and Theoretical Physics, Silver Street, Cambridge, CB3 9EW, England. *Telephone:* (01223) 337843.

HAWKINS, Paula; American politician; b. Salt Lake City, Utah; d. of Paul B. and Leoan (née Staley) Fickes; m. Walter Eugene Hawkins 1947; one s. two d.; ed. Utah State Univ.; mem. Republican Precinct Cttee., Orange Co., Fla. 1965–74, Rep. Nat. Comm. for Fla. 1968–87; Speakers Chair. Fla. Republican Exec. Cttee. 1967–69, mem. Fla. Republican Nat. Convention 1972, S. Regional Rep., Republican Nat. Cttee. 1972–; Republican Senator, Fla. 1981–87; Pres. Paula Hawkins and Assocs. 1988–; mem. Maitland Civic Cen. 1965–76; Charter mem. Bd. of Dirs. Fla. Americans Constitutional Action Cttee. of 100 1966–68, Sec.-Treas. 1966–68; mem. Gov. of Fla. Comm. on Status of Women 1968–71; Public Service Commr. Fla., Tallahassee 1972–80; mem. Perm. Sub-Cttee. on Narcotics Control and Terrorism OAS 1981–; U.S. Del. to U.N. Narcotics Convention, Vienna 1987, U.S. Del. to U.N. Convention N.Y. 1994; Chair. Nat. Cttee. on Responsibilities for Financing Postsecondary Educ. 1990–92; mem. bd. dirs. Freedom Foundation 1981–; fmr. Chair. Legis. Comm. Orange Co. Drug Abuse Council, fmr. co-Chair. Orange Co. March of Dimes; del. UN Conv. 1994–; fmr. mem. Cen. Fla. Museum Speakers Bureau; Citation for Service, Fla. Republican Party; Above and Beyond Award (Outstanding Woman in Fla. politics); Dr. h.c. (Nova Univ.), (St. Thomas Villa Nova), (Rollino Coll.). *Address:* P.O. Box 193, Winter Park, FL 32790, U.S.A.

HAWLEY, Sir Donald Frederick, K.C.M.G., M.B.E., M.A.; British diplomatist (retd.), company chairman and consultant; b. 22 May 1921, Essex; s. of the late F. G. and G. E. C. (née Hills) Hawley; m. Ruth Morwenna Graham 1964; one s. three d.; ed. Radley, New Coll., Oxford; Barrister-at-Law, Inner Temple; served with H.M. Forces 1941–44; Sudan Political Service 1944–47; Sudan Judiciary 1947–55; Foreign Office 1956–58; H.M. Political Agent, Trucial States 1958–61; Head of Chancery British Embassy, Cairo 1962–64; Counsellor, High Commission, Lagos 1965–67; Counsellor (Commercial), Baghdad 1968–71; Amb. to Sultanate of Oman 1971–75; Asst. Under Sec. of State, Foreign and Commonwealth Office 1975–77; High Commr. in Malaysia 1977–81; mem London Advisory Comm. Hongkong and Shanghai Banking Corpn. 1981–91; Chair. Ewbank Preece Ltd. 1982–86; Chair. The Centre for British Teachers 1987–91; Chair. Royal Soc. for Asian Affairs; Chair. Anglo-Omani Soc. 1975–77, Vice-Pres. 1981; Chair. British-Malaysian Soc. 1983 (Vice-Pres. 1993); Pres. of Council Reading Univ. 1987–94; Chair. Sudan Pensioners Asscn. 1992–; Hon.D.Litt. (Reading) 1994; Hon. D.C.L. (Durham) 1997. *Publications:* Courtesies in the Trucial States 1965, The Trucial States 1970, Oman and its Renaissance 1977, 1995, Courtesies in the Gulf Area 1978, Manners and Correct Form in the Middle East 1983, Sandtracks in the Sudan 1995, Sudan Canterbury Tales 1998. *Leisure interests:* gardening, walking, tennis. *Address:* Little Cheverell House, Devizes, Wilts., SN10 4JS, England. *Telephone:* (01380) 813322.

HAWLEY, Robert, C.B.E., F.R.S.E., F.ENG., D.SC., PH.D.; British business executive and engineer; b. 23 July 1936, Wallasey; s. of William Hawley and Eva Hawley; m. Valerie Clarke 1961; one s. one d.; ed. Wallasey Grammar School, Wallasey Tech. Coll., Birkenhead Tech. Coll. and King's Coll., Univ. of Durham; joined C. A. Parsons 1961, Electrical Designer, Generator Dept. 1964, Chief Electrical Eng. 1970, Dir. of Production and Eng. 1973–74; Man. Dir. NEI Parsons 1976; Man. Dir. Power Eng. Group, NEI PLC 1986–88, Man. Dir. Operations 1989–92; Main Bd. Dir. Rolls Royce PLC 1989–92; Chief Exec. Nuclear Electric PLC 1992–95, British Energy PLC 1995–97; Chair. INBIS PLC, ERAtech PLC; Dir. (non-exec.) Tricorder PLC; Pres. Partnership Korea, Inst. of Electrical Engineers 1996–97; Advisor HSBC Investment Bank PLC; Chair. Council Durham Univ. *Publications:* co-author of Dielectric Solids 1970, Conduction and Breakdown in Mineral Oil 1973, Fundamentals of Electromagnetic Field Theory 1974, Vacuum as an Insulator. *Leisure interests:* philately, gardening. *Address:* Summerfield, Rendcomb, nr. Cirencester, Glos., GL7 7HB, England.

HAWN, Goldie; American actress; b. 21 Nov. 1945, Washington, D.C.; d. of Edward Rutledge Hawn and Laura Hawn; m. 1st Gus Trikonio 1969 (divorced); m. 2nd Bill Hudson (divorced); two s. one d.; ed. American Univ., Washington, D.C.; began career as chorus-line dancer, World's Fair, New York 1964. *Stage appearances include:* Romeo and Juliet (Williamsburg), Kiss Me Kate, Guys and Dolls (New York). *TV series include:* Good Morning, World, Rowan and Martin's Laugh-In, Goldie and Kids—Listen to Us. *Films include:* Cactus Flower, There's a Girl in my Soup, Butterflies are Free, The Sugarland Express, $, The Girl from Petrovka, Shampoo, The Duchess and the Dirtwater Fox, Foul Play, Seems Like Old Times, Private Benjamin, Best Friends, Protocol, Swing Shift, Overboard, Bird On A Wire, Housesitter, Deceived, Death Becomes Her, Something to Talk About (exec. producer only), The First Wives Club 1996, Everybody Says I Love You 1996. *Address:* c/o Ed Limato, ICM, 8942 Wilshire Boulevard, Beverly Hills, CA 90211, U.S.A.

HAWORTH, Lionel, O.B.E., F.R.S., R.D.I., F.ENG.; British aeronautical engineer; b. 4 Aug. 1912, Edenburg, S. Africa; s. of John B. and Anna S. (née Ackerman) Haworth; m. Joan I. Bradbury 1956; one s. one d.; ed. Rondebosch Boys' High School and Univ. of Cape Town; Graduate apprenticeship with Associated Equipment Co. 1934; Designer Rolls-Royce Ltd., Derby 1936, Asst. Chief Designer 1944; Deputy Chief Designer, Aero Division 1951, Chief Designer (Civil Engines), Aero Div. 1954, Chief Engineer (Propeller Turbines), Aero Div. 1962; Chief Design Consultant, Bristol Siddeley Engines Ltd. 1963, Chief Designer 1964; Dir. of Design, Bristol Siddeley Engines Ltd., Bristol Engine Div. 1965; Dir. of Design, Rolls-Royce Ltd., Bristol Engine Div. 1968, Dir. of Design, Rolls-Royce (1971) Ltd., Bristol Engine Div. 1971–77, Eng. Consultant, Rolls-Royce Ltd., Aero Div., Bristol 1977–81; Eng. Consultant, Lionel Haworth and Assocs. 1977, now Sr. Partner; Founder Fellow, Fellowship of Eng. 1975; Bronze Medal, Royal Aeronautical Soc., British Gold Medal for Aeronautics 1971, Royal Designer for Industry (R.D.I.) 1976. *Leisure interest:* sailing. *Address:* 10 Hazelwood Road, Sneyd Park, Bristol, BS9 1PX, England. *Telephone:* (0117) 9683032.

HAWTHORNE, James Burns, C.B.E.; British management consultant; b. 27 March 1930, Belfast; s. of Thomas Hawthorne and Florence Burns; m. Patricia King 1958; one s. two d.; ed. Queen's Univ. Belfast; Asst. master, Sullivan Upper School 1951–60; radio and TV producer and publr., BBC 1960–68; Chief Asst. BBC N. Ireland 1969–70; Controller TV, Govt. of Hong Kong 1970–72, Dir. of Broadcasting 1972–78; Controller, BBC N. Ireland 1978–88; Chair. Health Promotion Agency for N. Ireland 1988–, N. Ireland Community Relations Council 1990–96; Visiting Prof. Univ. of Ulster 1993–; Fellow, Royal TV Soc.; Winston Churchill Fellowship 1968; Royal TV Soc. Special Award 1986; Hon. LL.D. (Queen's, Belfast) 1988. *Publications:* Two Centuries of Irish History (ed.) 1966, Broadcasting to a Divided Community 1982; contribs. to various publs. *Leisure interests:* angling, caravanning, music, building restoration. *Address:* The Long Mill, Lissara, 67 Kilmore

Road, Crossgar, Co. Down, BT30 9HJ, Northern Ireland. *Telephone:* (01396) 831830. *Fax:* (01396) 831840.

HAWTHORNE, Sir Nigel Barnard, Kt., C.B.E.; British actor; b. 5 April 1929, Coventry; s. of Charles B. Hawthorne and Agnes Rice; ed. Christian Brothers' Coll. Cape Town; commenced acting career 1950; has worked mainly in England since 1951; stage appearances include: Otherwise Engaged 1976, Privates on Parade 1978, Peer Gynt and Tartuffe with RSC 1983–84, Across from the Garden of Allah 1986, Jacobowksi and the Colonel (Nat. Theatre) 1986, The Magistrate (Nat. Theatre) 1986, Hapgood (Aldwych) 1988, Shadowlands 1989–90, The Madness of George III (Olivier Award 1992, Evening Standard Award 1992) 1992, The Clandestine Marriage (Queen's) (also Dir.) 1994; numerous TV appearances including Marie Curie 1977, Destiny 1978, Edward and Mrs Simpson 1978, The Knowledge 1979, Yes Minister 1980–83, 1985–86, The Critic 1982, The Barchester Chronicles 1982, Mapp and Lucia 1984–86, Yes Prime Minister 1986, 1987, The Miser 1988, The Shawl 1989, Relatively Speaking 1989, The Trials of Oz 1991, Flea-Bites 1992; Late-Flowering Lust 1994, The Fragile Heart 1996 (B.A.F.T.A. Award for Best TV Actor); Forbidden Territory 1997; film appearances include: Firefox 1981, Gandhi 1981, Golda 1981, John Paul II 1983, The House 1984, Turtle Diary 1984, The Chain 1985, The Madness of King George 1994, Richard III 1995, Twelfth Night 1996, Murder in Mind 1997, Amistad 1997, Madeline 1997, The Object of My Affection 1997, At Sachem Farm 1998; Hon. M.A. (Sheffield) 1987, (Leicester) 1994.

HAWTHORNE, Sir William (Rede), Kt., C.B.E., M.A., SC.D., F.R.S., F.ENG., F.INST.MECH.E.; British professor of applied thermodynamics; b. 22 May 1913, Benton, Newcastle-on-Tyne; s. of William Hawthorne and Elizabeth Curle Hawthorne; m. Barbara Runkle 1939 (died 1992); one s. two d.; ed. Westminster School, London, Trinity Coll., Cambridge, and Mass. Inst. of Tech., U.S.A.; Devt. Eng., Babcock & Wilcox Ltd. 1937–39; Scientific officer, Royal Aircraft Establishment 1940–44, seconded to Sir Frank Whittle 1940–41; British Air Comm., Washington, D.C. 1944–45; Deputy Dir. of Engine Research, Ministry of Supply (U.K.) 1945–46; Assoc. Prof. of Mechanical Eng. M.I.T. 1946–48; George Westinghouse Prof. of Mechanical Eng., M.I.T. 1948–51; Prof. of Applied Thermodynamics Univ. of Cambridge 1951–80, Head of Eng. Dept. 1968–73; Fellow, Trinity Coll., Cambridge 1951–68; Master of Churchill Coll., Cambridge 1968–83; Hunsaker Prof. of Aeronautical Eng., M.I.T. 1955–56; Visiting Inst. Prof., M.I.T. 1962–68, 1973–78, Sr. Lecturer 1978–; mem. of Corpn. of M.I.T. 1969–73; Chair. Home Office Scientific Advisory Council 1967–76, Advisory Council on Energy Conservation 1974–79; Dir. Cummins Engine Co., Inc. 1974–86, Dracone Developments Ltd. 1957–87; Foreign Assoc. U.S. Nat. Acad. of Sciences, U.S. Nat. Acad. of Eng.; Vice-Pres. Royal Soc. 1969–70, 1979–81; mem. Electricity Supply Research Council 1953–83, Comm. on Energy and the Environment 1978–81; Hon. Fellow, Royal Aeronautical Soc., A.I.A.A.; Fellow of the Fellowship of Eng. 1976; Hon. mem. A.S.M.E. 1982; Hon. Fellow Royal Soc. of Edinburgh 1983, Fellow Imperial Coll. London 1983; Hon. D.Eng. (Sheffield) 1976, (Liverpool) 1982, Hon. D.Sc. (Salford) 1980, (Strathclyde, Bath) 1981, (Oxford) 1982, (Sussex) 1984; Medal of Freedom (U.S.A.) 1957, Royal Medal (Royal Soc.) 1982, Dudley Wright Prize (Harvey Mudd Coll., Calif.) 1985, Tom Sawyer Award (A.S.M.E.) 1992. *Publications:* (Ed.) Aerodynamics of Compressors and Turbines, vol. X, (Co-Ed.) Design and Performance of Gas Turbine Power Plants, vol. XI, High Speed Aerodynamics and Jet Propulsion; numerous papers in scientific and tech. journals. *Address:* Churchill College, Cambridge, CB3 0DS, England; 19 Chauncy Street, Cambridge, MA 02138, U.S.A. *Telephone:* (01223) 362601 (England); (617) 253-2479 (U.S.A.).

HAY, Andrew Osborne, O.B.E., B.A.; Australian business executive; b. 9 June 1945, Melbourne; s. of Sir David Osborne Hay and Lady Alison Marion Parker Hay; m. Marianne Perrott 1981; three d.; ed. Geelong Grammar School, New York Univ. and Australian Nat. Univ.; Lieut. Royal Australian Infantry 1968–69; Exec. ICI Australia Ltd. 1970–71; Man. Dir. Chapman Hay Ltd 1979–95; Chair. Adroyal Ltd. 1987–95, Lease Plan Australia Ltd. 1988–95, Berklee Ltd. 1988–; Pvt. Sec. to Minister for the Environment 1972, to Deputy Leader of the Opposition 1973–75, Prin. Pvt. Sec. to Treasurer 1975–77, to Minister for Industry and Commerce 1977–78; Pres. Melbourne Chamber of Commerce 1985–87; Chair. Australian Fed. of Employers 1986–87; Pres. Australian Chamber of Commerce 1987–88; Chair. Moorland Hire Ltd. 1989–94; Dir. Oakford Group Ltd. 1987–91; Hon. Treas. Royal Humane Soc. of Australasia 1984–. *Leisure interests:* tennis, golf, sailing, reading, horse racing. *Address:* Apt. 5, Amesbury House, 237 Domain Road, South Yarra, Vic. 3141, Australia. *Fax:* (03) 9821 4908.

HAY, Sir David Russell, Kt., C.B.E., M.D.(N.Z.), F.R.C.P., F.R.A.C.P.; New Zealand cardiologist; b. 8 Dec. 1927, Christchurch; s. of Sir James Hay and Lady Davidina Hay; m. Dr. Jocelyn V. Bell 1958; two d.; ed. St. Andrew's Coll., Christchurch and Otago Univ.; Physician, N. Canterbury Hosp. Bd. 1959–64; Cardiologist, Canterbury Hosp. Bd. 1964–89, Head, Dept. of Cardiology 1969–78, Chair. of Medical Services and Head of Dept. of Medicine 1978–84; Medical Dir. Nat. Heart Foundation of N.Z. 1977–92; Clinical Reader, Christchurch Clinical School of Univ. of Otago 1980–88; mem. WHO Working Group on Tobacco or Health, Western Pacific 1994; mem. WHO Advisory Panel on Tobacco or Health 1977–, and other professional appts.; Vice-Pres. R.A.C.P. 1988–92; Pres. Nat. Heart Foundation of N.Z. 1996–99; N.Z. 1990 Commemoration Medal, R.A.C.P. Coll. Medal 1993, WHO Tobacco or Health Medal 1995. *Publications:* 95 publs. in scientific journals. *Leisure interests:* golf, writing. *Address:* 20 Greers Road, Christchurch 4, New Zealand. *Telephone:* 3585 482.

HAY, Raymond A., B.S., M.B.A.; American business executive; b. New York; m. Grace Mattson; two c.; ed. Long Island and St. John's Univs.; fmr. Exec. Vice-Pres., Pres. of U.S. Operations and mem. Bd. of Dirs. and Exec. Cttee. Xerox Corpn.; Pres. and C.O.O. LTV Corpn. 1975, C.E.O. 1982–91, Chair. of Bd. 1983–91; mem. Bd. of Dirs. Shamrock Corpn., Dallas, Nat. Medical Enterprises, Inc., Los Angeles and MCorp, Dallas; mem. Exec. Cttee. Pres Reagan's Pvt. Sector Survey on Cost Control, Pres.'s Council for Int. Youth Exchange; holder of many other civic offices in Dallas. *Address:* c/o The LTV Corporation, 25 West Prospect Avenue, Cleveland, OH 44115, U.S.A.

HAYAISHI, Osamu, M.D., PH.D.; Japanese institute director; b. 8 Jan. 1920, Stockton, Calif., U.S.A.; s. of Jitsuzo and Mitsu Hayaishi; m. Takiko Satani 1946; one d.; ed. Osaka High School, Osaka Univ.; Asst. Prof., Dept. of Microbiology, Washington Univ. School of Medicine, St. Louis, Mo., U.S.A., 1952–54; Chief, Toxicology, Nat. Inst. of Arthritis and Metabolic Diseases, Nat. Insts. of Health, Bethesda, Md., U.S.A. 1954–58; Prof., Dept. of Medical Chemistry 1958–83, Prof., Dept. of Molecular Biology, Inst. for Chemical Research, Kyoto Univ. 1959–76; Prof. Dept. of Physiological Chem. and Nutrition, Univ. of Tokyo 1970–74; Prof. Inst. of Scientific and Industrial Research, Osaka Univ. 1975–76; Dean Faculty of Medicine, Kyoto Univ. 1979–81; Prof. Emer. Kyoto Univ. 1983–; Pres. Osaka Medical Coll. 1983–89; Dir. Osaka Bioscience Inst. 1987–98, Dir. Emer. 1998–; mem. Scientific Council Int. Inst. of Cellular and Molecular Pathology (Belgium) 1979–; Foreign Hon. mem. of American Acad. of Arts and Sciences 1969, Foreign Assoc. of the U.S. Nat. Acad. of Sciences 1972; Dunham Lecture (Harvard) 1980, Pfeizer Lecture, Albert Einstein School of Medicine 1980; mem. Japan Acad. 1974, New York Acad. of Sciences 1975; Hon. mem. American Soc. of Biological Chemists 1974, Int. Soc. on Clinical Entymology 1988, Soc. for Free Radical Research 1988; Hon. D.Sc. (Michigan) 1980; Hon. M.D. (Karolinska Institutet, Sweden) 1985; Dr. h.c. (Padua) 1988; Award of Japan Soc. of Vitaminology 1964, Award of Matsunaga Science Foundation 1964, Asahi Award for Science and Culture 1965, Award of Japan Acad. 1967, Order of Culture 1972, Award of Fujiwara Science Foundation 1975, Médaille de Bronze de la Ville de Paris 1975, CIBA Foundation Gold Medal 1976, Louis and Bert Freedman Foundation Award for Research in Biochemistry 1976, Deutsche Akademie der Naturforscher Leopoldina (F.R.G.) 1978, Jiménez Díaz Memorial Award (Spain) 1979, Wolf Foundation Prize in Medicine, Israel 1986, Jaroslav Heyrovský Gold Medal, Czechoslovak Acad. of Sciences 1988, Special Achievement Award, Miami Biotech. Winter Symposium 1989, Distinguished Lecturer in Neuroscience Awards, La. State Univ. Medical Center, U.S.A. 1990, Distinguished Visitor Awards, Univ. of New Orleans, U.S.A. 1990; 4th Vaajasalo Lecture, 5th Nordic Neuroscience Meeting, Finland 1991, Invited Lecture, Founding Congress of World Fed. of Sleep Research Socs., France 1991, Luigi Musajo Award, Italy 1995; Hon. Citizen of Kyoto 1984, Int. Hon. Citizen of New Orleans, U.S.A. 1990, 1st Order of Merit Grand Cordon of Sacred Treasure. *Publications:* Oxygenases 1962, Molecular Mechanisms of Oxygen Activation 1974, Molecular Oxygen in Biology 1974, and 510 scientific reviews and articles. *Leisure interest:* golf. *Address:* Osaka Bioscience Institute, 6-2-4 Furuedai Suita, Osaka 565-0874 (Office); Royal Court Shimogamo 205, 1–29 Izumigawa-cho, Shimogamo, Sakyo-ku, Kyoto 606-0807, Japan 606 (Home). *Telephone:* 06-872-4833 (Office); 075-781-1089 (Home).

HAYAMI, Masaru; Japanese banker and economist; joined Bank of Japan 1947, with br. offices in New York and London, Man. Foreign Office, Tokyo, Exec. Dir. 1978, now Gov.; assoc. Nissho Iwai Corpn., 1981, later Pres.; Chair. bilateral econ. cooperation groups with Brazil, U.A.E. and Belgium; fmr. Head Japan Inst. of Corp. Execs. and many int. business asscns. *Publication:* The Day the Yen Wins Respect. *Address:* Bank of Japan, 2-1-1, Hongoku-cho, Nihonbashi, Chuo-ku, Tokyo 103, Japan. *Telephone:* (3) 3279-1111. *Fax:* (3) 5200-2256.

HAYAMI, Yujiro, PH.D.; Japanese professor of economics; b. 26 Nov. 1932, Tokyo; s. of Kannosuke Hayami and Chiyoko Hayami; m. Takako Suzuki 1962; one s. two d.; ed. Univ. of Tokyo and Iowa State Univ.; economist, Japan Nat. Research Inst. of Agricultural Econs. 1956–66; Assoc. Prof. of Econs. Tokyo Metropolitan Univ. 1966–72, Prof. 1972–86; economist, Int. Rice Research Inst. 1974–76; Prof. of Int. Econs. Aoyama-Gakuin Univ. 1986–. *Publication:* Development Economics: From the Poverty to the Wealth of Nations 1997. *Leisure interest:* tennis. *Address:* 6-8-14 Okusawa, Setagaya-ku, Tokyo 158, Japan. *Telephone:* 03-3701-1345.

HAYASHIDA, Yukio; Japanese politician; b. 26 Nov. 1915, Kyoto Pref.; s. of Nobumaru and Yurie Hayashida; m. Yoko Takahata 1942; two s.; ed. Tokyo Imperial Univ.; joined Ministry of Agric. and Forestry 1939, Chief, Fisheries Admin. Dept. Fisheries Agency 1959, Chief Sec. to Minister of Agric. and Forestry 1962; Chief, Kinki Agric. Admin. Bureau 1963; Head, Horticulture Bureau 1964; mem. House of Councillors 1966–78; Parl. Vice-Minister for Int. Trade and Industry 1971; Gov. of Kyoto 1978–86; mem. House of Councillors 1986–; Minister of Justice 1987–88. *Publications:* The Countries of Oceania, Discovering the New History of Kyoto. *Leisure interests:* painting, calligraphy. *Address:* 1-9-18 Wakabayashi, Setagayaku, Tokyo, Japan. *Telephone:* (03) 3413-2200.

HAYCRAFT, Anna Margaret (pseudonym Alice Thomas Ellis); British writer; b. 9 Sept. 1932; d. of John Lindholm and Alexandra Lindholm; m.

Colin Haycraft 1956 (died 1994); four s. one d. (also one s. one d. deceased); ed. Bangor Co. Grammar School for Girls and Liverpool School of Art; columnist The Spectator, The Universe, Catholic Herald, The Oldie. *Publications include:* (as Alice Thomas Ellis) The Sin Eater 1977, The Birds of the Air 1980, The Twenty-Seventh Kingdom 1982, The Other Side of the Fire 1983, Unexplained Laughter 1985, Secrets of Strangers (with Tom Pitt-Aikens) 1986, Home Life 1986, More Home Life 1987, The Clothes in the Wardrobe 1987, The Skeleton in the Cupboard 1988, Home Life Three 1988, The Loss of the Good Authority (with Tom Pitt-Aikens) 1989, Wales: an anthology (ed.) 1989, Home Life Four 1989, The Fly in the Ointment 1989, A Welsh Childhood 1990, The Inn at the Edge of the World 1990, Pillars of Gold 1992, Serpent on the Rock 1994, The Evening of Adam (short stories) 1994, Cat Among the Pigeons 1994, Fairy Tale 1996, The Sin Eater 1998; (as Anna Haycraft) Natural Baby Food 1977, Darling, You Shouldn't Have Gone to So Much Trouble (with Caroline Blackwood) 1980. *Address:* 22 Gloucester Crescent, London, NW1 7DS, England. *Telephone:* 0171-485 7408. *Fax:* 0171-482 6632.

HAYDAR, Mohammad Haydar; Syrian politician; b. 1931; ed. secondary schools, Lattakia, Univ. of Damascus; teacher, Lattakia, Hama 1951–60; with Ministry of Agrarian Reform 1960–63; Dir. Alghab Establishment, Hama 1963; Dir. Agrarian Reform, Damascus, Daraa, Alsuweidaa 1964; Dir. Legal and Admin. Affairs, Ministry of Agric. and Agrarian Reform 1965; Gov. Alhasakeh 1966; teacher, Damascus 1968; mem. Command., Damascus Branch of Baath Arab Socialist Party (BASP) 1968; Temporary Regional Command of BASP 1970; mem. of both Regional and Nat. Commands of BASP, mem. of Cen. Command, Progressive Nat. Front of Syria and Minister of Agric. and Agrarian Reform until 1973; Deputy Premier for Econ. Affairs 1973–76; mem. of Nat. Command of BASP 1980–; mem. of the Nat. Progressive Front 1980–. *Address:* Foreign Relations Bureau, Baath Arab Socialist Party, Damascus, Syria.

HAYDÉE PEREIRA DA SILVA, Marcia; Brazilian ballet dancer and choreographer; b. 18 April 1937, Niterói; d. of Dr. Alcides Pereira da Silva and Margarita Haydée Salaverry Pereira da Silva; m. Günther Schöberl 1996; ed. Royal Ballet School, London and in Paris under Olga Preobrajendska and Lubov Egorova; mem. Grand Ballet du Marquise de Cuevas 1951–61; Prin. Dancer, Stuttgart Ballet 1961, Artistic Dir. 1976–96; Artistic Dir. Ballet de Santiago de Chile 1992–96; creator of roles in numerous ballets by John Cranko, John Neumeier and Maurice Béjart. *Address:* Stuttgart Ballet, Direktion, Oberer Schlossgarten 6, 70173 Stuttgart, Germany. *Telephone:* 49-711-20 32 235. *Fax:* 49-711-20 32 491.

HAYDEN, William George, A.C., B.ECONS.; Australian politician; b. 23 Jan. 1933, Brisbane, Queensland; m. Dallas Broadfoot 1960; one s. two d.; ed. Brisbane State High School, Univ. of Queensland; Police constable, Queensland 1953–61; mem. Parl. for Oxley 1961–88; Parl. Spokesman on Health and Welfare 1969–72; Treasurer 1975; Minister of Social Security 1972–75, of Foreign Affairs 1983–88, of Trade 1987–88; Gov.-Gen. 1989–96; Leader Parl. Labor Party (Opposition) 1977–83; Adjunct Prof. Queensland Univ. of Tech.; Hon. Dr. Univ. (Griffith), Hon. LL.D. (Univ. of Queensland); Hon. D.Litt. (Univ. of S. Queensland) 1997; Gwangha Medal (Korean Order of Diplomatic Merit), K.St.J.; Australian Humanist of the Year 1996. *Leisure interests:* reading, music, golf, riding, fishing, skiing, bush walking. *Address:* G.P.O. Box 7829, Waterfront Place, Brisbane, Queensland 4001, Australia.

HAYE, Colvyn Hugh, C.B.E., B.A.; British civil servant, educator and administrator; b. 7 Dec. 1925, Tundla, U.P., India; s. of Colvyn Hugh Haye and Avis Rose Kelly; m. Gloria Mary Stansbury 1949; two d.; ed. Oak Grove School, Sherwood Coll., Melbourne Teachers' Coll., Univ. of Melbourne, Australia, Christ Church, Oxford; served R.N.V.R. 1944–46; joined Colonial Service (now H.M. Overseas Civil Service), posted Hong Kong as Educ. Officer 1953, Sr. Educ. Officer 1962, Asst. Dir. of Educ. 1969, Deputy Dir. of Educ. 1975, Dir. of Educ. 1980, Sec. Admin. Grade and Commr., London 1984–87; Council and Exec. Overseas Service Pensioners' Asscn. 1988–97; Jardine Visitor to Univs. of Oxford and Cambridge 1989–97. *Leisure interests:* reading, writing, walking and talking. *Address:* Balmenoch, Gwydyr Road, Crieff, Perthshire, PH7 4BS, Scotland. *Telephone:* (01764) 656626. *Fax:* (01764) 656626.

HAYEK, His Beatitude Ignace Antoine II, D.PHIL.; Syrian ecclesiastic; b. 14 Sept. 1910; s. of Naum Hayek and Chafica Sciamsi; ed. Séminaire Patriarcal, Charfé, Lebanon, Pontifical Coll., of Propaganda Fide, Rome, and Oriental Pontifical Inst., Rome; ordained priest 1933, successively or concurrently Dir. of School, Curate and Vicar-Gen., Aleppo; Archbishop of Aleppo 1959–68; Syrian Patriarch of Antioch 1968. *Address:* c/o Patriarcat Syrien Catholique d'Antioche, B.P. 116-5087, rue de Damas, Beirut, Lebanon.

HAYEK, Nicolas G.; Swiss business executive; b. 19 Feb. 1928, Beirut; of American-Lebanese parentage; m.; one s. one d.; founded consultancy firm Hayek Eng. 1963; firm acts as adviser to govts and business concerns in Europe, U.S.A., China and notably to Swiss watch and high precision industry; co-founder, Chair and C.E.O., SMH (high-tech. co.) 1986; alt. Chair. Bd. of Dirs. MCC. Micro Compact Car Ltd. (Biel), SMH/Swatch and Chair. Swatch-Telecom (Biel); Pres. French govt. Reflection Group on Econ. Strategy 1996–; mem. Council for Research, Tech. and Innovation (Germany) 1995–; Dr. h.c. Neuchâtel Univ. (Switzerland) 1996. *Leisure interests:* swimming, tennis. *Address:* SMH, Seevorstadt 6, 2502 Biel, Switzerland. *Telephone:* 32-3436811. *Fax:* 32-3436911.

HAYES, Sir Brian, G.C.B.; British civil servant; b. 5 May 1929, Norwich; s. of Charles Hayes and Flora Hayes; m. Audrey Jenkins 1958; one s. one d.; ed. Norwich School, Corpus Christi Coll., Cambridge; joined Ministry of Agric., Fisheries and Food 1956, Deputy Sec. for Agricultural Commodity Policy 1973–78, Perm. Sec. 1979–83; Jt. Perm. Sec., Dept. of Trade and Industry 1983–85, Perm. Sec. 1985–89; Advisory Dir. Unilever 1990–; Dir. Tate and Lyle PLC 1989–, Guardian Royal Exchange PLC 1989–, SANE 1990–; Lloyd's Mems'. Ombudsman 1994–. *Leisure interests:* reading, watching cricket. *Address:* c/o Unilever House, Blackfriars, London, E.C.4, England.

HAYES, Cheryl Davis, M.B.A., M.A.; American researcher and administrator; b. 27 Oct. 1950, Ia.; d. of James G. Davis and Gloria Westerberg Davis; m. John C. Hayes Jr. 1972; two s. one d.; ed. Skidmore Coll., Georgetown Univ. and The Wharton School, Univ. of Pa.; Research Fellow, Smithsonian Inst. 1972–74; Study Dir. Study Project on Children's Service, N.A.S./N.R.C. (Nat. Research Council) 1978–80, Panel for Study of Policy Formation Process 1978–80, Panel on Work, Family and Community, Panel on Adolescent Pregnancy and Childbearing 1984; Exec. Officer, Cttee. on Child Devt. Research and Public Policy 1980; Exec. Dir. Nat. Comm. on Children; mem. Bd. of Trustees, Nat. Child Research Center; mem. Bd. Beauvoir School. *Publications:* several books on aspects of social policy research. *Address:* 4347 Forest Lane, N.W., Washington, DC 20007, U.S.A. (Home). *Telephone:* 202-364-0742.

HAYES, Colin Graham Frederick, M.A., R.A., F.R.C.A.; British artist; b. 17 Nov. 1919, London; s. of G. Hayes, and Winifred Yule; m. 1st Jean Law 1949; m. 2nd Marjorie Berry 1992; three d.; ed. Westminster School, Christ Church, Oxford and Ruskin School of Drawing, Oxford; R.E. Field Survey 1940, invalided out (Capt.) 1945; Tutor, Sr. Tutor, Reader, Royal Coll. of Art 1949–84, now Hon. Fellow; Pres. Royal Soc. of British Artists 1993–98; De Laszlo Medal. *Publications:* Renoir, Stanley Spencer, Landscape Painting in Oils, Robert Buhler. *Leisure interest:* travel. *Address:* 26 Cleveland Avenue, London, W4 1SN, England. *Telephone:* 0181-994 8762.

HAYES, Francis Mahon, B.A., D.P.A., B.L.; Irish diplomatist; b. 2 March 1930, Cork; s. of Francis Mahon Hayes and Aileen Hayes née Walsh; m. Kathleen O'Donoghue 1958; one s. three d.; ed. Nat. Univ. of Ireland, King's Inn, Dublin; Asst. Legal Adviser, Dept. of Justice 1957–65; Asst. Legal Adviser, First Sec. Dept. of Foreign Affairs 1965–70, Legal Adviser, Counsellor 1970–74, Legal Adviser, Asst. Sec. 1974–77; Amb. to Denmark, Norway and Iceland 1977–81; Perm. Rep. to UN Office at Geneva 1981–87; Deputy Sec. Dept. of Foreign Affairs 1987–89; Perm. Rep. to UN, New York 1989–95; mem. Int. Law Comm. 1986–91, The Constitution Review Group 1995–96. *Leisure interests:* travel, sport spectating, reading, theatre, golf. *Address:* Tara, 28 Knocknashee, Goatstown, Dublin 14, Ireland. *Telephone:* (353-1) 2983787. *Fax:* (353-1) 2983787.

HAYES, John Philip, C.B., M.A.; British economist; b. March 1924, Fleet, Hants.; ed. Corpus Christi Coll., Oxford; with Political and Econ. Planning (PEP), London 1950–53; with OEEC 1953–58; Econ. Dept., IBRD 1958–64; Head, Econ. Devt. Div. OECD 1964–67; Dir. World Economy Div., Econ. Planning Staff, Ministry of Overseas Devt. 1967–69, Deputy Dir.-Gen. of Econ. Planning 1969–71, Overseas Devt. Ministry, then Overseas Devt. Admin.; Dir. Econ. Program and Econ. Analysis and Projections Depts., IBRD 1971–73; Dir. Trade and Finance Div., Commonwealth Secr. 1973–75; Asst. Under-Sec. of State FCO 1975–84; Sr. Fellow, Trade Policy Research Centre 1984–89. *Publications:* Economic Effects of Sanctions on Southern Africa 1987, Making Trade Policy in the European Community 1993. *Address:* 223 Hoylake Crescent, Ickenham, Middx., UB10 8JL, England (Home). *Telephone:* (01895) 633 023.

HAYES, John Trevor, C.B.E., M.A., PH.D., F.S.A.; British art administrator and art historian; b. 21 Jan. 1929, London; s. of the late Leslie Thomas Hayes and Gwendoline (née Griffiths) Hayes; ed. Ardingly, Keble Coll., Oxford, Courtauld Inst. of Art, London, Inst. of Fine Arts, N.Y.; Asst. Keeper, London Museum 1954–70, Dir. 1970–74; Dir. The Nat. Portrait Gallery 1974–94; Commonwealth Fund Fellow, N.Y. Univ. 1958–59; Visiting Prof. in History of Art, Yale Univ. 1969; Chair. Walpole Soc. 1981–96; Hon. Fellow, Keble Coll., Oxford. *Publications:* London, A Pictorial History 1969, The Drawings of Thomas Gainsborough 1970, Catalogue of oil paintings in the London Museum 1970, Gainsborough as Printmaker 1971, Rowlandson, Watercolours and Drawings 1972, Gainsborough, Paintings and Drawings 1975, The Art of Graham Sutherland 1980, Catalogues of Gainsborough exhbns. for the Tate Gallery and the Grand Palais 1980–81, Landscape Paintings of Thomas Gainsborough 1982, Gainsborough Drawings (with Lindsay Stainton) 1983, The Art of Thomas Rowlandson 1990, The Portrait in British Art 1991, Catalogue of the British Paintings in the National Gallery of Art, Washington 1992, London in Paint (with Mireille Galinou) 1996, Catalogue of Gainsborough exhbn. at Ferrara Arte 1998, Gainsborough and Rowlandson: A New York Private Collection 1998. *Leisure interests:* music, walking, gardening, travel. *Address:* 61 Grantham Road, Chiswick, London, W4 2RT, England. *Telephone:* 0181-747 9768.

HAYES, Roger Peter, B.SC. (ECON.), M.A.; British public relations company director; b. 15 Feb. 1945, Hampton; s. of Patricia Hall and Peter Hall; m.

Margaret Jean Eales 1974; one s.; ed. Isleworth Grammar School, London Univ., Univ. of Southern Calif., U.S.A.; Reuters Corresp., Paris and London 1967–72; Vice-Pres. and Dir. Buson-Marsteller 1972–79; Man. P.A. Consulting Group 1979–83; Dir. Corp. Communications, Thorn-EMI PLC 1983–87; Chair. Hayes-MacLeod; Dir. Carma Int. Ltd.; Sec.-Gen. Int. Public Relations Asscns. (Bd. mem. 1984–88); Dir. (non-exec.) IT World 1985–; Chair. Int. Foundation for Public Affairs Studies 1986–89; Pres. Int. Public Relations Assen. 1997; Dir. Matrix Corp. Communications Strategist 1993–; Dir.-Gen. British Nuclear Industry Forum 1993–97; Vice-Pres. (Public Affairs and Govt. Relations) Ford of Europe 1991–93; Fellow Inst. of Public Relations (U.K.). *Publications:* (Co-author) Corporate Revolution 1986, Experts in Action 1988, Systematic Networking 1996. *Leisure interests:* books, music, cinema, int. politics, tennis, travel. *Address:* 75 Ellerby Street, London, SW6 6EL; 11c Tavistock House South, Tavistock Square, London, WC1H 9LF, England. *Telephone:* 0171-731 1255 (Ellerby Street); 0171-388 0671 (Tavistock Square).

HAYES, William, PH.D., M.A., D.PHIL.; Irish physicist and university administrator; b. 12 Nov. 1930, Killorglin; s. of Robert Hayes and Eileen Tobin; m. Joan Ferriss 1962 (died 1996); two s. one d.; ed. Univ. Coll. Dublin and St. John's Coll. Oxford; Official Fellow, St. John's Coll. Oxford 1960–87, Prin. Bursar 1977–87, Pres. 1987–; Univ. lecturer in Physics, Univ. of Oxford 1962–87; Dir. Clarendon Lab. Oxford 1985–87; Pro-Vice-Chancellor, Univ. of Oxford 1990–; Chair. Curators of Oxford Univ. Chest 1992–; Sr. Foreign Fellow, American Nat. Science Foundation, Purdue Univ. 1963–64; Visiting Prof. Univ. of Ill. 1971; mem. Tech. Staff, Bell Labs., N.J. 1974; Hon. mem. Royal Irish Acad. 1998; Hon. D.Sc. (Nat. Univ. of Ireland), (Purdue Univ.) 1996. *Publications:* Scattering of Light by Crystals (with R. Loudon) 1978, Defects and Defect Processes in Non-Metallic Solids (with A. M. Stoneham) 1985; research papers in professional journals. *Leisure interests:* walking, reading, listening to music. *Address:* President's Lodgings, St. John's College, Oxford, OX1 3JP, England. *Telephone:* (01865) 277419. *Fax:* (01865) 277482.

HAYMAN, Walter Kurt, M.A., SC.D., F.R.S.; British mathematician; b. 6 Jan. 1926, Cologne, Germany; s. of Franz Samuel Haymann and Ruth Therese Hensel; m. 1st Margaret Riley Crann 1947 (died 1994); three d.; m. 2nd Waficka Katifi 1995; ed. Gordonstoun School, Cambridge Univ.; Lecturer, Kings Coll., Newcastle, and Fellow, St. John's Coll., Cambridge 1947; Lecturer 1947–53, and Reader, Univ. of Exeter 1953–56; Visiting Lecturer, Brown Univ., U.S. 1949–50, Stanford Univ. Summer 1950, 1955, American Math. Soc. 1961; Prof. of Pure Math., Imperial Coll. of Science and Technology, London 1956–85 (Prof. Emer. 1985–, Sr. Research Fellow 1995–), Univ. of York 1985–93 (Prof. Emer. 1993–); mem. London Math. Soc.; mem. Cambridge Philosophical Soc.; Fellow Imperial Coll. 1989; Foreign mem. Finnish Acad. of Science and Letters, Accademia dei Lincei; Corresp. mem. Bavarian Acad. of Science; Hon. D.Sc. (Exeter) 1981, (Birmingham) 1985, (Giessen) 1992, (Uppsala) 1992, (Nat. Univ. of Ireland) 1997; first organizer (1964–68) British Math. Olympiad; 1st Smiths Prize 1948, shared Adams Prize, Cambridge Univ. 1949, Junior Berwick Prize 1955, Senior Berwick Prize of the London Math. Soc. 1964, de Morgan Medal 1995. *Publications:* Multivalent Functions 1958, 1994, Meromorphic Functions 1964, Research Problems in Function Theory 1967, Subharmonic Functions I 1976, II 1989, and over 180 articles in various scientific journals. *Leisure interests:* music, travel, television. *Address:* Department of Mathematics, Imperial College, 180 Queen's Gate, London, SW7 2BZ, England (University). *Telephone:* 0171-589 5111 (Ext. 58609).

HAYNES, Desmond Leo; Barbadian cricketer; b. 15 Feb. 1956, Holders Hill, Barbados; m. Dawn Haynes 1991; ed. Fed. High School, Barbados; right-hand opening batsman, teams: Barbados 1976–95 (Capt. 1990–91), Scotland (Benson & Hedges Cup) 1983, Middx. 1989–94, W. Prov. 1994–97; 116 Tests for W. Indies 1977–94 (4 as Capt.), scoring 7,487 runs (average 42.2) including 18 hundreds; scored 26,030 first-class runs (61 hundreds); toured England 1979 (World Cup), 1980, 1983 (World Cup), 1984, 1988, 1991; 238 limited-overs ints., scoring record 8,648 runs including record 17 hundreds.

HAYS, Adm. Ronald Jackson, B.S.; American naval officer; b. 19 Aug. 1928, Urania, La.; s. of George H. Hays and Fannie E. (née McCartney) Hays; m. Jane M. Hughes 1951; two s. one d.; ed. Northwestern State Univ., U.S. Naval Acad.; Commdt. ensign U.S. Navy 1950, Destroyer Officer Atlantic Fleet 1950–51, Attack Pilot Pacific Fleet 1953–56; Test Pilot 1956–59, Squadron Leader 1961–63; Air Warfare Officer 7th Fleet Staff 1967–68; Tactical Aircraft Planning Officer, Office Chief Naval Operations 1969–71; C.-in-C. U.S. Naval Force Europe, London 1980–83; Vice-Chief Naval Operations Dept., Washington 1983–85; C.-in-C. U.S. Pacific Command 1985–88; rank of Adm. 1983; Pres. and C.E.O. The Pacific Int-Center for High Tech. Research 1988–92, Tech. Consultant 1992–; D.S.M. with three gold stars, Silver Star with two gold stars, D.F.C. with gold and silver star; Legion of Merit, and numerous other awards and medals. *Leisure interest:* golf. *Address:* 869 Kamoi Place, Honolulu, HI 96825, U.S.A. (Home).

HAYWARD, Sir Jack (Arnold), Kt., O.B.E., F.R.G.S.; British business executive; b. 14 June 1923, Wolverhampton; s. of the late Sir Charles Hayward and Hilda Arnold; m. Jean Mary Forder 1948; two s. one d.; ed. Northaw Preparatory School, Stowe School, Buckingham; joined R.A.F. 1941, active service as pilot officer in S.E. Asia Command, demobilized with rank of Flight-Lieut. 1946; joined Rotary Hoes Ltd. 1947, with S. Africa br. –1950; f. U.S. arm Firth Cleveland Group of Cos. 1951; joined Grand Bahama Port Authority 1956, Chair. Grand Bahama Devt. Co. Ltd. and Freeport Commercial and Industrial Ltd. 1976–; Pres. Lundy Field Soc., Wolverhampton Wanderers F.C.; Vice-Pres. S.S. Great Britain Project; Hon. Life Vice-Pres. Maritime Trust 1971; Paul Harris Fellow (Rotary) 1983; Hon. LL.D. (Exeter) 1971, Hon. D.B.A. (Wolverhampton) 1994; William Booth Award, Salvation Army 1987. *Leisure interests:* sport, watching cricket, amateur dramatics. *Address:* Seashell Lane, P.O. Box F-40099, Freeport, Grand Bahama Island, Bahamas. *Telephone:* (242) 3525165.

HAZELHOFF, Robertus, LL.M.; Netherlands banker; b. 21 Oct. 1930, Delft; s. of Hendricus Hazelhoff and Rinske van Terwisga; m. G. M. van Huet 1960; ed. Univ. of Leiden; Man. Banco Tornquist, Buenos Aires 1965; Man. Algemene Bank Nederland, New York Office 1968, mem. Man. Bd. Algemene Bank Nederland N.V. 1971–, Chair. 1985–90, Vice-Chair. 1990; Vice-Chair. Man. Bd. ABN AMRO Holding N.V. 1991–92, Chair. 1992; Vice-Chair. Amsterdam-Rotterdam Bank N.V. 1990–; Vice-Chair. ABN AMRO Bank N.V. 1991–92; , Chair. 1992–94; Chair. Supervisory Bd. Heineken NV, NV Koninklijke Bijenkorf Beheer KBB, Stork NV; mem. Supervisory Bd. Nedlloyd NV, Kon. Nederlandsche Hoogovens en Staalfabrieken NV, and various other cos. *Leisure interest:* playing golf. *Address:* Nw. Bussummerweg 208, 1272 CN Huizen, Netherlands (Home).

HAZELTINE, Richard Deimel, M.S., PH.D.; American professor of physics; b. 12 June 1942, Jersey City, N.J.; s. of late Alan Hazeltine and of Elizabeth Barrett Hazeltine; m. Cheryl Pickett 1964; one s. one d.; ed. Harvard Coll. and Univ. of Michigan; mem. Inst. for Advanced Study 1969–71; research scientist, Univ. of Texas, Austin 1971–82, Prof. of Physics 1986–, Asst. Dir. Inst. for Fusion Studies 1982–86, Acting Dir. 1987–88, 1991, Dir. 1991–; Assoc. Ed. Reviews of Modern Physics 1990–; Fellow, American Physical Soc. *Publications:* articles in scientific journals. *Address:* University of Texas at Austin, Moore Hall Room 11. 222–61500, 26th & Speedway, Austin, TX 78712, U.S.A. *Telephone:* (512) 471-1322. *Fax:* (512) 471-6715.

HAZEN, Paul Mandeville, M.B.A.; American banker; b. 1941; m.; ed. Univ. of Ariz. and Univ. of Calif. (Berkeley); Asst. Man. Security Pacific Bank 1964–66; Vice-Pres. Union Bank 1966–70; Chair. Wells Fargo Realty Advisors 1970–76; with Wells Fargo Bank, San Francisco 1979–, Exec. Vice-Pres. and Man. Real Estate Industries Group 1979–80, mem. Exec. Office 1980, Vice-Chair. 1980–84, Pres. and C.O.O. 1984–94, Chair. 1995–, also Dir.; Pres. and Treas. Wells Fargo Mortgage & Equity Trust 1977–84; with Wells Fargo & Co. (parent), San Francisco 1979–, Exec. Vice-Pres., then Vice-Chair., Pres., C.O.O. and Dir. 1978–95, Chair., C.E.O. 1995–; Trustee, Wells Fargo Mortgage and Equity Trust; mem. Bd. of Dirs. Pacific Telesis Group. *Address:* Wells Fargo Bank N.A., 420 Montgomery Street, San Francisco, CA 94163, U.S.A.

HAZIM, Mgr. Ignatius IV; Lebanese ecclesiastic; b. 1920, Mharde; ed. Beirut Univ. and l'Institut Saint-Serge, Paris; Dir. of a secondary Theological Inst., Beirut, Lebanon; Rector of Theological Inst. Balamand Monastery then elected Bishop of Lattakia, Syria 1966, took up post 1970; Greek Orthodox Patriarch of Antioch and All the East 1979–; several times Pres. Middle East Council of Churches, Geneva; Founder Univ. of Balamand, Lebanon 1987, Pres. Bd. of Trustees; lectures in European and Middle-Eastern univs. *Publications:* La résurrection et l'homme d'aujourd'hui and in Arabic: I Believe, The Telling of Your Word Enlightens, Words on Pastoral Matters, The Church in the Middle East (trans. of the work by Père Corbon), God's Design (trans. of the work by Suzanne de Dietrich). *Address:* P.O. Box 9, Damascus, Syria. *Telephone:* 11 542 44 00. *Fax:* 11 542 44 04.

HAZZARD, Shirley, F.R.S.L.; author; b. 30 Jan. 1931, Sydney, Australia; d. of Reginald Hazzard and Catherine Hazzard; m. Francis Steegmuller 1963 (died 1994); ed. Queenwood School, Sydney; Combined Services Intelligence, Hong Kong 1947–48; U.K. High Commr.'s Office, Wellington, N.Z. 1949–50; UN, New York (Gen. Service Category) 1952–61; novelist and writer of short stories and contrib. to The New Yorker 1960–; Guggenheim Fellow 1974; mem. Nat. Acad. of Arts and Letters, American Acad. of Arts and Sciences; U.S. Nat. Acad. of Arts and Letters Award in Literature 1966; First Prize, O. Henry Short Story Awards 1976; Nat. Critics Circle Award for Fiction 1981; Boyer Lecturer, Australia 1984, 1988. *Publications:* short stories: Cliffs of Fall 1963; novels: The Evening of the Holiday 1966, People in Glass Houses 1967, The Bay of Noon 1970, The Transit of Venus 1980; History: Defeat of an Ideal: A Study of the Self-destruction of the United Nations 1973, Countenance of Truth: The United Nations and the Waldheim Case 1990. *Leisure interest:* Parthenophile. *Address:* 200 East 66th Street, New York, NY 10021, U.S.A.

HE CHUNLIN; Chinese politician; b. Aug. 1933, Wuxi City, Jiangsu Prov.; joined CCP 1951; ed. Northeast China Agricultural Coll.; Dir. Special Econ. Zones Office of State Council 1984–93; Deputy Sec. Gen. State Council 1988–98, Sec. Gen. Standing Cttee. of Nat. People's Congress March 1998–; mem. 14th CCP Cen. Cttee. 1992, 15th CCP Cen. Cttee. 1997–. *Address:* State Council, Beijing, People's Republic of China.

HE GUANGWEI; Chinese civil servant; Deputy Dir. China Nat. Tourism Admin. 1986–95, Dir. Nov. 1995–. *Address:* China National Tourism Administration, 9A Jian Guo Men Nei Dajie, Beijing 100740, China. *Telephone:* (10) 513 8866. *Fax:* (10) 601 2013.

HE GUANGYUAN; Chinese state official; b. 1930, Anxin Co., Hebei Prov.; Vice-Minister of Machinery and Electronics Industry 1982–88, Minister

1988–93, of Machine-Bldg. Industry 1993–96; alt. mem. 12th CCP Cen. Cttee. 1982–87, 13th Cen. Cttee. 1987–92; mem. 8th NPC 1993–, 14th CCP Cen. Cttee. 1992–97; Chair. Motions Cttee., 9th Nat. Cttee. of CPPCC. *Address:* c/o National Committee of Chinese People's Political Consultative Conference, 23 Taipingqiao Street, Beijing, People's Republic of China.

HE GUOQIANG; Chinese politician, b. Oct. 1943, Xiangxiang Co., Hunan Prov.; ed. Beijing Chemical Eng. Inst.; joined CCP 1966; Dir. and CCP Sec. Shandong Petro-Chemical Dept. 1984; alt. mem. 12th CCP Cen. Cttee. 1985, 13th CCP Cen. Cttee. 1987, 14th CCP Cen. Cttee. 1992; mem. of the Standing Cttee. of CCP Shandong Provincial Cttee., Vice-Sec., Sec. CCP Ji'nan City Cttee. 1986; Vice-Minister of Chemical Industry 1991; Vice-Sec. CCP Fujian Provincial Cttee., Acting Gov. Fujian Prov. 1996, Gov. 1997–; mem. 15th CCP Cen. Cttee 1997–. *Address:* Office of the Governor, Fuzhou City, Fujian Province, People's Republic of China.

HE KANG; Chinese government and party official; b. 26 Feb. 1923, Hebei Prov.; m. Miao Shixia 1945; two s.; ed. Agric. Coll. of Guangxi Univ.; Chief Dir. of Agric. and Forestry under Shanghai Mil. Control Cttee.; Deputy Head Dept. of Agric. and Forestry under E. China Mil. and Political Cttee. 1950–52; Dir. Dept. of Special Forestry of Cen. Ministry of Forestry 1952–54; Dir. Dept. of Tropical Plants, Ministry of Agric. 1954–57; Dir. S. China Tropical Crop Science Research Inst. and Tropical Crop Coll. 1957–72; Deputy Dir. Gen. Bureau of Land Reclamation, Guangdong Prov. 1972–77; Vice-Minister of Agric. and Forestry 1978; Deputy Dir. Nat. Comm. on Agric. and Vice-Minister of Agric. 1979; mem. 12th Cen. Cttee. CCP 1982–87, mem. 13th Cen. Cttee. 1987–93; mem. 8th NPC 1993–, Financial and Econ. Cttee.; Minister of Agriculture, Animal Husbandry and Fishery 1983–90; Deputy Dir. Nat. Planning Comm. 1983–85; NPC Deputy for Guangxi Zhuang Autonomous Region; Vice-Chair. Nat. Cttee., China Asscn. for Science and Tech. 1986–; Acting Vice-Chair. Nat. Agric. Regional Planning Cttee. 1979; Vice-Chair. All China Agric. Zoning Cttee. 1989; Pres. Chinese Village & Township Enterprise Asscn. 1990–, Agric. Econs. Soc. 1990–, China-Bangladesh Friendship Asscn.; Scientific Adviser to Nat. Environment Protection Cttee. 1992; Deputy to 3rd Nat. People's Congress 1964; Hon. Vice-Chair. Zhongkai Inst. of Agric. Tech.; World Food Prize 1993. *Address:* Ministry of Agriculture, Nun Zen Nan Li, Beijing, People's Republic of China. *Telephone:* 5001359.

HE LULI; Chinese administrator and paediatrician; b. 7 June 1934, Shandong Prov.; d. of late He Siyuan and He Yiwen; m. Rong Guohuang 1958; two s.; ed. Beijing Coll. of Medicine; paediatrician, Beijing Children's Hospital 1957–; Vice-Mayor Beijing Municipality 1988–96; Vice-Chair. Women and Youth Cttee., Revolutionary Cttee. of the Chinese Kuomintang 1988–96, Chair. 1997–; mem., Vice-Chair. CPPCC 8th Nat. Cttee. 1993–98; Vice-Chair. Standing Cttee. of 9th NPC 1998–; Vice-Pres. All China Women's Fed. 1993–. *Address:* Standing Committee of National People's Congress, Beijing, People's Republic of China.

HE LUTING; Chinese musician and composer; b. 20 July 1903, Jiulong Town, Shaodong Co., Hunan Prov.; s. of He Shengchun and Mrs. He Shengchun; m. Jiang Ruizhi 1932 (died 1997); three d. (one deceased); composed Buffalo Boy's Flute; Vice-Chair. Chinese Musicians' Asscn. 1950–66, 1979–85, Hon. Chair. 1985–; in political disgrace 1966–76; mem. Presidium CPPCC 6th Nat. Cttee. 1983–88, 7th Nat. Cttee. 1988; Vice-Chair. China Fed. of Literature and Art Circles 1979–89, Hon. mem. 1989; Hon. Chair. Shanghai Musicians Asscn. 1989–; Hon. Pres. Shanghai Conservatory 1986–; Hon. Chair. Shanghai Musicians' Asscn. 1989; Hon. mem. Int. Music Council 1983–. *Publications:* Selected Essays on Music, Vol I, Vol II, Complete Works Vols I, II, III. *Leisure interests:* literature, Chinese poetry, gouache painting. *Address:* Lane 76/4 Tai An Road, Shanghai 200052, People's Republic of China. *Telephone:* 86-021-62836074. *Fax:* 86-021-62836074.

HE QIZONG, Maj.-Gen.; Chinese army officer; b. 1943, Yingshan Co., Sichuan Prov.; joined PLA 1961; joined CCP 1965; Deputy Commdr. Kunming Mil. Region 1979–85; Chief of Staff of Div. 1982–83, Div. Commdr. 1983, Deputy Commdr. of Army 1983–84, Commdr. 1984–85, Deputy Chief of Gen. Staff, PLA 1985; alt. mem. 13th CCP Cen. Cttee. 1987–92; alt. mem. 14th Cen. Cttee. 1992–; Deputy Commdr. Nanjing Mil. Region 1993–; rank Maj.-Gen. 1988. *Address:* People's Liberation Army General Staff Headquarters, Beijing, People's Republic of China.

HE YONG; Chinese politician; b. Oct. 1940, Qianxi Co., Hebei Prov.; joined CCP 1958; ed. Tianjin Univ.; Vice-Dir. Org. Dept. of CCP Cen. Cttee.; Vice-Minister of Supervision 1988–98, Minister 1998–; mem. Standing Cttee. of CCP Cen. Comm. for Discipline Inspection 1992; mem. 15th CCP Cen. Cttee. 1997–; Vice-Sec. CCP Cen. Comm, for Discipline Inspection 1997–. *Address:* Ministry of Supervision, 35 Huayuan Bei Lu, Haidian Qu, Beijing, People's Republic of China.

HE ZEHUI, ENG.D.; Chinese physicist; b. 5 March 1914, Suzhou City, Jiangsu Prov.; m. Qian Sanqiang (deceased); three d.; ed. Qinghua Univ., Berlin Univ.; researcher Curie Inst., France 1941–48; researcher Modern Physics Inst., Academia Sinica 1953–; won 3rd prize of Academia Sinica Science Awards for paper Research into the Process of Preparing Nuclear Emulsoid, 1957; Vice-Dir. Inst. of Atomic Energy, Academia Sinica 1964–66; in disgrace during Cultural Revolution 1966–76; rehabilitated 1977; Deputy Dir. Inst. of High Energy Physics, Academia Sinica 1978–; mem., Dept. of Math. and Physics, Academia Sinica 1985–. *Address:* Room 203, Bldg. 14, Zhong Guan Cun, Beijing 100080, People's Republic of China. *Telephone:* 284314 (Beijing).

HE ZHENLIANG; Chinese government official; b. 29 Dec. 1929, Zhejiang Prov.; m. 1953; one s. one d.; ed. Aurora Univ., Shanghai; Sec.-Gen. the Chinese Olympic Cttee. 1982–86, Vice-Pres. 1986–89, Pres. 1989–94, Hon. Pres. 1994–; Dir. Int. Liaison Dept., State Comm. of Physical Culture and Sports 1982–85, Vice Minister 1985–94; Vice-Pres. Int. Ass. for the Nat. Org. of Sports 1984; mem. IOC 1981–, Exec. Bd. 1985–89, 1994–98, Vice-Pres. 1989–93, Pres. Cultural Comm. 1995–; Vice-Chair. All-China Sports Fed. 1986, Councillor 1997–; mem. CPPCC 1988–92, Standing Cttee. of CPPCC 1993–; Pres. Athletic Asscn. of P.R.C. 1992–96, Rowing Asscn. of P.R.C. 1986–, Rowing Fed. of Asia 1990–94. *Address:* 9 Tiyuguan Road, Beijing, People's Republic of China.

HE ZHIQIANG; Chinese government official and engineer; b. 1934, Lijiang Co., Yunnan Prov.; ed. Chongqing Univ.; joined CCP 1956; Deputy Chief Engineer of Yunnan Prov. Geological Bureau 1979–83; Vice-Gov. of Yunnan Prov. 1983–85; Gov. 1985–98; Deputy Sec., CPC 6th Yunnan Prov. Cttee. 1996–; NPC Deputy for Yunnan Prov.; mem. 14th CCP Cen. Cttee. 1992–97. *Address:* Yunnan Provincial Government, 5 Wuchua Shan Road, Kunming City, Yunnan Province, People's Republic of China.

HE ZUOXIU; Chinese physicist; b. 27 July 1927, Shanghai; m. Qing Chengrui 1962; one s.; ed. Shanghai Jiaotong Univ., Qinghua Univ.; researcher, Beijing Modern Physics Inst. and Atomic Energy Inst., Academia Sinica 1951–80; Deputy Dir. of Theoretical Physics Inst. Academia Sinica 1980–; mem. Dept. of Math. and Physics, Academia Sinica 1985–. *Publications:* A New Possible Quantized Field Theory of Composite Particles. *Address:* Theoretical Physics Institute, P.O. Box 2735, Beijing 100080, People's Republic of China. *Telephone:* (086) 1-2555248.

HEAD, Alan Kenneth, A.O., D.SC., F.A.A., F.R.S.; Australian physicist and mathematician; b. 10 Aug. 1925, Melbourne; s. of Rowland H. J. and Elsie M. (née Burrell) Head; m. Gwenneth N. Barlow 1951; ed. Univ. of Melbourne and Univ. of Bristol; Research Scientist CSIRO Div. of Aeronautics 1947–50, Aeronautical Research Labs. 1953–57, Div. of Tribophysics 1957–81, Div. of Chemical Physics 1981–86, Div. of Materials Science 1987–; Visiting Prof. Brown Univ. 1961–62, Univ. of Fla. 1971; Christensen Fellow, St. Catherine's Coll., Oxford 1986; Syme Research Medal 1965. *Publications:* Computed Electron Micrographs and Defect Identification 1973, numerous scientific papers. *Address:* C.S.I.R.O., Division of Manufacturing Science, Private Bag 33, Clayton South MDC, Vic. 3169 (Office); 10 Ellesmore Court, Kew, Vic. 3101, Australia (Home). *Telephone:* (03) 9544 2801 (Office); (03) 9853 0673 (Home). *Fax* (03) 9544 1128.

HEAD, Tim David, B.A.; British artist; b. 22 Oct. 1946, London; s. of Percy Head and Muriel Head; m. Vivian Katz 1973; two d.; ed. Dept. of Fine Art, Univ. of Newcastle upon Tyne, St. Martin's School of Art, London; Lecturer, Goldsmith's Coll. School of Art, London 1971–79; Lecturer, Slade School of Fine Art, Univ. Coll. London 1976–; Fellowship at Clare Hall and Kettle's Yard, Cambridge 1977–78; *comms.:* Sculpture, Nat. Museum of Photography, Film and TV, Bradford, Yorks. 1985, Floor Design, Science Museum, London 1995 Installation, Chatham Historic Dockyard, Rochester, Kent, Sculpture, Dance Performance with Laurie Booth Co. 1997–98, Light Screen, Artezium Arts and Media Centre, Luton 1998; *solo exhbns:* Museum of Modern Art, Oxford 1972, Gallery House, London 1973, Whitechapel Art Gallery and Garage Gallery, London 1974, Rowan Gallery, London 1975, 1976, 1978, Arnolfini Gallery, Bristol 1975, Anthony Stokes Gallery, London 1977, Kettle's Yard, Cambridge, Henie-Onstad Kunstcenter, Oslo 1978, I.C.A., Brisbane, Paola Betti Gallery, Milan, Serpentine Gallery, London, Third Eye Centre, Glasgow 1979, Gallery Bama, Paris, British Pavilion, Venice Biennale 1980, Locus Solus, Genoa 1981, Prov. Museum, Hasselt 1983, I.C.A., London 1985, Anthony Reynolds Gallery, London 1986, Whitechapel Art Gallery, London 1992, Frith Street Gallery, London 1992, 1995, City Art Gallery, Manchester 1993, Kunstverein Freiburg 1995, Kunstverein Heilbronn 1995, Stadtgalerie Saarbrücken 1995, Kunstverein Braunschweig 1995, Osterwalder Art Office Hamburg 1995, 1997; numerous group exhbns. in Milan, Kassel, Paris, Brussels, Sydney, New York, Vienna, London, Pa., Basle, Regensburg, Leeds, Montreal and Swansea; Gulbenkian Foundation Visual Arts Award 1975, First Prize, John Moores Liverpool Exhbn. 15, Walker Art Gallery, Liverpool 1987. *Address:* 17 Belsize Park Gardens, London, NW3 4JG, England.

HEALEY, Baron (Life Peer) cr. 1992, of Riddlesden in the County of West Yorkshire, **Denis Winston Healey,** P.C., C.H., M.B.E., F.R.S.L.,; British politician; b. 30 Aug. 1917, Mottingham; s. of William Healey; m. Edna May (née Edmunds) Healey 1945; one s. two d.; ed. Bradford Grammar School and Balliol Coll., Oxford; Maj., Royal Engineers 1945; Sec. Labour Party Int. Dept. 1945–52; M.P. 1952–92; Sec. of State for Defence 1964–70; Chancellor of the Exchequer 1974–79; Opposition Spokesman for Treasury and Econ. Affairs 1979–80, for Foreign and Commonwealth Affairs 1980–87; Chair. Interim Ministerial Cttee. of IMF 1977–79; Deputy Leader of Labour Party 1980–83; Pres. Birkbeck Coll. London 1993–; Hon. Fellow, Balliol Coll. Oxford 1980; Hon. D.Litt. (Bradford) 1983; Hon. LL.D., (Sussex) 1989, (Leeds) 1991; Grand Cross of Order of Merit, Germany 1979; Freeman of Leeds 1991. *Publications:* The Curtain Falls 1951, New Fabian Essays 1952, Neutralism 1955, Fabian International Essays 1956, A Neutral Belt in

Europe 1958, NATO and American Security 1959, The Race Against the H Bomb 1960, Labour Britain and the World 1963, Healey's Eye (photographs) 1980, Labour and a World Society 1985, Beyond Nuclear Deterrence 1986, The Time of My Life (autobiog.) 1989, When Shrimps Learn to Whistle (Collection of Essays) 1990, My Secret Planet 1992, Denis Healey's Yorkshire Dales 1995. *Address:* House of Lords, London, SW1A 0PW; Pingles Place, Alfriston, East Sussex BN26 5TT, England.

HEALY, Thomas William, PH.D., F.R.A.C.I., F.A.A., F.T.S.E.; Australian professor of physical chemistry; b. 1 June 1937; s. of W. T. Healy and C. M. Healy; m. Beverley M. L. Fay 1960; four s.; ed. St. Kilda, Univ. of Melbourne and Columbia Univ., N.Y., U.S.A.; lecturer, Univ. of Calif. (Berkeley) 1964–65; Sr. Lecturer in Physical Chem., Univ. of Melbourne 1967–75, Reader 1975–77, Prof. 1977–, Dean Faculty of Science 1985–90, Dir. Advanced Mineral Product Special Research Centre 1991–, Pres. Academic Bd. and Pro-Vice-Chancellor 1997–98; Assoc. Prof., Univ. of Calif., U.S.A. 1970; Sr. Assoc. Corp. Lab., I.C.I. (U.K.) 1981; Chair. Australian Landscape Trust 1997–; Queen Elizabeth II Fellow, Univ. of Melbourne 1965–67, Visiting Research Fellow, Univ. of Bristol, England 1975, Fulbright Sr. Fellow, Clarkson Univ., N.Y., U.S.A. 1981; Gov. Ian Potter Foundation; American Chem. Soc. Certificate of Merit 1967, Rennie Medal RACI 1968, Grimwade Prize, Univ. of Melbourne 1974, Royal Soc. of Vic. Medalist 1993. *Publications:* 200 research papers in physical chem., colloid and surface science, mineral processing, textbooks. *Leisure interests:* sailing, photography, reading. *Address:* 98 Barkly Street, Carlton, Vic. 3053, Australia.

HEANEY, Seamus; Irish poet and author; b. 13 April 1939, Northern Ireland; s. of Patrick and Margaret (née McCann) Heaney; m. Marie Devlin 1965; two s. one d.; ed. St. Columb's Coll., Londonderry, Queen's Univ. of Belfast; Lecturer St. Joseph's Coll. of Educ., Belfast 1963–66, Queen's Univ. of Belfast 1966–72; freelance writer 1972–75, Lecturer, Carysfort Coll. 1975–81, Sr. Visiting Lecturer, Harvard Univ. 1982–84, Boylston Prof. of Rhetoric and Oratory 1985–; Prof. of Poetry, Oxford Univ. 1989–94; Hon. D.Litt. (Oxford) 1997; W. H. Smith Prize 1975, Bennet Award 1982, Sunday Times Award for Excellence in Writing 1988, Lannan Literary Award 1990, Nobel Prize for Literature 1995, Whitbread Book of the Year Award 1997 (for The Spirit Level); Commdr. Ordre des Arts et des Lettres. *Publications:* Poems: Death of a Naturalist 1966, Door into the Dark 1969, Wintering Out 1972, North 1975, Field Work 1979, Sweeney Astray 1984, Station Island 1984, The Haw Lantern 1987, New Selected Poems 1966–1987 1990, Seeing Things 1991, Sweeney's Flight 1992, The Spirit Level 1996, Opened Ground: Poems 1966–96 1998. Prose: Preoccupations 1980, The Government of the Tongue 1988, The Place of Writing 1990, The Redress of Poetry (lectures) 1995. Anthology: The School Bag 1997 (co-ed. with Ted Hughes); Play: The Cure at Troy 1991; Translation: Laments, by Jan Kochanowski (with Stanislaw Baranczak). *Address:* c/o Faber and Faber, 3 Queen Square, London, WC1N 3AU, England.

HEAP, Robert Brian, C.B.E., M.A., C.CHEM., PH.D., F.R.S., F.R.S.C., F.I.BIOL.; British director of research; b. 27 Feb. 1935, Derbyshire; s. of late Bertram Heap and Eva M. Melling; m. Marion P. Grant 1961; two s. one d.; ed. New Mills Grammar School, Univ. of Nottingham and King's Coll. Cambridge; univ. demonstrator, Cambridge 1960; Lalor Research Fellow, ARC Babraham, Cambridge, staff mem. 1964, Head, Dept. of Physiology 1976, Head Cambridge Research Station 1986; Dir. of Research, AFRC (Agricultural and Food Research Council) Inst. of Animal Physiology and Genetics Research, Cambridge and Edin. 1989–93, Acting Dir. of Science, AFRC 1991–94, Dir. of Research, Babraham Inst. 1993–94; Visiting Prof. Univ. of Nairobi 1974; Visiting Research Fellow, Murdoch Univ. 1976; Visiting Sr. Fellow School of Clinical Medicine, Cambridge Univ. 1994–, Babraham Inst. 1995–, Master St. Edmund's Coll., Cambridge 1996–; Special Prof. Univ. of Nottingham 1988–; Pres. Inst. of Biology 1996–98; mem. Council Royal Soc. 1994– (Foreign Sec. and Vice-Pres. 1996–); mem. Nuffield Council on Bioethics 1997–; other professional appts. and distinctions. *Publications:* papers on reproductive biology endocrinology, growth and lactation in biological and medical journals. *Leisure interests:* music, walking, travel. *Address:* St. Edmund's College, Cambridge, CB3 0BN; Lincoln House, 8 Fendon Road, Cambridge, CB1 4RT, England (Home). *Telephone:* (01223) 248509 (Home). *Fax:* (01223) 415868 (Home).

HEARNE, Sir Graham James, Kt., C.B.E.; British business executive and solicitor; b. 23 Nov. 1937, Birmingham; s. of Frank Hearne and Emily (née Shakespeare) Hearne; m. Carol Jean Brown 1961; one s. three d.; ed. George Dixon Grammar School, Birmingham; admitted solicitor 1959; with Pinsent & Co. Solicitors 1959–63, Fried, Frank, Harris, Shriver & Jacobson Attorneys, New York 1963–66, Herbert Smith & Co., Solicitors 1966–67, Industrial Reorganization Cttee. 1967–68, N. M. Rothschild & Sons Ltd. 1968–77; Finance Dir. Courtaulds Ltd. 1977–81; Chief Exec. Tricentrol 1981–83; Group Man. Dir. Carless, Capel & Leonard 1983–84; non-exec. Dir. N. M. Rothschild & Sons Ltd. 1977–, Courtaulds PLC 1991–98, Gallaher Group PLC 1997–, BTR PLC 1998–; Chief Exec. Enterprise Oil PLC 1984–91, Chair. 1991–; High Sheriff of Greater London 1995–96. *Address:* 5 Crescent Place, London, SW3 2EA, England. *Telephone:* 0171-925-4000.

HEARNS, Thomas; American boxer; b. 18 Oct. 1958, Grand Junction, Tenn.; professional boxer 1977–; won WBA World Welterweight Championship 1980, lost it to Sugar Ray Leonard (q.v.) 1981, drew rematch June 1989; WBA World Super-Welterweight Champion 1982–86; unsuccessfully challenged Marvelous Marvin Hagler (q.v.) for World Middleweight Championship 1985; won World Light-Heavyweight Championship from Dennis Andries 1987, 1993; boxed at cruiserweight 1992; won WBO Super Middleweight Championship 1988; won WBA Light-Heavyweight Championship 1991, lost it to Ivan Barkley 1992; won World Boxing Union Cruiserweight title 1995; Golden Gloves Champion 1977. *Address:* 19244 Bretton Drive, Detroit, MI 48223, U.S.A.

HEARST, George Randolph, Jr.; American newspaper executive; b. 13 July 1927, San Francisco; s. of George Randolph Hearst and Blanche Wilbur; m. 1st Mary Thompson 1951 (died 1969); two s. two d.; m. 2nd Patricia Ann Bell 1969 (divorced 1985); Staff Los Angeles Examiner 1948–50, San Francisco Examiner 1954–56, Los Angeles Evening Herald-Express 1956– (Business Man. 1957, Publr. 1960–); Publr. Los. Angeles Herald-Examiner 1962–; Vice-Pres. The Hearst Corpn. 1977–96, Chair. 1996–; Dir., Trustee The Hearst Foundation. *Address:* Hearst Corporation, 1150 South Olive Street, Suite 2620, Los Angeles, CA 90015, U.S.A.

HEARST, Randolph Apperson; American newspaper executive; b. 2 Dec. 1915, New York; s. of William R. Hearst and Millicent V. Willson; brother of William R. Hearst, Jr. (q.v.); m. 1st Catherine Campbell 1938 (divorced 1982); five d.; m. 2nd Maria Scruggs 1982 (divorced 1986); m. 3rd Veronica de Uribe 1987; ed. Harvard Univ.; Asst. to Ed. Atlanta Georgian 1934–38; Asst. to Publr., San Francisco Call-Bulletin 1938–41, Exec. Editor 1947–49, Publr. 1950–53; Ed. and Pres. San Francisco Examiner 1972–; Pres., Dir. and Chief Exec. Hearst Consolidated Publications Inc.; Pres. Hearst Publishing Co. Inc. 1953–64; Chair. Dir. The Hearst Corpn. 1965–96, Chair. Exec. Cttee. 1965–73; Trustee, William Randolph Hearst Foundation; Pres. The Hearst Foundation 1972–. *Address:* Hearst Corporation, 959 8th Avenue, New York, NY 10019, U.S.A.

HEATH, Rt. Hon. Sir Edward Richard George, K.G., P.C., M.B.E., M.P.; British politician and conductor; b. 9 July 1916, Thanet; s. of William George Heath and Edith Anne Pantony; ed. Chatham House School, Ramsgate and Balliol Coll., Oxford; fmr. Pres. Oxford Univ. Conservative Asscn.; fmr. Chair. Fed. of Univ. Conservative Asscns.; fmr. Pres. Oxford Union; served in R.A. during Second World War, rising to rank of Lieut.-Col.; Commdr. 2nd Regt. HAC 1947–51; Master Gunner within Tower of London 1951–54; Civil Service 1946–47; M.P. for Bexley 1950–74, for Bexley, Sidcup 1974–83, for Old Bexley and Sidcup 1983–; Asst. Opposition Whip 1951; Lord Commr. of the Treasury (Sr. Govt. Whip) 1951, Jt. Deputy Chief Whip 1952–53, Deputy Chief Whip 1953–55, Parl. Sec. to Treasury and Govt. Chief Whip 1955–59; Minister of Labour 1959–60; Lord Privy Seal with Foreign Office responsibilities 1960–63, Sec. of State for Industry, Trade and Regional Devt. and Pres. Bd. of Trade 1963–64; Leader British Del., Brussels Conf. for countries seeking entry into Common Market 1961–63; Leader British Del. to first UN Conf. on Trade Aid and Devt. 1964; Leader of Conservative Party 1965–75; Leader of Opposition 1965–70, 1974–75; Prime Minister 1970–74; completed negotiations for Britain's entry into EEC 1971, signed Treaty 1972; mem. Independent Comm. on Int. Devt. Issues (Advisory Cttee. to Brandt Comm.) 1977–80; mem. Public Review Bd. Arthur Andersen & Co. 1978–; Chair. IRIS 1981–83; Devt. Adviser to China Investment and Devt. Fund, Kleinwort Benson China Man.; Chair. London Symphony Orchestra (LSO) Trust 1963–70, mem. Trust 1974–, Hon. mem. LSO 1974–, has conducted LSO in London, Cologne, Bonn; has conducted numerous orchestras worldwide, including Liverpool Philharmonic, English Chamber, Berlin Philharmonic, Chicago Symphony, Philadelphia Symphony, Jerusalem Symphony, Shanghai Philharmonic and Beijing Cen. Symphony Orchestras; Vice-Pres. Bach Choir 1970–; co-f., Pres. European Community Youth Orchestra 1977–80; has conducted on several records; Visiting Chubb Fellow, Yale 1975, Montgomery Fellow, Dartmouth Coll. 1980; Hon. F.R.C.M., Hon. F.R.C.O., Hon. Fellow Balliol Coll., Oxford, Nuffield Coll., Inst. of Devt. Studies, Sussex, Royal Canadian Coll. of Organists, (Univ. of London) 1994, Goldsmiths' Coll., Univ. of London 1996; Hon. D.C.L. (Oxford, Kent), Hon. D.Tech. (Bradford), Dr. h.c. (Sorbonne), Hon. LL.D. (Westminster Coll., Salt Lake City), (Wales) 1998, Hon. D.L. (Westminster Coll., Miss.), Hon. D.P.A. (Wesleyan Coll., Ga.), Dr. h.c. (Univ. of London) 1990, (Open Univ.) 1997; Hon. Bencher, Gray's Inn, Scholar of Gray's Inn 1938; Hon. Fellow Queen Mary and Westfield Coll., London; Charlemagne Prize 1963, Freiherr von Stein Foundation Award 1971, Estes J. Kefauver Foundation Award, Stresemann Medal 1971, Gold Medal (City of Paris) 1978, European Peace Cross 1979, World Humanity Award 1980, Gold Medal, European Parl. 1981, Schuman Medal 1996; Grand Cross of Merit with Star and Sash (Germany); Grand Cordon, Order of the Rising Sun; "Pro Arte" of the Förderergemeinschaft der Europäischen Wirtschaft 1997; Conservative. *Publications:* One Nation: a Tory Approach to Social Problems (co-author) 1950, Old World, New Horizons 1970, Sailing—a Course of My Life 1975, Music—a Joy for Life 1976, revised edn. 1997, Travels—People and Places in My Life 1977, Carols—the Joy of Christmas 1977, Our Europe 1990, The Course of My Life (memoirs) 1998. *Leisure interests:* music, sailing (Capt. British Admiral's Cup Team 1971, 1979, Capt. British Sardinia Cup Team 1980). *Address:* House of Commons, London, SW1A 0AA, England. *Telephone:* 0171-219 3561/2. *Fax:* 0171-219 5919.

HEATH-STUBBS, John (Francis Alexander), O.B.E., F.R.S.L.; British poet; b. 9 July 1918; s. of Francis Heath Stubbs and Edith Louise Sara Marr; ed. Bembridge School, Worcester Coll. for the Blind, The Queen's Coll., Oxford; English tutor 1944–45; Editorial Asst., Hutchinson's 1945–46; Gregory

Fellow in Poetry, Univ. of Leeds 1952–55; Visiting Prof. of English, Univ. of Alexandria 1955–58, Univ. of Mich. 1960–61; Lecturer in English Literature, Coll. of St. Mark and St. John, Chelsea 1963–73; Pres. The Poetry Soc. 1991–94; Queen's Gold Medal for Poetry 1973, Oscar Williams—Jean Durwood Award 1977, Howard Sergeant Memorial Award 1989. *Publications: poetry:* Wounded Thammuz, Beauty and the Beast, The Divided Ways, The Swarming of the Bees, A Charm Against the Toothache, The Triumph of the Muse, The Blue Fly in his Head, Selected Poems, Satires and Epigrams, Artorius, A Parliament of Birds, The Watchman's Flute, Birds Reconvened, Buzz Buzz, Naming of the Beast, The Immolation of Adelph, Collected Poems, Cats' Parnassus, A Partridge in a Pear Tree, Time Pieces, The Game of Love and Death 1990, A Ninefold of Charms 1991, Selected Poems 1991, Selected Poems 1992, Sweet Apple Earth 1993, Chimeras 1994, Galileo's Salad 1996, Torriano Sequences 1997; *autobiography:* Hindsights 1993; *drama:* Helen in Egypt; *criticism:* The Darkling Plain, Charles Williams, The Pastoral, The Ode, The Verse Satire; *translations:* Hafir of Shiraz, The Rubaiyyat of Omar Khayyam (both with Peter Avery), Leopardi: Selected Prose and Poetry (with Iris Origo), The Poems of Anyte (with Carol A. Whiteside); Ed. Selected Poems of Jonathan Swift, of Tennyson, of Alexander Pope, The Forsaken Garden, Faber Book of Twentieth Century Verse (both with David Wright), Images of Tomorrow, Homage to George Barker on his Sixtieth Birthday, Selected Poems of Thomas Gray, Poems of Science (with Philips Salman), In the Shadows, David Gray 1991. *Leisure interest:* taxonomy. *Address:* 22 Artesian Road, London, W2 5AR, England. *Telephone:* 0171-229 6367.

HEATON, Brian Thomas, D.SC., C.CHEM., D.PHIL., F.R.S.C.; British professor of chemistry; b. 16 Feb. 1940, Broughton-in-Furness; s. of William Edwin Heaton and Mabel Heaton (née Benson); m. Wendy Janet Durrant 1964; three d.; ed. Ulverston Grammar School, Hatfield Polytechnic, Univ. of Sussex; lecturer in Chem. Univ. of Kent at Canterbury 1968–81, Sr. Lecturer 1981–84, Reader 1984, Prof. 1984–85; Grant Prof. of Inorganic Chem. Univ. of Liverpool 1985–, Head of Dept. of Chem. 1988–97; Nuffield Fellowship 1981; Chair. SERC Inorganic Cttee. 1990–93; Sec. and Treas. Dalton Div. Royal Soc. of Chem. 1990–93; Tilden Lectureship and Prize Royal Soc. of Chem. 1986; Fellowship Japanese Soc. for Promotion of Science 1989; Leverhulme Foundation Research Fellowship 1997. *Publications:* articles in journals. *Leisure interests:* rugby, walking, listening to and playing music, eating and drinking (especially wine). *Address:* Department of Chemistry, University of Liverpool, P.O. Box 147, Liverpool, L69 3BX, England. *Telephone:* 0151-794 3524. *Fax:* 0151-794 3540.

HEATON, Frances Anne, B.A., LL.B.; British finance executive; b. 11 Aug. 1944, Winchester, Hants.; d. of John Ferris Whidborne and Marjorie Annie Maltby; m. Martin Heaton 1969; two s.; ed. Trinity Coll., Dublin, Civil Service Coll., London Business School; with Dept. of Econ. Affairs 1967–70; joined H.M. Treasury 1970, asst. sec. 1979–80; seconded to S. G. Warburg & Co. Ltd. 1977–79; with Corp. Finance Div., Lazard Bros. & Co. Ltd 1980, Dir. 1987–; Dir. W. S. Atkins PLC 1990–, Deputy Chair. (non-exec.) 1996–; Dir.-Gen. The Panel on Takeovers and Mergers 1992–94; Dir. Bank of England 1993–, Elementis PLC 1994–; mem. Cttee. on Standards in Public Life -1997; N.E. Dir. BUPA 1998–. *Leisure interests:* bridge, gardening, riding. *Address:* c/o Lazard Brothers & Co. Ltd, 21 Moorfields, London, EC2P 2HT, England. *Telephone:* 0171-588 2721.

HECHE, Anne; American actress; b. 25 May 1969. *Films:* An Ambush of Ghosts 1993, The Adventures of Huck Finn 1993, A Simple Twist of Fate 1994, Milk Money 1994, I'll Do Anything 1994, The Wild Side 1995, Pie in the Sky 1995, The Juror 1996, Walking and Talking 1996, Donnie Brasco 1997, Volcano 1997, Subway Stories, Wag the Dog 1997, Six Days Seven Nights 1998, A Cool Dry Place 1998. *TV:* (series) Another World; (films) O Pioneers! 1992, Against the Wall 1994, Girls in Prison 1994, Kingfish: A Story of Huey P. Long 1995, If These Walls Could Talk 1996.

HECHT, Anthony Evan, M.A.; American poet and professor of English; b. 16 Jan. 1923, New York; s. of Melvyn Hahlo and Dorothea (née Holzman) Hecht; m. 1st Patricia Harris 1954 (divorced 1961); two s.; m. 2nd Helen d'Alessandro 1971; one s.; ed. Bard Coll. and Columbia Univ.; Teacher, Kenyon Coll. 1947–48, State Univ., Iowa 1948–49, New York Univ. 1949–56, Smith Coll. 1956–59; Assoc. Prof. of English, Bard Coll. 1961–67; Faculty mem., Univ. of Rochester 1967, John H. Deane Prof. of Rhetoric and Poetry 1968; Hurst Prof., Washington Univ. 1971; Prof. Graduate School, Georgetown Univ., Washington D.C. 1985–93; Visiting Prof., Harvard Univ. 1973, Yale Univ. 1977; Consultant in Poetry, Library of Congress 1982–84; Trustee, American Acad., Rome; mem. Nat. Inst. of Arts and Letters, American Acad. of Arts and Science; Guggenheim Fellow 1954, 1959, Ford Foundation Fellow 1967, Rockefeller Foundation Fellow 1967; Fellow Acad. of American Poets, Chancellor 1971; Prix de Rome 1950; Brandeis Univ. Creative Arts Award 1965; Bollingen Prize 1983, Eugenio Montale Prize for Poetry 1985, Hariet Monroe Award 1987, Ruth B. Lilly Award 1988, Aiken Taylor Award, Nat. Educ. Asscn. 1989, Tanning Prize 1997. *Publications:* (poetry) A Summoning of Stones 1954, The Seven Deadly Sins 1958, A Bestiary 1960, The Hard Hours (Pulitzer Prize, Miles Poetry Award, Wayne Univ. 1968, Russell Loines Award, Nat. Inst. of Arts and Letters) 1968, Millions of Strange Shadows 1977, Collected Earlier Poems 1990; Jiggery Pokery (co-author and co-auditor) 1967; Seven Against Thebes (trans. with Helen Bacon) 1973, The Venetian Vespers 1979, Obbligati: Essays in Criticism 1986, The Transparent Man 1990, The Hidden Law: The Poetry of W. H. Auden 1993, On the Laws of the Poetic Art 1995, The Presumptions of Death 1995, Flight Among the Tombs 1996. *Address:* 4256 Nebraska Avenue, N.W., Washington, DC 20016, U.S.A. (Home).

HECHTER, Daniel; French couturier; b. 30 July 1938, Paris; s. of Raymond Hechter and Rosy Mendelsohn; m. 1st Marika Stengl Diez Deaux (deceased); one d.; m. 2nd Jennifer Chambon 1973; ed. Lycées Voltaire and Chaptal, Paris; designer 1954–; designer at House of Pierre d'Alby 1959–62; Founder and Dir.-Gen. Vêtements Hechter 1962–; Pres. Fed. Française du Pret-à-Porter Féminin 1984–87; Pres. Festival de la Mode 1987; Pres. Strasbourg Racing Club 1987. *Leisure interests:* football, tennis, swimming, skiing, curling, golf. *Address:* 4 ter avenue Hoche, 75008 Paris, France.

HECKER, François, L. EN D.; French banker; b. 27 Aug. 1919, Paris; m. Geneviève Poves 1945; two s.; ed. Law Faculty, Paris, and Ecole Nat. d'Organisation Economique et Sociale; with Banque Nat. pour le Commerce et l'Industrie (B.N.C.I.) 1945–65, Asst. in Gen. Secr. 1956, Asst. Sec.-Gen. 1963, Sec.-Gen. Banque Nat. de Paris (after merger with Comptoir Nat. d'Escompte de Paris) 1964, Controller-Gen. 1966, Dir. of foreign branches and subsidiaries 1969, Prin. Dir. in charge of int. div. 1973–79, Asst. Dir.-Gen. 1979–83, Hon. Dir. Gen. and Consultant 1983; Pres. Banque Arabe 1984–86; Officier, Légion d'honneur. *Leisure interests:* golf, cycling. *Address:* 61 boulevard de la Saussaye, 92200 Neuilly-sur-Seine, France (Home).

HECKER, Zvi, B.ARCH.; Israeli architect; b. 31 May 1931, Cracow, Poland; m. Deborah Houchman 1957; one s. one d.; ed. Cracow Polytechnic School of Architecture, Israel Inst. of Tech. Haifa and Avni Acad. Tel Aviv; worked in office of Arieh Sharon and Benjamin Idelson, Tel Aviv 1957–58; in partnership with Eldar Sharon, Tel Aviv 1959–65, with Alfred Neumann, Tel Aviv 1960–68; Visiting Prof. Laval Univ. Quebec 1968–69, Adjunct Prof. 1969–72; Visiting lecturer, McGill Univ. Montreal and Univ. of Pa. 1969–72; pvt. practice, Tel Aviv 1972–; work includes housing projects, synagogues, public bldgs. etc. *Publications:* exhbn. catalogues, articles in professional journals. *Address:* 19 Elzar Street, Tel Aviv 65157, Israel.

HEDELIUS, Tom Christer, M.B.A.; Swedish banker; b. 3 Oct. 1939, Lund; s. of Curt Hedelius and Brita (Påhlsson) Hedelius; m. Ulla Marianne Ericsson 1964; three s.; ed. Univ. of Lund; industrial expert, Svenska Handelsbanken 1967–69, Credit Man. 1969–74, Head, Regional Unit (Stockholm City) 1974–76, Head, Cen. Credit Dept. 1976–78, Pres. 1978–, Chair. of Bd. 1991–; Chair. Bd. Bergman & Beving AB, Svenska AB Le Carbone, Anders Sandrews Stiftelse; Vice-Chair. AGA AB, Telefon AB LM Ericsson 1991–, AB Industrivarden 1991–; mem. Bd. Svenska Cellulosa AB, AB Volvo, SAS Ass. of Reps.; Hon. Dr. Econ. (Umeå) 1989. *Address:* Svenska Handelsbanken, Kungsträdgårdsgatan 2, 106 70 Stockholm (Office); Sturegatan 38, 11436 Stockholm, Sweden (Home). *Telephone:* (8) 229220. *Fax:* (8) 7013331.

HEDER BAI; Chinese politician; b. 1930, Jeminay, Xinjiang; ed. Cen. Party School, Beijing; joined CCP 1951; Dir. Finance Comm. of Xinjiang 1980–82; Vice-Chair., People's Govt. of Xinjiang Autonomous Region 1983, Xinjiang Uygur Autonomous Regional 8th People's Congress 1993–. *Address:* People's Government of Xinjiang Autonomous Region, Urumqi, People's Republic of China.

HEDSTRÖM, Per Göran, M.SC.E.E.; Swedish business executive; b. 27 March 1943, Norsjö; m. Gunnel I. Hedström 1965; one s. one d; ed. Royal Inst. of Tech. of Stockholm; Lab. Man. Svenska Radio AB 1967; Lab. Man. Husqvarna AB 1972, Dir. Product Devt. 1975; Vice-Pres. Operations, The Tappan Co. 1980; Tech. Dir. Electrolux France 1983, Pres. White Goods Div. 1984, Product Line Man. of Sterilization and Disinfection 1985; Corporate Tech. Dir. and Sr. Vice-Pres. Electrolux Group Tech. 1989–94, Chair. 1994–98, Man. Dir. 1994–96. *Address:* c/o Electrolux SA, 43 avenue Felix Loreat, 60300 Senlis, France.

HEESCHEN, David Sutphin, PH.D.; American radio astronomer; b. 12 March 1926, Davenport, Iowa; s. of Richard G. and Emily S. Heeschen; m. Eloise St. Clair 1950; two s. one d.; ed. Univ. of Illinois, Harvard Univ.; Lecturer, Wesleyan Univ. 1954–55; Research Assoc. Harvard Univ. 1955–56; Astronomer, Nat. Radio Astronomy Observatory 1956–77, Dir. 1962–78, Sr. Scientist 1977–92, Emer. Sr. Scientist 1992–; consultant to NASA 1960–61, 1968–72, to Univs. Space Research Asscn. 1996–99, Nat. Radio Astronomy Observatory 1997–99; mem. Nat. Acad. of Sciences, American Astron. Soc. (Vice-Pres. 1969–71, Pres. 1980–82), Int. Astron. Union (Vice-Pres. 1976–82), Int. Scientific Radio Union, American Acad. of Arts and Sciences, American Philosophical Soc., A.A.A.S.; Research Prof. of Astronomy Univ. of Va. 1980–92; Nat. Science Foundation Distinguished Public Service Award 1980, Alexander von Humboldt Sr. Scientist Award 1985, Karl Jansky Lecturer 1993. *Leisure interests:* sailing, scuba diving, amateur radio. *Address:* 702 Copa D'Oro, Marathon, FL 33050, U.S.A. (Home). *Telephone:* (305) 289-0911 (Home).

HEFFER, Simon James, M.A.; British journalist; b. 18 July 1960; s. of late James Heffer and of Joyce Mary Clements; m. Diana Caroline Clee 1987; two s.; ed. King Edward VI School Chelmsford, Corpus Christi Coll. Cambridge; medical journalist 1983–85; freelance journalist 1985–86; Leader Writer Daily Telegraph 1986–91, Deputy Political Corresp. 1987–88, Political Sketch Writer 1988–91, Political Columnist 1990–91, Deputy Ed. 1994–96; Deputy Ed. The Spectator 1991–94; columnist Evening Standard 1991–93, Daily Mail 1993–94, 1995–. *Publications:* A Tory Seer (Jt. Ed. with C. Moore) 1989, A Century of County Cricket (Ed.) 1990, Moral Desperado: a Life of

Thomas Carlyle 1995, Power and Place: The Political Consequences of King Edward VII 1998, Like the Roman: The Life of Enoch Powell 1998. *Leisure interests:* cricket, music, ecclesiology, bibliophily. *Address:* The Daily Mail, 2 Derry Street, London, W8 5TT, England. *Telephone:* 0171-938 6000.

HEFNER, Hugh Marston, B.S.; American publisher; b. 9 April 1926, Chicago, Ill.; s. of Glenn L. and Grace (née Swanson) Hefner; m. 1st Mildred Williams 1949 (divorced 1959); one s. one d.; m. 2nd Kimberley Conrad 1989; two s.; ed. Univ. of Illinois; Ed.-in-Chief Playboy Magazine 1953–, Oui Magazine 1972–81; Chair. Emer. Playboy Enterprises 1988–; Pres. Playboy Club Int. Inc. 1959–86; Int. Press Directory Int. Publisher Award 1997; *Leisure interests:* cinema, jazz. *Address:* Playboy Enterprises Inc., 9242 Beverly Boulevard, Beverly Hills, CA 90210, U.S.A.

HEGARTY, Anthony Francis, D.SC., PH.D.; Irish professor of chemistry; b. 5 Aug. 1942, Cork; s. of Daniel F. Hegarty and Patricia Doyle; m. Ann M. Fleming 1967; two s. two d.; ed. Univ. Coll. Cork (Nat. Univ. of Ireland) and Univs. of Paris and Calif.; lecturer in Chem., Univ. Coll. Cork 1970–79; Prof. of Organic Chem., Univ. Coll. Dublin (UCD) 1980–, Dean of Postgraduate Studies 1989–95, mem. Governing Body of UCD 1990–, Vice-Pres. UCD 1997–; Visiting Prof. Brandeis Univ. 1975, Kuwait Univ. 1983, Univ. of Paris VII 1987; Chair. Nat. Trust for Ireland 1984–87; Chair. Royal Soc. of Chem. in Ireland 1987–90; mem. Senate, Nat. Univ. of Ireland 1992–; mem. Royal Irish Acad. 1981, Council mem. 1982–96, Sec. for Science 1986–88, Treas. 1988–96. *Publications:* 170 papers in int. journals in area of organic reaction mechanisms and bioorganic chem. *Leisure interests:* sailing, walking, classical music. *Address:* Department of Chemistry, University College, Dublin, Belfield, Dublin 4, Republic of Ireland. *Telephone:* (01) 7062305. *Fax:* (01) 7062029.

HEGAZY, Abdel Aziz Muhammad, D.PHIL.; Egyptian politician; b. 3 Jan. 1923; ed. Fuad Univ., Cairo, Birmingham Univ.; Dean, Faculty of Commerce, Ain Shams Univ. 1966–68; mem. Nat. Assembly 1969–75; Minister of the Treasury 1968–73; Deputy Prime Minister, Minister of Finance, Econ. and Foreign Trade 1973–74; First Deputy Prime Minister April-Sept. 1974, Prime Minister 1974–75; Chair. Allied Arab Bank 1985; teaching and working as a management consultant and certified accountant in Cairo, Jeddah and Beirut.

HEGDE, Rama Krishna; Indian politician; b. 29 Aug. 1927, Doddamane, Siddapur Taluk, Uttara Kannada Dist.; m. Saraswati Hegde; three c.; ed. Kashi Vidyapeeta, Benares and Lucknow Univs.; active in Quit India movement, imprisoned twice; organized Ryots' (Tenants') movt., Uttara Kannada Dist.; Pres. Dist. Congress Cttee., Uttara Kannada Dist. 1954–57; entered State Legis. as Deputy Minister for Planning and Devt. 1957; Gen. Sec. Mysore Pradesh Congress 1958–62; Minister in charge of Rural Devt., Panchayatraj and Co-operation, Nijalingappa's Cabinet 1962–65, Minister for Finance, Excise, Prohibition, Information and Publicity 1965–67, for Finance, Excise and Planning 1967–68, for Finance, Planning and Youth Services 1968, 1971, of Commerce 1998–; Leader of Opposition 1971–77; imprisoned during Emergency; elected Gen. Sec. All India Janata Party 1977; elected to Rajya Sabha from Karnataka Ass. 1978; Leader, Karnataka Janata Legislature Party 1983; first-ever non-Congress Chief Minister in the State; continued as head of caretaker ministry 1984; following State Legislature by-election, Chief Minister of Karnataka 1985–88; Deputy Chair. Planning Comm. 1989–90; Pres. World Fed. U.N. Asscns. *Address:* Ministry of Commerce, Udyog Bhavan, New Delhi 110011, India.

HEGEDÜS, Loránt, D.THEOL.; Hungarian ecclesiastic; b. 1930, Hajdunánás; s. of Géza Hegedüs and Magdolna Szabó; m. Zsuzsa Illés; two s. two d.; ed. Theological Acad., Budapest, Basel; asst. minister Bicske, Budapest 1956, Komló Nagykörös, Alsónémedi 1954–63, Hidas 1963–65; presbyter Hidas 1965–68, Szabadság tér, Budapest 1983–96, Kálvin tér, Budapest 1996–; Bishop 1990–; Prof. 1993–; acting Chair. Hungarian Presbyterian Churches Ecumenical Council 1994; mem. Presidium of European Churches Conf. 1992–97, Council of Hundreds 1997–; Prof. h.c. (Budapest, Veszprém); Bocskai Díj Award 1997. *Publications include:* Aspekte der Gottesfrage 1979, Nyitás a Végtelenre (Opening for Eternity) 1989, The Concept of Transcendence 1991, Kálvin teológiája (Calvin's Theology) 1996, Isten szuverenitása és az ember felelössége (The Sovereignty of God and the Responsibility of Man) 1996, Jézus és Europa (Jesus and Europe) 1998. *Leisure interests:* reading, listening to music. *Address:* 1054 Budapest, Szabadság tér 23, Hungary. *Telephone:* (1) 311-8695. *Fax:* (1) 311-8695.

HEGEL, Eduard, DR.PHIL., DR.THEOL.; German theologian; b. 28 Feb. 1911, Wuppertal-Barmen; s. of Albert and Maria (née Ommer) Hegel; ed. Univs. Bonn, Münster and Munich; Prof. for Middle and New Church History, Trier 1949, Münster 1953, Bonn 1966–76, Prof. Emer. 1976; mem. Historical Comm. for Westphalia 1958, Rheinisch-Westfälische Akademie der Wissenschaften 1973–; Apostolic Protonotar, Prelate. *Publications include:* Die Kirchenpolitischen Beziehungen Hannovers 1934, Kirchliche Vergangenheit im Bistum Essen 1960, Geschichte der Katholisch-Theologischen Fakultät Münster (2 vols.) 1966, 1971, Geschichte des Erzbistums Köln, Bd. 4–5 1979, 1987, Ecclesiastica Rhenana 1986, St. Kolumba in Köln. Eine mittelalterliche Grossstadtpfarrei in ihren Werden und Vergehen 1996. *Address:* Gregor-Mendel-Strasse 29, 53115 Bonn, Germany. *Telephone:* (0228) 23 22 73.

HEIDE, Ola Mikal, M.SC., DR.AGR.; Norwegian professor of botany; b. 26 April 1931, Trondenes; s. of Hans Kr. Heide and Marit Heide; m. Gerd Lillebakk 1955; three s. two d.; ed. Agricultural Univ. of Norway and Univ. of Wisconsin; Research Fellow, Agric. Univ. of Norway 1961–70; Prof. of Plant Sciences, Makerere Univ. of Kampala, Uganda 1970–72; Prof. of Plant Physiology, Univ. of Tromsö 1972–76; Prof. of Botany, Agric. Univ. of Norway 1976–, Head, Dept. of Biology and Nature Conservation 1990–95, Rector 1978–83; Vice-Chair. Agric. Research Council of Norway 1979–84; mem. various advisory cttees., etc.; mem. Norwegian Acad. of Sciences, Royal Soc. of Sciences of Uppsala 1991, Finnish Acad. of Science and Letters 1994; Pres. Scandinavian Soc. of Plant Physiology 1976–82, 1988–94, Fed. of European Socs. of Plant Physiology 1988–90; Kellogg Foundation Fellowship 1965; Norsk Varekrigsforsikrings Fund Science Prize 1968. *Publications:* more than 90 primary scientific publs. in the field of plant physiology and ecophysiology. *Leisure interests:* sport, especially cross country skiing and running. *Address:* Agricultural University of Norway, Dept. of Biology and Nature Conservation, 1432 Ås-NLH (Office); Skogvegen 34, 1430 Ås, Norway (Home). *Telephone:* 64 94 84 86 (Office); 64 94 16 01 (Home). *Fax:* 64 94 85 02 (Office).

HEIGERT, Hans A., DR.PHIL.; German journalist; b. 21 March 1925, Mainz; m. Hildegard Straub 1951; three s. two d.; ed. Ludwigburg High School, Univs. of Stuttgart, Heidelberg and Oklahoma; served with army 1943–45 before resuming education; worked as a journalist in newspapers, radio and television from 1950, becoming Chief Editor, Süddeutsche Zeitung 1970–85; mem. Presidium Goethe Inst., Munich 1984–93 (Pres. 1989–93); winner of Theodor Heuss Preis 1969; Bayerischer Verdienstorden 1974, Bundesverdienstkreuz 1979. *Publications:* Stätten der Jugend 1958, Sehnsucht nach der Nation 1966, Deutschlands falsche Träume 1968. *Address:* 82110 Germering/Oberbayern, Eichenstrasse 12, Germany.

HEIGHTON, (John) Steven, M.A.; Canadian author; b. 14 Aug. 1961, Toronto, Ont.; s. of John Heighton and Lambie Stephanopoulos; m. Mary Huggard 1988; one d.; ed. Silverthorn Coll. Inst., Queen's Univ.; Ed. Quarry magazine 1988–94; Gerald Lampert Award for Best First Book of Poetry 1990, Air Canada Award 1990, Gold Medal for Fiction, Nat. Magazine Awards 1992. *Publications include:* Stalin's Carnival (poetry) 1989, Foreign Ghosts (travelogue/poetry) 1989, Flight Paths of the Emperor (fiction) 1992, Théâtre de revenants (French translation of Flight Paths of the Emperor) 1994, The Ecstasy of Skeptics (poetry) 1994, On Earth As It Is (fiction) 1995, The Admen Move on Lhasa: Writing and Culture in a Virtual World (essays) 1997, La rose de l'érèbe (French translation of On Earth As It Is) 1998; poetry, fiction and critical articles in nat. and int. periodicals and anthologies 1984–. *Address:* Box 382, Kingston, Ont. K7L 4W2, Canada. *Telephone:* (613) 546 9677.

HEIKAL, Mohamed Hassanein; Egyptian journalist; b. 1923; m.; three s.; Reporter The Egyptian Gazette 1943, Akher Sa'a magazine 1945; Ed. Al-Akhbar daily newspaper 1956–57; Ed. Al-Ahram 1957, Chair. Bd. dirs. 1961–74; mem. Central Cttee. Socialist Union 1968; Minister of Information and Foreign Affairs 1970; arrested Sept. 1981, released Nov. 1981. *Publications:* Nahnou wa America 1967, Nasser: The Cairo Documents 1972, The Road to Ramadan 1975, Sphinx and Commissar 1979, The Return of the Ayatollah 1981, Autumn of Fury 1983, Cutting the Lion's Tail 1986, Suez Through Egyptian Eyes 1986, Boiling Point 1988, (The) Explosion 1990, Illusions of Triumph 1992, Arms and Politics 1993, Secret Channels 1996. *Address:* c/o HarperCollins Publishers, 77-85 Fulham Palace Road, Hammersmith, London, W6 8JB, England.

HEILBRONER, Robert L., PH.D., LL.D.; American economist; b. 24 March 1919, New York; s. of Louis and Helen (née Weiller) Heilbroner; m. 1st Joan Knapp 1952 (divorced 1975); two s.; m. 2nd Shirley Davis 1975; ed. Harvard Univ., New School for Social Research, New York; Norman Thomas Professor, Dept. of Econs., Graduate Faculty, New School for Social Research 1966–72, Norman Thomas Prof. Emer. 1972–; hon. degrees from La Salle Coll., Philadelphia, Pa., Long Island Univ., Ripon Coll., Wis. and Wagner Coll., State Univ. of New York. *Publications:* numerous articles and books, including The Worldly Philosophers 1953, The Future as History 1959, An Inquiry into the Human Prospect 1975, Beyond Boom and Crash 1978, Marxism: For and Against 1980, Five Economic Challenges (with Lester Thurrow) 1981, Economics Explained 1982, The Nature and Logic of Capitalism 1985, Behind the Veil of Economics 1988, Twenty-First Century Capitalism 1993, Visions of the Future 1995, Teachings from the Worldly Philosophy 1996. *Leisure interest:* piano. *Address:* c/o New School for Social Research, 66 West 12th Street, New York, NY 10011, U.S.A.

HEILBRONNER, François; French government official; b. 17 March 1936, Paris; s. of Paul Heilbronner and Elsie Schwob; m. Nathalie Ducas 1966; two s. two d.; ed. Lycée Charlemagne, Paris, Inst. d'Etudes Politiques, Paris and Ecole Nat. d'Admin.; Insp. des Finances 1964; apptd. to secr. of interministerial cttee. on questions of European econ. cooperation 1966, Deputy Sec.-Gen. 1969–72; Adviser to Minister of Foreign Affairs 1968–69; Deputy Dir. Office of Minister of Agric. 1972–73, Dir. 1973–74; econ. and financial adviser to Prime Minister Jacques Chirac 1974, Deputy Dir. of Office of Prime Minister Chirac 1975–76, 1986; Insp.-Gen. des Finances 1983; Pres. Groupe des assurances nationales (Gan) 1986, Banque pour l'industrie française, Phénix Soleil S.p.A. (Italy) (now Gan Italia S.p.A.) 1986–94; consultant FH Conseil 1995–; Pres. HL Gestion; Dir. Fondation Médecins sans Frontières, COJYP; Chevalier, Légion d'honneur, du Mérite maritime; Officier, Ordre Nat. du Mérite; Commdr. du Mérite agricole. *Address:* 12 rue Théodule Ribot, 75017 Paris, France.

HEILBRUN, Carolyn Gold, PH.D.; American author and professor of English literature; b. 13 Jan. 1926, East Orange, N.J.; d. of Archibald Heilbrun and Estelle (Roemer) Gold; m. James Heilbrun 1945; one s. two d.; ed. Wellesley Coll., Columbia Univ.; Instructor, Brooklyn Coll. 1959–60; Instructor, Columbia Univ., New York 1960–62, Asst. Prof. 1962–67, Assoc. Prof. 1967–72, Prof. of English Literature 1972–; Avalon Foundation Prof. of Humanities, Columbia Univ. 1986–93, Prof. Emer. 1986–93; mem. Mystery Writers of America (mem. Exec. Bd. 1982–84); Guggenheim Fellow 1966; Rockefeller Fellow 1976; several hon. degrees including Hon. D.H.L. (Pace) 1996, (Brown) 1997; Nero Wolfe Award 1981. *Publications:* The Garnett Family 1961, Christopher Isherwood 1970, Towards Androgyny 1973, Reinventing Womanhood 1979, Writing A Woman's Life 1988, Hamlet's Mother and Other Women 1990, The Education of a Woman: The Life and Times of Gloria Steinem 1995, The Last Gift of Time 1997, Collected Stories 1997; (as Amanda Cross) eleven novels. *Address:* c/o Eilen Levine Literary Agency, Suite 1801, 15 East 26th Street, New York 10010, U.S.A.

HEINDORFF, Michael, M.A., F.R.C.A.; German artist; b. 26 June 1949, Braunschweig; s. of Hans Heindorff and Sigrid Bootz (née Hampe); m. Monica Buferd 1983; one s. one d.; ed. Art Coll. and Univ. of Braunschweig, Royal Coll. of Art; has been represented in numerous group exhbns. internationally 1976–, also numerous solo exhbns. 1977–; sr. tutor in painting, R.C.A. 1980–; various comms. 1986–; life mem. Chelsea Arts Club 1988–; John Moore's Liverpool Award 10 1976; Schmidt-Rotluff Prize 1981, Villa Massimo Prize 1981. *Address:* 33 Charlotte Road, Shoreditch, London, EC2A 3PB; 2 Shrubland Road, London, E8 4NN, England. *Telephone:* 0171-739 1096 (Shoreditch); 0171-254 9241 (Shrubland Road). *Fax:* 0171-254 2193 (Shrubland Road).

HEINE, Volker, PH.D., F.R.S.; British professor of theoretical physics (retd.); b. 19 Sept. 1930, Germany; m. Daphne Hines 1955; one s. two d.; ed. Wanganui Collegiate School, Otago and Cambridge Univs.; Demonstrator, Lecturer and Reader, Cambridge 1958–76, Prof. in Theoretical Physics 1976–97; Visiting Prof. Univ. of Chicago 1965–66; Visiting Scientist Bell Labs., U.S.A. 1970–71; Fellow, Clare Coll., Cambridge 1960–; Fellow, American Physics Soc.; Foreign mem. Max Planck Gesellschaft; Maxwell Medal, Inst. of Physics, Royal Medal, Royal Soc., Dirac Medal, Inst. of Physics. *Publications:* Group Theory in Quantum Mechanics 1960, Solid State Physics (Vol. 24) 1970, (Vol. 35) 1980; articles in Journal of Physics, Physical Review, etc. *Address:* Cavendish Laboratory, Madingley Road, Cambridge, CB3 0HE, England. *Telephone:* (01223) 337258.

HEINEKEN, Alfred Henry; Netherlands industrialist; b. 4 Nov. 1923, Amsterdam; s. of H. P. Heineken and C. Breitenstein; m. Martha Lucille Cummins 1948; one d.; ed. Kennemer Lyceum; mem. Supervisory Council Heineken N.V. (brewing) 1951, del. mem. 1958, mem. Exec. Bd. 1964, Vice-Chair. 1969, Chair. 1971–89, Chair. and del. mem. Supervisory Council 1989–95, Chair. and mem. Bd. of dirs.; Heineken Holding N.V. 1979–; Kt., Order of the Lion of The Netherlands; Commdr. Order of Orange-Nassau; Officier, Légion d'honneur. *Address:* Pentagon B.V., 2e Weteringplantsoen 5, 1017 ZD Amsterdam, Netherlands.

HEINONEN, Olavi Ensio; LL.D.; Finnish judge; b. 12 Sept. 1938, Kuopio; s. of Eino Ensio Heinonen and Aili Vesa; m. Marjatta Rahikainen 1962; two s. two d.; ed. Univ. of Helsinki; Asst. Prof. of Law, Univ. of Helsinki 1969–70; Justice, Supreme Court of Finland 1970–86; Parl. Ombudsman 1986–89; Chief Justice, Supreme Court of Finland 1989–; Grand Cross, Order of White Rose of Finland; Hon. LL.D. (Turku). *Publications:* books and articles on criminal justice and criminal policy. *Leisure interests:* cycling, basketball. *Address:* Supreme Court, Pohjoisesplanadi 3, P.O. Box 301, 00171 Helsinki, Finland. *Telephone:* (09) 12381. *Fax:* (09) 1238354.

HEINTEL, Erich, DR. PHIL.; Austrian professor of philosophy; b. 29 March 1912, Vienna; s. of Rudolf Heintel and Luise Kästner; m. 1st Margarete Weininger 1939 (died 1982); two s. two d.; m. 2nd Waltraud Sammet 1984; ed. Univ. of Vienna; Dozent Univ. of Vienna 1940, Prof. of Philosophy 1952–82, Prof. Emer. 1982–; mem. Austrian Acad. of Sciences, Allgemeine Gesellschaft für Philosophie in Deutschland, Humboldt-Gesellschaft, Internationale Hegel-Vereinigung; Hon. Pres. Vienna Philosophical Soc.; Grosses Ehrenzeichen für Verdienste um die Republik Österreich; Ehrenmedaille der Bundeshaupstadt Wien in Gold; Bundesverdienstkreuz (Fed. Republic of Germany); Goldene František Palacky-Medaille (C.S.S.R. Acad. of Sciences) 1989; other awards and decorations; D. Theol. h.c. (Hamburg) 1986. *Publications include:* Hegel und die analogia entis 1958, Die beiden Labyrinthe der Philosophie 1968, Einführung in die Sprachphilosophie 1972, Grundriss der Dialektik (2 vols.) 1984, Was kann ich wissen? Was soll ich tun? Was darf ich hoffen? Versuch einer gemeinverständigen Einführung in das Philosophieren 1986, Gesammelte Abhandlungen (6 vols.) 1988–96, Die Stellung der Philosophie in der "universitas litterarum" 1990. *Leisure interests:* philosophy, collecting mushrooms, swimming. *Address:* 1190 Vienna, Bauernfeldgasse 7/1/6, Austria. *Telephone:* (1) 368 15 62.

HEISBOURG, François, F.R.S.A.; French business executive; b. 24 June 1949, London, England; s. of Georges Heisbourg and Hélène Pinet; m. Elyette Levy 1989; two s.; ed. Coll. Stanislas, Paris, Inst. d'Etudes Politiques, Cycle Supérieur d'Aménagement et d'Urbanisme, Ecole Nat. d'Admin.; Asst. to Dir. of Econ. Affairs, Ministry of Foreign Affairs 1977–78; policy planning staff, Ministry of Foreign Affairs 1978–79; First Sec. Perm. Mission of France to UN 1979–81; Int. Security Adviser to Minister of Defence 1981–84; Vice-Pres. Thomson Int. 1984–87; Dir. Int. Inst. for Strategic Studies (IIIS), London 1987–92; Sr. Vice-Pres. Matra Défense Espace 1992–98; now Chair. Geneva Center for Security Policy; Head French Interministerial Group on teaching of, and research in, strategic and int. affairs; Visiting Prof. in Political Science; Chevalier, Ordre nat. du Mérite; decorations from Spain, Germany and Togo. *Publications:* La Puce, les Hommes et la Bombe (with P. Boniface) 1986, Les Volontaires de l'an 2000 1995, The Future of Warfare 1997; numerous articles in int. media and scholarly journals. *Leisure interests:* hiking, chess, collecting atlases. *Address:* 88 rue de Sèvres, 75007 Paris, France.

HEITSCH, Ernst, D.PHIL.; German professor of classics; b. 17 June 1928, Celle; s. of Ernst Heitsch and Luise Meineke; m. Paula Sötemann 1961; two s. one d.; ed. Univ. Göttingen; Univ. Lecturer in Classical Linguistics Univ. Göttingen 1960–66, Professor 1966–67; Prof. of Classical Linguistics Univ. of Regensburg 1967–; mem. Akad. der Wissenschaften und der Literatur zu Mainz, Deutsches Archäologisches Institut. *Publications:* Die griechischen Dichterfragmente der römischen Kaiserzeit 1963, Epische Kunstsprache und Homer 1968, Parmenides 1974, 1995, Parmenides und die Anfänge der Erkenntniskritik und Logik 1979, Xenophanes 1983, Antiphon aus Rhamnus 1984, Willkür und Problembewusstsein in Platons Kratylos 1984, Platon über die rechte Art zu reden und zu schreiben 1987, Überlegungen Platons im Theaetet 1988, Wollen und Verwirklichen 1989, Wege zu Platon 1992, Platon Phaidros 1993, Erkenntnis und Lebenstührung 1994, Geschichte und Situationen bei Thukydides 1996, Grenzen philologischer Echtheitskritik 1997; numerous articles in periodicals. *Leisure interest:* sailing. *Address:* Mattinger Strasse 1, 93049 Regensburg, Germany. *Telephone:* (0941) 31944.

HEJDUK, John Quentin, M.ARCH., F.A.I.A.; American architect and professor of architecture; b. 19 July 1929, New York; m. Gloria Fiorentino 1951; one s. one d.; ed. The Cooper Union, Univ. of Cincinnati, Harvard Univ. Grad. School of Design, Univ. of Rome School of Architecture, Italy (Fulbright Scholar); worked in various architectural offices New York 1947–52; instructor in Architectural Design, Univ. of Tex., Austin 1954–56; worked in office of I.M. Pei and Partners, New York 1956–58; Asst. Prof. of Architecture, School of Architecture, Cornell Univ., Ithaca, New York 1958–60; Critic of Architectural Design, Grad. School of Design, Yale Univ. 1961–64; Prof. of Architecture, The Irwin S. Chanin School of Architecture of The Cooper Union 1964– (Chair. Architecture Dept. (1964–75), Dean and Prof. of Architecture 1975–; Prin. own firm 1966–; numerous awards and prizes including: (for Cooper Union Foundation Bldg. Renovation) Municipal Arts Soc. Award 1975, New York State Council on the Arts Award 1975, New York Soc. of Architects Award 1977, Honor Award, American Inst. of Architects 1990, Innovation in Design Award, Chrysler Corpn. 1993. *Publications include:* Education of an Architect (with Roger Canon) 1971, Fabrications 1975, The Silent Witnesses and Other Poems 1980, Mask of Medusa 1986, Victims 1987, Bovisa 1987, Collapse of Time 1988, Riga 1988, Vladivostok 1989, Aesop's Fables (illustrations) 1991, Lancaster/Hanover Masque 1992, Soundings 1993, Architectures in Love 1995, Adjusting Foundations 1995, Pewter Wings, Golden Horns, Stone Veils 1997, Such Places as Memory 1998. *Address:* The Irwin S. Chanin School of Architecture of the Cooper Union, 30 Cooper Square, New York, NY 10003; 5271 Huxley Avenue, Bronx, NY 10471, U.S.A.

HEKMATYAR, Gulbuddin; Afghanistan politician and fmr. guerrilla leader; leader Hezb-i-Islam Mujahideen Movt. against Soviet-backed regime; Prime Minister of Afghanistan 1993–94, 1996–97; returned from exile in Iran 1998.

HELD, Al; American artist; b. 12 Oct. 1928, New York; ed. Art Students League, New York, and Acad. de la Grande Chaumière, Paris; Prof. of Art, Yale Univ. 1962–78, Adjunct Prof. of Painting 1978–; one-man shows at André Emmerich Gallery, New York, 1965, 1967, 1968, 1970, 1972, 1973, 1975, 1976, 1978, 1979, 1980, 1982, 1984–92, 1995, 1996, 1997, Inst. of Contemporary Art, Boston 1978, Robert Miller Gallery, New York 1980, 1982, 1987, 1990, 1994, Richard Gray Gallery, Chicago 1984, Pace Editions, New York 1984 and also in Zürich, Amsterdam, Stuttgart, London etc.; has participated in numerous group shows and work appears in many permanent collections inc. Whitney Museum, Museum of Modern Art, New York, San Francisco Museum of Art, Nat. Gallery Berlin, Hirshhorn Museum and Sculpture Gardens, Washington; co-founder Brata Gallery, New York 1965; Guggenheim Fellow 1966; Logan Medal, Art Inst. of Chicago 1964, Brandeis Univ. Creative Arts Award 1983. *Publications:* articles in professional journals. *Address:* c/o Andre Emmerich Gallery, 41 E. 57th Street, New York, NY 10022, U.S.A.

HELD, Heinz Joachim, DR. THEOL.; German theologian; b. 16 May 1928, Wesseling/Rhein; s. of Heinrich Held and Hildegard Röhrig; m. Anneliese Novak 1959; one s. three d.; ed. Wuppertal, Göttingen, Heidelberg, Bonn and Austin, Tex.; research asst. Wuppertal Theological Seminary 1953–56; clergyman, Friedrichsfeld/Niederrhein 1957-64; Prof. of Theology, Buenos Aires Lutheran Seminary 1964–68; Pres. River Plate Evangelical Church, Buenos Aires 1968–74; mem. Cen. Cttee. World Council of Churches 1968–91; Moderator of Cen. Cttee. and Exec. Cttee. 1983–91; Pres. Office for Foreign Relations of Evangelical Church in Germany 1975–93; Bishop 1991; Chair. Nat. Council of Churches, Fed. Repub. of Germany 1982–88, 1992–95; Hon. Dr.theol. (Lutheran Theological Acad. Budapest) 1985; Hon. D.D. (Acad. of Ecumenical Indian Theology and Church Admin., Madras)

1988. *Leisure interests:* stamp collecting, amateur music (piano), photography. *Address:* Bussilliatweg 32, 30419 Hannover, Germany. *Telephone:* (0511) 271 43 08.

HELD, Richard M., M.A., PH.D.; American professor of psychology; b. 10 Oct. 1922, New York; s. of Lawrence Walter Held and Tessie Klein Held; m. Doris Bernays 1951; three c.; ed. Columbia and Harvard Univs. and Swarthmore Coll.; Research Asst. Dept. of Psychology, Swarthmore Coll. 1946–48; Research Asst., Teaching Fellow, and N.I.H. Postdoctoral Fellow, Dept. of Psychology, Harvard Univ. 1949–53; Instructor, Asst. Prof., Assoc. Prof., Prof. and Chair. Dept. of Psychology, Brandeis Univ. 1953–62; mem. Inst. for Advanced Study, Princeton 1955–56; Sr. Research Fellow of Nat. Science Foundation and Visiting Prof. Dept. of Psychology, M.I.T. 1962–63, Prof., Dept. of Brain and Cognitive Sciences 1963–93, Dept. Chair. 1977–86, Prof. Emer. and Sr. Lecturer 1994–; Prof. of Vision Science and Dir. of Research, New England Coll. of Optometry; Fellow, American Acad. of Arts and Sciences; mem. N.A.S. and many other learned socs.; numerous other professional appointments; Glenn A. Fry Award 1979, H. C. Warren Medal 1983, Kenneth Craik Award 1985; Dr. h.c. (Free Univ. of Brussels) 1984, (New England Coll. of Optometry). *Leisure interests:* tennis, theatre, visual arts. *Address:* c/o Department of Brain and Cognitive Sciences, E10-237A, Massachusetts Institute of Technology, 79 Amherst Street, Cambridge, MA 02139, U.S.A. *Telephone:* (617) 253-5745. *Fax:* (617) 253-9767.

HELÉN, N. Gunnar, PH.D.; Swedish politician; b. 5 June 1918, Vingåker; s. of Gustaf Helén and Ingeborg Helén (née Andersson); m. Ingrid Rying 1938; one s. one d.; with Swedish Broadcasting Corpn. 1939–49; Literary Ed. of Stockholms-Tidningen 1949–55; mem. Parl. 1953–66, 1970–76; mem. Nordic Council 1954–64, 1970–76; Asst. Prof. Univ. of Stockholm 1956–; Gov. of Prov. of Kronoberg 1965–70; Chair. Liberal Party of Sweden 1969–75; mem. Bd. of Govs. Swedish Nat. Debt Office 1974–77; Gov. of Stockholm 1977–84; Chair. Swedish Broadcasting Corpn. 1978–83; Chair. Liberal Newspapers K.B. 1976–93. *Publications:* Birger Sjöberg Kriser och kransar i stilhistorisk belysning 1946, Röst i Radion 1950, Friheten och de två systemen 1954, Skola, yrke, samhälle i USA 1955, 7 år av skolreformer 1957, Rätt till utbildning 1960, Svenska författare 1964, Politik för ett mänskligare samhälle 1970, Frihet i gemenskap 1974, Fröken på Tagel 1977, Bättre Svenska 1984, Alltför många jag 1991. *Address:* Jakob Dubbes väg 8, 13150 Saltsjöduvnäs, Sweden. *Telephone:* 0468-7168245 (Home).

HELFT, Jorge Santiago; Argentinian arts foundation director; b. 10 June 1934, France; s. of late Jacques Helft and Marianne Loevi; m. Mariana Eppinger 1955; three s.; ed. New York Univ. and Columbia Univ., U.S.A.; lived in Paris until 1940, New York 1940–47, Buenos Aires 1947–; business exec. with Continental Grain Co. 1956–74, Vesuvio S.A. 1974–82; Trustee and Dir. Fundación Antorchas 1985–, Fundación Lampadia, Vaduz, Liechtenstein; Pres. Fundación San Telmo 1980–; Founding mem. and Dir. Fundación Teatro Colón 1978–; Oficial, Ordem de Rio Branco (Brazil). *Leisure interests:* arts and music. *Address:* Fundación Antorchas, Chile 300 (1098), Buenos Aires (Office); Defensa 1364 (1143), Buenos Aires, Argentina (Home).

HELINSKI, Donald Raymond, PH.D.; American professor of biology; b. 7 July 1933, Baltimore, Md.; s. of George L. Helinski and Marie M. Helinski; m. Patricia M. Doherty 1962; one s. one d.; ed. Univ. of Maryland, Case Western Reserve Univ., Cleveland, Ohio, Stanford Univ.; U.S. Public Health Service Postdoctoral Fellow Stanford Univ. 1960–62; Asst. Prof., Princeton Univ. 1962–65; Assoc. Prof. Dept. of Biology, Univ. of Calif., San Diego 1965–70, Prof. 1970–, Chair. Dept. of Biology 1979–81, Dir. Center for Molecular Genetics 1984–95, Assoc. Dean of Natural Sciences 1994–97; mem. Nat. Inst. Health Advisory Cttee. on DNA Recombinant Research 1975–78; mem. N.A.S., A.A.A.S. *Publications:* over 150 publications and 50 review articles in the fields of biochemistry, molecular genetics and microbiology. *Address:* c/o Center for Molecular Genetics, 9500 Gilman Drive, University of California, San Diego, La Jolla, CA 92093, U.S.A.

HELLAWELL, Keith, Q.P.M., M.SC., LL.D.; English anti-drugs coordinator and police officer; b. 18 May 1942, Yorks.; s. of Douglas Hellawell and Ada Alice Hellawell; m. Brenda Hey 1963; one s. two d.; ed. Kirkburton Secondary Modern School, Dewsbury Tech. Coll., Cranfield Inst. of Tech. and London Univ.; worked for five years as a miner before joining Huddersfield Borough Police; progressed through every rank within W. Yorks. Police to Asst. Chief Constable; Deputy Chief Constable of Humberside 1985–90, Chief Constable of Cleveland Police 1990–93, Chief Constable of W. Yorks. Police 1993–98; first U.K. Anti Drugs Coordinator 1998–; Asscn. of Police Officers Spokesman on Drugs; mem. Advisory Council on the Misuse of Drugs, Bd. Community Action Trust; Trustee Nat. Soc. for the Prevention of Cruelty to Children; mem. Editorial Advisory Bd. Journal of Forensic Medicine; Dir. (non-exec.) Evans of Leeds. *Leisure interests:* gardening, design. *Address:* Government Offices, Great George Street, London, SW1A 2AL, England. *Telephone:* 0171-270 5385. *Fax:* 0171-270 5857.

HELLER, Joseph, M.A.; American writer; b. 1 May 1923, Brooklyn; m. 1st Shirley Held 1945; one s. one d.; m. 2nd Valerie Humphries 1987; ed. New York Univ., Columbia Univ., New York, Univ. of Oxford; Instructor, Pa. State Univ. 1950–52; advertisement writer, Time magazine 1952–56, Look magazine 1956–58; Promotion Man. McCall's magazine 1958–61; fmr. teacher of writing, Yale Univ., Univ. of Pa., City Univ., New York; Nat. Inst. of Arts and Letters grant for Literature 1963; served in U.S.A.A.F., rank of Lieut., World War II; Prix Médicis Etranger 1985. *Publications:* Catch 22 (novel) 1961, We Bombed in New Haven (play) 1968, Something Happened (novel) 1974, Clevinger's Trial (play) 1974, Good as Gold (novel) 1979, God Knows (novel) 1984, No Laughing Matter (with Speed Vogel) 1985, Poetics (novel) 1987, Picture This (novel) 1988, Closing Time 1994, Best of Playboy Fiction 1997, As Good as Gold 1997, Now and Then: A Memoir, From Coney Island to Here 1998. *Address:* c/o Simon and Schuster, 1230 Ave of the Americas, New York, NY 10020, U.S.A.

HELLER, Michał Kazimierz; Polish professor of philosophy of science and ecclesiastic; b. 12 March 1936, Tarnów; ed. Inst. of Theology, Tarnów; Catholic Univ. of Lublin, Pontifical Acad. of Theology, Kraków; Extraordinary Prof. 1985; Ordinary Prof. 1990; ordained Priest 1959; Prof. of Cosmology and Philosophy of Science Pontifical Acad. of Theology, Kraków; jt. mem. Vatican Astronomical Observatory; ordinary mem. Pontifical Acad. of Sciences, Rome 1991; mem. Petersburg Acad. of Sciences 1997; mem. Int. Astronomical Union, Int. Soc. for General Relativity and Gravitation, European Physical Soc., Int. Soc. of the Study of Time, Polish Physical Soc., Polish Astronomical Soc., Science Soc. of Catholic Univ. of Lublin; Dr. h.c. (Acad. of Mining and Metallurgy, Kraków) 1996. *Publications:* The Singular Universe—An Introduction to the Classical Singularity Theory 1991, Theoretical Foundations of Cosmology—Introduction to the Global Structure of Space-Time 1992, Physics of Space-Time and Motion 1993, and over 600 publs. on relativistic physics, cosmology, history and philosophy of science and relations between science and theology and articles in journals. *Address:* Papieska Akademia Teologiczna, Wydział Filozoficzny, ul. Franciszkańska 1, 30-004 Kraków, Poland.

HELLMAN, Peter S., M.B.A., B.ECONS.; American business executive; b. 16 Oct. 1949, Cleveland, Ohio; m. Alyson Dulin Ware 1976; one s. one d.; ed. Hobart Coll. and Case Western Reserve Univ.; with The Irving Trust Co., New York 1972–79; Financial Planning Assoc., BP America 1979–82, Man. Financial Planning 1982–84, Dir., Operations Analysis 1984–85, Asst. Treas. 1985–86, Corp. Treas. 1986–89; Vice-Pres. and Treas. TRW Inc. 1989–91, Exec. Vice-Pres. and Chief Financial Officer 1991–94, Exec. Vice-Pres. and Asst. Pres. 1994–95, Pres. and C.O.O. 1995–; Dir. Arkwright Mutual Insurance Co.; mem. Soc. of Automotive Engineers, Cttee. on Foreign Relations of Cleveland Council of World Affairs; Trustee Cleveland Zoological Soc. *Address:* TRW Inc., 1900 Richmond Road, Cleveland, OH 44124, U.S.A.

HELLMUTH, George Francis, M.ARCH.; American architect; b. 5 Oct. 1907, St. Louis, Mo.; s. of George William and Harriet Fowler Hellmuth; m. Mildred Lee Henning 1941; four s. one d.; ed. Washington Univ., St. Louis, Mo., Ecole des Beaux Arts, Fontainebleau; Gen. practice in father's firm (George W. Hellmuth) 1935–40; Asst. to Pres. Smith, Hinchman & Grylls, Detroit, Mich. 1940–49; Partner Hellmuth, Yamasaki & Leinweber 1949–55; Chair. Bd. Hellmuth, Obata & Kassabaum, Inc. 1955–78, HOK-International Inc. 1977–86; Vice-Pres. Plannet Corpn. 1986–; f. and Chair. Datacon Techs. Inc. 1987–; Co-f. Helmuth Dunn Inc., Designers, Hellmuth Dunn and Co., St Louis 1994–; principal int. work includes: King Saud Univ.; King Khaled Int. Airport, Riyadh; Nile Tower, Cairo; Univ. of West Indies, Trinidad; American Embassy, El Salvador; Taipei World Trade Center, Taiwan; Air Defence Command H.Q., Saudi Arabia; Burgan Bank, Kuwait, Burger King Headquarters, Miami; Pres. Bald Eagle Co.; Steedman Travelling Fellowship 1930; First Honor Award, A.I.A. 1956; Coll. of Fellows A.I.A. 1973. *Address:* One Metropolitan Square, 211 North Broadway, Saint Louis, MO 63102; 5 Conway Lane, St. Louis, MO 63124, U.S.A. (Home).

HELLSTRÖM, Mats, B.A.; Swedish politician; b. 12 Jan. 1942, Stockholm; m. Elisabeth Hellström; two c.; ed. Univ. of Stockholm; lecturer in Econs. Univ. of Stockholm 1965–69; mem. Parl. 1968; mem. Exec. Cttee. Social Democratic Party Youth League 1969–72; mem. Bd. Social Democratic Party 1969–96; Special Adviser, Ministry of Labour 1973–76; Minister with special responsibility for foreign trade issues at Ministry of Foreign Affairs 1983–86; Minister of Agric. 1986–91, for Foreign Trade and European Union Affairs 1994–96; mem. of Parl. 1969–96; Amb. to Germany 1996–. *Address:* Swedish Embassy, 53113 Bonn, Allianzplatz, Haus 1, Heussallee 2-10, Germany. *Telephone:* (228) 260020. *Fax:* (228) 223837.

HELLSVIK, Gun, LL.B.; Swedish politician; b. Lund; m.; one s.; ed. Lund Univ.; fmr. lecturer in Commercial Law, Lund Univ.; mem. Bd. Lund Inst. of Tech., IDEON Research Park; Municipal Commr. and Chair. Municipal Exec. Bd., Lund 1982; mem. Nat. Bd. Moderate Party 1985–; leader municipal opposition group 1988; Minister of Justice 1991–94. *Leisure interests:* cooking. *Address:* c/o Moderata Samlingsparteit, P.O. Box 1243, 111 82 Stockholm, Sweden.

HELLWIG, Fritz, DR.PHIL.HABIL.; German politician and economist; b. 3 Aug. 1912, Saarbrücken; s. of Friedrich H. and Albertine (Christmann) Hellwig; m. Dr. Margarete Werners 1939; two s. one d.; ed. Marburg, Vienna and Berlin Univs.; Staff mem. of the Saarbrücken Chamber of Industry and Commerce 1933–39; Dir. of the Saarwirtschaftsarchiv 1936–39; Man. of the Dist. Orgs. of the Iron and Steel Industry at Düsseldorf and Saarbrücken, 1940–43; war service 1943–47; Econ. Adviser and Dir. of Deutsches Industrieinstitut, Cologne 1951–59; Substitute del., Consultative Assembly of Council of Europe 1953–56; mem. of Bundestag 1953–59; Chair. of the Econ. Affairs Cttee. of the Bundestag 1956–59; mem. of European Parl. 1959; mem. of High Authority of the European Coal and Steel Community, Luxembourg 1959–67; Vice-Pres. of the Comm. of the European Communities, Brussels 1967–70; Exec. mem. Bd. of German Shipowners' Asscn. 1971–73; Hon. Prof.

Univ. of Trier (History of Cartography); Grosses Bundesverdienstkreuz mit Stern und Schulterband 1971. *Publications:* Westeuropas Montanwirtschaft, Kohle und Stahl beim Start der Montan-Union 1953, Saar zwischen Ost und West, Die wirtschaftliche Verflechtung 1954, 10 Jahre Schumanplan 1960, Gemeinsamer Markt und Nationale Wirtschaftspolitik 1961, Montanunion zwischen Bewährung und Belastung 1963, Politische Tragweite der europäischen Wirtschaftsintegration 1966, Das schöne Buch und der Computer 1970, Die Forschungs- und Technologiepolitik der Europäischen Gemeinschaften 1970, Verkehr und Gemeinschaftsrecht: Seeschiffahrt und Europäische Wirtschaftgemeinschaft 1971, Die deutsche Seeschiffahrt: Strukturwandel und künftige Aussichten 1973, Zur älteren Kartographie der Saargegend I 1977, II 1981, Alte Pläne von Stadt und Festung Saarlouis 1980, Die Hogenberg-Geschichtsblätter 1983, Landkarten der Pfalz am Rhein (with W. Reiniger and K. Stopp) 1984, Mittelrhein und Moselland im Bild alter Karten 1985, Überwindung der Grenzen. Robert Schuman zum Gedenken 1986, Caspar Dauthendeys Karte des Herzogtums Braunschweig 1987. *Leisure interests:* collecting old maps, views and illustrated books. *Address:* Klosterbergstrasse 117C, 53177 Bonn, Germany. *Telephone:* (0228) 32 20 17.

HELLYER, Hon. Paul Theodore, P.C., B.A.; Canadian politician; b. 6 Aug. 1923, Waterford, Ont.; s. of Audrey S. Hellyer and Lulla M. Anderson; m. Ellen Jean Ralph; two s. one d.; ed. Waterford High School, Curtiss Wright Tech. Inst., California, and Univ. of Toronto; Fleet Aircraft Manufacturing Co., Fort Erie 1942–44; Royal Canadian Air Force 1944–45; Owner, Mari-Jane Fashions, Toronto 1945–56; Treas. Curran Hall Ltd. 1950, Pres. 1951–62; Pres. Trepil Realty Ltd. 1951–62; Pres. Hendon Estates Ltd. 1959–62; mem. House of Commons 1949–57, 1958–74, Parl. Asst. to Minister of Nat. Defence 1956–57, Assoc. Minister April–June 1957, Minister of Nat. Defence 1963–67, of Transport 1967–69, responsible for Central Mortgage and Housing Corpn. 1968–69; Chair. Task Force on Housing and Urban Devt. 1968; Acting Prime Minister 1968–69; joined Progressive Conservative Party July 1972; re-joined Liberal Party 1982; Leader Canadian Action Party 1997–; Opposition spokesman on Industry, Trade and Commerce 1973; Distinguished visitor, Faculty of Environmental Studies, York Univ. 1969–70; Founding Chair. Action Canada 1971; Syndicated Columnist, Toronto Sun 1974–84; Exec. Dir. Canada UNI Asscn. 1991–95; Fellow Royal Soc. for Encouragement of the Arts. *Publications:* Agenda: A Plan for Action 1971, Exit Inflation 1981, Jobs For All: Capitalism on Trial 1984, Canada at the Crossroads 1990, Damn the Torpedos 1990, Funny Money: A Common Sense Alternative to Mainline Economics 1994, Surviving the Global Financial Crisis: The Economics of Hope for Generation X 1966, Arundel Lodge; A Little Bit of Old Muskoka 1996, The Evil Empire: Globalization's Darker Side 1997, Stop: Think 1999. *Leisure interests:* swimming, skin and scuba diving, stamp collecting. *Address:* Suite 506, 65 Harbour Square, Toronto, Ont. M5J 2L4, Canada.

HELME, Mart; Estonian diplomatist; b. 31 Oct. 1949, Parnu, Estonia; ed. Tartu Univ.; ed. Eesti Raamat Publishing House 1973–75; reporter Harju Elu (newspaper) 1975–77; sr. ed. Literature section Pioneer magazine 1977–86; farmer 1986–89; publisher 1989–91; acting dir. Union of Publishers of Estonia, political observer Paeveleht (daily) 1991–93; Head Fourth Bureau (Asia, Africa, S. America) Political Dept., Ministry of Foreign Affairs Feb.–May 1994; Head Third Bureau (Russia, C.I.S., E. and Cen. Europe) Political Dept., Ministry of Foreign Affairs 1994–95; Amb. to Russian Fed. 1995–. *Address:* Maly Kislovsky per. 5, 103009 Moscow, Russia. *Telephone:* (095) 290 50-13 (Office).

HELMFRID, Staffan, PH.D.; Swedish professor of human geography; b. 13 Dec. 1927, Stockholm; s. of Hartwig E. W. Helmfrid and Greta Helmfrid (née Kristiansson); m. Antje Teichmann 1954; three d.; ed. Stockholm Univ.; Asst., Dept. of Geography, Stockholm Univ. 1951, Asst. Prof. 1955, Assoc. Prof. 1962, Research Fellow 1967, Prof. of Human Geography 1969–92, Dean of Faculty of Social Sciences 1970, Pro-Rector (Vice-Pres.) Stockholm Univ. 1974, Rektor 1978–88; Chair. Bank of Sweden Tercentenary Foundation 1980–86, Fulbright Comm. in Sweden 1984–85; CC-PU, Council of Europe 1983–88; Chair. Swedish Nat. Cttee. of Geography 1988–94; mem. Royal Acad. of Letters, History and Antiquities (Sec.-Gen. 1993–98), Royal Acad. of Science (Vice.-Pres. 1988–91), Academia Europaea; Dr. h.c. (Helsinki) 1988; Kt., Royal Order of North Star; H.M. Gold Medal, 12th size; Lord in Waiting 1987. *Publications:* Östergötland Västanstång. Studien über die ältere Agrarlandschaft und ihre Genese 1962; books and articles on agrarian and historical geography; textbooks on geography and social science, National Atlas of Sweden. *Leisure interests:* mountain hiking, folk dance. *Address:* Stockholm University, 10691 Stockholm; Björkhagsvägen 40, 18635 Vallentuna, Sweden (Home). *Telephone:* (08) 51174833 (Home). *Fax:* (08) 339022 (Univ.).

HELMS, Jesse; American politician; b. 18 Oct. 1921, Monroe, N.C.; s. of Mr. and Mrs. J. A. Helms; m. Dorothy Jane Coble 1942; one s. two d.; ed. Wingate Coll. and Wake Forest Coll. (now Wake Forest Univ. at Winston-Salem); served U.S. Navy 1942–45; subsequently became city editor, The Raleigh Times and Dir. of news and programmes for Tobacco Radio Network and Radio Station WRAL; Admin. Asst. to Senators Willis Smith and Alton Lennon; Exec. Dir. N.C. Bankers Asscn. and Ed., The Tarheel Banker 1953–60; editorial writer and presenter, WRAL-TV and Tobacco Radio Network 1960; Exec. Vice-Pres., Vice-Chair. of Bd. and Asst. C.E.O., Capitol Broadcasting Co. (which operates WRAL-TV and Tobacco Radio Network) 1960–72; Senator from North Carolina 1973–, Chair. Senate Agric. Cttee. 1981–87, mem. Foreign Relations Cttee. 1981– (Chair. 1995–), Ranking Repub. 1987–; Republican. *Leisure interests:* reading, community service, fishing. *Address:* U.S. Senate, 403 Dirksen Senate Office Building, Washington, DC 20510, U.S.A. *Telephone:* (202) 224-6342 (Office).

HELMS, Richard M.; American government official and international consultant; b. 30 March 1913, St. Davids, Pa.; s. of Herman Helms and Marion McGarrah; m. 1st Julia Bretzman Shields 1939 (divorced 1968); one s.; m. 2nd Cynthia McKelvie 1968; ed. high schools in U.S.A., Switzerland and Germany, and Williams Coll.; worked for United Press and The Indianapolis Times 1935–42; joined U.S. Navy 1942, in Office of Strategic Service, Second World War; Central Intelligence Group 1946–47, Cen. Intelligence Agency 1947–73, Deputy Dir. for Plans 1962, Deputy Dir. 1965, Dir. 1966–73; Amb. to Iran 1973–76; int. consultant 1976–; Pres. Safeer Co., Washington 1977–97; Nat. Security Medal 1983. *Address:* c/o Safeer Co., 4649 Garfield Street, N.W., Washington, DC 20007, U.S.A.

HELØE, Leif Arne; Norwegian politician and dentist; b. 8 Aug. 1932, Harstad; ed. Univ. of Oslo; school and dist. dentist, Harstad region 1957; Prof. of Community Dentistry, Univ. of Oslo 1975; mem. Harstad City Council 1960–69, mem. Municipal Exec. Bd. 1968–69, Mayor of Harstad 1968–69; proxy mem. Storting (Parl.) 1965–73; Minister of Health and Social Affairs 1981–86; Dir.-Gen. Norwegian Research Council for Science and Humanities 1988–91; Co. Gov. of Troms; Conservative. *Address:* Strandveien 13, 9000 Tromsø, Norway.

HÉLOU, Charles; Lebanese politician, lawyer and journalist; b. 1911; ed. St. Joseph (Jesuit) Univ. and Ecole Française de Droit, Beirut; Barrister, Court of Appeal and Cassation, Beirut 1936; founded newspaper L'Eclair du Nord, Aleppo, Syria 1932; founded Le Jour, Beirut 1934, Political Dir. until 1947; Lebanese Minister to Vatican 1947; Minister of Justice and Health, Lebanon 1954–55, of Educ. Feb.-Sept. 1964; Pres. of Lebanon 1970; Min. of State July-Aug. 1979; Pres. Association des Parlementaires de Langue Française 1973; fmr. Sec.-Gen. Catholic Action of Lebanon. *Address:* Kaslik, Jounieh, Lebanon.

HELTAU, Michael; Austrian actor; b. 5 July 1938, Ingolstadt; s. of Georg Heltau and Jakobine Heltau; ed. gymnasium and Reinhardt Seminar; appeared at Würzburg and Bayerische Staatstheater, Munich 1953, Schillertheater, Berlin and Hamburg Schauspielhaus 1964–68, Théâtre du Châtelet, Paris 1968, Theater in der Josefstadt, Vienna 1957–69, Volkstheater, Vienna 1970, Salzburg Festival 1965–75; Kammerschauspieler, Burgtheater, Vienna 1972–, Doyen of the Burgtheater; noted for appearances in Shakespearean roles including Hamlet, Romeo, Richard II, Henry VI, Schnitzler's Anatol, von Hofmannsthal's Der Schwierige, Schiller's Wallenstein, etc.; second career as singer, especially songs of Jacques Brel (in German) and Viennese songs; numerous one-man shows on stage and television; Karl Skraup Prize; Kainz Medal/Goldener Rathausmann; Gold Award of City of Vienna. *Leisure interests:* reading, swimming. *Address:* Sulzweg 11, 1190 Vienna, Austria.

HELWIG, David Gordon, M.A.,; Canadian writer; b. 5 April 1938, Toronto; s. of William Helwig and Ivy Helwig; m. Nancy Keeling 1959; two d.; ed. Univs. of Toronto and Liverpool; lecturer, then Asst. Prof. Queen's Univ., Kingston, Ont. 1962–74, also Asst. Prof. 1976–80; literary man. CBC 1974–76; CBC Poetry Award 1983. *Publications:* collections of poetry and novels including Figures in a Landscape 1968, Close to the Fire 1999. *Leisure interests:* choral music, gardening. *Address:* Belfast, PE1 C0A 1A0, Canada. *Telephone:* (902) 659-2942.

HELY-HUTCHINSON, Timothy Mark, M.A.; British publisher; b. 26 Oct. 1953, London; s. of Earl of Donoughmore and Countess of Donoughmore (née Parsons); ed. Eton Coll., Oxford Univ.; Man. Dir. Macdonald & Co. (Publrs.) Ltd. 1982–86, Headline Book Publishing PLC 1986–93; Group Chief Exec. Hodder Headline PLC 1993–; Venturer of the Year (British Venture Capital Asscn.) 1990, Publr. of the Year (British Book Awards) 1992. *Leisure interests:* opera, racing. *Address:* Hodder Headline PLC, 338 Euston Road, London, NW1 3BH (Office); 25 Royal Crescent, London, W11 4SN, England.

HEMINGWAY, Gerardine; British fashion designer; b. 7 Dec. 1961; m. Wayne Hemingway (q.v.); two s. two d.; together with husband started in business with market stall in Camden, London; cr. footwear, clothing and accessory label Red or Dead 1992; collection retailed through eight Red or Dead shops in U.K. and three Red or Dead shops in Japan, and wholesaled to int. network of retailers; currently with Pentland Group PLC; Street Designers of the Year, British Fashion Awards 1995, 1996, 1997. *Publication:* Red or Dead: The Good, The Bad and the Ugly 1998. *Address:* Red or Dead Ltd., Building 201, Courtney Road, GEC East Lane Estate, Wembley, Middx., HA9 7PP, England.

HEMINGWAY, Wayne; British fashion designer; b. 19 Jan 1961; s. of Billy Two Rivers (Mohawk Indian chief); m. Gerardine Hemingway (q.v.); two s. two d.; together with wife started in business with market stall in Camden, London; cr. footwear, clothing and accessory label Red or Dead 1992; collection retailed through eight Red or Dead shops in U.K. and three Red or Dead shops in Japan, and wholesaled to int. network of retailers; jt. venture with Pentland Group PLC 1996–; Street Designers of the Year, British Fashion Awards 1995, 1996, 1997. *Address:* Red or Dead Ltd., Building

201, Courtney Road, GEC East Lane Estate, Wembley, Middx., HA9 7PP, England. *Telephone:* 0181-904 4774. *Fax:* 0181-908 4659.

HEMMING, John Henry, C.M.G., M.A., D.LITT., F.S.A.; Canadian author and publisher; b. 5 Jan. 1935, Vancouver, B.C.; s. of H. Harold Hemming, O.B.E., M.C. and Alice L. Hemming, O.B.E.; m. Sukie Babington-Smith 1979; one s. one d.; ed. Eton Coll. and McGill and Oxford Univs.; Dir. and Sec. Royal Geographical Soc. 1975–96; Jt. Chair. Hemming Publishing Ltd. 1976–; Chair. Brintex Ltd., Newman Books Ltd.; explorations in Peru and Brazil 1960, 1961, 1971, 1972, 1986–88; Hon. D.Litt. (Warwick) 1989, (Stirling) 1991; Pitman Literary Prize 1970, Bolton Prize for Latin American History 1971, Christopher Award (U.S.A.) 1971, Founder's Medal, Royal Geographical Soc. 1989, Bradford Washburn Medal, Boston Museum of Science 1989, Mungo Park Medal, Royal Scottish Geographical Soc. 1988; Orden al Mérito (Peru), Special Award, Instituto Nacional de Cultura (Peru) 1996, Citation of Merit, Explorers' Club (New York) 1997, Order of Southern Cross (Brazil) 1998. *Publications:* The Conquest of the Incas 1970, Tribes of the Amazon Basin in Brazil (with others) 1973, Red Gold: The Conquest of the Brazilian Indians 1978, The Search for El Dorado 1978, Machu Picchu 1982, Monuments of the Incas 1983, Change in the Amazon Basin, 2 vols. (Ed.) 1985, Amazon Frontier: The Defeat of the Brazilian Indians 1987, Maracá 1988, Roraima, Brazil's Northernmost Frontier 1990, The Rainforest Edge (Ed.) 1993, Royal Geographical Society Illustrated (Ed.) 1997, The Golden Age of Discovery 1998. *Leisure interests:* exploration, writing. *Address:* Hemming Publishing Ltd., 32 Vauxhall Bridge Road, London, SW1V 2SS, England. *Telephone:* 0171-973 6404. *Fax:* 0171-233 5049.

HEMMINGS, David Leslie Edward; British actor and feature film director; b. 18 Nov. 1941; m. 1st Genista Ouvry 1960; one d.; m. 2nd Gayle Hunnicutt 1969 (dissolved 1975); one s.; m. 3rd Prudence J. de Casembroot 1976; two s.; ed. Glyn Coll., Epsom; in entertainment industry 1949–, Dir. Int. Home Video FGH Pty. Ltd., Melbourne, Film and General Holdings Inc., Calif.; appeared in The Turn of the Screw (English Opera Group) 1954. *Films include:* Five Clues to Fortune 1957, Saint Joan 1957, The Heart Within 1957, Men of Tomorrow 1958, In The Wake of a Stranger 1958, No Trees in the Street 1959, Some People 1962, Play it Cool 1962, Live it Up 1963, Two Left Feet 1963, The System 1964, Be My Guest 1965, Eye of the Devil 1966, Blow Up 1966, Camelot 1967, Barbarella 1967, Only When I Larf 1968, The Charge of the Light Brigade 1968, The Long Day's Dying 1968, The Best House in London 1968, Alfred the Great 1969, Fragment of Fear 1970, The Walking Stick 1970, Unman, Wittering & Zigo 1971, The Love Machine 1971, Voices 1973, Don't Worry Momma 1973, Juggernaut 1974, Quilp 1974, Profundo Rosso 1975, Islands in the Stream 1975, The Squeeze 1976, Power Play 1978, Harlequin 1980, Beyond Reasonable Doubt 1982, The Rainbow 1989; Jeeves (musical), Her Majesty's Theatre, London 1975; Scott Fitzgerald, BBC TV 1975, The Rime of the Ancient Mariner 1978 and Charlie Muffin 1979, ITV; Dir. feature films Running Scared 1972, The 14 1973 (Silver Bear Award, Berlin Film Festival 1973), Just a Gigolo 1978, David Bowie Stage 1979, Murder by Decree 1979, Survivor 1979, Race to the Yankee Zephyr 1980, Dark Horse; Produced: Strange Behaviour 1981, Turkey Shoot 1981. *Leisure interest:* painting. *Address:* c/o Michael Whitehall Ltd., 125 Gloucester Road, London, S.W.7, England.

HEMPEL, Rt. Rev. Johannes, C.B.E., D.THEOL.; German ecclesiastic; b. 23 March 1929, Zittau; s. of Albert Hempel and Gertrud (née Buchwald) Hempel; m. Dorothea Schönbach 1956; two s. one d.; ed. Univs. of Tübingen, Heidelberg, Kirkliche Hochschule, Berlin; Rev. Evangelical Lutheran Church, Saxony 1952–57, Bishop 1972–94; Student Pastor and teacher of theology, Leipzig 1957–72; a Pres. of WCC; 3 hon. degrees. *Address:* Hutbergstr. 78, 01326 Dresden, Germany. *Telephone:* 0351-2683142. *Fax:* 0351-2683142.

HEMPSTONE, Smith; American journalist, author and diplomatist; b. 1 Feb. 1929, Washington, D.C.; s. of Smith Hempstone and Elizabeth Noyes; m. Kathaleen Fishback 1954; one d.; ed. St. Albans School for Boys, Washington, D.C., Culver Mil. Acad., Ind., and Univ. of the South, Sewanee, Tenn.; Fellow, Inst. of Current World Affairs (in Africa), New York 1956–60; African corresp. (Nairobi), Chicago Daily News 1960–64; Nieman Fellow, Harvard Univ. 1964–65; Latin American corresp. The Washington Star 1965–67, European corresp. (London) 1967–70, Assoc. Ed. 1970–75; Ed.-in-Chief, The Washington Times 1982–85; syndicated newspaper columnist 1970–75, 1975–82, 1982–89; Amb. to Kenya 1989–93; Amb.-in-Residence, Univ. of the South, Sewanee, Tenn. 1993, Virginia Mil. Inst., Lexington, Va. 1994; Hon. Ph.D. (Univ. of the South); Hon. LL.D. (Westminster Coll.). *Publications:* Africa, Angry Young Giant 1961, Rebels, Mercenaries & Dividends 1962, A Tract of Time (novel) 1966, In the Midst of Lions (novel) 1968, Rogue Ambassador 1997; numerous magazine articles, newspaper columns etc. *Leisure interests:* hunting, fishing, reading, travel, boating. *Address:* 7611 Fairfax Road, Bethesda, MD 20814, U.S.A. *Telephone:* (301) 907-3961 (winter); (207) 594-4176 (summer).

HEN, Józef; Polish author and playwright; b. 8 Nov. 1923, Warsaw; s. of Roman Hen and Ewa Hen; m. Irena Hen 1946; one s. one d.; self-educated; lecturer Sorbonne, France 1993 and Univ. of Warsaw 1995–96; mem. Académie des Sciences, Belles Lettres et des Beaux Arts, Bordeaux, France. *Publications include:* Kwiecień (April) 1960 (Book of the Year, 1961), Skromny chłopiec w haremie (A modest boy in a harem) 1957, Bokser i śmierć (The boxer and death) 1975, Niebo naszych ojców (Sky of our fathers) 1997, Teatr Heroda (Herod's theatre) 1966, Crimen, Królewskie sny, Oko Dajana (Crimen, Royal dreams, and Dajan's Eye), Milczące między nami (Silent between us) 1985, Odejście Afrodyty (Aphrodite's Departure), Nowolipie, Najpiękniejsze lata (The most beautiful years), Ja, Michał z Montaigne (I, Michel de Montaigne) 1978, Nie boję się bezsennych nocy (I'm not afraid of sleepless nights) 1987, 1992, Błazen-Wielki Maż (Jester – The Great Man). *Film screenplays include:* Kwiecień (April), Krzyż walecznych (Cross of the brave), Nikt nie woła (Nobody's calling), Bokser i śmierć (The boxer and death), Prawo i pięść (Law and the Fist), and Don Gabriel. *Screenplays for TV serials:* Życie Kamila Kuranta (The Life of Kamil Kurant), Crimen and Królewskie Sny (Royal Dreams). *Theatre plays:* Ja, Michał z Montaigne (I, Michel de Montaigne), Justyn! Justyn!, Popołudnie kochanków (Lovers' Afternoon). *Leisure interests:* historical and literary monographs, watching sports programmes on television, films. *Address:* Al. Ujazdowskie 8 m. 2, 00-478 Warsaw, Poland. *Telephone:* (22) 629-19-03.

HENARE, Tau; New Zealand politician; m.; five c.; fmr. Advisory Officer in Maori Devt., Waitakere City Council, Youth Educ. Co-ordinator, Race Relations Conciliator, Advisory Officer, Dept. of Internal Affairs; M.P. for Northern Maori (now Te Tai Tokerau) 1993–; Minister of Maori Affairs 1997–, for Racing, Assoc. Minister for Sport, Fitness and Leisure; Deputy Leader N.Z. First Party, Spokesperson on Cultural Affairs and Treaty of Waitangi Negotiations. *Address:* Ministry of Maori Affairs, P.O. Box 3943, Wellington 6015, New Zealand. *Telephone:* (04) 494-7000. *Fax:* (04) 494-7010.

HENDERSON, Sir Denys (Hartley), Kt., M.A., LL.B., F.R.S.A.; British business executive and solicitor; b. 11 Oct. 1932, Colombo, Sri Lanka; s. of late John Hartley Henderson and Nellie Henderson (née Gordon); m. Doreen Mathewson Glashan 1957; two d.; ed. Aberdeen Grammar School and Univ. of Aberdeen; Commercial Asst. ICI 1957–58, Chair. Paints Div. 1977–80, Main Bd. Dir. 1980, Deputy Chair. 1986–87, Chair. 1987–95; Chancellor Univ. of Bath 1993–98; Chair. Zeneca Group PLC 1993–95; Dir. (non-exec.) Rank 1994– (Chair. 1995–), Barclays Bank PLC 1983–97, Barclays PLC 1985–97, RTZ Corpn. PLC 1990–96, MORI 1995–, Dalgety PLC 1996–98 (Chair. 1997–98); mem. Law Soc. of Scotland 1955–; Chair. Court of Govs. of Henley Man. Coll. 1989–96; mem. Pres.'s Cttee., CBI 1987–96; First Crown Estate Commr. 1995–; Trustee, The Natural History Museum 1989–98; Chair. Univ. of Aberdeen Quincentenary Appeal Cttee. 1993–96; Pres. and Chair. Bd. British Quality Foundation 1993–97; Hon. D.Univ. (Brunel) 1987, (Strathclyde) 1993; Hon. LL.D. (Aberdeen) 1987, (Nottingham) 1990, (Manchester) 1991, (Bath) 1993; Hon. D.Sc. (Cranfield Inst. of Tech.) 1989, (Teesside) 1993; Hon. Fellow City and Guilds of London Inst. 1990, Soc. of Chemical Industry Centenary Medal 1993. *Leisure interests:* family life, swimming, reading, travel, gardening and "unskilled but enjoyable" golf.

HENDERSON, Donald Ainslie, M.D., M.P.H.; American professor of epidemiology and international health; b. 7 Sept. 1928, Cleveland, Ohio; s. of David A. Henderson and Grace E. McMillan; m. Nana I. Bragg 1951; two s. one d.; ed. Oberlin Coll., Univ. of Rochester and Johns Hopkins Univ.; Intern, Mary Imogene Bassett Hospital, Cooperstown, New York 1954–55, Resident 1957–59; various posts at Communicable Diseases Center, Dept. of Health, Educ. and Welfare 1955–66, Chief Smallpox Eradication Program 1965–66; Asst. Prof. of Preventive Medicine and Community Health, Emory Univ. School of Medicine 1960–66; Chief Medical Officer, WHO Smallpox Eradication 1966–77; Dean and Prof. of Epidemiology and Int. Health, Johns Hopkins Univ. School of Hygiene and Public Health 1977–90; Assoc. Dir., Office of Science and Tech. Policy, Exec. Office of the Pres. 1991–93; Deputy Asst. Sec. Dept. of Health and Human Services, Wash. 1993–94, Sr. Scientific advisor 1994–95; Prof. Johns Hopkins Univ. School of Public Health, Baltimore 1995–, Dir. Civilian Biodefense Studies Center; mem. numerous professional socs., cttees. and advisory panels, etc. and recipient of numerous scientific awards and recognitions from orgs. in U.S.A., Canada, U.K., Japan, Uruguay, Switzerland, Republic of China, Ethiopia, Afghanistan, Germany, India and Pakistan; thirteen hon. degrees. *Publications:* more than 100 dealing primarily with smallpox eradication, epidemiology and immunization. *Address:* Johns Hopkins University School of Public Health, 624 N. Broadway, Baltimore, MD 21205 (Office); Candler Building, Suite 850, 111 Market Place, Baltimore, MD 21202, U.S.A. (Home). *Telephone:* (410) 223 1667. *Fax:* (410) 223 1665.

HENDERSON, Horace Edward; American public affairs consultant; b. 30 July 1917, Henderson, N.C.; s. of Thomas Brantley Henderson M.D. and Ethel Maude Duke; m. Vera Schubert 1966; two d.; ed. Coll. of William and Mary, and Yale Univ.; Army Capt., Second World War; Owner, Henderson Real Estate, Williamsburg, Va. 1947–52; Vice-Pres. Jr. Chamber Int. 1951–52; Nat. Pres. U.S. Jr. Chamber of Commerce 1952–53; Asscns. Coordinator, Nat. Auto Dealers Asscn., Wash. 1954–55; Dir. Chamber of Commerce of the U.S.A. 1954; Exec. Cttee. U.S. Cttee. for the UN 1954; Trustee, Freedoms Foundation 1955; Vice-Chair. Operation Brotherhood 1954–56; Republican Party cand. for Congress 1956, Lieut.-Gov. of Va. 1957, Independent cand. for Senate 1972; Dir. Office of Special Liaison and Special Asst., Deputy Under-Sec. of State 1958; U.S. Del. to ILO 1959–60, WHO 1959–60, UNESCO 1960, FAO 1959, High Comm. for Refugees 1959, ECOSOC 1959, U.S. Del. to UN 1960; Deputy Asst. Sec. of State for Int. Orgs., Dept. of State, Washington, D.C. 1959–60; Chair. Republican Party of Virginia 1962–64; mem. Republican Nat. Cttee. 1962–64; Chair. of Bd., Henderson Real Estate Agency McLean, Va. 1965–69; Dir.-Gen. World

Peace Through Law Center, Geneva 1965–69; Pres. and Chair. Community Methods Inc. 1969–75; Chair. World Peace Treaty 2000 Campaign; Pres. Int. Domestic Devt. Corps 1975, Chair. Asscn. for Devt. of Educ. 1977–78; Exec. Dir. World Asscn. of Judges 1968; Chair. Congressional Reform Cttee. 1976; Exec. Vice-Pres. American Lawmakers Asscn. 1977; Real Estate and Man. Consultant 1978–86; Pres. Williamsburg Vacations Inc. 1983–84, Nat. Asscn. for Free Trade 1986; mem. St. Andrews Soc.; Elder, Presbyterian Church. *Address:* 1100 Gough Street 15F, San Francisco, CA 94109, U.S.A. (Home). *Telephone:* (415) 928-3924 (Home).

HENDERSON, Sir (John) Nicholas, G.C.M.G., K.C.V.O., M.A.; British diplomatist (retd.); b. 1 April 1919, London; s. of Prof. Sir Hubert Henderson; m. Mary Barber 1951; one d.; ed. Stowe School and Hertford Coll., Oxford; Asst. Pvt. Sec. to British Foreign Sec. 1944–47; served in British Embassies in Washington, Athens, Vienna, Santiago; Prin. Pvt. Sec. to Foreign Sec. 1963–65; Minister, Madrid 1965–69; Amb. to Poland 1969–72, to Fed. Germany 1972–75, to France 1975–79, to U.S.A. 1979–82; Dir. Hambros PLC 1982–89, Foreign and Colonial Investment Trust 1982–89, Mercantile and Gen. Reinsurance Co. Ltd. 1982–89, Tarmac 1983–89, F & C Eurotrust 1984–90, Eurotunnel PLC 1986–88, Sotheby's 1989–, F. & C. German Investment Trust 1990–94; Fuel Tech Europe 1990–; mem. supervisory bd. Fuel Tech NV 1987–90, Lord Warden of the Stanneries and Keeper of the Privy Seal of the Duke of Cornwall 1985–90; Chair. Channel Tunnel Group 1985–86; Trustee, Nat. Gallery 1985–89; mem. Council Duchy of Cornwall 1985–90; Hon. Fellow, Hertford Coll., Oxford Univ.; Hon. D.C.L. (Oxford). *Publications:* Prince Eugen (biography), The Birth of NATO, The Private Office 1984, Channels and Tunnels 1987, Mandarin: The Diary of an Ambassador 1994; various articles and stories in Horizon, New Writing, History Today, Country Life, The Economist. *Leisure interests:* tennis, gardening. *Address:* 6 Fairholt Street, London, SW7 1EG, England. *Telephone:* 0171-589 4291.

HENDERSON, Patrick David, C.M.G., M.A.; British economist and international official; b. 10 April 1927, Sheffield; s. of late David Henderson and Eleanor Rowbotham; m. Marcella Kodicek 1960; one s. one d.; ed. Ellesmere Coll., Shropshire and Corpus Christi Coll., Oxford; Fellow and tutor in econs., Lincoln Coll., Oxford 1948–64; Commonwealth Fund Fellow, Harvard Univ. 1952–53; Econ. Adviser, H.M. Treasury 1957–58; Chief Economist, Ministry of Aviation 1964–66; Adviser, Harvard Devt. Advisory Service (Greece and Malaysia) 1967–68; Visiting Lecturer, Econ. Devt. Inst., World Bank 1968–69; with World Bank (IBRD) 1969–75, Dir. Econs. Dept. 1972–73; Prof. of Political Economy, Univ. Coll., London 1975–83; mem. Nat. Ports Council 1979–81; Special Adviser, Sec. of State for Wales 1978–79; mem. Bd. Commonwealth Devt. Corpn. 1980–83; Head, Dept. of Econs. and Statistics, OECD 1984–92; Visiting Fellow, Devt. Centre, OECD 1992, Centre for European Policy Studies; Visiting Prof. Melbourne Business School; Reith Lecturer, BBC 1985, Copland Memorial Lecture 1989. *Publications:* Nyasaland: The Economics of Federation (co-author) 1960, Economic Growth in Britain (Ed. and contrib.) 1965, The Energy Sector in India 1975, Innocence and Design: the Influence of Economic Ideas on Policy 1986, Economic Policies for the 1990s 1991, Trade Blocs: The Future of Regional Integration (Jt. Ed.) 1994. *Leisure interests:* reading, walking, swimming, looking at buildings.

HENDERSON, Richard, PH.D., F.R.S.; British molecular biologist; b. 19 July 1945, Edinburgh; s. of John W. and Grace S. (Goldie) Henderson; m. 1st Penelope Fitzgerald 1969 (divorced 1988); one s. one d. (one d. deceased); m. 2nd Jade Li 1995; ed. Hawick High School, Boroughmuir Secondary School, Univs. of Edinburgh and Cambridge; professional interest in structure and function of protein molecules, especially in biological membranes; Helen Hay Whitney Postdoctoral Fellow, Yale Univ., U.S.A. 1970–73; Fellow, Darwin Coll., Cambridge 1982–; mem. research staff, MRC Lab. of Molecular Biology 1973–, Dir. 1996–; Ernst Ruska Prize for Electron Microscopy 1981; Lewis S. Rosenstiel Award, Brandeis Univ. 1991, Louis Jeantet Award 1993. *Publications:* many scientific articles in books and journals. *Leisure interests:* canoeing, wine. *Address:* Medical Research Council Laboratory of Molecular Biology, Hills Road, Cambridge, CB2 2QH, England. *Telephone:* (01223) 248011.

HENDERSON, Robert Alistair; British business executive; b. 4 Nov. 1917; s. of Robert E. Henderson and Beatrice J. E. Henderson; m. Bridget E. Lowther 1947; two s. (one s. deceased) one d.; ed. Eton Coll. and Magdalene Coll. Cambridge; mil. service 1940–45; Jessel Toynbee & Co. Ltd. 1945–48; Borneo Co. Ltd. 1948–51; Robert Benson, Lonsdale & Co. Ltd. 1951, Dir. 1957; Dir. Kleinwort, Benson Ltd. 1961, Vice-Chair. 1970–71, Deputy Chair. 1971–75, Chair. 1975–83; Dir. Equitable Life Assurance Soc. 1958–81; Chair. Kleinwort Devt. Fund PLC (fmrly. Cross Investment Trust, Ltd.) 1969–91, Kleinwort, Benson, Lonsdale PLC 1978–88, Merchants Trust PLC 1985–94, MT Oil & Gas, Ltd. 1985–87; Deputy Chair. Cadbury Schweppes PLC 1983–92, British Airways 1985–89. *Leisure interests:* gardening, shooting, fishing. *Address:* 7 Royal Avenue, London, SW3 4QE; North Ecchinswell Farm, Ecchinswell, nr. Newbury, Berks., RG15 8UJ, England. *Telephone:* (01635) 268244 (Berks.).

HENDERSON, Sir William MacGregor, D.SC., F.R.C.V.S., F.R.S.E., F.R.S.; British veterinary surgeon; b. 17 July 1913, Edinburgh, Scotland; s. of the late William Simpson Henderson and Catherine Alice Macus Berry; m. Alys Beryl Goodridge 1941; four s.; ed. George Watson's Boys' Coll., Royal Veterinary Coll., Edinburgh, Univ. of Edinburgh; Research Officer Animal Virus Inst., Pirbright 1939–56, Deputy Dir. 1955–56; Dir. Pan-American Foot-and-Mouth Disease Center, Rio de Janeiro, Brazil 1957–65; Dir. Agricultural Research Council Inst. for Research on Animal Diseases, Compton 1967–1972, Sec. to the Agricultural Research Council 1972–78; Chair. U.K. Genetic Manipulation Advisory Group 1979–82; mem. Bd. Dirs. Celltech Ltd. 1981–84, Wellcome Biotech. Ltd. 1983–90, Pacific Aqua Foods Ltd. 1986–; Pres. Zoological Soc. of London 1984–89, Royal Asscn. British Dairy Farmers 1985–87; Dalrymple-Champneys Award 1974, Massey-Ferguson Nat. Award 1980, Underwood-Prescott Award 1981; Corresp. mem. Argentinian Acad. Agronomy and Veterinary Science 1980–; Hon. D.M.V. (Edinburgh) 1974, Hon. Dr. Veterinary Science (Liverpool) 1977, Hon. D.Sc. (Bristol) 1985; Dr. (Univ. of Stirling) 1989. *Publications:* Quantitative Study of Foot-and-Mouth Disease Virus 1949, Man's Use of Animals 1981, British Agricultural Research and the Agricultural Research Council 1981, A Personal History of Testing Foot-and-Mouth Disease Vaccines in Cattle 1985, A Man of the Country 1994; numerous papers in scientific journals. *Leisure interests:* fauna and flora, gardening, walking. *Address:* Culvers, Croft Road, Goring-on-Thames, Reading, RG8 9ES, England.

HENDRICKS, Barbara, B.SC., B.MUS.; American soprano; b. 20 Nov. 1948, Stephens, Ark.; d. of M. L. and Della Hendricks; m. Martin Engström 1978; one s. one d.; ed. Univ. of Neb. and Juilliard School of Music, New York, studying with Jennie Tourel; operatic début, San Francisco Opera (L'Incoronazione di Poppea) 1976; has appeared with opera companies of Boston, Santa Fe, Glyndebourne, Hamburg, La Scala (Milan), Berlin, Paris, Los Angeles, Florence and Royal Opera, Covent Garden (London), Vienna; recitals in most maj. centres in Europe and America; has toured extensively in U.S.S.R. and Japan; concert performances with all leading European and U.S. orchestras; has appeared at many maj. music festivals including Edin., Osaka, Montreux, Salzburg, Dresden, Prague, Aix-en-Provence, Orange and Vienna; nearly 50 recordings; nominated Goodwill Amb. for Refugees at UN 1987; Hon. mem. Inst. of Humanitarian Law, San Remo, Italy 1990; Hon. D. Mus. (Nebraska Wesleyan Univ.) 1988, Dr. h.c. (Univ. of Louvain, Belgium) 1990; Commdr. des Arts et des Lettres. *Film appearance:* La Bohème 1988. *Leisure interest:* reading. *Address:* c/o Harrison Parrott Ltd, 12 Penzance Place, London, W11 4PA, England; IMG Artists North America, 22E 71st Street, New York, NY 10021, U.S.A.

HENDRICKSE, Rev. Helenard Joe (Alan), B.A.; South African politician and religious official; b. 22 Oct. 1927, Uitenhage, Cape; m. Patricia Heber (Terry) 1957; two s. two d.; ed. Univ. of Fort Hare, Rhodes Univ.; ordained Minister of Uitenhage Congregational Church of Southern Africa 1986–; f. Blacks School Uitenhage 1951; elected Head United Congregational Church of Southern Africa 1972; teacher 1951–69; elected to Coloured Persons Rep. Council 1969, to Exec., responsible for Educ. 1975; Leader Labour Party of S.A. 1978–94; elected to House of Reps. (Coloured Chamber) 1984–94, Chair. Ministers' Council 1984–86, Minister Without Portfolio and Chair. Ministers' Council, House of Reps. 1986–87; ANC Senator E. Cape Region 1994–. *Address:* 16 Jubilee Crescent, Uitenhage 6230, South Africa.

HENDRICKSE, Ralph George, M.D., F.R.C.P., F.M.C. (PAED.); British consultant paediatrician (retd.); b. 5 Nov. 1926, Cape Town, S. Africa; s. of William G. Hendrickse and Johanna T. (Dennis) Hendrickse; m. Begum Johanahara Abdurahman 1948; one s. four d; ed. Livingstone High School, Cape and Univ. of Cape Town Medical School; Sr. Medical Officer, McCord Zulu Hosp. Durban 1949–54; Sr. Registrar, Univ. Coll. Hosp. Ibadan, Nigeria 1956–57; Lecturer, Sr. Lecturer, Univ. of Ibadan 1957–62, Prof. and Head, Dept. of Paediatrics 1962–69, Dir. Inst. of Child Health 1964–69; Sr. Lecturer and Dir. Diploma in Tropical Child Health Course, Univ. of Liverpool and Liverpool School of Tropical Medicine 1969–75, Prof. of Tropical Paediatrics 1975–91, Dean Liverpool School of Tropical Medicine 1988–91, Prof. and Head of newly created Dept. of Tropical Paediatrics and Int. Child Health, Liverpool Univ. 1988–91, Prof. Emer. 1991–; Hon. Consultant Paediatrician, Liverpool Health Authority 1969–; founder and Ed.-in-Chief, Annals of Tropical Paediatrics 1981–; mem. Advisory Expert Panel on Tropical Pediatrics of Int. Pediatric Asscn.; mem. Standing Panel of Experts in Public Health Medicine of London Univ. 1990–93, 1993–; Hon. Fellow Coll. of Paediatrics and Child Health 1996; Hon. D.Sc. (Cape Town) 1998; Frederick Murgatroyd Memorial Prize, Royal Coll. of Physicians 1970. *Publications:* Tropical Paediatrics: Update and Current Review 1981, Paediatrics in the Tropics 1991, Mycotoxins and Human Health; over 150 articles in scientific journals (1954–86). *Leisure interests:* swimming, golf, gardening, painting, travel. *Address:* Beresford House, 25 Riverbank Road, Heswall, Wirral, Merseyside, L60 4SQ, England. *Telephone:* (0151) 342 5510. *Fax:* (0151) 342 5510.

HENDRY, Stephen Gordon, M.B.E.; British snooker player; b. 13 Jan. 1969, Edinburgh; s. of Gordon J. Hendry and Irene Anthony; m. Amanda Elizabeth Teresa Tart 1995; one s.; ed. Inverkeithing High School; commenced professional career 1985; Scottish Champion 1986, 1987, 1988; winner, Rothmans Grand Prix 1987; world doubles Champion 1987; Australian Masters Champion 1987; British Open Champion 1988; New Zealand Masters Champion 1988; Benson & Hedges Masters Champion 1989, 1990, 1991, 1992, 1993, 1996; U.K. Professional Champion 1989, 1990, 1994, 1995, 1996; Asian Champion 1989; Regal Masters Champion 1989; Dubai Classic Champion 1989; Embassy World Champion 1990, 1992, 1993, 1994, 1995, 1996; Irish Masters 1992; Int. Open 1993. *Publication:* Snooker Masterclass

1994. *Leisure interests:* golf, music. *Address:* Stephen Hendry Snooker Ltd., Kerse Road, Stirling, FK7 7SG, Scotland. *Telephone:* (01786) 462634. *Fax:* (01786) 450068.

HENG SAMRIN; Cambodian politician; b. 25 May 1934; Political Commissar and Commdr. of Khmer Rouge 4th Infantry Div. 1976–78; led abortive coup against Pol Pot and fled to Viet Nam 1978; Pres. Nat. Front for Nat. Salvation of Kampuchea 1978; Pres. People's Revolutionary Council 1979 (took power after Vietnamese invasion of Kampuchea); Chair. Council of State of Cambodia 1991; Sec. Gen. People's Revolutionary Party of Kampuchea (KPRP) 1981–91; mem. Politburo of Cambodia 1991–. *Address:* Council of State, Phnom-Penh, Cambodia.

HENKEL, Hans-Olaf; German business executive; b. 14 March 1940, Hamburg; European Head Int. Business Machines (IBM) -1995, Chair. IBM Germany; Pres. Bundesverband der Deutschen Industrie eV (BDI) 1995–. *Address:* Gustav-Heinemann-Ufer 84–88, 50968 Cologne, Germany.

HENKIN, Louis, LL.D., L.H.D.; American professor of law; b. 11 Nov. 1917, Russia; s. of Yoseph Henkin and Frieda Kreindel; m. Alice Hartman 1960; three s.; ed. Yeshiva Coll. and Harvard Univ.; admitted New York Bar 1941, U.S. Supreme Court Bar 1947; law clerk 1940–41, 1946–47; mil. service 1941–45; with State Dept. 1945–46, 1948–57; UN Legal Dept. 1947–48; lecturer in law, Columbia Univ. 1956–57; Visiting Prof. Univ. of Pa. 1957–58, Prof. of Law 1958–62; Prof. Columbia Univ. 1962, mem. Inst. for War and Peace Studies 1962–, Hamilton Fish Prof. of Int. Law and Diplomacy 1963–78, Harlan Fiske Stone Prof. of Constitutional Law 1978–79, Univ. Prof. 1979–88, Univ. Prof. Emer. and Special Service Prof. 1988–; Chair. Directorate, Columbia Univ. Center for Study of Human Rights 1986–; Pres. U.S. Inst. of Human Rights 1970–93; Vice-Pres. Lawyers' Cttee. on Human Rights, Immigration and Refugee Services 1994–; numerous professional and public appts., affiliations and distinctions etc.; Fellow, American Acad. of Arts and Sciences; mem. American Philosophical Soc., Council on Foreign Relations, American Soc. of Int. Law, Int. Law Asscn., Inst. de Droit Int., U.S. Asscn. of Constitutional Law etc.; Guggenheim Fellow 1979–80. *Publications:* numerous books and articles on constitutional law, constitutionalism, int. law, Law of the Sea and human rights including: How Nations Behave (2nd edn.) 1979, Constitutionalism and Rights: The Influence of the United States Abroad 1989, Foreign Affairs and the U.S. Constitution 1990, International Law: Politics and Values 1995. *Address:* 460 Riverside Drive, New York, NY 10027, U.S.A. (Home). *Fax:* (212) 854-7946.

HENLE, Christian-Peter; German business executive; b. 9 Nov. 1938, Duisburg; s. of Günter and Anne-Liese (née Küpper) Henle; brother of Jörg Alexander Henle (q.v.); m. Dr. Susanne Beitz 1967; two s.; ed. High School, Duisburg, Institut d'Etudes Politiques, Paris; joined Klöckner Eisenhandel GmbH, Düsseldorf 1963–64; with Klöckner and Co., Duisburg 1964–65, Vice-Pres. Klöckner Inc., New York 1965–67; Pres. Klöckner Industrie-Anlagen GmbH, Duisburg 1967–70; mem. Bd. of Dirs. responsible for depts. for liquid fuels, motor fuels and lubricants, gas, chemicals, industrial plants, Klöckner and Co., Duisburg 1971–, partner 1977–; Chair. Supervisory Bd. Klöckner-Humboldt-Deutz AG (KHD), Cologne, Mietfinanz GmbH, Mülheim/Ruhr; mem. Supervisory Bd. KHD Humboldt Wedag AG, Cologne, Deutsche Babcock AG, Oberhausen, Gerling-Konzern Welt-Versicherungs-Pool AG, Cologne, Gerling-Konzern Globale Rückversicherungs-AG, Cologne, Knipping-Dorn GmbH, Herne; Chair. Advisory Bd. Fisser & v. Doornum, Hamburg, Montan Brennstoffhandel und Schiffahrt GmbH & Co. KG, Munich; mem. Advisory Bd. Dresdner Bank AG, Frankfurt, Arnold Knipping GmbH, Gummersbach; mem. of Bd. Mineralölwirtschaftsverband e.V., Hamburg; mem. Int. Advisory Bd. The American Univ., Washington, D.C., U.S.A.; Pres. Deutsche Gesellschaft für Auswärtige Politik e.V., Bonn; Verdienstkreuz am Bande des Verdienstordens (Fed. Repub. of Germany); Chevalier de l'Ordre du Mérite (Senegal). *Publication:* Auf dem Weg in ein neues Zeitalter (Ed. and Co-Author) 1985. *Leisure interests:* music, sports (tennis, golf), collecting contemporary works of art. *Address:* Klöckner & Co. AG, Klöckner Haus, Neudorfer Strasse 3–5, 47057 Duisburg, Germany. *Telephone:* 203/18 22 53.

HENLE, Jörg Alexander; German business executive; b. 12 May 1934, Aachen; s. of Dr. Günter and Anne-Liese (née Küpper) Henle; brother of Christian-Peter Henle (q.v.); one s. three d.; ed. Cologne, Munich, Princeton (N.J.), Stanford, Geneva and Berlin Univs.; joined Klöckner-Werke AG 1962; Man. Establecimientos Klöckner S.A., Buenos Aires 1964–65; Deputy mem. directorate of Klöckner Mannstaedt-Werke, Troisdorf 1965–67; mem. directorate, Klöckner-Werke AG, Hütte Bremen 1967–68; mem. Man.Bd. Klöckner-Werke AG 1968–71, Chair. Supervisory Bd. 1979–92; Chair. Bd. of Man. Klöckner & Co. AG 1971–92; Chair. Bd. Peter-Klöckner-Stiftung, Duisburg; mem. Bd. Stichting Verenigt Bezit, The Hague, Int. Yehudi Menuhin Foundation, Brussels; fmr. mem. Supervisory Bd. Allianz Lebensversicherungs-AG, Mietfinanz GmbH, AG, Robert Bosch GmbH, Readymix AG; fmr. mem. Advisory Bd. HERMES Kreditversicherungs-Aktiengesellschaft; fmr. Vice-Pres. Niederrheinische Industrie- und Handelskammer Duisburg-Wesel-Kleve zu Duisburg. *Leisure interests:* plastic arts, theatre, music. *Address:* Karlsbader Strasse 1, 14193 Berlin, Germany. *Telephone:* (030) 8252244. *Fax:* (030) 8265228.

HENLEY, Elizabeth Becker, B.F.A., PH.D.; American playwright and actress; b. 8 May 1952, Jackson, Miss.; d. of Charles and Lydy Henley; ed. Univ. of Illinois; Pulitzer Prize for Drama 1981, N.Y. Drama Critics Circle Best Play Award 1981, George Oppenheimer/Newsday Playwriting Award 1980–81. *Publications:* Crimes of the Heart 1981, The Wake of Jamey Foster 1982, Am I Blue 1982, The Miss Firecracker Contest, The Debutante Ball 1985, The Lucky Spot 1987, Abundance 1989, The Debutante Ball 1991, Beth Henley: Monologues for Women 1992; screenplays: Nobody's Fool 1986, Crimes of the Heart 1986, Miss Firecracker 1989, Signatures (stage, film) 1990, Control Freaks (stage) 1993, Revelers (stage, film) 1994. *Address:* The William Morris Agency, 151 El Camino Drive, Beverly Hills, CA 90212, U.S.A.

HENN, Walter, DR.ING; German architect; b. 20 Dec. 1912, Reichenberg/Bez. Dresden; s. of Karl Henn and Hedwig Bretschneider; m. Dr. med. Hilde Leistner 1938; two s. three d.; ed. Technische Hochschule Dresden and Akad. der Bildenden Künste, Dresden; Prof. of Bldg. and Industrial Construction, Technische Hochschule, Dresden 1946, Technische Hochschule, Braunschweig 1953; founder and dir. of first inst. for industrial construction in Germany 1957; mem. Deutsche Wissenschaftsrat 1969; Foreign mem. Acad. of Eng. of the Russian Fed. Nov. 1992–; mem. numerous comms., working parties etc; has undertaken bldgs. in Germany and elsewhere including industrial, admin. and school bldgs., research centres, electricity and water works etc.; mem. Mainz Acad., Braunschweig Scientific Soc.; Dr. techn. h.c. (T.U. Vienna); Dr.-Ing. h.c. (T.U. Dresden). *Publications:* several books (translated in 11 languages) and more than 200 articles in professional journals. *Address:* Ramsachleite 13, 82418 Murnau, Germany. *Telephone:* (08841) 9531. *Fax:* (08841) 99390.

HENNEKINNE, Loïc; French diplomatist; b. 20 Sept. 1940, Caudéran, Gironde; s. of Michel Hennekinne and Elisabeth Declemy; m. 2nd Marie Bozelle 1987; one d.; two s. (by first m.); ed. Ecole Nat. d'Admin.; First Sec. French embassies in Vietnam 1969–71, Chile 1971–73; Minister-Counsellor, Japan 1979–81; del. for external action, Ministry of Industry 1981–82; Dir. of Cabinet of Minister of Research and Industry 1982; Dir. of Personnel and Admin. Ministry of Foreign Affairs 1983–86; Amb. to Indonesia 1986–88; Gen. Sec. summit conf. of Western industrialized nations, Paris 1989; Diplomatic Adviser to Pres. Mitterrand 1989–91; Amb. to Japan 1991–93, to Canada 1997–98; Sec.-Gen. Ministry of Foreign Affairs 1998–; Inspector-Gen. of Foreign Affairs 1993–96; Chevalier, Ordre nat. du Mérite; Chevalier, Légion d'honneur. *Leisure interest:* tennis. *Address:* Ministry of Foreign Affairs, 37 quai d'Orsay, 75007 Paris; 15 avenue Frochot, 75009 Paris, France (Home).

HENNESSY, Edward L., Jr., B.S.; American business executive; b. 22 March 1928, Boston, Mass.; s. of Edward L. Hennessy and Celina Mary Doucette; m. Ruth F. Schilling 1951; one s. one d.; ed. Fairleigh Dickinson Univ., Rutherford, N.J., and New York Univ. Law School; Asst. Controller, Textron 1950–55; Group Controller, Eastern Electronics Group, Lear Siegler Inc. 1956–60; Controller, Int. Electronic Corpn., Int. Telephone & Telegraph Corpn. 1960–61, Controller, Corporate Staff 1961–62, Controller, ITT Europe 1962–64; Dir. of Finance, Europe, Middle East and Africa, Colgate Palmolive Co. 1964–65; Vice-Pres. Finance, Heublein Inc. 1965–68, Sr. Vice-Pres. Admin. and Finance 1969–72; Dir. United Technologies Corpn. 1972–79, Sr. Vice-Pres. Finance and Admin. 1972–77, Exec. Vice-Pres., Group Vice-Pres. Systems & Equipment Group, and Chief Financial Office 1977–79; Chair., C.E.O. and Pres. Allied Corpn. 1979–; Chair. and C.E.O. Allied-Signal Inc. 1985–91; Dir. Martin Marietta Corpn., Bank of New York, Coast Guard Foundation; Trustee, Fairleigh Dickinson Univ, Catholic Univ. of America. *Leisure interests:* sailing, tennis, reading. *Address:* P.O. Box 3000 R, Morristown, NJ 07960, U.S.A.

HENNESSY, John Basil, A.O., D.PHIL., D.LITT., F.S.A., F.A.H.A.; Australian archaeologist; b. 10 Feb. 1925, Horsham Vic.; s. of Thomas B. Hennessy and Nellie M. Poultney; m. Ruth M. R. Shannon 1954; one s. two d.; ed. Villa Maria & St. Patrick's Coll. Ballarat, Univ. of Sydney and Magdalen Coll. Oxford; lecturer, Near Eastern Archaeology, Univ. of Sydney 1955–61; Asst. Dir. British School of Archaeology, Jerusalem 1965–66, Dir. 1966–70; Edwin Cuthbert Hall Visiting Prof. of Middle Eastern Archaeology, Univ. of Sydney 1970–72, Edwin Cuthbert Hall Prof. 1973–90, Prof. Emer. 1991–, also Hon. Assoc. School of Archaeology, Classics and Ancient History; Dir. Australian Foundation for Near Eastern Archaeology 1973–91, Gov. 1992–; Gov. Cyprus Research Centre 1992–; Dir. of Excavations Sphagion, Stephania (Cyprus) 1951, Damascus Gate, Jerusalem 1964–66, Amman 1966, Teleilat Ghassul (Jordan) 1967–77, Samaria 1968, Pella (Jordan) 1978–88. *Publications:* Stephania 1964, The Foreign Relations of Palestine During the Early Bronze Age 1967, World Ceramics, The Ancient Near East 1968, The Arab States in the Modern World 1977–79, Masterpieces of Western Ceramics 1978, Pella in Jordan 1982, Archaeology of Jordan I 1986, Ayia Paraskevi and Vasilia 1988, Archaeology of Jordan II 1989. *Address:* 497 Old Windsor Road, Kellyville, N.S.W., 2153, Australia. *Telephone:* 629-1514 (Home).

HENRICH, Dieter, D.PHIL.; German professor of philosophy; b. 5 Jan. 1927, Marburg; s. of Hans Harry Henrich and Frieda Henrich; m. Dr Bettina von Eckardt 1975; two d.; ed. Univ. of Heidelberg; Prof. Freie Univ. Berlin 1960–65, Univ. of Heidelberg 1965–81; now. Prof. of Philosophy, Univ. of Munich; Visiting Prof. Columbia Univ. 1968–72, Univ. of Mich. 1969, Harvard Univ. 1973–86, Tokyo Univ. 1979, Yale Univ. 1987; Hon. Prof. Humboldt Univ., Berlin 1997; mem. Heidelberg and Bavarian Acads; Hon. Foreign mem. American Acad. of Arts and Sciences. *Publications:* Der ontologische Gottesbeweis 1960, Fichtes ursprüngliche Einsicht, 1967, Hegel im Kontext 1971, Identität und Objektivität 1976, Fluchtlinien 1982, Der Gang des

Andenkens 1986, Konzepte 1987, Ethik zum nuklearen Frieden 1990, Konstellationen 1991, Der Grund im Bewusstsein 1992, The Moral Image of the World 1992, The Unity of Reason 1994, I. C. Diez 1997. *Address:* Gerlichstrasse 7a, 81245 Munich, Germany. *Telephone:* 089/811 91 31. *Fax:* 089/811 79 878.

HENRY, André Armand; French politician and teacher; b. 15 Oct. 1934, Fontenoy-le-Château; s. of Alice Henry; m. Odile Olivier 1956; one s. one d.; ed. Bains-les-Bains, Ecole normale d'instituteurs, Mirecourt; teacher, Fontenoy-le-Château 1955–56, Thaon-les-Vosges 1956–69; began trade union career with Syndicat Nat. des Instituteurs (S.N.I.), Training Coll. Rep. (Vosges) 1954, mem Exec. Comm. (Vosges) 1955–69, Asst. Sec.-Gen. (Vosges) 1960–63, Sec.-Gen. (Vosges) 1963–69, mem. Nat. Council, S.N.I. 1965–74, Perm. Sec. 1969–74; in charge of youth, then gen. admin. section of S.N.I.; mem. Fed. Council, in charge of culture, youth and leisure sections, Fédération de l'Education Nationale (F.E.N.) 1971, Perm. Sec. and Sec.-Gen. 1974–81; Minister for Free Time 1981–83; Délégué Général à l'économie sociale 1983–; Chair. and Man. Dir. Caisse Nat. de l'Energie 1984–87; Inspecteur Général de l'administration de l'Education Nat. 1989-95; Nat. Vice-Prés. Association laïque pour l'éducation et la formation professionelle des adolescents (ALEFPA) 1995–; Délégué départemental de l'Education Nationale; Vice-Pres. Mission Laïque française; Commdr., Ordre du mérite; Chevalier, Légion d'honneur, Chevalier des palmes académiques. *Publications:* Dame l'école 1977, Serviteurs d'idéal (2 vols), Conquérir l'Avenir 1992, Le Ministre qui voulait changer la vie 1996. *Leisure interests:* football, volleyball, photography, flying light aircraft. *Address:* 1 bis rue de l'Espérance, 94000 Créteil, France (Home). *Telephone:* (01) 48-99-37-79.

HENRY, Rev. Dr. Carl F. H., TH.D., PH.D.; American theologian and author; b. 22 Jan. 1913, New York; s. of Karl F. and Johanna (Vaethroeder) Henry; m. Helga I. Bender 1940; one s. one d.; ed. Wheaton Coll., Ill., Northern Baptist Theological Seminary, Boston Univ., New Coll., Edinburgh, and King's Coll., Cambridge; Prof. of Theology, Northern Baptist Theological Seminary, Chicago 1942–47; Prof. of Theology and Christian Philosophy, Fuller Theological Seminary 1947–56; Ed. Christianity Today 1956–68; Visiting Prof. of Theology, Eastern Baptist Theological Seminary 1968–70, Prof.-at-large 1970–74; Lecturer-at-large, World Vision Int. 1974–87; Visiting Prof. of Theology, Calvin Theological Seminary 1986, Trinity Evangelical Divinity School 1987–96, Tyndale Seminary, Netherlands 1990; Sr. Research Prof., Southern Baptist Theological Seminary 1994–96; Corresp. World Magazine 1995–; Chair. World Congress on Evangelism, Berlin 1966; Program Chair. Jerusalem Conf. on Biblical Prophecy 1971; Pres. Evangelical Theological Soc. 1969–70, American Theological Soc. 1974–75, Inst. for Advanced Christian Studies 1971–74, 1976–79; Vice-Pres. Inst. for Religion and Democracy 1984–96; Sec. Carl F. H. Henry Study and Resource Centre; mem. Bd. M.E. Foundation, Prison Fellowship Ministries 1991–98, Riverside Foundation; mem. Bd. of Judges, Amy Foundation, writing awards 1989–; Fellow Christianity Today Inst. 1987–94; numerous hon. degrees; Religious Heritage of America Gold Award for 50 years of spiritual and moral leadership 1993; Distinguished Alumnus Award for contrib. in Theology, Boston Univ. 1998. *Publications:* author of 45 books, including God, Revelation and Authority (6 vols.). *Leisure interests:* writing, browsing in antique shops. *Address:* 1141 Hus Drive (Apt. 206), Watertown, WI 53094, U.S.A. *Telephone:* (920) 262-2251. *Fax:* (920) 262-2251.

HENRY, Sir Geoffrey Arama, K.B.E.; Cook Islands politician; b. 16 Nov. 1940, Aitutaki; s. of Arama Henry and Mata Uritaua; m. Louisa Olga Hoff 1965; four s. two d.; ed. Wanganui Collegiate School, Victoria Univ., Wellington, N.Z.; school teacher 1965–67; active in politics 1965–68; public service 1970–72; returned to politics, Cabinet Minister 1972–78; Leader of Opposition 1978–89; Prime Minister 1983, Deputy Prime Minister in Coalition Govt. 1984, Prime Minister 1989–; organizer Jt. Commercial Comm., U.S.A. and Pacific Islands 1990; Chair. Econ. Summit of Small Island States 1992; Chancellor Univ. of S. Pacific 1992; Silver Jubilee Medal 1977, N.Z. Commemoration Medal 1990. *Leisure interests:* golf, rugby and other sports, reading, music. *Address:* P.O. Box 281, Rarotonga, Cook Islands.

HENRY, Lenny, C.B.E.; British comedian and actor; b. 29 Aug. 1958; m. Dawn French (q.v.); numerous tours including Loud! 1994, Australia 1995. *Television includes:* New Faces (debut), Tiswas, Three of a Kind 1981–83, The Lenny Henry Show, Alive and Kicking 1991, Bernard & the Genie 1991, In Dreams 1992, The Real McCoy 1992, Chef (title role) (three series), Lenny Hunts the Funk, New Soul Nation, White Goods 1994, Funky Black Shorts 1994, Comic Relief, Lenny Go Home 1996, British Acad. Awards (host) 1997, Lenny's Big Amazon Adventure 1997, Lenny Goes to Town 1998. *Films include:* True Identity 1991. *Video:* Lenny Henry Live and Unleashed 1989, Lenny Henry Live and Loud 1994; toured Australia with Large! show 1998; awards include: Monaco Red Cross Award, The Golden Nymph Award (for Alive and Kicking) 1992, BBC Personality of the Year, Radio and Television Industry Club 1993. *Publications:* The Quest for the Big Woof (autobiographical) 1991, Charlie and the Big Chill (children's book) 1995. *Address:* c/o PBJ Management Ltd., 5 Soho Square, London, W1V 5DE, England. *Telephone:* 0171-287 1112. *Fax:* 0171-287 1448.

HENRY, Pierre; French composer; b. 9 Dec. 1927, Paris; s. of Georges Henry and Germaine Mazet; m. Isabelle Warnier 1971; one d. and one s. by previous m.; ed. Conservatoire Nat. Supérieur de Musique and studies with Nadia Boulanger, Olivier Messiaen and Félix Passerone; head of group researching concrete music, ORTF 1950–58; founder and Dir. Studio Apsome 1959–; founder, asscn. for electro-acoustic composition and research 1972; cr. Son et Recherche asscn. 1982; Officier, Légion d'honneur, Officier, Ordre Nat. du Mérite, Commdr. des Arts et des Lettres; Grand Prix, Acad. du Disque 1966; Grand Prix, Acad. Charles Cros 1970; Grand Prix Nat. de la Musique 1985; Grand Prix de la Musique Symphonique (Sacem) 1987; Victoires de la Musique 1998, Grand Prix Karl Sczuka 1997, etc. *Works include:* Symphonie pour un homme seul 1950, Messe de Liverpool 1967, Messe pour le temps présent 1970, Deuxième Symphonie 1972, Nijinsky, Clown de Dieu (ballet by Maurice Béjart) 1973, Dieu, action de voix, de sons et de gestes (spectacular, Lille 1977, Paris 1978), Hommage à Beethoven 1979, Les Noces chymiques, rituel féerique en 12 journées (Opéra comique) 1980, Paradis Perdus 1982, Berlin, symphonie d'une grande ville (film, concert) 1987, Livre des morts égyptien 1988, Une Maison de Sons 1990, Maldoror-Feuilleton 1992, L'Homme à la Caméra (film/concert) 1993, Une Ample Comédie à Cent Actes Divers: Hommage à La Fontaine 1995, Intérieur/Extérieur 1996, Schubert 97 (1997), Histoire Naturelle 1997, La Xème Remix 1998, L'homme au microphone 1999. *Address:* 32 rue Toul, 75012 Paris, France.

HENRY de VILLENEUVE, Xavier, L. EN D.; French banker; b. 8 July 1932, Quintin; s. of Jacques Henry de Villeneuve and Yvonne de la Motte de la Motte Rouge; m. Simone de Vigneral 1963; two s. one d.; ed. Ecole des Frères, Quintin, Coll. des Cordeliers, Dinan, Coll. St. Charles, St. Brieuc and Faculté de Droit, Rennes; joined Banque de Bretagne 1959, Asst. Dir.-Gen. 1971, Dir.-Gen. 1979, Pres. and Man. Dir. 1986; Pres. and Man. Dir., Banque de la Cité 1978–82, Pres. 1983–85, Hon. Pres., Admin. 1991; Pres. Comm. des Affaires Sociales of Asscn. Française des Banques 1988, Pres. Compagnie Financière de Participation 1988, Ronceray 1991–93, ACLPME 1995–98, ACLPME Finances 1997–98; Vice-Prés. Asscn. d'Eloge 1995–96, Résidences ACL 1997–98; Chevalier, Légion d'honneur, des Arts et des Lettres. *Publication:* Contes et nouvelles des quatre vents. *Leisure interests:* the arts, reading, old wars, hunting. *Address:* 19 rue de la Convention, 75015 Paris; Kerbic, 22200 Pommerit-le-Vicomte, France (Homes).

HENRYSSON, Haraldur; Icelandic judge; b. 17 Feb. 1938, Reykjavik; m. Elisabet Kristinsdóttir 1972; one s.; ed. Reykjavik High School, Univ. of Iceland; Asst. Judge 1964–73; Judge Criminal Court, Reykjavik 1973–89, Supreme Court 1989–, Pres. 1996–97; Chair. cttee. investigating accidents at sea 1973–83; Pres. Nat. Life Saving Asscn. 1982–90; Vice-mem. Althing 1967–71; Kt. Grand Cross of Icelandic Falcon. *Leisure interests:* outdoor sports. *Address:* Hæstirettur Islands, Domhus v. Arnarhol, 150 Reykjavik, Iceland. *Telephone:* 510-3030. *Fax:* 562-3995.

HENSON, Lisa; American film company executive; b. 1961; d. of late Jim Henson and of Jane Henson; ed. Harvard Univ.; joined Warner Bros. as Exec. Asst. to Head of Production 1983, apptd. Dir. of Creative Affairs 1985, Exec. Vice-Pres. (Production) 1992; Pres. (Production) Columbia Pictures 1993, Studio Pres. 1994–. *Address:* Columbia Pictures, 3400 Riverside Drive, Burbank, CA 91505, U.S.A.

HENZE, Hans Werner; German composer and conductor; b. 1 July 1926, Gütersloh; s. of Franz Henze and Margarete Geldmacher; ed. Staatsmusikschule, Brunswick, Kirchenmusikalisches Institut, Heidelberg; Musical Dir. Heinz Hilpert's Deutsches Theater in Konstanz 1948; Artistic Dir. Ballet of the Hessian State Theatre in Wiesbaden 1950; living in Italy as an independent artist since 1953; Prof. of Composition, Mozarteum, Salzburg 1961; Prof. of Composition, Hochschule für Musik, Cologne 1980–81; Artistic Dir. Accad. Filarmonica Romana 1982–91; Prof. of Composition Royal Acad. of Music, London 1987–91; mem. Akademie der Künste, Berlin 1960–68, Bayerische Akademie der Schönen Künste, Munich; Dr. Mus. (Edinburgh) 1971; Robert Schumann Prize 1952, North-Rhine-Westphalia Art Prize 1956, Prix d'Italia 1954, Sibelius Gold Medal, Harriet Cohen Awards, London 1956, Music Critics Prize, Buenos Aires 1958, Kunstpreis, Berlin, Niedersächsischer Kunstpreis 1962, Ludwig-Spohr-Preis 1976, Heidelberg-Bach-Preis 1983, Siemens-Preis 1990, Preis des Internationales Theaterinstituts 1991, Grosses Bundesverdienst-Kreuz 1991, Kultureller Ehrenpreis 1996, numerous other awards and prizes. *Composition:* Operas: Das Wundertheater, Boulevard Solitude, König Hirsch, Der Prinz von Homburg, Elegy for Young Lovers 1961, Der Junge Lord 1964, Die Bassariden 1965, La Cubana, We Come to the River, The English Cat 1983, Das verratene Meer 1990; Radio Operas: Ein Landarzt, Das Ende einer Welt; Ballets: Jack Pudding, Tancred under Cantylene, Variationen, Labyrinth, The Idiot, Apoll und Hyazinth, Maratona, Undine, Nachtigall, Orpheus; Oratorio: Novae de Infinito Laudes 1962; Cantatas: Being Beauteous 1963, Ariosi 1963, Cantata della Fiaba Estrema 1963; Choral works: Chorfantasie 1964, Musen Siziliens 1966; Oratorio: The Raft of the Medusa 1968; seven Symphonies, Violin and Piano and Violoncello Concertos, Double Concerto for Oboe, Harp and Strings, five String Quartets, Wind Quintet, Kammermusik 1958 (tenor and ensemble), El Cimarron 1969, The Tedious Way to the Place of Natasha Ungeheuer 1970, Heliogabalus Imperator 1971, La Cubana 1972, Voices 1973, Tristan 1974, Ragtime and Habanera 1975, The English Cat 1983; film music for Muriel, etc. *Publications:* Das Ende einer Welt 1953, Tagebuch eines Balletts 1959, Musik und Politik 1976, Die Englische Katze—Ein Arbeitsbuch 1979–82 1983, Reiselieder mit böhmischen Quinten 1996. *Leisure interests:* poetry, botany. *Address:* c/o Schott Musik International GmbH, Weihergarten 5, 55116 Mainz, Germany.

HEPBURN, Katharine; American actress; b. 12 May 1907, Hartford, Conn.; d. of the late Dr. Thomas N. Hepburn and Katharine Houghton; m. Ludlow Ogden Smith (divorced); ed. Bryn Mawr Coll., Pa.; professional stage actress since 1928; film actress since 1932; also appears on TV; received gold medal for best film actress, Venice 1934, Whistler Soc. award 1957; Lifetime Achievement Award (Annual American Comedy Awards) 1989; four Acad. Awards (Oscars). *Stage plays include:* The Lake, The Philadelphia Story, Without Love 1942, As You Like It 1950, The Millionairess 1952, The Taming of the Shrew 1955, The Merchant of Venice 1955, Much Ado About Nothing 1955, Coco (musical) 1970 (on tour 1971), A Matter of Gravity 1976 (on tour 1977), The West Side Waltz 1981. *Films include:* A Bill of Divorcement 1932, Morning Glory 1933 (Acad. Award 1934), Little Women 1933, Alice Adams 1935, Sylvia Scarlett 1935, Mary of Scotland 1936, A Woman Rebels 1936, Quality Street 1937, Stage Doors 1937, Bringing Up Baby 1938, Holiday 1938, The Philadelphia Story (N.Y. Critics' Award) 1940, Woman of the Year 1942, Keeper of the Flame 1942, Undercurrent 1946, Sea of Grass 1947, State of the Union 1948, Adam's Rib 1949, The African Queen 1951, Pat and Mike 1952, Summer Madness 1955, The Rainmaker 1956, Desk Set 1957, Suddenly Last Summer 1959, Long Day's Journey Into Night 1962, Guess Who's Coming to Dinner? 1967 (Acad. Award 1968), The Lion in Winter 1968 (Acad. Award 1969), The Madwoman of Chaillot 1969, The Trojan Women 1971, A Delicate Balance 1973, The Glass Menagerie (TV) 1973, Love Among the Ruins (TV) 1975, Rooster Cogburn 1975, Olly Olly Oxen Free 1976, The Corn is Green (TV) 1979, Christopher Strong 1980, On Golden Pond 1981 (Acad. Award 1982), The Ultimate Solution of Grace Quigley 1984, Mrs. Delafield Wants to Marry (TV) 1986, Laura Lansing Slept Here (TV) 1988, The Man Upstairs (TV) 1992, Love Affair 1993, This Can't Be Love (TV) 1994, One Christmas 1994. *Publication:* The Making of The African Queen 1987, Me (autobiog.) 1991. *Address:* c/o William Morris Agency, 151 El Camino Drive, Beverly Hills, CA 90212, U.S.A.

HEPPELL, (Thomas) Strachan, C.B.; British public service official; b. 15 Aug. 1935, Teesside; s. of late Leslie Heppell and Doris Potts; m. Felicity Rice 1963; two s.; ed. Acklam Hall Grammar School, Middlesbrough and Queen's Coll. Oxford; Asst. Prin. Nat. Assistance Bd. (NAB) 1958; Prin. NAB, Cabinet Office, Dept. of Health and Social Security (DHSS) 1963; Asst. Dir. of Social Welfare, Hong Kong 1971–73; Asst. Sec. DHSS 1973, Under-Sec. 1979; Deputy Sec. DHSS, Dept. of Health 1983; Chair. Man. Bd. European Medicines and Evaluation Agency (EMEA) 1994–; consultant, Dept. of Health 1995–; mem. Broadcasting Standards Comm. 1996–; Chair. Family Fund Trust 1997–; Visting Fellow L.S.E. 1996–. *Publications:* contribs. to publs. on social security, social welfare, health and pharmaceuticals. *Address:* Department of Health, Richmond House, 79 Whitehall, London, SW1A 2NS; European Medicines Evaluation Agency, 7 Westferry Circus, Canary Wharf, London, E14 4HB, England. *Telephone:* 0171-210 5559; 0171-418 8400. *Fax:* 0171-210 5023; 0171-418 8416.

HERB, Raymond George, PH.D.; American professor of physics; b. 22 Jan. 1908, Navarino, Wis.; s. of Joseph and Annie Herb; m. Anne Williamson 1945; two s. three d.; ed. Univ. of Wisconsin.; Research Assoc. in Physics, Univ. of Wis. 1935–39, Research Assoc. and Asst. Prof. in Physics 1939–40, Assoc. Prof. 1941–45, Prof. 1945–61, Charles Mendenhall Prof. of Physics 1961–72; Pres. and Chair of Bd. Nat. Electrostatics Corp. 1965–; mem. N.A.S.; Distinguished Service Citation for Coll. of Engineers, Univ. of Wis.; Dr. h.c. (Univs. of Basel and São Paulo), Hon. Ph.D. (Lund) 1993; Tom W. Bonner Award 1968. *Publication:* Van de Graaf Generators in Handbuch der Physik XLIV 1959. *Address:* National Electrostatics Corporation, 7450 Graber Road, P.O. Box 620310, Middleton, WI 53562 (Office); P.O. Box 223A, Rural Route 1, Mazomanie WI 53560, U.S.A. (Home). *Telephone:* (608) 831-7600 (Office).

HERBERT, Rt. Rev. Christopher William, F.R.S.A., B.A.; British ecclesiastic; b. 7 Jan. 1944, Lydney, Glos.; s. of Walter Herbert and late Hilda Dibben; m. Janet Turner 1968; two s.; ed. Monmouth School, Univ. of Wales, Lampeter, Univ. of Bristol and Wells Theological Coll.; Curate, St. Paul's, Tupsley, Hereford 1967–71; Adviser in Religious Educ. Diocese of Hereford 1971–76, Dir. of Educ. 1976–81; Vicar, St. Thomas on the Bourne, Diocese of Guildford 1981–90; Dir. of Post-Ordination Training, Diocese of Guildford 1984–90; Archdeacon of Dorking 1990–95; Bishop of St. Albans 1995–. *Publications include:* Be Thou My Vision 1985, This Most Amazing Day 1986, The Question of Jesus 1987, Alive to God 1987, Ways Into Prayer 1987, Help in Your Bereavement 1988, Prayers for Children 1993, Pocket Prayers 1993, The Prayer Garden 1994, Words of Comfort 1994, A Little Prayer Diary 1996, Pocket Prayers for Children 1999. *Leisure interests:* cycling, reading, writing, walking. *Address:* Abbey Gate House, St. Albans, Herts., AL3 4HD, England. *Telephone:* (01727) 853305. *Fax:* (01727) 846715.

HERBERT, (Dennis) Nicholas; 3rd Baron Hemingford, M.A.; British journalist; b. 25 July 1934, Watford, Herts.; s. of Dennis George Ruddock Herbert, 2nd Baron Hemingford and Elizabeth McClare (née Clark); m. Jennifer Mary Toresen Bailey 1958; one s. three d.; ed. Oundle School, Clare Coll., Cambridge; Sports Desk, Reuters 1956–57, Diplomatic Desk 1957–60, Washington Bureau 1960–61; Asst. Washington Corresp., The Times 1961–65, Middle East Corresp. 1966–68, Deputy Features Ed. 1968–70; Ed. Cambridge Evening News 1970–74; Editorial Dir. Westminster Press 1974–92, Deputy Chief Exec. 1992–95; Pres. Guild of British Newspaper Eds. 1980–81, Media Soc. 1982–84; Sec. Asscn. of British Eds. 1985–95; mem. E. Anglian Regional Cttee., Nat. Trust 1984–, Chair. 1990–; Trustee Bell Educational Trust 1985–90. *Publications:* Jews and Arabs in Conflict 1969, Press Freedom in Britain (with David Flintham) 1991. *Leisure interests:* Victorian military history, computers, genealogy, destructive gardening. *Address:* The Old Rectory, Hemingford Abbots, Huntingdon, Cambs., PE18 9AN, England. *Telephone:* (01480) 466234. *Fax:* (01480) 380275.

HERBERT, Walter William (Wally); British explorer; b. 24 Oct. 1934; s. of Capt. W. W. J. Herbert and Helen Manton; m. Marie McGaughey 1969; two d.; trained as surveyor, Royal Engineers 1950–53, Egypt 1953–54; Surveyor with Falklands Islands Dependencies Survey based at Hope Bay, Antarctica 1955–58; travelled in S. and N. America 1958; Expedition to Lapland and Spitsbergen 1960; Surveyor with N.Z. Antarctic Expedition mapping routes of Capt. Scott and Capt. Amundsen 1960–62; Leader Expedition to N.W. Greenland 1967–68; Leader of British Trans-Arctic Expedition 1968–69, which made first surface crossing of Arctic Ocean from Alaska to Spitzbergen via North Pole by dog sledges; Leader Expedition to N.W. Greenland 1971–73, to Lapland 1974, several expeditions to N.W. Greenland 1975–87; second visit to N. Pole April 1987, third visit Aug. 1991; Jt. Hon. Pres., World Expeditionary Asscn; Hon. mem. British Schools Exploring Soc.; Polar Medal 1962 and clasp 1969, Livingstone Gold Medal, Royal Scottish Geographical Soc. 1969, Founder's Gold Medal, Royal Geographical Soc. 1970, City of Paris Medal 1983, French Geographical Soc. Medal 1983, Explorer's Medal, Explorer's Club 1985, Finn Ronne Award for Antarctic exploration 1985. *Film:* The Noose of Laurels 1988. *Exhibitions:* First one-man-show of paintings at the Royal Geographical Soc. 1994, Explorers Club, New York 1994, QE-2 1994, 1995, Australian Geographical Soc. 1995, Traveller's Club, London 1997. *Publications:* A World of Men 1968, Across the Top of the World 1969, The Last Great Journey on Earth 1971, Polar Deserts 1971, Eskimos 1976, North Pole 1978, Hunters of the Polar North 1982, The Noose of Laurels 1989 and contribs. to several other books. *Leisure interest:* painting. *Address:* c/o Royal Geographical Society, 1 Kensington Gores, London, SW7 2AR, England; Rowan Cottage, Catlodge, Laggan, Inverness-shire, PH20 1AH, Scotland. *Telephone:* (01582) 544396 (Home). *Fax:* (01582) 544396.

HERBERT, William Valentine, LL.M., PH.D.; Saint Christopher and Nevis diplomatist and lawyer; b. 1936, Basseterre, St. Kitts; m.; three c.; ed. London Univ., England; called to Bar (Middle Temple) 1959; founding mem. and first Pres. People's Action Movt.; acted as Constitutional Adviser to Govts. of Turks and Caicos, Anguilla and St. Kitts and Nevis; fmr. Man. Dir. Caribbean Commercial Bank (Anguilla) and Man. Dir. Anguilla Trust Co.; mem. Bar Asscn. of St. Kitts-Nevis, Org. of Caribbean Bar Asscns., World Peace Through Law and Council of Legal Educ. for the Caribbean; Perm. Rep. to UN 1983–90. *Publication:* Natural Justice, the Ammunthodo Case. *Address:* c/o Government Headquarters, Church Street, Basseterre, Saint Christopher and Nevis.

HERBIG, George Howard, PH.D.; American astronomer; b. 2 Jan. 1920, Wheeling, W. Va.; s. of George A. Herbig and Glenna Howard; m. 1st Delia McMullin 1943; three s. one d.; m. 2nd Hannelore Tillmann 1968; ed. Univ. of California (Los Angeles and Berkeley); Junior Astronomer, Lick Observatory, Mount Hamilton, Calif. 1948–50, Asst. Astronomer 1950–55, Assoc. Astronomer 1955–60, Astronomer 1960–87; Asst. Dir. Lick Observatory 1960–63, Acting Dir. 1970–71; Prof. of Astronomy, Univ. of Calif. (Santa Cruz) 1967–87; Astronomer, Inst. for Astronomy, Univ. of Hawaii 1987–; Visiting Prof. and lecturer Chicago 1959, Mexico 1961, Observatoire de Paris 1965, Max-Planck-Institut für Astronomie, Heidelberg 1969, Stockholm 1973, Hawaii 1976–77; mem. N.A.S., astronomy del. to People's Repub. of China 1977; Henry Norris Russell Lecturer, American Astronomical Soc. 1975; lectured in U.S.S.R. and Poland under exchange agreement, U.S.-U.S.S.R. Acads. of Science 1965, 1987; U.S. Nat. Science Foundation Sr. Postdoctoral Fellow 1965; mem. N.A.S., American Acad. of Arts and Sciences; Corresp. mem. Société scientifique Royale de Liège, Max-Planck-Inst. für Astronomie, Heidelberg; mem. numerous boards, comms., consultancies, etc.; Warner Prize, American Astronomical Soc. 1955, medal from Univ. of Liège 1969, Catherine Wolfe Bruce Gold Medal, Astronomical Soc. of the Pacific 1980, Petrie Prize and Lecture, Canadian Astronomical Soc. 1995. *Publications:* Ed. of and contributor to Non-Stable Stars 1957, Spectroscopic Astrophysics 1970; approximately 220 scientific papers, articles and reviews. *Leisure interests:* none.

HERBIG, Gunther; German conductor; b. 30 Nov. 1931, Aussig, Czechoslovakia; s. of Emil Herbig and Gisela (née Hieke) Herbig; m. Juttta Czapski 1958; one s. one d.; ed. Franz Liszt Conservatory for Music, Weimar; Conductor Nat. Theatre, Weimar 1957–62; Music Dir. Hans Otto Theatre, Potsdam 1962–66; Conductor Berlin Symphony Orchestra, Berlin, G.D.R. 1966–72, Gen. Music Dir. 1977–83; Gen. Music Dir. Dresden Philharmonic, Dresden, G.D.R. 1972–77; Music Dir. Detroit Symphony Orchestra, Detroit, Mich, U.S.A. 1984–90, Toronto Symphony Orchestra 1988–94, Toronto, Ont., Canada 1990–91; Prin. Guest Conductor Dallas Symphony Orchestra, Dallas Tex. 1979–81, BBC Philharmonic Orchestra, Man., England 1981–84; Theodor Fontane Prize 1964, Cultural Award (G.D.R.) 1970. *Leisure interests:* walking, swimming, reading. *Address:* Toronto Symphony Orchestra, 60 Simcoe Street, C116, Toronto, Ont. M5J 2H5, Canada.

HERBST, Axel, LL.D.; German fmr. European Economic Community official and diplomatist; b. 9 Oct. 1918, Mülheim; m. Elfe Bretschneider 1943; two d.; ed. Univs. of Berlin, Cologne and Münster, Acad. of Int. Law, The Hague, and Law Society's School of Law, London; German Foreign Service 1951, German Embassy, Washington; Head, North American Desk, Fed. Ministry of Foreign Affairs 1957–60; Deputy Exec. Sec. Comm. of the European Economic Community (EEC) 1960–63, Dir.-Gen. External Relations 1963–68; Ministerial Dir. and Head of Foreign Trade and Devt. Div. Fed. Ministry of Foreign Affairs 1969–73; Amb., Perm. Rep. to UN, Geneva 1973–76; Amb. to France 1976–83; Consultant for Int. Affairs 1983–. *Address:* Adenauerallee 99-103, 53113 Bonn, Germany. *Telephone:* 34-2747.

HERCUS, Luise Anna, PH.D.; Australian academic; b. 16 Jan. 1926, Munich, Germany; d. of Alfred Schwarzschild and Theodora Schwarzschild; m. Graham Robertson Hercus 1954; one s.; ed. Oxford Univ., U.K. and Australian Nat. Univ., Canberra; tutor and lecturer St. Anne's Coll., Oxford 1946–54; Research Fellow Univ. of Adelaide 1965–68; Sr. Lecturer Asian Studies Australian Nat. Univ. 1969–71, Reader 1972–91, now Visiting Fellow in Linguistics; much work on recording nearly extinct Aboriginal languages 1963–. *Publications:* The Languages of Victoria: A Late Survey 1969, The Bagandji Language 1982, This is What Happened, Historical Narratives by Aborigines (Co-Ed.) 1986, Nukunu Dictionary 1992, Wembawemba Dictionary 1992, Paakanyi Dictionary 1993; articles on Middle Indo-Aryan and on oral traditions of S. Australian Aborigines. *Leisure interest:* raising orphaned marsupials. *Address:* Kintala via Gundaroo, Dick's Creek Road, N.S.W. 2620, Australia. *Telephone:* 062-368145.

HERCUS, Dame Margaret Ann, D.B.E., P.C., B.A., LL.B.; New Zealand politician; b. 24 Feb. 1942, Hamilton; d. of Horace and Mary (née Ryan) Sayers; m. John Hercus; two s.; ed. Victoria, Auckland and Canterbury Univs.; Lawyer and Staff Training Officer, Beath & Co., Christchurch 1969–70; mem. Price Tribunal and Trade Practices Comm. 1973–75; Deputy Chair. Commerce Comm. 1975–78; Chair. Consumer Rights Campaign 1975; M.P. for Lyttelton 1978–87; Opposition Spokesperson on Social Welfare, Consumer Affairs and Women's Affairs 1978–84; Minister of Social Welfare, Police and Women's Affairs 1984–87; Perm. Rep. of N.Z. to the UN 1989–90; int. consultant 1991–; Labour. *Leisure interests:* collecting original New Zealand prints, theatre, reading. *Address:* 2 Ribbonwood Road, Geraldine 8751, New Zealand.

HERCZEGH, Géza Gábor, PH.D.; Hungarian judge; b. 17 Oct. 1928, Nagykapos; s. of the late Károly Herczegh and Jolán Olchvary; m. Melinda Petnehazy 1961; one s. one d.; ed. French Grammar School, Gödöllö, Univ. of Szeged; Research Fellow in public int. law Inst. of Political Science, Budapest 1951–67; Prof. of Law, Head Int. Law Dept., Univ. of Pécs 1967–90; Judge, Vice-Pres. Constitutional Court 1990–93; Judge Int. Court of Justice, The Hague 1994–; mem. Hungarian Acad. of Sciences 1985; Dr. h.c. (Marburg) 1990. *Publications:* The Colonial Question and International Law 1962, General Principles of Law and the International Legal Order 1969, Development of International Humanitarian Law 1984, Foreign Policy of Hungary 896–1919 1987. *Leisure interests:* history, archaeology. *Address:* International Court of Justice, Peace Palace, Carnegieplein 2, 2517 KJ The Hague, Netherlands.

HERINCX, Raimund (Raymond Frederick); British opera and concert singer, voice teacher and therapist; b. 23 Aug. 1927, London; s. of Florent Herincx and Marie Cheal; m. Margaret J. Waugh (known as Astra Blair) 1954; one s. two d.; ed. Thames Valley Grammar School and Univ. of London; Educ. Officer, Household Cavalry 1946–48; studied singing in Antwerp, Brussels, Barcelona and London with Giovanni Valli, Samuel Worthington and Harold Williams 1949–53; mem. Royal Opera House chorus; joined Welsh Nat. Opera 1956; Prin. Baritone, Sadler's Wells Opera 1957–67; début Royal Opera House, Covent Garden 1968; joined Metropolitan Opera House, New York 1976, subsequently appearing in most major U.S. opera houses mainly in works of Wagner and Richard Strauss; Prof. of Voice Royal Acad. of Music 1970–77; Sr. Voice Teacher, North East of Scotland Music School 1979–; voice therapist 1979–; voice teacher Trinity Coll. of Music, London 1993–; lecturer, Univ. Coll., Cardiff 1984–87; Music Critic for Music and Musicians; Opera Medal, Int. Music Awards 1968; Hon. R.A.M. 1971. *Leisure interests:* Artists' Asscn. Against Aids, vineyard man., plant breeding (begonias and geraniums), wine and its history, wildfowl. *Address:* Monks' Vineyard, Larkbarrow, East Compton, Pilton, Shepton Mallet, Somerset, BA4 4NR, England. *Telephone:* (01749) 344462.

HERING, Gerhard F.; German theatrical director and author; b. 28 Oct. 1908, Rogasen; ed. Humanistisches Gymnasium, Stettin, Univs. of Berlin and Heidelberg; Asst., Preussisches Staatstheater Berlin; joined Magdeburgische Zeitung 1933, theatre critic and literary editor 1934–37; theatre critic Kölnische Zeitung 1937–42; forced to resign for political reasons; editor Vision 1946–48; chief producer Deutsches Theater, Konstanz 1946–50; Dir. Otto-Falckenberg-Schauspielschule der Kammerspiele, Munich 1950–52; chief opera and drama producer, Württembergische Staatstheater, Stuttgart 1952–54; freelance writer and producer for radio, television and theatre in Munich, Stuttgart, Frankfurt, Göttingen 1954–60; Head of W.D.R.—Studios Kultur, Düsseldorf 1960–61; Dir. Landestheater, Darmstadt 1961–71; Hon. Prof. Theaterwissenschaft, Univ. of Giessen 1967–; productions have included plays of Sophocles, Euripides, Goethe, Schiller, Grillparzer, Lessing, Gerhart Hauptmann, Georg Kaiser, Konrad Wünsche, Sartre, Genet; mem. Deutsche Akad. für Sprache und Dichtung; mem. Deutsche Akad. der Darstellenden Künste (Vice-Pres. 1966, Pres. 1970). *Publications include:* Porträts und Deutungen—Von Herder zu Hofmannsthal 1948, Klassische Liebespaare 1948, 1950, Ein Brunnen des Lebens 1950, Gerhart Hauptmann 1955, Der Ruf zur Leidenschaft 1959, Ein grosser Herr: Das Leben des Fürsten Pückler (with Vita Huber) 1969; introductions and contributions to numerous books and texts. *Address:* Park Rosenhöhe, Edschmidweg 25, 64287 Darmstadt, Germany.

HERING, Jürgen; German librarian; b. 15 Sept. 1937, Chemnitz; s. of late Karl Hering and of Margot (Schubert) Hering; m. Inge Rich 1961; one s. two d.; ed. Univs. of Stuttgart, Munich and Tübingen; Library Asst. Stuttgart Univ. Library 1968, Library Adviser 1971, Sr. Library Adviser 1972, Librarian 1974, Chief Librarian 1975–96; Dir. Sächsische Landesbibliothek-Staats and Dresden Univ. Library 1997–; Chair. Verein Deutscher Bibliothekare 1979–83, First Deputy Chair. 1983–85; Dir. Max-Kade-Stiftung Stuttgart 1982–, Wissenschaftliche Beirat Bibliothek für Zeitgeschichte, Stuttgart 1986–, Kuratorium Deutsches Biblioteksinstitut Berlin 1990–95; mem. Exec. Cttee. German Libraries Asscn. 1992–95 (Chair. 1989–92). *Leisure interests:* photography, travel. *Address:* Eichenparkstr. 34, 70619 Stuttgart, Germany. *Telephone:* (0351) 463-4308. *Fax:* (0351) 463-7173.

HERKE, Horst W., DR.RER.POL.; German business executive; b. 2 Dec. 1931, Mainz; m. Barbara Herke; one d.; Man. of financial analyses, Adam Opel AG 1959–74, Asst. to Chair. of Bd. 1976–77, Treasurer 1977–82, Dir. of Purchasing 1982–84, Chair. of Bd. 1986–89; Financial Staff of Gen. Motors overseas org. 1974–76, Gen. Man. Gen. Motors Espana 1984–86.; Vice-Pres. Econ. Affairs, Gen. Motors Europe 1989–. *Leisure interests:* theatre, gardening, cycling.

HERKSTRÖTER, Cornelius Antonius Johannes, B.SC.; Netherlands petroleum company executive; b. 21 Aug. 1937, Venlo; m. Regina Maria Haske 1959; two s. one d.; qualified as chartered accountant; joined Billiton as business economist 1967, following acquisition of Billiton by Shell Petroleum, apptd. Head Dept. Financial and Econ. Affairs 1971, various sr. posts in Billiton cos., Switzerland and Netherlands 1972–80, Area Co-ordinator S.E. Asia, Shell Int. Petroleum Co. Ltd. 1980, Vice-Pres. (Finance) Shell Française S.A. 1982, Chair. Bd. of Man. Deutsche Shell A.G. 1985, Regional Co-ordinator Europe, Dir. Shell Internationale Petroleum Mij. B.V. 1988, Man. Dir. The Shell Petroleum Co. Ltd., Chair. Supervisory Bd. Shell Nederland B.V., Group Man. Dir 1989, Chair. Supervisory Bd. Deutsche Shell A.G. 1990, Dir. Shell U.K. Ltd., Chair. Bd. of Dirs. Billiton Int. Metals B.V. 1991, Pres. N.V. Koninklijke Nederlandsche Petroleum Maatschappij (Royal Dutch Petroleum Co.) 1992–; Dir. numerous cos. in group; Verdienstkreux (First Class) (Germany); Kt. Order of Netherlands Lion. *Address:* Royal Dutch Petroleum Company, P.O. Box 162, 2501 AN The Hague, Netherlands. *Telephone:* (070) 377-4895. *Fax:* (070) 377-2616.

HERLING GRUDZIŃSKI, Gustaw; Polish writer, literary critic and journalist, b. 20 May 1919, Kielce; ed. Univ. of Warsaw; prisoner in Russian labour camps 1940–42, participant battle of Monte Cassino, literary head weekly Orzeł Biały, Rome 1945–46, assoc. Literary Inst. in Paris, joint ed. Parisian publ. Kultura 1947–55, assoc. ed. 1956–; in London 1948–51, worked for weekly Wiadomości; employee Free Europe Polish Radio, Munich 1952–55; in Italy since 1955. *Publications:* Żywi i umarli (The living and the dead) 1945, Inny świat (A World Apart) 1953, Skrzydła ołtarza (Wings of the altar) (short stories) 1960, Drugie przyjście (Second coming) (short stories) 1963, Upiory rewolucji (Phantoms of the revolution) (literary sketch) 1969, Dziennik pisany nocą (Diary written at night) (from 1973–93), Opowiadania zebrane (Collected tales) 1988. *Address:* Via Crispi 69, 801211 Naples, Italy.

HERMAN, Alexis M.; American politician and administrator; b. 16 July 1947, Mobile, Ala.; ed. Xavier Univ.; founder, fmr. C.E.O. H.M. Herman & Assocs., Washington; Nat. Dir. Minority Women's Employment Program until 1977; dir. Women's Bureau Dept. of Labor 1977–81; Chief of Staff, Deputy Chair. Democratic Nat. Convention Cttee. until 1991, C.E.O. 1991–92; Deputy Dir. Clinton-Gore Presidential Transition Office 1992–93; Asst. to Pres. of U.S.A., Public Liaison Dir. White House 1993–96; mem. Nat. Council of Negro Women; Secretary of Labor 1997–. *Address:* Office of the Secretary, U.S. Department of Labor, Washington, DC 20210, U.S.A.

HERMANNSSON, Steingrímur, M.SC.; Icelandic central bank governor, engineer and politician; b. 22 June 1928; s. of the late Hermann Jónasson and Vigdís Steingrímsdóttir; m. 1st Sara Jane Hermannsson 1951; m. 2nd Gudlaug Edda Gudmundsdóttir 1962; four s. two d.; ed. Reykjavik Coll., Illinois and California Insts. of Tech.; engineer, City of Reykjavik Electrical Power Works 1952–53; electrical engineer, Fertilizer Plant Inc., Iceland 1953–54; engineer S. Calif. Edison Co. 1954–56; Dir. Nat. Research Council, Iceland 1957–78; M.P. 1971–94; Minister of Justice, Ecclesiastical Affairs and Agric. 1978–79; Minister of Fisheries and Communications 1980–83; Prime Minister of Iceland 1983–87, 1988–91, also Minister of Econ. Planning; Minister of Foreign Affairs and Foreign Trade 1987–88; Gov. Cen. Bank of Iceland 1994–98; Chair. Progressive Party 1979–91 (Sec. 1971–79), Caltech's Alummi Distinguished Service Award 1986, IIT's Professional Achievement Award 1991, Icelandic Athletics Asscn. Gold Medal, Paul Harris Rotary Fellow. *Leisure interests:* outdoor sports, skiing, golf, forestry, carpentry. *Address:* Mavanes 19, 210 Gardaba, Iceland (Home). *Telephone:* (354) 564 1509.

HERMANS, Christopher, M.A.; Botswana banker; b. 23 Dec. 1936, Cape Town, South Africa; s. of Henry Hodgson Hermans and Marjorie Stanhope

Hermans; m. 1st Janet Gallagher 1960 (divorced 1987); one s. two d.; m. 2nd Vonna Deulen 1987; two d.; ed. Diocesan Coll., Rondebosch, Cape Town, Trinity Coll., Oxford, Howard Univ., Wash., Vanderbilt Univ., Nashville, Tenn.; Asst. Sec. for Devt., Bechuanaland Protectorate Admin. 1961–66; Perm. Sec., Ministry of Devt. Planning, Botswana Govt. 1966–70, Ministry of Finance and Devt. Planning 1970–75; Gov. Bank of Botswana 1975–77, 1987–; Sr. Planning Adviser/Loan Officer, World Bank 1977–82, C.E.O. Thailand and Indonesia Programs Div., 1982–84; C.E.O. of World Bank Regional Mission, Bangkok 1984–87; Presidential Order of Meritorious Service. *Leisure interests:* tennis, wildlife, windsurfing, gardening. *Address:* Bank of Botswana, P.O. Box 712, Gaborone, Botswana.

HERMASZEWSKI, Gen. Mirosław; Polish astronaut and air force officer; b. 15 Sept. 1941, Lipniki (now Ukraine); s. of Roman Hermaszewski and Kamila Hermaszewska; m. 1965; one s. one d.; ed. Air Force Officers' School, Dęblin 1961–64, Gen. Staff Acad., Warsaw; served in Nat. Air Defence 1964–76; 1st class pilot 1966, supersonic MiG-21 pilot 1967, flight leader 1971–72, deputy squadron leader 1972–75, regt. commdr. 1975–76; master's class pilot; in Cosmonauts' Training Centre, Zvezdnoy Gorodok, nr. Moscow 1976–78; space flight on board Soyuz-30 and space-station SALUT-6 June–July 1978; service in HQ of Nat. Air Defence 1978–80; student, Gen. Staff Acad., Moscow 1980–82; Second-in-Command, Air Forces and Air Defence of Polish Repub. 1990–91; Commdr. Air Force Officers' School, Dęblin 1984–90; mem. Space Research Cttee. of Polish Acad. of Sciences 1978–, Assn. of Space Explorers 1985–; Pres. Gen. Bd. Polish Astronautical Soc. 1983–87; Maj.-Gen. 1988; Gold Cross of Merit 1976, Cross of Grunwald Order (1st Class) 1978, Gold Star of Hero of U.S.S.R. 1978, Order of Lenin 1978, Mil. Champion Pilot 1978, Cosmonaut of Polish People's Repub. 1978, Int. Order of Smile 1991. *Leisure interests:* literature, hunting, tourism, dogs. *Address:* ul. Czeczota 25, 02-607 Warsaw, Poland.

HERMON, Sir John (Charles), Kt., O.B.E., Q.P.M.; British police officer; b. 23 Nov. 1928, Belfast; s. of late William Rowan Hermon and Agnes Hermon; m. 1st Jean Webb 1954 (died 1986); one s. one d.; m. 2nd Sylvia Paisley 1988; two s.; ed. Larne Grammar School; accountancy training and business 1946–50; joined Royal Ulster Constabulary 1950, Chief Constable 1980–89; Pres. Int. Professional Security Assn. 1993–96; C.St.J. 1984. *Publication:* Holding the Line (autobiog.) 1997. *Leisure interests:* boating, reading and walking. *Address:* Warren Road, Donaghadee, Co. Down, Northern Ireland.

HERNÁNDEZ ALCERRO, Jorge Ramón; Honduran diplomatist; b. 29 Aug. 1948; m.; two c.; ed. Inst. Européen de Hautes Etudes Internationales, France, Univ. of Nice and Universidad Nacional Autónoma de Honduras; former attorney and lecturer at Univ. Nacional Autónoma de Honduras; fmr. Judge, Inter-American Court of Human Rights; fmr. Gen. Sec. Inovación y Unidad Party, Deputy to Nat. Ass. and Deputy to Nat. Congress; fmr. Deputy Foreign Minister; fmr. Amb. on Special Assignment in Latin America, U.S.A. and at UN General Ass.; Perm. Rep. to UN 1987–89. *Address:* c/o Ministry for Foreign Affairs, Avda la Paz, Edif. Atala, Tegucigalpa, Honduras.

HERNÁNDEZ CERVANTES, Héctor; Mexican politician; b. Dec. 1923, Mexico City; ed. Nat. Univ. of Mexico, Colegio de México and Univ. of Melbourne; fmrly. taught econ. theory, Univ. of Mexico and Centre of Latin American Monetary Studies; economist, Banco de México; Asst. Dir. of Financial Studies, Ministry of Finance; Dir.-Gen. of Industry and Commerce, Ministry of Commerce Dir.-Gen. of Financial and Int. Studies, Ministry of Finance; Under-Sec. of Foreign Trade, Ministry of Commerce and Industrial Devt. 1982–83, Sec. of Commerce and Industrial Devt. 1983–88. *Address:* c/o Secretaría de Industria y Comercio, Avenida Cuauhtémoc 80, México, D.F., Mexico.

HERNÁNDEZ COLÓN, Rafael, A.B., LL.B.; Puerto Rican politician and lawyer; b. 24 Oct. 1936, Ponce; s. of Rafael Hernández Matos and Dorinda Colón Clavell; m. Lila Mayoral 1959; three s. one d.; ed. Valley Forge Mil. Acad., Wayne Pa., Johns Hopkins Univ., Univ. of Puerto Rico Law School; private law practice 1959–69, 1977–84; Assoc. Commr. of Public Service 1960–62; lecturer in Law, Catholic Univ. of Puerto Rico 1961–65; Sec. of Justice 1965–67; Senator at Large, Popular Democratic Party 1968; Pres. of Senate 1969–73; Leader of Popular Democratic Party 1969; Gov. of Puerto Rico 1972–76, 1989–93; Trustee Carnegie Foundation for Int. Peace; mem. Inter American Bar Assn.; Dr. h.c. (Johns Hopkins Univ., Catholic Univ. of Puerto Rico), Harvard Foundation Award 1987, Great Cross of Isabel la Católica (Spain), Order of El Libertador (Venezuela). *Publications:* Text on Civil Procedure 1968, and many articles on topics of law. *Address:* c/o Popular Democratic Party, 403 Ponce de León Avenue, P.O. Box 5788, Puerta de Tierra, San Juan 00906, Puerto Rico.

HERNÁNDEZ MANCHA, Antonio; Spanish politician and lawyer; state lawyer; mem. Andalusian Parl.; Leader Alianza Popular 1987–89. *Address:* c/o Alianza Popular, Génova 13, Madrid 4, Spain.

HERRERA, Luis Felipe; Chilean banker, lawyer and economist; b. 17 June 1922, Valparaíso; s. of Joaquín Herrera and Inés Lane; m. Inés Olmo 1961; two s.; ed. Colegio Alemán de Santiago, Escuela Militar, Univs. of Chile and London; Legal Dept., Central Bank of Chile 1943–47; Attorney for Central Bank of Chile and private law practice 1947–52; Prof. of Econs., Schools of Law and Sociology, Univ. of Chile 1947–58; Under-Sec. for Economy and Commerce 1952; Minister of Finance April–Oct. 1953; Gen. Man. Central Bank of Chile 1953–58; Gov. Int. Bank for Reconstruction and Development, IMF 1953–58, Exec. Dir. 1958–60; Pres. Inter-American Development Bank 1960–71; Pres. Soc. for Int. Development 1970–71; Co-ordinator-Gen. ECIEL Program (Jt. Studies for Latin American Econ. Integration) 1974–, Perm. Consultant 1981–; Pres. Admin. Council, Int. Fund for Promotion of Culture (UNESCO) 1976–; Chair. Bd. of Trustees, UN Inst. for Training and Research 1976–; Pres. World Soc. of Ekistics, Inst. for Int. Co-operation 1977–80, Corporación Investigaciones para el Desarrollo (CINDE) 1986, Chilean Chapter of S.I.D. 1986; mem. Bd. of Govs. Int. Devt. Research Centre (IDRC) 1980; mem. Bd. of Trustees, Third World Foundation; mem. Hon. Bd., Raul Prebisch Foundation 1986; Perm. Consultant Emer. Int. American Devt. Bank; Dr. h.c. (Santiago de Chile) 1993, and numerous other hon. degrees; Bronfman Award, American Public Health Assn. 1969, Condecoración al Mérito, Minas Gerais State, Brazil 1969, Premio "Diego Portales", Chile 1971, Premio Serfin de Integración Mexico 1987, Premio ONU: Medalla Plata a la Paz, Cepal, Santiago 1988, U.N. Personnel Peace Prize 1989, Universidad Austral de Chile: Condecoración al Mérito Universitario 1990; and numerous other awards and prizes; Great Cross for Distinguished Service, Fed. Repub. of Germany 1958, Kt. Grand Cross, Order of Merit, Italy 1966, Medalla Cívica "Camilo Torres", Colombia 1968, Grand Cross for Educational Merit, Brazil 1969, Gran Cruz de la Orden del Sol, Peru 1971, Gran Cruz Placa de Plata, Dominican Repub. 1971, Gran Cruz Orden Rubén Darío, Nicaragua 1971, Orden Boyacá, Colombia 1971, do Cruzeiro do Sul, Brazil 1971, de la Orden Manuel Amador Guerrero, Panama 1971, Orden Abdón Calderón, Ecuador 1971, al Mérito Nacional, Paraguay 1971, Orden del Aguila Azteca, Mexico 1972, Antonio José de Irisarri, Guatemala 1975, Orden al Mérito Cultural "Andrés Bello", Venezuela 1978, Officier de l'Ordre du Mérite, France 1979, Gran Cruz de Isabel La Católica, Spain 1980. *Publications:* El Banco Central de Chile 1945, Política económica 1950, Fundamentos de la Política Fiscal 1951, Manual de Política Económica 1952, Elementos de Economía Monetaria 1955, ¿Desarrollo Económico o Estabilidad Monetaria? 1958, América Latina Integrada 1964, El Desarrollo Latinoamericano y su Financiamiento 1967, Nacionalismo Latinoamericano 1968, Chile en América Latina 1969, Internacionalismo, Regionalismo, Nacionalismo 1970, América Latina: Experiencias y Desafíos 1974, América Latina: Viejas y Nuevas Fronteras 1978, El Escenario Latinoamericano y el Desafío Cultural 1981, Despertar de un Continente: América Latina 1960–1980 1983, Comunidad Latinoamericana de Naciones: presencia de Chile 1983, Visión de América Latina: 1974–1984, 1985, América Latina: Desarollo e Integración 1986. *Address:* Calle El Cerro 1991, Santiago 9, Chile (Home). *Telephone:* 232-8097 (Home).

HERRERA CAMPÍNS, Luis, D.IUR.; Venezuelan politician; b. 4 May 1925, Acarigua, Portuguesa State; mem. Partido Social Cristiano (COPEI) 1946–; represented COPEI at first World Conf. of Christian Democrat Parties 1956; Deputy for Lara State 1958; Pres. COPEI 1961; elected Deputy for Lara 1963, 1968; elected Senator for Portuguesa 1963; Pres. of Venezuela 1979–83. *Address:* c/o Partido Social Cristiano, esq. San Miguel, Avda. Pantéon cruce con Fuerzas Armadas, San José, Caracas 1010, Venezuela.

HERRERO RODRIGUEZ DE MIÑON, Miguel; Spanish politician and barrister; b. 18 June 1940; s. of Miguel Herrero and Carmen Rodríguez de Miñon; m. Cristina de Jáuregui; one s. two d.; ed. Univs. of Madrid, Oxford, Luxembourg, Geneva, Paris and Louvain; Lecturer in Int. Law, Univ. of Madrid 1963–65; Sr. Legal Adviser to Spanish Admin. 1966; Gen. Sec. Ministry of Justice 1976; mem. Parl. 1977–93; Leader, Parl. Group of UCD in Govt. 1980–81; Vice-Leader of Parl. Group of A.P., major opposition Group in Parl. 1982–87; mem. Real Academia de Ciencias Morales y Políticas, Trilateral Comm.; Gran Cruz de Isabel la Católica, Gran Cruz de San Raimundo de Peñafort. *Publications:* several books on constitutional law and int. relations. *Address:* Calle Mayor 70, bajo, 28013 Madrid, Spain (Office). *Telephone:* (1) 559 5405. *Fax:* (1) 541 7092.

HERRING, (William) Conyers, PH.D.; American physicist; b. 15 Nov. 1914, Scotia, N.Y.; s. of Dr. W. Conyers Herring and Mary Joy Herring; m. Louise C. Preusch 1946; three s. one d.; ed. Univ. of Kansas and Princeton Univ.; Nat. Research Council Fellow, M.I.T. 1937–39; Instructor in Math., and Research Assoc. in Math. Physics, Princeton Univ. 1939–40; Instructor in Physics, Univ. of Missouri 1940–41; mem. Scientific Staff, Columbia Univ. Div. of War Research 1941–45; Prof. of Applied Mathematics, Univ. of Texas 1946; Research Physicist, Bell Telephone Laboratories 1946–78; Prof. of Applied Physics, Stanford Univ. 1978–, Prof. Emer. 1981–; mem. Inst. for Advanced Study, Princeton 1952–53; mem. N.A.S.; Fellow, American Acad. of Arts and Sciences; Oliver E. Buckley Solid State Physics Prize, American Physical Soc. 1959, Distinguished Service Citation, Univ. of Kansas 1973, James Murray Luck Award for Excellence in Scientific Reviewing, Nat. Acad. of Sciences 1980, Von Hippel Award, Materials Research Soc. 1980, Wolf Prize in Physics 1985. *Publication:* Exchange Interactions among Itinerant Electrons (Vol. 4 of series Magnetism) 1966. *Leisure interests:* church and cultural activities. *Address:* Department of Applied Physics, Stanford University, Stanford, CA 94305 (Office); 3945 Nelson Drive, Palo Alto, CA 94306, U.S.A. (Home). *Telephone:* 415-723-0686 (Office); 415-856-9649 (Home).

HERRMANN, Siegfried, DR. THEOL., DR. PHIL.; German theologian; b. 15 May 1926, Dresden; s. of Martin Herrmann and Emma Herrmann (née Hammer); m. Ruth Hoffmann 1957; one s. one d.; ed. Univ. of Leipzig; Asst. in Old Testament Studies, Univ. of Leipzig 1951–59; Dozent, Humboldt

Univ. Berlin 1960–66; Prof. of Old Testament, Evangelical Theology Dept., Univ. of Bochum 1966–91, Prof. Emer. 1991–; Fellow Inst. for Advanced Studies of Hebrew Univ., Jerusalem 1983–84; mem. Nordrhein-Westfälische Akad. Wissenschaften, Düsseldorf 1973–. *Publications:* Untersuchungen zur Überlieferungsgestalt mittelägyptischer Literaturwerke 1957, Die prophetischen Heilserwartungen im Alten Testament 1965, Israel in Egypt 1973, Time and History 1977, A History of Israel in Old Testament Times 1980, Jeremia 1986, Studien zur Geschichte und Theologie des Alten Testaments 1986, Jeremia: Der Prophet und das Buch 1990, Die Geschichte Israels (with Walter Klaiber) 1996, Die Schriften der Bibel (with Walter Klaiber) 1996. *Address:* Paracelsusweg 14, 44801 Bochum, Germany. *Telephone:* 0234/70 17 75.

HERRON, Very Rev. Andrew, M.A., B.D., LL.B.; Scottish clergyman; b. 29 Sept. 1909, Glasgow; s. of John Todd Herron and Mary Skinner Herron (née Hunter); m. Joanna Fraser Neill 1935; four d.; ed. Strathbungo and Albert Road Acad., Glasgow Univ., Trinity Coll., Glasgow; Minister (Church of Scotland) of Linwood 1936–40, of Houston and Killellan 1940–59; Clerk to the Presbytery of Paisley 1953–59, of Glasgow 1959–81; Moderator of the Gen. Ass. of the Church of Scotland 1971–72, Convener of the Business Cttee. of the Gen. Ass. 1972–76, Convener Dept. of Publicity and Publ. 1959–69; Special Lecturer in Practical Theology, Univ. of Glasgow 1968–85; Ed. Church of Scotland Year Book 1961–92; Baird Lecturer 1985; Barclay Lecturer 1990; Hon. D.D. (St. Andrews) 1975, (Glasgow) 1989; Hon LL.D. (Strathclyde) 1983. *Publications:* Record Apart 1972, Guide to the General Assembly 1976, Guide to Congregational Affairs 1979, Guide to the Presbytery 1982, Kirk by Divine Right (Baird Lecture) 1985, Guide to the Ministry 1987, Guide to Ministerial Income 1987, Minority Report 1990, Houston and Killellan, A Handful of Yesterdays 1993, The Law and the Practice of the Kirk 1995, Inter Alia 1995. *Address:* 44 McLaren Court, Fenwick Place, Glasgow, G46 6UF, Scotland. *Telephone:* (0141) 638 0791.

HERSCHBACH, Dudley Robert, B.S., M.S., A.M., PH.D.; American professor of chemistry; b. 18 June 1932, San José, Calif.; s. of Robert Dudley Herschbach and Dorothy Edith Beer; m. Georgene Lee Botyos 1964; two d.; ed. Stanford and Harvard Univs.; Asst. Prof. Univ. of Calif., Berkeley 1959–61, Assoc. Prof. 1961–63; Prof. of Chem., Harvard Univ. 1963–76, Frank B. Baird, Jr., Prof. of Science 1976–, Chair. Dept. of Chem. 1977–80, Faculty Council 1980–83, Co-Master of Currier House 1981–86, Fellow, Exxon Faculty 1980–; Assoc. Ed., Journal of Physical Chem. 1980–88; Fellow, American Acad. of Arts and Sciences; mem. N.A.S. American Chemical Soc.; Hon. D.Sc. (Toronto) 1977, (Adelphi) 1990; shared Nobel Prize for Chemistry; Pure Chem. Prize, American Chemical Soc. 1965, Spiers Medal, Faraday Soc. 1976, Pauling Medal, American Chem. Soc. 1978, Polanyi Medal Royal Soc. of Chem. 1982, Langmuir Prize, American Physical Soc. 1983, Sierra Nevada Distinguished Chemist Award 1993, Kosolapoff Medal 1994, William Walker Prize 1994. *Publications:* Research papers in Journal of Chemical Physics, Proceedings of the National Academy, Review of Scientific Instruments. *Leisure interests:* viola, running. *Address:* Department of Chemistry, Harvard University, 12 Oxford Street, Cambridge, MA 02138, U.S.A.

HERSHEY, Barbara; American actress; b. 5 Feb. 1948, Hollywood, Los Angeles; one s.; m. Stephen Douglas 1992; ed. Hollywood High School; début in TV series The Monroes. *Film appearances include:* With Six you get Eggroll, The Last Summer, The Baby Maker, Boxcar Bertha, The Stuntman, The Entity, The Right Stuff, The Liberation of Lord Byron Jones, Love Comes Quietly, The Pursuit of Happiness, Passion Flower, The Natural, Hannah and Her Sisters, Tin Men, Shy People 1987 (Best Actress, Cannes Film Festival), The Last Temptation of Christ 1988, A World Apart 1988 (Best Actress, Cannes Film Festival), Beaches 1989, Defenceless 1989, Aunt Julia and the Scriptwriter 1990, Paris Trout 1990, A Killing in a Small Town 1990 (Best Actress Emmy and Golden Globe), The Public Eye 1991, Defenseless 1991, Swing Kids 1993, Splitting Heirs, Falling Down 1993, A Dangerous Woman 1994, Last of the Dogmen, Portrait of a Lady, The Pallbearer 1996, A Soldier's Daughter Never Cries 1998; TV films include: Just a Little Inconvenience, A Killing in a Small Town (Emmy and Golden Globe Awards 1990), The Bible 1993, Portrait of a Lady 1996. *Address:* CAA, 9830 Wilshire Boulevard, Beverly Hills, CA 90212, U.S.A.

HERSOM, Naomi Louisa, M.ED., PH.D.; Canadian academic; b. 4 Feb. 1927, Winnipeg; d. of Frederick Hersom and Anna Hersom; ed. Univs. of Manitoba and Alta; teacher and prin., Winnipeg 1954–67; Prof. of Curriculum Studies, Univ. of Alta 1969–75; Dir. of Undergraduate Programmes and Assoc. Dean (Academic), Univ. of B.C. 1975–79, Prof. of Educational Admin. 1979–81; Dean, Coll. of Educ. Univ. of Sask. 1981–86; Pres. Mt. St. Vincent Univ. 1986–91; Visiting Scholar Univ. of Ottawa 1991–92; Vice-Pres. Int. Fellowship of Evangelical Students (IFES) 1991–96; Dir. and Vice-Pres. Social Science Fed. of Canada 1979–82; Pres. Canadian Educ. Asscn. 1989–90; mem. numerous comms., task forces etc.; Hon. LL.D. (McGill, York) 1988, (Manitoba) 1989, (Ottawa) 1990, (St. Mary's Univ. and Univ. of Vic.) 1991, (Alberta) 1992, (Providence Coll.) 1998; George Croskery Memorial Award 1985; Grand Dame of Merit, Kts. of Malta. *Publications:* co-author: Curriculum Development for Classroom Teachers 1971, Locally Initiated School Evaluation 1973, Developing Evaluation Systems in Schools: Organizational Strategies 1975, A Study of Open Area Schools in the Edmonton Public School System 1978, Women and the Canadian Labour Force 1982, contrib. to Educational Leadership 1992. *Leisure interest:* bird-watching. *Address:* 405 Quebec Street, #301, Victoria, B.C., V8V 4ZZ, Canada. *Telephone:* (250) 360 1892. *Fax:* (250) 360 1892.

HERSOV, Basil Edward, D.M.S., M.A., LL.D, F.R.S.A.; South African business executive; b. 18 Aug. 1926, Johannesburg; s. of Abraham Sundel Hersov and Gertrude Hersov (née Aronson); m. Antoinette Herbert 1957; two s. two d.; ed. Michaelhouse, Natal and Christ's Coll., Cambridge; pilot in S.A. Air Force 1944–46; joined Anglovaal Ltd. as Learner Official on gold mine 1949, later holding a number of sr. positions with Anglovaal Group: Deputy Chair. 1970, Chair. and Man. Dir. 1973–; Chair. Hartebeestfontein Gold Mining Co. Ltd., Anglovaal Industries Ltd., The Associated Manganese Mines of S.A. Ltd.; mem. bd. of many other cos. within and outside Anglovaal Group; Dir. Mutual and Fed. Insurance Co. Ltd.; Pres. and Fellow Inst. of Dirs. (S.A.); Hon. Pres., mem. Council, S.A. Foundation; Gov. Rhodes Univ. Bd. of Trustees, Business S. Africa, Nat. Business Initiative; mem. Council, S.A. Chamber of Mines; Fellow, S.A. Inst. of Mining and Metallurgy, S.A. Inst. of Man.; Hon. LL.D. (Rhodes); Hon. Col. 21 Squadron S.A.A.F.; Decoration for Meritorious Service. *Leisure interests:* skiing, horse racing, tennis, flying and sailing. *Address:* 'Springwaters", Box 65097, Benmore 2010, South Africa (Home). *Telephone: Fax:* (011) 634-0038.

HERTELEER, Vice-Adm. Willy Mauritz; Belgian military officer; b. 1 Oct. 1941, Assenede; m. Jacqueline Liekens 1962; one s. three d.; ed. Royal Cadet School, Brussels, Merchant Navy Acad., Belgian Staff Coll., Brussels, Ecole Supérieure de Guerre Navale, Paris; commissioned Belgian Navy 1962, as ensign served on minesweepers and a supply/command ship 1963-68, became mine warfare specialist 1969–70, Staff Officer Mine Countermeasures, Operational Command 1970–72; Commdr. coastal minesweeper 1975, ocean minesweeper/hunter 1978, (instructor Belgian-Dutch School for Mine Warfare, Ostend between these postings); rank of Lieut.-Commdr. 1979; apptd. to Planning section, Belgian Naval Staff, also mem. Naval Bd., NATO Mil. Standardization Agency 1979–82; Second-in-Command frigate Westdiep 1982–84, Commdg. Officer 1984–85; Asst. Chief of Staff Operations, Naval Operations Command 1986, Chief of Staff 1986–87; Head Belgian-Dutch School for Mine Warfare 1987–89; mem. Audit Team, Belgian Naval Staff, Brussels 1989, Staff Officer, Operations 1990, Commdr. Naval Operations 1990–92; rank of Rear-Adm. 1992; joined Gen. Staff Headquarters, Brussels 1992, Chief of Naval Staff 1993–95; rank of Vice-Adm. 1995; Chief of the Gen. Staff 1995–. *Address:* Rue d'Evère, 1140 Brussels, Belgium. *Telephone:* (02) 701 3150. *Fax:* (02) 701 6625.

HERTZ, Roy, PH.D., M.D.; American professor of pharmacology and of obstetrics and gynaecology; b. 19 June 1909, Cleveland, Ohio; s. of Aaron D. Hertz and Bertha Lichtman; m. 1st Pearl Ruby Fennell 1934 (died 1962); one s. one d.; m. 2nd Dorothy Oberdorfer 1965; ed. Univ. of Wisconsin, Johns Hopkins Univ.; U.S. Public Health Service, Div. on Physiology, Nat. Insts. of Health 1941–44; Nat. Cancer Inst. 1944–51; Chair., Endocrinology Section Nat. Cancer Inst. 1946–51; Asst. Clinical Prof. of Medicine, The George Washington Univ. Medical School 1948–66; Nat. Cancer Inst., Nat. Insts. of Health, Bethesda, Md., Chief, Research Medicine, 1951–53, Chief Endocrinology, 1953–65; Scientific Dir., Nat. Inst. of Child Health and Human Devt., Nat. Inst. of Health, Bethesda, Md. 1965–66; Professor of Obstetrics and Gynaecology, The George Washington Univ. School of Medicine, Washington 1966–67; Chief, Reproduction Research, Nat. Inst. of Child Health and Human Devt., Nat. Insts. of Health, Bethesda, Md. 1967–69; Assoc. Dir., the Population Council, The Rockefeller Univ., New York 1969–72, Visiting Scientist 1972–; Prof. of Obstetrics and Gynaecology and of Medicine, Dir. of Clinical Research, New York Medical Coll. Valhalla, N.Y. 1972–73; Research Prof. of Pharmacology and Obstetrics/Gynaecology, George Washington Univ. Medical School 1973–83, Prof. Emer. 1983–; Scientist Emer. N.I.H., Bethesda, Md. 1987–; mem. N.A.S. 1972–; Fellow, American Coll. of Obstetrics and Gynaecology 1970–; mem. numerous other learned societies; Hon. D.Sc. (Wis.) 1986; Lasker Foundation Medical Research Award 1972, Cancer Research Award, Int. Coll. of Surgeons 1969. *Publications:* numerous articles on fertility regulation and cancer research. *Leisure interests:* linguistics, gardening. *Address:* 25006 Half Pone Point Rd., Hollywood, MD 20636, U.S.A. (Home).

HERTZBERGER, Herman; Netherlands architect and professor of architectural design; b. 6 July 1932, Amsterdam; m. J. C. Van Seters 1959; one s. two d.; ed. Delft Tech. Univ.; pvt. practice, Amsterdam 1958–; Co-Ed. (Dutch) Forum 1959–63; Prof. of Architectural Design, Delft 1970–, Univ. of Geneva 1982–93; Chair. Berlage Inst. 1990–95; Hon. mem. Acad. Royale de Belgique 1975, Bund Deutscher Architecten 1983, R.I.B.A. 1991, Akad. der Künste 1993, Acad. d'Architecture de France 1997; architectural award of the town of Amsterdam 1968, Eternit Award 1974, Fritz Schumacher Award 1974, Architecture Award of the City of Amsterdam 1985, Premio Europa 1991, BNA Award 1991, Concrete Award 1991, Prix Rhénan 1993, Architecture Award, City of Breda 1998. *Major works:* office bldg., Centraal Beheer, Apeldoorn 1972, housing for old and disabled people "De Drie Hoven", Amsterdam 1974, music centre, Vredenburg (concert hall), Utrecht 1979, Ministry of Social Welfare 1990, Theatre Centre Spui, The Hague 1992, library and art school, Breda 1993, Chassé Theater, Breda 1995, Theater Markant, Uden 1996, residential buildings, Düren 1996, Berlin 1997, extension to Vanderveen Department Store, Assen 1997, YKK Dormitory, Kurobe City 1998, Bijlmer Monument (with Georges Descombes) 1998. *Publications:* Homework for More Hospitable Form (Dutch), Forum XXIV 1973, Lessons for Students in Architecture 1991. *Leisure interest:* music.

Address: Architectuurstudio Herman Hertzberger, Gerard Doustraat 220, P.O. Box 74665, 1070 BR Amsterdam, Netherlands. *Telephone:* 31 20 676 58 88. *Fax:* 31 20 673 55 10.

HERVÉ, Edmond; French politician; b. 3 Dec. 1942, La Bouillie, Côtes du Nord; m. Jeannine Le Gall 1978; two s. one d.; Prof. of Constitutional Law, Rennes Univ.; Conseiller général, Ille-et-Vilaine 1973–82; Deputy for Ille-et-Vilaine to Nat. Ass. 1986–93; Mayor of Rennes 1977–; fmr. Minister of Health; Minister Del. to Minister of Industry for Energy 1981–83; Sec. of State for Health 1983–86; Regional Councillor, Brittany 1986–88; Pres. regional hosp. centre and univ. hosp. centre, both in Brittany 1977–; Pres., District Urbain de L'agglomeration rennaise (Audiar) 1989, Conférence permanente du tourisme urbain 1989; mem. Conseil de Surveillance du Crédit local de France 1990, City Scientific Cttee. on Science and Industry of La Villette 1990, Nat. Council on Towns and Urban Social Devt. 1991; charged with manslaughter arising from the use of HIV-contaminated blood in transfusions Feb. 1999, found guilty but court ruled he should not be punished; Parti Socialiste. *Address:* Assemblée nationale, 75355 Paris; Mairie, P.O. Box 26A, 35031 Rennes, France.

HERWARTH VON BITTENFELD, Hans; German diplomatist; b. 14 July 1904, Berlin; s. of Hans Richard and Ilse (von Tiedemann) Herwarth von Bittenfeld; m. Elisabeth, Baroness von Redwitz 1935; one d.; ed. Univs. of Berlin, Breslau and Munich; entered Foreign Office 1927; Attaché, Paris 1930; Second Sec. and Personal Sec. to Amb. Moscow 1931–39; mil. service 1939–45; Govt. Counsellor, Dir., Bavarian State Chancellery 1945–49; Ministerialdirigent and Chief of Protocol, Fed. German Govt. 1950; apptd. Minister 1952; Amb. to U.K. 1955–61; State Sec., Chief of Office of Fed. Pres. 1961–65; Amb. to Italy 1965–69; State Sec. Foreign Office, Bonn. March 1969, now retd.; Chair. Comm. for Reform of Foreign Service 1969–71, Supervisory Bd. Deutsche Unilever GmbH 1969–77, Venice Cttee. German UNESCO Comm.; Pres. Goethe-Inst., Munich 1971–77, Int. Advisory Cttee. to Save Venice; Hon. Pres Deutsch–Englische Gesellschaft, Düsseldorf; Grand Cross 2nd Class, Order of Merit (Fed. Germany), Hon. G.C.V.O. and other decorations. *Publications:* Against Two Evils 1931–45, Von Adenauer zu Brandt 1945–1989. *Leisure interest:* antiques. *Address:* Schloss, 96328 Küps, Germany.

HERZOG, Maurice; French fmr. mountaineer, civil servant and businessman; b. 15 Jan. 1919, Lyons (Rhône); s. of Robert Herzog and Germaine Beaume; m. 1st Comtesse Marie Pierre de Cossé Brissac 1964 (divorced 1976), one s. one d.; m. 2nd Elisabeth Gamper 1976, two s.; ed. Collège Chaptal, Paris, Faculty of Science, Lyon and Faculty of Law, Paris; Leader, French Himalayan Expedition 1950; fmr. Dir. Kléber-Colombes Soc.; High Commr. for Youth and Sport 1958–63, Sec. of State 1963–66; mem. UN Econ. and Social Council 1966–67; mem. Int. Olympic Cttee. 1970, Chief of Protocol 1975; fmr. Deputy, Haute Savoie, Mayor of Chamonix; Pres. Financial Comm. Rhône-Alpes Regional Council; Pres. Spie-Batignolles Int., Spie-Loisirs; Dir. Spie-Capag, Triton-Europe (London), Tractebel-Finance (Geneva), Tractebel (Belgium), Caixa Bank (Paris); Hon. Pres. Société du tunnel du Mont-Blanc 1984–; Pres. Triton-France 1984–94; Commdr., Légion d'honneur; Croix de guerre, and other French and foreign decorations. *Publications:* Annapurna premier 8000, Regards sur L'Annapurna, L'Expédition de l'Annapurna, La Montagne, Les grandes aventures de l'Himalaya, L'Autre Annapurna. *Leisure interests:* history, literature, science. *Address:* IPR, 5 rue du Louvre, 75001 Paris (Office); 21 boulevard Richard Wallace, 92200 Neuilly-sur-Seine; La Tournette, 84 chemin de la Tournette, 74400 Chamonix-Mont-Blanc, France (Homes).

HERZOG, Roman, DR. JUR.; German politician; b. 5 April 1934, Landshut; m. Christiane Krauss 1958; ed. Univ. of Munich, Freie Univ. Berlin and Hochschule für Verwaltungswissenshaft, Speyer; mem. Bd. Evangelische Kirche in Deutschland Chamber for Public Accountability 1971–80; Rep. of Rhineland-Palatinate in Bundestag 1973–78; Chair. Evangelical Working Party, CDU/CSU 1978–83; Minister for Culture and Sport, Baden-Württemberg 1978–80, for Interior 1980–83; mem. Fed. Cttee. CDU 1979–83; Vice-Pres. Fed. Constitutional Court 1983–87, Pres. 1987–94; Pres. of Germany 1994–99; Hon. Prof. Hochschule für Verwaltungswissenschaft, Speyer, Univ. of Tübingen; Hon. D.C.L. (Oxford) 1996. *Publications include:* Kommentar zur Grundgesetz (co-author) 1968, Staaten der Frühzeit: Ursprünge und Herrschaftsformen 1988. *Address:* Schloss Bellevue, Spreeweg 1, 10557 Berlin, Germany (Home). *Telephone:* (0228) 2001 (Office).

HERZOG, Werner; German film director; b. 5 Sept. 1942, Munich; *Films directed:* Signs of Life 1967, Even Dwarfs Started Small 1970, Fata Morgana 1971, The Land of Darkness and Silence 1971, Aguirre Wrath of God 1973, The Enigma of Kaspar Hauser 1974, The Great Ecstasy of Woodcutter Steiner 1974, How Much Wood Would Woodchuck Chuck 1976, Heart of Glass 1976, Stroszek 1976–77, Woyzeck 1979, Nosferatu 1979, Le pays du silence et de l'obscurité 1980, Fitzcarraldo 1982, Where the Green Ants Dream 1984, Cobra Verde 1987, Scream from Stone 1991; *opera directed:* Lohengrin (Bayreuth) 1987.

HESBURGH, Rev. Theodore M., S.T.D.; American ecclesiastic and fmr. university president; b. 25 May 1917; s. of Anna Hesburgh and Theodore Hesburgh; ed. Univ. of Notre Dame, Gregorian Univ., Rome, and Catholic Univ. of America; ordained priest of Congregation of Holy Cross 1943; joined Univ. of Notre Dame 1945, Head of Theology Dept. 1948–49, Exec. Vice-Pres. of Univ. 1949–52, Pres. 1952–87, Pres. Emer. 1987–; mem. U.S. Comm. on Civil Rights 1957–72 (Chair. 1969–72), President's Comm. on All-Volunteer Armed Force, Carnegie Comm. on the Future Structure and Financing of Higher Educ., Comm. on the Future of Private and Independent Higher Educ. in New York State, Presidential Clemency Bd. 1974–75; Perm. Rep. of Holy See to Int. Atomic Energy Agency, Vienna 1957; Pres. Int. Fed. of Catholic Univs.; Trustee, Rockefeller Foundation, Chair. Bd. of Trustees 1977–82, Carnegie Foundation for Advancement of Teaching (Pres. 1963–64); Chair. Acad. Council, Ecumenical Inst. for Advanced Theological Studies in Jerusalem; Chair. with rank of Amb. U.S. Del. to UN Conf. on Science and Tech. for Devt. 1977–79; Chair. Select Comm. on Immigration and Refugee Policy 1979–81; Dir. U.S. Inst. of Peace 1991; fmr. Dir. American Council on Educ.; Fellow, American Acad. of Arts and Sciences; 124 hon. degrees; Distinguished Service Medal, U.S. Navy; Presidential Medal of Freedom 1964, Jefferson Award 1976. *Publications:* God and the World of Man 1950, Patterns for Educational Growth 1958, Thoughts for Our Times 1962, More Thoughts for Our Times 1965, Still More Thoughts for Our Times 1966, Thoughts IV 1968, Thoughts V 1969, The Humane Imperative: A Challenge for the Year 2000 1974, The Hesburgh Papers: Higher Values in Higher Education 1979, God, Country, Notre Dame 1990, Travels with Ted and Ned 1992. *Address:* c/o 1315 Hesburgh Library, University of Notre Dame, Notre Dame, IN 46556, U.S.A. *Telephone:* (219) 631-6882.

HESELTINE, Rt. Hon. Michael Ray Dibdin, P.C., M.P.; British politician; b. 21 March 1933, Swansea, Wales; s. of the late Col. Rupert and of Eileen Ray Heseltine; m. Anne Edna Harding Williams 1962; one s. two d.; ed. Shrewsbury School, Pembroke Coll., Oxford (Hon. Fellow 1986); Pres. Oxford Union 1954; Chair. Haymarket Press 1965–70; M.P. for Tavistock 1966–74, for Henley 1974–; Parl. Sec. Ministry of Transport 1970; Parl. Under-Sec. of State, Dept. of the Environment 1970–72; Minister of Aerospace and Shipping 1972–74; Opposition Spokesman for Industry 1974–76, for the Environment 1976–79; Sec. of State for the Environment 1979–83, 1990–92, for Defence 1983–86, Sec. of State for Industry and Pres. of the Bd. of Trade 1992–95; Deputy Prime Minister and First Sec. of State 1995–97; Dir. Haymarket Publishing Group 1997–; Pres. Asscn. of Conservative Clubs 1982–83; Hon. LL.D. (Liverpool) 1990. *Publications:* Reviving the Inner Cities 1983, Where There's a Will 1987, The Challenge of Europe: Can Britain Win? 1988 (Bentinck Prize 1989), Mightier than the Sword: A Study of Japanese Economic Imperialism 1990. *Address:* House of Commons, Westminster, London, SW1A 0AA; Thenford House, nr. Banbury, Oxon., England (Home).

HESS, Benno, M.D.; German medical research director; b. 22 Feb. 1922, Berlin; s. of Ludwig Hess and Herta Hess; m. Ulrike Hess 1955; one s. four d.; ed. Heidelberg Univ.; Dir. and Scientific mem. Max-Planck-Inst. Dortmund 1965–; Prof. Ruhr Univ. Bochum 1970–; Vice-Pres. Max-Planck-Gesellschaft zur Förderung der Wissenschaften, Munich 1980–90; mem. European Molecular Biology Org.; Special Adviser, Comm. for Science and Tech. of European Community; mem. Deutsche Akad. der Naturforscher Leopoldina, Düsseldorf and Heidelberg Acads.; Hon. mem. American Soc. of Biological Chemists; mem. A.A.A.S. and other learned socs. etc. *Publications:* articles in scientific journals. *Leisure interests:* nonlinear dynamics and organization of biology, structure and function of biomembranes, science as a historical process. *Address:* c/o Max-Planck-Institut für medizinische Forschung, Jahnstrasse 29, 69120 Heidelberg, Germany (Office). *Telephone:* 06221/486341. *Fax:* 06221/486340.

HESSEL, Stephane F., M.B.E.; French diplomatist; b. 20 Oct. 1917, Berlin; s. of Franz Hessel and Helen (née Grund) Hessel; m. 1st Vitia Mirkine-Guetzevitch 1939 (died 1986); two s. one d.; m. 2nd Christiane Chabry 1987; war service 1941–45; Admin. Dir. Secr. Gen., UN 1946–50; served in Foreign Ministry 1950–54; Asst. to the Pres. 1954–55; Adviser to High Commr., Saigon 1955–57, Foreign Affairs Adviser, Algiers 1964–69; Asst. Admin. UNDP 1970–72; Perm. Rep. to UN Office, Geneva 1977–81; mem. High Authority for Audiovisual Communication 1982–85; Chair. Asscn. France-Algérie 1985; mem. Haut conseil à l'intégration 1990–94; Commdr., Légion d'honneur 1982, Grand Officier, Ordre Nat. du Mérite, Croix de guerre 1939–45, Médaille des Evadés, Commdr. des palmes académiques. *Leisure interest:* Greek mythology. *Address:* 6 rue Antoine Chantin, 75014 Paris, France. *Telephone:* (01) 45.43.47.80. *Fax:* (01) 45.43.47.80.

HESTER, James McNaughton, D.PHIL.; American university official; b. 19 April 1924, Chester, Pa.; s. of James Montgomery Hester and Margaret (McNaughton) Hester; m. Janet Rodes 1953; three d.; ed. Princeton and Oxford Univs.; Capt., U.S. Marine Corps 1943–46, 1951–52; Civil Information Officer, Fukuoka Mil. Govt. Team, Japan 1946–47; Rhodes Scholar, Oxford Univ. 1947–50; Asst. to Rhodes Trustees Princeton 1950; Asst. to Pres., Handy Assocs. Inc. (Management Consultants) N.Y. 1953–54; Account Supervisor, Gallup & Robinson Inc. 1954–57; Provost, Brooklyn Center, L.I. Univ. 1957–60, Vice-Pres., Trustee L.I. Univ.; Prof. of History, Exec. Dean Arts and Sciences, Dean Grad. School of Arts and Sciences, N.Y. Univ. 1960–61, Trustee 1962, Pres. 1962–75; Rector, UN Univ., Tokyo 1975–80; Pres. New York Botanical Garden 1980–89; Dir. Union Carbide Corpn. 1963–96, Alliance Fund and related funds 1983; Chair. Pres. Nixon's Task Force on Priorities in Higher Educ. 1969; mem. Asscn. of American Rhodes Scholars 1962, Council on Foreign Relations 1962; Pres. Harry Frank Guggenheim Foundation 1989–; Trustee Lehman Foundation 1973; Hon. LL.D. (Princeton, Moorehouse Coll., Hofstra Univ., Lafayette Coll., Hahnemann Medical Coll., Fordham); Hon. L.H.D. (Hartwick Coll., Pace Univ., Colgate,

Pittsburgh, New York); Hon. D.C.L. (Alfred Univ.); Chevalier, Légion d'honneur, First Class Order of the Sacred Treasure. *Leisure interest:* painting. *Address:* Harry Frank Guggenheim Foundation, 527 Madison Avenue, New York, NY 10022-4304 (Office); 45 E. 89th Street, Apt. 39C, New York, NY 10128, U.S.A. (Home). *Telephone:* (212) 289-1673.

HESTER, Ronald Ernest, PH.D., D.SC., F.R.S.C.; British professor of chemistry; b. 8 March 1936, Slough, Bucks.; s. of Ernest Hester and Rhoda Lennox; m. Bridget Maddin 1958; two s. two d.; ed. Royal Grammar School, High Wycombe, Univs. of London and Cambridge, and Cornell Univ., U.S.A.; Asst. Prof. Cornell Univ. 1962–65; lecturer, sr. lecturer, Reader, Univ. of York 1965–85, Prof. of Chem. 1985–; European Ed. BioSpectroscopy 1994–; mem. Council and various bds., Science & Eng. Research Council (SERC). *Publications:* Physical Inorganic Chemistry 1964, Understanding Our Environment 1986, Advances in Spectroscopy (26 vols.) 1975–98, Spectroscopy of Biological Molecules 1991, Issues in Environmental Science and Technology 1994–; more than 300 research papers in int. journals. *Leisure interests:* squash, skiing, tennis, golf, travel. *Address:* Department of Chemistry, University of York, York, YO1 5DD (Office); The Old Rectory, Crayke, York, YO6 4TA, England (Home).

HESTON, Charlton; American actor; b. 4 Oct. 1924, Evanston, Ill.; s. of Russell Carter and Lilla Charlton Heston; m. Lydia Clark 1944; one s. one d.; ed. Northwestern Univ., Evanston; first Broadway appearance in Antony and Cleopatra 1948; has starred in more than 50 films, Hollywood 1950–; Pres. Screen Actors Guild 1965–71; mem. Nat. Council of Arts 1967; Trustee American Film Inst. 1971–, Chair 1973; Chair. on Arts, Presidential Task Force on Arts and Humanities 1981–; Vice-Pres. Nat. Rifle Asscn. 1997–98, Pres. 1998–; Acad. Award for Best Actor, Ben Hur 1959, Veterans of Foreign Wars Citizenship Medal 1982, Golden Medal of the City of Vienna 1995; Commdr. Ordre des Arts et des Lettres. *Stage appearances include:* Macbeth 1954, 1959, 1976 (London), Mister Roberts 1954, Detective Story 1956, A Man for All Seasons 1965, 1987, Caine Mutiny Court Martial (also Dir.), London 1985. *Television includes:* Chiefs (CBS) 1983, Nairobi Affair (CBS) 1984, The Colbys (ABC-TV), A Thousand Heroes 1991. *Films include:* Julius Caesar 1950, Dark City 1950, The Greatest Show on Earth 1952, The Savage 1952, Ruby Gentry 1952, The President's Lady 1953, Pony Express 1953, Arrowhead 1953, Bad for Each Other 1953, The Naked Jungle 1953, Secret of the Incas 1954, The Far Horizons 1955, Lucy Gallant 1955, The Private War of Major Benson 1955, Three Violent People 1956, The Ten Commandments 1956, Touch of Evil 1958, The Big Country 1958, The Buccaneer 1958, Ben Hur 1959, The Wreck of the Mary Deare 1959, El Cid 1961, The Pigeon that Took Rome 1962, Diamond Head 1962, 55 Days at Peking 1962, Major Dundee 1964, The Greatest Story Ever Told 1965, The Agony and the Ecstasy 1965, The War Lord 1965, Khartoum 1966, Counterpoint 1967, Will Penny 1967, Planet of the Apes 1967, Beneath the Planet of the Apes 1969, The Hawaiians 1970, Julius Caesar 1970, The Omega Man 1971, Antony and Cleopatra 1972, Skyjacked 1972, The Call of the Wild 1972, Soylent Green 1973, The Three Musketeers 1973, The Four Musketeers 1974, Earthquake 1974, Airport 1975, Midway 1975, Two Minute Warning 1976, The Last Hard Men 1976, The Prince and the Pauper 1976, Gray Lady Down 1978, The Awakening 1980, Mother Lode 1981, Caine Mutiny Court Martial (also Dir.) 1988, Treasure Island 1989, Almost an Angel (cameo), Solar Crisis, Wayne's World 2 (cameo), True Lies 1994, In the Mouth of Madness, Alaska (also Dir.), Hercules (voice) 1997. *Publications:* The Actor's Life 1979, In the Arena 1995, Charlton Heston Presents the Bible 1997. *Leisure interests:* sketching, tennis. *Address:* c/o Jack Gilardi, ICM, 8942 Wilshire Boulevard, Beverly Hills, CA 90211, U.S.A.

HETHERINGTON, Sir Arthur Ford, Kt., D.S.C., B.A.; British business executive and engineer; b. 12 July 1911; s. of the late Sir Roger Gaskell Hetherington and Lady (Honoria) Hetherington; m. Margaret Lacey 1937; one s. one d.; ed. Highgate School, London, Trinity Coll., Cambridge; Deputy Chair. Southern Gas Bd. 1956–61, Chair. 1961–64; Chair. East Midlands Gas Bd. 1964–66; Deputy Chair. Gas Council 1967–72, Chair. 1972–73; Chair. British Gas Corpn. 1973–76, British Standards Inst. 1976–79; Hon. D.Sc. (London) 1974. *Address:* 32 Connaught Square, London, W2 2HL, England. *Telephone:* 0171-723 3128.

HETHERINGTON, (Hector) Alastair, M.A.; British journalist; b. 31 Oct. 1919, Llanishen, Glamorganshire, Wales; s. of late Sir Hector Hetherington and Lady Hetherington; m. 1st Helen Miranda Oliver 1957 (divorced 1978); two s. two d.; m. 2nd Sheila Cameron 1979; ed. Gresham's School, Holt, and Corpus Christi Coll., Oxford; served in Royal Armoured Corps 1940–46; on staff The Glasgow Herald 1946–50; joined (Manchester) Guardian 1950, Foreign Ed. 1953, Ed. 1956–75, Dir. Guardian Newspapers Ltd. 1967–75; with BBC 1975–80, Controller BBC Scotland 1975–78, Man. BBC Highland 1979–80; Research Prof., Stirling Univ. 1982–87, Emer. Prof. 1987–; mem. Peacock Cttee.; Fellow, Nuffield Coll., Oxford 1973–80; Hon. Fellow Corpus Christi Coll. Oxford; Hon. Fellow RIAS; Dr. h.c. (Lille) 1989; Journalist of the Year, Nat. Press Awards 1970, Bank of Scotland Special Award 1992. *Publications:* Guardian Years 1981, News, Newspapers and Television 1985, News in the Regions 1989, Cameras in the Commons 1990, Highlands and Islands—A Generation of Progress 1990, Inside BBC Scotland 1975–1980 1992, Walker's Guide to Arran 1995. *Leisure interest:* hill walking. *Address:* Tigh na-Fraoich, High Corrie, Isle of Arran, KA27 8JB; Green Hill House, 38 Chalton Road, Bridge of Allan, Stirling, FK9 4EF, Scotland. *Telephone:* (01770) 810652 (Arran); (01786) 833316 (Stirling).

HEWISH, Antony, PH.D., F.R.S., F.R.A.S.; British radio astronomer; b. 11 May 1924, Fowey, Cornwall; s. of Ernest W. Hewish and of the late Grace F. L. Hewish (née Pinch); m. Marjorie E. C. Richards 1950; one s. one d.; ed. King's Coll., Taunton and Gonville and Caius Coll., Cambridge; war service 1943–46; Research Fellow, Gonville and Caius Coll., Cambridge 1951–54, Supernumerary Fellow 1956–61; Univ. Asst. Dir. of Research 1953–61, lecturer 1961–69; Fellow, Churchill Coll. Cambridge 1962–; Reader in Radio Astronomy, Univ. of Cambridge 1969–71, Prof. 1971–89, Prof. Emer. 1989–; Prof. Royal Inst. 1977; Dir. Mullard Radio Astronomy Observatory, Cambridge 1982–88; Vikram Sarabhai Prof., Ahmedabad 1988; Foreign Hon. mem. American Acad. of Arts and Sciences 1970; Foreign Fellow Indian Nat. Science Acad.; Hon. Sc.D. (Leicester) 1976, (Exeter) 1977, (Manchester) 1989, (Santa Maria, Brazil) 1989, (Cambridge) 1996, (Univ. Teknologi Malaysia) 1997; Hamilton Prize (Cambridge) 1951, Eddington Medal, Royal Astronomical Soc. 1968, Boys Prize, Inst. of Physics 1970, Dellinger Medal, Int. Union of Radio Science, Hopkins Prize, Cambridge Philosophical Soc. 1972, Michelson Medal, Franklin Inst. 1973, Holweck Medal and Prize, Soc. Française de Physique 1974, Nobel Prize for Physics (jointly with Sir Martin Ryle) 1974, Hughes Medal, Royal Soc. 1977. *Publications:* many papers in scientific journals; Editor: Seeing Beyond the Invisible. *Leisure interests:* listening to good music, swimming, sailing. *Address:* Pryor's Cottage, Kingston, Cambridge, CB3 7NQ, England. *Telephone:* (01223) 262657.

HEWSON, John, PH.D.; Australian politician, professor of economics and business executive; b. 28 Oct. 1946, Carlton N.S.W.; m. 1st Margaret Hewson; two s. one d.; m. 2nd Carolyn Hewson 1988; one d.; ed. Univ. of Sydney, Univ. of Saskatchewan, Canada and Johns Hopkins Univ. U.S.A.; Economist IMF; Research Economist Reserve Bank; Prof. of Econs. Univ. of N.S.W. 1978–87, Head School of Econs. 1983–86; Dir. Japanese Man. Studies Cen. 1984–87; M.P. for Wentworth (Sydney) 1987–95; Leader of the Opposition 1990–94; Shadow Treas., Shadow Minister for Finance 1989, Shadow Minister for Industry, Commerce, Infrastructure and Customs 1994–95; Chair. ABN AMRO Australia Ltd. 1995–, The John Hewson Group 1995–, Network Entertainment Ltd.; Vice-Chair. TV Shopping Network; Dir. Churchill Resources. *Publications:* Liquidity Creation and Distribution in the Eurocurrency Market 1975, The Eurocurrency Markets and their Implications (jtly.) 1975, Offshore Banking in Australia 1981. *Leisure interests:* golf, classic cars, jazz music, gardening, antiques. *Address:* c/o ABN Amro Australia Ltd, Flat 14, 10 Spring Street, Sydney, N.S.W. 2000, Australia.

HEY, John Denis, M.A., M.SC.; British professor of economics and statistics; b. 26 Sept. 1944; s. of G. B. Hey and E. H. Hey; m. Marlene Bissett 1968 (divorced 1997); one s. two d.; ed. Univs. of Cambridge and Edinburgh; econometrician, Hoare & Co. London 1968–69; lecturer in Econs. Univ. of Durham 1969–74, Univ. of St. Andrews 1974–75; lecturer in Economic Statistics, Univ. of York 1975, Sr. lecturer, Prof. of Econs. and Statistics 1984– (part-time 1998–), Co-Dir. Centre for Experimental Econs. 1986–; Hon. Prof. of Econs. and Econometrics, Univ. of Vienna; Prof. Ordinario, Univ. of Bari 1998–. *Publications:* Statistics in Economics 1974, Uncertainty in Microeconomics 1979, Economics in Disequilibrium 1981, Data in Doubt 1984, Experiments in Economics 1991, Experimental Economics (Ed.) 1995, Economics of Risk 1997. *Leisure interests:* eating, drinking, walking, squash. *Address:* Department of Economics and Related Studies, University of York, Heslington, York, YO1 5DD, England; Università degli Studi di Bari, via Camillo Rosalba 53, 70124 Bari, Italy. *Telephone:* (01904) 433786 (York). *Fax:* (01904) 433759 (York).

HEYDE, Christopher Charles, PH.D., F.A.A.; Australian university professor and statistician; b. 20 April 1939, Sydney; s. of G. C. Heyde and A. D. Wessing; m. Elizabeth James 1965; two s.; ed. Barker Coll., Hornsby, Sydney Univ. and Australian Nat. Univ.; Asst. Prof. Mich. State Univ. 1964–65; lecturer Univ. of Sheffield, U.K. 1965–67; Special Lecturer Univ. of Manchester, U.K. 1967–68; Reader, Australian Nat. Univ. 1968–75; Chief Research Scientist CSIRO 1975–83; Prof. and Chair. Dept. of Statistics, Univ. of Melbourne 1983–86; Prof. and Head Dept. of Statistics, Inst. of Advanced Studies 1986–88, Dean School of Math. Sciences 1989–91; Prof. of Statistics, Inst. of Advanced Studies, Australian Nat. Univ. 1992–; Visiting Prof. Stanford Univ., Calif. 1972–73; Ed. Australian Journal of Statistics 1973–78, Stochastic Processes and Their Applications 1983–89, Journal of and Advances in Applied Probability 1990–; Fellow Inst. of Mathematical Statistics 1973; Pres. Statistical Soc. of Australia 1979–80, also Hon. Life mem.; mem. Int. Statistical Inst. (Vice-Pres. 1985–87, 1993–95), Australian Acad. of Science (Vice-Pres. 1988–89, Treas. 1989–93); Pitman Medallist, Statistical Soc. of Australia 1988, Thomas Ranken Lyle Medal, Australian Acad. of Sciences 1994, Inaugural Hannan Medal Australian Acad. of Sciences 1995. *Publications:* I. J. Bienaymé: Statistical Theory Anticipated (with E. Seneta) 1977, Martingale Limit Theory and Its Application (with P. Hall) 1980, Quasi-Likelihood and Its Application 1997; plus 170 articles on probability theory and mathematical statistics. *Address:* Department of Statistics, Institute of Advanced Studies, Australian National University, Canberra, A.C.T. 0200; 22 Nungara Place, Aranda, A.C.T. 2614, Australia (Home). *Telephone:* (02) 6249 2962.

HEYERDAHL, Thor, PH.D.; Norwegian explorer and anthropologist; b. 6 Oct. 1914, Larvik; s. of Thor Heyerdahl and Alison Heyerdahl (née Lyng); m. 1st Liv Coucheron Torp 1936; two s.; m. 2nd Yvonne Dedekam-Simonsen 1948; three d.; ed. Univ. of Oslo; specialized in zoology and geography at univ. but changed to anthropology during field researches among Polynesians in Marquesas Is. 1937–38; research in N.W. Indian territory of Brit. Columbia (ref. theory of two separate American Indian movements into Pacific) 1939–40; served free Norwegian Mil. Forces 1941–45; research in Europe and U.S.A. 1945–47; led Kon-Tiki expedition from Callao, Peru to Raroia, Polynesia (covering 4,300 miles in 101 days and thus proving Peruvian Indians could have settled in Polynesia) 1947; founded (with Knut Haugland) Kon-Tiki Museum, Oslo 1949; research and lectures in Europe and U.S.A. 1948–52; led Norwegian Archaeological Expedition to Galapagos (establishing evidence of pre-European visits by South American Indians), Field Research in Bolivia, Peru and Colombia 1954; led Norwegian Archaeological Expedition to Easter Island and the East Pacific 1955–56; attempted to cross Atlantic in papyrus boat Ra I 1969 (covering 2,800 miles in 56 days); sailed from Safi, Morocco, in papyrus boat Ra II May 1970, in attempt to cross Atlantic and prove that ancient Mediterranean civilization could have sailed a reed boat to America, and arrived in Barbados July 1970; led expedition of Sumerian-type reed boat, Tigris, to test navigational capabilities of such ancient craft from Asia to Africa 1977–78; archaeological excavations, Maldive Islands 1982–83; led archaeological expeditions to Easter Island 1986, 1987; organizer jt. Norwegian/Chilean archaeological expdn. Easter Island 1986–88; organizer Kon-Tiki Museum, Museo Brürung archaeological project Tacume, Peru 1988–; Vice-Pres. World Asscn. of World Federalists 1966–, Worldview Int. Foundation 1982–; Int. Patron United World Colls. 1973–; Int. Trustee, World Wildlife Fund 1977–; mem. Norwegian Acad. of Science 1958; Fellow, New York Acad. of Sciences 1960; Hon. Ph.D. (Oslo) 1961; Commdr. of the Order of St. Olav, Officer Servicio del Mérito Distinguido of Peru 1952, Grande Ufficiale dell' Ordine al Merito della Repubblica Italiana 1965, Order of Merit First Class, Egypt 1971, Grand Officer Royal Alaouites Order, Morocco 1971, and many other awards including Acad. First Award ("Oscar") for Kon-Tiki film 1951; Vega Medal (Swedish Soc. of Anthropology and Geography) 1962, Patron's Gold Medal (Royal Geographical Soc., London) 1964, shared UN Pahlavi Environmental Prize 1978. *Publications:* På Jakt Efter Paradiset 1938, Kon-Tiki Ekspedisjonen (trans. 64 languages) 1948, American Indians in the Pacific: The Theory behind the Kon-Tiki Expedition 1952, Archaeological Evidence of Pre-Spanish Visits to the Galapagos Islands 1956, Aku-Aku: Påskeøoyas Hemmelighet (trans. 32 languages) 1957, Reports of the Norwegian Archaeological Expedition to Easter Island and the East Pacific, (Vol. I Archaeology of Easter Island 1961, Vol. II Miscellaneous Reports 1965) (with E. N. Ferdon), Indianer und Alt-Asiaten im Pazifik 1966, Sea Routes to Polynesia 1968, The Ra Expeditions 1971, Fatuhiva: Back to Nature 1974, Zwischen den Kontinenten 1975, The Art of Easter Island 1975, Early Man and the Ocean 1978, The Tigris Expedition 1980, The Maldive Mystery 1986, Easter Island—The Mystery Solved 1989, The Kon-Tiki Man (with Christopher Ralling) 1990, Pyramids of Tucume (jtly.) 1995, Green Was the Earth on the Seventh Day 1996, and many articles. *Leisure interest:* outdoor life. *Address:* Kon-Tiki Museum, Bygdøynesveien 36, 0286 Oslo, Norway.

HEYLIN, Angela Christine; British public relations consultant; b. 17 Sept. 1943; d. of the late Bernard Heylin and Ruth Victoria Heylin; m. Maurice Minzly 1971; one s.; ed. Apsley Grammar School, Watford Coll.; C.E.O. Charles Barker Lyons 1984, Charles Barker Watney & Powell 1986–, Charles Barker Traverse-Healy 1987–; Dir. Charles Barker Group 1984, Chair. and C.E.O. 1988; C.E.O. Charles Barker PLC 1992–96, Chair. 1996–; Dir. Corporate Communications 1989, Young Vic 1992–; mem. Citizen's Charter Advisory Panel 1993–97; Award for Outstanding Contrib. to the Industry 1988. *Leisure interests:* theatre, piano, entertaining. *Address:* Charles Barker PLC, 56 Dean Street, London, W1V 6HX (Office); 46 St. Augustine's Road, London, NW1 9RN, England (Home). *Telephone:* 0171-494 1331 (Office); 0171-485 4815 (Home).

HEYM, Stefan, PH.D.; American/German writer; b. 10 April 1913, Chemnitz; ed. Berlin Univ. and Chicago Univ., U.S.A.; fled to Czechoslovakia 1933; journalist 1933–35; moved to U.S.A. 1935; waiter and ed. of anti-fascist newspaper, New York 1937–39; served in American Army 1943–45; co-f. Neue Zeitung, Munich 1945; leader American Del. to Second World Peace Congress, Warsaw 1950; returned to GDR 1952; mem. Bd. GDR Writers' Assoc. Exec. Bd., expelled 1979, SDP mem. Bundestag 1994–96. *Publications include:* Hostages 1942, The Crusaders 1949, The Eyes of Reason 1955, Cannibals and Other Stories 1953, Goldsborough 1953, The Glasemapp Case 1959, Shadows and Lights 1960, The Lenz Papers 1964, The King David Report 1972, Five Days in June 1974, Ways and Detours 1980, Ahasuer 1981, Obituary 1988, Radek 1995, The Winter of Our Discomfort 1996, Women Always Disappear 1997. *Address:* c/o Bertelsmann Publishers, 81678 Munich, Germany.

HEYMAN, Ira Michael, J.D.; American professor of law; b. 30 May 1930, New York City; s. of Harold A. Heyman and Judith Sobel; m. Therese Thau 1950; two s. (one deceased); ed. Dartmouth Coll. and Yale Law School; Legislative Asst. to Senator Irving M. Ives, Washington, D.C. 1950–51; mem. State Bar of N.Y. 1956; Assoc. Carter, Ledyard & Milburn, New York 1956–57; Law Clerk, Court of Appeals for Second Circuit, New Haven, Conn. 1957–58; Chief Law Clerk, U.S. Supreme Court 1958–59; Acting Assoc. Prof. of Law, Univ. of Calif. (Berkeley) 1959–61, Prof. 1961–94, Prof. of Law and City and Regional Planning 1966–93, Prof. Emer. 1993–, Vice-Chancellor 1974–80, Chancellor 1980–90; Sec. Smithsonian Inst. 1994–99; mem. State Bar. of Calif. 1961–; Visiting Prof. Yale Law School 1963–64, Stanford Law School 1971–72; Trustee Lawyers' Comm. for Civil Rights Under Law 1977, Chair. 1991; Chair. Dartmouth Coll. 1991; mem. Bd. of Dirs., Pacific Gas & Electric Co. 1985–; other professional appts. and consultancies; Chevalier, Légion d'honneur; Hon. LL.D. (Univ. of Pacific) 1981, (Maryland) 1986; Hon. D.Hum.Litt. (Hebrew Union Coll.) 1984. *Publications:* numerous articles in journals, papers and legal documents in areas of civil rights, constitutional law, land planning, metropolitan govt., housing, environmental law and man. *Leisure interests:* tennis, opera. *Address:* c/o Smithsonian Institution, 1000 Jefferson Drive, S.W., Washington, DC 20560, U.S.A.

HEYMANN, Daniel, PH.D.; Argentinian professor of economics; b. 30 Dec. 1949, Buenos Aires; s. of Gunther Heymann and Marta Weil; m. Cristina Bramuglia 1976; two s.; ed. Coll. Français de Buenos Aires, Univ. of Buenos Aires and Univ. of Calif. Los Angeles; Asst. Prof. Univ. of Buenos Aires 1973–75; Research Asst. ECLA, Buenos Aires Office 1974–78, Sr. Economist 1982–; Prof. Instituto Torcuato Di Tella, Buenos Aires 1982–; Visiting Assoc. Prof. Univ. of Calif. Los Angeles 1987, Visiting Prof. 1991; Prof. Univ. of Buenos Aires 1987–. *Publications:* Fluctuations of the Argentine Manufacturing Industry 1980, Three Essays on Inflation and Stabilization 1986, The Austral Plan 1987, Notes on High Inflation and Stabilization 1990, Distributive Conflict and the Fiscal Deficit: Some Inflationary Games (jtly.) 1991, On the Interpretation of the Current Account 1994, High Inflation (jtly.) 1995, Business Cycles from Misperceived Trends (jtly.) 1996. *Address:* Paraguay 1178, 2do. Piso, 1057 Buenos Aires, Argentina.

HEYSSEL, Robert Morris, M.D.; American physician; b. 19 June 1928, Jamestown, Mo.; s. of Clarence C. Heyssel and Meta (Reusser) Heyssel; m. Maria McDaniel 1955; five c.; ed. Univ. of Missouri and St. Louis Univ.; postgraduate training, St. Louis Univ. Hosp. 1953–56, Barnes Hosp., St. Louis 1953–56; Haematologist, Acting Dir. Dept. of Medicine, Atomic Bomb Comm., Nagasaki and Hiroshima 1956–58; mem. Faculty, School of Medicine, Vanderbilt Univ. 1959–68, Dir. Div. of Nuclear Medicine 1962–68, Assoc. Prof. of Medicine 1964–68; Assoc. Dean, School of Medicine, Johns Hopkins Univ. 1968–72, Prof. of Medicine 1971–, Prof. Health Care Org. 1972–83; Exec. Vice-Pres., Dir. Johns Hopkins Hospital 1972–83, Pres. 1983–92; Pres. Johns Hopkins Health System 1986–92; mem. numerous local, state and nat. comms. on health, medicine, medical educ. etc.; mem. Inst. of Medicine, N.A.S.; Fellow American Coll. of Physicians; Hon. D.Sc. (St. Louis) 1985, and other awards. *Publications:* articles in professional journals. *Leisure interests:* hunting, fishing. *Address:* 230 Stony Run Lane, Baltimore, MD 21210, U.S.A.

HIBBEN, Sally, B.A.; British film producer; b. 3 July 1953, London; d. of Eric Hibben and Nina Hibben; ed. Keele Univ. and Univ. Coll., London Univ.; researcher and sub-ed. The Movie 1978–81; freelance journalist (film and sports) 1981–93; documentary producer 1982–87; drama producer 1988–; founder mem. and Dir. Parallax Pictures Ltd. *Documentaries:* Live a Life 1982, The Road to Gdansk, Great Britain United. *TV and film productions:* A Very British Coup (B.A.F.T.A. and Emmy awards) 1987, Riff Raff (FELIX European Film award) 1991, Raining Stones 1993, Bad Behaviour (exec. producer) 1993, Ladybird, Ladybird 1994, I.D. 1995, Land and Freedom (exec. producer) 1995, The Englishman Who Went Up a Hill But Came Down a Mountain (exec. producer) 1995, Carla's Song 1996; Jt. Business Award, Women in TV and Film 1994. *Publications:* Politics, Ideology and the State (ed.) 1978, The Making of Licence to Kill 1989, The Making of The Official History of the James Bond Films 1987, 1989, Back to the Future III 1990, The Official History of the Carry On Films 1988; contribs. to various film journals, magazines and collections. *Leisure interests:* walking, cooking, Tottenham Hotspur Football Club. *Address:* Parallax Pictures Ltd., 7 Denmark Street, London, W.C.2, England. *Telephone:* 0171-836 1478. *Fax:* 0171-497 8062.

HIBBERT, Christopher, M.C., M.A., F.R.S.L.; British author; b. 5 March 1924, Enderby, Leics.; s. of late Canon H.V. Hibbert; m. Susan Piggford 1948; two s. one d.; ed. Radley Coll., Oriel Coll. Oxford; served Second World War, Capt. London Irish Rifles (twice wounded) 1943–45; partner firm of land agents and auctioneers 1949–58; Hon. D.Litt.; Heinemann Award for Literature 1962, McColvin Medal Library Asscn. 1989. *Publications:* The Destruction of Lord Raglan 1961, Corunna 1961, Benito Mussolini 1962, The Battle of Arnhem 1962, The Court at Windsor 1964, The Roots of Evil 1964, Agincourt 1965, Garibaldi and his Enemies 1966, The Making of Charles Dickens 1967, London: Biography of a City 1969, The Dragon Wakes: China and the West 1970, The Personal History of Samuel Johnson 1971, George IV (Vol. I) 1972, (Vol. II) 1973, The Rise and Fall of the House of Medici 1974, Edward VII 1976, The Great Mutiny: India 1857 1978, The French Revolution 1980, Rome: Biography of a City 1985, The English: A Social History 1986, The Grand Tour 1987, Venice: The Biography of a City 1988, The Encyclopaedia of Oxford (Ed.) 1988, The Virgin Queen: The Personal History of Elizabeth I 1990, Redcoats and Rebels: The War for America 1770–1781 1990, Cavaliers and Roundheads: The English at War, 1642–1649 1993, Florence: The Biography of a City 1993, Nelson: A Personal History 1994, Corunna (Great Battles) 1996, A Soldier of the 71st 1996, Wellington: A Personal History 1997, No Ordinary Place: Radley College and the Public School System 1847–1997 1997, George III: A Personal History 1998. *Leisure interests:* gardening, cooking. *Address:* 6 Albion Place, West Street, Henley-on-Thames, Oxfordshire, RG9 2DT, England. *Telephone:* (01491) 575235.

HIBBERT, Sir Reginald Alfred, G.C.M.G.; British diplomatist (retd.); b. 21 Feb. 1922, London; m. Ann Alun Pugh 1949; two s. one d.; ed. Queen

Elizabeth's Grammar School, Barnet, Worcester Coll., Oxford; war service with Special Operations Executive in Albania, and 4th Queen's Own Hussars in Italy; joined Diplomatic Service 1946, served in Romania, Austria, Guatemala, Turkey, Belgium, and in Foreign Office; Chargé d'affaires, Resident Mission to Mongolian People's Repub. 1964–66; Counsellor, Office of the Political Adviser to C.-in-C. Far East, Singapore 1967–69, Political Adviser 1969–71; Minister, Bonn Embassy 1972–75, Asst. Under-Sec. of State, Foreign and Commonwealth Office 1975–76; Deputy Under-Sec. of State for European Affairs and U.K. Political Dir. in Political Cttee. of the Nine 1976–79; Amb. to France 1979–82; Dir. Ditchley Foundation 1982–87; Chair. Franco-British Soc. 1990–95; Pres. Féd. Britannique des Alliances Françaises 1997–; Visiting Fellow Nuffield Coll., Oxford 1984–88; Hon. Research Fellow Univ. Coll. of Swansea 1988–; Hon. Fellow Worcester Coll. 1991–; Cmmdr. Légion d'honneur. *Publication:* The Albanian National Liberation Struggle: The Bitter Victory 1991. *Leisure interests:* gardening, reading, music. *Address:* Frondeg, Pennal, Machynlleth, Powys, SY20 9JX, Wales. *Telephone:* (01654) 791220.

HICK, Graeme Ashley; Zimbabwean cricketer; b. 23 May 1966, Salisbury (now Harare); s. of John and Eve Hick; ed. Banket Primary School, Prince Edward Boys' High School; right-hand batsman, off-break bowler, slip fielder; teams: Zimbabwe 1983–86, Worcs. 1984–, Northern Dists. 1987–89, Queensland 1990–91; scored his first hundred when aged six (for Banket primary school); youngest player (17) to appear in 1983 World Cup and youngest to rep. Zimbabwe; 53 Tests for England 1991–99, scoring 2,993 runs (average 34.4), including 5 hundreds; scored 30,189 first-class runs (average 55.2), with 104 hundreds (including 9 doubles, one triple and one quadruple (405 not out) to 1 April 1999); youngest to score 2,000 in a season (1986); scored 1,019 runs before June 1988, including a record 410 runs in April; fewest innings for 10,000 runs in county cricket (179); youngest (24) to score 50 first-class hundreds; toured Australia 1994–95; mem. England World Cup Squad 1996; 75 limited-overs ints. by Dec. 1998. *Publication:* My Early Life (autobiog.) 1992. *Leisure interests:* golf, tennis, squash, indoor hockey, cinema, television, listening to music. *Address:* c/o Worcestershire County Cricket Club, New Road, Worcester, WR2 4QQ, England. *Telephone:* (01905) 748474.

HICK, John Harwood, PH.D., D.PHIL., D.LITT.; British university teacher; b. 20 Jan. 1922, Scarborough, Yorks.; s. of Mark Day Hick and Mary Aileen Hirst; m. Joan Hazel Bowers 1953; three s. one d.; ed. Bootham School, York, Edinburgh Univ., Oxford Univ., Westminster Theological Coll., Cambridge; Minister, Belford Presbyterian Church, Northumberland 1953–56; Asst. Prof. of Philosophy, Cornell Univ., U.S.A. 1956–59; Stuart Prof. of Christian Philosophy, Princeton Theological Seminary, U.S.A. 1959–64; Lecturer in Divinity, Cambridge Univ. 1964–67; H. G. Wood Prof. of Theology, Birmingham Univ. 1967–80; Danforth Prof. of Philosophy of Religion, Claremont Graduate School, U.S.A. 1980–92, Prof. Emer. 1992–, Chair., Dept. of Religion, Dir. Blaisdell Programs in World Religions and Cultures 1983–92; Gifford Lecturer, Edin. Univ. 1986–87; Guggenheim Fellow 1963–64, 1986–87; S.A. Cook Bye-Fellow, Gonville and Caius Coll., Cambridge 1963–64; Vice-Pres. World Congress of Faiths, British Soc. for the Philosophy of Religion; Hon. Prof., Univ. of Wales; Hon. Theol. Dr. (Uppsala); Grawemeyer Award in Religion 1991. *Publications include:* Faith and Knowledge, Evil and the God of Love, God and the Universe of Faiths, Death and Eternal Life, Arguments for the Existence of God, Problems of Religious Pluralism, God Has Many Names, Philosophy of Religion, The Second Christianity, An Interpretation of Religion, Disputed Questions in Theology and the Philosophy of Religion, The Metaphor of God Incarnate, The Rainbow of Faiths; Ed. The Myth of God Incarnate, The Many-Faced Argument, The Myth of Christian Uniqueness, The Existence of God, Truth and Dialogue, Christianity and Other Religions, Faith and the Philosophers. *Address:* 144 Oak Tree Lane, Selly Oak, Birmingham, B29 6HU, England. *Telephone:* 0121-689 4803.

HICKEL, Walter Joseph; American fmr. state governor and business executive; b. 18 Aug. 1919, nr. Claflin, Kan.; s. of Robert A. Hickel and Emma Zecha; m. 1st Janice Cannon 1941 (died 1943); one s.; m. 2nd Ermalee Strutz 1945; five s.; ed. public schools in Claflin; builder/owner, Traveler's Inn, Anchorage 1953–82, Fairbanks, Alaska 1955–82, Hickel Investment Co., Anchorage 1947–, Hotel Captain Cook, Anchorage, Northern Lights Shopping Center, Univ. Shopping Center, Anchorage, Valley River Shopping Center; Chair. Bd. Hickel Investment Co.; Founder and fmr. Chair. Yukon Pacific Corpn.; Founder Inst. of the North, Alaska Pacific Univ. 1996; fmr. mem. Bd. of Dirs. Rowan Cos., Inc.; fmr. mem. world advisory council, Int. Design Science Inst.; fmr. mem. cttee. on scientific freedom and responsibility A.A.A.S.; fmr. mem. Bd. of Dirs. Salk Inst.; mem. Republican Nat. Cttee. 1954–64; Sec. U.S. Dept. of Interior 1969–70; Gov. of Alaska 1966–69, 1990–94; Sec. Gen. The Northern Forum 1994–; several hon. degrees and other honours and distinctions; Order of Kts. of Malta; Independent. *Address:* P.O. Box 101700, Anchorage, AK 99510; 1905 Loussac Drive, Anchorage, AK 99517, U.S.A.

HICKEY, H.E. Cardinal James Aloysius; American ecclesiastic; b. 11 Oct. 1920, Midland; s. of James P. Hickey and Agnes Ryan Hickey; ordained 1946, elected to the titular Church of Taraqua 1967, consecrated bishop 1967, transferred to Cleveland 1974, prefect 1980; Archbishop of Washington 1980–; Chancellor, Catholic Univ. America 1980–; Chair. bd. trustees Nat. Shrine of Immaculate Conception 1980–, Bishop's Cttee. on N. American Colls. 1988–92, 1994–97; Episcopal Moderator Holy Childhood Asscn. 1984–93; cr. Cardinal 1988. *Address:* Archdiocesan Pastoral Center, P.O. Box 29260, Washington, DC 20017, U.S.A. *Telephone:* (301) 853-3800.

HICKOX, Richard Sidney, M.A., F.R.C.O., L.R.A.M.; British conductor; b. 5 March 1948, Stokenchurch, Bucks.; s. of Rev. S. E. Hickox and Jean Millar; m. 1st Frances Ina Sheldon-Williams 1976; one s.; m. 2nd Pamela H. Stephen 1995; one s.; ed. Royal Grammar School, High Wycombe, R.A.M., London and Queens' Coll. Cambridge (Organ Scholar); Dir. of Music, High Wycombe Parish Church 1970–71, St. Margaret's, Westminister 1972–82, Barbican Summer Festival 1984–85; Artistic Dir. Wooburn Festival 1967–, Christ Church Spitalfields Festival 1978–94, St. Endellion Festival 1974–, Truro Festival 1981–, Chester Summer Festival 1989–, City of London Festival 1994–; Artistic Dir. Northern Sinfonia 1982–90, Prin. Guest Conductor 1990–; Music Dir., City of London Sinfonia and Richard Hickox Singers (now City of London Sinfonia Singers) 1971–, Bradford Festival Choral Soc. 1978–, London Symphony Chorus 1976–; Assoc. Conductor, London Symphony Orchestra 1985–; co-f. Opera Stage 1985; has conducted opera at Covent Garden, English Nat. Opera, Opera N. and Scottish Opera; has recorded Bach Masses, Albinoni Adagio, music by Finzi, Delius and Duruflé, Burgon Requiem, Haydn Nelson Mass (all for Decca, Argo Label); Gluck Armide, Handel Alcina, music by Vaughan Williams, Gilbert and Sullivan, Elgar Miniatures, Delius Miniatures and Berkeley Or Shall We Die? (all for EMI). *Leisure interests:* football, tennis, politics. *Address:* 35 Ellington Street, London, N7 8PN, England (Home). *Telephone:* 0171-607 8984 (Home).

HIDE, Raymond, C.B.E., M.A., SC.D., C.PHYS., F.INST.P., F.R.S.; British research geophysicist; b. 17 May 1929, Bentley near Doncaster; s. of late Stephen Hide and late Rose Edna Hide (née Cartlidge, later Mrs T. Leonard); m. Phyllis Ann Licence 1958; one s. two d.; ed. Percy Jackson Grammar School, Doncaster, Manchester and Cambridge Univs.; Research Assoc. in Astrophysics, Yerkes Observatory, Univ. of Chicago 1953–54; Sr. Research Fellow, Gen. Physics Div. A.E.R.E., Harwell 1954–57; lecturer in Physics, King's Coll. Univ. of Durham 1957–61; Prof. of Geophysics and Physics at M.I.T. 1961–67; Head of the Geophysical Fluid Dynamics Lab., Chief Scientific Officer (Individual Merit), Meteorological Office, Bracknell 1967–90; Gresham Prof. of Astronomy, Gresham Coll., City of London 1985–90; Dir. Robert Hooke Inst. 1990–92 and Visiting Prof. of Physics, Oxford Univ. 1990–92, Research Prof., Dept. of Physics 1992–94, Prof. Emer. of Physics, Oxford Univ. 1994–; Visiting Prof. Dept. of Math., Univ. Coll., London 1969–84; Adrian Visiting Fellow, Univ. of Leicester 1981–83; Fellow Jesus Coll., Oxford 1983–97, Hon. Fellow 1997–; mem. Council, Royal Soc. of London 1988–90; mem. Pontifical Acad. of Sciences, American Acad. of Arts and Sciences, Academia Europaea, Royal Astronomical Soc. (Pres. 1983–85), Royal Meteorological Soc. (Pres. 1974–76, Hon. mem. 1989), European Geophysical Soc. (Pres. 1982–84, Hon. mem. 1988), American Geophysical Union, Inst. of Physics, Int. Astronomical Union and numerous other socs. and cttees.; Chair. British Nat. Cttee. for Geodesy and Geophysics, U.K. Chief Del. to Int. Union of Geodesy and Geophysics 1979–85; Hon. D.Sc. (Leicester) 1985, (UMIST) 1994, (Paris) 1995; Charles Chree Medal and Prize of Inst. of Physics 1975, Holweck Medal and Prize, Société Française de Physique and Inst. of Physics 1982, Gold Medal, Royal Astronomical Soc. 1989, William Bowie Medal, American Geophysical Union 1997, Hughes Medal, Royal Soc. 1998, L. F. Richard Medal, European Geophysical Soc. 1999. *Publications:* numerous scientific articles and papers. *Address:* Jesus College, Oxford, OX1 3DW, England.

HIEBERT, Erwin Nick, PH.D.; American professor of history of science; b. 27 May 1919, Saskatchewan, Canada; s. of Cornelius N. and Tina Hiebert; m. Elfrieda Franz 1943; one s. two d.; ed. Bethel Coll., N. Newton, Kan., Univs. of Chicago and Wisconsin-Madison; Research Chemist, Standard Oil Co. of Indiana and the Manhattan Project 1943–46; Research Chemist, Inst. for Study of Metals, Univ. of Chicago 1947–50; Asst. Prof. of Chem., San Francisco State Coll. 1952–55; Instr. in History of Science, Harvard 1955–57; Asst. Prof., Assoc. Prof., Prof., History of Science, Univ. of Wis.-Madison 1957–70; Prof. of History of Science, Harvard 1970–90, Chair. 1977–84, Emer. Prof. 1990–; Pres. Div. of History of Science, Int. Union of History and Philosophy of Science 1982–84; Fellow, American Acad. of Arts and Sciences, Acad. Int. d'Histoire des Sciences; mem. Sächsische Akad. der Wissenschaften, Leipzig 1989–. *Publications:* Impact of Atomic Energy 1961, Historical Roots of the Principle of Conservation of Energy 1962, The Conception of Thermodynamics in the Scientific Thought of Mach and Planck 1967, and papers on history and philosophy of physics and chem. since 1800. *Leisure interests:* music, gardening. *Address:* c/o Harvard University, Widener Library 172, Cambridge, MA 02138, U.S.A. *Telephone:* (617) 495-0325. *Fax:* (617) 495-3344.

HIGGINS, George Vincent, M.A., J.D.; American author and lawyer; b. 13 Nov. 1939, Brockton, Mass.; s. of John T. Higgins and Doris (née Montgomery) Higgins; m. 1st Elizabeth Mulkerin 1965 (divorced 1979); one s. one d.; m. 2nd Loretta L. Cubberley 1979; ed. Boston Coll., Stanford Univ., Westfield State Coll.; Barrister 1967; Reporter Providence Journal 1962–63; corresp. A.P. Springfield, Mass. 1963–64, Boston 1964–66; Asst. Attorney Gen., Mass. 1967–70, Asst. U.S. Attorney, Mass. 1970–73; legal practice in Boston 1973–; Prof. Boston Univ. 1988–; columnist Boston Herald 1977–79, Boston Globe 1979–85, Wall Street Journal 1984–87; mem. Writers Guild. *Publications:* The Friends of Eddie Coyle 1972, The Digger's Game 1973, Cogan's Trade 1974, A City on a Hill 1975, The Friends of Richard Nixon

1975, The Judgment of Deke Hunter 1976, Dreamland 1977, A Year or So With Edgar 1979, Kennedy for the Defense 1980, The Rat on Fire 1981, The Patriot Game 1982, A Choice of Enemies 1984, Penance for Jerry Kennedy 1985, Impostors 1986, Wonderful Years, Wonderful Years 1988, The Sins of the Fathers 1988, Trust 1989, On Writing 1990, Victories 1990, The Mandeville Talent 1991, Defending Billy Ryans 1992, Bomber's Law 1993, Swan Boats at Four 1995, Sandra Nichols Found Dead 1996, A Change of Gravity 1997. *Address:* Boston University Creative Writing Program, 236 Bay State Road, Boston, MA 02215, U.S.A.

HIGGINS, Jack (see Patterson, Harry).

HIGGINS, Michael D., B.COMM., M.A.; Irish politician and writer; b. April 1941, Limerick; m. Sabina Coyne; three s. one d.; ed. Univ. Coll. Galway, Indiana Univ. and Univ. of Manchester; fmr. lecturer in Sociology and Politics, Univ. Coll. Galway; Senator 1973–77; mem. Galway Co. Council 1974–85; Alderman, Galway Borough Council 1974–85, Mayor of Galway 1982–83; mem. Galway City Council 1985–93; many other public appts.; mem. Dáil 1981–82, 1987–; Chair. The Labour Party 1978–87; Minister for Arts, Culture and the Gaeltacht 1993–97; mem. Sociological Asscn. of Ireland, American Sociological Asscn, PEN, Irish Writers' Union. *Address:* c/o Department of Arts, Culture and the Gaeltacht, 43–49 Mespil Road, Dublin 4, Ireland. *Telephone:* (01) 6670788. *Fax:* (01) 6670825.

HIGGINS, Dame Rosalyn, D.B.E., J.S.D., Q.C., F.B.A.; British judge and professor of international law; b. 2 June 1937; d. of late Lewis Cohen and of Fay Inberg; m. Rt. Hon. Terence L. Higgins 1961; one s. one d.; ed. Burlington Grammar School, London, Girton Coll. Cambridge and Yale Law School; U.K. Intern, Office of Legal Affairs, UN 1958; Commonwealth Fund Fellow 1959; Visiting Fellow, Brookings Inst. Washington, D.C. 1960; Jr. Fellow in Int. Studies, L.S.E. 1961–63; staff specialist in int. law, Royal Inst. of Int. Affairs 1963–74; Visiting Fellow, L.S.E. 1974–78; Prof. of Int. Law, Univ. of Kent at Canterbury 1978–81; Prof. of Int. Law, L.S.E. 1981–95; Judge of Int. Court of Justice 1995–; mem. UN Cttee. on Human Rights 1985–; Visiting Prof. Stanford Univ. 1975, Yale Univ. 1977; Vice-Pres. American Soc. of Int. Law 1972–74; Dr. h.c. (Paris XI); Hon. D.C.L. (Dundee) 1994, (Durham, L.S.E.) 1995, (Cambridge, Sussex, Kent, City Univ., Greenwich, Essex) 1996, (Birmingham, Leicester, Glasgow) 1997; Ordre des Palmes Académiques, Yale Law School Medal of Merit 1997, Manley Hudson Medal (ASIC) 1998. *Publications include:* The Development of International Law through the Political Organs of the United Nations 1963, Conflict of Interests 1965, The Administration of the United Kingdom Foreign Policy through the United Nations 1966, Law in Movement—essays in memory of John McMahon (ed., with James Fawcett) 1974, UN Peacekeeping: documents and commentary: (Vol. I) Middle East 1969, (Vol. II) Asia 1971, (Vol. III) Africa 1980, (Vol. IV) Europe 1981, Problems and Process—International Law and How We Use It 1994; articles in law journals and journals of int. relations. *Leisure interests:* sport, cooking, eating. *Address:* International Court of Justice, Peace Palace, 2517 KJ, The Hague, Netherlands; Essex Court Chambers, 24 Lincoln's Inn Fields, London, WC2A 3ED, England.

HIGGINS, Stuart; British journalist: b. 26 April 1956; m. Jenny Higgins; one s. one d.; ed. Chase School for Boys, Filton Tech. Coll., Arblaster's of Bristol, Cardiff Coll. of Food, Tech. and Commerce; dist. reporter, The Sun, Bristol 1979, fmr. N.Y. corresp., Royal reporter Features Ed., Exec. News Ed., Deputy Ed. 1991–93, Ed. 1994–98; consultant 1998–; Acting Ed. News of the World 1993–94.

HIGGINSON, John, M.D., F.R.C.P.; American professor of pathology; b. 16 Oct. 1922, Belfast, N. Ireland; s. of William Higginson and Ellen Margaret Rogers; m. Nan Russell McKee 1949; two d.; ed. Royal Belfast Academical Inst., Belfast, and Univ. of Dublin; Pathologist, S. African Inst. for Medical Research, Baragwanath Hosp., S. Africa 1950–58; Head, Geographical Pathology Unit and Cancer Registry, S. African Inst. for Medical Research 1954–58; Assoc. Prof. of Pathology and Oncology, Univ. of Kansas Medical Center 1958–62; American Cancer Soc. Career Professorship, Univ. of Kansas 1961–66; Prof. of Pathology, Univ. of Kansas Medical Center 1962–66; Dir. Int. Agency for Research on Cancer, Lyons, France 1966–82; Sr. Consultant Scientist, Univs. Associated for Research and Educ. in Pathology Inc. 1982–84; Research Prof. Univ. North Carolina 1982–84; Visiting Prof. Univ. Md. 1983–85; Clinical Prof. of Family Medicine, Georgetown Univ. Medical Center; Hon. Fellow Royal Acad. of Medicine in Ireland, Fellow, Royal Coll. of Physicians, London, etc. *Publications:* Human Cancer: Epidemiology and Environmental Causes 1992; over 200 scientific papers in field of environmental biology and cancer research. *Leisure interests:* golf, antique maps, painting. *Address:* 16 Sundew Road, Savannah, GA 31411, U.S.A.

HIGGS, Peter Ware, PH.D., F.R.S.E., F.R.S.; British professor of theoretical physics; b. 29 May 1929, Newcastle upon Tyne; s. of Thomas W. Higgs and Gertrude M. (née Coghill) Higgs; m. Jo Ann Williamson 1963; two s.; ed. Cotham Grammar School, Bristol and King's Coll. London; Sr. Research Fellow, Univ. of Edin. 1955–56; ICI Research Fellow, Univ. Coll. London 1956–57, Imperial Coll. London 1957–58; Lecturer in Math. Univ. Coll., London 1958–60; Lecturer in Math. Physics, Univ. of Edin. 1960–70, Reader 1970–80, Prof. of Theoretical Physics 1980–96; Hon. D.Sc.; Hughes Medal, Royal Soc. 1981, Rutherford Medal, Inst. of Physics 1984, James Scott Prize, Royal Soc. of Edin. 1994, Paul Dirac Medal and Prize, Inst. of Physics 1997, High Energy and Particle Physics Prize, European Physical Soc. 1997. *Publications:* papers in scientific journals. *Leisure interests:* walking, swimming, listening to music. *Address:* 2 Darnaway Street, Edinburgh, EH3 6BG, Scotland. *Telephone:* 0131-225 7060.

HIGHAM, John, PH.D.; American professor of history; b. 26 Oct. 1920, New York; s. of Lloyd Stuart Higham and Margaret (née Windred) Higham; m. Eileen Moss 1948; two s. two d.; ed. Johns Hopkins Univ. and Univ. of Wisconsin; Instructor in History, Univ. of Calif., Los Angeles 1948–50, Asst. Prof. 1950–54; Assoc. Prof., Rutgers Univ. 1954–58, Prof. 1958–60; Prof. Univ. of Mich., Ann Arbor 1961–67, Moses Coit Tyler Univ. Prof. 1968–71, 1972–73; John Martin Vincent Prof. of History, Johns Hopkins Univ. 1971–72, 1973–89, Emer. Prof. 1989–; Newman Prof. of American Civilization, Cornell Univ. 1991–92; Pres. Immigration History Soc. 1979–82, Org. of American Historians 1973–74; Assoc. Dir. of Studies, Ecole des Hautes Etudes en Sciences Sociales 1981–82; mem. American Acad. of Arts and Sciences; Dunning Prize, American Historical Asscn. 1956; Fulbright-Hays Lecturer, Kyoto American Studies Seminar 1974, Mellon Sr. Fellow, Nat. Humanities Center 1988–89. *Publications include:* Strangers in the Land 1955, History: Humanistic Scholarship in America 1965, Writing American History 1970, Send These to Me 1975, The Politics of Ethnicity (with others) 1982, American Immigrants and Their Generations 1990, Civil Rights and Social Wrongs 1997. *Address:* Department of History, The Johns Hopkins University, Baltimore, MD 21218; 309 Tuscany Road, Baltimore, MD 21210, U.S.A. (Home). *Telephone:* (410) 243-0112 (Home).

HIGHTOWER, John B.; American museum director; b. 23 May 1933, Atlanta, Georgia; s. of Edward A. and Margaret K. Hightower; m. 2nd Martha Ruhl 1984; one s. one d. (from 1st marriage); ed. Yale Univ.; Gen. Asst. to Pres. and Publisher, American Heritage Publishing Co. 1961–63; Exec. Dir. New York State Council on the Arts 1964–70; Dir. Museum of Modern Art, New York 1970–72; Pres. Assoc. Councils of Arts, New York 1972–74; Pres. South St. Seaport 1977–84; Exec. Dir. Richard Tucker Music Foundation 1977–89, The Maritime Center, Norwalk 1984–89; adviser to arts councils throughout U.S.A., Cultural Adviser to Presidential Latin American Comm. 1969; Founder and Chair., Advocates for the Arts 1974–77; Instructor, Arts Man., Wharton School 1976–77, New School 1976–77; Chair. Planning Corpn. for the Arts; Dir. Planning and Devt. of the Arts, Univ. of Va. 1989–93; Interim Dir. Bayly Museum, Univ. of Va. 1990–91; Pres., C.E.O. The Mariners' Museum, Va. 1993–; N.Y. State Award 1970. *Leisure interests:* gardening, cooking, travel. *Address:* 101 Museum Parkway, Newport News, VA 23606, U.S.A. (Home).

HIGHTOWER, Rosella; American/French dance teacher, choreographer and artistic director; b. 30 Jan. 1920, Ardmore, U.S.A.; d. of Charles Hightower and Ula Fanning; m. Jean Robier 1955; one d.; worked with Léonide Massine at Ballets Russes from 1938; later soloist, American Ballet Theater; created roles in Balanchine's Apollo, Tudor's Pillar of Fire, etc.; leading dancer with Marquise de Cuevas' Ballet 1947–61; founder, Centre de Danse Int. (for training of dancers from around the world) 1961; Artistic Dir. Ecole Supérieure de Danse de Cannes Rosalind Hightower 1991–; also dir. of ballet at Marseilles Opera, Grand Théâtre de Nancy, Paris Opéra and La Scala, Milan; Officier, Légion d'honneur, Commdr. Ordre nat. du Mérite; other awards include Prix Porselli 1993, Lys d'Or 1994, Oklahoma Treasures 1997. *Address:* Centre de Danse International Rosella Hightower, Le Gallia, 27 boulevard Montfleury, 06400 Cannes (Office); Villa Piège de Lumière, Parc Fiorentina, avenue de Vallauris, 06400 Cannes, France (Home). *Telephone:* (4) 93 06 79 79 (Office). *Fax:* (4) 93 06 79 78 (Office).

HIJIKATA, Takeshi; Japanese business executive; b. 18 March 1915, Ena City, Gifu Prefecture; s. of Kikusaburo and Sue Hijikata; m. Michiko Kumakura; two s. one d.; ed. Tokyo Imperial Univ.; joined Sumitomo Chemical Co. Ltd. 1941, Dir. 1971, Man. Dir. 1973, Exec. Vice-Pres. 1977, Pres. 1977, Chair. 1985–93, Counsellor 1993–; Chair. Japan Tobacco Inc.; Dir. Fuji Oil Co. Ltd., Sumitomo Seika Chemicals Co. Ltd., Japan Cttee. for Econ. Devt.; Dir. and Counsellor Sumitomo Pharmaceuticals Co. Ltd.; Dir. Sumitomo Bakelite Co. Ltd., Inabata and Co. Ltd.; Adviser and Hon. mem. Fed. of Econ. Orgs. (Keidanren); Adviser Japan Chem. Industry Asscn.; Standing Dir. Japan Fed. of Employees' Asscn., Kansai Econ. Fed.; mem. Trade Conf., Prime Minister's Office, Atomic Energy Comm., Science and Tech. Agency, Japan Singapore Asscn. *Leisure interests:* golf, reading. *Address:* Sumitomo Chemical Co. Ltd., 5-33 Kitahama, 4-chome, Chuo-ku, Osaka 541; 27-1, Shinkawa, 2-chome, Chuo-ku, Tokyo 104, Japan.

HILALY, Agha, M.A., S.PC.; Pakistani diplomatist; b. 20 May 1911, Bangalore; s. of late Agha Abdulla; m. Malek Taj Kazim 1938; three s.; ed. Madras and Cambridge Univs.; entered Civil Service 1936; apptd. Under-Sec. to Finance Ministry, Govt. of Bengal; transferred to pre-partition Govt. of India and served as Under-Sec. in Ministries of Agriculture, Food and Commerce 1941–47; Deputy Sec. Pakistan Foreign Ministry 1947–51, Joint Sec. 1951–54; attended several Int. Confs. as Sec.-Gen. of Pakistan dels.; Amb. to Sweden, Norway, Denmark and Finland 1956–59, to U.S.S.R. (concurrently Minister to Czechoslovakia) 1959–61; High Commr. in India and Amb. to Nepal 1961–63; High Commr. in U.K. and Amb. to Repub. of Ireland 1963–66; Amb. to U.S.A. (concurrently to Mexico, Venezuela and Jamaica) 1966–71; mem. Bd. of Dirs. State Bank of Pakistan 1973–, Fed. Bank of Co-operatives (Islamabad) 1973–; Chair. Bd. of Govs. Pakistan Inst. of Strategic Studies 1973–; Leader Pakistan del. to Human Rights Comm. 1981–85, UN Working Group on Missing Persons 1983–; Hilal-i-Quaid-i-Azam, Grand Cross of

Order of Northern Star (Sweden), Grand Cross of Order of Gurkha (Nepal). *Leisure interests:* photography, hunting. *Address:* 22B Circular Street, Phase 2, Defence Housing Society, Karachi 6, Pakistan. *Telephone:* 540 202 (Home).

HILBE, Alfred J., DR.ECON.; Liechtenstein politician; b. 22 July 1928, Gmunden, Austria; s. of Franz and Elisabeth (née Glatz) Hilbe; m. Virginia Joseph 1951; one d.; ed. classical secondary schools in Vaduz and Zürich, Ecole Nationale des Sciences Politiques, Paris and Univ. of Innsbruck; several posts in private business 1951–54; in foreign service 1954–65, Counsellor, Liechtenstein Embassy, Berne until 1965; Deputy Head of Govt. of Liechtenstein 1965–70, Head of Govt. 1970–74; Financial Consultant 1974–; Grosskreuz of Liechtenstein Order of Merit, Grosses Silbernes Ehrenzeichen am Bande (Austria) 1975, Order of St. Gregory (Vatican); Fatherland Union Party. *Leisure interests:* skiing, tennis, photography. *Address:* 9494 Schaan, Garsill 11, Principality of Liechtenstein. *Telephone:* 075-232 2002 (Home); 232 8320 (Office).

HILDENBRAND, Werner; German professor of economics; b. 25 May 1936, Göttingen; lecturer Univ. of Heidelberg 1964–66; Visiting Asst. Prof. Univ. of Calif., Berkeley 1966–67, Visiting Assoc. Prof. 1967–68; Research Prof. Univ. of Louvain, Belgium 1968–76; Prof. of Econs. Univ. of Bonn 1969–; Visiting Prof. of Econs., Berkeley and Stanford 1970, Berkeley 1973–74, Visiting Ford Prof. Berkeley 1985–86, European Univ. Inst., Florence 1989–, Univ. of Calif., San Diego 1986–91; Fellow Econometric Soc. 1972; mem. Rhein-West Akademie der Wissenschaften 1981–, Academia Europaea 1985–; Leibniz-Preis Deutsche Forschungsgemeinschaft 1987; Max-Planck-Forsch-Preis 1995; Dr. h.c. Univ. Louis Pasteur (Strasbourg) 1988. *Publications:* Core and Equilibria of a Large Economy 1974, Lineare ökonomische Modelle (with K. Hildenbrand) 1975, Introduction to Equilibrium Analysis (with A. Kirman) 1976, Equilibrium Analysis (with A. Kirman) 1988, Market Demand: Theory and Empirical Evidence 1993; numerous papers. *Address:* University of Bonn, Wirtschaftstheorie II, Lennestr. 37, 53113 Bonn 1, Germany. *Telephone:* 0228 73 92 42.

HILDRETH, Eugene A., B.S., M.D., F.A.C.P., F.R.S.M.; American physician and university professor; b. 11 March 1924, St. Paul, Minn.; s. of Eugene A. Hildreth and Lila K. Hildreth; m. Dorothy Ann Meyers 1946; two s. two d.; ed. Washington and Jefferson Coll., Univ. of Virginia School of Medicine, Johns Hopkins Hosp., Baltimore, Md., Univ. of Pennsylvania; Research in Dept. of Research Medicine, Univ. of Pa., Philadelphia 1957–60, Markle Scholar in Academic Medicine 1958–63, Assoc. Dean, Univ. of Pa. 1964–67, Prof. of Clinical Medicine 1971–90, Prof. Emer. 1990–; Dir. Dept. of Medicine, The Reading Hosp. and Medical Center, Reading, Pa.; Chair. Allergy and Immunology Subspeciality Bd. 1966–72, American Bd. of Allergy and Immunology 1971–72, American Bd. of Internal Medicine 1975–82, Federated Council of Internal Medicine 1981–82, American Coll. of Physicians (ACP) Cttee. on Developing Criteria and Standards for Delineation of Clinical Privileges 1986–90, Regent ACP 1985–92, Chair. Bd. of Regents 1989–91, Pres. ACP 1991–92, Master 1992–, mem. nominating cttee. 1997–; mem. Federated Council of Internal Medicine, Fed. of the American Socs. for Experimental Biology, A.A.A.S., ACP Cttee. on Ethics, ACP Cttee. on Int. Medicine, Inst. of Medicine (I.O.M.), N.A.S., Council of I.O.M., Nominations Cttee. of I.O.M., Bower Award Cttee. of Franklin Inst. 1994–, working group on disability of U.S. Presidents 1994–. *Publications:* numerous scientific papers, chapters in books, reviews etc. *Leisure interests:* reading, white water kayaking, backpacking, museums, farming. *Address:* R.R. 3, Box 3960, Mohnton, PA 19540, U.S.A. (Home).

HILDREW, Bryan, C.B.E., M.SC., D.I.C., F.C.G.I., F.ENG.; British engineer; b. 19 March 1920, Sunderland, Co. Durham; s. of Alexander William and Sarah Jane Hildrew; m. Megan Kathleen Lewis; two s. one d.; ed. Bede Collegiate School, Sunderland, Sunderland Tech. Coll., City and Guilds Coll., London Univ.; Principal Surveyor Engineering Investigations, Lloyds Register of Shipping 1961–65, Deputy Chief Engineer Surveyor 1965–67, Chief Engineer Surveyor 1967–70, Tech. Dir. 1970–77, Man. Dir. 1977–85; Pres. Inst. Mech. Engs. 1980–81; Chair. Council of Eng. Insts. 1981–82; Pres. Inst. Marine Engs. 1983–85; Chair. Abbeyfield Orpington Soc. 1985–; D.Eng. h.c. (Newcastle upon Tyne) 1987; D. Univ. h.c. (Surrey) 1994. *Leisure interests:* walking, orienteering. *Address:* 8 Westholme, Orpington, Kent. BR6 0AN, England.

HILFIGER, Tommy; American men's fashion designer; b. Elmira, N.Y.; m. Susie Hilfiger; four c.; opened first store, People's Place, Elmira 1969; owned ten clothes shops throughout N.Y. State by 1978; became full-time designer 1979; launched own sportswear label 1984; acquired fashion business from Mohan Muranji, cr. Tommy Hilfiger Corpn. 1989; mem. Bd. Fresh Air Fund, Race to Erase Multiple Sclerosis; winner From the Catwalk to the Sidewalk award, VH-1 Fashion and Music Awards 1995, Menswear Designer of the Year, Council of Fashion Designers of America 1995. *Leisure interests:* fishing, scuba diving, skiing. *Address:* Tommy Hilfiger U.S.A. Inc., 485 Fifth Avenue, New York, NY 10017, U.S.A. (Office); c/o Lynne Franks PR, 327–329 Harrow Road, London, W9 3RB, England. *Telephone;* 0171-724 6777. *Fax:* 0171-724 8484.

HILGARD, Ernest Ropiequet, PH.D.; American professor of psychology and education; b. 25 July 1904, Belleville, Ill.; s. of Dr. George E. Hilgard and Laura Ropiequet Hilgard; m. Josephine Rohrs 1931; one s. one d.; ed. Univ. of Illinois and Yale Univ.; Instructor in Psychology, Yale Univ. 1928–33; Asst. Prof. to Prof. of Psychology and Educ., Stanford Univ. 1933–69, Exec. Head, Dept. of Psychology 1942–51, Dean of Grad. Div. 1951–55, Emer. Prof. of Psychology and Educ. 1969–; Past Pres. American Psychological Asscn.; mem. N.A.S., Nat. Acad. of Educ., American Philosophical Soc., American Acad. of Arts and Sciences; Hon. Fellow, British Psychological Asscn.; Hon. D.Sc. (Kenyon Coll.) 1964, (Colgate) 1987, (Northwestern) 1987; Hon. LL.D. (Centre Coll.) 1974; Hon. PH.D. (Oslo) 1994; Warren Medal, Distinguished Scientific Contribution Award, Gold Medal, American Psychological Foundation, Gold Medal, Int. Soc. of Hypnosis, N.A.S. Scientific Reviewing Award 1984. *Publications:* Conditioning and Learning 1940, Theories of Learning 1948, Introduction to Psychology 1953, Hypnotic Susceptibility 1965, Hypnosis in the Relief of Pain 1975, Divided Consciousness 1977, American Psychology in Historical Perspective 1978, Psychology in America: A Historical Survey 1987, Fifty Years of Psychology 1988 and articles in professional journals. *Address:* Apartment 226, 850 Webster Street, Palo Alto, CA 94301, U.S.A. (Home).

HILGER, Wolfgang, DR.RER.NAT.; German business executive; b. 16 Nov. 1929, Leverkusen; ed. Univ. of Bonn; joined Hoechst AG 1958, mem. Bd. 1974, Deputy Chair. 1983, Chair. 1985–94; Pres. Advisory Bd. Cassella, Hoechst Holland, Hoechst CeramTec, Riedel de Haën, Messer Griesheim GmbH; Hon. Prof. Univ. of Frankfurt. *Address:* c/o Hoechst AG, Postfach 80 03 20, 65903 Frankfurt, Germany.

HILL, Anthony; British artist and mathematician; b. 23 April 1930, London; s. of Adrian Hill and Dorothy Whitley; m. Yuriko Kaetsu 1978; ed. Bryanston School, St. Martin's School of Art, Cen. School of Arts and Crafts; one-man exhbn. Inst. of Contemporary Arts (ICA), London 1958, exhbn. (with Gillian Wise) 1963; exhbn. Kasmin Gallery, London 1966, 1969, exhbns. (with Redo) 1969, 1980; retrospective exhbn. Haywood Gallery, London 1983; one-man exhbn. Mayor Gallery 1994; works in nat. collections G.B., U.S.A., France, Israel, Denmark; Leverhulme Fellowship 1971–72, Hon. Research Fellow, Dept. of Mathematics, Univ. Coll. 1971–72, Hon. Research Assoc. 1972–; mem. The London Math. Soc. 1979–. *Publications:* Data: Directions in Art, Theory and Aesthetics (Ed.) 1968, Duchamp: Passim 1994; numerous articles in art and mathematical journals. *Leisure interest:* erotology. *Address:* 24 Charlotte Street, London, W.1, England.

HILL, (Arthur) Derek, C.B.E., F.R.G.S.; British artist and author; b. 6 Dec. 1916, Bassett, Hants.; s. of A. J. L. Hill and Grace L. Mercer; ed. Marlborough Coll.; designer of sets and costumes for Covent Garden and Sadler's Wells; one-man exhbns. Nicholson Gallery, London 1943, Leicester Galleries, London, 1947, 1950, 1953, 1956; retrospective exhbn. Whitechapel Gallery, London 1961, Arts Council of N. Ireland, Belfast 1970, Mun. Gallery, Dublin 1971; work represented in exhbns. in Europe and USA 1957–, and in public collections in U.K., Ireland, Denmark, Liechtenstein, U.S.A. and Canada; organiser of exhbns. at Tate Gallery, Royal Acad. etc. 1934–. *Publications:* Islamic Architecture and Its Decoration (with O. Grabar) 1965, Islamic Architecture in North Africa (with L. Golvin) 1976; articles in magazines and journals. *Leisure interests:* gardening, travel. *Address:* c/o National Art Collections Fund, 20 John Islip Street, London, S.W.1, England.

HILL, Christopher (see Hill, (John Edward) Christopher).

HILL, Rt. Rev. Christopher John, B.D., M.TH.; British ecclesiastic; b. 10 Oct. 1945; s. of Leonard Hill and Francis Hill; m. Hilary Ann Whitehouse 1976; three s. one d.; ed. Sebright School, Worcs. and King's Coll., London; ordained (Diocese of Lichfield) 1969; Asst. Chaplain to Archbishop of Canterbury for Foreign Relations 1974–81, Sec. for Ecumenical Affairs 1981–89; Anglican Sec. Anglican-Roman Catholic Int. Comm. I and II 1974–91; Anglican-Lutheran European Comm. 1981–82; Hon. Canon Canterbury Cathedral 1982–89; Canon Residentiary of St. Paul's Cathedral, London 1989–96; Chaplain to Queen 1987–96; Area Bishop of Stafford, Diocese of Lichfield 1996–, Hon. Canon Lichfield Cathedral 1996–; Assoc. King's Coll., London; mem. Church of England-German Churches Conversations 1987–89, Church of England-Nordic-Baltic Conversations 1989–93, Church of England Legal Advisory Comm. 1991–, Faith and Order Advisory Group of Gen. Synod 1997–; mem. Council for Christian Unity 1992–97; Co-Chair. London Soc. of Jews and Christians 1991–96, Church of England-French Protestant Conversations 1993–98; Vice-Chair. Ecclesiastical Law Soc. 1993–; Chair. Cathedrals' Precentors Conf. 1994–96; Anglican Co-Chair. Meissen Theological Conf. 1999; mem. London Soc. for the Study of Religion 1990–. *Publications:* Anglicans and Roman Catholics: the Search for Unity (Co-Ed.), The Documents in the Debate. A Retrospect on the Papal Decision on Anglican Orders 1896 (Co-Ed.) 1996; ecumenical articles. *Leisure interests:* music, walking, reading. *Address:* Ash Garth, 6 Broughton Crescent, Barlaston, Stoke-on-Trent, ST12 9DD, England. *Telephone:* (01782) 373308. *Fax:* (01782) 373705.

HILL, Damon Graham Devereux, O.B.E.; British motor racing driver; b. 17 Sept. 1960, Hampstead, London; s. of late Graham Hill (fmr. Formula One World Champion) and of Bette Hill; m. Georgie Hill 1988; two s. two d.; ed. Haberdashers' Aske's School, London; first drove a car aged 5 years; first drove in motorcycle racing 1979; driver with Canon Williams team 1993, Rothmans Williams Renault team 1994–96, Arrows Yamaha team 1997, Benson and Hedges Jordan team 1998–; first motor racing victory in Formula Ford 1600, Brands Hatch 1984; first Formula One Grand Prix, Silverstone 1992; winner, driving Williams-Renault FW15C, Hungarian Grand Prix 1993, winner, Belgian and Italian Grands Prix 1993, 1994; third place, Drivers' World Championship 1993; winner, Spanish Grand Prix,

Barcelona 1994, British Grand Prix, Silverstone 1994, Portuguese Grand Prix 1994, Japanese Grand Prix 1994, 1996, French Grand Prix 1996, Spanish Grand Prix 1996, Argentine Grand Prix 1995, 1996, San Marino Grand Prix 1995, 1996, Hungarian Grand Prix 1995, Brazilian Grand Prix 1996, German Grand Prix 1996, Australian Grand Prix 1995, 1996, Canadian Grand Prix 1996; second place, Drivers' World Championship 1994, 1995, World Champion 1996; British Competition Driver of the Year Autosport Awards 1995; 84 Grand Prix starts, 21 wins, 20 pole positions, 19 fastest laps, 41 podium finishes; numerous racing and sports personality awards. *Publications:* Damon Hill Grand Prix Year 1994, Damon Hill: My Championship Year 1996. *Leisure interests:* motorcycles, golf, guitar playing, music, skiing, training. *Address:* c/o Edward Lewis, Verulam Gardens, 70 Gray's Inn Road, London, WC1X 8NF, England.

HILL, David, M.ECON.; Australian sports administrator; b. 20 June 1946, Sussex, England; s. of Kathleen Hill; m. Emily Booker 1985; ed. East Sydney Tech. Coll. and Univ. of Sydney; Dir. N.S.W. Govt. Ministerial Advisory Unit 1976–80; mem. Public Transport Comm. 1979; Chief Exec. State Rail Authority 1980–86; mem. Senate, Univ. of Sydney 1983; Commr. Australian Nat. Airlines 1984; Chair. Australian Broadcasting Corpn. 1986, Man. Dir. 1986–95; Chair. Australian Soccer Fed., Rockdale, N.S.W. 1995; Chair. Sydney Water Corpn. Ltd. 1997–. *Leisure interests:* soccer, reading, chess, opera. *Address:* Australian Soccer Federation, P.O. Box 175, Paddington, N.S.W. 2021, Australia.

HILL, Debra; American film director, producer and scriptwriter; b. Philadelphia, Pa.; began film career as script supervisor and asst. dir.; producer and co-scriptwriter, Halloween 1980, The Fog, Halloween II; work for TV includes Adventures in Babysitting, El Diablo, Monsters, Dream On, Girls in Prison. *Films:* Halloween, The Fog, Escape from New York, Halloween II, Halloween III, Season of the Witch, The Dead Zone, Head Office, Adventures in Babysitting, Big Top Pee-Wee, Heartbreak Hotel, Gross Anatomy, The Fisher King.

HILL, Geoffrey (William), M.A., F.R.S.L.; British poet and university professor; b. 18 June 1932; s. of late William George Hill and Hilda Beatrice Hill (née Hands); m. 1st Nancy Whittaker 1956 (divorced 1983); three s. one d.; m. 2nd Alice Goodman 1987; one d.; ed. County High School, Bromsgrove and Keble Coll., Oxford; mem. acad. staff Univ. of Leeds 1954–80, Prof. of English Literature 1976–80; Univ. Lecturer in English and Fellow of Emmanuel Coll., Cambridge 1981–88; Univ. Prof. of Literature and Religion Boston Univ. 1988–; Co-Dir. Editorial Inst., Boston Univ. 1998–; Churchill Fellow Univ. of Bristol 1980; Clark Lecturer Trinity Coll., Cambridge 1986; Fellow American Acad. of Arts and Sciences; Hon. Fellow Keble Coll., Oxford 1981, Emmanuel Coll., Cambridge 1990; Hon. D.Litt. (Leeds) 1988; Whitbread Award 1971, R.S.L. Award (W. H. Heinemann Bequest) 1971, Loines Award, American Acad. and Inst. of Arts and Letters 1983, Ingram Merrill Foundation Award in Literature 1985, Kahn Award 1998. *Publications:* poetry: For the Unfallen 1959 (Gregory Award 1961), King Log 1968 (Hawthornden Prize 1969, Geoffrey Faber Memorial Prize 1970), Mercian Hymns 1971 (Alice Hunt Bartlett Award 1971), Somewhere is Such a Kingdom: Poems 1952–71 1975, Tenebrae 1978 (Duff Cooper Memorial Prize 1979), The Mystery of the Charity of Charles Péguy 1983, Collected Poems 1985, New and Collected Poems 1952–1992 1994, Canaan 1996; poetic drama: Henrik Ibsen, Brand: a version for the English stage 1978 (produced at Nat. Theatre, London 1978), 3rd (revised) edn. 1996; criticism: The Lords of Limit: essays on literature and ideas 1984, The Enemy's Country 1991; poetry: The Triumph of Love 1998. *Address:* University Professors, Boston University, 745 Commonwealth Avenue, Boston, MA 02215, U.S.A.

HILL, George Roy, B.A.; American film and theatre producer and director; b. 20 Dec. 1921, Minneapolis, Minn.; s. of George Roy and Helen (Owens) Hill; m. Louisa Horton 1951; two s. two d.; ed. Yale Univ. and Trinity Coll., Dublin; Directed first stage production Biography, Gate Theatre, Dublin 1948. *Other productions include:* Look Homeward, Angel 1957, The Gang's All Here 1959, Green-willow, Period of Adjustment 1960, Moon on a Rainbow Shawl 1962, Henry, Sweet Henry 1967; directed first film 1962. *Other films include:* Period of Adjustment 1963, Toys in the Attic 1963, The World of Henry Orient 1964, Hawaii 1966, Thoroughly Modern Millie 1967, Butch Cassidy and the Sundance Kid 1969, Slaughterhouse-Five 1972, The Sting 1973 (Oscar, Best Dir.), The Great Waldo Pepper 1975, Slap Shot 1976, A Little Romance 1979, The World According to Garp 1982, The Little Drummer Girl 1984, Funny Farm 1988; first television production 1954. *Other productions include:* A Night to Remember, Helen Morgan, Child of our Time, Judgement at Nuremberg; Academy Award (The Sting) 1973. *Address:* Pan Arts Productions, 59 East 54th Street, New York, N.Y. 10022, U.S.A.

HILL, Graham Starforth, M.A., F.R.S.A.; British solicitor and banker (retd.); b. 22 June 1927, Oxford, England; s. of late Capt. H. V. J. Hill and late Mrs. H. D. Hill (née Starforth); m. Margaret Elise Ambler 1952 (divorced 1962); one s. one d.; ed. Winchester and St. John's Coll., Oxford; Flying Officer, R.A.F. 1948–50; called to Bar (Gray's Inn) 1951; admitted advocate and solicitor Singapore, W. Malaysia, advocate Brunei, solicitor Hong Kong 1955; admitted solicitor England 1961; Crown Counsel, Colonial Legal Service, Singapore 1953–56; partner (finally sr. partner) Rodyk and Davidson, solicitors, Singapore 1957–76, Consultant 1985–96; Pres. Law Soc. of Singapore 1969–73; mem. Council of Int. Bar Asscn. 1970–78; Hon. Legal Adviser, British High Comm., Singapore 1957–76; Dir. Guinness Mahon & Co. Ltd. 1977–83, Chair. 1979–83; Resident Consultant to Milan and Rome Offices of Frere Cholmeley Bischoff, solicitors 1990–94; Dir. Phelan, Lewis and Peat Ltd. 1984–86; mem. Disciplinary Cttee., Inst. of C.A. 1980–85; Trustee, Southwark Cathedral Devt. Trust 1980–85, Royal Opera House Trust 1982–85; Cavaliere della Stella della Solidarietà; Commendatore al Merito della Repubblica Italiana. *Publication:* Report of the Constitutional Commission of Singapore. *Leisure interests:* music, books, Italy. *Address:* 36 Terrazze del Porto, P.O. Box 24, 07020 Porto Cervo, Sardegna, Italy; 10 St. Thomas Street, Winchester, Hants., SO23 9HE, England. *Telephone:* (0789) 92626 (Italy); (01962) 854146 (Winchester). *Fax:* 0789 92615 (Italy); (01962) 867674 (Winchester).

HILL, (John Edward) Christopher, M.A., D.LITT., F.B.A.; British historian; b. 6 Feb. 1912, York; s. of Edward H. and Janet A. Hill; m. 1st Inez Waugh 1944; one d. (deceased); m. 2nd Bridget Irene Sutton 1956; one s. one d. (one d. deceased); ed. St. Peter's School, York, and Balliol Coll., Oxford; Fellow of All Souls Coll., Oxford 1934–38; Asst. Lecturer, Univ. Coll., Cardiff 1936–38; Fellow and Tutor in Modern History, Balliol Coll., Oxford 1938–65, Master of Balliol Coll. 1965–78; Army and Foreign Office Service 1940–45; Univ. Lecturer in 16th and 17th Century History, Oxford 1959–65; Visiting Prof. Open Univ. 1978–80, Preston Polytechnic 1982–84; mem. Editorial Bd. Past and Present 1952–68, Yale Edition of Milton's Complete Prose; Foreign Hon. mem. American Acad. of Sciences 1973; Hon. D.Litt. (Glasgow, Hull, Norwich, Wales, Exeter, Sheffield, St. Alfred's Coll., Winchester, Leicester), Hon. LL.D. (Bristol), Hon. D.Univ. (York), (Open), Hon. Dr. (Sorbonne Nouvelle); shared Heinemann Award for Books 1978; James Holly Hanford Award; Milton Soc. of America Award 1978. *Publications:* The English Revolution, 1640 1940, Lenin and Russian Revolution 1947, The Good Old Cause (documents, edited jointly with E. Dell) 1949, Economic Problems of the Church 1956, Puritanism and Revolution 1958, The Century of Revolution 1603-1714 1961, Society and Puritanism in Pre-Revolutionary England 1964, Intellectual Origins of the English Revolution 1965, Reformation to Industrial Revolution 1967, God's Englishman 1970, Antichrist in 17th Century England 1971, The World Turned Upside Down 1972, The Law of Freedom and Other Selected Writings of Gerrard Winstanley (editor) 1973, Change and Continuity in 17th Century England 1975, Milton and the English Revolution 1977, Some Intellectual Consequences of the English Revolution 1980, The World of the Muggletonians (co-author) 1983, The Experience of Defeat: Milton and Some Contemporaries 1984, Writing and Revolution in 17th Century England 1985, Religion and Politics in 17th Century England 1986, People and Ideas in 17th Century England 1986, A Turbulent, Seditious and Factious People: John Bunyan and his Church (W. H. Smith Literary Prize) 1988, A Nation of Change and Novelty: Radical Politics, Religion and Literature in 17th-Century England 1990, The English Bible and the 17th Century Revolution 1993, Liberty Against the Law 1996, The Origins of the English Revolution Revisited 1997. *Address:* Woodway House, Sibford Ferris, Banbury, Oxon., OX15 5RA, England.

HILL, Sir John McGregor, Kt., F.R.S., F.R.ENG.; British atomic energy official; b. 21 Feb. 1921, Chester; s. of the late John Campbell Hill and of Margaret Elizabeth Park; m. Nora Eileen Hellett 1947; two s. one d.; ed. Richmond County Grammar School, King's Coll., London, and St. John's Coll., Cambridge; Flight Lieut., R.A.F., Second World War; research at Cavendish Laboratory, Cambridge 1946–48; Lecturer, London Univ. 1948–50; U.K. Atomic Energy Authority 1950–81, mem. for Production 1964–67, Chair. 1967–81; Chair. British Nuclear Fuels Ltd. 1971–83, Aurora Holdings PLC 1983–88, Rea Bros. 1987–95; mem. Energy Comm. Dept. of Energy 1978–79, Nuclear Power Advisory Bd. 1973–81; Foreign Assoc. mem., Nat. Acad. of Engineering of the U.S.A. 1976; Hon. D.Sc. (Bradford) 1981; Hon. F.I.Chem.E. 1977; Hon. F.I.E.E. 1981. *Leisure interests:* golf, gardening. *Address:* Dominic House, Sudbrook Lane, Richmond, Surrey, TW10 7AT, England (Home). *Telephone:* 0181-940 7221. *Fax:* 0181-940 7221.

HILL, Michael William, M.A., B.SC.; British information consultant; b. 27 July 1928, Ross-on-Wye; s. of Geoffrey Hill and Dorothy Hill; m. 1st Elma Jack Forrest (died 1967); one s. one d.; m. 2nd Barbara Joy Youngman; ed. King Henry VIIIth School, Coventry, Nottingham High School, Lincoln Coll., Oxford; Research Chemist, Laporte Chemicals Ltd. 1953–56; Tech. and Production Man., Morgan Crucible Group 1956–64; Asst. Keeper, British Museum 1964–68, Deputy Librarian Nat. Reference Library of Science and Invention (NRLSI) 1965–68, Keeper 1968–73; Dir., Science Reference Library, British Library 1973–86; Assoc. Dir. Science. Tech. and Industry, British Library 1986–88; Hon. Pres. Fed. Int. d'Information et de Documentation 1985–90; fmr. Chair. Circle of State Librarians; fmr. Vice-Pres. Int. Asscn. of Tech. Univ. Librarians; Co-founder Western European Round Table on Information and Documentation. *Publications:* Patent Documentation (with Wittmann and Schiffels) 1979, Michael Hill on Science, Technology and Information 1988, National Surveys of Library and Information Services: 2: Yugoslavia (with Tudor Silovic), National Information Policies and Strategies 1994; Jt. Series Ed. Bowker Saur Guides to Information Sources. *Leisure interests:* golf, theatre, music, Scottish dancing. *Address:* Jesters, 137 Burdon Lane, Cheam, Surrey, SM2 7DB, England. *Telephone:* 0181-642 2418.

HILL, Polly, PH.D.; British economic anthropologist; b. 10 June 1914, Cambridge; d. of A. V. Hill, C.H. and Margaret N. Hill (née Keynes); m. Kenneth Humphreys 1953 (divorced 1961, died 1985); one d.; ed. Newnham

Coll., Cambridge; mem. editorial staff Economic Journal, Cambridge 1936–38; Research Asst., Fabian Soc., London 1938–39; temporary civil servant successively Treasury, Bd. of Trade and Colonial Office 1940–51; mem. editorial staff West Africa, London 1951–53; mem. academic staff Univ. of Ghana, Legon 1954–65; field work in northern Nigeria, writing in Cambridge 1966–72; Smuts Reader in Commonwealth Studies, Univ. of Cambridge 1973–79, Emer. Reader 1979–; field work in India 1977–78, as Leverhulme Emer. Fellow 1981–82; Fellow Clare Hall, Cambridge 1966–81, Emer. Fellow 1981–; Hon. Fellow S.O.A.S. 1998. *Publications:* The Unemployment Services 1940, The Gold Coast Farmer 1956, The Migrant Cocoa Farmers of Southern Ghana 1963, Studies in Rural Capitalism in West Africa 1970, Rural Hausa: A Village and a Setting 1972, Population, Prosperity and Poverty: Rural Kano, 1900 and 1970 1977, Dry Grain Farming Families: Hausaland (Nigeria) and Karnataka (India) compared 1982, Development Economics on Trial: the Anthropological Case for a Prosecution 1986, Lydia and Maynard: The Letters of L. Lopokova and J. M. Keynes (Ed. with R. Keynes) 1989, Who Were the Fen People? 1993 and many other publs. *Leisure interest:* embroidery. *Address:* 4 Earl Street, Cambridge, CB1 1JR, England. *Telephone:* (01223) 315151.

HILL, Robert Lee, PH.D.; American university professor; b. 8 June 1928, Kansas City, Mo.; s. of William Alfred Hill and Geneva Eunice Sculock Hill; m. 1st Helen Root Hill 1948 (divorced); m. 2nd Deborah Anderson Hill 1982; one s. three d. (from previous marriage); ed. Kansas Univ.; Research Instructor, Univ. of Utah, Salt Lake City 1956–57, Asst. Research Prof. 1957–60, Assoc. Research Prof. 1960–61; Assoc. Prof., Duke Univ., Durham, N.C. 1961–65, Prof. 1965–74, Chair. Dept. of Biochemistry 1969–93, James B. Duke Prof. 1974–; Fellow, American Acad. of Arts and Sciences 1974–; mem. N.A.S. 1975–; Pres. American Soc. of Biological Chemists 1976–77; Pres. Asscn. of Medical Depts. of Biochemistry 1982–83; Gen. Sec. Int. Union of Biochemistry 1985–91. *Publications:* Co-Author: Principles of Biochemistry 1978, Co-Ed. The Proteins (vol.1 1975, vol. V 1982). *Address:* Department of Biochemistry, Duke University Medical Center, Durham, NC 27710, U.S.A. *Telephone:* (919) 684-5326.

HILL, Robert Murray, B.A., LL.M.; Australian politician; b. 25 Sept. 1946; s. of C. M. Hill; m. Diana Jacka 1969; two s. two d.; ed. Scotch Coll., S. Australia, Univ. of Adelaide, Univ. of London, U.K.; barrister and solicitor 1970–; Liberal Party Campaign Chair. 1975–77, Chair. Constitutional Cttee. 1977–81; Vice-Pres. Liberal Party, S. Australian Div. 1977–79; Senator for S. Australia 1981–; Shadow Minister for Foreign Affairs –1993, for Defence 1993–94, for Public Admin. 1993–94, for Educ., Science and Tech. 1994–96; Leader of Opposition in Senate 1993–96; Minister for the Environment, Leader of Govt. in Senate March 1996–; mem. Law Soc., S. Australia. *Leisure interests:* Australian and Asian history. *Address:* Commonwealth Parl. Offices, 100 King William Street, Adelaide, S.A. 5000; Parliament House, Canberra, A.C.T. 2600, Australia.

HILL, Rodney, M.A., SC.D., F.R.S.; British professor of mechanics of solids; b. 11 June 1921; s. of Harold H. Hill; m. Jeanne K. Wickens 1946; one d.; ed. Leeds Grammar School and Pembroke Coll., Cambridge; Armament Research Dept. 1943–46; Cavendish Lab. Cambridge 1946–48; British Iron and Steel Research Asscn. 1948–50; Research Fellow, Univ. of Bristol 1950–53, Reader 1953; Prof. of Applied Math. Univ. of Nottingham 1953–62; Professorial Research Fellow 1962–63; Berkeley Bye-Fellow, Gonville and Caius Coll. Cambridge 1963–69, Fellow 1972–88, Life Fellow 1988–; Reader, Univ. of Cambridge 1969–72, Prof. of Mechanics of Solids 1972–79; Hon. D.Sc. (Manchester) 1976, (Bath) 1978; Von Karman Medal, American Soc. of Civil Engineers 1978, Gold Medal and Int. Modesto Panetti Prize, Turin Acad. of Sciences 1988, Royal Medal, The Royal Soc., London 1993. *Publications:* Mathematical Theory of Plasticity 1950, Principles of Dynamics 1964. *Address:* c/o Department of Applied Mathematics and Theoretical Physics, Silver Street, Cambridge, CB3 9EW, England.

HILL, S. Richardson, Jr., M.D.; American university president and physician; b. 19 May 1923, Greensboro, N.C.; s. of Samuel Richardson Hill and Nona Sink Hill; m. Janet Redman 1950; one s. three d.; ed. Riverside Mil. Acad., Gainesville, Ga., Duke Univ. and Bowman Gray School of Medicine of Wake Forest Univ.; Intern in Medicine, then Asst. Resident, Asst. in Medicine, Peter Bent Brigham Hosp., Boston, Mass. and Teaching Fellow, then Research Fellow in Medicine, Harvard Medical School 1947–50; Chief Resident in Medicine, N.C. Baptist Hosp. and Instructor, Bowman Gray School of Medicine 1950–51; Chief, Medical Service, U.S.A.F. Hosp., Keesler, Miss. 1951–53; Asst. in Medicine, Harvard Medical School and Peter Bent Brigham Hosp. 1953–54; Asst. Prof. of Medicine and Dir. Metabolic and Endocrine Div., Medical Coll. of Ala. (later Univ. of Ala. School of Medicine), Birmingham, Ala. 1954–57, Assoc. Prof. 1957–62, Prof. 1962–94, Dean 1962–68, Vice-Pres. for Health Affairs and Dir. of Medical Center, Univ. of Ala. in Birmingham 1968–77, Pres. Univ. of Ala. at Birmingham 1977–87, Distinguished Prof. 1987–94, Distinguished Prof. Emer. 1994–; Fellow A.A.A.S., American Coll. of Physicians, Royal Soc. of Medicine, New York Acad. of Sciences; mem. Asscn. for Acad. Health Centers (Pres. 1973), N.A.S. Inst. of Medicine, American Fed. for Clinical Research (Pres. 1961–62), Bd. of Regents of Nat. Library of Medicine (Chair. 1979–80). *Leisure interests:* sailing, swimming and reading. *Address:* University of Alabama at Birmingham, UAB Station, Birmingham, AL 35294; 109 Mount Brook Park Drive, Birmingham, AL 35213, U.S.A. (Home). *Telephone:* (205) 934-3493 (Univ.); (205) 870 8755 (Home).

HILL, Susan Elizabeth, B.A., F.R.S.L.; British author and playwright; b. 5 Feb. 1942; d. of late R. H. Hill and Doris Hill; m. Prof. Stanley W. Wells 1975; two d. (and one d. deceased); ed. grammar schools in Scarborough and Coventry and King's Coll. London; literary critic, various journals 1963–; numerous plays for BBC 1970–; Fellow, King's Coll. London 1978; presenter, Bookshelf, BBC Radio 1986–87; f. and publr. Long Barn Books 1996–. *Publications include:* The Enclosure 1961, Do Me a Favour 1963, Gentleman and Ladies 1969, A Change for the Better 1969, I'm the King of the Castle 1970, The Albatross 1971, Strange Meeting 1971, The Bird of the Night 1972, A Bit of Singing and Dancing 1973, In the Springtime of the Year 1974, The Cold Country and Other Plays for Radio 1975, The Ramshackle Company (play) 1981, The Magic Apple Tree 1982, The Woman in Black 1983 (stage version 1989), One Night at a Time (for children) 1984, Through the Kitchen Window 1984, Through the Garden Gate 1986, Mother's Magic (for children) 1986, The Lighting of the Lamps 1987, Lanterns Across the Snow 1987, Shakespeare Country 1987, The Spirit of the Cotswolds 1988, Can it be True? (for children) 1988, Family (autobiog.) 1989, Susie's Shoes (for children) 1989, Stories from Codling Village (for children) 1990, I've Forgotten Edward (for children) 1990, I Won't Go There Again (for children) 1990, Pirate Poll (for children) 1991, The Glass Angels 1991, Beware! Beware! 1993, King of Kings 1993, Reflections from a Garden (with Rory Stuart) 1995, Contemporary Women's Short Stories 1995 (Ed., with Rory Stuart), Listening to the Orchestra 1996 (short stories), The Second Penguin Book of Women's Short Stories 1997, The Service of Clouds 1998. *Leisure interests:* walking in the English countryside, friends, reading, broadcasting. *Address:* Longmoor Farmhouse, Ebrington, Chipping Campden, Glos., GL55 6NW, England. *Telephone:* (01386) 593352. *Fax:* (01386) 593443.

HILL, Terrell Leslie, PH.D.; American biophysicist and chemist; b. 19 Dec. 1917, Oakland, Calif.; s. of George Leslie and Ollie Moreland Hill; m. Laura Etta Gano 1942; one s. two d.; ed. Univ. of California at Berkeley and Harvard Univ.; Instructor in Chem., Western Reserve Univ. 1942–44; Research Assoc., Radiation Lab., Univ. of Calif. at Berkeley 1944–45; Research Assoc. in Chem., then Asst. Prof. of Chem., Univ. of Rochester 1945–49; Chemist, U.S. Naval Medical Research Inst. 1949–57; Prof. of Chem., Univ. of Oregon 1957–67; Prof. of Chem., Univ. of Calif. at Santa Cruz 1967–71, Vice-Chancellor, Sciences 1968–69, Adjunct Prof. of Chem. 1977–89, Prof. Emer. 1989–; Sr. Research Chemist, Nat. Insts. of Health 1971–88, Scientist Emer. 1988–; mem. Nat. Acad. of Sciences, American Chemical Soc., Biophysical Soc., American Civil Liberties Union, Nat. Asscn. for Advancement of Coloured People, etc.; Guggenheim Fellow, Yale 1952–53; Sloan Foundation Fellow 1958–62; Arthur S. Flemming Award, U.S. Govt. 1954, Dist. Civilian Service Award, U.S. Navy 1955, Award of Washington Acad. of Sciences 1956, Kendall Award, American Chemical Soc. 1969, Superior Service Award, U.S. Public Health Service 1981, Distinguished Service Award, Univ. of Oregon 1983. *Publications:* Statistical Mechanics 1956, 1987, Statistical Thermodynamics 1960, 1986, Thermodynamics of Small Systems Vol. I 1963, 1994, Vol. II 1964, 1994, Matter and Equilibrium 1965, Thermodynamics for Chemists and Biologists 1968, Free Energy Transduction in Biology 1977, Cooperativity Theory in Biochemistry 1985, Linear Aggregation Theory in Cell Biology 1987, Free Energy Transduction and Biochemical Cycle Kinetics 1989; also research papers. *Leisure interests:* reading, walking, music. *Address:* 433 Logan Street, Santa Cruz, CA 95062, U.S.A. (Home).

HILL SMITH, Marilyn, A.G.S.M.; British soprano opera singer; b. 9 Feb. 1952, Carshalton, Surrey; d. of George and Irene Smith; ed. Nonsuch High School, Ewell and Guildhall School of Music and Drama; cabaret, pantomime, concerts 1971–74; toured Australia and N.Z. with Gilbert & Sullivan for All 1974, U.S.A. and Canada 1976; Prin. Soprano, English Nat. Opera 1978–84; Covent Garden début in Peter Grimes 1981; has appeared at several major European music festivals including Versailles, Granada, Aldeburgh, London Promenade Concerts etc., also with New Sadlers Wells Opera, Canadian Opera Co., Welsh Nat. Opera, Scottish Nat. Opera, New D'Oyly Carte Opera, Lyric Opera of Singapore, etc. and on television and radio and has made several recordings particularly of operetta; Young Musician of the Year 1975 and other prizes. *Leisure interests:* cooking, gardening, sleeping. *Address:* c/o Music International, 13 Ardilaun Road, Highbury, London, N5 2QR, England. *Telephone:* 0171-359 5183/4.

HILLARY, Sir Edmund Percival, K.G., K.B.E.; New Zealand explorer, bee farmer and diplomatist; b. 20 July 1919, Auckland; s. of Percival Augustus and Gertrude Hillary; m. 1st Louise Mary Rose 1953 (died 1975); one s. two d. (one deceased); m. 2nd June Mulgrew 1989; ed. Auckland Grammar School and Univ. of Auckland; served R.N.Z.A.F. (on Catalinas in the Pacific) 1944–45; went to Himalayas on N.Z. Garwhal expedition 1951, when he and another were invited to join the British reconnaissance over Everest under Eric Shipton; took part in British expedition to Cho Oyu 1952, and in British Mount Everest Expedition under Sir John Hunt 1953, when he and Tenzing reached the summit on May 29th; Leader N.Z. Alpine Club Expedition to Barun Valley 1954; N.Z. Antarctic Expedition 1956–58, reached South Pole Dec. 1957; Leader Himalayan Expeditions 1961, 1963, 1964; Pres. Volunteer Service Abroad in New Zealand 1963–64; built a hospital for Sherpa tribesmen, Nepal 1966; Leader climbing expedition on Mount Herschel, Antarctica 1967; River Ganges Expedition 1977; High Commr. to India (also accred. to Bangladesh and Nepal) 1984; Hon. Pres. Explorers Club of New York; Consultant to Sears Roebuck & Co., Chicago; UNICEF Special Rep.

Children of the Himalayas 1991–; Hubbard Medal 1954, Polar Medal 1958; Gurkha Right Hand (1st Class), Star of Nepal (1st Class), Founders' Gold Medal, Royal Geographical Soc.; James Wattie Book of the Year Award, N.Z. 1975; Hon. LL.D. (Victoria Univ., B.C., Canada, Victoria Univ., New Zealand) and other hon. degrees. *Publications:* High Adventure 1955, The Crossing of Antarctica (with Sir Vivian Fuchs) 1958, No Latitude for Error 1961, High in the Thin Cold Air (with Desmond Doig) 1963, Schoolhouse in the Clouds 1965, Nothing Venture, Nothing Win (autobiog.) 1975, From the Ocean to the Sky: jet-boating up the Ganges 1979, Two Generations (with Peter Hillary) 1983, Sagarmatha, The View from the Summit 1998. *Leisure interests:* walking, fishing, camping. *Address:* 278A Remuera Road, Auckland 5, New Zealand (Home).

HILLEBRECHT, Rudolf Friedrich Heinrich, DIPL. ING.; German architect and town planner; b. 26 Feb. 1910, Hanover; s. of Ernst and Bertha (née Arning) Hillebrecht; m. 1st Ruth Frommhold 1937; m. 2nd Oxana Saweljewa 1967; one d.; ed. Humanistisches Gymnasium, Hanover, and Technische Hochschulen, Hanover and Berlin; worked with Walter Gropius, Berlin 1933–34; Building Inspector, Travemünde, Hamburg and Hanover 1934–37; Office Manager, architectural practice of Konstanty Gutschow, Hamburg 1937–45; worked in Dept. for Replanning of Hamburg 1937–44; Army Service 1944–45; worked with Werner Kallmorgen, Hamburg 1945–46; Deputy Chief, Building Div., British Occupied Zone 1946; Sec. for Building Affairs, German Advisory Council of British Zone 1946–48; Municipal Town Planner and Architect, City of Hanover 1948–75; Pres. Gottfried-Wilhelm-Leibniz-Gesellschaft 1969–85; Pres. German Acad. for Town and Country Planning 1973–79, and other orgs.; Grosses Bundesverdienstkreuz mit Stern und Schulterband, and many other decorations; Hon. Citizen of Hanover 1980. *Leisure interests:* arts, literature, music. *Address:* Gneiststrasse 7, 30169 Hanover, Germany (Home). *Telephone:* 885862.

HILLEL, Shlomo; Israeli politician; b. 1923, Baghdad, Iraq; s. of Aharom Hillel and Hanini Hillel; m. Tmima Rosner 1952; one s. one d.; ed. Herzliah High School, Tel-Aviv and Hebrew Univ., Jerusalem; mem. Ma'agan Michael Kibbutz 1942–58; Jewish Agency for Palestine—mission to countries in Middle East 1946–48, 1949–51; Israel Defence Forces 1948–49; Prime Minister's Office 1952–53; mem. of Knesset 1953–59, 1974–; Amb. to Guinea 1959–61, to Ivory Coast, Dahomey, Upper Volta and Niger 1961–63; mem. Perm. Mission to UN with rank of Minister 1964–67; Asst. Dir.-Gen. Ministry of Foreign Affairs 1967–69; Minister of Police 1969–77; Co-ordinator of political contacts with Arab leadership in administered territories 1970–77; Minister of the Interior June-Oct. 1974, 1996–97; Chair. Ministerial Cttee. for Social Welfare 1974–77, Cttee. of the Interior and Environment 1977–81, of Foreign Affairs and Defence 1981–84; Perm. Observer to Council of Europe 1977–84; Speaker of the Knesset Sept. 1984–88; Chair. Sephardi Fed. 1976–; World Chair. Keren Hayesod United Israel Appeal 1989–; Pres. Council for Preservation of Historical Sites in Israel 1996–; Chair. Zalman Shazar Center, Jerusalem; Israel Prize for Life Achievement 1998; Commdr. Nat. Order of Repubs. of Ivory Coast, Upper Volta and Dahomey. *Publication:* Operation Babylon 1988. *Leisure interests:* tennis, gardening. *Address:* 14 Gelber Street, Jerusalem 96755, Israel. *Telephone:* (2) 6411-416 (Home). *Fax:* (2) 6436612.

HILLEMAN, Maurice Ralph, PH.D.; American virologist; b. 30 Aug. 1919, Miles City, Mont.; s. of Robert A. and Edith M. (Matson) Hilleman; m. 1st Thelma L. Mason 1943 (deceased); m. 2nd Lorraine Witmer 1963; two d.; ed. Montana State Coll. and Univ. of Chicago; Asst. Bacteriologist, Univ. of Chicago 1942–44; Research Assoc., Virus Laboratories, E.R. Squibb & Sons 1944–47; Chief Virus Dept. 1947–48; Medical Bacteriologist and Asst. Chief, Virus and Rickettsial Diseases, Army Medical Service Graduate School, Walter Reed Army Medical Center 1948–56; Chief, Respiratory Diseases, Walter Reed Army Inst. of Research, Washington 1956–57; Dir. Virus and Cell Biology Research, Merck Inst. for Therapeutic Research, Merck & Co. Inc. 1957–66, Exec. Dir. 1966–70; Dir. Virus and Cell Biology Research, Vice-Pres. Merck Sharp and Dohme Research Laboratories 1970–78, Sr. Vice-Pres. 1978–84; Dir. Merck Inst. for Therapeutic Research 1984–; Visiting lecturer in Bacteriology, Rutgers Univ. 1947; Visiting Investigator, Hospital of Rockefeller Institute for Medical Research 1951; Visiting Prof. Department of Bacteriology, Univ. of Maryland 1953–57; Adjunct Prof. of Virology in Pediatrics, School of Med., Univ. of Pa. 1968–; Consultant, Surgeon-Gen. U.S. Army 1958–63; Children's Hosp. of Philadelphia 1968–; mem. Expert Advisory Panel on Virus Diseases, WHO 1952–, Cttee. on Influenza 1952, Cttee. on Respiratory Diseases 1958, Scientific Group on Measles Vaccine Studies 1963, on Viruses and Cancer 1964, on Human Viral and Rickettsial Vaccines 1965, on Respiratory Diseases 1967; mem. Study Section, Microbiology and Immunology Grants-in-Aid Program 1953–61; mem. Editorial Bd. Int. Soc. of Cancer 1964–71, Inst. for Scientific Information 1968–70, American Journal of Epidemiology 1969–75, Infection and Immunity 1970–76, Excerpta Medica 1971–, Proceedings of the Soc. for Experimental Biology and Medicine 1976, Editorial and Publs. Cttee. 1977–; mem. Council, Tissue Culture Asscn. 1977–; mem. Council for Div. of Biological Sciences, Pritzker School of Medicine 1977–; mem. American Type Culture Collection Virology Dept. Review Cttee. 1980; mem. Overseas Medical Research Labs. Cttee., Dept. of Defense 1980; Editorial Bd., Antiviral Research 1980–; mem. Bd. of Dirs., W. Alto Jones Cell Science Center 1980–82, The Joseph Stokes Jr. Research Inst., Univ. of Pa. 1986–, Nat. Foundation for Infectious Diseases; mem. Advisory Bd. Inst. of Biomedical Sciences, Taiwan, 1982–; mem. N.A.S. Cttee. on a Nat. Strategy for AIDS 1986–87, Nat. Vaccine Advisory Cttee. of Nat. Vaccine Program 1988–; mem. Cttee. on New Vaccine Development Nat. Acad. of Sciences 1983–; mem. AIDS Vaccine R & D Working Group, N.I.H. 1992–; mem. Scientific Council of Paul Ehrlich Foundation 1993–; mem. numerous U.S. and Int. Medical Socs.; John Herr Musser Lecturer, Tulane Univ. School of Med. 1969; 19th Graugnard Lecturer 1978; Fellow, American Acad. of Microbiology, American Acad. of Arts and Sciences; mem. N.A.S.; Foreign Corresp. mem. Académie Nationale de Pharmacie, Paris; Hon. D.Sc. (Montana Univ.) 1966, (Maryland Univ.) 1968, (Washington and Jefferson Coll.) 1992; Dr. h.c. (Univ. Leuven) 1984; many awards including Distinguished Civilian Service Award given by Sec. of Defense 1957, Washington Acad. of Sciences Award for Scientific Achievement in the Biological Sciences 1958, Walter Reed Army Medical Center Incentive Award 1960, Merck Dirs. Scientific Award 1969, 1984, Dean M. McCann Award for Distinguished Service 1970, Procter Award 1971, American Acad. of Achievement, Golden Plate Award 1975, Industrial Research Inst. Achievement Award 1975, Gold Medal for Service to Humanity, Hellenic Red Cross 1982, American Medical Asscn. Scientific Achievement Award 1983, Albert Lasker Medical Research Award 1983, Howard Taylor Ricketts Award, Univ. Chicago 1983, Sabin Medal, German Soc. for Social Paediatrics 1988, Nat. Medal of Science, Pres. of U.S.A. 1988, Alumni Medal, Univ. of Chicago 1989, Robert Koch Gold Medal, Germany 1989, San Marino Medical Award 1989, Special Lifetime Achievement Award Children's Vaccine Initiative of WHO 1996, Sabin Gold Medal, Lifetime Achievement Award, Sabin Vaccine Foundation 1997, Maxwell Finland Award, Nat. Foundation for Infectious Diseases 1998. *Publications:* more than 460 original publications on virology, immunology and public health. *Leisure interest:* work. *Address:* Merck Institute, Merck Research Laboratories, WP 53C-350, West Point, PA 19118, U.S.A. *Telephone:* (215) 652-8913. *Fax:* (215) 652-2154.

HILLENBRAND, Martin Joseph, PH.D.; American diplomatist; b. 1 Aug. 1915, Youngstown, Ohio; s. of Joseph and Maria Hillenbrand; m. Faith Stewart 1941; two s. one d.; ed. Univs. of Dayton and Columbia; Vice-Consul, Zürich 1939, Rangoon 1940, Calcutta 1942, Lourenço Marques 1944, Bremen 1944; Consul, Bremen 1946; Bureau of German Affairs, State Dept. 1950–52; First Sec., Paris 1952–56; U.S. Political Adviser, Berlin 1956–58; Dir. Office of German Affairs, State Dept. 1958–62; Head of "Berlin Task Force" 1962–63; Deputy Chief of Mission, Bonn 1963–67; Chair. Fulbright Comm. for Germany 1963–67; Amb. to Hungary 1967–69; Asst. Sec. of State for European Affairs 1969–72; Amb. to Fed. Repub. of Germany 1972–76; Dir.-Gen. Atlantic Inst. for Int. Affairs, Paris 1977–82; Dean Rusk Prof. of Int. Relations, Univ. of Ga. 1982–97, Prof. Emer. 1997–, Dir. Global Policy Studies 1983–91; Chair. Bd., Southern Centre for Int. Studies, Atlanta 1988–90; Co-Dir. Center for Int. Trade and Security (fmrly. Center for East-West Trade Policy), Univ. of Ga. 1987–97; Dir Mercedes-Benz NA 1990–94; Grand Order of Merit (Fed. Repub. of Germany) and many other honours. *Publications:* Power and Morals 1948, Zwischen Politik und Ethik (co-author) 1968, The Future of Berlin (co-author and ed.) 1980, Global Insecurity: A Strategy for Energy and Economic Growth (co-ed.) 1982, Germany in an Era of Transition 1983, Fragments of Our Time: Memoirs of a Diplomat 1998, and numerous articles. *Leisure interests:* reading, walking, golf. *Address:* Center for International Trade and Security, University of Georgia, Athens, GA 30602, U.S.A. *Telephone:* (706) 542-2111. *Fax:* (706) 542-4421.

HILLER, Susan, M.A.; American artist; b. 7 March 1940; d. of Paul Hiller and Florence Ehrich; m. David Coxhead 1962; one s.; ed. Smith Coll. and Tulane Univ.; one-woman exhbns. at galleries in London and other British cities, Toronto, Zürich, Warsaw, Adelaide, Sydney, etc. since 1973; has participated in numerous group shows in Britain and abroad, also numerous solo exhbns.; lecturer, Slade School of Art, London 1982–; Artist-in-Residence, Univ. of Sussex 1975; Assoc. Prof. of Arts, Dept. of Fine and Applied Arts, Univ. of Ulster 1991–; Gulbenkian Foundation Visual Artists Award 1976, 1977. *Publications:* Dreams—Visions of the Night (co-author), The Myth of Primitivism (Ed.). *Address:* 83 Loudoun Road, London, NW8 0DL, England. *Telephone:* 0171-372 0438.

HILLER, Dame Wendy, D.B.E.; British actress; b. Stockport; d. of Frank Hiller and Marie Stone; m. Ronald Gow 1937 (died 1993); one s. one d.; ed. Winceby House, Bexhill; trained as an actress Manchester Repertory Theatre; Hon. LL.D (Manchester) 1984; Acad. Award for Best Actress, Separate Tables 1959; numerous stage and film roles. *Plays include:* Love on the Dole (London and New York) 1935, Cradle Song, The First Gentleman 1945, Tess of the d'Urbervilles, The Heiress (London and New York) 1947, Ann Veronica 1949, The Night of the Ball 1955, Waters of the Moon 1955, Moon for the Misbegotten (New York) 1957, Flowering Cherry 1958, Toys in the Attic 1960, Aspern Papers (New York) 1962, The Wings of the Dove 1963, The Sacred Flame 1967, When We Dead Awaken (Edinburgh Festival) 1968, The Battle of Shrivings 1970, Crown Matrimonial 1972, John Gabriel Borkman (London) 1975, Lies 1976, The Aspern Papers 1984, Driving Miss Daisy 1988. *Films include:* Pygmalion 1938, Major Barbara 1940, I Know Where I'm Going 1945, Separate Tables 1958, Sons and Lovers 1960, A Man for All Seasons 1966, David Copperfield 1969, Murder on the Orient Express 1975, Voyage of the Damned 1976, Cat and the Canary 1977, The Elephant Man 1979, Making Love 1981, The Kingfisher 1982, The Lonely Passion of Miss Judith Hearne 1987. *Television:* The Importance of Being Earnest 1986, All Passion Spent 1987, A Taste for Death 1988, Ending Up 1989, The

Best of Friends 1991, The Countess Alice 1992. *Leisure interest:* gardening. *Address:* c/o Chatto & Linnit, Prince of Wales Theatre, Coventry Street, London, W1V 7FE, England.

HILLERY, Patrick John, B.SC., M.B., B.CH., B.A.O., D.P.H., M.R.I.A.; Irish fmr. Head of State and politician; b. 2 May 1923, Miltown Malbay, Co. Clare; s. of Dr. Michael Joseph Hillery and Ellen Hillery (née McMahon); m. Mary Beatrice Finnegan 1955; one s. one d.; ed. Miltown Malbay National School, Rockwell Coll., Cashel and Univ. Coll., Dublin; worked in General Children's Tuberculosis and Psychiatric Hospital; mem., Health Council 1955–57; Medical Officer, Miltown Malbay 1957–59; Coroner for West Clare 1958–59; mem. Dáil 1951–73; Minister for Educ. 1959–65, for Industry and Commerce 1965–66, for Labour 1966–69, of Foreign Affairs 1969–72; Vice-Pres. Comm. of European Communities with special responsibility for Social Affairs 1973–76; Pres. of Ireland 1976–90; mem. Royal Irish Acad. 1963; Hon. Fellow Royal Coll. of Surgeons (Ireland), Faculty of Dentistry, Royal Coll. of Surgeons (Ireland), All-India Inst. of Medical Sciences, Royal Coll. of Physicians (Ireland), Royal Coll. of Gen. Practitioners, Pharmaceutical Soc. of Ireland 1984; Hon. LL.D. (Nat. Univ. of Ireland, Trinity Coll., Dublin, Univ. of Melbourne, Pontifical Univ. of Maynooth, Limerick); Robert Schumann Gold Medal (France), Grand Croix, Légion d'honneur, Freeman City of Dublin, and other decorations. *Leisure interests:* golf, painting, reading, travel. *Address:* Grasmere, Greenfield Road, Sutton, Dublin 13, Ireland.

HILLIER, Bevis, F.R.S.A.; British writer and editor; b. 28 March 1940; s. of Jack Ronald Hillier and Mary Louise Palmer; ed. Reigate Grammar School and Magdalen Coll., Oxford; Editorial Staff, The Times 1963–68, Antiques Corresp. 1970–84, Deputy Literary Ed. 1981–84; Ed. British Museum Soc. Bulletin 1968–70; Guest Curator, Minn. Inst. of Arts 1971; Ed. the Connoisseur 1973–76; Assoc. Ed., Los Angeles Times 1984–88; Ed. Sotheby's Preview 1990–93. *Publications:* Master Potters of the Industrial Revolution: The Turners of Lane End 1965, Pottery and Porcelain 1700–1914 1968, Art Deco of the 1920s and the 1930s 1968, Posters 1969, Cartoons and Caricatures 1970, The World of Art Deco 1971, 100 Years of Posters 1972, Austerity-Binge 1975, The New Antiques 1977, Greetings from Christmas Past 1982, The Style of the Century 1900–1980 1983, John Betjeman: A Life in Pictures 1984, Young Betjeman 1988, Early English Porcelain 1992; Co-Ed. A Tonic to the Nation: The Festival of Britain 1951 1976. *Leisure interests:* piano, collecting, awarding marks out of ten for suburban front gardens. *Address:* c/o The Maggie Noach Literary Agency, 21 Redan Street, London, W14 0AB, England.

HILL-NORTON, Baron (Life Peer) cr. 1979, of South Nutfield in the County of Surrey; **Admiral of the Fleet Peter John Hill-Norton,** G.C.B.; British naval officer; b. 8 Feb. 1915, Germiston; s. of Martin J. and Margery B. Norton; m. Margaret E. Linstow 1936; one s. one d.; ed. Royal Naval Coll., Dartmouth and Royal Naval Coll., Greenwich; went to sea 1932; commissioned 1936; served Arctic convoys, N.W. Approaches and Admiralty Naval Staff, Second World War 1939–45; Commdr. 1948; Captain 1952; Naval Attaché, Argentine, Uruguay, Paraguay 1953–55; in command H.M.S. Decoy 1956–57, H.M.S. Ark Royal 1959–61; Asst. Chief of Naval Staff 1962–64; Flag Officer, Second-in-Command Far East Fleet 1964–66; Deputy Chief of the Defence Staff (Personnel and Logistics) 1966; Second Sea Lord and Chief of Naval Personnel Jan.-Aug. 1967; Vice-Chief of Naval Staff 1967–68; Commander-in-Chief, Far East 1969–70; Chief of Naval Staff and First Sea Lord 1970–71; Chief of the Defence Staff 1971–74; Chair. North Atlantic Mil. Cttee. 1974–77; Pres. Sea Cadet Asscn. 1977–84; Vice-Pres. Royal United Service Inst. 1977; Pres. Friends of Osborne House 1980; Chair. Partridge, Muir & Warren 1982–; Pres. British Maritime League 1982–85; Liveryman, Worshipful Company of Shipwrights 1973; Freeman of the City of London 1974. *Publications:* No Soft Options 1978, Sea Power 1982. *Leisure interests:* golf, shooting. *Address:* Cass Cottage, Hyde, Fordingbridge, Hampshire, SP6 2QH, England.

HILLS, Carla Anderson, A.B., LL.D.; American government official and lawyer; b. 3 Jan. 1934, Los Angeles; d. of Carl and Edith (Hume) Anderson; m. Roderick Maltman Hills 1958; one s. three d.; ed. Stanford Univ., Calif., St. Hilda's Coll., Oxford, U.K., Yale Law School; Asst. U.S. Attorney, Civil Div., Los Angeles, Calif. 1958–61; Partner, Munger, Tolles, Hills & Rickershauser (law firm) 1962–74; Adjunct Prof., School of Law, Univ. of Calif., Los Angeles 1972; Asst. Attorney-Gen. Civil Div., U.S. Dept. of Justice 1974–75; Sec. of Housing and Urban Devt. 1975–77; Partner, Latham, Watkins & Hills (law firm) 1978–86, Weil, Gotshal and Manges, Washington 1986–88, Mudge Rose Gutherie Alexander & Ferdon 1994; Chair., C.E.O. Hills & Co. 1993–; U.S. Trade Rep., Exec. Office of the Pres. 1989–93; Co-Chair. Alliance to Save Energy 1977–89; Vice-Chair. Bar of Supreme Court of the U.S., Calif. State and D.C. Bars, Council Section of Anti-trust Law, American Bar Asscn. 1974, American Law Inst. 1974–, Fed. Bar Asscn. (Los Angeles Chapter, Pres. 1963), Women Lawyers Asscn. (Pres. 1964), Los Angeles County Bar Asscn., Chair. of various cttees. including Standing Cttee. on Discipline, Calif. 1970–74; mem. Bd. of Dirs. Int. Business Machines, The Signal Co. Inc., Standard Oil Co. of Calif., American Airlines Inc., Int. Exec. Service Corpns., Time-Warner Inc. 1993–, Chevron Corp. 1993–; mem. Carnegie Comm. on the Future of Public Broadcasting 1977–78, Sloan Comm. on Govt. and Higher Educ. 1977–79, Advisory Cttee. Woodrow Wilson School of Public and Int. Affairs 1977–80, Yale Univ. Council 1977–80, Fed. Accounting Standards Advisory Council 1978–80, Trilateral Comm. 1977–82, 1993–, American Cttee. on East-West Accord 1977–79, Int. Foundation for Cultural Cooperation and Devt. 1977, Editorial Bd., National Law Journal 1978, Calif. Gov.'s Council of Econ. Policy Advisers 1993–, Council on Foreign Relations 1993–; Vice-Chair. Nat. Cttee. on U.S.-China Relations 1993–; mem. bd. dirs. U.S.-China Business Council, Vice-Chair. 1995–; Contributing Editor, Legal Times 1978–88; Fellow, American Bar Foundation 1975; Trustee, Pomona Coll. 1974–79, Norton Simon Museum of Art 1976–80, Brookings Inst. 1977, Univ. of S. Calif. 1977–79; Advisor, Annenberg School of Communications, Univ. of S. Calif. 1977–78; Chair. Urban Inst. 1983; Dir. Time Warner 1993; Hon. degrees from Pepperdine Univ., Calif. 1975, Washington Univ., Mo. 1977, Mills Coll., Calif. 1977, Lake Forest Coll. 1978. *Publications:* Federal Civil Practice (co-author) 1961, Antitrust Adviser (editor and co-author) 1971. *Leisure interest:* tennis. *Address:* Hills and Hills, 1200 19th Street, N.W., Suite 201, Washington, DC 20036; 3125 Chain Bridge Road, N.W., Washington, DC 20016, U.S.A. (Home).

HILLS, Sir Graham (John), Kt., PH.D., F.R.S.E., F.R.S.C.; British university vice-chancellor; b. 9 April 1926; s. of Albert Hills and Marjorie Harper; m. 1st Brenda Stubbington 1950 (died 1974); one s. three d.; m. 2nd Mary J. McNaughton 1980; ed. Birkbeck Coll. London; lecturer in Physical Chem. Imperial Coll. London 1949–62; Prof. of Physical Chem. Univ. of Southampton 1962–80; Prin. and Vice-Chancellor, Univ. of Strathclyde 1980–91; Scottish Gov. of BBC 1989–94; Visiting Prof. Univ. of W. Ont. 1968, Case Western Reserve Univ. 1969, Univ. of Buenos Aires 1977; Pres. Soc. of Chemical Industry 1991–93; other professional appts.; Hon. Fellow Birkbeck Coll. London, Univ. of N.E. London; Hon. Sc.D. (Tech. Univ. of Łódź); Hon. D.Sc. (Southampton, Waterloo, Lisbon); Hon. LL.D. (Glasgow); Hon. Medal, Univ. of Pavia 1988; Commdr. Polish Order of Merit, Royal Norwegian Order of Merit; Hon. F.C.S.D. 1996. *Publications:* Reference Electrodes 1961, Polarography 1964; contributions to Faraday Transactions. *Leisure interests:* country life, European political history, rocking the boat. *Address:* 2 Holm Burn Place, Inverness, IV1 2WT, Scotland.

HILLY, Francis Billy; Solomon Islands politician; b. 1947; ed. Univ. of S. Pacific; joined pre-independence govt. working under Solomon Mamaloni (q.v.); later worked for a pvt. co. in Gizo; mem. Parl. 1976–84, 1993–; fmr. Premier of Western Prov.; Prime Minister of the Solomon Islands 1993–94. *Address:* c/o Office of the Prime Minister, Legakiki Ridge, Honiara, Solomon Islands.

HILSMAN, Roger, PH.D.; American diplomatist and educator; b. 23 Nov. 1919, Waco, Texas; s. of Colonel Roger Hilsman and Emma Prendergast Hilsman; m. Eleanor Hoyt 1946; two s. two d.; ed. West Point and Yale Univ.; U.S. Army 1943–53; Center for Int. Studies, Princeton Univ. 1953–56; Chief Foreign Affairs Div. of Legislative Reference Service, Library of Congress 1956–58, Deputy Dir. (for Research) 1958–61; Dir. Bureau of Intelligence and Research, Dept. of State 1961–63; Asst. Sec. of State for Far Eastern Affairs 1963–64; Prof. of Govt., Columbia Univ. 1964–89, now Prof. Emer.; Fulbright Distinguished Lecturer to India 1985; mem. Nat. Security Educ. Bd. 1994–. *Publications:* Strategic Intelligence and National Decisions 1956, To Move a Nation 1967, The Politics of Policy Making in Defense and Foreign Affairs 1971, The Crouching Future, International Politics and U.S. Foreign Policy, A Forecast 1975, To Govern America 1979, The Politics of Governing America 1985, Conceptual Models and the Politics of Policy Making 1986, American Guerrilla, My War behind Japanese Lines 1990, George Bush vs Saddam Hussein: Military Success! Political Failure? 1992, The Cuban Missile Crisis, The Struggle over Policy 1996, From Nuclear Military Strategy to a World Without War 1998; co-author: Military Policy and National Security 1956, Foreign Policy in the 60s 1965; contributor to Alliance Policy in the Cold War 1959, NATO and American Security 1959, The Guerrilla—and How to Fight Him 1962, Modern Guerrilla Warfare 1962. *Leisure interest:* designing toys. *Address:* 251 Hamburg Cove, Lyme, CT 06371, U.S.A. (Home). *Telephone:* (860) 434-9912.

HILSUM, Cyril, C.B.E., PH.D., F.ENG., F.INST.P., F.I.E.E., F.I.E.E.E., F.R.S.; British research scientist; b. 17 May 1925, London; s. of Ben and Ada Hilsum; m. Betty Hilsum 1947 (died 1987); one d. (one d. deceased); ed. Raines School, London, and Univ. Coll., London; H.Q. Admiralty 1945–47; Admiralty Research Lab., Teddington 1947–50; Services Electronics Research Lab., Baldock 1950–64; Royal Signals and Radar Establishments, Malvern 1964–83; Visiting Prof., Univ. Coll., London 1988–; Chief Scientist, Gen. Electric Co. (GEC) Research Labs. 1983–85; Dir. of Research, GEC PLC 1985–92, Corporate Research Adviser 1992–96; Pres. Inst. of Physics 1988–90; mem. Science and Eng. Research Council 1984–88; recipient of several awards; Hon. D.Eng. (Sheffield) 1992, (Nottingham Trent) 1998. *Publications:* Semiconducting III-V Compounds 1961; over 100 scientific and technical papers. *Leisure interests:* tennis, chess, ballroom dancing. *Address:* 12 Eastglade, Moss Lane, Pinner, Middx., HA5 3AN, England. *Telephone:* 0181-866 8323. *Fax:* 0181-933 6114.

HILTON, Janet; British musician; b. 1 Jan. 1945, Liverpool; d. of H. Hilton and E. Hilton; m. David Richardson 1968; two s. (one deceased) one d.; ed. Belvedere School, Liverpool, Royal Manchester Coll. of Music, Vienna Konservatorium; BBC concerto début 1963; appearances as clarinet soloist with maj. British orchestras including Royal Liverpool Philharmonic, Scottish Nat., Scottish Chamber, City of Birmingham Symphony, Bournemouth Symphony, Bournemouth Sinfonietta, City of London Sinfonia, BBC Scottish and Welsh Symphony, BBC Philharmonic; guest at Edin., Aldeburgh, Bath, Cheltenham, City of London Festivals, Henry Wood Promenade concerts;

appearances throughout Europe and N. America; Prin. Clarinet Scottish Chamber Orchestra 1974–80, Kent Opera 1984–88; teacher Royal Scottish Acad. of Music and Drama 1974–80, Royal Northern Coll. of Music 1983–87; Head of Woodwind, Birmingham Conservatoire 1992–; Head of Woodwind, Royal Coll. of Music, London 1998–; Prof., Univ. of Cen. England (U.C.E.) 1993; Dir. Camerata Wind Soloists; several recordings for Chandos, including all Weber's music for clarinet with the C.B.S.O., Lindsay Quartet and Keith Swallow, the Neilsen and Copland Concertos with the S.N.O., Stanford Clarinet Concerto with Ulster Orchestra, Mozart Clarinet Quintet with the Lindsay Quartet 1998; dedicatee of works by Iain Hamilton, John McCabe, Edward Harper, Elizabeth Maconchy, Alun Hoddinott, Malcolm Arnold. *Leisure interests:* cookery, reading. *Address:* Holly House, East Downs Road, Bowdon, Altrincham, Cheshire, WA14 2LH, England. *Telephone:* 0161-928 3471.

HIMMELFARB, Gertrude, PH.D., F.B.A.; American professor of history and author; b. 8 Aug. 1922; d. of Max Himmelfarb and Bertha (Lerner) Himmelfarb; m. Irving Kristol 1942; one s. one d.; ed. Brooklyn Coll. and Univ. of Chicago; Distinguished Prof. of History, Graduate School, City Univ. New York 1965–88, Prof. Emer. 1988–; Fellow, American Philosophical Soc., American Acad. of Arts and Sciences, Royal Historical Soc., etc.; many public and professional appts.; Rockefeller Foundation Award 1962–63; Guggenheim Fellow 1955–56, 1957–58, Nat. Endowment for the Humanities Fellowship 1968–69, American Council of Learned Socs. Fellowship 1972–73, Woodrow Wilson Int. Center Fellowship 1976–77, Rockefeller Foundation, Humanities Fellowship 1980–81 and other fellowships; numerous hon. degrees including Hon. D.Hum.Litt. (Boston) 1987, (Yale) 1990, Hon. D.Litt. (Smith Coll.) 1977. *Publications:* Lord Acton: A Study in Conscience and Politics 1952, Darwin and the Darwinian Revolution 1959, Victorian Minds 1968, On Liberty and Liberalism: The Case of John Stuart Mill 1975, The Idea of Poverty 1984, Marriage and Morals Among the Victorians 1986, The New History and the Old 1987, Poverty and Compassion: The Moral Imagination of the Late Victorians 1991, On Looking Into the Abyss: Untimely Thoughts on Culture and Society 1994, The De-Moralization of Society From Victorian Virtues to Modern Values 1995. *Address:* City University of New York, 33 West 42nd Street, New York, NY 10036 (Office); 2510 Virginia Avenue, N.W., Washington, DC 20637, U.S.A. *Telephone:* (202) 338-7207.

HINAULT, Bernard; French cyclist; b. 14 Nov. 1954, Yffiniac, Côtes du Nord; s. of Joseph and Lucie (Guernion) Hinault; m. Martine Lessard 1974; two s.; competitive cycling début 1971; French junior champion 1972; French Champion 1978; World Champion 1980; winner, Tour de France 1978, 1979, 1981, 1982, 1985, Tour d'Italie 1980, 1982, 1985, Tour d'Espagne 1978, 1983, Grand Prix des Nations 1978, 1982, 1984, Luis Puig Trophy 1986, Coors Classic, U.S.A. 1986 and many other int. racing events; retd. from racing 1986; Technical Adviser, Tour de France 1986–; Sports Dir. French team 1988–; Dir.-Gen. Ouest Levure 1992–; Chevalier, Légion d'honneur, Ordre Nat. du Mérite. *Publications:* Moi, Bernard Hinault (with others) 1979, Le Pentolou des souvenirs, Cyclisme sur route, technique, tactique, entraînement, Vélo tout terrain, découverte, technique et entraînement. *Address:* Ouest Levure, 7 rue de la Sauvaie, Z1 Sud-est, 35000 Rennes, France.

HINCH, Edward John, PH.D., F.R.S.; British academic; b. 4 March 1947, Peterborough; s. of Joseph Edward Hinch and Mary Grace Hinch (née Chandler); m. Christine Bridges 1969; one s. one d.; ed. Cambridge Univ.; Fellow Trinity Coll., Cambridge 1971–; asst. lecturer Cambridge Univ. 1972–75, lecturer 1975–94, Reader in Fluid Mechanics 1994–98, Prof. 1998–; Chevalier, Order nat. du Mérite 1997. *Publications:* Perturbation Methods 1991, various papers in learned journals on fluid mechanics and its application. *Address:* Trinity College, Cambridge, CB2 1TQ, England. *Telephone:* (01223) 338427. *Fax:* (01223) 338564.

HINCHCLIFFE, Peter Robert Mossom, C.V.O., C.M.G., M.A.; British diplomatist (retd.); b. 9 April 1937, Mahableshwar, India; s. of Peter Hinchcliffe and Jeannie Hinchcliffe; m. Archbold Harriet Siddall 1965; three d.; ed. Radley Coll., Trinity Coll., Dublin; British Army 1955–57; H.M.O.C.S. Aden Protectorate 1961–67; First Sec. FCO 1969–71; mem. U.K. Mission to UN 1971–74; Head of Chancery, British Embassy, Kuwait 1974–76, FCO 1976–78, Deputy High Commr., Dar es Salaam 1978–81, Consul Gen., Dubai 1981–85; Head of Information Dept. FCO 1985–87, Amb. to Kuwait 1987–90; High Commr. in Zambia 1990–93; Amb. to Jordan 1993–97; Hon. Fellow, Edin. Univ.; Senior Research Fellow, Queen's Univ., Belfast. *Publication:* Time to Kill Sparrows (anthology of diplomatic verse) 1998. *Leisure interests:* golf, tennis, cricket. *Address:* Antrim House, Kirk Lane, Hutton, Berwick upon Tweed, TD15 1TS, England. *Telephone:* (01289) 386121. *Fax:* (01289) 386122.

HINCK, Walter, D.PHIL.; German professor of language and literature; b. 8 March 1922, Selsingen; s. of Johann and Anna (née Steffens) Hinck;. m. Sigrid Graupe 1957; one d.; ed. Univ. of Göttingen; Prof. of Modern German Language and Literature, Literary Criticism, Univ. of Cologne 1964–; mem. Rheinisch-Westfälischen Akad. der Wissenschaften 1974–, (Vice-Pres. 1986–87), Sektion Bundesrepublik Deutschland des Internationalen PEN-Clubs 1986–. *Publications:* Die Dramaturgie des späten Brecht 1959, Das deutsche Lustspiel des 17. und 18. Jahrhunderts und die italienische Komödie 1965, Die deutsche Ballade von Bürger bis Brecht 1968, Das moderne Drama in Deutschland 1973, Von Heine zu Brecht—Lyrik im Geschichtsprozess 1978, Goethe—Mann des Theaters 1982, Germanistik als Literaturkritik 1983, Heinrich Böll: Ausgewählte Erzählungen 1984, Das Gedicht als Spiegel der Dichter 1985, Theater der Hoffnung, Von der Aufklärung bis zur Gegenwart 1988, Die Wunde Deutschland, Heinrich Heines Dichtung 1990, Walter Jens. Un homme de lettres 1993, Magie und Tagtraum. Das Selbstbild des Dichters in der deutschen Lyrik 1994, Geschichtsdichtung 1995, Im Wechsel der Zeiten: Leben und Literatur (autobiog.) 1998. *Address:* Am Hammergraben 13/15, 51503 Rösrath, (Hoffnungsthal) bei Cologne, Germany. *Telephone:* 02205-5147.

HINDE, Robert Aubrey, D.PHIL., SC.D., F.R.S.; British biologist and psychologist; b. 26 Oct. 1923, Norwich; s. of Ernest B. Hinde and Isabella Hinde; m. 1st Hester Cecily Coutts (divorced); two s. two d.; m. 2nd Joan Stevenson 1971; two d.; ed. Oundle School, St. John's Coll., Cambridge, Balliol Coll., Oxford; pilot, R.A.F. Coastal Command 1940–45; Curator, Ornithological Field Station, Dept. of Zoology, Univ. of Cambridge 1960–64, Fellow of St. John's Coll. 1951–54, 1958–, Master 1989–94; Royal Soc. Research Prof. 1963–89; Hon. Dir. MRC Unit of Devt. and Integration of Behaviour 1970–89; Hitchcock Prof., Univ. of Calif. 1979; Foreign Hon. mem. A.A.A.S. 1974; Hon. Fellow American Ornithologists' Union 1976; Hon. Foreign Assoc. N.A.S. 1978; Hon. Fellow Royal Coll. of Psychiatry 1988; mem. Acad. Europaea 1990; numerous awards; Hon. Fellow, British Psychological Soc. 1981; Hon. Fellow Balliol Coll. Oxford 1986, Trinity Coll. Dublin 1990; Hon. Sc.D. (Univ. Libre, Brussels) 1974, (Nanterre) 1978, (Gothenborg) 1991; Dr. h.c. (Stirling) 1991, (Edin.) 1992, (W. Ont.) 1996, (Oxford) 1998; Croonian Lecturer (Royal Soc.) 1990, Frink Medal, Zoological Soc. of London 1992, Royal Medal, Royal Soc. 1996, Soc.'s Medal, Asscn. for the Study of Animal Behaviour 1997. *Publications:* Animal Behaviour: A Synthesis of Ethology and Comparative Psychology 1966, Social Behaviour and its Development in Sub-human Primates 1972, Biological Bases of Human Social Behaviour 1974, Towards Understanding Relationships 1979, Ethology 1982, Individuals, Relationships and Culture 1987; Ed. Bird Vocalizations 1969, Primate Social Behaviour 1983; Jt. Ed. Short-term Changes in Neural Activity and Behaviour 1970, Constraints on Learning 1973, Growing Points in Ethology 1976, Social Relationships and Cognitive Development 1985, Relationships Within Families (Ed.) Mutual Influences 1988, Aggression and War: Their Biological and Social Bases (Ed.) 1988, Education for Peace (Ed.), Co-operation and Prosocial Behaviour (Jt. Ed.) 1991, The Institution of War (Ed.) 1991, War: a cruel necessity? (Jt. Ed.) 1994, Relationships: a dialectical perspective 1997,Why Gods Persist 1999; numerous articles in learned journals. *Leisure interests:* ornithology, reading. *Address:* St. John's College, Cambridge, CB2 1TP, England. *Telephone:* (01223) 339356. *Fax:* (01223) 337720.

HINDE, Thomas (see Chitty, Sir Thomas Wiles).

HINDERY, Leo Joseph, Jr., M.B.A.; American business executive; b. 31 Oct. 1947, Springfield, Ill.; s. of Leo Joseph Hindery and E. Marie Whitener; m. Deborah Diane Sale 1980; one s.; ed. Seattle Univ. and Stanford Univ.; U.S. Army 1968–70; Asst. Treasurer Utah Int., San Francisco 1971–80; treasurer Natomas Co., San Francisco 1980–82; Exec. Vice-Pres. Finance Jefferies and Co., L.A. 1982–83; Chief Finance Officer A.G. Becker Paribas, New York 1983–85; Chief Officer Planning and Finance Chronicle Publishing Co., San Francisco 1985–88; Man. Gen. Partner Intermedia Partners, San Francisco 1988–; Pres. TCI Cable Vision 1998–; mem. Bd. dirs. DMX Inc., NETCOM On-Line Comm. Services Inc., Nat. Cable TV Asscn., Cable Telecommunications Asscn., C-Span. *Leisure interest:* golf. *Address:* TCI Cable Vision, 1855 Folsom Street, No. 546, San Francisco, CA 94103, U.S.A.

HINDLIP, 6th Baron (cr. 1886); **Sir Charles Henry Allsopp;** British business executive; b. 5 April 1940; s. of late Baron Hindlip and of Cecily Valentine Jane Borwick; m. Fiona Victoria Jean Atherley McGowan 1968; one s. three d.; ed. Eton Coll.; served in Coldstream Guards 1959–62; joined Christie's 1962, Gen. Man. New York 1965–70, Chair. 1996–; Dir. Christie Manson & Wood 1970–, Deputy Chair. 1985–86, Chair. 1986–96. *Leisure interests:* painting, shooting. *Address:* Christie's, 8 King Street, St. James's, London, SW1Y 6QT (Office); 18 Chester Square, London, SW1W 9HS; The Cedar House, Inkpen, Berks., RG15 0DT, England. *Telephone:* 0171-839 9060 (Office); 0171-730 8844.

HINDS, Samuel Archibald Anthony, B.SC.; Guyanese politician; b. 27 Dec. 1943, Mahaicony, E. Coast, Demerara; m.; three c.; ed. Queen's Coll. Georgetown and Univ. of New Brunswick; various positions with Bauxite Co., Linden, Guyana 1967–92; mem. Science and Industry Cttee. Nat. Science Research Council 1973–76; fmr. Chair. Guyanese Action for Reform and Democracy (GUARD); Prime Minister of Guyana 1992–, also Minister of Public Works. *Address:* Office of the Prime Minister, Georgetown, Guyana.

HINE, Air Chief Marshal Sir Patrick, G.C.B., G.B.E., F.R.AE.S., C.B.I.M.; British air force officer; b. 14 July 1932, Chandlers Ford, Hants.; s. of Eric Graham Hine and Cecile Grace Hine (née Philippe); m. Jill Adèle Gardner 1956; three s.; ed. Sherborne House Preparatory School 1937–41, Peter Symonds School, Winchester 1942–49; fighter pilot and mem. R.A.F. 'Black Arrows' and 'Blue Diamonds' Formation Aerobatic Teams 1957–62; Commdr. No. 92 Squadron 1962–64 and 17 Squadron 1970–71, R.A.F. Germany Harrier Force 1974–75; Dir. R.A.F. Public Relations 1975–77; Asst. Chief of Air Staff for Policy 1979–83; C.-in-C. R.A.F. Germany and Commdr. NATO's 2nd Allied Tactical Air Force 1983–85; Vice-Chief of the Defence Staff 1985–87; Air mem. for Supply and Organisation, Air Force Bd. 1987–88; Air

Officer Commanding-in-Chief, Strike Command, C.-in-C. U.K. Air Forces 1988–91; Jt. Commdr. British Forces in Gulf Conflict, Aug. 1990–April 1991; with reserve force, rank of Flying Officer 1991–; Mil. Adviser to British Aerospace 1992–; King of Arms, Order of the British Empire 1997–. *Leisure interests:* golf, mountain walking, skiing, photography, caravanning, travel.

HINGIS, Martina; Swiss tennis player; b. 30 Sept. 1980, Košice, Czechoslovakia; d. of Mélanie Hingis; competed in first tennis tournament 1985; family moved to Switzerland at age seven; winner French Open Jr. championship 1993, Wimbledon Jr. Championship 1994; has competed in the Italian Open, U.S. Open, Chase Championship (N.Y.) and Wimbledon; won first professional tournament Filderstadt (Germany) 1996; winner Australian Open 1997 (youngest winner of a Grand Slam title in Twentieth Century), U.S. Open 1997; Wimbledon Singles Champion 1997, winner Australian Open 1998. *Leisure interests:* horse-riding, roller-blading.

HINO, Ichiro; Japanese politician and lawyer; fmr. lawyer; Minister of Posts and Telecommunications Jan.–Oct. 1996; mem. House of Reps.; mem. Social Democratic Party of Japan (SDPJ). *Address:* c/o Social Democratic Party of Japan, 1-8-1, Nagata-cho, Chiyoda-ku, Tokyo 100, Japan.

HINSON, David R.; American airline executive; m. Ursula Hinson; three c.; fighter pilot U.S.N. 1956–60, airline and eng. pilot 1960–72; founder, Dir. Midway Airlines Inc. 1979–, Chair., C.E.O. 1985–; Admin. Fed. Aviation Admin. 1993–96; Dir. several cos. *Address:* Midway Airlines Inc., 5700 Cicero Avenue, Chicago, IL 60638, U.S.A.

HINTEREGGER, Gerald; Austrian United Nations official; m.; two s.; joined Austrian diplomatic service 1957; Deputy Chief of Mission, Washington, D.C. 1965–70; Chef de Cabinet, Minister of Foreign Affairs 1970–75; Amb. to Spain 1975–78, to U.S.S.R. 1978–81; Sec.-Gen. for Foreign Affairs and Perm. Rep. to UN, Vienna 1981–87; Exec. Sec. UN Econ. Comm. for Europe (ECE) 1987–93; Acting UN High Commr. for Refugees 1989. *Address:* c/o United Nations Economic Commission for Europe, Palais des Nations, 1211 Geneva 10, Switzerland.

HIQUILY, Philippe; French sculptor; b. 27 March 1925, Paris; s. of Jules Hiquily and Madeleine Velvet; m. Meei-Yen Wo 1985; two s.; ed. secondary school and Ecole Nat. Supérieure des Beaux-Arts Paris; mil. service in Indochina 1943–47; since 1951 has concentrated on sculpture in metal, influenced by primitive art; Chevalier des Arts et des Lettres; Ordre Royal de Louang-Brabang (Laos). *Leisure interests:* fishing, agriculture, viticulture. *Address:* 21 rue Olivier-Noyer, Paris, France. *Telephone:* 45.39.30.25.

HIRAI, Takushi; Japanese politician; b. 1931; previous posts include Parl. Vice-Minister of Int. Trade and Industry and of Justice; Chair. Cttee. on Foreign Affairs, House of Councillors; Dir. Judicial Affairs Div., Liberal Democratic Party (LDP) Policy Research Council; Minister of Labour 1986–87; Dir. House of Councillors Cttee. on the Budget 1990–. *Address:* c/o Liberal Democratic Party, 1-11-23, Nagata-cho, Chiyoda-ku, Tokyo 100, Japan.

HIRAMATSU, Morihiko, LL.B.; Japanese civil servant; b. 12 March, 1924, Oita; s. of late Oriji Hiramatsu and Kun Hiramatsu; m. 1st Chizuko Ueda 1949; m. 2nd Teruko Mihara 1976; two d.; ed. Kumamoto No. V. High School and Tokyo Univ.; employee Ministry of Commerce and Industry 1949–64; Dir. Industrial Pollution Div. Enterprises Bureau, Ministry of Int. Trade and Industry 1964–65, Petroleum Planning Div. Mining Bureau 1965–67, Export Insurance Div. Trade Promotion Bureau 1967–69, Electronics Policy Div. Heavy Industries Bureau 1969–73, Co-ordination Office Basic Industries Bureau 1973–74; Counsellor Secr. Land Agency 1974–75; Vice-Gov. of Oita Pref. 1975–79, Gov. 1979–; Chair. Kyushu Govs'. Asscn. 1991–; Ramon Magsaysay Award for Govt. Service (Philippines) 1995; Gran Cruz da Legião de Honra Giuseppe Garibaldi (Brazil) 1987. *Publications:* Talks on Software, Exhortations to One Village One Product, Challenging Technopolis, Age of Decentralised Management, Let's Try What's Impossible in Tokyo, Think Globally and Act Locally, Locally Generated Ideas. *Leisure interests:* reading, golf, early morning walks. *Address:* Governor's Official Residence, 8-20 Niage-machi, Oita City, Oita Prefecture 870-0046, Japan. *Telephone:* 097-532-2001.

HIRANUMA, Takeo; Japanese politician; fmr. Parl. Vice-Minister of Finance; Deputy Chair. LDP Policy Research Council, Chair. LDP Nat. Org. Cttee.; mem. House of Reps.; Minister of Transport 1995–96. *Address:* c/o Liberal Democratic Party, 1-11-23, Nagata-cho, Chiyoda-ku, Tokyo 100, Japan.

HIROSE, Shin-ichi, B.LAWS; Japanese business executive; b. 25 Jan. 1913; ed. Tokyo Imperial Univ.; Govt. official 1938–65, Vice-Minister, Ministry of Transport 1964–65, Senior Man. Dir. of Nippon Express Co. Ltd. 1968–72, Exec. Vice Pres. 1972–76, then Pres. 1976. Cttee. of Overall Nat. Land Devt. Council, 1975–; Dir., Japan Fed. of Employers' Asscns., 1975–, Fed. of Economic Orgs., 1975–. *Address:* 1-29-12, Amanuma, Suginami-ku, Tokyo, Japan (Home).

HIRSCH, Georges-François; French opera administrator; b. 5 Oct. 1944, Paris; s. of George Hirsch; stage-hand, Théâtre des Capucines 1960; later stage man. Théâtre de la Culture de l'Ile de France; Dir. Théâtre de Limoges 1969–74; directed various productions especially in U.S.A. 1974–79; Dance Admin. Paris Opéra 1979–82; mem. directing team, RTLN 1982–83; Dir. Théâtre des Champs-Elysées 1983–89; Gen. Admin. Opéra Bastille 1989–92, Opéra de Paris (Garnier Bastille) 1991–92; mem. council CSA 1993–96; Gen. Dir. Orchestre de Paris 1996–; Officier, Légion d'honneur; Chevalier, Ordre Nat. du Mérite; Commdr. des Arts et Lettres. *Address:* Orchestre de Paris, 252, rue du Faubourg Saint-Honoré, 75008 Paris, France. *Telephone:* 01-45-61-65-60. *Fax:* 01-42-89-24-49.

HIRSCH, Judd, B.S.; American actor; b. 15 March 1935, New York; s. of Joseph S. Hirsch and Sally Kitzis; m. Bonni Chalkin 1992; ed. City Coll. of New York; appearances in Barefoot in the Park 1966, Knock Knock 1975 (Drama Desk Award), Scuba Duba 1967–69, King of the United States 1972, Mystery Play 1972, Hot L Baltimore 1972–73, Prodigal 1973, Chapter Two 1977–78, Talley's Folly 1979 (Obie Award), The Seagull 1983, I'm Not Rappaport 1985–86 (Tony Award), Conversations with my Father (Tony Award) 1992, A Thousand Clowns 1996, Below the Belt 1996, Death of a Salesman 1997; has appeared in numerous television plays, series, films etc; mem. Screen Actors Guild. *Films include:* King of the Gypsies 1978, Ordinary People 1980, Without a Trace 1983, Teachers 1984, The Goodbye People 1986, Running on Empty 1988, Independence Day 1996. *Address:* c/o J. Wolfe Provident Financial Management, 10395 West Olympic Boulevard, Los Angeles, CA 90064, U.S.A.

HIRSCH, Leon; American business executive; b. 20 July 1927, Bronx, New York; s. of late Roslyn Hirsch and Isidor Hirsch; m. 2nd Turi Josefsen 1969; two s. one d. from 1st m.; ed. Bronx School of Science; Chair. and C.E.O. United States Surgical Corpn. 1964–; inventor and developer of Auto Suture surgical staplers; Chair. Advisory Bd. American Soc. of Colon and Rectal Surgeons Research Foundation; mem. American Business Conf.; Dir. Americans for Medical Progress; mem. Bd. of Trustees, Boston Univ.; Gordon Grand Fellow, Yale Univ.; Surgery Award Nessim Habif, Univ. of Geneva. *Leisure interests:* fishing, horseback riding, skiing, tennis. *Address:* 150 Glover Avenue, Norwalk, CT 06856, U.S.A. *Telephone:* (203) 845-1401. *Fax:* (203) 845-4133.

HIRSCH, Sir Peter Bernhard, Kt., PH.D., F.R.S.; British professor of metallurgy; b. 16 Jan. 1925, Berlin; s. of Ismar Hirsch and Regina Meyersohn; m. Mabel A. Kellar (née Stephens) 1959; one step-s. one step-d.; ed. Univ. of Cambridge; Lecturer in Physics, Univ. of Cambridge 1959–64, Reader 1964–66; Fellow, Christ's Coll., Cambridge 1960–66, Hon. Fellow 1978; Isaac Wolfson Prof. of Metallurgy, Univ. of Oxford 1966–92, Prof. Emer. 1992, Fellow, St. Edmund Hall 1966–92, Fellow Emer. 1992–; Chair. Metallurgy and Materials Cttee., Science Research Council 1970–73; mem. Council, Inst. of Physics 1968–72, Inst. of Metals 1968–73, Electricity Supply Research Council 1969–82, Council for Scientific Policy 1970–72, Metals Soc. Council 1978–82, Council Royal Soc. 1977–79; mem. Bd. (part-time) UKAEA 1982–94, Chair. 1982–84; mem. Tech. Advisory Cttee. Advent 1982–89; Dir. Cogent 1985–89, Rolls-Royce Assocs. 1994–98; mem. Tech. Advisory Cttee. Monsanto Electronic Materials 1985–88; Chair. Isis Innovation Ltd. 1988–96, Tech. Advisory Group on Structural Integrity 1993–, Materials and Processes Advisory Bd. Rolls-Royce PLC 1996–; Hon. Fellow, St. Catharine's Coll., Cambridge 1982, Royal Microscopical Soc. 1977, Japan Soc. of Electron Microscopy 1979; Assoc. mem. Royal Acad. of Sciences, Letters and Fine Arts of Belgium; Hon. D.Sc. (Newcastle Univ.) 1979, (City Univ.) 1979, (Northwestern Univ.) 1982, (East Anglia Univ.) 1983, Hon. D.Eng. (Liverpool) 1991, (Birmingham) 1993); Rosenhain Medal, Inst. of Metals 1961, Boys' Prize, Inst. of Physics and Physical Soc. 1962, Clamer Medal, Franklin Inst. 1970, Wihuri Int. Prize 1971, Hughes Medal of the Royal Soc. 1973, Platinum Medal of the Metals Soc. 1976, Royal Medal of Royal Soc. 1977, A.A. Griffith Medal, Inst. of Materials 1979, Arthur Von Hippel Award, Materials Research Soc. 1983, Wolf Prize in Physics 1984, Distinguished Scientist Award, Electron Microscopy Soc. of America 1986, Holweck Prize, Inst. of Physics and French Physical Soc. 1988, Gold Medal, Japan Inst. of Metals 1989, Acta Metallurgica Gold Medal 1997. *Publications:* Electron Microscopy of Thin Crystals (jt. author) 1965, The Physics of Metals, 2, Defects (ed.) 1975 and numerous articles in learned journals. *Leisure interest:* walking. *Address:* Department of Materials, University of Oxford, Parks Road, Oxford, OX1 3PH (Office); 104A Lonsdale Road, Oxford, OX2 7ET, England (Home). *Telephone:* (01865) 273773 (Office). *Fax:* (01865) 273764.

HIRSCH, Robert Paul; French actor; b. 26 July 1925; s. of Joachim Hirsch and Germaine Anne Raybois; mem. Comédie Française 1952–74; Prix Jean-Jacques Gautier 1987; numerous stage appearances include: La belle aventure, Le prince travesti, Monsieur de Pourceaugnac, Les temps difficiles, La double inconstance, Le dindon, Amphitryon, Britannicus, Crime et Châtiment, La faim et la soif, Monsieur Amilcar, L'abîme et la visite, le Piège, Deburau, Chacun sa vérité, Les dégourdis de la 11e 1986, Mon Faust 1987, Moi, Feuerbach 1989, le Misanthrope 1992, Une Folie 1993. *Films include:* Le dindon, Votre dévoué Blake, En effeuillant la marguerite, Notre-Dame de Paris, Maigret et l'affaire Saint-Fiacre, 125 rue Montmartre, Par question le samedi, Monnaie de singe, Martin soldat, Toutes folles de lui, les Cracks, Appelez-moi Mathilde, Traitement de choc, Chobizenesse, La crime 1983, Hiver 54 1989; Officier des Arts et des Lettres, Jean-Jacques Goutier Prize 1987, César best supporting actor (for Hiver 54) 1990, Brig. d'honneur 1992. *Address:* Agence JFPM, 11 rue Chanez, 75016 Paris; 1 place du Palais Bourbon, 75007 Paris, France.

HIRSCH BALLIN, Ernst; Netherlands politician and lawyer; b. 15 Dec. 1950; s. of Ernst D. Hirsch Ballin and Maria Koppe; m. Pauline van de Grift

1974; two c.; mem. Faculty of Law, Amsterdam Univ. 1974–77; Legal Expert, Ministry of Justice 1977–81; Prof. of Constitutional and Admin. Law, Tilburg Univ. 1981–89, Prof. of Int. Law 1994–; Minister of Justice and Netherlands Antillean and Aruban Affairs 1989–94; M.P. (Lower House) 1994–95, (Upper House) 1995–; Vice-Pres. Catholic Radio and TV Org. (KRO); Pres. Catholic Univ. of Theology, Utrecht; Christian Democrat. *Address:* Bruggenrijt 12, 5032 BH Tilburg, Netherlands. *Telephone:* (13) 4668246.

HIRSCHFIELD, Alan J., B.S., M.B.A.; American business executive; b. 10 Oct. 1935, Oklahoma City; ed. Univ. of Okla. and Harvard Univ.; Vice-Pres. Allen and Co. 1959–67; Vice-Pres. (Finance) and Dir. Warner Bros. Seven Arts Inc. 1967–68; Vice-Pres. and Dir. American Diversified Enterprises Inc. 1968–73; Pres. and C.E.O., Columbia Pictures Industries Inc. 1973–79; Consultant, Warner Communications Inc. 1979; Vice-Chair. and C.O.O., 20th Century-Fox Film Corpn. 1979–81, Chair., C.E.O. and C.O.O. 1981–84; C.E.O. Data Broadcasting Corpn. 1990–; Pres. Jackson Hole Land Trust, Cantel, Inc., CPP Belwin, Conservation Int., Trout Unlimited; Dir. Straight Arrow Publishing Co., John B. Coleman Co., Motion Picture Assen. of America, New York State Motion Picture and TV Advisory Bd., Film Soc. of Lincoln Cen., Will Rogers Memorial Fund, George Gustav Heye Center, Nat. Museum of the American Indian 1997–; Trustee, Cancer Research Inst. (Sloan-Kettering). *Address:* P.O. Box 7443, Jackson, WY 83002, U.S.A.

HIRSCHMAN, Albert Otto, DR.ECON.SC.; American political economist; b. 7 April 1915, Berlin, Germany; s. of Carl Hirschmann and Hedwig Marcuse; m. Sarah Chapiro 1941; two d.; ed. Lycée Français, Berlin, Ecole des Hautes Etudes Commerciales, Paris, London School of Econs., Univ. of Trieste, Italy; Research Fellow in Int. Econs., Berkeley, Calif., U.S.A. 1941–43; Economist, Fed. Reserve Bd., Washington, D.C. 1946–52; Econ. Adviser and Consultant, Bogotá, Colombia 1952–56; Prof. of Econs., Yale Univ. 1956–58, Columbia Univ. 1958–64, Harvard Univ. 1964–74; Prof. of Social Science, Inst. for Advanced Study, Princeton 1974–85, Prof. Emer. 1985–; mem. N.A.S.; Distinguished Fellow American Econ. Assen.; Corresp. Fellow British Acad.; Foreign mem. Accademia Nazionale dei Lincei, Italy; 15 hon. degrees and several prizes and awards including Toynbee Prize 1998. *Publications include:* National Power and the Structure of Foreign Trade 1945, The Strategy of Economic Development 1958, Journeys towards Progress: Studies of Economic Policy-Making in Latin America 1963, Development Projects Observed 1967, Exit, Voice, and Loyalty 1970, A Bias for Hope: Essays on Development and Latin America 1971, The Passions and the Interests 1977, Essays in Trespassing 1981, Shifting Involvements: Private Interest and Public Action 1982, Getting Ahead Collectively: Grassroots Experiences in Latin America 1984, Rival Views of Market Society and Other Recent Essays 1986, The Rhetoric of Reaction: Perversity, Futility, Jeopardy 1991, A Propensity to Self-Subversion 1995, Crossing Boundaries: Selected Writings and an Interview 1998. *Leisure interests:* art and art history. *Address:* c/o Institute for Advanced Study, Princeton, NJ 08540 (Office); 16 Newlin Road, Princeton, NJ, U.S.A. (Home). *Telephone:* (619) 734-8252 (Office). *Fax:* (609) 951 4457.

HIRST, Damien; British artist; b. 1965, Bristol; ed. Goldsmiths Coll., London; winner Turner Prize 1995; one-man exhbns. include: Inst. of Contemporary Arts (ICA), London 1991, Emmanuel Perrotin, Paris 1991, Cohen Gallery, New York 1992, Regen Projects, L.A. 1993, Galerie Jablonka, Cologne 1993, Milwaukee Art Museum 1994, Dallas Museum 1994, Kukje Gallery, Seoul 1995, White Cube/Jay Jopling, London 1995, Prix Eliette von Karajan 1995, Max Gandolph-Bibliothek, Salzburg, Gasogian Gallery, New York 1996, Bruno Bischofberger, Zurich 1997, Astrup Fearnley, Oslo 1997. Group exhbns. include: ICA, London 1989, Glasgow 1989, Building One, London 1990, The Cornerhouse, Manchester 1991, Serpentine Gallery, London 1991, 1993, 1994, Saatchi Collection, London 1992, Arolsen, Germany 1992, Rome 1992, Karsten Schubert, London 1992, Luis Campaña Gallery, Frankfurt 1992, Anthony d'Offay Gallery, London 1992, Barbara Gladstone Gallery, New York 1992, Tate Gallery, London 1992, Istanbul 1992, Galerie Metropol, Vienna 1992, Museum Fridericianum, Kassel 1993, Aperto Section, Venice 1993, Cohen Gallery, New York 1993, Nat. Gallery of Australia, Canberra 1994, Reina Sofia, Madrid 1994, Centre for Contemporary Art, Glasgow 1994, South Bank Centre, London 1994, Irish Museum of Modern Art, Dublin 1994, Kunsthaus, Zurich 1995, Contemporary Fine Arts, Berlin 1995, Museum Sztuki, Poland 1995, Tate Gallery (Turner Prize exhbn.), South Bank Centre, Waddington Galleries, London 1995, Musée d'Art Moderne, Jeu de Paume, Paris 1996, ICA, Hayward Gallery, London 1996, R.A., London 1997, Museum of Contemporary Art, Sydney 1997, Bohen Foundation, New York 1997 and many others. *Publication:* I Want to Spend the Rest of My Life Everywhere, One to One, Always, Forever 1997. *Address:* c/o Julia Royse, The White Cube Gallery, 44 Duke Street, St. James's, London, SW1Y 6DD, England. *Telephone:* 0171-930 5373. *Fax:* 0171-930 9973.

HIRST, Paul Heywood, M.A.; British academic; b. 10 Nov. 1927, Huddersfield; s. of Herbert Hirst and Winifred Hirst; ed. Huddersfield Coll., Trinity Coll. Cambridge and Univ. of London; school teacher of math. 1948–55; Lecturer and Tutor, Dept. of Educ., Univ. of Oxford 1955–59; Lecturer in Philosophy of Educ., Inst. of Educ., Univ. of London 1959–65; Prof. of Educ., King's Coll., Univ. of London 1965–71; Prof. of Educ. and Head Dept. of Educ., Univ. of Cambridge 1971–88, Emer. Prof. 1988–; Fellow Wolfson Coll., Cambridge 1971–88, Emer. Fellow 1988–; Visiting Prof., Univs. of B.C., Alberta, Malawi, Otago, Melbourne, Sydney, Puerto Rico, London 1988–; Vice-Chair. Cttee. for Educ., C.N.A.A. 1975–81, Chair. Cttee. for Research 1988–92; Chair. Univs. Council for Educ. of Teachers 1985–88; Hon. Vice-Pres. Philosophy of Educ. Soc. 1979–; mem. Swann Cttee. on Educ. of Children of Ethnic Minorities 1981–85; Hon. D.Ed. (C.N.A.A.) 1992. *Publications:* Logic of Education (with R. S. Peters) 1970, Knowledge and the Curriculum 1974, Moral Education in a Secular Society 1974, Educational Theory and its Foundation Disciplines (Ed.) 1983, Initial Teacher Training and the Role of the School (with others) 1988, Philosophy of Education: Major Themes in the Analytic Tradition (Jt. Ed.), 4 vols. 1998; numerous articles in educational and philosophical journals. *Leisure interest:* music (especially opera). *Address:* Flat 3, 6 Royal Crescent, Brighton, BN2 1AL, England (Home). *Telephone:* (01273) 684118.

HIRZEBRUCH, Friedrich Ernst Peter, DR. RER. NAT.; German professor of mathematics; b. 17 Oct. 1927, Hamm, Westf.; s. of Dr. Fritz Hirzebruch and Martha Hirzebruch (née Holtschmit); m. Ingeborg Spitzley 1952; one s. two d.; ed. Westfälische Wilhelms-Univ., Münster, and Technische Hochschule, Zürich; Scientific Asst. Univ. of Erlangen 1950–52; mem. Inst. for Advanced Study, Princeton, N.J., U.S.A. 1952–54; Dozent, Univ. of Münster 1954–55; Asst. Prof., Princeton Univ., N.J. 1955–56; Full Prof., Bonn Univ. 1956–, Dean, Faculty of Math. and Natural Sciences 1962–64; Dir. Max-Planck-Inst. für Mathematik, Bonn 1981–95; Pres. German Math. Soc. 1961–62, 1990, European Math. Soc. 1990–94; mem. Leopoldina, Heidelberg, Mainz, Netherlands and Nordrheinwestf. Acads., N.A.S. (U.S.A.), Bayerische Akad. der Wissenschaften, Finnish Acad. of Sciences, Russian (fmrly. U.S.S.R.) Acad. of Sciences, Acad. des Sciences (Paris), Akad. der Wissenschaften, Göttingen, American Acad. of Arts and Sciences, Ukrainian Acad., Sächsische Akad., Berlin-Brandenburgische Akad., Royal Soc., Royal Irish Acad., Polish Acad. of Sciences, Acad. Europaea, European Acad. of Arts and Sciences; Dr. h.c. (Univs. of Warwick, Göttingen, Wuppertal, Notre Dame, Trinity Coll. Dublin, Athens, Potsdam), Hon. D.Sc. (Oxford) 1984; Silver Medal, Swiss Fed. Inst. of Technology 1950, Wolf prize in Mathematics 1988, Lobachevskii Prize, U.S.S.R. Acad. of Sciences 1989, Seki Prize, Japanese Mathematical Soc. 1996, Cothenius Gold Medal Leopoldina 1997, Lomonosov Gold Medal, Russian Acad. of Sciences 1997; Orden pour le Mérite 1991, Grosses Verdienstkreuz mit Stern 1993, Order of the Holy Treasure, Gold and Silver (Japan) 1996. *Publications:* Neue topologische Methoden in der algebraischen Geometrie 1956, Collected Papers (2 vols.) 1987. *Address:* Max-Planck-Institut für Mathematik, Gottfried-Claren-Strasse 26, 53225 Bonn (Office); Thüringer Allee 127, 53757 St. Augustin, Germany (Home). *Telephone:* 0228-4020 (Office); 02241-332377 (Home).

HISLOP, Ian David, B.A.; British editor, writer and broadcaster; b. 13 July 1960; s. of the late David Atholl Hislop and of Helen Hislop; m. Victoria Hamson 1988; one s. one d.; ed. Ardingly Coll. and Magdalen Coll., Oxford; joined Private Eye (satirical magazine) 1981, Deputy Ed. 1985–86, Ed. 1986–; Columnist The Listener magazine 1985–89, The Sunday Telegraph 1996–; TV critic The Spectator magazine 1994–96. *Radio:* The News Quiz 1985–, Fourth Column 1992–, Lent Talk 1994, Gush (scriptwriter, with Nick Newman) 1994. *TV scriptwriting:* Spitting Image 1984–89, The Stone Age (with Nick Newman) 1989, Briefcase Encounter 1990, The Case of the Missing 1991, He Died a Death 1991, Harry Enfield's Television Programme 1990–92, Harry Enfield and Chums 1994–97, Mangez Merveillac 1994, Dead on Time 1995, Gobble 1996; TV performer Have I Got News for You 1990–. *Publications:* various Private Eye collections 1985–, contribs. to newspapers and magazines on books, current affairs, arts and entertainment. *Address:* c/o Private Eye, 6 Carlisle Street, London, W1V 5RG, England. *Telephone:* 0171-437 4017.

HITAM, Dato' Mohd. Yusof, B.A.; Malaysian diplomatist; b. 1 Jan. 1936, Mentakab; m. Datin Michiyo Noor Azian Binti Mustakim 1966; three s.; ed. Univs. of Singapore and Malaya; Amb. to Vietnam 1976–78; High Commr. to New Zealand 1978–80; Dir.-Gen. Ministry of Foreign Affairs, Assen. of South East Asian Nations Nat. Secr. 1980; Perm. Rep. to UN 1986–88 (also accred. to Cuba); Sec.-Gen. Ministry of Foreign Affairs 1988; Amb. to Switzerland 1989–90; Perm. Rep. to UN, Geneva 1989; Amb. to various confs.; Pingat Peringatan Malaysia-Gansa 1968, Johan Setia Mahkota 1976, Darjah Indera Mahkota 1986. *Leisure interests:* reading, golf, shooting. *Address:* c/o Ministry of Foreign Affairs, Wisma Putra, Jalan Wisma Putra, 50602 Kuala Lumpur; No. 25, Lorong 2C, Taman Hillview, Ukay Hights, Kuala Lumpur, Malaysia (Home). *Telephone:* 4560918 (Home).

HITAM, Tan Sri Dato' Musa bin; Malaysian politician (retd.); b. 18 April 1934, Johor; ed. English Coll., Johor Baharu Univ. of Malaya and Univ. of Sussex; assoc. sec. Int. Student Conf. Secr. (COSEC), Leiden 1957–59; civil servant 1959–64; political sec. to Minister of Transport 1964; M.P. 1968–90; Asst. Minister to Deputy Prime Minister 1969; studied in U.K. 1970, subsequently lectured at Univ. of Malaya; Chair. Fed. Land Devt. Authority 1971; Deputy Minister of Trade and Industry 1972–74; Minister of Primary Industries 1974–78, of Educ. 1978–81; Deputy Prime Minister and Minister of Home Affairs 1981–86; Deputy Pres. UMNO 1981–86; Special Envoy to UN 1990–91; Malaysia's Chief Rep. to UN Comm. on Human Rights 1994–; Special Envoy of the Prime Minister to Commonwealth Ministerial Action Group (C.M.A.G.). *Address:* No. 12, Selekoh Tunku, Bukit Tunku, 50480, Kuala Lumpur, Malaysia.

HITE, Shere D., M.A.; American writer; b. St. Joseph, Mo.; m. Friedrich Hoericke 1985; ed. Univ. of Florida, Columbia Univ.; Dir. feminist sexuality project NOW, New York 1972–78; Dir. Hite Research Int., New York 1978–; instructor in female sexuality, New York Univ. 1977–; lecturer Harvard Univ., McGill Univ., Columbia Univ., also numerous women's groups, int. lecturer 1977–89; mem. Advisory Bd. Foundation of Gender and Genital Medicine, Johns Hopkins Univ.; consultant editor Journal of Sex Educ. and Therapy, Journal of Sexuality and Disability; mem. NOW, American Historical Asscn., American Sociological Asscn., A.A.A.S., Acad. of Political Science, Women's History Asscn., Society for Scientific Study of Sex, Women's Health Network; Visiting Prof. Nihon Univ., Japan 1998; f. Nike Prize for Women's Non-Fiction Writing, Frankfurt 1997. *Publications:* Sexual Honesty: By Women For Women 1974, The Hite Report: A Nationwide Study of Female Sexuality 1976, The Hite Report on Male Sexuality 1981, Hite Report on Women and Love: A Cultural Revolution in Progress 1987, Good Guys, Bad Guys (with Kate Colleran) 1989, Women as Revolutionary Agents of Change: The Hite Reports and Beyond 1993, The Hite Report on the Family: Growing Up Under Patriarchy 1994, The Divine Comedy of Ariadne and Jupiter 1994, The Hite Report on Hite: A Sexual and Political Autobiography 1996, How Women See Other Women 1998. *Address:* 2 Soho Square, London, W1V, England (Office).

HITTMAIR, Otto, DR.PHIL.; Austrian professor of physics (retd.); b. 16 March 1924, Innsbruck; s. of Dr. Rudolf and Margarete (née Schumacher) Hittmair; m. Anna Rauch 1956; one s. three d.; ed. Univ. of Innsbruck, Univ. of Basel, Dublin Inst. for Advanced Studies, M.I.T.; with C.N.R.S., France 1952–54; Fellow, Univ. of Sydney 1954–56; with Comisión Nacional de Energía Atómica, Argentina 1957, Atomic Inst., Vienna 1958–60; Head and Prof., Inst. of Theoretical Physics, Technical Univ. of Vienna 1960–92, Dean 1968–69, Rector 1977–79; Vice-Pres. Int. Soc. of Eng. Educ. 1974–97, Ring of Honour; Pres. Austrian Acad. of Sciences 1987–91, Vice-Pres. 1991–97; mem. Royal Soc. of Sciences of Uppsala; Dr. techn. h.c. (Budapest); Jubilee Medal, Univ. of Innsbruck, Erwin Schrödinger Prize 1974, Wilhelm Exner Medal 1980, Science Prize, Vienna 1982, Johann Josef Ritter von Prechtl Medal 1996. *Publications:* Nuclear Stripping Reactions (with S. T. Butler) 1957, Wärmetheorie (with G. Adam) 1988, Lehrbuch der Quantentheorie 1972, Supraleitung (with H. W. Weber) 1979, Akademie der Wissenschaften: Entwicklung einer österreichischen Forschungsinstitution (ed. with H. Hunger) 1997. *Leisure interests:* mountaineering, chamber music. *Address:* Schlossfeld 9, A-6020 Innsbruck, Austria.

HJELM-WALLÉN, Lena, M.A.; Swedish politician; b. 14 Jan. 1943, Sala; d. of Elly Hjelm-Wallén and Gustaf Hjelm; m. Ingvar Wallén 1965; one d.; ed. Univ. of Uppsala; teacher in Sala 1966–69; active in Social Democratic Youth League; elected to 2nd Chamber of Parl. 1968; mem. Exec. Cttee. Västmanland branch of Socialdemokratiska Arbetarepartiet (Social Democratic Labour Party—SDLP) 1968, mem. SDLP Parl. Exec. 1976–82, SDLP spokeswoman on schools, mem. Bd. SDLP 1978–87, SDLP Spokeswoman on Educ. 1991–94; Minister without Portfolio, with responsibility for schools 1974–76; Minister of Educ. and Cultural Affairs 1982–85, of Int. Devt. Co-operation 1985–91, for Foreign Affairs 1994–98; Deputy Prime Minister 1998–. *Leisure interests:* nature, books, gardening, family. *Address:* c/o Cabinet Office, Rosenbad 4, 103 33 Stockholm, Sweden.

HJÖRNE, Lars Goran; Swedish newspaper editor and publisher; b. 20 Oct. 1929, Gothenburg; s. of late Harry Hjörne; one s. one d.; Chief Ed. Göteborgs-Posten 1969–89, Chair. 1969–95, Hon. Chair. 1995–; Hon. British Consul-Gen. in Gothenburg 1991–98. *Address:* Polhemsplatsen 5, 405 02 Gothenburg (Office); Stora Vägen 43, 26043 Arild, Sweden (Home). *Telephone:* (031) 62-40-00 (Office); (042) 34-68-03 (Home).

HJÖRNE, Peter Lars; Swedish newspaper editor and publisher; b. 7 Sept. 1952, Gothenburg; s. of Lars Hjörne and Anne Gyllenhammar; m. 2nd Karin Linnea Tuvesson 1995; three d.; ed. Göteborgs Högre Samskola and Univ. of Gothenburg; Man. Trainee John Deere Co., U.S.A. 1978–79; Exec. Asst. Göteborgs-Posten 1979–82, Deputy Man. Dir. 1983–85, Man. Dir. 1985–93, Publisher and Chief Ed. 1993–. *Leisure interests:* sailing, literature, music, art. *Address:* Göteborgs-Posten, Polhemsplatsen 5, 405 02 Gothenburg, Sweden.

HJORTH, Poul Lindegård, DR. PHIL.; Danish philologist; b. 24 July 1927, Holmstrup; s. of Georg L. and Agnes (née Thygesen) Hjorth; m. Karen-Louise Balsløv 1952; one s. one d.; ed. Univ. of Copenhagen; Lecturer in Danish, Univ. of Lund, Sweden 1956–62; Prof. of Danish Language, Royal Danish Acad. of Educational Studies 1965–78; Prof. of Scandinavian Philology, Univ. of Copenhagen 1978–92; mem. Royal Danish Acad. of Sciences and Letters 1974–; Chair. Selskab for nordisk Filologi 1963–68, Dansk Sprognaevn (Danish Language Bd.) 1966–73, Universitets-Jubilaeets danske Samfund 1977–. *Publications:* Nordsamsisk Bøjningslaere 1958, Karl Magnus Krønike 1960, Filologiske Studier over Karl Magnus Krønike 1965, Sjaelens og Kroppens Traette 1971, Forvandlingerne, Uddrag af Matthias Moths Oversaettelse af Ovids Metamorphoses 1979, Matthias Moth og Ovids Metamorfoser 1997. *Address:* Anemonevej 25, 2970 Hørsholm, Denmark. *Telephone:* 45 86 26 27.

HLA HAN, Col., M.B., B.S., D.P.H.; Myanma politician; b. 26 Sept. 1918; ed. Rangoon and Liverpool Univs.; served in Burma National Army and Resistance 1942–45; joined Burma Medical Corps 1949; Dir. Medical Services, Ministry of Defence 1955; promoted Col. 1958; mem. Revolutionary Council and Minister for Health and Educ. 1962–74; Minister for Foreign Affairs 1970–72; mem. Council of State 1974–78; Star of Independent Sithu (First Class). *Address:* c/o Council of State, Yangon, Myanmar.

HLAWITSCHKA, Eduard, DR.PHIL.; German university professor; b. 8 Nov. 1928, Dubkowitz; s. of Ernst Hlawitschka and Emilie Tschwatschal; m. Eva-Marie Schuldt 1958; one s. one d.; ed. Univs. of Freiburg i. Br. and Saarbrücken; Prof. Univ. of Düsseldorf 1969, Univ. of Munich 1975–; Pres. Sudetendeutsche Akademie der Wissenschaften und Künste 1991–94, Sudetendeutscher Kulturpreis für Wissenschaft 1987. *Publications:* ten books including: Franken, Alemannen, Bayern und Burgunder in Oberitalien 1960, Studien zur Äbtissinnenreihe von Remiremont 1963, Lotharingien und das Reich an der Schwelle der deutschen Geschichte 1968, Die Anfänge des Hauses Habsburg-Lothringen 1969, Libri memoriales I 1970, Vom Frankenreich zur Formierung der europäischen Staaten- und Völkergemeinschaft 840–1046 (1986), Untersuchungen zu den Thronwechseln der ersten Hälfte des ll. Jahrhunderts und zur Adelsgeschichte Süddeutschlands 1987, Stirps Regia 1988. *Address:* Panoramastrasse 25, 82211 Herrsching/Ammersee, Germany. *Telephone:* 08152 4991.

HLAWKA, Edmund, DR.PHIL.; Austrian professor of mathematics; b. 5 Nov. 1916, Bruck a.d. Mur; m. Rosa Reiterer; ed. Univ. of Vienna; Asst. Math. Inst., Univ. of Vienna 1938–48, Lecturer 1946, Prof. 1948–81; Prof. Tech. Univ. of Vienna 1981–87, Emer. 1987–; Dannie-Heinemann Prize 1963, Ehrenzeichen für Kunst und Wissenschaften 1964, City of Vienna Prize 1969, Gauss-Medaille 1977, Grosses Goldenes Ehrenzeichen, Repub. of Austria 1987; mem. Austrian Acad. of Sciences, Acad. Leopoldina, Rheinisch-Westfälische Akad., Bayerische Akad. der Wissenschaften, Accad. di Bologna. *Publications:* Theory of Uniform Distribution 1974, Zahlentheorie 1979, Grundbegriffe der Mathematik 1979, Zahlentheoretische Methoden in der Numerischen Mathematik 1981, Zahlentheoretische Analysis I 1985, II 1987, III 1990, Geometrische und Analytische Zahlentheorie 1986, Ungleichungen 1990; more than 140 articles in scientific journals. *Leisure interest:* reading. *Address:* c/o Institut für Analysis, Technische Universität Wien, Wiedner Hauptstrasse 8-10, Vienna 1040 (Office); Margaretenstrasse 27, Vienna 1040, Austria (Home).

HNATYSHYN, Rt. Hon. Ramon John, P.C., C.C., C.M.M., C.D., B.A., LL.B., Q.C.; Canadian politician and lawyer; b. 16 March 1934, Saskatoon, Saskatchewan; s. of John Hnatyshyn and Helen Constance Pitts; m. Gerda Andreasen 1960; two s.; ed. Nutana Collegiate Inst., Saskatoon, Univ. of Saskatchewan; fmr. lecturer in Law, Univ. of Saskatchewan; served in R.C.A.F. 1951–58; called to Bar of Saskatchewan 1957, to Ont. Bar 1986; Pvt. Sec. and Exec. Asst. to Govt. Leader in Senate 1958–60; returned to law practice, Saskatoon 1960; apptd. Q.C., Saskatchewan 1973; Sr. Partner, Gowling, Strathy and Henderson; mem. House of Commons 1974–88; apptd. Deputy House Leader of Opposition 1976; Minister of State for Science and Tech. 1979, Minister of Energy, Mines and Resources 1979–80, Govt. House Leader 1984–86, Pres. of Queen's Privy Council for Canada 1985–86, Minister responsible for Regulatory Affairs 1986, Minister of Justice and Attorney-Gen. 1986–88; Gov. Gen. of Canada 1990–95; served on several Commons standing cttees. 1974–79, 1980–84; apptd. Q.C. for Canada 1988; past Pres. UNA of Canada (N. Saskatchewan Branch), Law Soc. of Saskatchewan (Hon. Life mem. 1989), Saskatoon Gallery and Conservatory Corpn.; mem. Saskatoon and Canadian Bar Asscns.; Hon. LL.D. (Univ. of Sask.) 1990, (Open Univ., B.C.) 1991, (Royal Mil. Coll., Kingston) 1991, (Queen's Univ.) 1991, (McGill Univ.) 1992, (State Univ. of Chernivtsi, Ukraine) 1992, (Univ. of Man.) 1992, (Carleton Univ., Ottawa) 1992, (Royal Roads Mil. Coll.) 1994, (Univ. of Northern B.C.) 1994, (Alberta) 1994, (Memorial Univ.) 1994, (Law Soc. of Upper Canada) 1996; Hon. D.Cn.L. (Univ. of Emmanuel Coll., Saskatoon) 1993; Hon. D.C.L. (Bishop's Univ., Lennoxville, Quebec) 1993; D.Univ. (Ottawa) 1991; Hon. D.Phil. (Yonsei, Korea) 1994; Hon. Fellow of Royal College of Physicians and Surgeons of Canada; St. Volodymyr Medal Award, World Congress of Ukrainians 1989. *Address:* Suite 2600, 160 Elgin Street, Ottawa, Ont., K1P 1C3, Canada (Office).

HO, Edmund; Macau business executive and politician; mem. Legis. Ass. of Macau; Vice-Pres. Macau Chamber of Commerce; Gen. Man. Banco Tai Fung. *Address:* Tai Fung Bank Bldg., Av. Almeida Ribeiro 296; Legislative Assembly, Macau. *Telephone:* 322323 (Banco Tai Fung). *Fax:* 570737 (Banco Tai Fung).

HO, Peng-Yoke, PH.D., D.SC., C.PHYS., F.INST.P., F.A.H.A.; Australian professor of Chinese; b. 4 April 1926, Malaysia; s. of late Tih-Aun Ho and Yeen-Kwai Ng; m. Lucy Mei-Yiu Fung 1955; one s. four d.; ed. Raffles Coll., Singapore and Univ. of Malaya, Singapore; Asst. Lecturer in Physics Univ. of Malaya, Singapore 1951–54, lecturer in Physics 1954–60, Reader Dept. of Physics 1960–64; Prof. of Chinese Studies, Univ. of Malaya, Kuala Lumpur 1964–73, Dean of Arts 1967–68; Foundation Prof. Griffith Univ., Queensland 1973–89, Foundation Chair. School of Modern Asian Studies 1973–78, Prof. Emer. 1989–; Prof. of Chinese, Univ. of Hong Kong 1981–87, Master Robert Black Coll. 1984–87; mem. Acad. Sinica; Dir. Needham Research Inst., Cambridge; Professorial Research Assoc., S.O.A.S., London Univ.; Hon. Prof., Chinese Acad. of Science, Beijing, Univ. of Science and Tech., Beijing, North-West Univ., Xian, China; Hon.D.Litt. (Edin.). *Publications:* The Astronomical Chapters of the Chin Shu 1966, Li, Qi and Shu: An Introduction to Chinese Science and Civilization 1985, Science and Civilization in China (with Joseph Needham), Vol. 5, Part 3 1976, Part 4 1980, Part 7 1986. *Leisure interest:* chess. *Address:* 2B Sylvester Rd., Cambridge, CB3 9AF, England; 8 Holdway

Street, Kenmore, Queensland 4069, Australia. *Telephone:* (01223) 311545 (Cambridge).

HO, Stanley; Macau business executive; b. 25 Nov. 1921; Group Exec. Chair. Shun Tak Holdings Ltd. (operator of world's largest jetfoil fleet); founder and Man. Dir. Sociedade de Turismo e Diversões de Macau (STDM), controlling ferry services, dock terminal, casinos, hotels and 40 per cent of Macau's airport; business interests in Hong Kong and Macau include airline, tourism and entertainment, hotels, banking, property and TV broadcasting; funds Orient Foundation (org. dedicated to preserving colonial architecture and Portuguese Chinese culture); Vice-Pres. Basic Law Drafting Cttee., Macau Special Admin. Region 1988, Vice-Pres. Preparatory Cttee., Macau Special Admin. Region 1998; mem. Selection Cttee. for First Govt. of Hong Kong Special Admin. Region 1996, 9th NPC Election Council, Hong Kong Special Admin. Region 1997; mem. Standing Cttee. CPPCC 1998; Co-Chair. Int. Cttee. Franklin Delano Roosevelt Memorial Capital Campaign; Hon. D.Sc. (Univ. of Macau) 1984, (Univ. of Hong Kong) 1987; O. St. J. 1983, Chevalier, Légion d'honneur 1984, Order of the Sacred Treasure (Japan) 1987, Cavaleiro Comendador, Ordem Equestre de S. Gregorio Magno 1989, Sri Paduka Mahkota Perak (Malaysia) 1990, Gra Cruz, Ordem do Infante D. Henrique 1995. *Address:* Sociedade de Turismo e Diversões de Macau (STDM) SARL, Macau. *Telephone:* (852) 2859-3111 (Hong Kong); (853) 566065 (Macau). *Fax:* (852) 2858-1014 (Hong Kong); (853) 371981 (Macau).

HO, Tao, B.A., M.ARCH., L.H.D.; British architect; b. 17 July 1936, Shanghai, China; s. of Ping-Yin Ho and Chin-Hwa Chiu; m. 1st Chi-Ping Lu 1960, one s. two d.; m. 2nd Irene Lo 1978, one d.; ed. Pui Ching Middle High School, Hong Kong 1950–56, Williams Coll., Williamstown, Mass., and Harvard Univ., U.S.A.; Research Asst., Albright-Knox Art Gallery, Buffalo, N.Y. 1959; Architectural Asst. to Walter Gropius 1963–64; Visiting lecturer, Fine Arts Dept., Chinese Univ., Hong Kong 1965–67; founded own practice, TAOHO Design Architects, Hong Kong 1968–; co-founder, Hong Kong Arts Centre 1969, Chair. Visual Arts Cttee., Hong Kong Arts Centre 1972–77; Visiting Critic, Harvard Univ. Graduate School of Design 1975; External Examiner of Art, Chinese Univ., Hong Kong 1975–79; Visiting Critic, Design Dept., Hong Kong Polytechnic 1979–; Hon. lecturer, School of Architecture, Hong Kong Univ. 1979–; Chair. Hong Kong Designers Asscn. 1981; Hon. Adviser, City Hall Museum, Hong Kong 1981–; Chinese Govt. Advisor for Hong Kong Affairs 1995; mem. Bd. of Architects, Singapore 1981–; Assoc. mem. Chartered Inst. of Arbitrators 1979–; core mem. Asian Planning and Architectural Consultants Ltd. 1975–; Founder, Dir. Vision Press Ltd., Hong Kong 1982–; Fellow, Hong Kong Inst. of Architects 1971–; Hon. Fellow, American Inst. of Architects 1988–; Hon. Fellow, Philippines Inst. of Architects 1993–; mem. Singapore Inst. of Architects 1988; L'Ordre des Architectes, France, 1992; founding mem. Hong Kong Artists' Guild 1987; f. Philharmonic Soc. of Hong Kong Professionals 1991; has organized more than 20 exhbns. for Hong Kong Arts Centre 1972–; Arthur Lehman Fellow, Harvard Univ. 1960–63; Hon Fellow American Inst. of Architects 1988; Hon. D.Hum.Litt. (Williams Coll., Mass., U.S.A.) 1979; Design Merit Award (Chinese Manufacturers' Asscn.), Silver Medal (Hong Kong Inst. of Architects), Bicentennial Medal (Williams Coll., U.S.A.). *Prin. works include:* Hong Kong Govt. Pavilion, C.M.A. Exhbn., Hong Kong 1969; Hong Kong Int. Elementary School 1975, Hong Kong Arts Centre 1977, residential devt., Shouson Hill, Hong Kong (with K. C. Lye) 1979, Planning and Urban design of 3 major Chinese cities: Xiamen, Qingdao and Harigzhou 1985–86, 6A Bowen Road Apt 1983 (HKIA Silver Medal), Bayview Residential Devt. 1988, (HKIA Design Award), Hong Kong Baptist Coll. Redevt. 1988–89; revitalization of Western Market, Hong Kong 1992; Eng. Bldg., Chinese Univ. of Hong Kong 1993; renovation of Hong Kong Govt. House 1993; designed commemorative stamps for Hong Kong Govt. 1975; commissioned by SWATCH to design art clock tower to represent Hong Kong at 1996 Olympic Games, Atlanta, U.S.A.; one-man painting exhbns. at China Art Gallery, Beijing 1993, La Maison de Verre, Paris 1993, Hong Kong Univ. Museum 1995. *Publications:* numerous papers on theory and practice of art and architecture. *Leisure interests:* collecting art, writing about art, listening to music, painting, reading in cosmology and philosophy of science, sculpture. *Address:* Upper Deck, North Point (West), Passenger Ferry Pier, North Point, Hong Kong, Special Administrative Region, People's Republic of China. *Telephone:* (852) 28118780. *Fax:* (852) 28110337.

HOAGLAND, Edward; A.B.; American author; b. 21 Dec. 1932, New York; s. of Warren Eugene Hoagland and Helen Kelley Morley; m. 1st Amy J. Ferrara 1960 (divorced 1964); m. 2nd Marion Magid 1968 (died 1993); one d.; ed. Harvard Univ.; faculty mem. New School for Social Research, New York 1963–64, Rutgers Univ. 1966, Sarah Lawrence Coll., Bronxville, New York 1967, 1971, City Univ. 1967, 1968, Iowa Univ. 1978, 1982, Columbia Univ. 1980, 1981, Brown Univ. 1988, Bennington Coll., Bennington, Vt. 1987–94, Univ. of Calif. at Davis 1990, 1992; Gen. Ed. Penguin Nature Library 1985–; Houghton Mifflin Literary Fellow 1954; American Acad. of Arts and Letters Travelling Fellow 1964; Guggenheim Fellow 1964, 1975; mem. American Acad. of Arts and Letters; Longview Foundation Award 1961; O. Henry Award 1971; New York State Council on Arts Award 1972; American Acad. of Arts and Letters Harold D. Vursell Award 1981; Nat. Endowment Arts Award 1982, Lannan Foundation Award 1993; Brandeis Univ. Citation in Literature 1972. *Publications:* Cat Man 1956, The Circle Home 1960, The Peacock's Tail 1965, Notes from the Century Before: A Journal from British Columbia 1969, The Courage of Turtles 1971, Walking the Dead Diamond River 1973, The Moose on the Wall: Field Notes from the Vermont Wilderness 1974, Red Wolves and Black Bears 1976, African Calliope: A Journey to the Sudan 1979, The Edward Hoagland Reader 1979, The Tugman's Passage 1982, City Tales 1986, Seven Rivers West 1986, Heart's Desire 1988, The Final Fate of the Alligators 1992, Balancing Acts 1992; numerous essays and short stories. *Address:* P.O. Box 51, Barton, VT 05822, U.S.A. (Home).

HOAR, Gen. Joseph P., M.A.; American army officer (retd.); b. 30 Dec. 1934, Boston, Mass.; s. of Joseph J. Hoar (deceased) and Marion J. Hoar; m. Charlene Hoar 1956; one s. four d.; ed. Tufts Univ., George Washington Univ.; 2nd Lieut. Marine Corps 1957, rifle platoon commdr. 5th Marines, battalion staff officer 1st bn. 1st Marines, platoon commdr., later guard company commdr. Marine Barracks Yorktown, VA., asst. G-1 Marine Corps Base, Camp Lejeune, N.C., bn. operations officer 2nd Marine Div., bn. and brigade advisor Vietnamese Marines 1966–68, special asst. to asst. commandant Marine Corps, exec. officer 1st Battalion 9th Marines 1968–71, instructor Marine Corps Command and Staff Coll. 1972–76, served Personnel Management Div. HQ U.S. Marine Corps 1976–77; commdr. 3rd Battalion 1st Marines 1977–79, promoted Col. regimental commdr. 1st Marines 1979–81; commanded 31st Marine Amphibious Unit on board U.S.S. Belleau Wood 1981–84; Asst. Chief-of-Staff G-1 Marine Corps Recruit Depot, San Diego 1984–85; rank of Brig. Gen. 1984; asst. div. commdr. 2nd Marine Div., Dir. Facilities and Services Div. Installations and Logistics Dept. HQ Marine Corps Washington 1985–87; commanding Gen. Marine Corps Recruit Depot and Eastern Recruiting Region Parris Island 1987–88; promoted Maj. Gen. 1987, Chief-of-Staff U.S. Cen. Command 1988–90; Deputy Chief-of-Staff Plans, Policies and Operations 1990–91; rank of Lieut. Gen. 1990; C.-in-C. U.S. Cen. Command 1991–94; Pres. J. P. Hoar and Assoc. Inc. 1994–; Co-Chair. Middle East Panel, Council on Foreign Relations 1994–; rank of Gen. 1991; Fellow World Econ. Forum; three Defense Distinguished Service Medals, Bronze Star Medal with Combat "V" and Gold Star, Meritorious Service Medal with Gold Star and other decorations; awards from nine foreign governments. *Leisure interest:* tennis. *Address:* 386 13th Street, Del Mar, CA 92014, U.S.A. *Telephone:* (619) 794-0546. *Fax:* (619) 794-0531.

HOARE, Charles Antony Richard, F.R.S.; British professor of computation; b. 11 Jan. 1934, Colombo, Ceylon (now Sri Lanka); s. of Henry S. M. and Marjorie F. (née Villiers) Hoare; m. Jill Pym 1962; one s. one d.; ed. Dragon School, Oxford, King's School, Canterbury, Merton Coll., Oxford, Unit. of Biometry, Oxford, and Moscow State Univ.; with Elliott Bros. (London) Ltd. 1960–68; Prof. of Computing Science, Queen's Univ. of Belfast 1968–77; Prof. of Computation, Univ. of Oxford 1977–; James Martin Prof. of Computing, Univ. of Oxford 1993–; Fellow Wolfson Coll. 1977–; mem. Acad. Europea; Foreign mem. Acad. Lincei, Italy; corresp. mem. Bavarian Acad. of Sciences; Hon. D.Sc. (Univ. of S. Calif., Warwick, Pennsylvania, Queens, Belfast) 1987; Hon. D.Univ. (York) 1989, (Essex) 1991, (Bath) 1993; A.M. Turing Award, Harry Goode Memorial Award, Distinguished Fellow of British Computer Soc., Faraday Medal 1985. *Publications:* Structured Programming (co-author) 1972, Communicating Sequential Processes 1985, Essays in Computing Science 1989, Unifying Theories of Programming (co-author) 1998. *Leisure interests:* walking, music, reading. *Address:* Oxford University Computing Laboratory, Programming Research Group, Wolfson Building, Parks Road, Oxford, OX1 3QD, England. *Telephone:* (01865) 273841.

HOBAN, Russell Conwell; American author; b. 4 Feb. 1925, Lansdale, Pa.; s. of Abram Hoban and Jenny (née Dimmerman) Hoban; m. 1st Lillian Aberman 1944 (dissolved 1975); one s. three d.; m. 2nd Gundula Ahl 1975; three s.; ed. Lansdale High School and Philadelphia Museum School of Industrial Art; served U.S. Infantry, Italy 1943–45; held various jobs including general illustration with Wexton co., New York 1945–51; TV Art Dir. BBDO Advertising, N.Y. 1951–56; freelance illustrator 1956–65; copywriter, Doyle Dane Bernbach, New York 1965–67; novelist and author of children's books 1967–; Whitbread Prize for How Tom Beat Captain Najork and His Hired Sportsmen (children's book) 1974; John W. Campbell Memorial Award and Australian Science Fiction Achievement Award for Riddley Walker 1983. *Publications and other works:* novels: The Mouse and His Child 1967, The Lion of Boaz-Jachin and Jachin-Boaz 1973, Kleinzeit 1974, Turtle Diary 1975, Riddley Walker 1980, Pilgermann 1983, The Medusa Frequency 1987, Fremder 1996, The Trokeville Way 1996, Mr Rinyo-Clacton's Offer 1998, and 62 children's picture books and two books of verse for children since 1959; collection of poems The Last of the Wallendas 1997; text for The Carrier Frequency (theatre piece, Impact Theatre Co-operative) 1984; stage version of Riddley Walker (Manchester Royal Exchange Theatre Co.) 1986; The Moment under the Moment (a collection including stories, essays and a libretto) 1992; The Second Mrs Kong (opera text, music by Birtwistle) 1994 (premiere Glyndebourne 1994); radio play: Perfect and Endless Circles 1995; short stories performed on Radio 3 and 4; various essays and pieces for Granta and The Fiction Magazine. *Address:* 6 Musgrave Crescent, London, SW6 4PT, England. *Telephone:* 0171-731 3997. *Fax:* 0171-731 2531.

HOBDAY, Sir Gordon (Ivan), Kt., PH.D., F.R.S.C.; British business executive (retd.); b. 1 Feb. 1916, Derbyshire; s. of the late Alexander Thomas Hobday and Frances Cassandra Hobday (née Meads); m. Margaret Jean Joule 1940; one d.; ed. Long Eaton Grammar School, Univ. Coll., Notts.; joined The Boots Co. Ltd. 1939, Dir. of Research 1952–68, Deputy Man. Dir. 1968–70,

Man. Dir. 1970–72, Chair. 1973–81; Dir. The Metal Box Co. Ltd. 1976–81; Dir. Lloyds Bank 1981–86; Deputy Chair. Price Comm. 1977–78; Chair. Cen. Independent Television Co. Ltd. 1981–85; Chancellor Univ. of Nottingham 1979–91 (Pres. of the Council 1973–82); Pres. Portland Tring Coll. for the Disabled 1990–93; Lord Lieut. and Keeper of the Rolls for Nottinghamshire 1983–91; Hon. LL.D. *Leisure interests:* handicrafts, gardening. *Address:* Newstead Abbey Park, Nottingham, NG15 8GD, England.

HOBHOUSE, Rt. Hon. Sir John Stewart, Kt., P.C.; **Lord Justice Hobhouse**; British judge; ed. Christ Church Coll., Oxford; called to Bar Inner Temple 1955, Q.C. 1973; Judge of High Court, Queen's Bench Div. 1982–93; Lord Justice of Appeal 1993–. *Address:* Royal Courts of Justice, Strand, London, WC2 2LL, England.

HOBSBAWM, Eric John Ernest, C.H., PH.D., F.B.A.; British university professor; b. 9 June 1917, Alexandria; s. of Leopold Percy Hobsbawm and Nelly Gruen; m. Marlene Schwarz 1962; one s. one d.; ed. Cambridge Univ.; Lecturer, Birkbeck Coll. 1947–59, Reader 1959–70, Prof. of Econ. and Social History 1970–82, Prof. Emer. 1982–; Fellow, King's Coll., Cambridge 1949–55; Andrew D. White Prof.-at-Large, Cornell Univ. 1976–82; Prof., New School for Social Research, New York 1984–; Hon. Foreign Mem. American Acad. of Arts and Sciences; Foreign Mem. Hungarian Acad. of Sciences; Dr. h.c. (Stockholm) 1970, (Chicago) 1976, (East Anglia) 1982, (New School) 1982, (York Univ., Canada) 1986, (Pisa) 1987, (London) 1993, (Essex) 1996, (Columbia Univ.) 1997, (Buenos Aires, Univ. of ARCIS, Santiago, Chile) 1998; Chevalier, Palmes Académiques, Order of the Southern Cross (Brazil) 1996. *Publications:* Primitive Rebels 1959, The Age of Revolution 1962, Labouring Men 1964, Industry and Empire 1968, Captain Swing 1969, Bandits 1969, Revolutionaries 1973, The Age of Capital 1975; Ed. Storia del Marxismo (5 vols.) 1978–82, Worlds of Labour 1984, The Age of Empire 1875–1914 1987, Politics for a Rational Left: Political Writing 1989, Nations and Nationalism since 1780 1990, Echoes of the Marseillaise 1990, The Jazz Scene 1992, The Age of Extremes 1914–1991 1994, On History (essays) 1997, Uncommon People: Resistance, Rebellion and Jazz 1998. *Address:* Birkbeck College, Malet Street, London, WC1E 7HX, England.

HOCH, Orion, PH.D.; American business executive; b. 1928, Canonsburg, Pa.; m. 1st Jane Lee Ogan 1952 (died 1978); one s. two d.; m. 2nd Catherine Nan Richardson 1980; one s.; ed. Carnegie Mellon Univ., Univ. of Calif. Los Angeles and Stanford Univ.; engaged in research and devt. Hughes Aircraft 1952–54; various positions, Electron Devices Div. Litton Industries Inc. 1957–68; Vice-Pres. Litton Components Group 1968–70; Corp. Vice-Pres. Litton Industries Inc. 1970, Sr. Vice-Pres. 1971, Deputy Head, Business Systems and Equipment Group 1973–74; Pres. Advanced Memory Systems (later Intersil Inc.) 1974–81; Pres. Litton Industries Inc. 1982–88, Dir. and C.O.O. 1982, C.E.O. 1986–93, Chair. 1988–94, Chair. Emer. 1994–; Chair. Exec. Cttee., Dir. Western Atlas Inc. 1994–98. *Address:* UNOVA Incorporated, 360 North Crescent Drive, Beverly Hills, CA 90210, U.S.A.

HOCHHUTH, Rolf; Swiss playwright; b. 1 April 1931; m.; three s; fmr. publisher's reader; Resident Municipal Playwright, Basel 1963; mem. PEN of Fed. Repub. of Germany. *Publications:* Plays: The Representative 1962, The Employer 1965, The Soldiers 1966, Anatomy of Revolution 1969, The Guerillas 1970, The Midwife 1972, Lysistrata and the NATO 1973, A German Love Story (novel) 1980, Judith 1984, The Immaculate Conception 1989. *Address:* P.O. Box 661, 4002 Basel, Switzerland.

HOCINE; Algerian photographer; fmrly. photojournalist Reuters; photojournalist Agence France-Presse, Algiers 1993–; World Press Photo of the Year Award 1997. *Exhibition:* "Algeria: A Country in Mourning", Newseum, Arlington, Va. 1998. *Address:* c/o Agence France-Presse, 6 rue Abd al-Karimel-Khettabi, Algiers, Algeria.

HOCKIN, Thomas, P.C., M.P., PH.D.; Canadian politician and businessman; b. 5 March 1938, London, Ont.; s. of Thomas Munro Hockin and Margaret Marion McKillop; m. Marion Schaefer 1967; one s. two d.; ed. Medway Secondary School, Univ. of Western Ont., Harvard Univ.; Pres. Markham Imports; Prof. Univ. of Western Ont. School of Business; Pres. Sotheby's Canada 1981–83; mem. Ont. Police Comm. 1980–84, Albany Royal Canadian Mil. Inst.; M.P. 1984–93; Minister of State for Finance 1986–89, for Small Businesses and Tourism 1989–93; Pres., C.E.O. Investment Funds Inst. of Canada 1994–; Progressive Conservative. *Leisure interests:* baseball watching, golf, tennis.

HOCKNEY, David, C.H., R.A.; British artist; b. 9 July 1937, Bradford; s. of Kenneth and Laura Hockney; ed. Bradford Coll. of Art and Royal Coll. of Art; taught at Maidstone Coll. of Art 1962, Univ. of Iowa 1964, Univ. of Colo. 1965, Univ. of Calif. (Los Angeles) 1966, (Berkeley) 1967; has travelled extensively in Europe and U.S.A.; first one-man exhbn., Kasmin Gallery, London 1963; subsequent one-man exhbns. at Museum of Modern Art, New York 1964, 1968, Laundau-Alan Gallery, New York 1964, 1967, Kasmin Gallery 1965, 1966, 1968, 1969, 1970, 1972, Stedeljik Museum, Amsterdam 1966, Palais des Beaux-Arts, Brussels 1966, Studio Marconi and Galleria dell'Ariete, Milan 1966, Galerie Mikro, Berlin 1968, Whitworth Art Gallery, Manchester 1969, André Emmerich Gallery, New York 1969, 1972, 1979, 1980, 1982, 1983, 1984, 1985, Gallery Springer, Berlin 1970, Kestner-Ges., Hanover 1970, Whitechapel Gallery (retrospective exhbn.), London 1970, Kunsthalle, Bielefeld 1971, Musée des Arts Décoratifs, Louvre, Paris 1974, Galerie Claude Bernard, Paris 1975, Nicholas Wilder, Los Angeles 1976, Galerie Neundorf, Hamburg 1977, Warehouse Gallery 1979, Knoedler Gallery 1979, 1981, 1982, 1983, 1984, 1986, Tate Gallery (retrospective exhbn.) 1980, 1986, 1988, Hayward Gallery (Photographs) 1983, 1985, L.A. County Museum (retrospective) 1988, The Metropolitan Museum of Art (retrospective) N.Y. 1988, Knoedler Gallery, London 1988, A Emmerich Gallery, N.Y. 1988, 1989, L.A. Louver Gallery, Venice 1982, 1983, 1985, 1986, 1988, Nishimura Gallery, Tokyo, Japan 1988, Manchester City Art Galleries (retrospective exhbn.) 1996; Assoc. mem. Royal Acad. 1985; group exhbns. include ICA, Second and Third Paris Biennales of Young Artists, Musée d'Art Moderne 1961, 1963, Third Inst. Biennale of Prints, Nat. Museum of Art, Tokyo 1962, London Group Jubilee Exhbn. 1914–1964, Tate Gallery 1964, Painting and Sculpture of a Decade, Gulbenkian Foundation, Tate Gallery, London 1964, Op and Pop, Stockholm and London 1965, Fifth Int. Exhbn. of Graphic Art, Ljubljana 1965, First Int. Print Biennale, Cracow 1966, São Paulo Biennale 1967, Venice Biennale 1968, Pop Art Redefined, Hayward Gallery, London 1969, 150 Years of Photography, Nat. Gallery, Wash., D.C. 1989–90; touring show of prints and drawings Munich, Madrid, Lisbon, Teheran 1977, Saltaire, Yorks, New York, L.A. 1994, Royal Acad. (drawings) 1995–96; designed sets for Rake's Progress, Glyndebourne 1975, La Scala 1979, The Magic Flute, Glyndebourne 1978, L'Enfant et les sortilèges, Nightingale, Covent Garden 1983, Tristan and Isolde, L.A. Music Centre Opera, L.A. 1987; designer of costumes and sets, Metropolitan Opera House, New York 1980, of sets Varii Capricci 1983; appeared in autobiographical documentary film A Bigger Splash 1974; Guinness Award 1961, Graphic Prize, Paris Biennale 1963, First Prize 8th Int. Exhbn. of Drawings and Engravings, Lugano 1964, prize at 6th Int. Exhbn. of Graphic Art, Ljubljana 1965, Cracow 1st Int. Print Biennale 1966; Hon. Ph.D. (Royal Coll. of Art) 1992; Hon. D.Litt. (Oxford) 1995; First Prize 6th John Moores Exhbn. 1967, Hamburg Foundation Shakespeare Prize 1983, Praemium Imperiale, Japan Art Asscn. 1989, Fifth Annual Gov.'s Award for Visual Arts in Calif. 1994. *Publications:* Hockney by Hockney 1976, David Hockney, Travel with Pen, Pencil and Ink 1978 (autobiography), Photographs 1982, China Diary (with Stephen Spender, q.v.) 1982, Hockney Paints the Stage 1983, David Hockney: Cameraworks 1984, Hockney on Photography: Conversations with Paul Joyce 1988, David Hockney: A Retrospective 1988, Hockney's Alphabet (ed. by Stephen Spender) 1991, That's the Way I See It 1993 (autobiog.), Off the Wall: Hockney Posters 1994, David Hockney's Dog Days 1998, Hockney on Art: Photography, Painting and Perspective 1998. *Address:* c/o 7508 Santa Monica Boulevard, Los Angeles, CA 90046, U.S.A.; Tradhart Ltd., 19B Buckingham Avenue, Slough, SL1 4QB, Berks., England.

HOCQ, Nathalie; French business executive; b. 7 Aug. 1951, Neuilly (Hauts-de-Seine); d. of Robert Hocq and Christiane Arnoult; m. Patrick Choay; ed. École Mary Mount, Neuilly, Cours Victor-Hugo, Paris and Univ. of Paris-Dauphine; Publicity Asst., Havas-conseil 1970; in charge of duty-free network, Briquet Cartier 1970; Exec. Cartier S.A. 1974, Gen. Man. 1977, Man. Dir. Devt. 1979–81; Vice-Chair. Cartier Int. 1981; Pres., Dir.-Gen. Poiray Joalliers Paris 1988–. *Leisure interests:* riding, tennis, skiing and swimming. *Address:* Poiray Joailliers, 1 rue de la Paix, 75002 Paris, France.

HODDINOTT, Alun, D.MUS., C.B.E.; Welsh composer; b. 11 Aug. 1929, Bargoed, S. Wales; s. of Thomas Ivor Hoddinott and Gertrude Jones; m. Beti Rhiannon Huws 1953; one s.; ed. Gowerton Grammar School and Univ. Coll., Cardiff; Lecturer, Cardiff Coll. of Music and Drama 1951–59; Lecturer Univ. Coll., Cardiff 1959–65, Reader 1965–67, Prof. of Music 1967–87; Artistic Dir. Cardiff Festival of Twentieth Century Music 1966–89, Pres. 1989–; Hon. mem. Royal Acad. of Music; Fellow, Royal Northern Coll. of Music 1980, Univ. Coll., Cardiff 1981, Welsh Coll. of Music and Drama 1990; Hon. D.Mus. (Sheffield) 1993; Walford Davies Prize 1954, Bax Medal 1957, Hopkins Medal of the St. David's Soc. of New York 1981, Glyndŵr Medal 1997. *Works include:* seven symphonies 1955–77; four sinfoniettas, eleven concertos 1951–69, six piano sonatas 1959–72, four violin sonatas 1969–76, sonatas for harp, cello, clarinet, horn, sonata for Cello and Piano 1977, Welsh Dances, Investiture Dances, Black Bart, Dives and Lazarus 1965, Variants 1966, Fioriture 1968, The Tree of Life 1971, Ritornelli 1974, The Beach at Falesa (opera) 1974, The Magician (opera), Ancestor Worship, Five Landscapes (song cycles), A Contemplation upon Flowers (songs for soprano and orchestra), What the Old Man Does is Always Right (opera), Passaggio for orchestra 1977, Dulcia Iuventutis 1977, Sonata for Organ, Voyagers (for baritone solo, male voices and orchestra) sonatina for guitar, sonatina for two pianos, The Rajah's Diamond (opera), scena for string quartet, ritornelli for brass quintet, Hymnus Ante Somnum, nocturnes and cadenza for solo 'cello, The Heaventree of Stars (for violin and orchestra) 1980, The Trumpet Major (opera in three acts) 1981, nocturnes and cadenzas for solo flute, ritornelli for four double basses, Te Deum (for mixed voices and organ), Lanterne des Morts (for orchestra), Six Welsh Folk Songs (soprano and piano), Doubles (for oboe, harpsichord and strings), Five Studies (for orchestra), Four Scenes from the Trumpet Major (for orchestra), Quodlibet for orchestra 1982, Quodlibet for brass quintet 1983, Masks (oboe, bassoon and piano) 1983, Ingravescentem aetatem (chorus and piano duet) 1983, Lady and Unicorn: Cantata for mixed voices and piano, Piano Trio No. 2, Bagatelles for oboe and harp, String Quartet No. 2, Piano Sonata No. 7, Scenes and Interludes: Concertante for trumpet, harpsichord and strings, Symphony No. 6, Hommage à Chopin (orchestra), Bells of Paradise: Cantata for baritone, mixed chorus and orchestra 1984, Welsh Dances, Third Suite (orchestra), Divertimenti for flute, bassoon, double bass and percussion, Scena for string orchestra, Sonata for two pianos, The Silver Hound: Cycle for tenor and piano, Passacaglia and Fugue for organ, Fanfare with Variants for brass band, Green Broom: Ballad for male voices and piano, Sonata for four clarinets, Sing a New Song (anthem for mixed voices and organ) 1985, Flower Songs (women's voices and piano), Concerto for violin, cello and orchestra, Sonata No. 8 for piano, Divisions: Concertante for horn, harpsichord and strings, Concerto for orchestra, Concerto for clarinet and orchestra 1986, Aspiciens A Longe (anthem for mixed voices and organ) 1987, Welsh dances (for brass band) 1987, Cantata: Legend of St. Julian 1987, String Quartet No. 3 1988, Dr. Faustus: Scena (for mixed voices and brass) 1988, lines from Marlowe's Dr. Faustus 1988, Noctis Equi (cello and orchestra), Songs of Exile, Piano Sonata No. 9, Star Children, Piano Sonata No. 10, Symphony for organ and orchestra 1989, Emynau Pantycelyn (cantata) 1990, Three Advent Carols 1990, Novelette for flute, oboe and piano 1991, Sonata for flute and piano 1991, Sonata No. 5 for violin and piano 1992, Vespers Canticle 1992, Symphony for brass and percussion 1992, Chorales, Variants and Fanfares for organ and brass quintet 1992, Gloria 1992, A Vision of Eternity 1992, Three Motets for chorus and organ 1993, Wind Quintet 1993, Sonata No. 11 for piano 1993, Mass for St David 1994, Sonata No. 12 for piano 1994, Six Bagatelles for string quartet 1994, Three Hymns for mixed chorus and organ 1994, Shakespeare Songs for unaccompanied chorus 1994, The Silver Swimmer for soprano and ensemble 1994, Five Poems of Gustavo Adolfo Bécquer for baritone and piano 1994, One Must Always Have Love (song for high voice and piano) 1994, Mistral (concerto for violin and orchestra) 1995, Shining Pyramid (concerto for trumpet and orchestra) 1995, Sonata for oboe and harp 1995, Ty Mhorav (for poems for Gwyn Thomas for baritone and piano) 1995, The Poetry of Earth (songs for mixed choir and piano duet) 1995, Camargue Mass 1996, Sonata No. 3 (cello and piano) 1996, Magnificat and Nunc Dimittis 1996, String Quartet No. 4 1996, Piano Trio No. 3 1996, Sonata No. 2 (clarinet and piano) 1996, Sonata No. 6 (violin and piano) 1997, Tempi: Sonata for Harp 1997, The Poetry of Earth (songs for baritone and harp) 1997, Island of Dragons (variants for cello) 1998, Dragon Fire (concertante for timpani, percussion and orchestra), Grongor Hill (scena for baritone, string quartet and piano), Lizard (variants for recorder), Tower (opera in three acts) 1998–99. *Leisure interest:* travelling. *Address:* 64 Gowerton Road, Three Crosses, Swansea, SA4 3PX, Wales.

HODDLE, Glenn; British professional footballer and football manager; b. 27 Oct. 1957; s. of Derek Hoddle and Teresa Roberts; m. Christine Anne Stirling (divorced); one s. two d.; ed. Burnt Mill School, Harlow; player with Tottenham Hotspur 1976–86, AS Monaco, France 1986; (12 under 21 caps, 53 full caps on England Nat. Team 1980–88, played in World Cup 1982 and 1986); player/man. Swindon Town 1991–93 (promoted to FA Premier League 1993); player/man. Chelsea 1993–96; coach English Nat. Team 1996–99; FA Cup winners' Medal (Tottenham Hotspur) 1981 and 1982, UEFA Cup winners' Medal (Tottenham Hotspur) 1984, French Championship winners' Medal (Monaco) 1988. *Publications:* Spurred to Success (autobiog.), Glenn Hoddle: The 1998 World Cup Story 1998. *Leisure interests:* tennis, golf, reading. *Address:* c/o The Football Association, 16 Lancaster Gate, London, W2 3LW, England. *Telephone:* 0171-262 4542.

HODEL, Donald Paul, J.D.; American government official; b. 23 May 1935, Portland, Ore.; s. of Philip E. and Theresia R. (Brodt) Hodel; m. Barbara B. Stockman 1956; two s. (one deceased); ed. Harvard Coll. and Univ. of Oregon; admitted to Oregon Bar 1960; attorney, Daview, Biggs, Strayer, Stoel & Boley 1960–63; Georgia Pacific Corpn. 1963–69; Deputy Admin., Bonneville Power Admin. 1969–72, Admin. 1972–77; Pres. Nat. Elec. Reliability Council, Princeton, N.J. 1978–80; Pres. Hodel Assocs. Inc. 1978–81; Under-Sec. Dept. of Interior 1981–83; Sec. of Energy 1982–85, of the Interior 1985–89; Republican.

HODGE, Patricia; British actress; b. Grimsby; m. Peter Owen; two s.; ed. London Acad. of Music and Dramatic Art; won Eveline Evans Award for Best Actress; Hon.D.Litt. (Hull) 1996. *Stage appearances include:* No-one Was Saved, All My Sons, Say Who You Are, The Birthday Party, The Anniversary, Popkiss, Two Gentlemen of Verona, Pippin, Maudie, Hair, The Beggar's Opera, Pal Joey, Look Back in Anger, Dick Whittington, Happy Yellow, The Brian Cant Children's Show, Then and Now, The Mitford Girls, As You Like It, Benefactors, Noel and Gertie, Separate Tables, The Prime of Miss Jean Brodie, A Little Night Music (Royal Nat. Theatre), Heartbreak House 1997. *Film appearances:* The Disappearance, Rose Dixon—Night Nurse, The Waterloo Bridge Handicap, The Elephant Man, Heavy Metal, Betrayal, Sunset, Just Ask for Diamond, The Secret Life of Ian Fleming, The Leading Man 1996, Prague Duet 1996, Jilting Joe 1997. *TV appearances:* Valentine, The Girls of Slender Means, Night of the Father, Great Big Groovy Horse, The Naked Civil Servant, Softly, Softly, Jackanory Playhouse, Act of Rape, Crimewriters, Target, Rumpole of the Bailey, The One and Only Mrs Phyllis Dixey, Edward and Mrs Simpson, Disraeli, The Professionals, Holding the Fort, The Other 'Arf, Jemima Shore Investigates, Hayfever, The Death of the Heart, Robin of Sherwood, O.S.S., Sherlock Holmes, Time for Murder, Hotel du Lac, The Life and Loves of a She Devil, Rich Tea and Sympathy 1991, The Cloning of Joanna May 1991, The Legacy of Reginald Perrin 1996, The Moonstone 1996. *Address:* c/o I.C.M., Oxford House, 76 Oxford Street, London, W1R 1RB, England.

HODGKIN, Sir Howard, Kt., C.B.E., D.LITT.; British painter; b. 6 Aug. 1932; m. Julia Lane 1955; two s.; ed. Camberwell School of Art and Bath Acad. of Art; Trustee, Tate Gallery 1970–76, Nat. Gallery 1978–85; first one-man show of paintings Arthur Tooth & Sons, London 1962 since when numerous one-man shows of paintings and prints in U.K., U.S.A., Europe and Australia, including Galerie Lawrence Rubin, Zurich 1997, Gaposian Gallery, New York 1998, Haas and Fuchs Galerie, Berlin 1998, Anthony d'Offay Gallery 1999; retrospective exhbn. Metropolitan Museum of Art, New York 1995, then Modern Art Museum, Fort Worth, Der Kunstverein, Düsseldorf and Hayward Gallery, London 1995–97; has participated in numerous group exhbns. worldwide; British rep., Venice Biennale 1984; works in many public collections including Tate Gallery, London, Museum of Modern Art, New York, Nat. Gallery of Washington, Metropolitan Museum of Art, New York, Nat. Gallery of S. Australia, Adelaide, Walker Art Center, Minneapolis; mem. Cttee. Nat. Art Collections Fund 1989–90; Hon. Fellow, Brasenose Coll., Univ. of Oxford 1988; Tate Gallery Turner Prize 1985; Hon. D.Litt. (Birmingham) 1997. *Address:* c/o Anthony d'Offay Gallery, 9, 21, 23 and 24 Dering Street, London, W1R 9AA, England. *Telephone:* 0171-499 4100. *Fax:* 0171-493 4443.

HODGSON, Sir Maurice Arthur Eric, Kt., M.A., B.SC., F.I.CHEM.E., F.ENG., C.CHEM., F.R.S.C.; British company executive; b. 21 Oct. 1919, Bradford; s. of Walter and Amy (née Walker) Hodgson; m. Norma Fawcett 1945; one s. one d.; ed. Bradford Grammar School and Merton Coll., Oxford; joined ICI Ltd., Fertilizer and Synthetic Products Group 1942; seconded to ICI (New York) Ltd. 1955–58; Head of Technical Dept., ICI Ltd. 1958, Devt. Dir. Heavy Organic Chemicals Div. 1960 (Deputy Chair. 1964), Gen. Man. Co. Planning 1966, Commercial Dir. and Planning Dir. 1970, Deputy Chair. 1972–78, Chair. 1978–82; Dir. Carrington Viyella Ltd. 1970–74, Imperial Chemicals Insurance Ltd. 1970–78 (Chair. 1972–78), Chair. British Home Stores PLC 1982–87; Dir. (non-exec.) Storehouse PLC 1985–89; Nominated mem. Council of Lloyd's 1987–94; mem. Court of British Shippers' Council 1978–82, Council, CBI 1978–82, Pres.'s Cttee., The Advertising Asscn. 1978–90, Int. Council, The Salk Inst. 1978–97, Int. Advisory Cttee., Chase Manhattan Bank 1980–83, Int. Advisory Bd. AMAX Inc. 1982–85, European Advisory Council Air Products and Chemicals Inc. 1982–84; Dir. (non exec.) Dunlop Holdings PLC 1982–83, Chair. Jan.–Nov. 1984; Visiting Fellow, School of Business and Organizational Studies, Univ. of Lancaster 1970–80; Hon. Fellow, Merton Coll., Oxford 1979; Hon. Fellowship UMIST 1979; Trustee, The Civic Trust 1978–82; mem. of Court, Univ. of Bradford 1979–94; Gov., London Graduate School of Business Studies 1978–87; Pres. Merton Soc. 1986–89; Chair. Civil Justice Review Advisory Cttee. 1985–88; Hon. D.Univ. (Heriot-Watt) 1979, Hon. D.Tech. (Bradford) 1979, Hon. D.Sc. (Loughborough Univ. of Technology) 1981; Messel Medal, Soc. of Chemical Industry 1980, George E. Davis Medal, Inst. of Chemical Eng. 1982. *Leisure interests:* horse-racing, swimming, fishing. *Address:* Suite 75/76, Kent House, 87 Regent Street, London, W1R 7HF, England. *Telephone:* 0171-734 7777.

HODGSON, Thomas R., M.S.E., M.B.A.; American business executive; b. 17 Dec. 1941, Lakewood, Ohio; s. of Thomas J. Hodgson and Dallas L. Hodgson; m. Susan Cawrse 1963; one s. two d.; ed. Purdue Univ., Univ. of Mich. and Harvard Univ.; devt. eng. DuPont 1964; Assoc. Booz-Allen & Hamilton 1969–72; with Abbott Labs. 1972–, Gen. Man. Faultless Div. 1976–78, Vice-Pres. and Gen. Man. Hosp. Div. 1978–80, Pres. Hosp. Div. 1980–83, Group Vice-Pres. and Pres. Abbott Int. Ltd. 1983–84, Exec. Vice-Pres. 1985–80, Pres. and C.O.O. Abbott Labs. Oct. 1990–; Visiting Prof. Purdue Univ. 1996–. *Leisure interests:* skiing, scuba, wind-surfing, racquetball, tennis, kayaking. *Address:* Abbott Laboratories, 100 Abbott Park Road, Abbott Park, North Chicago, IL 60064 (Office); 1015 Ashley Road, Lake Forest, IL 60045, U.S.A. (Home). *Telephone:* (708)-688-8288.

HOEKMAN, Johan Bernard (Joop); Netherlands diplomatist; b. 11 Sept. 1931, Groningen; m. Jeanne van Gelder 1957; three s. one d.; ed. Univ. of Groningen; joined Foreign Service 1961, Attaché, Baghdad 1962–65, Second Sec., Washington 1965–68, Chargé d'Affaires, Jeddah 1968–72, Counsellor, Cairo 1972–74, Deputy, later Head Dept. for Financial and Econ. Devt. Co-operation, Ministry of Foreign Affairs 1974–80, Dir.-Gen. for Int. Co-operation 1984–88; Amb. to Senegal 1980–81, to Suriname 1981–84, 1988–90, to U.K. (also accred. to Iceland) 1990–94; Kt. Order of Netherlands Lion, Officer, Order of Orange Nassau, and several foreign decorations. *Address:* Staten Laan 102, 2582 GV The Hague, Netherlands.

HOFFENBERG, Sir Raymond, K.B.E., M.A., M.D., PH.D., F.R.C.P.(U.K.), F.R.C.P.(E.), F.R.C.P.(I.); British physician; b. 6 March 1923, Port Elizabeth, S. Africa; s. of Benjamin Hoffenberg and Dora Hoffenberg; m. Margaret Rosenberg, 1949; two s.; ed. Grey High School, Port Elizabeth, Univ. of Cape Town Medical School; Sr. Lecturer in Medicine, Groote Schuur Hosp., Cape Town 1955–68; MRC Sr. Scientist and Consultant Physician, Nat. Inst. for Medical Research and Royal Free Hosp., London, England 1968–70, at MRC Clinical Research Centre and Northwick Park Hosp. 1970–72; Prof. of Medicine Univ. of Birmingham 1972–85; Pres. Royal Coll. of Physicians, London 1983–89, Wolfson Coll. Oxford 1985–93, Mental Health Foundation 1989–; Prof. of Medical Ethics Univ. of Queensland 1993–95; Hon. Fellow, American Coll. of Physicians; Hon. F.R.A.C.P.; Hon. F.A.C.P.; Hon. F.R.C.P.C.; Hon. F.F.O.M.; Hon. F.F.P.M.; Hon. F.R.C.Psych.; Hon. F.R.C.S. (Ed.); Hon. F.R.C.P.C.H.; Hon. mem. Acad. of Medicine of Malaysia; Hon. D.Sc. (Leicester, City Univ., London, Witwatersrand, Cape Town, Imperial Coll., London Univ.); Hon. M.D. (Bristol). *Publications:* numerous chapters and articles on plasma protein metabolism, thyroid function and other aspects of endocrinology. *Leisure interests:* walking, golf. *Address:* 1 Sherborne House, Sherborne, Glos., GL54 3DZ, England. *Telephone:* (01451) 844545. *Fax:* (01451) 844874.

HOFFMAN, Alan Jerome, A.B., PH.D.; American mathematician and educator; b. 30 May 1924, New York; s. of Jesse and Muriel Hoffman; m. 1st Esther Walker 1947 (died 1988); two d.; m. 2nd Elinor Hershaft 1990; ed. George Washington High School, Columbia Univ.; mem. U.S. Army Signal Corps 1943–46; mem. Inst. for Advanced Study 1950–51; Mathematician, Nat. Bureau of Standards 1951–56; Scientific Liaison Officer, Office of Naval Research, London 1956–57; Consultant, Gen. Electric Co. 1957–61; Adjunct Prof. City Univ. of New York 1965–75; Research Staff mem. IBM Research Center 1961–; IBM Fellow 1977–; Visiting Prof., Yale Univ. 1975–80, Rutgers Univ. 1990–, Georgia Inst. of Tech. 1992–93; Consulting Prof., Stanford Univ. 1981–91; Fellow, New York Acad. of Sciences, American Acad. of Arts and Sciences; mem. Nat. Acad. of Sciences; Hon. D.Sc. (Technion) 1986; Von Neumann Prize (Operations Research Soc. and Inst. of Man. Science) 1992. *Publications:* numerous articles in mathematical journals. *Leisure interests:* table tennis, music. *Address:* IBM T.U. Watson Research Center, Box 218, Yorktown Heights, NY 10598, U.S.A.

HOFFMAN, Dustin Lee; American actor; b. 8 Aug. 1937, Los Angeles, Calif.; s. of Harry Hoffman; m. 1st Anne Byrne 1969 (divorced); two d.; m. 2nd Lisa Gottsegen 1980; two s. two d.; ed. Santa Monica City Coll.; worked as an attendant at a psychiatric inst.; demonstrator Macy's toy dept.; First stage role in Yes is for a Very Young Man (Sarah Lawrence Coll., Bronxville, N.Y.); Broadway debut in A Cook for Mr. General 1961; Officier Ordre des Arts et des Lettres; Britannia Award (B.A.F.T.A.) 1997. *Other stage appearances in:* Harry, Noon and Night 1964, Journey of the Fifth Horse (Obie Award) 1966, Star Wagon 1966, Fragments 1966, Eh? (Drama Desk, Theatre World, Vernon Rice Awards) 1967, Jimmy Shine 1968, Death of a Salesman 1984, The Merchant of Venice 1989; Asst. Dir. A View from the Bridge; Dir. All Over Town 1974. *Film appearances in:* The Tiger Makes Out 1966, Madigan's Millions 1966, The Graduate 1967, Midnight Cowboy 1969, John and Mary 1969, Little Big Man 1970, Who is Harry Kellerman ...? 1971, Straw Dogs 1971, Alfredo Alfredo, Papillon 1973, Lenny 1974, All the President's Men 1975, Marathon Man 1976, Straight Time 1978, Agatha 1979, Kramer vs. Kramer 1979 (Acad. Award 1980, New York Film Critics Award), Tootsie (New York Film Critics Award, Nat. Soc. of Film Critics Award) 1982, Ishtar 1987, Rain Man (Acad. and Golden Globe Awards) 1988, Family Business 1989, Dick Tracy 1990, Hook 1991, Billy Bathgate 1991, Hero 1992, Outbreak 1995, American Buffalo, Sleeper 1996, Wag the Dog 1997, Mad City 1997, Sphere 1997. *TV appearance in:* Death of a Salesman 1985. *Leisure interests:* tennis, piano, photography, reading. *Address:* Punch Productions, 1926 Broadway, Suite 305, New York, NY 10023, U.S.A.

HOFFMAN, Grace; American mezzo-soprano singer; b. 14 Jan. 1925, Cleveland, Ohio; d. of Dave and Hermina Hoffman; ed. Western Reserve Univ. and Manhattan School of Music, New York; completed musical studies in Italy (Fulbright Scholarship); appeared at Maggio Musicale, Florence; guest performance as Azucena (Il Trovatore) Zürich Opera and subsequently mem. of this company for two years; debut at La Scala, Milan as Fricka (Die Walküre); with Stuttgart Opera 1955–; given titles Württembergische Kammersängerin 1960, Austrian Kammersängerin 1980; has appeared at Edinburgh and Bayreuth festivals; numerous guest appearances in leading roles at Teatro Colón, Buenos Aires, San Francisco Opera, Chicago Lyric Opera, Covent Garden, Metropolitan Opera, the Vienna Opera, in Berlin, Brussels, etc.; numerous oratorio and concert appearances in the major European music centres; Prof. of Voice, Hochschule für Musik, Stuttgart 1978; Vercelli Prize, Medal of State of Baden-Württemberg 1978. *Leisure interests:* her house and furnishing it. *Address:* Bergstrasse 19, 72666 Neckartailfingen, Germany (Home).

HOFFMANN, Baron (Life Peer) cr. 1995, of Chedworth in the County of Gloucestershire, **Rt. Hon. Leonard Hubert Hoffmann,** Kt., M.A., P.C.; British judge; b. 8 May 1934; s. of B. W. Hoffmann and G. Hoffmann; m. Gillian Sterner 1957; two d.; ed. South African Coll. School, Cape Town, Univ. of Cape Town and Queen's Coll. Oxford; Advocate, Supreme Court of S. Africa 1958–60; called to Bar, Gray's Inn, London 1964, Bencher 1984; Q.C. 1977; Judge, Courts of Appeal of Jersey and Guernsey 1980–85; Judge, High Court of Justice, Chancery Div. 1985–92; Lord Justice of Appeal 1992–95; a Lord of Appeal in Ordinary 1995–; Judge Court of Final Appeal, Hong Kong Special Admin. Region 1997–; Dir E.N.O. 1985–90, 1991–94; Stowell Civil Law Fellow, Univ. Coll. Oxford 1961–73; Hon. Fellow, Queen's Coll. Oxford; Hon D.C.L. (City) 1992, (Univ. of West of England) 1995. *Publication:* The South African Law of Evidence 1963. *Address:* Surrey Lodge, 23 Keats Grove, London, NW3 2RS, England.

HOFFMANN, Luc, PH.D.; Swiss biologist; b. 23 Jan. 1923, Basel; s. of Dr. Emanuel Hoffmann and Marie-Anne Hoffmann (née Stehlin); m. Daria Razumovsky 1953; one s. three d.; ed. Gymnasium Flim, Grisons, Univ. of Basel; f. Station Biologique de la Tour du Valat 1954, Man. Dir. 1954–84, Chair. of Bd. Fondation Tour du Valat 1974–; f. World Wildlife Fund (WWF) (later World Wide Fund for Nature) 1961, Vice-Pres. of Bd. 1961–88 (Exec. Vice-Pres. 1971–78); Vice-Pres. of Bd. Int. Union for Conservation of Nature (IUCN) 1966–69; Hon. Dir. Int. Waterfowl and Wetlands Research Bureau (IWRB) 1962–68; mem. Exec. Cttee. Int. Council for Bird Preservation (ICBP) 1984–90, Vice-Pres. Bd. of Dirs. Hoffmann-La Roche and Co., Basel 1990–96; Commdr. Order of the Golden Ark (Netherlands) 1988, Dr. h.c. Univ. of Basel. *Publications:* 60 publs. in the fields of ornithology, wetland ecology and conservation, (with K. Weber) Camargue 1968. *Leisure interests:* contemporary art, bird watching. *Address:* La Tour du Valat, 13200 Le Sambuc, France (Office); Le Petit Essert, 1147 Montricher, Switzerland (Home). *Telephone:* 021 864 5977 (Office); 90 97 20 13 (Home).

HOFFMANN, Roald, PH.D.; American professor of chemistry; b. 18 July 1937, Złoczow, Poland; s. of Hillel Safran and Clara Rosen, step s. of Paul Hoffmann; m. Eva Börjesson 1960; one s. one d.; ed. Columbia and Harvard Univs.; Jr. Fellow, Soc. of Fellows, Harvard Univ. 1962–65; Assoc. Prof. of Chem., Cornell Univ. 1965–68, Prof. 1968–74, John A. Newman Prof. of Physical Science 1974–96, F.M.T. Rhodes Prof. of Humane Letters 1996–; mem. American Acad. of Arts and Sciences, Nat. Acad. of Sciences, American Philosophical Soc.; Foreign mem. Royal Soc., Indian Nat. Acad. of Sciences, Royal Swedish Acad. of Sciences; mem. Acad. of Sciences of the U.S.S.R., Societas Scientarum Fennica 1986; Hon. D. Tech. (Royal Inst. of Technology, Stockholm) 1977, Hon. D.Sc. (Yale) 1980, (Columbia) 1982, (Hartford) 1982, (City Univ. of New York) 1983, (Puerto Rico) 1983, (Uruguay) 1984, (La Plata) 1984, (Colgate) 1985, (State Univ. of New York at Binghamton) 1985, (Ben Gurion Univ. of Negev) 1989, (Lehigh) 1989, (Carleton) 1989, (Md.) 1990, (Ariz.) 1991, (Bar-Ilan Univ.) 1991, (Central Fla.) 1991, (Athens) 1991, (Thessaloniki) 1991, (St. Petersburg) 1991, (Barcelona) 1992, (Northwestern Univ.) 1996, (The Technion) 1996; American Chem. Soc. Award 1969, Fresenius Award 1969, Harrison Howe Award 1969, Annual Award of Int. Acad. of Quantum Molecular Sciences 1970, Arthur C. Cope Award, A.C.S. 1973, Linus Pauling Award 1974, Nichols Medal 1980, shared Nobel Prize for Chemistry 1981, Inorganic Chemistry Award A.C.S. 1982, Nat. Medal of Science 1984, Nat. Acad. of Sciences Award, in Chemical Sciences 1986, Priestley Medal 1990. *Publications:* Conservation of Orbital Symmetry 1969, The Metamict State 1987, Solids and Surfaces 1988, Gaps and Verges 1990, Chemistry Imagined 1993, The Same and Not the Same 1995, Old Wine, New Flasks 1997. *Address:* Department of Chemistry, Cornell University, Ithaca, NY 14853, U.S.A. *Telephone:* 607-255-3419 (Office).

HOFMANN, Peter; German tenor; b. 12 Aug. 1944, Marienbad; ed. Hochschule für Musik, Karlsruhe; operatic début as Tamino, Lübeck 1972; mem. Stuttgart Opera 1973–; sang Siegmund, centenary production of The Ring, Bayreuth 1976, Covent Garden London 1976; U.S. début as Siegmund, San Francisco Opera 1977; début Metropolitan New York (Lohengrin) 1980; pop artist 1984–. *Address:* c/o Fritz Höfman, Schloss Schönreuth 8581, Germany.

HOFMANN, Werner, D.PHIL.; Austrian museum administrator and author; b. 8 Aug. 1928, Vienna; s. of Leopold Hofmann and Anna (née Visvader) Hofmann; m. Jacqueline (née Buron) Hofmann 1950; ed. Univ. of Vienna; Asst. Albertina, Vienna 1950–55; Dir. Museum of the 20th Century, Vienna 1962–69, Hamburger Kunsthalle 1969–90; Guest lecturer Barnard Coll., N.Y. 1957; Guest Prof. Berkeley, Calif. 1961, Harvard Univ. 1981, 1982, Columbia Univ. 1984, New York Univ. 1991, Vienna Univ. 1991; Commdr. Ordre des Arts et des Lettres; Gold Ehren-Medaille City of Vienna 1988, Sigmund-Freud-Preis 1991. *Publications:* Die Plastik des 20. Jahrhunderts 1958, Das irdische Paradies-Kunst im 19. Jahrhundert 1960, Grundlagen der modernen Kunst 1966, Turning Points in 20th Century Art 1969, Gustav Klimt und die Wiener Jahrhundertwende 1970, Nana, Mythos und Wirklichkeit 1973, Kataloge der Ausstellungsreihe "Kunst um 1800" 1974–80, Edouard Manet: Das Frühstück im Atelier 1985, Ausstellungskatalog "Zauber der Medusa" 1987, Une Époque en rupture 1750–1830 1995, Die Moderne im Rück-Spiegel. Hauptwege der Kunstgeschichte 1998. *Address:* Sierichstr. 154, 22299 Hamburg, Germany (Home). *Telephone:* 46 47 11. *Fax:* 46 47 11.

HOFMEISTER, Paul Emil Julius; German business executive; b. 28 April 1909, Bremen; s. of Heinrich Hofmeister and Dora Meijer; m. Elisabeth Sommer 1934 (deceased); one d.; ed. commercial school; joined Norddeutsche Affinerie 1927, mem. man. 1947, Pres. 1961–76, Chair. 1976–81, Hon. Chair. 1981–; Hon. Chair. Otavi Minen AG, Eschborn 1985; Orden al Mérito Bernardo O'Higgins (Chile). *Leisure interests:* riding, golf, collecting art. *Address:* Borchlingweg 11, 22605 Hamburg, Germany (Home). *Telephone:* 880-41-34 (Home).

HOFMEKLER, Ori, B.F.A.; Israeli painter; b. 12 March 1952, Israel; s. of Daniel Hofmekler and Rina Kune; m. Ilana Wellisch 1977; one s. one d.; ed. Bezalel Acad., Jerusalem and Jerusalem Univ.; Shtrouk Prize 1976. *Publications:* Hofmekler's People 1983; contribs. to Penthouse Magazine since 1983, and to magazines in France, Germany and U.S.A. *Leisure interests:* reading, sports and travel.

HOGAN, Linda; American poet, novelist and essayist; Assoc. Prof. Univ. of Colo. *Publications include:* Mean Spirit, Savings, Red Clay (poems and stories), Solo Storms (novel), Stories We Hold Secret, Book of Medicines (poetry), From Women's Experience to Feminist Theology. *Address:* University of Colorado, Central Office, Boulder, CO 80309, U.S.A.

HOGAN, Paul, A.O.; Australian film actor; m. 1st Noelene Hogan (dissolved 1989); five c.; m. 2nd Linda Kozlowski 1990; former rigger on Sydney Harbour Bridge; host of TV shows A Current Affair, The Paul Hogan Show; filmed TV specials on location in England 1983; commercials for Australian Tourist Comm., Fosters Lager; Dir. Lightning Jack Film Trust. *Films:* Crocodile Dundee 1986, Crocodile Dundee II 1989, Almost An Angel 1993,

Lightning Jack 1994, Flipper 1996. *TV:* Anzacs: The War Down Under. *Address:* c/o Silverstream Associates, Level 1, NAB House, 225 George Street, Sydney, N.S.W. 2000, Australia.

HOGARTH, (Arthur) Paul, O.B.E., R.A.; British artist; b. 4 Oct. 1917, Kendal, Cumbria; s. of Arthur Hogarth and Janet Bownass Hogarth; m. 1st Doreen Courtman 1940; m. 2nd Phyllis Pamplin 1953; m. 3rd Patricia Douthwaite 1961 (divorced 1981); m. 4th Diana Marjorie Cochran 1986; one s.; ed. St. Agnes School, Manchester, Manchester Coll. of Art and St. Martin's School of Art, London; Sr. Tutor, R.C.A. 1964–71; painter in watercolours, draughtsman, illustrator and printmaker; rep. in many perm. collections including: (U.K.) British Museum, Tate Gallery, Royal Acad. of Arts, Fitzwilliam Museum, Cambridge, Whitworth Art Gallery, Manchester, Carlisle Art Gallery and Victoria and Albert Museum; (U.S.A.) Boston Public Library, Logan Library, Philadelphia and Library of Congress, Washington D.C.; retrospective exhbns. include The World of Paul Hogarth, 1953–69, at R.C.A. 1971, Travels through the Seventies, Kyle Gallery, London 1980, The Other Hogarth: Drawings, Lithographs and Watercolours, 1954–84 (Northern Arts Council), at art galleries in N. England 1984–85, Ports of Call, Kyle Gallery 1991, Travels in D. H. Lawrence Country 1994, Travels in Croatia 1995; Royal Designer for Industry 1979, Francis Williams Illustration Award 1982. *Publications:* Creative Pencil Drawing 1964, Artist as Reporter 1967 (revised and enlarged 1986), Creative Ink Drawing 1968, Artists on Horseback 1972, Arthur Boyd Houghton 1983, Graham Greene Country 1986, The Mediterranean Shore 1988, In Praise of Churches (with John Betjeman) 1996, Drawing on Life: the Autobiography of Paul Hogarth 1997. *Address:* c/o Tessa Sayle, 11 Jubilee Place, London, SW3 3TE, England. *Telephone:* 0171-823 3883. *Fax:* 0171-823 3363.

HOGG, Sir Christopher Anthony, Kt., M.A., M.B.A.; British business executive; b. 2 Aug. 1936, London, England; s. of Anthony Wentworth Hogg and Monica Mary Gladwell; m. Anne Patricia Cathie 1961 (dissolved 1997); two d.; ed. Marlborough Coll., Trinity Coll., Oxford, and Harvard School of Business Administration U.S.A.; Nat. Service, Parachute Regt. 1955–57; Research Assoc. Institut pour l'Etude des Méthodes de Direction de l'Entreprise (business school), Lausanne, Switzerland 1962–63; with Philip Hill, Higginson, Erlangers Ltd. (later Hill Samuel & Co. Ltd.) 1963–66; staff mem. Industrial Reorganisation Corpn. 1966–68; joined Courtaulds Group 1968, Man. Dir. 1971, non-exec. Dir. British Celanese Ltd. 1971–72, Chair. 1972–75, Dir. Courtaulds Ltd. 1973–, a Deputy Chair. 1978–80, Chief Exec. 1979–, Chair. Courtaulds PLC 1980–96, Courtaulds Textiles PLC 1990–95; Deputy Chair. Allied Domecq 1995–96, Chair. 1996–; Dir. Reuters Group PLC 1984–, (Chair. 1985–), Smithkline Beecham 1993–; Chair. (non-exec.) Royal Nat. Theatre 1995–; Trustee Ford Foundation 1987–; mem. Dept. of Industry Industrial Devt. Advisory Bd. 1976–81, Cttee. of Award for Harkness Fellowships 1980–86, Int. Council J.P. Morgan 1988–, Court, Bank of England 1992–96; Hon. Fellow Trinity Coll. Oxford 1982; Hon. F.C.S.D. 1987; Hon. D.Sc. (Cranfield Inst. of Tech.) 1986, (Aston) 1988; B.I.M. Gold Medal 1986, Centenary Medal, Soc. of Chemical Industry 1989. *Publication:* Masers and Lasers 1962. *Leisure interests:* theatre, reading, walking. *Address:* Reuters Group PLC, 85 Fleet Street, London, EC4P 4AJ, England (Offices).

HOGG, Baroness (Life Peer) cr. 1995, of Kettlethorpe in the County of Lincolnshire; **Sarah Elizabeth Mary Hogg;** British economist; b. 14 May 1946; d. of Lord Boyd-Carpenter; m. Rt. Hon. Douglas M. Hogg Q.C., M.P. 1968; one s. one d.; ed. St. Mary's Convent, Ascot and Lady Margaret Hall, Oxford Univ.; staff writer, The Economist 1967, Literary Ed. 1970, Econs. Ed. 1977; Econs. Ed. Sunday Times 1981; Presenter, Channel 4 News 1982–83; Econs. Ed. and Deputy Exec. Ed. Finance and Industry, The Times 1984–86; Asst. Ed. and Business and City Ed. The Independent 1986–89; Econs. Ed. The Daily Telegraph 1989–90; Head Policy Unit, 10 Downing Street (rank Second Perm. Sec.) 1990–95; Chair. London Econs. 1997– (Dir. 1995–97); mem. Int. Advisory Bd., Nat. Westminster Bank 1995–, Advisory Bd., Bank Inter 1995–, House of Lords Select Cttee. on Science and Tech. 1995–, Council, Royal Econ. Soc. 1996–, Council, Hansard Soc. 1996–; Dir. London Broadcasting Co. 1982–90, Royal Nat. Theatre 1988–91, Foreign & Colonial Smaller Cos. Investment Trust 1995– (Chair. 1997–), Nat. Provident Inst. 1996–, GKN 1996–; Fellow, Eton Coll. 1996–; Hon. Fellow, Lady Margaret Hall, Oxford 1994; Gov. Centre for Econ. Policy Research 1985–92; Hon. M.A. (Open Univ.) 1987; Hon. D.Litt. (Loughborough Univ.) 1992; Wincott Foundation Financial Journalist of the Year 1985. *Publication:* Too Close to Call (with Jonathan Hill) 1995. *Address:* House of Lords, London, SW1A 0PW, England.

HOGGART, Richard, M.A., D.LITT.; British educator and writer; b. 24 Sept. 1918, Leeds; s. of Tom Longfellow Hoggart and Adeline Emma Hoggart (née Long); m. Mary Holt France 1942; two s. one d.; ed. Leeds Univ.; Royal Artillery 1940–46; Staff Tutor and Sr. Staff Tutor, Univ. Coll. of Hull and Univ. of Hull 1946–59; Sr. Lecturer in English, Univ. of Leicester 1959–62; Visiting Prof. Univ. of Rochester, N.Y. 1956–57; Prof. of English, Birmingham Univ. 1962–73; Pres. British Asscn. of fmr. UN Civil Servants 1978–86; Chair. European Museum of the Year Award Cttee. 1977–, Broadcasting Research Unit 1980–90; mem. Albemarle Cttee. on Youth Services 1958–60, Youth Service Devt. Council 1960–62, Pilkington Cttee. on Broadcasting 1960–62; Gov. Birmingham Repertory Theatre 1963–70; Dir. Centre for Contemporary Cultural Studies 1964–73; mem. BBC Gen. Advisory Council 1959–60, 1964–70, Arts Council of G.B. 1976–81, Culture Advisory Cttee. of U.K. Nat. Comm. to UNESCO 1966–70, Communications Advisory Cttee. of U.K. Nat. Comm. to UNESCO 1977–79, Wilton Park Academic Council 1983–; Chair. Arts Council Drama Panel 1977–80, Vice-Chair. Arts Council 1980–81, Chair. Advisory Council for Adult and Continuing Educ. 1977–83, The Statesman and Nation Publishing Co. Ltd. 1978–81; Gov. Royal Shakespeare Theatre 1966–88; Asst. Dir.-Gen. for Social Sciences, Humanities and Culture UNESCO 1970–75; Warden of Goldsmiths' Coll. 1976–84; Chair. Book Trust 1995–97; Pres. Nat. Book Cttee. 1997–; Hon. Visiting Prof., Univ. of E. Anglia 1985–, Univ. of Surrey 1985–; Hon. Fellow Sheffield City Polytechnic 1983, Goldsmiths' Coll. 1987, Ruskin Coll. Oxford 1994; BBC Reith Lecturer 1971; Hon. D.Univ. (Open Univ.) 1972, (Surrey) 1981; Hon. D.-ès-L. (Bordeaux) 1974, (Paris) 1987; Hon. LL.D. (C.N.A.A.) 1982, (York Univ., Toronto) 1988; Hon. Litt.D. (E. Anglia) 1986, Hon. D.Litt. (Leicester Univ.), (Hull Univ.) 1988, (Univ. of Keele) 1995, (Metropolitan Univ. of Leeds) 1995, (Univ. of Westminster) 1996; Hon. Ed.D. (Univ. of E. London) 1998. *Publications:* Auden 1951, The Uses of Literacy 1957, W. H. Auden—A Selection 1961, Teaching Literature 1963, How and Why Do We Learn 1965, Essays in Literature and Culture 1969, Speaking to Each Other 1970, Only Connect 1972, An Idea and Its Servants 1978, An English Temper 1982, The Future of Broadcasting (ed. with Janet Morgan) 1978, An Idea of Europe (with Douglas Johnson) 1987, A Local Habitation 1988, Liberty and Legislation (Ed.) 1989, A Sort of Clowning 1990, An Imagined Life 1992, Townscape with Figures 1994, The Way We Live Now 1995. *Leisure interests:* family, reading, writing. *Address:* Mortonsfield, Beavers Hill, Farnham, Surrey, GU9 7DF, England. *Telephone:* (01252) 715740. *Fax:* (01252) 715740.

HOGWOOD, Christopher Jarvis Haley, C.B.E., M.A., F.R.S.A.; British musician; b. 10 Sept. 1941, Nottingham; s. of Haley Evelyn and Marion Constance (née Higgott) Hogwood; ed. Cambridge Univ., Charles Univ., Prague, Czechoslovakia; founder-mem. Early Music Consort of London 1965–76; f. and Dir. Acad. of Ancient Music 1973–; mem. Faculty of Music, Cambridge Univ. 1975–; Dir. Handel and Haydn Soc., Boston, U.S.A. 1986–; Hon. Prof. of Music, Keele Univ. 1986–90; Dir. of Music, St. Paul Chamber Orchestra, Minn., U.S.A. 1987–92, Prin. Guest Conductor 1992–98; Int. Prof. of Early Music Performance, R.A.M., London 1992–; Visiting Prof. Dept. of Music, King's Coll., London 1992–96; Artistic Dir. Summer Mozart Festival, Nat. Symphony Orchestra, U.S.A. 1993–; Assoc. Dir. Beethoven Acad., Antwerp 1998–; Hon. Fellow, Jesus Coll., Cambridge 1989, Pembroke Coll., Cambridge 1992; Hon. D.Mus. (Keele) 1991; Walter Willson Cobbett Medal (Worshipful Co. of Musicians) 1986, Freeman Worshipful Co. of Musicians 1989, Distinguished Musician Award (Inc. Soc. of Musicians) 1997. *Publications:* Music at Court 1977, The Trio Sonata 1979, Haydn's Visits to England 1980, Music in Eighteenth Century England (co-author) 1983, Handel 1984, Holmes' Life of Mozart (ed.) 1991; many editions of musical scores; contribs. to The New Grove Dictionary of Music and Musicians 1980; numerous recordings. *Address:* 10 Brookside, Cambridge, CB2 1JE, England. *Telephone:* (01223) 363975.

HOHENFELLNER, Peter, D.IUR.; Austrian diplomatist; b. 1939, Vienna; ed. Univ. of Vienna; joined Ministry for Foreign Affairs 1967; served Austrian Legation, Prague 1969–70, Cabinet of Fed. Chancellor 1970, Embassies in Tunis 1972–74, Algiers 1974–75, Budapest 1975–78; Amb. to Cuba 1978–81, to Lebanon 1982–84; Dir. Dept. for Int. Orgs. 1985–88; Deputy Political Dir. Ministry for Foreign Affairs, Vienna 1986–88; Perm. Rep. to UN 1988–94. *Address:* c/o Ministry of Foreign Affairs, Ballhausplatz 2, 1014 Vienna, Austria.

HOHLER, Erla Bergendahl, PH.D., F.S.A.; Norwegian archaeologist and art historian; b. 20 Nov. 1937, Oslo; m. Christopher Hohler 1961; three c.; ed. Univ. of Oslo; Asst. Prof. Inst. of Art History, Univ. of Oslo 1975; Keeper Medieval Dept., Univ. Museum of Nat. Antiquities, Oslo 1987; Prof. Inst. of Archaeology, Art History and Numismatics, Oslo Univ. 1993–; Prof. of Art History Univ. of Tromsø 1994; mem. Det Norske Videnskapsakademi 1994. *Publications:* The Capitals of Urnes Church 1975, Stavkirkene 1981, Stilentwicklung in der Holzkirchen Architektur 1981, Norwegian Stave Church Carving 1989, Norwegian Stave Church Carving Catalogue Raisonné 1997. *Address:* Lyder Sagens Gt. 23, 0358 Oslo, Norway. *Telephone:* 47 22 85 18 52.

HOHOFF, Curt, DR.PHIL.; German writer; b. 18 March 1913, Emden; s. of Caspar Hohoff and Elisabeth (née Waterman) Hohoff; m. Elfriede Federhen 1949; four s. one d.; ed. Univs. of Münster, Munich, Cambridge and Berlin; journalist Rheinischer Merkur, Koblenz 1948–49, Süddeutsche Zeitung, Munich 1949–50, freelance 1950–; mem. Akad. der Künste, Berlin 1956, Bayerische Akad. der Künste, Munich 1958; Bundesverdienstkreuz 1992. *Publications:* Woina-Woina, Russisches Tagebuch 1951, Geist und Ursprung (essays) 1954, Heinrich von Kleist (biog.) 1957, Schnittpunkte (essays) 1963, Die Märzhasen (novel) 1966, München 1970, Jakob M. R. Lenz (biog.) 1977, Grimmelshausen (biog.) 1978, Unter den Fischen (memoirs) 1982, Die verbotene Stadt (novel) 1986, Besuch bei Kalypso, Landschaften und Bildnisse 1988, J. W. von Goethe, Dichtung und Leben (biog.) 1989, Scheda—im Flug vorbei (novel) 1993, Veritas christiana (essays) 1994, Glanz der Wirklichkeit, Gelehrte Prosa (essays) 1998. *Address:* Adalbert-Stifter-Strasse 27, 81925 Munich, Germany. *Telephone:* (089) 9828980.

HOLBOROW, Leslie Charles, B.PHIL., M.A.; New Zealand university vice-chancellor; b. 28 Jan. 1941, Auckland; s. of George Holborow and Ivah V. Holborow; m. Patricia L. Walsh 1965; one s. two d.; ed. Henderson High School, Auckland Grammar School and Univs. of Auckland and Oxford; Jr.

lecturer, Univ. of Auckland 1963; lecturer, Sr. Lecturer, Univ. of Dundee (until 1967 Queen's Coll. Univ. of St. Andrews) 1965–74; Prof. of Philosophy, Univ. of Queensland, Brisbane 1974–85, Pres. Professorial Bd. 1980–81, Pro-Vice-Chancellor (Humanities) 1983–85; Vice-Chancellor, Victoria Univ. of Wellington 1985–98; Chair. N.Z. Vice-Chancellors' Cttee. 1990, 1996; Council mem. Asscn. of Commonwealth Univs. 1990–91, 1996; Pres. Australasian Asscn. of Philosophy 1977; Nat. Pres. N.Z. Inst. of Int. Affairs 1987–90; mem. N.Z. Cttee. for Pacific Econ. Co-operation 1986–94, Education Sub-Cttee. of N.Z. Nat. Comm. for UNESCO 1996–; Trustee N.Z. String Quartet 1990–. *Publications:* articles in philosophical journals. *Leisure interests:* tramping, sailing, listening to music. *Address:* 11 Kinross Street, Wellington, New Zealand (Home).

HOLBROOKE, Richard C.; American diplomatist; b. 24 April 1941, New York; s. of Dan Holbrooke and Trudi Moos Kearl; two s.; m. 2nd Kati Morton 1995; ed. Brown Univ. and Woodrow Wilson School, Princeton Univ.; Foreign Service Officer in Vietnam and related posts 1962–66; White House Vietnam staff 1966–67; Special Asst. to Under-Secs. of State Katzenbac and Richardson and mem. U.S. del. to Paris peace talks on Vietnam 1967–69; Dir. Peace Corps, Morocco 1970–72; Man. Dir. Foreign Policy (quarterly magazine) 1972–76; consultant, Pres.'s Comm. on Org. of Govt. for Conduct of Foreign Policy and contributing Ed. Newsweek 1974–75; coordinator of nat. security affairs, Carter-Mondale campaign 1976; Asst. Sec. of State for E. Asian & Pacific Affairs 1977–81; Vice-Pres. of Public Strategies 1981–85; Man. Dir. Lehman Brothers 1985–93; Amb. to Germany 1993–94; Asst. Sec. of State for European and Canadian Affairs 1994–96; Vice-Chair. C-S First Boston Corpn. 1996–98; Adviser Baltic Sea Council 1996–98; Special Presidential Envoy for Cyprus 1997–98, to Yugoslavia (on Kosovo crisis); nominated as Perm. Rep. to UN 1999. *Publications:* Counsel to the President (co-author) 1991, To End a War 1998; articles and essays. *Leisure interest:* tennis. *Address:* c/o Department of State, 2201 C Street, N.W., Washington, DC 20520; 799 United Nations Plaza, New York, NY 10017, U.S.A.

HOLDEN, Roberto; Angolan nationalist leader; b. 1925, São Salvador, Northern Prov.; ed. Belgian Congo (now Democratic Republic of the Congo); worked in Finance Dept., Belgian Admin., Léopoldville (now Kinshasa), Stanleyville (now Kisangani) and Bukavu; founded União das Populações de Angola (UPA) 1954; travelled widely in Africa and Europe; attended first and second All African Peoples Confs. Accra 1958, Tunis 1960; elected to the Steering Cttee., Tunis; founded La voix de la nation angolaise, a fortnightly newspaper; assumed leadership of guerrilla liberation operations against the Portuguese in Angola; made several trips to U.S.A. 1961; became leader of Frente Nacional de Libertação de Angola (FNLA) when UPA merged with Partido Democrático Angolano (PDA) March 1962; Premier of Angolan govt. in exile, Governo Revolucionário de Angola no Exílio (GRAE) 1962; leader of defeated FNLA forces in Angolan civil war after Portuguese withdrawal Nov. 1975; exiled to Zaire then Senegal; expelled from Senegal 1979; living in Paris 1980.

HOLDEN-BROWN, Sir Derrick, Kt.; British business executive; b. 14 Feb. 1923, Surrey; s. of Harold Walter and Beatrice Florence (née Walker) Holden-Brown; m. Patricia Mary Ross Mackenzie 1950; one s. one d.; ed. Westcliff; served Royal Navy 1941–46; Chartered Accountant 1948; joined Hiram Walker and Sons, (distillers) 1949; Man. Dir., Cairnes Ltd., (brewers), Ireland 1954, Grants of St. James's Ltd. 1960; Dir. Ind Coope Ltd. 1962; Chair. Victoria Wine Co. 1964; Dir. Allied Breweries Ltd. 1967–91, Finance Dir. 1972, Vice-Chair. 1975–82, Chair. Beer Div. 1978–86; Chair. Brewers' Soc. 1978–80, Vice-Pres. 1980–; Chair. Allied-Lyons PLC 1982–91, C.E.O. 1982–88; Deputy Chair. Sun Alliance and London Insurance PLC 1985–92; Dir. Midland Bank PLC 1984–88, FIDC 1984– (Deputy Chair. 1974–76); Pres. Food and Drink Fed. 1984–86; mem. Inst. of Chartered Accountants of Scotland. *Leisure interests:* sailing, offshore cruising. *Address:* Copse House, Milford-on-Sea, Lymington, Hants., England. *Telephone:* (01590) 642247.

HOLDERNESS, Baron (Life Peer), cr. 1979, of Bishop Wilton in the County of Humberside; **Richard Frederick Wood,** P.C., D.L.; British politician; b. 5 Oct. 1920, London; s. of 1st Earl of Halifax and Lady Dorothy Onslow; m. Diana Kellett 1947; one s. one d.; ed. Eton and New Coll., Oxford; Attaché, British Embassy, Rome 1940; army 1940–43, wounded; M.P. 1950–79; Parl. Pvt. Sec. to Minister of Pensions 1951–53, to Minister of State, Bd. of Trade 1953–54, to Minister of Agric. and Fisheries 1954–55; Joint Parl. Sec. Ministry of Pensions and Nat. Insurance 1955–58; Parl. Sec. Ministry of Labour 1958–59; Minister of Power 1959–63, of Pensions and Nat. Ins. 1963–64, of Overseas Devt. 1970–74; Dir. Yorks. Conservative Newspapers 1947–55, Hulton Press 1953–55, F. J. C. Lilley and Co. Ltd. 1967–70, Hargreaves Group PLC 1974–86; Gov. Queen Elizabeth's Foundation for the Disabled 1946–; Pres. 1983–96; Chair. Disablement Services Authority 1987–91, Advisory Group on Rehabilitation 1991–96; Regional Dir. Yorks. and Humberside Regional Bd., Lloyds Bank Ltd. 1981–90; Deputy Lieut. County of Humberside; Hon. Col. 4th Battalion, Royal Green Jackets 1967–89; Hon. LL.D. (Sheffield, Hull and Leeds Univs.). *Leisure interest:* travel. *Address:* Flat Top House, Bishop Wilton, York, YO4 1RY; 43 Lennox Gardens, London, SW1X 0DF, England. *Telephone:* (01759) 368266 (Bishop Wilton), 0171-225 2151 (London). *Fax:* (01759) 368727 (Bishop Wilton), 0171-589 4356 (London).

HOLDGATE, Sir Martin Wyatt, Kt., C.B., M.A., PH.D.; British biologist; b. 14 Jan. 1931, Horsham; s. of the late Francis W. Holdgate and Lois M. (née Bebbington) Holdgate; m. Elizabeth M. Weil (née Dickason) 1963; two s.; ed. Arnold School, Blackpool and Queens' Coll. Cambridge; Research Fellow, Queens' Coll. Cambridge 1953–56; Jt. leader Gough Island Scientific Survey 1955–56; lecturer in Zoology, Univ. of Manchester 1956–57, Univ. of Durham 1957–60; leader, Royal Soc. Expedition to southern Chile 1958–59; Asst. Dir. of Research, Scott Polar Research Inst. Cambridge 1960–63; Chief Biologist, British Antarctic Survey 1963–66; Deputy Dir. (Research), The Nature Conservancy (U.K.) 1966–70; Dir. Central Unit on Environmental Pollution, Dept. of Environment 1970–74; Dir. Inst. of Terrestrial Ecology 1974–76; Dir.-Gen. of Research, Dept. of Environment 1976–81; Chief Scientist and Deputy Sec. (Environment Protection), Dept. of Environment and Chief Scientific Adviser, Dept. of Transport 1981–88; Dir.-Gen. Int. Union for Conservation of Nature and Natural Resources (now World Conservation Union) 1988–94; Pres. Zoological Soc. of London 1994–; Co-Chair. Intergovernmental Panel on Forests, UN Comm. on Sustainable Devt. 1995–97; mem. Royal Comm. on Environmental Pollution 1994–; Chair. Int. Inst. for Environment and Devt. 1994–, Governing Council, Arnold School 1997–; Hon. D.Sc. (Durham) 1991, Sussex (1993), (Lancaster) 1995; Bruce Medal, Royal Soc. of Edinburgh and Royal Scottish Geog. Soc., Silver Medal, UNEP, UNEP Global 500 1988, Commdr. Order of the Golden Ark 1991, Patrons Medal, Royal Geographical Soc. 1992; Livingstone Medal, Royal Scottish Geographical Soc., Int. Conservationist of the Year Award, Nat. Wildlife Fed., U.S.A. 1993. *Publications include:* Mountains in the Sea: The Story of the Gough Island Expedition 1958, A Perspective of Environmental Pollution 1979, From Care to Action 1996, The Green Web: A Union for World Conservation 1998. *Leisure interests:* natural history, climbing hills. *Address:* 35 Wingate Way, Trumpington, Cambridge, CB2 2HD, England. *Telephone:* (01223) 840086. *Fax:* (01223) 512131.

HOLDING, Clyde, LL.B.; Australian politician; b. 27 April 1931, Melbourne; m. 1st Margaret Sheer (divorced); two s. one d.; m. 2nd Judith Crump; one d.; ed. Melbourne Univ.; solicitor; mem. Victorian Parl. for Richmond 1962–77; Leader State Parl. Labor Party and Leader of Opposition 1967–77; mem. Fed. Parl. for Melbourne Ports 1977–; Minister for Aboriginal Affairs 1983–86, for Arts and Territories 1988–89, of Employment Services and Youth Affairs, and Minister Assisting the Treasurer 1987–88, Minister, assisting the Minister for Immigration, Local Govt. and Ethnic Affairs 1988–89, assisting the Prime Minister 1988–89; Minister for Arts, Tourism and Territories 1989–90; Pres. Victorian Labor Party 1977–79. *Address:* 117 Fitzroy Street, St Kilda, Vic. 3183, Australia. *Telephone:* (3) 9534 8126. *Fax:* (3) 9534 1575.

HOLDSWORTH, Sir (George) Trevor, Kt., C.V.O., F.C.A.; British business executive and accountant; b. 29 May 1927, Bradford; m. 1st Patricia June Ridler 1951 (died 1993); three s.; m. 2nd Jenny Watson 1995; ed. Keighley Grammar School, Bradford; with Rawlinson, Greaves and Mitchell (accountants), Bradford 1944–51; with Bowater Corpn. 1952–63, becoming Dir. and Controller of U.K. paper making subsidiaries; Deputy Chief Accountant, Guest Keen and Nettlefolds Ltd. 1963–64, Group Chief Accountant 1965–67, Chair. 1980–88; Gen. Man. Dir., GKN Screws and Fasteners Ltd. 1968–70, Dir. and Group Controller 1970–72, Group Exec. Vice-Chair., Corpn. Controls and Services 1973–74, Deputy Chair. 1974, Man. Dir. and Deputy Chair. 1977, Chair. 1980–88; Chair. British Satellite Broadcasting 1987–90; Dir. Thorn EMI PLC 1977–86, Equity Capital for Industry Ltd. 1976–83, Midland Bank PLC 1979–88, Prudential Corpn. 1986–96 (Deputy Chair. 1988–92); Chair. Allied Colloids Group PLC 1983–96; Dir. Opera Now Enterprises Ltd. 1988; Dir. (non-exec.) Owens-Corning 1994–98; mem. Council, British Inst. of Man. 1974–84, Vice-Chair. 1978–80, Chair. 1980, Vice-Pres. 1982; mem. Council C.B.I. 1974–, Econ. and Financial Policy Cttee. C.B.I. 1976–80, Pres. C.B.I. 1988–90; Chair. (part-time) Nat. Power 1990–95, Beauford PLC 1991–; Chancellor Bradford Univ. 1992–97; Council, Inst. of Dirs. 1978–80, Steering Group on Unemployment 1982, Programmes Unit 1982, Bd. of Govs. Ashridge Man. Coll. 1978–92; Chair. Tax Reform Working Party 1984–86 (Deputy Pres. 1987–88), Lambert Howarth Group PLC 1993–98; Chair. Wigmore Hall Trust 1992–; Vice-Pres. Eng. Employers' Fed. 1980; mem. Exec. Cttee. Soc. of Motor Mfrs. and Traders 1980–83; mem. Eng. Industries Council 1980; mem. Advisory Bd. LEK Partnerships 1992–; Trustee, Anglo-German Foundation for the Study of Industrial Soc. 1980–92; mem. British North American Cttee. 1981–85, European Advisory Council AMF Inc. 1982–85, Council Royal Inst. of Int. Affairs 1983–88; Vice-Pres. Ironbridge Gorge Museum Devt. Trust 1981–; Trustee, Royal Opera House Trust 1981–84; mem. Duke of Edinburgh's Award (Business and Commercial Enterprises Group) 1980, Int. Trustee 1987–94; mem. Council Foundation for Mfg. and Industry; Freeman, City of London; Liveryman, Worshipful Co. of Chartered Accountants in England and Wales; Hon. D. Tech. (Loughborough) 1981, Hon. D.Sc. (Aston) 1982, Hon. D. Business Admin. (Inst. Man. Centre from Buckingham) 1986; Hon. D.Sc. Univ. Sussex; Hon. D.Eng. (Birmingham) 1992; British Inst. Man. Gold Medal 1987; City and Guilds Insignia Award in Tech. (h.c.) 1989; Chartered Accountants Founding Societies' Centenary Award 1983. *Leisure interests:* music, theatre. *Address:* The Athenaeum, Pall Mall, London SW1, England.

HOLKERI, Harri Hermanni, M.POL.SC.; Finnish politician; b. 6 Jan. 1937, Oripää; s. of Antti Edvard Holkeri and Maire Kyllikki Ahlgren; m. Marja-Liisa Lepisto 1960; one s. one d.; Sec. Nat. Coalition Party Youth League 1959–60, Information Sec. 1960–62; Information Sec. Nat. Coalition Party 1962–64, Research Sec. 1964–65, Party Sec. 1965–71, Chair. 1971–79; mem.

Helsinki City Council 1969–88, Chair. 1981–87; mem. Parl. 1970–78; mem. Bd. Bank of Finland 1978–; Chair. of Standing Finnish-Soviet Intergovernmental Comm. for Economic Co-operation 1989–91; Prime Minister of Finland 1987–91; Hon. K.B.E. *Address:* Bank of Finland, P.O. Box 160, 00101 Helsinki, Finland. *Telephone:* (90) 1831.

HOLLÁN, R. Susan; Hungarian professor of haematology; b. 26 Oct. 1920, Budapest; d. of Dr. Henrik Hollán and Dr. Malvin Hornik; m. Dr. György Révész; one s. one d.; ed. Univ. Medical School, Budapest; Internal Med., Rokus Hospital, Budapest 1945–50; Research Fellow, Univ. Med. School, Budapest 1950–54; Science Adviser, Inst. for Experimental Medical Research 1954–91; Dir. Nat. Inst. of Haematology and Blood Transfusion 1959–85, Dir.-Gen. 1985–90; Prof. of Haematology, Postgraduate Med. School 1970–90; Corresp. mem. Hungarian Acad. of Sciences 1973, mem. 1982– (mem. of Presidium 1976–84); fmr. Pres. Int. Soc. of Haematology and Vice-Pres. Int. Soc. of Blood Transfusion; mem. WHO Global AIDS Research Steering Cttee.; mem. WHO Expert Cttee. on Biological Standardization; mem. Clinical and Immunological Work Cttee. of Hungarian Acad. of Sciences; mem. Bd. of Special Cttee. for Clinical Sciences; Exec. mem. Hungarian Medical Research Council; Editor-in-Chief Hungarian Medical Encyclopaedia and Haematologia (quarterly); mem. HSWP Cen. Cttee. 1975–89; Hon. mem. American Soc. of Hematology, Polish Soc. of Haematology, German Soc. of Haematology (Fed. Repub. of Germany), Purkinje Soc. (Czechoslovakia), Turkish Soc. of Haematology, All-Union Scientific Soc. of Haematology and Blood Transfusion (U.S.S.R.); Foreign Corresp. mem. Soc. de Biologie, Collège de France, Paris; Vice-Pres. Nobel Prize Award, Int. Physicians Prevention of Nuclear War 1983–89; Hon. Pres. Hungarian Soc. of Human Genetics; Hungarian Academic Award 1970; State Prize 1974; Socialist Hungary Medal. *Publications:* Basic Problems of Transfusion 1965, Haemoglobins and Haemoglobinopathies 1972, Genetics, Structure and Function of Blood Cells 1980, Management of Blood Transfusion Services 1990; over 300 papers in Hungarian and international medical journals. *Leisure interest:* fine arts, sport. *Address:* Daróczi ut 24, 1113 Budapest (Office); Palánta u. 12, 1025 Budapest, Hungary (Home). *Telephone:* (1) 4669-350; 372-4210 (Office). *Fax:* (1) 4666-004; 372-4352.

HOLLAND, Agnieszka; Polish film director and screenwriter; b. 28 Nov. 1948, Warsaw; m. Laco Adamik; one d.; ed. FAMU film school, Prague; asst. to Kryzstof Zanussi in filming of Illumination 1973; mem. production group 'X' led by Andrzej Wajda in Warsaw 1972–81; dir. first TV film 1973; subsequently worked in theatre in Cracow; co-dir. (with Jerzy Domaradzki and Paweł Kędzierski) film Screen Test 1977; co-scripted Wajda's film Rough Treatment 1978; also worked with Wajda on A Love in Germany, Man of Marble, Man of Iron, The Orchestra Conductor, Korczak, Danton 1982; wrote screenplay for Yurke Bocayevicz's Anna; has also made documentaries for French TV. *Films directed include:* Provincial Actors 1979, The Fever 1980, The Lonely Woman 1981, Angry Harvest (Germany) 1985, To Kill A Priest (France) 1988, Europa Europa (Germany, France) 1990, Oliver, Oliver (France) 1993, Secret Garden (U.S.A.) 1993, Total Eclipse (England, France) 1995, Washington Square (U.S.A.) 1997. *Address:* Agence Nicole Cann, 1 rue Alfred de Vigny, 75008 Paris, France. *Telephone:* (1) 44-15-14-21.

HOLLAND, Charles Hepworth, M.A., PH.D.; British professor of geology and mineralogy; b. 30 June 1923, Southport; s. of William and Elizabeth Holland; m. Eileen Storey 1952; one d.; ed. Univ. of Manchester; Asst. lecturer, Univ. of Manchester 1951–52; Lecturer in Palaeontology and Stratigraphy, Bedford Coll. London 1953–64, Sr. Lecturer in Geology 1965–66; Prof. of Geology and Mineralogy and Head, Dept. of Geology Trinity Coll. Dublin 1966–93, Fellow Emer. 1993–, Dean of Science 1980–84; Pres. Palaeontological Assn. 1974–76, Geological Soc. of London 1984–86; mem. Royal Irish Acad., Academia Europaea; Hon. Corresp. mem. Geol. Soc. of Sweden; T. N. George Medal, Glasgow Geological Soc. 1982, Major Edward Coke Medal, Geological Soc. of London 1991. *Publications:* A Geology of Ireland (ed. and contrib.) 1981, A Global Standard for the Silurian System (ed. and contrib.) 1989, Trinity College Dublin and the Idea of a University (Ed. and contrib.) 1991, The Idea of Time 1999; numerous professional papers. *Leisure interests:* literature, travel, gardening. *Address:* Department of Geology, Trinity College, Dublin 2, Ireland.

HOLLAND, Julian Miles (Jools); British pianist and broadcaster; b. 24 Jan. 1958; s. of Derek Holland and June Rose Lane; one s. two d.; ed. Invicta Sherington School, Shooters' Hill School; pianist 1975–78; keyboard player with pop group Squeeze (hits: Take Me I'm Yours, Cool for Cats, Up The Junction etc.) 1978–; regularly tours U.K. and U.S.A., concerts at Madison Square Garden and Royal Albert Hall. *Solo albums:* A World of His Own 1990, Full Compliment 1991, A–Z of Piano 1993, Live Performance 1995, Solo Piano 1995; guest performances with numerous artists including Elvis Costello, George Harrison; TV Presenter The Tube 1981–86, Juke Box Jury 1989, Sunday Night (with David Sanborn) 1990, The Happening 1990, Later With Jools Holland (series) 1993–; actor and writer TV play The Groovy Fellers 1988; wrote and produced TV films Walking to New Orleans 1985 and Mr Roadrunner 1991. *Publication:* Beat Route 1998. *Leisure interests:* sketching, giving advice. *Address:* Helicon Mountain Ltd., Helicon Mountain, Station Terrace Mews, London, SE3 7LP, England. *Telephone:* 0181-858 0984. *Fax:* 0181-293 4555.

HOLLANDER, John, PH.D.; American poet and professor of English; b. 28 Oct. 1929, New York; s. of Franklin and Muriel (Kornfeld) Hollander; m. 1st Anne Loesser 1953 (divorced 1977); two d.; 2nd Natalie Charkow 1981; ed. Columbia Univ., Harvard Univ., and Indiana Univ.; Lecturer in English, Connecticut Coll. 1957–59; Instructor in English, Yale Univ. 1959–61, Asst. Prof. of English 1961–64, Assoc. Prof. 1964–66, Prof. 1977–85, A. Bartlett Giamatti Prof. 1986–95, Sterling Prof. of English 1995–; Prof. of English, Hunter Coll., New York 1966–77; Christian Gauss Seminarian, Princeton Univ. 1962; Visiting Prof., School of Letters and Linguistic Inst., Indiana Univ. 1964; Visiting Prof. Seminar in American Studies, Salzburg, Austria 1965; editorial assoc. for poetry Partisan Review 1959–65; mem. poetry bd. Wesleyan Univ. Press 1959–62; mem. Editorial Bd. 1981–; Fellow, American Acad. of Arts and Sciences; mem. American Acad. of Arts and Letters; Fellow Ezra Stiles Coll., Yale Univ. 1961–64; Overseas Fellow Churchill Coll., Univ. of Cambridge 1967–68; Fellow Nat. Endowment for Humanities 1973–, Silliman Coll. 1977–; Hon. D.Litt (Marietta Coll.) 1982; Hon. D.H.L. (Indiana) 1990; Levinson Prize 1964, Nat. Inst. of Arts and Letters Award 1963, Guggenheim Fellow 1979–80, Chancellor, Acad. of American Poets 1981–, Bollingen Prize 1983; MacArthur Fellow 1990. *Publications include:* A Crackling of Thorns 1958, The Untuning of the Sky 1961, Movie-Going and Other Poems 1962, Visions from the Ramble 1965, Types of Shape 1969 (enlarged edn.) 1991, The Night Mirror 1971, Town and Country Matters 1972, Selected Poems 1972, The Head of the Bed 1974, Tales Told of the Fathers 1975, Vision and Resonance 1975, Reflections on Espionage 1976, Spectral Emanations 1978, In Place 1978, Blue Wine 1979, The Figure of Echo 1981, Rhyme's Reason 1981 (enlarged edn.) 1989, Powers of Thirteen 1983, In Time and Place 1986, Harp Lake 1988, Some Fugitives Take Cover 1988, Melodious Guile 1988, William Bailey 1991, Tesserae 1993, Selected Poetry 1993, The Gazer's Spirit 1995, The Work of Poetry 1997, The Poetry of Everyday Life 1998, Figurehead 1999; contributor of numerous poems and articles to journals; editor and contributing editor of numerous books including: Poems of Ben Jonson 1961, The Wind and the Rain 1961, Jiggery-Pokery 1966, Poems of Our Moment 1968, Modern Poetry: Essays in Criticism 1968, American Short Stories since 1945 1968, The Oxford Anthology of English Literature (with Frank Kermode, q.v.) 1973, For I. A. Richards: Essays in his Honor 1973, Literature as Experience (with Irving Howe and David Bromwich) 1979, The Essential Rossetti 1990, American Poetry: the Nineteenth Century 1993, Animal Poems (ed.) 1994, Garden Poems (ed.) 1996, Marriage Poems (Ed.) 1997, Frost (Ed.) 1997, Committed to Memory (Ed.) 1999; contributing editor Harper's magazine 1969–71. *Address:* c/o Dept of English, Yale University, P.O. Box 208302, New Haven, CT 06520-8302, U.S.A. *Telephone:* (203) 432-2231. *Fax:* (203) 387-3497.

HOLLANDER, Samuel, O.C., PH.D., F.R.S.C.; British/Canadian professor of economics; b. 6 April 1937, London, England; s. of Jacob Hollander and Lily Hollander; m. Perlette Kéroub 1959; one s. one d.; ed. Gateshead Talmudical Acad., Hendon Tech. Coll., Kilburne Polytechnic, London School of Econs., Princeton Univ., N.J.; emigrated to Canada 1963; Asst. Prof., Univ. of Toronto 1963–67, Assoc. Prof. 1967–70, Prof. 1970–84, Univ. Prof. 1984–98, Univ. Prof. Emer. 1998–; Visiting Prof. Florence Univ., Italy 1973–74, London Univ. 1974–75, Hebrew Univ, Jerusalem 1979–80, 1988, La Trobe Univ., Melbourne, Australia 1985, Auckland Univ., N.Z. 1985, 1988, Sorbonne 1997; several guest lectureships; Fulbright Fellowship 1959; Guggenheim Fellowship 1968–69; Social Science Fed. of Canada 50th Anniversary Book Award 1990. *Publications:* The Sources of Increased Efficiency 1965, The Economics of Adam Smith 1973, The Economics of David Ricardo 1979, The Economics of J. S. Mill 1985, Classical Economics 1987, Ricardo—The New View: Collected Essays I 1995, The Economics of T. R. Malthus 1997, The Literature of Political Economy: Collected Essays II 1998. *Address:* Department of Economics, University of Toronto, 150 St. George Street, Toronto, Ont. M5S 1A1, Canada. *Telephone:* (416) 978-5105. *Fax:* (416) 978-6713.

HÖLLDOBLER, Berthold Karl, DR.RER.NAT.; German professor of zoology; b. 25 June 1936, Erling-Andechs; s. of Dr. med. Karl Hölldobler and Maria Russmann; m. Friederike M. Probst; three s.; ed. Univs. of Würzburg and Frankfurt-am-Main; Asst. Prof. Univ. of Frankfurt 1966–69, Prof. of Zoology 1972; Research Assoc. Harvard Univ. 1969–71, Prof. of Biology 1973–90, Alexander Agassiz Prof. of Zoology 1982–90, Scientific Assoc. 1991–; Prof. of Zoology, Univ. of Würzburg 1989–; Adjunct Prof. of Neurobiology, Univ. of Ariz., Tucson 1989–; mem. German Acad. of Natural Sciences (Leopoldina), American Acad. of Arts and Sciences, Bavarian Acad. of Sciences, Academia Europaea, Berlin-Brandenburgische Akad. der Wissenschaften, Frankfurt Scientific Soc.; Fellow, American Animal Behavior Soc.; Fellow, A.A.A.S.; Guggenheim Fellow 1980; Foreign Fellow, American Philosophical Soc.; Humboldt Foundation Award 1987, G. W. Leibniz Prize 1990, Pulitzer Prize 1991, Karl V. Frisch Prize, Kôrker Prize for European Science. *Publications:* The Ants 1990, Journey to the Ants 1994; 180 scientific publs. *Leisure interests:* painting, graphic arts, music. *Address:* Zoologie II, Biozentrum, Am Hubland, 97074 Würzburg, Germany. *Telephone:* (0931) 8884307. *Fax:* (0931) 8884309.

HOLLENDER, Louis François, M.D.; professor of clinical surgery; b. 15 Feb. 1922, Strasbourg; s. of Emile Hollender and Clotilde Fritsch; m. Nicole Ziegler 1957; two d.; ed. Medical Faculties of Strasbourg and Paris, Harvard Medical School, Boston, Washington Univ., St. Louis, Univ. of Ill., Chicago, U.S.A.; Resident, Strasbourg Univ. Hosp. 1945–52, Chief Resident 1953–55, Assoc. Prof. of Gen. Surgery 1955–59, Chief Surgeon 1959–69, Prof. of Digestive and Gen. Surgery and Head of Dept. 1969–92; Prof. Emer., Univ.

Louis Pasteur, Strasbourg 1992; Dr. h.c. (Athens), (Córdoba), (L'Aquila); mem. Nat. Acad. of Surgery of France (Past Pres.), Nat. Acad. of Medicine, Acad. of Athens; Hon. F.A.C.S., Hon. F.R.C.S. (England). *Publications:* treatises on digestive surgery and surgery of the pancreas and of the colon, numerous scientific papers on visceral and general surgery. *Leisure interests:* golf, skiing, tennis. *Address:* 2 rue Blessig, 67000 Strasbourg, France (Home). *Telephone:* 3-88-35-31-84.

HÖLLERER, Walter Friedrich, DR.PHIL.; German writer and critic; b. 19 Dec. 1922, Sulzbach-Rosenberg, Bavaria; s. of Hans and Christine Höllerer, née Pürkner; m. Renate von Mangoldt 1965; two s.; ed. Univs. of Erlangen, Göttingen and Heidelberg; Dozent in German Studies, Frankfurt/Main Univ. 1958, Münster Univ. 1959; Ord. Prof. of Literature, Berlin Technical Univ. 1959–, Dir. Inst. für Sprache im technischen Zeitalter 1961–; Steuben Visiting Prof., Univ. of Wis. 1960; Dir. Literarisches Colloquium, Berlin 1963; Prof. Univ. of Ill., Urbana 1973–; Ed. Akzente: Zeitschrift für Dichtung 1954 (now co-publr.), Sprache im technischen Zeitalter 1961 (now publr.); publr. Literatur als Kunst; mem. German PEN Club, Akad. für Sprache und Dichtung, Berlin Acad. of Arts, Group 1947, Communità Europea degli Scrittori, Schutzverband der Schriftsteller deutscher Sprache; Fontane Prize, Johann Heinrich Merck Prize, Horst-Bienek-Preis für Lyrik, Ernst Reuter Plakette. *Publications:* Der andere Gast (poems) 1952, 1964, Transit: Lyrikbuch der Jahrhundertmitte (anthology) 1956, Zwischen Klassik und Moderne: Lachen und Weinen in der Dichtung einer Übergangszeit (essays) 1958, Junge amerikanische Lyrik 1961, Spiele in einem Akt 1962, Gedichte 1964, Theorie der modernen Lyrik 1965, Modernes Theater auf kleinen Bühnen 1966, Ein Gedicht und sein Autor (poems and essays) 1967, Ausserhalb der Saison (poems) 1967, Systeme (poems) 1969, Elite und Utopie 1969, Dramaturgisches (correspondence with Max Frisch q.v.) 1969, Die Elephantenuhr (novel) 1973, 1975, Hier wo die Welt anfing 1974, Geschichte, die nicht im Geschichtsbuch steht 1976, Alle Vögel alle (comedy) 1978, Berlin: Übern Damm und durch die Dörfer (essays) 1978, Gedichte 1942–82 1982, Autoren im Haus, Zwanzig Jahre Literatur in Berlin 1982, Die Leute von Serendip erkunden die Giftfabrik, Sprache 97 1986, Walter Höllerers Oberpfälzische Weltei-Erkundungen 1987, Zurufe, Widerspiele (essays) 1992. *Address:* Heerstrasse 99, 14055 Berlin, Germany. *Telephone:* 304-58-79.

HOLLICK, Baron (Life Peer) cr. 1991, of Notting Hill in the Royal Borough of Kensington and Chelsea, **Clive Richard Hollick,** B.A.; British business executive; b. 20 May 1945, Southampton; s. of Leslie George Hollick and Olive Mary (née Scruton) Hollick; m. Susan Mary Woodford 1977; three d.; ed. Univ. of Nottingham; joined Hambros Bank 1968, Dir. 1973; C.E.O. MAI PLC (fmrly. Mills & Allen Int. PLC) 1974–96, Shepperton Studios 1976–84, Garban Ltd. (U.S.A.) 1983–97, United News & Media PLC 1996–; Dir. Logica PLC 1987–91, Meridian Broadcasting 1991–96, British Aerospace 1992–97, Anglia TV Ltd. 1994–; mem. Nat. Bus Co. 1984–91, Applied Econs. Dept. Advisory Cttee. (Univ. of Cambridge) 1989–97, Financial Law Panel 1993–97; Special Adviser to Dept. of Trade and Industry 1997–; Trustee Inst. for Public Policy Research 1988–; Hon. LL.D. (Nottingham) 1993. *Leisure interests:* cinema, countryside, reading, tennis, theatre. *Address:* House of Lords, London, SW1A 0PW, England.

HOLLIDAY, Charles O., Jr., B.S.; American business executive; b. 9 March 1948, Nashville; m. Ann Holliday; two s.; ed. Univ. of Tenn.; joined DuPont Fibers Dept. as engineer, Old Hickory, Tenn. 1970, Business Analyst, Wilmington, Del. 1974, later product planner, Asst. Plant Man., Seaford, Del. 1978; joined DuPont Corp. Planning Dept. 1984, Global Business Man. for Nomex 1986, Global Business Dir. for Kevlar 1987; Dir. of Marketing DuPont Chemicals and Pigments Dept. 1988; Vice-Pres., then Pres. DuPont Asia-Pacific 1990, Chair. 1995; Sr. Vice-Pres. DuPont 1992, Exec. Vice-Pres., mem. Office of Chief Exec. 1995, Dir. July 1997–, Pres. Oct. 1997–, C.E.O. Feb. 1998–, Chair. Dec. 1998–; Dir. DuPont Photomasks Inc., Pioneer Hi-Bred Int. Inc., Analog Devices Inc.; sr. mem. Inst. of Industrial Engineers; mem. Chancellor's Advisory Council for Enhancement Univ. of Tenn., Knoxville. *Address:* E.I. DuPont De Nemours and Co., 1007 Market Street, Wilmington, DE 19898, U.S.A. *Telephone:* (302) 774-1000.

HOLLIDAY, Sir Frederick (George Thomas), Kt., C.B.E., F.I.BIOL., F.R.S.E.; British fmr. university vice-chancellor, zoologist and business executive; b. 22 Sept. 1935; s. of late Alfred Holliday and Margaret Holliday; m. Philippa Davidson 1957; one s. one d.; ed. Bromsgrove County High School and Univ. of Sheffield; Fisheries Research Training Grant (Devt. Comm.), Marine Lab. Aberdeen 1956–58, Scientific Officer 1958–61; lecturer in Zoology, Univ. of Aberdeen 1961–66; Prof. of Biology, Univ. of Stirling 1967–75, Deputy Prin. 1972, Acting Prin. 1973–75; Prof. of Zoology, Univ. of Aberdeen 1975–79; Vice-Chancellor and Warden, Univ. of Durham 1980–90; Dir. Shell U.K. 1980–; mem. Bd. Northern Investors Ltd. 1984–90, BRB 1990–94 (Chair. BR (Eastern) 1986–90), Union Railways 1992–97, Lyonnaise des Eaux 1996–97, Wise Speke PLC 1997–; mem. Northern Regional Bd. Lloyd's Bank 1985–91, Chair. 1986–89, Deputy Chair. 1989–91; Independent Chair. Jt. Nature Conservation Cttee. 1991; mem. numerous cttees. etc.; Chair. Northumbrian water Group PLC 1993–, Council, Water Aid 1995–, Northern Venture Capital Fund 1996–; Pres. British Trust for Ornithology 1996; Hon. D.Univ. (Stirling) 1984; Hon. D.Sc. (Sheffield) 1987, (Cranfield) 1991. *Publications:* Wildlife of Scotland (ed. and contrib.) 1979; numerous publs. on fish biology and wildlife conservation in Advanced Marine Biology, Fish Physiology, Oceanography and Marine Biology etc. *Leisure interests:* walking, gardening. *Address:* Northumbrian Water, Regent Centre, P.O. Box 4, Gosforth, Newcastle upon Tyne, NE3 3PX, England. *Telephone:* 0191-284 3151. *Fax:* 0191-284 0378.

HOLLIDAY, Robin, PH.D., F.R.S.; British geneticist; b. 6 Nov. 1932, Palestine; s. of Clifford Holliday and Eunice Holliday; m. 1st Diana Collet Parsons 1957 (divorced 1983); one s. three d.; m. 2nd Lily I. Huschtscha 1986; one d.; ed. Hitchin Grammar School and Univ. of Cambridge; mem. scientific staff, Dept. of Genetics, John Innes Inst. Bayfordbury, Herts 1958–65; mem. scientific staff, Div. of Microbiology, Nat. Inst. for Medical Research 1965–70, Head, Div. of Genetics 1970–88; Chief Research Scientist CSIRO 1988–1997. *Publications:* The Science of Human Progress 1981, Genes, Proteins and Cellular Ageing 1986, Understanding Ageing 1995; about 250 research publs. *Leisure interests:* sculpture, writing. *Address:* 12 Roma Court, West Pennant Hills, N.S.W. 2125, Australia (Home). *Telephone:* (02) 9873-3476 (Home). *Fax:* (02) 9871-2159.

HOLLIGER, Heinz; Swiss oboist and composer; b. 1939, Langenthal; m. Ursula Holliger; ed. in Berne, Paris and Basel under Emile Cassagnaud (oboe) and Pierre Boulez (composition); Prof. of Oboe, Freiberg Music Acad. 1965–; has appeared at all the major European music festivals and in Japan, U.S.A., Australia, Israel, etc.; recorded over 80 works, mainly for Philips and Deutsche Grammophon; recipient of several international prizes. *Compositions include:* Der magische Tänzer, Trio, Siebengesang, Wind Quintet, Dona nobis pacem, Pneuma, Psalm, Cardiophonie, Kreis, String Quartet, Atembogen, Die Jahreszeiten, Come and Go, Not I. *Address:* Konzertgesellschaft, Hochstrasse 51/Postfach, 4002 Basel, Switzerland.

HOLLINGHURST, Alan James, B.A., M.LITT.; British writer; b. 26 May 1954, Stroud; s. of the late James Kenneth Hollinghurst and of Elizabeth Lilian Hollinghurst (née Keevil); ed. Canford School, Dorset, Magdalene Coll., Oxford; with Times Literary Supplement 1982–95, Deputy Ed. 1985–90; Somerset Maugham Award 1988; American Acad. of Arts and Letters E.M. Forster Award 1989; James Tait Black Memorial Prize 1994. *Publications include:* The Swimming-Pool Library 1988, The Folding Star 1994, the Spell 1998. *Leisure interests:* music, architecture. *Address:* 15 Tanza Road, London, NW3 2UA, England.

HOLLINGS, Ernest F., B.A., LL.B.; American politician and lawyer; b. 1 Jan. 1922; m. 2nd Rita Liddy 1971; two s. two d. (by previous marriage); ed. Charleston Public Schools, The Citadel and Univ. of S. Carolina; served U.S. Army 1942–45; admitted to S. Carolina Bar 1947; mem. S. Carolina House of Reps. 1948–54, Speaker *pro tem.* 1951–53; Lieut.-Gov. of S. Carolina 1955–59, Gov. of S. Carolina 1959–63; law practice, Charleston 1963–66; Senator from S. Carolina 1966–; Chair. Democratic Senatorial Campaign Cttee. 1971–73; mem. Hoover Comm. on Intelligence Activities 1954–55, President's Advisory Comm. on Intergovernmental Relations 1959–63, on Federalism 1981–; mem. Senate Cttees. on Appropriations, Commerce, Budget, Chair. Budget Cttee. 1980, Commerce Cttee. 1982; mem. Democratic Policy Cttee., Office of Tech. Assessment, Nat. Ocean Policy Study; numerous awards; Democrat. *Publication:* The Case against Hunger: A Demand for a National Policy 1970. *Address:* U.S. Senate, 125 Russell Senate Office Building, Washington, DC 20510, U.S.A. (Office).

HOLLINGS, (George) Leslie, A.M.; British/Australian journalist; b. 25 Feb. 1923, Hull; s. of late John Hollings and Elizabeth (Singleton) Hollings; m. Joan Gwendoline Pratt 1951; two s.; ed. N.E. Tech. School of Art, Colchester, Essex; Sub-Ed. The Daily Telegraph, London 1957–59; Sub-Ed. The Times, London 1959–65; Ed. The Australian 1975–80, Man. Ed. 1980–82, Ed.-in-Chief 1983–88; Dir. News Ltd. 1987–89; Deputy Chair. The Sydney Inst. 1989–93; Counsellor Cttee. for Econ. Devt. of Australia 1993–; mem. Policy Cttee., Bureau of Meteorology 1983–87; mem. Council of Australian Nat. Gallery 1985–92, Deputy Chair. 1987–92. *Leisure interests:* reading, opera, ballet, gardening, walking. *Address:* c/o The Sunday Telegraph, News Ltd., GPO Box 4245, Sydney, N.S.W. 2001, Australia.

HOLLINGWORTH, Clare, O.B.E.; British journalist; b. 10 Oct. 1911; d. of John Albert Hollingworth and Daisy Gertrude Hollingworth; m. 1st Vyvyan Derring Vandeleur Robinson 1936 (divorced 1951); m. 2nd Geoffrey Spence Hoare 1952 (died 1966); ed. Girls' Collegiate School, Leicester, Grammar School, Ashby de la Zouch, School of Slavonic Studies, Univ. of London; mem. staff League of Nations Union 1935–38; worked in Poland for Lord Mayor's Fund for Refugees from Czechoslovakia 1939; Corresp. for Daily Telegraph Poland, Turkey, Cairo (covered Desert Campaigns, troubles in Persia and Iraq, Civil War in Greece and events in Palestine) 1941–50, for Manchester Guardian (covered Algerian War and trouble spots including Egypt, Aden and Vietnam), based in Paris 1950–63; Guardian Defence Corresp. 1963–67; foreign trouble-shooter for Daily Telegraph (covering war in Vietnam) 1967–73, Corresp. in China 1973–76, Defence Corresp. 1976–81; Far Eastern Corresp. in Hong Kong for Sunday Telegraph 1981–; Research Assoc. (fmrly. Visiting Scholar), Centre for Asian Studies, Univ. of Hong Kong 1981–; Hon. D.Litt. (Leicester) 1993; Journalist of the Year Award and Hannan Swaffer Award 1963; James Cameron Award for Journalism 1994. *Publications:* Poland's Three Weeks War 1940, There's A German Just Behind Me 1945, The Arabs and the West 1951, Mao and the Men Against Him 1984, Front Line 1990. *Leisure interests:* visiting second-hand furniture and bookshops, collecting modern pictures and Chinese porcelain, music. *Address:* 19 Dorset Square, London, NW1 6QB, England; 302 Ridley House, 2 Upper Albert Road, Hong Kong, Special Administrative Region, People's

Republic of China. *Telephone:* 0171-262 6923 (London); 2868-1838 (Hong Kong).

HOLLINGWORTH, Most Rev. Peter, A.O., O.B.E., M.A., L.TH., F.A.I.M.; Australian ecclesiastic; b. 10 April 1935, Adelaide; m. Kathleen Ann Turner 1960; three d.; ed. Trinity Coll. Univ. of Melbourne; Deacon-in-Charge then Priest-in-Charge, St. Mary's, N. Melbourne; Chaplain to the Brotherhood of St. Laurence 1965, Assoc. Dir. 1970, later Dir. of Social Services, Exec. Dir. 1980–90; Hon. Curate, St. Silas's, N. Balwyn, later Hon. Curate at St. Faith's, Burwood, and Priest-in-Charge, St. Mark's, Fitzroy; recipient of travelling bursary 1967; elected Canon, St. Paul's Cathedral 1980; Bishop of the Inner City 1985–90, Archbishop of Brisbane 1990–; Chaplain to Order of St. John of Jerusalem; Nat. chaplain to Order of St. Lazarus of Jerusalem; Chair. Int. Year of Shelter for the Homeless, Nat. Cttee. of Non-Governmental Orgs. 1986–88, Anglican Social Responsibilities Comm. of Gen. Synod 1990–97, Anglicare in diocese of Brisbane; Pres. Victorian Council of Social Services 1969; mem. Centenary of Fed. Council, Constitutional Convention (as non-parl. Rep.); Fellow Trinity Coll. Melbourne; Hon. LL.D. (Monash Univ.) 1986, (Melbourne) 1990; Hon. D.Univ. (Griffith Univ.) 1993, (Queensland Univ. of Tech.) 1994, (Cen. Queensland) 1995; Victorian Rostrum Award of Merit 1985, Advance Australia Award 1988, Paul Harris Fellowship, Rotary Club 1989, Australian Achiever Award, Australian of the Year 1992, Nat. Living Treasure of Australia (Nat. Trust) 1997. *Publications:* The Powerless Poor 1972, Victims of Affluence 1974, Australians in Poverty 1979, Public Thoughts of an Archbishop 1996. *Address:* G.P.O. Box 421, Brisbane 4001, Queensland, Australia. *Telephone:* (7) 3835 2222. *Fax:* (7) 3832 5030.

HOLLÓ, Janos; Hungarian chemical engineer; b. 20 Aug. 1919, Szentes; s. of Gyula Holló and Margit Mandl; m. 1st Hermina Milch (1944); m. 2nd Vera Novák 1956; two s. one d.; ed. Tech. Univ., Budapest; Tech. Dir. Budapest Breweries 1948; Prof. Agricultural and Chemical Tech., Budapest Tech. Univ. 1952–90, Dean Chemical Eng. Faculty 1955–57, 1963–72, Prof. Emer. 1991–; Dir. Hungarian Acad. of Sciences Cen. Research Inst. of Chemistry 1972–91, Prof. of Research 1991–; Pres. Comm. Int. des Industries Agricoles et Alimentaires (CIIA); Chair. Cereals and Pulses Cttee., Int. Org. for Standardization (ISO) 1960–, Agricultural and Food Products Cttee. 1971–; Gen. Sec. Scientific Asscn. of Hungary Food Industry 1949, Chair., Pres. 1981–91, Hon. Pres. 1991–; Pres. Int. Soc. for Fat Research (ISF) 1964–66, 1982–83, Exec. mem. 1964–; Chief Ed. Acta Alimentaria, Journal of Food Investigations, Biotechnology and Environmental Protection Today and Tomorrow; mem. numerous editorial bds.; mem. Hungarian Acad. of Sciences 1967; Hon. mem. Polish Science Asscn. of Food Industries 1971, Austrian Soc. for Food and Biochemistry 1983; foreign mem. Finnish Acad. of Tech. Sciences 1984, German Acad. of Sciences 1984, Polish Acad. of Sciences 1991, New York Acad. of Sciences 1994, Int. Acad. of Food Science Tech. 1998; Dr. h.c. (Tech. Univ. of Vienna) 1973, (Berlin, Charlottenburg) 1984, (Tech. Univ. Budapest) 1991, (Univ. of Horticulture and Food Industry, Budapest) 1991; Commandeur Ordre du mérite pour la recherche et l'invention 1962; medal of French Starch Syndicate 1963; Chevalier des Palmes académiques 1967; Labour Order of Merit 1971, 1979; Saare medal 1972; Premio d'oro Interpetrol 1973; Copernicus Medal 1974; State Prize 1975; Prix d'honneur de l'Acad. Int. du Lutèce 1978; Chevreul medal 1986; Normann medal 1986; Award for Outstanding Paper Presentation (American Oil Chem. Soc.) 1992. *Publications:* numerous books (with others) including Technology of Malting and Brewing, Biotechnology of Food and Feed Production, Bioconversion of Starch, Aliments non-conventionnels à destination humaine, Automatization in the Food Industry, The Application of Molecular Distillation; co-author of some 600 articles for professional journals. *Address:* Central Research Institute for Chemistry of the Hungarian Academy of Sciences, 1025 Budapest, Pusztaszeri ut 59/67, Hungary. *Telephone:* (1) 325-7750. *Fax:* (1) 325-7750.

HOLLOM, Sir Jasper (Quintus), K.B.E.; British banker b. 16 Dec. 1917, Bromley, Kent; s. of Arthur Hollom and Kate Louisa Hollom; m. Patricia Elizabeth Mary Ellis 1954; ed. King's School, Bruton; entered Bank of England 1936, Deputy Cashier 1956–62, Chief Cashier 1962–66, Exec. Dir. 1966–70, Deputy Governor 1970–80, Dir. 1980–84; Chair. Panel on Takeovers and Mergers 1980–87; Dir. Portals Holdings 1980–88, Gen. Accident, Fire and Life Assurance Corpn. 1980–85; External Dir. BAT Industries 1980–87; Chair. Commonwealth Devt. Finance Co. 1980–86; Pres. Council of Foreign Bondholders 1983–89; Chair. Council for the Securities Industry 1985–86; Chair. Eagle Star Holdings PLC 1985–87, Eagle Star Insurance Co. Ltd. 1985–87; Dir. (non-exec.) Corp. Finance Advisory Ltd. 1991–96. *Address:* The Long Barn, Alexanders Lane, Privett, Alton, Hants., GU34 3PW, England. *Telephone:* (01730) 828417.

HOLLOWAY, Bruce William, A.O., PH.D., D.SC., F.A.A., F.T.S.E.; Australian professor of genetics; b. 9 Jan. 1928, Adelaide; s. of Albert Holloway and Gertrude C. Walkem; m. Brenda D. Gray 1952; one s. one d.; ed. Scotch Coll., Adelaide, Univ. of Adelaide and Calif. Inst. of Tech.; Lecturer in Plant Pathology, Waite Agric. Research Inst. 1949–50; Research Fellow in Microbial Genetics, John Curtin School of Medicine, Australian Nat. Univ. 1953–56; Sr. Lecturer 1956–60, then Reader in Microbial Genetics, Univ. of Melbourne 1956–67; Foundation Prof. of Genetics, Monash Univ. 1968–93, Head Dept. of Genetics and Devt. Biology 1968–93, Hon. Professorial Fellow 1994–; Chair. Bd. CRC for Vertebrate Biological Control 1994–; Project Coordinator, Crawford Fund 1994–; Visiting Lecturer in Microbiology and Fellow, M.I.T. 1962–63; Sec. Biological Sciences, Australian Acad. of Science 1982–86; Visiting Prof. Univ. of Newcastle-upon-Tyne 1977–78; Chair. Nat. Biotechnology Program Research Grants Scheme 1983–86; mem. Industry and Research Devt. Bd. 1986–89. *Publications:* over 160 papers on genetics and microbiology in scientific journals and conf. proc. *Leisure interests:* music, reading, tennis. *Address:* 22 Reading Avenue, North Balwyn, Vic., 3104, Australia (Home). *Telephone:* 03-9819-7383 (Home). *Fax:* 03-9857 8756 (Home)

HOLLOWAY, Admiral James Lemuel, III; American naval officer (retd.); b. 23 Feb. 1922, Charleston, S. Carolina; s. of Admiral James L. Holloway, Jr and late Jean Hagood; m. Dabney Rawlings 1942; one s. (died 1964), two d.; ed. U.S. Naval Acad., Md; Commissioned Ensign in U.S. Navy 1942, served on destroyers in Atlantic and Pacific Theatres, World War II; Gunnery Officer U.S.S. Bennion, took part in Battle of Surigao Straits; Exec. Officer of Fighter Squadron Fifty-two, U.S.S. Boxer, Korean War 1952–54; Commdr. Attack Squadron Eighty-three, U.S.S. Essex, Sixth Fleet during Lebanon landings 1958; Nat. War Coll. 1961; Nuclear training under Admiral Rickover 1963; Commdg. Officer U.S.S. Enterprise (first nuclear-powered carrier) Vietnam War 1965–67; promoted to rank of Rear-Admiral 1967; Dir. Strike Warfare Div., Program Coordinator Nuclear Attack Carrier Program, Office of Chief of Naval Operations; Commdr. Sixth Fleet Carrier Striking Force, directed operations in E. Mediterranean during Jordanian crisis 1970; Deputy C.-in-C. Atlantic and U.S. Atlantic Fleet, Vice-Admiral 1971; Commdr. Seventh Fleet during combat operations in Viet Nam 1972–73; Vice-Chief of Naval Operations 1973–74; Chief of Naval Operations 1974–78; mem. Jt. Chiefs of Staff 1974–78; Chair. Special Operations Review Group, Iranian Hostage Rescue 1981; Special Envoy of Vice-Pres. of U.S.A. to Bahrain 1986; mem. Pres.'s Comm. on Merchant Marine and Defense 1986; Pres. Council of American Flagship Operators 1981–87; Chair. of Bd. Asscn. of Naval Aviation; Chair. Academic Advisory Bd. to U.S. Naval Acad.; Exec. Dir., Vice-Pres.'s Task Force on Combating Terrorism 1985; Pres.'s Blue Ribbon Comm. on Defense Man. 1985–86; Commr., Comm. on Merchant Marine and Defense 1987, Comm. on Integrated Long-Term Strategy 1987; mem. Bd. of Dirs. U.S. Life Insurance Co. 1985–, UNC Inc. 1987–, George Marshall Foundation 1988–, Atlantic Council 1990–; mem. Bd. of Govs., St. John's Coll. 1996–; Pres. Naval Historical Foundation 1984–; Chair. Bd. Historic Annapolis Foundation 1990–; Chair. and Pres. Naval Acad. Found. 1994–, Chair. Bd. of Trustees Naval Acad. Endowment Trust 1997–; Pres. Bd. of Trustees, St. James School, Md.; Tech. Adviser for film Top Gun 1986; awarded numerous medals for meritorious service including Defense Distinguished Service Medal (twice), Navy Distinguished Service Medal (four times), Legion of Merit, Distinguished Flying Cross, Bronze Star Medal with Combat "V", Air Medal (four times), Modern Patriot Award 1994, U.S. Navy League Annual Award for Distinguished Civilian Leadership 1997, Sons of the Revolution Distinguished Patriot Award 1999, and many foreign decorations. *Publications:* numerous articles on aviation, sealift and defence organization. *Leisure interest:* sailing. *Address:* 1694 Epping Farms Lane, Annapolis, MD 21401, U.S.A. *Telephone:* (410) 849-2115. *Fax:* (410) 849-2115.

HOLLOWAY, John, D.LITT., LITT.D., F.R.S.L.; British professor of modern English (retd.); b. 1 Aug. 1920, Croydon; s. of George Holloway and Evelyn Astbury; m. 1st Audrey Gooding 1946; one s. one d.; m. 2nd Joan Black 1978; ed. New Coll., Oxford; war service, commissioned in artillery, seconded to Intelligence; temp. lecturer in Philosophy, New Coll. 1945; Fellow of All Souls Coll., Oxford 1946–60; Lecturer in English, Univ. of Aberdeen 1949–54; Lecturer in English, Cambridge Univ. 1954–66, Reader in Modern English 1966, Fellow of Queens' Coll. 1955–82, Life Fellow 1982–, Prof. of Modern English 1972–82; Visiting Prof., Chicago 1965, Johns Hopkins Univ. 1972, Charlottesville, Va. 1979, N.Y. Univ. (Berg Prof.) 1987; Visiting Fellow, Univ. of Wellington 1984, Univ. of Kyoto 1986; various univ. admin. positions. *Publications:* Language and Intelligence 1951, The Victorian Sage 1953, The Charted Mirror (essays) 1960, (ed.) Poems of the Mid-Century 1957, (ed.) Selections from Shelley 1960, Shakespeare's Tragedies 1961, The Colours of Clarity (essays) 1964, The Lion Hunt 1964, Widening Horizons in English Verse 1966, A London Childhood 1966, Blake, The Lyric Poetry 1968, The Establishment of English 1972, Later English Broadside Ballads Vol. I 1975, Vol. II 1979 (both vols. with Joan Black), The Proud Knowledge 1977, Narrative and Structure 1979, The Slumber of Apollo 1983, Oxford Book of Local Verses 1987; contribs. to journals; verse: The Minute 1956, The Fugue 1960, The Landfallers 1962, Wood and Windfall 1965, New Poems 1970, Planet of Winds 1977, Civitatula (Cambridge, the Little City) 1993. *Address:* c/o Queens' College, Cambridge, CB3 9ET, England. *Telephone:* (01223) 335511.

HOLLOWAY, Most Rev. Richard Frederick, B.D., S.T.M., F.R.S.E.; British ecclesiastic; b. 26 Nov. 1933, Glasgow; s. of Arthur Holloway and Mary Holloway; m. Jean Holloway 1963; one s. two d.; ed. Kelham Theological Coll., Edinburgh Theological Coll. and Union Theological Seminary, New York; Curate, St. Ninian's, Glasgow 1959–63; Priest-in-charge, St. Margaret's and St. Mungo's, Gorbals, Glasgow 1963–68; Rector, Old St. Paul's, Edinburgh 1968–80, Church of the Advent, Boston, Mass. 1980–84; Vicar, St. Mary Magdalen's, Oxford 1984–86; Bishop of Edin. 1986–; Primus, Scottish Episcopal Church 1992–; mem. Human Fertilisation and Embryology Authority, U.K. 1991; Hon. D.Univ. (Strathclyde) 1994; Hon. D.D. (Aberdeen) 1994; Winifred M. Stanford Award for The Killing 1984. *Publications include:* Beyond Belief 1981, The Killing 1984, Paradoxes of Christian

Faith and Life 1984, The Sidelong Glance 1985, The Way of the Cross 1986, Seven to Flee, Seven to Follow 1986, Crossfire 1988, Another Country, Another King 1991, Who Needs Feminism? 1991, Anger, Sex, Doubt and Death 1992, The Stranger in the Wings 1994, Churches and How To Survive Them 1994, Behold Your King 1995, Limping towards the Sunrise 1996, Dancing on the Edge 1997. *Leisure interests:* walking, movies, reading, cooking. *Address:* The Diocesan Centre, 21A Grosvenor Crescent, Edinburgh, EH12 5EL (Office); 3 Eglinton Crescent, Edinburgh, EH12 5DH, Scotland (Home). *Telephone:* 0131-538 7044 (Office); 0131-226-5099 (Home). *Fax:* 0131-538 7088.

HOLLOWAY, Robin Greville, PH.D., D.MUS.; British composer, writer on music and university teacher; b. 19 Oct. 1943, Leamington Spa; s. of Robert Charles Holloway and Pamela Mary Holloway (née Jacob); ed. St. Paul's Cathedral Choir School, King's Coll. School, Wimbledon, King's Coll., Cambridge and New Coll., Oxford; Lecturer in Music, Univ. of Cambridge 1975–; Fellow of Gonville and Caius Coll., Cambridge 1969–; compositions include Garden Music opus 1 1962, Scenes from Schumann opus 13 1970, Evening with Angels opus 17 1972, Domination of Black opus 23 1973, Clarissa opus 30 1976, Second Concerto for Orchestra opus 40 1979, Brand opus 48 1981, Women in War opus 51 1982, Seascape and Harvest opus 55 1983, Viola Concerto opus 56 1984, Double Concerto opus 68, The Spacious Firmament opus 69, Violin Concerto opus 70 1990, Frost at Midnight opus 78, Third Concerto for Orchestra opus 80 1994, Clarinet Concerto opus 82 1996, Peer Gynt opus 84 1984–97, Scenes from Antwerp opus 85 1997. *Publications:* Wagner and Debussy 1978; numerous articles and reviews. *Leisure interest:* cities. *Address:* Gonville and Caius College, Cambridge, CB2 1TA, England. *Telephone:* (01223) 335424. *Fax:* (01223) 335424.

HOLM, Erik, M.A., PH.D.; Danish foundation director and political economist; b. 6 Dec. 1933, Hobro; s. of Carl Holm and Anne Margrethe Holm (née Nielsen); m. Annie Jacoba Kortleven 1960 (died 1984); two s. two d.; ed. Univ. of Copenhagen; Economist, Cen. Statistical Office, Copenhagen 1961–65, IMF, Washington, D.C. 1965–69; Sr. Economist, Ministry of Econ. Affairs, Copenhagen 1969–72; Adviser on European Affairs to Prime Minister 1972–82; Prin. Adviser (econ. and financial affairs), EC Comm., Brussels 1982–87; Visiting Scholar, Inst. of Int. Studies, Univ. of Calif., Berkeley 1987–89; Dir. The Eleni Nakou Foundation, London 1989–; lecturer in Econs., Univ. of Copenhagen 1962–65, in Political Science 1971–81. *Publications:* Stabilitet og Uligevagt 1986, Money and International Politics 1991, Union eller Nation 1992, Europe, a Political Culture? Fundamental Issues for the 1996 IGC 1994; articles in Danish and int. publications on European econ. and political affairs. *Address:* 38 Montagu Mansions, London, W1H 1LD, England; Xylografensvej 4, 3220 Tisvildeleje, Denmark. *Telephone:* 0171-935 0729 (London); 4870 9715 (Tisvildeleje). *Fax:* 0171-935 0729 (London); 4870 9315 (Tisvildeleje).

HOLM, Sir Ian, Kt., C.B.E.; British actor; b. 12 Sept. 1931, Ilford; s. of Dr. James Harvey Cuthbert and Jean Wilson Cuthbert; m. 1st Lynn Mary Shaw 1955 (divorced 1965); one s. three d.; m. 2nd Sophie Baker 1982 (divorced 1986); one s.; m. 3rd Penelope Wilton 1991; one step-d.; ed. Chigwell Grammar School, Essex, RADA (Royal Acad. of Dramatic Art); joined Shakespeare Memorial Theatre 1954; Worthing Repertory 1956; on tour with Lord Olivier in Titus Andronicus 1957; mem. R.S.C. 1958–67; Laurence Olivier Award 1998. *Roles include:* Puck, Ariel, Lorenzo, Henry V, Richard III, The Fool (in King Lear), Lennie (in The Homecoming); appeared in Moonlight 1993, King Lear 1997. *Films include:* Young Winston, Oh! What a Lovely War, Alien, All Quiet on the Western Front, Chariots of Fire, The Return of the Soldier, Greystoke 1984, Laughterhouse 1984, Brazil 1985, Wetherby 1985, Dance with a Stranger 1985, Dreamchild 1985, Henry V 1989, Another Woman 1989, Hamlet 1990, Kafka 1991, The Hour of the Pig 1992, Blue Ice 1992, The Naked Lunch 1992, Frankenstein 1993, The Madness of King George 1994, Loch Ness 1994, Big Night 1995, Night Falls on Manhattan 1995, The Fifth Element 1996, A Life Less Ordinary 1996, The Sweet Hereafter 1997, The Fifth Element 1997. *Television appearances include:* The Lost Boys 1979, We, the Accused 1980, The Bell 1981, Strike 1981, Inside the Third Reich 1982, Mr. and Mrs. Edgehill 1985, The Browning Version 1986, Game, Set and Match 1988, The Endless Game 1989, The Last Romantics 1992, The Borrowers 1993, The Deep Blue Sea 1994, Landscape 1995. *Leisure interest:* tennis. *Address:* c/o Julian Belfrage Assocs., 46 Albemarle Street, London, W1X 4PP, England.

HOLM, Richard H., PH.D.; American professor of chemistry; b. 24 Sept. 1933, Boston, Mass.; m. Florence L. Jacintho 1958; four c.; ed. Univ. of Mass. and M.I.T.; Asst. Prof. of Chem., Harvard Univ. 1960–65; Assoc. Prof. of Chem. Univ. of Wisconsin 1965–67; Prof. of Chem. M.I.T. 1967–75, Stanford Univ. 1975–80; Prof. of Chem. Harvard Univ. 1980–83, Higgins Prof. 1983–, Chair. Dept. of Chem. 1983–86; mem. American Acad. of Arts and Sciences, N.A.S.; several awards for research in inorganic chem.; A.M. (h.c.); D.Sc. (h.c.); Chemical Sciences Award 1993. *Publications:* numerous research papers in professional journals in the fields of inorganic chemistry and biochemistry. *Address:* Department of Chemistry, Harvard University, Cambridge, MA 02138 (Office); 483 Pleasant Street, #10, Belmont, MA 02139, U.S.A. (Home).

HOLMAN, Ralph Theodore, PH.D.; American professor of biochemistry; b. 4 March 1918, Minneapolis, Minn.; s. of Alfred Theodore Holman and May Carlia Anna Nilson; m. Karla Calais 1943; one s.; ed. Univ. of Minnesota and Rutgers Univ., New Brunswick, New Jersey; Instructor, Physiological Chem., Univ. of Minn. 1944–46; Medical Nobel Inst., Stockholm, Sweden 1946–47; American-Scandinavian Foundation Fellow, Univ. of Uppsala, Sweden 1947; Assoc. Prof. of Biochemistry and Nutrition, Texas A. & M. Univ. 1948–51; Assoc. Prof. of Biochemistry, Hormel Inst., Univ. of Minn. 1951–56, Prof. 1956–88, Exec. Dir. Hormel Inst. 1975–85, Emer. Exec. Dir. 1985, Prof. Emer. 1988–; Prof. of Biochemistry, Univ. of Minn. Medical School; Adjunct Prof. of Biochemistry, Mayo Medical School 1977–; Pres. Mower County Council of Churches 1952–56, American Oil Chem. Soc. 1974–75; Sr. Ed., Omega 3 News Online 1997–; Fellow American Inst. of Nutrition; mem. N.A.S., Hormel Foundation; Pres. and Organizer, Golden Jubilee Int. Congress, Essential Fatty Acids Prostaglandins 1980; Sinclair Memorial Lecturer, Third Int. Congress on Essential Fatty Acids and Eicosanoids, Adelaide 1992; Borden Award 1966; Bailey Award, American Oil Chem. Soc.; Award in Lipid Chem., American Oil Chem. Soc. and other prizes; research interests: essential polyunsaturated fatty acids, their quantified requirements, role in liver function and abnormalities in disease. *Publications:* 400 publs. on lipid biochemistry and nutrition; Ed. Lipids 1974–85, Founding Ed. Progress in Lipid Research 1951–. *Leisure interests:* writing, history, orchids, orchid research, gardening and construction. *Address:* 1403 Second Avenue S.W., Austin, MN 55912, U.S.A. (Home). *Telephone:* (507) 437-3504 (Home).

HOLME OF CHELTENHAM, Baron, cr. 1990 (Life Peer), of Cheltenham in the County of Gloucestershire, **Richard Gordon Holme,** C.B.E., M.A.; British politician, publisher and business executive; b. 27 May 1936, London; s. of Jack Richard Holme and Edna (Eggleton) Holme; m. Kay Powell 1958; two s. two d.; ed. Royal Masonic School, St. John's Coll. Oxford, Harvard Business School, U.S.A.; served in 10th Gurkha Rifles in Malaya 1954–56; Marketing Man., Unilever 1959–64; Dir. Penguin Books 1964–66; Chair. BPC Publishing 1966–70; Pres. CRM Books, Calif., U.S.A. 1970–74; Dir. Nat. Cttee. for Electoral Reform 1976–84; Chair. Constitutional Reform Centre 1985, Threadneedle Publishing Group 1988–, Hollis Directories 1989–, Prima Europe 1992–1995, Brasseys Ltd. 1996–98; Pres. Liberal Party 1980–81; Liberal Democrat Parl. Spokesman on Northern Ireland, House of Lords 1992–; Chair. of Govs. English Coll., Prague; Vice-Chair. Hansard Soc. for Parl. Govt.; Dir. RTZ-CRA (now Rio Tinto PLC) 1996–98; mem. Bd. Campaign for Oxford; Liberal Democrat. *Publications:* No Dole for the Young 1975, A Democracy Which Works 1978, The People's Kingdom (Jt. Ed.) 1987, 1688–1988: Time for a New Constitution 1988. *Leisure interests:* walking, opera. *Address:* House of Lords, London, SW1A 0PW, England. *Telephone:* 0171-753 2454.

HOLMES, George Arthur, PH.D., F.B.A.; British historian; b. 22 April 1927, Aberystwyth, Wales; s. of the late John Holmes and Margaret Holmes; m. Evelyn Anne Klein 1953; two s. (one deceased), two d.; ed. Ardwyn County School, Aberystwyth, Univ. Coll. Aberystwyth and St. John's Coll. Cambridge; Fellow, St. John's Coll. Cambridge 1951–54; Tutor, St. Catherine's Coll. Oxford 1954–62, Fellow and Tutor 1962–89, Vice-Master 1969–71; Chichele Prof. of Medieval History and Fellow, All Souls Coll., Oxford 1989–94; Visiting Prof., Harvard Univ. Center for Italian Renaissance Studies, Florence 1995–; mem. Inst. for Advanced Study, Princeton, N.J., U.S.A. 1967–68; Chair. Victoria County History Cttee., Inst. of Historical Research 1979–89; Jt. Ed. English Historical Review 1974–81; Del., Oxford Univ. Press 1982–92; Emer. Fellow, Leverhulme Trust 1996–98; Serena Medal for Italian Studies, British Acad. 1993. *Publications:* The Estates of the Higher Nobility in Fourteenth-Century England 1957, The Later Middle Ages 1962, The Florentine Enlightenment 1400–1450 1969, Europe: Hierarchy and Revolt 1320–1450 1975, The Good Parliament 1975, Dante 1980, Florence, Rome and the Origins of the Renaissance 1986, The Oxford Illustrated History of Medieval Europe (ed.) 1988, The First Age of the Western City 1300–1500 1990, Art and Politics in Renaissance Italy (Ed.) 1993, Renaissance 1996, The Oxford Illustrated History of Italy (Ed.) 1997. *Address:* Highmoor House, Primrose Lane, Weald, Bampton, Oxon., OX18 2HY, England. *Telephone:* (01993) 850408.

HOLMES, Sir John Eaton, K.B.E., M.A., C.V.O., C.M.G.; British diplomatist; b. 29 April 1951, Preston; s. of Leslie Holmes and Joyce Holmes; m. Penelope Morris 1976; three d.; ed. Preston Grammar School, Balliol Coll., Oxford; joined FCO 1973; with Embassy, Moscow 1976–78; First Sec. FCO 1978–82; Asst. Pvt. Sec. to Foreign Sec. 1982–84; First Sec. Embassy, Paris 1984–87; Asst. Head Soviet Dept., FCO 1988–89; seconded to Thomas De La Rue & Co. 1989–91; counsellor British High Comm., India 1991–95; Prin. Pvt. Sec. to Prime Minister 1996–99; Amb. to Portugal Aug. 1999–. *Leisure interests:* reading, music, sport. *Address:* c/o Foreign and Commonwealth Office, King Charles Street, London, SW1A 2AH, England.

HOLMES, Kenneth Charles, M.A., PH.D., F.R.S.; British research biophysicist; b. 19 Nov. 1934, London; s. of Sidney C. and Irene M. (née Penfold) Holmes; m. Mary Lesceline Scruby 1957; one s. three d.; ed. Chiswick County School, St. John's Coll., Cambridge, and Birbeck Coll., London; Research Asst., Birkbeck Coll. 1955–59; Research Assoc., Children's Hosp., Boston 1960–62; scientific staff, MRC Lab. of Molecular Biology, Cambridge 1962–68; Dir. Dept. of Biophysics, Max-Planck-Inst. for Medical Research, Heidelberg 1968–; Prof. of Biophysics, Heidelberg Univ. 1972–. *Publications:* articles in scientific books and journals. *Leisure interests:* rowing, singing. *Address:* Max-Planck-Institute for Medical Research, Abt. Biophysik, Jahnstrasse 29, 69120 Heidelberg (Office); Mühltalstrasse 117b, 6900 Heidelberg, Germany (Home). *Telephone:* (6221) 486270 (Office); 06221/471313 (Home).

HOLMES, Larry; American boxer; b. 3 Nov. 1949, Cuthbert, Georgia; s. of John and Flossie Holmes; m. Diana Holmes; one s. four d.; ed. Easton, Pa.; amateur boxer 1970–73; 22 amateur fights, 19 wins; lost by disqualification to Duane Bobick in finals of American Olympic trials 1972; won World Boxing Council version of world heavyweight title from Ken Norton June 1978; has made nine defences, all won inside scheduled distance (breaking previous record held by Joe Louis); became first man to stop Muhammad Ali Oct. 1980; stripped of World Boxing Council version 1983; lost Int. Boxing Fed. version to Michael Spinks 1985, beaten again by Spinks 1986; defeated by Mike Tyson (q.v.) in attempts to win WBA, WBC and IBF Heavyweight titles 1988; beaten by Evander Holyfield (q.v.) 1992, and by Oliver McCall 1995; undefeated for record 13 years. *Leisure interests:* food, sport and self-education. *Address:* c/o Holmes Enterprises Inc., 704 Alpha Bldg., Easton, PA 18042, U.S.A.

HOLMES, Sir Peter F., Kt., M.C., M.A.; British petroleum executive; b. 27 Sept. 1932, Athens, Greece; s. of Gerald Holmes and Caroline Morris Holmes; m. Judith M. Walker 1955 (separated 1997); three d.; ed. Malvern Coll., Trinity Coll., Cambridge; with the Shell Group of Cos. 1956–, C.E.O. Shell Markets (Middle East) Ltd. 1965–68, C.E.O. Shell Cos. in Libya 1970–73; Man. Dir. and C.E.O. Shell Petroleum Devt. Co. of Nigeria Ltd. 1977–81, Pres. Shell Int. Trading Co. 1981–83, Dir. Shell Transport and Trading Co. PLC 1982–, Chair. 1985–93; Man. Dir. Royal Dutch/Shell Group 1982–93 (Chair. Cttee. 1992–93); Pres. Hakluyt Foundation 1997–; Dir. (non-exec.) Norman-Broadbent Int. 1993–; Trustee WWF-U.K. 1989–96; Hon. D.Sc. (Cranfield) 1993. *Publications:* Mountains and a Monastery 1958, Nigeria, Giant of Africa 1985, Turkey, A Timeless Bridge 1988. *Leisure interests:* mountaineering, travel in remote areas, 19th century travel literature. *Address:* c/o Shell Centre, London, SE1 7NA, England.

HOLMES À COURT, Janet, A.O., B.SC.; Australian business executive; b. 1943, Perth; one d. three s.; ed. Perth Modern School and Univ. of Western Australia; fmr. science teacher; Exec. Chair. Heytesbury Pty. Ltd. (family-owned co. which includes Heytesbury Beef Ltd., Vasse Felix (Vineyards), Heytesbury Thoroughbreds, John Holland Group, Stoll Moss Theatres and Key Transport); Chair. John Holland Group, Australian Children's TV Foundation, Black Swan Theatre Co., W. Australian Symphony Orchestra; fmr. Pro-Chancellor, Univ. of W. Australia; mem. Bd. Man. Festival of Perth. *Address:* c/o Stoll Moss Theatres Ltd., Manor House, 21 Soho Square, London, W1V 5FD, England. *Telephone:* 0171-494 5200.

HOLOMISA, Maj.-Gen. Bantubonke Harrington (Bantu); South African politician and army officer; b. 25 July 1955, Mqandull, Transkei; s. of the late Chief B. Holomisa; m. Tunyelwa Dube 1981; one s. two d.; joined Transkei Defence Force 1976, Lieut. Platoon Commdr. 1978–79, Capt. Training Wing Commdr. 1979–81, Lieut.-Col. Bn. Command 1981–83, Col. SS01 Operations and Training 1984–85, rank of Brig., Chief of Staff, Transkei Defence Force 1985–87, Commdr. 1987–94; Leader of Transkei 1987–94; mem. A.N.C. Nat. Exec. Cttee. 1994; Deputy Minister of Environmental Affairs, Govt. of Nat. Unity 1994–96; leader United Democratic Movt. 1997–. *Address:* National Assembly, Cape Town, South Africa.

HOLOUBEK, Gustaw; Polish theatre director and actor; b. 21 April 1923, Cracow; s. of Gustaw and Eugenia Holoubek; m. 1st Danuta Kwiatkowska; m. 2nd Maria Wachowiak, m. 3rd Magdalena Zawadzka; one s. two d.; ed. State Higher Dramatic School, Cracow; actor in Cracow theatres 1947–49; at Wyspiański Theatre, Katowice, Artistic Man. 1954–56; at Polish Theatre, Warsaw 1958–59; actor Dramatic Theatre, Warsaw 1959–63 and 1969–82, Dir. and Artistic Man. 1972–82, Nat. Theatre, Warsaw 1963–68, Polish Theatre, Warsaw 1969–82, Ateneum Theatre, Warsaw 1989–96, Dir. and Artistic Man. 1997–; Assoc. Prof. State Higher Theatrical School; Vice-Chair. SPATIF (Asscn. of Polish Theatre and Film Actors) 1963–70, Chair. 1970–81; Hon. Pres. of ZASP (Union of Polish Stage Artists) 1981; Deputy to Sejm (Parl.) 1976–82; Senator 1989–91; mem. Presidential Council for Culture 1992–95. *Roles include:* Judge Caust in Leprosy at the Palace of Justice, Baron Goetze in Le diable et le bon Dieu (Sartre), Gustaw-Konrad in Dziady (A. Mickiewicz), Violinist in Rzeźnia (S. Mrożek), Beggar in Electra (J. Giraudoux), Hick in The Iceman Cometh (O'Neill), King Lear, Oedipus, Hamlet, Richard II and Hadrian VII (Peter Luke), Gen. Wincenty Krasiński in November Night (Wyspiański), Count Szarma in Operetka (Gombrowicz); also appears in films and television plays; Dir. Mazepa (film) 1976, A Book of Great Wishes (film) 1997; numerous decorations including State Prize 1953, 1966, 1978 (1st Class), Order of Banner of Labour 2nd Class, Knight's Cross of Polonia Restituta, Award Meritorius Activist of Culture 1972, Warsaw City Prize 1975, Cttee. for Polish Radio and TV Award 1980, Prix Italia 1994. *Leisure interest:* sports. *Address:* ul. Dragonów 4 m. 49, Warsaw, Poland.

HOLROYD, Michael, C.B.E.; British author; b. 27 Aug. 1935, London; s. of Basil and Ulla (née Hall) Holroyd; m. Margaret Drabble (q.v.) 1982; ed. Eton Coll.; Chair. Soc. of Authors 1973–74, Nat. Book League 1976–78; Pres. English Centre of PEN 1985–88; Chair. Strachey Trust 1990–95, Public Lending Right Advisory Cttee. 1997–, Royal Soc. of Literature 1998–; mem. Arts Council (Chair. Literature Panel) 1992–95; Governor, Shaw Festival Theatre, Niagara-on-the-Lake 1993–; Hon. D.Litt. (Ulster) 1992, (Sheffield, Warwick) 1993, (East Anglia) 1994, (London School of Econs.) 1998. *Publications:* Hugh Kingsmill 1964, Lytton Strachey 1967–68, Unreceived Opinions 1973, Augustus John 1974–75 (new edn. 1996), Bernard Shaw: Vol. 1: The Search for Love 1988, Vol II: The Pursuit of Power 1989, Vol. III: The Lure of Fantasy 1991, Vol. IV: The Last Laugh 1992, Vol. V: The Shaw Companion 1992, Bernard Shaw 1997 (one-vol. biog.), Basil Street Blues 1999. *Leisure interests:* music, stories. *Address:* c/o A. P. Watt Ltd., 20 John Street, London, WC1N 2DL, England. *Telephone:* 0171-405 6774.

HOLST, Per; Danish film producer; b. 28 March 1939, Copenhagen; s. of Rigmor Holst and Svend Holst; m. 1st Anni Møller Kjeldsen 1962–72; m. 2nd Kristina Holst 1976; four s.; entered film industry with Nordisk Film 1957; Film Man. and copywriter, WA Advertising Agency 1962; Nordisk Film 1965; established Per Holst Filmproduktion ApS 1965; numerous film awards including Palme d'Or, Cannes Film Festival and Acad. Award (Oscar) for Pelle the Conqueror 1988. *Films:* Afskedens Time 1967, Benny's Bathtub 1967, Kaptajn Klyde og Hans Venner vender tilbage 1981, The Tree of Knowledge 1982, Zappa 1983, Beauty and the Beast 1983, The Boy Who Disappeared 1984, Twist and Shout 1984, Element of Crime 1984, Up on Daddy's Hat 1985, Coeurs Flambes 1986, Pelle the Conqueror 1987, The Redtops 1988, Aarhus by Night 1989, Sirup 1990, War of the Birds 1990, Cassanova 1990, The Hideaway 1991, Pain of Love 1992, Jungle Jack 1993. *Leisure interest:* golf.

HOLSTENER-JØRGENSEN, Helge, M.SC., DR. AGRON.; Danish scientist; b. 10 Dec. 1924, Tingsted; s. of Edgon and Eva Holstener-Jørgensen; m. Agnete Buemann 1949; one s. one d.; ed. Royal Veterinary and Agricultural Univ., Copenhagen; Scientist, Danish Forest Experiment Station 1950–62, Head 1962–92; Sr. Research Fellow, Forestry Research Inst., N.Z. 1967–68; Prof. of Silviculture, Royal Veterinary and Agricultural Univ., Copenhagen 1973–74; Council Chair. Royal Agricultural Soc. of Denmark 1982–90; Fellow, Royal Danish Acad. of Sciences and Letters 1980–; Foreign Fellow, Royal Swedish Acad. of Agric. and Forestry 1983–; Knight of Dannebrog. *Publications:* numerous publs. on soil science, tree nutrition, irrigation and decoration greenery. *Leisure interests:* literature, gardening. *Address:* Solbjerget 44, 3460 Birkerød, Denmark (Home). *Telephone:* 45 81 20 51.

HOLT, Sir James Clarke, Kt., D.PHIL., F.B.A.; British historian and university professor; b. 26 April 1922, Bradford, Yorks.; s. of the late Herbert Holt and Eunice Holt; m. Alice Catherine Elizabeth Suley 1950 (died 1998); one s.; ed. Bradford Grammar School and Queen's Coll., Oxford; served in army 1942–45; Harmsworth Sr. Scholar, Merton Coll., Oxford 1947–49; Lecturer, Univ. of Nottingham 1949–62, Prof. of Medieval History 1962–66; Prof. of History, Univ. of Reading 1966–78, Dean of Faculty of Letters and Social Sciences 1972–76; Professorial Fellow, Emmanuel Coll., Cambridge 1978–81, Prof of Medieval History, Cambridge Univ. 1978–88, Master of Fitzwilliam Coll., Cambridge 1981–88; Visiting Prof., Univ. of Calif., Santa Barbara, U.S.A. 1977; Visiting Hinkley Prof., Johns Hopkins Univ., U.S.A. 1983; Raleigh Lecturer, British Acad. 1975; Visiting Prof., Japan 1986; mem. Advisory Council on Public Records 1974–81; Pres. Royal Historical Soc. 1980–84; Vice-Pres. British Acad. 1986–88; Pres. Lincoln Record Soc. 1987–96; Corresp. Fellow Medieval Acad. of America; Hon. Fellow, Emmanuel Coll. 1985–, Fitzwilliam Coll. 1988–, The Queen's Coll., Oxford 1996–; Hon. D.Litt. (Reading) 1984, (Nottingham) 1996; Comendador de la Orden del Mérito Civil 1988. *Publications:* The Northerners: A Study in the Reign of King John 1961, Praestia Rolls 14–18 John 1964, Magna Carta 1965, The Making of Magna Carta 1966, Magna Carta and the Idea of Liberty 1972, The University of Reading: The First Fifty Years 1977, Robin Hood 1982, War and Government in the Middle Ages (Ed. with John Gillingham), Magna Carta and Medieval Government 1985; Hand-list of Acta Henry II and Richard I surviving in British Repositories (with Richard Mortimer) 1986, Domesday Studies (Ed.) 1987, Colonial England 1066–1215 1997; papers in English Historical Review, Past and Present, Economic History Review, trans. Royal Historical Soc. *Leisure interests:* music, mountaineering, cricket, fly-fishing. *Address:* 5 Holben Close, Barton, Cambridge, CB3 7AQ. *Telephone:* (01223) 332041.

HOLT, Peter Malcolm, D.LITT., F.B.A., F.S.A., F.R.HIST.S.; British professor of history; b. 28 Nov. 1918, Leigh, Lancs.; s. of Rev. Peter Holt and Elizabeth Holt; m. Nancy Bury (née Mawle) 1953; one s. one d.; ed. Univ. Coll., Oxford; Sudan Civil Service, Ministry of Educ. 1941–53, Govt. Archivist 1954–55; joined S.O.A.S. 1955, Prof. of Arab History 1964–75, Prof. of the History of the Near and Middle East 1975–82, Prof. Emer. 1982–, Hon. Fellow 1985. *Publications:* The Mahdist State in the Sudan 1958, 1970, Studies in the History of the Near East 1973, The Memoirs of a Syrian Prince 1983, The Age of the Crusades 1986, Early Mamluk Diplomacy 1995, The Sudan of the three Niles 1999; Co-Ed. The Cambridge History of Islam 1970. *Leisure interest:* walking. *Address:* Dryden Spinney, Bletchington Road, Kirtlington, Kidlington, Oxford, OX5 3HF, England. *Telephone:* (01869) 350477.

HOLTHUSEN, Hans Egon, D.PHIL.; German writer; b. 15 April 1913, Rendsburg, Schleswig-Holstein; s. of Johannes Holthausen and Alma Holthusen, née Hagelstein; m. 1st Lori Holthusen 1950; m. 2nd Inge Holthusen 1952; one s. one step-d.; ed. Tübingen, Berlin and Munich Univs.; served in the army 1939–45; writer 1945–; Dir. Goethe House, New York 1961–64; Del. Biennale Int. de Poésie, Knokke (Belgium) 1951–52; Perm. Prof. German Literature, Northwestern Univ. Evanston, Ill. 1968–81; Pres. Bavarian Acad. of Fine Arts 1968–74; Kiel Kulturpreis 1956, Bavarian Order of Merit 1973, Bayerisches Literaturpreis (Jean Paul Preis) 1983, Bayerische Maximiliansorden 1984, Kunstpreis des Landes Schleswig-Holstein 1984, Grosses Bundesverdienstkreuz 1987. *Publications:* essays: Rilkes Sonette an Orpheus—Versuch einer Interpretation 1937, Der späte Rilke 1949, Der unbehauste Mensch 1951 and 1955, Ja and Nein 1954, Das Schöne und das Wahre 1958, Kritisches Verstehen 1961, Avantgardismus 1964, Plädoyer für den Einzelnen 1967, Kreiselkompass 1976, Amerikaner und Deutsche, Dialog zweier Kulturen 1977, Opus 19 Reden und Widerreden aus 25 Jahren 1983; poems: Hier in der Zeit 1949, Labyrinthische Jahre 1952; novel: Das Schiff 1956; biographies: R. M. Rilke in Selbstzeugnissen und Bilddokumenten 1958, Eduard Mörike in Selbstzeugnissen und Bilddokumenten 1971, Sartre in Stammheim 1982, Opus 19: Reden und Widerreden aus 25 Jahren 1983, Gottfried Benn: Leben, Werk, Widerspruch 1986; also: Indiana Campus: ein amerikanisches Tagebuch 1969, Chicago: Metropolis am Michigansee 1981, Vom Eigensinn der Literatur—Kritische Versuche aus der achtziger Jahren 1989. *Leisure interests:* hiking, swimming, music. *Address:* Agnesstrasse 48, 8000 Munich 40, Germany. *Telephone:* (089) 271 2161.

HOLTON, A. Linwood, Jr., B.A., LL.B.; American politician and lawyer; b. 21 Sept. 1923, Big Stone Gap, Va.; s. of Abner Linwood and Edith (Van Gorder) Holton; m. Virginia Harrison Rogers 1953; two s. two d.; ed. public schools in Big Stone Gap, Washington and Lee Univ., and Harvard Law School; Partner, Eggleston, Holton, Butler and Glenn (law firm); served submarine force during Second World War; fmr. Chair. Roanoke City Republican Cttee.; Vice-Chair. Virginia Republican State Cen. Cttee. 1960–69; del. to Republican Nat. Convention 1960, 1968, 1972; mem. Nat. Nixon for Pres. Cttee. March 1967; Regional Co-ordinator for Nixon for Pres. Cttee.; Gov. of Virginia 1970–74; Asst. Sec. of State for Congressional Relations, Dept. of State 1974–75; partner in law firm of Hogan and Hartson 1975–78; Vice-Pres., Gen. Counsel American Council Insurance, Washington 1978–84; Chair. Burket Miller Center for Public Affairs, Univ. of Va. 1979–; Pres. Supreme Court Historical Soc. 1980–89; Pres. Centre for Innovative Tech., Herndon, Va. 1988–94; partner in law firm of Mezzullo and McCandlish 1994–; Republican. *Address:* Mezzullo and McCandlish, 1111 East Main Street, Suite 1500, P.O. Box 796, Richmond, VA 23206 (Office); 6010 Claiborne Drive, McLean, VA 22101, U.S.A. (Home). *Telephone:* (804) 775-3817 (Office); (703) 821-2745.

HOLTON, Gerald, PH.D.; American physicist and historian of science; b. 23 May 1922, Berlin, Germany; s. of Dr. Emanuel and Regina (Rossman) Holton; m. Nina Rossfort 1947; two s.; ed. Wesleyan Univ., Middletown, Conn., Harvard Univ.; Harvard Univ. staff, officers' radar course and lab. for Research on Sound Control 1943–45, various faculty posts 1945–, Mallinckrodt Prof. of Physics and Prof. of History of Science 1975; Visiting Prof., MIT 1976–94; Nat. Science Foundation Faculty Fellow, Paris 1960–61; Exchange Prof., Leningrad Univ. 1962; founder and Ed.-in-Chief, Daedalus 1958–61; Morris Loeb lecturer Oxford Univ. 1993; Rothschild Lecturer Harvard Univ. 1997; Dir WHO Collaborating Center in Mental Health for Texas and Mexico 1993–; mem. Council, History of Science Soc. 1959–61, Pres. 1982–84; Fellow, American Physical Soc. (Chair. Div. History of Physics 1992–93), American Acad. of Arts and Sciences (mem. Council 1991–95), Académie Internationale d'Histoire des Sciences (Vice-Pres. 1982–89), Deutsche Akademie der Naturforscher Leopoldina, Académie Internationale de Philosophie des Sciences; Visiting mem. Inst. for Advanced Study, Princeton 1964, 1967; mem. Nat. Acad. of Sciences Cttee. on Communication with Scholars in the People's Repub. of China 1969–72, U.S. Nat. Comm. on IUHPS 1982–88 (Chair. 1988); mem. German American Acad. Council Kuratorium 1997–; mem. Bd. of Govs., American Inst. of Physics 1969–74; Fellow, Center for Advanced Study in Behavioral Sciences, Stanford, Calif. 1975–76; mem. U.S. Nat. Comm. on UNESCO 1975–80, Library of Congress Council of Scholars 1979–, U.S. Nat. Comm. on Excellence in Educ. 1981–83, Nat. Humanities Center 1989–93; Herbert Spencer Lecturer, Oxford 1979, Jefferson Lecturer 1981; Robert A. Millikan Medal 1967, Oersted Medal 1980, Guggenheim Fellowship 1980–81, Presidential Citation for Service to Educ. 1984, McGovern Medal 1985, Andrew Gemant Award 1989, George Sarton Medal 1989, Bernal Prize 1989, Joseph Priestley Award 1994. *Publications:* Introduction to Concepts and Theories in Physical Science 1958, Thematic Origins of Scientific Thought 1973, 1988, Scientific Imagination 1978, Limits of Scientific Inquiry (Ed.) 1979, Albert Einstein, Historical and Cultural Perspectives (Ed.) 1982, The Advancement of Science, and its Burdens 1986, Science and Anti-Science 1993, Einstein, History, and Other Passions 1995, Gender Differences in Science Careers (Co-author) 1995, Who Succeeds in Science? The Gender Dimension (Co-author) 1995; mem. Editorial Bd., Collected Papers of Albert Einstein. *Leisure interests:* music, kayaking. *Address:* c/o Jefferson Physics Laboratory, Harvard University, Cambridge, MA 02138 (Office); 64 Francis Avenue, Cambridge, MA 02138, U.S.A. (Home).

HOLTZMAN, Wayne H(arold), M.S., PH.D.; American psychologist; b. 16 Jan. 1923, Chicago, Ill.; s. of Harold H. Holtzman and Lillian Manny; m. Joan King 1947; four s.; ed. Northwestern and Stanford Univs.; Asst. Prof. Univ. of Texas at Austin 1949–53, Assoc. Prof. 1954–59, Prof. of Psychology 1959–, Dean Coll. of Educ. 1964–70, Hogg Prof. of Psychology and Educ. 1964–; Assoc. Dir. Hogg Foundation for Mental Health 1955–64, Pres. 1970–93, Special Counsel 1993–; Dir. Science Research Assocs. 1974–89; Population Resource Center 1980–; Pres. Int. Union of Psychological Science 1984–88; other professional affiliations; Faculty Research Fellow, Social Science Research Council 1953–54, Center for Advanced Study in Behavioral Sciences 1962–63; Hon. L.H.D. (Southwestern) 1980. *Publications:* Tomorrow's Parents (with B. Moore) 1964, Computer Assisted Instruction, Testing and Guidance 1971, Personality Development in Two Cultures (with others) 1975, Introduction to Psychology 1978, School of the Future (with others) 1992. *Leisure interests:* travel, photography, gardening. *Address:* Hogg Foundation for Mental Health, The University of Texas, P.O. Box 7998, Austin, TX 78713-7998 (Office); 3300 Foothill Drive, Austin, TX 78731, U.S.A. (Home). *Telephone:* (512) 471-5041 (Office); (512) 452-8296 (Home).

HOLUM, John; American government official; b. 4 Dec. 1940, Highmore, S. Dak.; m. Barbara P. Pedersen; one c.; ed. Northern State Teachers' Coll. and George Washington Univ.; mem. staff of Sen. George McGovern 1965–79; mem. Policy and Planning Staff, U.S. State Dept. 1979–81; attorney, O'Melveny & Myers (law firm) 1981–93; defence and foreign policy adviser to Bill Clinton during 1992 presidential campaign; Dir. Arms Control and Disarmament Agency (ACDA) 1993–97; Acting Under Sec. of State for Arms Control and Int. Security 1997–; Democrat. *Address:* Office of the Under Secretary, 2201 C Street, N.W., Room 7208, Washington, DC 20520, U.S.A.

HOLYFIELD, Evander; American boxer; b. 19 Oct. 1962, Atlanta, Ga.; Bronze Medal, 1984 Olympic Games; World Boxing Assen. (WBA) cruiserweight title 1986; Int. Boxing Fed. cruiserweight title 1987; World Boxing Council (WBC) cruiserweight title 1988; world heavyweight champion 1990–92, 1993–94, 1996– (following defeat of Mike Tyson (q.v.) Nov. 1996), defended title against Tyson 1997 (Tyson disqualified for biting off part of Holyfield's ear); defended IBF Heavyweight title against Michael Moorer 1997; defended WBA and IBF titles, and contested WBC title, against Lennox Lewis (q.v.) March 1999, bout declared a draw; f. Real Deal Record Label 1999. *Address:* Main Event Boxing Federation, 811 Totowa Road, Totowa, NJ 07512, U.S.A.

HOLZACH, Robert, DR.IUR.; Swiss banker; b. 28 Sept. 1922, Zürich; ed. Univs. of Zürich and Geneva; admitted to the bar, Thurgau 1951; Trainee, Union Bank of Switzerland, Geneva and London 1951–53, mem. Secr. Commercial Div. Head Office 1953–56, Asst. Man. Commercial Div. 1956–62, Man. Commercial Div. 1962–66, Deputy Gen. Man. responsible for credit operations in German-speaking Switzerland 1966–67, Gen. Man. 1968–80, Head, Admin. Div. 1971–76, responsible for Gen. Management Staff Depts. 1976–80, Chair. Bd. of Dirs. 1980–88, Hon. Chair. 1988–96; Rep. of Union Bank of Switzerland on Bd. of Dirs. and Advisory Bds., major firms in Switzerland and Germany; Col. in Swiss Army, in command of Infantry Reg. 31 1966–69. *Publication:* Herausforderungen 1988. *Address:* c/o Union Bank of Switzerland, Bahnhofstrasse 45, 8001 Zürich, Switzerland.

HOLZER, Jenny, M.F.A.; American artist; b. 29 July 1950, Gallipolis, Ohio; d. of Richard Vornholt Holzer and Virginia Beasley Holzer; m. Michael Andrew Glier 1984; one d.; ed. Ohio Univ., Rhode Island School of Design, Whitney Museum of American Art Ind. Study Program; became working artist in New York 1977; solo exhbns. 1978– include Rüdiger Schöttle Gallery, Munich, Germany 1980, Barbara Gladstone Gallery, New York 1983, Dallas Museum of Art, Texas 1984, Des Moines Art Center, Iowa 1986, Am Hof, Vienna, Austria 1986, Rhona Hoffman Gallery, Chicago 1987, Contemporary Arts Museum, Houston 1987, Brooklyn Museum, New York 1988, American Pavilion, 44th Venice Biennale, Italy 1990, Art Tower Mito, Japan 1994, Bergen Museum of Art, Norway 1994, Williams Coll. Museum of Art, Williamstown, Mass. 1995, Kunstmuseum Kartause Ittingen, Warth, Switzerland 1996, Index Gallery, Osaka, Japan 1997, Yvon Lambert Gallery, Paris 1998, Inst. Cultural Itau, São Paulo 1998; special projects and comms. 1978– include "Green Table", Univ. of Calif., San Diego 1993, "Lustmord", Süddeutsche Zeitung Magazin, no. 46, Germany, "Black Garden", Nordhorn, Germany 1994, "Allentown Benches", Allentown, Pa. 1995, "Erlauf Peace Monument", Erlauf, Austria 1995, installation at Schiphol Airport, Amsterdam, Netherlands 1995, Biennale di Firenze, Florence, Italy 1996, installation for Hamburger Kunsthalle, Hamburg, Germany 1996, perm. installation at Guggenheim Museum, Bilbao, Literaturhaus Munich, Germany, Oskar Maria Graf Memorial 1997, Kunsthalle Zürich, Switzerland; numerous group exhbns. 1978– include Museum of Modern Art, New York 1988, 1990, 1996, Guggenheim Museum, New York 1996, Centre Pompidou, Paris, France 1996; Hon. D.Arts (Ohio Univ.) 1994; Golden Lion Award for Best Pavilion, 44th Venice Biennale, Italy 1990, Gold Medals for Title and Design, Art Directors' Club of Europe 1993, Skowhegan Medal for Installation, New York 1994, Crystal Award, for outstanding contrib. to cross-cultural understanding, World Econ. Forum, Switzerland 1996. *Publications:* A Little Knowledge 1979, Black Book 1980, Eating Through Living 1981, Truisms and Essays 1983. *Leisure interests:* reading, riding. *Address:* 80 Hewitts Road, Hoosick Falls, NY 12090, U.S.A. *Telephone:* (518) 686-9323 (Office). *Fax:* (518) 686-9019 (Office).

HOMBACH, Bodo; German politician and business executive; b. 19 Aug. 1952, Mülheim; m. 1977; ed. Düsseldorf Polytechnic, Duisberg Comprehensive Univ., Hagen Correspondence Univ.; fmrly. trainee telecommunications worker, youth affairs spokesman and youth worker; Sec. German TU Fed. (DGB) North Rhine Westphalia 1974–76; Educ. Policy Sec. Educ. and Sciences TU North Rhine Westphalia 1976–77, Regional Business Man. 1977–79; Deputy State Business Man. German Social Democratic Party (SPD) North Rhine Westphalia 1979–81, Business Man. 1981–91, Deputy Chair. Mülheim Dist. 1993, Deputy Chair. Niederrhein Dist. 1998; Fed. Minister Without Portfolio and Head Fed. Chancellery Oct. 1998–; mem.

North Rhine Westphalia Landtag 1990–98, Chair. Parl. Inquiry Comm. 1992–94, Parl. Econ. Affairs Spokesman 1994–98, State Minister for Econ. and Medium Industry, Tech. and Transport June–Oct. 1998; Dir. Marketing, Org. and Co. Strategy Preussag Handel GmbH (fmrly. Salzgitter Stahl AG), Man. 1992–98, Business Man. Preussag Int. GmbH 1995–98. *Publications include:* Der SPD von innen, Die Zukunft der Arbeit, Aufruf für eine Geschichte des Volkes in Nordrhein-Westfalia, Die Lokomotive in voller Fahrt der Räder wechseln, Anders Leben, Sozialstaat 2000, Die Kraft der Region: Nordrhein-Westfalia in Europa. *Address:* Federal Chancellery, Adenauerallee 139–141, 53113 Bonn; Schwannstrasse 12, 40476 Düsseldorf, Germany. *Telephone:* (228) 560 (Bonn). *Fax:* (228) 56-23-57 (Bonn).

HONDROS, Ernest Demetrios, C.M.G., D.SC., F.R.S.; British scientist; b. 18 Feb. 1930, Kastellorizo, Dodecanese, Greece; s. of Demetrios Hondros and Athanasia Paleologos; m. Sissel Kristine Garder-Olsen 1968; two s.; ed. Univ. of Melbourne, Australia, Univ. of Paris; CSIRO Tribophysics Lab., Melbourne 1955–59; Research Fellow, Laboratoire de Chimie Minérale, Univ. of Paris 1959–62; Sr. Research Fellow, Nat. Physical Lab. 1962, Prin. Research Fellow 1965, Sr. Prin. Research Fellow 1974, Supt. Materials Div. 1979–85; Dir. Petten Establishment, EC (now EU) Jt. Research Centre, Netherlands 1985–95, Dir. Inst. for Advanced Materials 1989–95; Visiting Prof. Imperial Coll. of Science, Tech. and Medicine 1988–; Hatfield Memorial Lecturer, Univ. of Sheffield 1986; Hon. mem. Soc. Française de Metallurgie; Hon. D.Sc. (Univ. of London) 1997; Rosenhain Medal, Howe Medal, Griffiths Medal. *Publications:* Energetics of Solid-Solid Interfaces 1969, Grain Boundary Segregation (with M. P. Seah) 1973. *Leisure interest:* reading. *Address:* 37 Ullswater Crescent, London, SW15 3RG, England. *Telephone:* 0181-549 9526. *Fax:* 0181-549 9526.

HONECKER, Margot; German politician; b. (as Margot Feist) 17 April 1927, Halle; m. Erich Honecker 1953 (deceased); one d.; Co-Founder Anti-Fascist Youth Cttee., Halle 1945; mem. CP 1945–89; Sec., Freie Deutsche Jugend (FDJ) Cttee., Sachsen-Anhalt; Chair. Young Pioneers and Sec., Cen. Council, FDJ 1949–53; mem. Volkskammer 1949–54, 1967–89; mem. Cen. Cttee. Socialist Unity Party (SED) 1963–89; univ. training in U.S.S.R. 1953–54; Head Teacher Training Dept., Ministry of Educ. 1955–58, Deputy Minister of Educ. 1958–63, Minister of Educ. 1963–89; with husband in Moscow 1991, sought asylum in Chilean Embassy, Moscow Dec. 1991; left Embassy for Chile July 1992; mem. Acad. of Pedagogical Sciences; Dr. h.c.; Karl-Marx-Orden, Vaterländischer Verdienstorden in Gold, Held der Arbeit, and other decorations. *Publication:* On Educational Policy and Pedagogics in the German Democratic Republic 1986.

HONEGGER, Fritz; Swiss politician; b. 25 July 1917, Bischofszell; s. of Fritz Honegger and Elisabeth Honegger Brunnschweiler; m. Lucienne Jacot 1944; two s.; ed. Univ. of Zürich; Cantonal Councillor, Zürich 1957–75, Pres. Cantonal Parl., Zürich 1965–66; Deputy from Canton of Zürich to Council of States 1967–78; Chair. Radical Democratic Party of Switzerland 1974–78; elected Fed. Councillor Dec. 1977; Head Fed. Dept. of Public Economy 1978–82; Vice-Pres. of Switzerland Jan.–Dec. 1981, Pres. Jan.–Dec. 1982. *Leisure interests:* reading and travelling. *Address:* Schloss-Strasse 29, 8803 Rüschlikon, Switzerland (Home).

HONEYCOMBE, Sir Robert William Kerr, Kt., PH.D., D.SC., F.ENG., F.R.S.; Australian professor of metallurgy; b. 2 May 1921, Melbourne; s. of William Honeycombe and Rachael (Kerr) Honeycombe; m. June Collins 1947; two d.; ed. Geelong Coll. and Univ. of Melbourne; research officer CSIRO (Australia) 1942–47; ICI Research Fellow, Cavendish Lab., Cambridge 1948–49; Royal Soc. Armourers and Brasiers' Research Fellow, Cavendish Lab. 1949–51; Sr. Lecturer in Physical Metallurgy, Univ. of Sheffield 1951–55, Prof. 1955–66; Goldsmiths' Prof. of Metallurgy, Univ. of Cambridge 1966–84, Prof. Emer. 1984–; Fellow, Trinity Hall, Cambridge 1966–73, Hon. Fellow 1975–; Pres. Clare Hall, Cambridge 1973–80, Fellow 1980–88, Emer. Fellow 1988–; Pres. Inst. of Metallurgists 1977, Metals Soc. 1980–81; Treasurer and Vice-Pres. Royal Soc. 1986–92; recipient of several medals and hon degrees. *Publications:* The Plastic Deformation of Metals 1968, Steels: Microstructure and Properties 1981. *Leisure interests:* walking, gardening, music, photography. *Address:* Department of Materials Science and Metallurgy, University of Cambridge, Pembroke Street, Cambridge, CB2 3QZ; 46 Main Street, Hardwick, Cambridge, CB3 7QS, England. *Telephone:* (01223) 334356; (01954) 210501.

HONEYMAN, Janice Lynne; South African actress, director and writer; b. 14 Jan. 1949, Cape Town; d. of Frank Gordon Honeyman and Marie Evelyn Honeyman; ed. Univ. of Cape Town (performers diploma); dir. and actress with Market Theatre Co. and Performing Arts Council of Transvaal 1970–; Dir. Dogge's Troupe-Interaction, London 1977–78; founder mem. Market Theatre Co., Resident Dir. 1984–85, Trustee Market Theatre Foundation 1985–; Trustee Foundation for Equality 1993–; Exec. and Artistic Dir. Johannesburg Civic Theatre 1993–; freelance dir. R.S.C. 1988–89, and of opera, operetta and musicals; Assoc. Artist PACT; Ernest Oppenheimer Award for Resident Dir., Market Theatre, S.A. Young Artists Award; Breytenbach Epathalon, A.A. Vita Award for directing; Gallo Award for Best Performance, Johnnie Walker Black Label Achievers Award. *Leisure interests:* reading, opera, swimming, snorkelling, travelling. *Publications:* This is for Keeps (with V. Cooke and D. Keogh) 1984, Knickerbocker Knockabout 1988. *Address:* 8A Seymour Street, Westdene, Johannesburg 2092, South Africa. *Telephone:* 011-403 3408 (Office); 011-477 7626 (Home). *Fax:* 011-403 3412.

HONG HU; Chinese politician; b. June 1940, Jinzhai Co., Anhui Prov.; ed. Beijing Industrial Inst.; joined CCP 1965; Vice-Sec.-Gen., Sec.-Gen. State Comm. for Econ. Restructuring 1982–91; Vice-Dir. State Comm. for Econ. Restructuring 1991–98; mem. Comm. of Securities of the State Council 1992–98; mem. CCP Cen. Cttee. for Discipline Inspection 1992; mem. 15th CCP Cen. Cttee. 1997–; Acting Gov. Jilin Prov. 1998–. *Address:* Jilin Provincial People's Government, Changchun, Jilin Province, People's Republic of China.

HONG JAE-HYONG; Korean politician; b. Chongju City, N. Chungchong Prov.; ed. Seoul Nat. Univ.; joined Foreign Exchange Bureau, Ministry of Finance 1963; later worked at IBRD, Washington, D.C.; Admin., Korean Customs Admin.; Pres. Export-Import Bank of Korea, Korea Exchange Bank; Minister of Finance 1993; Deputy Prime Minister, Minister of Finance and Econs. 1994–96. *Address:* c/o Ministry of Finance, 1 Jungang-dong, Gwachon City, Kyonggi Province, Republic of Korea.

HONG QIAN, (Tscha Hung), PH.D.; Chinese philosopher and university professor; b. 21 Oct. 1909, Fuki; mem. Vienna Circle 1931–36; Research Fellow, New Coll. Oxford, U.K. 1945–47, Visiting Fellow Queen's Coll. 1980, 1984, Trinity Coll. 1982; Dir. Philosophy Inst., Beijing Univ. 1984–; Hon. Pres. Chinese Soc. of Contemporary Foreign Philosophy 1980–, Sino-British Summer Coll. in Beijing 1988–; mem. Editorial Advisory Bd. Vienna Circle Collection, Dordrecht, Netherlands 1990–; Dr. h.c. (Vienna) 1984. *Publications:* Ayer and The Vienna Circle, in The Philosophy of Ayer 1992, Das Kausalproblem in der heutigen Physick, in Studien zur Österreichen Philosophie Verlag. *Address:* 2nd Apt. No. 232, Zhong Quan Yuan, Beijing University, 100871 Beijing, People's Republic of China.

HONG XUEZHI, Gen.; Chinese army officer; b. 1913, Jinzhai Co., Anhui Prov.; joined CCP 1929; Deputy Commdr., army corps, 4th Field Army 1949; Commdr. Guangdong Mil. Region 1949–50; mem. Guangzhou Mil. Control Comm. 1949–50; Political Commissar, 16th Corps 1950; Dir. Logistics Dept. Chinese People's Volunteers in Korea 1952; mem. Nat. Defence Council 1954–59; Deputy Dir. PLA Logistics Dept. 1954–56, Dir. 1956–59; alt.-mem. 8th Cen. Cttee. of CCP 1956; mem. Standing Cttee., 5th NPC 1978; Dir., Gen. Office for Nat. Defence Industry 1978–79; Dir. 2nd Office of Nat. Defence 1979–80; Vice-Chair. Cttee. to Examine Proposals, 2nd Session, 5th NPC 1979; mem. 11th Cen. Cttee. of CCP 1979; mem. 12th Cen. Cttee. CCP 1982–85; Dir. PLA Gen. Logistics Dept. 1980–85, Political Commr. 1985–87; mem. and Deputy Sec.-Gen. Cen. Mil. Comm. 1982–; mem. Cen. Party Consolidation Guidance Comm. 1983; Vice-Chair. Cen. Patriotic Public Health Campaign Cttee. 1983; Head Leading Group of All-Army Financial and Econ. Discipline Inspection, CCP Cen. Mil. Comm. 1986; Chair. PLA Greening Cttee. 1984; Vice-Chair. Cen. Greening Cttee. 1983; Hon. Vice-Pres. Beijing Social Welfare Foundation 1984; promoted Gen. PLA 1988; Sr. Adviser China Soc. of Mil. Sciences 1991–; mem. Presidium 14th CCP Nat. Congress 1992, Vice-Chair. 8th Nat. Cttee. CPPCC 1993–98, Hon. Pres. Handball Asscn. *Address:* Office of the Director, People's Liberation Army General Logistics Department, Beijing, People's Republic of China.

HONG, Tae-Shik, B.L.; South Korean banker; b. 20 Dec. 1934; ed. Korea Univ. and Univ. of Ottawa; joined Korea Devt. Bank 1957, Man. Research Dept. 1972, Deputy Gen. Man. Foreign Loan Dept. 1977, Chief Rep. London office 1981, Gen. Man. Business Control Dept. 1984, Gen. Man. Fund Man. Dept. 1986, Asst. Gov. 1987, Deputy Gov. 1990. *Leisure interests:* golf, computer.

HONIG, Edwin, M.A.; American professor of comparative literature and poet; b. 3 Sept. 1919, New York; s. of Abraham David Honig and Jane Freundlich; m. 1st Charlotte Gilchrist 1940 (died 1963); m. 2nd Margot S. Dennes 1963 (divorced 1978); two s.; ed. Univ. of Wis.; Instructor in English Purdue Univ. 1942–43, New York Univ. and Ill. Inst. Tech. 1946–47, Univ. of N.M. 1947–48, Claremont Coll. 1949, Harvard Univ. 1949–52, Briggs-Copeland Asst. Prof. of English, Harvard 1952–57; mem. Faculty Brown Univ. 1957, Prof. of English 1960–82, of Comparative Literature 1962–82, Chair. Dept. of English 1967, Prof. Emer. 1983–; Visiting Prof. Univ. of Calif., Davis 1964–65; Mellon Prof. Boston Univ. 1977; Dir. Copper Beech Press; Guggenheim Fellow 1948, 1962; Amy Lowell Travelling Poetry Fellow 1968; Golden Rose Award New England Poetry Club 1961; Poetry Prize, Saturday Review 1956; NEA Award (in poetry) 1980, (in transl.) 1983; Columbia Univ. Translation Center Nat. Award 1985. *Publications include: poems:* The Moral Circus 1955, The Gazabos 1960, Survivals 1964, Spring Journal 1968, Four Springs 1972, Shake a Spear With Me, John Berryman 1974, At Sixes 1974, The Affinities of Orpheus 1976, Selected Poems (1955–1976) 1979, Interrupted Praise 1983, Gifts of Light, The Imminence of Love: Poems 1962–92 1993; *plays:* The Widow 1953, The Phantom Lady 1964, Life is a Dream, Calisto and Melibea (play/libretto) 1972, Ends of the World and Other Plays 1983, Calderón: Six Plays 1993; *prose:* Always Astonished 1988; *criticism:* García Lorca 1944, Dark Conceit: The Making of Allegory 1959, Calderón and the Seizures of Honor 1972, The Poet's Other Voice 1985; *stories:* Foibles and Fables of an Abstract Man 1979; *anthologies* (with Oscar Williams): The Mentor Book of Major American Poets 1961, The Major Metaphysical Poets 1968; Spenser 1968; also translations of works by García Lorca, Calderón de la Barca, Fernando Pessoa, Miguel Hernández and Lope de Vega; produced opera Calisto and Melibea 1979, play Life is a Dream 1988. *Address:* Brown University, Box 1852, Providence, RI 02912 (Office); 99 Post Road, F-5, Warwick, RI 02888, U.S.A. (Home). *Telephone:* (401) 461-2363.

HONJO, Tasuku, M.D., PH.D.; Japanese academic; b. 27 Jan. 1942, Kyoto; s. of Shoichi Honjo and Ryu Honjo; m. Shigeko Kotani 1969; one s. one d.; ed. Ube High School and Kyoto Univ.; Fellow, Carnegie Inst. of Washington, Baltimore 1971–73; Visiting Fellow and Assoc. Lab. of Molecular Genetics, Nat. Insts. of Health 1973–74; Asst. Prof. Dept. of Physiological Chem. and Nutrition, Faculty of Medicine, Univ. of Tokyo 1974–79; Prof. Dept. of Genetics, Osaka Univ. School of Medicine 1979–84; Prof. Dept. of Medical Chem. Faculty of Medicine Kyoto Univ. 1984–, Dir. Center for Molecular Biology and Genetics 1989–97; Hon. mem. American Asscn. of Immunologists; Asahi Award 1981; Erwin von Baelz Award 1985; Takeda Medical Award 1988; Behring-Kitsato Prize 1992, Japan Acad. Award 1996. *Publications:* Immunoglobulin Genes (ed.) 1989, Seppuku and Autoimmunity 1992. *Address:* Department of Medical Chemistry, Kyoto University, Yoshida, Sakyo-ku, Kyoto 606, Japan. *Telephone:* 81-75-753-4371. *Fax:* 81-75-753-4388.

HONKAPOHJA, Seppo Mikko Sakari, D.SOC.SC.; Finnish professor of economics; b. 7 March 1951, Helsinki; m. Sirkku Anna-Maija Honkapohja 1973; one s. one d.; ed. United World Coll. of the Atlantic, U.K., Univ. of Helsinki; Scientific Dir. Yrjö Jahnsson Foundation 1975–87; Prof. of Econs., Turku School of Econs. and Business Admin. 1987–91, Prof.-at-Large (Dosent) 1992–; Prof.-at-Large (Dosent) of Econs., Univ. of Helsinki 1981–91, Acting Prof. of Econs. (Econometrics) 1985–87, Prof. of Econs. 1992–; Visiting Lecturer and Scholar, Harvard Univ., U.S.A. 1978–79; Visiting Assoc. Prof. of Econs., Stanford Univ., U.S.A. 1982–83; Sr. Fellow Acad. of Finland 1982–83, Acad. Prof. 1989–95; Man. Ed. Scandinavian Journal of Econs. 1984–88; Ed. European Econ. Review 1993–; mem. Bd. Finnish Econ. Asscn. 1989–91, Finnish Soc. For European Studies 1994–; mem. Council, European Econ. Asscn. 1985–86; Vice-Chair. Kansallis Foundation for Financial Research 1989–96; mem. Governing Body The Finnish Cultural Foundation 1994–, Chair. 1997–; mem. Advisory Bd. Journal of Econ. Surveys 1994–; mem. Supervisory Bd., Okopankki Ltd. 1996–, Chair 1997–; mem. Finnish Acad. of Science and Letters, Academia Europaea. *Publications:* Limits and Problems of Taxation 1985; Ed. several books including The State of Macroeconomics 1990, Macroeconomic Modelling and Policy Implications 1993; numerous articles in journals. *Leisure interest:* fishing. *Address:* Department of Economics, P.O. Box 54, University of Helsinki, FIN-00014, Finland. *Telephone:* 191 8876. *Fax:* 191 8877.

HOOD, Leroy Edward, M.D., PH.D.; American biologist; b. 10 Oct. 1938, Missoula, Mon.; m. Valerie A. Logan 1963; one s. one d.; ed. Calif. Inst. of Tech. and Johns Hopkins School of Medicine; NIH Predoctoral Fellowship, Calif. Inst. of Tech. 1963–64, NIH Postdoctoral Fellowship 1964–67; Sr. Investigator, Immunology Branch, GL&C, Nat Chemical Industries, Nat. Insts. of Health, Bethesda, Md. 1967–70; Asst. Prof. of Biology Calif. Inst. of Tech. 1970–73, Assoc. Prof. 1973–75, Prof. 1975–77, Bowles Prof. of Biology 1977–92, Chair. Div. of Biology 1980–89, Dir. Cancer Center 1981; Gates Prof. of Molecular Biotech. Univ. of Wash. 1992–, Chair. School of Medicine 1992–; Dir. N.S.F. Science and Tech. Center for Molecular Biotechnology 1989–; mem. N.A.S., American Acad. of Arts and Sciences; numerous awards and honours. *Publications:* co-author of five books on immunology and biochemistry. *Leisure interests:* mountaineering, climbing, running, photography, science fiction. *Address:* University of Washington, School of Medicine, Department of Molecular Biotechnology, P.O. Box 35 7730, Seattle, WA 98195, U.S.A.

HOOD, William Clarence, PH.D., F.R.S.C.; Canadian economist; b. 13 Sept. 1921, Yarmouth, N.S.; s. of Percy Alexander Hood and Vida Barr (née Webster) Hood; m. Alville Mary Lennox 1948; one s. one d.; ed. Mount Allison Univ., Sackville, N.B., Univ. of Toronto; Economist, Wartime Prices and Trade Bd., Ottawa 1941; Govt. Meteorologist 1943–44; Instructor in Econs., Univ. of Saskatchewan 1944–46; Asst., Assoc. and Full Prof. of Econs., Univ. of Toronto 1946–64; Adviser to Bank of Canada, Ottawa 1964–69; Asst. Deputy Minister of Finance with responsibility for Econ. Analysis, Fiscal Policy and Int. Finance 1970–74, Assoc. Deputy Minister of Finance 1975–79, Deputy Minister of Finance 1979; Econ. Counsellor and Dir. of Research Dept., IMF, Washington, D.C. 1980–86; Econ. Consultant, Washington, D.C. 1986–; Pres. Canadian Econs. Asscn. 1969–70; Fellow of Royal Soc. of Canada 1963–, of Econometric Soc. 1975–; Hon. LL.D. (Mount Allison Univ.) 1970, (McMaster Univ., Hamilton, Ont.) 1980. *Publications:* Studies in Econometric Method (with T. C. Koopmans, q.v.) 1953, Output, Labour and Capital in the Canadian Economy (with A. D. Scott) 1958, Financing of Economic Activity in Canada 1959 and various articles in journals. *Leisure interests:* particle physics, cycling, skiing. *Address:* 9513 Liberty Tree Lane, Vienna, VA 22182, U.S.A. *Telephone:* (703) 938-0098.

't HOOFT, Gerardus; Netherlands professor of theoretical physics; b. 5 July 1946, Den Helder; s. of H. 't Hooft and M.A. van Kampen; m. Albertha A. Schik 1972; two d.; ed. Dalton Lyceum Gymnasium beta, The Hague, Rijks Universiteit, Utrecht; Fellow C.E.R.N. (Theoretical Physics Div.), Geneva 1972–74; Asst. Prof., Univ. of Utrecht 1974–77, Prof. 1977–; mem. Koninklijke Acad. van Wetenschappen, Letteren en Schone Kunsten v. België, Koninklijke Nederlandse Acad. van Wetenschappen; Foreign Assoc. N.A.S. (U.S.A.); Foreign Hon. mem. American Acad. of Arts and Sciences, Académie des Sciences; Dr. h.c. (Chicago) 1981, (Leuven) 1996, (Bologna) 1998; W. Prins Prize 1974, Akzo Prize 1977, Dannie Heineman Prize 1979, Wolf Prize 1982, Spinoza Premium 1995; Pius XI Medal 1983, Lorentz Medal 1986, Franklin Medal 1995, G. C. Wick Medal 1997. *Publications:* Under the Spell of the Gauge Principle 1994, In Search of the Ultimate Building Blocks 1996; papers on Renormalization of Yang-Mills Fields, Magnetic monopoles, Instantons, Gauge theories, quark confinement, quantum gravity and black holes. *Leisure interests:* piano, painting. *Address:* University of Utrecht, Spinoza Institute, P.O. Box 80.195, 3508 TD Utrecht, Netherlands. *Telephone:* (30) 253 7549; 253 5928. *Fax:* (30) 253 5937.

HOOGLANDT, Jan Daniel, D.SC.; Netherlands steel manufacturing executive; b. 15 Feb. 1926, Tangier, Morocco; m.; four c.; ed. Hilversum Gymnasium, Municipal Univ. of Amsterdam; joined Koninklijke Nederlandsche Hoogovens en Staalfabrieken NV 1954 as Asst. in Econ. Dept. 1954; retd. May 1988 as Chair. Bd. Hoogovens Groep BV; Chair. Supervisory Bd. ABN/AMRO –1996, Ned. Participatie Maatschappij NV; mem. Supervisory Bd. Koninklijke Nederlandsche Hoogovens en Staalfabrieken NV –1996, NV Koninklijke Nederlandse Petroleum Maatschappij –1996, Heineken NV; Order of the Netherlands Lion 1976; Commdr. Order Oranje Nassau 1988. *Address:* Zwartweg 16, 2111 AJ Aerdenhaut, Netherlands.

HOOKER, Charlie (Charles Raymond); British artist; b. 1 June. 1953, London; s. of Raymond C. and Daphne Hooker; m. Stephanie J. Burden 1980; one s.; ed. Purley Grammar School, Croydon Coll. of Art and Brighton Polytechnic; founder mem. The Artistics (music ensemble) 1972–75, 2B Butlers Wharf (art space) 1974–75; Visiting lecturer, Chelsea, Croydon, Winchester, Trent, Cardiff, Central, Brighton, Newport, Newcastle, Camberwell Schools of Art/Polytechnics 1977–; part-time lecturer Brighton Polytechnic 1990–92; external examiner, Chelsea School of Art 1995–; Sr. lecturer Camberwell Coll. 1990–92; Sr. lecturer/Area Leader—Sculpture, Univ. of Brighton 1992–; Artist in Residence at Amherst Jr. and Hatcham Wood Secondary Schools 1985; Co-ordinator, Artists' Open Week, Camberwell School of Art 1989; several one-man and group shows of maquettes and drawings and numerous installations and performances in U.K., Europe, America and Australia 1975–; works in Arts Council collection and private collections, and perm. public outdoor work in U.K.; Art/Science projects with Science Museum, London and Herstmonceux Science Centre 1995; published discussions in Performance and in Aspects 1980, 1984, 1986, De Appel 1987; *radio interviews:* BBC Radio Nottingham 1981, BBC Radio Cambridge 1986, Warsaw Radio 1988; *TV interviews:* BBC Look North 1983, Anglia TV 1985, W. Australia TV News 1985; published video recording 'Charlie Hooker Talks to Mike Archer' (Havering Educational) 1988; *audio recordings:* Restricted Movement 1982, Transitions 1984, Charlie Hooker and Performers 1987, Wave-Wall/Dust and a Shadow 1991 for Audio Arts, Separate Elements 1992. *Leisure interest:* walking. *Address:* 28 Whippingham Road, Brighton, Sussex, BN2 3PG, England. *Telephone:* (01273) 600048. *Fax:* (01273) 643128.

HOOKER, John Lee; American blues singer and guitarist and songwriter; b. 22 Aug. 1917, Clarksdale, Miss.; studied guitar under Will Moore; extensive tours across N. America 1951–, Europe and U.K. 1961–; appeared at Newport Folk Festival 1959, 1960, 1963, Newport Jazz Festival 1964, American Blues Festival 1964, 1965, 1968, Ann Arbor Blues Festival 1969, 1970, 1973, 1974, at Carnegie Hall 1971, 1983, 1986; W.C. Handy Award 1986, 1989, 1990, 1993, 1996; TV appearances include Midnight Special 1971, Don Kirsher's Rock Concert 1978; writer of numerous blues songs including She's Long, She's Tall, Boom Boom, Boogie Chillen; has recorded over 100 albums including Folklore of John Lee Hooker 1962, Big Soul of John Lee Hooker 1964, Best of John Lee Hooker 1974, This is Hip 1980, Tantalising With The Blues 1982, Solid Sender 1984, Black Rhythm and Blues 1984, The Healer 1988, Never Get Out of These Blues Alive 1990, John Lee Hooker 1990, I'm in the Mood 1991, More Real Folks Blues/The Missing Album 1991, That's My Story 1991, Mr Lucky 1991, That's Where It's At, Boom Boom 1992, Get Back Home 1992, Graveyard Blues 1992, Hobo Blues 1992, The Early Years 1994, Simply the Truth 1994, One Way 1994, Chill Out 1995; has also recorded under names Delta John, John Lee Booker, Birmington Sam, Texas Slim, John Williams; Folk Heritage Award, Smithsonian Inst. 1983, Rhythm and Blues Foundation Lifetime Achievement Award 1998, and other awards. *Film:* The Blues Brothers 1980. *Address:* c/o Rosebud Agency, P.O. Box 170429, San Francisco, CA 94117, U.S.A.

HOOKER, Morna Dorothy, D.D., M.A., PH.D.; British professor of divinity; b. 19 May 1931, Surrey; d. of P. F. Hooker and L. Riley; m. Rev. Dr. W. D. Stacey 1978 (died 1993); ed. Univ. of Bristol; Research Fellow, Univ. of Durham 1959–61; lecturer in New Testament, King's Coll. London 1961–70, Fellow 1979–; lecturer in Theology, Univ. of Oxford 1970–76, Keble Coll. Oxford 1972–76; Fellow, Linacre Coll. Oxford 1970–76, Hon. Fellow 1980–; Visiting Fellow, Clare Hall, Cambridge 1974; Lady Margaret Prof. of Divinity, Univ. of Cambridge 1976–98; Fellow, Robinson Coll. Cambridge 1977–; Jt. Ed. Journal of Theological Studies 1985–; Pres. Soc. for New Testament Studies 1988–89; Visiting Prof. McGill Univ. 1968, Duke Univ. N.C. 1987, 1989; Hon. Fellow, Westminster Coll., Oxford 1995–; Hon. D.Litt. (Bristol) 1994, Hon. D.D. (Edin.) 1997. *Publications:* Jesus and the Servant 1959, The Son of Man in Mark 1967, Pauline Pieces 1979, Studying the New Testament 1979, The Message of Mark 1983, Continuity and Discontinuity 1986, From Adam to Christ 1990, A Commentary on the Gospel According to St. Mark 1991, Not Ashamed of the Gospel 1994, The Signs of a Prophet 1997, Beginnings: Keys that Open the Gospels 1997. *Leisure interests:* molinology, music, walking. *Address:* Robinson College, Cambridge, CB3 9AN, England. *Telephone:* (01223) 339149. *Fax:* (01223) 351794.

HOOKWAY, Sir Harry Thurston, Kt., PH.D.; British administrator and librarian; b. 23 July 1921, London; s. of William and Bertha Hookway; m. Barbara Butler 1956; one s. one d.; ed. Trinity School of John Whitgift and London Univ.; Asst. Dir. Nat. Chem. Lab. 1959; Dir. U.K. Scientific Mission (N. America), Scientific Attaché, Embassy, Washington, Scientific Adviser, High Comm., Ottawa 1960–64; Head, Information Div. Dept. of Scientific and Industrial Research 1964–65; Chief Scientific Officer, Dept. of Educ. and Science 1966–69, Asst. Under-Sec. of State 1969–73; Deputy Chair. and Chief Exec. British Library Bd. 1973–84; Pro-Chancellor Loughborough Univ. of Tech. 1987–93; mem. Royal Comm. on Historical Monuments (England) 1981–88; Chair. Publrs. Data Bases Ltd. 1984–87, L.A. Publishing Ltd. 1986–89; Pres. The Library Asscn. 1985; Dir. Arundel Castle Trustees 1976–; Hon. Fellow Inst. of Information Scientists; Hon. LL.D., Hon D. Litt., Hon. F.L.A.; Gold Medal Int. Asscn. of Library Asscns. 1985. *Publications:* papers in learned and professional journals. *Leisure interests:* music, travel. *Address:* 3 St. James Green, Thirsk, North Yorks., YO7 1AF, England.

HOOLEY, Christopher, PH.D., F.R.S.; British university professor; b. 7 Aug. 1928, Edinburgh; s. of Leonard Joseph Hooley and Barbara Hooley; m. Birgitta Kniep 1954; two s.; ed. Abbotsholme School and Corpus Christi Coll. Cambridge; Capt., Royal Army Educational Corps 1948–49; Fellow, Corpus Christi Coll. 1955–58; Lecturer in Math., Univ. of Bristol 1958–65; Prof. of Pure Math., Univ. of Durham 1965–67; Prof. of Pure Math. 1967–95, Distinguished Research Prof. 1995–, Head of Dept. of Math. Wales Univ., Coll. of Cardiff (fmrly. Univ. Coll. Cardiff) 1988–96, Dean of Faculty of Science 1973–76, Deputy Prin. Univ. Coll. Cardiff 1979–81, Wales Univ. Coll. of Cardiff 1991–94; Visiting mem., Inst. for Advanced Study, Princeton, U.S.A. on several occasions since 1970, Institut des Hautes Etudes Scientifiques, Paris 1984; Adam's Prize, Cambridge 1973; Sr. Berwick Prize, London Math. Soc. 1980. *Publications:* Applications of Sieve Methods to the Theory of Numbers 1976, Recent Progress in Analytic Number Theory (Ed. with H. Halberstam) 1981. *Leisure interests:* antiquities and classic cars. *Address:* Rushmoor Grange, Backwell, Bristol, BS19 3BN, England. *Telephone:* (01275) 462363.

HOOPER, Anthony Sidney Colchester, B.SC., M.S.; South African librarian; b. 16 Sept. 1943, Pretoria; s. of Winifred Hooper and Henry John Colchester Hooper; m. 1st Adriana Holleman 1969 (divorced 1991); one s. one d.; m. 2nd Valerie Anne Loubser 1992; ed. Ellis Robins High School, Harare, Univ. of Cape Town and Catholic Univ. of America; Research Asst., Univ. Coll. of Rhodesia 1965; Head, Reference and Translations Service, Council for Scientific and Industrial Research, Pretoria 1969–74; Chief Librarian, Natal Soc. Library, Pietermaritzburg 1974–80; Univ. Librarian, Dir. of Libraries, Univ. of Cape Town 1980–98; Pres. S. African Inst. for Librarianship and Information Science 1984–86; mem. Bd. S. African Bibliographic and Information Network (Sabinet) 1984–; Fellow, S. African Inst. for Librarianship and Information Science; Pres. Owl Club 1992–93. *Publications:* numerous professional publs. on libraries and librarianship. *Leisure interests:* reading, carpentry, running and cooking. *Address:* c/o University of Cape Town Libraries, Rondebosch, Cape Town 7700, South Africa.

HOOYKAAS, Reijer, D.SC.; Netherlands university professor; b. 1 Aug. 1906, Schoonhoven; m. Ilona Van Asselt 1936; one s. four d.; ed. Utrecht Univ.; chem. teacher, Amsterdam 1930, Zeist 1932; Extraordinary Prof. of History of Science, Free Univ. of Amsterdam 1945–48, Prof. 1948–66, and of Mineralogy 1948–60; Prof. of History of Science, Univ. of Utrecht 1967–76; Visiting Prof. Open Univ. (U.K.) 1973–74; fmr. Pres. Int. Comm. History Geological Sciences; mem. Royal Netherlands Acad. of Sciences and Letters, Int. Acad. of History of Science, Hollandsche Maatschappij der Wetenschappen; Assoc. mem. Comité belge d'Histoire des Sciences; Foreign mem. Royal Belgian Acad. of Sciences and Acad. da Cultura Portuguesa; Corresp. mem. Inst. de Coimbra; Hon. D.Sc. (Coimbra), Dr. h.c. (Open Univ.); Knight Order of Nederlandse Leeuw, Commdr. Order of Polonia Restituta, Grande-Oficial Order of Infante D. Henrique. *Publications:* The Concept of Element, Its Historical-Philosophical Development 1933, Robert Boyle: A Study in Science and Christianity 1943, The Chemical Revolution: A. L. Lavoisier 1952, Humanisme, science et réforme, Pierre de la Ramée 1958, The Principle of Uniformity in Geology, Biology and Theology 1959, Physik und Mechanik in historischer Hinsicht 1963, Introdução à História das Ciências 1965, Nature and History 1966, Catastrophism in Geology 1970, History of Science, from Babel to Bohr 1971, Religion and the Rise of Modern Science 1972, Humanism and 16th Century Portuguese Science and Letters 1979, Science in Manueline Style: The Historical Context of D. João de Castro's Scientific Works 1980, Selected Studies in History of Science 1983, G. J. Rheticus' Treatise on Holy Scripture and the Motion of the Earth 1984, Sciences in the Service of the Common Weal 1987, The History and Philosophical Background of Hauy's Theory of Crystal Structure 1994; numerous articles in international historical and scientific journals. *Address:* Krullelaan 35, 3701TB Zeist, Netherlands. *Telephone:* 03404-22488.

HOPE, Alec Derwent, A.C., O.B.E., B.A.; Australian poet; b. 21 July 1907, Cooma, N.S.W.; s. of Rev. Percival Hope and Florence Ellen Scotford; m. Penelope Robinson 1938 (died 1988); two s. one d. (deceased); ed. Sydney and Oxford Univs.; fmr. Lecturer Sydney Teachers' Coll. and Sr. Lecturer Melbourne Univ.; Prof. of English, School of Gen. Studies, Australian Nat. Univ. 1951–68, Prof. Emer. 1968–; Library Fellow, Australian Nat. Univ. 1969–72; retd. 1973; Visiting Fellow, Clare Hall, Cambridge 1986; Hon. Fellow, Univ. Coll., Oxford 1986; Fellow, Australian Acad. of the Humanities; Hon. D.Litt. (Australian Nat. Univ.) 1972, (New England) 1973, (Monash) 1976, (Melbourne) 1976; Arts Council Prize 1965, Britannica-Australia Award 1966, Levinson Prize for Poetry (Chicago) 1969, Ingram Merrill Award for Literature 1969, Robert Frost Award for Poetry 1976; Hon. mem. American Acad. and Inst. of Arts and Letters 1989. *Publications:* The Wandering Islands 1955, Poems 1960, The Cave and the Spring 1965, Collected Poems 1966, New Poems 1965–69, Dunciad Minor 1970, A Midsummer Eve's Dream 1970, Collected Poems 1930–1970 1972, Selected Poems 1973, Native Companions 1974, A Late Picking 1975, A Book of Answers 1978, The New Cratylus 1979, The Pack of Autolycus 1979, The Drifting Continent 1979, Antechinus 1981, Doctor Faustus 1982, Tre Volti dell'Amore 1982, The Age of Reason 1985, Selected Poems 1986, Ladies from the Sea 1987, The Shorter Lyrics of Catullus (trans.) 1989, The Lyrics of Luis Vaz de Camoens, A Selection (with Isabel Martinho, trans.) 1989, Orpheus (poems) 1991, Chance Encounters (memoirs), verse and criticism in numerous magazines, including Meanjin, Southerly, M.U.M., Hermes, Quadrant, Westerly, Overland and The Southern Review. *Leisure interests:* camping, travel, reading, music. *Address:* c/o Andrew Hope, P.O. Box 7949, Alice Springs, N.T. 0871, Australia.

HOPE, Bob; American comedian; b. 29 May 1903, Eltham, England; m. Dolores Reade 1934; two adopted s. two adopted d.; first film 1938; since then has appeared in numerous films and radio and television productions; numerous hon. degrees and awards including American Congressional Medal of Honor 1963, Award of Entertainment Hall of Fame 1975, four special Academy Awards, American Hope Award 1988, Medal of Liberty, Hon. K.B.E. and 48 hon. doctorates (1999), Nat. Medal of Arts 1995; Order of St. Gregory the Great. *Films include:* College Swing, Big Broadcast, Give Me A Sailor, Thanks for the Memory 1938, Never Say Die, Some Like it Hot, Cat and the Canary 1939, Road to Singapore 1940, Nothing But the Truth, Road To Zanzibar, Louisiana Purchase, Caught in the Draft 1941, My Favourite Blonde, Star Spangled Rhythm, Road to Morocco 1942, They've Got Me Covered, Let's Face It 1943, Princess and the Pirate 1944, Road to Utopia 1945, Monsieur Beaucaire 1946, My Favourite Brunette 1947, Road To Rio, The Paleface 1948, Sorrowful Jones, The Great Lover 1949, Fancy Pants 1950, My Favourite Spy, Lemon Drop Kid 1951, Son of Paleface 1952, Off Limits, Here Come the Girls 1951, Road to Bali 1953, Casanova's Big Night 1954, Seven Little Foys 1955, Iron Petticoat, That Certain Feeling 1956, Beau James 1957, Paris Holiday 1958, Alias Jesse James 1959, The Facts of Life 1960, Bachelor in Paradise 1961, Road to Hong Kong 1962, Call Me Bwana 1963, A Global Affair 1964, I'll Take Sweden 1965, Boy, Did I Get a Wrong Number! 1966, Eight on the Lam 1967, Private Life of Sgt O'Farrell 1968, How to Commit Marriage 1969, The Road to Ruin 1972, Cancel My Reservation 1972, The Bob Hope Christmas Special 1987, The Bob Hope Birthday Special 1988, Bob Hope's Yellow Ribbon Party 1991, Bob Hope: A 90th Birthday Celebration 1993. *Publications:* They've Got Me Covered 1941, I Never Left Home 1944, So This Is Peace 1946, Have Tux, Will Travel 1954, I Owe Russia $1200 1963, Five Women I Love 1966, The Last Christmas Show 1974, Road to Hollywood 1977, Confessions of a Hooker 1985, Don't Shoot, It's Only Me 1990. *Address:* Hope Enterprises Inc., 3808 Riverside Drive, Burbank, CA 91505, U.S.A. (Office).

HOPE, Christopher, M.A., F.R.S.L.; South African writer; b. 26 Feb. 1944, Johannesburg; s. of Dudley Mitford Hope and Kathleen Mary Hope; m. Eleanor Marilyn Klein; two s.; Cholmondeley Award 1972, David Higham Award 1981, Whitbread Prize for Fiction for Kruger's Alp 1985, C.N.A. Literary Award (S. Africa) 1989. *Publications:* A Separate Development 1981, Private Parts 1982, The King, the Cat and the Fiddle (with Yehudi Menuhin) 1983, Kruger's Alp 1984, The Dragon Wore Pink 1985, The Hottentot Room 1986, Black Swan 1987, White Boy Running 1988, My Chocolate Redeemer 1989, Moscow! Moscow! 1990, Serenity House 1992, The Love Songs of Nathan J. Swirsky 1993, Darkest England 1996. Poetry: Cape Drives 1974, In the Country of the Black Pig 1981, Englishman 1985, Me, the Moon and Elvis Presley 1997. *Leisure interest:* getting lost. *Address:* c/o Rogers, Coleridge & White, 20 Powis Mews, London, W11 1JN, England. *Telephone:* 0171-221 3717. *Fax:* 0171-229 9084.

HOPE, Most Rev. and Rt. Hon. David Michael, K.C.V.O., D.PHIL.; British ecclesiastic; b. 14 April 1940; ed. Wakefield Grammar School, Nottingham Univ., Linacre Coll. Oxford; Curate, St. John's, Tuebrook, Liverpool 1965–70; Chaplain, Church of Resurrection, Bucharest 1967–68; Vicar, St. Andrew's, Warrington 1970–74; Prin. St. Stephen's House, Oxford 1974–82; Warden, Community of St. Mary the Virgin, Wantage 1980–87; Vicar, All Saints', Margaret Street, London 1982–85; Bishop of Wakefield 1985–91, of London 1991–95, of York 1995–; Prelate of the Order of the British Empire 1991–95; Dean of the Chapels Royal 1991–95. *Publications:* The Leonine Sacramentary 1971, Living the Gospel 1993. *Address:* Bishopthorpe, York, YO23 2GE, England. *Telephone:* (01904) 707021. *Fax:* (01904) 709204.

HOPE OF CRAIGHEAD, Baron (Life Peer) cr. 1995, of Bamff in the District of Perth and Kinross; **Rt. Hon. James Arthur David Hope,** P.C., M.A., LL.B.; British judge; b. 22 June 1938, Edinburgh, Scotland; s. of Arthur Henry Cecil Hope, and Muriel Ann Neilson Hope; m. Katharine Mary Kerr 1966; two s. one d.; ed. The Edinburgh Acad., Rugby School, St. John's Coll. Cambridge; nat. service, Seaforth Highlanders 1957–59; admitted to Faculty of Advocates, to practise at Scottish bar 1965; Standing Jr. Counsel to Bd. of Inland Revenue in Scotland 1974–78; apptd. Q.C. in Scotland 1978;

Advocate-Depute, Crown Office, Edin. 1978–82; Chair. and Legal Chair. Medical Appeal Tribunals 1985–86; Dean Faculty of Advocates 1986–89; Lord Justice Gen. of Scotland and Lord Pres. of Court of Session 1989–; a Lord of Appeal in Ordinary 1996–; Pres. Stair Soc. 1993–; Chancellor, Univ. of Strathclyde 1998–; Hon. Prof. of Law, Univ. of Aberdeen 1994–; Hon. Fellow St. John's Coll., Cambridge 1995; Hon. LL.D. (Aberdeen) 1991, (Strathclyde) 1993, (Edin.) 1995. *Publications:* Gloag & Henderson's Introduction to the Laws of Scotland (Jt. Ed.) 1968, (Asst. Ed.) 1980, 1987, Armour on Valuation for Rating (Jt. Ed.) 1971, 1985, The Rent (Scotland) Act (jtly.) 1984, 1986, Stair Memorial Encyclopedia of Scots Law. *Leisure interests:* walking, ornithology, music. *Address:* House of Lords, London, SW1A 0PW, England; 34 India Street, Edinburgh, EH3 6HB, Scotland. *Telephone:* 0171-219 3202 (London); (0131) 225 8245 (Edinburgh).

HOPE, Maurice; British boxer; b. 6 Dec. 1951, Antigua, West Indies; s. of Norris and Sarah Andrew Hope; m. Patricia Hope; one s. two d.; came to Britain 1961; ed. Hackney Secondary Modern School, London; rep. England and Great Britain as amateur boxer with Repton Amateur Boxing Club; quarter-finalist at Olympic Games, Munich 1972; professional boxer June 1973–; won British light-middleweight title from Larry Paul Nov. 1974, retained it v. Paul (Sept. 1975) and Tony Poole (April 1976); won Lonsdale Belt outright and became Commonwealth champion by beating Poole; lost to Bunny Sterling for vacant British middleweight title, June 1975; won European light-middleweight title from Vito Antuofermo, Rome Oct. 1976; drew with Eckhard Dagge for World Boxing Council (WBC) version of world light-middleweight title, Berlin March 1977; retained European title v. Frank Wissenbach, Hamburg (May 1977) and Joel Bonnetaz, Wembley (Nov. 1977); relinquished European title Sept. 1978; won WBC version of world light-middleweight title from Rocky Mattioli, San Remo March 1979; retained it v. Mike Baker (Sept. 1979), Mattioli (July 1980) and Carlos Herrera (Nov. 1980), lost it to Wilfredo Benitez (May 1981); 34 fights, 30 wins, one draw; now a trainer. *Leisure interests:* table tennis, snooker, pool.

HOPE-CROSBY, Polly, F.R.S.A.; British artist, designer, writer and photographer; b. 21 June 1933, Colchester; d. of Gen. Sir Hugh Stockwell and Lady Stockwell; m. 1st John Hope 1953; m. 2nd Theo Crosby 1990; one s.; ed. Heatherley, Chelsea and Slade Schools of Art; numerous solo exhbns.; has completed various commissions including pointillist mural for Barbican Centre, London, four life-size terracotta figures for Shakespeare's Globe Theatre; collaborated on bldg. Shakespeare's Globe Theatre; works with several composers writing librettos; has composed Greek song cycles; has written film scripts, made videos, films and animated films. *Publications include:* Here Away From it All 1969, Us Lot 1970, The Immaculate Misconception 1972, A Baker's Dozen of Greek Folk Songs 1994, Songs My Parrot Taught Me 1994. *Animated film:* Memories 1995. *Leisure interest:* music. *Address:* 5A & B Heneage Street, Spitalfields, London, E1 5LJ, England. *Telephone:* 0171-247 3450. *Fax:* 0171-247 3450.

HOPKINS, Sir Anthony, Kt., C.B.E.; British actor; b. 31 Dec. 1937, Port Talbot, Wales; s. of Richard Hopkins and Muriel Hopkins; m. 1st Petronella Barker 1967 (divorced 1972); one d.; m. 2nd Jennifer Lynton 1973; ed. Cowbridge Grammar School, S. Wales, Welsh Coll. of Music and Drama, Cardiff, Royal Acad. of Dramatic Art; mil. training and service: clerk Royal Artillery Unit, Bulford 1958–60; joined Manchester Library Theatre, Asst. Stage Man. 1960; then at Nottingham Repertory Co.; joined Phoenix Theatre, Leicester 1963; then Liverpool Playhouse, then Hornchurch Repertory Co.; joined Nat. Theatre Co. 1967; Film debut The Lion in Winter 1967; film, TV, stage actor in U.K. and U.S.A. 1967–, in U.S.A. 1974–84; Commandeur, Ordre nat. des Arts et Lettres; Hon. Fellow St. David's Coll., Lampeter 1992; Hon. D.Litt. (Univ. of Wales) 1988; B.A.F.T.A. TV Actor Award 1972, Emmy Awards 1976, 1981, Variety Club Film Actor of the Year (The Bounty) 1984, Stage Actor of the Year (Pravda) 1985, S.W.E.T. The Observer Award for Pravda 1985, Best Actor, Moscow Film Festival, for 84 Charing Cross Road 1987, B.A.F.T.A. Award and Acad. Award for Best Actor for The Silence of the Lambs 1992, B.A.F.T.A. Award for Best Actor in The Remains of the Day 1994, U.S. Film Advisory Bd. Special Career Achievement Award for U.S. Work 1994, B.A.F.T.A. (U.S.) Britannia Award for Outstanding Contrib. to the Int. Film and TV Indsutry 1995, and numerous others worldwide. *Stage appearances include:* title role in Macbeth, Nat. Theatre 1972, Dr. Dysart in Equus, Plymouth Theatre, New York 1974, 1975, Huntingdon Hartford Theatre, Los Angeles (also Dir.) 1977, Prospero in The Tempest, Los Angeles 1979, Old Times, New York 1983, The Lonely Road, Old Vic Theatre, London 1985, Pravda, Nat. Theatre 1985, King Lear (title role), Nat. Theatre 1986, Antony and Cleopatra (title role), Nat. Theatre 1987, M. Butterfly 1989, Dir., Dylan Thomas: Return Journey (Edin.) 1991, August (also Dir.) 1994. *Film appearances include:* The Looking Glass War 1967, Claudius in Hamlet 1969, When Eight Bells Toll 1969, Torvald in A Doll's House 1972, The Girl from Petrovka 1973, Juggernaut 1974, A Bridge Too Far 1976, Audrey Rose 1976, International Velvet 1977, Magic 1978, The Elephant Man 1979, A Change of Seasons 1980, Capt. Bligh in The Bounty 1983, The Good Father 1985, 84 Charing Cross Road 1987, The Old Jest 1987, A Chorus of Disapproval 1988, The Tenth Man 1988, Desperate Hours 1989, The Silence of the Lambs 1990, Spotswood 1990, One Man's War 1990, Howard's End 1991, Freejack 1991, Bram Stoker's Dracula 1991, Chaplin 1992, The Trial 1992, The Innocent 1992, Remains of the Day 1992, Shadowlands 1993, Legends of the Fall 1993, The Road to Wellville 1993, August (also Dir.) 1994, Nixon 1995, Surviving Picasso 1995, Bookworm 1996, Valley Girls 1996, The Sweet Hereafter 1997, Meet Joe Black 1998, Amistad 1998, Titus Andronicus 1999, Instinct 1999. *TV appearances include:* A Heritage and its History, A Company of Five 1968, The Three Sisters, The Peasants Revolt 1969, title roles in Dickens, Danton, Astrov in Uncle Vanya, Hearts and Flowers 1970, Pierre in War and Peace 1971–72, title role in Lloyd George 1972, QB VII 1973, A Childhood Friend, Possessions, All Creatures Great and Small, The Arcata Promise 1974, Dark Victory, The Lindbergh Kidnapping Case (Emmy Award) 1975, Victory at Entebbe 1976, title role in Kean 1978, The Voyage of the Mayflower 1979, The Bunker (Emmy Award), Peter and Paul 1980, title role in Othello, Little Eyolf, The Hunchback of Notre Dame 1981, A Married Man 1982, Strangers and Brothers 1983, Old Times, The Arch of Triumph, Mussolini and I, Hollywood Wives, Guilty Conscience 1984, Blunt (role of Guy Burgess) 1987, Heartland 1989, Across the Lake (Donald Campbell) 1989, Great Expectations (Magwitch) 1989, To Be the Best 1990, A Few Selected Exits (Gwyn Thomas) 1993, Big Cats 1993. *Leisure interests:* music, playing the piano, reading philosophy and European history. *Address:* c/o 25 St. George's Court, 258 Brompton Road, London, SW3 2AT, England.

HOPKINS, Antony, C.B.E., F.R.C.M.; British musician, author and broadcaster; b. 21 March 1921, London; s. of the late Hugh and Marjorie Reynolds; m. Alison Purves 1947 (died 1991); ed. Berkhamsted School and Royal Coll. of Music; composed incidental music for theatre (Old Vic, Stratford-upon-Avon), radio and cinema; composed music for winning entries, Italia Prize 1952 and 1957; radio broadcaster in series Talking about Music; Hon. Fellow R.A.M., Robinson Coll. (Cambridge) 1980; Hon. D.Univ. (Stirling) 1980; City of Tokyo Medal 1973, Grand Prix, Besançon Film Festival for John and the Magic Music Man, Chappell Gold Medal, Cobbett Prize, Royal Coll. of Music. *Compositions:* Five studies for voices, Psalm 42, songs, recorder pieces, two ballets, Magnificat and Nunc Dimittis (for girls' choir), A Time for Growing, Early One Morning, Three's Company, Dr. Musikus, Partita (for solo violin), John and the Magic Music Man (for narrator and orchestra; filmed 1976), three piano sonatas and others. *Publications:* Talking about Symphonies 1961, Talking about Concertos 1964, Talking about Sonatas 1971, Music Face to Face, Downbeat Guide 1977, Understanding Music 1979, The Nine Symphonies of Beethoven 1980, Songs for Swinging Golfers 1981, Sounds of Music 1982, Beating Time (autobiog.) 1982, Pathway to Music 1983, The Concertgoer's Companion Vol. I 1984, Vol. II 1986, The Seven Concertos of Beethoven 1997. *Leisure interests:* golf, motoring. *Address:* Woodyard Cottage, Ashridge, Berkhamsted, Herts., HP4 1PS, England. *Telephone:* (01442) 842257.

HOPKINS, Godfrey Thurston; British photojournalist and writer; b. 16 April 1913, London; s. of Sybil Beatrice Bately and Robertson Thurston Hopkins; m. Grace Fyfe Robertson 1955; one s. one d.; ed. Salesian R.C. School, Burwash, Sussex, Montpelier Coll., Brighton, Brighton Coll. of Art; trained as magazine illustrator, then as photographer; photographer with R.A.F. Italy and N. Africa 1939–45; freelance photographer in Europe 1946–49; mem. staff Picture Post, assignments worldwide 1949–57 and particular interest in aspects of British life; worked for London advertising agencies 1958–68; tutor, Studies in Photojournalism, Guildford School of Photography, W. Surrey Coll. of Art and Design 1970–78; one-man exhbn., Arts Council of G.B., toured U.K. 1976–77, Zelda Cheatle Gallery, London 1993; group exhbn. British Art 1940–80, Hayward Gallery, London 1980, Vic. and Albert Museum, London 1994; All Human Life: Great Photographs from the Hulton Deutsch Collection, Barbican Art Gallery, London 1994; Europa de Posguerra 1945–65, Barcelona, 1995; work in public collections including Victoria and Albert Museum, Arts Council, Museum of London, Metropolitan Museum of Art, New York, Helmut Gernsheim Collection, Switzerland, J. Paul Getty Museum, U.S.A.; Encyclopaedia Britannica award (twice). *Publication:* Thurston Hopkins 1977. *Leisure interests:* painting, writing. *Address:* Wilmington Cottage, Wilmington Road, Seaford, East Sussex, BN25 2EH, England. *Telephone:* (01323) 897656. *Fax:* (01323) 897656.

HOPKINS, Sir Michael John, Kt., C.B.E., F.R.I.B.A., R.A.; British architect; b. 7 May 1935; s. of late Gerald Hopkins and Barbara Hopkins; m. Patricia Wainwright 1962; one s. two d.; ed. Sherborne School, Architectural Asscn. and R.I.B.A.; partnership with Norman Foster (q.v.) 1969–75; f. Michael Hopkins & Partners 1976–; consultant architect Vic. & Albert Museum 1985; Vice-Pres. Architectural Asscn. 1987–93, Pres. 1997–; mem. Royal Fine Art Comm. 1986–; Trustee Thomas Cubitt Trust 1987–, British Museum 1993–; mem. R.I.B.A. Council, London Advisory Cttee. to English Heritage, Architectural Advisory Group, Arts Council; R.I.B.A. Award 1977, 1980, 1988, 1989, 1994, 1996; Civic Trust Award 1979, 1988, 1990, 1997; Financial Times Award 1980, 1982; Structural Steel Award, 1980, 1988; Royal Acad. Architectural Award 1982, co-winner (with wife Patricia Hopkins) R.I.B.A. Gold Medal for Architecture 1994. *Major works include:* Patera Bldg. System 1984, Residential Centre for Schlumberger, Cambridge 1984, Bicentenary Stand, Lord's Cricket Ground 1987, redevelopment of Bracken House for Ohbayashi Corpn. 1987–91, R&D Centre, Solid State Logic 1988, Glyndebourne Opera House 1987–94, M.C.C. 1987, New Parl. Bldg., Westminster 1989–, Inland Revenue Centre, Nottingham 1992–95, Office building for IBM at Bedfont Lakes, The Queen's Bldg., Emmanuel Coll., Cambridge 1993–95, Redevelopment of Tottenham Court Road and Marylebone stations, Saga Group Headquarters 1994–, The William Younger Centre 1990–, Wildscreen World 1996–, Bristol 2,000–; Hon. mem. Bund Architekten; Hon.

F.A.I.A. 1996, Hon. Fellow, Royal Incorporation of Architects of Scotland 1996; Hon. D.Litt. (Nottingham) 1995, Hon. D.Tech. (London Guildhall). *Leisure interests:* sailing, Catureglio. *Address:* 27 Broadley Terrace, London, NW1 6LG (Office); 49A Downshire Hill, London, NW3 1NX, England (Home). *Telephone:* 0171-724 1751 (Office); 0171-794 1494 (Home).

HOPKINS, P. Jeffrey, PH.D.; American professor of religious studies; b. 30 Sept. 1940, Providence, R.I.; s. of Charles E. Hopkins and Ora Adams; m. Elizabeth S. Napper 1983 (divorced 1990); ed. public schools in Barrington, R.I., Pomfret School, Conn., Harvard Univ., Univ. of Wis.-Madison and Lamaist Buddhist Monastery of America; Asst. Prof. of Religious Studies, Univ. of Va. 1973–77, Assoc. Prof. 1977–89, Prof. 1989–, Dir. Center for South Asian Studies 1979–82, 1985–94; Pres. Inst for Asian Democracy 1994–; Visiting Prof. Univ. of B.C. 1983–84; Yehan Numata Distinguished Visiting Prof. of Buddhist Studies, Univ. of Hawaii 1995; Chief Interpreter to Dalai Lama (q.v.) on overseas tours 1979–89; Fulbright Scholar, India and Germany 1971–72, 1982. *Publications:* Meditation on Emptiness 1973, Emptiness Yoga 1987, Fluent Tibetan 1993, Emptiness in the Mind-Only School of Buddhism 1999; author or translator of 20 other books including eight in collaboration with the Dalai Lama; several articles. *Leisure interests:* meditation, walking in woods. *Address:* Department of Religious Studies, University of Virginia, 104 Cocke Hall, Charlottesville, VA 22903 (Office); Rt. 1 Box 65A, Dyke, VA 22935, U.S.A. (Home). *Telephone:* (804) 924-6716 (Office); (804) 973-3256 (Home). *Fax:* (804) 924-1467.

HOPPER, Dennis; American actor, author, photographer and film director; b. 17 May 1936, Dodge City, Kan.; m. 3rd Katherine La Nasa 1989; one s.; two d. (from previous marriages); ed. public schools in San Diego; numerous TV appearances include Loretta Young Show. *Film appearances include:* Rebel without a Cause 1955, I Died a Thousand Times 1955, Giant 1956, Story of Mankind, Gunfight at the O.K. Corral 1957, Night Tide, Key Witness, From Hell to Texas 1958, Glory Stompers 1959, The Trip 1961, The Sons of Katie Elder 1962, Hang 'Em High 1966, Cool Hand Luke 1967, True Grit 1968, The American Dreamer 1971, Kid Blue 1973, The Sky is Falling 1975, James Dean—The First American Teenager 1976, Mad Dog Morgan 1976, Tracks 1979, American Friend 1978, Apocalypse Now 1979, Wild Times 1980, King of the Mountain 1981, Human Highway 1981, Rumble Fish 1983, The Osterman Weekend 1984, Black Widow 1986, Blue Velvet 1986, River's Edge 1987, Blood Red 1989, Flashback 1989, The American Wars 1989, Chattahoochie 1990, Motion and Emotion 1990, Superstar: The Life and Times of Andy Warhol 1990, Hot Spot 1990, True Romance, Boiling Point, Super Mario Bros 1993, Chasers 1994, Speed 1994, Waterworld 1995, Search and Destroy 1995, Basquiat 1996, Carried Away 1996; actor, writer, dir. Easy Rider 1969, The Last Movie 1971, Paris Trout 1990, The Indian Runner 1991; actor, dir. Out of the Blue 1980; dir. Colors 1988, The Hot Spot 1990, Catchfire 1991, Nails 1991; has held several public exhbns. of photographs; named Best New Dir., Cannes 1969; Best Film awards at Venice 1971, Cannes 1980. *Publication:* Out of the Sixties (photographs) 1988. *Address:* c/o Creative Artists Agency, 9830 Wilshire Blvd., Beverly Hills, CA 90212, U.S.A.

HOPPER, Wilbert Hill (Bill), O.C., B.SC., M.B.A.; Canadian business executive; b. 14 March 1933, Ottawa, Ont.; s. of the late Wilbert C. and Eva (Hill) Hopper; m. Patricia M. Walker 1957; two s.; ed. American Univ. and Univ. of Western Ontario; Petroleum Geologist, Imperial Oil 1955–57; Petroleum Economist, Foster Assocs. 1959–61; Sr. Energy Economist, Nat. Energy Bd. 1961–64; Sr. Petroleum Consultant, Arthur D. Little, Cambridge, Mass. 1964–73; Asst. Deputy Minister, Energy Policy, Dept. of Energy, Mines and Resources 1973–75; Pres., C.E.O. and Dir. Petro-Canada 1976–79, Chair., C.E.O. and Dir. 1979–; Chair. and Dir. Westcoast Energy Inc.; Vice-Chair. and Dir. Panartic Oils Ltd.; mem. Bd. of Bi-Provincial Upgrader Joint Venture; Dir. Syncrude Canada Ltd, Canada-China Trade Council, Petro-Canada Int. Assistance Corpn.; mem. Bd. of Govs. Acadia Univ., N.S., Schooner Bluenose Foundation, Oxford Inst. for Energy Studies, Ashbury Coll., Ottawa; Int. Advisory Council, Centre for Global Energy Studies; Hon. LL.D. (Wilfrid Laurier); mem. numerous socs., cttees., and asscns. *Address:* 500 Eau Claire Ave., South West, Apartment H302, Calgary, Alberta, T2P 3R8, Canada.

HOPWOOD, Sir David (Alan), Kt., F.R.S.; British professor of genetics; b. 19 Aug. 1933, Kinver, Staffs.; s. of Herbert Hopwood and Dora Grant; m. 1962 Joyce Lilian Bloom; two s. one d.; ed. Purbrook Park County High School, Hants., Lymm Grammar School, Cheshire, St. John's Coll., Cambridge; John Stothert Bye-Fellow, Magdalene Coll., Univ. of Cambridge 1956–58, Research Fellow, St. John's Coll. 1958–61, Univ. Demonstrator 1957–61; Lecturer in Genetics, Univ. of Glasgow 1961–68; Emer. Prof. of Genetics, Univ. of E. Anglia, and Genetics Dept., John Innes Centre 1968–; Hon. Prof., Chinese Acad. of Medical Science, Inst. of Microbiology and Plant Physiology, Chinese Acad. of Sciences, Huazhong Agricultural Univ., Wuhan, China; fmr. Pres. Genetical Soc. of G.B.; Fellow, Inst. of Biology; Foreign Fellow, Indian Nat. Science Acad.; Hon. mem. Hungarian Acad. of Sciences, Soc. for Gen. Microbiology, Spanish Soc. of Mircobiology; Hon. Dr. ETH (Zürich, Switzerland); Hon. Fellow UMIST, Magdalene College Cambridge. *Publications:* Genetics of Bacterial Diversity 1989 (Ed. D. A. Hopwood and K. F. Chater); numerous articles and chapters in scientific journals and books. *Leisure interests:* gardening and cooking. *Address:* John Innes Centre, Norwich Research Park, Colney, Norwich, NR4 7UH (Office); 244 Unthank Road, Norwich, NR2 2AH, England (Home). *Telephone:* (01603) 452571. *Fax:* (01603) 456844.

HORÁK, Jiří, PH.D.; Czech politician; b. 24 April 1924, Hradec Králové; m. Zdena Letáková 1948; ed. Univ. of Commerce, Prague, Columbia Univ., New York; press secretary to Minister of Industry of Czechoslovakia 1946–47; defected from Czechoslovakia Feb. 1948; Gen. Sec., Asscn. of Czechoslovak Political Exiles in Germany; Co-founder of Masaryk Coll. at Univ. of Ludwigsburg, Germany; Sec. of Cen. Cttee. of Czechoslovak Social Democratic Youth, Germany 1950–51; left Germany for U.S.A. 1951; lecturer on State Law, Manhattan Univ., later Head of Dept. of Politics, Riverdale, N.Y. 1961–89; co-founder and publr. magazine Evidence 1972–; Chair. Exec. Cttee., Council of Free Czechoslovakia, U.S.A. 1974–; holds many honorary posts in U.S.A.; mem. advisory board on ethnic issues to the Mayor of New York; Vice-Pres., American Fund for Exiles from Czechoslovakia, U.S.A.; returned to Czechoslovakia 1990; Chair. Czechoslovak Social Democratic Party 1990; Deputy to Fed. Ass. June–Dec. 1992; Chair. Social Democratic Deputies' Club at Fed. Ass. June–Dec. 1992; lives in U.S.A.

HORECKER, Bernard L., B.S., PH.D.; American biochemist; b. 31 Oct. 1914, Chicago, Ill.; s. of Paul Horecker and Bessie Horecker; m. Frances Goldstein 1936; three d.; ed. Univ. of Chicago; Research Assoc., Dept. of Chem., Univ. of Chicago 1939–40; Examiner U.S. Civil Service Comm., Washington, D.C. 1940–41; Biochemist U.S. Public Health Service (U.S.P.H.S.) Nat. Insts. of Health (N.I.H.) Industrial Hygiene Research Lab. 1941–47, Nat. Inst. of Arthritis and Metabolic Diseases 1947–53, Chief, Section on Enzymes and Cellular Biochemistry, N.I.H. Nat. Inst. of Arthritis and Metabolic Diseases 1953–56; Head Lab. of Biochemistry and Metabolism 1956–59; Prof. and Chair. Dept. of Microbiology, New York Univ. School of Medicine 1959–63, Dept. of Molecular Biology Albert Einstein Coll. of Medicine 1962–71, Dir. Div. of Biol. Sciences 1970–72, Assoc. Dean for Scientific Affairs 1971–72; Vice-Chair. Div. of Biological Chem., A.C.S. 1975–76, Chair. 1976–77; mem. Roche Inst. of Molecular Biology 1972–84, Head Lab. of Molecular Enzymology 1977–84; professorial lecturer on Enzymes, George Washington Univ. 1950–57; Visiting Prof., Univ. of Calif. 1954, Univ. of Ill. 1957, Univ. of Paraná, Brazil, 1960, 1963, Cornell Univ. 1964, Univ. of Rotterdam 1970; Visiting Investigator, Pasteur Inst. 1957–58, Indian Inst. of Science, Bangalore 1971; Ciba Lecturer, Rutgers Univ. 1962; Phillips Lecturer, Haverford Coll. 1965; Reilly Lecturer, Notre Dame Univ. 1969; Visiting Prof., Albert Einstein Coll. of Medicine 1972–84; Adjunct Prof., Cornell Univ. Medical Coll. 1972–84, Prof. of Biochemistry 1984–89, Prof. Emer. 1989, Dean Graduate School of Medical Sciences 1984–92; Hon. Prof. Fed. Univ. of Paraná, Brazil 1981–; Ed. Biochemical and Biophysical Research Communications 1959–89; Chair. Editorial Cttee. Archives of Biochemistry and Biophysics 1968–84; Ed. Current Topics in Cellular Regulation 1969–89; mem. Scientific Advisory Bd., Roche Inst. of Molecular Biology 1967–70, Chair. 1970–72; Dir. Academic Press 1968–73; mem. Comm. on Personnel, American Cancer Soc. 1969–73; Medical Scientist Training Program Study Section N.I.H. 1970–72; mem. Scientific Advisory Comm. for Biochem. and Chemical Carcinogenesis, American Cancer Soc. 1974–78, Council for Research and Clinical Investigation Awards, American Cancer Soc.; Pres. American Soc. of Biological Sciences 1968–69, Harvey Soc. of New York 1970–71; Vice-Chair. Pan American Asscn. of Biochemical Socs. 1971, Chair. 1972; mem. Nat. Acad. of Sciences; Hon. mem. of Swiss, Japanese, Spanish Socs., Hellenic Biochemical and Biophysical Soc., Greece, Brazilian Acad. Sciences; Fellow, American Acad. of Arts and Sciences; mem. Indian Nat. Acad. of Science; Corresp. mem. Argentine Acad. of Science; Prof. h.c. (Univ.of Paraná, Brazil) 1982; Hon. D.Sc. (Univ. of Urbino, Italy); Paul Lewis Labs. Award in Enzyme Chem. 1952, Fed. Security Agency's Superior Accomplishment Award 1952, Hillebrand Prize, A.C.S. 1954, Washington Acad. of Sciences Award in Biological Sciences 1954, Rockefeller Public Service Award 1957, Fulbright Travel Award 1963, Commonwealth Fund Fellow 1967, Merck Award (American Soc. of Biological Chemists) 1981, Carl Neuberg Medal (Virchow-Pirquet Med. Soc.) 1981. *Leisure interests:* gardening, ornithology. *Address:* 1621 Sand Castle Road, Sanibel Island, FL 33957, U.S.A.

HORINOUCHI, Hisao; Japanese politician; mem. House of Reps.; fmr. Minister of Agric., Forestry and Fisheries; Minister of Posts and Telecommunications 1996–98. *Address:* c/o Ministry of Posts and Telecommunications, 1-3-2, Kasumigaseki, Chiyoda-ku, Tokyo 100, Japan (Office).

HORLOCK, Sir John Harold, Kt., SC.D., F.ENG., F.R.S.; British university administrator and engineer; b. 19 April 1928, Edmonton; s. of Harold E. and Olive M. Horlock; m. Sheila J. Stutely 1953; one s. two d.; ed. Latymer School, Edmonton, and St. John's Coll., Cambridge; design engineer, Rolls-Royce Ltd. 1949–51; Demonstrator, Lecturer in Eng., Univ. of Cambridge 1952–58, Prof. of Eng. 1967–74; Harrison Prof. of Mech. Eng., Univ. of Liverpool 1958–67; Vice-Chancellor, Univ. of Salford 1974–80, Open Univ. 1981–90; Fellow, Open Univ. 1991–; Treas. and Vice-Pres. Royal Soc. 1992–97; Hon. Prof. Warwick Univ. 1990–; Pro-Chancellor Univ. of Manchester Inst. of Science and Tech. 1995–; Hon. Fellow UMIST, St. John's Coll. Cambridge; Hon. D.Sc. (Heriot Watt, Salford, C.N.A.A., East Asia, De Montfort, Cranfield); Hon. D.Eng. (Liverpool); Hon. D.Univ. (Open Univ.); Hawksley Gold Medal (Inst. of Mech. Eng.), R. T. Sawyer Award (American Soc. of Mech. Eng.) 1997. *Publications:* Axial Flow Compressors 1958, Axial Flow Turbines 1967, Actuator Disc Theory 1978, Thermodynamics and Gas Dynamics of I.C. Engines (Ed.) Vol. I 1982, Vol. II 1986, Cogeneration:

Combined Heat and Power 1987, Combined Power Plants 1992. *Leisure interests:* music, sport. *Address:* 2 The Avenue, Ampthill, Bedford, MK45 2NR, England (Home). *Telephone:* (01525) 841307.

HORN, Gabriel, M.A., M.D., SC.D., F.R.S.; British zoologist and university administrator; b. 9 Dec. 1927, Birmingham; s. of late Abraham Horn and Anne Horn; m. 1st Ann L. D. Soper 1952 (divorced 1979); two s. two d.; m. 2nd Priscilla Barrett 1980; ed. Handsworth Tech. School and Coll., Univ. of Birmingham; served in R.A.F. 1947–49; house appts. in Birmingham hosps. 1955–56; demonstrator in Anatomy, Univ. of Cambridge 1956–62, Lecturer 1962–72, Reader in Neurobiology 1972–74, Fellow, King's Coll. 1962–74, 1978–92; Prof. and Head Dept. of Anatomy, Univ. of Bristol 1974–77; Prof. of Zoology, Univ. of Cambridge 1978–95, Head of Dept. 1979–94, Emer. Prof. 1995–; Master Sidney Sussex Coll., Cambridge 1992–99; Deputy Vice-Chancellor, Univ. of Cambridge 1994–98; Chair. Animal Sciences and Psychology Research Cttee. Biotech. and Biochemistry Research Council 1994–96; Sr. Research Fellow in Neurophysiology, Montreal Neurological Inst., McGill Univ. 1957–58; Leverhulme Research Fellow Laboratoire de Neurophysiologie Cellulaire, France 1970–71; visiting professorships and lectureships Canada, Hong Kong, U.S.A., U.K. and Uganda 1963–90; mem. Biological Sciences Cttee., SRC 1973–75, Research Cttee. Mental Health Foundation 1973–78; Dir. Co. of Biologists 1980–93; mem. Agricultural and Food Research Council 1991–94; Chair. Cttee. on Biology of Spongiform Encephalopathies 1991–94; Hon. mem. Anatomical Soc.; Foreign mem. Georgian Acad. of Sciences; Kenneth Craik Award 1962. *Publications:* Short-Term Changes in Neural Activity and Behaviour (Ed. with R. A. Hinde) 1970, Memory, Imprinting and the Brain 1985, Behavioural and Neural Aspects of Learning and Memory (Ed. with J. R. Krebs) 1991; papers in scientific journals, mainly on neuroscience topics. *Leisure interests:* walking, cycling, riding, music, wine. *Address:* Sidney Sussex College, Cambridge, CB2 3HU, England. *Telephone:* (01223) 330868. *Fax:* (01223) 338884.

HORN, Gyula, D.ECON.; Hungarian politician and economist; b. 5 July 1932, Budapest; s. of Géza Horn and Anna (née Csörnyei) Horn; m. Anna Király; one s. one d.; ed. Rostov Coll. of Econs. (U.S.S.R.) and Political Acad. of Hungarian Socialist Workers' Party; staff mem., Ministry of Finance 1954–59; Desk Officer, Ministry of Foreign Affairs 1959–61, Perm. Sec. 1985–89, Minister for Foreign Affairs 1989–90; Embassy Sec., Sofia 1961–63, Belgrade 1963–69; staff mem. to Head of Int. Dept., Hungarian Socialist Workers' Party 1969–85; mem. of Parl. 1990–; Chair. Foreign Affairs Standing Cttee. of Parl. 1990–93; Prime Minister of Repub. of Hungary 1994–98, 1998–; founding mem. of Hungarian Socialist Party 1989, Pres. 1990–; mem. European Honorary Senate 1991–; Regional Vice-Pres., Socialist Int. (New York) 1996; Golden Order of Labour, Grand Cross of Germany, Sharp Blade Award, Solingen 1991, Humanitarian Award of German Freemasons 1992, Gold Europe Award 1994, Kassel Glass of Understanding Award 1995. *Publications:* Yugoslavia: Our Neighbour, Social and Political Changes in Albania since World War II, Development of East–West Relations in the 70s, Pikes (autobiog.) 1991; co-author of over 100 articles published in tech. journals. *Leisure interests:* tennis, swimming, jogging. *Address:* Hungarian Parliament, 1055 Budapest, Kossuth Lajos tér 1/3, Hungary. *Telephone:* (1) 268-3398.

HORN, Heinz, DR.RER.POL.; German company executive; b. 17 Sept. 1930, Duisberg; s. of Heinrich and Elisabeth (née Eckernkamp) Horn; m.; two s. two d.; ed. Univ. of Frankfurt, Univ. of Munster; fmrly. with Mannesmann for 6 years; Financial Dir., Erschweiler Bergweks-Verein 1965–68, mem. Bd. and later Pres. 1974–83; mem. Bd., Krupp 1968–72; Deputy Chair. of the Bd., Ruhrkohle AG, Essen 1983–85, Chair. Man. Bd. 1985–95; Chair. Supervisory Bd. Rütgerswerke AG, EBV 1989–95.

HORNBY, Sir Simon (Michael), Kt.; British business executive; b. 29 Dec. 1934; s. of late Michael Hornby and Nicolette Ward; m. Sheran Cazalet 1968; ed. Eton Coll., New Coll. Oxford and Harvard Business School; entered W. H. Smith & Son 1958, Dir. 1965; Dir. W. H. Smith & Son (Holdings) 1974–, Group Chief Exec. 1978–82; Chair. W. H. Smith Group PLC 1982–94; Dir. Pearson PLC 1978–97, Lloyds Bank 1988–; Chair. Lloyds Abbey Life 1992–97; Chair. Nat. Book League 1978–80 (Deputy Chair. 1976–78), Pres. Book Trust 1990–96, Chelsea Soc. 1994–; Chair. Design Council 1986–92, Asscn. for Business Sponsorship of the Arts 1988–97; mem. Council, Royal Horticultural Soc. 1992, Hon. D.Univ. (Stirling) 1992, Hon. D.Litt. (Hull) 1994, Hon. LL.D. (Reading) 1996. *Leisure interests:* gardening, golf. *Address:* 8 Ennismore Gardens, London, SW7 1LN; The Ham, Wantage, Oxon, OX12 9JA, England. *Telephone:* 0171-584 1597.

HORNE, Colin James, A.M., M.A., M.LITT., DIP.ED., F.A.H.A.; Australian professor of English; b. 31 Oct. 1912, Bendigo, Vic.; s. of Thomas J. Horne and Nellie Horne; m. 1st Margaret E. Parsons 1939 (died 1962); four s.; m. 2nd Cynthia N. Werfel 1968; ed. Melbourne Univ. and Balliol Coll., Oxford; Asst. and Lecturer in English, Queen's Univ., Belfast 1939–48; Lecturer and Sr. Lecturer in English, Univ. of Leicester 1948–57; Jury Prof. of English Language and Literature, Univ. of Adelaide 1957–77, Dean, Faculty of Arts 1969–70, Emer. Prof. 1977–; Chair. Arts Enquiry Comm., S.A. 1960–62, Writers Week, Adelaide Festival of Arts 1969–74, mem. Cttee. 1960–80, Hon. life mem. 1980; Pres. Australasian and Pacific Soc. for 18th Century Studies 1976–80, Mt. Lofty Dist. Historical Soc. 1980–91, Friends of State Library of S. Australia 1982–93; mem. Cttee. Int. Asscn. of Univ. Profs. of English 1965–83; Fellow Australian Acad. of the Humanities 1972–, Vice-Pres. 1977–78; Patron S. Australia English Teachers' Asscn. 1960–. *Publications:* Swift on His Age 1953, Four Hundred Years of Shakespeare 1964, The Progress of Poetry 1965, Studies in the Eighteenth Century 1968, The Dunstan Decade 1981, The Classical Temper in Western Europe 1983, Comedy 1993. *Leisure interests:* travelling, reading, book-collecting. *Address:* Woodstock, 12 Bracken Road, Stirling, South Australia 5152, Australia (Home). *Telephone:* (8) 8339-2303 (Home).

HORNE, Donald Richmond, A.O.; Australian author and lecturer; b. 26 Dec. 1921, Sydney; s. of David Horne and Florence Carpenter; m. Myfanwy Gollan 1961; one s. one d.; ed. Univ. of Sydney, Univ. Coll., Canberra; Ed. The Observer 1958–61, The Bulletin 1961–62, 1967–72; Co-Ed. Quadrant 1963–66; Contributing Ed. Newsweek Int. 1973–77; Advisory Bd. The Australian Encyclopedia 1973–89, Chair. 1987–89; served Advisory Council for N.S.W. Cultural Affairs 1976–80; Council, Soc. of Authors 1982–, Pres. 1984–85; Chair. Copyright Agency Ltd. 1983–84; Chair. The Australia Council 1985–90; Research Fellow, Univ. of N.S.W. 1973–74, Sr. Lecturer 1975–79, Assoc. Prof. 1980–84, Prof. 1984–86, Prof. Emer. 1987–, Chair. Arts Faculty 1982–86, Council 1983–86; Chancellor Univ. of Canberra 1991–95; Chair. Ideas for Australia Programme 1991–94; Fellow, Australian Acad. of Humanities; Hon. D.Litt. (Univ. of N.S.W.) 1986; Hon. D. Univ. (Griffith Univ.). *Publications:* The Lucky Country 1964, The Permit 1965, The Education of Young Donald 1967, God is an Englishman 1969, The Next Australia 1970, But What If There Are No Pelicans? 1971, The Australian People 1972, Death of the Lucky Country 1976, Money Made Us 1976, His Excellency's Pleasure 1977, Right Way, Don't Go Back 1978, In Search of Billy Hughes 1979, Time of Hope 1980, Winner Take All 1981, The Great Museum 1984, Confessions of a New Boy 1985, The Public Culture 1986, The Lucky Country Revisited 1987, Portrait of an Optimist 1988, Ideas for a Nation 1989, The Coming Republic 1992, The Intelligent Tourist 1993, The Avenue of the Fair Go 1997, An Interrupted Life 1998. *Leisure interest:* writing. *Address:* 53 Grosvenor Street, Woollahra, N.S.W. 2025, Australia (Home). *Telephone:* 389 4212 (Home).

HORNE, Marilyn; American mezzo-soprano; b. 16 Jan. 1934, Bradford, Pa.; d. of Bentz and Berneice Horne; m. 1st Henry Lewis (divorced); one d.; m. 2nd Nicola Zaccaria; ed. Univ. of Southern California (under William Vennard); performed with several German opera cos. in Europe 1956; debut, San Francisco Opera 1960; has since appeared at Covent Garden, London, the Chicago Lyric Opera, La Scala, Milan, Metropolitan Opera, New York; repertoire includes Eboli (Don Carlo), Marie (Wozzeck), Adalgisa (Norma), Jane Seymour (Anna Bolena), Amneris (Aida), Carmen, Rosina (Barbiere di Siviglia), Fides (Le Prophète), Mignon, Isabella (L'Italiana in Algeri), Romeo (l Capuletti ed i Montecchi), Tancredi (Tancredi), Orland (Orlando Furioso); many recordings; numerous hon. doctorates; Nat. Medal of Arts 1992, Kennedy Center Honor 1995, Musical American Musician of the Year 1995. *Leisure interests:* needlepoint, swimming, reading, sightseeing. *Address:* c/o Colombia Artists Management Inc., Wilford Division, 165 West 57th Street, New York, NY 10019, U.S.A.

HORNER, James; American film music composer; b. Los Angeles, Calif.; ed. Royal Coll. of Music, London, Univ. of S. Carolina, Univ. of Calif. at Los Angeles. *Film scores:* The Lady in Red, Battle Beyond the Stars, Humanoids from the Deep, Deadly Blessing, The Hand, Wolfen, The Pursuit of D. B. Cooper, 48 Hours, Star Trek II: The Wrath of Khan, Something Wicked This Way Comes, Krull, Brainstorm, Testament, Gorky Park, The Dresser, Uncommon Valor, The Stone Boy, Star Trek III: The Search for Spock, Heaven Help Us, Cocoon, Volunteers, Journey of Natty Gann, Commando, Aliens, Where the River Runs Black, The Name of the Rose, An American Tail (Grammy Award for song Somewhere Out There), P.K. and the Kid, Project X, Batteries Not Included, Willow, Red Heat, Vibes, Cocoon: The Return, The Land Before Time, Field of Dreams, Honey I Shrunk the Kids, Dad, Glory (Grammy Award for instrumental composition), I Love You to Death, Another 48 Hours, Once Around, My Heroes Have Always Been Cowboys, Class Action, The Rocketeer, An American Tail: Fievel Goes West, Thunderheart, Patriot Games, Unlawful Entry, Sneakers, Swing Kids, A Far Off Place, Jack the Bear, Once Upon a Forest, Searching for Bobby Fischer, The Man without a Face, Bopha!, The Pelican Brief, Clear and Present Danger, Legend of the Fall, Braveheart, Casper, Apollo 13, Jumanji, Courage Under Fire, Ransom, To Gillian on her 37th Birthday. *Address:* c/o Gorfaine Schwartz Agency, 3301 Barham Boulevard, Suite 201, Los Angeles, CA 90068, U.S.A.

HORNHUES, Karl-Heinz, DR.RER.POL.; German politician; b. 10 June 1939, Stadtlohn; m. Ellen Buss 1965; two s.; ed. Univ. of Münster; Adviser, Catholic Adult Educ. Center, Ludwig-Windthorst-Hause, Holthausen 1966–71, Dir. 1970–71; Educ. and Teaching Dir. Hofmann-La Roche AG, Grenzbach 1971; Assoc. Prof. of Social Econs. and Political Science 1974, Prof. 1977; mem. Bundestag 1972–; Deputy Chair. of CDU/CSU Parl. Party in Bundestag in charge of foreign policy, defence policy and European affairs 1989–94; Chair. Selection Cttee. in Bundestag 1994–; Chair. German African Foundation. *Address:* Piusstr. 19, 49134 Wallenhorst, Germany. *Telephone:* 05407-2187.

HÖRNLUND, Börje; Swedish politician; b. 17 June 1935, Nordmaling, Västerbotten; Regional Forestry Man. Forest Owners' Asscn. Västerbotten 1963–67, Inspector of Forests; mem. Exec. Cttee. Centre Party Youth League 1963, Centre Party Nat. Bd. 1977–; Municipal Councillor Skellefteå and mem. Västerbotten County Council 1966; mem. Bd. Swedish Fed. of County Councils 1972–, Chair. 1977–80; M.P. 1976–; Minister of Labour 1991–94; fmr. Chair. Official Cttee. on Health and Medical Care, mem. Regional Econ. Cttee.; mem. Bd. of Govs. Bank of Sweden. *Address:* c/o Ministry of Labour, Drottninggt. 21, 103 33 Stockholm, Sweden.

HOROVITZ, Joseph, M.A., B.MUS., F.R.C.M.; British composer-conductor; b. 26 May 1926, Vienna; ed. New Coll., Oxford Univ. and Royal Coll. of Music, London, and studied with Nadia Boulanger, Paris; resident in U.K. 1938–; Music Dir. Bristol Old Vic 1949–51; Conductor Festival Gardens Orchestra and open-air ballet, London 1951; Co-conductor Ballets Russes, English season 1952; Assoc. Dir. Intimate Opera Co. 1952–63; Asst. Conductor Glyndebourne Opera 1956; Prof. of Composition, Royal Coll. of Music 1961–; mem. Council, Composers' Guild 1970–, Council, Performing Right Soc. 1969–96; Pres. Int. Council of Composers and Lyricists of Int. Fed. of Socs. of Authors and Composers 1981–89; Commonwealth Medal Composition 1959, Leverhulme Music Research Award 1961, Gold Order of Merit of Vienna 1996. *Compositions:* 16 ballets including Alice in Wonderland, Les Femmes d'Alger, Miss Carter Wore Pink, Concerto for Dancers; One-act operas: The Dumb Wife, Gentlemen's Island; concertos for violin, trumpet, jazz harpsichord, oboe, clarinet, bassoon, percussion, tuba; other orchestral works include Horizon Overture, Jubilee Serenade, Sinfonietta for Light Orchestra, Fantasia on a Theme of Couperin, Toy Symphony; brass band music includes a euphonium concerto, Sinfonietta, Ballet for Band, Concertino Classico, Theme and Co-operation, The Dong with a Luminous Nose; music for wind band includes a divertimento Bacchus on Blue Ridge, Windharp, Fête Galante, Commedia dell'Arte, Dance Suite, and Ad Astra in commemoration of the Battle of Britain; choral music includes Samson, Captain Noah and his Floating Zoo (Ivor Novello Award for best British music for children 1976), Summer Sunday, Endymion, Sing unto the Lord a New Song, 3 choral songs from As You Like It; vocal music includes Lady Macbeth (mezzo-soprano and piano) and works for the King's Singers (e.g. Romance); chamber music includes 5 string quartets, oboe sonatina, oboe quartet and clarinet sonatina; contribs. to Hoffnung Concerts: Metamorphoses on a Bed-Time Theme and Horrortorio for chorus, orchestra and soloists; numerous scores for theatre productions, films and TV series (Ivor Novello Award for best TV theme of 1978 for the series Lillie); productions of Son et Lumière include St. Paul's Cathedral, Canterbury Cathedral, Brighton Pavilion, English Harbour Antigua, Bodiam Castle. *Address:* Royal College of Music, Prince Consort Road, London, SW7 2BS, England.

HOROWITZ, Norman Harold, PH.D.; American biologist; b. 19 March 1915, Pittsburgh, Pa.; s. of Joseph Horowitz and Jeanette Miller; m. Pearl Shykin 1939 (died 1985); one s. one d.; ed. Univ. of Pittsburgh and Calif. Inst. of Technology; National Research Council Fellow 1939–40; Research Fellow, Calif. Inst. of Technology, Pasadena 1940–42, Assoc. Prof. of Biology 1947–53, Prof. 1953–, Prof. Emer. 1982–, Chair., Division of Biology 1977–80; Research Assoc. Stanford Univ. 1942–46; Chief, Bioscience Section, Jet Propulsion Lab., Pasadena 1965–70; Fulbright and Guggenheim Fellow, Univ. of Paris 1954–55; mem. Nat. Acad. of Sciences; Fellow, American Acad. of Arts and Sciences. *Publications:* To Utopia and Back: The Search for Life in the Solar System 1986, numerous technical articles on genetics, biochemistry and space exploration. *Leisure interests:* gardening, music. *Address:* Biology Division, California Institute of Technology, Pasadena, CA 91125, U.S.A. *Telephone:* (626) 395-4926.

HORROCKS, Jane; British actress; b. Lancs.; one c.; stage appearances include The Rise and Fall of Little Voice. *TV:* (film) Hunting Venus; (series) Red Dwarf, Absolutely Fabulous. *Film:* Little Voice 1998.

HORROCKS, Raymond, C.B.E., C.INST.M., F.I.M.I., F.R.S.A.; British business executive; b. 9 Jan. 1930, Bolton, Lancs. (now Greater Manchester); s. of Cecil and Elsie Horrocks; m. Pamela F. Russell 1953; three d.; ed. Bolton Grammar School, Wigan Tech. Coll., Univ. of Liverpool; man. trainee, textile industry, Bolton and Manchester 1944–48, 1950–51; Army Intelligence Corps 1948–50; sales rep. Proctor and Gamble 1951–52; merchandiser, Marks and Spencer 1953–58; Buying Controller, Littlewoods Mail Order Stores 1958–63; Man. Replacement Parts, Ford Motor Co. 1963, Man. Warranty and Customer Relations 1964, Man. Car Supply 1965, Divisional Man. Engine and Special Equipment Operations 1966, Marketing Man. Cars 1967, Man. Advanced Vehicle Operations 1968–72; Regional Dir. (Europe and Middle East), Materials Handling Group, Eaton Corpn. 1972–77; Deputy Man. Dir. Leyland Cars, British Leyland Ltd./BL PLC 1977–78, Chair. and Man. Dir. Austin Morris Ltd. 1978–80, Man. Dir. BL Cars Ltd. 1980–81, Dir. BL Ltd. 1981–86; Chair. and Chief. Exec. BL Cars Ltd. 1981–82, ARG Holdings Ltd. 1981–86; Chair. Unipart Group Ltd. 1981–86; Group Chief Exec. Cars, BL PLC 1982–86; Chair. Jaguar Cars Holdings Ltd. 1982–84, Exide Europe 1986–88, Owenbell Ltd. 1986–, Chloride Group PLC 1988–, SMAC Group PLC 1988–89; Dir. (non-Exec.) Kay Consultancy Group Ltd. 1988–89, Chair. 1989–91; Dir. Nuffield Services Ltd. 1982–86; Dir. (non-exec.) Electrocomponents 1986–, Lookers 1986–, The Caravan Club 1983–87, Jaguar PLC 1984–85, Image Interiors (Wessex) Ltd. 1985–86, Chloride Group PLC 1986–88; Deputy Chair. Applied Chemicals Ltd. 1987–96; mem. CBI Council 1981–86, CBI Europe Cttee. 1985–86; Trustee, British Motor Industry Heritage Trust 1983–86. *Leisure interests:* fly fishing, caravanning, steam engines. *Address:* Far End, Riverview Road, Pangbourne, Reading, Berks., RG8 7AU, England. *Telephone:* (0118) 984 4623; (0118) 984 5124. *Fax:* (0118) 984 3592.

HORTON, Frank Elba, M.S., PH.D.; American university president; b. 19 Aug. 1939, Chicago; s. of Elba E. Horton and Mae P. Prohaska; m. Nancy Yocom 1960; four d.; ed. Western Ill. and Northwestern Univs.; mem. Faculty, Univ. of Ia. 1966–75, Prof. of Geography 1966–75, Dir. Inst. of Urban and Regional Research 1968–72, Dean of Advanced Studies 1972–75; Vice-Pres. for Acad. Affairs and Research, Southern Ill. Univ. 1975–80; Chancellor, Univ. of Wis., Milwaukee 1980–85; Pres. Univ. of Oklahoma 1985–88; Pres. and Prof. of Geography and Higher Educ., Univ. of Toledo 1988–; Trustee Toledo Symphony Orchestra 1989–, Toledo Hosp. 1989–, Public Broadcasting Foundation, NW Ohio 1989–93, Soc. Bank and Trust 1990–; Vice-Chair. Toledo Chamber of Commerce 1991–93; mem. Bd. of Dirs. Inter-State Bakeries. *Publications:* Geographic Perspectives on Urban Systems with Integrated Readings (with B. J. L. Berry) 1970, Urban Environmental Management Planning for Pollution Control 1974. *Leisure interests:* hiking, skiing, golf, jogging. *Address:* The University of Toledo, 2801 W. Bancroft Street, Toledo, OH 43606 (Office); 3883 W. Bancroft Street, Toledo, OH 43606, U.S.A. (Home). *Telephone:* (419) 537-2211 (Office).

HORTON, Sir Robert Baynes, Kt., S.M., F.I.CHEM.E., F.R.S.A., C.B.I.M.; British business executive; b. 18 Aug. 1939, London; s. of the late William H. Horton and of Dorothy Joan Baynes; m. Sally Doreen Wells 1962; one s. one d.; ed. King's School, Canterbury, St. Andrews Univ., Massachusetts Inst. of Technology; with British Petroleum Ltd. (now BP PLC) 1957–86, 1988–92, Gen. Man. BP Tankers 1975–76, Gen. Man. Corporate Planning 1976–79, Man. Dir. and C.E.O. BP Chemicals 1979–83, B.P. Bd. 1983–86, Deputy Chair. 1989–90, Chair. and C.E.O. 1990–92; Chair., C.E.O. Standard Oil Co. 1986–88; Vice-Chair. British Railways Bd. 1992–94; Chair. Railtrack PLC 1993–99, JKX Oil & Gas PLC 1995–97; Chancellor, Kent Univ. 1990–95; Pres. Chemical Industries Asscn. 1982–84, BESO 1993–97; Vice-Chair. B.I.M. 1984–90, ABSA 1992–; Dir. (non-exec.) ICL PLC 1982–84, Pilkington Bros. 1985–86, Emerson Electric 1987–, Partner Re 1993–, Farnell Electronics PLC 1995–; Gov. King's School, Canterbury 1984–; Chair. Sloan School (M.I.T.) Visiting Cttee.; mem. M.I.T. Corpn. 1987–97; Chair. Business in the Arts, Tate Gallery Foundation 1988–92; Hon. LL.D. (Dundee) 1988, Hon. D.C.L. (Kent) 1990, Hon. D.C.L. (Aberdeen) 1992, Hon. D.Sc. (Cranfield Inst. of Tech.) 1992, (Kingston) 1993, Hon. D.B.A. (N. London) 1991, Hon. D. Univ., Open Univ. 1993, Hon. F.C.G.I., F.I.Chem.E., C.I.Mgt; Corporate Leadership Award, M.I.T. 1987. *Leisure interests:* music, country activities, reading. *Address:* c/o The Athenaeum, 107 Pall Mall, London, S.W.1, England.

HORVAT, Branko, DIPL. in ECON., PH.D., D.SC.; Croatian university professor and economist; b. 1928, Petrinja; s. of Artur and Dolores (Stöhr) Horvat; m. Ranka Peašinović 1952; two d.; ed. Zagreb Univ., Victoria Univ. of Manchester, Harvard Univ., M.I.T.; partisan 1944–45; Researcher, Inst. of Petroleum, Inst. of Econ., Zagreb 1952–55; Research Dir. Fed. Planning Bureau, Belgrade 1958–62; Visiting Research Fellow, Inst. of Int. Econs. Stockholm 1973–74; f. and Dir. Inst. of Econ. Sciences, Belgrade 1963–70; mem. Fed. Econ. Council, Fed. Cttee. for Market and Prices 1963–71; Econ. Adviser, govts. of Yugoslavia, Peru and Turkey 1970–74, 1979–80; Visiting Prof. in Econ. Theory, Planning or Comparative Social Systems, Univs. of Belgrade, Ljubljana, Mich., Fla., Stockholm, Paris, Dar es Salaam, American Univ., Univ. Católica de Chile, Univ. of Notre Dame, Yale Univ., Cambridge Univ.; Prof. of Econs., Univ. of Zagreb 1975–; Regents Prof., Univ. of Calif. at Berkeley 1993; Pres. Asscn. for Yugoslav Democratic Initiative 1989–90, Social-Democratic Union 1992–; mem. shadow cabinet 1990; Bd. mem. Econ. Soc.; Founder Pres. Int. Asscn. for the Econ. of Self-Man.; f. Ed. Econ. Analysis and Workers' Man.; mem. Yugoslav govt. dels. on planning to UN, Poland, U.S.S.R., Int. Foundation for Devt. Alternatives, Centre International de Coordination des Recherches sur l'Autogestion; councils of various int. asscns. and ed. bds.; lecturer at over 70 int. educational establishments; Ford Foundation Fellowship 1964; Fulbright Prof. 1978, 1984–85; Medal of Merit, May Festival Prizes, Zagreb 1948, 1949, 1950, Manchester Statistical Soc. Prize. *Publications include:* Economics of the Petroleum Industry (4 vols.) 1954–65, Towards a Theory of Planned Economy 1961, Interindustry Analysis 1962, Economic Models 1962, Economic Science and National Economy 1968, An Essay of Yugoslav Society 1969, Business Cycles in Yugoslavia 1969, Economic Analysis 1972, Economic Policy of Stabilization 1976, Self-Governing Socialism (co-author) 1976, Political Economy of Socialism 1982, Yugoslav Economy 1967–83, 2 vols. 1984, Social Crisis 1985, The Labour Theory of Prices and Other Unsolved Problems of Economic Theory 1986, The Kosovo Question 1988, Foundations of Yugoslav Socialism 1989, Entrepreneurship and the Market Transformation of 'Social' Ownership 1990, The Theory of Value, Interest and Capital 1994, The Theory of International Trade 1998 and 250 articles in numerous int. prof. journals; works have been translated into 17 languages. *Leisure interest:* manual labour. *Address:* 32 Gornji Lukšić, Zagreb, Croatia. *Telephone:* 381 137 38411. *Fax:* 381 137 38411.

HOSKING, Geoffrey Alan, PH.D., F.B.A., F.R.HIST.S.; British academic; b. 28 April 1942, Troon, Ayrshire; s. of Stuart Hosking and Jean Smillie; m. Anne Lloyd Hirst 1970; two d.; ed. Maidstone Grammar School, Moscow State Univ., Kings Coll., Cambridge, St. Antony's Coll., Oxford; lecturer in Govt. Univ. of Essex 1966–71, lecturer in History 1972–76, Sr. Lecturer and Reader in History 1976–84; Prof. of Russian History, School of Slavonic Studies, Univ. of London 1984–99, Leverhulme Research Prof. 1999–; Deputy Dir. School of Slavonic and East European Studies, Univ. of London 1996–98;

Visiting Prof. in Political Science Univ. of Wis. (Madison), U.S.A. 1971–72, Slavisches Institut, Univ. of Cologne, Germany 1980–81; L.A. Times History Book Prize 1986, BBC Reith Lecturer 1988; mem. Booker Prize Jury for Russian Fiction 1993. *Publications:* The Russian Constitutional Experiment 1973, Beyond Socialist Realism 1980, The First Socialist Society: a History of the Soviet Union from Within 1985, The Awakening of the Soviet Union 1990, The Road to Post-Communism: Independent Political Movements in the Soviet Union 1985–91 (with J. Aves and P. Duncan) 1992, Russia: People and Empire (1552–1917) 1997, Ed. (with George Schöpflin) Myths and Nationhood 1997, Ed. (with Robert Service) Russian Nationalism Past and Present 1998. *Leisure interests:* music, walking, chess. *Address:* School of Slavonic and East European Studies, University of London, Senate House, Malet Street, London, WC1E 7HU, England. *Telephone:* 0171-637 4934.

HOSKINS, Bob (Robert William); British actor; b. 26 Oct. 1942; s. of Robert Hoskins and Elsie Lillian Hoskins; m. 1st Jane Livesey 1970; one s. one d.; m. 2nd Linda Banwell 1984; one s. one d.; ed. Stroud Green School; several stage roles at Nat. Theatre. *Films include:* National Health 1973, Royal Flash 1974, Zulu Dawn 1980, The Long Good Friday 1980, The Wall 1982, The Honorary Consul 1983, Lassiter 1984, The Cotton Club 1984, Brazil 1985, The Woman Who Married Clark Gable 1985, Sweet Liberty 1985, Mona Lisa 1986 (New York Critics Award, Golden Globe Award, Best Actor Award, Cannes Festival), A Prayer for the Dying 1987, The Lonely Passion of Judith Hearne 1987, Who Framed Roger Rabbit? 1987, The Raggedy Rawney (dir., acted in and wrote) 1988, Mermaids 1989, Shattered 1990, Heart Condition 1990, The Projectionist 1990, The Favour, The Watch and the Very Big Fish 1990, Hook 1991, The Inner Circle 1992, Super Mario Brothers 1992, Nixon 1995, The Rainbow 1996 (also Dir.), Michael 1996, Cousin Bette 1996, Twenty-four-seven 1998, The Secret Agent 1998. *TV appearances include:* Omnibus–It Must be Something in the Water 1971, Villains 1972, Thick as Thieves 1972, Schmoedipus 1974, Shoulder to Shoulder 1974, Pennies from Heaven 1975, Peninsular 1975, Sheppey 1980, Flickers 1980, Othello 1981, The Beggars' Opera 1983, Mussolini and I 1984, The Changeling 1993, World War Two: Then There Were Giants 1993. *Stage:* Old Wicked Songs 1996. *Leisure interests:* photography, gardening, playgoing. *Address:* c/o ICM, Oxford House, 76 Oxford Street, London, W1N 0AX, England.

HOSKYNS, Sir John Austin Hungerford Leigh, Kt.; British business executive; b. 23 Aug. 1927, Farnborough, Hants.; s. of late Lieut.-Col. Chandos Hoskyns and Joyce Hoskyns; m. Miranda Jane Marie Mott 1956; two s. one d.; ed. Winchester Coll.; Capt. British Army 1945–57; with IBM U.K. Ltd. 1957–64; Chair. and Man. Dir. Hoskyns Group Ltd. 1964–75; Part-time Policy Adviser to Opposition 1975–77, Full-time Adviser to Rt. Hon. Margaret Thatcher (q.v.) and Shadow Cabinet 1977–79, Head, Prime Minister's Policy Unit 1979–82; Dir.-Gen. Inst. of Dirs. 1984–89; Chair. Burton Group 1990–98 (Dir. 1990–98), EMAP 1994–98 (Dir. 1993–98), Arcadia Group PLC 1998–; Dir. ICL PLC 1982–84, AGB Research PLC 1983–88, Clerical Medical and Gen. Life Assurance Soc. 1983–98, McKechnie Brothers PLC 1983–93, Ferranti PLC 1986–94; Hon. D.Sc. (Salford) 1986; Dr. h.c. (Essex) 1987. *Leisure interests:* opera, shooting. *Address:* c/o Child & Co., 1 Fleet Street, London, EC4Y 1BD, England.

HOSNI, Naguib, D. EN D.; Egyptian professor of criminal law and politician; b. 5 Nov. 1928, Cairo; m. Fawzia Ali 1957; two s. one d.; ed. Cairo Univ. and Univ. of Paris, France; Asst. Prof. of Criminal Law, Cairo Univ. 1959, Prof. 1964–, Vice-Dean Faculty of Law 1970–73, Dean 1977–83, Pres. 1987–89; Visiting Prof., Arab Univ. of Beirut, Lebanon, 1967–70, Univ. of U.A.E. 1974–76, Univ. of Paris (12) 1991; Pres. Bd. of Legal Studies 1987–, African Univs. 1989–; Dir. Centre for the Prevention of Crime and Treatment of Offenders, Cairo Univ. 1993–; mem. Int. Soc. of Penal Law, Int. Soc. of Criminology, Int. Soc. of Social Defence; Senator 1989–; State Prize 1961, 1967; Medal of Science 1960, 1979; Medal of the Republic 1976; State Award 1991; Palmes Académiques (France) 1979. *Publications include:* International Criminal Law 1960, Abnormal Criminals 1967, Criminal Participation 1969, Criminal Intent 1988, Treatment of Mentally Ill Offenders 1992, The Constitution and Criminal Law 1992. *Leisure interests:* reading, music. *Address:* 30 Aden Street, Mohandessin, Giza, Egypt. *Telephone:* 3490 555; 3490 857.

HOSOKAWA, Morihiro; Japanese politician; b. 14 Jan. 1938, Tokyo; m. Kayoko Hosokawa; one s. two d.; ed. Sophia Univ., Tokyo; reporter The Daily Asahi Shimbun; mem. House of Councillors 1971–83; Gov. of Kumamoto 1983–91; founder, Chair. Japan New Party 1992; Prime Minister 1993–94; fmr. mem. Liberal Democratic Party (LDP). *Leisure interests:* skiing, golf. *Address:* House of Representatives, Chiyoda-ku, Tokyo 100, Japan.

HOSPITAL, Janette Turner, M.A.; Australian author; b. 12 Nov. 1942, Melbourne; d. of Adrian Charles Turner and Elsie Turner (née Morgan); m. Clifford Hospital 1965; one s. one d.; ed. Univ. of Queensland and Queen's Univ., Canada; High School teacher, Queensland 1963–66; librarian, Harvard Univ. 1967–71; lecturer in English, St. Lawrence Coll., Kingston, Ont., in maximum and medium-security fed. penitentiaries for men 1971–82; professional writer 1982–; Writer-in-Residence and lecturer Writing Program, M.I.T. 1985–86, 1987, 1989, Writer-in-Residence Univ. of Ottawa, Canada 1987, Univ. of Sydney, Australia 1989, Queen's Univ. at Herstmonceux Castle, U.K. 1994; Adjunct Prof. of English, La Trobe Univ., Melbourne 1990–93; Visiting Fellow and Writer-in-Residence Univ. of E. Anglia, U.K. 1996; O'Connor Chair. in Literature, Colgate Univ., Hamilton, N.Y. 1999–; Dr. h.c. Griffith Univ. (Queensland) 1995; several awards for novels and short stories; Gold Medal, Nat. Magazine Awards (Canada) 1991 (for travel writing), First Prize, Magazine Fiction, Foundation for the Advancement of Canadian Letters 1982. *Publications:* The Ivory Swing (Seal First Novel Award) 1982, The Tiger in the Tiger Pit 1983, Borderline 1985, Charades 1988, The Last Magician 1992, Oyster 1996; (short story collections) Dislocations (Fiction Award, Fellowship of Australian writers 1988) 1986, Isobars 1990, Collected Stories 1995; crime thriller (under pseudonym Alex Juniper) A Very Proper Death 1991; numerous articles. *Address:* c/o Jill Hickson, P.O. Box 271, Woollahra, Sydney, N.S.W. 2025, Australia; c/o Mic Cheetham, 11–12 Dover Street, London, W1X 3PH, England; c/o Elaine Markson, 44 Greenwich Ave., New York, NY 10011, U.S.A.

HOSS, Dr. Selim al–; Lebanese politician and professor of economics; b. 1930; m. Leila Hoss (died 1990); Chair. Banking Control Comm. 1967–73; Chair. Nat. Bank for Industrial and Tourist Devt. 1973–76; Prime Minister 1976–80, remaining as Prime Minister in caretaker capacity July–Oct. 1980, Minister of the Econ. and Trade and Information 1976–79, of Industry and Petroleum 1976–77, of Labour, Fine Arts and Educ. 1984–85 (resgnd.), 1985; Acting Prime Minister 1987–90, also Minister of Foreign and Expatriate Affairs; Prime Minister of Lebanon Dec. 1998–; Chair. Compagnie Arabe et Internationale d'Investissement 1981–; Dir. Banque Arabe et Int. d'Investissement 1983–. *Publications:* The Development of Lebanon's Financial Markets 1974, Nafiza Ala Al Mustakbal (Window on the Future) 1981. *Address:* Office of the Prime Minister, Beirut; B.A.I.I. Centre Géfinor, Bloc B, Apartment 1401, 14th Floor, P.O. Box 11-9692, Beirut; Doha, Na'meh, Beirut, Lebanon.

HOSSAIN, Kemaluddin, LL.B.; Bangladeshi judge; b. 31 March 1923, Calcutta, India; ed. Ballygunge Govt. High School, Calcutta, St. Xavier's Coll. and Calcutta Univ. Law Coll.; Advocate, High Court, Dacca 1950–69; Sr. Advocate Supreme Court, Pakistan 1966–69; Deputy Attorney-Gen., Pakistan 1968–69; Judge, High Court, Dacca 1969–72; Judge, High Court, Bangladesh 1972–75, Appellate Div. 1975–78; Chief Justice, Bangladesh 1978–82; Negotiator, Indus Water Treaty 1960; part-time law lecturer, City Law Coll., Dacca 1956–68; Chair. Law Cttee. 1978; attended several int. law confs. incl. Commonwealth Chief Justices Conf., Canberra May 1980. *Address:* c/o Chief Justice's House, 19 Hare Road, Dhaka, Bangladesh. *Telephone:* 243585 (Office); 404849 (Home).

HOSSAIN, Shah Moazzem, M.A.; Bangladeshi politician; b. 10 Jan. 1939, Munsigonj Dist.; m.; one s. one d.; ed. Dhaka Univ.; Gen. Sec. East Pakistan Students League 1959–60, Pres. 1960–63; Chair. the All-Party Action Cttee. 1962; political prisoner for many years between 1953 and 1978; Chief Whip, Bangladesh Parliament 1972–73; co-f. Democratic League 1976, Gen. Sec. 1977–83; Minister of Land Admin. and Land Revenue 1973–75, in charge of Ministry of Labour and Manpower 1984–85, of Information 1985–86, of Local Govt., Rural Devt. and Co-operatives 1986–88, of Labour and Manpower 1988–90, of Food 1990; Deputy Prime Minister 1987–90. *Publications:* Nitta Keragarey 1976.

HOSSEIN, Robert; French actor and director; b. 30 Dec. 1927, Paris; s. of Amin Hossein and Anna Mincovschi; m. 1st Marina de Poliakoff 1955 (divorced); two s.; m. 2nd Caroline Eliacheff 1962 (divorced); one s.; m. 3rd Candice Patou 1976; one s.; stage actor, dir. and playwright, film dir. and producer, scriptwriter and actor; Chair. and Man. Dir. Sinfonia Films 1963–; Founder and Dir. Théâtre populaire de Reims and of Théâtre-Ecole de Reims 1971; Artistic Dir. Théâtre de Paris-Théâtre moderne 1975–; *plays include:* La neige était sale, Haute surveillance, Les voyous (writer), La P. respectueuse, Huis-Clos, Vous qui nous jugez (writer), Les six hommes en question (co-writer with Frédéric Dard and producer), La moitié du plaisir (producer), Crime et châtiment, Les bas-fonds, Roméo et Juliette, Pour qui sonne le glas, La maison des otages, Hernani (produced for the Comédie Française) 1974, La maison de Bernada (produced at the Odéon) 1975, Le cuirassé Potemkine (dir. at Palais des Sports) 1975, Des souris et des hommes, Shéhérazade (ballet) 1975, Procès de Jeanne d'Arc (producer) 1976, Pas d'orchidées pour Miss Blandish (producer and actor) 1977, Notre-Dame de Paris (producer) 1978, Le cauchemar de Bella Manningham (producer) 1978, Danton et Robespierre (producer) 1979, Lorna et Ted 1981, Un grand avocat 1983, Les brumes de Manchester 1986, Liberty or Death and the Heritage of the French Revolution (Dominique Prize for Best Dir.) 1988, Dans la nuit la liberté (producer) 1989, Cyrano de Bergerac (producer) 1990, Jésus était son nom 1991, Les bas-fonds 1992, Je m'appelais Marie-Antoinette 1993, La nuit du crime (producer and actor) 1994, Angélique, Marquise des anges (director and actor) 1995, Ouragan sur le Caine 1997, La Vie en bleu 1997, Surtout ne coulez pas (producer) 1997; *films include:* Quai des blondes, Du rififi chez les hommes, Crime et châtiment, Toi le venin (script-writer and producer), Le jeu de la vérité (writer), Le goût de la violence (script-writer and producer), Le repos du guerrier, Le vice et la vertu, Les yeux cernés, Angélique marquise des anges, Banco à Bangkok, Le vampire de Düsseldorf, Le tonnerre de Dieu, La seconde vérité, J'ai tué Raspoutine (writer and producer), Indomptable Angélique, Don Juan 1973, Prêtres interdits, Le protecteur, Le faux cul 1975, Les uns et les autres, Le professionnel 1981, Les Misérables (producer) 1982, Un homme nommé Jésus (director) 1983, Jules César 1985, Les brumes de Manchester 1986, Un homme et une femme, vingt ans déjà 1986, Les Enfants du désordre 1989, l'Affaire 1994, la Nuit du Crime 1994; Prix Orange 1963; Chevalier, Ordre Nat. du Mérite,

Chevalier, Légion d'honneur, Commdr. des Arts et des Lettres, Médaille de Vermeil de la Ville de Paris, Molière d'honneur 1995. *Leisure interest:* skiing. *Publications:* La sentinelle aveugle 1978, Nomade sans tribu 1981, En désespoir de cause (memoirs) 1987. *Address:* c/o Mme. Ghislaine de Wing, 10 rue du Docteur Roux, 75015 Paris, France.

HOTTEL, Hoyt Clarke, A.B., S.M.; American professor of chemical engineering and engineering consultant; b. 15 Jan. 1903, Salem, Ind.; s. of Louis Weaver and Myrtle Clarke Hottel; m. Nellie Louise Rich 1929; one s. three d.; ed. Indiana Univ. and Massachusetts Inst. of Technology (M.I.T.); Asst. Prof., Prof. M.I.T. 1927–41, Prof. of Fuel Eng. 1941–66, Carbon Dubbs Prof. of Chemical Eng. 1966–68, Prof. Emer. 1968–; Dir. Fuels Research Lab. 1934–68; Section Chief on Fire Warfare, Nat. Defense Cttee. 1942–45; Chair. Nat. Acad./Nat. Research Council Cttee. on Fire Research 1955–67, American Flame Research Cttee. 1952–73; Hon. Chair. 1973–; Vice-Pres. Combustion Inst. 1952–64; Chemical Eng. Consultant, Winchester, 1968–; mem. Advisory Panel for Fire Research 1985–91; Lecture series on radiative tranfer and furnaces, Budapest, Naples, Beijing, Xian 1985–86; mem. numerous other scientific cttees. and comms.; mem. Nat. Acad. of Sciences, Nat. Acad. of Eng., American Acad. of Arts and Sciences, A.C.S., A.I.Ch.E.; Fellow, American Inst. of Chemical Engineers; numerous medals and awards including U.S. Medal for Merit, Egerton Gold Medal, King's Medal for Service in the Cause of Freedom (U.K.), Jakob Award, A.S.M.E./A.I.Ch.E., Daniels Award, Int. Solar Energy Soc., Melchett Medal, Inst. of Energy (U.K.), Gold Medal, Royal Soc., Founders Award, Nat. Acad. of Eng. 1980, John Fritz Medal 1994, Chair. in Chem. Eng., M.I.T., named in his honour 1995. *Publications:* Thermodynamic Charts for Combustion Processes (with others) 1949, Radiative Transfer (with A. F. Sarofim) 1967, New Energy Technology—Some Facts and Assessments (with J. B. Howard) 1971, Reaction Kinetics of Carbon Dioxide with Electrode Carbon Particles, in Fuel 1988; sections in handbooks and about 150 papers on combustion, thermodynamics, jet and flame structure, radiative transfer, solar energy utilization, energy conversion, industrial furnace Design. *Leisure interests:* gardening, books, grandchildren. *Address:* 27 Cambridge Street, Winchester, MA 01890, U.S.A. *Telephone:* (617) 729-3873.

HOTTER, Hans; German singer; b. 19 Jan. 1909, Offenbach; m. Helga Fischer 1936; one s. one d.; ed. Munich; concert debut 1929, opera debut 1930; mem. Vienna, Hamburg and Munich Opera cos.; has appeared in concerts and operas in major cities in Europe, Australia and the U.S.A., and in Festivals at Salzburg, Bayreuth and Edinburgh; renowned for Wagnerian roles; retd. 1974. *Address:* c/o Bayerische Staatsoper, 80539 Munich, Germany.

HOU, Hsiao-hsien; Taiwanese film director; b. 8 April 1947, Meihsien, Canton Prov.; ed. Taipei Nat. Acad. of Arts film and drama dept.; worked as an electronic calculator salesman; entered film industry in 1973; asst. to several dirs. from 1974. *Films include:* Chiu shih liu-liu-te t'a (Cute Girl) 1981, Feng-erh t'i-t'a-ts'ai (Cheerful Wind) 1982, Tsai na ho-pan ch'ing-ts'ao-ch'ing (Green Grass of Home) 1982, Erh-tzu-te ta wan-ou (The Sandwich Man) 1983, Feng-kuei-lai-te jen (The Boys from Fengkuei/All the Youthful Days) 1983, Tung-tung-te chia-ch'i (A Summer at Grandpa's) 1984, T'ung-nien wang-shih (The Time to Live and the Time to Die) 1985, Lien-lien feng-ch'en (Dust in the Wind/Rite of Passage) 1986, Ni-lo-ho nü-erh (Daughter of the Nile) 1987, Pei-ch'ing ch'eng-shih (A City of Sadness) 1989 (winner of Golden Lion at the Venice Film Festival).

HOU JIE; Chinese politician; b. 1931, Luan Co., Hebei Prov.; joined CCP 1948; Vice-Chair. Revolutionary Cttee., Heilongjiang Prov. 1977–78; Vice-Gov., Heilongjiang 1979–85, Gov. 1985–89; Sec. CCP Cttee., Heilongjiang 1982–83, Deputy Sec. 1985–88; Vice-Minister of Water Resources 1988–93; Minister of Construction 1993–98; fmr. Vice-Dir. Nat. Greening Cttee. and Capital Planning Cttee.; Vice-Chair. Nat. Afforestation Cttee.; mem. 12th CCP Cen. Cttee. 1985, 13th Cen. Cttee. 1987–92, 14th CCP Cen. Cttee. 1992–97; Chair. Population, Resource and Environment Cttee., 9th Nat. Cttee. of CPPCC 1998–. *Address:* c/o National Committee of Chinese People's Political Consultative Conference, 23 Taipingqiao Street, Beijing, People's Republic of China.

HOU RUNYU; Chinese orchestral conductor; b. 6 Jan. 1945, Kunming; s. of Hou Zhu and Zhu Bangying; m. Su Jia 1971; one s. one d.; ed. Music Middle School of Shanghai Conservatory, Shanghai Conservatory (conducting); studied at Musikhochschule, Cologne, Fed. Repub. of Germany, and Mozarteum, Salzburg, Austria 1981–85; started playing piano aged 7, debut, Kunming 1954; Prin. Conductor Shanghai Symphony Orchestra 1990–. *Leisure interest:* sport. *Address:* 1710-3-602 Huai-Hai-Zhong Road, Shanghai, People's Republic of China. *Telephone:* 64316474.

HOU XUEYUE, PH.D.; Chinese politician and botanist; b. Hexian Co., Anhui Prov.; ed. in U.S.A.; Prof. Beijing Univ.; mem. Chinese Acad. of Sciences; mem. 8th Standing Cttee. NPC 1993–. *Address:* National People's Congress, Tian An Men Square, Beijing 100805, People's Republic of China.

HOU ZONGBIN; Chinese administrator; b. 1929, Nanhe Co., Hebei Prov.; one s. one d.; joined CCP 1946; Vice-Gov., Gansu Prov. 1983–88; Deputy Sec. of Gansu Prov. CP 1986–88; Deputy Sec. Shaanxi Prov. CP 1989–90; Gov. Shaanxi Prov. 1989–90; Sec. Henan Prov. CP 1990–92; a Deputy Sec. Cen. Comm. for Discipline Inspection; Chair. Internal Affairs and Judicial Cttee. of 9th NPC 1998–; mem. 14th CCP Cen. Cttee. 1992–97. *Address:* c/o Standing Committee of National People's Congress, Beijing, People's Republic of China.

HOUGH, Richard; British author; b. 15 May 1922, Brighton; s. of George Hough and Margaret Hough; m. 1st Helen Charlotte Woodyatt 1943; m. 2nd Judy Taylor 1980; four d.; ed. Frensham Heights School, Farnham; served Second World War R.A.F. pilot fighter command 1941–46; Publr., The Bodley Head 1947–55; Dir. Hamish Hamilton 1955–70; mem. of Council 1970–84; Vice-Pres. Navy Records Soc. 1977–82; Chair. Auxiliary Hosp. Cttee. King Edward's Hosp. Fund 1975–80, mem. Council 1970–86; Best Book of the Sea Award 1972. *Publications include:* The Fleet that had to Die 1958, Admirals in Collision 1959, First Sea Lord (Admiral Fisher) 1969, Captain Bligh and Mr. Christian 1972, Louis and Victoria: the First Mountbattens 1974, One Boy's War (memoirs) 1975, Mountbatten: Hero of our Time 1980, Edwina: Countess Mountbatten of Burma 1983, The Great War at Sea 1914–18 1983, The Longest Battle 1986, The Battle of Britain: The Jubilee History (with Denis Richards) 1989, Winston and Clementine 1990, Bless Our Ship: Mountbatten and the Kelly 1991, Other Days Around Me: a Memoir 1992, Edward and Alexandra 1992, Captain James Cook 1994, Victoria and Albert 1996, Sister Agnes 1998, also author of books for children under pseudonym Bruce Carter. *Address:* 31 Meadowbank, London, NW3 1AY, England. *Telephone:* 0171-722 5663. *Fax:* 0171-722 7750.

HOUGH, Stephen Andrew Gill, F.R.N.C.M., M.MUS.; British pianist; b. 22 Nov. 1961, Heswall, Cheshire; ed. Chetham's School of Music, Royal Northern Coll. of Music and Juilliard School, New York; regular guest performer with London Symphony, Philharmonia, Royal Philharmonic, London Philharmonic and City of Birmingham Symphony Orchestras; regular appearances with maj. orchestras in U.S.A., Europe, Australia, Far East and at int. music festivals; Dayas Gold Medal (Royal Northern Coll. of Music), Terence Judd Award 1982, Naumburg Int. Piano Competition 1983. *Recordings include:* complete Beethoven violin sonatas (with Robert Mann), Hummel piano concertos, recitals of Liszt and Schumann, Brahms concerto no. 2, The Piano Album vols. I, II, Britten Music for One and Two Pianos, Scharwenka and Sauer concertos, Grieg, Liszt, Rubinstein cello sonatas (with Steven Isserlis), Brahms violin sonatas (with Robert Mann), York Bowen piano music, Franck piano music, Mompou piano music, Liebermann piano concertos, Mendelssohn piano and orchestral works, Schubert sonatas and New York Variations. *Leisure interest:* reading. *Address:* c/o Harrison Parrott Ltd., 12 Penzance Place, London, W11 4PA, England.

HOUGHTON, James Richardson, A.B., M.B.A.; American business executive (retd.); b. 6 April 1936, Corning, New York; s. of the late Amory Houghton and Laura Richardson Houghton; m. May Kinnicutt 1962; one s. one d.; ed. St. Paul's School, Concord, N.H., Harvard Coll. and Harvard Univ. Business School; worked in investment banking, Goldman, Sachs and Co., New York 1959–61; in production and finance, Corning Glass Works, Danville, Ky. and Corning, New York 1962–64; Vice-Pres. and Area Man., Corning Glass Int., Zurich and Brussels 1964–68; Vice-Pres. and Gen. Man. Consumer Products Div., Corning Glass Works (Corning Inc. since 1989), Corning, New York 1968–71, Vice-Chair. of Bd. 1971–83, Chair. of Bd. and C.E.O. 1983–96, also fmr. Chair. Exec. Cttee.; Dir. Exxon Corpn., Corning Inc., Metropolitan Life Insurance Co., J. P. Morgan Co. Inc.; Trustee Corning Glass Works Foundation, Corning Museum of Glass, Metropolitan Museum of Art, Pierpont Morgan Library; mem. Council on Foreign Relations, The Business Council, Harvard Corpn. *Address:* c/o Corning Inc., 80 E. Market Street, Suite 201, Corning, NY 14830; The Field, 36 Spencer Hill Road, Corning, NY 14830, U.S.A. (Home).

HOUGHTON, Sir John, Kt., C.B.E., M.A., D.PHIL., F.R.S.; British physicist; b. 30 Dec. 1931, Dyserth, Clwyd; s. of Sidney and Miriam (née Yarwood) Houghton; m. 1st Margaret E. Broughton 1962 (died 1986); one s. one d.; m. 2nd Sheila Thompson 1988; ed. Rhyl Grammar School and Jesus Coll., Oxford; Research Fellow, Royal Aircraft Establishment. Farnborough 1954–57; Lecturer in Atmospheric Physics, Univ. of Oxford 1958–62, Reader 1962–76, Prof. 1976–83, Fellow. Jesus Coll. 1960–83, Hon. Fellow 1983–; Dir. Appleton, Science and Eng. Research Council 1979–83; Chair. Earth Observation Advisory Cttee., European Space Agency 1980–93; Chair. Jt. Scientific Cttee., World Climate Research Prog. 1981–83; Dir.-Gen. Meteorological Office 1983–90, Chief Exec. 1990–91; mem. Exec. Cttee. WMO 1983–91, Vice-Pres. 1987–91; Pres. Royal Meteorological Soc. 1976–78; Chair. (or Co-Chair.) Scientific Assessment Working Group, Intergovernmental Panel on Climate Change 1988–, Royal Comm. on Environmental Pollution 1992–98, Jt. Scientific and Technical Cttee., Global Climate Observing System 1992–95; mem. U.K. Govt. Panel on Sustainable Devt. 1994–; Hon. Scientist Rutherford Appleton Lab. 1992–; Hon. mem. Royal Meteorological Soc., American Meteorological Soc.; Fellow Optical Soc. of America; mem. Acad. Europaea; Hon. D.Sc. (Univ. of Wales) 1991, (Stirling) 1992, (East Anglia) 1993, (Leeds) 1995, (Heriot-Watt) 1997, (Greenwich) 1997; Charles Chree Medal and Prize (Inst. of Physics) 1979, Jt. recipient Rank Prize for opto-electronics 1989, Glazebrook Medal (Inst. of Physics) 1990, Symonds Gold Medal, Royal Meteorological Soc. 1991, Bakerian Lecturer, Royal Soc. 1991, Global 500 Award, UNEP 1994, Gold Medal, Royal Astronomical Soc. 1995, Int. Meteorological Org. Prize 1998. *Publications:* Infra Red Physics (with S. D. Smith) 1966, The Physics of Atmospheres 1977, 1986, Remote Sounding of Atmospheres (with F. W. Taylor and C. D. Rodgers) 1984, Does God Play Dice? 1988, The Search for God: Can Science Help? 1995, Global Warming: the Complete Briefing 1997. *Address:* IPCC

Unit, Hadley Centre, Meteorological Office, Bracknell, Berks., RG12 2SY, England. *Telephone:* (01344) 856 888. *Fax:* (01344) 856 912.

HOUGRON, Jean (Marcel), L. EN D.; French writer; b. 1 July 1923, Caen; s. of Jean Hougron and Denise Grude; m. 1st Noëlle Desgouille (divorced); two s. two d.; m. 2nd Victoria Sanchez 1974; one s.; ed. Faculty of Law, Univ. of Paris; schoolmaster 1943–46; commercial employment in export-import firm, Saigon 1946–47; lorry driver 1947–49; translator in American Consulate 1950; news ed. Radio France Asie 1951; returned to France to write 1952; bookseller in Nice 1953–54; lived in Spain 1958–60; Grand Prix du Roman, Acad. Française 1953, Prix Populiste 1965; Grand Prix de la Science-Fiction for Le Naguen 1982; Chevalier des Arts et des Lettres. *Publications:* Tu récolteras la tempête 1950, Rage blanche 1951, Soleil au ventre 1952, Mort en fraude (film) 1953, La nuit indochinoise 1953, Les portes de l'aventure 1954, Les Asiates 1954, Je reviendrai à Kandara (film) 1955, La terre du barbare 1958, Par qui le scandale 1960, Le signe du chien 1961, Histoire de Georges Guersant 1964, Les humiliés 1965, La gueule pleine de dents 1970, L'homme de proie 1974, L'anti-jeu 1977, Le Naguen 1979, La chambre (novel) 1982, Coup de soleil 1984, Beauté chinoise 1987. *Address:* Hachette Littérature, 79 boulevard Saint-Germain, 75006 Paris (Office); 1 rue des Guillemites, 75004 Paris, France (Home).

HOUMADI, Halifa; Comoran politician; Prime Minister of Comoros 1994–95; mem. Rassemblement pour la démocratie et le renouveau (RDR). *Address:* c/o Office of the Prime Minister, BP 421, Moroni, Comoros.

HOUNGBEDJI, Adrien; Benin politician and lawyer; sentenced to death in absentia March 1975 after alleged involvement in attempted coup; Speaker of Nat. Ass. 1991–96; Prime Minister 1996–98; Leader Parti du renouveau démocratique (PRD). *Address:* c/o Office of the Prime Minister, Cotonou, Benin.

HOUNSFIELD, Sir Godfrey Newbold, Kt., C.B.E., F.R.S.; British research scientist; b. 28 Aug. 1919; s. of Thomas Hounsfield; ed. Magnus Grammar School, Newark, City and Guilds Coll., London, and Faraday House Electrical Eng. Coll.; served R.A.F. 1939–46; with EMI Ltd. 1951–, Head of Medical Systems section 1972–76, Chief Staff Scientist 1976–77, Senior Staff Scientist, Central Research Labs. of EMI (now THORN EMI Central Research Labs.) 1977–86, Consultant to Labs. 1986–; inventor EMI-scanner computerized transverse axial tomography system for X-ray examination; Professorial Fellow in imaging sciences, Univ. of Manchester 1978–; Consultant (part-time) Nat. Heart and Chest Hospitals 1986–; MacRobert Award 1972; Wilhelm-Exner Medal, Austrian Industrial Asscn. 1974; Ziedses des Plantes Medal, Physikalisch-Medizinische Gesellschaft, Würzburg 1974; Prince Philip Medal Award, City and Guilds of London Inst. 1975; ANS Radiation Award, Georgia Inst. of Tech. 1975; Lasker Award 1975; Duddell Bronze Medal, Inst. of Physics 1976; Golden Plate, American Acad. of Achievement 1976; Churchill Gold Medal 1976; Gairdner Foundation Award 1976; shared Nobel Prize in Medicine and Physiology 1979 with Prof. A. M. Cormack (q.v.) for development of computer-assisted tomography; Dr.Med. h.c. (Basel) 1975; Hon. D.Sc. (City Univ., London) 1976, (London) 1976; Hon. D. Tech. (Loughborough) 1976; Dr. h.c. (Cambridge) 1992; Hon. F.R.C.P., Hon. Fellow Royal Coll. of Radiologists and other awards and prizes. *Publications:* articles in professional journals. *Leisure interests:* mountain walks and country rambles, music, playing piano. *Address:* Thorn EMI Central Research Laboratories, Dawley Road, Hayes, Middx., UB3 1HH (Office); 15 Crane Park Road, Whitton, Twickenham, TW2 6DF, Middx., England (Home). *Telephone:* 0181-848 6404 (Office); 0181-894 1746 (Home).

HOUSE, Lieut-Gen. Sir David George, G.C.B., K.C.V.O., C.B.E., M.C.; British army officer; b. 8 Aug. 1922; s. of A. G. House; m. Sheila Betty Darwin 1947; two d.; ed. Regent's Park School, London; war service in Italy and then various regimental appointments with the King's Royal Rifle Corps, 1st Bn. The Royal Green Jackets and staff appointments; Commanded 51st Gurkha Brigade in Borneo 1965–67; Chief, BRIXMS 1967–69; Deputy Mil. Sec. 1969–71; Chief of Staff, HQ British Army of the Rhine 1971–73; Dir. of Infantry 1973–75; Gen. Officer Commdg. Northern Ireland 1975–77; Col. Commdt. The Light Div.; Col. Commdt. Small Arms School Corps 1974–77; Dir. Yorks & Humberside, Lloyds Bank 1985–91; Gentleman Usher of the Black Rod, House of Lords 1978–85. *Leisure interests:* music, gardening. *Address:* Dormer Lodge, Aldborough, North Yorks., YO5 9EP, England.

HOUSE, Lynda Mary; Australian film producer; b. 30 April 1949, Tasmania; d. of Graeme House and Patricia House; m. Tony Mahood 1993; mem. Bd. Film Vic. 1993–96, Australian Film Finance Corpn. 1997–. *Films include:* Proof (Australian Film Inst. Best Film 1991), Muriel's Wedding (Australian Film Inst. Best Film 1994). *Leisure interests:* watching films, reading, gardening. *Address:* 117 Rouse Street, Port Melbourne, Vic. 3121, Australia. *Telephone:* (3) 9646-4025. *Fax:* (3) 9646-6336.

HOUSHIARY, Shirazeh, B.A.; British sculptor; b. 15 Jan. 1955, Iran; ed. Tehran Univ., Chelsea School of Art and Cardiff Coll. of Art; sculptor at the Lisson Gallery, London; Jr. Fellow Cardiff Coll. of Art 1979–80; Prof. London Inst. 1997–; one-person exhbns. include: Chapter Arts Centre 1980, Galleria Massimo Minini, Milan 1983, Valentina Moncada, Rome 1992, Camden Arts Centre, London, Fine Arts Centre, Univ. of Mass. 1993–94, Islamic Gallery, British Museum 1997; group exhbns. include: The Sculpture Show (Arts Council of G.B., Hayward Gallery, Serpentine Gallery), New Art (Tate Gallery London) 1983, Bruges La Morte Gallery, Belgium 1992, Sculptors' Drawings The Body of Drawing (Univ. of Warwick, Coventry and The Mead Gallery) 1993, Tate Gallery, London 1994, Sculpture at Goodwood 1994, 1997, Dialogues of Peace, Palais des Nations, Geneva 1995, Negotiating Rapture, Museum of Contemporary Art, Chicago 1996. *Address:* Lisson Gallery London Ltd, 67 Lisson Street, London, NW1 5DA, England. *Telephone:* 0171-724 2739. *Fax:* 0171-724 7124.

HOUSLAY, Miles Douglas, PH.D., F.R.S.E., F.R.S.A.; British professor of biochemistry; b. 25 June 1950, Wolverhampton; s. of Edwin Douglas Houslay and Georgina Marie Houslay (née Jeffs); m. Rhian Mair Gee 1972; two s. one d.; ed. The Grammar School, Brewood, Staffs., Univ. Coll., Cardiff, King's Coll., Cambridge; ICI Postdoctoral Research Fellow, Univ. of Cambridge 1974–76, Research Fellow, Queen's Coll. 1975–76; Lecturer in Biochemistry, UMIST 1976–82, Reader 1982–84; Gardiner Prof. of Biochemistry, Univ. of Glasgow 1984–; Hon. Sr. Research Fellow, Calif. Metabolic Research Foundation, La Jolla, U.S.A. 1980–91; Deputy Chair. Editorial Bd. Biochemical Journal; Ed.-in-C., Cellular Signalling; mem. Editorial Bd. Progress in Growth Factor Research 1988–93; external assessor Univ. of Malaysia 1991–; mem. Cttee., Biochemical Soc. 1982–86; Chair. MRC Cell Bd. Research Grant Cttee. A 1990–92, British Heart Foundation Research Grant Cttee. 1996–; mem. MRC Cell Bd. 1989–94; mem. Scottish Home and Health Dept. Research Cttee. 1991–94, Wellcome Trust Biochem. Cell Biology Grant Panel 1996–; Trustee British Heart Foundation 1996–; Colworth Medal, Biochemical Soc. *Publications:* Dynamics of Biological Membranes, and over 300 scientific articles. *Leisure interests:* walking, music, cycling, sailing, driving. *Address:* Molecular Pharmacology Group, Division of Biochemistry and Molecular Biology, IBLS, Wolfson Building, University of Glasgow, Glasgow, G12 8QQ, Scotland. *Telephone:* (0141) 330 5903.

HOUSTON, Whitney; American singer; b. 9 Aug. 1963, East Orange, N.J.; d. of John Houston and Cissy Houston; m. Bobby Brown 1992; one d.; trained under direction of mother; mem. Hew Hope Baptist Jr. Choir 1974; background vocalist, Chaka Khan 1978, Lou Rawls 1978, Cissy Houston 1978; appeared in Cissy Houston night club act; record debut, Hold Me (duet with Teddy Pendergrass) 1984. *Albums include:* Whitney Houston 1985, Whitney 1986, I'm Your Baby Tonight 1990. *Songs include:* Greatest Love of All, Saving My Love For You, Didn't We Almost Have It All, You're Still My Man. *Films:* The Bodyguard 1992, Waiting to Exhale 1996, The Preacher's Wife 1997; Grammy Award for Best Female Pop Performance 1985, 1987; seven American Music Awards; other music awards; Hon. H.H.D. (Grambling Univ.). *Address:* c/o John Houston Nippi Inc., 2160 N. Central Road, Fort Lee, NJ 07024, U.S.A.

HOUTHAKKER, Hendrik Samuel; American economist; b. 31 Dec. 1924, Amsterdam, Netherlands; s. of Bernard and Marion (née Lichtenstein) Houthakker; m. Anna-Teresa Tymieniecka 1955; two s. one d.; ed. Univ. of Amsterdam; Research Staff mem., Dept. of Applied Econs., Univ. of Cambridge 1949–51; on Research Staff, Cowles Comm. for Research in Econs., Univ. of Chicago 1952–53; Prof. of Econs., Stanford Univ. 1954–60, Harvard Univ. 1960–94, Prof. Emer. 1994–, Chair. 1987–88; Sr. Staff Economist, Council of Econ. Advisers 1967–68, mem. 1969–71; Vice-Pres. American Econ. Asscn. 1972; Dir. New York Futures Exchange 1979–; Fellow, Econometric Soc. (Past Pres. and Council mem.); mem. Nat Acad. of Sciences; Corresp. mem. Royal Netherlands Acad. of Sciences; Dr. h.c. (Amsterdam) 1972, (Fribourg) 1974; John Bates Clark Medal of American Econ. Asscn. 1963. *Publications:* The Analysis of Family Budgets (with S. J. Prais) 1955, Consumer Demand in the United States (with L. D. Taylor) 1966, Economic Policy for the Farm Sector 1967, The World Price of Oil, 1976; also articles. *Address:* 348 Payson Road, Belmont, MA 02178 (Home); Department of Economics, Littauer Bldg., Harvard University, Cambridge, MA 02138 (Office); 348 Payson Road, Belmont, MA 02178, U.S.A. *Telephone:* 617-495-2111 (Office).

HOUTTE, Baron Jean van, D. EN D.; Belgian politician and emeritus university professor; b. 17 March 1907, Ghent; s. of Hubert van Houtte; m. Cécile de Stella 1932; one s. three d.; ed. Univ. of Ghent; Prof. Univ. of Liège 1931, Univ. of Ghent 1937; Head of Secretariat, Ministry of the Interior 1944–45; co-opted Senator 1949–68; Minister of Finance 1950–52; Prime Minister 1952–54; Minister of Finance 1958–61; Minister of State 1966; Hon. Pres. Sabena Airlines; various Belgian and foreign decorations. *Publications:* Traité des sociétés de personnes à responsabilité limitée 1935, 1950, 1962, La responsabilité civile dans les transports aériens 1940, La réparation des dommages de guerre aux biens privés 1948, Formulierboek voor notarissen 1947, Principes du droit fiscal belge 1958, 1966, 1979. *Address:* 54 Boulevard St. Michel, Brussels, Belgium. *Telephone:* 733-62-94.

HOVE, Andrew C., Jr.; American finance official; b. 9 Nov. 1934, Minden, Neb.; s. of late Andrew C. Howe and Rosalie Vopat; m. Ellen Matzke 1956; one s. two d.; ed. Univ. of Nebraska and Univ. of Wisconsin Grad. School of Banking; U.S. Navy 1956–60; Neb. Nat. Guard 1960–63; officer, Minden Exchange Bank & Trust Co. 1960–81, Chair. and C.E.O. 1981–90, Vice-Chair. 1990–92; Vice-Chair. Fed. Deposit Insurance Corpn. 1990–92, 1994–97, 1998–, Chair. 1992–94, 1997–98. *Address:* Federal Deposit Insurance Corporation, 550 17th Street, N.W., Washington, DC 20429, U.S.A.

HOVERS, Joannes Coenradus Maria, PH.D.; Netherlands business executive; b. 29 July 1943, Beek; m. Ineke van der Heijde 1971; three s.; ed. Michiel Lyceum, Geleen, Tilburg Univ.; with Océ NV 1967–76, Chair. Bd. of Exec. Dirs. May 1998–; Chair. Man. Bd. Teewen Group (bldg. materials), later Chair. Man. Bd. Synres (synthetic resins) 1976–83; mem. Man. Bd. Stork NV 1983–88, Exec. Vice-Pres. Man. Bd. 1988–89, C.E.O. Man. Bd. 1989–98; Chair. Comm. of Int. Econ. Relations; Supervisory Dir. De Nederlandsche Bank NV, Hoechst AG, Koninklijke Grolsch NV, Ericsson Telecommunicatie BV, Randstad Holding NV; mem. Supervisory Bd. TIAS Training Inst., Gooi-Noord Regional Hosp.; Asscn. of European Man. Publrs. Award 1973. *Address:* Océ NV, P.O. Box 101, 5900 MA Venlo, Netherlands. *Telephone:* (77) 359 2205. *Fax:* (77) 359 5436.

HOVEYDA, Fereydoun, LL.D.; Iranian diplomatist; b. 21 Sept. 1924, Damascus; ed. Univ. of Paris; various positions, Imperial Iranian Embassy, Paris 1946–51; Programme Specialist, Mass Communications Dept., UNESCO 1952–64; Under-Sec. of State for Int. and Econ. Affairs, Ministry of Foreign Affairs 1965–71; Perm. Rep. to UN 1971–79; del to various int. confs. including UN Gen. Assembly 1948, 1951, 1965, UNESCO Confs. 1966, 1968, 1970 and ECOSOC sessions 1966–69; Léopold Sédar Senghor Literary Prize 1973. *Publications:* studies: Le plan septennal iranien 1948, La nationalisation du pétrole en Iran 1951, Histoire du roman policier 1968, The Fall of the Shah 1979; novels: Les quarantaines 1962, L'aérogare 1965, Dans une terre étrange 1968, Le losange 1969, Les neiges du Sinai 1973.

HOVING, Thomas, PH.D.; American author and cultural administrator; b. 15 Jan. 1931, New York; s. of Walter Hoving and Mary Osgood Field; m. Nancy Bell 1953; one d.; ed. The Buckley School, New York, Eaglebrook School, Deerfield, Mass., Exeter Acad., Exeter N.H., The Hotchkiss School, Lakeville, Conn., and Princeton Univ.; Curatorial Asst. of Medieval Art and The Cloisters, Metropolitan Museum of Art 1959–60, Asst. Curator 1960–63, Assoc. Curator 1963–65, Curator of Medieval Art and The Cloisters 1965; Commr. of Parks, New York 1966; Admin. of Recreation and Cultural Affairs, New York 1967; Dir. Metropolitan Museum of Art 1966–77; Ed.-in.-Chief Connoisseur Magazine 1981–90; Arts and Entertainment Corresp. ABC News 20/20 1978–84; Pres. Hoving Associates Inc. cultural affairs consulting; Fellowship, Nat. Council of Humanities 1955, Kienbusch and Haring Fellowship 1957; Hon. LL.D. (Pratt Inst.) 1967, Hon. D.F.A. (New York) 1968, Hon. D.Hum. (Princeton) 1968, Hon. D. Litt. (Middlebury Coll.) 1968; Distinguished Citizen's Award, Citizen's Budget Cttee. 1967, Creative Leadership in Educ. Award, New York Univ. 1975, Woodrow Wilson award, Princeton 1975. *Publications:* Guide to the Cloisters 1962, Tutankhamun, The Untold Story 1978, Two Worlds of Andrew Wyeth 1978, King of the Confessors 1981, Masterpiece 1986, Discovery 1989, Making the Mummies Dance, Inside the Metropolitan Museum of Art 1992, False Impressions: The Hunt for Big-Time Art Fakes 1996, Andrew Wyeth: Autobiography 1996, Greatest Works of Art of Western Civilization 1997. *Leisure interests:* sailing, skiing, bicycling, flying. *Address:* Hoving Associates Inc., 150 East 73rd Street, New York, NY 10021, U.S.A. *Fax:* (212) 570-0348.

HOWARD, Alan Mackenzie, C.B.E.; British actor; b. 5 Aug. 1937, London; s. of Arthur John and Jean (Compton Mackenzie) Howard; m. 1st Stephanie Hinchcliffe Davies 1965; m. 2nd Sally Beauman 1976; one s.; ed. Ardingley Coll.; National Service with R.A.F. in Germany 1956–58; Stage Hand, Asst. Stage Man., Actor, Belgrade Theatre Coventry 1958–60; London West End debut, Duke of York's Theatre in Roots 1959; played in London at Royal Court, Arts, Mermaid, Strand, Phoenix theatres, also outside London 1960–65; with Royal Shakespeare Co. 1966–, Assoc. Artist 1967–; Plays and Players London Theatre Critics most promising Actor Award 1969, Best Actor Award 1977; Soc. of West End Theatre Managers Best Actor in a Revival Award 1976, 1978; Evening Standard Drama Award for Best Actor 1978, 1981; Variety Club of Great Britain Best Actor Award 1980. *Plays include:* Twelfth Night, Revenger's Tragedy, As You Like It, The Relapse, King Lear, Troilus and Cressida, Much Ado About Nothing, Bartholomew Fair, Dr. Faustus, Hamlet, Midsummer Night's Dream, Enemies, Man of Mode, The Balcony, The Bewitched, Henry IV parts 1 and 2, Henry V, Wild Oats, Henry VI parts 1, 2 and 3, Coriolanus, Antony and Cleopatra, Children of the Sun, Richard II, Richard III, The Forest, Good 1981, 1982–83, Breaking the Silence 1985, The Silver King 1990, Scenes from a Marriage 1990, Pygmalion 1992, Macbeth 1993, La Grande Magia 1995, Rosencrantz and Guildenstern Are Dead 1995, Oedipus Plays 1996, Waiting for Godot 1997, King Lear 1997, Khludov in Flight 1998. *Films include:* The Return of the Musketeers, The Cook, The Thief, His Wife and Her Lover. *TV appearances include:* Coriolanus, Sherlock Holmes, A Perfect Spy. *Leisure interests:* reading, music. *Address:* c/o Julian Belfrage Associates, 46 Albemarle Street, London, W1X 4PP, England.

HOWARD, Ann; British mezzo-soprano opera singer; b. 22 July 1936, Norwood, London; d. of William A. and Gladys W. Swadling; m. Keith Giles 1954; one d.; ed. with Topliss Green and Rodolfa Lhombino, London, and Dominic Modesti, Paris; repertoire includes Carmen, Dalila (Samson et Dalila), Dulcinée (Don Quichotte), Hélène (La Belle Hélène), Eboli (Don Carlos), Azucena (Il Trovatore), Amneris (Aida), Isabella (Italiana in Algeri), Proserpina (Orfeo), Ortrud (Lohengrin), Brangaene (Tristan und Isolde), Fricka (Das Rheingold and Die Walküre), Baba the Turk (The Rake's Progress), Katisha (The Mikado), Czipra (Gipsy Baron), Lilli Vanessi (Kiss Me Kate), Clytemnestra (Electra), La Grande Duchesse de Gerolstein, Stepmother (Into The Woods), Prince Orlofsky (Die Fledermaus), Old Lady (Candide), Auntie (Peter Grimes), Hostess (Boris Godunov), Jezi Baba (Rusalka), Marcellina (Marriage of Figaro), Emma Jones (Street Scene), performed in world premières of Mines of Sulphur (Bennett) 1970, Rebecca (Josephs) 1982, The Tempest (Eaton, U.S.A.) 1985, The Plumber's Gift (Blake) 1989, The Doctor of Myddfai (Maxwell Davies) 1996 and in U.K. première of Le Grand Macabre 1981; series of Gilbert and Sullivan operas Performing Arts Centre, NY State Univ. 1993–98; has appeared in U.K., France, Canada, U.S.A., Mexico, Chile, Portugal, Germany, Austria and Italy and on BBC radio and TV. *Leisure interests:* gardening, cooking. *Address:* c/o Stafford Law Associates, 6 Barham Close, Weybridge, Surrey, KT13 9PR, England. *Telephone:* (01932) 854489. *Fax:* (01932) 858521.

HOWARD, Anthony Michell, C.B.E., M.A.; British journalist; b. 12 Feb. 1934, London; s. of the late Canon W. G. Howard and Janet (née Rymer) Howard; m. Carol Anne Gaynor 1965; ed. Westminster School and Christ Church, Oxford; on editorial staff Manchester Guardian 1959–61; Political Corresp. New Statesman 1961–64; Whitehall Corresp. Sunday Times 1965; Washington Corresp. Observer 1966–69; Asst. Ed. New Statesman 1970–72, Ed. 1972–78; Ed. The Listener 1979–81; Deputy Ed. The Observer 1981–88; Presenter Face the Press, Channel Four 1982–85; Presenter, reporter BBC TV 1989–92; Obituaries Ed., The Times 1993–99; Harkness Fellow, U.S.A. 1960. *Publications:* The Making of the Prime Minister (with Richard West) 1965, ed. The Crossman Diaries 1964–70, 1979, Rab: The Life of R. A. Butler 1987, Crossman: The Pursuit of Power 1990, ed. The Times Lives Remembered 1993. *Address:* 11 Campden House Court, Gloucester Walk, London, W8 4HU; Dinham Lodge, Ludlow, Shropshire, SY8 1EH, England. *Telephone:* 0171-937 7313 (London); (01584) 878457 (Shropshire).

HOWARD, Elizabeth Jane, F.R.S.L.; British novelist; b. 26 March 1923; d. of David Liddon and Katharine M. Howard; m. 1st Peter M. Scott 1942; one d.; m. 2nd James Douglas-Henry 1959; m. 3rd Kingsley Amis 1965 (divorced 1983, deceased); ed. at home and at London Mask Theatre School; BBC TV modelling 1939–46; Sec. Inland Waterways Asscn. 1947; then professional writer including plays for TV; John Llewellyn Rhys Memorial Prize 1950; Hon. Artistic Dir. Cheltenham Literary Festival 1962; Artistic Co-Dir. Salisbury Festival of Arts 1973. *Publications:* The Beautiful Visit 1950, The Long View 1956, The Sea Change 1959, After Julius 1965, Something in Disguise 1969 (TV series 1982), Odd Girl Out 1972, Mr. Wrong 1975; Ed. A Companion for Lovers 1978; Getting it Right 1982 (Yorkshire Post Prize) (film script 1985), The Attachment (film script) 1986, Howard and Maschler on Food: cooking for occasions (jtly.) 1987, The Light Years (1st vol. of The Cazalet Chronicle), Green Shades (gardening anthology) 1991, Marking Time (2nd vol. of The Cazalet Chronicle) 1991, Confusion (3rd vol. of The Cazalet Chronicle) 1993, Casting Off (4th vol. of the Cazalet Chronicle) 1995. *Leisure interests:* music, gardening, enjoying all the arts, travelling, natural history. *Address:* c/o Jonathan Clowes, Iron Bridge House, Bridge Approach, London, NW1 8BD, England.

HOWARD, Hon. John Winston, LL.B.; Australian politician; b. 26 July 1939, Sydney; s. of Lyall Falconer and Mona Jane Howard; m. Alison Janette Parker 1971; two s. one d.; ed. Univ. of Sydney; solicitor to Supreme Court, N.S.W. 1962; partner, Sydney solicitors' firm 1968–74; Liberal M.P. for Bennelong, N.S.W., Fed. Parl. 1974–; Minister for Business and Consumer Affairs 1975–77, Minister Assisting Prime Minister 1977, Fed. Treas. 1977–83; Deputy Leader of Opposition 1983–85, Leader 1985–89; Leader Liberal Party Sept. 1985–89; Prime Minister of Australia March 1996–; Shadow Minister for Industrial Relations, Employment and Training, Shadow Minister assisting the Leader on the Public Service and Chair. Manpower and Labour Market Reform Group 1990–95; mem. State Exec., N.S.W. Liberal Party 1963–74; Vice-Pres., N.S.W. Div., Liberal Party 1972–74; Leader Liberal Party 1995–. *Leisure interests:* reading, cricket, tennis. *Address:* Department of the Prime Minister and Cabinet, 3–5 National Circuit, Barton, A.C.T. 2600; G.P.O. Box 36, Sydney, N.S.W. 2001, Australia. *Telephone:* (2) 6271-5111 (A.C.T.). *Fax:* (2) 6271-5415 (A.C.T.).

HOWARD, Ken (James Kenneth), R.A., R.W.S., R.W.A., A.R.C.A.; British painter; b. 26 Dec. 1932, London; s. of Frank Howard and Elizabeth Howard; m. 1st Ann Popham (divorced 1974); m. 2nd Christa Gaa (née Köhler; died 1992); ed. Kilburn Grammar School, Hornsey School of Art, Royal Coll. of Art; British Council Scholarship to Florence 1958–59; taught in various London art schools 1959–73; Official Artist for Imperial War Museum, Northern Ireland 1973, 1978; painted for British Army in Northern Ireland, Germany, Cyprus, Oman, Hong Kong, Brunei, Nepal, Canada, Norway, Belize, Beirut 1973–83; one-man exhbns. including New Grafton Gallery, London 1971–, Lowndes Lodge Gallery 1987–, Everard Read Gallery, Johannesburg 1998, Jersey, Hong Kong, Nicosia, Delhi; works in public collections including Plymouth City Art Gallery, Ulster Museum, Imperial War Museum, Nat. Army Museum, Hove City Art Gallery, Guildhall Art Gallery; comms. for UN, B.A.O.R., Stock Exchange, London, States of Jersey, Banque Paribas, Drapers Co., Royal Hosp. Chelsea; Hon. mem. Royal Inst. of Oil Painters, Royal Soc. of British Artists; First Prize Lord Mayor's Art Award 1965, Hunting Group Award 1982, Sparkasse Karlsruhe 1983; Prizewinner John Moores 1978. *Publications:* The Paintings of Ken Howard 1992, Ken Howard: A personal viewpoint 1998. *Leisure interests:* opera, cinema. *Address:* 8 South Bolton Gardens, London, SW5 0DH; St. Clements Studio, Paul Lane, Mousehole, Cornwall, TR19 6TR, England. *Telephone:* 0171-373 2912 (London); (01736) 731596 (Cornwall). *Fax:* 0171-244 6246.

HOWARD, Melvin, M.S.; American business executive; b. 5 Jan. 1935, Boston; s. of John Howard and Molly Sagar; m. Beverly Kahan 1957; one s. one d.; ed. Univ. of Mass. and Columbia Univ.; Financial Exec. Ford Motor Co. Dearborn, Mich. 1959–67; Vice-Pres. Admin. Shoe Corpns. of America,

Columbus, Ohio 1967–70; Asst. Controller, Business Products Group, Xerox Corpn. Rochester, N.Y. 1970–72, Vice-Pres. (Finance), Business Devt. Group 1972–74, Sr. Vice-Pres., Sr. Staff Officer 1974–75, Corp. Vice-Pres. and Controller 1975–77, Corp. Vice-Pres. (Finance) 1977–78, Sr. Corporate Vice-Pres. (Finance) 1978–81, Sr. Vice-Pres. and Chief Financial Officer 1981–84, Exec. Vice-Pres. and Pres. Financial Services 1984–86, Vice-Chair. 1986; Chair. Xerox Financial Services, Inc.; Pres., C.E.O. Ehrlich Boben Financial Corpn. 1990–92; Man. Dir. Taurus Advisory Group 1993–94; mem. Bd. Xerox Corpn., LMH Fund Ltd., Crum & Forster Inc., Van Kampen Merritt Inc., Gould Pumps Inc., Xerox Credit Corpn., Bond Investors Group, VMS Realty Partners. *Address:* 42 Red Coat Road, Westport, CT 06880, U.S.A.

HOWARD, Rt. Hon. Michael, P.C., Q.C.; British politician and barrister; b. 7 July 1941; s. of Bernard Howard and Hilda Howard; m. Sandra Clare Paul 1975; one s. one d. one step-s.; ed. Llanelli Grammar School, Peterhouse, Cambridge; Pres. Cambridge Union 1962; called to Bar, Inner Temple 1964, Master of the Bench of Inner Temple 1992; Jr. Counsel to the Crown (Common Law) 1980–82; a Recorder 1986–; Conservative parl. cand., Liverpool (Edge Hill) 1966, 1970; Chair. Bow Group 1970–71; M.P. for Folkestone and Hythe 1983–; Parl. Pvt. Sec. to Solicitor-Gen. 1984–85; Under-Sec. of State, Dept. of Trade and Industry, Minister for Corporate and Consumer Affairs 1985–87; Minister of State, Dept. of the Environment 1987–88, Minister of Water and Planning 1988–90; Sec. of State for Employment 1990–92, for the Environment 1992–93, Home Sec. 1993–97; Opposition Front-Bench Spokesman on Foreign and Commonwealth Affairs 1997–99; Chair. Soc. of Conservative Lawyers 1985. *Leisure interests:* watching football and baseball. *Address:* House of Commons, London, SW1A 0AA, England. *Telephone:* 0171-219 3000. *Fax:* 0171-219 5322.

HOWARD, Sir Michael Eliot, Kt., C.B.E., M.C., D.LITT., F.B.A.; British historian; b. 29 Nov. 1922, London, England; s. of the late Geoffrey Eliot Howard and of Edith Howard (née Edinger); ed. Wellington Coll., Christ Church, Oxford; served in army 1942–45; Asst. lecturer, lecturer in History, King's Coll., London 1947–53; lecturer, Reader in War Studies, Univ. of London 1953–63; Prof. of War Studies, Univ. of London 1963–68; Fellow in Higher Defence Studies, All Souls Coll., Oxford 1968–77; Chichele Prof. of the History of War, Univ. of Oxford 1977–80; Regius Prof. of Modern History, Univ. of Oxford 1980–89, Emer. Prof. 1989–, Hon. Fellow, Oriel Coll. 1990; Hon. Student Christ Church 1990; Robert A. Lovett Prof. of Mil. and Naval History, Yale Univ. 1989–93; Leverhulme Lecturer 1996; Lee Kuan Yew Distinguished Visitor, Nat. Univ. of Singapore 1996; Pres. Int. Inst. for Strategic Studies; Foreign mem. American Acad. of Arts and Sciences; Hon. Litt.D. (Leeds) 1979; Hon. D. Litt. (London) 1988; Duff Cooper Memorial Prize 1961, Wolfson Literary Award 1972, NATO Atlantic Award 1989; Chesney Memorial Gold Medal, R.U.S.I. *Publications:* The Franco-German War 1961, Grand Strategy, Vol. IV (in UK History of Second World War) 1972, The Continental Commitment 1973, War in European History 1976, trans. (with Peter Paret) Clausewitz on War 1976, War and the Liberal Conscience 1978, Restraints on War 1979, The Causes of Wars 1983, Clausewitz 1983, Strategic Deception: British Intelligence in the Second World War 1990, The Lessons of History (essays) 1991. *Leisure interests:* music, gardening. *Address:* The Old Farm, Eastbury, Newbury, Berks., RG16 7JN, England (Home). *Telephone:* (01488) 71387 (England).

HOWARD, Ron; American film actor and director; b. 1 March 1954, Duncan, Okla; s. of Rance Howard and Jean Howard; m. Cheryl Alley 1975; two s. two d.; ed. Univ. of S. Calif. and Los Angeles Valley Coll.; Dir., co-author, star, Grand Theft Auto 1977; regular TV series The Andy Griffith Show 1960–68, The Smith Family 1971–72, Happy Days 1974, and many other television appearances. *Films directed include:* Night Shift 1982, Splash 1984, Cocoon 1985, Gung Ho 1986, Return to Mayberry 1986, Willow 1988, Parenthood 1989, Backdraft 1991, Far and Away (also co-producer) 1992, The Paper 1994, Apollo 13 1995 (Outstanding Directorial Achievement in Motion Picture Award from Directors' Guild of America 1996). *Film appearances include:* The Journey 1959, Five Minutes to Live 1959, Music Man 1962, The Courtship of Eddie's Father 1963, Village of the Giants 1965, Wild County 1971, Mother's Day, American Graffiti 1974, The Spikes Gang, Eat My Dust 1976, The Shootist 1976, More American Graffiti 1979, Leo and Loree (TV), Act of Love 1980, Skyward 1981, Through the Magic Pyramid (dir., exec. producer) 1981, When Your Lover Leaves (co-exec. producer) 1983, Return to Mayberry 1986, Ransom 1996. *Address:* c/o Peter Dekom Bloom, Dekom & Hergott, 150 S. Rodeo Drive, Beverly Hills, CA 90212; Imagine Entertainment, 1925 Century Park East, Suite 230, Los Angeles, CA 90067, U.S.A.

HOWARTH, Elgar, A.R.A.M., D.MUS.; British musician; b. 4 Nov. 1935, Cannock, Staffs.; s. of Oliver Howarth and Emma Wall; m. Mary Bridget Neary 1958; one s. two d.; ed. Eccles Grammar School and Manchester Univ.-Royal Manchester Coll. of Music (jt. course); orchestral player 1958–70; Chair. Royal Philharmonic Orchestra 1968–70; Prin. Guest Conductor Opera North 1985–88; freelance orchestral conductor 1970–; Musical Adviser Grimethorpe Colliery Brass Band 1972–; compositions: Trumpet Concerto 1968, Trombone Concerto 1962, Music for Spielberg 1984, Songs for B.L. for brass band; Fellow, Royal Northern Coll. of Music, Welsh Coll. of Music; Hon. Fellow, Univ. Coll. Salford; D. Univ. (Cen. England); Hon. D. Mus. (Keele) 1996; Eddison Award 1977, Olivier Award for Outstanding Achievement in Opera 1997; Fellow Welsh Coll. of Music and Drama. *Leisure interests:* hypochondria, cricket, football. *Address:* 27 Cromwell Avenue, London, N6 5HN, England.

HOWARTH, Judith; British opera singer; b. 11 Sept. 1962, Ipswich; m. 1986; ed. Royal Scottish Acad. of Music and Drama and studies with Patricia Macmahon; recipient of special bursary to join Royal Opera House, Covent Garden as prin. soprano in 1985–86 season; maj. roles with Royal Opera include Musetta, Ännchen (Der Freischütz), Gilda, Adela, Marguerite de Valois (Les Huguenots), Liu, Norina, Marzelline and Morgana (Alcina) 1989–96; now freelance; numerous concert and recital engagements in U.K., U.S.A., Far East, Australia and N.Z.; debut at Salzburg Festival in Mozart's Der Schauspieldirektor 1991; has also appeared with Florida Grand Opera, Drottningholm Festival, Opera North and Glyndebourne Touring Opera; debut with Deutsche Staatsoper, Berlin in Cavalli's La Didone 1996. *Leisure interest:* cooking. *Address:* c/o Lies Askonas Ltd., 6 Henrietta Street, London, WC2E 8LA, England. *Telephone:* 0171-379 7700. *Fax:* 0171-242 1831.

HOWARTH, Thomas, PH.D., F.R.I.B.A., F.R.A.I.C.; British/Canadian architect, planning consultant and university professor; b. 1 May 1914, Wesham, Lancs.; s. of Lawrence Howarth and Agnes (née Cornall) Howarth; m. Edna Marland 1940 (separated 1971); one s. one d.; ed. Kirkham Grammar School, Univs. of Manchester and Glasgow; Lecturer in Architecture, Glasgow School of Arch. and Glasgow School of Art 1939–46; Lecturer, then Sr. Lecturer in Arch., Manchester Univ. 1946–58; Dir. and Prof. School of Architecture, Univ. of Toronto 1958–83, Dean. Faculty of Architecture, Urban and Regional Planning and Landscape Architecture 1967–74, Prof. Emer. 1982–; Planner, Glendon Coll. Campus and Adviser to Bd. of Govs., York Univ., Ont. 1960–87; Master Planner, Laurentian Univ., Ont. 1962–; served as Commr. (2 terms) and on Advisory Design and Planning Cttees. of Nat. Capital Comm. 1964–80; has contributed to educ. and professional affairs in various parts of world especially N. America, Europe, Asia and the Caribbean; Vice-Pres. Commonwealth Asscn. of Architects 1963–89, Regional Rep. for the Americas 1981–87; Founder mem. and Past Pres. Canadian Soc. of the Decorative Arts 1981–; Hon. Fellow, American Inst. of Architects; Hon. mem. Ont. Asscn. of Landscape Architects, Ont. Asscn. of Architects; R.I.B.A. Alfred Bossom Research Fellow 1952; U.S. Soc. of Architectural Historians Book Award 1953; Killam Sr. Research Scholar, Univ. of Calgary 1977; Dr. h.c. (Stirling) 1981. *Publications:* Charles Rennie Mackintosh and the Modern Movement 1952, Poems 1996. *Leisure interests:* interior design, travel, collecting art nouveau, lecturing, writing. *Address:* 131 Bloor Street West, Apt. 1001, Toronto, M5S 1R1, Ont., Canada (Home). *Telephone:* (416) 920 5171.

HOWATCH, Susan, LL.B.; British writer; b. 14 July 1940, Leatherhead, Surrey; d. of G. S. Sturt; m. Joseph Howatch 1964; one d.; ed. Sutton High School, King's Coll., London Univ.; emigrated to U.S.A. 1964, lived in Ireland 1976–80, returned to U.K. 1980; first book published 1965. *Publications:* (novels) Penmarric 1971, Cashelmara 1974, The Rich are Different 1977, Sins of the Fathers 1980, The Wheel of Fortune 1984, Glittering Images 1987, Glamorous Powers 1988, Ultimate Prizes 1989, Scandalous Risks 1991, Mystical Paths 1992, Absolute Truths 1994, A Question of Integrity (U.S. title: The Wonder Worker) 1997. *Leisure interest:* theology. *Address:* c/o Gillon Aitken Associates, 29 Fernshaw Road, London, SW10 0TG, England. *Telephone:* 0171-351 7561.

HOWDEN, Timothy Simon; British business executive; b. 2 April 1937, London; s. of Phillip Alexander Howden and Rene Howden; m. Penelope Mary Howden 1958 (divorced 1984); two s. one d.; ed. Tonbridge School; on staff of Reckitt & Colman in France, Fed. Repub. of Germany and U.K., ending as Dir. Reckitt & Colman Europe 1962–73; Dir. RHM Flour Mills 1973–75, Man. Dir. RHM Foods Ltd. 1975–80, Chair. and Man. Dir. British Bakeries Ltd. 1980–85, Planning Dir. RHM PLC 1985–89, Man. Dir. RHM PLC 1989–92; Group Chief Exec. for Europe, The Albert Fisher Group 1992–96, C.E.O. for N. America 1996–97; Dir. (non-exec.) Scholl PLC 1994–, Saltire PLC 1996–, Fimming Int. 1998–. *Leisure interests:* skiing, scuba diving, tennis, sailing. *Address:* Flat 72, Berkeley House, Hay Hill, London, W1X 7LH, England. *Telephone:* (01628) 484121.

HOWE, Brian Leslie, B.A.; Australian politician; b. 28 Jan. 1936, Melbourne; s. of John Percy Howe and Lilian May Howe; m. Renate Morris 1962; one s. two d.; ed. Melbourne Univ., McCormick Theological Seminary, Chicago; worked as Uniting Church Minister, Melbourne and Morwell, Victoria; fmr. Sr. Lecturer in Sociology and Chair. Dept. of Social and Political Studies, Swinburne Inst. of Tech., Melbourne; joined Australian Labor Party 1961; M.P. for Batman, House of Reps. 1977–96; Minister for Defence Support 1983–84, for Social Security and assisting the Prime Minister for Social Justice 1984–90, for Health, Housing and Community Services and assisting the Prime Minister for Social Justice 1990–93, for Housing, Local Govt. and Community (now Human) Services 1993–94, for Housing and Regional Devt. 1994–96; Deputy Prime Minister 1991–95; Minister assisting the Prime Minister for Commonwealth Relations 1991–93; Professional Assoc. Centre for Public Policy and Dept. of Social Work, Univ. of Melbourne 1996–; Visiting Research Fellow Woodrow Wilson School of Public Policy and Int. Affairs 1997; fmr. Chair. Caucus Econs. Cttee.; fmr. mem. Caucus Resources Cttee., Urban and Regional Affairs Cttee., House of Reps. Standing Cttee. on the Environment, Jt. House Cttee. on Publs. *Address:* 48 High Street, Northcote, Vic. 3070, Australia.

HOWE, Harold, II; American educator (retd.); b. 1918, Hartford, Conn.; s. of Margaret Armstrong and Arthur Howe; m. Priscilla Foster Lamb 1940; one s. two d.; ed. Yale and Columbia Univs., Univ. of Cincinnati, and Harvard Univ; history teacher, Darrow School, New Lebanon, New York 1940–42; Lt. U.S. Naval Reserve 1942–45; history teacher, Phillips Acad., Andover, Mass. 1947–50; Prin., Andover High School and Junior High School 1950–53; Prin., Walnut Hills High School, Cincinnati, Ohio 1953–57; Prin., Newton High School, Newton, Mass. 1957–60; Supt. of Schools, Scarsdale, N.Y. 1960–64; Exec. Dir. Learning Inst. of N. Carolina, Chapel Hill, N. C. 1964–65; U.S. Commr. of Educ. 1965–68; Adviser on Educ., Ford Foundation, India 1968–70; Vice-Pres. for Educ., Ford Foundation 1971–79, for Educ. and Public Policy 1979–81; Sr. Lecturer, Harvard Graduate School of Educ. 1981–94, Prof. Emer. 1989–94; fmr. Trustee, Vassar Coll., Yale Univ., Teachers' Coll. Columbia Univ.; Trustee Educational Testing Services 1986–95 (Chair. 1990–92); Trustee and Vice-Chair. Coll. Entrance Examination Bd. 1963–65; Visiting Cttee. of Harvard Graduate School of Educ. 1980; Chair. William T. Grant Foundation Comm. on Work, Family and Citizenship 1986–88; Hon. LL.D. (Univ. of Notre Dame, Shaw Univ., N. Carolina, Princeton Univ., Adelphi Univ., N.Y., St. Louis Univ., Missouri, Hunter Coll. of City Univ. of New York, Univ. of Hartford, Tulane Univ.); James Bryant Conant Award, Educ. Comm. of the States, for contribs. to American Educ. 1986, Harold W. McGraw, Jr. Prize in Education 1994. *Publication:* Picking up the Options 1968, Thinking about Our Kids 1993. *Leisure interest:* outdoor activities. *Address:* 80 Lyme Road, Hanover, NH 03755, U.S.A. *Telephone:* (617) 369-8265.

HOWE OF ABERAVON, Baron (Life Peer), cr. 1992, of Tandridge in the County of Surrey, **(Richard Edward) Geoffrey Howe,** C.H., P.C., Q.C.; British politician and lawyer; b. 20 Dec. 1926, Port Talbot, Glam.; s. of late B. Edward and of E. F. Howe; m. Elspeth R. M. Shand 1953; one s. two d.; ed. Winchester Coll. and Trinity Hall, Cambridge; called to the Bar, Middle Temple 1952, Bencher 1969; Deputy Chair. Glamorgan Quarter Sessions 1966–70; M.P. for Bebington 1964–66, for Reigate 1970–74, for East Surrey 1974–92; Solicitor-Gen. 1970–72; Minister for Trade and Consumer Affairs 1972–74; Opposition Spokesman for Social Services 1974–75, for Treasury and Econ. Affairs 1975–79; Chancellor of the Exchequer 1979–83; Sec. of State for Foreign and Commonwealth Affairs 1983–89; Lord Pres. of the Council, Leader of House of Commons and Deputy Prime Minister 1989–90; Visitor S.O.A.S. Univ. of London 1991; Special Adviser on European and Int. Affairs to int. law firm Jones, Day, Reavis & Pogue 1991–; Herman Phleger Visiting Prof. Stanford Law School, U.S.A. 1992–93; Pres. G.B.-China Centre 1992–; Chair. Framlington Russian Investment Fund 1994–; a Gov. IMF 1979–83; Chair. Int. Cttee. 1983; fmr. Pres. British Overseas Trade Bd.; Dir. Sun Alliance and London Insurance Group 1974–79, BICC 1991–97, Glaxo 1991–96; fmr. Dir. EMI Ltd., AGB Research Ltd.; mem. Int. Advisory Council, J. P. Morgan, Stanford Univ. Inst. for Int. Studies, Bertelsmann Foundation, Fuji Wolfensohn Int. European Advisory Bd. 1996–, Carlyle European Advisory Bd. 1996–; Hon. Fellow Trinity Hall 1992; Hon. LL.D. (Wales) 1988; Hon. D.C.L. (City Univ.) 1993; Joseph Bech Prize 1993; Grand Cross of the Order of Merit (Germany) 1992; Conservative. *Publication:* Conflict of Loyalty 1994. *Leisure interests:* photography, gardening. *Address:* House of Lords, London, SW1A 0PW, England.

HOWE YOON CHONG, B.A., D.S.O.; Singaporean politician and banker; b. 1923, China; m.; three c.; ed. St. Francis' Inst. Malacca, Raffles Coll. and Univ. of Malaya in Singapore; fmr. civil servant; Sec. to Public Service Comm.; C.E.O. Housing and Devt. Bd. 1960; Perm. Sec. Ministries of Finance and Nat. Devt.; Deputy Chair. Econ. Devt. Bd.; Chair. and Pres. Devt. Bank of Singapore, concurrently Chair. and Gen. Man. Port of Singapore Authority; Perm. Sec. Prime Minister's Office and Head of Civil Service; mem. Parl. 1979–84; Minister of Defence 1979–82, of Health 1982–84; Chair. and Chief Exec. Devt. Bank of Singapore 1985–90, Straits Trading Co., Ltd. 1992–; Chair. Great Eastern Life Assurance Co. Ltd. 1992–; mem. Bd. of Trustees, Eisenhower Exchange Fellowships Inc. 1980–90; Malaysia Medal, Meritorious Service Medal; Hon. D. Litt. (Singapore). *Address:* c/o Straits Trading Company Ltd., 9 Battery Road, 21-00 Straits Trading Building, Singapore 049910.

HOWELL, Francis Clark, PH.D.; American professor of anthropology; b. 27 Nov. 1925, Kansas City, Mo.; s. of E. Ray and Myrtle M. Howell; m. Betty Ann Tomsen 1955; one s. one d.; ed. Univ. of Chicago; Instructor in Anatomy, Washington Univ. 1953–55; Asst. Prof. of Anthropology, Univ. of Chicago 1955–59, Assoc. Prof. of Anthropology 1959–62, Prof. of Anthropology 1962–70; Prof. of Anthropology, Univ. of Calif., Berkeley 1970–92, Emer. Prof. 1992–; mem. N.A.S., American Philosophical Soc.; Fellow American Acad. of Arts and Sciences; Foreign mem. Acad. des Sciences Paris; Trustee, Fellow and fmr. Pres., Calif. Acad. of Science. *Publications:* African Ecology and Early Man (ed.) 1963, Early Man 1965, Earliest man and environments in the Rudolf Basin (ed.) 1975; numerous papers on anthropology in professional journals. *Address:* Laboratory for Human Evolutionary Studies, Museum of Vertebrate Zoology, University of California, Berkeley, CA 94720; 1994 San Antonio, Berkeley, CA 94707, U.S.A. (Home). *Telephone:* (510) 642-1393 (Office); (510) 524-6243 (Home).

HOWELL, Margaret, DIP.A.D.; British couturier; b. 5 Sept. 1946, Tadworth; d. of E. H. Howell; m. Paul Renshaw 1974 (divorced 1987); one s. one d.; ed. Tadworth Primary School, Deburgh Co-Educational, Goldsmith's Coll., London; 1st Margaret Howell Collection 1972; opened first London shop 1977; opened flagship shop, Beauchamp Place, London 1987; opened Margaret Howell (France) 1996; over 50 retail outlets worldwide by end of 1996; Co. Dir. Margaret Howell Ltd. 1985–; Designer of the Year. *Leisure interests:* films, art exhbns., visiting country houses and gardens, walking, the countryside. *Address:* Margaret Howell (87), Ltd., 5 Garden House, 8 Battersea Park Road, London, SW8 4BG, England.

HOWELL OF GUILDFORD, Baron (Life Peer) cr. 1997, of Penton Mewsey in the County of Hampshire; **David Arthur Russell Howell,** P.C., B.A.; British politician, journalist and economist; b. 18 Jan. 1936, London; s. of the late Col. Arthur Howell and of Beryl Howell; m. Davina Wallace 1967; one s. two d.; ed. Eton Coll., King's Coll., Cambridge; Lieut. Coldstream Guards 1954–56; Econ. Section, H.M. Treasury 1959, resgnd. 1960; Leader-writer The Daily Telegraph 1960; Chair. Bow Group 1961–62; fmr. ed. Crossbow; M.P. for Guildford 1966–97; a Lord Commr. of Treasury 1970–71; with Civil Service Dept. 1970–72; Parl. Under-Sec. Dept. of Employment 1971–72; Minister of State, Northern Ireland Office 1972–74, Dept. of Energy Jan.-Feb. 1974; Sec. of State for Energy 1979–81, for Transport 1981–83; Chair. House of Commons Foreign Affairs Cttee. 1987–97, One Nation Group of Conservative M.Ps 1987–97; U.K.-Japan 2000 Group 1990–97; Dir. Conservative Political Centre 1964–66; Dir. Monks Investment Trust, John Laing Investments PLC; Advisory Dir. SBC-Warburg, Dillon Read; Visiting Fellow, Nuffield Coll., Oxford 1993–; Gov. Sadler's Wells Foundation. *Publications:* Principle in Practice (co-author) 1960, The Conservative Opportunity 1965, Freedom and Capital 1981, Blind Victory 1986. *Leisure interests:* family life, writing. *Address:* House of Lords, Westminster, London, SW1A 0PW; Chalkcroft Farm, Penton Mewsey, Andover, Hampshire, SP11 0RL, England.

HOWELLS, Anne Elizabeth; British opera and concert singer; b. 12 Jan. 1941, Southport, Lancs.; d. of Trevor and Mona Howells; m. 1st Ryland Davies (q.v.) 1966 (divorced 1981); m. 2nd Stafford Dean 1981; one s. one d.; ed. Sale County Grammar School, Royal Manchester Coll. of Music; three seasons in Chorus with Glyndebourne Festival Opera 1964–66, took leading role at short notice in L'Ormindo (Cavalli) 1967, subsequent roles include Dorabella in Così fan tutte, Cathleen in world premiere Rising of the Moon (Nicholas Maw), Composer in Ariadne, Diana in Calisto; with Royal Opera House, Covent Garden 1969–71, appearing as Lena in world premiere of Victory (Richard Rodney Bennett), Rosina in The Barber of Seville, Cherubino in The Marriage of Figaro; Guest Artist with Royal Opera House 1973–; has also appeared with Welsh Nat. Opera, Scottish Opera, English Nat. Opera, Chicago Opera, Geneva Opera, Metropolitan Opera, New York, Lyons Opera, Marseilles Opera, Nantes Opera, Netherlands Opera, and in Naples, San Francisco and in Belgium and at La Scala, and Salzburg Festival 1976 and 1980 (Tales of Hoffmann and film version of Clemenza di Tito), and in Hamburg and Berlin; Fellow Royal Manchester Coll. of Music. *Leisure interests:* cinema, reading. *Address:* c/o IMG Artists, Media House, 3 Burlington Lane, London, W4 2TH, England.

HOWELLS, William White, D.SC., PH.D., F.S.A.; American anthropologist; b. 27 Nov. 1908, New York; s. of John Mead Howells and Abby MacDougall White; m. Muriel Gurdon Seabury 1929; one s. one d.; ed. St. Paul's School, Concord, N.H. and Harvard Univ; Asst. Prof. to Prof., Univ. of Wis. 1939–54; Ed. American Journal of Physical Anthropology 1949–54; Prof. of Anthropology, Harvard Univ. 1954–74, Emer. 1974–; Curator of Somatology, Peabody Museum 1955–75, Honorary Curator 1975–; Pres. American Anthropological Asscn. 1951; F.S.A.; mem. N.A.S., American Acad. of Arts and Sciences; Corresp. mem. Royal Soc. of S.A., Austrian Acad. of Sciences, Anthropological Socs. of Paris and Vienna, Soc. of Antiquaries of London, Geographical Soc. of Lisbon, Spanish Soc. for Biological Anthropology; Hon. Foreign Fellow, Indian Anthropological Asscn.; Viking Fund Medal in Physical Anthropology 1955, Hon. D.Sc. (Beloit College) 1975, (Witwatersrand Univ.) 1985; Hon. Fellow, School of American Research 1975; Distinguished Service Award, American Anthropological Asscn. 1978, Darwin Lifetime Achievement Award, Physical Anthropologists Asscn. 1992; Broca Prix du Centenaire, Anthropological Soc. of Paris 1980, Viking Fund Medal and Award 1954. *Publications:* Mankind So Far 1944, The Heathens 1948, Back of History (British edn. Man in the Beginning) 1954, Mankind in the Making 1959, Ideas on Human Revolution (ed.) 1962, The Pacific Islanders 1973, Cranial Variation in Man 1973, Evolution of the Genus Homo 1973, Multivariate Statistical Methods in Physical Anthropology 1984 (Ed.), Skull Shapes and the Map 1989, Getting Here 1993, Who's Who in Skulls 1995. *Leisure interest:* travel. *Address:* 11 Lawrence Lane, Kittery Point, ME 03905, U.S.A. *Telephone:* (207) 439-1302. *Fax:* (207) 439-1380.

HOWIE, Archibald, C.B.E., PH.D., F.R.S.; British university professor and research physicist; b. 8 March 1934, Kirkcaldy, Scotland; s. of Robert Howie and Margaret Marshall McDonald; m. Melva Jean Scott 1964; one s. (deceased), one d.; ed. Kirkcaldy High School, Univ. of Edinburgh, California Inst. of Tech., U.S.A., Univ. of Cambridge; ICI Research Fellow (Cavendish Lab.) and Research Fellow (Churchill Coll., Cambridge) 1960–; Demonstrator in Physics (Cavendish Lab.) 1961–65; Teaching Fellow and Dir. of Studies in Physics (Churchill Coll.) 1961–, Lecturer 1965–79, Reader 1979–86, Prof. 1986–, Head of Dept. of Physics 1989–97; part-time Consultant Union Carbide Corpn. 1977–78, World Bank China Univ. Devt. Programme 1984, Norwegian Research Council 1986; Dir. (non-exec.) NPL Man. Ltd. 1995–; Pres. Royal Microscopical Soc. 1984–86, Int. Fed. of Socs. for Electron Microscopy 1999–; Hon. Fellow Royal Soc. of Edin. 1995; Hon. Dr. of Physics

(Univ. of Bologna) 1989, (Univ. of Thessaloniki) 1995; C. V. Boys Prize (jtly), Guthrie Medal, Inst. of Physics 1992; Hon. Fellow, Royal Microscopical Soc.; Hughes Medal (jtly), Royal Soc., Distinguished Scientist Award and Hon. mem. Electron Microscopy Soc. of America. *Publications:* Electron Microscopy of Thin Crystals (Jt. author) 1965 and numerous articles on electron microscopy and related subjects in scientific journals. *Leisure interest:* making wine. *Address:* 194 Huntingdon Road, Cambridge, CB3 0LB, England (Home). *Telephone:* (01223) 570977 (Home). *Fax:* (01223) 363263 (Office).

HOWIE, J. Robert, B.A., B.C.L., Q.C.; Canadian politician; b. 29 Oct. 1929, Fredericton, New Brunswick; s. of James R. Howie and Mary L. Pond; m. Nancy Goulding 1955; one s. three d.; ed. University of New Brunswick; solicitor, Oromocto 1962–72; Clerk of the New Brunswick Legislature 1970–72; mem. House of Commons 1972, 1974; Minister of State (Transport) 1979–80, 1984; Presiding mem. Veterans' Appeal Board 1990–93; lawyer, pvt. practice 1993; Progressive Conservative. *Leisure interests:* curling, hockey, theatre, swimming. *Address:* 678 Churchill Row, Fredericton, New Brunswick, Canada.

HOWLIN, Brendan; Irish politician; b. 9 May 1956, Wexford; ed. St. Patrick's Teachers' Training Coll. Dublin; fmr. school teacher; mem. Wexford Co. Council 1985; Alderman, Wexford Borough Council 1985–, Mayor 1986–87; Senator 1982–87; Deputy to Dáil 1987–, Chief Whip, Labour Party 1987; Minister of Health 1993–94, for Transport, Energy and Communications 1994, of the Environment 1994–97. *Address:* c/o Department of the Environment, Custom House, Dublin 1, Ireland.

HØYEM, Tom, M.A.; Danish politician, teacher, journalist and fmr. businessman; b. 10 Oct. 1941, Nykøbing, Falster; s. of Ove Charles Høyem and Karen Høyem; m. Inge-Lise Bredelund 1969; one s. one d.; ed. Univ. of Copenhagen; schoolteacher 1960–64; teacher, Skt Jørgens Gymnasium 1964–80; sr. master, Foreningen Norden, Sweden 1967–68; businessman 1968–75; co-founder, Chair. Centre Democratic Party 1973; Asst. Prof. of Danish Language and Literature, Univ. of Stockholm 1975–79; Danish corresp. for the Berlingske Tidende in Sweden 1975–80; headmaster Høng Gymnasium 1979; Sec. of State for Greenland 1982–87; Headmaster European School, Culham 1987–94; Headmaster European School, Munich 1994–; co-founder of European Folk High School, Møn, Denmark and of similar insts. in Sicily, Austria, Ireland and Luxembourg; leader of European Movt. West Zeeland, Denmark 1980–82; Hon. Pres. European Inst. Luxembourg 1983; election observer in Albania and Bosnia 1996; mem. "Let Bosnia Live" Goodwill Amb. for Copenhagen; mem. Ausländerbeirat, Munich 1997–; Kt. of the Dannebrog. *Publications:* Avisens spiseseddel-avisens ansigt 1975, Tabloidetik i Norden 1976, Mulighedernes Samfund 1985, Laegaest 1985, Dagens Grønland 1986, There is Something Wonderful in the State of Denmark 1987, Gud, Konge, Faedreland 1987, Nordisk i Europa 1988. *Leisure interests:* politics, reading. *Address:* European School, Elise Aulinger Strasse 21, 81739 Munich, Germany.

HOYLAND, John, R.A.; British artist; b. 12 Oct. 1934, Sheffield; s. of John Kenneth and Kathleen Hoyland; m. Airi Karkainen 1958 (dissolved 1968); one s.; ed. Sheffield Coll. of Art and Crafts and Royal Acad. Schools; taught Hornsey School of Art 1960–61; Chelsea School of Art 1962–70, Prin. Lecturer 1965–69; St. Martin's School of Art 1974–77; Slade School of Fine Art 1974–77, 1979–89; Charles A. Dana Prof., Colgate Univ., Hamilton, N.Y., U.S.A. 1972; Artist in Residence, Studio School, New York 1978, Melbourne Univ., Australia 1979; has exhibited all over the world; exhibited ceramic and glass sculptures 1994; recent one-man exhbns. include Annandale Gallery, Sydney, Australia 1997, Royal Acad., London 1999; Selector, Hayward Annual and Silver Jubilee R.A. Exhbns. 1979; Faculty mem. and Visitor, British School at Rome 1984; Curator, Hans Hofman Exhbn., Tate Gallery, London 1988; Young Artist Int. Award, Tokyo 1963; Gulbenkian Foundation Award 1963; Peter Stuyvesant Travel Award 1964; John Moores Exhbn. Prize 1965; First Prize Edin. Open 100 1969; Chichester Nat. Art Award 1975; Arts Council of G.B. Purchase Award 1979; First Prize John Moores Exhbn. 1982; Order of the Southern Cross (Brazil) 1986; First Prize Athena Award, Barbican Gallery, London 1987; Charles Wollaston Award 1998. *Address:* 41 Charterhouse Square, London, EC1M 6EA, England.

HOYLE, Sir Fred, Kt., M.A., F.R.S.; British astronomer, mathematician and author; b. 24 June 1915, Gilstead, Bingley, Yorks.; s. of Ben and Mabel (née Pickard) Hoyle; m. Barbara Clark 1939; one s. one d.; ed. Bingley Grammar School and Emmanuel Coll. and St. John's Coll., Cambridge; Fellow, St. John's Coll. 1939–72, Hon. Fellow 1973–; Univ. lecturer in Mathematics, Cambridge 1945–58; Staff mem. Mount Wilson and Palomar Observatories, Calif., U.S.A. 1956–62; Plumian Prof. of Astronomy and Experimental Philosophy, Cambridge Univ. 1958–72, Dir. Inst. of Theoretical Astronomy 1966–72; Visiting Prof. of Astrophysics at Calif. Inst. of Technology 1963–; Hon. Research Prof. of Physics and Astronomy, Manchester Univ. 1972–; Visiting Prof. at Large, Cornell Univ. 1973–79; Hon. research Prof. Cardiff Univ. 1975–; Prof. of Astronomy Royal Institution 1969–72; Hon. mem. American Acad. of Arts and Sciences 1964, Royal Irish Acad. 1977, Mark Twain Soc. 1978; Foreign Assoc. Nat. Acad. of Sciences 1969; Vice-Pres. Royal Soc. 1970–71; Pres. Royal Astronomical Soc. 1971–73; Foreign Mem. American Philosophical Soc. 1980; Hon. Fellow, Emmanuel Coll., Cambridge 1983, Inst. of Astronomy, Cambridge Univ. 1996; Hon. Sc.D. (East Anglia) 1967, Hon. D.Sc. (Leeds) 1969, (Bradford) 1975, (Newcastle) 1976; Mayhew Prizeman 1936, Smith's Prizeman 1938, Goldsmith Exhibitioner 1938, Sr. Exhibitioner Royal Comm. of 1851 1938, Kalinga Prize 1968, Balzan Prize 1994, Annenberg Award in Astronomy Educ., American Astronomical Soc. 1996, Gold Medal, Royal Astronomical Soc. 1968, Bruce Medal, Astronomical Soc. of the Pacific 1970, Royal Medal, Royal Soc. 1974, Dorothea Klumpke Roberts Award, Astronomical Soc. of the Pacific 1977, Dag Hammarskjöld Gold Medal, Académie Diplomatique de la Paix 1986, Karl Schwarzchild Medal, German Astronomical Soc. 1992, Balzan Prize 1994, Annenberg Award for Astronomy Educ. American Astronomical Soc. 1996, Crafoord Prize 1997. *Publications:* Recent Research in Solar Physics 1949, Nature of the Universe 1950, Decade of Decision 1953, Frontiers of Astronomy 1955, The Black Cloud (novel) 1957, Ossian's Ride 1958, A for Andromeda (television series with John Elliot) 1962, Astronomy 1962, Fifth Planet (with Geoffrey Hoyle) 1963, Of Men and Galaxies 1964, Galaxies, Nuclei and Quasars 1965, October First is too late 1966, Man in the Universe 1966, Rockets in Ursa Major (with Geoffrey Hoyle) 1969, Seven Steps to the Sun (with Geoffrey Hoyle) 1970, The Molecule Men (with Geoffrey Hoyle) 1971, From Stonehenge to Modern Cosmology 1972, The Inferno (with Geoffrey Hoyle) 1972, Nicolaus Copernicus 1973, Into Deepest Space (with Geoffrey Hoyle) 1974, Action at a Distance in Physics and Cosmology 1974, Highlights in Astronomy (U.S.)/Astronomy Today (U.K.) 1975, Astronomy and Cosmology 1975, Ten Faces of the Universe 1977, On Stonehenge 1977, The Incandescent Ones (with Geoffrey Hoyle) 1977, Energy or Extinction: the case for Nuclear Energy 1977, Lifecloud (with N. C. Wickramasinghe) 1978, The Westminster Disaster (novel, with Geoffrey Hoyle) 1978, Diseases from Space (with N. C. Wickramasinghe) 1979, Physics-Astronomy Frontier (with J. V. Narlikar) 1980, Common Sense in Nuclear Energy (with Geoffrey Hoyle) 1980, Space Travellers, the Origins of Life (with N. C. Wickramasinghe) 1980, Evolution from Space (with N. C. Wickramasinghe), Ice: The Ultimate Human Catastrophe 1981, The Giants of Universal Park, The Frozen Planet of Azuron, The Energy Pirate, The Planet of Death (children's stories) 1982, The Intelligent Universe 1983, Comet Halley 1985, The Small World of Fred Hoyle 1986, Cosmic Life Force (jtly.) 1988, The Theory of Cosmic Grains (jtly.) 1991, Our Place in the Cosmos (jtly.) 1993, Home is Where the Wind Blows (autobiog.) 1994. *Leisure interests:* music, mountaineering. *Address:* c/o The Royal Society, 6 Carlton House Terrace, London, SW1Y 5AG, England.

HOYTE, Hugh Desmond, S.C., B.A., LL.B.; Guyanese politician; b. 9 March 1929, Georgetown; s. of George Alphonso Hoyte and Gladys Marietta Hoyte; m. Joyce Noreen (née De Freitas) Hoyte 1965; two d. (deceased); ed. Progressive High School, Univ. of London and Middle Temple, London; master at Grenada Boys' Secondary School 1955–57; mem. Legal Practitioners' Cttee. 1964–68; Sec. Guyana Bar Asscn. 1962–66, Vice-Pres. 1967–68; Chair. Customs Tariff Tribunal 1966–69; Chair. Timber Grants Wages Council 1967–68; mem. Elections Comm. 1967–68; elected M.P. 1968; Minister of Home Affairs 1969–70, of Finance 1970–72, of Works and Communications 1972–74, of Econ. Devt. 1974; then mem. Admin. Cttee., Cen. Exec. Cttee. and Gen. Council of the People's Nat. Congress, Vice-Pres., responsible for Econ. Planning and Finance and subsequently Production, Leader 1985–92; First Vice-Pres. and Prime Minister 1984; Pres. Co-operative Repub. of Guyana 1985–92, also responsible for Home Affairs and Public Information. *Leisure interests:* music, reading. *Address:* 14 North Road, Bourda, Georgetown, Guyana. *Telephone:* 60182. *Fax:* 60871.

HRAWI, Elias; Lebanese politician and businessman; b. 1930, Zahle; President of Lebanon 1989–98; fmr. Maronite Christian deputy. *Address:* c/o Office of the President, Baabda, Beirut, Lebanon.

HRIVŇÁK, Ivan, DR.SC.; Slovak professor of physical metallurgy and materials science; b. 23 Dec. 1931, Komárno; s. of Ján Hrivňák and Margita Hrivňáková (née Kocisová); m. Dása Hrivnáková 1953; one s. one d.; ed. Faculty of Mechanical Eng. Slovak Tech. Univ. Bratislava; Head, Div. of Fundamental Labs. in Welding Research Inst., Bratislava; Prof. of Physical Metallurgy and Material Science; Rector of Tech. Univ. Košice 1991–94; Pres. Slovak Acad. of Sciences 1989–90; Vice-Pres. Int. Inst. of Welding 1992–94; mem. Czechoslovak Acad. of Sciences, Slovak Acad. of Sciences, Ukraine Acad. of Sciences. *Publications:* numerous articles on physics of metallurgy and welding. *Leisure interests:* motor-boating, gardening. *Address:* Department of Materials Science, Faculty of Materials Science and Technology, Slovak University of Technology, ul. J. Bottu 23, 917 24 Trnava, Slovakia. *Telephone:* (805) 552 1002 ext. 28. *Fax:* (805) 552 1119.

HROUDA, Barthel, DR.PHIL.; German academic; b. 28 June 1929, Berlin; s. of Fritz Hrouda and Frieda Hrouda; m. Helma Plugge 1957; two s. one d.; ed. Gymnasium Graues Kloster Berlin and Freie Universität Berlin; Lecturer, Univ. of Saarbrücken 1963; Prof. Univ. of Munich 1963–64, 1969–94, Univ. of Berlin 1964–69; mem. German Inst. of Archaeology, Munich and Brussels Acads. *Publications:* Kulturgeschichte assyrischen Flachbildes 1965, Handbuch der Archaeologie, Vorderasien 1971, Isin-Išān Bahrīyāt I-IV 1977, 1981, 1987, 1991, Der Alte Orient 1991, Mesopotamien 1997. *Leisure interest:* travel. *Address:* Sternstrasse 4B, 82110 Germering, Germany. *Telephone:* 845549.

HSIAO WAN-CH'ANG (Vincent C. Siew), M.A.; Taiwanese politician and civil servant; b. 3 Jan. 1939; m. Susan Chu; three d.; ed. Nat. Chengchi Univ.; Vice-Consul, Kuala Lumpur 1966–69, Consul 1969–72; Section Chief Ministry of Foreign Affairs 1972; Deputy Dir., Dir. 4th Dept. Bd. of Foreign Trade 1972–77, Deputy Dir.-Gen. 1977–82, Dir.-Gen. 1982–88; Vice-Chair.

Council for Econ. Planning and Devt. 1988–89, Chair. 1993–94; Dir. Kuomintang Cen. Cttee. Dept. of Organisational Affairs 1989–90; Minister of Econ. Affairs 1990–93; mem. Kuomintang Cen. Cttee., Cen. Standing Cttee. 1993–; Chair. Mainland Affairs Council 1994; rep. for Chiayi, Legis. Council; Eisenhower Exchange Fellow 1985. *Publication:* Research on Improvement of the Foreign Trade Structure. *Address:* 16th Floor, 4 Chung Hsiao W. Road, Section 1, Taipei, Taiwan.

HSÜ, Kenneth Jinghwa, M.A., PH.D.; Swiss professor of geology; b. 28 June 1929, China; s. of Sin-wu Hsü and Su-lan; m. 1st Ruth Grunder 1958 (deceased); two s. one d.; m. 2nd Christine Eugster 1966; one s.; ed. Chinese Nat. Univ., Nanking, Ohio State Univ., Univ. of Calif. at Los Angeles and ETH, Zürich; Research Geologist and Research Assoc. Shell Devt. Co., Houston, Tex. 1954–63; Assoc. Prof. State Univ. of New York, Binghamton, N.Y. 1963–64; Assoc. Prof. Univ. of Calif. Riverside 1964–67; Prof. Swiss Fed. Inst. of Tech. (ETH), Zürich 1967–94; Pres. Tarim Assocs. AG; Pres. Int. Asscn. of Sedimentologists 1978–82; Chair. Int. Marine Geology Comm. 1980–89; Hon. Prof. Chinese Acad. of Sciences; Foreign Assoc. N.A.S.; mem. Acad. Sinica (Taiwan); Fellow, Inst. of Advanced Studies, Berlin 1995–96; Assoc. Fellow Third World Acad. of Sciences; Dr. h.c. (Nanjing Univ.) 1994; Wollaston Gold Medal, Geological Soc. of London; Twenhofel Medal, American Sedimentological Soc. *Publications:* Ein Schiff revolutioniert die Wissenschaft 1982, The Mediterranean was a Desert 1984, The Great Dying 1986, Challenger at Sea 1994, Geology of Switzerland 1995, Tectonic Facies Map of China 1996; other books and more than 300 scientific articles. *Leisure interest:* Chinese aerophilately. *Address:* Frohburgstr. 96, 8006 Zürich, Switzerland. *Telephone:* (1) 362 1462. *Fax:* (1) 364 3231.

HSU CHING-CHUNG, D.AGRIC.; Taiwanese politician (retd.); b. 19 July 1907, Taipei; s. of Teh An Hsu and Shyh Iuan Hung; m. Huang Tsen; two s. one d.; ed. Taipei Acad., Taipei Imperial Univ; Prof., Nat. Taiwan Univ. 1945–47; Dir. Agricultural and Forestry Admin., Taiwan Provincial Govt. 1947–49; Commr. Dept. of Agric. and Forestry, Taiwan Provincial Govt. 1949–54, Commr. 1954–57; mem. Cen. Planning and Evaluation Cttee., China Nationalist Party 1955–61, Deputy Sec.-Gen. Cen. Cttee. 1961–66; Minister of the Interior 1966–72; Vice-Premier of Exec. Yuan 1972–81; mem. Standing Cttee., Taiwan Land Bank 1946–67, China Farmers' Bank 1967–72; Medal of Clouds and Banner. *Publications:* several studies on agricultural problems in Taiwan. *Leisure interests:* horticulture, reading, painting, golf. *Address:* 180 Yenping S. Road, Taipei, Taiwan.

HSU LI-TEH, LL.M, M.P.A.; Taiwanese politician; b. 6 Aug. 1931, Loshan County, Honan; m.; two s.; ed. Taiwan Provincial Coll. of Law and Commerce, Nat. Chengchi Univ. and Harvard Univ.; Dir. Fifth Dept. Exec. Yuan 1972–76; Admin. Vice-Minister of Finance 1976–78; Commr. Dept. of Finance, Taiwan Provincial Govt. 1978–81; Minister of Finance 1981–84, of Econ. Affairs 1984–85; Chair. Lien-ho Jr. Coll. of Tech., Global Investment Holding Co. Ltd. 1986–88; Chair. Finance Comm. Cen. Cttee. Kuomintang 1988–93; Deputy Sec.-Gen. and Exec. Sec. Policy Coordination Comm. Cen. Cttee. Kuomintang 1990–93; Vice-Premier of Taiwan 1993–97. *Address:* c/o National Assembly, Taipei, Taiwan.

HSU SHUI-TEH, M.A.; Taiwanese politician; b. 1 Aug. 1931, Kaohsiung City; m. Yang Shu-hua; two s.; ed. Nat. Taiwan Normal Univ., Nat. Chengchi Univ. and Japan Univ. of Educ.; official, Pingtung County Govt. 1968–70, Kaohsiung City Govt. 1970–75; Commr. Dept. of Social Affairs, Taiwan Provincial Govt. 1975–79; Dir. Dept. of Social Affairs, Cen. Cttee., Kuomintang 1979; Sec.-Gen. Kaohsiung City Govt. 1979–82; Mayor of Kaohsiung 1982–85, of Taipei 1985–88; Minister of the Interior 1988–91; Rep. Taipei Econ. and Culture Rep. Office in Japan 1991–93; Hon. LL.D. (Lincoln Univ.) 1985. *Publications:* The Childhood Education of Emile, My Compliments—Recollections of Those Days Serving as Kaohsiung Mayor, A Thousand Sunrises and Midnights, My Scoopwheel Philosophy, A Study of Welfare Administration for the Aged, several works on psychology and educ. *Address:* c/o Kuomintang, 53 Jen Ai Road, Section 3, Taipei, Taiwan.

HU, Jason Chih-chiang, PH.D.; Taiwanese official; b. 15 May 1948, Kirin Prov., China; m. Shirley S. Hu; one s. one d.; ed. Nat. Chengchi Univ., Univ. of Southampton, Univ. of Oxford; Exec. Sec. Nat. Union of Students 1966–68; Youth Rep. del. to second conf. of World League for Freedom and Democracy 1968; led del. to U.N. World Youth Congress 1970; fmr. instructor Inst. of Int. Studies, Univ. of S.C., U.S.A.; taught Oxford Overseas Studies Prog. 1982–83, Research Fellow St. Antony's Coll., Univ. of Oxford 1985; Assoc. Prof. Nat. Sun Yat-sen Univ. 1986–90; Chief Nat. Unification Council Conf. Dept. 1990; Deputy Dir. First Bureau, Office of the Pres. concurrently Presidential Press Officer 1991; fmr. Dir.-Gen. Govt. Information Office, Exec. Br. and Govt. Spokesman; fmr. Rep. of Taipei Econ. and Cultural Office, Washington, D.C.; Minister of Foreign Affairs Oct. 1997–; Deputy Sec.-Gen. Asian Pacific League for Freedom and Democracy 1986–89; Sec.-Gen. Repub. of China Chapter of World League for Freedom and Democracy 1989–91; Deputy Sec.-Gen. for Strategic Studies 1989. *Publications include:* On the Role of PLA in Post-Mao Chinese Politics, Chinese Politics After Mao 1977, numerous articles on Chinese and strategic affairs. *Address:* Ministry of Foreign Affairs, 2 Chiehshou Road, Taipei 10016, Taiwan. *Telephone:* (2) 3119292. *Fax:* (2) 3144972.

HU CHUANZHI; Chinese business executive; b. 1932; joined CCP 1957; a Vice-Chair. Shanghai Municipal 10th People's Congress, Standing Cttee. 1990–; Gen. Man. of China State Shipbldg. Corpn. 1993. *Address:* China State Shipbuilding Corporation, 5 Yuetan Beijie Street, Beijing 100861, People's Republic of China.

HU FUGUO; Chinese administrator and engineer; b. 1937, Changzi Co., Shanxi Prov.; ed. Fuxin Mining Coll.; Dir. Xishan Coal Mining Admin. of Shanxi Prov., 1978–82, Gov. (a.i.) of Shanxi Prov. 1992–93; Sec. CPC 6th Shanxi Provincial Cttee. 1993–; Chair. CPC 7th Shanxi Provincial Ctte. 1994–; Vice-Minister of Coal Industry 1982–88; Vice-Minister of Energy 1988; mem. State Econ. Examination Cttee. 1983; mem. 14th CCP Cen. Cttee. 1992–97, 15th CCP Cen. Cttee. 1997–. *Address:* Shanxi Provincial Committee of CCP, Taiyuan, People's Republic of China.

HU HAN, PH.D.; Chinese academic; s. of Hu Yen Bo and Xiao Shi Xun; m. Dong Yu Shen; one d.; ed. Central Univ., Zhongqing; Lab. of Genetics & Breeding, Dept. of Biology Univ. of Leningrad, U.S.S.R.; Asst. Prof. of Inst. of Genetics, Academia Sinica 1964–78; Assoc. Prof. 1977–87, Dir. 1978–96, Prof. 1992–; Chair. of Scientific Cttee. of State Key Lab. of Plant Cell & Chromosome Eng.; Vice-Pres. Genetics Soc. of China 1991; Ed. of Science in China and Chinese Sciences Bulletin 1978–91, of Theoretical Applied Genetics 1982–, of Plant Science 1992–; Nat. Science Congress Prize 1978, Maj. Prize, Academia Sinica 1978. *Publications:* (co-ed.) Haploids of Higher Plants in Vitro. 1986, Plant Somatic Genetics & Crop Improvement 1988, Plant Cell Manipulation & Breeding 1990, numerous articles on androgenesis in cereals and chromosome eng. of pollen-derived plants in wheat. *Address:* Institute of Genetics, Academia Sinica, Bei Sha Tan Building, Beijing 100101, People's Republic of China.

HU JINTAO; Chinese party and state official; b. Dec. 1942, Jixi Co., Anhui Prov.; ed. Qinghua Univ.; joined CCP 1964; alt. mem. 12th CCP Cen. Cttee. 1982, mem. 1985; Dir. Construction Comm., Gansu Prov. Govt. 1980–82; Sec. Gansu Prov. Branch Communist Youth League 1982; Sec. Communist Youth League 1982–85; mem. Standing Cttee., 6th NPC, mem. Presidium and mem. Standing Cttee., CPPCC 6th Nat. Cttee. 1983–98; Vice-Pres. of People's Repub. of China 1998–; Sec. CCP Cttee., Guizhou 1985–88, Tibet 1988–92; mem. 13th CCP Cen. Cttee. 1987–92, 14th CCP Cen. Cttee. 1992–97, Sec., Secr. 1992–; mem. 15th CCP Cen. Cttee. 1997–; Pres. Cen. Party School 1993–; mem. CCP Politburo Standing Cttee. 1992–, Head Cen. Leading Group for Party Bldg. Work. *Address:* Central Committee of the Chinese Communist Party, 1 Zhong Nan Hai, Beijing, People's Republic of China.

HU JIWEI; Chinese journalist; b. 1916, Weiyuan, Sichuan Prov.; Deputy Dir. Information Bureau, North-West China Mil. and Admin. Council 1950; Ed.-in-Chief and Deputy Dir. The Masses Daily, Xian 1950; Ed.-in-Chief N.W. Branch Xinhua News Agency and N.W. People's Broadcasting Station 1950; Deputy Ed.-in-Chief People's Daily 1953–66, Ed.-in-Chief 1977–82, Dir. 1982–83; Pres. Beijing Journalism Studies Soc. 1980–89; mem. Standing Cttee. 6th and 7th NPC 1983–90; Vice-Chair. Educ., Science, Culture and Public Health Cttee., NPC 1983–90; Pres. Chinese Confed. of Societies of Journalism 1984–90. *Address:* Renmin Ribao, Jin Tai Xi Lu, Beijing, People's Republic of China.

HU KEHUI; Chinese politician; b. Feb. 1944, Anshun, Guizhou Prov.; ed. Southwest Univ. of Political Science and Law; joined CCP 1971; Chief Procurator of Guizhou Prov. People's Procuratorate 1993–98; Vice-Chair. Supreme People's Procuratorate 1998–. *Address:* Supreme People's Procuratorate, Beijing, People's Republic of China.

HU LIJIAO; Chinese party official; b. 1914, Jiangxi; m. Gu Ming; one s.; joined CCP 1930; took part in Long March as mem. Little Devils 1934; Deputy Dir. Org. Dept. E. China Bureau 1950; Vice-Chair. People's Control Cttee., E. China Mil. and Admin. Council (ECMAC) 1951, Dir. Personnel Dept. ECMAC 1951, Vice-Chair. Labour Employment Cttee. ECMAC 1952; Vice-Minister of Finance 1954–58; Sec. CCP Cttee. Ministry of Finance 1954–58; Prin. Cadres School, Ministry of Finance 1957–58; 1st Sec. Secr., Songjiang Dist., Heilongjiang CP 1958; Deputy Dir. People's Bank of China 1961–66, Acting Pres. 1966; disappeared during Cultural Revolution; Deputy Sec. CCP Cttee., Henan 1975–77, 2nd Sec. 1977–; Vice-Chair. Prov. Revolutionary Cttee., Henan 1977–79; mem. 11th CCP Cen. Cttee. 1977; Chair. Standing Cttee. People's Congress, Henan 1979; 2nd Sec. CCP Cttee., Shanghai 1981–85; Chair. Municipal People's Congress, Shanghai 1981–; mem. 12th CCP Cen. Cttee. 1982–85; Deputy to 3rd, 5th and 6th NPC; mem. Presidium 6th NPC 1986; mem. Cen. Advisory Comm. CCP 1987–. *Leisure interests:* tennis, swimming, chess. *Address:* 200 The People's Square, Shanghai, People's Republic of China. *Telephone:* 289977.

HU PING; Chinese government official; b. 1930, Jiaxing Co., Zhejiang Prov.; ed. Jiangsu Industry Inst.; joined CCP 1950; Vice-Gov. of Fujian 1981–83; Sec. CCP Prov. Cttee. Fujian 1982; Deputy Sec. CCP Prov. Cttee., Fujian 1982; Dir. Fujian Cttee. for Econ. Reconstruction 1983; alt. mem. 12th CCP Cen. Cttee. 1982, mem. 1985; mem. 13th CCP Cen. Cttee. 1987–92, 14th CCP Cen. Cttee. 1992–; Sec. CCP Prov. Cttee. 1982–83; Acting Gov. of Fujian 1983, Gov. 1983–87 (removed from post); Vice-Minister, State Planning Comm. 1987–88; Minister of Commerce 1988–93; Dir. Special Econ. Zones Office 1993–96; Chair. Bd. of Regents, Overseas Chinese Univ. 1986. *Address:* c/o Ministry of Commerce, 45 Fuxingmen Nei Dajie, Beijing 100801, People's Republic of China.

HU QIHENG; Chinese scientist and administrator; b. 15 June 1934, Beijing; d. of Shu Wei Hu and Wen Yi Fan; m. Yuan Jian Lian 1959; one s. one d.;

ed. in U.S.S.R.; Dir. Inst. of Automation, Academia Sinica 1980–89; a Vice-Pres., Chinese Acad. of Sciences 1988–96; mem. CPPCC 1993–; Vice-Pres., China Asscn. for Science and Tech. 1996. *Leisure interests:* reading novels, growing flowers, pets (kittens and guinea-pigs), bicycling, computer drawing. *Address:* Chinese Academy of Sciences, 52 Sanlihe Road, Beijing 100864, People's Republic of China. *Fax:* (10) 62624476; 68512458.

HU QILI; Chinese politician; b. 1929, Yulin Co., Shaaxi Prov.; one s. one d.; Sec. Communist Youth League (CYL) Cttee., Beijing Univ. 1954; Vice-Chair. Students' Fed. 1954; mem. Standing Cttee., Youth Fed. 1958; Sec. CYL 1964, 1978; Vice-Chair. Youth Fed. 1965; purged 1967; Vice-Pres. Qinghua Univ., Beijing 1978; Sec. CYL 1978; Chair. Youth Fed. 1979–80; mem. Standing Cttee., 5th CPPCC 1979–83; Mayor, Tianjin 1979–82; Sec. CCP Cttee., Tianjin 1981–82; Dir. Gen. Office Cen. Cttee. CCP 1982–87; mem. 12th CCP Cen. Cttee. 1982–87, 13th CCP Cen. Cttee. 1987–92, Politburo 1982–89, Politburo Standing Cttee. 1987–89; Sec. Secr. CCP 1982–89; Vice-Chair. Cen. Party Consolidation Comm. 1983–89; mem. Presidium, 1st session 7th NPC; Vice-Minister of Electronics Industry and Machine-Bldg. Industry 1991–93; Minister of Electronics Industry 1993–98; mem. 14th CCP Cen. Cttee. 1992–97; Vice-Chair. 9th Nat. Cttee. of CPPCC 1998. *Leisure interests:* tennis, cycling. *Address:* National Committee of Chinese People's Political Consultative Conference, 23 Taipingqiao Street, Beijing 100823, People's Republic of China.

HU SHENG; Chinese party official, historian and philosopher: b. 11 Jan. 1918, Suzhou City, Jiangsu Prov.; ed. Beijing Univ.; joined CCP 1938; newspaper and book ed. 1938–48; Sec.-Gen. Propaganda Dept., CCP 1951; in political disgrace 1966–73; Dir. CCP History Research Centre 1982–; Pres. Soc. of Research into the History of the CCP 1983–; Deputy Sec.-Gen., Constitution Revision Cttee. 1982; mem. 12th Cen. Cttee., CCP 1982–87; Vice-Chair. CPPCC 7th Nat. Cttee. 1988–93, 8th Nat. Cttee. 1993–98; mem. Presidium 14th CCP Nat. Congress Oct. 1992; Pres. Sun Yat-sen Soc. 1984; Vice-Chair. Cttee. for Drafting Basic Law of Hong Kong Special Admin. Region 1985; Pres. Chinese Acad. of Social Sciences 1985–; Deputy Dir. Comm. for Commemorating 40th Anniversary of UN 1985; Pres. Postgraduate School, Chinese Acad. of Social Sciences 1985–90; Vice-Chair. Nat. Academic Degrees Cttee. 1988; Deputy Dir. Leading Group for Party History Work 1994–; Academician, European Acad. of Sciences 1990; Hon. Adviser, Soc. for Study of Mao Zedong's Poetry. *Publications:* Reason and Freedom 1946, Systems of Thought and Study 1946, Imperialism and Chinese Politics 1948, From Opium War to May 4th Movement 1981, Collected Works of Hu Sheng (9 vols.) 1996. *Address:* Chinese Academy of Social Sciences, Jianguo Mennei Dajie 5, 100732 Beijing, People's Republic of China. *Fax:* 86-10-5138154.

HU TSU TAU, Richard, PH.D.; Singaporean politician; b. 30 Oct. 1926; m. Irene Tan Dee Leng; one s. one d.; ed. Anglo-Chinese School, Univ. of California (Berkeley), U.S.A., Univ. of Birmingham, U.K.; Lecturer in Chemical Eng., Univ. of Manchester, U.K. 1958–60; joined Shell (Singapore and Malaysia) 1960, Dir. Marketing and Gen. Man. Shell (KL) 1970, with Shell Int. Petroleum Co., Netherlands 1973, Chief Exec. Shell Cos. (Malaysia) 1974, Chair. and Chief Exec. Shell Cos. (Singapore) 1977, Chair. 1982; Man. Dir. The Monetary Authority of Singapore and Man. Dir. Govt. of Singapore Investment Corpn. Pte. Ltd. 1983–84; elected M.P. (People's Action Party) 1984; Chair. The Monetary Authority of Singapore, Chair. Bd. of Commrs. of Currency 1985; Minister for Trade and Industry Jan.–May 1985, for Health 1985–87, for Finance 1985–, of Nat. Devt. 1992. *Leisure interests:* golf, swimming. *Address:* Ministry of Finance, 100 High Street, 09-01 The Treasury, Singapore 179434. *Telephone:* 2259911. *Fax:* 3327435.

HU YIZHOU; Chinese aviation administrator (retd.); b. 1928, Shanghai; engineer, Civil Aviation Admin. of China (CAAC) 1949–80; joined CCP 1960; Deputy Dir. Beijing Regional Admin. of CAAC 1980–82; Deputy Dir.-Gen. Civil Aviation Admin. 1982–85, Dir.-Gen. 1985–91, Advisor 1991–94. *Address:* c/o General Administration of Civil Aviation of China, 155 Dongsi Street West, Beijing 100710, People's Republic of China.

HUA GUOFENG; Chinese politician; b. 1920, Shanxi; m. Han Chih-chun; Vice-Gov. Hunan 1958–67; Sec. CCP Hunan 1959; Vice-Chair. Hunan Revolutionary Cttee. 1968, Chair. 1970; mem. 9th Cen. Cttee. of CCP 1969; First Sec. CCP Hunan 1970–77; Political Commissar Guangzhou Mil. Region, People's Liberation Army 1972; First Political Commissar Hunan Mil. District, PLA 1973; mem. Politburo, 10th Cen. Cttee. of CCP 1973; Deputy Premier and Minister of Public Security 1975–76, Acting Premier Feb.–April 1976, Premier 1976–81, Deputy Premier 1981; First Vice-Chair. Cen. Cttee. of CCP April–Oct. 1976, Chair. 1976–81; Chair. CCP Military Affairs Comm. 1976–81; Chair. and mem. Politburo, 11th Cen. Cttee. CCP 1977–81, Vice-Chair. 1981–82; mem. 12th CCP Cen. Cttee. 1982–87, 13th CCP Cen. Cttee. 1987–92, 14th CCP Cen. Cttee. 1992–97, 15th CCP Cen. Cttee. 1997–. *Address:* Central Committee, Zhongguo Gongchan Dang, Beijing, People's Republic of China.

HUANG, Rayson Lisung, C.B.E., J.P., D.SC., D.PHIL., F.R.C.P. (EDIN.); Chinese university vice-chancellor and retd. professor of chemistry; b. 1 Sept. 1920, Shantou, China; s. of Rufus and Roseland Huang; m. Grace Wei Li 1949; two s.; ed. Munsang Coll., Hong Kong, Univs of Hong Kong and Oxford; Demonstrator in Chemistry, Nat. Kwangsi Univ., Kweilin, China 1943; Post-Doctoral Fellow and Research Assoc., Univ. of Chicago 1947–50; lecturer in Chem. Univ. of Malaya, Singapore 1951–54, Reader in Chem. 1955–59; Prof. of Chem. Univ. of Malaya, Kuala Lumpur 1959–69, Dean of Science 1962–65; Vice-Chancellor, Nanyang Univ., Singapore 1969–72, Univ. of Hong Kong 1972–86; Pres. Asscn. of Southeast Asian Insts. of Higher Learning 1970–72, 1981–83; Chair. Council, Asscn. of Commonwealth Univs. 1980–81; unofficial mem. Legis. Council of Hong Kong 1977–83; Vice-Chair. of Council, Shantou Univ., China 1987–94; mem. Drafting Cttee. and Vice-Chair. Consultative Cttee. for Basic Law of the Hong Kong Special Admin. Region of the People's Repub. of China 1985–90; Life mem. of Court, Univ. of Hong Kong; Life mem. Bd. of Trustees Croucher Foundation, Hong Kong; Dir. Ming Pao Enterprise Corpn. Ltd., Hong Kong 1990–94; Hon. D.Sc. (Hong Kong); Hon. LL.D. (E. Asia, Macao); Order of the Rising Sun (Japan) 1986. *Publications:* Organic Chemistry of Free Radicals 1974; about 50 research papers on chemistry of free radicals, molecular rearrangements and synthetic oestrogens. *Leisure interests:* opera, ballet, concerts, violin-playing. *Address:* Raycrest II, 10 The Stables, Selly Park, Birmingham B29 7JW, England.

HUANG AN-LUN, M.M., F.T.C.L.; Chinese composer; b. 15 March 1949, Guangzhou City, Guangdong Prov.; s. of Huang Fei-Li and Zhao Fang-Xing; m. Ouyang Rui-Li 1974; one s.; ed. Central Conservatory of Music, Beijing, Univ. of Toronto, Canada, Trinity Coll. of Music, London and Yale Univ., U.S.A.; started piano aged 5; studied with Shaw Yuan-Xin and Chen Zi; works have been widely performed in China, Hong Kong, Philippines, northern Africa, Australia, Europe, U.S.A. and Canada; Resident Composer, Cen. Opera House of China 1976–; Deputy Dir. State Bureau of Materials and Equipment 1987–88; Vice-Minister of Materials 1990; Fellowship in Composition, Trinity Coll. of Music, London 1983; Yale Alumni Asscn. Prize, Yale Univ. 1986; *compositions:* operas: Flower Guardian op. 26 1979, Yeu Fei op. 37 1986 and 6 others; symphonic, chamber, vocal, choral and film music, including: Symphonic Concert op. 25, Symphonic Overture, The Consecration of the Spring in 1976 op. 25a 1977, Piano Concerto in G op. 25b 1982, Symphony in C op. 25c 1984, The Sword (symphonic poem) op. 33 1982, Easter Cantata (text by Semuel Tang) op. 38 1986; Psalm 22-A Cantata in Baroque Style op. 43c. 1988, Piano Concerto in G; ballets: The Little Match Girl op. 24 1978, A Dream of Dun Huang op. 29 1980, and 7 other records. *Leisure interests:* reading, sport. *Address:* The Central Opera House of China, Zuojia Zhuang, Out of Dongzhimen Gate, Beijing, People's Republic of China. *Telephone:* (416) 423-6396.

HUANG ANREN; Chinese artist; b. 8 Oct. 1924, Yangjiang County, Guandong; s. of Huang Ting Jin and Lin Fen; m. Tan Su 1941; two s. two d.; fmr. Vice-Sec.-Gen. Guangdong Branch, Chinese Artists' Asscn.; Chair. Guangzhou Hairi Research Inst. of Painting and Calligraphy; Adviser, Guangdong Writers' Asscn. of Popular Science. *Publications:* Selected Paintings of Huang Anren, Album of Sketches by Huang Anren, On Arts: Collection of Commentaries by Huang Anren. *Leisure interests:* literature, music. *Address:* Room 602, No 871-2 Renminbei Road, Guangzhou, People's Republic of China.

HUANG DA, M.A.; Chinese economist and academic; b. 22 Feb. 1925, Tianjin; m. Shu-zhen Luo 1952; two s.; ed. Northern China United Univ. 1946; Dir. Finance Dept. Renmin Univ. of China 1978–83, Vice-Pres. 1983–91, Pres. 1991–94; mem. Nat. People's Congress (NPC), NPC Cttee. on Finance & Econ. 1993–98; mem. and head of econ. group, Academic Degrees Cttee. of the State Council 1988–; mem. Monetary Policy Cttee. of People's Bank of China 1997–; Dir. Expert Advisory Cttee. on Humanities and Social Sciences Studies, State Educ. Comm. 1997–; currently in charge of the Eighth 5-Year Plan key projects: Marketization of Income, Distribution & Social Security and Restructuring Mechanism of Transition from Saving to Investment in Socialist Market Economic Systems; Vice-Chair. Chinese Soc. for Finance and Banking 1984–95 (Chair. 1995–), Chinese Soc. for Public Finance 1983–, Chinese Soc. for Prices 1986–, Chinese Soc. for Materials Circulation 1990–; Vice-Pres. China Enterprise Man. Asscn. and the Securities Asscn. of China 1987–; Council mem., Chinese Asscn. for Int. Understanding 1982–; Chair. Chinese Cttee. on Econs. Educ. Exchange with U.S.A. 1985–. *Publications include:* Money & Money Circulation in the Chinese Socialist Economy 1964, Socialist Fiscal & Financial Problems 1981, Introduction to the Overall Balancing of Public Finance and Bank Credit 1984, The Price Scissors on the Price Parities between Industrial and Agricultural Products 1990, The Economics of Money and Banking 1992, Macro-economic Control and Money Supply 1997. *Leisure interests:* calligraphy, running. *Address:* Office of the President, Renmin University of China, Beijing 100872, People's Republic of China.

HUANG DUFENG; Chinese artist; b. 1913, Jieyang Co., Guangdong; taught by Gao Jianfu; studied in Japan; returned to China from Indonesia 1960; taught fine arts in China; Prof. Guangxi Inst. of Fine Arts; Deputy Dir. Guangxi Branch, Chinese Artists' Asscn. Vice-Chair. Autonomous Regional Guangxi CPPCC 4th Cttee. 1979–82, 5th Cttee. 1983–88, 6th Cttee. 1988–. *Address:* Guangxi Institute of Fine Arts, Nanning City, Guangxi Province, People's Republic of China.

HUANG FANZHANG; Chinese economist; b. 8 Feb. 1931, Jiang-Xi; s. of Qi-Kun Huang and Yun-Jin Hua; m. Yue-Fen Xue 1959; two s.; ed. Peking Univ.; Researcher, Inst. of Econs. Chinese Acad. of Social Science (CASS) 1954–, Sr. Researcher and Prof. 1979–, Deputy Dir. 1982–85; Visiting Scholar, Harvard Univ. 1980–82, Stockholm Univ. 1982; Exec. Dir. for China, IMF 1985–86; Visiting Research Assoc. Center for Chinese Studies, Univ. of Mich. 1986–87; Consultant to World Bank 1987–88; Dir. Dept. of

Int. Econ. Studies, State Planning Comm. of PRC 1988–90; Vice-Pres. Economic Research Centre, State Planning Comm. 1990–; Consultant for a series of 100 books on current Chinese Economy 1994; CASS Prize 1985. *Publications:* Modern Economics in Western Countries (with others) 1963, The Evolution of Socialist Theories of Income Distribution 1979, Swedish Welfare State in Practice and its Theories 1987, The Reform in Banking System and The Role of Monetary Policy in China 1989, Joint Stock System – An Appropriate Form to China's Socialist Public Ownership 1989, The Characteristics of the World Economy in the 1980s, its prospects for the 1990s, and China's counter-measures 1990, China's Exploration of the Theories of Economic Reform in the last Ten Years (1979–89) 1991, Stock Ownership, Privatization, Socialization and other Topics 1992, Foreign Direct Investment in China since 1979 1992, On the Trend and Pattern of Economic Growth in East Asia and the Asia-Pacific Region 1993, East Asian Economies: Development, Prospects for Co-operation and China's Strategy 1993, China's Transitional Inflation 1994, China's Use of Foreign Direct Investment and Economic Reform 1995, Selected Works of Huang Fan-Zhang (1980–93) 1995, White Paper on East Asian Economies 1996. *Leisure interest:* classical music. *Address:* Apartment 801, Building 13, Mu-Xi-Di, Bei-Li, Beijing 100038, People's Republic of China. *Telephone:* (10) 6326-1950. *Fax:* (10) 6850-1708.

HUANG HUA; Chinese diplomatist; b. 1913, Cixian Co., Hebei Prov.; m. He Liliang; two s. one d.; ed. Yanqing Univ., Beijing; joined CCP 1936; fmr. Dir., Foreign Affairs Bureau of Tianjin, Nanking and Shanghai; later Dir., West European Dept., Ministry of Foreign Affairs; Chief. Chinese del. at Panmunjom (Korean War political negotiations) 1953; Political adviser to Premier Zhou En-lai, spokesman of Chinese del. to Geneva Conf. on Indo-China and Korea 1954, First Afro-Asian Conf., Bandung 1955; Adviser, Sino-American negotiations, Warsaw 1958; Amb. to Ghana 1960–66, to Egypt 1966–69, to Canada July-Nov. 1971; Perm. Rep. to UN 1971–76; Minister of Foreign Affairs 1976–83; mem. 10th Cen. Cttee. CCP 1974, 11th 1978, 12th 1983–87; a Vice-Premier, State Council 1980–82; State Councillor 1982–83; Vice-Chair. Standing Cttee., 6th NPC 1983–88; mem. Standing Cttee. of Cen. Advisory Comm. 1987; mem. Presidium, 14th CCP Nat. Congress Oct. 1992; Pres. Exec. Cttee., China Welfare Inst. 1988; Pres. Chinese Asscn. for Int. Friendly Contacts 1992–; Hon. Pres. China Int. Public Relations Asscn. 1991–, Chinese Environmental Protection Foundation 1993–; Chair. Soong Ching Ling Foundation 1992–; Adviser Chinese Asscn. for Promotion of the Population Culture; Head several int. dels.; Hon. Pres. Yenching Alumnae Assoc.; Pres. Smedley, Strong, Snow Soc. of China; mem. Policy Board Interaction Council; Hon. D.Hum.Litt. (Missouri). *Leisure interests:* fishing, jogging. *Address:* Standing Committee, National People's Congress, Beijing, People's Republic of China.

HUANG HUANG; Chinese party official; b. 1933, Lianshui Co., Jiangsu Prov.; joined PLA 1946, CCP 1949; Leading Sec. CCP Cttee., Anhui Prov. 1983–86; mem. 12th CCP Cen. Cttee. 1985–87; mem. Presidium 6th NPC 1986–; Deputy Gov. Jianxi Prov. 1987–90; Sec. CPC 7th Ningxia Hui Autonomous Regional Cttee. 1990–; Political Commissar 1990–96; mem. 14th CCP Cen. Cttee. 1992–. *Address:* Ningxia Hui Autonomous Region, Yinchuan, People's Republic of China.

HUANG JIANXIN; Chinese film director; b. 1954, Shenxian, Hebei Prov.; ed. Northwest Univ., Beijing Motion Picture Acad. *Films include:* The Black Cannon Incident, Samsara, Stand Straight, Don't Collapse, Back to Back, Face to Face. *Address:* Xi'an Film Studio, Xi'an, People's Republic of China.

HUANG JU; Chinese party and government official; b. 1938; Deputy Dir. First Bureau, Mechanical and Electrical Industry of Shanghai 1979–82; mem. Standing Cttee. of Shanghai Municipal CCP Cttee. 1983–, Deputy Sec. 1985–94; Vice-Mayor Shanghai 1986–91, Mayor 1991–95; alt. mem. 13th CCP Cen. Cttee. 1987–92; Chair. People's Armament Cttee. 1992–; mem. 14th CCP Cen. Cttee. 1992–97, 15th CCP Cen. Cttee. 1997–; mem. CCP Politburo 1994–; Sec. CPC 6th Shanghai Municipal Cttee. 1994–. *Address:* c/o Shanghai Municipal People's Government, Shanghai, People's Republic of China.

HUANG KUN; Chinese university professor; b. 1919, Zhejiang Prov.; Prof. of Physics, Beijing Univ. 1959; Deputy to NPC 1964; Dir. Inst. of Semi-Conductors of the Chinese Acad. of Sciences 1977; mem. Standing Cttee. of 5th, 6th and 7th CPPCC 1978; Pres. Chinese Soc. of Physics 1987–; mem. Science and Tech. Cttee. 7th CPPCC 1988; Standing Cttee. mem. CPPCC 8th Nat. Cttee. 1993–; mem. Royal Swedish Acad. *Publications:* Dynamical Theory of Crystal Lattices (with Max Born), The Physics of Semiconductors (with Xie Xide), The Physics of Solid State. *Address:* P.O. Box 912, Beijing, People's Republic of China.

HUANG QITAO; Chinese government official; fmr. Vice-Minister of Nuclear Industry; fmr. Vice-Dir. State Science and Tech. Comm., Dir. State Bureau of Nuclear Safety Feb. 1994–. *Address:* State Science and Technology Commission, 15B Fuxing Road, Haidian District, Beijing, People's Republic of China. *Telephone:* 10-8515544.

HUANG QIZAO; Chinese politician; b. Nov. 1933, Baxian Co., Sichuan Prov.; ed. Southwest Teachers' Coll.; joined CCP 1952; Sec. Communist Youth League Chongqing City Cttee.; Vice-Dir. Dept. of Culture of Chongqing City 1980; Vice-Dir. Dept. of Educ. of Chongqing City; Vice-Dir. Dept. of Culture of Sichuan Prov.; Dir. CCP United Front Work Dept. of Sichuan Prov.; Vice-Pres. Political Consultative Conf. Sichuan Prov.; Sec.-Gen. CCP Sichuan Provincial Cttee. 1988; Vice-Pres. of 6th Exec. Cttee. and Sec. Secr. of All-China Women's Fed. 1988; First Sec. Secr. of All-China Women's Fed. 1990–; Vice-Dir. Co-ordination Cttee. for Women's and Children's Work of State Council 1990–; mem. 14th CCP Cen. Cttee. 1992, 15th CCP Cen. Cttee. 1997–. *Address:* All-China Women's Federation, Beijing, People's Republic of China.

HUANG WEILU; Chinese engineer; b. 1916; ed. Cen. Univ., Beijing, London Univ. in Great Britain; one of the pioneers of rocket science in China and later of earth satellites 1959–; Chief Engineer of the Ministry of Astronautics Industry 1982–; Vice-Chair. Science and Tech. Cttee. 1982–; Deputy 6th NPC 1983–87, 7th NPC 1988; Corresp. mem. Int. Acad. of Astronautics 1986–. *Address:* Science and Technology Committee, Beijing, People's Republic of China.

HUANG XUEMIN; Chinese businessman; Pres. Asscn. of Pvt. Enterprises of Guangdong; Vice-Pres. Guangdong Asscn. of Industry and Commerce. *Address:* Association of Private Enterprises of Guangdong, Guangzhou, Guangdong Province, People's Republic of China.

HUANG YONGYU; Chinese artist and poet; b. 1924, Fenghuang Co., Hunan Prov.; best known for his satirical picture of an owl with its left eye closed, produced during the 'Gang of Four' era; Vice-Chair. Chinese Artists' Asscn. 1985–; mem. Nationalities Cttee. 7th CPPCC; Commendatore (Italy) 1986. *Address:* Central Academy of Fine Arts, Beijing, People's Republic of China.

HUANG ZHENDONG; Chinese politician; b. 1940; joined CCP 1981; Vice-Minister of Communications 1985–91, Minister 1991–; mem. 14th CCP Cen. Cttee. 1992–97, 15th CCP Cen. Cttee. 1997–. *Address:* c/o Ministry of Communications, 10 Fuxing Road, Haidian District, Beijing 100845, People's Republic of China.

HUBBARD, John, B.A.; American painter; b. 26 Feb. 1931, Ridgefield, Conn.; s. of G. Evans Hubbard and Dorothea Denys Hubbard; m. Caryl Whineray 1961; one s. one d.; ed. Milton Acad., Harvard Univ. and Art Students' League; served U.S. army in Counter-Intelligence 1953–56; exhbns. include nine at New Art Centre, London 1961–75, four at Fischer Fine Art, London 1979–91, Ten Americans, Rome 1959, British Painting in the Sixties, European Tour 1963, British Painting 1974, Hayward Gallery, London 1974, Jubilee Exhbn., R.A., London 1977, Yale Center for British Art 1986, Purdy Hicks Gallery, London 1994, McLauren Gallery, Ayr, Scotland 1996 and others in London, Oxford and elsewhere; designed décor and costumes for Le Baiser de la Fée, Dutch Nat. Ballet 1968, Midsummer, Royal Ballet, London 1983 and Sylvia Pas de Deux, Royal Ballet, London 1985; mem. Advisory Panel, Tate Gallery, St. Ives 1993–. *Publication:* Second Nature 1984. *Leisure interests:* walking and gardening. *Address:* Chilcombe House, Chilcombe, nr. Bridport, Dorset, England. *Telephone:* (01308) 482234.

HUBEL, David Hunter, M.D.; American professor of neurobiology; b. 27 Feb. 1926, Windsor, Ont., Canada; s. of Jesse H. Hubel and Elsie M. Hunter; m. S. Ruth Izzard 1953; three s.; ed. McGill Univ; Prof. of Neurophysiology, Harvard Medical School 1965–67, George Packer Berry Prof. of Physiology and Chair. Dept. of Physiology 1967–68, George Packer Berry Prof. of Neurobiology 1968–82; John Franklin Enders Univ. Prof. 1982–; George Eastman Prof., Univ. of Oxford 1991–92; First Annual George A. Miller Lecture, Cognitive Neuroscience Soc. 1995; mem. N.A.S., Leopoldina Acad., Bd. of Syndics, Harvard Univ. Press 1979–83; Foreign mem. Royal Soc., London; Sr. Fellow, Harvard Soc. of Fellows 1971–; Fellow American Acad. of Arts and Sciences; Hon. A.M. (Harvard) 1962, Hon. D.Sc. (McGill) 1978, (Manitoba) 1983, (Oxford), (Univ. of Western Ont.) 1993, (Gustavus Adolphus Coll.) 1994, (Ohio State Univ.) 1995, Hon. D.Hum.Litt. (Johns Hopkins Univ.) 1990; Lewis S. Rosenstiel Award for Basic Medical Research (Brandeis Univ.) 1972, Friedenwald Award (Asscn. for Research in Vision and Ophthalmology) 1975, Karl Spencer Lashley Prize (American Philosophical Soc.) 1977, Louisa Gross Horwitz Prize, (Columbia Univ.) 1978, Dickson Prize in Medicine, Univ. of Pittsburgh 1979, Soc. of Scholars, Johns Hopkins Univ. 1980, Ledlie Prize (Harvard Univ.) 1980, Nobel Prize in Medicine or Physiology 1981, New England Ophthalmological Soc. Award 1983, Paul Kayser Int. Award of Merit in Retina Research 1989, City of Medicine Award 1990, Gerald Award (Soc. for Neuroscience) 1993, Charles F. Prentice Medal (American Acad. of Optometry) 1993, Helen Keller Prize (Helen Keller Eye Research Foundation) 1995. *Publications:* Eye, Brain and Vision 1987; articles in scientific journals. *Leisure interests:* music, photography, astronomy, languages, weaving, amateur radio. *Address:* Department of Neurobiology, Harvard Medical School, 220 Longwood Avenue, Boston, MA 02115; 98 Collins Road, Newton, MA 02168, U.S.A. (Home). *Telephone:* (617) 432-1655 (Office); (617) 527-8774 (Home). *Fax:* (617) 432-0210 (Office).

HUBER, Karl, PH.D.; Swiss government official; b. 18 Oct. 1915, Häggenschwil; s. of Carl Huber and Mathilde Haessig; m. Elizabeth Fink 1945; one s. two d.; ed. high school, St. Gall, and Univ. of Berne; entered Fed. Admin. 1941, mem. staff of Gen. Secr. of Ministry of Political Econ.; Sec.-Gen. Ministry of Political Econ. 1954; Fed. Chancellor of Swiss Confederation 1967–81. *Leisure interests:* history, swimming, walking. *Address:* Steingrubenweg 23, 3028 Spiegel, Switzerland.

HUBER, Robert, DR.RER.NAT.; German biochemist; b. 20 Feb. 1937, Munich; s. of Sebastian Huber and Helene Huber; m. Christa Huber 1960; two s. two d.; fmr. external Prof. Tech. Univ. Munich; Dir. Max-Planck-Inst. für

Biochimie 1972–; Assoc. Prof. Munich Tech. Univ. 1976–; Ed. Journal of Molecular Biology 1976–; Scientific mem., Max-Planck-Gesellschaft; mem. Bavarian Acad. of Sciences, Accad. Nazionale dei Lincei and numerous socs.; Dr. h.c. (Louvain) 1987, (Ljubljana) 1989, (Tor Vergata, Rome) 1990; E. K. Frey Prize (German Surgical Soc.) 1972; Otto Warburg Medal (Soc. for Biological Chemistry) 1977; Emil von Behring Prize (Univ. of Marburg) 1982; Keilin Medal (Biochem. Soc. London); Richard Kuhn Medal (Soc. of German Chemists) 1987; E. K. Frey-E. Werle Medal 1989, Kone Award (Asscn. of Clinical Biochemists) 1990; Orden Pour le Mérite; Nobel Prize for Chemistry 1988; Sir Hans Krebs Medal 1992, Bayerischer Maximiliansorden für Wissenschaft und Kunst 1993, Linus Pauling Medal 1993, Distinguished Service Award (Miami Winter Symposia) 1995. *Leisure interests:* hiking, biking, skiing. *Address:* Max Planck Institut für Biochemie, Am Klopferspitz 18A, 82152 Martinsried, Germany. *Telephone:* (089) 8578-2677. *Fax:* 8578-3516.

HUCKABEE, Michael Dale, B.A.; American state governor and ecclesiastic; b. 24 Aug. 1955, Hope, Ark.; m. Janet McCain 1974; three s. one d.; ed. Ouachita Baptist Univ., Arkadelphia, Ark., Southwestern Baptist Theological Seminary, Fort Worth; ordained to ministry 1974; pastor various Baptist churches 1974–, Beech St. 1st Baptist Church, Texarkana, Ark. 1986–; Lieut. Gov. State of Ark. 1994–96, Gov. of Arkansas 1996–; Founder, Past-Pres. American Christian TV System, Pine Bluff; Pres. Ark. Baptist Convention 1989–; columnist weekly newspaper Positive Alternatives. *Address:* Office of the Governor, State Capitol, Little Rock, AR 72201 (Office); 1800 Center Street, Little Rock, AR 72206, U.S.A. (Home).

HUCKNALL, Mick; British singer and songwriter; b. 8 June 1960; formerly with own punk band Frantic Elevators; founder, lead singer, Simply Red 1984–; world tours 1989–90, 1992; singles include: Money's Too Tight To Mention, Holding Back The Years (reached No. 1, U.S.A. 1985), The Right Thing, A New Flame, Something Got Me Started; albums: Picture Book 1985, Men and Women 1987, A New Flame 1989, Stars (has sold 9 million copies, one of UK's best-selling albums of all time) 1991, Life 1995; mem. Govt. Task Force on the Music Industry 1997–; Hon. M.Sc. (UMIST) 1997. *Address:* c/o East West Records, Electric Lighting Station, 46 Kensington Court, London, W8 5DA, England. *Telephone:* 0171-938 2181. *Fax:* 0171-937 6645.

HUCKSTEP, Ronald Lawrie, C.M.G., F.T.S.E., M.A., M.D., F.R.C.S., F.R.C.S.E., F.R.A.C.S., F.A.ORTH.A.; British/Australian consultant orthopaedic surgeon and university professor; b. 22 July 1926, Chefoo, China; s. of Herbert George Huckstep and Agnes Huckstep (née Lawrie-Smith); m. Ann Macbeth 1960; two s. one d.; ed. Cathedral School, Shanghai, Queens' Coll., Cambridge, Middlesex, Royal Nat. Orthopaedic and St. Bartholomew's Hosps., London; Registrar and Chief Asst., Orthopaedic Dept., St. Bartholomew's Hosp. and various surgical appts., Middx. and Royal Nat. Orthopaedic Hosps. 1952–60; Hunterian Prof., Royal Coll. of Surgeons 1959–60; Lecturer, Sr. Lecturer and Reader in Orthopaedic Surgery, Makerere Univ., Kampala, Uganda 1960–67, Prof. 1967–72; Hon. Consultant Orthopaedic Surgeon, Mulago and Mengo Hosps. and Round Table Polio Clinic, Kampala 1960–72; Hon. Orthopaedic Surgeon to all Govt. and Mission hosps. in Uganda and Adviser on Orthopaedic Surgery to Ministry of Health, Uganda 1960–72; Prof. and Head, Dept. of Traumatic and Orthopaedic Surgery Univ. of N.S.W. 1972–92 and fmr. Rotating Chair., School of Surgery; Chair. Dept. of Traumatic and Orthopaedic Surgery and Dir. of Accident Services, Prince of Wales/Prince Henry Hosps. 1972–92, Consultant Orthopaedic Surgeon, Royal S. Sydney and Sutherland Hosps., Sydney 1974–92; Emer. Prof. of Traumatic and Orthopaedic Surgery, Univ. of N.S.W. and Consultant Orthopaedic Surgeon, Prince of Wales and Prince Henry Hosps. 1993–; Visiting Prof. Univ. of Sydney 1995–; Hon. Adviser, Rotary Int., The Commonwealth Foundation, WHO and UN on starting services for the disabled in developing countries 1970–; Sr. Medical Disaster Commdr., Dept. of Health, N.S.W. and Chair. and mem. of various disaster and emergency cttees. in Australia 1972–; Corresp. Ed. British and American Journals of Bone and Joint Surgery 1965–72, Injury, British Journal of Accident Surgery 1972; mem. Traffic Authority of N.S.W. 1982–; Consultant to Archives of Orthopaedic Surgery 1984; Founder World Orthopaedic Concern 1973, Hon. Fellow 1978; Patron Medical Soc. of Univ. of N.S.W. 1976; Hon. Dir. Orthopaedic Overseas, U.S.A. 1978; Vice-Pres. Australian Orthopaedic Asscn. 1982; Pres. Coast Medical Asscn., Sydney 1985–86; Hon. Fellow Western Pacific Orthopaedic Asscn. 1968, Asscn. of Surgeons of Uganda 1993; Chair. or mem. of numerous other bodies; Hon. M.D. (Univ. of N.S.W.) 1988; Irving Geist Award, Int. Soc. for Rehabilitation of the Disabled 1969, Melsome Memorial Prize, Cambridge 1948, Raymond Horton Smith Prize, Cambridge 1957, Betts Memorial Medal, Australian Orthopaedic Asscn. 1983, James Cook Medal, Royal Soc. of N.S.W. 1984, K. L. Sutherland Medal, Australian Acad. of Tech. Sciences 1986, Paul Harris Fellow and Medal, Rotary Int. and Rotary Foundation 1987, Humanitarian Award (Orthopaedics Overseas, U.S.A.) 1991, Vocational Service Award, Rotary Club of Sydney 1994; numerous orthopaedic inventions including Huckstep nail, hip, femur, knee, shoulder, humerus, staple, circlip, plate, bone screw, caliper, wheelchairs and skelecasts. *Publications:* Typhoid Fever and other Salmonella Infections 1962, A Simple Guide to Trauma 1970, Poliomyelitis: A Guide for Developing Countries, including appliances and rehabilitation 1975, A Simple Guide to Orthopaedics 1993, Picture Tests–Orthopaedics and Trauma 1994, numerous chapters in books and papers. *Leisure interests:* photography, designing orthopaedic appliances and implants, swimming and travel. *Address:* 108 Sugarloaf Crescent, Castlecrag, Sydney, N.S.W. 2068, Australia (Home). *Telephone:* (612) 9958-1786. *Fax:* (612) 9967-2971.

HUDEČEK, Václav; Czech violinist; b. 7 June 1952, Rožmitál pod Třemšínem, Příbram Dist.; m. Eva Trejtnarova 1977; ed Faculty of Music, Acad. of Musical Arts, Prague 1968–73; worked with David Oistrakh, Moscow 1970–74; worked as musician 1974–; mem., Union of the Czech Composers and Concert Artists 1977–; individual concerts, 1967–; soloist with Czech Philharmonic Orchestra 1984–90; freelance musician 1990–; concert tours to Austria, G.D.R., Norway, Hungary, U.S.S.R., Switzerland, Turkey, U.S.A., Yugoslavia, Japan, Italy, Iceland, Finland, Jordan; also gramophone recordings; Concertino Praga int. radio competition 1967, Award for Outstanding Labour 1978, Artist of Merit 1981, Supraphon Gold Record Prize 1994. *Address:* Euroconcert, Bellebern 10a, 78234 Engen, Germany (Office); Londynska 25, 120 00 Prague 2, Czech Republic (Home). *Telephone:* (07733) 3256 (Office); (02) 255172 (Home). *Fax:* (07733) 3259.

HUDEK, Ľudovít, LL.D.; Slovak politician and lawyer; b. 30 May 1948, Bratislava; one s. one d.; ed. Komenský Univ., Bratislava 1967–72; co. lawyer; teacher, Faculty of Investigation, Police Force School, Bratislava 1976–92; expert with Ministry of Justice of Czechoslovakia (later of Slovak Repub.) on penal and constitutional law 1992–94; commercial lawyer June–Nov. 1994; Public Prosecutor Gen. Nov.–Dec. 1994; Minister of Interior, Slovak Repub. 1994–96; Chair. Govt. Comm. for Combating Antisocial Activities 1995. *Publications:* essays, articles and professional studies. *Leisure interests:* tennis, swimming. *Address:* Slovak National Council, Mudroňova 1, 812 80 Bratislava, Slovakia (Office). *Telephone:* (7) 534 1111 (Office).

HUDSON, Hugh; British film director and producer; b. 25 Aug. 1936; s. of late Michael Donaldson-Hudson and Jacynth Ellerton; m. Susan Caroline Michie 1977; one s.; ed. Eton. *Films include:* Chariots of Fire 1980 (5 BAFTA Awards, 4 Oscars, other awards), Greystoke: The Legend of Tarzan 1984, Revolution 1985 (BFI Anthony Asquith Award for Music), Lost Angels 1989, Son of Adam 1996, A Life So Far 1997; numerous documentaries, political films (for Labour Party) and advertisements. *Address:* Hudson Film Ltd., 61 Eaton Mews West, London, SW1W 9ET, England. *Telephone:* 0171-235 1220. *Fax:* 0171-235 1220.

HUDSON, Robert Francis, PH.D., F.R.S.; British professor of organic chemistry; b. 15 Dec. 1922; s. of late John F. Hudson and Ethel Hudson; m. Monica A. Stray 1945; one s. two d.; ed. Brigg Grammar School and Imperial Coll., London; Asst. Lecturer, Imperial Coll. 1945–47; Consultant, Wolsey Ltd., Leicester 1945–50; Lecturer, Queen Mary Coll., London 1947–59; Research Fellow, Purdue Univ. 1954; Group Dir. Cyanamid European Research Inst., Geneva 1960–66; Prof. of Organic Chem. Univ. of Kent at Canterbury 1967–85, Prof. Emer. 1985–; Consultant British Petroleum 1983–87; Visiting Prof. at univs. in U.S.A., Canada, France, Germany etc. *Publications:* Wool—Its Physics and Chemistry (with P. Alexander) 1954, Structure and Mechanism in Organophosphorus Chemistry 1965; papers in scientific journals. *Address:* 37 Puckle Lane, Canterbury, Kent, CT1 3LA, England. *Telephone:* (01227) 761340.

HUE, Robert; French politician and nurse; b. 19 Oct. 1946, Cormeilles-en-Parisis; s. of René Hue and Raymonde Gregorius; m. Marie-Edith Solard 1973; one s. one d.; ed. Coll. d'Enseignement Technique and Ecole d'Infirmier; mem. Young Communists 1962; mem. French CP Party 1963–, mem. Secr. Fed. of Val d'Oise 1970–77, mem. Cen. Cttee. 1987, mem. Politburo 1990, Nat. Sec. 1994–; Cand. of CP, French Presidential Election May 1995; Mayor of Montigny-les-Cormeilles 1977–; Conseiller-Gén. Val d'Oise 1988–97; Deputy for Argenteuil-Bezons 1997–; Pres. Nat. Asscn. of communist and republican elected mems. 1991–94; *Publications:* Histoire d'un village du Parisis des origines à laRévolution 1981, Du village à la ville 1986, Montigny pendant la Révolution 1989, Communisme: la mutation 1995, Il faut qu'on se parle 1997. *Leisure interests:* reading, painting, cinema, music (jazz and rock), walking. *Address:* Parti Communiste Françaíse, 2 place du Colonel Fabien, 75167 Paris, France.

HUERTA DÍAZ, Vice-Admiral Ismael; Chilean diplomatist (retd.) and naval officer; b. 13 Oct. 1916; s. of Rear-Adm. Ismael Huerta Lira and Lucrecia Díaz Vargas; m. Guillermina Wallace Dunsmore Aird 1942; two s. two d.; ed. Sacred Heart School, Valparaíso, Naval Acad., Ecole Supérieure d'Electricité, Paris, Naval Polytechnic Acad., Chile; successive posts in Chilean Navy include Dir. of Armaments, Dir. of Instruction, Dir. of Scientific Investigation, Dir. of Naval Polytechnic Acad., Dir. of Shipyards, Dir.-Gen. of Army Services; Prof. of Electronics, Univ. de Concepción 1954, 1955, 1956; Prof. of Radionavigation, Univ. Católica de Valparaíso 1962–67; mem. Org. Cttee., Pacific Conf., Viña del Mar 1970, Pres. Centre of Pacific Studies 1970–72; Dir. Compañía de Acero del Pacífico (CAP) 1970, 1971, 1972; Pres. Nat. Transport Cttee. 1972; Minister of Public Works 1973, of Foreign Affairs 1973–74; Perm. Rep. to UN 1974–77; Rector Univ. Técnica Federico Santa María 1977–85; Chair. Bd. Empresa Marítima del Estado 1978–; mem. Coll. of Chilean Engineers. Inst. of Mechanical Engineers of Chile; Decoration of Pres. of the Repub. (Chile), Grand Officer Order of Léopold II (Belgium), Gran Cruz de la Orden del Libertador San Martín (Argentina), Gran Cruz Extraordinaria de la Orden Nacional al Mérito (Paraguay), Medall Kim-Kank (Repub. of Viet Nam). *Publications:* The Role of the Armed

Forces in Today's World 1968, Volvería a ser Marino (memoirs) 1988, and various technical articles.

HUET, Pierre, D. en D.; French civil servant; b. 12 Nov. 1920, Paris; m. Catherine Viénot 1944; one s. two d.; ed. Paris Law Faculty and Ecole des Sciences Politiques; Special Asst., French Govt. Refugee Del. 1940, Asst. to Sec. of State, Ministry of Food 1944; Jr. mem. Conseil d'Etat, mem. Legal Cttee. of French Union 1946; Asst. to Sec.-Gen., Cttee. for European Econ. Co-operation 1947; Legal Adviser, OEEC 1948; Gen. Counsel, OEEC 1956; Dir.-Gen. European Nuclear Energy Agency 1958–64; Sec.-Gen. Council of State 1966–70; Councillor of State 1970; Chair. Bd., Asscn. Technique pour l'Energie Nucléaire 1965–75; Pres. Centre d'Informatique Juridique 1971–75; Vice-Chair. European Atomic Forum (FORATOM) 1973–75; Chair. Comm. Interministérielle des radioéléments artificiels, Comm. Nationale des Sondages, Comm. Nationale des Réseaux Cablés, Comm. de la télématiques, Comm. Consultative des services télématiques; mem. Comm. Nat. de la Communication et des Libertés (CNCL) 1986–89; Counsel, Telecommunications and Computer Law, Bd. mem. S.I. de conseil en communication électronique 1989–; Corresp. mem. Institut de France (Acad. des sciences morales et politiques); Commdr., Ordre de Léopold (Belgium); Grosses Goldenes Ehrenzeichen für Verdienste (Austria), Officier, Légion d'honneur, Commdr., Ordre nat. du Mérite. *Address:* 128 boulevard Malesherbes, 75017 Paris, France.

HUG, Michel, PH.D.; French civil engineer; b. 30 May 1930, Courson; s. of René and Marcelle (née Quenee) Hug; m. Danielle Michaud; one s. two d.; ed. Ecole Polytechnique, Ecole Nationale des Ponts et Chaussées, State Univ. of Iowa; joined Electricité de France 1956, various positions at the Chatou Research and Test Centre 1956–66, Regional Man. (Southern Alps) 1967–68, Research and Devt. Man. 1969–72, Planning and Construction Man. 1972–82; Gen. Man. Charbonnages de France (French Coal Bd.) 1982–86; Prof. of Fluid Mechanics, Ecole Nationale des Ponts et Chaussées 1963–80; Chair. Bd. Ecole Nationale Supérieure d'Electrotechnique, d'Electronique, d'Informatique et d'Hydraulique de Toulouse 1980–90; Chair. Bd. CdF Chimie 1985–86; Deputy Admin. Org. des Producteurs d'Energie Nucléaire (OPEN) 1992–; mem. Applications Cttee. of Acad. des Sciences 1987; Hon. mem. Int. Assoc. of Hydraulics Research; Foreign mem. U.S. Nat. Acad. of Eng. 1979–; mem. American Nuclear Soc.; Lauréat de l'Institut (Prix des Laboratoires) 1964; Commdr. Ordre nat. du Merite 1980; Officier, Légion d'honneur 1977; Officier des Palmes Académiques (Ministry of Educ.) 1986; Chevalier des Arts et Lettres 1981, du mérite agricole. *Publications:* Mécanique des fluides appliquée aux problèmes d'aménagement et d'énergétique 1975, Organiser le changement dans l'entreprise—une expérience à E.D.F. 1975. *Leisure interests:* tennis, shooting, swimming, flying. *Address:* 57 avenue Franklin Roosevelt, 75008 Paris, France.

HUGH SMITH, Sir Andrew Colin, Kt., B.A.; British stockbroker; b. 6 Sept. 1931; s. of late Lt.-Commdr. Colin Hugh Smith; m. Venetia Flower 1964; two s.; ed. Ampleforth Coll. and Trinity Coll., Cambridge; called to Bar (Inner Temple) 1956; with Courtaulds Ltd. 1960–68; joined Capel-Cure Carden (subsequently Capel-Cure Myers) 1968, became Partner 1970, Sr. Partner 1979; Deputy Chair. ANZ McCaughan Merchant Bank 1985–90; Chair. Holland & Holland PLC 1987–95; elected to Council, The Stock Exchange 1981; Chair. The Int. Stock Exchange (now London Stock Exchange), London 1988–94; Chair. Penna PLC 1995–, Microtransfer Ltd. 1995–, European Advisory Bd. Andersen Consulting 1995–; Dir. Matheson Lloyds Investment Trust 1994–97, (non-exec.) J. Bibby & Sons (now Barlow Int.) 1995–, Barbour Ltd. 1998–; mem. Hon. Treasurer Malcolm Sargent Cancer Fund for Children 1992–. *Leisure interests:* gardening, shooting, fishing, reading. *Address:* c/o European Advisory Board, Andersen Consulting, 2 Arundel Street, London, W.C.2, England.

HUGHES, Anthony Vernon, M.A.; Solomon Islands banking executive and civil servant; b. 29 Dec. 1936, England; s. of Henry Norman Hughes and Marjorie Hughes; m. 1st Carole Frances Robson 1961 (divorced 1970); one s.; m. 2nd Kuria Vaze Paia 1971; one s. one d. two adopted d.; ed. Queen Mary's Grammar School, Walsall, England, Pembroke Coll., Oxford and Bradford Univ.; Commr. of Lands, Registrar of Titles, Solomon Islands 1969–70, Head of Planning 1974–76, Perm. Sec. Ministry of Finance 1976–81, Gov. Cen. Bank 1982–93; Devt. Sec., Gilbert and Ellice Islands 1971–73; Regional Econ. Advisor UN Econ. and Social Comm. for Asia and the Pacific Jan. 1994–; Cross of Solomon Islands 1981. *Publications:* numerous articles on land tenure, econ. planning, devt. admin., foreign investment, especially jt. ventures, with special emphasis on small countries. *Leisure interests:* working outside, sculling, sailing. *Address:* ESCAP, Pacific Operations Centre, PMB 004, Port Vila, Vanuatu; P.O. Box 486, Honiara, Solomon Islands (Home).

HUGHES, Catherine Eva, C.M.G., M.A.; British fmr. diplomatist and college principal; b. 24 Sept. 1933, London; d. of Edmund Pestell and Isabella Pestell; m. J. T. Hughes 1991; ed. Leeds Girls' High School and St. Hilda's Coll. Oxford; joined Foreign Office 1955; served The Hague, Bangkok, Vientiane, OECD Del., Paris 1955–75; Counsellor, E. Berlin 1975; seconded to Cabinet Office 1978; Inspector H.M. Diplomatic Service 1981–83; Minister (Econ.), Bonn 1983–87; Asst. Under-Sec. FCO 1987–89; Prin., Somerville Coll. Oxford 1989–96. *Address:* 2 Bishop Kirk Place, Oxford, OX2 7HJ, England.

HUGHES, Rev. Gerard Joseph, M.A., S.T.L., PH.D.; British ecclesiastic; b. 6 June 1934, Wallington, Surrey; s. of Henry Hughes and Margaret Hughes; ed. St. Aloysius Coll. Glasgow, London Inst. of Educ., Campion Hall, Univ. of Oxford, Heythrop Coll. Oxford and Univ. of Mich.; Chair. Dept. of Philosophy, Heythrop Coll. Univ. of London 1973–, Vice-Prin. 1986–; mem. Senate and Academic Council, Univ. of London 1987–; Vice-Provincial, British Prov. of Soc. of Jesus 1982–88; Austin Fagothey Prof. of Philosophy, Univ. of Santa Clara, Calif. 1988, 1992. *Publications:* Authority in Morals 1978, Moral Decisions 1980, The Philosophical Assessment of Theology (ed.) 1987. *Leisure interests:* music, computer programming, crosswords, walking. *Address:* Heythrop College, Kensington Square, London, W8 5HQ (Office); 221 Goldhurst Terrace, London, NW6 3EP, England (Home). *Telephone:* 0171-795 6600 (Office); 0171-328 2868 (Home). *Fax:* 0171-795 4200 (Office).

HUGHES, H. Richard; British architect; b. 4 July 1926, London; s. of Major Henry and Olive (née Curtis) Hughes; m. Anne Hill 1951; one s. two d.; ed. Kenton Coll., Nairobi, Kenya, Hilton Coll., Natal, S.A., Architectural Asscn. School of Architecture, London; Corporal, Kenya Regt., attached to Royal Engineers 1944–46; Asst. Architect Kenya and Uganda 1950–51; Architect, Hartford, Conn., U.S.A. 1953–55, Nairobi, Kenya 1955–57; Prin. Richard Hughes and Partners 1957–86; Chair. Kenya Branch, Capricorn Africa Soc. 1958–61, Environment Liaison Cen. 1976–78, Lamu Soc. 1977–79; UN Environment Programme (UNEP) Consultant on Human Settlements Tech. 1978; UN Cen. for Human Settlements Consultant on building materials, construction tech. in developing countries 1979; Ed., Fireball Int. 1986–92; mem. Exec. Cttee., Friends of the Elderly, London 1987–92; Trustee, Zebra Trust, London 1988 (Vice-Chair. 1994); Guide, The Tate Gallery, London 1988; NADFAS lecturer 1995. *Publications:* joint author (with Graham Searle) Habitat Handbook 1982, In the Frame 1989, Capricorn – A History 1999 and many contribs. to books on architecture and articles in New Commonwealth, Architectural Review, Architects Journal and Modern Painters; Ed. Living Paintings Trust Albums of Architecture for the Blind 1991, 1994. *Leisure interests:* collecting modern art, dinghy sailing. *Address:* 47 Chiswick Quay, London, W4 3UR, England. *Telephone:* 0181-995 3109. *Fax:* 0181-995 3109.

HUGHES, John Lawrence, B.A.; American publisher; b. 13 March 1925, New York; s. of John C. Hughes and Margaret Kelly; m. Rose M. Pitman 1947; three s. one d.; ed. Yale Univ.; reporter, Nassau Review Star, Rockville Centre, Long Island, N.Y. 1949; Asst. Sr. Ed., Pocket Books, Inc. New York 1949–59; Vice-Pres. Washington Square Press 1958; Sr. Ed., Vice-Pres., Dir. William Morrow & Co. 1960–65, Pres. and C.E.O. 1965–85; Pres. The Hearst Trade Book Group 1985–87, Chair., C.E.O. 1988–90, Ed.-at-large, Group Advisor 1990–; Trustee, Yale Univ. Press, Pierpont Morgan Library, Library of America, Acad. of American Poets; mem. Bd. Asscn. of American Publishers 1986–90 (Chair. 1988–90); mem. Bd. Nat. Book Awards 1982–94 (Chair. 1988–89); mem. Publrs. Hall of Fame 1989. *Leisure interest:* golf. *Address:* The Hearst Book Group, 1350 Sixth Avenue, New York, N.Y. 10019 (Office); P.O. Box 430, Southport, CT 06490, U.S.A. (Home). *Telephone:* (212) 261-6552 (Office); (203) 259-8957 (Home).

HUGHES, John W.; American film producer, screenplay writer and director; b. 18 Feb. 1950, Detroit, Mich.; m. Nancy Ludwig; two s.; ed. Univ. of Arizona; copywriter and Creative Dir. Leo Burnett Co.; Ed. Nat. Lampoon magazine which led to writing screenplay of Nat. Lampoon's Class Reunion; f. and Pres. Hughes Entertainment 1985–. *Films:* National Lampoon's Class Reunion (screenplay) 1982, National Lampoon's Vacation (screenplay) 1983, Mr. Mom (screenplay) 1983, Nate and Hayes (screenplay) 1983, Sixteen Candles (screenplay and dir.) 1984, National Lampoon's European Vacation (screenplay) 1985, Weird Science (screenplay and dir.) 1985, The Breakfast Club (screenplay, dir. and producer) 1985, Ferris Bueller's Day Off (screenplay, dir. and producer) 1986, Pretty in Pink (screenplay and producer) 1986, Some Kind of Wonderful (screenplay and producer) 1987, Planes, Trains and Automobiles (screenplay, dir. and producer) 1987, The Great Outdoors (screenplay and producer) 1988, She's Having a Baby (screenplay, dir. and producer) 1988, National Lampoon's Christmas Vacation (screenplay and producer) 1989, Uncle Buck (screenplay, dir. and producer) 1989, Home Alone (screenplay and producer 1990, Career Opportunities (screenplay and producer) 1990, Dutch (screenplay and producer) 1991, Curly Sue (screenplay, dir. and producer) 1991, Only the Lonely (co-producer) 1991, Beethoven (screenplay, as Edmond Dantes) 1992, Home Alone 2: Lost in New York (screenplay and producer) 1992, Dennis the Menace (screenplay and producer) 1993, Baby's Day Out (screenplay and producer) 1994, Miracle on 34th Street (screenplay and producer) 1994, 101 Dalmatians (screenplay) 1996; Commitment to Chicago Award 1990, NATO/ShoWest Producer of the Year 1990. *Address:* c/o Jacob Bloom, Bloom and Dekom, 150 South Rodeo Drive, Beverly Hills, CA 90212; Hughes Entertainment, 10201 West Pico Boulevard, Los Angeles, CA 90064, U.S.A.

HUGHES, Leslie Ernest, M.B., D.S., F.R.C.S., F.R.A.C.S.; Australian professor of surgery; b. 12 Aug. 1932, Parramatta; s. of Charles J. Hughes and Vera D. (Raines) Hughes; m. Marian Castle 1955; two s. two d.; ed. Parramatta High School and Univ. of Sydney; surgical trainee, Sydney 1955–59; Registrar, Derby and London, U.K. 1959–61; British Empire Cancer Research Campaign Research Fellow, King's College Hospital, London 1962–63; Reader in Surgery, Univ. of Queensland 1964–71; Eleanor Roosevelt Int. Scholar, Roswell Park Memorial Inst., Buffalo, N.Y. 1969–71; Prof. of Surgery, Univ. of Wales Coll. of Medicine, Cardiff 1971–92, Emer. Prof. 1992–;

Visiting Prof. Univs. of Queensland, Allahabad, Sydney, Witwatersrand, Cairo, Melbourne, Lund, Albany, New York and N.S.W.; Pres. Welsh Surgical Soc. 1991–93, Surgical Research Soc. 1992–94; Chair. Editorial Cttee., European Journal of Surgical Oncology 1992–97. *Publications:* Benign Disorders and Diseases of the Breast 1989; more than 200 papers and book chapters dealing mainly with tumour immunology, disease of the breast, inflammatory bowel disease, surgical oncology, surgical pathology and wound healing. *Address:* Brook House, 14 Millwood, Lisvane, Cardiff, CF4 5TL, Wales.

HUGHES, Louis R., M.B.A.; American motor executive; b. 10 Feb. 1949, Cleveland, O.; m. Candice Ann Hughes 1972; two c.; ed. Gen. Motors Inst. Flint, Mich. and Harvard Univ.; began career with Gen. Motors on financial staff in New York; Asst. Treas 1982; Vice-Pres. of Finance, Gen. Motors of Canada 1985–86; Vice-Pres. for Finance, Gen. Motors (Europe), Zürich 1987–89; Chair., Man. Dir. Adam Opel AG 1989–92; Exec. Vice-Pres. Gen. Motors Corpn. (responsible for int. operations) 1992–; Pres. Gen. Motors (Europe) AG 1992–94; Chair. Bd. Saab Automobile AB 1992–; Pres. Gen. Motors Int. Operations, Inc. 1994–; mem. Supervisory Bd. Deutsche Bank 1993–; mem. Bd. of Dirs. AB Electrolux; Pres. Swiss-American Chamber of Commerce; Chair. European Council of American Chambers of Commerce; Order of Merit (Germany). *Leisure interests:* skiing, mountain climbing, antiques. *Address:* General Motors International Operations, Inc., Stelzenstrasse 4, 8152 Glattbrugg, Switzerland. *Telephone:* (1) 8282600. *Fax:* (1) 8282675.

HUGHES, Mervyn Gregory; Australian cricketer; b. 23 Nov. 1961, Euroa, Vic.; s. of Ian Hughes and Freda Hughes; m. Sue Hughes 1991; one d.; right-arm fast bowler and right-hand lower-order batsman; played for Victoria 1981–95, Essex 1983; 53 Test matches for Australia 1985–94, eighth Australian to achieve Test Double, taking 212 wickets (average 28.3) and scoring 1,032 runs (average 16.6), took hat-trick v. W. Indies, Perth 1988; toured England 1989, 1993; 33 limited-overs ints. *Leisure interests:* golf, relaxing at home, going to the beach. *Address:* c/o Australian Cricket Board, 90 Jolimont Street, Jolimont, Vic. 3002, Australia.

HUGHES, Sean Patrick Francis, M.S., F.R.C.S., F.R.C.S.(E.), F.R.C.S.I.; British orthopaedic surgeon; b. 2 Dec. 1941, Farnham, Surrey; s. of Patrick J. Hughes and Kathleen E. Hughes; m. Felicity M. Anderson 1971; one s. two d.; ed. Downside School and St. Mary's Hosp. Medical School, Univ. of London; Asst. Lecturer in Anatomy, St. Mary's Hosp. Medical School 1969; Research Fellow, Mayo Clinic, U.S.A. 1975; Sr. Registrar in Orthopaedics, Middlesex Hosp. London 1977; Sr. Lecturer in Orthopaedics, Royal Postgraduate Medical School, London 1979; Prof. of Orthopaedic Surgery, Univ. of Edinburgh 1979–91, Royal Postgrad. Medical School 1991–; Hon. Consultant Orthopaedic Surgeon Hammersmith Hosp. and Ealing Hosp. 1991–; Clinical Dir. Surgery and Anaesthetics Hammersmith Hosps. NHS Trust 1998–; Prof. of Orthopaedic Surgery, Head of Div. Surgery Anaesthetics and Intensive Care, Imperial Coll. School of Medicine 1997; Hon. Civilian Consultant to R.N.; Hon. Consultant, Nat. Hosp. for Nervous Diseases, London 1994–. *Publications:* several books and papers on orthopaedics, particularly bone blood flow, musculoskeletal infection, fractures and spinal injury. *Leisure interests:* sailing, golf, walking, skiing. *Address:* Imperial College School of Medicine, Charing Cross Campus, Fulham Palace Road, London, W6 8RF (Office); 24 Fairfax Road, London, W4 1EW, England (Home). *Telephone:* 0181-846 1477 (Office).

HUI, Ann; Hong Kong film director; b. 1949, Anshan, N.E. China; ed. Univ. of Hong Kong and London Film School. *Films include:* The Secret 1979, Boat People 1982, Romance of Book and Sword 1987, Yakuza Chase 1991, Summer Snow 1995.

HUI LIANGYU; Chinese provincial governor and economist; b. 1944, Yushu Co., Jilin Prov.; ed. Jilin Agricultural School; joined CCP 1966; Deputy Sec. CCP Yushu Co. Cttee. 1974–77; Deputy Dir. Jilin Prov. Agricultural Bureau, Prov. Agricultural and Animal Husbandry Dept. 1977–84; Deputy Sec. CCP Baichengzi Prefectural Cttee., Commr. Baichengzi Admin. Office 1984–85; elected mem. Standing Cttee. CCP Jilin Prov. Cttee. 1985; Dir. Rural Policy Research Office, Dir. Rural Work Dept. CCP Jilin Prov. Cttee. 1985–87; apptd. Vice-Gov. Jilin Prov. 1987; Deputy Dir. CCPCC Policy Research Office 1991–93; Deputy Sec. CCP Hubei Prov. Cttee. 1992–94; Chair. 7th Hubei Prov. CPPCC Cttee; alt. mem. 14th CCP Cen. Cttee. 1992–99; Vice-Gov. and Acting Gov. Anhui Prov. 1994–95, Gov. 1995–98; Deputy Sec. CCP Anui Prov. Cttee. 1994–; mem. 15th CCP Cen. Cttee. 1997–. *Address:* Office of the Governor of Anhui Province, Hefei, Anhui Province, People's Republic of China.

HUISGEN, Rolf, PH.D.; German academic; b. 13 June 1920, Gerolstein, Eifel; s. of Edmund Huisgen and Maria Flink; m. Trudl Schneiderhan 1945; two d.; ed. Univs. of Bonn and Munich; Lecturer, Univ. of Munich 1947–49, Full Prof. of Organic Chem. 1952–88, Prof. Emer. 1988–; Assoc. Prof., Univ. of Tübingen 1949–52; Rockefeller Fellow, U.S.A. 1955; numerous guest professorships, U.S.A., Israel, Japan, Spain and Switzerland; Hon. Fellow, Royal Soc. of Chem., London; mem. Bavarian Acad. of Science, Deutsche Akad. der Naturforscher Leopoldina; Foreign Assoc. N.A.S., Washington; Corresp. mem. Real Acad. de Ciencias Exactas, Madrid, Heidelberg Acad. of Sciences, Polish Acad. of Sciences; Hon. mem. American Acad. of Arts and Sciences, Soc. Chimique de France, Pharmaceutical Soc. of Japan, Gesellschaft Deutscher Chemiker, Accad. Nazionale dei Lincei (Italy), Istituto Lombardo; Dr. h.c. (Univ. Complutense de Madrid) 1975, Dr. rer. nat. h.c. (Freiburg) 1977, (Erlangen-Nuremberg) 1980, (Würzburg) 1984, (Regensburg) 1985, (St. Petersburg) 1993; Liebig Medal, Gesellschaft Deutscher Chemiker 1961, Médaille Lavoisier, Soc. Chimique de France 1965, Roger Adams Award in Organic Chem., American Chemical Soc. 1975, Otto Hahn Award for Chem. and Physics 1979, Adolfo Quilico Medal, Italian Chemical Soc. 1987 and other awards; Bavarian Order of Merit; Bavarian Maximilian Order for Science and Art. *Publications:* The Adventure Playground of Mechanisms and Novel Reactions (autobiog.) 1994; more than 500 research papers on organic reaction mechanisms and cycloadditions. *Leisure interests:* modern art, archaeology. *Address:* Institut für Organische Chemie der Universität München, Karlstr. 23, 80333 Munich (Office); Kaulbachstr. 10, 80539 Munich, Germany (Home). *Telephone:* (89) 5902211 (Office); (89) 281645 (Home). *Fax:* (89) 5902604 (Office).

HUISMANS, Sipko, B.A.; British business executive; b. 28 Dec. 1940, Ede, Netherlands; s. of Jouko Huismans and Roelofina Huismans; m. Janet Durston 1969; two s. one d.; ed. Stellenbosch Univ., S. Africa; joined Courtaulds as shift chemist with Ustu Pulp Co., Ltd. 1961; Sales Man., later Gen. Man. Springwood Cellulose Co., Ltd. 1968; Exec. responsible for Courtaulds trading interests in Eastern Europe and Far East 1974; apptd. to Courtaulds Fibres Bd. 1980, Man. Dir. of Fibres 1982; apptd. to Int. Paint Bd. 1986, Chair. 1987; Chair. Courtaulds Chemical and Industrial Exec. 1988–; responsible for films and packaging 1989; mem. Courtaulds Group Exec. 1986–; Man. Dir. Courtaulds PLC 1990–91, Chief Exec. 1991–96; Dir. (non-exec.) Vickers PLC 1994–, Imperial Tobacco Group PLC 1996–. *Leisure interests:* motor racing, sailing and 'competition'. *Address:* Latchmore House, Brockenhurst, Hants., SO42 7UE, England.

HUIZENGA, Harry Wayne; American entertainment corporation executive; b. 29 Dec. 1939, Evergreen Park, Ill.; s. of G. Harry Huizenga and Jean (Riddering) Huizenga; m. Martha Jean Pike 1972; three s. one d.; ed. Calvin Coll.; Vice-Chair., Pres., C.O.O. Waste Man. Inc., Oak Brook, Ill. 1968–84; Prin. Huizenga Holdings. Inc., Fort Lauderdale, Fla. 1984–; Chair. and C.E.O. Blockbuster Entertainment Corpn., Fort Lauderdale 1987–94; owner Florida Marlins, Miami 1992–; co-owner Miami Dolphins, Joe Robbie Stadium; mem. Team Republican Nat. Cttee., Washington, D.C. 1988–90; Man of Year, Billboard/Time Magazine 1990 and numerous other awards. *Leisure interests:* golf, collecting antique cars. *Address:* Huizenga Holdings, Inc., 200 S. Andrews Ave, Fort Lauderdale, FL 33301, U.S.A.

HUIZENGA, John R., PH.D.; American nuclear chemist and educator; b. 21 April 1921, Fulton, Ill.; s. of Harry M. and Josie B. (Brands) Huizenga; m. Dorothy J. Koeze 1946; two s. two d.; ed. Calvin Coll., Grand Rapids, Mich. and Univ. of Illinois, Urbana, Ill.; Lab. Supervisor, Manhattan Wartime Project, Oak Ridge 1944–46; Assoc. Scientist, Argonne Nat. Lab., Chicago 1949–57, Sr. Scientist 1958–67; Prof of Chem. and Physics Univ. of Rochester, New York 1967–78, Tracy H. Harris Prof. of Chem. and Physics 1978–91, Prof. Emer. 1991–, Chair. Dept. of Chem. 1983–88; Fulbright Fellow, Netherlands 1954–55; Guggenheim Fellow, Paris 1964–65, Berkeley, Munich and Copenhagen 1973–74; E. O. Lawrence Award, Atomic Energy Comm. 1966, Award for Nuclear Application in Chem., A.C.S. 1975; mem. N.A.S., A.C.S.; Fellow American Acad. of Arts and Sciences, American Physical Soc., A.A.A.S. *Publications:* Nuclear Fission (with R. Vandenbosch) 1973, Damped Nuclear Reactions (with W. U. Schröder), Treatise on Heavy-Ion Science, Vol. 2 1984, Cold Fusion: the Scientific Fiasco of the Century 1992; 275 articles in professional journals. *Leisure interests:* tennis, golf. *Address:* 43 McMichael Drive, Pinehurst, NC 28374, U.S.A. *Telephone:* (910) 295-9539.

HULCE, Tom; American actor; b. 6 Dec. 1953, Detroit; ed. N. Carolina School of Arts. *Plays include:* The Rise and Rise of Daniel Rocket, Eastern Standard, A Few Good Men. *Films:* September 30th 1955, National Lampoon's Animal House, Those Lips Those Eyes, Amadeus 1985, Echo Park 1985, Slam Dance 1987, Nicky and Gino 1988, Parenthood 1989, Shadowman, The Inner Circle, Fearless, Mary Shelley's Frankenstein 1994, Wings of Courage 1995, The Hunchback of Notre Dame (voice). *TV includes:* Emily Emily, St. Elsewhere, Murder in Mississippi 1990, Black Rainbow. *Address:* c/o CAA, 9830 Wilshire Boulevard, Beverly Hills, CA 90212, U.S.A.

HULL, Jane Dee, M.SC.; American lawyer and politician; b. 8 Aug. 1935, Kansas City; d. of Justin D. Bowersock and Mildred Swenson; m. Terrance Ward Hull 1954; two s. two d.; ed. Kansas and Arizona Univs.; house maj. whip, Ariz. House of Reps. 1987–88, Speaker of House 1989–93; Chair. Ethics Cttee., Econ. Devt. Cttee. 1993; mem. Legis. Council, Gov.'s Int. Trade and Tourism Advancement Bd., Gov.'s Strategic Partnership for Econ. Devt., Employment Implementation Task Force 1993; fmr. Sec. of State of Arizona, Gov. 1997–; mem. Bd. dirs. Morrison Inst. for Public Policy, Ariz. Town Hall, Ariz. Econ. Council; mem. Nat. Org. of Women Legislators, Nat. Repub. Legislators Asscn.; Nat. Legislator of the Year Award 1989, Econ. Devt. Award of Ariz. Innovation Network 1993; Republican. *Address:* Office of the Governor, State Capitol, West Wing, 1700 West Washington Street, Phoenix, AZ 85007, U.S.A.

HULL, John Folliott Charles, C.B.E., M.A.; British banker; b. 21 Oct. 1925, London; s. of Sir Hubert and Lady Hull; m. Rosemarie Waring 1951; one s. three d.; ed. Downside, Jesus Coll., Cambridge; Cap. Royal Artillery 1944–48, serving with Royal Indian Artillery; called to Bar, Inner Temple 1952; Dir. Schroders PLC 1969–72, 1974–85, Deputy Chair. 1977–85; J. Henry

Schroder Wagg & Co. Ltd. 1957–72, 1974–85, Dir. 1961–72, Deputy Chair. 1974–77, Chair. 1977–83, Dir. 1984–85; Dir.-Gen. City Panel on Take-overs and Mergers 1972–74, Deputy Chair. 1987–; Deputy Chair. Land Securities PLC 1976–97, 1998– (Chair. 1997–98); Dir. Lucas Industries PLC 1975–90, Legal & Gen. Group PLC 1976–90, Goodwood Racecourse Ltd. 1987–93; Chair. Bank of England's City Co. Law Cttee. 1976–78; mem. Council Manchester Business School 1974–86, Lay mem. of the Council of the Stock Exchange 1983–84. *Leisure interests:* reading political history and 19th-century novelists. *Address:* 33 Edwardes Square, London, W8 6HH, England. *Telephone:* 0171-603 0715.

HULME, Keri; New Zealand novelist; b. 9 Mar. 1947, Christchurch, N.Z.; worked as tobacco picker, fish and chip cook, TV dir. and woollen mill worker and studied law, before becoming full-time writer 1972; writer-in-residence Otago Univ. 1978, Univ. of Canterbury, Christchurch 1985. *Publications:* The Bone People 1984, The Windeater 1987, Strands (poems) 1991, Bait 1992; awarded Booker McConnell Prize for Fiction, U.K. 1985. *Address:* c/o Hodder & Stoughton Ltd., 338 Euston Road, London, NW1 3BH, England.

HULSE, Russell Alan, PH.D.; American research physicist; b. 28 Nov. 1950; s. of Alan Earle Hulse and Betty Joan Wedemeyer; ed. The Cooper Union, New York and Univ. of Massachusetts; worked at Nat. Radio Astronomy Observatory 1975–77; researcher at Plasma Physics Lab., Princeton Univ. 1977–, Prin. Research Physicist 1992–, Head Advanced Modelling Sciences Lab. 1994–; Fellow American Physical Soc. 1993, Distinguished Resident Fellow, Princeton Univ. 1994; Nobel Prize in Physics (jt. winner) 1993. *Publications:* papers in professional journals and conf. proceedings in fields of pulsar astronomy, controlled fusion plasma physics and computer modelling. *Leisure interests:* cross-country skiing, canoeing, nature photography, bird watching, other outdoor activities, target shooting, music. *Address:* Princeton University, Plasma Physics Laboratory, James Forrestal Research Campus, P.O. Box 451, Princeton, NJ 08543, U.S.A. *Telephone:* (609) 243-2621.

HULST, Hendrik Christoffel van de, PH.D.; Netherlands astronomer; b. 19 Nov. 1918, Utrecht; m. Wilhelmina Mengerink 1946; two s. two d.; ed. Utrecht Univ.; Post-Doctoral Fellow Chicago Univ. 1946–48; lecturer in Astronomy, Leiden Univ. 1948–52, Prof. of Astronomy 1952–84; Pres. Comm. 1934 (Interstellar Matter) Int. Astronomical Union 1952–58, Nederland Astronomen Club 1953–56, Cttee. on Space Research (COSPAR) 1958–62; Chair. Netherlands Comm. for Geophysical and Space Research 1960–83; Vice-Chair. European Space Research Org. (ESRO) 1960–65, Chair. 1968–70; mem. Royal Neths. Acad. of Sciences; Eddington Medal, Royal Astronomical Soc. (U.K.) 1955, Draper Medal, Nat. Acad. of Sciences (U.S.A.) 1956, Rumford Medal, Royal Soc. (U.K.) 1964, Bruce Medal of the Astronomical Soc. of the Pacific 1978, Massey Medal, Royal Soc. 1990. *Publications:* A Course of Radio Astronomy 1951, Phaenomenologie en Natuurwetenschap (with C. A. van Peursen) 1953, Light Scattering by Small Particles 1957, Multiple Light Scattering 1980; numerous articles and papers, particularly on interstellar matter. *Address:* Sterrewacht Leiden, Huygens Laboratorium, P.O. Box 9513, 2300 RA Leiden; Sterrewacht 8, Leiden, Netherlands. *Telephone:* 071-131192 (Home).

HULTQVIST, Bengt Karl Gustaf, PH.D.; Swedish space physicist; b. 21 Aug. 1927, Hemmesjö; s. of Eric Hultqvist and Elsa Hultqvist; m. Gurli Gustafsson 1953; two s. one d.; ed. Univ. of Stockholm; Dir. Kiruna Geophysical Observatory 1956–73, Kiruna Geophysical Inst. 1973–87, Swedish Inst. of Space Physics 1987–94, Int. Space Science Inst. (ISSI), Berne, Switzerland 1995–; Chair. Swedish Space Science Cttee. 1972–97, Swedish Nat. Cttee. for Geodesy and Geophysics, EISCAT Council 1987–88, Nordic Soc. for Space Research 1989–92; Kt. of the Northern Star Award, Royal Swedish Acad. of Science 1968, 1972; Gold Medal, Royal Swedish Acad. of Eng. Sciences, King's Medal 1991, Berzelius Medal, Royal Swedish Acad. of Science 1994, Julius Bartels Medal, European Geophysical Soc. 1996. *Publications include:* Introduction to geocosmophysics 1967, High latitude space plasma physics (ed.) 1983, Space, Science and I 1997; 185 scientific papers on radiation and space physics. *Address:* Swedish Institute of Space Physics, Box 812, 981 28 Kiruna, Sweden (Office). *Telephone:* (46) 980 79000.

HUME, H.E. Cardinal (George) Basil, M.A. (Oxon)., S.T.L. (Fribourg); British ecclesiastic; b. 2 March 1923, Newcastle upon Tyne; s. of the late Sir William and Lady Hume; ed. Ampleforth Coll., York, St. Benet's Hall., Oxford, and Fribourg Univ., Switzerland; ordained as a Catholic priest 1950; Sr. Master in Modern Languages, Ampleforth Coll., York 1952–63, Housemaster of St. Bede's 1955–63; Prof. of Dogmatic Theology at Ampleforth Abbey 1955–63; Magister Scholarum, English Benedictine Congregation 1957–63; Abbot of Ampleforth 1963–76; Archbishop of Westminster March 1976–; cr. Cardinal May 1976; Pres. Bishops' Conf. of England and Wales 1979–, Council of European Bishops' Confs. 1978–87; Jt. Pres. Churches Together in England 1990–; mem. Pontifical Council for the Promotion of Christian Unity, Congregation for Religious and Secular Insts., Congregation for the Sacraments and Divine Worship, Congregation for Eastern Churches, Pontifical Council for Pastoral Assistance to Health Care Workers; Hon. D.D. (Newcastle) 1979, (Cambridge) 1979, (London) 1980, (Oxford) 1981, (York) 1982, (Kent) 1983, (Hull) 1989, (Keele) 1990; Dr. h.c. (Durham) 1987, (San Anselmo, Rome) 1987, (Surrey) 1992; Hon. LL.D. (Univ. of Northumbria at Newcastle) 1992; Hon. Bencher of Inner Temple 1976; Hon. Freeman of City of Newcastle 1980, City of London 1980, Worshipful Co. of Skinners. *Publications:* Searching for God 1977, In Praise of Benedict 1981, To be a Pilgrim 1984, Towards A Civilization of Love 1988, Light in the Lord 1991, Remaking Europe 1994, Footprints of The Northern Saints 1996, The Mystery of Love 1996, Basil in Blunderland 1997, The Mystery of the Cross 1998. *Leisure interest:* angling. *Address:* Archbishop's House, Westminster, London, S.W.1, England. *Telephone:* 0171-798 9033.

HUME, John, M.A.; Irish politician and fmr. teacher; b. 18 Jan. 1937, Londonderry, N. Ireland; s. of Samuel and Anne (née Doherty) Hume; m. Patricia Hone 1960; two s. three d.; ed. St. Colomb's Coll., Londonderry, St. Patrick's Coll., Maynooth, Nat. Univ. of Ireland; Research Fellow, Trinity Coll., Assoc. Fellow, Centre for Int. Affairs, Harvard; Founder mem. Credit Union in N. Ireland, Pres. 1964–68; Non-violent Civil Rights leader 1968–69; rep. Londonderry in Northern Ireland Parl. 1969–72, in N. Ireland Assembly 1972–73; Minister of Commerce, Powersharing Exec. 1974; rep. Londonderry in N. Ireland Convention 1975–76; elected to European Parl. June 1979–; Leader, Social Democratic and Labour Party (SDLP) Dec. 1979–; mem. N. Ireland Ass. 1982–86; M.P. for Foyle 1983–; mem. for Foyle, N.I. Ass. 1998–; mem. SDLP New Ireland Forum 1983–84, Irish Transport and General Workers Union, Bureau of European Parliament Socialist 1979–, Regional Policy and Regional Planning Cttee. 1979–, EEC, A.C.P.-EEC Joint Ass. 1979–, Socialist Co.-Chair. Intergroup on Minority Cultures and Languages; Co-Leader Int. Democratic Observers for 1986 Philippines Election; mem. Advisory Cttee. on Pollution of the Sea (ACOPS) 1989; shared Nobel Peace Prize 1998. Dr. h.c. (Massachusetts) 1985; Sponsor, Irish Anti-Apartheid Movement; Dr. h.c. (Catholic Univ. of America) 1986, (St. Joseph's Univ., Phila.) 1986; Hon. Dr. (Univ. of Mass., Catholic Univ. of America, Wash. D.C., St. Joseph's Univ., Phila., Tusculum Coll., Tenn.); Hon. LL.D. (Queen's) 1995, (Wales) 1996, Hon. D.Litt. (Ulster) 1998. *Address:* 5 Bayview Terrace, Derry, BT48 7EE, Northern Ireland. *Telephone:* (01504) 363423 (Office).

HUMMEL, Arthur William, Jr., M.A.; American diplomatist; b. 1 June 1920, Fenzhou (Fenchow), China; s. of Arthur William Hummel and Ruth Emily Bookwalter; m. Betty L. Fristenberger 1951; two s.; ed. Antioch Coll., Coll. of Chinese Studies, Beijing, Univ. of Chicago: English teacher Fu Jen Middle School, Beijing 1941; interned by Japanese 1941–44, escaped 1944; mem. Chinese guerrilla unit 1944–45; Liaison Officer UNRRA, Tianjin, China 1945–46; Staff Lecturer, United Service to China, New York 1946–47; Intelligence Analyst Officer, Naval Intelligence 1950; Foreign Affairs Officer, Dept. of State 1950–52; Consul, Deputy Public Affairs Officer, Hong Kong 1952, Public Affairs Officer 1953–55; Attaché, Deputy Public Affairs Officer, U.S. Embassy, Tokyo 1955–57; Attaché, Public Affairs Officer, Rangoon, Burma 1957–60; Nat. War Coll. 1960–61; Deputy Dir. Voice of America 1961–63; Deputy Asst. Sec. of State for Cultural and Educational Affairs 1963–65; Deputy Chief of Mission, Taipei, Taiwan 1965–68; Amb. to Burma 1968–71; Deputy Asst. Sec. of State for Far Eastern and Pacific Affairs 1971–75; Amb. to Ethiopia 1975–76; Asst. Sec. of State for Far Eastern and Pacific Affairs 1976–77; Amb. to Pakistan 1977–81, to People's Repub. of China 1981–85; Dir. Exploration Co. of La. 1994–; Arthur S. Fleming Award 1959, Sec. of State's Distinguished Honor Award 1985; mem. Far Eastern Asscn. *Address:* 4923 Essex Avenue, Chevy Chase, MD 20815, U.S.A.

HUMPHREYS, James Charles, B.COM., M.SC.; Australian diplomatist; b. 6 Oct. 1934, Melbourne; s. of James Thomas and Mary Charlotte Humphreys; m. Diane May Dummett 1962; two d.; ed. Scotch Coll., Melbourne, Univs. of Melbourne and London; with Dept. of Trade and Customs 1951–62; Dept. of Treasury 1963–71; Counsellor (Financial), Tokyo 1972–74; Dept. of Foreign Affairs, Canberra 1974–78; Amb. to Denmark 1978–80, to OECD, Paris 1980–83; First Asst. Sec. (Econ.) Dept. of Foreign Affairs, Canberra 1984–86; First Asst. Sec., Dept. of Foreign Affairs and Trade, Canberra 1987–88; High Commr. in Canada, also accred. to Bermuda 1989–91; Exec. Dir. EBRD, London 1991–94; Consul-Gen. in U.S.A., New York 1994–96; Chief Exec. Global Econs. Ltd. 1997–. *Leisure interests:* sailing, tennis, reading, music. *Address:* P.O. Box 335, Double Bay, N.S.W. 2028, Australia.

HUMPHRIES, (John) Barry, A.O.; Australian entertainer and author; b. 17 Feb. 1934; s. of J. A. E. Humphries and L. A. Brown; m. 1st Rosalind Tong 1959; two d.; m. 2nd Diane Millstead; two s.; m. 3rd Lizzie Spender 1990; ed. Melbourne Grammar and Univ. of Melbourne; repertory seasons Union Theatre, Melbourne 1953–54, Phillip Street Revue Theatre, Sydney 1956, Demon Barber Lyric, Hammersmith 1959, Oliver, New Theatre 1960; one-man shows (author and performer): A Nice Night's Entertainment 1962, Excuse I 1965, Just a Show 1968, A Load of Olde Stuffe 1971, At Least You Can Say That You've Seen It 1974, Housewife Superstar 1976, Isn't It Pathetic at His Age 1979, A Night with Dame Edna 1979, An Evening's Intercourse with Barry Humphries 1981–82, Tears Before Bedtime 1986, Back with a Vengeance, London 1987–88, Look at Me when I'm Talking to You 1993–94, Edna: The Spectacle 1998, Dame Edna: The Royal Tour, San Francisco 1998, Remember You're Out 1999; numerous plays, films and broadcasts; best-known for his comic characterisations of Dame Edna Everage, Sir Les Patterson and Sandy Stone; Pres. Frans de Boewer Soc. (Belgium). *Publications:* Bizarre 1964, Innocent Austral Verse 1968, The Wonderful World of Barry McKenzie (with Nicholas Garland) 1970, Bazza Holds His Own (with Nicholas Garland) 1972, Dame Edna's Coffee Table Book 1976, Les Patterson's Australia 1979, Treasury of Australian Kitsch 1980, A Nice Night's Entertainment 1981, Dame Edna's Bedside Companion 1982, The Traveller's Tool 1985, The Complete Barry McKenzie 1988, My Gorgeous Life: the autobiography of Dame Edna Everage 1989, The Life and Death of Sandy Stone 1991, More Please: An Autobiography 1992,

Women in the Background (novel) 1996. *Leisure interests:* reading second-hand booksellers' catalogues in bed, inventing Australia. *Address:* c/o PBJ Management Ltd., 5 Soho Square, London, W1V 5DE, England.

HUMPHRYS, John; British broadcaster; b. 17 Aug. 1943; s. of Edward George Humphrys and Winifred Matthews; m. (divorced); one s. one d.; ed. Cardiff High School; Washington corresp. BBC TV 1971–77, Southern Africa corresp. 1977–80, Diplomatic corresp. 1981; presenter, BBC Nine o'Clock News 1981–87; presenter, BBC Radio 4 Today Programme 1987–, On the Record, BBC TV 1993–, John Humphrys Interview Radio 4 1995–; Hon. Fellow Cardiff Univ. 1998; Hon. D.Litt. (Dundee) 1996; Hon. M.A. (Univ. of Wales) 1998. *Publication:* Devil's Advocate 1999. *Leisure interests:* cello, trees, books. *Address:* BBC, News Centre, Wood Lane, London, W. 12, England.

HUN SEN; Cambodian politician; b. 1952, Kompang-Cham Prov.; m. Binn Sam Hieng 1976; three s. three d.; ed. Phnom Penh; joined Khmer Rouges 1970, rising to Commdt.; in Viet Nam with pro-Vietnamese Kampucheans 1977, returned to Kampuchea (now Cambodia) after Vietnamese-backed take-over; Minister for Foreign Affairs 1979–85; Deputy Prime Minister 1981; Chair. Council of Ministers of Cambodia (Prime Minister) 1985–93, Second Prime Minister Royal Govt. of Cambodia 1993–98, Prime Minister of Cambodia 1998–; Vice-Chair. Cambodian People's Party (CPP). *Address:* Council of Ministers, Phnom Penh, Cambodia.

HUNDERTWASSER, Friedensreich (Friedrich Stowasser); Austrian artist; b. 15 Dec. 1928, Vienna; s. of the late Ernst and Elsa Stowasser; m. 1st 1958 (dissolved 1960); m. 2nd Yuko Ikewada 1962 (dissolved 1966); first one-man exhbn. at Art Club, Vienna 1952; evolved theory of "Transautomatism" and developed it into a "Grammar of Vision"; exhbns. at Studio Paul Facchetti, Paris 1954, Galleria del Naviglio, Milan 1955, Galerie H. Kamer, Paris 1957–60, Aberbach Fine Art, New York 1973, Vienna 1974, at galleries in Milan, Tokyo, at Venice Biennale, etc.; travelling exhbns. Albertina Graphic 1974–, Austria Presents Hundertwasser to the Continents 1975– (shown in 32 museums in 4 continents by 1981), Hundertwasser is Painting 1979–, Creative Architecture—Eternal Longing 1992–; architecture: construction of apt. house for the City of Vienna 1983–85, redesign of a church in Bärnbach 1987–88, redesign of an incinerator in Vienna 1988–92, construction of a children's day care centre in Frankfurt 1988–93, Kunst Haus in Vienna (a Hundertwasser Museum) 1989–91, construction of a thermal village in Blumau 1994–97; Guest Lecturer Kunsthochschule, Hamburg 1959; Head of a School of Painting, Acad. of Fine Arts, Vienna 1981–; has travelled extensively round the world; nude demonstration against sterile architecture, Munich and Vienna 1968; has designed postage stamps for numerous countries; Prix du Syndicat d'Initiative, Bordeaux, 1957, Sanbra Prize, São Paulo Biennale 1959, Mainichi Prize, Sixth Int. Art Exhbn., Tokyo 1961, Austrian State Prize (from Kunstsenat) 1980, Austrian Environment Award 1981, Gross Preis der deutschen Beufsphilatelie 1998, numerous other awards. *Publications:* issued manifestos: Mouldiness Manifesto: Against Rationalism in Architecture 1958, Individual Building Alteration Law and Architecture Boycott Manifesto 1968, Los von Loos 1968, Your Right to Windows—Your Duty to the Trees 1972, The Colour in Town Architecture 1981; portfolios: Look at It on a Rainy Day 1971–72, Midori No Namida 1975, Nana Hyaku Mizu 1973, Joy of Man 1988; ed. Brockhaus Encyclopedia 1989; Hundertwasser's Rainy Day (film) 1972. *Address:* P.O. Box 28, 1182 Vienna, Austria.

HUNGER, Herbert, D.PHIL.; Austrian professor of Byzantine studies; b. 9 Dec. 1914, Vienna; s. of Dr. Hermann and Johanna (née Kölbl) Hunger; m. Ruth Friedrich 1941; two s. one d.; ed. Humanistisches Gymnasium and Univ. of Vienna; Librarian Austrian Nat. Library 1948–56, Dir. Papyrus Collection 1956–62; Prof. of Byzantine Studies, Univ. of Vienna 1962–85; Pres. Austrian Acad. of Sciences 1973–82; hon. or corresp. mem. of 18 foreign Acads.; Österreichisches Ehrenzeichen für Wissenschaft und Kunst and many other awards and prizes; Dr. h.c. (Chicago, Thessalonika, Helsinki, Athens, Ioannina). *Publications:* Lexikon der griechischen und römischen Mythologie 1953, 1988, Byzantinische Geisteswelt 1958, Katalog der griechischen Handschriften der Österreichischen Nationalbibliothek (6 vols.) 1961–94, Prooimion 1964, Reich der Neuen Mitte 1965, Johannes Chortasmenos 1969, Byzantinistische Grundlagenforschung 1973, Die hochsprachliche profane Literatur der Byzantiner (2 vols.) 1978, Anonyme Metaphrase zu Anna Komnene, Alexias XI-XIII 1981, Des Nikephoros Blemmydes "Basilikos Andrias" und dessen Metaphrase (with I. Ševčenko) 1986, Schreiben und Lesen in Byzanz 1989. *Leisure interest:* chamber music. *Address:* Weissgerberlände 40, 1030 Vienna, Austria.

HUNLÉDÉ, Ayi Houénou, L. en D.; Togolese politician; b. 2 Feb. 1925, Anécho; ed. Univ. of Montpellier, France; Asst. Insp. of schools, Northern Togo, then teacher at Ecole Normale d'Atakpamé 1953–56; worked for French Overseas Territories Admin. 1958; Asst. Admin. Mayor, Lomé; Chief, admin. subdivision of Tabligbo; Admin. Mayor of Tsévié 1958–60; Amb. to France, U.K., EEC 1960–65; High Commr. for Planning 1965–67; Minister of Foreign Affairs 1967–76; ordained pastor in Togolese Evangelical Church Aug. 1977; Commdr., Légion d'honneur, Great Cross of Merit (Fed. Repub. of Germany), Commdr., Order of Liberia. *Address:* c/o Togolese Evangelical Church, Lomé, Togo.

HUNT, Caroline Rose, PH.D.; American business executive; b. 8 Jan. 1923, El Dorado; d. of H. L. Hunt and Lyda Bunker; divorced; four s. one d.; ed. Mary Baldwin Coll., Univs. of Texas and Charleston; beneficiary of Caroline Hunt Trust Estate which includes Corpn., Rosewood Properties, Rosewood Resources with interests in oil and gas properties, luxury hotels, office devts. in maj. cities; owner Lady Primrose's Shopping English Countryside; Hon. Chair. and Chair. numerous socs. and cttees.; Award for Excellence in Community Service in the Field of Business, Dallas Historic Soc. 1984, Les Femmes du Monde Award 1988, Grande Dame d'Escoffier 1989, Nat. Fragrance Council Award 1994, British American Commerce Award 1994. *Publication:* The Compleat Pumpkin Eater. *Leisure interests:* antiques, writing. *Address:* 100 Crescent Court, Ste. 1700, Dallas, TX 75201, U.S.A.

HUNT, Helen; American actress; b. 15 June 1963, L.A.; d. of Gordon Hunt. *Stage appearances include:* Been Taken, Our Town, The Taming of the Shrew, Methusalem. *Films include:* Rollercoaster, Girls Just Want to Have Fun, Peggy Sue Got Married, Project X, Miles From Home, Trancers, Stealing Home, Next of Kin, The Waterdance, Only You, Bob Roberts, Mr Saturday Night, Kiss of Death, Twister, As Good As It Gets (Acad. Award for Best Actress 1998), Twelfth Night. *TV includes:* Swiss Family Robinson, Mad About You (Emmy Award 1996, 1997, Golden Globe Award 1997). *Address:* c/o Connie Tavel, 9171 Wilshire Boulevard, Suite 436, Beverly Hills, CA 90210, U.S.A.

HUNT, James Baxter, Jr., B.S.(EDUC.), M.S.(ECONS.); American politician; b. 16 May 1937, Guilford Co., N.C.; s. of James Baxter and Elsie (Brame) Hunt; m. Carolyn Joyce Leonard 1958; one s. three d.; ed. North Carolina State Univ., Univ. of North Carolina; called to Bar of N.C. 1964; Econ. Adviser to Govt. of Nepal for Ford Foundation 1964–66; partner with Kirby, Webb and Hunt 1966–72, Poyner and Spruill, Raleigh, N.C. 1985–93; Lieut.-Gov. North Carolina 1973–77, Gov. of North Carolina 1977–85, Jan. 1993–; Democrat; mem. Bd. of Dirs. Nat. Center for Educ. and the Economy; 1st Annual Harry S. Truman Award Nat. Young Democrats 1975, Soil Conservation Honors Award 1986, Outstanding Govt. Leader in U.S. Conservation, Nat. Wildlife Fed. 1983 and other awards. *Address:* Office of the Governor, 116 West Jones Street, Raleigh, NC 27603, U.S.A.

HUNT, Jonathan Lucas, P.C., M.A.; New Zealand politician; b. 2 Dec. 1938, Lower Hutt; s. of H. Lucas and A. Z. Hunt; ed. Auckland Grammar School, Auckland Univ.; teacher Kelston Boys' High School 1961–66; tutor, Univ. of Auckland 1964–66; mem. for New Lynn 1966–; Jr. Govt. Whip 1972, Chair. of Cttees. and Deputy Speaker of House of Reps. 1974–75, Acting Speaker 1975; Labour Opposition Spokesman on Health 1976–79, Constitution and Parl. Affairs 1978–81; Sr. Opposition Whip 1980–84; Shadow Minister of Broadcasting 1982; Minister of Broadcasting and Postmaster-Gen. 1984–87, Minister of State 1987–89, Leader of the House 1987–90, Minister of Broadcasting 1988–90; Minister for Tourism 1988–89, of Housing 1989, of Communications Jan.–Oct. 1990; Senior Opposition Whip 1990–96; Shadow Leader of the House 1996–. *Leisure interests:* music, international affairs, cricket, literature. *Address:* Parliament Buildings, Wellington; P.O. Box 15180, New Lynn, Auckland (Office); Lone Kauri Road, Kare Kare, R.D.I., New Lynn, Auckland, New Zealand (Home). *Telephone:* (04) 4719831 (Office); (09) 8128864.

HUNT, Pierre; French diplomatist; b. 3 Sept. 1925, Paris; two d.; ed. Lycée Janson-de-Sailly, Faculté de Droit de Paris and Ecole nat. de la France d'outre-mer; Deputy Dir. Services de Presse et d'Information 1965; Sec.-Gen. Comité interministeriel pour l'Information 1969; Admin. SOFIRAD and Radio Monte Carlo 1970; Amb. to Congo 1972–76, to Madagascar 1976–78, to Tunisia 1980–83, to Egypt 1985–89, to Portugal 1989–90; Ambassadeur de France 1990; Spokesman for the Pres. 1978–80; Officier Légion d'honneur, Ordre national du Mérite. *Leisure interests:* tennis, golf, swimming, painting, photography. *Address:* 12 rue de la Comète, 75007 Paris, France (Home).

HUNT, Sir Rex Masterman, Kt., C.M.G., B.A.; British diplomatist (retd.); b. 29 June 1926; s. of the late H. W. Hunt and of Ivy Masterman; m. Mavis Buckland 1951; one s. one d.; ed. Coatham School, St. Peter's Coll., Oxford; service with R.A.F. 1944–48; with Overseas Civil Service 1951; Dist. Commr., Uganda 1962; in Commonwealth Relations Office 1963–64; First Sec., Kuching, Malaysia 1964–65, Jesselton (now Kota Kinabalu), Malaysia 1965–67, Brunei 1967; First Sec., (Econ.), Embassy, Turkey 1968–70; First Sec. and Head of Chancery, Embassy, Indonesia 1970–72; Asst., Middle East Dept., FCO 1972–74; Counsellor, Embassy, S. Viet Nam 1974–75, Deputy High Commr., Malaysia 1976–79; Gov. and C.-in-C. Falkland Islands and Dependencies 1980–82, expelled after Argentine seizure of Falkland Islands April 1982, returned as Civil Commr. June, after UK recapture of Islands; Civil Commr. Falkland Islands 1982–Sept. 1985, Gov. Oct. 1985, High Comm. British Antarctic Territory 1980–85. *Publication:* My Falkland Days 1992. *Leisure interests:* gardening, golf. *Address:* Old Woodside, Broomfield Park, Sunningdale, Berks., SL5 0JS, England. *Telephone:* (01344) 625563.

HUNTEN, Donald Mount, PH.D.; American astronomer and physicist; b. 1 March 1925, Montreal, Canada; s. of Kenneth William Hunten and Winnifred Binnmore Mount; m. Isobel Ann Rubenstein 1949 (divorced 1995); two s.; ed. Univ. of Western Ontario, McGill Univ.; Research Assoc. to Prof. Univ. of Sask., Saskatoon 1950–63; Physicist Kitt Peak Nat. Observatory 1963–78; Consultant to NASA 1964–, Science Adviser to NASA Assoc. Admin. for Space Science 1977–78; Prof. of Planetary Science Univ. of Ariz., Tucson 1978–88, Regents Prof. 1988–; mem. N.A.S.; numerous awards. *Publications:*

Introduction to Electronics 1964, Theory of Planetary Atmospheres (with J. W. Chamberlain) 1987, several NASA publs., numerous papers in scientific journals. *Leisure interest:* music. *Address:* Department of Planetary Sciences, University of Arizona, Tucson, AZ 85721; 3445 W. Foxes Den Drive, Tucson, AZ 85745, U.S.A. (Home). *Telephone:* (602) 621-4002 (Office). *Fax:* (602) 621-4933.

HUNTER, Evan, B.A.; American author; b. 15 Oct. 1926, New York; s. of Charles and Marie Lombino; m. 1st Anita Melnick 1949; three s.; m. 2nd Mary Vann Finley 1973 (divorced); one step d.; m. 3rd Dragica Dimitrijevic 1997; ed. Cooper Union and Hunter Coll.; *Publications:* The Blackboard Jungle 1954, Second Ending 1956, Strangers When We Meet 1958 (screenplay 1959), A Matter of Conviction 1959, Mothers and Daughters 1961, The Birds (screenplay) 1962, Happy New Year, Herbie 1963, Buddwing 1964, The Easter Man (play) 1964, The Paper Dragon 1966, A Horse's Head 1967, Last Summer 1968, Sons 1969, The Conjurer (play) 1969, Nobody Knew They Were There 1971, Every Little Crook and Nanny 1972, The Easter Man 1972, Come Winter 1973, Streets of Gold 1974, The Chisholms 1976, Me and Mr. Stenner 1976, Love, Dad 1981, 87th Precinct Mysteries, Far From the Sea 1983, Lizzie 1984, Criminal Conversation 1994, Privileged Conversation 1996, Me and Hitch 1997; under pseudonym Ed McBain: Cop Hater 1956, The Mugger 1956, The Pusher 1956, The Con Man 1957, Killer's Choice 1957, Killer's Payoff 1958, Lady Killer 1958, Killer's Wedge 1959, 'Til Death 1959, King's Ransom 1959, Give the Boys a Great Big Hand 1960, The Heckler 1960, See Them Die 1960, Lady, Lady, I Did It 1961, Like Love 1962, The Empty Hours (three novelettes) 1962, Ten plus One 1963, Ax 1964, He Who Hesitates 1965, Doll 1965, The Sentries 1965, Eighty Million Eyes 1966, Fuzz 1968 (screenplay 1972), Shotgun 1969, Jigsaw 1970, Hail, Hail, The Gang's All Here 1971, Sadie When She Died 1972, Let's Hear It for the Deaf Man 1972, Hail to the Chief 1973, Bread 1974, Where There's Smoke 1975, Blood Relatives 1975, So Long as You Both Shall Live 1976, Long Time No See 1977, Goldilocks 1977, Calypso 1979, Ghosts 1980, Rumpelstiltskin 1981, Heat 1981, Ice 1983, Beauty and the Beast 1983, Jack and the Beanstalk 1984, Lightning 1984, Snow White and Rose Red 1985, Eight Black Horses 1985, Cinderella 1986, Another Part of the City 1986, Poison 1987, Puss in Boots 1987, Tricks 1987, McBain's Ladies 1988, The House that Jack Built 1988, Lullaby 1989, Downtown 1989, Vespers 1990, Three Blind Mice 1990, Widows 1991, Kiss 1992, Mary, Mary 1992, Mischief 1993, There Was a Little Girl 1994, And All through the House 1994, Romance 1995, Gladly the Cross-Eyed Bear 1996, Nocturne 1997. *Leisure interest:* travel.

HUNTER, Holly, B.F.A.; American actress; b. 20 March 1958, Atlanta, Ga.; d. of Charles Hunter and Opal M. Catledge; m. Janusz Kaminski 1995; ed. Carnegie-Mellon Univ.; Broadway appearances include Crimes of the Heart, The Wake of Jamey Foster, The Miss Firecracker Contest; other stage appearances include A Weekend Near Madison, The Person I Once Was, Battery (all in New York), A Lie of the Mind (Los Angeles) and in regional productions; Emmy Award for TV production Roe vs. Wade 1989; Best Actress Award, American TV Awards, for cable TV production of The Positively True Adventures of the Alleged Texas Cheerleader Murdering Mom 1993; Best Actress Award, Cannes Film Festival Award 1993 and Acad. Award 1994 for role in The Piano; Dir. Calif. Abortion Rights Action League. *Films:* Broadcast News 1987, Raising Arizona 1987, Miss Firecracker 1989, Always 1989, Once Around 1990, The Piano 1993, The Firm 1993, Home for the Holidays, Copycat 1995, Crash 1996, Living Out Loud 1998.

HUNTER, Robert John, PH.D., F.A.A., F.R.A.C.I., C.CHEM.; Australian research chemist; b. 26 June 1933, Abermain, N.S.W.; s. of Ronald J. Hunter and Elizabeth Dixon; m. Barbara Robson 1954 (divorced 1995); one s. one d.; ed. Cessnock High School, N.S.W., New England Univ. Coll. and Univ. of Sydney; secondary school teacher 1953–54; Tech. Officer, CSIRO 1954–57, Research Officer 1960–64; lecturer, Univ. of Sydney 1964, Assoc. Prof. of Physical Chemistry 1972–90, Head, School of Chem. 1987–90, Hon. Research Assoc. 1990–; Dir. Colloidal Dynamics Pty. Ltd. 1988–96; Chair. Nat. Science and Industry Forum 1991–93; Pres. Int. Asscn. of Colloid and Interface Scientists 1992–94; Nat. Pres. Scientists for Global Responsibility (fmrly. Scientists Against Nuclear Arms) 1986–88, 1990–92, 1996–; Alexander Memorial Lecturer 1987, Liversidge Lecturer of Royal Soc. of N.S.W. 1988; Archibald Ollé Prize 1982, 1993. *Publications:* Chemical Science 1976, Zeta Potential in Colloid Science 1981, Foundations of Colloid Science, (Vol. I) 1987, (Vol. 2) 1989, Introduction to Modern Colloid Science 1993. *Leisure interests:* music, drama, reading. *Address:* School of Chemistry, The University of Sydney, N.S.W. 2006 (Office); 26/20A Austin Street, Lane Cove, N.S.W. 2066, Australia (Home). *Telephone:* (02) 9351-2220 (Office); (02) 9427-6261 (Home). *Fax:* (02) 9351-3329.

HUNTER, Tony (Anthony Rex), M.A., PH.D. F.R.S.; British molecular biologist and virologist; b. 23 Aug. 1943, Ashford; s. of Ranulph Rex Hunter and Nellie Ruby Elsie Hitchcock; m. 1st Philippa Charlotte Marrack 1969 (divorced 1974); m. 2nd Jennifer Ann Maureen Price 1992; two s.; ed. Felsted School, Essex and Gonville and Caius Coll., Cambridge; Research Fellow Christ's Coll., Cambridge 1968–71, 1973–75; Research Assoc. Salk Inst., San Diego, Calif. 1971–73, Asst. Prof. 1975–78, Assoc. Prof. 1978–82, Prof. 1982–; Adjunct Assoc. Prof. Dept. of Biology Univ. of California, San Diego 1979–82, Adjunct Prof. 1982–; American Acad. of Arts and Sciences 1992; Assoc. mem. EMBO 1992; American Cancer Soc. Research Prof. 1992–; Fellow Royal Soc. for Encouragement of Arts, Manufactures and Commerce (RSA) 1989; Foreign Assoc. Nat. Acad. of Sciences (U.S.A.) 1998; American Business Foundation for Cancer Research Award 1988; Katherine Berkan Judd Award (Memorial Sloan-Kettering Cancer Center) 1992, Hopkins Medal (Biochemical Soc.) 1994, Gairdner Foundation Int. Award 1994, General Motors Cancer Research Foundation Mott Prize 1994. *Publications:* 350 papers and journal articles. *Leisure interests:* white water rafting, desert camping. *Address:* Molecular Biology and Virology Laboratory, The Salk Institute, P.O. Box 85800, San Diego, CA 92186, U.S.A. *Telephone:* (619) 453-4100 (Ext. 1385) (Office). *Fax:* (619) 457-4765 (Office).

HUNTINGTON, Samuel Phillips, M.A., PH.D.; American political scientist; b. 18 April 1927, New York; s. of Richard Huntington and Dorothy S. Phillips; m. Nancy Arkelyan 1957; two s.; ed. Harvard and Yale Univs. and Univ. of Chicago; Instructor in Govt. Harvard Univ. 1950–53, Asst. Prof. 1953–58; Assoc. Dir. Inst. of War and Peace Studies, Columbia Univ. 1959–62; Prof. of Govt. Harvard Univ. 1962–67, Frank G. Thomson Prof. of Govt. 1967–81, Clarence Dillon Prof. of Int. Affairs 1981–82, Eaton Prof. of Science of Govt. 1982–95, Albert J. Weatherhead III Univ. Prof. 1995–; Dir. John M. Olin Inst. for Strategic Studies 1989–; Chair. Harvard Acad. for Int. and Area Studies 1996–; Co-ordinator of Security Planning for Nat. Security Council, White House, Washington, DC 1977–78; Fellow, Center for Advanced Study of Behavioral Sciences, Stanford Univ. 1969–70; Visiting Fellow, All Souls Coll. Oxford 1973; Fellow, Woodrow Wilson Int. Center for Scholars, Washington, D.C. 1983–84; Sr. Research Assoc. Int. Inst. for Strategic Studies, London 1990; Guggenheim Fellow 1972–73; many other academic and professional appts. *Publications:* author or ed. of over a dozen books including The Third Wave: Democratization in the Late Twentieth Century 1991, The Clash of Civilizations and the Remaking of World Order 1996; ninety scholarly articles, contribs. to books, monographs. *Address:* Olin Institute for Strategic Studies, Harvard University, 1737 Cambridge Street, Cambridge, MA 02138, U.S.A. *Telephone:* (617) 495-4432. *Fax:* (617) 495-1384.

HUO YINGDONG (also known as Henry Fok Ying-tung); Chinese politician and business executive; b. 10 May 1923, Panyu Co., Guangdong Prov.; Perm. mem. 5th and 6th CPPCC 1983–88; Perm. mem. 7th Standing Cttee. NPC 1988–92; mem. Preparatory Cttee. of the Hong Kong Special Admin. Region 1985–97; Vice-Chair. 8th Nat. Cttee. CPPCC 1993–98, 9th Nat. Cttee. 1998–; Vice-Chair. PWC; Chair. Yau Wing Co. Ltd.; Chair. Henry Fok Estates Ltd. 1955–; Dir. China Int. Trust and Investment Corpn. 1979–; Pres. Real Estate Developers Asscn. of Hong Kong, Hong Kong Football Asscn.; Vice-Pres. Chinese Gen. Chamber of Commerce, China Asscn. for Advancement of Int. Friendship, All China Sports Fed.; mem. Exec. Cttee. Fed. of Int. Football Asscns. *Address:* National Committee of Chinese People's Political Consultative Conference, 23 Taipingqiao Street, Beijing, People's Republic of China; Pedder Building, Central, Hong Kong Special Administrative Region, People's Republic of China.

HUONG, Tran Van (see Tran Van Huong).

HUPPERT, Herbert Eric, M.A., PH.D., SC.D., F.R.S.; Australian scientist; b. 26 Nov. 1943, Sydney; s. of Leo Huppert and Alice (née Neumann) Huppert; m. Felicia Ferster 1966; two s.; ed. Sydney Boys High School, Univ. of Sydney, Australian Nat. Univ. and Univ. of California, San Diego; ICI Research Fellow Cambridge Univ. 1968–69, Asst. Dir. Research Dept. Applied Math. and Theoretical Physics 1970–81, Univ. Lecturer 1981–88, Reader Geophysical Dynamics 1988–89, Prof. of Theoretical Geophysics 1989–; Prof. of Math., Univ. of N.S.W. 1991–95; BP Venture Unit Sr. Research Fellow 1983–89; Fellow King's Coll., Cambridge 1970–; fmr. Visiting Research Scientist Univs. of Calif., Canterbury, New South Wales and Australian Nat. Univ., M.I.T., Woods Hole Oceanographic Inst. and California Inst. of Tech.; Vice-Chair. Scientists for the Release of Soviet Refuseniks 1985–88, Co-Chair. 1988–92; mem. Council NERC 1993–98, Scientific Council, the Earth Centre 1995–; Ed. Journal of Soviet Jewry 1986–92; Assoc. Ed. Journal of Fluid Mechanics 1971–90; mem. Editorial Bd. Philosophical Transactions of the Royal Soc. A, Reports on Progress in Physics; Evnin Lecturer, Princeton University 1995; Mid-West Mechanics Lecturer 1996–97. *Publications:* c. 150 papers on fluid motions associated with the atmosphere, oceans, volcanoes and the interior of the earth. *Leisure interests:* his children, squash, mountaineering, lawn tennis. *Address:* Institute of Theoretical Geophysics, Department of Applied Mathematics and Theoretical Physics, University of Cambridge, Silver Street, Cambridge, CB3 9EW (Office); 46 De Freville Avenue, Cambridge, CB4 1HT, England (Home). *Telephone:* (01223) 337853 (Office); (01223) 356071. *Fax:* (01223) 337918.

HUPPERT, Isabelle Anne; French actress; b. 16 March 1953, Paris; d. of Raymond Huppert and Annick Beau; one s. one d.; ed. Lycée de Saint-Cloud, Ecole nat. des langues orientales vivantes; Pres. Comm. d'avances sur recettes 1994–; Prix Susanne Blanchetti 1976, Prix Bistingo 1976, Prix César 1978, and for Best Actress (for la Cérémonie) 1996, Gold Palm, Cannes 1978, Prix d'interpretation, Cannes 1978. *Films include:* Le bar de la Fourche, César et Rosalie, Les valseuses, Aloïse, Dupont la joie, Rosebud, Docteur Françoise Gailland, Le juge et l'assassin, Le petit Marcel 1976, Les indiens sont encore loin 1977, La dentellière, Violette Nozière 1978, Les soeurs Brontë 1978, Loulou 1980, Sauve qui peut (la vie), Les Héritières 1980, Heaven's Gate 1980, Coup de Torchon 1981, Dame aux Camélias 1981,

Les Ailes de la Colombe 1981, Eaux Profondes 1981, Passion, travail et amour, La Truite 1982, Entre Nous 1984, My Best Friend's Girl 1984, La Garce 1984, Signé Charlotte, Sac de noeuds 1985, Cactus 1986, Sincerely Charlotte 1986, The Bedroom Window 1986, The Possessed 1988, Story of Women 1989, Milan Noir 1990, Madame Bovary 1991, Malina 1991, Après l'amour 1992, La Séparation 1994, Amateur 1994, L'Inondation 1994, La Cérémonie 1995, Les Affinités électives 1996, Rien ne va Plus 1997, les Palmes de M. Schutz 1997; several theatre appearances including Mary Stuart (London) 1996. *Address:* c/o VMA, 10 avenue George V, 75008 Paris, France.

HUQ, Muhammad Shamsul, M.A.; Bangladeshi social scientist and educationist; b. 2 Dec. 1910, Comilla; s. of the late M. Karimul Huq and Mahmuda Khatoon; m. Tayyeba Huq 1938; two s.; ed. Univs. of Calcutta, Dhaka and London; Scholar-in-Residence, Advanced Projects, East-West Centre, Honolulu 1963–64; Vice-Chancellor Rajshahi Univ. 1965–69; Minister for Educ., Scientific and Technological Research of fmr. Pakistan 1969–71; led Del. 25th Anniversary of ECOSOC, Paris 1970; mem. UNESCO Int. Experts Cttee. on formulation of policy of training abroad, Paris 1971; Fellow, Woodrow Wilson Int. Center for Scholars, Smithsonian Inst., Washington, D.C. 1971–73; Vice-Chancellor Dhaka Univ. 1975–76; Chair. Planning Cttee. Social Science Research Council 1977–82; mem. Pres.'s Council of Advisers in charge of Ministry of Foreign Affairs 1977–78; Foreign Minister 1978–82; Chair., Trustee Bangladesh Nat. Museum, Dhaka 1983–86; Chair. Bd. Govs. Bangladesh Inst. of Int. and Strategic Studies 1982–89; Pres. Foundation for Research on Educational Planning and Devt. 1973; Chair. Nat. Advisory Group, Asia-Pacific Network in Social Sciences 1988; led Del. to UN 1977, 1978, 1979, 1980, 1981; active in negotiation of Ganges Water Agreement with India 1977, repatriation of 200,000 Burmese refugees 1978, election of Bangladesh to Security Council, UN 1979–80, Commonwealth Conf. initiative on Zimbabwe, Lusaka 1978–79, the Middle East issue (mem. Ministerial Cttee. on Jerusalem) and preparations for Cancun Summit March 1981 (attended Summit Oct. 1981); B.B. Gold Medal, Univ. of Calcutta 1933. *Publications:* Changing Education in England 1948, Compulsory Education in Pakistan 1954, Education and Development Strategy in South and South East Asia 1965, Education, Manpower and Development in South and South East Asia 1975, Higher Education and Employment in Bangladesh (jointly) 1983, The Patterns of Education in South and South East Asia (in Encyclopaedia Britannica and German encyclopaedia Lexikon der Pedagogik), Tragedy in Lebanon, Geo-political Implications, Cancún and after: from Hope to Despair, Education and Development 1986, International Politics: A Third World Perspective 1987, The Dilemmas of the Weak States: Bangladesh in International Politics 1992, Aid, Development and Diplomacy: The Need for an Aid Policy (jtly.) 1999. *Leisure interests:* reading, writing, gardening. *Address:* Reema, 10 Eskatan Garden Road, Dhaka 1000, Bangladesh. *Telephone:* 503485 (Office); 414045 (Home).

HUQ, Maj.-Gen. Shamsul; Bangladeshi politician and army officer; b. 1 Sept. 1931, Shugandhi, Comilla Dist.; m.; two s. two d.; ed. Sengarchar High School, Dhaka Coll.; commissioned Army Medical Corps 1955, served Army and Air Force Medical Services, then joined War of Liberation, organised Medical Services, achieved rank of Lieut.-Col. 1971, then Dir.-Gen. Medical Services, rank of Col., then Brig. 1983, rank of Maj.-Gen. 1979; Minister of Health and Population Control 1982–86, of Relief and Rehabilitation 1986–87, of Commerce 1990–91. *Leisure interest:* gardening. *Address:* c/o Ministry of Commerce and Industry, Shilpa Babour, Motijheel, Dhaka, Bangladesh.

HURD OF WESTWELL, Baron (Life Peer) cr. 1997, of Westwell in the County of Oxfordshire; **Douglas Richard Hurd,** C.H., C.B.E., P.C.; British politician and diplomatist; b. 8 March 1930, Marlborough; s. of the late Baron Hurd and Stephanie Corner; m. 1st Tatiana Elizabeth Michelle Eyre 1960 (dissolved 1982); three s.; m. 2nd Judy Smart 1982; one s. one d.; ed. Eton Coll., Trinity Coll., Cambridge; joined diplomatic service 1952; served in Beijing 1954–56, U.K. Mission to UN 1956–60, Private Sec. to Perm. Under-Sec. of State, Foreign Office 1960–63, in British Embassy, Rome 1963–66; joined Conservative Research Dept. 1966, Head of Foreign Affairs Section 1968; Private Sec. to Leader of the Opposition 1968–70, Political Sec. to the Prime Minister 1970–74; M.P. for Mid-Oxon 1974–83, for Witney 1983–97; Opposition Spokesman on European Affairs 1976–79, Minister of State, FCO 1979–83, Home Office 1983–84; Sec. of State for N. Ireland 1984–85; Home Sec. 1985–89; Sec. of State for Foreign and Commonwealth Affairs 1989–95; mem. Royal Comm. for Lords Reforms 1999–; Deputy Chair. NatWest Markets 1995–98; Dir. NatWest Group 1995–99; Chair. British Invisibles 1997–; Deputy chair. Coutts and Co. 1998–; and for Conservative Leadership 1990; Chair. Prison Reform Trust; Chair. Booker Prize Cttee. 1998; Spectator Award for Parliamentarian of the Year 1990. *Publications:* The Arrow War 1967, Send Him Victorious (with Andrew Osmond) 1968, The Smile on the Face of the Tiger 1969, Scotch on the Rocks 1971, Truth Game 1972, Vote to Kill 1975, An End to Promises 1979, War Without Frontiers (with Andrew Osmond) 1982, Palace of Enchantments (with Stephen Lamport) 1985, The Last Day of Summer 1992, The Search for Peace 1997, The Shape of Ice 1998. *Leisure interests:* writing and broadcasting. *Address:* House of Lords, Westminster, London, SW1A 0PW; c/o Hawkpoint Partners Ltd., Crosby Court, 4 Great St. Helens, London, EC3A 6HA, England. *Telephone:* 0171-665 4536/4538. *Fax:* 0171-665 4694.

HURFORD, Christopher John, A.O., B.SC. (ECON.), F.C.A.; Australian company director and public affairs consultant; b. 30 July 1931; m. Lorna Seedsman 1960; two s. three d.; ed. L.S.E.; served Royal Australian Navy Reserve 1951–52; M.P. for Adelaide, House of Reps. 1969–87; Minister for Housing and Construction and Minister Assisting the Minister for Industry and Commerce 1983–84, Minister Assisting the Treas. 1983–87, Minister for Immigration and Ethnic Affairs 1984–87; Minister for Community Services Feb.–July 1987; Consul-Gen. of Australia, New York 1988–91; Dir. of External Relations, Univ. of South Australia 1991–93; Dir. South Australia Econ. Devt. Bd. 1993–94, Commonwealth Funds Man. Ltd. 1993–96, Techsearch Inc. (Univ. of S. Australia) 1993–96; Chair. Child Health Research Inst. Inc. 1997–, Gropep Pty. Ltd. 1997–; Exec. Chair. Hurford Pty. Ltd. 1993–; Treas. Aboriginal Educ. Foundation 1965–67, S. Australian Council of Civil Liberties 1967–68; Appeal Chair. Austcare 1968–70; Fellow, Inst. of Chartered Accountants in Australia; Australian Labor Party. *Leisure interests:* golf, cinema, reading. *Address:* 65 Hackney Road, Hackney (Adelaide), South Australia 5069, Australia. *Telephone:* (8) 8363-2982. *Fax:* (8) 8363-9022.

HURFORD, Peter (John), O.B.E., M.A., MUS.B., F.R.C.O.; British organist; b. 22 Nov. 1930, Minehead, Somerset; s. of Hubert John Hurford and Gladys Winifred James; m. Patricia Mary Matthews 1955; two s. one d.; ed. Blundell's School, Royal Coll. of Music (Open Foundation Scholar), Jesus Coll. Cambridge (organ scholar) and private studies with André Marchal, Paris; commissioned Royal Signals 1954–56; Organist and Choirmaster Holy Trinity Church, Leamington Spa 1956–57; Dir. of Music, Bablake School, Coventry 1956–57; Master of the Music, Cathedral and Abbey Church of St. Alban 1958–78; freelance concert and recording organist 1978–; Visiting Prof., Coll. Conservatory of Music, Cincinnati, U.S.A. 1967–68, Univ. of Western Ont., Canada 1976–77; Visiting Artist-in-Residence, Sydney Opera House 1980–82; Prof. R.A.M. 1982–88; John Betts Fellow, Univ. of Oxford 1992–93; Hon. Fellow in Organ Studies, Univ. of Bristol 1997–; Decca recording artist 1977–: over 70 records, including complete organ works of J. S. Bach, Handel, F. Couperin, P. Hindemith and music of Franck, Mendelssohn, etc.; concerts in U.S.A., Canada, Australia, N.Z., Japan, Far East, E. and W. Europe 1960–; f. Int. Organ Festival 1963, Artistic Dir. 1963–79, Hon. Pres. 1981–; Pres. Inc. Asscn. of Organists 1995–97; Council mem. Royal Coll. of Organists 1963–, Pres. 1980–82; Hon. mem. R.A.M. 1982; Fellow Royal School of Church Music 1977; Hon. F.R.C.M. 1987; Hon. D.Mus. (Baldwin-Wallace Coll., Ohio, U.S.A.) 1981, (Bristol Univ.) 1992; Gramophone Award 1979. *Compositions include:* (organ music) Suite—Laudate Dominum, Chorale Preludes, (choral music) The Communion Service, Series III, The Holy Eucharist, Rite 2 (for American Episcopal Church). *Publications:* Making Music On The Organ 1988, sundry forewords, contribs. to journals. *Leisure interests:* walking and wine. *Address:* Broom House, St. Bernard's Road, St. Albans, Herts., AL3 5RA, England.

HURLEY, Alfred Francis, PH.D.; American university president and professor of history; b. 16 Oct. 1928, Brooklyn, N.Y.; s. of Patrick F. Hurley and Margaret C. Hurley; m. Joanna Leahy Hurley 1953; four s. one d.; ed. St. John's Univ., New York and Princeton Univ.; U.S. Air Force Navigator, Planner and Educator; enlisted as Pvt., retd. as Brig.-Gen.; served in Tex., Colo. and Germany with brief assignments in Washington, D.C. and Vietnam 1950–80; Instructor, Asst. Prof. and Research Assoc. U.S.A.F. Acad. 1958–63; Perm. Prof. of History and Head of History Dept., U.S.A.F. 1966–80; Chair. Humanities Div. and mem. Acad. Bd. U.S.A.F. Acad. 1977–80; Vice-Pres. for Admin. Affairs, Univ. of N. Tex. 1980–82, Prof. of History 1982–, Chancellor and Pres. 1982–, Guggenheim Fellow 1971–72; Eisenhower Inst. Fellow, Smithsonian Inst. 1976–77; Legion of Merit, U.S.A.F. 1972; Oak Leaf Cluster 1980; Pres.'s Medal, St. John's Univ. 1990. *Publications:* Billy Mitchell: Crusader for Air Power 1964, Air Power and Warfare (ed.) 1979. *Leisure interests:* jogging, reading, international travel. *Address:* Office of the President, University of North Texas, Denton, TX 76203 (Office); 828 Skylark Drive, Denton, TX 76205, U.S.A. (Home). *Telephone:* (817) 565-2904 (Office).

HURLEY, Denis Eugene, PH.L., S.T.L.; South African ecclesiastic (retd.); b. 9 Nov. 1915, Cape Town; s. of Denis Hurley and Theresa May (née O'Sullivan) Hurley; ed. St. Charles' Coll., Pietermaritzburg, St. Thomas' Univ., Rome, Gregorian Univ., Rome; ordained priest 1939; Curate, Emmanuel Cathedral, Durban 1940–43; Superior of St. Joseph's Scholasticate Prestbury (now Cedera) 1944–46; Vicar Apostolic of Natal with rank of Bishop March 1947; Archbishop of Durban 1951–92; Pres. S.A. Catholic Bishops' Conf. 1952–60, 1981–87; attended Second Vatican Council 1962–65; Pres. S.A. Inst. of Race Relations 1965–66; Chair. Int. Comm. on English in the Liturgy 1975–92; founded ecumenical agency for social concern known as Diakonia in Durban 1976; Hon. Dr. Iur. (Notre Dame) 1978, (De Paul Univ.) 1986; Hon. D. Litt. (Natal) 1978; Hon. D.Hum. Litt. (Catholic Univ. of America) 1982, (Georgetown Univ.) 1987; Hon. D.S.T. (Univ. of Santa Clara) 1986; Hon. Dr. (Univ. of Louvain) 1988; Hon. D.Sc. (Univ. of Cape Town) 1988; Hon. LL.D. (Witwatersrand) 1988; Hon. D.Th. (Catholic Theological Union of Chicago) 1993; civic honours, City of Durban 1972; Freedom of the City (Durban) 1992, (Pietermaritzburg) 1993; Chevalier, Légion d'honneur 1975, Order of Merit of the Italian Repub. 1997. *Publication:* Facing the Crisis 1997. *Leisure interests:* reading, following cricket and rugby on radio and TV. *Address:* Emmanuel Cathedral, Cathedral Road, Durban 4001, South Africa. *Telephone:* (31) 3063595. *Fax:* (31) 3063597.

HURLEY, Elizabeth Jane; British actress, producer and model; b. 10 June 1965; d. of the late Roy Leonard Hurley and of Angela Mary Hurley; producer for Simian Films and producer of Extreme Measures 1996, Mickey Blue Eyes 1998; Spokeswoman and model for Estee Lauder. *Theatre includes:* The Cherry Orchard—A Jubilee (Russian and Soviet Arts Festival), The Man Most Likely To (Middle East tour). *Television includes:* title role in Christabel (series), The Orchid House, Act of Will, The Resurrector, Rumpole, Inspector Morse, The Good Guys, The Young Indiana Jones Chronicles, Sharpe's Enemy, Cry of the City. *Films include:* Aria 1987, Rowing With the Wind 1987, The Skipper 1989, The Long Winter of 39, Passenger '57 1992, Bedlam, Mad Dogs and Englishmen 1994, Dangerous Ground 1995, Samson and Delilah 1996, Austin Powers: International Man of Mystery (ShoWest Award for Best Supporting Actress 1997) 1996, Permanent Midnight 1997, My Favourite Martian 1997, Ed TV 1998, Austin Powers: The Spy Who Shagged Me 1998. *Leisure interest:* gardening. *Address:* Simian Films, 3 Cromwell Place, London, SW7 2JE, England. *Telephone:* 0171-589 6822. *Fax:* 0171-589 9405.

HURLEY, Rev. Michael Anthony, S.J., S.T.D.; Irish ecumenical theologian and Jesuit priest; b. 10 May 1923, Ardmore, Co. Waterford; s. of Johanna Foley and Martin Hurley; ed. Mount Melleray Seminary, Cappoquin, Univ. Coll., Dublin, Jesuit Theological Faculty, Louvain, Pontifical Gregorian Univ., Rome; entered Soc. of Jesus 1940; ordained priest 1954; lecturer in Dogmatic Theology, Jesuit Theological Faculty, Dublin 1958–70; Dir. Irish School of Ecumenics, Dublin 1970–80; mem. Columbanus Community of Reconciliation, Belfast 1983–93 (Leader 1983–91); Hon. LL.D. (Queen's Univ., Belfast) 1993, (Trinity College, Dublin) 1995. *Publications:* Church and Eucharist (Ed.) 1966, Ecumenical Studies: Baptism and Marriage (Ed.) 1968, Theology of Ecumenism 1969, John Wesley's Letter to a Roman Catholic (Ed.) 1968, Irish Anglicanism (Ed.) 1970, Beyond Tolerance: The Challenge of Mixed Marriage (Ed.) 1975, Reconciliation in Religion and Society (ed.) 1994, Christian Unity: An Ecumenical Second Spring? 1998; articles in various periodicals. *Leisure interest:* reading. *Address:* Jesuit Community, Milltown Park, Dublin 6, Ireland. *Telephone:* 269 8411. *Fax:* 260 0371.

HURLEY, Dame Rosalinde, D.B.E., LL.B, M.D., F.R.C.PATH, F.R.C.O.G.; British professor of microbiology and barrister; b. 30 Dec. 1929, London; d. of late William Hurley and Rose Hurley; m. Peter Gortvai 1963; ed. Acad. of the Assumption, Wellesley Hills, Mass., Queen's Coll., London, Univ. of London, Inns of Court; Consultant Microbiologist 1962–75; Prof. of Microbiology, Royal Postgraduate Medical School's Inst. of Obstetrics and Gynaecology 1975–95, Prof. Emer. 1995–; Consultant Microbiologist, Queen Charlotte's Maternity Hosp., London 1963–95, Hon. Consultant 1995–; Vice-Chair. Cttee. on Dental and Surgical Materials 1975–78, Chair. 1979–81; Chair. Medicines Comm. 1982–94; Pres. Asscn. of Clinical Pathologists 1984–; Chair. Asscn. of Profs. of Medical Microbiology 1987–94; European Parl. Rep., Man. Bd. European Medicines Evaluation Agency 1994–; mem. Advisory Bd., Sheffield Inst. of Biotech. Law and Ethics 1995; Hon. F.F.P.M. 1990; Hon. D. Univ. (Surrey) 1984. *Publications:* Candida Albicans 1964; numerous papers on candidosis, and infections in pregnant women and the newborn. *Leisure interests:* reading, gardening. *Address:* 2 Temple Gardens, Temple, London, EC4Y 9AY, England. *Telephone:* 0171-353 0577.

HÜRLIMANN, Hans, LL.D.; Swiss politician and lawyer; b. 6 April 1918, Walchwil, Zug; m. Marie Theres Duft 1947; two s. one d.; ed. Univs. of Fribourg and Berne; Barrister, Zug 1946; Legal Adviser, Zug 1946, Town Clerk 1949; mem. Legis. Chamber, Zug Canton 1946, mem. Cantonal Govt. as Head of Dept. of Justice, Police and Mil. Affairs 1954–62, of Educ., Cultural and Mil. Affairs 1962–73; mem. Council of States 1966–73; mem. Fed. Council as Head of Dept. of Home Affairs (the Interior) 1974–82, Vice-Pres. Jan.-Dec. 1978, Pres. Jan.–Dec. 1979; Chair. Conf. of Heads of Cantonal Mil. Depts. 1960–68, Conf. of Heads of Cantonal Educ. Depts. 1968–73; mem. Council of Swiss Fed. Insts. of Tech. 1970–73; fmr. mem. Exec. Bd., Christian-Democratic People's Party. *Publications:* Das Recht der Stadtgemeinde Zug, and many publications on juridical, educational and military topics. *Leisure interests:* music, books, theatre, skiing, hiking. *Address:* Schönbühl 3, 6300 Zug, Switzerland.

HURN, David; British photographer and lecturer; b. 21 July 1934, Redhill, Surrey; s. of Stanley Hurn and Joan Maynard; m. Alita Naughton 1964 (divorced 1971); one d.; ed. Hardy's School, Dorchester and Royal Mil. Acad., Sandhurst; Asst. Photographer to Michael Peto and George Vargas, Reflex Agency, London 1955–57; Freelance Photographer for The Observer, Sunday Times, Look, Life, etc. 1957, working from Wales 1971; mem. Magnum Photos co-operative agency, New York, Paris, London and Tokyo 1967; Editorial Adviser Album Photographic magazine, London 1971; Head, School of Documentary Photography, Gwent Coll. of Higher Educ., Newport, Gwent 1973–90; Distinguished visiting artist and Adjunct Prof., Arizona State Univ., U.S.A. 1979–80; mem. Photographic Cttee., Arts Council of G.B. 1972–77, Arts Panel 1975–77, C.N.A.A. 1978–87; numerous individual and group exhbns., U.K., France, Fed. Repub. of Germany, The Netherlands, Spain, Sweden, Belgium, U.S.A., Japan 1971; works in collections of Welsh Arts Council, Arts Council of G.B., British Council, Bibliothèque Nationale, Paris, Int. Center of Photography, New York, San Francisco Museum of Modern Art, Museum of Modern Art, New York and others; Welsh Arts Council Award 1971; Kodak Photographic Bursary 1975; U.K./U.S.A. Bicentennial Fellowship 1979–80; Imperial War Museum Arts Award 1987–88; Bradford Fellow 1993–94; Arts Council of Wales Bursary 1995. *Publication:* David Hurn: Photographs 1956–1976 1979. *Leisure interests:* music, looking, meeting people. *Address:* Prospect Cottage, Tintern, Gwent, Wales. *Telephone:* (01291) 689 358. *Fax:* (01291) 689 464.

HURN, Sir (Francis) Roger, Kt., British business executive; b. 9 June 1938; s. of Francis James Hurn and Joyce Elsa Bennet; m. Rosalind Jackson 1980; one d.; ed. Marlborough Coll.; eng. apprentice, Rolls Royce Motors; joined Smiths Industries PLC 1958, Corp. Staff Dir. for Overseas Operations 1969–74, Man. Dir. Int. Operations 1974–75, Div. Man. Dir. 1975–76, Exec. Dir. 1976–, Man. Dir. 1978–91, Chief Exec. 1981–96, Chair. 1991–98; Chair. (non-exec.) GEC; Deputy Chair., Dir. (non-exec.) Glaxo Wellcome PLC 1997–; Chair. Gen. Electric Co. PLC 1998–; Dir. (non-exec.) ICI PLC 1993–; Hon. D.Sc. (Cranfield Inst. of Tech.) 1991; Young Businessman of the Year (Guardian Newspaper) 1980. *Address:* General Electric Company PLC, 1 Bruton Street, London, W1X 8AQ, England.

HURNÍK, Ilja; Czech pianist and composer; b. 25 Nov. 1922, Ostrava-Poruba; m. Jana Hurníková 1966; one s.; ed. Conservatoire, Prague; composition; Acad. of Music and Dramatic Arts, Prague 1948–52; self-employed artist 1942–; one-man concerts since 1942, Poland, Switzerland, Fed. Repub. of Germany, Cuba, U.S.A.; Dr. h.c. (Univ. of Ostrava) 1992; Czech Musical Fund Prize 1967, Supraphon Prize 1971, Grand Prix, Piano Duo Asscn. of Japan 1990; *Works:* piano compositions: The First Melodies 1931, Concert for Oboe and Strings 59, Preludes for piano 1943, Studies for four hands 1975; chamber compositions: Sonata for viola and piano, Four Seasons of the Year for 12 instruments 1952, Sonata da camera, Moments musicaux for 11 wind instruments 1955, Esercizii for wind quartet 1963; vocal works: cantata Maryka 1948, Children's Tercets 1956, oratorio Noah 1959, Choirs about Mothers for mixed choir 1962, cantata Aesop, songs for alto and orchestra Sulamit 1965, Seasonal Madrigals 1984, Water, Water 1986, Oratorio for children's chorus and orchestra 1990; ballet: Ondráš 1950, Faux pas de quatre 1979; opera: The Lady and Robbers 1966; recorded complete works of Debussy. *Publications:* The Journey with a Butterfly, Marshland, Childhood in Silesia (memoirs), Laurel Leaves 1987; children's books, including Kterak psáti a řečniti (How to Write and speak) 1997. *Address:* Český rozhlas, Vinohradská 12, 120 99, Prague 2; Národní Třída 35, 110 00, Prague 1, Czech Republic. *Telephone:* (2) 24 09 44 34; 24 21 42 26.

HURT, John; British actor; b. 22 Jan. 1940, Chesterfield; s. of Rev. Arnould Herbert and Phyllis (née Massey) Hurt; m. 1st Donna Peacock 1984 (divorced 1990); m. 2nd Jo Dalton 1990 (divorced 1995); two s.; ed. The Lincoln School, Lincoln and Royal Acad. of Dramatic Art; began as painter; stage debut, Arts Theatre, London 1962; Dir. United British Artists 1982. *Stage appearances include:* Chips With Everything, Vaudeville Theatre 1962, The Dwarfs, Arts 1963, Hamp (title role), Edinburgh Festival 1964, Inadmissible Evidence, Wyndhams 1965, Little Malcolm and his Struggle against the Eunuchs, Garrick 1966, Belcher's Luck, (RSC), Aldwych 1966, Man and Superman, Gaiety, Dublin 1969, The Caretaker, Mermaid 1972, The Only Street, Dublin Festival and Islington 1973, Travesties (RSC), Aldwych and The Arrest, Bristol Old Vic 1974, The Shadow of a Gunman, Nottingham Playhouse 1978, The London Vertigo, Dublin 1991, A Month in the Country, Albery 1994. *Films include:* The Wild and the Willing 1962, A Man for All Seasons 1966, Sinful Davey 1968, Before Winter Comes 1969, In Search of Gregory 1970, Mr. Forbush and the Penguins 1971, 10 Rillington Place, The Ghoul 1974, Little Malcolm 1974, East of Elephant Rock 1977, The Disappearance, The Shout, Spectre, Alien, Midnight Express 1978, Heaven's Gate 1980, The Elephant Man 1980, Champions 1983, The Hit 1983, 1984 1984, Jake Speed 1985, Rocinante 1986, Aria 1987, White Mischief 1987, Scandal 1988, From the Hip 1989, Frankenstein Unbound, The Field 1989, Windprints 1990, King Ralph 1991, Lapse of Memory 1991, Dark at Noon 1992, Monolith 1994, Even Cowgirls Get the Blues 1994, Wild Bill 1994, Rob Roy 1994, Dead Man 1996, Wild Bill 1996, Contact 1997, Love and Death on Long Island 1998. *TV appearances include:* The Waste Places 1968, The Naked Civil Servant (Emmy Award 1976) 1975, Caligula in I, Claudius 1976, Treats 1977, Raskolnikov in Crime and Punishment 1979, Poison Candy 1988, Deadline 1988, Who Bombed Birmingham? 1990, Journey to Knock 1991, Red Fox 1991, Six Characters in Search of an Author 1992, Prisoner in Time 1995, Saigon Baby 1995. *Address:* c/o Julian Belfrage & Associates, 46 Albemarle Street, London, W1X 4PP, England. *Telephone:* 0171-491 4400.

HURT, William; American actor; b. 20 March 1950, Wash.; m. 1st Mary Beth Hurt; m. 2nd Heidi Henderson 1989; two s.; ed. Tufts Univ., Juilliard School; appeared with Ore. Shakespeare Festival production of A Long Day's Journey Into Night, N.Y.; *stage appearances include:* Henry V 1976, Mary Stuart, My Life, Ulysses in Traction, Lulu, Fifth of July, Childe Byron, The Runner Stumbles, Hamlet, Hurlyburly, Beside Herself 1989, Ivanov 1991, others; *films include:* Altered States, Eyewitness, Body Heat (Theatre World Award 1978), The Big Chill, Gorky Park, Kiss of the Spider Woman (Best Actor Award Cannes Film Festival 1985, Acad. Award for Best Actor 1985), Children of a Lesser God, Broadcast News 1987, A Time of Destiny 1988, The Accidental Tourist 1989, The Plastic Nightmare, I Love You to Death 1990, The House of Spirits 1990, The Doctor 1991, Until the End of the World 1991, Mr. Wonderful 1993, The Plague 1993, Trial by Jury 1994, Second Best 1994, Jane Eyre 1995, Secrets Shared With a Stranger, Smoke 1995, Michael, Loved; mem. Circle Repertory Co., N.Y.; recipient 1st Spencer Tracy Award 1988, for outstanding screen performances and professional achievement.

HURTADO LARREA, Oswaldo, B.RER.POL., D.IUR.; Ecuadorean politician; b. 26 June 1939, Riobamba; s. of José Hurtado and Judith Larrea de Hurtado; m. Margarita Pérez de Hurtado; three s.; two d.; ed. Catholic Univ. of Quito; founded Ecuadorian Christian Democratic Party 1964; Pres. of Congress 1966; Prof. of Political Sociology, Catholic Univ., Quito; Dir. Instituto Ecuatoriano de Desarrollo Social (INEDES) 1966; Under-Sec. of Labour 1969; Sub-Dean, Faculty of Econs. and Dir. Inst. of Econ. Research, Catholic Univ., Quito 1973; invited to form part of World Political Council of Christian Democracy 1975; joined with other political groups to form Popular Democracy 1978; Pres. Org. of Christian Democrats of America, Vice-Pres. Int. Christian Democrats; Pres. Comm. to prepare Law of Referendum of Elections and Political Parties 1977; Vice-Pres. of Ecuador and Pres. Consejo Nacional de Desarrollo (Nat. Devt. Council) 1979–81; Pres. of Ecuador 1981–84; Pres. Nat. Ass. 1998; Pres. Cordes (org. for study of Latin American devt. problems) (Quito); fmr. Vice-Pres. Inst. for European Latinamerican Relations, Madrid; mem. Council of ex-Pres. Atlanta, Interamerican Dialogue Washington, South American Peace Comm. Santiago, Raúl Prebisch Foundation Buenos Aires, Latin American Popular Foundation Caracas, Centre for Research and Promotion of Latin America-European Relations Madrid; mem. various environmental comms.; Dr. h.c. (Georgetown) and various foreign decorations. *Publications include:* El poder político en Ecuador 1977. *Leisure interests:* tennis and gardening. *Address:* Suecia 277 y Av. Los Shyris, Quito, Ecuador. *Telephone:* (5932) 455701/454406. *Fax:* (5932) 446414.

HURVICH, Leo M., PH.D.; American sensory psychologist; b. 11 Sept. 1910, Malden, Mass.; s. of Julius S. Hurvich and Celia Chikinsky; m. Dorothea Jameson 1948; ed. Harvard Coll. and Harvard Univ.; Asst., Dept. of Psychology, Harvard Univ. 1936–37, Instructor and Tutor 1937–40, Research Asst., Div. of Research, Graduate School of Business Admin. 1941–47; Research Psychologist, Color Tech. Div., Eastman Kodak Co. 1947–57; Prof. of Psychology, New York Univ. 1957–62; Prof. of Psychology, Dept. of Psychology and Inst. of Neurological Sciences, Univ. of Pa. 1962–79, Prof. Emer., mem. Inst. of Neurological Sciences, Dir. Vision Training Program 1979–91; Visiting Prof. Columbia Univ. 1971–72, Univ. of Rochester, N.Y. 1974; fmr. Chair. Washington Square Coll.; mem. Research Advisory Cttee., Lighthouse 1993–; mem. N.A.S., Int. Brain Research Org., Int. Research Group in Colour Vision Deficiencies, Asscn. for Research in Vision and Ophthalmics; Fellow, Center for Advanced Study in the Behavioral Sciences, Stanford 1981–82; Fellow American Acad. of Arts and Sciences, American Psychological Asscn., Soc. of Experimental Psychologists, Optical Soc. of America; Guggenheim Fellow 1964–65, William James Fellow American Psychological Soc. 1989; Hon. D.Sc. State Univ. of N.Y.; several awards including Howard Crosby Warren Medal for Outstanding Research, Soc. of Experimental Psychologists 1971, I. H. Godlove Award, Inter-Soc. Color Council, Distinguished Scientific Contrib. Award, American Psychological Asscn. 1972, Edgar D. Tillyes Medal, Optical Soc. of America, Deane B. Judd-AIC Award, Asscn. Internationale de la Couleur 1985, Helmholtz Prize 1987 (Cognitive Neuroscience Institute). *Publications:* The Perception of Brightness and Darkness (with D. Jameson) 1966, Outlines of a Theory of the Light Sense (trans., with D. Jameson) 1964, Handbook of Sensory Physiology (Ed., with D. Jameson) 1972, Color Vision 1981, Color, Research and Application (Topical Ed.) 1992–94. *Address:* Department of Psychology, University of Pennsylvania, 3815 Walnut Street, Philadelphia, PA 19104, U.S.A. *Telephone:* (215) 898-7313.

HURWITZ, Emanuel, C.B.E, F.R.A.M., F.R.S.A.M.D.; British violinist; b. 7 May 1919, London; s. of Isaac Hurwitz and the late Sarah Gabrilovitch; m. Kathleen Crome 1948; one s. one d.; ed. Royal Acad. of Music, London; Leader, Hurwitz String Quartet 1946–53, Melos Ensemble 1956–74; Leader Goldsborough Orchestra 1947–57, English Chamber Orch. 1957–69, New Philharmonia Orch. 1968–70, Aeolian String Quartet 1970–81; Prof. Royal Acad. of Music 1968–; Visiting Lecturer Royal Scottish Acad. of Music and Drama 1987–, Univ. of Mich. 1995; recorded complete Haydn Quartets with Aeolian Quartet 1972–76; now active internationally in chamber music master classes; f. Emanuel Hurwitz Chamber Music Trust 1993; Pres. Inc. Soc. of Musicians 1995–96; Gold Medal, Worshipful Company of Musicians 1965. *Leisure interests:* collecting books and antique violin bows, listening to Beethoven piano works, Mozart operas and Schubert songs. *Address:* 25 Dollis Avenue, London, N3 1DA, England. *Telephone:* 0181-346 3936. *Fax:* 0181-343 1595.

HUSAIN, Maqbool Fida; Indian painter; b. 17 Sept. 1915, Sholapur, Maharashtra State; s. of Fida and Zainub Husain; m. Fazila Abbasi 1943; four s. two d.; joined Progressive Artists Group, Bombay 1948; first one-man exhbn., Bombay 1950, later at Rome, Frankfurt, London, Zürich, Prague, Tokyo, New York, New Delhi, Calcutta, Kabul and Baghdad; mem. Lalit Kala Akademi, New Delhi 1954, Gen. Council Nat. Akademi of Art, New Delhi 1955; mem. Rajya Sabha 1986; First Nat. Award for Painting 1955; Int. Award, Biennale Tokyo 1959. *Major works:* Murals for Air India Int. at Hong Kong, Bangkok, Zürich and Prague 1957, and WHO Building, New Delhi 1963; Mural in Mosaic for Lever Bros. and Aligarh Univ. 1964; High Ceramic Mural for Indian Govt. Building, New Delhi; Exhibitor "Art now in India" exhbn., London 1967; world's largest painting on canvas (240 ft. × 12 ft.) 1985; India through the Lens of a Painter (photographic show), U.S.S.R. 1988. *Publications:* Husain's Letters 1962, Husain 1971, Poetry to be seen 1972, Triangles 1976, Tata's book Husain 1988. *Film:* Through the Eyes of the Painter 1967 (Golden Bear Award, Berlin 1967). *Address:* 23 Canning Lane, New Delhi 11001, India.

HUSÉN, Torsten, PH.D.; Swedish educationist; b. 1 March 1916, Lund; s. of Johan and Betty (née Prawitz) Husén; m. Ingrid Joensson 1940 (died 1991); two s. one d.; ed. Univ. of Lund; Research Asst., Inst. of Psychology, Univ. of Lund 1938–43; Sr. Psychologist, Swedish Armed Forces 1944–51; Reader in Educational Psychology, Univ. of Stockholm 1947–52, Prof. 1953–56; Prof. of Educ. and Dir. Inst. of Educ. Research, Univ. of Stockholm 1956–71, Prof. of Int. Educ. 1971–82; Fellow, Center for Advanced Study in the Behavioural Sciences, Stanford, Calif. 1965–66, 1973–74, Wissenschaftskolleg, Berlin 1984; Expert in Royal Comms. on Swedish School Reform 1957–65; mem. Panel of Scientific Advisers to Swedish Govt. 1962–69; Chair. Int. Asscn. for the Evaluation of Educ. Achievement 1962–78; Consultant to OECD and the World Bank 1968–85, United Nations Univ.; Co-Ed. in Chief, Int. Encyclopedia of Educ.; Chair. Governing Bd., Int. Inst. Educ. Planning, Paris 1970–81; mem. Governing Bd. Max Planck Inst., Berlin 1964–82, Int. Council for Educ. Devt. 1971–93; Chair. Int. Acad. of Educ. 1986–95, 1996–97; Chair. Int. jury, Gravemeyer award in Educ. 1988–90; Chair. Acad. Europaea Task Force on Educ. 1988–91; Visiting Prof., Univs. of Chicago 1959, Hawaii 1968, Ontario Inst. for Studies in Educ. 1971, Stanford Univ. 1981, California 1984; mem. Swedish Royal Acad. of Sciences 1972–, U.S. Nat. Acad. of Educ. 1967–; Hon. mem. American Acad. of Arts and Sciences, Acad. Europaea, U.S.S.R. (now Russian) Acad. of Pedagogical Sciences; LL.D. h.c. (Chicago) 1967, (Glasgow) 1974, D.Tech. (Brunel Univ.) 1974; L.H.D. (Rhode Island Univ.) 1975; D.Ed. (Joensuu) 1979, (Amsterdam) 1982, (Ohio State Univ.) 1985; Hon. Prof. (East China Normal Univ.) 1984; Medal for Distinguished Service in Int. Educ., Teachers Coll., Columbia Univ. 1970, Comenius Medal 1993. *Publications:* Psychological Twin Research 1959, Problems of Differentiation in Swedish Compulsory Schooling 1962, International Study of Achievement in Mathematics I-II 1967, Educational Research and Educational Change 1968, Talent, Opportunity and Career 1969, Talent, Equality and Meritocracy 1974, Social Influences on Educational Attainment 1975, The School in Question 1979, An Incurable Academic (autobiog.) 1983, Educational Research and Policy 1984, Becoming Adult in a Changing Society (with James Coleman) 1985, The Learning Society Revisited 1986, Higher Education and Social Stratification 1987, Educational Research and School Reforms 1988, Education and the Global Concern 1990, Schooling in Modern European Society 1992, The Role of the University 1994, School and University Facing the 21st Century 1995, The Information Society 1998. *Leisure interest:* book collecting (old books). *Address:* Institute for International Education, Stockholm University, 10691 Stockholm; Armfeltsgatan 10, 11534 Stockholm, Sweden (Home). *Telephone:* 08-16-43-24 (Office); 08-664-19-76 (Home).

HUSSEIN, Abdirizak Haji; Somali politician and diplomatist; b. 1924, Galkayo District; joined Somali Youth Club which became Somali Youth League 1944, Pres. 1956–58; Pres. of Univ. Inst., Mogadishu 1956–59, mem. Nat. Assembly 1959–69, later formed Popular Movt. for Democratic Action; Minister of Interior, later of Works and Communications 1960–64; Prime Minister 1964–67; detained following coup 1969, released April 1973; Perm. Rep. to UN 1974–80. *Address:* c/o Ministry of Foreign Affairs, Mogadishu, Somalia.

HUSSEIN, Abdul-Aziz; Kuwaiti politician and diplomatist; b. 1921, Kuwait; m. 1948; two s. one d.; ed. Teachers Higher Inst., Cairo and Univ. of London; fmr. Dir. "House of Kuwait", Cairo, Dir.-Gen. Dept. of Educ., Kuwait; Amb. to the U.A.R. 1961–62; Perm. Rep. to Arab League Council; State Minister in Charge of Cabinet Affairs 1963–64; Minister of State for Cabinet Affairs Feb. 1971–85; Counsellor of H.M. the Amir of Kuwait 1985–. *Publication:* Lectures on Arab Society in Kuwait 1960. *Address:* Amari Diwan, Seif Palace, Kuwait City, Kuwait.

HUSSEIN, Saddam (see Saddam Hussein).

HUSSEINOV, Col. Suret Davud ogly; Azerbaijani politician; b. 1959; m.; two s.; ed. Gyanja Inst. of Tech.; worker, asst. foreman carpet factory, Gyanja 1982–83, sorter procurement station, Sheki 1984–86; sr. controller, foreman wool processing factory, Yevlakh 1987–, Dir. 1989–; Pres. Consortium Azersherstprom 1983; mem. Parl. 1990, Vice-Prime Minister, plenipotentiary of Pres. in Nagorny Karabakh, Comm. of Nat. Army Corps 1992–93; rank of Col. 1992; Nat. Hero of Azerbaijan 1992; deprived of all his posts by order of the Pres. Feb. 1993; Prime Minister of Azerbaijan 1993–94; dismissed after organizing an abortive coup d'état 1994; lives in exile.

HUSSEY OF NORTH BRADLEY, Baron (Life Peer), cr. 1996, of North Bradley in the County of Wiltshire; **Marmaduke James Hussey,** M.A.; British business executive; b. 29 Aug. 1923; s. of late E. R. J. Hussey, C.M.G. and Christine Hussey; m. Lady Susan K. Waldegrave 1959; one s. one d.; ed. Rugby School and Trinity Coll., Oxford; served with Grenadier Guards, Italy 1939–45; joined Associated Newspapers 1949, Dir. 1964; Man. Dir. Harmsworth Publs. 1967–70; mem. Thomson Org. Exec. Bd. 1971; Chief. Exec. and Man. Dir. Times Newspapers Ltd. 1971–80, Dir. 1982–86; Chair. Royal Marsden Hosp. 1985–, Bd. of Govs. BBC 1986–96; a Rhodes Trustee 1972–91; mem. Bd. British Council 1983–96; Trustee Royal Acad. Trust 1988–96; Vice-Chair. Appeals Cttee. B.L.E.S.M.A.; Dir. Colonial Mutual Group PLC 1982–97, Wm. Collins PLC 1985–89; Jt. Chair. Great Western Radio 1985–86; Chair. Ruffer Investment Man. Ltd. 1995–, Cadweb 1996–; mem. Govt. Working Party on Artificial Limb and Appliance Centres in

England 1984–86, Man. Cttee. and Educ. Cttee. King Edward's Hosp. Fund for London 1987–. *Address:* Waldegrave House, Chewton Mendip, near Bath, Somerset, BA3 4PD; Flat 15, 45/47 Courtfield Road, London, SW7 4DB, England. *Telephone:* 0171-370 1414 (London).

HUSSON, Philippe Jean Louis Marie, D. EN D.; French diplomatist; b. 22 July 1927, Nouméa, New Caledonia; s. of Jean Husson and Antoinette Leclerc; m. Christiane Marchand 1956; three s. two d.; ed. Inst. d'Études Politiques; Ecole nat. d'admin.; Contrôleur Civil, Morocco 1954–56; Moroccan Desk, Foreign Ministry, Paris 1956–58; First Sec., French Embassy, Bucharest 1958–61, Moscow 1961–64, Second Counsellor, Washington, D.C. 1964–67; Deputy Dir. Cultural and Scientific Relations, Foreign Ministry 1967–71; First Counsellor, French Embassy, Ottawa 1971–74, Minister-Counsellor, Moscow 1974–77; Deputy Perm. Rep. to the UN, New York 1977–81; Amb. to Finland 1981–84; Deputy Inspector-Gen., Foreign Ministry 1984–87; Amb. to Canada 1987–89; Dir. Archives and Documentation, Foreign Ministry 1990–92; Govt. Diplomatic Advisor 1992; mem. Comm. on publ. of French diplomatic documents 1992–, Comm. on archives of Ministry of Foreign Affairs 1995–; Officier, Légion d'honneur; Commdr., Ordre nat. du Mérite. *Address:* 7 promenade Venezia, Grand Siècle, 78000 Versailles, France (Home).

HUSTON, Anjelica; American actress; b. 8 July 1951, Los Angeles, Calif.; d. of late John Huston and Enrica Huston (née Soma); m. Robert Graham 1992; stage appearances include Tamara, Los Angeles 1985; TV appearances include: The Cowboy and the Ballerina (NBC-TV film) 1984, Faerie Tale Theatre, A Rose for Miss Emily (PBS film), Lonesome Dove (CBS mini-series). *Films include:* Sinful Davey, A Walk with Love and Death 1969, The Last Tycoon 1976, The Postman Always Rings Twice 1981, Swashbuckler, This is Spinal Tap 1984, The Ice Pirates 1984, Prizzi's Honor (Acad. Award for Best Supporting Actress 1985, New York and Los Angeles Film Critics' Awards 1985), Gardens of Stone, Captain Eo, The Dead, Mr North, A Handful of Dust, The Witches, Enemies, A Love Story, The Grifters, The Addams Family, Addams Family Values, The Player, Manhattan Murder Mystery, The Crossing Guard 1995, The Perez Family 1995, Buffalo '66 1997, Phoenix 1997; dir. Bastard out of Carolina 1995, Phoenix 1997. *Address:* c/o International Creative Management, 8942 Wilshire Boulevard, Beverly Hills, CA 90211, U.S.A.

HUTCHINSON, (John) Maxwell; British architect; b. 3 Dec. 1948; s. of late Frank M. Hutchinson and Elizabeth R. M. Wright; ed. Oundle, Scott Sutherland School of Architecture, Aberdeen and Architectural Asscn. School of Architecture; founder, Hutchinson & Partners (Chartered Architects) 1972, Chair. Hutchinson & Partners Architects Ltd. 1987–92; Dir. The Hutchinson Studio Architects 1992–; Visiting Prof. of Architecture, Queen's Univ., Belfast 1988–93; Special Prof. of Architectural Design, Nottingham Univ. 1993–96; Chair. Permarock Products Ltd, Loughborough 1985–96, London Br. Elgar Soc. 1987–93, East Midlands Arts Bd. 1991–94, British Architectural Library Trust 1991–, Schools of Architecture Accreditation Bd. 1991–; Vice-Pres. Industrial Bldg. Bureau 1988–91; mem. Council, Royal Inst. of British Architects (RIBA) 1978–93, Sr. Vice-Pres. 1988–89, Pres. 1989–91; Fellow Greenwich Univ.; mem. Council Royal School of Church Music 1997—; Hon. Fellow Royal Soc. of Ulster Architects 1992; regular broadcaster on TV and radio. *Publication:* The Prince of Wales, Right or Wrong: An Architect Replies 1989. *Compositions:* The Kibbo-Kift 1979, The Ascent of Wilberforce 111 1984, Requiem in a Village Church 1988, Christmas Cantata 1990. *Leisure interests:* composing, recording, playing the guitar loudly, cooking, champagne. *Address:* Flat 61, Cavendish Mansions, Clerkenwell Road, London, EC1R 5DH, England. *Telephone:* (0973) 795210.

HUTCHISON, Clyde A., Jr., PH.D.; American university professor; b. 5 May 1913, Alliance, Ohio; s. of Clyde A. and Bessie G. Hutchison; m. Sarah Jane West 1937; two s. one d.; ed. Ohio State Univ.; Nat. Research Council Fellow, Columbia Univ. 1937–38; Asst. Prof. of Chem., Univ. of Buffalo 1939–45; Research Assoc., Univ. of Va. 1942–43, Manhattan District Project 1943–45; Asst. Prof. Enrico Fermi Inst., Univ. of Chicago 1945–50, Dept. of Chem. 1948–50, Assoc. Prof. 1950–54, Prof. 1954–63, Carl William Eisendrath Prof. 1963–69, Carl. W. Eisendrath Distinguished Service Prof. of Chem. 1969–83, Emer. 1983–, Chair. Dept. of Chem. 1959–62; Consultant Argonne Nat. Lab. 1946–; Ed., Journal of Chemical Physics, American Inst. of Physics 1953–59; Visiting Prof. sponsored by Japan Soc. for the Promotion of Science 1975; Eastman Prof., Oxford Univ. 1981–82; Visiting Lecturer, Chinese Acad. of Sciences 1986; mem. N.A.S., A.C.S.; Fellow, American Acad. of Arts and Sciences, American Physical Soc. (mem. Council 1967–71); Guggenheim Fellow, Oxford Univ. 1955–56, 1972–73; Hon. D.Sc. (Cedarville); Ohio State Univ. Centennial Achievement Award 1970; Peter Debye Award, A.C.S. 1972. *Publications:* 110 scientific papers, documents and contribs. to books. *Address:* Searle Laboratory, University of Chicago, 5735 Ellis Avenue, Chicago, IL 60637, U.S.A. *Telephone:* (312) 702-7069. *Fax:* (312) 702-0805.

HUTCHISON, Kay Bailey, LL.B.; American politician; b. 22 July 1943, Galveston, Tex.; d. of Allan Bailey and Kathryn Bailey; m. Ray Hutchison; ed. Univ. of Tex.; TV news reporter, Houston 1969–71; pvt. law practice 1969–74; Press Sec. to Anne Armstrong (q.v.) 1971; Vice-Chair. Nat. Transport Safety Bd. 1976–78; Asst. Prof. Univ. of Tex. Dallas 1978–79; Sr. Vice-Pres., Gen. Counsel, Repub. of Tex. Corpn. Dallas 1979–81; counsel, Hutchison, Boyle, Brooks & Fisher, Dallas 1981–91; mem. Tex. House of Reps. 1972–76; elected Treas. of Tex. 1990; Senator from Texas 1993–; Fellow, American Bar Foundation, Tex. Bar Foundation; mem. American Bar Asscn., State Bar of Tex.; Republican. *Address:* U.S. Senate, 370 Russell Senate Building, Washington, DC 20510, U.S.A.

HUTT, Peter Barton, B.A., LL.M.; American lawyer; b. 16 Nov. 1934, Buffalo, N.Y.; s. of Lester Ralph Hutt and Louise Rich Fraser; m. Eleanor Jane Zurn 1959; two s. two d; ed. Phillips Exeter Acad., Yale and Harvard Univs.; Assoc., Covington and Burling (law firm) 1960–68, Partner 1968–71, 1975–; lecturer on Food and Drug Law, Harvard Law School 1994–, Stanford Law School 1998—; Chief Counsel, U.S. Food and Drug Admin. 1971–75; Counsel, Soc. for Risk Analysis, American Coll. of Toxicology; Chair. Alcoholic Beverage Medical Research Foundation 1986–92; Vice-Chair. Legal Action Center, New York 1984–, Foundation for Biomedical Research 1988–; mem. Inst. of Medicine, N.A.S. 1970–, Advisory Bd., Tufts Center for Study of Drug Devt. 1976–, Univ. Va. Center for Advanced Studies 1982–, Nat. Cttee. on New Drugs for Cancer and AIDS 1988–90; Inst. of Medicine Round Table on Drugs and Vaccines against AIDS 1988–95; mem. Bd. of Dirs. of numerous cos.; mem. Advisory Bd. Inst. of Medicine 1970 and of numerous other scientific orgs.; Underwood-Prescott Award, M.I.T. 1977. *Publications:* Dealing with Drug Abuse (with Patricia M. Wald) 1972, Food and Drug Law: Cases and Materials (with Richard A. Merrill) 1980. *Leisure interests:* research on the history of govt. regulation of food and drugs. *Address:* Covington & Burling, 1201 Pennsylvania Avenue, N.W., Washington, DC 20004 (Office); 5325 Chamberlin Avenue, Cherry Chase, MD 20815, U.S.A. (Home). *Telephone:* (202) 662-5522 (Office). *Fax:* (202) 662-6291 (Office).

HUTTON, Baron (Life Peer) cr. 1997, of Bresagh in the County of Down, **Rt. Hon. Sir (James) Brian Edward Hutton,** Kt., P.C.; British judge; b. 29 June 1931, Belfast, Northern Ireland; s. of late James Hutton and Mabel Hutton; m. Mary Gillian Murland 1975; two d.; ed. Shrewsbury School, Balliol Coll. Oxford, Queen's Univ. of Belfast; called to Northern Ireland Bar 1954, Q.C. (Northern Ireland) 1970, Bencher, Inn of Court of Northern Ireland 1974, Sr. Crown Counsel 1973–79, Judge of High Court of Justice 1979–88, Lord Chief Justice of Northern Ireland 1988–97; a Lord of Appeal in Ordinary 1997–; mem. Jt. Law Enforcement Comm. 1974, Deputy Chair. Boundary Comm. for N. Ireland 1985–88; Pres. Northern Ireland Asscn. for Mental Health 1983–; Hon. Fellow, Balliol Coll., Hon. Bencher, Inner Temple, King's Inns, Dublin. *Publications:* articles in Modern Law Review. *Address:* House of Lords, Westminster, London, SW1A 0PW, England.

HUTTON, Timothy; American actor; b. 22 Aug. 1960, Malibu, Calif.; s. of Jim Hutton and Maryline Hutton; m. Debra Winger (q.v.) 1986 (divorced); one s. *TV appearances include:* Zuma Beach 1978, Best Place to Be, Baby Makes Six, Sultan and the Rock Star, Young Love, First Love, Friendly Fire 1979. *Films include:* Ordinary People 1980 (Oscar for Best Supporting Actor), Taps 1981, Daniel 1983, Iceman 1984, Turk 1985, The Falcon and the Snowman 1985, Made in Heaven 1987, A Time of Destiny 1988, Everybody's All-American 1988, Betrayed 1988, Torrents of Spring 1990, Q & A 1990, The Temp 1993, The Dark Half 1993, French Kiss 1995, City of Industry, Scenes From Everyday Life 1995, The Substance of Fire 1996, Mr and Mrs Loving 1996, Beautiful Girls 1996; plays: Prelude to a Kiss, Broadway 1990, Babylon Gardens 1991. *Address:* c/o William Morris Agency, 151 El Camino Drive, Beverly Hills, CA 90212, U.S.A.

HUTTON, Will Nicholas, M.B.A.; British newspaper editor; b. 21 May 1950, London; s. of William Hutton and Dorothy Haynes; m. Jane Atkinson 1978; one s. two d.; ed. Chislehurst and Sidcup Grammar School, Univ. of Bristol and INSEAD; with Phillips & Drew (stockbrokers) 1971–77; Sr. Producer Current Affairs, BBC Radio 4 1978–81; Dir. and Producer Money Programme, BBC2 1981–83; econs. corresp. Newsnight, BBC2 1983–88; Ed. European Business Channel 1988–90; Econs. Ed. The Guardian 1990–95, Asst. Ed. 1995–96; Ed. The Observer 1996–98, Ed.-in-Chief 1998–; Visiting Fellow Nuffield Coll., Oxford 1995; Political Journalist of the Year, What the Papers Say 1993; Hon. D. Litt. (Kingston) 1995, (De Montfort) 1996. *Publications:* The Revolution That Never Was: an assessment of Keynesian economics 1986, The State We're In 1994, The State to Come 1997. *Leisure interests:* family, reading, squash, tennis, cinema, writing. *Address:* The Observer, 119 Farringdon Road, London, EC1R 3ER, England. *Telephone:* 0171-713 4309. *Fax:* 0171-713 4437.

HUXLEY, Sir Andrew Fielding, Kt., O.M., SC.D., F.R.S.; British physiologist; b. 22 Nov. 1917, London; s. of Leonard and Rosalind (née Bruce) Huxley; m. Jocelyn Richenda Gammell Pease 1947; one s. five d.; ed. Univ. Coll. School, Westminster School and Trinity Coll., Cambridge; Operational Research, Anti-Aircraft Command 1940–42, Admiralty 1942–45; Fellow of Trinity Coll., Cambridge 1941–60, 1990–, Dir. of Studies 1952–60, Hon. Fellow 1967–90, Master, Trinity Coll. 1984–90; Demonstrator, Dept. of Physiology, Cambridge Univ. 1946–50, Asst. Dir. of Research 1951–59, Reader in Experimental Biophysics 1959–60; Jodrell Prof. of Physiology, Univ. Coll., London 1960–69; Royal Soc. Research Prof. 1969–83, Prof. Emer. of Physiology, Univ. of London 1983–; Pres. British Asscn. for the Advancement of Science 1976–77; Chair. Medical Research Cttee. of the Muscular Dystrophy Group 1974–80, Vice-Pres. Muscular Dystrophy Group 1980–; mem. Govt.'s Scientific Authority for Animals 1976–77, Agric. Research Council 1977–81, Nature Conservancy Council 1985–87, Home Office Animal Procedures Cttee. 1987–95; mem. Council, Royal Soc. 1960–62, 1977–79, 1980–85; Pres. Royal Soc. 1980–85, Int. Union of Physiological Sciences 1986–93; mem.

Leopoldina Acad. 1964; Emer. mem. Acad. Europaea 1989; Trustee, British Museum (Natural History) 1981–91, Science Museum 1983–88; Croonian Lecturer, Royal Soc. 1967; First Florey Lecturer, Australia 1982; Romanes Lecturer, Oxford 1982–83; Fenn Lecturer, Sydney 1983; Davson Lecturer, American Physiological Soc. 1998; Fellow, Imp. Coll. of Science and Tech. 1980; Hon. Fellow, Univ. Coll., London 1980, Inst. of Biology 1981, Darwin Coll., Cambridge 1981, Royal Soc. of Edinburgh 1983, Fellowship of Eng. 1986, Queen Mary Coll. 1987; Hon. mem. Royal Irish Acad. 1986, Japan Acad. 1988; Hon. Research Fellow, Dept. of Physiology, Univ. Coll., London 1983; Foreign Fellow Indian Nat. Science Acad. 1985; Assoc. mem. Royal Acad. of Sciences, Letters and Fine Arts, Belgium 1978; Hon. mem. American Soc. of Zoologists 1985; Foreign Assoc. N.A.S. 1979; Foreign mem. Dutch Soc. of Sciences 1984; Hon. Foreign mem. American Acad. of Arts and Sciences 1961, Royal Acad. of Medicine, Belgium 1978; Hon. M.D. (Saar) 1964, (Charles Univ., Prague) 1998; Hon. D.Sc. (Sheffield) 1964, (Leicester) 1967, (London) 1973, (St. Andrews) 1974, (Aston) 1977, (Oxford) 1983, (Keele) 1985, (Md.) 1987, (Brunel) 1988, (Hyderabad) 1991, (Glasgow) 1993, (Witwatersrand) 1998; Hon. Sc.D. (Cambridge) 1978, (Pennyslvania) 1984, (East Anglia) 1985; Hon. LL.D. (Birmingham) 1979, (Dundee) 1984; Dr. h.c. (Marseilles) 1979, (York) 1981, (W. Australia) 1982, (Harvard Univ.) 1984, (Humboldt Univ.) 1985, (Toyama) 1995; Hon. D.H.L. (New York) 1982; Nobel Prize for Physiology or Medicine 1963, Copley Medal (Royal Soc.) 1973, Swammerdam Medal (Soc. for Natural Science, Medicine and Surgery, Amsterdam) 1997; Grand Cordon of Sacred Treasure (Japan) 1995. *Publications:* papers chiefly in Journal of Physiology, Reflections on Muscle (Sherrington Lectures, Liverpool Univ.). *Leisure interests:* walking, design of scientific instruments. *Address:* Manor Field, 1 Vicarage Drive, Grantchester, Cambridge, CB3 9NG, England. *Telephone:* (01223) 840207. *Fax:* (01223) 840207.

HUXLEY, George Leonard, M.A., F.S.A., M.R.I.A.; British professor; b. 23 Sept. 1932, Leicester; s. of Sir Leonard Huxley and Lady Molly Huxley; m. Davina Iris Best 1957; three d.; ed. Blundell's, Magdalen Coll., Oxford; Fellow All Souls Coll., Oxford 1955–61; Prof. of Greek, Queen's Univ., Belfast 1962–83, Prof. Emer. 1988–; Pres. Classical Asscn. of Ireland 1999–; Dir. Gennadius Library, American School of Classical Studies, Athens 1986–89, mem. Man. Cttee. A.S.C.S.A. 1991–; mem. Irish Advisory Bd., Int. Irish Studies, Liverpool Univ. 1997–; Hon. Prof. Trinity Coll., Dublin 1989–; Sr. Vice-Pres. Fédération Int. des Sociétés d'Etudes classiques 1984–89; Irish mem., Humanities Cttee. of European Science Foundation 1978–86; Vice-Pres. Royal Irish Acad. 1984–85, 1997–98, Hon. Librarian 1990–94, Special Envoy 1994–; mem. Acad. Europaea 1990; Patron Irish Inst. of Hellenic Studies, Athens 1998–; Litt.D. h.c. (Dublin); Hon. D.Litt. (Belfast); Cromer Greek Prize 1963. *Publications:* Early Sparta 1962, Achaeans and Hittites 1960, The Early Ionians 1966, Greek Epic Poetry 1969, Kythera (jt. ed.) 1972, Pindar's Vision of the Past 1975, On Aristotle and Greek Society 1979, Homer and the Travellers 1988. *Leisure interest:* sidero-dromophilia. *Address:* School of Classics, Trinity College, Dublin 2, Ireland (Office); Forge Cottage, Church Enstone, Oxfordshire, OX7 4NN, England (Home). *Telephone:* 6764222 (Office); (01608) 677595 (Home).

HUXLEY, Hugh Esmor, M.B.E., F.R.S., PH.D., SC.D.; British scientist; b. 25 Feb. 1924, Birkenhead, Cheshire; s. of Thomas Hugh Huxley and Olwen Roberts; m. Frances Fripp 1966; one d.; two step-s., one step-d.; ed. Park High School, Birkenhead and Christ's Coll., Cambridge; Radar Officer, R.A.F. Bomber Command and Telecommunications Research Establishment, Malvern 1943–47; Research Student, Medical Research Council Unit for Molecular Biology, Cavendish Lab., Cambridge 1948–52; Commonwealth Fund Fellow, Biology Dept., M.I.T. 1952–54; Research Fellow, Christ's Coll., Cambridge 1953–56; mem. of External Staff of Medical Research Council and Hon. Research Assoc., Biophysics Dept., Univ. Coll. London 1956–61; mem. of Scientific Staff, Medical Research Council Lab. of Molecular Biology, Cambridge 1962–87, Jt. Head, Structural Studies Div. 1976–87, Deputy Dir. 1977–87; Prof. of Biology, Rosenstiel Basic Medical Sciences Research Center, Brandeis Univ., Boston, Mass. 1987–97, Prof. Emer. 1997– (Dir. 1988–94); Fellow, King's Coll., Cambridge 1961–67, Churchill Coll., Cambridge 1967–87; Harvey Soc. Lecturer, New York 1964–65; Sr. Visiting Lecturer, Physiology Course, Woods Hole, Mass. 1966–71; Wilson Lecturer, Univ. of Tex. 1968; Dunham Lecturer, Harvard Medical School 1969; Croonian Lecturer, Royal Soc. of London 1970; Ziskind Visiting Prof. of Biology, Brandeis Univ. 1971; Penn Lecturer, Univ. of Pa. 1971; Mayer Lecturer, M.I.T. 1971; Miller Lecturer, State Univ. of N.Y. 1973; Carter-Wallace Lecturer, Princeton Univ. 1973; Pauling Lecturer, Stanford Univ. 1980; Jesse Beams Lecturer, Univ. of Va. 1980; Ida Beam Lecturer, Univ. of Ia. 1981; mem. Advisory Bd. of Rosenstiel Basic Medical Sciences Center, Brandeis Univ. 1971–77; mem. Council of Royal Soc. of London 1973–75, 1984–86; mem. Scientific Advisory Cttee., European Molecular Biology Lab. 1975–81; mem. Bd. of Trustees, Associated Univs. Inc. 1987–90; mem. German Acad. of Science, Leopoldina 1964; Foreign Hon. mem. American Acad. of Arts and Sciences 1965, Danish Acad. of Sciences 1971, American Soc. of Biological Chemists 1976, Foreign Assoc. N.A.S. 1978, American Asscn. of Anatomists 1981, American Physiological Soc. 1981, American Soc. of Zoologists 1986; Hon. Fellow, Christ's Coll., Cambridge 1981; Hon. D.Sc. (Harvard) 1969, (Univ. of Chicago) 1974, (Univ. of Pa.) 1976, (Leicester) 1988; Feldberg Award for Experimental Medical Research 1963, William Bate Hardy Prize of the Cambridge Philosophical Soc. 1965, Louisa Gross Horwitz Prize 1971, Int. Feltrinelli Prize for Medicine 1974, Int. Award, Gairdner Foundation 1975, Baly Medal, Royal Coll. of Physicians 1975, Royal Medal, Royal Soc. of London 1977, E. B. Wilson Medal, American Soc. for Cell Biology 1983, Albert Einstein World Award of Science 1987, Franklin Medal 1990, Distinguished Scientist Award, Electron Microscopy Soc. of America 1991, Copley Medal Royal Soc. of London 1997. *Publications:* articles in scientific journals. *Leisure interests:* skiing, sailing. *Address:* Rosenstiel Basic Medical Sciences Research Center, Brandeis University, Waltham, MA 02254, U.S.A. *Telephone:* (617) 736-2490.

HUXTABLE, Ada Louise, A.B.; American writer and critic; b. New York; d. of Michael Louis and Leah (Rosenthal) Landman; m. L. Garth Huxtable 1942; ed. Hunter Coll., and Inst. of Fine Arts, New York Univ.; Asst. curator of architecture and design, Museum of Modern Art, New York 1946–50; Fulbright Scholarship to study contemporary Italian architecture and design 1950, 1952; contributing ed. Progressive Architecture, Art in America, freelance writer on architecture and design 1952–63; architecture critic, New York Times 1963–82; mem. Times Editorial Bd. 1973–82; independent architectural consultant and critic 1982–96; Architecture Critic, The Wall Street Journal 1996–; mem. Corpn. Visiting Cttees. on Architecture, Harvard Univ., M.I.T., Rockefeller Univ. Council, Smithsonian Council; mem. Soc. of Architectural Historians, American Acad. of Arts and Letters, American Philosophical Soc.; Hon. mem. American Inst. of Architects; Hon. Fellow Royal Inst. of British Architects; Fellow of American Acad. of Arts and Sciences; Guggenheim fellowship for studies in American architecture 1958; numerous hon. degrees; numerous prizes and awards including: Frank Jewett Mather Award of Coll. Art Asscn. for art criticism 1967, Pulitzer Prize for Distinguished Criticism 1970, Architectural Criticism Medal of American Inst. of Architects 1969, Special Award of Nat. Trust for Historic Preservation 1970, Nat. Arts Club Medal for Literature 1971, Diamond Jubilee Medallion of the City of New York 1973, U.S. Sec. of Interiors' Conservation Award 1976, Thomas Jefferson Medal for Architecture 1977, Jean Tschumi Prize for Architectural Criticism, Int. Union of Architects 1987, Medal for Architectural Criticism (Acad. d'Architecture Française) 1988, MacArthur Prize Fellowship 1981–86, Henry Allen Moe Prize in the Humanities (American Philosophical Soc.) 1992. *Publications:* Pier Luigi Nervi 1960, Classical New York 1964, Will They Ever Finish Bruckner Boulevard? 1970, Kicked a Building Lately? 1976, The Tall Building Artistically Reconsidered: The Search for a Skyscraper Style 1985, Architecture, Anyone? 1986, Goodbye History, Hello Hamburger 1986, The Unreal America: Architecture and Illusion 1997. *Address:* 969 Park Avenue, New York, NY 10028, U.S.A.

HUYDECOPER, Jonkheer (Jan Louis) Reinier, LL.M.; Netherlands diplomatist; b. 23 Feb. 1922, Utrecht; s. of Jonkheer Louis Huydecoper and Jonkvrouwe Laurence B. W. Ram; m. Baroness Constance C. van Wassenaer 1944; one s. two d.; ed. Univ. of Utrecht; banking 1942–44; Legal Dept., Ministry of Finance 1945–46; entered Ministry of Foreign Affairs 1946; served UN, New York 1946, Ottawa 1947–48, Military Mission, Berlin 1949–50, Bonn 1950–52, London 1952–56, Djakarta 1956–59, Washington 1959–62, Rome 1962–66, Ministry of Foreign Affairs 1966–70, London 1970–73; Amb. and Head. of Del. to European Security Conf., Helsinki and Geneva 1973–74; Amb. to U.S.S.R. 1974–77, to Portugal 1978–80; Insp. of Foreign Service 1981–82; Amb. to U.K. (also accred. to Iceland) 1982–86; Chevalier, Order of Netherlands Lion, Commdr. Order of Orange Nassau; Hon. G.C.V.O. and other foreign decorations. *Address:* Wassenaarseweg 132, The Hague, Netherlands.

HUYGENS, Robert Burchard Constantijn, PH.D.; Netherlands professor of medieval Latin (retd.); b. 10 Dec. 1931, The Hague; m. Caroline Sprey 1962; one s. two d.; ed. Leiden Univ.; army service 1952–54; lecturer in Medieval Latin, Univ. of Leiden 1964, Prof. 1968–96; Fellow, Dumbarton Oaks, Washington, D.C. 1982, Inst. for Advanced Study, Jerusalem 1983–84, Inst. for Advanced Study, Princeton, N.J. 1986–87, Herzog August Bibliothek, Wolfenbüttel 1987; mem. Royal Netherlands Acad., Soc. des Antiquaires de France, Monumenta Germaniae Historica. *Publications include:* Jacques de Vitry 1960, Accessus ad Auctores 1970, Vézelay 1976, William of Tyre 1986, Berengar of Tours 1988, Guibert of Nogent 1992. *Address:* Witte Singel 28, 2311 BH Leiden, Netherlands. *Telephone:* 071-5143798.

HVEDING, Vidkunn; Norwegian engineer, economist and politician; b. 27 March 1921, Orkdal; s. of Johan and Ida Marie (née Songlid) Hveding; m. 1st Ellen Palmstrom 1948 (divorced 1963); m. 2nd Tone Barth 1963 (died 1980); m. 3rd Grete Blydt Quisler 1986; one s. three d.; ed. Norwegian Inst. of Tech. (N.T.H.), Univ. of Trondheim; eng. (design and supervision), various hydro-power projects 1946–54; Assoc. Prof. of Hydroelectric Eng., N.T.H. 1954–56, Prof. 1958–61; Adviser, Ethiopian Electric Light and Power Authority 1956–57; Man. Project Dept., Noreno Brasil SA, São Paulo 1957–58; Asst. Dir.-Gen. Norwegian Water Resources and Elec. Bd. 1961–63; Adviser, Kuwait Fund for Arab Econ. Devt. 1963–65; Sec.-Gen. Norwegian Ministry of Industry 1967–68; Chair. and Chief Exec., Norwegian Water Resources and Electricity Bd. 1968–75; Planning Man. Industrial Bank of Kuwait 1975–77; dir. of various cos. in banking industry, shipping, consulting 1977–81, 1983–; Minister of Petroleum and Energy 1981–83; Commdr., Royal Order of St. Olav. *Publications:* Comprehensive Energy Analysis Norway 1969, Hydropower Development in Norway 1992, articles on hydroelectric power tech., energy econs., resource conservation and political philosophy. *Leisure interests:* skiing, sailing, woodwork. *Address:* Voksenkollv.

23B, 0393 Oslo, Norway (Home). *Telephone:* 221 42 810 (Home). *Fax:* 221 42 810.

HVISTENDAHL, Finn Arild, M.S.; Norwegian banker; b. 12 Feb. 1942, Oslo; m. Anne-Lise Vandsemb 1963; one s. two d.; ed. Norwegian Inst. of Tech. Trondheim; Head, Petrochemical Div. Norsk Hydro 1980–84; Chief Financial Officer, Norsk Hydro 1984–87, Pres.-Dir.-Gen. Cofaz/Hydro Azote, Paris 1987–89, Exec. Vice-Pres. Norsk Hydro 1989–91; Pres. and C.E.O. Den Norske Bank 1991–98. *Address:* c/o Den Norske Bank, Stranden 21, P.O. Box 1171, 0107 Oslo, Norway.

HVOROSTOVSKY, Dmitri; Russian opera singer; b. 16 Oct. 1962; m.; one s. one d.; ed. Krasnoyarsk High School of Arts; Western début in 'Pique Dame', Nice Opera; U.S. début in 'La Traviata', Chicago Lyric Opera 1993; has appeared at Royal Opera House, Covent Garden, London, Metropolitan Opera, N.Y., La Scala, Milan, Salzburg Festival, Edin. Festival, Pacific Music Festivals; winner First Prize Toulouse Singing Competition 1988, Cardiff Singer of the World 1989. *Leisure interests:* keeping fit. *Address:* c/o Lies Askonas Ltd., 6 Henrietta Street, London, WC2E 8LA, England.

HWANG IN-SUNG; Korean politician; b. 9 Jan. 1926; ed. Korea Mil. Acad. and Seoul Nat. Univ.; army officer 1960–68; Asst. Minister without Portfolio 1970; Chief Sec. to Prime Minister 1973; Gov. N. Cholla Prov. 1973–78; Minister, Ministry of Transport 1978; Pres. KNTC 1980; mem. Nat. Ass. 1981, 1985, 1992; Minister, Ministry of Agric., Forestry and Fisheries 1985–87; Chair. Asiana Air Lines 1988–93; Pres. Kumho Air Lines 1989–93; Chair. Political Cttee. Democratic Liberal Party 1992; Prime Minister of Repub. of Korea March–Dec. 1993. *Address:* c/o Office of the Prime Minister, Seoul, Republic of Korea.

HYMAN, Joe, F.R.S.A.; British textile executive; b. 14 Oct. 1921; m. 1st Corrine I. Abrahams 1948 (marriage dissolved); one s. one d.; m. 2nd Simone Duke 1963; one s. one d.; ed. North Manchester Grammar School; entered father's General Textile Merchanting Co. 1937; founder Portland Woollen Co. 1946; owner Melso Fabrics Ltd., now Gainsborough Cornard Ltd. (Cornard Knitting Mills Ltd., Fine Jersey Ltd., and Cooper Bros.) 1957; Gainsborough Cornard and William Hollins Ltd. merged to form Viyella Int. Ltd. 1961, Chair. 1962–69, Dir. 1961–70; Chair. John Crowther and Sons (Milnsbridge) Ltd. 1971–81; mem. Lloyds; Trustee, Pestalozzi Children's Village Trust 1967–; mem. Textile Council 1968; Gov. Bedales School 1966, L.S.E. 1968; British Inst. of Man.; Companion of Textile Inst.; Pres. Textile Benevolent Asscn. *Leisure interests:* music, golf, gardening. *Address:* 24 Kingston House North, Prince's Gate, London, SW7 1LN, England.

HYMAN, Timothy; British painter and writer on art; b. 17 April 1946, Hove; s. of Alan Hyman and Noreen Gypson; m. Judith Ravenscroft 1982; ed. Charterhouse and Slade School of Fine Art; mounted Narrative Paintings at Arnolfini and ICA Galleries, etc. 1979–80; started to exhibit at Blond 1980, one-man exhbns. 1981, 1983 and 1985; Austin/Desmond (one-man exhbn. 1990), Castlefield, Manchester 1993, Gallery Chemould, Bombay 1994, Gallery M, Flowers East 1994; group exhbns. at Royal Acad., Hayward Gallery, Whitechapel Art Gallery, Nat. Portrait Gallery; public collections include Arts Council, Bristol City Art Gallery, Museum of London, Contemporary Art Soc., British Museum, Govt. Art Collection; Visiting Prof. at Baroda, two British Council lecture tours 1981–83; Artist in Residence at Lincoln Cathedral 1983–84, Sandown Racecourse 1992; Purchaser for Arts Council Collection 1985; selector, John Moores Prize 1995; Hon. Research Fellow, Univ. Coll., London; Leverhulme Award 1992, Rootstein Hopkins Foundation Award 1995, Wingate Award 1998. *Publications:* Hodgkin 1975, Kitaj 1977, Beckmann 1978, Balthus 1980, Narrative Paintings 1979, Inquisitioning Our Realisms 1981, English Romanesque 1984, In Their Circumstances 1985, Kiff 1986, Domenico Tiepolo 1987, Ensor 1990, Spencer 1991, Bhupen Khakhar (monograph) 1998, Bonnard (monograph) 1998; numerous articles on contemporary figurative painting in London Magazine, Artscribe, Times Literary Supplement 1975–. *Leisure interests:* the novels of John Cowper Powys, reading, travel, cinema. *Address:* 62 Myddelton Square, London, E.C.1, England. *Telephone:* 0171-837 1933.

HYND, Ronald; British choreographer; b. 22 April 1931, London; s. of William John Hens and Alice Louisa Griffiths; m. Annette Page 1957; one d.; ed. Holloway Co., numerous wartime emergency schools, England; trained with Marie Rambert 1946; joined Ballet Rambert 1949, Royal Ballet (then K/A Sadlers Wells Ballet) 1952 (Prin. dancer 1959–70); Ballet Dir. Bavarian State Opera 1970–73, 1984–86; freelance choreographer; ballets presented by numerous int. ballet cos., including English Nat. Ballet, Royal Sadler's Wells, La Scala Milan, Deutsche Oper Berlin, Vienna State Opera, Bavarian State Opera, American Ballet Theater, Australian Ballet, Tokyo Ballet, Canadian Nat. Ballet, Grands Ballets Canadiens, Dutch Nat. Ballet, Slovenian Nat. Ballet, South African State Theatre Ballet, Royal Danish Ballet, etc.; TV productions of Merry Widow, Nutcracker and Sanguine Fan. *Leisure interests:* gardens, music, travel. *Publications:* Three Act Ballets: Merry Widow 1975, The Nutcracker 1976, Rosalinda 1978, Papillon 1979, Le Diable à Quatre 1984, Coppelia 1985, Ludwig II 1986, The Hunchback of Notre Dame 1988, The Sleeping Beauty 1993; One Act Ballets include: Dvorak Variations 1970, Fairy's Kiss 1967, Sanguine Fan 1976, La Chatte 1978, La Valse 1981, Seasons 1982, Fanfare 1985. *Address:* Fern Cottage, Upper Somerton, Bury St. Edmonds, Suffolk, IP29 4ND, England. *Telephone:* (01284) 789284. *Fax:* (01284) 789284.

HYNDE, Chrissie; American singer, songwriter and musician; b. 7 Sept. 1951, Akron, Ohio; one d. with Ray Davies; m. Jim Kerr (divorced); one d.; contrib. to New Musical Express; co-f. Chrissie Hynde and the Pretenders 1978, singer, songwriter and guitarist, new band formed 1983; tours in Britain, Europe and U.S.A.; platinum and gold discs in U.S.A. *Singles include:* Stop Your Sobbing (debut) 1978, Kid, Brass in Pocket, I Go to Sleep 1982, Back on the Chain Gang 1982, Middle of the Road 1984. *Albums include:* Pretenders (debut) 1980, Pretenders II 1981, Extended Play 1981, Learn to Crawl 1985, Get Close 1986, The Singles 1987.

HYNES, Garry, B.A.; Irish theatre director; b. 10 June 1953, Ballaghaderreen, Co. Roscommon; d. of Oliver Hynes and Carmel Hynes; ed. Dominican Coll., Galway, Univ. Coll. Galway; founded Druid Theatre Co. 1975, Artistic Dir. 1994–; Artistic Dir. Abbey Theatre, Dublin 1991–94; plays directed at Druid include The Playboy of the Western World, Conversations on a Homecoming, Bailegangaire (with Siobhán McKenna), plays directed at Abbey include A Whistle in the Dark, The Plough and the Stars, The Power of Darkness, Famine; directed R.S.C., Stratford and London 1988, 1989; Hon. LL.D. (Nat. Council for Educ. Awards) 1987; Fringe First, Edin. 1980, Harveys Award for Best Dir. 1983, Time Out (London) Award for Direction 1988, People of the Year Award 1989. *Publication:* Island Protected by a Bridge of Glass 1979 (premiere Druid Theatre Co., Galway). *Leisure interests:* books, poker, food. *Address:* Druid Theatre Company, Chapel Lane, Galway, Ireland. *Telephone:* (91) 568617.

HYNES, Samuel, D.F.C., PH.D., F.R.S.L.; American educator and author; b. 29 Aug. 1924, Chicago; s. of Samuel Lynn and Margaret (Turner) Hynes; m. Elizabeth Igleheart 1944; two d.; ed. Univ. of Minnesota, Columbia Univ.; served U.S.M.C.R. 1943–46, 1952–53; mem. faculty, Swarthmore Coll. 1949–68, Prof. of English Literature 1965–68; Prof. of English Northwestern Univ., Evanston, Ill. 1968–76, Princeton Univ. 1976–90, Woodrow Wilson Prof. of Literature 1978–90, Prof. Emer. 1990–; Fulbright Fellow 1953–54; Guggenheim Fellow 1959–60, 1981–82; Bollingen Fellow 1964–65; American Council of Learned Socs. Fellow 1969, 1985–86; Nat. Endowment for Humanities Sr. Fellow 1973–74, 1977–78. *Publications:* The Pattern of Hardy's Poetry (Explicator award 1962), William Golding 1964, The Edwardian Turn of Mind 1968, Edwardian Occasions 1972, The Auden Generation 1976, Flights of Passage: Reflections of a World War Two Aviator 1988; Ed.: Further Speculations by T. E. Hulme 1955, The Author's Craft and Other Critical Writings of Arnold Bennett 1968, Romance and Realism 1979, Complete Poetical Works of Thomas Hardy, Vol. I 1982, Vol. II 1984, Vol. III 1985, Vols. IV, V 1995, Thomas Hardy 1984, A War Imagined 1990, Complete Short Fiction of Joseph Conrad (Vol. I–III) 1992, (Vol. IV) 1993. *Address:* 130 Moore Street, Princeton, NJ 08540, U.S.A.

HYTNER, Nicholas Robert, M.A.; British theatre director; b. 7 May 1956, Manchester; s. of Benet A. Hytner and Joyce Myers; ed. Manchester Grammar School and Trinity Hall, Cambridge; staff producer, English Nat. Opera (ENO) 1978–80; Assoc. Dir. Royal Exchange Theatre, Manchester 1985–89; Assoc. Dir. Royal Nat. Theatre 1989–97; *theatre and opera productions include:* Wagner's Rienzi (ENO) 1983, Tippett's King Priam (Kent Opera) 1984, Handel's Xerxes (ENO), The Scarlet Pimpernel (Chichester Festival) 1985, As You Like It, Edward II, The Country Wife, Schiller's Don Carlos, (Royal Exchange) 1986, Handel's Giulio Cesare (Paris Opera), Measure for Measure (Royal Shakespeare Co. (RSC)) 1987, Tippett's The Knot Garden (Royal Opera), The Magic Flute (ENO), The Tempest (RSC) 1988, The Marriage of Figaro (Geneva Opera), Joshua Sobol's Ghetto (Nat. Theatre), Miss Saigon (Theatre Royal, Drury Lane) 1989, King Lear (RSC) 1990, The Wind in the Willows (Nat. Theatre) 1990, Volpone (Almeida) 1990, The Madness of George III (Nat. Theatre) 1991, The Recruiting Officer (Nat. Theatre) 1992, Carousel (Nat. Theatre) 1992, The Importance of Being Earnest, Aldwych 1993, Don Giovanni (Bavarian State Opera) 1994, The Cunning Little Vixen (Paris) 1995, The Cripple of Inishmaan 1997, The Crucible 1997. *Films:* The Madness of King George 1994, The Crucible 1996, Chicago 1999; Laurence Olivier Award for Xerxes 1985, Evening Standard Opera Award 1985, Evening Standard Best Dir. Award 1989, Tony Award Best Dir. of a Musical (for Carousel) 1994. *Address:* c/o The Royal National Theatre of Great Britain, South Bank, London, SE1 9PX, England. *Telephone:* 0171-452 3333 (Office).

I

IACOCCA, Lee A.; American automobile executive; b. 15 Oct. 1924, Allentown, Pa.; s. of Nicola Iacocca and Antoinette Perrotto; m. 1st Mary McCleary 1956 (died 1983); two d.; m. 2nd Peggy Johnson 1986 (divorced); m. 3rd Darrien Earle 1991; ed. Lehigh and Princeton Univs.; with Ford Motor Co. 1946; District Sales Man., Washington 1956; Ford Div. Truck Marketing Man. 1956; Car Marketing Man. 1957; Vice-Pres. and Gen. Man., Ford Div. 1960–65; Vice-Pres. Car and Truck Group 1965; Exec. Vice-Pres., North American Automotive Operations 1967; Exec. Vice-Pres., Ford Motor Co. and Pres. Ford North American Automotive Operations 1969–70, Pres. Ford Motor Co. 1970–78; Pres., C.O.O., Chrysler Corpn. 1978–79, Chair. 1979–93, C.E.O. 1979–93, Dir. –1993; prin. Iacocca Partners 1994–; Acting Chair. Kro Koo Roo Inc. 1998–; Pres. Iacocca Assocs., L.A.; mem. Soc. Automotive Engineers, Hon. doctorates, Muhlenberg Coll. and Babson Inst.; Chair. of Presidential Comm. to restore Statue of Liberty 1982–86; Detroit's Man of the Year 1982; Jefferson Award 1985; Kt., Order of Labour (Italy) 1989. *Publication:* Iacocca, An Autobiography (with William Novak) 1984, Talking Straight 1988.

IACOVOU, Georgios, M.A., M.SC.; Cypriot politician and diplomatist; b. 19 July 1938; s. of Kyriacos Iacovou and Maria Michalopoulou; m. Jennifer Bradley 1963; one s. three d.; ed. Greek Gymnasium for Boys, Famagusta, and Univ. of London; Eng., Cyprus Building and Road Construction Corpn. Ltd 1960–61; Man. Electron Ltd., Nicosia 1961–63; with Operations Research and Finance Depts., British Railways Bd., London 1964–68; Sr. Consultant (Management), Price Waterhouse Assocs., London 1968–72; Dir. Cyprus Productivity Centre, Nicosia 1972–76; Dir. Special Service for Care and Rehabilitation of Displaced Persons 1974–76; Chief, E. African Region, UNHCR, Geneva 1976–79; Amb. to Fed. Repub. of Germany (also accred. to Austria and Switzerland) 1979–83; Dir.-Gen. Ministry of Foreign Affairs Jan.–Sept. 1983; Minister of Foreign Affairs 1983–93; Pres. Cttee. of Ministers, Council of Europe Nov. 1983; participated in Commonwealth Heads of State and Govt. Confs. in Delhi 1983, Bahamas 1985, Vancouver 1987, Kuala Lumpur 1989 and non-Aligned Summit, Harare 1986, Belgrade 1989; Chair. Ministerial Conf. of Non-Aligned Movt., Nicosia 1988; Hon. M.A. (Boston); Hon. D.I.C. B.Sc. (London); Grosses Verdienstkreuz mit Stern und Schulterband (Fed. Repub. of Germany), Grosses Goldenes Ehrenzeichen (Austria), Grand Cross, Order of Phoenix (Greece), Grand Cross of the Order of Isabella the Catholic (Spain), Grand Cross of the Order of Honour (Greece), Order of the Flag with Sash (Yugoslavia), Order of the Repub. First Class (Egypt), Grand Cross of Infante D. Henrique (Portugal). *Address:* c/o Ministry of Foreign Affairs, 18–19 Dem. Severis Avenue, Nicosia, Cyprus. *Telephone:* (02) 302101.

IAKOVOS, Archbishop; American ecclesiastic; b. 29 July 1911, Island of Imbros, Turkey; s. of Maria and Athanasios Coucouzis; baptismal name Demetrios; ed. Theological School of Halki, Istanbul; Deacon 1934; ordained priest in Lowell, Mass., U.S.A. 1940; Dean Cathedral of the Annunciation, Boston 1942–54; Bishop of Malta 1954; Rep. of Patriarch of Constantinople to World Council of Churches, Geneva 1955; Primate, Archbishop, Greek Orthodox Church in North and South America 1959–96; Exarch, Ecumenical Patriarchate of Constantinople; Pres. World Council of Churches 1959–68; fmr. Dean Holy Cross Orthodox Theological School, Mass., now Pres.; Presidential Medal of Freedom 1980, Inaugural Award New York Univ. 1981, Great Cross of the Holy Sepulchre, Patriarchate of Jerusalem 1982, Gold Medal of Acad. of Athens 1985, numerous hon. degrees. *Address:* 31 Park Drive, South Rye, New York, NY 10021, U.S.A.

IANNELLA, Egidio, C.P.N.; Argentinian banker and consultant; b. 16 May 1921, Buenos Aires; s. of Antonio and Carmen Bárbaro; m. Isabel Rodríguez; one s. one d.; ed. Escuela Nacional de Comercio, Buenos Aires, Univ. Nacional de Buenos Aires and Centro de Estudios Monetarios Latinoamericanos, Mexico; various positions in Banco Central de la República Argentina 1939–56, Gen. Man. 1967–69, Pres. 1969–70, 1981–82, 1989, Dir. 1978–81; Gen. Man. Banco Argentino de Comercio 1956–66; Exec. Vice-Pres. Banco Federal Argentino 1971–77; Pres. Banco Nacional de Desarrollo 1978–81; Pres. Asociación Latinoamericana de Instituciones Financieras de Desarrollo (ALIDE), Lima 1979–81, 1989–90; mem. Bd. Bolsa de Comercio de Buenos Aires 1992–98, Counsellor, Foundation of the Bolsa 1993–99; Prof., Pontificia Univ. Católica Argentina 1966–95; Pres. VISA Argentina S.A. 1983–99; Dir. VISA Int., Miami, U.S.A. 1985–99; Pres. Rotary Club of Buenos Aires 1991–92. *Address:* Calle Tucumán 540, 6°A (1049), Buenos Aires, Argentina. *Telephone:* (541) 325-1403; (541) 325-3091. *Fax:* (541) 325-3091.

IBBS, Sir (John) Robin, Kt., K.B.E., M.A., D.SC., LL.D., F.C.I.B.; British industrialist; b. 21 April 1926, Birmingham; s. of late Prof. T. L. Ibbs and of Marjorie Bell; m. Iris Barbara Hall 1952; one d.; ed. Gresham's School, Upper Canada Coll., Toronto, Univ. of Toronto, Trinity Coll., Cambridge, and Lincoln's Inn; called to Bar 1952; Instructor Lieut., R.N. 1947–49; C. A. Parsons & Co. Ltd. 1949–51; joined ICI 1952, held various eng., tech., production, commercial and gen. man. appointments at Head Office, Gen. Chemicals Div. and Metals Div.; Man. Planning Dept., Imperial Metal Industries Ltd. 1969–74, Exec. Dir. 1972–74, Non-Exec. Dir. 1974–76; Gen. Man. Planning, ICI 1974–76, Exec. Dir. 1976–80, 1982–88; Dir. ICI Americas Inc. 1976–80; Dir. ICI Australia Ltd. 1982–87; Dir. Lloyds Bank PLC 1985–97, Deputy Chair. 1988–93, Chair. 1993–97; Chair. Lloyds TSB Group PLC 1995–97; Chair. Lloyds Merchant Bank Holdings Ltd. 1989–92; mem. Industrial Devt. Advisory Bd., Dept. of Industry 1978–80, Head Central Policy Review Staff, Cabinet Office 1980–82; mem. Council, Chemical Industries Asscn. 1976–80, 1982–88, Vice-Pres. 1983–87, Hon. mem. 1987; mem. Governing Body and Council, British Nat. Cttee., ICC 1976–80, Chair. Finance and Gen. Purposes Cttee. 1976–80; mem. Top Salaries Review Body 1983–88; mem. Council, Royal Inst. of Int. Affairs, Chatham House 1983–89; mem. Court, Cranfield Inst. of Tech. 1983–88; Adviser to the Prime Minister on Efficiency and Effectiveness in Govt. 1983–88; Trustee and Deputy Chair. Isaac Newton Trust 1988–; Leader of review of House of Commons services 1990; Chair. Council, Univ. Coll., London 1989–95; Hon. Fellow Univ. Coll., London 1993; Hon. D.Sc. (Bradford) 1986, Hon. LL.D. (Bath) 1993. *Leisure interests:* walking, natural history, gardening, social history, music and arts. *Address:* c/o Lloyds TSB Group, 71 Lombard Street, London, EC3P 3BS, England.

IBERS, James Arthur, PH.D.; American professor of chemistry; b. 9 June 1930, Los Angeles; s. of Max Ibers and Esther Imerman; m. Joyce Henderson 1951; one s. one d.; ed. Calif. Inst. of Tech.; NSF Post-doctoral Fellow, Melbourne, Australia 1954–55; chemist, Shell Devt. Co. 1955–61, Brookhaven Nat. Lab. 1961–64; mem. faculty Northwestern Univ. 1964–, Prof. of Chem. 1964–85, Charles E. and Emma H. Morrison Prof. of Chem. 1986–; mem. N.A.S., American Acad. of Arts and Sciences, American Crystallographic Asscn., American Chem. Soc. (Inorganic Chem. Award 1978); Distinguished Service Award 1992, Pauling Medal 1994. *Address:* Department of Chemistry, Northwestern University, Evanston, IL 60208–3113 (Office); 2657 Orrington Avenue, Evanston, IL 60201, U.S.A. (Home). *Telephone:* (847) 491-5449 (Office). *Fax:* (847) 491-7713.

IBRAHIM, Maj. Abu al-Qassim Mohammed; Sudanese politician and army officer; b. 1937, Omdurman; ed. Khartoum Secondary School and Military Coll.; commissioned 1961; mem. Revolutionary Council 1969; Minister of Local Govt. 1969–70; Asst. Prime Minister for Services 1970; Minister of Interior 1970–71, of Health and Social Welfare 1971–73, of Agric., Food and Natural Resources 1974–76; mem. Political Bureau of Sudanese Socialist Union 1971–79, Deputy Sec.-Gen. 1975–76, Sec.-Gen. 1976–79; Commr. for Khartoum Prov. 1976–79; First Vice-Pres. of Sudan 1977–79.

IBRAHIM, Encik Anwar bin, B.A.; Malaysian politician; b. 10 Aug. 1947; ed. Univ. of Malaya; Pres. UMNO Youth Movt. 1982–; Vice-Pres. UMNO 1982–; Head UMNO Permatang Pauh Div. 1982–; Deputy Minister, Prime Minister's Dept. 1982; Minister of Sport, Youth and Culture 1983, of Agric. 1984–86, of Educ. 1986–91, of Finance 1991–98; Deputy Prime Minister 1993–98; arrested Sept. 1998; sentenced to six years imprisonment for corruption April 1999.

IBRAHIM, Izzat; Iraqi politician; b. 1942, al-Dour Shire; ed. secondary schools; Ed. Voice of the Peasant 1968, Head Supreme Cttee., for People's Work 1968–70; Minister of Agrarian Reform 1970–74; Vice-Pres. Supreme Agric. Council 1970–71, Head 1971–79; Minister of Agriculture 1973–74; Minister of Interior 1974–79; mem. Revolutionary Command Council, Vice-Chair. 1979–; Deputy Sec.-Gen. Regional Command of Arab Baath Socialist Party July 1979–; mem. Nat. Command Arab Baath Socialist Party. *Address:* Arab Baath Socialist Party, Office of the Deputy Secretary-General, P.O. Box 6012, Al-Mansour, Baghdad (Office); Karkh, Baghdad, Iraq (Home).

IBRAHIM, Sid Moulay Abdullah; Moroccan politician; b. 1918; ed. Ben Youssef Univ., Marrakesh and the Sorbonne, Paris; mem. Istiqlal (Independence) Party 1944–59; mem. Editorial Cttee. Al Alam (Istiqlal organ) 1950–52; imprisoned for political reasons 1952–54; Sec. of State for Information and Tourism, First Moroccan Nat. Govt. 1955–56; Minister of Labour and Social Affairs 1956–57; Prime Minister and Minister of Foreign Affairs 1958–60; leader Union Nationale des Forces Populaires 1959–72.

ICAHN, Carl C.; American business executive; b. 1936, Queens; m. Liba Icahn; two c.; ed. Princeton Univ. and New York Univ. School of Medicine; apprentice broker, Dreyfus Corpn., New York 1960–63; Options Man. Tessel, Patrick & Co., New York 1963–64, Gruntal & Co. 1964–68; Chair. and Pres. Icahn & Co., New York 1968–; Chair. and C.E.O. ACF Industries Inc., Earth City, Mo. 1984–; Chair. Trans World Airlines Inc. 1986–. *Address:* TWA Inc., 605 Third Ave, New York, NY 10158, U.S.A.

ICE-T (Tracy Marrow); American rap singer and actor; b. Newark, N.J.; m. Darlene Ortiz; one c. *Albums:* Rhyme Pays 1987, The Iceberg/Freedom of Speech, Just Watch What You Say 1989, O.G. Original Gangster 1991, Havin' a "T" Party (with King Tee) 1991, Body Count 1992, Home Invasion 1993, The Classic Collection 1993, Born Dead (with Body Count) 1994. *Films (actor):* Breakin' 1984, New Jack City 1991, Ricochet 1991, Trespass 1992, Surviving the Game 1994, Tank Girl 1995, Johnny Mnemonic 1995. *Publication:* The Ice Opinion 1994. *Address:* Priority Records, 6430 W. Sunset Blvd., Los Angeles, CA 90028, U.S.A.

ICHIKAWA, Kon; Japanese film director; b. 1915; ed. Ichioka Commercial School, Osaka. *Films include:* Poo-San 1953, A Billionaire 1954, The Heart

1954, Punishment Room 1955, The Burmese Harp 1956, The Men of Tohoku 1956, Conflagration 1958, Fires on the Plain 1959, The Key 1959, Bonchi 1960, Her Brother 1960, The Sin 1961, Being Two Isn't Easy 1962, The Revenge of Yuki-No-Jo 1963, Alone on the Pacific 1963, Tokyo Olympiad 1964, Seishun 1970, To Love Again 1971, The Wanderers 1973, Visions of Eight (co-dir.) 1973, Wagahai wa Neko de Aru 1975, The Ingunami's 1976, Gokumon-to 1977, Joobachi 1978, Byoin-zaka no Kubikukuri no le 1979, Ancient City 1980, The Makioka Sisters 1983, Actress 1987, Fusa 1993, The Forty-Seven Ronin 1994.

IDE, Shoichi; Japanese politician; fmr. Parl. Vice-Minister Econ. Planning Agency; Minister of Health and Welfare 1994–95; mem. House of Reps. for Nagano; Chair. Sakigake Party in House of Reps.; Dir. Budget Cttee. *Address:* c/o Ministry of Health and Welfare, 1-2-2, Kasumigaseki, Chiyoda-ku, Tokyo 100, Japan.

IDEI, Nobuyuki; Japanese business executive; m. Teruyo Idei; one d.; ed. Waseda Univ.; joined Sony, est. Sony of France, fmrly. Head of Corp. Communications and Brand Image, Pres. 1995–. *Leisure interests:* music, cinema. *Address:* Sony, 7-35 Kitashinagawa 6-chome, Shinagawa-ku, Tokyo 141, Japan (Office). *Telephone:* 3-5448-2111. *Fax:* 3-5448-2244.

IDEMITSU, Yuji; Japanese business executive; b. 1 Jan. 1927, Fukuoka; m. Yoko Idemitsu 1956; two s.; ed. Kyushu Teikoku Univ.; joined Idemitsu Kosan Co. 1948, Gen. Man. London Office 1974–77, Man. Dir. and Gen. Man. Overseas Operations Dept. 1981–83, Sr. Man. Dir. & Gen. Man. Chiba Refinery 1985–86, Exec. Vice-Pres. 1986–93, Pres. 1993–98; mem. Petroleum Asscn. of Japan (Pres. 1995–), Fed. Econ. Orgs. (mem. Exec. Bd. 1993–). *Leisure interests:* reading, golf, calligraphy. *Address:* c/o Idemitsu Kosan Co. Ltd., 1-1, 3 chome, Marunouchi, Chiyoda-ku, Tokyo 100, Japan. *Telephone:* 03-3213-3110. *Fax:* 03-3213-9340.

IDRIS, Kamil E., B.A., PH.D.; Sudanese diplomatist and lawyer; ed. Univs. of Cairo, Khartoum, Ohio and Geneva and Inst. of Public Admin., Khartoum; part-time journalist El-Ayam and El-Sahafa newspapers in Sudan 1971–79; lecturer Univ. of Cairo 1976–77, Ohio Univ. 1978, Univ. of Khartoum 1986; Asst. Dir. Arab Dept., Ministry of Foreign Affairs, Khartoum 1977–78, Asst. Dir. Research Dept. Jan.–June 1978, Deputy Dir. Legal Dept. July–Dec. 1978; mem. Perm. Mission of Sudan to UN Office, Geneva 1979–82; Vice-Consul of Sudan, Switzerland 1979–82; Sr. Program Officer, Devt. Cooperation and External Relations Bureau for Africa, WIPO 1982–85, Dir. Devt. Cooperation and External Relations Bureau for Arab and Cen. and Eastern European Countries 1985–94, Deputy Dir.-Gen. WIPO 1994–97, Dir.-Gen. Nov. 1997–; mem. UN Int. Law Comm. (ILC) 1991–96 (Vice-Chair. 45th session 1993); served on numerous cttees. of int. orgs. including WHO, ILO, ITU, UNHCR, OAU, Group of 77 etc. and Sudanese del. to numerous int. and regional confs.; Prof. of Public Int. Law, Univ. of Khartoum; mem. African Jurists Asscn.; Scholars and Researchers State Gold Medal (Sudan) 1983, Scholars and Researchers Gold Medal, Egyptian Acad. of Scientific Research and Tech. 1985. *Publications include:* State Responsibility in International Law 1977, North-South Insurance Relations: The Unequal Exchange 1984, The Law of Non-navigational Uses of International Water Courses; the ILC's draft articles: An Overview 1995, The Theory of Source and Target in Child Psychology 1996 and articles on law, economics, jurisprudence and aesthetics in newspapers and periodicals. *Address:* World Intellectual Property Organization, 34 chemin des Colombettes, 1211 Geneva 20, Switzerland. *Telephone:* (22) 338 9111. *Fax:* (22) 733 5428.

IENG SARY; Cambodian politician; m. Khieu Thirith; ed. Paris; fmr. teacher; active in left-wing movts. and forced to flee Phnom-Penh 1963; prominent in Khmer Rouge insurgent movement 1963–75; Khmer Rouge liaison officer to Royal Govt. of Nat. Union of Cambodia (GRUNC) in exile 1971–75; mem. Politburo Nat. United Front of Cambodia (FUNC) 1970–79; Second Deputy Prime Minister of Democratic Kampuchea (now Cambodia) with special responsibility for Foreign Affairs, GRUNC 1975–79; charged with genocide by Heng Samrin regime and sentenced to death *in absentia* Aug. 1979; Deputy Prime Minister in charge of Foreign Affairs of Democratic Kampuchean Govt. in exile (Khmer Rouge) fighting Vietnamese forces 1979–82; rep. for Finance and Econ. Affairs (in coalition in exile) 1982–92; mem. Co-ordination Cttee. Nat. Govt. of Cambodia for Finance and Economy 1991; defected from Khmer Rouge Aug. 1996; granted amnesty Sept. 1996.

IGARASHI, Kozo; Japanese politician; mem. House of Reps.; fmr. Mayor Asahika-wa City; mem. Social Democratic Party of Japan (SDPJ), Dir. Public Information; Minister of Construction 1993–94; Chief Sec. to CAST 1994–95. *Address:* House of Representatives, Tokyo, Japan.

IGGO, Ainsley, PH.D., D.SC., F.R.C.P.(E.), F.R.S.E., F.R.S.; British professor of veterinary physiology; b. 2 Aug. 1924; s. of the late Lancelot G. Iggo and Catherine J. Fraser; m. Betty J. McCurdy 1952; three s.; ed. Gladstone School, New Zealand, Southland Tech. High School, N.Z., Lincoln Coll., N.Z. and Univs. of Otago and Aberdeen; Asst. Lecturer in Physiology, Otago Univ. Medical School 1948–50; N.Z. McMillan Brown Travelling Fellow, Rowett Inst. 1950–51; Lecturer in Physiology, Univ. of Edin. Medical School 1952–60; Nuffield Royal Soc. Commonwealth Fellow, Australian Nat. Univ. 1959; Royal Soc. Locke Research Fellow 1960–62; Prof. of Veterinary Physiology, Univ. of Edin. 1962–90, Dean, Faculty of Veterinary Medicine 1974–77, 1986–90; Visiting Prof. Univ. of Ibadan 1968, Univ. of Kyoto 1970, Univ. of Heidelberg 1972. *Publications:* articles in scientific journals. *Leisure interests:* bee-keeping, gardening. *Address:* 5 Relugas Road, Edin. EH9 2NE, Scotland. *Telephone:* 0131-667 4879.

IGLESIAS, Enrique V.; Uruguayan international official; b. 26 July 1931, Asturias, Spain; s. of Isabel García de Iglesias; ed. Univ. de la República, Montevideo; held several positions including Prof. Agregado, Faculty of Political Economy, Prof. of Econ. Policy and Dir. Inst. of Econs., Univ. de la República, Montevideo 1952–67; Man. Dir. Unión de Bancos del Uruguay 1954; Technical Dir. Nat. Planning Office of Uruguay 1962–66; Pres. (Gov.), Banco Central del Uruguay 1966–68; Chair. Council, Latin American Inst. for Econ. and Social Planning (ILPES), UN 1967–72, Interim Dir. Gen. 1977–78; Head, Advisory Mission on Planning, Govt. of Venezuela 1970; Adviser UN Conf. on Human Environment 1971–72; Exec. Sec. Econ. Comm. for Latin America and the Caribbean (ECLAC) 1972–85; Minister of External Affairs 1985–88; Pres. Inter-American Devt. Bank (IDB) April 1988–; Acting Dir.-Gen. Latin American Inst. for Econ. and Social Planning 1973–78; Pres, Third World Forum 1973–76; mem. Steering Cttee., Soc. for Int. Devt. 1973–92, Pres. 1989, Selection Cttee., Third World Prize 1979–82; Sec.-Gen. UN Conf. on New and Renewable Sources of Energy Feb.–Aug. 1981; Chair. UN Inter-Agency Group on Devt. of Renewable Sources of Energy; mem. North-South Round Table on Energy; Chair. Energy Advisory Panel, Brundtland Comm. 1984–86; Hon. LL.D. (Liverpool) 1987; Prince of Asturias Award 1982. *Leisure interests:* music, art. *Address:* Inter-American Development Bank, 1300 New York Avenue, N.W., Washington, DC 20577, U.S.A.

IGNATENKO, Vitaly Nikitich; Russian journalist; b. 19 April 1941, Sochi; m. Svetlana Ignatenko; one s.; ed. Moscow Univ.; ed., corresp., Deputy Ed.-in-C. Komsomolskaya Pravda 1963–75; Deputy Dir.-Gen. TASS (U.S.S.R. Telegraph Agency) 1975–78; Deputy Head of Int. Information Section, CPSU Cen. Cttee. 1978–86; Ed.-in-C. Novoe Vremya 1986–90; Asst. to fmr. Pres. Gorbachev, Head of Press Service 1990–91; Dir.-Gen. Agency ITAR-TASS 1991–; Deputy Chair. Council of Ministers 1995–97; Pres. Russian Public TV (ORT) 1998–; mem. Int. Acad. of Information Science, Russian Fed. Comm. on UNESCO Affairs, Union of Russian Journalists, Union of Russian Cinematographers; Lenin's Prize 1978, Prize of U.S.S.R. Journalists' Union 1975; Order of the Friendship of Peoples (twice) 1996. *Publications:* several books and more than 30 film scripts. *Leisure interest:* tennis. *Address:* ITAR-TASS, Tverskoy blvd. 10–12, 103009 Moscow, Russia. *Telephone:* 229-79-25. *Fax:* 203-31-80.

IGNATIUS ZAKKA I IWAS, His Holiness Patriarch; Iraqi ecclesiastic; b. 21 April 1933, Mosul, Iraq; ed. St. Aphrem Syrian Orthodox Theol. Seminary, Mosul, Gen. Theol. Seminary, New York and New York Univ.; ordained 1957; consecrated Metropolitan for Archdiocese of Mosul 1963, transferred to Archdiocese of Baghdad 1969; Patriarch of Antioch and All the East (Supreme Head of Universal Syrian Orthodox Church) 1980–; fmr. mem. Iraq Acad. of Science, Arabic Acad. of Jordan; fmr. mem. Cen. Cttee. WCC; Fellow, Faculty of Syriac Studies, Lutheran School of Theol., Chicago 1981; Hon. D.D. (Gen. Theol. Seminary, N.Y.). *Publications:* several books and articles. *Address:* Syrian Orthodox Patriarchate, Bab Toma, PB 22260, Damascus, Syria. *Telephone:* 5432401. *Fax:* 5432400.

IHAMUOTILA, Jaakko, M.S.ENG.; Finnish business executive; b. 15 Nov. 1939, Helsinki; s. of Veikko Artturi Ihamuotila and Anna-Liisa (née Kouki) Ihamuotila; m. Tuula Elina Turja 1965; two s. one d.; ed. Univ. of Tech., Helsinki; Asst. in Reactor Tech. 1963–66, Acting Asst. to Prof. of Physics 1964–66; with Canadian Gen. Electric Co. Ltd., Toronto 1966; Imatran Voima Oy 1966–68; Valmet Oy 1968–70, Asst. Dir. 1970–72, Dir. of Planning 1972–73, Man. Dir. 1973–79, mem. Bd. 1980–82; mem. Bd. Neste Oy 1979–, Chair. and Chief Exec. 1980–; Chair. Bd. of Dirs. Asko Oy, Silja Oy Ab, Chemical Industry Fed. of Finland; mem. Bd. Pohjola Insurance Co.; mem. Supervisory Bd. Merita Bank Ltd., MTV Finland, Finnish Cultural Foundation a.o.; mem. Bd. Finnair, Confed. of Finnish Industry and Employers; mem. Council Econ. Orgs. in Finland, Nat. Bd. of Econ. Defence, Council of Univ. of Tech.; Hon. Dr. Tech. *Leisure interests:* tennis, outdoor pursuits. *Address:* Neste Oy, Keilaniemi, 02150 Espoo, Finland (Office). *Telephone:* (20) 4501.

IHSANOĞLU, Ekmeleddin, PH.D.; Turkish professor of history of science and international administrator; b. 1943, Cairo, Egypt; m. Füsun Bilgiç 1971; three s.; instructor and researcher Ain Shams Univ. and Al-Azhar Univ., Cairo 1966–70, Exeter Univ., England 1975–77; Assoc. Prof. Univ. of Ankara 1979; Prof. and Head Dept. of History of Science Univ. of Istanbul; Dir. Gen. Research Centre for Islamic History, Art and Culture, Org. of the Islamic Conf., also Sec. Int. Comm. for Preservation of Islamic Cultural Heritage; Founder and Chair. Turkish History of Science Asscn. 1989; mem. numerous orgs. concerned with study of Islamic issues, including Middle E. Studies Asscn. of N. America, Royal Acad. of Islamic Civilisation Research, Jordan, Nat. Council for Translation of Studies and Research, Tunisia, Inst. of Islamic Research, Istanbul, Int. Soc. for History of Arabic and Islamic Sciences and Philosophy, Paris, Al-Furqan Islamic Heritage Foundation, U.K., CMES, Harvard Univ., etc.; mem. Tunisian Acad. of Sciences, Letters and Arts, Acad. Int. d'Histoire des Sciences; Dr. h.c. (Mimar Sinan Univ.) 1993; Distinction of the First Order Medal (Egypt) 1990. *Publications:* has written, edited and translated several books on Islamic culture and science; over 70 articles and papers. *Leisure interests:* reading and music. *Address:* Research Centre for Islamic History, Art and Culture, Yıldız Sarayı, Seyir Köşkü, Barbaros Bulvarı, 80700 Beşiktaş, İstanbul, Turkey. *Telephone:* (212) 259 1742. *Fax:* (212) 258 4365.

IIDA, Keizo; Japanese retail executive; b. 13 April 1900, Osaka City; m. Miyoko 1931; one s.; ed. Keio Univ.; Osaka Br., Takashimaya Dept. Store 1926, Man. 1941, Dir. Takashimaya 1942–, Man. Dir. 1943–52, Pres. 1952–60, now Chair. *Leisure interest:* painting. *Address:* 1-2-18, Hibarigaoka, Takarazuka City, Hyogo Pref., Japan.

IIDA, Yotaro; Japanese business executive; b. 25 Feb. 1920; ed. Univ. of Tokyo; joined Mitsubishi Heavy Industries Ltd. 1943, Gen. Man. Utility Power Systems 1973–76, Gen. Man. Utility and Industrial Power Systems 1976–77, Gen. Man. Utility Power Systems 1977, Dir. and Deputy Gen. Man. of Power Systems 1977–81, Man. Dir. and Gen. Man. of Power Systems 1981–83, Exec. Vice-Pres. and Gen. Man. of Power Systems 1983–85, Pres. 1985–86, 1988–91; Chair. 1991–95; Chair. Soc. of Japanese Aerospace Cos. Inc. *Address:* c/o Mitsubishi Heavy Industries Ltd., 5-1, 2-chome Marunouchi, Chiyoda-ku, Tokyo, Japan.

IKAWA, Motomichi, PH.D.; Japanese banking and finance executive; b. 2 Oct. 1947, Tokyo; m. Yoshiko Ikawa; ed. Tokyo Univ., Univ. of California at Berkeley; economist Balance of Payments Div., OECD, Paris 1976–79; various man. posts Ministry of Finance, Tokyo 1979–85; Asst. Regional Commr., C.I.D., Osaka Taxation Bureau 1985–86; Dir. Budget, Personnel and Man. Systems Dept., Asian Devt. Bank 1986–89; Asst. Vice-Minister of Finance, Int. Affairs 1989–90; Dir. Int. Org. Div., Int. Finance Bureau, Ministry of Finance 1990–91, Foreign Exchange and Money Market Div. 1991–92, Devt. Policy Div. 1992–93, Co-ordination Div. 1993–94; Man. Dir. Co-ordination Dept., Overseas Econ. Co-operation Fund 1994-96; Deputy Dir.-Gen. Int. Finance Bureau 1996–97, Sr. Deputy Dir.-Gen. 1997–98; Exec. Vice-Pres. Multilateral Investment Guarantee Agency (MIGA), World Bank Group 1998–. *Publications:* Exchange Market Interventions during the Yen Depreciation 1980 1982, IMF Handbook 1990, The Role of the Overseas Economic Co-operation Fund towards 2010 1994. *Leisure interests:* tennis, golf, hiking. *Address:* Multilateral Investment Guarantee Agency, 1818 H Street, N.W., U12-001, Washington, D.C. 20433, U.S.A. *Telephone:* (202) 473-6138. *Fax:* (202) 522-2620.

IKEDA, Daisaku; Japanese philosopher and author; b. 2 Jan. 1928, Tokyo; s. of Nenokichi and Ichi Ikeda; m. Kaneko Shiraki 1952; two s.; ed. Fuji Coll.; Pres. Soka Gakkai 1960–79, Hon. Pres. 1979–, Pres. Soka Gakkai Int. 1975–; founder of Soka Univ., Soka Univ. of America, Soka Women's Junior Coll., Tokyo, Kansai Soka Schools, Soka Kindergartens (Sapporo, Hong Kong, Sinagapore and Malaysia), Inst. of Oriental Philosophy, Boston Research Center for the 21st Century, Toda Inst. for Global Peace and Policy Research, Tokyo, Shinzuoka Fuji Art Museum, Min-On Concert Asscn. and Victor Hugo House of Literature; Poet Laureate, World Acad. of Arts and Culture, U.S.A. 1981–; Hon. Professorship Nankai Univ. 1998; Foreign mem., Brazilian Acad. of Letters 1993–; Hon. mem., Club of Rome 1996–, Inst. of Oriental Studies of Russian Acad. of Sciences 1996–; Hon. Senator, European Acad. of Sciences and Arts 1997–; Official Patron, World Congress of Poets 1998; Dr. h.c. (Moscow State Univ.) 1975, (Sofia) 1981, (Buenos Aires) 1990, (Univ. of the Philippines) 1991, (Nairobi) 1992, (Ankara) 1992, (Glasgow) 1994, (Tribhuvan) 1995, (Hong Kong) 1996, (Denver) 1996, (Havana) 1996, (Univ. of Ghana) 1996, (Nat. Univ. of Mongolia) 1997, (Delhi) 1999, (Cheju Nat. Univ.) 1999 and others; Hon. Prof. Nat. Univ. of San Marcos 1981, Beijing Univ. 1984, Fudan Univ. 1984, Nat. Univ. of Lomas de Zamora 1993, Jilin Univ. 1997; UN Peace Award 1983, Kenya Oral Literature Award 1986, UNHCR Humanitarian Award 1989, Rosa Parks Humanitarian Award (U.S.A.) 1993, Simon Wiesenthal Center Int. Tolerance Award (U.S.A.) 1993, Tagore Peace Award, The Asiatic Soc. (India) 1997, and others; Order of the Sun of Peru with Grand Cross 1984, Grand Cross, Order of Merit in May (Argentina) 1990, Nat. Order of Southern Cross (Brazil) 1990, Kt. Grand Cross of the Most Noble Order of the Crown (Thailand) 1991, Hon. Cross of Science and the Arts (Austria) 1992, Kt. Grand Cross of Rizal (Philippines) 1996. *Publications:* The Human Revolution Vols. I–VI 1972–99, The Living Buddha 1976, Choose Life 1976, Buddhism: The First Millennium 1977, Glass Children and Other Essays 1979, La Nuit Appelle L'Aurore 1980, A Lasting Peace vols. I–II 1981, 1987, Life: An Enigma, a Precious Jewel 1982, Before It Is Too Late 1984, Buddhism and Cosmos 1985, The Flower of Chinese Buddhism 1986, Human Values in a Changing World 1987, Unlocking the Mysteries of Birth and Death 1988, The Snow Country Prince 1990, The Princess and the Moon 1992, A Lifelong Quest for Peace 1992, Choose Peace 1995, A New Humanism: The University Addresses of Daisaku Ikeda 1996, Ikeda-Gorbachev Dialogue (in Japanese) 1996, The Wisdom of the Lotus Sutra, Vols. I–VI (in Japanese) 1996–99, Ikeda-Aylwin Dialogue (in Japanese) 1997, New Human Revolution, Vol. I (in Japanese) 1998, New Human Revolution, Vols. I–IX (in Japanese) 1998–2000, and other writings on Buddhism, civilization, life and peace. *Leisure interest:* photography. *Address:* 32 Shinano-machi, Shinjuku-ku, Tokyo 160-8583, Japan. *Telephone:* (3) 5360-9831. *Fax:* (3) 5360-9885.

IKEDA, Yukihiko; Japanese politician; b. 13 May 1937, Kobe City, Hyogo Pref.; ed. Univ. of Tokyo; Overall Co-ordination Div. Minister's Secr., Ministry of Finance 1961; seconded to Ministry of Foreign Affairs (served four years as Vice-Consul, New York) 1964; Pvt. Sec. to Minister of Finance 1974; mem. House of Reps. 1976–; Deputy Chief Cabinet Sec. 1981; Chair. Prime Minister's Office Div., Policy Research Council of LDP 1983; Chair. Cttee. on Finance, House of Reps. 1986; Dir.-Gen. Man. and Co-ordination Agency June–Aug. 1989; Deputy Sec.-Gen. LDP March–Dec. 1990; Dir.-Gen. Defence Agency 1990–91; Minister for Foreign Affairs 1996–97. *Address:* c/o Liberal-Democratic Party, 1-11-23, Nagata-cho, Chiyoda-ku, Tokyo 100, Japan.

IKEHATA, Seiichi; Japanese politician; mem. House of Reps., fmr. Dir. Cttee. on Social and Labour Affairs; fmr. Chair. Special Cttee. on Disasters; Minister of State, Dir.-Gen. Nat. Land Agency 1995–96; mem. Social Democratic Party of Japan (SDPJ). *Address:* c/o Social Democratic Party of Japan, 1-8-1, Nagata-cho, Chiyoda-ku, Tokyo 100, Japan.

IKLÉ, Fred Charles, PH.D.; American government official and social scientist; b. 21 Aug. 1924, Samaden, Switzerland; m. Doris Eisemann 1959; two d.; ed. Univ. of Chicago; research scholar, Bureau of Applied Social Research, Columbia Univ. 1950–54; Consultant to Nat. Research Council 1950–54; mem. Social Science Dept., Rand Corpn. 1955–61, Head of Dept. 1968–73; Research Assoc. in Int. Relations, Centre for Int. Affairs, Harvard Univ. 1962–63; Assoc. Prof., then Prof. of Political Science, M.I.T. 1963–67; Dir. U.S. Arms Control and Disarmament Agency 1973–77; Under-Sec. of Defense for Policy 1981–88; Distinguished Scholar, Centre for Strategic Int. Studies 1988–; Co-Chair. U.S. Comm. on Integrated Long Term Strategy 1987–88; mem. Bd. Int. Peace Acad. 1977–81; Chair. Council on Nat. Security of Republican Nat. Cttee. 1977–79; Chair. Conservation Man. Corpn. 1978–81, 1988–, Telos Corpn. 1995–; Dir. Zürich-American Insurance; Dir. Nat. Endowment for Democracy 1992–; U.S. Defense Dept. Distinguished Public Service Awards 1975, 1987, 1988. *Publications:* The Social Impact of Bomb Destruction 1958, After Detection...What? 1961, How Nations Negotiate 1964, Every War Must End 1971, Can Social Predictions be Evaluated? 1967, Can Nuclear Deterrence Last Out The Century? 1973, and many articles on int. affairs and negotiations. *Address:* CSIS, 1800 K Street, N.W., Washington, DC 20006; 7010 Glenbrook Road, Bethesda, MD 20814, U.S.A. (Home). *Telephone:* (202) 775-3155 (Office).

ILETO, Rafael M.; Philippine politician; b. 24 Oct. 1920, Sn. Isidro, Nueva Ecija; s. of Francisco Ileto and Lorenza Manio; m. Olga Clemena Ileto 1945; three s. four d.; ed. Univ. of the Philippines, Philippine and U.S. Mil. Acads.; served U.S. Army World War II; Officer in Philippine Army 1950, f. and Head Scout Rangers 1950–55; Mil. Attaché in Laos and S. Vietnam 1955–59; Operations Chief, Nat. Intelligence Co-ordinating Agency 1959; fmr. Commanding Gen. of Philippine Army and Deputy Chief of Staff; rank of Lieut.-Gen.; Amb. to Iran 1975, later Amb. to Thailand; Deputy Defence Minister Feb.–Nov. 1986, Defence Minister 1986–88; Pres. Adviser on Nat. Security Affairs Feb. 1989–. *Leisure interests:* golf, swimming. *Address:* c/o Office of the President, San Miguel, Metro Manila, The Philippines.

ILIĆ, Venceslav; Bosnia and Herzegovina judge; b. 10 Sept. 1937, Sarajevo; s. of Anto Ilić and Ema Ilić (née Uršić); m. Bogdanka Ilić (née Mioković); two d.; District Court Judge 1972–78; Public Prosecutor 1978–84; Supreme Court Judge 1984–87, 1992–96; Pres. Dist. Court 1987–92; Pres. Supreme Court, Fed. of Bosnia and Herzegovina Sept. 1996–; Medallion of the City of Sarajevo. *Publications:* work on educ. of juridical personnel. *Leisure interests:* work for sports orgs., walking in the countryside. *Address:* Trg Merhemića 14/I, Sarajevo, Federation of Bosnia and Herzegovina. *Telephone:* 664-186. *Fax:* 664-755.

ILIESCU, Ion; Romanian politician; b. 3 March 1930, Oltenița, Ilfov District; m. Elena Iliescu 1951; ed. Bucharest Polytechnic Inst., and Energy Inst., Moscow; researcher, Energy Eng. Inst., Bucharest 1955; Pres. Union of Student Asscns. 1957–60; Alt. mem. Cen. Cttee. of RCP 1965–68, mem. 1968–84; First Sec. Cen. Cttee. of Union of Communist Youth and Minister for Youth 1967–71; Sec. RCP Cen. Cttee. 1971; Vice-Chair. Timiș County Council 1971–74; Chair Iași County Council 1974–79; accused of 'intellectual deviationism' and kept under surveillance; Chair. Nat. Water Council 1979–84; Dir. Tech. Publishing House, Bucharest 1984–89; Pres. Nat. Salvation Front 1989–90, Pres. Provisional Council for Nat. Unity Feb.–May 1990, Pres. of Romania 1990–96, Senator 1996–. *Publications:* Global Problems and Creativity, Revolution and Reform, Romania in Europe and in the World; studies on water man. and ecology, political power and social relations. *Address:* Romanian Senate, 1 Piața Revoluției, 71243 Bucharest, Romania.

ILLICH, Ivan PH.D.; American educator and writer; b. 4 Sept. 1926, Vienna, Austria; ed. Gregorian Univ., Rome, Univ. of Salzburg; went to U.S.A. 1951; Asst. Pastor in New York; Vice-Rector Catholic Univ. of Puerto Rico 1956–60; Lecturer, Dept. of Political Science, Fordham Univ. 1960–76; Co-Founder Center for Intercultural Documentation (CIDOC), Cuernavaca, Mexico 1961–76, Pres. of Bd. 1963–68, mem. 1968–76; Guest Prof. of Medieval History, Univ. of Kassel, 1979–81, Univ. of Calif., Berkeley 1982, Univ. of Marburg 1983–84; Prof. of the Humanities and Sciences, Pa. State Univ. 1986–97; Guest Prof., Doctoral Program in Architecture, Univ. of Pa., Phila. 1990–95; Karl Jasper's Professorship, Univ. of Oldenburg, Germany 1990–91; Guest Prof., Univ. of Bremen 1991–; mem. Berlin Inst. of Advanced Studies 1981–82. *Publications:* Celebration of Awareness 1969, Deschooling Society 1971, Tools for Conviviality 1973, Energy and Equity 1973, Medical Nemesis 1975, The Right to Useful Unemployment 1979, Toward a History of Needs 1979, Shadow-Work 1981, Gender 1982, H_2O and the Waters of Forgetfulness 1985, ABC: The Alphabetization of the Popular Mind 1988, In the Mirror of the Past 1991, In the Vineyard of the Text: A Commentary to Hugh's Didascalicon 1993; contributed to Esprit, Temps Modernes, Kursbuch, New York Review of Books, New York Times, Le Monde. *Address:* Apdo. 1-479, 62000 Cuernavaca, Morelos, Mexico.

ILLUECA, Jorge E., LL.D.; Panamanian politician and diplomatist; b. 17 Dec. 1918, Panama City; m.; four c.; ed. Univ. de Panamá, Harvard Law School, Univ. of Chicago; Prof., Univ. de Panamá 1962–63, 1966–68; Pres. Nat. Bar Asscn. 1963–64, 1966–68; Dir. El Panamá América (newspaper) 1963–64, 1967–68; Special Amb. to U.S.A. to begin negotiations for new Panama Canal Treaty 1964, Special Envoy for negotiations on the treaty 1972; mem. del. to UN Gen. Assembly 1957, 1961, 1975, also to 3rd Special Emergency Session; Head of del. to 1st Session of 3rd UN Conf. on Law of the Sea 1974, mem. del to 4th Session 1976; Deputy Perm. Rep. to UN 1957, Perm. Rep. 1960, 1976–81, 1994–97, Pres. 38th Session of UN Gen. Ass. Sept.–Dec. 1983; mem. Perm. Court of Arbitration, The Hague, Netherlands 1974–76; fmr. Foreign Minister; Vice-Pres. of Panama 1982–83, Pres. Feb.–Oct. 1984; U Thant Award 1983. *Address:* c/o Ministry of Foreign Affairs, Panamá 4, Panama.

ILLYA II, Catholicos-Patriarch of all Georgia; Georgian ecclesiastic; b. 4 Dec. 1933, Sno, Kazbegi Region; ed. Moscow Theological Seminary, Moscow Theological Acad.; took monastic vows 1957; Father-Superior 1960; Archimandrite 1961; Vicar of Cathalicos-Patriarch 1963; entrusted with Tsum-Abkhaz diocese 1977; Tsum-Abkhaz Mitropolite 1969; Rector Mtskheta Theological Acad. 1963–72; awarded second panagya 1972; enthroned as Cathalicos-Patriarch of all Georgia 1977–; Pres. World Council of Churches 1978–83; Dr. of Theology American St.-Vladimir Theological Acad.; holder of highest awards of churches of Georgia, Constantinople, Alexandria, Antiochia, Jerusalem, Russia, Czechoslovakia and Poland; Order of Friendship of Peoples.

ILVES, Toomas Hendrik, M.A.; Estonian fmr. government minister, diplomatist and scientist; b. 1953, Stockholm, Sweden; m. Merry Bullock; two c.; ed. Columbia Univ., New York, U.S.A., Univ. of Pennsylvania, U.S.A.; Research Asst., Dept. of Psychology, Columbia Univ. 1974–76, 1979; Asst. to Dir. and English Teacher, Centre for Open Educ., Englewood, N.J. 1979–81; Arts Admin. and Dir. Vancouver Literary Centre, Canada 1981–82; lecturer in Estonian Literature and Linguistics, Dept. of Interdisciplinary Studies, Simon Fraser Univ., Vancouver 1983–84; Research Analyst, Radio Free Europe, Munich, Germany 1984–88, Dir. Estonian Service 1988–93; Amb. of Estonia to U.S.A. (also accred. to Canada and Mexico) 1993–96; Minister of Foreign Affairs 1996–98. *Address:* c/o Ministry of Foreign Affairs, Rävala pst 9, EE0100 Tallinn, Estonia. *Telephone:* (6) 442559; 443266.

ILYENKO, Yuriy Gerasimovich; Ukrainian cinematographer; b. 9 May 1936, Ukraine; s. of Gerasim and Maria Ilyenko; m. Liudmyla Yefymenko 1977; two s.; ed. VGIK, Moscow; Head Sub-Faculty of Directing and Dramatic Composition, State Inst. of Theatrical Arts, Kiev. *Films include:* Shadows of Our Forgotten Ancestors (by Paradzhyanov) 1964 (16 int. prizes); (as director), A Spring for the Thirsty 1965, On the Eve of Ivan Kupalo Day 1968, A White Bird with a Black Mark 1971, In Defiance of All 1972, To Dream and to Live 1974, Baked Potato Festival 1977, The Forest Song 1981, Strip of Wild Flowers 1982, Legend of Queen Olga 1983, Straw Bells 1985, Swan Lake-The Zone 1990 (2 prizes, Cannes Film Festival). *Leisure interest:* painting (exhibited in Kiev, Munich and Vienna). *Address:* 9 Michail Kotzybinksy Str., Apt. 22, Kiev 252030, Ukraine. *Telephone:* (044) 2247540 (Home). *Fax:* (044) 2247540 (Home).

IL'YIN, Leonid Andreyevich, D.MED.; Russian toxicologist; b. 1928; ed. First Leningrad Medical Inst.; worked as dr. in the navy, Head of lab. of irradiation protection, Deputy Dir. Leningrad Inst. of Irradiation Protection, U.S.S.R. Ministry of Public Health 1961–67; Dir. Inst. of Biophysics, U.S.S.R. Ministry of Public Health 1968–89; Dir. Inst. of Radiation Medicine 1989–; mem. Russian Acad. of Medical Sciences 1982, Vice Pres. 1984–90; Deputy Chair. Soviet Cttee. Doctors Against the Nuclear Threat 1984–90; Hero of Socialist Labour; U.S.S.R. State Prize, Pirogov Prize. *Publications:* more than 100 works on problems of toxicology and radiation medicine, including A Threat of Nuclear War (together with E. Chazov). *Address:* Institute of Radiation Medicine, Zhivopisnaya Street 46, 123182 Moscow, Russia. *Telephone:* 190-56-51.

ILYUMZHUNOV, Kirsan Nikolayevich; Kalmyk politician, b. 5 April 1962, Elista; m.; one s.; ed. Moscow Inst. of Int. Relations; later man. Japanese cos. in Russia; f. a number of maj. enterprises in Kalmykya; Pres. Int. Corp. SAN 1991; Peoples' Deputy of Russian Fed. 1990–93; Pres. of Kalmyk Repub. (Khalmg Tangch) 1993, mem. Russian Council of Fed. 1993–; Pres. Int. Chess Fed. (FIDE) 1995–. *Address:* Office of the President, Elista, Kalmykya; Council of Federation, Bolshaya Dmitrovka 26, 103031 Moscow, Russia. *Telephone:* (87322) 2-33-07 (Elista); (095) 292-42-27, 926-67-92 (Moscow). *Fax:* (87322) 334-20-39.

ILYUSHIN, Viktor Vasilyevich; Russian politician; b. 4 June 1947, Nizhny Tagil; m.; one s. one d.; ed. Urals Polytech. Inst., G. Plekhanov Acad. of Nat. Econ.; worked as metalworker Nizhnevartovsk metallurgy plant; master Nizhny Tagil metallurgy plant; First Sec. Sverdlovsk City Komsomol cttee., then regional cttee., First Sec. Sverdlovsk regional CPSU Cttee.; on staff Cen. CPSU Cttee.; counsellor Cen. Cttee. Afghanistan People's Democratic Party; asst. to Boris Yeltsin on staff of Cen. CPSU Cttee. and Moscow City Exec. Cttee.; asst. to Chair. Russian Supreme Soviet 1990–91; Head, Pres. Yeltsin's Secr. 1991–92; First Asst. Pres. of Russian Fed. 1991–96, First Deputy Prime Minister 1996–97; Chair. Bd. of Dirs. Gazprom-Media 1997–. *Leisure interest:* tennis. *Address:* Gazprom, Nametkina str. 16, 117887 Moscow, Russia. *Telephone:* 719-30-01.

IMADY, Mohammed, PH.D.; Syrian economist and planner; b. 1 Dec. 1930, Damascus; s. of Jawdat Imady and Yosra Hawasly; m. Mildred Elain Rippey 1958; one s. two d.; ed. Damascus Secondary School, Damascus Univ. and New York Univ.; Deputy Minister of Planning 1968–72, Minister 1972; Minister of Economy and Foreign Trade 1972–79; Pres. Arab Econ. Soc. 1974–75, Syrian Econ. Soc. 1976; Chair. Bd. of Govs. IMF, IBRD 1975–76; Dir.-Gen. and Chair. Arab Fund for Econ. and Social Devt. 1979–85; Minister of Economy and Foreign Trade 1985; Founders Day Award (New York Univ.). *Publication:* Economic Development and Planning (textbook in Arabic for Damascus Univ.) 1968.

IMAI, Nobuko; Japanese viola soloist; b. 18 March 1943, Tokyo; m. Aart van Bochove 1981; one s. one d.; ed. Toho School of Music, Tokyo, Juilliard School and Yale Univ., U.S.A.; mem. Vermeer Quartet 1974–79; soloist with Berlin Philharmonic, London Symphony Orchestra, Royal Philharmonic, the BBC orchestras, Detroit Symphony, Chicago Symphony, Concertgebouw, Montreal Symphony, Boston Symphony, Vienna Symphony, Orchestre de Paris, Stockholm Philharmonic; festival performances include Marlborough, Salzburg, Lockenhaus, Casals, South Bank, Summer Music, Aldeburgh, BBC Proms, Int. Viola Congress (Houston), New York "Y", Festival d'Automne, Paris; conceived Int. Hindemith Viola Festival (London, New York, Tokyo) 1995; Prof. High School of Music, Detmold 1985–; Artistic Adviser, Casals Hall, Tokyo; over 20 recordings; First Prize Munich, Second Prize Geneva Int. Viola Competitions; Avon Arts Award 1993, Japanese Educ. Minister's Art Prize for Music 1993, Mobil Japan Art Prize 1995, Suntory Hall Prize 1996. *Leisure interest:* cooking. *Address:* c/o Irene Witmer Personal Management in Classical Music, Kerkstraat 97, 1017 GD Amsterdam, The Netherlands. *Telephone:* (20) 524 4040. *Fax:* (20) 524 4044.

IMAI, Takashi; Japanese business executive; b. 1929, Kamakura; ed. Univ. of Tokyo; joined Fuji Iron & Steel 1952, Man. Raw Materials 1963; Deputy Gen. Man. Fuel and Ferrous Metals, Nippon Steel (formed by merger of Fuji Iron & Steel and Yawata Steel) 1970, Gen. Man. Iron Ore 1973, Man. Dir. 1983, Exec. Vice-Pres. 1989, Pres. Nippon Steel 1992–. *Leisure interest:* go. *Address:* Nippon Steel Corporation, 6-3 2-chome Otemachi, Chiyoda-ku, Tokyo, Japan.

IMAM, Zafar; Bangladeshi politician; b. 1940, Feni; ed. Punjab Univ.; joined Pakistan Army 1966, C.O. 10th Bengal Regt. 1971, Lieut.-Col. 1975; mem. Bangladesh Nationalist Party Exec. Cttee. 1978; M.P. 1979; Deputy Minister of Relief and Rehabilitation 1980, Minister 1985–86, Minister of Jute 1986–88, of Textiles 1988–89, of Forests and the Environment 1990–91; Bir Birkram Award. *Address:* c/o Ministry of Forests and the Environment, Dhaka, Bangladesh.

IMAMURA, Shohei; Japanese film director; b. 15 Sept. 1926, Tokyo; ed. Waseda Univ.; entered film industry in 1951 as an asst. dir.; started directing 1958; opened film school Yokohama Hoso Eiga Seimon Gako where he teaches. *Films include:* The Stolen Desire, Lights of Night, The Endless Desire 1958, My Second Brother 1959, Hogs and Warships/The Flesh is Hot/ The Dirty Girls 1961, The Insect Woman 1963, Unholy Desire 1964, The Pornographer/ The Amorists 1966, A Man Vanishes 1967, Kuragejima—Legends from a Southern Island 1968, Postwar Japanese History 1970, The Ballad of Narayama (Golden Palm at Cannes) 1983, Zegen, Black Rain (Grand Prize for Tech. Excellence, Cannes Film Festival 1989) 1989, The Eel (Golden Palm at Cannes). *Address:* Toei Company Ltd., 3-2-17 Ginza, Chuo-Ku, Tokyo 104, Japan.

IMAN (Iman Abdul Majid); Somali model; b. 1956; m. 1st Spencer Haywood; m. 2nd David Bowie (q.v.) 1992; one d.; ed. Nairobi Univ.; fashion model 1976–90, has modelled for Claude Montana and Thierry Mugler; signed Revlon Polish Ambers contract (first black model to be signed by int. cosmetics co.) 1979; has made numerous TV appearances and has appeared in a Michael Jackson video. *Films include:* Star Trek VI: The Undiscovered Country, Houseparty II, Exit to Eden. *Address:* c/o Elite Model Management, 40–42 Parker Street, London WC2B 5PQ, England. *Telephone:* 0171-333 0888.

IMANAGA, Fumio; Japanese business executive; b. 22 Feb. 1928; s. of Fumihiko Imanaga; m. 1953; two c.; ed. Moji Middle School and First Imperial Fisheries Inst.; joined Nippon Suisan Kaisha Ltd. 1948, mem. Bd. of Dirs. 1977, Man. Dir. 1980, Sr. Man. Dir. 1983, Exec. Vice-Pres. 1985, Pres. 1986. *Leisure interests:* golf, reading.

IMANAKA, Hiroshi, LL.D.; Japanese university professor; b. 2 Dec. 1930, Fukuoka City; s. of late Tsugumaro Imanaka; ed. Univs. of Hiroshima and Nagoya; lecturer, Faculty of Educ., Miyazaki Univ. 1960–65; Lecturer, Dept. of Gen. Educ., Hiroshima Univ. 1965–67, Assoc. Prof. 1967–78, Prof. of Political Science, Faculty of Integrated Arts and Sciences 1978–81, Faculty of Law 1981–91, Prof. Emer. 1991–; Dean and Prof., Kinjogakuin Univ. 1991–. *Publications:* Constitutional Law (co-author) 1971, George Lawson's Political Theory of Civil Government 1976, A Study of the History of English Political Thought 1977, Parliamentarism and its Origin in the Era of English Revolution. *Address:* 11-8-403 Kitayama-Minami, Moriyama-ku, Nagoya Shi, Japan. *Telephone:* (052) 791-7933.

IMANALIYEV, Muratbeck Sansyzbayevich, CAND. HIST.; Kyrgyzstan politician; b. 1956, Frunze (now Bishkek); m.; two c.; ed. Inst. of Asian and African Countries, Moscow State Univ., Leningrad br. Inst. of Oriental Studies U.S.S.R. Acad. of Sciences; Second Sec. on Press and Information

Ministry of Foreign Affairs Kyrgyz S.S.R. 1982–88, Head of Protocol Consulate Div. 1988–89, Head Consular Div. 1989–90, Minister of Foreign Affairs Kyrgyz Repub. 1991–93; Amb. to China 1993–96; Head Int. Div. Presidential Admin. 1996–97; Minister of Foreign Affairs June 1997–. *Address:* Ministry of Foreign Affairs, Erkindik blvd. 54, 720021 Bishkek, Kyrgyz Republic (Office). *Telephone:* (3312) 22 05 45 (Office).

IMBERT, Jean Raoul Léon, DIP.; French university professor; b. 23 June 1919, Calais; s. of Léon Imbert and Maria (née Decobert) Imbert; m. Thérèse Chombart 1945; two s. (and one s. deceased) one d.; ed. Faculté de Droit de Paris (Sorbonne); mem. Faculty of Law, Nancy 1947–58; Prof. of History of Law, Paris 1958–88; Tech. Adviser to the Ministry of Health 1958; Dean of the Faculty of Law, Phnom-Penh, Cambodia 1959–61; Rector of the Univ. of Yaoundé, Cameroon 1971–73; Rector of the Acad. of Versailles 1973–75; Dir. of Higher Studies, Ministry of Univs. 1976–79; Dir. Centre Nat. des Oeuvres Universitaires et Scolaires 1979–82; Pres. of the Univ. of Law, Econs. and Social Sciences, Paris 1984–88; Lauréat de l'Acad. des Inscriptions et Belles Lettres 1948, Lauréat de l'Acad. Française 1983; mem. Acad. des Sciences morales et politiques 1982–, Inst. de France; Foreign mem. Acad. of Science and Letters, Milan 1983–; Commdr. Légion d'honneur, Ordre nat. du Mérite, Chevalier du Mérite militaire, Croix de la valeur militaire, Commdr. des Palmes académiques; Silver Medal Int. Asscn. of Univ. Presidents 1972. *Publications:* Histoire du droit privé 1950 (trans. into Japanese), Le droit hospitalier de la Révolution et de l'Empire 1954, Le droit antique 1960 (trans. into Greek and Portuguese), Histoire des institutions khmères 1961, Histoire économique des origines à 1789 1965 (trans. into Spanish), La peine de mort 1967, La France et les droits de l'homme 1968, Le pouvoir, les juges et les bourreaux 1972, Le Cameroun 1973, Le procès de Jésus 1980, Histoire des hôpitaux de France 1982, L'Eglise catholique dans la France contemporaine 1990, Les temps carolingiens 1994. *Leisure interest:* flying. *Address:* 57 boulevard Poniatowski, 75012 Paris, France.

IMBERT, Baron (Life Peer), cr. 1999, of New Romney in the County of Kent, **Peter Michael Imbert;** British police officer and business executive; b. 27 April 1933, Folkestone, Kent; s. of late William Henry Imbert and of Frances May Hodge; m. Iris Rosina Dove 1956; one s. two d.; ed. Harvey Grammar School; Metropolitan Police 1953–93, Asst. Chief Constable, Surrey Constabulary 1976–77, Deputy Chief Constable 1977–79, Chief Constable, Thames Valley Police 1979–85, Deputy Commr. Metropolitan Police 1985–87, Commr. 1987–93; Metropolitan Police Anti-Terrorist Squad 1973–75; Police negotiator in Balcombe Street (London) IRA Siege Dec. 1975; Sec. Nat. Crime Cttee., ACPO Council 1980–83, Chair. 1983–85; Chair. Vehicle Security Installation Bd. 1994–96; Chair. (non-exec.) Retainagroup 1995–; Chair. Capital Eye Security Ltd. 1997–; Dir. (non-exec.) Securicor 1993–, Camelot Gp. 1994–; consultant CDR Int. 1997–; mem. Gen. Advisory Council, BBC 1980–87, Criminal Justice Consultative Cttee. 1992–93; Chair. Surrey Co. Cricket Club Youth Trust 1993–96; mem. Ministerial Advisory Bd. on Royal Parks 1993–, Public Policy Cttee. of Royal Automobile Club 1993–; Trustee Help the Aged 1993–95, St. Catherine's Foundation Cumberland Lodge; Hon. D.Litt (Reading Univ.), Hon. M.B.A. (Int. Management Centre); D.L. Greater London 1994–98, J.P. 1998; Lord Lieut. of Greater London 1998–. *Leisure interests:* golf, bad bridge, watching good cricket, talking about his grandchildren. *Address:* The Lieutenancy Office, City Hall, P.O. Box 240, Victoria Street, London, SW1E 6QP, England. *Telephone:* 0171-641 3259.

IMBUSCH, George Francis, D.SC., PH.D., F.INST.P., F.A.I.P., F.I.E.E.; Irish professor of experimental physics; b. 7 Oct. 1935, Limerick; s. of George Imbusch and Alice Neville; m. Mary Rita O'Donnell 1961; one s. one d.; ed. Christian Brothers' School, Limerick, Univ. Coll. Galway and Stanford Univ.; mem. tech. staff, Bell Labs. U.S.A. 1964–67; lecturer in Physics, Univ. Coll. Galway 1967–74, Prof. of Experimental Physics 1974–, Head, Dept. of Physics 1986–89, Vice-Pres. Univ. Coll. Galway 1992–98; Science Sec., Royal Irish Acad. 1989–93; Visiting Prof. Univ. of Wis. 1978, Regensburg 1981, Utrecht 1988, Canterbury, N.Z. 1995, Georgia 1998. *Publications:* Optical Spectroscopy of Inorganic Solids (co-author) 1989; 100 scientific papers in journals. *Leisure interests:* painting, reading. *Address:* Forramoyle West, Barna, Co. Galway, Republic of Ireland. *Telephone:* (91) 592159.

IMRAN KHAN NIAZI; Pakistani cricketer; b. 25 Nov. 1952, Lahore; m. Jemima Goldsmith 1995; one s.; ed. Aitchison Coll. and Cathedral School, Lahore, Worcester Royal Grammar School, England, Keble Coll. Oxford; right-arm fast bowler, middle-order right-hand batsman; played for Lahore 1969–71, Worcs. 1971–76, Oxford Univ. 1973–75 (Capt. 1974), Dawood 1975–76, PIA 1975–81, Sussex 1977–88, N.S.W. 1984–85; 88 Test matches for Pakistan 1971–92, 48 as Capt., scoring 3,807 runs (average 37.6) and taking 362 wickets (average 22.8); toured England 1971, 1974, 1975 (World Cup), 1979 (World Cup), 1982, 1983 (World Cup), 1987; scored 17,771 first-class runs and took 1,287 first-class wickets; 175 limited-overs ints., 139 as Capt. (including 1992 World Cup victory); second player to score a century and take 10 wickets in a Test 1983; only third player to score over 3,000 Test runs and take 300 wickets; Special Rep. for Sports, UNICEF 1989; Ed.-in-Chief Cricket Life 1989–90; f. Imran Khan Cancer Hosp. Appeal 1991–; Hon. Fellow Keble Coll. Oxford 1988; Hilal-e-Imtiaz 1993. *Publications:* Imran 1983, All-Round View (autobiog.) 1988, Indus Journey 1990, Warrior Race 1993; writes syndicated newspaper column. *Address:* c/o Shankat Khanum Memorial Trust, 29 Shah Jamal, Lahore 546000, Pakistan.

IMRAN TUANKU JAAFAR, Tunku; Malaysian business executive; ed. The King's School, Canterbury and Univ. of Nottingham; formerly worked for nat. oil co.; with father opened own co. in partnership with Jardine Matheson Holdings 1977; founder and Man. Dir. Antah Holdings (with holdings in Arab-Malaysian Bank, Pepsi-Cola Bottling, joint venture rural water supply, leasing cos., insurance cos., security, tech. products and real estate) 1983–. *Address:* Antah Holdings, Berhad, Complex Bejabat Damansaia, Kuala Lumpur, Malaysia.

IMRAY, Sir Colin Henry, K.B.E., C.M.G., K.ST.J., M.A.; British diplomatist; b. 21 Sept. 1933, Newport, Mon.; s. of Henry Gibbon Imray and Frances Olive Badman; m. Shirley Margaret Matthews 1957; one s. three d.; ed. Highgate School, London, Hotchkiss School, Conn., U.S.A. and Balliol Coll., Oxford; Second Lieut. Seaforth Highlanders, Royal W. African Frontier Force 1952–54; Asst. Prin. Commonwealth Relations Office 1957–58, 1961–63; Third then Second Sec. British High Comm., Canberra 1958–61; First Sec., Nairobi 1963–66; Asst. Head Personnel Dept. FCO 1966–70; British Trade Commr., Montreal 1970–73; Counsellor, Consul Gen. and Head of Chancery, Islamabad 1973–77; Royal Coll. of Defence Studies 1977; Commercial Counsellor British Embassy, Tel Aviv 1977–80; Deputy High Commr., Bombay 1980–84; Asst. Under-Sec. of State (Chief Inspector and Deputy Chief Clerk) 1984–85; High Commr. in Tanzania 1986–89, in Bangladesh 1989–93; Sec. Gen. O.St.J. 1993–97, Dir. Overseas Relations 1997–98; mem. Cen. Cttee. Royal Over-Seas League 1998–; Freeman City of London 1994. *Leisure interests:* travel, walking. *Address:* Holbrook House, Reading Road, Wallingford, Oxon., OX10 9DT, England.

IMRU HAILE SELASSIE, Lij Mikhail; Ethiopian politician; b. 1930; ed. Oxford Univ., England; fmr. Dir.-Gen. Ministry of Defence and mem. Planning Bd., Ministry of Agriculture; fmr. Amb. to U.S., then to U.S.S.R.; Head Ethiopian mission to UN Office, Geneva until 1974; Minister of Commerce and Industry March 1974; Minister in the Prime Minister's Office in charge of Econ. and Social Affairs April-July 1974, Prime Minister July-Sept. 1974; Minister of Information 1974–75; Chief Political Adviser to Head of State 1975–76.

INAGAKI, Jitsuo; Japanese politician; mem. House of Reps.; fmr. Parl. Vice-Minister of Health and Welfare; Dir. Gen. Hokkaido Devt. Agency and Okinawa Devt. Agency (State Minister) Nov. 1996–. *Address:* Hokkaido Development Agency, 3-1-1, Kasumigaseki, Chiyoda-ku, Tokyo 100, Japan (Office). *Telephone:* 3-3581-9111 (Office). *Fax:* 3-3581-1208 (Office).

INAGAKI, Masao; Japanese advertising executive; b. 27 Oct. 1922, Aichi Pref.; s. of Gonpachi and Katsu Inagaki; m. Teruko Inagaki 1949; one d.; ed. Training Inst., Ministry of Foreign Affairs; with Civil Property Bureau, Ministry of Foreign Affairs 1948–50; joined Sekai-Sha, apptd. Gen. Man., Advertising Div. 1950; f. and Dir. Daiichi-Tsushinsya; f. Asatsu Inc., C.E.O. and Pres. 1956–. *Leisure interest:* writing poems. *Address:* 7-16-12, Ginza, Chuo-ku, Tokyo 104 (Office); 2-32-7 Matusgaoka, Nakano-ku, Tokyo 165, Japan (Home). *Telephone:* (03) 3547-2111 (Office); (03) 3951-8644 (Home). *Fax:* (03) 3547-2345 (Office).

INBAL, Eliahu; British/Israeli conductor; b. 16 Feb. 1936, Jerusalem; s. of Jehuda Joseph and Leah Museri Inbal; m. Helga Fritzsche 1968; three s.; ed. Acad. of Music, Jerusalem, Conservatoire National Supérieur, Paris; from 1963 guest conductor with numerous orchestras including Milan, Rome, Berlin, Munich, Hamburg, Stockholm, Copenhagen, Vienna, Budapest, Amsterdam, London, Paris, Tel-Aviv, New York, Chicago, Toronto and Tokyo; Chief Conductor, Radio Symphony Orchestra, Frankfurt 1974–90, Hon. Conductor 1995–, Teatro La Fenice 1984–87; Hon. Conductor, Nat. Symphony Orchestra, RAI Torino 1996–; has made numerous recordings, particularly of Mahler, Bruckner, Berlioz and Shostakovich. *Leisure interests:* music reproduction, photography. *Address:* Hessischer Rundfunk, Bertramstrasse 8, 6000 Frankfurt, Germany. *Telephone:* 0611/ 1552371.

INDIANA, Robert, B.F.A.; American artist; b. 13 Sept. 1928, New Castle Ind.; ed. John Herron School of Art, Indianapolis, Munson-Williams-Proctor Inst., Utica, New York, Art Inst. of Chicago, Skowhegan School of Painting and Sculpture, Univ. of Edinburgh and Edinburgh Coll. of Art; served U.S.A.A.F. 1946–49; Artist-in-Residence, Center of Contemporary Art, Aspen, Colo. 1968; Hon. D.F.A. (Franklin and Marshall Coll., Lancaster, Pa.) 1970. One-man exhbns.: Stable Gallery, New York 1962, 1964, 1966, Walker Art Center, Minneapolis 1963, Inst. of Contemporary Art, Boston 1963, Rolf Nelson Gallery, Los Angeles 1965, Dayton's Gallery 1912, Minneapolis 1966, Galerie Alfred Schmela, Düsseldorf 1966, Stedelijk van Abbemuseum, Eindhoven 1966, Museum Hans Lange, Krefeld (Fed. Repub. of Germany) 1966, Württembergischer Kunstverein, Stuttgart 1966, Inst. of Contemporary Art, Univ. of Pennsylvania 1968, Marion Koogler McNay Art Inst., San Antonio, Tex. 1968, Herron Museum of Art, Indianapolis 1968, Toledo Museum of Art, Ohio 1968, Hunter Gallery, Aspen, Colo. 1968, Creighton Univ., Omaha 1969, St. Mary's Coll., Notre Dame, Ind. 1969, Colby Coll. Art Museum, Waterville, Maine 1969–70, Currier Gallery of Art, Manchester, N.H. 1970, Hopkins Center, Dartmouth Coll. Hanover, N.H. 1970, Bowdoin Coll. Museum of Art, Brunswick, Maine 1970, Brandeis Univ., Waltham, Mass. 1970, Heron Art Museum, Indianapolis 1977, Univ. of Texas 1977, Osuna Gallery, Washington 1981, Tex. Art Centre 1982, William A. Farnsworth Library and Art Museum, Maine 1982. *Major group exhbns. include:* Painting and Sculpture of a Decade, Tate Gallery, London 1964, Twenty-ninth Biennial Exhbn. of American Painting, Corcoran Gallery of Art, Washington, D.C. 1965, Pop Art and the American Tradition, Milwaukee 1965, White House Festival of the Arts, Washington 1965, American Painting Now, Expo 67, Montreal 1967, Annual Exhbns. of American Painting, Documenta IV, Kassel 1968, Art in the Sixties, Cologne 1969, San Francisco Museum of Art 1975, Royal Acad., London 1991, Museo Nacional Reina Sofia, Madrid 1992, numerous others. *Address:* Press Box 464, Vinalhaven, ME 04863, U.S.A.

INDJOVA, Reneta, PH.D.; Bulgarian economist and politician; b. 6 July 1953, Nova Zgora; m. Boyan Slavenkov 1977 (divorced 1990); one d.; ed. Sofia Univ. of Nat. and World Economy; Univ. Asst. Prof. of Political Economy and Econs. 1975–89; a founder of Union of Democratic Forces (UDF), co-author UDF's platform 1990; Econ. Counsellor to Great Nat. Ass. 1990–91; Expert, govt.'s Agency for Econ. Devt. 1991–93; Head of Privatization Agency 1993, Exec. Dir. 1994; Prime Minister 1994–95; Founder and Nat. Chair. political party "For Real Reforms" 1997; Fellow, Eisenhower Exchange Program, Phila. 1995; Trustee American Univ. of Blagoevgrad 1996–; Distinguished Speaker, Atlantic Club of Bulgaria 1995. *Leisure interests:* literature, music, tailoring. *Address:* "Hadji Dimitar" bl. 142, A, ap. 4, Sofia 1510, Bulgaria.

INDURÁIN, Miguel; Spanish cyclist; b. 16 July 1964, Villava, Navarre; m. Marisa Induráin; one d.; mem. Reynolds team 1984–89, Banesto team 1989–96; five successive times winner, Tour de France 1991–95, 1995 winning time, 92 hrs. 44 min. 59 sec.; Gold Medal, Atlanta Olympics 1996; ranked No 1 cyclist 1992, 1993; announced retirement Jan. 1997. *Address:* Villava, Pamplona, Spain.

ING HUOT; Cambodian politician; Minister of Educ. 1993, of Foreign Affairs and Int. Co-operation 1995–98, First Prime Minister 1997–98. *Address:* c/o Ministry of Foreign Affairs, Phnom-Penh, Cambodia.

INGAMELLS, John, B.A.; British museum director and art historian; b. 12 Nov. 1934, Northampton; s. of the late George H. Ingamells and Gladys L. (Rollett) Ingamells; m. Hazel Wilson 1964; two d.; ed. Hastings and Eastbourne Grammar Schools and Fitzwilliam House, Cambridge; Art Asst. York Art Gallery 1959–62; Asst. Keeper of Art, Nat. Museum of Wales 1963–67; Curator, York Art Gallery 1967–77; Asst. to Dir. Wallace Collection 1977–78, Dir. 1978–92; mem. Exec. Cttee. Nat. Art Collections Fund 1992–97. *Publications;* The Davies Collection of French Art 1967, The English Episcopal Portrait 1981, Wallace Collection, Catalogue of Pictures (Vol. I) 1985, (Vol. II) 1986, (Vol. III) 1989, (Vol. IV) 1992, Dictionary of British Visitors to Italy in the 18th Century 1996, A Dictionary of British and Irish Travellers in Italy 1701–1800 1998; numerous museum catalogues, exhibition catalogues and articles in learned journals. *Address:* 39 Benson Road, London, SE23 3RL, England (Home).

INGE, Baron (Life Peer) cr. 1997, of Richmond in the County of North Yorkshire; **Field Marshal Peter Anthony Inge,** G.C.B.; British army officer; b. 5 Aug. 1935; s. of Raymond Albert Inge and late Grace Maud Caroline Inge; m. Letitia Marion Beryl Thornton-Berry 1960; two d.; ed. Summer Fields, Wrekin Coll., Royal Mil. Acad. Sandhurst; commissioned Green Howards 1956, ADC to G.O.C. 4 Div. 1960–61, Adjutant 1st Green Howards 1963–64, student Staff Coll. 1966, Ministry of Defence 1967–69, Co. Commdr. 1st Green Howards 1969–70, student Jt. Service Staff Coll. 1971, Brigade Maj. 11th Armoured Brigade 1972, Instructor Staff Coll. 1973–74, C.O. 1st Green Howards 1974–76, Commdt. Jr. Div. Staff Coll. 1977–79, Commdr. 4th Armoured Brigade 1980–81, Chief of Staff HQ 1st (BR) Corps 1982–83, G.O.C. NEDIST and Commdr. 2nd Infantry Div. 1984–86, Dir.-Gen. Logistic Policy (Army) 1986–87, Commdr. 1st (BR) Corps 1987–89, Commdr. NORTHAG and Commdr. in Chief BAOR 1989–92, Chief of Gen. Staff 1992–94, of the Defence Staff 1994–97, Constable of the Tower of London 1996–; ADC Gen. to the Queen 1991–94, Deputy Lieut. of N. Yorks. 1994; Col. The Green Howards 1982–94, Col. Commdt. RMP 1987–92, Col. Commdt. APTC 1988–97; Dir. (non-exec.) Racal Electronics PLC; Freeman City of London 1994. *Leisure interests:* cricket, walking, music, reading, military history. *Address:* House of Lords, London, SW1A 0PW, England.

INGELMAN-SUNDBERG, Axel, M.D., PH.D.; Swedish gynaecologist and university professor; b. 22 Dec. 1910, Uppsala; s. of Isidor Sundberg and Maria Ingelman; m. 1st Anna Brandberg 1937; m. 2nd Mirjam Furuhjelm 1946; three s. one d.; ed. Uppsala Univ. and Royal Caroline Inst., Stockholm; Asst. in Gen. Chemistry, Uppsala Univ. 1929, in Histology 1930–31, in Pathology 1937; Asst. Prof. of Obstetrics and Gynaecology, Royal Caroline Inst. 1947–49, Assoc. Prof. 1949–58, Royal Prof. 1958–77; Chair. Univ. Dept. of Obstetrics and Gynaecology, Sabbatsberg Hosp. 1958–79; Scientific Consultant, Swedish Defence Forces 1969–79; Swedish Nat. Bd. of Health and Welfare 1960–79; Consultant, Sophiahemmet Hosp. 1979–88, Ersta Hosp. 1983–88; Chief Ed. Acta Obstetricia et Gynaecologica Scandinavica 1970–77, Assoc. Ed. Int. Journal of Fertility 1972–77, Int. Journal of Gynaecology and Obstetrics 1974–86; Hon. Prof., Univs. of Montevideo and Buenos Aires; Visiting Prof. at numerous univs.; Pres. Swedish Gynaecological Soc. 1961–69, Scandinavian Asscn. of Obstetricians and Gynaecologists 1966–68, 5th World Congress on Fertility and Sterility 1966, Int. Fertility Asscn. 1968–74, Int. Urogynaecological Asscn. 1976–81; Vice-Pres. Int. Fed. of Gynaecologists and Obstetricians 1973–76; F.R.C.O.G. (ad eundem); Hwasser Prize 1934, Figo Medal 1994. *Publications:* The Childbearing Years 1951; Co-author: A Child Is Born 1965–82; 200 scientific papers. *Leisure interest:* salmon fishing. *Address:* Fjalarstigen 1A, 182 64, Djursholm, Sweden. *Telephone:* (8) 755 44 18. *Fax:* (8) 753 21 34.

INGHAM, Sir Bernard, Kt.; British fmr. civil servant; b. 21 June 1932, Halifax, Yorkshire; s. of Garnet Ingham and Alice Ingham; m. Nancy Hilda Hoyle 1956; one s.; ed. Hebden Bridge Grammar School; reporter Hebden Bridge Times 1948–52, The Yorkshire Post and Yorkshire Evening Post, Halifax 1952–59; with The Yorkshire Post, Leeds 1959–61, Northern Industrial Corresp. 1961; with The Guardian 1962–67, Labour Staff, London 1965–67; Press and Public Relations Adviser Nat. Bd. for Prices and Incomes 1967–68; Chief Information Officer, Dept. of Employment and Productivity 1968–72; Dir. of Information Dept. of Employment 1973; with Dept. of Energy 1974–79, Dir. of Information 1974–77, Under-Sec. and Head of Energy Conservation Div. 1978–79; Chief Press Sec. to the Prime Minister 1979–90; columnist, Daily Express 1991–98; Chair. Bernard Ingham Communications 1990–; Pres. British Franchise Asscn. 1993–; Vice-Pres. Country Guardian 1991–; non-exec. Dir. McDonald's Restaurants Ltd. 1991–, Hill and Knowlton 1991–; Hon. Dir. Government-Enterprise Communication Unit, Univ. of Newcastle upon Tyne 1991–; mem. council Univ. of Huddersfield 1994–; Visiting Prof. Middlesex Univ. Business School 1997–; Dr. h.c. (Buckingham) 1997. *Publication:* Kill the Messenger 1991. *Leisure interests:* walking, reading, gardening, visiting Yorkshire. *Address:* 9 Monahan Avenue, Purley, Surrey, CR8 3BB, England. *Telephone:* 0181-660 8970. *Fax:* 0181-668 4357.

INGHRAM, Mark Gordon, PH.D.; American professor and physicist; b. 13 Nov. 1919, Livingstone, Mont.; s. of Mark G. and Luella McNay Inghram; m. Evelyn M. Dyckman 1946; one s. one d.; ed. Olivet Coll. and Univ. of Chicago; Physicist, Univ. of Minn. 1942, Manhattan Project, Columbia Univ. 1943–45; Sr. Physicist Argonne Nat. Lab. 1945–49; Instructor in Physics, Univ. of Chicago 1947–49, Asst. Prof. 1949–51, Assoc. Prof. 1951–57, Prof. of Physics 1957–69, Samuel K. Allison Distinguished Service Prof. of Physics 1969–84, Chair. Dept. of Physics 1959–70, Assoc. Dean Div. of Physical Sciences 1964–71, 1981–84, Assoc. Dean, The College 1981–84, Master, Physical Sciences Collegiate Div. 1981–84, Samuel K. Allison Distinguished Service Prof. Emer. 1985–; mem. N.A.S.; Lawrence Smith Medal of N.A.S. 1957. *Publications:* Over 150 research papers in scientific journals. *Address:* 3077 North Lakeshore Drive, Holland, MI 49424, U.S.A. *Telephone:* (616) 399-8638.

INGLIS, Kenneth Stanley, M.A., D.PHIL.; Australian professor and university administrator; b. 7 Oct. 1929, Melbourne; s. of Stanley W. Inglis and Irene (née Winning) Inglis; m. 1st Judy Betheras 1952 (deceased 1962); one s. two d.; m. 2nd Amirah Gust 1965; ed. Univs. of Melbourne and Oxford; Sr. Lecturer Univ. of Adelaide 1956–60, Reader 1960–62; Reader Australian Nat. Univ. 1963–65, Prof. 1965–66; Prof. Univ. of Papua New Guinea 1967–72, Vice-Chancellor 1972–75; Professorial Fellow Australian Nat. Univ. 1975–76, Prof. of History, Research School of Social Sciences 1977–94, Prof. Emer. 1994–; Overseas Visiting Fellow St. John's Coll., Cambridge 1990–91; Hon. D.Litt. (Melbourne) 1996; Ernest Scott Prize for History 1983–84. *Publications:* Churches and the Working Classes in Victorian England 1963, The Australian Colonists 1974, This is the ABC: The Australian Broadcasting Comm. 1932–1983, 1983, The Rehearsal 1985, Australians: A Historical Library, 11 vols. (Gen. Ed.) 1987–88, Nation: The Life of an Independent Journal and Opinion 1958–72, (ed.) 1989, Sacred Places: War Memorials in the Australian Landscape 1998. *Address:* P.O. Box 5, O'Connor, A.C.T. 2602, Australia.

INGOLD, Keith Usherwood, O.C., PH.D., F.R.S., F.R.S.C., F.C.I.C.; Canadian research chemist; b. 31 May 1929, Leeds, England; s. of Sir Christopher Kelk Ingold and Lady Edith Hilda Usherwood; m. Carmen Cairine Hodgkin 1956; two s. one d.; ed. Univ. Coll., Univ. of London, Oxford Univ.; Postdoctoral Fellow Nat. Research Council of Canada 1951–53, Research Officer Div. of Chem. 1955–90, Head Hydrocarbon Chem. Section 1965–90, Assoc. Dir. 1977–90; Postdoctoral Fellow Univ. of B.C. 1953–55; Distinguished Research Scientist, Steacie Inst. for Molecular Sciences 1990–; Adjunct Prof. Dept. of Biochemistry, Brunel Univ., U.K. 1983–94; Adjunct Prof. Dept. of Chem. and Biochem. Univ. of Guelph, Ont. 1985–89; Adjunct Research Prof., Carleton Univ., Ottawa 1991–; Adjunct Prof. Dept. of Chem., Univ. of St. Andrews, Scotland 1997–; visiting scientist to numerous univs., numerous lectureships; Sr. Carnegie Fellowship Univ. of St. Andrews (Scotland) 1977; Fellow Univ. Coll. London 1987; mem. Royal Soc. of Chem. (U.K.), American Chem. Soc.; Vice-Pres. Canadian Soc. for Chem. 1985–87, Pres. 1987–88; Hon. mem. Sociedad Argentina de Investigaciones en Química Orgánica; Hon. D.Sc. (Guelph, Ontario) 1985, (St. Andrews) 1989, (Carleton Univ.) 1992, (McMaster Univ., Ontario) 1995, (Dalhousie Univ., N.S.) 1996; Hon. LL.D. (Mount Allison) 1987; numerous awards including Chem. Inst. of Canada Medal 1981, Syntex Award in Physical Organic Chem. 1983, Royal Soc. of Canada Centennial Medal 1982, Henry Marshall Tory Medal, Royal Soc. of Canada 1985, Pauling Award, A.C.S. 1988, Alfred Bader Award in Organic Chem., Canadian Soc. for Chem. 1989, Humboldt Research Award 1989, Davy Medal, Royal Soc. 1990, Arthur C. Cope Scholar Award, A.C.S. 1992, Izaak Walton Killam Memorial Prize, Canada Council 1992, James Flack Norris Award in Physical Organic Chem., A.C.S. 1993, Angelo Mangini Medal, Italian Chemical Soc. 1997, Canada Gold Medal for Science and Eng., Natural Science and Eng. Research Council 1998. *Publications:* Free-Radical Substitution Reactions (with B. P. Roberts) 1971, Nitrogen-centered Radicals, Aminoxyl and Related Radicals (with J. C. Walton) 1994; over 450 publications in the open scientific literature. *Leisure interests:* skiing, water skiing. *Address:* Steacie Institute for Molecular Sciences, National Research Council of Canada, Ottawa, Ont., K1A 0R6, Canada. *Telephone:* (613) 990-0938. *Fax:* (613) 941-8447.

INGÓLFSSON, Thorsteinn; Icelandic diplomatist; b. 9 Dec. 1944, Reykjavík; s. of Ingólfur Thorsteinsson and Helga Gudmundsdóttir; m. 1st Gudrún Valdís Ragnarsdóttir (divorced 1986); one s. one d.; m. 2nd Hólmfrídur Kofoed-Hansen 1994; ed. Commercial Coll. of Iceland, Univ. of Iceland; First Sec. and Deputy Chief of Mission, Washington D.C. 1973–78; Chief of Div., Ministry of Foreign Affairs 1978–85; Minister Counsellor 1981; Deputy Perm. Rep. to Int. Orgs., Geneva 1985–87, Acting Perm. Rep. Feb.–June 1987; rank of Amb. 1987; Dir. Defence Dept. Ministry for Foreign Affairs, 1987–90; Chair. Icelandic-American Defence Council 1987–90; Perm. Under-Sec. for Foreign Affairs 1990–94; Perm. Rep. to North Atlantic Council and WEU 1994–; Grand Cróix, Legion d'honneur, Hon. G.C.M.G., numerous decorations. *Address:* Icelandic Delegation to North Altantic Council, NATO-OTAN, Boulevard Leopold III 39, 1110 Brussels, Belgium. *Telephone:* 2-726-5084. *Fax:* 2-726-4531.

INGRAHAM, Hubert Alexander; Bahamian politician; b. 4 Aug. 1947, Pine Ridge, Grand Bahama; m. Delores Velma Miller; six c.; ed. Cooper's Town Public School, Southern Sr. School and Govt. High School Evening Inst. Nassau; called to the Bar, Bahamas 1972; Sr. Partner, Christie, Ingraham & Co. (law firm); fmr. mem. Air Transport Licensing Authority; fmr. Chair. Real Property Tax Tribunal; mem. Nat. Gen. Council Progressive Liberal Party (PLP) 1975; Nat. Chair. and mem. Nat. Exec. Cttee. PLP 1976; elected to House of Ass. as PLP mem. 1977, 1982; Minister of Housing, Nat. Insurance and Social Services 1982–84; Chair. Bahamas Mortgage Corpn. 1982; alt. del. conf. of IDB, Uruguay 1983, IMF/IBRD 1979–84; expelled from PLP 1986; elected to Nat. Assembly as independent 1987; Parl. Leader, Official Opposition 1990–92; Leader, Opposition Free Nat. Movt. and of Official Opposition May 1990; Prime Minister of the Bahamas Aug. 1992–, also of Housing and Local Govt. 1995–97, and Trade and Industry 1995–97; fmrly. Minister of Finance and Planning. *Leisure interests:* reading, swimming. *Address:* Office of the Prime Minister, Cecil V. Wallace-Whitfield Centre, P.O. Box CB-10980, Nassau, Bahamas.

INGRAM, David John Edward, C.B.E.; British university vice-chancellor; b. 6 April 1927, Wimbledon; s. of late John Ingram and Marie Weller; m. Ruth McNair 1952; two s. one d.; ed. King's Coll. School, Wimbledon and New Coll., Oxford; Research Fellow and lecturer, Univ. of Southampton 1952–57, Reader in Electronics 1957–59; Prof. and Head Dept. of Physics, Univ. of Keele 1959–73, Deputy Vice-Chancellor 1964–65, 1968–71; Prin. Chelsea Coll., Univ. of London 1973–80; Vice-Chancellor Univ. of Kent at Canterbury 1980–94, Prof. Emer. 1994–; Hon. Treas. Cttee. of Vice-Chancellors and Prins. 1987–94; Chair., British Council Cttee. on Europe 1989–91, Univs.' Staff Training and Devt. Cttee. 1989–95, Univ. Cen. Council on Admissions 1991–94, British Council Cttee. on Higher Educ. 1991–95; mem. Governing Body, South Bank Univ., Wye Coll., King's School Canterbury, West Heath School, S.P.C.K., Carnegie U.K. Trust 1980–, British Council Main Bd. 1991–95, Thanet Healthcare Trust 1992–95, Taunton and Somerset N.H.S. Trust 1995–; Pres. Victoria Inst. 1986–; Fellow, Chelsea Coll., Roehampton Inst.; Hon. D.Sc. (Clermont-Ferrand) 1965, (Keele) 1983; Hon. D.C.L. (Kent) 1994; D.L. *Publications:* Spectroscopy at Radio & Microwave Frequencies 1955, Free Radicals as Studied by Electron Spin Resonance 1958, Biological and Biochemical Applications of Electron Spin Resonance 1969, Radiation and Quantum Physics 1973, Radio and Microwave Spectroscopy 1976; various publs. in proceedings of Royal Soc. and learned journals. *Leisure interests:* sailing, debating, do-it-yourself. *Address:* Cordwainers Cottage, Maundown, Wiveliscombe, Somerset, TA4 2BU, England (Home).

INGRAM, James Charles, A.O., B.A.(ECON.); Australian diplomatist and international civil servant; b. 27 Feb. 1928, Warragul; m. Odette Koven 1950; one s. two d.; ed. De la Salle Coll., Melbourne Univ.; joined Dept. of External Affairs 1946; Third Sec., Tel-Aviv 1950; First Sec., Washington 1956; Chargé d'Affaires, Brussels 1959; Counsellor, Djakarta 1962, Australian Mission to UN 1964; Asst. Sec. External Affairs, Canberra 1967; Amb. to Philippines 1970–73; High Commr. in Canada, Jamaica, Barbados, Guyana, Trinidad and Tobago 1973–74; First Asst. Sec. Australian Devt. Assistance Agency 1975–76; Dir.-Gen. Australian Devt. Assistance Bureau, Dept. of Foreign Affairs 1977–82; Exec. Dir. UN World Food Programme 1982–92; Dir. Australian Inst. of Int. Affairs 1992–93; Visiting Fellow, Centre for Int. and Public Law, A.N.U. 1993–94, Nat. Centre for Development Studies, A.N.U. 1995–98; Chair., Australian Govt. Advisory Cttee. on Non-Govt. Devt. Orgs. 1995–; mem. Bd. of Trustees, Int. Food Policy Research Inst. 1991– (Chair. 1996–), Crawford Fund for Int. Agric. Research, Melbourne 1994–, Int. Crises Group, Brussels 1995–; mem. Gov. Council, Soc. for Int. Devt. 1988–94; mem. Commonwealth Intergovernmental Group on the Emergence of a Global Humanitarian Order, London 1994–95; Alan Shawn Feinstein World Hunger Award (Brown Univ.) 1991. *Leisure interests:* music, reading, gardening. *Address:* 4 Stokes Street, Manuka, A.C.T. 2603, Australia. *Telephone:* 6295 0446. *Fax:* 6295 0552.

INGRAM, Vernon M., F.R.S., F.A.A.A.S., PH.D., D.SC.; British professor of biochemistry; b. 19 May 1924, Breslau, Germany; s. of Kurt and Johanna Immerwahr; m. 1st Margaret Young 1950; one s. one d.; m. 2nd Elizabeth Hendee 1984; ed. Birkbeck Coll., Univ. of London; Research Chemist, Thos. Morson and Son 1941–45; Lecture Demonstrator, Birkbeck Coll., London 1945–47, Asst. Lecturer 1947–50; Rockefeller Foundation Fellow, New York 1950–51; Coxe Fellow, Yale Univ. 1951–52; mem. staff, Molecular Biology Unit, Cavendish Lab., Cambridge 1952–58; Visiting Assoc. Prof. M.I.T. 1958–59; Assoc. Prof. M.I.T. 1959–61, Prof. of Biochem. 1961–, John and Dorothy Wilson Prof. of Biology 1988–; Guggenheim Fellow, Univ. of London 1967–68; Fellow American Acad. of Arts and Sciences. *Publications:* Haemoglobin and its Abnormalities 1961, The Haemoglobins in Genetics and Evolution 1963, The Biosynthesis of Macromolecules 1965, 1971. *Leisure interest:* music. *Address:* Department of Biology, Massachusetts Institute of Technology, 77 Massachusetts Avenue, Cambridge, MA 02139, U.S.A. *Telephone:* 617-253-3706.

INGRAMS, Richard Reid; British journalist; b. 19 Aug. 1937, London; s. of Leonard St. Clair and Victoria (née Reid) Ingrams; m. Mary Morgan 1962 (divorced 1993); two s. (one deceased) one d.; ed. Shrewsbury School, Univ. Coll., Oxford; joined Private Eye 1962; Ed. 1963–86, Chair. 1974–; Ed. The Oldie 1992–; TV critic The Spectator 1976–84; columnist, The Observer 1988–90, 1992–. *Publications:* Private Eye on London (with Christopher Booker and William Rushton) 1962, Private Eye's Romantic England 1963, Mrs. Wilson's Diary (with John Wells) 1965, Mrs. Wilson's Second Diary 1966, The Tale of Driver Grope 1968, The Bible for Motorists (with Barry Fantoni) 1970, The Life and Times of Private Eye (Ed.) 1971, Harris in Wonderland (as Philip Reid with Andrew Osmond) 1973, Cobbett's Country Book (Ed.) 1974, Beachcomber; the works of J. B. Morton (Ed.) 1974, The Best of Private Eye 1974, God's Apology 1977, Goldenballs 1979, Romney Marsh (with Fay Godwin) 1980, Dear Bill: the collected letters of Denis Thatcher (with John Wells) 1980, The Other Half 1981, Piper's Places (with John Piper) 1983, Dr. Johnson by Mrs. Thrale (Ed.) 1984, Down the Hatch (with John Wells) 1985, Just the One (with John Wells) 1986, John Stewart Collis: a memoir 1986, The Best of Dear Bill (with John Wells) 1986, Mud in Your Eye (with John Wells) 1987, The Eye Spy Look-alike Book (ed.) 1988, The Ridgeway 1988, You Might As Well Be Dead 1988, England: An Anthology 1989, No. 10 1989, On and On .... Further Letters of Denis Thatcher (with John Wells) 1990, ed. The Oldie Annual 1993, The Oldie Annual II 1994, Malcolm Muggeridge 1995; ed. I Once Met 1996. *Leisure interests:* music, book selling. *Address:* c/o The Oldie, 45 Poland Street, London, W1V 3DF, England.

INGRAO, Pietro; Italian politician and journalist; b. 30 March 1915, Lenola, Latina; m. Laura Lombardo Radice 1944; one s. four d.; ed. Univ. of Rome; began career as a journalist; active in anti-fascist student groups at Univ. of Rome 1939; joined Italian Communist Party (PCI) 1940; joined editorial staff of l'Unità (PCI newspaper) 1943; took part in resistance movement in Rome and Milan 1943–45; Ed. l'Unità 1947–57; mem. Nat. Exec. and Secretariat of PCI 1956; mem. Chamber of Deputies (lower house of Parl.) for Rome, Latino, Frosinone, Viterbo 1948–58, for Perugia, Terni, Rieti 1958–63, 1968–, for Ancona and Perugia 1963–68; Pres. of PCI Parl. Group 1972–76; Pres. of Chamber of Deputies 1976–79; Pres. of Centre of Studies and Activities for the Reform of the State 1979. *Publications:* essays on political and social subjects in periodicals, incl. Rinascita, Critica Marxista 1945–, Masse e Potere 1977, Crisi e Terzavia 1978, Tradizione e Progetto 1982, Il Dubbio dei Vincitori (poetry) 1987. *Address:* Centro Studie Iniziative per la Riforma dello Stato, via Della Vite, Rome, Italy. *Telephone:* 6784101.

INGSTAD, Helge Marcus; Norwegian explorer and author; b. 30 Dec. 1899, Meråker; s. of Olav and Olga Marie (née Qvam) Ingstad; m. Anne Stine (née Moe) 1941 (deceased); one d.; Barrister, Levanger, Norway 1922–25; lived as trapper N.E. of Great Slave Lake, Arctic Canada 1926–30; Norwegian Gov., N.E. Greenland 1932–33; Norwegian Gov. of Svalbard (Spitsbergen) 1933–35; studied Apache Indians, Arizona, and made expedition to Sierra Madre Mountains, Mexico, in search of some primitive Apache Indians 1936–38; studied Eskimo group Nunamiut, Brooks Range, N. Alaska 1949–50; made expedition with wife to W. Greenland to study old Norse settlements 1953; made eight archaeological expeditions to N. America, where at N. tip of Newfoundland (L'Anse aux Meadows) a Norse pre-Columbian site was discovered and excavated 1960–68; made expedition to Eastern Coast of Baffin Island and located Helluland, mentioned in Vinland Saga 1970; Hon D.Sc. (St. Olaf Coll., Minn.) 1965, (Memorial Univ. St. John's Newfoundland) 1969, (McGill Univ., Montreal) 1975, (Oslo) 1976, (Calgary) 1977, (Bergen Univ.) 1993; Hon. mem. Acad. of Sciences and Letters, Oslo 1991; numerous awards including Franklin L. Burr Award (Nat. Geographic Soc., Washington) 1964, The Wahlberg Award 1968, The Gunnerus Award, Fridtjof Nansen Award 1977, Royal Geographical Soc. Patron's Medal (U.K.) 1991, Grand Cross of the Royal Order of St. Olav (Norway) 1991. *Publications:* Pelsjegerliv blant Nord-Kanadas Indianere (Land of Feast and Famine) 1931, Øst for Den Store Bre (East of the Great Glacier) 1935, Apache—Indianerne. Jakten pa den tapte stamme 1939, Klondyke Bill 1945, Siste Båt (play) 1946, Landet med De Kalde Kyster 1948, Nunamiut. Blant Alaskas Innlands-eskimoer (Nunamiut-Among Alaska's Inland Eskimos) 1951, Landet under Leidarstjernen (Land under the Pole Star) 1959, Vesterveg til Vinland (Westward to Vinland) 1965, The Norse Discovery of America (vol. II) 1985, Nunamiut Stories 1987, The Land of Feast and Famine 1992. *Leisure interest:* chess. *Address:* Vettalivei 24, 0389 Oslo 3, Norway. *Telephone:* 02-14-21-35.

INGVARSSON, Ingvi S.; Icelandic diplomatist (retd.); b. 12 Dec. 1924, Reykjavík; m.; one d.; ed. Akureyri Coll., Glasgow Univ. and London School of Econs.; entered diplomatic service 1956; First Sec., Moscow 1958–62, Washington, D.C. 1962–66; Deputy Perm. Rep. to NATO 1966–71, concurrently Counsellor, Paris and Brussels; Deputy Sec.-Gen. Ministry of Foreign Affairs 1971–72; Perm. Rep. to UN 1973–77; Amb. to Sweden, concurrently to Finland and Yugoslavia 1977–82, to Albania 1978–82, to Saudi Arabia 1981–82; Perm. Under-Sec. Ministry of Foreign Affairs, Reykjavík 1982–86; Amb. to U.S.A. 1986–91 (also accred. to Canada, Argentina, Chile, Brazil and Mexico), to Denmark 1991–94 (also accred. to People's Repub. of China, Israel, Italy, Lithuania and Turkey); Pres. UNA of Iceland 1998. *Address:* Thorragata 5, 101 Reykjavík, Iceland.

INHOFE, James Mountain, B.A.; American politician; b. 17 Nov. 1934, Des Moines, Ia.; s. of Perry Inhofe and Blanche Mountain; m. Kay Kirkpatrick 1958; two s. two d.; ed. Univ. of Tulsa; mem. Okla. House of Reps. 1966–68; mem. Okla. State Senate 1968–76, Minority Leader 1970–76; Mayor of Tulsa 1978–84; mem. U.S. House of Reps., 1st Dist. Okla. 1987–94; Senator from Oklahoma Jan. 1995–; Pres. Fly Riverside Inc. 1978, Quaker Life Insurance Co.; Republican. *Address:* U.S. Senate, 453 Russell Senate Building, Washington, DC 20510, U.S.A.

INK, Claude; French business executive; b. 17 March 1928, Hussigny; s. of Gilbert Ink and Paule Rollin; m. Annie Beaurain-Verdollin 1952; two s. one d.; ed. Ecole Polytechnique; engineer, Sollac 1952, Asst. Dir.-Gen. 1966, Vice-Pres., Dir.-Gen. Sollac 1978; Dir.-Gen. SCAC 1969; Pres. Bd. of Dirs., Solmer 1980, Dir. Gen. 1985; Pres. and Dir.-Gen. Solnetal, Vice-Pres. Sollac; Dir.-Gen. Sacilor; Pres. Chambre syndicale Fer blanc 1986; Del. Gen. Fondation Ecole Polytechnique 1987–95, Conseilleur 1996; Pres. Asscn. Professionnelle des Producteurs Européens de l'Acier pour l'Emballage Léger (A.P.E.A.L.) 1988–90; Pres. Comité Int. du titre de L'ingénieur 1996–; Officier, Légion d'honneur. *Address:* Fondation de l'Ecole Polytechnique, place des Corolles, 92080 Paris-la-Defense (Office); 65 bis avenue du Belloy, 78110 Le Vesinet, France (Home). *Telephone:* (3) 9524503 (Home).

INKELES, Alex, PH.D.; American professor of sociology; b. 20 April 1920, Brooklyn, New York; s. of Meyer Inkeles and Ray Gewer Inkeles; m. Bernadette Mary Kane 1942; one d.; ed. Cornell and Columbia Univs., Washington School of Psychiatry; Social Science Research Analyst, Dept. of State 1942–46, Int. Broadcasting Div. 1949–51; Instructor in Social Relations, Harvard Univ. 1948–49, Lecturer in Sociology 1948–57, Prof. 1957–71, Dir. Russian Research Center Studies in Social Relations 1963–71, Dir. Center of Int. Affairs Studies on Social Aspects of Econ. Devt. 1963–71; Margaret Jacks Prof. of Educ., Stanford Univ. 1971–78, Prof. of Sociology and, by Courtesy, Educ. 1978–90, Emer. Prof. of Sociology 1995–; Sr. Fellow, Hoover Inst. on War, Revolution and Peace 1978–, Prof. Emer. 1990–; numerous fellowships including Inst. for Advanced Study, Princeton, Guggenheim, Fulbright, Rockefeller Foundation, Bellagio, Italy, N.A.S. Exchange Program with People's Repub. of China, Nankai Univ. 1983; mem. American Acad. of Arts and Sciences, N.A.S., A.A.A.S., American Philosophical Soc., American Psychology Asscn.; numerous awards. *Publications:* Public Opinion in Soviet Russia 1950, How the Soviet System Works 1956, The Soviet Citizen: Daily Life in a Totalitarian Society 1959, What is Sociology? 1964, Social Change in Soviet Russia 1968, Becoming Modern: Individual Change in Six Developing Countries 1974, Exploring Individual Modernity 1983, On Measuring Democracy: Its Consequences and Concomitants 1991, National Character: A Psycho-Social Perspective 1996, One World Emerging? Convergence and Divergence in Industrial Societies 1998. *Leisure interests:* travel, East Asian art collection, biking, swimming. *Address:* Hoover Institution, HHMB-112, Stanford University, Stanford, CA 94305-6010; 1001 Hamilton Avenue, Palo Alto, CA 94301, U.S.A. (Home). *Telephone:* (415) 723-4856 (Office); (415) 327-4197 (Home). *Fax:* (415) 723-1687 (Office).

INMAN, Bobby Ray, B.A.; American politician, former naval officer and business executive; b. 4 April 1931, Rhonesboro, Tex.; s. of Herman Inman and Mertie Hinson; m. Nancy Russo 1958; two s.; ed. Univ. of Texas and Nat. War Coll.; commissioned Ensign, U.S. Navy 1952, Adm. 1981; Asst. Naval Attaché, Stockholm 1965–67; exec. asst., sr. aide to Vice-Chief of Naval Operations, Washington, D.C. 1972–73; Asst. Chief of Staff (Intelligence) on staff of C.-in-C., U.S. Pacific Fleet 1973–74; Dir. Naval Intelligence, Dept. of Navy 1974–76; Vice-Dir. Defence Intelligence Agency 1976–77; Dir. Nat. Security Agency, Fort Meade, Md. 1977–81; Deputy Dir. CIA 1981–82; Chair., Pres., C.E.O. Microelectronics and Computer Tech. Corpn., Austin, Tex. 1983–86; Chair. Bd., C.E.O. Westmark Systems Inc., Austin 1986–89; pvt. investor Austin 1990–; nominated as Sec. for Defense 1993, withdrew 1994; Legion of Merit and numerous service decorations. *Address:* 701 Brazos Street, Suite 500, Austin, TX 78701, U.S.A.

INNES OF EDINGIGHT, Sir Malcolm Rognvald, K.C.V.O.; b. 25 May 1938; s. of the late Sir Thomas Innes of Learney and of Lady Lucy Buchan; m. Joan Hay 1963; three s.; ed. Edinburgh Acad., Univ. of Edinburgh; Falkland Pursuivant Extraordinary 1957; Carrick Pursuivant 1958; Lyon Clerk and Keeper of the Records 1966; Marchmont Herald 1971, Lord Lyon King of Arms 1981–; Secretary to Order of the Thistle 1981–; mem. Queen's Body Guard for Scotland (Royal Company of Archers) 1971; Pres. Heraldry Soc. of Scotland; Grand Officer of Merit, Sovereign Mil. Order, Malta, K. St. J. *Leisure interest:* visiting places of historic interest. *Address:* 35 Inverleith Row, Edinburgh, EH3 5QH, Scotland. *Telephone:* 0131-552 4924.

INNIS, Roy Emile Alfredo; American human rights organization executive and chemist; b. 6 June 1934, St. Croix, Virgin Islands; s. of Alexander and Georgianna Innis; m. Doris Funnye 1965; six s. (two deceased) two d.; ed. City Coll., New York; joined U.S. Army 1950, Sergeant 1951, discharged 1952; pharmaceutical research work, Vick Chemical Co., then medical research Montefiore Hosp. until 1967; active in Harlem chapter of Congress of Racial Equality (CORE) 1963–, Chair. Harlem Educ. Cttee. 1964, Chair. Harlem CORE 1965–67, Second Nat. Vice-Chair. 1967–68, Assoc. Nat. Dir. CORE Jan-Sept. 1968, Nat. Dir. Sept. 1968–70; Founder Harlem Commonwealth Council, First Exec. Dir. 1967–68, now mem. of Bd.; Res. Fellow, Metropolitan Applied Research Center 1967–; Co-Publisher The Manhattan Tribune 1968–71; mem. Bd. and Steering Cttee. Nat. Urban Coalition; mem. of Bd. New York Coalition, Haryou Inc., Bd. of Dirs. New Era Health Educ. and Welfare, Bd. of Advisers Pan-African Journal; mem. Editorial Staff Social Policy Magazine; Publr. The Correspondent; Co-Chair. Econ. Devt. Task Force, New York Urban Coalition; founder CORE Community School, South Bronx 1977. *Publications:* The Little Black Book 1971; chapters in: The Endless Crisis, Black Economic Development 1970, Integrating America's Heritage: A Congressional Hearing to Establish A National Commission on Negro History and Culture 1970, Profiles in Black 1976; articles and editorials in Manhattan Tribune, CORE Magazine, Business Weekly, etc. *Leisure interests:* reading, sports, music. *Address:* 817 Broadway, New York, NY 10003, U.S.A. (Office).

INNOCENTI, H.E. Cardinal Antonio; Italian ecclesiastic; b. 23 Aug. 1915, Poppi, Fiesole, Tuscany; ordained 1938; consecrated Bishop, Titular See of Aeclanum 1968, then Archbishop; fmr. Apostolic Nuncio in Spain; cr. Cardinal 1985; fmr. Prefect of Congregation for the Clergy; Pres. of the Pontificial Comm. for the Conservation of the Artistic and Historic Heritage of the Church 1988–91; Pres. Pontifical Comm. 'Ecclesia Dei' 1991–. *Address:* Piazza della Città Leonina 9, 00193 Rome, Italy.

INNOCENTI, Luigi; Italian industrialist; b. 19 Dec. 1923; ed. Massimo Coll., Rome and School of Engineering, Rome; Manager, Innocenti 1948–51, Gen. Vice-Dir. 1951–58, Vice-Chair. 1958–66, Chair 1966–. *Address:* Via Senato 19, Milan, Italy.

İNÖNÜ, Erdal, PH.D.; Turkish politician; b. 1926, Ankara; s. of late İsmet Inönü (fmr. Prime Minsiter and Pres. of Turkey); m.; ed. Ankara Univ., California Inst. of Tech., U.S.A.; Prof. of Physics, Middle East Tech. Univ. 1960–74, also served as Dean, Science-Literature Faculty and Rector; Chair. Social Democratic Party (SODEP), subsequently Social Democratic Populist Party (SHP) 1963, merged with Repub. Peoples' Party 1995; elected deputy from Izmir 1986, 1987; Deputy Prime Minister and State Minister 1991–94; Minister of Foreign Affairs March–Sept. 1995. *Address:* c/o Ministry of Foreign Affairs, Yeni Hizmet Binası, 06520 Balgat, Ankara, Turkey.

INOSE, Hiroshi, DR.ENG.; Japanese professor of electronic engineering; b. 5 Jan. 1927, Tokyo; s. of Yoshikazu and Kyo Inose; m. Mariko Inose 1960; no c.; ed. Univ. of Tokyo; Assoc. Prof., Univ. of Tokyo 1956–61, Prof. of Electronic Eng. 1961–87; Dir. of Educ. Computer Center, Univ. of Tokyo 1974–78, Dir. of Computer Center (for nationwide service) 1977–81, Dean, Faculty of Eng. 1986–87; Science Adviser to Minister of Educ., Science and Culture 1978–82; Special Adviser to Minister for Science and Tech. 1979; Special Asst. to Minister for Foreign Affairs 1983; Dir. Centre for Bibliographic Information 1983–86; Dir.-Gen. Nat. Centre for Science Information System 1987–; Chair. Cttee. for Scientific and Technological Policy, OECD, 1984–87; Chair. Cttee. for Information, Computer and Communications Policy, OECD 1987–90; Foreign Assoc., Nat. Acad. of Sciences (U.S.A.), Nat. Acad. of Eng. (U.S.A.); Foreign mem. American Philosophical Soc., Royal Swedish Acad. of Eng. and Sciences, Royal Acad. of Eng. (U.K.); Fellow, I.E.E.E.; Hon. mem. Royal Inst. of G.B.; Marconi Int. Fellowship; Japan Acad. Prize; I.E.E.E. Award in Int. Communication. *Publications:* Road Traffic Control 1977, An Introduction to Digital Communications Systems 1979, Information, Technology and Civilisation (with J. R. Pierce) 1984. *Leisure interests:* reading Japanese classics, gardening, travelling. *Address:* 3-29-1 Otsuka, Bunkyo-ku, Tokyo 112 (Office); 39-9, Jingumae 5-chome, Shibuya-ku, Tokyo 150, Japan (Home). *Telephone:* 03-942 6901 (Office); 03-5468 7123 (Home).

INOUE, Issei; Japanese politician and civil servant; fmr. Mayor of Settsu City; mem. House of Reps., fmr. Dir. Cttee. on Foreign Affairs; fmr. Vice-Chair. Social Democratic Party of Japan (SDPJ); Minister of Posts and Telecommunications 1995–96. *Address:* c/o Social-Democratic Party of Japan, 1-8-1, Nagata-cho, Chiyoda-ku, Tokyo 100, Japan.

INOUE, Kichio; Japanese politician; b. 1923, Kagoshima Pref.; worked as tech. expert with a mining firm; fmr. mem. city and pref. assemblies; mem. House of Councillors; fmr. Leader of LDP del. in Upper House; Dir.-Gen. Hokkaido and Okinawa Devt. Agencies 1998–. *Leisure interests:* kendo, golf, reading. *Address:* Hokkaido Development Agency, 3-1-1, Kasumigaseki, Chiyoda-ku, Tokyo 100; Okinawa Development Agency, 1-6-1, Nagata-cho, Chiyoda-ku, Tokyo 100, Japan. *Telephone:* (03) 3581-9111 (Hokkaido); (03) 3581-2361 (Okinawa). *Fax:* (03) 3581-1208 (Hokkaido).

INOUYE, Daniel Ken, A.B., J.D.; American politician and lawyer; b. 7 Sept. 1924, Honolulu, Hawaii; s. of Hyotaro and Kame Imanaga Inouye; m. Margaret Shinobu Awamura 1949; one s.; ed. Univ. of Hawaii and George Washington Univ. Law School.; U.S. Army 1943–47; Majority Leader, Territorial House of Reps. 1954–58, mem. Territorial Senate 1958–59; mem. U.S. Congress 1959–62; U.S. Senator from Hawaii 1963–; Democrat; mem. Senate Cttee. on Appropriations, Commerce Cttee., Asst. Majority Whip 1964–76; mem. Dem. Senatorial Campaign Cttee., Senate Select Cttee. on Indian Affairs; Chair. Senate Appropriations Subcttee. on Foreign Operations; Chair. Senate Commerce Subcttee. on Merchant Marine and Tourism; Chair. Senate Select Cttee. on Intelligence 1976–77; Chair. Senate Sub-Cttee. on Budget Authorizations 1979–84, Head Special Cttee. on Iran Affair 1986; Temp. Chair. and Keynoter 1968 Dem. Nat. Convention; Sec. Dem. Conf. 1977; Purple Heart with Cluster; Horatio Alger Award 1989, Medal of Honour with Blue Ribbon, (Japan) 1989. *Address:* U.S. Senate, 722 Hart Senate Office Building, Washington, DC 20510 (Office); 469 Ena Road, Honolulu, HI 96815, U.S.A. *Telephone:* 202-224-3934 (Office).

INOUYE, Kaoru; Japanese banker; b. 13 May 1906, Chiba Pref.; s. of Jiro and Masa Inouye; m. Mitsuko Shibuya 1932; three c.; ed. Tokyo Univ.; joined Dai-Ichi Bank, Ltd. 1929, Dir. 1954, Deputy Pres. 1961, Pres. 1962–66, Chair. 1966–69, Pres. 1969–71; Chair. Dai-Ichi Kangyo Bank 1971–76, Dir., Hon. Chair. 1976–82, Hon. Chair. 1982; fmr. Dir. Asahi Mutual Life Insurance Co., Taisei Fire and Marine Insurance Co.; Sr. Adviser, Kawasaki Heavy Industries Ltd., Isuzu Motors Ltd., Furukawa Co. Ltd., Furukawa Electric Co. Ltd. *Address:* c/o The Dai-Ichi Kangyo Bank, 1–5 Uchisaiwaicho 1-chome, Chiyoda-ku, Tokyo 100, Japan.

INOUYE, Minoru, B.L.; Japanese banker; b. 1924, Tokyo; m.; one s.; ed. Univ. of Tokyo; joined Bank of Tokyo 1947, Deputy Agent, New York 1964–66, Deputy Gen. Man. Int. Funds and Foreign Exchange Div. 1966–67, Deputy Gen. Man. Planning and Co-ordination Div. 1967–70, Gen. Man. 1970–72, Dir. and Gen. Man. London Office 1972–75, Resident Man. Dir. for Europe 1975, Man. Dir. 1975–79, Sr. Man. Dir. 1979–80, Deputy Pres. 1980–85, Pres. 1985–90, Adviser 1990, Adviser, Bank of Tokyo-Mitsubishi, Ltd. 1996–; Orden Mexicana del Aguila Azteca, Mexico 1986, Medal of Honour, with Blue Ribbon, Japan 1989, Ordem Nacional de Cruzeiro do Sul, Brazil 1989, Chevalier, Légion d'honneur 1990, Order of the Rising Sun, Gold and Silver Star, Japan 1994. *Leisure interests:* golf, travel. *Address:* The Bank of Tokyo-Mitsubishi, Ltd., 3–2 Nihombashi Hongokucho 1-chome, Chuo-ku, Tokyo 103-002, Japan (Office).

INSANALLY, Samuel Rudolph, B.A.; Guyanese diplomatist; b. 23 Jan. 1936; ed. Univs. of London and Paris; teacher of modern languages Kingston Coll., Jamaica, Queen's Coll., Guyana and Univ. of Guyana 1959–66; Counsellor at Guyanese Embassy, Washington D.C. 1966–69; Chargé d'affaires at Embassy, Venezuela 1970, Amb. 1972–78; Deputy Perm. Rep. of Guyana to UN, New York 1970–72, Perm. Rep. 1987–; Perm. Rep. to EEC 1978–81; Amb. to Belgium (also accred to Sweden, Norway and Austria) 1978–81, to Colombia 1982–86; Head of Political Div. I Ministry of Foreign Affairs of Guyana 1982–86; High Commr. to Barbados, Trinidad and Tobago and the Eastern Caribbean 1982–86; mem. Bd. of Governors Inst. of Int. Relations, Trinidad and Tobago 1982–86. *Address:* Permanent Mission of Guyana to the United Nations, 866 United Nations Plaza, Suite 555, New York, NY 10017, U.S.A.; c/o Ministry of Foreign Affairs, 254 New Garden Street and South Road, Georgetown, Guyana.

INSULZA SALINAS, José Miguel; Chilean politician and lawyer; b. 1943; m. Georgina Núñez V.; four c.; ed. St. George's Coll., Santiago, Law School, Universidad de Chile, Facultad Latinoamericana de Ciencias Sociales and Univ. of Michigan, U.S.A.; Prof. of Political Theory, Universidad de Chile, of Political Sciences, Pontificia Universidad Católica de Chile –1973; Political Adviser to Ministry of Foreign Relations, Dir. Diplomatic Acad. –1973; researcher, then Dir. Instituto de Estudios de Estados Unidos, Centro de Investigación y Docencia Económicas, Mexico 1981–88; Prof., Universidad Autónoma de México; Head Multilateral Econ. Affairs Dept., Ministry of Foreign Relations, Deputy Chair. Int. Co-operation Agency 1990–94; Under-Sec. for Foreign Affairs 1994, Minister Sept. 1994–; mem. Bd. of Dirs. Instituto de Fomento de Desarrollo Científico y Tecnológico; mem. Consejo Chileno de Relaciones Internacionales, Consejo de Redacción, Nexos Magazine, Mexico, Corporación de Desarrollo Tecnológico Empresarial. *Address:* Ministro de Relaciones Exteriores, Morandé 441, Casilla 91, Correo 21, Santiago, Chile. *Telephone:* 698 2501. *Fax:* 699 4202.

INTRILIGATOR, Michael David, PH.D.; American economist and educator; b. 5 Feb. 1938, New York; s. of Allan Intriligator and Sally Intriligator; m. Devrie Shapiro 1963; four s.; ed. M.I.T., Yale Univ.; Asst. Prof. Econs. Univ. of Calif. at L.A. (UCLA) 1963–66, Assoc. Prof. 1966–72, Prof. Dept. of Political Econs. 1972–, Prof. Dept. of Political Science 1981–, Prof. Dept. of Political Studies 1994–, Dir. Center for Int. and Strategic Affairs 1982–92; Dir. Jacob Marschak Interdisciplinary Coll. 1977–; mem. Council on Foreign Relations (NY), Int. Inst. for Strategic Studies (London), Fellow Econometric Soc. *Publications include:* Mathematical Optimization and Economic Theory 1971, Economic Models, Techniques and Applications 1978, A Forecasting and Policy Simulation Model of the Health Care Sector 1979, East-West Conflict: Elite Perceptions and Political Opinions (jtly.) 1988. *Leisure interests:* travel and art collecting, classical music. *Address:* Department of Economics, UCLA, Los Angeles, CA 90095 (Office); 140 Foxtail Drive, Santa Monica, CA 90402, U.S.A. (Home). *Telephone:* (310) 825-4144 (Office); (310) 395-7909 (Home). *Fax:* (310) 825-9528 (Office).

IOANNIDES, George X.; Cypriot politician; b. 1924, Ktima Paphos; m.; ed. Greek Gymnasium, Paphos, Middle Temple, London; called to bar, London 1947; law practice, Paphos 1948–70; mem. House of Reps. (Patriotic Front Group) for Paphos 1960–70; Minister of Justice 1970–72, of the Interior and Defence 1972–74, of Justice and Health 1976–78, Minister to the Presidency 1978–80; mem. of Cyprus del. to many int. meetings.

IOFFE, Boris Lazarevich; Russian theoretical physicist; b. 6 July 1926, Moscow; s. of Lazar and Pesia Ioffe; m. 1st Svetlana Mikhailova 1957 (divorced 1974); one s.; m. 2nd Nina Libova 1990; ed. Moscow Univ.; Jr. Scientist, Inst. of Theoretical and Experimental Physics (ITEP), Moscow 1950–55, Sr. Scientist 1955–77, Head of Lab. 1977–, Chair. ITEP Scientific Council 1990–97; Deputy Ed. Moscow Physics Soc. Journal; mem. High Energy Physics Scientific Policy Cttee. (Russia) 1992, Russian Nuclear Soc. –1990; Corresp. mem. U.S.S.R. (now Russian) Acad. of Sciences 1990; Fellow American Physical Soc. 1995; Order of Honour of U.S.S.R. 1954, 1974, U.S.S.R. Award for Discovery 1988, 1990, Alexander von Humboldt Award (Germany) 1994. *Publications:* Hard Processes 1984, several articles. *Leisure interests:* mountaineering (especially in Cen. Asia and Far East), skiing. *Address:* Institute of Theoretical and Experimental Physics, Bolshaya Cheremushkinskaya 25, 117218 Moscow (Office); Bolotnikovskaya Street 40, Korp 4, Apt. 16, 113209 Moscow, Russia (Home). *Telephone:* (095) 123-31-93 (Office); 121-44-38 (Home). *Fax:* (095) 883-96-01.

IORDACHE, Ştefan; Romanian actor; b. 3 Feb. 1941, Bucharest; s. of Traian Iordache and Elena Iordache; m. Michaela Tonitza 1970; ed. Theatre and Cinema Art Inst., Bucharest; with Nat. Theatre, Craiova and Nottara Theatre, Bucharest. *Stage roles include:* Hamlet 1977, Apemantus in Timon of Athens 1978, Master in Master and Margaret 1980, Richard III 1982, Titus in Titus Andronicus 1992, Cearnota in The Run (Bulgakov) 1995. *Films:* The Stranger 1964, Glissando 1982, Luxurious Hotel 1991, The Most Beloved on Earth 1992, My Name Is Adam 1996, The Man of Today 1997; Karlovy Vary Award (Best Actor) 1967, Romanian Academy Prize (Best Actor) 1993. *Leisure interest:* life. *Address:* 16 George Cantilli Street, Bucharest, Romania (Home). *Telephone:* (1) 211.82.42.

IOSELIANI, Dzhaba, D.PHIL.; Georgian politician, professor, writer and playwright; b. 10 July 1926, Khashuri; s. of Alexander Ioseliani and Constantine Ioseliani; m. Venera Bolkradze 1967; one s.; fmr. academic; leader Rescue Corps group (est. 1989, fmrly. called Mkhedrioni), barred from standing in 1991 elections owing to arrest for illegal possession of firearms Feb. 1991; released by anti-Gamsakhurdia forces Dec. 1991; jt. Head Mil. Council on assumption of power 1992; mem. State Council March–Oct. 1992; M.P. 1992–; Head, Comm. for Conflict Resolution 1994–; arrested Nov. 1995, charged with conspiracy to assassinate Pres. Shevardnadze, sentenced to 11 years' confinement 1998. *Publications include:* Country Limonia (novel) 1995. *Leisure interest:* books.

IOSIFESCU, Marius Vicenţiu Viorel, PH.D., D.SC.; Romanian mathematician; b. 12 Aug. 1936, Piteşti; s. of the late Victor and Ecaterina Iosifescu; m. Ştefania Eugenia Zamfirescu 1973; one s.; ed. Bucharest Univ.; consultant Cen. Statistical Bd. 1959–62; Asst. Prof. Bucharest Polytech. Inst. 1961–63; Research Mathematician Inst. of Math. and Centre for Math. Statistics, Bucharest 1963–76, head Centre for Math. Statistics 1976–; Visiting Prof. Univs. of Paris 1974, 1991, 1996, 1998, Mainz 1977–78, Frankfurt am Main 1979–80, Bonn 1981–82, Melbourne 1991, Lille 1997, Bordeaux 1998; Overseas Fellow Churchill Coll., Cambridge Univ. 1971; mem. editorial bds. Bulletin Mathématique de la Soc. des Sciences Mathématiques de Roumanie, Mathematica, Revue d'Analyse Numérique et de Théorie de l'Approximation; Deputy Chief Ed. Revue Roumaine de Mathématiques Pures et Appliquées; mem. Int. Statistical Inst., Bernoulli Soc. for Mathematical Statistics and Probability (mem. council 1975–79), American Math. Soc.; Corresp. mem. Romanian Acad. 1991; Romanian Acad. Prize 1965, 1972; Bronze Medal Helsinki Univ. 1975; Chevalier, Ordre des Palmes Académiques 1993. *Publications:* Random Processes and Learning (with R. Theodorescu) 1969, Stochastic Processes and Applications in Biology and Medicine, Vol. I Theory, Vol. II Models (with P. Tăutu) 1973, Finite Markov Processes and Their Applications 1980, ed. Proceedings of Braşov Conference on Probability Theory 1971, 1974, 1979, 1982, Dependence with Complete Connections and its Applications (with Ş. Grigorescu) 1982, 1990, ed. Studies in Probability and Related Topics 1983, Elements of Stochastic Modelling (with Ş. Grigorescu, G. Oprişan and G. Popescu) 1984, From Real Analysis to Probability: Autobiographical Notes 1986. *Leisure interests:* music, playing violin. *Address:* Str. Dr. N. Manolescu 9-11, 76222 Bucharest 35, Romania (Home). *Telephone:* (401) 4103523 (Home).

IRAN, fmr. Empress of (see Pahlavi, Farah Diba).

IRANI, Jamshed Jiji, PH.D.; Indian business executive; b. 2 June 1936, Nagpur; s. of Jiji D. Irani and Khorshed Irani; m. Daisy Irani 1971; one s. two d.; ed. Sheffield Univ.; worked for British Iron and Steel Research Asscn. 1963–67; Tata Iron and Steel Co. Ltd. 1968–, Gen. Man. 1979–81, Deputy Man. Dir. 1981–83, Vice-Pres. (Operations) 1983–85, Pres. 1985–88, Jt. Man. Dir. 1988–92, Man. Dir. 1992–; Dir. of numerous cos.; Nat. Metallurgist Award 1974, Platinum medal of I.I.M. 1988; Hon. K.B.E. 1997. *Publications:* numerous tech. papers. *Leisure interests:* philately, photography. *Address:* 3 C Road, Northern Town, Jamshedpur, 831001 Bihar, India. *Telephone:* 431024 (Office); 431025 (Home). *Fax:* 431818 (Office).

IRANI, Ray R., D.SC.; American business executive; b. 15 Jan. 1935, Beirut, Lebanon; s. of Rida Irani and Naz Irani; m. Ghada Irani; two s. one d.; ed.

Univ. of S. Calif.; Sr. Research Leader, Monsanto Co. 1957–67; Assoc. Dir. New Products, later Dir. of Research, Diamond Shamrock Corpn. 1967–73; joined Olin Corpn. 1973, Pres. Chemicals Group 1978–80, Dir. and Corp. Pres. 1980–83; Exec. Vice-Pres. Occidental Petroleum Corpn., Los Angeles 1983–84, Pres. and C.O.O. 1984–91, Chair., C.E.O., Pres. 1991–96, Chair. and C.E.O. 1996–, also Dir.; C.E.O. Occidental Chemical Corpn., 1983–91, Chair. 1983–94; Chair. Canadian Occidental Petroleum, Ltd., Calgary 1987–; mem. Bd. of Dirs., American Petroleum Inst.; mem. American Chem. Soc., American Inst. of Chemists, Scientific Research Soc., American Industrial Research Inst. *Publications:* Particle Size; numerous papers in field of particle physics. *Address:* Occidental Petroleum Corporation, 10889 Wilshire Blvd., Los Angeles, CA 90024, U.S.A.

IREDALE, Randle W., F.R.A.I.C., B.ARCH.; Canadian architect; b. 1 June 1929, Calgary, Alberta; s. of William E. Iredale and Isobel M. Fielden; m. Kathryn Margaret Bahr 1953; two s. one d.; ed. Univ. of British Columbia; Registered Architect, British Columbia 1957; established practice 1958; formed Rhone & Iredale, Architects 1960; Chair. of Bd. and Dir. of Research, Fabtec Structures 1969–72; established Canadian Environmental Services 1968; Dir. Cancon-Canadian Eng. Services 1969–74, Canadian Construction Information Corpn. 1972–74; Guest lecturer on architectural practice and design methods (for American Inst. of Architects), Seattle 1969, Sun Valley 1971, Chicago 1972; Guest Lecturer, Pa. State Univ. 1971, Univ. of Wis. 1972; Adjunct Assoc. Prof., Univ. of British Columbia School of Architecture 1980–; mem. Vancouver City Design Panel 1963–65, Council, Architectural Inst. of British Columbia 1973–80; f. The Iredale Partnership for urban design and planning, Man. Partner 1990–; Professional Advisor, Royal Architectural Inst. of Canada Gov.-Gen. Awards Program 1986, 1990; Fellow, Royal Canadian Architectural Inst. 1977; Canadian Housing Design Council Awards 1966, 1975; American Public Power Asscn. Awards 1971, 1973; American Iron & Steel Inst. Citation 1971; Canadian Architect Award of Excellence 1970; Royal Architectural Inst. of Canada Award 1974. *Publications:* articles in specialized journals. *Leisure interests:* skiing, gardening, carpentry. *Address:* 1151 West 8th Avenue, Vancouver, B.C., V6H 1C5 (Office); 1537 Westbrook Crescent, Vancouver, B.C., Canada (Home). *Telephone:* (604) 736 5581 (Office); (604) 224-7003 (Home).

IRELAND, Norman Charles, C.A., F.C.M.A.; British business executive; b. 1927, Aden; s. of Charles Ireland and Winifred A. Ireland; m. Gillian M. Harrison 1953; one s. one d.; ed. in U.K., U.S.A. and India; Chartered Man. Accountant with Richard Brown & Co. 1944–50, Brown Fleming & Murray 1950–54, Avon Rubber Co. 1955–64; Chief Accountant, United Glass 1964–66; Finance Dir. BTR PLC 1967–87, Chair. 1993–96; Chair. Bowater PLC 1987–93, The Housing Finance Corpn. 1988–93, Intermediate Capital Group 1989–93, Meggitt 1987–93. *Leisure interests:* gardening, ballet, opera, music.

IRHAYIM, Tarik al-, PH.D.; Iraqi petroleum engineer and business executive; b. 3 Feb. 1937, Mosul; m. Amel Ahmed Omar 1962; four s. two d.; ed. Al-Idadyia High School, Guildford Tech. Coll., Univ. of Birmingham; Chief Petroleum Engineer North Oil Co. 1971–80, Project Man. Underground Storage 1980–87, Man. Laboratories 1987–90, Deputy Fields Dir. 1990–92, Fields Dir. 1992–95, Consultant 1995; Dir. Euphrates Consulting Bureau 1996–; Order of Merit. *Publications:* Bulk Storage of Crude Oil 1963, Thermal Analogue Studies 1966, Quality Assurance in Oil Field Operations 1989. *Leisure interests:* bridge, swimming, reading, world affairs. *Address:* Euphrates Consulting Bureau, Sector 101, Sadoon, Street 87, Ahmed Bldg. No. 21, Suite 14H/9, Bataween, Baghdad, Iraq. *Telephone:* 718-1927. *Telex:* 212252.

IRIANI, Abdul Karim al-, PH.D. ECONS.; Yemeni politician and economist; b. 12 Oct. 1934, Eryan; m.; three s. three d.; ed. Univ. of Georgia, Yale Univ., U.S.A.; worked in an agricultural project in Yemen 1968–72; Chair. Cen. Planning Org. 1972–76; Minister of Devt. 1974–76, of Educ. and Rector San'a Univ. 1976–78; Adviser, Kuwait Fund for Arab Econ. Devt. 1978–80; Prime Minister 1980–83; Deputy Prime Minister and Minister of Foreign Affairs 1984–90, 1994–98; Prime Minister of Yemen 1998–; Minister of Foreign Affairs 1990–93, of Planning and Devt. 1993–94; Chair. Council for the Reconstruction of Earthquake Areas 1983–84. *Address:* Office of the Prime Minister, San'a, Republic of Yemen.

IRIBARRÉN BORGES, Ignacio; Venezuelan diplomatist and lawyer; b. 1912, Valencia, Venezuela; s. of late Ignacio Iribarrén and Mary Borges; m. Carolina Terrero 1938; two s. one d.; ed. Don Bosco Coll., Valencia and Univ. Central de Venezula; District Attorney, Valencia 1936; Judge, Primary Court of Claims, Valencia 1936–39; Prof. of Roman Law, Miguel José Sanz School of Law, Valencia 1938–39; Asst. Prof. of Civil Law, Univ. Central de Venezuela 1940–44; Counsellor Cen. Univ. City Inst. 1945–47; mem. Univ. Council 1946–47; later Pres. Compañía Conahotu Ltda; Sec. Governing Junta (under Presidency of Dr. Edgard Sanabria) 1958–59; Amb. to U.K. 1959–64, to U.S.A. 1976–79; Minister of Foreign Affairs 1964–69, of Information and Tourism (acting) 1984–85, Minister of State and Minister of Culture 1984–87; Grand Cordon, Order of the Liberator and numerous other decorations. *Leisure interests:* literature, history. *Publications:* La Poesía de Vicente Gerbasi 1972, A Literary Revolution: Yeats, Joyce, Pound, Eliot 1980, On Theatre, Poetry, and Novel 1980.

IRIGOIN, Jean, D. ÈS L.; French professor; b. 8 Nov. 1920, Aix-en-Provence; s. of Paul Irigoin and Isabelle Gassier; m. Janine Garaud 1954; two s. two d.; ed. Collège St.-Louis-de-Gonzague, Paris, Sorbonne and Ecole pratique des Hautes Etudes, Paris; Prof. Univ. of Poitiers 1953–65, Univ. of Paris X 1965–72, Univ. of Paris IV 1972–85; Collège de France (chaire de Tradition et critique des textes grecs) 1985–92; mem. Institut de France 1981, Acads. of Athens, Göttingen, Munich, Naples, Rome; Pres. Fédération Internationale des Etudes Classiques 1989–94. *Publications:* Histoire du texte de Pindare 1952, Règles et recommandations pour les éditions critiques 1972, Bacchylide 1992, Tradition et critique des textes grecs 1997. *Address:* 11 Place Marcelin-Berthelot, 75231 Paris Cedex 05, France. *Telephone:* (01) 44-27-10-18. *Fax:* (01) 44-27-11-09.

IRIMESCU, Ion; Romanian sculptor; b. 27 Feb. 1903, Preuţesti, Suceava County; s. of Petru and Maria Irimescu; m. Eugenia Melidon 1932; ed. School of Fine Arts, Bucharest and Académie Grande Chaumière, Paris; Prof. Fine Arts Inst. N. Grigorescu, Bucharest 1966–; Vice-Chair. Romanian Artists' Union 1963–68; Chair. Romanian Artists' Union 1978–90; exhbns. in Bucharest, Cluj-Napoca, Iaşi, Athens, Oslo, Moscow, Anvers-Middleheim, Paris, Barcelona, Zürich, Sofia, Budapest, Berlin, Ankara, Cairo, Belgrade; perm. sculptures in Modern Art Museum, Tel Aviv, Pushkin Art Museum, Moscow, and numerous works (sculptures and drawings) in Romanian museums, including 450 works at the Ion Irimescu Museum at Fălticeni, Suceava County; Citizen of Honour of Fălticeni, Iaşi and Cluj; Dr. h.c. ('George Enercu' Superior Acad. of Art, Iaşi); State Prize 1954, 1955; Prize of Romanian Acad. 1943; People's Artist 1964. *Leisure interest:* classical music. *Address:* Uniunea Artistilor Plastici, Str. Nicolae Iorga 42, Bucharest; Str. Zambaccian 12, Sector 1, Bucharest, Romania. *Telephone:* 6332751.

IROBE, Yoshiaki; Japanese banker; b. 18 July 1911, Tokyo; s. of Tsuneo and Tsuneko (Hirohata) Irobe; m. Kiyoko Kodama 1939; three s. one d.; ed. Tokyo Imperial Univ.; Man., Matsuyama Branch, The Bank of Japan 1954, Deputy Chief, Personnel Dept. 1956, Chief Sec. and Chief, Foreign Relations Dept. 1959, Chief, Personnel Dept. 1962, Man. Nagoya Branch 1963; Sr. Man. Dir., The Kyowa Bank Ltd. (now Asahi Bank) 1966, Deputy Pres. 1968, Pres. 1971–80; Chair. 1980–86, Adviser 1986–, Hon. Chair. 1986–. *Leisure interests:* 'Go', travel, reading. *Address:* 26-6, Saginomiya 6-chome, Nakano-ku, Tokyo, Japan (Home). *Telephone:* 999-0321 (Home).

IRONS, Jeremy; British actor; b. 19 Sept. 1948, Isle of Wight; m. 2nd Sinead Cusack (q.v.) 1978; two s.; TV debut 1968; Officier Ordre des arts et des lettres. *TV appearances include:* Notorious Woman, Love for Lydia, Langrishe Go Down, Voysey Inheritance, Brideshead Revisited, The Captain's Doll, Tales from Hollywood 1991. *Films:* Nijinsky 1980, The French Lieutenant's Woman 1980, Moonlighting 1981, Betrayal 1982, The Wild Duck 1983, Swann in Love 1983, The Mission 1986, A Chorus of Disapproval 1988, Dead Ringers (New York Critics Best Actor Award 1988) 1988, Australia 1989, Danny, The Champion of the World 1989, Reversal of Fortune (Acad. Award 1991) 1990, Kafka 1991, Damage 1991, Waterland 1992, M. Butterfly 1994, House of the Spirits 1994, Die Hard with a Vengeance 1995, Stealing Beauty 1996, Lolita 1996, The Man in the Iron Mask 1997, Chinese Box 1998. *Stage appearances:* The Real Thing, Broadway 1984 (Tony Award), Rover 1986, The Winter's Tale 1986, Richard II, Stratford 1986. *Address:* c/o Hutton Management, 200 Fulham Road, London, SW10 9PN, England. *Telephone:* 0171-352 4825.

IRSHAIDAT, Salah, B.A.; Jordanian lawyer; b. 1919, Irbid; s. of Al Jaibari; m. Lamis Sulaiman 1959; one s. two d.; ed. Damascus Coll., Univ. of Syria; conciliation judge 1942; land settlement judge, later Public Prosecutor, Asst. Attorney Gen., Pres. Attorney Gen., mem. Court of First Instance; mem. Court of Appeal, Pres.; Deputy Minister of Justice; Judge Supreme Court of Justice; Pres. Court of Cassation and High Justice 1989–. *Publication:* publ. on history of Andalusia. *Leisure interest:* reading law books.

IRVINE, Ian, F.C.A., C.B.I.M., F.R.G.S., F.R.S.A.; British business executive; b. 2 July 1936; ed. Surbiton County Grammar School and London School of Econs.; joined Touche Ross & Co. 1961, partner 1965; Man. Dir. Fleet Holdings PLC 1982–85, also Dir. Express Newspapers PLC and Morgan-Grampian PLC (subsidiaries); consultant to United Newspapers PLC until 1985; Dir. non-exec. Capital Radio 1982–, Chair 1992–; Dir. TV-AM PLC 1983, Chair. 1988–90; Dir. British Satellite Broadcasting 1990–91, MEPC PLC 1992–95; Chair. British Sky Broadcasting 1990–91; Chief Exec. Octopus Publishing Group 1986, with responsibility for Butterworths 1989; Chief Exec. Reed Int. Books 1990–94; Dir. Reed Int. PLC 1987, Chair. 1994–97; mem. Exec. Cttee. Reed Elsevier 1993–96, Chair. 1994–96, Co-Chair. 1996–; Chair. (non-exec.) Video Networks 1997–. *Address:* Reed Elsevier PLC, Quadrant House, The Quadrant, Sutton, Surrey, SM2 5AS, England.

IRVINE, John Maxwell, PH.D., C.PHYS., F.INST.P., F.R.A.S., F.R.S.A., F.R.S.E., C.I.M.; British theoretical physicist; b. 28 Feb. 1939, Edinburgh; s. of John MacDonald Irvine and Joan Paterson Irvine; m. Grace Ritchie 1962; one s.; ed. George Heriot's School, Edin., Univs. of Edin., Manchester, Michigan; Asst. Lecturer in Theoretical Physics, Univ. of Manchester 1964–66, lecturer 1968–73, Sr. Lecturer 1973–76, Reader 1976–83, Prof. 1983–91, Dean of Science 1989–91; Prin. and Vice-Chancellor Univ. of Aberdeen 1991–96; Prin. and Vice-Chancellor Univ. of Birmingham 1996–; Chair. Scottish Advisory Group on the Acad. Year 1993–96, Cttee. of Scottish Univ. Principals 1994–96; Research Assoc., LNS, Cornell Univ., U.S.A. 1966–68; Head of Nuclear Theory, SERC Daresbury Lab. 1974–78; Dir. Rowett Research Inst. 1992–96, Cobuild Ltd. 1996–, Barber Trust 1996–; mem. Bd. Scottish Council Devt. and Industry 1991–96, Grampian Enterprise Ltd. 1992–96;

Council mem. Inst. of Physics 1981–87, 1988–92 (Vice-Pres. 1982–87), European Physical Soc. 1989–92; mem. Nuclear Physics Bd. and Chair. Nuclear Structure Cttee. SERC 1984–88; mem. Scottish Econ. Council 1993–96, Council Asscn. of Commonwealth Univs. 1993–96 (Chair. 1994–95), BT Scottish Advisory Forum 1993–96, British Council (Scotland) 1993–96, Council CVCP 1995–, Bd. HEQC 1994–97, UCEA, UCAS 1995–; Hon. D.Sc. (William and Mary) 1995; Hon. D.Ed. (RGU) 1995; Hon. D.Univ. (Edin.) 1995; Hon. LL.D. (Aberdeen) 1997; Hon. F.R.C.S. (E.) 1995. *Publications:* The Basis of Modern Physics 1967, Nuclear Structure Theory 1972, Heavy Nuclei, Superheavy Nuclei and Neutron Stars 1975, Neutron Stars 1978; more than 100 research publs. on physics. *Leisure interests:* hill walking, tennis. *Address:* Vice-Chancellor's Office, University of Birmingham, Edgbaston, Birmingham, B15 2TT, England. *Telephone:* (0121) 414 4536. *Fax:* (0121) 414 4534.

IRVINE OF LAIRG, Baron (Life Peer) cr. 1987, of Lairg in the District of Sutherland, **Alexander Andrew Mackay Irvine,** Q.C., M.A., LL.B.; British lawyer; b. 23 June 1940; s. of Alexander Irvine and Margaret Christina Irvine; m. 1st Margaret Veitch (divorced 1973); m. 2nd Alison Mary McNair 1974; two s.; ed. Inverness Acad., Hutchesons' Boys' Grammar School, Univ. of Glasgow, Christ's Coll., Cambridge; lecturer, L.S.E. 1965–69; called to the Bar, Inner Temple 1967, Bencher 1985; a Recorder 1985–88; Deputy High Court Judge 1987–97; Shadow Lord Chancellor 1992–97, Lord Chancellor May 1997–; Trustee Whitechapel Art Gallery 1990–, Hunterian Collection 1997–; Hon. LL.D. (Glasgow) 1997. *Leisure interests:* cinema, theatre, art, travel. *Address:* House of Lords, Westminster, London, SW1A 0PW, England.

IRVING, Amy; American actress; b. 10 Sept. 1953, Palo Alto, Calif.; m. Steven Spielberg (q.v.) 1985 (divorced); one s.; one s. by Bruno Barreto; ed. American Conservatory Theater and London Acad. of Dramatic Art; stage appearances include Juliet in Romeo and Juliet, Seattle Repertory Theater 1982–83, on Broadway in Amadeus 1981–82, Heartbreak House 1983–84, off Broadway in The Road to Mecca 1988; frequent TV appearances. *Films include:* Carrie, The Fury, Voices, Honeysuckle Road, The Competition, Yentl, Mickey and Maude, Rumpelstiltskin, Crossing Delancey, A Show of Force, Benefit of the Doubt, Kleptomania, Acts of Love (also co-exec. producer), I'm Not Rappaport, Carried Away.

IRVING, Edward, SC.D., F.R.S.C., F.R.A.S., F.R.S.; Canadian research scientist; b. 27 May 1927; s. of George E. Irving and Nellie Irving; m. Sheila A. Irwin 1957; two s. two d.; ed. Colne Grammar School and Univ. of Cambridge; army service 1945–48; Research Fellow, Fellow and Sr. Fellow, Australian Nat. Univ. 1954–64; Dominion Observatory, Canada 1964–66; Prof. of Geophysics, Univ. of Leeds 1966–67; Research Scientist, Dominion Observatory, later Earth Physics Br. Dept. of Energy, Mines and Resources, Ottawa 1967–81; Research Scientist, Pacific Geoscience Centre, Sidney, B.C. 1981–92, Emer. Research Scientist 1992–; Adjunct Prof. Carleton Univ. Ottawa 1975–81, Univ. of Vic. 1985–95; Fellow, American Geophysical Union; Foreign Assoc. Nat. Acad. of Science (U.S.A.); several awards and medals. *Publications:* Palaeomagnetism 1964; contributions to learned journals. *Leisure interests:* gardening, carpentry, choral singing. *Address:* Pacific Geoscience Centre, 9860 West Saanich Road, Box 6000, Sidney, B.C., V8L 4B2; 9363 Carnoustie Crescent, R.R.2, Sidney, B.C., V8L 5G7, Canada (Home). *Telephone:* (250) 363 6404 (Office); (250) 656-9645 (Home).

IRVING, John Winslow, B.A., M.F.A.; American author; b. 2 March 1942, Exeter, N.H.; s. of Colin F. N. Irving and Frances Winslow; m. 1st Shyla Leary 1964 (divorced 1981); two s.; m. 2nd Janet Turnbull 1987; one s.; ed. Univs. of Pittsburgh, Vienna, New Hampshire and Iowa; Asst. Prof. of English, Mt. Holyoke Coll. 1967–72, 1975–78; writer-in-residence, Univ. of Iowa 1972–75; with Bread Loaf Writers' Conf. 1976; Rockefeller Foundation grantee 1971–72; Nat. Endowment for Arts Fellow 1974–75, Guggenheim Fellow 1976–77. *Publications:* novels including: Setting Free the Bears 1969, The Water-Method Man 1972, The 158-Pound Marriage 1974, The World According to Garp 1978, The Hotel New Hampshire 1981, The Cider House Rules 1985, An Introduction to Great Expectations 1986, A Prayer for Owen Meany 1989, A Son of the Circus 1994, Trying to save Piggy Sneed 1996 (a collection of memoirs, short stories and essays), An Introduction to A Christmas Carol 1996, A Widow for One Year 1998, short stories and reviews in other publs. *Address:* c/o Turnbull Agency, P.O. Box 757, Dorset, VT 05251, U.S.A.

IRWIN, Flavia, (Lady de Grey), R.A.; British artist; b. 15 Dec. 1916, London; d. of Clinton Irwin and Everilda Irwin; m. Sir Roger de Grey 1942; two s. one d.; ed. Hawnes School, Ampthill, Beds. and Chelsea School of Art; taught gen. design at Medway Coll. of Art 1970–75; Sr. tutor, Decorative Arts Course, City & Guilds of London Art School, Kennington, London 1975–; solo exhbn. Ansdell Gallery; several group exhbns. including Royal Acad. of Arts Summer Exhbn.; work in collections including Westminster Conf. Centre, London, Midland Montague Morgan Grenfell, Carlisle City Art Gallery, Dept. of the Environment, Govt. Art Collection; Hon. Academician, Royal West of England Acad., Bristol. *Leisure interests:* swimming, reading. *Address:* 5 Camer Street, Meopham, Kent, DA13 0XR, England. *Telephone:* (01474) 812327.

ISA, Pehin Dato Haji; Brunei politician; trained as barrister in U.K.; fmrly. Gen. Adviser to Sultan of Brunei, now Special Adviser, with ministerial rank in Prime Minister's Office; Minister of Home Affairs 1988–95, Special Adviser to the Prime Minister –1995. *Address:* c/o Ministry of Home Affairs, Bandar Seri Begawan, Brunei.

ISAACS, Sir Jeremy Israel, Kt. M.A.; British arts administrator; b. 28 Sept. 1932; s. of Isidore Isaacs and Sara Jacobs; m. 1st Tamara (née Weinreich) 1958 (died 1986); one s. one d.; m. 2nd Gillian Widdicombe 1988; ed. Glasgow Acad., Merton Coll., Oxford; TV Producer, Granada TV (What the Papers Say, All Our Yesterdays) 1958, Associated Rediffusion (This Week) 1963, B.B.C. TV (Panorama) 1965; Controller of Features, Associated Rediffusion 1967; with Thames TV 1968–78, Producer, The World at War 1974, Cold War 1998; Dir. of Programmes 1974–78; special independent consultant TV series Hollywood, ITV, A Sense of Freedom, ITV, Ireland, a Television Documentary, B.B.C., Battle for Crete, N.Z. TV, Cold War, Turner Broadcasting; C.E.O., Channel Four TV Co. 1981–88; Gen. Dir. Royal Opera House 1988–96 (Dir. 1985–97); Chief Exec. Jeremy Isaacs Productions 1998–; Gov. British Film Inst. 1979–; Chair., British Film Inst. Production Bd. 1979–81; James MacTaggart Memorial Lecturer, Edinburgh TV Festival 1979; Fellow, Royal Television Soc. 1978, B.A.F.T.A. 1985, B.F.I. 1986; Hon. D.Litt. (Strathclyde) 1983, (Bristol) 1988; Dr. h.c. (Council for Nat. Academic Awards) 1987, (R.C.A.) 1988; Hon. LL.D. (Manchester) 1998; Desmond Davis Award for outstanding creative contrib. to TV 1972; George Polk Memorial Award 1973; Cyril Bennett Award 1982; Lord Willis Award for Distinguished Service to TV 1985. *Publications:* Storm Over Four: A Personal Account 1989, Cold War (jtly.) 1999. *Leisure interests:* books, walks, sleep. *Address:* Jeremy Isaacs Productions, 8 Shelton Street, London, WC2H 9JR, England.

ISAACSON, Walter Seff, M.A.; American journalist; b. 20 May 1952, New Orleans; s. of Irwin Isaacson and Betsy Isaacson; m. Cathy Wright 1984; one d.; ed. Harvard Univ., Univ. of Oxford; reporter Sunday Times, London 1976–77, States-Item, New Orleans 1977–78; staff writer Time magazine, New York 1978–79, political corresp. 1979–81, Assoc. Ed. 1981–84, Sr. Ed. 1985–91, Asst. Man. Ed. 1991–93, Man. Ed. 1996–; Ed. New Media Time, Inc. 1993–96; mem. Council on Foreign Relations, Century Asscn.; received Overseas Press Club Award, NY 1981, 1984, 1987. *Publications:* Pro and Con 1983, Kissinger: A Biography 1992, The Wise Men (jtly.) 1986 (Harry Truman Book Prize 1987). *Address:* Time Magazine, Time-Life, Rockefeller Center, New York, NY 10020, U.S.A.

ISAAKOV, Yuri Fedorovich, D.M.; Russian surgeon; b. 28 June 1923, Kovrov, Vladimir Region; s. of Fedor Fedorovich and Kladvia Fedorovna Isaakov; m. Tamara Gennadievna Isaakov; one s.; ed. Russian State Medical Univ.; asst., docent, prof. 1953–65, Head of Chair of Children Surgery Russian State Medical Univ. 1966–; Vice-Pres. Russian Acad. of Medical Sciences; Chair. Russian Asscn. of Children Surgeons; mem. Int. Soc. of Surgeons; mem. Presidium of Russian Soc. of Surgeons; expert of WHO on scientific directions in public health. *Publications:* more than 300 scientific works, including 13 monographs on plastic and reconstructive surgery, surgery of intestine and lungs. *Leisure interests:* sports. *Address:* Russian Academy of Medical Sciences, Solyanka str. 14, 103001 Moscow, Russia (Office); Frunzenskaya nab. 50, apt. 89, 119270 Moscow, Russia (Home). *Telephone:* 254 10 77 (Office); 242 46 15 (Home).

ISARANGKUN NA AYUTHAYA, Chirayu; Thai economist and politician; b. 12 Nov. 1942, Bangkok; m.; two s.; ed. St. Gabriel's School, Bangkok, King's Coll. School, Wimbledon, England, Univ. of London and Australian Nat. Univ.; joined Dept. of Tech. and Econ. Co-operation 1964; transferred to Nat. Inst. of Devt. Admin. (NIDA) 1967, Assoc. Dean School of Devt. Cons. 1974–76, Dean 1976–80, Acting Vice-Rector 1981; Adviser to Prime Minister in third govt. of Gen. Kriangsak Chomanan and first govt. of Gen. Prem Tinsulanonda; Deputy Minister of Industry in second, third and fourth Prem govts.; Minister in the Prime Minister's Office 1986–87; fmr. Chair. Bank of Asia Ltd. *Address:* 191 South Sathorn Road, Khet Yannawa, Bangkok 10120; c/o Bank of Asia, Bangkok 10300, Thailand.

ISARD, Walter, PH.D.; American economist; b. 19 April 1919, Philadelphia, Pa.; s. of Lazar and Anna (Podolin) Isard; m. Caroline Berliner 1943; four s. four d.; ed. Temple, Harvard and Chicago Univs.; Instructor Wesleyan Univ. 1945, M.I.T. 1947; Visiting Lecturer Tufts Coll. 1947; Assoc. Prof. of Econs., Assoc. Dir. of Teaching, Inst. of Econs., American Univ. 1948–49; Research Fellow and Lecturer, Harvard Univ. 1949–53; Assoc. Prof. of Regional Econs., Dir. Urban and Regional Studies, M.I.T. 1953–56; Prof. of Econs., Chair. Dept. of Regional Science, Univ. of Pa. 1956–75, Head Dept. of Peace Science 1975–77; Visiting Prof. of Regional Science, Yale Univ. 1960–61, of Landscape Architecture and Regional Science, Harvard Univ. 1966–71; Chair. Graduate Group in Peace Research and Peace Science Unit 1970–78; Sr. Research Assoc., Visiting Prof. of Econs., Regional Science and Policy Planning, Cornell Univ. 1971–79, Prof. 1979–; Distinguished Visiting Prof., Inst. für Regionalwissenschaft, Karlsruhe 1972; Consultant, Tenn. Valley Authority 1951–52, Resources for the Future Inc. 1954–58, Ford Foundation 1955–56; Founder Regional Science Asscn. 1954, Editor, Co-Ed. Papers 1954–58, Pres. 1959, Hon. Chair. 1960–; Ford Foundation Fellow in Econs. and Business Admin. 1959–60; Editor, Co-Ed., Journal of Regional Science 1960–; Chair. OEEC Econ. Productivity Agency Conf. on Regional Econs. and Planning, Bellagio, Italy 1960; Founder Peace Science Soc. (Int.) 1963, Co-Ed. Papers 1963–, Exec. Sec. 1964–, Pres. 1968; Pres. World Acad. of Art and Science 1977–81; Dir. ECAAR 1989–; Assoc. Ed. Quarterly Journal of Economics 1968–71, Peace Economics, Peace Science and Public Policy 1994–; mem. Editorial Bd. Journal of Conflict Resolution 1972–; mem.

N.A.S.; Fellow, American Acad. of Art and Sciences 1980; Fellow A.A.A.S. 1987; Dr. h.c. (Poznań Acad. of Econ.) 1976, (Erasmus Univ.) 1978, (Karlsruhe) 1979, (Umeå) 1980, (Univ. of Ill.) 1982, (Binghamton Univ.) 1997; Hon. Prof. (Peking Univ., Northwest Univ.) 1993; August Lösch Ring 1988. *Publications:* Atomic Power: An Economic and Social Analysis 1952, Location Factors in the Petrochemical Industry 1955, Location and Space Economy 1956, Municipal Costs and Revenues resulting from Community Growth 1957, Industrial Complex Analysis and Regional Development 1959, Methods of Regional Analysis 1960, Regional Economic Development 1961, General Theory: Social, Political, Economic and Regional 1969, Regional Input-Output Study 1971, Ecologic-Economic Analysis for Regional Planning 1971, Spatial Dynamics and Optimal Space-Time Development 1979, Conflict Analysis and Practical Conflict Management Procedures 1982, Arms Races, Arms Control and Conflict Analysis 1988, Practical Methods of Regional Science and Empirical Applications 1990, Location Analysis and General Theory 1990, Economics of Arms Production and the Peace Process 1992, The Science of Peace 1992, Commonalities in Art, Science and Religion 1997, Methods of Interregional and Regional Analysis 1998. *Leisure interest:* music. *Address:* Department of Economics, 476 Uris Hall, Cornell University, Ithaca, NY 14853 (Office); 3218 Garrett Road, Drexel Hill, PA 19026, U.S.A. (Home). *Telephone:* (607) 255-3306 (Office). *Fax:* (607) 255-2818.

ISĂRESCU, Constantin Mugurel, PH.D.; Romanian economist; b. 1 Aug. 1949, Drăgăşani, Vâlcea Co.; s. of Constantin Isărescu and Aritina Isărescu; m. Elena Isărescu; one s. one d.; ed. Acad. of Econs; research fellow Inst. for World Econ. 1971–90; asst. lecturer Acad. of Econs., Bucharest 1975–89, Prof. 1996–; Prof. Timişoara West Univ. 1994–96; fmrly. Prof. Banking Coll. of Romanian Banking Inst.; fmrly. First Sec. Embassy, Washington; Gov. Nat. Bank of Romania Sept. 1990–; Chair. Romanian Chess Fed.; Chair. for Romania, Club of Rome; Vice-Pres. Central Banks' Govs.' Club; mem. Bd. Romanian American Enterprise Fund; Honour Medal (Architects' World Forum). *Publications:* Financial Crisis 1979, Gold, Myth and Reality 1980, Stock Exchange 1982, Recent Developments in Romania 1990, Monetary Policy, Macroeconomic Stability and Banking Reform in Romania 1995, Banking System in Romania: Recent Developments and Prospects 1996, Reform of Financial System in Romania and European Integration 1996, Monetary Policy After 1989 1997. *Leisure interest:* vine growing. *Address:* National Bank of Romania, 25 Lipscani Street, Bucharest 70421, Romania. *Telephone:* (1) 312-62-32. *Fax:* (1) 312-49-34.

ISAYEV, Alexander Sergeyevich; Russian biologist and forester; b. 26 Oct. 1931, Moscow; m. Lidia Pokrovskaya 1953; two d.; ed. Leningrad Forestry Acad.; mem. CPSU 1965–91; Deputy Chair. Council for Protection of the Environment and Rational Exploitation of Resources in U.S.S.R. Supreme Soviet 1979–89; mem. U.S.S.R. (now Russian) Acad. of Sciences 1984; Dir. V. N. Sukachev Forestry Inst., Krasnoyarsk, Chair. Krasnoyarsk Div., Siberian Dept. of U.S.S.R. Acad. of Sciences 1977–88; Pres. GOSKOMLES (State Comm. on Forestry) 1988–91; Chair. Higher Ecological Council at Russian Fed. Supreme Soviet 1992–93; Dir. Centre for Ecological Problems and Productivity of Forests 1991–; Pres. Int. Forestry Inst. 1991–; Gold Medal (Int. Union of Forestry Research Orgs.) 1976; Hon. Diploma (UNEP Programme) 1989; Gold Medal (Russian Acad. of Sciences) 1992. *Publications:* eight books, 250 articles. *Leisure interests:* fishing, hunting. *Address:* Novocheremushkinskaya str. 69, 117418 Moscow, Russia. *Telephone:* (095) 332-86-52. *Fax:* (095) 332-29-17.

ISHIBASHI, Kanichiro; Japanese business executive; b. 1 March 1920, Kurume-shi, Fukuoka-ken; s. of Shojiro and Masako Ishibashi; m. Saeko Ishibashi 1944; one s. two d.; ed. Faculty of Law, Univ. of Tokyo; naval service 1943–45; joined Bridgestone Tire Co. Ltd. (now called Bridgestone Corpn.) 1945, Dir. 1949–, Vice-Pres. 1950–63, Pres. 1963–73, Chair. 1973–85, Hon. Chair. Feb. 1985–; Exec. Dir. Fed. of Econ. Orgs., Japan Fed. of Employers' Asscns.; Pres. Japan Rubber Mfrs. Asscn. *Leisure interests:* pictures, photography, music, golf. *Address:* 10-1, Kyobashi 1-chome, Chuo-ku, Tokyo (Office); 1 Nagasaka-cho, Azabu, Minato-ku, Tokyo, Japan (Home). *Telephone:* 03-567-0111 (Office); 03-583-0150 (Home).

ISHIGURO, Kazuo, O.B.E., M.A.; British author; b. 8 Nov. 1954, Nagasaki, Japan; s. of Shizuo Ishiguro and Shizuko Ishiguro; m. Lorna Anne Macdougall 1986; one d.; ed. Woking Grammar School, Univs. of Kent and East Anglia; fmr. community worker, Renfrew; writer 1980–. *Publications include:* A Pale View of Hills (Winifred Holtby Prize) 1982, An Artist of the Floating World (Whitbread Book of the Year Fiction Prize) 1986, A Profile of Arthur J. Mason (TV Play), The Remains of the Day (Booker Prize 1989) 1989, The Saddest Music in the World (screenplay) 1989, The Unconsoled (Cheltenham Prize 1995) 1995. *Address:* c/o Rogers, Coleridge and White Ltd., 20 Powis Mews, London, W11 1JN, England. *Telephone:* 0171-221 3717. *Fax:* 0171-229 9084.

ISHIHARA, Shintaro; Japanese politician; b. Sept. 1932, Kobe; m.; four s.; ed. Hitotsubashi Univ.; mem. House of Councillors 1972; mem. House of Reps. 1972–95; Minister of State, Dir.-Gen. Environment Agency 1976; Minister of Transport 1987–88; Akutagawa Prize for Literature; Liberal-Democratic Party. *Publications include:* The Season of the Sun, The Tree of the Young Man, The Forest of Fossils, The Japan that Can Say No (with Akio Morita, q.v.) 1989, etc. *Leisure interests:* yachting, skiing. *Address:* Room 606, Sanno Grand Bldg., 2-14-2 Nagata-cho, Chiyoda-ku, Tokyo, Japan.

ISHII, Hajime; Japanese politician; b. 17 Aug. 1934, Kobe; m. Tomoko Sugiguchi 1961; one s.; ed. Konan Univ., Stanford Univ. Graduate School; mem. House of Reps. 1969–; fmr. Parl. Vice-Minister of Transport; Minister of State, Dir.-Gen. Nat. Land Agency 1989–90; Minister of Home Affairs May–June 1994; fmr. Chair. Liberal-Democratic Party Nat. Org. Cttee.; fmr. Chair. LDP Research Comm. on Foreign Affairs; Exec. mem. Japan Renewal Party; Chair. Special Cttee. on Political Reform (House of Reps.). *Address:* No. 1 Diet Bldg., Room 220, 2-2-1 Nagata-cho, Chiyoda-ku, Tokyo 100, Japan. *Telephone:* (3) 3508-7220 (Office).

ISHII, Kazuhiro; Japanese architect; b. 1 Feb. 1944, Tokyo; s. of Toshio Ishii and Kyoko Ishii; m. Noriko Nagahama 1988; two d.; ed. Univ. of Tokyo and Yale Univ.; lecturer, Waseda Univ. 1991–, Univ. of Tokyo 1992–; Japan Inst. of Architecture Prize 1989; main works: Noshima Educational Zone 1970–82, Tanabe Agency Bldg. 1983, Gyro-Roof 1987, Sukiya Mura 1989, Kitakyu-shu City Hall 1991. *Publications:* Rebirth of Japanese-style Architecture 1985, Thought on Sukiya 1985, My Architectural Dictionary 1988. *Leisure interests:* golf, music (playing saxophone). *Address:* 4-14-27 Akasaka, Minato-ku, Tokyo 107 (Office); 7-5-1-303 Akasaka, Minato-ku, Tokyo 107, Japan (Home). *Telephone:* 03-3505-0765 (Office); 03-3584-0779 (Home).

ISHII, Maki; Japanese composer and conductor; b. 28 May 1936, Tokyo; m. Christa Frauke Meinecke 1963; one s. one d.; ed. Hochschule für Musik, Berlin; invited by DAAD (German Academic Exchange Service) to take part in Berliner Künstlerprogramm 1969; has since travelled widely in Europe, USA and Asia as composer and conductor of contemporary music; founded Japanese Tokk Ensemble 1973; lived with percussion group Ondeko-Za on Sado Island and composed several important works for group 1975–76; appeared at Berlin Metamusik Festival 1978; Maki Ishii Concert, Paris Festival 1978, Eté Japonais, Geneva 1983; presenter and dir. of series Here Comes the Orchestra for TBS-TV, Japan 1978–84; conducting debut with New Japan Philharmonic Orchestra 1979; Artistic Dir. Tokyo Summer Festival 1985–89; lecturer, Hochschule für Kunste Berlin 1988, San Francisco 1989; organizer, Asian Music Festival, Tokyo 1990; dir. production of his ballets in Rotterdam, The Hague and Paris 1991; recipient of several music and recording awards and other distinctions. *Compositions include:* Kyô-Sô (for percussion and orchestra) 1969, Sô-Gû II (for Gagaku and orchestra) 1971, Monochrome (for Japanese drums and gongs) 1976, Mono-Prism (for Japanese drums and orchestra) 1976, Afro-Concerto (for percussion and orchestra) 1982, Thirteen Drums (for percussion solo) 1985, Kaguyahime (ballet score) 1985, Floating Wind (symphonic linked works) 1992, String Quartet 1992. *Leisure interest:* taking a stroll. *Address:* 1-24-3 Jiyugaoka, Meguro-ku, Tokyo 152, Japan. *Telephone:* (03) 3718 00 59. *Fax:* (03) 3725 01 23.

ISHII, Michiko; Japanese politician; mem. House of Councillors; fmr. Parl. Vice-Minister of Labour; Dir. Gen. Environment Agency (State Minister) 1996–98. *Address:* c/o Environment Agency, 1-2-2, Kasumigaseki, Chiyoda-ku, Tokyo, Japan (Office).

ISHIKAWA, Shigeru, D.ECON.; Japanese economist; b. 7 April 1918; ed. Tokyo Univ. of Commerce (now Hitotsubashi Univ.); attached to Jiji Press News Agency 1945–56, Hong Kong Corresp. 1951–53; Asst. Prof., Inst. of Econ. Research, Hitotsubashi Univ. 1956–63, Prof. 1963–82, Dir. 1972–74, Prof. Emer. 1982–; Far Eastern Fellow, East Asian Research Center, Harvard Univ. 1957–58; Visiting Prof. School of Oriental and African Studies, Univ. of London 1980, Hon. Fellow 1991; Prof. School of Int. Politics, Econs. and Business, Aoyama Gakuin Univ. 1982–94, Prof. Emer. 1994–; Visiting Prof. Josai Univ. 1994–; Order of Friendship (Vietnam) 1997–. *Publications:* National Income and Capital Formation in Mainland China 1965, Economic Development in Asian Perspective 1967, Agricultural Development Strategies of Asia 1970, Labor Absorption in Asian Agriculture 1978, Essays on Technology, Employment and Institutions in Economic Development: Comparative Asian Experience 1981. *Address:* 19-8, 4 chome Kugayama, Suginami-ku, Tokyo 168-0082, Japan. *Telephone:* (3) 3332-8376. *Fax:* (3) 3332-0877.

ISHIKAWA, Tadao, LL.D.; Japanese academic; b. 21 Jan. 1922, Tokyo; s. of Chukichi Ishikawa and Yoshi Ishikawa; m. Yoshiko Ishikawa (deceased); one s. three d.; ed. Keio Univ., Harvard Univ. and Univ. of Calif. at Berkeley, U.S.A.; mem. Faculty of Law, Keio Univ., 1946–87, Prof. 1955–87, Dean 1971–77, Vice-Pres. Keio Univ. 1965–69, Pres. 1977–93; mem. Bd. Int. Asscn. of Univ. Pres. 1980–85; Pres. Japan Asscn. of Pvt. Univs. and Colls. 1983–88; Vice-Chair. Prov. Council on Educ. Reform 1984–87; Chair. Univ. Council, Ministry of Educ. 1987–, Tokyo Metropolitan Bd. of Educ. 1988–, The Juvenile Problem Council 1989–; Chair. Japan-China Friendship Cttee. for the 21st Century 1984–; Chair. Lower House Election Redistricting Council 1994–; Dr. h.c. (Western Mich. Univ., U.S.A.); Hon. LL.D. (York Univ., Toronto); Award for Cultural Merit, Japanese Govt. 1991, Grand Cordon, Order of the Rising Sun 1995, and many other awards. *Publications include:* A History of the Chinese Constitution 1952, A Study of the History of the Chinese Communist Party 1959, International Politics and Red China 1968, Contemporary Issues of Present Day China 1970, My Dreams and My Choice 1993; numerous articles. *Address:* Ishikawa Doko-Bunseki Kenkyujo, Izumikan Kioi-cho Building 5F, 4-9 Kioi-cho, Chiyoda-ku, Tokyo 102 (Office); 4-1-10-209 Hiroo, Shibuya-ku, Tokyo 150, Japan (Home). *Telephone:* (03) 3288-3496 (Office); (03) 3486-4317 (Home).

ISHIMARU, Akira, PH.D., F.I.E.E.E.; American professor of electrical engineering; b. 16 March 1928, Fukuoka, Japan; s. of Shigezo Ishimaru and Yumi Ishimaru (née Yamada); m. Yuko Kaneda 1956; two s. two d.; ed. Univ. of Tokyo, Univ. of Washington, U.S.A.; Asst. Prof., Univ. of Washington 1958–61, Assoc. Prof. 1961–65, Prof. of Electrical Eng. 1965; Boeing Martin Prof. 1993, also Adjunct Prof. of Applied Math.; Visiting Assoc. Prof. Univ. of Calif. at Berkeley 1963–64; Ed. Radio Science 1978–82; mem. Editorial Bd. Proc. I.E.E.E. 1973–83; mem. Nat. Acad. of Eng. 1996–; Ed.-in-Chief Waves in Random Media 1990–; Fellow Optical Soc. of America 1982; I.E.E.E. Centennial Medal 1984, Distinguished Achievement Award 1995, 1998. *Publications:* Wave Propagation and Scattering in Random Media, vols. 1 and 2 1978, Electromagnetic Wave Propagation, Radiation and Scattering 1991. *Address:* c/o Department of Electrical Engineering, University of Washington, P.O. Box 352500, Seattle, WA 98195 (Office); 2913 165th Place, N.E., Bellevue, WA 98008, U.S.A. (Home).

ISHIOKA, Eiko; Japanese designer; ed. Nat. Univ. of Fine Arts, Tokyo; fmr. Art Dir. Shiseido cosmetics co.; designer of advertising posters, television commercials and stage sets; created designs for film Mishima, play M. Butterfly and opera The Making of the Representative for Planet 8; designed cover for a Miles Davis album (Grammy award). *Publication:* Eiko by Eiko: Eiko Ishioka, Japan's Ultimate Designer 1990.

ISHIZAKA, Kimishige, M.D., PH.D.; Japanese biomedical research scientist; b. 12 March 1925, Tokyo; m. Teruko Ishizaka 1949; one s.; ed. Univ. of Tokyo; Chief, Dept. of Serology, Div. of Immunoserology, Tokyo 1953–62; Chief, Dept. of Immunology, Children's Asthma Research Inst. and Hosp., Denver, Colo. 1962–70; Assoc. Prof. of Medicine and Microbiology, Johns Hopkins Univ. 1970–81, Dir. Subdept. of Immunology 1981–88, O'Neill Prof. of Immunology and Medicine 1981–89; Scientific Dir. and Head, Div. of Immunobiology, La Jolla Inst. of Allergy and Immunology, La Jolla, Calif. 1989–; Emperor's Award 1974; Pioneer of Modern Allergy Award 1982; Distinguished Scientist Award, Japanese Medical Soc. of America 1989. *Publications:* numerous contribs. to scientific journals. *Address:* La Jolla Institute for Allergy and Immunology, 11149 North Torrey Pines Road, La Jolla, CA 92037, U.S.A. *Telephone:* (619)-558-3540.

ISHLINSKY, Aleksandr Yulyevich; Russian applied mathematician; b. 6 Aug. 1913, Moscow; s. of Yuliy Eduardovich Ishlinsky and Sofia Ivanovna Kirillova; m. Natalia Vladimirovna Zaporozhets 1943; ed. Moscow Univ.; mem. CPSU 1940–91; Prof., Moscow Univ. 1944–48, Prof. and Head of Dept. 1955–64; Prof. Kiev Univ. 1949–55; Dir. Inst. for Problems in Mechanics, U.S.S.R. (now Russian) Acad. of Sciences 1964–88, Hon. Dir. 1989–; mem. Ukrainian Acad. of Sciences 1948, U.S.S.R. (now Russian) Acad. of Sciences 1960–; Chair. U.S.S.R. Union of Scientific and Eng. Socs. 1970; Regional mem. Int. Fed. Scientific Workers; Deputy to Supreme Soviet U.S.S.R. 1974–89; Pres. World Fed. of Eng. Orgs. 1987; Foreign mem. Mexican Eng. Acad. 1976, Czechoslovakia Acad. 1977, Polish Acad. 1977; Hon. mem. Int. Acad. of Science History 1981; Lenin Prize 1960, Hero of Socialist Labour 1961, and other decorations. *Publications:* The Dynamics of Ground Masses 1954, The Theory of the Horizon Compass 1956, On the Equation of Problems Determining the Position of Moving Objects by Using a Gyroscope and Measuring Acceleration 1957, The Mechanics of Gyroscopic Systems 1963, Inertial Guidance of Ballistic Rockets 1968, Orientation, Gyroscopes and Inertial Navigation 1976, Applied Problems in Mechanics 1986, Classical Mechanics and Inertia Forces 1987. *Leisure interests:* radiotechnique, chess. *Address:* Institute for Problems in Mechanics, Russian Academy of Sciences, prospekt Vernadskogo 101, Korp. 1, Moscow 117526, Russia. *Telephone:* (095) 434-34-65.

ISKANDER, Fazil Abdulovich, Russian/Abkhaz author; b. 6 March 1929, Sukhumi, Georgian SSR; m.; one s. one d.; ed. Maxim Gorky Inst. of Literature, Moscow; first works publ. 1952; U.S.S.R People's Deputy 1989–91; Pres. Assen. of Authors and Publrs. against Piracy; Head, World of Culture; Dr. h.c. (Norwich Univ., U.S.A.); U.S.S.R. State Prize 1989, State Prize of Russia 1993, A. Sakharov Prize, A. Pushkin Prize (Germany) 1994, Malaparti Prize (Italy) 1995, Moscow-Penne Prize (Italy) 1996, Triumph Prize 1998. *Publications include:* Green Rain 1960, Youth of the Sea 1964, Forbidden Fruit 1966 (English trans. 1972), Summer Forest 1969, Time of Lucky Finds 1970, Tree of Childhood & Other Stories 1970, Sandro from Chegem 1978, Metropol (co-ed.) 1979, Small Giant of the Big Sex 1979, Rabbits and Boa Constrictors 1987, The Path (poems) 1987, Poets and Tsars 1991, Man and His Surroundings 1992, Pshada 1993, Sofichka 1996, The One Who Thinks about Russia and the American 1997. *Address:* Leningradski prosp. 26, korp. 2, Apt. 67, 125040 Moscow, Russia. *Telephone:* (095) 212-73-60.

ISLAM, A.K.M. Nurul; Bangladeshi politician and judge; b. 1925, Khajilpur, Dhaka Dist. m. Jahanara Arjoo; two s. two d.; ed. in Calcutta; Advocate, Dhaka High Court 1951, Supreme Court 1956; Additional Judge, Dhaka High Court 1968, Judge 1970; Chief Election Commr. of Bangladesh 1977, 1982; founder and Sr. Prof. City Law Coll. Dhaka; active in independence movt. 1971; Vice-Pres. of Bangladesh 1986–88, 1989, also Minister of Law and Justice 1986–89. *Address:* c/o Office of the Vice President, Dhaka, Bangladesh.

ISLAM, Nurul, PH.D.; Bangladeshi economist; b. 1 April 1929, Chittagong; s. of Abdur Rahman and Mohsena Begum; m. Rowshan Ara 1957; one s. one d.; ed. Univ. of Dhaka and Harvard Univ.; Reader in Econs. Dhaka Univ. 1955–60, Prof. 1960–64; Dir. Pakistan Inst. of Devt. Econs., Karachi 1964–72; Visiting Prof. Econ. Devt. Inst., World Bank 1967–68; Professorial Research Assoc., Yale Econ. Growth Cen. 1968 and 1971; Deputy Chair. Bangladesh Planning Comm. (with ministerial status) 1972–75; Chair. Bangladesh Inst. of Devt. Studies, Dhaka 1975–77; mem. Bd. of Trustees Int. Rice Research Inst., Manila 1973–77, Exec. Cttee. Third World Forum 1974–, Bd. of Govs. Int. Food Policy Research Inst. 1975–, UN Cttee. on Devt. Planning 1975–77; Asst. Dir.-Gen. Econ. and Social Policy Dept., Food and Agric. Org. of UN 1977–; mem. Editorial Bd. The World Economy, London, Research Advisory Cttee., World Bank 1980, Advisory Group, Asian Devt. Bank, Manila 1981–82, Advisory Cttee., Inst. of Int. Econ., Washington, D.C.; Consultant with various UN Cttees, ESCAP, UNESCO, UNCTAD etc.; Nuffield Foundation Fellow at Univs. of London and Cambridge 1958–59; Rockefeller Fellow, Netherlands School of Economics 1959. *Publications:* A Short-Term Model of Pakistan's Economy: An Econometric Analysis 1964, Studies in Foreign Capital and Economic Development 1960, Studies in Consumer Demand 1965, Studies in Commercial Policy and Economic Growth 1970, Development Planning in Bangladesh—A Study in Political Economy 1977, Development Strategy of Bangladesh 1978, Interdependence of Developed and Developing Countries 1978, Foreign Trade and Economic Controls in Development: The Case of United Pakistan 1980, Aid and Influence: The Case of Bangladesh (co-author) 1981; Co-Author: Agriculture Towards 2000 1981, The Fifth World Food Survey 1985, Agriculture Price Policies 1985. *Leisure interests:* reading political and historical books, movies. *Address:* FAO, 00153 Rome, Italy (Office). *Telephone:* 5797.3001 (Office).

ISMAEL, Dr. Julius Emanuel: Indonesian banker and economist; b. 16 July 1927, Jakarta; m. Hermien S. Hardjodiwirjo 1957; two s. one d.; ed. Univ. of Indonesia, Cornell Univ., Univ. of Pittsburgh; Ass. to the Chair. Nat. Planning Agency 1968–70; Pres. Bank Ekspor-Impor Indonesia 1970–73; Man. Dir. Bank of Indonesia 1973–83; Prof. of Financial Man. Univ. of Indonesia 1974; Exec. Dir. IMF 1983. *Address:* c/o International Monetary Fund, 700 19th Street, N.W., Washington, DC 20431, U.S.A. *Telephone:* (202) 623-7430.

ISMAIL, Mohamed Ali, M.A.; Malaysian investment banker; b. 16 Sept. 1918, Port Kelang, Selangor; s. of Haji Mohamed Ali bin Taib and Hajjah Khadijah binti Haji Ahmad; m. Maimunah binti Abdul Latiff 1949; two s.; ed. Univ. of Cambridge and Middle Temple, London; joined Malayan Civil Service 1946; Asst. State Sec., Selangor State 1948–50; Asst. Sec. Econ. Div. of Fed. Treasury 1950–53; Econ. Officer, Penang 1954–55; Controller, Trade Div., Ministry of Commerce and Industry 1955–57; Minister Malaysian Embassy, Washington 1957–58, Econ. Minister 1958–60; Exec. Dir. IBRD, Int. Finance Corpn., Int. Devt. Assen. 1958–60; Deputy Gov. Cen. Bank of Malaysia 1960–62, Gov. 1962–80; Chair. Capital Issues Cttee. 1968–80, Malaysian Industrial Devt. Finance Bhd. 1969–; Pres. Malaysian Inst. of Man. 1966–68; Chair. Nat. Equity Corpn. 1978–; Chair. of Council, Malaysia Inst. of Bankers 1978–80; mem. Nat. Devt. Planning Cttee. 1962–80, Council of Univ. of Malaya 1962–72; Adviser, Nat. Corpn. (PERNAS) 1971–80; mem. Foreign Investment Cttee 1974–80; mem. Bd. of Govs., Asian Inst. of Man., Manila 1971–; Dir. Sime, Darby Berhad 1980–; Chair. Guthrie Corpn. Ltd. April 1982–, Harrisons Malaysian Plantations Berhad 1982–; Malaysian Nat. Reinsurance Berhad 1985, Commodities Trading Comm. 1981–, Panglima Mangku Negara 1964, Order of Panglima Negara Bintang Sarawak 1976; Hon. LL.D. (Univ. of Malaya) 1973, (Univ. of Singapore) 1982; Hon. D.Econ. (Univ. Kebangsaan Malaysia) 1982; Seri Paduka Mahkota Selangor award 1977; Seri Paduka Mahkota Johor Award 1979; Tun Abdul Razak Foundation Award 1980. *Leisure interests:* golf, swimming. *Address:* Office of the Chairman, Malaysian Industrial Development Finance Bhd., 195A Jaslan Tun Razak, P.O. Box 12110, 50939 Kuala Lumpur; National Equity Corporation, P.O.B. 745, Kuala Lumpur (Offices); 23 Jalan Natesa, off Cangkat Tunku, Kuala Lumpur, Malaysia (Home). *Telephone:* 03-2613313 (Office); 03-2425597 (Home).

ISMAIL, Dato Razali, B.A.; Malaysian diplomatist; b. 1939, Kedah; m.; three c.; joined Ministry of Foreign Affairs 1962; served Delhi 1963–64; Asst. High. Commr. in Madras 1964–66; Second Sec. Paris 1966–68; Prin. Asst. Sec. Ministry of Foreign Affairs 1968–70; Counsellor, London 1970–72; various posts at Ministry of Foreign Affairs and Chargé d'Affaires, Vientiane 1972–78; Amb. to Poland 1978–82; High Commr. in India 1982; Deputy Sec.-Gen. Ministry of Foreign Affairs 1985–88; Perm. Rep. to UN 1988, Pres. UN Gen. Ass. 1996–97. *Address:* c/o Ministry of Foreign Affairs, Wisma Putra, Jalan Wisma Putra, 50602 Kuala Lumpur, Malaysia.

ISMAIL, Sabri, D.IUR.; Egyptian economist; b. 1924, Malawi; m; lecturer in Law Faculty, Alexandria Univ., Egypt, later Prof. of Econ.; Sec.-Gen. of the Egyptian CP 1955; mem. of the Egyptian Econ. Org. 1958; Econ. Adviser to the Pres. 1959; mem. Arab Socialist Union Sec. and Ed. in Chief Dar Al-Maarifa Publishing House 1966; Dir. al-Ahram Econ. Research Org. 1968; Dir. Egyptian Nat. Planning Inst. 1970; Deputy Minister of Planning 1971 then Minister of State for Planning 1972; Minister of Planning 1974–75; Sec.-Gen. Scientific Conference of Egyptian Economists; mem. Academic Advisory Board, UN African Inst. of Devt. and Planning, Dakar, Senegal 1971–; mem. Academic Cttee., UN African Inst. of Devt. and Planning, Kuwait; founding mem. of the Third World Forum; Deputy Chair. Council for the Devt. of Economies and Social Research in Africa; Deputy Gen. Man. Nasser Social Bank, Cairo. *Publications:* Economie et Structure Economique 1952, Lectures in Economics 1954, Organization of the Public Sector, Confrontation with Israel 1969, Political Papers 1972. *Address:* 36 Kasr El-Nil Street, P.O. Box 2552, Egypt. *Telephone:* 979-030.

ISMAIL AMAT; Chinese politician; b. 1935, Xinjiang; active in People's Commune Movt. -1960; Deputy Sec. CCP Cttee., a country admin., Xinjiang 1960; Deputy Dir. Dept. of Political Work in Culture and Educ. Xinjiang 1960; mem. 10th CCP Cen. Cttee. 1973–77; Sec. CCP Cttee., Xinjiang 1974–79; Vice-Chair. Aubnavan Regional Revolutionary Cttee., Xinjiang 1974–79; Political Commissar, Xinjiang Mil. Region 1976–85; First Deputy Dir. Party School, Xinjiang 1977–85; Chair People's Govt., Xinjiang 1979–85; mem. 12th CCP Cen. Cttee. 1982–87, 13th CCP Cen. Cttee. 1987–92, 14th CCP Cen. Cttee. 1992–97, 15th CCP Cen. Cttee. 1997–; Minister of State Nationalities Affairs Comm. 1986–98; State Councillor 1993–; Minister in charge of State Nat. Affairs Comm. 1993–; Pres. China-Turkey Friendship Asscn.; Hon. Pres. Chinese Asscn. of Ethnic Minorities for External Exchanges. *Address:* State Nationalities Affairs Commission, 25 Taipingqiao Street, West District, Beijing 100800, People's Republic of China.

ISMAIL MAHSUT; Chinese politician; b. 1940, Xinjiang; joined CCP 1963; Mayor of Urumqi, Xinjiang Uygur Autonomous Region 1990. *Address:* c/o Office of Mayor, Urumqi City, People's Republic of China.

ISOKALLIO, Kaarlo, M.SC.; Finnish business executive; b. 13 May 1948, Helsinki; m. Ammi Kristiina; one d.; ed. Univ. of Tech., Helsinki; Project Engineer Wärtsilä Corpn. 1972–74; Marketing Dir. IBM (Finland) 1974–81; Man. Dir. Kabmatik AB, Sweden 1981–83; with Nokia Corpn. 1983– Dept. Man. Cables Dept., Machinery Div., 1983–85, Pres. Electronics, Information Systems 1985–86, Pres. Information Systems 1986–88, Exec. Pres. Nokia Data Group 1988–90, Pres. and C.O.O. Nokia Corpn. 1990–91, Deputy to C.E.O., Vice-Chair. Group Exec. Bd. 1990; mem. Bd. of Dirs. Oy Lindell Ab 1987–, Taloudellinen Tiedotustoimisto 1991–; mem. Supervisory Bd. Mecrastor Oy 1987–, Oy Rastor Ab 1987–, Helsinki Univ. Cen. Hosp. Foundation 1991–; mem. Bd. Econ. Information Bureau 1991–, ICL PLC 1991–; mem. Tech. Del., Ministry of Trade and Industry 1990–; Chair. Bd. MTV (Finnish commercial TV) 1991–; mem. Acad. for Tech. Sciences 1991. *Address:* c/o Technical Delegation, Ministry of Trade and Industry, Aleksanterinkatu 4, P.O. Box 230, 00171 Helsinki, Finland.

ISOMURA, Hisanori; Japanese broadcasting executive; b. 9 Aug. 1929, Tokyo; one s. one d.; ed. Gakushuin Univ.; joined Nippon Hoso Kyokai (NHK) (Japan Broadcasting Corpn.) as special correspondent Indochina, France 1953, Chief Washington Bureau 1965–71, Dir. Int. News Div., Tokyo Head Office 1971–82, Dir.-Gen. News and Current Affairs 1982–88, Gen. Man. Dir. 1988; special adviser to Dir.-Gen. of UNESCO; Pres. asscn. to construct Japanese cultural centre, Paris; Prof. Japanese Cultural Inst.; Nippon Kisha Club Award 1977. *Leisure interest:* golf.

ISOZAKI, Arata; Japanese architect; b. 23 July 1931, Oita City; s. of Soji Isozaki and Tetsu Isozaki; m. Aiko Miyawaki 1974; two s.; ed. Univ. of Tokyo; with Kenzo Tange's team 1954–63; Pres. Arata Isozaki and Assocs. 1963–; juror, Pritzker Architecture Prize 1979–84, Concours Int. de Parc de la Villette 1982, The Peak Int. Architectural Competition 1983, R. S. Reynolds Memorial Award 1985, The Architectural Competition for the New Nat. Theatre of Japan 1986, competitions for Passenger Terminal Bldg., Kansai Int. Airport 1988, Triangle de la Folie, Paris 1989, Int. Architects' competition, Vienna EXPO '95 1991, Kyoto Station Bldg. Renovation Design competition 1991; visiting prof. at numerous univs. including Harvard, Yale and Columbia; numerous prizes; *works include:* Expo '70, Osaka 1966–70, Oita Medical Hall 1959–69, Annex 1970–72, Oita Prefectural Library 1962–66, head office of Fukuoka Mutual Bank 1968–71, Museum of Modern Art, Gunma 1971–74, Kitakyushu City Museum of Art 1972–74, Kitakyushu Cen. Library 1972–74, Shuko-sha Bldg. 1974–75, Kamioka Town Hall 1975–78, Gymnasium and Dining Hall, NEG Co. 1978–80, Los Angeles Museum of Contemporary Art 1981–86, Tsukuba Centre Building 1978–83, Palladium, New York 1983–85, Sports Hall, Barcelona 1983–90, Brooklyn Museum 1986, Art Tower, Mito 1986–90, Bond Univ., Australia 1987–89, Hara Museum—ARC 1987–88, Kitakyushu Int. Conf. Center 1987–90, Team Disney bldg. 1987–90, Tokyo Univ. of Art and Design 1986–90, Guggenheim Museum, U.S.A. 1991–92, Centre for Advanced Science and Tech., Hyogo 1993, Japanese Art and Tech. Centre, Krakow 1994, Museum of Contemporary Art, Nagi 1994, B-Con Plaza (int. conf. centre) 1995, Toyonokuni Libraries for Cultural Resources 1995, Kyoto Concert Hall 1995, Domus: la casa del hombre, La Coruña, Spain 1995; Hon. Fellow Acad. Tiberina, A.I.A., R.I.B.A. 1994–; Hon. Academician Royal Acad. of Arts 1994; Hon. mem. B.D.A.; Chevalier Ordre des Arts et des Lettres. *Publications include:* Kukane 1971, Kenchiku no Kaitai 1975, Shūho ga 1979, Kenchiku no Shūji 1979, Kenchiku no Seijigaku 1989, Image Game 1990, Arata Isozaki Architecture 1960–90 1991, Kenchiku to iu Keishiki 1991, GA Architect 6—Arata Isozaki (Vol. 1) 1991, Arata Isozaki—Works 30 1992. *Address:* Arata Isozaki and Associates, 6-17, Akasaka 9-chome, Minato-ku, Tokyo 107, Japan. *Telephone:* (03) 3405-1526. *Fax:* (03) 3475-5265.

ISRAEL, Werner, O.C., PH.D., F.R.S.C., F.R.S.; Canadian professor of physics; b. 4 Oct. 1931, Berlin, Germany; s. of Arthur Israel and Marie Kappauf; m. Inge Margulies 1958; one s. one d.; ed. Univ. of Cape Town, S.A. and Trinity Coll., Dublin, Ireland; Asst. Prof., then Full Prof. of Math., Univ. of Alberta 1958–71, Prof. of Physics 1971–96, Univ. Prof. 1986–; Adjunct Prof. of Physics, Univ. of Vic., B.C. 1997–; Pres. Int. Soc. of General Relativity and Gravitation 1997–(2000); Research Scholar, Dublin Inst. for Advanced Studies 1956–58; Fellow Canadian Inst. for Advanced Research 1986–; Hon. D.Sc. (Queen's Univ.) 1987; Dr. h.c. (Univ. de Tours) 1994; Izaak Walton Killam Prize 1983, Tomalla Prize (Tomalla Foundation for Gravitational Research, Switzerland) 1996. *Publications:* (Co-Ed. with S. W. Hawking, q.v.) General Relativity, an Einstein Centenary Survey 1979, 300 Years of Gravitation 1987; numerous papers on black hole theory, general relativity, statistical mechanics. *Leisure interest:* music. *Address:* Department of Physics and Astronomy, University of Victoria, P.O. Box 3055, Victoria, B.C., V8W 3P6; Suite 401, 2323 Hamiota Street, Victoria, B.C., V8R 2N1, Canada (Home). *Telephone:* (250) 721-7708 (Office).

ISRAELACHVILI, Jacob Nissim, PH.D., F.A.A., F.R.S.; Australian/Israeli university professor; b. 19 Aug. 1944, Tel Aviv; s. of Haim Israelachvili and Hela Israelachvili; m. Karin Haglund 1971; two d.; ed. Univ. of Cambridge; Postdoctoral Research Fellow, Cavendish Lab. Cambridge 1971–72; European Molecular Biology Org. (EMBO) Research Fellow, Univ. of Stockholm 1972–74; Professorial Fellow, Inst. of Advanced Studies, Australian Nat. Univ., Canberra 1974–86; Professor of Chemical Eng. and Materials Science, Univ. of Calif. Santa Barbara 1986–; Debye Lecturer, Cornell Univ. 1987; Foreign Assoc. Nat. Acad. of Eng. (U.S.A.) 1996; Pawsey Medal, Australian Acad. of Science 1977. *Publications:* Intermolecular and Surface Forces 1985; numerous scientific publs. on surface forces in liquids and biological membrane structure and interactions. *Leisure interests:* history, backgammon. *Address:* Department of Chemical Engineering, University of California, Santa Barbara, CA 93106 (Office); 2233 Foothill Lane, Santa Barbara, CA 93105, U.S.A. (Home). *Telephone:* (805) 893-8407 (Office); (805) 963-9545 (Home).

ISSELBACHER, Kurt Julius, M.D.; American professor of medicine; b. 12 Sept. 1925, Wirges, Germany; s. of Albert and Flori Isselbacher; m. Rhoda Solin 1950; one s. three d.; ed. Harvard Univ. and Harvard Medical School; Chief. Gastrointestinal Unit, Mass. Gen. Hosp. 1957–88, Chair. Research Cttee. 1967, Dir. Cancer Centre 1987–; Prof. of Medicine Harvard Medical School 1966–, Mallinckrodt Prof. of Medicine 1972, Chair. Exec. Cttee. Medicine Depts. 1968–, Chair. Univ. Cancer Cttee. 1972–87; mem. governing bd. Nat. Research Council 1987–90; Ed.-in-Chief, Harrison's Principles of Internal Medicine 1991–; mem. N.A.S. (Chair. Food and Nutrition Bd. 1983–88, Exec. Cttee. and Council 1987–90); Distinguished Achievement Award, American Gastroenterological Asscn. (AGA) 1983; Friedenwald Medal, AGA 1985, John Phillips Memorial Award, American Coll. of Physicians 1989, Bristol-Myers Squibb Award for Distinguished Achievement in Nutrition Research 1991. *Leisure interest:* tennis. *Address:* Massachusetts General Hospital Cancer Centre, 139 13th Street, Charlestown, MA 02129 (Office); 20 Nobscot Road, Newton Center, MA 02159, U.S.A. (Home). *Telephone:* (617) 726-5610 (Office).

ISSERLIS, Steven John, C.B.E.; British cellist; b. 19 Dec. 1958, London; s. of George Isserlis and Cynthia Isserlis; m. Pauline Mara; one s.; ed. City of London School, Int. Cello Centre, Scotland, Oberlin Coll., Ohio, U.S.A.; London début Wigmore Hall 1977; London concerto début 1980; concerts and recitals throughout the world; artistic dir. IMS Prussia Cove; featured soloist in Channel 4 TV series with Dudley Moore; TV documentary about Schuman and performance of Schuman's cello concerto, Channel 4 TV; numerous recordings; hon. mem. R.A.M.; Piatigorsky Award 1993, Royal Philharmonic Soc. Award. *Publications:* transcription Beethoven Variations in D arranged for violin or cello and piano or harpsichord, edn. of Saint-Saëns pieces for cello and piano. *Leisure interests:* videos, books, gossiping, eating, avoiding practising, sleeping, telling everybody how sleepy I am. *Address:* c/o Harrison & Parrott Ltd., 12 Penzance Place, London, W11 4PA, England. *Telephone:* 0171-229 9166. *Fax:* 0171-221 5042.

ISSING, Otmar, PH.D.; German economist and banker; b. 27 March 1936, Würzburg; s. of Hans Issing and Josefine Issing; m. Sieglinde Issing 1960; Prof. of Econs. Univ. of Erlangen-Nuremberg 1967–73, Univ. of Würzburg 1973–90; mem. Advisory Council, Fed. Ministry of Econs. 1980–90; mem. German Council of Econ. Experts 1988–90; mem. Bd. Deutsche Bundesbank, European Cen. Bank 1998; mem. Cen. Bank Council; mem. Acad. of Sciences and Literature, Mainz, Acad. Europaea, Salzburg; Hon. Prof. Univ. of Würzburg. *Publications:* Introduction to Monetary Policy (6th edn.) 1996, Introduction to Monetary Theory (10th edn.) 1995. *Address:* Georg-Sittig-Strasse 8, 97074 Würzburg, Germany.

ISSOUFOU, Mahamadou; Niger politician; b. 1952, Illéla; Pres. Parti Nigérien pour la Démocratie et le Socialisme (PNDS); Prime Minister of Niger 1993–94. *Address:* c/o Office of the Prime Minister, Niamey, Niger.

ISTOMIN, Eugène George; American pianist; b. 26 Nov. 1925, New York; s. of George T. Istomin and Assia Chavin; m. Marta Montanez Casals 1975; ed. Curtis Inst., Philadelphia; studied under Kyriena Silote, Rudolf Serkin; Concert pianist 1943–; toured with Adolf Busch Chamber Players 1944–45; first European appearance 1950; charter mem. Casals Prades and Puerto Rico festivals 1950–; several world tours; founded Trio with Isaac Stern and Leonard Rose 1961; numerous recordings of solo, orchestral and chamber works; Leventritt Award 1943. *Leisure interests:* archaeology, history, painting, baseball. *Address:* c/o ICM Concerts, 40 West 57th Street, New York, NY 10019, U.S.A. (Office).

ITO, Kosuke; Japanese politician; mem. House of Reps.; fmr. Parl. Vice-Minister for Nat. Land Agency; Dir. Gen. Nat. Land Agency 1996.

IVANCHENKO, Aleksander Vladimirovich, D. JUR.; Russian lawyer; b. 8 Jan. 1954, Krasnodar; m.; one d.; ed. Higher School of Ministry of Internal Affairs; worked in Moscow militia forces; lecturer, Higher School of Ministry of Internal Affairs 1983–88; on staff Supreme Soviet Russian Fed. 1988–93; Deputy Chair., Cen. Election Comm. of Russian Fed. 1993–96, Chair. 1996–. *Publications:* papers and articles on problems of political rights and freedom, on election law. *Leisure interests:* tennis, walks in the countryside. *Address:* Centre of Election Commission, Ilyinka str. 10, Moscow, Russia. *Telephone:* (095) 206 8480 (Office).

IVANIŠEVIĆ, Goran; Croatian tennis player; b. 13 Sept. 1971, Split; s. of Srdjan Ivanišević and Gorana Ivanišević; won US Open jr. doubles with Nargiso 1987; turned professional 1988; joined Yugoslav Davis Cup squad 1988; runner-up, Wimbledon Championship 1992, 1994, 1998; semi-finalist, ATP World Championship 1992; Bronze medal, men's doubles, Barcelona Olympic Games 1992; winner of numerous ATP tournaments, including Kremlin Cup, Moscow 1996.

IVANOV, Igor Sergeyevich; Russian diplomatist; b. 23 Sept. 1945, Moscow; m.; one d.; ed. Moscow Pedagogical Inst. of Foreign Languages; jr. researcher Inst. of World Econs. and Int. Relations, U.S.S.R. Acad. of Sciences 1969–73; diplomatic service 1973–; Second, then First Sec., Counsellor, Counsellor-Envoy U.S.S.R. Embassy, Spain 1973–83; expert First European Dept., Ministry of Foreign Affairs 1983–84; Counsellor of Minister 1984–85; Asst. Minister 1985–86; Deputy Chief, then Chief of Dept. 1987–92; Chief Gen. Sec., mem. of Bd. 1989–91; Russian Amb. to Spain 1991–93; First Deputy Minister of Foreign Affairs 1994–98, Minister Sept. 1998–. *Address:* Ministry of Foreign Affairs, Smolenskaya-Sennaya 32/34, Moscow, Russia. *Telephone:* (095) 244-40-56; 244-41-19.

IVANOV, Mikhail Vladimirovich; Russian microbiologist; b. 6 Dec. 1930; m.; ed. Moscow State Univ.; researcher Inst. of Microbiology, U.S.S.R. Acad. of Sciences, head of lab., Deputy Dir. Inst. of Biochem. and Physiology of Plants and Micro-organisms; Dir. Inst. of Microbiology 1984–; corresp. mem. U.S.S.R. (now Russian) Acad. of Sciences 1981, mem. 1987; research in geochem. activities of microorganisms and biotech., marine microbiology, global ecology and biogeochem.; S. Vernadsky Prize; Ed.-in-Chief Microbiology journal. *Leisure interest:* coin collecting. *Address:* Institute of Microbiology, Russian Academy of Sciences, 60-letiya Oktyabrya pr., 7 kor. 2, 117811 Moscow, Russia. *Telephone:* (095) 135-21-39 (Office); 299-63-17 (Home).

IVANOV, Vadim Tikhonovich; Russian biochemist; b. 18 Sept. 1937; s. of Tikhon Timofeevitch Ivanov and Lidia Ivanovna Ivanovna; m. Raisa Alexandrovna (née Osadchaya) Ivanovna; one s. one d.; ed. Moscow State Univ.; jr., sr. researcher, head of lab., Deputy Dir., Dir. Shemyakin-Ovchinnikov Inst. of Bio-organic Chem. Russian Acad. of Sciences; corresp. mem. U.S.S.R. (now Russian) Acad. of Sciences 1976, mem. 1987, Academician-Sec. Dept. of Biochem. and Biophysics 1996–; research in chem. of proteins and peptides, structure and functions of neuropeptides, synthetic vaccines; Chair. Council New Problems of Bioeng.; Lenin Prize, U.S.S.R. State Prize. *Publications include:* Membrane active complexones 1974, The way to Protein Synthesis 1982. *Leisure interests:* chess, nature. *Address:* Institute of Bio-organic Chemistry, Russian Academy of Sciences, Miklukho-Maklay str. 16/10, 117437 Moscow, Russia. *Telephone:* (095) 330 56 38 (Office). *Fax:* (095) 310 70 07.

IVANOV, Vladimir; Bulgarian physician; b. 6 June 1923, Simeonovgrad; s. of Boris Ivanov and Maria Ivanova; m. Liliana Kirova 1948; one s.; ed. Univ. of Sofia, Acad. of Medical Sciences, Moscow and Univ. of London; Deputy Dir. Scientific Psychoneurological Inst. Sofia 1956–63; Asst. Prof. and Head Dept. of Psychiatry and Medical Psychology, Varna 1963–67, Prof. 1967–85; Deputy Rector, Higher Medical Inst. Varna, 1964–66, Rector 1966–72; Dir. Scientific Inst. of Neurology, Psychiatry and Neurosurgery, Medical Acad. Sofia and Head, First Psychiatric Clinic 1985–88; Ed.-in-Chief Neurology, Psychiatry and Neurosurgery 1987–91; Adviser to Bulgarian Medical Acad. 1988; Pres. Bulgarian Scientific Soc. of Psychosomatic Medicine 1989; mem. Admin. Bd., Union of Scientific Medical Socs. of Bulgaria 1991–95; mem. Council, Neurosciences and Behaviour Foundation 1991–; Ed.-in-Chief Psychosomatic Medicine 1993–; mem. Bulgarian Nat. Acad. of Medicine; several awards and medals. *Publications:* some 14 monographs and numerous articles in professional journals. *Leisure interests:* philosophy, poetry. *Address:* Bulgarian Medical Academy, 1 Psychiatric Clinic, Sofia 1431 (Office); Praga 26, Sofia 1606, Bulgaria (Home). *Telephone:* 52-03-33 (Office); 52-42-68 (Home).

IVANOV, Vyacheslav Vsevolodovich, D.PHIL.; Russian philologist and translator; b. 21 Aug. 1929, Moscow; s. of Vsevolod Vyacheslavovich Ivanov; m.; one s.; ed. Moscow State Univ.; Dir. of the Library of Foreign Literature in Moscow 1991–94; People's Deputy of the U.S.S.R. 1989–91; Dir. Inst. of World Culture 1990–94; Prof. U.C.L.A. 1994–; Lenin Prize 1988; Hon. mem. American Linguistics Soc. 1968. *Publications:* works on Indo-european linguistics, Slavic and general linguistics, semiotics, including: Indo-european, Praslavic and Anatolian linguistic systems 1965, Slavic Linguistic Modelling Systems (with V. Toporov) 1965, Studies in the field of Slavic antiquities (with V. Toporov) 1974, Indo-european language and Indo-europeans v. 1–2 (with T. Gamrekelidze) 1984, Balkan Peninsula in the Mediterranean Context 1986, The Ethnolinguistics of the Text 1988, The Category of Passivity in Slavic and Balkan Languages 1989, Novelties in Linguistics 1990; ed. works on Balto-slavic spiritual culture. *Address:* Slavic Department, University of California at Los Angeles, Los Angeles, CA 90024, U.S.A. *Telephone:* (310) 825-4321.

IVANOVA, Ludmila Nikolayevna; Russian geneticist; b. 10 Feb. 1929; ed. Novosibirsk Inst. of Med.; Head of lab., Inst. of Cytology and Genetics Siberian br. Russian Acad. of Sciences 1971–; corresp. mem., Russian Acad. of Sciences 1991, mem. 1997–; main research in cellular and molecular mechanisms of regulation of permeability of biological membranes. *Address:* Institute of Cytology and Genetics, Akademika Lavretyeva prosp. 10, Novosibirsk, Russia. *Telephone:* (3832) 35 54 74 (Office).

IVANS, Dainis; Latvian politician; b. 25 Sept. 1955, Madona; s. of Evalds Ivans and Ilga Ivans; m. Elvira Chrschenovitch 1979; two s. two d.; school teacher and journalist; Reporter Latvian TV 1980–85; organised opposition to hydro-electric scheme nr. Daugavpils 1986; Ed. School and family magazine 1986–88; Pres. of Latvian People's Front 1988–90; U.S.S.R. People's Deputy 1989–90; Mem. Latvian Supreme Soviet 1990–, Vice-Chair. 1990–91; Gen. Sec. Latvian Comm. of UNESCO 1992–, Sec. Writers Union 1994–. *Leisure interests:* Oriental philosophy, literature, fishing. *Address:* Bruninieku Str. 89, Apt. 6, Riga, Latvia. *Telephone:* (2) 323142 (Office); 274644 (Home).

IVANTER, Ernest Viktorovich; Russian biologist; b. 15 Nov. 1935, Moscow; s. of Victor S. Ivanter and Irina F. Riss; m. Tatjana Matusevich 1960; one s. one d.; ed. Moscow K. Timiryazev Acad. of Agric.; sr. lab., jr. researcher Kivach Karelian br. U.S.S.R. Acad. of Sciences 1958–60; jr. researcher Inst., of Biology Karelian branch of U.S.S.R. Acad. of Sciences 1960–63; asst., docent, Prof. dean Petrozavodsk Univ. 1965–; Chair. Dept. of Zoology and Ecology Petrozavodsk Univ. 1987–; corresp. mem. U.S.S.R. (now Russian) Acad. of Sciences 1991; research in ecology, biocenology, morphophysiology and evolutional ecology of animals; mem. Scientific Council for Biological fundamentals of protection and rational use of Fauna; mem. U.S.A. Zoological Soc.; Hon. mem. Finnish Soc. of Teriologues. *Publications include:* Population Ecology of Small Mammals 1975, Adaptive peculiarities of mammals 1985, Fauna of Karelia 1988, Statistical Methods for Biologists 1992, Zoogeography 1993; numerous articles in scientific journals. *Leisure interests:* books, sport, tourism. *Address:* Petrozadovsk University, Lenin pr. 33, 185640 Petrozavodsk, Russia. *Telephone:* (8142) 7-17-41; 9-99-51 (Office). *Fax:* (8142) 7-21-08.

IVANY, J.W. George, M.A., PH.D.; Canadian university president; b. 26 May 1938, Grand Falls, Newfoundland; s. of Gordon Ivany and Stella Skinner; m. Marsha Gregory 1983; one s. three d.; ed. Memorial Univ. of Newfoundland, Columbia Univ. and Univ. of Alberta; Head of Science Dept. Prince of Wales Coll. St. John's, Newfoundland 1960–63; Grad. Teaching Fellow, Univ. of Alberta 1963–64, Asst. Prof. of Elementary Educ. 1965–66; Asst. Prof. of Natural Science, Teachers Coll. Columbia Univ. 1966–68, Assoc. Prof. 1968–74, Head, Dept. of Science Educ. 1972–74; Visiting Fellow, Inst. of Educ., Univ. of London 1972–73; Dean and Prof. Faculty of Educ., Memorial Univ. of Newfoundland 1974–77; Dean and Prof. Faculty of Educ., Simon Fraser Univ. 1977–84, Vice-Pres. (Academic) 1984–89; Pres. and Vice-Chancellor, Univ. of Sask. 1989–; Chair. Bd. Nat. Inst. of Nutrition 1995–98; various public appts.; Hon. LL.D. (Memorial Univ. Newfoundland) 1991. *Publications include:* High School Teaching: A Report on Current Practices 1972, Today's Science: A Professional Approach to Teaching Elementary School Science 1975, Who's Afraid of Spiders: Teaching Science in the Elementary School 1988; textbooks; articles in professional journals. *Address:* University of Saskatchewan, 105 Administration Place, Saskatoon, Saskatchewan, S1N 5A2, Canada. *Telephone:* (306)-966-6612. *Fax:* (306)-975-1026.

IVEROTH, C. Axel; Swedish business executive; b. 4 Aug. 1914, Ekerö; s. of Carl Carlsson Iveroth and Jenny Iveroth; m. Inger Dorthea Iveroth; two s. two d.; ed. Stockholm School of Econ.; Producer, Swedish Broadcasting Corpn. 1937–41; Sec. Industrial Inst. for Econ. and Social Research 1939–44; Industrial Counsellor, Swedish Embassy, Washington 1944–45; Man. Dir. Cementa 1945–52; Chair. and Man. Dir. Cembureau (Cement Statistical and Tech. Asscn.) 1949–57; Dir.-Gen. Fed. of Swedish Industries 1957–77, Vice-Chair. 1977; Chair. Int. Council of Swedish Industry 1977–81; Ed.-in-Chief Industria 1946, Swedish-American News Exchange 1952–66; Chair. and Founder Industrial Council for Social and Econ. Studies 1948–60; Chair. Advisory Bd. European Productivity Agency, Paris 1954–56; Chair. Swedish Productivity Council 1957–65; Bd. mem. Gen. Export Asscn. of Sweden 1961, Chair. and Exec. Bd. mem. 1971–81; Chair. Sweden-America Foundation 1970–88; Chair. Integration Cttee. of European Industrial Feds. 1958–; Sec.-Gen. Business and Industry Advisory Cttee. to OECD (BIAC) 1962–63, Vice-Chair. 1974–82; Chair. Swedish Nat. Cttee. of the European League for EEC Co-operation 1965; Vice-Chair. Union des Industries de la Communauté européenne, Brussels 1977–79; mem. Bd. Royal Swedish Acad. of Eng. Sciences 1957–; Chair. Securitas Int. AB 1950–83, Banque nat. de Paris, Sweden 1986–88, AIM AB 1985–, Sweden-Japan Foundation 1979–87 (Hon. Chair. 1987–); Chair. Asscn. of Swedish Chambers of Commerce Abroad 1979–; Int. Adviser Swedish Business Group, Japan 1987–; Chair. Swedish Section of the European League for Econ. Co-operation 1975–, Swedish Mastership in Exports 1985–; Knight Commdr. of the Royal Order of Vasa (Sweden), Hon. C.B.E., Officier Ordre de la Couronne (Belgium), Officier, Légion d'honneur, Commdr. Ordine al Merito della Repubblica Italiana, Order of the White Rose of Finland, Third Degree of the Rising Sun (Japan). *Publications:* Handicraft and Small Industries in Sweden 1943, The Good

Society 1980; numerous articles on politics and economics in press and professional journals. *Leisure interests:* angling, skiing.

IVERSEN, Leslie Lars, PH.D., F.R.S.; British scientist; b. 31 Oct. 1937; s. of Svend and Anna Caia Iversen; m. Susan Diana (née Kibble) Iversen 1961; one s. one d. (one d. deceased); ed. Cambridge, Harkness Fellow, U.S.A.; with Nat. Inst. of Mental Health and Dept. of Neurobiology, Harvard Medical School 1964–66; Locke Research Fellow of Royal Soc., Dept. of Pharmacology, Cambridge 1967–71, Dir. MRC Neurochemical Pharmacology Unit 1971–82; Exec. Dir. Merck, Sharp and Dohme Neuroscience Research Centre 1982–95; Visiting Prof., Dept. of Pharmacology, Univ. of Oxford 1995–96, Visiting Prof. of Pharmacology 1996–99; Fellow Trinity Coll., Cambridge 1964–84; Foreign Assoc. N.A.S. 1986. *Publications:* The Uptake and Storage of Noradrenaline in Sympathetic Nerves (with S. D. Iversen) 1967, Behavioural Pharmacology 1975. *Leisure interests:* reading, gardening. *Address:* Department of Pharmacology, University of Oxford, Mansfield Road, Oxford, OX1 3QT, England. *Telephone:* (01865) 271850. *Fax:* (01865) 271882.

IVERSON, Ann; American retail executive; b. 1944; d. of John Earl Van Eenenaam and Dorothy Ann Knight; ed. Arizona State Univ.; m. 4th (divorced); one s. one d.; ed. Arizona Univ.; with Bullock's Dept. Store, L.A., Harzfield's, Kan. City, T.H. Mandy, Va.; Operating Vice-Pres. Bloomingdale's (two main brs.) 1984; Sr. Vice-Pres. of Stores, Region Vice-Pres. Bonwit Teller, NY 1989–90; joined Storehouse (U.K. retailer group) 1989, Stores Dir. British Home Stores (BHS), Chief Exec. Mothercare; Chief Exec. Kay-Bee Toys, Laura Ashley 1995–97.

IVORY, James Francis, M.F.A.; American film director; b. 7 June 1928, Berkeley, Calif.; s. of the late Edward Patrick Ivory and Hallie Millicent De Loney; ed. Univs. of Oregon and Southern California; began to work independently as a film maker 1952; dir., writer and cameraman in first films; Partner (with Indian producer Ismail Merchant (q.v.)) Merchant Ivory Productions 1962–; has collaborated on screenplay of numerous films with author Ruth Prawer Jhabvala (q.v.); Guggenheim Fellow 1974; D. W. Griffith Award (Dirs. Guild of America) 1995; Commdr. Ordre des arts et des lettres. *Films:* documentaries: Venice, Theme and Variations 1957, The Sword and the Flute 1959, The Delhi Way 1964; feature films: The Householder 1963, Shakespeare Wallah 1965, The Guru 1969, Bombay Talkie 1970, Savages 1972, The Wild Party 1975, Roseland 1977, The Europeans 1979, Quartet 1981, Heat and Dust 1983, The Bostonians 1984, A Room with a View 1986, Maurice 1987, Slaves of New York 1989, Mr and Mrs Bridge 1990, Howards End 1992, The Remains of the Day 1993, Jefferson in Paris 1995, Surviving Picasso 1996, A Soldier's Daughter Never Cries 1998, Cotton Mary 1998; TV films: Adventures of a Brown Man in Search of Civilisation 1971, Autobiography of a Princess 1975 (also published as a book 1975), Hullabaloo over Georgie and Bonnie's Pictures 1978, The Five Forty-Eight 1979, Jane Austen in Manhattan 1980. *Leisure interest:* looking at pictures. *Address:* 18 Patroon Street, Claverack, NY 12513, U.S.A. *Telephone:* (212) 582-8049 (Office); (518) 851-7808 (Home).

IWAN, Dafydd, B.ARCH.; Welsh politician, singer-composer and record company manager; b. 24 Aug. 1943, Brynaman, Wales; s. of Rev. Gerallt and Elizabeth Jane Jones; m. 1st Marion Thomas 1968 (divorced 1986); two s. one d.; m. 2nd Bethan Jones 1988; two s.; ed. Aman Valley Grammar School, Ysgol Ty Tan Domen, Y Bala, Univ. Coll. of Wales, Aberystwyth and Welsh School of Arch., Cardiff; f. Sain (Recordiau) Cyf (now Wales' leading record co.) 1969; Man. Dir. 1983–; f. Tai Gwynedd Housing Asscn. 1971; founder-trustee, Nant Gwrtheyrn Language Centre 1975; mem. Nat. Eisteddfod of Wales Council; Chair. Welsh Language Soc. 1968–71; parl. cand. 1974, 1983, 1984; Chair. Plaid Cymru (Nationalist Party of Wales) 1982–84, Vice-Pres. 1984–95; Plaid Cymru mem. of Gwynedd Unitary Authority 1995–; Chair. Planning and Economic Devt. Cttee., Cyngor Gwynedd Council 1995–; Gold Disc for services to Welsh music; hon. mem. Gorsedd of Bards for services to Welsh language; over 40 records, cassettes, CDs and video of live concert 1965–; nonconformist lay preacher. *Publications:* Dafydd Iwan (autobiog.) 1982, 100 O Ganeuon (collection of songs) 1983, Caneuon Dafydd Iwan (2nd collection of songs) 1991. *Leisure interests:* composing songs, sketching, reading. *Address:* SAIN, Llandwrog, Caernarfon, Gwynedd, LL54 5TG (Office); Carrog, Rhos-Bach, Caeathro, Caernarfon, Gwynedd, LL55 2TF, Wales (Home). *Telephone:* (01286) 831-111 (Office); (01286) 76004 (Home). *Fax:* (01286) 831497.

IWATARO, Sukio; Japanese politician; fmr. labour union official; Minister of State and Dir.-Gen. Environment Agency Jan.–Nov. 1996; mem. House of Reps.; mem. Social Democratic Party of Japan (SDPJ). *Address:* c/o Social Democratic Party of Japan, 1-8-1, Nagata-cho, Chiyoda-ku, Tokyo 100, Japan.

IYANAGA, Shokichi; Japanese professor of mathematics; b. 2 April 1906; s. of Katsumi Iyanaga and Kiyono (née Shidachi) Iyanaga; m. Sumiko Kikuchi 1936; three s. one d.; ed. First High School, Univ. of Tokyo and Athénée Français, Tokyo; Assoc. Prof., Univ. of Tokyo 1935–42, Prof. 1942–67, Prof. Emer. 1967–; Visiting Prof., Chicago Univ. 1960–61; Dean Faculty of Science, Univ. of Tokyo 1965–67; Prof., Gakushuin Univ. 1967–77; Assoc. Prof., Univ. of Nancy 1967–68; Pres. Math. Soc. of Japan, Int. Comm. on Math. Instruction 1975–78, Vice-Pres. Council of Admin. Maison franco-japonaise 1978–91; Adviser, Maison franco-japonaise 1991–; Pres. Council of Admin. Tsuda Coll. 1993–95; mem. Science Council of Japan 1948–58, Exec. Cttee. Int. Math. Union 1952–55, Japan Acad. 1978–, Council of Admin. Tsuda Coll. 1995–; Officier, Ordre Palmes Académiques, Officier Légion d'honneur, Order of Rising Sun (2nd Class) 1976. *Publications:* Introduction to Geometry 1968, Theory of Numbers (ed.) 1969, Encyclopaedic Dictionary of Mathematics (editor in chief) 1954, Collected Papers 1994. *Leisure interests:* literature and western music. *Address:* 12-4 Otsuka 6-chome, Bunkyo-ku, Tokyo 112-0012, Japan. *Telephone:* (03) 3945-5977. *Fax:* (03) 3945-9246.

IZETBEGOVIĆ, Alija, PH.D.; Bosnia and Herzegovina politician; b. 8 Aug. 1925, Bosanski Šamac; m.; one s. two d.; ed. Sarajevo Univ.; legal adviser PUT Co., Traffic Inst., Sarajevo; imprisoned for nationalist activities for 3 years 1945, for pan-Islamic activities 1983, released 1988; f. and Chair. Party of Democratic Action (PDA) 1990; elected to Presidency of Bosnia and Herzegovina Nov. 1990, Pres. of the Presidency 1990–96, Co-Pres. 1996–. *Publications:* Islamic Declaration 1970, Islam between East and West 1976, Problems of Islamic Revival 1981, Meditation in Prison 1995, several articles and essays. *Address:* Office of the President, 71000 Sarajevo, Bosnia and Herzegovina.

IZMEROV, Nikolay Fedotovich, M.D.; Russian medical official; b. 19 Dec. 1927, Frunze, Kirghizia; ed. Tashkent Medical School and Moscow Cen. Inst. for Advanced Medical Training; worked as doctor in Khavast rural areas, Tashkent Dist.; Postgraduate training, Moscow 1952–53; Sr. Insp. U.S.S.R. Ministry of Health 1953–55; Postgraduate training (Municipal Hygiene) 1955–58; doctor in Moscow City Sanitary Epidemiological Station 1956–59; Deputy Dir. (Int. Health), Dept. of External Relations, U.S.S.R. Ministry of Health 1960–62; Vice-Minister of Health of R.S.F.S.R., Moscow and Chief Sanitary Insp. 1962–64; Asst. Dir.-Gen. WHO 1964–71; Dir. Inst. of Occupational Health of the U.S.S.R. (now Russian) Acad. of Medical Sciences 1971–; Corresp. mem. Russian Acad. of Medical Sciences 1980, mem. 1986, Acad.-Sec. Dept. of Preventive Medicine 1990–. *Address:* Institute of Occupational Health of the Russian Academy of Medical Sciences, 31 Prospekt Budennogo, Moscow 105275, Russia. *Telephone:* 365-02-09. *Fax:* 365-02-09.

IZRAEL, Yuri Antonievich, DR. PHYS.-MATH. SC.; Russian geophysicist and ecologist; b. 15 May 1930, Tashkent; s. of Antony I. Izrael and Antonina S. Shatalina; m. Elena Sidorova 1958; one s. one d.; ed. Tashkent State Univ.; engineer, research assoc. Geophysics Inst. of U.S.S.R. Acad. of Sciences 1953–63; Deputy Dir., Dir. of Inst. of Applied Geophysics 1963–70; Head of Main Admin. of Hydrometeorological Service of U.S.S.R. 1974–78; First Deputy Head 1970–74, Prof. 1973; Corresp. mem. U.S.S.R. (now Russian) Acad. of Sciences 1974, mem. 1994, Acad.-Sec., Dept. of Oceanography, Atmospheric Physics and Geography 1996–; mem. Russian Acad. of Ecology 1994; Chair. U.S.S.R. State Cttee. for Hydrometeorology and Environmental Control 1978–88; Chair. U.S.S.R. State Cttee. for Hydrometeorology 1988–91, Dir. Research Inst. of Global Climate and Ecology 1990–; Deputy to Supreme Soviet 1979–89; Sec. and First Vice-Pres. World Meteorological Org. 1975–87; Vice-.Chair. Intergovernmental Panel on Climate Change; Mem. Int. Acad. of Astronautics 1990; State Prize in the field of Environment 1981, Gold medal of U.S.S.R. Acad. of Sciences in the field of Ecology 1983, Gold Medal (per Chernobyl) of Int. Centre "Ettore Majorana" (Italy) 1990, Gold Medal of Soviet State Exhbn. 1991, UN-UNEP Sasakawa Environmental Prize 1992, Gold Medal and Prize of Int. Meteorological Org. 1992; state orders. *Publications:* Peaceful Nuclear Explosions and Environment 1974, Ecology and Control of Environment 1983, Global Climatic Catastrophes 1986, Antropogenic Climate Change 1987, Antropogenic Ecology of the Ocean 1989, Chernobyl: Radioactive Contamination of the Environment 1990, Earth's Ozone Shield and its Changes (co-author) 1992, Radioactive Fallout after Nuclear Explosions and Accidents 1996, and numerous other scientific books and articles. *Leisure interests:* organ music, mountaineering, philately. *Address:* Institute of Global Climate and Ecology, Glebovskogo str. 20B, 107258 Moscow (Office); Apt. 84, Romanov per. 3, 84, Moscow, Russia (Home). *Telephone:* (095) 169-24-30 (Office); 203-81-59 (Home). *Fax:* (095) 160-08-31.

IZRAELEWICZ, Erik, D.ECON.; French journalist; b. 6 Feb. 1954, Strasbourg; ed. Haute Ecole de Commerce, Centre de Formation des Journalistes and Univ. de Paris I; journalist, L'Expansion 1981–85; Banking Finance Ed. Le Monde 1986–88, Head of Econ. Service 1989–92, Deputy Ed.-in-Chief 1992–94, New York corresp. 1993–94, econs. reporter, Europe 1994–95, leader writer 1994, Ed.-in-Chief 1996. *Address:* c/o Le Monde, 21 bis rue Claude Bernard, Paris, Cedex 05, France.

IZZO, Lucio; Italian economist and financial executive; b. 5 April 1932, Rome; m. Marga Berg; two d.; ed. Univ. of Oxford and M.I.T.; Econ. Research Dept., Bank of Italy 1958–60, 1962–63; Rockefeller Fellow, Dept. of Econs., M.I.T. 1960–62; Asst. Prof. of Econs., Univ. of Rome 1963–66; Assoc. Prof., then Prof. of Econs., Univ. of Siena 1966–74; Visiting Prof. of Econs., L.S.E. 1971–72; Prof. of Econs., Univ. of Rome 1975; Econ. Adviser to Minister of the Budget 1974–78, to Minister of the Treasury 1980–82; Vice-Pres. and Vice-Chair. Bd. of Dirs. European Investment Bank (EIB) 1982; Italian Rep. OECD Working Party 3, Econ. Policy Cttee. 1976–81; mem. American Econ. Asscn., American Finance Asscn., Econometric Soc.; Pres. of Italy's Gold Medal for studies in field of public finance 1978.

J

JAAKSON, Ernst; Estonian diplomatist; b. 11 Aug. 1905, Riga, Latvia; s. of Jaan Jaakson and Marie Jaakson; m. (wife deceased); ed. German Gymnasium, Riga, Univs. of Latvia and Tartu and Columbia Univ., New York; served at Estonian Legation in Riga and at Ministry of Foreign Affairs, Tallinn; Sec. Estonian Consulate, San Francisco 1929, New York 1932; later Vice-Consul and Consul of Estonia, New York; Consul-Gen. of Estonia in charge of Legation, New York 1965–91; Perm. Rep. of Estonia to UN 1991–94, Special Adviser to Mission of Estonia 1994–; Amb. to U.S.A. 1991–93, Consul-Gen. at UN 1993–. *Address:* Permanent Mission of Estonia to the United Nations, Suite 2415, 630 Fifth Avenue, New York, NY 10111, U.S.A.

JABŁOŃSKI, Henryk, PH.D.; Polish politician and historian; b. 27 Dec. 1909, Waliszew; s. of Władysław Jabłoński and Pelagia Jabłońska; m. Jadwiga Wierzbicka 1946; one s. one d.; ed. Univ. of Warsaw; Prof. Acad. of Political Sciences, Warsaw 1946–50, Warsaw Univ. 1950–80; mem. Nat. Council 1945–47, Deputy to Sejm (Parl.) 1947–89; Deputy Minister of Educ. 1947–53; Sec. Polish Socialist Party 1946–48; mem. Polish United Workers' Party (PZPR) 1948–90, mem. Cen. Cttee. 1948–81, 1986–90, Deputy mem. Political Bureau 1970–71, mem. 1971–81; Minister of Higher Educ. 1965–66; Minister of Educ. and Higher Educ. 1966–72; Pres. Council of State (Head of State) 1972–85; Maj.-Gen. 1988; corresp. mem. Polish Acad. of Sciences 1952–56, mem. 1956–, Vice-Pres. 1966–71; mem. Presidium of All-Polish Cttee. of Nat. Unity Front 1972–76, Chair. 1976–83; Chair. of the Supreme Council of the Asscn. of Fighters for Freedom and Democracy 1983–90; mem. Acad. of Romanian Repub. 1965–; mem. Czech. Acad. of Sciences 1965–; Foreign mem. U.S.S.R. (now Russian) Acad. of Sciences 1966–; mem. Mongolian Acad. of Sciences 1975–; corresp. mem. Mexican Acad. of History 1979–; Hon. mem. Club of Rome; Hon. L.H.D. (Moscow), Dr. h.c. (Bucharest Univ., Higher School of Econs., Wrocław) 1972, (Loránd Eötvös Univ.) 1973, (Łódź) 1975, (Wrocław) 1975, (Jagellonian Univ., Cracow) 1980, (Higher School of Pedagogics, Cracow) 1985; State Prize (2nd class) 1955, (1st class) 1964, Special State Prize 1979; Grand Cross, Order of Polonia Restituta 1974, Order of Banner of Labour (First Class) 1959, Order of the Builders of People's Poland 1964, Order of Friendship of Nations, Grand Croix Légion d'honneur, Great Ribbon, Order of Leopold (Belgium) and numerous other orders and decorations. *Publications:* The Military Criminal Court in 1794 1935, Aleksander Waszkowski—Warsaw's Last Military Chief in the Insurrection of 1863-64 1937, Public Opinion, Parliament and the Press, At the Origins of the Present Day 1947, Polish National Autonomy in the Ukraine in 1917–18, 1948, The Policy of the Polish Socialist Party during the First World War 1958, The Birth of the Second Republic 1918–19 1962, School, Teacher, Education 1972, Independence and National Traditions 1978, International Importance of Polish Fights for National Independence in XVIII and XIX Centuries 1978, Selected Works Vols. I-III 1986, Vols. IV-VI 1988. *Leisure interests:* reading, walking. *Address:* ul. Filtrowa 61 m. 4, 02-056 Warsaw, Poland. *Telephone:* (22) 825 47 52.

JACK, Kenneth Henderson, O.B.E., F.R.S.; British professor of applied crystal chemistry; b. 12 Oct. 1918, North Shields, Northumberland (now Tyne and Wear); s. of late John Henderson Jack and Emily Jack (née Cozens); m. Alfreda Hughes 1942 (died 1974); two s.; ed. Tynemouth Municipal High School, King's Coll., Univ. of Durham, Fitzwilliam Coll., Univ. of Cambridge; Experimental Officer Ministry of Supply 1940–41; Lecturer in Chem., Univ. of Durham 1941–45, 1949–52, 1953–57; Sr. Scientific Officer British Iron and Steel Research Asscn. 1945–49; Research at Cavendish Lab., Cambridge 1947–49; Research Engineer Westinghouse Electrical Corpn., Pittsburgh, Pa., U.S.A. 1952–53; Research Dir. Thermal Syndicate Ltd., Wallsend 1957–64; Prof. of Applied Crystal Chem. Univ. of Newcastle-upon-Tyne 1964–84, Prof. Emer. 1984–; Consultant Cookson Group PLC 1986–94; Hon. Prof. Univ. of Wales, Swansea 1996–; Dir. Wolfson Research Group for High-Strength Materials 1970–84; Fellow American Ceramic Soc. 1984; Hon. mem. Soc. Française de Métallurgie 1984; mem. Acad. of Ceramics 1989; hon. mem. Materials Research Soc. (India) 1991, Ceramics Soc. of Japan 1991; numerous awards and prizes including Prince of Wales Award for Industrial Innovation and Production 1984, Royal Soc. Armourers and Brasiers Award 1988, Inst. of Metals Griffith Medal 1989, American Ceramic Soc. Sosman Lecturer 1989. *Publications:* papers on solid state chem., crystallography, metallurgy, ceramic science and glass tech. in scientific journals and conference proceedings. *Leisure interest:* walking. *Address:* Cookson House, Willington Quay, Wallsend, Tyne and Wear, NE28 6UQ (Office); 147 Broadway, Cullercoats, North Shields, Tyne and Wear, NE30 3TA, England (Home). *Telephone:* (0191) 2622211 (Office); (0191) 2573664 (Home). *Fax:* (0191) 2633847.

JACKAMAN, Michael Clifford John, M.A.; British businessman; s. of Air Commodore Clifford Thomas Jackaman and Lily Margaret Jackaman; m. Valerie Jane Pankhurst 1960; one s. one d.; ed. Felsted School, Essex, Jesus Coll., Cambridge; with Yardley Ltd. 1959–60, Beecham Foods Ltd. 1960–63, John Harvey & Sons Ltd. 1963–65, Findus Ltd. 1965, Harveys of Bristol 1966–92 (Chair. 1969–92); Marketing Dir. Allied Breweries Ltd. 1978–80, Deputy Man. Dir. 1978–83; Chair. Allied Vintners Ltd. 1983–88; Chair. and C.E.O. Hiram Walker–Allied Vintners Ltd. 1988–91; Chair. Allied-Lyons (now Allied Domecq) PLC 1991–96; Chair. Grand Appeal, Royal Hosp. for Sick Children, Bristol 1996–; Dir. Rank Group PLC 1992–97, Kleinwort Benson Group 1994–98. *Leisure interests:* opera, gardening, tennis, walking, oriental antiques. *Address:* Appeal Office, Royal Hospital for Children, 24 Upper Maudlin Street, Bristol, BS2 8DJ, England. *Telephone:* (0117) 928 3850. *Fax:* (0117) 929 3718.

JACKLIN, Bill, M.A., R.A.; British artist and painter; b. 1 Jan. 1943, Hampstead; s. of Harold Jacklin and Alice Jacklin; m. 1st Lesley Berman 1979 (divorced 1993); m. 2nd Janet Russo 1993; ed. Walthamstow School of Art, London and Royal Coll. of Art; teacher at numerous art colls. 1967–75; moved to New York 1985. *One-man shows include:* Nigel Greenwood, Inc. 1970, 1971, 1975, Hester van Royen Gallery 1973, 1977, Marlborough Fine Art 1980, 1983, 1988, 1992, 1997, Marlborough Gallery, New York 1985, 1987, 1990, 1997, "Urban Portraits", Museum of Modern Art, Oxford 1992, Hong Kong Art Centre 1995. *Paintings included in following collections:* Arts Council of G.B., British Council, British Museum, Metropolitan Museum of Art, New York, Museum of Modern Art, New York, Tate Gallery, Victoria and Albert Museum; Artist-in-Residence British Council, Hong Kong 1993-95. *Leisure interest:* walking. *Address:* c/o Marlborough Fine Art, 6 Albemarle Street, London, W1X 4BY, England.

JACKLIN, Tony, C.B.E.; British golfer; b. 7 July 1944, Scunthorpe; s. of Arthur David Jacklin and Doris Lillian Jacklin; m. Vivien Jacklin 1966 (died 1988); two s. one. d.; m. 2nd Astrid May Waagen 1988; one s. one step-s. one step-d.; Lincolnshire Open champion 1961; professional 1962–85, 1988–; won British Asst. Professionals' title 1965; won Dunlop Masters 1967, 1973; first British player to win British Open since 1951 1969; U.S. Open Champion 1970; first British player to win U.S. Open since 1920 and first since 1900 to hold U.S. and British Open titles simultaneously; Greater Greensboro Open champion, U.S.A. 1968, 1972; won Italian Open 1973, German Open 1979, Venezuelan Open 1979, Jersey Open 1981, British P.G.A. champion 1982 and 15 major tournaments in various parts of the world; played in eight Ryder Cup matches and four times for England in World Cup; Capt. of 1983 G.B. and Europe Ryder Cup Team; Capt. of victorious European Ryder Cup Team 1985 (first win for Europe since 1957), 1987; BBC TV golf commentator; moved to Sotogrande, Spain from Jersey Oct. 1983, Commr. of Golf, Las Aves Club, Sotogrande 1983–; Dir. of Golf, San Roque Club 1988–; Hon. Life Pres. British Professional Golfers' Asscn.; Hon. Fellow, Birmingham Polytechnic 1989. *Publications:* Golf With Tony Jacklin 1969, The Price of Success 1979, Jacklin's Golfing Secrets (with Peter Dobereiner), The First Forty Years (with Renton Laidlaw) 1985. *Address:* c/o IMG, 1 Erieview Plaza, Cleveland, Ohio 44114, U.S.A.

JACKSON, Betty, M.B.E.; British couturier; b. 24 June 1949, Lancashire; d. of Arthur Jackson and Phyllis Gertrude Jackson; m. David Cohen 1985; one s. one d.; ed. Bacup and Rawtenstall Grammar School and Birmingham Coll. of Art and Design; Chief Designer Quorum 1975–81; f. Betty Jackson Ltd. 1981, Dir. 1981–; opened Betty Jackson retail shop 1991; Fellow Birmingham Polytech. 1989, Univ. of Cen. Lancashire 1993; Hon. Fellow RCA 1989, part-time tutor 1982–; Designer of the Year 1985, Royal Designer for Industry (Royal Soc. of Arts) 1988, 1989, Fil d'Or, Int. Linen 1989. *Leisure interests:* reading, listening to music. *Address:* Betty Jackson Ltd., 1 Netherwood Place, Netherwood Road, London, W14 0BW, England. *Telephone:* 0171-602 6023. *Fax:* 0171-602 3050.

JACKSON, Colin Ray, M.B.E.; British athlete; b. 18 Feb. 1967; mem. Brecon Athletics Club; honours (110m. hurdles) include: Silver Medal European Jr. Championships 1985, Gold Medal World Jr. Championships 1986, Silver Medal Commonwealth Games 1986, Silver Medal European Cup 1987, Bronze Medal World Championships 1987, Silver Medal Olympic Games 1988, Silver Medal World Cup 1989, Gold Medal European Cup 1989, 1993, Gold Medal Commonwealth Games 1990, Gold Medal World Cup 1992, Gold Medal (and new world record) World Championships 1993 (Silver Medal 4 x 100m. relay); honours (60m. hurdles): Silver Medal World Indoor Championships 1989, 1993, Gold Medal European Indoor Championships 1989 (Silver Medal 1987), 1994, Gold Medals European and Commonwealth Championships 1994; Gold Medal European Championships 1998; mem. Brecon Athletics Club, U.K. Int. 1985–; numerous Welsh, U.K., European and Commonwealth records.

JACKSON, Daryl Sanders, A.O., DIP.ARCH., B.ARCH., L.F.R.A.I.A., A.R.I.B.A.; Australian architect; b. 7 Feb. 1937, Clunes, Victoria; s. of Cecil John Jackson and Doreen May Sanders; m. Kay Parsons 1960; one s. three d.; ed. Wesley Coll., Melbourne, Royal Melbourne Inst. of Tech., Univ. of Melbourne; Asst., Edwards, Madigan and Torzillo, Sydney 1959, Don Henry Fulton, Melbourne 1960, Chamberlin, Powell and Bon, London 1961–63, Paul Rudolph, New Haven, Conn. 1963–64, Skidmore, Owings and Merrill, San Francisco 1964; Partner, Daryl Jackson, Evan Walker Architects, Melbourne 1965–79; Dir. Daryl Jackson Pty. Ltd. Architects 1979–; Dir. Daryl Jackson, Robin Dyke Pty. Ltd. (Sydney) 1985–; Prof. Assoc. Architecture Melbourne Univ. 1985–; Pres. Wesley Coll. Council, Melbourne 1993–; Dir. Daryl Jackson Alastair Swayn Pty. Ltd. (Canberra); Dir. Daryl Jackson Int. Ltd. (London) 1989–;

Dir. RAIA Victorian Chapter Housing Service 1966–69; mem. RAIA Victorian Chapter Council 1967–77, Victorian Tapestry Workshop Cttee. 1975–84, Parl. House Construction Authority, Canberra 1985–89, Victorian Arts Centre Trust 1991, Melbourne Cricket Club 1992– (Vice-Pres. 1997–); Trustee, Nat. Gallery of Vic. 1983–95; Chair. Australian Film Inst. 1990–94, Melbourne Major Events Co. Ltd. 1991–; Assoc. R.I.B.A.; Life Fellow Royal Australian Inst. of Architects; Hon. F.A.I.A.; numerous architectural and design awards. *Publications:* Daryl Jackson Architecture: Drawings and Photos 1984, Daryl Jackson, The Master Architect 1996, numerous articles and papers. *Major works:* Y.W.C.A. Community Resource Centre, Suva, Fiji 1973, Princes Hill High School, Melbourne 1973, Methodist Ladies' Coll., Library Resource Centre, Melbourne 1973, City Edge Housing Devt., Melbourne 1976, School of Music, Canberra 1976, Asscn. for Modern Educ. School, Canberra 1977, Emu Ridge Govt. Housing Devt., Canberra 1978, School of Art, Canberra 1980, McLachlan Offices, Canberra 1980, The Walter and Eliza Hall Inst. of Medical Research, Melbourne 1982, Nat. Sports Centre, Swimming Training Hall, Bruce, A.C.T. 1982, Australian Chancery Complex, Riyadh, Saudi Arabia 1987, Hyatt Hotel, Canberra, Bond Univ., Gold Coast 1989, Commercial Union Office Bldg., Melbourne 1990, Melbourne Cricket Ground Southern Stand 1991, 120 Collins Street, Melbourne, Methodist Ladies' Coll. Music School, Kew 1994, Subiaco Oval Redevelopment, Perth 1994, Wesley Coll. Pre-Preparatory School, Prahran 1995, Brisbane Cricket Ground Redevelopment, 'The Gabba' 1995. *Address:* 161 Hotham Street, East Melbourne, Vic. 3002, Australia (Home).

JACKSON, Edwin Sydney, F.S.A., F.C.I.A., B.COM.; Canadian financial executive; b. 17 May 1922, Regina, Sask.; s. of late Edwin and Dorothy Hazel (née Bell) Jackson; m. Nancy Joyce (née Stovel) 1948; three d.; ed. Univ. of Manitoba; joined Mfrs. Life Insurance Co. 1948, Pres. and CEO 1972, Chair. and C.E.O. 1985–87, Chair. 1987–90, Vice-Chair. 1990–; Pres. Canadian Inst. of Actuaries 1966–67; Chair. Life Office Man. Asscn. 1982–83; Chair. Canadian Life and Health Insurance Asscn. 1977–78; Dir. American Coll. of Life Insurance; Dir. Manufacturers Life Capital Corpn. Inc.; mem. Soc. of Actuaries; Past Pres. Ont. Div. Canadian Arthritis and Rheumatism Soc.; Dir. Canadian Centre for Philanthropy. *Leisure interests:* skiing, curling, golf. *Address:* 101 Stratford Crescent, Toronto, Ont. M4N 1C7, Canada.

JACKSON, Francis Alan, D.MUS., F.R.C.O.; British organist and composer; b. 2 Oct. 1917, Malton, Yorks.; s. of William Altham Jackson and Eveline May (née Suddaby); m. Priscilla Procter 1950; two s. one d.; ed. York Minster Choir School and with Sir Edward Bairstow; Organist Malton Parish Church 1933–40; war service with 9th Lancers in N. Africa and Italy 1940–46; Asst. Organist York Minster 1946, Master of the Music 1946–82, Organist Emer. 1988–; Conductor York Musical Soc. 1947–82, York Symphony Orchestra 1947–80; now freelance organist and composer; published works include Symphony in D minor 1957, Organ Concerto 1985, Eclogue for piano and organ 1987, organ music including 4 sonatas, 3 duets, church music, songs and monodramas, Blessed City: The Life and Works of Edward C. Bairstow 1996; Patron, Whitlock Trust; Hon. D.Univ. (York) 1983; Hon. Fellow Royal School of Church Music, Westminster Choir Coll., Princeton, N.J., U.S.A., Royal Northern Coll. of Music; Order of St. William of York 1983. *Leisure interests:* gardening, art and architecture. *Address:* Nether Garth, East Acklam, Malton, North Yorkshire, YO17 9RG, England. *Telephone:* (01653) 658395.

JACKSON, Frank Cameron, PH.D., F.A.H.A.; Australian professor of philosophy; b. 31 Aug. 1943, Melbourne; s. of Allan C. Jackson and Ann E. Jackson; m. Morag E. Fraser 1967; two d.; ed. Melbourne and La Trobe Univs.; Prof. of Philosophy, Monash Univ., Vic. 1978–86, 1991; Prof. of Philosophy, A.N.U. 1986–90, 1992–, Dir. Inst. of Advanced Studies 1998–. *Publications:* Perception 1978, Conditionals 1986, The Philosophy of Mind and Cognition 1996, From Metaphysics to Ethics 1998, Mind, Method and Conditionals 1998. *Leisure interests:* reading, tennis. *Address:* Chancelry, Australian National University, A.C.T. 0200; 33 David Street, O'Connor, A.C.T. 2602, Australia. *Telephone:* (2) 6279 8487 (Office). *Fax:* (2) 6279 9614.

JACKSON, Glenda, C.B.E.; British actress and politician; b. 9 May 1936, Birkenhead, Cheshire; d. of Harry and Joan Jackson; m. Roy Hodges 1958 (divorced 1976); one s.; ed. Royal Acad. of Dramatic Art; fmr. mem. Royal Shakespeare Co. where roles included Ophelia in Hamlet and Charlotte Corday in Marat/Sade (in London and New York); played Queen Elizabeth I in television series Elizabeth R; Pres., Play Matters (fmrly Toy Libraries Asscn.) 1976–; Dir. United British Artists 1983–; Hon. D.Litt (Liverpool) 1978, Hon. LL.M. (Nottingham) 1992; Hon. Fellow, Liverpool Polytechnic 1987; Acad. Award ("Oscar") for Women in Love 1971, for A Touch of Class 1974; Labour M.P. for Hampstead and Highgate 1992–; Parl. Under-Sec. of State, Dept. for the Environment and Transport May 1997–. *Plays include:* Marat/Sade, New York and Paris 1965, The Investigation 1965, Hamlet 1965, US 1966, Three Sisters 1967, Collaborators 1973, The Maids 1974, Hedda Gabler 1975, The White Devil 1976, Antony and Cleopatra 1978, Rose 1980, Strange Interlude 1984, Phaedra 1984, 1985, Across from the Garden of Allah 1986, Strange Interlude 1986, The House of Bernarda Alba 1986, Macbeth 1988, Scenes from an Execution 1990, Mermaid 1990, Mother Courage 1990, Mourning Becomes Electra 1991. *Films include:* Marat/Sade 1966, Negatives 1968, Women in Love 1969, The Music Lovers 1970, Sunday, Bloody Sunday 1971, The Boy Friend 1971, Mary, Queen of Scots 1971, The Triple Echo 1972, Bequest to the Nation 1972, A Touch of Class 1973, The Romantic Englishwoman 1975, The Tempter 1975, The Incredible Sarah 1976, The Abbess of Crewe 1976, Stevie 1977, Hedda 1977, House Calls 1978, The Class of Miss McMichael 1978, Lost and Found 1979, Hopscotch 1980, The Return of the Soldier 1982, Giro City 1982, Summit Conference 1982, Great and Small 1983, And Nothing But the Truth 1984, Turtle Diary 1985, Beyond Therapy 1985, Business as Usual 1986, Salome's Last Dance 1988, The Rainbow 1989, The Secret Life of Sir Arnold Bax 1992. *Television appearances include:* Elizabeth R 1971, Sakharov 1984; Dir. United British Artists 1983–. *Leisure interests:* gardening, reading, listening to music. *Address:* House of Commons, London, SW1A 0AA, England.

JACKSON, Rev. Jesse Louis; American clergyman and civic leader; b. 8 Oct. 1941, Greenville, N. Carolina; s. of Charles Henry and Helen Jackson; m. Jacqueline Lavinia Brown 1964; three s. two d.; ed. Univ. of Illinois, Illinois Agricultural and Tech. Coll., Chicago Theological Seminary; ordained to Ministry Baptist Church 1968; active Black Coalition for United Community Action 1969; Co-Founder Operation Breadbasket S. Christian Leadership Conf.; Co-ordinating Council Community Orgs., Chicago 1966, Nat. Dir. 1966–77; Founder and Exec. Dir. Operation PUSH (People United to Save Humanity), Chicago 1971–; unsuccessful cand. for Democratic nomination for U.S. Presidency 1983–84, 1987–88; TV Host, Voices of America 1990–; Pres. Award Nat. Medical Asscn. 1969; Humanitarian Father of the Year Award Nat. Father's Day Cttee. 1971. *Address:* c/o Rainbow PUSH Coalition, 930 E. 50th Street, Chicago, IL 60615, U.S.A.

JACKSON, (Kevin) Paul, B.A., F.I.D.; British television producer and executive; b. 2 Oct. 1947, London; s. of T. Leslie Jackson and Jo Spoonley; m. Judith E. Cain 1981; two d.; ed. Gunnersbury Grammar School and Univ. of Exeter; stage man. Marlowe Theatre, Canterbury 1970, Thorndike Theatre, Leatherhead 1971; production work for BBC TV: Two Ronnies, 3 of a Kind, Carrott's Lib, The Young Ones, Happy Families 1971–82; freelance producer and dir. Canon and Ball, Girls on Top 1982–84; Producer and Chair. Paul Jackson Productions: Red Dwarf, Don't Miss Wax, Saturday Live 1984–86; Exec. Producer, Appointments of Dennis Jennings (Acad. Award 'Oscar' for Best Live Action Short 1989); Man. Dir. NGTV 1987–91; Dir. of Progs. Carlton TV 1991–93, Man. Dir. Carlton TV 1993–94, Carlton U.K. Productions 1994–96; now Controller BBC Entertainment; Chair. Comic Relief 1987–98; Vice-Chair. Charity Projects 1990–92, Chair. 1992–98; Chair. RTS 1994–96; Stanford Exec. Programme; Fellow Inst. of Dirs.; BAFTA 1983, 1984. *Leisure interests:* theatre, rugby, travel, food and wine, friends and family. *Address:* Room 4152, BBC Television Centre, Wood Lane, London, W12 7RJ, England.

JACKSON, Michael, B.A.; British broadcasting executive; b. 11 Feb. 1958; s. of Ernest Jackson and Margaret Jackson (née Kearsley); ed. King's School, Macclesfield, Polytechnic of Cen. London; Organiser Channel 4 Group 1979; Producer The Sixties 1982; ind. producer Beat Productions Ltd. 1983–87; Ed. The Late Show, BBC TV (B.F.I. Award) 1988–90; with Late Show Productions 1990–91; Head of Music and Arts BBC TV 1991–93, Controller BBC2 1993–96, Controller BBC1 and BBC Dir. of TV 1996–97; C.E.O., Dir. of Programmes Channel 4 1997–; programmes produced include: Whose Town is it Anyway?, Open the Box, The Media Show, The Nelson Mandela Tribute, Tales from Prague (Grierson Documentary Award), Moving Pictures, The American Late Show (Public Broadcasting Service, U.S.A.), Naked Hollywood (B.A.F.T.A. Best Factual Series Award), Sounds of the Sixties, The Lime Grove Story, TV Hell; Hon. D. Litt. (Westminster) 1995. *Leisure interests:* reading, walking. *Address:* Channel 4 Television, 124 Horseferry Road, London, SW1P 2TX, England. *Telephone:* 0171-396 4444.

JACKSON, Michael Joseph; American singer; b. 29 Aug. 1958, Gary, Ind.; s. of Joseph W. and Katherine E. (Scruse) Jackson; m. 1st Lisa Presley 1994 (divorced 1996); m. 2nd Debbie Rowe 1996; one s.; ed. privately; lead singer, Jackson Five (group now called Jacksons) 1969; records for Epic Records; recordings include Off The Wall 1979, Thriller (listed in Guinness Book of Records as the most successful LP in record history) 1982, BAD, Dangerous 1991, HIStory: Past, Present and Future, Book 1 1995; appeared in films The Wiz 1978, Moonwalker 1988 and has made numerous television appearances; performed at Silver Jubilee of H.M. Queen Elizabeth II 1977; leader of Jackson's US Tour; recipient of gold and platinum record awards; numerous other awards. *Publication:* Moonwalk (autobiog.) 1988, Dancing the Dream, Poems and Reflections 1992. *Address:* c/o Bob Jones, 9255 Sunset Boulevard, # 1100, Los Angeles, CA 90069, U.S.A.

JACKSON, Peter; film director; b. New Zealand. *Films:* Meet the Feebles, Bad Taste, Dead Alive, Heavenly Creatures, The Frighteners. *Address:* c/o ICM, 8942 Wilshire Boulevard, Beverly Hills, CA 90211, U.S.A.

JACKSON, Peter John, B.S.C.; British business executive; b. 16 Jan. 1947, Sheffield; two s. one d.; ed. Univ. of Leeds; personnel and industrial relations positions at British Steel, Comm. on Industrial Relations, Guthrie Industries 1968–76; Dir. Personnel and Employee Relations, Deputy Man. Dir. Perkins Engines (Shrewsbury), Perkins Engines Group 1976–87; Personnel Dir. British Sugar PLC 1987–88, Deputy Man. Dir. 1988–89, Man. Dir. 1989–93, Chief Exec. 1994–; Dir. Assoc. British Foods PLC 1992–, C. Czarnikow Sugar Ltd. 1993–. *Address:* British Sugar PLC, Oundle Road, Peterborough, PE2 9QU, England. *Telephone:* (01733) 563171.

JACKSON, Rashleigh Esmond; Guyanese diplomatist; b. 12 Jan. 1929, New Amsterdam, Berbice; two s. two d.; ed. Queen's Coll., Georgetown, Univ. Coll., Leicester, England, Columbia Univ., New York.; entered public service 1948; Master, Queen's Coll. 1957; Prin. Asst. Sec., Ministry of Foreign Affairs 1965, Perm. Sec. 1969–73; Perm. Rep. to UN 1973–78; Minister for Foreign Affairs 1978–90; consultant 1992–; Pres. UN Council for Namibia 1974; Chair. Caribbean Task Force on Environment 1991–92; Man. Dir. Public Affairs Consulting Enterprise (PACE) 1993–; mem. Bd. of Dirs. Environmental Protection Agency Guyana 1997–. *Address:* 182 Republic Park, East Bank, Demerara, Guyana. *Telephone:* 72847. *Fax:* (2) 55512.

JACKSON, Samuel L.; American actor; b. 1949, Washington; m. LaTanya Richardson; one d.; ed. Morehouse Coll.; co-f. and mem. Just Us theatre co., Atlanta. *Stage appearances:* Home, A Soldier's Story, Sally/Prince, Colored People's Time, Mother Courage, Spell No. 7, The Mighty Gents, The Piano Lesson, Two Trains Running, Fences. *TV appearances:* (series) Movin' On 1972, Ghostwriter 1992; (films) The Trial of the Moke 1978, Uncle Tom's Cabin 1987, Common Ground 1990, Dead and Alive: The Race for Gus Farace 1991, Simple Justice 1993, Assault at West Point 1994, Against the Wall 1994. *Film appearances include:* Together for Days 1972, Ragtime 1981, Eddie Murphy Raw 1987, Coming to America 1988, School Daze 1988, Do The Right Thing 1989, Sea of Love 1989, A Shock to the System 1990, Def by Temptation 1990, Betsy's Wedding 1990, Mo' Better Blues 1990, The Exorcist III 1990, GoodFellas 1990, Return of the Superfly 1990, Jungle Fever 1991 (Best Actor Award, Cannes Int. Film Festival, New York Film Critics' Award), Strictly Business 1991, Juice 1992, White Sands 1992, Patriot Games 1992, Johnny Suede 1992, Jumpin' at the Boneyard 1992, Fathers and Sons 1992, National Lampoon's Loaded Weapon 1 1993, Amos & Andrew 1993, Menace II Society 1993, Jurassic Park 1993, True Romance 1993, Hail Caesar 1994, Fresh 1994, The New Age 1994, Pulp Fiction 1994, Losing Isaiah 1995, Kiss of Death 1995, Die Hard With a Vengeance 1995, The Great White Hype 1996, A Time to Kill 1996, The Long Kiss Goodnight, Jackie Brown, Trees Lounge, Hard Eight, Out of Sight, The Negotiator, Deep Blue Sea, Sphere, Eve's Bayou (also producer). *Address:* c/o ICM, 8942 Wilshire Boulevard, Beverly Hills, CA 90211, U.S.A.

JACOB, François, M.D., D.SC.; French professor of genetics; b. 17 June 1920, Nancy; m. Lise Bloch 1947 (died 1984); three s. one d.; ed. Lycée Carnot and Univ. de Paris à la Sorbonne; Officer Free French Forces 1940–45; with Inst. Pasteur 1950–, Asst. 1950–56, Head of Laboratory 1956–60, Head of Cellular Genetics Unit 1960–91, Pres. 1982–88; Prof. of Cellular Genetics Coll. de France 1965–92; mem. Acad. des Sciences 1977, Acad. française 1996; Foreign mem. Royal Danish Acad. of Sciences and Letters 1962, American Acad. of Arts and Sciences 1964; Foreign Assoc. Nat. Acad. of Sciences (U.S.A.) 1969; Foreign mem. Royal Soc., London 1973, Acad. Royale Médicale Belgique 1973, Acad. of Sciences of Hungary 1986, Royal Acad. of Sciences of Madrid 1987; Prix Charles Léopold Mayer, Acad. des Sciences 1962, Nobel Prize for Medicine (jointly with A. Lwoff and J. Monod) 1965; Croix de la Libération, Grand Croix Légion d'honneur. *Publications:* The Logic of Life 1970, The Possible and the Actual 1981, The Statue Within 1987, la Souris, la mouche et l'homme 1997, and over 200 scientific papers. *Address:* Institut Pasteur, 25 rue de Dr. Roux, 75724 Paris Cedex 15; 15 rue de Condé, 75006 Paris, France (Home).

JACOB, Mathew Mundakaal, B.ECON., LL.B., M.A.; Indian politician; ed. Univs. of Madras and Lucknow; advocate High Court of Cochin, specialising in taxation; involved in youth training in various parts of India for Bhoodan Movt. for redistribution of land; Sec. Gen. Bharat Sevak Samaj org. to encourage popular participation in nat. devt., Kerala 1956–66; led youth Work Camp movt. in India and co-leader int. work camps in Bangalore and Calcutta overseen by UNESCO; Indian Rep. World Youth Festival, Moscow 1957, World Ass. of Youth Conf., Delhi 1958; Convenor Student and Youth Affairs Cttee. for Nat. Defence, Kerala State Govt. 1962; State Sec. Sadachar Samiti, Kerala; mem. Exec. Cttee. India Red Cross, Kerala State; Organiser Youth Hostel Movt., Kerala State and served as Sec. Gen. Youth Hostel Asscn. of India; experience as social worker; mem. Bd. of Govs. Inst. of Social Work directly after inception; Chair. Plantation Corpn. of Kerala 1974–78; first Chair. Oil Palm India Ltd. (jt. P.C.K.-Govt. initiative); Pres. Kerala State Co-operative Rubber Marketing Bd., Cochin for six years; Dir. Indian Overseas Bank 1976–82; f. and Dir. then Chair. Chitralekha Film Cooperative, Trivandrum; Publr. Bharat Sevak social work journal 1958–67; Man. Dir. and Publr. Congress Review newspaper 1977–86; Man. Dir. Veekshanam (Malayalam daily) newspaper 1978–82; fmr. Sec. Gen. Congress Party, Kerala State; fmr. mem. All India Congress Cttee. (AICC); mem. Indian Parl. (Senate) 1982–94; Chair. Parl. Cttee. on Subordinate Legislation 1983–85; Deputy Chair. Senate 1986–87; Minister of State for Parl. Affairs 1987–93, Minister of State for Water Resources 1988–89, Minister of State for Home Affairs, Council of Ministers 1991–93, Chair. Parl. Standing Cttee. on Home Affairs 1993–94; Gov. of Meghalaya, Shillong 1995–, of Arunachal Pradesh 1996; Del. to UN Gen. Ass. 1985, 1993, to UN/IPU World Disarmament Symposium 1985, UN World Human Rights Conf. 1993, to Commonwealth, IPU and rubber producers' confs. *Address:* Office of the Governor of Meghalaya, Raj Bhavan, Shillong-793001, India.

JACOBI, Sir Derek George, Kt., C.B.E., M.A.; British actor; b. 22 Oct. 1938, London; s. of Alfred George Jacobi and Daisy Gertrude Masters; ed. Leyton County High School and St. John's Coll., Cambridge; Birmingham Repertory Theatre 1960–63 (first appeared in One Way Pendulum 1961); National Theatre 1963–71; Prospect Theatre Co. 1972, 1974, 1976–78, Artistic Assoc. 1976–91; Old Vic Co. 1978–79; joined R.S.C. April 1982; Vice-Pres., Nat. Youth Theatre 1982–; Artistic Dir. Chichester Festival Theatre 1995–96; Hon. Fellow St. John's Coll., Cambridge; Variety Club Award 1976, British Acad. Award 1976, Press Guild Award 1976, Royal Television Soc. Award 1976, Hamburg Shakespeare Award 1998. *TV appearances include:* She Stoops to Conquer, Man of Straw, The Pallisers, I Claudius, Philby, Burgess and Maclean, Tales of the Unexpected, A Stranger in Town, Mr. Pye, Brother Cadfael 1994. *Films:* Odessa File, Day of the Jackal, The Medusa Touch, Othello, Three Sisters, Interlude, The Human Factor, Charlotte 1981, The Man who went up in Smoke 1981, The Hunchback of Notre Dame 1981, Inside the Third Reich 1982, Little Dorrit 1986, The Tenth Man 1988, Henry V, The Fool 1990, Dead Again, Hamlet 1996, Love is the Devil (Evening Standard Award for Best Actor 1998) 1997. *Plays Include:* The Lunatic, Lover and the Poet 1980, The Suicide 1980, Much Ado about Nothing, Peer Gynt, The Tempest 1982, Cyrano de Bergerac 1983, Breaking the Code 1986, Richard II 1988, Richard III 1989, Kean 1990, Becket 1991, Mad, Bad and Dangerous to Know, Ambassadors 1992, Macbeth 1993, Hadrian VII, Playing the Wife 1995, Uncle Vanya 1996; dir. Hamlet 1988. *Leisure interests:* gardening, reading, looking for the next job. *Address:* c/o ICM Ltd., Oxford House, 76 Oxford Street, London, W1N 0AX, England.

JACOBOVITS de SZEGED, Adriaan; Netherlands diplomatist; b. 27 Dec. 1935, Vienna, Austria; s. of Giulio Jacobovits de Szeged and Eveline Tak van Poortvliet; m. Françoise S. Montant 1968; two s.; ed. Univ. of Leyden; Ministry of Finance 1963; joined Foreign Service 1964; postings at Embassy Moscow, Perm. Mission to UN and other int. orgs., Geneva, Embassy, London, Embassy, Nairobi, Perm. Del. to EC, Brussels; Dir. Econ. Cooperation, Ministry of Foreign Affairs 1978–82; Dir.-Gen. Political Affairs 1982–86; Perm. Rep. to UN, New York 1986–89; Perm. Rep. NATO, Brussels 1989–93; Amb. to U.S.A. 1993. *Address:* c/o Ministry of Foreign Affairs, Bezuidenhoutseweg 67, P.O. Box 20061, 2500 EB The Hague, Netherlands.

JACOBS, Adrianus Gerardus, M.ECON.; Netherlands business executive; b. 28 May 1936, Rotterdam; m. C. M. M. de Haas 1963; two s. one d.; ed. Univ. of Rotterdam; joined De Nederlanden van 1845 1962 (Nationale-Nederlanden since 1963), Gen. Man. 1979, mem. Exec. Bd. 1988, mem. Exec. Bd. ING Group 1991, Vice-Chair. Exec. Bd. ING Group July 1992, Chair. Sept. 1992–; Chair. Exec. Bd. ING Insurance N.V. July 1992–; Dir. Nederlandse Participatie Mij. N.V., N.V. Struktongroep, Nat. Investeringsbank N.V.; Kt. Order of Netherlands Lion. *Address:* ING Group, Strawinskylaan 2631, P.O. Box 810, 1000 AV, Amsterdam, Netherlands. *Telephone:* 541-5411. *Fax:* 541-5444.

JACOBS, Albertus Stephanus (Japie); D.COM.; South African banker and economist; b. 27 June 1927, Wolmaransstad; s. of Jacobus J. Jacobs and Cornelia (née Geldenhuys) Jacobs; m. Elizabeth M. Combrink 1953; two s. two d.; ed. Lydenburg High School; with Dept. of Forestry 1946–49; Pres. Afrikaanse Handelsinstituut 1949; Deputy Econ. Adviser Econ. Advisory Council 1966–68; Chief Economist Volkskas 1968–71; Advisor South African Reserve Bank 1971–78, Gen. Man. 1978–80, Deputy Gov. 1981–85, Sr. Deputy Gov. 1986–90; Advisor to Minister of Finance 1990–94, to Deputy Pres. 1994–95; financial and economic consultant 1995–; mem. Nat. Econ. Forum 1994–; Fellow, Inst. of Bankers (Pres. 1989). *Leisure interests:* golf, hunting.

JACOBS, Francis Geoffrey, D.PHIL.; British lawyer; b. 8 June 1939, Cliftonville; s. of the late Cecil Sigismund Jacobs and Louise (née Fischhof) Jacobs; m. 1st Ruth Freeman 1964; m. 2nd Susan Felicity Gordon Cox 1975; two s. three d.; ed. City of London School, Christ Church, Oxford and Nuffield Coll., Oxford; lecturer in Jurisprudence, Univ. of Glasgow 1963–65; lecturer in Law, L.S.E. 1965–69; Prof. of European Law, King's Coll., London 1974–88, Fellow, King's Coll. 1990; Secr. European Comm. of Human Rights and Legal Directorate, Council of Europe 1969–72; Legal Sec. Court of Justice of the EC 1972–74, Advocate Gen. 1988–; Barrister, Middle Temple 1964, Q.C. 1984, Bencher 1990; Gov. Inns of Court School of Law 1996–; Hon. LL.D. (Univ. of Birmingham) 1996; Hon. D.C.L. (City Univ., London) 1997; Commdr., Ordre de Mérite 1983. *Publications include:* several books on European law and Yearbook of European Law (founding Ed.) 1981–88. *Address:* Court of Justice of the European Communities, Kirchberg, 2925 Luxembourg; Wayside, 15 St. Alban's Gardens, Teddington, Middx., TW11 8AE, England. *Telephone:* 43031 (Luxembourg); 0181-943 0503 (England).

JACOBS, Louis, C.B.E., PH.D.; British rabbi; b. 17 July 1920, Manchester; s. of Harry Jacobs and Lena Jacobs; m. Sophie Lisagorska 1944; two s. one d.; ed. Manchester Cen. High School, Manchester Talmudical Coll. and Univ. Coll. London; Rabbi, Cen. Synagogue, Manchester 1948–54, New West End Synagogue 1954–60; Dir. Soc. for Study of Jewish Theology 1960–64; Rabbi, New London Synagogue 1964–; Visiting Prof. Lancaster Univ. 1987–; Hon. LL.D.; Hon. D.H.L. *Publications include:* Principles of the Jewish Faith, A Jewish Theology, God, Torah, Israel, Jewish Mystical Testimonies, The Structure and Form of the Babylonian Talmud, Hasidic Prayer, Religion and the Individual, The Jewish Religion: a companion, Concise Companion to Judaism 1999, Beyond Reasonable Doubt 1999. *Leisure interests:* walking, theatre, cinema. *Address:* 27 Clifton Hill, St. John's Wood, London, NW8 0QE, England.

JACOBS, Peter Alan, B.SC.; British business executive; b. 22 Feb. 1943, Ayrshire; m. Eileen Dorothy Naftalin 1966; two s. one d.; ed. Glasgow and Aston Univs.; Production Man. Pedigree Petfoods 1981–83; Sales Dir. Mars Confectionery 1983–86; Man. Dir. British Sugar PLC 1986–91; Dir. S. and W. Berisford PLC 1986–91; C.E.O. British United Provident Asscn. 1991–98;

Chair. Healthcall 1998–; Dir. (non-exec.) Hillsdown Holdings 1998–, Bank Leumi (U.K.) 1998–, Allied Domecq 1998–. *Leisure interests:* tennis, squash, music, theatre, fund-raising. *Address:* 2 Norfolk Road, London, NW8 6AX. England.

JACOBS, Sir Piers, Kt.; British business executive; b. 27 May 1933, London; s. of Selwyn Jacobs and Dorothy Jacobs; m. Josephine Lee 1964; one d.; joined Hong Kong civil service, Registrar Gen.'s Office 1962; Registrar Gen. 1976; Sec. for Econ. Services 1982–86; Financial Sec. 1986–91; Vice-Chair. China Light & Power Co. 1992–, Dir. Sir Elly Kadoorie & Sons Ltd. 1992–, Chair. 1995–. *Leisure interests:* walking, reading. *Address:* c/o St. George's Building 24th Floor, 2 Ice House Street, Hong Kong Special Administrative Region, People's Republic of China.

JACOBSON, Dan, B.A., F.R.S.L.; British (b. South African) writer; b. 7 March 1929, Johannesburg; s. of Hyman Michael and Liebe (Melamed) Jacobson; m. Margaret Pye 1954; two s. one d.; ed. Boys' High School, Kimberly, Univ. of Witwatersrand, S. Africa; worked in business and journalism in S. Africa, settled in England 1955; Fellow in Creative Writing, Stanford Univ., Calif. 1956–57; Prof. of English, Syracuse Univ., New York 1965–66; Visiting Fellow, State Univ. of N.Y. 1971, Humanities Research Centre, Australian Nat. Univ., Canberra 1981; Lecturer Univ. Coll., London 1975–79; Reader in English, Univ. of London 1979–87; Prof. of English, Univ. Coll., London 1988–94, Prof. Emer. 1995–; Hon. D. Litt. (Witwatersrand) 1997; John Llewelyn Rhys Award 1958, W. Somerset Maugham Award 1961, Jewish Chronicle Award 1971, H. H. Wingate Award 1978, J. R. Ackerley Award for Autobiography 1986. *Publications:* novels: The Trap 1955, A Dance in the Sun 1956, The Price of Diamonds 1957, The Evidence of Love 1960, The Beginners 1965, The Rape of Tamar 1970, The Wonder-Worker 1973, The Confessions of Josef Baisz 1977, Her Story 1987, Hidden in the Heart 1991, The God-Fearer 1992; short stories: Inklings 1973; criticism: The Story of the Stories 1982; Adult Pleasures 1988; autobiography: Time and Time Again 1985; travel: The Electronic Elephant 1994, Heshel's Kingdom 1998. *Address:* c/o A. M. Heath & Co., 79 St. Martin's Lane, London, W.C.2, England. *Telephone:* 0171-836 4271.

JACOBSON, Nathan, PH.D.; American professor of mathematics; b. 8 Sept. 1910, Warsaw, Poland; s. of Charles Jacobson and Pauline Ida Rosenberg; m. Florence Dorfman 1942; one s. one d.; ed. Univ. of Alabama, Princeton Univ.; Asst. Inst. for Advanced Study, Princeton 1933–34, Lecturer Bryn Mawr Coll. 1935–36; Nat. Research Council Postdoctoral Fellow, Chicago 1936–37; Instructor Univ. of North Carolina 1937–38, Asst. Prof. 1938–40, Assoc. Prof. 1940–43; Assoc. Ground School Instructor, Navy Preflight School 1942–43; Assoc. Prof. Johns Hopkins Univ. 1943–47; Assoc. Prof. Yale Univ. 1947–49, Prof. 1949–81, Prof. Emer. 1981–, Henry Ford II Prof. of Maths 1964; Visiting Prof. Univ. of Calif. at Berkeley and at Los Angeles, Univ. of Chicago, Tata Inst., Bombay, ETH Zürich; Hon. Prof. Univ. of Alabama 1981; Guggenheim Fellow 1951–52, Fulbright Fellow 1951–52; Visiting Lecturer Japan, Italy, Israel, Australia, Taiwan, People's Repub. of China; Pres. American Mathematical Soc. 1971–73; Vice-Pres. Int. Mathematical Union 1972–74; hon. mem. London Mathematical Soc.; mem. Nat. Acad. of Sciences, American Acad. of Arts and Sciences; Hon. D.Sc. (Chicago) 1972. *Publications:* Theory of Rings 1943, Lectures in Abstract Algebra (3 vols.) 1953–64, Structure of Rings 1956, Lie Algebras 1962, Structure and Representations of Jordan Algebras 1968, On Quadratic Jordan Algebras 1969, Exceptional Lie Algebras 1971, Basic Algebra I 1974, PI—Algebras 1975, Basic Algebra II 1980, Structure Theory of Jordan Algebras 1981, and numerous articles. *Leisure interests:* travel, tennis, gardening. *Address:* Department of Mathematics, Yale University, New Haven, CT 06520 (Office); 2 Prospect Court, Hamden, CT 06517, U.S.A. (Home). *Telephone:* (203) 432-4194 (Office).

JACOBY, Ruth; Swedish international civil servant; b. 13 Jan. 1949, New York, U.S.A.; d. of Erich Jacoby and Lotte Jacoby; m. Bjorn Meidal 1976; two s.; ed. Univ. of Uppsala; First Sec., Ministry for Foreign Affairs, Stockholm 1972, Deputy Asst. Under-Sec. 1984–88, Asst. Under-Sec. and Head of Dept. 1990–94; mem. Swedish del. to OECD, Paris 1980–84; Deputy Asst. Under-Sec., Ministry of Finance 1988–90; Exec. Dir. World Bank 1994–97; Amb. 1997–. *Address:* Malmgardsvagen 6, 11638 Stockholm, Sweden. *Telephone:* (8) 6412787. *Fax:* (8) 641 2787.

JACOMB, Sir Martin Wakefield, Kt., M.A.; British banker; b. 11 Nov. 1929, Chiddingfold, Surrey; s. of Felise Jacomb and Hilary W. Jacomb; m. Evelyn Heathcoat Amory 1960; two s. one d.; ed. Eton Coll. and Worcester Coll. Oxford; practised at the Bar 1955–68; Kleinwort, Benson Ltd. 1968–85, Vice-Chair. 1976–85; Dir. Hudson's Bay Co., Canada 1971–86; Chair. The Merchants Trust PLC 1974–85, Transatlantic Fund Inc. 1978–85; Dir. Christian Salvesen PLC 1974–88, British Gas PLC 1981–88; Deputy Chair. Securities and Investments Bd. Ltd. 1985–87; a Deputy Chair. Barclays Bank PLC 1985–93; Chair. Barclays de Zoete Wedd 1986–91, British Council 1992–98; Dir. Commercial Union Assurance Co. PLC 1984–93 (Deputy Chair. 1988–93); Dir. Bank of England 1986–95, Daily Telegraph 1986–95, RTZ Corpn. PLC (now Rio Tinto PLC) 1988–; Chair. Postel Investment Man. Ltd. 1991–95; Dir. Marks and Spencer 1991–; Deputy Chair. (non-exec.) Delta PLC 1993–94, Chair. 1994–; Chair. Prudential Corpn. 1995–; Dir. Royal Opera House Covent Garden Ltd. 1987–92, Oxford Playhouse Trust Ltd. 1994, Oxford Playhouse Ltd. 1994; External mem., Finance Cttee., Oxford Univ. Press 1971–95; Hon. Master of the Bench of the Inner Temple 1987; Trustee, Nat. Heritage Memorial Fund 1982–97; Hon. Fellow Worcester Coll. Oxford 1994; Dr. h.c. (Buckingham, Oxford) 1997. *Leisure interests:* theatre, family, bridge, tennis. *Address:* Prudential Corporation PLC, 142 Holborn Bars, London, EC1N 2NH, England. *Telephone:* 0171-548 3901.

JACQUEMARD, Simonne; French novelist; b. 6 May 1924, Paris; d. of André and Andrée (Raimondi) Jacquemard; m. 2nd Jacques Brosse 1955; ed. Inst. Saint-Pierre, Univ. of Paris; Teacher of music, Latin and French; collaborator, Laffont-Bompiani Dictionaries; contributor to Figaro littéraire, La table ronde; travelled in U.S.S.R., Egypt, Greece, Italy, N. Africa and Spain; Prix Renaudot 1962, Grand prix Thyde-Monnier 1984; Officier Ordre des Arts et des Lettres. *Publications:* Les fascinés 1951, Sable 1952, La leçon des ténèbres 1954, Judith Albarès 1957, Planant sur les airs 1960, Compagnons insolites 1961, Le veilleur de nuit 1962 (Prix Renandot 1962), L'oiseau 1963, L'orangerie 1963, Les derniers rapaces 1965, Dérive au zénith 1965, Exploration d'un corps 1965, Navigation vers les îles 1967, A l'état sauvage 1967, L'éruption du Krakatoa 1969, La thessalienne 1973, Des roses pour mes chevreuils 1974, Le mariage berbère 1975, Danse de l'orée 1979, Le funambule 1981, Lalla Zahra 1983, La fête en éclats 1985, Les belles échappées 1987, L'huître dans la perle 1993, Le Jardin d'Hérodote 1995, l'Éphebe couronné de lierre 1995, la Gloire d'Ishawara 1996, Vers l'estuaire ébloui 1996, Trois mystiques grecs 1997; studies on music (with Lucette Descave), and on bird life and observation of wild animals. *Address:* 12 bis avenue des Gobelins, 75005 Paris, France.

JACQUES, Paula; French author and broadcaster; b. 8 May 1949, Cairo; d. of Jacques Abadi and Esther Sasson; m. (divorced 1970); worked as comedienne in Africa; joined Radio France Internationale as reporter, worked on Apres-midi de France-Culture, L'Oreille en coin 1975–90; presenter Nuits-noires France-Inter radio Sept. 1997–; sometime writer F Magazine; mem. Prix Femina jury 1996–. *Publications:* Lumiere de l'oeil 1980, Un baiser froid comme la lune 1983, L'Heritage de Tante Carlotta 1987, Deborah et les anges dissipes (Prix Femina 1991), La Descente au Paradis 1995, Les femmes avec leur amour 1997. *Address:* France-Inter, 116 avenue du Président Kennedy, 75220 Paris cedex 16, France.

JACQUES, Yves Henri, M.A.; French diplomatist; b. 31 Aug. 1929, Marseille; s. of Ivan Jacques and Fernande (née Fabrega) Jacques; m. Monique Serre 1956; two s.; ed. Ecole Nat. d'Admin.; French Embassy, Bonn 1960–63, Washington 1966–70, Rabat 1970–72; Foreign Office 1972–74, 1977–83; Ministry of Industry and Research 1974–77; OECD 1983–86; Defence Studies Inst. 1987–89; Pres. Asscn. Pour le Devt. d'Echanges Int. de Produits et de Tech. Agro-Alimentaires 1988–94; Chair. Franco-Soviet Working Group for Agri-food Business 1988–94; Foreign Trade Counsellor 1990–; Légion d'honneur, Ordre du Mérite, Bundesverdienst, Germany. *Publications:* Poèmes des Années 50 1963, L'Eternel Septembre 1976. *Leisure interests:* sport (jogging, skiing, surfing), music. *Address:* 69 rue de l'Université, 75007 Paris; 90 avenue des Mimosas, 83110 Sanary, France. *Telephone:* (01) 44.18.08.97.

JACQUET, Michel Antoine Paul Marie; French business executive; b. 28 March 1936, Dijon; s. of André Jacquet and Marie-Antoinette Baut; m. 2nd Marie-Agnès Corbière 1976; one s. and one s. one d. by first m.; ed. Lycée Rouget de Lisle, Lons-le-Saulnier, Lycée du Parc, Lyons and Ecole Polytechnique; Dir.-Gen. Crédit Lyonnais d'Espagne 1971–77; Dir.-Gen. Paribas Gabon and Pres. Sogapar 1977–79; Deputy Dir. Banque Paribas 1980–84; C.E.O. Paribas New York 1985–88; Pres. Nord-Est and Magnésia 1989–95; now Man. Ledo-Salina; Croix de Valeur militaire. *Address:* Ledo-Salina, 46-48 rue Lauriston, 75116 Paris (Office); 15 rue Raynouard, 75016 Paris, France (Home).

JACQUINOT, Pierre, D. ÈS SC.; French academic; b. 18 Jan. 1910, Frouard; s. of Georges Auguste Jacquinot and Eugénie Louise Vicq; m. Françoise Touchot 1937 (died 1986); three s. one d.; ed. Univ. of Nancy; Researcher C.N.R.S. 1933–42, Dir.-Gen. 1962–69; Prof. Univ. of Clermont Ferrand 1942–46; Prof. Univ. of Paris 1946–79, Emer. Prof. 1979–; mem. Acad. des Sciences 1966–, Pres. 1980–82; Commdr. Légion d'honneur, Grand-Croix, Ordre Nat. du Mérite; Holweck Prize (London-Paris) 1950; Golden Medal C.N.R.S. 1978; Grand Prix des Sciences de la ville de Paris. *Publications:* more than 150 articles on optics and atomic physics in scientific journals. *Address:* chemin du Merisier-Noir, 91400 Orsay, France (Home).

JAENICKE, Lothar, D.PHIL., DIPL.CHEM.; German biochemist; b. 14 Sept. 1923, Berlin; s. of Johannes Jaenicke and Erna (née Buttermilch) Jaenicke; m. Dr Doris Heinzel 1949; two s. two d.; ed. Univs. of Marburg, Tübingen; taught Univ. of Marburg 1946–57, Munich 1957–62, Cologne 1962, apptd. Prof. Cologne Univ. 1963, also Dir. Inst. of Biochem. 1988; Prof. Freie Universität Berlin; Visiting Scientist All India Inst. of Medicine, New Delhi 1961, Univ. of Texas, Austin 1977, 1992; Visiting Prof. American Univ. of Beirut 1971, Ain Shams Univ., Cairo 1974, Indian Inst. of Science, Bangalore 1980; mem. Rheinisch-Westfälische Akademie der Wissenschaften, Deutsche Akademie der Naturforscher Leopoldina; corresp. mem. Bayerische Akad. der Wissenschaften, Academia Europea; Fellow, Wissenschaftskolleg Berlin 1986–87; Paul Ehrlich/Ludwig-Darmstaedter-Preis 1963, Otto Warburg Medal 1979, Richard Kuhn Medal 1984. *Publications: c.* 250 original papers on enzymology and biochemical signalling in scientific journals. *Address:* Kaesenstrasse 13, 50677 Cologne, Germany.

JAFFE, Harold W., A.B., M.D.; American epidemiologist; b. 26 April 1946, Newton, Mass.; ed. Univ. of California at Berkeley, and at Los Angeles; jr. doctor at Univ. of Calif. at L.A. Hosp. 1971–74; Clinical Research Investigator, Venereal Disease Control Div., Centers for Disease Control (CDC), Atlanta 1974–77, 1980–81, Epidemic Intelligence Service Officer for AIDS Activity 1981–83, f. (with James W. Curran and others) Kaposi's Sarcoma-Opportunistic Infections Task Force, Center for Infectious Diseases to study causes of immune-deficiency disease in homosexual men 1981, Chief, Epidemiology Br. of AIDS Programme, CDC 1983–; Fellow in Infectious Diseases, Univ. of Chicago 1977–80; Visiting Prof., Chester Beatty Labs., Inst. of Cancer Research and Dept. of Medicine, Hammersmith Hosp., London, U.K. 1988–90; Clinical Instructor of Medicine, Emory Univ. School of Medicine, Atlanta; Assoc. Ed. American Journal of Epidemiology, mem. Editorial Bd. AIDS journal, Commendation Medal for work on HIV/AIDS, U.S. Public Health Service 1984, Meritorious Service Medal 1986, Distinguished Service Medal 1992. *Publications:* book chapters and over 90 articles in scientific journals, including Epidemiologic Aspects of the Current Outbreak of Kaposi's Sarcoma and Opportunistic Infections, in New England Journal of Medicine Jan. 1982, The Epidemiology of AIDS: Current Status and Future Prospects, in Science Sept. 1985 (co-author), HIV Infection and AIDS in the United States, in Science, Feb. 1989 (co-author). *Address:* Centers for Disease Control, Mailstop G-29, 1600 Clifton Road, Atlanta, GA 30333, U.S.A.

JAFFE, Stanley Richard, B.ECONS.; American film producer and director; b. 31 July 1940, New York; s. of Leo Jaffe and Dora Bressler; m. Melinda Long; two s. two d.; ed. Wharton School, Univ. of Pa.; with Seven Arts Assoc. Corpn. 1962–67, exec. asst. to Pres. 1964; Dir. E. Coast programming, Seven Arts TV 1963–64, Dir. programming 1965–67; Exec. Vice-Pres., Chief. Corp. Officer, Paramount Pictures Corpn. 1969–70, Pres. Corpn. also Pres. Paramount TV 1970–71; Pres. Jaffilms Inc. 1971; Exec. Vice-Pres. worldwide production, Columbia Pictures Corpn. 1965–76; Pres. and C.O.O. Paramount Communications, New York 1991–94; Gov., Pres., C.O.O. N.Y. Knicks 1991–94; Gov. N.Y. Rangers 1991–94; owner Jaffilms LLC 1994–. *Films include:* The Professionals 1963, Goodbye Columbus 1968, Bad Company 1971, Man on A Swing 1973, Bad News Bears 1974, Kramer vs Kramer 1979, Taps 1981, Without a Trace 1983, Racing with the Moon 1984, Firstborn 1984, Fatal Attraction 1987, The Accused 1988, Black Rain 1989, School Ties 1992, The Firm 1993. *Address:* Lean Building 119, 10202 Washington Boulevard, Culver City, CA 90232, U.S.A.

JAFFRÉ, Philippe Serge Yves, L. EN D.; French business executive; b. 2 March 1945, Charenton-le-Pont; s. of Yves-Frédéric Jaffré and Janine Alliot; m. Elisabeth Coulon 1974; one s. two d.; ed. Inst. d'Etudes Politiques, Paris and Ecole Nat. d'Admin.; Inspecteur des Finances 1974–; Dept. of Treasury 1977–88; Gen. Sec. Comité Interministériel pour l'Aménagement des Structures Industrielles (CIASI) 1978; Tech. Adviser to Minister of Economy 1979; Deputy Dir. Dept. of Govt. Holdings 1984; Head, Dept. for Monetary and Financial Affairs 1986; Dir. Banque Stern 1988; Pres. C.E.O., Caisse Nat. de Crédit Agricole 1988; Chair. and C.E.O. Elf Aquitaine 1993–; Insp.-Gen. of Finances 1994; Chevalier, Légion d'Honneur, Chevalier, Ordre du Mérite, Officier, Ordre du Mérite Agricole. *Leisure interest:* golf. *Address:* Elf Aquitaine, 2 place de la Coupole, 92078 Paris la Défense, Cedex 45, France. *Telephone:* (1) 47.44.45.46.

JAGAN, Janet, O.E.; Guyanese politician and author; b. 20 Oct. 1920, Chicago, Ill., U.S.A.; d. of Charles and Kathryn Rosenberg; m. Cheddi Jagan 1943 (died 1997); one s. one d.; Gen. Sec. People's Progressive Party (PPP) 1950–70; Ed. Thunder 1950–56; Deputy Speaker House of Assembly 1953; six months' political imprisonment 1954; Minister of Labour, Health and Housing 1957–61; Minister of Home Affairs 1963–64; mem. Elections Comm. 1967–68; Ed. Mirror 1969–72, 1973–97; Int. Sec. PPP 1970–84, Exec. Sec. 1984–90; mem. Nat. Assembly 1976–97; Amb. at Large and acting Amb. to the UN Oct.–Dec. 1993; First Lady of Guyana 1992–97; Prime Minister of Guyana March–Dec. 1997; Pres. of Guyana Dec. 1997–; Pres. Women's Progressive Org., Union of Guyanese Journalists; fmr. Chair. Comm. on Rights of the Child, Man. Cttee. Castellani House (nat. art collection); Outstanding Woman Award, Univ. of Guyana 1989, Mahatma Gandhi Award, UNESCO, for contrib. to democracy, peace and women's rights; Order of Excellence 1993, Order of the Liberator (Venezuela) 1998. *Publications:* History of the People's Progressive Party 1971, Army Intervention in the 1973 Elections in Guyana 1973, An Examination of National Service 1976, When Grandpa Cheddi Was a Boy and other stories (children's) 1993; children's books: Patricia the Baby Manatee and other stories 1995, Children's Stories of Guyana's Freedom Struggles 1995, Anastasia, the Ant Eater, and other stories 1997. *Leisure interests:* swimming, writing children's stories. *Address:* Office of the President, New Garden Street and South Road, Georgetown, Guyana. *Telephone:* (2) 51330. *Fax:* (2) 63395.

JAGENDORF, André Tridon, PH.D.; American professor of plant physiology; b. 21 Oct. 1926, New York; s. of Moritz A. and Sophie S. Jagendorf; m. Jean Whitenack 1952; one d. two s.; ed. Cornell and Yale Univs.; Postdoctoral Fellow, Univ. of Calif., Los Angeles 1951–53; Asst. Prof., Johns Hopkins Univ. 1953–58, Assoc. Prof. 1958–65, Prof. of Biology 1966; Prof. of Plant Physiology, Cornell Univ. 1966–, Liberty Hyde Bailey Prof. of Plant Physiology 1981–96, Emer. Prof. 1997–; mem. N.A.S. 1980; Pres. American Soc. of Plant Physiologists; Merck Fellow in Natural Sciences 1951–53; Weizmann Fellow 1962; A.A.A.S. Fellow 1964; Fellow American Acad. of Arts and Sciences 1972; Outstanding Young Scientist Award, Md. Acad. of Sciences 1961, Kettering Research Award 1963, C. F. Kettering Award in Photosynthesis, American Soc. of Plant Physiologists 1978, Charles Reid Barnes Award 1989. *Publications:* 162 papers in scientific journals. *Address:* c/o Plant Biology Section, Plant Sciences Building, Cornell University, Ithaca, NY 14853 (Office); 309 Brookfield Road, Ithaca, NY 14850, U.S.A. (Home).

JAGGER, Mick; British singer, song writer and actor; b. 26 July 1943, Dartford, Kent; s. of Joe Jagger and Eva Jagger; m. 1st Bianca Pérez Morena de Macías 1971 (divorced 1979); one d.; m. 2nd Jerry Hall (q.v.) 1990; two s. two d.; one d. by Marsha Hunt; ed. London School of Econs., London Univ.; began singing career with Little Boy Blue and the Blue Boys while at L.S.E.; appeared with Blues Inc. at Ealing Blues Club, Singer with Blues Inc. at London Marquee Club 1962; formed Rolling Stones 1962; wrote songs with Keith Richards under pseudonyms Nanker, Phelge until 1965, without pseudonyms 1965–; first own composition to reach no. 1 in U.K. charts The Last Time 1965; first major U.K. tour 1964; major U.S. tours 1964, 1966, 1969, 1972, 1973, 1975, 1981; toured Europe 1973, 1982, the Americas 1975; recent tours with Rolling Stones 1989, 1994; title role in film Ned Kelly 1969, appeared in Performance 1969, Gimme Shelter 1972, Free Jack 1991; lived in France for some years; Pres. L.S.E. Students' Union 1994–. Records: singles include: Come On 1963, I Wanna Be Your Man 1963, It's All Over Now 1964, Little Red Rooster 1964, Satisfaction 1965, Jumping Jack Flash 1968, Honky Tonk Women 1969, Brown Sugar 1971, Miss You 1978, Emotional Rescue 1980, Beast of Burden, She's So Cold, Dancing in the Street (with David Bowie for Live Aid Appeal) 1985, Voodoo Lounge 1994; albums include: The Rolling Stones 1964, The Rolling Stones No. 2 1965, Out of Our Heads 1965, Aftermath 1966, Between the Buttons 1967, Their Satanic Majesties Request 1967, Beggar's Banquet 1968, Let it Bleed 1969, Get Yer Ya-Ya's Out 1969, Sticky Fingers 1971, Exile on Main Street 1972, Goat's Head Soup 1973, It's Only Rock'n'Roll 1974, Black and Blue 1976, Some Girls 1978, Emotional Rescue 1980, Still Life 1982, She's the Boss (solo) 1985, Primitive Cool 1987, Steel Wheels 1989 (also co-producer), Flashpoint 1991, Bent 1997; producer Enigma (film) 1996. *Address:* c/o Marathon Music, 5 Church Row, Wandsworth Plain, London SW18 1ES, England.

JAGIELIŃSKI, Roman; Polish politician; b. 2 Jan. 1947, Wichradz, Radom Prov.; m.; two s.; ed. Horticulture Dept. Main School of Farming; runs fruit farm in village of Świniokierz Dworski, Piotrków Trybunalski Prov.; Pres. Polish Fruit-Growers' Union; mem. United Peasants' Party (ZSL) 1970–89; mem. Polish Peasants' Party "Rebirth" 1989–90; mem. Polish Peasants' Party (PSL) 1990–97; co-f. and leader Peasant Democratic Party 1997–; Deputy to Sejm (Parl.) 1991–; Vice-Pres. Polish Peasants' Party Parl. Club 1991-96; Deputy Prime Minister and Minister of Agric. and Food Economy 1995–97; Vice-Chair. Parl. Comm. for Small and Medium Enterprises 1997–. *Address:* Sejm RP, ul. Wiejska 4/6/8, 00-902 Warsaw, Poland. *Telephone:* (22) 694 16 02.

JAGLAND, Thorbjørn; Norwegian politician; b. 5 Nov. 1950; m. Hanne Grotjord 1975; two c.; ed. Univ. of Oslo; Exec. Sec. Norwegian Labour League of Youth (AUF) 1977–81; Project and Planning Officer, Norwegian Labour Party 1981–86, Acting Gen. Sec. 1986, Gen. Sec. 1987, Chair. 1992–; mem. Storting; Chair. Labour Party Parl. Group; Prime Minister of Norway 1996–97. *Publications include:* Min europeiske drøm 1990, Ny solidaritet 1993, Brev 1995, co-author For det blir for sent 1982; articles on defence, nat. security and disarmament. *Address:* Stortinget, N-0026 Oslo, Norway. *Telephone:* 22 31 30 50. *Fax:* 22 31 38 44.

JAHN, Gerhard; German politician and lawyer; b. 10 Sept. 1927, Kassel; s. of Ernst and Lilly (née Schlüchterer) Jahn; m. 1st Anna Waas 1950; one s. two d.; m. 2nd Ursula Müller 1986; ed. Humanistisches Friedrichs Gymnasium, Kassel and Univ. Marburg; qualified as lawyer 1956; mem. Parl. Sozial-Demokratische Partei (SPD) 1948; mem. Bundestag 1957–90; Parl. State Sec. to Minister of Foreign Affairs 1967; Minister of Justice 1969–74; Pres. Deutscher Mieterbund 1979–95; Freeman of Marburg 1977; Grosses Bundesverdienstkreuz mit Stern und Schulterband 1984. *Leisure interest:* photography. *Address:* Bismarckstrasse 15, 35037 Marburg, Germany.

JAHN, Helmut, F.A.I.A.; architect; b. 4 Jan. 1940, Nuremberg; m. Deborah Lampe 1970; one s.; ed. Technische Hochschule, Munich and Illinois Inst. of Tech.; C. F. Murphy Assocs. 1967–73, Exec. Vice-Pres. and Dir. of Planning and Design 1973; corporate mem. American Inst. of Architects 1975; registered architect, NCARB 1975; mem. German Chamber of Architects, State of Hesse 1986; Prin. Murphy/Jahn 1981, Pres. 1982, Pres. and C.E.O. 1983–; Visiting Prof. Harvard Univ. 1981, Yale Univ. 1983; numerous other lectureships at univs. and professional socs. 1989–93; participant in numerous architectural exhbns.; completed bldgs. include libraries, exhbn. halls, court bldgs., office and leisure bldgs., university bldgs., hotels, apts. and airport terminals in U.S.A., Europe and Far East; Hon. D.F.A. (St. Mary's Coll. Notre Dame, Ind.); Chevalier, Ordre des Arts et des Lettres (France), Bundesverdienstkreuz Erster Klasse (Germany); numerous professional awards. *Leisure interests:* sailing, skiing. *Address:* Murphy/Jahn, Inc., 35 East Wacker Drive, Chicago, IL 60601, U.S.A. *Telephone:* (312) 427-7300. *Fax:* (312) 332-0274.

JAHN, Robert George, M.A., PH.D.; American professor of aerospace sciences; b. 1 April 1930, Kearny, N.J.; s. of George Jahn and Minnie Holroyd; m. Catherine Seibert 1953; one s. three d.; ed. Princeton Univ.; Teaching

Asst. Princeton Univ. 1953–55; Instructor. Lehigh Univ. Bethlehem, Pa. 1955–56, Asst. Prof. 1956–58; Asst. Prof. of Jet Propulsion, Calif. Inst. of Tech. Pasadena 1958–62; Asst. Prof. of Aeronautical Eng. Princeton Univ. 1962–64, Assoc. Prof. 1964–67, Prof. of Aerospace Sciences 1967–, Dean, School of Eng. and Applied Science 1971–86; mem. various NASA research cttees.; numerous professional appts. etc.; Fellow, American Physics Soc., American Inst. of Aeronautics and Astronautics; Hon. Sc.D. (Andrha) 1986. *Publications:* Physics of Electric Propulsion 1968, Margins of Reality (with B. J. Dunne) 1987. *Address:* Department of Aerospace Sciences, Princeton University, Princeton, NJ 08544, U.S.A. (Home).

JAKHAR, Bal Ram; Indian politician; b. 23 Aug. 1923, Panjkosi, Ferozepur Dist., Punjab; s. of Chaudhri Raja Ram Jakhar; m. Rameshwari Jakhar; three s. two d.; elected to Punjab Ass. 1972, Deputy Minister of Co-operatives and Irrigation 1972–77, Leader of Opposition 1977–79; Speaker, Lok Sabha (House of the People) 1980–89; Pres. Indian Parl. Group, Indian Group of IPU, Indian Branch, CPA 1979–; Minister of Agric. 1991–96; Chair. Bharat Krishak Samaj 1979; led numerous Indian parl. dels. overseas 1980. *Publication:* People, Parliament and Administration. *Address:* 11 Race Course Road, New Delhi 110011, India.

JAKI, Stanley L., S.T.D., PH.D.; American university professor and ecclesiastic; b. 17 Aug. 1924, Györ, Hungary; s. of Imre Jaki and Etelka Szabo; ed. Pontifical Atheneum San Anselmo, Rome and Fordham Univ., New York; mem. of staff Seton Hall Univ., S. Orange, N.J. 1965–72, Prof. of Physics 1972–75, Distinguished Univ. Prof. 1975–; R.C. Priest of Benedictine Order; Gifford Lecturer Univ. of Edinburgh 1974–76; Fremantle Lecturer Oxford Univ. 1977, Forwood Lecturer, Liverpool Univ. 1992; Corresp. mem., Acad. des Sciences de Bordeaux 1985; Hon. mem. Pontifical Acad. of Sciences 1991; Lecomte du Nouy Prize 1970; Templeton Prize 1987, Farmington Inst. Lecturer, Oxford 1988, 1989. *Publications include:* The Relevance of Physics 1966, Brain, Mind and Computers 1969, The Milky Way: An Elusive Road for Science 1972, Science and Creation 1974, The Road of Science and the Ways to God 1978, Planets and Planetarians: A History of Theories of the Origin of Planetary Systems 1978, The Origin of Science and the Science of its Origin 1978, Cosmos and Creator 1980, Uneasy Genius: The Life and Work of Pierre Duhem 1984, Chance or Reality and Other Essays 1986, The Keys of the Kingdom: A Tool's Witness to Truth 1986, The Absolute Beneath the Relative and Other Essays 1988, The Savior of Science 1988, And on this Rock: The Witness of One Land and Two Covenants 1978, Miracles and Physics 1989, God and the Cosmologists 1989, The Only Chaos and Other Essays 1990, The Purpose of It All 1990, Catholic Essays 1990, Cosmos in Transition: Studies in the History of Cosmology 1990, Scientist and Catholic: Pierre Duhem 1991, Universe and Creed 1992, Genesis 1 through the Ages 1992, Is there a Universe? 1993; (trans.) The Ash Wednesday Supper (Giordano Bruno) 1975, Universal Natural History and Theory of the Heavens (Kant) 1981. *Address:* P.O. Box 167, Princeton, NJ 08542, U.S.A. (Home). *Telephone:* (609) 896 3979 (Home). *Fax:* (609) 896-9307.

JAKOBOVITS, Baron (Life Peer), cr. 1987, of Regents Park in Greater London, **Immanuel Jakobovits,** Kt., PH.D.; British rabbi; b. 8 Feb. 1921, Königsberg, Germany (now Kaliningrad, Russia); s. of Rabbi Dr. Julius Jakobovits and Paula Wreschner; m. Amélie Munk 1948; two s. four d.; ed. Jews' Coll. London, Yeshivah Etz Chaim, London, Univ. of London; Minister of Brondesbury Synagogue, London 1941–44, of S.E. London Synagogue 1944–47, of Great Synagogue, London 1947–49; Chief Rabbi of Ireland 1949–58; Rabbi of Fifth Avenue Synagogue, New York 1958–67; Chief Rabbi of the United Hebrew Congregations of the British Commonwealth of Nations, London 1967–91; Fellow, Univ. Coll., London 1984; Hon. D.D. (Lambeth) 1987, (Univ. of Wales) 1993; Hon. D.Litt. (City Univ., London) 1986; Hon Fellow Queen Mary Coll., 1987; Templeton Prize for Progress in Religion 1991. *Publications:* Jewish Medical Ethics 1959, Journal of a Rabbi 1966, Jewish Law Faces Modern Problems 1966, The Timely and the Timeless 1977, If Only My People . . . Zionism in My Life 1985, Ed. Centenary Edn. Authorised Daily Prayer Book 1990, Dear Chief Rabbi 1995. *Address:* Jews' College, 44A Albert Road, London, NW4 2SJ, England. *Telephone:* 0181-203 8667. *Fax:* 0181-203 8826.

JAKOBSEN, Mimi; Danish politician; b. 19 Nov. 1948, Copenhagen; d. of Erhard Jakobsen; Lecturer in German Philology and Phonetics, Univ. of Copenhagen; M.P. 1977–, Minister for Cultural Affairs. 1982–86; Minister for Social Affairs 1986–88, of Business Affairs 1993–96, of Industry 1994–96; Leader Centre Democrat Party 1989–. *Address:* Centrum-Demokraterne, Folketinget, Christiansborg, 1240 Copenhagen K, Denmark.

JAKOBSON, Max; Finnish diplomatist and journalist; b. 1923, Viipuri; s. of Jonas and Helmi (née Virtanen) Jakobson, m. Marilyn S. Medney 1954; two s. one d.; journalist until 1953; Press Attaché, Finnish Embassy, Washington 1953–59; Chief of Press Dept., Ministry of Foreign Affairs 1959–62; Asst. Dir. for Political Affairs, Ministry of Foreign Affairs 1959–62, Dir. 1962–65; Perm. Rep. of Finland to UN 1965–72; Amb. to Sweden 1972–75; Man. Dir. Council of Econ. Orgs. in Finland 1975–84, independent consultant 1985–. *Publications include:* The Diplomacy of the Winter War, Finnish Neutrality, Finland: Myth and Reality. *Address:* Rahapajankatu 3B 17, 00160, Helsinki 16, Finland. *Telephone:* 651884.

JALAL, Mahsoun B., PH.D.(ECON.); Saudi Arabian businessman; b. 26 June 1936; m. Michæle Marie Garein 1967; three s. one d.; ed. Univ. of Cairo, Egypt, Rutgers Univ., New Brunswick, N.J., U.S.A., Univ. of California, U.S.A.; Prof., Chair. Dept. of Econs., Riyadh Univ. 1967–75; Consultant to various Govt. agencies 1967–75; formed the Consulting Centre 1969 (Pres. 1981–); Vice-Chair. and Man. Dir. Saudi Fund for Devt. 1975–79; mem. Civil Service Council 1977–78; Dir. Saudi Int. Bank, London 1975–; Chair. Saudi Int. Bank, Nassau, Bahamas 1979–81; Chair. Saudi Investment Banking Corpn. 1977–82, OPEC Special Fund (now OPEC Fund) 1979–82; Dir. Saudi Basic Industries Corpn. 1975–87; Exec. Dir. IMF 1978–81; Chair. Saudi United Commercial Bank 1983–85; Chair. Eastern Petrochemical Co. 1981–86; Chair. Tunisian-Saudi Devt. Investment Co. 1981–; Chair. and CEO Nat. Industrialization Co. 1984–90, Man. Dir. 1990–94; Chair. and Man. Dir Nat. Co. for Glass Industries 'Zoujaj' 1990–; Man. Dir. Motazah Le Cote de Cartage Co., Tunis 1995; Chair. various investment cos.; Golden Star, First Class (Taiwan) 1973, Tanda Mahputera (Indonesia) 1978, Chevalier Ordre National (Mali) 1978, Order of the Repub., First Class (Tunisia) 1985. *Publications:* Principles of Economics, other books and articles on econ. devt. and econ. theory. *Leisure interests:* travel, sports. *Address:* P.O. Box 88646, Riyadh 11672, Saudi Arabia (Office). *Telephone:* 4770045-6 (Office). *Fax:* 4770087.

JALAN, Bimal, PH.D.; Indian economist; ed. Cambridge, Oxford and Bombay Univs.; various positions at IMF, World Bank, Pearson Comm. 1964–70; chief economist, Industrial Credit and Investment Corpn. of India 1970–73; econ. adviser, Ministry of Finance and of Industry, India 1973–79; Chief Econ. Adviser, Ministry of Finance 1981–88, Sec. for Banking 1985–88; Dir. Econ. Affairs, Commonwealth Secr., London 1979–81; Exec. Dir. IMF 1988–90; fmr. Exec. Dir. IBRD; Gov. Reserve Bank 1997–. *Publications include:* Essays in Development Policies, Problems and Policies in Small Economies (ed.). *Address:* Reserve Bank of India, P.O. Box 406, Mumbai, 400 023, India.

JALLOUD, Major Abdul Salam Ahmed; Libyan politician and army officer; b. 15 Dec. 1944; ed. Secondary School, Sebha, Mil. Acad., Benghazi.; mem. of Revolutionary Command Council 1969–77, Gen. Secr. of Gen. People's Congress 1977–79; Minister of Industry and the Econ., Acting Minister of the Treas. 1970–72; Prime Minister 1972–77; Second-in-Command to Revolutionary Leader Col. Gaddafi (q.v.) 1997–. *Address:* c/o General Secretariat of the General People's Congress, Tripoli, Libya.

JAMAL, Amir Habib, B.COMM. (ECON.); Tanzanian politician; b. 26 Jan. 1922, Dar es Salaam; s. of Habib Jamal and Kulsum Thawer; m. 1st Zainy Kheraj; m. 2nd Shahsultan Cassam 1967; three s. one d.; ed. primary school, Mwanza, secondary school, Dar es Salaam, and Univ. of Calcutta, India; elected mem. Tanganyika Legis. Council 1958; Minister of Urban Local Govt. and Works 1959, of Communication, Power and Works 1960; Minister of State, President's Office, Directorate of Devt. 1964; re-elected M.P. 1965; Minister of Finance 1965–72; Minister for Commerce and Industries 1972–75, of Finance and Econ. Planning 1975–77, of Communications and Transport 1977–79, of Finance 1979–83, without Portfolio 1983–84, Minister of State for Cabinet Affairs, Pres.'s Office 1984–85; Head, Perm. Mission to the UN, Geneva Nov. 1985–; Chair. Interpress Service, Third World, Rome; Chair. Governing Council Sokoine Univ. of Agric., Morogoro; Hon. Exec. Dir. South Centre, Geneva; mem. Nat. Exec. CCM Party; Dr. h.c. (Uppsala) 1973, (Dar es Salaam) 1980; mem. Brandt Comm. 1977–80, Trustee Dag Hammarskjold Foundation; mem. Advisory Panel, World Inst. for Devt. Economics Research. *Leisure interests:* gardening, reading, bridge, swimming. *Address:* 47 avenue Blanc, 1202 Geneva, Switzerland.

JÁMBOR, Ági; American pianist; b. 4 Feb. 1909, Budapest, Hungary; d. of Vilmos Jámbor and Olga Riesz; ed. Budapest Acad. of Music under Kodály and Weiner, and Musikhochschule, Berlin; regular concert tours throughout U.S.A.; Full Prof., Dept. of Music and Anthropology/Ethno-Musicology, Bryn Mawr Coll., Pa. 1958–77, Prof. Emer. 1977–; Curator of Music Instruments, Univ. Museum, Pa.; Brahms Prize, Deutsche Akad., Berlin 1928, Int. Chopin Prize, Warsaw 1937.

JAMBREK, Peter, M.A., PH.D.; Slovenian judge; b. 14 Jan. 1940, Ljubljana; ed. Grammar School, Ljubljana, Ljubljana Univ. and Univ. of Chicago; Prof. Dept. of Theory of Law and State, Ljubljana; Judge, Constitutional Court of Repub. of Slovenia 1990, Pres. 1991–95; Judge, European Court of Human Rights 1993–. *Publications:* Development and Social Change in Yugoslavia: Crises and Perspectives of Building a Nation 1975, Participation as a Human Right and as a Means for the Exercise of Human Rights 1982, Contributions for the Slovenian Constitution 1988, Constitutional Democracy 1992. *Address:* Ceste v Megre 4, 64260 Bled, Slovenia (Home). *Telephone:* (386) (64) 77-449 (Home).

JAMES, Clive Vivian Leopold; Australian author, broadcaster and journalist; b. 7 Oct. 1939; s. of Albert A. James and Minora M. Darke; ed. Sydney Technical High School, Sydney Univ. and Pembroke Coll. Cambridge; Pres. of Footlights at Cambridge; television critic, The Observer 1972–82, feature writer 1972–; Dir. Watchmaker Productions 1994–; as lyricist for Pete Atkin, record albums include: Beware of the Beautiful Stranger, Driving Through Mythical America, A King at Nightfall, The Road of Silk, Secret Drinker, Live Libel, The Master of the Revels; also songbook, A First Folio (with Pete Atkin). *Television series include:* Cinema, Up Sunday, So It Goes, A Question of Sex, Saturday Night People, Clive James on Television, The Late Clive James, The Late Show with Clive James, Saturday Night Clive, Fame in the 20th Century, Sunday Night Clive, The Clive James Show; numerous TV documentaries. *Publications:* non-fiction: The Metropolitan Critic 1974,

The Fate of Felicity Fark in the Land of the Media 1975, Peregrine Prykke's Pilgrimage through the London Literary World 1976, Britannia Bright's Bewilderment in the Wilderness of Westminster 1976, Visions Before Midnight 1977, At the Pillars of Hercules 1979, First Reactions 1980, The Crystal Bucket 1981, Charles Charming's Challenges on the Pathway to the Throne 1981, From the Land of Shadows 1982, Glued to the Box 1982, Flying Visits 1984, Snakecharmers in Texas 1988, The Dreaming Swimmer 1992, Fame 1993; novels: Brilliant Creatures 1983, The Remake 1987; autobiography: Unreliable Memoirs 1980, Falling Towards England: Unreliable Memoirs Vol. II 1985, May Week was in June 1990, Brrm! Brrm! or The Man from Japan or Perfume at Anchorage 1991, Fame in the 20th Century 1993, The Metropolitan Critic 1993; three vols. of poetry; criticism: Clive James on Television 1993, The Silver Castle 1996 (novel).

JAMES, Rt. Rev. Colin Clement Walter, M.A.; British ecclesiastic; b. 20 Sept. 1926, Cambridge; s. of late Canon Charles C.H. James and Gwenyth M. James; m. Margaret J. (Sally) Henshaw 1962; one s. two d.; ed. Aldenham School, King's Coll. Cambridge and Cuddesdon Theological Coll.; Asst. Curate, Stepney Parish Church 1952–55; Chaplain, Stowe School 1955–59; BBC Religious Broadcasting Dept. 1959–67; Religious Broadcasting Organizer, BBC South and West 1960–67; Vicar of St. Peter with St. Swithin, Bournemouth 1967–73; Bishop Suffragan of Basingstoke 1973–77; Canon Residentiary of Winchester Cathedral 1973–77; Bishop of Wakefield 1977–85; Bishop of Winchester 1985–95; Pres. Woodward Corpn. 1978–93, RADIUS 1980–93; Chair. Central Religious Advisory Cttee., BBC and IBA 1979–84, Liturgical Comm. 1986–93; Hon. D. Litt. (Southampton) 1996. *Leisure interests:* theatre, travelling. *Address:* 5 Hermitage Road, Lansdown, Bath, BA1 5SN, England. *Telephone:* (01225) 312720.

JAMES, Sir Cynlais (Kenneth) Morgan, K.C.M.G., M.A.; British diplomatist (retd.); b. 29 April 1926, Resolven; s. of Thomas Ellis James and Lydia Ann (Morgan) James; m. Teresa Girouard 1953; two d.; ed. St. Marylebone Grammar School, Durham Univ., Trinity Coll., Cambridge; in R.A.F. 1944–47; Sr. Branch of Foreign Service 1951, in Tokyo 1953, Brazil 1956, Cultural Attaché, Moscow 1959, Foreign Office 1962, Paris 1965, Saigon 1969; FCO, Head of Western European Dept. 1971–75; NATO Defence Coll. 1975–76; Minister, Paris 1976–81; Amb. to Poland 1981–83; Asst. Under-Sec. of State 1983; Amb. to Mexico 1983–86; Dir. Thomas Cook Group 1986–91; Dir.-Gen. Canning House 1987–92; Dir. Darwin Instruments; Dir. (non-exec.) Latin American Investment Trust 1991–96; Dir. Foreign and Colonial Emerging Markets Investment Trust PLC, Euro Principals Ltd.; Adviser to Amerada Hess; Chair. British Inst., Paris, British-Mexican Soc. 1987–90, Inst. of Latin-American Studies 1992–; mem. Franco-British Council; Dr. h.c. (Mexican Acad. of Int. Law); Order of the Aztec Eagle (Mexico), Order of Andres Bello (Venezuela), Order of Merit (Chile), Chevalier, Légion d'honneur. *Leisure interests:* history, music, tennis, cricket. *Address:* 63 Eccleston Square, London, SW1V 1PH, England. *Telephone:* 0171-828 8527.

JAMES, Edison Chenfil, M.SC.; Dominican politician and agronomist; b. 18 Oct. 1943, Marigot, s. of David James and Patricia James; m.; one s. two d.; ed. North East London Polytechnic, Reading Univ., Imperial Coll. (Univ. of London); teacher St. Mary's Acad. Sept.–Dec. 1973; agronomist Ministry of Agric. 1974–76; Farm Improvement Officer Caribbean Devt. Bank (attached to Dominica Agricultural and Industrial Devt. Bank) 1976–80, Loans Officer 1976–80; Co-ordinator Coconut Rehabilitation and Devt. Project; Chief Exec. (Gen. Man.) Dominica Banana Marketing Corpn. 1980–87; Adviser to Dirs. Bd. of Windward Islands Banana Growers Asscn. (WINBAN) 1980–87; Man. Dir. Agricultural Man. Corpn. Ltd. (AMCROP) 1987–95; Leader Dominica United Workers Party (UWP) and Parl. Leader of the Opposition 1990–95; Prime Minister of Dominica 1995–, also Minister of Legal and Foreign Affairs and Labour; leading negotiator with several int. aid agencies; served on numerous public service cttees. *Leisure interests:* cricket, football, int. affairs, politics, table tennis. *Address:* Office of the Prime Minister, Kennedy Avenue, Roseau, Dominica. *Telephone:* 4482401.

JAMES, Forrest Hood, Jr., B.S.; American politician and business executive; b. 15 Sept. 1934, Lanett, Ala.; s. of Forrest Hood James Sr. and Rebecca Ellington James; m. Bobbie Mooney James 1955; three s.; ed. Auburn Univ., Ala.; Founder, Pres., Chair. Bd. Diversified Products Corpn., Opelika, Ala. 1962–78; Gov. of Alabama 1979–82, 1996–99; Democrat. *Leisure interests:* duck hunting, reading, history. *Address:* c/o The Governor's Office, 600 Dexter Ave, Montgomery, AL 36130, U.S.A.

JAMES, Geraldine; British actress; b. 6 July 1950; d. of Gerald Trevor Thomas and Annabella Doogan Thomas; m. Joseph Sebastian Blatchley 1986; one d.; ed. Downe House, Newbury, Drama Centre London Ltd.; *stage appearances*: repertory, Chester 1972–74, Exeter 1974–75, Coventry 1975, Passion of Dracula 1978, The White Devil 1981, Turning Over 1984, When I was a Girl I used to Scream and Shout 1987, Cymbeline 1988, Merchant of Venice 1989 (and Broadway 1990), Death and the Maiden 1992, Lysistrata 1993, Hedda Gabler 1993, Give Me Your Answer Do 1998; *TV series*: The History Man 1980, Jewel in the Crown 1984, Blott on the Landscape 1985, Echoes 1988, Stanley and the Women 1991, Kavanagh Q.C. 1995, 1998, Band of Gold 1995, Over Here 1995, Band of Gold 1996, Drovers' Gold 1996, Gold 1997, Kavanagh QC 1997; *TV films*: Dummy 1977, She's Been Away 1989, Inspector Morse 1990, The Doll's House 1991, Ex 1991, The Healer 1994, Doggin Around 1994, Rebecca 1996, See Saw 1997; *films*: Sweet William 1978, Night Cruiser 1978, Gandhi 1981, The Storm 1985, Wolves of Willoughby Chase 1988, The Tall Guy 1989, If Looks Could Kill 1990, The Bridge 1990, Losing Track 1991, Prince of Shadows 1991, No Worries 1992, Words on the Window Pane 1993, Moll Flanders 1996, The Man Who Knew Too Little 1996. *Leisure interest:* music. *Address:* c/o Julian Belfrage Associates, 46 Albemarle Street, London, W.1, England.

JAMES, Harold, PH.D.; British professor of history; b. 19 Jan. 1956, Bedford; s. of Leslie James and Else James; m. Marzenna Kowalik 1991; one s.; ed. Perse School, Cambridge and Gonville & Caius Coll. Cambridge; Fellow of Peterhouse, Cambridge 1978–86; Fellow, Inst. for European History, Mainz, Germany 1981; Asst. Prof. of History, Princeton Univ. 1986–91, Assoc. Prof. 1991–95, Prof. 1995; Prof. of History, Grad. Inst. of Int. Studies, Geneva 1996; Ellen Macarthur Prize for Econ. History 1982. *Publications:* The Reichsbank and Public Finance in Germany 1985, The German Slump: Politics and Economics 1924–36 1986, A German Identity 1770–1990 1989, Vom Historikerstreit zum Historikerschweigen 1993, The Deutsche Bank 1870–1890 1995, International Monetary Co-operation Since Bretton Woods 1995. *Leisure interests:* travel, music. *Address:* c/o 129 Dickinson Hall, Princeton University, Princeton, NJ 08544 (Office); 10 Dickinson Street, Princeton, NJ 08540, U.S.A. (Home).

JAMES, Harold L., PH.D.; American geologist; b. 11 June 1912, Nanaimo, B.C., Canada; s. of Evan James and Blodwen James; m. Ruth Graybeal 1936; four s.; ed. Washington State Univ. and Princeton Univ.; Geologist, U.S. Geological Survey 1941–, Chief Geologist 1965–71, Research Geologist 1971–; Visiting Lecturer, Northwestern Univ. 1953, 1954; Prof., Univ. of Minnesota 1961–65; mem. Nat. Acad. of Sciences; Pres. Soc. of Econ. Geologists 1970. *Publications:* About 70 papers in professional journals and in U.S. Geological Survey. *Leisure interests:* reading, fishing, writing. *Address:* 1320 Lakeway Drive 121, Bellingham, WA 98226, U.S.A. *Telephone:* (360) 671-7943 (Home).

JAMES, Ioan Mackenzie, M.A., D.PHIL., F.R.S.; British professor of geometry; b. 23 May 1928; s. of Reginald D. James and Jessie A. James; m. Rosemary G. Stewart 1961; no c.; ed. St. Paul's School and Queen's Coll. Oxford; Commonwealth Fund Fellow, Princeton, Univ. of Calif. Berkeley and Inst. for Advanced Study 1954–55; Tapp Research Fellow, Gonville & Caius Coll. Cambridge 1956; Reader in Pure Math. Univ. of Oxford 1957–69, Sr. Research Fellow, St. John's Coll. 1959–69, Savilian Prof. of Geometry 1970–95, Prof. Emer. 1995–, Fellow, New Coll. 1970–95, Emer. Fellow 1995–, Leverhulme Emer. Fellow 1996–98; Ed. Topology 1962–; Hon. Fellow, St. John's Coll., Oxford 1988; Hon. Prof. Univ. of Wales 1989; Whitehead Prize and Lecturer 1978; Hon. D.Sc. (Aberdeen) 1993. *Publications:* The Mathematical Works of J.H.C. Whitehead 1963, The Topology of Stiefel Manifolds 1976, Topological Topics 1983, General Topology and Homotopy Theory 1984, Aspects of Topology 1984, Topological and Uniform Spaces 1987, Fibrewise Topology 1988, Introduction to Uniform Spaces 1989, Handbook of Algebraic Topology 1995, Fibrewise Homotopy Theory 1998, papers in mathematical journals. *Address:* Mathematical Institute, 24–29 St. Giles, Oxford, OX1 3LB, England. *Telephone:* (01865) 273541.

JAMES, Michael Leonard, M.A., F.R.S.A., (pen-name Michael Hartland); British government official, writer and broadcaster; b. 7 Feb. 1941; s. of the late Leonard James and Marjorie James; m. Jill Elizabeth Tarján 1975; two d.; ed. Christ's Coll., Cambridge; entered govt. service (GCHQ) 1963; Pvt. Sec. to Rt. Hon. Jennie Lee, Minister for the Arts 1966–68; Prin. D.E.S. 1968–71; Planning Unit of Rt. Hon. Margaret Thatcher, Sec. of State for Educ. and Science 1971–73, Asst. Sec. 1973; Deputy Chief Scientific Officer 1974; Adviser to OECD, Paris, and U.K. Gov., Int. Inst. for Man. of Tech., Milan 1973–75; Int. negotiations on non-proliferation of nuclear weapons 1975–78; Dir., IAEA Vienna 1978–83; Adviser Int. Relations 1983–85 (Consultant 1985–) to Comm. of the European Communities, Brussels; a Chair. Civil Service Selection Bds. 1983–93; Chair. The Hartland Press Ltd. 1985–, Wade Hartland Films Ltd. 1991–; Hon. Fellow Univ. of Exeter 1985–; Gov. East Devon Coll. of Further Educ., Tiverton 1985–91, Colyton Grammar School 1985–90, Sidmouth Community Coll. 1988–, Chair. Bd. of Govs. 1998; Chair. Bd. of Govs. Axe Vale Further Educ. Unit, Seaton 1987–91; mem. Exeter Social Security Appeal Tribunal 1986–, Immigration Appeal Tribunal 1987–; Devon and Cornwall Rent Assessment Panel 1990–; Feature Writer and Book Reviewer for The Times (resident thriller critic 1990–91), Sunday Times, Guardian and Daily Telegraph (resident thriller critic 1993–). *TV and radio include:* Sonja's Report (ITV documentary) 1990, Masterspy: interviews with KGB defector Oleg Gordievsky (BBC Radio 4) 1991. *Publications:* Internationalization to Prevent the Spread of Nuclear Weapons (Co-author) 1980; novels (under pen-name Michael Hartland): Down Among the Dead Men 1983, Seven Steps to Treason 1985 (South West Arts Literary Award, dramatized for BBC Radio 4 1990), The Third Betrayal 1986, Frontier of Fear 1989, The Year of the Scorpion 1991, (under pen-name Ruth Carrington) Dead Fish 1998; articles on int. relations and nuclear energy. *Address:* Cotte Barton, Branscombe, Devon, EX12 3BH, England. *Telephone:* (01297) 680382. *Fax:* (01297) 680381.

JAMES, P. D. (See James of Holland Park).

JAMES, Thomas Garnet Henry, C.B.E., M.A., F.B.A.; British museum curator (retd.); b. 8 May 1923, Neath, Wales; s. of Thomas Garnet James and Edith James (née Griffiths); m. Diana Margaret Vavasseur-Durell 1956; one s.; ed. Neath Grammar School and Exeter Coll. Oxford; served in army

(R.A.) 1942–45; Asst. Keeper, British Museum 1951–74; Laycock Student, Worcester Coll. Oxford 1954–60; Keeper of Egyptian Antiquities, British Museum 1974–88; Chair. Egypt Exploration Soc. 1983–89, Vice-Pres. 1990; Chair. Advisory Cttee., Freud Museum 1987–98; Wilbour Fellow, The Brooklyn Museum 1964; Visiting Prof., Collège de France 1983; Visiting Prof. Memphis State Univ. 1990; mem. German Archaeological Inst; Hon. Fellow Exeter Coll. Oxford 1998. *Publications:* The Mastaba of Khentika 1953, The Hekanakhte Papers 1962, Hieroglyphic Texts in the British Museum, I (revised) 1961, 9 1970, Archaeology of Ancient Egypt 1972, Corpus of Hieroglyphic Inscriptions in The Brooklyn Museum, 1 1974, Pharaoh's People 1984, Egyptian Painting 1985, Ancient Egypt: The Land and Its Legacy 1988, Egypt: The Living Past 1992, Howard Carter: The Path to Tutankhamun 1992, A Short History of Ancient Egypt 1995, Egypt Revealed: Artist-Travellers in an Antique Land 1997. *Leisure interests:* music, cooking. *Address:* 113 Willifield Way, London, NW11 6YE, England (Home). *Telephone:* 0181-455 9221 (Home). *Fax:* 0181-731 6303.

JAMES OF HOLLAND PARK, Baroness (Life Peer) cr. 1991, of Southwold in the County of Suffolk, **P(hyllis) D(orothy) James,** O.B.E., J.P., F.R.S.L., F.R.S.A.; British author; b. 3 Aug. 1920, Oxford; d. of Sidney Victor James and Dorothy Amelia Hone; m. Connor Bantry White (deceased) 1941; two d.; ed. Cambridge Girls' High School; Admin., Nat. Health Service 1949–68; Prin., Home Office 1968; Police Dept. 1968–72; Criminal Policy Dept. 1972–79; J.P., Willesden 1979–82, Inner London 1984; Chair. Soc. of Authors 1984–86, Pres. 1997–; a Gov. of BBC 1988–93; Assoc. Fellow Downing Coll., Cambridge 1986; mem. Bd. of British Council 1988–93, Arts Council; Chair. Arts Council Literary Advisory Panel 1988–92; mem. Detection Club; mem. Church of England Liturgical Comm. 1991–; Hon. Fellow, St. Hilda's Coll., Oxford 1996; Hon. D.Litt. (Buckingham) 1992, (Herts.) 1994, (Glasgow) 1995, (Durham) 1998; Hon. Lit.D. (London) 1993; Dr. h.c. (Essex) 1996. *Publications:* Cover Her Face 1962, A Mind to Murder 1963, Unnatural Causes 1967, Shroud for a Nightingale 1971, The Maul and the Pear Tree (with T. A. Critchley) 1971, An Unsuitable Job for a Woman 1972, The Black Tower 1975, Death of an Expert Witness 1977, Innocent Blood 1980, The Skull beneath the Skin 1982, A Taste for Death 1986, Devices and Desires 1989, The Children of Men 1992, Original Sin 1994, A Certain Justice 1997. *Leisure interests:* exploring churches, walking by the sea. *Address:* c/o Greene & Heaton Ltd, 37A Goldhawk Road, London, W12 8QQ, England.

JAMIR, S. C., B.A., LL.B.; Indian politician; b. 17 Oct. 1931; s. of Shri Senayangba; m. Alemia Jamir 1959; three s. two d.; ed. Univ. of Allahabad; mem. Interim Body of Nagaland, then Jt. Sec. Naga People's Convention; Vice-Chair. Mokokchung Town Cttee. 1959–60; M.P. 1961–70; Parl. Sec., Ministry of External Affairs, Govt. of India 1961–67; Union Deputy Minister of Railways, of Labour and Rehabilitation, of Community Devt. and Co-operation, Food and Agric. 1968–70; elected mem. to Nagaland Legis. Ass. 1971–73, re-elected mem. from Aonglenden Constituency 1974; subsequently apptd. Minister of Finance, Revenue and Border Affairs; re-elected 1977 and apptd. Deputy Chief Minister in UDF Ministry; Chief Minister of ULP Ministry April 1980; resgnd. when NNDP Ministry came to power June 1980; Leader of Opposition Congress (I) in State Legis. Ass. 1980–82; elected from 26 Aonglenden Constituency, Gen. Elections 1982; unanimously elected Leader Congress (I) Legislature Party, Chief Minister Nagaland 1982–86, 1989–92, 1993–; M.P. Rajya Sabha 1987–89. *Address:* Chief Minister's Secretariat, Kohima, Nagaland, India.

JAMMEH, Col. Yahya A. J. J.; Gambian Head of State and army officer (retd.); b. 25 May 1965, Kanilai Village, Foni Kansala Dist., Western Div., m. Tuti Faal-Jammeh; ed. Gambia High School; joined fmr. Gambia Nat. Gendarmerie as Pvt. 1984; with Special Intervention Unit, Gambia Nat. Army 1984–86, Sergeant 1986, Escort Training Instructor, Gendarmerie Training School 1986–89, Cadet Officer 1987, commissioned 1989, Second Lieut. 1989, in charge of Presidential Escort, Presidential Guards 1989–90, C.O. Mobile Gendarmerie Jan.–June 1991, Mil. Police Unit June–Aug. 1991, Lieut. 1992, Commdr. Gambia Nat. Army Mil. Police Aug.–Nov. 1992, Capt. 1994, Col. 1996; became Chair. Armed Forces Provisional Ruling Council, Head of State 1994; elected Pres. of The Gambia Sept. 1996–; numerous awards. *Leisure interests:* playing tennis, soccer, hunting, reading, correspondence, driving and riding motorcycles, music, films, animals. *Address:* Office of the President, State House, Banjul, The Gambia.

JANABIL; Chinese party official; b. April 1934, Khaba Co., Xinjiang; s. of Simagul Janabil and Ajikhan Janabil; m. Zubila Janabil 1955; two s. two d.; alt. mem. 10th CCP Cen. Cttee. 1973; Vice-Chair. Revolutionary Cttee., Xinjiang Autonomous Region 1975–79; Chair. Revolutionary Cttee., and First Sec. CCP Cttee., Ili Autonomous Kazakh Pref. 1975–80; Deputy Sec. CCP Cttee., Xinjiang 1977–83, Sec. 1983–85; Vice-Chair. Xinjiang 1979–83; Deputy Sec. CCP 4th Xinjiang Uyghur Autonomous Regional Cttee. 1983–; Chair. CPPCC 7th Xinjiang Uygur Autonomous Regional Cttee. 1993; Pres. Xinjiang Br. Futurology Soc. 1980; alt. mem. 12th CCP Cen. Cttee. 1982, 13th Cen. Cttee. 1987, 14th Cen. Cttee. 1992–. *Address:* c/o Xinjiang Autonomous Regional Chinese Communist Party, Urumqi, Xinjiang, People's Republic of China.

JANCSÓ, Miklós; Hungarian film director; b. 27 Sept. 1921, Vác; s. of Sándor Jancsó and Angela Poparád; m. 1st Katalin Wowesny 1949; one s. one d.; m. 2nd Márta Mészáros 1958; one s. ; m. 3rd Zsuzsa Csákány 1981; one s.; studied legal sciences and ethnography at Kolozsvár (now Cluj), Romania, and Budapest Coll. of Cinematographic Art; worked at newsreel studio 1953–58; Documentary film studio 1962; Chief Producer, Hunnia Film Studio 1963–; Grand Prix of San Francisco 1961, Prize of Fédération Internationale de la Presse Cinématographique (FIPRESCI), Balázs Béla prize 1965, Merited artist 1970, Eminent Artist of the Hungarian People's Repub. 1980, Best Dir. Award, Cannes Festival 1972, Kossuth Prize (2nd Degree) 1973, Prize for Oeuvre Complet (Cannes) 1982, Prize for Oeuvre Complet (Venice) 1990, Best Dir. Award, Montreal 1992. *Films:* A harangok Rómába mentek (The Bells have gone to Rome) 1959, Oldás és Kötés (Cantata) 1963, Igy Jöttem (My Way Home) 1965, Szegény Legények (The Round-Up) 1966, Csillagosok—Katonák (The Red and the White) 1967, Csend és Kiáltás (Silence and Cry) 1968, Fényes Szelek (The Confrontation) 1969, Sirókkó (Winter Wind) 1969, La Pacifista 1970, Agnus Dei 1971, Red Psalm 1972, Elektreia (Electra) 1975, Private Vices, Public Virtues 1976, Hungarian Rhapsody 1978, Allegro Barbaro 1978, The Tyrant's Heart or Boccaccio in Hungary 1981, Omega 1984, The Dawn 1985, Season of Monsters 1987, The God is Going Backwards 1990, The Blue Danube Waltz 1991; For Italian TV: Il Tecnico e il Rito, Roma rivuole Cesare, La Pacifista; *Stage productions:* Jack the Ripper (Budapest) 1977, Nostoi (Seoul) 1988; *Opera directed:* Otello (Florence) 1980. *Address:* Eszter u. 17, 1022 Budapest, Hungary (Home). *Telephone:* 135-3761 (Home).

JANDA, Krystyna; Polish actress, film and theatre director; b. 18 Dec. 1952, Starachowice; m.; two s. one d.; ed. State Higher School of Drama, Warsaw; actress Atheneum Theatre, Warsaw 1976–93, Powszechny Theatre, Warsaw 1993–; acting in TV and cabarets; numerous awards in Poland and abroad; above 30 leading roles in classic and contemporary plays. *Films include:* Man of Marble 1976, Without Anaesthetic 1978, The Border 1978, The Conductor 1979, Die Grune Vogel 1979, Golem 1979, Mephisto 1980, War Between Worlds 1980, Man of Iron 1981, Interrogation 1982, Espion lève Toi 1981, Bella Donna 1983, Ce fut un Bel Eté 1982, Gluth 1983, Der Bulle und das Madchen 1984, Vertige 1985, My Mother's Lovers 1985, Laputa 1986, Short Film About Killing 1987, II Decalogue, V Decalogue 1988, Ownership 1989, Polish Kitchen 1991, Relieved of the Life 1992, Pestka (actress and dir.) 1995, As 1995, Mother's Mother 1996, Unwritten Principles 1997, Last Chapter 1997. *Stage appearances include:* Bal manekinów 1974, Edukacja Rity 1984, Z zycia glist 1984, Biała bluzka 1987, Medea 1988, Shirley Valentine 1990, Kobieta zawieckiona 1996, Kotka na gorącym blaszanym dachu 1997, Maria Callas Lelicja śpiewa 1997. *TV series:* Mierzejewska 1989. Best Actress 40th Int. Film Festival, San Sebastián. *Address:* Teatr Powszechny, ul. Zamoyskiego 20, Warsaw, Poland.

JANDL, Ernst, D.PHIL.; Austrian poet and dramatist; b., 1 Aug. 1925, Vienna; s. of Viktor and Luise (née Rappel) Jandl; ed. Univ. of Vienna; teacher at grammar schools 1946–79; writer 1952–; Visiting Prof., Univ. of Texas, Austin 1971; Lecturer in Poetics, Johann Wolfgang Goethe Univ., Frankfurt am Main, winter term 1984; Georg-Trakl-Prize for Poetry 1974; Great Austrian State Prize 1984; Georg-Büchner-Prize 1984; Frankfurter Hörspiel Prize 1989; Peter Huchel Prize for Poetry 1990; H. von Kleist Prize 1993; Friedrich Hölderlin Prize 1995; Grosses Goldenes Ehrenzeichen (Austria) 1996, Austrian Insignia for Arts and Letters. *Publications:* poetry: Andere Augen 1956, Laut und Luise 1966, Sprechblasen 1968, Der künstliche Baum 1970, Dingfest 1973, Die Bearbeitung der Mütze 1978, Der gelbe Hund 1980, Selbstporträt des Schachspielers als trinkende Uhr 1983, Idyllen 1989, Stanzen 1992, Lechts und Rinks 1995, Peter und die Kuh 1996; play: Aus der Fremde 1980; lectures and essays: Die schöne Kunst des Schreibens 1976, Das Öffnen und Schliessen des Mundes 1985; Collected Works (3 vols.) 1985; Poetical Works (10 vols.) 1997. *Leisure interest:* jazz. *Address:* P.O. Box 227, A-1041 Vienna, Austria. *Telephone:* 505-80-22.

JANEWAY, Elizabeth Hall, A.B.; American author; b. 7 Oct. 1913, Brooklyn, New York; d. of Charles H. and Jeannette F. (Searle) Hall; m. Eliot Janeway 1938 (died 1993); two s.; ed. Barnard Coll.; Assoc. Fellow Yale Univ.; educator's award Delta Kappa Gamma, 1972; mem. Council, Authors Guild, Council Authors League America, PEN; Chair. N.Y. State Council for the Humanities; Assoc. Fellow Yale; Hon. Ph.D. (Simpson Coll., Cedarcrest Coll., Villa Maria Coll.), Hon D.H.L. (Russell Sage Coll., Fla. Int. Univ., Simmons Coll. 1989); Medal of Distinction, Barnard Coll. 1981, Fellow A.A.A.S. *Publications:* The Walsh Girls 1943, Daisy Kenyon 1945, The Question of Gregory 1949, The Vikings 1951, Leaving Home 1953, Early Days of the Automobile 1956, The Third Choice 1959, Angry Kate 1963, Accident 1964, Ivanov Seven 1967, Man's World, Women's Place 1971, Between Myth and Morning: Women Awakening 1974, Harvard Guide to Contemporary American Writing 1979, Powers of the Weak 1980, contributions to Comprehensive Textbook of Psychology 1974, 1980, Cross Sections from a Decade of Change 1982, Improper Behaviour 1987. *Address:* 350 East 79th Street, New York, NY 10021, U.S.A.

JANEWAY, Richard, A.B., M.D.; American physician and medical school administrator; b. 12 Feb. 1933, Los Angeles, Calif.; s. of VanZandt and Grace Eleanor Bell Janeway; m. Katherine Esmond Pillsbury 1955; one s. two d.; ed. Colgate Univ., Univ. of Pennsylvania School of Medicine; Instructor in Neurology, Bowman Gray School of Medicine of Wake Forest Univ. (now Wake Forest Univ. School of Medicine) 1966–67, Asst. Prof. 1967–70, Assoc. Prof. 1970–71, Prof. 1971–, Dean 1971–85, Exec. Dean 1985–94, Vice-Pres. for Health Affairs 1983–90, Exec. Vice-Pres. 1990–97, Univ. Prof. of Medicine and Man. 1997–, Exec. Vice-Pres. Emer. for Health Affairs 1997–; mem. Bd. of Dirs. Castle Springs, Inc. 1993–, Qual Choice of N.C. 1994–; Chair. Asscn.

of American Medical Colls. 1984–85; mem. Bd. Dirs. BB&T Corpn. 1995–, S. Nat. Corpn. 1989–95; mem. Nat. Asscn. for Biomedical Research 1993–96, Americans for Medical Progress Inc. 1993–97; mem. Bd. of Trustees Colgate Univ., 1988–95, Winston-Salem State Univ. 1991–95; John and Mary R. Markle Scholar in Acad. Medicine; mem. Inst. of Medicine of N.A.S., American Medical Asscn., A.A.A.S., American Heart Asscn., American Neurological Asscn., Soc. for Neuroscience, Soc. of Medical Admins., American Clinical and Climatological Asscn.; Fellow American Acad. of Neurology; Life Fellow American Coll. of Physicians. *Leisure interests:* golf, photography, gardening, travel. *Address:* Wake Forest University, School of Medicine, Medical Center Blvd., Winston-Salem, NC 27157 (Office); 2710 Old Town Club Road, Winston-Salem, NC 27106, U.S.A. (Home). *Telephone:* (336) 716-1825 (Office); (336) 727-7537 (Home). *Fax:* (336) 716-1822.

JANICOT, Daniel Claude Emmanuel, L. EN D.; French international official; b. 20 May 1948, Neuilly; s. of François-Xavier Janicot and Antoinette Mauxion; m. 2nd Catherine Lachenal 1991; one s.; two d. from previous marriage; ed. Ecole Nat. d'Admin., Inst. d'Etudes Politiques and Faculté de Droit, Paris; Auditeur, Conseil d'Etat 1975–, Deputy Sec.-Gen. 1978–82, Maître des requêtes 1979; Maître de Confs. Insts. d'Etudes Politiques, Paris and Bordeaux and Ecole Nat. des Ponts et Chaussées; mem. Admin. Council, Public Information Library, Beaubourg 1979; Del. Gen. American Center 1980–90; Vice-Pres. Bibliothèque Nationale 1981; Maître de séminaire, Ecole Nat. d'Admin. 1982–83; Del. Gen. Union Centrale des Arts Décoratifs 1982–86; Special Adviser Office of Dir.-Gen. of UNESCO 1990–91, Dir. of Exec. Office of Dir.-Gen. 1991–94, Asst. Dir.-Gen. 1994–; State Councillor 1995–; Chair. Bd., Centre Nat. d'Art Contemporain de Grenoble 1995–; Vice-Chair. Bd., Institut Français de Gestion 1996–; Chevalier, Ordre Nat. du Mérite, Ordre des Arts et des Lettres. *Address:* UNESCO, 7 place de Fontenoy, 75007 Paris (Office); 6 rue Casimir-Périer, 75007 Paris, France (Home). *Telephone:* (1) 45 68 13 00 (Office). *Fax:* (1) 47 34 85 87.

JANKLOW, William John, B.S., J.D.; American politician and lawyer; b. 13 Sept. 1939, Chicago, Ill.; s. of Arthur and LouElla Janklow; m. Mary Dean Thom 1960; one s. two d.; ed. Flandreau High School, South Dakota, Univ. of South Dakota; Staff Attorney and Chief Officer, S. Dakota Legal Services 1966–67; Directing Attorney and Chief Officer, S. Dakota Legal Services 1967–72; Chief Trial Attorney, S. Dakota Attorney Gen.'s Office 1973–74; Attorney Gen. of S. Dakota 1975–79; Gov. of S. Dakota 1979–87, 1995–; apptd. Bd. of Dir. of Nat. Legal Services Corpn.; Nat. award for legal excellence and skill; various awards; mem. Exec. Cttee. of the Nat. Governors' Asscn.; Republican. *Leisure interests:* waterskiing, collecting 1950s music. *Address:* Office of the Governor, 500 E. Capitol Avenue, Pierre, SD 57501, U.S.A.

JANKOWITSCH, Peter, D.D.L.; Austrian diplomatist and politician; b. 10 July 1933, Vienna; s. of Karl and Gertrude (née Ladstaetter) Jankowitsch; m. Odette Prevor 1962; one s.; ed. Vienna Univ. and The Hague Acad. of Int. Law; fmr. lawyer; joined foreign service 1957, worked in Int. Law Dept.; Private Sec., Cabinet of Minister of Foreign Affairs 1959–62; posted to London 1962–64; Chargé d'affaires, Dakar, Senegal 1964–66; Head of Office of Bruno Kreisky, Chair. Austrian Socialist Party 1967; Chief of Cabinet of Fed. Chancellor (Kreisky) 1970–72; Perm. Rep. to UN 1972–78; Perm. Rep. to OECD 1978–82; Deputy Perm. Under-Sec., Chief of Cabinet, Fed. Ministry of Foreign Affairs 1982–83; Fed. Minister for Foreign Affairs 1986–87; mem. Austrian Nat. Ass. (Nationalrat) 1983–90 (Chair. Foreign Relations Cttee. 1987–90), 1992–93; Minister of State for Integration and Devt. Co-operation 1990–92; Perm. Rep. to OECD and ESA 1993–98; Chair. OECD Devt. Centre 1994–98; Chair. Jt. Cttee. European Parl.–Austrian Parl.; Chair. UN Cttee. on Peaceful Uses of Outer Space 1972–91; Vice-Chair. of Bd., Int. Energy Agency 1979–83; Rep. for Austria to UN Security Council 1973–75, Pres. Security Council Nov. 1973, Vice-Pres. 29th Gen. Assembly; Vice-Pres. 7th Special Session of Gen. Assembly Sept. 1975; mem. UN Security Council Mission to Zambia 1973; Sec.-Gen. Franco-Austrian Centre for East-West Encounters 1998–; Int. Sec. Soc. Dem. Party of Austria 1983–90; Chair. Human Rights Cttee. Socialist Int. 1987–97; Pres. Cttee. of Parliamentarians of EFTA 1989–90; Hon. Pres., Austrian Soc. for European Policy 1996–; mem. Bd. Austrian Foreign Policy Soc, Austrian Inst. for Int. Politics, Vienna Inst. for Devt., Austrian UN League (fmrly Vice-Pres.); Vice-Chair. Socialist Int. Cttee. on Econ. Affairs 1997–; Pres. Austrian Nat. Cttee. for Unispace 1999; Hon. mem. Bd. Int. Inst. of Space Law. *Publications:* Kreisky's Era in Austrian Foreign Policy (Ed. with E. Bielka and H. Thalberg) 1982, Red Markings—International (Ed. with H. Fischer) 1984 and papers and articles on Austria and on econ. and political devt. of the Third World; contrib. to Wörterbuch des Völkerrechts 1960. *Leisure interests:* history and baroque music. *Address:* Salzgries 19, 1010 Vienna, Austria. *Telephone:* (1) 535 23 35. *Fax:* (1) 533 89 27.

JANKOWSKA-CIEŚLAK, Jadwiga; Polish actress; b. 15 Feb. 1951, Gdańsk; m.; one s. one d.; ed. State Higher School of Drama, Warsaw; numerous awards including prize for best actress of Cannes Film Festival 1982. *Leisure interests:* knitting, fishing. *Address:* Film Polski, ul. Mazewiecka 6/8, 00-950 Warsaw, Poland.

JANNUZZI, Giovanni; Italian diplomatist; b. 6 Nov. 1935, Rome; s. of Senator Onofrio Jannuzzi and Renata Calzolari; m. Princess Anne de Looz-Corswarem and de Corswarem-Looz; ed. St. Joseph Coll. Rome and Univ. of Rome; Amb. to Nigeria 1980–82; Deputy Perm. Rep. to UN, New York 1982–85; Deputy Political Dir. Ministry of Foreign Affairs 1985–86; Head Secr. of European Political Cooperation, EC, Brussels 1987–91; Dir.-Gen. of Econ. Affairs, Ministry of Foreign Affairs 1991–93; Dir. Cabt. of Minister of Foreign Affairs 1992; now Perm. Rep. of Italy to North Atlantic Council, Brussels; Assoc. Prof. Univ. of Rome Law School 1993; Grand Officer, Order of Repub. of Italy; decorations from Spain, Belgium, Brazil, Austria, Qatar. *Publications:* poetry: Stazione di Frontiera 1989, Il Bel Tempo 1991. *Leisure interests:* poetry, journalism. *Address:* NATO Headquarters, Evère, 1110 Brussels, boulevard Léopold III (Office); 9 avenue des Sorbiers, 1180 Uccle, Belgium (Home). *Telephone:* 322-707.62.11 (Office); 322-375.62.56 (Home).

JANOT, Raymond Marcel Louis, L. EN D., L. ÈS L.; French civil servant; b. 9 March 1917, Paris; s. of Gaston Janot and Madeleine Paumier; m. Catherine de Brunel de Serbonnes 1940; two s. two d.; ed. Coll. Stanislas, Lycée Henry-IV, Paris Univ. and Ecole Libre des Sciences Politiques; Auditeur, Conseil d'Etat 1946, Maître des Requêtes 1948; Legal Counsellor, Présidence de la République 1947–51; Econ. Counsellor French High Comm. in Indo-China 1951–52; Dir. du Cabinet, Minister for Relations with Associated States 1952–53; Sec.-Gen. Conseil d'Etat 1956–59; Mayor of Serbonnes, Conseiller général of canton of Sergines 1959, 1961, 1967, 1979, 1985; Tech. Counsellor, Gen. de Gaulle 1958–59; Sec.-Gen. French Community 1959–60; Dir.-Gen. Radiodiffusion-Télévision française 1960–62; mem. Conseil d'Etat 1962; Pres. Econ. Devt. Cttee. of Yonne 1964–; mem. Econ. and Social Comm. Bourgogne 1964–73; Pres. Admin. Council of the commune and dept. of Paris 1983; Vice-Pres. Syndicat Nat. de l'Industrie Pharmaceutique 1975–; Pres. Superior Admin. Council of the Commune and Dept. of Paris 1983–; Pres. Conseil régional de Bourgogne 1989–92; Commandeur Légion d'honneur; Croix de guerre, Médaille des Evadés, Commdr. Ordre nationale du Mérite. *Address:* 11 avenue d'Eylau, 75116 Paris; le Petit Varennes, 89140 Serbonnes, France. *Telephone:* (1) 47-27-72-89.

JANOWITZ, Gundula; Austrian opera singer; b. 2 Aug. 1937, Berlin, Germany; d. of Theodor and Else (née Neumann) Janowitz; m.; one d.; ed. Acad. of Music and Performing Arts, Graz; Début with Vienna State Opera 1960; has sung with Deutsche Oper, Berlin 1966, Metropolitan Opera, New York 1967, Teatro Colón, Buenos Aires 1970, Munich State Opera 1971, Grand Opera, Paris 73, Covent Garden Opera 1976, La Scala 1978; concerts in major cities throughout the world, appearances at Bayreuth, Aix-en-Provence, Glyndebourne, Spoleto, Salzburg, Munich Festivals; mem. Vienna State Opera, Deutsche Oper, Berlin; recordings with Deutsche Grammophon, EMI, Decca. *Leisure interest:* modern literature. *Address:* 3072 Kasten 75, Austria.

JANOWSKI, Gabriel, D.AGRIC.; Polish politician and farmer; b. 22 April 1947, Konstantów; s. of Jan Janowski and Józefa Janowska; m. Elżbieta Radomyska 1974; one s. two d.; ed. Lycée, Błonie, Warsaw Agric. Univ., Int. Agric. Center, Wageningen, Netherlands; scientific worker and tutor, Warsaw Agric. Univ., 1971–80, 1983–89; Founder and Vice-Pres., Solidarity Workers' Union of Farmers 1980–81, Pres. 1989–91; interned 1981–82; Co-organizer, Farmers' Pastorate 1983–89; lecturer, people's univs. 1983–89; Co-organizer and Vice-Pres., Warsaw Econ. Soc. 1986; Founder and Vice-Chair., Econ. Union 1989; Senator 1989–91; Vice-Pres., Citizens' Parl. Club 1989–91; Founder, Bank of Econ. Union 1990; Deputy to Sejm (Parl.) 1991–93, 1997–; Minister of Agric. and Food Economy 1991–93; Pres. Polish Peasants' Party—People's Alliance (PSL—PL) 1992; Chair. Parl. Cttee. on Agric. and Rural Devt. 1997–; mem. Parl. Ass., Council of Europe 1997–. *Leisure interests:* history, gardens. *Address:* 02-958 Warsaw, ul. Stanisława Kostki 5 m. 3 (Home); 05-870 Błonie, Faszczyce Stare 18, Poland. *Telephone:* 642 01 49 (Home); 725 47 54 (Farm).

JANOWSKI, Jan Stanislaw, D.SC.; Polish politician and professor of metallurgy; b. 20 June 1928, Kielce; s. of Franciszek Janowski and Kazimiera Cudek; m. Maria Włoch 1962; one s. one d.; Projects Office of Cement and Lime Industry, Cracow 1951–54; Head, Sub-Dept. of Pig Iron Metallurgy, Univ. of Mining and Metallurgy, Cracow 1954–69, Asst. Prof. 1969–72, Extraordinary Prof. 1972–78, Ord. Prof. 1978–, Dean Metallurgical Faculty 1972–78, Dir. Inst. of Metallurgy 1974–78, Vice-Rector 1978–81, Head, Blast Furnace Dept., Inst. of Metallurgy 1980–88, Rector 1987–93; mem. Inst. of Metals (U.K.) and other scientific bodies; mem. Presidium, Cen. Cttee. 1976–81, 1985–90; Pres. Democratic Party (SD) 1993–; Deputy to Sejm (Parl.) 1976–91; Chair. SD Deputies' Club 1989, Vice-Pres. 1976–81, Pres. Science and Tech. Progress Cttee. 1981–82; Vice-Pres. Foreign Affairs Cttee. and Polish Group of Interparl. Union 1980–82, 1985–89; participant Round Table plenary debates Feb.–April 1989; Deputy Prime Minister, Vice-Chair. Council of Ministers and Minister-Head of the State Office for Scientific-Technological Progress and Implementation 1989–91; Pres. Cttee. on Scientific and Tech. Devt. of Council of Ministers 1989–91; Vice-Pres. Econ. Cttee. Council of Ministers 1989–91; mem. Presidential Science Council 1992–95; State Prize (1st class) 1972; Commdr.'s with Star, Commdr.'s and Officer's Cross, Order of Polonia Restituta; Gold Cross of Merit and other decorations. *Leisure interests:* sport, tourism, bridge, historical books, playing with grandson. *Address:* c/o Stronnictwo Demokratyczne, 00-021 Warsaw, ul. Chmielna 9; 30-047 Cracow, ul. Szymanowskiego 1 m. 10, Poland. *Telephone:* 33.26.13 (Office); 33.58.35 (Home). *Fax:* 33.36.73.

JANOWSKI, Marek; German conductor; b. 18 Feb. 1939; studied in Italy and Fed. Repub. of Germany; Music Dir. Freiburg and Dortmund operas 1973–79; regular Guest Conductor Paris, West Berlin, Hamburg, Cologne and Munich opera houses; has also conducted at Metropolitan Opera, New York and Chicago, San Francisco, Dresden and Vienna State operas and Teatro Colon, Buenos Aires and Orange Festival, France; has conducted concerts with Berlin Philharmonic, Chicago Symphony, London Symphony Orchestra, Philharmonia, NHK (Tokyo), Dresden Staatskapelle, Boston Symphony Orchestra, Stockholm Philharmonic and BBC Symphony Orchestra; fmr. Artistic Adviser, Royal Liverpool Philharmonic Orchestra; Chief Conductor Orchestre Philharmonique de Radio France 1984–; and Gurzenich-Orchester, Cologne 1986–; recordings include Wagner's Der Ring des Nibelungen, Weber's Euryanthe and Die Schweigsame Frau, Penderecki's The Devil of London and Bruckner's Symphony No. 6.

JANSEN, Jan Kristian Schøning, DR.MED.; Norwegian professor of physiology; b. 16 Jan. 1931, Oslo; s. of Jan Jansen and Helene Schøning; m. Helen Troye 1981; three s. two d.; ed. Oslo Univ.; Rockefeller Foundation Research Fellow, Univ. of Oxford 1959–60; Asst. Prof. Dept. of Physiology, Oslo Univ. 1968–79, Prof. of Physiology 1979–96; Visiting Prof. Harvard Medical School 1970–71; Sr. Research Fellow, Norwegian Research Council 1995–; Anders Jahres Prize 1967, Monrad Krohn Legat 1982, Fridtjof Nansen Award 1996. *Publications:* articles in professional journals. *Address:* c/o Institute of Physiology, University of Oslo, P.B. 1103, Blindern, 0317 Oslo 3, Norway.

JANSONS, Maris; Latvian conductor; b. 14 Jan. 1943, Riga, Latvia; s. of Arvid Jansons and Erhaida Jansons; m. Irina Jansons 1967; one d.; ed. by father (also conductor), then Leningrad Conservatory (under N. Rabinovich), Vienna Conservatory (with Hans Swarovsky) and Salzburg (under von Karajan); Prin. Guest Conductor of Leningrad (now St. Petersburg) Philharmonic Orchestra, Chief Conductor of Oslo Philharmonic 1979–; Guest Conductor of Welsh Symphony Orchestra 1985–88; Prin. Guest Conductor of London Philharmonic Orchestra -1997; Chief Conductor of Pittsburgh Symphony Orchestra 1997–; has appeared all over world, with Berlin Philharmonic, Royal Concertgebouw Orchestra, Montreal Symphony, Toronto Symphony and maj. British orchestras; world-wide tours with Oslo Philharmonic and Leningrad Philharmonic; R.S.F.S.R. People's Artist 1986; Royal Norwegian Order of Merit 1988. *Leisure interests:* arts, theatre, films, sports. *Address:* c/o Oslo Philharmonic Orchestra, P.O. Box 1607, 0119 Oslo, Norway; c/o IMG Artists Europe, Media House, 3 Burlington Lane, London, W.4., England. *Telephone:* (812) 315-03-06 (St. Petersburg, Russia).

JANSSEN, Baron Daniel, ING., LIC., M.B.A.; Belgian business executive; b. 15 April 1936, Brussels; s. of Baron Charles-E. Janssen and Marie-Anne (née Boël) Janssen; m. Thérèse Bracht 1970; three s.; ed. Univ. of Brussels, Harvard Univ.; Asst. Sec. Euratom Comm., Brussels 1959–60; Prof. Brussels Univ. 1965–71; mem. Club of Rome 1968–87; Bd. of Dirs. Brussels Univ. 1969–70; mem. of Bd. Inst. pour l'Encouragement de la Recherche Scientifique dans l'Industrie et l'Agriculture (IRSIA) 1971–77, Vice-Chair. 1974–77; mem. of Bd. Belgian Fed. of Chemical Industries 1972–76, Chair. 1976–79; mem. European Cttee. for R & D, EEC 1974–79; Chair. Exec. Cttee. UCB 1975–84, Fed. of Belgian Enterprises 1981–84; C.E.O., Solvay & Cie. S.A. 1986–, now Chair. Bd.; holds non-exec. functions on numerous enterprises; recipient of Alumni Achievement Award, Harvard Business School. *Leisure interests:* tennis, skiing, shooting. *Address:* Solvay & Cie S.A., 33 rue du Prince Albert, 1050 Brussels (Office); La Roncière, 108 avenue Ernest Solvay, 1310 La Hulpe, Belgium (Home).

JANSSEN, Paul-Emmanuel, (Baron Janssen), LL.D.; Belgian banker; b. 22 Feb. 1931; m. Cecilia Löfgren; one s. one d.; ed. Univ. Libre de Bruxelles, Harvard Business School of Admin., Boston, U.S.A.; Chair. Generale de Banque S.A., Soc. Immobilière du Brabant, Atlas Copco Airpower, Belgium, United World Coll., Belgium; Dir. Solvac, Atlas Copco AB, Sweden, Union Financière Boël, Usines Gustave Boël, Groupe Lhoist; Commdr. Ordre de la Couronne. *Leisure interests:* riding, hunting, forestry, music. *Address:* Generale de Banque, S.A., Montagne du Parc 3, 1000 Brussels, Belgium.

JANSSON, Jan-Magnus, PH.D.; Finnish professor and publisher; b. 24 Jan. 1922, Helsinki; s. of Carl Gösta and Anna-Lisa Jansson (née Kuhlefelt); m. 1st Kerstin Edgren 1948 (divorced 1970); m. 2nd Marita Hausen 1970 (divorced 1975); m. 3rd Siv Dahlin 1976; two d.; ed. Helsinki Univ.; Prof. of Political Science, Helsinki Univ. 1954–74; Minister of Trade and Industry 1973–74; Ed.-in-Chief Hufvudstadsbladet 1974–87; Chair. Bd. Finnish Inst. of Foreign Affairs 1959–85; Chair. Paasikivi Soc. 1964–66, 1975–85, Swedish People's Party in Finland 1966–73, Parl. Defence Comms. 1970–71, 1975–76, 1980–81, mem. Governmental Comm.'s for Constitutional Reform 1983–90; mem. Bd. Int. Political Science Assoc. 1966–73; Chancellor Åbo Akad. (Swedish Univ. of Finland) 1985–90; Commdr. Order of the White Rose of Finland, Commdr. Grand Cross of the Order of the Lion of Finland, Cross of Liberty. *Publications:* Hans Kelsens statsteori 1950, Frihet och jämlikhet 1952, Politikens teori 1969, Idé och verklighet i politiken 1972, Ledare 1981, Från splittring till samverkan: parlamentarismen i Finland 1992, Tidiga Möten (memoirs) 1996 and two collections of poetry. *Leisure interest:* literature. *Address:* Linnankoskigatan 15 B 16, 00250 Helsinki 25, Finland (Home). *Telephone:* 493424 (Home).

JANVIER, Gen. Bernard Louis Antonin; French army officer; b. 16 July 1939, La Voulte-sur-Rhône, Ardèche; s. of Pierre Janvier and Eugénie Bernard; m. Denise Diaz 1963; two s. one d.; ed. Lycée de Nice, Coll. d'Orange, Lycée Bugeaud, Algiers, Univ. of Rennes and Ecole Spéciale Militaire de Saint-Cyr; commissioned 2nd Lieut. 1960; served in Algeria 1962–64, Madagascar and Comoros 1964–67; Co. Commdt. 9th Parachute Regt. 1968–70; Commdt. in charge of trainee officers, Ecole Spéciale Militaire de Saint-Cyr 1970–72; Bn. Chief 1974; training course, Ecole Supérieure de Guerre 1974–76; Lieut.-Col. 1978; Second-in-Command, Bureau of Operations-Instruction 1981; Col. 1982; Chef de Corps, 2nd Overseas Parachute Regt. 1982–84; Head, Office of Personnel, Chief of Ground Forces 1984–87; Deputy to Gen. Commdt. 6th Armoured Div. 1987–89; Brig.-Gen. 1988; Chief. Org.-Logistic Div. of Army Chief of Staff 1989–91; Commdt. Operation Requin, Port Gentil, Gabon 1991; Commdt. Daguet Div. Saudi Arabia and Iraq 1991; Div. Gen. 1991; Commdt. 6th Armoured Div. Nîmes 1991–93; Army Chief of Staff, Operational Planning (Emia) 1993–95; Gen. Army Corps 1994; Army Chief of Staff 1995–; Dir. Centre des hautes études militaires, Inst. des hautes études de la défense national 1996–; Commdt. UN Peace Forces in fmr. Yugoslavia 1995; Commdr. Légion d'honneur, Ordre Nat. du Mérite, Legion of Merit (U.S.A.); numerous other decorations including medals from Kuwait and Saudi Arabia. *Leisure interests:* history of Provence, running. *Address:* Institut des hautes études de la défense nationale — Centre des hautes études militaires, Ecole militaire, 17–21 place Joffre, 00450 Armées (Office); 6 place de l'Eglise, 83310 Grimaud, France (Home).

JANZEN, Daniel Hunt, PH.D.; American professor of biology; b. 18 Jan. 1939, Millwaukee, Wis.; s. of Daniel Hugo Janzen and Floyd Foster Janzen; twice m., twice divorced; one s. one d. from 1st marriage; ed. Univ. of Minnesota and Univ. of California, Berkeley; Asst. and Assoc. Prof., Univ. of Kansas 1965–68; Assoc. Prof., Univ. of Chicago 1969–72; Assoc. Prof. and Prof. of Ecology and Evolutionary Biology, Univ. of Mich. 1972–76; Prof. of Biology, Univ. of Pa., Philadelphia 1976–; teacher Org. for Tropical Studies in Costa Rica 1965–; field research in tropical ecology, supported mainly by grants from Nat. Science Foundation, U.S.A. 1963; MacArthur Fellow 1989; Gleason Award, American Botanical Soc. 1975; Crafoord Prize, Coevolutionary Ecology, Swedish Royal Acad. of Sciences 1984. *Publications:* Herbivores (Ed., with G. A. Rosenthal) 1979, Costa Rican Natural History (Ed.) 1983 and over 250 papers in scientific journals. *Leisure interest:* tropical ecology. *Address:* Department of Biology, University of Pennsylvania, Philadelphia, PA 19104, U.S.A.; Parque Nacional Santa Rosa, Apdo. 169, Liberia, Guanacaste Province, Costa Rica. *Telephone:* (215) 898-5636 (U.S.A.); 69-55-98 (Costa Rica).

JAPAN, Emperor of (see Akihito).

JARAY, Tess, D.F.A.; British artist, b. 31 Dec. 1937, Vienna; d. of Dr Francis F. and Pauline Jaray; m. 1960 (divorced 1983); two d.; ed. Alice Ottley School, Worcester, St. Martin's School of Art and Slade School of Fine Art; French Govt. scholarship 1961; teacher Hornsey Coll. of Art 1964–88, Slade School of Art 1968–; commissioned to paint mural for British Pavilion, Expo '67, Montreal, terrazzo floor Victoria Station, London 1985, Centenary Square, Birmingham 1988, Cathedral Precinct Wakefield 1989, Hosp. Square, Leeds 1998; individual exhbns. Grabowski Gallery, London 1963, Hamilton Galleries, London 1965, 1967, Axiom Gallery, London 1969, Whitechapel Gallery, London 1973, Adelaide Festival Centre 1980, Whitworth Art Gallery, Manchester, and Ashmolean Museum, Oxford 1984, Serpentine Gallery 1988; numerous group exhbns. in Rome, Liverpool, London, Bern, etc. *Address:* 29 Camden Square, London, N.W.1, England. *Telephone:* 0171-485 5057.

JARMAN, Franklin Maxey; American business executive; b. 10 Nov. 1931, Nashville, Tenn.; s. of late Walton Maxey Jarman and of Sarah (Anderson) Jarman; m. 1st Nancy M. Smith 1970; m. 2nd Julia W. Lipscomb 1976; three s.; ed. Montgomery Bell Acad. and M.I.T.; joined GENESCO 1957, mem. Bd. of Govs. 1960, Advisory Bd. 1960, Bd. of Dirs. 1961, Treas. 1962, Financial Vice-Pres. 1964, Exec. Vice-Pres. mem. Finance and Exec. Cttees. 1966, Pres 1969–77, Chair. GENESCO 1969, C.E.O. 1973–77; Chair. North American Financial Co. 1977; Pres. Phillips & Brooks/Gladwyn Inc. 1977; Dir. Stanadyne 1970–90, Seabord World Airlines 1975–85. *Leisure interests:* water sports, flying. *Address:* Phillips/Gladwin Inc., P.O. Box 267, Cumming, GA 30130 (Office); 601 Bowling Avenue, Nashville, TN 37215, U.S.A. (Home). *Telephone:* (404) 887-9901 (Office). *Fax:* (404) 781-8076 (Office).

JARMUSCH, Jim; American film director; b. 1953, Akron, O.; ed. Medill School of Journalism, Northwestern Univ., Evanston, Ill., Colombia Coll., S.C.; Teaching Asst. to Nicholas Ray at New York Univ. Graduate Film School 1976–79; has worked on several films as sound recordist, cameraman and actor; with 12 Gauge Productions, Inc. 1996; directed: (shorts) Stranger than Paradise (Part one: The New World) 1982, The Lady don't Mind 1985, Coffee and Cigarettes 1986, Sightsee 1988, Coffee and Cigarettes Part Two 1988; (feature length) Permanent Vacation 1980, Stranger than Paradise (Camera D'Or, Cannes Film Festival 1984) 1984, Down By Law 1986, Mystery Train 1989, Night on Earth, In the Soup (actor only), Tigrero: A Film That Was Never Made, Dead Man 1995, Year of the Horse 1997. *Address:* Exoskeleton Inc., 208 E. 6th Street, New York, NY 10003, U.S.A.

JAROCKI, Jerzy; Polish theatre director; b. 11 May 1929, Warsaw; s. of Bohdan Jarocki and Leokadia Jarocka; m. 1st 1962; one d.; m. 2nd Danuta Maksymowicz 1980; ed. State Higher School of Drama, studies in drama production in Cracow and in U.S.S.R.; directs plays mainly by Polish writers S. Witkiewicz, W. Gombrowicz, T. Różewicz and S. Mrożek, also by Shakespeare and Chekov; with Old Theatre, Cracow 1962–; mem. Presidential Council for Culture 1992–95; mem. Polish Acad. of Arts and Skills, Cracow;

productions abroad, including Amsterdam, Zürich, Munich, Chelyabinsk, Nuremberg, Wuppertal, Belgrade, Novi Sad 1972–; teacher, State Higher School of Drama, Cracow 1963–, Asst. Prof. 1965–85, Extraordinary Prof. 1985–; has directed over 90 plays including: Ślub (The Wedding) 1960, 1973, 1974, 1991, Cymbeline 1967, Moja Córeczka (My Little Daughter) 1968, Stara Kobieta Wysiaduje (Old Woman Brooding) 1969, Three Sisters 1969, 1974, Pater Noster 1971, Szewcy (The Shoemakers) 1972, On All Fours 1972, Matka (The Mother) 1966, 1974, The Trial 1973, The Cherry Orchard 1975, Rzeźnia (The Slaughterhouse) 1975, Bal Manekinów (Mannequins Ball) 1976, King Lear 1977, White Glove 1978, Twilight 1979, The Dream of the Sinless 1979, The Inspector General 1980, Murder in the Cathedral 1982, Pieszo (On Foot) 1981, La Vida es Sueño 1983, Sceny z Jaffy (Scenes from Jaffa) 1984, Samobójca (The Suicide) 1987, Portret (Portrait) 1988, (in Germany) 1996, Słuckaj Izraelu (Listen, Israel) 1989, Prilapka (Trap) 1992, Sen Srebrny Salomei (Silver Dream of Salomea) 1993, Płatonow 1993, Kasia z Heilbromu (Kate from Heilbrom) 1994, Grzebanie 1996, Płatonow alitpominięty (Płatonow the Missed Act) 1996, Faust 1997, Historia PRL wg Mrożka (PPR History by Mrożek) 1998; Gold Cross of Merit, Commdr.'s Cross, Order of Polonia Restituta, Gold Award of City of Cracow, Minister of Culture and Arts Prize (1st Class) 1971, 1997, State Prize (2nd Class) 1976, Contact-Int. Theatre Festival (3rd Prize) 1994, Baltic House Int. Film Festival, St. Petersburg 1997, and others. *Address:* ul. Moniuszki 33, 31-523 Cracow, Poland.

JAROUDI, Saeb, M.A.; Lebanese international official; b. 25 Nov. 1929, Beirut; m. Leila Salam 1963; one s. one d.; ed. Int. Coll. Beirut, Univ. of California at Berkeley, Columbia Univ.; Instructor in Econs. and Research Economist, American Univ. of Beirut 1953–56; Econ. Officer UN Secr., New York 1956–65, detailed from UN as Econ. Adviser to Govt. of Kuwait 1962–64; Chief Economist, Kuwait Fund for Econ. and Social Devt. 1966–69; Minister of Nat. Econ., Lebanon 1970–72; Pres. Arab Fund for Econ. and Social Devt. 1972–79; Chair. Saudi Finance Group 1980–. *Leisure interest:* numismatics. *Address:* c/o Arab Fund for Economic and Social Development, P.O. Box 21923, Kuwait.

JARRATT, Sir Alexander Anthony, Kt., C.B.; British company executive; b. 19 Jan. 1924, London; s. of Alexander and Mary Jarratt; m. (Mary) Philomena Keogh 1946; one s. two d.; ed. Royal Liberty Grammar School, Essex, and Birmingham Univ.; mil. service in Fleet Air Arm; Asst. Prin. Ministry of Power 1950–53, Prin. 1953–54; Treasury 1954–55; Prin. Pvt. Sec. to Minister of Fuel and Power 1955–59; Asst. Sec. in Oil Div. of Ministry 1959–63, Under-Sec. in Gas Div. 1963–64; Cabinet Office 1964–65; First Sec., Nat. Bd. for Prices and Incomes 1965–68; Deputy Under-Sec. of State, Dept. of Employment and Productivity 1968; Deputy Sec. Ministry of Agric. 1970; mem. Bds. of IPC and Reed Int. Ltd. 1970; Man. Dir. IPC 1970–74, Chair. 1974–, also of IPC Newspapers 1974; Chair. and C.E.O. Reed Int. Ltd. 1974–85; mem. Supervisory Bd., Thyssen-Bornemisza 1972–89; non-exec. Dir. ICI Ltd. 1975–91, Smith's Industries 1984–96 (Chair. (non-exec.) 1985–91); Dir. and Deputy Chair. Midland Bank 1980–91; Jt. Deputy Chair. Prudential Corpn. 1987–91, 1992–94 (Dir. 1985–94); Chair. Admin. Staff Coll., Henley 1976–89, Centre for Dispute Resolution 1990–; Pres. Advertising Asscn. 1979–83; Chair. C.B.I. Employment Policy Cttee. 1982–86; Pres. Periodical Publishers Asscn. 1983–85; Vice-Pres. Inst. of Marketing 1982; Chancellor Birmingham Univ. Sept. 1983–; Gov. Ashridge Man. Coll.; mem. Council Confed. of British Industries; Hon. D.Sc. (Cranfield), Hon. D. Univ. (Brunel, Essex), Hon. D.L.I. (Birmingham). *Leisure interests:* countryside pursuits, theatre, music, reading. *Address:* Barn Mead, Fryerning, Essex, CM4 0NP, England.

JARRE, Jean Michel André, L. ÈS L.; French composer; b. 24 August 1948, Lyon; s. of Maurice Jarre (q.v.) and France (née Pejot) Jarre; m. 2nd Charlotte Rampling (q.v.) 1978; two s. one d.; ed. Lycée Michelet, Université de la Sorbonne, Conservatoire de musique de Paris; composer of electronic music 1968–; int. concerts include shows in China, Europe and U.S.A.; shows incorporate state-of-the-art sound and vision tech.; Composer for ballet Aor, and Opera de Paris 1971. *Albums include:* Oxygène 1976, Equinoxe 1978, Magnetic Fields 1980, The China Concerts 1982, Music for Supermarkets 1983, Zoolook 1984, Rendez-vous 1986, Revolutions 1987, Jarre Live 1989, (Best Instrumental Album, Victoire de la Musique 1986); Concert d'Images 1989 (Exhibition), Waiting for Cousteau 1990, Chronologie 1993, Oxygène 7–13 1997; Officier des Arts et des Lettres; Officer, Legion d'honneur; UNESCO Goodwill Amb. 1993; Soc. des auteurs, compositeurs et éditeurs de musique Gold Medal 1980. *Publications:* Concert d'Images 1989, Paris-la-Défense, une ville en concert 1990, Europe in Concert 1994, Paris-Tour Eiffel, Concert pour la Tolérance 1995. *Address:* B.P. 58, 78290 Croissy-sur-Seine, France.

JARRE, Maurice Alexis; French composer; b. 13 Sept. 1924, Lyons; s. of André Jarre and Gabrielle Boullou; m. 1st France Pejot 1946; one s.; m. 2nd Dany Saval 1965; one d.; m. 3rd Laura Devon 1967; m. 4th Khong Fui Fong 1984; ed. Lycée Ampère, Lyons and Conservatoire Nat. Supérieur de Musique; musician attached to Radiodiffusion Française 1946–50; Dir. of Music, Théâtre Nat. Populaire (TNP) 1950–63; work includes symphonic music, music for theatre and ballet including Roland Petit's Notre-Dame de Paris (created at Paris Opéra 1966) and numerous film scores including: Lawrence of Arabia (Acad. Award) 1963, Dr Zhivago (Acad. Award) 1965, Ryan's Daughter 1970, Shogun 1980, Doctors in Love 1982, A Passage to India (Acad. Award) 1985, The Mosquito Coast 1987, Tai-pan 1987, Gaby 1988, Gorillas in the Mist 1989, Dead Poets Society 1990, Fatal Attraction, Ghost, les Vendanges de feu 1994, Sunchaser 1996; Officier, Légion d'honneur, Commdr. des Arts et des Lettres; Prix Italia 1955, 1962; Grand Prix du Disque, Acad. Charles Cros 1962; Hollywood Golden Globe 1965, 1984, People's Choice Award 1988, etc. *Address:* Sacem, 225 avenue Charles de Gaulle, 92521 Neuilly-sur-Seine, France.

JARRETT, Keith; American pianist and composer; b. 8 May 1945, Allentown, Pa.; gave first solo concert aged 7, followed by professional appearances; 2 hour solo concert of own compositions 1962; led own trio in Boston; worked with Roland Kirk, Tony Scott and others in New York; joined Art Blakely 1965; toured Europe with Charles Lloyd 1966; with Miles Davis 1970–71; soloist and leader of own groups 1969–; Officier, Ordre des Arts et des Lettres. *Albums include:* Personal Mountains, Nude Ants, The Cure 1990, Bye Bye Black 1991, At the Dear Head Inn 1992, Bridge of Light 1993, At the Blue Note 1994, La Scala 1995. *Address:* Vincent Ryan, 135 West 16th Street, New York, NY 10011, U.S.A.

JARRETT, William Fleming Hoggan, PH.D., F.R.C.V.S., F.R.C.PATH., F.R.S.E., F.R.S.; British professor of veterinary pathology; b. 2 Jan. 1928; s. of James Jarrett and Jessie Jarrett; m. Anna F. Sharp 1952; two d.; ed. Lenzie Acad., Glasgow Veterinary Coll. and Univ. of Glasgow; A.R.C. Research Student 1949–52; Lecturer, Dept. of Veterinary Pathology, Univ. of Glasgow Veterinary School 1952–53; Head of Hosp. Pathology Dept. of Veterinary Hosp., Univ. of Glasgow 1953–61; Reader in Pathology, Univ. of Glasgow 1962–65, Prof. of Veterinary Pathology 1968–91, Sr. Research Fellow 1991–; seconded to Univ. of E. Africa 1963–64; Hon. D.M.V. (Edin.) 1989; Feldberg Prize 1987, Saltire Award 1989. *Publications:* articles in scientific journals. *Leisure interests:* skiing, sailing, mountaineering, music. *Address:* Auchineden House, Blanefield, Glasgow, G63 9AX, Scotland. *Telephone:* (01360) 770112.

JARRING, Gunnar, PH.D.; Swedish diplomatist; b. 12 Oct. 1907, Brunnby; m. Agnes Charlier 1932; one d.; ed. Lund Univ.; Assoc. Prof. Turkic Languages Lund Univ. 1933–40; Attaché Ankara 1940–41; Chief Section B Teheran 1941; Chargé d'affaires a.i. Teheran and Baghdad 1945, Addis Ababa 1946–48; Minister to India 1948–51, concurrently to Ceylon 1950–51, to Iran, Iraq and Pakistan 1951–52; Dir. Political Div. Ministry of Foreign Affairs 1953–56; Perm. Rep. to UN 1956–58; rep. on Security Council 1957–58; Amb. to U.S.A. 1958–64, to U.S.S.R. 1964–73, and to Mongolia 1965–73; Special Envoy of UN Sec.-Gen. on Middle East Situation Nov. 1967–91; Grand Cross Order of the North Star. *Publications:* Studien zu einer osttürkischen Lautlehre 1933, The Contest of the Fruits—An Eastern Turki Allegory 1936, The Uzbek Dialect of Qilich, Russian Turkestan 1937, Uzbek Texts from Afghan Turkestan 1938, The Distribution of Turki Tribes in Afghanistan 1939, Materials for the Knowledge of Eastern Turkestan (Vols.I–IV) 1947–51, An Eastern Turki-English Dialect Dictionary 1964, Literary Texts from Kashghar 1980, Return to Kashghar 1986, Prints from Kashghar 1991, Central Asian Turki Place-names 1997. *Address:* Pontus Ols vaeg 7, 26040 Viken, Sweden.

JARUZELSKI, Gen. Wojciech; Polish politician and army officer; b. 6 July 1923, Kurów, Lublin Prov.; s. of Władysław Jaruzelski and Wanda Jaruzelska; m. Barbara Jaruzelska 1961; one d.; ed. Infantry Officers' School and Karol Świerczewski Gen. Staff Acad., Warsaw; served with Polish Armed Forces in U.S.S.R. and Poland 1943–45; various sr. army posts 1945–65; Chief of Cen. Political Bd. of the Armed Forces 1960–65; Deputy Minister of Nat. Defence 1962–68, Minister 1968–83; Chair. Council of Ministers 1981–85; First Sec. Cen. Cttee. PZPR 1981–89; Chief of Gen. Staff 1965–68; Brig.-Gen. 1956, Divisional-Gen. 1960, Gen. of Arms 1968, Gen. of Army 1973; mem. PZPR 1948–90, mem. PZPR Cen. Cttee. 1964–89, mem. Political Bureau 1971–89; Deputy to Sejm (Parl.) 1961–89; Vice-Pres. Chief Council of Union of Fighters for Freedom and Democracy 1972–88; Chair. Comm. for Econ. Reform 1981–86; Chair. Mil. Council for Nat. Salvation 1981–83; mem. Presidium All-Poland Cttee. of Nat. Unity Front 1981–83, Provisional Nat. Council of Patriotic Movt. for Nat. Rebirth (PRON) 1982–83, mem. Nat. Council PRON 1983–89; Chair. Country Defence Cttee. 1983–90, Supreme Commdr. of the Armed Forces of Polish People's Repub. for Wartime 1983–90; Chair. Council of State (Head of State) 1985–89, Pres. of Polish People's Repub. (Polish Repub.) 1989–90; decorations include Order of Builders of People's Poland, Order of Banner of Labour (First Class), Kt.'s Cross of Order of Polonia Restituta, Silver Cross of Virtuti Militari and Cross of Valour, Medals of 30th and 40th Anniversary of People's Poland, Hon. Miner of People's Repub., Order of Lenin 1968, 1983, Commdr.'s Cross Order of the Crown (Belgium) 1967, Order of the October Revolution (U.S.S.R.) 1973, Scharnhorst Order (G.D.R.) 1975, Grand Cross Order of Henry the Navigator (Portugal) 1975, Order of the State Banner (Dem. People's Repub. of Korea) 1977, Order of Suche Bator (Mongolia) 1977, Order of the Red Banner (Hungary) 1977, Order of the Red Banner (U.S.S.R.) 1978, Order of the White Lion (Czechoslovakia) 1979, Order of Klement Gottwald (Czechoslovakia) 1983, Karl Marx Order (G.D.R.) 1983, Order of the Star of the Socialist Repub. (First class with Riband) (Romania) 1983, Order of the Golden Star (Vietnam) 1983, Order of Georgi Dimitrov (Bulgaria) 1983, Order of the Red Battle Banner (Mongolia) 1983, Order of the Banner (First Class with Diamonds) (Hungary) 1983, Order of José Martí (Cuba) 1983, Grand Cross of Order of the Holy Saviour (Greece) 1987. *Publication:* Stan Wojenny: Dlaczego 1993. *Leisure interests:* history, military affairs. *Address:* Biuro Byłego Prezydenta RP Wojciecha Jaruzelskiego, Al. Jerozolimskie 91, 02-001 Warsaw, Poland. *Telephone:* (22) 684 22 60.

JÄRVI, Neeme; Estonian conductor; b. 7 June 1937, Tallinn, Estonia; s. of Elss and August Järvi; m. Liilia Järvi 1961; two s. one d.; ed. Tallinn Music School, Leningrad Conservatorium and Leningrad Post-Graduate Studium; studied with N. Rabinovich and Y. Mravinsky; Conductor Estonian Radio Symphony Orchestra –1963; Chief Conductor Estonian State Opera House 1963–76; Chief Conductor Estonian State Symphony Orchestra 1976–80; emigrated to U.S.A. 1980; Principal Guest Conductor City of Birmingham Symphony Orchestra, England 1981–83; Prin. Conductor Royal Scottish Nat. Orchestra 1984–88, Conductor Laureate 1988–; Prin. Conductor Gothenburg Orchestra, Sweden 1982–; Music Dir. Detroit Symphony Orchestra, U.S.A. 1990–; Guest Conductor of many int. symphony orchestras including New York Philharmonic, Boston, Chicago, Royal Concertgebouw, Philharmonia, London Symphony, London Philharmonic; conducted Eugene Onegin 1979, 1984, Samson and Delilah 1982 and Khovanshchina 1985 at Metropolitan Opera House, New York; many recordings including all Prokoviev, Sibelius, Grieg, Nielsen, Dvorak, Shostakovich, Franz Berwald and Stenhammar symphonies; Hon. mem. Royal Swedish Acad. of Music; First Prize, Accademia Nazionale di Santa Cecilia Conductors' Competition 1971, Gramophone Magazine's Artist of the Year 1991; Kt. Commdr. of North Star Order, Sweden. *Address:* c/o Columbia Artists' Management Ltd., 28 Cheverton Road, London, N19 3AY, England. *Telephone:* 0171-272 8020. *Fax:* 0171-272 8991.

JÄRVI, Osmo Henrik, M.D.; Finnish pathologist; b. 1 Jan. 1911, Helsinki; s. of Prof. Toivo Henrik Järvi and Helfrid Helena (née Soderman-Siutila); m. Dr. Enne-Maija Kinnunen 1937 (died 1990); one s. three d.; ed. Helsinki and Utrecht Univs. and Karolinska Inst., Stockholm; Asst. Anatomy Dept., Helsinki Univ. 1932–38; Asst., Dept. of Pathological Anatomy 1938–44; Lecturer, Microscopical Anatomy, 1940–45, Prof. of Pathological Anatomy, Turku Univ. 1944–77; Dean, Faculty of Medicine 1945–54, Rector 1954–60; Chair. Finnish Medical Research Council 1961–67; mem. Finnish Acad. of Science and Letters 1960 (Chair. 1980; Hon. mem. 1992), Finnish Medical Soc. "Duodecim", Hon. mem. Finnish Medical Soc. "Läkaresällskapet" 1960, Finnish Soc. of Gastroenterology 1986, Finnish Soc. of Cytology 1987, Finnish Otolaryngological Asscn. 1992; mem. Swedish Medical Soc., Finnish Asscn. of Pathologists (Chair. 1956–62), Swedish Asscn. of Pathologists, Scandinavian Asscn. of Pathologists (Chair. 1958–61), Pathological Soc. of G.B. and Ireland, American Soc. of Clinical Pathologists, Int. Acad. of Pathology, New York Acad. of Sciences, Cancer Asscn. of Finland (Chair. of Del. 1967–69 and 1978–80, Chair. of Bd. 1969–75), Cancer Foundation of Finland (Chair. 1960–66), Fellow, Int. Acad. of Cytology, etc.; Hon. mem. Finnish Cultural Foundation 1978; Hon. Ph.D. (Åbo Acad., Finland) 1968, Hon. M.D. (Turku Univ.) 1980, (Oulu Univ.) 1983; Pohjola Medical Award 1983, Finnish Acad. of Science and Letters Award 1986. *Publications:* works on secretion process and Golgi apparatus, morbid pathology of respiratory and gastrointestinal tract, especially neoplasms, etc., exfoliated cytology; Pohdintaa (Meditations) 1967. *Leisure interest:* the fine arts. *Address:* Yliopistonkatu 2K, 20110 Turku, Finland. *Telephone:* 2317390.

JARVIK, Robert Koffler, M.D.; American physician; b. 11 May 1946, Midland, Mich.; s. of Norman Eugene and Edythe (née Koffler) Jarvik; m. Marilyn vos Savant 1987; one s. one d.; ed. Syracuse Univ., New York, Univ. of Bologna, New York Univ., Univ. of Utah; research asst., Div. of Artificial Organs, Univ. of Utah 1971–77; Acting Dir. Old St. Mark's Hosp., Div. of Artificial Organs 1977–78, Asst. Dir. 1978–82; Pres. Symbian Inc., Salt Lake City 1981–87, Jarvik Research Inc. 1987–; Asst. Research Prof. of Surgery, Univ. of Utah 1979–87; awards include Inventor of the Year 1983, Outstanding Young Men of America 1983, Gold Heart Award 1983, Par Excellence Award (Univ. of Utah); Hon. D.Sc. (Syracuse) 1983, (Hahnemann Univ.) 1985; mem. American Soc. for Artificial Internal Organs, Int. Soc. for Artificial Organs. *Publication:* Ed. (U.S. Section) The International Journal of Artificial Organs. *Address:* c/o Department of Surgery, College of Medicine, University of Utah, Salt Lake City, Utah, U.S.A.

JASKIERNIA, Jerzy Andrzej, D.JUR.; Polish diplomatist and politician; b. 21 March 1950, Kudowa Zdrój; s. of Zofia Jaskiernia and Mieczysław Jaskiernia; m. Alicja Słowińska 1980; one s. one d.; ed. Jagellonian Univ., Cracow; academic teacher Law and Admin. Faculty of Jagellonian Univ., Cracow 1972–81; mem. Main Bd. of Socialist Youth Union 1973–76; mem. Polish Socialist Youth Union (ZSMP) 1976–85; mem. Main Arbitration Bd. 1976–80, Chair. 1980–81, Chair. ZSMP Gen. Bd. 1981–84; mem. Polish United Workers' Party (PZPR) 1970–90, deputy mem. PZPR Cen. Cttee. 1982–86, Vice-Chair., Youth Comm. of PZPR Cen. Cttee. 1981–86; mem. Inter-party Problems Comm. of PZPR Cen. Cttee. 1986–88, Nat. Council of Patriotic Movt. for Nat. Rebirth 1983–89; Sec.-Gen. 1984–87; Adviser to Minister of Foreign Affairs 1987–88; Counsellor, Embassy in Washington 1988–90; mem. Scientific Bd., Research Inst. of Youth Problems (Warsaw) 1984–89; mem. Social Democracy of the Repub. of Poland (SdRP) 1990–, SdRP Cen. Exec. Cttee. 1991–92 (Head Parl. and Self-Govt. Affairs Dept. 1990–91), SdRP Presidium of the Main Council 1993–97, Chair. Cttee. on Int. Co-operation 1998–; Deputy to Sejm (Parl.) 1985–89, 1991–; mem. Nat. Ass. Constitutional Cttee. 1992–95; Chair. Legis. Cttee. of the Sejm 1993–95, 1996–97; Minister of Justice and Attorney-Gen. 1995–96; Prof. Higher Pedagogical School, Kielce 1995–; Deputy Chair. Democratic Left Alliance (SLD), Parl. Caucus 1996–; mem. Parl. Ass. of Council of Europe 1994–, Chair. Subcttee. on Human Rights 1998–; Chair. Polish-British Parl. Group 1993–; Deputy Chair. Jt. Parl. Cttee. of Repub. of Poland and EU 1997–. *Publications:* Pozycja stanów w systemie federalnym USA 1979, Dylematy młodych 1984, Dialog naszą szansą 1985, (co-author) System polityczny PRL w procesie przemian 1988, Problemy pluralizmu, porozumienia narodowego i consensusu w systemie politycznym PRL 1989, Stany Zjednoczone a współczesne procesy i koncepcje integracji europejskiej 1992, Zasada równości w prawie wyborczym USA 1992, Wizja parlamentu w nowej Konstytucji Rzeczypospolitej Polskiej 1994. *Address:* ul. Wiejska 4/6/8, 00-902 Warsaw, Poland. *Telephone:* (22) 694 22 55.

JASON, David, O.B.E.; British actor; b. 2 Feb. 1940; s. of Arthur Jason and Olwyn White; started acting career in repertory. *Theatre includes:* Under Milk Wood 1971, The Rivals 1972, No Sex Please . . . We're British! 1972, Darling Mr London (tour) 1975, Charley's Aunt (tour) 1975, The Norman Conquests 1976, The Relapse 1978, Cinderella 1979, The Unvarnished Truth (Mid/Far East tour) 1983, Look No Hans! (tour and West End) 1985. *Films:* Under Milk Wood 1970, Royal Flash 1974, The Odd Job 1978, Only Fools and Horses, Wind in the Willows 1983. *TV includes:* Do Not Adjust Your Set 1967, The Top Secret Life of Edgar Briggs 1973–74, Mr Stabbs 1974, Ronnie Barker Shows 1975, Open All Hours 1975, Porridge 1975, Lucky Feller 1975, A Sharp Intake of Breath 1978, Del Trotter in Only Fools and Horses 1981–91, Porterhouse Blue 1986, Jackanory 1988, A Bit of A Do 1988–89, Single Voices: The Chemist 1989, Amongst Barbarians 1989, Pa Larkin in The Darling Buds of May 1990–92, A Touch of Frost 1992. *Voice work:* Dangermouse, Count Duckula, The Wind in the Willows. Awards include Best Actor Award, B.A.F.T.A. 1988. *Leisure interests:* diving, flying, motorcycles. *Address:* c/o Richard Stone Partnership, 25 Whitehall, London, SW1A 2BS, England.

JASRAI, Puntsagiin; Mongolian politician; b. 26 Nov. 1933; ed. Moscow Inst.; teacher then headmaster of primary school, Gobi-Altai Aimag (Prov.) 1950–54; Insp. of the Exec. Bd. People's deputies of Gobi-Altai Aimag 1954–56; lecturer at the Inst. of Econs. 1961–65; Deputy Chief Cen. Statistical Bd. of the MPR 1966–70; Chair. State Prices Cttee. 1970–75, State Prices and Standard 1975–76; Head Dept. of the Cen. Cttee. of the MPRP 1976–78; First Deputy Chair. State Planning Comm. MPRP 1978–84; Deputy Chair. Council of Ministers, Chair. State Planning Comm. 1984; Deputy Chair. Council of Ministers, Chair. State Planning and Economy Cttee. 1988; Prime Minister of Mongolia 1992–96; mem. MPRP Conf.; mem. State Great Hural (Parl.); Dir. Asscn. of Mongolian Consumers' Co-operatives 1990. *Address:* c/o Office of the Prime Minister, Ulan Bator, Mongolia.

JASTROW, Robert; American physicist and writer; b. 7 Sept. 1925, New York; s. of Abraham Jastrow and Marie Jastrow; Asst. Prof., Yale Univ. 1953–54, Consultant nuclear physics, U.S. Naval Research Lab. 1958–62; Head Theoretical Div., Goddard Space Flight Centre, NASA 1958–61, Chair. Lunar Exploration Comm. 1959–60, Dir. Goddard Inst. Space Studies 1961–81; Adjunct Prof. of Astronomy, Columbia Univ., New York 1961–77, of Earth Sciences, Dartmouth Coll., Hanover, N.H. 1973–92, of Geology and Astronomy, Columbia Univ. 1977–81; Pres. G. C. Marshall Inst. 1985–; Chair., Dir. Mount Wilson Inst. 1991–; Hon. D.Sc. (Manhattan Coll.) 1980; Arthur S. Flemming Award 1965; NASA Medal for exceptional scientific achievement 1968. *Publications:* Red Giants and White Dwarfs, The Origin of the Solar System 1963, The Evolution of Stars, Planets and Life 1967, Astronomy: Fundamentals and Frontiers 1972, The Venus Atmosphere 1969, Until the Sun Dies 1977, God and the Astronomers 1978, The Enchanted Loom 1981, How to Make Nuclear Weapons Obsolete 1985, Journey to the Stars 1989. *Address:* Mount Wilson Observatory, Hale Solar Laboratory, 740 Holladay Road, Pasadena, CA 91106, U.S.A.

JATOI, Ghulam Mustafa; Pakistani politician and landowner; b. 14 Aug. 1932, New Jatoi; s. of Ghulam Rasool Jatoi; m. 1st 1951; m. 2nd 1965; five s. three d.; Sind Prov.; elected Pres. Nawabshah Dist. Council 1954; elected mem. W. Pakistan Ass. 1956, Nat. Ass. of Pakistan 1962, 1965, 1970, 1977, 1989, 1990, 1993, 1997; del. to UN Gen. Ass. 1962, 1965, to IPU Conf., Ottawa (elected Vice-Pres. of Conf.) 1965; Fed. Minister for Communications, Political Affairs, Railways and Natural Resources 1971; Special Envoy of Pres. to Indonesia, Malaysia, Japan 1972, of Prime Minister to Turkey 1976; founder mem. People's Party (PPP); fmr. aide to late Zulfikar Ali Bhutto, Prime Minister of Pakistan; fmr. Chief Minister of Sind; imprisoned for political activities 1977; led Movt. for Restoration of Democracy against mil. regime; founder, Nat. People's Party (NPP); Leader of Opposition 1988; Leader of Combined Opposition Parties (COP) 1990; Leader of Islamic Democratic Alliance for 1990 election; caretaker Prime Minister of Pakistan Aug.–Nov. 1990. *Leisure interest:* hunting. *Address:* Jatoi House, 18 Khayaban-e-Shamsheer Defence Housing Authority, Phase V, Karachi, Pakistan.

JATTI, Basappa Danappa, B.A., LL.B.; Indian politician; b. 10 Sept. 1912, Savalgi, Bijapur District; m. Sangamma Jatti; three s. one d.; ed. Bijapur Govt. High School, Rajaram Coll., Sykes Law Coll., Kolhapur; practised law at Jamkhandi; State Minister, Jamkhandi, later Chief Minister; mem. Legis. Assembly, Bombay, later Mysore; Deputy Minister of Health and Labour, Bombay 1952; Chair. Land Reforms Cttee., Chief Minister, Mysore 1958–62; Minister of Finance, Mysore 1962–65, of Food, Mysore 1965–67; Lieut.-Gov. of Pondicherry 1968; Gov. of Orissa 1972–74; Vice-Pres. of India 1974–79, Acting Pres. Feb.–July 1977; Chair. Rajya Sabha 1974–79; LL.D. h.c. (Karnatak Univ., Guru Nanak Dev Univ.). *Address:* Shivanand, 224 Bellary Road, Bangalore, India.

JAUDEL, Jean Emmanuel; French publisher; b. 6 Jan. 1910, Strasbourg; s. of Armand Jaudel and Lucie Jaudel; m. Nicole Weill 1946; one s. one d.; ed. Faculty of Law of Paris Univ., Ecole libre des sciences politiques, Ecole des hautes etudes internationales, Geneva; Man. Dir. Atlantique française 1945–; Chair. La Revue des Deux Mondes, publrs. of La Revue des Deux Mondes (monthly review) 1969, Pres. Supervisory Bd. 1988–; Pres. Asscn. Presse-Enseignement 1981–; Officier Légion d'honneur, Commdr. Ordre nat. du Mérite, Médaille militaire, Croix de guerre, other French and foreign awards. *Leisure interest:* riding. *Address:* 31 rue de Penthièvre, 75008 Paris, France (Home). *Telephone:* 359-68-36 (Home).

JAUHO, Pekka Antti Olavi; Finnish scientist and consultant; b. 27 April 1923, Oulu; s. of Antti Arvid Jauho and Sylvi (née Pajari) Jauho; m. Kyllikki Hakala 1948; one s.; ed. Univ. of Helsinki; Chief Mathematician, Insurance Co. Kansa 1951–54; Assoc. Prof., Tech. Univ. of Helsinki 1955–57 (now Helsinki Univ. of Tech.), Prof. of Tech. Physics 1957–70; Dir.-Gen. The State Inst. for Tech. Research (Tech. Research Centre of Finland since 1972) 1970–87; consultant to many Finnish and foreign cos.; mem. Acad. of Finland, American Nuclear Soc., European Physical Soc., RILEM, Finnish Acad. of Sciences, IVA (Swedish Acad. of Tech. Sciences), and several Finnish socs.; Hon. Prize of YDIN Power Asscn., Hon. Prize of VILAMO Foundation 1996. *Publications:* about 120 articles. *Leisure interest:* music. *Address:* Otakaari 1, 02150 Espoo 15 (Office); Tuohikuja 9E, 02130 Espoo, Finland (Home). *Telephone:* (9) 4513132 (Office); (9) 427705 (Home). *Fax:* (9) 427705.

JAUMOTTE, Baron André; Belgian university official and mechanical engineer; b. 8 Dec. 1919, Jambes; s. of Jules Jaumotte and Marie Braibant; m. Valentine Demoulin 1946; ed. Free Univ. of Brussels; Head Depts. of Applied Mechanics and Aerodynamics, Free Univ. of Brussels 1958–86, Rector 1968–73, Pres. 1974–81; Pres. A-VN; mem. Bd. UN Univ., Tokyo 1980–86; Hon. Pres. Asscn. des Universités partiellement ou entièrement de langue française (AUPELF) 1981–84; mem. Royal Acad., Belgium, Royal Acad. of Overseas Science, European Acad. of Sciences, Letters and Arts, Int. Acad. of Astronautics, Academia Europaea; Foreign mem. Czechoslovak Acad. of Science; mem. Nat. Acad. of Air and Space, France; Foreign mem. Acad. des Sciences (Paris) 1989, Romanian Acad. 1994; Hon. Dr. h.c. (Free University, Brussels), (Laval Univ., Quebec), (Univ. of Cluj, Romania), (Tech. Univ., Bucharest); Commdr. Légion d'honneur 1981, Grand Officier Ordine al Merito della Repubblica Italiana 1973, Commdr. Ordre du Mérite (Gabon), Grand Officier Ordre de la Couronne (Belgium) 1983, Grand Officier Ordre de Léopold 1988, Order of the Sacred Treasure, Gold and Silver Stars (Japan) and various other awards. *Publications:* Rocket Propulsion 1967, Choc et Ondes de Choc 1971, 1973, Un demi-siècle de nucléaire en Belgique 1994, and 300 articles on internal aerodynamics and thermodynamics of turbomachines. *Leisure interests:* painting and sculpture. *Address:* Université Libre de Bruxelles, avenue Jeanne 44, CP 120, 1050 Brussels; 33 avenue Jeanne Bte. 17, B1050 Brussels, Belgium (Home). *Telephone:* 650-3271 (Office); 647-5413 (Home). *Fax:* (2) 650-4599.

JAUNARENA, José Horacio, D.JUR.; Argentinian politician; b. 29 Nov. 1942, Pergamino; m. Ana O'Ana; one d.; ed. Univ. Nacional de Buenos Aires, also law studies in Madrid; practised law in Buenos Aires and Pergamino; lecturer-in-charge Democratic Educ., Inst. Superior del Prof. Joaquín V. González, Pergamino 1976; Dir. Sunday Supplement, La Opinión de Pergamino; mem. Unión Cívica Radical, Pergamino 1973–76; Under-Sec. of Defence, Ministry of Defence 1983–84, Sec. 1984–86, Minister of Defence 1986–89.

JAVED MIANDAD KHAN; Pakistani cricketer; b. 12 June 1957, Karachi; m.; ed. CMS Secondary School, Karachi; Asst. Vice-Pres. Habib Bank of Pakistan; right-hand middle-order batsman, leg-break and googly bowler; played for Karachi 1973–76, Sind 1973–76, Sussex 1976–79, Habib Bank 1976–94, Glamorgan 1980–85; 124 Test matches for Pakistan 1976–94, 34 as capt., scoring 8,832 runs (average 52.5) including 23 hundreds; scored 28,647 first-class runs (80 hundreds); toured England 1975, 1979 (World Cup), 1982, 1983 (World Cup), 1987, 1992 (capt.); 233 limited-overs ints. *Leisure interests:* hockey, soccer, swimming, reading sports books, television, spending time with family. *Address:* c/o Pakistani Board of Control for Cricket, Gaddafi Stadium, Lahore, Pakistan.

JAVIERRE ORTAS, H.E. Cardinal Antonio María, S.D.B.; Vatican ecclesiastic; b. 21 Feb. 1921, Siétamo, Huesca, Spain; ordained 1949, elected 1976, consecrated titular Archbishop of Meta 1976; Sec. of the Congregation for Catholic Educ.; cr. Cardinal 1988; Archivist and Librarian of the Holy Roman Church 1988–91; Prefect of Congregation for Divine Worship and the Discipline of the Sacraments 1991; mem. Congregations for Doctrine of Faith, of Bishops, of Catholic Educ., Pontificial Council for the Laity. *Address:* Via Rusticucci 13, 00193 Rome, Italy.

JAWARA, Hon. Alhaji Sir Dawda (Kairaba), Kt., M.R.C.V.S., D.T.V.M.; Gambian politician; b. 16 May 1924, Barajally; s. of Almamy and the late Mama Jawara; ed. Achimota Coll., Glasgow Univ.; Principal Veterinary Officer, Gambian Civil Service 1957–60; entered politics 1960; Minister of Educ. 1960–61; Premier 1962–65; Prime Minister 1965–70; Pres. of Repub. of The Gambia 1970–94 (overthrown in coup); Vice-Pres. of Confed. of Senegambia Feb. 1982; Minister of Defence 1985; Pres. Comité Inter-Etats de Lutte contre la Sécheresse du Sahel; mem. Board, Peutinger Coll. (Fed. Repub. of Germany); Hon. G.C.M.G. 1974; decorations from Senegal, Mauritania, Lebanon, Grand Master Nat. Order of the Repub. of Gambia 1972, Peutinger Gold Medal 1979; numerous other decorations. *Leisure interests:* golf, gardening, sailing.

JAWORSKI, Zbigniew, M.ENG.; Polish politician; b. 12 Jan. 1940; m. Jolanta Jaworska; one s., one d.; ed. Warsaw Univ. of Tech.; worked at Gen. Man. of Public Roads, Warsaw 1968–92, 1994–, recently Dir. of Supervision Dept.; active mem. Christian National Union (ZChN) 1990–; Minister of Transport and Maritime Economy 1992–93. *Leisure interests:* sightseeing, travel. *Address:* Generalna Dyrekcja Dróg Publicznych, ul. Wspólna 1/3, 00-921 Warsaw, Poland. *Telephone:* (22) 622 35 23.

JAY, Sir Michael Hastings, K.C.M.G., M.A., M.SC.; British diplomatist; b. 19 June 1946, Shawford, Hants.; s. of late Alan Jay and of Felicity Vickery; m. Sylvia Mylroie 1975; ed. Winchester Coll., Magdalen Coll. Oxford and S.O.A.S., Univ. of London; Ministry of Overseas Devt. 1969–73, 1976–78; U.K. Del. IMF, IBRD, Washington, D.C. 1973–75; First Sec. New Delhi 1978–81; FCO 1981–85; Cabinet Office 1985–87; Counsellor, Paris 1987–90; Asst. Under-Sec. of State for EC Affairs, FCO 1990–93, Deputy Under-Sec. of State (Dir. for EC (now EU) and Econ. Affairs) 1994–96; Amb. to France 1996–. *Address:* British Embassy, 35 rue du Faubourg Saint Honoré, 75383 Paris Cédex 08, France.

JAY, Peter, M.A.; British economic journalist and fmr. diplomatist; b. 7 Feb. 1937; s. of late Lord Jay; m. 1st Margaret Ann Callaghan, d. of Lord Callaghan (q.v.), 1961 (divorced 1986); one s. two d.; one s. by Jane Tustian; m. 2nd Emma Thornton 1986; three s.; ed. Winchester Coll. and Christ Church, Oxford; Midshipman and Sub-Lieut., R.N.V.R. 1956–57; Asst. Prin., H.M. Treasury 1961–64, Private Sec. to Jt. Perm. Sec. 1964, Prin. 1964–67; Econs. Ed. The Times 1967–77, Assoc. Ed. Times Business News 1969–77; Presenter, Weekend World, ITV 1972–77, The Jay Interview 1975–77; Amb. to U.S.A. 1977–79; Consultant, Economist Group 1979–81; Dir. The Economist Intelligence Unit (EIU) 1979–83; Columnist The Times 1980; Dir. New Nat. Theatre, Washington, D.C. 1979–81; Chair. TV-AM 1980–83, TV-AM News 1982–83, Pres. TV-AM 1983; Presenter, A Week in Politics, Channel 4 1983–86; Chief of Staff to Robert Maxwell 1986–89; Econs. Ed., BBC 1990–; Sr. Ed. Consultant, Man. Dir. Banking World BPCC, Editor Banking World 1983–86, Supervising Ed. 1986–89; Chair. United Way of G.B. 1982–83, Feasibility Study 1982–83; Chair. Nat. Council for Voluntary Orgs. 1981–86; Visiting Scholar, Brookings Inst., Washington, D.C. 1979–80; Copland Memorial Lecturer, Australia 1980; Gov. Ditchley Foundation 1982–; Hon. D.H. (Ohio State Univ.) 1978; Political Broadcaster of Year 1973, Royal TV Soc.'s Male Personality of Year (Pye Award) 1974, Shell Int. TV Award 1974, Wincott Memorial Lecturer 1975. *Publications:* The Budget 1972, Foreign Affairs, America and the World 1979 (Contrib.) 1980, The Crisis for Western Political Economy and other essays 1984, Apocalypse 2000 (with Michael Stewart) 1987; numerous newspaper and magazine articles. *Leisure interest:* sailing. *Address:* Hensington Farmhouse, Woodstock, Oxon, OX20 1LH, England. *Telephone:* (01993) 811222. *Fax:* (01993) 812861.

JAYAKUMAR, Shunmugam, LL.M.; Singaporean diplomatist; b. 12 Aug. 1939, Singapore; m. Dr. Lalitha Rajahram 1969; two s. one d.; ed. Univ. of Singapore and Yale Univ.; Dean, Law Faculty, Univ. of Singapore 1974–80, Prof. of Law; Perm. Rep. of Singapore to UN 1971–74, High Commr. to Canada 1971–74; M.P. 1980–; Minister of State for Law and Home Affairs 1981–83; Minister of Labour 1983–85, of Home Affairs 1985–94, of Foreign Affairs 1994–, also of Law. *Publications:* Constitutional Law Cases from Malaysia and Singapore 1971, Public International Law Cases from Malaysia and Singapore 1974, Constitutional Law (with documentary material) 1976, and articles in journals. *Address:* Ministry of Foreign Affairs, 250 North Bridge Road, #07-00 Raffles City Tower, Singapore 179101.

JAYALALITHA, C. Jayaram; Indian politician and fmr. film actress; b. 24 Feb. 1948, Mysore City; d. of R. Jayaram; has appeared in over 100 films; joined All-India Anna Dravida Munnetra Kazhagam (AIADMK) 1982, Propaganda Sec. 1983, Deputy Leader, Leader; elected mem. Rajya Sabha (parl.) 1984; Chief Minister, Tamil Nadu 1991–96; Kalaimamani Award 1971–72; several publs. *Address:* c/o Chief Minister's Secretariat, Madras, India.

JAYSTON, Michael; British actor; b. 29 Oct. 1935, Nottingham; s. of Aubrey Jayston and Edna Myfanwy Llewelyn; m. 1st Lynn Farleigh 1965 (divorced 1970); m. 2nd Heather Mary Sneddon (divorced 1977); m. 3rd Elizabeth Ann Smithson 1978; three s. one d.; with the RSC 1965–69, Nat. Theatre 1976–79. *Films include:* Cromwell 1970, Nicholas and Alexandra 1971, Follow Me 1972, Bequest to the Nation 1972, Tales That Witness Madness 1973, Craze 1973, The Internecine Project 1974. *TV appearances include:* Power Game, Charles Dickens, Beethoven, Solo—Wilfred Owen, Quiller 1975, Tinker, Tailor, Soldier, Spy 1979, Dr. Who 1986, A Bit of a Do 1988, Kipling's Sussex 1989, About Face 1989, Darling Buds of May 1992, Outside Edge 1995–96, Only Fools and Horses 1996. *Theatre appearances include:* Private Lives 1980, Sound of Music 1981, Way of the World 1984–85, Woman in Mind, Beethoven Readings with Medici String Quartet 1989, Dancing at Lughnasa 1992, Wind in the Willows, Nat. Theatre 1994, Racing Demon, Chichester Prod. in Toronto 1998. *Leisure interests:* cricket, darts, chess. *Address:* c/o Michael Whitehall Ltd., 125 Gloucester Road, London, SW7 4TE, England.

JAZAIRY, Idriss; Algerian international administrator and diplomatist; b. 29 May 1936, Neuilly-sur-Seine, France; three s. one d.; Chief Econ. and

Social Dept. Algiers 1963–71; Dir. Int. Co-operation, Ministry of Foreign Affairs 1963–71; Adviser to Pres. of Repub. 1971–77; Under-Sec.-Gen. Ministry of Foreign Affairs 1977–79; Amb. to Belgium, Luxembourg and EEC 1979–82; Amb.-at-large specializing in int. econ. affairs, Ministry of Foreign Affairs 1982–84; Pres IFAD 1984–93; Exec. Dir. Agency for Co-operation and Research in Devt. (ACORD) 1993–; Pres. Bd. of Govs. African Devt. Bank 1971–72; Chair. UN Gen. Ass. Cttee. on North-South Dialogue 1978–79. *Leisure interests:* jogging, skiing, riding. *Address:* ACORD, 52 Horseferry Road, London, SW1P 2AF, England. *Telephone:* 0171-227 8600. *Fax:* 0171-799 1868.

JEAMBAR, Denis; French journalist; mem. staff Paris-Match 1970–73, Le Point 1973–95 (Ed. 1993–95); Ed. Radio station Europe 1 1995–96; Ed.-in-Chief weekly L'Express 1996–. *Publications:* several books including Sur la route de Flagstaff, George Gershwin, Dieu s'amuse, Le poisson pourrit par la tête, Daisy. *Leisure interests:* painting, cinema, literature, travel. *Address:* L'Express, 61 avenue Hoche, 75411 Paris cedex 08, France. *Telephone:* (1) 40-54-30-00. *Fax:* (1) 42-67-72-93.

JEAN BENOÎT GUILLAUME MARIE ROBERT LOUIS ANTOINE ADOLPHE MARC D'AVIANO, H.R.H. Grand Duke of Luxembourg, Duke of Nassau, Prince of Bourbon-Parma; b. 5 Jan. 1921, Colmar Berg; m. Princess Josephine-Charlotte of Belgium April 1953; three s. two d.; Lieut.-Rep. of Grand Duchess 1961–64; became Grand Duke of Luxembourg on abdication of Grand Duchess Charlotte Nov. 1964; Col. of the Irish Guards; mem. Int. Olympic Cttee.; Chief Scout, Luxembourg Boy Scouts' Asscn.; Col. Regt. Irish Guards 1984–; Dr. h.c. (Strasbourg, Miami). *Leisure interests:* photography and natural history. *Address:* Grand Ducal Palace, 2013 Luxembourg.

JEANCOURT-GALIGNANI, Antoine; French business executive; b. 12 Jan. 1937, Paris; s. of Paul Jeancourt-Galignani and Germaine Verley; m. 1st Brigitte Auzouy 1961 (divorced 1983); three s. one d.; m. 2nd Hannelore Wagner 1983; one d.; ed. Mount St. Mary's Coll. Spinkhill, U.K., Ecole Saint Louis de Gonzague, Faculté de Paris, Ecole Nat. d'Admin.; Inspecteur de Finances 1965; Asst. Sec., Office of Minister of Finance 1968–70, Treasury Dept. of Ministry of Finance 1970–71; with Chase Manhattan Bank, New York 1972; Sr. then Exec. Vice-Pres. in charge of int. and corp. banking, Crédit Agricole 1973–79; joined Banque Indosuez 1979, Pres. 1980–81, 1982–88, Chair. and C.E.O. 1981–82, 1988–94; Chair. Assurances Générales de France 1994–; Dir. Paribas, Société Générale, Bouygues, Total, Euro Disney (Chair. Supervisory Bd. 1995–); Chair. French-Korean Cttee. of MEDEF; Officier, Légion d'honneur, Ordre nat. du Mérite, Chevalier du Mérite agricole, Croix de la valeur militaire. *Address:* 87 rue de Richelieu, 75002 Paris (Office); 3 avenue Bosquet, 75007 Paris, France (Home).

JEANMAIRE, Renée Marcelle (Zizi); French actress, dancer and singer; b. 29 April 1924; m. Roland Petit (q.v.) 1954; one d.; student, Paris Opera Ballet 1933–40, Dancer 1940–44; with Ballets de Monte-Carlo, Ballets Colonel de Basil, Ballets Roland Petit; Dir. (with Roland Petit) Casino de Paris 1969–; Chevalier Légion d'honneur, Chevalier des Arts et des Lettres, Officier, Ordre nat. du Mérite; leading roles in Aubade, Piccoli, Carmen, La Croqueuse de Diamants, Rose des Vents, Cyrano de Bergerac, La Dame dans la Lune, La Symphonie Fantastique 1975, Le loup, La chauve-souris 1979, Hollywood Paradise Show 1985, Java for ever 1988, Marcel et la Belle Excentrique 1992. *Films:* Hans Christian Andersen, Anything Goes, Folies Bergères, Charmants Garçons, Black Tights, la Revue, Zizi je t'aime; musical: The Girl in Pink Tights (Broadway); music hall appearances. *Address:* c/o Ballets Roland Petit, 20 boulevard Gabès, 13008 Marseille, France.

JEANNENEY, Jean-Marcel, L. ÈS L., D. EN D.; French politician and economist; b. 13 Nov. 1910, Paris; s. of Jules Jeanneney (fmr. Pres. of the Senate and Minister); m. Marie-Laure Monod 1936; two s. (and one s. deceased) five d.; ed. Ecole Libre des Sciences Politiques, Paris; Prof. of Political Economy, Grenoble Univ. 1937–51, Dean of Law Faculty 1947–51; Prof. of Social Econs. Paris Univ. 1951–56, of Financial Econs. 1957–59, of Political Econs. 1970–80; Dir. du Cabinet of his father, Jules Jeanneney, Minister of State, de Gaulle Prov. Govt. 1944–45; mem. Admin. Council, Ecole nat. d'admin. 1945–58; Dir. Econ. Activity Study Service, Fondation Nat. des Sciences politiques 1952–58; Consultant to OEEC 1953; mem. Rueff Cttee. 1958; Rapporteur and del. to numerous confs.; Minister of Industry, (Debré Cabinet) 1959–62; Amb. to Repub. of Algeria 1962–63; Chair. French Cttee. on Co-operation with Developing Countries 1963; mem. and French Rep. to UN Econ. and Social Council 1964–66; Minister of Social Affairs 1966–68; Deputy June 1968; Minister of State 1968–69; Pres. L'Observatoire français des Conjonctures économiques 1981–89; Dir. Nat. Foundation for Political Sciences 1981–; Commdr. Légion d'honneur, Grand Croix Ordre Nat. du Mérite, Commdr. des Palmes académiques. *Publications:* Essai sur les mouvements des prix en France depuis la stabilisation monétaire (1927–1935) 1936, Economie et droit de l'électricité (with C. A. Colliard) 1950, Les commerces de détail en Europe occidentale 1954, Forces et faiblesses de l'économie française 1945–1956, Textes de droit économique et social français 1789-1957 (with Perrot), Documents économiques (2 Vols.) 1958, Economie politique 1959, Essai de comptabilité interrégionale française pour 1954, 1969, Régions et sénat 1969, A mes amis gaullistes 1973, Pour un nouveau protectionnisme 1978, Les economies occidentales du XIXème siècle à nos jours 1985, L'Economie française depuis 1967, la traversée des turbulences mondiales 1989, Vouloir l'emploi 1994, Ecoute la France qui gronde 1996, Une Mémoire Républicaine 1997. *Address:* 69 quai d'Orsay, 75007 Paris (Office); 102 rue d'Assas, 75006 Paris; Rioz 70190, France (Homes). *Telephone:* (01) 43-26-39-46 (Paris); (03) 84-91-82-52 (Rioz).

JEANNENEY, Jean-Noël, D. ÈS L.; French politician and professor; b. 2 April 1942, Grenoble; s. of Jean-Marcel Jeanneney (q.v.) and Marie-Laure (née Monod) Jeanneney; m. 2nd Annie-Lou Cot 1985; two s.; ed. Lycées Champollion and Louis-le-Grand, Ecole normale supérieure, Inst. d'études politiques de Paris; Lecturer in Contemporary History, Univ. de Paris X 1969–77, lecturer 1968; Univ. Prof. Inst. d'études politiques de Paris 1977–; Pres., Dir.-Gen. Radio-France and Radio-France Int. 1982–86; Pres. Bicentenary of the French Revolution 1988–89; mem. Bd. of Dirs., Agence France-Presse 1982–84, Télédiffusion de France 1982–86, La Sept 1986, Seuil Publs. 1987–91, 1993–; Chair. Scientific Council, Inst. d'Histoire du Temps Présent 1991–; Sec. of State for External Trade 1991–92, for Communication 1992–93; Regional Councillor, Franche-Comté 1992–98; Chair. Advisory Cttee for "Histoire" (cable TV) 1997–; Pres. Europartenaires 1998–; historical films for French TV: Léon Blum ou la fidélité 1973, Eamon de Valera 1975, Le Rhin 1996, Les Grandes Batailles de la République 1996–98, Senghor entre deux mondes 1998. *Publications:* le Riz et le Rouge, cinq mois en Extrême-Orient 1969, le Journal politique de Jules Jeanneney 1939–42 1972, François de Wendel en République, l'Argent et le Pouvoir 1976, Leçon d'histoire pour une gauche en pouvoir, la Faillite du Cartel 1924–26 1977, le Monde de Beuve-Méry ou le métier d'Alceste (co-author) 1979, l'Argent caché, milieux d'affaires et pouvoirs politiques dans la France du XXe Siècle 1981, Télévision nouvelle mémoire, les magazines de grand reportage 1959–68 (with others) 1982, Echec à Panurge, l'audiovisuel public au service de la différence 1986, Concordances des temps, chroniques sur l'actualité du passé 1987, Georges Mandel, l'Homme qu'on attendait 1991, l'Avenir vient de loin 1994, Une histoire des médias des origines à nos jours 1996, le Passé dans le prétoire, l'historien, le juge et le journaliste 1998. *Address:* 27 rue Saint-Guillaume, 75007 Paris (Office); 48 rue Galande, 75005 Paris, France (Home). *Fax:* 01.40.51.09.40.

JEANNIOT, Pierre Jean, O.C., M.SC.; Canadian air transport official; b. 9 April 1933, Montpellier, France; ed. Sir George Williams Univ., McGill Univ. and Univ. de Montréal; designer of aircraft and marine instrumentation, Sperry Gyroscope of Canada 1952–55; various positions in research, devt. and man., Air Canada 1955–68; contributed to devt. of the "black box"; Vice-Pres. Computers and Communications, Univ. du Québec 1969; Vice-Pres. Computer and Systems Services, Air Canada 1970–76; subsequently held other sr. positions in Air Canada; Exec. Vice-Pres. and C.O.O. Air Canada 1983, Pres. and C.E.O. 1984–90; Pres. and C.E.O. JINMAG Inc. 1990–92; Dir.-Gen. IATA 1993–; Dir. Bank of Nova Scotia; Chair. Bd. Univ. of Quebec 1971–77; Dr. h.c. (Quebec) 1988, (Concordia) 1997; Man. Achievement Award, McGill Univ. 1989; many other professional and public appts.; Chevalier, Légion d'honneur, Independence Medal of First Order (Jordan). *Publications:* numerous technical papers. *Address:* International Air Transport Association, Route de l'Aéroport 33, P.O. Box 416, 1215 Geneva 15-Airport, Switzerland.

JEELOF, Gerrit; Netherlands business exective; b. 13 May 1927, Leeuwarden; m. Jantje Aleida Plinsinga (died 1992); two d.; ed. Univ. for Business Admin., Nyenrode; joined Philips Electronics N.V. 1950, posts in S. America, Italy, U.K. and U.S.A.; retd. as Vice-Chair. Bd. of Man. 1990, mem. Supervisory Bd.; mem. Bd. Dirs. V.N.U. Publishing, ROBECO Investment Funds, Centraal Beheer Insurance, Cabot Corpn., Boston, U.S.A.; Chair. Bd. Dirs. European-American Chamber of Commerce, Washington, D.C. 1990–; Commdr. del Ordine al Merito della Repubblica Italiana 1974, Hon. C.B.E. 1981, Officer Orde van Oranje Nassau 1985, Kt. Order of Netherlands Lion, Commdr. Order of Leopold II (Belgium). *Leisure interests:* sailing, golf. *Address:* Apt. 3F, Long Island Apts., Le Zoute, Zwinlaan 11, 8300 Knocke-Heist, Belgium. *Telephone:* 5061-0085.

JEEVES, Malcolm Alexander, C.B.E., M.A., PH.D.; British professor of psychology and author; b. 16 Nov. 1926, Stamford; s. of Alexander Frederic Thomas Jeeves and Helena May Jeeves (née Hammond); m. Ruth Elisabeth Hartridge 1955; two d.; ed. Stamford School, St. John's Coll., Cambridge, Harvard Univ.; commd. Royal Lincs. Regt., served with 'Desert Rats' in First Bn. Sherwood Foresters, B.A.O.R. 1945–48; Research Exhibitioner St. John's Coll., Cambridge 1952; Rotary Foundation Fellow, Harvard Univ. 1953; lecturer Leeds Univ. 1956; Prof. of Psychology Adelaide Univ. 1959–69, Dean 1962–64; Vice-Prin. St. Andrews Univ. 1981–85; Dir. MRC Cognitive Neuroscience Research Group, St. Andrews 1984–89; Hon. Research Prof. St. Andrews Univ. 1993–; Ed.-in-Chief Neuropsychologia 1990–93; mem. Psychology Cttee. S.S.R.C. 1972–76, Biology Cttee. S.E.R.C. 1980–84, Science Bd. 1985–89, Council 1985–89, Neuroscience and Mental Health Bd., MRC 1985–89, Manpower Sub-Cttee., A.B.R.C. 1991–93, Council Royal Soc. of Edin. 1984–88, Exec. 1985–87, Vice-Pres. Royal Soc. of Edin. 1990–93, Pres. 1996–99; Pres. Section J, B.A.A.S. 1988; Founding Fellow Acad. of Medical Sciences 1998; Abbie Memorial Lecture, Adelaide Univ. 1981, Cairns Memorial Lecture, 1986, 1987; Hon. Sheriff Fife 1986–; Hon. D.Sc. (Edin.); Burney Student, Kenneth Craik Award (St. John's Coll., Cambridge); Gregg Bury Prize. *Publications:* Thinking in Structures (with Z. P. Dienes) 1965, The Effects of Structural Relations upon Transfer (with Z. P. Dienes) 1968, The Scientific Enterprise and Christian Faith 1969, Experimental Psychology: An Introduction for Biologists 1974, Psychology and Christianity: The View Both Ways 1976, Analysis of Structural Learning (with G. B.

Greer) 1983, Free to be Different (with R. J. Berry and D. Atkinson) 1984, Behavioural Science: a Christian Perspective 1984, Psychology — Through the Eyes of Faith (with D. G. Myers) 1987, Mind Fields 1994, Callosal Agenesis (ed. with M. Lassonde) 1994, Human Nature at the Millennium 1997, Science, Life and Christian Belief (with R. J. Berry) 1998, papers on neuropsychology and cognition in scientific journals. *Leisure interests:* music, fly fishing, walking. *Address:* School of Psychology, University of St. Andrews, St. Andrews, Fife, KY16 9JU; The Royal Society of Edinburgh, 22–24 George Street, Edin., EH2 2PQ, Scotland. *Telephone:* (01334) 462057 (Univ.); (0131) 225 6057 (Royal Soc.). *Fax:* (01334) 463042 (Univ.); (0131) 220 6889 (Royal Soc.).

JEEWOOLALL, Ramesh, LL.B.; Mauritius politician and lawyer; m.; two c.; ed. Middle Temple, London; lawyer 1969–71; magistrate 1971–72; Chair. Tea Devt. Authority 1976; elected to Legis. Ass. (Labour Party) 1976, Deputy Speaker 1976–79, Speaker 1979–82, 1996–; elected to Legis. Ass. (Alliance Party) 1987; Minister of Housing, Lands and Environment 1987–90. *Address:* National Assembly, Port Louis, Mauritius; 92 Belle Rose Avenue, Quatre Bornes, Mauritius. *Telephone:* 4645371.

JEFFARES, Alexander Norman, A.M., M.A., PH.D., D.PHIL.; British professor of English; b. 11 Aug. 1920, Dublin; s. of Cecil N. Jeffares and Agnes (née Fraser) Jeffares; m. Jeanne A. Calembert 1947; one d.; ed. The High School, Dublin, Trinity Coll., Dublin and Oriel Coll., Oxford; Lecturer in Classics, Trinity Coll., Dublin 1943–45; lector in English, Groningen Univ., Netherlands 1946–48; lecturer in English Literature, Univ. of Edinburgh 1949–51; Prof. of English Language and Literature, Univ. of Adelaide 1951–57; Prof. of English Literature, Univ. of Leeds 1957–74; Prof. of English, Univ. of Stirling 1974–86, Hon. Prof. 1986–; Hon. Research Fellow Royal Holloway Coll., Univ. of London 1997–; Man. Dir. Academic Advisory Services Ltd. 1974–; Dir. Colin Smythe Ltd. 1975–; mem. Scottish Arts Council 1979–84, Vice-Chair. 1980–84; Chair. Book Trust, Scotland 1986–89; Pres. Scottish PEN 1986–89; mem. Arts Council of G.B. 1980–84; mem. Council, Royal Soc. of Edinburgh 1986–89, Vice-Pres. 1988–89; Dir. Edinburgh Book Festival 1982–90; mem. Exec. Cttee. Scots Australian Council 1992–; Hon. Fellow, Trinity Coll. Dublin; Hon. D. de l'Univ. (Lille); Hon. D.Litt. (Ulster). *Publications:* W. B. Yeats: man and poet 1949, Seven Centuries of Poetry 1955, The Circus Animals 1970, Restoration Drama (4 vols.) 1974, A History of Anglo-Irish Literature 1982, Poems of W. B. Yeats: a new selection 1984, A New Commentary on the Poems of W. B. Yeats 1984, Brought up in Dublin (poems) 1987, Brought up to Leave (poems) 1987, An Irish Childhood (with A. Kamm) 1987, A Jewish Childhood (with A. Kamm), W. B. Yeats: A New Biography 1988, Yeats's Poems 1989, Yeats's Vision 1990, W. B. Yeats, The Love Poems 1990, W. B. Yeats, Poems of Place 1991, Always your Friend: Letters between Maud Gonne and W. B. Yeats 1893–1938 (with Anna MacBride White) 1992, Jonathan Swift, Selected Poems 1992, Joycechoyce (with Brendan Kennelly) 1992, Ireland's Women: Writings Past and Present (with Katie Donovan and Brendan Kennelly) 1994, Maud Gonne MacBride, A Servant of the Queen (with Anna MacBride White) 1994, Collins Dictionary of Quotations (with Martin Gray) 1995, Images of Invention: Essays on Irish Writing 1996, Victorian Love Poems 1996, A Pocket History of Irish Literature 1997, Irish Love Poems 1997, The Secret Rose: Love Poems by W. B. Yeats 1998, Wonder and a Wild Desire: Love Poems from Ireland 1999, The Poems and Plays of Oliver St. John Gogarty 1999. *Leisure interests:* drawing, restoring old houses. *Address:* Craighead Cottage, Fife Ness, Crail, Fife, KY10 3XN, Scotland. *Telephone and fax:* (01333) 450898.

JEFFERSON, Sir George Rowland, Kt., C.B.E., F.ENG., F.I.E.E., F.R.AE.S., F.R.S.A., C.B.I.M., F.C.G.I.; British business executive; b. 26 March 1921; s. of Harold Jefferson and Eva Elizabeth Ellen; m. Irene Watson-Browne 1943 (died 1998); three s.; ed. Dartford Grammar School, Kent; eng. apprentice, Royal Ordnance Factory, Woolwich 1937–42; with R.A.O.C. and R.E.M.E. 1942; Anti-Aircraft Command and Armament Design Dept., Fort Halstead 1942–45; Ministry of Supply, Fort Halstead 1945–52; joined Guided Weapons Div., English Electric Co. Ltd. 1952, Chief Research Engineer 1953, Deputy Chief Engineer 1958; Dir. English Electric Aviation Ltd. 1961; with British Aircraft Corpn. (BAC), Dir. and C.E.O., BAC (Guided Weapons) Ltd. 1963, Deputy Man. Dir. 1964, mem. Bd. 1965–77; Dir. British Aerospace, Chair. and C.E.O. its Dynamics Group 1977–80; Chair. BAC (Anti-Tank) 1968–78; Deputy Chair. Post Office 1980–87; Chair. British Telecommunications 1981–87, C.E.O. –1986; Dir. Babcock Int. 1980–87, Lloyds Bank 1986–89; Chair. Matthew Hall PLC 1987–88; Chair. City Centre Communications Ltd. 1988–90, Videotron Corpn. 1990–97; Dir. AMEC PLC 1988–90; mem. Nat. Enterprise Bd. 1979–80, Governing Council Business in the Community Ltd. 1984–87; Freeman of the City of London; Hon. F.I.Mech.E., Hon. D.Sc. (Bristol), Hon. D.Univ. (Essex). *Address:* 449 Kingsway, Landsdale, Perth, WA 6065, Australia.

JEFFORDS, James Merrill, B.S., LL.B.; American politician; b. 11 May 1934, Rutland, Vt.; s. of Olin M. Jeffords and Marion Hausman; m. Elizabeth Daley; one s. one d.; ed. Yale and Harvard Univs.; admitted to Vermont Bar 1962; law clerk, Judge Ernest Gibson, Vt. District 1962; Partner, Bishop, Crowley & Jeffords 1963–66, Kinney, Carbine & Jeffords 1967–68; mem. Vt. Senate 1967–68; Attorney-Gen. State of Vt. 1969–73; Partner, George E. Rice, Jr. and James M. Jeffords 1973–74; mem. 94th–100th Congresses from Vt.; Senator from Vermont 1989–; Republican. *Address:* US Senate, 728 Hart Building, Washington, DC 20510, U.S.A.

JEFFREY, Richard Carl, PH.D.; American university professor; b. 5 Aug. 1926, Boston, Mass.; s. of Mark M. Jeffrey and Jane Markovitz; m. Edith Kelman 1955; one s. one d.; ed. Univs. of Boston, Chicago and Princeton; lecturer in computer design M.I.T. 1952–55, Asst. Prof. of Electrical Eng., M.I.T. 1958–59, Asst. Prof. of Philosophy, Stanford Univ. 1959–63, visiting mem. Inst. for Advanced Study 1963, Assoc. Prof. of Philosophy City Coll. of New York 1964–67, Prof. of Philosophy, Univ. of Pa. 1967–74, Princeton Univ. 1974–. *Publications:* The Logic of Decision 1965, Formal Logic: Its Scope and Limits 1967, Computability of Logic (jtly. with Geo Borlos) 1974, Studies in the Inductive Logic of Probability (Vol. I) 1970, (Vol. II) 1979 (Jt. Ed.), Probability and the Art of Judgement 1991. *Address:* 55 Patton Avenue, Princeton, NJ 08540, U.S.A. *Telephone:* (609) 924 9139.

JEFFREYS, Sir Alec John, Kt., M.A., F.R.C.PATH., F.R.S.; British university professor; b. 9 Jan. 1950, Oxford; s. of Sidney Victor Jeffreys and Joan Jeffreys (née Knight); m. Susan Miles 1971; two d.; ed. Luton Grammar School, Luton Sixth Form Coll., Merton Coll., Oxford; European Molecular Biology Org. Postdoctoral Research Fellow, Univ. of Amsterdam 1975–77; lecturer, Dept. of Genetics, Univ. of Leicester 1977–82, Lister Inst. Research Fellow 1982–91, Reader in Genetics 1984–87, Prof. of Genetics 1987–, Royal Soc. Wolfson Research Prof. 1991–; Inventor of Genetic Fingerprinting; Hon. mem. American Acad. of Forensic Sciences 1998; Colworth Medal Biochemical Soc. 1985, Linnean Bicentenary Medal for Zoology, Linnean Soc. 1987, Carter Medal, Clinical Genetics Soc. 1987, Davy Medal, Royal Soc. 1987, Analytica Prize, German Soc. of Clinical Chemistry 1988, Press, Radio and TV awards for the Midlander of the Year 1988, 1989, Albert Einstein World of Science Award, World Cultural Council 1996, Baly Medal, Royal Coll. of Physicians 1997; Hon. D.Univ. (Open Univ.) 1991, F.F.Sc. (India). *Publications:* numerous articles on human molecular genetics. *Leisure interests:* walking, swimming, postal history, reading unimproving novels. *Address:* Department of Genetics, Adrian Building, University of Leicester, University Road, Leicester, LE1 7RH, England. *Telephone:* (0116) 2523374.

JEFFRIES, Lionel; British actor and director; b. 10 June 1926; s. of Bernard Jeffries and Elsie (née Jackson) Jeffries; m. Eileen Walsh; one s. two d.; began career in film industry 1947; writer and dir. The Railway Children, The Amazing Mr Blunden, Wombling Free; dir. Baxter, The Water Babies. *Stage appearances include:* (London) Hello Dolly 1983–84, See How They Run, Two into One 1984–85, The Wild Duck 1990, (New York) Pygmalion 1989. *Films include:* Bhowani Junction, The Nun's Story, Law and Disorder, Life is a Circus, Idle on Parade, Jazzboat, Please Turn Over, Two-Way Stretch, Trials of Oscar Wilde, Fanny, The Hellions, Operation Snatch, Mrs Gibbon's Boys, Wrong Arm of the Law, Call Me Bwana, The Long Ships, First Men in the Moon, Secret of my Success, Murder Ahoy, You Must be Joking, Journey to the Moon, Camelot, Chitty Chitty Bang Bang, Ménage à trois, Danny Champion of the World; *TV films include:* Ending Up 1989, First and Last, Heaven on Earth 1997. *Leisure interest:* oil painting. *Address:* c/o Samira Higham, ICM, Oxford House, 76 Oxford Street, London, W1R 1RB, England. *Telephone:* 0171-636 6565 (Agent).

JEKER, Robert A.; Swiss business executive; b. 26 Aug. 1935, Basel; m. Vreni Jeker 1967; one s. two d.; ed. Univ. of Massachusetts, Amherst; head Spalenberg br. Credit Suisse, Basel 1968–72, Head Credit Suisse, Basel 1972–76, mem. Exec. Bd. 1976–83, Pres. Zurich 1983–93; Man. Dir. Unotec, Anora and Nueva Holdings 1993–96; now Chair. Bd. ABB AG, Baden, Georg Fischer, Schaffhouse, Swiss Steel, Emmenbrücke, Bertigroup AG, Basel. *Leisure interests:* sports, concerts. *Address:* c/o Messe Basel, 4021 Basel, Switzerland. *Telephone:* (61) 686-2010. *Fax:* (61) 686-2009.

JELE, Khiphusizi Josiah; South African diplomatist; b. 1 May 1930, Johannesburg; m. 1976; one s. two d.; ed. Mil. Acad. Odessa, and Moscow Political Science Acad., U.S.S.R.; studied public admin., Great Britain and U.S.A.; African Nat. Congress (ANC) Political Commissar, Dir. of Broadcasting, Chief Rep., Dar es Salaam, Tanzania 1967–71, ANC Rep. World Peace Council Secr., Helsinki, Finland 1971–77, Dir., ANC Int. Affairs Dept., Lusaka, Zambia 1978–83, Chair. ANC Political Cttee., Lusaka 1983–85, Sec. to ANC Political Mil. Council, Lusaka 1985–91, mem. ANC Nat. Elections Comm. 1991–92, mem. ANC Civil Service Unit 1992–94; mem. ANC Exec. Cttee. 1977–94; M.P. 1994; Perm. Rep. of South Africa to UN 1994–; mem. Hon. Ambassadorial Cttee., Congress of Racial Equality; Phelps-Stokes Fund Annual Award 1995 (Hon. mem. bd. of Fund); Freedom of City of Memphis. *Publications:* (papers) Racism in South Africa 1973, Population Explosion in Africa 1974; Western Military Collaboration with South Africa (booklet). *Leisure interests:* soccer, boxing, jazz, classical music, reading. *Address:* Permanent Mission of South Africa to the United Nations, 333 East 38th Street, New York, NY 10016, U.S.A. *Telephone:* (212) 692-2465.

JELINEK, Otto John; Canadian politician; b. 1940, Prague, Czechoslovakia; m. Leata Mary Bennett 1974; two s.; ed. Oakville, Ont., Swiss Alpine Business Coll., Davos, Switzerland; business exec.; M.P. 1972–93; apptd. Parl. Sec. to Minister of Transport 1979; fmr. mem. Caucus Cttee. on Trade, Finance, Econ. Affairs, fmr. mem. Standing Cttee. on Transport and Communications, on External Affairs; fmr. mem. Parl. Cttee. on Miscellaneous Estimates, Minister of State (Fitness and Amateur Sport) 1984–88, for Multiculturalism 1985–86, of Supply and Services and Receiver Gen. of Canada 1988–89; Acting Minister of Public Works 1988–89, Minister of Nat. Revenue 1989–93; Pres. Jelinek Int. Inc. 1993–; mem. Bd. Dirs. Hummingbird Communications Ltd., Canbra Foods Ltd.; Chair. Canada-Taiwan Friendship Cttee.; mem. Big Brothers' Asscn. of Canada, Olympic Club of Canada, Canadian Sports Hall of Fame; Fed. Progressive Conservative Party. *Address:* 182 Brookfield Crescent, Oakville, Ont., L6K 1A9, Canada (Home).

JELJASZEWICZ, Janusz, PH.D.; Polish microbiologist ; b. 8 Aug. 1930, Wilno; s. of Aleksander and Helena Jeljaszewicz; m. 1st (divorced); one d.; m. 2nd Anna Dąbrowska 1995; ed. Medical Acad., Poznań; Asst., Microbiology Research Centre of Medical Acad., Poznań 1952–60; Lecturer, Microbiology Research Centre of Medical Acad., Warsaw 1960–63; with State Inst. of Hygiene, Warsaw 1963–94; Head, Lab. of Bacterial Metabolites 1963–96, Asst. Prof. 1965, Extraordinary Prof. 1973, Ordinary Prof. 1978–; Chair. Scientific Council attached to Minister of Health and Social Welfare 1979–88; Chair. Section of Chemotherapy, Polish Medical Asscn. 1980–96; Chair. Scientific Council attached to State Inst. of Hygiene 1981–96; Dir. State Inst. of Hygiene 1996–; Corresp. mem. Polish Acad. of Sciences (PAN) 1994–, Chair. Cttee. on Human Infections 1996, Medical Faculty Societas scientiarum varsouiensis; Chair. Polish-American Cttee. for Health Research Co-operation 1975–91; WHO expert on bacterial infections 1973–; in charge of Polish-American scientific project "Pathogenesis of Staphylococcal and Streptococcal Infections" 1963–80; mem. numerous medical socs.; Kt.'s Cross of Order of Polonia Restituta, Gold Cross of Merit; State Award for Achievements in Science 1976, Certificate of Appreciation U.S. Public Health Service. *Publications:* Bacterial Toxins and Cell Membranes 1978, Bacteria and Cancer 1983, Staphylococci and Staphylococcal Infections (6 vols.) 1965–85, Medical Microbiology (5 vols.) 1983–85, Chemotherapy and Immunity 1985, Bacterial Protein Toxins 1984–90 (4 vols.); about 400 research works in Polish and foreign professional journals. *Leisure interests:* collecting bibliophile editions, history, human motivation. *Address:* Państwowy Zakład Higieny, ul. Chocimska 24, 00–791 Warsaw, Poland. *Telephone:* (22) 49 76 12; (22) 49 77 81.

JELLICOE, 2nd Earl, (cr. 1925); **George Patrick John Rushworth Jellicoe,** K.B.E., D.S.O., M.C., F.R.S.; British politician, diplomatist and businessman; b. 4 April 1918, Hatfield; s. of 1st Earl Jellicoe (Admiral of the Fleet); m. 1st Patricia O'Kane 1944; m. 2nd Philippa Ann Bridge 1966; three s. four d.; ed. Winchester and Trinity Coll., Cambridge; mil. service (Coldstream Guards, Special Air Service and Special Boat Service) 1939–45; joined Foreign Office 1947; First Sec. Washington, Brussels, Baghdad; Deputy Sec.-Gen. Baghdad Pact; Lord-in-Waiting 1961; Jt. Parl. Sec., Ministry of Housing and Local Govt. 1961–62; Minister of State, Home Office 1962–63; First Lord of Admiralty 1963–64; Minister of Defence for the Royal Navy 1964; Deputy Leader of the Opposition, House of Lords 1967–70; Lord Privy Seal and Leader of House of Lords 1970–73; Dir. S. G. Warburg 1966–70, 1973–88, Smiths Industries 1973–87, Tate & Lyle 1974–93 (Chair. 1978–83), Chair. Booker Tate Ltd. 1988–91; Chair. Davy Corpn. 1985–90, European Capital 1991–95; Dir. Morgan Crucible 1974–88; Sotheby's (Holdings) 1973–93; Pres. London Chamber of Commerce and Industry 1979–82, Parl. and Scientific Cttee. 1980–83, Crete Veterans Asscn. 1990–, British Heart Foundation 1992–95, Royal Geographical Soc. 1993–97, SAS Asscn. 1996–; Chancellor Univ. of Southampton 1984–96; Chair. Council of King's Coll., Univ. of London 1977–84, Medical Research Council 1982–90, British Overseas Trade Bd. 1983–86; Pres. East European Trade Council (Chair. 1986–90); Pres. Kennet and Avon Canal Trust 1980–93; Croix de guerre, Légion d'honneur, Grand Commdr. Greek Order of Honour, Greek War Cross. *Leisure interests:* skiing and travel. *Address:* Tidcombe Manor, Tidcombe, Nr. Marlborough, Wilts, SN8 3SL; 97 Onslow Square, London, S.W.7, England. *Telephone:* (01264) 731 225 (Wilts.); 0171-584 1551 (London). *Fax:* (01264) 731-418.

JELVED, Marianne, M.ED.; Danish politician; b. 5 Sept. 1943, Charlottenlund; m.; teacher in public schools 1967–89, Royal Danish School of Educ. Studies 1979–87; Deputy Mayor of Gundsø 1982–85; mem. Folketing 1988–; Chair. Social Liberal mems. of Parl. 1988; Minister for Econ. Affairs 1993–, also for Nordic Cooperation 1994–. *Publications:* BRUD: Radikale vaerdier i en forandret tid (co-author) 1994. *Address:* Ministry of Economic Affairs, Ved Stranden 8, 1061 Copenhagen K, Denmark. *Telephone:* 33 92 41 74. *Fax:* 33 93 60 20.

JENCKS, William Platt, M.D.; American biochemist; b. 15 Aug. 1927, Bar Harbor, Me.; s. of Gardner Jencks and Elinor Melcher Cheetham; m. Miriam Ehrlich Jencks 1950; one s. one d.; ed. Harvard Coll. and Harvard Medical School; Intern, Peter Bent Brigham Hosp., Boston, Mass. 1951–52; mem. staff, Dept. of Pharmacology, Army Medical Service Graduate School 1953–54, Chief, Dept. of Pharmacology 1954–55; Life Insurance Medical Research Fund Postdoctoral Fellow, Mass. Gen. Hosp. 1955–56; U.S. Public Health Service Postdoctoral Fellow, Dept. of Chem., Harvard 1956–57; Asst. Prof. of Biochem., Brandeis Univ. 1957–60, Assoc. Prof. of Biochem. 1960–63, Prof. of Biochem. 1963–96, of Biochem. and Molecular Pharmacodynamics 1977–96, Prof. Emer. 1996–; Guggenheim Memorial Foundation Fellow 1973–74; Fellow A.A.A.S., American Acad. of Arts and Sciences; mem. Nat. Acad. of Sciences, American Soc. of Biological Chemists, American Philosophical Soc.; Foreign mem. Royal Soc. (U.K.); American Chem. Soc. Award in Biological Chem. 1962, American Soc. of Biological Chemists Merck Award 1993, James Flack Norris Award 1995, Repligen Award 1996. *Publications:* Catalysis in Chemistry and Enzymology 1969, Biochemistry (co-author) 1992, and over 380 articles in journals. *Leisure interest:* music. *Address:* Brandeis University, Graduate Department of Biochemistry, Waltham, MA 02254 (Office); 11 Revere Street, Lexington, MA 02420, U.S.A. (Home). *Telephone:* (781) 736-2315 (Office); (781) 862-8875 (Home). *Fax:* (781) 736-2349.

JENKIN OF RODING, Baron (Life Peer), cr. 1987, of Wanstead and Woodford in Greater London; **(Charles) Patrick Fleeming Jenkin,** P.C., M.A., F.R.S.A.; British politician; b. 7 Sept. 1926, Edinburgh; s. of late C. O. F. Jenkin and Margaret E. Jenkin (née Sillar); m. Alison Monica Graham 1952; two s. two d.; ed. Clifton Coll., Bristol, Jesus Coll., Cambridge; called to the Bar, Middle Temple 1952; Adviser Distillers Co. Ltd. 1957–70; Hornsey Borough Council 1960–63; M.P. for Wanstead and Woodford 1964–87; Opposition Spokesman on Finance, Econs. and Trade 1965–66, 1967–70; Financial Sec. to Treasury 1970–72, Chief Sec. 1972–74; Minister for Energy Jan.–March 1974; mem. Shadow Cabinet 1974–79; Opposition Spokesman on Energy 1974–76, on Social Services 1976–79; Sec. of State for Social Services 1979–81, for Industry 1981–83, for the Environment 1983–85; mem. House of Lords Select Cttee. on Science and Tech. 1997–; Non-Exec. Dir. Tilbury Contracting Group Ltd. 1974–79, Royal Worcs. Co. Ltd. 1975–79; Dir. Continental and Industrial Trust Ltd. 1975–79; Adviser Arthur Andersen 1985–96; Dir. Friends Provident Life Office 1986–88, Chair. 1988–98; Chair. Lamco Paper Sales Ltd. 1987–93; Dir. U.K.-Japan 2000 Group 1986– (Chair. 1986–90); Chair. Crystalate Holdings PLC 1988–90, Target Finland Ltd. 1991–96 (Dir. 1989–91); Vice-Pres. Asscn. of Metropolitan Authorities 1987–, Nat. Asscn. of Local Councils 1987–, Greater London Area Conservatives 1987–89, Pres. 1989–92; mem. U.K. Advisory Bd. Nat. Econ. Research Assocs. Inc. 1985–; Dir. U.K. Council for Econ. and Environmental Devt. Ltd. 1987–; Council mem. Guide Dogs for the Blind Asscn. 1987–97; Chair. Westfield Coll. Trust 1988–; Adviser Sumitomo Trust and Banking Co. Ltd. 1989–; Pres. British Urban Regeneration Asscn. 1990–96; Chair. Forest Healthcare NHS Trust 1991–97; mem. Advisory Bd. PPRU, Queen Mary and Westfield Coll. 1991–97 (Fellow 1991–), Supervisory Bd. Achmea Holding NV 1991–98; Council mem. Imperial Cancer Research Fund 1991–97, (Deputy Chair. 1994–97; Patron Stort Trust 1991, St. Clare West Essex Hospice Care Trust 1991–; Jt. Pres. MIND (Nat. Asscn. of Mental Health) 1991–93, Asscn. of London Govt. 1995–; Vice-Pres., Nat. Housing Fed. 1991–; Sr. Vice-Pres. World Congress on Urban Growth and Devt. 1992–94; Pres. London Boroughs Asscn. 1992–95; Adviser Thames Estuary Airport Co. Ltd. 1992–; mem. Int. Advisory Bd. Marsh & McLennan Cos. Inc. (US) 1993–, Nijenrode Univ., Netherlands 1994–98; Vice-Pres., Foundation for Science and Tech. 1996–97, Chair. 1997–; Hon. LL.D. (Univ. of the South Bank); Freeman City of London, Hon. Freeman London Borough of Redbridge; Conservative. *Leisure interests:* music, gardening, sailing, D.I.Y. *Address:* House of Lords, London, SW1A 0PW, England. *Telephone:* 0171-219 6966. *Fax:* 0171-219 0759.

JENKINS, Sir Brian Garton, G.B.E., M.A., F.C.A.; British business executive; b. 3 Dec. 1935, Beckenham; m. (Elizabeth) Ann Jenkins; one s. one d.; ed. Tonbridge, Trinity Coll., Oxford; with R.A., Gibraltar 1955–57; partner Coopers & Lybrand 1960–95; Chair. Woolwich PLC 1995–; Pres. Inst. of Chartered Accountants in England and Wales 1985–86, London Chamber of Commerce and Industry 1996–98, British Computer Soc. 1997–98; Chair. Charities Aid Foundation 1998–; Lord Mayor of London 1991–92; Hon. Bencher Inner Temple; Hon. mem. Baltic Exchange. *Publication:* An Audit Approach to Computers 1978. *Address:* 12 Devereux Court, Strand, London, WC2R 3JJ, England. *Telephone:* 0171-353 6775. *Fax:* 0171-353 6778.

JENKINS, (David) Clive; British trade unionist (retd.); b. 2 May 1926, Port Talbot; s. of David Samuel and Miriam Harris (née Hughes) Jenkins; m. Moira McGregor Hilley 1963 (divorced 1989); one s. one d.; ed. Port Talbot Central Boys' School, Port Talbot County School and Swansea Tech. Coll.; employed in metallurgical test house 1940; mem. Port Talbot Co-operative Soc. Educ. Cttee. 1945; Branch Sec. and Area Treas., Asscn. of Scientific Workers 1946; Asst. Midlands Div. Officer, Asscn. of Supervisory Staffs, Execs. and Technicians (ASSET) 1947, Transport Industrial Officer 1949, Nat. Officer 1954, Gen. Sec. ASSET 1961–68; Jt. Gen. Sec. Asscn. of Scientific, Tech. and Man. Staffs 1968–70, 1988–89, Gen. Sec. 1970–88, Gen. Sec. Emer. 1989–; Metropolitan Borough Councillor 1954–60; Chair. Nat. Jt. Council for Civil Air Transport 1967–68, London Enterprise Devts. 1984–89; Ed. Trade Union Affairs 1961–63; mem. Gen. Council of Trades Union Congress 1974–89; Dir. Unity Trust 1984–86, Green Independents Goshawk Trust 1990–; mem. Nat. Research Devt. Corpn. 1974–80; mem. British Overseas Trade Bd.; mem. Cttee. of Enquiry on Industrial Democracy 1976; mem. Cttee. to Review the Functioning of Financial Insts. 1977; mem. TUC Econ. Cttee. 1978–89, TUC Gen. Purposes and Finance Cttee. 1979–89, TUC-Labour Party Liaison Cttee. 1979–89, Comm. of Inquiry into Labour Party 1979; mem. Int. Cttee., Social Insurance and Ind. Welfare Cttee., Employ and Org. Cttee.; mem. NEDC 1983–89; mem. Bd. BNOC 1979–82; mem. Advisory, Conciliation and Arbitration Service (ACAS) 1986–89; Trustee, Nat. Heritage Memorial Fund 1980–88; Gov. Royal Sadlers Wells Foundation 1985–88; Chair. Roosevelt Memorial Trust, Educ. Trust, Friends of the Earth Trust 1984–86; Gov. Commonwealth Inst.; Fellow Woodrow Wilson Centre, Wash., D.C. 1975; Australian Commonwealth Govt. Scholarship 1989; Pres. TUC 1987–88; Gold Badge of Congress 1988, 1989. *Publications:* Power at the Top 1959, Power Behind the Screen 1961, British Trade Unions Today (with J. E. Mortimer) 1965, The Kind of Laws the Unions Ought to Want (with J. E. Mortimer) 1968, Computers and the Unions (with

Barrie Sherman) 1977, Collective Bargaining (with Barrie Sherman) 1977, The Collapse of Work (with Barrie Sherman) 1979, White Collar Unionism: The Rebellious Salariat (with Barrie Sherman) 1979, The Leisure Shock (with Barrie Sherman) 1981, All Against the Collar (autobiog.) 1990; pamphlets and essays; Daily Mirror and Tribune Columnist. *Leisure interests:* working with environmentalists, particularly the case of Fairy Penguins and keeping an eye on multinational exploiters.

JENKINS, Rt. Rev. David Edward, M.A.; British ecclesiastic; b. 26 Jan. 1925, London; s. of Lionel C. Jenkins and Dora K. (née Page) Jenkins; m. Stella M. Peet 1949; two s. two d.; ed. St. Dunstan's Coll., Catford, Queen's Coll., Oxford, Lincoln Theological Coll.; Capt. R.A. 1945–47; priest 1954; Succentor Birmingham Cathedral 1953–54; Fellow and Chaplain and Praelector in Theology, Queen's Coll., Oxford 1954–69; Hon. Fellow 1990; Dir. Humanum Studies, WCC, Geneva 1969–73; Dir. William Temple Foundation, Manchester 1973–78; Prof. of Theology Leeds Univ. 1979–84, Prof. Emer. 1984–; Bishop of Durham 1984–94; Asst. Bishop of Ripon 1994–; Hon. Prof. of Divinity, Durham 1994–; Hon. Fellow, Sunderland Univ.; Hon. D.D. (Durham, Aberdeen, Trinity Coll., Toronto, Leeds, Birmingham); Hon. D.Lit. (Teesside); Hon. D.C.L. (Northumbria). *Publications:* The Glory of Man 1967, Living With Questions 1969, What is Man? 1970, The Contradiction of Christianity 1979, God, Miracles and the Church of England 1987, God, Politics and the Future 1988, God, Jesus and Life in the Spirit 1988, Still Living With Questions 1990, Free to Believe (with Rebecca Jenkins) 1991. *Leisure interests:* music (opera and church music), walking, birdwatching, nature and conservation, travel and books. *Address:* Ashbourne, Cotherstone, Barnard Castle, Co. Durham, DL12 9PR, England.

JENKINS, Elizabeth, O.B.E.; British writer; b. 31 Oct. 1905; ed. Newnham Coll. Cambridge. *Publications:* The Winters 1931, Lady Caroline Lamb: a Biography 1932, Portrait of an Actor 1933, Harriet (Femina Vie Heureuse Prize) 1934, The Phoenix Nest 1936, Jane Austen—a Biography 1938, Robert and Helen 1944, Young Enthusiasts 1946, Henry Fielding, English Novelists Series 1947, Six Criminal Women 1949, The Tortoise and the Hare 1954, Ten Fascinating Women 1955, Elizabeth the Great 1958, Elizabeth and Leicesster 1961, Brightness 1963, Honey 1968, Dr. Gully 1972, The Mystery of King Arthur 1975, The Princes in the Tower 1978, The Shadow and the Light: A Life of Daniel Dungla Home 1983. A Silent Joy (novel) 1992. *Address:* 121 Greenhill, Hampstead, London, NW3 5TY, England. *Telephone:* 0171-435 4642.

JENKINS, Harold, M.A., D.LITT., F.B.A.; British university professor (retd.); b. 19 July 1909, Shenley, Bucks.; s. of Henry Jenkins and Mildred (Carter) Jenkins; m. Gladys Puddifoot 1939 (died 1984); ed. Wolverton Grammar School and Univ. Coll. London; Quain Student, Univ. Coll. London 1930–35; William Noble Fellow, Univ. of Liverpool 1935–36; Jr. Lecturer in English, Univ. of the Witwatersrand 1936–38, Lecturer 1939–44, Sr. Lecturer 1945; Lecturer in English, Univ. Coll. London 1945–46, Reader 1946–54; Prof. of English, Westfield Coll, Univ. of London 1954–67; Regius Prof. of Rhetoric and English Literature Univ. of Edin. 1967–71, Prof. Emer. 1971–; Visiting Prof. Duke Univ. 1957–58, Univ. of Oslo 1974; Gen. Ed. Arden Shakespeare 1958–82; Pres. Malone Soc. 1989–; Hon. D.Litt. (Iona Coll., U.S.A.) 1983, Sr. Fellow British Acad. 1989; Shakespeare Prize, FVS Foundation, Hamburg 1986. *Publications:* Henry Chettle 1934, Edward Benlowes: Biography of a Minor Poet 1952, Hamlet (Arden Shakespeare) 1982. *Address:* 22 North Crescent, Finchley, London, N3 3LL, England.

JENKINS, Dame (Mary) Jennifer, D.B.E.; British administrator; b. 18 Jan. 1921; d. of the late Sir Parker Morris; m. Roy Jenkins, now Lord Jenkins of Hillhead (q.v.) 1945; two s. one d.; ed. St. Mary's School, Calne, Girton Coll., Cambridge; with Hoover Ltd. 1942–43; Ministry of Labour 1943–46; Political and Econ. Planning 1946–48; part-time extra-mural lecturer 1949–61; part-time teacher Kingsway Day Coll. 1961–67; Chair. Consumers Asscn. 1965–76; mem. Exec. Bd. British Standards Inst. 1970–73, Design Council 1971–74, Cttee. of Man. Courtauld Inst. 1981–84, Exec. Cttee., Nat. Trust 1985–91 (Chair. 1986–90), Ancient Monuments Bd. 1982–84, Historic Bldgs. and Monuments Comm. 1984–85; Chair. Historic Bldgs. Council for England 1975–84, Royal Parks Review Group 1991–96, Architectural Heritage Fund 1994–97, Expert Panel, Heritage Lottery Fund 1995–; Pres. Ancient Monuments Soc. 1985– (Sec. 1972–75); Chair. N. Kensington Amenity Trust 1974–77; Trustee Wallace Collection 1977–83; Dir. J. Sainsbury Ltd. 1981–86, Abbey Nat. PLC 1984–91; J.P. London Juvenile Courts 1964–74; Hon. Fellow Landscape Inst. 1995; Hon. F.R.I.B.A., Hon. F.R.I.C.S., Hon. M.R.T.P.I.; Hon. LL.D. (Univ. of London) 1988, (Bristol) 1990, Hon. D.C.L. (Univ. of Newcastle Upon Tyne) 1992, Hon. D.Univ. (York) 1990, (Strathclyde) 1993; Hon. D.Arch. (Oxford Brookes) 1993, (Greenwich). *Publication:* From Acorn to Oak Tree: The Growth of the National Trust 1994. *Address:* 2 Kensington Park Gardens, London, W11 3HB; St. Amand's House, East Hendred, Oxon., OX12 8LA, England.

JENKINS, Sir Michael Romilly Heald, K.C.M.G., B.A.; British diplomatist and business executive; b. 9 Jan. 1936, Cambridge; s. of Prof. Romilly Jenkins and Celine J. (née Haeglar) Jenkins; m. Maxine L. Hodson 1968; one s. one d.; ed. King's Coll., Cambridge; entered Foreign (subsequently Diplomatic) Service 1959; served in Paris, Moscow and Bonn; Deputy Chef de Cabinet 1973–75, Chef de Cabinet to George Thomson, EEC 1975–76; Prin. Adviser to Roy Jenkins (now Lord Jenkins q.v.) Jan.-Aug. 1977; Head, European Integration Dept. (External), FCO 1977–79; Head, Cen. Advisory Group, EEC 1979–81; Deputy Sec.-Gen., Comm. of the European Communities 1981–83; Asst. Under-Sec. of State (Europe), FCO 1983–85; Minister, British Embassy, Washington 1985–87; Amb. to the Netherlands 1988–93; Exec. Dir. Kleinwort Benson Group PLC 1993–, Exec. Dir. Kleinwort Benson Ltd. 1993–, Vice-Chair. Dresdner Kleinwort Benson 1996–; Chair. British Group, Trilateral Comm. 1995–, Action Centre for Europe (ACE) 1995–; Dir. Aegon NV 1994–; Advisor Sage Int. Ltd. 1998–. *Publications:* Arakcheev, Grand Vizir of the Russian Empire 1969, A House in Flanders 1992. *Leisure interest:* tennis. *Address:* c/o Dresdner Kleinwort Benson, 20 Fenchurch Street, London, EC3P 3DB, England.

JENKINS, Simon David, B.A.; British journalist; b. 10 June 1943, Birmingham; s. of Daniel Jenkins; m. Gayle Hunnicutt 1978; one s. one step-s.; ed. Mill Hill School, St. John's Coll., Oxford; worked for Country Life Magazine 1965; News Ed. Times Educ. Supplement 1966–68; Leader-Writer, Columnist, Features Ed. Evening Standard 1968–74; Insight Editor, Sunday Times 1974–76; Ed. Evening Standard 1977–78; Political Ed. The Economist 1979–86; columnist Sunday Times 1986–90, The Spectator 1992–95, The Times 1992–; Ed. The Times 1990–92; Dir. Faber and Faber (Publrs.) Ltd. 1981–90; mem. Bd., Old Vic Co. 1979–81; Part-time mem. British Rail Bd. 1979–90, London Regional Transport Bd. 1984–86; founder and Dir. Railway Heritage Trust 1985–90; Gov. Museum of London 1984–87, Bryanston School 1986–94; Dir. The Municipal Journal 1980–90; Deputy Chair. Historic Bldgs. and Monuments Comm. 1985–90, English Heritage; Trustee World Monuments Funds 1995–; mem. South Bank Bd. 1985–90; mem. Millennium Comm. 1994–; Chair. Comm. for Local Democracy 1993–95, Bldg. Books Trust 1994–; Rio Tinto David Watt Memorial Prize 1998. *Publications:* A City at Risk 1971, Landlords to London 1975, Newspapers: The Power and the Money 1979, The Companion Guide to Outer London 1981, Images of Hampstead 1982, The Battle for the Falklands 1983, With Respect, Ambassador 1985, The Market for Glory 1986, The Selling of Mary Davies and other writings 1993, Against the Grain 1994, Accountable to None: the Tory nationalization of Britain 1995. *Leisure interests:* architecture, history of London. *Address:* c/o The Times, 1 Pennington Street, London, E1 9XN, England.

JENKINS OF HILLHEAD, Baron (Life Peer), cr. 1987, of Pontypool in the County of Gwent; **Roy Harris Jenkins,** O.M., F.B.A., P.C.; British politician, Chancellor of Oxford University, writer and former President of the European Commission; b. 11 Nov. 1920; s. of Arthur Jenkins, M.P.; m. Jennifer Morris (q.v.) 1945; two s. one d.; ed. Abersychan Grammar School and Balliol Coll., Oxford; Royal Artillery 1942–46; mem. Staff of Industrial and Commercial Finance Corpn. 1946–48; M.P. (Labour) for Cen. Southwark, London 1948–50, for Stechford, Birmingham 1950–77; M.P. (S.D.P.) for Glasgow Hillhead 1982–87; Parl. Private Sec. to Sec. of State for Commonwealth Relations 1949–50; Gov. British Film Inst. 1955–58; mem. Cttee. of Man., Soc. of Authors 1956–60; Chair. Fabian Soc. 1957–58; mem. Council, Britain in Europe; Chair. Britain in Europe Campaign for referendum of 1975; Dir. of Financial Operations, John Lewis Partnership Ltd. 1962–64; Minister of Aviation 1964–65; Sec. of State for Home Dept. 1965–67, 1974–76; Chancellor of the Exchequer 1967–70; Deputy Leader of Labour Party 1970–72; Pres. Comm. of the European Communities 1977–81; mem. Council for Social Democracy Jan.–March 1981; co-founder Social Democratic Party (SDP) March 1981, Leader 1982–83; Leader Liberal Democratic Party Peers House of Lords 1988–98; Pres. Royal Soc. of Literature 1988–; Co-Pres. Royal Inst. of Int. Affairs 1993–; Chancellor, Oxford Univ. March 1987–; Chair. Comm. on Electoral Reform 1998; Adviser (part-time) Morgan Grenfell 1981–82, Dir. Morgan Grenfell Holdings Ltd. 1981–82; Hon. Foreign mem. American Acad. of Arts and Sciences 1973; Hon. Fellow, Berkeley Coll., Yale, Balliol Coll., Oxford, St. Antony's Coll., Oxford, University Coll., Cardiff; Hon. LL.D. (Leeds) 1971, (Harvard) 1972, (Pennsylvania) 1973, (Dundee) 1973, (Loughborough) 1975, (Bath) 1978, (Michigan) 1978, (Essex) 1978, (Wales) 1978, (Reading) 1979, (Bristol) 1980, (Georgetown) 1988, Hon. D.Litt. (Glasgow) 1972, (City University, London) 1976, Hon. D.C.L. (Oxford) 1973, Hon. D.Sc. (Warwick) 1978, (Univ. of Aston in Birmingham) 1977, (Kent) 1992, Hon. Doctor of Univ. of Keele 1977; Dr. h.c. (Open Univ.) 1979, (Louvain) 1979, (Urbino) 1979, (West Va.) 1992, (Glamorgan) 1994, (Bologna) 1994; Charlemagne Prize 1972, Robert Schuman Prize 1972, Prix Adolph Bentinck 1978. *Publications:* Purpose and Policy (Editor) 1947, Mr. Attlee: An Interim Biography 1948, New Fabian Essays (contributor) 1952, Pursuit of Progress 1953, Mr. Balfour's Poodle 1954, Sir Charles Dilke: A Victorian Tragedy 1958, The Labour Case 1959, Asquith 1964, Essays and Speeches 1967, Afternoon on the Potomac? 1972, What Matters Now 1973, Nine Men of Power 1974, Partnership of Principle 1985, Truman 1986, Baldwin 1987, Gallery of Twentieth Century Portraits 1988, European Diary 1977–81, 1989, A Life at the Centre (autobiog.) 1991, Portraits and Minatures 1993, Gladstone 1995 (Whitbread Biography Award 1995), The Chancellors 1998. *Address:* 2 Kensington Park Gardens, London, W11 3BH; St. Amand's House, East Hendred, Oxon., OX12 8LA, England.

JENNINGS, Elizabeth, C.B.E., M.A.; British poet and critic; b. 18 July 1926, Boston, Lincs.; d. of Dr. H. C. Jennings; ed. Oxford High School, St. Anne's Coll., Oxford; Asst. at Oxford City Library 1950–58; Reader for Chatto & Windus Ltd. 1958–60; freelance writer 1960–; Arts Council Prize for Poems, 1953, Somerset Maugham Award for A Way of Looking 1956, Richard Hillary Prize for The Mind has Mountains 1966, Arts Council Award 1981, Paul Hamlyn Foundation Award 1997. *Publications:* Poetry: Poems 1953, A Way of Looking 1955, A Sense of the World 1958, a translation of Michelangelo's Sonnets 1961, Song for a Birth or Death 1961, Recoveries 1963, The Mind has Mountains 1966, The Secret Brother (for children) 1966, Collected Poems 1967, The Animals' Arrival 1969, Lucidities 1971, Relationships 1972, Growing Points 1975, Consequently I Rejoice 1977, After the Ark (for children) 1978, Moments of Grace 1979, Celebrations and Elegies 1982, Extending the Territory 1985, Collected Poems 1953–86 1986 (W.H. Smith Award 1987), Tributes 1989, Times and Seasons 1992, Familiar Spirits 1994; Criticism: Every Changing Shape 1961, Seven Men of Vision 1976; ed. Batsford Book of Religious Verse 1982, In Praise of Our Lady 1982, Extending the Territory 1985, Collected Poems 1953–86 1986 (W. H. Smith Award 1987), Tributes 1989, Times and Seasons 1992, Familiar Spirits 1994, A Spell of Words 1997, Praises 1998; writings also include contributions to New Yorker, Southern Review, Poetry (Chicago), Botteghe Oscure, Daily Telegraph, Encounter, New Statesman, Observer, Scotsman, Country Life, Listener and others. *Leisure interests:* theatre, music, looking at pictures, conversation. *Address:* c/o David Higham Assocs. Ltd., 5–8 Lower John Street, London, W1R 4HA, England.

JENNINGS, Hon. Mr. Justice John R. R., B.A., LL.B., Q.C.; Canadian judge; b. 10 July 1937, Toronto, Ont.; s. of Robert D. Jennings and Mary Rogers; m. Eyton Margaret Embury 1964; two s.; ed. Upper Canada Coll., Univ. of Toronto and Osgoode Hall Law School, Toronto; Past mem. York Co. Legal Aid Area Cttee.; mem. and past mem. Council, Medico-Legal Soc.; Chair. Nat. Family Law Section 1974–76; Pres. Co. of York Law Asscn. 1976; Chair. Bd., Windsor-Essex-Mediation Centre 1981–85; Dir. Canadian Bar Insurance Asscn 1987–89; Pres. Advocates' Soc. 1987, Canadian Bar Asscn. 1989–90, Canadian Bar Foundation 1989–90, CBANET Inc. 1989–90; Judge, Gen. Div., Ont. Court 1991–; Fellow, American Coll. of Trial Lawyers. *Leisure interests:* tennis, travel. *Address:* Court House, 361 University Avenue, Toronto, Ont., M5G 1X9 (Office); 70 Montclair Avenue, Apartment 703, Toronto, Ont., M5P 1P7, Canada (Home). *Telephone:* (416) 486-0562 (Office).

JENNINGS, Sir John (Southwood), Kt., C.B.E., PH.D., F.R.S.E., F.G.S.; British business executive; b. 30 March 1937, Oldbury, Worcs.; s. of the late George Southwood Jennings and of Irene Beatrice (née Bartlett) Jennings; m. 1st Gloria Ann Griffiths 1961 (dissolved 1996); one s. one d.; m. 2nd. Linda Elizabeth Baston 1997; ed. Oldbury Grammar School, Univs. of Birmingham and Edin.; joined Royal Dutch/Shell 1958, various posts, including Gen. Man. and Chief Rep. of Shell cos. in Turkey 1976–78, Man. Dir. Shell UK Exploration and Production 1979–84, Exploration and Production Co-ordinator, Shell Internationale Petroleum Mij., The Hague 1985–90; Dir. The Shell Transport and Trading Co. PLC 1987– (Man. Dir. Royal Dutch/Shell Group of Cos. 1987–97, Chair. Shell Transport and Trading Co. 1993–97); Dir. Det Norske Veritas 1997–, Robert Fleming Holdings Ltd. 1998–, the Mitie Group 1998–, Norseman Tectonics 1998–; Vice-Chair. Governing Body London Business School 1993–97 (mem. 1992–97); Vice-Pres. Liverpool School of Tropical Medicine 1991–97; mem. Council Royal Inst. of Int. Affairs 1994–97; Trustee, Edin. Univ. Devt. Trust 1996, Exeter Univ. Council 1997–, Int. Advisory Bd. Toyota Corpn. 1997–, Bd. of Counsellors Bechtel Corpn. 1997–; Hon. D.Sc. (Edin.) 1991, (Birmingham) 1997; Commdr., Ordre Nat. du Mérite (Gabon). *Leisure interests:* fishing, travel, music, wine. *Address:* c/o Shell Centre, London, SE1 7NA, England (Office).

JENNINGS, Sir Robert Yewdall, M.A., LL.B.; British judge of the International Court of Justice (retd.); b. 19 Oct. 1913, Idle, Yorks; s. of Arthur Jennings and Edith Schofield Jennings; m. Christine Dorothy Bennett 1955; one s. two d.; ed. Belle Vue Grammar School, Bradford, Downing Coll., Cambridge, Harvard Univ.; war service (army) 1940–46; Asst. Lecturer in Law, L.S.E. 1938–39, Lecturer 1946–55; called to the Bar, Lincoln's Inn 1943, Hon. Bencher 1970–; Q.C. 1969; Whewell Prof. of Int. Law, Cambridge Univ. 1955–81; Reader in Int. Law, Council of Legal Educ. 1959–70; Ed. Int. and Comparative Law Quarterly 1957–59, British Yearbook of Int. Law 1959–81, Sr. Ed. 1974–81; Assoc. Inst. of Int. Law 1957, mem. 1967, Vice-Pres. 1979–81, Pres. 1981–83, Hon. mem. 1985–; Judge, Int. Court of Justice, The Hague 1982–95 (Pres. 1991–94); mem. Perm. Court of Arbitration 1982–; Hon. mem. American Soc. of Int. Law 1989; fmr. legal consultant to numerous govts.; Counsel in several int. arbitrations; Fellow Jesus Coll., Cambridge 1939–, Sr. Tutor 1949–55, fmr. Pres., Hon. Fellow 1982–; Hon. Fellow Downing Coll. 1982–, L.S.E. 1994–; Hon. LL.D. (Hull) 1987, (Cambridge) 1993, (Leicester) 1995; Hon. Dr. Juris (Saarland), (Rome—Sapientia) 1990; Hon. D.C.L. (Oxford) 1996; Manley O. Hudson Medal 1993. *Publications:* The Acquisition of Territory 1963, General Course on International Law 1967, Oppenheim's International Law (9th ed. with Sir Arthur Watts) 1992, Collected Writings (2 vols.) 1998 and numerous articles and monographs. *Leisure interests:* music, walking in Lake District. *Address:* 61 Bridle Way, Grantchester, Cambridge, CB3 9NY, England.

JENRETTE, Richard Hampton, M.B.A.; American insurance executive; b. 5 May 1929, Raleigh, N.C.; s. of Joseph M. Jenrette and Emma Love; ed. Univ. of N. Carolina and Harvard Grad. School of Business Admin.; New England Life Insurance Co. 1951–53; Brown Bros. Harriman & Co. 1957–59; with Donaldson, Lufkin & Jenrette Inc. 1959–, Chair. 1986–; Chair. Bd. of Dirs. Equitable Life Assurance Soc. 1987–94, Chair Exec. Cttee. May 1994–, Chair., C.E.O. Equitable Investment Corpn. 1986–90; Dir. Advanced Micro Devices, Sunnyvale, Calif.; Trustee, The Rockefeller Foundation, many other public affiliations and appts.; Hon. D.Litt. (Univ. of S.C.) and other awards. *Address:* Donaldson, Lufkin & Jenrette, 140 Broadway, New York, NY 10005; Equitable Life Assurance Society, 787 7th Avenue, New York, NY 10019 (Offices); 67 East 93rd Street, New York, NY 10128, U.S.A. (Home).

JENS, Walter, D.PHIL.; German critic, philologist and novelist; b. 8 March 1923, Hamburg; s. of Walter and Anna (Martens) Jens; m. Inge Puttfarcken 1951; two s.; ed. Hamburg and Freiburg im Breisgau Univs.; Asst. Hamburg and Tübingen Univs. 1946–50; Dozent, Tübingen Univ. 1950–56, Prof. of Classical Philology and Rhetoric 1956–67; Prof. Univ. of Hamburg 1986; mem. German PEN (Pres. 1976–82), Berliner Akad. der Künste, Deutsche Akad. für Sprache und Dichtung; D.Phil., h.c.; Lessingpreis der Hansestadt Hamburg 1968, TV Prize, Trade Union of German Employees 1976, Heinrich Heine Prize 1981, Hamburger Medaille für Kunst und Wissenschaft 1984, Theodor-Heuss-Preis 1988, Hermann-Sinsheimer-Preis der Stadt Freinsheim. *Publications include:* Nein—Die Welt der Angeklagten (novel) 1950, Der Blinde (novel) 1951, Vergessene Gesichter (novel) 1952, Der Mann, der nicht alt werden wollte (novel) 1955, Die Stichomythie in der frühen griechischen Tragödie 1955, Hofmannsthal und die Griechen 1955, Das Testament des Odysseus (novel) 1957, Statt einer Literaturgeschichte (Essays on Modern Literature) 1957, Moderne Literatur—moderne Wirklichkeit (essay) 1958, Die Götter sind sterblich (Diary of a Journey to Greece) 1959, Deutsche Literatur der Gegenwart 1961, Zueignungen 1962, Herr Meister (Dialogue on a Novel) 1963, Euripides-Büchner 1964, Von deutscher Rede 1969, Die Verschwörung (TV play) 1970, Am Anfang der Stall, am Ende der Galgen 1973, Fernsehen-Themen und Tabus 1973, Der tödliche Schlag (TV play) 1974, Der Prozess Judas (novel) 1975, Der Ausbruch (libretto) 1975, Republikanische Reden 1976, Eine deutsche Universität, 500 Jahre Tübinger Gelehrtenrepublik 1977, Zur Antike 1979, Die Orestie des Aischylos 1979, Warum ich Christ bin (Ed.) 1979, Ort der Handlung ist Deutschland (essays) 1979, Die kleine grosse Stadt Tübingen 1981, Der Untergang (drama) 1982, In letzter Stunde (Ed.) 1982, Aufruf zum Frieden 1983, In Sachen Lessing 1983, Kanzel und Katheder 1984, Momos am Bildschirm 1984, Dichtung und Religion (with H. Küng) 1985, Roccos Erzählung 1985, Die Friedensfrau 1986, Theologie und literatur 1986, Das A und das O—die Offenbarung der Johannes 1987, Deutsche Lebensläufe 1987, Feldzüge eines Republikaners 1988, Juden und Christen in Deutschland 1988, Reden 1989, Schreibschule 1991, Die sieben letzten Worte am Kreuz 1992, Die Friedensfrau 1992, Mythen der Dichter 1993, Am Anfang das Wort 1993, Menschenwürdig sterben 1995. *Address:* Sonnenstrasse 5, 72076 Tübingen, Germany. *Telephone:* 07071 292114.

JENSEN, Arthur Robert, PH.D.; American educational psychologist; b. 24 Aug. 1923, San Diego; s. of Arthur Alfred Jensen and Linda Schachtmayer; m. Barbara Jane Delarme 1960; one d.; ed. Calif. (Berkeley), Columbia and London Univs.; Asst. in Medical Psychology, Univ. of Maryland 1955–56; Research Fellow, Inst. of Psychiatry, London Univ. 1956–58; Asst. Prof. to Prof. of Educational Psychology, Univ. of Calif., Berkeley 1958–; Research Psychologist, Inst. of Human Learning 1962–; Guggenheim Fellow 1964–65; Fellow, Center for Advanced Study in the Behavioral Sciences 1966–67; Visiting Lecturer, Melbourne, La Trobe, Adelaide and Sydney Univs. 1977, various univs. in India 1980. *Publications:* Genetics and Education 1972, Educability and Group Differences 1973, Educational Differences 1973, Bias in Mental Testing 1980, Straight Talk About Mental Tests 1981, The *g* Factor 1998. *Address:* School of Education, University of California, Berkeley, CA 94720, U.S.A. (Office). *Telephone:* (510) 642-4201 (Office).

JENSEN, Brikt, PH.D.; Norwegian writer; b. 15 Sept. 1928, Bergen; m. Anne-Grethe Rønnow Jensen; two s. one d.; lecturer Univ. of Strasbourg 1957; research scholar 1961; office man. Univ. of Oslo 1962; Asst. Man. Gyldendal Norsk Forlag publr. 1965, Pres. 1970, main reader 1980–95; mem. Int. Publrs. Comm.; appeared on literary radio and TV programmes 1972–78. *Publications:* Diktning Eller Psykologi? 1963, Brev Fra Et Steinhus 1975, Hverdag 1979, Loggbok 1981, Arbok 1983, Selvangivelse 1993, Min Korsikanske Landsby 1996; ed. several anthologies. *Address:* 20113 Olmeto, Corse du Sud, France; Frederik Stangs Gate 40, 0264 Oslo, Norway. *Telephone:* 4-95-74-62-41 (France); 22-44-01-90 (Norway). *Fax:* 4-95-74-62-41 (France).

JENSEN, Elwood V., PH.D.; American academic and director of research; b. 13 Jan. 1920, Fargo, N.D.; s. of Eli A. and Vera Morris Jensen; m. 1st Mary Collette 1941 (died 1982); one s. one d.; m. 2nd Hiltrud Herborg 1983; ed. Wittenberg Coll. and Univ., of Chicago; Guggenheim Fellowship E.T.H. Zürich 1946–47; Asst. Prof. Dept. of Surgery, Univ. of Chicago 1947–51, Asst. Prof. Ben May Lab. for Cancer Research and Dept. of Biochemistry 1951–54, Assoc. Prof. 1954–60, Prof. Ben May Lab. for Cancer Research 1960–63, American Cancer Soc. Research Prof. Ben May Lab. and Dept. of Physiology 1963–69, Prof. Dept. of Physiology 1969–73, Dept. of Biophysics and Theoretical Biology 1973–84, Dept. of Physiological and Pharmacological Sciences 1977–84, Dept. of Biochemistry 1980–90, Dir. Ben May Lab. for Cancer Research 1969–82, Charles B. Huggins Distinguished Service Prof. Univ. of Chicago 1981–90, Prof. Emer. 1990–; Research Dir. Ludwig Inst. for Cancer Research, Zürich 1983–87; scholar-in-residence Fogarty Int. Center N.I.H. 1988, Cornell Univ. Medical Coll. 1990–91; Visiting Scientist Inst. for Hormone and Fertility Research, Hamburg, Germany 1991–97; Visiting Prof. Karolinska Inst., Sweden 1998–; mem. research advisory bd. Clinical Research Inst., Montreal 1987–; mem. scientific advisory bd. Klinik für Tumorbiologie, Freiburg 1993–, Strang Cancer Prevention Center, New

York 1994–; mem. N.A.S. (mem. Council 1981–84), American Acad. of Arts and Sciences; Hon. D.Sc. (Wittenberg Univ.) 1963, (Acadia Univ.) 1976, (Medical Coll. Ohio) 1991; Hon. M.D. (Hamburg Univ.) 1995; Nobel Ass. Fellowship 1998, and numerous other awards and prizes. *Publications:* 223 articles and reviews since 1945. *Leisure interests:* tennis, squash, riding. *Address:* Department of Medical Nutrition, Karolinska Institute, 760 Novum, S-141 86 Huddinge, Sweden. *Telephone:* (8) 5858-3702 (Office); (8) 779-5544 (Home). *Fax:* (8) 779-8795.

JENSEN, Hans Peter, PH.D., D.SC.; Danish university rector; b. 11 June 1943, Copenhagen; m. Helle Rønnow Olesen 1965; two s. one d.; ed. Univ. of Copenhagen, Chalmers Univ. of Tech., Gothenburg; Asst. Prof. Tech. Univ. of Denmark 1969, Assoc. Prof. 1972, Head of Chem. Dept. A. 1980–83, Dean of Chem. Faculty 1983–86, Rector 1986–; Research Assoc. Univ. of Oregon 1974–75, Visiting Prof. 1978, 1984; mem. Danish Natural Science Research Council 1984–92, Danish Acad. of Tech. Sciences, Cttee. on Higher Educ. and Research (Council of Europe), Evaluation Group of European Postgraduate Training Programme 1989–93, Cultural Foundation between Denmark and Finland 1989–97, Fulbright Commission of Denmark; Chair. Danish Rectors' Conf.; Chair. Bd. Danish Research Acad.; Chair. UNESCO Int. Cttee. on Eng. Educ.; Dr. h.c. (Shenandoah Univ., U.S.A.) 1993, (Helsinki Univ. of Tech.) 1998, (State Univ. of N.Y.) 1998. *Publications:* General Chemistry (textbook) 1985; articles in professional journals. *Leisure interests:* music, literature. *Address:* Technical University of Denmark, Building 101A, 2800 Lyngby (Office); Resedavej 9, 2820 Gentofte, Denmark (Home). *Telephone:* 45 25 10 00 (Office); 39 65 34 29 (Home). *Fax:* 4593 4028 (Office); 39 65 34 77 (Home).

JENSEN, Ole Vig; Danish politician; b. 17 May 1936, Frederikssund; fmr. teacher; mem. Folketing (Parl.) 1971–73, 1978–, mem. Presidium 1984–; mem. Gen. Council, Social Liberal Party 1968–, Exec. Council 1974–, Deputy Chair. Parl. Group 1979–; mem. Cen. Land Bd. 1983–; Chair. Parl. Cttee. for Agric. and Fisheries 1979–84; Deputy Chair. Parl. Educ. Cttee. 1979–82; Minister of Cultural Affairs 1988–90, of Educ. 1993–98. *Address:* c/o Ministry of Education and Research, Frederiksholms Kanal 21–25, 1220 Copenhagen K, Denmark.

JERIE, Jan, D.SC.; Czech scientist; b. 21 Aug. 1913, Prague; s. of Prof. Josef Jerie and Gisela (née Opitzová) Jerie; m. Eva Kozáková 1939; two s. one d.; ed. Univ. of Tech., Prague; designer Skoda Works 1938–47, research worker 1947–69; co-founder State Research Inst. of Machine Designing 1947–69; Prof. Dept. of Internal Combustion Turbines, Faculty of Tech. 1969–75; Head Dept. of Aviation, Faculty of Tech. 1976–80, consulting Prof. 1980–84, adviser 1984–, Prof. Emer. 1997–; lecturer at seminars in China, India, Korea, Argentina, Canada; mem. and chair. numerous int. scientific socs. and cttees.; Hon. mem. Czech. Soc. for Mechanics 1982–; State Prize 1961, Golden Křižík Medal 1973, Golden Felber Medal of Czech. Acad. of Sciences 1978. *Publications:* 80 research reports, 50 scientific articles and textbooks, author of many patented inventions. *Leisure interests:* photography, classical music, gardening. *Address:* Kat. let. FS-ČVUT, Karlovo nám. 13, 121 35 Prague 2 (Office); Nad Komornickou 3, 160 00 Prague 6, Czech Republic (Home). *Telephone:* 02-24357433.

JEROME, Rt. Hon. James Alexander, P.C., B.A.; Canadian politician and judge; b. 4 March 1933, Kingston, Ont.; s. of Joseph Leonard Jerome and Phyllis Devlin; m. Barry Karen Hodgins 1958; three s. (one s. deceased) two d.; ed. St. Michael's Coll., Univ. of Toronto and Osgoode Hall; Lawyer; Alderman, Sudbury 1966–67; M.P. 1968–80; Parl. Sec. to Pres. of Privy Council; Speaker House of Commons 1974–80; Assoc. Chief Justice, Fed. Court of Canada 1980–; Liberal. *Address:* Federal Court of Canada, Kent and Wellington Streets, Ottawa, Ont., K1A 0H9, Canada.

JERUSALEM, Siegfried; German tenor; b. 17 April 1940, Oberhausen; m. 1980; one s. one d.; studied violin and piano at Folkwang Hochschule, Essen; played bassoon in German orchestras, including Stuttgart Radio Symphony Orchestra; studied voice and started singing career in Zigeunerbaron 1975; début Metropolitan New York 1980, La Scala 1981, Vienna State Opera 1979; sang Loge and Siegfried, Wagner's Ring Cycle, Metropolitan New York 1990, Tristan, Bayreuth 1993, Wagner's Ring Cycle, Vienna 1994, Wagner's Rienzi, Vienna 1997; Bundesverdienstkreuz (1st Class) 1996. *Leisure interests:* video, tennis, photography, golf. *Address:* c/o Dr G. Hilbert (Agent), Maximillianstrasse 22, 80539 Munich, Germany.

JERVIS, Simon Swynfen, M.A., P.S.A., F.R.S.A.; British museum director; b. 9 Jan. 1943, Yoxford; s. of late John Swynfen Jervis and of Diana (née Marriott) Parker; m. Fionnuala MacMahon 1969; one s. one d.; ed. Downside School, Corpus Christi Coll., Cambridge; with Leicester Museum and Art Gallery 1964–66; Asst. Keeper, Furniture Dept., Vic. and Albert Museum 1966–75, Deputy Keeper 1975–79, Acting Keeper 1989, Curator 1989–90; Dir. Fitzwilliam Museum, Cambridge 1990–95; Dir. of Historic Bldgs., Nat. Trust 1995–; mem. Council, Soc. of Antiquaries 1986–88 (Pres. 1995–), Royal Archaeological Inst. 1987–91; Chair. Nat. Trust Arts Panel 1987–95; Ed. Furniture History Soc. 1987–91, Chair. 1998–; Dir. Burlington Magazine 1993–, Trustee 1997–; Guest Scholar, J. Paul Getty Museum 1988–89; Trustee, Royal Collection Trust 1993–, Sir John Soane's Museum 1999–. *Publications:* Victorian Furniture 1968, Victorian and Edwardian Decorative Art: the Handley Read Collection 1972, Printed Furniture Designs Before 1650 1974, High Victorian Design 1974, The Penguin Dictionary of Design and Designers 1984, Furniture from Austria and Hungary in the Victoria and Albert Museum 1986. *Leisure interests:* churches, tennis. *Address:* The National Trust, 36 Queen Anne's Gate, London, SW1H 9AS, England. *Telephone:* 0171-222 9251.

JESIH, Boris; Slovenian artist and poet; b. 8 Aug. 1945, Škofja Loka; s. of Svetoslav and Kristina Jesih; m. Bojana Žokalj 1970 (divorced 1981); one s. one d.; ed. Acad. of Fine Arts, Ljubljana, Berlin; works appear in numerous collections; major exhbns. include: 37th Biennale, Venice 1978, Premio le Arti 1971, 11–15th Biennale of Graphic Arts, Ljubljana 1975–83, 6–10th Biennale of Graphic Art, Cracow 1976–84, Premio Biella 1976, British Print Biennale, Bradford 1980, 1982, 1984, Die Kunst vom Stein, Vienna 1985; 10 nat. and 10 int. Awards; has published several books of poetry. *Leisure interests:* basketball, fishing. *Address:* Valjavčeva 17, 61000 Ljubljana, Slovenia.

JESZENSZKY, Géza, PH.D.; Hungarian historian and politician; b. 10 Nov. 1941, Budapest; s. of Zoltán Jeszenszky and Pálma Miskolczy-Simon; m. Edit Héjj; one s. one d.; ed. Eötvös Loránd Univ. Budapest; subject specialist with Nat. Széchényi Library 1968–76; Sr. lecturer 1976–81, reader 1981–; Dean of the School of Political and Social Sciences, Budapest Univ. of Econs. 1989–90, Head, Faculty of Int. Relations 1990–91; Visiting Prof. Univ. of Santa Barbara, Calif. 1984–86 and Univ. of Calif. at L.A. 1986; Visiting De Roy Prof., Univ. of Michigan, Ann Arbor 1996; Founding mem. Hungarian Democratic Forum 1988–96, Head Foreign Affairs Cttee. 1988–90, mem. Presidency 1990–94; Minister of Foreign Affairs 1990–94; mem. Parl. 1994–98; Amb. to U.S.A. 1998–. *Publications:* Prestige Lost, The Changing Image of Hungary in Great Britain 1894–1918 1986, The Hungarian Question in British Politics 1848–1914 1986, István Tisza: Villain or Tragic Hero? 1987, Lessons of Appeasement 1994, More Bosnias? National and Ethnic Tensions in the Post-Communist World 1997; other studies in Hungarian and English. *Leisure interests:* literature, jazz, dedicated skier. *Address:* Embassy of Hungary, 3910 Shoemaker Street, N.W., Washington, DC 20008, U.S.A. *Telephone:* (202) 362-3284. *Fax:* (202) 966-8135.

JEWISON, Norman Frederick, O.C., B.A.; Canadian film director; b. 21 July 1926, Toronto; s. of Percy Joseph and Dorothy Irene (née Weaver) Jewison; m. Margaret Dixon 1953; two s. one d; ed. Malvern Collegiate High School, Toronto, Victoria Coll., Univ. of Toronto; stage actor, Toronto; TV actor 1950–52; TV dir. for CBC 1953–58, CBS 1958–61; film dir. 1961–; Faculty mem. Inst. for American Studies, Salzburg, Austria 1969; Pres. D'Avoriaz Film Festival 1981–; Dir. Centre for Advanced Film Studies 1987–; mem. Electoral Bd., Dirs. Guild of America; mem. Canadian Arts Council; Acad. of Canada Special Achievement Award 1988; Emmy Award 1960; Golden Globe Award 1966; Best Dir., Berlin Film Festival for Moonstruck 1988; Hon. LL.D. (Univ. of Western Ont.) 1974; Irving Thalberg Memorial Prize 1999. *Films Include:* Forty Pounds of Trouble, The Thrill of It All 1963, Send Me No Flowers 1964 (all for Universal Studios), Art of Love, The Cincinnati Kid 1965, The Russians are Coming (also producer) 1966, In the Heat of the Night (Acad. Award 1967), The Thomas Crown Affair (also producer) 1967, Gaily, Gaily 1968, The Landlord (producer) 1969, Fiddler on the Roof (also producer) 1970, Jesus Christ Superstar (also producer) 1972, Billy Two Hats (producer) 1972, Rollerball 1974, F.I.S.T. (also producer) 1977, And Justice for All 1979, Best Friends 1982, A Soldier's Story 1984, Agnes of God 1985, Moonstruck 1987, In Country 1989, Other People's Money 1991, Only You 1994, Bogus 1996; dir. TV shows for Harry Belafonte, Andy Williams, Judy Garland and Danny Kaye. *Leisure interests:* skiing, yachting, tennis. *Address:* Yorktown Productions Ltd., 300 West Olympic Boulevard, Santa Monica, CA 90404; c/o ICM, 8942 Wilshire Boulevard, Beverly Hills, CA 90211, U.S.A.

JEWKES, Sir Gordon Wesley, K.C.M.G.; British diplomatist; b. 18 Nov. 1931; s. of the late Jesse Jewkes; m. Joyce Lyons 1954; two s.; ed. Barrow Grammar School, Magnus Grammar School, Newark-on-Trent and elsewhere; joined Colonial Office 1948; with army 1950–52; with Gen. Register Office 1950–63, 1965–68; mem. Civil Service Pay Research Unit 1963–65; joined FCO 1968; Commercial Consul, Chicago 1969–72, Consul-Gen. 1982–85; Deputy High Commr. Port of Spain 1972–75; Head of Finance Dept., FCO and Finance Officer of Diplomatic Service 1975–79; Consul-Gen. Cleveland 1979–82; Gov. Falkland Islands, Commr. South Georgia and South Sandwich Islands, High Commr. British Antarctic Territory 1985–88; Consul-Gen., N.Y. and Dir.-Gen. Trade and Investment, U.S.A. 1989–91; mem. Bd. of Dirs. Hogg Group PLC 1992–94, Slough Estates PLC 1992–; Exec. Dir. The Walpole Cttee. 1992–96; mem. Council Univ. of Buckingham 1996–, Marshall Aid Commemoration Comm. 1996–, Salvation Army London Advisory Bd. 1996–. *Leisure interests:* music, travel, walking. *Address:* 19 Furzefield Road, Beaconsfield, Bucks., HP9 1PG, England.

JEYARETNAM, J. B., LL.B.; Singaporean politician and lawyer; b. 5 Jan. 1926, Ceylon; ed. Muar, Johore, Malaysia, St. Andrew's School, Singapore, Univ. Coll. London; joined Singapore legal service 1952; First District Judge until 1963; legal practice 1963–87 (disbarred 1987); Sec.-Gen. Workers' Party 1971–; M.P. for Anson 1981–87; fined and jailed for one month on charge of fraud; first opposition M.P. for 15 years. *Address:* Workers' Party, 411B Jalan Besar, Singapore 0820.

JHABVALA, Ruth Prawer, C.B.E., M.A.; British writer; b. 7 May 1927, Cologne, Germany; d. of Marcus Prawer and Eleonora Cohn; sister of Siegbert Salomon Prawer (q.v.); m. C. S. H. Jhabvala 1951; three d.; ed. Hendon Co. School and London Univ.; born in Germany of Polish parentage;

refugee to England 1939; lived in India 1951–75, in U.S.A. 1975–; Neill Gunn. Int. Fellowship 1979; Booker Award for best novel 1975; MacArthur Foundation Award 1984. *Publications:* novels: To Whom She Will 1955, Nature of Passion 1956, Esmond in India 1958, The Householder 1960, Get Ready for Battle 1962, A Backward Place 1962, A New Dominion 1971, Heat and Dust 1975, In Search of Love and Beauty 1983, The Nature of Passion 1986, Poet and Dancer 1993, Shards of Memory 1995; short story collections: A Stronger Climate 1968, An Experience of India 1970, How I Became a Holy Mother 1976, Out of India: Selected Stories 1986, Three Continents 1987, Poet and Dancer 1993, Shards of Memory 1995, East into Upper East 1998; film scripts (for James Ivory q.v.): Shakespeare Wallah 1965, The Guru 1969, Bombay Talkie 1971, Autobiography of a Princess 1975, Roseland 1977, Hullabaloo over Georgie and Bonnie's Pictures 1978, Jane Austen in Manhattan 1980, Quartet 1981, A Room with a View 1986, Madame Sousatzka 1988, Mr and Mrs Bridge 1989, Howards End 1992, The Remains of the Day 1993, Jefferson in Paris 1995, Surviving Picasso 1996. *Address:* 400 East 52nd Street, New York, NY 10022, U.S.A.

JI CHAOZHU, B.SC.; Chinese diplomatist; b. 30 July 1929, China; s. of Prof. Chi Kungchuan; m. Wang Xiangtong 1957; two s.; ed. Harvard Univ., U.S.A., Tsinghua Univ., Peking; stenographer and typist at Panmunjom for Chinese People's Volunteers 1952–54; English interpreter for Mao Zedong, Zhou Enlai and others 1955–73; Counsellor at Liaison Office of China in Washington, D.C. 1973–75; Deputy Dir. Dept. for Int. Orgs. and Confs., Ministry of Foreign Affairs 1975–79, Deputy Dir. of American and Oceanic Affairs 1979–82; Minister-Counsellor of Chinese Embassy in Washington, D.C. 1982–85; Amb. to Fiji, Kiribati and Vanuatu 1985–87; Amb. to the U.K. 1987–91; UN Under-Sec. for Tech. Co-operation for Devt. 1991–92; Under Sec.-Gen., Dept. of Econ. Devt. 1992–96 (now Dept. for Devt., Support and Man. Services). *Leisure interests:* swimming, archaeology, history. *Address:* c/o Ministry of Foreign Affairs, 225 Chaoyangmennei Dajie, Dongsi, Beijing 100701, People's Republic of China.

JI PENGFEI (JI LUO); Chinese politician; b. 1910, Yongji Co., Shanxi Prov.; m. Xu Hanbing; three s. three d.; ed. Mil. Medical Coll.; joined CCP 1933; on Long March in Medical Dept., Red Army 1935; Deputy Political Commissar, Army Corps, 3rd Field Army 1950; Amb. to German Dem. Repub. 1950–55; Vice-Minister of Foreign Affairs 1955–72; Acting Minister of Foreign Affairs 1968–72, Minister 1972–74; Sec.-Gen. Standing Cttee., Nat. People's Congress 1975–79; Vice-Premier, State Council 1979–82, Sec.-Gen. 1980–81, State Councillor 1982–; Head of CP Liaison Office 1981–82; mem. Political and Legal Affairs Group, Cen. Cttee., CCP 1978–; mem. 10th Cen. Cttee., CCP 1973, 11th Cen. Cttee. 1977; Dir. State Council Hong Kong and Macao Affairs 1983–90, Chair. Cttee. for Drafting Basic Law of Hong Kong Special Admin. Region 1985–90; Hon. Pres. China-Germany Friendship Asscn. 1992–; Pres. Asscn. for Well Known Chinese Figures 1993–; Hon. Chair. China Foundation for Int. and Strategic Studies 1989–; mem. Standing Cttee. of Cen. Advisory Comm. 1987–92; mem. Presidium 14th CCP Nat. Congress 1992. *Address:* State Council, Zhong Nan Hai, Beijing, People's Republic of China.

JI XIANLIN; Chinese university professor; b. 6 Aug. 1911, Shandong Prov.; one s. one d.; ed. Tsinghua Univ., Beijing, Univ. of Göttingen, Fed. Repub. of Germany; Prof., Dir. Dept. of Oriental Languages, Beijing Univ. 1946; disappeared during Cultural Revolution; Vice-Pres. Beijing Univ. 1978–84; Dir. South Asian Inst., Chinese Acad. of Social Sciences 1978–85; Pres. Foreign Languages Research Soc. 1981; Pres. Soc. of Linguistics 1986, Soc. for Study of Africa and Asia, Dunhuang-Turpan Soc.; Vice-Pres. China Educ. Asscn. for Int. Exchanges 1988–; Adviser, Chinese Writers' Asscn. 1996–. *Publications include:* Collected Papers on the History of Cultural Relations Between China and India 1982, Studying the Ramayana 1981, Selected Papers on the Languages of Ancient India 1982, and trans. of various Indian classics including 7 vols. of Valmiki's Ramayana 1980, Problems of the Language of Primitive Buddhism 1985. *Address:* Department of Oriental Studies, Beijing University, Beijing, People's Republic of China. *Telephone:* 2501578.

JI YUNSHI: Chinese politician; b. Sept. 1945, Haimen, Jiangsu Prov.; ed. Shandong Univ.; joined CCP 1975; Vice-Gov. Jiangsu Prov. 1989–99; Gov. 1999–. *Address:* Jiangsu Provincial People's Government, Nanjing, Jiangsu Province, People's Republic of China.

JIA CHUNWANG; Chinese state official; b. 1938, Beijing; ed. Qinghua Univ.; Vice-Chair. Tibet Autonomous Regional People's Govt. 1984–85; Minister of State Security 1985–98; Minister of Public Security 1998; mem. 12th CCP Cen. Cttee. 1985, 13th Cen. Cttee. 1987–92; mem. Cen. Comm. of Political Science and Law 1991–, 14th CCP Cen. Cttee. 1992–97, 15th CCP Cen. Cttee. 1997–. *Address:* Ministry of Public Security, 14 Dongchangan Jie, Beijing, People's Republic of China.

JIA LANPO; Chinese archaeologist and palaeontologist; b. 25 Nov. 1908, Yutian Co., Hebei Prov.; ed. Huiwen High School; joined Peking Man excavation work at Zhoukoudian 1931–37; researcher, Inst. of Vertebrate Palaeontology and Palaeoanthropology, Academia Sinica 1949–; Vice-Pres., Society for Pacific Region History 1984–; mem. Dept. of Earth Sciences, Academia Sinica 1985–; Senior Fellow Chinese Acad. of Sciences 1998–. *Publications:* The Land of Peking Man 1950, Prehistoric Residents on China's Mainland 1978, China's Old Stone Age 1984. *Address:* Chinese Academy of Sciences, Beijing 100864, People's Republic of China.

JIA PINGWA; Chinese writer; b. 21 Feb. 1952, Danfeng Co., Shaanxi Prov.; s. of Jia Yanchun and Zhouzhue; m.; one d.; ed. Dept. of Chinese Language, Northwest Univ., Xian; Ed., Shaanxi People's Publishing House 1975–; Chief Ed. magazine Mei Wen (Beautiful Essays); mem. Writers' Asscn. 1979–; Prize for Nat. Literature (3 times), Pegasus Prize for Literature. *Publications:* more than 60 works; including novels Turbulence, The Corrupt and Waning, White Night; short stories and essays; works have been translated in many languages. *Leisure interest:* painting, collecting antiques. *Address:* No. 2 Lian Hu Xiang, Xian City, Shaanxi, People's Republic of China.

JIA QINGLIN; Chinese engineer and government official; b. 1940, Jiaohe Co., Hebei Prov.; ed. Hebei Coll. of Eng.; joined CCP 1959; Deputy Sec. Fujian Prov. CCP Cttee. 1985–93, Sec. 1993–; Gov. of Fujian Prov. 1991–94; Mayor of Beijing 1997–; Chair. Standing Cttee. Fujian Provincial 8th People's Congress 1994–; mem. 14th Cen. Cttee. CCP 1992–97, 15th CCP Cen. Cttee. 1997–; Sec. CCP Beijing Municipal Cttee. 1997–; mem. CCP Politburo 1997–. *Address:* Office of Mayor, Beijing, People's Republic of China.

JIA ZHIJIE; Chinese party and government official; b. 1935, Fuyu Co., Jilin Prov.; ed. Soviet Union; joined CCP 1960; Dir. Lanzhou Petrochemical Machinery Plant; Deputy Sec. Plant CCP Cttee.; Deputy Sec. Gansu Prov. CCP Cttee. 1983–92; Gov. Gansu Prov. 1986–92; Gov. of Hubei Prov. 1992–94; Sec. CCP Cttee. Hubei Prov. 1994–; Sec.-in-Chief Hubei Mil. District CCP Cttee. 1994–; alt. mem. CCP 13th Cen. Cttee. 1987–92; mem. 14th CCP Cen. Cttee. 1992–97, 15th CCP Cen. Cttee. 1997–. *Address:* Office of Provincial Governor, 1 Beihuan Road, Wuhan, Hubei Province, People's Republic of China. *Telephone:* (27) 87814585. *Fax:* (27) 87816148.

JIAGGE, Annie Ruth, LL.D.; Ghanaian judge and voluntary worker; b. 7 Oct. 1918, Lomé, Togo; d. of the late Rev. R. D. Baëta and Henrietta L. Baëta; m. F. K. A. Jiagge 1953; ed. Achimota Training Coll., London School of Econs., Lincoln's Inn; Headmistress of Keta Presbyterian Sr. Girls' School for 5 years; admitted to bar, Ghana 1950, practised law 1950–55; Dist. Magistrate 1955–57, Sr. Magistrate 1957–59; Judge, Circuit Court 1959–61, High Court 1961–69, Court of Appeal 1969–83 (Pres. 1980–83); Ghanaian Rep. on UN Comm. on the Status of Women 1962–72, Chair. 1968; author of basic draft of 1968 UN Declaration on Elimination of Discrimination against women; Chair. Comm. on Investigation of Assets 1966, Ghana Council on Women and Devt. 1975–80; Moderator WCC Programme to Combat Racism 1984–91; Pres. Cttee. of Churches' Participation in Devt. 1985–93; mem. Court, Univ. of Legon 1968–; fmr. Pres. Y.W.C.A. of Ghana, mem. Exec. Cttee. for 12 years and fmr. Vice-Pres. of World Y.W.C.A.; mem. Presidium World Council of Churches 1975–83; mem. Int. Advisory Bd., Noel Foundation 1990–; mem. Cttee. of Experts to prepare the draft of the 1992 Constitution of Ghana; mem. Pres.'s Transitional Cttee. 1993; mem. Council of State 1993–; Hon LL.D. (Legon) 1974; Gimbles' Int. Award for Humanitarian Work 1969, Ghana Grand Medal 1969. *Leisure interests:* music, gardening, crafts. *Address:* No. 8 Onyasia Crescent, Roman Ridge, P.O. Box 5511, Accra North, Ghana. *Telephone:* 772046.

JIANG, Li-Jin, PH.D.; Chinese organic chemist and academician; b. 15 April 1919, Beijing; d. of Jiong-Shang Jiang and Shu-Duan Li; m. Guo-Zhi Xu 1954; two s.; ed. Univ. of Minnesota, U.S.A.; Prof. and Sr. Research Fellow, Inst. Photographic Chem., Acad. Sinica 1978–; mem. Standing Cttee. 6th CPPCC 1983–87, 7th CPPCC 1988–92, 8th CPPCC 1993–97; mem. Standing Cttee. of Chem. Div., Acad. Sinica 1981–93, Academician Acad. Sinica 1994–. *Publications:* The Chemistry and Phototherapeutic Mechanism of Hypocrellins (Second Prize, Natural Science Award, Acad. Sinica 1990), The Relationship between the Structures of the Phycobiliproteins and the Evolution of the Algal Species, The Study of the Mechanism of Energy Transfer (Second Prize, Natural Science Award, Acad. Sinica 1993), The Photochemical, Photophysical and Photodynamical Actions of the Naturally Occurring Perylenohydroxylquinones (Second Prize, Natural Science Award, Acad. Sinica 1996). *Leisure interests:* tennis, travelling. *Address:* Institute of Photographic Chemistry, Academia Sinica, Bei Sha Tan, De Wai, Beijing 100101 (Office); Apartment 804, Building 812, Huang Zhuang, Haidian Qu, Beijing 100080, People's Republic of China (Home). *Telephone:* (010) 64888068 (Office); (010) 62569291 (Home). *Fax:* (010) 62029375.

JIANG BAOLIN; Chinese artist; b. 20 Jan. 1942, Penglai Co., Shandong Prov.; s. of the late Jiang Chunfu and Dai Shuzhi; m. Ling Yunhua 1970; one s. one d.; ed. Dept. of Traditional Chinese Painting, Inst. of Fine Arts, Zhejiang, Cen. Acad. of Fine Arts, Beijing; worked in Cultural House, Fenghua Co. 1967–79; Dir. Zhejiang Artists' Gallery 1982–84; Vice-Pres. Zhejiang Landscape Painting Research Inst. 1982–; mem. Council of Zhejiang Br. of Chinese Painters' Asscn. 1984–; mem. Bd. Zhejiang Painting Acad. 1984–; Prof. Beijing Cen. Fine Arts Acad. 1996–; mem. Council, Cui Zifan Art Foundation Int.; Hon. Adviser, Research Bd. of Advisers, American Biographical Inst. 1992–; mem. Chinese Artists' Asscn.; numerous exhbns. 1987–, including Contemporary Chinese Paintings in celebration of Hong Kong's return to China, Beijing, Shanghai, Tianjin 1997. *Paintings include:* Spring in Remote Valley 1972, Pear Blossoms in Spring Rain 1981, He Lan Mountain 1983, Cottages in Si Ming 1983, Autumn Jubilation in She Village, Mountains and Rocks in Home Village, Rainy Season, Autumn Flavour 1984, Grapes 1986, Moonlight, Hurricane, Bumper Harvest 1987. *One-man exhibitions:* Beijing 1987, Taipei, Taiwan 1987, Gaoxiong, Taiwan 1989, Bonn 1991, Paris 1991, Hong Kong 1994, Seoul, Korea 1996. *Group exhibitions:* Chinese Ink-Wash Paintings, Beijing 1988 (Prize for outstanding works), Selected Chinese Ink-Wash Paintings, Hong Kong 1989, Monte

Carlo 1992 (Prince's Prize), Shenzheng 1992, 8th Nat. Art Exhbn. (mem. Adjudicators' Cttee.), Nat. Symposium of City Landscape, Shenzheng 1995; 72 paintings in collection Asian Art Gallery, Seoul, Korea. *Publications:* Collections of Jiang Baolin's Paintings 1984, Jiang Baolin's ink-wash paintings 1989, Signatur Objekt 15, Jiang Baolin 1991, Jiang Baolin's Paintings (publ. in France) 1991, A selection of Jiang Baolin's Bird and Flower Paintings 1992, The World of Jiang Baolin's Ink & Wash Painting 1994, The Art World of Jiang Baolin (publ. in Korea) 1996. *Leisure interests:* Beijing Opera, literature, music, gardening. *Address:* 201 Building 11, 2nd District, Nandu Huaynan Wenyi Road, Hangzhou, People's Republic of China. *Telephone:* (0571) 8850096. *Fax:* (0571) 8850096.

JIANG BOJU; Chinese mathematician; b. 4 Sept. 1937, Tianjin City; m. Chuanrong Xu 1968; two d.; ed. Peking Univ.; Assoc. Prof. Math. Peking Univ. 1978–82, Prof. 1983–, Dean School of Math. Sciences 1995–98; mem. Chinese Acad. of Sciences 1980; Fellow, Third World Acad. of Sciences 1985; HLHL Mathematics Prize 1996; Nat. Scientific Award of China 1982, 1987; S.S. Chern Mathematics Award 1988. *Address:* Department of Mathematics, Peking University, Haidian Road, Beijing 100871, People's Republic of China. *Telephone:* (86-10) 6275-1804. *Fax:* (10) 6275-1801.

JIANG CHUNYUN; Chinese party official; b. April 1930, Laixi Co., Shandong Prov.; joined CCP 1947; Dir. of Gen. Office Laixi Co. CCP Cttee. 1957–60; Deputy Section Chief Qingdao branch, China Export Corpn. for Local Products 1957–60; with Foreign Trade Bureau, Qingdao City 1957–60; instructor and inspector, and Deputy Dir. of Gen. Office, Propaganda Dept. Shandong Prov. CCP Cttee. 1960–66; manual work in village in Huimin Co. during Cultural Revolution, sent to cadre school, Qihe Co. 1969; worked under Revolutionary Cttee. Shandong Prov. 1970–75; Deputy Dir., Gen. Office Shandong Prov. CCP Cttee. 1975–77, Deputy Sec.-Gen., then Sec.-Gen. 1977–83, Deputy Sec. 1983–84; Sec. Ji'nan Municipal CCP Cttee. 1984–87; Acting Gov. Shandong Prov. 1987–88, Gov. 1988–89; Pres. Shandong Prov. Party School 1989–92; First Sec. Shandong Mil. Dist. CCP Cttee. 1989–94; Vice-Premier of State Council (in charge of agricultural work) 1995–; mem. CCP Politburo 1992–, CCP Cen. Cttee. Secr. 1994–98; Head State Flood-Control and Drought Relief H.Q.; mem. 13th CCP Cen. Cttee., 14th CCP Cen. Cttee., 15th CCP Cen. Cttee. 1997–, Vice-Chair. Standing Cttee. of 9th NPC 1998–. *Address:* Standing Committee of National People's Congress, Beijing, People's Republic of China.

JIANG DANING; Chinese administrator; b. 1929, Shanghai; Man. Shanghai Municipality Cigarette, Wine and Confection Co. 1983–; Sec.-Gen. China Democratic Nat. Construction Asscn. 1984–; mem. Nat. Cttee. of 7th CPPCC 1988.

JIANG ENZHU; Chinese diplomatist; b. 1938, Jiangsu Prov.; entered Ministry of Foreign Affairs as translator 1965; Third, later Second Sec. London during 1970s; fmr. Dir. Dept. of West European Affairs, Ministry of Foreign Affairs, Vice-Minister 1994–95; Amb. to UK 1995–97; Chief Negotiator for People's Repub. of China in Sino-British talks over future of Hong Kong; a Deputy Head Preliminary Working Cttee. of Preparatory Cttee. of Hong Kong Special Admin Region; Dir. Hong Kong br. Xinhua News Agency 1997–; mem. 15th CCP Cen. Cttee. 1997–. *Address:* Xinhua News Agency, 387 Queen's Road East, Wanchai, Hong Kong Special Administrative Region, People's Republic of China.

JIANG FUTANG, Lieut.-Gen.; Chinese army officer; b. Oct. 1941, Rongcheng Co., Shandong Prov.; joined PLA 1959; joined CCP 1960; ed. PLA Political Acad.; Vice-Divisional Political Commissar; Dir. Army Political Dept. 1980; Army Political Commissar 1980; Dir. Political Dept. of PLA Ji'nan Mil. Area Command; Vice-Political Commissar and Dir. Political Dept. of PLA Chengdu Mil. Area Command 1985–95; Commissar PLA Shenyang Mil. Area Command 1995–; rank of Maj. Gen. 1988, Lieut. Gen. 1993–; mem. 15th Cen. Cttee. 1997–. *Address:* PLA Shenyang Military Area Command, Shenyang City, Liaoning Province, People's Republic of China.

JIANG MINKUAN; Chinese party and state official; b. 1930, Wuxian Co., Jiangsu Prov.; ed. Shanghai Polytechnic School; joined CCP 1961; fmr. technician, workshop dir., factory dir. and chief engineer; Deputy Sec. CCP Cttee., Sichuan Prov. 1983–88; Vice-Gov., Sichuan 1983–85, Gov. 1985–88; Vice-Chair. State Science and Tech. Comm. 1988–90; mem. 12th CCP Cen. Cttee. 1985, 13th CCP Cen. Cttee. 1987–92; mem. 14th Cen. Cttee. CCP 1992–97; Dir. State Patent Bureau 1988–89; Deputy Dir. United Front Work Dept., CCP Cen. Cttee. 1990–95, now Exec. Deputy Head United Front Work Dept.; Vice-Pres. China Asscn. of Inventions 1991–; Vice-Chair. All China Fed. of Industry and Commerce, China Chamber of Commerce 1993–; Vice-Chair. Science, Educational Culture, Public Health and Physical Culture Cttee., 9th Nat. Cttee. of CPPCC 1998–. *Address:* c/o National Committee of Chinese People's Political Consultative Conference, 23 Taipingqiao Street, Beijing, People's Republic of China.

JIANG QINGXIANG: Chinese economist; b. 1918; m.; three s. four d.; Prof., Econs. Dept., Law School, Sun Yat-sen Univ. 1944–45; Prof. Chongqing Univ., Researcher Sichuan Prov. Bank 1945–46; Prof. Nat. Coll. of Commerce 1947–49; Dir. and Prof. Great China Univ. 1949–52; Prof. Fu Tan Univ. 1952–57; Prof. and Research Fellow, Inst. of Econs., Shanghai Acad. of Social Sciences 1957–; mem. Nat. Cttee. People's Political Consultative Conf. *Publications:* China's Wartime Economy (co-author), An Investigative Report on the Silk Industry in Sichuan Province, Principles of National Economy Planning, Glimpses of Urban Economy in Bianjing.

JIANG WEN; Chinese actor and film director; b. 1963, Tangshan, Hebei Prov.; ed. Cen. Acad. of Drama; joined China Youth Arts Theatre 1984; now actor at Cen. Acad. of Drama; acted in Furong Town, Red Sorghum, directed The Days of Splendid Sunshine. *Address:* Central Academy of Drama, Beijing, People's Republic of China.

JIANG XI; Chinese government official; b. Jan. 1923, Shanghai; fmr. Vice-Minister of Commerce; Pres. China Gen. Commercial 1994–. *Address:* c/o Ministry of Commerce, 45 Fuxingmennei Street, Beijing 100801, People's Republic of China.

JIANG XIESHENG; Chinese engineer and business executive; b. 1928, Danyang Co., Jiangsu Prov.; ed. Qinghua Univ.; alt. mem. 12th CCP Cen. Cttee. 1982, 13th Cen. Cttee. 1987; Chief Engineer and Man. Machine Building Factory, Xindu, Sichuan 1982; Vice-Minister of Aviation Industry 1984–88, of Aeronautics and Astronautics Industry 1988–93; mem. CPPCC 8th Nat. Cttee. *Address:* c/o Ministry of Aeronautics and Astronautics Industry, Beijing, People's Republic of China.

JIANG XINXIONG; Chinese party and government official; b. 6 July 1931; ed. Nankai Univ., Tianjin; joined CCP 1956; Dir. nuclear fuel plant 1979–82; Vice-Minister of Nuclear Industry 1982–83, Minister 1983; Chair. Bd. of Dirs., China Isotopes Co. 1983–98; Pres. Nat. Nuclear Corpn. 1988–98; Chair. China Atomic Energy Authority 1994–; Deputy Head Leading Group for Nuclear Power Plants; Vice-Chair Finance and Econ. Cttee. of 9th NPC 1998–; alt. mem. 12th Cen. Cttee. CCP 1982, 13th Cen. Cttee. 1985–92, 14th Cen. Cttee. CCP 1992–97. *Address:* c/o Standing Committee of National People's Congress, Beijing, People's Republic of China. *Telephone:* 868381.

JIANG ZEMIN; Chinese party and government official and head of State; b. 17 Aug. 1926, Yangzhou City, Jiangsu Prov.; ed. Jiaotong Univ., Shanghai; joined CCP 1946; worked in Shanghai Yimin No. 1 Foodstuffs Factory, Shanghai Soap Factory, First Ministry of Machine-bldg. Industry; trainee, Stalin Automobile Plant, Moscow, U.S.S.R. 1955–56; Deputy Chief Power Div., Deputy Chief Power-Engineer, Dir., Power Plant, Changchun No. 1 Auto Works 1957–62; Deputy Dir. Shanghai Electric Equipment Research Inst., Dir., and Acting Party Sec. Wuhan Thermo-Tech. Machinery Research Inst., Deputy Dir., Dir. Foreign Affairs Bureau of First Ministry of Machine-bldg. Industry 1962–80; Vice-Chair. and Sec.-Gen. State Comm. on Admin. of Imports and Exports and State Comm. on Admin. of Foreign Investment 1980–82; First Vice-Minister Electronics Industry 1982–83, Minister 1983–85; Mayor of Shanghai 1985–88; Deputy Sec., Sec. Shanghai Municipal Party Cttee. 1985–89; mem. 12th Nat. Congress CCP Cen. Cttee. 1982, Politburo 1st Plenary Session of 13th Cen. Cttee. 1987, Gen. Sec. 4th Plenary Session 1989, Chair. Mil. Cttee. 5th Plenary Session 1989; mem. Standing Cttee. Politburo, Gen. Sec. and Chair. Mil. Cttee. 14th and 15th CCP Cen. Cttees. 1992–; Chair. Cen. Mil. Comm. 1990–; Pres. People's Repub. of China 1993–; Hon. Chair. Red Cross Soc. of China; Hon. Pres. Software Industry Asscn. *Address:* Office of the President, Beijing, People's Republic of China.

JIANG ZHENGHUA; Chinese politician; b. Oct. 1937, Hangzhou City, Zhejiang Prov.; ed. Xi'an Jiaotong Univ., Int. Population Science Coll., Bombay, India 1982; Vice-Dir. State Family Planning Comm. 1991–; joined Chinese Peasants' and Workers' Democratic Party 1992; Vice-Chair. Chinese Peasants' and Workers' Democratic Party 1992, Chair. 1997–; mem. Standing Cttee. 8th CPPCC 1993–98; Vice-Chair. Standing Cttee. of 9th NPC 1998–. *Address:* Standing Committee of National People's Congress, Beijing, People's Republic of China.

JIANG ZHUPING; Chinese engineer and administrator; b. 1937, Yixing Co., Jiangsu Prov.; ed. Faculty of Missile Eng., Harbin Mil. Eng. Inst.; joined CCP 1960; with Design Inst. of Ministry of Nat. Defence 1963–65; Deputy Dir. Design Inst. of Nanchang Aircraft. Mfg. Plant 1978–82, Deputy Sec. plant's Party Cttee. 1982–84; Sec. Party Cttee. of Depts. under Ministry of Aeronautics Industry 1984–85; Vice-Gov. of Jiangxi Prov. 1985–88; Deputy Sec. CCP Jiangxi Prov. Cttee. 1988–95; Gov. of Hubei Prov. 1995–; Deputy Sec. CCP 6th Hubei Provincial Cttee.; mem. 14th CCP Cen. Cttee. 1992–97, 15th CCP Cen. Cttee. 1997–. Deputy Dir. Civil Aviation Gen. Admin. of China 1991–95. *Address:* Hubei Provincial Government, Wuhan, Hubei Province, People's Republic of China.

JIANG ZILONG; Chinese writer; b. 2 June 1941, Cang Xian, Hebei; s. of Jiang Junsan and Wei Huanzhang; m. Zhang Qinglian 1968; one s. one d.; worker Tianjin Heavy Machinery Plant 1958; navy conscript 1960–65; Vice-Chair. 5th Nat. Cttee. Chinese Writers' Asscn. 1996–; Nat. Short Story Prize 1979. *Publications:* A New Station Master 1965, One Day for the Chief of the Bureau of Electromechanics 1976, Manager Qiao Assumes Office 1979, Developer 1980, Diary of a Plant Secretary 1980, All the Colours of the Rainbow 1983, Yan-Zhao Dirge 1985, Serpent Deity 1986. *Address:* Tianjin Writers' Association, Tianjin, People's Republic of China. *Telephone:* 334980 (Office); 398250 (Home).

JIAO LINYI; Chinese party official; b. 1920, Pingshan Co., Hebei Prov.; m. 1935; four c.; joined CCP 1937; Deputy Mayor, Guangzhou 1955; Deputy for Guangdong Prov. to 2nd NPC 1958; Sec. CCP Cttee., Guangzhou Municipality 1958, Second Sec. 1965–73, Acting First Sec. 1966, First Sec. 1973–79, Vice-Chair. Revolutionary Cttee. 1969–73, Chair. 1973–78; alt. mem. CCP Cen. Cttee. 1969; Vice-Chair. Revolutionary Cttee. Guangdong Prov. 1973–79; mem. 10th CCP Cen. Cttee. 1973; Sec. CCP Cttee. Guangdong 1975–79; Deputy for Guangdong to 5th NPC 1978; Sec. CCP Cttee. Hunan

Prov. 1979–85, Sec. of CPC Hinan Prov. Comm. 1986; Vice-Chair. CPC Guangdong Prov. Advisory Comm. 1988–. *Leisure interest:* calligraphy. *Address:* Guangdong Provincial Chinese Communist Party, Canton, Guangdong, People's Republic of China.

JIČINSKÝ, Zdeněk, DR.JUR.; Czech politician, university professor and jurist; b. 26 Feb. 1929, Ostřešany; m. Nada Jičínská 1961; two s.; ed. Charles Univ., Prague; mem. Czech. CP 1951–69; on staff of Inst. of Social Sciences, Cen. Cttee. of Czech. CP 1954–60; Prof., Law Faculty, Charles Univ. 1964–70; mem. Scientific Law Council, Charles Univ. 1962–69; mem. Legal Comm., Cen. Cttee. of Czech. CP 1964; mem. Expert Comm. of Govt. Cttee. for Constitutional Regulation of Repub. 1968; Deputy Chair. Czech. Nat. Council 1968; mem. Chamber of Nations, Fed. Ass. of C.S.S.R. 1969; forced to leave public life and university 1969; lawyer in insurance co. 1969–77; signed Charter 77; Rep. Civic Forum 1989; Deputy Chair. Fed. Ass. 1989–90, First Deputy Chair. 1990–92; Deputy and mem. Presidium Fed. Ass. 1992–; mem. Civic Movt. 1991–92; mem. Czechoslovak Social Democratic Party 1992–; M.P. 1996–, Deputy Chair., Parl. Constitutional Juridical Cttee. 1996–; mem. Standing Del. to Interparl. Union 1996–98; political commentator, Právo newspaper (fmrly. Rudé Právo) 1992–. *Publications:* On the Development of Thinking in Czechoslovakia in the Sixties 1991, Developments in Czechoslovak Parliament since November 1989 1993, The Extinction of Czechoslovakia in 1992 from a Constitutional Viewpoint 1993, Problems of Czech Politics 1994, Charter 77 and Society Governed by the Law 1995, Constitutional and Political Problems of the Czech Republic 1995; numerous works on politics, theory of state and law and institutional law. *Address:* Parliament of the Czech Republic, Sněmovní 4, 118 26 Prague 1 (Office); Pařížská 12, 110 00 Prague 1, Czech Republic (Home). *Telephone:* (2) 5717 1111, 2459 2111 (Office); (2) 231-25-60 (Home).

JIMENEZ, Menardo R., B.SC.(COM); Philippine business executive; b. 6 Dec. 1932, Manila; s. of late Marcelo A. Jimenez and Emiliana Rodriguez-Jimenez; m. Carolina L. Gozon 1962; two s. two d.; ed. Far Eastern Univ., qualified as certified accountant; worked for Abaca Corpn. of Philippines (Abacorp) 1956–70; Pres. and C.E.O. Repub. Broadcasting Inc. (GMA-7); Chair. M.A. Jimenez Enterprises Inc., Majalco Finance & Investment Corpn., Cable Entertainment Corpn.; Pres. Albay-Agro Industrial Devt. Corpn., Justitia Realty & Devt. Corpn., GMA Marketing & Productions Inc.; dir. many cos.; Chair. and Trustee Kapwa Ko Mahal Ko Foundation; Chair. Bd. Philippine Constitution Asscn.; Chair. Prison Fellowship Philippines Inc.; Gov. Philippine Nat. Red Cross; Dir. Philippine Chamber of Commerce and Industry; Dir. or Trustee many other bodies. *Leisure interest:* stamp collection. *Address:* Republic Broadcasting System Inc., 2nd Floor, Saggitarius Bldg., H.V. dela Costa Street, Salcedo Village, Makati City, 1200, Philippines. *Telephone:* 8163883; 8122922. *Fax:* 8133223; 8163042.

JIMÉNEZ-BELTRÁN, Domingo; Spanish environmental executive; b. 2 April 1944, Zaragoza; s. of Mariano Jiménez and María Gloria Beltrán; m. Elin Solem; one c.; ed. High Tech. School of Industrial Engineers and Polytechnic Univ. Madrid; lecturer, Polytechnic Univ. Madrid 1978–86; Exec. Adviser to Minister for Public Works and Planning 1983–85; Deputy Dir.-Gen. for Int. and EU Relations and with Ministry of Public Works and Urban Planning 1985–86; Attaché for Environment and Public Works, Perm. mission to EU, Brussels 1986–87; Head of Div. Health, Physical Safety and Quality, Consumers Policy Service, European Comm. 1987–91; Dir.-Gen. for Environmental Policy, Sec. of State for Environment and Housing, Ministry of Public Works, Transport and Environment 1991–94; Exec. Dir. European Environment Agency, Copenhagen 1994–. *Publications:* author and ed. of various publs. and articles. *Address:* European Environment Agency, Kongens Nytorv 6, 1050 Copenhagen K, Denmark. *Telephone:* (45-33) 36.71.00. *Fax:* (45-33) 36.71.99.

JIN BAOSHENG; Chinese party official; b. Oct. 1927, Jinxiu, Guangxi; m. Wu Jianzhen 1954; one s. one d.; Deputy for Guangxi Prov. to 1st NPC 1954, 2nd NPC 1958; Deputy for Guangxi Autonomous Region to 3rd NPC 1964, 5th NPC 1978–82, 6th NPC 1983–87, 7th NPC 1988–; mem. State Nationalities Affairs Comm. 1979–83; Vice-Chair., Guangxi 1979–83; alt. mem. 12th CCP Cen. Cttee. 1982–87; Deputy Sec. CCP Cttee. Guangxi 1983–; Vice-Dir. Standing Cttee. of People's Congress of Guangxi Zhuang Autonomous Region 1988–. *Publication:* My Beloved Yao Mountains, The Nationality Problems of Guangxi in the Primary Stage of Socialism, The Village Committee's Construction, Handbook of Nationalities Work. *Address:* Guangxi Autonomous Regional Chinese Communist Party, Nanning, Guangxi, People's Republic of China.

JIN JIAN; Chinese party official; b. 1932, Beijing; joined CCP 1932; Deputy Sec. Beijing Municipal CCP Cttee. 1984–86; Vice-Minister of Justice 1988–93; Chair. Nationalities Comm. CPPCC; alt. mem. CCP Cen. Cttee. 1985; mem. CPPCC 8th Nat. Cttee. *Address:* Ministry of Justice, Beijing, People's Republic of China.

JIN LUXIAN, Rt. Rev. Louis; Chinese Catholic bishop; b. 20 June 1916, Shanghai; s. of Luc Jin and Lucy Chang; ed. Xuhui seminary in Shanghai, seminaries in France and Rome; Bishop, Shanghai diocese 1984–; Dir. Sheshan Catholic Seminary in Shangai 1985–; mem. Standing Cttee. CPPCC 8th Nat. Cttee. 1993. *Leisure interest:* collecting stamps. *Address:* Sheshan Catholic Seminary, Shanghai; Bishop's Residence, 158 Pu Xi Road, Shanghai 200030, People's Republic of China. *Telephone:* (021) 64398913. *Fax:* (021) 64398913.

JIN RENQING; Chinese politician; b. July 1944, Suzhou, Jiangsu Prov.; ed. Cen. Inst. of Finance and Banking; joined CCP 1972; Vice-Minister of Finance; Vice-Mayor of Beijing; Vice-Sec. CCP Beijing Municipal Cttee. 1991–98; Dir. State Tax Bureau 1998–; alt. mem. CCP 15th Cen. Cttee. 1997–. *Address:* State Tax Bureau, Beijing, People's Republic of China.

JIN SHANGYI; Chinese artist; b. 1934 Jiaozuo City, Henan Prov.; ed. Cen. Fine Arts Acad., Beijing; known as the forerunner of classicism in Chinese Art; Pres. Cen. Inst. of Fine Arts 1987–. *Works include:* Mao Zedong Leads the Red Army on the Long March 1964, A Maiden 1981, A Tajik Girl 1983. *Address:* Central Institute of Fine Arts, 5 Xiaowei Hutong, East District, Beijing 100730, People's Republic of China.

JIN SHUI; Chinese writer (b. Shi Tiesheng); b. 1951, Beijing; graduated from middle school 1967; paralysed while working in countryside. *Publications:* The Professor of Law and His Wife, Half Hour Lunch Break, Brothers, My Far Away Qingpingwan. *Address:* China Federation of Art and Literature, Beijing, People's Republic of China.

JIN XIANGWEN; Chinese administrator; b. Oct. 1939, Shanghai; ed. Wuhan Surveying and Mapping Inst.; joined CCP 1966; Dir. State Bureau of Surveying and Mapping 1988–. *Address:* State Bureau of Surveying and Mapping, Beijing, People's Republic of China.

JIN YONG; (b. Cha Liangyong); Chinese writer and newspaper publisher; b. 1923, Haining, Zhejiang Prov.; ed. Dongwu Law School; founder of Ming Bao newspaper in Hong Kong. *Publications:* 14 kung-fu novels.

JIN YONGJIAN; Chinese diplomatist and international official; b. 15 Sept. 1934; s. of Jin Zhiying and Bo Canzhang; m. Wang Youping 1955; two s.; ed. Beijing Univ. of Foreign Studies; officer People's Inst. of Foreign Affairs of China 1954–63; Attaché Embassy, Nairobi 1964–67; officer African Dept. Ministry of Foreign Affairs, Beijing 1967–71, Deputy Dir.-Gen., Dir.-Gen. 1984–88, Dir.-Gen. Dept. of Int. Orgs. and Conferences 1988–90; Third Sec., Second Sec. Embassy, Lagos 1971–76; Second Sec., First Sec., Counsellor Perm. Mission to UN, N.Y., Alt. Rep. to UN Security Council, Rep. to Security Council Special Cttee. on Decolonization, UN Council for Namibia 1977–84, Deputy Perm. Rep., Amb. to UN, Deputy Rep. to Security Council 1990–92; Amb., Perm. Rep. to UN, Geneva, also accred. to other int. orgs. in Switzerland 1992–96; Under-Sec.-Gen. for Devt. Support and Man. Services, UN 1996–97, for Gen. Ass. Affairs and Conf. Services June 1997–. *Leisure interests:* walking, Chinese chess, bridge. *Address:* United Nations Headquarters, Room S-2963-A, New York, NY 10017 (Office); 8 Peter Cooper Road, Apartment 8H, New York, NY 10010, U.S.A. (Home). *Telephone:* (212) 963-8362. *Fax:* (212) 963-8196.

JING SHUPING; Chinese industrialist; b. 1918, Shangyu Co., Zheijiang Prov.; ed. St. John's Univ., Shanghai; Deputy Man. Xinzhong Factory, Shanghai 1940–42; Man. Changxing Trade Co. 1943–50; Deputy Sec.-Gen. Fed. of Industry and Commerce 1963; mem. Bd. of Dirs. China Int. Trust and Investment Corpn. (CITIC) 1979, Vice-Pres. 1984–89, Exec. Dir., Chair. Bd. Dirs. 1988–; Chair. Bd. Dirs. China Minsheng Banking Corpn. 1993–; Pres. China Int. Econ. Consultants Inc. 1981–; Vice-Chair. Exec. Cttee. of All-China Fed. of Industry and Commerce 1988–93, Chair. 1993–; mem. Standing Cttee. 6th NPC 1986; Deputy Sec.-Gen. 8th Nat. Cttee. of CPPCC 1993–98; Vice-Chair. 9th Nat. Cttee. of CPPCC 1998–; mem. NPC Preliminary Working Cttee. of Preparatory Cttee. of Hong Kong Special Admin. Region 1993–97; Vice-Chair. Asscn. for Relations Across the Taiwan Straits 1991–; Vice-Pres. Taiwan Studies Soc. 1988–. *Address:* China International Trust and Investment Corporation (CITIC), Beijing, People's Republic of China.

JISCHKE, Martin, C., PH.D.; American administrator; b. 8 July 1941, Chicago, Ill.; m. Patricia Fowler Jischke; one s. one d.; ed. Ill. Tech. Inst. Chicago, Ill., M.I.T. Cambridge; asst. to Transportation Sec. U.S. Transportation Dept. 1975–76; Dir., Prof. School of Aerospace, Mechanical & Nuclear Eng. 1977–81; Dean Eng. Coll. Okla. Univ. 1981–86, Acting Pres. 1985; Chancellor Mo.-Rolla Univ. 1986–91; Pres. Iowa State Univ. 1991–, Asscn. of Big Twelve Univs. 1994–. *Publications:* articles in specialist journals. *Leisure interests:* golf, reading, travel. *Address:* Office of the President, Iowa State University, Ames, IA 50011 (Office); The Knoll, Iowa State University, Ames, IA 50011, U.S.A. (Home).

JOBERT, Michel; French politician and lawyer; b. 11 Sept. 1921, Meknès, Morocco; s. of Jules and Yvonne (Babule) Jobert; m. Muriel Frances Green; one s.; ed. Meknès Lycée, Ecole Libre des Sciences Politiques, Paris, and Nat. School of Admin., Paris; Auditor Court of Accounts 1949, Counsel 1953, Conseiller-Maître 1971, Conseiller honoraire Cour des Comptes 1986; attached to Departmental Staff of Sec. of State for Finance 1952; Tech. Adviser, Ministry of Labour and Social Security 1952–54; attached to the Office of Pierre Mendès-France 1954–55 and Feb.-May 1956; Dir. of Cabinet to the High Commr. for French W. Africa 1956–58, to M. Lecourt, Minister of State 1959–61; Deputy Dir. of Cabinet to Prime Minister Georges Pompidou 1963–66, Prin. Private Sec. 1966–68; Sec.-Gen. of the Presidency 1969–73; Minister of Foreign Affairs 1973–74; Minister of State for Foreign Trade 1981–83; founder and leader Mouvement des Démocrates 1974–; fmr. mem. Bd. of SOFIRAD (Radio Monte-Carlo), Havas Agency and French Radio and Television Org.; Chair. Bd. of Dirs. Nat. Forestry Office 1966–73; Conseiller maître, Cour des Comptes 1971–86, Magistrate, Cour des Comptes; practised at Paris Bar 1990–; Arbitrator ICC French Nat. Cttee. 1991; Publr. of monthly newsletter La Lettre de Michel Jobert 1974–84; Prix de la Langue de France 1989; Commdr. Légion d'honneur, Croix de guerre 1939–45. *Publications:* Mémoires d'avenir 1974, Les Idées simples de la vie 1975, L'autre regard 1976, Lettre ouverte aux femmes politiques 1976, Parler aux français 1977, La vie d'Hella Schuster 1977, Maroc, extrême Maghreb du soleil couchant 1978, Chroniques du Midi libre 1982, La rivière aux grenades 1982, Vive l'Europe libre 1984, Par trente-six chemins 1984, Maghreb, à l'ombre de ses mains 1985, Les Américains 1987, Journal immédiat 1987, Vandales! 1990, Journal du Golfe: Août 1990–Août 1991 1991, Ni dieu ni diable 1993, Chroniques de l'Espérance 1988–1992 1993, Horizons méditerranéens 1993, l'Aveuglement du monde occidental: Chroniques de politique internationale 1993–1996, 1997. *Address:* 108 Quai Louis Blériot, 75016 Paris (Office); 21 quai Alphonse-Le Gallo, 92100 Boulogne-Billancourt, France (Home).

JOBS, Steven Paul; American business executive; b. 1955; adopted s. of Paul J. and Clara J. Jobs; m. Laurene Powell 1991; ed. Reed Coll.; with Hewlett-Packard, Palo Alto, Calif.; designer, video games, Atari Inc. 1974; Chair. of Bd. Apple Computer Inc., Cupertino, Calif. 1975–85, Consultant 1997–; Interim C.E.O. 1997–; Pres. NeXT Inc., Calif. 1985–96; C.E.O. Pixar Animation Studios; co-designer (with Stephan Wozniak), Apple I Computer 1976. *Address:* Apple Computer Inc., 1 Infinite Loop, Cupertino, CA 95014, U.S.A.

JOCELYN, Henry David, PH.D., F.B.A.; Australian classical scholar; b. 22 Aug. 1933, Bega, N.S.W.; s. of John Daniel Jocelyn and Phyllis Irene Burton; m. Margaret Jill Morton 1958; two s.; ed. Canterbury Boys' High School, Univ. of Sydney and St. John's Coll., Cambridge, U.K.; mem. teaching staff, Univ. of Sydney 1960–73, Prof. of Latin 1970–73; Hulme Prof. of Latin, Univ. of Manchester 1973–96; Visiting Prof. Yale Univ., U.S.A. 1967, Australian Nat. Univ. 1979, Univ. of Cape Town 1985, Univ. of Fribourg, Switzerland 1989, Univ. of Catania, Italy 1994, Cornell Univ., U.S.A. 1995; Hon. Litt.D. (Sydney). *Publications:* The Tragedies of Ennius 1967, Regnier de Graaf on the Human Reproductive Organs 1972, Philology and Education 1988, (ed.) Studies in Latin Literature and its Tradition 1989, (ed.) FRD. Goodyear, Papers on Latin Literature 1992, (ed.) Tria Lustra 1993, (ed.) Aspects of Nineteenth-Century British Classical Scholarship 1996; contribs. on Greek and Latin philology to periodicals 1964–. *Address:* The Bent House, 56–60 Lyne Road, Kidlington, Oxon., OX5 1AD, England. *Telephone:* (01865) 842754.

JOEL, Billy (William Martin Joel); American pop singer; b. 9 May 1949, Bronx, New York; s. of Howard Joel and Rosalind Nyman; m. Christie Brinkley 1985 (divorced 1994); one. d.; popular recording artist 1972–; first tour of U.S.S.R. by American popular music artist 1987; Summer tour with Elton John (q.v.) 1994, Spring tour with Elton John 1995, Asian and European Tour with Elton John 1998; songs include Just the Way You Are 1978, Honesty 1979, We Didn't Start the Fire 1989; albums include Piano Man, Streetlife Serenade, Turnstiles, The Stranger, 52nd Street, Glass Houses 1980, Songs in the Attic, The Nylon Curtain 1982, An Innocent Man, Greatest Hits (Vols. I & II) 1985, The Bridge 1986, Live From the Soviet Union (concert) 1987, Storm Front 1989, River of Dreams 1993; recipient of numerous Grammy Awards; Dr. h.c. (Berkee Coll. of Music) 1993. *Address:* Maritime Music Inc., 2nd Floor, 280 Elm Street, Southampton, NY 11968, U.S.A.

JOFFE, Roland I. V.; British film director; b. 17 Nov. 1945, London; m. Jane Lapotaire (divorced); one s.; ed. Carmel Coll., Berks. and Univ. of Manchester. *Films:* The Killing Fields 1984, The Mission 1986, Fat Man and Little Boy 1989, City of Joy 1991, Super Mario Bros (producer only), The Scarlet Letter. *Television Films:* Spongers 1978, No Mama No 1980, United Kingdom 1981, 'Tis Pity She's a Whore 1982, Shadow Makers 1990, The Stars Look Down (series); Prix Italia 1978, Prix de la Presse, Prague 1978, Premio San Fidele 1985. *Address:* Lightmotive, Suite 1020, 2934 1/2 North Beverly Glen Circle, # 270, Los Angeles, CA 90077, U.S.A.

JOHANES, Jaromir; Czech diplomatist and politician (retd.); b. 21 Aug. 1933, Dobra nad Sazavou, E. Bohemia; ed. Moscow Inst. of Int. Relations; joined Ministry of Foreign Affairs 1958; served London; later Consul-Gen. Australia; Amb. to U.S.A. and Canada; Deputy Foreign Minister 1982, First Deputy Foreign Minister 1987; Minister of Foreign Affairs 1988–89; Counsellor-Envoy to Turkey 1990–93, Amb. to Turkey 1993–95.

JÓHANNSON, Kjartan, C.E., PH.D.; Icelandic politician; b. 19 Dec. 1939, Reykjavík; s. of Jóhann and Astrid Dahl Thorsteinsson; m. Irma Karlsdóttir 1964; one d.; ed. Reykjavík Coll., Tech. Univ. of Stockholm, Sweden, Univ. of Stockholm, Illinois Inst. of Tech., Chicago; Consulting Eng. in Reykjavík 1966–78; Teacher in Faculty of Eng. and Science, later Prof. in Faculty for Econs. and Business Admin., Univ. of Iceland 1966–78, 1980–89; Chair. Org. for Support of the Elderly, Hafnarfjördür; mem. Bd. of Dir. Icelandic Aluminium Co. Ltd. 1970–75; Chair. Fisheries Bd. of Municipal Trawler Co., Hafnarfjördür 1970–74; mem. Municipal Council, Hafnarfjördür 1974–78; mem. Party Council and Exec. Council, Social Democratic Party 1972–89, Vice-Chair. of Social Democratic Party 1974–80, Chair. 1980–84; mem. Althing (Parl.) 1978–89, Speaker of the Lower House 1988–89; Minister of Fisheries 1978–80, also Minister of Commerce 1979–80; Amb. Perm. Rep. to UN and other int. orgs. Geneva 1989–94; Sec.-Gen. EFTA 1994–. *Address:* European Free Trade Association, 9–11 rue de Varembé, 1211 Geneva 20, Switzerland. *Telephone:* 74 91 335.

JOHANSEN, Hans Christian, DR.OEC.; Danish professor of economic history; b. 27 June 1935, Aarhus; s. of Vilhelm Johansen and Clara Andersen; m. Kirstine Madsen 1967; one s. one d.; ed. Univ. of Aarhus; Danish Foreign Service 1963–64; Sr. Lecturer, Univ. of Aarhus 1964–70; Prof. of Econ. History, Univ. of Odense 1970–. *Publications:* books and articles on Danish and int. econ. and social history in the 18th, 19th and 20th centuries. *Address:* Anne Maries Alle 4A, 5250 Odense SV, Denmark. *Telephone:* 66-172105.

JOHANSEN, John MacLane, M.ARCH.; American architect; b. 29 June 1916, New York; s. of John C. and Jean MacLane Johansen; m. 1st Mary Lee Longcope 1945; m. 2nd Beate Forberg 1981; one s. one d.; ed. Harvard Coll. and Harvard Grad. School of Design; self-employed architect 1947, est. office in New York 1950, est. firm of Johansen-Bhavnani 1973, pvt. practice, New York 1989–; Pres. Architectural League 1968–70; Prof. Pratt Inst.; Prof. of Architecture at Yale Univ. at various times and has taught for short periods at M.I.T., Columbia and Harvard Univs., and Univ. of Pa.; Architect in Residence, American Acad. in Rome 1975; mem. Nat. Inst. of Arts and Letters; Brunner Award 1968; Gold Medal, New York Chapter, American Inst. of Architects 1976; Hon. D.F.A. (Maryland Inst. and Clark Univ.). *Publication:* An Architecture for the Electronic Age, The Three Imperatives of Architecture, Observations and Deductions. *Leisure interests:* painting, writing, music, building construction, sport, travel. *Address:* 821 Broadway, New York, NY 10003, U.S.A.

JOHANSEN, Peter, PH.D.; Danish professor of computer science; b. 29 Jan. 1938, Copenhagen; s. of Paul Johansen and Grethe (née Smith) Johansen; m. Jytte Jepsen 1963; one s. two d.; ed. Univ. of Copenhagen; Asst. Prof. Tech. Univ. 1964–67; mem. Research Staff M.I.T. 1967–69; Asst. Prof. of Computer Science, Univ. of Copenhagen 1969–74, Prof. 1974–, Dean of Faculty 1988–90; Visiting Prof. Univ. of Manoa, Hawaii 1977–78; mem. Danish Natural Science Research Council 1981–84, Royal Danish Acad. of Sciences 1984–. *Publications:* An Algebraic Normal Form for Regular Events 1972, The Generating Function of the Number of Subpatterns 1979, Representing Signals by their Toppoints in Scale Space 1986, Inductive Inference of Ultimately Periodic Sequences 1988, On the Classification of Toppoints in Scale Space 1994, On-line string matching with feedback 1995, Adaptive Pattern Recognition 1997. *Address:* Ornebakken 72, 2840 Holte, Denmark. *Telephone:* 45 805302.

JOHANSON, Donald Carl, PH.D.; American physical anthropologist; b. 28 June 1943, Chicago; s. of Carl Torsten and Sally Eugenia (Johnson) Johanson; m. 1st Susan Whelan 1981 (divorced); one step-s. one step-d.; m. 2nd Lenora Carey 1988; one s.; ed. Univ. of Illinois, Univ. of Chicago; mem. Dept. of Physical Anthropology, Cleveland Museum of Natural History 1972–81, Curator 1974–81; Adjunct Prof. Case Western Reserve Univ. 1982; Prof. of Anthropology, Stanford Univ. 1983–89, Ariz. State Univ. 1997; host, Nature series, Public Broadcasting Service TV 1982, host-narrator three-part Nova series In Search of Human Origins 1994; Pres. Inst. of Human Origins, Berkeley 1981–97; Dir. Inst. of Human Origins, Tempe, Ariz. 1997–; Fellow, A.A.A.S., Royal Geographical Soc., California Acad. of Sciences; Hon. D.Sc. (John Carroll) 1979, (The College of Wooster) 1985; Fregene Prize 1987, American Book Award 1982, Distinguished Service Award, American Humanist Assсn. 1983, Golden Plate American Acad. of Achievement 1976, Professional Achievement Award 1980, Outstanding Achievement Award 1979, Golden Mercury Int. Award 1982, Alumni Achievement Award, Univ. of Ill. 1995. *Films produced:* The First Family 1981, Lucy in Disguise 1982. *Publications:* The Beginnings of Humankind (with M. A. Edey) 1981 (American Book Award), Dating of South Africa Hominids Sites 1982, Blueprints: Solving the Mystery of Evolution (with M. A. Edey) 1989, Lucy's Child: The Discovery of a Human Ancestor (with James Shreeve) 1989, Journey from the Dawn (with Kevin O'Farrell) 1990, Ancestors: In Search of Human Origins (with L. E. Johanson and Blake Edgar) 1994, From Lucy to Language (with Blake Edgar) 1997; many scientific articles, papers, and reviews. *Leisure interests:* photography, tennis, fly-fishing, classcal music (including opera). *Address:* Institute of Human Origins, Arizona State University, P.O. Box 874101, Tempe, AZ 85287, U.S.A.

JOHANSSON, (Erik) Lennart Valdemar; Swedish industrialist; b. 3 Oct. 1921, Gothenburg; s. of Waldemar and Alma Johansson (née Nordh); m. Inger Hedberg 1944; two s. one d.; ed. Tech. Coll.; Production Engineer AB SKF 1943, Man. of Mfg. 1961, Gen. Man. 1966, Deputy Man. Dir. 1969, Pres. and Group C.E.O. 1971–95, Chair. 1985–92, Hon. Chair. 1992–; mem. Royal Swedish Acad. of Eng. Sciences 1971; D. Tech. h.c. (Chalmers Univ. of Tech., Gothenburg) 1979; Hon. D.Tech. (Sarajevo) 1983; King of Sweden's Medal; Commdr. Merito della Repub. Italiana, Commdr. Royal Order of Vasa, Yugoslav Star Medal with Golden Garland, Das grosse Bundesverdienstkreutz, Kt. Commdr.'s Cross (1st Class), Finnish Order of the Lion, John Ericsson Medal 1986. *Leisure interests:* sailing, swimming. *Address:* Götabergsgatan 22, 411 34 Gothenburg, Sweden (Home).

JOHANSSON, Leif; Swedish business executive; joined Electrolux 1978, Chief Exec. 1994.

JOHANSSON, Olof; Swedish politician; b. 1937, Ljungby, Kalmar; m. Inger Johansson; two s.; non-commissioned reserve officer 1959; farm-worker, journalist, office worker, teacher 1953–65; mem. Stockholm City Council 1966–70; Sec. Centre Party's Parl. Group 1966–69, Chair. Youth League 1969–71; M.P. 1971–; mem. Nat. Bd. Centre Party 1971–, Asst. Deputy

Leader 1979–86, Deputy Leader 1986–87, Leader 1987; Minister for Energy and Tech. Devt. 1976–78, for Civil Service Affairs and Personnel 1979–82, for the Environment 1991–94; mem. Council of Europe 1986–, Nordic Council 1986–, Advisory Council on Foreign Affairs 1987–. *Address:* c/o Centre Party, Bergsgt. 7B, P.O. Box 22107, 104 22 Stockholm, Sweden.

JOHN, David Glyndwr, M.A., M.B.A.; British business executive; b. 20 July 1938, Pontypridd; s. of William G. John and Marjorie John; m. Gillian Edwards 1964; one s. one d.; ed. Christ's Coll. Cambridge, Columbia Univ. New York and Harvard Univ.; trainee man. British Steel; later worked for RTZ and Redland; joined Gray Mackenzie (Inchcape Group) 1981, Chief Exec. 1986; Chief Exec. Inchcape Berhad 1987, Chair. 1990; mem. Bd. Inchcape PLC 1988–95; Exec. Chair. Inchcape Toyota Motors 1995, Premier Oil PLC 1998–; Dir. non-exec. BOC Group PLC 1993–, Chair. Jan. 1996–; Dir. British Biotech PhC 1996–, The St. Paul Cos. Inc., Minn., U.S.A. 1996–. *Leisure interests:* sailing, skiing. *Address:* c/o Coutts and Co., 2 Lower Sloane Street, London, SW1W 8BJ, England.

JOHN, Sir Elton Hercules, Kt., C.B.E.; British musician; b. (as Reginald Kenneth Dwight) 25 March 1947, Pinner, Middx.; s. of Stanley Dwight and Sheila Farebrother; m. Renata Blauel 1984 (divorced 1988); ed. Pinner Co. Grammar School; began piano lessons 1951; played piano in Northwood Hills Hotel bar 1964; joined local group Bluesology 1965; began writing songs with Bernie Taupin 1967; recording contract with DJM Records 1967; first single I've Been Loving You 1968, first LP Empty Sky 1969; concerts in Los Angeles 1970; engaged Man. John Reid 1971–; formed Rocket Record Co. with Bernie Taupin 1973; frequent tours in U.K., U.S.A., Japan, Australia 1971–76; Vice-Pres. Nat Youth Theatre of G.B. 1975–; first int. star to perform concerts in U.S.S.R. 1979; first album released by Rocket Record Co. 1976; produced records with Clive Franks for Kiki Dee, Blue, Davey Johnstone's China 1976–77; Chair. Watford Football Club 1976–90, 1997–, Life Pres. 1990–; visited China with Watford Football Club 1983; f. Elton John AIDS Foundation 1993; Hon. mem. Royal Acad. of Music 1997; Ivor Novello Awards 1976, 1977, and silver and gold discs in various countries for singles and albums; U.S. Grammy Awards 1991, 1998; Acad. Award for Best Original Song 1995. *Records:* singles: Lady Samantha, It's Me That You Need, Border Song, Rock and Roll Madonna, Your Song, Friends, Rocket Man, Honky Cat, Crocodile Rock, Daniel, Saturday Night's Alright (for fighting), Goodbye Yellow Brick Road, Step into Christmas, Candle in the Wind, Don't Let the Sun Go Down on Me, The Bitch is Back, Lucy in the Sky with Diamonds, Philadelphia Freedom, Someone Saved My Life Tonight, Island Girl, Grow Some Funk of Your Own, Pinball Wizard, Don't Go Breaking My Heart (with Kiki Dee), Sorry Seems to be the Hardest Word, Crazy Water, Bite Your Lip, Ego, Part Time Love, Song for Guy, Are You Ready for Love, Victim of Love, Johnny B. Goode, Little Jeanie, Sartorial Eloquence, Nobody Wins, Just like Belgium, Blue Eyes, I'm Still Standing, Empty Garden, Princess, All Quiet on the Western Front, I Guess that's Why They Call It the Blues, Sad Songs (Say So Much), Passengers, Who Wears these Shoes, Breaking Hearts, Act of War, Nikita, Wrap Her Up, Cry to Heaven, Heartache All Over the World, Slow Rivers, Your Song, Candle in the Wind, I Don't Wanna Go On With You Like That, Healing Hands, Sacrifice; albums: Empty Sky, Elton John, Tumbleweed Connection, Friends (film soundtrack), 17-11-70, Madman Across the Water, Honky Chateau, Don't Shoot Me I'm Only the Piano Player, Goodbye Yellow Brick Road (double), Caribou, Elton John's Greatest Hits (2 vols.), Captain Fantastic and the Brown Dirt Cowboy, Rock of the Westies, Here and There, Blue Moves (double), A Single Man, Victim of Love, Lady Samantha, 21 at 33, The Fox, Jump Up, Love Songs, Too Low for Zero, Breaking Hearts, Ice on Fire 1985, Leather Jackets 1986, Live in Australia 1987, Reg Strikes Back 1988, Sleeping with the Past 1989, The Very Best of Elton John 1990, The One 1992, Made in England 1995. *Films:* Goodbye to Norma Jean 1973, To Russia with Elton 1980, The Rainbow 1989; played Pinball Wizard in Tommy 1973. *Leisure interests:* football, collecting records, tennis, all sports. *Address:* Elton John Management, 7 King Street Cloisters, Clifton Walk, London, W6 0GY, England.

JOHN, Patrick; Dominican politician; b. 7 Jan. 1937; fmr. mem. Parl.; Leader Dominica Labour Party 1974–83, Deputy Leader 1983–84; Minister of Communications and Works 1970–73, Deputy Premier and Minister of Finance 1974, Premier of Dominica 1974–78, Prime Minister 1978–79, Minister for Housing, Security and Devt. 1978–79; Gen. Sec. Labour Party of Dominica 1985; M.P. July–Nov. 1985; arrested 1981, tried and acquitted May 1982, re-tried Oct. 1985; sentenced to 12 years' imprisonment for conspiracy to overthrow govt.

JOHN PAUL II, His Holiness Pope (Karol Wojtyła); Polish ecclesiastic; b. 18 May 1920, Wadowice; s. of Karol Wojtyła and Emilia Kaczorowska; ed. Jagiellonian Univ., Cracow, Angelicum, St Thomas Pontifical Univ., Rome; ordained Priest 1946; Prof. of Moral Theology at Jagiellonian Univ. and Metropolitan Ecclesiastic Seminary, Cracow, Catholic Univ. of Lublin (KUL); Chair. Dept. of Ethics, Catholic Univ. of Lublin; Titular Bishop of Ombi and Vicar-Gen. of Archdiocese of Cracow 1958–64, Archbishop of Cracow 1964–78; cr. Cardinal by Pope Paul VI 1967; elected Pope Oct. 1978; Hon. Freeman of Dublin 1979; Hon. Citizen of Warsaw 1996; Dr. h.c. (Mainz) 1977, (Coimbra) 1982, (Salamanca) 1982, (Cracow) 1983, (Lublin) 1983. *Publications:* (as Karol Wojtyła) Love and Responsibility 1960, In Front of the Jeweller's Shop (play) 1960, The Acting Person 1969, Sources of Renewal–The Implementation of the Second Vatican Council 1972, Sign of Contradiction 1976, Brother of Our Lord (play) 1979, Collected Poems 1982, The Collected Plays and Writings on Theater (transl. B. Taborski) 1987; (as John Paul II) The Redeemer of Man 1979, On the Mercy of God 1980, On Human Work 1981, The Role of the Christian Family in the Modern World 1981, Be Not Afraid 1982, On Reconciliation and Penance 1984, Christian Meaning of Human Suffering 1984, The Apostles of the Slavs 1985, The Lord, the Giver of Life 1986, Virgin Mary 1987, The Anxiety for Social Causes 1987, Missionary Mandate 1990, Centesimus Annus 1991, Formation of Priests 1992, Catholic Catechism 1992, The Shine of Truth 1993, Letter to Families 1994, Priestly Ordination 1994, The Jubilee of 2000 1994, Crossing the Threshold of Hope 1994, Letter to Children 1994, The Gospel of Life 1995, Eastern Church 1995, They Should Be One 1995, Letter to Women 1995, Church in Africa 1995, The Union of Brest 1995, The Gift and Mystery 1996, On Consecrated Life 1996, New Hope for Lebanon 1997, Faith and Mind. *Leisure interests:* skiing, rowing, sport. *Address:* Palazzo Apostolico Vaticano, 00120 Città del Vaticano, Rome, Italy.

JOHNS, Anthony Hearle, PH.D.; Australian professor of Islamic studies; b. 28 Aug. 1928, Wimbledon, U.K.; s. of late Frank Charles Johns and of Ivy Doris Kathleen Johns (née Hearle); m. Yohanni Bey 1956; four s. one d.; ed. St. Boniface's Coll., Plymouth, U.K. and School of Oriental and African Studies, Univ. of London; lecturer Ford Foundation-sponsored Training Project, Indonesia 1954–58; Sr. Lecturer in Indonesian Languages and Literatures, Australian Nat. Univ. 1958–63, Prof. 1963–, Chair. and Head. Dept. 1963–83, Dean Faculty of Asian Studies 1963–64, 1965–67, 1975–79, 1988–91, Head Southeast Asia Centre 1983–88; Visiting Prof., Univ. of Toronto (Dept. of Religious Studies and Dept. of Middle East and Islamic Studies) 1989; Special Foreign Visiting Prof. in Islamic Studies Chiba Univ., Tokyo 1991; Visiting Scholar, Oxford Centre for Hebrew and Jewish Studies, U.K. 1993–94; Visiting Fellow, Research School Pacific and Asian Studies, Australian Nat. Univ., Canberra 1994–96, 1997– (2000); Fellow Inst. for Advanced Studies, Hebrew Univ. of Jerusalem 1984–85; Fellow Australian Acad. of Humanities 1972; Univ. of London Sr. Studentship 1953–54, Rhuvon Guest Prize in Islamic Studies, S.O.A.S. 1953–54. *Publications:* The Gift Addressed to the Spirit of the Prophet 1965, A Road with No End (trans. and Ed.) 1968, Cultural Options and the Role of Tradition 1981, Islam in Asia II Southeast and East Asia (Ed. and contrib. with R. Israeli) 1984. *Leisure interests:* music, literature. *Address:* 70 Duffy Street, Ainslie, Canberra, A.C.T. 2602, Australia. *Telephone:* (02) 62496574.

JOHNS, David John, C.B.E., D.SC., F.ENG., F.R.AE.S.; British university vice-chancellor; b. 29 April 1931, Bristol; ed. St. Brendan's Coll. Bristol, Univ. of Bristol; lecturer in Aircraft Design, Coll. of Aeronautics, Cranfield 1958–64; Reader in Aeronautics, Loughborough Univ. of Tech. 1964–68, Prof. 1968–72, Prof. and Head of Dept. of Transport Tech. 1972–82, Dean, School of Eng. 1975–78, Sr. Pro-Vice-Chancellor 1982–83; Foundation Dir., City Polytechnic of Hong Kong 1983–89; Vice-Chancellor and Prin. Univ. of Bradford 1989–98; Fellow Hong Kong Inst. of Engineers, Aeronautical Soc. of India. *Publications:* Thermal Stress Analyses 1965; book chapters and more than 120 articles in professional journals. *Leisure interests:* theatre, music, bridge.

JOHNS, Jasper; American painter; b. 15 May 1930, Augusta; s. of Jasper Johns Sr. and Jean Riley; ed. Univ. of South Carolina; works in following collections: Tate Gallery, London, Museum of Modern Art, New York, Albright-Knox Art Gallery, Buffalo, N.Y., Museum Ludwig, Cologne, Hirshhorn Museum and Sculpture Garden, Washington, D.C., Whitney Museum of American Art, Stedelijk Museum, Amsterdam, Moderna Museet, Stockholm, Dallas Museum of Fine Arts, Art Inst. of Chicago, Baltimore Museum of Art, Kunstmuseum Basel, Cleveland Museum of Art, Nat. Gallery of Art, Washington, D.C., San Francisco Museum of Modern Art, Va. Museum of Fine Arts, Walker Art Center, Minneapolis; one-man exhibitions: Leo Castelli Gallery, New York 1958, 1960, 1961, 1963, 1966, 1968, 1976, 1981, 1984, 1987, 1991, Nat. Acad. of Design, New York 1996, and numerous other galleries in Canada, France, Germany, Italy, Japan, Spain, Switzerland, U.K. and U.S.A., Nat. Acad. of Design, N.Y. 1996; mem. American Acad. of Arts and Letters; Hon. R.A. (London); Prize, Pittsburgh Int. 1958, Wolf Foundation Prize 1986, Gold Medal (American Acad. and Inst. of Arts and Letters) 1986, Int. Prize, Venice Biennale 1988, Nat. Medal of Arts 1990, Officier, Ordre des Arts et des Lettres 1990, Praemium Imperiale Award (Japan) 1993. *Address:* c/o Leo Castelli Gallery, 420 W. Broadway, New York, NY 10012, U.S.A.

JOHNS, Air Chief Marshal Sir Richard Edward, G.C.B., C.B.E., L.V.O., F.R.AE.S.; British air force officer; b. 28 July 1939, Horsham, Sussex; s. of late Lt. Col. Herbert Edward Johns and Marjory Harley Johns (née Everett); m. Elizabeth Naomi Anne Manning 1965; one s. two d.; ed. Portsmouth Grammar School, R.A.F. Coll. Cranwell; commissioned 1959; Night Fighter/Night Reconnaissance Squadrons, U.K., Cyprus, Aden 1960–67; Flying Instructor 1968–71, Flying Instructor to H.R.H. the Prince of Wales 1970–71; Officer Commanding 3 (Fighter) Squadron (Harrier) 1975–77; Dir. Air Staff Briefing 1979–81; Station Commdr. and Harrier Force Commdr., R.A.F. Gütersloh 1982–84; ADC to H.M. The Queen 1983–84; at Royal Coll. of Defence Studies 1985; Sr. Air Staff Officer R.A.F. HQ, Germany 1985–88; Sr. Air Staff Officer HQ Strike Command 1989–91; Air Officer Commanding No. 1 Group 1991–93; Chief of Staff, Deputy C.-in-C. Strike Command and U.K. Air Forces 1993–94; Air Officer Commanding in Chief Strike Command 1994; C.-in-C. Allied Forces N.W. Europe 1994–97; Chief of Air Staff and Air ADC to H.M. The Queen 1997–. *Leisure interests:* military history, rugby, cricket, equitation. *Address:* Room 6249, Ministry of Defence, Main Building, Whitehall, London, SW1A 2HB, England. *Telephone:* 0171-218 7220. *Fax:* 0171-218 3834.

JOHNSEN, Sigbjørn; Norwegian politician; b. 1 Oct. 1950, Lillehammer; m. Helle Laier Johnsen; ed. Norwegian School of Man.; Deputy Rep. for Hedmark Co., Storting (Parl.) 1973–; Vice-Pres. Norwegian Labour League of Youth (AUF) 1975–77; Deputy Chair. Equal Status Council 1976–83; Minister of Finance 1990–96; Del. to Council of Europe's Parl. Ass. 1985–; mem. Storting (Parl.) Standing Cttee. on Justice 1976–77, on Local Govt. and the Environment 1977–80, on Finance 1981– (Deputy Chair. 1986–), Nat. Council for Open-Air Recreation 1984–. *Address:* Ministry of Finance, Akersgt. 42, P.O. Box 8008 Dep., 0030 Oslo, Norway. *Telephone:* 22-34-90-90. *Fax:* 22-34-95-05.

JOHNSON, Barry Edward, PH.D., F.R.S.; British mathematician; b. 1 Aug. 1937, Woolwich, London; s. of Edward and Evelyn May (née Bailey) Johnson; m. 1st Jennifer Pat Johnson 1961 (divorced 1979); two s. one d.; m. 2nd Margaret Blyth Johnson 1991; ed. Epsom County Grammar School, Hobart State High School, Univs. of Tasmania and Cambridge; Instructor Univ. of Calif. 1961–62, Visiting Lecturer Yale Univ. 1962–63, Visiting Prof. 1970–71, Lecturer Exeter Univ. 1963–65, Univ. of Newcastle upon Tyne 1965–68, Reader 1968–69, Head of Dept. of Pure Mathematics 1976–84, Prof. of Pure Mathematics 1969–, Head of School of Mathematics 1983–86, Dean Faculty of Science 1986–89; Visiting Prof. Univ. of Calif., Los Angeles 1990–91; mem. London Mathematical Soc. Council 1974–78, Pres. 1981–82; Auditor Higher Educ. Quality Council (Div. of Quality Audit) 1993–. *Publications:* Cohomology of Banach algebras 1972 and numerous scientific papers. *Leisure interests:* reading, travel. *Address:* 63 Montagu Court, Gosforth, Newcastle upon Tyne, NE3 4JL, England. *Telephone:* Tyneside (0191) 213 1013.

JOHNSON, Ben, M.A.; British artist; b. 24 August 1946, Llandudno, Wales; s. of Harold Johnson and Ivy Lloyd Jones; m. Sheila Kellehar 1976; two s.; ed. Royal Coll. of Art; has exhibited internationally since 1969; has undertaken direct commissions from Centre Pompidou, Paris and Museum of London; work represented in public and corp. collections at Boymans van Beuningen Museum, Rotterdam, British Council, London, Tate Gallery, London, Contemporary Arts Soc., London, R.I.B.A., London, City Art Gallery, Glasgow, Whitworth Gallery, Manchester, Centre Pompidou, Paris, Victoria & Albert Museum, London, Deutsche Bank, British Petroleum, Guildhall Art Gallery, Corpn. of London, Special Admin. Regional Govt. of Hong Kong, New Convention & Exhbn. Centre, Hong Kong, Regional Services Council Museum, Hong Kong. *Leisure interests:* architecture, cities. *Address:* 4 St. Peter's Wharf, Hammersmith Terrace, London, W6 9UD, England. *Telephone:* 0181-563 8768. *Fax:* 0181-563 8768.

JOHNSON, Ben; Canadian (b. Jamaican) athlete; b. 30 Dec. 1961, Falmouth, Jamaica; emigrated with family to Canada 1976; began athletics career coached by Charlie Francis 1977; finished last, Commonwealth Games 100 metres trial, Canada 1978; won Canadian jr. title, became Canadian citizen 1979; selected for Olympic Games, Moscow, but Canada boycotted Games 1980; came sixth in 100 metres, Pan-American Jr. Games 1980, second, Commonwealth Games 1982; semi-finalist, World Championships 1983; bronze medallist, Olympic Games, L.A., U.S.A.; won World Cup 1985, Commonwealth title 1986, indoor 60 metres in record time 1987; gold medallist, World Championships, with time of 9.83 seconds, Rome 1987; came first in final, Olympic Games, in world record 9.79 seconds, Seoul 1988; medal withdrawn after allegations concerning drug-taking; stripped of World Record Sept. 1989, life ban from Canadian nat. team lifted Aug. 1990; failed second drugs test and banned from athletics for life March 1993.

JOHNSON, Betsey Lee, B.A.; American fashion designer; b. 10 Aug. 1942, Hartford, Conn.; d. of John Herman Johnson and Lena Virginia Johnson; m. 1st John Cale 1966; one d.; m. 2nd Jeffrey Olivier 1981; ed. Pratt Inst., New York, Syracuse Univ.; editorial asst. Mademoiselle magazine 1964–65; partner and co-owner Betsey, Bunky & Nini, New York 1969–; shops in New York, L.A., San Francisco, Coconut Grove, Fla., Venice, Calif., Boston, Chicago, Seattle; Prin. Designer for Paraphernalia 1965–69; designer Alvin Duskin Co., San Francisco 1970; Head Designer Alley Cat by Betsey Johnson (div. of LeDamor, Inc.) 1970–74; freelance designer for Jr. Womens' div., Butterick Pattern Co. 1971, Betsey Johnson's Kids Children's Wear (div. of Shutterbug Inc.) 1974–77, Betsey Johnson for Jeanette Maternities, Inc. 1974–75; designer for Gant Shirtmakers Inc. (women's clothing) 1974–75, Tric-Trac by Betsey Johnson (women's knitwear) 1974–76, Butterick's Home Sewing Catalog 1975– (children's wear); Head Designer jr. sportswear co.; designed for Star Ferry by Betsey Johnson and Michael Miles (children's wear) 1975–77; owner and Head Designer B.J., Inc., designer wholesale co., New York 1978; Pres. and Treas. B.J. Vines, New York; opened Betsey Johnson store, New York 1979; mem. Council of Fashion Designers, American Women's Forum; Merit Award, Mademoiselle magazine 1970, Coty Award 1971, two Tommy Print Awards 1971. *Address:* Betsey Johnson Company, 209 West 38th Street, New York, NY 10018; 110 East 9th Street, Suite A889, Los Angeles, CA 90079, U.S.A.

JOHNSON, Brian Frederick Gilbert, PH.D., F.R.S., F.R.S.C.; British professor of inorganic chemistry; b. 11 Sept. 1938; s. of Frank Johnson and Mona Johnson; m. Christine Draper 1962; two d.; ed. Northampton Grammar School, Univ. of Nottingham; Reader in Chem., Cambridge Univ. 1978–90, Fellow Fitzwilliam Coll. 1970–90, Hon. Fellow 1990–; Crum Brown Prof. of Inorganic Chem., Edin. Univ. 1991–95, Prof. of Chemistry, Univ. of Cambridge 1995–; Tilden Lecturer, R.S.C.; Corday Morgan Medal, R.S.C. *Publications:* Transition Metal Clusters 1980. *Leisure interests:* walking, painting, riding. *Address:* Department of Chemistry, Lensfield Road, Cambridge, CB2 1EW, England.

JOHNSON, Charles Richard, M.A.; American author; b. 23 April 1948, Evanston, Ill.; m. Joan New 1970; one s. one d.; ed. Southern Illinois Univ.; fmr. cartoonist and filmmaker; lecturer, Univ. of Washington, Seattle 1975–79, Assoc. Prof. of English 1979–82, Prof. 1982–; Co.-Dir. Twin Tigers (martial arts studio); recipient of U.S. Nat. Book Award for Middle Passage 1990. *Publications include:* novels: Faith and the Good Thing 1974, Oxherding Tale 1982, Middle Passage 1990; The Sorcerer's Apprentice (short stories); Being and Race: Black Writing Since 1970 1988, The Middle Passage 1990, All This and Moonlight 1990, In Search of a Voice (with Ron Chernow) 1991; Black Humor, Half-Past Nation Time (drawings); Booker, Charlie Smith and the Fritter Tree (broadcast plays); numerous reviews, essays and short stories. *Address:* c/o Antheneum Publishers, Macmillan Publishing Company, 866 3rd Avenue, New York, NY 10022; c/o University of Washington, Department of English, Engl. G N-30, Seattle, WA 98105, U.S.A.

JOHNSON, David Gale; American economist; b. 10 July 1916, Vinton, Iowa; s. of Albert D. Johnson and Myra Jane Reed; m. Helen Virginia Wallace 1938; one s. one d.; ed. Iowa State Coll., Univs. of Wisconsin and Chicago; Research Assoc. Iowa State Coll. 1941–42, Asst. Prof. of Econs. 1942–44; Dept. of Econs., Univ. of Chicago 1944–, Asst. Prof. 1944–54, Prof. 1954– (now Emer.), Assoc. Dean Div. of Social Sciences 1957–60, Dean 1960–70, Chair. Dept. of Econs. 1971–75, 1980–84, Dir. Office of Econ. Analysis 1975–80, Vice-Pres. and Dean of Faculties 1975–76, Provost 1976–80; Economist, Office of Price Admin. 1942, Dept. of State 1946, Dept. of Army 1948; Office of the President's Special Rep. for Trade Negotiations 1963–64; Agency for Int. Devt. 1961–62; Tenn. Valley Authority 1950–55; RAND Corpn. 1953–71; Dir. Social Science Research Council 1954–57; Pres. American Farm Econ. Asscn. 1964–65, Nat. Opinion Research Center 1962–75, 1979–85, Southeast Chicago Comm. 1980– (Pres. 1980–); Treas. American Asscn. for the Advancement of Slavic Studies (AAASS) 1980–82; mem. President's Nat. Advisory Comm. on Food and Fibre 1965–67; Adviser, Policy Planning Council, U.S. Dept. of State 1966–69; mem. Nat. Research Council, mem. Exec. Cttee. Div. of Behavioural Sciences, Nat. Research Council 1969–73, Asscn. for Comparative Econ. Studies (ACES) 1982; mem. Bd. of Dirs., William Benton Foundation 1981; mem. Nat. Comm. on Population Growth and the American Future 1970–72; Acting Dir. Univ. of Chicago Library 1971–72; mem. Council on Int. Econ. Policy 1972–75; mem. Steering Cttee., Nat. Acad. of Sciences World Food and Nutrition Study 1975–77; Co-Chair. Cttee. on Population and Econ. Growth, Nat. Research Council 1984–86; mem. Comm. for Econ. Educ. and Research in China 1984–94, Int. Advisory Cttee. China Centre for Econ. Research, Beijing Univ. 1995–; Dir. Center for E. Asian Studies 1994–; Fellow, American Acad. of Arts and Sciences 1976; mem. N.A.S. *Publications:* Forward Prices for Agriculture 1947, Trade and Agriculture 1950, Grain Yields and the American Food Supply 1963, World Food Problems and Prospects 1975, Prospects for Economic Reform in the People's Republic of China 1982, The People's Republic of China 1978–1900 1990, World Agriculture in Disarray (revised edn.) 1991, Long Term Agricultural Policies for Cen. Europe 1996. *Leisure interests:* reading, travel. *Address:* Department of Economics, The University of Chicago, 1126 E. 59th Street, Chicago, IL 60637 (Office); 5617 S. Kenwood Avenue, Chicago, IL 60637, U.S.A. (Home). *Telephone:* (312) 702-8251 (Office); (312) 493-4015 (Home).

JOHNSON, David Willis, B.ECONS., M.B.A.; Australian business executive; b. 7 Aug. 1932, Tumut, N.S.W.; s. of Alfred Ernest Johnson and Eileen Melba Johnson (née Burt); m. Sylvia Raymonda Wells 1966; three s.; ed. Univs. of Sydney and Chicago; Exec. Trainee Ford Motor Co., Geelong; Man. Trainee Colgate-Palmolive, Sydney 1959–60, Product Man. 1961, Asst. to Man. Dir. 1962, Brands Man. 1963, Gen. Products Man. 1964-65; Asst. Gen. Man. and Marketing Dir., Colgate-Palmolive, Johannesburg 1966, Chair. and Man. Dir. 1967–72; Pres. Warner-Lambert/Parke Davis Asia, Hong Kong 1973–76, Personal Products Div., Warner-Lambert Co., Morris Plains, N.J. 1977, Exec. Vice-Pres. and Gen. Man. Entenmann's Div., Bay Shore, N.Y. 1979, Pres. Speciality Foods Group, Morris Plains, N.J. 1980-81, Vice-Pres. 1980–82; Pres. and C.E.O. Entenmann's Div., Bay Shore 1982, Vice-Pres. Gen. Foods Corpn., White Plains, N.Y. 1982–87, Pres., C.E.O. Entenmann's Inc., Bay Shore 1982–87; Chair., Pres. and C.E.O. Gerber Products Co., Fremont, Mich. 1987–89, Chair. and C.E.O. 1989–90; Pres., C.E.O. and Dir. Campbell Soup Co., Camden, N.J. 1990–97, Chair. Bd. of Dirs. 1993–; mem. Bd. Dirs. Colgate-Palmolive Co., Exec. Advisory Bd. Donaldson, Lufkin & Jenrette Merchant Banking Partners; mem. Advisory Council Univ. of Notre Dame Coll. of Business Admin., Univ. of Chicago Grad. School of Business; Distinguished Alumnus Award, Univ. of Chicago 1992; Dir. of Year Award, Nat. Asscn. of Corp. Dirs 1997; fmr. Dir. American Bakers Asscn., Nat. Food Producers' Asscn., Grocery Mfrs. America. *Address:* Campbell Soup Company World Headquarters, Campbell Place, Camden, NJ 08103, U.S.A. *Telephone:* (609) 342-4800.

JOHNSON, Douglas William John, B.A., B.LITT.; British historian; b. 1 Feb. 1925, Edinburgh; s. of John Thornburn Johnson and Christine Douglas-Mair; m. Madeleine Rébillard 1950; one d.; ed. Royal Grammar School, Lancaster, Worcester Coll. Oxford, Ecole Normale Supérieure, Paris; lecturer in History, Univ. of Birmingham 1949–63, Prof. of Modern History and Head History Dept. 1963–68; Prof. of French History, Univ. Coll. London 1968–90, Prof. Emer. 1990–, Dean of Faculty of Arts 1979–82; Visiting Prof. French Dept., King's Coll. 1993–; mem. Franco-British Council 1973–; Hon. D.Sc. (Univ. of Aston) 1997; Officier, Légion d'honneur, Chevalier, Ordre nat. du mérite, Commdr. des Palmes économiques. *Publications:* Guizot: Aspects of French History 1963, France and the Dreyfus Affair 1966, A Concise History of France 1970, The Age of Illusion (with Madeleine Johnson) 1987, The Permanent Revolution (with Geoffrey Best) 1988, Michelet and the French Revolution 1990, How European are the French? 1996. *Leisure interests:* French politics, music. *Address:* 29 Rudall Crescent, London, NW3 1RR, England; 12 rue Delambre, 75014 Paris, France. *Telephone:* 0171-435 6668 (London); (1) 43.27.69.81 (Paris).

JOHNSON, Earvin (Magic Johnson); American professional basketball player; b. 14 Aug. 1959, Lansing, Mich.; s. of Earvin Johnson and Christine Johnson; m. Cookie Kelly; one s.; ed. Mich. State Univ.; professional basketball player Los Angeles Lakers Nat. Basketball Asscn. (NBA) 1979–91 (retd.), returned to professional sport 1992, later announced abandonment of plans to resume sporting career; Vice-Pres., co-owner Los Angeles Lakers 1994–, Head Coach 1994, resumed career Feb. 1996, retd. July 1996; presenter TV show The Magic Hour 1998–; mem. NCAA Championship Team 1979, Nat. Basketball All-Star Team 1980, 1982–89, Nat. Basketball Asscn. Championship Team 1980, 1982, 1985, 1987, 1988; named most valuable player NBA Playoffs 1980, 1982, 1987, NBA 1987, 1989, 1990; fmr. mem. Nat. Aids Asscn., rejoined 1993; commentator NBC-TV 1995–96; Player of the Year (Sporting News) 1987. *Publications:* Magic 1983, What You Can Do to Avoid AIDS 1992, My Life (autobiog.) 1992. *Address:* c/o Los Angeles Lakers, Great Western Forum, 3900 West Manchester Blvd., P.O. Box 10, Inglewood, CA 90306, U.S.A.

JOHNSON, Frank Robert; British journalist; b. 20 Jan. 1943; s. of late Ernest Johnson and of Doreen Johnson (née Skinner); ed. Chartesey Secondary School, Shoreditch Secondary School; messenger boy, Sunday Express 1959–60; reporter local and regional newspapers 1960–69; mem. political staff Sun newspaper 1969–72; parl. sketch writer and leader writer Daily Telegraph 1972–79; columnist Now! magazine 1979–81; parl. sketch writer The Times 1981–83, 1986–87, Paris diarist 1984, Bonn Corresp. 1985–86, Assoc. Ed. 1987–88; Assoc. Ed. The Sunday Telegraph 1988–93, Deputy Ed. (Comment) 1993–94, Deputy Ed. 1994–95; Ed. The Spectator 1995–; Parl. Sketch Writer of the Year, Granada, What The Papers Say 1977, Columnist of the Year, British Press Awards 1981. *Publications:* Out of Order 1982, Frank Johnson's Election Year 1983. *Leisure interests:* opera, ballet. *Address:* The Spectator, 56 Doughty Street, London, WC1N 2LL, England. *Telephone:* 0171-405 1706.

JOHNSON, Frederick Ross, B.COMM., M.B.A.; Canadian business executive; b. 13 Dec. 1931, Winnipeg, Man.; s. of Frederick H. Johnson and Caroline Green; m. Laurie A. Graumann 1979; two s. (from previous marriage); ed. Univs. of Manitoba and Toronto; Vice-Pres. Merchandising, T. Eaton Co. (Canada) 1965–66; Exec. Vice-Pres. and C.O.O., GSW Ltd. 1966–71; Pres. and C.E.O., Standard Brands Ltd., Canada 1971–74; Dir. Standard Brands Inc. 1974–, Sr. Vice-Pres. 1974–75, Pres. 1975–76, Chair. and C.E.O. 1977–81; Pres. and C.O.O. Nabisco Brands Inc. 1981–83, Vice-Pres. and C.E.O. 1984–85, Chief Exec. R.J.R. Nabisco 1987–89 (after take over of Nabisco by Reynolds), Pres. and C.O.O. R. J. Reynolds Industries 1985–87, Pres. and C.E.O. 1987–89; Chair. and C.E.O. RJM Group Inc. 1989–; Dir. Wosk's Ltd., Vancouver, Bank of Nova Scotia, Toronto; mem. Advisory Council, Columbia Univ., New York; Trustee, Econ. Club of New York; Chair. Multiple Sclerosis Soc., New York branch; Hon. Dr. (St. Francis Xavier Univ., Antigonish, N.S.) 1978, (Univ. of Newfoundland) 1980. *Leisure interests:* golf, skiing, tennis. *Address:* RJM Group, 200 Galleria Parkway, Suite 970, Atlanta, GA 30339, U.S.A.

JOHNSON, Gabriel Ampah, D.D'ÉTAT; Togolese professor of biology and administrator; b. 13 Oct. 1930, Aneho; s. of William K. A. Johnson and Rebecca A. Ekue-Hettah; m. Louise Chipan 1962; three s. three d.; ed. Univ. of Poitiers, France; Teaching Asst., Univ. of Poitiers until 1956; Research Fellow, C.N.R.S., France 1958–60; Deputy Dir. of Educ., Togo 1959-60; Asst. Prof. Nat. Univ. of Ivory Coast, Abidjan 1961–64, Assoc. Prof. 1965–66, Prof., Chair. of Biology 1966–, Asst. Dean, Faculty of Science 1963–68, Founding Dir. Nat. Centre for Social Services 1964–68; Founding Rector, Univ. du Bénin, Lomé, Togo 1970–86; Dir. of Higher Educ., Togo 1970–75; Pres. Nat. Planning Comm. of Togo 1973; Pres. Asscn. of African Univs. 1977–80; mem. Exec. Bd. UNESCO 1997–; mem. Bd. of Admin., Asscn. of Partially or Fully French-Speaking Univs. 1975–, Pan African Inst. for Devt. 1977–; mem. Cen. Cttee. Togo People's Rally (ruling party) 1976–; Founding Pres. Africa Club for an Integrated Devt. 1980–; mem. Zoological Soc. of France 1956, Biological Soc. of France 1962, Endocrinological Soc. of France 1966; Medal of Honour, Univ. of São Paulo, Brazil 1980; Hon. Vice-Pres. Gold Mercury Int. 1983; Hon. Dr. Sherbrooke, Canada) 1979, (Lille) 1983, (Bordeaux) 1986; Gold Mercury Int. Award 1982, Chevalier Ordre nationale de la Côte d'Ivoire 1966; Officier Ordre du Mono (Togo), Officier Légion d'honneur 1971, Commdr. Order of Cruzeiro do Sul (Brazil) 1976, Commdr. Order of Merit (France) 1983, Commdr. of Academic Palms (France) 1986; Gold Medal of Honour, Univ. of Benin. *Publications:* several articles in scientific journals. *Leisure interests:* reading, classical and modern music, swimming, farming (cattle breeding). *Address:* B.P. 7098, Lomé, Togo. *Telephone:* 21-53-65 (Home).

JOHNSON, Gary Earl, B.A.; American business executive and politician; b. 1 Jan. 1953, Minot, N.D.; s. of Earl W. Johnson and Lorraine B. Bostow; m. Dee Sims 1976; one s. one d.; ed. Univ. of New Mexico; Pres. and C.E.O. Big J Enterprises, Albuquerque 1976–; Gov. of New Mexico 1995–; mem. Bd. dirs. Entrepreneurship Studies programme Univ. of N.M., Albuquerque Chamber of Commerce 1993–95; Entrepreneur of the Year 1995; Republican. *Leisure interests:* rock and mountain-climbing, skiing, flying, athletics. *Address:* Office of the Governor, Room 400, State Capitol, Santa Fe, NM 87503, U.S.A.

JOHNSON, Graham Rhodes, O.B.E., F.R.A.M., F.G.S.M.; British concert accompanist; b. 10 July 1950; s. of late John Edward Donald Johnson and of Violet May Johnson; ed. Hamilton High School, Bulawayo, Rhodesia, Royal Acad. of Music, London; Artistic Adviser, accompanist Alte Oper Festival, Frankfurt 1981–82; Prof. of Accompaniment, Guildhall School of Music 1986–; Song Adviser, Wigmore Hall 1992–; Artistic Dir. The Speakers' Almanac; guest lecturer in several countries; writer, presenter BBC Radio 3 series on Poulenc, BBC TV series on Schubert 1978, Liszt 1986; concert début, Wigmore Hall 1972; has accompanied numerous singers including Dame Elisabeth Schwarzkopf, Jessye Norman, Victoria de los Angeles, Dame Janet Baker, Sir Peter Pears, Felicity Lott, Felicity Palmer, John Shirley Quirk, Thomas Hampson, Robert Holl, Tom Krause; has appeared at festivals in Edin., Munich, Hohenems, Salzburg, Bath, Hong Kong, Bermuda; numerous recordings; Gramophone Award 1989. *Publications:* contrib. The Britten Companion 1984, Gerald Moore: The Unashamed Accompanist, The Spanish Song Companion 1992, articles and reviews. *Leisure interest:* dining out. *Address:* 83 Fordwych Road, London, NW2 3TL, England. *Telephone:* 0181-452 5193.

JOHNSON, Hugh Eric Allan, M.A.; British author, editor and broadcaster; b. 10 March 1939, London; s. of Guy F. Johnson and Grace Kittel; m. Judith Eve Grinling 1965; one s. two d.; ed. Rugby School, King's Coll., Cambridge; feature writer Condé Nast Magazines 1960–63; Ed. Wine and Food Magazine 1963–65; wine corresp. Sunday Times 1965–67, Travel Ed. 1967; Ed. Queen Magazine 1968–70; Wine Ed. Gourmet Magazine 1971–72; Wine Ed. Cuisine Magazine (New York) 1983–84; Chair. Winestar Productions Ltd. 1984–, The Hugh Johnson Collection Ltd., The Movie Business; Hon. Chair. 'Wine Japan' 1989–93; Pres. Sunday Times Wine Club 1973–, Circle of Wine Writers 1997–, Vinopolis Soc. 1999–; founder mem. Tree Council 1974–; Dir. Château Latour 1986–; Consultant, Jardines Wines and Spirits K.K., British Airways; Editorial Consultant The Garden (Royal Horticultural Soc. Journal) 1975–; Sec. Wine and Food Soc. 1962–63; TV series Wine—A User's Guide 1986, Vintage—A History of Wine 1989; TV programme Return Voyage 1992; Gardening Corresp. New York Times 1986–87; Dr. h.c. (Essex) 1998; André Simon Prize 1967, 1989, Glenfiddich Award 1972, 1984, 1989, Marqués de Cáceres Award 1984, Wines and Vines Trophy 1982, Grand Prix de la Communication de la Vigne et du Vin 1992, 1993, Decanter Magazine Man of the Year 1995 etc. *Publications:* Wine 1966, Frank Schoonmaker's Encyclopaedia of Wine (Ed. of English edn.) 1967, The World Atlas of Wine 1971, The International Book of Trees 1973, The California Wine Book (with Bob Thompson) 1975, Understanding Wine (Sainsbury Guide) 1976, Hugh Johnson's Pocket Wine Book (annually since 1977), The Principles of Gardening 1979, revised edn. with new title, Hugh Johnson's Gardening Companion 1996, Hugh Johnson's Wine Companion 1983, How to Handle a Wine (video) 1984; Hugh Johnson's Cellar Book 1986, The Atlas of German Wines 1986, How to Enjoy Your Wine 1985, The Wine Atlas of France (with Hubrecht Duijker) 1987, The Story of Wine 1989, The Art and Science of Wine (with James Halliday) 1992, Hugh Johnson on Gardening: The Best of Tradescant's Diary 1993, The New German Wine Atlas (with Stuart Pigott) 1995. *Leisure interests:* travel, trees, gardening, pictures. *Address:* 73 St. James's Street, London, SW1A 1PH; Saling Hall, Great Saling, Essex, CM7 5DT, England; Domaine des Boutons, 03190 Hérisson, Allier, France.

JOHNSON, Adm. Jay; American naval officer; b. 1946, Great Falls, Mont.; m. Garland Hawthorne; one c.; ed. U.S. Naval Acad.; joined U.S. Navy 1968; fmr. Asst. to Chief of Naval Personnel; fmr. Commdr. Naval Group Eight, Theodore Roosevelt Battle Group 1992; Commdr. Second Fleet Striking Fleet Atlantic, Jt. Task Force 120 1994; fmr. Vice-Chief Naval Operations; aircraft-carrier combat pilot during Vietnam war; Chief of Naval Operations 1996–. *Address:* The Pentagon, Washington, DC 20350, U.S.A. *Telephone:* (202) 697-5737. *Fax:* (202) 695-1219.

JOHNSON, John H.; American publisher; b. 19 Jan. 1918, Arkansas; m. Eunice Johnson; one s. (deceased) one d.; ed. DuSable High School and Chicago and Northwestern Univs.; Asst. Ed. 1936, later Man. Ed. of employees' publication, Supreme Life Insurance Co. of America; C.E.O., Chair. Johnson Publishing Co. 1942–; founded Ebony 1945, Jet 1951; first Black businessman to be selected as one of the "ten outstanding young men of the year" by U.S. Jr. Chamber of Commerce 1951; accompanied Vice-Pres. Nixon at Ghana Independence celebrations 1957, appointed Special Amb. representing the U.S. at Ivory Coast Independence celebrations 1961, and Kenya Independence ceremony 1963; Chair. and C.E.O. Supreme Life Insurance Co.; Dir. Marina City Bank of Chicago, Service Fed. Savings and Loan Asscn., Chicago, Greyhound Corpn., Zenith, Bell & Howell, Arthur D. Little Corpn., 20th Century-Fox Corpn., United Negro Coll. Fund, etc.;

Trustee, Inst. of Int. Educ., Tuskegee Inst., Howard and Fisk Univs.; Dir. Chicago Asscn. of Commerce; Hon. LL.D. of several univs. and colls.; Horatio Alger Award 1966, named Publr. of the Year by Magazine Publrs.' Asscn. 1972, and numerous other awards. *Publication:* Succeeding Against the Odds 1989. *Address:* 1270 Avenue of the Americas, New York, NY 10020; 1750 Pennsylvania Avenue, N.W., Washington, DC 20006, U.S.A.

JOHNSON, III, Joseph Eggleston, M.D.; American professor of medicine and administrator; b. 17 Sept. 1930, Elberton, Ga.; s. of Joseph Eggleston Johnson and Marie (Williams) Johnson; m. Judith H. Kemp 1956; one s. two d.; ed. Vanderbilt Univ., Nashville, Tenn., Johns Hopkins Univ.; Instructor in Medicine, Johns Hopkins Univ. School of Medicine 1961–62, Physician, Johns Hopkins Hosp 1961–66, Asst. Prof. of Medicine 1962–66, Asst. Dean for Student Affairs 1963–66; Assoc. Prof. of Medicine, Univ. of Fla. Coll. of Medicine 1966–68, Chief, Div. of Infectious Disease 1966–72, Prof. of Medicine 1968–72, Assoc. Dean 1970–72; Prof. and Chair. Dept. of Medicine, Bowman Gray School of Medicine 1972–85; Chief of Medicine, N.C. Baptist Hosp. 1972–85; Dean, Univ. of Mich. Medical School 1985–90, Prof. of Internal Medicine 1985–93; Sr. Vice-Pres. American Coll. of Physicians 1993–, interim exec. Vice-Pres. 1994–95; mem. accreditation comm. on grad. medical educ. 1988–93; Markle Scholar, Royal Soc. of Medicine; mem. Johns Hopkins Soc. of Scholars. *Publications:* 100 articles and book chapters on infectious disease, immunology and internal medicine. *Address:* American College of Physicians, Independence Mall West, Sixth Street at Race, Philadelphia, PA 19106 (Office); 15-C-44, The Philadelphian, 2401 Pennsylvania Avenue, Philadelphia, PA 19130, U.S.A. (Home). *Telephone:* (215) 351-2690 (Office).

JOHNSON, Kenneth Langstreth, PH.D., F.R.S., F.ENG.; British engineer and university professor; b. 19 March 1925, Barrow-in-Furness, Lancs.; s. of F. H. Johnson and E. H. Langstreth; m. Dorothy Rosemary Watkins 1954; one s. two d.; ed. Barrow-in-Furness Grammar School for Boys, Univ. of Manchester; Tech. Asst. Messrs. Rotol Ltd., Gloucester 1945–49; Asst. Lecturer Mechanical Eng., Manchester Coll. of Tech. 1949–54; Lecturer, then Reader in Eng., Univ. of Cambridge 1954–77, Prof. 1977–92, Prof. Emer. 1992–; Fellow Jesus Coll. 1957–; Fellow Inst. Mechanical Engs. 1948; prize papers, Inst. Mechanical Engs. 1961, 1969, 1975, 1986, 1987; Gold Medal, Inst. Mechanical Eng. 1985. *Publications:* One Hundred Years of Hertz Contact 1982, Contact Mechanics 1985; over 100 papers in scientific and eng. journals. *Leisure interests:* music, swimming, mountain walking. *Address:* 1 New Square, Cambridge, CB1 1EY, England. *Telephone:* (01223) 355287.

JOHNSON, Hon. Leslie Royston, A.M.; Australian politician; b. 22 Nov. 1924, Sydney; s. of W. C. Johnson and M. H. English; m. Gladys Jones 1948; one s. two d.; mem. House of Reps. for Hughes, N.S.W. 1955, 1958, 1961, 1963, 1969, 1972, 1974, 1975, 1977, 1980, 1983; Minister of Housing 1972–73, for Housing and Construction 1973–75, of Aboriginal Affairs June–Nov. 1975; Opposition Whip 1977–83; Deputy Speaker and Chair. of Cttees. 1983; High Commr. in New Zealand 1984–87; Parl. Adviser to Australian Del. to UN 1981; Chair. Australia-N.Z. Foundation 1989–, Ausdef Friendly Soc. 1993–; Pres. (Vice-Pres. 1988–91) Asscn. of fmr. mems. of Australian Parl. 1991–; mem. Council for Australia Abroad 1990; mem. Bd. Nelson Bay R.S.L. and Citizens Retirement Village Ltd. *Leisure interests:* swimming, photography. *Address:* 2/434 Port Hacking Road, Caringbah, N.S.W. 2229, Australia. *Telephone:* (2) 9525 0028. *Fax:* (2) 9525 0028.

JOHNSON, Manuel H., Jr.; American economist; b. 10 Feb. 1949, Troy, Alabama; s. of Manuel Holman Johnson Sr. and Ethel Lorraine Jordan; m. Mary Lois Wilkerson 1972; two s.; ed. Troy State Univ., Florida State Univ., George Mason Univ., Fairfax, Va.; Asst. Sec. of Treasury for Econ. Policy 1982–86; mem. Fed. Reserve Bd. 1985–90, Vice-Chair. 1986–90; Dir. Centre for Global Market Studies, Mason Univ., Fairfax, Va. 1990–94; Co-Chair., Sr. Partner Johnson Smick Int., Washington 1990–. *Publications: Co-author:* Political Economy of Federal Government Growth 1980, Better Government at Half Price 1981, Deregulating Labor Relations 1981. *Address:* Johnson Smick International, 1133 Connecticut Avenue, N.W., # 901, Washington, DC 20036, U.S.A.

JOHNSON, Michael; American athlete; b. 13 Sept. 1967, Dallas; ed. Baylor Univ.; world champion 200m. 1991, 400m. and 4 x 400m. 1993, 200m., 400m. and 4 x 400m. (world record) 1995, 400m. 1997; Olympic champion 4 x 400m. (world record) 1992, 200m., 400m. 1996, world record holder 400m. (indoors) 44.63 seconds 1995, 4 x 400m. (outdoors) 2:55.74 1992, 2:54.29 1993; undefeated at 400m. from 1989–97; first man to be ranked world no. 1 at 200m. and 400m. simultaneously 1990, 1991, 1994, 1995; world record holder for 400m. relay 42.93 seconds; Olympic champion 200m. (world record), 400m., Atlanta 1996. *Address:* U.S.A. Track and Field, P.O. Box 120, Indianapolis, IN 46206, U.S.A.

JOHNSON, Paul (Bede), B.A.; British journalist, historian and broadcaster; b. 2 Nov. 1928, Barton; s. of William Aloysius and Anne Johnson; m. Marigold Hunt 1957; three s. one d.; ed. Stonyhurst and Magdalen Coll., Oxford; Asst. Exec. Ed. Réalités, Paris 1952–55; Asst. Ed. New Statesman 1955–60, Deputy Ed. 1960–64, Ed. 1965–70, Dir. 1965; DeWitt Wallace Prof. of Communications, American Enterprise Inst., Washington, D.C. 1980; mem. Royal Comm. on the Press 1974–77, Cable Authority 1984–90; free-lance writer; Book of the Year Prize, Yorkshire Post 1975, Francis Boyer Award for Services to Public Policy 1979; King Award for Excellence (Literature) 1980. *Publications:* The Offshore Islanders 1972, Elizabeth I: a Study in Power and Intellect 1974, Pope John XXIII 1975, A History of Christianity 1976, Enemies of Society 1977, The National Trust Book of British Castles 1978, The Civilization of Ancient Egypt 1978, Civilizations of the Holy Land 1979, British Cathedrals 1980, Ireland: Land of Troubles 1980, The Recovery of Freedom 1980, Pope John Paul II and the Catholic Restoration 1982, Modern Times 1983 (revised 1991), History of the Modern World: From 1917 to the 1980s 1984, The Pick of Paul Johnson 1985, Saving and Spending: The working-class economy in Britain 1870–1939 1986, The Oxford Book of Political Anecdotes (ed.) 1986, The History of the Jews 1987, Intellectuals 1988, The Birth of the Modern World Society 1815–1830 1991, 20th Century Britain: Economic Social and Cultural Change 1994, Wake Up Britain! 1994, The Quest for God 1996, To Hell with Picasso and other essays 1996, A History of the American People 1997. *Leisure interests:* painting, mountaineering. *Address:* 29 Newton Road, London, W2 5JR; The Coach House, Over Stowey, nr. Bridgwater, Somerset, TA5 1HA, England. *Telephone:* 0171-229 3859 (London); (01278) 732393 (Somerset).

JOHNSON, Philip Cortelyou, A.B.; American architect; b. 8 July 1906; ed. Harvard Univ.; Dir. Dept. of Architecture and Design, Museum of Modern Art 1932–54, Trustee 1958–; with Johnson/Burgee Architects 1967–; works include the Annexe and Sculpture Court, Museum of Modern Art, and the Glass House, New Canaan, Conn., Lincoln Center Theater; assoc. with the late Mies van der Rohe in design of Seagram Building, New York; mem. Acad. of Arts and Letters; Bronze Medallion (City of New York) 1980; Pritzker Prize 1979, Fellows Award R.I. School of Design 1983. *Publications:* The International Style, Architecture since 1922 (with H. R. Hitchcock, Jr.) 1932, Machine Art 1934, Mies van der Rohe 1947, Architecture 1949–1965 1966. *Address:* 885 Third Avenue, # 300, New York, NY 10022 (Office); Ponus Ridge Road, New Canaan, CT 06840, U.S.A. (Home).

JOHNSON, Pierre Marc, B.A., LL.L., M.D., F.R.S.C.; Canadian politician and lawyer; b. 5 July 1946, Montreal; s. of late Daniel Johnson and Reine (Gagné) Johnson; m. Marie-Louise Parent 1973; one s. one d.; ed. Coll. Jean-Brébeuf, Montreal, Univ. de Montréal and Univ. de Sherbrooke; called to Quebec Bar 1971; admitted Quebec Coll. of Physicians and Surgeons 1976; elected to Quebec Nat. Ass. 1976; mem. Nat. Exec. Council, Parti Québécois 1977–79, Pres. Parti Québécois 1985–87; Minister of Labour and Manpower, Quebec 1977–80, of Consumer Affairs, Cooperatives and Financial Insts. 1980–81, of Social Affairs 1981–84, of Justice, Attorney-Gen. and Minister Responsible for Canadian Intergovernmental Affairs 1984–85; Premier of Quebec Oct.-Dec. 1985; Leader of Opposition, Quebec Nat. Ass. 1985–87; Sr. Counsel Heenan Blaikie Attorneys, Montreal; Dir. Unimedia, Innovitech Inc., CRC Sofema, EETINA (Mexico), Int. Union for Conservation of Nature (Geneva); Hon. Ph.D. (Lyon). *Publication:* The Environment and NAFTA: implementing and understanding New Continental Law 1995. *Leisure interests:* skiing, swimming, music. *Address:* 1250 René Levesque blvd West, Suite 2500, Montreal, Que., H3B 4Y1, Canada. *Telephone:* (514) 846-2200. *Fax:* (514) 846-3427.

JOHNSON, Richard Keith; British actor; b. 30 July 1927, Upminster, Essex; s. of Keith Holcombe and Frances Louisa Olive (Tweed) Johnson; m. 1st Sheila Ann Sweet 1957 (divorced); one s. one d.; m. 2nd Kim Novak 1965 (divorced); m. 3rd Marie-Louise Nordlund 1982 (divorced); one s. one d.; ed. Parkfield School, Felsted School, Royal Acad. of Dramatic Art; Nat. Theatre Player, Assoc. Artist R.S.C.; first stage appearance in Hamlet, Opera House, Manchester 1944; major parts include Marius Tertius (The First Victoria) 1950, Pierre (The Madwoman of Chaillot) 1951, Demetrius (A Midsummer Night's Dream) 1951, George Phillips (After My Fashion) 1952, Beauchamp, Earl of Warwick (The Lark) 1955, Laertes (Hamlet) 1955, Jack Absolute (The Rivals) 1956, Lord Plynlimmon (Plaintiff in a Pretty Hat) 1956, Orlando (As You Like It), Mark Antony (Julius Caesar), Leonatus (Cymbeline), Ferdinand (The Tempest), Romeo (Romeo and Juliet), Sir Andrew Aguecheek (Twelfth Night), title-role in Pericles, Don Juan (Much Ado About Nothing) 1957–58, Ferdinand (The Tempest) 1957, Romeo (Romeo and Juliet), Sir Andrew Aguecheek (Twelfth Night), Moscow and Leningrad; Charles (Blithe Spirit), Pinchwife (The Country Wife), Pilate (The Passion), title-role in The Guardsman all at Nat. Theatre 1975–78; U.K. tour, Death Trap 1982, in Long Day's Journey Into Night 1996, Uncle Vanya 1996, Staying On 1997, To Kill a Mockingbird 1997, Plenty 1999; first film appearance in Captain Horatio Hornblower 1950; films include Never so Few 1959, The Haunting 1963, The Pumpkin Eater 1964, Operation Crossbow 1965, Khartoum 1966, Deadlier Than the Male 1966, Hennessy 1975, Turtle Diary 1984, Treasure Island 1989, Oedipus the King, wrote and acted in Hennessy; first appeared on TV 1949; TV films include: Man for All Seasons 1988, Voice of the Heart 1988, The Camomile Lawn, Anglo-Saxon Attitudes 1992; leading roles in productions including Rembrandt, Antony and Cleopatra, Hamlet (Claudius), The Member for Chelsea (Sir Charles Dilke), Cymbeline; founder, Chair. and C.E.O. United British Artists 1982–, Dir. 1983–; mem. Council British Acad. Film and Television Arts 1976–78; recent productions include: The Biko Inquest, Serjeant Musgrave's Dance, The Playboy of the Western World, Old Times, Turtle Diary, Castaway, The Lonely Passion of Judith Hearne, The Rivals, An Inspector Calls, Aldwych. *Publication:* Hennessy 1974. *Leisure interests:* gardening, music, travel. *Address:* c/o Conway, Van Gelder, Robinson Ltd., 18–21 Jermyn Street, London, SW1Y 6HP, England.

JOHNSON, Thomas S., A.B., M.B.A.; American bank executive; b. 19 Nov. 1940, Racine, Wis.; m. Margaret Ann Werner 1970; two s. one d.; ed. Trinity Coll., Harvard; Head Graduate Business Program, Instructor Finance and

Control Ateneo de Manila Univ. 1964–66; Special Asst. to Controller, Dept. of Defense 1966–69; with Chemical Bank and Chemical Banking Corpn. 1969–89, Exec. Vice-Pres. 1979, Sr. Exec. Vice-Pres. 1981, Pres. 1983–89; Pres., Dir. Corp. and Mfrs. Hanover Trust Co. 1989–91, Olympia and York Devts. Ltd. 1992–; Chair. Pres. C.E.O. GP Financial Corpn., GreenPoint Savings Bank, Flushing, N.Y. 1993–; Chair. Bd. of Dirs. Union Theological Seminary, Harvard Business School Club of Greater New York; Bank Capital Market Asscn's Cttee. for Competitive Securities Market; Dir. Bond Club of New York Inc.; Vice-Pres. and Bd. mem. Cancer Research Inst. of America; Bd. mem. Texas Commerce Bancshares Inc., Pan Atlantic Re, Inc., Phelps Stokes Fund, Montclair Art Museum; mem. Council on Foreign Relations, Inc., Financial Execs. Inst. Asscn. of Reserve City Bankers, The Group of Thirty. Trustee Trinity Coll.; mem. Business Cttee., Museum of Modern Art, Consultative Group on Int. Econ. and Monetary Affairs. *Address:* GreenPoint Financial Corporation, 90 Park Avenue, New York, NY 10016, U.S.A.

JOHNSON, Timothy Peter, M.A., J.D.; American politician; b. 28 Dec. 1946, Canton, S.D.; s. of Vandal Johnson and Ruth Ljostveit; m. Barbara Brooks 1969; two s. one d.; ed. Univ. of S. Dakota and Michigan State Univ.; called to bar, S. Dakota 1975, U.S. Dist. Court, S. Dakota 1976; fiscal analyst, Legis. Fiscal Agency, Lansing, Mich. 1971–72; sole practice, Vermillion, S. Dak. 1975–86; mem. S. Dakota House of Reps. 1978–82, S. Dakota Senate 1982–86; mem. 101st-103rd U.S. Congresses 1987–97; Senator from S. Dakota 1997–; Democrat. *Address:* United States Senate, 502 Hart Senate Office Building, Washington, DC 20510, U.S.A.

JOHNSON, William, D.SC., F.R.S., F.ENG., F.I.MECH.E.; British professor of engineering (retd.); b. 20 April 1922, Manchester; s. of James Johnson and Elizabeth Riley; m. Heather Marie Thornber 1946; three s. two d.; ed. Univ. of Manchester; Prof. of Mechanical Eng. UMIST 1960–75, Visiting Prof. of Mechanical Eng. and History of Science 1992–94; Prof. of Mechanics, Eng. Dept. Univ. of Cambridge 1975–82 (retd.); Visiting Prof., Industrial Eng. Dept., Purdue Univ., Ind., U.S.A. 1984–85, United Technologies Distinguished Prof. of Eng. 1988–89; Founder of Int. Journal of Mechanical Sciences 1960–87, Int. Journal of Impact Eng. 1983–87; Foreign Fellow Acad. of Athens 1982; Foreign mem. Russian Acad. of Science (Ural Br.) 1993; Fellow of Univ. Coll. London 1981; Hon. D. Tech. (Bradford) 1976, Hon. D.Eng. (Sheffield) 1986, (UMIST) 1995; T. Bernard Hall Prize 1965, 1966, James Clayton Fund Prize 1972, 1977, Safety in Mech. Eng. Prize 1980, 1991, James Clayton Prize, Inst. Mechanical Engineers 1987, Silver Medal Inst. Sheet Metal 1987. A.M.P.T. Gold Medal, Dublin 1995. *Publications:* (with various co-authors) Plasticity for Mechanical Engineers 1962, Mechanics of Metal Extrusion 1962, Bibliography of Slip Line Fields 1968, Impact Strength of Materials 1972, Engineering Plasticity 1973, Engineering Plasticity: Metal Forming Processes 1978, Crashworthiness of Vehicles 1978, Bibliography of Slip Line Fields 1982. *Leisure interests:* gardening, walking, music, reading. *Address:* Ridge Hall, Chapel-en-le-Frith, High Peak, SK23 9UD; 62 Beach Road, Carlyon Bay, St. Austell, Cornwall, PL25 3PJ, England. *Telephone:* (01298) 812441 (High Peak); (01726) 813179 (St. Austell).

JOHNSON SIRLEAF, Ellen; Liberian politician and civil servant; ed. Harvard Univ.; Asst. Minister of Finance 1964–69, Deputy Minister of Finance 1977–80; Sr. Loan Officer, IBRD, Washington, D.C. 1973–77, 1980–81; fmr. Pres. Liberian Bank for Devt. Investment; Vice-Pres. Citibank Regional Office for Africa, Nairobi 1981–85; Vice-Pres. and mem. Bd. of Dirs. Equator Holders, Equator Bank Ltd., Washington, D.C. until 1992; Asst. Admin. UNDP and Dir. Regional Bureau for Africa 1992–. *Address:* c/o United Nations Development Programme, 1 United Nations Plaza, New York, NY 10017, U.S.A.

JOHNSON-LAIRD, Philip Nicholas, PH.D., F.R.S., F.B.A.; British psychologist; b. 12 Oct. 1936, Leeds, Yorks.; s. of Eric Johnson-Laird and Dorothy Johnson-Laird (née Blackett); m. Maureen Mary Sullivan 1959; one s. one d.; ed. Culford School, Univ. Coll., London; left school at age 15 and worked as quantity surveyor and in other jobs before univ.; Asst. Lecturer, Dept. of Psychology, Univ. Coll., London 1966, Lecturer 1967–73; Visiting mem. Inst. for Advanced Study, Princeton, U.S.A. 1971–72; Reader in Experimental Psychology, Univ. of Sussex 1973, Prof. 1978–82; Asst. Dir., MRC Applied Psychology Unit, Cambridge 1982–89; Fellow Darwin Coll. Cambridge 1984–89; Visiting Fellow, Cognitive Science, Stanford Univ., U.S.A. 1980, Visiting Prof. of Psychology 1985, Visiting Prof. of Psychology, Princeton Univ., U.S.A. 1986, Prof. 1989–, Stuart Prof. of Psychology 1994–; Dr. h.c. (Gothenburg) 1983; Laurea h.c. (Padua) 1997; Rosa Morison Memorial Medal, Univ. Coll. London, James Sully Scholarship; Spearman Medal, British Psychological Soc. 1974, Pres.'s Award 1985. *Publications:* Thinking and Reasoning (Ed. with P. C. Wason) 1968, Psychology of Reasoning (with P. C. Wason) 1972, Language and Perception (with G. A. Miller) 1976, Thinking (Ed. with P. C. Wason) 1977, Mental Models 1983, The Computer and the Mind 1988, Deduction (with R. M. J. Byrne) 1992, Human and Machine Thinking 1993; numerous articles in psychological journals; reviews. *Leisure interests:* arts and music, talking and arguing. *Address:* Department of Psychology, Princeton University, Princeton, NJ 08544, U.S.A. *Telephone:* (609) 258 4432.

JOHNSTON, Allen Howard, C.M.G., L.TH., LL.D.; New Zealand ecclesiastic; b. 2 Sept. 1912, Auckland; s. of Joseph Howard Johnston and Clara Johnston; m. Joyce Rhoda Grantley 1937; four d.; ed. Univ. of Auckland, St. John's Coll., Auckland; Asst. Curate in Anglican Church, St. Mark's, Remuera 1935; Vicar of Northern Wairoa 1937, of Otahuhu 1944, of Whangarei 1949; Archdeacon of Waimate 1949; Bishop of Dunedin 1953–69, Waikato 1969–80; Primate and Archbishop of New Zealand 1972–80; Chaplain and Sub-Prelate, Order of St. John of Jerusalem 1974–; Chair. N.Z. Church Pension Bd. 1973–88; mem. Royal Comm. of Inquiry into Arthur Allan Thomas Case 1979; Fellow of St. John's Coll., Auckland; Hon. LL.D. (Otago). *Leisure interest:* gardening. *Address:* 3 Wymer Terrace, Hamilton, New Zealand. *Telephone:* 8553238.

JOHNSTON, David Lloyd, C.C., LL.B.; Canadian professor of law; b. 28 June 1941, Sudbury, Ont.; s. of Lloyd Johnston and Dorothy Stonehouse; m. Sharon Downey 1964; five d.; ed. Sault Collegiate Inst., Sault Ste. Marie, Ont., Harvard Univ., Univ. of Cambridge and Queen's Univ., Kingston; Asst. Prof. Faculty of Law, Queen's Univ., Kingston; 1966–68; Asst. Prof. Faculty of Law, Univ. of Toronto 1968–69, Assoc. Prof. 1969–72, Prof. 1972–74; Dean and Prof. Faculty of Law, Univ. of W. Ont. 1974–79; Prof. of Law, McGill Univ. 1979–, Prin. and Vice-Chancellor 1979–94; Pres. Harvard Univ. Bd.of Overseers 1997–98; recipient of ten hon. degrees. *Publications:* Computers and the Law 1968, Canadian Securities Regulation 1977, The Law of Business Associations (with R. Forbes) 1979, Canadian Companies and the Stock Exchange 1980, If Quebec Goes: The Real Cost of Separation (with Marcel Côté) 1995, Getting Canada On Line: Understanding the Information Highway (co-author) 1995, Cyberlaw 1997; numerous articles in academic journals. *Leisure interests:* jogging, skiing. *Address:* Centre for Medicine, Ethics and Law, McGill University, 3690 Peel Street, Montreal, Québec, H3A 2T5 (Office); 18 Sunnyside Avenue, Westmount, Québec, H3Y 1C9, Canada (Home). *Telephone:* 398-7402 (Office); 485-2166 (Home). *Fax:* 398-4668.

JOHNSTON, Rt. Hon. Donald J., P.C., Q.C., B.A., LL.B.; Canadian politician, lawyer and international civil servant; b. 1936, Cumberland, Ont.; m. Heather Bell Maclaren; four d.; ed. McGill Univ. and Univ. of Grenoble; joined Stikeman, Elliott (int. law firm) 1961; subsequent f. own law firm, Johnston, Heenan & Blaikie; teacher of law, McGill Univ. 1963–76; mem. Parl. 1978–88; Pres. Treasury Bd. 1980–82; Minister for Econ. Devt. and Minister of State for Science and Tech. 1982–83; Minister of State for Econ. Devt. and Tech. 1983–84; Minister of Justice and Attorney-Gen. June–Sept. 1984; elected Pres. Liberal Party of Canada 1990, re-elected 1992; Counsel, Heenan, Blaikie (law firm), Montreal 1988–96; Sec.-Gen. OECD 1996–. *Publications:* Up the Hill (political memoirs) 1986; one book on taxation; numerous professional papers. *Leisure interests:* tennis, piano, writing. *Address:* Organization for Economic Co-operation and Development, 2 rue André-Pascal, 75775 Paris Cedex 16, France. *Telephone:* (1) 45.24.80.10. *Fax:* (1) 45.24.80.12.

JOHNSTON, J(ohn) Bennett, Jr.; American politician; b. 10 June 1932, Shreveport, La.; s. of J. Bennett Johnston; m. Mary Gunn; two s. two d.; ed. Byrd High School, Washington and Lee Univ., U.S. Mil. Acad. and Louisiana State Univ. Law School; School of Law; Mil. service in Judge Advocate Gen. Corps La.; State Senator 1968–72; Senator from Louisiana 1972–96; Chair. Democratic Senatorial Campaign Cttee. 1975–76; mem. Senate Cttee. on Energy and Natural Resources, on Appropriations, Senate Budget Cttee., mem. Senate Bldg. Cttee.; partner Johnston & Assocs. 1996–; Democrat. *Leisure interest:* tennis. *Address:* Johnston & Associates, 1455 Pennsylvania Avenue, N.W., Suite 200, Washington, DC, 20004, U.S.A.

JOHNSTON, Ronald John, PH.D.; British geographer; b. 30 March 1941, Swindon; s. of Henry Louis Johnston and Phyllis Joyce (née Liddiard) Johnston; m. Rita Brennan 1963; one s. one d.; ed. The Commonweal Co. Secondary Grammar School, Swindon, Univ. of Manchester; Teaching Fellow, then lecturer, Dept. of Geography, Monash Univ., Australia 1964–66; lecturer then Reader, Dept. of Geography, Univ. of Canterbury, N.Z. 1967–74; Prof. of Geography, Univ. of Sheffield 1974–92, Pro-Vice-Chancellor for Academic Affairs 1989–92; Vice-Chancellor Univ. of Essex 1992–95; Prof. of Geography, Univ. of Bristol 1995–; Co-Ed. Environment and Planning 1979–, Progress in Human Geography 1979–; Murchison Award, Royal Geographical Soc. (R.G.S.) 1985, Victoria Medal (R.G.S.) 1990, Hons. Award for Distinguished Contribs., Asscn. of American Geographers 1991. *Publications:* author or co-author of more than 30 books, including Geography and Geographers, Philosophy and Human Geography, City and Society, The Geography of English Politics, A Nation Dividing?, Bell-ringing: the English Art of Change-Ringing, An Atlas of Bells; Ed. or Co-ed. of more than 20 books, including Geography and the Urban Environment (six vols.), The Dictionary of Human Geography; author or co-author of more than 300 articles in academic journals. *Leisure interests:* bell-ringing, walking. *Address:* Department of Geography, University of Bristol, Bristol, BS8 1SS (Office); 123 The Close, Salisbury, SP1 2EY, England (Home). *Telephone:* (0117) 928 9116 (Office); *Fax:* (0117) 928 7878.

JOHNSTON, Thomas Lothian, PH.D., C.I.MGT., F.I.P.D., F.R.S.A., F.R.S.E.; British fmr. university principal, consultant and fmr. business executive; b. 9 March 1927, Whitburn; s. of late T. B. Johnston and Janet B. Lothian; m. Joan W. Fahmy 1956; two s. three d.; ed. Hawick High School and Univs. of Edinburgh and Stockholm; lecturer in Political Econ. Univ. of Edin. 1953–65; Prof. of Econs. Heriot-Watt Univ. 1966–76; Chair. Manpower Services Cttee. for Scotland 1977–80; Prin. and Vice-Chancellor, Heriot-Watt Univ. 1981–88; Chair. inquiry into staff representation, London Clearing Banks 1978–79, water workers' dispute 1983; mem. Scottish Milk

Marketing Bd. 1967–72, Scottish Telecommunications Bd. 1977–81; Dir. First Charlotte Assets Trust 1981–92, Hodgson Martin Ltd. 1989–97, Scottish Life Assurance Co. 1989–97; editorial adviser, Royal Bank of Scotland Review 1985–92; numerous visiting academic appts.; Pres. Scottish Econ. Soc. 1978–81; Pres. Royal Soc. of Edin. 1993–96; Chair. in Scotland, Royal Soc. of Arts 1991–95; Trustee Nat. Galleries of Scotland 1989–95; D.L., City of Edin.; foreign mem. Royal Swedish Acad. of Eng. Science; Commdr. Royal Swedish Order of Polar Star; Dr. h.c. (Edin.); Hon. LL.D. (Glasgow); D.Ed. (C.N.A.A.); D. Univ. (Heriot-Watt); Hon. D.Litt. (Napier); Fellow Educational Inst. of Scotland. *Publications:* Collective Bargaining in Sweden 1962, The Structure and Growth of the Scottish Economy (jtly.) 1971, Introduction to Industrial Relations 1981; numerous translations from Swedish. *Leisure interests:* gardening, walking. *Address:* 14 Mansionhouse Road, Edin., EH9 1TZ, Scotland. *Telephone:* (0131) 667 1439.

JOHNSTON, Very Rev. William Bryce, M.A., B.D., D.D., D.LITT.; British ecclesiastic; b. 16 Sept. 1921, Edinburgh; s. of William B. Johnston and Isabel W. Highley; m. Ruth M. Cowley 1947; one s. two d.; ed. George Watson's Coll. Edinburgh and Univ. of Edinburgh; Chaplain to H.M. Forces 1945–49; Minister, St. Andrew's Bo'ness 1949–55, St. George's Greenock 1955–64, Colinton Parish Church, Edinburgh 1964–91; Chaplain to H.M. The Queen in Scotland 1981–91, Extra Chaplain 1991–; Moderator of Gen. Ass. of Church of Scotland 1980–81, Chair. Judicial Comm. 1987–91; Visiting Lecturer in Social Ethics, Heriot-Watt Univ. 1966–87; Cunningham Lecturer, New Coll. Edinburgh 1968–71. *Leisure interests:* organ music, bowls. *Address:* 15 Elliot Road, Edin., EH14 1DU, Scotland. *Telephone:* (0131) 441 3387.

JOHNSTONE, D. Bruce, PH.D.; American university administrator and educator; b. 13 Jan. 1941, Minneapolis, Minn.; s. of Donald Bruce and Florence Elliott Johnstone; m. Gail Eberhardt 1965; one s. one d.; ed. Harvard Univ. and Univ. of Minnesota; Admin. Asst. to Senator Walter F. Mondale (q.v.) 1969–71; Project Specialist, Ford Foundation 1971–72; Exec. Asst. to Pres. and Vice-Pres., Univ. of Pa. 1972–77, Adjunct Assoc. Prof. of Educ. 1976–79, Vice-Pres. for Admin. 1977–79; Pres. State Univ. Coll., Buffalo 1979–88; Chancellor State Univ. of New York 1988–94; Prof., Univ. at Buffalo 1994–. *Publications:* Sharing The Costs of Higher Education: Student Financial Assistance in The United Kingdom, The Federal Republic of Germany, France, Sweden, and the United States 1986, other works on the econs. and man. of higher educ. *Leisure interests:* writing, wilderness canoeing, wildflower botany. *Address:* 468 Baldy Hall, University at Buffalo, Buffalo, NY 12246, U.S.A. *Telephone:* (716) 645-3168. *Fax:* (716) 645-2481.

JOHNSTONE, John W., Jr., B.A.; American business executive (retd.); b. 19 Nov. 1932, Brooklyn, New York; s. of John W. Johnstone Sr. and Sarah J. (Singleton) Johnstone; m. Claire Lundberg 1956; three s.; ed. Hartwick Coll., Oneonta, New York and Harvard Univ.; Hooker Chemical Corpn. 1954–75, Group Vice-Pres., Niagara Falls, New York 1973–75; Pres. Airco Alloys, Div. of Airco Inc., Niagara Falls, New York 1976–79; Vice-Pres. and Gen. Man., Industrial Products, Olin Corpn., Stamford, Conn. 1979–80, Sr. Vice-Pres., Chemicals Group 1980, Pres. and Vice-Pres. Olin Corpn. 1980, Exec. Vice-Pres. 1983, Dir. 1984, Pres. Olin Corpn. 1985–96, C.O.O. 1986–87, C.E.O. 1987–96; Chair., Pres. and C.E.O. Olin Corpn. 1988–96, Chair. of Bd. 1990–96, mem. Bd. Dirs. 1996–, Chair. Exec. Finance Cttee. 1996–; Dir. Phoenix Home Life Insurance Co. 1986–, Research Corpn. 1987–96, American Brands Inc. 1989–; McDermott Int., Inc. 1995–, Research Corpn. Technologies 1996–; Chair. Bd. Dirs. Chemical Mfrs. Asscn. 1991; Trustee Hartwick Coll. 1983–91, 1992–; mem. Bd. Dirs. American Productivity and Quality Center; mem. Policy Cttee. Business Roundtable 1992–; Hon. D.Sc. (Hartwick Coll.) 1990. *Leisure interests:* golf and shooting—Trap/skeet. *Address:* Olin Corporation, 501 Merritt 7, Norwalk, CT 06851, U.S.A. *Telephone:* (203) 703-3000 (Office).

JOHORE, H.H. Sultan of, Sultan Mahmood Iskandar ibni Al-Marhum Sultan Ismail; Malaysian Ruler; b. 8 April 1932, Johore Bahru, Johore; s. of Sultan Tengku Ismail of Johore; m. 1st Josephine Trevorrow 1956; m. 2nd Tengku Zanariah Ahmad Zanariah Ahmad 1961; ed. Sultan Abu Bakar English Coll., Johore Bahru, Trinity Grammar School, Sydney, Australia, Devon Tech. Coll., Torquay, U.K.; Tengku Makota (Crown Prince) 1959–61, 1981; Raja Muda (second-in-line to the throne) 1966–81; fifth Sultan of Johore 1981–; Col.-in-Chief, Johore Mil. Forces 1981–; Yang di-Pertuan Agung (Supreme Head of State) 1984–89; f. Mado's Enterprises and Mados-Citoh-Daiken (timber cos.). *Leisure interests:* hunting, tennis, golf, flying, water sports.

JOKIPII, Liisa, M.D.; Finnish university teacher and medical doctor; b. 26 March 1943, Helsinki; m. Anssi Jokipii 1968; two s. two d.; ed. Univ. of Helsinki; Asst., Dept. of Serology and Bacteriology, Univ. of Helsinki 1973, Dozent in Clinical Microbiology and Immunology 1977–; Prof. of Clinical Microbiology and Immunology, Univ. of Oulu 1977; Prof. of Bacteriology and Serology, Univ. of Turku 1978. *Publications:* scientific articles on cell-mediated immunity, bacteriology and parasitology; textbook chapters on parasitology. *Leisure interests:* classical music (opera), old Finnish handicrafts and design. *Address:* Vanhaväylä 37, 00830 Helsinki, Finland (Home). *Telephone:* 358-0-783 827 (Home).

JOKLIK, Wolfgang Karl, D.PHIL.; American professor of microbiology and immunology; b. 16 Nov. 1926, Vienna, Austria; s. of Karl F. Joklik and Helene (née Giessl) Joklik; m. 1st Judith V. Nicholas 1955 (died 1975); one s. one d.; m. 2nd Patricia H. Downey 1977; ed. Sydney and Oxford Univs.; Research Fellow, Australian Nat. Univ. 1954–56, Fellow 1957–62; Assoc. Prof. of Cell Biology, Albert Einstein Coll. of Medicine, New York 1962–65, Siegfried Ullman Prof. 1966–68; Prof. and Chair. Dept. of Microbiology and Immunology Duke Univ. 1968–92, James B. Duke Distinguished Prof. 1972–; Pres. Virology Div. American Soc. for Microbiology 1966–69; Chair. Virology Study Section Nat. Insts. of Health 1973–75; Pres. American Medical School Microbiology Chairs.' Asscn. 1979; Pres. American Soc. for Virology 1982–83; Ed.-in-Chief Virology 1975–93, Microbiological Reviews 1991–95; Assoc. Ed. Journal of Biological Chem. 1978–88; mem. N.A.S., mem. N.A.S. Inst. of Medicine. *Publications:* Contrib. to and Sr. Ed. specialist books, including Zinsser Microbiology, Principles of Animal Virology, The Reoviridae, more than 200 articles in specialist journals. *Leisure interests:* travel, photography, music, golf, tennis and squash. *Address:* Department of Microbiology, P.O. Box 3020, Duke University Medical Center, Durham, NC 27710, U.S.A. *Telephone:* (919) 684-2042. *Fax:* (919) 684-8735.

JOKŪBONIS, Gediminas; Lithuanian sculptor; b. 8 March 1927, Kupiškis; s. of Albinas Jokūbonis and Domicėlė Jokūbonienė; m. Bronė Valantinaitė 1953; two s. one d.; ed. Kaunas Inst. of Decorative and Applied Arts, Inst. of Arts, Lithuanian S.S.R.; lecturer, Vilnius Inst. of Arts (now Acad. of Arts) 1965–, Prof. 1974–; mem. U.S.S.R. (now Russian) Acad. of Arts 1983; People's Artist of Lithuania 1977; author of monumental sculptures in Lithuania, including Mother (Memorial Complex, Pirciupiai) 1960, Monuments to the singer Kipras Petrauskas, Vilnius 1974, to the poet Maironis, Kaunas 1977, to A. Miczkevic, Vilnius 1984, to poet Vienažindys Mažeikiai 1987, to Grand Duke of Lithuania Vytautas, Vytautas church in Kaunas 1991, to Martynas Mažvydas, Nat. Library, Vilnius 1996; Lithuanian State Prize, Lenin Prize. *Leisure interests:* archaeology, history. *Address:* VDA, Maironio str. 6, 2600 Vilnius (Office); V. Kudirkos 4–3, 2009 Vilnius, Lithuania. *Telephone:* (2) 613433 (Office); 630714 (Home).

JOLIF, Claude Emmanuel, L. EN D.; French diplomatist; b. 19 May 1933, Nancy; s. of Pierre Jolif and Marie-Liliane Le Gac; m. Annie Abgrall 1959; one s. two d.; ed. Coll. Saint-François-Xavier, Vannes and Ecole Nat. d'Admin.; joined Ministry of Foreign Affairs 1962; served New Delhi 1963–65, Tel Aviv 1966–69, Moscow 1973–77, Rabat 1977–80; Deputy Dir. UN and int. orgs. service 1980; Under-Sec. Ministry of Foreign Affairs 1980–83; Dir.-Gen. Int. Centre for Children 1983–88; Head of Francophone Affairs, Ministry of Foreign Affairs 1989–91; Amb. to Belarus 1992–97; Chevalier, Légion d'honneur. *Address:* 21 rue du Bouloi, 75001 Paris, France (Home).

JOLIOT, Pierre Adrien, D. ÈS SC.; French scientist; b. 12 March 1932, Paris; s. of Frédéric Joliot and Irène Joliot Curie; m. Anne Gricourouff 1961; two s.; ed. Faculté des Sciences de Paris; researcher, Centre Nat. de la Recherche Scientifique 1954–81, Dir. of Research 1974–; Prof., Collège de France 1981–; Chef de Service, Institut de Biologie Physico-Chimique 1975–94, Admin. 1994–; Dir. Dept. of Biology, Ecole Normale Supérieure 1987–92; Scientific Adviser to Prime Minister 1985–86; mem. Comité nat. d'évaluation de la recherche, CNER, 1989–92; mem. de l'Institut (Acad. des Sciences, Paris) 1982; mem. N.A.S. (U.S.A.), Academia Europaea, Acad. Européenne des Sciences, des Arts et des Lettres; Prix André Policard-Lacassagne 1968, Charles F. Kettering Award for excellence in photosynthesis 1970, Prix du Commisariat à l'Energie Atomique 1980, Gold Medal C.N.R.S. 1982; Officier Légion d'honneur; Commdr. de l'Ordre du mérite. *Publications:* scientific works on bioenergetics and photosynthesis. *Leisure interests:* tennis, sailing, skiing. *Address:* Institut de Biologie Physico-Chimique, 13 rue Pierre et Marie Curie, 75005 Paris (Office); 16 rue de la Glacière, 75013 Paris, France (Home). *Telephone:* (1) 43.25.26.09 (Office); (1) 43.37.22.56 (Home).

JOLLEY, Elizabeth Monica, A.O.; British/Australian writer and lecturer; b. 4 June 1923, Birmingham; d. of Charles Knight and Margarethe Knight; m. Leonard Jolley 1945; one s. two d.; ed. Friends' School, Sibford; trained as a nurse Queen Elizabeth Hosp., Birmingham 1940–46; moved to W. Australia with family 1959; held a variety of occupations; lecturer School of Communication and Cultural Studies, Curtin Univ. of Tech.; Hon. D.Tech. (W.A.I.T., now Curtin), Hon. D.Litt. (Macquarie Univ.), (Queensland) 1997; novels Mr. Scobie's Riddle and My Father's Moon won Age Book of the Year Award, novel The Well won Miles Franklin Award (film 1997), novel The Sugar Mother won France-Australia Literary Translation Award, novel Milk and Honey won Premier of N.S.W. Prize and the collection of essays Central Mischief won Premier of W.A. Prize; ASAL Gold Medal for contrib. to Australian Literature. *Publications:* thirteen novels including The Orchard Thieves 1995, Lovesong 1997, one vol. of poetry, one vol. of essays, one vol. of radio plays. *Address:* 28 Agett Road, Claremont 6010, Western Australia. *Telephone:* (8) 9384 7879.

JOLLY, Robert Dudley, B.V.SC., PH.D., D.SC., F.R.S.N.Z.; New Zealand veterinary pathologist; b. 1 Oct. 1930, Hamilton; s. of Thomas D. Jolly and Violet Mills; m. Aline C. Edwards 1958; two s. two d.; ed. King's Coll., N.Z. and Univs. of Auckland and Sydney; mixed veterinary practice, Rotorua 1955–59; Teaching Fellow, Univ. of Sydney 1960–63; Assoc. Prof. Univ. of Guelph, Canada 1963–65; Sr. Lecturer, Massey Univ. 1965–68, Reader 1968–85, Prof. in Veterinary Pathology and Public Health 1985–96, Prof. Emer. 1997–; Hon. mem. American Coll. of Veterinary Pathologists; Hon. Fellow Australian Coll. of Veterinary Science; Hon. F.R.C.P.A. *Publications:* 130 publs. in scientific books and journals. *Leisure interests:* gardening, trout fishing. *Address:* Institute of Veterinary, Animal and Biomedical Science, Massey University, Palmerston North (Office); 136 Buick Crescent, Palmerston North, New Zealand (Home). *Telephone:* (6) 3569099 (Office); (6) 3545852 (Home).

JOLOWICZ, John Anthony, Q.C., M.A.; British professor of law; b. 11 April 1926, London; s. of H. F. Jolowicz and Ruby Wagner; m. Poppy Stanley 1957; one s. two d.; ed. Oundle School and Trinity Coll., Cambridge; army service 1944–48; called to the Bar 1952; Q.C. 1990; Fellow, Trinity Coll. Cambridge 1952–; Asst. lecturer, lecturer in law, Univ. of Cambridge 1955–72, Reader in Common and Comparative Law 1972–76, Prof. of Comparative Law 1976–93, Prof. Emer. 1993–, Chair. Faculty of Law 1985–87; Visiting Prof. Chicago 1957, Mexico 1965, 1968, Paris 1976, Bologna 1992, Trento 1995; a Vice-Pres. Int. Acad. of Comparative Law; Corresp. mem. Acad. des Sciences Morales et Politiques; other professional affiliations, etc.; Dr. h.c. (Nat. Univ. Mexico) 1985. *Publications:* Winfield & Jolowicz on Tort, H. F. Jolowicz's Lectures on Jurisprudence 1963, Public Interest Parties and the Active Role of the Judge (with M. Cappelletti) 1975, Droit Anglais (with others) 1992; numerous legal articles. *Leisure interests:* music, reading, winter sports, grandchildren. *Address:* Trinity College, Cambridge CB2 1TQ; Brick Court Chambers, 7–8 Essex Street, London, WC2R 3LD (Offices); West Green House, Barrington, Cambs., CB2 5SA, England (Home). *Telephone:* (01223) 338400; 0171-379 3550 (Offices); (01223) 870495 (Home). *Fax:* (01223) 338564 (College); 0171-379 3558 (Office); (01223) 872852 (Home).

JOLY, Alain; French business executive; b. 18 April 1938, Nantes; s. of Albert Joly and Yvonne Poyet Rolin; m. Marie-Helène Capbern-Gasqueton 1966; two s. one d.; ed. Lycée Louis Le Grand, Paris and Ecole Polytechnique Paris; Engineer, L'Air Liquide 1962–67; Dir. of Operations, Canadian Liquid Air 1967–73; Dir. Corp. Planning, Société L'Air Liquide 1973–76, Regional Man. 1976–78, Gen. Sec. 1978–81, Vice-Pres. 1981, Dir. 1982, Chair. and C.E.O. 1995–; Dir. Lafarge Coppée (now Lafarge) 1993–, Banque Nat. de Paris 1995–; Croix de la Valeur Militaire, Chevalier, Légion d'honneur. *Leisure interests:* tennis, sailing, golf. *Address:* L'Air Liquide S.A., 75 Quai d'Orsay, 75007 Paris, France. *Telephone:* (1) 40.62.55.55.

JONAS, Peter, C.B.E., B.A., L.R.A.M., F.R.C.M., F.R.S.A.; British arts administrator and opera company director; b. 14 Oct. 1946, London; s. of Walter Adolf and Hilda May Jonas; m. Lucy Hull 1989; ed. Worth School, Univ. of Sussex, Royal Northern Coll. of Music, Manchester, Royal Coll. of Music, London, Eastman School of Music, Univ. of Rochester, U.S.A.; Asst. to Music Dir., Chicago Symphony Orchestra 1974–76, Artistic Admin. 1976–85; Dir. of Artistic Admin., The Orchestral Asscn., Chicago 1977–85; Gen. Dir. English Nat. Opera 1985–93; Staatsintendant (Gen. Dir.) Bavarian State Opera, Munich 1993–; mem. Bd. of Man. Nat. Opera Studio 1985–93; mem. Council Royal Coll. of Music 1988–95; mem. Council of Man., London Lighthouse 1990–92; mem. Kuratorium Richard Strauss Gesellschaft 1993–; mem. Advisory Bd. Bayerische Vereinsbank 1994–; Hon. D. Mus. (Sussex) 1993. *Leisure interests:* 20th century architecture, cinema, theatre, skiing, mountains, wine. *Address:* c/o Bayerische Staatsoper, Nationaltheater, Max-Joseph-Platz 2, 80539 Munich, Germany. *Telephone:* (89) 21851000. *Fax:* (89) 21851003.

JONES, Alan Stanley, O.B.E.; Australian racing driver; b. 2 Nov. 1946, Melbourne; s. of Stan Jones (fmr. Australian champion racing driver); m. Beverly Jones 1971; one adopted s.; ed. Xavier Coll., Melbourne; began racing in 1964 in Australia, raced in Britain from 1970; World Champion 1980, runner-up 1979; CanAm Champion 1978. *Grand Prix wins:* 1977 Austrian (Shadow-Ford), 1979 German (Williams-Ford), 1979 Austrian (Williams-Ford), 1979 Dutch (Williams-Ford), 1979 Canadian (Williams-Ford); 1980 Argentine (Williams-Ford), 1980 French (Williams-Ford), 1980 British (Williams-Ford), 1980 Canadian (Williams-Ford), 1980 U.S. (Williams-Ford), 1981 U.S. (Williams-Ford); announced retirement in 1981. *Leisure interests:* collecting interesting cars, farming in Australia.

JONES, Allen, R.A.; British artist; b. 1 Sept. 1937, Southampton; s. of William and Madeline Jones; m. 1st Janet Bowen 1964 (divorced 1978); two d.; m. 2nd Deirdre Morrow 1994; ed. Hornsey School of Art, Royal Coll. of Art; Sec., Young Contemporaries, London 1961; lived in New York 1964–65; Tamarind Lithography Fellowship, Los Angeles 1966; Guest Prof. Dept. of Painting, Univ. of S. Florida 1969; Hochschule für Bildende Künste, Hamburg 1968–70, Hochschule der Künste, Berlin 1982–83; Guest Lecturer Univ. of Calif. 1977; first one-man exhbn., London 1963, one-man exhbns. in U.K., U.S.A., Switzerland, Germany, Italy, Australia, Japan, Netherlands, Belgium, Austria, Spain, China, Argentina, Brazil, Czech Repub., Cyprus, Norway 1963–; many group exhbns. of paintings and graphic work, worldwide 1962–; first travelling retrospective, Europe 1979–80; Welsh Arts Council-sponsored sculpture exhbn. 1992; Commercial Mural Project, Basel 1979; designs for TV and stage in Fed. Repub. of Germany and U.K.; sculptures commissioned for Liverpool Garden Festival 1984, Cotton's Atrium, Pool of London 1987, Sterling Hotel, Heathrow 1990, Riverside Health Authority, Westminster and Chelsea Hosp., London 1993, Swire Properties, Hong Kong 1997, Goodwood 1998; works in many public and pvt. collections in U.K. and elsewhere including Tate Gallery, London, Victoria & Albert Museum, London, Museum of 20th Century, Vienna, Stedelijk Museum, Amsterdam, Museum of Modern Art, New York, Hirshhorn Museum, Washington D.C.; Trustee British Museum 1990; Prix des Jeunes Artistes, Paris Biennale 1963, Art and Work Award, Wapping Arts Trust 1989, Heitland Foundation Award 1995. *Publications:* Allen Jones Figures 1969, Allen Jones Projects 1971, Waitress 1972, Ways and Means 1977, Sheer Magic (Paintings 1959–79) 1979, U.K. 1980, Allen Jones (painting and sculpture) 1963–93 1993, Allen Jones Prints 1995, Allen Jones 1997. *Address:* 41 Charterhouse Square, London, EC1M 6EA, England. *Fax:* 0171-600 1204.

JONES, Alwyn Rice, M.A.; Welsh ecclesiastic; b. 25 March 1934, Capel Curig, Gwynedd; s. of the late John Griffith Jones and Annie Jones (née Roberts); m. Meriel Ann Jones 1967; one d.; ed. Llanrwst Grammar School, Univ. of Wales, Lampeter, Fitzwilliam Coll., Cambridge; ordained Diocese of Bangor, deacon 1958, priest 1959; asst. curate Llanfairisgaer, Bangor 1958–62; sec. and chaplain Student Christian Movt. Colls. Wales 1962–65; chaplain St. Winifred's School, Llanfairfechan 1965–67; Diocesan Dir. of Educ. Diocese of Bangor 1965–75, youth chaplain 1967–72, warden of ordinands 1970–75; asst. tutor in Religious Studies Univ. Coll. of North Wales 1973–76; Hon. Canon Bangor Cathedral 1975; vicar of St. Mary's with Battle 1979–82; Bishop of St. Asaph 1982–; Archbishop of Wales 1991–; Chair. Religious Panel S4C TV 1987; Pres. Council of Churches for Britain and Ireland 1997–; mem. Religious Advisory Panel IBA 1973–75. *Leisure interests:* music, walking. *Address:* Esgobty, St. Asaph, Denbighshire, LL17 0TW, Wales. *Telephone:* (01745) 583503. *Fax:* (01745) 584301.

JONES, Rt. Hon. Aubrey, B.SC.; British politician, economist and industrialist; b. 20 Nov. 1911, Merthyr Tydfil; s. of Evan and Margaret Aubrey Jones; m. Joan Godfrey-Isaacs 1948; two s.; ed. London School of Econs.; on foreign and editorial staff The Times 1937–39 and 1947–48; served with Army Intelligence Staff, War Office and Mediterranean 1940–46; joined British Iron and Steel Fed. as Special Asst. to Chair. 1949, Econ. Dir. 1954 and Gen. Dir. 1955; M.P. for Birmingham (Hall Green) 1950–65; Minister of Fuel and Power 1955–57, of Supply 1957–59; mem. Council of Asscn. with European Coal and Steel Community 1955–57; fmr. Dir. Guest, Keen & Nettlefolds Steel Co. Ltd., fmr. Chair. Staveley Industries Ltd., fmr. Dir. Courtaulds Ltd.; Chair. Nat. Bd. for Prices and Incomes 1965–70; Chair. Laporte Industries (Holdings) Ltd. 1970–72; Dir. Thomas Tilling Ltd. 1970–82, Inbucon Int. Ltd. 1975–79, Black and Decker Ltd. 1977–81; Dir. Cornhill Insurance Co. Ltd. 1971–82, Chair. 1971–73; Hon. Fellow, London School of Econs. 1959, mem. Court of Govs. 1964; Hon. Fellow Commoner, Churchill Coll., Cambridge 1972–73, 1982–86; Regent Lecturer, Univ. of Calif., Berkeley 1968; Visiting Fellow, New Coll. Oxford 1978, Science Policy Research Unit, Univ. of Sussex 1986–92, Hon. Fellow 1993–; Sr. Research Assoc., St. Antony's Coll., Oxford 1979–81; Gov. Nat. Inst. Econ. and Social Research 1967; Hon. Vice-Pres. Consumers' Asscn. 1967–72; Adviser to Public Service Review Comm. of Nigerian Govt. 1973–74; mem. Council Int. Inst. for Strategic Studies 1962–74, Int. Council for Settlement of Investment Disputes, Washington D.C. 1974–81; Leading Adviser to Iranian Govt. on Agricultural Devt. Plan 1974–75; UN Adviser to Iranian Govt. on Public Sector Problems 1975–79, on Productivity, Prices and Incomes 1976–79; Hon. Pres. Oxford Energy Policy Club 1977–88; fmr. Conservative, joined Liberal Party 1980, Pres., Fulham Liberal Democrats 1988. *Publications:* The Pendulum of Politics 1946, Right and Left 1944, Industrial Order 1950, The New Inflation—The Politics of Prices and Incomes 1973, Oil: The Missed Opportunity 1981, Britain's Economy: The Roots of Stagnation 1985. *Leisure interests:* sailing, skiing. *Address:* "Arnen", 120 Limmer Lane, Felpham, Bognor Regis, W. Sussex, PO22 7LP, England. *Telephone:* (01243) 58 2722.

JONES, Barry Owen, A.O., M.A., LL.B., D.SC., D.LITT., D.UNIV., F.A.A., F.A.H.A., F.T.S.E., F.R.S.A.; Australian politician, fmr. public servant, teacher, university lecturer and lawyer; b. 11 Oct. 1932, Geelong, Vic.; s. of Claud Edward Jones and Ruth Marion (née Black) Jones; m. Rosemary Hanbury 1961; M.P. Victorian Parl. 1972–77, House of Reps. 1977–98; Minister for Science 1983–90, Minister for Technology 1983–84, Minister Assisting the Minister for Industry, Tech. and Commerce 1984–87, Minister for Science, Customs and Small Business 1988–90; Minister Assisting the Prime Minister for Science and Tech. 1989–90; Visiting Prof. Wollongong Univ. 1991–, Victoria Univ. of Tech. 1994–; mem. Nat. Comm. for UNESCO 1990–, Exec. Bd. of UNESCO, Paris 1991–95; Chair. House of Reps. Cttee. on Long Term Strategies 1990–96; Nat. Pres. Australian Labor Party 1992–; Chair. Australian Film and TV School 1973–75, Australian Film Inst. 1974–80; Deputy Chair. Australian Council for the Arts 1969–73, Australian Constitutional Convention 1997–98; Vice-Pres., World Heritage Cttee. 1995–96, Australia ICOMOS Inc. 1998–; mem. Australian Film Devt. Corpn. 1970–75, Australian Nat. Library Council 1996–98; Raymond Longford Award (Australian Film Inst.) 1986, Redmond Barry Award (ALIA) 1996; Australian Labor Party. *Publications include:* Macmillan Dictionary of Biography 1981, Sleepers, Wake!: Technology and the Future of Work 1982, Managing Our Opportunities 1984, Living by Our Wits 1986, Dictionary of World Biography 1994. *Leisure interests:* films, music, travel, collecting autographed documents, antique terracottas and paintings, reading. *Address:* GPO Box 496H, Melbourne, Victoria 3001, Australia. *Telephone:* (3) 9500 9231. *Fax:* (3) 9500 9231.

JONES, Ben Joseph, LL.B.; Grenadian politician and lawyer; b. 5 Aug. 1924, St. Andrews; ed. Belair Presbyterian School, Chiswick Polytechnic, London, Gray's Inn, London and Univ. of London; attached to firm of solicitors, London 1962–64; private practice, Grenada 1964–65; magistrate, St. George's, Grenada 1965–66; est. and Dir. Dept. (later Ministry) of External Affairs 1966–67; Opposition Senator 1967–79; Minister of External

Affairs and Legal Affairs 1984–87, of Legal Affairs, External Affairs, Tourism, Agric., Land and Forestry, Attorney Gen. 1987–88, of External Affairs, Agric., Lands, Forestry and Tourism 1988–89; Deputy Prime Minister Jan.–Dec. 1989; Prime Minister 1989–90; Minister of Agric., Lands, Forestry and Fisheries 1990. *Leisure interests:* tennis, gardening, reading. *Address:* Victoria Street, Grenville, St. Andrew's; Moyah, St. Andrew's, Grenada. *Telephone:* 442-7355 (Victoria Street); 442 7844 (Moyah).

JONES, Bill T.; American dancer and choreographer; b. 15 Feb. 1952, Bunnell, Fla.; ed. State Univ. of New York, Binghamton; Co-Founder American Dance Asylum 1973; Co-Founder, Artistic Dir. Bill T. Jones/Arnie Zane Dance Co. 1982–; Choreographer (with Arnie Zane) Pas de Deux for Two 1974, Across the Street 1975, Whosedebabedolbabedoll 1977, Monkey Run Road 1979, Blauvelt Mountain 1980; Choregrapher Negroes for Sale (soloist) 1973, Track Dance 1974, Everybody Works/All Beasts Count 1976, De Sweet Streak to Loveland 1977, The Runner Dreams 1978, Stories, Steps and Stomps 1978, Progresso 1979, Echo 1979, Naming Things Is Only the Intention to Make Things 1979, Floating the Tongue 1979, Sisyphus Act I and II 1980, Open Spaces 1980, Tribeca, Automation, Three Wise Men, Christmas 1980, Secret Pastures 1984, History of Collage 1988, D-Man in the Waters 1989, Dances 1989, Last Supper at Uncle Tom's Cabin/The Promised Land 1991, Love Defined 1991, Aria 1992, Last Night on Earth 1992, Fête 1992, Still/Here 1993 (Edin. Festival 1995), Achilles Loved Patroclus 1993, War Between the States 1993, Still/Here 1994, We Set Out Early . . . Visibility Was Poor 1997; Dir., Choreographer of operas include: New Year 1990 (Co-Dir. BBC TV production), The Mother of Three Sons, Lost in the Stars; Dir. Guthrie Theatre, Minneapolis 1994; Assoc. Choreographer Lyons Opera Ballet 1995–; N.Y. Dance and Performance (Bessie) Award (with Arnie Zane) 1986, Bessie Award for D-Man in the Waters 1989, Dorothy B. Chandler Performing Arts Award 1991, Dance Magazine Award 1993, Edin. Festival Critics' Award (presented to Jones/Zane Dance Co.) 1993, MacArthur Foundation Grant. *Publication:* Last Night on Earth 1995. *Address:* Bill T. Jones/Arnie Zane Dance Company, 853 Broadway, Suite 1706, New York, NY 10003, U.S.A.

JONES, Bryn Terfel; British bass baritone singer; b. 9 Nov. 1965, Pantglas, Snowdonia; s. of Hefin Jones and Nesta Jones; m. Lesley Haliday 1987; two s.; ed. Ysgol Duffryn Nantlle, Pengroes, Gwynedd and Guildhall School of Music and Drama; has appeared in role of Mozart's Figaro at world's leading opera houses including Royal Opera House, Covent Garden, Metropolitan Opera, New York and La Scala, Milan; other roles at Royal Opera House include Masetto, Balstrode, Jochanaan and Falstaff; many concert appearances in Europe, U.S.A. Canada, Japan and Australia; frequent guest soloist with Berlin Philharmonic Orchestra; numerous recordings include The Marriage of Figaro, Britten's Gloriana, Beethoven's Ninth Symphony, Brahms' Requiem; Pres. Nat. Youth Choir of Wales, Festival of Wales; Vice-Pres. Llangollen Int. Eisteddfod; Hon. Fellow, Univ. of Wales, Aberystwyth, Welsh Coll. of Music and Drama, Univ. of Wales, Bangor; Hon. D.Mus. (Glamorgan) 1997; White Robe, Gorsedd; recipient, Kathleen Ferrier Scholarship 1988; Gold Medal Award 1989; Lieder Prize, Cardiff Singer of World Competition 1989; Young Singer of the Year, Gramophone magazine 1992; British Critics' Circle Award 1992; Newcomer of Year, Int. Classic Music Awards 1993; Caecillia Prize for recording of Vagabond 1995; Grammy Award for best classical vocal performance for recording of opera arias 1996; People's Award, Gramophone awards for recording of Vagabond 1996; Britannia Record Club Members' Award for recording of Something Wonderful 1997. *Leisure interests:* golf, collecting fob watches, supporting Manchester United. *Address:* c/o Harlequin Agency, 203 Fidlas Road, Cardiff, CF4 5NA, Wales. *Telephone:* (01222) 750821. *Fax:* (01222) 755971.

JONES, Catherine Zeta; British actress; d. of David James Jones. *Stage appearances include:* The Pyjama Game, Annie, Bugsy Malone, 42nd Street, Street Scene. *Television appearances include:* Darling Buds of May, Out of the Blue, Cinder Path 1994, Return of the Native 1995, Titanic 1996. *Film appearances include:* Scheherazade, Coup de Foudre, Splitting Heirs 1993, Blue Juice 1995, The Phantom 1996, The Mask of Zorro 1997, Entrapment 1998. *Address:* c/o ICM Ltd., Oxford House, 76 Oxford Street, London, W1N 0AX, England. *Telephone:* 0171-636 6565. *Fax:* 0171-323 0101.

JONES, Gen. David Charles, D.F.C.; American air force officer (retd.); b. 9 July 1921, Aberdeen, S. Dak.; s. of Maurice Jones and Helen Meade; m. Lois M. Tarbell 1942; one s. two d.; ed. Univ. of North Dakota and Minot State Coll., N. Dak., U.S.A.F. Flying School, Nat. War Coll.; Commdr. 22nd Air Refueling Squadron 1953–54, 33rd Bomb Squadron 1954; Operations Planner, Bomber Mission Branch, HQ Strategic Air Command Sept.–Dec. 1954, Aide to C.-in-C., SAC 1955–57; Dir. of Material, later Deputy Commdr. for Maintenance, 93rd Bomb Wing 1957–59; Chief, Manned Systems Branch, Deputy Chief and later Chief, Strategic Div., DCS/Operations, HQ U.S.A.F. 1960–64; Commdr. 33rd Tactical Fighter Wing March–Oct. 1965; Insp.-Gen. HQ United States Air Forces in Europe 1965–67, Chief of Staff Jan.–June 1967, Deputy Chief of Staff, Plans and Operations 1967–69; Deputy Chief of Staff, Operations, HQ 7th Air Force, Repub. of Viet Nam 1969, Vice-Commdr. 7th Air Force, Tan Son Nhut Airfield, Repub. of Viet Nam 1969; Commdr. 2nd Air Force 1969–71; Vice-C.-in-C. U.S.A.F.E., later C.-in-C. U.S.A.F.E. and Commdr. 4th Allied Tactical Air Forces, Ramstein Air Base, Fed. Repub. of Germany 1971–74; Chief of Staff, U.S. Air Force 1974–78, Chair. Jt. Chiefs of Staff 1978–82; Dir. USAir, Radio Corpn. of America, Nat. Broadcasting Co., Kemper Group 1982–, US Steel, Nat. Educ. Corpn.; Chair. Bd. Hay Systems Inc.; Hon. D. Hum. Litt. (Nebraska) 1974; Hon. D. Laws (Louisiana Tech. Univ.) 1975; Distinguished Service Medal with Oak Leaf Cluster, Legion of Merit, Distinguished Flying Cross, Bronze Star Medal, Air Medal W/I OLC, and many other decorations. *Leisure interests:* jogging, skiing, racquetball, flying, historical novels.

JONES, (David) Huw, M.A.; British broadcasting executive; b. 5 May 1948, Manchester; s. of late Idris Jones and of Olwen Edwards; m. Siân Marylka Miarczynska 1972; one s. one d.; ed. Cardiff High School for Boys, Jesus Coll., Oxford; pop singer, recording artist, TV presenter 1968–76; Dir., Gen. Man. Sain Recording Co. 1969–81; Chair. Barcud Cyf (TV Facilities), Caernarfon 1981–93; Man. Dir., Producer Teledu'r Tir Glas Cyf (ind. production co.) 1982–93; first Chair. Teledwyr Annibynnol Cymru (Welsh Ind. Producers) 1984–86; Chief Exec. S4C (Welsh Fourth Channel) 1994–; Hon. Fellow Univ. of Wales, Aberystwyth. *Leisure interests:* reading, cycling, walking. *Address:* S4C, Parc Ty Glas, Llanishen, Cardiff, CF4 5DU, Wales. *Telephone:* (1222) 741400. *Fax:* (1222) 754444.

JONES, Dean Mervyn; Australian cricketer (retd.); b. 24 March 1961, Coburg, Vic.; m. Jane Jones 1986; one d.; ed. Mt. Waverley High School, Vic.; right-hand batsman; played for Victoria 1981–82 to 1997–98; (Capt. 1993–94 to 1995–96), Durham 1992, Derbyshire (Capt.) 1996 to 1997, resigning mid-way through season and returning home; played in 52 Tests for Australia 1983–84 to 1992–93, scoring 3,631 runs (average 46.5) including 11 hundreds; toured England 1989; scored 19,188 first-class runs (55 hundreds); 164 limited-overs internationals. *Publication:* Deano: My Call 1995. *Leisure interests:* golf, baseball, looking after his two Rottweilers.

JONES, Douglas Samuel, M.B.E., C.MATH., C.ENG., F.R.S., F.R.S.E.; British professor of mathematics; b. 10 Jan. 1922, Corby, Northants.; s. of Jesse Dewis Jones and Bessie Streather; m. Ivy Styles 1950; one s. one d.; ed. Wolverhampton Grammar School, Corpus Christi Coll., Univ. of Oxford; Flight Lieut., R.A.F. Volunteer Reserve 1941–45; Commonwealth Fellow, Mass. Inst. of Tech. 1947–48; Asst. Lecturer, then Lecturer, Univ. of Manchester 1948–54, Sr. Lecturer 1955–57; Visiting Prof., New York Univ. 1955, 1962–63; Prof. of Math., Univ. of Keele 1957–64; Ivory Prof. of Math., Univ. of Dundee 1965–92, Emer. Prof. 1992–; mem. Univ. Grants Cttee. 1976–86, Chair. Math. Sciences sub-cttee. 1976–86; mem. Computer Bd. 1976–82; mem. Open Univ. Visiting Cttee. 1982–87; mem. Council, Inst. of Math. and its applications 1982–97 (Pres. 1988–90); Hon. Fellow, Corpus Christi Coll., Univ. of Oxford; Hon. D.Sc. (Strathclyde); Van Der Pol Gold Medal, Int. Scientific Radio Union; Keith Prize, R.S.E., Naylor Prize of London Math, Soc. *Publications include:* Electrical and Mechanical Oscillations 1961, The Theory of Electromagnetism 1964, Introductory Analysis (vol.1) 1969, (vol.2) 1970, Methods in Electromagnetic Wave Propagation 1979, 1994, Elementary Information Theory 1979, The Theory of Generalised Functions 1982, Differential Equations and Mathematical Biology 1983, Acoustic and Electromagnetic Waves 1986, Assembly Programming and the 8086 Microprocessor 1988, 80 × 86 Assembly Programming 1991, Introduction to Asymptotics 1997. *Address:* Department of Mathematics, The University, Dundee, DD1 4HN (Office); 1 The Nurseries, St. Madoes, Glencarse, Perth, PH2 7NX, Scotland (Home). *Telephone:* (01382) 344486 (Office); (01738) 860544 (Home).

JONES, (Everett) Le Roi (Imamu Baraka); American poet and dramatist; b. 7 Oct. 1934, Newark, N.J.; s. of Coyette L. Jones and Anna Lois (Russ) Jones; m. 1st Hettie R. Cohen 1958 (divorced 1965); two step-d.; m. 2nd Sylvia Robinson (Bibi Amina Baraka) 1966; five c.; one step-c.; ed. Howard Univ., New School and Columbia Univ.; served with U.S.A.F.; taught poetry at New School Social Research, drama at Columbia Univ., literature at Univ. of Buffalo; Visiting Prof., San Francisco State; began publishing 1958; founded Black Arts Repertory Theater School, Harlem 1964, Spirit House, Newark 1966; Whitney Fellowship 1963, Guggenheim Fellowship 1965; Fellow, Yoruba Acad. 1965; Visiting Lecturer, Afro-American Studies, Yale Univ. 1977–78; Asst. Prof. of African Studies State Univ. of New York 1980–83, Assoc. Prof. 1983–85, Prof. 1985–; mem. Int. Co-ordinating Cttee. of Congress of African Peoples; mem. Black Acad. of Arts and Letters. *Publications include:* Preface to a Twenty Volume Suicide Note 1961, Dante 1962, Blues People 1963, The Dead Lecturer 1963, Dutchman 1964, The Moderns 1964, The System of Dante's Hell 1965, Home 1965, Jello 1965, Experimental Death Unit 1965, The Baptism—The Toilet 1966, Black Mass 1966, Mad Heart 1967, Slave Ship 1967, Black Music 1967, Tales 1968, Great Goodness of Life 1968, Black Magic, Four Black Revolutionary Plays 1969, Black Art 1969, In Our Terribleness 1970, Junkies are Full of Shhh ..., Bloodrites 1970, Raise 1971, It's Nation Time 1971, Kawaida Studies 1972, Spirit Reach 1972, Afrikan Revolution 1973, Hard Facts: Excerpts 1975, Spring Song 1979, AM/TRAK 1979, In the Tradition: For Black Arthur Blythe 1980, Reggae or Not! Poems 1982, The Autobiography of Le Roi Jones/Amiri Baraka 1984, Thornton Dial: Images of the Tiger 1993, Shy's, Wise, Y's: The Griot's Tale 1994; several film scripts; ed. Hard Facts 1976. *Address:* c/o State University of New York, Department of African Studies, Stony Brook, NY 11794, U.S.A.

JONES, George; American country music singer; b. 12 Sept. 1931, Saratoga, Texas; s. of George Jones and Clara Washington Jones; m. 3rd Tammy Wynette 1969 (divorced 1975, died 1998); m. 4th Nancy Sepulvado 1983; began singing for money on streets in Beaumont aged 11; performed on local radio and bars; began recording career with single No Money in This Deal 1954; has recorded over 200 albums. *Publication:* I Lived to Tell It All (autobiography). *Address:* Razor & Tie, 214 Sullivan Street, Suite 4A, New York, NY 10012, U.S.A.

JONES, Grace; American singer, model and actress; b. 19 May 1952, Spanishtown, Jamaica; d. of Robert and Marjorie P. Jones; one s.; m. Atila Altaunbay 1996; went to New York at age of 12; abandoned Spanish studies at Syracuse Univ. for first stage role, Phila.; became fashion model in New York, then Paris; made first album, Portfolio, for Island Records 1977; debut as disco singer New York 1977; films include: Conan the Destroyer, A View to a Kill 1985, Vamp, Straight to Hell, Siesta, Boomerang 1991; albums include: Fame, Muse, Island Life, Slave to the Rythymn; opened La Vie en Rose restaurant, New York 1987.

JONES, Dame Gwyneth, D.B.E., F.R.C.M.; British soprano; b. 7 Nov. 1936, Pontnewynydd, Mon., Wales; d. of Edward George Jones and Violet Webster; m. Till Haberfeld; one d.; ed. Royal Coll. of Music, London, Accad. Chigiana, Siena, Zürich Int. Opera Centre; with Zürich Opera House 1962–63; a Prin. Dramatic Soprano Royal Opera House, Covent Garden 1963–; with Vienna State Opera House 1966–, Deutsche Oper Berlin 1966–, Bavarian State Opera 1967–; guest performances in numerous opera houses throughout the world including La Scala, Milan, Rome Opera, Berlin State Opera, Munich State Opera, Hamburg, Paris, Metropolitan Opera, New York, San Francisco, Los Angeles, Zürich, Geneva, Dallas, Chicago, Teatro Colón, Buenos Aires, Tokyo, Bayreuth Festival, Salzburg Festival, Arena di Verona, Edinburgh Festival and Welsh Nat. Opera; Kammersängerin in Austria and Bavaria; known for many opera roles including Leonara, Il Trovatore, Desdemona, Otello, Aida, Aida (Verdi), Leonore, Fidelio (Beethoven), Senta, The Flying Dutchman (Wagner), Medea, Medea (Cherubini), Sieglinde, Die Walküre (Wagner), Lady Macbeth, Macbeth (Verdi), Elizabeth, Don Carlos (Verdi), Madame Butterfly (Puccini), Tosca (Puccini), Donna Anna, Don Giovanni (Mozart), Salome (R. Strauss), Kundry, Parsifal and Isolde, Tristan und Isolde (Wagner), Helena, Aegyptische Helena (R. Strauss), Färberin, Frau ohne Schatten, Elektra, Elektra (R. Strauss), Elizabeth/Venus, Tannhäuser (Wagner), Marschallin, Der Rosenkavalier (R. Strauss), Brünnhilde, Der Ring des Nibelungen (Wagner), Ortrud, Lohengrin (Wagner), Minnie, Fanciulla del West (Puccini), Norma (Bellini), Erwartung (Schoenberg), La voix humaine (Poulenc); TV films: Fidelio, Aida, Flying Dutchman, Beethoven 9th Symphony, Tannhäuser, Poppea (Monteverdi), Rosenkavalier (R. Strauss), Die Walküre, Siegfried, Götterdämmerung, Die lustige Witwe; recordings for Decca, DGG, Philips, Chandos, EMI, CBS; Hon. D.Mus. (Wales); hon. mem. Vienna State Opera 1989; Shakespeare Prize, Hamburg 1987, Bundesverdienstkreuz (Germany) 1988, Commdr. des Arts et Lettres (France) 1993. *Address:* P.O. Box 556, 8037 Zürich, Switzerland.

JONES, James Earl; American actor; b. 17 Jan. 1931, Miss.; m. Cecilia Hurt 1982; ed. Univ. of Mich.; numerous stage appearances on Broadway and elsewhere include Master Harold . . . And the Boys, Othello, King Lear, Hamlet, Paul Robeson, A Lesson From Aloes, Of Mice and Men, The Iceman Cometh, A Hand is on the Gate, The Cherry Orchard, Danton's Death, Fences; frequent TV appearances; cast as voice of Darth Vader in films Star Wars, The Empire Strikes Back and The Return of the Jedi; Tony Award for role in stage version and Golden Globe Award for role in screen version of The Great White Hope; Hon. D.F.A. (Princeton, Yale, Mich.); numerous awards. *Films include:* Matewan, Gardens of Stone, Soul Man, My Little Girl, The Man, The End of the Road, Dr Strangelove, Conan the Barbarian, The Red Tide, A Piece of the Action, The Last Remake of Beau Geste, The Greatest, The Heretic, The River Niger, Deadly Hero, Claudine, The Great White Hope, The Comedians, Coming to America, Three Fugitives, Field of Dreams, Patriot Games, Sommersby, The Lion King (voice), Clear and Present Danger, Cry the Beloved Country, Lone Star, A Family Thing, Gang Related, Rebound. *Address:* c/o Richard Bauman & Associates, 5757 Wilshire Boulevard, Suite 473, Los Angeles, CA 90036, U.S.A.

JONES, James Larkin (Jack), C.H., M.B.E.; British trade unionist; b. 29 March 1913, Liverpool; s. of George and Anne Sophie Jones; m. Evelyn Mary Taylor 1938; two s.; ed. Liverpool; worked in eng. and dock industries 1927–39; served in Spanish Civil War; Midlands Official, Transport and Gen. Workers' Union 1939–63, Exec. Officer 1963–69, Gen. Sec. 1969–78; Dist. Sec. Confed. of Shipbuilding and Eng. Unions 1939–63; mem. Labour Party Nat. Exec. Cttee. 1964–67; Deputy Chair. Nat. Ports Council 1967–78; mem. Council, Trades Union Congress 1968–78; Chair. Int. Cttee., TUC 1972–78; mem. Exec. Bd. Int. Confed. of Free Trade Unions, European Trade Union Confed., Pres. EFTA Trade Union Council 1973–; British Overseas Trade Bd. 1975–78, Advisory, Conciliation and Arbitration Service (ACAS) 1975–78; mem. Royal Comm. on Criminal Procedure 1978–; mem. NEDC 1969–78; mem. Econ. and Social Cttee., EEC 1975–78; Pres. Retd. Mems. Asscns., TGWU 1978–, Nat. Pensioners' Convention 1992–; Vice-Pres. Int. Transport Workers Fed. 1974–80, Age Concern (England), Anti-Apartheid Movement, European Fed. of Retd. and Elderly Persons 1990–; Chair. Nat. Museum of Labour History 1990–; Hon. mem. Int. Longshoremen's Asscn. (U.S.A.) 1973, Union Gen. de Trabajadores de España (Spain) 1975; Hon. D.Litt. (Warwick); Fellow, Nuffield Coll., Oxford 1970–78, Chartered Inst. of Transport 1971; Assoc. Fellow L.S.E. 1978; Hon. Fellow John Moore Univ., Liverpool 1988, Lancashire Cen. Univ. 1993; City of Coventry Medal of Merit; Freeman City of London; Dimbleby Lecture, BBC-TV 1977. *Publications:* Incompatibles 1968, A to Z of Trade Unionism and Industrial Relations 1982, A Union Man (autobiog.) 1986. *Leisure interests:* walking, painting. *Address:* 74 Ruskin Park House, Champion Hill, London, SE5 8TH, England (Home). *Telephone:* 0171-274 7067.

JONES, James Robert, LL.B.; American diplomatist; b. 5 May 1939, Muskogee, Okla.; s. of Robert Jones and Margaret Wich; m. Olivia Barclay 1968; two s.; ed. Univ. of Oklahoma and Georgetown Univ.; Asst. to Pres. Johnson, White House, Washington, D.C. 1965–69; practising lawyer and business consultant, Tulsa, Okla. 1969–73; mem. U.S. Congress 1973–87; partner, Dickstein, Shapiro & Moran (law firm), Washington, D.C. 1987–89; Chair. and C.E.O. American Stock Exchange, New York 1989–93; Amb. to Mexico 1993–97; Pres. Warnaco Int. 1997–98; Steiger Award 1979. *Leisure interests:* golf, reading. *Address:* 544 East 86th, # 14E, New York, NY 10028, U.S.A.

JONES, Rt. Rev. James Stuart, B.A.; British ecclesiastic; b. 18 Aug. 1948; s. of Maj. James Stuart Anthony Jones and Helen Deans Dick Telfer (née McIntyre); m. Sarah Caroline Rosalind Marrow 1980; three d.; ed. Univs. of Exeter and Keele; asst. master Sevenoaks School 1971–75; producer Scripture Union 1975–81; asst. curate Christ Church, Clifton 1982–84, Assoc. Vicar 1984–90; Vicar Emmanuel Church, Croydon 1990–94; Bishop of Hull 1994–98; Bishop of Liverpool 1998–. *Publications include:* Following Jesus 1984, Finding God 1987, Why Do People Suffer? 1993, The Power and the Glory 1994. *Leisure interests:* swimming, opera and holidays in France. *Address:* Bishop's Lodge, Woolton Park, Woolton, Liverpool, L25 6DT, England. *Telephone:* (0151) 421 0831. *Fax:* (0151) 428 3055.

JONES, Le Roi (see Jones, (Everett) Le Roi).

JONES, Michael Frederick; British journalist; b. 3 July 1937, Gloucester; s. of late Glyn F. Jones and Elizabeth Coopey; m. Sheila Dawes 1959; three s.; ed. Crypt Grammar School, Gloucester; reporter on provincial newspaper 1956–64; Financial Times 1964–65; Daily Telegraph 1965–67; Business News Asst. Ed. The Times 1967–70; Man. Ed. The Asian, Hong Kong 1971; News Ed. Sunday Times 1972, Political Corresp. 1975, Political Ed. 1984, Assoc. Ed. 1990–95, Assoc. Ed. (Politics) 1995–; Chair. Parl. Press Gallery, House of Commons 1989–91. *Leisure interests:* exploring Britain, reading history. *Address:* The Sunday Times, 1 Pennington Street, London, E1 9XW, England. *Telephone:* 0171-782 5000. *Fax:* 0171-782 5237.

JONES, Philip James, D.PHIL., F.B.A.; British historian and academic; b. 19 Nov. 1921, London; s. of John David Jones and Caroline Susan Jones (née Davies); m. Carla Susini 1954; one s. one d.; ed. St. Dunstan's Coll., London and Wadham Coll., Oxford; Asst. Lecturer in Modern History, Glasgow Univ. 1949–50; Lecturer in Medieval History, Leeds Univ. 1950–61, Reader 1961–63; Fellow and Tutor in Modern History, Brasenose Coll., Oxford 1963–89, Librarian 1965–89, Emer. Fellow 1989–; Eileen Power Memorial Studentship 1956–57; Corresp. mem. Deputazione Toscana di Storia Patria 1975–; Serena Medal for Italian Studies 1988. *Publications:* The Malatesta of Rimini 1974, Economia e Società nell'Italia medioevale 1980; contribs. to Cambridge Economic History I 1966, Storia d'Italia, II 1974, Storia d'Italia, Annali, I 1978, The Italian City-State: from commune to signoria 1997, articles. *Address:* 167 Woodstock Road, Oxford, OX2 7NA, England. *Telephone:* (01865) 557953.

JONES, Philip Mark, C.B.E., F.R.N.C.M., F.R.C.M., F.G.S.M., F.R.S.A.; British musician; b. 12 March 1928, Bath; s. of John and Mabel Jones; m. Ursula Strebi 1956; ed. Battersea Grammar School, London, Royal Coll. of Music; Prin. Trumpet, all major London orchestras 1949–72; pioneer of chamber music for brass ensembles; Founder and Dir. Philip Jones Brass Ensemble 1951–86; Head of School of wind and percussion, Royal Northern Coll. of Music, Manchester 1975–77; Head, Wind and Percussion Dept., Guildhall School of Music and Drama, London 1983–88; Prin. Trinity Coll. of Music, London 1988–94; mem. Arts Council of G.B. 1984–88; Gov. Chetham's School, Manchester 1988–94; Chair. Musicians' Benevolent Fund 1995–; mem. Royal Soc. of Musicians, Worshipful Co. of Musicians, Park Lane Group Artistic Cttee.; Hon. R.A.M., Hon. F.T.C.L.; Grand Prix du Disque 1977, Composers Guild Award 1979, Cobbett Medal of the Worshipful Company of Musicians 1986, Cesare Bendinelli Award, Verona 1993; Freeman, City of London 1988. *Recordings:* over 50 gramophone records with Philip Jones Brass Ensemble. *Publications:* Just Brass music series (Ed.) 1973–89. *Leisure interests:* history, mountain walking, skiing. *Address:* 14 Hamilton Terrace, London, NW8 9UG, England. *Telephone:* 0171-286 9155. *Fax:* 0171-286 9155.

JONES, Quincy; American composer, arranger, conductor and trumpeter; b. 14 March 1933, Chicago; s. of Quincy Delight and Sarah Jones; m. 2nd Peggy Lipton; two d.; three c. by previous m.; one d. by Nastassia Kinski (q.v.); ed. Seattle Univ., Berklee School of Music and Boston Conservatory; trumpeter, arranger, Lionel Hampton Orchestra 1950–53; arranger for orchestras and singers inc. Frank Sinatra, Dinah Washington, Count Basie, Sarah Vaughan and Peggy Lee; organizer and trumpeter, Dizzy Gillespie Orchestra, Dept. of State tour of Near and Middle East and S. America 1956; Music Dir. Barchlay Disques, Paris; led own European tour 1960; Music Dir. Mercury Records 1961, Vice-Pres. 1964; conductor of numerous film scores; composer, actor in film Blues for Trumpet and Koto; albums include Body Heat 1974, The Dude 1981, Back on the Block 1989; producer recordings of Off the Wall 1980 by Michael Jackson (q.v.), Thriller 1982, Bad, videotape Portrait of An Album: Frank Sinatra with Quincy Jones and Orchestra 1986; German Jazz Fed. Award; Edison Int. Award (Sweden); Downbeat Critics Poll award; Downbeat Readers Poll award; Billboard

Trendsetters award 1983; Martell Foundation Humanitarian award 1986, Lifetime Achievement Award, Nat. Acad. Songwriters 1989, Jean Hersholt Humanitarian Award 1995; several Grammy awards etc.; Dr. h.c. (Berklee Music Coll.) 1983; Scopus Award (Hebrew Univ.) 1993, (Clark Univ.) 1993. *Address:* Rogers and Cowan, 3800 Barham Boulevard, Suite 503, Los Angeles, CA 90068, U.S.A.

JONES, Stephen John Moffat, B.A. (HONS); British milliner; b. 31 May 1957, West Kirby, Cheshire; s. of Gordon Jones and Margaret Jones; ed. Liverpool Coll., St. Martins School of Art; milliner 1980–, collaborating with int. designers including Jean-Paul Gaultier, Comme des Garçons, Claude Montana, John Galliano, Christian Dior (Paris) 1997–; colour creator for Shiseido Cosmetics; licences in Japan for gloves, sunglasses, kimonos. *Leisure interest:* sculpture. *Address:* 36 Great Queen Street, London, WC2B 5AA, England. *Telephone:* 0171-242 0770. *Fax:* 0171-242 0796.

JONES, Steve; British scientist; b. 24 March 1944, Aberystwyth, Wales; ed. Wirral Grammar School; fmr. Head Galton Lab.; Prof. of Genetics Univ. Coll., London; column writer The Daily Telegraph; Reith Lecturer 1991. *Publications:* The Language of the Genes, In the Blood. *Address:* c/o University College, London, Gower Street, London, WC1E 6BT, England. *Telephone:* 0171-387 7050. *Fax:* 0171-383 2048.

JONES, Sir Thomas Philip, Kt., C.B.; British business executive; b. 13 July 1931, Erith; s. of Mary Elizabeth Jones and William Ernest Jones; m. Mary Phillips 1955; two s.; ed. Cowbridge Grammar School, Jesus Coll., Oxford; Asst. Prin., Ministry of Supply 1955; Prin., Ministry of Aviation 1959; on loan to H.M. Treasury 1964–66; Prin. Private Sec. to Minister of Aviation 1966–67; Asst. Sec., Ministry of Tech., then to Ministry of Aviation Supply 1967–71; Under-Sec., Dept. of Trade and Industry 1971, Under Sec., Dept. of Energy 1974, Deputy Sec. 1976–83; mem. BNOC 1980–82; Chair. Electricity Council 1983–90, Total Oil Marine PLC 1990–98, Total Oil Holdings Ltd. 1990–98; Dir. IVO Energy 1990–97, Gas Transmission 1990–92. *Leisure interests:* walking, watching rugby, football, reading. *Address:* 62 Tachbrook Street, London, SW1V 2NA, England. *Telephone:* 0171-233 7107.

JONES, Tom, O.B.E.; British singer; b. (as Thomas Jones Woodward) 7 June 1940, Treforest, Glamorgan; m. Melinda Trenchard 1956; one s.; made first hit record It's Not Unusual 1965; other records include Once Upon A Time, Green Green Grass of Home, I'll Never Fall in Love Again, I'm Coming Home, Delilah, Help Yourself, I Who Have Nothing, Close Up, Body and Soul, A Boy From Nowhere 1987, Kiss 1988, Carrying A Torch 1991; appeared in TV shows Beat Room, Top Gear, Thank Your Lucky Stars, Sunday Night at the London Palladium; toured U.S.A. 1965; appeared in Ed Sullivan Show at Copacabana, New York, and in variety show This Is Tom Jones in U.K. and U.S.A. 1969; acted and sang in live performance of Dylan Thomas' Under Milkwood 1992; made 26 singles with Decca, 16 albums, including The Complete Tom Jones 1992; appeared in film Mars Attacks! 1996; Hon. Fellow Welsh Coll. of Music and Drama 1994; Britain's Most Popular Male Singer in Melody Maker Poll 1967, 1968; Hon. Fellow Welsh Coll. of Music and Drama 1994. *Address:* c/o Tom Jones Enterprises, 10100 Santa Monica Blvd., Suite 348, Los Angeles, CA 90067, U.S.A.

JONES, Tommy Lee; American actor; b. 15 Sept. 1946, San Saba, Tex.; m. Kimberlea Cloughley 1981; ed. Harvard Univ.; Broadway debut in A Patriot for Me; other Broadway appearances include Four in a Garden, Ulysses in Night Town, Fortune and Men's Eyes; Emmy Award for TV role as Gary Gilmon in The Executioner's Song; other TV appearances include The Amazing Howard Hughes, Lonesome Dove, The Rainmaker, Cat on a Hot Tin Roof, Yuri Nosenko, KGB, April Morning. *Films include:* Love Story 1970, Eliza's Horoscope, Jackson County Jail, Rolling Thunder, The Betsy, Eyes of Laura Mars, Coal Miner's Daughter, Back Roads, Nate and Hayes, River Rat, Black Moon Rising, The Big Town, Stormy Monday, The Package, Firebirds, JFK, Under Siege, House of Cards, The Fugitive, Blue Sky, Heaven and Earth, Natural Born Killers, The Client, Blue Sky, Cobb, Batman Forever, Men In Black 1997, Volcano 1997, Marshals 1997, Small Soldiers (voice) 1998.

JONG, Erica Mann, M.A.; American author and poet; b. 26 March 1942, New York; d. of Seymour Mann and Eda (Mirsky) Mann; m. 1st Allan Jong (divorced 1975); m. 3rd Jonathan Fast 1977 (divorced 1983); one d.; m. 4th Kenneth David Burrows 1989; ed. Barnard Coll. and Columbia Univ., New York; mem. Faculty, English Dept. City Univ. of New York 1964–65, 1969–70; Overseas Div. Univ. of Md. 1967–69; mem. Literature Panel, N.Y. State Council on Arts 1972–74; mem. Faculty Salzburg Seminar, Salzburg, Austria 1993; Bess Hokin Prize, Poetry magazine 1971, Alice Faye di Castagnola Award, Poetry Soc. of America 1972, Prix Littéraire, Deauville Film Festival 1997; Nat. Endowment Arts grantee 1973; Hon. Fellow (Welsh Coll. of Music and Drama) 1994. *Publications:* poems: Fruits & Vegetables 1971, Half-Lives 1973, Loveroot 1975, At the Edge of the Body 1979, Ordinary Miracles 1983, Becoming Light 1991; novels: Fear of Flying 1973, How to Save Your Own Life 1977, Fanny 1980, Parachutes and Kisses 1984, Serenissima; a Novel of Venice 1987 (reissued as Shylock's Daughter 1995), Any Woman's Blues 1990, Inventing Memory 1997; non-fiction: Witches 1981, Megan's Book of Divorce (for children) 1984, The Devil at Large: Erica Jong on Henry Miller 1993, Fear of Fifty 1994, What Women Want 1998; Composer Zipless: Songs of Abandon from the Erotic Poetry of Erica Jong 1995. *Leisure interests:* sailing, flying. *Address:* Erica Jong Productions, c/o K. D. Burrows, 425 Park Avenue, New York, NY 10019, U.S.A. *Telephone:* (212) 980-6922. *Fax:* (212) 421-5279.

JONG, Petrus J. S. de, D.S.C.; Netherlands politician and naval officer; b. 3 April 1915, Apeldoorn; m. Anna Geertriida Jacoba Henriette Bartels; three c.; ed. Royal Naval Coll.; entered Netherlands Royal Navy 1931, commissioned 1934; submarine commdr. during Second World War; Adjutant to Minister for Navy 1948; Capt. of frigate De Zeeuw 1951; Staff Officer on staff Allied Commdr.-in-Chief, Channel, Portsmouth 1953; Adjutant to Queen of Netherlands 1955; Capt. of destroyer Gelderland 1958; State Sec. for Defence 1959–63; Minister of Defence 1963–67; Prime Minister and Minister of Gen. Affairs 1967–71; mem. First Chamber (Parl.) 1971–74; Catholic Party.

JONSEN, Albert R., M.A., PH.D., S.T.M.; American professor of ethics in medicine; b. 4 April 1931, San Francisco; s. of Albert R. Jonsen and Helen C. Sweigert; m. Mary E. Carolan 1976; ed. Gonzaga Univ., Spokane, Wash., Santa Clara Univ., Calif. and Yale Univ.; Instructor in Philosophy, Loyola Univ. of Los Angeles 1956–59; Instructor in Divinity, Yale Univ. 1966–67; Asst., Assoc. Prof. in Philosophy and Theology, Univ. of San Francisco 1968–73, Pres. 1969–72; Prof. of Ethics in Medicine and Chief, Div. of Medical Ethics, Univ. of Calif., San Francisco 1973–87; Prof. of Ethics in Medicine, Chair. Dept. of Medical History and Ethics, Univ. of Wash., Seattle 1987–; Commr. US Nat. Comm. for Protection of Human Subjects of Biomedical and Behavioral Research 1974–78; Commr. President's Comm. for Study of Ethical Problems in Medicine and in Biomedical and Behavioral Research 1979–82; mem. Artificial Heart Assessment Panel, Nat. Heart and Lung Inst. 1972–73, 1984–86; mem. Nat. Bd. of Medical Examiners 1985–88; Consultant American Bd. of Internal Medicine 1978–84; mem. N.A.S. Inst. of Medicine; mem. Cttee. on AIDS Research N.A.S.; Chair. N.A.S. Panel on the Social Impact of AIDS 1989–92, Nat. Advisory Bd. on Ethics and Reproduction 1991–96; Pres. Soc. for Health and Human Values 1986; Guggenheim Fellowship 1986–87. *Publications:* Responsibility in Modern Religious Ethics 1968, Ethics of Newborn Intensive Care 1976, Clinical Ethics (with M. Siegler and W. Winslade) 1982, The Abuse of Casuistry (with S. Toulmin) 1986, The Old Ethics and the New Medicine 1990, The Impact of AIDs on American Society (with J. Stryker) 1993, The Birth of Bioethics: An Historical Memoir of the Origins and Growth of Bioethics in the United States 1947–87 1997. *Leisure interests:* sketching, swimming, walking, music. *Address:* Department of Medical History and Ethics, Box 357120, University of Washington, Seattle, WA 98195, U.S.A.

JOPLIN, Graham Frank, M.B., CH.B., F.R.C.P., PH.D.; British professor of clinical endocrinology; b. 11 May 1927, Wellington, N.Z.; s. of the late Frank Joplin and Mary Joplin; m. Helen Logan 1959; two d.; ed. Wellington Boys' Coll., Victoria Univ., Wellington and Otago Univ. Medical School, Dunedin; rotating internship Wellington Hosp. 1952–53; Pathology Registrar, Palmerston North Hosp. 1954; House Physician Hammersmith, Cen. Middx., and Brompton Hosps. London 1955–56; Registrar, Sr. Registrar, Hammersmith Hosp. 1957–63, Hon. Consultant Physician 1963–89, Sr. Lecturer, Reader, Prof. of Clinical Endocrinology; Wellcome Clinical Research Fellowship 1963–67. *Publications:* approx. 300 research papers on mostly endocrine topics, published in medical journals. *Leisure interests:* gardening, travel. *Address:* Woodview, Warren Road, Kingston, Surrey, KT2 7HN, England. *Telephone:* 0181-942 8435.

JOPLING, Baron (Life Peer), cr. 1997, of Ainderby Quernhow in the County of North Yorkshire, **(Thomas) Michael Jopling,** P.C., B.SC., D.L.; British politician and farmer; b. 10 Dec. 1930, Ripon, Yorks.; s. of Mark Bellerby Jopling; m. Gail Dickinson 1958; two s.; ed. Cheltenham Coll. and King's Coll., Newcastle upon Tyne; mem. Thirsk Rural Dist. Council 1958–64; Conservative M.P. for Westmorland 1964–83, Westmorland and Lonsdale 1983–97; Jt. Sec. Conservative Parl. Agric. Cttee. 1966–70; Parl. Pvt. Sec. to Minister of Agric. 1970–71; an Asst. Govt. Whip 1971–73; Lord Commr. of the Treasury 1973–74; an Opposition Spokesman on Agric. 1974–75, 1976–79; Shadow Minister of Agric. 1975–76; Parl. Sec. to H.M. Treasury and Chief Whip 1979–83; Minister of Agric., Fisheries and Food 1983–87; mem. Nat. Council, Nat. Farmers' Union 1962–64, U.K. Exec., Commonwealth Parl. Assen. 1974–79, 1987–97, Vice-Chair. 1977–79, Int. Exec. 1988–89; Hon. Sec. British American Parl. Group 1987–, Select Cttee. on Foreign Affairs 1987–97; Chair. Select Cttee. on Sittings of the House 1991–92; Pres. Auto-Cycle Union 1989–; Hon. D.C.L. (Newcastle) 1992; D. L. Cumbria 1991–97, N. Yorks. 1998–. *Address:* Ainderby Hall, Thirsk, North Yorks., YO7 4HZ, England. *Telephone:* (01845) 567224.

JÖRBERG, Lennart, PH.D.; Swedish professor of economic history; b. 26 Jan. 1927, Varberg; ed. Lund and Harvard Univs.; Assoc. Prof. Lund Univ. 1961–70; Research Fellow, Council for Social Sciences, Stockholm 1970–73; Prof. of Econ. History, Lund Univ. 1973–92; mem. Royal Acad. of Sciences, Stockholm. *Publications:* Growth and Fluctuations of Swedish Industry 1869–1912 1961, A History of Prices in Sweden 1732–1914 (2 vols.) 1972, Swedish Entrepreneurs during the Industrial Breakthrough 1870–1885, 1988. *Address:* c/o Department of Economic History, School of Economics and Management, P.O. Box 7083, 220 07 Lund, Sweden.

JORDAN, Hamilton (see Jordan, W. H. M.).

JORDAN, Michael Hugh, M.S.CHEM.E.; American broadcasting and media executive; b. 15 June 1936, Kansas City, Mo.; m. Kathryn Hiett 1961; one

s. one d.; ed. Yale and Princeton Univs.; consultant prin. McKinsey & Co. 1964–74; Dir. Financial Planning PepsiCo 1974–76, Sr. Vice-Pres. Planning and Devt. 1976–77, Sr. Vice-Pres. Mfg. Operations Frito-Lay Div. PepsiCo Int. 1977–82, Pres., C.E.O. 1983–85, Pres. PepsiCo Foods Int. 1982–83, Exec. Vice-Pres., Chief Financial Officer PepsiCo Inc. 1985–86, Pres. 1986, also Bd. Dirs., Pres., C.E.O. PepsiCo Worldwide 1987–92; Chair., C.E.O. Westinghouse Electric Corpn. 1993–; Chair. Centre for Excellence in Ed. 1988–92; Chair., Bd. Dirs., partner Clayton, Dubilier and Rice 1992–93; now Chair. CBS; mem. Bd. Dirs. Melville Corpn., Rhone-Poulenc Rorer, Aetna, Dell Computers Inc., United Negro Coll. Fund 1986–. *Address:* CBS Gateway Center, 51 West 52nd Street, New York, NY 10019, U.S.A.

JORDAN, Michael Jeffery; American basketball and baseball player; b. 17 Feb. 1963, Brooklyn, N.Y.; s. of the late James Jordan and of Delores Jordan; m. Juanita Vanoy 1989; two s. one d.; ed. Univ. of N.C.; player for Chicago Bulls, Nat. Basketball Asscn. (NBA) 1984–93 1995–98 (NBA Champions 1991, 1992, 1993, 1996, 1997, 1998), Birmingham Barons baseball team 1993; mem. NCAA championship team 1982, U.S. Olympic team 1984, NBA All-Star team 1985–91; with Nashville Sounds 1994–95; holds record for most points in NBA playoff game with 63; Seagram's NBA Player of the Year 1987; Most Valuable Player, NBA All-Star Game 1988, NBA Most Valuable Player 1988, 1991, 1992, 1996, 1998; named world's highest paid athlete, Forbes Magazine 1992; retd. 1998. *Publications:* Rare Air: Michael on Michael (autobiog.) 1993, I Can't Accept Not Trying: Michael Jordan on the Pursuit of Excellence. *Address:* c/o Chicago Bulls, 1901 W. Madison Street, Chicago, IL 60612, U.S.A.

JORDAN, Neil, B.A.; Irish writer and director; b. 25 Feb. 1950, Sligo; two d.; ed. St. Paul's Coll. Raheny, Dublin and Univ. Coll. Dublin; founded Irish Writers' Cooperative 1974. *Directed films:* Angel 1981, Company of Wolves 1984, Mona Lisa 1986, High Spirits 1988, We're No Angels 1989, The Miracle 1991, The Crying Game 1992, Interview with a Vampire 1994, Michael Collins 1995 (Golden Lion, Venice 1996), The Butcher Boy 1997, In Dreams 1999; many awards including Guardian Fiction Award, London Critics' Circle, Evening Standard Award. *Publications:* novels, plays and film-scripts including Night in Tunisia and Other Stories 1976, The Past 1980, The Dream of a Beast 1983, Sunrise with Sea Master 1995, Nightlines 1995. *Leisure interest:* music. *Address:* 2 Martello Terrace, Bray, Co. Wicklow, Ireland.

JORDAN, Vernon Eulion, Jr.; American lawyer; b. 15 Aug. 1935, Atlanta; s. of Vernon Eulion Jordan and Mary (Griggs) Jordan; m. 1st Shirley M. Yarbrough 1958 (died 1985); one c.; m. 2nd Ann Dibble Cook 1986; ed. DePauw Univ., Howard Univ.; mem. Bar, Ga. 1960, Ark. 1964; law practice, Atlanta 1960–61; Ga. Field Dir. N.A.A.C.P. 1961–63; law practice, Pine Bluff, Ark. 1964–65; Dir. Voter Educ. Project Southern Regional Council 1964–68; Attorney Office of Econ. Opportunity, Atlanta 1969; Exec. Dir. United Negro Coll. Fund 1970–71; Pres. Nat. Urban League 1972–81; Sr. Partner Akin, Gump, Strauss, Hauer & Feld; Chair. Clinton Pres. Transition Bd.; fmr. mem., trustee and dir. numerous orgs. including Presidential Clemency Bd., Urban Inst., American Express Co., Revlon Group Inc.; over 50 hon. degrees, including Princeton Univ., Harvard Univ. *Address:* Akin, Gump, Strauss, Hauer & Feld L.L.P., Suite 400, 1333 New Hampshire Avenue, N.W., Washington, DC 20036, U.S.A. (Office).

JORDAN, William Brian, C.B.E.; British trade union official; b. 28 Jan. 1936; s. of Walter Jordan and Alice Jordan; m. Jean Livesey 1958; three d.; ed. Secondary Modern School, Birmingham; convenor of shop stewards, Guest Keen & Nettlefolds 1966; full-time organizer for AUEW 1976; Pres. Amalgamated Eng. and Electrical (fmrly. Amalgamated and Eng.) Union 1986–95; mem. TUC Gen. Council 1986–95 (Chair. Cttee. on European Strategy 1988–95); mem. NEDC 1986–92, Energy Industry Training Bd. 1986–91, Council, Industrial Soc. 1987–, Advisory, Conciliation & Arbitration Service (ACAS) 1987–95, Nat. Training Task Force 1989–92, Eng. Training Authority 1991–, etc.; Gen. Sec. ICFTU Dec. 1994–; Dr. h.c. (Univ. of Cen. England) 1993, (Univ. of Cranfield) 1995. *Leisure interests:* reading, Birmingham City Football Club supporter. *Address:* ICFTU, 155 blvd. Emile Jacqmain, 1210 Brussels, Belgium. *Telephone:* (2) 224 02 11.

JORDAN, (William) Hamilton (McWhorter), B.A.; American politician; b. 21 Sept. 1944, Charlotte, N.C.; s. of Richard and Adelaide Jordan; m. 1st Nancy Jordan (divorced); m. 2nd Dorothy A. Henry 1981; one s.; served in S. Viet Nam with Int. Voluntary Services 1967–68; Youth Co-ordinator in Jimmy Carter's campaign for Governorship of Ga. 1966, Man. 1970; Campaign Dir. for Nat. Democratic Party Campaign Cttee. 1973–74, for Carter's Pres. Campaign 1975–76, for Carter's re-election campaign 1980; an Asst. to Pres. 1977–81; White House Chief of Staff 1979–81; Distinguished Visiting Fellow, Emory Univ. 1981–82; political commentator Cable News Network 1981–; consultant in Corp. and int. communications 1984–; Pres., C.O.O. Whittle Communications 1991–92, Vice-Chair. 1992–. *Publication:* Crisis: The Last Year of the Carter Presidency 1982.

JORDAN, (Zweledinga) Pallo, PH.D.; South African politician; b. 22 May 1942, Kroonstad, O.F.S.; s. of Dr Archibald Jordan and Priscilla Ntantala; m. Carolyn Roth 1972; one d.; ed. Athlone High School, Cape Town, Univs. of Cape Town and Wisconsin and London School of Econs.; joined African Nat. Congress (ANC) 1960; worked full time for ANC in London 1975–77, Head, Radio Freedom, Luanda, Angola 1977–79, in Lusaka, Zambia 1980–90; elected to ANC Nat. Exec. Cttee. (NEC) 1985; Deputy Sec. of Information 1985, Admin. Sec. of NEC Secr. –1988; Sec. of Information 1989; mem. Nat. Exec. Cttee. ANC; Minister of Posts, Telecommunications and Broadcasting 1994–96, of Environmental Affairs and Tourism May 1996–. *Publications:* articles and papers on South African political questions. *Address:* Ministry of Environmental Affairs and Tourism, 240 Vermeulen Street, Pretoria 0002, South Africa.

JØRGENSEN, Anker; Danish politician and trade unionist; b. 13 July 1922, Copenhagen; s. of Johannes Jørgensen; m. Ingrid Jørgensen 1948; four c.; ed. School for Orphans and evening classes; messenger, shipyard worker, warehouse worker 1936–50; Vice-Pres. Warehouse Workers' Union 1950, Pres. 1958–62; Group Sec. Transport and Gen. Workers' Union 1962–68, Pres. 1968–72; mem. Folketing (Parl.) 1964–94; mem. Bd. of Dirs., Workers' Bank of Denmark 1969–; Prime Minister 1972–73; Parl. Leader, Social Democratic Group 1973–75; Prime Minister 1975–82; Chair. Social Democratic Party, Social Democratic Parl. Group 1972–87; mem. European Cttee. Against Racism 1994–. *Publication:* Memoirs (Vol. I) 1994. *Address:* Borgbjergsvej 1, 2450 S.V. Copenhagen, Denmark.

JØRGENSEN, Bo Barker, PH.D.; Danish biologist; b. 22 Sept. 1946, Copenhagen; s. of Carl C. B. Jørgensen and Vibeke Balslev Smidt; m. Inga M. Vestergaard 1971; two s. one d.; ed. Univs. of Copenhagen and Aarhus; lecturer, Dept. of Ecology and Genetics, Univ. of Aarhus 1973–77, Sr. lecturer 1977–87, Prof. 1987–92; Dir. Max Planck Inst. for Marine Microbiology, Bremen, Germany 1992–97; Prof., Univ. of Bremen, Germany 1993; Adjunct Prof., Univ. of Aarhus 1993–; research, Marine Biology Lab., Eilat, Israel 1974, 1978, NASA—ARC, Moffett Field, Calif. 1984–85. *Publications:* about 100 scientific publs. in int. journals in the field of ecology, microbiology and geochemistry. *Leisure interests:* photography, music. *Address:* Auf den Hornstücken 25, 28359 Bremen, Germany. *Telephone:* 421-24 23 36.

JØRGENSEN, Sven-Aage, M.A.; Danish professor of German philology; b. 22 July 1929, Herstedvester; s. of Aage Julius Jørgensen and Emma Lydia (née Eriksen) Jørgensen; m. Elli Andresen 1957 (divorced 1985); two s. one d.; ed. Birkerød Statsskole, Univ. of Copenhagen, Univ. of Würzburg and Warburg Inst., London; lecturer Univ. of Copenhagen 1961, Prof. of German Philology 1968–; Research Prof. Univ. of Bielefeld 1980–81; Visiting Prof. Heidelberg 1973, Regensburg 1985, Kiel 1986, Cologne 1990; Visiting Fellow A.N.U. 1975; mem. Royal Danish Acad. of Sciences and Letters 1986, Akad. der Wissenschaften in Göttingen 1998; Univ. Gold Medal 1957, Kt. of Order of Dannebrog. *Publications:* J. G. Hamann's Fünf Hirtenbriefe 1962, J. G. Hamann's Sokratische Denkwurdigkliten und Aesthetica in Nuce 1962, Th. Fontane's Unwiederbringlich 1971, J. G. Hamann 1976, Deutsch-dänische Literaturbeziehungen im 18. Jhdrt. (co-ed.) 1977, Dänische 'guldalderliteratur' und deutsche Klassik (co-ed.) 1982, Tysk et sprog Fire Stater—Fire Kulturer 1989, Wieland's Oberon 1990, Geschichte der deutschen Literatur 1740–1789 (co-author) 1990, Zentren der Aufklärung: Kopenhagen—Kiel Altona (co-ed.) 1992, Verfilmte Litteratur (co-ed.) 1993, Fortschritt ohne Ende—Ende des Fortschritts? (ed.) 1994, Wieland Epoche-Werk-Wirkung (co-author) 1994; numerous articles. *Leisure interests:* jogging, swimming. *Address:* Institut for germansk filologi, Københavns universitet, Njalsgade 80, Tr. 16, 2300 Copenhagen S.; Ny Kongensgade 20, 3, 1557 Copenhagen V, Denmark. *Telephone:* 35 32 81 64 (Office); 33 15 76 04 (Home). *Fax:* 35 32 81 71 (Office).

JORGENSON, Dale W., PH.D.; American economist; b. 7 May 1933, Bozeman, Mont.; s. of Emmett B. Jorgenson and Jewell T. Jorgenson; m. Linda Ann Mabus 1971; one s. one d.; ed. Reed Coll. and Harvard Univ.; Asst. Prof. of Econs. Univ. of Calif., Berkeley 1959–61, Assoc. Prof. 1961–63, Prof. 1963–69; Prof. of Econs. Harvard Univ. 1969–80, Frederic Eaton Abbe Prof. of Econs. 1980–; Frank William Taussig Research Prof. of Econs. 1992–94; Dir. Program on Tech. and Econ. Policy, Kennedy School of Govt., Harvard Univ. 1984–; Visiting Prof. of Econs. Hebrew Univ., Jerusalem 1967, Stanford Univ. 1973; Visiting Prof. of Statistics Oxford Univ. 1968; Consulting Ed., North-Holland Publishing Co., Amsterdam, Netherlands 1970; Fellow, A.A.A.S., American Acad. of Arts and Sciences, American Statistical Asscn., Econometric Soc. (Pres. 1987); mem. N.A.S., American Econ. Asscn., Royal Econ. Soc., Econ. Study Soc., Conf. on Research in Income and Wealth, Int. Asscn. for Research in Income and Wealth; Foreign mem. Royal Swedish Acad. of Sciences; several fellowships including Nat. Science Foundation Snr. Postdoctoral Fellowship, Netherlands School of Econs., Rotterdam 1967–68; lectures include Shinzo Koizumi, Keio Univ., Tokyo, Japan 1972, Fisher-Schultz, 3rd World Congress, Econometric Soc. 1975, Frank Paish, Asscn. of Univ. Teachers of Econs. Conf., U.K. 1980, Erik Lindahl Lectures, Uppsala Univ. 1987; Hon. D.Phil. (Oslo), (Uppsala) 1991; prizes include John Bates Clark Medal, American Econ. Asscn. 1971. *Publications:* Technology and Economic Policy (with R. Landau) 1986, Productivity and U.S. Economic Growth 1987, Technology and Capital Formation 1989, General Equilibrium Modeling and Economic Policy Analysis 1990, Tax Reform and the Cost of Capital (with K.-Y. Yun) 1991, Tax Reform and the Cost of Capital: An International Comparison (with R. Landau) 1993, Postwar U.S. Economic Growth 1995, International Comparisons of Economic Growth 1995, Capital Theory and Investment Behavior 1996, Tax Policy and the Cost of Capital 1996, Improving America's Schools 1996, Aggregate Consumer Behaviour 1997, Measuring Social Welfare 1997, Econometric General Equilibrium Modelling 1998, Energy, the Environmental and Economic Growth 1998; over 190 papers and contribs. to learned journals and collections of essays. *Address:* Department of Economics, Harvard University, Littauer 122, Cambridge, MA 02138 (Office); 1010 Memorial Drive, Cambridge, MA 02138, U.S.A. (Home). *Telephone:* (617) 495-0833 (Office); (617) 491-4069 (Home).

JORTNER, Joshua, PH.D.; Israeli professor of physical chemistry; b. 14 March 1933, Tarnow, Poland; s. of Arthur Jortner and Regina Jortner; m. Ruth Sanger 1960; one s. one d.; ed. Hebrew Univ. of Jerusalem; Instructor Dept. of Physical Chemistry, Hebrew Univ. of Jerusalem 1961–62, Sr. lecturer 1963–65; Research Assoc. Univ. of Chicago 1962–64, Prof. 1965–71; Assoc. Prof. of Physical Chem., Tel-Aviv Univ. 1965–66, Prof. 1966–, Head Inst. of Chem. 1966–72, Deputy Rector 1966–69, Vice-Pres. 1970–72, Heinemann Prof. of Chem. 1973–; Visiting Prof. H.C. Orsted Inst., Univ. of Copenhagen 1974, Visiting Prof. of Chem. 1978; Visiting Prof. UCLA-Berkeley 1975; Vice-Pres. Israeli Acad. of Sciences and Humanities 1980–86, Pres. 1986–; Int. Acad. of Quantum Science Award 1972, Weizmann Prize 1973, Rothschild Prize 1976, Kolthof Prize 1976, Israel Prize in Chem. 1982, Wolf Prize 1988, Hon. J. Hejrovsky Gold Medal. *Publications:* Intramolecular Radiationless Transitions (with M. Bixon) 1968, Energy Gap Law for Radiationless Transitions (with E. Englman) 1970, Electronic Excitations in Condensed Rare Gases (with N. Schwentner and E. E. Koch) 1985, Cluster Size Effects 1992; The Jerusalem Symposia on Quantum Chemistry and Biochemistry (Ed. with Bernard Pullman) Vols. 15-27 1982–93. *Leisure interests:* reading, writing. *Address:* School of Chemistry, Tel Aviv University, Ramat Aviv, 69978 Tel Aviv, Israel. *Telephone:* (972) 3 6408322. *Fax:* (972) 3 6415054.

JORY, Edward John, PH.D, F.A.H.A.; British/Australian professor of classics; b. 20 June 1936, England; s. of E. Jory; m. Marie McGee 1965; three s.; ed. Humphry Davy Grammar School, Penzance and Univ. Coll., London; lecturer Dept. of Classics and Ancient History, Univ. of Western Australia 1959–65, Sr. Lecturer 1966–73, Assoc. Prof. 1974–78, Dean of Faculty of Arts 1976–79, Prof. and Head of Dept. 1979–84, 1988–89, Head of Div. of Arts and Architecture 1990–93, Exec. Dean Faculty of Arts 1994–; Visiting Prof. Institute of Classical Studies, Univ. of London 1990; Fellow Australian Acad. of Humanities, Alexander von Humboldt Fellow, Kommission für Alte Geschichte und Epigraphik, Munich 1974. *Publications:* contrib. to Corpus Inscriptionum Latinarum 1974, 1989, numerous articles on the Roman theatre. *Leisure interests:* cricket, skin diving, golf. *Address:* 36 Marita Road, Nedlands, 6009 W. Australia, Australia. *Telephone:* 9386-2714.

JOSEPH, Cedric Luckie, M.A.; Guyanese diplomatist (retd.); b. 14 May 1933, Georgetown; s. of late Frederick McConnell Joseph and Cassie Edith Joseph, née Austin; m. Dona Avril Barrett 1973; two s. (adopted); ed. L.S.E., Univ. Coll. of Wales, Aberystwyth; taught history at a London Comprehensive School 1962–66; Lecturer in History, Univ. of the W. Indies, Kingston, Jamaica 1966–71; Prin. Asst. Sec., Ministry of Foreign Affairs, Guyana 1971–74; Deputy High Commr. for Guyana in Jamaica 1974–76, Counsellor, Embassy of Guyana, Washington, D.C. 1976, Deputy Perm. Rep., Perm. Mission of Guyana to the UN 1976–77; High Commr. for Guyana in Zambia (also accred. to Angola, Botswana, Mozambique, Tanzania and Zimbabwe) 1977–82, in the U.K. (also accred. as Ambassador to France, the Netherlands, Yugoslavia and UNESCO) 1982–86; Chair. Commonwealth Cttee. on Southern Africa 1983–86, Head of the Presidential Secretariat 1986–91, Sec. to the Cabinet 1987–91, Sr. Amb., Ministry of Foreign Affairs 1991–94; Foreign policy analyst 1995–; Cacique's Crown of Honour 1983. *Publications include:* The Manning Initiative 1993; in Guyana Review: Intervention in Haiti 1994, Reconstruction of the Caribbean Community 1994, Dependency and Mendicancy 1995, Transition and Guyana 1995, Caribbean Community—Security and Survival 1997, Anglo-American Diplomacy and the Reopening of the Guyana/Venezuela Boundary Controversy 1961–1966 1998. *Leisure interests:* tennis, walking. *Address:* 332 Republic Park, Peter's Hall, East Bank Demerara, Guyana. *Telephone:* (2) 54451. *Fax:* (2) 54451.

JOSEPHSON, Brian David, PH.D., F.INST.P., F.R.S.; British physicist; b. 4 Jan. 1940, Cardiff; s. of Abraham and Mimi Josephson; m. Carol Anne Olivier 1976; one d.; ed. Cardiff High School, Cambridge Univ.; Fellow, Trinity Coll., Cambridge 1962–; Research Asst. Prof. Univ. of Illinois 1965–66; Asst. Dir. of Research, Cambridge Univ. 1967–72, Reader in Physics 1972–74, Prof. of Physics 1974–; faculty mem. Marharishi European Research Univ. 1975; Hon. mem. Inst. of Electrical and Electronic Engineers; Foreign Hon. mem. American Acad. of Arts and Sciences; New Scientist Award 1969, Research Corpn. Award 1969, Fritz London Award 1970, Hughes Medal Royal Soc. 1972, shared Nobel Prize for Physics 1973. *Publications:* Co-ed. Consciousness and the Physical World 1980; research papers on superconductivity, critical phenomena, theory of intelligence, science and mysticism. *Leisure interests:* walking, ice skating, photography, astronomy. *Address:* Cavendish Laboratory, Madingley Road, Cambridge, CB3 0HE, England. *Telephone:* (01223) 337260. *Fax:* (01223) 337356.

JOSEPHSON, Erland; Swedish actor and theatre director; b. 15 June 1923; at Municipal Theatre, Helsingborg 1945–49, Gothenburg 1949–56, Royal Dramatic Theatre, Stockholm 1956–; Dir. of Royal Dramatic Theatre, Stockholm 1966–75; American stage début in The Cherry Orchard 1988. *Film appearances include:* Montenegro 1981, Fanny and Alexander 1983, After the Rehearsal 1984, The Unbearable Lightness of Being 1988, Hanussen 1989, Meeting Venus, The Ox, Sofie, Ulysses' Gaze. *Publications include:* Cirkel 1946, Spegeln och en portvakt 1946, Spel med bedrövade artister 1947, Ensam och fri 1948, Lyssnarpost 1949, De vuxna barnen 1952, Utflykt 1954, Sällskapslek 1955, En berättelse om herr Silberstein 1957, Kungen ur leken 1959, Doktor Meyers sista dagar 1964, Kandidat Nilssons första natt 1964, Lejon i Övergångsåldern (pjas Dromaten) 1981, En talande tystnad (pja's Dramaten) 1984, Loppaus Kvällsvard 1986, Kameleonterna 1987, Järgen 1988, Rollen 1989. *Address:* c/o Royal Dramatic Theatre, Nybroplan, Box 5037, 102 41 Stockholm, Sweden.

JOSHI, Damayanti, B.A.; Indian classical dancer; b. 5 Dec. 1932, Bombay; d. of Ramchandra Joshi and Vatsala Joshi; ed. numerous Schools of Classical Dancing; leading exponent of Kathak Dance; has choreographed numerous productions, holding dance seminars throughout India and touring extensively in Asia, Africa and Europe; acts as examiner in music and dance for numerous Indian univs.; holds numerous public service posts connected with the dance; Chair. Dancers' Guild, Bombay; Life mem. numerous dance socs.; Visiting Prof. IndiraKala Sangeet Vishwavidyalaya, Khairagarh, also conducts teachers' workshops; has performed before Heads of State of Nepal, Afghanistan, U.S.S.R., Laos, Yugoslavia, Indonesia, Philippines, Mexico; TV appearances and film Damayanti Joshi on Kathak Dance; lecture demonstrations in G.B., Germany, China and India; Sangeet Nathak Award 1968. *Publications:* Madame Menaka (monograph), articles for art magazines, weeklies, dailies. *Leisure interests:* reading, writing, sitar. *Address:* D-1, Jeshtharam Baug, Tram Terminus, Dadar, Bombay 400013, India. *Telephone:* 4141589.

JOSPIN, Lionel Robert; French politician; b. 12 July 1937, Meudon, Hauts-de-Seine; s. of Robert Jospin and Mireille Dandieu; m. 2nd Sylviane Agacinski 1994; one s. one d. (from previous m.), one step-s.; ed. École nat. d'administration; Sec. Ministry of Foreign Affairs 1965–70; Prof. Econ. Inst. universitaire de tech. de Paris-Sceaux, also attached to Univ. de Paris XL 1970–81; Nat. Sec. Socialist Party, mem. steering cttee. 1973–75, spokesman on Third World Affairs 1975–79, Int. Relations 1979–81, First Sec. 1981–88; Head 1995–97; Councillor for Paris (18e arrondissement) 1977–86; Socialist Deputy to Nat. Ass. for Paris (27e circ.) 1981–86, for Haute-Garonne 1986–88; mem. Gen. Council Haute-Garonne 1988–; Conseiller régional, Midi-Pyrénées 1992–; Minister of State, Nat. Educ., Research and Sport May–June 1988; Minister of State, Nat. Educ., of Youth and Sport 1988–91, attached to the Ministry of Educ. Nat. 1991–92; Presidential Cand. 1995; Prime Minister of France June 1997–. *Publication:* l'invention du Possible 1991. *Leisure interest:* basketball. *Address:* Office of the Prime Minister, Hôtel Matignon, 57 rue de Varenne, 75700 Paris, France.

JOSSELIN, Charles; French politician; b. 31 March 1938, Pleslin-Trigavou; m. 2nd Evelyne Besnard 1987; four c.; fmr. attaché, financial secr., Banque de l'Union Parisienne, economist, Soc. centrale pour l'équipement du territoire; Parti Socialiste (PS) Nat. Ass. Deputy for 2nd Côtes d'Armor Constituency (Dinan) 1973–78, 1981–; Minister of State for Transport 1985–86, for the Sea 1992–93; Sec. of State attached to Minister of Foreign Affairs, with responsibility for Co-operation 1997, for Co-operation and Francophonie 1997–98, Minister of State 1998–; Mayor of Pleslin-Trigavou 1977–97; mem. European Parl. 1979–81; Chair. Nat. Council for Regional Economies and Productivity 1982–86, Nat. Ass.'s EC Select Cttee. 1981–85, 1988–92, Vice-Chair. EU Select Cttee. 1993–; Chair. Parl. Study Group on int. aid orgs.; mem. Côtes d'Armor Gen. Council for Ploubalay canton 1973–, Chair. 1976–; mem. Nat. Council for Town and Country Planning, Local Finance Cttee., EU Cttee. of the Regions. *Address:* Ministry of Co-operation, 20 rue Monsieur, 75700 Paris, France. *Telephone:* (1) 47.83.10.10. *Fax:* (1) 43.06.97.40.

JOULWAN, Gen. George Alfred, B.S., M.A.; American army officer; b. 16 Nov. 1939, Pottsville, Pa.; m. Karen E. Jones; three d.; ed. U.S. Mil. Acad. West Point, Loyola Univ., Chicago, U.S. Army War Coll., Washington, D.C.; served in Vietnam as Co. Commdr. and Operations Officer, 1st Bn., 26th Infantry, 1st Infantry Div. and as Brigade Operations Officer and Deputy Div. Operations Officer, 101st Airborne Div. (Air Assault); Aide-de-Camp to Vice-Chief of Staff, U.S. Army; Special Asst. to the Pres. 1973–74, to Supreme Allied Commdr., Europe 1974–75; Bn. Commdr., U.S. Army, Europe 1975–77; Dir. Political and Economic Studies, U.S. Army War Coll., Pa. 1978–79; Commdr. 2nd Brigade, 3rd Infantry Div. (Mechanized), U.S. Army, Europe 1979–81, Chief of Staff 1981–82; Exec. Officer to Chair., Jt. Chiefs of Staff, Washington, D.C. 1982–85; Dir. Force Requirements (Combat Support Systems), Office of Deputy Chief of Staff for Operations and Plans, Washington, D.C. 1985–86; Deputy Chief of Staff for Operations, U.S. Army, Europe and Seventh Army 1986–88, Commdg. Gen., 3rd Armored Div. 1988–89, V Corps, 1989–90; C.-in-C., U.S. Southern Command, Quarry Heights, Panama 1990–93, U.S. European Command, Stuttgart/Vaihingen, Germany 1993–97; Supreme Allied Commdr., Europe, SHAPE, Belgium Oct. 1993–; numerous decorations including Defense Distinguished Service Medal (with Oak Leaf Cluster), Defense Superior Service Medal, Silver Star (with Oak Leaf Cluster); numerous orders including Légion d'honneur, Hessian Order of Merit (Germany). *Address:* Supreme Headquarters, Allied Powers Europe, B7010 SHAPE, Belgium. *Telephone:* 65 44 4113/4088. *Fax:* 65 44 3540.

JOUVEN, Pierre Jean Antoine; French industrialist; b. 29 March 1908, Paris; s. of Alphonse Jouven and Jeanne Bouhey; m. Madeleine Huguet 1931; three s. three d.; ed. Ecole Polytech. and Ecole des Mines, Paris; Engineer, Corps des Mines 1931–42; with Compagnie Pechiney, Paris 1943–72, Chair. of Bd. 1968–72; Chair. Pechiney Ugine Kuhlmann 1972–75,

Hon. Pres. 1975–; Chair. Int. Primary Aluminium Inst. 1972–74; Pres. Fondation Franco-Americaine 1976–81, now Hon. Pres.; Commdr. Légion d'honneur, Grand Officier, Ordre nat. du Mérite. *Address:* 34 rue Guynemer, 75006 Paris, France (Home). *Telephone:* 45-48-01-98.

JOVANOVIĆ, Vladislav, LL.B.; Serbian diplomatist; b. 9 June 1933, Prokuplje; s. of Milorad Jovanović and Dragica Jovanović; m. Mirjana Jovanović (née Borić) 1985; one s.; ed. Belgrade Univ.; joined Foreign Service 1957; served in Belgium, Turkey and U.K. 1960–79, Amb. to Turkey 1985–89; various sr. posts in Fed. Ministry for Foreign Affairs 1990–91; Head Yugoslav Dels. to Disarmament and Human Dimension confs. of CSCE 1990–91; Minister of Foreign Affairs, Repub. of Serbia 1991–92; Fed. Minister for Foreign Affairs of Yugoslavia 1992, 1993–95; Amb. and Perm. Rep. of Yugoslavia to UN 1995–; Légion d'honneur and other decorations. *Publications:* two books of poetry. *Leisure interest:* chess. *Address:* Permanent Mission of Yugoslavia to the United Nations, 854 Fifth Avenue, New York, N.Y. 10021, U.S.A. *Telephone:* (212) 879 8700. *Fax:* (212) 879 8705.

JOVANOVIĆ, Živadin; Serbian politician; b. 14 Nov. 1938, Oparic, Rekovać Dist.; ed. Belgrade Univ.; legal adviser, Novi Beograd Dist. Council 1961–64; with Ministry of Foreign Affairs 1964–; Yugoslavian Amb. to Angola 1988–93; Asst. to Minister of Foreign Affairs 1994–97; Deputy Chair. Socialist Party of Serbia 1997–; mem. Parl. (Narosna Skuptina) of Serbia 1997–; Minister of Foreign Affairs of Yugoslavia 1998. *Address:* Ministry of Foreign Affairs, Kneza Milosa 24, 11000 Belgrade, Yugoslavia. *Telephone:* (38111) 68 25 55 (Office). *Fax:* (38111) 68 26 68.

JOXE, Pierre Daniel, L. EN D.; French politician; b. 28 Nov. 1934, Paris; s. of Louis Joxe and Françoise-Hélène Halevy; m. 3rd Valérie Cayeux 1981; two s. two d. from previous marriage; ed. Lycée Henri IV, Faculté de droit and Ecole Nat. d'Admin.; Mil. Service 1958–60; Auditor, later Counsellor Cour des Comptes; mem. Exec. Bureau and Exec. Cttee., Socialist Party 1971–; Deputy for Saône and Loire 1973, 1978, 1981, 1986, 1988; Minister of Industry and Admin. May–June 1981, of the Interior, Decentralization and Admin. July 1984 and March 1986, of the Interior 1988–91, of Defence 1991–93; First Pres. Cour des Comptes (audit court) 1993–; mem. European Parl. 1977–79; Pres. Regional Council, Burgundy 1979–82, Socialist Parl. Group 1981–84, 1986–88; Commdr. ordre nat. du Mérite, Hon. K.B.E. *Publications:* Parti socialiste 1973, Atlas du Socialisme 1973, L'édit de Nantes 1998. *Address:* Cour des comptes, 13 rue Cambon, 75100 Paris, RP, France (Office).

JOYNER-KERSEE, Jacqueline; American athlete; b. 3 March 1962, E. St. Louis, Ill.; m. Bobby Kersee 1986; ed. Univ. of Calif. at Los Angeles (UCLA); specializes in heptathlon; coached by husband; now asst. basketball coach, UCLA; world record heptathlon scores: 7,158 points, Houston, 1986; 7,215 points, US Olympic trial, Indianapolis 1988; 7,291 points, Seoul 1988; 7,044 points (Gold Medal), Olympic Games, Barcelona 1992; 3 Olympic Gold Medals, 4 World Championships (Sept. 1994); 2 Gold Medals (Olympic Games) 1996; with Richmond Rage in American Basketball League; winner IAAF Mobil Grand Prix 1994; Jim Thorpe Award 1993, Jackie Robinson Robie Award 1994. *Publication:* A Kind of Grace (autobiog.) 1997. *Address:* Elite International Sports Marketing Inc., 701 Market Street, Suite 1575, St. Louis, MO 63101, U.S.A.

JOY-WAY ROJAS, Victor, B.ENG., M.A., M.ECON.; Peruvian politician; ed. Univ. Nac. de Ingeniería, Escuela Superior de Admin. Pública, Peru, Williams Coll., Mass. and Harvard Univ., U.S.A.; Man. Dir. number of overseas trade and int. business cos.; consultant to UN and OAS on foreign trade; Head Andean Plan for the Promotion of Exports, Cartagena Accord Group; Pres. Org. of Peruvian Importers and Exporters; Co-ordinator China-Latin America Econ. Cooperation Programmes; Dir. Corpn. Andina de Fomento; Ministry of Industry, Tourism, Integration and Int. Commercial Negotiations 1991–92; mem. Democratic Constituent Congress 1992–, Third Vice-Pres. 1993, Second Vice-Pres. 1994–95, First Vice-Pres. 1995–96, Pres. 1996–97, 1998; fmr. Vice-Pres. Amazonian Parl; Pres. Council of Ministers and Minister of the Economy Jan. 1999–; Rep. of Pres. of Peru to External Debt Cttee.; Pres. Econ. Comm. 1995–96, Foreign Affairs Comm. 1997–98, Peruvian Congress; Pres. Peru-China Friendship League, Peru-Brazil Friendship League; mem. Privatization Cttee. (COPRI). *Address:* Oficina del Presidente, Lima, Peru.

JU MING; Taiwanese sculptor; b. 20 Jan. 1938, Taiwan; began career as woodcarver and potter; more recently worked in bronze; numerous one-man shows in U.S.A. and Far East; major exhbn. of ceramic pieces in Hong Kong 1988; produced three series, The Living World, the first being an extension of wood-carving technique to include colour, the second being a series of life-size (or larger) bronzes and the third being created from rolled steel, shown at Hakone Open-Air Museum, Japan 1995; exhbn. of bronzes inspired by t'ai chi (Chinese shadow boxing) shown at South Bank, London 1991, Hakone Open-Air Museum, Japan 1995, place Vendôme, Paris 1997; Sculpture Award Chinese Sculptors and Artists Asscn. 1976, Award for the Ten Outstanding Youths 1987, Nat. Culture Award, Republic of China Nat. Culture Foundation 1976. *Address:* 28 Lane 460, Chih Shan Road, Section 2, Taipei, Taiwan.

JUAN CARLOS I; King of Spain; b. 5 Jan. 1938, Rome; s. of the late H.R.H. Don Juan de Borbón y Battenberg, Count of Barcelona, and of H.R.H. Doña María de las Mercedes de Borbón y Orleans, and grandson of King Alfonso XIII and Queen Victoria Eugenia of Spain; m. Princess Sophia, d. of the late King Paul of the Hellenes and of Queen Frederica, 1962; heir, Crown Prince Felipe, b. Jan. 1968; daughters Princess Elena, Princess Cristina; ed. privately in Fribourg (Switzerland), Madrid, San Sebastián, Inst. of San Isidro, Madrid, Colegio del Carmen, Gen. Mil. Acad., Zaragoza and Univ. of Madrid; spent childhood in Rome, Lausanne, Estoril and Madrid; commissioned into the three armed forces and undertook training in each of them 1957–59; has studied the organization and activities of various govt. ministries; named by Gen. Franco as future King of Spain 1969, inaugurated as King of Spain 22 Nov. 1975, named as Capt.-Gen. of the Armed Forces Nov. 1975; Foreign mem. Académie des sciences morales et politiques, Assoc. mem. 1988; Dr. h.c. (Strasbourg) 1979, (Madrid), (Harvard) 1984, (Sorbonne) 1985, (Oxford) 1986, (Trinity Coll., Dublin) 1986, (Bologna) 1988, (Cambridge) 1988, (Coimbra) 1989, (Tokyo, Bogotá, Limerick, Tufts, Chile) 1990, (Toronto) 1991, (Jerusalem) 1993; Charlemagne Prize 1982, Bolívar Prize (UNESCO) 1983, Gold Medal Order 1985, Candenhove Kalergi Prize, Switzerland 1986, Nansen Medal 1987, Humanitarian Award Elie Wiesel, U.S.A. 1991, shared Houphouët Boigny Peace Prize (UNESCO) 1995, Franklin D. Roosevelt Four Freedoms Award 1995. *Address:* Palacio de la Zarzuela, Madrid, Spain.

JUCKER, Hans, D.SC.; Swiss business executive (retd.); b. 1927, Kusnacht; ed. Fed. Polytechnic, Zürich and Univ. of London; chemical research, Ciba Co., Basle; later head of research at two Swiss precision instrument cos.; Head of Research Alusuisse 1969; Chief Exec. Lonza (subsidiary of Alusuisse), Basle 1974; Chief Exec. Alusuisse 1986–91; Chair. 1991–97. *Address:* c/o Alusuisse, Feldegstrasse 4, 8034 Zürich, Switzerland.

JUDA, Annely, C.B.E.; German art dealer; b. 23 Sept. 1914, Kassel; d. of Kurt Brauer and Margarete Brauer; m. Paul A. Juda 1939 (dissolved 1955); one s. two d.; ed. grammar school; opened Molton Gallery, London 1960; founded Hamilton Gallery 1963; started (with her son David) under her own name Annely Juda Fine Art 1967; Cologne Prize 1993. *Publications:* numerous art catalogues. *Leisure interests:* theatre, music. *Address:* Annely Juda Fine Art, 23 Dering Street, London, W1R 9AA (Office); 74 Windermere Avenue, London, N3 3RA, England (Home). *Telephone:* 0171-629 7578 (Office). *Fax:* 0171-491 2139 (Office).

JUGNAUTH, Rt. Hon. Sir Anerood, K.C.M.G., P.C., Q.C.; Mauritian politician and lawyer; b. 29 March 1930, Palma; m. Sarojini Devi Ballah; one s. one d.; ed. Church of England School, Palma, Regent Coll., Lincoln's Inn, London; called to Bar 1954; won seat on Legis. Ass., Mauritius 1963; Minister of State and Devt. 1965–67, of Labour 1967; Dist. Magistrate 1967; Crown Counsel and Sr. Crown Counsel 1971; co-founder and Pres. Mouvement Militant Mauricien with Paul Bérenger (q.v.) Dec. 1971–; Leader of Opposition 1976; Prime Minister of Mauritius 1982–95, also Minister of Finance 1983–84, also fmrly. of Defence and Internal Security and Reform Insts., fmrly of Information, Internal and External Communications and the Outer Islands, Attorney-Gen. and Minister of Justice; Order of the Rising Sun (Japan) 1988, Officier, Légion d'honneur 1990. *Leisure interests:* football, swimming. *Address:* La Caverne No. 1, Vacoas, Mauritius.

JULESZ, Bela, PH.D.; American experimental psychologist and university professor; b. 19 Feb. 1928, Budapest, Hungary; s. of Jeno Julesz and Klementin Fleiner; m. Margit Fasy 1953; ed. Tech. Univ. Budapest and Hungarian Acad. of Sciences; Asst. Prof. Dept. of Communication, Tech. Univ. Budapest 1950–51; mem. tech. staff, Telecommunication Research Inst. Budapest 1951–56; mem. tech. staff, Bell Labs, Murray Hill, N.J. 1956–64, head, sensory and perceptual processes 1964–83; research head, visual perception research, AT & T Bell Labs. Murray Hill, N.J. 1984–89; Prof. of Psychology, Dir. Lab. of Vision Research, Rutgers Univ., N.J. 1989–; Visiting Prof. Dept. of Biology Calif. Inst. of Tech. 1985–; Fellow, American Acad. of Arts and Sciences, A.A.A.S.; mem. N.A.S.; corresp. mem. Göttingen Acad.; hon. mem. Hungarian Acad.; MacArthur Fellow Award, H.P. Heineken prize, Royal Netherlands Acad. of Arts and Sciences 1985. *Publications:* Foundations of Cyclopean Perception, Dialogues on Perception; 200 scientific papers on visual perception. *Address:* Laboratory of Vision Research, Rutgers University, Psychology Building, Busch Campus, Piscataway, NJ 08854, U.S.A. *Telephone:* (732) 445-6520.

JULIANA Louise Emma Marie Wilhelmina, H.R.H., former Queen of the Netherlands; Princess of the Netherlands, Princess of Orange-Nassau, Duchess of Mecklenburg, Princess of Lippe-Biesterfeld; b. 30 April 1909; daughter of Queen Wilhelmina and Prince Henry of Mecklenburg-Schwerin; married Prince Bernhard of Lippe-Biesterfeld 1937; daughters Princess Beatrix Wilhelmina Armgard (now Queen Beatrix, q.v.), b. Jan. 1938, Princess Irene Emma Elisabeth, b. Aug. 1939, Princess Margriet Francisca, b. Jan. 1943, Princess Maria Christina, b. Feb. 1947; went to Canada after German occupation 1940; in England 1944; returned to Netherlands 1945; Princess Regent Oct.–Dec. 1947, May-Aug. 1948; Queen of Netherlands 1948–80 (abdicated 30 April 1980). *Address:* c/o Palace of Soestdijk, Amsterdamsestraatweg 1, 3744 AA Baarn, Netherlands.

JULIEN, Claude Norbert; French journalist; b. 17 May 1925, Saint-Rome de Cernon; s. of Henri Julien and Léontine (née Gau); m. Jacqueline Tannery 1949; two s. two d.; ed. Ecole primaire de Labruguière, Univ. of Notre Dame, Ind., U.S.A.; Ed.-in-Chief Vie catholique illustrée 1949–50, Dépêche Marocaine à Tanger 1950–51; Foreign Ed. Le Monde 1951, Asst. Head Foreign Service 1960–69, Head 1969–73, Ed.-in-Chief Le Monde diplomatique 1973–82, Dir. 1982–90 (Man. Le Monde 1981–82); Admin. Canadian

Inst. for Int. Peace and Security (Ottawa), la Maison de l'Amérique latine; Pres. Cercle Condorcet, Paris, Ligue française de l'enseignement, Paris, Festival international des francophonies, Paris and Limoges; Foreign mem. Royal Soc. of Canada; Dr. h.c. (Univ. de Mons-Hainaut, Belgium) 1996; Officier, Légion d'honneur; Prix Aujourd'hui for book L'Empire américain. *Publications:* L'Amérique en révolution (with J. Julien) 1956, Le Nouveau Nouveau Monde 1960, La Révolution cubaine 1962, God's Trombones 1960, Le Canada—dernière chance de l'Europe 1968, L'Empire américain 1968, Le suicide des démocraties 1972, Le Rêve et l'histoire—deux siècles d'Amérique 1976, Le devoir d'irrespect 1979. *Leisure interest:* gardening. *Address:* Le Buguet-Haut, 47500 Sauveterre-la-Lémance, France (Home). *Telephone:* (5) 53.40.62.71. *Fax:* (5) 53.40.62.41.

JULIEN, Michael Frederick, F.C.A., F.C.T.; British business executive and accountant; b. 22 March 1938, London; s. of late Robert A.F. Julien and Olive R. Evans; m. Ellen Martinsen 1963; one s. two d.; ed. St. Edward's School, Oxford; Price Waterhouse & Co. 1958–67; other commercial appts. 1967–76; Group Finance Dir. BICC 1976–83; Exec. Dir. Finance and Planning, Midland Bank 1983–86; Man. Dir. Finance and Admin. Guinness PLC 1987–88, Dir. (non-exec.) 1988–97; Group Chief Exec. Storehouse PLC 1988–92; Chair. Owners Abroad PLC (now First Choice Holidays PLC) 1993–97; Dir. Medeva PLC 1993–98. *Leisure interests:* family, travel. *Address:* Bendochy, Ellesmere Road, Weybridge, Surrey, KT13 0HQ, England. *Telephone:* (01932) 844663. *Fax:* (01932) 859677.

JULIUS, DeAnne, PH.D.; American economist; b. 14 April 1949; d. of Marvin Julius; m. Ian A. Harvey 1976; one s. one d.; ed. Iowa State Univ. and Univ. of California at Davis; Econ. Adviser for Energy, IBRD 1975–82; Man. Dir. Logan Assocs., Inc. 1983–86; Dir. of Econs. Royal Inst. of Int. Affairs, London 1986–89; Chief Economist Shell Int. Petroleum Co., London 1989–93, British Airways 1993–97; mem. Monetary Policy Cttee., Bank of England 1997–; Chair. British Airways Pension Investment Man. Ltd. 1995–97; Amex Bank Prize for essay Is Manufacturing Still Special in the New World Order? (with R. Brown) 1993. *Leisure interests:* skiing, windsurfing. *Publications:* The Economics of Natural Gas 1990, Global Companies and Public Policy: The Growing Challenge of Foreign Direct Investment 1990 and articles on int. economics. *Address:* Bank of England, Threadneedle Street, London, EC2R 8AH, England. *Telephone:* 0171-601 4313. *Fax:* 0171-601 4610.

JULLIEN, François, D. ÈS L.; French professor of philosophy; b. 2 June 1951, Embrun, Hautes-Alpes; s. of Raymond Jullien and Marie Cler; m. Odile Sournies 1974; one s. two d.; ed. Ecole normale supérieure and Univ. of Shanghai; Head French Sinology Unit, Hong Kong 1978–81; Resident Maison franco-japonaise, Tokyo 1985–87; Sr. Lecturer Univ. de Paris VIII-Saint-Denis 1981–87, Prof. 1987–90, Prof. Univ. de Paris VII-Denis Diderot 1990–; Pres. Asscn. française des études chinoises 1988–90; Pres. Collège Int. de philosophie Oct. 1995–; Dir. Oriental collection, P.U.F.; mem. Editorial Cttee. Critique journal. *Publications:* Fleurs du matin cueillies le soir 1976, Sous le dais fleuri 1978 (both translations of the Chinese texts of Lu Xun), La Valeur allusive 1985, Procès cu création 1989, Eloge de la fadeur 1991, La Propension des choses 1991, Figures de l'immanence 1993, Le Détour et l'accès 1995, Fonder la morale 1995, Traité de l'efficacité 1997, Un sage est sans idée ou l'autre de la philosophie 1998. *Address:* Université Paris VII-Denis Diderot, 2 place Jussieu, 75251 Paris cedex 05 (University); 26 bis blvd. de Port Royal, 75005 Paris, France (Home).

JULLIEN, Mgr. Jacques; French ecclesiastic; b. 7 May 1929, Brest; s. of Pierre Jullien and Jeanne Maudon; ed. Grand-Séminaire de Quimper, Univ. Catholique d'Angers, Univ. Catholique de Paris et Hautes-Etudes, Paris; ordained priest 1954; Vicar, Locmaria-Quimper; Prof. of Moral Theology, Grand-Séminaire de Quimper 1957–69; Curé, Saint-Louis de Brest 1969–78; Bishop of Beauvais 1978–84; Coadjutor Bishop to Cardinal Gouyon 1984; Archbishop of Rennes, Dol and Saint-Malo 1985; Chevalier, Légion d'honneur. *Publications:* Le Chrétien et la politique 1963, Les Chrétiens et l'état (Co-author) 1967, La régulation des naissances, Humanae Vitae 1968, Pour vous, qui est Jésus-Christ? (Co-author) 1968, Faire vivre, livre blanc sur l'avortement (Co-author) 1969, Les prêtres dans le combat politique 1972, L'homme debout 1980, En paroles et en actes 1983, La Procréation artificielle: des motifs d'espérer (Co-author), Demain la Famille 1992, Trop Petit pour ta grâce 1996. *Address:* Evêché, 45 rue de Brest, 35042 Rennes Cedex, France. *Telephone:* 99.54.06.06.

JULY, Serge; French journalist; b. 27 Dec. 1942, Paris; one s.; journalist Clarté 1961–63; Vice-Pres. Nat. Union of Students 1965–66; French teacher Coll. Sainte-Barbe, Paris 1966–68; Asst. Leader Gauche prolétarienne 1969–72 (disbanded by the Govt.); f. with Jean-Paul Sartre, Jean-Claude Vernier and Philippe Gavi Libération Feb. 1973, Chief Ed. 1973–, Publ. Dir. 1974–75, Jt. Dir. Nov. 1981, Man. Dir. Jan. 1987–; Reporter Europe 1 April 1983; mem. Club de la presse Europe 1 Oct. 1976–. *Publications:* Vers la guerre civile (with Alain Geismar and Erlyne Morane) 1969, Dis maman, c'est quoi l'avant-guerre? 1980, Les Années Mitterrand 1986, La Drôle d'Année 1987, Le Salon des artistes 1989, La Diagonale du Golfe 1991. *Address:* Libération, 11 rue Beranger, 75003 Paris, France (Office). *Telephone:* 42.76.19.78 (Office).

JUMA, Omar Ali; Tanzanian politician; fmr. govt. official; Chief Minister of Zanzibar 1988–95; Vice-Pres. of Tanzania Nov. 1995–. *Address:* Office of the Vice-President, P.O. Box 776, Zanzibar, Tanzania. *Telephone:* (54) 20511.

JUMBE, (Mwinyi) Aboud; Tanzanian politician (retd.); b. 14 June 1920, Zanzibar; s. of Jumbe Mwinyi and Sanga Mussa; m. Khadija Ibrahim 1947, Zeyena Rashid 1976, Fatma Muhammed 1980; fourteen s. four d.; ed. secondary school, Zanzibar and Makerere Univ. Coll., Uganda; Teacher 1946–60; fmr. mem. Zanzibar Township Council; mem. Afro-Shirazi Party (ASP) 1960–77, later Organizing Sec., Head 1972–77; Vice-Chair. Chama Cha Mapinduzi (formed by merger of TANU and ASP) 1977–84; mem. Nat. Assembly of Zanzibar (ASP) 1961–84; Opposition Whip 1962–64; Minister of Home Affairs, Zanzibar Jan.-April 1964; Minister of State, First Vice-President's Office, Tanzania 1964–72, concurrently responsible for Ministry of Health and Social Services 1964–67; First Vice-Pres. of Tanzania 1972–77, Vice-Pres. 1977–84; Chair. Zanzibar Revolutionary Council 1972–84; fmr. Vice-Chair. Revolutionary Party of Tanzania; has resgnd. all govt. and party positions and now resides as a villager; engaged in small-scale fishing, animal husbandry and land cultivation. *Leisure interests:* reading and writing Islamic materials. *Address:* Mjimwema, P.O. Box 19875, Dar es Salaam, Tanzania. *Telephone:* 33969; 31359.

JUMBE, Philbert Alexander; Zimbabwean business executive; b. 22 Oct. 1946, Bindura; m. Bernadette Stembeni 1974; one s. five d.; ed. Bradley Inst., Bindura; Man. Dir. Zimbabwe Bearings (Pvt) Ltd., Harare 1980–; Chief Exec. PAJ Holdings (Pvt) Ltd., Zimbabwe Bearings Manufacturing (Pvt) Ltd.; Pres. Zimbabwe Nat. Chamber of Commerce (ZNCC) 1989–90, 1990–91 (Chair. Harare Branch 1986); mem. Council, Zimbabwe Asscn. of Pension Funds 1980–81; Chair. Machembere Creche, Highfield 1978; Chair. and Founder-mem. Rusununguko School Students' Asscn. 1987; Life mem. Jairosi Jiri Asscn. 1985, Zimbabwe Council for Welfare of Children 1986; Award for outstanding services to ZNCC 1985, 1989. *Leisure interests:* tennis, squash, jogging. *Address:* Zimbabwe Bearings (Pvt) Ltd., P.O. Box 4600, Harare, Zimbabwe. *Telephone:* (4) 792688, 729248, 729249.

JUMINER, Bertène Gaëtan, LIC.MED.; French professor of medicine; b. 6 Aug. 1927, Cayenne, French Guiana; s. of Félix Juminer and Marie-Léone Placide; m. 2nd Bernadette Stephenson 1977; one s. one d.; (two s. three d. from previous marriage); Head Lab. of Exotic Pathology, Faculty of Medicine, Montpellier 1956–58; Head of Lab. Inst. Pasteur, Tunis 1958–66; Maître de Conf. Agrégé and Hosp. Biologist, Faculty of Medicine, Meched, Iran 1966–67; Prof. and Hosp. Biologist, Faculty of Medicine, Dakar, Senegal 1967–73; Prof. and Hosp. Biologist Faculty of Medicine, Amiens, Univ. of Picardie 1972–81; Rector of Acad. des Antilles et de la Guyane and Chancellor of Univ. 1982–87; Prof., Head of Univ. Hosp. Centre Point-à-Pitre 1988–97; Pres. Société immobilière de la Guadeloupe; mem. Int. Human and Animal Mycology Asscn. Comm. of French Repub. for Educ., Science and Culture (UNESCO), Nat. Council of Univs. 1992–98, other nat. and int. professional bodies; Chevalier, Légion d'honneur; Officier de l'Ordre national du Mérite; Prix des Caraibes 1981. *Publications:* Les Bâtards 1961, Au seuil d'un nouveau cri 1963, La revanche de Bozambo 1968, Les héritiers de la presqu'île 1979, La fraction de seconde 1990, about 120 articles on parasitology, epidemiology, medical mycology and medical entomology. *Leisure interests:* music, jazz. *Address:* la Bertenière, Bellemont, 97114 Trois-Rivières, Guadeloupe.

JUNCKER, Jean-Claude; Luxembourg politician; b. 9 Dec. 1954, Redange-sur-Attert; s. of Jos Juncker and Marguerite Hecker; m. Christiane Frising 1979; ed. Univ. of Strasbourg; Parl. Sec. to Christian Social Party 1979–82; Sec. of State for Labour and Social Affairs 1982–84, Minister of Labour, Minister in charge of Budget 1984–89, Minister of Labour, of Finance 1989–94; Prime Minister of Luxembourg Jan. 1995–, also Minister of State, of Finance and the Treasury, of Labour and Employment; Chair. Christian Social Party 1990–95. *Leisure interest:* reading. *Address:* Hôtel de Bourgogne, 4 rue de la Congrégation, 2910 Luxembourg. *Telephone:* 478-1. *Fax:* 46-17-20.

JUNEAU, Pierre, O.C., LL.D.; Canadian public servant; b. 17 Oct. 1922, Verdun, Que.; s. of Laurent Edmond and Marguerite (Angrignon) Juneau; m. Fernande Martin 1947; two s. one d.; ed. Coll. Ste-Marie, Montreal and Inst. Catholique, Paris; joined Nat. Film Bd. 1949, Head of European Office 1952, Sec. 1954, Senior Asst. to Commr. and Dir. of French Language Productions 1964, Vice-Chair. Bd. of Govs. 1966; Chair. Canadian Radio-TV Comm. 1968; Pres. Montreal Int. Film Festival 1959–68; Ministry of Communications 1975; special policy adviser, Office of Prime Minister 1975; Chair. Nat. Capital Comm. 1976; Under-Sec. of State 1978; Deputy Minister of Communications 1980; Pres. Canadian Broadcasting Corpn. 1982–89; Visiting Prof. Univ. of Montreal; Chair. Center for Int. Studies and Co-operation, Canadian Radio and TV Inst.; Pres. World Radio and TV Council; mem. Royal Soc. of Canada, Club of Rome; Hon. LL.D. (York Univ., Toronto) 1973, (Trent Univ., Peterborough) 1987. *Leisure interests:* tennis, music, reading. *Address:* Chemin Sainte Catherine, Apt. PH-1, Outremont, Quebec, H2V 2A7, Canada.

JÜNGEL, Eberhard Klaus, DR.THEOL.; German professor of theology; b. 5 Dec. 1934, Magdeburg; s. of Kurt Jüngel and Margarete Rothemann; ed. Humboldtschule, Magdeburg, Katechetisches Seminar, Naumburg/Saale, Kirchliche Hochschule, Berlin and Univs. of Zürich and Basel; Asst. Kirchliche Hochschule (Sprachenkonvikt), East Berlin 1959–61, lecturer in New Testament 1961–63, lecturer in Systematic Theology 1963–66; ordained priest of the Evangelical Church 1962; Prof. of Systematic Theology and History of Dogma, Univ. of Zürich 1966–69; Prof. of Systematic Theology and Philosophy of Religion and Dir. Inst. für Hermeneutik (interpretation of scripture), Univ. of Tübingen 1969–, Dean, Faculty of Evangelical Theology 1970–72, 1992–94; Ephorus Evangelisches Stift, Tübingen 1987–; Guest Prof. of Systematic Theology, Univ. of Halle-Wittenberg 1990–93, Univ. of Berlin 1994; various appts. within Evangelical Church, etc.; mem. Heidelberg and Norwegian Acads. and Academia Scientiarum et Artium Europaea, Salzburg; Hon. D.D. (Aberdeen) 1985; Karl Barth Prize 1986; Orden pour le mérite 1992, Grosses Verdienstkreuz mit Stern des Verdienstordens 1994. *Publications:* 20 books including Paulus und Jesus 1962, Gottes Sein ist im Werden 1965, Unterwegs zur Sache 1972, Gott als Geheimnis der Welt 1977, Entsprechungen 1980, Glauben und Verstehen, Zum Theologiebegriff Rudolf Bultmanns 1985, Wertlose Wahrheit. Zur Identität und Relevanz des christlichen Glaubens 1990, Das Evangelium von der Rechtfestigung des Gottlosen als Zentrum des Glaubens 1998, (Ed.) Religion in Geschichte und Gegenwart, and four vols. of sermons. *Address:* Institut für Hermeneutik, Liebermeisterstrasse 12, 72076 Tübingen; Schwabstrasse 51, 72074 Tübingen, Germany.

JUNGERIUS, Pieter Dirk, D.SC.; Netherlands professor of geography; b. 10 June 1933, Rÿnsburg; ed. Gymnasium B, Leiden and Univ. of Amsterdam; Asst. Univ. of Amsterdam 1955–59; Scientific Officer, Soil Survey of England and Wales 1959–63; on secondment to Soil and Land Use Survey, Ghana 1959, Ministry of Agric. E. Nigeria 1960–63; Sr. Lecturer in Physical Geography, Univ. of Amsterdam 1963–70; seasonal staff mem. Ministry of Mines and Tech. Surveys, Canada 1965–67; Prof. of Physical Geography, Climatology and Cartography, Univ. of Amsterdam 1970–; mem. Royal Netherlands Acad. of Sciences 1987. *Publications:* Soil Evidence of Tree Line Fluctuations, Alberta, Canada 1969, Quarternary Landscape Developments, Río Magdalena, Colombia 1976, Soils and Geomorphology 1985, Perception and Use of the Physical Environment in Peasant Societies 1986, Dunes of the European Coast: Geomorphology, Hydrology, Soils.

JUNID, Datuk Seri Sanusi bin, A.I.B.; Malaysian politician; b. 10 July 1943, Jerlun Langkawi, Kedah; m. Nila Inangda Manjam Keumala; three c.; ed. City of London Coll., Univ. of London and Berlitz School of Languages, Hamburg; fmr. bank manager for seven years; Deputy Minister of Home Affairs 1978–81; Minister of Rural and Nat. Devt. 1981–86, of Agric. 1986–95; mem. UMNO Supreme Council 1981–83. *Address:* c/o Ministry of Agriculture, Wisma Tani, Jalan Mahameru, 50624 Kuala Lumpur, Malaysia.

JUNZ, Helen B., M.A.; American economist and consultant; d. of Samson Bachner and Dobra Bachner; ed. Univ. of Amsterdam and New School of Social Research; Acting Chief, Consumer Price Section, Nat. Industrial Conf. Bd., New York 1953–58; Research Officer, Nat. Inst. of Social and Economic Research, London 1958–60; Economist, Bureau of Economic Analysis, Dept. of Commerce, Washington 1960–62; Advisor, Div. of Int. Finance, Bd of Govs., Fed. Reserve System 1962–77; Adviser, OECD, Paris 1967–69; Sr. int. economist, Council of Econ. Advisers, The White House, Washington 1975–77; Deputy Asst. Sec., Office of Asst. Sec. for Int. Affairs, Dept. of the Treasury, Washington, 1977–79; Vice-Pres. and Sr. Advisor, First National Bank of Chicago 1979–80; Vice-Pres. Townsend Greenspan and Co. Inc., New York 1980–82; Sr. Advisor, European Dept., IMF, Washington 1982–87, Deputy Dir. Exchange and Trade Relations Dept. 1987–89, Special Trade Rep. and Dir., Geneva Office 1989–94, Dir. Gold Econ. Service, World Gold Council, Geneva and London 1994–96; Pres. HBJ Int., London 1996–. *Publications:* numerous articles in professional journals. *Address:* HBJ International, 23 Warwick Square, London, SW1V 2AB, England. *Telephone:* 0171-630 9727. *Fax:* 0171-630 9727.

JUPPÉ, Alain Marie; French politician and government finance official; b. 15 Aug. 1945, Mont-de-Marsan, Landes; s. of Robert Juppé and Marie (Darroze) Juppé; m. 1st Christine Leblond 1965; one s. one d.; m. 2nd Isabelle Legrand-Bodin 1993; one d; ed. Lycée Louis-le-Grand, Paris, Ecole normale supérieure, Inst. d'études politiques, Paris and Ecole Nat. d'Amin.; Insp. of Finance 1972; Office of Prime Minister Jacques Chirac (q.v.) June–Aug. 1976; Technical adviser, Office of Minister of Cooperation 1976–78; Nat. del. of R.P.R. 1976–78; Tech. Adviser, Office of Mayor of Paris (Jacques Chirac, q.v.) 1978; Dir.-Gen. with responsibility for finance and econ. affairs, Commune de Paris 1980; Councillor, 18th arrondissement, Paris 1983–95; Second Asst. to Mayor of Paris in charge of budget and financial affairs 1983–95; Deputy to Nat. Ass. from Paris 1988–97, from Gironde 1997–; Mayor of Bordeaux June 1995–; Nat. Sec. of R.P.R. with responsibility for econ. and social recovery 1984–88, Sec.-Gen. 1988–95, Acting Pres. 1994–95, Pres. 1995–97; M.E.P. 1984–86, 1989–93; Deputy to Minister of Economy, Finance and Privatization with responsibility for budget 1986–88; Minister of Foreign Affairs 1993–95; Prime Minister of France 1995–97; cleared of embezzlement charges 1999; Grand Cross of Merit, Sovereign Order of Malta. *Publications:* la Tentation de Venise 1993, *Entre Nous 1996. Address:* Assemblée nationale, 75355 Paris; Mairie, place Pey-Berland, 33077 Bordeaux cedex, France.

JURINAC, Sena; Austrian singer; b. 24 Oct. 1921; m. Dr. Josef Lederle; studied under Milka Kostrencíc; first appearance as Mimi, Zagreb 1942; mem. Vienna State Opera Co. 1944–82; now works as a voice teacher; has sung at Salzburg, Glyndebourne Festivals, etc.; sang in Der Rosenkavalier 1966 and 1971, Tosca 1968, Iphigénie en Tauride 1973, Covent Garden; Austrian State Kammersängerin 1951; numerous tours and recordings; Ehrenkreuz für Wissenschaft und Kunst 1961; Grosses Ehrenzeichen für Verdienste um die Republik Österreich 1967; Ehrenring der Wiener Staatsoper 1968; Ehrenmitglied der Wiener Staatsoper 1971. *Address:* c/o Vienna State Opera, 1010 Vienna, Austria.

JURKOVIČ, Pero, PH.D.; Croatian economist; b. 4 June 1936, Brštanica, Neum, Bosnia and Herzegovina; ed. Univs. of Sarajevo, Skopje and Zagreb; chief accountant, construction materials industry Neretva, Čapljina 1956–57; Officer for Planning, Municipality of Čapljina 1960–61, Chief Officer for Agric. 1961–63; Dir. Inst. of Economy, Mostar 1963–67; Assoc. to Adviser, Econ. Inst., Zagreb (also Assoc. Prof., Foreign Trade School, and Faculties of Econs. Zagreb and Mostar) 1967–80; Prof., Faculty of Econs., Zagreb 1980–92; Gov. Nat. Bank of Croatia 1992–96; Chief Econ. Adviser to Pres. of Croatia 1997–; mem. Int. Inst. for Financing, Saarbrücken, Int. Asscn. of Economists; Guest Lecturer, Univs. of Rotterdam, London, Lexington and Fla.; B. Adžija and M. Mirkovic awards. *Publications:* about 150 including System of Public Financing (with Ksente Bogoev) 1977, Introduction to the Theory of Economic Policy 1984, Fundamentals of the Economics of Public Services 1987, Commercial Finances 1987, Fiscal Policy 1989. *Address:* c/o Presidential Palace, Pautovčak 241, 10000 Zagreb, Croatia.

JUSYS, Oskaras; Lithuanian diplomatist; b. 13 Jan. 1954, Anyksciai Region; m.; one s.; ed. Vilnius Univ., V. Lomonosov Univ., Moscow; Scientific Scholarship, IREX Exchange Programme, Law School, Columbia Univ., New York, U.S.A. 1985–86; Sr. Lecturer, Faculty of Law, Vilnius Univ. 1981–1985, Assoc. Prof. 1986–90; Dir. Legal Dept., Ministry of Foreign Affairs 1990–92, Counsellor to Minister of Foreign Affairs 1993–94, Amb., Perm. Rep. of Lithuania to UN 1994–; Dir. Lithuanian Br. of U.S. law firm McDermott, Will & Emery 1993–94. *Leisure interests:* jazz, basketball. *Address:* Permanent Mission of Lithuania to the United Nations, 420 Fifth Avenue, 3rd Floor, New York, NY 10018, U.S.A. *Telephone:* (212) 354-7820. *Fax:* (212) 354-7833.

JUTIKKALA, Eino Kaarlo Ilmari, PH.D.; Finnish historian; b. 24 Oct. 1907, Sääksmäki; s. of Kaarle Fredrik Rinne and Hilma Maria Hagelberg; ed. Helsinki Univ.; Docent, Helsinki Univ. 1933, Prof. of Finnish History 1947–50, 1954–74, Prof. of Econ. History 1950–54, Dean of Faculty of Arts 1966–69; Chair. State Comm. for the Humanities 1967–70; mem. Culture Foundation for Finland and Sweden 1960–71; Academician, Finnish Acad. 1972; Ph.D. h.c. (Stockholm), Pol.D. h.c. (Helsinki), D. h.c. (Helsinki Commercial Univ.), D. h.c. (Tampere). *Publications include:* Suomen talonpojan historia 1942, Atlas of Finnish History 1949, Turun kaupungin historia 1856-1917 1957, A History of Finland 1962, Pohjoismaisen yhteiskunnan historialliset juuret 1965, Bonden adelsmannen kronan i Norden 1550–1750 1979, Tampereen kaupungin historia 1905–45 1979, Desertion in the Nordic Countries 1300–1600 (with others) 1982, Kuolemalla on aina syynsä 1987, Valtion tiedoituslaitoksen salainen sotakronikka 1997; studies dealing with demographic, agrarian and parliamentary history, the history of communications, etc.; editor of several historical works and learned journals (Historiallinen Aikakauskirja 1970–82). *Address:* Merikatu 3B, Helsinki 14, Finland.

JUTTERSROEM, Christina, B.A.; Swedish journalist and academic; b. 4 March 1927, Stockholm; d. of Siri Lewell and Gosta Lewell; m. 1st Stig Jutterstroem 1962; m. 2nd Ingemar Odlander 1978; two d.; political reporter Swedish Radio and TV 1967–75, Africa Corresp. 1975–77, Man. Ed. Radio News and Commentaries 1977–81; Ed.-in-Chief Dagens Nyheter 1982–95, Expressen 1995–96; Prof. of Journalism, Univ. of Gothenburg 1997. *Address:* Baltzar Platens 63, 11242 Stockholm, Sweden. *Telephone:* (8) 653-5447. *Fax:* (8) 651-7474.

JYRÄNKI, Antero, D.IUR.; Finnish professor of constitutional law; b. 9 Aug. 1933, Hamina; two s. one d.; ed. Univ. of Helsinki; Assoc. Prof. of Public Law, Univ. of Tampere 1966–70; Gen. Sec. to the Pres. of the Repub. 1970–73; Sr. Research Fellow, Acad. of Finland 1974–77; Vice-Chair., Comm. on the Revision of the Constitution 1970–74; Assoc. Prof. of Public Law, Univ. of Tampere 1977–79; Prof. of Constitutional and Int. Law, Univ. of Turku 1980–98, Dean, Law Faculty 1981–83, 1991–93; Research Prof., Acad. of Finland 1983–87; Pres. Finnish Asscn. of Constitutional Law 1982–88; mem. Council of the Int. Asscn. of Constitutional Law 1983–, mem. Exec. Cttee. 1993–; mem. Admin. Bd. Finnish Broadcasting Corpn. 1983–, Finnish Acad. of Science 1987–; Perm. Expert for the Constitutional Comm. of Parl. 1982–. *Publications:* Sotavoiman ylin päällikkyys (The Command-in-Chief of the Armed Forces) 1967, Yleisradio ja sananvapaus (The Freedom of Expression and Broadcasting) 1969, Perustuslaki ja yhteiskunnan muutos (The Constitution and the Change of Society) 1973, Presidentti (The President of the Republic) 1978, Lakien laki (The Law of the Laws) 1989, Kolme vuotta linnassa (Three Years in the Presidential Castle) 1990, Valta ja vapaus (Power and Freedom) 1994. *Leisure interests:* languages, literature, problems of mass communication. *Address:* Faculty of Law, University of Turku, 20014 Turku, Finland.

K

KAAS, Patricia; French pop singer; b. Stiring Wendel, nr. Forbach; tea-dance and night-club appearances aged 13; first single, Jalousie, aged 17; first major success with Mademoiselle Chante le Blues; albums include Je Te Dis Vous; produces records throuugh her own co. Note de Blues; toured Vietnam and Cambodia 1994. *Address:* c/o Talent sorcier, 3 rue des Petites, Ecuries, 75010 Paris, France.

KABAKOV, Alexander Abramovich; Russian writer and journalist; b. 22 Oct. 1943, Novosibirsk; m.; one d.; ed. Dniepropetrovsk Univ.; engineer space rocket production co. 1965–70; journalist Gudok 1972–88; columnist, then Deputy Ed.-in-Chief Moscow News 1988–97; special corresp. Commerstant publr. 1997–; first literary publ. 1975; Moscow Journalists' Union Prize 1989. *Publications:* Cheap Novel 1982, Cafe Yunost 1984, Oil, Comma, Canvas 1986, Approach of Kristapovich (triology) 1985, Obviously False Fabrications (collection of short stories) 1989, No Return 1989, Story-Teller 1991, Imposter 1992, The Last Hero (novel) 1995, Selected Prose 1997, One Day from the Life of a Fool 1998. *Leisure interest:* jazz. *Address:* Moscow News, Tverskaya 16/2, 103829 GSP, Moscow, Russia (Office). *Telephone:* 200-33-05 (Office); 251-82-25 (Home).

KABANDA, Célestin; Rwandan diplomatist; b. 1936, Rusagara; ed. Petit Séminaire de Kabgayi, Grand Séminaire de Nyakibanda, Univ. of Lovanium (now campus of Kinshasa, Zaire); Pvt. Sec. to Pres. of Rwanda 1961; served in Legislation Bureau, Office of the Pres. and as Sec. of the Council of Ministers 1962–64; Amb. to U.S.A. 1964–69; Amb. to Canada and Perm. Rep. to UN 1966–69; Amb. to France, Italy and Spain and Perm. Rep. to UNESCO, Paris 1969–72; Dir. of Telecommunications, Ministry of Posts, Telecommunications and Transport 1973; Préfet, Ruhengeri 1973–74; Préfet, Gikongoro 1975–77; Amb. to Libya 1977–79, to Ethiopia and to OAU, Addis Ababa 1979–84; Perm. Rep. to UN 1984–89. *Address:* c/o Ministry of Foreign Affairs, BP 179, Kigali, Rwanda.

KABANOV, Victor Aleksandrovich; Russian chemist; b. 15 Jan. 1934, Moscow; s. of Alexander Nikolaevich Kabanov and Brainina Matilda Yakovlevna; m. Nersesova Aramovna 1961; one s.; ed. Moscow State Univ.; jr. researcher, Head of Lab. Moscow State Univ. 1956–70, Prof., Head of Chair 1970; Corresp. mem. U.S.S.R. (now Russian) Acad. of Sciences 1968, mem. 1987; Academician Sec. Dept. of Gen. and Tech. Chemistry; Ed.-in-Chief Doklady Akademii Nauk (periodical); Ed.-in-Chief Encyclopedia of Polymers; Chair. Scientific Council on High-Molecular Compounds; mem. American Chemical Soc.; Foreign mem. Royal Acad. of Sciences of Belgium; mem. Acad. Europea; Lenin Prize and other distinctions. *Publications include:* scientific works on polymerization mechanisms, polyelectrolyte complexes, polymers of medical application, including Polymerization of Ionizing Polymers 1975, New Class of Complex Water-Soluble Polyelectrolites 1982, Complex Radial Polymerization 1987. *Address:* School of Chemistry, Moscow State University, Leninskie Gory, 117899 Moscow, Russia (Office). *Telephone:* 938 1739 (Office).

KABARITI, Abdul Karim A., B.A.; Jordanian politician; b. 15 Dec. 1949, Amman; m.; two c.; ed. St. Edward's Univ., Austin, Tex., U.S.A., American Univ. of Beirut, Lebanon; licensed financial adviser, New York –1986; proprietor of a money exchange co.; mem. bd. of dirs. of many cos.; mem. House of Reps. for Governorate of Ma'an 1989–93, 1993–95, Minister of Tourism 1989–92, of Labour 1992–93, of Foreign Affairs 1995–96, Prime Minister, Minister of Defence and of Foreign Affairs 1996–97; Chair. Foreign Relations Cttee. of House of Reps. 1994–; Chair. Bd. Social Security Corpn. 1992–93; Chair. Bd. Vocational Training Corpn. 1992–93. *Leisure interests:* water skiing, music. *Address:* House of Representatives, Amman, Jordan.

KABAT, Elvin Abraham, B.S., A.M. PH.D.; American microbiologist and geneticist; b. 1 Sept. 1914, New York; s. of Harris Kabat and Doreen Otesky; m. Sally Lennick 1942; three s.; ed. Coll. of City of New York and Columbia Univ.; Lab. Asst. in Immunochemistry, Presbyterian Hosp., New York 1933–37; Rockefeller Foundation Fellow at Inst. of Physical Chem., Uppsala, Sweden 1937–38; Instructor in Pathology, Cornell Medical Coll. 1938–41; mem. of Faculty, Columbia Univ. 1941–, Asst. Prof. of Bacteriology 1946–48, Assoc. Prof. of Bacteriology 1948–52, Prof. of Microbiology 1952–85, Prof. of Human Genetics and Devt. 1969; Higgins Prof. of Microbiology 1984–85, Emer. 1985–; Arthur A. Hirata Memorial Lecturer, Univ. of Kansas 1988; Microbiologist, Medical Service, Presbyterian Hosp., Neurological Inst. 1956–; Expert Nat. Cancer Inst. 1975–82, Nat. Insts. of Allergy and Infectious Diseases 1982–89; Expert O.D. Nat. Insts. of Health 1989–93; Pres. American Asscn. of Immunologists 1965–66; Pres. Harvey Soc. 1976–77; mem. World Health Org. (WHO) Advisory Panel on Immunology 1965–80, Editorial Bd. Journal of Immunology 1961–76, Editorial Bd. Immunochemistry, Carbohydrate Research; consultant, Nat. Cancer Inst. 1975–79; mem. N.A.S.; Fellow, American Acad. of Arts and Sciences; Fogarty Scholar, Nat. Insts. of Health 1974–75; Third Alexander S. Wiener Lecture, New York Blood Center 1979; Hon. LL.D. (Glasgow) 1976, Hon. Ph.D. (Weizmann Inst. of Science, Israel) 1982, (Northwestern Univ.) 1994, Hon. Dr. (Univ. d'Orléans) 1982; Eli Lilly Award in Bacteriology and Immunology 1949, Golden Hope Chest Award Nat. Multiple Sclerosis Soc. 1962, Karl Landsteiner Memorial Award, American Asscn. of Blood Banks 1966, Claude Bernard Medal, Univ. of Montreal 1968, City of Hope Annual Research Award 1974, Award of Fifth Int. Convocation on Immunology 1976, Louisa Gross Horwitz Prize 1977, R. E. Dyer Lecture Award, Nat. Insts. of Health 1979, Townsend Harris Medal, City Coll., New York, Graduate Faculties Alumni Award for Excellence (Pure Sciences) Columbia Univ. 1982, Philip Levine Award, American Soc. of Clinical Pathologists 1982, Dickson Prize in Medicine, Univ. of Pittsburgh 1986, 1st Pierre Grabar Lecturer Société Française d'Immunologie and German Soc. of Immunology, Distinguished Service Award, Columbia Univ. 1988, Acad. Medal, N.Y. Acad. of Medicine 1989, Hon. mem. Japanese Electrophoresis Soc. 1989, Nat. Medal of Science 1991, Lifetime Award, American Asscn. of Immunologists 1995. *Publications:* Experimental Immunochemistry (with M. Mayer) 1948, Blood Group Substances, Their Chemistry and Immunochemistry 1956; (with Tai Te Wu) Structural Concepts in Immunology and Immunochemistry 1968, Variable Regions of Immunoglobulin Chains, Tabulations and Analyses of Amino Acid Sequences 1976, Sequences of Immunoglobulin Chains, Tabulation and Analysis of Amino Acid Sequences of Precursors, V-regions, C-regions, J-Chain and β2-Microglobulins 1979, Sequences of Proteins of Immunological Interest 1987; and numerous scientific papers. *Address:* 70 Haven Avenue, Room 1212, New York, NY 10032, U.S.A. (Home). *Telephone:* 212-WA-7-6807 (Home).

KABBA, Alhaji Ahmed Tejan; Sierra Leonean Head of State and civil servant; b. 16 Feb. 1932, Pendembu, Kailahun Dist., Eastern Prov.; m. Patricia Tucker; ed. St. Edward's School, Freetown, Univ. Coll. of Wales; called to the Bar (Gray's Inn), London; fmr. Dist. Commr. Moyamba, Kono, Bombali and Kambia Dists., Deputy Sec., Ministry of Social Welfare and Perm. Sec., Ministries of Educ. and of Trade and Industry; joined staff of UN, served as UNDP Rep. Lesotho 1973, Tanzania and Uganda 1976, temporarily assigned to Zimbabwe 1980, apptd. head of Eastern and Southern Africa Div. 1979, Deputy Personnel Dir., then Dir., Div. of Admin. and Man. 1981; mem. Sierra Leone People's Party (SLPP) 1954–; Pres. of Sierra Leone 1996–97, March 1998–, also Minister of Defence. *Address:* Office of the President, Freetown, Sierra Leone.

KABBAJ, Omar; Moroccan business executive; mem. Exec. Bd. IMF; econ. affairs specialist Prime Minister's Office; Exec. Pres., Chair. Bd. of Dirs. African Devt. Bank (ADB) Sept. 1995–. *Address:* African Development Bank, 01 BP 1387, Abidjan 01, Côte d'Ivoire. *Telephone:* 20-40-00. *Fax:* 22-12-63.

KABBARAH, Muhammad Bashar, PH.D.; Syrian banker and economist; b. 1944, Damascus; s. of M. Jamil Kabbarah and Hikmat Kouatly; m. 1968; three c.; ed. American Univ. Washington, D.C., Western Illinois Univ. and American Univ. of Beirut; Section Head, Office of Gen. Studies, The Presidency 1973–74; Economist, Econ. Bureau, The Presidency 1974–77, Sr. Economist 1977–82; Adviser/Dir. Econ. Bureau of Pres. of Syria 1982–95; Gov. Cen. Bank of Syria 1995–; Chief Ed. The Syrian Econ. Journal 1975–84. *Publications:* more than 20 papers and articles in professional journals and contribs. to The Arabic Encyclopedia. *Leisure interests:* historical reading, antiquities, agronomy, sports. *Address:* Central Bank of Syria, P.O. Box 2254, Altajrida Al-Mughrabia Square, Damascus, Syria. *Telephone:* 2212642; 2220550. *Fax:* 2227109.

KABILA, Laurent; Democratic Republic of Congo Head of State and fmr. guerrilla leader; b. S. Shaba Prov.; one s.; ed. in France; fmr. Leader Parti de la révolution populaire (P.R.P.); Leader Alliance des forces démocratiques pour la libération du Congo (AFDL); overthrew govt. of fmr. Pres. Mobutu after guerrilla war; Pres. Democratic Repub. of Congo May 1997–. *Address:* Office of the President, Hôtel du Conseil Exécutif, avenue des 3Z, Kinshasa, Gombe, Democratic Republic of the Congo. *Telephone:* (12) 30892.

KABORÉ, Roch Marc Christian; Burkinabè politician; Minister of State in Charge of Relations with Insts. 1990–94; Prime Minister of Burkina Faso 1994–96; mem. Organisation pour la démocratie populaire Mouvement du travail (ODP/MT), First Vice-Pres. Congrès pour la démocratie et le progrès (CDP) (new party f. 1996 as successor to ODP/(MT) 1996–. *Address:* Congrès pour la démocratie et le progrès, Ouagadougou, Burkina Faso.

KACHORNPRASART, Maj.-Gen. Sanan; Thai politician; b. 7 Sept. 1944, Phichit; ed. Chulachomklao Royal Mil. Acad.; aide-de-camp to Gen. Chalard Hiranyasiri; involved in attempted coup 1981; Democrat Party M.P. for Phichit 1983, 1986, 1988; Deputy Communications Minister 1986; Minister of Agric. and Co-operatives 1989; Deputy Prime Minister 1990–91. *Address:* c/o House of Representatives, Bangkok, Thailand.

KACZMAREK, Jan, DR.T.SC.; Polish scientist; b. 2 Feb. 1920, Pabianice; s. of Władysław and Zofia Kaczmarek; m. Olga Steranka 1946; one s. one d.; ed. Acad. of Mining, Cracow; Asst. to Asst. Prof. Acad. of Mining and Metallurgy, Cracow 1947–58; Head, Dept. of Metal Working, Cracow Tech. Univ. 1958–68, Asst. Prof. 1958–62, Prof. 1962–89, Pro-Rector and Rector 1966–68; with Research Inst. of Metal Cutting (IOS) 1949–68, Dir. 1958–68; Pres. State Cttee. for Science and Tech. 1968–72; deputy to Sejm (Parl.) 1972–75, 1985–89; Minister of Science, Higher Educ. and Tech. and mem.

Govt. Presidium 1972–74; Prof. Inst. for Fundamental Problems of Tech. 1978–, Head Dept. of Mechanical Systems 1980–90, Leader State research projects 1975–, Head Lab. for Surface Layer of Solids 1990–; Pres. Supervisory Bd. SIGMA-NOT Ltd. (publrs.), Warsaw) 1991–; Corresp. mem. Polish Acad. of Sciences (PAN) 1962, Ordinary mem. 1971–, Scientific Sec. 1972–80, mem. Presidium 1972–80, 1984–87, Chair. Scientific Cttee. of Machines Construction 1982–93; Chair. Gen. Council Fed. of Polish Scientific-Tech. Asscns. (NOT) 1972–90, Vice-Chair. 1976–80, Vice-Pres. 1982–84, Pres. 1984–90; mem. Polish Acad. of Art and Science (PAU) 1989–, Polish Acad. of Eng. 1991– (mem. Exec. Cttee. 1991–); Foreign mem. Nat. Acad. of Eng. (U.S.A.) 1976–, Bulgarian Acad. of Sciences 1977–, Royal Acad. of Sciences, Literature and Arts, Belgium 1978–; Foreign Hon. mem. Groupement pour l'Avancement des Mécaniques Industrielles (GAMI), France 1979–; mem. Int. Inst. for Production Eng. Research (CIRP) 1961–, Pres. 1973–74, mem. Senate 1975–, Hon. mem. 1990–; Hon. mem. Polish Soc. of Mechanical Eng. 1972–; and mem. numerous other Polish, foreign and int. scientific socs.; Dr. h.c. (Tech. Univ. Chemnitz) 1973, (Moscow Tech. Univ.) 1974; Kt.'s and Commdr.'s Cross of Polonia Restituta, Gold Order of Palmes Académiques 1971, Grand Officier Légion d'honneur 1972, and other decorations. *Publications:* numerous publs. on production engin., and theory of machining and science of science, incl. (in Polish) Principles of Metals Cutting 1956, Theory of Machining by Cutting: Abrasion and Erosion 1970, (in English) 1976, On Principles of Science Policy 1972, (in French) 1972. *Leisure interests:* gardening and classical music. *Address:* al. J. Ch. Szucha 16 m. 46, 00-582 Warsaw, Poland. *Telephone:* (22) 826 98 06 (Office).

KACZMAREK, Zdzisław; Polish scientist; b. 7 Aug. 1928, Poznań; s. of Edward and Klara Kaczmarek; m. Imelda Kaczmarek 1950; two s. one d.; ed. Warsaw Univ. of Tech.; scientific worker in Warsaw Univ. of Tech. 1947–78, Doctor of Tech. Sciences 1958, Assoc. Prof. 1961–67, Extraordinary Prof. 1967–72, Ordinary Prof. 1972–; fmr. Dir. of Inst. of Environmental Eng. in Dept. of Water and Sanitary Eng.; Chief of Div. in the State Hydro-Meteorological Inst. (PIH-M), Warsaw 1957–60, Vice-Dir. 1960–63, Gen. Dir. of Hydro-Meteorological Inst. 1963–66; Dir. of Inst. for Meteorology and Water Economy, Warsaw 1976–80; Head, Water Resources Dept., Inst. of Geophysics, Warsaw 1981–; Chair. of Cttee. of Water Economy, Polish Acad. of Sciences (PAN); mem. Polish United Workers' Party (PZPR) 1951–90; Deputy mem. of Warsaw Cttee. of PZPR 1955–57, worked in Dept. of Science and Educ. of Central Cttee of PZPR, Senior Instructor 1960–63, Deputy Chief of Dept. 1966–71; mem. of Comm. of Science in Cen. Cttee. of PZPR, mem. of Cen. Cttee. 1986–89; former mem. of Gen. Bd. of Polish Teachers' Asscn. (ZNP); First Deputy Minister of Science, Higher Educ. and Tech. 1972–74; Project Leader, Int. Inst. of Applied Systems Analysis, Austria 1974–76, 1989–91; Deputy Chair. of Cen. Qualifying Comm. for Scientific Personnel, attached to Chair. of Council of Ministers –1989; Chair. State Council for Environmental Protection 1981–86; Poland 2000 Cttee. for Prognosis on Country Devt. 1984–88, Nat. Cttee. of Int. Council of Scientific Unions, Cttee. on Water Resources; mem. Comm. for Hydrology, WMO 1993–; mem. Cttee. for Research on World Socialist System's Countries, Cttee. for Peaceful Research; Corresp. mem. Polish Acad. of Sciences 1969–80, mem. 1980–, Deputy Scientific Sec. Polish Acad. of Sciences 1971–72, Sec. of VII Dept. of Polish Acad. of Sciences 1978–80, Sec.-Gen. Polish Acad. of Sciences 1981–88; Foreign mem. Acad. of Sciences of German Democratic Repub.; Int. Hydrological Prize 1990; Silver and Gold Cross of Merit, Commdr.'s Cross and Officer's Cross of Order of Polonia Restituta, Order of Banner of Labour (1st Class), Order of Friendship of Nations (U.S.S.R.), Silver Star of Order of Friendship (G.D.R.), and other decorations. *Publications:* numerous works on hydrology and water resources, on organization of scientific research and on co-operation of science and national economy. *Leisure interests:* sightseeing and tourism. *Address:* al. J. Ch. Szucha 16 m. 51, 00-582 Warsaw, Poland. *Telephone:* (22) 629 10 57.

KACZYŃSKI, Jarosław Aleksander, D.JUR.; Polish politician and lawyer; brother of Lech Kaczyński (q.v.); b. 18 June 1949, Warsaw; s. of Rajmund Kaczyński and Jadwiga Kaczyńska; ed. Warsaw Univ.; asst., sr. asst. in Inst. of Science and Higher Educ. 1971–76; collaborator, Workers' Defence Cttee. (KOR) 1976–80; scientific worker, Białystok br. of Warsaw Univ. 1977–81; ed. Głos (independent magazine) 1980–82; warehouseman 1982; mem. Solidarity Trade Union 1980–; Sec. Nat. Exec. Comm. of Solidarity 1986–87; took part in Round Table talks in Comm. for Political Reforms Feb.–April 1989; Ed.-in-Chief Solidarność (weekly) 1989–91; Dir. Office of Pres. and Minister of State 1990–91; deputy to Senate 1989–91; deputy to Sejm (Parl.) 1991–93, 1997–; Chair. Centre Alliance 1990–97; mem. Helsinki Comm. in Poland 1982–89. *Leisure interests:* reading, history of Poland. *Address:* Sejm RP, ul. Wiejska 4/6/8, 00-902 Warsaw, Poland. *Telephone:* (22) 694 2500.

KACZYŃSKI, Lech Aleksander, PH.D.; Polish civic trade union leader and lawyer; brother of Jarosław Kaczyński (q.v.); b. 18 June 1949, Warsaw; s. of Rajmund Kaczyńska and Jadwiga Kaczyńska; m. Maria Mackiewicz 1978; one d.; ed. Warsaw, Gdańsk Univ.; Asst., sr. asst. in Labour Law Dept., Gdańsk Univ. 1971–; adviser to striking workers in Gdańsk Aug. 1980; mem. Solidarity Ind. Self-governing Trade Union 1980–; head Group for Current Analysis and Intervention Bureau of Founding Cttee. of Solidarity Trade Union, then head regional Centre for Social and Professional Work, Gdańsk 1980–81; mem. Regional Bd. of Solidarity, Gdańsk 1981; interned 1981–82; assoc. of Lech Wałęsa 1982–91 and Provisional Co-ordinating Comm. of Solidarity 1983–84, its rep. in Gdańsk Jan.–July 1986, Sec. July 1986–; sec. Nat. Exec. Comm. of Solidarity 1988–90; took part in Round Table talks in Comm. for Trade Union Pluralism Feb.–April 1989; mem. Presidium Nat. Exec. Comm. of Solidarity 1989–90, First Deputy Chair. Nat. Comm. May 1990–91, Assoc. Workers' Defence Cttee. (KOR) 1977–78, Free Trade Unions on the Seacoast 1978–; Citizens' Cttee. of Solidarity Chair. 1988–91; Senator 1989–91, Minister of State for Nat. Security Affairs in Chancellery of Pres. of Poland March–Nov. 1991; Pres. Cen. Audit Comm. 1992–95; deputy to Sejm (Parl.) 1991–93, Chair. Comm. of Admin. and Interior Affairs; Vice-Leader Programme Bd. of Public Affairs Inst., Warsaw 1996–; mem. EUROSAT Governing Bd. 1993–, Admin. Bd. of ILO. *Publications:* Social Pension 1989, and some 15 works on labour law and social insurance. *Leisure interests:* reading, family, history, philosophy. *Address:* ul. Mierosławskiego 3 m. 2, 80-430 Sopot, Poland.

KADANNIKOV, Vladimir Vasilievich; Russian manager; b. 3 Sept. 1941, Gorky (now Nizhny Novgorod); m.; two d.; ed. Gorky Polytech. Inst.; fitter, foreman, then area man., Gorky Automotive Plant 1959–67; Deputy Workshop Man., Volga Automotive Works 1967–76; Deputy Dir.-Gen. PO AvtoVAZ in charge of production 1976–86, First Deputy Dir.-Gen., then Dir. R&D Centre 1986–88, Dir.-Gen. PO AvtoVAZ 1988–93, Pres. and Dir.-Gen. joint stock co. AvtoVAZ Inc. 1993–96; First Deputy Prime Minister of Russia Jan.–Aug. 1996; Chair., Bd. of Dirs. AvtoVAZ Inc. 1996–; Chair. Council for Industrial Policy; Hon. Prof. Samara State Univ.; mem. Presidential Consultative Council; mem. Int. Eng. Acad., Russian Eng. Acad.; fmr. People's Deputy of the U.S.S.R.; Hero of Socialist Labour. *Publications:* scientific articles on cold sheet stamping by stretch forming, book chapters. *Leisure interest:* reading. *Address:* Yuzhnoe Shosse 36, 445633 Tol'yatti, Russia. *Telephone:* (8482) 37 71 25. *Fax:* (848) 378 74 50.

KADANOFF, Leo Philip, PH.D.; American physicist; b. 14 Jan. 1937, New York; s. of Abraham Kadanoff and Celia (Kibrick) Kadanoff; m. Ruth Ditzian 1979; three d.; ed. Harvard Univ.; postdoctoral research at Bohr Inst. for Theoretical Studies, Copenhagen 1960–62; Asst. Prof. of Physics, Univ. of Ill. 1962–63, Assoc. Prof. 1963, Prof. 1965–69; Visiting Prof., Cambridge Univ., England 1965; Univ. Prof. of Physics, Brown Univ. 1969–78, Prof. of Eng. 1971–78; Prof. of Physics, Univ. of Chicago 1978–82, John D. and Catherine T. MacArthur Distinguished Service Prof. of Physics and Math. 1982–; Alfred P. Sloan Foundation Fellow 1962–67; mem. Ed. bd. Annals of Physics 1982–, Nuclear Physics 1980–; Fellow American Acad. of Arts and Sciences, American Physical Soc., mem. N.A.S., Buckley Prize, American Physical Soc. 1977; Wolf Foundation Award 1980, IUPAP Boltzmann Medal 1989. *Publications:* Quantum Statistical Mechanics (with G. Baym) 1962, Scaling Laws for Ising Models near Tc, in Physics *2* 263 1966. *Address:* James Franck Institute, University of Chicago, 5840 South Ellis Avenue, Chicago, IL 60637 (Office); 5421 South Cornell Avenue, Chicago, IL 60615, U.S.A. (Home).

KÁDÁR, Béla, PH.D.; Hungarian politician and economist; b. 21 March 1934, Pécs; s. of Lajos Kádár and Teréz Schmidt; m. Patricia Derzső; one s.; ed. Budapest Univ. of Economy; with int. econ. dept. Nat. Bank of Hungary; Elektro-impex Foreign Trading Co.; dept. head and research man. Business and Market Research Inst.; Hungarian Acad. of Sciences Research Inst. of World Economy 1965–88; lecturer Eötvös Loránd Univ. of Budapest; Visiting Prof. Santiago de Chile and San Marcos Univ. of Lima; Grand Prix Hungarian Acad. of Sciences; Dir. Econ. Planning Inst. 1988–90; Minister of Int. Econ. Relations 1990–94; mem. Parl. 1994–; Chair. Cttee. on Budget and Finances; Vice-Chair. Hungarian Asscn. of Economists 1990–; Univ. Prof. 1998–; Pres. Hungarian Import-Export Bank 1998–; Vice-Pres. Hungarian Soc. of Foreign Affairs 1998–. *Publications:* author of 8 books, 400 papers. *Leisure interests:* music, literature. *Address:* Budapest 1124, Mártonhegyi u. 38/B, Hungary. *Telephone:* (1) 3557-987. *Fax:* (1) 3557-987.

KADAR, Rabia; Chinese business executive; b. 1948, Aletai, N. Xinjiang; m. Stick Aji; eleven c.; launched March 8th Store 1987; Chair. Akdar Industrial and Trade Co. 1992; est. leather-processing factory, Xinjiang, Rabia Store, Kazakstan, garment factory 1994, knitting mill 1994; Vice-Chair. Xinjiang All-Fed. of Industries and Commerce, Xinjiang Women Entrepreneurs Asscn.; mem. nat. and regional cttees. of CPPCC.

KADARÉ, Ismail; Albanian author; b. 28 Jan. 1936, Gjirokaster; s. of Halit Kadaré; m. Elena Gushi 1963; two c.; ed. Univ. of Tirana, Gorky Inst. Moscow; full-time writer since 1963; works translated into more than 30 languages; sought political asylum in Paris Oct. 1990; mem. Albanian Acad.; corresponding then Assoc. foreign mem. Académie des sciences morales et politiques; mem. Acad. of Arts, Berlin, Acad. Mallarmé, Dr. h.c. (Grenoble III) 1992, (St. Etienne) 1997; prix Mondial Cino del Duca 1992. *Publications include:* Chronicle in Stone (novel) 1971, The Great Winter (novel) 1973, The Twilight 1978, The Three-Arched Bridge 1978, The Niche of Shame 1978, The Palace of Dreams 1981, Broken April 1982, Invitation to an official concert and other Stories 1985, Who Brought Back Doruntine? 1986, The Concert 1988, Eschyle or The Eternal Loser 1988, The H Dossier 1989, Albanian Spring 1991, Le Monstre 1991, La Pyramide 1992, La grande Muraille 1993, Le Firman aveugle 1993, Clair de Lune 1993, L'Ombre 1994, L'Aigle 1996, Spiritus 1996, Oeuvres 1993–97 (5 vols.) 1997; poetry including The Sixties, Insufficient Time. *Address:* 63 blvd. Saint-Michel, 75005 Paris, France.

KADDOUR, Mohammed Ghassan el; Syrian civil engineer; b. 1952, El-Bab; m. Myriam Koudsi; one s. two d.; ed. Univ. of Aleppo; with Milihouse Corpn. 1976–80; in business 1981–83; Chair.-Dir. Gen. Syrian Railways 1983–. *Leisure interest:* sport. *Address:* Syrian Railways, P.O. Box 182, Aleppo, Syria. *Telephone:* (21) 221 3900/01/02. *Fax:* (21) 222 8480, 222 5697.

KADHAFI, Col. Mu'ammar Muhammed al- (see Gaddafi, Col. Mu'ammar Muhammed al-).

KADUMA, Ibrahim Mohamed, B.SC.(ECON.), B.PHIL.; Tanzanian politician and economist; b. 1937, Mtwango Njombe, Iringa Region; s. of the late Mohamed Maleva Kaduma and of Mwanaidza Kaduma; m. Happiness Y. Mgonja 1969; four s. one d.; ed. Makerere Univ. Coll. Uganda, and Univ. of York, U.K.; Accounts Clerk, the Treasury 1959–61, Accounts Asst. 1961, Asst. Accountant 1962–65, Economist 1965–66, Dir. of External Finance and Technical Co-operation 1967–69, Deputy Sec. Treasury 1969–70; Principal Sec. Ministry of Communications, Transport and Labour, 1970–72, Treasury 1972–73; Dir. Inst. of Devt. Studies, Univ. of Dar es Salaam 1973–75, Centre on Integrated Rural Devt. for Africa 1982–85; Minister for Foreign Affairs 1975–77, of Trade 1980–81, of Communications and Transport 1981–82; Vice-Chancellor Univ. of Dar es Salaam 1977–80; Gen. Man. Tanzania Sisal Devt. Bd. 1985–; Arts Research Prize, Makerere Univ., Uganda 1964–65. *Leisure interests:* tennis, squash, gardening, dairy farming. *Address:* P.O. Box 277, Tanga, Tanzania. *Telephone:* (53) 44401 (Office); 46224 (Home).

KAEL, Pauline; American author and film critic; b. 19 June 1919, Sonoma County, Calif.; d. of Isaac P. Kael and Judith (née Friedman) Kael; one d.; ed. Univ. of California, Berkeley; film critic on The New Yorker 1968–91; Guggenheim Fellow 1964, George Polk Memorial Award for Criticism 1970, Nat. Book Award (Arts and Letters) 1974 for Deeper into Movies, Best Magazine Column Award 1974, Distinguished Journalism Award 1983; Hon. D.LL. (Georgetown) 1972, D. Arts & Lit. (Columbia Coll.) 1972, D. Lit. (Smith Coll.) 1973, D. Hum. Litt. (Kalamazoo Coll.) 1973, (Reed Coll.) 1975, (Haverford Coll.) 1975, D. Lit. (Allegheny Coll.) 1979, D. Fine Arts (New York School of Visual Arts) 1980. *Publications:* I Lost it at the Movies 1965, Kiss Kiss Bang Bang 1968, Going Steady 1970, Raising Kane (in The Citizen Kane Book) 1971, Deeper into Movies 1973, Reeling 1976, When the Lights Go Down 1980, 5001 Nights at the Movies 1982, Taking It All In 1984, State of the Art 1985, Hooked 1989, 5001 Nights at the Movies Expanded 1991, Movie Love 1991, For Keeps 1994, Raising Kane and other essays 1996. contrib. to Partisan Review, Vogue, The New Republic, McCall's, The Atlantic, Harpers, etc. *Address:* c/o The New Yorker, 20 West 43rd Street, New York, NY 10036, U.S.A.

KAESTLE, Carl F., PH.D.; American historian of education; b. 27 March 1940, Schenectady, New York; s. of Francis L. Kaestle and Regina Perreault Kaestle; ed. Scotia-Glenville High School, Yale and Harvard Univs.; Prin. American School of Warsaw, Poland 1964–66; Teaching Fellow, History Dept., Harvard Univ. 1969–70; Asst. Prof. of Educational Policy Studies and History, Univ. of Wis.-Madison 1970–73, Assoc. Prof. 1973–78, Prof. 1978; Vilas Prof. 1988; Visiting Lecturer in American Studies, Flinders Univ., Adelaide, Australia 1981; John Simon Guggenheim Fellowship 1977–78; Pres. History of Ed. Soc. 1980–81; Vice-Pres. American Educational Research Assen. 1985–87; Dir. Wis. Center for Educ. Research 1986–88; mem. Nat. Acad. of Educ., Vice-Pres. 1987–89, Pres. 1993–(97). *Publications:* The Evolution of an Urban School System: New York City, 1750–1850 1973, Joseph Lancaster and the Monitorial School Movement 1973, Education and Social Change in 19th Century Massachusetts (with Maris Vinovskis) 1981, Pillars of the Republic: Common Schools and American Society 1983, Literacy in the United States: Readers and Reading since 1880 1991; many articles on history of American educ. and history of literacy, in Journal of Interdisciplinary History, The Harvard Educational Review and other journals. *Leisure interests:* vocal and piano music. *Address:* Department of Educational Policy Studies, 221 Education Building, University of Wisconsin, Madison, WI 53706; Department of History, 3211 Humanities Building, University of Wisconsin, Madison, WI 53706, U.S.A. *Telephone:* (608) 262-1760 and (608) 263-1800 (Offices).

KAFELNIKOV, Yevgeny Aleksandrovich; Russian tennis player; b. 18 Feb. 1974, Sochi; student Krasnodar Pedagogical Inst.; started playing tennis in Sochi Children sports school 1982; later with coach Anatoly Lepeshin; ATP professional since 1992; won 17 ATP tournaments including Milan, St. Petersburg, Gstaad, Long Island; won French Open (singles and doubles) 1996; won Moscow Kremlin Cup 1997; won Australian Open 1999; mem. Russian Fed. Davis Cup Championship Team 1993; highest ATP rating 1st (May 1999); runner-up World Championship, Hanover 1997. *Address:* All-Russian Tennis Association, Luzhnetskaya nab. 8, 119871 Moscow, Russia. *Telephone:* (095) 201 1095 (Office).

KAFI, Ali; Algerian politician and army officer; b. Al Harroch; rank of col. in independence movt., controlled a dist. 1954–62; Sec. Gen. Nat. Assoc. of War Veterans; fmr. Amb. to Egypt, Tunisia; mem. State Council Jan. 1992–; Pres. of Algeria 1992–94; mem. Nat. Liberation Front; Sec.-Gen. Nat. Asscn. of War Veterans. *Address:* c/o Front de libération nationale, 7 rue du Stade, Hydra, Algiers, Algeria.

KAFKA, Alexandre; Brazilian professor of economics; b. 25 Jan. 1917; s. of late Bruno and Jana Kafka (née Bondy de Bondrop); m. Rita Petschek 1947; two d.; Prof. of Econs., Univ. de São Paulo 1941–46; Adviser to Brazilian Del. to Preparatory Cttee. and Conf. of Int. Trade Org. 1946–48; Asst. Div. Chief, Int. Monetary Fund (IMF) 1949–51, Exec. Dir. 1966–98, Vice-Chair. Deputies of Cttee. on Reform of Int. Monetary System and Related Matters 1972–74; Adviser, Superintendency of Money and Credit (now Banco Central do Brasil); Dir. of Research, Brazilian Inst. of Econs. 1951–56, Dir. 1961–63; Chief Financial Inst. and Policies Section, UN 1956–59; Prof. of Econs., Univ. of Va., U.S. 1959–60, 1963–75, Lecturer Law School 1977–87; lecturer, George Washington Univ. 1989, Visiting Prof. of Econs., Boston Univ. 1975–79; Adviser to Minister of Finance 1964; Ordem do Rio Branco, Comendador 1973, and other decorations. *Publication:* IMF Governance, in G-24: commemorating 50th year after Bretton Woods Conf. 1994. *Address:* c/o International Monetary Fund, 700 19th Street, N.W., Room 13-210, Washington, DC 20431; 4201 Cathedral Avenue, N.W., Washington, DC 20016 (Apt. 805-E), U.S.A. *Telephone:* (202) 623 7880 (Office); (202) 362 1737 (Home).

KAFRAWY, Hasaballah El-; Egyptian politician; b. 22 Nov. 1930; s. of Mohamed El-Kafrawy; m. Elham Abd El-Aziz Fouad 1961; three s.; ed. Alexandria Univ.; with southern region of High Dam electricity lines until 1966; Chair. Canal Gen. Contracting Co.; Vice-Pres. of exec. organ for reconstruction of Suez Canal region 1974, Pres. 1975; Gov. of Damietta 1976; Deputy Minister for Reconstruction, then Minister of Devt., Housing and Land Reclamation 1977–86; supervised planning of satellite cities and public utilities of Sadat, Ramadan 10, October 6, May 15, Cairo Sanitary Project, Damietta Port etc.; Minister of Devt., New Communities, Housing and Public Utilities 1986–93; mem. Egyptian People's Ass. 1979–; Pres, Egyptian Eng. Asscn. 1990–; Perm. mem. Int. Org. of Metropolis; UN Prize for Housing 1992; Nile Sash. *Address:* 21 Gamal Eldin Aboulmahasen Street, Garden City, P.O. Box 11451, Cairo, Egypt. *Telephone:* (202) 3555505. *Fax:* (202) 3556255.

KAGAMI, Hideo; Japanese diplomatist; b. 1923, Yamanashi Pref.; m.; two s.; ed. Tokyo Univ.; joined Ministry of Foreign Affairs 1948; Dir.-Gen. Public Information and Cultural Affairs Bureau, Middle Eastern and African Affairs Bureau, Research and Planning Dept., European and Oceanic Affairs Bureau; Counsellor Perm. Mission to UN 1969–71; Embassy Counsellor, Cambodia 1971–74; Amb. to Iraq 1979–82, to the EEC 1982–88; Perm. Rep. to UN 1988–90. *Address:* c/o Ministry of Foreign Affairs, 2-2 Kasumigaseki, Chiyoda-ku, Tokyo, Japan. *Telephone:* (03) 3580-3311.

KAHALANI, Avigdor, B.A.; Israeli politician and army officer; b. 1944, Israel; m.; three c.; ed. Tel-Aviv Univ., Haifa Univ., Command and Gen. Staff Coll.; Fort Leavenworth, Kan., U.S.A., Nat. Defence Coll.; fmr. career officer in Israeli Defence Forces, to rank of Brig.-Gen.; mem. Knesset (Parl.) 1992– (Labour Party 1992–96, The Third Way party 1996–), mem. Knesset Foreign Affairs and Defence Cttee., Educ. and Culture Cttee. 1992–96; a founder-mem. The Third Way, led party in 1996 elections; Minister of Internal Security 1996–; D.S.M., Medal of Valour. *Publications:* The Heights of Courage: A Tank Leader's War, On the Golan 1975, A Warrior's Way 1989. *Address:* Ministry of Internal Security, P.O. Box 18182, Kiryat Hamemshala, Jerusalem 91181, Israel. *Telephone:* (2) 530-8003. *Fax:* (2) 584-7872.

KÄHLER, Erich Ernst, DR.PHIL.; German mathematician; b. 16 Jan. 1906, Leipzig; s. of Ernst and Elsa Kähler (née Götsch); m. 1st Luise Günther 1938 (died 1970); two s. (one deceased) one d. (deceased); m. 2nd Charlotte Schulze 1972; ed. Leipzig Univ.; Lecturer Hamburg 1930; Prof. Univ. Königsberg 1936; Prof. (with Chair) Univ. Leipzig 1948; Prof. Tech. Univ. Berlin 1958; Prof. Univ. Hamburg; Hon. Prof. Tech. Univ. Berlin 1964, Emer. 1974–; mem. Sächsische Akad. der Wissenschaften 1948–, Deutsche Akad. der Naturforscher Leopoldina 1957–; Foreign mem. Accad. Nazionale dei Lincei 1961–, Istituto Lombardo 1987–. *Publications:* Einführung in die Theorie der Systeme von Differentialgleichungen 1934, Geometria Aritmetica 1958, Der innere Differentialkalkül 1963, Wesen und Erscheinung als mathematische Prinzipen der Philosophie 1965, Saggio di una dinamica della vita 1973, Monadologie (Vol. I) 1975, (Vol. II) 1978, (Vol. III) 1983, Also sprach Ariadne 1984, Die Poincaré-Gruppe 1985, Raum Zeit Individuum 1993. *Leisure interests:* philosophy, theology. *Address:* Mozartstrasse 42, 22880 Wedel, Germany. *Telephone:* (04103) 86535.

KAHN, Alfred E., PH.D.; American economist and government official; b. 17 Oct. 1917, Paterson, N.J.; s. of the late Jacob M. and Bertha Orlean Kahn; m. Mary Simmons 1943; one s. two d.; ed. New York Univ. and Graduate School, Univ. of Missouri, Yale Univ.; Research Staff of Brookings Inst. 1940, 1951–52; joined U.S. Govt. Service with Antitrust Div., Dept. of Justice, Dept. of Commerce, War Production Bd. 1941–43; Research Staff, 20th Century Fund 1944–45; Asst. Prof. Dept. of Econs., Ripon Coll., Wis. 1945–47; joined Dept. of Econs., Cornell Univ., Ithaca, N.Y., as Asst. Prof. 1947, Chair. Econs. Dept. 1958–63, Robert Julius Thorne Prof. of Econs. 1966–89, Emer. Prof. 1989–, mem. Bd. of Trustees 1964–69, Dean Coll. of Arts and Sciences 1969–74; Chair. New York Public Service Comm. 1974–77, Civil Aeronautics Bd. 1977–78; Adviser to the Pres. on Inflation and Chair. Council on Wage and Price Stability 1978–80; Special Consultant, Nat. Econ. Research Associates 1980–; Chair. Int. Inst. for Applied Systems Analysis Advisory Cttee. on Price Reform and Competition in the U.S.S.R. 1990–91; Vice-Pres. American Econ. Asscn. 1981–82; mem. American Acad. of Arts and Sciences; Hon. LL.D. (Colby Univ., Ripon Coll., Univ. of Mass., Northwestern Univ., Colgate Univ.), Hon. D.H.L. (State Univ. of New York)

1985. *Publications:* Great Britain in the World Economy 1946, (co-author) Fair Competition, the Law and Economics of Antitrust Policy 1954, (co-author) Integration and Competition in the Petroleum Industry 1959, The Economics of Regulation (two vols.) 1970, 1971, 1988, Letting Go: Deregulating the Process of Deregulation 1998. *Leisure interests:* sports, dramatics, music. *Address:* 221 Savage Farm Drive, Ithaca, NY 14850, U.S.A. (Home). *Telephone:* (607) 277-3007 (Office); (607) 266-8340 (Home).

KAHN, Jacob Meyer, B.A., M.B.A.; South African business executive; b. 29 June 1939, Pretoria; m. Lynette Sandra Asher 1968; two d.; ed. Brits High School, Univ. of Pretoria; joined O.K. Bazaars (1929) Ltd. 1966, Man. Dir. 1978, Exec. Chair. 1981; Dir. South African Breweries Ltd. 1981, Exec. Chair. and Group Man. Dir. 1990–97; Chair. Edgars Stores Ltd., Southern Sun Hotel Holdings Ltd., Amalgamated Retail Ltd.; Dir. Amalgamated Beverage Industries Ltd., Assoc. Furniture Cos. Ltd., Da Gama Textile Co. Ltd., Consolidated Investment Co. Ltd., First Nat. Trust, Johannesburg, Iscor Ltd., Liberty Life Asscn. of Africa Ltd., Liberty Holdings Ltd., The Lion Match Co. Ltd.; mem. State Pres.'s Econ. Advisory Council. *Leisure interests:* reading, playing tennis. *Address:* South African Breweries Ltd., 2 Jan Smuts Avenue, P.O. Box 1099, Johannesburg, South Africa.

KAHN-ACKERMANN, Georg; German politician, journalist and broadcaster; b. 4 Jan. 1918, Berlin-Charlottenburg; s. of Lucian Kahn-Ackermann and Maria Gretor; m. Rosemarie Müller-Diefenbach 1945; one s. two d.; ed. Starnberg Grammar School; mem. Social Democratic Party (Sozialdemokratische Partei Deutschlands—SPD) 1946; mem. Bundestag 1953–57, 1962–69, 1970–74; Vice-Pres. Admin. Council Deutschlandfunk; Pres. Political Comm., Western European Union; Vice-Pres. Assembly, Council of Europe 1973–74: Sec.-Gen. Council of Europe 1974–79; Pres. V. G. Wort 1979; Vice-Pres. Deutsche Welthungerhilfe 1968–89; mem. Bd. Asscn. of fmr. mems. of Bundestag 1982–; Pres. European Comm. of German Journalists Asscn. 1991–. *Leisure interests:* cookery. *Address:* Sterzenweg 3, 82541 Münsing, Germany. *Telephone:* 08177 206. *Fax:* 08177 1303.

KAIFU, Toshiki; Japanese politician; b. 1932; m. Sachiyo Kaifu; elected to House of Reps. six times; Parl. Vice-Minister of Labour; Chair. Steering Cttee. of House of Reps.; various posts in admin. of the late Takeo Miki 1974–76, incl. Deputy Chief Cabinet Sec., Chair. of Diet Policy Cttee. of Liberal Democratic Party (LDP); Minister of Educ. 1976–77, 1985–86; Prime Minister of Japan 1989–91; leader New Frontier Party (opposition coalition) 1994–95. *Address:* House of Representatives, Tokyo, Japan.

KAIN, Karen, C.C.; Canadian ballet dancer; b. 28 March 1951, Hamilton, Ont.; d. of Charles A. Kain and Winifred Mary Kelly; m. Ross Petty 1983; ed. Nat. Ballet School; joined Nat. Ballet 1969, Prin. 1970; has danced most of major roles in repertoire; appeared as Giselle with Bolshoi Ballet on U.S.S.R. tour, Aurora in the Sleeping Beauty with London Festival Ballet in U.K. and Australia, in Swan Lake with Vienna State Opera Ballet; toured Japan and Korea with Ballet national de Marseille 1981; created roles of Chosen Maiden in The Rite of Spring for Nat. Ballet 1979, Giuletta in Tales of Hoffman for Ballet national de Marseille 1982, the Bride in The Seven Daggers/Los Siete Punales and roles in Glen Tetley's Alice 1986, La Ronde 1987, Daphnis and Chlöe 1988, Tagore 1989; appeared in CBC-TV productions of Giselle, La Fille Mal Gardée, The Merry Widow, Alice, La Ronde; Pres. The Dancer's Transition Centre; hon. patron Kidney Foundation of Canada; hon. degrees, York, McMaster and Trent Univs., Silver Medal, Second Int. Ballet Competition, Moscow 1973. *Publication:* Movement Never Lies 1994. *Address:* c/o The National Ballet of Canada, 470 Queens Quay, Toronto, Ont., M5V 3K4, Canada.

KAISER, Karl, PH.D.; German professor of political science; b. 8 Dec. 1934, Siegen; s. of Walther Kaiser and Martha Müller; m. Deborah Strong 1967; two s. one d.; ed. Univs. of Cologne, Bonn and Grenoble and Nuffield Coll. Oxford; lecturer, Harvard Univ. 1963–67, Univ. of Bonn 1968–69, Johns Hopkins Univ. Bologna Center 1968–69; Prof. of Political Science, Univ. of the Saarland 1969–74, Univ. of Cologne 1974–91, Univ. of Bonn 1991–; Dir. Research Inst. of German Soc. for Foreign Affairs, Bonn 1973–; Prix Adolphe Bentinck 1973; NATO Atlantic Award 1986; Hon. C.B.E. 1989; Officier, Légion d'honneur. *Publications:* EEC and Free Trade Area 1963, German Foreign Policy in Transition 1968, Europe and the U.S.A. 1973, New Tasks for Security Policy 1977, Reconciling Energy Needs and Proliferation 1978, Western Security: What Has Changed, What Can be Done? 1981, Atomic Energy Without Nuclear Weapons 1982, German-French Security Policy 1986, British-German Cooperation 1987, Space and International Politics 1987, Germany's Unification, The International Aspects 1991, Germany and the Iraq Conflict 1992, Foreign Policies of the New Republics in Eastern Europe 1994, Germany's New Foreign Policy, Vol. 1 1994, Vol. 2 1995, Vol. 3 1996, The Foreign Policies of the New Democracies in Central and Eastern Europe 1994, Acting for Europe, German-French Co-operation in a Changing World 1995, World Politics in a New Era 1996. *Leisure interests:* music, sailing. *Address:* Forschungsinstitut der Deutschen Gesellschaft für Auswärtige Politik e.V., 53113 Bonn, Adenauerallee 131; 10787 Berlin, Rauchstrasse 18 (Offices); 53173 Bonn, Kronprinzenstrasse 68, Germany (Home). *Telephone:* 0228/2675-150 (Bonn); 030/254231-00 (Berlin) (Offices). *Fax:* 0228/2675-173.

KAISER, Michael M., M.A.; American arts administrator; ed. Brandeis Univ. and Sloan School of Man., M.I.T.; f. and Dir. Michael M. Kaiser Assocs. (consultancy) 1981–85, Kaiser/Engler (arts man. consultancy) 1994, Pres. 1994–95; Exec. Dir. Alvin Ailey Dance Theater Foundation 1991–93, American Ballet Theatre 1995–98, Royal Opera House, London Nov. 1998–; Adjunct Prof. of Business Admin., Rockhurst Coll., Kan. 1985–86, then Adjunct Prof. of Arts Admin., New York Univ.; U.S. Del. advisory comm. on arts funding policies of S. African govt. 1994–95; Visiting Prof. of Arts Admin., Univ. of Witwatersrand 1995; Assoc. Dir. State Ballet of Mo. 1985–87, Pierpoint Morgan Library 1987–89; mem. Bd. dirs. New York Foundation for the Arts; fmr. dir. Washington Opera, Ensemble Studio Theater, PS 122. *Publications:* Understanding the Competition: A Practical Guide to Competitive Analysis 1981, Developing Industry Strategies: A Practical Guide to Industry Analysis 1983, Strategic Planning in the Arts: A Practical Guide 1995. *Address:* Royal Opera House, Covent Garden, London, WC2E 9DD, England. *Telephone:* 0171-240 1200. *Fax:* 0171-212 9502.

KAISER, Philip M., A.B., M.A.; American diplomatist, publisher and banker; b. 12 July 1913, New York; s. of Morris and Temma Kaiser; m. Hannah Greeley 1939; three s.; ed. Univ. of Wisconsin and Balliol Coll., Oxford (Rhodes Scholar); Fed. Reserve System 1939–42, Bd. of Econ. Warfare 1942–46; joined Research Planning Div. Dept. of State 1946; Exec. Asst. to Asst. Sec. of Labor (Int. Labor Affairs) 1946–47; Dir. Office of Int. Labor Affairs, Dept. of Labor 1947–49; Asst. Sec. of Labor 1949–53; U.S. Govt. mem., Governing Body, Int. Labor Org. 1949–53; Labor Adviser, Comm. for Free Europe 1953–54; Special Asst. to Gov. of New York 1955–58; Prof. of Int. Relations, American Univ. 1958–61; Amb. to Senegal and Mauritania 1961–64; Minister, American Embassy in London 1964–69; Amb. to Hungary 1977–80, to Austria 1980–81; Professorial Lecturer Johns Hopkins School for Advanced Int. Studies 1981–83; Chair. and Man. Dir. Encyclopaedia Britannica Int. Ltd., London 1969–75; Sr. Consultant SRI Int. 1981–97; mem. Bd., Guinness Mahon Holdings Ltd. 1975–77, Weidenfeld and Nicolson 1969–77, American Ditchley Foundation 1981–, Soros Foundation 1983–, Council of American Ambs. 1984–, Franklin & Eleanor Roosevelt Inst. 1985–, Weizmann Inst. of Science, Asscn. of Diplomatic Studies 1987–, Partners for Democratic Change, American Acad. of Diplomacy 1996–; mem. Council on Foreign Relations, Washington Inst. of Foreign Affairs. *Publication:* Journeying Far and Wide: A Political and Diplomatic Memoir 1993. *Leisure interests:* tennis, swimming, music, ballet, theatre. *Address:* 2101 Connecticut Avenue, N.W., Washington, DC 20008, U.S.A. (Home). *Telephone:* (202) 667-6095 (Home).

KAJANTIE, Keijo Olavi, PH.D.; Finnish professor of physics; b. 31 Jan. 1940, Hämeenlinna; m. Riitta Erkiö 1963; one s. one d.; ed. Univ. of Helsinki; Visiting Scientist C.E.R.N., Geneva 1966–67, 1969–70; Assoc. Prof. of Physics, Univ. of Helsinki 1970–72, Prof. 1973–; Visiting Prof., Univ. of Wis., Madison 1975; Research Prof. Acad. of Finland 1985–90. *Publications:* approx. 100 publs. in the field of elementary particle physics. *Address:* Department of Theoretical Physics, University of Helsinki, P.O. Box 33, Hallituskatu 8, 00014 Helsinki; Liisankatu 12D 26, 00170 Helsinki, Finland (Home). *Telephone:* (90) 1911 (Univ.); (358-0) 1352232 (Home).

KAJIYAMA, Seiroku; Japanese politician; b. 27 March 1926, Ibaragi Pref.; m. Harue Kajiyama; one s. one d.; ed. Nihon Univ.; mem. Ibaraki Prefectural Ass. 1955–69, Speaker 1967–69; mem. House of Reps. 1969–; Deputy Chief Cabinet Sec. 1974; Parl. Vice-Minister for Construction 1976, for Int. Trade and Industry 1979; Chair. House of Reps. Standing Cttee. on Commerce and Industry 1983; Chair. Exec. Council of Liberal Democratic Party (LDP) 1986; Minister of Home Affairs 1987–88, of Trade and Industry 1989; Chief Cabinet Sec. 1996–97. *Leisure interests:* golf, shogi (4th dan), reading. *Address:* Kudun Shukusha, 2-14-3 Fujimi, Chiyoda-ku, Tokyo 102, Japan.

KAKHIDZE, Djansug Ivanovich; Georgian conductor; b. 10 Jan. 1936, Tbilisi, Georgia; s. of Ivan Kakhidze and Margaret Kakhidze; m. Kakabadze Vanda 1957; one s. one d.; graduated from Tbilisi Conservatoire 1958; postgraduate work 1958–64; Chief Conductor Georgian State Chapel Choir 1955–62; Conductor Paliashvili Opera and Ballet Theatre, Tbilisi 1962–71, Chief Conductor 1982–; Chief Conductor of Georgian Symphony Orchestra 1973–; leading conductor, first American Festival of Soviet Music, Boston 1988; Pres. Tbilisi Music Centre 1989–; Chief Conductor and Artistic Dir. Tbilisi Symphony Orchestra 1993–; Pres. Int. Music Festival 'Autumn Tbilisi' 1998; guest conductor of many int. symphony orchestras in Europe and U.S.A.; teacher, Prof. Tbilisi Conservatoire 1978–; Rustaveli Georgian S.S.R. State Prize 1977; U.S.S.R. People's Artist 1985. *Leisure interest:* football. *Address:* Tbilisi Centre for Music and Culture, D. Agmashenebeli Avenue 125, 380064 Tbilisi (Office); Leselidze Street 18, 380005 Tbilisi, Georgia (Home). *Telephone:* (32) 96 06 20 (Office); (32) 98 44 46 (Home). *Fax:* (32) 95 89 96 (Office).

KAKLAMANIS, Apostolos; Greek politician and lawyer; b. 7 Sept. 1936, Lefkas; s. of Christos Kaklamanis and Evageloula Kaklamanis; m. Athina-Anna Gavera 1972; one s. one d.; Gen. Sec. Ministry of Welfare 1964–65; political prisoner during colonels' dictatorship; founding mem. Pasok and mem. Cen. Cttee.; M.P. 1974–; Minister of Labour 1981–82, of Educ. and Religious Affairs 1982–86, of Justice 1986–87, Minister in charge of the Prime Minister's Office 1987–88, Minister of Health, Welfare and Social Services 1988–89, of Labour 1989–90; Pres. Parl. 1993–. *Address:* Parliament Building, Athens, Greece.

KÁKOSY, László; Hungarian Egyptologist; b. 15 Aug., 1932, Budapest; s. of Károly Kákosy and Ilona Vámos; m. Éva Grigássy; ed. Eötvös Loránd

Univ. of Arts and Sciences; lecturer Eötvös Loránd Univ. of Arts and Sciences, head Dept. of Egyptology 1972, Prof. 1960; lecturer, Pázmány Peter Catholic Univ. 1996–; Chair. of Working Cttee. on History of Ancient Sciences Hungarian Acad. of Sciences 1987; mem. Cttee. of Oriental Studies; Pres. Soc. of Classical Studies 1997–, research in religion, culture, archaeology of Ancient Egypt, Egyptian-Greek Relations; mem. of the Nubian Expedition of Hungarian Acad. of Sciences 1964; participated in the planning of a new museum for Cairo 1983; dir. Hungarian excavations in Thebes 1983–; Corresp. mem. Acad. of Sciences, Heidelberg, Germany 1996–; Research Fellow of the Lexikon der Ägyptologie of Wiesbaden 1975; Kuzsinszky Commemorative Medal, Ábel Jenő Commemorative Medal, Széchenyi Award 1992. *Publications:* Varázslás az ókori Egyiptomban Magic in Ancient Egypt 1969, Egy évezred a Nilus völgyében with Edith Varga, A Millennium in the Nile Valley 1970, Egyiptom és antik csillaghit Egypt and Ancient Belief in Stars 1978, Ré fiai Sons of Re 1979, Fény és káosz Light and Chaos 1984, La magia in Egitto ai tempi dei faraoni 1985, Dzsehutimesz sirja Thébában The Tomb of Djehutimes in Thebes 1989, Zauberei im alten Ägypten 1989. *Leisure interests:* astronomy, chess. *Address:* Eötvös Loránd University of Arts and Sciences, 1088 Budapest, Múzeum krt. 4., B. ép. Hungary. *Telephone:* (1) 266-0860/2933.

KAKOURIS, Constantine; Greek judge; b. 16 March 1919, Pyrgos; s. of Nicolas and Helen Kakouris; ed. Univs. of Athens and Paris; called to Bar, Athens 1942; Auxiliary Judge, Supreme Admin. Court 1951–62, Asst. Judge 1962–70, Judge 1970–83; Judge, Court of Justice of EEC 1983–97; several times mem. or Pres. High Council of the Judiciary and High Council of Diplomatic Corps, Chief Inspector for Admin. Tribunals; Pres. or mem. several cttees.; Corresp. mem. Acad. of Athens 1996–; Dr. h.c. (Univ. of Athens Law School) 1992. *Publications:* A study of General Theory of Law on Judiciary Power and the Mission of the Courts; articles and reviews in legal and philosophical journals. *Leisure interest:* philosophy. *Address:* 52, Skoufa Street, 106.72 Athens, Greece. *Telephone:* (1) 363 5588.

KAKU, Ryuzaburo; Japanese businessman; b. 19 May 1926, Aichi-Ken; m. Meiko Kaku; one s. one d.; ed. Kyushu Univ.; joined Canon Inc. 1954, mem. Bd. of Dirs. 1972–, Gen. Man. Finance and Accounting Div. 1972–74, Man. Dir. 1974–77, Pres. and Rep. Dir. 1977–84, Chair. Canon U.S.A. Inc. 1984–, Chair. and Rep. Dir. Canon Inc. 1989–97, fmr. C.E.O., now Hon. Chair.; Officier Légion d'honneur, Medal of Honour with Blue Ribbon. *Leisure interest:* reading. *Address:* Canon Inc., 30-2, Shimomaruko 3-chome, Ohla-ku, Tokyo 146, Japan.

KALANTARI, Issa, PH.D.; Iranian politician and agriculturalist; b. 1952, Marand; s. of Mohammad Hussein Kalantari and Kobra Kalantari (née Esfandi); m. 1982; one s. one d.; ed. Univs. of Urmiya, Nebraska and Iowa State; Head Agricultural Extension Org. 1982, Plant and Seed Improvement Research Inst. 1983, Deputy Minister for Agricultural Research, Educ. and Extension 1983–85, Man. Dir. and Head Bd. of Dirs. Moghan Stock-farming and Agro-Industry Complex, Ministry of Agric. 1985–88; Minister of Agric. 1988–; Pres. World Food Council 1991–95. *Publications:* A Policy for Reforming Nutrition Patterns: Nutrition Physiology and Foodstuff Economics 1997; series of articles in journal Agricultural Economics and Development. *Leisure interests:* reading, sport. *Address:* Ministry of Agriculture, Keshavarz Blvd., Tehran, Iran. *Telephone:* 0098 21 654209. *Fax:* 0098 21 651030.

KALASHNIKOV, Anatoliy Ivanovich; Russian wood-engraver; b. 5 April 1930, Moscow; s. of Ivan Nikoforovich Kalashnikov and Vera Alekseevna Kalashnikova; m. 1st Iulia Kaizer 1957 (died 1980); m. 2nd Ludmila Chembrovskaya 1980 (died 1994); m. 3rd Ludmila Fyodorova 1994; ed. Moscow Art Inst. (fmrly. Stroganoff Art School), pupil of Ivan Pavlov, Dmitry Sobolev and Mikhail Matorin; freelance designer for many Soviet publishing houses and Ministry of Communications (postal designs) 1950–90; designed over 100 postage stamps, 500 commemorative envelopes and over 950 bookplates; 160 solo exhbns. worldwide; elected Academician, Int. Acad. of the Book and Art of the Book, Moscow 1992; Hon. mem. Royal Society of Painter-Etchers and Engravers, London 1988, Soc. of Wood Engravers, London 1991; Merited Artist of Russia 1983; 20 prizes in int. bookplate design competitions, Italy, Spain, Hungary, Denmark, Poland, Germany, U.S.A. *Publications include:* Canton Ticino 1978, Anglo-Russian Relations 1983, Lombardia 1991, War and Peace: A suite of Wood Engravings based on the novel by Leo Tolstoy 1991, 500 Exlibris 1993, Frankonia 1993, The Dostoyevsky Suite 1994, Omar Khayam in Wood engravings by A. Kalashnikov 1994, Sensuality and the Bookplate 1996, Golden Ring of Russia 1997; many albums and suites. *Leisure interests:* travelling. *Address:* Leninsky prospekt 44, Apt. 124, 117334 Moscow, Russia. *Telephone:* (095) 137-37-30.

KALASHNIKOV, Maj.-Gen. Mikhail Timofeyevich, D.TECH.SC.; Russian military engineer; b. 10 Nov. 1919, Kurya, Altaiskii Kpai Region; s. of Timofei Aleksandrovich Kalashnikov and Aleksandra Frolovna; m. (deceased); one s. two d.; served World War II; inventor of new types of armaments since 1940s, of machine guns RPK, PK, PKT and of automatic machine carbines AK, AKM (total number of machine carbines produced designed by Kalashnikov exceeds 55 million); Deputy of U.S.S.R. Supreme Soviet 1950–54, 1966–69, 1970–73, 1974–78, 1979–83, 1984–88; U.S.S.R. State Prize 1949; Lenin Prize 1964; Hero of Socialist Labour 1958, 1976. *Leisure interests:* hunting, fishing, gardening. *Address:* AO "Izhmash", Izhevsk, Russia. *Telephone:* 49 52 49 (Office); 52 41 85 (Home).

KALASHNIKOV, Sergey Vyacheslavovich; Russian politician; b. 3 July 1951, Akmolinsk, Kazakh S.S.R.; m.; two c.; ed. Leningrad State Univ., Inst. of Psychology, U.S.S.R. (now Russian) Acad. of Sciences, Acad. of Nat. Econs. U.S.S.R. Council of Ministers; Head, Social-Psychological service U.S.S.R. Ministry of Defence, concurrently Head, Chair of Scientific Foundation of Man., Moscow Higher Energy School, Prorector, Inst. of Oil and Chem. Industry (Neftekhim) also Dir., U.S.S.R. Ministry of Oil Industry 1979–91; Chair., Bd. Dirs. European-Asian Bank; Dir.-Gen. Int. Asscn. of Defence against Unemployment and Poverty; mem. Liberal Democratic Party; mem. State Duma 1993–98, Chair. Cttee. on Labour and Social Support, Chair., Perm. Comm. on Social Policy, Interparl. Ass. of C.I.S. 1993–98; Minister of Labour and Social Devt. Sept. 1998–; mem., Int. Acad. of Informatics. *Publications:* over 50 works including 2 monographs and textbook on social psychology. *Address:* Ministry of Labour and Social Development, Birzhevaya pl. 1, 103706 Moscow, Russia. *Telephone:* (095) 928 0683 (Office). *Fax:* (095) 230 2407 (Office).

KALETSKY, Anatole, M.A.; journalist; b. 1 June 1952, Moscow, Russia; s. of Jacob Kaletsky and Esther Kaletsky; m. Fiona Murphy 1985; two s. one d.; ed. Melbourne High School, Westminster City School, King's Coll., Cambridge and Harvard Univ.; Hon. Sr. Scholar King's Coll., Cambridge 1973–74; Kennedy Scholar Harvard Univ. 1974–76; financial writer The Economist 1976–79; leader writer Financial Times 1979–81, Washington Corresp. 1981–83, Int. Econs. Corresp. 1984–86, Chief New York Bureau 1986–90, Moscow Assignment 1990; Econs. Ed. The Times 1990–96, Assoc. Ed. and econ. commentator 1992–; Dir. Kaletsky Econ. Consulting 1997–; mem. Advisory Bd. U.K. Know-How Fund for E. Europe and fmr. Soviet Union; Specialist Writer of the Year, British Press Awards 1980, 1992, Commentator of the Year, What the Papers Say 1996, Financial Journalist of the Year, Wincott Foundation Award 1997. *Publications:* The Costs of Default 1985, In the Shadow of Debt 1992. *Leisure interests:* playing the violin, cinema, family life. *Address:* The Times, 1 Pennington Street, London, E1 9XN, England. *Telephone:* 0171-782 5000.

KALICHSTEIN, Joseph, M.SC.; American/Israeli concert pianist; b. 15 Jan. 1946, Tel Aviv; s. of Isaac Kalichstein and Mali Kalichstein; m. Rowain (née Schultz) Kalichstein; two c.; ed. Juilliard School, New York; New York debut 1967; European debut 1970; appearances with all the world's leading orchestras; mem. Piano Faculty of Juilliard School 1985–; First Prize, Leventritt Int. Competition 1969, Edward Stevermann Memorial Prize 1969. *Leisure interests:* reading, chess.

KALILOMBE, Rt. Rev. Patrick-Augustine, S.T.L., S.S.L., PH.D.; Malawi ecclesiastic and lecturer; b. 28 Aug. 1933, Dedza; s. of Pierre Kalilombe and Helena Mzifei; ed. Kasina Seminary, Kachebere Theological Coll., Gregorian Univ., Rome, Graduate Theological Union, Berkeley, U.S.A.; trained as White Father, Algeria and Tunisia 1954–58; ordained priest 1958; teacher and Rector, Kachebere Major Seminary 1964–72; Bishop of Lilongwe 1972–78; Fellow and Lecturer in Third World Theologies, Selly Oak, Birmingham, U.K. 1982–86, Dir. Centre for Black and White Christian Partnership Selly Oak 1985–, Sr. Lecturer, Third World Theologies 1982–87; Vice-Pres. East African Episcopal Confs. 1974–76, Ecumenical Asscn. of Third World Theologians 1976–78, Ecumenical Asscn. of African Theologians 1985–; Cttee. mem. Symposium of Episcopal Confs. of Africa and Madagascar 1974–76; mem. Council, Malawi Univ. 1974–76. *Publications:* Christ's Church in Lilongwe 1973, From Outstations to Small Xtian Communities 1983. *Address:* Selly Oak Colleges, Bristol Road, Birmingham, B29 61Q (Office); Flat 10, Elizabeth Court, 107 Metchley Lane, Harborne B17 0JH, England (Home). *Telephone:* (0121) 472-4231; 472-7952; (0121) 426-1738 (Home).

KALLAS, Siim; Estonian politician and banker; b. 2 Oct. 1948, Tallinn; s. of Udo Kallas and Rita Kallas; m. Kristi Kallas (née Kartus) 1972; one s. one d.; ed. Tartu Univ.; Chief Specialist Ministry of Finance Estonian S.S.R. 1975–79; Gen. Man. Estonian Savings Banks 1979–86; Deputy Ed. Rahva Haal 1986–89; Chair. Asscn. of Estonian Trade Unions 1989–91; Pres. Eesti Pank (Bank of Estonia) 1991–95; Founder and Leader Reform Party-Liberals: elected to Riigikogu (Parl.) 1995–; Minister of Foreign Affairs 1995–96. *Leisure interests:* tennis, swimming. *Address:* c/o Riigikogu, Lossi plats 1a, Tallinn 0100, Estonia.

KALLIO, Heikki Olavi, LL.M.; Finnish administrator; b. 9 June 1937, Turku; m. 1st Liisa Toivonen 1961 (divorced 1995); three s. one d.; m. 2nd Anneli Hämäläinen 1997; ed. Helsinki Univ.; Chief Admin. Officer Univ. of Turku 1963–71; Admin. Dir. Acad. of Finland 1971–72, Vice-Pres. (Admin.) 1973–; Admin. Dir. State Tech. Research Centre 1973. *Leisure interests:* sailing, navigation, safety and security at sea. *Address:* Vilhonvuorenkatu 6, 00500 Helsinki, Finland. *Telephone:* (9) 7748 8230. *Fax:* (9) 7748 8379.

KALMAN, Jozef, RS.DR.; Slovak politician and trade union official; b. 18 April 1951, Pohorelá, Banská Bystrica Dist.; s. of Jozef Kalman and Lucia Kalmanová; m. Mária Kalmanová 1972; two d.; official of Metal Workers' Trade Union; Vice-Prime Minister, Govt. of Slovak Repub. 1994–98. *Address:* Movement for Democratic Slovakia (HZDS), Tomášikova 32A, Bratislava, Slovakia. *Telephone:* (7) 23 01 44, 23 47 42.

KALORKOTI, Panayiotis; British artist; b. 11 April 1957, Cyprus; one s.; ed. Univ. of Newcastle upon Tyne, R.C.A., Koninklijke Akad. voor Kunst en Vormgeving, 's-Hertogenbosch; artist in residence Leeds Playhouse 1985,

Cleveland Co. 1992, The Grizedale Soc., Cumbria 1994; Bartlett Fellow in Visual Arts, Univ. of Newcastle upon Tyne 1988; commissioned by Imperial War Museum, London 1988, Nat. Garden Festival, Gateshead 1989–90; now part-time tutor and visiting lecturer at various Art Depts.; has exhibited at Hatton Gallery, Newcastle upon Tyne 1988–89 (also touring exhbn.), Imperial War Museum 1990, Cleveland Gallery, Middlesbrough 1992 (also touring exhbn.), Gallery K, London 1994 (also touring exhbn.), Gallery in the Forest, Grizedale 1995, Design Works, Gateshead 1997, Shipley Art Gallery, Gateshead 1998–99 (also touring exhbn.); Granada Prize for Northern Young Contemporaries, Whitworth Art Gallery, Manchester 1983. *Publications include:* Kalorkoti 1988, A Retrospective of Etchings and Screenprints 1990, A Retrospective View 1985–91 1992, Etchings and Drawings 1992, Retrospective (Etchings 1983–93) 1994, Reflections of Grizedale (Acrylics, Watercolours, Etchings) 1995, An Exhibition of Acrylics, Watercolours and Etchings 1997, Heads, Faces and Figures 1998. *Leisure interests:* music, films, malt whisky, travel. *Address:* 6 Burdon Terrace, Newcastle upon Tyne, NE2 3AE, England.

KALPAGÉ, Stanley, PH.D.; Sri Lankan diplomatist and agricultural chemist; b. 30 Aug. 1925, Colombo; s. of late Andrew Christopher Perera Kalpagé and Gimara Agnes Kalpagé (née Perera); m. Chithranganie Herat 1963; two s.; ed. Univ. of Ceylon, Colombo, Univs. of Leeds and London, U.K.; held academic posts, Depts. of Agric. and Agricultural Chem., Univ. of Peradeniya 1951–74; mem. Upper House 1965–71; Adviser to Ministry of Educ. 1977–78; Sec. Ministry of Higher Educ. and Chair. Univ. Grants Comm. 1978–89; High Commr. in India 1989–91; Perm. Rep. to UN, New York 1991–94; Chair. Sri Lanka's del. to 46th (1991) and 47th (1992) Gen. Ass., Special Political and Decolonization Cttee. of 48th Gen. Ass., Open-ended Working Group on Revitalization of Work of Gen. Ass., Special Comm. to Investigate Israeli Practices affecting the Human Rights of the Palestinian People and other Arabs of the Occupied Territories, ad hoc Comm. of Gen. Ass. on Indian Ocean as a Zone of Peace, Sri Lanka's del. to 10th Ministerial Meeting of Non-Aligned Movt., Accra, Ghana 1991; Rep. of Sri Lanka, UN Gen. Ass. Third Cttee. (Social, Humanitarian and Cultural) 1967, 1968, 1969; mem. Jt. Select Cttee. of Parl. for Revision of Constitution 1968–69; mem. UN Univ. Council 1980–86, Bd. of Trustees Asian Inst. of Tech. 1980–89; mem. Bd. of Man., Postgraduate Inst. of Archaeology, Postgrad. Inst. of Man. 1986–89; columnist The Sunday Island newspaper; Gen. Pres. Sri Lanka Asscn. for the Advancement of Science 1993; Visiting Prof. Bandaranaike Center for Int. Studies, Bandaranaike Int. Diplomatic Training Inst., Ranjan Wijeratne Acad. for Political Educ.; Fellow Nat. Acad. of Sciences of Sri Lanka 1986–, Inst. of Chem., Sri Lanka 1977–; Nuffield Fellowship in Natural Sciences, U.K. 1961, Int. Cooperation Admin. Fellowship, U.S.A. 1961, Int. Visitor Program Fellowship, U.S.A. 1985; Hon. D.Sc. (Peradeniya) 1985, (Ruhuna) 1987; Deshamanya Award for outstanding and distinguished service to the Nation 1993. *Publications:* Tropical Soils—Their Classification, Fertility and Management, 1974, 1976, 1983, Soils and Fertilizer Use in Malaysia 1979, Higher Education: Themes and Thoughts 1988, Mission to India: From Confrontation to Co-operation; numerous scientific articles. *Leisure interests:* public speaking, farming, writing, reading, walking. *Address:* 33/1 Pagoda Road, Nuge-godo, Sri Lanka. *Telephone:* (1) 853754. *Fax:* (1) 853754.

KALPOKAS, Donald; Ni-Vanuatu politician; fmr. Minister of Educ. and Judicial Services; Pres. Vanuaaku Pati (VP); Prime Minister of Vanuatu Sept.–Dec. 1991, 1998–, also Minister of Comprehensive Reform Programme 1998–, Deputy Prime Minister and Minister of Educ. 1996–97. *Address:* Vanuaaku Pati, P.O. Box 472, Port Vila, Vanuatu.

KALUGIN, Maj.-Gen. Oleg Danilovich; Russian intelligence officer and politician; b. 6 Sept. 1934, Leningrad; m.; two d.; ed. Leningrad Univ., Columbia Univ.; on staff of KGB 1958–89; corresp. Soviet Radio, New York 1959–65; Second, then First Sec. Embassy, Washington 1965–70; Chief Dept. of External Intelligence Service KGB 1973–80; First Deputy Chief of KGB for City of Leningrad and Leningrad Region 1980–87; returned to Moscow 1987, forced to retire for participation in democratic movt. and criticism of KGB 1989, deprived of all decorations and titles by order of Pres. Gorbachev 1990; prosecuted, all charges lifted at end of 1991; U.S.S.R. People's Deputy 1990–91; gave evidence on activities of KGB in courts and mass media; consultant, Information Service Agency; mem. Fed. Democratic Movt. 1995–; now works as publr. in U.S.A.; ed. Economics, Politics and Law in Russia; awarded many decorations. *Publications:* A Look from Lubianka, My 32 Years of Espionage Against the West; numerous articles. *Leisure interests:* hunting, fishing. *Telephone:* (202) 347-2624 (Office); (301) 431-0093 (Home).

KALULE, Ayub; Ugandan boxer; b. 16 July 1953, Kampala; m.; three d.; amateur boxer 1967–76; lightweight gold medal, Commonwealth Games 1974; inaugural winner of world amateur light-welterweight championship 1974; professional boxer April 1976–; won Commonwealth middleweight title May 1978 (first Ugandan to win a Commonwealth championship); defended it Sept. 1978; won World Boxing Asscn. version of world light-middleweight title from Masashi Kudo, Akita, Japan Oct. 1979; retained title v. Steve Gregory Dec. 1979, Emiliano Villa April 1980, Marijan Benes June 1980 and Bushy Bester Sept. 1980; first Ugandan to win a world title; won all 35 fights before losing to Sugar Ray Leonard (q.v.) 1981. *Leisure interest:* table tennis. *Address:* c/o Palle, Skjulet, Bagsvaert 12, Copenhagen 2880, Denmark.

KALVODA, Jan; Czech politician and lawyer; b. 30 Oct. 1953, Prague; m.; one c.; ed. Charles Univ., Prague; jr. clerk, Lawyers' Office, Rokycany 1979–83; mem. Regional Asscn. of Lawyers, Plzeň 1983–; lawyer 1983–90; organizer of Civic Forum, Rokycany Nov. 1989; Deputy to Czech Nat. Council (mem. Civic Forum then Civic Democratic Alliance) 1990–92; mem. Presidium, Czech Nat. Council 1990–92, Chair. Standing Comm. for Security Policy 1990; Vice-Pres., Czech Nat. Council 1991–92; mem. Civic Democratic Alliance 1991–, Chair. 1992–96; Vice-Premier of Czech Repub. 1992–96 (resgnd.); Chair. Legis. Council of Czech Republic 1992–96; Head, Office for Legislation and Public Admin. of Czech Repub. 1992–96; Minister of Justice July–Dec. 1996 (resgnd.); lawyer 1998–. *Address:* Občanská Demokratická Aliance, Rytířská 16, 11000 Prague 1, Czech Republic. *Telephone:* 242 11179, 242 14390 (Office).

KALYAGIN, Aleksander Aleksandrovich; Russian actor; b. 25 May 1942, Malmysh, Kirov Region; m. Glushenko Yevgeniya Konstantinovna; one s. one d.; ed. Shchukin Higher School of Theatre Art; actor Taganka Theatre and Yermolova Theatre in Moscow 1966–71; Moscow Art Theatre 1971–93. *Roles in productions:* Old New Year by Roshchin, Notes of the Lunatic by N. Gogol, Galileo by Brecht, Tartuffe by Molière, several plays by A. Gelman, M. Shatrov and other contemporary dramatists; in cinema since 1967. *Films include:* Untimely Man 1973, One's Own Among Strangers 1974, Slave of Love 1976, Interrogation 1979, Aesop 1982, Prokhindiada or Run on the Spot 1985, How Are You Doing, Crucians? 1992; f. and artistic dir. Et Cetera Theatre in Moscow 1992–; People's Artist of Russia 1983, State Prize 1981, 1983; master classes in Russia and in Europe; Chair. Union of Theatre Workers of Russia 1996–. *Leisure interests:* collecting art books, museums. *Address:* Union of Theatre Workers, Strastnoy blvd. 10, 103031 Moscow, (Office), 1905 Goda str., 3 Apt. 91, 123100 Moscow, Russia (Home). *Telephone:* (095) 229 8894 (Office); (095) 205 2654 (Home).

KAMALI, Norma; American fashion designer; b. 27 June 1945, New York; d. of Sam Arraez and Estelle Galib; m. M. H. Kamali (divorced); independent fashion designer, New York 1965–; opened first shop in East 53rd Street 1968, moving to Madison Ave. 1974; retitled business OMO (On My Own) and moved to 56th St. 1978; second boutique opened Spring Street, New York 1986; OMO Home opened 1988; collaboration with Bloomingdale's on production of exclusive collections 1988–; OMO Tokyo opened 1990; awards include Coty American Fashion Critics' Winnie Award 1981, 1982, Outstanding Women's Fashion Designer of the Year Award, Council of Fashion Designers of America 1982, American Success Award 1989. *Address:* 11 West 56th Street, New York, NY 10019, U.S.A.

KAMANDA WA KAMANDA, L. EN D.; Democratic Republic of the Congo politician, administrator and lawyer; b. 10 Dec. 1940, Kikwit; s. of Raphaël Kamanda and Germaine Kukikidika; two s. one d.; ed. Coll. St. Ignace de Kiniati, Coll. Notre Dame de Mbansa Boma, Univ. Lovanium, Kinshasa; Lawyer, Court of Appeal 1964–; Legal Adviser, Féd. congolaise des travailleurs 1964–65; Prof. Inst. Nat. d'Etudes Politiques 1965–66; Legal Adviser to Presidency of Repub. 1965–66, Sec.-Gen. 1966–67; Principal Adviser with responsibility for legal, administrative, political and diplomatic affairs to Presidency of Repub.; Dir. de Cabinet to Sec.-Gen. of Org. of African Unity 1967–72, Asst. Sec.-Gen. 1972–78; Perm. Rep. to UN 1979–82; State Commr. for Foreign Affairs and Int. Co-operation 1982–83, for Justice 1983–84; Deputy Sec.-Gen. MPR 1987; f. Mouvement populaire de la revolution (MPR) 1997; Assoc. mem. Office Nat. de la Recherche Scientifique et du Développement; Vice-Pres. Zairian section, Soc. Africaine de la Culture; del. to several int. confs; Deputy Prime Minister 1994–97, in charge of Institutional Reforms, Justice and Keeper of the Seals 1994–96, of Interior 1996–97. *Publications:* Essai-critique du système de la criminalité d'emprunt 1964, Négritude face au devenir de l'Afrique 1967, L'université aujourd'hui en Afrique 1969, L'intégration juridique et le développement harmonieux des nations africaines 1969, L'incidence de la culture audio-visuelle sur le phénomène du pouvoir 1970, Les organisations africaines Vol. I: L'OUA ou la croisade de l'unité africaine 1970, Vol. II: 1970, Le défi africaine—une puissance économique qui s'ignore 1976, L'enracinement—culture et progrès 1976. *Address:* Mouvement populaire de la revolution, Kinshasa, Democratic Republic of the Congo.

KAMARCK, Andrew Martin, B.S., M.A., PH.D.; American international bank official; b. 10 Nov. 1914, Newton Falls, New York; s. of Martin Kamarck and Frances Earl; m. Margaret Goldenweiser Burgess 1941; one s. two d.; ed. Harvard Univ.; Int. Section, Fed. Reserve Bd. 1939–40; U.S. Treasury 1940–42; U.S. Army 1942–44; Allied Control Comm., Italy 1943–44; Allied Control Council, Germany 1945; Office of Int. Finance, U.S. Treasury, Chief of Nat. Advisory Council on Int. Monetary and Financial Problems (N.A.C.) Div., Financial Policy Cttee. preparing Marshall Plan 1945–48; U.S. Treasury Rep., Rome 1948–50; Chief of Africa section, Econ. Dept., World Bank 1950–52; Econ. Adviser, Dept. of Operations, Europe, Africa and Australasia, World Bank, Chief of Econ. Missions to 14 countries, 1952–64; Dir. Econ. Dept., World Bank 1965–71; Dir. Econ. Devt. Inst. 1972–77, Sr. Fellow 1977–78; mem. American Econ. Asscn., Council on Foreign Relations; Dir. African Studies Asscn. 1961–64; Visiting Fellow, Harvard Inst. Int. Devt. 1977–86; Regents Prof., Univ. of Calif. 1964–65; mem. Council, Soc. for Int. Devt. 1967–70, 1973–76; Pres. Housing Assistance Corpn. of Cape Cod 1980–83. *Publications:* The Economic Development of Uganda (co-author) 1961, The Economics of African Development 1967, The Tropics and Economic Development 1976, La Politica Finanziaria degli Alleati in Italia 1977,

Economics and the Real World 1983, Donato Menichella (contrib.) 1986, The Role of the Economist in Government (co-author) 1989, The Bretton Woods-GATT System (co-author) 1995, The Art of Economics 1996, The Economics of the 21st Century 1998. *Address:* 118 Pine Ridge Road, Brewster, MA 02631, U.S.A. *Telephone:* (508) 385-8221.

KAMBA, Walter Joseph, B.A., LL.B., LL.M.; Zimbabwean administrator and professor; b. 6 Sept. 1931, Marondera; s. of Joseph Mafara and Hilda Kamba; m. Angeline Saziso Dube 1960; three s. (one deceased); ed. Univ. of Cape Town, Yale Law School; Attorney High Court of Rhodesia (now Zimbabwe) 1963–66; Research Fellow Inst. of Advanced Legal Studies, London Univ. 1967–68; Lecturer then Sr. Lecturer in Comparative Law and Jurisprudence, Univ. of Dundee 1969–80, Dean Faculty of Law 1977–80; Legal Adviser ZANU (PF) 1977–80; Professor of Law, Univ. of Zimbabwe 1980, Vice-Prin. 1980–81, Vice-Chancellor 1981–91; Vice-Chair. Zimbabwe Broadcasting Corpn. 1980–87, Chair. 1987; Inaugural UNESCO Africa Prof., Univ. of Utrecht 1992–96; Founding Dean and UNESCO Prof. of Human Rights, Democracy and Law, Univ. of Namibia 1994–; Trustee Zimbabwe Mass Media Trust 1981–, Conservation Trust of Zimbabwe 1981–87, Zimbabwe Cambridge Trust 1987–; mem. bd. Gov.'s Rauche House Coll. Harare 1980–; mem. Working Party on Future Policy of Asscn. of Commonwealth Univs. 1981; mem. Council, Exec. Cttee. and Budget Review Cttee. Asscn. of Commonwealth Univs. 1981–83; mem. Council UN Univ. for Peace, Costa Rica 1982–86, Univ. of Zambia 1982–86, Commonwealth Standing Cttee. on Student Affairs 1982–88, UN Univ., Tokyo 1983–89, Zimbabwe Nat. Comm. for UNESCO 1987–, Bd. of Govs. Zimbabwe Inst. of Devt. Studies 1982–, Chair. 1986–, Exec. Bd. Asscn. African Univs. 1984–; Chair. Electoral Supervisory Comm. 1984, Kingston's (Booksellers and Distributors) 1984–, Asscn. of Eastern and Southern African Univs.1984–87; Chair. Council UN Univ., Tokyo 1985–87; Vice-Pres. Int. Asscn. of Univs. 1985–1990, Pres. 1990–; Trustee, African-American Inst. (New York) 1985–; mem. Int. Bd., United World Colls. 1985–87, Bd. of Govs., Int. Devt. Research Centre, Canada 1986–, Nat. Cttee. Law and Population Studies Project 1986–, Swaziland Univ. Planning Comm. 1986, Bd., Commonwealth of Learning 1988, Int. Cttee. for Study of Educ. Exchange 1988–; Patron, Commonwealth Legal Education Asscn. 1986–; Hon. LL.D. (Dundee) 1982, (Natal) 1995, (Zimbabwe) 1998; Officer, Ordre des palmes académiques. *Publications:* articles in law journals. *Leisure interest:* tennis. *Address:* Faculty of Law, University of Namibia, Private Bag 13301, 340 Mandume Ndemufayo Avenue, Pioneerspark, Windhoek, Namibia.

KAMEI, Masao; Japanese business executive; b. 20 April 1916, Kobe City, Hyogo Pref.; s. of Einosuke Kamei and Sei Kamei; m. Hanae Kamei; two s. one d.; ed. Tokyo Univ.; Director Sumitomo Electric Industries Ltd. 1964–66, Man. Dir. 1966–69, Senior Man. Dir. 1969–71, Exec. Vice-Pres. 1971–73, Pres. 1973–82, Chair. 1982–91, Sr. Adviser 1991–; Exec. Dir. Fed. of Econ. Orgs. (Keidanren) 1973–91, Kansai Econs. Fed. 1974–; Vice-Pres. Japan Fed. of Employers' Asscns. (Nikkeiren) 1977–91; Commr. Local Govt. System Investigation Council 1977–88, Employment Council 1986–, Advisory Council on Election System 1989–91; Chair. Cttee. for the Promotion of Political Reform 1992–; Chair. Japanese Nat. Railways Reform Comm. 1983–87; Chair. Assets Disposal Council of Japan Nat. Railways Settlement Corpn. 1991–; Vice-Chair. Japan Productivity Center 1987–92, Chair. 1992–; Chair. Kansai Int. Airport Co. Ltd., Osaka, Japan 1988–95; Chair. Housing and Bldg. Land Council 1988–, New Media Devt. Asscn. 1989–, Japan Housing Asscn. 1991–; Blue Ribbon Medal 1976, Order of the Sacred Treasure (First Class) 1986. *Leisure interests:* paintings, golf. *Address:* 34-11, Kyodo 1-chome, Setagaya-ku, Tokyo 156, Japan.

KAMEI, Shizuka; Japanese politician; Parl. Vice-Minister of Transport, Minister 1994–95, of Construction 1996; mem. House of Reps. for Hiroshima; Chair. LDP Nat. Org. Cttee, and Acting Chair. LDP Policy Research Council. *Address:* c/o Liberal-Democratic Party, 1-11-23, Nagata-cho, Chiyoda-ku, Tokyo 100, Japan.

KAMEI, Yoshiyuki; Japanese politician; fmr. Parl. Vice-Minister of Transport, Minister Jan.–Nov. 1996; mem. House of Reps.; mem. LDP. *Address:* c/o Liberal-Democratic Party, 1-11-23, Nagata-cho, Chiyoda-ku, Tokyo 100, Japan.

KAMEL AHMED, Kamal El-Din, M.B., CH.B., D.M.SC., M.D.; Egyptian pathologist; b. 20 Jan. 1927, Mehella El-Kobra; m. Naguia Abd-El Khalek Safwat 1954; one s.; ed. medical schools of Cairo and Ain Shams Univs. and Max Planck Inst., Fed. Repub. of Germany; WHO mission, Iran; Prof. and Head Dept. of Pathology, Mansoura Medical School 1969–80, Dean of Medical School 1971–80; Vice-Pres. Mansoura Univ. 1980–82, Pres. 1983–87; Prof. Emer. Mansoura Medical School 1987–; Distinguished Service Medal 1987, Mansoura Univ. Award 1988. *Publications:* A Study of Carcinoma of the Urinary Bladder 1958, A New Application of Van Gieson Stain in the Diagnosis of Tumours of the Nervous System 1962, A Scheme for the Histological Diagnosis of Tumours of the Nervous System during Operations 1965, Modern Pathology 1989. *Leisure interest:* member of Gezira Sporting Club, Cairo. *Address:* 33 Ramsis Street, Apartment 144, Cairo, Egypt. *Telephone:* 5741307.

KAMEN, Martin D., B.S., PH.D.; American professor of chemistry; b. 27 Aug. 1913, Toronto, Canada; s. of Harry Kamen and Goldie Achber; m. 1st Beka Doherty (died 1963); m. 2nd Dr. V. L. Swanson 1967 (died 1987); one s.; ed. elementary and secondary schools, Chicago, and Univ. of Chicago; Research Chemist (Assoc.), Radiation Lab., Univ. of Calif. (Berkeley) 1937–44; Assoc. Prof. of Biochemistry and Research Assoc., Inst. of Radiology, Washington Univ. Medical School, St. Louis 1945–57; Prof. of Biochemistry, Brandeis Univ., Waltham, Mass. 1957–61, Univ. of Calif., La Jolla 1961, Univ. of Southern Calif., Los Angeles 1975–78, Prof. Emer. 1978–; Prof. Emer. Univ. of Calif. (San Diego Campus), La Jolla 1978–; Dir. Laboratoire de Photosynthèse C.N.R.S., France 1967–69; mem. N.A.S., American Acad. of Science and Letters, American Philosophical Soc.; Fellow, American Inst. of Chemists; Sr. Fellow Humboldt Foundation; American Chemical Soc. Award for Applications of Nuclear Science to Chem. 1963; American Soc. of Plant Physiologists, Kettering Award 1968, American Soc. of Biological Chem., Merck Award 1981; Dr. h.c. (Sorbonne, Paris) 1969, Hon. D.Sc. (Chicago) 1969, (Washington Univ., St. Louis, Illinois (Circle Campus) 1977, (Freiburg) 1979, (Weizmann Inst., Rehovoth, Israel) 1987, (Brandeis Univ., Waltham, Mass.) 1988; Alumni Medal, Univ. of Chicago 1973; Sr. Scientist Award, von Humboldt Foundation, Univ. of Freiburg 1974; Patten Prof., Indiana Univ. 1975; John Scott Award, Phila. City Council 1989; Einstein Award, Consejo Cultural Mondial 1989. *Publications:* Isotopic Tracers in Biology 1961, Primary Processes in Photosynthesis 1963, A Tracer Experiment 1964; and over 300 papers on chemical microbiology, photosynthesis and nuclear chemistry. *Leisure interest:* music. *Address:* Casa Dorinda, Apt. B-58, 300 Hot Springs Road, Montecito, CA 93108, U.S.A.

KAMILOV, Abdulaziz Khufizovich, C.HIS.SC.; Uzbekistan diplomatist; b. 16 Nov. 1947, Yangiyul; m.; one s.; ed. Moscow Inst. of Oriental Languages; Diplomatic Acad. U.S.S.R. Ministry of Foreign Affairs; diplomatic service 1972; Attache U.S.S.R. Embassy, Lebanon 1973–76; Second Sec. U.S.S.R. Embassy Syria 1980–84; mem. Div. of Near E., U.S.S.R. Ministry of Foreign Affairs 1984–88; sr. researcher Inst. of World Econs. and Int. Relations, U.S.S.R. Acad. of Sciences 1988–91; Counsellor Uzbekistan Embassy, Russian Fed. 1991–92; Deputy Chair. Security Service of Uzbekistan Repub. 1992–94; First Deputy Minister of Foreign Affairs Jan.–Aug. 1994, Minister Aug. 1994–. *Address:* Ministry of Foreign Affairs, Uzbekistansky prosp. 9, 700029 Tashkent, Uzbekistan. *Telephone:* (993) 139-15-17, 133-64-75.

KAMIŃSKI, Gen. Józef; Polish army officer and politician; b. 3 March 1919, Brzèzany, Tarnopol Dist.; s. of Antoni and Tekla (née Szpakowska) Kamińska; m. Krystyna Kamińska (née Podlaszewska); one s. one d.; ed. Infantry Training Centre, Rembertów; during Second World War in U.S.S.R., served in Red Army unit in the Far East 1940–43 in Polish Army 1943–, soldier of Tadeusz Kościuszko First Infantry Div. Platoon Commdr., subsequently Co. and Battalion Commdr.; Deputy C.-in-C., 34th Infantry Regt., 8th Infantry Div.; took part in fighting against armed underground Ukrainian org. in Bieszczady Mountains 1946; Commdr. of Regt. then of Infantry Div. and Armoured Div.; Brig.-Gen. 1954; Armoured Corps Commdr. 1954–64; Commdr., Pomeranian Mil. Dist. 1964–71, Silesian Mil. Dist. 1971–76; rank of Gen. 1974; Deputy Chief of Staff of United Armed Forces of Warsaw Treaty, then Commdt. of Karol Świerczewski Gen. Staff Acad. of Polish Army, Warsaw; mem. Union of Fighters for Freedom and Democracy (ZBoWiD), fmr. mem. ZBoWiD Voivodship Bd., Bydgoszcz, mem. ZBoWiD Chief Council, Pres. ZBoWiD Gen. Bd.; Pres. Union of Veterans of Polish Repub. and Fmr. Political Prisoners 1990–; Order of Banner of Labour (1st and 2nd Class), Grunwald Cross (3rd Class), Order Polonia Restituta (4th and 5th Class), Order of Lenin, Order of Friendship among the Nations, Virtuti Militari Cross (5th Class). *Leisure interest:* military history. *Address:* Zarząd Główny Związku Kombatantów Rzeczypospolitej Polskiej i byłych Więźniów Politycznych, Aleje Ujazdowskie 6a, 00-461 Warsaw, Poland. *Telephone:* 29 30 33 (Office).

KAMIŃSKI, Marek; Polish explorer; b. 24 March 1964, Gdańsk; *expeditions to:* Mexico, Guatemala, crossing of Spitsbergen, crossing of Greenland; attempted solo crossing of Antarctica; first man who reached alone both North and South Poles in the same year 1995; Finalist World Young Business Achiever 1994; Man of the Year 1995, "Życie Warszawy" daily. *Publication:* My Poles. Diaries from Expeditions 1990–98 1998. *Leisure interests:* travelling to the coldest places in the world, sailing, philosophy. *Address:* ul. Dickmana 14/15, 80-339 Gdańsk, Poland. *Telephone:* 58-5522513. *Fax:* 58-5523315.

KAMLANG-EK, Gen. Arthit; Thai politician; b. Bangkok; ed. Chulachomklao Royal Mil. Acad.; Supreme Commdr. of the Armed Forces and C.-in-C. of the Army 1983–86; Senator 1977, 1986; Thai People's Party M.P. for Loei 1988; Deputy Prime Minister Sept. 1990–91. *Address:* c/o Government House, Nakhom Pathan Road, Bangkok 10300, Thailand.

KAMMERER, Hans, F.R.I.B.A.; German architect; b. 25 Feb. 1922, Frankfurt; ed. Univ. of Stuttgart; Asst. Prof. Univ. of Stuttgart 1951–52; Visiting Prof. Kingston School of Art 1952–53; teaching, professional practice etc. 1953–63; Prof. of Design, Dept. of Architecture, Stuttgart 1973–86; Guest Prof. Univ. of Calif. Berkeley 1978; teaching, Univ. of Arizona, Phoenix 1983, 1986; mem. Akad. der Künste Berlin; numerous nat. and int. awards and prizes. *Leisure interests:* painting, sports. *Address:* Hardtstrasse 39, 71394 Kernen, Germany. *Telephone:* (07151) 42974. *Fax:* (07151) 48618.

KAMOUGUE, Lt.-Col. Wadal Abdelkader; Chadian politician and army officer; b. 20 May 1939, Bitam, Gabon; s. of Terkam Kamougue and Jeannette Kinel; m. 1st Eve-Marie Baba 1967; m. 2nd Martine Rondoh 1983; Minister of Foreign Affairs and Co-operation, mem. of Supreme Mil. Council in Govt. of Brig.-Gen. Félix Malloum 1975–78; Commdr. of Gendarmerie 1978–79;

mem. Provisional State Council following Kano peace agreement March–May 1979, in charge of Agric. and Animal Resources; Leader of Front Uni du Sud (later Forces Armées Tchadiennes) 1979–; Vice-Pres. of Transitional Gov. of Nat. Unity (GUNT) Nov. 1979–82; now Vice-Pres. in exile; Leader Mouvement révolutionnaire du peuple; Pres. of State Council June–Sept. 1982; fled to Cameroon, then Gabon Sept.–Oct. 1982, after defeat by forces of FAN; returned to N'Djamena Feb. 1987; Minister of Agric. 1987–89, of Trade and Industry 1989–90; mem. Conseil Provisoire de la République (CPR) 1991–92; Pres. Union pour le Renouveau et la Démocratie (URD) 1992–; Minister of Civil Service and Labour –1994; Général de Brigade 1992. *Leisure interests:* volleyball, basketball, reading, table tennis, athletics. *Address:* B.P. 92, N'Djamena, Chad. *Telephone:* 51-44-23. *Fax:* 51-41-87.

KAMP, Norbert, DR. PHIL.; German academic; b. 24 Aug. 1927, Niese; s. of Otto Kamp and Valerie (née Steier) Kamp; m. Rosemarie Füllner 1958; two s. one d.; ed. Univs. of Göttingen and Münster; Research Asst. Universität Göttingen 1957; mem. Istituto Storico Germanico Rome 1957–61; Research Asst. Univ. of Münster 1961–69; Asst. Prof. of Medieval History, Tech. Univ. of Berlin 1969–70; Ordinary Prof. of Medieval History, Tech. Univ. of Brunswick 1970–92, Rector 1976–78; Pres. Georg-August-Univ., Göttingen 1979–92, Ord. Prof. of Medieval History 1992–95, Prof. Emer. 1995–; mem. Akad. der Wissenschaften Göttingen 1986, Accademia Pontaniana Napoli 1986. *Publications:* Moneta Regis 1957, Kirche und Monarchie im staufischen Königreich Sizilien I, 1-4 1973–82. *Address:* Leipziger Strasse 236B, 38124 Braunschweig-Stöckheim, Germany (Home). *Telephone:* 61 00 55 (Home).

KAMPELMAN, Max M., J.D., PH.D.; American diplomatist; b. 7 Nov. 1920, New York; s. of Joseph Kampelmacher and Eva Gottlieb; m. Marjorie Buetow 1948; two s. three d.; ed. New York and Minnesota Univs.; Partner, Fried, Frank Harris, Shriver and Kampelman, Washington 1956–85, Fried, Frank Harris, Shriver and Jacobson 1989–91, Counsellor 1991–; Visiting Prof. Political Science, Claremont Coll., Calif. 1963; Sr. Advisor, U.S. Del. to the U.N. 1966–67; Chair. Emer., Greater Washington Telecommunications Asscn. (WETA-TV); Co-Chair., U.S. Del. to observe the Elections in El Salvador 1984; Bd. of Dirs., U.S. Inst. of Peace 1985–86; Amb., Head of U.S. Del. to the Negotiations on Nuclear and Space Arms 1985–89; Counselor Dept. of State 1987–89; Amb. and Chair. U.S. Del. to the Conf. on Security and Co-operation in Europe, Madrid 1980–83; Amb., Head U.S. del. to Geneva Meeting on Ethnic Minorities of the CSCE 1991; Amb., Head U.S. del. to Moscow Meeting of Conf. on Human Dimension of the CSCE 1991; Legis. Counsel to Sen. H. H. Humphrey 1949–55; Bd. of Trustees Woodrow Wilson Int. Center for Scholars 1979–90 (Chair. 1979–81); Chair. Freedom House 1983–85, 1989–; Dr. h.c. (Hebrew Univ. of Jerusalem) 1982, (Hebrew Union Coll.) 1984, (Georgetown Univ.) 1984, (Bates Coll.) 1986, (Minn.) 1987, (Bar Ilan) 1987, (Adelphi Univ.) 1988, (Yeshiva Univ.) 1990, (Ben Gurion Univ.) 1992, (Florida Int. Univ.) 1993, (Brandeis Univ.) 1993; D.lur. h.c. (Jewish Theological Seminary of N.Y.) 1988, (N.Y. Univ.) 1988; The Anatoly Scharansky Award 1981; Vanderbilt Gold Medal, New York Univ. Law Center 1982; Human Rights Award, American Fed. of Teachers 1983; Masaryk Award, Czechoslovak Nat. Council of America 1983; Golden Plate Award, American Acad. of Achievement 1984; Kt. Commdr's Cross of the Order of Merit (Fed. Repub. of Germany) 1984; Henry M. Jackson Award (JINSA) 1987; Sec. of State's Distinguished Service Award 1988; Trainar Award for Distinction In The Conduct of Diplomacy, Georgetown Univ. 1988 Pres.'s Citizens' Medal 1989. *Publications:* The Communist Party vs. the C.I.O.: A Study in Power Politics 1957, Three Years at the East-West Divide 1983; Co-Author: The Strategy of Deception 1963; contrib. to Congress Against the President 1976, Entering New Worlds: The Memoirs of a Private Man in Public Life 1991. *Address:* Fried, Frank Harris, Shriver and Jacobson, Suite 800, 1001 Pennsylvania Avenue, N.W., Washington, DC 20004 (Office); 3154 Highland Place, N.W., Washington, DC 20008, U.S.A. (Home). *Fax:* (202) 639-7008.

KAMPOURIS, Emmanuel Andrew, M.A.; Greek business executive; b. 14 Dec. 1934, Alexandria, Egypt; s. of Andrew G. Kampouris and Euridice A. Caralli; m. Myrto Stellatos 1959; two s.; ed. King's School, Bruton, U.K., Oxford Univ. and N. Staffs. Coll. of Tech.; Plant Man. and Dir. KEREM, Athens 1962–64; Dir. HELLENIT, Athens 1962–65; Vice-Pres. and Group Exec. (Int. and Export), American Standard Inc., Piscataway, N.J. 1979–84, Sr. Vice-Pres. (Bldg. Products) 1984–89; Pres. and C.E.O. American Standard Inc. New York 1989–, Chair. 1993–. *Leisure interests:* golf, tennis, classical music. *Address:* American Standard Inc., 1 Centennial Avenue, Piscataway, NJ 08854, U.S.A.

KAMU, Okko; Finnish conductor and violinist; b. 7 March 1946, Helsinki; m. Susanne Kamu 1987; three s. three d.; ed. Sibelius Acad.; leader, Suhonen Quartet 1964; began professional career with Helsinki Philharmonic Orchestra 1965; subsequently appointed leader, Finnish Nat. Opera Orchestra, Third Conductor 1967; guest conductor, Swedish Royal Opera, Stockholm 1969; Chief Conductor, Finnish Radio Symphony Orchestra 1971; Music Dir. Oslo Philharmonic 1975–79, Helsinki Philharmonic 1981–89; Prin. Conductor, Netherlands Radio Symphony 1983–86; Prin. Guest Conductor, City of Birmingham Symphony Orchestra 1985–88; Prin. Conductor, Sjaelland Symphony Orchestra, Copenhagen 1988–94; Music Dir. Stockholm Sinfonietta 1989–93, Helsingborg Symphony Orchestra 1991–; First Guest Conductor, Singapore Symphony Orchestra 1995–; Music Dir. Finnish Nat. Opera, Helsinki 1996–; Prin. Guest Conductor Lausanne Chamber Orchestra 1999–; conducted world premières of Sallinen's operas The Red Line and The King Goes Forth to France; numerous engagements with orchestras and opera houses worldwide; mem. Royal Swedish Acad. of Music 1996; First Prize, First Int. Karajan Conductor Competition, Berlin 1969. *Leisure interests:* sailing, fishing, underwater photography, diving, golf, gastronomy, family life. *Address:* Villa Arcadia, Calle Mozart 7, Rancho Domingo, 29639 Benalmedina Pueblo, Spain.

KAN, Naoto; Japanese politician; fmr. patent attorney; Minister of Health and Welfare Jan.–Nov. 1996; mem. House of Reps.; mem. New Party Sakigake (NPS), now Sakigake. *Address:* c/o Ministry of Health and Welfare, 1-2-2, Kasumigaseki, Chiyoda-ku, Tokyo 100, Japan.

KAN, Yuet Wai, M.D., D.SC., F.R.C.P., F.R.S.; American physician and investigator; b. 11 June 1936, Hong Kong; s. of Tong Po Kan and Lai Wai Li; m. Alvera Lorraine Limauro 1964; two d.; ed. Wah Yan Coll., Hong Kong and Univ. of Hong Kong Medical School; Asst. Prof. of Pediatrics, Harvard Medical School, U.S.A. 1970–72; Assoc. Prof., Dept. of Medicine, Univ. of Calif., San Francisco 1972–77, Prof., Depts. of Lab. Medicine, Medicine 1977–, Louis K. Diamond Prof. of Hematology 1983–, Investigator, Howard Hughes Medical Inst. 1976–; Head Div. of Molecular Medicine and Diagnostics 1989–; Dir. and Hon. Prof. Inst. of Molecular Biology, Univ. of Hong Kong 1991–94; mem. Research Grants Council, Hong Kong 1990–94; mem. N.I.H. Blood Diseases and Resources Advisory Cttee. 1985–89, Nat. Inst. of Digestive and Kidney Disease Advisory Council, NIH 1991–95; mem. Scientific Advisory Bd., St Jude's Children's Hosp. 1994–97, Qiu Shi Science and Technologies Foundation, Hong Kong 1994–, Nat. Heart, Lung & Blood Inst. 1995–96, Thalassemia Int. Fed. 1995–; Trustee Croucher Foundation 1992–, Chair. 1997–; mem. N.A.S.; Assoc. Fellow, Third World Acad. of Sciences, Academia Sinica (Chinese Acad. of Sciences); Damashek Award, American Soc. of Hematology 1979, Stratton Lecture Award, Int. Soc. of Hematology 1980, George Thorn Award, Howard Hughes Medical Inst. 1980, Gairdner Foundation Int. Award 1984, Allan Award, American Soc. of Human Genetics 1984, Lita Annenberg Hazen Award for Excellence in Clinical Research 1984, Waterford Award in Biomedical Sciences 1987, N.I.H. Merit Award 1987, American Coll. of Physicians Award 1988, Sanremo Int. Award for Genetic Research 1989, Warren Alpert Foundation Prize 1989, Albert Lasker Clinical Medical Research Award 1991, Christopher Columbus Discovery Award in Biomedical Research 1992, City of Medicine Award 1992, Cotlove Award, Acad. of Clinical Lab. Physicians and Scientists 1993, Merit Award, Fed. of Chinese Canadians Educ. Foundation 1994, Helmut Horten Research Award 1995. *Publications:* more than 240 articles and chapters in many scientific journals and books. *Address:* Room U-426, University of California, Parnassus Avenue, San Francisco, CA 94143-0793, U.S.A. *Telephone:* (415) 476-5841.

KANAAN, Taher Hamdi, PH.D.; Jordanian politician, economist and civil servant; b. 1 March 1935, Nablus, Palestine; s. of Hamdi and Najiah (née Quttainah) Kanaan; m. Ilham Kahwaji 1960; three s.; ed. American Univ. of Beirut, Trinity Coll., Cambridge; Econ. Adviser, Ministry of Planning, Iraq 1964–65; Dir. of Programmes at Arab Fund for Econ. and Social Devt., Kuwait 1973–76; Consultant in Industrial Devt., Ministry of Planning, Morocco 1977–78; Chief External Financing and Devt., UNCTAD, Geneva 1979–83; Dir. and Econ. Adviser Arab Fund 1983–85; Minister of Occupied Territories Affairs 1985, of Planning 1986–89; Gen. Man. Industrial Devt. 1989–92; World Bank Resident Rep. in Ghana 1992–94; Hon. Prof. Univ. of Warwick 1994; World Bank Chief Thought Forum, Bd. of Higher Educ., Jordan, Bd. of Dirs., Arab Soc. for and Chief Economist 1996–97; T. H. Lee Prof. of World Affairs and Prof. of Econs. Cornell Univ., Ithaca, N.Y. 1997–; American Agricultural Econs. Asscn. Research 1960–63, Direction of and Contribution to Arab Fund, Basic Programme for *Leisure interest:* watching TV. *Address:* 248 Warren Hall, Cornell University, Ithaca, NY 14853, U.S.A. *Telephone:* (607) 255-7966. *Fax:* (607)0, 1971, 1972, UNCTAD Trade and Development Report 1981, 1982, 1983. *Leisure interests:* swimming, music, history and philosophy. *Address:* Industrial Development Bank, P.O. Box 1982, Amman, Jordan. *Telephone:* (6) 644645. *Fax:* (6) 647821.

KANAKARATNE, Neville, M.A., LL.B.; Sri Lankan fmr. diplomatist and provincial governor; b. 19 July 1923, Colombo; s. of A. de S. Kanakaratne and Mildred de Silva; ed. Royal Coll., Colombo, Univs. of Ceylon and Cambridge and Middle Temple, London; Crown Counsel, Dept. of Attorney-Gen. 1951–57; First Sec. and Legal Adviser, Perm. Mission of Ceylon at UN 1957–61; Legal Adviser to Special Rep. of UN Sec.-Gen. in the Congo 1961–62; Legal and Political Adviser to Commdr., UN Emergency Force, Gaza 1962–64; Legal Adviser to Commdr. UN Peace Keeping Force, Cyprus and to Special Rep. of UN Sec.-Gen. 1964–65; Sr. Fellow, Centre for Int. Studies, New York Univ. 1965–66; Minister for Econ. Affairs, Ceylon High Comm., London 1967–70; Amb. to U.S.A. 1970–78, to U.S.S.R. 1982–88; High Commr. in India 1991–94 (also accred. to Bhutan); Gov. Southern Prov. of Sri Lanka 1995–; del. to numerous int. confs. and several sessions of UN Gen. Assembly; U.N. Survey Mission to Namibia Aug. 1978, Deputy Special Rep. to Namibia Office of Sec.-Gen. 1978–81; Hon. LL.D. (George Washington Univ.). *Leisure interests:* theatre, music, reading. *Address:* 50 Castle Street, Colombo 8, Sri Lanka.

KANANIN, Roman Grigorevich; Russian architect; b. 19 June 1935, Moscow; s. of Grigoriy Kananin and Maria Kananin; m. 1959; one d.; ed. Moscow Architectural Inst. *Works include:* Patrice Lumumba Univ. (now Univ. of People's Friendship), Moscow (with others) 1969–73, residential blocks on Lenin Prospekt, Moscow 1965–70, multi-storey brick residential complex, Noviye Cheremushky 1973–84, memorial complex to war veterans in Novorossiysk 1982, various monuments in Moscow and Magnitogorsk, including monument to Gerzen and Ogarev, Vorobyevy Hils, Moscow, Palace of Youth, Moscow 1978, IRIS Pulman Hotel and apts., Moscow 1991, Parus Business Centre, Tverskaya-Yamskaya St., Moscow 1994; Head of Atelier No. 3. of 'Mosproyekt-1' 1972–; Lenin Prize 1984; Honoured Architect of Russia 1993. *Leisure interest:* sport. *Address:* Joint-Stock Company Mosprojekt, 13/14, 1-st Brestkaya str., GSP, 125190 Moscow, Russia. *Telephone:* (095) 209-61-22, 250-46-99. *Fax:* (095) 209-50-02.

KANAWA, Dame Kiri, (see Te Kanawa, Dame Kiri).

KANBUR, Ravi, M.A., D.PHIL.; British economist; b. 28 Aug. 1954, Dharwar, India; s. of Prof. M.G. Kanbur and M.M. Kanbur; m. Margaret S. Grieco 1979; ed. King Edward VII Camp Hill School, Birmingham, Gonville & Caius Coll. Cambridge and Merton and Worcester Colls. Oxford; Prize Fellow, Nuffield Coll. Oxford 1978–79; Fellow in Econs. Clare Coll. Cambridge 1979–83; Prof. of Econs. Univ. of Essex 1983–85; Visiting Prof. Princeton Univ. 1985–87; Prof. of Econs. and Dir. Devt. Econs. Research Centre, Univ. of Warwick 1987–89; Sr. Adviser and Ed. World Bank Economic Review and World Bank Research Observer, IBRD, Washington, D.C. 1989–92; World Bank Resident Rep. in Ghana 1992–94; Hon. Prof. Univ. of Warwick 1994; World Bank Chief Economist for Africa 1994–96; World Bank Prin. Adviser to Sr. Vice-Pres. and Chief Economist 1996–97; T. H. Lee Prof. of World Affairs and Prof. of Econs. Cornell Univ., Ithaca, N.Y. 1997–; American Agricultural Econs. Asscn. Research Award (jtly. with L. Haddad) 1991. *Publications:* articles in learned journals. *Leisure interest:* watching TV. *Address:* 309 Warren Hall, Cornell University, Ithaca, NY 14853, U.S.A. *Telephone:* (607) 255-7966. *Fax:* (607) 255-9984.

KANCHELI, Giya (Georgy); Georgian composer; b. 10 Aug. 1935, Tbilisi; s. of Alexander Kancheli and Agnessa Kancheli; m. Valentina Djikia; one s. one d.; ed. Tbilisi State Conservatory with I. Tuskia; Prof. Tbilisi Conservatory 1970–90; Music Dir. Rustaveli Drama Theatre 1971–; First Sec. Georgian Composers' Union 1984–89; Composer in Residence, Berlin (German Academic Exchange Service) 1991–92; Composer in Residence, Royal Flemish Philharmonic Orchestra, Antwerp 1995–96. *Compositions include:* symphonies: First 1967, Second 1970, Third 1973, Fourth (in Memoriam Michelangelo) 1975, Fifth 1977, Sixth (In Memory of Parents) 1980, Seventh (Epilogue) 1986; other symphonic works: Mourned by the Wind for orchestra and viola 1989, Lament (in memory of Luigi Nono), for violin, soprano and orchestra 1995; opera: Music for the Living 1984; chamber works: Life Without Christmas 1989–90 (cycle of four works for chamber ensembles), Magnum Ignotum, for wind ensemble and tape 1994, Exil, for soprano, small ensemble and tape 1994; music to plays by Shakespeare King Lear, Richard III and other productions of Rustaveli Drama Theatre, incidental music; U.S.S.R. State Prize 1976, U.S.S.R. People's Artist 1988, State Prize of Georgia 1982, Nika Prize for film music 1987, Triumph Prize Moscow 1998. *Address:* Tovstonogov str. 6, 380064 Tbilisi, Georgia; Consience Straat 14, 2018 Antwerp, Belgium. *Telephone:* 883/95 03 39 (Tbilisi); 3232/308553 (Antwerp).

KANE, Edward R., PH.D.; American business executive; b. 13 Sept. 1918, Schenectady, N.Y.; s. of Edward and Elva Kane; m. Doris Peterson 1948; two d.; ed. Union Coll., M.I.T.; joined E. I. du Pont de Nemours & Co. 1943; Textile Fibres 1943–66; Asst. Gen. Man. Industrial and Biochemicals Dept. 1966, Gen. Man. 1967, Dir. 1969–89; Vice-Pres., Dir., mem. Exec. Cttee. E. I. du Pont de Nemours & Co. 1969–73, mem. Finance Cttee. and Vice-Chair. Exec. Cttee. 1971–79, Pres. and C.O.O. 1973–79; Dir. J. P. Morgan and Morgan Guaranty Trust 1978–88; (Dir. Advisory Council 1989–), Mead Corpn. 1980–87, INCO Ltd. 1981–89, Texas Instruments 1980–89; mem. Nat. Acad. of Eng. (Treas., Council mem. 1986–94), Corpn. M.I.T. 1979–89; American Chemical Soc., Soc. Chemical Industry (Chair. American Section 1973–74, Pres. London Soc. 1980–81); mem. Governing Bd. Nat. Research Council 1986–94; Int. Palladium Medal (American Section) Soc. de Chimie Industrielle 1979. *Address:* Old Kennett Road, Wilmington, DE 19807, U.S.A.

KANEKO, Hisashi, M.SC.; Japanese business executive; ed. Tokyo Univ., Univ. of California, Berkeley; joined NEC Corpn. 1956, Pres. NEC America 1989–91, NEC Corpn. 1994–. *Address:* NEC Corporation, 7-1 Shiba 5-chome, Minato-ku, Tokyo 108-01, Japan.

KANERVA, Ilkka Armas Mikael, M.POL.SC.; Finnish politician; b. 28 Jan. 1948, Lokalahti; mem. Turku City Council 1972–; Party Man., Nat. Coalition Party 1972–93 (mem. Exec. Cttee. 1975–93), Chair. Nat. Coalition Party Youth League 1972–76; M.P. 1975–, Minister of State (attached to Office of the Council of State) 1987–90; Minister at the Ministry of Finance 1989–91, 1991; Minister of Transport and Communications 1990–91, of Labour 1991–94. *Address:* c/o National Coalition Party, Kansakoulukiya 3, 00100 Helsinki, Finland.

KANG, Dong-Suk; American violinist; b. 28 April 1954, S. Korea; m. Martine Kang; one s. one d.; ed. Juilliard School, New York and Curtis Inst. Philadelphia (under Ivan Galamian); prize winner, Queen Elisabeth of the Belgians, Montréal, San Francisco Foundation and Carl Flesch competitions; has appeared with maj. orchestras throughout U.S.A., U.K., Europe and Far East and at music festivals around the world including BBC Promenade concerts (debut 1987); recordings include complete repertoire for violin and orchestra by Sibelius, Nielsen Violin Concerto, Elgar Violin Concerto, Bruch Violin Concerto, Walton Violin Concerto. *Address:* c/o Clarion/Seven Muses, 47 Whitehall Park, London, N19 3TW, England. *Telephone:* 0171-272 4413. *Fax:* 0171-281 9687.

KANG, Young Hoon, M.A., PH.D.; Korean politician and diplomatist; b. 30 May 1922; m. Hyo-Soo Kim 1947; two s. one d.; ed. Univs. of Manchuria and Southern California; Mil. Attaché to Embassy, Washington, D.C. 1952–53; Div. Commdr. 1953, Corps Commdr. 1959–60; retd. rank of Lieut.-Gen. 1961; Asst. Minister of Defence 1955–56; Staff mem. Research Inst. on Communist Strategy and Propaganda, Univ. of S. California 1968–69; Dir. Research Inst. on Korean Affairs, Silver Spring, Md. 1970–76; Dean Graduate School, Hankuk Univ. of Foreign Studies 1977–78; Chancellor Inst. of Foreign Affairs and Nat. Security, Ministry for Foreign Affairs 1978–80; Amb. to U.K. 1981–84, to the Holy See 1985–88; Prime Minister of the Repub. of Korea 1988–91; numerous mil. medals.

KANI, John; South African actor; fmrly. worked on a car ass. line; began acting in amateur production; Tony Award for Broadway performance in Athol Fugard's Sizwe Banzi is Dead; many stage tours abroad and appearances in S. Africa particularly at Market Theatre, Johannesburg; appeared in Waiting for Godot, Miss Julie, Othello (Market Theatre, Johannesburg) 1987. *Address:* c/o Market Theatre, Johannesburg, South Africa.

KANIA, Madhukar Hiralal, LL.B.; Indian judge; b. 18 Nov. 1927, Bombay; s. of Hiralal J. Kania and Bhanumati Kania; m. Rupa Kania; two d.; Fellow, Govt. Law Coll. Bombay 1949–50, part-time Prof. 1956–62; Asst. Govt. Pleader of Maha 1964–67, Govt. Pleader 1967–69, Additional Judge, Bombay High Court 1969, Judge 1971, Acting Chief Justice 1985; Chief Justice 1986; Judge, Supreme Court of India 1987–91, Chief Justice 1991. *Address:* c/o Supreme Court of India, Tilak Marg, New Delhi 110001, India. *Telephone:* 301 4989 (Home).

KANIS, Pavol, D.PHIL., C.SC.; Slovak politician; b. 27 Aug. 1948; m.; two c.; ed. Charles Univ., Prague; has held various positions in Party of the Democratic Left; Minister of Defence 1998–. *Leisure interests:* reading, gardening. *Address:* Ministry of Defence, Kutuzovova 7, 832 28 Bratislava, Slovakia.

KANN, Peter Robert; American journalist; b. 13 Dec. 1942, New York; s. of Robert Kann and Marie Breuer; m. 1st Francesca Mayer 1969 (died 1983); m. 2nd Karen House 1984; one s. two d.; ed. Harvard Univ.; with The Wall Street Journal 1964–; journalist, New York 1964–67, Vietnam 1967–68, Hong Kong 1968–75, Publr. and Ed. Asian edn. 1976–79, Assoc. Publr. 1979–88; Exec. Vice-Pres. Dow Jones & Co. 1986, Pres. int. and magazine groups 1986–89, mem. Bd. of Dirs. 1987; Publr. and Editorial Dir. The Wall Street Journal 1989–; Pres. Dow Jones & Co. New York 1989–91, Chair., C.E.O. 1991–; Chair. Bd. Far Eastern Econ. Review 1987–89; Dir. Group Expansion Prize Bd. 1987–; Trustee Asia Soc. 1989–94, Inst. for Advanced Study, Princeton 1990–, Aspen Inst. 1994–; mem. Pulitzer Prize Bd. 1987; recipient, Pulitzer Prize for int. reporting 1972. *Address:* Wall Street Journal, 200 Liberty Street, New York, NY 10281, U.S.A.

KANOVITZ, Howard, B.S.; American painter; b. 9 Feb. 1929, Fall River, Mass.; s. of Meyer J. Kanovitz and Dora (Rems) Kanovitz; m. Mary Rattray 1961 (divorced 1992); one d.; ed. Providence Coll., Rhode Island School of Design, New School for Social Research, New York Univ. Inst. of Fine Arts; one-man exhbns. New York, Fall River, Cologne, Malmö, Utrecht, Duisburg, Berlin, Hanover, Freiburg, Rottweil, Chicago, Frankfurt, Seoul 1962–; numerous group exhbns. 1953–; works in numerous public collections; D.A.A.D. Fellowship Berlin 1979. *Leisure interests:* music, fishing. *Address:* 463 Broome Street, New York, NY 10013, U.S.A. *Telephone:* (212) 226-2294.

KANTARAT, Air Chief Marshal Panieng; Thai air force officer (retd.) and politician; b. 1 April 1921, Samut Prakan; m. Khunying Suranooch; three s. one d.; ed. Wat Thep Sirin School, Bangkok, Royal Thai Army Tech. Mil. Acad., Flying Training School, Air Command and Staff Coll., Thailand Air Command. and Staff Coll., U.S.A., Army War Coll., Bangkok, Nat. Defence Coll.; attended courses R.A.F. Cen. Flying School, U.K., Combat Crew Training School, U.S.A.; Sr. Officer Defense Man. Course, U.S.N.; started air force career as Pilot Officer, Lop Buri, Commdr., Wing 2, Lop Buri 1956, Wing 1, Bangkok and Acting Deputy Dir. of Operations, Tactical Air Command 1957; Air Attaché, Thai Embassy, London 1958; Deputy Dir. of Air Operations 1961; Deputy Chief of Staff, Tactical Air Command 1962; Dir., Directorate of Operations 1963; Deputy Chief of Air Staff for Operations 1971; Vice-Chief of Air Staff 1974, Chief 1975; Deputy Minister of Defence 1979–86, Minister 1986–88; C.-in-C. Royal Thai Air Force 1977–81. *Leisure interests:* golf, gardening. *Address:* 74/20 Soi Khangkhan 2, Paholyothin Road, Patum-Dhany Province 12130, Thailand.

KANTER, Rosabeth Moss, M.A., PH.D.; American professor of management, consultant and writer; b. 15 March 1943, Cleveland; d. of Nelson Nathan Moss and Helen (née Smolen) Moss; m. 1st Stuart Alan Kanter 1963 (died 1969); m. 2nd Barry Alan Stein 1972; one s.; ed. Bryn Mawr Coll., Univ. of Michigan and Harvard Univ. Law School; Asst. then Assoc. Prof. Brandeis Univ. 1967–77; Prof. Yale Univ. 1977–86; Class of 1960 Prof. of Man. Harvard Univ. Business School 1986–; Visiting Prof. Harvard Univ. 1973–74, M.I.T. 1979–80; Ed. Harvard Business Review 1989–92; Chair. Bd. Goodmeasure Inc., Cambridge, Mass. 1977–; consultant to numerous cos.; mem. Bd. NOW Legal Defence and Educ. Fund, New York 1979–86, 1993–,

Malcolm Baldridge Nat. Quality Award 1994–, American Production and Quality Center 1989–, Econ. Policy Inst. 1993–; mem. Gov.'s Council for Econ. Growth, Mass. 1994–, Co-Chair. int. trade task force 1995–; mem. American Sociological Asscn. (Exec. Council 1982–85), Eastern Sociological Soc. (Exec. Council 1975–78, Gellman Award 1978), Acad. of Man., Cttee. of 200 (also f.); Incorporator Babson Coll. 1984–87, Boston Children's Museum 1984–; Trustee Coll. Retirement Equities Fund, New York 1985–89; Guggenheim Fellow; many hon. degrees; Woman of the Year, New England Women's Business Owners 1981, Int. Asscn. Personnel Women 1981, MS Magazine 1985, Working Woman AT & T Hall of Fame 1986, McFeely Award, YMCA 1995, and other awards. *Publications:* Work and Family in the U.S. 1977, Men and Women of the Corporation 1977 (C. Wright Mills Award), The Change Masters 1983, Creating the Future: The Massachusetts Comeback and Its Promise for America (with M. S. Dukakis) 1988, When Giants Learn to Dance 1989 (Johnson, Smith, Knicely Award), The Challenge of Organization Change (with B. A. Stein and T. D. Jick) 1992, World Class: Thriving Locally in the Global Economy 1995, Rosabeth Moss Kanter on the Frontiers of Management 1997, and six other books; also over 200 articles in professional journals, magazines, books etc. *Leisure interests:* tennis, swimming. *Address:* Harvard University Graduate School of Business Administration, Soldiers Field, Boston, MA 02163, U.S.A. (Office). *Telephone:* (617) 495-6053. *Fax:* (617) 496-5271.

KANTHER, Manfred; German politician; b. 26 May 1939, Schweidnitz; six c.; ed. Univs. of Marburg and Bonn; served articles, Lüdenscheid, Westphalia; Sr. legal counsellor, Plettenberg 1967–70; mem. Hesse Landtag 1970–; Gen. Sec. CDU Hesse 1970–87; Minister of Finance, Hesse 1987–91; mem. Bundesrat 1987–; Minister of the Interior, Fed. Govt. 1994–98. *Address:* c/o Ministry of the Interior, Graurheindorfer Strasse 198, 53117 Bonn, Germany.

KANTOR, Mickey; American politician and corporate lawyer; b. 1939; m. 1st (died 1978); one s. (died 1988); m. 2nd 1982; one d.; ed. Vanderbilt Univ., Georgetown Univ. Law School; served U.S.N.; began career as lawyer protecting rights of migrant farm workers; partner L.A. law firm 1993; mem. Bd. of Legal Services Corpn. in Carter Admin.; mem. Comm. investigating L.A. Riots 1992; Dir. Bill Clinton's Presidential Campaign 1992; U.S. Trade Rep. 1993–97; Sec. of Commerce 1996–. *Address:* Department of Commerce, Office of the Secretary, 14th & Constitution Avenue, N.W., Washington, DC 20230, U.S.A. *Telephone:* (202) 219-3605. *Fax:* (202) 482-6007.

KANTROWITZ, Adrian, M.D.; American heart surgeon; b. 4 Oct. 1918, New York City; s. of Bernard Abraham and Rose Esserman Kantrowitz; m. Jean Rosensaft 1947; one s. two d.; ed. New York Univ. and Long Island Coll. of Medicine; Cleveland Teaching Fellow in Physiology, Western Reserve Univ. School of Medicine 1951–52; Instructor in Surgery, New York Medical Coll. 1952–55; Asst. Prof. of Surgery, New York Downstate Medical Center 1955–57, Assoc. Prof. of Surgery 1957–64, Prof. of Surgery 1964–70; Adjunct Surgeon, Montefiore Hospital, Bronx, New York 1951–55; Dir. (full-time) Cardiovascular Surgery, Maimonides Hospital 1955–64; Attending Surgeon, Maimonides Medical Center 1955–64; Dir. Surgical Services (full-time), Maimonides Medical Center and Coney Island Hospital, Brooklyn 1964–70; Chair. Dept. of Surgery, Sinai Hospital, Detroit 1970–73, Chair. Dept. of Cardiovascular-Thoracic Surgery 1973; Prof. Surgery, Wayne State Univ. School of Medicine 1970–; Pres. Brooklyn Thoracic Soc. 1967–68; Pres. American Soc. of Artificial Internal Organs 1968–69; mem. Editorial Bd. Journal of Biomedical Materials Research 1966–, mem. Scientific Review Bd. Medical Research Engineering 1966–; Henry L. Moses Research Prize 1949; New York State Medical Soc., First Prize, Scientific Exhibit 1952, First Prize Maimonides Hospital Research Soc. for work in Bladder Stimulation 1963, Gold Plate Award, American Acad. of Achievement 1966, Max Berg Award for Outstanding Achievement in Prolonging Human Life 1966, Brooklyn Hall of Fame Man of Year Award for Science 1966, Theodor and Susan B. Cummings Humanitarian Award, American Coll. of Cardiology 1967; performed first human implantation of a partial mechanical heart 1966; performed first U.S. human heart transplantation 1967 and first human intra-aortic balloon pump 1968. *Publications:* numerous articles and films on heart surgery. *Leisure interests:* flying, skiing, sailing, music. *Address:* 300 River Place, Detroit, MI 48207 (Office); 70 Gallogly Road, Auburn Hills, MI 48326, U.S.A. *Telephone:* (313) 446-2800 (Office). *Fax:* (313) 446-2801.

KANTROWITZ, Arthur Robert, PH.D.; American physicist and university professor; b. 20 Oct. 1913, New York; s. of Bernard A. Kantrowitz and Rose (née Esserman) Kantrowitz; m. 1st Rosalind Joseph 1943 (divorced 1973); three d.; m. 2nd Lee Stuart 1980; ed. Columbia Univ.; Physicist and Chief of Gas Dynamics Section Nat. Advisory Cttee. for Aeronautics 1935–46; Prof. Aero Eng. and Eng. Physics Cornell Univ. 1946–56; Fulbright and Guggenheim Fellow Cambridge and Manchester Univs. (U.K.) 1953–54; Founder and C.E.O. Avco Everett Research Lab. Inc., Everett, Mass. 1955–78, Sr. Vice-Pres. and Dir. Avco Corpn. 1956–79; Prof. of Eng. Thayer School of Eng., Dartmouth Coll. 1978–; mem. Presidential Advisory Group on Anticipated Advances in Science and Tech., "Science Court" Task Force Chair. 1975–76; mem. Bd. of Dirs. Hertz Foundation; Hon. Prof. Huazhong Inst. of Tech., Wuhan, People's Repub. of China 1980; mem. N.A.S., Nat. Acad. of Eng., American Inst. of Physics; Fellow American Acad. of Arts and Sciences, American Physical Soc., American Inst. of Aeronautics and Astronautics, Int. Acad. of Astronautics, American Inst. for Medical and Biological Eng.; Theodore Roosevelt Medal of Science 1967, Messenger Lecturer, Cornell Univ. 1978; Hon. Life mem. Bd. of Govs., The Technion; M. H. D. Faraday Medal, UNESCO 1983; achievements include high-energy lasers, heart assist devices, MHD generators, re-entry from space, notable early work in fusion and molecular beams. *Publications:* co-author Fundamentals of Gas Dynamics 1958, author or co-author of more than 200 scientific and professional articles. *Address:* 4 Downing Road, Hanover, NH 03755, U.S.A. (Home). *Telephone:* (603) 643-3639 (Home).

KANZAKI, Takenori; Japanese politician; mem. House of Reps.; mem. Komeito, Chair. Foreign Affairs Cttee.; Chair. Diet Policy Cttee.; Minister of Posts and Telecommunications 1993–94. *Address:* House of Representatives, Tokyo, Japan.

KAO, Charles, PH.D.; American (b. Chinese) academic; b. 4 Nov. 1933, Shanghai, China; s. of Chun-Hsian Kao and of late Tisung-Fong King; m. May-Wan Wong 1959; one s. one d.; ed. Univ. of London; engineer, Standard Telephones and Cables Ltd., U.K. 1957–60, Research Scientist/Research Man., Standard Telecommunications Labs. Ltd./ITT Cen. European Lab., Essex, U.K. 1960–70; Chair. Dept. of Electronics, Chinese Univ. of Hong Kong 1970–74; Chief Scientist and Dir. of Eng. Electro-Optical Products Div. ITT, Roanoke, Va. 1974–81, Vice-Pres. and Dir. of Eng. 1981–88; Exec. Scientist and Corporate Dir. of Research, ITT Advanced Tech. Centre, Conn. 1983–87; Vice-Chancellor The Chinese Univ. of Hong Kong 1987–96; Chair. and C.E.O. Transtech Services Ltd. 1996–; Hon. D.Sc. (Chinese Univ. of Hong Kong) 1985, (Sussex) 1990, (Durham) 1994; Dr. h.c. (Soka) 1991; Hon. D.Eng. (Glasgow) 1992; Hon. Dr. of Telecommunications Eng. (Padova, Italy) 1996; numerous awards and prizes including Alexander Graham Bell Medal, Inst. of Electrical & Electronic Engs. (USA) 1985, Marconi Int. 1985, Faraday Medal, Inst. of Electronic Engs. (U.K.) 1989; Hon. C.B.E. 1993, Japan Prize 1996. *Publications:* Optical Fiber Technology II 1981, Optical Fiber Systems: Technology, Design and Applications 1982, Optical Fibre 1988, A Choice Fulfilled—The Business of High Technology 1991. *Leisure interests:* tennis, hiking, pottery-making. *Address:* Transtech Services Ltd., Room 1641, Telecom House, 3 Gloucester Road, Wanchai, Hong Kong Special Administrative Region, People's Republic of China. *Telephone:* 2888 8772. *Fax:* 2827 9922.

KAO, Chin-Yen; Chinese business executive; b. 24 May 1929, Taiwan; m. Lai-Kwan Kao; one d.; ed. Tainan Co. Tienchow Elementary School; Sales Man. Tainan Fabric Corpn. 1957–67; Pres. Enterprises Corpn. 1967–89, Vice-Chair and Pres. 1989–, C.E.O. Pres. Enterprises Group 1989–, Chair. Pres. Enterprises Chain Store Corpn. 1986–; Chair. Ztong Yee Industrial Co. Ltd. 1977–, Ton Yi Industrial Corpn. 1979–; mem. Cen. Standing Cttee, Kuomintang 1994–; Hon. Ph.D. (Lincoln) 1983. *Address:* 301 Chung Cheng Road, Yungkang, Tainan County, Taiwan.

KAO, Henry Yu-shu; Chinese politician (retd.); b. 3 Sept. 1913, Taipei; s. of Ching-Ho Kao and Shih Lee; m. Tsui-Yung Huang 1941; three s.; ed. Waseda Univ., Tokyo; Mayor of Taipei 1954–57, 1964–72; Minister of Communications 1972–76, without Portfolio 1976–89; Sr. Advisor to Pres. of Taiwan. *Leisure interest:* golf. *Address:* 5 Ching-tao West Road, Taipei, Taiwan. *Telephone:* 311-9898. *Fax:* 311-3928.

KAPARTIS, Costas, M.A.; Cypriot labour relations official; b. 28 Sept. 1933, Nicosia; m. Anna Kapartis; three c.; ed. Webster and Cornell Univs.; various positions in Ministry of Labour and Social Insurance 1957–65; Dir.-Gen. Cyprus Employers' Fed. 1965–75; Exec. Sec. Int. Org. of Employers (IOE) 1975, Deputy Sec.-Gen. 1980–90, Sec.-Gen. 1990–. *Address:* International Organisation of Employers, 26 chemin de Joinville, 1216 Cointrin/Geneva (Office); 9 chemin A. Pasteur, 1209 Geneva, Switzerland (Home).

KAPIL DEV; Indian cricketer; b. 6 Jan. 1959, Chandigarh; m.; ed. Punjab Univ.; right-hand middle-order batsman, right-arm fast-medium bowler; played for Haryana 1975–76 to 1991–92, Northamptonshire 1981–83, Worcestershire 1984–85; played in 131 Tests for India 1978–79 to 1993–94, 34 as Capt., scoring 5,248 runs (average 31.0) including 8 hundreds and taking record 434 wickets (average 29.6); youngest to take 100 Test wickets (21 years 25 days); hit four successive balls for six v. England, Lord's 1990; scored 11,356 runs (18 hundreds) and took 835 wickets in first-class cricket; toured England 1979, 1982, 1983 (World Cup), 1986 and 1990; 224 limited-overs internationals. *Publication:* Kapil Dev—Triumph of the Spirit 1995. *Leisure interests:* hunting, riding, dancing. *Address:* c/o Board of Control for Cricket in India, E-4, Radio Colony, Indore (M.P.), India.

KAPLAN, Jeremiah; American publishing executive; b. 15 July 1926, New York; s. of Samuel Kaplan and Fannie Brafman; m. Charlotte R. Larsen 1945; one s. three d.; Vice-Pres. Free Press Glencoe Inc., Ill. 1947–60, Pres. 1960–64; Editorial Dir. Gen. Publishing Div. Crowell Collier Publishing Co. 1960–62, Vice-Pres. 1962–67, Sr. Vice-Pres. 1967–; Chair. Bd. Science Materials Inc. 1962–63; Vice-Pres. Macmillan Co. 1960–63, Exec. Vice-Pres. 1963–65, Pres. 1965–73, 1977–86, Chair. 1983–87; Exec. Vice-Pres. Crowell Collier Div. Macmillan Inc. 1968–86; Head, Product Devt. Corp. Marketing Planning, Crowell Collier & Macmillan Inc. 1972–, also mem. Bd. Dirs.; Chair. Collier Macmillan Int. 1973; Exec. Vice-Pres. and Dir. Macmillan Inc. 1979–86; Chair. Bd. Macmillan Publishing Co., Inc. 1980–86; Special Adviser to Chair. Simon & Schuster, Inc. New York 1987, Pres. 1987–90.

KAPLAN, Jonathan Stewart; American film writer and director; b. 25 Nov. 1947, Paris; s. of Sol Kaplan and Frances Heflin; m. Julie Selzer 1987;

one d.; ed. Univ. of Chicago, New York Univ. and New World Pictures Roger Corman Postgrad. School of Film Making, Hollywood; mem. tech. staff, Bill Graham's Fillmore East, New York 1969–71; appeared in The Dark at the Top of the Stairs, Broadway 1956–57. *Films:* Night Call Nurses 1972, Student Teachers 1973, The Slams 1973, Truck Turner 1974, White Line Fever 1974, Mr Billion 1976, Over the Edge 1978, 11th Victim 1979, Muscle Beach 1980, Gentleman Bandit 1981, White Orchid 1982, Heart Like a Wheel 1983, Project X 1986, The Accused 1987, Immediate Family 1989, Love Field 1990, Unlawful Entry 1992, Bad Girls 1994; dir. Rebel Highway 1994, Picture Windows 1995. *Address:* c/o Meschures, 760 N. La Cienega Blvd., Los Angeles, CA 90069, U.S.A.

KAPLANSKY, Irving, B.A., M.A., PH.D.; American mathematician; b. 22 March 1917, Toronto, Canada; s. of Samuel Kaplansky and Anna Zuckerman; m. Rachelle Brenner 1951; two s. one d.; ed. Univ. of Toronto and Harvard Univ.; Instructor, Harvard Univ. 1941–44; Research Mathematician, Columbia Univ. 1945; Instructor, Univ. of Chicago 1945–47, Asst. Prof. 1947–52, Assoc. Prof. 1952–56, Prof. 1956–84, Chair. Dept. of Maths. 1962–67; Pres. American Math. Soc. 1984; Dir. Berkeley Math. Sciences Research Inst. 1984–92; mem. N.A.S. 1966; apptd. to George Herbert Mead distinguished service Professorship 1969; Hon. Dr. of Maths. (Waterloo) 1968, Hon. LL.D. (Queen's) 1969. *Publications:* numerous research papers and books on mathematics. *Leisure interests:* music, swimming. *Address:* c/o Mathematical Sciences Research Institute, 1000 Centennial Drive, Berkeley, CA 94720, U.S.A. *Telephone:* 642-0143.

KAPLICKY, Jan; Czech architect; b. 1937, Prague; living in U.K. 1968–; Co-founder (with David Nixon) of design studio—Future Systems 1979; with partner Amanda Levete 2nd in competition for the Bibiothèque de France (Paris); exhbn. in Prague 1998.

KAPNICK, Harvey Edward, Jr., B.S., C.P.A.; American business executive (retd.); b. 16 June 1925, Palmyra, Mich.; s. of Harvey E. and Beatrice Bancroft Kapnick; m. 1st Jean Bradshaw 1947 (died 1962); m. 2nd Mary Redus Johnson 1963; three s.; ed. Cleary Coll. and Univ. of Michigan; joined Arthur Andersen & Co. (Accountants) 1948, Partner 1956, Man. Partner, Cleveland Office 1962, mem. Bd. of Dirs. 1966, Chair. and Chief Exec. 1970–79, Deputy Chair. and C.O.O., First Chicago Corpn., First Nat. Bank, Chicago 1979–80; Pres. Kapnick Investment Co. 1980–84, 1989–; Chair., Pres. and C.E.O. Chicago Pacific Corpn. 1984–89; Vice-Chair. Gen. Dynamics 1991–94; Dir. Dearborn Park Corpn., Chicago Council on Foreign Relations, Lyric Opera of Chicago, United Way of Metropolitan Chicago; Chair. U.S. Treasury Advisory Cttee. on Fed. Consolidated Financial Statements; mem. Iran-U.S. Business Council (Chair. U.S. Section), U.S. Advisory Cttee. for Trade Negotiations, U.S. Advisory Cttee. on Transnational Enterprises; mem. American Inst. of Certified Public Accountants; mem. U.S. del. to Ad Hoc Working Group on Accounting Standard, OECD Cttee. on Int. Investment and Multinational Enterprises; mem. Bd. of Trustees Menninger Foundation, Orchestral Asscn., Logistics Man. Inst., Museum of Science and Industry Northwestern Univ.; Hon. D.Sc. (Cleary Coll.) 1971, Hon. D.H.L. (DePauw Univ.) 1979. *Address:* 1300 Third Street, Naples, FL 33940 (Office); 4000 Run Row, Naples, FL 33940, U.S.A. (Home).

KAPOOR, Anish, M.A.; Indian sculptor; b. 12 March 1954, Bombay; s. of Rear-Adm. and Mrs. D. C. Kapoor; m. Susanne Spicale 1995; one d. one s.; ed. Hornsey Coll. of Art, Chelsea Coll. of Art and Design, London; teacher, Wolverhampton Polytechnic 1979; Artist-in-Residence, Walker Art Gallery, Liverpool 1982; one-man exhbns. in Paris 1980, 1998, London 1981, 1982, 1983, 1985, 1988, 1989–90, 1990–91 (Anish Kapoor Drawings, Tate Gallery, London), 1993, 1995–96, 1998, Liverpool 1982, 1983, Rotterdam, Lyon 1983, New York 1984, 1986, 1989, 1990, 1993, Basel 1985, Oslo, Univ. of Mass. Amherst 1986, Sydney 1987, Nagoya, Japan 1989, 1994, Venice 1990, Grenoble 1990–91, Madrid 1991, 1992, Hanover 1991, Ushimado, Japan 1991, Cologne 1991, 1996–97, Los Angeles 1992, San Diego 1992–93, Tel Aviv 1993, Ljubljana 1994, Tokyo 1995, Tillburg 1995, Milan 1995–96, Turku, Finland 1996, Cambridge, England 1996, Brescia, Italy 1996, 1998, San Francisco 1996, Bordeaux 1998, Santiago de Compostela, Spain 1998; travelling exhbn. U.S.A. and Canada 1992–93; and has participated in group exhbns. since 1974 throughout Britain and in Europe, North America, Japan, Australia, New Zealand, Mexico, Morocco and Brazil; works in public collections including Tate Gallery, London, Hirshhorn Museum and Sculpture Garden, Washington, D.C., Museum of Modern Art, New York, Art Gallery of N.S.W., Australia, Contemporary Art Soc., London, Nat. Gallery, Ottawa, Hara Museum of Contemporary Art, Tokyo, Auckland City Art Gallery, N.Z., Tel Aviv Museum of Art, and many others; public comms.: Cast Iron Mountain, Tachikawa Art Project, Tokyo 1994, outdoor comms., Toronto 1995, Israel Museum, Jerusalem 1997, Bordeaux 1998–99; Hon. Fellow London Inst. 1997; Hon. D.Litt. (Leeds) 1993; Premio Duemila, Venice Biennale 1990, Turner Prize, Tate Gallery, London 1991. *Address:* c/o Lisson Gallery, 67 Lisson Street, London, NW1 5DA, England. *Telephone:* 0171-724 2739. *Fax:* 0171-724 7124.

KAPOOR, Shashi; Indian actor and producer; b. 18 March 1938, Calcutta; s. of Prithviraj Kapoor; m. Jennifer Kendal 1958 (died 1984); three c.; joined Shakespeareana co. 1955, and toured India, Pakistan and Malaysia; producer 1978–. *Films include:* Awaara 1951, Char Diwari 1960, Householder 1962, Shakespeare Wallah 1965, Jab Jab Phool Khile 1965, Wagt 1967, Aa Gale Lag Jaa 1973, Deewar 1975, Siddartha 1978, Heat and Dust 1983, Ustav 1984, Sammie and Rosie Get Laid 1987, The Deceivers, Nomads, Ajuba 1988, In Custody 1994; *films produced include:* Junoon 1979 (Nat. Award), Kalyug, 36 Chowringhee Lane 1981, Vijeta 1982. *Address:* Film Vilas, Janki Kutir, Juhu Church Road, Bombay 400049, India. *Telephone:* 577476.

KAPRIO, Leo, M.D., M.P.H., DR.P.H., F.A.P.H.A. ; Finnish international public health officer; b. 28 June 1918, Tuusula, Finland; s. of Dr. Arthur J. T. M. and Mrs. K. Molander; m. Aini Korhonen, M.PH.ED. 1943; two s. one d.; ed. Helsinki, Johns Hopkins and Harvard Univs.; Finnish Army Medical Corps during Second World War; Chief Medical Adviser to Finnish Population Asscn. (Vaestoliitto) 1944–49; Chief Medical Adviser, Finnish Red Cross 1951–56; Chair. of State Cttee. to reorganize Finnish Health Services 1953–54; mem. of WHO Advisory Panel on Public Health Admin. 1951–56, 1985–(99); Chief, Div. of Public Health, Nat. Health Service 1952–56; Regional Officer, E. Mediterranean and Europe, WHO 1956–63; Finnish del. to WHO 1953–54; Bd. mem. WHO of UN R.I.S.D. (Geneva) 1964–67; WHO rep. at World Population Conf. 1965; Dir. Div. of Public Health Services 1963–67; Regional Dir. for Europe 1967–85; Special Adviser to Dir.-Gen. WHO 1985–88; Chair. of Global Advisory Group of WHO Expanded Programme of Immunization 1986–90; lecturer on Int. Health Helsinki Univ. 1989–93; Chair. Finnish Cttee. of the Club of Rome 1991–94; Hon. mem. Schools Public Health Asscn. for the European Region 1978, Int. Epidemiological Asscn. 1987; Foreign Corresp. mem. Div. des Sciences, Acad. des Sciences, Inscriptions et Belles Lettres de Toulouse 1977; Dr. h.c. (Leuven), Dr. Med. h.c. (Uppsala), Prof. h.c. (Govt. of Finland). Dr. h.c. (Cracow Medical Acad.) 1976, LL.D. h.c. (Leeds) 1982, Hon. F.F.C.M. (U.K.); J. E. Purkyne Medal (Czechoslovakia), Johan Peter Frank Medal (Fed. Repub. of Germany), Commdr. of the Order of the Finnish White Rose 1982, Commdr.'s Cross of the Icelandic Order of the Falcon 1982, Commdr.'s Cross of the Swedish Royal Order of North Star 1984, The Nordic Public Health Award 1989, The Amdriia Stampar Medal of ASHER 1993, and numerous other awards and medals. *Publications:* Primary Health Care in Europe 1979, Forty Years of WHO in Europe 1991 (in English and French), Thirty Years in International Service (in Finnish) 1994, WHO in the UN System (in English and French) 1995; over 100 health policy documents, articles and scientific publs. in Finnish, Swedish, English and German. *Leisure interest:* history. *Address:* P. Hesperiamkatu 7, 00260 Helsinki, Finland. *Telephone:* (9) 406752.

KAPTEYN, Paul Joan George, LL.D.; Netherlands lawyer; b. 31 Jan. 1928, Laren, N.H.; s. of Paul J. and Picaine (Schröder) Kapteyn; m. Ieteke Streef 1956; one s. one d.; ed. Univ. of Leiden, Inst. des Hautes Etudes Int., Paris; Asst. Prof. of Int. Law, Univ. of Leiden 1953–60; with Foreign Office, The Hague 1960–63; Prof. of Law of Int. Orgs., Univ. of Utrecht 1963–74, Univ. of Leiden 1972–76; mem. Council of State 1976–90, Pres. Judicial Section 1984–90; mem. Int. Comm. of Jurists 1976–90; Pres. Netherlands Asscn. of Int. Law 1987–93; Judge, Court of Justice of the EC 1990–; mem. Royal Netherlands Acad. of Sciences. *Publications:* The Common Assembly of the European Coal and Steel Community 1960; Co-author: An Introduction to the Law of the European Communities 4 edns. 1970–87. *Leisure interests:* tennis, reading, travelling. *Address:* Court of Justice of the European Communities, Palais de la Cour de Justice, L-2925 Luxembourg (Office); 16 rue Bellevue, L-1227 Luxembourg (Home). *Telephone:* 461-757. *Fax:* 4303-2800.

KAPUŚCIŃSKI, Ryszard, M.A.; Polish journalist; b. 4 March 1932, Pińsk; s. of Józef Kapuściński and Maria Bobka Kapuścińska; m. Alicja Mielczarek 1952; one d.; ed. Faculty of History, Warsaw Univ.; began career with Sztandar Młodych 1951, with Polityka 1957–61; later Corresp. Polish Press Agency (PAP) in Africa and Latin America 1962–72; Kultura 1974–81; Deputy Chair. Poland 2000 Cttee., Polish Acad. of Sciences 1981–85; mem. Presidential Council of Culture 1992–95; mem. Polish Journalists Asscn. –1982; Sr. Assoc. mem. St. Antony's Coll., Oxford 1985; Visiting Scholar Bangalore Univ. 1973, Univ. of Caracas 1978, Columbia Univ. 1983, Temple Univ., Phila. 1988; mem. Bd. PEN Club Polish Centre, Bd. of Advisers, New Perspectives Quarterly; mem. European Acad. of Science and Art 1993–; mem. Polish Acad. of Art and Science 1998–; Dr. h.c. (Silesian Univ.) 1997; B. Prus Prize 1975, Julian Brun Prize, Int. Prize of Int. Journalists Org. five times, State Prize (Second Class) 1976, Prize of German Publishers and Booksellers for European Understanding, Leipzig 1994, Prix d'Astrolab, Paris 1995, Jan Parandowski PEN Club Prize 1996; Alfred Jurzykowski Foundation Award in the Field of Literature, New York 1994, Turański Foundation Award, Toronto 1996, Josef Conrad Literature Award (J. Piłsudski Inst. of America), New York 1997; Gold Cross of Merit, Kt.'s Cross, Order of Polonia Restituta 1974. *Publications:* Busz po polsku 1962, Czarne gwiazdy 1963, Kirgiz schodzi z konia 1968, Gdyby cała Afryka... 1969, Dlaczego zginął Karl von Spreti 1970, Chrystus z karabinem na ramieniu 1975, Jeszcze dzień życia 1976, Cesarz 1978, Wojna futbolowa 1978, Szachinszach 1982, Notes (poems) 1986, Lapidarium 1990, Vol. II 1995, Vol. III 1997, Imperium 1992, Lapidaria 1997, Heban 1998. *Leisure interest:* photography. *Address:* ul. Prokuratorska 11 m. 2, 02-074 Warsaw, Poland. *Telephone:* (22) 825 22 23. *Fax:* (22) 825 22 23.

KARADJORDJEVIC, H.R.H. Crown Prince Alexander (see **ALEXANDER KARADJORDJEVIC,** H.R.H. Crown Prince).

KARADŽIĆ, Radovan; Serbian political leader and psychiatrist; b. 19 June 1945, Montenegro; m. Lilyan Karadžić; one s. one d.; worked in state hosps. (specialised in neuroses and depression); with Unis Co.; Co.-f. Serbian Democratic Party 1990; leader of self-declared Serbian Repub. (in Bosnia and Herzegovina), elected Pres., resgnd. 1996, int. arrest warrant issued for him July 1996; attended ceasefire talks in London Aug. 1992, Geneva Jan. 1993, after outbreak of hostilities; named as war crimes suspect by UN Tribunal for fmr. Yugoslavia April 1995; formally charged with genocide and crimes against humanity by Int. War Crimes Tribunal for fmr. Yugoslavia 1995; now in hiding; mem. Order of St. Dionysus of Xanthe (First Rank); received main literary award of Montenegro for book of poetry Slavic Guest 1993; Risto Ratkovic Prize for Literature; Mikhail Sholokhov prize for Poetry (Russian Writers' Union) 1994. *Leisure interest:* composes music. *Publications:* three books, children's poetry.

KARAGANOV, Sergei Aleksandrovich, DR.HAB.; Russian defence and foreign affairs specialist; b. 12 Sept. 1952, Moscow; m. Irina O. Karaganova 1980; one d.; Jr. Fellow, Sr. Fellow, Head of Section, U.S.A. and Canada Studies Inst. 1978–88; Research Fellow, Perm. Mission of U.S.S.R. at UN 1976–77; Head of Dept., Deputy Dir. Inst. of Europe of Russian Acad. of Sciences 1988–; mem. Foreign Policy Council, Ministry of Foreign Affairs of Russia 1991–; founder and Chair. Bd. Council of Foreign and Defence Policy 1991–; mem. Presidential Council of Russia 1992–; mem. Consulting Council to Security Council of Russia 1993–; mem. Consultative Council of Fed. 1996–. *Publications:* Tactical Nuclear Weapons in Europe 1990, Security of the Future Europe 1991, Russia: The New Foreign Policy and Security Agenda. A View from Moscow 1993, What Has Gone Wrong With Western Aid to Russia? 1993, Damage Limitation or Crisis? Russia and the Outside World, Russia's Economic Role in Europe 1995. *Leisure interests:* athletics, literature, cooking. *Address:* Mohovaja Street 8-3B, 103873 Moscow (Office); Chernyahovskogo, 9/5 Apt. 387, 125139 Moscow, Russia (Home). *Telephone:* 203-68-34; 203-7348 (Office); 152-99-82 (Home). *Fax:* (095) 200-42-98.

KARAGEORGHIS, Vassos, PH.D., F.S.A., F.R.S.A.; Cypriot archaeologist; b. 29 April 1929, Trikomo; s. of George and Panagiota Karageorghis; m. Jacqueline Girard 1953; one s. one d.; ed. Pancyprian Gymnasium, Nicosia, Univ. Coll., and Inst. of Archaeology, London Univ.; Asst. Curator, Cyprus Museum 1952–60, Curator 1960–63, Acting Dir., Dept. of Antiquities, Cyprus 1963–64, Dir. 1964–89; Dir. Archaeological Research Unit, Prof. of Archaeology, Univ. of Cyprus 1992–96; excavations at Salamis 1952–73, Akhera and Pendayia 1960, Kition 1962–81, Maa-Palaeokastro, Pyla-Kokkinokremos 1979–87; Dir. d'Etudes, Ecole Pratique des Hautes Etudes, Sorbonne, Paris 1983–84; Adjunct. Prof. of Classical Archaeology, State Univ. of New York, Albany 1973–; Geddes-Harrower Prof. of Classical Art and Archaeology, Univ. of Aberdeen 1975; Visiting Mellon Prof., Inst. for Advanced Study, Princeton 1989–90; adviser to the Pres. of Cyprus on cultural heritage 1989–92; mem. Council, A. G. Leventis Foundation (mem. Governing Body 1997–), Cultural Foundation of the Bank of Cyprus; mem. Royal Swedish Acad., Accademia dei Lincei, Acad. des Inscriptions et Belles Lettres, German Archaeological Inst., Acad. of Athens; Corresp. mem. Austrian Acad. of Sciences; Hon. mem. Soc. for Promotion of Hellenic Studies, Archaeological Inst. of America, Council, Greek Archaeological Soc.; Visiting Fellow, Merton Coll., Oxford 1979, 1988, Sr. Research Fellow 1980, Hon. Fellow 1990; Visiting Fellow, All Souls Coll., Oxford 1982; Fellow, Royal Soc. of Humanistic Studies, Lund, Univ. Coll., London, Royal Soc. of Arts; Corresp. Fellow, British Acad.; Hon. Fellow, Soc. of Antiquaries, London; Dr. h.c. (Lyon, Göteborg, Athens, Birmingham, Toulouse, Brock, Brussels, Oxford); Prix de la Soc. des Etudes Grecques, Sorbonne 1966, R. B. Bennett Commonwealth Prize 1978, Onassis Prize 'Olympia' 1991, Premio Internazionale 'I Cavalli d'Oro di San Marco' 1996; Chevalier, Légion d'honneur 1971, Order of Merit (1st Class), Fed. Repub. of Germany 1980, Commdr. Royal Order of Polar Star (Sweden) 1990, Commdr. Ordre des Arts et des Lettres 1990, Commdr. Order of Merit (Italy) 1990, Austrian Decoration for Arts and Sciences 1997. *Publications include:* Treasures in the Cyprus Museum 1962, Corpus Vasorum Antiquorum 1963, 1965, Nouveaux documents pour l'étude du bronze récent à Chypre 1964, Sculptures from Salamis, Vol. I 1964, Vol. II 1966, Excavations in the Necropolis of Salamis, Vol. I 1967, Vol. II 1970, Vol. III 1973, Vol. IV 1978, Mycenaean Art from Cyprus 1968, Cyprus (Archaeologia Mundi) 1968, Salamis in Cyprus 1969, Altägäis und Atlkypros (with H. G. Buchholz) 1971, Cypriot Antiquities in the Pierides Collection, Larnaca, Cyprus 1973, Fouilles de Kition I 1974, Kition, Mycenaean and Phoenician discoveries in Cyprus 1976, The Civilization of Prehistoric Cyprus 1976, La céramique chypriote de style figuré I-III (with Jean des Gagniers) 1974–79, Vases et figurines de l'Age du Bronze (with Jean des Gagniers) 1976, Fouilles de Kition II (with J. Leclant and others) 1976, Hala Sultan Tekké I (with P. Åström, D. M. Bailey) 1976, Fouilles de Kition III (with M. G. Guzzo Amadasi) 1977, Two Cypriot sanctuaries of the end of the Cypro-Archaic period 1977, The Goddess with Uplifted Arms in Cyprus 1977, Cypriot Antiquities in the Medelhavsmuseet, Stockholm (with C. G. Styrenius and M.-L. Winbladh) 1977, Mycenaean Pictorial Vase Painting (with Emily Vermeule) 1981, Excavations at Kition IV (with J. N. Coldstream and others) 1981, Cyprus from the Stone Age to the Romans 1982, Palaepaphos-Skales. An Iron Age Cemetery in Cyprus 1983, Pyla-Kokkinokremos—A late 13th Century B.C. fortified settlement in Cyprus (with M. Demas) 1984, Cyprus at the close of the Late Bronze Age (with J. D. Muhly, eds.) 1984, Ancient Cypriot Art in the Pierides Foundation Museum (with others) 1985, Archaeology in Cyprus 1960–85 (ed.) 1985, Excavations at Kition V (with M. Demas) 1985, La Nécropole d'Amathonte III: Les Terres Cuites 1987, Excavations at Maa-Palaeokastro 1979–86, 1988 (with M. Demas), Blacks in Ancient Cypriot Art 1988, The end of the Late Bronze Age in Cyprus 1990, Tombs at Palaepaphos 1990, Les anciens Chypriotes: entre orient et occident 1990, The Coroplastic Art of Ancient Cyprus (Vol. I) 1991, (Vol. II) 1993, (Vol. III) 1993, (Vol. IV) 1995, (Vol. VI) 1996, Cyprus in the Eleventh Century B.C. (Ed.) 1994, Cyprus and the Sea (Ed. with D. Michaelides) 1995, The Evolution of the Economy of Cyprus from the Prehistoric Period to the Present Day (Ed. with D. Michaelides) 1996, and articles in Greek, German, American, English and French journals. *Leisure interest:* gardening. *Address:* c/o Foundation Anastasios G. Leventis, 40 Gladstonos Street, 1095 Nicosia, Cyprus. *Telephone:* (2) 461706, 475018. *Fax:* (2) 475002.

KARAMANOV, Alemdar Sabitovich; Ukrainian/Crimean Tatar composer; b. 10 Sept. 1934, Simferopol; ed. Moscow State Conservatory (pupil of S. Bogatyrev and D. Kabalevsky); author of numerous symphonic compositions including 24 symphonies 1954–94, vocal-orchestral compositions of secular and religious character, including Requiem 1991, Mysteria of Khersones 1993, 3 piano concertos, 2 violin concertos, Nat. Anthem of Crimea Repub. 1992, chamber ensembles, piano music, choruses and vocal compositions; most of his music not performed up to late 1980s. *Address:* Voykova str. 2, Apt. 4, Simferopol, Crimea, Ukraine (Home). *Telephone:* (0652) 462 00 (Home).

KARAMI, Omar; Lebanese politician; fmr. Minister of Educ. and the Arts; Prime Minister of Lebanon 1990–92. *Address:* c/o Office of the Prime Minister, Beirut, Lebanon.

KARAN, Donna; American fashion designer; b. 2 Oct. 1948, Forest Hills, New York; m. 1st Mark Karan (divorced 1978); one d.; m. 2nd. Stephan Werss 1983; ed. Parsons School of Design, New York; designer, Anne Klein & Co., then Addenda Co. until 1968; returned to Anne Klein 1968, Assoc. Designer 1971, Dir. of Design (in collaboration with Louis Dell'Olio, q.v.) 1974–84; owner, designer Donna Karan Co., New York 1984–96, designer Donna Karan Int. (public co.) 1996–; mem. Fashion Designers of America; Coty Awards 1977, 1981, Fashion Designers of America Women's Wear Award 1996. *Address:* Donna Karan International, 550 Seventh Avenue, New York, NY 10018, U.S.A.

KARAOSMANOGLU, Attila, PH.D.; Turkish economist; b. 20 Sept. 1932, Manisa; s. of Ibrahim Ethem Karaosmanoglu and Fatma Eda Karaosmanoglu; m. Sukriye Ozyet 1960; one s.; ed. Univs. of Ankara and Istanbul, Harvard and New York Univs., U.S.A.; faculty mem. Middle East Tech. Univ. and Ankara Univ. 1954–63; Head Econ. Planning Dept., State Planning Org. of Turkey 1960–62; Adviser, Fed. of Turkish Trade Unions, Consultant, Turkish Scientific and Tech. Research Council 1963–65; Consultant, Directorate for Scientific Affairs, OECD 1965–66; Economist, then Sr. Economist, World Bank 1966–71; Deputy Prime Minister in Charge of Econ. Affairs and Chair. of the High Planning Council, Turkish Govt. 1971; mem. Exec. Bd., Is Bank, Turkey 1972; Chief Economist, World Bank 1973–75, Dir. of Devt. Policy 1975–79, Dir. of Europe, Middle East and N. Africa Region Country Programmes 1979–82, Vice-Pres. E. Asia and Pacific Region 1983–87, Asia Region 1987–91 (IBRD), Man. Dir. World Bank (IBRD) 1991–95; Chief Adviser, Istanbul Chamber of Industry 1995–; mem. Bd. Scientific and Technological Research Council of Turkey 1995–, Alt. Bank of Turkey 1996–; Chair. Bd. Nat. Inst. of Metrology 1997–. *Publication:* Towards Full Employment and Price Stability (OECD publ., with others) 1977, Poverty and Prosperity—The Two Realities of Asian Development 1989, Diversity and Consensus—The Emergence of an Asian Development Paradigm 1991. *Address:* Dr Faruk Ayanoglu Cad. 37 D.5, 81030 Fenerbahce, Istanbul, Turkey. *Telephone:* (216) 363 6953. *Fax:* (216) 369 4076.

KARASAWA, Shunjiro; Japanese politician; b. 1930; previous posts include: Parl. Vice-Minister of Finance and of Educ.; Deputy Chief Cabinet Sec.; Chair. Cttee. on Social and Labour Affairs, House of Reps.; Deputy Chair. Liberal Democratic Party (LDP) Policy Research Council; Minister of Posts and Telecommunications 1986–87. *Address:* c/o Liberal-Democratic Party, 1-11-23, Nagata-cho, Chiyoda-ku, Tokyo 100, Japan.

KARASIN, Grigory Borisovich; Russian diplomatist; b. 23 Aug. 1949, Moscow; m.; two d.; ed. Moscow Inst. of Oriental Languages, Moscow State Univ.; diplomatic service since 1972; translator, attaché U.S.S.R. Embassy, Senegal 1972–76; attaché First African Div., U.S.S.R. Ministry of Foreign Affairs 1976–77; sec. to Deputy Minister of Foreign Affairs 1977–79; Sec. Embassy, Australia 1979–85; First Sec., Counsellor Second European Div. Ministry of Foreign Affairs 1985–88; Counsellor U.S.S.R. Embassy, U.K. 1988–92; Head of Dept. of Africa, Ministry of Foreign Affairs of Russia 1992–93; Head. Dept. of Information and Press 1993–96; Deputy Minister of Foreign Affairs 1996–. *Address:* Ministry of Foreign Affairs, Smolenskaya-Sennaya 34/32, Moscow, Russia. *Telephone:* (095) 244 9221 (Office).

KARAYEV, Tamerlan; Azerbaijani politician; b. 1952, Gasimly, Agdam Region; s. of Yelmar Karayev and Khalida Karayeva; m. Farida Karayeva 1976; two s.; ed. Azerbaijan Univ.; public prosecutor 1973–78; lecturer, Azerbaijan Univ. 1978–91; became involved in opposition politics late 1980s; leader moderate wing Popular Front, elected Deputy to Supreme Soviet 1990, Deputy Chair., First Deputy Chair. 1991–93; Amb. to China 1993–. *Leisure interest:* golf. *Address:* Embassy of Azerbaijan, San Li Tun Diplomatic Office Building 1-32, Beijing 100600 (Office); San Li Tun Diplomatic Apartments 3-2-32, Beijing 100600, People's Republic of China. *Telephone:* 65324614 (Office); 65324712 (Home). *Fax:* 65324615 (Office).

KARCZEWSKI, Witold Andrzej, M.D.; Polish neurophysiologist; b. 30 Aug. 1930, Lvov; s. of Stanisław Karczewski and Aniela Karczewska; m. Elżbieta

Węgrzyn 1962; one s.; ed. Medical Acad., Warsaw; scientific worker Polish Acad. of Sciences (PAN), Medical Research Centre, Warsaw 1954–95, Asst., Sr. Asst. 1954–65, independent researcher 1965–, Head of Research Unit, Head of Neurophysiology Dept. 1968–92; Extraordinary Prof. 1971–79, Ordinary Prof. 1979–95, Prof. Emer. 1995–; mem. Scientific Councils; Pres. Polish Foundation for Advancement of Science 1990–; Chair. State Cttee. for Scientific Research 1991–95; mem. WHO Global Advisory Cttee. for Health Research 1992–; mem. numerous scientific socs.; State Prize (2nd class), Kt.'s and Officer's Crosses of Polonia Restituta. *Publications:* more than 80 articles on neurophysiology and science policy, published in Polish and foreign journals. *Leisure interests:* reading, yachting. *Address:* ul. Włościańska 16 m. 56, 01-710 Warsaw, Poland. *Telephone:* (22) 663 24 13.

KARDASHEV, Nikolai Semenovich; Russian astronomer; b. 25 April 1932; m.; one d.; ed. Moscow State Univ.; lab., sr. lab., jr., sr. researcher State Astronomical Inst. 1955–67; head of lab., Deputy Dir. Inst. of Space Studies U.S.S.R. Acad. of Sciences 1967–90; Dir. Astronomical Cen. Lebedev Physical Inst., U.S.S.R. Acad. of Sciences 1990–; corresp. mem. U.S.S.R. (now Russian) Acad. of Sciences 1976, mem. 1994; research in radiophysics, radioastronomy, radio radiation of galaxies and quasars; U.S.S.R. State Prize. *Publications include:* Pulsars and nonthermal Radio Sources 1970, Strategy and Future Projects 1977, numerous articles in scientific journals. *Address:* Astronomical Centre of Lebedev Physical Institute, Russian Academy of Sciences, Profsoyuznaya str. 84/32, 117810 Moscow, Russia. *Telephone:* (095) 333 2189 (Office).

KAREFA-SMART, John Musselman, B.A., B.SC., M.D., C.M., D.T.M., M.P.H., F.R.S.H., F.A.P.H.A., F.R.S.A.; Sierra Leonean politician and physician; b. 17 June 1915, Rotifunk; s. of Rev. James Karefa-Smart and May Karefa-Smart (née Caulker); m. Rena Joyce Weller 1948; one s. two d.; ed. Fourah Bay and Otterbein Colls., McGill and Harvard Univs.; lecturer, Union Coll., Bunumbu 1936–38; ordained Elder of Evangelical United Brethren Church 1938; Medical Officer, R.C.A.M.C. 1943–45; Sierra Leone Missions Hospitals 1946–48; Lecturer, Ibadan Univ. Coll. (Nigeria) 1949–52; Health Officer, WHO 1952–55, Leader del. to WHO 1956 and 1959; mem. House of Reps. 1957–64; Minister of Lands and Survey 1957–59; Africa Consultant, World Council of Churches 1955–56; Minister for External Affairs 1960–64; Asst. Prof. Columbia Univ. 1964–65; Asst. Dir.-Gen. WHO, Geneva 1965–70; Visiting Prof. of Int. Health, Harvard Univ. 1971–73, Lecturer Harvard Medical School 1973–; Medical Dir. Roxbury Health Centre 1973–78, Health and Devt. Consultant 1978–; Clinical Prof. Boston Univ. 1976–; Visiting Prof. Harvard Univ. 1977–; returned to Sierra Leone 1990; f. United Democratic Party; now Pres. United Nat. People's Party (UNPP); mem. of Parl., Leader of Opposition 1996–; Hon. LL.D. (Otterbein, McGill, Boston); Commdr. Order of Star of Africa (Liberia), Kt. Grand Band, Order of African Redemption (Liberia), Grand Cordon, Order of the Cedar (Lebanon). *Publications:* The Halting Kingdom 1959, Evaluating Health Program Impact 1974. *Leisure interests:* private flying, photography, stamps. *Address:* 20 Pipe Line, Juba, P.O. Box 1015, Freetown, Sierra Leone. *Telephone:* (22) 232.403. *Fax:* (22) 220.050.

KARGBO, Tom Obakeh, B.A., DIP.ED., M.SC., PH.D.; Sierra Leonean diplomatist; b. 17 July 1945, Mabonto; s. of Pa Yamba Kargbo and Leah Susannah Kargbo; m. Mary Kargbo 1980; one s. two d.; ed. Fourah Bay Coll., Univ. of Sierra Leone and Univ. of Salford, Manchester, England; Lecturer St. Augustine's Teachers' Coll., Makeni 1969–72; Sr. teacher Muslim Brotherhood Secondary School, Freetown 1973–75; Lecturer Dept. of Environmental Studies and Geography, Njala Univ. Coll., Univ. of Sierra Leone 1984–87; Perm. Rep. of Sierra Leone to UN, New York 1987–92; Amb. to U.S.A. 1993–94. *Publications:* numerous papers including two for UNICEF (on disability) and one for FAO (on rural issues). *Leisure interests:* reading, games (outdoor). *Address:* c/o Department of Foreign Affairs and International Cooperation, Gloucester Street, Freetown, Sierra Leone.

KARHILO, Aarno, LL.M.; Finnish diplomatist; b. 22 Nov. 1927, Helsinki; m.; two c.; ed. Univ. of Helsinki; entered diplomatic service 1952, served in Helsinki, Washington and Rio de Janeiro; First Sec., Rome 1961; Counsellor and Deputy Chief of Mission, UN 1963–65, Moscow 1966–68; Adviser to del. at UN Gen. Ass. 1959–60, 1963–65, 1969–71, Vice-Chair. 1972–76, 1988–92; Amb. to Japan 1971–72; Perm. Rep. to UN 1972–77; Perm. Rep. to UNESCO and Amb. to France 1977–82, to U.S.S.R. 1983–88; Under-Sec. of State for Political Affairs, Ministry for Foreign Affairs, Helsinki 1988–92, Acting Sec. of State 1992–93; Vice-Pres. ECOSOC 1973, Pres. 1974; Chair. Finnish del. for ECOSOC Sessions 1972–74; Pres. Bd. of Finnish Nat. Opera 1990–95; Chair. Council of Finnish Design Forum 1989–95; mem. Council for Naantali Music Festival 1985–, Ed. Bd. Nat. Defence (periodical) 1989–, Council, Red Cross of Finland 1990–. *Publications:* articles on foreign policy and cultural policy. *Leisure interest:* the arts. *Address:* P.O. Box 176, Helsinki, Finland.

KARIEVA, Bernara; Uzbekistan ballerina; b. 28 Jan. 1936, Tashkent; d. of Rakhim Kariev; m. Kulakhmat Rizaev; two d.; ed. Tashkent Choreography School (under N. A. Dovgelli and L. A. Zass) 1947–51, and Moscow School of Choreography (under M. A. Kozhukhova); Prin. ballerina with Navoi Theatre, Tashkent 1955–86, coach 1986–, Dir. Bolshoi Navoi Theatre of Opera and Ballet 1994–; mem. CPSU 1967–91; dances frequently with the Bolshoi and has given many performances abroad; Prof. Tashkent School of Choreography; Pres. Bd. Uzbek Union of Theatre Workers; U.S.S.R. People's Deputy 1989–91; mem. UNESCO Nat. Comm. on Culture, Uzbekistan. *Roles include:* Odette/Odile (Giselle), Francesca da Rimini, Young Lady (Young Lady and Hooligan by Shostakovich), Anna Karenina (by Shchedrin), Donna Anna (Don Juan), Zarrina (Love and the Sword by Ashrafi), Cinderella; awards include Uzbek State Prize 1970, People's Artist of U.S.S.R. 1973, U.S.S.R. State Prize 1982. *Leisure interests:* piano music, visually discovering the world. *Address:* Navoi Opera Theatre, Tashkent; 28 Mustafo Kamol Otaturk Street, Tashkent 700029, Uzbekistan.

KARIM, Mustai (pseudonym of Mustafa Safich Karimov); Bashkir writer and poet; b. 20 Oct. 1919, Kliashevo, Bashkiria; s. of Safa Karimov and Vazifa Karimova; m. Rauza Saubanova 1941; one s. one d.; ed. Bashkir Pedagogical Inst. 1940; mem. CPSU 1944–91, Soviet Army 1941–45; Chair. Bashkir Writers' Union 1962–; first publ. 1935; Order of Lenin, State Prize (U.S.S.R.) 1972, Hero of Socialist Labour 1979, Lenin Prize 1984. *Publications include:* The Detachment Moves Off 1938, Spring Voices 1941, December Song 1942, The Girls from Our Kolkhoz 1948, Sabantui 1953, Europe-Asia 1951–54, Poems on Viet Nam 1956–57, The Wedding Feast Goes On 1947, Lonely Birch 1950, Viet Nam Is Not Far 1958, Abduction of a Girl 1959, A Song Unsung 1961, On the Night of the Lunar Eclipse 1964, Selected Works (2 vols.) 1969, Year by Year 1971, Salavat 1973, Prometheus 1975, A Long-Long Childhood 1972–78, A Horse to Dictator 1 1980, Collected Works 1983, Homeland, Bread, Love 1985, Forgiveness 1985, The Village Advocates 1989, Flashes of Life 1991, Evening Meal 1993, The Return 1994, Daddy Yalaletdin 1996, Collected Works (five vols.) 1996–98. *Leisure interests:* fishing, playing preference. *Address:* Lenin St. 31/33, Fl. 20, Ufa 450000, Russia. *Telephone:* (3472) 22-10-38.

KARIM-LAMRANI, Mohammed; Moroccan politician and government official; b. 1 May 1919, Fez; m.; four c.; economic adviser to H.M. King Hassan II; Dir.-Gen. Office Chérifien des Phosphates 1967–90; Chair. Crédit du Maroc; Minister of Finance April-Aug. 1971; Prime Minister 1971–72, 1983–86, 1992–94; Pres. Crédit du Maroc, Phosphates de Boucraa, Société Marocaine de Distillation et Rectification; Econ. Adviser to King Hassan II of Morocco (q.v.); f. and Pres. Soc. Nat. d'Investissements 1966–; Ouissam de Grand Officier de l'Ordre du Trône, Légion d'honneur, Order of Rising Sun (Japan). *Address:* Rue du Mont Saint Michel, Anfa Supérieur, Casablanca 21300, Morocco.

KARIMOV, Dzhamshed Khilolovich, D.ECON.; Tajikistan politician; b. 4 Aug. 1940, Dushanbe; ed. Moscow Technological Inst. of Light Industry; researcher Cen. Research Inst. of Econs. and Math., U.S.S.R. Acad. of Sciences; Asst. Chair of Econ. of Industry Tajik State Univ., jr. researcher, Head of Div. of Optimal Planning Inst. of Econ., Tajik Acad. of Sciences 1962–72, Deputy Dir., Dir Research Inst. of Econ. and Econ.-Mathematical Methods of Planning, State Planning Cttee., Tajik S.S.R. 1972–81; Corresp. mem Tajik Acad. of Sciences; Deputy Chair. State Planning Cttee. 1981–88; Deputy Chair. Council of Ministers, Chair. State Planning Cttee. 1988–89; First Sec. Dushanbe City Cttee. of CP Tajikistan 1989–91; U.S.S.R. People's Deputy 1989–92; Deputy, First Deputy Chair. Council of Ministers Tajik Repub. 1991–92; represented Repub. of Tajikistan in Russia 1992–93; Chief Advisor on Econ. to Pres. Sept.–Nov. 1994; Prime Minister of Tajikistan 1994–96; Adviser to Pres. Rakhmonov 1996–97; Amb. to China 1997–. *Address:* c/o Office of the Prime Minister, Dushanbe, Tajikistan.

KARIMOV, Islam, CAND.ECON.SC.; Uzbekistan politician; b. 30 Jan. 1938, Samarkand; m. Tat'yana Karimova; two d.; ed. Cen. Asian Polytechnic and Tashkent Econs. Inst.; mem. CPSU 1964–91; work in Tashkent aviation construction factory 1960–66; sr. specialist, head of section, Vice-Chair. of Uzbekistan Gosplan 1966–83; Minister of Finance, Deputy Chair. of Council of Ministers, Uzbek S.S.R. 1983–86; First Sec. of Kashkadarinsk Dist. Cttee. (obkom) 1986–89; First Sec. Cen. Cttee. Uzbek CP 1989–91; U.S.S.R. People's Deputy 1989–91; Mem. Cen. Cttee. CPSU and Politburo 1990–91; Pres. of Uzbek S.S.R. 1990; Chair. People's Democratic Party of Uzbekistan 1991–96; Pres. of Uzbekistan 1991–, concurrently Chair. Cabinet of Ministers; Hon. Chair. Fund of Friendship of Cen. Asia and Kazakhstan; various decorations. *Publications:* Uzbekistan's Way of Restoration and Progress, To Complete the Noble Cause, Uzbekistan's Way of Strengthening Economic Reforms 1995, Stability and Reforms 1996, Uzbekistan on the Threshold of the Twenty-First Century 1997. *Address:* Office of the President, Uzbekistansky prosp. 45, 700163 Tashkent, Uzbekistan. *Telephone:* (993) 139 53 00; (993) 139 54 56. *Fax:* (993) 139-55-25.

KARINA, Anna (Hanne Karin Bayer); French film actress; b. 22 Sept. 1940, Fredriksburg, Solbjerg, Denmark; d. of Carl Johann Bayer and of Elva Helvig Frederiksen; m. 1st Jean-Luc Godard (q.v.) (divorced); m. 2nd Pierre-Antoine Fabre 1968 (divorced); m. 3rd Daniel Georges Duval 1978; Prix Orange. *Films include:* She'll Have To Go 1961, Une femme est une femme 1961, Vivre sa vie 1962, Le petit soldat 1963, Bande à part 1964, Alphaville 1965, Made in the USA 1966, La religieuse 1968, The Magus 1968, Before Winter Comes 1968, Laughter in the Dark 1969, Justine 1969, The Salzburg Connection 1972, Living Together 1974, L'assassin musicien 1975, Les oeufs brouillés 1976, Boulette chinoise 1977, L'ami de Vincent 1983, Ave Maria 1984, Dernier été à Tanger 1987, Cayenne Palace 1987, L'Oeuvre au noir 1988, Last Song 1989, L'Homme qui voulait être coupable 1990; has also appeared on television and in theatre. *Publications:* Golden City 1983, On n'achète pas le soleil (novel) 1988. *Address:* Orban éditions, 76 rue Bonaparte, 75006 Paris, France.

KARK, Austen Steven, C.B.E., M.A.; British writer and broadcaster; b. 20 Oct. 1926, London; s. of Maj. Norman Kark and late Ethel Kark; m. 1st Margaret Solomon 1949 (dissolved 1954); two d.; m. 2nd Nina Bawden (q.v.) 1954; two step-s. (one deceased) one d.; ed. Upper Canada Coll., Toronto, Nautical Coll., Pangbourne, Royal Naval Coll. and Magdalen Coll., Oxford; dir. first production in U.K. of Sartre's The Flies, Oxford 1948; trained as journalist with Belfast Telegraph and L'Illustré, Switzerland; freelance journalist and broadcaster, London and New York 1952–54; joined BBC as scriptwriter European Productions 1954; Head S. European Services 1964, E. European Services 1972, Controller English Services and Ed. World Service 1974, Deputy Man. Dir. External Broadcasting (now World Service) 1981–85, Man. Dir. 1985–86, Broadcasting Consultant 1987–; Chair. CPC Guidebooks 1988–; Adviser to Lord Soames on broadcasting during independence elections, Rhodesia 1980, later returned to Zimbabwe to advise Prime Minister on radio and television in Zimbabwe 1980, mem. of U.K. del. CSCE London Information Forum 1989; fmr. Trustee Research Fund for Complementary Medicine; Trustee Commonwealth Journalists Asscn. Trust 1992–. *Publication:* Attic in Greece 1994. *Leisure interests:* real tennis, mosaics, grandchildren. *Address:* 22 Noel Road, London, N1 8HA, England; 19 Kapodistriou, Nauplion 21100, Greece.

KARL, Elfriede; Austrian politician; b. 14 Sept. 1933, Salzburg; ed. Acad. for Social Studies; completed commercial apprenticeship 1950; saleswoman 1950–53; shorthand typist, Building and Timber Workers Union, Salzburg office 1953–60; joined Salzburg Chamber of Labour 1961, Sec. to Econs. Dept. 1968; State Sec. for Family Affairs Policy, Kreisky Govt. 1971–79; State Sec., Fed. Ministry of Finance 1979–83; Fed. Minister for Family Affairs 1983–84; mem. Austrian Socialist Party (now Social-Democratic Party of Austria). *Address:* c/o Social-Democratic Party of Austria, Löwelstrasse 18, 1014 Vienna, Austria.

KARLE, Isabella, PH.D.; American chemist; b. 2 Dec. 1921, Detroit, Mich.; d. of Zygmunt A. and Elizabeth (Graczyk) Lugoski; m. Jerome Karle (q.v.) 1942; three d.; ed. Univ. of Michigan; Assoc. Chemist, Univ. of Chicago 1944; Instructor in Chem., Univ. of Mich. 1944–46; Physicist, Naval Research Lab., Washington, D.C. 1946–; mem. N.A.S., American Crystallographic Asscn. American Chem. Soc., American Physical Soc., American Biophysical Soc.; Hon. D.Sc. (Mich.) 1976, (Wayne State) 1979, (Md.) 1986; Hon. D. Hum. Lett. (Georgetown) 1984, Lifetime Achievement Award (Women in Science and Eng.) 1986, Gregori Aminoff Prize (Swedish Royal Acad. of Sciences) 1988, Bijvoet Medal (Univ. of Utrecht, The Netherlands) 1990, Bower Award in Science (Franklin Inst.) 1993, Chemical Sciences Award (N.A.S.) 1995, Nat. Medal of Science (Pres.'s Award, U.S.A.) 1995, and other awards and honours. *Leisure interests:* swimming, ice skating, needlework. *Publications:* over 300 scientific articles, chapters and reviews. *Address:* Naval Research Laboratory, Code 6030, Washington, DC 20375 (Office); 6304 Lakeview Drive, Falls Church, VA 22041, U.S.A. (Home). *Telephone:* (202) 767-2624 (Office).

KARLE, Jerome, PH.D.; American government scientist; b. 18 June 1918, Brooklyn, New York; s. of Louis Karfunkle and Sadie Helen Kun; m. Isabella (née Lugoski) Karle (q.v.) 1942; three d.; ed. Abraham Lincoln High School, City Coll. of New York, Harvard Univ. and Univ. of Mich.; Head, Electron Diffraction Section, Naval Research Lab. 1946–58, Head, Diffraction Branch 1958–68, Chief Scientist, Lab. for the Structure of Matter 1968–; Prof. (part-time), Univ. of Maryland 1951–70; Pres. American Crystallographic Asscn. 1972; Chair. U.S. Nat. Cttee. for Crystallography of N.A.S. and Nat. Research Council 1973–75; Pres. Int. Union of Crystallography 1981–84; Charter mem. Sr. Exec. Service 1979; Fellow, American Physical Soc.; mem. N.A.S.; jt. recipient of Nobel Prize for Chemistry 1985, for development of methods to determine the structures of crystals, and several other awards. *Publications:* one book and about 200 research and review articles on theoretical and experimental topics associated with the study of the structures of materials by diffraction methods. *Leisure interests:* stereo-photography, swimming, ice-skating. *Address:* Laboratory for the Structure of Matter, Code 6030, Naval Research Laboratory, Washington, DC 20375, U.S.A. *Telephone:* (202) 767-2665.

KARLIN, Samuel, PH.D.; American mathematician; b. 8 June 1924, Poland; m. Elsie Karlin (divorced); two s. one d.; ed. Illinois Inst. of Technology and Princeton Univ.; Calif. Inst. of Tech., Bateman Research Fellow 1947–48, Asst. Prof. 1949–51, Assoc. Prof. 1951–55, Prof. 1955–56; Visiting Asst. Prof. Princeton Univ. 1950; Prof. Stanford Univ. 1956–; Guggenheim Fellow to Israel and France 1960–61; Guest Mathematical Soc. of Japan 1964; Head, Dept. of Pure Mathematics, Weizmann Inst. of Science, Rehovot, Israel 1970–73, Dean, Faculty of Mathematics 1973; Consultant Rand Corpn., Santa Monica; Chief Ed. Theoretical Population Biology; Ed. or Assoc. Ed. Journal of Mathematical Analysis, Logistics Journal, Journal of Applied Probability, Journal d'analyse, Journal of Mathematics and Mechanics, Journal of Mathematical Biosciences, Journal of Approximation Theory and Advances in Mathematics; Fellow, Inst. of Mathematical Statistics 1956, American Acad. of Arts and Sciences 1981; fmr. mem. Int. Statistics Inst., American Acad. of Arts and Sciences and Council of American Mathematical Soc.; mem. of American Mathematical Soc., Applied Mathematics, panel Nat. Research Council, N.A.S.; Pres.-elect. Inst. of Mathematical Statistics 1977, Pres. 1978–79; Procter Fellow, Princeton Univ. 1946; Wald Memorial Lecturer 1957; Henry and Bertha Benson Chair of Mathematics 1971; Andrew D. White Prof.-at-Large, Cornell Univ. 1975–81; Wilks Lecturer at Princeton 1977; Seymour Sherman Memorial Lecturer 1978; Commonwealth Lecturer, Univ. of Mass. 1980; Gibbs Lectures, American Mathematical Soc. 1983; Mahalanobis Memorial Lectures, Indian Statistical Inst. 1983; Fisher Memorial Lectures 1983; Robert Grimmitt Chair, Stanford 1978. *Publications:* Sex Ratio Evolution (with Sabin Lessard) 1986, Evolutionary Processes and Theory (Ed. with E. Nevo) 1986, over 300 articles in various journals on topics of pure and applied probability theory, game theory, decision theory and statistical methodology, mathematical analysis and mathematical biology. *Address:* Department of Mathematics, Stanford University, Building 380, Stanford, CA 94305, U.S.A. *Telephone:* (415) 723-2204.

KARMAZIN, Mel; American media executive; b. 1944; stage man. CBS Radio 1960–70, Chair., C.E.O. CBS Station Group 1996–, now Pres., C.O.O. CBS Corpn.; Vice Pres., Gen. Man. Metromedia Inc. 1970–81; Pres. Infinity Broadcasting Corpn. 1981–96, C.E.O. 1988–96. *Address:* CBS Station Group, 40 West 57th Street, Floor 14, New York, NY 10019, U.S.A.

KARMEL, Peter Henry, A.C., C.B.E., B.A., PH.D.; Australian academic administrator; b. 9 May 1922, Melbourne; s. of Simeon and Ethel Karmel; m. Lena Garrett 1946; one s. five d.; ed. Univ. of Melbourne, Trinity Coll., Cambridge; Research Officer, Commonwealth Bureau of Census and Statistics 1943–45; Lecturer in Econs., Univ. of Melbourne 1946, Sr. Lecturer 1948–49; George Gollin Prof. of Econs. and Dean of Faculty of Econs., Univ. of Adelaide 1950–62, Prin. (desig.), Univ. of Adelaide at Bedford Park (later Flinders Univ. of S. Australia) 1961–66, Vice-Chancellor 1966–71; Visiting Prof., Queen's University, Belfast 1957–58; Chair., Interim Council, Univ. of Papua New Guinea 1965–69, Chancellor 1969–70; Chair., Australian Univs. Comm. 1971–77, Australia Council 1974–77, Commonwealth Tertiary Educ. Comm. 1977–82; Pres., Australian Council for Educational Research 1979–; Vice-Chancellor, Australian Nat. Univ. 1982–87; Chair., Commonwealth Govt. Quality of Educ. Review Cttee. 1984–85, Australian Inst. of Health 1987–92; Pres. Acad. of Social Sciences in Australia 1987–90; Exec. Chair., Canberra Inst. of the Arts 1988–91; Chair. Australian Nat. Council on AIDS 1988–91, Bd. of Inst. of the Arts, Australian Nat. Univ. 1992–; Mackie Medal 1975, Australian Coll. of Educ. Medal 1981. *Address:* 4/127 Hopetoun Circuit, Yarralumla, A.C.T. 2600, Australia. *Telephone:* (02) 62852414. *Fax:* (02) 62495705.

KARMI, Ram; Israeli architect; b. 1931, Jerusalem; m.; three s. three d.; ed. Architectural Asscn. School, London; joined father's architectural office in partnership Karmi-Meltzer-Karmi 1956; est. (with sister) office of Ram Karmi, Ada Karmi-Melamed, Karmi Assoc. 1962; est. Karmi Assoc. (br. office), New York 1972; Chief Architect, Ministry of Housing 1975–79; Partner, Karmi Architects & Co., Tel Aviv 1979–; various teaching posts at Faculty of Architecture and Town Planning, Technion since 1964, Assoc. Prof. 1987–94; Visiting Prof. Princeton Univ. 1969, M.I.T. 1972; projects include univ. bldgs. (Faculty of Humanities, Hebrew Univ., Mt. Scopus), schools, hotels (Holyland Compound, Jerusalem), pvt. homes, large housing projects (Giloh, Jerusalem), public bldgs. (Museum of Children of the Holocaust, Supreme Court, Jerusalem) and industrial complexes; numerous awards and competition prizes. *Publications:* articles in professional journals. *Address:* Ram Karmi Architects, 17 Kaplan Street, Tel-Aviv 64734, Israel. *Telephone:* (3) 6913646. *Fax:* (3) 6913508.

KARMOKOV, Khachim Mukhamedovich, DR. ECON.; Russian medical official; b. 2 May 1941, Zayukovo, Kabardin-Balkar Autonomous Repub.; m.; one d.; ed. Kabardin-Balkar State Univ.; master construction team, head tech. div. Kabbalkmezhkolkhozstroi 1963–64; architect Construction Trust Sevkavkoopstroi 1964–66; teacher, asst., sr. teacher, docent Kabardin-Balkar State Univ. 1966–67, 1971–78; Head Construction Dept. Kabbalkarstroi 1978–81; docent Kabardino-Balkar State univ. 1981–83; Deputy Man. Trust Kabbalpromstroi 1983–90; deputy to Supreme Soviet Kabardin-Balkar Autonomous Repub. 1990; Deputy Chair. Council of Ministers, Chair. Comm. on Econ. Reform 1990; Deputy Chair, then Chair. Supreme Soviet Kabardin-Balkar Repub. 1991–94; Chair. Accountant Chamber of Russian Fed. Jan. 1994–; mem. State Duma Russian Fed. 1993–94. *Address:* Accountant Chamber, Guilyarovskogo str. 31, Suite 1, 129090 Moscow, Russia (Office). *Telephone:* (095) 284 8797 (Office).

KARMOUL, Akram Jamil, PH.D.; Jordanian business executive and consultant; b. 13 Aug. 1939, W. Bank; m. Huda Abu-Errub 1964; two s. two d.; ed. Assiut Univ., Strathclyde Univ., Imperial Coll., London; geologist, geophysicist and mining engineer 1961–72; Dir. Industry, later Dir. Science and Tech. Ministry of Planning 1972–80; Dir. Gen. of Industry Ministry of Industry and Trade 1980–87; Dir., Man. Industrial, Commercial and Agric. Co. 1987; Exec. Dir., Asst. Man. Dalla-Al-Baraka Saudi Group, Jeddah 1988–89; Dir. of Industry Dept. UN-ESCWA Comm. for W. Asia 1989–93; Gen. Man. United Textile Group 1995; Assoc. Consultant Arab Consulting Centre and Assignments UNDP 1996–; Cand. Gen. Man. for a public firm 1996–; Science Award for Outstanding Persons. *Leisure interests:* reading, swimming. *Publications:* numerous works on mineral wealth and industrial tech. of Jordan, public enterprises.

KARNAD, Girish, M.A.; Indian playwright, film-maker and actor; b. 19 May 1938, Matheran; s. of Raghunath Karnad and Krishnabai Karnad; m. Saraswathy Ganapathy 1980; one s. one d.; ed. Karnatak Coll., Dharwad and Univ. of Oxford; Pres. Oxford Union Soc. 1963; Asst. Man. Oxford Univ. Press, Madras 1963–69, Man. 1969–70; Homi Bhabha Fellow 1970–72; Dir. Film & TV Inst. of India, Pune 1974, 1975; Visiting Prof. and Fulbright

Scholar-in-Residence Univ. of Chicago 1987–88; Indian Co-chair., Media Cttee., Indo-U.S. Subcomm. 1984–93; Chair. Sangeet Natak Akademi (Nat. Acad. of Performing Arts) 1988–93; Hon. D.Litt. (Univ. of Karnataka) 1994; several awards for film work; Padma Shri; Padma Bhushan 1992. *Plays:* Yayati 1961, Tughlaq 1964, Hayavadana 1971, Anjumallige 1976, Hittina Hunja 1980, Nagamandala 1988, Taledanda 1990, Agni Mattu Male 1995. *Films:* Vamsha Vriksha 1971, Kaadu 1973, Tabbaliyu Neenade Magane 1977, Ondanondu Kaaladalli 1978, Utsav 1984, Cheluvi 1992. *Address:* 301 Silver Cascade, Mount Mary Road, Bombay 400 050; 697, 15th Cross, J.P. Nagar Phase II, Bangalore 560 078, India. *Telephone:* (022) 642 0988 (Bombay); (080) 663 0463 (Bangalore). *Fax:* (080) 665 6319.

KAROUI, Hamed, PH.D.; Tunisian politician; b. 30 December 1927, Sousse; m.; four c.; ed. Faculté de Médecine de Paris; doctor at Sousse Regional Hosp. 1957–; active in the Destour movt. from 1942, including responsibility for Al Kifah journal; Pres. Féd. Destourienne de France; Municipal Councillor, Sousse 1957–72, Mayor 1985; Deputy to the Nat. Ass. 1964, re-elected 1981 and 1989; Vice-Pres. Chamber of Deputies 1983–86; Minister for Youth and Sports 1986–87; Dir. Parti Socialiste Destourien (renamed Rassemblement Constitutionnel Démocratique, 1988) 1987, Vice-Pres.; Minister for Justice 1988–89; Prime Minister Sept. 1989–; grand cordon de l'ordre de l'Indépendance et de la République (Tunisia). *Address:* Office of the Prime Minister, Tunis; Rassemblement Constitutionnel Démocratique, boulevard 9 Avril 1938, Tunis, Tunisia.

KARP, David, B.S.S.; American writer; b. 5 May 1922, New York; s. of Abraham Karp and Rebecca Levin; m. 1st Lillian Klass 1944 (died 1987); two s.; m. 2nd Claire Leighton 1988; ed. City Coll. of the City of New York; Continuity Dir. Station W.N.Y.C., New York 1948–49; free-lance writer 1949–; Guggenheim Fellowship for creative writing 1956–57; mem. editorial board Television Quarterly 1965–71, 1972–; mem. Council, Writers' Guild of America, West, Inc. 1967–74; Pres. Leda Productions, Inc. 1968–; film and television producer (20th Century Fox, Metro-Goldwyn-Mayer, Paramount Pictures) 1970–; Emmy Award by Acad. of Television, Arts and Sciences 1964–65; mem. PEN Club; mem. Acad. of Motion Picture Arts and Sciences; Pres. Television-Radio Branch, Writers' Guild of America, West 1969–71; Trustee, Producer-Writers' Guild Pension Fund 1970–, Vice-Chair. 1976, Sec. 1977, Chair. 1978–79, Chair. Finance Cttee. 1975; Trustee, Writers' Guild Health Fund 1974–; Chair. Benefits Comm. Health Fund 1978; Sec. Health Fund 1979, Chair. 1980–; Co-Chair. Building Cttee. Pension Plan 1980–; Chair. Pension and Health Funds 1996–; mem. The Players 1988–92 (resgnd.). *Publications:* One 1953, The Day of the Monkey 1955, All Honorable Men 1956, Leave Me Alone 1957, The Sleepwalkers 1960, Vice-President in Charge of Revolution (with M. D. Lincoln) 1960, The Last Believers 1964, Café Univers (play) 1967; also contributed many articles and reviews to magazines and has written for radio, cinema and television. *Leisure interests:* reading, photography. *Address:* 300 East 56th Street, Apt. 3C, New York, NY 10022; 1136 Barker Road, M-34, Pittsfield, MA 01201, U.S.A. (Summer).

KARPLUS, Martin, PH.D.; American professor of chemistry; b. 15 March 1930, Vienna, Austria; m. Marci Hazard 1981; one s. two d.; ed. Harvard Univ. and Calif. Inst. of Technology; Nat. Science Foundation Postdoctoral Fellow, Mathematical Inst., Oxford; Asst. Prof., Dept. of Chem., Univ. of Illinois 1955–59; Assoc. Prof. 1960; Prof. of Chem., Columbia Univ. 1960–66, Harvard Univ. Cambridge, Mass. 1966–, Theodore William Richards Prof. of Chem., Harvard Univ. 1979–; Visiting Prof. Univ. of Paris 1972–73, 1980–81 (Prof. 1974–75), Collège de France 1980–81, 1987–88; Prof. Conventionné Louis Pasteur Univ. 1992, 1994–; mem. European Acad. of Arts, Sciences and Humanities, N.A.S., American Acad. of Arts and Sciences, Int. Acad. of Quantum Molecular Science; Foreign mem. Netherlands Acad. of Arts and Science; Harrison Howe Award, American Chem. Soc. (Rochester Section), Phi Lambda Upsilon Frensenius Award, Distinguished Alumnus Award (Calif. Inst. of Tech.), Irving Langmuir Award (American Physical Soc.), Nat. Lecturer (Biophysics Soc.), Theoretical Chem. Award, A.C.S. (first recipient). *Publications:* Atoms and Molecules (with R. N. Porter) 1970, A Theoretical Perspective of Dynamics, Structure and Thermodynamics (with C. L. Brooks III and B. M. Pettitt) 1988; over 500 articles in the field of theoretical chemistry. *Address:* Department of Chemistry, Harvard University, 12 Oxford Street, Cambridge, MA 02138, U.S.A.

KARPOV, Anatoliy Yevgenievich; Russian chess player; b. 23 May 1951, Zlatoust; s. of Yevgeniy Stepanovich Karpov and Nina Karpov; m. 1st Irina Karpov; one s.; m. 2nd Natalia Bulanova; ed. Leningrad Univ.; mem. CPSU 1980–91; U.S.S.R. Candidate Master 1962, Master 1966; European Jr. Champion 1967, 1968, World Jr. Champion 1969; Int. Master 1969, Int. Grandmaster 1970; U.S.S.R. Champion 1976, 1983, 1988; World Champion 1975–85; became World Champion when the holder Bobby Fischer (q.v.) refused to defend the title and he retained his title against Viktor Korchnoi in 1978 and in 1981; defended against Garry Kasparov (q.v.) in Moscow Sept. 1984, the match later adjourned due to the illness of both players; lost to the same player in 1985; unsuccessfully challenged Kasparov 1986, 1987, 1990; won World Championship title under FIDE after split in chess orgs. 1993, 1997, 1998; winner of over 140 int. competitions 1966–; People's Deputy of U.S.S.R. 1989–91; Pres. Soviet Peace Fund (now Int Asscn. of Peace Funds) 1982–; mem. Soviet (now Russian) UNESCO Affairs Comm.; mem. Bd. Int. Chess Fed.; Ed.-in-Chief Chess Review 64 (magazine) 1980–91; winner of Oscar Chess Prize 1973–77, 1979–81, 1984, 1994. *Publications:* Chess is My Life 1980, Karpov Teaches Chess 1987, Karpov on Karpov 1991. *Address:* International Peace Fund, Prechistenka 10, Moscow, Russia. *Telephone:* 202-41-71, 202-42-36.

KARPOV, Viktor Pavlovich; Russian diplomatist (retd.); b. 9 Oct. 1928; m.; one d.; ed. Moscow State Inst. for Int. Relations; scientific work 1951–55; joined U.S.S.R. Ministry of Foreign Affairs 1955, with Soviet Embassy, Washington 1962–66; participated in Soviet-U.S. Strategic Arms Limitation Talks SALT-1 and SALT-2 (headed Soviet Del. at SALT-2 1978), Head, Soviet Del., Soviet-U.S. Arms Talks 1982–83, Geneva 1985–87; Deputy Minister of Foreign Affairs of the U.S.S.R. 1988–91; Amb.-at-Large, Ministry of Foreign Affairs of the Russian Fed. 1992–. *Address:* c/o Ministry of Foreign Affairs of the Russian Federation, 34/32 Smolenskaya-Sennaya pl., Moscow, Russia. *Telephone:* (095) 244-46-91.

KARPOV, Vladimir Vasilyevich; Russian author and editor; b. 28 July 1922, Orenburg; s. of Vasiliy Karpov and Lydia Karpov; m. Evgenia Vasilievna Karpov 1956; one s. two d.; ed. Military Acad., Moscow and Gorky Literary Inst.; arrested 1941, sent to camp, released to join a penal battalion, subsequently distinguishing himself in military reconnaissance work; mem. CPSU 1943–91; started publishing (novels, stories, essays) 1948–; Deputy Ed. of Oktyabr 1974–77; Sec. of Presidium of U.S.S.R. Union of Writers 1981–86, First Sec. 1986–91; Chief Ed. of Novy mir 1981–86; Deputy to the Presidium of the U.S.S.R. Supreme Soviet 1984–89; mem. CPSU Cen. Cttee. 1988–90, U.S.S.R. People's Deputy 1989–91; Academician (Russian Acad.); Hon. D.Litt (Strathclyde Univ.); State Prize 1986; Hero of Soviet Union 1944. *Publications:* The Marshal's Baton 1970, Take Them Alive 1975, The Regimental Commander 1982–84, The Eternal Struggle 1987, Marshal Zhukov, (Vol. I) 1989, (Vol. II) 1992, (Vol. III) 1995, Selected Works (3 vols.). *Leisure interests:* collecting books, especially on mil. history. *Address:* Kutozovsky prosp. 26, Apt. 94, Moscow, Russia. *Telephone:* 249-26-12. *Fax:* (095) 200-02-93.

KARSENTI, René, M.S., M.B.A., PH.D.; French international finance official; b. 27 Jan. 1950, Tlemcen, Algeria; s. of Leon Karsenti and Mireille Benhaim; m. Hélène Dayan 1978; two d.; ed. ESCIL, Lyons, Paris Business School and Sorbonne, Paris; researcher in finance and econs. Univ. of Calif. Berkeley 1973; investment analyst/portfolio man. Caisse des Dépôts, Paris 1975–79; Finance Officer, World Bank (IBRD), Washington, D.C. 1979–83, Financial Adviser 1983–85, Div. Chief 1985–87, Sr. Man. Finance Dept. Treasury 1987–89; Treas., Dir. Financial Policy Dept. Int. Finance Corpn. World Bank Group, Washington, D.C. 1989–91; Treas. European Bank for Reconstruction and Devt. (EBRD) 1991–95; Dir.-Gen. of Finance European Investment Bank 1995–. *Publication:* Research in Pharmaceutical Industry 1977, various financial lectures and articles. *Leisure interests:* swimming, antiques, travel. *Address:* European Investment Bank, 100 Blvd Konrad Adenauer, 2950 Luxembourg.

KARSH, Yousuf, C.C.; Canadian photographer; b. 23 Dec. 1908, Mardin, Armenia-in-Turkey; s. of Bahia and Amsih Karsh; m. 1st Solange Gauthier 1939 (died 1961); m. 2nd Estrellita Nachbar 1962; ed. Sherbrooke, Quebec and School of Art and Design, Boston, Mass.; Photo apprenticeship to John Garo of Boston; arrived in Canada from Armenia-in-Turkey 1925; specialized in portrait photography; Canadian citizen 1947; Visiting Prof. of Photography, Ohio Univ. 1967–69; Photographic Adviser to Expo 1970, Osaka, Japan 1969; Visiting Prof. of Fine arts, Emerson Coll., Boston 1972–73; numerous one-man exhbns., North America 1967–; touring exhbn. Men Who Make Our World Japan 1970, U.S.A. 1971–68, France, Germany, Netherlands 1971–73, Belgium, Arles 1974–75, Athens 1978 (now in perm. collection Museum of Contemporary Art, Tokyo, Nat. Gallery of Australia and Province of Alberta, Canada), Bradford, England 1983, Int. Center of Photography, New York 1983, 1992–93, Nat. Portrait Gallery, London 1984, Nat. Gallery Edinburgh, Scotland 1984, Nat. Portrait Gallery, Helsinki 1985, Beijing, China 1985, Muscarelle Museum of Art, Coll. of William and Mary 1986, 80th Birthday Celebration, Barbican Centre, London 1988, retrospective exhbn. Nat. Gallery of Canada 1989, subsequently on tour; other exhbns. include Washington, D.C. 1993, Lausanne 1993, 85th Birthday Tribute exhbn., Bradford, England 1993, "American Legends", Int. Center of Photography 1993, Corcoran Gallery 1993, Mint Museum, Charlotte, N.C., "Karsh: Selected Portraits", Canadian Embassy, Washington, D.C. 1994, retrospective, Museum of Fine Arts, Boston, U.S.A. 1996, Detroit Inst. of Arts 1996–97, Tower Gallery, Yokohama, Japan 1997–98, 90th Birthday Tribute, Nat. Gallery, Ottawa 1998, "Karsh in London", Canada House, London 1998; film: Karsh: The Searching Eye 1986; eponymous annual lecture inaugurated at Museum of Fine Arts, Boston 1998; fmr. Nat. Vice-Pres. now corp. mem. Muscular Dystrophy Asscns. of America 1970–; mem. Royal Acad. Arts and Sciences, Canada 1975; Trustee, Photographic Arts and Sciences Foundation 1970–; Hon. LL.D. (Queen's Univ., Kingston, Ont., Carleton Univ. and Savannah Coll. of Art and Design), Hon. D.H.L. (Dartmouth Coll. at Hanover, New Hampshire, Emerson Coll., Boston, Mass., Mount Allison Univs.), Hon. D.C.L. (Bishop's Univ., Quebec), LL.D. h.c. (Brooke Inst.) 1973, (Univ. of Mass.) 1978, (Hartford Univ.) 1980, (Tufts Univ.) 1982, D.F.A. (Syracuse Univ.) 1986, (Yeshiva Univ. N.Y.) 1989, (Columbia Coll.) 1990, (Univ. of British Columbia) 1990; Jerusalem Prize for Arts and Letters, Bezalel Acad., Israel 1997; Canada Council Medal 1965, Centennial Medal 1967, Gold Medal Americas Soc. 1989, Lotos Medal of Merit 1989; Univ. of Detroit President's Cabinet Annual Award 1979, Encyclopaedia Britannica Achievement in Life Award 1979, Silver Shingle Award, Boston Univ. Law School 1982, Creative Edge Award 1989, Master

Photographer Award 1990, Medal of Canadian Confed. (125th anniversary) 1992. *Publications:* Faces of Destiny 1946, This is the Mass (English and French editions), This is Rome 1959, Portraits of Greatness 1959, This is the Holy Land 1961, In Search of Greatness (autobiog.) 1962, These are the Sacraments (co-author) 1963, The Warren Court 1964 (co-author), Karsh Portfolio 1967, Faces of our Time 1971, Karsh Portraits 1976, Karsh Canadians 1978, Karsh: A Fifty-Year Retrospective 1983, revised and augmented edn. 1996, American Legends 1992. *Leisure interests:* tennis, reading, archaeology, music. *Address:* 2 Commonwealth Avenue, Boston, MA 02116, U.S.A.

KARTASHKIN, Vladimir Aleksandrovich, DR. JUR.; Russian politician; b. 4 March 1934; m. Elena Kovanova 1991; one s. one d.; ed. Moscow State Univ.; Chief Scientific Researcher Inst. of State and Law 1957–63; with Div. of Human Rights UN 1969–73; Consultant UN Dir.-Gen. on Juridical Problems 1979–85; researcher Inst. of State and Law 1985–; Chair. Comm. on Human Rights Russian Presidency May 1996–; Prof. Int. Inst. of Human Rights, Strasbourg, Cornell Univ., Santa-Clair Univ. *Publications:* over 150 books on articles including Human Rights in International and State Law. *Leisure interests:* tennis, swimming. *Address:* Commission on Human Rights, Varvarka str. 7, Moscow, Russia (Office). *Telephone:* (095) 206 49 14 (Office).

KARTOMI, Margaret Joy, A.M., F.A.H.A., DR. PHIL., B.MUS., A.U.A.; Australian musicologist; b. 24 Nov. 1940, Adelaide; d. of George Hutchesson and Edna Hutchesson; m. Hidris Kartomi 1961; one d.; ed. Univ. of Adelaide; Lecturer Monash Univ. Music Dept. 1969–70, Sr. Lecturer 1971–73, Reader 1974–88, Prof. of Music 1989–, Head of Music Dept. 1989–97; Dir. Inst. of Contemporary Asian Studies, Monash Univ. 1989–91; Dir. Monash-ANZ Centre for Int. Briefing 1988–, Monash Asia Inst. 1988–; Dir.-at-large Int. Musicology Soc. 1993–; Visiting Prof., Univ. of Calif., Berkeley 1986–87; Fellow Acad. of the Humanities 1982–; Dir. Symposium of Int. Musicological Soc., Melbourne 1988; Alexander Clarke Prize for Pianoforte Performance 1960, Dr. Ruby Davy Prize for Musical Composition 1961, Fed. German Record Critics' Prize 1983, 1998; A.M. 1991. *Publications:* On Concepts and Classifications of Musical Instruments 1990, five other books (author or Ed.), numerous articles and 300 articles in the New Grove Dictionary of Musical Instruments 1989. *Leisure interests:* tennis, badminton, concerts, theatre. *Address:* Department of Music, Monash University, Wellington Rd. Clayton, Vic. 3168, Australia (Office). *Telephone:* (03) 9905 3230 (Office). *Fax:* 9905 3241.

KARUKUBIRO-KAMUNANWIRE, Perezi, PH.D.; Ugandan diplomatist; b. 25 July 1937, Mbarara; m.; two c.; ed. Columbia Univ.; Chair. Uganda People's Congress Youth League 1958–63; Pres. and Chair. Pan-African Students' Org. in the Americas 1965–70; Prof. City Univ. of New York 1974–86; Amb. to Austria, Fed. Repub. of Germany and the Holy See, and Perm. Rep. to int. orgs. in Vienna 1986–88; Perm. Rep. to UN, New York 1988–95; Chair. UN Gen. Ass. Special Political Cttee. 1990–95. *Address:* c/o Ministry of Foreign Affairs, P.O. Box 7048, Kampala, Uganda.

KARUNAKARAN, Shri Kannothu.; Indian politician; b. July 1918; s. of K. Rammuny Marar; m. Kalliani Amma; one s. one d.; active in Freedom Movt. while a student and imprisoned many times; founder mem. of INTUC, Kerala, fmr. Pres. INTUC, Kerala; fmr. Vice-Chair. Rubber Bd.; mem. Trichur Municipality 1945–47, Cochin Legis. Ass. 1948–49; elected to Kerala Legis. Ass. 1965; Chief Whip, Congress Legislature Party 1952–53, 1954–56; Leader Congress Legislature Group 1967–70; Chair. Cttee. on Public Accounts 1968–69, 1969–70; Minister for Home Affairs 1971–77, of Industry 1995–96; Chief Minister of Kerala March 1977, resgnd. April 1977; Leader of Opposition 1978, 1980–81; Chief Minister of Kerala 1981–87; mem. AICC Working Cttee., Parl. Bd.; Leader Opposition, Kerala Legis. Ass. *Address:* c/o Ministry of Industry, Udyog Bhavan, New Delhi 110 011, India. *Telephone:* (11) 3011815.

KARUNANIDHI, Muthuvel (known as Kalaignar); Indian politician and playwright; b. 3 June 1924, Thirukkuvalai, Thanjavur; s. of Muthuvel Karunanidhi and Anjuham Karunanidhi; m. Dayalu Karunanidhi; four s. one d.; ed. Thiruvarur Bd. High School; Editor-in-Charge Kudiarasu; journalist and stage and screen playwright in Tamil, acting in his own plays staged to collect party funds; has written over 35 film-plays including the screen version of the Tamil classic Silappadhikaram, stage plays and short stories; started first student wing of the Dravidian movement called Tamilnadu Tamil Manavar Mandram; one of the founder mems. of Dravida Munnetra Kazhagam Legislative Party (D.M.K.) 1949, Treas. 1961, Deputy Leader 1968, Pres. 1969–; founder-editor of the Tamil daily organ of the D.M.K. Murasoli; represented Kulittalai in State Assembly 1957–62, Thanjavur 1962–67, Saidapet 1968; led the Kallakkudi Agitation and was imprisoned for six months; fmr. Minister of Public Works; Chief Minister of Tamil Nadu (Madras) 1969–76 (presidential rule imposed), 1989–90; Thamizha Vell (Patron of Tamil), Asscn. of Research Scholars in Tamil 1971; Hon. D.Litt. (Annamalai Univ., Tamil Nadu) 1971. *Address:* 7A S. Gopalapuram, IV Street, Madras 600086, India.

KARYAKIN, Yuri Fedorovich; Russian literary scholar and sociologist; b. 22 July 1930, Perm; ed. Moscow Univ.; mem. CPSU, expelled 1968; jr. researcher Inst. of History, U.S.S.R. Acad. of Sciences 1956–57; Head of Div. History of U.S.S.R. 1957–60; ed., consultant, deputy head of div. Problems of Peace and Socialism 1960–65; admin. asst., researcher Inst. of Problems of Workers' Movt., Acad. of Sciences (now Inst. of Comparative Politology) 1966–; mem. Higher Coordination Council, Supreme Soviet of Russia 1991; U.S.S.R. People's Deputy 1989–91. *Publications:* Self-Deception of Raskolnikov, The Banned Book Gets Freedom, Dostoevsky and the Eve of XXI Century, literary essays, criticism, articles on political issues. *Address:* Institute of Comparative Politology, Kolpachny per. 9-a, 101831 Moscow, Russia. *Telephone:* 916-03-97.

KASAHARA, Yukio, B.ENG.; Japanese business executive; b. 27 Jan. 1925, Tokyo; m. Yuri Tsumura 1983; no c.; ed. Tokyo Univ.; joined Nippon Mining Co. 1949, mem. Bd. of Dirs. 1974, Man. Dir. and Gen. Man. Petroleum Group 1976, Sr. Man. Dir. and Gen. Man. Petroleum Group 1979, Exec. Vice-Pres. and Gen. Man. of Planning and Devt. Group and Petroleum Group 1981, Pres. and Rep. Dir. 1983–89, Chair. and Rep. Dir. June 1989–; fmr. Chair. Japan Energy Corpn. *Leisure interests:* reading, model railroading. *Address:* Nippon Mining Co. Ltd., 10-1, Toranomon 2-chome, Minato-ku, Tokyo, 107 (Office); 3–6–1201, Okubo 2-chome, Shinjuku-ku, Tokyo 169, Japan (Home). *Telephone:* (03) 3505-8111 (Office); (03) 202-3119 (Home).

KASARAVALLI, Girish; Indian film script writer and director; b. 3 Dec. 1950, Karasavalli, Karnataka; s. of Ganesh Rao and Laxmi Devi; m. Vaishali Kasaravalli 1978; one s. one d.; studied pharmacy and film direction; began film career 1977; Prin. Adarsh Film Inst. 1978–86; Hon. Ed. Chitravihari 1986–87; mem. advisory panel, Deep Focus, Rujuvathu (literary and cultural quarterly); mem. film advisory cttee. to Govt. of Karnataka 1979; mem. Gov. Council, Film and TV Inst. of India, Poona 1981–84. *Films:* Avashesh (The Ruins, Golden Lotus Award) 1975, Ghatashraddha (The Ritual Excommunication, Golden Lotus Award, Int. Catholic Jury Award, Ducats Award, Mannheim) 1977, Akramana (Siege, Moitra Award) 1978, Mooru Darigalu (Three Pathways) 1981, Tabarana Kathe (Story of Tabara, Golden Lotus Award) 1986, Bannada Vesha (The Mask) 1988 (Nat. Award, Silver Lotus), Mane 1990 (Nat. Silver Lotus Award), Ek Ghar 1991. *Address:* 1015 Drishya, 8th Cross, 16th Main B.T.M. Layout, I stage, I phase, Bangalore 560 029, India. *Telephone:* 64 10 15.

KASATKINA, Natalya Dmitriyevna; Russian ballet dancer and choreographer; b. 7 June 1934, Moscow; d. of Dmitriy A. Kasatkin and Anna A. Kardashova; m. Vladimir Vasilyov 1956; one s.; ed. Bolshoi Theatre Ballet School; with Bolshoi Theatre Ballet Company 1954–76, main roles including Frigia (Spartacus), Fate (Carmen), The Possessed (Rites of Sacred Spring); Choreographer (with V. Vasilyov) of Vanina Vanini 1962, Geologists 1964, Rites of Sacred Spring 1965, Tristan and Isolde 1967, Preludes and Fugues 1968, Our Yard 1970, The Creation of the World 1971, Romeo and Juliet 1972, Prozrienie 1974, Gayane 1977, Mayakovsky (opera) 1981, Adam and Eve (film ballet) 1982, The Magic Cloak 1982, The Mischiefs of Terpishore 1984, Blue roses for a ballerina (film ballet) 1985, Pushkin 1986, The Faces of Love 1987, Petersburg's Twilights 1987, The Fairy's Kiss 1989, Don Quixote (film ballet) 1990; TV Film: Choreographic Novels; Head (with V. Vasilyov); Moscow State Classical Ballet Theatre 1977–; wrote libretto and produced operas Peter I 1975, Così fan Tutte (with V. Vasilyov) 1978; State Prize of U.S.S.R. 1976, People's Actress of RSFSR 1984. *Leisure interests:* drawing, cooking. *Address:* Karetny Riad 5/10, Apt. 37, 103006 Moscow, Russia. *Telephone:* (095) 299-9524. *Fax:* (095) 921-3127.

KASATONOV, Adm. Igor Vladimirovich; Russian naval officer; b. 10 Feb. 1939, Vladivostok; s. of Vladimir Afanaseyvich Kasatonov and Tamara Kirilovna; m. Julia Alexandrovna 1971; twin s. one d.; ed. Black Sea Nakhimov Higher Navigation School, Mil. Navigation Acad., Gen. Staff Acad.; commdr. of battery, combat unit, sr. asst.-commdr., commdr. of ship 1960–75, Head of staff div. of ships 1975–80, commdr. of div. 1980–82, commdr. of small fleet 1982–88, First Deputy Commdr. of North Navy 1988–91, Commdr. of Black Sea Navy 1991–92, First Deputy C.-in-C. of Russian Navy 1992–; mem. St. Peter's Acad. of Sciences and Arts. *Leisure interests:* history, collecting badges and stamps with a naval theme, table tennis, lawn tennis. *Address:* Ministry of Defence, Novy Arbat 19, Moscow (Office); Bolshoi Kozlovsky Per. 6, 103175 Moscow, Russia (Home). *Telephone:* 293 39 14 (Office).

KASDAN, Lawrence Edward, B.A., M.A.; American film director and screenwriter; b. 14 Jan. 1949, Miami Beach, Florida; s. of Clarence Norman Kasdan and Sylvia Sarah (née Landau) Kasdan; m. Meg Goldman 1971; two s.; ed. Univ. of Mich.; copywriter W.B. Doner and Co. (Advertising), Detroit 1972–75, Doyle, Dane Berbach, L.A. 1975–77; Freelance Screenwriter 1977–80; Motion Picture Dir., screenwriter, L.A. 1980–; Co-Screenwriter, The Empire Strikes Back 1980; Screenwriter, Continental Divide 1981, Raiders of the Lost Ark 1981; Writer, Dir., Body Heat 1981; Co-screenwriter, Return of the Jedi 1982; Co-screenwriter, Dir., Exec. Producer, The Big Chill 1983, Silverado 1985, The Accidental Tourist 1989, I Love You to Death 1989; Producer, Cross My Heart 1987; Grand Canyon (dir., co-screenwriter), The Body Guard (screenwriter exec. producer), Wyatt Earp (dir., co-producer, co-screenwriter), French Kiss (dir.); recipient Clio awards for Advertising, Writers Guild Award for The Big Chill 1983; mem. Writers Guild, American West, Dirs. Guild, American West. *Address:* United Talent Agency, 9560 Wilshire Boulevard, Floor 5, Beverly Hills, CA 90212, U.S.A.

KASER, Michael Charles, M.A., D.LITT.; British economist; b. 2 May 1926, London; s. of Joseph Kaser and Mabel Blunden; m. Elizabeth Anne Mary Piggford 1954; four s. one d.; ed. King's Coll., Cambridge; with Econs. Section Ministry of Works, London 1946–47; H.M. Foreign Service 1947–51, Second Sec., Moscow 1949; UN Econ. Comm. for Europe, Geneva 1951–63; lecturer in Soviet Econs., Univ. of Oxford 1963–72, Chair. Faculty Bd. 1974–76, mem. Gen. Bd. of Faculties 1972–78, Chair. Advisory Council of Adult Educ. 1972–78, Univ. Latin Preacher 1982; Gov. Plater Coll., Oxford 1968–95, Emer. Gov. 1995–; Visiting Prof. of Econs., Univ. of Mich., U.S.A. 1966; Visiting lecturer, European Inst. of Business Admin., Fontainebleau 1959–82, 1988–92, Univ. of Cambridge 1967–68, 1977–78, 1978–79; Reader in Econs. and Professorial Fellow, St. Antony's Coll., Oxford 1972–93, Sub-Warden 1986–87, Reader Emer. 1993–; Dir., Inst. of Russian, Soviet and E. European Studies, Univ. of Oxford 1988–93; Assoc. Fellow Templeton Coll., Oxford 1983–; Visiting Fellow Henley Man. Coll. 1987–; Vice-Chair. Social Science Research Council Int. Activities Cttee. 1980–84; Special Adviser House of Commons Foreign Affairs Cttee. 1985–87; Chair. Co-ordinating Council, Area Studies Asscns. 1986–88 (mem. 1980–93, 1995), Wilton Park Academic Council (FCO) 1986–92 (mem. 1985–); Pres. British Asscn. of Slavonic and E. European Studies 1988–91, Vice-Pres. 1991–93; Prin. Charlemagne Inst., Edin. 1993–94, Hon. Fellow Divinity Faculty, Univ. of Edin. 1993–96; Hon. Prof., Inst. for German Studies, Univ. of Birmingham 1994–; mem. Int. Social Science Council (UNESCO) 1980–91, Council Royal Inst. of Int. Affairs 1979–85, 1986–92, Royal Econ. Soc. 1975–86, 1987–90, School of Slavonic and East European Studies 1981–87, Cttee. Nat. Asscn. for Soviet and East European Studies 1965–88, Steering Cttee. Königswinter Anglo-German Confs. 1969–90, Exec. Cttee. Int. Econ. Asscn. 1974–83, 1986– (Gen. Ed.), also various editorial bds., Anglo-Soviet, British-Mongolian, Anglo-Polish, British-Bulgarian, British-Yugoslav (Chair.), Canada-U.K., British-Romanian and U.K.-Uzbek Round Tables, British-Polish Mixed Comm.; Sec. British Nat. Cttee. of A.I.E.S.E.E 1988–93; Pres. British Asscn. of Fmr. UN Civil Servants 1994–, Albania Soc. of Britain 1992–95; Chair. Council, the Keston Inst., Oxford 1994–; Trustee Foundation of King George VI and Queen Elizabeth, St. Catharine's (Chair. Academic Consultative Cttee. 1987–); Sir Heinz Koeppler Trust (Chair. 1992–); mem. Higher Educ. Funding Council for England Advisory Bd. on E. European Studies 1995–; Hon. D.Soc.Sc. (Birmingham) 1996; Kt. Order of St. Gregory the Great 1990. *Publications:* Comecon: Integration Problems of the Planned Economies 1965, Planning in East Europe (with J. Zielinski) 1970, Soviet Economics 1970, Health Care in the Soviet Union and Eastern Europe 1976, Economic Development for Eastern Europe 1968, Planning and Market Relations 1971, The New Economic Systems of Eastern Europe 1975, The Soviet Union since the Fall of Khrushchev 1975, Soviet Policy for the 1980s 1982, Economic History of Eastern Europe, Vols. I-III 1985–86, Early Steps in Comparing East-West Economies 1991, Reforms in Foreign Economic Relations of Eastern Europe and the Soviet Union 1991, The Economics of Transition in Eastern Europe 1992, The Central Asian Economies after Independence (with S. Mehrotra) 1992, 1996, Education and Economic Change in Eastern Europe and the Former Soviet Union 1992, Cambridge Encyclopedia of Russia and the Former Soviet Union 1994, Privatization in the CIS 1996, The Economies of Kazakstan and Uzbekistan 1997; articles in econ. and Slavic journals. *Address:* 7 Chadlington Road, Oxford, OX2 6SY, England (Home). *Telephone:* (01865) 515581. *Fax:* (01865) 516781.

KASHIWAGI, Yusuke, LL.B.; Japanese banker; b. 17 Oct. 1917, Dalian, China; s. of Hideshige Kashiwagi and Kiyo Yamada; m.; two s. two d.; ed. Tokyo Imperial Univ.; entered Ministry of Finance 1941; Foreign Exchange Bureau 1941, Minister's Secr. 1945, Budget Bureau 1948, Sr. Budget Examiner 1951, Dir. Research Section of Foreign Exchange Bureau 1954, Dir. Planning Section 1956; Financial Sec. Embassy in Washington, D.C. 1958; Financial Counsellor, Ministry of Finance 1961; Financial Commr. 1965; Dir.-Gen. Int. Finance Bureau 1966; Vice-Minister of Finance for Int. Affairs 1968; resgnd. from Ministry of Finance 1971; Special Adviser to Minister of Finance 1971–72; Deputy Pres. Bank of Tokyo Ltd. 1973–77, Pres. 1977–82, Chair. Bd. of Dirs. 1982–92, Sr. Adviser 1992–96, Sr. Adviser Bank of Tokyo-Mitsubishi 1996–; Dir. Sony Corpn. 1976–92; mem. Exec. Cttee. Trilateral Comm. 1973–92; Adviser, Int. Finance Corpn., Washington, D.C. 1979–92; mem Int. Monetary Conf. 1977–92; mem. business advisory cttee. EBRD 1991–; Dir. Meiji Seika Kaisha, Tokyo 1983–97; Chair. BIAC Japan 1985–93, BIAC OECD 1988–90; Adviser Robeco Group, Rotterdam 1985–; Grand Cordon, Order of the Sacred Treasure 1989. *Address:* The Bank of Tokyo-Mitsubishi Ltd., 3-2, Nihombashi Hongokucho 1-Chome Chuo-ku, Tokyo 103-0021, Japan 103-0021.

KASHLEV, Yuriy Borisovich, D.HIST; Russian diplomatist; b. 13 April 1934, Tejen; s. of Boris and Olga Kashlev; m. 1957; one s. one d.; ed. Moscow Inst. of Int. Relations; fmr. mem. CPSU; worked for Soviet Cttee. for Youth Orgs. 1961–65; CPSU Cen. Cttee. 1965–68; Counsellor, U.S.S.R. Ministry of Foreign Affairs 1968–70; served in Embassy, U.K. 1970–71, Counsellor, Head of Sector, Deputy Head, Dept. of Information, Ministry of Foreign Affairs 1971–78, Head Dept. 1982–86; Sec.-Gen. U.S.S.R. Comm. for UNESCO 1978–82; Head Dept. of Humanitarian and Cultural Relations 1986–89, Deputy First Vice-Minister, U.S.S.R. Ministry of Foreign Affairs 1986–90; mem. or head of Soviet dels. to CSCE confs. Geneva, Berne, Vienna, Paris; Russian Amb. to Poland 1990–96; Rector Diplomatic Acad., Foreign Ministry 1996–. *Publications:* Détente in Europe: from Helsinki to Madrid, International Information Exchange, After Fourteen Thousand Wars, Mass Media and International Relations, Ideological Struggle or Psychological War, and other books on int. affairs. *Leisure interests:* tennis, journalism. *Address:* Diplomatic Academy, Ostozhenka str. 53/2, 119021, Moscow, Russia. *Telephone:* (095) 246-18-44.

KASICH, John R., B.A.; American politician; b. 13 May 1952, McKees Rocks, Pa.; ed. Ohio State Univ.; Admin. Asst. Ohio State Senate 1975–77; mem. Ohio Legislature 1979–82; mem. 98th–104th Congress from 12th Ohio Dist., Washington 1983–; mem. Nat. Security Cttee.; mem. House Budget Cttee., now Chair. *Address:* House of Representatives, 1111 Longworth, Washington, D.C. 20515, U.S.A.

KASMIN, John; British art dealer; b. 24 Sept. 1934, London; m. Jane Nicholson 1959 (divorced 1975); two s.; ed. Magdalen Coll. School, Oxford; worked for Gallery One, Soho, London; Dir. New London Gallery, Bond St. 1960–61; f. Kasmin Gallery, Man. Dir. Kasmin Ltd. 1961–, Knoedler Kasmin Ltd. 1977–92. *Leisure interest:* books. *Address:* c/o Kasmin Ltd., 34 Warwick Avenue, London, W9 2PT, England. *Fax:* 0171-289 0746.

KASPAROV, Garri Kimovich; Russian-Azerbaijani chess player; b. (as Harry Weinstein) 13 April 1963, Baku; s. of late Kim Weinstein and of Clara Kasparova; m. 1st Masha Kasparova (divorced); one d.; m. 2nd Yulia Kasparova; one s.; ed. Azerbaijan Pedagogical Inst. of Foreign Languages; Azerbaijan Champion 1975; U.S.S.R. Jr. Champion 1975; Int. Master 1979, Int. Grandmaster 1980; World Jr. Champion 1980; won U.S.S.R. Championship 1981, subsequently replacing Anatoliy Karpov (q.v.) at top of world ranking list; won match against Viktor Korchnoi, challenged Karpov for World Title in Moscow, Sept. 1985, the match being adjourned due to the illness of both players; won rescheduled match to become the youngest ever World Champion in 1985; successfully defended his title against Karpov 1986, 1987, 1990; series of promotional matches in London Feb. 1987; won Times World Championship against Nigel Short 1993; stripped of title by World Chess Fed. 1993; winner Oscar Chess Prize 1982–83, 1985–89, World Chess Cup 1989; highest-ever chess rating of over 2800 1992–; f. Professional Chess Asscn. (PCA) 1993; won PCA World Championship against V. Anand 1995; won match against Deep Blue computer 1996, lost 1997; Deputy Leader Democratic Party of Russia 1990–91. *Publication:* Child of Change (with Donald Trelford) 1987. *Address:* c/o Russian Chess Federation, Gogolevski blvd. 11, 121019 Moscow, Russia. *Telephone:* (095) 291-97-55, 290-17-93.

KASPER, Walter Josef, DR.THEOL.; German Catholic theologian; b. 5 March 1933, Heidenheim/Brenz; s. of Josef Kasper and Theresia Bacher; ed. Univs. of Tübingen and Munich; ordained Priest 1957; Prof. of Dogmatic Theology, Univ. of Münster 1964–70, Univ. of Tübingen 1970–89; Bishop of Rottenburg-Stuttgart 1989–; Chair. Comm. for World Church Affairs 1991–, Comm. for Doctrine of Faith, German Bishops Conf. 1996–; Special Sec. Synod of Bishops 1985; mem. Heidelberger Akad. der Wissenschaften, Academia Scientiarum et Artium Europaea; mem. Congregation for the Doctrine of Faith, Pontifical Council for Culture 1998; Dr. h.c. (Catholic Univ. of America, Washington, D.C.) 1990, (St. Mary's Seminary and Univ., Baltimore) 1991; Bundesverdienstkreuz. *Publications:* Die Tradition in der Römischen Schule 1962, Das Absolute in der Geschichte 1965, Glaube und Geschichte 1970, Einführung in den Glauben 1972 (An Introduction to Christian Faith 1980), Jesus der Christus 1974, Der Gott Jesu Christi 1982, Theologie und Kirche 1987 (Theology and Church 1989), The Christian Understanding of Freedom and the History of Freedom in the Modern Era 1988, Wahrheit und Freiheit in der Erklärung über die Religionsfreiheit des II. Vatikanischen Konzils 1988, Lexicon für Theologie und Kirche 1993–. *Leisure interest:* climbing. *Address:* Bischöfliches Ordinariat, 72101 Rottenburg, Germany. *Fax:* 07472-169556.

KASPSZYK, Jacek; Polish conductor; b. 1952; conducting debut at age 14; studied conducting, theory and composition, and psychology, Warsaw; debut Warsaw Opera 1975, Visiting First Conductor Deutsche Oper am Rhein, Düsseldorf 1976; Prin. Conductor Polish Nat. Radio Symphony Orchestra 1976–80, Music Dir. 1980–82; debut Berlin Philharmonic and New York 1978, London (with Philharmonia) 1982; conducted French Nat., Stockholm Philharmonic, Bavarian Radio Symphony, Rotterdam, Czech Philharmonic Orchestras; conducted Detroit Opera and San Diego Symphony Orchestra 1982; concerts at La Scala, Milan 1982; Australian tour with Chamber Orchestra of Europe 1983; conducted U.K. orchestras 1983–; debut Henry Wood Promenade Concerts 1984; Prin. Conductor and Artistic Adviser North Netherlands Orchestra 1991–95; Prin. Guest Conductor English Sinfonia 1992–; Prin. Guest Conductor Polish Philharmonic 1996; Artistic and Musical Dir. Great Theatre—Nat. Opera Warsaw 1998–; operas conducted include: A Midsummer Night's Dream (Lyon), Eugene Onegin (Bordeaux), The Magic Flute (Opéra Comique, Paris, and Stockholm), Seven Deadly Sins (Lyons), Fledermaus (Scottish Opera), Flying Dutchman (Opera North, U.K.), Barber of Seville (English Nat. Opera); recordings with London Symphony, London Philharmonic, Royal Philharmonic, Philharmonic Orchestras, Warsaw Symphony Orchestra, several other recordings. *Address:* c/o Harold Holt Ltd., 31 Sinclair Road, London, W14 0NS, England; Teatr Wielki, pl. Teatralny 1, 00-077, Warsaw, Poland. *Telephone:* 0171-603 4600 (England); (22) 827 5640 (Poland).

KASRASHVILI, Makvala; Georgian soprano; b. 13 March 1948, Kutaisi; d. of Nina Nanikashvili and Filimon Kasrashvili; m. (divorced); ed. Tbilisi Conservatory; joined Bolshoi Co., Moscow 1968; has performed internationally, including Covent Garden London, Metropolitan Opera New York, Verona, Vienna State Opera etc.; People's Artist of the U.S.S.R. 1986; Grand Prix, Montreal Vocal Competition. *Roles include:* Lisa, Tatyana, Maria, Tosca, Lauretta, Donna Anna, Leonora, Aida, Turandot, Amelia. *Leisure* *interest:* car driving. *Address:* Bolshoi Theatre, Teatralnaya Pl. 1, Moscow, Russia. *Telephone:* 200-58-00 (Home).

KASSEBAUM, Nancy Landon, M.A.; American politician; b. 29 July 1932, Topeka; d. of Alfred M. Kassebaum and Theo Landon; three s. one d.; m. 2nd Howard Baker (q.v.) 1996; ed. Univs. of Kansas and Mich.; mem. Washington staff of Senator James B. Pearson of Kansas 1975–76; Senator from Kansas 1979–97; mem. several senate cttees.; mem. Bd. Trustees Robert Wood Johnson Foundation 1997–; Republican. *Address:* c/o Robert Wood Johnson Foundation, College Road East, P.O. Box 2316, Princeton, NJ 08543, U.S.A.

KASSEM, Abdul-Rauf al-, D.ARCH.; Syrian politician; b. 1932, Damascus; ed. Damascus Univ. School of Arts, Istanbul and Geneva Univs.; teacher of architecture, School of Fine Arts Damascus, Dean 1964–70, Head, Architecture Dept., School of Civil Engineering Damascus Univ. 1970–77, Rector 1977–79; concurrently engineer 1964–77; Gov. of Damascus 1979–80; elected mem. Baath party Regional Command Dec. 1979, Cen. Command of Progressive Nat. Front April 1980; Prime Minister 1980–87; mem. Higher Council for Town Planning 1968–; mem. Nat. Union of Architects' Perm. Comm. on Town Planning 1975–; Hon. Prof. Geneva Univ. 1975–. *Address:* c/o Office of the Prime Minister, Damascus, Syria.

KASTEN, Robert W., Jr., B.A.; American politician; b. 19 June 1942, Milwaukee, Wis.; s. of Robert W. and Mary (Ogden) Kasten; m. Eva J. Nimmons 1986; one d.; ed. Univ. of Arizona and Columbia Univ., New York; with Genesco, Nashville, Tenn. 1966–68; Dir. and Vice-Pres. Gilbert Shoe Co., Thiensville, Wis. 1968–75; mem. Wis. Senate 1972–75; Joint Finance Cttee. 1973–75, Chair. Joint Survey Cttee. on Tax Exemptions 1973–80; Designee Eagleton Inst. of Politics 1973; mem. House of Reps. 1975–79 from 9th Dist., Wis., mem. Govt. Operations Cttee., Small Businesses Cttee.; alt. del. Republican Nat. Convention 1972, del. 1976, Co-Chair. 1988; Senator from Wisconsin 1980–93; founder Kasten & Co, Thiensville, Wis. 1993–; sr. assoc. Strategic and Int. Studies Center, Washington 1993–; served on Appropriations, Budget, Commerce, Science and Transportation Cttee., and Small Business Cttee. *Address:* Kasten & Co., #800, 815 Connecticut Ave, NW, Washington, DC 20006; Strategic and International Studies Center, 1800 K Street NW, Washington DC 20006, U.S.A.

KASTNER, Elliott; American film producer; b. 7 Jan. 1933, New York; s. of Jack Kastner and Rose Kastner; m. Tessa Kennedy; four s. one d.; produced numerous films: Harper (The Moving Target), Kaleidoscope 1965, The Bobo, Laughter in the Dark, Night of the Following Day, Where Eagles Dare 1968, The Walking Stick, A Severed Head, When Eight Bells Toll, Tam Lin, Villain, X Y and Zee, The Nightcomers, Big Truck and Poor Clare, Face to the Wind, Fear is the Key, The Long Goodbye, Cops and Robbers, Jeremy, 11 Harrowhouse, Spot, Rancho Deluxe, 92 in the Shade, Farewell My Lovely, Russian Roulette, Breakheart Pass, The Missouri Breaks, The Swashbuckler, A Little Night Music, Equus, Black Joy, The Stick-Up, The Medusa Touch, The Big Sleep, Absolution, Golden Girl, Yesterday's Hero, North Sea Hijack, The First Deadly Sin, Death Valley, Man Woman and Child, Oxford Blues, Garbo Talks, Nomads, White of the Eye, Heat, Angel Heart, Zits, The Blob, Jack's Back, Never on Tuesday, Zombie High, A Chorus of Disapproval, Homeboy, The Last Party. *Address:* Winkast Film Productions Ltd., Pinewood Studios, Iver Heath, Iver, Bucks., SL0 0NH, England.

KATANANDOV, Sergey Leonidovich; Russian politician and businessman; b. 21 April 1955; m.; two s.; ed. Petrozavodsk State Univ.; worked as Head of sector, sr. engineer, Petrozavodskstroi; mem. Petrozavodsk City Exec. Cttee., Chair. City Soviet, Mayor of Petrozavodsk 1994–98; Chair. Karelian Govt. 1998–. *Leisure interests:* fishing, hunting. *Address:* Government of Karelia, Lenina prosp. 19, Petrozavodsk 185020, Karelia, Russia. *Telephone:* (8142) 76 41 41 (Office). *Fax:* (8142) 77 41 48 (Office).

KATES, Robert William, PH.D.; American professor of geography; b. 31 Jan. 1929, Brooklyn, New York; s. of Simon J. Kates and Helen G. Brener; m. Eleanor C. Hackman 1948; one s. two d.; ed. Univ. of Chicago; Asst. Prof. Graduate School of Geography, Clark Univ. 1962–65, Assoc. Prof. 1965–67, Prof. 1968–92, Univ. Prof. 1974–80, Univ. Prof. and Dir. Alan Shawn Feinstein World Hunger Program 1986–92, Prof. Emer. 1992–; Dir. Bureau of Resource Assessment and Land Use Planning, Univ. Coll., Dar es Salaam 1967–68; Hon. Research Prof. Univ. of Dar es Salaam 1970–71; Fellow, Woodrow Wilson Int. Center for Scholars 1979; mem. Asscn. of American Geographers (Pres. 1993–94); many other professional appointments; mem. N.A.S., A.A.A.S., American Acad. of Arts and Sciences etc.; several awards. *Publications include:* Risk Assessment of Environmental Hazard 1978, The Environment as Hazard (with Ian Burton and Gilbert F. White) 1978; co-ed. of 18 books; monographs and articles on environmental topics.

KATHRADA, Ahmed, B.A., B.BIBLIOGRAPHY; South African politician; b. 21 Aug. 1929, Schweizer Reneke; joined Young Communist League 1941; first imprisoned for participation in Passive Resistance 1946, subsequently imprisoned several times during 1950s and 1960s; first banned in 1954, accused in treason trial 1956–61, placed under house arrest Oct. 1962; sentenced to life imprisonment, Rivonia Trial 1964, unconditionally released 1989; rep. S.A. in World Fed. of Democratic Youth 1951–52; involved in Defiance Campaign 1952, Congress of People's Campaign 1955; Sec. first Free Mandela Cttee. 1962; mem. ANC del. to Talks about Talks with South African Govt. 1990, Nat. Exec. Cttee. ANC 1991–, Internal Leadership Cttee. of ANC, Head Public Relations Dept.; M.P. Govt. of Nat. Unity 1994–; Parl. Counsellor in Office of Pres. 1994–; Chair. Robben Island Museum Council; Chair. Ex-Political Prisoners' Cttee; Fellow Mayibuye Centre, Univ. of Western Cape; Patron Trauma Centre, Cape Town. *Address:* House of Assembly, Cape Town, South Africa. *Telephone:* (021) 464 2121 (Cape Town); (012) 319 1620 (Pretoria). *Fax:* (021) 464 2123 (Cape Town); (012) 325 1270 (Pretoria).

KATIN, Peter, F.R.A.M., A.R.C.M.; British pianist; b. 14 Nov. 1930, London; s. of Jerrold and Gertrude Katin; m. Eva Zweig 1954; two s.; ed. Henry Thornton School, Royal Acad. of Music, Westminster Abbey; London debut, Wigmore Hall 1948; extensive concert tours in U.K., Europe, Africa, Canada, U.S.A. and Far East; special interest in Chopin; recordings for Decca, EMI, Unicorn, Everest, Philips, CFP, Lyrita and Pickwick Int., Claudio, Olympia, Simax, Athene; Prof. Royal Acad. of Music 1956–60, Univ. of Western Ont. 1978–84, Royal Coll. of Music 1992–; Founder Katin Centre for Advanced Piano Studies 1991, Katin Trio 1997; Pres. Surrey Sinfonietta 1994–; Chopin Arts Award (New York) 1977; Hon.D.Music (De Montfort) 1994. *Leisure interests:* writing, tape-recording, theatre, reading, photography. *Address:*c/o TRANSART, & Bristol Gardens, London, W9 2JG, England. *Telephone:* 0171-286 7526. *Fax:* 0171-266 2687.

KATO, Koichi; Japanese politician; b. 17 June 1939, Tsuruoka, Yamagata Pref.; m. Aiko Sugiura 1967; one s. three d.; ed. Univ. of Tokyo, Harvard Univ.; entered Ministry of Foreign Affairs 1964, Vice-Consul, Japanese Consulate Gen., Hong Kong 1967–69, Deputy Dir., Chinese Div., Asian Affairs Bureau 1969–71; M.P. for 2nd Dist., Yamagata Pref., House of Reps. 1972–, Deputy Chief Cabinet Sec. 1978–80, Minister of State for Defence 1984–86; Minister of State, Chief Cabinet Sec. 1991–92; Dir. House Cttee. on Rules and Admin. 1980–81, on Agric., Forestry and Fisheries 1981–83; Vice-Chair., Diet Policy Cttee. of the Liberal Democratic Party (LDP) 1980–81; Dir., Agric. and Forestry Div., LDP Policy Affairs Research Council 1981–83; Dir.-Gen., LDP Gen. Affairs Bureau 1983–84; Chief Deputy Chair. of Political Research Council LDP 1986–87, Chair. 1994–95; Acting Chair. Research Comm. on Comprehensive Agric. 1987–88; Acting Sec.-Gen. LDP 1992–94, Sec.-Gen. 1995. *Address:* c/o Liberal-Democratic Party, 1-11-23 Nagata-cho, Chiyoda-ku, Tokyo 100, Japan.

KATO, Mutsuki; Japanese politician; b. 1926; elected to House of Reps. from Okayama Pref. six times; fmr. Parl. Vice-Minister for Transport; fmr. Vice-Chair. Liberal-Democratic Party Policy Affairs Research Council; Minister of State and Dir.-Gen. Nat. Land Agency 1982–83, of Agric., Forestry and Fisheries 1986–87, May–July 1994. *Address:* c/o Liberal-Democratic Party, 1-11-23, Nagata-cho, Chiyoda-ku, Tokyo 100, Japan.

KATO, Susumu, PH.D.; Japanese professor of atmospheric physics; b. 27 Aug. 1928, Saitama; s. of Nimpei Kato (deceased) and Minoru Kato; m. Kyoko Kojo; ed. Kyoto Univ.; lecturer, Faculty of Eng., Kyoto Univ. 1955–61, Asst. Prof. Ionosphere Research Lab. 1961–62, Assoc. Prof. 1964–67, Prof. 1967–81, Dir. and Prof. Radio Atmospheric Science Center 1981–92, Prof. Emer. 1992–; Research Officer, Upper Atmosphere Section, CSIRO, N.S.W., Australia 1962–64; Visiting Scientist, High Altitude Observatory, NCAR, Colo. 1967–68, 1973–74; Visiting Prof., Dept. of Meteorology, UCLA, Los Angeles 1973–74, Bandung Inst. of Tech., Indonesia 1992–; Vice-Chair. Japan-Indonesia Science and Tech. Forum 1992–; AGU Fellow 1991; Tanakadate Prize 1959, Yamaji Science Prize 1974, Appleton Prize 1987, Hasegawa Prize 1987, Fujiwara Prize 1989, Japan Acad. Award 1989. *Publications:* Dynamics of the Upper Atmosphere 1980; over 100 scientific papers on atmospheric tidal theory, observation of atmospheric waves by MST radar. *Leisure interests:* reading, music, jogging, swimming, Japanese calligraphy. *Address:* Japan-Indonesia Science and Technology Forum, Rokko Building No. 2, 5th Floor, 1-3-7, Shinkawa, Chuo-ku, Tokyo 104 (Office); 22-15 Fujimidai, Otsu, Shiga Prefecture 520, Japan (Home). *Telephone:* 0775-34-1177 (Home). *Fax:* 0775-33-4013 (Home).

KATONA, Tamás; Hungarian politician and historian; b. 2 Feb. 1932, Budapest; s. of Tibor Katona and Magdolna Halász; m. Klára Barta; one s. two d.; ed. Archiepiscopal Highschool (Rákóczianum), Budapest, Eötvös Loránd Univ. Budapest; Head public libraries 1954–61; ed. Magyar Helikon Publishing House and Európa Publishing House 1961–86; lecturer on 19th-century Hungarian History at Eötvös Coll. 1980–85, at József Attila Univ. of Szeged 1986–90; joined Hungarian Democratic Forum, later joined Hungarian Democratic People's Party; mem. of Parl. 1990–; Sec. of State for Foreign Affairs 1990–92; Sec. of State, Prime Minister's Office 1992–94; First Vice-Pres. IPU, Hungary; Mayor First Dist. (Castle Hill) Budapest 1994–; Ed. serial publs. Bibliotheca Historica and Pro Memoria (pocket library of history and cultural history). *Publications:* Az aradi vértanúk 1979, 1983, 1991 (The Martyrs of Arad), A korona kilenc évszázada (Nine Centuries of the Crown) 1979, A tatárjárás emlékezete (The Mongol Invasion) 1981, 1987, Budavár bevételének emlékezete, 1849 (Capture of Fort Buda in 1849) 1991, Csány László erdélyi főkormánybiztos (László Csány High Commissioner of Transylvania) 1991. *Leisure interests:* tennis, music. *Address:* Fortuna-utca 13, 1014 Budapest, Hungary. *Telephone:* 201-13-65.

KATRITZKY, Alan Roy, M.A., D.PHIL., PH.D., SC.D., F.R.S.; British/American professor of chemistry, researcher and consultant; b. 18 Aug. 1928, London; s. of Frederick C. and Emily C. (Lane) Katritzky; m. Agnes Kilian 1952; one s. three d.; ed. Oxford and Cambridge Univs.; Univ. Lecturer, Cambridge

1958–63; Fellow Churchill Coll., Cambridge 1959–63; Prof. of Chem., Univ. of East Anglia 1963–80, Dean, School of Chemical Sciences 1963–70, 1976–80; Kenan Prof. Univ. of Fla. 1980–; Dir. Florida Inst. of Heterocyclic Compounds 1986–; Foreign mem. Polish Acad. of Sciences, Royal Catalan Acad. of Sciences; Hon. Fellow, Italian Chem. Soc., Polish Chem. Soc.; Hon. Prof. Beijing Inst. of Tech., Xian Modern Univ.; Hon. D.Sc. (Madrid, Poznań, Gdansk, E. Anglia, Toulouse, St. Petersburg, Bucharest); Tilden Lecturer, Chem. Soc.; Heterocyclic Award, Royal Soc. of Chem., Sr. Humboldt Award (Germany); Cavaliere ufficiale (Italy); Heyrowsky Medal, Czech Acad. of Science. *Publications:* five books and 1300 papers in heterocyclic chemistry; Ed. Advances in Heterocyclic Chemistry (70 vols.) and Comprehensive Heterocyclic Chemistry, 1st edn. (8 vols.), 2nd edn. (10 vols.), Organic Functional Group Transformations (7 vols.). *Leisure interests:* walking, wind surfing. *Address:* Department of Chemistry, University of Florida, Gainesville, FL 32611 (Office); 1221 SW 21st Avenue, Gainesville, FL 32601, U.S.A. (Home). *Telephone*: (904) 392-0554 (Office); (904) 378-1221 (Home). *Fax:* (904) 392-9199.

KATSIFARAS, Georgios; Greek politician; b. 1935, Kallentsi, Peloponnese; ed. Univ. of Athens; arrested and deported to remote areas 1968–71; in Canada with Andreas Papandreou 1971–74; mem. Cen. Cttee. Panhellenic Socialist Movement (PASOK) 1974–, mem. Econ. Cttee. 1977–; M.P. 1981–89, 1991–; Minister for Merchant Marine 1982–85, 1993–96, of Commerce 1986–87. *Address:* c/o Ministry of Merchant Marine, Odos Gregoriou Lambraki 150, Piraeus, Greece.

KATTAN, Mohammed Imad, B.SC., M.C.D.; Jordanian architect and planner; b. 3 Sept. 1951, Amman; s. of Mahmoud Kamal and Ilham Hamzah; m. 1st Leen M. Halawa 1983; m. 2nd Nawal Radi Abdulla 1987; one s.; ed. Bath and Liverpool Univs., U.K.; architect-planner, CH2M Hill, Portland, Ore., U.S.A. 1977–81; lecturer, Jordan Univ., Amman 1981–84; Dir. UBMC, Amman 1982–95; Chair. and Man. Dir. UDC, Amman 1982–; Man. Dir. ASCO (Architectural Systems Co. Ltd.), Amman 1997–. *Leisure interests:* tennis, jogging, photography, scuba diving. *Address:* P.O. Box 950846, Amman 11195, Jordan. *Telephone:* (6) 5692669, 4648043. *Fax:* (6) 4648043.

KATTAN, Naim, O.C., F.R.S.C.; Canadian writer; b. 26 Aug. 1928, Baghdad, Iraq; s. of Nessim and Hela Kattan; m. Gaetane Laniel 1961; one s.; ed. Univ. of Baghdad and Sorbonne, Paris; newspaper corresp. in Near East and Europe, broadcaster throughout Europe; emigrated to Canada 1954; Int. Politics Ed. for Nouveau Journal 1961–62; fmr. teacher at Laval Univ.; fmr. Sec. Cercle Juif de langue française de Montréal; freelance journalist and broadcaster; Prof., Univ. of Quebec, Montreal; Assoc. Dir. Canada Council; mem. Académie Canadienne-Française; Pres. Royal Soc. of Canada; Officier Ordre des Arts et Lettres de France; Chevalier Ordre Nat. du Québec. *Publications: novels:* Adieu Babylone 1975, Les Fruits arrachés 1981, La Fiancée promise 1983, La Fortune du passager 1989, La Célébration 1997; *essays:* Le réel et le théâtral 1970, Ecrivains des Amériques, Tomes I-III, Le Repos et l'Oubli 1987, La fortune du passager 1989, Le Père 1990, Farida 1991, La Reconciliation 1992, A. M. Klein 1994, La distraction 1994, Culture: Alibi ou liberté 1996, Idoles et images 1996, Figures bibliques 1997; also numerous short stories and criticisms. *Address:* 2463 rue Sainte Famille No. 2114, Montreal, Quebec, H2X 2K7, Canada. *Telephone:* (514) 499-2836. *Fax:* (514) 499-9954.

KATZ, Sir Bernard, M.D., D.SC., F.R.C.P., F.R.S.; British professor of biophysics; b. 26 March 1911, Leipzig, Germany; s. of Max Katz; m. Marguerite Penly 1945; two s.; ed. Univs. of Leipzig and London; Biophysical Research, Univ. Coll. London 1935–39, Beit Memorial Fellow 1938–39; Carnegie Research Fellow, Sydney Hospital, Sydney, N.S.W. 1939–42; Royal Australian Air Force 1942–45; Asst. Dir. of Research in Biophysics and Henry Head Research Fellow, Royal Soc. 1946–50; Reader in Physiology, Univ. Coll. London 1950–51; Prof. of Biophysics and Head of Dept., Univ. Coll. London 1952–78, Prof. Emer. 1978–; mem. Royal Soc., Sec. 1968, and Vice-Pres. 1970–76; mem. Agricultural Research Council 1967–77; Herter Lecturer, Johns Hopkins Univ. 1958; Dunham Lecturer, Harvard Univ. 1961; Croonian Lecturer, Royal Soc. 1961; Foreign mem. Accademia Nazionale Dei Lincei, Royal Danish Acad. of Sciences 1968, American Acad. Arts and Sciences 1969, N.A.S. 1976, Japanese Pharmacological Soc. 1977, American Physiological Soc. 1985; Corresp. mem. Australian Acad. of Science 1987; Hon. D.Sc. (Southampton, Melbourne Univs.) 1971, (Cambridge Univ.) 1980, Hon. Ph.D. (Weizmann Inst. Science) 1979, Hon. M.D. (Leipzig) 1990; Baly Medal, Royal Coll. of Physicians 1967, Copley Medal, Royal Soc. 1967, Nobel Prize (jtly.) for Physiology or Medicine 1970, Cothenius Medal, Deutsche Akademie der Wissenschaften, Leopoldina 1989; Foreign mem. Orden pour le mérite für Wissenschaften und Künste 1982. *Publications:* Electric Excitation of Nerve 1939, Nerve, Muscle and Synapse 1966, The Release of Neural Transmitter Substances 1969. *Address:* c/o Department of Physiology, University College, Gower Street, London, WC1E 6BT, England.

KATZ, Michael, A.B., M.D.; American pediatrician and educator; b. 13 Feb. 1928, Lwow, Poland; s. of Edward Katz and Rita Gluzman; m. Robin J. Roy 1986; one s.; ed. Univ. of Pennsylvania, State Univ. of New York, Brooklyn, Columbia Univ. School of Public Health; Intern, Univ. of California, Los Angeles, Medical Center 1956–57; Resident, Presbyterian Hosp. New York 1960–62, Dir. Pediatric Service 1977–92; Hon. Lecturer in Paediatrics, Makerere Univ. Coll., Kampala, Uganda 1963–64; Instructor in Pediatrics, Columbia Univ. 1964–65, Prof. in Tropical Medicine, School of Public Health 1971–92, Prof. Emer. 1992–, Prof. of Pediatrics, Coll. of Physicians and Surgeons 1972–77, Reuben S. Carpentier Prof. and Chair. Dept. of Pediatrics 1977–92, Prof. Emer. 1992–; Asst. Prof. of Pediatrics, Univ. of Pa. 1966–71; Vice-Pres. for Research, March of Dimes, Birth Defects Foundation 1992–; Pres. World Alliance of Orgs. for the Prevention of Birth Defects 1995–; Assoc. mem. Wistar Inst., Philadelphia 1965–71; Consultant, WHO regional offices, Guatemala, Venezuela, Egypt, Yemen; mem. U.S. Del. to 32nd World Health Ass., Geneva 1979; Consultant, UNICEF, New York and Tokyo; Jurzykowski Foundation Award in Medicine 1983; mem. numerous medical socs. including Inst. of Medicine, N.A.S.; Alexander von Humboldt Foundation Sr. U.S. Scientist Award 1987. *Publications:* contributions to numerous journals and medical works. *Address:* 1275 Mamaroneck Avenue, White Plains, NY 10605, U.S.A. *Telephone:* (914) 997 4555. *Fax:* (914) 997-4560.

KATZ, Samuel Lawrence, M.D.; American professor of pediatrics; b. 29 May 1927, Manchester, N.H.; s. of Morris Katz and Ethel Lawrence Katz; m. 1st Betsy Jane Cohan 1950 (divorced 1971); four s. (one s. deceased) three d.; m. 2nd Catherine Minock Wilfert 1971; two step-d.; ed. Dartmouth Coll. and Harvard Univ.; hosp. appts., Boston, Mass. 1952–56; Exchange Registrar, Pediatric Unit, St. Mary's Hosp. Medical School, London, England 1956; Research Fellow in Pediatrics, Harvard Medical School at Research Div. of Infectious Diseases, Children's Hosp. Medical Center, Boston 1956–58, Research Assoc. 1958–68; Pediatrician-in-Chief, Beth Israel Hosp., Boston 1958–61, Visiting Pediatrician 1961–68; Assoc. Physician, Children's Hosp. Medical Center, Boston 1958–63, Sr. Assoc. in Medicine 1963–68, Chief, Newborn Div. 1961–67; Instructor in Pediatrics, Harvard Medical School, Boston 1958–59, Assoc. 1959–63, Tutor in Medical Sciences 1961–63, Asst. Prof. of Pediatrics 1963–68; Co-Dir. Combined Beth Israel Hosp.-Children's Hosp. Medical Center, Infectious Disease Career Training Program 1967–68; Prof. and Chair. Dept. of Pediatrics, Duke Univ. School of Medicine, Durham, N.C. 1968–90, Wilburt C. Davison Prof. of Pediatrics 1972–97; prin. activities involve research on children's vaccines and on pediatric AIDS; mem. Bd. of Dirs. Georgetown Univ. 1987–93, Hasbro Foundation 1988–, Burroughs Wellcome Fund 1991–, (Chair. Bd. of Dirs. 1995–(99)); Consultant, Nat. Insts. of Health (NIH), AIDS Exec. Cttee. 1986–89, mem. NIH Pediatric AIDS Exec. Cttee. 1994–97; mem. Editorial Bd. Pediatric Infectious Diseases Report; fmr. mem. Editorial Bd. Annual Review in Medicine, Postgraduate Medicine, Reviews of Infectious Diseases, Current Problems in Pediatrics, Ped Sat (TV Educ.); Fellow American Acad. of Pediatrics, Infectious Diseases Soc. of America; mem. A.A.A.S., Soc. for Pediatric Research, American Soc. for Microbiology, American Asscn. of Immunologists, American Public Health Asscn., American Soc. for Clinical Investigation, American Pediatric Soc., American Epidemiological Soc., American Soc. for Virology, American Fed. for Clinical Research, Inst. of Medicine; Hon. D.Sc. (Georgetown Univ.) 1996; Presidential Medal of Dartmouth Coll. for Leadership and Achievement 1991, Distinguished Physician Award (Pediatric Infectious Diseases Soc.) 1991, Bristol Award and Soc. Citation Infectious Diseases Soc. of America 1993, Needleman Medal and Award, American Public Health Asscn. 1997, and other awards. *Publications:* numerous articles in scientific journals, textbooks of pediatrics and infectious diseases. *Leisure interests:* jazz drumming, cycling, reading, opera. *Address:* Duke University Medical Center, P.O. Box 2925, Durham, NC 27710 (Office); 1917 Wildcat Creek Road, Chapel Hill, NC 27516, U.S.A. (Home). *Telephone:* (919) 684-3734 (Office); (919) 968-0008 (Home). *Fax:* (919) 681-8934 (Home); (919) 968-0447 (Home).

KATZAV, Moshe; Israeli politician and economist; b. 1945, Iran; m.; five c.; ed. Hebrew Univ., Jerusalem; Mayor, Kiryat Malachi 1969, 1974–81; mem. Knesset 1977–; mem. Cttee. on Interior Affairs and the Environment 1977–81, Cttee. on Educ. and Culture 1977–81, Cttee. on Defence, Cttee. on Foreign Affairs; Deputy Minister of Housing 1981–83; Minister of Labour and Social Affairs 1984–88, of Transport 1988–92; mem. Inner Cabinet 1990–; Deputy Prime Minister, Minister of Tourism 1996; Chair. Likud Faction in Knesset (parl.) 1992–; mem. Likud Party. *Address:* c/o Ministry of Tourism, P.O. Box 1018, 24 King George Street, Jerusalem 91009, Israel.

KATZENBACH, Nicholas deBelleville; American government official and lawyer; b. 17 Jan. 1922, Philadelphia; s. of Edward and Marie Katzenbach; m. Lydia King Phelps Stokes 1946; two s. two d.; ed. Philips Exeter Acad., Princeton and Yale Univs. and Balliol Coll., Oxford; U.S. Army Air Force 1941–45; admitted to N.J. Bar 1950, Conn. Bar 1955, New York Bar 1972; with firm Katzenbach Gildea and Rudner, Trenton, N.J. 1950; Attorney-Adviser, Office of Gen. Counsel, Air Force 1950–52, part-time Consultant 1952–56; Assoc. Prof. of Law, Yale Univ. 1952–56; Prof. of Law, Univ. of Chicago 1956–60; Asst. Attorney-Gen., U.S. Dept. of Justice 1961–62, Deputy Attorney-Gen. 1962–64, Attorney-Gen. 1965–66; Under-Sec. of State 1966–69; Sr. Vice-Pres. and Gen. Counsel, IBM Corpn. 1969–86; Partner Riker, Danzig, Scherer, Hyland and Perretti 1986–91, Counsel 1991–; mem. American Bar Asscn., American Judicature Soc., American Law Inst.; hon. degrees from Rutgers Univ., Univ. of Bridgeport (Conn.), Tufts Univ., Georgetown Univ., Princeton, Northeastern Univ., Brandeis Univ.; Democrat. *Publications:* The Political Foundations of International Law (with Morton A. Kaplan) 1961, Legal Literature of Space (with Prof. Leon Lipson) 1961. *Address:* 33 Greenhouse Drive, Princeton, NJ 08540, U.S.A.

KATZENBERG, Jeffrey; American film executive; b. 1950; m. Marilyn Siegal; one s. one d.; Asst. to Chair., C.E.O. Paramount Pictures, New York 1975–77; Exec. Dir. Marketing, Paramount TV, Calif. 1977, Vice-Pres.

Programming 1977–78; Vice-Pres. feature production, Paramount Pictures 1978–80, Sr. Vice-Pres. production, motion picture div. 1980–82, Pres. production, motion pictures and TV 1982–94; Chair. Walt Disney Studios, Burbank, Calif. 1994–; Co-founder Dream works SKG 1995–. *Address:* Dreamworks SKG, 100 Universal Terrace Parkway, Suite 477, North Hollywood, CA 91608, U.S.A.

KATZIR, Ephraim, M.SC., PH.D.; Israeli fmr. Head of State, scientist, teacher and administrator; b. (as Ephraim Katchalski) 16 May 1916, Kiev, Russia; s. of Yehuda and Tsila Katchalski; m. Nina Gotlieb 1938 (deceased); one s.; ed. Hebrew Univ., Jerusalem; Prof. and Head, Dept. of Biophysics, Weizmann Inst. of Science 1951–73; Chief Scientist, Ministry of Defence 1966–68; Pres. of Israel 1973–78; Prof. Weizmann Inst. of Science 1978–, Prof. Tel Aviv Univ. 1978–; first incumbent Herman F. Mark Chair in Polymer Science, Polytechnic Inst. of New York 1979; Pres. World ORT Union (Org. for Rehabilitation Through Training) 1987–90, COBIOTECH Int. Scientific Cttee. for Biotech. 1989–95; mem. Israel Acad. of Sciences and Humanities, N.A.S., U.S.A., Leopoldina Acad. of Science, German Democratic Repub., American Soc. of Biological Chemists (Hon.), The Royal Soc. of London (Foreign mem.), American Acad. of Arts and Sciences (Foreign Hon. mem.), Int. Union of Biochemistry, Acad. des Sciences, France (Foreign mem.), Royal Inst. of Great Britain (Hon. mem.), American Acad. of Microbiology and many other orgs.; Hon. Prof. Polytechnic Inst., New York; Hon. Ph.D. (Brandeis, Michigan, Harvard, Northwestern, Jerusalem Hebrew, McGill, Thomas Jefferson, Oxford, Miami Univs., Weizmann Inst., Israel Technion and Hebrew Union Coll., Jerusalem, Eidgenossische Technische Hochschule, Univ. of Buenos Aires); Tchernikhovski Prize 1948; Weizmann Prize 1950; Israel Prize Natural Sciences 1959; Rothschild Prize Natural Sciences 1961; Linderstrøm-Lang Gold Medal 1969; Hans Krebs Medal 1972; Underwood Prescott Award, M.I.T. 1982; first recipient of Japan Prize, Science and Tech. Foundation of Japan 1985; Enzyme Eng. Award 1987; Commdr. Légion d'honneur, France 1990. *Publications:* numerous papers and articles on proteins and polyamino acids, polymers structure and function of living cells and enzyme engineering. *Leisure interest:* swimming. *Address:* Department of Biological Chemistry, Weizmann Institute of Science, P.O. Box 26, Rehovot 76100, Israel.

KATZ-OZ, Avraham, M.SC.; Israeli politician; b. 1934, Tel Aviv; m.; three c.; ed. Hebrew Univ.; mem. Kibbutz Nahal Oz; served as Kibbutz Sec. and held various offices in Kibbutz movt.; mem. Labour Alignment Party; mem. Knesset 1981–; Minister of Agric. 1988–90. *Address:* c/o Ministry of Agriculture, P.O.B. 7011, Hakirya, Tel Aviv 61070, Israel.

KAUFMAN, Rt. Hon. Gerald Bernard, P.C., M.A., M.P.; British politician; b. 21 June 1930; s. of Louis and Jane Kaufman; ed. Leeds Grammar School and Queen's Coll., Oxford; Asst. Gen. Sec. Fabian Soc. 1954–55; political staff, Daily Mirror 1955–64; political corresp. New Statesman 1964–65; Parl. Press Liaison, Labour Party 1965–70; M.P. for Manchester, Ardwick 1970–83; for Manchester, Gorton 1983–; Under-Sec. of State for the Environment 1974–75, for Industry 1975; Minister of State, Dept. of Industry 1975–79; mem. Parl. Cttee. of Labour Party 1980–92; Opposition Spokesman for Home Affairs 1983–87; Shadow Foreign Sec. 1987–92; Chair. House of Commons Nat. Heritage Select Cttee. 1992–97, Culture, Media and Sport Select Cttee. 1997–; mem. Labour Party Nat. Exec. Cttee. 1991–92. *Publications:* How to Live under Labour (co-author) 1964, To Build the Promised Land 1973, How to be a Minister 1980 (revised edn. 1997), Renewal: Labour's Britain in the 1980's 1983, My Life in the Silver Screen 1985, Inside the Promised Land 1986, Meet Me in St Louis 1994. *Leisure interests:* cinema, opera, records, theatre, concerts, travel. *Address:* House of Commons, London, S.W.1; 87 Charlbert Court, Eamont Street, London, N.W.8, England. *Telephone:* 0171-219 5145. *Fax:* 0171-219 6825.

KAUFMAN, Henry, B.A., M.S., PH.D.; American banker; b. 20 Oct. 1927, Wenings, Germany; s. of Gustav and Hilda (née Rosenthal) Kaufman; m. Elaine Reinheimer 1957; three s.; ed. New York and Columbia Univs.; went to U.S.A. 1937; Asst. Chief Economist, Research Dept., Fed. Reserve Bank of New York 1957–61; with Salomon Bros., New York 1962–88, Gen. Partner 1967–88, mem. Exec. Cttee. 1972–88, Man. Dir. 1981–88, also Chief Economist, in charge Bond Market Research, Industry and Stock Research, and Bond Portfolio Analysis Research Depts.; f. Henry Kaufman & Co., N.Y. 1988–; Pres. Money Marketeers, New York Univ. 1964–65; Dir. Lehman Bros. 1995–; Trustee, Hudson Inst.; mem. Bd. of Govs., Tel-Aviv Univ.; mem. American Econ. Assn., American Finance Assn., Conf. of Business Economists, Econ. Club, New York (also Dir.), UN Assn. (also Dir), Council on Foreign Relations. *Publication:* Interest Rates, the Markets and the New Financial World 1986. *Address:* Henry Kaufman & Co., 65 E. 55th Street, New York, NY 10022, U.S.A.

KAUFMAN, Philip; American film writer and director; b. 23 Oct. 1936, Chicago, Ill.; s. of Nathan Kaufman and Betty Kaufman; m. Rose Kaufman; one s.; ed. Univ. of Chicago and Harvard Law School; fmr. teacher in Italy. *Films:* Goldstein (co-screenplay, co-dir. and co-producer) (Prix de la Nouvelle Critique, Cannes 1964), Fearless Frank 1965, The Great Northfield Minnesota Raid 1971, The White Dawn (dir. only) 1973, Invasion of the Body Snatchers (dir. only) 1977, The Wanderers (co-screenplay and dir.) 1979, The Right Stuff (dir. and screenplay) 1983 (winner of four Acad. Awards), The Unbearable Lightness of Being (dir. and co-screenplay) 1988, (Orson Welles Award for Best Filmmaker-Writer/Dir. 1988, Nat. Soc. of Film Critics Award for Best Dir. 1988), Henry & June (dir. and co-scriptwriter) 1990, Rising Sun (dir. and co-screenplay) 1993. *Address:* c/o William Morris Agency, 151 El Camino Drive, Beverly Hills, CA 90212, U.S.A.

KAUFMANN, Arthur, DR.IUR.; German university professor; b. 10 May 1923, Singen; s. of Edmund Kaufmann and Elisabeth (née Gsell) Kaufmann; m. Dorothea Helffich 1949; one s. three d.; ed. Univs. of Frankfurt and Heidelberg; judge at Landgericht Karlsruhe 1951–57; Docent Univ. of Heidelberg 1957–60; Ordinary Prof. Univ. of Saarbrücken 1960–69, Univ. of Munich 1969–, now emer.; fmr. Dir. Inst. for Legal Philosophy and Legal Information, Univ. of Munich; Ordinary mem. Bayerische Akademie der Wissenschaften 1980–; mem. many other academies and orgs.; Hon. Pres. German Section Int. Assn. for Philosophy of Law and Social Philosophy 1982–, Hon. Pres. Int. Assn. for Philosophy of Law and Social Philosophy 1991–; numerous hon. degrees; Dr. h.c. (Munich); Hon. mem. Inst. for Advanced Studies in Jurisprudence, Univ. of Sydney. *Publications:* Naturrecht und Geschichtlichkeit 1957, Das Schuldprinzip 1976, Analogie und 'Natur der Sache' 1982, Schuld und Strafe 1983, Strafrecht zwischen Gestern und Morgen 1983, Rechtsphilosophie im Wandel 1984, Beiträge zur Juristischen Hermeneutik 1984, Gerechtigkeit, der vergessene Weg zum Frieden 1986, Gustav Radbruch 1987, Rechtsphilosophie in der Nach Neinzeit 1990, Vom Ungehorsam gegen die Obrigkeit 1991, Das Gewissen und das Problem der Rechtsgeltung 1991, Über Gerechtigkeit 1993, Grundprobleme der Rechtsphilosophie 1994, Einführung in Rechtsphilosophie und Rechtstheorie der Gegenwart 1994; more than 600 articles and trans. into 16 languages. *Leisure interests:* music, literature, theology. *Address:* Longinusstrasse 3, 81247 Munich, Germany. *Telephone:* 089/8111723.

KAUL, Pratap Kishen, M.A.; Indian diplomatist; b. 3 July 1929, Calcutta; s. of late K. K. Kaul; m. Usha Kaul; three d.; ed. Allahabad and Harvard Univs.; Deputy Sec., Ministries of Home Affairs and Finance 1965–66, Joint Sec. Ministry of Finance 1967–73, Finance Sec. and Sec. Economic Affairs 1983–85; Joint Sec. Ministry of Steel and Mines 1975–76; Chief Controller, Imports and Exports, Ministry of Commerce Jan.–July 1976, Additional Sec. 1976–80, Sec. (Export Devt.) Feb.–May. 1980, Sec. (Textiles) July–Sept. 1980, Sec. 1980–81; Chair. State Trading Corpn. 1980–81; Defence Sec. Ministry of Defence 1981–83; Cabinet Sec. 1985–86; Amb. to the U.S.A. 1986–89. *Leisure interests:* reading, sports. *Address:* c/o Ministry of External Affairs, South Block, New Delhi 110011, India.

KAUL, Triloki Nath; Indian diplomatist; b. 18 Feb. 1913, Baramulla, Kashmir; s. of T. Kaul Jalali and Gunwanti Kaul; m. Sati Kaul 1931 (deceased); one s. one d.; ed. Univs. of Punjab, Allahabad, London; joined Indian Civil Service 1936; served in United Provinces as Joint Magistrate and Collector 1937–47; Sec. Indian Council of Agricultural Research, New Delhi 1947; First Sec. Indian Embassy, Moscow 1947–49, Washington 1949–50, Counsellor 1950–52, and Minister 1952–53, Beijing; Joint Sec. Ministry of External Affairs, New Delhi 1953–57; Chair. Int. Comm. for Supervision and Control, Viet Nam 1957–58; Amb. to Iran 1958–60; Deputy High Commr. U.K. 1960–61, Acting High Commr. 1961–62; Amb. to U.S.S.R. and Mongolia 1962–66; Sec. to Govt. of India, Ministry of External Affairs, New Delhi, 1966–68; Sec.-Gen. Ministry of External Affairs 1968–73; Amb. to U.S.A. 1973–76; Pres. Indian Council for Cultural Relations 1977 (resigned April 1977); Pres. World Affairs Foundation, Himalaya Research and Cultural Foundation, STAND (Science and Tech. for Nat. Devt.); Vice-Pres. CRRID (Centre for Research in Rural and Industrial Devt.); Founder, World Affairs; mem. Exec. Bd. UNESCO 1980–85; Amb. to U.S.S.R. 1986–89; Hon. Fellow, King's Coll., London 1962; Hon. Prof. Kashmir Univ. 1978; Hon. LL.D. (Avadh Univ.) 1977. *Publications:* Diplomacy in Peace and War: Recollections and Reflections 1978, India, China and Indochina 1979, The Kissinger Years—Indo-U.S. Relations 1980, Reminiscences—Discreet and Indiscreet 1981, Life in a Himalayan Hamlet 1982, Ambassadors Need not Lie (3 vols.) 1986–89, Stalin to Gorbachev and beyond 1991, Future of CIS 1992, My Years Through Raj to Swaraj 1993. *Leisure interests:* reading, writing, gardening, photography, music. *Address:* 7 Poorvi Marg, Vasant Vihar, New Delhi-110057; Hermitage, Care Post Master, Rajgarh (H.P.) 173101, India. *Telephone:* (11) 6146169, 6142554, 6142920 (New Delhi); (01799) 68222 (Rajgarh). *Fax:* (11) 6891930 (New Delhi).

KAULA, Prithvi Nath, M.A., M.LIBR.SC.; Indian professor of library science; b. 13 March 1924, Srinagar; s. of Damodar Kaula; m. Asha Kaula 1941; two s. three d.; ed. S.P. Coll., Srinagar, Punjab Univ., Delhi Univ., Banaras Hindu Univ.; mem. Council, Indian Library Assn. 1949–53, 1956–62; Man. Ed. Annals, Bulletin and Granthalaya of Indian Library Assn. 1949–53; Sec. Ranganathan Endowment for Library Science 1951–61; Gen. Sec. Delhi Library Assn. 1953–55, 1958–60, Vice-Pres. 1956–58; Visiting lecturer in Library Science, Aligarh Muslim Univ. 1951–58; Reader Dept. of Library Science, Univ. of Delhi 1958–60; Vice-Pres. Govt. of Indian Libraries Assn. 1958–61; mem. Review Cttee. on Library Science, Univ. Grants Comm. 1961–63, mem. Panel on Library and Information Science 1978–80, 1982–, Chair. 1990–92, Chair. Curriculum Devt. Cttee. 1991–93; Visiting lecturer Documentation, Research and Training Centre, Bangalore 1962, 1965; Ed. Library Herald 1958–61, Herald of Library Science 1962; Chair. Fed. of Indian Library Assns. 1966, Pres. 1974–; mem. Governing Council, Nat. Library of India 1966–69; UNESCO Expert, UNESCO Regional Centre in the Western Hemisphere, Havana 1967–68; Gen. Sec. Indian Assn. of Teachers of Library Science 1969, Pres. 1973–85, Patron 1986–; Ed. Granthalaya Vijnana 1970–; Librarian, Banaras Hindu Univ., and Prof. of Library

Science 1971–78, Dean Faculty of Arts 1980–82; Prof. Emer. Kashi Vidyapith 1983–, UGC Prof. Emer. Lucknow Univ. 1985–; Ed. Research Journal of the Banaras Hindu Univ. 1980–, Ed. Progress in Library and Information Science 1980–; Ed.-in-Chief International Information, Communication and Education 1982–; Chair. Council of Literacy and Adult Educ. 1971–; Pres. Indian Library Asscn. 1996–; Vice-Pres. Indian Asscn. of Special Libraries and Information Centres; Dir. UNESCO Training Programme on Library Science and Documentation, Havana, Cuba 1968, Modernisation of Library and Information Service, Nat. Library, Bangkok, Thailand 1978; Bureau for Promotion of Urdu Library Science 1980–84; mem. State Library Cttee., Uttar Pradesh 1981–85, Acad. Council, Aligarh Muslim Univ. 1996–, Acad. Council, Dr. Ambedkar Univ. 1997–; Hon. Adviser, Libraries, AP Govt.; mem. Raja Rammohun Roy Library Foundation 1974–77, 1996–; Bd. of Studies in Library and Information Science of 16 univs.; Expert mem. UNESCO Advisory Group on Comparability of Higher Degrees in Library Science 1973–, Nat. Review Cttee. on Univ. and Coll. Libraries 1996–; Dir. Int. Inst. of Higher Studies in Educ., Knowledge and Professional Training 1992–; Patron Indian Coll. Library Asscn., Nat. Music Acad., Library Council; Visiting Prof. 35 Indian Univs., 7 American Univs., Univ. of Havana, Hebrew Univ., Jerusalem, and Univs. in France, Cuba, Canada, the G.D.R., Hungary, Mexico, Spain, Thailand, the U.S.S.R. and the U.K.; Consultant and Adviser on Library Science to several int. orgs. and nat. asscns.; Organizing Sec. and Pres. of numerous confs.; f. several professional bodies, trusts, journals etc., est. Kaula Endowment for Library and Information Science 1974; Kaula Gold Medal awarded to 15 int. recipients 1975–, Ranganathan-Kaula Gold Medal 1980–; Hon. Fellow Int. Council for Professional Educ. 1992; honoured by Int. Festschrift Cttee. 1984, 1994; Indian Library Movement Award 1974; Pro Mundi Beneficio Medal 1975; Deutsche Bucherei Medal 1981; Commemorative Medal of Honour 1985, and numerous other awards. *Publications:* 58 books and monographs and numerous other publs. including over 800 technical papers and book reviews on library science, labour problems and student unrest. *Leisure interests:* reading, writing, the study of library and information science. *Address:* Lucknow University, C-239 Indira Nagar, Lucknow 226016, India. *Telephone:* 381497.

KAUNDA, Dr. Kenneth David: Zambian politician; b. 28 April 1924, Lubwa; m. Betty Banda 1946; six s. (one s. deceased) two d. one adopted s.; ed. Lubwa Training School and Munali Secondary School; Schoolteacher at Lubwa Training School 1943, Headmaster 1944–47; Sec. Chinsali Young Men's Farming Asscn. 1947; welfare officer, Chingola Copper Mine 1948; school teaching 1948–49; Founder-Sec. Lubwa branch, African Nat. Congress (ANC) 1950, district organizer 1951, prov. organizer 1952, Sec.-Gen. for N. Rhodesia 1953; imprisoned for possession of prohibited literature Jan.-Feb. 1954; broke away from ANC to form Zambia African Nat. Congress 1958; imprisoned for political offences May 1959–Jan. 1960; Pres. United Nat. Independence Party 1960–92, 1995–; Minister of Local Govt. and Social Welfare, N. Rhodesia 1962–64; Prime Minister of N. Rhodesia Jan.–Oct. 1964; Pres. Pan-African Freedom Movement for East, Central and South Africa (PAFMECSA) 1963; First Pres. of Zambia 1964–91, and Minister of Defence 1964–70, 1973–78; Head of Sub-Cttee. for Defence and Security 1978–91; Minister of Foreign Affairs 1969–70, also of Trade, Industry, Mines and State Participation 1969–73; Chair. Mining and Industrial Devt. Corpn. of Zambia 1970; Chair. Org. of African Unity (OAU) 1970–71, 1987–88, Non-Aligned Nations Conf. 1970–73, fmr. Chair. ZIMCO; Chancellor, Univ. of Zambia 1966–91, Copperbelt Univ. 1988; f. Peace Foundation 1992; charged with "misprision of treason" over alleged involvement in attempted coup d'état 1997; freed after 5 months of house arrest after charges dropped June 1998; deprived of citizenship March 1999; Hon. Dr. of Laws (Fordham, Dublin, Windsor (Canada), Wales, Sussex, York and Chile Univs.), Dr. h.c. (Humboldt State Univ., Calif.) 1980; Order of the Collar of the Nile, Kt. of the Collar of the Order of Pius XII, Order of the Queen of Sheba, Jawaharlal Nehru Award for Int. Understanding, Quaide Azam Human Rights Inst. Prize (Pakistan) 1976. *Publications:* Black Government 1961, Zambia Shall Be Free 1962, A Humanist in Africa (with Colin Morris) 1966, Humanism in Zambia and its Implementation 1967, Letter to my Children 1977, Kaunda On Violence 1980. *Address:* United National Independence Party, P.O. Box 30302, Lusaka, Zambia.

KAUR, Prabhjot (see Prabhjot Kaur).

KAURISMÄKI, Aki; Finnish film maker; b. 4 April 1957; co-founder film production co-operative Filmtotal; Man. Dir. and jt. owner (with brother Mika Kaurismäki) film production co. Villealfa; jtly. runs distribution co. Senso Film. *Films:* (Co-writer and Asst. Dir.) The Liar 1980, The Worthless 1982, The Clan: Tale of the Frogs 1984, Rosso 1985; (Co-Dir.) The Saimaa Gesture 1981; (Dir.) Crime and Punishment 1983, Calamari Union 1985 (Special Award, Hong Kong Int. Film Festival), Shadows in Paradise 1986 (Jussi Award for Best Finnish Film), Hamlet 1987, Ariel 1988, Leningrad Cowboys Go Home 1989, The Match Factory Girl 1989, I Hired a Contract Killer 1990, La Vie de Boheme, Leningrad Cowboys Meet Moses 1993, Take Care of Your Scarf, Tatiana 1995. *Rock videos:* Rock'y VI, Thru', The Wire, L.A. Woman 1986. *Address:* c/o The Finnish Film Foundation, K.13, Kanavakatu 24, SF-00160 Helsinki, Finland.

KAUZMANN, Walter Joseph, PH.D.; American professor of chemistry; b. 18 Aug. 1916, Mount Vernon, New York; s. of Albert Kauzmann and Julia Kahle; m. Elizabeth Flagler 1951; two s. one d.; ed. Cornell, Princeton Univs.; Research Fellow, Westinghouse Co.; with Nat. Defense Council Explosives Research Lab.; worked on Atomic Bomb project, Los Alamos Labs., New Mexico 1944–46; Asst. Prof. Princeton Univ. 1946–51, Assoc. Prof. 1951–60, Prof. 1960–83, David B. Jones Prof. of Chem. 1963–83, Chair. Dept. of Chemistry 1963–68, Dept. of Biochemical Sciences 1980–82; Visiting Scientist, Nat. Resources Council of Canada, Halifax 1983; mem. N.A.S., American Acad. of Arts and Sciences, American Chem. Soc., American Physical Soc., A.A.A.S., Fed. of American Scientists, American Soc. of Biochemists, American Geophysical Union, Mathematical Asscn. of America; Guggenheim Fellow 1957, 1974–75; Visiting Lecturer Kyoto Univ. 1974, Ibadan Univ. 1975; Hon. Ph.D. (Stockholm Univ.) 1992; first recipient Kaj Ulrik Linderstrøm-Lang Medal 1966; Stein and Moore Award (Protein Soc.) 1993. *Publications:* Introd. to Quantum Chemistry 1957, Thermal Properties of Matter (2 vols.) 1966, 1967, Structure and Properties of Water 1969. *Address:* c/o Department of Chemistry, Princeton University, Princeton, NJ 08544, U.S.A.

KAVAN, Jan Michael, B.SC.; Czech politician and journalist; b. 17 Oct. 1946, London; s. of Pavel Kavan and Rosemary Kavanová (née Edwards); m. Lenka Mazlová 1991; one s. three d.; ed. Charles Univ., Prague, London School of Econs. and St. Antony's Coll., Oxford; journalist Universita Karlova, Prague 1966–68; Ed. East European Reporter, London 1985–90; Dir. Palach Press Ltd., London 1974–90, Deputy Dir. Jan Palach Information and Research Trust 1982–90; Vice-Pres. East European Cultural Foundation, London 1985–90; mem. Parl., Foreign Affairs Cttee., Fed. Ass., Czech Repub. 1990–92; Chair. Policy Centre for the Promotion of Democracy, Prague 1992–98; Senator Parl. of Czech Repub. 1996–; Minister of Foreign Affairs 1998–; lecturer Adelphi Univ., New York 1993, Amherst Coll., Mass. 1994. *Publications:* Czechoslovak Socialist Opposition 1976, Voices of Czechoslovak Socialists 1977, Voices from Prague 1983, Justice with a Muzzle 1996. *Leisure interests:* international politics, good literature, film, theatre. *Address:* Ministry of Foreign Affairs, Loretánské nám 5, Prague 1, 118 000, Czech Republic. *Telephone:* (4202) 24182555. *Fax:* (4202) 24182041.

KAWAI, Ryoichi; Japanese business executive; b. 18 Jan. 1917; s. of Yoshinari Kawai and Chieko Kawai; m. 1st Kiyoko Kawai 1942 (died 1973); 3 s.; m. 2nd Junko Kawai 1976; ed. Tokyo Univ.; fmr. Pres. Komatsu Ltd., Chair. 1982–95, Dir. and Counsellor June 1995–. *Leisure interest:* golf. *Address:* c/o Komatsu Building, 3-6, Akasaka 2-chome, Minato-ku, Tokyo, Japan.

KAWAKUBO, Rei; Japanese couturier; b. 1943; ed. Keio Univ., Tokyo; joined Asahikasei 1964; freelance designer 1966; launched Comme des Garçons Label 1969; f. and Pres. Comme des Garçons Co. Ltd. 1973; Japan Comme des Garçons Collection presented twice a year, Tokyo; 395 outlets in Japan, 5 Comme des Garçons shops and 550 outlets outside Japan; currently has 11 lines of clothing, 1 line of furniture, and a perfume; opened 1st overseas Comme des Garçons Boutique in Paris 1982; joined Fed. Française de la Couture 1982; f. Six magazine 1988; cr. costumes and stage design for Merce Cunningham's Scenario 1997; Dr. h.c. (R.C.A., London) 1997; Mainichi Newspaper Fashion Award 1983, 1988; Chevalier Ordre des Arts et des Lettres. *Address:* c/o Comme des Garçons Co. Ltd., 5-11-5 Minamiaoyama, Minatoku, Tokyo, Japan.

KAWALEROWICZ, Jerzy; Polish film director and screenwriter; b. 19 Jan. 1922, Gwoździec; m.; one s. two d.; ed. Acad. of Fine Arts, Kraków 1946, Film Inst., Kraków 1948; Film dir. 1950–; Artistic Man. Film Group KADR 1956–68, 1989–; Assoc. Prof. State Higher Film, TV and Theatre School, Łódź 1980; mem. Nat. Council of Culture 1986–90; mem. ZASP (Union of Polish Stage Artists) 1960–; Chair. of SFP (Polish Film Union) 1966–78; Hon. Chair. of SFP 1978; mem. PUWP 1954–90; Deputy to Sejm 1985–89; numerous State distinctions. *Films:* Gromada 1951, Celuloza 1953, Pod gwiazdą Frygijską 1954, Cień 1956, Prawdziwy koniec wielkiej wojny 1957, Pociąg 1959, Matka Joanna od Aniołów 1960, Faraon 1965, Gra 1968, Magdalena 1971, Śmierć prezydenta 1977, Spotkanie na Atlantyku 1980, Austeria 1982, Jeniec Europy 1989, Bronsteins Kinder 1990, Za co? 1995. *Leisure interest:* sport. *Address:* Studio Filmowe KADR, ul. Puławska 61, 02-595 Warsaw (Office); ul. Marconich 5 m. 21, 02-954 Warsaw, Poland (Home). *Telephone:* (22) 845 49 23 (Office). *Fax:* (22) 845 4923 (Office).

KAWAMATA, Tadashi, M.F.A.; Japanese visual artist; b. 1953, Hokkaido; ed. Tokyo Nat. Univ. of Fine Art and Music; works exhibited at Venice Biennale 1982, Int. Youth Triennale of Drawing, Nuremberg 1983, Documenta 8 1987, São Paulo Biennale 1987, Tyne Int. Exhbn. for Contemporary Art, Newcastle upon Tyne and Gateshead, U.K. 1990; apartment projects: Takara House Room 205, Tokyo 1982, Slip in Tokorozawa 1983, Tetra House N-3 W-26, Sapporo 1983; construction site projects: Spui Project, The Hague 1986, La Maison des Squatters, Grenoble 1987, Nove de Julho Cacapave, São Paulo 1987, Fukuroi Project 1988; urban projects: P.S.1 Project, New York 1985, Destroyed Church, Kassel 1987, Toronto Project at Colonial Tavern Park, Toronto 1989, Project at Begijnhof St. Elisabeth, Kortrijk, Belgium 1989–90; projects are the subject of several catalogues; Asian Cultural Council Fellowship Grant (worked in New York 1984–86); Grand Prix Int. Youth Triennale 1983.

KAWASAKI, Jiro; Japanese politician; b. Mie; s. of Hideji Kawasaki; ed. Keio Univ.; with Matsushita Electric Industrial Co. 1973–80; mem. for Tokai, House of Reps. 1980–; fmr. Parl. Vice-Minister of Posts and Telecommunications; Minister of Transport 1988–; fmr. Head Public Relations Dept. of LDP. *Leisure interests:* reading, tennis. *Address:* Ministry of Transport,

2-1-3, Kasumigaseki, Chiyoda-ku, Tokyo 100, Japan. *Telephone:* (03) 3580-3111. *Fax:* (03) 3580-7982.

KAWASAKI, Seiichi; Japanese banker; b. 13 Nov. 1922, Tokyo; s. of Hachiroemon Kawasaki and Mine Kawasaki; m. Ruriko Yamaguchi 1957; three d.; ed. Tokyo Univ.; joined Mitsui Trust 1946; Dir. and Gen. Man. Marunouchi branch 1974, Osaka branch 1975; Man. Dir. 1977, Sr. Man. Dir. 1979, Deputy Pres. 1980, Pres. 1982, Chair. Mitsui Trust 1987–94, Pres. 1990. *Publication:* Knowledge of Trusts 1957. *Leisure interests:* walking, reading. *Address:* 5-18 Minami Aoyama 4-chome, Minato-ku, Tokyo, Japan (Home). *Telephone:* (03) 401-4095 (Home).

KAWASAKI, Teruo, B.ECONS.; Japanese business executive; b. 11 June 1918; m. Miyoko Kawasaki 1951; one s.; ed. Keio Univ.; joined Nihon Kasei 1943; mem. Bd Dirs. Mitsubishi Rayon 1971–, Man. Dir. 1975–79, Exec. Man. Dir. 1979–82, Exec. Vice-Pres. 1982–83, Pres. 1983–88, Chair. 1988–93, Sr. Adviser 1993–; Pres. Japan Chemical Fibres Asscn. 1990. *Address:* 18–37 Higashiashiya-cho, Ashiya City, Hyogo Prefecture, Japan.

KAWAWA, Rashidi Mfaume; Tanzanian politician; b. 1929, Songea; ed. Tabora Secondary School; fmr. Pres. of the Tanganyikan Fed. of Labour; Minister of Local Govt. and Housing 1960–61; Minister without Portfolio 1961–62; Prime Minister Jan.-Dec. 1962, Vice-Pres. 1962–64; Second Vice-Pres., United Republic of Tanzania 1964–77, also Prime Minister 1972–77; Minister of Defence and Nat. Service 1977–80, Minister without Portfolio 1980; fmr. Vice-Pres. of TANU (Tanganyika African Nat. Union); Sec.-Gen. Chama Cha Mapinduzi 1982–93.

KAY, John Anderson, M.A., F.B.A.; British professor of economics; b. 3 Aug. 1948, Edinburgh; s. of James Kay and Allison Kay; m. Deborah Freeman 1986 (divorced 1995); ed. Royal High School, Edin., Univ. of Edinburgh and Nuffield Coll. Oxford; Fellow, St. John's Coll. Oxford 1970–; lecturer in Econs. Univ. of Oxford 1971–79; Research Dir. Inst. for Fiscal Studies 1979–82, Dir. 1982–86; Dir. Centre for Business Strategy, London Business School 1986–91; Chair. London Econs. 1986–96; Dir. Said Bus. School, Univ. of Oxford 1997–, Undervalued Assets Trust PLC 1994–; Dir. (non-exec.) Halifax Bldg. Soc. 1991–97, Foreign & Colonial Special Utilities Investment Trust PLC 1993–, Value and Income Trust PLC 1994–, Halifax PLC 1997–. *Publications:* The Business of Economics, The British Tax System, Foundations of Corporate Success, Why Firms Succeed; co-author of Concentration in Modern Industry, The Reform of Social Security, The Economic Analysis of Accounting Profitability; articles in scholarly journals. *Address:* Said Business School, University of Oxford, Radcliffe Infirmary, Woodstock Road, Oxford, OX2 6HE, England (Home). *Telephone:* (01865) 228470. *Fax:* (01865) 228471.

KAYE, Harvey Jordan, PH.D.; American professor of social change and development; b. 9 Oct. 1949, Englewood, N.J.; s. of Murray N. Kaye and Frances Kaye; m. Lorna Stewart 1973; two d.; ed. Paramus High School, Rutgers Univ., Univ. of Mexico, Univ. of London, U.K. and Louisiana State Univ.; Asst. Prof. of Interdisciplinary Studies, St. Cloud Univ., Minn. 1977–78; Asst. Prof. of Social Change and Devt., Univ. of Wis., Green Bay 1978–83, Assoc. Prof. 1983–86, Head of Dept. 1985–88, Prof. 1986–; Ben and Joyce Rosenberg Prof. of Social Change and Devt. 1990–; Dir. Center for History and Social Change 1991–; Visiting Fellow, Univ. of Birmingham, U.K. 1987; mem. Editorial Bd. Marxist Perspectives 1978–80, The Wisconsin Sociologist, Wis. Sociological Asscn. 1985–87, Rethinking History 1996–; Consulting Ed., Verso Publishers, London 1988–94, NYU Press 1996–; Series Ed., American Radicals (Routledge) 1992–; columnist Times Higher Educational Supplement 1994–, Tikkun magazine 1996–, Index on Censorship 1996–; mem. Exec. Bd., Center for Democratic Values 1996–, Scholars, Artists and Writers for Social Justice 1997–; mem. American Historical Asscn., American Sociological Asscn., American Studies Asscn., Org. of American Historians; Founders' Award for Scholarship 1985, Isaac Deutscher Memorial Prize 1993 (for The Education of Desire). *Publications:* The British Marxist Historians 1984, The Powers of the Past 1991, The Education of Desire 1992, Why do Ruling Classes Fear History? 1996, Thomas Paine 1999; (Ed.) History, Classes and Nation-States 1988, The Face of the Crowd: Studies in Revolution, Ideology and Popular Protest 1988, Poets, Politics and the People 1989, E. P. Thompson: Critical Perspectives (with K. McClelland) 1990, The American Radical (with M. Buhle and P. Buhle) 1994, Imperialism and its Contradictions 1995, Ideology and Popular Protest 1995; numerous articles on history and historians. *Leisure interests:* travel, films, friendship and conversation. *Address:* Social Change and Development Department, University of Wisconsin-Green Bay, 2420 Nicolet Drive, Green Bay, WI 54301, U.S.A. (Office). *Telephone:* (920) 465-2355/2755 (Office). *Fax:* (920) 465-2791.

KAYENKIKO, Anatole; Burundian politician and engineer; b. Ngozi Prov.; ed. Caen Univ.; fmr. Mayor of Bujumbura; Minister of Public Works and Equipment –1994; Prime Minister of Burundi 1994–95; mem. Union pour le Progrès Nat. (UPRONA). *Address:* c/o Union pour le Progrès national, BP 1810, Bujumbura, Burundi.

KAYLA, Ziya; Turkish economist; b. 1912, Istanbul; s. of Col. Sevki Kayla and Zehra Vefkioglu; m. Sevinc Cenk 1967; ed. School of Political Sciences, Istanbul; Ministry of Finance 1934–63, Asst. Inspector, Inspector and Chief Inspector of Finance 1934–60, Deputy Minister of Finance 1960–63; Chair. Bd. of Dirs. and Dir.-Gen. Central Bank of Turkey 1963–66; Alternate Gov. for Turkey, IBRD 1961–65; Pres. Banks' Asscn. of Turkey 1963–66; Sec.-Gen. Comm. of Regulation of Bank Credits 1963–66; Head of Foreign Investment Encouragements Cttee. 1963–66; mem. Bd. of Controllers of the Prime Ministry 1966–70; Chair. Türkiye Vakiflar Bankasi 1971–76; mem. Bd. Central Bank of Turkey 1978–80; mem. Higher Educ. Council 1981–82; Auditor Türkiyė Iş Bankasi 1983–88. *Publications:* Emission Movements in Turkey 1967, Treasury and Central Banks Relations 1970, Knowledge of Economic Situation by Central Bank's Bulletin of Statistics 1978, Central Bank's Operations 1981. *Leisure interest:* writing articles on economics for newspapers. *Address:* Mesnevi Sokak 8/8 Çankaya, Ankara, Turkey. *Telephone:* 438-71-09.

KAYSEN, Carl, A.B., M.A., PH.D.; American economist; b. 5 March 1920, Philadelphia; s. of Samuel and Elizabeth Resnick; m. 1st Annette Neutra 1940 (died 1990); two d.; m. 2nd Ruth A. Butler 1994; ed. Overbrook High School, Philadelphia, Univ. of Pennsylvania and Harvard Univ.; Nat. Bureau of Econ. Research 1940–42; Office of Strategic Services, Washington, D.C. 1942–43; U.S. Army (Intelligence) 1943–45; Teaching Fellow in Econs., Harvard Univ. 1947, Jr. Fellow, Soc. of Fellows 1947–50, Asst. Prof. in Econs. 1950–55, Assoc. Prof. 1955–57, Prof. 1957–66, Assoc. Dean, Graduate School of Public Admin. 1960–66, Lucius N. Littauer Prof. of Political Economy 1964–66; Dir., Inst. of Advanced Study, Princeton 1966–76, Dir. Emer. 1976–, Prof. of Social Science 1976–77; David W. Skinner Prof. Political Econ., M.I.T. 1976–90, Prof. Emer. 1990–, Sr. Research Scientist 1992–; Dir. Program in Science, Tech. and Soc. 1981–86; Vice-Chair. and Dir. Research, Sloan Comm. on Govt. and Higher Educ. 1977–79; Sr. Fulbright Research Scholar, London School of Econs. 1955–56; Econ. Consultant to Judge Wyzanski, Fed. District Court of Mass. 1950–52; Deputy Special Asst. to Pres. for Nat. Security Affairs 1961–63. *Publications:* United States v. United Shoe Machinery Corporation, an Economic Analysis of an Anti-Trust Case 1956, The American Business Creed (with others) 1956, Anti-Trust Policy (with D.F. Turner) 1959, The Demand for Electricity in the United States (with Franklin M. Fisher) 1962, The Higher Learning, the Universities and the Public 1969, Nuclear Power, Issues and Choice, Nuclear Energy Policy Study Group Report (with others) 1977, A Program for Renewed Partnership, Report of the Sloan Commission on Government and Higher Education (with others) 1980, Emerging Norms of Justified Intervention 1993, Peace Operations by the United Nations (with George Rathjens) 1996, The American Corporation Now (ed.) 1996. *Address:* Massachusetts Institute of Technology in Defense and Arms Control Studies, 292 Main Street, E38-603 Cambridge, MA 02139, U.S.A. *Telephone:* (617) 253-4054. *Fax:* (617) 253-9330.

KAZAN, Elia (Elia Kazanjoglous), A.B., M.F.A.; American film and stage director; b. 7 Sept. 1909, Istanbul, Turkey; s. of George and Athena (Sismanoglou) Kazan; m. 1st Molly Day Thacher 1932 (died 1963); two s. two d.; m. 2nd Barbara Loden 1967 (died 1980); one s.; m. 3rd Frances Rudge 1982; ed. Williams Coll. and Yale Dramatic School; Apprentice and Stage Man. with Group Theatre; acted on stage 1935–41 in Waiting for Lefty, Golden Boy, Gentle People, Fire-Alarm Waltz, Liliom and in two films City for Conquest and Blues in the Night 1941; stage dir. Skin of Our Teeth (Drama Critics Award), One Touch of Venus, Harriet, Jacobowsky and the Colonel (Drama Critics Award), Streetcar Named Desire, Death of a Salesman (Drama Critics Award), Tea and Sympathy, Cat on a Hot Tin Roof (Drama Critics Award), The Dark at the Top of the Stairs, J. B., Sweet Bird of Youth, for Lincoln Center Repertory Theatre After the Fall, But for Whom Charlie, The Changeling; *directed films:* A Tree Grows in Brooklyn 1945, Gentlemen's Agreement (Academy Award) 1947, Boomerang 1947, Pinky 1949, Panic in the Streets 1950, Streetcar Named Desire 1951, Viva Zapata 1952, Man on a Tightrope 1953, On the Waterfront (Acad. Award) 1954, East of Eden 1955, Baby Doll 1956, A Face in the Crowd 1957, Wild River 1960, Splendor in the Grass 1961, America, America 1963, The Arrangement 1969, The Visitors 1972, The Last Tycoon 1976; Best Picture of Year Award, New York Film Critics 1948, 1952, 1955; D. W. Griffith Award, Dirs. Guild of America 1987, Hon. Golden Bear Award 1996, Hon. Acad. Award 1999; fmr. Dir. of Actors Studio. *Publications:* America, America 1962, The Arrangement 1967, The Assassins 1972, The Understudy 1974, Acts of Love 1978, The Anatolian 1982, A Life (autobiog.) 1988, Beyond the Aegean 1994.

KAZANKINA, Tatyana; Russian athlete; b. 17 Dec. 1951, Petrovsk, Saratov Region; d. of Vasily Kazankin and Maria Kazankina; m. Alexandre Kovalenko 1974; one d.; int. athlete since 1972; competed Olympic Games Montreal 1976, winning Gold Medals at 800 m. and 1500 m., Moscow 1980, won Gold Medal at 1500 m.; European Indoor Silver Medallist 1975; World records at 800 m., 1500 m. (three times), 2000 m., 3000 m., 4 × 800 m.; World Bronze Medal 1983; suspended for life by IAAF 1984, reinstated 1985; economist, Leningrad; Asst. Prof., St. Petersburg Acad. of Physical Culture; Pres. St. Petersburg Union of Athletes; Hon. Master of Sport 1976; Hon. Ph.D. 1992. *Leisure interests:* travelling, human contacts. *Address:* c/o Light Athletic Federation, Millionnaia 22, St. Petersburg (Office); Hoshimina Street 11-1-211, St. Petersburg, Russia (Home). *Telephone:* 114-69-31 (Office); 595-09-40 (Home). *Fax:* (812) 315-97-95.

KAZANNIK, Aleksei Ivanovich, D.IUR.; Russian lawyer; b. 26 July 1941; m.; two s.; ed. Irkutsk Univ.; teacher Irkutsk Univ. 1975–79; Prof., Head of Chair, Omsk Univ. 1979–89, 1994–; forbidden to give public lectures because of criticism of Soviet invasion into Afghanistan; U.S.S.R. People's Deputy 1989–91; fmr. mem. U.S.S.R. Supreme Soviet; active participant Movt.

Democratic Russia; mem. Interregional Group of Deputies; mem. Cttee. on ecology problems and rational use of natural resources, U.S.S.R. Supreme Soviet; mem. Pres.'s Council 1993–94; Chair. Cttee. on problems of nationalities, religions and public orgs. of Omsk Region; Prosecutor-Gen. of Russia 1993–94; Founder and Chair. Party of People's Conscience 1995–. *Publications:* legal aspects of regional problems of nature preservation, numerous articles on ecology, law, pamphlets. *Address:* c/o Omsk University, Prosp. Mira 55A, 644077 Omsk, Russia.

KAZARNOVSKAYA, Lubov Yurievna; Russian soprano; b. 18 July 1956; m. Robert Rossik; ed. Moscow Gnessin School of Music and Moscow State Conservatory; as student became soloist Moscow Nemirovich-Danchenko Musical Theatre 1981–86; soloist Leningrad Kirov (now Mariinsky) Opera Theatre 1986–89; debut outside U.S.S.R. in Un Ballo in Maschera, Zürich Opera 1989, Desdemona in Otello, Covent Garden, London March 1990; moved to Vienna 1989, performs in maj. opera houses of the world, in opera productions with Herbert von Karajan, Carlos Kleiber, Claudio Abbado, Riccardo Muti, Daniel Barenboim, James Conlon; also performs in concerts, including Requiem (Verdi), La Voix humaine by Poulenc, and at festivals in Salzburg, Bregenz, Edin. and others; roles include leading parts in Eugene Onegin, Iolanthe, La Bohème, Pagliacci, Faust, Marriage of Figaro, Falstaff, Force of Destiny, Boris Godunov, La Traviata, Salome; prize winner All-Union competition of singers 1981, Int. competition in Bratislava 1984. *Address:* Hohenbergstrasse 50, A-1120 Vienna, Austria. *Telephone:* (01) 83 91 06 (Home).

KAZHEGELDIN, Akezhan Magzhanovich; Kazakhstan politician and economist; b. 27 March 1952, Georgiyevka, Semipalatinsk Region: m.; two c.; ed. Semipalatinsk Pedagogical Inst., Almaty Inst. of Nat. Econs.; Chair. Regional Exec. Cttee. of Semipalatinsk 1983; Dir. Ore-enriching Factory, Deputy Head Admin. of Semipalatinsk Region 1991–94; Pres. Kazakstan Union of Industrialists and Entrepreneurs 1992–; First Deputy Prime Minister of Kazakstan 1993–94, Prime Minister 1994–97. *Publications include:* Kazakstan in the Conditions of Reforms, Problems of State Regulation in the Conditions of Socio-Economic Transformation, Socio-Economic Problems of Development of Kazakstan in the Conditions of Reforms. *Address:* c/o Respubliki sq. 4, Almaty, Kazakstan. *Telephone:* (3272) 620090.

KAZIM, Parvez, M.A.; Pakistani author and publisher; b. 21 April, Rangoon, Burma; s. of Ali Khan Kazim and Begum (née Shaheda) Kazim; m. 1992; ed. Univs. of Punjab and Karachi; Exec. mem. S.W.O. 1975–76; formed S.W.P.S. Islamabad 1975–76, C.A.O. 1980–83; Consultant P.Q.F. Islamabad 1982–83; Exec. Dir. Teenage Publishers, Karachi 1981–82; Patron-in-Chief Gen. Knowledge Acad., Karachi 1981–82; Man. Dir. Pixy Publishers 1986–87; Dir. (Admin.) Parvez Acad. 1985–86; Chair. Fantasia Group of Publication F.G.P., Karachi 1987–; Exec. Dir. Sports and Games Acad. 1987–91; Man. Dir. Intermedia Communications (Pvt.) Ltd 1994–95; Publr. and Exec. Ed. Fashion Craze Int. 1995–; Man. Ed. Men's Wear Classics 1994–95; Aria and I.P.A. Excellence Awards. *Publications:* Pakistan, a Land of Many Faces, Safina-e-Maloomat, Islam, the Greatest Religion in the World, Jazira-e-Maloomat, Karachi, A City of Lights, Jeeway Pakistan, Archaeological Sites of Pakistan, Ganjina-e-Maloomat, Mohammed, the Messenger of God, Uks-e-Quran, Treasure of Knowledge; Compiler and Ed. Who is Who in Pakistan, Who is Who in the Muslim World, 200 Great Scientists, Ocean of Knowledge and Universal Encyclopaedia; numerous articles for newspapers and magazines. *Leisure interests:* collecting rare antiques, postcards and coins, cricket, badminton, draughts. *Address:* III/F/8/14A Nazimabad, Karachi.

KAZMIN, Andrei Ilyich; Russian banker; b. 1958, Moscow; m.; ed. Moscow Inst. of Finance; economist br. U.S.S.R.. Savings bank (Sberbank) 1983–84; asst., then Deputy Dean Moscow Inst. of Finance 1984–88; on staff U.S.S.R. (now Russian) Acad. of Sciences 1988–91; training in European banks 1991–93; on staff Ministry of Finance Russian Fed. 1993–96; Pres., mem. Supervising Council Savings Bank of Russian Fed.; mem. Supervising Cttee. Agency on Housing Credits 1996–. *Leisure interest:* sports. *Address:* Sberbank, Seleznevskaya str. 40, 103473 Moscow, Russia (Office). *Telephone:* (095) 284 4043 (Offfice).

KE TING-SUI (Ge Tingsui), PH.D.; Chinese scientist; b. 3 May 1913, Shantung; m. He Yizhen 1941; one s. one d.; ed. Univ. of Calif. Berkeley; mem. staff Spectroscopy and Radiation Lab. M.I.T. 1943–45; Research Assoc. Inst. for the Study of Metals, Univ. of Chicago 1945–49; Prof. Physics, Tsinghua Univ. 1949–52; Prof., Deputy Dir. Inst. Metal Research, Acad. Sinica 1952–80; f., Prof., Dir. Inst. of Solid State Physics 1980–86, Prof. and Hon. Dir. 1986–, Dir. Lab. of Internal Friction and Defects in Solids 1985–93; current research: grain boundary relaxation, point defect-dislocation interaction, monlinear anelasticity; Prof. of Physics, Univ. of Science and Tech. of China 1987–93, concurrently Prof., Tsinghua Univ. 1993–95; Guest Research Prof., Inst. Metal Research, Shenyang, Chinese Acad. of Sciences 1995–; Visiting Prof. Max-Planck Inst. for Metals, Stuttgart 1979–80; Guest Prof. Nat. Inst. of Applied Science, Lyon 1980–81; lecturer TMS Inst. of Metals; Deputy 3rd NPC 1963–74, 5th NPC 1978–83, 6th NPC 1983–88, 7th NPC 1988–93; Sr. mem. Chinese Acad. of Sciences; Hon. mem. Japan Inst. of Metals; R. R. Hasiguti Prizes 1996, Ho Leung Ho Lee Prize 1996; C. Zener Medallist 1989; Robert Franklin Mahl Award 1999. *Publications:* 250 scientific papers, Proceedings of Ninth Int. Conference on Internal Friction and Ultrasonic Attenuation in Solids (ed.) 1990, Grain Boundary Relaxation and Grain Boundary Structure 1998, Internal Friction and Defects in Solids 1999, Materials Damping 2000. *Address:* Institute of Solid State Physics, Chinese Academy of Sciences, Hefei 230031, Anhui, People's Republic of China. *Telephone:* (0551) 5591415; (0551) 5591429. *Fax:* (0551) 5591434.

KEACH, Stacy; American actor and director; b. June 1942, Savannah, Ga.; m. Malgossia Tomassi 1986; two d.; stage debut in Joseph Papp's production of Hamlet, Cen. Park 1964; other stage appearances include A Long Day's Journey into Night, Macbird (Vernon Rice Drama Desk Award), Indians, Deathtrap, Hughie, Barnum, Cyrano de Bergerac, Peer Gynt, Henry IV (Parts I & II), Idiot's Delight, The King and I 1989, Love Letters 1990–93, Richard III 1991, Stieglitz Loves O'Keefe 1995; numerous TV appearances; dir. Incident at Vichy and Six Characters in Search of an Author for TV; recipient of three Obie Awards, Pasadena Playhouse Alumni Man of the Year 1995, Pacific Pioneers Broadcasters' Asscn. Diamond Circle Award 1996. *Films include:* The Heart is a Lonely Hunter, End of the Road, The Travelling Executioner, Brewster McCloud, Doc, Judge Roy Bean, The New Centurions, Fat City, The Killer Inside Me, Conduct Unbecoming, Luther, Street People, The Squeeze, Gray Lady Down, The Ninth Configuration, The Long Riders, Road Games, Butterfly, Up in Smoke, Nice Dreams, That Championship Season, The Lover, False Identity, The Forgotten Milena, John Carpenter's Escape from LA 1996, Prey of the Jaguar 1996, The Truth Configuration 1998. *Publication:* Keach, Go Home! 1996 (autobiog.).

KEAN, Thomas H., M.A.; American fmr. politician and university president; b. 21 April 1935, New York; m. Deborah Bye; two s. one d.; fmr. teacher of history and govt.; mem. N.J. Ass. 1967–77, Speaker 1972, Minority Leader 1974; Acting Gov. of N.J. 1973, Gov. 1982–90; Pres. Drew Univ., Madison, N.J. 1990–; mem. White House Conf. on Youth 1970-71. *Address:* Office of the President, Drew University, Madison, NJ 07940, U.S.A.

KEANE, Fergal Patrick, O.B.E.; Irish journalist and broadcaster; b. 6 Jan. 1961; s. of the late Eamon Brendan Keane and of Mary Hasset; m. Anne Frances Flaherty 1986; one s.; ed. Terenure Coll., Dublin and Presentation Coll., Cork; trainee reporter Limerick Leader 1979–82; reporter Irish Press Group, Dublin 1982–84, Radio Telefis Eireann, Belfast 1986–89 (Dublin 1984–86); Northern Ireland Corresp. BBC Radio 1989–91, South Africa Corresp. 1991–94, Asia Corresp. 1994–97, Special Corresp. 1997–; Reporter of the Year Sony Silver Award 1992 and Sony Gold Award 1993, Int. Reporter of the Year 1993, Amnesty Int. Press Awards, RTS Journalist of the Year 1994. *Publications:* Irish Politics Now 1987, The Bondage of Fear 1994, Season of Blood: A Rwandan Journey 1995, Letter to Daniel 1996. *Leisure interests:* fishing, golf, poetry. *Address:* c/o BBC Television, Wood Lane, London, W12 7RJ, England.

KEANE, John Brendan; Irish writer; b. 21 July 1928, Listowel, Co. Kerry; s. of William B. Keane and Hannah (née Portill) Keane; m. Mary O'Connor 1955; three s. one d.; ed. Listowel Boys' Nat. School, St. Michael's Coll., Listowel; Pres. Irish PEN 1970–72, now Pres. Irish Consultative Council PEN; mem. Irish Arts Council 1973–74; Irish American Fund Award for Literature, Sunday Ind. Award for Literature, Sunday Tribune Award for Literature. *Publications:* Plays: Sive 1959, Sharon's Grave 1960, The Field 1965, Big Maggie 1969, Moll 1972; Books of Letters series: 8 vols. including Letters of a Successful T.D. 1967, of a Parish Priest 1972, of a Civic Guard 1976, of an Irish Minister of State 1978; Man of the Triple Name (biography) 1984; Essays series: 6 vols. including Unlawful Sex 1978, Owl Sandwiches 1985; novels: The Bodhran Makers 1986, Durango 1992, The Contractors 1993, Christmas Tales 1993. *Leisure interest:* walking. *Address:* 37 William Street, Listowel, Co. Kerry, Ireland. *Telephone:* 068-21127.

KEAR, David, C.M.G., B.SC.ENG., PH.D., A.R.S.M., F.R.S.NZ.; British/New Zealand geologist, administrator and consultant; b. 29 Oct. 1923, London; s. of Harold and Constance May (née Betteridge) Kear; m. Joan Kathleen Bridges 1948; two s. one d.; ed. Sevenoaks School, Imperial Coll., London; served in Royal Navy 1944–47; Prospecting Officer, Ministry of Fuel and Power, U.K. 1947; Geologist, N.Z. Geological Survey 1948, Dist. Geologist, Ngaruawahia 1949–58, Auckland 1958–65, Chief Econ. Geologist 1963–67, Dir. N.Z. Geological Survey 1967–74; Asst. Dir.-Gen. Dept. of Scientific and Industrial Research, N.Z. 1974–80, Dir.-Gen. 1980–83; with FAO, W. Samoa 1969–74; with Ministry of Energy, N.Z. 1978; Pres. Geological Soc. of N.Z. 1959–60; Vice-Pres. Royal Soc. of N.Z. 1975–79 (Fellow 1973); Pres. N.Z. Exec. Man. Club 1978–79; mem. N.Z. Liquid Fuels Trust Bd. 1978–83; Dir. Circum-Pacific Council for Energy and Mineral Resources 1983–, Cluff Oil (N.Z.) N.L. 1984–88; Consultant Geothermal Energy N.Z. Ltd. for Kenya, Indonesia and N.Z. 1985–88; mem. UN Advisory Cttee. on Science and Tech. for Devt. 1988–90; Consultant to ESCAP 1991–; Consultant to S. Pacific Applied Geoscience Comm. 1991–; Warrington-Smyth Prize 1949; Frecheville Prize 1952. *Publications:* approx. 125 bulletins, scientific papers and maps on New Zealand geology, volcanology, including N.Z. Volcanoes–Their Story 1999, mineral resources and energy prospects, also on Western Samoa geology, volcanology and water supply. *Leisure interests:* golf, theatre, New Zealand and Pacific science, family history. *Address:* 34 West End, Ohope, New Zealand (Home). *Telephone:* (Whakatane) 7-312-4635.

KEATING, Francis Anthony, II, J.D.; American politician and lawyer; b. 10 Feb. 1944, St. Louis; s. of Anthony Francis Keating and Anne Martin; m. Catherine Dunn Heller 1972; one s. two d.; ed. Georgetown and Oklahoma Univs.; called to the bar, Okla. 1969; Special Agent with FBI 1969–71; Asst. Dist. Attorney, Tulsa Co. 1971–72; mem. Okla. House of Reps. 1972–74, Okla. Senate 1974–81; attorney, Northern Dist., Okla. 1981–84; Asst. Sec.

U.S. Treasury Dept., Washington 1985–88, Assoc. Attorney-Gen. Dept. of Justice 1988–89, Gen. Counsel and Acting Deputy Sec. Dept. of Housing and Urban Devt. 1989–93; attorney in pvt. practice, Tulsa 1993–95; Gov. of Oklahoma 1995–; mem. Okla. Bar Asscn. *Address:* Office of the Governor, 212 State Capitol Bldg., Oklahoma City, OK 73105, U.S.A.

KEATING, Henry Reymond Fitzwalter, F.R.S.L.; British writer; b. 31 Oct. 1926, St. Leonards-on-Sea, Sussex; s. of John Hervey Keating and Muriel Keating; m. Sheila Mary Mitchell 1953; three s. one d.; ed. Merchant Taylors' School, Trinity Coll., Dublin; Journalist 1952–59; Chair. Crime Writers Asscn. 1970–71, Soc. of Authors 1983, 1984; Pres. The Detection Club 1985; Gold Dagger Award 1964, 1980, Diamond Dagger Award 1996. *Publications:* Death and the Visiting Firemen 1959, The Perfect Murder 1964, Inspector Ghote's Good Crusade 1966, Inspector Ghote Caught in Meshes 1967, Inspector Ghote Hunts the Peacock 1968, Inspector Ghote Plays a Joker 1969, Inspector Ghote Breaks an Egg 1970, Inspector Ghote Goes by Train 1971, The Strong Man 1971, Inspector Ghote Trusts the Heart 1972, Bats Fly Up for Inspector Ghote 1974, The Underside 1974, Murder Must Appetize 1976, Filmi, Filmi Inspector Ghote 1976, A Long Walk to Wimbledon 1978, Sherlock Holmes, the Man and his World 1979, The Murder of the Maharajah 1980, Go West, Inspector Ghote 1981, The Lucky Alphonse 1982, The Sheriff of Bombay 1983, Under a Monsoon Cloud 1984, Dead on Time 1988, Inspector Ghote, His Life and Crimes 1989, The Iciest Sin 1990, Cheating Death 1992, The Rich Detective 1993, Doing Wrong 1994, The Good Detective 1995, Asking Questions 1996, The Soft Detective 1997, Bribery, Corruption 1999. *Address:* 35 Northumberland Place, London, W2 5AS, England. *Telephone:* 0171-229 1100.

KEATING, Hon. Paul John; Australian politician; b. 18 Jan. 1944, Sydney; s. of Matthew Keating and Min Keating; m. Annita van Iersel 1975; one s. three d.; ed. De la Salle Coll., Bankstown; elected to the House of Reps. for the Fed. Seat of Blaxland 1969–96; Minister for N. Australia Oct.–Nov. 1975; Opposition Spokesman on Agric. Jan.-March 1976; on Minerals and Energy 1976–83, on Treasury Matters Jan.-March 1983; Fed. Treas. 1983–91; Leader Australian Labor Party 1991–96, Prime Minister of Australia 1991–96; Pres. of N.S.W. Branch Labor Party 1979–83; Visiting Prof. in Public Policy Univ. of N.S.W. 1996–. *Address:* Keating Associates, Level 2, 31 Bligh Street, Sydney, N.S.W. 2000, Australia.

KEATINGE, William Richard, M.A., M.B., B.CHIR., PH.D., M.R.C.P.; British professor of physiology; b. 18 May 1931, London; s. of Edgar Mayne Keatinge and Katherine Lucille Keatinge; m. Margaret Ellen Annette Hegarty 1955; one s. two d.; ed. Univ. of Cambridge, St. Thomas's Hosp. Medical School; Dir. of Studies in Medicine, Pembroke Coll., Cambridge 1956–60; Fellow of Cardiovascular Research Inst., San Francisco 1960–61; Dept. of Regius Prof. of Medicine, Oxford, M.R.C. appt. 1961–68; Fellow and Tutor in Physiology, Pembroke Coll., Oxford 1956–68; Reader in Physiology, London Hosp. Medical Coll. 1968–71, Prof. 1971–90; Prof. of Physiology, Queen Mary and Westfield Coll. 1990–; Oliver-Sharpey Lecturer, Royal Coll. of Physicians 1986. *Publications:* Survival in Cold Water: The Physiology and Treatment of Immersion Hypothermia and Drowning 1970, Local Mechanisms Controlling Blood Vessels (with C. Harman) 1980, numerous articles and papers. *Leisure interests:* archaeology, sailing. *Address:* Biomedical Sciences, Queen Mary and Westfield College, Mile End Road, London, E1 4NS, England.

KEATON, Diane; American actress; b. 5 Jan. 1946, Calif.; student Neighbourhood Playhouse, New York; New York stage appearances in Hair 1968, Play It Again Sam 1971, The Primary English Class 1976; *films include:* Lovers and Other Strangers 1970, Play It Again Sam 1972, The Godfather 1972, Sleeper 1973, The Godfather Part 2 1974, Love and Death 1975, I Will-I Will-For Now 1975, Harry and Walter Go To New York 1976, Annie Hall 1977, (Acad. Award for Best Actress and other awards), Looking for Mr. Goodbar 1977, Interiors 1978, Manhattan 1979, Reds 1981, Shoot the Moon 1982, Mrs Soffel 1985, Crimes of the Heart 1986, Trial and Error 1986, Radio Days 1987, Heaven (Dir.) 1987, Baby Boom 1988, The Good Mother 1988, The Lemon Sisters 1989, Running Mates 1989, The Godfather III, Wildflower (Dir.) 1991, Heaven (Dir.), Secret Society (Dir.), Manhattan Murder Mystery 1993, Unsung Heroes (Dir.) 1995, Father of the Bride 2 1995, Marvin's Room, The First Wives Club 1996, The Only Thrill 1997. *Publications:* Reservations, Still Life (Ed.). *Address:* c/o John Burnham, William Morris Agency, 151 El Camino Drive, Beverly Hills, CA 90212, U.S.A.

KEATON, Michael; American actor; b. 9 Sept. 1951, Pittsburgh; m. Caroline MacWilliams (divorced); one s.; ed. Kent State Univ.; with comedy group, Second City, Los Angeles; TV appearances include All in the Family, Maude, Mary Tyler Moore Show, Working Stiffs, Report to Murphy, Roosevelt and Truman (TV film). *Films:* Night Shift 1982, Mr Mom 1983, Johnny Dangerously 1984, Touch and Go 1987, Gung Ho 1987, Beetlejuice 1988, Clean and Sober 1988, The Dream Team 1989, Batman 1989, Much Ado About Nothing 1992, My Life, The Paper 1994, Speechless 1994, Multiplicity, Jackie Brown 1997, Desperate Measures 1998, Jack Frost 1999. *Address:* c/o Creative Artists Agency, 9830 Wilshire Boulevard, Beverly Hills, CA 90212, U.S.A.

KEAVENEY, Raymond, M.A.; Irish gallery director and art historian; b. 1947, Carlanstown, Co. Meath; ed. Franciscan Coll., Gormanston, University Coll. Dublin; worked and studied abroad 1976–79; Curator, Nat. Gallery of Ireland, Dublin 1979–81, Asst. Dir. 1981–88, Dir. 1988–; specializes in Italian art and Old Master drawings. *Publications:* exhbn. catalogues, including Master European Drawings (for U.S. tour 1984), Views of Rome (U.S. tour and Nat. Gallery Ireland 1989–90). *Address:* National Gallery of Ireland, Merrion Square West, Dublin 2, Ireland. *Telephone:* 6615133. *Fax:* 6615372.

KEBICH, Vyacheslau Frantsavich (Vyacheslav Frantsevich); Belarus politician; b. 10 June 1936, Konyushevshchina, Minsk Dist.; s. of Frants Karlovich Kebich and Tatyana Vasilyevna Kebicha; m. Yelena Kebicha 1970; one s. one d.; ed. Belarus Polytechnic Inst., Higher Party School; mem. CPSU 1962–91, Cen. Cttee. 1980–91; engineer, man. in Minsk 1973–80; party official 1980–85; Deputy Chair. Council of Ministers, Chair. State Planning Cttee. 1985–90; U.S.S.R. People's Deputy 1989–91; Chair. Council of Ministers (Prime Minister) of Byelorussia (now Belarus) 1990–94; Presidential Cand. 1994; mem. Supreme Soviet (Parl.) 1980–96, M.P. 1996–; Corresp. mem. Int. Eng. Acad.; Belarus State Prize. *Leisure interest:* fishing. *Address:* National Assembly, K. Marksa str. 38, Dom Urada, 220016 Minsk, Belarus. *Telephone:* (017) 229-33-13.

KEDAH, H.R.H. The Sultan of; Tuanku Haji Abdul Halim Mu'adzam Shah ibni Al-Marhum Sultan Badishah, D.K., D.K.H., D.K.M., D.M.N., D.U.K., D.K. (KELANTAN), D.K. (PAHANG), D.K. (SELANGOR), D.K. (PERLIS), D.K. (JOHORE), D.K. (TRENGGANU), D.P. (SARAWAK), S.P.M.K., S.S.D.K., D.H.M.S.; Ruler of Kedah, Malaysia; b. 28 Nov. 1927, Alor Setar; m. Tuanku Bahiyah binti Al-marhum, Tuanku Abdul Rahman, d. of 1st Yang di Pertuan Agong of Malaya, 1956; three d.; ed. Sultan Abdul Hamid Coll., Alor Setar and Wadham Coll., Oxford; Raja Muda (Heir to Throne of Kedah) 1949, Regent of Kedah 1957, Sultan 1958–; Timbalan Yang di Pertuan Agong (Deputy Head of State of Malaysia) 1965–70, Yang di Pertuan Agong (Head of State) 1970–75; Col. Commdt. Malaysian Reconnaissance Corps 1966; Col.-in-Chief of Royal Malay Regiment 1975; First Class Order of the Rising Sun (Japan) 1970, Bintang Maha Putera, Klas Satu (Indonesia) 1970, Knight Grand Cross of the Bath (U.K.) 1972, Kt. of the Order of St. John 1974, Most Auspicious Order of the Rajamithrathorn (Thailand) 1973. *Leisure interests:* golf, billiards, photography, tennis. *Address:* Istana Anak Bukit, Alor Setar, Kedah, Darul Aman, Malaysia.

KEDDAFI, Col. Mu'ammar al- (see Gaddafi, Col. Mu'ammar al-).

KEE, Robert, C.B.E., M.A.; British journalist, author and broadcaster; b. 5 Oct. 1919, Calcutta, India; s. of late Robert and Dorothy F. Kee; m. 1st Janetta Woolley 1948; one d.; m. 2nd Cynthia Judah 1960 (divorced 1989); one s. (and one s. deceased) one d.; m. 3rd Catherine M. Trevelyan 1990; ed. Rottingdean School, Stowe School and Magdalen Coll., Oxford; journalist, Picture Post 1948–51; picture ed. WHO 1952; foreign corresp. Observer 1956–57, Sunday Times 1957–58; literary ed. Spectator 1957; with BBC 1958–62, 1979–82, ITV 1964–78; Presenter 7 Days (Channel 4) 1984–88, TV series include: Ireland: a television history (13 parts), The Writing on the Wall; numerous BBC radio broadcasts 1946–97. *Publications:* A Crowd Is Not Company 1947, 1989, The Impossible Shore, A Sign of the Times, Broadstrop in Season, Refugee World, The Green Flag 1972, Ireland: A History 1980, The World We Left Behind 1939, 1984, 1945: The World We Fought For 1985, Trial and Error 1986, Munich: The Eleventh Hour 1988, The Picture Post Album 1989, The Laurel and the Ivy 1993, Parnell and Irish Nationalism 1993. *Leisure interests:* swimming, music. *Address:* c/o Rogers, Coleridge and White, 20 Powis Mews, London, W11 1JN, England.

KEEBLE, Sir (Herbert Ben) Curtis, G.C.M.G.; British diplomatist (retd.); b. 18 Sept. 1922, London; s. of Herbert and Gertrude Keeble; m. Margaret Fraser 1947; three d.; ed. Clacton County High School, London Univ.; served Royal Irish Fusiliers 1942–47; entered Foreign Service 1947; served in Batavia (now Jakarta, Indonesia) 1947–49; Foreign Office 1949–51, 1958–63; Berlin 1951–54; Washington 1954–58; Counsellor and Head of European Econ. Orgs. Dept. 1963–65; Counsellor (Commercial), Berne 1965–68; Minister, Canberra 1968–71; Asst. Under-Sec. of State, FCO 1971–74; Amb. to G.D.R. 1974–76; Deputy Under-Sec. of State, FCO 1976–78; Amb. to U.S.S.R. 1978–82; Chair. G.B.-U.S.S.R. Asscn. 1985–92, Britain-Russia Centre 1993–, Foundation for Accountancy and Financial Man. 1993–; Gov. of BBC 1985–90; mem. Council of Royal Inst. of Int. Affairs 1984–90, Council of the School of Slavonic and East European Studies; Consultant to FCO 1984–97. *Publications:* The Soviet State: The Domestic Roots of Soviet Foreign Policy 1985, Britain and the Soviet Union 1917–1989 1990. *Leisure interests:* sailing, painting. *Address:* Dormers, St. Leonards Road, Thames Ditton, Surrey, England.

KEEFFE, Barrie Colin; British dramatist, novelist and director; b. 31 Oct. 1945, London; s. of the late Edward Thomas Keeffe and Constance Beatrice Keeffe (née Marsh); m. 1st Sarah Dee (Truman) 1969 (dissolved 1975); m. 2nd Verity Eileen Bargate 1981 (died 1981); two step-s.; m. 3rd Julia Lindsay 1983 (dissolved 1991); ed. East Ham Grammar School; fmrly. actor with Nat. Youth Theatre, journalist; has written plays for theatre, TV and radio; currently resident writer Shaw Theatre, London, R.S.C.; assoc. writer Theatre Royal, Stratford East, also mem. bd.; Assoc. Soho Theatre Co.; French Critics Prix Révélation 1978; Giles Cooper Award Best Radio Plays; Mystery Writers of America Edgar Alan Poe Award 1982. *Theatre plays include:* Only a Game 1973, A Sight of Glory 1975, Scribes 1975, Here Comes the Sun 1976, Gimme Shelter 1977, A Mad World My Masters 1977, Barbarians 1977, Frozen Assets 1978, Sus 1979, Bastard Angel 1980, She's So Modern 1980, Black Lear 1980, Chorus Girls 1981, Better Times 1985,

King of England 1988, My Girl 1989, Not Fade Away 1990, Wild Justice 1990, I Only Want to Be With You 1995. *Plays directed include:* A Certain Vincent, A Gentle Spirit, Talking of Chekov (Amsterdam and London), My Girl (London and Bombay), The Gary Oldman Fan Club (London). *Film:* The Long Good Friday (screenplay). *Television plays include:* Substitute 1972, Not Quite Cricket 1977, Gotcha 1977, Nipper 1977, Champions 1978, Hanging Around 1978, Waterloo Sunset 1979, King 1984. *Publications:* (novels) Gadabout 1969, No Excuses 1983. *Leisure interests:* playing tennis, watching soccer. *Address:* 110 Annandale Road, London, SE10 0JZ, England. *Telephone:* 0181-858 7764.

KEEFFE, Bernard, B.A.; British conductor, broadcaster and professor; b. 1 April 1925, London; s. of Joseph Keeffe and Therea Keeffe (née Quinn); m. Denise Walker 1954; one s. one d.; ed. St. Olave's Grammar School and Clare Coll., Cambridge; served in Intelligence Corps 1943–47; mem. Glyndebourne Opera Co. 1951–52; BBC Music Staff 1954–60; Asst. Music Dir., Royal Opera House 1960–62; Conductor BBC Scottish Orchestra 1962–64; Prof., Trinity Coll. of Music 1966–; freelance conductor and broadcaster on radio and TV, concerts with leading orchestras 1966–; mem. int. juries, competitions in Sofia, Liège, Vienna and London; Warden solo performers section, Inc. Soc. of Musicians 1971; mem. Exec. Cttee. Anglo-Austrian Music Soc.; Hon. Fellow Trinity Coll. of Music. *Leisure interest:* photography. *Address:* 153 Honor Oak Road, London, SE23 3RN, England. *Telephone:* 0181-699 3672.

KEEGAN, John; British military historian and journalist; b. 1934, London; m. Susanne Keegan; two s. two d.; ed. privately and Balliol Coll. Oxford; awarded travel grant to study American Civil War in U.S.A.; writer of political reports for U.S. Embassy, London, 1957–59; lecturer, sr. lecturer War Studies Dept. Royal Mil. Acad. Sandhurst 1959–86; war correspondent for Daily Telegraph, Beirut 1984; Defence and mil. correspondent, Daily Telegraph 1986–; Delmas Prof. of History, Vassar Coll. 1996–98; contributing ed. U.S. News and World Report 1986–; Dir. E. Somerset NHS Trust 1991–97; Samuel Eliot Morrison Prize U.S. Soc. for Mil. History 1996; Hon. LL.D. (New Brunswick) 1997. *Publications include:* The Face of Battle 1976, The Nature of War 1981, Six Armies in Normandy: From D-Day to the Liberation of Paris 1982, Zones of Conflict: An Atlas of Future Wars 1986, Soldiers: A History of Men in Battle 1986, The Mask of Command 1987, Who's Who in Military History (with A. Wheatcroft) 1987, The Price of Admiralty: The Evolution of Naval Warfare 1989, The Second World War 1990, Churchill's Generals (ed.) 1991, The Face of Battle 1991, A History of Warfare 1993, Warparths: travels of a military historian in North America 1995, Who's Who in World War 2 1995, The Battle for History: Re-fighting World War II 1995, Who's Who in Military History (with Andrew Wheatcroft) 1996, Warpaths 1996, The Battle for History 1996; ed. and co-ed. of several mil. reference works. *Address:* The Manor House, Kilmington, nr. Warminster, Wilts, BA12 6RD, England. *Telephone:* (01985) 844856.

KEEL, Alton G., Jr., PH.D.; American diplomatist and civil servant; b. 8 Sept. 1943, Va.; s. of Alton G. Keel and Ella Kennedy; m. Franmarie Kennedy-Keel 1982; one d.; ed. Univ. of Virginia and Univ. of California, Berkeley; Facility Man. Naval Weapons Center 1971–77; Sr. Official Senate Armed Services Cttee., US Senate 1977–81; Asst. Sec. Air Force for Research, Devt. and Logistics, The Pentagon 1981–82; Assoc. Dir. Nat. Security and Int. Affairs 1982–86; Exec. Dir. Pres. Comm. on Space Shuttle Challenger Accident 1986; Acting Asst. to the Pres. for Nat. Security Affairs 1986; Perm. Rep. to NATO 1987–89; Pres., Man. Dir. Carlyle Int., The Carlyle Group 1992–94; Chair. Carlyle SEAG 1994–95, Chair., Man. Dir. Atlantic Partners L.L.C. Washington 1992–; Nat. Congressional Science Fellow A.I.A.A. 1977; Air Force Decoration Exceptional Civilian Service 1982; NASA Group Achievement Award 1987, Distinguished Alumnus Award (Univ. of Va.) 1987. *Publications:* numerous scientific and tech. articles, foreign policy and nat. security publs. *Leisure interests:* running, golf, sailing, physical fitness. *Address:* Atlantic Partners, P.O. Box 12206, Arlington, VA 22219, U.S.A.

KEGEL, Gerhard Theodor Otto, DR.; German professor of law; b. 26 June 1912, Magdeburg; s. of Martin Kegel and Wilhelmine Schönbach; m. Irmgard Vethake 1940; one s. three d.; ed. Joachimsthalsches Gymnasium and Univs. of Erlangen, Göttingen and Berlin; Prof. of Law 1950–78, Prof. Emer. 1978–; Pres. German Council of Private Int. Law 1964–85; Berkeley Citation 1981; Grosses Bundesverdienstkreuz. *Publication:* Internationales Privatrecht. *Leisure interest:* music. *Address:* Am Steinrausch 3, 54576 Hillesheim, Germany. *Telephone:* 06593-334.

KEILIS-BOROK, Vladimir Isaakovich, D.SC.; Russian geophysicist and applied mathematician; b. 31 July 1921, Moscow; s. of Isaak Moiseyevich and Kseniya Ruvimovna; m. L. N. Malinovskaya 1955; one d.; ed. S. Ordzhonikidze Inst. of Geological Prospecting, O. Schmidt Inst. of Earth Physics, U.S.S.R. Acad. of Sciences; Chair. Dept. of Computational Geophysics 1960–89; Dir. Int. Inst. Earthquake Prediction Theory and Mathematical Geophysics 1989–98, Hon. Dir. 1998–; mem. U.S.S.R. (now Russian) Acad. of Sciences 1987–; Foreign Assoc. N.A.S.; Foreign Hon. mem. American Acad. of Arts and Sciences; Assoc. Royal Astronomical Society; mem. ed. bd. of several int. journals 1987–91; fmr. Pres. Int. Union of Geodesy and Geophysics. *Publications:* Computational Seismology series, Vols. 1–24 1966–91, other works on global seismology and tectonics. *Leisure interests:* mountaineering, sociology. *Address:* International Institute of Earthquake Prediction Theory and Mathematical Geophysics, Moscow 113556, Warshavskoye sh. 79, Kor. 2, Russia. *Telephone:* (095) 110-77-95 (Office); (095) 936 55 88 (Home). *Fax:* (095) 956-70-95.

KEILLOR, Garrison Edward, B.A.; American writer and broadcaster; b. 7 Aug. 1942, Anoka, Minn.; s. of John P. Keillor and Grace R. (Denham) Keillor; m. Jenny Lind Nilsson; ed. Univ. of Minnesota; cr. radio show A Prairie Home Companion 1974–87, American Radio Co. 1989; Grammy Award for best non-musical recording (Lake Wobegon Days) 1987, Ace Award for best musical host (A Prairie Home Companion) 1988. *Publications:* Happy to Be Here 1982, Lake Wobegon Days 1985, Leaving Home 1987, We Are Still Married: Stories and Letters 1989, WLT: A Radio Romance 1991, The Book of Guys 1993, Cat, You Better Come Home (children's book) 1995, The Man Who Loved Cheese 1996, The Sandy Bottom Orchestra 1996, Wobegon Boy 1997. *Address:* 45 7th Street East, Saint Paul, MN 55101, U.S.A.

KEINÄNEN, Eino, M.POL.SC.; Finnish fmr. civil servant and business executive; b. 17 Nov. 1939; ed. Univ. of Helsinki; credit official, Kansallis-Osake-Pankki 1962–64; Head of Section, Finnish State Computer Centre and Planning Organ for State Accounting 1965–68; various posts, Budget Dept., Ministry of Finance 1969–85, Head Budget Dept. 1985–87, Perm. Under-Sec. 1987–89, Perm. State Sec. 1989–95; Gen. Man. and mem. Bd. Postipankki Ltd. 1995–96, Chair and Chief Exec. March 1996–; mem. Bd. of Dirs. Finnish State Treasury 1985–89, Finnish Tourist Bd. 1985–89, Finnish Foreign Trade Asscn. 1985–89, Cen. Statistical Office of Finland 1985–89; mem. Investment Fund of Finland 1985–89; Vice-Pres. Supervisory Bd. Finnish Export Credit Ltd. 1987–, Finnish Fund for Industrial Devt. Co-operation Ltd. (Finnfund) 1994–; Pres. Bd. of Dirs. State Computer Centre 1988–; mem. Supervisory Bd. Slot Machine Asscn. 1989–, Regional Devt. Fund of Finland Ltd. 1989–, Finnish Grain Bd. 1989–; mem. Bd. of Admin. Alko Ltd. 1989–; Pres. Supervisory Bd. Finnish Ice-Hockey Asscn. 1989–. *Address:* Postipankki Ltd., Unioninkati 22, 00007 Helsinki, Finland. *Fax:* (0) 6221019.

KEITA, Ibrahima Boubacar; Malian politician; Minister of Foreign Affairs 1993–94; Prime Minister of Mali Feb. 1994–; Sec. External Relations Alliance pour la Démocratie au Mali (ADEMA). *Address:* Office of the Prime Minister, B.P. 97, Bamako, Mali.

KEITEL, Harvey; American actor; b. 13 May 1939; m. Lorraine Bracco (divorced); one d.; ed. Actors Studio; served U.S. Marines; starred in Martin Scorsese's student film Who's That Knocking at My Door?; stage appearances in Death of a Salesman, Hurlyburly. *Films:* Mean Streets, Alice Doesn't Live Here Anymore, That's the Way of the World, Taxi Driver, Mother Jugs and Speed, Buffalo Bill and the Indians, Welcome to L.A., The Duellists, Fingers, Blue Collar, Eagle's Wing, Deathwatch, Saturn 3, Bad Timing, The Border, Exposed, La Nuit de Varennes, Corrupt, Falling in Love, Knight of the Dragon, Camorra, Off Beat, Wise Guys, The Men's Club, The Investigation, The Pick-up Artist, The January Man, The Last Temptation of Christ, The Two Jakes, Two Evil Eyes (The Black Cat), Thelma & Louise, Tipperary, Bugsy, Reservoir Dogs, Bad Lieutenant, Mean Streets, The Assassin, The Young Americans, The Piano, Snake Eyes, Rising Sun, Monkey Trouble, Clockers, Dangerous Game, Pulp Fiction, Smoke, Imaginary Crimes, Ulysses' Gaze 1995, Blue in the Face 1995, City of Industry, Cop Land 1996, Head Above Water, Somebody to Love 1996. *Address:* c/o William Morris Agency, 151 El Camino Drive, Beverly Hills, CA 90212, U.S.A.

KEITH, Sir Kenneth James, K.B.E., LL.M., Q.C.; New Zealand judge; b. 19 Nov. 1937; s. of Patrick James Keith and Amy Irene Keith (née Witheridge); m. Jocelyn Margaret Buckett 1961; two s. two d.; ed. Auckland Grammar School, Auckland Univ., Victoria Univ. of Wellington, Harvard Law School; with Dept. of External Affairs, Wellington 1960–62; with Law Faculty, Vic. Univ. 1962–64, 1966–91, Prof. 1973–91, Dean 1977–81; UN Secr. Office of Legal Affairs 1968–70; with N.Z. Inst. of Int. Affairs 1971–73; Judge Courts of Appeal of Samoa 1982–, Cook Islands 1982–, Niue 1995–, N.Z. 1996–; mem. N.Z. Law Comm. 1986–91, Pres. 1991–96; awarded 1990 Commemoration Medal. *Publications:* Advisory Jurisdiction of the International Court 1971, Essays on Human Rights (Ed.) 1968, numerous Law Comm. publs. and papers on constitutional law in legal journals. *Leisure interests:* family, walking, reading. *Address:* Court of Appeal, P.O. Box 1606, Wellington; 11 Salamanca Road, Kelburn, Wellington, New Zealand. *Telephone:* (4) 9158200 (Court of Appeal); (4) 4726664. *Fax:* (4) 9158250 (Court of Appeal); (4) 472664.

KEITH, Penelope Anne Constance, O.B.E.; British actress; b. 2 April 1940, Sutton, Surrey; d. of Frederick Hatfield and Constance Mary Keith; m. Rodney Timson 1978; ed. Annecy Convent, Seaford, Sussex, Convent Bayeux, Normandy, Webber Douglas School, London; first professional appearance, Civic Theatre, Chesterfield 1959; repertory, Lincoln, Salisbury, Manchester 1960–63, Cheltenham 1967; R.S.C., Stratford 1963, Aldwych 1965; Pres. Actors Benevolent Fund 1990–; Gov. Queen Elizabeth's Foundation for the Disabled 1989–, Guildford School of Acting 1991–; Trustee Yvonne Arnaud Theatre 1992–. *Stage appearances include:* Suddenly at Home 1971, The Norman Conquests 1974, Donkey's Years 1976, The Apple Cart 1977, The Millionairess 1978, Moving 1980, Hobson's Choice, Captain Brassbound's Conversion 1982, Hay Fever 1983, The Dragon's Tail 1985, Miranda 1987, The Deep Blue Sea 1988, Dear Charles 1990, The Merry Wives of Windsor 1990, The Importance of Being Earnest 1991, On Approval 1992, Relatively Speaking 1992, Glyn and It 1994, Monsieur Amilcar 1995, Mrs Warren's Profession 1997. *Film appearances include:* Rentadick, Take a Girl Like You, Every Home Should Have One, Sherlock Holmes, The Priest of Love; *TV appearances include:* The Good Life (Good Neighbors in U.S.A.) 1974–77, Private Lives 1976, The Norman Conquests 1977, To the Manor Born 1979–81, On Approval 1980, Spider's Web, Sweet Sixteen, Waters of the Moon, Hay Fever, Moving, Executive Stress, What's my Line? 1988, Growing Places, No Job for a Lady 1990, Law and Disorder 1994, Next of Kin; Best Light Entertainment Performance (British Acad. of Film and TV Arts) 1976, Best Actress 1977, Show Business Personality (Variety Club of G.B.) 1976, BBC TV Personality 1979, Comedy Performance of the Year (Soc. of West End. Theatre) 1976, Female TV Personality, T.V. Times Awards 1976–78, BBC TV Personality of the Year 1978–79, TV Female Personality (Daily Express) 1979–82. *Leisure interest:* gardening. *Address:* London Management, 2 Noel Street, London, W1V 3RB, England. *Telephone:* 0171-287 9000.

KEITH OF CASTLEACRE, Baron (Life Peer), cr. 1980, of Swaffham in the County of Norfolk; **Kenneth Alexander Keith,** F.R.S.A.; British industrialist and banker; b. 30 Aug. 1916; s. of late Edward Charles Keith; m. 1st Lady Ariel Olivia Winifred Baird 1946 (divorced 1958); one s. one d.; m. 2nd Nancy (Slim) Hayward (née Gross) 1962 (divorced 1972); m. 3rd Marie-Luz Hanbury (née Dennistoun-Webster) 1973; ed. Rugby and Dresden; trained as Chartered Accountant, London 1934–39; Army Service 1939–45; Asst. to Dir.-Gen. Political Intelligence Dept., Foreign Office 1945–46; Asst. to Man. Dir. Philip Hill & Partners, London 1946–48, Dir. 1947; Dir. Philip Hill Investment Trust 1949, Man. Dir. 1951; Man. Dir. Philip Hill, Higginson & Co. Ltd. 1951–59, Philip Hill, Higginson, Erlangers Ltd. 1959–62, Chair. 1962–65; Deputy Chair. and Chief Exec. Hill Samuel & Co. 1965–70, Group Chair. 1970–80; Chair. and Chief Exec. Rolls-Royce 1972–80; Chair. Arlington Securities PLC 1982–90; mem. Bd. Standard Telephone and Cables 1977–85, Chair. 1985–89; Vice-Chair. Beecham Group Ltd. 1970–85, Chair. 1985–87; Vice-Chair. BEA 1964–71, Dir. British Airways 1971–72; Dir. Bank of Nova Scotia 1958–86, Eagle Star Insurance Co. 1955–75, Nat. Provincial Bank 1967–69, Times Newspapers Ltd. 1967–81, Guinness Peat Aviation Group 1983; Pres. British Standards Inst. 1989–94; mem. Nat. Econ. Devt. Council 1964–71; Chair. Econ. Planning Council for East Anglia 1965–70; Gov. Nat. Inst. of Econ. and Social Research; Council mem. Manchester Business School; Pres. Royal Norfolk Agricultural Asscn. 1989, RoSPA 1989–92; Hon. Companion Royal Aeronautical Soc.; Croix de Guerre with Silver Star. *Leisure interests:* shooting, farming, golf. *Address:* The Wicken House, Castle Acre, Norfolk, PE32 2BP, England. *Telephone:* (01760) 755225.

KEKILBAYEV, Abish Kekilbayevich (pseudonym Abish Tagan); Kazakhstan politician and writer; b. 6 Dec. 1939, Ondy, Mangystau Region, Kazakhstan; s. of Kekilbay Kokimov and Aysaule Kokimova; m. Klara Zhumabaeva; four c.; ed. Kazakh State Univ.; schoolteacher of Kazakh language; worked for newspapers Kazakh Adebieti and Leninshil Zhas; Ed.-in-Chief Studio Kazakhfilm; CP official in Alma-Ata; Deputy Minister of Culture Kazakh S.S.R.; Sec. Man. Cttee. Kazakh Writers' Union; Chair. Presidium of Kazakh Soc. for Protection of Monuments of History and Culture 1962–89; Chair. Cttee. on Nat. Policy, Language and Culture Devt., Kazakhstan Supreme Soviet 1991–93; Ed.-in-Chief Egemen Kazakhstan (newspaper) 1992–93; State Counsellor 1993–94; Chair., Supreme Council of Repub. 1994–95; State Counsellor to Pres. of Repub. 1995–; Deputy to Majlis (Parl.) 1995–; State Sec. Rep. of Kazakhstan 1996–. *Publications:* author of novels, short stories, critical reviews, translations. *Address:* House of Government, Astora (Office); Markova str. 13, Apt. 7, 480013 Almaty, Kazakhstan (Home). *Telephone:* (3172) 32-27-04 (Office); (3272) 692329.

KELDYSH, Leonid Venyaminovich, D.PHYS. MATH.SC.; Russian physicist; b. 7 April 1931, Moscow; s. of Benjamin L. Granovskii and Lyudmila V. Keldysh; m. Galina S. Krasnikova 1983; one s.; ed. Moscow State Univ.; jr. then sr. researcher, Head of Sector, Head of Dept., Lebedev Physical Inst. U.S.S.R. (now Russian) Acad. of Sciences 1954–89, Dir. 1989–93, Sr. researcher 1993–; Prof. Moscow State Univ. 1965–; Pres. Physical Soc. of Russian Fed. 1998–; Corresp. mem. U.S.S.R. Acad. of Sciences 1968, mem. 1976; main research on solid state theory, physics of semiconductors, interaction of radiation with matter; Fyzika i Tekhnika Poluprovodnikov; Foreign Assoc. Nat. Acad. of Sciences (U.S.A.) 1995–; Lenin Prize, Lomonosov Prize, Hewlett-Packard Prize 1975; A. V. Humboldt Research Award 1975. *Publications:* Coherent Exciton States 1972, Absorption of Ultrasound by Electron-Hole Drops 1976, articles in scientific journals. *Address:* P.N. Lebedev Physical Institute, Leninski Prospect 53, 117924 Moscow V-333, Russia. *Telephone:* (095) 135 3033. *Fax:* (095) 938 2251.

KELETI, György; Hungarian politician and army officer; b. 18 May 1946, Losonc; m. Erzsébet Petrik; three c.; ed. Zalka Máté Mil. Tech. Coll., Zrinyi Miklós War Coll.; co. commdr., then later deputy commdr. of a bn. in Vác Dist. 1969–74; posts in Ministry of Defence 1980; Press Spokesman of Ministry of Defence 1977; mem. Hungarian Socialist Party (HSP) 1992; mem. Parl. 1992–; mem. of Nat. Security Cttee. of Parl.; Minister of Defence 1994–98; rank of Col. in army reserve; Order of Star (with swords), Silver Cross of Merit. *Address:* c/o Honvédelmi Minisztérium, 1055 Budapest, Balaton u. 711, Hungary.

KELLER, Andrew, PH.D., F.INST.P., F.R.S.; British research scientist; b. 22 Aug. 1925; s. of Imre Keller and Margit Klein; m. Eva Bulhack 1951 (died 1997); one s. one d.; ed. Univs. of Budapest and Bristol; Technical Officer, ICI Ltd. Manchester 1948–55; Ministry of Supply research appt. Univ. of Bristol 1955–57, Research Asst. 1957–63, Lecturer 1963–65, Reader 1965–69, Research Prof. in Polymer Science 1969–91, Prof. Emer. 1991–; mem. Acad. Europaea 1994; Foreign mem. Hungarian Acad. of Sciences 1998; High Polymer Prize, American Physics Soc. 1964; Swinburne Award, Plastics Inst. 1974; Max Born Medal, Inst. of Physics and Deutsche Physik Gesellschaft 1983; Rumford Medal (Royal Soc.) 1994. *Publications:* numerous papers in scientific journals. *Leisure interests:* outdoor sports, mountain walking, concerts. *Address:* 41 Westbury Road, Bristol, BS9 3AU, England. *Telephone:* (0117) 9629767.

KELLER, Joseph Bishop, PH.D.; American professor of mathematics and mechanical engineering; b. 31 July 1923, Paterson, N.J.; s. of Isaac Keller and Sally Bishop; m. Evelyn Fox 1963 (divorced 1976); one s. one d.; ed New York Univ.; Prof. of Math. Courant Inst. of Math. Sciences, New York Univ. 1948–79, Chair. Dept. of Math., Univ. Coll. of Arts and Sciences and Graduate School of Eng. and Sciences 1967–73; Prof. of Math. and Mechanical Eng. Stanford Univ. 1979–; Hon. Prof. of Math. Sciences (Univ. of Cambridge) 1990–; mem. N.A.S., Foreign mem. Royal Soc.; Hon. D.Tech. (Tech. Univ. of Denmark) 1979; Hon. D.Sc. (Northwestern Univ.) 1988, (Crete) 1993, (New Jersey Inst. Tech.) 1995, (Carlos Tercero de Madrid) 1995; Nemmers Prize 1996, shared Wolf Prize 1997; Nat. Medal of Science 1988, N.A.S. Award in Applied Math. and Numerical Analysis 1995, numerous awards and lectureships. *Publications:* about 400 articles in professional journals. *Leisure interests:* hiking, skiing. *Address:* Department of Mathematics, Stanford University, Stanford, CA 94305 (Office); 820 Sonoma Terrace, Stanford, CA 94305, U.S.A. (Home). *Telephone:* (415) 723-0851 (Office).

KELLEY, Harold H., PH.D.; American professor of psychology; b. 16 Feb. 1921, Boise Idaho; s of Harry H. Kelley and Maude M. Kelley; m. Dorothy Drumm 1942; one s. two d; ed. Univ. of Calif., Berkeley and M.I.T.; Study Dir. and lecturer, Dept. of Psychology, Univ. of Mich. 1948–50; Asst. Prof., Dept. of Psychology, Yale Univ. 1950–55; Assoc Prof., then Prof., Dept. of Psychology, Univ. of Minn. 1955–61; Prof. Dept. of Psychology, Univ. of Calif., Los Angeles 1961–91, Prof. Emer. 1991–; Fellow N.A.S., American Acad. of Arts and Sciences; Distinguished Sr. Scientist Soc. for Experimental Social Psychology; Distinguished Scientific Contribution Award, American Psychological Asscn.; Kurt Lewin Memorial Award (Soc. for the Psychological Study of Social Issues). *Publications:* The Social Psychology of Groups (with J. W. Thibaut) 1959, Attribution (co-author) 1972, Interpersonal Relations (with J. W. Thibaut) 1978, Personal Relationships 1979, Close Relationships (co-author) 1983. *Leisure interests:* music, backpacking. *Address:* 21634 Rambla Vista Street, Malibu, CA 90265, U.S.A.

KELLOU, Mohamed; Algerian diplomatist and lawyer; b. 27 March 1931, Mansoura; s. of Arezki Kellou and Zehoua Kellou; m. Annyssa Abdelkader 1965; three d.; ed. Univs. of Algiers and Montpellier; Lawyer, Algiers; fmr. Vice-Pres. Union Générale des Etudiants Musulmans Algériens (U.G.E.M.A.) (in charge of Foreign Affairs); Front de Libération Nationale (F.L.N.) Rep. in U.K. 1957–61; Chief of Provisional Govt. of Algeria Diplomatic Mission to Pakistan 1961–62; Dir. of African, Asian and S. American Affairs, Ministry of Foreign Affairs, Repub. of Algeria 1962–63; Amb. to U.K. 1963–64, to Czechoslovakia 1964–70, to Argentina 1970–75, to People's Repub. of China 1975–77, to Fed. Repub. of Germany 1979–82, to Zimbabwe 1982–84; Minister Plenipotentiary, Ministry of Foreign Affairs, Algiers 1984–88; mem. People's Nat. Ass. and Chair. Foreign Affairs Cttee. 1977–79; lawyer, Court of Appeal, specializing in int. affairs 1988–. *Leisure interests:* reading, tennis, swimming. *Address:* 4 rue Nafaa Haffaf, 16000 Algiers (Office); 40 Boulevard des Martyrs, 16000 Algiers, Algeria (Home). *Telephone:* (2) 734681, 734682 (Office); (2) 609104 (Home). *Fax:* (2) 736793.

KELLS, Ronald (Ronnie) David, D.L., B.SC.(ECON.), F.C.I.S., F.I.B.; British banker; b. 14 May 1938, Belfast; s. of Robert Kells and Frances Beckett; m. Elizabeth A. Hanna 1964; one s. one d.; ed. Bushmills Grammar School, Sullivan Upper School, Holywood, Queen's Univ. Belfast and Babson Coll., Boston, Mass.; joined Ulster Bank Ltd. 1964, Investment Man. 1969, Deputy Head, Related Banking Services 1976, Head of Planning and Marketing 1979; seconded to Nat. Westminster Bank 1982; Dir. and Head of Br. Banking Div. Ulster Bank Ltd. 1984, Chief Exec. 1994–. *Leisure interests:* golf, winter sports, gardening, walking. *Address:* The Moyle, 10 Upper Knockbreda Road, Belfast, BT6 9QA, Northern Ireland. *Telephone:* (01232) 797912.

KELLY, Anthony, PH.D., F.ENG., F.R.S.; British fmr. university administrator and metallurgist; b. 9 Jan. 1929, Hillingdon, Middx.; s. of Group Capt. V. G. Kelly and Violet E. M. Kelly; m. Christina M. Dunleavie 1956 (died 1997); three s. one d.; ed. Presentation Coll., Reading, Univ. of Reading and Trinity Coll., Cambridge; Research Assoc. Univ. of Ill. 1953–55; Univ. of Birmingham 1955; Founding Fellow, Churchill Coll., Cambridge and Lecturer in Metallurgy 1958–67, Life Fellow Churchill Coll. 1985; Supt. of Div., later Deputy Dir. Nat. Physical Lab. 1967–75; Vice-Chancellor, Univ. of Surrey 1975–94, Univ. Prof. 1987; Chair. Eng. Materials Requirements Board, Dept. of Industry 1976–80; Dir. Johnson Wax UK 1981–97, QUOTEC 1984–, NPL Man. Ltd. 1995–; fmr. Dir. Teddington Devts.; Chair. Surrey Satellite Tech. 1985–94; mem. Academia Europaea; Foreign Assoc. U.S. Acad. of Eng.; Fellow Churchill Coll., Cambridge; awards include William Hopkins Prize 1967, Beilby Medal 1967, A. A. Griffith Medal (Univ. of Del.) 1974, Medal of Excellence (Univ. of Del.) 1984; Int. Gold Medal (American Soc. for Materials) 1991. *Publications:* Strong Solids 1966, Crystallography and

Crystal Defects (with G. W. Groves) 1970; many papers in journals of physical sciences. *Leisure interests:* science of materials, sailing. *Address:* 29 Madingley Road, Cambridge, CB3 0EG, England. *Telephone:* (01223) 313222. *Fax:* (01223) 363691.

KELLY, Donald P.; American business executive; b. 24 Feb. 1922, Chicago; m. Byrd M. Sullivan 1952; two s. one d.; ed. De Paul, Loyola and Harvard Univs.; Man. Data Processing, Swift & Co. 1953, Asst. Controller 1965, Controller 1967, Vice-Pres. Corp. Devt. 1968, Financial Vice-Pres. and Dir. 1970–; Financial Vice-Pres. and Dir. Esmark April-Oct. 1973, Pres., C.O.O. 1973–77, Pres. and C.E.O. 1977–82, Chair., Pres. and C.E.O. 1982–84; Chair. Kelly Briggs and Assocs., Inc. 1984–86; Chair., C.E.O. BCI Holdings Corpn. 1986–87; Chair. and C.E.O. EII Holdings Inc. 1987–88; Chair. Beatrice Co., Chicago March–Oct. 1988; Pres. and C.E.O. D.P. Kelly Assocs. L.P. Nov. 1988–; Dir., Chair., Pres., C.E.O. Envirodyne Industries Inc. 1989–96. *Address:* D.P. Kelly and Associates, 701 Harger Road, Suite 190, Oak Brook, IL 60521, U.S.A.

KELLY, Ellsworth; American painter and sculptor; b. 31 May 1923, Newburgh, N.Y.; ed. Boston Museum Fine Arts School and Ecole des Beaux Arts, Paris; one-man shows including Galerie Arnaud 1951, Betty Parsons Gallery, New York 1956, 1957, 1959, 1961, 1963, Galerie Maeght, Paris 1958, 1964, Tooth Gallery, London 1962, Washington Gallery of Modern Art 1964, Inst. of Contemporary Art, Boston 1964, Sidney Janis Gallery, New York, 1965, 1967, 1968, 1971, Dayton's Gallery 12, Minn. 1971, Albright Art Gallery 1972, Leo Castelli Gallery, New York, 1973, 1975, 1977, 1981, 1982, 1984, 1985, 1989, 1990, New York Museum of Modern Art 1973, 1978, Blum/ Helman Gallery, New York, 1975, 1977, 1979, 1981, 1982, 1984, 1985, 1986, 1988, 1989, 1992, Stedelijk Museum, Amsterdam 1979, Hayward Gallery, London 1980, Whitney Museum of Modern Art, New York 1982, St. Louis Museum of Art 1983, Anthony d'Offay Gallery, London 1992, 1994; works exhibited, Salon de Réalités Nouvelles, Paris 1950, 1951, Carnegie Int. 1958, 1961, 1964, 1967, São Paulo Biennale 1961, Tokyo Int. 1963, Documenta III and IV, Germany 1964, 1968, Venice Biennale 1966, Guggenheim Int. 1967, Corcoran Annual, Washington, D.C. 1979, etc.; works in numerous permanent collections including Museum of Modern Art, Whitney Museum, Carnegie Inst., Chicago Art Inst., Guggenheim Museum, Tate Gallery, London, Musée d'Art Moderne, Paris, Stedelijk Museum, Amsterdam; mem. Nat. Inst. of Arts and Letters; recipient of numerous art prizes; Chevalier Ordre des Arts et des Lettres 1993.

KELLY, Gregory Maxwell, PH.D., F.A.A.; Australian professor of pure mathematics; b. 5 June 1930, Sydney; s. of Owen S. Kelly and Rita M. (née McCauley) Kelly; m. 1960; three s. one d.; ed. Univs. of Sydney and Cambridge, England; Lecturer in Pure Math. Univ. of Sydney 1957–60, Sr. Lecturer 1961–65, Reader 1965–66; Prof. of Pure Math. Univ. of N.S.W. 1967–72, Univ. of Sydney 1973–94, Emer. Prof. and Professorial Fellow 1995–. *Publications:* An Introduction to Algebra and Vector Geometry 1972, Basic Concepts of Enriched Category Theory 1981, numerous learned papers. *Leisure interests:* bridge, music, tennis, swimming. *Address:* University of Sydney, School of Mathematics and Statistics, FO7, Sydney, N.S.W. 2006 (Office); 319 Mona Vale Road, St. Ives, N.S.W. 2075, Australia (Home). *Telephone:* (02) 9351-3796 (Office); (02) 9983-9985 (Home).

KELLY, John Hubert, B.A.; American diplomatist; b. 20 July 1939, Fond du Lac, Wis.; m. Helena Marita Ajo; one s. one d.; ed. Emory Univ., Atlanta; Second Sec. U.S. Embassy, Ankara 1966–67; American Consul, Songkhla, Thailand 1969–71; First Sec. U.S. Embassy, Paris 1976–80; Deputy Exec. Sec., Dept. of State, Washington D.C. 1980–81, Sr. Deputy Asst. Sec. of State for Public Affairs 1982–83, Prin. Deputy Asst. Sec. of State for European Affairs 1983–85; Amb. to Lebanon 1986–88, to Finland 1991–94; Prin. Deputy Dir. of Policy Planning Staff 1988–89; Asst. Sec. for Near Eastern and S.E. Asian Affairs 1989–93; Man. Dir. Int. Equity Partners, Atlanta 1995–; Dir. Finnish-American Chamber of Commerce 1998; Trustee Lebanese-American Univ. 1997. *Address:* International Equity Partners, 1808 Over Lake Drive S.E., Suite D, Conyers, GA 30013, U.S.A.

KELLY, John Philip, L.V.O., M.B.E.; British diplomatist; b. 25 June 1941, Tuam, Ireland; s. of William Kelly and Norah Kelly (née Roche); m. Jennifer Anne Buckler 1964; one s.; joined H.M. Diplomatic Service 1959; worked at Embassies in Kinshasa (fmrly. Léopoldville) 1962–65, Cairo 1965–67, Bonn 1967–70; with FCO 1970–73, 1986–89, 1994–96; with High Comm. Canberra 1973–76, Consulate-Gen. Antwerp 1977–78; with Dept. of Trade 1980–82; Rep. to Grenada 1982–86; Deputy Gov. of Bermuda 1989–94; Gov. Turks and Caicos Islands 1996–. *Leisure interests:* golf, reading, walking. *Address:* Waterloo, Government House, Grand Turk, Turks and Caicos Islands. *Telephone:* 946-2309. *Fax:* 946-2903.

KELLY, Most Rev. Patrick Altham, S.T.L., PH.L.; British ecclesiastic; b. 23 Nov. 1938, Morecambe; s. of John Kelly and Mary (née Altham) Kelly; ed. Preston Catholic Coll., Venerable English Coll., Rome; Asst. Priest, Lancaster Cathedral 1964–66; Prof. of Dogmatic Theology, Oscott Coll., Birmingham 1966–79, Rector 1979–84; Bishop of Salford 1984–96; Archbishop of Liverpool, Metropolitan of the Northern Prov. 1996–. *Address:* Lowood, Carnatic Road, Mossley Hill, Liverpool L18 8BY, England. *Telephone:* 0151-724 6398.

KELLY, Ros, B.A.; Australian politician; b. 25 Jan. 1948, Sydney; d. of M. Raw and P. Raw; m. David Morgan; one s. one d.; ed. Univ. of Sydney; high-school teacher, N.S.W. and A.C.T. 1969–74; consultant and mem. A.C.T. Consumer Affairs Council 1974–79; mem. A.C.T. Legal Aid Comm. 1976–79; fmr. mem. A.C.T. Legis. Ass.; mem. Fed. Parl. 1980–95; Sec. Fed. Labor Party Parl. Caucus 1981–87; Minister for Defence Science and Personnel 1987–89, for Telecommunications and Aviation Support 1989–90, for Sport, the Environment, and Territories 1990–94, for the Arts 1990–93, Assisting the Prime Minister for the Status of Women 1993–94; Group Exec., Dames and Moore, Australia and Asia 1995–; mem. Int. Advisory Bd. Normandy Poseidon Ltd. 1995–; mem. Bd. Normandy Minerals. *Leisure interests:* reading, films, aerobics. *Address:* c/o Dames and Moore, 1/41 McLaren Street, North Sydney, NSW 2060, Australia. *Telephone:* (2) 9955 7772. *Fax:* (2) 9955 7324.

KELLY, Sharon Pratt, B.A., J.D.; American politician and lawyer; b. 30 Jan. 1944, Washington, D.C.; d. of Carlisle E. Pratt; m. 1st Arrington L. Dixon 1967 (divorced 1982); two d.; m. 2nd James Kelly III 1991; ed. Roosevelt High School, Washington, D.C. and Howard Univ.; Assoc. Pratt & Queen (law firm) 1971; teaching post, Antioch School of Law, Washington, D.C. 1972–76; Assoc. Gen. Counsel, Potomac Electric Power Co. (PEPCO) 1976, Dir. of Consumer Affairs 1979, Vice-Pres. 1983, Vice-Pres. for Public Policy 1986–89; mem. Democratic Nat. Cttee. 1977; Treas. Democratic Party 1989; Mayor of Washington, D.C. 1991–95; Dr. h.c. (Howard, George Washington and Georgetown Univs. and St. Mary's Coll.). *Address:* 1525 Iris Street, N.W., Washington, DC 20012, U.S.A.

KELMAN, Arthur, PH.D.; American plant pathologist and university professor; b. 11 Dec. 1918, Providence, R.I.; s. of Philip Kelman and Minnie Kollin; m. Helen Moore Parker 1949; one s.; ed. Univ. of Rhode Island and North Carolina State Univ.; served U.S. Signal Corps 1942–45; Asst. Prof., N.C. State Univ. 1949–53, Assoc. Prof. 1954–57, Prof. 1957–62, W.N. Reynolds Distinguished Prof. of Plant Pathology and Forestry 1962–65, Univ. Distinguished Scholar 1990–; Chief Scientist Competitive Grants Program, Nat. Research Initiative, USDA 1991–93; Visiting Scientist, Rockefeller Inst. for Medical Research, New York 1953–54; Chair. and Prof., Dept. of Plant Pathology, Univ. of Wis. at Madison 1965–75, L.R. Jones Prof. 1975–89, WARF (Wis. Alumni Research Foundation) Sr. Distinguished Prof. of Plant Pathology and Bacteriology 1984–89; N.S.F. Sr. Postdoctoral Fellowship, Cambridge Univ., England 1971–72; Pres. American Phytopathological Soc. 1967, Int. Soc. for Plant Pathology 1973–78; Chair. Div. of Biological Sciences, Comm. on Life Sciences, Nat. Research Council 1979–82, Bd. on Basic Biology 1984–85; mem. Council, N.A.S. 1986–89, Cttee. on Science Eng. and Public Policy, N.A.S. 1986–89; Fellow American Phytopathological Soc., Award of Distinction; mem. N.A.S., American Acad. of Arts and Sciences; Fellow American Acad. of Microbiology; Dr. h.c. (Rhode Island) 1977. *Publication:* The Bacterial Wilt caused by Pseudomonas Solanacearum 1953. *Leisure interests:* gardening, wood carving. *Address:* 615 Yarmouth Road, Raleigh, NC 27607, U.S.A. (Home). *Telephone:* (919) 881-7763 (Home).

KELMAN, Charles D., B.S., M.D.; American ophthalmologist; b. 23 May 1930, Brooklyn, New York; s. of Eva and David Kelman; m. 2nd Ann Gur-Arie 1989; one s. and one s. two d. from previous marriage; ed. Tuft's Univ., Univ. of Geneva Medical School, Switzerland; Residency in Ophthalmology, Wills Eye Hosp., Pa. 1956–60; Attending Surgeon, Manhattan Eye, Ear and Throat Hosp., New York 1967–, New York Eye and Ear Infirmary 1983–; Attending Ophthalmologist, Riverside Gen. Hosp., Secaucus, N.J. 1979; developed new techniques for cataract removal and lens implantation and invented surgical instruments for these operations 1962–67; has taught method to over 4,000 ophthalmologists from hospitals throughout world; Founder and Pres. Autogenesis Technologies Inc. (medical research co.); Pres. David J. Kelman Research Foundation; Clinical Prof. N.Y. Medical Coll., Valhalla 1980–; Hon. Chair. European Soc. for Phaco- and Related Techniques; Arthur J. Bedell Memorial Lecturer 1991; Co-founder Aura Medical Systems (medical tech. co.); Hon. Pres. World Congress on Lens Implant Surgery 1994; Physician's Recognition Award, American Medical Asscn., American Acad. of Achievement Gold Plate Award, American Acad. of Ophthalmology Sr. Honor Award, Ridley Medal, Int. Congress of Ophthalmology, Nat. Medal of Tech. award, and numerous other awards. *Publications:* Atlas of Cryosurgical Techniques in Ophthalmology 1966, Phacoemulsification and Aspiration: The Kelman Technique of Cataract Removal 1975, Cataracts—What You Must Know About Them 1982, Through My Eyes (autobiography) 1985 and numerous articles. *Leisure interests:* golf, saxophone, composing, flying. *Address:* Eye Centre, 220 Madison Avenue, New York, NY 10116, U.S.A.

KELMAN, James; British author; b. 1946, Glasgow; m.; two d.; Cheltenham Prize for Greyhound for Breakfast 1987, James Tait Black Memorial Prize for A Disaffection 1989, Scottish Arts Council Book Award for The Burn, Booker Prize for How Late It Was, How Late. *Publications include:* Not Not While the Giro (short stories), The Bus Conductor Hines, A Chancer, Greyhound for Breakfast, A Disaffection (novel), The Burn (short stories), How Late It Was, How Late (novel). *Address:* c/o Weidenfeld and Nicolson Ltd., Orion House, Upper St. Martin's Lane, London, WC2H 9EA, England. *Telephone:* 0171-240 3444.

KELSO, Adm. Frank Benton II; American naval officer; b. 11 July 1933, Fayetteville, Tenn.; s. of Thomas Benton Kelso and Wista Muse; m. Landess McCown 1956; four c.; ed. US Naval Acad.; Commdr. ensign U.S.N. 1956; Office of Program Appraisal 1983; Office, Sec. for the Navy 1985; rank of

Adm. 1986; Commdr. U.S. Sixth Fleet 1985–86; Commdr.-in-Chief, U.S. Atlantic Fleet, Norfolk, Va. 1986–88; Supreme Allied Commdr., Atlantic Commdr.-in-Chief, Atlantic Command, Norfolk 1988–90; Chief of Naval Operations, Washington, D.C. 1990–94; Acting Sec. of Navy 1993; retd. 1994.

KELTOŠOVÁ, Olga, B.SC.; Slovak politician; b. 27 Feb. 1943, Pezinok; ed. Komenský Univ. Bratislava; collaborated with various students' magazines later banned in 1968; worked as translator and interpreter 1970–89; Press Sec. Democratic Party 1989; Deputy Chair. to Slovak Nat. Council 1990–92; expelled from Democratic Party 1991; joined Movt. for Democratic Slovakia 1991–; Minister of Labour, Social Affairs and Family Matters 1992–94, 1995–98; Chair. Co-ordination Cttee. for Issues of Handicapped 1995, Co-ordinating Body for Problems of Women 1996–. *Address:* Movement for Democratic Slovakia (HZDS), Tomášikova 32/A, Bratislava 1, Slovakia (Office). *Telephone:* (7) 23 01 44, 23, 47 42.

KELVEDON OF ONGAR, Baron (Life Peer) cr. 1997, **(Henry) Paul Guinness Channon,** P.C., M.A.; British politician; b. 9 Oct. 1935; s. of late Sir Henry Channon and Lady Honor (née Guinness) Svejdar; m. Ingrid Olivia Georgia Wyndham 1963; one s. two d. (one d. deceased); ed. Eton Coll., Oxford Univ.; 2nd Lieut. Royal Horse Guards; M.P. for Southend West 1959–97; Parl. Pvt. Sec. to Minister of Power 1960, to the Home Sec. and later to the Foreign Sec. 1961–64; Opposition Spokesman on the Arts 1967–70; Parl. Sec., Ministry of Housing 1970–72; Minister of State, Northern Ireland Office April–Nov. 1972; Minister for Housing and Construction 1972–74; Opposition Spokesman on Prices and Consumer Affairs June–Oct. 1974, on the Environment 1974–75; Minister of State, Civil Service Dept. 1979–81; Minister of State, Dept. of Education and Science (responsible for the Arts 1981–83; Minister of State for Trade, Dept. of Trade and Industry 1983–86; Sec. of State for Trade and Industry 1986–87, for Transport 1987–89; Chair. House of Commons Finance and Services Cttee. 1992–97, Transport Select Cttee. 1993–97; Sponsor, Royal Comm. on Historical Monuments 1983–; Conservative. *Address:* c/o Iveagh Trustees Ltd., 41 Harrington Gardens, London, SW7 4JU; Kelvedon Hall, Brentwood, Essex, England. *Telephone:* (01277) 362180.

KEMAL, Yashar; Turkish writer and journalist; b. 1923, Adana; m. Thilda Serrero 1952; one s.; self-educated; mem. Académie Universelle des Cultures, Paris; Dr. h.c. (Strasbourg) 1991, (Akdeniz Univ., Antalya) 1991, (Mediterranean Univ.) 1992; Prix Mondial Cino del Duca 1982, VIII Premi Internacional Catalunya, Barcelona 1996, Peace Prize of German Book Trade 1997, Hellman-Hammett Award, New York 1996; Commdr., Légion d'honneur 1984. *Publications:* (in English) Memed, My Hawk 1961, The Wind from the Plain 1963, Anatolian Tales 1968, They Burn the Thistles 1973, Iron Earth, Copper Sky 1974, The Legend of Ararat 1975, The Legend of the Thousand Bulls 1976, The Undying Grass 1977, The Lords of Akchasaz (Part I), Murder in the Ironsmiths' Market 1979, The Saga of a Seagull 1981, The Sea-Crossed Fisherman 1985, The Birds Have Also Gone 1987, To Crush the Serpent 1991; novels, short stories, plays and essays in Turkish. *Leisure interest:* folklore. *Address:* P.K. 14, Basinköy, Istanbul, Turkey.

KEMOULARIA, Claude de; French international administrator and diplomatist; b. 30 March 1922, Paris; m. Chantal Julia de Kemoularia 1951; one d.; ed. Coll. Carnot, Fontainebleau, Faculté de Droit, Univ. de Paris and Ecole Libre des Sciences Politiques; early career with Ministry of Interior 1945, Office of Gov.-Gen. French Zone of Occupied Germany 1946–47, Ministry of Finance 1948; Parly. Sec. to Paul Reynaud 1948–56; Personal Asst. to Sec.-Gen. of UN, Dag Hammarskjöld 1957–61, in charge of World Refugee Year 1959–60; Dir. European Information Services of UN 1961; entered private business 1962; Dir. Forges de Chatillon-Commentry 1962–79, Paribas North America 1979–82, S. G. Warburg 1980–82; Sr. Consultant to Administrator, UN Devt. Programme 1964–82; Private Adviser to Prince Rainier of Monaco 1965–67; financial adviser for int. operations (Banque de Paris et des Pays-Bas) 1968–82; Hon. Chair. Soc. Néo-Calédonienne de Dévt. et Participations, Soc. Gabonaise de Participations; Amb. to Netherlands 1982–84; Perm. Rep. to UN 1984–87; U.N. Goodwill Amb. for Population Matters 1987–92, Vice-Chair. SGS Holding France 1994–; Dir. Société générale de surveillance 1987–94, Nina Ricci, Eurocopter, Bank Dofar Al Omani Al Fransi, Baiduri Bank Brunei; Pres. Paribas Netherlands 1988–92, Hon. Pres. 1992; Dir. Revue politique et parlementaire 1989–; mem. Nat. Cttee. European Movement; Hon. Pres. French UN Asscn.; Chair. Friends of the French Repub. Asscn.; Officier Légion d'honneur, Commdr. des Arts et des Lettres and other decorations. *Address:* 41 boulevard du Commandant Charcot, 92200 Neuilly-sur-Seine; Lascours, 24200 Carsac-Aillac, France.

KEMP, Rt. Rev. Eric Waldram, M.A., D.D., D.LITT., F.R.HIST.S.; British ecclesiastic; b. 27 April 1915, Grimsby; s. of Tom Kemp and Florence L. Waldram; m. Leslie Patricia Kirk 1953; one s. four d.; ed. Brigg Grammar School, Lincs., Exeter Coll., Oxford and St. Stephen's House; ordained Deacon 1939; Priest 1940; Curate St. Luke's, Southampton 1939–41; Librarian Pusey House, Oxford 1941–46; Chaplain Christ Church, Oxford 1941–46; Acting Chaplain St. John's Coll., Oxford 1943–45; Fellow, Chaplain, Tutor and Lecturer in Theology and Medieval History Exeter Coll. 1946–69; Dean of Worcester 1969–74; Lord Bishop of Chichester 1974–; Canon and Prebendary of Caistor in Lincoln Cathedral 1952; Hon. Provincial Canon of Cape Town 1960; Bampton Lecturer 1959–60; Chaplain to the Queen 1967–69; Chanoine d'honneur Chartres Cathedral 1998; Hon. D. Litt. (Sussex) 1986, Hon. D.D. (Berne) 1987. *Publications:* Canonization in the Western Church 1948, 25 Papal Decretals Relating to the Diocese of Lincoln 1954, An Introduction to Canon Law in the Church of England 1957, Life and Letters of K. E. Kirk 1959, Counsel and Consent 1961, Man: Fallen and Free 1969, Square Words in a Round World 1980. *Leisure interests:* music and travel. *Address:* The Palace, Chichester, W. Sussex, PO19 1PY, England. *Telephone:* (01243) 782161. *Fax:* (01243) 531332.

KEMP, Jack F., B.A.; American politician; b. 13 July 1935, L.A.; m. Joanne Main; two s. two d.; ed. Occidental Coll., Long Beach State Univ., Calif., Western Univ.; special Asst. to Gov. of Calif. 1967, to Chair. Republican Nat. Cttee. 1969; mem. 92nd–100th congresses from 31st N.Y. Dist. 1971–89; professional football player for thirteen years; Public Relations officer Marine Midland Bank, Buffalo; Cand. for Republican Pres. nomination 1987–88; Republican Cand. for Vice-Pres. 1996; Sec. of Housing and Urban Devt. 1989–93; Co-Chair. Empower America 1993–; mem. Pres. Council on Physical Fitness and Sports, Exec. Cttee. Player Pension Bd., Nat. Football League, Nat. Asscn. Broadcasters, Engineers and Technicians, Buffalo Area Chamber of Commerce, Sierra Club, American Football League Players Asscn. (co-founder, Pres. 1965–70). *Address:* Empower America, 1776 I Street, N.W., Washington, DC 20006, U.S.A.

KEMP, Martin John, M.A., D.LITT., F.B.A., F.R.S.A., F.R.S.E.; British historian of art and science; b. 5 March 1942, Windsor; s. of Frederick Maurice Kemp and Violet Anne (née Tull) Kemp; m. Jill Lightfoot 1966 (separated 1995); one s. one d.; ed. Windsor Grammar School, Downing Coll., Cambridge and Courtauld Inst. of Art, London Univ.; lecturer in History of Western Art, Dalhousie Univ., N.S., Canada 1965–66; lecturer in History of Fine Art, Univ. of Glasgow 1966–81; Prof. of Fine Arts, Univ. of St. Andrews 1981–90; Prof. of History, Royal Scottish Acad. 1985–; Prof. of History and Theory of Art, Univ. of St. Andrews 1990–95; Prof. of History of Art, Univ. of Oxford 1995–; Fellow Trinity Coll. Oxford 1995–; Provost St. Leonard's Coll., Univ. of St. Andrews 1991–95; mem. Inst. for Advanced Study, Princeton, N.J., U.S.A. 1984–85; Slade Prof., Univ. of Cambridge 1987–88; Benjamin Sonenberg Visiting Prof., Inst. of Fine Arts, New York Univ. 1988; Wiley Visiting Prof., Univ. of N. Carolina, Chapel Hill 1993; British Acad. Wolfson Research Prof. 1993–98; Trustee Nat. Galleries of Scotland 1982–87, Vic. and Albert Museum, London 1986–89, British Museum 1995–, Ashmolean Museum 1995–; Pres. Leonardo da Vinci Soc. 1988–97; Chair. Asscn. of Art Historians 1989–92; mem. Exec. Scottish Museums Council 1990–95; Dir. and Chair. Graeme Murray Gallery 1990–92; mem. Bd. Interalia 1992–, Bd. Museum Training Inst. 1993–98, Council British Soc. for the History of Science 1994–97; mem. Visual Arts Advisory Panel, Arts Council of England 1996–; Hon. mem. American Acad. of Arts and Sciences 1996–; Mitchell Prize 1981; Armand Hammer Prize for Leonardo Studies 1992. *Publications:* Leonardo da Vinci, The Marvellous Works of Nature and Man 1981, Leonardo da Vinci (Co-Author) 1989, The Science of Art, Optical Themes in Western Art from Brunelleschi to Seurat 1990, Behind the Picture. Art and Evidence in the Italian Renaissance 1997. *Leisure interest:* sport, especially hockey. *Address:* Trinity College, Oxford, OX1 3BH, England. *Telephone:* (01865) 278290. *Fax:* (01865) 278299.

KEMPTHORNE, Dirk Arthur, B.S.; American politician; b. 29 Oct. 1951, San Diego; s. of James Henry Kempthorne and Maxine Jesse (Gustason) Kempthorne; m. Patricia Jean Merrill 1977; one s. one d.; ed. Univ. of Idaho; Exec. Asst. to Dir. Idaho Dept. Lands, Boise 1975–78; Exec. Vice-Pres. Idaho Home Builders' Asscn. 1978–81; Campaign Man., Batt for Gov., Boise 1981–82; Idaho Public Affairs Man. FMC Corpn., Boise 1983–86; Mayor of Boise 1986–93; Senator from Idaho 1993–99; Gov. of Idaho 1999–; Chair. U.S. Conf. of Mayors Standing Cttee. on Energy and Environment 1991–93, mem. Advisory Bd. 1991–93; Sec. Nat. Conf. of Republican Mayors and Municipal Elected Officials 1991–93; mem. Bd. of Dirs. Parents and Youth Against Drug Abuse 1987–; Republican. *Address:* Office of the Governor, P.O. Box 83720, Boise, ID 83720, U.S.A.

KEMP-WELCH, John, F.R.S.A.; British stock exchange executive; b. 31 March 1936, Hertford; s. of Peter Kemp-Welch and Peggy Kemp-Welch; m. Diana Leishman 1964; one s. three d.; ed. Winchester Coll.; Hoare & Co. 1954–58; Cazenove & Co. 1959–93, Jt. Sr. Partner 1980–93; Dir. Savoy Hotel PLC 1985–; Dir. London Stock Exchange 1991–, Chair. July 1994–; Chair. Scottish Eastern Investment Trust 1994–, Claridge's Hotel 1995–97; Deputy Chair. Financial Reporting Council 1994–; Vice-Chair. Fed. of European Stock Exchanges 1996–; Dir. Royal and Sun Alliance Insurance Group PLC 1994–, British Invisibles 1994–, Securities and Futures Authority 1994–, ProShare 1995–97. *Address:* 12 Tokenhouse Yard, London, EC2R 7AN, England.

KENDAL, Felicity, C.B.E.; British actress; b. 25 Sept. 1946; d. of Geoffrey and Laura Kendal; m. 1st (divorced); one s.; m. 2nd Michael Rudman 1983 (divorced 1991); one s.; ed. six convents in India; first appeared on stage 1947, at age nine months in A Midsummer Night's Dream; grew up touring India and Far East with parents' theatre co., playing pageboys at age eight and Puck at age nine, graduating to roles such as Viola in Twelfth Night, Jessica in The Merchant of Venice and Ophelia in Hamlet; returned to England 1965; London debut as Carla in Minor Murder, Savoy Theatre 1967. *Other stage roles include:* Katherine in Henry V, Lika in The Promise, Leicester 1968, Amaryllis in Back to Methuselah, Nat. Theatre, Hermia in A Midsummer Night's Dream, Hero in Much Ado About Nothing, Regent's

Park, London 1970, Anne Danby in Kean, Oxford 1970, London 1971; Romeo and Juliet, 'Tis Pity She's a Whore and The Three Arrows 1972; The Norman Conquests, London 1974, Viktosha in Once Upon a Time, Bristol 1976, Arms and The Man, Greenwich 1978, Mara in Clouds, London 1978; Constanza Mozart in Amadeus, Desdemona in Othello; On the Razzle 1981, The Second Mrs. Tanqueray, The Real Thing 1982, Jumpers 1985, Made in Bangkok 1986, Hapgood 1988, Ivanov 1989, Much Ado About Nothing 1989, Hidden Laughter 1990, Tartuffe 1991, Heartbreak House 1992, Arcadia 1992, An Absolute Turkey 1994, Indian Ink 1995, Mind Millie for Me 1996, The Seagull 1997, Waste 1997, Alarms and Excursions 1998. *TV appearances include:* four series of The Good Life; Solo; The Mistress; Honey for Tea; Viola in Twelfth Night 1979, plays and serials including The Camomile Lawn 1992. *Films:* Shakespeare Wallah 1965, Valentino 1976; Variety Club Most Promising Newcomer 1974, Best Actress 1979, Clarence Derwent Award 1980, Evening Standard Best Actress Award 1989. *Publication:* White Cargo (memoirs) 1998. *Address:* c/o Chatto and Linnit, Prince of Wales Theatre, Coventry Street, London, W1V 7FE, England. *Telephone:* 0171-930 6677.

KENDALL, David George, D.SC., SC.D., F.R.S.; British mathematician; b. 15 Jan. 1918, Ripon, Yorkshire; s. of Fritz Ernest Kendall and Emma Taylor; m. Diana Louise Fletcher 1952; two s. four d.; ed. Ripon Grammar School, The Queen's Coll., Oxford; Experimental Officer, Ministry of Supply 1940–45, Fellow, Magdalen Coll., Oxford 1946–62, Emer. Fellow 1989, Prof. of Mathematical Statistics, Univ. of Cambridge 1962–85, Emer. Prof. 1985, Fellow of Churchill Coll. 1962–; Pres. London Mathematical Soc. 1972–74, Bernoulli Soc. 1975, Sections for Mathematics and Physics, British Asscn. 1982; mem. of Council, Royal Soc. 1967–69, 1982–83; mem. Academia Europaea 1991; Hon. mem. Romanian Acad. 1992; Milne Lecturer (Oxford) 1983; Hotelling Lecturer (N. Carolina) 1985; Hon. Fellow Queen's Coll., Oxford 1985; Hon. D. de l'U. (Paris-René Descartes) 1976; Hon. D.Sc. (Bath) 1986; Royal Statistical Soc. Silver Medal 1955, Gold Medal 1981, Weldon Prize and Medal, Oxford Univ. 1974, Royal Soc. Sylvester Medal 1976, London Mathematical Soc. Whitehead Prize 1980, De Morgan Medal 1989, Inst. Math. Statistics Rietz Lecturer 1989, Bernoulli Soc. Kolmogorov Lecturer 1990. *Publications:* Jt. Editor: Mathematics in the Archaeological and Historical Sciences 1971, Stochastic Analysis 1973, Stochastic Geometry 1974, Analytic and Geometric Stochastics 1986. *Leisure interests:* rocketry, astronomy, genealogy, geology. *Address:* Statistical Laboratory, 16 Mill Lane, Cambridge, CB2 1SB (Office); 37 Barrow Road, Cambridge, CB2 2AR, England (Home). *Telephone:* (01223) 337948 (Office); (01223) 353991 (Home).

KENDALL, David William, F.C.A.; British business executive; b. 8 May 1935; s. of William Jack Kendall and Alma May Kendall; m. 1st Delphine Hitchcock 1960 (divorced); one s. one d.; m. 2nd Elisabeth Rollison 1973; one s. one d.; ed. Enfield Grammar School, Southend High School; with Elles Reeve & Co. 1955–62, Shell-Mex & BP Ltd. 1963–68; Finance Dir. Irish Shell & BP Ltd. 1969–70; Crude Oil Sales Man. British Petroleum Co. Ltd. 1971–72, Man. Bulk Trading Div. 1973–74, mem. Org. Planning Cttee. 1975; Gen. Man. BP N.Z. Ltd. 1976–79, Man. Dir. and C.E.O. 1980–82; Chair. BP South West Pacific 1979–82; Finance and Planning Dir. BP Oil Ltd. 1982–85, Man. Dir. and C.E.O. 1985–88; Dir. BP Chemicals Int. 1985–88, BP Oil Int. 1985–88, BP Detergents Int. 1985–88; Deputy Chair. British Coal Corpn. 1989–90; Dir. (non-exec.) Bunzl PLC 1988–90, Chair. 1990–93; Dir. STC PLC 1988–90; Chair. Ruberoid PLC 1993–, Whitecroft PLC 1993–, Meyer Int. PLC 1994–95, Celtic Energy Ltd. 1994–, Wagon Industrial Holdings PLC 1997–; Non-exec. Dir. Blagden Industries PLC 1993–94, Chair. 1994–; Dir. Danka Business Systems PLC 1993–, Gowrings 1993–, South Wales Electricity PLC 1993–96; Pres. U.K. Petroleum Industries Asscn. 1987–88, Oil Industries Club 1988. *Leisure interests:* golf, music. *Address:* 41 Albion Street, London, W2 2AU, England. *Telephone:* 0171-258 1955.

KENDELL, Robert Evan, C.B.E., M.A., M.D., F.R.C.P., F.R.C.P. (E), F.R.C.PSYCH., F.R.S.E., F.MED.SCI; British psychiatrist, civil servant and university teacher; b. 28 March 1935, Rotherham, Yorks.; s. of Robert Owen Kendell and Joan Evans; m. Ann Whitfield 1961; two s. two d.; ed. Mill Hill School, Peterhouse, Cambridge, King's Coll. Hosp. Medical School, London; psychiatric training, Maudsley Hosp., London 1962–66; Visiting Prof., Univ. of Vermont Coll. of Medicine, U.S.A 1969–70; Reader in Psychiatry, Inst. of Psychiatry, Univ. of London 1970–74; Prof. of Psychiatry, Univ. of Edin. 1974–91, Dean of Faculty of Medicine 1986–90; Chief Medical Officer, Scottish Office Home and Health Dept. 1991–96; Pres., Royal Coll. of Psychiatrists 1996–; mem. WHO Expert Advisory Panel on Mental Health 1979–91; Chair. WHO Expert Cttee. on Problems related to Alcohol Consumption 1979; mem. MRC 1984–88; H.B. Williams Travelling Prof. of Royal Australian and N.Z. Coll. of Psychiatrists 1981; Gaskell Gold Medal, Royal Coll. of Psychiatrists 1967; Paul Hoch Medal of the American Psychopathological Asscn. 1988. *Publications:* The Classification of Depressive Illnesses 1968, Psychiatric Diagnosis in New York and London 1972, The Role of Diagnosis in Psychiatry 1975, Companion to Psychiatric Studies (Ed.) 1983, 1988, 1993. *Leisure interests:* over-eating, walking up hills. *Address:* Royal College of Psychiatrists, 17 Belgrave Square, London, SW1X 8PG, England (Office); 3 West Castle Road, Edin., EH10 5AT, Scotland. *Telephone:* 0171-235 2351 (Office); (0131) 229 4966 (Home). *Fax:* 0171-245 1231 (Office).

KENEALLY, Thomas Michael, A.O., F.R.S.L.; Australian author; b. 7 Oct. 1935, Sydney; s. of Edmund Thomas and Elsie Margaret Keneally; m. Judith Mary Martin 1965; two d.; Lecturer in Drama, Univ. of New England, Armidale, N.S.W. 1968–70; Visiting Prof. Univ. of Calif., Irvine 1985; Berg Prof., Dept. of English, New York Univ. 1988; Pres. Nat. Book Council of Australia –1987; Chair. Australian Soc. of Authors 1987–90, Pres. 1990–; Prof. Dept. of English and Comparative Literature, Univ. of Calif. at Irvine 1991–95; mem. Literary Arts Bd. 1985–; mem. Australia-China Council; mem. American Acad. of Arts and Sciences; Founding Chair. Australian Republican Movt. 1991–93; Hon. D.Lit. (Univ. of Queensland), (Univ. of Ireland) 1994; Hon. D.Litt (Fairleigh Dickenson Univ., U.S.A.) 1996, (Rollins Coll., U.S.A.) 1996; Royal Soc. of Literature Prize, Booker Prize 1982 (for Schindler's Ark), Los Angeles Times Fiction Prize 1983. *Publications:* Bring Larks and Heroes 1967, Three Cheers for the Paraclete 1968, The Survivor 1969, A Dutiful Daughter 1970, The Chant of Jimmie Blacksmith 1972, Blood Red, Sister Rose 1974, Gossip from the Forest 1975, Season in Purgatory 1976, A Victim of the Aurora 1977, Passenger 1978, Confederates 1979, Schindler's Ark 1982, Outback 1983, The Cut-Rate Kingdom 1984, A Family Madness 1985, Australia: Beyond the Dreamtime (contrib.) 1987, The Playmaker 1987, Towards Asmara 1989, Flying Hero Class 1991, Now and in Time to Be: Ireland and the Irish 1992, Woman of the Inner Sea 1992, The Place Where Souls Are Born: A Journey into the American Southwest 1992, Jacko: The Great Intruder 1993, The Utility Player—the story of Des Hassler (non-fiction) 1993, Our Republic (non-fiction) 1993, A River Town 1995, Homebush Boy: A Memoir 1995, The Great Shame 1998. *Leisure interest:* cross-country skiing. *Address:* Hickson Associates, PO Box 271, Woollahra, N.S.W. 2025, Australia.

KENGO WA DONDO, Leon, LL.D.; Democratic Republic of the Congo politician, lawyer and diplomatist; b. 1935; fmr. Procurator-Gen. and Pres. of Judicial Council of Zaire; Minister of Justice 1979–80; Amb. to Belgium 1980–82; First State Commr. 1982–86, 1988–90; State Comm. for Foreign Affairs 1986–87; elected Prime Minister of Zaire (now Democratic Repub. of Congo) by Parl. of Transition and High Council of Repub. 1994–97.

KENILOREA, Rt. Hon. Sir Peter, DIP. ED.; Solomon Islands politician; b. 23 May 1943, Takataka, Malaita; m. Margaret Kwanairara 1971; two s. two d.; ed. Teachers' Coll. in New Zealand; Schoolmaster, King George VI Secondary School 1968–70; Asst. Sec. Finance 1971; Admin. Officer, district admin. 1971–73; Lands Officer 1973–74; Deputy Sec. to Cabinet and to Chief Minister 1974–75; District Commr., Eastern Solomons 1975–76; mem. Legis. Assembly 1976–78; M.P. for East Are–Are 1976–; Chief Minister of the Solomon Islands 1976–78; Prime Minister of Solomon Islands 1978–81, 1984–86; Deputy Prime Minister 1986–89, Minister of Foreign Affairs 1988–89, of Foreign Affairs and Trade Relations 1990; Ombudsman 1996–; Dir. S. Pacific Forum Fisheries Agency 1991–94; Queen's Silver Jubilee Medal 1977. *Publications:* numerous articles for political and scientific publications. *Leisure interests:* reading, sports. *Address:* Kalala House, P.O. Box 535, Honiara, Guadalcanal, Solomon Islands.

KENNAN, George Frost, A.B.; American diplomatist and scholar; b. 16 Feb. 1904, Milwaukee, Wis.; m. Annelise Sørensen 1931; one s. three d.; ed. Princeton Univ.; Vice-Consul Hamburg 1927, Tallin 1928; Third Sec. Riga, Kovno and Tallin 1929; Language Officer, Berlin 1929; Third Sec. Riga 1931, Moscow 1934; Consul Vienna 1935, Second Sec. 1935; Second Sec. Moscow 1935; Dept. of State 1937; Second Sec. Prague 1938, Consul 1939; Second Sec. Berlin 1939, First Sec. 1940; Counsellor, Lisbon 1942; Counsellor to U.S. del. European Advisory Comm. London 1944; Minister-Counsellor Moscow 1945; Deputy for Foreign Affairs, Nat. War Coll., Washington 1946; Policy Planning Staff, Dept. of State 1947; Chief, Policy Planning Staff, Dept. of State 1949–50; on leave, at Inst. for Advanced Study, Princeton, N.J. 1950–51, Prof. 1956; Amb. to U.S.S.R. 1952–53; retd. from Foreign Service 1953; Charles R. Walgreen Foundation Lecturer, Univ. of Chicago 1951; Stafford Little Lecturer, Princeton 1954; George Eastman Visiting Prof. Oxford Univ. 1957–58; Reith Lecturer on Russia, The Atom and the West 1957; Visiting Lecturer, History, Harvard Univ. 1960, Yale Univ. 1960; Amb. to Yugoslavia 1961–63; Prof. Inst. for Advanced Study, Princeton 1963–74, Prof. Emer. 1974–; Prof. Princeton Univ. 1964–66; mem. Nat. Inst. of Arts and Letters (Pres. 1965–68); American Acad. of Arts and Letters (Pres. 1967–71); Univ. Fellow in History and Slavic Civilizations; Harvard Univ. 1966–70; Fellow, All Souls Coll., Oxford 1969; Fellow, Woodrow Wilson Int. Center for Scholars, Smithsonian Inst. 1974–75; Nat. Book Award, Bancroft Prize, Pulitzer Prize history 1956, biography 1968, Francis Parkman Prize; LL.D. h.c. (Yale, Dartmouth, Colgate, Notre Dame, Kenyon, Princeton, Michigan, Northwestern, Brandeis, Denison, Harvard, Rutgers, Wisconsin Univs., Lake Forest, Clark, Oberlin, Brown, William & Mary Coll., Columbia, New York), Hon. D.C.L. (Oxford) 1969; Hon. degrees (Univ. of Helsinki) 1986, (Rider Coll.) 1988; Benjamin Franklin Fellow of the Royal Soc. of Arts, London 1968; Albert Einstein Peace Prize 1981; Grenville Clarke Prize 1981; Peace Prize of the W. German Book Trade 1982, Union Medal, Union Theological Seminary 1982, American Acad. and Inst. of Arts and Letters Gold Medal for History 1984, Freedom from Fear Medal, Franklin D. Roosevelt Foundation, Physicians for Social Responsibility Annual Award 1988, Toynbee Award 1988, Encyclopedia Britannica Award 1989, Presidential Medal of Freedom 1989, Gov.'s Award (of N.J.) 1989. *Publications:* American Diplomacy 1900-1950 1952, Das Amerikanisch-Russische Verhältnis 1954, Realities of American Foreign Policy 1954, Soviet-American Relations 1917–1920, Vol. I, Russia Leaves the War 1956, Vol. II, The Decision to Intervene 1958, Russia, The Atom and the West (Reith Lectures) 1958, Soviet Foreign Policy 1917–45 1960, Russia and the West under Lenin and Stalin 1961, On Dealing with the Communist World 1963, Memoirs 1925–1950 1967, Democracy and the Student Left 1968, From Prague After Munich: Diplomatic Papers 1938–1940 1968, The Marquis de Custine and his "Russia in 1839" 1971, Memoirs 1950–1963 1972, The Cloud of Danger 1977, The Decline of Bismarck's European Order: Franco-Russian Relations 1875–1890 1979, The Nuclear Delusion: Soviet-American Relations in the Atomic Age 1982, The Fateful Alliance 1984, Sketches from a Life 1989, Around the Cragged Hill, A Personal and Political Philosophy 1993, At a Century's Ending: Reflections 1982–95 1996. *Address:* Institute for Advanced Study, Princeton, NJ 08540, U.S.A.

KENNARD, Olga, SC.D., F.R.S., O.B.E.; British research scientist; b. 23 March 1924, Budapest, Hungary; d. of Joir Weisz and Catherina Weisz; m. 1st David Kennard 1948 (divorced 1961); two d.; m. 2nd Sir Arnold Burgen (q.v.) 1993; ed. schools in Hungary, Prince Henry VIII Grammar School, Evesham and Newnham Coll. Cambridge; Research Asst. Cavendish Lab. Cambridge 1944–48; MRC Scientific Staff, London 1948–61; MRC External Scientific Staff, Univ. of Cambridge 1961–89; Dir. Cambridge Crystallographic Data Centre 1965–97; MRC Special Appt. 1969–89; Visiting Prof., Univ. of London 1988–90; mem. Academia Europaea; Royal Soc. Chem. Prize for Structural Chem. 1980. *Publications:* about 200 papers in scientific journals and books on X-ray crystallography, molecular biology, information technology; 20 scientific reference books. *Leisure interests:* swimming, music, modern architecture and design. *Address:* Keelson, 8A Hills Avenue, Cambridge, CB1 4XA, England. *Telephone:* (01223) 415381.

KENNARD, William; American lawyer and government official; b. 19 Jan. 1957; m. Deborah D. Kennedy 1984; ed. Stanford and Yale Univs.; fmrly. with Nat. Asscn. of Broadcasters and in pvt. practice specialising in telecommunications law; Gen. Counsel to Fed. Communications Comm. 1993–97, Chair. Oct. 1997–. *Address:* Federal Communications Commission, 1919 M Street, NW, Washington, DC 20554, U.S.A.

KENNEDY, Anthony M., LL.B.; American judge; b. 23 July 1936, Sacramento; s. of Anthony J. Kennedy and Gladys Kennedy; m. Mary Davis; two s. one d.; ed. Stanford and Harvard Univs. and London School of Econs. and Political Science; mem. Calif. Bar 1962, U.S. Tax Court Bar 1971; Assoc. Thelen, Marrin, Johnson & Bridges, San Francisco 1961–63; sole practice, Sacramento 1963–67; partner, Evans, Jackson & Kennedy (law firm) 1967–75; Prof. of Constitutional Law, McGeorge School of Law, Univ. of Pacific 1965; Judge, U.S. Court of Appeals, 9th Circuit, Sacramento 1976–88; Judge Supreme Court of U.S.A. Jan. 1988–. *Address:* Supreme Court Building, 1 First Street, N.E., Washington, DC 20543, U.S.A.

KENNEDY, Charles Peter, M.A.; British politician, journalist and broadcaster; b. 25 Nov. 1959, Inverness; s. of Ian Kennedy and Mary McVarish MacEachen; ed. Lochaber High School, Fort William and Univ. of Glasgow; journalist, BBC Highland, Inverness 1982; Fulbright Scholar and Assoc. Instr. Dept. of Speech Communication, Indiana Univ. Bloomington Campus 1982–83; M.P. for Ross, Cromarty and Skye 1983–97, for Ross, Skye and Inverness W. 1997–; mem. Social Democratic Party 1983–88, Liberal Democrats 1988– (spokesperson on Trade and Industry 1988–89, on Health 1989–92, on Europe and E.-W. relations 1992–97, on Agric. and Rural Affairs 1997–); Pres. Liberal Democrats 1990–94. *Address:* House of Commons, London SW1A 0AA, England. *Telephone:* 0171-219 5090.

KENNEDY, Donald, M.A., PH.D.; American academic; b. 18 Aug. 1931, New York; s. of William D. and Barbara (Bean) Kennedy; m. 1st Barbara J. Dewey 1953; two d.; m. 2nd Robin Beth Wiseman 1987; two step-s.; ed. Harvard Univ.; Asst. Prof. Syracuse Univ. 1956–59, Assoc. Prof. 1959–60; Asst. Prof. Stanford Univ. 1960–62, Assoc. Prof. 1962–65, Prof. 1965–77, Chair. Dept. of Biological Sciences 1965–72, Benjamin Crocker Prof. of Human Biology 1974–77, Vice-Pres. and Provost 1979–80, Pres. 1980–92, Pres. Emer. and Bing Prof. of Environmental Science 1992–; Sr. Consultant, Office of Science and Tech. Policy, Exec. Office of the Pres. 1976–77; Commr. of Food and Drug Admin. 1977–79; Fellow, American Acad. of Arts and Sciences; mem. N.A.S.; Dinkelspiel Award 1976; Hon. D.Sc. (Columbia Univ., Williams Coll., Michigan, Rochester, Ariz.). *Publications:* The Biology of Organisms (with W. M. Telfer) 1965, Academic Duty 1997; over 60 articles in scientific journals. *Leisure interests:* skiing, fly fishing, natural history. *Address:* Stanford University, Institute for International Studies, Encina Hall 200, Stanford, CA 94305, U.S.A.

KENNEDY, Eamon, M.A., PH.D.; Irish diplomatist; b. 13 Dec. 1921, Dublin; s. of Luke W. and Ellen (née Stafford) Kennedy; m. Barbara J. Black 1960; one s. one d.; ed. Univ. Coll. Nat. Univ. of Ireland, Dublin; Third Sec., Dept. of Foreign Affairs, Dublin 1943; Consul, New York 1947; Second Sec., Ottawa 1947–49; First Sec., Washington 1949–50, Paris 1950–54; First Sec. and Acting Chief of Protocol, Dept. of Foreign Affairs 1954–56; Counsellor, Irish Mission to UN 1956–61; Irish del. to UN Gen. Assembly 1956–60; Amb. to Nigeria 1961–64, to Fed. Repub. of Germany 1964–70, to France 1970–74; Perm. Rep. to OECD, Perm. del. to UNESCO 1970–74; Perm. Rep. to UN 1974–78; Amb. to U.K. 1978–83, to Italy (also accred. to Turkey and Libya) 1983–86; Special Adviser, with rank of Amb., Perm. Mission of Ireland to the UN 1987–; Grosses Bundesverdienstkreuz mit Stern, Grand Croix de Mérite de la Répub. Française. *Leisure interests:* golf, languages, theatre, music. *Address:* 525 East 86th Street, Apartment 17-D, New York, NY 10028; 6730 Nassau Point Road, Cutchogue, NY 11935, U.S.A. *Telephone:* (212) 249-8262; (516) 734-7790.

KENNEDY, Edward Moore, A.B., LL.B.; American politician and lawyer; b. 22 Feb. 1932, Boston, Mass.; s. of late Joseph Kennedy and of Rose Kennedy; brother of late Pres. John F. Kennedy; m. 1st Virginia Joan Bennett 1958 (divorced 1982); two s. one d.; m. 2nd Victoria Annie Reggie 1992; ed. Milton Acad., Harvard Coll. and Univ. of Virginia Law School; U.S. Army, Infantry, Private 1st Class 1951–53; Reporter, Int. News Service, N. Africa 1956; Man. Western States, John F. Kennedy Presidential Campaign 1960; fmr. Asst. District Attorney, Mass.; U.S. Senator from Massachusetts 1962–; Asst. Majority Leader, U.S. Senate 1969–71; Chair. Senate Judiciary Comm. 1979–81, ranking Democrat Labour and Human Resources Cttee. 1981–; Pres. Joseph P. Kennedy Jr. Foundation 1961–; Trustee, Boston Univ., Boston Symphony, John F. Kennedy Library, Lahey Clinic, Boston, John F. Kennedy Center for the Performing Arts, Robert F. Kennedy Memorial Foundation; Bd. mem. Fletcher School of Law and Diplomacy, Mass. Gen. Hospital; mem. Bd. Advisers, Dunbarton Oaks Research Library and Collections; numerous hon. degrees; Order of the Phoenix (Greece) 1976; Harvard Univ. John F. Kennedy School of Govt. Medal 1986; Democrat. *Publications:* Decisions for a Decade 1968, In Critical Condition 1972, Our Day and Generation 1979, Freeze: how you can help prevent nuclear war (with Senator Mark Hatfield, q.v.) 1979. *Address:* U.S. Senate, Senate Office Building, 315 Russell Senate Building, Washington, DC 20510, U.S.A.

KENNEDY, Eugene Patrick, B.SC., PH.D.; American professor of biological chemistry; b. 4 Sept. 1919, Chicago; s. of Michael and Catherine Frawley Kennedy; m. Adelaide Majewski 1943; three d.; ed. De Paul Univ. and Univ. of Chicago; Asst. Prof., Ben May Lab., Univ. of Chicago 1952–55, Assoc. Prof. 1955–56, Prof. of Biological Chem. 1956–60; Prof. and Head, Dept. of Biological Chem., Harvard Medical School 1960–65, Hamilton Kuhn Prof. of Biological Chem., Harvard Medical School 1960–; Assoc. Ed. Journal of Biological Chemistry 1969; Pres. American Soc. of Biol. Chemists 1970–71; mem. N.A.S., American Acad. of Arts and Sciences, American Philosophical Soc.; Hon. D.Sc. (Chicago) 1977; Glycerine Research Award 1956; Paul-Lewis Award, American Chem. Soc. 1959; Lipid Chem. Award of the American Oil Chemists Soc. 1970, Josiah Macy, Jr. Foundation Faculty Scholar Award 1974, Gairdner Foundation Award 1976, George Ledlie Prize (Harvard) 1976, Sr. U.S. Scientist Award, Alexander von Humboldt Foundation 1983, Passano Award 1986, Heinrich Wieland Prize 1986. *Address:* Department of Biological Chemistry, Harvard Medical School, 25 Shattuck Street, Boston, MA 02115; 221 Mount Auburn Street, Cambridge, MA 02138, U.S.A.

KENNEDY, George Danner, B.A.,; American business executive; b. 30 May 1926, Pittsburgh, Pa.; s. of Thomas Reed and Lois (Smith) Kennedy; m. Valerie Putis 1972; three s. one d.; ed. Williams Coll.; Scott Paper Co. 1947–52; Champion Paper Co. 1952–65; Pres. Brown Co. 1965–71; Exec. Vice-Pres., IMCERA (fmrly. Int. Minerals & Chemical Corpn.) 1971–78, Dir. 1975, Pres. 1978–86, C.E.O. 1983–93, Chair. of Bd. IMCERA (now Mallinckrodt Group) 1986–; Dir. SCM Corpn. 1978–82; Dir. Brunswick Corpn. 1979; Dir., Exec. Cttee., Kemper Group and Foundation 1982; Dir. Ill. Tool Works 1988; Bd. Chair. Children's Memorial Hosp., Chicago; Vice-Pres., Dir. N.E. Ill. Boy Scout Council; Trustee Nat. Comm. Against Drunk Driving, Chicago Symphony. *Address:* P.O. Box 559, Winnetka, IL 60093, U.S.A.

KENNEDY, James C., B.B.A.; American publishing and media executive; b. 1947; m.; ed. Univ. of Denver; with Atlanta Newspapers 1976–79; Pres. Grand Junction Newspapers 1979–80; Publr. Grand Junction Daily Sentinel 1980–85; Vice-Pres. newspaper Div. Cox Enterprises Inc. 1985–86, Exec. Vice-Pres., Pres. 1986–87, C.O.O., Chair. 1987–; Chair., C.E.O. Cox Enterprises Inc. 1988–. *Address:* Cox Enterprises Inc., P.O. Box 105357, Atlanta, GA 30348 (Office); 1601 W. Peachtree Street North East, Atlanta, GA 30309, U.S.A. (Home).

KENNEDY, Sir Ludovic Henry Coverley, Kt., M.A., F.R.S.L.; British writer and broadcaster; b. 3 Nov. 1919, Edinburgh; s. of late Capt. E. C. Kennedy, R.N., and of Rosalind Kennedy; m. Moira Shearer King (q.v.) 1950; one s. three d.; ed. Eton Coll., Christ Church, Oxford; served in R.N. 1939–46 (attained rank of Lieut.); Pvt. Sec. and A.D.C. to Gov. of Newfoundland 1943–44; Librarian, Ashridge (Adult Educ.) Coll. 1949; Ed., feature, First Reading (BBC Third Programme) 1953–54; Lecturer for British Council, Sweden, Finland, Denmark 1955, Belgium, Luxembourg 1956; contested Rochdale by-election 1958, gen. election 1959 as Liberal candidate; Pres. Nat. League of Young Liberals 1959–61, mem. Liberal Party Council 1965–67; TV and radio: introduced Profile, ATV 1955–56; newscaster, ITV 1956–58; introducer On Stage, Associated Rediffusion 1957, This Week, Associated Rediffusion 1958–59; Chair. BBC features: Your Verdict 1962, Your Witness 1967–70; commentator BBC's Panorama 1960–63, Television Reports Int. (also producer) 1963–64; introducer BBC's Time Out 1964–65, World at One 1965–66; presenter Liberal Party's Gen. Election TV Broadcasts 1966, The Middle Years, ABC 1967, The Nature of Prejudice, ATV 1968, Face The Press, Tyne-Tees 1968–69, 1970–72, Against the Tide, Yorkshire TV 1969, Living and Growing, Grampian TV 1969–70, 24 Hours, BBC 1969–72, Ad Lib, BBC 1970–72, Midweek, BBC 1973–75, Newsday, BBC 1975–76, Tonight, BBC 1976–80, A Life with Crime BBC 1979, presenter Lord Mountbatten Remembers 1980, Change of Direction 1980, Did You See BBC 1980–88, Great Railway Journeys of the World BBC 1980, Chair. Indelible Evidence BBC 1987, 1990, A Gift of the Gab BBC 1989, Portrait BBC 1989; mem. Council Navy Records Soc. 1957–70; Pres. Sir Walter Scott Club, Edin. 1968–69; Chair. Royal Lyceum Theatre Co. of Edin. 1977–84; Chair. Judges,

NCR Book Award 1990–91; Pres. Voluntary Euthanasia Soc. 1995–; F.R.S.A. 1974–76; Voltaire Memorial Lecturer 1985; Hon. D.L. (Strathclyde) 1985, (Southampton) 1993; Dr. h.c. (Edin.) 1990, (Stirling) 1991; Richard Dimbleby Award (BAFTA) 1989, Bar Council Special Award 1992; Cross First Class, Order of Merit (Fed. Repub. of Germany). *Films include:* The Sleeping Ballerina, The Singers and the Songs, Scapa Flow, Battleship Bismarck, Life and Death of the Scharnhorst, U-Boat War, Target Tirpitz, The Rise of the Red Navy, Lord Haw-Haw, Who Killed the Lindbergh Baby?, Elizabeth: The First Thirty Years, A Life of Richard Dimbleby, Happy Birthday, dear Ma'am, Murder in Belgravia: The Lucan Affair, Princess to Queen. *Publications:* Sub-Lieutenant 1942, Nelson's Band of Brothers 1951, One Man's Meat 1953, Murder Story 1956, Ten Rillington Place 1961, The Trial of Stephen Ward 1964, Very Lovely People 1969, Pursuit: the Chase and Sinking of the Bismarck 1974, A Presumption of Innocence: the Amazing Case of Patrick Meehan 1975, The Portland Spy Case 1978, Wicked Beyond Belief: The Luton Post Office Murder Case 1980, A Book of Railway Journeys 1980, A Book of Sea Journeys 1981, A Book of Air Journeys 1982, Menace; The Life and Death of the Tirpitz 1979, The Airman and the Carpenter: The Lindbergh Case and the Framing of Richard Hauptmann 1985, On My Way to the Club (autobiog.) 1989, Euthanasia: The Good Death 1990, Truth to Tell (collected writings) 1991, In Bed with an Elephant: A Journey through Scotland's Past and Present 1995, All in the Mind: A Farewell to God 1999; Gen. Ed. The British at War 1973–77. *Address:* c/o Rogers, Coleridge and White, 20 Powis Mews, London, W11 1JN, England.

KENNEDY, Michael, C.B.E., M.A., F.R.N.C.M.; British journalist and critic; b. 19 Feb. 1926, Manchester; s. of Hew G. and Marian F. Kennedy; m. Eslyn Durdle 1947; ed. Berkhamsted School; staff music critic, The Daily Telegraph 1950–, Northern Ed. 1960–86; music critic, The Sunday Telegraph 1989–; Gov. Royal Northern Coll. of Music; Hon. mem. Royal Manchester Coll. of Music 1971; Hon. M.A. (Manchester) 1975. *Publications:* The Hallé Tradition 1960, The Works of Ralph Vaughan Williams 1964, Portrait of Elgar 1968, History of Royal Manchester College of Music 1971, Barbirolli 1971, Portrait of Manchester 1971, Mahler 1974, Strauss 1976, Britten 1980, Concise Oxford Dictionary of Music 1980, Oxford Dictionary of Music 1985, Adrian Boult 1987, Portrait of Walton 1989, Music Enriches All: The First 21 Years of the RNCM, Manchester 1973–94 1994, Richard Strauss, Man, Musician, Enigma 1999. *Leisure interest:* cricket. *Address:* 3 Moorwood Drive, Sale, Cheshire, M33 4QB, England. *Telephone:* (0161) 973-7225.

KENNEDY, Nigel; British violinist; b. 28 Dec. 1956; s. of John Kennedy and Scylla Stoner; partner Eve Westmore; one s.; ed. Yehudi Menuhin School, Juilliard School of Performing Arts; chosen by the BBC as the subject of a five-year documentary on the devt. of a soloist following his début with the Philharmonia Orchestra 1977; has since appeared with all the maj. British orchestras; has made appearances at all the leading U.K. festivals and in Europe at Stresa, Lucerne, Gstaad, Berlin and Lockenhaus; début at the Tanglewood Festival with the Boston Symphony under André Previn 1985, at Minn. with Sir Neville Marriner, at Montreal with Charles Dutoit; has given concerts in the field of jazz with Stephane Grappelli at Carnegie Hall and Edin. and runs his own jazz group; recordings include the Elgar Sonata with Peter Pettinger (Chandos Records), Tchaikovsky, Sibelius, Vivaldi, Mendelssohn, Bruch, Walton Viola and Violin Concertos, and the Elgar Concerto with the London Philharmonic Orchestra (EMI/Eminence); Sr. Vice-Pres. Aston Villa FC 1990–; Hon. D.Litt. (Bath) 1991; for his recording of the Elgar Concerto he received the Record of the Year nomination by Gramophone Magazine Feb. 1985 and received the Best Classical Disc of the Year award, London 1985. *Publication:* Always Playing 1991. *Address:* c/o Russells (Solicitors), Regency House, 1–4 Warwick Street, London, W1R 5WB, England.

KENNEDY, Paul Michael, M.A., D.PHIL., F.R.HIST.S.; British historian; b. 17 June 1945, Wallsend; s. of John Patrick Kennedy and Margaret (née Hennessy) Kennedy; m. Catherine Urwin 1967; three s.; ed. St. Cuthbert's Grammar School, Newcastle upon Tyne, Univ. of Newcastle and Oxford Univ.; Research Asst. to Sir Basil Liddell Hart 1966–70; lecturer, Reader and Prof., Univ. of E. Anglia 1970–83; J. Richardson Dilworth Prof. of History, Yale Univ. 1983–, Dir. Int. Security Studies 1988–; Visiting Fellow, Inst. for Advanced Study, Princeton 1978–79; Fellow, Alexander von Humboldt Foundation; Hon. D.H.L. (New Haven, Alfred, Long Island, Connecticut); Hon. D.Litt. (Newcastle, East Anglia); Hon. LL.D. (Ohio); Hon. M.A. (Yale). *Publications:* The Samoan Tangle 1974, The Rise and Fall of British Naval Mastery 1976, The Rise of the Anglo-German Antagonism 1980, The Realities Behind Diplomacy 1981, Strategy and Diplomacy 1983, The Rise and Fall of the Great Powers 1988, Grand Strategy in War and Peace 1991, Preparing for the Twenty-First Century 1993. *Leisure interests:* soccer, hill-walking, old churches. *Address:* Department of History, Yale Univ., P.O. Box 208324, New Haven, CT 06520, U.S.A. *Telephone:* (203) 432-6246 (Office).

KENNEDY, William Joseph, B.A.; American author and professor of English; b. 16 Jan. 1928, Albany, New York; s. of William J. Kennedy and Mary E. McDonald; m. Ana Segarra 1957; one s. two d.; ed. Siena Coll.; Asst. Sports Ed., columnist, Glens Falls Post Star, New York 1949–50; reporter, Albany Times-Union, New York 1952–56, special writer 1963–70; Asst. Man. Ed., columnist, P.R. World Journal, San Juan 1956; reporter, Miami Herald 1957; corresp. Time-Life Publs., Puerto Rico 1957–59; reporter, Knight Newspapers 1957–59; Founding Man. Ed. San Juan Star 1959–61; lecturer, State Univ. of New York, Albany 1974–82, Prof. of English 1983–; Visiting Prof. Cornell Univ. 1982–83; founder, N.Y. State Writers' Inst. 1983; Nat. Endowment for Arts Fellow 1981, MacArthur Foundation Fellow 1983, Gov. of New York Arts Award 1984, Creative Arts Award, Brandeis Univ. 1986; Pulitzer Prize and Nat. Book Critics Circle Award 1984 for Ironweed; several hon. degrees. *Publications include:* The Ink Truck 1969, Legs 1975, Billy Phelan's Greatest Game 1978, Ironweed 1983, O Albany! (non-fiction) 1983, Charlie Malarkey and the Belly Button Machine (children's book) 1986, Quinn's Book 1988, Very Old Bones 1992, Riding the Yellow Trolley Car 1993, Charlie Malarkey and the Singing Moose (children's book) 1994, The Flaming Corsage 1996, Grand View (play) 1996; film scripts, The Cotton Club 1984, Ironweed 1987; also short stories, articles in professional journals. *Address:* NYS Writers Institute, Washington Avenue, Albany, NY 12222, U.S.A.

KENNEDY OF THE SHAWS, Baroness (Life Peer) cr. 1997, of Cathcart in the City of Glasgow, **Helena Ann Kennedy,** Q.C., F.R.S.A.; British lawyer; b. 12 May 1950; d. of Joshua Kennedy and Mary Jones; partner (Roger) Iain Mitchell 1978–84; one s.; m. Dr Iain L. Hutchison 1986; one s. one d.; ed. Holyrood Secondary School, Glasgow and Council of Legal Educ.; called to the Bar, Gray's Inn 1972; mem. Bar Council 1990–93; mem. CIBA Comm. into Child Sexual Abuse 1981–83; mem. Bd. City Limits Magazine 1982–84, New Statesman 1990–96, Counsel Magazine 1990–; mem. Council, Howard League for Penal Reform 1989–, Chair. Comm. of Inquiry into Violence in Penal Insts. for Young People (report 1995); Commr. BAFTA inquiry into future of BBC 1990, Hamlyn Nat. Comm. on Educ. 1991–; Visiting lecturer, British Postgrad. Medical Fed. 1991–; Adviser, Mannheim Inst. on Criminology, L.S.E. 1992–; Leader of inquiry into health, environmental and safety aspects of Atomic Weapons Establishment, Aldermaston (report 1994); Chancellor, Oxford Brookes Univ. 1994–; Chair. British Council 1998–; author of official report (Learning Works) for Further Educ. Funding Council on widening participation in further educ. 1997; Hon. Fellow Inst. of Advanced Legal Studies, Univ. of London 1997; mem. Advisory Bd., Int. Centre for Prison Studies 1998; Chair. London Int. Festival of Theatre, Standing Cttee. for Youth Justice; fmr. Chair. Charter 88 (resgnd.); Pres. London Marriage Guidance Council, Birth Control Campaign, Nat. Children's Bureau, Hillcroft Coll.; Vice-Pres. Haldane Soc., Nat. Ass. of Women; mem. British Council's Law Advisory Cttee. Advisory Bd. for Study of Women and Gender, Warwick Univ.; Hon. mem. Council, Nat. Soc. for Prevention of Cruelty to Children; presenter of various programmes on radio and TV and creator of BBC drama series Blind Justice 1988; Patron, Liberty; 12 hon. degrees; Women's Network Award 1992, UK Woman of Europe Award 1995; Campaigning and Influencing Award, Nat. Fed. of Women's Insts. 1996, Times Newspaper Lifetime Achievement Award in the Law (jtly.) 1997; Hon. LL.D (Wolverhampton) 1997, (Leicester) 1998. *Publications:* The Bar on Trial (jtly.) 1978, Child Abuse Within the Family (jtly.) 1984, Balancing Acts (jtly.) 1989, Eve was Framed 1992; articles on legal matters, civil liberties and women. *Leisure interests:* theatre, spending time with family and friends. *Address:* House of Lords, London, SW1A 0PW, England. *Telephone:* (01708) 379482. *Fax:* (01708) 379482.

KENNET, (2nd Baron) cr. 1935, of the Dene; **Wayland Young,** F.R.I.B.A.; British politician and writer; b. 2 Aug. 1923, London; s. of Edward Hilton Young (Lord Kennet) and Kathleen Bruce; m. Elizabeth Ann Adams 1948; one s. five d.; ed. Stowe School, Trinity Coll., Cambridge; Royal Navy 1942–45; Foreign Office 1946–47, 1949–51; Corresp. for Observer newspaper in Western Mediterranean countries 1953–55; mem. Parl. Assembly Council of Europe and Western European Union 1962–65; Chair. British Cttee. for International Co-operation Year 1965; Parl. Sec. Ministry of Housing and Local Govt. 1966–70; Chair. Int. Parl. Confs. on the Environment 1971–78; Chair. Advisory Cttee. on Oil Pollution of the Sea 1970–74; Chair. Council for the Protection of Rural England 1971–72; Opposition Spokesman on Foreign Affairs and Science Policy, House of Lords 1971–74; Dir. Europe Plus Thirty Project 1974–75; mem. European Parl. 1978–79; Chief Whip S.D.P., House of Lords 1981–83, Spokesman on Foreign Affairs and Defence 1981–90; Vice-Chair. Parl. Office of Science and Tech. 1989–93; Vice-Pres. Parl. and Scientific Cttee. 1989–98; rejoined Labour Party 1990; Pres. Architecture Club 1984–94; mem. North Atlantic Ass. 1997–. *Publications:* The Italian Left 1949, The Deadweight 1952, Now or Never 1953, Old London Churches (with Elizabeth Young) 1956, The Montesi Scandal 1957, Still Alive Tomorrow 1958, Strategy for Survival 1959, The Profumo Affair 1963, Eros Denied 1965, Preservation 1972, The Futures of Europe 1976, London's Churches (with Elizabeth Young) 1986, Northern Lazio: An Unknown Italy (with Elizabeth Young) 1990; Ed. Disarmament and Arms Control 1963–65, The Rebirth of Britain 1982, Parliaments and Screening 1994, The Italian Encyclopedia 1998. *Leisure interests:* sailing, swimming, music. *Address:* House of Lords, London, SW1A 0PW, England.

KENNEY, Edward John, M.A., F.B.A.; British professor of Latin; b. 29 Feb. 1924, London; s. of George Kenney and Emmie Carlina Elfrida Schwenke; m. Gwyneth Anne Harris; ed. Christ's Hosp. and Trinity Coll. Cambridge; served in Royal Signals, U.K. and India 1943–46; Asst. Lecturer, Univ. of Leeds 1951–52; Research Fellow, Trinity Coll., Cambridge Univ. 1952–53, Fellow of Peterhouse 1953–91, Asst. Lecturer in Classics, Cambridge Univ. 1955–60, Lecturer 1960–70, Reader in Latin Literature and Textual Criticism 1970–74, Kennedy Prof. of Latin 1974–82, Emer. Prof. 1982–; Pres. Jt. Asscn. of Classical Teachers 1977–79, Classical Asscn.1982–83; Treas. and Chair. Council of Almoners, Christ's Hosp. 1984–86; Foreign mem. Royal

Netherlands Acad. of Arts and Sciences. *Publications:* P. Ovidi Nasonis Amores, etc. 1961, Lucretius, De Rerum Natura III 1971, The Classical Text 1974, The Cambridge History of Classical Literature, Vol. II, Latin Literature (Ed. and Contrib.) 1982, The Ploughman's Lunch (Moretum) 1984, Ovid, Metamorphoses—Introduction and Notes 1986, Ovid, The Love Poems—Introduction and Notes 1990, Apuleius, Cupid & Psyche 1990, Ovid, Sorrows of an Exile (Tristia)—Introduction and Notes 1992, Ovid, Heroides xvi–xxi 1996, Apuleius, The Golden Ass—Trans. with Introduction and Notes 1998. *Leisure interests:* cats, books. *Address:* Peterhouse, Cambridge, CB2 1RD, England.

KENNY, Sir Anthony John Patrick, Kt., D.PHIL., F.B.A.; British philosopher and university teacher; b. 16 March 1931, Liverpool; s. of John and Margaret (Jones) Kenny; m. Nancy Caroline Gayley 1966; two s.; ed. Gregorian Univ., Rome, St. Benet's Hall, Oxford; ordained Catholic priest, Rome 1955; Curate, Liverpool 1959–63; returned to lay state 1963; Asst. Lecturer, Univ. of Liverpool 1961–63; Lecturer in Philosophy, Exeter and Trinity Colls., Oxford 1963–64; Tutor in Philosophy, Balliol Coll, Oxford 1964, Fellow 1964–78, Sr. Tutor 1971–72, 1976–77, Master 1978–89; Warden Rhodes House 1989–99; Professorial Fellow St. John's Coll., Oxford 1989–; Pro-Vice-Chancellor, Univ. of Oxford 1984–99; Wilde Lecturer in Natural and Comparative Religion, Oxford 1969–72; Joint Gifford Lecturer, Univ. of Edin. 1972–73; Stanton Lecturer, Univ. of Cambridge 1980–83; Speaker's Lecturer in Biblical Studies, Oxford Univ. 1980–83; Visiting Prof. Stanford and Rockefeller Univs., Univs. of Chicago, Washington, Mich., Cornell; Vice-Pres. British Acad. 1986–88, Pres. 1989–93; Chair. Bd. British Library 1993–96 (mem Bd. 1991–96); Del. and mem. of Finance Cttee., Oxford Univ. Press 1986–93; Ed. The Oxford Magazine 1972–73; mem. Royal Norwegian Acad. 1993–, American Philosophical Asscn. 1994–; Hon. D.Litt. (Bristol) 1982, (Denison Univ.) 1986, (Liverpool) 1988, (Glasgow) 1990, (Lafayette) 1990, (Trinity Coll., Dublin) 1992, (Hull) 1993, (Belfast) 1994; Hon. D.C.L. (Oxford) 1987. *Publications:* Action, Emotion and Will 1963, Responsa Alumnorum of English College, Rome (2 vols.) 1963, Descartes 1968, The Five Ways 1969, Wittgenstein 1973, The Anatomy of the Soul 1974, Will, Freedom and Power 1975, Aristotelian Ethics 1978, Freewill and Responsibility 1978, The God of the Philosophers 1979, Aristotle's Theory of the Will 1979, Aquinas 1980, The Computation of Style 1982, Faith and Reason 1983, Thomas More 1983, The Legacy of Wittgenstein 1984, A Path from Rome 1985, The Logic of Deterrence 1985, The Ivory Tower 1985, Wyclif—Past Master 1985, Wyclif's De Universalibus 1985, Rationalism, Empiricism and Idealism 1986, Wyclif in His Times 1986, The Road to Hillsborough 1986, Reason and Religion (essays) 1987, The Heritage of Wisdom 1987, God and Two Poets 1988, The Metaphysics of Mind 1989, Mountains 1991, What is Faith? 1992, Aristotle on the Perfect Life 1992, Aquinas on Mind 1992, The Oxford Illustrated History of Western Philosophy (ed.) 1994, Frege 1995, A Life in Oxford 1997, A Brief History of Western Philosophy 1998. *Address:* Rhodes House, Oxford, OX1 3RG, England. *Telephone:* (01865) 270902.

KENNY, General Sir Brian (Leslie Graham), G.C.B., C.B.E.; British army officer; b. 18 June 1934; s. of late Brig. James W. Kenny, C.B.E. and Aileen A. G. Swan; m. Diana C. J. Mathew 1958; two s.; ed. Canford School; commissioned into 4th Hussars (later Queen's Royal Irish Hussars) 1954; served British Army of the Rhine (BAOR), Aden, Malaya, Borneo and Cyprus; pilot's course 1961; Ministry of Defence 1966–68; Instructor Staff Coll. 1971–73; C.O. Queen's Royal Irish Hussars, BAOR and UN, Cyprus 1974–76; Col. G.S. 4 Armoured Div. 1977–78; Command, 12 Armoured Brigade (Task Force D) 1979–80; Royal Coll. of Defence Studies 1981; Commdr. 1st Armoured Div. 1982–83; Dir. Army Staff Duties, Ministry of Defence 1983–85; Command, 1st British Corps 1985–87; C.-in-C. BAOR and Commdr. NATO's Northern Army Group 1987–89; Deputy Supreme Allied Commdr. Europe 1989–93; Col. Commandant RAVC 1983–95; Col. QRIH 1985–93; Col. Commandant RAC 1988–93; Gov. Royal Hosp. Chelsea 1993–99, Canford School 1988–; Chair. ABF 1993–99. *Leisure interests:* skiing, cricket, tennis, golf, shooting, racing. *Address:* c/o Lloyds Bank PLC, Camberley, Surrey, GU15 3SE, England. *Telephone:* 0171-730 0161.

KENNY, Douglas T., PH.D.; Canadian professor of psychology and fmr. university administrator; b. 20 Oct. 1923, Victoria, B.C.; s. of late John Ernest Kenny and Margaret (née Collins) Kenny; m. Margaret Lindsay Howieson; one s. one d.; ed. Victoria Coll., B.C., Univ. of British Columbia, Univ. of Washington, Seattle, Wash., U.S.A.; mem. then Prof., Dept. of Psychology, Univ. of British Columbia 1950–88, Head of Dept. 1965–69, Acting Dean of Faculty of Arts 1969–70, Dean 1970–75, Pres. and Vice-Chancellor of Univ. July 1975–83, Pres. Emer. and Prof. Emer. 1989–; Teacher of Psychology, Univ. of Washington 1947–50, Washington State Univ. 1953, Harvard Univ. 1963–65; mem. Bd. of Trustees Vancouver Gen. Hosp. 1976–78, Canada Council 1975–78, Social Sciences and Research Council 1978–83, Monterey Inst. of Int. Studies, Monterey, Calif. 1980–83, The Discovery Foundation (B.C.) 1979–83; Founding mem., Bd. of Govs., Arts, Sciences and Tech. Centre, Vancouver 1980; Past mem. of Commonwealth Asscn. of Univs., Int. Asscn. of Univ. Pres.; Hon. Patron The Int. Foundation of Learning 1983–; mem. American Psychological Asscn. 1950–; LL.D. h.c. (Univ. of B.C.) 1983; Queen's Silver Jubilee Medal 1977, Park O. Davidson Memorial Award for Outstanding Contribution to Devt. of Psychology 1984. *Publications:* numerous articles and chapters on psychology and educ. in Canada, U.S.A., and Japan. *Leisure interests:* collecting Chinese and Japanese art, painting. *Address:* 401–2128 West 43rd Avenue, Vancouver, B.C. V6M 2E1, Canada. *Telephone:* (604) 264-8615. *Fax:* (604) 264-9650.

KENNY, Michael, R.A., F.R.B.S.; British sculptor; b. 10 June 1941, Liverpool; s. of James and Ellen (née Gordon) Kenny; m. 1st Rosemary Flood; m. 2nd Angela Smith 1978 (divorced 1992); one s. one d., two step-d.; m. 3rd Susan Rowland 1993; ed. St. Francis Xavier's Coll., Liverpool, Liverpool Coll. of Art and Slade School of Fine Art, London; Dir. of Fine Art Studies, Goldsmiths Coll., Univ. of London 1983–88; Chair. Faculty of Sculpture, British School at Rome 1982–; Prin. City & Guilds School of Art 1995–; mem. Treasurer Royal Acad. 1995; mem. Bd. of Govs., London Inst. 1986, Cathedrals Advisory Comm. 1988–91; Trustee Royal Acad. of Arts; mem. Royal W. of England Acad.; *one-man exhbns.:* Oxford 1964, Southampton 1965, London 1966, 1969, 1977, 1978, 1979, 1981, 1984, 1989, 1994, 1995, 1996, 1997, in Manchester 1977, Liverpool, Birmingham, Portsmouth, Glasgow, Newcastle upon Tyne 1981, Aberdeen, Brighton 1982, Tokyo 1983, 1985, 1989, Duisburg (retrospective), Paris, Harrogate 1984, Frankfurt 1985, Royal Acad. 1986, Hong Kong, Galleria del Naviglio, Milan 1987, Royal Acad. 1995, Lancaster 1995; *numerous group exhbns.* in England, Europe, America, Australia and Japan, including Royal Acad. Summer Exhbn., Goldsmiths School of Art Centenary Exhbn. 1991; public sculptures commissioned for Lumsden, Scotland, Parc de la Courneuve, Paris, Addenbrookes Hosp., Cambridge, England, Yokohama Business Park, Japan, London Docklands (Limehouse Link Tunnel), Muraoka-cho, Hyogo Pref., Japan, Nene Coll., Northampton, Nene Coll., Northampton 1997, Greenham Common Enterprise Park 1998; has also produced drawings for P&O liner 'Orianna'; *works in public collections:* British Museum, Victoria & Albert Museum, Tate Gallery, Walker Art Gallery, Liverpool, Arts Council, British Council, Duisburg Museum, Germany, Nat. Gallery of Romania, Hara Museum, Japan, Leeds City Art Gallery, Hants. Co. Council, Muraoka-cho Town Council, Japan, Seine St. Denis, France etc. *Leisure interests:* ornithology, cosmology, physics, astronomy. *Address:* 71 Stepney Green, London, E1 3LE (Studio); 64 Randolph Avenue, London, W9 1BE, England (Home). *Telephone:* 0171-790 3409 (Studio); 0171-286 6672 (Home). *Fax:* 0171-790 3409.

KENSIT, Patsy, (Patricia Jude Kensit); British film actress; b. 4 March 1968, London; m. 1st Dan Donovan; m. 2nd Jim Kerr (divorced 1996); one s.; m. 3rd Liam Gallagher (q.v.) 1997; childhood film actress; also appeared in commercials; with brother James Kensit's band Eighth Wonder made successful pop album Fearless. *Films include:* The Great Gatsby, The Bluebird, Absolute Beginners, Chorus of Disapproval, The Skipper, Chicago Joe and The Showgirl, Lethal Weapon II, Twenty-One, The Skipper, Prince of Shadows, Does This Mean We're Married, Blame It On The Bellboy, The Turn of the Screw, Beltenebros, Bitter Harvest, Prince of Shadows, Angels and Insects, Grace of My Heart. *TV appearances:* Great Expectations, Silas Marner, Tycoon: The Story of a Woman, Adam Bede, The Corsican Brothers (U.S. TV). *Address:* Peters Fraser & Dunlop Ltd., 503 The Chambers, Chelsea Harbour, Lots Road, London, SW10 0XF, England. *Telephone:* 0171-352 4446. *Fax:* 0171-352 7356.

KENT, H.R.H. the Duke of; Prince Edward George Nicholas Paul Patrick, K.G., G.C.M.G., G.C.V.O., A.D.C.; the Earl of St. Andrews and the Baron Downpatrick; b. 9 Oct. 1935; s. of the late Duke of Kent (fourth s. of King George V) and Princess Marina (d. of late Prince Nicholas of Greece); m. Katherine Worsley 1961; two s. (George, Earl of St. Andrews, and Lord Nicholas Windsor) one d. (Lady Helen Windsor); ed. Eton Coll. and Le Rosey, Switzerland; Second Lieut., Royal Scots Greys 1955; attended Army Staff Course 1966, later on staff, G.O.C. Eastern Command, Hounslow, Major 1967; Lieut.-Col. Royal Scots Dragoon Guards 1972, Maj. Gen. 1983, Deputy Col.-in-Chief 1993–; rank of Field Marshal 1993; Ministry of Defence 1972–76; Chair. Nat. Electronics Council 1977–; Vice-Chair. British Overseas Trade Bd. 1976–; Pres. All-England Lawn Tennis Club 1969–, Commonwealth War Graves Comm., RNLI 1969–, Football Asscn. 1971–, Automobile Asscn. 1973–, RAF Benevolent Fund 1974–, Scout Asscn. 1975–, Royal Inst. of Great Britain 1976–, Business and Technicians Educ. Council 1984–, Eng. Council 1989–, British Menswear Guild 1989–; Hon. Pres. Royal Geographical Soc. 1969–; Dir. Vickers; Chancellor Univ. of Surrey 1977–; Patron Inst. of Export 1977–, Kent Opera 1978–, The London Philharmonic 1980–, Anglo-Jordanian Soc. 1982–, The Hanover Band 1992–, Anglo-German Asscn. 1994; as Queen's Special Rep. has visited Sierra Leone 1961, Uganda 1962, The Gambia 1965, Guyana and Barbados 1966, Tonga 1967; A.D.C. to H.M. The Queen 1967; Grand Master of the United Grand Lodge of England 1967–; Col.-in-Chief Royal Regt. of Fusiliers 1969–, Devonshire and Dorset Regt. 1978–, Lorne Scots Regt. 1978–; Col. Scots Guards 1974; decorations from Greece, Nepal, Liberia and Jordan; Hon. D.C.L. (Durham), Hon. LL.D. (Leeds), D.Univ. (York). *Leisure interests:* skiing, shooting, photography, opera. *Address:* York House, St. James's Palace, London, SW1A 1BQ, England.

KENT, Bruce Eric, PH.D.; Australian historian; b. 15 Feb. 1932, Melbourne; s. of Rev. Eric Deacon Kent and Beatrice Maude Kent; m. Ann Elizabeth Garland 1966; two s.; ed. Geelong Grammar School, Melbourne Univ., Univ. of Oxford, U.K., A.N.U.; Tutor in History, Melbourne Univ. 1954–55; lecturer in History, A.N.U. 1962–70, Sr. Lecturer 1970–90, Reader 1990–, Acting Head History Dept. 1984; Fulbright Visiting Fellow, Hoover Inst., Stanford Univ. and History Dept., Princeton Univ., U.S.A. 1970; Visiting Lecturer, E. China Normal Univ., Shanghai 1975–76; Pres. Australian Asscn. of European Historians 1984–86; Visiting Fellow, Center of Int. Studies,

Princeton Univ., U.S.A., 1996; Victorian Rhodes Scholar 1955. *Publication:* The Spoils of War: the Politics, Economics, and Diplomacy of Reparations, 1918–1932 1989. *Leisure interests:* violin, cricket, surfing. *Address:* History Department, Arts Faculty, Australian National University, Canberra, A.C.T. 2601; 70 Dominion Circuit, Deakin, A.C.T. 2600, Australia (Home). *Telephone:* 062492716 (Office); 062731019 (Home).

KENT, Francis William, PH.D., DIP.ED., F.A.H.A.; Australian university teacher; b. 30 March 1942, Melbourne; m. 1st Dale V. Kent 1964 (divorced 1984); one d.; m. 2nd Carolyn James 1987; one s. one d.; ed. Univ. of Melbourne and Univ. of London; lecturer, Sr. Lecturer and Reader in History, Monash Univ. 1971–, Personal Chair. 1989–; Fellow Harvard Univ. at Centre for Italian Renaissance Studies, Florence 1977–78, Visiting Scholar 1982, Visiting Prof. 1986–87; Robert Lehman Visiting Prof. 1995–96; Foundation Co-Ed. I Tatti Studies: Essays in the Renaissance 1982; Chair. Australian Foundation for Studies in Italy; Socio Straniero Deputazione di Storia Patria per la Toscana. *Publications:* Household and Lineage in Renaissance Florence 1977, A Florentine Patrician and His Palace (with others) 1981, Neighbours and Neighbourhood in Renaissance Florence (with D. V. Kent) 1982, Patronage, Art and Society in Renaissance Italy (ed. with P. Simons) 1987, Bartolomeo Cederni and his Friends (with G. Corti) 1991; numerous articles. *Leisure interests:* reading, gardening, travel. *Address:* 80 Somers Street, Burwood, Vic. 3125, Australia.

KENT, John Philip Cozens, PH.D., F.B.A., F.S.A.; British numismatist; b. 28 Sept. 1928, London; s. of late John Cozens Kent, D.C.M. and late Lucy Ella (née Binns) Kent; m. Patricia Eleanor Bunford 1961; one s. one d.; ed. Minchenden County Grammar School and Univ. Coll., London; Asst. Keeper Dept. of Coins and Medals, British Museum 1953–74, Deputy Keeper 1974–83, Keeper 1983–90; Hon. Lecturer in Numismatics, Univ. of Birmingham 1993; Hon. Adviser, Coin Collection, Barber Inst. of Fine Arts 1996; Pres. British Asscn. of Numismatic Socs. 1974–78, Royal Numismatic Soc. 1984–89, London and Middx. Archaeological Soc. 1985–88; mem., Inst. de Sintra 1986, Int. Numismatic Comm. 1986–91, Hon. mem. Int. Numismatic Comm. 1991, Monumental Brass Soc. 1991; Fellow Museums Asscn.; Reginald Taylor Prize, British Archaeological Asscn. 1948, Lhotka Memorial Prize, Royal Numismatic Soc. 1977, Derek Allen Prize, British Acad. 1996; Medal, Royal Numismatic Soc. 1990, Medal, American Numismatic Soc. 1994. *Publications:* Late Roman Bronze Coinage (with R. A. G. Carson and P. V. Hill) 1960, Wealth of the Roman World (with K. S. Painter) 1977, Roman Coins 1978, 2000 Years of British Coins and Medals 1978, Roman Imperial Coinage Vol. VIII: The Family of Constantine I (337–364) 1981, A Selection of Byzantine Coins in the Barber Inst. of Fine Arts 1985, A Catalogue of Celtic Coins in the British Museum (ed. with M. R. Mays) Vol. I 1987, Vol. II 1990, Roman Imperial Coinage Vol. X; the divided Empire and the fall of the western parts 395–491 1994. *Leisure interests:* local history and archaeology, monumental brasses, medieval music, railway history. *Address:* 16 Newmans Way, Hadley Wood, Barnet, Herts., EN4 0LR, England.

KENTRIDGE, Sydney, Q.C., M.A.; British lawyer; b. 5 Nov. 1922, Johannesburg, South Africa; s. of Morris Kentridge and May Kentridge; m. Felicia Geffen 1952; two s. two d.; ed. King Edward VII School, Johannesburg, Univ. of the Witwatersrand and Exeter Coll., Oxford; war service with S. African forces 1942–46; Advocate, S. Africa 1949, Sr. Counsel 1965; called to Bar, Lincoln's Inn, London 1977, Bencher 1986; Queen's Counsel, England 1984; Judge, Court of Appeal, Jersey and Guernsey 1988–92; mem. Court of Appeal, Botswana 1981–89, Constitutional Court, S.A. 1995–97; Roberts Lecturer, Univ. of Pa. 1979; Hon. Fellow American Coll. of Trial Lawyers 1998; Hon. Fellow Exeter Coll., Oxford 1986; Hon. LL.D. (Leicester) 1985, (Cape Town) 1987, (Natal) 1989, (London) 1995, (Sussex) 1997; Granville Clark Prize, U.S.A. 1978. *Leisure interest:* opera. *Address:* 7–8 Essex Street, London, WC2R 3LD, England. *Telephone:* 0171-379 3550. *Fax:* 0171-379 3558.

KENWRIGHT, Bill; British theatre producer; b. 4 Sept. 1945; s. of Albert Kenwright and Hope (née Jones) Kenwright; ed. Liverpool Inst.; actor 1964–70; theatre producer 1970–; Dir. Everton Football Club; Dr. h.c. (Liverpool John Moores) 1994; numerous awards. *Plays directed include:* Joseph and The Amazing Technicolor Dreamcoat 1979, The Business of Murder 1981, A Streetcar Named Desire 1984, Stepping Out 1984, Blood Brothers 1988, Shirley Valentine 1989, Travels With My Aunt 1993, Piaf 1993, Lysistrata 1993, Medea 1993, Pygmalion 1997. *Address:* Bill Kenwright Ltd., 55–59 Shaftesbury Avenue, London, W1V 7AA, England. *Telephone:* 0171-439 4466.

KENZHAYEV, Safarali, LL.M.; Tajikistan politician; b. 18 Feb. 1942, Lenin Dist.; ed. Tajik Univ.; fmr. mem. CP; public prosecutor, Dushanbe 1965–83; public prosecutor on transport matters 1983–91; Chair. Control Cttee. Presidium Tajikistan Feb.–Dec. 1991; Chair. Supreme Soviet of Tajikistan 1991–92, Nat. Security Cttee. April–May 1992, People's Front of Tajikistan 1992. Chiar Socialist Party of Tajikistan 1996–; Chair Legislation and Human Rights Cttee Majlis Oli (Parl.) 1995–. *Publications include:* Law and Human Rights 1984, The Rights and Freedoms of Citizens 1988, With a Heavy Heart 1991, Crime 1993, Upheaval in Tajikistan (3 vols.) 1995; numerous professional articles. *Address:* Committee on Legislation and Human Rights, Majlis Oli, Dunshanbe, Tajikistan. *Telephone:* (3772) 21-78-93.

KENZO (pseudonym of **Kenzo Takada**); Japanese fashion designer; b. 1940, Kyoto; ed. art school in Japan; after graduating designed patterns for a Tokyo magazine; moved to Paris 1964; created own freelance collections and sold designs to Louis Feraud 1964–70; opened own shop Jungle Jap 1970; noted for translating traditional designs into original contemporary garments and for ready-to-wear knitwear.

KEOGH, James; American government official and journalist; b. 29 Oct. 1916, Nebraska; s. of David J. Keogh and Edith Dwyer Keogh; m. Verna Marion Pedersen; one s. one d.; joined Omaha Herald 1938, rising to Ed. 1948–51; contrib. to Time 1951, Ed. 1956–68; chief of research, Presidential election campaign 1968; special asst. to Pres. Nixon 1969–70; Dir. U.S. Information Agency 1973–76; Exec. Dir., Business Roundtable 1976–86; Dir. The Philadelphia Fund 1987–; Trustee Taft Inst. 1987–92. *Publications:* This is Nixon 1956, President Nixon and the Press 1972, One of a Kind 1995. *Leisure interest:* duplicate bridge. *Address:* 202 West Lyon Farm Drive, Greenwich, CT 06831, U.S.A.

KEOGH, Lainey; Irish designer; b. 20 Sept. 1957; d. of Peter Keogh and Patricia Byrne; worked in medical sciences –1983; began to work with yarn in 1983; recognized for work by Int. Wool 1987; mem. Secr. Int. Festival du Lin 1989, British Fashion Council 1994; Man. Dir. Lainey Keogh 1986–; Lable Ace Award for Costume Design for film Two Nudes Bathing 1995; developed fabrics for Dior couture studio 1998; People of the Year Award (Ireland) 1987, Prix De Coeur (France) 1998. *Leisure interests:* sky, walking, looking. *Address:* 42 Dawson Street, Dublin 2, Ireland. *Telephone:* (01) 679 3299. *Fax:* (01) 679 4975.

KEOUGH, Donald Raymond, B.S.; American business executive (retd.); b. 4 Sept. 1926, Maurice, Ia.; s. of Leo H. Keough and Veronica (née Henkels) Keough; m. Marilyn Mulhall 1949; three s. three d.; ed. Creighton Univ.; with Butter-Nut Foods Co., Omaha 1950–61, Duncan Foods Co., Houston 1961–67; Vice-Pres. and Dir. Marketing Foods Div., The Coca-Cola Co., Atlanta, Ga. 1967–71, Pres. 1971–73; Exec. Vice-Pres. Coca-Cola U.S.A. 1973–74, Pres. 1974–76; Exec. Vice-Pres. The Coca-Cola Co., Atlanta, Ga. 1976–79, Sr. Exec. Vice-Pres. 1980–81, Pres., C.O.O. and Dir. 1981–93; Chair. Bd. of Dirs., Coca-Cola Enterprises Inc., Atlanta, Ga. 1986–93, Advisor to Bd. 1993–; Chair. Bd. Allen & Co., Inc. 1993–, Excalibur Techs., Inc. 1996–; Dir. IBM World Trade of Americas Group, Tex. Commerce Bancshares Inc.; Chair. Bd. of Trustees, Univ. of Notre Dame. *Address:* 200 Galleria Parkway, Suite 970, Atlanta, GA 30339, U.S.A.

KERDEL-VEGAS, Francisco, M.D., M.SC.; Venezuelan dermatologist, physician and diplomatist; b. 3 Jan. 1928, Caracas; s. of Osvaldo F. Kerdel and Soíia Vegas de Kerdel; m. Martha Ramos de Kerdel 1977; two s. four d.; ed. Liceo Andrés Bello, Caracas, Universidad Central de Venezuela, Harvard Univ. and New York Univ., U.S.A.; Prof. of Dermatology, Universidad Central de Venezuela 1954–77; Visiting Scientist, Dept. of Experimental Pathology, ARC Inst., Cambridge, U.K., mem. Trinity Coll. Cambridge, Scientific Attaché, Venezuelan Embassy, London 1966–67; Vice-Chancellor Simón Bolívar Univ. 1969–70; Amb. to U.K. 1987–92, to France (also accred. to UNESCO) 1995–; Visiting Prof. United Medical and Dental Schools of Guy's and St. Thomas's Hosps., Univ. of London 1990; mem. Nat. Research Council, Venezuela 1969–79; mem. Bd. Universidad Metropolitana, Caracas 1970–, Int. Foundation of Dermatology 1987– (fmr. Pres.); Co-Chair. Pan-American Medical Asscn. 1990; Prosser White Oration, Royal Coll. of Physicians 1972; Fellow Venezuelan Acad. of Medicine, Venezuelan Acad. of Sciences, American Coll. of Physicians, American Acad. of Dermatology; Hon. Fellow Acad. of Medicine, Brazil, Chile; Hon. mem. Royal Soc. of Medicine, British Asscn. of Dermatologists, and Socs. of Dermatology of 15 other countries; Hon. D.Sc. (Calif. Coll. of Podiatric Medicine) 1975, (Cranfield Inst. of Tech., U.K.) 1991; Orders of Andrés Bello, Cecilio Acosta, Francisco de Miranda, Diego de Losada, El Libertador; Hon. C.B.E.; Chevalier, Légion d'honneur. *Publications:* Tratado de Dermatología 1959; chapters in textbooks on dermatology. *Leisure interests:* travelling, swimming, photography, reading. *Address:* Venezuelan Embassy, 11 rue Copernic, 75016 Paris, France.

KÉRÉKOU, Brig.-Gen. Mathieu (Ahmed); Benin politician and army officer; b. 2 Sept. 1933, Natitingou; ed. Saint-Raphael Mil. School, France; served French Army until 1961; joined Dahomey Army 1961; Aide-de-camp to Pres. Maga 1961–63; took part in mil. coup d'état which removed Pres. Christophe Soglo 1967; Chair. Mil. Revolutionary Council 1967–68; continued studies at French mil. schools 1968–70; Commdr. Ouidah Paratroop Unit and Deputy Chief of Staff 1970–72; leader of the military coup d'état which ousted Pres. Ahomadegbe Oct. 1972; Pres. and Head of Mil. Revolutionary Govt., Minister of Nat. Defence 1972–91, fmr. Minister of Planning, of Co-ordination of Foreign Aid, Information and Nat. Orientation; Pres. of Benin 1996–; Chair. Cen. Cttee. Parti de la Révolution Populaire du Bénin. *Leisure interests:* cycling, football. *Address:* Présidence de la République, P.O. Box 1288, Cotonou, Benin. *Telephone:* 30-02-28.

KERIN, John Charles, B.ECONS.; Australian politician; b. 21 Nov. 1937, Bowral, N.S.W.; s. of late Joseph Sydney and Mary Louise (née Fuller) Kerin; m. 1st Barbara Elizabeth Large (divorced 1971); one d.; m. 2nd Dr. June Rae Verrier 1983; one s. two d.; ed. Univ. of New England, Australian Nat. Univ.; Econs. Research Officer in wool marketing, Bureau of Agricultural Econs. 1971, 1975–78; M.P. for Macarthur, House of Reps. 1972–75, for Werriwa 1978–93; Minister for Primary Industry 1983–86, for Primary

Industries and Energy 1987–89, of Trade and Overseas Devt. 1991–93; Chair. Australian Meat and Livestock Corpn. 1994–97; Deputy Coal Mines Australia Ltd. 1994–; Chair. Biologic Int. Ltd. 1996–; Deputy Chancellor Univ. of Western Sydney 1996–; Leader, Labor Party Del. to E. Timor 1975; mem. Australian Devt. Assistance Agency Bd. 1975, Commonwealth Scientific and Industrial Research Org. Advisory Council 1980, Industry and Econ. Policy Cttees. of Cabinet and Caucus 1983; Leader Australian Del. to U.S.A. 1986; Australian Labor Party. *Leisure interests:* opera, ballet, bush-walking, tennis, classical music. *Address:* 26 Harpur Place, Garran, A.C.T. 2605, Australia.

KERKORIAN, Kirk; American business executive; b. 6 June 1917, Fresno, Calif.; m. 1st Hilda Schmidt 1942 (divorced 1951); m. 2nd Jane Hardy 1954; two d.; commercial airline pilot 1940; Capt. Transport Command, R.A.F. 1942–44; f. L.A. Air Services (later Trans Int. Airlines Group) 1948, Int. Leisure Corpn. 1968; C.E.O. M.G.M. Inc. 1973–74, Chair. Exec. Cttee., Vice-Chair. M.G.M. 1974–79, controlling stockholder M.G.M./U.A. Communications Co., consultant 1979–; majority shareholder M.G.M. Grand. *Address:* M.G.M./U.A. Communications Co., 2500 Broadway Street, Santa Monica, CA 90404, U.S.A.

KERMODE, Sir (John) Frank, Kt., M.A., F.B.A., F.R.S.L.; British university professor; b. 29 Nov. 1919, Douglas, Isle of Man; s. of John Pritchard Kermode and Doris Kennedy; m. Maureen Eccles 1947 (divorced); one s. one d.; ed. Liverpool Univ.; John Edward Taylor Prof., Manchester Univ. 1958–65; Winterstoke Prof., Bristol Univ. 1965–67; Lord Northcliffe Prof., Univ. Coll., London 1967–74; King Edward VII Prof., Cambridge Univ. 1974–82; Julian Clarence Levi Prof., Humanities Dept., Univ. of Columbia New York 1983 and 1985; Charles Eliot Norton Prof. of Poetry, Harvard Univ. 1977–78; Foreign mem. American Acad. Arts and Sciences; Hon. D.H.L. (Chicago); Hon. D.Litt. (Liverpool) 1981, (Amsterdam), (Yale) 1995, (Wesleyan) 1997, (London) 1997; Officier de l'Ordre des Arts et des Sciences. *Publications:* Romantic Image 1957, Wallace Stevens 1960, The Sense of an Ending 1967, Lawrence 1973, The Classic 1975, The Genesis of Secrecy 1979, The Art of Telling 1983, Forms of Attention 1985, History and Value 1988, The Literary Guide to the Bible (ed. with Robert Alter) 1989, An Appetite for Poetry 1989, Poetry, Narrative, History 1989, The Uses of Error 1991, The Oxford Book of Letters (with Anita Kermode) 1995, Not Entitled: A Memoir 1995. *Leisure interests:* squash, music. *Address:* 9 The Oast House, Grange Road, Cambridge, CB3 9AP, England. *Telephone:* (01223) 357931. *Fax:* (01223) 303790.

KERNAN, Roderick Patrick, PH.D., M.R.I.A.; Irish professor of physiology; b. 20 May 1928, Dublin; s. of Dermod Kernan and Pauline (Hickey) Kernan; m. Mary Cecily Kavanagh 1956; one s. one d.; ed. Synge Street Boys' School, Univ. Coll. Dublin; Research Assoc., Dept. of Reproductive Physiology, Rockefeller Inst., New York, U.S.A. 1957–58; Sr. Fellow Medical Research Council of Ireland 1958–66; Rae Prof. of Biochemistry, Royal Coll. of Surgeons in Ireland 1965–67; Assoc. Prof. of Gen. Physiology Univ. Coll. Dublin 1966–93, Emer. Prof. 1993; Visiting Prof. of Physiology, George Washington Univ., Washington, D.C. 1969–70; elected mem. Royal Irish Acad. 1965, mem. Council 1977–81, 1986–90, 1993–, Vice-Pres. 1978, 1986, Sec. for Science 1993–; elected mem. Physiological Soc. 1963. *Publications:* Cell K 1965, Cell Potassium 1980. *Leisure interests:* hill walking, photography, gardening, painting, music. *Address:* Royal Irish Academy, 19 Dawson Street, Dublin 2 (Office); 37 Templeville Drive, Dublin 6W, Ireland (Home). *Telephone:* (01) 676 2570 (Office). *Fax:* (01) 676 2346.

KERR, Clark, PH.D.; American educator; b. 17 May 1911, Reading, Pa.; s. of Samuel W. and Caroline Clark Kerr; m. Catherine Spaulding 1934; two s. one d.; ed. Swarthmore Coll., Stanford Univ., and Univ. of California (Berkeley); Asst. later Assoc. Prof. of Industrial Relations, Univ. of Washington 1940–45; Assoc. Prof., later Prof. of Industrial Relations, Univ. of Calif. (Berkeley) 1945, Chancellor 1952–58; Pres. Univ. of Calif. 1958–67, Pres. Emer. 1974; Chair. of Carnegie Comm. on Higher Educ. 1967–73, Chair. Carnegie Council Studies in Higher Educ. 1973–79; Program Director, Strengthening Presidential Leadership Project, Asscn. of Governing Bds. of Univ. and Colls., 1982–85; Godkin Lecturer, Harvard 1963, Marshall Lecturer, Cambridge 1967–68; has held various public posts, mainly in the field of labour relations; mem. American Econ. Asscn., Industrial Relations Research Asscn., Nat. Acad. of Educ., American Acad. of Arts and Sciences; Hon. Fellow, London School of Econs. and Political Science; Harold W. McGraw Jr. Prize in Educ. 1990; many hon. degrees. *Publications:* Unions, Management, and the Public (with E. W. Bakke) 1948, revised 1960, 1967, Industrialism and Industrial Man (with Dunlop, Harbison and Myers) 1960, 1973, 1975, The Uses of University 1964, with new Postscripts 1972, 1982, with 1994 Commentaries on Past Developments and Future Prospects 1995, Labour and Management in Industrial Society 1964, Marshall, Marx and Modern Times 1969, Labor Markets and Wage Determination 1977, Education and National Development 1979, The Future of Industrial Societies 1983, The Many Lives of Academic Presidents (with M. L. Gade) 1986, Industrial Relations in a New Age (Co-Ed. with P. D. Staudohar) 1986, Economics of Labor in Industrial Society (Co-Ed. with P. D. Staudohar) 1986, The Guardians: Boards of Trustees of American Colleges and Universities (with M. L. Gade) 1989, The Great Transformation in Higher Education: 1960–1980 1991, Troubled Times for American Higher Education: the 1990s and beyond 1994, Higher Education Cannot Escape History: Issues for the Twenty-First Century 1994, Labor Economics and Industrial Relations: Markets and Institutions (co-ed. with P. D. Staudohar) 1994. *Leisure interest:* gardening. *Address:* 8300 Buckingham Drive, El Cerrito, CA 94530, U.S.A. (Home).

KERR, David Nicol Sharp, C.B.E., M.SC., F.R.C.P., F.R.C.P.E.; British physician; b. 27 Dec. 1927, London; s. of William Kerr and Elsie Ransted; m. (Mary) Eleanor Jones 1960; two s. one d.; ed. George Watson's Boys' School and Univs. of Edinburgh and Wisconsin; Surgeon-Lieut. R.N.V.R. 1953–55; Surgeon Lieut.-Commdr. R.N.R. 1993–95; Prof. of Medicine, Univ. of Newcastle-upon-Tyne 1968–83; Dean, Royal Postgrad. Medical School 1984–91; Prof. of Renal Medicine, Univ. of London 1986–93, Prof. Emer. 1993–; Postgrad. Medical Adviser, North Thames Regional Health Authority, later N.H.S. Exec. N. Thames Regional Office 1991–97; Medical Awards Admin. Commonwealth Scholarships Comm. 1993–98; Hon. consultant renal physician, Hammersmith Hosp.; Ed. Journal of Royal Coll. of Physicians 1994–98; mem. Council, British Heart Foundation 1991–97; Volhard Medal (German Medical Foundation), Distinguished Overseas Medal (Nat. Kidney Foundation of U.S.A.) etc. *Publications:* Oxford Textbook of Clinical Nephrology (ed.); other books, book sections and articles in professional journals. *Leisure interests:* walking, theatre, opera, church. *Address:* 22 Carbery Avenue, London, W3 9AL, England (Home). *Telephone:* 0181-992 3231 (Home). *Fax:* 0181-992 3231.

KERR, Deborah Jane, C.B.E.; British actress; b. 30 Sept. 1921, Helensburgh, Dunbarton, Scotland; d. of Arthur Kerr Trimmer and Colleen Smale; m. 1st Anthony Bartley 1945 (divorced 1959); two d.; m. 2nd Peter Viertel 1960; one step-d.; ed. Rossholme Prep., Weston-super-Mare, Northumberland House, Bristol; began acting career at Open Air Theatre, Regent's Park 1939; first film Contraband, first major role as Jenny Hill in film Major Barbara; went to Hollywood 1946; film awards include four New York Drama Critics' Awards, 1947 (two), 1957, 1960; Hollywood Foreign Press Asscn. Awards 1956 (for The King and I), 1958; Variety Club of G.B. Award 1961; six Acad. Award Nominations; awards for plays include Donaldson and Sarah Siddons Awards for Tea and Sympathy; BAFTA Special Award 1991; Hon. Acad. Award 1994. *Films include:* Major Barbara 1940, Love on the Dole 1940, Penn of Pennsylvania 1940, Hatter's Castle 1941, The Day Will Dawn 1941, The Life and Death of Colonel Blimp 1942, Perfect Strangers 1944, Black Narcissus 1945, I See a Dark Stranger 1945, The Hucksters 1946, If Winter Comes 1947, Edward My Son 1948, The Prisoner of Zenda 1948, Young Bess 1949, King Solomon's Mines 1950, Quo Vadis 1950, Rage of The Vulture 1951, Dream Wife 1952, From Here to Eternity 1953, The End of the Affair 1954, The Proud and the Profane 1955, The King and I 1956, Heaven Knows Mr. Allison 1957, An Affair to Remember 1957, Separate Tables 1957/58, The Journey 1958, The Blessing 1958, Beloved Infidel 1960, The Sundowners 1960, The Innocents 1961, The Chalk Garden 1963, The Night of the Iguana 1963, Marriage on the Rocks 1965, Gypsy Moths 1968, The Arrangement 1968/69, The Assam Garden 1984, Reunion at Fairborough 1984. *Plays:* Heartbreak House 1943, Tea and Sympathy 1953 (U.S. tour 1954/55), The Day After the Fair (U.S. tour 1973/74), Seascape 1974/75, Souvenir 1975, Long Day's Journey Into Night (U.S.) 1977, Candida (London) 1977, The Last of Mrs. Cheyney (U.S. tour 1978), The Day After the Fair (Australian tour 1979), Overheard (London and U.K. tour 1981), The Corn is Green (London) 1985. *Television:* A Song at Twilight 1981, Witness for the Prosecution (TV film) 1982, Ann & Debbie, 1984, A Woman of Substance 1984, Hold the Dream 1986. *Leisure interests:* painting, gardening. *Address:* Klosters, 7250 Grisons, Switzerland.

KERR, Jean; American writer; b. 10 July 1923, Scranton; d. of Thomas J. Collins and Kitty O'Neill; m. Walter Kerr 1943; five s. one d.; ed. Catholic Univ. of America; mem. Nat. Inst. of Arts and Sciences; Hon. L.H.D. (Northwestern Univ.) 1962, (Fordham Univ.) 1965; Campion Award 1971, Laetare Medal 1971. *Publications:* Jenny Kissed Me (play) 1949, Touch and Go (play) 1950, King of Hearts (with Eleanor Brooke) 1954, Please Don't Eat the Daisies 1957, The Snake Has All the Lines 1960, Mary, Mary (play) 1962, Poor Richard (play) 1963, Penny Candy 1970, Finishing Touches (play) 1973, How I Got to Be Perfect 1978, Lunch Hour (play) 1980. *Address:* 1 Beach Avenue, Larchmont, New York, NY 10538, U.S.A.

KERR, Sir John Olav, K.C.M.G.; British diplomatist; b. 22 Feb. 1942; s. of late Dr and Mrs J. D. O. Kerr; m. Elizabeth Kalaugher 1965; two s. three d.; ed. Glasgow Acad. and Pembroke Coll. Oxford; entered diplomatic service 1966; served Moscow and Rawalpindi; Pvt. Sec. to Perm. Under-Sec. FCO 1974–79; Head DM1 Div. H.M. Treasury 1979–81; Prin. Pvt. Sec. to Chancellor of Exchequer 1981–84; Head of Chancery, Washington, D.C. 1984–87; Asst. Under-Sec. of State, FCO 1987–90; Amb. and Perm. Rep. of UK to EC (now EU), Brussels 1990–95; Amb. to U.S.A. 1995–97; Perm. Under-Sec. of State and Head of H.M. Diplomatic Service 1997–. *Address:* c/o Foreign and Commonwealth Office, King Charles Street, London, SW1, England.

KERR, Philip Ballantyne, LL.B., LL.M.; British writer and novelist, b. 22 Feb. 1956, Edinburgh; s. of William Kerr and Ann Brodie; m. Jane Thynne 1991; two s.; ed. Northampton Grammar School and Birmingham Univ.; Prix de Romans L'Aventures, Deutsches Krimi Prize. *Publications:* March Violets 1989, The Pale Criminal 1990, The Penguin Book of Lies 1990, A German Requiem 1991, Fights, Feuds and Heartfelt Hatreds 1992, A Philosophical Investigation 1992, Dead Meat 1993, Gridiron 1993, Esau 1996, A Five Year Plan 1997, The Second Angel 1998. *Leisure interests:* exercise, fly fishing, cinema and fine wine. *Address:* c/o A.P. Watts Literary

Agents, 20 John Street, London, WC1N 2DR, England. *Telephone:* 0171-405 6774. *Fax:* 0171-430 1952.

KERREY, Bob (J. Robert), B.S.; American politician; b. 27 Aug. 1943, Lincoln, Neb.; s. of James Kerrey and Elinor Kerrey; one s. one d.; ed. Univ. of Nebraska; owner, founder, developer, outlets in Omaha and Lincoln, Grandmother's Skillet Restaurant 1972–75; owner, founder fitness enterprises, including Sun Valley Bowl and Prairie Life Fitness Center, Lincoln, Neb.; Gov. of Nebraska 1983–87; Partner, Printon, Kane & Co., Lincoln 1987; Senator from Nebraska 1989–; Medal of Honor; Bronze Star; Purple Heart; Democrat. *Address:* United States Senate, 303 Hart Building, Washington, DC 20510, U.S.A.

KERRUISH, Sir (Henry) Charles, Kt., O.B.E.; Manx politician and farmer; b. 23 July 1917, Isle of Man; s. of Henry Howard Kerruish and Clara May Kewin; m. 1st Margaret Gell 1944; one s. three d.; m. 2nd Kay Warriner 1975; three step-d.; ed. Ramsey Grammar School; mem. House of Keys, Isle of Man 1946–90, Speaker 1962–90; First Pres. of Tynwald and of Legislative Council, Isle of Man 1990–; fmr. Chair. Health Services Bd., Tynwald, and mem. Gov.'s Exec. Council; Regional Councillor Commonwealth Parl. Asscn. 1975–77, Pres. 1983–84; mem. Court, Liverpool Univ. 1974–; Pres. Manx Loaghtan Sheep Breed Soc.; D. Iur. h.c. (Lancaster Univ.) 1990; Capt. Parish of Maughold. *Leisure interests:* horse breeding, motor cycling, reading. *Address:* Ballafayle, Maughold, Isle of Man. *Telephone:* (01624) 812293.

KERRY, John Forbes, J.D.; American politician; b. 11 Dec. 1943, Denver; s. of Richard J. and Rosemary (Forbes) Kerry; m. 1st Julia S. Thorne 1970; two d.; m. 2nd Teresa Heinz 1995; ed. Yale Univ. and Boston Coll.; U.S. Navy 1966–70; awarded Bronze Star, Silver Star, 3 Purple Hearts; called to Bar, Mass. 1976; Nat. co-ordinator, Vietnam Veterans Against The War 1969–71; Asst. Dist. Attorney, Middx. County, Mass. 1976–79; Partner, Kerry & Sragow, Boston 1979–82; Lieut Gov. State of Mass. 1982–84; Senator from Massachussetts 1985–; Democrat. *Publications:* The New Soldier 1971, The New War: the Web of Crime That Threatens America's Security 1997. *Address:* United States Senate, 421 Russell Senate Office Building, Washington, DC 20510, U.S.A.

KERWIN, Larkin, C.C., D.SC., LL.D., F.R.S.C.; Canadian physicist; b. 22 June 1924, Quebec City; s. of Timothy and Catherine (née Lonergan) Kerwin; m. Maria G. Turcot 1950; five s. three d.; ed. St. Francis Xavier Univ., Massachusetts Inst. of Tech., Laval Univ.; research physicist, Geotech. Corpn., Cambridge 1945–46; Asst. Prof. of Physics, Laval Univ. 1948–51, Assoc. Prof. 1951–56, Prof. 1956, Chair. Physics Dept. 1961–67, Vice-Dean, Faculty of Sciences 1967–69, Vice-Rector 1969–72, Rector 1972–77, Prof. Emer. 1991–; Vice-Pres. Natural Sciences and Eng. Research Council, Canada 1978–80; Pres. Nat. Research Council of Canada 1980–89; Pres. Canadian Space Agency 1989; developed an ion optics theory; invented inflection mass spectrometer; developed electron selector; discovered P8 and numerous excited states in various atoms and molecules; research into determination of isotopic abundance ratios; Pres. Canadian Asscn. of Physicists 1954–55, Int. Scientific and Tech. Affiliations Cttee. of Nat. Research Council 1972–80, Acad. of Science, Royal Soc. of Canada 1973–74, Asscn. of Univs. and Colls. of Canada 1974–75, Royal Soc. of Canada 1976; Sec.-Gen. Int. Union of Pure and Applied Physics 1972–84, First Vice-Pres. 1984–87, Pres. 1987–90; mem. Bd. of Dirs., Canada-France-Hawaii Telescope Corpn. 1973–78; mem. Acad. des Grands Québecois 1995–; Fellow, Canadian Acad. of Engineers 1987; Allan Lecturer, Univ. of Alberta 1987; Hon. LL.D. (St. Francis Xavier) 1970, (Toronto) 1973, (Concordia) 1976, (Alberta) 1983; Hon. D.Sc. (British Columbia) 1973, (McGill) 1974, (Memorial, Newfoundland) 1978, (Ottawa) 1981, (Royal Mil. Coll.) 1982, (Winnipeg) 1983, (Windsor) 1984, (Moncton) 1985; Hon. D.C.L. (Bishop's) 1978; Hon. LL.D. (Dalhousie) 1983; Hon. D. Univ. (Montreal) 1991; Prix David 1951, Médaille Pariseau, A.C.F.A.S. 1965, Centennial Medal 1967, Medal of Canadian Asscn. of Physicists 1969, Jubilee Medal 1977, Laval Alumni Medal (Gloire de l'Escolle) 1978, Canadian Council of Professional Engineers Gold Medal 1982, Médaille Rousseau de l'ACFAS 1983; Ordre nat. du Québec 1988; Officier, Légion d'honneur 1989. *Publications:* Atomic Physics: An Introduction 1963, and 50 scientific articles. *Address:* 2166 Bourbonière Park, Sillery, Quebec, G1T 1B4, Canada (Home).

KERZNER, Sol(omon); South African business executive; b. 23 Aug. 1935, Johannesburg; s. of Morris Kerzner; two s. three d.; ed. Athlons High School, Univ. of Witwatersrand; Founder and C.E.O. Southern Sun Hotels 1969–83; C.E.O. Sun Int. Hotels (South Africa) 1983–87, Chair. 1994–; Chair. World Leisure Group 1989–94; rep. Univ. of Witwatersrand for boxing and wrestling 1954–55; Inst. of Marketing Man. Marketing Award of the Year 1978–80, Jewish Businessman of the Year 1993.

KESRI, Sitaram; Indian politician; Minister of State for Parl. Affairs 1985; Minister for Welfare 1991; Treas. All-India Congress Cttee.; Pres. Congress Party 1996–98, Parl. Leader 1997. *Address:* All-India Congress Committee, 24 Akbar Road, New Delhi 110011, India. *Telephone:* (11) 3019080.

KESSAR, Yisrael, M.A.; Israeli politician, economist and sociologist; b. 1931, Yemen; emigrated to Israel 1933; served in the Histadrut (Gen. Fed. of Labour) 1966–92, Chair. Manpower Dept. and Youth and Sports Dept. 1966–71, Treas. 1973–77, Chair. Trade Union Dept. and Deputy Sec.-Gen. 1977–84, Sec.-Gen. 1984–92; Minister of Transport 1992–96; mem. Knesset 1984–; Labour. *Address:* 7 Helmonit Street, Rishon LeZion, Israel.

KESTELMAN, Sara; British actress; ed. Cen. School of Speech and Drama; joined Liverpool Playhouse; subsequently moved to Library Theatre, Manchester; roles included Abigail in The Crucible and Cecily in The Importance of Being Earnest; joined Royal Shakespeare Co. (RSC) 1969; roles for RSC included Mariana in Measure for Measure, Jessie Tate in The Silver Tassle, Margaret in Much Ado About Nothing, Cassandra in Troilus and Cressida, Natasha in Subject to Fits, Titania in A Midsummer Night's Dream and Cleopatra in Gorky's Enemies; other stage appearances have included Messalina in I Claudius (Queen's Theatre, London), Lady Macbeth and Ruth in The Homecoming (Birmingham Repertory Theatre), Prudence in Plunder and Ilyena in Uncle Vanya (Bristol Old Vic), Nine (Donmar) 1996; has appeared in several TV plays. *Film:* Zardoz.

KESWICK, Sir Chippendale (Chips) (see Keswick, Sir J. C. L.).

KESWICK, Henry Neville Lindley; British business executive; b. 29 Sept. 1938; s. of late Sir William Keswick and of Mary Lindley; a brother of Sir (John) Chippendale Keswick (q.v.) and of Simon Lindley Keswick (q.v.); m. Lady Tessa Reay 1985; ed. Eton Coll., Cambridge Univ.; Nat. Service 1956–58; Dir. Sun Alliance and London Insurance PLC 1975–96, Sun Alliance Group PLC 1989–, Deputy Chair. 1993–96, Dir. Royal and Sun Alliance Insurance Group PLC 1996; Dir. Robert Fleming Holdings Ltd., Rothmans Int. 1988–94, Hongkong Land Co. 1988–, Mandarin Oriental Int. 1988–, Dairy Farm Int. Holdings 1988–, The Daily Telegraph 1990–; Chair. Matheson & Co. 1975–, Jardine Matheson Holdings Ltd., Hong Kong 1972–75, 1989– (Dir. 1967–), Jardine Strategic Holdings 1989– (Dir. 1988–); Chair. Hong Kong Asscn. 1988–; mem. 21st Century Trust 1987–; Propr. The Spectator 1975–81; Trustee Nat. Portrait Gallery 1982– (Chair. 1994–); Vice-Patron Royal Soc. of British Sculptors 1998–. *Leisure interest:* country pursuits. *Address:* Matheson & Co. Ltd., 3 Lombard Street, London, EC3V 9AQ, England. *Telephone:* 0171-816 8100.

KESWICK, Sir (John) Chippendale Lindley, (Chips) Kt.; British merchant banker; b. 2 Feb. 1940; s. of the late Sir William Keswick and of Mary Lindley; brother of Henry N. L. Keswick (q.v.) and Simon L. Keswick (q.v.); m. Lady Sarah Ramsay 1966; three s.; ed. Eton Coll.,, Univ. of Aix-Marseilles; with Glyn Mills & Co. 1961–65; Jt. Vice-Chair. Hambros PLC 1986, Jt. Deputy Chair. 1990–97, Group Chief Exec. 1995–97; Chair. Hambros Bank Ltd. 1986–95, Chair. (non-exec.) 1995–, Chair. Hambros PLC 1997–; Sr. Banking and Capital Markets Adviser Société Générale 1998–; Dir. Persimmon PLC, De Beers 1993–, Bank of England 1993–, Edin. Investment Trust PLC 1992–, IMI PLC 1994–, Anglo American Corpn. of S. Africa Ltd. 1995; Vice-Counsellor, Cancer Research Campaign; Hon. Treas. Children's Country Holidays Fund; mem. Queen's Body Guard for Scotland, Royal Co. of Archers. *Leisure interests:* bridge, country pursuits. *Address:* Hambros Bank, 41 Tower Hill, London, EC3N 4HA, England. *Telephone:* 0171-480 5000.

KESWICK, Simon Lindley, F.R.S.A.; British business executive; b. 20 May 1942; s. of Sir William and Lady Keswick; brother of Henry N. L. Keswick (q.v.) and Sir John Chippendale Lindley Keswick (q.v.); m. Emma Chetwode 1971; two s. two d.; ed. Eton Coll. and Trinity Coll., Cambridge; Dir. Fleetways Holdings Ltd., Australia 1970–72, Greenfriar Investment Co. 1979–82, Matheson & Co. Ltd. 1978–82; Chair. Jardine Matheson Insurance Brokers 1978–82; Dir. Jardine Matheson & Co. Ltd., Hong Kong 1972–, Man. Dir. 1982, Chair. 1983–89; Chair. Hongkong Land Holdings Ltd. 1983–, Hongkong & Shanghai Banking Corpn. 1983–88, Jardine Matheson Holdings Ltd. 1984–89, Mandarin Oriental Int. Ltd. 1984–, Dairy Farm Int. Holdings Ltd. 1984–, Jardine Strategic Holdings Ltd. 1987–89, (Dir. 1987–), Fleming Mercantile Investment Trust 1990– (Dir. 1988–), Jardine Int. Motor Holdings 1990–97, Trafalgar House PLC 1993–96; Dir. Hanson PLC 1991–; Dir. (non-exec.) Wellcome 1995–; Trustee British Museum 1989–. *Leisure interests:* country pursuits, Tottenham Hotspur. *Address:* No. 9, Shek O, Hong Kong; Rockcliffe, Upper Slaughter, Cheltenham, Glos., GL54 2JW, England. *Telephone:* (01451) 30648.

KESWICK, Tessa; British administrator and fmr. civil servant; b. 15 Oct. 1942; d. of 15th Lord Lovat and Rosamund Broughton; m. 1st Lord Reay 1964 (divorced 1978); two s. one d.; m. 2nd Henry Keswick (q.v.) 1985; ed. Sacred Heart Convent, Woldingham, Surrey; Conservative Councillor, Royal Borough of Kensington and Chelsea 1982–86; Conservative Cand. for Inverness 1987; special policy adviser to Rt. Hon. Kenneth Clarke (q.v.) at Dept. of Health 1989, Dept. of Educ., Home Office, Treasury –1995; Dir. Centre for Policy Studies 1995–. *Leisure interests:* art, music, breeding horses. *Address:* Centre for Policy Studies, 57 Tufton Street, London, SW1P 3QL, England. *Telephone:* 0171-222 4488. *Fax:* 0171-222 4388.

KETELAAR, Jan Arnold Albert, PH.D.; Netherlands university professor; b. 21 April 1908, Amsterdam; s. of Albert Jans Ketelaar and L. C. M. Struycken; m. Sytske Bessem 1949; three s.; ed. Univ. of Amsterdam and California Inst. of Technology, Pasadena; Priv. Doz. Chemical Crystallography, Univ. of Leiden 1936–40, Lecturer in Physical Chemistry 1940–41; Prof. of Physical Chemistry and Chemical Thermodynamics, Univ. of Amsterdam 1941–60; Visiting Prof. of Chemistry, Brown Univ., Providence, R.I. 1958–59; Prof. of Electrochemistry, Univ. of Amsterdam 1960–78; mem. Nat. Bd. of Educ. 1960–78; mem. Royal Netherlands Acad. of Sciences. *Publications:* Monomorphe overgangen in de kristalstructuren van zilverkwikjodide, natriumnitraat en aluminium fluoride 1933, De Chemische Binding 1947, 1952, 1966, Physische Scheikunde 1950, Chemical Constitution 1953, 1958, Liaisons et propriétés chimiques 1960, Chemische Konstitution 1964, Chemical History in Fuel Cell Systems 1993. *Leisure interests:* reading, travelling. *Address:* Park de Eschhorst 6, 7461 BN Rÿssen, Netherlands. *Telephone:* 0548-512841.

KETY, Seymour S., M.D.; American professor of neuroscience; b. 25 Aug. 1915, Philadelphia; s. of Louis and Ethel Kety; m. Josephine Gross 1940; one s. one d.; ed. Univ. of Pennsylvania, post-doctoral Harvard Medical School and Massachusetts General Hospital; Instructor, Asst. Prof., Univ. of Pa. Medical School 1943–48; Prof. of Clinical Physiology, Univ. of Pa. 1948–51; Scientific Dir., Nat. Insts. of Mental Health and Neurological Diseases 1951–56, Chief, Lab. of Clinical Sciences 1956–61, 1962–67; Henry Phipps Prof. of Psychiatry, Johns Hopkins School of Medicine 1961–62; Prof. of Psychiatry, Harvard Medical School 1967–80, Prof. of Neuroscience 1980–83, Prof. Emer. of Neuroscience in Psychiatry 1983–; Dir. Psychiatric Research Lab., Mass. Gen. Hospital 1967–77; Dir. Labs. for Psychiatric Research, Mailman Research Center, McLean Hosp., Belmont, Mass. 1977–83; Sr. Scientist Nat. Inst. Mental Health 1983–96, Sr. Scientist Emer. 1996–; Founding Ed. Journal of Psychiatric Research 1961–82; mem. N.A.S., American Philosophical Soc., American Soc. of Pharmacology and Experimental Therapeutics, American Acad. Arts and Sciences; Past Pres. Asscn. for Research in Nervous and Mental Disease, American Psychopathological Asscn.; Hon. Pres. Int. Soc. of Cerebral Circulation and Metabolism; Hon. Fellow, Royal Coll. of Psychiatrists, London; Distinguished Fellow, American Psychiatric Asscn.; Hon. M.A., Sc.D., M.D.; many awards including McAlpin Medal, Nat. Asscn. for Mental Health 1972, Kovalenko Award (N.A.S.) 1973, William Menninger Award, American Coll. of Physicians 1976, Passano Award, Baltimore, Mihara Award, Tokyo, Emil Kraepelin Award, Max Planck Inst., Munich 1984, Ralph Gerard Award, Soc. for Neuroscience, N.A.S. Neuroscience Award 1988, de Hevesy Pioneer Award, Soc. of Nuclear Medicine 1988, Karl Lashley Award (American Philosophical Soc.) 1992, Lifetime Achievement Award (Int. Soc. for Psychiatric Genetics) 1993. *Publications:* Measurement of human cerebral blood flow and metabolism 1948, Theory of exchange of diffusible substances between capillaries and tissues 1951, Biochemical studies in schizophrenia 1959, The heuristic aspect of psychiatry 1961, Genetic-environmental interactions in the transmission of schizophrenia 1968, The biogenic amines in arousal, emotion and learning 1969, The Harvey Lecture: Biological Roots of Mental Illness 1975, The 52nd Henry Maudsley Lecture: The Syndrome of Schizophrenia 1979. *Leisure interests:* music, art. *Address:* 10 Longwood Drive, Apartment 252, Westwood, MA 02090, U.S.A. *Telephone:* (781) 461-9264.

KEUTCHA, Jean; Cameroonian politician, civil servant and diplomatist; b. June 1923, Bangangté; m.; three c.; ed. Ecole Supérieure d'Agriculture de Yaoundé; Chef de Cabinet, Minister of State with Special Responsibilities 1957, subsequently Chef de Cabinet, Sec. of State with responsibility for Information, Posts and Telecommunications; Asst. to Chief of Bamiléké Region 1959; Sub-Prefect, Bafoussam 1960; Prefect of Mifi, subsequently of Menoua 1962–64; Sec. of State for Public Works 1964, subsequently Sec. of State for Rural Devt. and Sec. of State for Educ.; Minister of Foreign Affairs 1971–72, 1975–80, of Agric. 1972–75; Amb. to EEC 1984–85, to People's Repub. of China 1985–88; now Pres. Caisse Nationale de Réassurances (CNR); Commdr. Order Camerounais de la Valeur, Grand Officier, Légion d'honneur, Grand Officier de l'Ordre National Gabonais, etc. *Publication:* Le guide pratique pour la taille du Caféier Arabica. *Address:* CNR, avenue Foch, BP 4180, Yaoundé, Cameroon. *Telephone:* 22-37-99. *Fax:* 23-36-80.

KÉVÉS, György; Hungarian architect; b. 20 March 1935, Osi; s. of Sándor Kévés and Ványi Piroska; m. Éva Földvári 1966; ed. Tech. Univ., Budapest; designer for firms, Agroterv and Eliti, Budapest 1959–61, Iparterv, Budapest 1961–69, Studio 'R' 1983–; private practice with Éva Földvári 1966–; teacher, Faculty of Architecture, Tech. Univ., Budapest 1966–73; Sr. Architect and Prof., Architectural Masterschool, Budapest 1974–; with Káva Architects 1987–, Kévés Architects S.A.; organizes confs. and exhbns. Masterschool, including exhbns. of post-modern architecture and Mario Bottá's works 1980–; organized lectures by Rob Krier and Mario Bottá, Hungary 1980; Visiting Lecturer, Washington Univ., St. Louis, U.S.A. 1981; exhbns.: Budapest, Milano Triennale 1973, Stuttgart 1977, Canada 1978, Washington Univ. St. Louis 1983; Ybl Prize; Hungarian State Prize; several first prizes in architecture competitions. *Publications include:* Architecture of the 70s, Architecture of the 20th century; and numerous articles in architectural magazines. *Leisure interest:* all kinds of art. *Address:* Kévés és Építésztársai Rt. 1121 Budapest, Melinda u. 21, Hungary.

KEYES, Robert W., PH.D., F.I.E.E.E.; American physicist and engineer; b. 2 Dec. 1921, Chicago, Ill.; m. Sophie Skadorwa 1966; one s. one d.; ed. Univ. of Chicago; with Argonne Nat. Lab. 1946–50, Westinghouse Research Lab. 1953–60; research staff mem., IBM Research Div. 1960–; Consultant to N.A.S. Nat. Research Council Physics Survey Cttee. 1970–71; Assoc. Ed. Revs. Modern Physics 1976–; mem. Evaluation Panel for Inorganic Materials Div., Nat. Bureau of Standards 1970–73; Chair. Gordon Conf. on Chem. and Physics of Microstructure Fabrication 1976, American Physical Soc. Cttee. on Applications of Physics 1976–78, Nat. Materials Advisory Bd. ad hoc Cttee. on Ion Implantation 1979, Int. Conf. on Heavy Doping and the Metal-insulator Transition in Semiconductors, Santa Cruz, Calif. 1984; mem. Grad. Record Examination Bd. (Educational Testing Service) 1978–81, I.E.E.E. Awards Bd. 1984–85; Fellow American Physical Soc.; mem. Nat. Acad. of Eng.; IBM Outstanding Contribution Award 1963, I.E.E.E. W.R.G. Baker Prize 1976. *Publications:* Physics of VLSI Systems 1987; 140 papers in professional journals. *Leisure interest:* nature. *Address:* IBM Research Division, P.O. Box 218, Yorktown Heights, NY 10598, U.S.A. *Telephone:* (914) 945-2040.

KEYFITZ, Nathan, PH.D., F.R.S.C.; American demographer; b. 29 June 1913, Montreal, Canada; s. of Arthur Keyfitz and Anna (née Gerstein) Keyfitz; m. Beatrice Orkin 1939; one s. one d.; ed. McGill Univ. and Univ. of Chicago, U.S.A.; Statistician, then Sr. Research Statistician, Dominion Bureau of Statistics, Ottawa 1936–56; Lecturer in Sociology, McGill Univ. 1948–51; Adviser to Indonesian Planning Bureau, Jakarta 1952–53; Prof. of Sociology, Univ. of Montreal 1962–63, Univ. of Toronto 1959–63, Univ. of Chicago 1963–68, Chair. Dept. of Sociology 1965–67; Prof. of Demography, Univ. of Calif., Berkeley 1968–72; Andelot Prof. of Sociology and Demography, Harvard Univ. 1972–83, Prof. Emer. 1983–, Chair. Dept. of Sociology 1978–80; Lazarus Prof. of Social Demography, Ohio State Univ. 1981–83, Prof. Emer. 1983–; Visiting Fellow Statistics Canada 1983–; Leader Population Programme, Deputy Dir., Int. Inst. for Applied Systems Analysis, Laxenburg, Austria 1984–93; Consultant, Dept. of Finance, Jakarta, Indonesia 1984–90; researcher Initiatives on Children, American Acad. of Arts and Sciences 1994–; mem. N.A.S., Int. Statistical Inst.; hon. mem. Canadian Statistical Soc. 1980–; Fellow American Statistical Asscn.; Pres. Population Asscn. of America 1970; Life Trustee, Nat. Opinion Research Center; Hon. M.A. (Harvard), Hon. LL.D. (Western Ont., Montreal, McGill, Alberta, Edmonton, Siena, Carleton). *Publications:* Applied Mathematical Demography 1985, Introduction to the Mathematics of Population 1977. *Leisure interests:* computers, foreign languages. *Address:* Initiatives for Children, American Academy of Arts and Sciences, 136 Irving Street, Cambridge, MA 02138 (Office); 1580 Massachusetts Avenue, Apt. 7C, Cambridge, MA 02138, U.S.A. (Home). *Telephone:* (617) 576 5000 (Office); (617) 491 2845 (Home). *Fax:* (617) 576 5050 (Office); (617) 491 7396 (Home).

KEYNES, Richard Darwin, C.B.E., M.A., PH.D., SC.D., F.R.S.; British scientist; b. 14 Aug. 1919, London; s. of late Sir Geoffrey Keynes and Margaret Elizabeth Darwin; m. Anne Pinsent Adrian; four s. (one deceased); ed. Oundle School and Trinity Coll., Cambridge; Temporary Experimental Officer, Anti-Submarine Establishment and Admiralty Signals Establishment 1940–45; Demonstrator, later Lecturer in Physiology Univ. of Cambridge 1949–60; Research Fellow, Trinity Coll., Cambridge 1948–52; Fellow of Peterhouse, Cambridge, and Dir. of Studies in Medicine 1952–60; Head of Physiology Dept., Agricultural Research Council Inst. of Animal Physiology, Babraham 1960–65, Dir. of Inst. 1965–73; Prof. of Physiology, Univ. of Cambridge 1973–86; Sec.-Gen. of Int. Union for Pure and Applied Biophysics 1972–78, Vice-Pres. 1978–81, Pres. 1981–84; Chair. ICSU/UNESCO Int. Biosciences Networks 1982–93; Pres. Fed. European Physiological Socs. 1991–94; Fellow of Churchill Coll., Cambridge 1961–, Fellow of Eton 1963–78; Hon. Fellow Peterhouse 1989; Ed. The Beagle Record 1979. *Publications:* Nerve and Muscle (with D. J. Aidley) 1981, Charles Darwin's Beagle Diary 1988, Lydia and Maynard: the letters of Lydia Lopokova and John Maynard Keynes 1989. *Leisure interest:* pre-Columbian antiquities. *Address:* 4 Herschel Road, Cambridge, CB3 9AG; Primrose Farm, Wiveton, Norfolk, NR25 7TQ, England. *Telephone:* (01223) 353107; (01263) 740317.

KEYWORTH, George Albert, II, PH.D.; American scientist and government official; b. 30 Nov. 1939, Boston; s. of Robert Allen and Leontine Briggs Keyworth; m. Polly Lauterbach 1962; one s. one d.; ed. Deerfield Acad., Yale Univ., Duke Univ., Research Asst. Duke Univ. 1963–68, Research Assoc. 1968; Staff mem. Physics, Los Alamos Nat. Lab. 1968–73; Asst. Group Leader, Neutron Physics, Los Alamos 1973–74, Group Leader 1974–77, Deputy Physics Div. Leader 1978, Div. Leader 1978–81, Acting Laser Fusion Div. Leader 1980–81; Science Adviser to Pres. of U.S.A., Dir. Office of Science and Tech. Policy, Washington, D.C. 1981–85, Consultant 1985–86; Chair. The Keyworth Co. 1986–, Progress and Freedom Foundation, Washington 1995–; Dir. of Research, Hudson Inst. 1988–90, Distinguished Fellow 1990–; mem. American Physical Soc., A.A.A.S.; Hon. Prof. (Fudan Univ.) 1984; Hon. D.Sc. (Rensselaer Polytechnic Inst.) 1982, (Univ. of Alabama) 1985; Hon. D.Eng. (Mich. Tech. Univ.) 1984. *Publications:* numerous publs. on science and tech., nat. defence, and nuclear physics. *Leisure interests:* skiing, backpacking. *Address:* Progress and Freedom Foundation, 1250 H Street, N.W., Washington, DC 20005, U.S.A.

KHADDAM, Abdel Halim; Syrian politician; Minister of the Economy and Foreign Trade 1969–70; Deputy Prime Minister and Minister of Foreign Affairs 1970–84; Vice-Pres. for Political and Foreign Affairs 1984–; mem. Regional Command, Baath Party 1971–84. *Address:* Office of the President, Damascus, Syria.

KHADDURI, Majid, B.A., L.H.D., PH.D., LL.D.; Iraqi writer and educationist; b. 27 Sept. 1908, Mosul, Iraq; m. Majdia Khadduri 1942 (died 1972); one s. one d.; ed. American Univ. of Beirut and Univ. of Chicago; Sec.-Treas. Baghdad PEN Club; mem. American Soc. of Int. Law; Iraqi del. to the 14th Conf. of the PEN Clubs in Buenos Aires 1936; mem. the Iraq del. at the San Francisco Conf. 1945; Visiting Lecturer in Near Eastern Politics at Indiana Univ. 1947–48; fmr. Prof. Modern Middle-Eastern History at the Higher Teachers' Coll., Baghdad, Iraq 1938–49; taught Middle East politics at Chicago and Harvard Univs. 1949–50; Prof. Middle East Studies, Johns Hopkins Univ. 1950–80, Emer. 1980–; Dir. of Research and Education, Middle East Inst. 1950–80; Visiting Middle East Prof., Columbia Univ.;

mem. American Political Science Asscn. and Pres. Shaybani Soc. of Int. Law (Washington); Corresp. mem., Acad. of Arabic Language, Cairo, Iraqi Acad.; Order of Rafidain (Iraq), Order of Merit, 1st Class (Egypt). *Publications:* The Liberation of Iraq from the Mandate (in Arabic) 1935, The Law of War and Peace in Islam 1941, The Government of Iraq 1944, The System of Government in Iraq (in Arabic) 1946, Independent Iraq 1951, War and Peace in the Law of Islam 1955, Islamic Jurisprudence 1961, Modern Libya 1963, The Islamic Law of Nations 1966, Republican Iraq 1969, Political Trends in the Arab World 1970, Arab Contemporaries 1973, Socialist Iraq 1978, Arab Personalities in Politics 1981, The Islamic Conception of Justice 1983, The Gulf War 1988, War in the Gulf 1990–91 1997. *Leisure interest:* long-distance walking. *Address:* 4454 Tindall Street, N.W., Washington 20016, DC, U.S.A. *Telephone:* (202) 966-2702.

KHAIL, Muhammad Ali Aba al-; Saudi politician; b. 1935, Buraidah; ed. Cairo Univ.; worked with Ministry of Communications to est. Inst. of Public Admin. 1961; Dir.-Gen. Inst. of Public Admin. 1962–63; Deputy Minister of Finance and Nat. Economy 1964, Vice-Minister 1970, Minister of State 1971; mem. Council of Ministers 1971; Minister of Finance and Nat. Economy 1975–96; Chair. Saudi Int. Bank (London), Public Investment Fund, Inst. of Public Admin., Pension and Retirement Fund, Saudi Arabia- U.S. Joint Comm. on Econ. Co-operation, Saudi Arabian-German Joint Comm. on Econ. and Tech. Co-operation, Saudi Arabian-Sino Perm. Jt. Cttee. on Econ. and Tech. Co-operation; mem. several bds.; numerous medals and decorations. *Leisure interests:* reading, indoor sports. *Address:* c/o Ministry of Finance and National Economy, Airport Road, Riyadh 11177, Saudi Arabia.

KHAIN, Viktor Yefimovich, D.SC.; Russian geologist; b. 26 Feb. 1914, Baku; s. of Sophia and Yefim Khain; m. Valentina Kuzmina 1949; two s.; ed. Azerbaijan Industrial Inst.; geologist at oil fields, Azerbaijan 1935–39; Assoc. Azerbaijan Oil Research Inst. 1939–41; army service 1941–45; mem. CPSU 1943–90; Sr. Assoc., Inst. of Geology, Acad. of Sciences, Azerbaijan S.S.R. 1945–54; Prof. Azerbaijan Industrial Inst. 1949–54; Head of Dept. Museum of Earth Sciences, Moscow Univ. 1954–60; Senior Assoc., Vernadsky Inst. of Geochemistry and Analytical Chem., U.S.S.R. Acad. of Sciences 1957–71; Prof. Geology Dept., Moscow Univ. 1961–94, Prof. Emer. 1994–; Sec.-Gen. Subcomm. for the Tectonic Map of the World, Int. Geological Congress 1972–87, Pres. 1988–; Senior Assoc., Geological Inst., U.S.S.R. Acad. of Sciences 1972–91, Institute of the Lithosphere, Russian Acad. of Sciences 1991–; Corresp. mem. U.S.S.R. Acad. of Sciences 1966–87, mem. 1987; mem. New York Acad. of Sciences 1994; Hon. mem. Moscow Soc. of Naturalists, Bulgarian Geological Soc., Acad. Europaea 1994; Foreign mem. Soc. Géologique de France, Geological Soc. of London, Georgian Acad. of Sciences 1996; Hon. Prof. of Earth Sciences, Changchun Univ. 1996; Hon. D.Sc. (Univ. P. et M. Curie, Paris) 1977; State Prize, U.S.S.R. 1987, Prestwich Prize, Soc. Géologique de France 1990, Steinmann Medaille, Geologische Vereinigung (GDR) 1991, Karpinsky Gold Medal (U.S.S.R. Acad. of Sciences) 1991, Fourmarier Medaille d'Or (Acad. Royale de Belgique) 1993, Lomonosov Prize (Moscow Univ.) 1993, State Prize, Russia 1995. *Publications include:* Geotectonic Principles of Oil Prospecting 1954, The Geology of Caucasus (with E. E. Milanovsky) 1963, General Geotectonics 1964, Regional Geotectonics (5 vols.) 1971–85, Geology of U.S.S.R. 1985, General Geology 1988 (co-author), Historical Geotectonics (Vol. 1) 1988 (with N. A. Bozhko), (Vol. 2) 1991 (with K. B. Seslavinsky), (Vol. 3) 1993 (with A. N. Balukhovsky), Geology of Northern Eurasia 1994, Main Problems of Modern Geology 1994, Geotectonics and Principles of Geodynamics (with M. G. Lomize) 1995, History and Methodology of Geological Sciences (with A. G. Ryabunkin) 1996, Historical Geology (with N. V. Koronovsky and N. A. Yasamanov) 1997. *Address:* Department of Geology, Moscow State University, Moscow 119899, Russia. *Telephone:* 939-11-09; 203-81-23 (Office); 242-44-47 (Home). *Fax:* (095) 233-5590.

KHAIRAT, Taha al-; Syrian diplomatist; b. 1936, Daka'a; m. Khadija Salamat 1957; three s. three d.; ed. Univ. of Damascus; teacher, Ministry of Educ. 1957–69; Dir. of Social Affairs and Security 1969–70; Sec. Baath Party br. in Daraa 1970–71; mem. regional leadership, Baath Arab Socialist Party 1971–80; Minister of Local Admin. 1976–80; Amb. to Bulgaria 1982–89; Dir. Arab Dept. Ministry of Foreign Affairs 1990–96. *Leisure interests:* reading. *Address:* c/o Ministry of Foreign Affairs, Damascus, Syria. *Telephone:* 6110882 (Home).

KHAKAMADA, Irina Mutzuovna; CAND. ECON.; Russian politician; b. 13 April 1955, Moscow; m. 3rd Vladimir Sirotinsky; one s. one d.; ed. Univ. of Friendship of Peoples in Moscow; mem. Research Inst. State Planning Cttee. 1981–85; teacher Tech. Inst. of Automobile Factory 1985–89; sr. expert Russian Stock Exchange of Raw Materials 1990; mem. Party of Econ. Freedom 1992, Sec.-Gen and Co-Chair. 1992–94; Pres. Liberal Women's Foundation 1994; mem. State Duma 1993–97; leader pre-election union Obscheye Delo 1995; Chair. State Cttee. for Support of Small Enterprises 1997–98. *Address:* Myasnitskaya str. 35, 101959 Moscow, Russia (Office). *Telephone:* (095) 207-95-50 (Office). *Fax:* (095) 207-95-50.

KHALATNIKOV, Isaac Markovich, D.PHYS.MATH.SC.; Russian theoretical physicist; b. 17 Oct. 1919, Dniepropetrovsk; m. Valentina Nikolaevna Shchors; two d.; ed. Dniepropetrovsk State Univ., U.S.S.R. Acad. of Sciences; jr. researcher, sr. researcher, head of div. Inst. of Physical Problems U.S.S.R. Acad. of Sciences 1945–65; Dir. L.D. Landau Inst. of Theoretical Physics, U.S.S.R. (now Russian) Acad. of Sciences 1965–92, Hon. Dir. 1992–; Adviser Russian Acad. of Sciences 1993–; Prof. Moscow Inst. of Physics and Tech. 1954–; Prof., Tel Aviv Univ. School of Physics and Astronomy 1993–; f., Pres. Landau Network Centro Volta, Como, Italy 1995; Corresp. mem. U.S.S.R. Acad. of Sciences 1972, mem. 1984; Foreign mem. Royal Soc. 1994; U.S.S.R. State Prize 1953, Landau Prize in Physics 1976, Alexander von Humboldt Prize 1992. *Publications:* more than 150 papers on solid state physics, relativistic cosmology, quantum field theory. *Leisure interests:* chess, draughts. *Address:* Landau Institute, Kosygina str. 2, 117940 Moscow, Russia. *Telephone:* (095) 137-32-44.

KHALID, Mansour, LL.D.; Sudanese diplomatist and lawyer; b. 13 Dec. 1931, Omdurman; s. of Khalid Mohammed and Sara Sawi; ed. Univs. of Khartoum, Pennsylvania and Paris; began his career as an attorney, Khartoum 1957–59; Legal officer, UN, New York 1962–63; Deputy UN resident rep., Algeria 1964–65; Bureau of Relations with Member States, UNESCO, Paris 1965–69; Visiting Prof. of Int. Law, Univ. of Colo. 1968, Univ. of Khartoum 1982; Minister of Youth and Social Affairs, Sudan 1969–71; Chair. of del. of Sudan to UN Gen. Assembly, Special Consultant and Personal Rep. of UNESCO Dir.-Gen. for UNWRA fund-raising mission 1970; Perm. Rep. of Sudan to UN 1971; Pres. UN Security Council; Minister of Foreign Affairs 1971–75, of Educ. 1975–77, of Foreign Affairs Feb.-Sept. 1977; Asst. to Pres. for Co-ordination and Foreign Affairs 1976, Asst. to Pres. for Co-ordination 1977; fmr. mem. Political Bureau and Asst. Sec.-Gen., Sudan Socialist Union 1978; resgnd. from all political posts July 1978 but remained mem. of Gen. Congress of the Sudan Socialist Union; Chair. Bureau of Trilateral Co-operation, Khartoum 1978–80; Personal Rep. for Exec. Dir. of UNEP Anti-desertification Programme 1981–82; UN Special Consultant on Co-ordination of UN Information System 1982; Chair. Univ. Devt. Cttee., Univ. of Khartoum 1982; Fellow, Woodrow Wilson Center, Smithsonian Inst. 1978–80, Financial and Investment Consultant 1980–; Loyal Son of Sudan and numerous foreign decorations. *Publications:* Private Law in Sudan 1970, The Nile Basin, Present and Future 1971, Solution of the Southern Problem and its African Implications 1972, The Decision-Making Process in Foreign Policy 1973, Sudan Experiment with Unity 1973, A Dialogue with the Sudanese Intellectuals, Nimeiri and the Revolution of Dis-May 1985, 1985, The Government They Deserve: the role of the elite in Sudan's political evolution 1990. *Leisure interests:* music, gardening. *Address:* P.O. Box 2930, Khartoum, Sudan (Home); 9 Jubilee Palace, London, S.W.3, England.

KHALIFA, H. H. Sheikh Hamad bin Isa al-; Amir of Bahrain; b. 28 Jan. 1950, Bahrain; s. of the late Shiekh Isa bin Salman al- Khalifa; m. Sheikha Sabeeka bint Ibrahim Al-Khalifa 1968; six s. four d.; ed. Secondary School, Manama, Bahrain, Leys School, Cambridge Univ., Mons Officer Cadet School, Aldershot, England, and U.S. Army Command and Gen. Staff Coll., Fort Leavenworth, Kan., U.S.A.; formed Bahrain Defence Force 1968, Commdr.-in-Chief 1968–, also C.-in-C. Nat. Guard, raised Defence Air Wing 1978; mem. State Admin. Council 1970–71; Minister of Defence 1971–88; Deputy Pres. Family Council of Al-Khalifa 1974–; succeeded as Ruler on the death of his father March 1999; created Historical Documents Centre 1976; founder-mem. and Pres. Bahrain High Council for Youth and Sports 1975–; initiated Al-Areen Wildlife Parks Reserve 1976; f. Salman Falcon Centre 1977, Amiri Stud, Bahrain 1977; f. Bahrain Equestrian and Horse Racing Asscn., Pres. 1977–; Founder Bahrain Centre for Studies and Research 1989; Orders of the Star of Jordan (1st Class) 1967, Al-Rafidain of Iraq (1st Class) 1968, National Defence of Kuwait (1st Class) 1970, Al-Muhammedi of Morocco (1st Class) 1970, Al-Nahdha of Jordan (1st Class) 1972, Qiladat Gumhooreeya of Egypt (1st Class) 1974, The Taj of Iran (1st Class) 1973, King Abdul-Aziz of Saudi Arabia (1st Class) 1976, Repub. of Indonesia (1st Class) 1977, Repub. of Mauritania (1st Class) 1969, El-Fateh Al-Adheem of Libya (1st Class) 1979, Kuwait Liberation 1994, Hon. K.C.M.G. (U.K.), Ordre nationale du Mérite de la République Française (1st Class) 1980, Grand Cross of Isabel la Católica of Spain (1st Class) 1981; Freedom of the City of Kansas 1971, U.S. Army Certificate of Honour 1972; Hon. mem. Helicopter Club of G.B. *Leisure interests:* horse riding, golf, study of ancient history and prehistory of Bahrain, water skiing, swimming, fishing, falconry, shooting, football, tennis. *Address:* The Crown Prince's Court, Al-Zahir Palace, P.O. Box 28788, Bahrain. *Telephone:* 666333. *Fax:* 664587.

KHALIFA, Brig. Gen. Khalifa bin Ahmed al-; Bahraini army officer; b. 20 June 1945, Muharraq, Bahrain; ed. Royal Mil. Acad., Sandhurst; platoon commdr.; training co. commdr.; Infantry Co. Commdr.; Bn. second in command; Battalion Commdr.; fmr. Chief of Staff, Bahrain Defence Force. *Address:* c/o Ministry of Defence, P.O. Box 245, West Rifaa, Bahrain. *Telephone:* 661-656.

KHALIFA, Sheikh Khalifa bin Sulman al–; Bahraini politician; b. 1935; son of the late Sheikh Sulman and brother of the ruler, Sheikh Isa (q.v.); Dir. of Finance and Pres. of Electricity Bd. 1961; Pres. Council of Admin. 1966–70; Pres. State Council 1970–73, Prime Minister 1973–; Chair. Bahrain Monetary Agency. *Address:* Office of the Prime Minister, P.O. Box 1000, Government House, Government Road, Manama, Bahrain. *Telephone:* 225-522. *Fax:* 229-022.

KHALIFA, Sheikh Mohammed bin Mubarak al-, B.A.; Bahraini politician; b. 1935; s. of Sheikh Mubarak bin Hamad al-Khalifa; m.; two c.; ed. American Univ. of Beirut, Oxford Univ. and Univ. of London; attended Bahrain Courts as cand. for the bench, Dir. of Information 1962; head Political Bureau 1968 (now Dept. of Foreign Affairs); State Council 1970;

Minister of Foreign Affairs 1971–. *Address:* Ministry of Foreign Affairs, P.O. Box 547, Government House, Government Road, Manama, Bahrain. *Telephone:* 227-555. *Fax:* 212-603.

KHALIFA BIN HAMAD AL-THANI, Sheikh (see Thani, Sheikh Khalifa bin Hamad al-).

KHALIKYAR, Fazle Haq; Afghanistan politician; b. 1934, Shahr-e Naw, Herat; s. of Gholam Yahya; ed. Kabul Univ.; govt. employee in Ministry of Planning 1958–60; Ministry of Internal Affairs 1962–64, Ministry of Communications 1966–67; Gen. Auditor, Kabul Prov.; Admin. Pres. Ministry of Finance 1969; Gov. Baghlan Prov. 1971; Deputy Minister of Finance 1971–72, First Deputy Minister of Finance 1972–81; Minister Counsellor, Council of Ministers and Gov.-Gen. North-Western Zone 1981–90; Prime Minister of Afghanistan 1990; Hero of the Republic.

KHALIL, Mustafa, M.SC., D.PHIL.; Egyptian politician, engineer and banker; b. 18 Nov. 1920, El Kalyoubieh; ed. Univ. of Cairo, Illinois Univ., U.S.A.; served in Egyptian State Railways 1941–47, 1951–52; training with Chicago-Milwaukee Railways (U.S.A.) 1947; lecturer in Railways and Highway Engineering, Ain Shams Univ., Cairo 1952; Tech. Consultant to Transport Cttee., Perm. Council for Nat. Production 1955; Minister of Communications and Transport 1956–64, of Industry, Mineral Resources and Electricity 1965–66; Deputy Prime Minister 1964–65; resigned from Cabinet 1966; Head of Broadcasting Corpn. 1970; Prime Minister 1978–80, also Minister of Foreign Affairs 1979–80; Deputy Chair. Nat. Democratic Party May 1980; Chair. Arab Int. Bank, Cairo 1980–. *Leisure interest:* music. *Address:* Arab International Bank, P.O. Box 1563, 35 Abdel Khalek Sarwat Street, Cairo (Office); 9A El Maahad El Swisry Street, Zamalek, Cairo, Egypt (Home). *Telephone:* 3905765 (Office); 3416111 (Home). *Fax:* 3916356.

KHALILOV, Erkin Khamdamovich, CAND. JUR.; Uzbekistan politician; b. 1955, Bukhara, Uzbekistan; m.; three s.; ed. Tashkent State Univ.; engineer Research-Production Unit Cybernetics 1977–79; jr., sr. researcher, Head of Div. Inst. of Philosophy and Law Uzbek Acad. of Sciences, 1979–90; people's deputy Repub. of Uzbekistan; Chair. Cttee. on Law, Deputy Chair. Oliy Majlis (Supreme Soviet) 1990–93; Acting Chair. 1993–95, Chair. 1995–. *Address:* Oliy Majlis, 700008 Tashkent, Uzbekistan (Office).

KHAMENEI, Ayatollah Seyed Ali; Iranian politician and religious leader; b. 1940, Mashad, Khorassan; m. 1964; four s. one d.; ed. Qom; studied under Ayatollah Khomeini; returned to Meshed 1964; imprisoned six times 1964–78, once exiled in 1978; fmr, personal rep. of Ayatollah Khomeini, Supreme Defence Council; Friday Prayer Leader, Teheran 1980–; Sec.-Gen. (and Pres. Cen. Cttee.) Islamic Republican Party 1980–87; Pres. of Iran 1981–89; Wali Faqih (Religious Leader) June 1989–; mem. Revolutionary Council until its dissolution Nov. 1979; survived assassination attempt June 1981, Commdr. Revolutionary Guards 1980; Rep. of Revolutionary, Ministry of Defence. *Leisure interests:* traditional Persian athletics. *Address:* Office of the Religious Leader, Teheran, Iran.

KHAMSY, Saly; Laotian diplomatist; b. 13 Feb. 1931, Bane Khone; s. of Thao Liène and Nang Thong Thiep; m. Nang Boun Nhom 1959; two s. two d.; ed. Phnom Penh (legal studies) and Ecole des Sciences Politiques, Paris; began diplomatic service career 1958; served Paris, Moscow, Tokyo; First Sec. and Counsellor, Tokyo 1972–75; Ministry of Foreign Affairs 1976–79; Amb. to Japan 1980–83, to India 1983–88; Perm. Rep. to UN 1988–93. *Leisure interests:* fishing, gardening. *Address:* c/o Ministry of Foreign Affairs, rue That Luang, Vientiane, Laos.

KHAN, Ali Akbar; Indian classical musician; b. 14 April 1922, Shivpur (now in Bangladesh); s. of Dr. Allauddin Khan and Medina Khan; m. Mary J. Khan; début Allahabad 1936; world tours since 1955; Founder Ali Akbar Coll. of Music, Calcutta 1956, San Rafael, Calif. 1968, Basel, Switzerland 1982; Musical Dir. of many films including award-winning Hungry Stones; numerous appearances at concerts and major festivals, world-wide; musical collaboration with Yehudi Menuhin, Ravi Shankar (qq.v.), the late Duke Ellington and others; lecture recitals at major univs., incl. Montreal, McGill, Washington, San Diego and Tennessee; composer of concerti, orchestra pieces and several ragas, notably Chandranandan, Gauri Manjari, Alamgiri, Medhavi; Propr. Alam Madina Music Productions (record co.); f. Ali Akbar Khan Foundation 1994; MacArthur Foundation Fellowship 1991; Nat. Heritage Fellowship 1997; recipient Meet the Composer/Arts Endowment Commissioning Music grant 1996; Hon. D.Litt. (Rabindra Bharati Univ., Calcutta) 1974; Dr. Arts, Calif. Inst. of Arts 1991; Pres. of India Award 1963, 1966, Grand Prix du Disque 1968, Padma-bhibhushan Award 1989, Kalidas Award 1992, Bill Graham Lifetime Award, B.A.M. 1993, Asian Paints Shiromani Award 1997, Nat. Acad. of Recording Arts and Science Gov.'s Award for Outstanding Achievement 1998, Asiatic Soc. of Calcutta Indira Gandhi Gold Plaque 1998; Ustad Ali Akbar Khan Day f. San Francisco, 18 Oct. 1998. *Address:* Ali Akbar College of Music, 215 West End Avenue, San Rafael, CA 94901, U.S.A. *Telephone:* (415) 454-6264.

KHAN, Amjad Ali; Indian musician; b. 9 Oct. 1945, Gwalior, Madhya Pradesh; s. of the late Ustad Hafiz Ali Khan and Rahat Jahan Begum; m. Subhalakshmi Bardoah 1976; two s.; sarod player; numerous concert performances including Pakistan 1981, China 1981, Hong Kong Arts Festival 1982, Festival of India (London) 1982; numerous recordings for maj. recording cos. in India and abroad; recording Raag Bhairav named one of best CDs in world, BBC Music Magazine 1996; mem. World Arts Council, Geneva; Founder-Pres. Ustad Haviz Ali Khan Memorial Soc. (promotion of Indian classical music and dance); Visiting Prof. Univ. of York, U.K. 1995; Hon. D. Univ. (York) 1997, (Delhi) 1998; awards include UNESCO Award, Int. Music Forum 1970, 1975, Special Honour, Sahitya Kala Parishad, Delhi 1977, Musician of Musicians, Bhartiya Vidhya Bhavan, Nagpur 1983, Amjad Ali Khan Day (Mass.) 1984, Acad. Nat. Award (Tirupathi) 1987, Raja Ram Mohan Roy Teacher's Award 1988, Sangit Natak Acad. Award 1989, Tansen Award, Nat. Cultural Org., New Delhi 1989, Vijaya Ratna Award, India Int. Friendship Soc., New Delhi 1990, Crystal Award, World Econ. Forum 1997, and others; Hon. Citizen Nashville, Tenn. 1997, Houston, Tex. 1997; Padma Shree 1975, Padma Bhusan 1991, Sarod Samrat, Gwalior 1993. *Compositions include:* many ragas; music for Kathak ballets Shan E Mughal, Shahajahan Ka Khwab, Ganesh; orchestral compositions Ekta Se Shanti, Ekta Ki Shakti, Tribute to Hong Kong (for Hong Kong Philharmonic Orchestra). *Leisure interests:* music, television, light reading, long walks. *Address:* 3 Sadhna Enclave, Panchsheel Park, New Delhi 110 017, India. *Telephone:* 6216082, 6449062. *Fax:* 6489011.

KHAN, Ghulam Ishaq; Pakistani politician and civil servant; b. 1915, Bannu; s. of late Ghulam Muhammad Khan; m. Shamin Ishaq 1950; one s.; ed. Islamia Coll., Peshawar, and Punjab Univ.; North-West Frontier Province (N.W.F.P.) Civil Service (India) 1940–47, Sub-Divisional Officer, Treasury Officer and Magistrate First Class 1940–44; Bursar and Sec. to Council of Management of Islamia Coll., Peshawar; Sec. to Chief Minister, N.W.F.P. 1947; Home Sec. Food and Dir. Civil Supplies to Govt. N.W.F.P. 1948; Devt. and Admin. Sec. for Agriculture, Animal Husbandry, Forests, Industries, Co-operatives and Village Aid 1949–52; Devt. Commr. and Sec. to Devt. Dept., N.W.F.P. 1953–56; Sec. for Devt. and Irrigation, Govt. of W. Pakistan 1956–58; mem. W. Pakistan Water and Power Devt. Authority 1958–61, Chair. 1961–66; mem. Land Reforms Comm. 1958–59, Chair. 1978–; Sec. Finance, Govt. of Pakistan 1966–70; Cabinet Sec. Govt. of Pakistan 1970; Gov. State Bank of Pakistan 1971–75; Sec.-Gen. Ministry of Defence 1975–77; Sec.-Gen.-in-Chief (status of Fed. Minister), Adviser for Planning and Co-ordination 1977–78; Adviser to Chief Martial Law Administrator 1978; Minister for Finance and Co-ordination 1978–79, for Finance, Commerce and Co-ordination 1979–85; Chair. Econ. Co-ordination Cttee. of the Cabinet 1978–85; Chair. Exec. Cttee. Nat. Econ. Council 1978; Deputy Chair. of Planning Comm. 1979–82, Chair. 1982; Chair. of Senate 1985–88; Pres. of Pakistan (a.i.) Aug.–Nov. 1988, Pres. 1988–93; Chair. of Jt. Ministerial Cttee. of Bd. of Govs. of World Bank and IMF 1982–88; Chair. Org. of Islamic Conf. Standing Cttee. on Scientific and Technological Co-operation 1988; Life Pres. Soc. for Promotion of Eng. Sciences and Tech. in Pakistan; Pres. Bd. of Govs. G.I.K. Inst. of Eng. Sciences and Tech.; Tamgha-i-Pakistan 1959, Sitara-i-Pakistan 1962, Halal-i-Quaid-i-Azam 1968, Int. Asscn. of Lions Clubs Head of State Medal, Int. Sword of Islam Award, Islamic Foundation, U.S.A. 1993; Grand Croix, Légion d'honneur. *Leisure interest:* social work. *Address:* 3/B Jamrud Road, University Town, Peshawar, NWFP, Pakistan. *Telephone:* (521) 842216. *Fax:* (521) 841966.

KHAN, Imran (see Imran Khan Niazi).

KHAN, Inamullah; Pakistani religious leader; b. 17 Sept. 1914, Rangoon, Burma; s. of H. H. A. Karim Khan and Amanat Zohra Bibi; m. Khadija Khalik 1939; one s. five d.; ed. Rangoon Univ.; Ed.-in-Chief Burma Muslim Daily –1942; in India 1942–46; Pakistani citizen 1948–; f. Modern World Muslim Congress; Hon. Pres. World Conf. on Religion and Peace; First Muslim recipient of Niwano Peace Prize and Templeton Prize. *Leisure interests:* reading, writing. *Address:* D-26, Block 8, Gulshan-e-Iqbal, Karachi 75300, Pakistan. *Telephone:* (021) 460712 (Office); (021) 468737 (Home).

KHAN, Muhammad Ishtiaq, M.A., F.R.A.S., F.S.A.; Pakistani museum director and archaeologist; b. 1 May 1934, Jhajjar, Rohtak Dist., India; s. of late Haji Muhammad Ishaq Khan and Amna Khatoon; m. Perveen Ishtiaq 1964; one s. four d.; ed. Punjab and Harvard Univs.; went to Pakistan 1947; Univ. Research Scholar, Lahore 1956–57, Archaeological Scholar 1957–58; Custodian, Archaeological Museum, Moenjodaro 1959–61, Taxila 1961–65, Harappa 1965; Asst. Supt. of Archaeology, Directorate of Archaeology 1965–66; Asst. Supt. of Archaeology, Nat. Museum of Pakistan, Karachi 1966–70; Supt. of Archaeology, W. Pakistan Circle, Lahore 1970–73; Dir. of Archaeology and Museums, Govt. of Pakistan 1973–83, fmr. Dir.-Gen.; Chair. Pakistan ICOM Nat. Cttee.; Gold Medal, Mongol Acad., Lahore. *Publications:* Lahore Fort 1974, Archaeology of Sind 1975, Shalamar 1977; articles in various journals. *Leisure interest:* reading. *Address:* Department of Archaeology and Museums, 27-A, Al-Asif Building, Commercial Area, Shaheed-e-Millat Road, Karachi, Pakistan.

KHAN, Niazi Imran (see Imran Khan Niazi)

KHAN, Lieut.-Gen. Sahabzada Yaqub; Pakistani politician, diplomatist and retd. army officer; b. 1920; served Second World War, Middle East; joined Pakistan Army, Commdr. armoured regt. 1947; attended Army Staff Coll., Quetta 1949, Ecole Supérieure de Guerre, Paris 1953–54, later Imperial Defence Coll., London; Vice-Chief Gen. Staff, Pakistan Army 1958; Commdr. armoured div.; Commandant Army Staff Coll., Quetta; Chief Gen. Staff; Corps Commdr. and Commdr., Eastern Command until 1970; Amb. to France (also accred. to Ireland and Jamaica) 1972, to U.S.A. 1973–79, to U.S.S.R. 1979–80, to France 1980–82; Minister of Foreign Affairs 1982–87, 1988–91, Special Rep. of UN in Western Sahara 1992. *Address:* c/o Department of

Peace-keeping Operations, Room S-3727-B, United Nations, New York, N.Y. 10017, U.S.A.

KHANE, Abd-El Rahman, M.D.; Algerian politician, administrator, and physician; b. 6 March 1931, Collo; m. 1955; three s. one d.; ed. Univ. of Algiers; served as officer in Nat. Liberation Army until Algerian independence 1962; Sec. of State, provisional govt. (GPRA) 1958–60; Gen. Controller Nat. Liberation Front 1960–61; Head of Finance Dept., GPRA 1961–62; Pres. Algerian-French tech. org. for exploiting wealth of Sahara sub-soil 1962–65; Pres. Electricité et Gaz d'Algérie July-Oct. 1964; mem. Bd. Dirs. Nat. Petroleum Research and Exploitation Co. 1965–66; Minister of Public Works and Pres. Algerian-French Industrial Co-operation Org. 1966–70; Physician, Cardiology Dept., Univ. Hosp. of Algiers 1970–73; Sec.-Gen. OPEC 1973–74; Exec. Dir. UNIDO 1975–85; founding mem., mem. Bd. Worldwatch Inst. *Address:* 42 chemin B. Brahimi, El Biar, Algiers, Algeria. *Telephone:* (02) 924483.

KHANH, Emanuelle (pseudonym of Renée Nguyen); French fashion designer; b. 12 Sept. 1937; m. Manh Khanh Nguyen 1957; one s. one d.; fmr. fashion model for various Paris houses including Balenciaga and Givenchy; designer of jr. sportswear for Cacharel, Paris 1962–67; established own co., launching Missoni knitwear etc. Paris 1970; founded own label, specializing in embroidered clothes, accessories etc. 1971. *Address:* Emanuelle Khanh International, 39 Avenue Victor Hugo, 75116 Paris, France. *Telephone:* 01.44.17.31.00.

KHANI, Abdallah Fikri El-; Syrian politician, diplomatist and judge; b. 25 Jan. 1925, Damascus; s. of Saïd El-Khani and Jamilah El-Khani; m.; two d.; ed. Syrian Univ., Damascus, St. Joseph, Beirut, and American Univ., Beirut; lawyer 1947–49; various functions including Sec.-Gen. in Presidency of Repub. 1949–59; lecturer, School of Law, Syrian Univ. 1954–58; Minister Counsellor then Minister Plenipotentiary, Madrid, Brussels, Ankara, London and Paris 1959–69; Perm. Rep. to UNESCO 1966–69; Head del. to UN Gen. Assembly and Security Council 1970; Chair. Syro-Lebanese Perm. Comm. 1969–72; Minister for Tourism 1972–76; Sec.-Gen. of Ministry of Foreign Affairs 1969–72, Minister of Foreign Affairs (acting) 1973–74, Deputy Minister 1976–77; Amb. to India (also accred. to Bangladesh, Burma, Nepal and Sri Lanka) 1978–81; mem. and Vice-Chair. UN Sub.-Comm. on Prevention of Discrimination and Protection of Minorities 1978–81; mem. Int. Court of Justice, The Hague 1981–85; mem. Int. Court of Arbitration of ICC 1991–93; mem. American Soc. of Int. Law; Order of Merit (Syria, Egypt, Jordan, Indonesia), Order of the Egyptian Repub., Grand Cross of the Argentine Order of May, His Holiness Pope Paul VI Bronze Medal. *Leisure interests:* music, sport, reading, philately. *Address:* 46 Argentine Street, Damascus, Syria. *Telephone:* 214505.

KHARITONOV, Mark Sergeyevich; Russian writer; b. 31 Aug. 1937, Zhitomir, Ukraine; m. Galina Edelman; one s. two d.; ed. Moscow Pedagogical Inst.; teacher of secondary school; exec. sec. of newspaper; ed. of publishing house 1960–69; freelance 1969–; trans. Kafka, Stefan Zweig, Elias Canetti, Herman Hesse, Thomas Mann and others; works banned in official press until 1988; first Booker Russian Novel Prize for Lines of Fate or Milashevich's Trunk 1992. *Publications include:* Prokor Menshutin 1971 (published 1988), Provincial Philosophy 1977 (published 1993), Two Ivans 1980 (published 1988), Lines of Fate or Milashevich's Trunk 1985 (published 1992), Storozh 1994, The Voices 1994, Return from Nowhere 1995, Seasons of Life 1998, A Mode of Existence 1998. *Address:* Bazhova str. 15, corp. 1, Apt. 182, 129128 Moscow, Russia. *Telephone:* 187-56-92.

KHARRAT, Edwar al-, LL.B.; Egyptian author; b. 16 March 1926, Alexandria; m. 1958; two s.; ed. Alexandria Univ.; previously Asst. Sec.-Gen. Afro-Asian People's Solidarity Org., Afro-Asian Writers' Asscn.; translator and broadcaster for Egyptian Broadcasting Service; Assoc. Sr. mem. St. Antony's Coll. Oxford 1979; has lectured at S.O.A.S., London Univ.; Ed. The Lotus, Afro-Asian Writings; radio script writer and literary critic; Ali Al Owais Award (for fiction) 1995. *Publications include:* short stories: High Walls 1959, Hours of Pride 1972, Suffocations of Love and Mornings 1983; novels: Rama and the Dragon 1979, The Railway Station 1985, The Other Time 1985, City of Saffron 1986, The Ribs of Desert 1987, Girls of Alexandria 1990, Creations of Flying Desires 1990, Waves of the Nights 1991, Ruins of Bobello 1992, Penetrations of Passion and Perdition 1993, Fantasies on Fire 1994, Flying Edifices 1997, Certitude of Thirst 1997, Throes of Fact and Folly 1998; poetry: Cry of the Unicorn 1998; literary criticism: Transgeneric Writing, The New Sensibility, From Silence to Rebellion, Beyond Reality 1990, Hymn to Density 1995. *Address:* 45 Ahmad Hishmat Street, Zamalek, Cairo, Egypt. *Telephone:* 3416367. *Fax:* (202) 3416367.

KHARRAZI, Kamal; Iranian diplomatist and fmr. university professor; b. 1 Dec. 1944, Teheran; m.; two c.; ed. Teheran Univ., Univ. of Houston, U.S.A.; Teaching Fellow, Univ. of Houston 1975–76; Man. of Planning and Programming, Nat. Iranian Television 1979; Man. Dir. Centre for Intellectual Devt. of Children and Young Adults 1979–81; Deputy Foreign Minister for Political Affairs 1979–80; Man. Dir. Islamic Repub. News Agency 1980–89; mem. Supreme Defence Council, Head War Information HQ 1980–89; Prof. of Man. and Psychology, Teheran Univ. 1983–89; Perm. Rep. to UN, New York 1989–97; Founding mem. Islamic Research Inst., London; mem. American Asscn. of Univ. Profs. *Publications:* textbooks and articles in journals. *Address:* c/o Ministry of Foreign Affairs, Teheran, Iran.

KHASBULATOV, Ruslan Imranovich, D.ECON.SC.; Russian/Chechen politician and economist; b. 22 Nov. 1942, Grozny; m.; one s. one d.; ed. Kazan State Univ., Moscow State Univ.; instructor Cen. Cttee. of Comsomol 1970–72, head of sector Fundamental Library of Social Sciences U.S.S.R. Acad. of Sciences 1972–74, head of sector Research Inst. of Higher Educ. 1974–79, lecturer, prof., Head Chair. of Economy of Foreign Countries in Plekhanov Inst. (now Acad.) of Economy 1979–90, 1995–; People's Deputy of Russia 1990–93, First Vice-Chair., then Acting Chair. Supreme Soviet 1990–91, Chair. 1991–93; Chair. Interparl. Ass. of C.I.S. 1992–93; under arrest after failed coup d'état attempt Oct. 1993; charged with inciting mass disorder Oct. 1993; released Feb. 1994; one of the leaders of opposition to Pres. Dudaev in Chechen crisis 1994–95; stood as cand. for Pres. 1995, subsequently withdrew; Head, Chair. of Economy, Moscow Univ. 1995–; Corresp. mem. Russian Acad. of Sciences 1991. *Publications:* Bureaucracy and Socialism, Russia: Time of Change, Power, The Struggle for Russia 1993, Great Russian Tragedy 1995. *Address:* Russian G. Plekhanov Academy of Economy, Stremyanny per. 36, 113054 Moscow, Russia. *Telephone:* (095) 958-50-15.

KHASHOGGI, Adnan M.; Saudi Arabian business entrepreneur; b. 1935, Mecca; s. of Mohammad Khashoggi; m. 1st Soraya Khashoggi (divorced 1980); four s. one d.; m. 2nd Laura Biancolini 1978; one s.; ed. Victoria Coll., Egypt and Calif. State Univ.; businessman in Seattle 1953–56; contract to sell trucks to Saudi Arabian Army 1956; Sales Agent in Saudi Arabia for Chrysler, Fiat, Westland Helicopters Ltd. and Rolls-Royce 1962, for Lockheed, Northrop and Raytheon 1964; came to prominence with oil-boom in mid-1970s, founding his own co. Triad, based in the U.S.A.; owns houses in Marbella, Paris, Cannes, Madrid, Rome, Beirut, Riyadh, Jeddah, Monte Carlo and the Canary Islands; arrested in Berne over illegal property deals April 1989, acquitted 1990.

KHATAMI, Hojjatoleslam Seyyed Mohammad, B.PHIL; Iranian politician; b. 1943, Ardkan, Yazd; s. of Ayatollah Seyyed Rooh Allah Khatami (religious scholar); m. 1974; one s. two d.; ed. Qom and Isfahan seminaries and Univ. of Teheran; Man. Islamic Centre, Hamburg; mem. for Ardakan and Meibod, first Islamic Consultative Ass. (Parl.); rep. of Imam Khomeini and Dir. Kayhan newspaper; fmr. Minister of Culture and islamic Guidance; Cultural Deputy HQ of C.-in-C. and Head Defence Publicity Cttee.; fmr. Minister of Culture and Islamic Guidance; fmr. Adviser to Pres. Rafsanjani and Pres. Nat. Library of Iran; fmr. mem. High Council of Cultural Revolution; Pres. Islamic Repub. of Iran May 1997–. *Publications:* Fear of Wave, From World of City to World City, Faith and Thought Trapped by Selfishness and numerous articles and speeches. *Address:* Office of the President, Pastor Avenue, Teheran, Iran. *Telephone:* 616 2440. *Fax:* 616 2824.

KHATIB, Hisham, PH.D.; Jordanian energy and environmental consultant and former politician; b. 5 Jan. 1936, Acre, Palestine; s. of Mohamed Khatib and Fahima Khatib; m. Maha Khatib 1968; two s. one d.; ed. Univs. of Cairo, Birmingham, London; Chief Engineer Jerusalem Electricity Co. 1965–73; Deputy Dir. Gen. Jordanian Electricity Authority 1974–76; Sr. Energy Expert Arab Fund, Kuwait 1976–80; Dir. Gen. Jordan Electricity Authority 1980–84; Minister of Energy 1984–90; Vice-Chair. World Energy Council 1989–92; int. energy consultant 1990–93; Minister of Water and Planning 1993–95; Chair. Cttee. for Developing Countries World Energy Council 1992–95; int. consultant 1995–; now Hon. Vice-Chair. World Energy Council; Achievement Medal, Inst. of Electrical Engineers (U.K.) 1998; decorations from Jordan, Sweden, Italy, Indonesia and Austria. *Publications:* Economics of Reliability 1978, Financial or Economic Evaluation of Projects 1997, numerous articles in professional journals. *Leisure interest:* collecting Nineteenth Century Jerusalem and Holy Land artefacts. *Address:* P.O. Box 925387, Amman, Jordan. *Telephone:* 6-5621-532 (Office); 6-5815-316 (Home). *Fax:* 6-5698-556.

KHAVIN, Vladimir Yosifovich; Russian architect; b. 1931, Moscow; s. of Yosif Efimovich Khavin and Sophya Danilovna Khavina; m. Nadezhda Ermakova; one s.; ed. Moscow Architectural Inst.; Head of Workshop no. 12 of Mosproekt-1; teacher, Moscow Inst. of Architecture 1976–; Lenin Prize 1984. *Works include:* Circus Bldg. on Vernadsky St., Moscow 1963–71, October Square 1972, Intourist Hotel Complex by Kakhovskaya Metro Station 1980, Monument to Frunze, Frunze 1965, The Rear to the Front Monument, Magnitogorsk 1972–79, memorial complex To the Heroes of the Civil War and the Great Patriotic War, Novorosiysk 1982, Moscow town-building exhbn., Brestskaya St. 1985, Palace of Youth on Komsomolskaya Ave., Moscow 1988, new residential dist. Yushnoye Buruvo 1990–, reconstruction of Cheryomushkinski Dist., Moscow 1990–, Russian Jt.-Stock Co. complex GASPROM 1995, apt. houses, Namyotkina str. 1997; Honoured Architect of Russia 1988. *Leisure interest:* painting. *Address:* Glavmosarchitektura, Triumfalnaya Square 1, 103001 Moscow (Office); Novocheryomushkinskaya str. 71/82, Apt. 259, 123056 Moscow, Russia (Home). *Telephone:* 251-61-72 (Office); 719-97-16 (Home). *Fax:* 251-61-72.

KHAYATA, Abdul Wahab Ismail, PH.D.(ECONS.); Syrian economist; b. 24 Feb. 1924, Aleppo; s. of Ismail Khayata and Fatma Othman Hammami; m.; two s. two d.; ed. Ecole Française de Droit, Beirut, London School of Econs., U.K., Univ. of Louvain, Belgium; Lecturer, then Prof. of Econs. and Financial Analysis, Univ. of Damascus 1956–68; with Cen. Bank of Syria, rising to Deputy Gov. 1953–63; Under-Sec. Ministry of Planning 1963–68, Minister for Planning 1965; Deputy Dir. for Europe and the Middle East, UNDP,

New York 1971–73; Financial Adviser, UN, Beirut 1969–71, 1973–74; Gen. Man. FRAB Bank Int. Paris. 1974–78; Pres. and Deputy Chair. Cen. Bank of Oman 1978–90, Pres. 1990–91, Adviser to Deputy Chair. 1991–92; Pres. Syrian Centre for Services and Financial Consultancies 1993–; Order of Oman Award (Third Class) 1984. *Publications:* papers on finance in the Middle East and international economic co-operation, three books on economics. *Leisure interests:* swimming, chess. *Address:* P.O. Box 16006, Aleppo, Syria. *Telephone:* (21) 674 577. *Fax:* (21) 674 553.

KHAYOYEV, Izatullo; Tajikistan official; b. 22 June 1936, Khodzhaikhok, Kulyab Dist., Tajik S.S.R.; ed. Tajik Univ., Higher Party School; mem. CPSU 1961–91; worked in financial insts. 1954–61; Head of Dept., Ministry of Agric. 1961–63; Chair. of collective farm 1963–65; sr. posts in state and CP insts. 1966–78; Minister of Meat and Dairy Industry, Tajik S.S.R. 1978–83; First Sec. Kulyab Dist. 1983–86; Deputy, U.S.S.R. Supreme Soviet 1984–89; cand. mem. CPSU Cen. Cttee. 1986–91; Chair. Council of Ministers, Tajik S.S.R. 1986–90, Vice-Pres. Tajik S.S.R. 1990–91; Prime Minister 1991–92; Minister of Foreign Econ. Relations 1992–94; Head of Staff of Pres. Rakhmonov. *Address:* Office of the President, Dushanbe, Tajikistan.

KHAZANOV, Gennady Viktorovich; Russian comedian and actor; b. 1945, Moscow; m. Zlata Khazanov; one d.; ed. State High School of Circus and Variety Acts; worked in radio equipment factory; debut as actor Moscow Univ. Students' Theatre Nash Dom; compere L. Utyosov Orchestra; on professional stage since 1969 in solo productions, first production Trifles of Life 1981; variety programmes Evident and Unbelievable 1987, Little Tragedies 1987, Selected 1988; leading role Gamblers of XXI Century Moscow Art Theatre; leading role in film Little Giant of Large Sex; performed in America, Australia, Israel, Germany, Canada; First Prize All-Union Competition of Variety Artists; Artistic Dir. Variety Theatre Mono 1991–96; Dir., Artistic Dir. Moscow Variety Theatre 1997–; State Prize 1995. *Address:* Variety Theatre, Bersenevskaya Nab. 20/2, 109072 Moscow, Russia. *Telephone:* (095) 230-18-68.

KHIEM, Gen. Trân Thien (see Trân Thien Khiem, Gen.).

KHIEU, Samphan; Cambodian politician; b. 1932, Svay Rieng Prov.; m. Khieu Ponnary; ed. Paris Univ.; founded French-language journal, Observer, Cambodia; Deputy, Nat. Assembly in Prince Sihanouk's party, Sangkum Reastr Nyum (Popular Socialist Community); served as Sec. of State for Commerce; left Phnom-Penh to join Khmer Rouge 1967; Minister of Defence in Royal Govt. of Nat. Union of Cambodia (GRUNC) 1970–76, Deputy Prime Minister 1970–76 (in exile 1970–75, in Phnom-Penh 1975–76); mem. Politburo Nat. United Front of Cambodia (FUNC) 1970–79; C.-in-C. Khmer Rouge High Command 1973–79; Pres. of State Presidium (Head of State) 1976–79; Prime Minister of the Khmer Rouge opposition Govt. fighting Vietnamese forces 1979–91; Vice-Pres. of Govt. of Democratic Kampuchea (in exile) June 1982–91 (responsibility for Foreign Affairs); Pres. Khmer Rouge 1985–91, returned to Cambodia Nov. 1991; "Prime Minister" of illegal Provisional Govt. of Nat. Unity (fmrly. Khmer Rouge) 1994–; Chair. Party of Democratic Kampuchea; Pres. and founder Nat. Solidarity Party May 1997–; mem. Supreme Nat. Council 1991–97; Vice-Pres. in charge of Foreign Affairs, Nat. Govt. of Cambodia 1991; Chair. Cambodian Nat. Union Party (CNUP) 1993–97.

KHIZHA, Georgy Stepanovich, D.TECH.SC.; Russian politician and manager; b. 2 May 1938, Ashkhabad; m.; two d.; ed. Leningrad Polytech. Inst., Acad. of Nat. Econ.; engineer, head of div., Chief Engineer, Dir.-Gen. Leningrad Engels Factory (now Svetlana Asscn.) 1961–91; Deputy Prime Minister of Russia 1992–93, Chair. Expert Council 1993–, Int. Cttee. for Econ. Reforms and Co-operation 1993–96. *Publications:* more than 60 papers and a few dozen licensed inventions. *Address:* Expert Council, Krasnopresnenskaya nab. 2, 103274 Moscow, Russia. *Telephone:* (095) 205-59-67.

KHLEFAWI, Gen. Abdel Rahman; Syrian army officer; b. 1927, Damascus; m.; four c.; ed. schools in Damascus; entered Mil. Coll. 1949, graduated as Lieut. 1950; promoted to Maj.-Gen. 1971; attended courses abroad, especially in France and the U.S.S.R.; served in Syrian Arab Army; Gov. Deraa, Chair. of Municipality and Chief of its Police; later Gov. of Hama; Rep. of Syria, Joint Arab Command, Cairo 1965–67; Chief of Martial Court; Chief, Dept. of Officers' Affairs 1968–70; Minister of the Interior, Deputy Martial Judge 1970–71; mem. House of People 1971; Prime Minister 1971–72, 1976–78; mem. Progressive Nat. Front; elected as mem. in Regional Leadership of Socialist Arab Ba'ath Party and Chief of Econ. and Financial Bureau.

KHLYSTUN, Viktor Nikolayevich, DR. ECON.; Russian agricultural engineer and politician; b. 19 March 1946, Dmitrievka, Konchetav Region, Kazakhstan; m.; two c.; ed. Moscow Inst. of Agric. Eng. (MIIZ); metalworker, worker sovkhoz 1963–65; asst., sr. teacher, docent, Dean Moscow Inst. of Agric. Eng. 1971–77, Sec. CP Bureau 1977–80, Pro-rector 1980–90; Chair. R.S.F.S.R. State Cttee. on Land Reform 1990–91; Minister of Agric. 1991–93, 1995–98; Deputy Chair. of Russian Govt. responsible for agric. problems 1997–98; Dir.-Gen. Inst. of Agrarian Market Research, Moscow 1998–; Prof., Academician, Russian Acad. of Agricultural Sciences. *Address:* Moscow Institute of Land Planning Use Engineering, 6, 2nd Institutskaya str., 109428 Moscow, Russia (Office). *Telephone:* (095) 171-29-50. *Fax:* (095) 171-29-50.

KHODORKOVSKY, Mikhail Borisovich; Russian businessman; b. 26 June 1963; m.; two s.; ed. D. Mendeleev Moscow Inst. of Chemistry and Tech.; Head Center of Interfield Research Programmes (N.T.T.M.) U.S.S.R. State Cttee. for Science and Tech. (now Menatep Asscn.) 1986–93; Chair. Bd. of Dirs., Menatep Bank 1993–; Chair. Bd. Commercial Innovation Bank of Scientific Progress 1989–90; Econ. Counsellor to Chair. of Russian Council of Ministers 1990–91; Deputy Minister of Fuel and Energy Industry 1991; Chair. Bd. of Dirs. Rosprom co. 1995–; Vice-Pres. YUKOS Asscn. 1996, Pres. Rosprom-YUKOS 1996–. *Address:* Association Menatep, Dubininskaya 17a, Moscow, Russia. *Telephone:* 235-88-15, 935-90-03.

KHORANA, Har Gobind, PH.D., M.SC.; Indian-born scientist; b. 9 Jan. 1922, Raipur; m. Esther Elizabeth Sibler 1952; one s. two d.; ed. Punjab Univ.; began career as organic chemist; worked with Sir Alexander Todd on building nucleotides, Cambridge 1950–52; later worked with Nat. Research Inst., Canada, until 1960; Prof. and Co-Dir. Inst. of Enzyme Chem., Univ. of Wis. 1960–64, Conrad A. Elvehjem Prof. in Life Sciences 1964–70; Andrew D. White Prof.-at-Large, Cornell Univ., Ithaca 1974–80; Alfred P. Sloan Prof. M.I.T. 1970–; mem. N.A.S.; Foreign Academician U.S.S.R. Acad. of Sciences 1971; Foreign mem. Royal Soc. London 1978; Pontifical Acad. of Sciences 1978; numerous hon. degrees, Nobel Prize for Medicine and Physiology (with Holley and Nirenberg) for interpretation of genetic code and its function in protein synthesis 1968, Louisa Gross Horwitz Prize for Biochem. 1968, American Chem. Soc. Award for creative work in Synthetic Chem. 1968, Lasker Foundation Award 1968, American Acad. of Achievement Award 1971, Willard Gibbs Medal 1974, Gairdner Foundation Annual Award 1980, Nat. Medal of Science 1987, Paul Kayser Int. Award of Merit 1987. *Publications:* Some Recent Developments in the Chemistry of Phosphate Esters of Biological Interest 1961; articles on Biochemistry in various journals. *Leisure interests:* music, hiking. *Address:* Departments of Biology and Chemistry, Massachusetts Institute of Technology, 77 Massachusetts Avenue, Room 68-680, Cambridge, MA 02139. U.S.A.

KHOUNA, Cheikh el Avia Ould Mohamed; Mauritanian politician; mem. Democratic and Social Republican Party (DSRP); fmr. Minister of Fisheries and Marine Economy; Prime Minister of Mauritania 1996–97, Nov. 1998–. *Address:* Office of the Prime Minister, Nouakchott, Mauritania.

KHRENNIKOV, Tikhon Nikolayevich; Russian composer; b. 10 June 1913, Yelets, Lipetsk region; s. of Nikolay Khrennikov and Varvara Kharlamova; m. Klara Arnoldovna Vax (Khrennikova) 1936; one d.; ed. Moscow Conservatoire; Dir. of Music Central Theatre of Soviet Army 1941–54; Gen. Sec. Soviet Composers' Union 1948–57, First Sec., then Chair. 1957–91; Chair. Int. Asscn. of Composers Unions 1991–92, Hon. Chair. 1995–; Pres. Tchaikovsky Int. Competition 1978–90; Prof. Moscow Conservatory 1966–; mem. CPSU 1947–91; Deputy to U.S.S.R. Supreme Soviet 1962–89; mem. Cttee. U.S.S.R. Parl. Group; mem. Cen. Auditing Comm., CPSU 1961–76; cand. mem. CPSU Cen. Cttee. 1976–87; U.S.S.R. People's Deputy 1989–91; mem. Santa Cecilia 1983; State Prize 1942, 1946, 1951, 1967, 1979, People's Artist of the R.S.F.S.R. 1955, of the U.S.S.R. 1963; Hero of Socialist Labour 1973, Lenin Prize 1974, UNESCO Prize 1977, Glinka Prize 1979. *Principal compositions:* four piano concertos 1933, 1971, 1983, 1991, Five Pieces for Piano 1933, First Symphony 1935, Three Pieces for Piano 1935, Suite for Orchestra from Music for Much Ado About Nothing, In the Storm (opera) 1939, Second Symphony 1941, incidental music for play Long Ago 1942, Frol Skobeyev (opera) 1950, Mother (opera) 1956, Concerto for Cello and Orchestra 1959, A Hundred Devils and One Girl (operetta) 1961, two Concertos for Violin 1964, 1976, White Nights (operetta) 1967, Boy Giant (opera for children) 1969, Our Courtyard (ballet for children) 1970, Much Ado About Hearts (chamber opera) 1974, Third Symphony 1975, Love for Love (ballet) 1976, The Hussars' Ballad (Ballet) 1980, Dorothea (opera) 1982–83, The Golden Calf 1985 (opera), Napoleon Buonaparte (ballet) 1995, Captain's Daughter (ballet, after A. Pushkin) 1997. *Address:* Plotnikov per. 10/28, Apt. 19, 121200 Moscow, Russia. *Telephone:* 244-71-72.

KHRZHANOVSKY, Andrei Yurevich; Russian maker of animated films and scriptwriter; b. 30 Nov. 1939, Moscow; s. of Yuriy Borisovich Khrzhanovsky and Vera Mihayilovna; m. Mariya Newman 1972; one s.; ed. VGIK; worked with 'Soyuzmultfilm' since 1962; Chair. Bd. Higher Refresher Animation School-Studio; many prizes. *Films include:* Once upon a time there lived a man by the name of Kozyavin 1966, The Glass Harmonica 1968, The Cupboard 1971, The Butterfly 1972, In the World of Fables 1973, A Wonderful Day 1975, The House that Jack Built 1976, I Fly to You in Memory (trilogy of films based on Pushkin's doodles) 1977, 1981, 1982, The King's Sandwich 1985, The School of Fine Arts (part 1—A Landscape with Juniper 1987, part 2—The Return 1990), The Lion with the Grey Beard 1994, Oleg Kagan: Life After Life (documentary) 1996, The Long Journey (based on Federico Fellini's drawings) 1997, The Dreams About MKHAT (documentary) 1999, Etudys About Pushkin 1999. *Address:* Vasilyevskaya str. 7, Apt. 56, 123056 Moscow, Russia. *Telephone:* 254-51-75. *Fax:* 253-87-09.

KHUBLARYAN, Martin Gaykovich; Russian hydrologist; b. 5 March 1935; m. Servenik A. Gabrielyan 1968; two d.; ed. Armenian Inst. of Agric.; sr. researcher, head of lab., Deputy Dir. Inst. of Water Problems U.S.S.R., Acad. of Sciences 1968–88, Dir. 1988–; corresp. mem. U.S.S.R. (now Russian) Acad. of Sciences 1984, mem. 1994; research in hydromechanics, hydrology, hydrogeology; mem. American Soc. of Hydrology. *Publications include:* Chemical substance transport in soil and its effect on groundwater quality 1989, Water Streams: Models of flow and quality surface water 1991, numerous other publications. *Leisure interests:* reading memoirs, painting, classical music, chess. *Address:* Water Problems Institute of the Russian Academy of Sciences, 3 ul. Gubkina, 117971 Moscow, Russia. *Telephone:* (095) 135-54-56. *Fax:* (095) 135-54-15.

KHUDAIBERDYEV, Narmankhonmadi Dzhurayevich; Uzbekistan politician; b. 1928, Uzbekistan; ed. Uzbek Agric. Inst.; mem. CPSU 1948–91; dept. head, sec. of a Regional Uzbek Komsomol Cttee.; Lecturer, Assistant Prof. Agric. Inst., Samarkand 1943–54; leading CPSU and state posts 1954–; Sec. Bukhara Dist. Cttee. of Uzbek CP, Head Agric. Dept. of Cen. Cttee. of Uzbek CP; Second Sec. Bukhara Dist. Cttee. 1956–60; Deputy to Supreme Soviet of Uzbek S.S.R. 1959–63, 1967; mem. Cen. Cttee. of Uzbek CP 1960; Deputy Chair. Council of Ministers of Uzbek S.S.R. 1960–61; First Sec. Surkhan-Darya Dist. Cttee. of Uzbek CP 1961–62; Prime Minister of Uzbekistan 1971–85; cand. mem. Cen. Cttee. of CPSU 1961–66, mem. 1971; mem. Foreign Affairs Comm. of Soviet of the Union, U.S.S.R. Supreme Soviet 1962–66; Sec. and mem. Presidium of the Cen. Cttee. of the Uzbek CP 1962–65, Chair. Agric. Bureau 1962–64; Chair. Council of Ministers of Uzbek S.S.R. 1971–84; mem. Politburo of Cen. Cttee. of Uzbek CP 1971–84; sentenced to nine years in a labour camp for bribery Sept. 1989, released 1992.

KHUDONAZAROV, Davlatnazar; Tajikistan film director and politician; b. 13 March 1944; ed. All-Union Inst. of Cinematography; mem. CPSU 1981–91; film dir. and cameraman in documentary cinema 1965–77; début in feature film The First Morning of Youth 1979. *Films include:* Dzura Sarkor, Tale about Rustam, Rustam and Sokhrab, One Life is not Enough, Tale about Siyavush, A Brook Ringing in Melted Snow (Prize of All-Union Film Festival 1983); Chair. Confed. of Cinema Unions 1990–; U.S.S.R. People's Deputy, mem. of Supreme Soviet 1989–91; mem. Inter-regional Deputies' Group; Cand. for Pres. of Tajikistan; moved to Moscow after civil war 1992; State Prize of Tajikistan 1972 and other awards. *Address:* Confederation of Cinema Unions, Vasilyevskaya str. 13, 123825 Moscow, Russia. *Telephone:* (095) 250-41-14 (Office).

KHURANA, Sundar Lal, M.A.; Indian politician; b. 28 Feb. 1919, Jhang (now in Pakistan); s. of A. L. Khurana; ed. Govt. Coll., Lahore; m. 1955; two s.; joined Defence Forces as Civilian Officer in 1943, subsequently obtaining regular comm.; joined Indian Admin. Service 1949; various posts in Rajasthan 1950–55; Deputy Sec., Ministry of Community Devt., Govt. of India and mem. Exec. Cttee. Cen. Social Welfare Bd. 1955–59; Sr. UN Adviser to Govt. of Afghanistan 1959–62; Collector and Dist. Magistrate, Commr. for Border Dists., Rajasthan 1963–66; Chair. Rajasthan State Electricity Bd. 1966–70; Commr. for Home Affairs, Sec. for Jails, Transport and Information and Public Relations Depts., Rajasthan 1970–71; Chief. Sec. to Govt. and Sec. various Depts., Rajasthan 1971–75; Sec., Ministry of Home Affairs and Sec. Justice Dept., Govt. of India 1975–77; Exec. Pres. Hindustan Times Groups of Publs. 1979–80 and 1980–81; Adviser to Gov. of Rajasthan March–June 1980; Lieut.-Gov. of Delhi 1981–82; Gov. of Tamil Nadu 1982–88; Past Nat. Pres. All India Inst. of Marketing Man.; Vice-Pres. All India Inst. of Public Admin. *Publication:* Towards a New Order. *Address:* Raj Bhavan, Madras, Tamil Nadu, India.

KHUSH, Gurdev Singh, PH.D., F.R.S.; Indian agricultural research scientist and plant breeder; b. 22 Aug. 1935, Rurkee; s. of Kartar Singh and Pritam Kaur; m. Harwant Kaur Grewal 1961; one s. three d.; ed. Punjab Univ., Chandigarh, Univ. of California, Davis, U.S.A.; Research Asst., Univ. of Calif., Davis 1957–60, Asst. Geneticist 1960–67; Plant Breeder, Int. Rice Research Inst., Manila, Philippines, 1967–72, Head of Dept. of Plant Breeding 1972–; mem. Indian Nat. Science Acad., Third World Acad. of Sciences, N.A.S. (U.S.A.); Borlaug Award 1977, Japan Prize 1987, Agronomy Award 1989, World Food Prize 1996, Rank Prize 1998. *Publications:* Cytogenetics of Aneuploids 1974, Plant Breeding Lectures 1984, Host Plant Resistance to Insects 1995; 152 research papers and 40 book chapters. *Leisure interests:* world history, human rights. *Address:* International Rice Research Institute, P.O. Box 933, Manila, Philippines. *Telephone:* (2) 845-0563. *Fax:* (2) 891-1292.

KHUSSAIBY, Salim Bin Mohammed Bin Salim al-; Omani diplomatist; b. 11 March 1939; m.; three c.; ed. Teachers Coll., Zanzibar and Police Officers Coll., Kenya; teacher Secondary School, Dubai 1964–70; joined Royal Omani Police 1970, apptd. Deputy Inspector Gen. of Police and Customs; Minister Plenipotentiary Ministry of Foreign Affairs 1976, later Chargé d'affaires Omani Embassy, Nairobi; Consul Gen. Bombay 1979; Amb. to Kuwait 1980, to Pakistan, (also accred. to Nepal, Bangladesh, Brunei, Darussalem, Indonesia and Malaysia) 1982–87; Perm. Rep. to the UN Sept. 1987–. *Address:* Permanent Mission of Oman to the United Nations, 866 United Nations Plaza, Suite 540, New York, NY 10017, U.S.A. *Telephone:* 355-3505.

KHUWEITER, Abdul Aziz Abdallah al-; Saudi Arabian politician; b. 1927, Onaizah; s. of Abdullah Khuweiter and Moodi al-Khuweiter; m. Fatima al-Khuweiter 1963; one s. three d.; Vice-Rector King Saud Univ.; Head Directorate Supervision and Follow-up; fmr. Minister of Health; Minister of Educ. 1987–95, of State 1995–; King Abdulaziz Order of Merit (Second Class), Republican Order, Sudan (First Class). *Publications:* Fi Turuk al Bahth, Tarikh Shafi Ibn Ali (Ed.), Al-Malik al-Zahir Baybars (in Arabic and English), Al-Rawd al Zahir (Ed.), Min Hatab al-Layl, Ayy-Bunayy, Qiraah Fi Diwan al-Sha'ir Muh. Uthaymin. *Leisure interest:* reading. *Address:* Council of Ministers, Murabba Riyadh 11121, Saudi Arabia.

KHVOROSTOVSKY (Hvorostovsky), Dmitry Alexandrovich; Russian baritone; b. 17 Oct. 1962, Krasnoyarsk; m. Svetlana Khvorostovskaya; ed. Krasnoyarsk Inst. of Arts; début as opera singer 1984; soloist Krasnoyarsk Opera Theatre 1984–90; winner All-Union Glinka Competition 1987; winner int. competitions in Toulouse, Nice, Cardiff; has gained worldwide reputation after his recitals in London, New York 1989–90; début in Moscow 1990; performances in La Scala, Liceo, Metropolitan Opera and others; roles include Eugene Onegin, Figaro (Barber of Seville), Robert (Iolanthe), Germont (Traviata), Silvio (Pagliacci), Eletsky (The Queen of Spades); State Prize of Russia 1991; People's Artist of Russia 1995. *Address:* c/o Askonas Holt Company, 6 Henrietta, Street, London, WC2E 8LA; c/o Elen Victorova, Mosfilmovskaya 26, apt. 5, Moscow, Russia. *Telephone:* 0171-379 7700.

KIANO, Julius Gikonyo, M.A., PH.D.; Kenyan politician and economist; b. 1 June 1926, Weithaga, Kenya; s. of Jonathan Kiano and Damari Wanjiru Kiano; m. Jane Mumbi Kiano 1966; two s. three d.; ed. Alliance High School, Kikuyu, Makerere Univ. Coll., Uganda, Antioch Coll. Ohio, Stanford Univ. and Univ. of California at Berkeley, U.S.A.; lecturer in Econs. and Constitutional Law at Royal Tech. Coll., Kenya (now Univ. of Nairobi) 1956–58; elected mem. Kenya Legis. Council 1958–63; mem. Indian Govt. Cultural Scholarships Cttee. and U.S. Scholarship Cttee. 1959–62; mem. Kenya Advisory Council on Tech. Educ. and Vocational Training 1960–62; mem. Kenya Parl. 1963–79; Minister of Commerce and Industry 1963–66, Minister of Labour 1966–67, Minister of Educ. 1968–70, Minister of Local Govt. 1970–73, Minister of Commerce and Industry 1973–76, Minister of Water Devt. 1976–79; Chair. African Ministers of Educ. Conf. 1968, African Ministers of Industry Conf. 1975; mem. Common Market and Econ. Consultative Council of the East African Community 1973–76; Pres. UN Conf. on Desertification Aug.–Sept. 1977; Man. Dir. Industrial Devt. Bank of Kenya 1980–83; mem. Freedom from Hunger Council 1976–; mem. Governing Council UNEP 1977–79; mem. Exec. Cttee. Kenya African Nat. Union (KANU) 1978–79, Sec. KANU Parl. Group 1978–79; mem. exec. Cttee. Assoc. of African Devt. Finance Insts. 1981–83; Chair. Nat. Oil Corpn. of Kenya 1983–; Chair. Kenya Petroleum Refineries Ltd. 1988–89, Kenya Broadcasting Corpn. 1989–. *Leisure interest:* social welfare. *Address:* Kenya Broadcasting Corporation, Broadcasting House, P.O. Box 30456, Nairobi, Kenya.

KIAROSTAMI, Abbas; Iranian film director, producer, writer and editor; b. 22 June 1940, Teheran; m. (divorced); two s.; ed. Teheran Univ.; worked as designer and illustrator (commercials, film credit titles and children's books); involved in establishment of film making dept. at Inst. for Intellectual Devt. of Children and Young Adults (Kanoon); independent film maker from early 1990s; has made over twenty films including shorts, educational films, documentaries. *Films directed include:* Bread and Alley (short) 1970 (debut production of Kanoon film dept.), The Traveler 1973, So Can I (short) 1975, Two Solutions for One Problem (short) 1975, The Report (Gozaresh) 1977, The Toothache (public-service film) 1980, Chorus (short) 1982, Fellow Citizen 1983, First Graders (documentary) 1985, Earthquake Trilogy: Where Is the Friend's House? 1987, Homework (documentary) 1989, Close Up (documentary) 1990, And Life Goes On 1992 (Rossellini Prize, Cannes Film Festival), Through the Olive Trees 1994, The Taste of Cherry 1997 (Palme d'Or, Cannes Film Festival). *Film screenplays:* The Key 1987, The Journey 1995, The White Balloon 1995 (Caméra d'Or, Cannes Film Festival); more than 50 int. prizes including special prize of the Pasolini Foundation 1995. *Address:* c/o Zeitgeist Films Ltd., 247 Center Street, 2nd Floor, New York, NY 10013, U.S.A.

KIBAKI, Mwai, B.A., B.SC.(ECON.); Kenyan politician; b. 1931, Othaya; three s. one d.; ed. Makerere Univ. Coll., London School of Econs.; Lecturer in Econs., Makerere Univ. Coll. 1959–60; Nat. Exec. Officer Kenya African Nat. Union (KANU) 1960–64; elected by Legis. Council as one of Kenya's nine reps. in E. African Legis. Assembly of E. African Common Services Org. 1962; mem. House of Reps. for Nairobi Doonholm 1963–74; Parl. Sec. to Treasury 1963–64; Asst. Minister of Econ. Planning and Devt. 1964–66; Minister for Commerce and Industry 1966–69, of Finance 1969–70, of Finance and Econ. Planning 1970–78, of Finance 1978–82, of Home Affairs 1978–88, of Health 1988–91; Vice-Pres. of Kenya 1978–88; Vice-Pres. KANU 1978–91; Leader Democratic Party 1991, Official Opposition 1998–. *Leisure interests:* reading, golf. *Address:* Democratic Party, P.O. Box 72961, Nairobi, Kenya. *Telephone:* 216694; 217735. *Fax:* 230719.

KIBBLE, Thomas Walter Bannerman, C.B.E., M.A., PH.D., F.R.S.; British professor of physics; b. 23 Dec. 1932, Madras, India; s. of Walter F. Kibble and Janet C. W. (née Bannerman) Kibble; m. Anne R. Allan 1957; one s. two d.; ed. Melville Coll., Edinburgh and Univ. of Edinburgh; Commonwealth Fund Fellow, Calif. Inst. of Tech. 1958–59; NATO Fellow, Imperial Coll., London 1959–60, Lecturer in Physics 1961–65, Sr. Lecturer 1965–66, Reader in Theoretical Physics 1966–70, Prof. of Theoretical Physics 1970–98, Head, Dept. of Physics 1983–91, Emer. Prof. and Sr. Research Fellow 1998–; Sr. Visiting Research Assoc. Univ. of Rochester, N.Y. 1967–68; Chair. Scientists Against Nuclear Arms 1985–91; Hughes Medal 1981, Rutherford Medal 1984, Guthrie Medal 1993. *Publication:* Classical Mechanics 1966. *Address:* Blackett Laboratory, Imperial College, Prince Consort Road, London, SW7 2BZ, England. *Telephone:* 0171-594 7845. *Fax:* 0171-594 7844.

KIBEDI, Wanume, LL.B.; Ugandan politician and lawyer; b. 3 Aug. 1941, Busesa; s. of Mr. and Mrs. E.M. Kibedi; m. Elizabeth Kibedi (née Amin) 1970; one d.; ed. Busoga Coll. and Univ. of London; articled with Waterhouse and Co., London 1961–66, admitted solicitor 1966; worked in office of Attorney-Gen., Uganda 1968; Partner, Binaisa and Co. (advocates) 1969–70; Minister of Foreign Affairs Feb. 1971–73 (resigned); del. to UN Gen. Ass. 1971; Perm. Rep. to the UN 1986–89. *Leisure interests:* chess, tennis, reading. *Address:* c/o Ministry of Foreign Affairs, P.O.B. 7048, Kampala, Uganda.

KIBEDI VARGA, Aron, PH.D.; Netherlands professor of French literature and poet; b. 4. Feb. 1930, Szeged, Hungary; m. 1st T. Spreij 1954, 2nd K. Agh 1964, 3rd S. Bertho 1991; four s. one d.; ed. Univs. of Amsterdam, Leiden, Sorbonne; lecturer in French Literature, Free Univ. of Amsterdam 1954–66, Prof. 1971–; Prof. of French Literature, Univ. of Amsterdam 1966–71; Visiting Prof. Iowa Univ. 1971, Yale Univ. 1975, Princeton Univ. 1980, Rabat Univ. 1985, Coll. de France 1992; mem. Cttee. Int. Soc. for the History of Rhetoric 1979–83; Pres. Int. Asscn. Word and Image Studies 1987–93; mem. Royal Netherlands Acad. of Sciences 1981–; mem. Hungarian Acad. of Sciences 1990–. *Publications:* Criticisms: Les Constantes du Poème 1963, Rhétorique et Littérature 1970, Théorie de la Littérature (Ed.) 1981, Discours récit, image 1989, Les Poétiques du classicisme (Ed.) 1990; Poetry (in Hungarian): Kint és Bent 1963, Téged 1975, Szépen 1991. *Address:* Department of French, Vrije Universiteit, Amsterdam, Netherlands. *Telephone:* 4446456.

KIBIROV, Timur Yuryevich (b. Zapoyev); Russian poet; b. 15 Feb. 1955, Shepetovka; m. Yelena Ivanovna Borisova; one d.; ed. Krupskaya Moscow Regional Pedagogical Inst.; jr. researcher All-Union Research Inst. of Arts –1993; first poems published in Yunost and Continent 1989; Pushkin Prize (Germany) 1993, Prize of Druzhba Narodov (magazine) 1993. *Publications:* collections of poetry: Calendar 1990, Verses about Love 1993; Sentiments 1994, verses in leading literary journals. *Address:* Ostrovityanova str. 34, korp. 1, Apt. 289, Moscow, Russia (Home). *Telephone:* 420 6175 (Home).

KIBRIA, Shah A. M. S., M.A.; Bangladeshi politician and fmr. United Nations official; b. 1 May 1931, Sylhet; m.; one s. one d.; ed. Univ. of Dacca, Fletcher School of Law and Diplomacy, Boston, Mass., U.S.A.; joined diplomatic service of Pakistan 1954; served various embassies until 1971; declared allegiance to Bangladesh and joined Bangladesh mission, Washington, D.C. 1971; Dir.-Gen. Political Affairs Dept., Ministry of Foreign Affairs 1972; Sec. Ministry of Foreign Affairs 1972–73; High Commr. in Australia (also accred. to New Zealand and Fiji) 1973–76; Perm. Rep. to UN Offices, Geneva 1976–78; Chair. Preparatory Cttee., Group of 77 for UNCTAD V, Geneva 1978; Foreign Sec., Ministry of Foreign Affairs 1978–81; Exec. Sec. UN Econ. and Social Comm. for Asia and the Pacific (ESCAP) 1981–92; Special Rep. of UN Sec.-Gen. for Co-ordination of Cambodian Humanitarian Assistance Programmes 1987; Political Adviser to Pres. of Awami League 1994–; Minister for Finance 1996–. *Publications:* Mridhubason (essays on contemporary political, econ. and social issues) 1997, Bangladesh at the Crossroads (essays on int. and nat. issues) 1999. *Address:* House No. 58, Road No. 3/A, Dhanmondi Residential Area, Dhaka 5, Bangladesh.

KIBRICK, Anne, ED.D.; American professor of nursing; b. 1 June 1919, Palmer, Mass.; d. of Martin Karlon and Christine Grigas Karlon; m. Sidney Kibrick 1949; one s. one d.; ed. Boston Univ., Columbia Univ., Harvard Univ.; Head Nurse, Worcs. Hahnemann Hosp. 1941–43; Staff Nurse, Children's Hosp. Medical Center, Boston 1943–45; Educ. Dir., Charles V. Chapin Hosp., Providence, R.I. 1945–47; Asst. Educ. Dir., Veterans Admin. Hosp. 1948–49; Asst. Prof. Simmons Coll., Boston 1949–55; Dir. Graduate Programmes in Nursing, Boston Univ. 1958–63, Prof. and Dean 1963–70; Dir. Graduate Programs in Nursing, Boston Coll. 1970–74; Chair. School of Nursing Boston State Coll. 1974–82; Dean Coll. of Nursing Univ. of Mass., Boston 1982–88, Prof. 1988–93, Prof. Emer. 1993–; Consultant Nat. Student Nurses Asscn. 1985–88; Consultant, Hadassah Medical Org., Israel, Cumberland Coll. of Health Sciences, N.S.W., Australia, Menonfia Univ., Shebin El-Kam, Egypt; Fellow American Acad. of Nursing 1973–; mem. Inst. of Medicine, Nat. Acad. of Sciences 1970–, Brookline Town Meeting 1995–; Charter mem. Nat. Acads. of Practice 1985–; mem. Bd. of Dirs. Post-Grad. Medical Inst., Mass. Medical Soc. 1983–96, Exec. Cttee. 1988–96; dir. Landy-Kaplan Nurses Council 1992– (Treasurer 1994–); D.H.L. (St. Joseph's Coll.), Mary Adelaide Nutting Award, Distinguished Service Award and Isabel Stewart Award, Nat. League for Nursing, Service Award, Nat Hadassah Org. and other awards. *Publications:* (with H. Wechsler) Explorations in Nursing Research 1979, numerous professional articles. *Leisure interests:* reading, travel. *Address:* 381 Clinton Road, Brookline, MA 02445, U.S.A. (Home). *Telephone:* (617) 734-4751 (Home).

KIDD, Doug; New Zealand politician and lawyer; b. 1941, Levin; m.; three c.; partner, Wisheart MacNab & Partners (law firm) 1965–79; fmr. part-time mussel farmer, Marlborough Sounds; Nat. Party M.P. for Marlborough/Kaikoura 1978–; Minister of State-Owned Enterprises, of Fisheries, and Assoc. Minister of Finance 1990–91; Assoc. Minister of Finance and Minister of Maori Affairs 1991–94; Minister of Energy, of Fisheries, and of Labour 1994–96 and for Accident Rehabilitation and Compensation Insurance; elected Speaker of House of Reps. 1996; Chair. of Parl. Service Comm.; fmr. Foundation Pres. Marlborough Forest Owners' Asscn.; Hon. Col. of 2nd Bn. (Canterbury and Nelson Marlborough West Coast) Royal N.Z. Infantry Regt. *Address:* Parliament Buildings, Wellington, New Zealand.

KIDD, Jodie; British fashion model; b. 1979, Surrey; great granddaughter of late Lord Beaverbrook; ed. St. Michael's School, W. Sussex; spent much of childhood in Barbados; has modelled for numerous fashion magazines; also top int. catwalk model for designers including Gucci, Prada, Karl Lagerfeld, Yves Saint Laurent, Chanel, John Galliano, Calvin Klein and Yohji Yamamoto; make-up model for Chanel 1999 season; fmr. Nat. Jr. Athletics Champion; holder of Under-15s High Jump record for Sussex; many awards as a jr. show jumper. *Leisure interests:* riding, polo. *Address:* c/o IMG Models, 13–16 Jacob's Well Mews, George Street, London, W1H 5PD, England. *Telephone:* 0171-486 8011.

KIDMAN, Fiona Judith, D.N.Z.M., O.B.E.; New Zealand writer; b. 26 March 1940, Hawera; d. of Hugh Eric Eakin and Flora Cameron Eakin (née Small); m. Ian Kidman 1960; one s. one d.; ed. small rural schools in the north of N.Z.; Founding Sec./Organiser N.Z. Book Council 1972–75; Sec. N.Z. Centre, PEN 1972–76, Pres. 1981–83; Pres. N.Z. Book Council 1992–95, Pres. of Honour 1997–; founded Writers in Schools, Words on Wheels (touring writing co.), Writers Visiting Prisons; teaches creative writing; many literary prizes including N.Z. Book Awards (fiction category), Queen Elizabeth II Arts Council Award for Achievement, Victoria Univ. Writers' Fellow; N.Z. Scholarship in Letters. *Publications:* A Breed of Women 1979, Mandarin Summer 1981, Mrs. Dixon and Friend (short stories) 1982, Paddy's Puzzle 1983, The Book of Secrets 1986, Unsuitable Friends (short stories) 1988, True Stars 1990, Wakeful Nights (poems selected and new) 1991, The Foreign Woman (short stories) 1994, Palm Prints (autobiog. essays) 1995, Ricochet Baby 1996, The House Within 1997. *Leisure interests:* theatre, film, gardening. *Address:* P.O. Box 14-401, Kilbirnie, Wellington, New Zealand. *Fax:* 64 4 386 1895.

KIDMAN, Nicole; Australian actress; b. 1967, Hawaii; m. Tom Cruise (q.v.) 1990; one adopted s. and one adopted d.; ed. St. Martin's Youth Theatre, Melbourne, Australian Theatre for Young People, Sydney and Philip Street Theatre; acting début in Australian film aged 14; Australian Film Inst. Best Actress Award for role in TV mini-series Bangkok Hilton; voted Best Actress of Year in Australia for role in Vietnam. *Films include:* The Emerald City, The Year My Voice Broke, Flirting, Dead Calm, Days of Thunder, Far and Away, Billy Bathgate, Malice, My Life, Batman Forever, To Die For, Portrait of a Lady, The Peacemaker, Eyes Wide Shut 1998, Practical Magic 1999. *Play:* The Blue Room 1998–99. *Address:* c/o Creative Artists Agency, 9830 Wilshire Boulevard, Beverly Hills, CA 90212, U.S.A.

KIDWAI, Mohsina; Indian politician; b. 1 Jan. 1932, Banda Dist.; d. of Qutubuddin Ahmed; m. Khalilur Rahman Kidwai 1953; three d.; ed. Women's Coll., Aligarh; mem. U.P. Legis. Council 1960–74, Legis. Ass. 1974–77, Lok Sabha 1978–79, 1980–84; Minister of State for Food and Civil Supplies, Govt. of U.P. 1973–74, Minister of Harijan and Social Welfare 1974–75, of Small-Scale Industries 1975–77; Union Minister of State for Labour and Rehabilitation 1982–83, for Health and Family Welfare 1983–84, for Rural Devt. Aug.–Oct. and Nov.–Dec. 1984; Minister of Health and Family Welfare 1984–88, of Urban Devt. 1988–90; Pres. U.P. Congress Cttee. (I) 1976–80, 1982, now Pres. U.P. Congress Exec. (I); Founder Patron Nat. Girls' Higher Secondary School, Bara Banki and other insts. helping women, children and destitutes, including Harijans. *Leisure interests:* reading biographies and other literary works, music, badminton. *Address:* Civil Lines, Bara Banki, Uttar Pradesh, India.

KIEBER, Walter, D.JUR.; Liechtenstein politician and lawyer; b. 20 Feb. 1931, Feldkirch, Austria; s. of Alfons and Elisabeth Kieber; m. Selma Ritter 1959; one s. one d.; ed. Grammar School in Bregenz, Austria, Univ. of Innsbruck; lawyer in Vaduz 1955–59, 1981–; entered civil service as Head of the Govt. Legal Office 1959; Chief of Presidential Office 1965–; Sec.-Gen. of Govt. 1969, Deputy Head of Govt. 1970–74, Head of Govt. 1974–78, Deputy Head of Govt. 1978–80; Pres. Liechtenstein Bar Asscn. 1993–; Grand Cross, Liechtenstein Order of Merit, Grosses Goldenes Ehrenzeichen am Bande für Verdienste um die Republik Österreich (Austria); Progressive Citizens' Party. *Address:* Heiligkreuz 6, FL-9490 Vaduz (Office); Landstrasse 22, FL-9494 Schaan, Liechtenstein (Home). *Telephone:* 235 81 81 (Office); 232 25 29 (Home).

KIEFER, Anselm; German artist; b. 8 March 1945, Donaueschingen; m.; three c.; ed. Univ. of Freiburg and Freiburg Acad., Karlsruhe Acad.; first one-man exhbn., Galerie am Kaiserplatz, Karlsruhe 1969; first one-man exhbn. in U.S.A., Marian Goodman Gallery, New York; retrospective exhbns. Städtische Kunsthalle, Düsseldorf, Musée d'Art Moderne, Paris and Israel Museum, Jerusalem 1984, Stedelijk Museum, Amsterdam 1986, U.S. tour 1987–89; first group exhbn., Deutscher Künstlerbund, Kunstverein, Hanover 1969; has also exhibited Kunstverein, Frankfurt 1976, Kassel Documenta 1977, 1982, 1987, Biennale de Paris 1977, Venice Biennale 1980; other group exhbns. include Expressions: New Art from Germany, touring exhbn. U.S.A. 1983–84, touring exhbn. Moscow and Leningrad 1983, 1984 Museum of Modern Art survey of int. art, Fifth Biennale of Sydney, Australia 1984; works in many pvt. collections including Saatchi Collection, London, and in many public galleries including Art Inst. of Chicago, Museum of Modern Art, Phila. Museum of Art, Hirshhorn Museum, Washington, D.C., Los Angeles Museum of Contemporary Art and San Francisco Museum of Modern Art; Wolf Foundation Prize 1990. *Publication:* A Book by Anselm Kiefer 1988.

KIELMANSEGG, Gen. Johann Adolf, Graf von; German army officer (retd.); b. 30 Dec. 1906, Hofgeismar; s. of the late Adolf Graf von Kielmansegg and the late Eva Graefin von Kielmansegg (née von Werner); m. Mechthild Freiin von Dincklage 1933; two s. two d.; ed. Monastic School, Rossleben; Army Service 1926, Officer 1930; War Acad., Berlin 1937–39; Gen. Staff, 1st and 6th Panzer Div. 1939–42; OKH (High Command of the Army) 1942–44, C.O. Armed Infantry Regiment 111 1944–45; journalistic activities 1945–50; Office of the Fed. Chancellor 1950–55; Mil. Rep. of Fed. Repub. of Germany to SHAPE, Paris 1955–58; Second-in-Command, 5th Panzer Div. 1959–60, C.O. 10th Panzer Div. 1960–63; Defence Ministry, Bonn until 1963, promoted to rank of Gen. 1963; C.-in-C. Allied Land Forces, Cen. Europe 1963–66; C.-in.-C. Allied Forces, Cen. Europe 1966–68; now writer on politico-military matters; mem. Int. Inst. for Strategic Studies (London), German Asscn. for Foreign Affairs, Inst. for Foreign Policy Analysis, Cambridge, Mass.; fmr. mem. U.S. Strategic Inst. Washington, D.C.; fmr. Chair. Advisory Bd. Inst. for Research into Military History; Grand Cross of the Fed. Repub. with Ribbon and Star, Commdr. Légion d'honneur, Commdr. Legion of Merit. *Publications:* Der Fritsch—Prozess 1938, Unbesiegbar? China als Militärmacht 1985. *Leisure interests:* history, political science. *Address:* Parkstift St. Ulrich Hebelstr. 18, 79188 Bad Krozingen, Germany. *Telephone:* (07633) 403-325.

KIEP, Walther Leisler, C.B.E.; German politician and business executive; b. 5 Jan. 1926, Hamburg; s. of late Louis Leisler Kiep and Eugenie vom Rath; m. Charlotte ter Meer 1950; three s. (one deceased), two d.; ed. Hamburg, Istanbul, Frankfurt; with Ford Motor Co., then Insurance Co. of North America 1948–55, joined Gradmann and Holler 1955–, man. partner 1968–; Advisory Council of Deutsche Bank; mem. CDU 1961–, mem. Bundestag 1965–80, 1980–81; fmr. Chair. Parliamentary Cttee. on Foreign Aid, Treasurer, mem. Exec. Cttee. 1971–; Lower Saxony Minister for Econs. and Finance 1976–80, concurrently Special Envoy for Turkish aid; Deputy to Leader of Opposition 1980–81; Chair. Atlantik-Brücke, Bonn 1984–; mem. Int. European Advisory Bd. Fuji-Wolfensohn, New York 1989–; Chair. ZENECA GmbH, Plankstadt 1993–; Chair. Int. Advisory Bd., J. & H. Marsh & McLennan Cos. New York 1993–; Chair. Supervisory Bd. IABG, Ottobrunn 1994–; Pres. European Business School, Oestrich-Winkel 1994–; mem. Int. Advisory Bd., Coll. Univ., New York 1997–; Bundesverdienstkreutz mit Stern und Schulterband, Grosses Verdienstkreuz des Niedersächsischen Verdienstordens. *Publications:* Goodbye Amerika-Was Dann? 1972, A New Challenge for Western Europe 1974. *Leisure interest:* history. *Address:* Gradmann and Holler Holding Herriotstrasse 3, 60528 Frankfurt a.M., Germany. *Telephone:* (69) 6676-600. *Fax:* (69) 6676-602.

KIERANS, Eric William, O.C.; Canadian politician and economist; b. 2 Feb. 1914, Montreal; s. of Hugh Kierans and Lena (née Schmidt); m. Teresa Catherine Whelan 1938; one s. one d.; ed. Loyola Coll., Montreal, and McGill Univ., Montreal; Prof. of Commerce and Finance 1953–60; Dir. McGill School of Commerce 1953–60; Pres. Montreal and Canadian Stock Exchanges 1960–63; Minister of Revenue, Quebec 1963–65; Minister of Health, Quebec 1965–66; Pres. Quebec Liberal Fed. 1966–68; Postmaster-Gen. and Minister responsible for Dept. of Communications 1968–69; Minister of Communications 1969–71; Consultant to Manitoba Govt. on Resources Policy 1972; Dir. Savings and Trust Corpn. of B.C. 1975, Sidbec-Dosco Ltée 1978; Prof. of Econs., McGill Univ. 1972–80; Chair. Canadian Adhesives Ltd. 1980; Prof. of Econs., Dalhousie Univ., Halifax 1983–84; mem. Council N.S. Barristers' Soc. 1990–94; Hon. LL.D (McGill Univ.) 1981, (Concordia Univ.) 1987, (Dalhousie Univ.) 1991; Liberal. *Publications:* Challenge of Confidence: Kierans on Canada 1967, Natural Resources Policy in Manitoba 1973. *Leisure interest:* sports. *Address:* 1000 Winwick Road, Halifax, N.S. B3H 4L5, Canada.

KIJIMA, Torazo, B.ECONS.; Japanese business executive; b. 18 Dec. 1901; ed. Tokyo Imperial Univ. (now Univ. of Tokyo). Dir. Japanese Nat. Railways 1950–52; mem. House of Councillors 1953–59; Pres. Hinomaru Ceramic Industry Co. Ltd. 1953, Aito Vehicles Industries Co. Ltd.; Chair. Bd. of Dirs. Nippon Express Co. Ltd. 1968–; Second Grand Order of Sacred Treasure (Japan) 1972, Commdr., Grand Order (Madagascar) 1973.

KIKABIDZE, Vakhtang Konstantinovich; Georgian actor and singer; b. 19 July 1938, Tbilisi; s. of Konstantin Kikabidze and Manana Bagrationi; m. Irene Kebadze 1964; one s.; soloist and leader of Georgian pop-group Orero 1966–; film début in 1967 with Meeting in the Hills; U.S.S.R. State Prize 1978, People's Artist of Georgian S.S.R. 1980, Order of Honour, special award (Georgia) 1994. *Films include:* Meeting in the Hills 1967, Don't Grieve 1968, I'm a Detective 1969, The Stone of the First Water 1970, Pen-name Lukach, The Melodies of Verikysky Block 1973, Lost Expedition 1973, Completely Gone 1972, Mimino 1978, TASS is Authorized to Inform, Hi! Friend (TV film) 1981, To Your Health Dear (dir., scriptwriter, actor) 1983, Man and all the Others (scriptwriter, producer, actor) 1985. *Leisure interest:* fishing. *Address:* S. Chikovani Street 20, Apt. 38, 380015 Tbilisi, Georgia. *Telephone:* (8832) 99-06-49; (8832) 98-90-14 (Office); (8832) 36-36-16 (Home).

KIKHIA, Mansur Rashid; Libyan diplomatist and lawyer; b. 1 Dec. 1931, Benghazi; ed. Cairo and Paris Univs.; joined Diplomatic Service 1957; Asst. in Nationality and Consular Affairs Section, Ministry of Foreign Affairs 1957, Head, Treaties and Int. Confs. Section 1958–60, 1962–65; Second Sec. for Consular and Cultural Affairs, Paris 1960–62; Chargé d'affaires, Paris 1962, Algiers 1963; Consul-Gen., Geneva 1965–67; mem. Perm. Mission to UN 1967–69; Under-Sec. Ministry of Unity and Foreign Affairs 1969–72; Perm. Rep. to UN Jan.–July 1972, 1975–81; Minister of Foreign Affairs 1972–73; leader Libyan Nat. Alliance; private law practice in Tripoli 1973–75; mem. dels. to UN Gen. Assembly 1961, 1966–70, Chair. of del. 1970, 1972, 1975, 1976, Vice-Chair. 1977, 1978, Rep. Libyan del. UN Security Council 1976, 1977, Pres. Security Council Sept. 1976, Nov. 1977, Chair. Libyan del. Third UN Conf. Law of the Sea 1977, 1978, ad hoc comm. on drafting of int. convention against taking of hostages 1977, Chair. UN Security Council Sanctions Comm. 1977, Chair. Libyan del. to preparatory comm. for special session devoted to disarmament 1977–78. *Address:* 72 Baghdad Street, Tripoli, Libya.

KIKOIN, Konstantin Abramovich, PH.D.; Russian theoretical physicist; b. 9 Aug. 1945, Tver; s. of Abram Kikoin and Ekaterina Sosenkova; m. Larisa Markina 1969; one s. one d.; ed. Ural State Univ. (Sverdlovsk/Ekaterinburg), Physical-Tech. Inst. Moscow; Jr. Scientific Researcher, Inst. of Optical-Physical Measurements, Moscow 1971–74; Sr. Scientific Researcher I.V. Kurchatov Inst. of Atomic Energy, Moscow 1974–85, Leading Scientific Researcher Vice-Head Solid State Theory Dept. 1985–; Deputy Chair. Exec. Bd. Moscow Physical Soc. 1989–, Assoc. Ed. Journal of Moscow Physical Soc. 1990–; Assoc. Ed. Journal of Experimental and Theoretical Physics 1991–; Rep. of American Inst. of Physics in Moscow 1992–; mem. Expert Council of Supreme Attestation Cttee. 1994–. *Publications:* more than 70 papers in scientific journals. *Leisure interest:* translating poetry from Russian into English. *Address:* I.V. Kurchatov Institute, Kurchatov Square 46, 123182 Moscow (Office); Vasilevsky str. 9/5, Apt. 21, 123182 Moscow, Russia (Home). *Telephone:* (095) 1969348 (Office); (095) 1966087 (Home).

KIKUTAKE, Kiyonori, B.A., F.A.I.A.; Japanese architect; b. 1 April 1928, Kurume; s. of Kiyoshi and Masue Kikutake; m. Norie Sasaki 1953; one s. two d.; ed. Waseda Univ.; est. Kiyonori Kikutake & Assocs. (Architects) 1953, now Rep. Dir.; Prof. Dept. of Architecture, Waseda Univ. 1959; Vice-Pres. Japan Fed. of Professional Architects Asscns., Tokyo Professional Architects' Asscn., Japan Architects' Asscn. 1982–; now Exec. Dir. Tokyo YMCA Inst. of Design; mem. Bd. Architectural Inst. of Japan 1962–; Visiting Prof. Univ. of Hawaii 1971; del. to UNESCO Int. Conf., Zürich 1970; Hon. Fellow, American Inst. of Architects 1971. *Major works include:* Shimane Prefectural Museum 1958, Sky House 1958, Admin. Building for Izumo Shrine, Tatebayashi City Hall 1963, Hotel Tokoen, Yonago-City, Miyakonojo City Hall, Pacific Hotel, Chigasaki 1966, Iwate Prefectural Library 1967, Shimane Prefectural Library, Hagi Civic Centre 1968, Kurume Civic Centre 1969, Expo Tower for Expo 70, Osaka 1970, Pasadena Heights (tiered mass housing) 1974, Aquapolis (floating module for ocean), Ocean Expo 75 1975, Hagi City Hall 1975, Redevelopment of Yamaga city centre 1975, Tsukuba Academic New Town, Pedestrian Deck Network and the Symbol Tower 1976, Otsu Shopping Centre 1976, branches of Kyoto Community Bank 1971–, Tanabe Museum, Matsue City 1979, Darumaya-Seibu Dept. Store 1980, Treasury of Izumo Shrine 1981, Seibu-Yaow Shopping Centre 1981, Karuizawa Art Museum 1981, Kuamoto Pref. Arts and Crafts Centre 1982, Fukuoka City Hall (Assembly Hall) 1982; Edo Tokyo Museum 1992, Kurume City Hall 1994; several awards including Ministry of Educ. Arts Award 1964, Architectural Inst. of Japan Award 1964, Pan Pacific Architectural Citation of the Hawaii Chapter, AIA 1964, Cultural Merits of Kurume City 1975, Auguste Perret Award UIA 1978, XXI Mainichi Art Awards 1979. *Publications:* Metabolism 1960 1960, Taisha Kenchiku-ron (Metabolic Architecture) 1968, Ningen-no-Kenchiku (Human Architecture) 1970, Ningen-no-Toshi (A Human City) 1970, Essence of Architecture 1973, Floating City 1973, Kiyonori Kikutake—Works and Methods 1956–70 1973, Community and Civilization 1978, Kiyonori Kikutake-Concepts and Planning 1978, Ningen-no-Kankyo (Human Environment) 1978, Community and City 1978, Tight Spaces, Macro-Engineering 1982. *Leisure interests:* swimming, photography, reading, travel. *Address:* 1-11-15 Ohtsuka, Bunkyo-ku, Tokyo, Japan. *Telephone:* 03-941-9184; 03-941-0830.

KILAR, Wojciech; Polish composer; b. 17 July 1932, Lvov; m.; ed. State Higher School of Music in Katowice, (student of B. Woytowicz) Nadia Boulanger School; mem. Cttee. Int. Festival of Contemporary Music Warszewsa Jesień 1975, Polish Composers union 1953–, numerous awards in Poland and abroad. *Works include:* Mała uwertura 1955, I Symfonia 1955, II Symfonia 1956, Oda Bela Bartok in Memoriam 1957, Riff 62 1962, Générique 1963, Diphthongs 1964, Springfield Sonnet 1963, Solenne 1967, Upstairs Downstairs 1971, Przygrywke i Kolęda 1972, Krzesany 1974, Bogurodzica 1975, Kościelec 1909 1976, Siwa mgła 1979, Exodus 1981, Victoria 1983, Angelus 1984, Orawa 1986, Prelude for Strings 1988; music for about 30 plays and 100 films. *Leisure interests:* books about mountains and cats, travels. *Address:* ul. Kościuszki 165, 40-524 Katowice, Poland. *Telephone:* 51 49 65.

KILBURN, Tom, C.B.E., PH.D., D.SC., F.I.E.E., F.ENG., F.R.S.; British professor of computer science; b. 11 Aug. 1921; s. of John W. Kilburn and Ivy Kilburn; m. Irene Marsden 1943; one s. one d.; ed. Wheelwright Grammar School, Dewsbury and Sidney Sussex Coll. Cambridge and Manchester Univ.; Telecommunications Research Establishment, Malvern 1942–46; Lecturer, Univ. of Manchester 1949, Sr. Lecturer 1951, Reader in Electronics 1955, Prof. of Computer Eng. 1960, Prof. of Computer Science 1964–81, now Prof. Emer.; Hon. Fellow, UMIST 1984; Foreign Assoc. Nat. Acad. of Eng. of U.S.A.; Royal Medal, Royal Soc. 1978; Distinguished Fellow, British Computer Soc.; for hon. degrees and other awards and prizes. *Publications:* papers in professional journals. *Address:* 11 Carlton Crescent, Urmston, Greater Manchester, M41 9HZ, England. *Telephone:* 0161-748 3846.

KILGUS, Martin A., M.A., PH.D.; German journalist; b. 15 March 1963, Stuttgart; s. of Alfred Kilgus and Charlotte-Pauline Hofmann; ed. Wirtemberg-Gymnasium, Stuttgart, Univ. of Stuttgart and The American Univ., Washington, D.C.; traineeship, NBC Radio; joined Dept. for Ethnic Broadcasting, SDR Radio & TV, Stuttgart 1989; worked as ed. for migrants' audio broadcasts; 1991; now Ed. with SWR (fmrly. SDR) Radio & TV; special field of research and activity: Digital Audio Broadcasting (DAB) and multi-lingual broadcasts; Chair. Int. Educ. Information Exchange (IEIE e.V.), Stuttgart 1996–; mem. German Asscn. for the UN; Caritas Prize for Journalism. *Leisure interests:* arts, literature, cooking, snowboarding. *Address:* SWR Radio & TV, 70178 Stuttgart, Christophstrasse 10, Germany. *Telephone:* (711) 6075065. *Fax:* (711) 600499.

KILLICK, Sir John Edward, G.C.M.G.; British diplomatist; b. 18 Nov. 1919, Isleworth; s. of late Edward W. J. Killick and Doris M. Stokes; m. 1st Lynette de Preez 1949 (died 1984); m. 2nd Irene M. H. Easton, O.B.E. 1985 (died 1995); ed. Latymer Upper School, Univ. Coll., London and Univ. of Bonn; Mil. Service 1939–46; Control Comm. for Germany 1946; entered diplomatic service 1946; Foreign Office 1946–48, Berlin, Frankfurt and Bonn 1948–51; Foreign Office 1951–53; British Embassy, Addis Ababa 1953–57; Nat. Defence Coll. of Canada 1957–58; Foreign Office 1958–61; Imperial Defence Coll. 1962; British Embassy, Washington 1963–68; Asst. Under-Sec. of State, FCO 1968–71; Amb. to U.S.S.R. 1971–73; Deputy Under-Sec. of State, FCO 1973–75; Perm. Rep. to NATO 1975–79; Dir. Dunlop S. Africa 1980–85; Pres. British Atlantic Cttee. 1985–92; Vice-Pres. Atlantic Treaty Asscn. 1991–93; Chair. S.A. Club 1986–89. *Publication:* The United States and European Reconstruction 1998. *Address:* Challoner's Cottage, 2 Birchwood Avenue, Southborough, Kent, TN4 0VE, England.

KILLIP, Christopher David; British photographer; b. 11 July 1946, Isle of Man; s. of Allen Killip and Mary Quirk; one s.; ed. Douglas High School for Boys; photography in Isle of Man 1969–71; Prof. of Visual Studies, Harvard Univ. 1991–; exhbns. include: Isle of Man, Arts Council of G.B. (ACGB) Tour of U.K. 1980–82, Serpentine Gallery 1985, Nat. Museum of Photography, Bradford 1986, Art Inst. of Chicago 1986, Victoria & Albert Museum 1988, Landesmuseum, Munster 1988, Princesshof Museum, Netherlands 1989, IVAM, Valencia 1990, Palais de Tokyo, Paris 1990; group exhbns. include: Royal Acad. 1989, Barbican Centre, London 1989, Photography until now, Museum of Modern Art (MOMA), New York 1990; works in many public collections including Victoria & Albert Museum, George Eastman House, U.S.A., Stedelijk Museum, Amsterdam, Nat. Gallery of Australia; ACGB Photography Awards 1973–74; Northern Arts Photography Fellow 1975–76; ACGB Bursary Award 1977; Henri Cartier-Bresson Award, Paris 1989. *Publications:* Isle of Man (portfolio), Isle of Man (book) 1980, In flagrante 1988. *Address:* Harvard University, 24 Quincy Street, Cambridge, MA 02138, U.S.A.

KILLY, Jean-Claude; French Olympic skier and business executive; b. 30 Aug. 1943, Saint-Cloud, Seine-et-Oise; s. of Robert Killy and Madeleine de Ridder; m. Danièlle Gaubert 1973 (died 1987); one d., two step-c.; ed. Ecole de Val-d'Isère, Lycées in Chambéry, Grenoble, Saint-Jean-de-Maurienne, Bourg-Saint-Maurice; French Champion 1964, 1965, 1966; won three medals at Winter Olympics, Grenoble, France 1968; retd. from competitive skiing 1968; customs officer 1965–68; Publicity Agent Gen. Motors 1968; Marketing Consultant (concerning skiing information) United Air Lines 1969; Tech. Advisor Dynamic 1981–; Pres. World Sport Marketing (now Anaury Sport Org.) 1992–; mem. Admin Bd. Coca-Cola 1993–, Coca-Cola Enterprises 1997–, Int. Olympic Cttee. 1995–; Commdr., Légion d'honneur. *Publications:* Skiez avec Killy 1969, le Ski 1978. *Address:* Amaury Sport, 2 rue Rouget de Lisle, 92137 Issy-les-Moulineaux, France; 13 chemin Bellefontaine, 1223 Cologny-GE, Switzerland.

KILMER, Val; American actor; b. 31 Dec. 1959, Los Angeles; m. Joanne Whalley (q.v.) 1988 (divorced 1996); one d.; ed. Hollywood's Professional School, Juilliard; stage appearances include: Electra and Orestes, Henry IV Part One 1981, As You Like It 1982, Slab Boys (Broadway debut) 1983, Hamlet 1988, 'Tis Pity She's A Whore 1992; also appears on TV. *Films:* Top Secret 1984, Real Genius 1985, Top Gun 1986, Willow 1988, Kill Me Again 1989, The Doors 1991, Thunderheart 1991, True Romance 1993, The Real McCoy 1993, Tombstone 1993, Wings of Courage 1995, Batman Forever 1995, Heat 1995, The Saint 1996, The Island of Dr. Moreau 1996, The Ghost and the Darkness 1996, Dead Girl 1996, Joe the King 1999. *Address:* c/o CAA, 9830 Wilshire Boulevard, Beverly Hills, CA 90212, U.S.A.

KIM, Jung Won; Korean business executive; b. 3 March 1948; ed. Kyungnam Sr. High School, Guilford Coll., New York; joined Hanil Synthetic Fiber Ind. Co. Ltd. 1972, Exec. Man. Dir. 1974, Vice-Pres. 1975, Pres. 1979–; Pres. Hanhyo Co. Ltd. 1977, Chair. 1984–; Pres. Hanhyo Devt. Co. Ltd. 1978, Chair. 1984–; Pres. Kyungnam Woollen Textile Co. Ltd. 1979; First Chair. Hanhyo Acad. 1982; Pres. Korean Amateur Volleyball Asscn. 1983, Vice-Pres. Asian Volleyball Asscn. 1983; awarded Saemaul Decoration 1974; First Hon. Consul Kingdom of the Netherlands 1985. *Address:* Kukje-ICC Corpn., C.P.O. Box 747, Seoul, Republic of Korea.

KIM, H.E. Cardinal Stephen Sou-hwan; Korean ecclesiastic; b. 8 May 1922, Taegu; ed. Sophia Univ., Tokyo, Major Seminary, Seoul, and Sociology Dept., Univ. of Munster, Germany; ordained priest 1951; Pastor of Andong, Archdiocese of Taegu 1951–53; Sec. to Archbishop of Taegu 1953–55; Pastor of Kimchon (Taegu) 1955–56; Dir. Sung-Eui Schools, Kimchon 1955–56; sociology studies, Univ. of Munster, Germany 1956–64; Editor-in-Chief Catholic Shibo (weekly) 1964–66; Bishop of Masan 1966–68; Archbishop of Seoul 1968–; cr. Cardinal 1969; Pres. Bishops' Conf. of Korea until 1987, Pres. Follow-up Cttee. for Fed. of Asian Bishops' Conf. 1971–74; Apostolic Admin. for Pyongyang; Dr. h.c. (Sogang Univ. Seoul) 1974, (Notre Dame Univ., U.S.A.) 1977, (Sophia Univ., Tokyo) 1988, (Korea Univ.) 1990, (Seaton Hall Univ., U.S.A.) 1990, (Yonsei Univ.) 1994, (Fu-Jen Univ., Taiwan) 1995, (Ateneo Univ., Philippines) 1997. *Leisure interests:* music, literature. *Address:* Archbishop's House, 2-Ka 1, Myong-dong, Chung-ku, Seoul, Republic of Korea. *Telephone:* (02) 771-7600. *Fax:* 777-6660.

KIM DAE-JUNG, M.A., PH.D.; Korean politician; b. 3 Dec. 1925, Hugwang-ri, S. Cholla Prov.; m. Lee Lee Ho; ed. Mokpo Commercial High School, Korea and Kyunghee Univs., Diplomatic Acad. of Foreign Ministry of Russia; Pres. Mokpo Merchant Ship Co. 1948; arrested by N. Korean Communists, escaped from jail 1950; Pres. Mokpo Daily News 1950; Deputy Commdr. S. Cholla Region, Maritime Defence Force 1950; Pres. Heungkuk Merchant Shipping Co. 1951; Pres Dae-yang Shipbldg. Co. 1951; mem. Cen. Cttee. Democratic Party 1957, Spokesman 1960, Spokesman, Nat. Alliance to Protect Human Rights 1958; elected to 5th Nat. Ass. 1961, 6th Nat. Ass. 1963; Spokesman, People's Party 1965, Chair. Policy Planning Council and mem. Cen. Exec. Bd. 1966; Spokesman, New Democratic Party and mem. of Party Cen. Exec. Bd. 1967; elected to 7th Nat. Ass. 1967, 8th Nat. Ass. 1971; injured in assassination attempt 1971; in exile, organized anti-dictatorship movts. in Japan and U.S.A. 1972; abducted from Japan by Korean C.I.A. agents, survived two assassination attempts, forcibly returned to Seoul, placed under house arrest 1973; arrested for criticizing Constitution 1976; sentenced to five years' imprisonment 1977; sentence suspended, released from jail, placed under house arrest 1978; house arrest lifted 1979; amnesty granted, civil rights restored, rearrested, charged with treason, sentenced to death 1980; sentence commuted to life imprisonment 1981; sentence reduced to 20 years, later suspended 1982; went into exile in U.S.A. 1982; f. Korean Inst. for Human Rights, Va. 1983; returned to Korea 1985; under intermittent house arrest 1985–87; Co-Chair. Council for Promotion of Democracy 1985; Standing Adviser, Reunification Democratic Party 1987; f. Party for Peace and Democracy, Pres. 1987–91; reappointed to 13th Nat. Ass. 1988; f., Pres. New Democratic Party April-Sept. 1991; f. Democratic Party, Co.-Chair. 1991–92; reappointed to 14th Nat. Ass., later retd. from politics 1992; f. Kim Dae-Jung Peace Foundation for Asia-Pacific Region, Chair. Bd. of Dirs. 1994; ended retirement from politics 1995; f. Nat. Congress for New Politics 1995; Pres. of Repub. of Korea Dec. 1997–; Co-Pres. Forum of Democratic Leaders in Asia-Pacific 1994; Visiting Fellow Clare Hall Coll., Univ. of Cambridge, U.K. 1993, Life Fellow 1993; mem. Int. Ecological Acad. Moscow 1994–; Adviser, Int. Cttee. for Relief of Victims of Torture, U.S.A. 1984–, Union Theological Seminary, U.S.A. 1984–; Visiting Fellow, Centre for Int. Affairs, Harvard Univ., U.S.A. 1983–84; Trustee, Fed. of Unions of Korean Shipbldg. Agents 1951; Ed.-in-Chief, Centre for Study of Korean Labour 1995; Hon. Prof. (Moscow Univ.) 1992, (Chinese Acad. of Social Sciences, Nankai Univ., Fudan Univ., People's Repub. of China) 1994; Hon. LL.D. (Emory Univ., U.S.A.) 1983, (Catholic Univ. of America) 1992; Hon. Dr. of Political Science (Wonkwang Univ.) 1994; numerous honours and awards including Bruno Kreisky Human Rights Award, Austria 1981, Union Medal, Union Theol. Seminary, U.S.A. 1994. *Publications include:* Conscience in Action 1985, Prison Writings 1987, Building Peace and Democracy 1987, Kim Dae-jung's Views on International Affairs 1990, In the Name of Justice and Peace 1991, Korea and Asia 1994, The Korean Problem: Nuclear Crisis, Democracy and Reunification 1994, Unification, Democracy and Peace 1994, Mass Participatory Economy: Korea's Road to World Economic Power 1996. *Address:* Chong Wa Dae, 1 Sejongno, Chongno-gu, Seoul, Republic of Korea (Home).

KIM JONG IL, Marshal; Korean politician; b. 16 Feb. 1942, secret camp on Mt. Paekdu; s. of late Kim Il Sung (named Eternal Pres. 1998) and Kim Jung Sook; m.; one c.; ed. Kim Il Sung Univ., Pyongyang; Deputy Dir., then Dir. a Dept. of Cen. Cttee. Workers' Party of Korea 1964–73, Sec. Cen. Cttee. 1973; mem. Political Comm. Cen. Cttee. 1974, mem. Presidium of Politburo of Cen. Cttee. of Korean Workers' Party 1980–, Gen. Sec. 1997–; Chair. Nat. Defence Comm. (Head of State) Sept. 1998–; mem. Mil. Comm. Cen. Cttee. at Sixth Party Congress 1980; Deputy to Supreme People's Assembly 1982; First Vice-Chair. Nat. Defence Comm. 1990–93, Chair. 1993–; Supreme Commdr. Korean People's Army 1991–; Marshal of the Democratic People's Repub. of Korea 1992–; Hon. Dr. (Chiclayo Univ., Peru) 1986; Hon. Prof. Inca Garsilaso, Vega Univ., Peru 1986; Kim Il Sung Prize; Hero of Democratic People's Repub. of Korea (twice), Kim Il Sung Order (three times), title of Marshal 1992; Orden de Solidaridad, Cuba, Grand Croix de l'Ordre Nat. des Mille Collines, Rwanda, Necklace Order of Egypt and many other foreign and domestic awards and honours. *Publications include:* Selected Works of Kim Jong Il (8 vols.), For the Completion of the Revolutionary Cause of Juche (8 vols.). *Address:* Central Committee of the Workers' Party of Korea, Pyongyang, Democratic People's Republic of Korea.

KIM JONG PIL, Brig.-Gen.; Korean politician; b. 7 Jan. 1926, Puyo; m. Park Young Ok (niece of the late Pres. Park Chung Hee); one s. one d.; ed. High School, Kongju, Seoul Nat. Univ. and Korean Military Acad.; served in Korean war; Dir. Korean Central Intelligence Agency 1961–63; mem. Nat. Assembly 1963–68, 1971–80; Chair. Democratic Republican Party 1963–68; Senior Adviser to Pres. 1970; Vice-Pres. Democratic Republican Party 1971, Pres. 1979–80 (banned from political activity 1980); Pres. New Democratic Republican Party 1987; Jt. Pres. Democratic Liberal Party (DLP) 1990–93,

Chair. 1993; now Pres. United Liberal Democrats; Prime Minister 1971–75, Aug. 1998–; mem. Spanish Nat. Acad., Korean Acad.; numerous awards from Korean and foreign govts.; Hon. LL.D. (Long Island Univ., N.Y.) 1964, (Chungang Univ., Seoul) 1966, (Fairleigh Dickinson Univ.) 1968; Hon. D.Hum.Litt. (Westminster Coll., Fulton, Mo.) 1966; Hon. Ph.D. (Hongik Univ.) 1974. *Leisure interests:* painting, music. *Address:* Office of the Prime Minister, 77 Sejong-no, Chongno-ku, Seoul; 340-38, Sindang 4-dong, Chung-ku, Seoul, Republic of Korea (Home). *Telephone:* (02) 503-7209 (Office); (02) 783-7061-2 (Home). *Fax:* (02) 503-7249 (Office); (02) 782-9185 (Home).

KIM MAHN-JE, D.ECON.; Korean politician and economist; b. 3 Dec. 1934, Sonsan; ed. Univs. of Denver and Missouri, U.S.A.; Assoc. Prof., Sogang Univ., Seoul 1965–70, Prof. 1982–; mem. Legis. Ass. 1980–; Minister of Finance 1983–86; Deputy Prime Minister and Minister of Econ. Planning 1986–88; Pres. Korean Devt. Inst. 1971–82, Korean Int. Econ. Inst. (KIEI) 1981, Koram Bank 1983–84; Pres. Pohang Iron & Steel Co. 1994–; Sr. Policy Researcher, Policy Research Inst. of Democratic Justice Party (DJP) 1982; mem. Monetary Bd. 1975–, Econ. Planning Bd. Advisory Cttee. 1982. *Address:* Pohang Iron and Steel Co. Chong dam-dong Kangnam-ku, Seoul, Republic of Korea.

KIM MYUNG HO; Korean banker; joined Bank of Korea 1957, Vice-Gov. 1991–92, Head Office of Bank Supervision 1992–93, Gov. 1993–95. *Address:* c/o Bank of Korea, 110, 3-ka, Namdaemun-no, Chung-ku, Seoul 100-794, Republic of Korea.

KIM SUK-JOON, B.A.; Korean business executive; b. 9 April 1955, Kyungsang Prov.; m.; two s. one d.; ed. Korea Univ., Seoul; mil. service Repub. of Korea Marine Corps 1972–75; planning office SsangYong Corp. 1977–79, N.Y. and L.A. br. offices SsangYong (U.S.A.) Inc. 1979–82, Dir. Planning and Project Man. Div. SsangYong Eng. and Construction Co. Ltd. 1982–83, C.E.O. 1983–95, Pres. 1983–92, Chair. 1992–95, Vice-Chair. SsangYong Business Group 1991–93, 1994–95, C.E.O. 1991–93, 1994–, Chair. 1995–, Chair., C.E.O. SsangYong Motor Co. 1994–95, Chair., C.E.O. SsangYong Cement Industrial Co. 1995–; Co-Chair. Korean Party Korea-France High-Level Businessmens' Club, Korean Party Korea-Singapore Econ. Co-operation Cttee.; Vice-Chair. Korea-Japan Econ. Asscn., Fed. of Korean Industries, Korean Employers' Fed.; mem. Korea Chamber of Commerce and Industries; Dir. Bd. of Trustees Kookmin. Univ.; Baden-Powell World Fellow World Scout Foundation; Order of Industrial Service Merit Gold Tower 1991. *Address:* SsangYong Business Group, 24-1, 2-ga, Jeo-dong, Jung-gu, Seoul 100-748, Republic of Korea. *Telephone:* 2-267-2121. *Fax:* 2-270-5515.

KIM WOO-CHOONG, B.A.; Korean business executive; b. 19 Dec. 1936, Taegu; ed. Kyunggi High School, Seoul, Yonsei Univ.; with Econ. Devt. Council; with Hansung Industrial Co. Ltd., Dir. –1967 (resgnd.); Founder, Daewoo Industrial Co. Ltd. (textile co.) 1967, Chair. Daewoo Group, includes Daewoo Shipbldg. & Heavy Machinery Ltd., Daewoo Motor Co., etc.; Founder, Daewoo Foundation 1978; sentenced to two years' imprisonment for bribery Aug. 1996, received suspended sentence Dec. 1996; Dr. h.c. (Yonsei Univ., Korea Univ., George Washington Univ., U.S.A., Univ. of South Carolina, Russian Econ. Acad., Univ. Santiago de Cali/Univ. del Valle, Colombia); numerous honours and awards including Int. Business Award, Int. Chamber of Commerce 1984; Cmmdr., Légion d'honneur 1996. *Publication:* It's Big World and There's Lots To Be Done 1989. *Address:* Daewoo Corporation, 541 5-Ga Namdaemunno , Chung-Gu, Seoul, Republic of Korea.

KIM YONG NAM; Korean politician; mem. Cen. Cttee. Workers' Party of Korea (WPK) 1970, Political Commissar 1977, mem. Political Bureau 1980–; Vice-Premier and Minister of Foreign Affairs 1983–98; Del. to Supreme People's Ass. *Address:* c/o Ministry of Foreign Affairs, Pyongyang, Democratic People's Republic of Korea.

KIM YOUNG SAM, B.A.; Korean politician; b. 20 Dec. 1927, Koje-gun, South Kyongsang Prov.; s. of Kim Hong-Jo and late Park Bu-ryon; m. Myoung-Soon Sohn; two s. three d.; ed. Kyongnam High School, Pusan and Seoul Nat. Univ.; mem. Nat. Ass. 1954–79; Founder-mem. Democratic Party 1955; re-elected Pres. New Democratic Party 1974, 1979; expelled from Nat. Ass. for opposition to regime of Pres. Park. 1979; arrested under martial law 1980–81; banned from political activity Nov. 1980; again under house arrest 1982–83; staged 23-day hunger strike demanding democracy May–June 1983; Co-Chair. Council for Promotion of Democracy 1984; played leading role in org. of New Korea Democratic Party (absorbing Democratic Korea Party) which won large number of seats in 1985 election; political ban lifted May 1985; Presidential Cand. 1987 elections; Founder-Pres. Reunification Democracy Party 1987–90; Exec. Chair. Democratic Liberal Party (DLP) 1990–97, Pres. 1992–97; Pres. of Repub. of Korea 1992–97; Dr. h.c. (Towson State Univ., Baltimore) 1974; Martin Luther King Peace Prize 1995. *Publications:* There is No Hill We Can Depend On, Politics is Long and Political Power is Short, Standard-Bearer in his Forties, My Truth and My Country's Truth. *Leisure interests:* calligraphy, mountain climbing, jogging, swimming.

KIMBALL, Warren Forbes, PH.D.; American professor of history; b. 24 Dec. 1935, Brooklyn, New York; s. of Cyril S. Kimball and Carolyn F. Kimball; m. Jacqueline Sue Nelson 1959; one s. two d.; ed. Villanova and Georgetown Univs.; served U.S.N.R. 1958–65; Instructor, U.S. Naval Acad. 1961–65; Asst. Prof., Georgetown Univ. 1965–67, Univ. of Georgia 1967–70; Assoc. Prof., Rutgers Univ. 1970–85, Prof. II 1985–93, Robert Treat Prof. of History 1993–; Pitt Prof. of American History, Corpus Christi, Cambridge Univ., U.K. 1988–89. *Publications:* "The Most Unsordid Act": Lend-Lease, 1939–1941 1969, Swords or Ploughshares? The Morgenthau Plan 1976, Churchill and Roosevelt: The Complete Correspondence (3 vols.) 1984, The Juggler: Franklin Roosevelt as Wartime Statesman 1991, Forged in War: Roosevelt, Churchill and the Second World War 1997. *Address:* Department of History, Rutgers University, Newark, NJ 07102; 19 Larsen Road, Somerset, NJ 08873, U.S.A. (Home). *Telephone:* (201) 648-5410 (Office); (908) 247-0769 (Home).

KINCAID, Jamaica; Antigua and Barbuda writer; b. 25 May 1949, St. John's; d. of Annie Richardson; m. Allen Shawn 1979; one s. one d.; staff writer The New Yorker 1976; lives in Vt., U.S.A. *Publications include:* At the Bottom of the River (short stories; American Acad. and Inst. of Arts and Letters Morton Dauwen Zabel Award) 1983, Annie John (novel) 1985, A Small Place (non-fiction) 1988, Lucy (novel) 1990, My Brother 1997, My Favorite Plant 1998. *Address:* c/o Farrar Straus & Giroux, 19 Union Square West, New York, NY 10003, U.S.A.

KINCSES, Veronika; Hungarian soprano, opera and concert singer; d. of György Kincses and Etelka Angyal; m. József Vajda; one s.; ed. Liszt Ferenc Music Acad. Budapest and Accademia Santa Cecilia, Rome; soloist State Opera, Budapest; song-recitals, also oratorio performances; guest performances U.S.A., Argentina, Venezuela, Hong Kong, Singapore etc. 1997–98; operatic roles include Madame Butterfly, Mimi (La Bohème), Manon Lescaut, Liu (Turandot), Le Villi (Puccini), Contessa (Le nozze di Figaro), Fiordiligi (Cosí fan tutte), Vitellia (La Clemenza di Tito), Elvira (Don Giovanni), Amelia (Simone Boccanegra), Leonora (La forza del destino), Micaela (Carmen), Marguerita (Faust), Silvana (Fiamma—Respighi), Eva (Meistersinger von Nürnberg), Adriana (Adriana Lecouvreur), Tosca, Judit (Bluebeard's Castle); Liszt Prize, Kossuth Prize, Merited Artist title, Grand Prix du Disque, Paris. *Leisure interest:* teaching singers. *Address:* International Management of the Hungarian State Opera, Andrássy ut 22, 1061 Budapest, Hungary; Robert Lombardo Associates, 61 West 62nd Street, New York, NY 10023, U.S.A. *Telephone:* (1) 332-7372 (Hungary); (212) 586-4453 (New York).

KIND, Dieter Hans, DR. ING.; German electrical engineer; b. 5 Oct. 1929, Reichenberg, Bohemia; s. of Hans Kind and Gerta Kind; m. Waltraud Wagner 1954; three c.; ed. Technical Univ., Munich; Prof. and Dir. High-Voltage Inst., Technical Univ., Braunschweig 1962–75, Prof. Emer. 1975–; Pres. Physikalisch-Technische Bundesanstalt, Braunschweig and Berlin 1975–95, Comité Int. des Poids et Mésures, Sèvres/Paris 1975–95; Fellow, I.E.E.E.; Dr. h.c. (Tech. Univ. Munich); Bundesverdienstkreuz (First Class). *Publications:* An Introduction to High-Voltage Experimental Technique 1978, High-Voltage Insulation Technology 1985; about 50 scientific articles. *Leisure interests:* sport, literature. *Address:* Knappstrasse 4, 38116 Braunschweig, Germany. *Telephone:* (0531) 511497. *Fax:* (0531) 511497.

KINDLEBERGER, Charles Poor, M.A., PH.D.; American economist; b. 12 Oct. 1910, New York; s. of E. Crosby Kindleberger and Elizabeth Randall McIlvaine Kindleberger; m. Sarah Bache Miles 1937; two s. two d.; ed. Kent School, Univ. of Pa. and Columbia Univ.; research economist, U.S. Treasury 1936; Fed. Reserve Bank of New York 1936–39; Bank for Int. Settlements 1939–40; Fed. Reserve Bd. 1940–42; Office of Strategic Services 1942–45; Capt. and Maj. U.S. Army 1944–45; Dept. of State 1945–48; Assoc. Prof. and Prof. M.I.T. 1948–81, now Prof. Emer.; Visiting Prof. Middlebury Coll. 1982–83, Brandeis Univ. 1983–87; Consulting Fellow British Acad.; mem. American Philosophical Soc., American Acad. of Arts and Sciences; Dr. h.c. (Paris, Ghent, Pennsylvania, Basel); Harms Prize 1978; Bronze Star, Legion of Merit. *Publications:* 25 books including: The World in Depression 1929–39 1973, Manias, Panics and Crashes 1978, A Financial History of Western Europe 1984, The Life of an Economist: An Autobiography 1991, Mariners and Markets 1992, World Economic Primacy 1500–1990 1996. *Address:* Brookhaven at Lexington A-406, 1010 Waltham Street, Lexington, MA 02421, U.S.A.

KINELEV, Vladimir Georgiyevich, DR. TECH. SC.; Russian politician; b. 28 Jan. 1945; m.; one d.; ed. Bauman Higher Tech. School; worked Cen. Bureau of Experimental Machine-Construction, asst., Prof., Pro-rector Bauman Higher Tech. School; First Deputy Chair. State Cttee. on Science and Higher School 1990–91; Chair. Cttee. on Higher School Ministry of Science, Higher School and Tech. Policy of Russian Fed., concurrently First Deputy Minister 1992–93; Chair. State Cttee. on Higher Educ. 1993–96; Deputy Chair. Russian Govt. 1996; Minister of Gen. and Professional Educ. 1996–98; Dir. UNESCO Inst. 1998–; mem. Int. Acad. of Eng. *Address:* UNESCO Institute, Kedrova str. 8, 117096 Moscow, Russia (Office). *Telephone:* (095) 125-60-30 (Office).

KING, Angus S., Jr., J.D.; American lawyer, broadcaster and politician; b. 31 March 1944; m. Mary J. Herman; four s. one d.; ed. Dartmouth Coll. and Pennsylvania Univ.; called to the Bar, Maine 1969; staff attorney Pine Tree Legal Assistance, Showhegan, Me. 1969–72; Chief Counsel Office of Senator William D. Hathaway, U.S. Senate Subcttee. on Alcoholism and Narcotics, Washington 1972–75; fmr. partner Smith, Lloyd & King, Brunswick, Me.; Gov. of Maine 1995–; TV host Me. Watch 1977–; Vice-Pres. and Gen. Counsel Swift River/Hafslund Co. 1983; f. and Pres. N.E. Energy Man. Inc. 1989–94. *Address:* Office of the Governor, State House, Station 1, Augusta, ME 04333, U.S.A.

KING, B. B. (Riley B. King); American singer and guitarist; b. 16 Sept. 1925, Itta Bena, Miss.; began teaching himself guitar 1945, later studied

Schillinger System; fmr. disc jockey and singer, Memphis radio stations; numerous int. appearances; founding mem. John F. Kennedy Performing Arts Center 1971; Co-Chair. Foundation for Advancement of Inmate Rehabilitation and Recreation 1972–; toured U.S.S.R. 1979; performance at closing ceremonies, Summer Olympics, Atlanta, Ga. 1996; numerous awards including Grammy Lifetime Achievement Award 1987; Grammy Award: Best Traditional Blues Album (for Blues Summit 1994); Kennedy Center Honours 1995; Hon. L.H.D. (Tougaloo Coll. Miss.) 1973; Hon. D. Mus. (Yale) 1977; *albums include:* King of the Blues 1989, Indianola Mississippi Seeds 1989, Blues is King 1990, Live at the Apollo 1991, Spotlight on Lucille 1992, Singin' the Blues 1993, numerous other recordings. *Address:* c/o Sidney A. Seidenberg, 1414 Avenue of the Americas, New York, NY 10019, U.S.A.

KING, Billie Jean; American tennis player; b. 22 Nov. 1943, Long Beach, Calif.; d. of Willard J. Moffitt; m. Larry King 1965; ed. Los Angeles State Univ.; Amateur player 1958–67, professional 1967–; Australian Champion 1968; Italian Champion 1970; French Champion 1972; Wimbledon Champion 1966, 1967, 1968, 1972, 1973, 1975; U.S. Open Champion 1967, 1971, 1972, 1974; Fed. Repub. of Germany Champion 1971; South African Champion 1966, 1967, 1969; has won record 20 Wimbledon titles (6 singles, 10 doubles, 4 mixed) and played more than 100 matches; had won 1,046 singles victories by 1984; Top Woman Athlete of Year 1973; sports commentator, ABC-TV 1975–78; f. Women's Tennis Asscn. 1973; Publisher, Women Sports 1974–; Commr., U.S. Tennis Team 1981–; C.E.O. World TeamTennis 1985–; Capt. U.S. Fed. Cup Team 1995–96; Women's Olympic Tennis Coach 1996; Consultant Virginia Slims Championship Series. *Publications:* Tennis to Win 1970, Billie Jean (with Kim Chapin) 1974, We Have Come a Long Way: The Story of Women's Tennis 1988. *Address:* c/o World TeamTennis, 445 North Wells, Suite 404, Chicago, IL 60610, U.S.A.

KING, Coretta Scott, A.B., MUS.B.; American singer and civil rights campaigner; b. 27 April 1927, Marion, Ala.; d. of Obidiah Scott and Bernice McMurray; m. Martin Luther King, Jr. 1953 (assassinated 1968); two s. two d.; ed. Antioch Coll., New England Conservatory of Music; concert début as singer, Springfield, Ohio 1948; numerous concerts throughout U.S.A.; performed in India 1959, and at Freedom Concert, U.S.A.; Voice Instructor, Morris Brown Coll., Atlanta, Ga. 1962; Del. to White House Conf. on Children and Youth 1960; sponsor, Cttee. for Sane Nuclear Policy, Cttee. on Responsibility, Mobilization to End War in Viet Nam 1966–67; mem. Southern Rural Action Project, Inc.; Pres. Martin Luther King Jr. Foundation; Chair. Comm. on Econ. Justice for Women; mem. Exec. Cttee., Nat. Cttee. of Inquiry; Co-Chair. Clergy and Laymen Concerned about Viet Nam, Nat. Comm. for Full Employment 1974; Pres. Martin Luther King Jr. Center for Social Change; Co-Chairperson Nat. Cttee. for Full Employment; mem. Exec. Bd. Nat. Health Insurance Cttee.; mem. Bd. Southern Christian Leadership Conf., Martin Luther King Jr. Foundation, U.K.; Trustee, Robert F. Kennedy Memorial Foundation, Ebenezer Baptist Church; sponsor, Margaret Sanger Memorial Foundation; commentator, Cable News Network, Atlanta 1980–; lecturer and writer; numerous awards including Universal Love Award, Premio San Valentine Cttee. 1968, Wateler Peace Prize 1968, Dag Hammarskjöld Award 1969, Pacem in Terris Award, Int. Overseas Service Foundation 1969, Leadership for Freedom Award, Roosevelt Univ. 1971, Martin Luther King Memorial Medal 1971, Int. Viareggio Award 1971; Hon. L.H.D. (Boston Univ.) 1969, (Marymount-Manhattan Coll., New York) 1969, (Morehouse Coll., Atlanta) 1970; Hon. H.H.D. (Brandeis Univ., Waltham, Mass.) 1969, (Wilberforce Univ., Ohio) 1970, (Bethune-Cookman Coll., Daytona Beach, Fla.) 1970, (Princeton Univ.) 1970; Hon. LL.D. (Bates Coll., Lewiston, Me.) 1971; Hon. Mus.D. (New England Conservatory of Music, Boston) 1971. *Publications:* My Life With Martin Luther King, Jr. 1969; articles in magazines. *Address:* Martin Luther King Jr. Center for Nonviolent Social Change, 449 Auburn Avenue, N.E., Atlanta, GA 30312; 671 Beckwith Street, S.W., Atlanta, GA 30314, U.S.A.

KING, David Anthony, PH.D., SC.D., F.R.S.C., F.INST.P., F.R.S.; British professor of physical chemistry and research scientist; b. 12 Aug. 1939, Durban, South Africa; s. of Arnold King and Patricia Vardy; m. Jane Lichtenstein 1983; three s. one d.; ed. St. John's Coll., Johannesburg, Univ. of Witwatersrand, Johannesburg, Imperial Coll. London; lecturer in Chemical Physics, Univ. of E. Anglia, Norwich 1966–74; Brunner Prof. of Physical Chemistry, Univ. of Liverpool 1974–88, Head Dept. of Inorganic, Physical and Industrial Chem. 1983–88; 1920 Prof. of Physical Chem., Dept. of Chem., Cambridge Univ. 1988–, Head Dept. of Chem. 1993–; Fellow St. John's Coll. 1988–95; Master of Downing Coll. 1995–; Ed. Chemical Physics Letters 1990–; Pres. Asscn. of Univ. Teachers 1976–77; Chair. British Vacuum Council 1982–85; mem. Comité de Direction, Centre Cinétique et Physique, Nancy 1974–81, Research Awards Advisory Cttee. Leverhulme Trust 1980–91 (Chair. 1995–), Direction Cttee. (Beirat) Fritz Haber Inst., Berlin 1981–93; Chair. European Science Foundation Programme 'Gas—Surface Interactions' 1991–96, Kettle's Yard Gallery, Cambridge 1989–; Shell Scholar 1963–66; Royal Soc. of Chem. Awards, Surface Chem. 1978, Tilden Lectureship 1988, Liversidge Lectureship and Medal 1997–98. *Publications:* The Chemical Physics of Solid Surfaces and Heterogeneous Catalysis, 7 vols. (Ed. with D. P. Woodruff) 1980–94; over 300 original publs. in the scientific literature. *Leisure interests:* photography, art, philosophy. *Address:* Department of Chemistry, University of Cambridge, Lensfield Road, Cambridge, CB2 1EW (Office); The Master's Lodge, Downing College, Cambridge, CB2 1DQ, England (Home). *Telephone:* (01223) 336338 (Office); (01223) 315629 (Home). *Fax:* (01223) 336362.

KING, Francis Henry, C.B.E., O.B.E., M.A., F.R.S.L.; British writer; b. 4 March 1923, Adelboden, Switzerland; s. of the late Eustace Arthur Cecil King and Faith Mina Read; ed. Shrewsbury School and Balliol Coll., Oxford; served in British Council 1948–62, Regional Dir., Kyoto, Japan 1958–62; theatre critic Sunday Telegraph 1978–88; Pres. English PEN 1978–86, Int. PEN 1986–89; Somerset Maugham Prize 1952, Katherine Mansfield Short Story Prize 1965, Yorkshire Post Prize 1984. *Publications:* novels: To the Dark Tower 1946, Never Again 1947, The Dividing Stream 1951, The Widow 1957, The Man on the Rock 1957, The Custom House 1961, The Last of the Pleasure Gardens 1965, The Waves Behind the Boat 1967, A Domestic Animal 1970, Flights 1973, A Game of Patience 1974, The Needle 1975, Danny Hill 1977, The Action 1978, Act of Darkness 1983, Voices in an Empty Room 1984, Frozen Music (novella) 1987, The Woman Who Was God 1988, Punishments 1989, The Ant Colony 1991, Secret Lives 1991, The One and Only 1994, Ash on an Old Man's Sleeve 1996, Dead Letters 1997; short stories: So Hurt and Humiliated 1959, The Japanese Umbrella 1964, The Brighton Belle 1968, Hard Feelings 1976, Indirect Method 1980, One is a Wanderer 1985, A Hand at the Shutter 1996; biography: E. M. Forster and His World 1978, My Sister and Myself: The Diaries of J. R. Ackerley 1982; travel: Florence 1982, Florence: A Literary Companion 1991, Yesterday Came Suddenly (autobiog.) 1993. *Leisure interests:* ikebana, pictures and music. *Address:* 19 Gordon Place, London, W8 4JE, England. *Telephone:* 0171-937 5715.

KING, Ivan R(obert), PH.D.; American astronomer; b. 25 June 1927, New York; s. of Myram King and Anne (Franzblau) King; m. Alice Greene 1952 (divorced 1982); two s. two d.; ed. Woodmere Acad., Hamilton Coll., Harvard Univ.; served U.S.N.R. 1952–54; Methods Analyst, U.S. Dept. of Defence 1952–56; Asst. Prof., then Assoc. Prof., Univ. of Ill. 1956–64; Assoc. Prof. of Astronomy Univ. of Calif. at Berkeley 1964–66, Prof. 1966–; Chair. Astronomy Dept. 1967–70; Pres. American Astronomical Soc. 1978–80; mem. A.A.A.S., Chair. Astronomy Section 1973; mem. N.A.S., American Acad. of Arts and Sciences. *Publications:* The Universe Unfolding 1976, The Milky Way as a Galaxy 1990; 100 articles in scientific journals. *Address:* Astronomy Department, University of California, Berkeley, CA 94720, U.S.A.

KING, Larry; American broadcaster; b. 19 Nov. 1933, Brooklyn; s. of Eddie Zeiger and Jennie Zeiger; m. 1st Alene Akins 1961 (divorced 1963, remarried 1967, divorced 1971); one d.; m. 2nd Sharon Lepore 1976 (divorced 1982); m. 3rd Julia Alexander 1989; one s.; m. 4th Shawn Southwick 1997; disc jockey with various radio stations, Miami, Fla. 1957–71; freelance writer and broadcaster 1972–75; radio personality, Station WIOD, Miami 1975–78; writer, entertainment sections of Miami Herald for seven years; host, The Larry King Show (radio talk show) 1978–, 1990 Goodwill Games, WLA-TV Let's Talk, Washington, D.C.; columnist, USA Today, Sporting News; appeared in films Ghostbusters 1984, Lost in America 1985; recipient of numerous broadcasting and journalism awards. *Publications:* Mr King, You're Having a Heart Attack (with B. D. Colen) 1989, Larry King: Tell Me More, When You're from Brooklyn, Everything Else is Tokyo 1992, On the Line (jtly) 1993, Daddy Day, Daughter Day (jtly) 1997. *Address:* c/o CNN Larry King Live, 820 1st Street, N.E., Washington, DC 20002, U.S.A.

KING, Leonard James, A.C., LL.B.; Australian judge (retd.); b. 1 May 1925, Norwood, S. Australia; s. of Michael and Mary King; m. Sheila T. Keane 1953; two s. three d.; ed. Marist Brothers' School, Norwood and Univ. of Adelaide; admitted to bar 1950, Q.C. 1967; mem. House of Ass. 1970; Attorney-Gen. 1970–75; Minister of Social Welfare and Aboriginal Affairs 1970–72, of Community Welfare 1972–75, of Prices and Consumer Affairs 1973–75; Judge, Supreme Court of South Australia 1975-78, Chief Justice 1978–95. *Leisure interests:* reading, sport, theatre. *Address:* 19 Wall Street, Norwood, S.A. 5065, Australia. *Telephone:* (08) 8331 7220.

KING, Maurice Athelstan, LL.B.; Barbadian politician and lawyer; b. 1 Jan. 1936; s. of James Cliviston King and Caroline Constance King; m. Patricia A. Williams; one s. one d.; ed. Harrison Coll., Barbados, Univ. of Manchester and Gray's Inn, London; lawyer in pvt. practice 1960–; Chair. Natural Gas Corpn. 1964–76; mem. Barbados Senate 1967–75; Gen. Sec. Democratic Labour Party 1968–69; Amb. to U.S.A. and Perm. Rep. to O.A.S. Jan.–Sept. 1976; mem. Parl. 1981–; Attorney-Gen. and Minister of Legal Affairs 1986–91, Attorney-Gen. 1991–94, and Minister of Foreign Affairs 1991–93, of Justice and CARICOM Affairs 1993–94. *Leisure interests:* music, tennis, reading, swimming. *Address:* c/o Ministry of Justice, Marine House, Hastings, Christ Church, Barbados.

KING, Mervyn Allister, B.A., F.B.A.; British economist and professor of economics; b. 30 March 1948; s. of Eric Frank King and Kathleen Alice Passingham; ed. Wolverhampton Grammar School, King's Coll., Cambridge; Jr. Research Officer, Dept. of Applied Econs., Cambridge Univ., mem. Cambridge Growth Project 1969–73, Research Officer 1972–76, lecturer, Faculty of Econs. 1976–77; Esmée Fairbairn Prof. of Investment, Univ. of Birmingham 1977–84; Prof. of Econs., L.S.E. 1984–95; Exec. Dir. Bank of England 1991–98, Chief Economist 1991–98, Deputy Gov. 1998–; Sr. Vice-Pres., Aston Villa Football Club 1995–; Research Officer, Kennedy School at Harvard Univ., U.S.A. 1971–72, Visiting Prof. of Econs. 1982; Visiting Prof. of Econs. M.I.T. 1983–84, L.S.E. 1996–; Co-Dir. L.S.E. Financial Markets Group 1987–91; Man. Ed. Review of Economic Studies 1978–83; mem. City Capital Markets Cttee.; Bd. mem. The Securities Asscn.; mem. Council and Exec. Cttee. Royal Econ. Soc. 1981–86, 1992–; Fellow Econometric Soc.; mem. Acad. Europaea 1992; mem. Council, European Econ. Asscn. (Pres. 1993); Research Assoc. Nat. Bureau of Econ. Research; Assoc. mem. Inst. of Fiscal and Monetary Policy, Ministry of Finance, Japan; Hon. Sr. Scholarship and Richards Prize, King's Coll. Cambridge 1969; Wrenbury Scholarship, Cambridge Univ. 1969; Stevenson Prize, Cambridge Univ. 1970; Kennedy Scholarship and Harkness Fellowship 1971; Medal of Univ. of Helsinki 1982. *Publications:* Public Policy and the Corporation 1977, The British Tax System (with J. A. Kay), Indexing for Inflation (Ed. with T. Liesner) 1975, The Taxation of Income from Capital Growth (Co-Author) 1984; numerous articles in various journals. *Address:* Bank of England, Threadneedle Street, London, EC2R 8AH, England. *Telephone:* 0171-601 4950, 601 4119. *Fax:* 0171-601 3047.

KING, Michael, O.B.E., D.LITT., D.PHIL.; New Zealand writer and historian; b. 15 Dec. 1945, Wellington; s. of Lewis King and Eleanor King (née Smith); m. Maria Jungowska 1987; one s. one d.; ed. Victoria Univ., Wellington and Waikato Univ., Hamilton; Sr. Journalist Waikato Times, Hamilton 1968–71; tutor in Journalism, Wellington Polytechnic 1972–74; Lahara Lecturer in Journalism, Univ. of Papua New Guinea, Port Moresby 1976; Research Fellow Centre for Maori Studies and Research, Univ. of Waikato 1978; Postdoctoral Fellow in History, Univ. of Auckland 1980; Fellowship in Humanities, Univ. of Waikato 1991–93; Sr. Research Fellow in Humanities Univ. of Auckland 1996–97; Burns Fellow Otago Univ. 1998; Medal for Services to New Zealand Literature 1990, N.Z. Literary Fund Award for Achievement 1989, Buckland Literary Award 1996 and many other awards and writer's fellowships. *Publications:* Being Pakeha: An Encounter with New Zealand and the Maori Renaissance 1985, Death of the Rainbow Warrior 1986, New Zealand 1987, Nga Iwi O Te Motu: 1,000 Years of Maori History 1997. *Leisure interests:* reading, fishing, planting trees. *Address:* P.O. Box 109, Whangamata, New Zealand. *Telephone:* (07) 865 9095. *Fax:* (07) 865 9095.

KING, Phillip, C.B.E., M.A. (CANTAB); British sculptor; b. 1 May 1934, Tunis, Tunisia; s. of the late Thomas J. King and Gabrielle Liautard; m. 1st Lilian Odelle 1957 (divorced 1987); one s. (deceased); m. 2nd Judith Corbalis 1991; ed. Mill Hill School, Christ's Coll., Cambridge, St. Martin's School of Art, London; Asst. to Henry Moore 1957–59; taught at St. Martin's School of Art 1959–74; one-man exhbn., Whitechapel Gallery 1968, British Pavilion at Venice Biennale with Bridget Riley (q.v.) 1968, British Council touring exhbn., Kroller Muller (Netherlands), Düsseldorf, Bern, Paris and Belfast 1974–75, Arts Council Exhbn., Hayward Gallery 1981; Prof. of Sculpture, Royal Coll. of Art 1980–90, Prof. Emer. 1991–; Trustee, Tate Gallery 1967–69; mem. Art Panel, Arts Council 1977–79; Assoc. Royal Acad. 1977; 1st Prize Int. Sculpture Exhbn., Piestany (Czechoslovakia) 1968. *Leisure interest:* holidays in Corsica close to both land and sea. *Address:* c/o Bernard Jacobson Gallery, 14A Clifford Street, London, W1X 1RF, England.

KING, Stephen Edwin, B.S.; American author; b. 21 Sept. 1947, Portland, Me.; s. of Donald King and Nellie R. (Pillsbury) King; m. Tabitha J. Spruce 1971; two s. one d.; ed. Univ. of Maine; teacher of English, Hampden Acad., Me. 1971–73; writer-in-residence, Univ. of Maine at Orono 1978–79; mem. Authors' Guild of America, Screen Artists' Guild, Screen Writers of America, Writers' Guild. *Publications:* novels include Carrie 1974, Salem's Lot 1975, The Shining 1976, The Stand 1978, Fire Starter 1980, Danse Macabre 1981, Cujo 1981, Different Seasons 1982, The Dark Tower: The Gunslinger 1982, Christine 1983, Pet Sematary 1983, Cycle of the Werewolf 1985, Skeleton Crew 1986, It 1987, Misery 1988, Horror: 100 Best Books (Jt. Ed.) 1988, The Dark Half 1989, Four Past Midnight 1990, The Stand 1990, Needful Things 1991, Gerald's Game 1992, Dolores Claiborne 1992, Nightmares and Dreamscapes 1993, Rose Madder 1995, The Green Mile 1996, Desperation 1996, The Regulators 1996, Wizard and Glass 1997, Bag of Bones 1997; Night Shift (short story collection) 1978 and numerous other short stories; as Richard Bachman: Rage 1977, The Long Walk 1979, Roadwork 1981, The Running Man 1982, Thinner 1984, Insomnia 1993.

KING, Thea, O.B.E., F.R.C.M., A.R.C.M., F.G.S.M.; British clarinettist; b. 26 Dec. 1925, Hitchin, Herts.; m. Frederick J. Thurston 1953; ed. Bedford High School and Royal Coll. of Music; Sadler's Wells Orchestra 1950–52; Portia Wind Ensemble 1955–68; London Mozart Players 1956–84; Prof. Royal Coll. of Music 1961–87, Guildhall School of Music 1988–; now mem. English Chamber Orchestra, Melos Ensemble of London, Robles Ensemble; frequent soloist, broadcaster and recitalist; recordings include works by Mozart, Brahms, Spohr, Mendelssohn, Bruch, Finzi, Stanford and 20th Century British music. *Publications:* Clarinet Solos (Chester Woodwind Series) 1977, Arrangement of J. S. Bach: Duets for Two Clarinets 1979, Schumann for the Clarinet 1991, Mendelssohn for the Clarinet 1993, The Romantic Clarinet: A Mendelssohn Collection 1994, Tchaikovsky 1995. *Leisure interests:* skiing, cows, pillow-lace. *Address:* 16 Milverton Road, London, NW6 7AS, England. *Telephone:* 0181-459 3453.

KING, Rt. Hon. Thomas (Tom) Jeremy, C.H., M.A., M.P.; British politician; b. 13 June 1933, Glasgow; s. of John H. King and Mollie King; m. Elizabeth J. Tilney 1960; one s. one d.; ed. Rugby School and Emmanuel Coll., Cambridge; in packaging and printing industry 1958–70; M.P. for Bridgwater 1970–; Parl. Private Sec. to Rt. Hon. Christopher Chataway 1970–74; Shadow Spokesman for Energy 1976–79; Minister for Local Govt. 1979–83; Sec. of State for the Environment Jan.–June 1983 for Transport June–Oct. 1983, for Employment 1983–85, for Northern Ireland Sept. 1985–89, for Defence 1989–92; Chair. Intelligence and Security Cttee. 1994–97; Chair. London Int. Exhbn. Centre, Docklands; Dir. (non-exec.) Electra Investment Trust 1992–; mem. Nolan Cttee. on Standards in Public Life 1994–97; Conservative. *Leisure interests:* cricket, skiing. *Address:* House of Commons, Westminster, London, SW1A 0AA, England. *Telephone:* 0171-219 3000.

KING OF WARTNABY, Baron (Life Peer), cr. 1983, of Wartnaby in the County of Leicestershire; **John Leonard King,** Kt., F.B.I.M.; British business executive; b. 29 Aug. 1918; s. of Albert John and Kathleen King; m. 1st Lorna Kathleen Sykes 1941 (died 1969); three s. one d.; m. 2nd Isabel Monckton 1970; f. Whitehouse Industries Ltd. 1945, and Ferrybridge Industries Ltd. (subsequently Pollard Ball & Roller Bearing Co.), Man. Dir. 1945, Chair. 1961–69; Chair. Dennis Motor Holdings Ltd. 1970–72, FKI Babcock plc (fmrly. Babcock and Wilcox, subsequently Babcock Int. Group plc) 1970–94 (Hon. Pres. 1994–), British Airways 1981–93 (Pres. 1993–97, Pres. Emer. 1997–); Dir. SKF (U.K.) Ltd. 1976–89, R. J. Dick Inc. (U.S.A.), Dick Corpn. (U.S.A.), Dick Precismeca Inc. (U.S.A.), The Daily Telegraph PLC 1990–; mem. NEDC Cttee. on Finance for Investment 1976–78, Review Bd. for Govt. Contracts 1975–78; Chair., British Olympic Appeals Cttee. 1975–78; Vice-Pres. Nat. Soc. for Cancer Relief; Hon. Fellow The Coke Oven Man. Assoc.; Fellow Inst. of Chartered Transport; Commdr. Royal Order of the Polar Star (1983); Hon. Dr.Hum. (Gardner-Webb Coll., U.S.A.) 1980; Dr. h.c. (City Polytechnic) 1991. *Leisure interests:* hunting, field sports, racing. *Address:* Berkeley Square House, Berkeley Square, London, W1X 6BA, England. *Telephone:* 0171-930 4915.

KING-HELE, Desmond George, F.R.S.; British author and scientist; b. 3 Nov. 1927, Seaford, Sussex; s. of late S. G. King-Hele and Mrs. B. King-Hele; m. Marie Newman 1954 (separated 1992); two d.; ed. Epsom Coll. and Trinity Coll., Cambridge; Royal Aircraft Establishment, Farnborough 1948–88 (research on earth's gravity field and upper atmosphere by analysis of satellite orbits), Deputy Chief Scientific Officer, Space Dept. 1968–88; mem. Int. Acad. of Astronautics; Chair. British Nat. Cttee. for the History of Science, Medicine and Tech. 1985–89, History of Science Grants Cttee. 1990–93; Ed. Notes and Records of the Royal Soc. 1989–96; Bakerian Lecturer, Royal Soc. 1974, Wilkins Lecturer, Royal Soc. 1997; Hon. D.Sc. (Univ. of Aston) 1979, Hon. D. Univ. (Univ. of Surrey) 1986; Eddington Medal, Royal Astronomical Soc. 1971, Chree Medal, Inst. of Physics 1971, Nordberg Medal, Int. Cttee. on Space Research 1990. *Publications:* Shelley: His Thought and Work 1960, Satellites and Scientific Research 1960, Erasmus Darwin 1963, Theory of Satellite Orbits in an Atmosphere 1964, Observing Earth Satellites 1966, Essential Writings of Erasmus Darwin 1968, The End of the Twentieth Century? 1970, Poems and Trixies 1972, Doctor of Revolution 1977, Letters of Erasmus Darwin 1981, Animal Spirits 1983, The R.A.E. Table of Earth Satellites 1957–1989, 1990, Erasmus Darwin and the Romantic Poets 1986, Satellite Orbits in an Atmosphere 1987, A Tapestry of Orbits 1992, John Herschel 1992, Erasmus Darwin: A Life of Unequalled Achievement 1999, and more than 200 scientific or literary papers in various learned journals. *Leisure interests:* playing tennis, savouring the beauties of nature, cross-country running. *Address*: 7 Hilltops Court, 65 North Lane, Buriton, Hants., GU31 5RS, England. *Telephone:* (01730) 261646.

KINGMAN, Sir John Frank Charles, Kt., SC.D., F.R.S.; British university Vice-Chancellor and mathematician; b. 28 Aug. 1939, Beckenham; s. of the late Frank E. T. and Maud Elsie (née Harley) Kingman; m. Valerie Cromwell 1964; one s. one d.; ed. Christ's Coll., Finchley, London, Pembroke Coll., Cambridge; Asst. Lecturer in Math., Univ. of Cambridge 1962–64, Lecturer 1964–65; Reader in Math. and Statistics, Univ. of Sussex 1965–66, Prof. 1966–69; Prof. of Math., Univ. of Oxford 1969–85; Chair. Science and Eng. Research Council 1981–85; Vice-Chancellor Univ. of Bristol 1985–; mem. council British Tech. Group 1984–92; mem. bd. British Council 1986–91; Pres. London Math. Society 1990–92; Hon. Fellow, St. Anne's Coll., Oxford, Pembroke Coll., Cambridge; Hon. D.Sc. (Sussex) 1983, (Southampton) 1985, Hon. LL.D. (Bristol) 1989; Officier des Palmes Académiques. *Publications:* Introduction to Measure and Probability (with S. J. Taylor) 1966, The Algebra of Queues 1966, Regenerative Phenomena 1972, Mathematics of Genetic Diversity 1980, Poisson Processes 1993. *Address:* Senate House, Tyndall Avenue, Bristol, BS8 1TH, England. *Telephone:* (0117) 9303960.

KINGSDOWN, Baron, Life Peer (cr. 1993) of Pemberton in the County of Lancashire, **Robert (Robin) Leigh-Pemberton,** K.G., P.C., M.A., D.C.L.; British banker, barrister and landowner; b. 5 Jan. 1927, Lenham; s. of the late Robert Douglas Leigh-Pemberton, M.B.E., M.C., and Helen Isabel Payne-Gallwey; m. Rosemary Davina Forbes 1953; five s. (one deceased); ed. St. Peter's Court, Broadstairs, Eton Coll., Trinity Coll., Oxford; Oppidan Scholar, Eton 1940–45; Grenadier Guards 1945–48; practised at the Bar 1953–60; Dir. Univ. Life Assurance Soc. 1968–78; Dir. Birmid-Qualcast PLC, Deputy Chair. 1970–75, Chair. 1975–77; Dir. Redland PLC 1972–83, Equitable Life Assurance Soc. 1978–83, Vice-Pres. 1982; Dir. Nat. Westminster Bank PLC 1972–74, Deputy Chair. 1974–77, Chair. 1977–83; Gov. Bank of England 1983–93; Dir. BIS 1983–; mem. Kent County Council 1961–77, Leader 1964–69, Chair. 1972–75; J.P. for Kent 1961–76; Deputy Lieut. for Kent 1969, Vice-Lord Lieut. 1972–82, Lord Lieut. 1982–; Gov. Wye Coll., London Univ. 1968–77; Hon. Master of the Bench, Inner Temple 1983; Deputy Pro-Chancellor of Kent Univ. 1969–78, Pro-Chancellor 1977–83; mem. Medway Ports Authority 1972–77, S.E. Econ. Planning Council 1971–74, Prime Minister's Cttee. on Standards in Local Govt. 1973–74, Cttee. of Enquiry into Teachers' Pay 1974, Cttee. to review Police Conditions of Service 1977–79, NEDC 1981–; Chair. City Communications Centre 1979–82, Cttee. of London Clearing Bankers 1982–83; Pres. Royal Agric. Soc. of England 1989–90; Dir. (non-exec.) Glaxo Wellcome 1993–96, (non-exec.) Hambros 1993–98, Redland 1972–83, 1993–, (non-exec.) Foreign & Colonial Investment Trust; Hon. D.C.L. (Kent) 1983, Hon. M.A. (Trinity Coll, Oxford) 1984; Hon. D.Litt. (City of London) 1988, (Loughborough) 1989, (City Polytechnic) 1990; K.St.J. 1983, Order of Aztec Eagle, Mexico (First Class) 1985. *Leisure interests:* English country life, skiing, the arts. *Address:* Hambros PLC, 41 Tower Hill, London, EC3N 4HA; Torry Hill, Sittingbourne, Kent ME9 0SP, England (Home).

KINGSLEY, Ben; British actor; b. 31 Dec. 1943; s. of Rahimtulla Harji Bhanji and Anna Leina Mary Bhanji; m.; three s. one d.; ed. Manchester Grammar School; with R.S.C. 1970–80; Nat. Theatre 1977–78; Assoc. Artist, R.S.C. *Stage appearances include:* A Midsummer Night's Dream, Occupations, The Tempest, Hamlet (title role), The Merry Wives of Windsor, Baal, Nicholas Nickleby, Volpone, The Cherry Orchard, The Country Wife, Judgement, Statements After An Arrest, Othello (title role), Caracol in Melons, Waiting for Godot. *Television appearances include:* The Love School 1974, Kean, Silas Marner, The Train 1987, Murderous Amongst Us 1988, several plays. *Films:* Gandhi (two Hollywood Golden Globe Awards 1982, New York Film Critics' Award, two BAFTA Awards, Acad. Award, Los Angeles Film Critics' Award 1983), Betrayal 1982, Harem 1985, Turtle Diary 1985, Without A Clue 1988, Testimony 1988, Pascali's Island 1988, Bugsy 1991, Sneakers 1992, Innocent Moves 1992, Dave 1992, Schindler's List 1993, Death and the Maiden 1994, Species 1995, Twelfth Night 1996, Photographing Fairies 1997, The Assignment 1998, Weapons of Mass Destruction 1998, Sweeney Todd 1998, The Confession 1999; Hon. M.A. (Salford Univ.); awarded Padma Shri (Govt. of India); London Standard Best Film Actor 1983. *Leisure interests:* music, gardening. *Address:* c/o ICM, 76 Oxford Street, London, WIN 0AX, England.

KINGSTON, Arthur Edward, PH.D., F.R.A.S., F.INST.P.; British professor of physics; b. 18 Feb. 1936, Armagh, N. Ireland; s. of Arthur Kingston and Henrietta Duff; m. Helen McCann 1962; one s. one d.; ed. Royal School Armagh and Queen's Univ. Belfast; Research Fellow, Queen's Univ. 1959–60, Sr. Research Fellow 1960–61; Asst. Lecturer, Liverpool Univ. 1961–62, lecturer 1962–63; Visiting Fellow, Univ. of Colorado, U.S.A. 1963–64; lecturer, Queen's Univ. 1964–68, Sr. Lecturer 1968–71, Reader 1971–83, Prof. of Theoretical Atomic Physics 1983–, Dean, Faculty of Science 1989–94, Provost for Science and Agric. 1994; mem. Royal Irish Acad., Int. Acad. of Astronautics. *Publications:* more than 250 papers in atomic physics and astro-physics. *Address:* College of Science and Agriculture, The Queen's University of Belfast, University Road, Belfast, BT7 1NN, N. Ireland. *Telephone:* (01232) 245 133, Ext. 3105. *Fax:* (01232) 434454.

KINGSTON, Maxine Hong, B.A.; American author; b. 27 Oct. 1940, Stockton, Calif.; d. of Tom Kingston and Ying Lan (Chew) Hong; m. Earll Kingston 1962; one s.; taught English, Sunset High School, Hayward, Calif. 1965–66, Kahuku High School, Hawaii 1967, Kahaluu Drop-In School 1968, Kailua High School 1969, Honolulu Business Coll. 1969, Mid-Pacific Inst., Honolulu 1970–77; Prof. of English, Visiting Writer, Univ. of Hawaii, Honolulu 1977; Thelma McCandless Distinguished Prof., Eastern Mich. Univ., Ypsilanti 1986; Chancellor's Distinguished Prof., Univ. Calif., Berkeley 1990–; Mademoiselle Magazine Award 1977, Anisfield-Wolf Book Award 1978, Stockton (Calif.) Arts Comm. Award 1981, Hawaii Award for Literature 1982; NEA Writing Fellow 1980; Guggenheim Fellow 1981, named Living Treasure of Hawaii 1980, American Acad. and Inst. Award in Literature 1990. *Publications:* The Woman Warrior: Memoirs of a Girlhood Among Ghosts 1976 (Nat. Book Critics Circle Award for non-fiction), China Men 1981 (Nat. Book Award), Hawaii One Summer 1987, Through The Black Curtain 1988, Tripmaster Monkey—His Fake Books 1989; short stories, articles and poems. *Address:* Department of English, University of California, 322 Wheeler Hall, Berkeley, CA 94720, U.S.A.

KINIGI, Sylvie; Burundian politician and civil servant; fmr. exec. officer of structural adjustment programme; Prime Minister of Burundi 1993–94; fmr. mem. Union pour le progres nat. (UPRONA). *Address:* c/o Office of the Prime Minister, Bujumbura, Burundi.

KINKEL, Klaus, LL.D.; German politician and lawyer; b. 17 Dec. 1936, Metzingen; s. of Ludwig Kinkel and Charlotte Klaus; m. Ursula Vogel 1961; one s. three d.; ed. Bonn, Cologne, Tubingen Univs.; lawyer 1962–70; Personal Aide to Hans Dietrich Genscher (q.v.) 1970–79; State Sec. Justice Ministry 1982–83, 1987–91, Justice Minister 1991–92; Minister of Foreign Affairs 1992–98; Head of External Intelligence Service 1983–87; Chair. Free Democratic Party 1993–95. *Leisure interests:* jogging, tennis. *Address:* c/o Ministry of Foreign Affairs, Adenauerallee 99-103, 53113 Bonn, Germany.

KINNELL, Galway, M.A.; American writer; b. 1 Feb. 1927, Providence, R.I.; s. of James S. Kinnell and Elizabeth Mills; m. Inés Delgado de Torres 1965; one s. two d.; ed. Princeton Univ.; mem. Nat. Inst., Acad. of Arts and Letters; Guggenheim Fellow 1963–64, 1974–75, MacArthur Fellow 1984; Dir. Writing Programme New York Univ. 1981–84, Samuel F. B. Morse Prof. of Arts and Sciences 1985–92, Erich Maria Remarque Prof. of Creative Writing 1992–; Award of Nat. Inst. of Arts and Letters 1962, Cecil Hemley Poetry Prize 1969, Medal of Merit 1975, Pulitzer Prize 1983, American Book Award 1983; named Vt. State Poet 1989–93. *Publications:* poetry: What a Kingdom it Was 1960, Flower Herding on Mount Monadnock 1963, Body Rags 1966, The Book of Nightmares 1971, The Avenue Bearing the Initial of Christ into the New World 1974, Mortal Acts, Mortal Words 1980, Selected Poems 1982, The Past 1985, The Imperfect Thirst 1994; novel: Black Light 1966; children's story: How the Alligator Missed Breakfast 1982; trans.: The Poems of François Villon 1965, On the Motion and Immobility of Douve 1968, The Lackawanna Elegy 1970; interviews: Walking Down the Stairs 1977. *Address:* Department of English, New York University, New York, NY 10003, U.S.A.

KINNERSLEY, David John, M.A.; British water consultant; b. 28 May 1926, Essex; s. of Arthur Kinnersley and Doris Angier; m. Barbara Fair 1950; one s. two d.; ed. Westcliff High School for Boys, Essex and Corpus Christi Coll. Cambridge; Nat. Coal Bd. 1951–58; UKAEA 1959–64; Deputy Gen. Man., Gen. Man. British Waterways Bd. 1964–69; Dir. Asscn. of River Authorities 1970–73; Chief Exec. North West Water Authority 1973–76; Econ. Adviser, Nat. Water Council 1976–83; Research Fellow, Nuffield Coll. Oxford 1983–84; Bursar and Fellow, Mansfield Coll. Oxford 1984–86; Adviser to Sec. of State for Environment 1987–89; mem. Bd. Nat. Rivers Authority 1989–91; mem. Council, WaterAid 1981–98; mem. Monopolies and Mergers Comm. for Water References 1990–96; Consultant, IBRD 1991–96; consultant to regional and nat. govts.; Hon. Fellow, Inst. of Water and Environmental Man.; Churchill Fellowship 1973. *Publications:* Troubled Water 1988, Coming Clean, The Politics of Water and the Environment 1994. *Leisure interests:* books, art, countryside and coastline. *Address:* 111 Church Street, Chesham, Bucks., HP5 1JD, England.

KINNOCK, Rt. Hon. Neil Gordon, P.C., B.A., M.P.; British politician; b. 28 March 1942; s. of Gordon Kinnock and Mary Howells; m. Glenys Elizabeth Parry 1967; one s. one d.; ed. Lewis School, Pengam, Univ. Coll., Cardiff; Pres. Univ. Coll., Cardiff Students' Union 1965–66; Tutor Organizer in Industrial and Trade Union Studies, Workers' Educational Asscn. 1966–70; M.P. for Bedwellty 1970–83, for Islwyn 1983–95; mem. Welsh Hosp. Bd. 1969–71; Parl. Pvt. Sec. to Sec. of State for Employment 1974–75; mem. Nat. Exec. Cttee., Labour Party 1978–94 (Chair. 1987–88); Leader of Labour Party 1983–92; Leader of the Opposition 1983–92; EC Commr. with responsibility for Transport 1995–; Pres. Cardiff Univ. 1998–; Dir. (unpaid) Tribune Publs. 1974–82, 7:84 Theatre Co. Ltd. 1979–; Hon. Prof. Thames Valley Univ. 1993–; Hon. LL.D. (Wales) 1992. *Publications:* Wales and the Common Market 1971, Making Our Way 1986, Thorns and Roses 1992; contribs. in newspapers and periodicals. *Leisure interests:* male voice choral music, opera, theatre, reading, children, rugby, soccer, cricket. *Address:* Commission of the European Communities, 200 rue de la Loi, 1049 Brussels, Belgium.

KINSELLA, Thomas; Irish poet; b. 4 May 1928, Dublin; s. of John Paul and Agnes Casserly Kinsella; m. Eleanor Walsh 1955; one s. two d.; Irish Civil Service 1946–65, resgnd. as Asst. Prin. Officer, Dept. of Finance 1965; Artist-in-Residence, Southern Ill. Univ. 1965–67, Prof. of English 1967–70; Prof. of English, Temple Univ., Philadelphia 1970–90; Dir. Dolmen Press Ltd., Cuala Press Ltd., Dublin; founded Peppercanister (private publishing enterprise), Dublin 1972; mem. Irish Acad. of Letters 1965–; Guggenheim Fellowship 1968–69, 1971–72; Guinness Poetry Award 1958; Irish Arts Council Triennial Book Award 1960; Denis Devlin Memorial Award 1966, 1969, 1992; Hon. D.Litt. (Nat. Univ. of Ireland) 1985. *Publications:* Poems 1956, Another September 1958, Downstream 1962, Nightwalker and Other Poems 1966, Notes from the Land of the Dead 1972, Butcher's Dozen 1972, New Poems 1973, Selected Poems 1956–1968 1973, Song of the Night and Other Poems 1978, The Messenger 1978, Fifteen Dead 1979, One and Other Poems 1979, Poems 1956–1973, Peppercanister Poems 1972–1978 1979; Songs of the Psyche (poems) 1985, Her Vertical Smile (poem) 1985, St. Catherine's Clock (poem) 1987, Out of Ireland (poems) 1987, Blood and Family (collected poems from 1978) 1988, Poems from Centre City 1990, Personal Places (poems) 1990, One Fond Embrace (poem) 1990, Madonna and other Poems 1991, Open Court (poems) 1991, Butcher's Dozen (anniversary reissue) 1992, From Centre City (collected poems from 1990) 1994, The Dual Tradition: an Essay on Poetry and Politics in Ireland 1995, Collected Poems 1956–94, The Pen Shop (poem) 1997, The Familiar (poems) 1999, Godhead (poems) 1999; The Táin (trans.) 1968; ed. Selected Poems of Austin Clarke 1976; co-ed. Poems of the Dispossessed 1600–1900 (with 100 translations from the Irish) 1981; Ed. Ireland's Musical Heritage: Sean O'Riada's Radio Talks on Irish Traditional Music 1981, The New Oxford Book of Irish Verse (including all new trans. from the Irish) 1986. *Leisure interests:* history, publishing. *Address:* Killalane, Laragh, County Wicklow, Ireland. *Telephone:* (404) 45112.

KINSELLA, William Patrick, B.A., M.F.A.; Canadian author; b. 25 May 1935, Edmonton, Alberta; s. of John M. Kinsella and Olive M. Elliot; m. 1st Myrna Salls 1957, 2nd Mildred Heming 1965, 3rd Ann Knight 1978; three d.; ed. Eastwood High School, Edmonton and Univs. of Victoria and Iowa; recipient Houghton Mifflin Literary Fellowship 1982; Books in Canada First Novel Award 1982; Canadian Authors' Asscn. Award for Fiction 1982; Writers Guild Alberta Award for Fiction 1982, 1983; Vancouver Award for Writing 1987; Stephen Leacock Award for Humour 1987; Canadian Booksellers Asscn. Author of the Year 1987. *Publications:* stories: Dance Me Outside 1977, Scars 1978, Shoeless Joe Jackson Comes to Iowa 1980, Born Indian 1981, The Moccasin Telegraph 1983, The Thrill of the Grass 1984, The Alligator Report 1985, The Fencepost Chronicles 1986, Five Stories 1987, Red Wolf, Red Wolf 1987, The Further Adventures of Slugger McBatt (reissued as Go the Distance 1995) 1988, The Miss Hobbema Pageant 1988, Dixon Cornbelt League 1993, Brother Frank's Gospel Hour 1994, The Secret of the Northern Lights 1998, The Silas Stories 1998; novels: Shoeless Joe 1982, The Iowa Baseball Confederacy 1986, Box Socials 1991, The Winter Helen Dropped By 1995, If Wishes Were Horses 1996, Magic Time 1998; other works: The Ballad of the Public Trustee 1982, The Rainbow Warehouse (poetry, with Ann Knight) 1989, Two Spirits Soar: The Art of Allen Sapp 1990, Even at this Distance (poetry, with Ann Knight) 1993, Poems 1990–1994 1998, The Hunt 1998. *Leisure interests:* baseball, sumo wrestling, Scrabble. *Address:* P.O. Box 2162, Blaine, WA 98231-2162, U.S.A.

KINSKI, Nastassja (b. Nastassja Nakszynski); actress (b. German); b. 24 Jan. 1961, W. Berlin; d. of the late Klaus Kinski and of Ruth Brigitte Kinski; m. Ibrahim Moussa 1984; one s. one d.; one d. by Quincy Jones (q.v.); film début in Falsche Bewegung 1975; Bundespreis 1983. *Films include:* Stay As You Are 1978, Tess 1978, One From The Heart 1982, Cat People 1982, Moon In The Gutter 1983, Spring Symphony 1983, Unfaithfully Yours 1984, The Hotel New Hampshire 1984, Maria's Lovers 1984, Paris, Texas 1984, Revolution 1985, Harem, Torrents of Spring 1989, On a Moonlit Night 1989, Magdalene 1989, The King's Future 1989, The Secret, Night Sun 1991, Faraway, So Close!, Terminal Velocity 1994, One Night Stand 1997, Little Boy Blue 1997, Father's Day 1997, Somebody is Waiting 1997, Sunshine 1998, Your Friends and Neighbors 1999. *Address:* 888 Seventh Avenue, New York, NY 10106, U.S.A.

KINTANAR, Roman, M.A., PH.D.; Philippine scientist, government official and university professor; b. 13 June 1929, Cebu City; s. of Augustin Y. Kintanar and Pureza Lucero; m. Generosa Perez-Kintanar 1959; two s. one d.; ed. Univ. of the Philippines, Univ. of Texas; Prof. of Physics, Univ. of the Philippines 1955–56, Feati Univ. 1958–65; Professorial lecturer, Ateneo de Manila Univ. 1966–68; Chief Geophysicist, Philippine Weather Bureau 1953–58, Dir. 1958–72; Admin. Philippine Atmospheric, Geophysical and Astronomical Services Admin. (PAGASA) 1972–77, Dir.-Gen. 1977–; Chair. Scientific and Tech. Cttee., UN Int. Decade for Natural Disaster Reduction 1994; Chair. of Bd., Typhoon Cttee. Foundation 1996–; Pres. ROMAROSA Realty Devt. Corpn. Inc. 1996–; del. or invited participant to 57 Regional or Int. Scientific Confs. 1959–79; Co-ordinator, WMO/ESCAP Typhoon Cttee. Secr. 1967–79; Perm. Rep. to WMO 1958; Vice-Pres. Regional Asscn. V for S.-W. Pacific (WMO-RA V) 1966–74, Pres. 1974–78; Vice-Pres. WMO 1978–79, Pres. 1979; Vice-Chair. Manila Observatory Inc. 1996–; mem. Philippine Asscn. for the Advancement of Science, Nat. Research Council of the Philippines, Philippine Meteorological Soc., Int. Asscn. of Seismology and Physics of the Earth's Interior, UNESCO/UNDRO Int. Advisory Cttee. on Earthquake Damage and Mitigation, and many other scientific socs.; Int. Meteorological Org. Prize 1995; Fulbright Smidthmundt Scholarship (U.S. Educational Foundation), Office of the Pres. Ecology Award, Budiras Award for Outstanding Performance (Bureau Dirs. Asscn.), Parangal ng PAGASA Award, Lingkod Bayan Award 1982, Padre Faura Astronomy Medal 1982. *Publications:* A Study of Typhoon Microseisms 1958 and many articles in scientific journals. *Leisure interests:* playing golf, chess. *Address:* 100 Don Primitivo Street, Don Antonio Heights, Quezon City, Philippines. *Telephone:* 9317069. *Fax:* 9318484.

KIPKETER, Wilson; Kenyan/Danish athlete; b. 12 Dec. 1970, Kapchemoiywo, Kenya; specializes in 800m.; world record-holder for 800m. (one minute and 41.11 seconds) 1997; coached by Slawomir Nowak; resident in Denmark since 1990, qualified to compete for Denmark May 1995; Gold Medal World Championships 1995, 1997; Gold Medal World Indoor Championships 1997.

KIPPENHAHN, Rudolf; German astronomer; b. 24 May 1926, Bärringen; s. of Rudolf Kippenhahn and Alma Belz; m. Johanna Rasper 1955; three d.; ed. Graslitz and St. Joachimsthal Schools, Univs. of Halle and Erlangen; Scientific Asst. Bamberg Observatory 1951–57; staff mem. Max-Planck-Inst. für Physik und Astrophysik, Inst. für Astrophysik 1957–65, mem. of directorate 1963, Dir. 1975–91; Visiting Prof. Caltech, Pasadena and Princeton Univs. 1961–62; Prof. Univ. Observatory, Göttingen 1965–75; Visiting Prof. Univ. of Calif., L.A. 1968, Ohio State Univ. 1979, Univ. Observatory, Hamburg 1986–87; Hon. Prof. Univ. of Munich 1975–; Assoc. mem. Royal Astronomical Soc., London; mem. Bayerische Akademie der Wissenschaften, Munich; Carus-Medal (Leopoldina, Halle); Carus Prize (City of Schweinfurt); Verdienstkreuz (1st Class) (Fed. Repub. Germany); Lorenz-Oken-Medal (Gesellschaft Deutscher Naturforscher und Ärzte). *Publications:* One Hundred Billion Suns: The Birth, Life and Death of the Stars 1983, Licht vom Rande der Welt 1984, Light from the Depth of Time 1987, Unheimliche Welten 1987, Stellar Structure and Evolution 1990, Der Stern von dem wir Leben 1990, Abenteuer Weltall 1991, Discovering the Secrets of the Sun 1994, and numerous articles in astronomical and astrophysical journals. *Address:* Rautenbreite 2, 37077 Göttingen, Germany. *Telephone:* (0551) 24714. *Fax:* (0551) 22902.

KIRA, Tatuo, PH.D.; Japanese scientist; b. 1919, Osaka; s. of Tetumyo Kira and Hukue Kira; m. Yasuko Kametani 1948; ed. Kitano High School, Osaka, The Third High School (Junior Coll.), Kyoto Univ.; Asst. Prof. Kyoto Univ. 1948–49; Prof. Osaka City Univ. 1949–81; Pres. Ecological Soc. of Japan 1980–83; Dir. Lake Biwa Research Inst. 1982–94; Chair. Scientific Cttee., Int. Lake Environment Cttee. Foundation 1986–95, Pres. Japan Soc. of Tropical Ecology 1990–97; Prof. Emer. Osaka City Univ.; Hon. mem. British Ecological Soc. 1985, Ecological Soc. of Japan 1995; Int. Cosmos Prize 1995; Duke of Edin. Prize of Japan Acad. 1998; Purple Ribbon Medal 1984, Order of the Sacred Treasure (Second Class) 1990. *Publications:* Nature and Life in S.E. Asia, (Vols. I–VII) (Ed.) 1961–76, Primary Production of Japanese Forests (Ed.) 1977, Biological Production in a Warm-temperate Evergreen Oak Forest (Ed.) 1978, Data Book of World Lake Environments I–III (Ed.) 1989–91, ten textbooks and compiled essays, 100 scientific papers. *Leisure interest:* growing wild plants. *Address:* Lake Biwa Research Institute, 1-10 Uchidehama, Otsu, Shiga 520 (Office); Nango 2-21-9, Otsu, Shiga 520, Japan (Home). *Telephone:* 0775-26-4800 (Office); 0775-34-8229 (Home).

KIRBY, Anthony John, PH.D. (CANTAB.), F.R.S., F.R.S.C.; British university teacher and research scientist; b. 18 Aug. 1935, Welwyn Garden City, Herts.; s. of Samuel A. Kirby and Gladys R. (née Welch) Kirby; m. Sara Nieweg 1962; one s. two d.; ed. Eton Coll., Gonville and Caius Coll., Cambridge; NATO Research Fellow, Brandeis Univ., Mass. 1963–64; demonstrator, lecturer, Organic Chem., Univ. of Cambridge 1968–85, Reader 1985–95, Prof. of Bio-organic Chem. 1995–, Tutor 1967–75, Dir. of Studies in Natural Sciences, Gonville & Caius Coll., Cambridge 1968–96; Fellow Gonville and Caius Coll. 1962–; Royal Soc. of Chemistry Award in Organic Reaction Mechanisms 1983, Tilden Lecturer of Royal Soc. of Chem. 1987, Ingold Lecturer of Royal Soc. of Chem. 1996. *Publications:* The Organic Chemistry of Phosphorus (with S. G. Warren) 1967, Stereoelectronic Effects at Oxygen 1983, Stereoelectronic Effects 1996; over 250 articles on mechanistic bio-organic chemistry. *Address:* University Chemical Laboratory, Cambridge, CB2 1EW (Office); 14 Tenison Avenue, Cambridge, CB1 2DY, England (Home). *Telephone:* (01223) 336370 (Office); (01223) 359343 (Home). *Fax:* (01223) 336362 (Office).

KIRBY, Louis Albert Francis; British journalist; b. 30 Nov. 1928, Liverpool; s. of late William J. Kirby and Anne Kirby; m. 1st Marcia Teresa Lloyd 1952 (divorced 1976); two s. three d.; m. 2nd Heather Veronica Nicholson 1976; one s. one d.; m. 3rd Heather Margaret McGlone 1983; two d.; ed. Coalbrookdale High School; gen. reporter, then Court Corresp., Daily Mail 1953–60, Political Corresp. 1960–62; Chief Reporter, then Leader Writer and Political Ed., Daily Sketch 1962–64, Asst. Ed. 1964–67, Exec. Ed., then Acting Ed. 1967–71; Deputy Ed. Daily Mail 1971–76; Ed. Evening News 1976–80; Dir. Associated Newspapers Group Ltd. and Vice-Chair. Evening News 1976–80; Ed. The New Standard 1980–81, The Standard 1981–86; Dir. Evening Standard Co. Ltd. 1980–86; Ed. Dir. Associated Newspapers 1986–88; Political Consultant, Daily Mail 1988–93; Ed. UK Mail 1993–. *Leisure interests:* theatre, reading. *Address:* Northcliffe House, London, W.8, England.

KIRBY, Hon. Justice Michael Donald, A.C., C.M.G., LL.M., B.A., B.ECONS.; Australian judge; b. 18 March 1939, Sydney; s. of Donald and the late Jean (née Knowles) Kirby; ed. Fort Street Boys' High School and Univ. of Sydney; Fellow, Senate, Univ. of Sydney 1964–69; mem. N.S.W. Bar Council 1974; Deputy Pres., Australian Conciliation & Arbitration Comm. 1975–83; Chair. Australian Law Reform Comm. 1975–84, OECD Expert Group on Privacy and Int. Data Flows 1978–80, Cttee. of Counsellors, Human and People's Rights UNESCO 1985, UNESCO Expert Group on the Rights of Peoples 1989; mem. Admin. Review Council of Australia 1976–84; mem. Council, Univ. of Newcastle, N.S.W. 1977–83, Deputy Chancellor 1978–83; mem. Australian Nat. Comm. for UNESCO 1980–84, 1997–, Australian Inst. of Multicultural Affairs 1979–83; Judge Fed. Court of Australia 1983–84; mem. Exec. CSIRO 1983–86; Chancellor, Macquarie Univ., Sydney 1984–93; Pres. Court of Appeal, Supreme Court of N.S.W. 1984–96; Acting Chief Justice of N.S.W. 1988, 1990, 1993, 1995; Admin. (Acting Gov.) N.S.W. 1991; Justice, High Court of Australia 1996–; Commr. WHO Global Comm. on Aids 1989–91; mem. Int. Comm. of Jurists, Geneva 1985–, mem. Exec. Cttee. 1989–95, Chair. 1992–95, Pres. 1995–98, Pres. Australian Section 1989–96; Special Rep. of Sec.-Gen. of UN on Human Rights for Cambodia 1993–96; Pres. Court of Appeal of Solomon Islands 1995–96; mem. Ethics Cttee. of Human Genome Org. 1995–; mem. Council of the Australian Opera; mem. ILO Fact-Finding and Conciliation Comm. on Freedom of Asscn. Inquiry on South Africa 1991–92; mem. Perm. Tribunal of Peoples' Session on Tibet 1992; Trustee AIDS Trust of Australia 1987–93; Gov. Int. Council for Computer Communications, Washington 1984–; mem. UNESCO Jury for Prize for Teaching of Human Rights 1994–96, UNESCO Int. Bioethics Cttee. 1996–; Hon. Fellow, N.Z. Research Foundation; Hon. D. Litt. (Newcastle, N.S.W.) 1987, (Ulster) 1998; Hon. LL.D. (Macquarie Univ.) 1995, (Sydney Univ.) 1996; Loewenthal Medal, Sydney Univ., Australian Human Rights Medal 1991. *Publications:* Industrial Index to Australian Labour Law 1978, 1984, Reform the Law 1983, The Judges 1984, Jt. Ed. A Touch of Healing 1986. *Leisure interest:* work. *Address:* Judge's Chambers, High Court of Australia, Canberra, A.C.T. 2600 (Office); 2c Dumaresq Road, Rose Bay, N.S.W., 2029, Australia (Home). *Telephone:* (06) 2706969 (Office). *Fax:* (06) 2706970.

KIRBY, Peter Maxwell, M.A., M.B.A.; Australian business executive; b. 2 Aug. 1947, South Africa; s. of Robert Maxwell Kirby and May Kirby; m. Erica Anne Ebden; one s.; ed. Rhodes Univ., Natal Univ., Manchester Univ., Univ. of the Witwatersrand, Harvard Business School; Man. Dir. Dulux Paints 1991–92; C.E.O. ICI Paints Asia Pacific 1992–95, ICI Paints 1995–98; Man. Dir. and C.E.O. CSR Ltd. Jan. 1998–. *Leisure interests:* boating, cars. *Address:* CSR Ltd., Level 1, 9 Help Street, Chatswood, N.S.W. 2067, Australia. *Telephone:* (2) 9235 8080. *Fax:* (2) 9235 8130.

KIRBY, Ronald Hubert, B.ARCH.; Zambian architect and urban designer; b. 3 Jan. 1936, Lusaka, N. Rhodesia; s. of Hubert Rowland Kirby and May Elizabeth Kirby (née Hinds); m. Davina Anne Roderick 1985; one d.; ed. Muir Coll., Uitenhage, Univ. of Cape Town, Univ. of Witwatersrand; architect, commissions include: Queen Victoria Memorial Library, Zimbabwe 1960, Ndola Civic Centre, Zambia 1975, U.A.E. Nat. Ass., Abu Dhabi 1977, Oppenheimer Life Sciences Bldg., Johannesburg 1979, Zimbabwe Parl. Bldg., Harare 1984; external examiner Univs. of Cape Town and Pretoria 1985, rep. Zambia and Africa at confs. in various countries; Chair. Transvaal Prov. Inst. of Architecture P.R. and Press Commn. 1985–87; Prof. of Architecture and Head of Dept. Univ. of Witwatersrand 1991–94; Dir. Zambia Nat. Housing Authority 1991–92; mem. S. Africa Council of Architects Educational Inspection Comm. to Univ. of Witwatersrand 1985–, Asscn. of Arbiters, Transvaal Prov. Inst. of Architecture Commn. 1983–87; fmr. Pres. Zambia Inst. of Architecture; Zambia Inst. of Architecture Industrial Award 1964, Commercial Awards 1964, 1968, Civic Award 1968, Institutional Awards 1971, 1973, 1983, Inst. of S. African Architecture Awards of Merit 1983, 1987, RIBA Bronze Medal, Rhodesia 1963, Habitation Space Int. Award 1981. *Publications:* numerous articles in professional journals. *Address:* P.O. Box 337, Melville, 2109 Johannesburg, S. Africa. *Telephone:* 271 482-2323.

KIRCHNER, Alfred; German theatre director; b. 22 May 1937, Göppingen; s. of Julius Kirchner and Alice (née Bonatz) Kirchner; two d.; ed. Max Reinhardt Schule, Berlin; Chief Producer, Staatstheater, Stuttgart 1972–79; mem. Bd. of Dirs. and Chief Producer, Schauspielhaus, Bochum 1979–86, Burgtheater, Vienna 1986–89; Gen. Dir. Staatliche Schauspielbühnen, Berlin 1990–97; guest producer at Residenztheater, Munich, Hamburg Schauspielhaus, Hamburg State Opera, Frankfurt Opera, Holland Festival, Brussels Opera, Vienna State Opera, Santa Fé Opera, etc.; has directed operas by Udo Zimmermann, Bernd Alois Zimmermann, Hans Zender, Hans Werner Henze, Mozart, Verdi, Mussorgsky, Tchaikovsky; Dir. Der Ring des Niebelungen, Bayreuth 1994; producer of work for radio and TV. *Publications:* newspaper articles. *Address:* Staatliche Schauspielbühnen Berlin, Bismarckstrasse 110, 10625 Berlin, Germany. *Telephone:* (030) 319 51.

KIRCHSCHLÄGER, Rudolf, DR.JUR.; Austrian politician; b. 20 March 1915, Niederkappel, Upper Austria; s. of Johann and Anna Kirchschläger; m. Herma Sorger 1940; one s. one d.; ed. Univ. of Vienna; Judge until 1954; joined Ministry of Foreign Affairs 1954, Head Dept. of Int. Law 1956, Deputy Sec.-Gen. for Foreign Affairs 1962–67; Prin. Pvt. Sec. to the Minister of Foreign Affairs 1963–67; Minister to Czechoslovakia until 1970; Minister of Foreign Affairs 1970–74; Fed. Pres. of Austria 1974–86; has attended numerous int. confs. and been mem. of Austrian del. to UN Gen. Assembly. *Leisure interests:* music, walking. *Address:* Anderg. 9, A-1170, Vienna, Austria. *Telephone:* 485 1145. *Fax:* 485 1145-4.

KIRIYENKO, Sergey Vladilenovich; Russian politician; b. 27 July 1962, Sukhumi; m.; two c.; ed. Gorky (now Nizhny Novgorod) Inst. of Water Transport Eng.; mem. CPSU 1980–91; Sec. Comsomol Cttee. Krasnoye Sormovo shipyard, Gorky 1986–90; Pres. Nizhny Novgorod Bank Garantia 1991–96; Pres. Norsi Oil Co. 1996–97; First Deputy Minister of Fuel and Energy Aug.–Nov. 1997, Minister 1997–98; First Deputy Prime Minister, Acting Chair. of Govt. March–April 1998, Chair. (Prime Minister) April–Aug. 1998. *Address:* Government Offices, Krasnopresnenskaya 2 Moscow, Russia.

KIRK, Geoffrey Stephen, LITT.D., F.B.A., D.S.C.; British professor of Greek; b. 3 Dec. 1921, Nottingham; s. of Frederic T. Kirk and Enid H. Pentecost; m. 1st Barbara Helen Traill 1950 (divorced 1975); one d.; m. 2nd Kirsten Jensen Ricks 1975; ed. Rossall School and Clare Coll., Cambridge; Fellow, Trinity Hall, Cambridge 1946–70, Trinity Coll. 1974–82; Commonwealth Fund Fellow, Harvard 1949; Lecturer, then Reader in Classics, Univ. of Cambridge 1950–64, Regius Prof. of Greek 1974–82, Prof. Emer. 1982–; Prof. of Classics, Yale Univ. 1964–70, Bristol Univ. 1971–73; Sather Prof. in Classical Literature, Berkeley, Calif. 1969; Mellon Prof., Tulane Univ. 1979; Blegen Prof. Vassar Coll. 1986; Visiting Prof. Yale Univ. 1988; Corresp. mem., Acad. of Athens 1993–. *Publications:* Heraclitus, the Cosmic Fragments 1954, The Presocratic Philosophers (with J. E. Raven) 1957, The Songs of Homer 1962, Myth, its Meaning and Functions 1970, The Nature of Greek Myths 1974, Homer and the Oral Tradition 1977, The Iliad: a Commentary (Vol. I) 1985, (Vol. II) 1990, Towards the Aegean Sea 1997. *Leisure interests:* 18th century architecture. *Address:* 12 Sion Hill, Bath, BA1 2UH, England.

KIRK, Kent Sand; Danish politician and fishing captain; b. 29 Aug. 1948, Esbjerg; s. of Sand and Brynhild Kirk; m. Ruth Henriksen 1971; three s. one d.; Master's certificate; capt. of fishing boat 1971–; Gen. Man. K. and K. Kirk Ltd. 1973–; Chair. Bd. Fishermen's Asscn., Esbjerg 1975–; mem. Bd. Danish Deep Sea Fishing Fed., Danish Fishermen's Producers' Org., Esbjerg Harbour Council 1976–; mem. European Parl. 1979–; mem. Folketing 1984–89; Minister for Fisheries 1989–93; mem. Bd. Danish Conservative Party 1980–84; Vice-Pres. European Democratic Group 1981–83; Partner, Esvagt Ltd. (Stand-by vessels) 1981–; Chair. Bd. Int. School, Esbjerg 1982–. *Leisure interests:* skiing, reading. *Address:* c/o Ministry of Fisheries, Stormgade 2, 1470 Copenhagen K, Denmark. *Telephone:* 33963852.

KIRK, Paul Grattan, Jr., A.B., LL.B.; American political official and lawyer; b. 18 Jan. 1938, Newton, Mass.; s. of Paul G. Kirk and Josephine (née O'Connell) Kirk; m. Gail Loudermilk 1974; ed. Harvard Univ.; partner, Sullivan & Worcester, Boston and Washington 1977–90, Counsel 1990–; Chair. Kirk & Assocs. Inc. 1990–; Special Asst. to Senator Edward Kennedy (q.v.); Nat. Political Dir. Kennedy for Pres. Cttee. 1980; Treas. Democratic Nat. Cttee. 1983–85, Chair. 1985–89; Visiting Lecturer, Mass. Continuing Legal Educ. Program, New England Law Inst., J. F. Kennedy Inst. of Politics, Harvard Univ.; Chair., Bd. of Dirs. J. F. Kennedy Library Foundation, Nominating Cttee. Harvard Bd. of Overseers 1993, Nat. Democratic Inst. for Int. Affairs; mem. Bd. of Dirs. Bradley Real Estate Inc., ITT Corpn. 1989–97, ITT Hartford Life Insurance Co., Hartford Financial Services Group, Rayonier Corpn. 1993–; mem. Bd of Trustees, Stonehill Coll., St. Sebastian's School 1992–; Co-Chair. Comm. on Pres. Debates; etc.; W. Averell Harriman Democracy Award 1988. *Leisure interest:* athletics. *Address:* Sullivan and Worcester, One Post Office Square, Suite 2400, Boston, MA 02109, U.S.A. *Telephone:* (617) 338-2800.

KIRKBY, Emma, M.A., F.G.S.M.D.; British singer; b. 26 Feb. 1949, Camberley, Surrey; d. of Capt. Geoffrey Kirkby and Beatrice Daphne Kirkby; one s. by Anthony Rooley; ed. Sherborne School for Girls and Somerville Coll., Oxford and pvt. singing lessons with Jessica Cash; specialist singer of renaissance, baroque and classical repertoire; started full-time professional singing 1975; since mid-1970s involved in revival of performances with period instruments and the attempt to recreate the sounds the composers would have heard; performances at the Proms 1977–; works as freelance, particularly with Consort of Musicke (dir. Anthony Rooley) and Acad. of Ancient Music (dir. Christopher Hogwood); Hon. D.Litt. (Salford) 1985; Hon. D.Mus. (Bath) 1994. *Recordings include:* Complete songs of John Dowland 1976–77, Messiah (Handel) 1979, 1988, Madrigals by Monteverdi, Wert, Scarlatti and other Italians, Schütz, Grabbe, Wilbye, Ward and other English composers, Monteverdi Vespers, Mass in B Minor (Bach), Handel's Athalia, Joshua, Judas Maccabaeus, Sequences by Hildegarde of Bingen (Hyperion), Arie Antiche and Songs of Maurice Greene, Dido and Aeneas, Handel's German Arias, Italian Cantatas: Songs by Arne and Handel, Stabat Mater (Pergolesi), Haydn's Creation, Mozart Motets, Mozart Concert Arias, Vivaldi Opera Arias, Handel Opera Arias, Christmas Music with Westminster Abbey Choir. *Address:* c/o Consort of Musicke, 54a Leamington Road Villas, London, W11 1HT, England. *Telephone:* 0171-229 5142. *Fax:* 0171-221 1282.

KIRKEGAARD, Knud E.; Danish politician; b. 17 May 1942, Ringkobing Co.; ed. Norre-Nissum Coll.; teacher; ed. and vocational training consultant; mem. Folketing (Parl.) 1984–; Conservative Party Educ. spokesman 1984; Minister for Labour 1989–93. *Address:* c/o Ministry of Labour, Laksegade, 19, 1063 Copenhagen K, Denmark.

KIRKINEN, Heikki, PH.D.; Finnish university professor (retd.); b. 22 Sept. 1927, Liperi; s. of Sulo A. Kirkinen and Anna Hirvonen; m. Maire Mirjam Rehvonen 1953; one s.; ed. Joensuu Lycée, Univ. of Helsinki; lecturer in History and Finnish, Orthodox Seminary of Finland 1953–59; lecturer in History, Univ. of Jyvaskyla 1960–62; Researcher, Acad. of Finland 1962–66; Assoc. Prof. Sorbonne, Paris 1966–70; Prof. of History, Univ. of Joensuu 1970–, Rector 1971–81, Prof. and Dir. Inst. of History 1981–90; Assoc. Prof., Sorbonne Nouvelle 1984–85; Assoc. Dir. of Studies, Ecole Pratique des Hautes Etudes, Paris 1988–89; Hon. mem. Kalevala Soc.; mem. History Soc., Finnish Literature Soc., Acad. of Sciences of Finland; mem. Acad. Européenne des Sciences, des Arts et des Lettres; Commdr., Order of the White Rose; Commdr., Ordre des Palmes Académiques, Officier, Ordre Nat. du Mérite (France). *Publications:* Les origines de la conception moderne de l'homme-machine 1960, Karelia between East and West, I. Russian Karelia in the Renaissance (1478–1617) 1970, Karelia on the Battlefield. Karelia between East and West, II 1976, Problems of Rural Development in Finland and in France (Ed.) 1982, Europas födelse. Bonniers varldshistoria 7 1984, The Kalevala, an Epic of Finland and all Mankind (with H. Sihvo) 1985, History of Russia and the Soviet Union (Ed.-in-Chief) 1986, Le monde kalévaléen en France et en Finlande avec un regard sur la tradition populaire et l'épopée brétonnes (Ed. with Jean Perrot) 1987, Byzantine Tradition and Finland 1987, Structures and Forces in History 1987, The Roots of the Kalevala Tradition in North Karelia 1988, Europe of Regions and Finland 1991, History of the Karelian People (with others) 1994, Provincial Government 1996. *Leisure interests:* music, fishing. *Address:* University of Joensuu, B.P. 111, 80101 Joensuu (Office); Roskildenkatu 4D7, 80140 Joensuu, Finland (Home). *Telephone:* (13) 801143, Finland.

KIRKLAND, Gelsey; American ballerina; b. 1953, Bethlehem, Pa.; m. Greg Lawrence; ed. School of American Ballet; youngest mem. of New York Ballet at 15 in 1968, Soloist 1969–72, Prin. Dancer 1972–74; American Ballet Theater 1974–81, 1982–84, teacher, coach American Ballet Theatre 1992–; Guest Dancer, Royal Ballet, London 1980, 1986, Stuttgart Ballet 1980; performed in numerous ballets including: Firebird, The Goldberg Variations, Scherzo fantastique, An Evening's Waltzes, The Leaves are Fading, Hamlet, The Tiller in the Field, Four Bagatelles, Stravinsky Symphony in C, Song of the Nightingale Connotations, Romeo and Juliet and others; appeared in TV show The Nutcracker 1977. *Publications:* Dancing on My Grave (autobiog.) 1987, The Shape of Love (with Greg Laurence) 1990, The Little Ballerina and Her Dancing Horse 1993. *Address:* c/o Dubé Zakin Management Inc., 67 Riverside Drive, Apartment 3B, New York, NY 10024, U.S.A.

KIRKLAND, (Joseph) Lane, B.S.; American trade unionist; b. 12 March 1922, Camden, S.C.; s. of Randolph Withers Kirkland and Louise Richardson; m. 1st Edith Hollyday 1944 (divorced 1972); five c.; m. 2nd Irena Neumann 1973; ed. U.S. Merchant Marine Acad. and School of Foreign Service,

Georgetown Univ.; Deck Officer, U.S. Merchant Marine 1941–46; Nautical Scientist, Hydrographic Office, Navy Dept. 1947–48; mem. of research staff, AFL 1948–53; Asst. Dir. Social Security Dept., AFL and AFL-CIO 1953–58; Dir. Research and Educ., Int. Union of Operating Engineers 1958–60; Exec. Asst. to Pres. AFL-CIO 1961–69, Sec.-Treas. 1969–79, Pres. 1979–95; mem. Bd. Polish American Enterprise Fund; Hon. LL.D. (Duke Univ., Princeton Univ., Dartmouth Univ., Columbia Univ.); several awards. *Leisure interests:* reading, gardening, archaeology. *Address:* George Meany Center for Labor Studies, 10 000 New Hampshire Avenue, Silver Spring, MD 20903, U.S.A.

KIRKPATRICK, Clayton, A.B.; American newspaper editor; b. 8 Jan. 1915, Waterman, Ill.; s. of Clayton Matteson Kirkpatrick and Mable Rose Swift; m. Thelma Marie De Mott 1943; two s. two d.; ed. Univ. of Ill.; Reporter, City News Bureau, Chicago 1938; mem. staff Chicago Tribune 1938–, Day City Ed. 1958–61, City Ed. 1961–63, Asst. Man. Ed. 1963–65, Man. Ed. 1965–67, Exec. Ed. 1967–69, Ed. 1969–79; Vice-Pres. Chicago Tribune Co. 1967–77, Exec. Vice-Pres. 1977–79, Pres. 1979–81, Chair. 1981; Del. to 19th Gen. Conf., UNESCO, Nairobi 1976; Bronze Star Medal for service in World War II; Elijah Parish Lovejoy Award, Colby Coll. 1978; William Allen White Award, Univ. of Kansas 1977; Fourth Estate Award, Nat. Press Club 1979. *Address:* 471 Stagecoach Run, Glen Ellyn, IL 60137, U.S.A. (Home).

KIRKPATRICK, Jeane Duane Jordan, M.A., PH.D.; American diplomatist and professor of political science; b. 19 Nov. 1926, Duncan, Okla.; d. of Welcher F. and Leona (Kile) Jordan; m. Evron M. Kirkpatrick 1955; three s.; ed. Stephens Coll., Columbia, Mo., Barnard Coll., Columbia Univ., New York, and Inst. de Science Politique, Univ. of Paris; Research Analyst, Dept. of State 1951–53; Research Assoc., George Washington Univ., Washington, D.C. 1954–56, Fund for the Republic 1956–58; Asst. Prof. of Political Science, Trinity Coll., Washington, D.C. 1962–67; Assoc. Prof. of Political Science, Georgetown Univ., Washington, D.C. 1967–73, Prof. 1973–; Leavey Prof. in Foundations of American Freedom 1978–; Sr. Fellow American Enterprise Inst. for Public Policy Research 1977–; Perm. Rep. to UN 1981–85; fmr. mem. Democratic Nat. Comm.; Vice-Chair. Comm. on Vice-Presidential Selection 1972–74, mem. Nat. Comm. on Party Structure and Presidential Nomination 1975; mem. Int. Research Council Cen. for Strategic and Int. Studies, Georgetown Univ.; Earhart Fellow 1956–57; Hon. L.H.D. (Georgetown Univ., Univ. of Pittsburgh, Univ. of Mich., Tel Aviv Univ., Coll. of William and Mary, St. John's Univ., St. Anselm's Univ., Syracuse Univ.); Prix Politique (France) 1984; Distinguished Alumna Award, Stephens Coll. 1978, Distinguished Alumna Medal, Barnard Coll. 1983, B'nai B'nith Award 1982; Pres. Medal of Freedom 1985, Hubert Humphry Award (American Political Science Asscn.) 1988; fmr. Democrat; joined Republican Party 1985. *Publications:* Foreign Students in the United States: A National Survey 1966, Mass Behavior in Battle and Captivity 1968, Leader and Vanguard in Mass Society: The Peronist Movement in Argentina 1971, Political Woman 1974, The Presidential Elite 1976, Dismantling the Parties: Reflections on Party Reform and Party Decomposition 1978, Dictatorships and Double Standards 1982, The Reagan Phenomenon 1983, Legitimacy and Force (2 vols.) 1988, Foreign Affairs: America and the World 1989–90, The Withering Away of the Totalitarian State 1990; ed. and contributor to several others; also articles in political journals. *Leisure interests:* contemporary fiction, Bach, gourmet cooking. *Address:* American Enterprise Institute, 1150 17th Street, N.W., Washington, DC 20036, U.S.A.

KIRKUP, James, B.A., F.R.S.L.; British writer; b. 23 April 1918, South Shields; s. of James Harold Kirkup and Mary Johnson; ed. Durham Univ.; Gregory Fellow in Poetry, Leeds Univ. 1950–52; Visiting Poet, Bath Acad. of Art 1953–56; travelling lectureship from Swedish Ministry of Education 1956–57; Prof. of English Language and Literature, Salamanca (Spain) 1957–58; Prof. of English Literature, Tohoku Univ. 1959–61; Visiting Prof. of English Literature, Japan Women's Univ., Tokyo 1964–69; Visiting Prof. and Poet in Residence, Amherst Coll. Mass. 1968–69; Prof. of English Literature, Univ. of Nagoya, Japan 1969–72; Morton Visiting Prof. in Int. Literature, Ohio Univ. 1975–76; Playwright in Residence, Sherman Theatre, Univ. Coll., Cardiff 1976–77; Prof. of English Literature, Kyoto Univ. of Foreign Studies 1977–89; Tutor, Arvon Foundation 1979; obituarist for The Independent and The Guardian newspapers 1989–; Literary Ed. Orient-West Magazine, Tokyo 1963–65; founder Pres. The British Haiku Soc. 1991–; Atlantic Award in Literature (Rockefeller Foundation) 1959. *Publications:* The Cosmic Shape 1947, The Drowned Sailor 1948, The Creation 1950, The Submerged Village 1951, A Correct Compassion 1952, A Spring Journey 1954, Upon This Rock, The Dark Child, The Triumph of Harmony 1955, The True Mystery of the Nativity, Ancestral Voices, The Radiance of the King 1956, The Descent into the Cave, The Only Child (autobiography) 1957, The Peach Garden, Two Pigeons Flying High (TV plays), Sorrows, Passions and Alarms (autobiography) 1960, The True Mystery of the Passion, The Prodigal Son (poems) 1956–60, These Horned Islands (travel) 1962, The Love of Others (novel) 1962, Tropic Temper (travel) 1963, Refusal to Conform, Last and First Poems 1963, The Heavenly Mandate 1964, Japan Industrial, Vols. I and II 1964–65, Tokyo (travel) 1966, Bangkok (travel) 1967, Paper Windows 1967, Michael Kohlhaas 1967, Filipinescas (travel) 1968, One Man's Russia (travel) 1968, Streets of Asia (travel) 1969, Hong Kong (travel) 1969, White Shadows, Black Shadows: Poems of Peace and War 1969, The Body Servant: Poems of Exile 1971, Japan Behind the Fan 1970, Streets of Asia 1969, Insect Summer (novel) 1971, A Bewick Bestiary 1971, Transmental Vibrations 1972, Brand (Ibsen) 1972, The Magic Drum (play for children) 1972, (story for children) 1973, Peer Gynt 1973, The Winter Moon, Selected Poems of Takagi Kyozo, Cyrano de Bergerac 1974, Play Strindberg 1974, The Conformer 1975, Don Carlos 1975, Heaven, Hell and Hara-Kiri 1975, Background to English Literature 1975, An English Traveller in Japan 1975, Frank the Fifth, Portrait of a Planet 1976, Scenes from Sesshu 1977, Modern Japanese Poetry (anthology) 1978, Dengoban Messages: One-line Poems, Zen Contemplations, Enlightenment 1979, Cold Mountain Poems, The Guardian of the Word, Aspects of Europe, Countries and Customs, British Traditions and Superstitions 1980, James Kirkup's Tales from Shakespeare 1969–84, Scenes from Sutcliffe 1981, The British Lady and Gentleman, I am Count Dracula 1981, Ecce Homo 1981, To The Unknown God 1982, The Bush Toads 1982, Folktales Japanesque 1982, To the Ancestral North (poems for autobiog.) 1983, The Glory that was Greece 1984, The Sense of the Visit 1984, Hearn in my Heart 1984; An Actor's Revenge (opera) 1979, Friends in Arms, Shunkinsho 1980, No More Hiroshimas 1982, 1995, The Damask Drum (opera) 1984, Trends and Traditions 1985, Dictionary of Body Language 1985, English with a Smile 1986, Fellow Feelings (poems) 1986, Portraits and Souvenirs 1987, The Mystery and Magic of Symbols 1987, The Cry of the Owl: Native American Folktales and Legends 1987, I of All People, Scenes from American Life, I Remember America, Everyday English Superstitions 1988, The Best of Britain 1989, Everyday English Proverbs 1989, Gaijin on the Ginza 1992, A Poet Could Not But Be Gay 1992, Throwback (Poems) 1992, First Fireworks (Poems) 1992, Me All Over: Memoirs of a Misfit (autobiog.) 1993, Queens Have Died Young and Fair (novel) 1993, Strange Attractors (poems) 1994, Blue Bamboo (Haiku) 1994, Words or Contemplation (poems) 1993, Noems, Koans & A Navel Display 1995, A Certain State of Mind 1995, Blindsight (trans. Hervé Guibert) 1995, Paradise (trans. Hervé Guibert) 1996, Collected Longer Poems 1996, Selected Shorter Poems 1996, Counting to 9,999 1996, Look at it This Way! (Poems for young people) 1995, A Child of the Tyne (autobiography) 1996, A Book of Tanka 1996 (Japan Festival Foundation Award 1997), The Patient Obituarist: New Poems 1996, Burning Giraffes: Modern Japanese Poets 1996, Broad Daylight: Poems East and West 1996, Figures in a Setting 1996, Utsusemi (tanka) 1996, Two Classic German Dramas: Kleist's Prince of Homburg and Schiller's Don Carlos 1997, The Nativity and the Passion: Two Mystery Plays 1997, How to Cook Women: Selected Poetry and Prose by Takagi Kyozo 1997, He Dreamed He Was a Butterfly 1998, Pikadon: An Epic 1998, Tanka Tales 1998, One-Man Band: Poems Without Words 1999, Tokonoma (haiku and tanka, with woodcuts by Naoko Matsubara), and others; numerous poems, plays and essays and trans. from French, German, Japanese, Italian and Norwegian. *Leisure interests:* macrobiotic diet, Zen Buddhist meditation, listening to good jazz. *Address:* c/o British Monomarks, BM-Box 2780, London, WC1N 3XX, England.

KIRPAL, Prem Nath, M.A., LL.B.; Indian educationist; b. 30 April 1909, Moga, Punjab; s. of Raibahadur Ishwardas and Bibi Kesari; ed. Punjab Univ. and Balliol Coll., Oxford; Lecturer, then Prof. of History and Political Science 1934–45; Educ. Adviser, Indian High Comm., London 1945–48; Deputy Sec. Ministry of Educ. and Sec.-Gen. Indian Nat. Comm. for UNESCO 1948–52; Deputy Dir. then Dir. UNESCO Dept. of Cultural Activities 1952–57; Joint Sec. Ministry of Educ. and Joint Educ. Adviser to Govt. of India 1957–60; Sec. Ministry of Educ. 1960–69; Sr. Specialist, East-West Centre, Honolulu Hawaii 1969; Dir. Int. Study of Private Philanthropy 1969–; Pres. Exec. Board, UNESCO 1970–72; Founder, Pres., Inst. of Cultural Relations and Devt. Studies, New Delhi 1971–; Pres. Indian Council of Peace Research 1972–; Pres. Int. Educational Consortium, New Delhi 1979–81; Consultant, World Bank, Washington, D.C.; mem. Exec. Council, Delhi Univ.; Chair. Delhi Public Library, Delhi School of Social Work; Pres. Forum of Educ., India; Hon. LL.D. (Temple Univ.), Hon. D.Sc. (Leningrad), Hon. D.Litt. (Punjab Univ.); UNESCO Gold Medal 1972, 30th Anniversary Award, UNESCO 1976, and other awards; Orders of Repub. of Egypt and of U.A.R. 1972. *Publications:* East India Company and Persia 1800-1810: A Study in Diplomatic Relations, Memoirs of Wollebrant de Jong 1624, Life of Dyal Singh Majithia, Main Trends in Cultural Development of India, A Decade of Indian Education 1958–68, Indian Education—Twenty-five Years of Independence, Youth Values and Established Culture, Education and Development, In Quest of Humanity, The Cosmic Sea and other Poems 1980, Songs of Psyche, Spirit's Musings, Songs of Eternity (philosophical poems), Voices from the Deep 1986, From Near and Far (poems) 1988, Autumn offerings (poems) 1989, Foundations of Education for Free India 1990, Education and International Cooperation 1991, Dreams and Solitudes 1990, Mind and Modes 1990, Monsoon Breezes 1991, Roses in December 1991 (all poems), Quests and Celebrations (poems), Heart's Offerings (poems), A Decade of Education in India, Culture and Development, Reconstituting the Human Community, and over 20 articles on education, culture and international co-operation. *Leisure interests:* hiking, painting, poetry and meditation. *Address:* F-63, Sujan Singh Park, New Delhi 110003, India (Home).

KIRPICHNIKOV, Mikhail Petrovich, PH.D.; Russian politician; b. 9 Nov. 1945, Moscow; m.; one d.; ed. Moscow Inst. of Physics and Tech.; with Inst. of Molecular Biology 1972–89; Deputy Head, Head of Div., U.S.S.R. Cttee. on Science and Tech. 1989–91; Head of Div., Head of Dept., Ministry of Science and Tech. Policy of Russian Fed. 1991–93; Head, Div. of Science, Educ., High School and Tech., Russian Govt. 1993–94, Head, Dept. of Science and Educ. 1994–98; First Deputy Minister of Science and Tech. July–Sept. 1998, Minister Sept. 1998–; mem., Russian Acad. of Sciences 1997–. *Publications:* over 200 books, articles and papers on biology. *Address:* Ministry of

Science and Technology, Tverskaya str. 11, 103905 Moscow, Russia. *Telephone:* (095) 229 2501 (Office). *Fax:* (095) 230 2823 (Office).

KIRPICHNIKOV, Valery Aleksandrovich; Russian politician; b. 29 June 1946, Rostov-on-Don; m.; two c.; ed. Leningrad Polytech. Inst.; army service, Lieut., air defence forces 1969–71; engineer, sr. engineer, Deputy Head of lab., S. Vavilov State Inst. of Optics, Leningrad Region br. 1971–81; chief engineer, Research Inst. of Complex Tests 1981–88; Deputy Chair., Chair., Exec. Cttee. Sosnovy Bor Town Soviet 1988–92; R.S.F.S.R. Peoples' Deputy 1990, mem. Supreme Soviet 1990–93; mem. State Duma 1993–98; Pres. Union of Russian Towns 1993–; Minister of Regional Policy of Russian Fed. Sept. 1998–; was Deputy Gov. Leningrad Region; f., movt. Russian Union of Local Self-Man. *Publications:* scientific works, patents. *Address:* Ministry of Regional Policy, Trubnikovsky per. 19, Moscow, Russia. *Telephone:* (095) 248 8373 (Office).

KIRSCHSTEIN, Ruth L., A.B., M.D.; American physician and administrator; b. 12 Oct. 1926, Brooklyn, New York; d. of Julius and Elizabeth (Berm) Kirschstein; m. Alan S. Rabson 1950; one s.; ed. Long Island Univ., New York and Tulane Univ., New Orleans, La.; Hosp. intern and resident 1951–54; Instructor in Pathology, Tulane Univ. 1954–55; Medical Officer, Resident in Pathology, then Pathologist, Lab. of Viral Products, Nat. Insts. of Health 1956–60, Chief, Section of Pathology, Lab. of Viral Immunology 1960–62, Asst. Chief, Lab. of Viral Immunology 1962–64, Acting Chief, Lab. of Pathology 1964–65, Chief 1965–72; Asst. Dir. Div. of Biologics Standards, Nat. Insts. of Health 1971–72, Acting Deputy Dir., Bureau of Biologics 1972–73, Deputy Assoc. Commr. for Science 1973–74; Dir. Nat. Inst. of Gen. Medical Sciences, NIH 1974–93; Deputy Dir. NIH 1993–; mem. Inst. of Medicine of N.A.S.; Co-Chair. PHS Co-ordinating Comm. on Women's Health Issues 1990–; Co-Chair. Special Emphasis Oversight Comm. on Science and Tech. 1989–; Hon. LL.D. (Atlanta) 1985; D.Sc. h.c. (Mount Sinai School of Medicine) 1984, (Medical Coll. of Ohio) 1986; Hon. Dr. (School of Medicine, Tulane Univ.) 1997; Presidential Meritorious Exec. Rank Award 1980, Distinguished Exec. Service Award Sr. Exec. Asscn. 1985, Presidential Distinguished Exec. Rank Award 1985, 1995, and numerous other awards. *Publications:* numerous scientific papers. *Address:* National Institutes of Health, Building 1, Room 126, 1 Center Drive, MSC 0148, Bethesda, MD 20892 (Office); 6 West Drive, Bethesda, MD 20814, U.S.A. (Home). *Telephone:* (301) 496-7322. *Fax:* (301) 402-2700.

KIRST, Michael, M.P.A., PH.D.; American professor of education; b. 1 Aug. 1939, West Reading, Pa.; s. of Russell Kirst and Marian (Weile) Kirst; m. Wendy Burdsall 1975; one s. one d.; ed. Dartmouth Coll., and Harvard Univ.; Assoc. Dir. President's Comm. on White House Fellows, Nat. Advisory Council on Educ. of Disadvantaged Children 1966; Dir. Program Planning and Evaluation, Bureau of Elementary and Secondary Educ., U.S. Office of Educ. 1967; Staff Dir. U.S. Senate Sub-Cttee. on Manpower, Employment and Poverty 1968; Prof. of Educ. and Business Admin. Stanford Univ. 1968–; Pres. Calif. State Bd. of Educ. 1977–81; Chair. Bd. of Int. Comparative Studies in Educ., N.A.S. 1994–; mem. numerous other educ. bds., cttees., etc. *Publications include:* Schools in Conflict: Political Turbulence in American Education (with F. Wirt) 1992, Contemporary Issues in Education: Perspectives from Australia and U.S.A. (with G. Hancock and D. Grossman) 1983, Who Controls Our Schools: American Values in Conflict 1984, Political Dynamics of American Education 1997. *Address:* School of Education, Stanford University, Stanford, CA 94305, U.S.A. *Telephone:* (650) 723-4412. *Fax:* (650) 725-7412.

KIRSZENSTEIN-SZEWIŃSKA, Irena, M.ECON.; Polish athlete; b. 24 May 1946, Leningrad, U.S.S.R. (now St. Petersburg, Russia); m.; two s.; ed. Warsaw Univ.; athlete 1961–80 (100 m., 200 m., long jump, 4 × 100 m. relay, 4 × 400 m. relay); took part in Olympic Games, Tokyo 1964 (silver medals for long jump and 200 m., gold medal for 4 × 100 m. relay), Mexico City 1968 (bronze medal for 100 m., gold medal for 200 m.), Munich 1972 (bronze medal for 200 m.), Montreal 1976 (gold medal for 400 m.); ten times world record holder, for 100 m., 200 m. and 400 m.; Pres. Polish Women's Sport Asscn. 1994–, Polish Athletic Asscn. 1997–; Vice-Pres. Polish Olympic Cttee. 1988–, Polish Olympians Asscn. 1993–, World Olympians Asscn. 1995–; mem. Council European Athletic Asscn. 1995–, Women's Cttee., Int. Amateur Athletic Fed., Int. Olympic Cttee. (IOC) 1998–, IOC Co-ordination Cttee. 1998–; Pres. Irena Szewińska Foundation—Vita-Aktiva 1998–; Gold Cross of Merit 1964, Officer's Cross, Order of Polonia Restituta 1968, Commdr.'s Cross, Order of Polonia Restituta 1972, with Star 1999, Order of Banner of Labour (2nd Class) 1976. *Leisure interests:* jogging, books, theatre. *Address:* Polish Athletic Association, ul. Cegłowska 68/70, 01-809 Warsaw, Poland. *Telephone:* (22) 639 70 15. *Fax:* (22) 639 70 16.

KIRWAN, William E., PH.D.; American university president and professor of mathematics; b. 14 April 1938, Louisville, Ky.; s. of Albert Dennis Kirwan and Elizabeth H. Kirwan; m. Patricia Harper 1960; one s. one d.; ed. Univ. of Kentucky, Rutgers Univ.; Asst. Instructor, Rutgers Univ. 1963–64; Asst. Prof., Dept. of Math., Univ. of Maryland 1964–68; Visiting Lecturer, Royal Holloway Coll., London Univ., U.K. 1966–67; Assoc. Prof., Dept. of Math., Univ. of Md. at Coll. Park 1968–72, Prof. 1972–, Chair. Dept. of Math. 1977–81, Vice-Chancellor for Academic Affairs 1981–88, Acting Chancellor 1982, Vice-Pres. for Academic Affairs and Provost 1986–88, Acting Pres. 1988–89, Pres. 1989–98; Pres. Ohio State Univ. 1998–; Chair. Nat. Asscn. of State Univs. and Land Grant Colls. 1995–; several other appointments; Ed. Proc. of American Math. Soc. 1979–85; NDEA Fellow 1960–63; Nat. Science Foundation Grants 1965–82; Officier, Order of Leopold II, Belgium 1989. *Publications:* Advances in Complex Analysis (Co-Ed. with L. Zalcman) 1976; numerous published research articles and seminar talks. *Leisure interests:* classical music, tennis. *Address:* Ohio State University, 1800 Cannon Drive, Columbus, OH 43210, U.S.A.

KISEKKA, Samson; Ugandan politician and medical practitioner; Chief Spokesman for Nat. Resistance Army; Adviser to Yoweri Museveni (q.v.); Prime Minister of Uganda 1986–91, Vice-Pres. of Uganda 1991–94, also fmrly. Minister of Internal Affairs, also Minister of Gender and Community Devt.; mem. numerous asscns.; Paul Harris Fellow of Rotary Int.; Hon. LL.D. (Southwest Adventist Coll., Texas). *Address:* c/o Office of the Prime Minister, P.O. Box 341, Kampala, Uganda.

KISELEV, Yevgeny Alekseyevich; Russian broadcaster; b. 15 June 1956, Moscow; s. of Alexei and Anna Kiselev; m. Masha Shakhova 1974; one s.; ed. Inst. of Asian and African Studies, Moscow State Univ.; teacher of Persian (Farsi) language, Higher School of KGB 1981–84; corresp., Radio Moscow Middle Eastern dept. 1984–86; TV journalist 1987–; regular host "120 Minutes" breakfast show 1987–90, staff corresp. news div. Gosteleradio (fmr. U.S.S.R. State Cttee. for TV and radio broadcasting) 1989–90; made series of documentaries on everyday life in Israel 1989, 1990; joined newly-founded Russian TV 1991, anchorman "Vesti" late-night news programme; joined Ostankino State TV co. 1992; started "Itogi" weekly news and current affairs programme 1992; Co-founder and Vice-Pres. NTV independent broadcasting co. 1993–; Co-founder, NTV-Plus Co. (direct satellite broadcasting) 1996; mem. Acad. of Russian TV; Journalist of the Year, Moscow Journalistic Union 1993, included on list of 100 most influential people in Russia, publ. monthly by Nezavisimaya Gazeta 1993–; Int. Press Freedom Award, Cttee. to Protect Journalists, New York 1995. *Leisure interest:* playing tennis. *Address:* NTV Television Company, Novy Arbat 36, 121205 Moscow, Russia (Office). *Telephone:* (095) 290-87-87, 290-91-38, 217-93-92 (Office). *Fax:* (095) 217-89-34.

KISHLANSKY, Mark Alan, PH.D., F.R.HIST.S.; American professor of history; b. 10 Nov. 1948, Brooklyn, N.Y.; s. of Morris Kishlansky and Charlotte Katz; m. Jeanne Thiel 1975; two s.; ed. Commack High School, State Univ. of New York at Stony Brook and Brown Univ.; Prof. of History, Univ. of Chicago 1975–91, Northwestern Univ. 1983, Harvard Univ. 1991–, Frank Baird Jr. Prof. of History 1997–; Mellon Visiting Prof. of History, Calif. Inst. of Tech. 1990; mem. Cttee. on Social Thought 1990–91; various research awards and other distinctions. *Publications:* The Rise of the New Model Army 1979, Parliamentary Selection: Social and Political Choice in Early Modern England, Early Modern Europe: The Crisis of Authority (ed. with C.M. Gray and E. Cochrane) 1987, Civilization in the West (with P. Geary and P. O'Brien) 1991, Sources of the West (ed.) 1991, Societies and Cultures in World Civilizations (with P. Geary, P.O'Brien, R. B. Worg) 1995, A Monarchy Transformed 1996. *Leisure interests:* Shakespeare, baseball, comedy. *Address:* Department of History, Harvard University, Cambridge, MA 02138, U.S.A. *Telephone:* (617) 496-3427. *Fax:* (617) 496-3425.

KISHTMAND, Sultan Ali; Afghanistan politician; b. 1935; ed. univ.; mem. of Hazara ethnic minority; a founder mem. People's Democratic Party of Afghanistan (PDPA) and mem. Cen. Cttee. 1965; with Parcham faction when PDPA split 1967; Minister of Planning April–Aug. 1978; tried on charges of conspiracy and sentenced to death 1978; sentence commuted by Pres. Amin. Oct. 1978; fmr. Vice-Pres. of Revolutionary Council; Deputy Prime Minister and Minister of Planning after Soviet intervention Dec. 1979–81; Prime Minister of Afghanistan and Chair. Council of Ministers 1981–88, 1989–90; First Vice-Pres. 1990–91.

KISIM, Marwan al-, PH.D.; Jordanian politician; b. 12 May 1938, Amman; ed. Eastern Michigan, Columbia and Georgetown Univs., U.S.A.; joined Ministry of Foreign Affairs 1962; Consul-Gen., New York 1964–65; Deputy Dir. of Protocol 1966; Political Officer, Jordanian Embassy, Beirut 1967–68, U.S.A. 1968–72; Sec. to Crown Prince Hassan (q.v.) 1972–75; Dir.-Gen. Royal Hashemite Court 1975–76, Chief 1988; Minister of State 1976; Minister of Supply 1977–79; Minister of State for Foreign Affairs 1979–80, Minister of Foreign Affairs 1980–83; Deputy Prime Minister and Minister of Foreign Affairs 1988–90; Jordanian, Syrian, Mexican, Lebanese, Chinese and Italian decorations. *Address:* c/o Ministry of Foreign Affairs, Amman, Jordan.

KISLITSYN, Vyacheslav Aleksandrovich; Russian politician; b. 4 Sept. 1948, Kosolapovo, Mari Autonomous Repub.; m.; one d.; ed. Tomsk School of Railway Transport, Mari State Pedagogical Inst., Moscow Inst. of Politology, Russian State Social Inst.; Chair. Regional Cttee. on Sports; instructor Exec. Cttee. Medvedsk Dist. Soviet; Chair. Semenov, then Znamensk Dist. Soviet 1972–78; Chair. Bd. Pobeditel kolkhoz 1978–89; U.S.S.R. People's Deputy 1992–93; Chair., Head of Admin. Medvedsk Dist. 1989–93; elected Pres., Head of Govt. Mari El Repub. Jan. 1997–; mem. Russian Council of Fed. 1993–. *Address:* Office of the President, Leninsky prospect 29, 424001 Yoshkar-Ola, Mari-El Republic, Russia (Office). *Telephone:* (8362) 55 66 64, 55 67 46 (Office).

KISSIN, Yevgeny Igorevich; Russian pianist; b. 10 Oct. 1971, Moscow; ed. Moscow Gnessin Music School, studied piano with Anna Kantor; début with Moscow Philharmonic 1984, in Europe 1988; toured Europe, U.S.A., Japan as child prodigy, played and recorded with orchestras under Herbert von Karajan, Seiji Ozawa, Claudio Abbado, Mstislav Rostropovich, participates in numerous European festivals; lives in U.S.A.; returned to Moscow for concerts 1997. *Address:* c/o Harold Holt Ltd., 31 Sinclair Road, London, W14 0NS, England. *Telephone:* 0171-603 4600 (Agent); (212) 580-5296 (Home, New York).

KISSINGER, Henry Alfred, M.A., PH.D.; American government official, university professor and consultant; b. 27 May 1923, Fuerth, Germany; m. 1st Anne Fleisher 1949 (divorced 1964); one s. one d.; m. 2nd Nancy Maginnes 1974; ed. George Washington High School, Harvard Coll., Harvard Univ.; went to U.S.A. 1938; naturalized U.S. Citizen 1943; U.S. Army 1943–46; Dir. Study Group on Nuclear Weapons and Foreign Policy, Council of Foreign Relations 1955–56; Dir. Special Studies Project, Rockefeller Brothers Fund 1956–58; Consultant, Weapons System Evaluation Group, Joint Chiefs of Staff 1956–60, Nat. Security Council 1961–63, U.S. Arms Control and Disarmament Agency 1961–68, Dept. of State 1965–68, and to various other bodies; Faculty mem. Harvard Univ. 1954–71; Dept. of Govt. and Center for Int. Affairs (on leave of absence 1969–71); Assoc. Dir. Harvard Univ. Center for Int. Affairs 1957–60; Dir. Harvard Int. Seminar 1951–71, Harvard Defense Studies Program 1958–71, Asst. to Pres. of U.S.A. for Nat. Security Affairs 1969–75; Sec. of State 1973–77; prominent in American negotiations for the Viet Nam settlement of Jan. 1973, and in the negotiations for a Middle East ceasefire 1973, 1974; Counsellor, Center for Strategic and Int. Studies 1977–, Trustee 1987–; Chair. Kissinger Associates, Inc. 1982–; mem. Pres.'s Foreign Intelligence Advisory Bd. 1984–90; Chair. Nat. Bipartisan Comm. on Cen. America 1983–84; Counsellor to Chase Manhattan Bank and mem. of its Int. Advisory Cttee.; Hon. Gov. Foreign Policy Asscn.; Sr. Fellow, Aspen Inst., syndicated columnist L.A. Times 1984–; Adviser to Bd. of Dirs. American Express, Revlon Group Inc., Continental Grain Co., Freeport McMoRan Inc., Hollinger Int.; Guggenheim Fellowship 1965–66, Woodrow Wilson Book Prize 1958, American Inst. for Public Service Award 1973, Nobel Peace Prize 1973, American Legion Distinguished Service Medal 1974, Wateler Peace Prize 1974, Presidential Medal of Freedom 1977, Medal of Liberty 1986, Hon. K.C.M.G. 1995 and many other awards and prizes. *Publications:* Nuclear Weapons and Foreign Policy 1956, A World Restored: Castlereagh, Metternich and the Restoration of Peace 1812-22 1957, The Necessity for Choice: Prospects of American Foreign Policy 1961, The Troubled Partnership: A Reappraisal of the Atlantic Alliance 1965, American Foreign Policy (3 essays) 1969, White House Years 1979, For the Record 1981, Years of Upheaval 1982, Observations: Selected Speeches and Essays 1982–84 1985, Diplomacy 1994 and numerous articles on U.S. foreign policy, international affairs and diplomatic history. *Address:* 350 Park Avenue, New York, NY 10022; Suite 400, 1800 K Street, N.W., Washington, DC 20006, U.S.A.

KISTLER, Darci; American ballerina; b. 4 June 1964, Riverside, Calif.; d. of Jack B. Kistler and Alicia Kistler (née Kinner); m. Peter Martins (q.v.) 1991; ed. studied with Irina Kosmovska in Los Angeles, School of American Ballet; joined corps de ballet New York City Ballet as prin. dancer under Balanchine 1980; injured 1982–85; teacher School of American Ballet 1994–; performances include prin. role in Haydn Concerto 1979, Swan Queen in Lev Ivanov's choreographing of Swan Lake 1979, leading roles in Brahms-Schönberg Quartet, Divertimento no. 15, Symphony in C, Raymonda Variations, Walpurgisnacht Ballet, Valse fantaisie, Tchaikovsky Suite no. 3, Dew Drop and the Sugar Plum Fairy in The Nutcracker 1980; new roles created for her in Suite from Soldier's Tale and Tchaikovsky Symphony no. 1 1980; leading roles in Who Cares?, Balanchine's Chaconne, Jacques d'Amboise's Irish Fantasy, Robbins' Prélude à l'après-midi d'un Faune, Martin's The Magic Flute 1981–82; shepherdess in Jacques d'Amboise's Pastorale 1982, siren in Peter Martins' Piano Rag-Music 1982; returned to New York Theater in Prélude à l'après-midi d'un Faune 1985; subsequent roles include: Titania in Balanchine's A Midsummer Night's Dream and the siren in his Prodigal Son, strip-tease girl in Slaughter on Tenth Avenue, man-eating door in Variations pour une porte et un soupir, title role in La Sonnambula 1986; recent work includes: Balanchine's Serenade, Ivesiana, Danses Concertantes, Mozartiana and Jewels 1988–89; Jerome Robbins' The Four Seasons 1989; Balanchine's Allegro brillante, Tchaikovsky Suite no. 3, Robbins' The Goldberg Variations, Other Dances, Dances at a Gathering, In G Major 1989–90, Balanchine Celebration 1993, Symphonic Dances 1994, Apollo 1994; début in Balanchine's La valse Feb. 1991, Peter Martins' The Sleeping Beauty; film: The Nutcracker 1993. *Publication:* Ballerina: My Story 1993. *Address:* c/o The New York City Ballet Inc., New York State Theater, 20 Lincoln Center, New York, NY 10023, U.S.A.

KITAJ, R. B., R.A.; American artist; b. 29 Oct. 1932, Ohio; m.; three c.; m. 2nd Sandra Fisher 1983; ed. New York, Vienna and Royal Coll. of Arts, London; has lived in London since 1960; Guest Prof. Univ. of Calif., Berkeley 1967–68, Univ. of Calif., Los Angeles 1970–71; one-man exhbns. in Marlborough New London Gallery 1963, 1970, Marlborough Gerson Gallery, New York, Los Angeles County Museum of Art 1965, Stedelijk Museum, Amsterdam, Museum of Art, Cleveland and Univ. of Calif., Berkeley 1967, Berlin and tour of Fed. Germany 1969–70, Kestner Gesellschaft, Hanover, Boymans-van-Beuningen Museum, Rotterdam 1970, Cincinnati Art Museum, Ohio (with James Dine, q.v.) 1973, Marlborough, New York 1974, 1978, Marlborough, Zürich 1977, Marlborough, London 1977, 1980, 1985; retrospective tour Hirshhorn Museum, Washington, Cleveland Museum and Kunsthalle, Dusseldorf 1981; retrospective exhbns., Tate Gallery, London 1994, L.A. Co. Museum of Art 1994, Metropolitan Museum of Art, New York 1995; work in public collections in museums in Australia, Denmark, Germany, Netherlands, Norway, Sweden, Switzerland, U.K. and U.S.A.; mem. American Inst. of Arts and Letters 1982; Hon. L.H.D. (Univ. of London) 1982; Dr. h.c. (Royal Coll. of Art) 1991; Hon. Dr. (Calif. Coll. of Art and Craft) 1995, (Univ. of Durham) 1996; 1st Prize for Painting (Golden Lion), Venice Biennale 1995; Order of Arts and Letters (France) 1996. *Publications:* David Hockney: A Retrospective (with others) 1988, First Diasporist Manifesto 1989. *Address:* c/o Marlborough Fine Art Ltd., 6 Albemarle Street, London, W.1, England.

KITAMURA, Hiroshi; Japanese diplomatist and university president; b. 20 Jan. 1929, Osaka; m. Sachiko Kitamura 1953; two d.; ed. Tokyo Univ., Fletcher School of Law and Diplomacy, Mass., U.S.A.; joined Foreign Affairs Ministry 1953, served in Washington, New York, Delhi; First Sec. Japanese Embassy, London 1963–66; Exec. Asst. to Prime Minister 1974–76; Deputy Dir.-Gen. American Affairs Bureau 1977–79, Dir.-Gen. 1982–84, Deputy Vice-Minister of Foreign Affairs 1984–87, Deputy Minister 1987–88; Consul-Gen. San Francisco 1979–82, Amb. to Canada 1988–90, to the U.K. 1991–94; Corp. Adviser, Mitsubishi Corpn. 1994–; Pres. Shumei Univ. 1998–; with Japanese Mission to OECD, Paris; Prime Minister's Personal Rep. to Venice Summit 1987, Toronto Summit 1988; Fellow Center for Int. Affairs, Harvard Univ. 1970. *Publications:* Psychological Dimensions of US-Japanese Relations 1971. *Address:* 1-15-6 Jingumae, Shibuya-ku, Tokyo, Japan. *Telephone:* (03) 3470-4630. *Fax:* (03) 3470-4830.

KITAMURA, So; Japanese playwright; b. 5 July 1952, Ohtsu-shi; m. Konomi Kitamura; one d.; leader Project Navi 1986–; Awards include Kishida Gikyoku-sho 1984, Kinoleuni-ya engeki-sho 1989. *Publications:* plays include: Hogiuta, So-Ko Gingatetsudo no yoru. Novels include: Kaijin nijumenso den (Shincho sha), Seido no majin (Shincho sha), Kenji (Kadokawa). *Leisure interest:* movies. *Address:* Project Navi, 11–13 Imaike-Minami, Chikusa-ku, Nagoya-shi, Aichi 464, Japan. *Telephone:* 052 731 2867.

KITAYENKO, Dmitriy Georgievich; Russian conductor; b. 18 Aug. 1940, Leningrad; ed. Leningrad Conservatory; postgrad. study Moscow Conservatory (under Khazanov and Ginzburg); further study at Acad. of Music, Vienna 1966–67; conductor, Nemirovich-Danchenko Theatre 1969–, prin. conductor 1970–76; chief conductor, Moscow Philharmonic 1976–89; numerous appearances in Europe and USA; teacher at Moscow Conservatory 1969–, Prof. 1986–90; Music Dir., Frankfurt Radio Orchestra 1990–95; Berne Symphony Orchestra 1994–; Perm. Conductor, Music Adviser, Bergen Philharmonic Orchestra 1991–; U.S.S.R. People's Artist 1984; R.S.F.S.R. State Prize 1988. *Address:* Münzgraben 2, CH-3000 Berne 7 (Office); Chalet Kalimor, CH-1652 Botterens, Switzerland (Home). *Telephone:* (31) 311 8321. *Fax:* (31) 311 6257.

KITBUNCHU, H.E. Cardinal Michael Michai; Thai ecclesiastic; b. 25 Jan. 1929, Samphran, Nakhon Pathom; ordained priest 1959; Archbishop of Bangkok 1973–; cr. Cardinal 1983. *Address:* Bishop's Conference of Thailand, 122 Soi Naaksuwan, Thanon Nonsi, Yannawa, Bangkok 10120, Thailand. *Telephone:* (2) 681-5361. *Fax:* (2) 681-5370.

KITCHEN, Lawrence Oscar; American business executive; b. 8 June 1923, Fort Mill, S.C.; s. of Samuel Sumpter Kitchen and Ruby Azalee Grigg; m. 2nd Brenda Lenhart 1978; one s. two d. by 1st marriage; ed. Foothill Coll.; aeronautical engineer, U.S. Navy Bureau of Aeronautics, Washington 1946–58, Staff Asst. to Asst. Chief of Bureau 1958; with Lockheed Missiles and Space Co., Sunnyvale, Calif. 1958–70, Man. Product Support Logistics 1964–68, Dir. Financial Controls 1968–70; Vice-Pres. Finance Lockheed-Ga. Co., Marietta 1970–71, Pres. 1971–75; Pres. Lockheed Corpn., Burbank, Calif. 1975–85, C.O.O. 1976–85, Chair., C.E.O. 1986–88, Chair. Exec. Cttee, Bd. of Dirs. 1989; mem. Int. Bd. Security Pacific Nat. Bank 1976; mem. Bd. of Visitors, Emory Inst., Founders Bd. Hollywood Presbyterian Hosp.; mem. Nominating Cttee. Aviation Hall of Fame; mem. Nat. Asscn. of Accountants, American Inst. of Aeronautics Astronautics, etc. *Address:* Lockheed Corporation, 4500 Park Granada Boulevard, Calabasas, CA 91399, U.S.A. (Office).

KITE, Thomas O., Jr.; American golfer; b. 9 Dec. 1949, Austin, Tex.; m. Christy Kite; two s. one d.; won Walker Cup 1971; turned professional 1972; won Ryder Cup 1979, 1981, 1983, 1985, 1987, 1989, 1993, European Open 1980, U.S. Open, Pebble Beach, Calif. 1992; L.A. Open 1993; 10 U.S. PGA wins; appt. Capt. U.S. team for 1997 Ryder Cup, Valderrama, Spain. *Address:* c/o PGA Tour, 112 Tpc Boulevard Ponte Vedra Beach, FL 32082, U.S.A.

KITOVANI, Tengiz; Georgian politician and army officer; Commdr. Georgian Nat. Guard; fmr. supporter of fmr. Pres. Gamsakhurdia, but opposed subordination of his command to Ministry of Internal Affairs Sept. 1991; Head opposition mil. forces Dec. 1991, Jt. Head Mil. Council Jan. 1992–; Head Georgian Nat. Guard; mem. Georgian State Council Mar.–Oct. 1992; mem. Supreme Soviet 1992–; Minister of Defence 1992–93; arrested in 1995, charged with conspiracy against the State, sentenced to eight years' confinement 1996.

KITSIKIS, Dimitri, M.A., PH.D.; Canadian/French/Greek poet and university professor; b. 2 June 1935, Athens; s. of the late Nikolas Kitsikis and Beata Petychakis; m. 1st Anne Hubbard 1955 (divorced 1973); one s. one d.; m. 2nd Ada Nikolaros 1975; one s. one d.; ed. American Coll. Athens, Ecole des Roches, Normandy, Lycée Lakanal and Lycée Carnot, Paris and Sorbonne, Paris; Research Assoc. Grad. Inst. of Int. Studies, Geneva 1960–62, Centre for Int. Relations, Nat. Foundation of Political Science, Paris 1962–65, Nat. Centre for Scientific Research, Paris 1965–70; Assoc. Prof. of History of Int. Relations, Univ. of Ottawa 1970–83, Prof. 1983–96, Emer. Prof. 1996–; Sr. Research Scholar, Nat. Centre of Social Research, Athens 1972–74; founder, Ed. Intermediate Region (journal) 1996–; adviser to govts. of Greece and Turkey; numerous visiting professorships and other appts. *Publications:* author of 19 books including; Propaganda and Pressure in International Politics 1963, The Role of the Experts at the Paris Peace Conference of 1919 1972, A Comparative History of Greece and Turkey in the 20th Century 1978, History of the Greek-Turkish Area 1981, The Ottoman Empire 1985, The Third Ideology and Orthodoxy 1990, Turkish-Greek Empire 1996; co-author of 26 other books; six vols. of poetry; over 70 scholarly articles. *Leisure interests:* art, science fiction, study of languages. *Address:* Department of History, University of Ottawa, Ont. K1N 6N5, Canada; 29 Travlantoni, Zographou, Athens 157.72, Greece. *Telephone:* (613) 562-5735 (Ottawa); (1) 777-6937 (Athens). *Fax:* (613) 562-5995 (Ottawa).

KITSON, Linda Frances, M.A.; British artist and teacher; b. 17 Feb. 1945 London; grand d. of Capt. James B. Kitson and Hon. Frances Margaret Palmer (née Howard); ed. West Preston Manor School, Rustington, Tortington Park, Arundel, Ecole des Beaux Arts, Lyons, St. Martin's School of Art and Royal Coll. of Art; visiting tutor, Royal Coll. of Art, St. Martin's School of Art 1972–78, Chelsea School of Art, Camberwell School of Art and Crafts, City & Guilds of London Art School 1972–82; Lecturer, Royal Coll, of Art 1979–82, visiting tutor 1984; Official War Artist, Falkland Islands Task Force 1982; several one-man exhbns. and contrib. to Royal Acad. Summer Exbn. since 1971; Pres. Army Arts and Crafts Soc. 1983; South Atlantic Medal (with rosette) 1983. *Publication:* The Falklands War: A Visual Diary 1982, The Plague 1985, Sun, Wind, Sand and Stars 1989. *Leisure interests:* rock-dancing, music. *Address:* 1 Argyll Mansions, Kings Road, London, SW3 5ER, England. *Telephone:* 0171-584 5020, Ext. 238; 0171-352 9043.

KITT, Eartha Mae; American singer and actress; b. 26 Jan. 1928, North, S.C.; d. of John Kitt and Anna Kitt; m. William McDonald 1960 (divorced); one d.; ed. high school; soloist with Katherine Graham Dance Group 1948; night club singer 1949–; stage appearances in Dr Faustus, Paris 1951, New Faces of 1952, New York, Mrs Patterson, New York 1954, Shinbone Alley, New York 1957, Timbuktu 1978, Blues in the Night 1985; numerous TV appearances; Woman of the Year, Nat. Asscn. of Negro Musicians 1968; records for RCA. *Films include:* New Faces 1953, Accused 1957, St. Louis Blues 1957, Anna Lucasta 1958, Mark of the Hawk 1958, Saint of Devil's Island 1961, Synanon 1965, Up the Chastity Belt 1971, Dragonard, All By Myself (documentary) 1982, Boomerang 1992, Fatal Instinct 1993. *Publications:* Thursday's Child 1956, A Tart is Not a Sweet, Alone with Me 1976, I'm Still Here 1990, Confessions of a Sex Kitten 1991. *Address:* c/o Eartha Kitt Productions, Flat 37, 888 7th Avenue, New York, NY 10106, U.S.A.

KITTANI, Ismat; Iraqi diplomatist; b. 1929, Emadieh, Mesopotamia (now part of Iraq); m.; one s.; ed. Knox Coll., Galesburg, Ill., U.S.A.; taught English, high school, Iraq; with Ministry of Foreign Affairs, Baghdad; Embassy, Cairo 1952; Perm. Mission of Iraq to UN (Perm. Rep. 1961–64) 1957–64; joined UN Secr. 1964; mem. Social and Econ. Cttee., Geneva; Asst. Sec.-Gen. UN 1973–75; Deputy Minister of Foreign Affairs, Head Dept. of Int. Orgs. and Confs. 1975–80; Pres. 36th Gen. Assembly of UN 1981–82; Perm. Rep. to UN 1985–90, UN Sec.-Gen.'s Special Rep. to Somalia 1992–93, Special Envoy to Tajikistan 1993, Special Adviser to UN Sec.-Gen. 1994. *Address:* United Nations, Palais des Nations, Room 190, Avenue de la Paix 8-14, 1211 Geneva 10, Switzerland. *Telephone:* (22) 907 1160, 786 1951. *Fax:* (212) 963-2155.

KITTEL, Charles, PH.D.; American professor of physics and author; b. 18 July 1916, New York; s. of George Paul Kittel and Helen Lemler Kittel; m. Muriel Agnes Lister 1938; two s. one d.; ed. Massachusetts Institute of Technology and Univs. of Cambridge and Wisconsin; Prof. of Physics, Univ. of Calif. at Berkeley 1951–78, Prof. Emer. 1978–; mem. N.A.S., American Acad. of Arts and Sciences; Buckley Prize for Solid State Physics, Berkeley Distinguished Teaching Award, Oersted Medal, American Asscn. of Physics Teachers. *Publications:* Quantum Theory of Solids 1963, Thermal Physics 1980, Introduction to Solid State Physics 1996. *Leisure interests:* friends, wine. *Address:* Department of Physics, University of California, Berkeley, CA 94720-7300, U.S.A. *Telephone:* (510) 525-5356.

KITTIKACHORN, Field-Marshal Thanom; Thai politician and army officer; b. 11 Aug. 1911, Tak; ed. Wat Kokplu School (Tak) and Military Acad. Bangkok; entered Mil. Survey Dept. as student officer 1931, assigned to Planning Section 1934; Lieut. in Mil. Educ. Dept. 1935, Instructor 1936–38, 1939–41, 1944–46; Capt. 1938, student officer in Infantry School, active service in Shan State 1941; Major 1943, Lieut.-Col. 1944; Instructor Mil. Acad. technical branch 1946–47; Commdr. 21st Infantry Regt. 1947; Colonel, Commdr. 11th Infantry Regt. 1948; Deputy Commdr. 1st Infantry Div. 1949, Commdr. 1950; Major-Gen., Deputy Commdr. 1st Army 1951; Commdr. 1st Army 1954; Lieut.-Gen., mem. Defence Coll. 1955; Deputy Minister of Co-operatives 1955; Asst. C.-in-C. of Army 1957; Deputy Minister of Defence April 1957, Minister Sept. 1957; Prime Minister, Minister of Defence, General 1958; Deputy Prime Minister and Minister of Defence 1959–63; Prime Minister 1963–71, 1972–73; Minister of Defence and Foreign Affairs 1973; Chair. Nat. Exec. Council Dec. 1971–72; Special A.D.C. to King; Chair. United People's Party 1968–73; in U.S.A. 1973–74; detained upon return to Bangkok Dec. 1974; exile in Singapore 1976; returned to Bangkok Sept. 1976; served as monk Sept. 1976–Feb. 1977.

KITZHABER, John Albert, M.D.; American doctor and politician; b. 5 March 1947, Colfax, WA; s. of Albert Raymond Kitzhaber and Annabel Reed Wetzel; ed. Dartmouth Coll. and Univ. of Oregon; intern Gen. Rose Memorial Hosp., Denver 1976–77; Emergency Physician Mercy Hosp., Roseburg, Ore. 1974–75; mem. Oregon House of Reps. 1979–81, Ore. Senate 1981–95, Pres. 1985, 1987, 1989, 1991; Gov. of Oregon 1995–; Assoc. Prof. Ore. Health Science Univ. 1986–; mem. American Coll. of Emergency Physicians, Physicians for Social Responsibility, American Council of Young Political Leaders; Democrat. *Address:* Office of the Governor, Capitol Bldg., Room 254, Salem, OR 97310, U.S.A.

KITZINGER, Sheila Helena Elizabeth, M.B.E., M.LITT.; British birth educator, author and social anthropologist; b. 29 March 1929, Taunton, Somerset; d. of Alex Webster and Clare Webster; m. Uwe Kitzinger (q.v.) 1952; five d.; ed. Bishop Fox's Girls' School, Taunton, Ruskin Coll. and St. Hugh's Coll., Oxford; Research Asst. Dept. of Anthropology, Univ. of Edin. 1952–53; Course Team Chair. Open Univ. 1981–83; Man. Cttee. Midwives' Information and Resource Service 1985–87, Editorial Cttee. 1987–; Chair. Steering Cttee. Int. Homebirth Movt.; Consultant, Int. Childbirth Educ. Asscn.; Adviser, Baby Milk Coalition, Maternity Alliance; Hon. Prof., Thames Valley Univ. 1993–; Patron of the Seattle School of Midwifery; Pres. Oxfordshire Branch, Royal Coll. of Midwives; mem. Royal Soc. of Medicine; Joost de Blank Award for Research 1971–73. *Publications:* The Experience of Childbirth 1962, Giving Birth 1971, Education and Counselling for Childbirth 1977, Women as Mothers 1978, The Place of Birth (ed. with John Davis) 1978, Birth at Home 1979, The Good Birth Guide 1979, The Experience of Breastfeeding 1979, Pregnancy and Childbirth 1980, Sheila Kitzinger's Birth Book 1981, Some Women's Experiences of Episiotomy (with Rhiannon Walters) 1981, 1983, Episiotomy: physical and emotional aspects 1981, Birth Over Thirty 1982, The New Good Birth Guide 1983, Woman's Experience of Sex 1983, (ed. with Penny Simkin) Episiotomy and the Second Stage of Labor 1984, Being Born 1986, Celebration of Birth 1987, Freedom and Choice in Childbirth 1987, Some Women's Experiences of Epidurals 1987, Giving Birth: How it Really Feels 1987, The Midwife Challenge (ed.) 1988, The Crying Baby 1989, The New Pregnancy and Childbirth 1989, Breastfeeding Your Baby 1989, Talking with Children about Things that Matter (with Celia Kitzinger) 1989, Pregnancy Day by Day (with Vicky Bailey) 1990, Homebirth and Other Alternatives to Hospital 1991, Ourselves as Mothers 1993, Birth over Thirty-Five 1994, The Year after Childbirth 1994, The New Pregnancy and Childbirth 1997, Becoming a Grandmother 1997, Childbirth and Authoritative Knowledge (jtly.) 1997. *Leisure interests:* painting, talking. *Address:* The Manor, Standlake, Oxon., OX8 7RH, England. *Telephone:* (01865) 300266. *Fax:* (01865) 300438.

KITZINGER, Uwe, C.B.E., M.LITT., M.A.; British academic; b. 12 April 1928, Nuremberg, Germany; s. of late Dr. G. and Lucy Kitzinger; m. Sheila Helena Elizabeth Webster (Sheila Kitzinger, q.v.) 1952; five d.; ed. Watford Grammar School, Balliol and New Coll., Oxford; Foundation Scholar, New Coll., Oxford; Pres. of Oxford Union 1950; Econ. Section, Council of Europe 1951–58; Research Fellow, Nuffield Coll., Oxford 1956–62, Official Fellow and Investment Bursar 1962–76, Emer. Fellow 1976–; Dean, European Inst. of Business Admin. (INSEAD), Fontainebleau 1976–80; Dir. Oxford Centre for Man. Studies 1980–84; Pres. Templeton Coll., Oxford 1984–91; Founding Ed., Journal of Common Market Studies 1962–; Visiting Prof. Univ. of West Indies 1964–65; Visiting Prof. and Assoc., Centre for Int. Affairs, Harvard 1969–70; Visiting Prof. Univ. of Paris VIII 1970–73; Adviser to the late Baron Soames (Vice-Pres. Comm. of the European Communities), Brussels 1973–75; Sr. Research Fellow Atlantic Council 1993–; Visiting Scholar Harvard Univ. 1993–; Founding Chair. Cttee. on Atlantic Studies 1967–70; Founding Chair. Major Projects Asscn. 1981–86; Pres. Int. Asscn. of Macro-Eng. Socs. 1987–92, 1996–, Féd. Britannique des Alliances Françaises; Council mem. European Movt. 1974–76, Royal Inst. of Int. Affairs 1976–85, Oxfam 1981–84, Fondation Jean Monnet 1990–; Chair. Oxfordshire Radio Ltd. 1988; mem. Conflict Man. Group, Cambridge, Mass., Inst. for Transition to Democracy, Zagreb, British Univs. Cttee., Encyclopaedia Britannica; co-f. Lentils for Dubrovnik 1991; Hon. LL.D. *Publications:* German Electoral Politics 1960, The Challenge of the Common Market 1961, Britain, Europe and Beyond 1964, The Second Try 1968, Diplomacy and Persuasion 1973, Europe's Wider Horizons 1975, The 1975 Referendum (with David Butler) 1976, Macro-Engineering and the Earth (Jt. Ed. with Ernst Frankel). *Leisure interest:* cruising under sail. *Address:* The Manor, Standlake, Oxon., OX8 7RH, England; La Rivière, 11100 Bages, France; Lowell House, Cambridge, MA 02138, U.S.A. *Telephone:* (01865) 300266 (England); (04) 68.41.70.13 (France); (617) 495-3495 (U.S.A.). *Fax:* (01865) 300438 (England); (04) 68.41.70.13 (France); (617) 495-3495 (U.S.A.).

KJELLEN, Bo, M.POL.SC.; Swedish diplomatist; b. 8 Feb. 1933, Stockholm; s. of John Kjellen and Elsa Kjellen; m. 1st Margareta Lindblom 1959 (deceased 1978), 2nd Gia Boyd 1980; four c.; ed. Univ. of Stockholm; entered Foreign Service 1957, posted to Rio de Janeiro, Brussels, Stockholm 1959–69; Prin. Pvt. Sec. to Sec.-Gen., OECD 1969–72; Deputy Head of Mission Del. to EEC, Brussels 1972–74; Amb. to Viet Nam 1974–77; Head Multilateral Dept. for Devt. Co-operation, Ministry of Foreign Affairs 1977–81; Under-Sec. Admin. and Personnel 1981–85; Amb. to OECD and UNESCO 1985–91;

Chief Negotiator, Ministry of Environment 1991–98; Negotiator Climate Convention 1991–; Hon. D.Sc. (Cranfield, U.K.) 1997. *Address:* Ministry of Environment, Tegelbacken 2, 10333 Stockholm, Sweden. *Telephone:* 4052175. *Fax:* 468211690.

KJER, Bodil; Danish actress; b. 2 Sept. 1917; has appeared at Royal Theatre of Denmark in more than 100 roles; numerous awards including four awards from Danish film critics (Bodil award named after her). *Films include:* Elly Petersen, The Invisible Army, Jenny and the Soldier, Meet Me on Cassiopeia, The Missing Clerk, Copper, Mirror, Mirror, Tradition, Up Yours!, Babette's Feast (Academy Award), Sunset Boys; Commdr. Order of Dannebro. *Address:* Vestre Pavilion, Frydenlund, Frydenlunds Allé 19, 2950 Vedbaek, Denmark.

KJETSAA, Geir, DR.PHIL.; Norwegian professor of Russian literature; b. 2 June 1937, Oslo; s. of Thorleif Kjetsaa and Marit Kjetsaa; m. Gerd Margit 1959; one d.; ed. Univ. of Oslo and Moscow State Univ.; Asst. Dept. of Slavic and Baltic Studies, Univ. of Oslo 1966–70, Prof. 1971–; Pres. Asscn. of Norwegian Slavists 1977–80, 1982–87, Asscn. of Scandinavian Slavists 1984–87; Vice-Pres. Int. Dostoevsky Soc. 1983–; mem. Norwegian Acad. of Sciences and Letters; Bastian Prize 1978. *Publications:* Evgenij Baratynskij 1973, The Authorship of The Quiet Don 1984, Dostoevsky and His New Testament 1984, Prinadlezhnost Dostoevskomu 1986, Fyodor Dostoevsky: A Writer's Life 1987, Nikolaj Gogol: Den gåtefulle dikteren 1990, Maksim Gorkij: En dikterskjebne 1994. *Address:* Universitetet i Oslo, P.O. Box 1030, Blindern, 0315 Oslo; Lybekkveien 12a, Oslo 3, Norway.

KJØNSTAD, Asbjørn, D.JUR.; Norwegian professor of law; b. 6 Feb. 1943, Frol; s. of late Arne Kjønstad and of Nelly Stavern Kjønstad; m. 1st Lise-Lena Stubberød 1971–81 (dissolved); one d.; m. 2nd Ayala Orkan 1995; Legal Adviser, Nat. Insurance Admin. 1970–72; Research Fellow, Univ. of Oslo 1972–78, Prof. of Private Law 1978–84, Head, Inst. of Pvt. Law 1983–84, Prof. of Social Law 1985–, Dean of Faculty of Law 1986–88, mem. Bd. of Univ. of Oslo 1986–88; Chair. Royal Comm. on Social Security Law 1982–90; Vice-Pres. European Inst. of Social Security; mem. Bd. Nat. Council on Tobacco and Health 1972–93, 1997–; mem. Norwegian Acad. of Science; Ju. D. h.c. (Lund Univ., Sweden) 1996. *Publications:* 32 scientific reports and books and some 120 articles on social security law, medical law and tort law including: Social Security and Compensation for Personal Injuries 1977, The Industrial Injuries Insurance 1979, Constitutional Protection of Social Security 1984, Medical Law 1987, Norwegian Social Law 1987, A Simplified National Insurance Act 1990, The National Insurance Disablement Pension 1992, Health Priority and Patient's Rights (co-ed.) 1992, Social Services and the Rule of Law (co-author) 1993, Constitutional Protection of Social Security Benefits (co-author) 1994, Aspects of Health Law (co-author) 1994, Welfare Law (co-author) 1997, Introduction to Social Security Law 1998, Social Security Act 1998. *Leisure interests:* outdoor exercise. *Address:* Lillevannsveien 37c, 0393 Oslo, Norway. *Telephone:* 22-13-80-75.

KLAASTE, Aggrey Zola, B.A.; South African journalist; b. 6 Jan. 1940, Kimberley; s. of late T. P. Klaaste; m. Valetta Kubugane Makgele; three s.; ed. Madibane High School, Univ. of Witwatersrand; journalist Trust 1970–71; News Ed. The World 1974–77, Post 1978–82; Asst. Ed. The Sowetan 1982, now Ed.; mem. Ed. Bd. Black Focus 1985, Viewpoint 1985; mem. Shield Unit Salvation Army 1984–; Hon. Ph.D. et Litt. (Transkei). *Leisure interests:* martial arts, reading, music. *Address:* P.O. Box 6663, Johannesburg 2000, South Africa.

KLAS, Eri; Estonian conductor; b. 7 June 1939, Tallinn; s. of Eduard Klas and Anna Klas; m.; one d.; ed. Tallinn State Conservatory, Leningrad State Conservatory; asst. conductor to Boris Khaikin Bolshoi Theatre, Moscow 1960–72; conductor Orchestra of Estonian Radio 1964–70; conductor Nat. Opera Theatre Estonia 1965–, Music Dir. 1975–95, Laureate conductor 1996–; repertoire includes more than 50 operas, operettas, musicals and ballets; conducted more than 100 symphony orchestras in 40 different countries; Music Dir. Royal Opera, Stockholm 1985–89; Prin. Guest Conductor, Finnish Nat. Opera 1990–; Chief Conductor Aarhus Symphony Orchestra, Denmark 1991–96; Prof. Sibelius Acad. Helsinki 1994–; Music Dir. Orchestra of Dutch Radio 1996–; Chair. Bd. Estonia Nat. Cultural Foundation 1991–; conducted at the Nobel Prize Ceremonial Concert in Stockholm 1989; Dr. h.c. (Estonian Acad. of Music) 1994; Order of Nordsternier Sweden. *Address:* Nurme 54, 0016 Tallinn, Estonia. *Telephone:* 5043444.

KLAUS, Josef, LL.D.; Austrian politician and lawyer; b. 15 Aug. 1910, Mauthen, Carinthia; m. Erna Seywald 1936; five c.; ed. Univs. of Vienna, Marburg/Lahn; Sec., Vienna Chamber of Labour 1934–38 (Deputy-Chair. of Political Economy Dept.); with timber trade firm, Vienna 1938–39; war service 1939–45 (prisoner of war); lawyer, Hallein, Salzburg 1945–49; Gov. of Salzburg 1949–61; Fed. Minister of Finance 1961–63; Fed. Chancellor 1964–70; fmr. Chair. Austrian People's Party.

KLAUS, Václav, PH.D.; Czech politician and economist; b. 19 June 1941, Prague; s. of Václav Klaus and Marie Klausová; m. Livia Klausová 1968; two s.; ed. Prague School of Econs., Cornell Univ.; researcher Inst. of Econs. Czechoslovak Acad. of Sciences until 1970; various positions Czechoslovak State Bank 1971–86; head Dept. of Macroeconomic Policy, Inst. of Forecasting, Acad. of Sciences 1987–; f. Civic Forum Movt. (Chair. 1990–91); Minister of Finance 1989–92; Chair. Civic Democratic Party 1991–; Deputy Prime Minister 1991–92; Prime Minister of Czech Republic 1992–97; Chair. State Defence Council 1993–97; Chair. Govt. Cttee. for Integration of Czech Repub. in NATO 1997; Chair. of Parl. 1998–; mem. Scientific Council, Palacký Univ. 1997–; Hon. Prof. Univ. Guadalajará 1993; Hon. D.Hum.Litt. (Suffolk Univ.), Hon. Dr. (Rochester Inst. of Tech.), (Jacksonville, U.S.A.) 1995, (Buckingham, U.K.) 1996; Dr. h.c. (Univ. Francisco Marroquín, Guatemala) 1993, (Prague School of Econs.) 1994, (Belgrano Univ., Argentina) 1994, (Tufts Univ., U.S.A.) 1994, Univ. of Aix-Marseilles) 1994, (Tech. Univ. of Ostrava) 1997, (Toronto, Canada) 1997; Max Schmidheiny Freedom Prize, St. Gallen 1992, Schumpeter Prize for Econs., Freedom Award, Ludwig Erhard Prize, Germany 1993, Poeutinger Collegium Prize 1993, Hermann Lindrath Prize (Hanover) 1993, Konrad Adenauer Prize (Prague) 1993, Club of Europe Award 1994, Prix Transition (Foundation du Forum Universale) 1994, Adam Smith Award (Libertas, Copenhagen) 1995, Int. Democracy Medal (Center for Democracy, Washington, D.C.) 1995, Transatlantic Leadership Award (European Inst., Washington, D.C.) 1995, Prognos Award (Prognos Forum, Basel) 1995, James Madison Award (James Madison Inst., Jacksonville, U.S.A.) 1995, Karel Engliš Prize (Universitas Masarykiana Foundation, Brno) 1995. *Publications:* A Road to Market Economy 1991, Tomorrow's Challenge 1991, Economic Theory and Economic Reform 1991, Why am I a Conservative? 1992, Dismantling Socialism: A Road to Market Economy II 1993, The Year—How much is it in the History of the Country? 1993, The Czech Way 1994, Rebirth of a Country: Five Years After 1994, Counting Down to One 1995, Between the Past and the Future: Philosophical Reflections and Essays 1996, The Defence of Forgotten Ideas 1997, Tak pravil Václav Klaus (So Said Václav Klaus, conversations with J. Klusáková); numerous articles. *Leisure interests:* tennis, skiing. *Address:* Civic Democratic Party, Sněmovní 3, Malá Strana, 110 00 Prague 1, Czech Republic. *Telephone:* 311 48 00, 311 48 01, 311 48 09.

KLEBE, Giselher; German composer; b. 28 June 1925, Mannheim; s. of Franz Klebe and Gertrud Michaelis Klebe; m. Lore Schiller 1946; two d.; ed. Berlin Conservatoire and with Boris Blacher; Composer in Berlin until 1957; Prof. of Composition and Theory of Music, Nordwestdeutsche Musik-Akademie, Detmold 1957–; mem. Acad. of Arts, Berlin and Hamburg, Bavarian Acad. of Fine Arts 1978; Pres. Berlin Acad. of Arts 1986–89; Bundesverdienstkreuz (1st Class) 1975; several prizes for composition. *Principal works:* Operas: Die Räuber (Schiller) 1957, Die tödlichen Wünsche (Balzac) 1959, Die Ermordung Cäsars (Shakespeare) 1959, Alkmene (Kleist) 1961, Figaro lässt sich scheiden (Ödön von Horvath) 1963, Jacobowsky und der Oberst (Werfel) 1965, Das Märchen von der Schönen Lilie (nach Goethe) 1969, Ein wahrer Held (Synge/Böll) 1975, Das Mädchen aus Domrémy (Schiller) 1976, Rendezvous (Sostschenkow) 1977, Der jüngste Tag (Ödön von Horwath) 1980, Die Fastnachtsbeichte (nach Zuckmayer) 1983, Gervaise Macquart (after Zola) 1995; Ballets: Signale 1955, Menagerie 1958, Das Testament (nach F. Villon) 1970; Orchestral Works: Zwitschermaschine 1950, Deux Nocturnes 1952, 6 symphonies 1952, 1953, 1967, 1971, 1977, 1995, Adagio und Fuge (with theme from Wagner's Walküre) 1962, Herzschläge (for Beatband and Symphony Orchestra), Konzert für Cembalo mit elektrischen Klangveränderungen und kleines Orchester 1972, Orpheus (Dramatic scenes for orchestra) 1976, Salutations 1981, Boogie Agitato 1981, Concerto for Clarinet and Orchestra op. 92; Songs: Fünf Lieder 1962, Vier Vocalisen für Frauenchor 1963, La Tomba di Igor Strawinsky (for oboe and chamber orch.) 1979, Concerto for organ and orch. 1980, Concerto for harp and orch. 1988, Concerto for 'cello and orch. 1989; Church music: Missa (Miserere Nobis) 1964, Stabat Mater 1964, Messe (Gebet einer armen Seele) 1966, Beuge dich, du Menschenseele (after S. Lagerlöf) for Baritone and Organ, Choral und Te deum for Solo Soprano, Choir and Orchestra 1978, Weihnachtsoratorium 1989; Chamber Music: 3 String Quartets 1949, 1963, 1981, 2 Solo Violin Sonatas 1952 and 1955, 2 Sonatas for Violin and Piano 1953 and 1974, "Römische Elegien" 1953, Piano Trio Elegia Appassionata 1955, Introitus, Aria et Alleluja for Organ 1964, Quintet for Piano and Strings quasi una fantasia 1967, Fantasie und Lobpreisung (for organ) 1970, Variationen über ein Thema von Hector Berlioz (for organ and three drummers) 1970, Sonate für Kontrabass und Klavier 1974, "Nenia" for solo violin 1975, Der Dunkle Gedanke for Clarinets and Piano 1980, Klavierstücke für Sonya (piano) 1980, Feuersturz für Klavier (op. 91) 1983. *Leisure interest:* photography. *Address:* Bruchstrasse 16, 32756 Detmold, Germany (Home). *Telephone:* 030-3900070 (Office); (05231) 2 34 14 (Home).

KLEIHUES, Josef Paul; German architect and professor; b. 11 June 1933, Rheine; s. of Heinrich Kleihues and Paula Krüselmann Kleihues; m. Sigrid Müller 1961; two s. two d.; ed. Tech. Univs. Stuttgart and Berlin; in pvt. practice; Dir. New Construction Planning, Int. Bldg. Exhbns. Berlin 1979–87; Prof. of Design and Architectural Theory, Univ. of Dortmund 1973–86, of Design and Town Planning 1986–94; Prof. of Architecture, Kunstakademie Düsseldorf 1994–98, Prof. Emer. 1998–; Irwin S. Chanin Distinguished Int. Prof., The Cooper Union, New York 1986–90; Visiting Eero Saarinen Prof., Grad. School of Architecture, Yale Univ., U.S.A. 1987. *Principal works:* Cen. Workshops Municipal Dept. of Refuse Collection, Berlin 1969–74, Block 270, Berlin 1971–77, New Hosp., Berlin-Neukoelln 1973–86, German Blades Museum, Solingen 1979–89, Archaeological Museum, Frankfurt/Main 1980–88, Kant Triangle, Berlin-Charlottenburg 1984–94, Lütze Museum and Municipal Gallery, Sindelfingen 1986–89, Henninger Museum and Municipal Gallery, Kornwestheim 1987–89, House 7, Block 7, Berlin 1986–89, San Clemente, Santiago de Compostela, Spain 1988–94, Hamburger Bahnhof, Museum of Contemporary Art, Berlin 1989–96, Museum of Contemporary Art, Chicago 1991–96, Houses Sommer and Liebermann,

Pariser Platz, Berlin 1992–98, Media Port, Berlin-Wedding 1994–96, Ministry of Labour, Berlin 1996–99; Young Generation Art Prize, Berlin 1967, Berlin Architecture Prize 1994, German Natural Stone Prize 1995; Order of Fed. Repub. of Germany (1st Class) 1988. *Publications:* Berlin Atlas zu Stadtbild und Stadtraum (compiler) 1971–73, Dortmunder Architekturhefte (Ed.) 1975–, Park Lenné. Ein innerstädtische Wohnform 1977, Dokumente und Projekte, Die Neubaugebiete (Ed.) 1979–. *Address:* Helmholtzstrasse 42, 10587 Berlin (Office); Schlickweg 4, 14129 Berlin, Germany (Home). *Telephone:* (030) 399 7790 (Office).

KLEIN, Calvin Richard; American fashion designer; b. 19 Nov. 1942, New York; s. of Leo Klein and Flore Klein (née Stern); m. 1st Jayne Centre 1964 (divorced 1974); one d.; m. 2nd Kelly Rector 1986; ed. Fashion Inst. of Tech., New York, and High School of Art and Design; started own fashion business 1968; Pres./Designer Calvin Klein Ltd. 1969–; Consultant Fashion Inst. of Tech. 1975–; mem. Council Museum of Modern Art, Guggenheim Museum, Council of Fashion Designers; Coty Award 1973, 1974, 1975; Coty Hall of Fame. *Leisure interests:* yoga, gymnastics. *Address:* Calvin Klein Industries Inc., 205 West 39th Street, 12th Floor, New York, NY 10018, U.S.A.

KLEIN, George, M.D.; Swedish tumour biologist; b. 28 July 1925, Budapest, Hungary; s. of Henrik Klein and Ilona Engel; m. Eva Fischer 1947; one s. two d.; ed. medical schools at Pécs, Szeged and Budapest, Hungary, and Stockholm, Sweden; Instructor Histology, Budapest Univ. 1945, Pathology 1946; Research Fellow, Karolinska Inst. 1947–49, Asst. Prof. of Cell Research 1950–57; fmr. Prof. of Tumour Biology and Head of the Inst. for Tumour Biology, Karolinska Inst. Med. School, Stockholm; Guest Investigator, Inst. for Cancer Research, Philadelphia, Pa. 1950; Visiting Prof., Stanford Univ. 1961; Fogarty Scholar, NIH 1972; Dunham Lecturer, Harvard Med. School 1966; Visiting Prof., Hebrew Univ., Jerusalem 1973–83; Harvey Lecturer 1973; Donald Wae Waddel Lecturer, Univ. of Arizona 1991; mem. Scientific Advisory Council of Swedish Med. Bd., Royal Swedish Acad. of Sciences; Corresp. mem. American Asscn. of Cancer Research; Foreign Assoc. N.A.S. of United States; hon. mem. American Asscn. of Immunologists, of Cancer Research, French Soc. of Immunology, Hungarian Acad. of Sciences, American Acad. of Arts and Sciences; Fellow, New York Acad. of Science; Ed. Advances in Cancer Research; Hon. D.Sc. (Univ. of Chicago) 1966, (Univ. of Neb.) 1991; Hon. M.D. (Univ. of Debrecen) 1988; Hon. Ph.D. (Hebrew Univ., Jerusalem) 1989, (Tel Aviv Univ.) 1994; Bertha Goldblatt Teplitz Award (jointly) 1960; Rabbi Shai Shacknai Prize in Tumour Immunology 1972; Bertner Award 1973; Award of American Cancer Soc. 1973; Prize of Danish Pathological Soc.; Harvey Prize 1975; Prize of Cancer Research Inst. 1975; Gairdner Prize 1976; Behring Prize 1977; Annual Award Virus Cancer Program 1977, Gen. Motors Sloan Prize for Cancer Research, Björkén Award of Uppsala Univ. 1979, Award of the Santa Chiara Acad., Italy, 1979, Erik Fernström Prize (with Eva Klein) 1983, Anniversary Prize of the Swedish Med. Asscn. 1983, Letterstedt Prize, Royal Swedish Acad. of Sciences 1989, Doblong Prize, Swedish Acad. of Literature 1990, Lisl and Leo Eitinger Prize, Oslo Univ. 1990. *Publications:* more than 1,000 papers in fields of experimental cell research and cancer research; The Atheist and the Holy City 1990, Hack i häl på Minerva (with Lars Gyllensten) 1993, Pietà 1993, Live Now 1997. *Address:* MTC, Karolinska Institutet, Box 280, 171 77 Stockholm; Kottlavagen 10, 181 61 Lidingö, Sweden. *Telephone:* (8) 728 67 30 (Office). *Fax:* (8) 33 04 98.

KLEIN, Herbert George; American journalist and fmr. government official; b. 1 April 1918, Los Angeles; s. of George J. and Amy Cordes Klein; m. Marjorie Galbraith 1941; two d.; ed. Univ. of Southern Calif; Journalist 1940–42; U.S. Naval Reserve 1942–46; Political Reporter and News Ed., Post Advocate 1946; Feature Writer, San Diego Evening Tribune 1950, Editorial Writer 1951; Chief Editorial Writer, San Diego Union 1951, Ed. 1959; mem. office staff of Vice-Pres. Nixon 1959–60; Dir. of Communications for the Exec. Branch 1969–73; publicist and press sec. for many of Richard Nixon's election campaigns; Vice-Pres. Corporate Relations Metromedia Inc. 1973–77; Pres. H. G. Klein Media Consultants 1977–80; Ed.-in-Chief, Vice-Pres. Copley Newspapers, San Diego 1980–; Trustee, Univ. S. Calif., Los Angeles; Hon. Dr. (Univ. of San Diego). *Address:* Copley Press Inc., 350 Camino De La Reina, San Diego, CA 92108 (Office); 5110 Saddlery Square, P.O. Box 8935, Rancho, Santa Fé, CA 92067, U.S.A. (Home).

KLEIN, Lawrence Robert, PH.D.; American economist and lecturer; b. 14 Sept. 1920, Omaha, Neb.; s. of Leo Byron Klein and Blanche Monheit; m. Sonia Adelson 1947; one s. three d.; ed. Univ. of Calif. at Berkeley, M.I.T., Lincoln Coll., Oxford; joined Faculty, Univ. of Chicago 1944–47; Research Assoc., Nat. Bureau of Econ. Research, Cambridge, Mass. 1948–50; with Univ. Michigan 1949–54; Research Assoc., Survey Research Center 1949–54; Oxford Inst. Statistics 1954–58; mem. faculty, Univ. of Philadelphia 1958–; Prof. 1958–, Univ. Prof. 1964–; Benjamin Franklin Prof. 1968–; Visiting Prof., Osaka Univ. 1960, Univ. of Colorado 1962, City Univ., New York 1962–63, Hebrew Univ. of Jerusalem 1964, Princeton Univ. 1966, Stanford Univ. 1968, Univ. of Copenhagen 1974; Ford Visiting Prof. Univ. of Calif. at Berkeley 1968; Visiting Prof. Inst. for Advanced Studies, Vienna 1970–74; Econ. Consultant to Canadian Govt. 1947, UNCTAD 1966, 1967, 1975, McMillan Co. 1965–74, E. I. du Pont de Nemours 1966–68, State of N.Y. 1969, American Telephone and Telegraph Co. 1969, Fed. Reserve Bd. 1973, UNIDO 1973–75, Congressional Budget Office 1977–, Council of Econ. Advisers 1977–80; Advisor State Planning Comm., People's Repub. of China; Chair. Bd. of Trustees, Wharton Econometrics Forecasting Assoc. Inc. 1969–80, Chair. Professional Bd. 1980–; Dir. Uni-Coll Corpn.; Trustee, Maurice Falk Inst. for Econ. Research, Israel, 1969–75; mem. Advisory Council, Inst. for Advanced Studies, Vienna 1977–; Chair. Econ. Advisory Cttee. Gov. of Pa. 1976–78; mem. Cttee. on Prices, Fed. Reserve Bd. 1968–70; Principal Investigator, Econometric Model Project of Brookings Inst., Washington, D.C. 1963–72, Project LINK 1968–, Sr. Adviser Brookings Panel on Econ. Activity 1970–; co-ordinator Jimmy Carter's Econ. Task Force 1976; mem. Advisory Bd., Strategic Studies Center, Stanford Research Inst. 1974–76; Ed. International Economic Review 1959–65, Assoc. Ed. 1965–; mem. Editorial Bd. Empirical Economics 1976–; Fellow, Econometrics Soc., American Acad. of Arts and Sciences, N.A.S., Social Sciences Research Council, American Economists' Asscn., Eastern Econ. Asscn., American Asscn. of Univ. Profs.; Hon. LL.D. (Mich.) 1977; Hon. Sc.D. (Widener Coll.) 1977; Dr. h.c. (Univ. of Vienna) 1977; Hon. Dr. Ed. (Villanova) 1978; Dr. h.c. (Bonn Univ., Free Univ. of Brussels and Univ. of Paris) 1979, (Univ. of Madrid) 1980, Hon. D.Litt. (Glasgow) 1991; William F. Butler Award, New York Asscn. of Business Economists 1975; Golden Slipper Club Award 1977; Nobel Prize in Econ. Science for work on econometric models 1980. *Publications:* The Keynesian Revolution 1947, Textbook of Econometrics 1953, An Econometric Model of the United States 1929–1952 1955, Wharton Econometric Forecasting Model 1967, Essay on the Theory of Economic Prediction 1968, Brookings Quarterly Econometric Model of U.S. Econometric Model Performance (author-ed.) 1976, The Economics of Supply and Demand 1983. *Address:* University of Pennsylvania McNeil Bldg., Room 335, 3718 Locust Walk, Philadelphia, PA 19104 (Office); 1317 Medford Road, Wynnewood, Philadelphia, PA 19096, U.S.A. (Home).

KLEIN, Peter Wolfgang, PH.D.; Netherlands professor of history; b. 10 Dec. 1931, Vienna, Austria; ed. Netherlands School of Econs., Rotterdam; Asst. Prof. of Econ. History 1959–65; Reader in Social History 1965–67; Prof. of Econ. and Social History, Erasmus Univ., Rotterdam 1969–85, Part-time Prof. of Econ. History 1969–74, Vice-Chancellor 1974–75, Dean Faculty of Econs. 1977–78, Head History Dept. 1979–81; Prof. of Early Modern History, State Univ. Leiden 1985–, Head History Dept. 1986–88; Pres. Dutch Historical Soc. 1987–; mem. State Cttee. for Nat. History 1981–, Bd. State Inst. for History Second World War 1972–89, Scientific Cttee. Inst. of Econ. History Francesco Datini 1986–, Cttee. Int. Asscn. of Econ. History 1985–, Royal Netherlands Acad. of Arts and Sciences 1979 (Chair. Arts Dept.); Founding mem. Academia Europaea. *Publication:* Dr. Trippen in de 17e. eeuw 1965. *Address:* Vakgroep Geschiedenis, Doelensteeg 16, 2311VL Leiden (Office); Oude Herengracht 24, Leiden, Netherlands (Home). *Telephone:* 071-272759 (Office).

KLEINDIENST, Richard Gordon, LL.B.; American lawyer; b. 5 Aug. 1923, Winslow, Ariz.; s. of Alfred R. Kleindienst and the late Gladys Love; m. Margaret Dunbar 1948; two s. two d.; ed. Winslow High School, Univ. of Ariz., Harvard Coll. and Harvard Law School; Law Clerk, Ropes, Gray, Best, Coolidge and Rugg, Boston 1949–50; Partner, Jennings, Strouss, Salmon and Trask, Phoenix, Ariz. 1950–57; mem. Ariz. House of Reps. 1953–54; Partner, Shimmel, Hill, Kleindienst and Bishop, Phoenix 1958–68; Chair. Ariz. State Republican Cttee. 1956; mem. Republican Nat. Cttee. 1956–60, 1960–63; Nat. Dir. of Field Operations, Goldwater for Pres. 1964, Nixon for Pres. 1968; Deputy Attorney-Gen. of U.S.A. 1969–72, Attorney-Gen. 1972–73; Pres. Fed. Bar Asscn. 1974–. *Leisure interests:* golf, chess, classical music, art. *Publication:* Justice (memoirs) 1985. *Address:* 3103 Crestview Drive, Prescott, AZ 86305, U.S.A.

KLEMPERER, William, PH.D.; American professor of chemistry; b. 6 Oct. 1927, New York; s. of Paul Klemperer and Margit (Freund) Klemperer; m. Elizabeth Cole 1949; one s. two d.; ed. New Rochelle High School, N.Y., Harvard Univ. and Univ. of California, Berkeley; U.S. Navy Air Corps 1944–46; Instructor, Berkeley Feb.–June 1954; Instructor, Harvard Univ. 1954–57, Asst. Prof. 1957–61, Assoc. Prof. 1961–65, Prof. 1965–; Asst. Dir., Nat. Science Foundation (for math. and physical sciences) 1979–81; mem. American Physical Soc., N.A.S., American Acad. of Arts and Sciences, American Chemical Soc.; Wetherill Medal, Franklin Inst.; several memorial lectures; Hon. D.Sc. (Univ. of Chicago) 1996; Irving Langmuir Award, American Chemical Soc.; Earle Plyler Award, American Physical Soc.; Distinguished Service Medal, Nat. Science Foundation–; Bomem Michelson Award, Coblentz Soc.; Remsen Award, Maryland Section of American Chemical Soc.; Peter Debye Award in Physical Chem., American Chemical Soc.; Faraday Medal, Royal Soc. of Chem. *Address:* Department of Chemistry and Chemical Biology, Harvard University, 12 Oxford Street, Cambridge, MA 02138 (Office); 53 Shattuck Road, Watertown, MA 02172, U.S.A. (Home). *Telephone:* (617) 495-4904 (Office); (617) 924-5775 (Home). *Fax:* (617) 496-5175 (Office).

KLEPPE, Johan; Norwegian politician and veterinarian; b. 29 Sept. 1928, Bjørnskinn, Andøya; s. of Jon Kleppe and Alvhild Caroliussen Kleppe; m. Inger Johansen 1961; one s. one d.; ed. Veterinary Coll. of Norway; Veterinarian 1954–63, Dist. Veterinarian, Andøy 1963–76, Supervisory Veterinarian 1966–76; Regional Veterinary Officer of North Norway 1976–94; mem. Bjørnskinn Municipal Council 1956–64; Deputy Mayor of Andøy 1964–66, Mayor 1966–68, 1975–78, mem. Exec. Cttee. Andøy municipality 1964–78; Deputy mem. of Parl. 1967; Parl. Under-Sec. of State, Ministry of Agriculture 1968–69; Liberal mem. of Parl. for Nordland 1969–73, mem. Bd. of Liberal Parl. faction 1969–73; mem. Liberal Party's Cttee. on Oil Policy and EC Cttee., mem. Prin. Planning Cttee.; Minister of Defence 1972–73; mem. Liberal Nat. Exec. 1966–72; Leader, Norwegian del., FAO confs., Rome and

Malta 1969; Norwegian Del., UN Gen. Ass., New York 1971; fmr. Bd. mem. Nordland Co. Liberal Asscn.; fmr. Chair. Students Liberal Asscn., Oslo and Bjørnskinn and Andøy Liberal Asscn.; Chair. of Board, Directorate of State Forests 1969–77, Chair. Nat. Council on Sheep-breeding 1969–82; Chair. of Bd. Nordlandsbanken A/S, 8480 Andenes 1974–90, State Veterinary Laboratory for Northern Norway 1976–91, Vesteraalen Intermunicipal Planning Office 1978–88; Vice-Chair. Cttee. Norwegian Veterinary Asscn. 1981–84, Chair. 1984–91; Chair. of Bd. Andøyposten a/s 1981–90, Troms Population Acad. Asscn. 1987–94; mem. Bd. Norwegian Nat. Programme for Sea Ranching 1990–94. *Address:* 8484 Risøyhamn, Norway. *Telephone:* 76147630. *Fax:* 76147630.

KLEPPE, Per; Norwegian politician and economist; b. 13 April 1923, Oslo; s. of Knut Sigurd and Nathalie Kleppe; m. Margaretha Ström 1951; two d. one step-s. one step-d.; Sec., Ministry of Finance 1952–53; with Cen. Bureau of Statistics 1953–54; mem. Research Councils Joint Cttee. 1954–57; Asst. Sec. of State, Ministry of Finance 1957–62, Chair. and Sec. Finance Policy Cttee. 1962–63; Head, Econ. section, EFTA Secr., Geneva 1963–67; Dir. Labour Party Research Office 1967–71; Minister of Commerce and Shipping 1971–72, of Finance 1973–79, of Long-term Planning and Co-ordination 1980–81; Sec.-Gen. EFTA, Geneva 1981–88. *Publications:* EFTA-EEC-NORDEK 1970, Bank og Kredittvesen 1974, 1979, Norges vei til Europa 1989, Visionen Og Hverdagen 1990, numerous econ. and political articles. *Leisure interests:* skiing, gardening. *Address:* Bjornveien 52, N-0387, Oslo 3, Norway. *Telephone:* 22491259.

KLEPSCH, Egon Alfred, DR.PHIL.; German politician; b. 30 Jan. 1930, Bodenbach/Elbe; s. of Egon Klepsch and Hermine Hölzl; m. Anita Wegehaupt 1952; three s. three d.; joined CDU 1951, mem. Bureau 1984–; Fed. Chair. Young Christian Democrats 1963–69; Chair. European Union of Young Christian Democrats 1964–70; mem. Bundestag 1965–80; mem. Parl. Assemblies of Council of Europe and of WEU 1969–80; M.E.P. (not directly elected) 1973–79, elected M.E.P. 1979–, Vice-Pres. European Parl. 1982–84, Pres. 1992–95; Vice-Pres. European People's Party (EPP) 1977–92, mem. Bureau 1992–, Chair. EPP Group 1977–82, 1984–92; Chair. Europa-Union Deutschland 1989–; Vice-Chair. German Council of European Movement 1990–; mem. Bd. of Govs. Deutschlandfunk 1991–; Bundesverdienstkreuz mit Stern und Schulterband and decorations from Italy, Luxembourg, Argentina, Chile and Greece. *Publications:* several books on European policy and military topics. *Leisure interest:* chess. *Address:* c/o Christian-Democratic Union, Konrad-Adenauer-Haus, Friedrich-Ebert Allee 73–75, 53115 Bonn, Germany.

KLESTIL, Thomas, D.ECON.; Austrian Head of State and diplomatist; b. 4 Nov. 1932; m. 1st two s. one d.; m. 2nd Margot Joffler 1999; ed. Economic Univ., Vienna; Office for Econ. Co-ordination in Fed. Chancellery, Vienna 1957–59; mem. of Austrian Del. to OECD, Paris 1959–62; Embassy, Washington D.C. 1962–66; Sec. to Fed. Chancellor 1966–69; Consul Gen. of Austria in Los Angeles, Calif. 1969–74; Perm. Rep. of Austria to UN 1978–82; Amb. to U.S.A. 1982–87; Sec.-Gen. for Foreign Affairs 1987–92; Pres. of Austria July 1992–. *Address:* Präsidentschaftskanzlei, Hofburg, 1010 Vienna, Austria.

KLIBI, Chedli, B.A.; Tunisian politician and international official; b. 6 Sept. 1925, Tunis; s. of Hassouna Klibi and Habiba Bannani; m. Kalthoum Lasram 1956; one s. two d.; ed. Sadiki Coll., Tunis, Sorbonne, Paris; successively high school teacher, lecturer, Univ. of Tunis and journalist 1951–57; Dir.-Gen. Tunisian Radio and TV 1958–61; Minister of Information and Cultural Affairs 1961–64, 1969–73, of Cultural Affairs 1976–78, of Information Sept. 1978; Minister, Dir. Cabinet of Pres. 1974–76; Sec.-Gen. League of Arab States 1978–90; Mayor of Carthage 1963–; mem. Political Bureau and Cen. Cttee., Neo Destour (Parti Socialiste Destourien) June 1979–; mem. Cairo Arabic Language Acad.; Grand Cordon, Order of Independence and Order of Repub. (Tunisia) and several foreign decorations. *Publications include:* The Arabs and the Palestinian Question, Islam and Modernity, Culture is a Civilisational Challenge. *Leisure interest:* Reading. *Address:* Carthage, Tunisia. *Telephone:* 734 535. *Fax:* 734 820.

KLIMA, Ivan, M.A.; Czech author; b. 14 Sept. 1931, Prague; m. Helena Mala-Klimova 1958; one s. one d.; ed. Charles Univ., Prague; Ed. Ceskoslovensky spisovatel (publishing house) 1958–63; Ed. Literarni noviny 1963–67, Literarni Listy 1968, Listy 1968–69; Visiting Prof. Univ. of Mich. Ann Arbor 1969–70; freelance author publishing abroad 1970–89; mem. Council, Czech Writers 1989–, Ed.'s Council, Lidové noviny 1996–97; Exec. Pres. Czech PEN Centre 1990–93; Hostovsky Award, New York 1985; George Theiner Prize (U.K.) 1993. *Publications:* A Ship Named Hope 1968, A Summer Affair 1972, My Merry Mornings (short stories) 1979, My First Love (short stories) 1985, Love and Garbage 1987, Judge on Trial 1987, Waiting for the Dark, Waiting for the Light, My Golden Trades (short stories) 1992, The Island of Dead Kings 1992, The Spirit of Prague (essays, jtly.) 1994, The Ultimate Intimacy (novel) 1997; plays: The Castle 1964, The Master 1967, The Sweetshop Myriam 1968, President and the Angel, Klara and Two Men 1968, Bridegroom for Marcela 1968, The Games 1975, Kafka and Felice 1986, contribs. to magazines. *Telephone:* (2) 402 2618; (2) 402 2617.

KLIMA, Viktor; Austrian politician and business executive; b. 4 June 1947, Vienna; ed. Vienna Tech. Univ., Univ. of Vienna; worked at Inst. for Automation and Scientific Business Consultancy; joined staff of Österreichische Mineralöl-Verwaltungs AG (ÖMV) 1970, Head Organizational Div. 1980–85, Dir. Cen. Personnel Office and group's Prokuriet (holder of a gen. power of attorney) 1986–, mem. Man. Bd. with responsibility for finance, control, accountancy and acquisitions (subsequently also chemical div.) 1990–92; Minister of Public Economy and Transport 1992–96, of Finance 1996–97, Fed. Chancellor of Austria 1997–; mem. several supervisory and advisory bds., Governing Bd. Fed. of Public Economy and Utility Enterprises; Chair. Fed. Econ. Chamber's Petroleum Industry Labour Law Cttee., Cttee. on Public and Utility Enterprises. *Address:* Office of the Federal Chancellor, Ballhausplatz 2, 1014 Vienna, Austria. *Telephone:* (1) 53-11-50. *Fax:* (1) 535-03-380.

KLIMOV, Dmitri Mikhailovich; Russian expert on mechanics; b. 13 July 1933; m.; ed. Moscow State Univ.; sr. researcher Research Inst. of Applied Mech. 1958–67; head of lab., head of div.; Deputy Dir. Inst. for Problems in Mechanics U.S.S.R. Acad. of Sciences 1967–89, Dir. 1989–; Corresp. mem U.S.S.R. (now Russian) Acad. of Sciences 1981, mem. 1992, Academician-Sec. Div. for Problems of Machine Engineering, Mechanics, and Control Processes 1996–; main research in mechanics, gyroscopic and navigation systems, gen. and analytical mechanics, mechanics of deformable solid bodies; Deputy Chair. Scientific Council on problems of Man. of Navigation Movt.; U.S.S.R. State Prize 1976, Russian State Prize 1994. *Publications:* Inertial Navigation on the Sea 1984, Applied Methods in Oscillations Theory 1988, Methods of Computer Algebra in Problems of Mechanics 1989, numerous articles. *Leisure interest:* chess. *Address:* Institute for Problems in Mechanics, Vernadskogo prosp. 101, 117526 Moscow, Russia. *Telephone:* (095) 434 4610 (Office); 938 1404 (Academy). *Fax:* (095) 938 2048 (Office).

KLIMOV, Elem Germanovich; Russian film director; b. 9 July 1933; m. Larisa Shepit'ko (died 1981); ed. Aviation Inst., All-Union State Cinematography Inst. (VGIK), Moscow; First Sec. U.S.S.R. Union of Film Makers 1986–90. *Films include:* The Fiancée, Careful—Banality!, Look, the Sky! (shorts) 1962–64; Welcome 1964, Adventures of a Dentist 1967, Sport, Sport, Sport 1971, Agony (on Rasputin) 1981 (with Alexei Petrenko), Farewell 1983, Come and See 1985. *Address:* Frunzenskaya nab. 24/1, Apt. 30, 119146 Moscow, Russia. *Telephone:* 242-42-47.

KLIMOVSKI, Savo, LL.D.; Macedonian politician; b. 1947, Skopje; m. Radmila Klimovski; one s. one d.; ed. Skopje Univ., Ljubljana Univ.; lecturer, Asst. Prof., Prof., Dean of Law Faculty, Pres., St. Cyril and Methodius Univ., Skopje; mem. Exec. Council, Macedonian Ass.; Pres. Macedonian Cttee. for Educ., Culture and Physical Culture; f. Democratic Alternative (political party) 1998–; mem. Govt. Coalition For Changes; Pres. Ass. of Repub. Macedonia; Pres. Cttee. for Constitutional Issues, Council for Interethnic Relations. *Address:* Sobranje, Oktomyri blvd. 11, 91000 Skopje, Macedonia. *Telephone:* (3891) 22 71 11 (Office).

KLIMUK, Piotr Ilyich, Col.-Gen., D.TECH.SC.; Russian cosmonaut; b. 10 July 1942, Komarovka, Brest Region; m. Lilia Vladimirovna; one s.; ed. Chernigov Higher Mil. Aviation School, Air Force Acad., Lenin Mil. Political Acad.; three space flights 1973–78; Deputy Head Yuriy Gagarin Centre for Cosmonauts Training 1978–91, Head 1991–; Hero of Soviet Union 1973, 1975; Tsiolkovsky Gold Medal, U.S.S.R. State Prize; U.S.S.R. People's Deputy 1989–91. *Publications:* Next to the Stars, Attacking Weightlessness. *Address:* Yuriy Gagarin Centre for Cosmonauts Training, Zvezdny Gorodok, Moscow Region, Russia. *Telephone:* (095) 526.35.33.

KLINE, Kevin Delaney, B.A.; American actor; b. 24 Oct. 1947, St. Louis; s. of Robert J. Kline and Peggy Kirk; m. Phoebe Cates 1989; one s. one d.; ed. Indiana Univ. and Julliard School Drama Div. New York; founding mem. The Acting Co. New York 1972–76; Obie Award for sustained achievement, Will Award for classical theatre; Broadway appearances in On the Twentieth Century 1978 (Tony Award 1978), Loose Ends 1979, Pirates of Penzance 1980 (Tony Award 1980), Arms and the Man 1985; off-Broadway appearances in Richard III 1983, Henry V 1984, Hamlet (also dir.) 1990, 1997. *Films include:* Sophie's Choice, Pirates of Penzance, The Big Chill 1983, Silverado 1985, Violets are Blue 1985, Cry Freedom 1987, A Fish Called Wanda (Acad. Award for Best Supporting Actor 1989) 1988, January Man 1989, I Love You to Death 1989, Soapdish 1991, Grand Canyon 1991, Consenting Adults 1992, Chaplin 1992, Dave 1993, Princess Caraboo 1994, Paris Match 1995, French Kiss 1995, Fierce Creatures 1996, The Ice Storm 1997, In and Out 1997. *Address:* c/o Creative Artists Agency, 9830 Wilshire Boulevard, Beverly Hills, CA 90212, U.S.A.

KLINGENBERG, Wilhelm; German professor of mathematics; b. 28 Jan. 1924, Rostock; s. of Paul Klingenberg and Henny Klingenberg; m. Christine Kob 1953; two s. one d.; ed. Kiel Univ.; Asst. Hamburg Univ. 1952–55; Asst. Prof., Assoc. Prof. Göttingen Univ. 1955–63; Prof. Univ. of Mainz 1963–66; Prof. of Math. Univ. of Bonn 1966–; mem. Acad. of Science and Literature, Mainz. *Publications:* A Course in Differential Geometry 1978, Lectures on Closed Geodesics 1978, Riemannian Geometry 1982, 1995, Der weite Weg zum Kailas 1992, Tibet 1997. *Leisure interests:* piano, horseback riding, Chinese art, art of Albrecht Dürer. *Address:* Am Alten Forsthaus 42, 53125 Bonn, Germany. *Telephone:* 228/251529.

KLINSMANN, Jurgen; German footballer; b. 30 June 1964; began career with Stuttgarter kickers before moving to Stuttgart; mem. winning team, World Cup 1990, UEFA Cup with Inter Milan 1991; joined Real Madrid 1992–93; with Tottenham Hotspur 1994–95, 1997–98, played for Bayern Munich 1995–97, Sampdoria 1997, 1998–; voted European Footballer of Year 1988. *Address:* c/o Sampdoria Football Club, Genoa, Italy.

KLJUŠEV, Nikola, D.ECON.SC.; Macedonian politician, economist and poet; b. 2 Oct. 1927, Stip; s. of Emanuel Kljušev and Lenka Kljušev; m. 1956; one s. one d.; ed. Skopje Univ.; mem. Macedonian Acad. of Arts and Sciences; retd. lecturer in econs.; Ed.-in-Chief, Economic Interview 1971–78; Prime Minister of Macedonia 1991–92; independent. *Publications:* (books on econs.): Period of Activization of Investment 1963, Criteria and Methods for Evaluation of Economic Efficiency of Investments 1965, Usage of Productive Capacity in Industry 1967, Policy and Economics of Investment in Companies 1968, Efficiency of Investment in Macedonian Industry 1969, Selected Problems of Theory and Policy of Economic Development 1978, Theory and Policy of Economic Development 1979, Investments (Theory, Economics, Policy) 1980; (books of poetry): Stone Island 1994, Antithesis 1994, The Power of the Word 1994, Ode to the Word 1995, Non-germinated Seed 1996; Selected Works (6 vols.) 1997. *Leisure interests:* hunting, skiing. *Address:* Dimitar Mirasciev 19, Skopje, Macedonia. *Telephone:* (91) 230 127.

KLOSE, Hans-Ulrich; German politician and lawyer; b. 14 June 1937, Breslau; two s. two d.; ed. gymnasium in Bielefeld, High School, Clinton, Iowa and Univs. of Freiburg and Hamburg; fmr. lawyer in Hamburg; mem. Social Democratic Party (SPD) 1964–; mem. Hamburger Bürgerschaft 1970; Mayor of Hamburg 1974–81; mem. Bundestag 1983– (Vice-Pres. 1994–); Treas. SPD 1987–91; Chair. SPD Parl. Party 1991–94; Hon. Citizen of Lima 1981. *Leisure interests:* early American cultures, art and antiques, painting, literature. *Address:* Bundeshaus, 53113 Bonn, Germany (Office). *Telephone:* 0228/16-81222; 0228/16-83229.

KŁOSKOWSKA, Antonina, PH.D.; Polish sociologist; b. 7 Nov. 1919, Piotrków Trybunalski; d. of Wincenty Kłoskowski and Cecylia Kłoskowska; ed. Łódź Univ; Doctor 1950–54, Asst. Prof. 1954–66, Assoc. Prof. 1966–73, Prof. 1973–; Expert, UNESCO 1967–; Head, Sociology of Culture Dept., Sociology Inst., Warsaw Univ. 1977–90; Head, Research Unit on Culture and Politics, Inst. of Political Sciences, Polish Acad. of Sciences (PAN) 1991–; Ed.-in-Chief "Kultura i Społeczeństwo" 1981–; Chair. Cttee. of Sociological Sciences, PAN 1973–81; Corresp. mem. PAN 1974–83, Ordinary mem. 1983–, mem. of Bd. 1989–; mem. Nat. Cttee. of Int. Sociological Asscn. attached to Social Sciences Dept. of Polish Acad. of Sciences 1984; Chair. Scientific Council of Inst. of Culture, Warsaw 1978–86; Chair. Scientific Council of Inst. of Political Studies, Polish Acad. of Sciences 1990–96; Pres. Polish Sociological Asscn. 1989–94; mem. Bd., Cttee. of Communication, Culture and Science, Int. Sociological Asscn.; Commdr.'s Cross, Order of Polonia Restituta; Scientific Prize, City of Łódź; Meritorious Teacher of People's Poland 1978. *Publications:* Kultura masowa, Krytyka i obrona 1964, Z historii i socjologii kultury 1969, Społeczne ramy kultury 1973, Machiavelli jako humanista na tle włoskiego Odrodzenia 1954, Education in a Changing Society (Co-ed.) 1977, Socjologia kultury (Sociology of Culture) 1981, Oblicza polskości (Images of Polishness) (Ed. 1990); Encyclopaedia of Polish Culture in the 20th Century, vol. I: Concepts and Problems (Ed.) 1991, The Neighbourhood of Cultures 1994, Kultury narodowe u korzeni (National Cultures—Personal Identities) (Co-ed.) 1996. *Leisure interests:* reading, television, holidaying in the country. *Address:* Instytut Studiów Politycrnych PAN, Polna 18/20, 00-625 Warsaw, Poland. *Telephone:* (22) 625 52 21.

KLOSSOWSKI de ROLA, Comte Balthasar (pseudonym Balthus); French artist; b. 29 Feb. 1908, Paris; s. of Victor Klossowski de Rola and Dorothée Spiro; m. 1st Antoinette von Wattenwyl 1937, two c.; m. 2nd Setsuko Ideta 1967; one c.; exhibited Galerie Pierre, Paris 1934, Pierre Matisse Gallery, New York City 1938, 1939, 1949, 1956, Moos Gallery, Geneva 1943, Wildenstein Galleries, Paris 1946, 1956, Dunn Int. Exhbn., London 1963; Retrospective Exhbn. at Tate Gallery, London 1968, at Georges Pompidou Centre, Paris 1983; Dir. Accademia di Francia, Villa Medici, Rome 1961–77; Grand Prix Nat. des Arts, Premium Imperiale (Japan Art Asscn.) 1991, retrospective exhbn. at Musée des Beaux-Arts de Lausanne (Switzerland) 1993. *Works include:* Frescoes, Church of Beatenberg, Switzerland 1928; costumes and sets for Artaud's The Cenci 1935, for Così Fan Tutte, Aix-en-Provence 1950; numerous paintings. *Address:* Grand Chalet, 1836 Rossinière, Canton de Vaud, Switzerland.

KLOSTER, Einar, B.A.; Norwegian business executive; b. 22 Sept. 1937, Oslo; s. of Knut Utstein Kloster and Ingeborg (née Ihlen) Kloster; m. Elizabeth (née Hajan) Blake 1961; two d.; ed. Dartmouth Coll. and Harvard Univ.; Marketing Man. Philips Norway Jan. 1961–68, Philips Head Office, Holland 1968–70; Marketing Dir. Philips Japan 1970–74; C.E.O. Philips East Africa 1974–77, Philips Norway 1978–82, Philips Brazil 1982–85; Exec. Vice-Pres. North American Philips Corpn. 1985–86, Pres. 1989; Chair. and C.E.O. Kloster Cruise Ltd. 1986–88, Pres. and C.E.O. Jan. 1989–; Chair. Norsk Hydro June 1997–. *Leisure interests:* golf, tennis, skiing. *Address:* Norsk Hydro AS, Bygdoy Alle 2, 0240 Oslo, Norway. *Telephone:* 22-43-21-00. *Fax:* 22-43-27-25.

KLOTZ, Irving Myron, PH.D; American professor of chemistry and biochemistry; b. 22 Jan. 1916, Chicago, Ill.; s. of Frank and Mollie Nasatir Klotz; m. Mary S. Hanlon 1966; two s. one d.; ed. Univ. of Chicago; Research Assoc., Northwestern Univ. 1940–42, Instructor in Chem. 1942–46, Asst. Prof. of Chem. 1946–47, Assoc. Prof. of Chem. 1947–50; Prof. of Chem. and Biochemistry 1950–, Morrison Prof. 1963–; Fellow, American Acad. of Arts and Sciences; mem. N.A.S.; Eli Lilly Award 1949, Midwest Award 1970 (A.C.S.), W. C. Rose Award (American Soc. of Molecular Biology) 1993. *Publications:* Chemical Thermodynamics 1950, 1964, 1972, 1986, 1994, Energy Changes in Biochemical Reactions 1957, 1967, Introduction to Biomolecular Energetics 1986, Diamond Dealers, Feather Merchants: Tales from the Sciences 1986, Ligand-Receptor Energetics: A Guide for the Perplexed 1997; over 300 research papers. *Address:* c/o Department of Chemistry, Northwestern University, Evanston, IL 60208-3113 (Office); 2515 Pioneer Road, Evanston, IL 60201, U.S.A. (Home). *Telephone:* (847) 491-3546 (Office). *Fax:* (847) 491-7713 (Office).

KLUG, Sir Aaron, Kt., O.M., PH.D., F.R.S.; British biochemist; b. 11 Aug. 1926; s. of Lazar Klug and Bella Silin; m. Liebe Bobrow 1948; two s.; ed. Durban High School and Univs. of the Witwatersrand and Cape Town; Jr. Lecturer 1947–48; Research Student, Cavendish Lab., Cambridge 1949–52; Rouse-Ball Research Studentship, Trinity Coll., Cambridge 1949–52; Colloid Science Dept., Cambridge 1953; Nuffield Research Fellow, Birkbeck Coll., London 1954–57; Dir. Virus Structure Research Group, Birkbeck Coll. 1958–61; mem. staff, MRC Lab. of Molecular Biology, Cambridge 1962–, Jt. Head, Div. of Structural Studies 1978–86, Dir. 1986; Pres. Royal Soc. Nov. 1995–; Fellow of Peterhouse 1962–93; Hon. Fellow Peterhouse, Cambridge 1993–, Royal Coll. of Pathologists 1991, Birkbeck Coll. 1994; Hon. Prof. Univ. of Cambridge 1989; Foreign Assoc. N.A.S.; Foreign mem. Max Planck Gesellschaft 1984; Foreign Hon. mem. American Acad. of Arts and Sciences; Hon. Fellow, Trinity Coll., Cambridge, Royal Coll. of Physicians 1987; Hon. D.Sc. (Chicago) 1978, (Columbia) 1978, (Witwatersrand 1984), (Hull) 1985, (St. Andrews) 1987, (Western Ont.) 1991, (Warwick) 1994; Dr. h.c. (Strasbourg) 1978; Hon. Dr. Fil. (Stockholm) 1980; Heineken Prize, Royal Netherlands Acad. of Science 1979; Louisa Gross Horwitz Prize (Columbia Univ.) 1981; Nobel Prize for Chemistry 1982, Copley Medal, Royal Soc. 1985, Harden Medal, Biochemical Soc. 1985, Baly Medal, Royal Coll. of Physicians 1987; William Bate Hardy Prize, Cambridge Philosophical Soc. 1996. *Publications:* articles in scientific journals. *Leisure interests:* reading, gardening. *Address:* MRC Laboratory of Molecular Biology, Cambridge, CB2 2QH (Office); 70 Cavendish Avenue, Hills Road, Cambridge, CB1 4UT, England (Home). *Telephone:* (01223) 248011 (Office); (01223) 248959 (Home).

KLUGE, John Werner, B.A.; American broadcasting and advertising company executive; b. 21 Sept. 1914, Chemnitz, Germany; s. of Fritz Kluge and Gertrude (Donj) Kluge; one s. one d.; ed. Wayne and Columbia Univs.; with Otten Bros. Inc., Detroit 1937–41; served U.S. Army 1941–45; Pres., Dir. WGAY Radio Station, Silver Spring, Md. 1946–59, St. Louis Broadcasting Corpn., Brentwood, Mo. 1953–58, Pittsburgh Broadcasting Co. 1954–59; Pres., Treas., Dir. Capitol Broadcasting Co., Nashville 1954–59, Assoc. Broadcasters Inc., Fort Worth, Dallas 1957–59; partner, Western N.Y. Broadcasting Co., Buffalo 1957–60; Pres., Dir. Washington Planagraph Co. 1956–60, Mid-Fla. Radio Corpn., Orlando 1952–59; Treasurer, Dir. Mid-Fla. TV Corpn. 1957–60; owner, Kluge Investment Co., Washington, D.C. 1956–60; partner, Nashton Properties, Nashville 1954–60, Texworth Investment Co., Fort Worth 1957–60; Chair. Bd. Seaboard Service System Inc. 1957–58; Pres. New England Fritos, Boston 1947–55, New York Inst. of Dietetics 1953–60; Chair. Bd., Pres., Dir. Metromedia Inc., New York 1986–; Chair. Bd., Treas., Dir., Kluge, Finkelstein & Co., Baltimore; Chair. Bd., Treas., Tri-Suburban Broadcasting Corpn., Washington, Kluge & Co.; Chair. Bd., Pres., Treas., Silver City Sales Co., Washington; Dir. Marriott-Hot Shoppes Inc., Nat. Bank Md., Waldorf Astoria Corpn. and other cos.; Vice-Pres. Bd. Dirs. United Cerebral Palsy Research and Educational Foundation 1972–. *Address:* Metromedia Inc., 1 Meadowlands Plaza, East Rutherford, NJ 07073, U.S.A.

KLUTSE, Kwassi; Togolese politician; fmr. Minister of Planning and Territorial Devt.; Prime Minister, Minister of Planning and Territorial Devt. Aug. 1996–. *Address:* Office of the Prime Minister, Lomé, Togo.

KLUXEN, Wolfgang, DR.PHIL.; German professor of philosophy; b. 31 Oct. 1922, Bensberg; m. Rosemarie Schmitz 1960; one s. two d.; ed. Univs. of Cologne, Bonn and Louvain; Asst. Univ. of Cologne 1953–60; Visiting Prof. Villanova Univ. 1960–61; Prof. Pädagogische Hochschule Neuss 1962–64; Prof. Ruhr Univ. Bochum 1964–69, Univ. of Bonn 1969–88, Prof. Emer. 1988–; Pres. Int. Soc. for Study of Medieval Philosophy 1973–83, Allgemeine Gesellschaft für Philosophie in Deutschland 1978–84; mem. Rhineland-Westphalian Acad. of Sciences; Grosses Bundesverdienstkreuz, Order of St. Gregory (Vatican). *Publications:* Philosophische Ethik bei Thomas von Aquin 1964, Joh. Duns Scotus Tractatus de primo principio 1974, Ethik des Ethos 1974, Moral, Vernunft, Natur 1997; numerous articles. *Address:* Humboldtstrasse 9, 53115 Bonn, Germany. *Telephone:* 0228-636714.

KNACKSTEDT, Günter Wilhelm Karl, PH.D.; German diplomatist; b. 29 July 1929, Berlin; s. of Willi and Anni Knackstedt; m. (divorced); two s.; m. 2nd Marianne Fischbach 1984; ed. Univs. of Frankfurt, Paris, Cincinnati and Harvard; Ed. at Cincinnati Enquirer 1958–59; Chief Ed. You and Europe, Wiesbaden 1959–61; joined diplomatic service 1961; Press Attaché, Havana 1963, Caracas 1963–66; Ministry of Foreign Affairs 1966–74, Sec. for Parl. Affairs 1976–79; Political Counsellor, Madrid 1974–76; Amb. to Luxembourg 1979–84, to Council of Europe, Strasbourg 1985–88, to Chile 1988–89, to Poland 1989–92, to Portugal 1992–94. *Publications:* Compendium of World History 1954, Living with Venezuelans 1968. *Leisure interests:* skiing, tennis, collecting old clocks. *Address:* 295 rue de Luxembourg, 8077 Bertrange, Luxembourg. *Telephone:* 453701. *Fax:* 453706.

KNAIFEL, Alexander Aronovich; Russian composer; b. 28 Nov. 1943, Tashkent; s. of Aron Iosifovich Knaifel and Muza Veniaminovna Shapiro-

Knaifel; m. Tatiana Melentieva 1965, one d.; ed. Moscow and Leningrad Conservatoires; works as freelance; mem. Composers Union 1968–, Cinematographers Union 1987–; Honoured Art Worker of Russia 1996. *Compositions:* Diada (Two Pieces) 1962, Classical Suite 1963, Five Poems by Mikhail Lermontov 1964, Angel 1964, Musique militaire 1964, The Coming City of the Seeking After 1964, Passacaglia 1965, The Canterville Ghost 1965–66, Disarmament 1966, 150 000 000 1966, Lamento 1967, The Petrograd Sparrows 1967, Monodia 1968, Medea 1968, Argumentum de jure 1969, Joan 1970–78, A prima vista 1972, Status nascendi 1975, Ainana 1978, Rafferti 1980, Vera (Faith) 1980, Solaris 1980, Da (Yes) 1980, A Silly Horse 1981, A Chance Occurrence 1982, Pagan Fate 1982, Nika 1983–84, Counteraction 1984, God 1985, Agnus Dei 1985, Wings of a Serf 1986, Madness 1987, Through the Rainbow of Involuntary Tears 1987–88, Litania 1988, Shramy marsha (Scars of March) 1988, Voznosheniye (The Holy Oblation) 1991, Svete Tikhiy (O Gladsome Light) 1991, Postludia 1992, Once Again on the Hypothesis 1992, Scalae Iacobis 1992, Chapter Eight 1993, Maranatha 1993, Cantus 1993, Butterfly 1993, In Pure and Transparent Air 1994, Prayers to the Holy Spirit 1994–95, Psalm 51 (50) 1995, Amicta sole 1995, The Beatitudes 1996, Bliss 1997, Lux aeterna 1997, This Child 1997, Tabernacle 1998, With the White on the White 1998, Snowflake on a Spiderthread 1998; incidental music for 40 films. *Leisure interests:* photography, shooting video films. *Address:* Skobelevski pr. 5, apt. 130, 194214 St. Petersburg, Russia (Home). *Telephone:* (812) 553 8268 (Home). *Fax:* (812) 553 5397; (812) 443 4892.

KNAPP, Charles, M.A., PH.D.; American university president; b. 13 Aug. 1946, Ames, Ia.; s. of Albert B. Knapp and Anne Marie Knapp; m. Lynne Vickers Knapp 1967; one d.; ed. Iowa State Univ. and Univ. of Wisconsin; Asst. Prof. of Econs. Univ. of Tex., Austin 1972–76; Special Asst. to U.S. Sec. of Labor 1976–79; Deputy Asst. Sec. of Labor for Employment Training 1979–81; Visiting Faculty, George Washington Univ. 1981–82; Senior Vice-Pres. Tulane Univ. 1982–85, Exec. Vice-Pres. 1985–87; Pres., Prof. of Econs. Univ. of Georgia 1987–97; Pres. Aspen Inst. 1997–; Dir. AFLAC, Inc. *Publications:* A Human Capital Approach to the Burden of the Military Draft 1973, Earnings and Individual Variations in Postschool Human Investment 1976, Employment Discrimination 1978. *Address:* Aspen Institute, 1333 New Hampshire Avenue N.W., Washington, DC 20036, U.S.A.

KŇAŽKO, Milan; Slovak politician and actor; b. 28 August 1945, Horné Plachtince, Veľký Krtíš Dist.; m. Eugenia Kňažková; three s.; ed. Acad. of Performing Arts, Bratislava, Univ. of Nancy, France; mem. drama company, Theatre on the Promenade, Bratislava 1970–71; actor, New Theatre, Bratislava 1971–85; mem. Slovak Nat. Theatre Drama Company, Bratislava, 1985–; co-founder, Public Against Violence (political movt.) Nov. 1989, rally speaker 1989–90; adviser to Pres. of Czechoslovakia 1989–90; deputy to House of People, Fed. Ass. 1990–92; Minister of Slovak Repub. 1990; Minister for Foreign Affairs, Govt. of Slovak Repub. 1990–91; mem. Movt. for Democratic Slovakia 1991–93 (resgnd.) (Vice-Chair. June 1991–93); Deputy Prime Minister, Slovak Repub. 1992–93, Minister for Foreign Affairs 1992–93, of Culture 1998–; Chair. Govt. Council of Slovak Republic for Ethnic Groups 1992–93; Chair. Alliance of Democrats 1993–94, Independent Deputies Club 1993–; First Deputy Chair. Democratic Union of Slovakia 1994–; numerous roles on stage, in films, on TV, on radio; Merited Artist Award 1986 (returned award 1989). *Leisure interests:* family, sport, culture, theatre. *Address:* Democratic Union of Slovakia, Medená 10, 811 02 Bratislava; Úrad vlády SR, Nám. Slobody 1, 813 70 Bratislava 1, Slovakia. *Telephone:* (07) 534 1111 (Ministry of Culture).

KNEALE, (Robert) Bryan (Charles), R.A.; British sculptor; b. 19 June 1930; m. Doreen Lister 1956; one s. (deceased) one d.; ed. Douglas High School, Douglas School of Art, Isle of Man, Royal Acad. Schools; Tutor, R.C.A. Sculpture School 1964, Sr. Tutor 1980–85, Head Dept. of Sculpture 1985–90; Head of Sculpture School, Hornsey 1967; Assoc. Lecturer, Chelsea School of Art 1970; Fellow R.C.A. 1972, Sr. Tutor 1980–85, Head of Sculpture Dept. 1985–90; Prof. of Drawing, Royal Coll. of Art 1990–95, Sr. Fellow 1995; Master of Sculpture R.A. 1982–85, Prof. 1985–90; mem. Fine Art Panels, Nat. Council for Art Design 1964–71, Arts Council 1971–73, CNAA 1974–82; Chair. Air and Space 1972–73; organized Sculpture '72, R.A. 1972, Battersea Park Silver Jubilee Sculpture 1977, Sade Exhbn., Cork 1982; exhbns. at Redfern Gallery, John Moores, Sixth Congress of Int. Union of Architects, Art Aujourd'hui, Paris, Battersea Park Sculpture, Tate Gallery, Whitechapel Gallery, Hayward Gallery, Serpentine Gallery, Compass Gallery, Glasgow, 51 Gallery, Edin., Arts Council Tours 1966–71, Nat. History Museum, Royal Coll. of Art, Sala Uno, Rome, Royal West of England Acad., etc.; Collections Arts Council of G.B., Contemporary Art Soc., Manx Museum, Nat. Galleries of Victoria, S. Australia and N.Z., City Art Galleries York, Nottingham, Manchester, Bradford, Leicester, Tate Gallery, Beaverbrook Foundation, Fredericton, Museum of Modern Art, São Paulo, Brazil, Bahia Museum, Brazil, Oriel Coll., Oxford, Museum of Modern Art, New York, Fitzwilliam Museum, Cambridge, etc. *Address:* 10A Muswell Road, London, N10 2BG, England. *Telephone:* 0181-444 7617.

KNEF, Hildegard; British actress, singer and authoress; b. 28 Dec. 1925, Ulm, Germany; d. of Hans Theodor and Frieda Auguste (née Groehn) Knef; m. 2nd David Cameron; one d.; m. 3rd Paul Rudolph Schell 1977; ed. art studio, Ufa Babelsberg; acted at Schlossparktheater, Berlin 1945, 1960, Imperial Theatre, New York 1955–56, Berliner Schaubühne 1961, 1964–65; Edison Prize 1972, Bundesverdienstkreuz (First Class) 1975, award for best female role, Karlsbad film festival 1976, Bundesfilmpreis 1959, 1977, Golden Tulip, Amsterdam 1981 and other film awards. *Films include:* Die Mörder sind unter uns 1946, Film ohne Titel 1948, Die Sünderin 1950, Entscheidung vor Morgengrauen 1951, Schnee am Kilimandscharo 1952, Alraune 1952, Illusion in Moll 1952, The Man Between 1953, Svengali 1954, La Fille de Hambourg 1958, Der Mann der sich verkaufte 1958, Lulu 1962, Landru 1962, Dreigroschenoper 1962, Das Grosse Liebesspiel 1963, Wartezimmer zum Jenseits 1964, The Lost Continent 1967, Jeder Stirbt für sich allein 1975, Fedora 1977; numerous recordings and numerous TV appearances. *Publications:* Der Geschenkte Gaul 1970, Ich brauche Tapetenwechsel 1972, Das Urteil 1975, (Mark Twain Prize 1980), Heimwehblues 1978, Nicht als Neugier 1978, So nicht 1982, Romy 1983. *Leisure interests:* music, painting. *Address:* c/o Agentur Lentz, Holbeinstrasse 4, 81679 Munich, Germany.

KNEŽEVIĆ, Stojan, D. EN MED., D. ÈS SC.; Croatian professor of internal medicine; b. 6 Dec. 1923, Split; s. of Stevo Knežević and Marija Knežević; m. Jelena Konstantinović 1947; one s. one d.; ed. Univ. of Zagreb; country doctor DZ-Sisak 1952–54; Specialist in Internal Medicine 1954–57; Asst. Clinic for Internal Medicine, Zagreb 1957–63; interim St. Antoine Hosp., Paris; Asst. Prof., then Prof. of Medicine, Univ. of Zagreb-Croatia 1963–; Head of Gastroenterology Inst., Univ. of Zagreb; Ed.-in-chief, Acta Medica Croatica 1996–; mem. Senate; Hon. mem. Croatian Acad. of Medical Sciences; Hon. mem Hrvatski Liječnički Zbor; Hon. mem. Czecho-Slovak Medical Asscn.; mem. Soc. européene de culture. *Publications:* Klinička medicina 1959, Interna medicina 1970, Etika i medicina 1976, San je java snena 1977 (literary), Medicinske razglednice 1985, Slike koje pamtim 1989 (poetry), Medicinski susreti 1990, Medicina Starije Dobi 1990, Udzbenik Interne Medicine 1991, Veliki Medicinski Savjetnik, Misli i Poruke (Aforiemi) 1998. *Leisure interests:* writing, poetry, philosophy. *Address:* Smičiklasova 19, 41000 Zagreb, Croatia. *Telephone:* (1) 4614856.

KNIGHT, Andrew Stephen Bower, F.R.S.A.; British journalist and newspaper executive; b. 1 Nov. 1939; s. of M. W. B. Knight and S. E. F. Knight; m. 1st Victoria Catherine Brittain 1966 (marriage dissolved); one s.; m. 2nd Begum Sabiha Rumani Malik 1975 (divorced 1991); two d.; Ed. The Economist 1974–86; Chief Exec. Daily Telegraph 1986–89, Ed.-in-Chief 1987–89; Chair. News Int. PLC 1990–94; Chair. Ballet Rambert 1984–87; Chair. Times Newspaper Holdings 1990–94; Dir. News Corpn. 1991–, Murray Emerging Economies Trust 1995–, Murray Ventures 1995–, Rothschild Investment Trust CP 1996–; mem. Advisory Bd. Center for Econ. Policy Research, Stanford Univ., U.S.A. 1981–; Gov. mem. Council of Man. Ditchley Foundation 1982–; Dir. Murray Ventures 1995–; now farms in Warwicks. and Dannevirke, N.Z. *Address:* c/o News International PLC, P.O.B. 495, Virginia Street, London, E1 9XY, England.

KNIGHT, Douglas Maitland, PH.D.; American educational and corporate administrator; b. 8 June 1921, Cambridge, Mass.; s. of Claude Rupert and Fanny Sarah Douglas Brown Knight; m. Grace Wallace Nichols 1942; four s.; ed. Yale Univ; Instructor of English, Yale 1946–47; Asst. Prof. of English Literature, Yale 1947–53; Morse Research Fellow 1951–52; Pres. Lawrence Univ., Appleton, Wisconsin 1954–63; Pres. Duke Univ., Durham, N. Carolina 1963–69, Pres. Emer. 1992–; Chair. Woodrow Wilson Nat. Fellowship Foundation; Chair. Nat. Library Comm. 1966–67; Div. Vice-Pres. Educational Devt., RCA, New York 1969–71, Div. Vice-Pres. Educ. Services 1971–72, Staff Vice-Pres. Educ. and Community Relations 1972–73, Consultant 1973–75; Pres. RCA, Iran 1971–72, Dir. 1971–73; Pres. Social Econ. and Educ. Devt. Inc. 1973–76, Questar Corpn. 1976–; Dir. Near East Foundation 1975–80; Co-Founder and Trustee, Questar Library of Science and Art 1982– (Pres. 1996–); Pres. Delaware River Mill Soc., 1992–97, Emer. 1997; mem. Nat. Comm. on Higher Educ. Issues 1981–84; Trustee, Solebury School, American Asscn. for the Advancement of the Humanities; numerous hon. degrees. *Publications:* Alexander Pope and the Heroic Tradition 1951, The Dark Gate (poems) 1971; Ed. and contrib.: Medical Ventures and the University 1967; Ed. The Federal Government and Higher Education 1960; Joint Ed. Twickenham edn. of Iliad and Odyssey (trans. by Alexander Pope) 1965, Libraries at Large 1968, Street of Dreams: The Nature and Legacy of the 1960s 1989, Journeys in Time (poems) 1993, Education and the Civil Order: A History of the Woodrow Wilson National Fellowship Foundation 1995. *Leisure interests:* farming, sailing. *Address:* Questar Corporation, 6204 Ingham Road, New Hope, PA 18938 (Office); 68 Upper Creek Road, Stockton, NJ 08559, U.S.A. (Home). *Telephone:* (201) 996-2054 (Office).

KNIGHT, Sir Harold Murray, Kt., K.B.E., D.S.C., M.COMM.; Australian banker; b. 13 Aug. 1919, Melbourne; s. of W. H. P. Knight; m. Gwenyth Catherine Pennington 1951; four s. one d.; ed. Scotch Coll., Melbourne, and Melbourne Univ; Commonwealth Bank of Australia 1936–40, 1946–55; served Australian Imperial Forces and Royal Australian Navy 1940–45 (awarded D.S.C.); Statistics Div., Research and Statistics Dept. of IMF 1955–59, Asst. Chief 1957–59; Research Economist, Reserve Bank of Australia 1960, Asst. Man. Investment Dept. 1962–64, Man. Investment Dept. 1964–68, Deputy Gov. Reserve Bank of Australia and Deputy Chair. of Bank's Bd. 1968–75, Gov. and Chair. of Bd. 1975–82; Dir. Western Mining Corpn. 1982–91, Mercantile Mutual Group 1983–89, Chair. 1985–89; Chair. I.B.J. Australia Bank Ltd. 1985–92; Dir. Angus and Coote Holdings Ltd. 1986–93; mem. Police Bd., N.S.W. 1988–89, 1991–93; Pres. Scripture Union, N.S.W. 1983–; Hon. Visiting Fellow, Macquarie Univ. 1983–86, Councillor 1984–87, 1990–93. *Publication:* Introducción al Análisis Monetario 1959. *Address:* 76 Yarrara Road, West Pymble, N.S.W. 2073, Australia.

KNIGHT, Jeffrey Russell, M.A., F.C.A.; British chartered accountant; b. 1 Oct. 1936, Bristol; s. of late Thomas E. Knight and Ivy Cissie Russell; m. Judith Podger 1959; four d.; ed. Bristol Cathedral School and St. Peter's Hall, Oxford; grad. trainee, The De La Rue Co. Ltd. 1960–62; articled clerk, Fuller, Wise, Fisher & Co. (chartered accountants) 1962–67; with The Stock Exchange, London 1967–90, Deputy Chief Exec. 1975, Chief Exec. 1982–89; Special Adviser, Fed. of Stock Exchanges in the EC 1990–98. *Leisure interests:* music, cricket. *Address:* Lordsmeade, Hurtmore Road, Godalming, Surrey, GU7 2DY, England. *Telephone:* (01483) 424399.

KNILL, Sir John Lawrence, Kt., D.SC., F.I.C.E., F.ENG.; British engineering geologist; b. 22 Nov. 1934, Wolverhampton; s. of William C. Knill and Mary Dempsey; m. Diane C. Judge 1957; one s. one d.; ed. Whitgift School, Croydon and Imperial Coll. London; Asst. Lecturer, Imperial Coll., Univ. of London 1957–59, Lecturer 1959–65, Reader 1965–73, Prof. of Eng. Geology 1973–93, Prof. Emer. 1993–, Sr. Research Fellow 1993–; Dir. Donaldson Assocs. 1993–96; Head, Dept. of Geology 1979–88; Dean, Royal School of Mines 1980–83; mem. Nature Conservancy Council 1985–91, Jt. Nature Conservation Cttee. 1991–; Chair. Radioactive Waste Man. Advisory Cttee. 1987–95, Natural Environment Research Council 1988–93, SAUL Trustee Co. 1997–; Hon. D.Sc. (Kingston) 1992, (Exeter) 1995; Hon. D.Tech. (Nottingham Trent) 1996; British Geotechnical Soc. Prize 1966; Whitaker Medal (IWEM) 1969; Hon. FCGI 1988; Aberconway Medal (IGEOL) 1989, William Smith Medal (GEOLSOC) 1995. *Publication:* Industrial Geology 1977. *Leisure interest:* viticulture. *Address:* Highwood Farm, Long Lane, Shaw-cum-Donnington, Newbury, Berks., RG14 2TB, England (Home).

KNIPPING VICTORIA, Eladio, LL.B.; Dominican diplomatist; b. 28 June 1933, Santiago de los Caballeros; s. of Elpidio Knipping and Luz Victoria; m. Soledad Knipping 1963; one s. one d.; ed. Autonomous University of Santo Domingo, Diplomatic School of Spain, School of Int. Affairs, Madrid; Asst. to Madrid Consulate 1963–65, Econ. Attaché, Netherlands 1966–68; Sec. Consultative Comm. Ministry of Foreign Affairs; Minister-Counsellor and Deputy Chief of Div. of UN Affairs, OAS and Int. Orgs. 1966–68, 1969–74; Minister-Counsellor Perm. Mission to UN, New York 1968–69, Amb. to Honduras 1974–78; Perm. Rep. to OAS 1979–83, 1987–95; Amb. (non-resident) to Barbados, Jamaica, St. Lucia and Trinidad and Tobago 1990–, to Haiti 1995–97, to Panama 1997–; Perm. Rep. to UN, New York 1983–87; Pres. Juridical and Political Comm., OAS Perm. Council 1981–82, 1992–93; Dominican mem. Int. Court of Arbitration, The Hague; Del. UN III Conf. of Law of the Sea; Lecturer in Int. Law Pedro Henriquez Ureña Univ. 1969; f. Inst. Comparative Law; mem. Spanish-Portuguese-American and Philippine Inst. of Int. Law (Pres. 1990–92); UN Adlai Stevenson Fellow. *Leisure interests:* reading, listening to music. *Address:* Embassy of the Dominican Republic, Gerardo Ortega 7, Piso 7, Apartado Postal 6250, Cuidad Panama, Panama.

KNÍŽÁK, Milan; Czech multimedia artist, writer and art theorist; b. 19 April 1940, Plzeň; s. of Karel Knížak and Emilie Knížaková; m. 1st Soňa Švecová 1967, 2nd Jarka Charvátová 1970, 3rd Marie Geislerová 1975; ed. Acad. of Fine Arts, Charles Univ., Prague; in U.S.A. (at invitation of Floxus group of artists) 1968–70; founded Aktual group; prosecuted and imprisoned on numerous occasions 1957–89 mostly for his art activities; Univ. Prof.; Rector Acad. of Fine Arts, Prague 1990–97; released LP The Rite of a Burning Mind 1992; exhbn. paintings, Prague 1998; awards include DAAD Berlin, Barkenhoff Worpswede, Germany, Schloss Bleckede, Germany, Schloss Solitude, Germany, 5th Inter-Triennale Wrocław, Poland; Medal 1st Degree, Ministry for Educ. and Physical Training 1997. *Publications:* Zeremonien 1971, Action as a Life Style 1986, Neo Knížák 1991, New Paradise 1995–96, Without Reason 1996, Rozhovor s P. Wolfem (Talk with P. Wolf), and many others. *Leisure interests:* collecting old marionettes. *Address:* AVU, U. Akademie 4, 17000 Prague, Czech Republic.

KNOLL, József; Hungarian pharmacologist; b. 30 May 1925, Kassa; s. of Jakab Knoll and Blanka Deutscher; m. Dr. Berta Knoll; one d.; ed. Medical Univ., Budapest; asst. lecturer Univ. Pharmacological Inst.; lecturer Medical Univ. 1958, Prof. and Head 1962–95, Vice-Rector 1964–70; corresp. mem. Hungarian Acad. of Sciences 1970, mem. 1979–; Gen. Sec. Hungarian Pharmacological Soc. 1962–67, Pres. 1967–83, Hon. Pres. 1984–; Chair. Nat. Drug Admin. Cttee. and Drug Research Cttee. of the Acad. of Sciences; Vice-Pres. Medical Sciences Section, Hungarian Acad. of Sciences 1967–76; mem. Leopoldina Deutsche Akad. der Naturwissenschaften, Halle 1974–; councillor Int. Union of Pharmacological Sciences 1981–84, First Vice-Pres. 1984–87; Foreign mem., Polish Acad. of Arts and Sciences 1995; Hon. Dr. Medizinische Akad., Magdeburg 1984–, Bologna Univ. 1988; Hon. mem. Pharmacological Socs. of Czechoslovakia, Bulgaria, Poland and of Italy; Hon. F.R.S.M. 1990; mem. editorial bd. of numerous int. pharmacological periodicals; Nat. Prize of Hungary 1985. *Publications:* Theory of Active Reflexes 1969, Handbook of Pharmacology, nine editions since 1965; over 700 papers in int. trade journals. *Leisure interest:* visual arts. *Address:* Semmelweis University of Medicine, Department of Pharmacology, Budapest 1445, Nagyvárad tér 4, Hungary. *Telephone:* 210-4405 (Office); 329-3805 (Home). *Fax:* 210-4405.

KNOPF, Alfred, Jr., A.B.; American publisher (retd.); b. 17 June 1918, New York; s. of Alfred A. Knopf and Blanche Wolf; m. Alice Laine 1952; one s. two d.; ed. Union Coll.; with Atheneum Publishers 1959–88, Chair. 1964–88; fmr. Vice-Chair. Scribner Book Cos.; fmr. Sr. Vice-Pres. MacMillan Publishing Co. *Address:* Bayberry Ridge, Westport, CT 06880, U.S.A.

KNOPFLER, Mark; British guitarist and songwriter; b. 12 Aug. 1949; s. of late Erwin Knopfler and of Louisa Knopfler; m. Lourdes Salomone 1983; ed. Leeds Univ.; fmr. journalist Yorkshire Evening Post; f. Dire Straits 1977, guitarist; first concert 1977; group has since toured worldwide; albums include: Making Movies, Brothers in Arms, On Every Street; best-known songs include Romeo and Juliet, Money For Nothing, Calling Elvis; has also toured with Eric Clapton and recorded with Chet Atkins; formed own ad hoc band, Notting Hillbillies; Hon. D.Mus. (Leeds) 1995; awards: Ivor Novello, BRIT, MTV, Grammy. *Address:* c/o Damage Management, 16 Lambton Place, London, W11 2SH, England. *Telephone:* 0171-229 2992. *Fax:* 0171-229 2213.

KNOPOFF, Leon, M.S., PH.D., A.A.A.S.; American professor of physics and geophysics; b. 1 July 1925, Los Angeles, Calif.; s. of Max Knopoff and Ray Singer; m. Joanne Van Cleef 1961; one s. two d.; ed. Calif. Inst. of Tech; Asst. Prof., Assoc. Prof. of Physics, Miami Univ. 1948–50; mem. staff Univ. of Calif. (Los Angeles) 1950–, Prof. of Geophysics 1959–, of Physics 1961–, Research Musicologist 1963–, Assoc. Dir. Inst. of Geophysics and Planetary Physics 1972–86; Prof. of Geophysics, Calif. Inst. of Tech. 1962–63; Visiting Prof. Technische Hochschule, Karlsruhe (Germany) 1966; Chair. U.S. Upper Mantle Cttee. 1963–71, Sec.-Gen. Int. Upper Mantle Cttee. 1963–71; Nat. Science Foundation Sr. Postdoctoral Fellow 1960–61; Guggenheim Foundation Fellowship (Cambridge) 1976–77; Visiting Prof., Harvard Univ. 1972, Univ. of Chile, Santiago 1973; Chair. Int. Cttee. on Mathematical Geophysics 1971–75; H. Jeffreys Lecturer, Royal Astronomical Soc. 1976; mem. N.A.S., American Philosophical Soc., American Physical Soc., Royal Astronomical Soc.; Fellow, American Acad. of Arts and Sciences, American Geophysical Union; Hon. mem. Seismological Soc. of America; Int. Co-operation Year Medal (Canada) 1965, Wiechert Medal, German Geophysical Soc. 1978, Gold Medal of the Royal Astronomical Soc. 1979, Medal of the Seismological Soc. of America 1990. *Publications:* The Crust and Upper Mantle of the Pacific Area (co-ed.) 1968, The World Rift System (co-ed.); chapters in Physics and Chemistry of High Pressures (ed. R. L. Bradley) 1963, Physical Acoustics (ed. W. P. Mason) 1965, The Earth's Mantle (ed. T. Gaskell) 1967, The Megatectonics of Oceans and Continents (ed. H. Johnson and B. L. Smith); papers in professional journals. *Leisure interests:* mountaineering, gardening, playing piano and harpsichord. *Address:* Institute of Geophysics and Planetary Physics, University of California, Los Angeles, CA 90095, U.S.A. *Telephone:* (310) 825-1885.

KNORRE, Dmitri Georgievich; Russian chemist and biochemist; b. 28 July 1926, Leningrad; s. of Georgy F. Knorre and Elena A. Knorre; m. Valeria L. Knorre 1959; one s. two d.; ed. Moscow Chemical-Technological Inst.; worked in U.S.S.R. (now Russian) Acad. of Sciences Inst. of Chemical Physics 1947–61, then in all grades to Head Dept. of Biochem. at Acad. of Sciences, Inst. of Organic Chem. 1961–84, Dir. at Acad. of Sciences Inst. of Bio-organic Chem., Novosibirsk 1984–96; Adviser to Pres. Acad. of Sciences 1996–; also Prof. of Univ. of Novosibirsk 1961–, Dean 1961–83 (Hon. Dr. of Chemical Science 1967); Corresp. mem. of Acad. 1968–81, mem. 1981, Acad.-Sec. Dept. of Biochem. and Biophysics 1988–96; Lenin Prize, M. Shemyakin Prize and other awards. *Publications:* works on phosphorous-organic compounds, tauthometria. *Leisure interest:* hiking. *Address:* Institute of Bio-organic Chemistry, Prospekt Lavrenteva 8, 630090, Novosibirsk, Russia. *Telephone:* 35-64-41 (Office); 35-57-03 (Home).

KNOWLES, Jeremy Randall, C.B.E., M.A., D.PHIL., F.R.S.; British professor of chemistry and biochemistry; b. 28 April 1935; s. of the late Kenneth G. J. C. Knowles and of Dorothy H. Swingler; m. Jane S. Davis 1960; three s.; ed. Magdalen Coll. School, Balliol Coll., Merton Coll. and Christ Church Oxford; Research Assoc. Calif. Inst. of Tech. 1961–62; Fellow, Wadham Coll. Oxford 1962–74 (Hon. Fellow 1990); Univ. Lecturer, Univ. of Oxford 1966–74; Amory Houghton Prof. of Chem. and Biochem. (fmrly of Chem.), Harvard Univ. 1974–, Dean Faculty of Arts and Sciences 1991–; Fellow, American Acad. of Arts and Sciences 1982; Foreign Assoc. N.A.S. 1988; mem. American Philosophical Soc. 1988; Hon. Fellow Balliol Coll. 1984, Wadham Coll. 1990, Royal Soc. of Chem.; Dr. h.c. (Univ. of Edin.) 1992; Charmian Medal, Royal Soc. of Chem. 1980, Alfred Bader Award (U.S.A.) 1989, Cope Scholar Award (U.S.A.) 1989, Prelog Medal 1989, Davy Medal, Royal Soc. 1991, Repligen Award (U.S.A.) 1992, Robert A. Welch Award in Chem. 1995. *Publications:* research papers and reviews in learned journals. *Address:* Harvard University, Faculty of Arts and Sciences, University Hall, MA 02138; 7 Bryant Street, Cambridge, MA 02138, U.S.A.

KNOWLES, Tony, B.A.; American politician and retailer; b. 1 Jan. 1943, Tulsa, m. Susan Morris; two s. one d.; ed. Yale Univ.; U.S. Army, Vietnam 1961–65; owner and Man. The Works, Anchorage 1968–, Downtown Deli, Anchorage 1978–; Mayor Municipality of Anchorage 1981–87; Gov. of Alaska 1994–; mem. Citizen's Cttee. for Planned Growth and Devt. of Anchorage 1972, Borough Ass., Anchorage 1975–79; Bd. dirs. KAKM TV Station, Anchorage Chamber of Commerce; mem. numerous sports cttees. *Address:* Office of the Governor, P.O. Box 110001, Juneau, AK 99811, U.S.A.

KNOWLTON, Richard L., B.A.; American business executive (retd.); b. 1932; m.; ed. Univ. of Colorado; joined George A. Hormel & Co. (food and meat packing co.) 1948, Asst. Man. Austin Plant 1969, Gen. Man. 1974, Vice-Pres. Operations 1974, Group Vice-Pres. Operations 1975–79, Pres. and C.O.O. 1979, C.E.O. 1981–95, Chair. 1984–95; Pres. 1981–92; Dir. Nat. Livestock and Meat Bd., Hormel Foundation Bd., First Nat. Bank of Austin,

First Bank of Minn., Canada Packers; Chair. American Meat Inst.; Dir. Minn. Business Partnership. *Address:* c/o Hormel Foods Corp., 1 Hormel Place, Austin, MN 55912, U.S.A.

KNOX, George Alexander, M.B.E., M.SC., F.R.S.N.Z.; New Zealand professor of zoology, consultant and scientific writer; b. 1919, Pleasant Point; ed. Univ. of New Zealand; school teacher 1937–41, 1946–48; served with N.Z. armed forces in Middle East 1942–43; Asst. Lecturer Canterbury Univ. Coll. 1949–51, Lecturer, then Sr. Lecturer 1952–59, Prof. of Zoology and Head of Dept., Univ. of Canterbury 1958–78, Prof. of Zoology 1978–83, Prof. Emer. 1983–; Leader Chatham Island 1954 Expedition, mem. Royal Soc. of London Chile Expedition 1958–59, field expeditions to Snares Islands, Campbell Island and Auckland Islands, Dir. Univ. of Canterbury Antarctic Research Unit 1962–83, 12 field expeditions to McMurdo Sound region; mem. Freshwater Fisheries Advisory Council 1966–70, N.Z. Nat. Cttee. for UNESCO 1970–74, Nat. Research Advisory Council, Environment and Energy Cttee. 1973–77, N.Z. Nat. Cttee. for the Man and Biosphere Programme 1972–80; mem. Scientific Cttee. on Antarctic Research (SCAR) 1969–, Sec. 1974–78, Pres. 1978–84; mem. Special Cttee. on Oceanic Research (SCOR) 1971–75, Special Cttee. for Int. Biological Programme (SCIBP) 1965–72; Bd. mem. Int. Asscn. of Ecology (INTECOL) 1965–89, Sec. Gen. 1973–78, Pres. 1978–82; Foundation mem., Council mem. N.Z. Ecological Soc. 1952–54, N.Z. Marine Sciences Soc. 1961–64 (Pres. 1961–62); mem. N.Z. Limnological Soc., N.Z. Antarctic Soc., Ecological Soc. of America, A.A.A.S., Australian Marine Sciences Soc.; Fellows Councillor Royal Soc. of N.Z. 1970–76, Int. Sec. 1970–73; Hutton Medal, Royal Soc. of N.Z. 1979, Conservation Trophy, N.Z. Antarctic Soc. 1980, N.Z. Marine Sciences Soc. Award for Outstanding Contribution to Marine Science in N.Z. 1985, N.Z. Asscn. for the Advancement of Science, Sir Ernest Marsden Medal for Service to Science 1985. *Publications:* 6 books, 125 papers. *Address:* Department of Zoology, University of Canterbury, Private Bag 4800, Christchurch, New Zealand.

KNOX, Selby Albert Richard, PH.D., C.CHEM., F.R.S.C.; British professor of inorganic chemistry; b. 24 Sept. 1944, Newcastle-upon-Tyne; s. of George H. Knox and Elsie Knox; m. Julie D. Edwards 1979; one s. two d.; ed. Rutherford Grammar School, Newcastle upon Tyne and Univ. of Bristol; Research Fellow, Univ. of Calif. Los Angeles 1970–71; lecturer, Univ. of Bristol 1972–83, Reader 1983–90, Prof. of Inorganic Chem. 1990–96, Head of School of Chemistry 1992–, Alfred Capper Pass Prof. of Chemistry 1996–; Corday-Morgan Medal and Prize 1980; Royal Soc. of Chem. Award for Chem. of Noble Metals and their compounds 1986; Royal Soc. of Chem. Tilden Lecturer 1992–93. *Publications:* over 160 scientific papers in organometallic chemistry. *Leisure interests:* trout fishing, sailing, skiing. *Address:* School of Chemistry, University of Bristol, Bristol, BS8 1TS (Office); 50 Druid Stoke Avenue, Stoke Bishop, Bristol, BS9 1DQ, England (Home). *Telephone:* (0117) 928 8158 (Office); (0117) 9685397 (Home). *Fax:* (0117) 929 0376.

KNUDSEN, Conrad Calvert, J.D.; American company executive; b. 3 Oct. 1923, Tacoma, Wash.; s. of Conrad D. and Annabelle Callison Knudsen, m. Julia Lee Roderick 1950 (died 1990); three s. one d.; ed. Washington Univ. and Law School, Seattle, and Columbia Univ., New York, N.Y.; Partner, Bogle, Bogle & Gates law firm, Seattle 1951–60; Exec. Vice-Pres. and Dir. Aberdeen Plywood and Veneer Inc. 1961–63; Pres. and Dir. Evans Products Co. 1963–68; Sr. Vice-Pres. Weyerhaeuser Co. 1969–76; Dir. Rainier Nat. Bank, Rainier Bancorporation, Castle & Cooke Inc., Cascade Corpn., West Fraser Timber Co. Ltd., Safeco Corpn., Koninklijke Nederlandse Papierfabrieken N.V. 1969–80; Pres. and C.E.O. MacMillan Bloedel Ltd. Sept. 1976–80, Chair. and C.E.O. 1980–83, Vice-Chair. 1983–90, Dir. Emer.; mem. U.S. and Washington State Bar Asscns. *Address:* 602 36th Avenue, E. Seattle, WA 98112, U.S.A. (Home).

KNUSSEN, (Stuart) Oliver, C.B.E.; British composer and conductor; b. 12 June 1952, Glasgow; s. of Stuart Knussen and Ethelyn Jane Alexander; m. Susan Freedman 1972; one d.; ed. Watford Field School, Watford Boys Grammar School, Purcell School; pvt. composition study with John Lambert 1963–68; conducted first performance of his First Symphony with London Symphony Orchestra 1968; Fellowships to Berks. Music Center, Tanglewood, U.S.A. 1970, 1971, 1973; Caird Travelling Scholarship 1971; Composer-in-residence, Aspen Festival, U.S.A. 1976, Arnolfini Gallery, U.S.A. 1978; Instructor in Composition, Royal Coll. of Music 1977–82; Guest Teacher, Tanglewood 1981; Co-ordinator Contemporary Music Activities, Berkshire Music Center, Tanglewood 1986–90; Co-Artistic Dir. Aldeburgh Festival 1983–98; Composer-in-residence, Philharmonia Orchestra 1984–; guest conductor, London Sinfonietta, Philharmonia Orchestra and many other ensembles U.K. and abroad 1981–; Assoc. Guest Conductor BBC Symphony Orchestra 1989–; Dir. Almeida Ensemble 1986–; mem. Exec. Cttee., Soc. for Promotion of New Music 1978–85; mem. Leopold Stokowski Soc., Int. Alban Berg Soc., New York; Countess of Munster Awards 1964, 1965, 1967; Peter Stuyvesant Foundation Award 1965; Watney-Sargent Award for Young Conductors 1969; Margaret Grant Composition Prize (for Symphony No. 2), Tanglewood 1971; Koussevitzky Centennial Comm. 1974; BBC commission for Promenade Concerts 1979 (Symphony No. 3); Arts Council Bursaries 1979, 1981; winner, first Park Lane Group Composer Award (suite from Where the Wild Things Are) 1982; BBC commission for Glyndebourne Opera 1983. *Compositions include:* operas: Where the Wild Things Are 1979–81, Higglety Pigglety Pop! 1983–84; symphonies: No. 1 1966–67, No. 2 (soprano and small orchestra) 1970–71, No. 3 1973–79; other works: Concerto for Orchestra 1968–70, Ophelia Dances, Book I 1975; other works for chamber ensemble and for voice and ensemble, for orchestra and for piano. *Leisure interests:* cinema, foreign literature, record collecting, record producing. *Address:* c/o Faber Music Ltd., 3 Queen Square, London, WC1N 3AR, England.

KNUTH, Donald Ervin, M.S., PH.D.; American professor of computer science; b. 10 Jan. 1938, Milwaukee, Wis.; s. of Ervin Henry Knuth and Louise Marie (née Bohning) Knuth; m. Nancy Jill Carter 1961; one s. one d.; ed. Case Inst. of Tech., California Inst. of Tech.; Asst. Prof. Math. Calif. Inst. of Tech. 1963–66, Assoc. Prof. 1966–68; Prof. of Computer Science, Stanford Univ. 1968–77, Fletcher Jones Prof. of Computer Science 1977–89, Prof. of Art of Computer Programming 1990–93, Prof. Emer. 1993–; mem. N.A.S., Nat. Acad. of Eng.; Foreign mem. Acádemie Française; numerous hon. degrees, including (Paris) 1986, (Oxford) 1988, (St. Petersburg) 1992; Nat. Medal of Science 1979; Steele Prize, American Math. Soc. 1986; Franklin Medal, Franklin Inst. of Philadelphia 1988, Harvey Prize, Israel Inst. of Tech. 1995, Kyoto Prize 1996; numerous awards. *Publications:* The Art of Computer Programming, (Vol. 1) 1968, (Vol. 2) 1969, (Vol. 3) 1973, Surreal Numbers 1974, Mariages Stables 1976, Computers and Typesetting (5 vols.) 1986, Concrete Mathematics 1988, Mathematical Writing 1989, 3:16 Bible Texts Illuminated 1990, Literate Programming 1992. *Leisure interests:* piano and organ playing, browsing in libraries. *Address:* Computer Science Department, Stanford University, Stanford, CA 94305-2140, U.S.A. *Telephone:* 415-723-4367.

KOBAYASHI, Taiyu; Japanese company executive; b. 13 June 1912, Hyogo Prefecture; m. Nagae Sano 1938; two s.; ed. Kyoto Univ.; joined Fuji Electric Co. 1935; joined Fujitsu Ltd. 1935, Dir. 1964, Man. Dir. Nov. 1969, Exec. Dir. 1972, Exec. Vice-Pres. 1975, Pres. 1976–81, Chair 1981; Pres. Communications Industries Asscn. of Japan 1976–78; Pres. Japan Electronic Industry Devt. Asscn. 1979–; Chair. Eng. Research Asscn. of Opto-Electronics Applied System 1981–; Purple Ribbon Award with Medal of Honour, Blue Ribbon Award with Medal of Honour. *Leisure interests:* gardening, golf. *Address:* 674 Nitta Kannami-cho, Tagata-gun, Shizuoka, Japan (Home).

KÖBBEN, André J. F., PH.D.; Netherlands professor of cultural anthropology and administrator; b. 3 April 1925, 's-Hertogenbosch; m. Agatha M. van Vessem 1953; one s. two d.; ed. Municipal Gymnasium and Univ. of Amsterdam; Prof. of Cultural Anthropology, Univ. of Amsterdam 1955–76; Visiting Prof. Univ. of Pittsburgh 1972; Cleveringa Prof. Univ. of Leiden 1980–81; Prof. Erasmus Univ. 1981–90; Dir. Centre for the Study of Social Conflicts 1976–90; Curl Bequest Prize, Royal Anthropological Inst. 1952; mem. Royal Netherlands Acad. of Science 1975, Hon. mem. Anthropological Soc. 1986. *Publications:* Le planteur noir 1956, Van primitieven tot medeburgers 1964, Why exceptions? The logic of cross-cultural analysis 1967, De Weerbarstige Waarheid (The Stubborn Truth) 1991, Het Partiële Gelÿk (On Being Partially in the Right) 1992, Wetenschap as Amusement (Research as Amusement) 1993, Why Slavery? 1997, and many others. *Address:* Libellenveld 2, 2318 VG Leiden, Netherlands. *Telephone:* (071) 5215369.

KOBETS, Gen., Konstantin Ivanovich, D.SC.; Russian army officer; b. 16 July 1939, Kiev; m.; one s.; ed. Kiev Higher Mil. School of Telecommunications, Mil. Acad. of Telecommunications, U.S.S.R. Gen. Staff Mil. Acad.; mil. service 1959–; commdr. communications section, co., bn., deputy commdr. communications regt. 1959–72; regt. commdr. 1972–74; Commdr. signal troops of Odessa mil. command 1974–76; Deputy Commdr. signal troops of Baikal mil. command 1978–80, Commdr. 1980–82; Commdr. signal troops of Far East Mil. Command 1982–86; First Deputy Commdr. signal troops of U.S.S.R. Armed Forces 1986–87, Commdr., Deputy Head Gen. Staff 1987–91; People's Deputy of Russia 1989–91; Minister of Defence of Russian Fed., Chief Comm. analysing high command activities during coup d'etat Aug.–Nov. 1991; Chair. State Cttee. on Defence and Security, State Sec. of Defence, Chair. Cttee. on preparation and realization of mil. reform Sept.–Dec. 1991; Chief Mil. Inspector of Russian Fed., Chair. Mil. Legal Comm. of Russian Ministry of Defence; Deputy Minister of Defence, Chief of Mil. Inspection 1995–97; arrested, charged with corruption 1997. *Publications:* Putsch: Before and After, articles on mil. problems. *Address:* c/o Ministry of Defence, ul. Myasnitskaya 37, 103160 Moscow, Russia.

KOBZON, Iosif Davydovich; Russian singer and politician; b. 11 Sept. 1937, Chasov Yar, Ukraine, m. Nelly Kobzon; one s. one d.; ed. Moscow Gnessin Pedagogical Inst. of Music; army service 1956–59, soloist Ensemble of Dance and Song of Caucasian Mil. command 1957–59; soloist All-Union Radio and TV Co. 1959–62; soloist Moskonzert 1962–89; Artistic Dir. and Chair., Vocal and Variety Show Faculty Gnessin Inst. (now Acad.) of Music 1989–, Prof. 1992; soloist and Artistic Dir. Concert Co. Moskva; retd. from concert activity 1997; Pres. Jt. Stock Co. Moskva 1990–97; U.S.S.R. People's Deputy 1989–92; mem. State Duma (Parl.) 1997–98 (suspended membership in protest against anti-Semitic declarations by Communist deputies); People's Artist of U.S.S.R., Russia and Dagestan Autonomous Repub.; U.S.S.R. State Prize 1984. *Address:* State Duma, Okhotny Ryad 1, 103265 Moscow, Russia (Office). *Telephone:* 244 0558 (Home).

KOÇ, Rahmi M.; Turkish business executive; Chair. Koç Holdings A.S.; fmr. Pres. ICC. *Address:* Koç Holdings AS, Nakkaştepe Aziz Bey Sok. 1, 80207 Kuzguncuk, Istanbul, Turkey.

KOČÁRNIK, Ivan, C.SC.; Czech politician and business executive; b. 29 Nov. 1944, Třebonín, Kutna Hora Dist.; m.; two d.; ed. Prague Inst. of Econs.;

worked at Research Inst. of Financial and Credit System until 1985; Dir. Research Dept. Fed. Ministry of Finance 1985–89; Deputy Minister of Finance of Czechoslovakia 1990; mem. Civil Democratic Party (ODS); Vice-Premier and Minister of Finance of Czech Repub. 1992–97; Gov. World Bank 1992–93; Chair. Council of Econ. and Social Agreement 1992–97; mem. State Defence Council, Czech Repub. 1992; Gov. IBRD 1994–97; Chair. Bd. Czech Insurance Co. 1997–; Best Minister of Finance in 1994, awarded by magazine Central European 1995. *Leisure interests:* tennis, skiing, hiking, music. *Address:* Czech Insurance Company, Spálená 16, 110 00 Prague 1, Czech Republic. *Telephone:* (02) 672 22 411.

KOCH, Edward I., LL.B.; American politician, local government official and lawyer; b. 12 Dec. 1924, New York; s. of Louis Koch and Joyce Silpe; ed. City Coll. of New York and New York Univ. Law School; served Second World War in U.S. Army; admitted to New York bar 1949; sole practice law, New York 1949–64; Sr. partner Koch, Lankenau, Schwartz & Kovner 1965–69; mem. Council, New York 1967–68, Mayor 1978–90; partner Robinson, Silverman, Pearce, Aronsohn and Berman, New York 1990–; mem. U.S. House of Reps. from New York, 17th Dist. 1969–72, 18th District 1973–77; mem. House Appropriations Cttee.; Sec. New York Congressional Del.; Democratic District Leader, Greenwich Village 1963–65, mem. Village Ind. Democrats; Visiting Fellow, Urban Research Center, New York Univ. 1990–91; TV commentator for Fox 5; columnist New York Post 1990–; film critic for 4 newspapers; appears in film segment Oedipus Wrecks 1989. *Publications:* Mayor (autobiog.) 1984, Politics 1985, His Eminence and Hizzoner (with Cardinal J. O'Connor, q.v.) 1989, All the Best: Letters from a Feisty Mayor 1990, Citizen Koch 1991, Ed Koch on Everything 1994, Murder at City Hall 1995, Murder on Broadway 1996, Murder on 34th Street 1997. *Address:* Robinson, Silverman, Pearce, Aronsohn and Berman, 1290 Avenue of the Americas, New York, NY 10104, U.S.A.

KOCHARIAN, Robert Sedrakovich: Armenian politician; b. 31 Aug. 1954, Stepanakert; s. of Sedrack S. Kocharian and Enna A. Dhanian; m. Bella L. Kocharean; two s. one d.; ed. Yerevan Polytech. Inst.; engineer and electrotechnician Karabakh Silk Production Factory, Stepanakert 1981–87; concurrently sec. factory CP Cttee. 1987–89; one of founders Karabakh Movt.; Deputy to Armenian Supreme Council 1989–94; left CP 1989; after proclamation of "Nagorny-Karabakh Repub." in Azerbaijan 2 Sept. 1991 and Referendum 10 Dec. 1991 elected to Supreme Council "Nagorny-Karabakh Repub." in Azerbaijan; Chair. State Cttee. of Defence and leader of Repub. 1992–94; elected First Pres. of "Nagorny-Karabakh Repub." in Azerbaijan by Supreme Council 1994–; Prime Minister of Repub. of Armenia 1997–98, Pres. 1998–. *Leisure interests:* basketball, jazz. *Address:* House of Government, Marshal Bagramian prosp. 19, 375010 Yerevan, Armenia. *Telephone:* (2) 52-54-00; 52-02-04. *Fax:* (2) 15-11-52.

KOCHERGA, Anatoly Ivanovich; Ukrainian opera singer (bass); b. 9 July 1947, Vinnitsa; s. of Ivan Kocherga and Maria Kocherga; m. Lina Kocherga 1985; one d.; ed. Kiev Conservatoire; studied at La Scala, Milan; soloist with Shevchenko Opera and Ballet, Kiev 1972–, also Vienna Opera; Glinka Prize 1971, Tchaikovsky Prize 1974; *major roles include:* Boris Godunov, Galitsky (Borodin's Prince Igor), Don Basilio (Barber of Seville), Mephistopheles (Gounod's Faust), Don Carlos (Verdi), Don Juan (Mozart), Chowanschina (Mussorgsky), Dosiphey (Khovanshchina), Nilakanta (Lakwe); U.S.S.R. People's Artist 1983. *Leisure interest:* tennis. *Address:* Gogolevskaya 37, Korp. 2, Apt. 47, Kiev 254053, Ukraine.

KOCHERGIN, Eduard Stepanovich; Russian theatrical designer; b. 22 Sept. 1937, Leningrad; s. of Stepan Kochergin and Bronislava (née Odinets) Kochergina; m. Inna Gabai 1962; one s.; ed. Leningrad Theatre Art Inst., theatre production faculty (pupil of N. Akimov and T. Bruni); chief set designer in various Leningrad theatres 1960–; chief set-designer at Gorky (now Tovstonogov) Bolshoi Drama Theatre 1972; worked as set-designer, Maly Drama Theatre, and in Japan, U.S.A., Poland, Germany, Finland, Canada, France; Prof. Y.I. Repin Inst. of Painting 1983–; mem. Russian Acad. of Fine Arts 1991; State Prize 1974, 1978; three Golden and two Silver awards, int. exhbns. theatre design Novisad 1975, 1978, Prague 1975, 1979, 1987; Honoured Artist of Russia. *Leisure interest:* research in Russian pre-Christian culture and symbolism. *Address:* Tovstonogov Bolshoi Drama Theatre, Fontanka 65, 191023 St. Petersburg, Russia. *Telephone:* (812) 352 89 33 (Office); (812) 351 23 79 (Home). *Fax:* (812) 110 47 10.

KOCHETKOV, Nikolay Konstantinovich: Russian chemist; b. 18 May 1915, Moscow; s. of Konstantin Kochetkov and Marie Kochetkova; m. Dr. Vera Volodina 1945; one s. one d.; ed. M. V. Lomonosov Inst. of Light Chem. Tech.; Asst., Chemistry Dept. of Moscow Univ. 1945–52, Dozent 1952–56, Prof. 1956–60; Head of Dept. of Organic Synthesis, Inst. of Pharmacology 1953–60; Deputy Dir., Head of nucleic acids and carbohydrates laboratory, Inst. of Natural Products 1960–66; Dir., Head of carbohydrates laboratory, Zelinsky Inst. of organic chem. 1966–88, Hon. Dir. 1988–; Corresp. mem. U.S.S.R. (now Russian) Acad. of Medical Sciences 1957–; Corresp. mem. U.S.S.R. (now Russian) Acad. of Sciences 1960–79, mem. 1979–; mem. Soc. de Chimie 1972–, Polish Acad. of Sciences 1988; Haworth Medal (Royal Soc. of Chem.) 1989, Lenin Prize 1989, Nat. Prize of Demidov Foundation 1993; Order of Lenin, Hero of Socialist Labour, Lomonosov Great Gold Medal, Russian Acad. of Science 1995 and other decorations. *Publications:* Chemistry of Natural Products 1961, Chemistry of Carbohydrates 1967, Organic Chemistry of Nucleic Acids 1970, Radiation Chemistry of Sugars 1973, Carbohydrates in the Synthesis of Natural Products 1984, Synthesis of Polysaccharides 1995. *Address:* Zelinsky Institute of Organic Chemistry, Leninsky Prospekt 47, Moscow B-334, Russia. *Telephone:* (095) 137-61-48 (Office); 237-48-16 (Home). *Fax:* (095) 135-53-28.

KOCHI, Jay K., PH.D.; American professor of chemistry; b. 17 May 1927, Los Angeles; s. of Tsuruzo Kochi; m. Marion K. Kiyono 1961; one s. one d.; ed. Cornell and Iowa State Univs.; Instructor Harvard Univ. 1952–55; Nat. Inst. of Health Special Fellow, Univ. of Cambridge (U.K.) 1955–56; Shell Devt. Co. Emeryville, Calif. 1956–62; Case Western Univ., Cleveland, Ohio 1962–69; with Ind. Univ. 1969–84; Robert A. Welch Distinguished Prof. of Chem. Univ. of Houston, Tex. 1984–; chemical consultant 1964–; mem. N.A.S.; J. F. Norris Award, American Chem. Soc. 1981; A. C. Cope Scholar Award, American Chem. Soc. *Publications:* three books and more than 500 research papers. *Address:* Department of Chemistry, University of Houston, University Park, Houston, TX 77204-5641; 4372 Faculty Lane, Houston, TX 77004, U.S.A. (Home). *Telephone:* 713-749-7166 (Home).

KOCSIS, Zoltán; Hungarian pianist, conductor and composer; b. 30 May 1952, Budapest; s. of Ottó Kocsis and Mária Mátyás; m. 1st Adrienne Hauser 1986; one s. one d.; m. 2nd Erika Tóth 1997; one s.; ed. Budapest Music Acad. (under Pál Kadosa); has appeared with Berlin Philharmonic Orchestra, and performed in Germany, U.S.S.R., Austria and Czechoslovakia 1971; toured U.S.A. together with Dezsö Ranki (q.v.) and Budapest Symphony Orchestra (under George Lehel) 1971; recitals in Netherlands, Paris, London and Ireland 1972; concerts in Norway, with Svyatoslav Richter (q.v.) in France and Austria, with Claudio Abbado (q.v.) and London Symphony Orchestra and at BBC Promenade Concerts in London, and Festival Estival, Paris 1977, Edin. Festival 1978; Asst. Prof. Music Acad. Budapest 1976–79, Prof. 1979–; Producer of Archive Section of Hungaroton (record co.); Co-founder, Artistic Co-dir. Budapest Festival Orchestra 1983–96; Music Dir. Hungarian Nat. Philharmonic Orchestra 1998–; First Prize, Beethoven Piano Competition, Hungarian Radio and Television 1970, Liszt Prize 2nd Degree 1973, Kossuth Prize; Merited Artist's title 1984. *Publications:* Miscellaneous publs., Arrangements for Piano and 2 Pianos, etc. *Leisure interest:* photography. *Address:* H-1126 Budapest, Nárcisz u. 29; Hungarian National Philharmonic Orchestra, 1051 Budapest V, Vörösmarty tér I, Hungary. *Telephone:* (1) 327-4375. *Fax:* (1) 318-0162.

KODAMANOĞLU, Nuri, M.SC.; Turkish politician; b. 16 Aug. 1923, Ulukişla-Niğde; s. of Fazil and Hatice Kodamanoğlu; m. Ayten Unal Kodamanoğlu 1951; ed. Istanbul Univ.; fmr. civil servant, Ministry of Educ.; later Under-Sec. Ministry of Educ.; Deputy to Grand Nat. Assembly; Minister of Energy and Natural Resources 1972; Adviser to the Prime Ministry 1988–; Chief Adviser to the Pres. 1991–; mem. Business Admin. Inst., Faculty of Political Science, Univ. of Ankara; mem. Ataturk Research Centre; mem. Bd. of Dirs. Turkish Petroleum Corpn.; mem. Consultative Cttee. Asscn. of Turkish Parliamentarians 1995–; Consultant, Asscn. of Turkish Chambers of Commerce, Chambers of Ind. and Exchange. *Publications:* Principles of New Education 1954, Education in Turkey 1963; various articles and reports. *Leisure interests:* handicrafts, gardening. *Address:* Bükreş Sokak No. 6 Daire 8, Çankaya, 06680 Ankara, Turkey. *Telephone:* (312) 427-15-15.

KODEŠ, Jan; Czech tennis player; b. 1 March 1946, Prague; s. of Jan Kodeš and Vlasta Richterová-Kodešová; m. 1st Lenka Rösslerová-Kodešová 1967 (divorced 1988); one s. one d.; m. 2nd Martina Schlonzova; one d.; ed. Coll. of Econs., Prague; Wimbledon Singles Champion 1973, French Open Singles Champion 1970 and 1971, runner-up U.S. Championships 1971, 1973, Italian Championships 1970, 1971, 1972; mem. Czechoslovak Davis Cup Team 1964–80, incl. 1975 (runners-up), 1980 (winners), non-playing Capt. 1982–87; Czechoslovak No. 1 player 1966–77; Bd. mem. Czechoslovak Tennis Asscn. (CTA), 1982–98; mem. ETA Men's Cttee. 1990–93; mem. ITF Davis Cup European Cttee. 1997–; Founder and Tournament Dir. Czech Open, Prague 1982–98; Pres. Czech Tennis Asscn. 1994–98; Dir. Czechoslovak Tennis Centre 1986–92; owner KP Fashion Group sro 1994–; Meritorious Master of Sports 1971, State Decoration for Outstanding Work 1973, ITF Award for Services to the Game 1988, Int. Tennis Hall of Fame 1990. *Leisure interests:* football, other sports, stamp collecting, films. *Address:* Na Beránce 20, Prague 6, 160.00 Czech Republic. *Telephone:* (2) 3332-2714. *Fax:* (2) 3332-1535.

KODJO, Edem; Togolese politician and administrator; b. 23 May 1938, Sokodé; m. 1962; two s. two d.; ed. Coll. Saint Joseph, Univ. of Rennes, Ecole Nat. d'Administration, Paris; worked as administrator for Office de Radiodiffusion-Télévision Française (ORTF) 1964–67; returned to Togo 1967; Sec.-Gen., Ministry of Finance, Economy and Planning 1967–72; Administrator, Banque Centrale des Etats de l'Afrique de l'Ouest 1967–76, Pres. of Admin. Council 1973–76; Dir.-Gen. Société Nat. d'Investissement 1972–73; Minister of Finance and Economy 1973–76, of Foreign Affairs 1976–77, of Foreign Affairs and Co-operation 1977–78; Sec.-Gen. of the OAU 1978–84; Assoc. Prof. Sorbonne, Paris 1985–90; Prime Minister of Togo 1994–96; Founder and Chair. Pan-African Inst. of Int. Relations (IPRI); Ed. Afrique 2000; mem. Rassemblement du Peuple Togolaise (RPT), RPT Political Bureau (Sec.-Gen. 1967–71); leader Togolese Union for Democracy (UTD); mem. Club of Rome; Gov. for Togo, IMF 1973–76; fmr. Chair. OAU Council of Ministers, Afro-Arab Perm. Comm. on Co-operation, OAU Cttee. of Ten; Dr. h.c. (Univ. of Bordeaux I); Commdr., Ordre du Mono, Togo, Univ. of Sorbonne Medal, Officier, Légion d'honneur; decorations from many African countries. *Address:* c/o Office of the Prime Minister, B.P. 5618, Lomé, Togo.

KOENIG, Pierre, B.ARCH.; American architect; b. 17 Oct. 1925, San Francisco; s. of Harold Koenig and Blanche Chige; m. 1st Sue Thompson 1953 (divorced 1959); one s.; m. 2nd Gaile Carson 1960 (divorced 1975); one s.; m. 3rd Gloria Kaufman 1984; ed. Univ. of Utah, Pasadena City Coll. and Univ. of Southern Calif.; opened own architectural office, Glendale, Calif. 1952; Instr. Architectural Design Studio, Univ. of S. Calif. 1962–69, Assoc. Prof. of Architecture 1970–; Dir. Chemehuevi Reservation Comprehensive Planning Program 1971–76; visiting lecturer at numerous univs., insts. etc.; designed Case Study Houses No. 21 and 22 (Arts and Architecture Magazine Case Study House Program 1959–60); work exhibited at Whitney Museum 1985–86, Museum of Contemporary Art, Los Angeles 1989–90 and in many other architectural exhbns.; Fellow A.I.A.; prizewinner, São Paulo Bienal 1957; Architectural League of N.Y. Award 1957; American Inst. of Steel Award 1963; numerous awards from American Inst. of Architects etc. *Publications:* The Chemehuevi Project (with others) 1971, The Chemehuevi Future 1973, This Is Our Land 1974, Remaking the Homeland 1975, The Chemehuevi Today 1976, Graphic Communication 1977, Prefabricated Building Systems. *Leisure interests:* music, drawing, photography, running. *Address:* 12221 Dorothy Street, Los Angeles, CA 90049, U.S.A. *Telephone:* (310) 826-1414.

KOEPP, David; American screenplay writer; wrote screenplay for Apartment Zero 1989, Bad Influence 1990 (with Martin Donovan), Toy Soldiers (with Daniel Petrie, Jr) 1991, Death Becomes Her (with Martin Donovan) 1992, Jurassic Park (with Michael Crichton) 1993, Carlito's Way 1993, The Paper (with Stephen Koepp) 1994, The Shadow 1994. *Address:* U.T.A., 9560 Wilshire Blvd., Fl. 5, Beverly Hills, CA 90212, U.S.A.

KOFFIGOH, Joseph Kokou; Togolese politician; b. 1948, Kpele Dafo; m.; three s. one d.; ed. Univs. of Abidjan and Poitiers, France; called to the Bar, Poitiers, France; joined Viale Chambers, Togo; f. Togo Bar Asscn. 1980, Pres. 1990; founder mem. Observatoire panafricain de la démocratie (OPAD) 1991, Ligue togolaise des droits de l'homme 1990; founder mem. and Vice-Pres. FAR (asscn. for reform); Vice-Pres. Nat. Sovereign Conf.; Prime Minister of Togo 1991–94, also Minister of Defence; Pres. Coordination nat. des forces nouvelles. *Leisure interests:* lawn tennis, basketball, shadow-boxing. *Address:* c/o Coordination nat. des forces nouvelles, Lomé, Togo.

KOFLER, Georg; German (b. Italian) television executive; b. 26 April 1957, Brunico, Italy; m. José Kofler; two s.; fmrly. mem. staff Austrian state broadcasting co. Österreichischer Rundfunk (ORF); with Eureka TV 1987–89; co-founder (with Gerhard Ackermans and Thomas Kirch) and Chair. Pro 7 TV network 1989–. *Address:* Medienallee 7, 85767 Unterföhring, Germany. *Telephone:* (089) 95070.

KOGAN, Pavel Leonidovich; Russian violinist and conductor; b. 6 June 1952, Moscow; s. of Leonid Kogan and Elizaveta Gilels; m. (divorced); one s.; ed. Moscow State Conservatory; studied conducting in Leningrad with I. Mussin and in Moscow with Leo Ginzburg; performances 1970–; winner Int. Jean Sibelius Competition Helsinki, 1970, performed in maj. concert halls of Europe, America and Japan as soloist, also in ensembles with parents and pianist Nina Kogan (sister); Conductor Moscow Chamber Orchestra 1980–83; performed with symphony orchestras in U.S.S.R. (Russia), U.S.A. and countries of Europe and Asia since 1983; Chief Conductor and Music Dir. Zagreb Philharmonic 1988–90, Moscow State Academic Symphony Orchestra 1988–; Prin. Guest Conductor, Utah Symphony Orchestra, U.S.A. 1998–(99). *Leisure interests:* automobiles. *Address:* Bryusov per. 8/10, Apt. 103009 Moscow, Russia (Home). *Telephone:* 292 1395 (Home).

KOGAN, Richard Jay, M.B.A.; American business executive; b. 6 June 1941, New York; ed. City Coll. of City Univ. of New York and Stern School of Business, New York Univ.; fmr. Pres. U.S. Pharmaceuticals Div. Ciba-Geigy Corpn.; Exec. Vice-Pres. Pharmaceutical Operations, Schering-Plough Corpn. 1982–86, Pres. and C.O.O. 1986–95, Pres. and C.E.O. 1996–; mem. Bd. Dirs. Atlantic Mutual Cos., Colgate-Palmolive Co., Bank of New York Co. Inc.; mem. Council on Foreign Relations. *Address:* Schering-Plough Corporation, One Giralda Farms, Madison, NJ 07940, U.S.A. *Telephone:* (201) 822-7000. *Fax:* (201) 822-7000.

KOGURE, Gohei, B.ECONS.; Japanese business executive; b. 19 Sept. 1924, Gunma Pref.; s. of Goro Kogure and Hiro Kogure; m. Noriko Shigehara 1951; one s. one d.; ed. Univ. of Tokyo; joined Dentsu Inc. 1947, Exec. Dir. 1971–73, Man. Dir. 1973–79, Sr. Man. Dir. 1979–85, Pres. and C.E.O. 1985–93, Chair. 1993–; mem. Bd. of Dirs., Keidranen (Fed. of Econ. Orgs.) 1985–; Pres. Japan Advertising Agencies Asscn. 1987–; Trustee Keizai Doyukai (Japan Asscn. of Corporate Execs.); mem. Exec. Bd. and Council, Japan Nat. Cttee. of ICC; World Vice-Pres. and Area Dir. Asia/Pacific, Int. Advertising Asscn.; Kt. Commdr. Order of St. Sylvester Pope with Star (Vatican); All Japan Advertising Award 1989. *Leisure interests:* golf, haiku. *Address:* Dentsu Inc., 11 Tsukiji 1-chome, Chuo-ku, Tokyo 104 (Office); 3-4-14 Higashi Kaigan Kita, Chigasaki-shi, Kanagawa Pref. 253, Japan (Home). *Telephone:* 03-5551-5000 (Office); 0467-82-8826 (Home).

KOH, Kun, M.S.; Korean politician; b. 2 Jan. 1938, Okgu-gun, Jeonbuk-do; m.; three s.; ed. Kyung Ki High School, Seoul Nat. Univ.; Pres. Gen. Students Asscn. Seoul Nat. Univ. 1959; Asst. Jr. Official Ministry of Home Affairs 1962–65, Asst. Dir. Planning Office 1965–68; Dir. Interior Dept. Jeonbuk Prov. 1968–71; Commr. New Village Movt. 1971–73; Vice-Gov. Kangwon Prov. 1973; Gov. of Jeonnam Prov. 1975–79; Chief Sec. of Political Affairs, Chong Wa Dae (The Blue House); Chief Adviser Korea Research Inst. for Human Settlement 1980; Minister of Transportation 1980–81, of Agric. and Marine Affairs 1981–82; Visiting Fellow, Harvard Univ. 1983; Visiting Prof. M.I.T. 1984; mem. 12th Nat. Ass. 1985–88; Minister of Home Affairs 1987; Dir. Local Admin. Bureau 1973–75; Mayor Seoul Metropolitan Govt. 1988–90; Pres. Myong Ji Univ. 1994–97; Co-Pres. Korea Fed. for Environment Movt. 1996–97; Prime Minister of S. Korea 1997–98; Mayor of Seoul 1998–; Hon. LL.D. (Won Kwang Univ.) 1992. *Address:* 31 Taepyung-no 1ga, Chung-gu, Seoul 100-744, Korea. *Telephone:* 82-2-731-6351. *Fax:* 82-2-774-2122.

KOH, Tommy Thong Bee, LL.D.; Singaporean diplomatist and law professor; b. 12 Nov. 1937, Singapore; s. of Koh Han Kok and Tsai Ying; m. Siew Aing 1967; two s.; ed. Univ. of Singapore, and Harvard and Cambridge Univs.; Asst. lecturer, Univ. of Singapore 1962–64, lecturer 1964–71; Sub-Dean, Faculty of Law, Univ. of Singapore 1965–67, Vice-Dean 1967–68; Perm. Rep. of Singapore to UN 1968–71, concurrently High Commr. to Canada 1969–71; Assoc. Prof. of Law and Dean, Faculty of Law, Singapore Univ. 1971–74; Perm. Rep. to UN, (also accred. to Canada and Mexico) 1974–84; Amb. to U.S.A. 1984–90; Amb.-at-Large, Ministry of Foreign Affairs 1990–; Dir. Inst. of Policy Studies 1990–97; Exec. Dir. Asia-Europe Foundation 1997–; Pres. Third UN Law of the Sea Conf. (Chair. Singapore Del. to Conf.) 1981–82; Chair. Preparatory Cttee., Chair. Main Cttee. UN Conf. on Environment and Devt. 1990–92; UN Sec.-Gen.'s Special Envoy to Russian Fed., Latvia, Lithuania and Estonia Aug.–Sept. 1993; Chair. Nat. Arts Council 1991–96; Hon. LL.D. (Yale) 1984; Adrian Clarke Memorial Medal 1961, Leow Chia Heng Prize 1961, Public Service Star 1971, Meritorious Service Medal 1979, Wolfgang Friedman Award 1984, Jackson H. Ralston Prize 1985, Annual Award of the Asia Soc., New York, 1985, Int. Service Award, Fletcher School of Law and Diplomacy, Tufts Univ., U.S.A. 1987, Jit Trainor Award for Distinction in Diplomacy, Georgetown Univ., U.S.A. 1987, Elizabeth Haub Prize, Univ. of Brussels and Int. Council on Environmental Law 1997; Fok Ying Tung Southeast Asia Prize, Hong Kong 1998; Distinguished Service Order Award 1990, Commdr. Order of the Golden Ark, The Netherlands 1993, Grand Cross of Order of Bernardo O'Higgins, Chile 1997. *Publications:* United States and East Asia: Conflict and Cooperation 1995, The Quest for World Order: Perspectives of a Pragmatic Idealist 1998. *Leisure interests:* sport, reading, music. *Address:* c/o Ministry of Foreign Affairs, 250 North Bridge Road, # 39-00 Raffles City Tower, Singapore 179101. *Telephone:* 3305600. *Fax:* 3381908.

KOHÁK, Erazim, PH.D.; Czech philosopher; b. 21 May 1933, Prague; m. 3rd Dorothy Kohák; three d. from 1st m.; ed. Yale Univ.; emigrated with parents to U.S.A. 1948; lecturer Univ. of Boston 1969–72, Prof. 1972–90; returned to Czechoslovakia 1990; Prof. Charles Univ., Prague 1990–; mem. Metaphysical Soc. of America, American Theological Soc.; Josef Vavroušek Prize for Ecology 1997; Medal for Merit (Czech Repub.) 1998. *Publications include:* The Embers and the Stars, Masaryk on Marx, Ideas and Experience, The Czech Question and the Ideal of Humanity in the Time of Normalisation, Victors and Vanquished 1978, Jan Patočka: His Thought and Work 1989, Human Beings: The Good and the Evil 1993; various articles in philosophical journals. *Leisure interests:* hiking, railways, ecology. *Address:* Charles University, Ovocný trh 5, 110 00 Prague 1, Czech Republic. *Telephone:* (24) 49-11-11. *Fax:* (24) 22-94-87.

KOHL, Helmut, DR.PHIL.; German politician; b. 3 April 1930, Ludwigshafen; s. of Hans and Cäcilie (née Schnur) Kohl; m. Hannelore Renner 1960; two s.; ed. Univs. of Frankfurt and Heidelberg; Mem. of man. of an industrial union 1959; Chair. Christian Democrat Party (CDU), Rhineland-Palatinate 1966–73, Deputy Chair. CDU Deutschlands 1969–73, Chair. 1973–98; Minister-Pres. Rhineland-Palatinate 1969–76; Leader of the Opposition in the Bundestag 1976–82; Fed. Chancellor, Fed. Repub. of Germany 1982–98; mem. Bundestag 1998; Dr. h.c. (Cambridge) 1998, Prof. h.c. (Tongji Univ., China) 1993; numerous hon. degrees; Karlspreis (Aachen) 1988, 1991; Jawarhal Nehru Award 1990; Konrad Adenauer Prize 1994, Leo Baeck Prize 1996; Grosses Bundesverdienstkreuz 1979, Bundesverdienstkreuz 1998, Grand Cross of Dutch Lion 1999, Grand Cross, Order of Merit. *Leisure interests:* reading, music, walking and swimming. *Address:* Marbacher Strasse 11, 67071 Ludwigshafen/Rhein-Oggersheim, Germany (Home).

KÖHLER, Horst, DR. RER. POL.; German banker; b. 22 Feb. 1943, Skierbieszow, Poland; m.; two c.; Sec. of State, Ministry of Finance, Bonn until 1993; Pres. Deutsche Sparkassen-und-Giroverband, Bonn 1993–; mem. Advisory Bd. Treuhandanstalt; Deputy German Gov. IBRD and European Bank for Reconstruction and Devt. (EBRD), Pres. EBRD 1998–; Pres. European Asscn. of Savings Banks 1994–. *Address:* European Bank for Reconstruction and Development, 1 Exchange Square, London, EC2A 2EH, England.

KOHLHAUSSEN, Martin; German banker; b. 6 Nov. 1935, Marburg/Lahn; m.; three c.; ed. Univs. of Frankfurt-am-Main, Freiburg and Marburg; bank training, Deutsche Bank, Frankfurt-am-Main; Man. Lloyds Bank, Frankfurt-am-Main 1974–76; Man. Tokyo Br. Westdeutsche Landesbank Girozentrale 1976–78, New York Br. 1979–81; mem. Bd. Man. Dirs. Commerzbank AG 1982–, Chair. 1991–; Pres. Bundesverband deutscher Banken 1997–. *Address:* Commerzbank AG, Kaiserplatz, 60261 Frankfurt-am-Main, Germany. *Telephone:* (069) 1362-0.

KOHLMEY, Gunther, DR.RER.POL.; German professor of economics; b. 27 July 1913, Berlin; m. Gerda Dörfel 1951; one d.; ed. Berlin and Freiburg im

Breisgau; library asst., Univ. of Berlin 1937–39, Prof. of Econs. 1949; Dean of Econ. Faculty, Acad. of Admin. 1948–53; Dir. of Econ. Inst., Acad. of Sciences, G.D.R. 1953–58, Head of Staff Int. Econs. Dept. 1958–73, Chair. Nat. Cttee. of Econ. Sciences 1979–81; Co-Ed. Utopie Kreativ (journal) 1992–; mem. Acad. of Sciences 1964; Hon. mem. Hungarian Acad. of Sciences 1979; Dr. h.c. 1978; Nat. Prize 1955; Golden State Awards 1978, 1983. *Publications include:* several papers for Int. Econ. Assen. and workshops of East-West Steering Cttee.; (in German) The Democratic World Market 1954, The Monetary System of G.D.R. 1958, Karl Marx's Theory of International Values 1962, National Productivity, Dynamic Productions, International Division of Labour 1965, Planning as Regulation and Control 1968, Socialization and Integration 1973, Ed. and co-translator Production of Commodities by Means of Commodities (P. Sraffa) 1968. *Leisure interests:* literature, fine arts. *Address:* Kleine Homeyerstr. 2A, 13156 Berlin, Germany.

KOHN, Walter, PH.D.; American professor of physics; b. 9 March 1923, Vienna, Austria; s. of Solomon Kohn and Gusti Rappaport; m. 1st Lois Mary Adams 1948 (divorced); three d.; 2nd Mara Schiff 1978; ed. Toronto and Harvard Univs.; served with Canadian Infantry 1944–45; Instructor Harvard Univ. 1948–50; Asst. Prof., Assoc. Prof., then Prof., Carnegie Inst. of Tech. 1950–59; Prof. Univ. of Calif. at San Diego 1960–79, Chair. Dept. of Physics 1961–63, Dir. Inst. for Theoretical Physics July 1979–84; Prof. of Physics, Univ. of Calif. at Santa Barbara 1984–91, Prof. Emer. and Research Prof. 1991–, Research Physicist Centre for Quantized Electronic Structures 1991–; mem. revision cttee. reactor div. NIST, Md. 1994–; Visiting Prof., Univs. of Mich. and Pa. 1957–58, Imperial Coll. of Science and Tech. London 1960; Nat. Research Council Fellow, Inst. of Theoretical Physics, Copenhagen 1951–52; Guggenheim Fellow and Visiting Prof. Ecole Normale Supérieure Paris 1963–64; Nat. Science Foundation Sr. Postdoctoral Fellow Univ. of Paris 1967; Fellow A.A.A.S.; Councillor-at-Large, American Physical Soc. 1968–72; Visiting Prof. Hebrew Univ., Jerusalem 1970; Fellow American Acad. of Arts and Sciences; mem. Int. Acad. of Quantum Molecular Sciences; mem. N.A.S.; Hon. LL.D. (Toronto) 1967; Hon. D.Sc. (Univ. of Paris) 1980, (Queen's Univ., Canada) 1986, Hon. D.Phil. (Brandeis Univ.) 1981; (Hebrew Univ. of Jerusalem) 1981; Oliver E. Buckley Prize in Solid State Physics 1960; Davisson-Germer Prize in Surface Physics 1977, Nat. Medal of Science 1988, Feenberg Medal 1991, shared Nobel Prize for Chemistry 1998. *Publications:* 200 scientific articles 1945–92. *Leisure interests:* flute, reading, sports. *Address:* Dept. of Physics, University of California, Santa Barbara, CA 93106, U.S.A. *Telephone:* (805) 893-3061.

KOHONEN, Teuvo Kalevi, DR.ENG.; Finnish physicist; b. 11 July 1934, Lauritsala; s. of Väinö Kohonen and Tyyne E. Koivunen; m. Elvi Anneli Trast 1959; two s. two d.; ed. Helsinki Univ. of Tech.; Teaching Asst. in Physics, Helsinki Univ. of Tech. 1957–59; Research Assoc. Finnish Atomic Energy Comm. 1959–62; Asst. Prof. in Physics, Helsinki Univ. of Tech. 1963–65, Prof. of Tech. Physics 1965–93; on leave as Visiting Prof. Univ. of Washington, Seattle 1968–69; Research Prof. Acad. of Finland 1975–78, 1980–; Dr. h.c. (Univ. of York, Åbo Akademi, Univ. of Dortmund); Eemil Aaltonen Prize 1983; Cultural Prize, Finnish Commercial TV (MTV) 1984, I.E.E.E. Neural Networks Pioneer Award 1991, Int. Neural Network Soc. Lifetime Achievement Award 1992, Finnish Cultural Foundation Prize 1994, Tech. Achievement Award, I.E.E.E. Signal Processing Soc. 1995, King-Sun Fu Prize, Int. Assen. for Pattern Recognition 1996, Centennial Prize, Finnish Assen. of Grad. Engineers (TEK) 1996; Commdr. Order of Lion of Finland; Kt., Order of White Rose of Finland. *Publications:* Digital Circuits and Devices 1972, Associative Memory: A System Theoretical Approach 1977, Content-Addressable Memories 1982, Self-Organization and Associative Memory 1984, Self-Organizing Maps 1995. *Leisure interests:* philosophy of music, literature. *Address:* Helsinki University of Technology, Laboratory of Computer and Information Science, Rakentajanaukio 2 C, 02150 Espoo, Finland. *Telephone:* (0) 4513268.

KOIRALA, Girija Prasad; Nepalese politician; fmr. Gen. Sec. Nepal Congress Party (NCP); Prime Minister of Nepal, also responsible for Defence, Foreign Affairs and Royal Palace Affairs 1991–94; Prime Minister of Nepal April 1998–; Minister of Royal Palace Affairs, Defence and Foreign Affairs, numerous other portfolios. *Address:* Office of the Prime Minister, Central Secretariat, Singh Durbar, Kathmandu, Nepal.

KOIRALA, Matrika Prasad; Nepalese politician and diplomatist; b. 1 Jan. 1912; ed. Banares and Patna, India; fmr. Pres. Nepali Congress Party; Prime Minister and Minister of Gen. Admin. and Foreign Affairs 1951–52, 1953–55; nominated to Upper House of Parl.; Amb. to U.S. 1962–64; Perm. Rep. to UN 1962–64; fmrly. exiled in India; Pres. Nat. People's Council 1992–94.

KOIVISTO, Mauno Henrik, PH.D.; Finnish politician; b. 25 Nov. 1923, Turku; s. of Juho and Hymni Sofia (née Eskola) Koivisto; m. Taimi Tellervo Kankaanranta 1952; one d.; ed. Turku University; Man. Dir. Helsinki Workers' Savings Bank 1959–67; Gov. Bank of Finland 1968–82; Minister of Finance 1966–67; Prime Minister 1968–70, 1979–82; Minister of Finance and Deputy Prime Minister Feb.-Sept. 1972; Pres. of Finland 1982–94; Chair. Bd. of Postipankki 1970–82, Mortgage Bank of Finland Ltd. 1971–82, Bd. of Admin. of Co-operative Soc. ELANTO 1966–82; mem. Bd. of Admin. of Co-operative Union KK 1964–82; Gov. for Finland in the Int. Bank for Reconstruction and Devt. 1966–69; Gov. for Finland IMF 1970–79. *Publications:* Sosiaaliset suhteet Turun satamassa (doctoral thesis) 1956, Landmarks: Finland in the World 1985, Foreign Policy Standpoints 1985–92: Finland and Europe 1992, Witness to History 1997; nine books on econs. and social politics. *Leisure interest:* volleyball. *Address:* c/o Presidential Palace, Helsinki, Finland.

KOIVULEHTO, Jorma Juhani, PH.D.; Finnish professor of Germanic philology; b. 12 Oct. 1934, Tampere; m. Marja-Liisa Pakarinen 1963; one s. one d.; ed. Univ. of Helsinki and German Dialect Research Centre of Marburg/Lahn, Fed. Repub. of Germany; Assoc. Prof. of Germanic Philology, Univ. of Helsinki 1973–83, Prof. 1983–; Research Prof., Acad. of Finland 1988–93; mem. Finnish Acad. of Sciences; corresp. mem. Akad. der Wissenschaften, Gottingen, Österreichische Akad. der Wissenschaften. *Publications include:* 'Jäten' in deutschen Mundarten 1971, Idg. Laryngale und die finnisch-ugrische Evidenz 1988, Uralische Evidenz für die Laryngaltheorie 1991, Indogermanisch-Uralisch: Lehnbezie-hungen oder (auch) Urverwandtschaft? 1994. *Address:* University of Helsinki, Germanic Institute, Hallituskatu 11, 00100 Helsinki (Office); Sallatunturintie 1 D 24, 00970 Helsinki, Finland (Home). *Telephone:* (0) 1912578 (Office); 326081 (Home). *Fax:* (0) 1913069.

KOIZUMI, Jun'ichiro; Japanese politician; mem. House of Reps. from Kanagawa; fmr. Parl. Vice-Minister of Finance, and of Health and Welfare; Minister of Posts and Telecommunications 1992–93; Chair. House of Reps. Finance Cttee.; mem. Mitsuzuka Faction of LDP; Minister of Health and Welfare 1996–98. *Address:* c/o Ministry of Health and Welfare, 1-2-2 Kasumigaseki, Chiyoda-ku, Tokyo 100, Japan.

KOJIMA, Kiyoshi, PH.D.; Japanese economist; b. 22 May 1920, Nagoya; m. Keiko Kojima 1947; ed. Tokyo Univ. of Commerce and Econs., Leeds Univ. (U.K.) and Princeton Univ. (U.S.A.); Asst. Prof. of Int. Econs., Hitotsubashi Univ. 1945–60, Prof. 1960–84, Emer. Prof. 1984–; Secr. (Dir.) for UN Conf. on Trade and Devt. 1963; Prof. Int. Christian Univ. 1984–91, Surugadai Univ. 1991–97; mem. Science Council of Japan 1985; British Council Scholarship 1952–53, Rockefeller Foundation Fellowship 1953–55. *Publications:* (in Japanese): Theory of Foreign Trade 1950, Japan's Economic Development and Trade 1958, Japan in Trade Expansion for Developing Countries 1964 (in English), Japan and a Pacific Free Trade Area 1971, Japan and a New World Economic Order 1977, Direct Foreign Investment 1978, Japanese Direct Investment Abroad 1990, Trade, Investment and Pacific Economic Integration 1996; Ed. Papers and Proceedings of a Conference on Pacific Trade and Development 1968, 1969, 1973; also articles in English on int. trade. *Leisure interests:* golf, Noh (Utai). *Address:* 3-24-10 Maehara-cho, Koganei-shi, Tokyo, Japan. *Telephone:* 042-381-1041.

KOK, Wim; Netherlands politician; b. 29 Sept. 1938; ed. Netherlands School of Int. Business; Adviser to Bldg. Workers Union 1961–67, Sec. 1967–69; mem. Exec. Bd. of Netherlands Fed. of Trade Unions 1969–73, Chair. (later renamed Confed. Netherlands Trade Unions Movt.) 1973–85; Chair., European Trade Union Confed. 1979–82; mem. Parl. 1986–, Party Leader Labour Party 1986–; Deputy Prime Minister and Minister of Finance 1989–94; Prime Minister of the Netherlands 1994–. *Address:* Office of the Prime Minister, Binnenhof 20, P.O. Box 20001, 2500 EA The Hague, Netherlands.

KOKOSHIN, Andrei Afanasievich, D.HIS.SC.; Russian government official; b. 26 Oct. 1945; m.; two d.; ed. Bauman Moscow Higher Tech. Univ.; mem. CPSU 1968–90; scientific researcher, Head of Dept., Deputy Dir. Inst. of U.S.A. and Canada Acad. of Sciences 1974–90; First Deputy Minister of Defence 1992–97; Chair. Interagency Cttee. on Defence Security, Security Council of the Russian Fed. 1993–97; mem. Govt. Council on Industrial Policy 1993–; mem. Interagency Governmental Comm. on Creation of Industrial Stock Cos. and Industrial-Financial Groups 1993–96; mem. Interagency Comm. on the Promotion of Industrial Exports 1993–96; Sec. Council of Defence of Russian Fed., Asst. to Pres. of Russian Fed. 1997–98; Sec. Security Council of Russian Fed. March–Oct. 1998; mem. Org. Bd. Otechectvo (Fatherland) political movt. 1998–; Hon. Chair. Russian Rugby Football League 1992–; mem. Russian Acad. of Social Sciences 1993; mem. Russian Acad. of Artillery and Rocket Science and Eng. 1993–; *Publications:* 12 books (6 as co-author) on nat. security, int. affairs, Russian nat. industrial policy and econs. including Forecasting and Foreign Policy 1975–, The USA in the System of International Relations in the 1980s 1984–, Weapons in Space: Security Dilemma 1986, National Industrial Policy of Russia 1992. *Address:* c/o Council of Defence, Office of the President, Kremlin, korp. 14v Moscow, Russia. *Telephone:* (095) 910-06-67 (Office).

KOKOV, Valery Mukhamedovich, CAND.ECON.SC.; Russian politician; b. 18 Oct. 1941, Tyrnauz; s. of Mukhammed Kambotovich Kokov and Zamirat Akhmedovna Kokova; m. Violetta Taubievna Oshnokova 1968; one s. one d.; ed. Kabardino-Balkarian Univ., Higher School of Cen. CP Cttee. in Rostov; chief agronomist in kolkhoz 1964–66; postgrad. student All-Union Research Inst. of Econ. of Agric. 1966–70; sr. economist, head of div. Ministry of Agric. Kabardino-Balkar Autonomous Repub., dir. of sovkhoz Leskensky 1970–74; First Sec. Urvansk Regional CP Cttee. 1974–83; Chair. State Cttee. on Material-Tech. Provision of the Repub. 1983–85; Sec. Kabardino-Balkar Regional CP Cttee. 1985–88, Second Sec. 1988–90, First Sec. 1990–91; Chair. Supreme Soviet Kabardino-Balkar A.S.S.R. 1990–91; Pres. of Kabardino-Balkariya Repub. 1992–; mem. Pres. Council of Russia 1994–; People's Deputy of Russian Fed. 1990–93; mem. Council of Fed. of Russia 1993–, Deputy Chair. 1996–; mem. Cttee for Internal Affairs, mem. Parl. Ass. of Black Sea Econ. Co-operation 1996–. *Address:* Office of President Lenina

27, R-360028, Nalchik (Office); Karashaeva 15/23, R-360028 Nalchik, Kabardino-Balkariya, Russia (Home). *Telephone:* (86622) 220 64 (Office).

KOŁAKOWSKI, Leszek, DR. PHIL., F.B.A.; Polish professor of philosophy; b. 23 Oct. 1927, Radom; s. of Jerzy Kołakowski and Lucyna (née Pietrusiewicz) Kołakowska; m. Tamara Dynenson 1949; one d.; ed. Łódź and Warsaw Univs.; Asst. (logic), Łódź Univ. 1947–49; Asst. Warsaw Univ. 1950–54, Chair. Section of History of Philosophy 1959–68 (expelled by Govt. for political reasons); Visiting Prof. McGill Univ., Montreal 1968–69; Prof. Univ. of Calif., Berkeley 1969–70; Sr. Research Fellow, All Souls Coll., Oxford 1970–; Prof. Yale Univ. 1975, Univ. of Chicago 1981–; mem. American Acad. of Arts and Sciences, Bayerische Akad. der Künste, Institut Int. de Philosophie, Acad. Europaea, Acad. Universelle des Cultures; mem. PEN Club, Polish Philosophical Soc., Polish Writers Asscn.; mem. Philosophical Soc., Oxford, U.K.; Dr. h.c. (Bard Coll., New York, Reed Coll., Portland, U.S.A., State Univ. of New York, Adelphi Univ., New York, Łódź Univ.) 1992; several prizes including Alfred Jurzykowski Award 1969, Prix Européen d'Essai 1980, Prix d'Erasme and McArthur Foundation Prize 1983, Jefferson Award 1986, Prix Tocqueville 1994, White Eagle Order 1997. *Publications include:* Chrétiens sans église 1968, Positivist Philosophy 1970, Die Gegenwärtigkeit des Mythos 1973, Husserl and the Search for Certitude 1975, Leben trotz Geschichte 1977, Main Currents of Marxism 1976–78, Religion If There Is No God 1982, Metaphysical Horror 1988, God Owes Us Nothing 1994. *Address:* 77 Hamilton Road, Oxford, OX2 7QA, England.

KOLAR, Jiri; French writer; b. 24 Sept. 1914, Protivin, Czechoslovakia; s. of Frantisek Kolar and Anna (née Simakova) Kolar; m. Bela Helclova 1949; first exhbn. of collages, Prague 1937; founding mem. SKUPINA (Group) 42 with fellow writers and artists; arrested and imprisoned 1953; weekly diary in collages, Tydenik 1967–70; exhbns. Kassel 1968, Brasília 1969, Osaka 1970, New York 1975, 1985, Paris 1981, London 1990, Netherlands 1990, 1993, Rome, Malmö, Miró Foundation, Barcelona; retrospective exhbn., Centro de Arte Reina Sofía, Madrid 1996; French nationality 1984; Collages 1952–82 at Albermarle Gallery, London 1987; Gottfried von Herder Award 1971. *Publications:* Krestny List (poems) 1941, Limb a Jine Basne (poems) 1945, Sedm Kantat (poems) 1945, Dny v Roce (poems) 1947, Mistr Sun o Basnickem Umeni 1956, Novy Epiktet 1957, Mor v Athenach 1958, Basne Ticha (poems) 1961, Navod k Upotrebeni (poems) 1967, Slovnik Metod 1983, Odpovedi 1984, Prometheova Jatra 1985, Dictionnaire des méthodes 1992 etc.; many titles also published in French. *Address:* 61 rue Olivier-Métra, 75020 Paris, France. *Telephone:* 43.66.01.55.

KOLESNIKOV, Gen. Mikhail Petrovich; Russian army officer; b. 30 June 1939, Yeisk, Krasnodar Dist.; m.; one s.; ed. Omsk Tank Tech. School, Gen. Staff Acad.; started mil. service as commdr. of platoon 1975, then commdr. of co., bn., regt. 1975–77, Head of Staff and Deputy Commdr. of Div. 1977–79, Commdr. of tank div. 1979–83, Commdr. of corps, Commdr. of Army in Transcaucasian Command 1983–87, Head of Staff and First Deputy Commdr. of troops in Siberian Command 1987–89, Head of Staff and First Deputy-C.-in-C. of Southern Command 1988–90, Head of Gen. Staff and First Deputy C.-in-C. of land troops 1990–91, Deputy Head of Staff of Armed Forces of Russian Fed. 1991–92, First Deputy Minister of Defence, Head of General Staff of Russian Fed. 1992–96; Chair. Cttee. Heads of Staff CIC Armed Forces 1996–98, Pres.'s State Tech. Comm. 1998–. *Address:* Gostekhkomissiya, Znamenka str. 19, 103160 Moscow, Russia. *Telephone:* (095) 924-68-08 (Office).

KOLESNIKOV, Lieut-Gen. Vladimir Ilyich; Russian criminal investigator; b. 1938; m.; two c.; ed. Rostov State Univ., Acad. of Ministry of Internal Affairs; worked as investigator, Deputy Head, Dept. of Criminal Investigation; Deputy Head, Dept. of Internal Affairs; Head, Main Dept. of Criminal Investigation 1991–; First Deputy Minister of Internal Affairs 1995–. *Address:* Ministry of Internal Affairs, Zhitnaya str. 19, 117049 Moscow, Russia. *Telephone:* (095) 239 5219 (Office). *Fax:* (095) 293 5995 (Office).

KOLFF, Willem Johan, M.D., PH.D.; American professor of surgery; b. 14 Feb. 1911, Leiden, Netherlands; s. of Jacob and Adriana Pieternella Kolff; m. Janke Cornelia Huidekoper 1937; four s. one d.; ed. Univs. of Leiden and Groningen; Asst. Pathological Anatomy, Univ. of Leiden 1934–36; Asst. Medical Dept. Univ. of Groningen 1938–41; Head, Medical Dept., Municipal Hosp., Kampen 1941–50; Privaat Docent, Univ. of Leiden Medical School 1949–51; mem. of staff, Research Div., Cleveland Clinic Foundation 1950–63; Asst. Prof., later Prof. of Clinical Investigation, Educ. Foundation of Cleveland Clinic Foundation 1950–67; mem. staff, Surgical Div., Cleveland Clinic Foundation 1958–67, Head, Dept. of Artificial Organs 1958–67, Scientific Dir. Artificial Organs Program 1966–67; Prof. of Surgery, Head of Div. of Artificial Organs, Univ. of Utah Coll. of Medicine 1967–86, Distinguished Prof. of Medicine and Surgery 1979–, also Research Prof. of Eng., Prof. of Internal Medicine Oct. 1981–, Dir. Kolff's Lab. 1986–; Hon. mem. Peruvian Urological Soc., Greek Soc. of Cardiology, Sociedad Médica de Santiago, Austrian Soc. for Nephrology, Fundacion Favaloro, Buenos Aires, Argentina 1981–; developed artificial kidney for clinical use; mem. Nat. Acad. of Eng. 1989; Foreign mem. Hollandsche Maatschappij der Wetenschappen; Hon. D.Sc. (Allegheny Coll.) 1960, (Tulane Univ.) 1975, (City Univ. New York) 1982, (Temple Univ. Philadelphia) 1983, (Univ. of Utah) 1983; Hon. M.D. (Rostock) 1975, (Univ. of L'Aquila, Italy) 1981, (Univ. of Bologna) 1983; Commdr. Order of Orange-Nassau, Orden de Mayo al Mérito en el Grado de Gran Oficial (Argentina) 1974; numerous medals, awards and prizes from several countries including Francis Amory Award (American Acad. of Arts and Sciences) 1948, Cameron Prize (Univ. Edinburgh) 1964, Gairdner Prize (Gairdner Foundation, Toronto) 1966, Gold Medal (Netherlands Surgical Soc.) 1970, Benjamin Franklin Fellow (Royal Soc. of Arts, London) 1972, Leo Harvey Prize (Technion Inst. of Israel) 1972, Ray C. Fish Award and Medal Tex. Heart Inst. 1975, Senior U.S. Scientist Award, Alexander von Humboldt Foundation 1978, Gewerbevereins Wilhelm-Exner Award (Austria) 1980, American Medical Asscn.'s Scientific Achievement Award for Outstanding Work 1982, Japan Prize, Science and Tech. Foundation of Japan 1986, ANNA Hon. mem. 1987, First Jean Hamburger Award in Clinical Nephrology, Int. Soc. of Nephrology 1987, Christopher Columbus Award, Washington 1992, "Father of Artificial Organs" Award and Medal, World Conf. of ISAO, Montreal 1992, Legacy of Life Award, LDS Hosp.-Deseret Foundation's Heart and Lung Inst. 1995, numerous other awards. *Publications:* De Kunstmatige Nier 1946, New Ways of Treating Uraemia 1947; over 600 articles in learned journals and chapters in books on organ replacement, etc. *Leisure interests:* bird-watching, hiking, camping. *Address:* Kolff's Laboratory/Bioengineering, University of Utah, 2460-A Merrill Engineering Building, Salt Lake City, UT 84112 (Office); 2894 Crestview Drive, Salt Lake City, UT 84108, U.S.A. (Home). *Telephone:* (801) 581-6296 (Office); (801) 582-3056 (Home).

KOLINGBA, André; Central African Republic politician and army officer; fmr. Chief of Staff; overthrew Pres. David Dacko (q.v.) in coup Sept. 1981; Pres. Mil. Cttee. for Nat. Recovery 1981–85; Pres. of Cen. African Repub. 1981–93, Minister of Defence and of War Veterans 1981–83, 1984–85, Prime Minister and Minister of Defence and War Veterans 1985–91; Pres. Cand. in Aug. 1993 election; rank of Gen. revoked March 1994.

KOLLEK, Theodore (Teddy); Israeli politician and public administrator; b. 27 May 1911, Vienna; s. of S. Alfred and Margaret Fleischer Kollek; m. Tamar Schwartz 1937; one s. one d.; ed. secondary school, Vienna; founder mem. Kibbutz Ein Gev 1937; Political Dept. Jewish Agency for Palestine 1940; established Jewish Agency office, Istanbul, for contact with Jewish underground in Europe 1942; Mission to U.S.A. for Haganah 1947–48; Head of U.S. Div., Israel Foreign Ministry 1950; Minister, Washington 1951–52; Dir.-Gen. of Prime Minister's Office, Jerusalem 1952–65; Chair. Israel Govt. Tourist Corpn. 1955–65; Chair. Israel Govt. Water Desalination Joint Project with U.S. Govt. 1964–66; Chair. Bd. of Govs. Israel Museum, Jerusalem 1964–, Africa-Israel Investment Co. Ltd. 1964–65; Mayor of Jerusalem 1965–93; mem. Advisory Bd. Inst. on Global Conflict and Co-operation 1982–92; Hon. Doctorate (Hebrew Univ., Jerusalem) 1977, (Univ. of Notre Dame) 1981, (Brown Univ.) 1983, (Jewish Theological Seminary, Harvard Univ.) 1984, (Ben Gurion Univ.) 1985, (Hebrew Union Coll.) 1986, (Weizmann Inst. of Science) 1986, (Tel Aviv Univ.) 1989; numerous prizes and awards. *Publications:* Jerusalem: A History of Forty Centuries (Co-Author), Pilgrims to the Holy Land 1970 (Co-Author), For Jerusalem (autobiography) 1978, My Jerusalem; Twelve Walks in the World's Holiest City (Co-Author), 180 scientific articles. *Leisure interests:* archaeology, reading, collecting ancient maps and books on Holy Land. *Address:* 6 Rashba Street, Rechavia, Jerusalem 92265, Israel (Home). *Telephone:* 6751704 (Office); 5633147 (Home).

KOLLER, Arnold; Swiss politician; b. 29 Aug. 1933; m. Erica Brauder 1972; two c.; fmr. univ. prof.; mem. Bundesrat (Fed. Council) Dec. 1986–, Head of Fed. Mil. (Defence) Dept. 1986–89, Vice-Pres. 1989–90; Head Fed. Dept. of Justice and Police 1989–; Pres. of Switzerland 1990–91, 1998–99; Christian Democratic Party. *Address:* c/o Federal Chancellery Bundeshaus-West, 3003 Bern, Switzerland.

KOLLO, René; German opera singer; b. 20 Nov. 1937, Berlin; s. of the late Willi and of Marie-Louise Kollodzieyski; m. 1st Dorthe Larsen 1967; one d.; m. 2nd Beatrice Bouquet 1982; began career with Staatstheater, Brunswick 1965; First Tenor, Deutsche Oper am Rhein 1967–71; guest appearances with numerous leading opera cos. and at annual Bayreuth Wagner festival; Bundesverdienstkreuz. *Performances include:* The Flying Dutchman 1969, 1970, Lohengrin 1971, Die Meistersänger von Nürnberg 1973, 1974, Parsifal 1975, Siegfried 1976, 1977, Tristan (Zürich) 1980, (Bayreuth) 1981. *Publication:* Imre Fabian im Gespräch mit René Kollo 1982. *Leisure interests:* sailing, tennis, flying.

KOLOBOV, Yevgeny Vladimirovich; Russian conductor; b. 19 Jan. 1946, Leningrad; m. Natalia Popovich; one s. one d.; ed. Sverdlosk (now Ekaterinburg) Conservatory class of M. Paverman; debut 1969, conductor Sverdlovsk Opera Theatre 1974–77, Chief Conductor 1977–81, conductor of Leningrad Kirov Theatre of Opera and Ballet 1981–87; Artistic Dir. and Chief Conductor K. Stanislavsky and V. Nemirovich-Danchenko Musical Theatre, Moscow 1988–90; f. and Artistic Dir. Moscow Municipal Theatre New Opera 1990–. *Productions include:* Maria Stuardá, Il Pirata, La Wally, I Due Foscari, thematic productions devoted to Mozart, Salieri, Rossini; People's Artist of Russia 1983; Triumph Prize 1995. *Address:* Moscow Municipal Theatre New Opera, Karetny Ryad 3, 103006 Moscow, Russia (Office). *Telephone:* (095) 200-08-68 (Office), 251 5394 (Home).

KOLODKIN, Anatoliy Lazarevich, D.C.L.; Russian specialist on law of sea and int. law; b. 27 Feb. 1928, Leningrad; s. of Lazar Kolodkin and Nadezhda Kolodkina; m. Berta Levina 1958; one s.; ed. Leningrad Univ.; mem. numerous U.S.S.R. dels. to int. confs. on maritime affairs; headed

U.S.S.R. dels. at confs. of Int. Maritime Satellite Org. (INMARSAT) 1981; participated in creation of Russian maritime satellite org. "Morsvyassputnik"; Deputy Dir., Prof. Scientific Research Inst. of Maritime Transport 1981–; Spokesman and Co-ordinator Group D, E. European states, at UN Conf. for elaboration UN Convention on conditions of registration of ships 1982–86; co-author draft Convention on legal status of Ocean Data Acquisition Systems; Prof. of Law of Sea, Moscow State Legal Acad. 1994–; mem. Perm. Court of Arbitration, The Hague 1990–; mem. (Judge) UN Int. Tribunal for Law of Sea 1996–; has lectured extensively on law of sea in Russia and abroad; Pres. Maritime Law Assen. of U.S.S.R (now C.I.S.) 1981–, Russian Int. Law Assen. 1994–; Chair. Nat. Cttee. of Russian Fed. on UN Decade of Int. Law 1996–; Co-Chair. Consultative Council of State Duma (Parl.) for Int. Law 1996–; Hon. Vice-Pres., Int. Maritime Cttee. 1994–; Deputy Chair. "Peace for the Oceans" Cttee. 1990–, Union of Lawyers; mem. Council, Int. Oceanic Inst. "Pacem in Maribus", Malta 1971–; mem. acad. councils, Law Faculty, Moscow Univ. 1975–, Inst. of State and Law, Russian Acad. of Sciences 1993–; mem. Higher Degree Cttee., Expert Council on Legal Sciences of Russian Fed. 1985–; mem. World Acad. of Science and Art 1989–; mem. Council, Law of the Sea Inst. (U.S.A.) 1989–95; mem. group of experts of State Duma for elaboration of new Russian marine legislation 1994–; Hon. Medal of Free Univ. of Brussels. *Publications:* 226 scientific articles in Russia and other countries. *Address:* Bolshoy Koptevsky per. 3, 125319 Moscow, Russia. *Telephone:* (095) 151-75-88. *Fax:* (095) 152-09-16.

KOŁODKO, Grzegorz Witold; Polish politician and professor of economics; b. 28 Jan. 1949, Tczew; m.; two d.; ed. Main School of Planning and Statistics, Warsaw; Prof., Chair. of Political Economy and Chair. of Planning and Econ. Policy, Main Business Coll. (fmrly. Main School of Planning and Statistics), Dir. Inst. of Finance 1988–; has lectured at many foreign colls. and univs.; Adviser to Pres. Nat. Bank of Poland 1982–88; fmr. consultant, World Inst. for Planning Econ. Growth of UN, Helsinki; IMF expert 1991–92; mem. Polish United Workers' Party (PZPR) 1969–90; currently holds no political affiliation; Deputy Prime Minister and Minister of Finance 1994–97; World Bank expert 1998–; mem. Polish Econ. Soc., Int. Inst. of Public Finance 1989–; Commdr.'s Cross, Order of Polonia Restituta. *Publications:* more than 200 publications on econ. theory and policy, including: Strategy for Poland 1994, The Polish Alternative. Old Myths, Hard Facts and New Strategies in Successful Transformation of the Polish Economy 1997, Equity Issues in Policy-making in Transition Economies 1998, From Shock to Therapy. The Political Economy of Post-socialist Transformations 1998. *Leisure interests:* music, reading, swimming, travelling, antique civilizations. *Address:* ul Małcużyńskiego 7 m. 12, 02-793 Warsaw, Poland.

KOŁODZIEJCZYK, Piotr; Polish politician and naval officer; b. 8 June 1939, Poznań; m.; two s.; ed. Naval Acad., Gdynia, and Acad. of Gen. Staff, Warsaw; began service in navy as volunteer 1956; promoted to rank of First Officer 1959; served at sea and in Navy H.Q. 1960–83; Commdr. Polish Army unit, Golan Heights 1977–78; Chief of Staff, Navy 1983; Commdr. of Navy and Dir. Main Educ. and Training Bd. of Polish Army; Vice-Adm. 1989; Minister of Nat. Defence 1990–91, 1993–95; rank of Adm. 1993. *Leisure interest:* sailing.

KOLOKOLOV, Boris Leonidovich; Russian diplomatist; b. 9 Nov. 1924; m.; one d.; ed. Moscow Inst. of Int. Relations; army service, took part in mil. operations 1942–50; diplomatic service, UN, Geneva 1956–62; mem. Protocol dept. U.S.S.R. Ministry of Foreign Affairs 1962–69, Chief of Protocol Dept. 1969–73; Amb. to Tunisia 1973–81; Deputy Minister of Foreign Affairs of R.S.F.S.R. (now Russia) 1981–96, Amb. Extraordinary and Plenipotentiary, and consultant on int. problems, Ministry of Foreign Affairs 1996–. *Address:* Ministry of Foreign Affairs, Sadovaya-Sennaya 32/34, Moscow, Russia. *Telephone:* 244-92-30. *Fax:* 253-90-81.

KOLPAKOVA, Irina Aleksandrovna; Russian ballerina; b. 22 May 1933, Leningrad; m. Vladlen Semeonov 1955; one d.; ed. Leningrad Choreographic School; Prima Ballerina, Kirov Theatre of Opera and Ballet, Leningrad (now Mariinsky Theatre, St. Petersburg) 1957–91; coach, American Ballet Theatre 1991–, Indianapolis ballet school 1995–; People's Artist of the U.S.S.R. 1965, Grand Prix de Ballet, Paris 1966, U.S.S.R. State Prize 1980, Hero of Socialist Labour 1983; prin. roles: Aurora (Sleeping Beauty), Juliet (Romeo and Juliet), Desdemona (Othello), Tao Khao (The Red Poppy), Maria (Fountain of Bakhchisarai), Giselle, Zolushka, Raymonda, La Sylphide, Les Sylphides, Don Quixote, Pushkin Creation of the World; cr. role of Katerina (The Stone Flower) and Shirin (Legends of Love). *Address:* c/o American Ballet Theatre, 890 Broadway, New York, NY 10003, U.S.A.

KOLTAI, Ralph, C.B.E.; British stage designer; b. 31 July 1924, Berlin, Germany; s. of Alfred Koltai and Charlotte Koltai (née Weinstein); m. Annena Stubbs 1954 (divorced 1976); ed. Cen. School of Art and Design, London; Head of Theatre Design Dept., Cen. School of Art and Design 1965–72; Assoc. Artist R.S.C. 1964–66, 1976–; Opera Dir. The Flying Dutchman, Hong Kong Arts Festival 1987 and La Traviata 1990; Designer, musical Metropolis 1989 (London), The Planets (Royal Ballet) 1990, The Makropulos Affair (Norwegian Opera) 1992, My Fair Lady (New York) 1993, La Traviata (Stockholm) 1993, Hair (London) 1993, Othello (Essen) 1994, (Tokyo) 1995, Madam Butterfly (Tokyo) 1995, Twelfth Night (Copenhagen) 1996, Carmen (Royal Albert Hall, London) 1997, Simon Boccanegra (Wales) 1997, Timon of Athens (Chicago) 1997, Nabucco (Festival Orange, France) 1998, Suddenly Last Summer (also dir., Nottingham Playhouse) 1998, Dalibor (Edin. Festival) 1998, A Midsummer Night's Dream; retrospective exhbn. London 1997, touring Asia, Israel, Europe 1998–99; over 190 productions of opera, drama and dance throughout Europe, the U.S.A., Canada and Australia. *Leisure interest:* wildlife photography. *Address:* c/o London Management, 2-4 Noel Street, London W.1.; 14A Soho Street, London, W1V 5DA, England. *Telephone:* 0171-287 9000. *Fax:* 0171-287 3236.

KOLVENBACH, Peter-Hans, S.J.; Netherlands ecclesiastic; b. 30 Nov. 1928, Druten (Gelderland); s. of Gerard A. J. Kolvenbach and Jacqueline J. P. Domensino; ed. Canisius Coll., Nijmegen, language studies in Netherlands and in Beirut, Inst. of Oriental Languages, Paris, Schools of Ancient Oriental Languages, Sorbonne; theological studies in Beirut, spiritual theology in Pomfret, Conn.; entered Soc. of Jesus 1948, ordained as a priest 1961; Prof. of General Linguistics and Armenian, Inst. of Oriental Languages and Faculty of Humanities, St Joseph's Univ., Beirut 1968–81; Prof. of Gen. Linguistics, then, Dir. Inst. of Philosophical Studies and Prof. of Hermeneutics, St. Joseph's Univ. 1968–74; del. to 32nd Gen. Congregation of Society of Jesus 1974; Provincial, Jesuit Vice-Province of the Near East 1974–81; Rector, Pontifical Oriental Inst., Rome 1981–83; Superior Gen. of the Society of Jesus Sept. 1983–. *Publications:* Men of God: Men for Others, A Most Pleasant Mission, El Padre Kolvenbach en Colombia, Kolvenbach en México, Cinco mensajes universitarios; numerous articles and reviews primarily in the field of linguistics and spiritual theology. *Address:* Borgo Santo Spirito 4, C.P. 6139, 00195 Rome, Italy. *Telephone:* 689771.

KOLVENBACH, Walter; German solicitor; b. 28 Jan. 1922, Düsseldorf; s. of Jean Kolvenbach and Henriette Kolvenbach; m. Irmgard Schmidt 1954; two s.; ed. Univs of Cologne and Frankfurt/Main; Gen. Counsel Henkel KG aA 1972–85; Chair. Legal Cttee. Verband der Chemischen Industrie e.v. 1977–85; Pres. European Co. Lawyers Assen. 1984–87; partner Law offices of Heuking, Kuhn, Düsseldorf 1987; Chair. Legal Cttee. Industrie und Handelskammer 1987–95; Hon. Prof. of Law, Univ. of Cologne 1988; mem. Int. Bar Assen., Treas. 1990–94, Hon. Life Mem. 1994; Hon. Senator, Heinrich-Heine-Univ. Düsseldorf 1990; Verdienstkreuz (1st Class) 1981, Grosses Verdienstkreuz der Verdienstordens 1987. *Publications include:* Workers' Participation in Europe 1977, Employee Councils in European Companies 1978, Privatrechtlicher Schutz für Auslands-vermögen 1985, Kolvenbach-Hanau, Handbook on European Employee Co-Management 1987, Protection of Foreign Investments 1988. *Address:* Peter-Roos-Strasse 6, 40547 Düsseldorf, Germany. *Telephone:* 0211/588774. *Fax:* 0211/5590436.

KOMAR, Vitaliy; Russian artist; b. 11 Sept. 1943, Moscow; initial artistic training at Moscow Stroganov Art School; originator with Aleksander Melamid (q.v.) of 'Sots-art'; mem. of U.S.S.R. Union of Artists, expelled for "distortion of Soviet reality and non-conformity with the principles of Socialist realism" 1972; emigrated to U.S.A. 1979. *Principal works include:* Young Marx 1976, Colour Writing 1972, Quotation 1972, Post Art 1973, Factory for Producing Blue Smoke 1975, Poster Series 1980; some work shown at Ronald Feldman Gallery, New York 1976; two-man exhbns. with Melamid at Tel Aviv Museum, Metropolitan, Modern Art and Guggenheim Museums in New York, Sydney Museum, Neue Gesellschaft für Bildende Kunst Berlin.

KOMAROV, Igor Sergeyevich, DR.SC.; Russian geologist; b. 29 Jan. 1917, Kiev; s. of Sergey Ivanovich Komarov and Nathalia Josifovna Komarova; m. Nathalya Khaime 1968; one s. one d.; ed. Moscow Geological Prospecting Inst.; prospecting work 1938–43; served in Soviet Army 1943–47; on staff of Moscow Geological Prospecting Inst., Asst. Prof., Dean, then Prof. 1948–; Lenin Prize for work on Eng. Geology of the U.S.S.R., 8 vols., published 1976–80. *Publications:* Engineering Geology of the Earth 1989, Engineering Geology of Platform Regions of the U.S.S.R. 1991. *Leisure interests:* skiing, bridge. *Address:* Moscow Geological-Prospecting Institute, 23 Micklucho–Macklai Street, 117873 Moscow (Office); 15–198 Millionshchikova Street, 115487 Moscow, Russia (Home). *Telephone:* 433-64-66 (Office); 112-05-90 (Home).

KOMATSU, Koh, B.ECONS.; Japanese banker; b. 14 March 1921, Kobe City; s. of Masanori and Sumi Komatsu; m. Setsuko Itoh 1948; one s. two d.; ed. Tokyo Univ.; joined Sumitomo Bank Ltd. 1946, Dir. 1971–, Man. Dir. 1973–77, Sr. Man. Dir. 1977–81, Deputy Pres. 1981–83, Pres. 1983–87, Deputy Chair. 1987; Dir. Fed. of Bankers Asscns. of Japan 1983–; Standing Dir. Kansai Econ. Fed. 1984–. *Leisure interest:* literature. *Address:* Sumitomo Bank, 3-2 Marunouchi 1-chome, Chiyoda-ku, Tokyo 100 (Office); 301 Higashi-matsubara Terrace, 24-15, Daita 4-chome, Setagaya-ku, Tokyo, Japan (Home). *Telephone:* (03) 282-5111 (Office); (03) 323-3154 (Home).

KOMER, Robert William, S.B., M.B.A.; American diplomatist and social scientist; b. 23 Feb. 1922, Chicago, Ill.; s. of Nathan A. Komer and Stella D. Komer; m. Geraldine M. Peplin 1961 (deceased); two s. one d.; ed. Harvard Coll., Harvard Graduate School of Business Admin. and Nat. War Coll.; U.S. Army 1943–46; Lieut.-Col. in U.S. Army Reserves 1946–81; Foreign Affairs Analyst, Central Intelligence Agency 1947–60; Senior Staff Asst., White House 1961–65; Deputy Special Asst. to Pres. for Nat. Security Affairs 1965–66; Special Asst. to Pres. 1966–67; Deputy to COMUSMACV for Civil Operations and Revolutionary Devt. with rank of Amb. (pacification in Viet Nam) 1967–68; Amb. to Turkey 1968–69; Senior Social Science Researcher, Rand Corpn. 1970–76; Adviser to Sec. of Defense for NATO Affairs 1977–79; Under-Sec. of Defense 1979–81; Consultant Rand Corpn. 1982–; Visiting Prof. George Mason Univ. 1991–92, George Washington Univ. 1992–94;

Presidential Medal of Freedom, Sec. of State's Distinguished Honor Award, Dept. of Defense Medal for Distinguished Public Service, U.S. Bronze Star, Vietnamese Orders, Grosses Bundesverdienstkreuz (Fed. Repub. of Germany) 1984. *Publications:* Civil Affairs and Military Government in the Mediterranean Theater (2 vols.) 1949, Establishment of ACC in Italy 1950, Treating NATO's Self-Inflicted Wound 1973, Origins of NATO Long Term Defense Program 1978, Maritime Strategy v. Coalition Defense 1984, Strategy-Making in the Pentagon (in Reorganizing America's Defense) 1985, Bureaucracy at War: U.S. Performance in the Vietnam Conflict 1986, Blowtorch 1995, and many articles. *Leisure interests:* tennis, swimming, military history. *Address:* RAND Corporation, 2100 M Street, N.W., Washington, DC 20037, U.S.A. (Office).

KOMISSAR, Mikhail Vitalyevich; Russian businessman and journalist; b. 27 Jan. 1953, Kharkov; m.; two d.; ed. Kharkov State Univ.; engineer, researcher Kharkov State Univ. 1975–79; army officer 1979–85; Sr. Ed., Deputy Head of Dept., U.S.S.R. State TV and Radio; Founder and Pres. First Independent Information Agency Interfax 1989–97, 1998–; Deputy Head of Admin., Head Information Service of Pres. Yeltsin 1997–. *Address:* Interfax, Tverskaya-yamskaya 1, 103006 Moscow, Russia. *Telephone:* (095) 250-98-40.

KOMLEVA, Gabriela Trofimovna; Russian ballerina; b. 27 Dec. 1938, Leningrad; d. of Trofim Ivanovich Komlev and Lucia Petrovna Komleva; m. Arkady Andreevich Sokolov-Kaminsky 1970; ed. Leningrad Ballet School (teacher Kostrovitskaya) and Leningrad Conservatoire; with Kirov (now Mariinsky) Ballet 1957–, teacher 1978–; teacher Leningrad Conservatoire 1987–, Prof. 1994; regular masterclasses in Europe and U.S.A. 1994–; Presenter Terpsichore's Finest Points, Leningrad TV 1985–89; numerous awards including People's Artist of U.S.S.R. 1983. *Major roles:* Odette-Odile in Swan Lake, Aurore in Sleeping Beauty, Nikiya in Bayadere, Raimonda, Giselle, Kitry in Don Quixote, Cinderella, Sylphide, Sylphides, Fire-Bird, Paquita, Pas de Quatre, and many modern ballets; *films:* Don Quixote, La Bayadère, The Sleeping Beauty, Paquita, Pas de Quatre, Cinderella, Moor's Pavana. The Firebird, Leningrad Symphony, Furious Isadora. *Leisure interests:* painting, music. *Address:* Fontanka River 116, Apt. 34, 198005 St. Petersburg, Russia. *Telephone:* 316-30-77. *Fax:* 316-30-77.

KOMLÓS, Péter; Hungarian violinist; b. 25 Oct. 1935, Budapest; s. of László Komlós and Franciska Graf; m. 1st Edit Fehér 1960, two s.; m. 2nd Zsuzsa Árki 1984, one s.; ed. Budapest Music Acad.; f. Komlós String Quartet 1957; First Violinist, Budapest Opera Orchestra 1960; Leader Bartók String Quartet 1963; extensive concert tours to U.S.S.R., Scandinavia, Italy, Austria, German Democratic Repub. Czechoslovakia 1958–64, U.S.A., Canada, N.Z. and Australia 1970, including Human Rights Day concert, UN H.Q. New York, Japan, Spain and Portugal 1971, Far East, U.S.A. and Europe 1973; performed at music festivals of Ascona, Edinburgh, Adelaide, Spoleto, Menton, Schwetzingen, Lucerne, Aix-en-Provence; recordings of Beethoven's string quartets for Hungaroton, Budapest and of Bartók's string quartets for Erato, Paris; 1st Prize, Int. String Quartet Competition, Liège 1964, Liszt Prize 1965, Gramophone Record Prize of Germany 1969, Kossuth Prize 1970, 1997, Eminent Artist Title 1980, UNESCO Music Council Plaque 1981; Order of Merit, Middle Cross of Repub. of Hungary 1995. *Leisure interests:* watching sports. *Address:* 1025 Budapest, Törökvész út 94, Hungary. *Telephone:* 200-91-02.

KOMMANDEUR, Jan, PH.D.; Netherlands professor of physical chemistry; b. 29 Nov. 1929, Amsterdam; s. of Jan Kommandeur and Rika Jorna; m. Elizabeth Eickholz 1951; two s.; ed. Univ. of Amsterdam; Postdoctoral Fellow, Research Council, Ottawa 1955–57; research scientist, Union Carbide Corpn., Cleveland, Ohio 1958–61; Prof. of Physical Chem. Univ. of Groningen 1961–; mem. Royal Netherlands Acad. of Science 1981, Science Advisory Council of the Netherlands. *Publications:* Photoconductivity in Aromatic Hydrocarbons 1958, Electric Conductivity in Organic Complexes 1961, Ions in Iodine 1966, Natural Gas in Europe: How much, for how long? 1977, Radiationless Transitions 1988. *Leisure interests:* literature, theatre, popularizing science. *Address:* Laboratory for Physical Chemistry, 9747 AG, Groningen (Office); Lekstraat 18, 9725 KM, Groningen, Netherlands (Home). *Telephone:* 050-634322.

KOMPLEKTOV, Viktor Georgiyevich; Russian politician and diplomatist; b. 8 Jan. 1932; m.; one d.; ed. Moscow Inst. of Int. Relations; diplomatic corps 1955–; work in Americas Dept. of U.S.S.R. Ministry of Foreign Affairs 1955–56, 1959–63; mem. CPSU 1962–91; mem. of CPSU Cen. Auditing Cttee. 1986–91; counsellor, Embassy, U.S.A. 1956–59, 1962–68; counsellor, Deputy Head USA Section 1970–76, Head of Section 1978–82; U.S.S.R. Deputy Minister of Foreign Affairs 1982–91; Russian Amb. to U.S.A. 1991–92; Amb.-at-Large, Special Rep. of Russian Fed. 1992–94; Amb. to Spain 1994–. *Address:* Embajada de Rusia, C/Velázquez 155, 28002 Madrid, Spain. *Telephone:* (1) 5622264. *Fax:* (1) 5629712.

KOMURA, Masahiko; Japanese politician; fmr. Parl. Vice-Minister Defence Agency; Minister of State, Dir.-Gen. Econ. Planning Agency 1994–95; mem. House of Reps. for Yamaguchi; Deputy Sec.-Gen. LDP, Chair. LDP Special Cttee. on Disasters. *Address:* c/o Economic Planning Agency, 3-1, Kasumigaseki, Chiyoda-ku, Tokyo, Japan.

KONARÉ, Alpha Omar, PH.D.; Malian politician; b. 1946, Kayes; m. Adam Ba; four c.; ed. Ecole Nat. Supérieure, Univ. of Warsaw, Poland; teacher; Dir. Inst. for Human Sciences, Bamako 1974, Historic and Ethnographic Div., Ministry of Culture 1975–78; Minister for Youth, Sports and Culture 1978–80 (resgnd.); Research Fellow, Institut Supérieur de Formation et de Recherche Appliquée, Bamako 1980–89; f. Jamana, a cultural co-operative 1983; f. daily Les Echos, monthly for young people, Grin Grin and news service on tape cassettes for rural population 1989; elected Pres. of Mali 1992–. *Publications:* Le Concept du Pouvoir en Afrique, Bibliographie archéologique du Mali, Les Grandes Dates du Mali (with Adam Ba), Sikasso Tata, Les Constitutions du Mali, Les Partis politiques au Mali. *Address:* Office of the President, B.P. 1463, Bamako, Mali. *Telephone:* 22-24-61.

KONDIĆ, Novak, M.A.; Serb politician and economist; b. 20 July 1952, Banja Luka; s. of Vlado Kondić and Gospa Kondić; m. Nevenka Predragović 1980; two s.; ed. Univ. of Banja Luka; Head Co. Accountancy Dept., Serbian Devt. Bank, Banja Luka 1977–86, Head of Inspectorate Control and Information Analysis 1986–90, Dir. Municipal Admin. of Public Revenues 1990–92, mem. Municipal Exec. Bd. 1990–92; Deputy Dir.-Gen. Payment Transaction Services for Repub. of Srpska 1992–95, for Banja Luka 1997–; Minister of Finance Repub. of Srpska 1995–97, 1998–; Rep. of Bosnia and Herzegovina to IMF 1998; Medal for Mil. Valour. *Leisure interests:* beekeeping, gardening, vineyard cultivation, fruit farming. *Address:* Kolubarska 11, 78 000 Banja Luka, Republic of Srpska, Bosnia and Herzegovina. *Telephone:* (78) 212 871.

KONDO, Jiro, DR.ENG.; Japanese professor of engineering; b. 23 Jan. 1917, Otsu City; s. of Shuzo Kondo; m. Kei Kondo 1944; one s. one d.; ed. Kyoto Univ., Tokyo Univ.; Prof. of Applied Mathematics and Gas Dynamics, Tokyo Univ. 1958–77, Dean Eng. Faculty 1975–77; Dir.-Gen. Nat. Inst. of Environmental Studies 1977–85; Pres. Science Council of Japan 1985–94, Central Council for Environmental Pollution Control 1988–; Deming Prize 1967, Purple Ribbon Medal 1982, Grand Cordon of the Order of the Sacred Treasure 1990, Person of Cultural Merit 1995. *Publications:* Integral Equations 1991, ed. Super Computing 1991. *Leisure interest:* swimming. *Address:* 9-2 Kizugawadai, Kizu-cho, Soraku-gun, Kyoto 619-02, Japan. *Telephone:* 774-75-2303. *Fax:* 774-75-2314.

KONDRATYEV, Col.-Gen. Georgy Grigorievich; Russian army officer; b. 17 Nov. 1944, Klintsy, Bryansk Region; m.; two c.; ed. Kharkov Guards Tank School, Mil. Acad. of Armoured Forces, U.S.S.R. Gen. Staff Acad.; served as commdr. of tank platoon, bn., Commdr. Regt., Gen. Staff 1973–74; Regt. Commdr. 1974–76; Deputy Commdr., Div. Commdr. 1976–85; Deputy C.-in-C. Turkestan Army Mil. Command 1985–87, Commdr. 1987–89; First Deputy C.-in-C. Turkestan Mil. Command 1989–91, Commdr. 1991–92; Deputy Minister of Defence of Russian Fed. 1992–95; Chief Mil. Expert, Deputy Minister Ministry of Emergencies and Natural Disasters 1995–. *Address:* Ministry of Emergencies and Natural Disasters, Teatralny per. 4, 103012 Moscow, Russia. *Telephone:* (095) 926-35-23.

KONDRAT'YEVA, Marina Viktorovna; Russian ballet dancer; b. 1 Feb. 1934; ed. Bolshoi Theatre Ballet School; with Bolshoi Ballet Co. 1953–80; People's Artist of R.S.F.S.R. 1976; coach at Bolshoi Theatre 1980–; Main roles include: Cinderella (Cinderella), Maria (Fountain of Bakchisarai), Aurora (Sleeping Beauty), Juliet (Romeo and Juliet), Katerina (Stone Flower), Giselle (Giselle), Gayane (Gayane), Odette-Odile (Swan Lake), Shirin (Legend of Love). *Address:* c/o Bolshoi Theatre, Teatralnaya Ploshchad 1, Moscow, Russia. *Telephone:* 291-27-97.

KONG JIESHENG; Chinese writer; b. 1952, Guangzhou City, Guangdong Prov.; Vice-Chair., Guangzhou Br. of Writers' Asscn. 1985–. *Publications:* My Marriage 1978, Story Investigations 1985. *Address:* Guangzhou Branch of Writers' Association, Guangzhou City, Guangdong Province, People's Republic of China.

KONG LINGREN; Chinese politician; b. Nov. 1924, Qufu Co., Shandong Prov.; ed. Tsinghua Univ.; joined Chinese Democratic League 1952; lecturer, Assoc. Prof., Prof. Shandong Univ.; Vice-Chair. Shandong Provincial CPPCC; Vice-Chair. China Confucius Foundation; mem. 7th CPPCC 1988; mem. Standing Cttee. 8th CPPCC 1993–; Vice-Chair. 7th Exec. Cttee. All-China Women's Fed. 1993–; Vice-Chair. 8th Chinese Democratic League Cen. Cttee. 1997–. *Address:* All-China Women's Federation, Beijing, People's Republic of China.

KONIDARIS, Ioannis (John), DR.IUR.; Greek professor of law; b. 10 Sept. 1948, Chios; s. of Marinos Konidaris and Ioanna Konidaris; m. Ersi Mantakas 1975, one d.; ed. Univs. of Athens, Thessaloniki and Munich; mil. service 1971–73; mem. Bar Asscn. of Athens 1974–; Asst. Faculty of Law, Univ. of Frankfurt 1978–81; lecturer in Ecclesiastical Law 1985; mem. editorial Bd. of official journal of Bar Asscn. of Athens 1985–; Prof. of Ecclesiastical Law, Univ. of Athens 1989–; Research Scholarship, Max Planck Inst. for European History of Law, Frankfurt-am-Main 1989–90; Dir. Research Centre for the History of Greek Law, Acad. of Athens 1994–, Ed. the Centre's Yearbook (Vol. 31) 1995, (Vol. 32) 1996, (Vol. 33) 1997, (Vol. 34) 1998. *Publications include:* Monastic Property Law Between 9th and 12th Centuries 1979, Legal Aspects of Monastery "Typika" 1984, Legal Theory and Praxis concerning Jehovah's Witnesses in Greece 1987, 1988, 1991, Law 1700/1987 and the Recent Crisis Between the Orthodox Church and the Greek State 1988, 1991, Subjects of Byzantine and Ecclesiastical Law 1991, Church and State in Greece 1993, The Conflict between Law and Canon and the Establishment of Harmony between them 1994, Ekklesiastika Atakta 1999; numerous articles on ecclesiastical law and history of law, especially Byzantine law.

Address: 3 Sina Street, 10679 Athens (University); 14 Anagnostopoulou Street, 10673 Athens (Acad. Research Centre); 107 Asklipiou Street, 11472 Athens (Private Office); 20 Bizaniou Street, 15237 Filothei/Athens, Greece (Home). *Telephone:* 3610313 (University); 3623565 (Acad. Research Centre); 3630391 (Private Office); 6742896 (Home). *Fax:* 3630391 (Private Office).

KÖNIG, H.E. Cardinal Franz; Austrian ecclesiastic; b. 3 Aug. 1905, Rabenstein, Pielach; ed. Univs. of Rome, Vienna and Lille; ordained 1933; Dozent, Vienna Univ. 1946; Prof., Faculty of Theology, Salzburg 1948; Titular Bishop of Livias 1952; Archbishop of Vienna 1956–85; cr. Cardinal by Pope John XXIII 1958; fmr. Pres. Secr. for Non-Believers, Rome; Pres. Pax Christi Int. 1985–90. *Publications include:* Christus und die Religionen der Erde, Religionswissenschaftliches Wörterbuch, Zarathustras Jenseitsvorstellungen und das Alte Testament 1964, Die Stunde der Welt 1971, Aufbruch zum Geist 1972, Das Zeichen Gottes 1973, Der Mensch ist für die Zukunft angelegt 1975, Kirche und Welt 1978, Glaube ist Freiheit 1981, Der Glaube der Menschen (Herausgeber) 1985, Der Weg der Kirche 1986, Lexikon der Religionen 1987, Juden und Christen haben eine Zukunft 1988 (König/Ehrlich). *Address:* Wollzeile 2, 1010 Vienna, Austria.

KONO, Yohei; Japanese politician; b. 15 Jan. 1937; ed. Waseda Univ., Stanford Univ.; mem. House of Reps. from Kanagawa; fmr. Parl. Vice-Minister of Educ., Dir.-Gen. Science and Tech. Agency; Chief Cabinet Sec. (State Minister) 1992–93; Chair. LDP Research Comm. on Foreign Affairs, Pres. 1993–; Deputy Prime Minister and Minister of Foreign Affairs 1994–96; left LDP to co-found New Liberal Club (now defunct) 1976–86; mem. Miyazawa faction of LDP. *Address:* Liberal Democratic Party (Jiyu-Minshuto), 1-11-23, Nagata-cho, Chiyoda-ku, Tokyo 100, Japan. *Telephone:* (03) 3581-0111.

KONOVALOV, Aleksander Nikolayevich, M.D.; Russian neurosurgeon; b. 12 Dec. 1933, Moscow; s. of Nikolai Konovalov and Ekaterina Konovalova; m. Inna Konovalova 1957, one s.; ed. First Moscow Medical Inst.; intern, researcher, Deputy Dir. Burdenko Research Inst. of Neurosurgery 1957–75, Dir. 1975–; mem. Russian Acad. of Medical Sciences; conducted unique operation on separation of the heads of Siamese twins 1989; Ed.-in-Chief Voprosi Neurochirurgii; U.S.S.R. State Prize; Orden Druzba Narodov. *Publications:* more than 215 works on problems of surgery. *Leisure interests:* tennis, skiing. *Address:* Institute of Neurosurgery, ul. Fadeeva 5, 125047 Moscow (Office); Novoslobodskaya str. 57/65, f. 33, 103055 Moscow, Russia (Home). *Telephone:* 251-65-26 (Office); 978-76-18 (Home). *Fax:* (095) 975-22-28.

KONRÁD, György; Hungarian novelist and essayist; b. 2 April 1933, Debrecen; s. of József Konrád and Róza Klein; m. Judit Lakner; three s. one d.; ed. Eötvös Loránd Univ., Budapest; Ed. Életképek 1956; social worker, Budapest 7th Dist. Council 1959–65; Ed. Magyar Helikon 1960–66; urban sociologist on staff of City Planning Research Inst. 1965–73; full-time writer 1973–; numerous scholarships; visiting Prof. of Comparative Literature, Colorado Springs Coll. 1988; Corresp. mem. Bayerische Akad., München; fmr. Pres. Int. PEN. *Awards include:* Herder, Vienna-Hamburg 1984, Charles Veillon European Essay, Zürich 1986, Fredfonden Peace Foundation, Copenhagen 1986, Fed. German Critic Prize for the Year's Novel 1986, Kossuth Prize. *Publications include:* (novels): A látogató (The Case Worker) 1969, A városlapító (The City Builder) 1977, A cinkos (The Loser) 1983, Kerti mulatságok (Feast in the Garden) 1987, Kőóra (Stone Clock) 1994; *(Essays):* Az értelmiség utja az osztályhatalomhoz (The Intellectuals on the Road to the Class Power) 1978, Az autonómia kisértése (The Temptation of Autonomy) 1980, Antipolitics 1986, The Melancholy of Rebirth 1991, Esszék 91–93 (Essays 1991–93) 1993, Várakozás (Expectation) 1995. *Address:* 1026 Budapest, Torockó utca 3, Hungary. *Telephone:* 36 /1/ 560-425.

KONSALIK, Heinz G.; German author; b. 28 May 1921 (as Heinz Günther), Cologne; s. of Heinz Arno Max Günther and Wanda Günther (née Konsalik); m. Elsbeth Langenbach 1948; two d.; ed. Univ. of Munich; worked as war corresp. 1939–45; Chief Ed. Liberator publishing co., Cologne 1946–48; Ed. Lustige magazine 1950. *Publications:* 131 novels including Der Arzt von Stalingrad, Strafbataillon 999, Russische Sinfonie, Die Rollbahn, Schicksal aus zweiter Hand, Rostende Ruhm, Der letzte Gefangene, Manöver im Herbst, Liebe am Don, Palmen I, II, Ein Sommer mit Danica, Heiss wie der Steppenwind, Die weisse Front, Liebe ist stärker als der Tod, Promenadendeck 1985, Sibirisches Roulette 1986, Das Golde Meer 1987, Das Bernsteinzimmer 1988, Tal ohne Sonne 1989. *Leisure interests:* Asian art, opera, travel, animals. *Address:* Elizabethenhof, 53604 Bad Honnef am Rhein, Germany.

KONTIĆ, Radoje, DR.TECH.SC.; Yugoslav (Montenegrin) politician and engineer; b. 31 May 1937, Nikšić, Montenegro; s. of Milivoje Kontić and Vidoslava Kontić; m. Mara Kontić; three c.; ed. High School of Chemical Eng.; specialized in France in ferrous metallurgy; Tech. Dir. Niksic Steel Co.; Prof. School of Tech. and Metallurgy Univ. of Podgorica; Minister Fed. Govt.; Prime Minister of Yugoslavia 1993–97. *Publications include:* univ. textbook on metallurgy. *Address:* Vlada Savezne Republike Jugoslavije, Lenjina blvd 2, 11070 Belgrade, Yugoslavia. *Telephone:* (11) 334 281 (Office).

KONTOGEORGIS, Georgios; Greek politician and public servant; b. 21 Nov. 1912; m.; Prin. Admin., Ministry of Economy and of Trade 1941–52; Dir.-Gen. Ministry of Trade until 1967; Sec. of State for Econ. Co-ordination and Planning 1974–77; mem. Parl. (New Democracy Party) 1977; Minister for Relations with the EEC 1977 (led negotiations for Greece's entry); Commr. for Transport, Fisheries and Co-ordination of Tourism, Comm. of European Communities 1981–85; Minister for Nat. Economy and Tourism 1989–90. *Publication:* The Association of Greece with the European Community 1961, Greece in Europe 1985, The European Idea: The European Union, Greece: History, Present, Perspectives 1995. *Address:* 26-28 Anagnostopoulou Street, 106 73 Athens, Greece. *Telephone:* 3616-844.

KONTOS, Constantine William; American government official; b. 10 Aug. 1922, Chicago, Ill.; s. of William C. and Irene Thomas Kontos; m. Joan Fultz 1948; two s.; ed. Univ. of Chicago and London School of Econs.; Special Asst. to Dir. of Econ. Co-operation Admin., Mission to Greece 1949–53; Program Budget Officer, Foreign Operations Admin., Washington, D.C. 1953–55; Sr. Man. Officer Int. Co-operation Admin., Washington, D.C. 1955–57; Exec. Officer, Bureau of Africa and Europe 1957–59; Deputy Dir. U.S. Agency for Int. Devt. (USAID) Mission, Ceylon 1959–61; Deputy Dir. USAID Mission, Nigeria 1961–64; attended Nat. War Coll. 1964–65; Dir. Personnel USAID 1965–67; Dir. USAID Mission, Pakistan 1967–69; Dir. Office of Program Evaluation, USAID 1969–72; Deputy Commr.-Gen. UN Relief and Works Agency (UNRWA) 1972–74; mem. policy planning staff, State Dept., Washington 1974–76; special rep. of Pres., Dir. Sinai support mission, Washington 1976–80; Amb. to Sudan 1980–83; mem. Policy Planning Council, Dept. of State 1983–86, Exec. Dir. of Advisory Cttee. to Sec. of State on South Africa 1986–87, Policy Planning Staff 1987; Sr. Vice-Pres. Exec. Council on Foreign Diplomats 1988–90; independent consultant 1990–; Vice-Pres. Global Business Access Inc. 1992–; Dept. of State Superior Honor Award 1971. *Address:* 3606 Warren Street, N.W., Washington, DC 20008, U.S.A. *Telephone:* (202) 966-8578 (Home).

KONUK, Nejat; Turkish-Cypriot politician, lawyer and writer; b. 1928, Nicosia; unmarried; ed. Turkish Lycée, Cyprus, and Law Faculty of Ankara Univ., Turkey; Legal Adviser in Turkish Civil Service, Turkey; Sec.-Gen. and Acting Dir.-Gen. of Turkish Communal Chamber, Cyprus; Under-Sec. to Rauf Denktaş (q.v.) 1968–69; Minister of Justice and Internal Affairs, Turkish Cypriot Admin. 1969–75; mem. for Nicosia, Turkish Communal Chamber, Constituent Assembly, Turkish Cypriot Legislative Assembly 1970–; founder mem. Nat. Unity Party 1975, Leader 1976–78; Prime Minister "Turkish Federated State of Cyprus" 1976–78; Leader of the Democratic People's Party 1979–82 (resgnd.); Pres. Legis. Assembly "Turkish Federated State of Cyprus" July–Dec. 1981, 1982–83; Prime Minister "Turkish Repub. of N. Cyprus" 1983–85. *Publications:* essays on literature, various papers on Cyprus, political articles 1953–77. *Leisure interests:* reading, swimming. *Address:* Kumsal, Lefkoşa, Mersin 10, Turkey.

KONUMA, Michiji, D.S.; Japanese professor of physics; b. 25 Jan. 1931, Tokyo; s. of Haruo Konuma and Taka Konuma; m. Masae Shinohara 1960; one s. one d.; ed. Musashi High School and Univ. of Tokyo; Research Assoc. Univ. of Tokyo 1958–67 (leave of absence 1963–67); Research Fellow, Consiglio Nazionale Ricerche, Italy and Visiting Prof. Scuola Normale Superiore, Pisa 1963–65; Visiting Prof. Catholic Univ. of Louvain, Belgium 1965–67; Assoc. Prof. Kyoto Univ. 1967–83; Prof. Keio Univ. 1983–96, Prof. Emer. 1996–; Prof. and Dean, Faculty of Environmental and Information Studies, Musashi Inst. of Tech., Yokohama 1996–; Visiting Prof. Univ. of the Air 1992–; mem. Physics Action Council, UNESCO; mem. and fmr. Pres. Physical Soc. of Japan; Pres. Asscn. of Asia Pacific Physical Socs.–1997; mem. Council, Pugwash Confs. on Science and World Affairs; other professional appts. *Publications:* numerous articles on theoretical particle physics, history of modern physics and physics educ. *Address:* Musashi Institute of Technology, Ushikubonishi 3-3-1, Tsuzuki-ku, Yokohama 224-0015 (Office); 200-9 Kudencho, Sakaeku, Yokohama 247-0014, Japan (Home). *Telephone:* (45) 910-2501 (Office); 81-45-891-8386 (Home). *Fax:* (45) 910-2502.

KONWICKI, Tadeusz; Polish writer and film director; b. 22 June 1926, Nowa Wilejka, fmrly. in U.S.S.R., now in Lithuania; m. Danuta Lenica; ed. Jagiellonian Univ., Cracow, Warsaw Univ.; Partisan, Home Army detachment 1944–45; mem. Polish Writers' Asscn. 1949–, Editorial Staff of Nowa Kultura (weekly) 1950–57; Mondello Prize for Literature 1981, and many other awards and prizes at int. film festivals, including Venice 1958; State Prize, 3rd Class 1950, 1954, 1st Class 1966, Kt.'s Cross, Order of Polonia Restituta 1954, Officer's Cross 1964. *Films directed:* Ostatni dzień lata (Last Day of Summer) 1958, Zaduszki 1962, Salto 1965, Jak daleko stąd, jak blisko 1972, Dolina Issy 1982, Lawa 1989. *Publications:* novels: Władza 1954, Godzina smutku 1954, Z oblężonego miasta 1955, Rojsty 1956, Dziura w niebie 1959, Sennik współczesny (A Dreambook of Our Time) 1963, Ostatni dzień lata (film scripts) 1966, Wniebowstąpienie 1967, Zwierzocztekoupiór 1969, Nic albo nic 1971, Kronika wypadków miłosnych 1974, Kalendarz i klepsydra (The Calendar and the Sand-Glass) 1976, Kompleks polski 1977, Mała Apokalipsa 1979, Wschody i zachody Księżyca 1982, Rzeka podziemna Podziemne ptaki 1985; Nowy Świat i okolice 1986, Bohiń 1987, Pamflet na samego siebie 1995, film scripts: Zimowy zmierzch (Winter Twilight), Matka Joanna od Aniołów, Faraon, Jowita, Austeria 1988. *Address:* ul. Górskiego 1 m. 68, 00-033 Warsaw, Poland.

KONYUKHOV, Fedor Filippovich; Russian explorer; b. 12 Dec. 1951, Chkalovo, Zaporizhye Region, U.S.S.R. (Now Ukraine); m.; two c.; ed. Kronstadt Marine Higher School, Bobruysk School of Arts; completed solo expedition to N. Pole 1989; completed project Seven Mountain Peaks of the World (one-man ascent of seven peaks of seven continents); f. School of Travellers 1991; Plenipotentiary Rep. of UNEP (UN programme on Environmental

Protection) 1997–; mem. Russian Union of Artists; Hon. Citizen Terpii, Italy 1991, Taipei, Taiwan 1995, Nakhodka, Russia 1996; Order of Friendship of Peoples, UNESCO Order; Merited Master of Sports. *Address:* Tourism and Sports Union of Russia, Studeniy proyezd 7, 129282 Moscow, Russia. *Telephone:* (095) 478 6302 (Office).

KOOIJMANS, Pieter Hendrik, D.JUR.; Netherlands politician and lawyer; b. 6 July 1933, Heemstede; m. A. Kooijmans-Verhage; four c.; ed. Free Univ. Amsterdam; mem. Faculty of Law, Free Univ. of Amsterdam 1960–65, Prof. of European Law and Public Int. Law 1965–73; State Sec. for Foreign Affairs 1973–77; Prof. of Public Int. Law, Univ. of Leiden 1978–92, 1995–; Minister for Foreign Affairs 1993–94; mem. (Judge) Int. Court of Justice 1997–; Chair. or mem. numerous orgs. including Chair. Bd. Carnegie Foundation, Netherlands Disaster Relief Agency; Head Netherlands del. to UN Comm. on Human Rights 1982–85, 1992, Chair. Comm. 1984–85, Special Rapporteur on questions relevant to torture 1985–92; mem. various UN and CSCE missions to fmr. Yugoslavia 1991–92. *Publications:* various textbooks and articles on int. law and human rights. *Address:* c/o International Court of Justice, Peace Palace, Carnegieplein 2, 2517 KJ The Hague, The Netherlands. *Telephone:* (70) 392-44-11. *Fax:* (70) 364-99-28.

KOONTZ, Dean R(ay); American author; b. 9 July 1945, Everett, Pa.; also writes under pseudonyms David Axton, Brian Coffey, Deanna Dwyer, K. R. Dwyer, John Hill, Leigh Nichols, Anthony North, Richard Paige and Owen West; s. of Raymond Koontz and Florence Logue; m. Gerda Ann Cerra 1966; fmr. teacher of English; freelance author 1969–; work includes novels, short stories, science fiction/fantasy, social commentary/phenomena and journalism. *Publications:* recent work (under various names) includes: The Voice of the Night 1980, Whispers 1980, The Funhouse 1980, The Eyes of Darkness 1981, The Mask 1981, House of Thunder 1982, Phantoms 1983, Darkness Comes 1984, Twilight 1984, Strangers 1986, Shadow Fires 1987, Watchers 1987, Twilight Eyes 1987, Oddkins 1988, Servants of Twilight 1988, Midnight 1989, The Bad Place 1990, Moon 1993, The House of Thunder 1993, Dark Rivers of the Heart 1994, Mr Murder 1994, Fun House 1994, Strange Highways 1994, Icebound 1995, Intensity 1995, The Key to Midnight 1995, Ticktock 1996, Sole Survivor 1996, Fear Nothing 1997, Demon Seed 1997, Seize the Night 1998. *Address:* William Morris Agency, 1325 Avenue of the Americas, New York, NY 10019, U.S.A.

KOOP, C. Everett, A.B., M.D., SC.D.; American surgeon; b. 14 Oct. 1916, New York; s. of J. Everett Koop and Helen Apel; m. Elizabeth Flanagan 1938; three s. one d.; ed. Dartmouth Coll., Cornell Medical School and Graduate School of Medicine, Univ. of Pennsylvania; Surgeon-in-Chief, Children's Hospital of Philadelphia 1948–81; Prof. of Pediatric Surgery, Univ. of Pa. 1959–85; Prof. of Pediatrics 1976–85; U.S. Surgeon Gen. 1985–89; Deputy Asst. Sec. for Health and Dir. Office of Int. Health, U.S. Public Health Service (U.S.P.H.S.) 1982; Consultant, U.S.N. 1964–84; Ed. of various medical journals 1961–; now with C. Everett Koop Inst.; McInery Prof., Dartmouth Coll. 1994–; mem. Asscn. Mil. Surgeons (Pres. 1982, 1987); 35 hon. degrees; Hon. F.R.C.S.; Denis Browne Gold Medal (British Asscn. of Paediatric Surgeons) 1971, Duarte, Sanchez and Mella Award of the Dominican Repub., Drexel Univ. Eng. and Science Day Award 1975, Chevalier, Légion d'honneur 1980, U.S.P.H.S. Distinguished Service Medal 1983, Department of Health and New Human Services, Secretary's Recognition Award 1986, Harry S. Truman Award 1990, Presidential Medal of Freedom 1995, Heinz Foundation Award 1995, and other U.S.P.H.S. awards. *Publications:* 230 papers and monographs, several books including Koop: The Memoirs of the Former Surgeon General 1991, Let's Talk 1992. *Leisure interest:* lapidary art. *Address:* 6707 Democracy Blvd., Suite 107, Bethesda, MD 20817, U.S.A. (Office). *Telephone:* (301) 493-6603 (Office). *Fax:* (301) 493-8160.

KOOPMAN, Antonius (Ton) Gerhardus Michael; Netherlands musician and professor of harpsichord; b. 2 Oct. 1944, Zwolle; m. Christine H. H. Mathot 1975; three d.; ed. Amsterdam Conservatory and Univ. of Amsterdam; Prof. of Harpsichord, Royal Conservatory, The Hague; f. Amsterdam Baroque Orchestra 1979; appears on concert platforms around the world and on radio and TV; has made over 200 recordings of harpsichord and organ works by Bach, Handel etc.; Hon. mem. Royal Acad. of Music, London; winner of several prizes. *Publications:* Interpretation of Baroque Music 1985 and a small book about J. S. Bach 1985; (co-ed.) The Harpsichord in Dutch Paintings. *Leisure interests:* art and culture of the renaissance and baroque period. *Address:* Meerweg 23, 1405 BC Bussum, Netherlands. *Telephone:* (0) 35 6913 676. *Fax:* (0) 35 6939 752.

KÖÖRNA, Arno; Estonian economist; b. 2 Feb. 1926, Tartu; s. of Artur and Anna Köörna; m. Eha Lind 1946; two c.; ed. Tartu Univ.; lecturer Tartu Univ. 1953–65; Prof. 1971; Corresp. mem. Estonian Acad. of Sciences 1972, mem. 1975; Scientific Dir. Inst. of Econs. Estonian Acad. of Sciences 1965–66, Dir. 1966–73; Chief Scientific Sec. Presidium of Estonian Acad. of Sciences 1973–82, Vice Pres. 1978–82, Pres. 1990–94. *Address:* Estonian Academy of Sciences, Kohtu str. 6, EE0001 Tallinn (Office); Kapi str. 9-22, EE0001 Tallinn, Estonia (Home). *Telephone:* (3726) 45 17 46 (Office); (3726) 45.14.17 (Home).

KÖPECZI, Béla; Hungarian politician and historian; b. 16 Sept. 1921, Nagyenyed (Aiud in Romania); s. of Árpád Köpeczi and Anna Tomai; m. Edit Bölcskei 1951; ed. Budapest and Paris Univs.; Publr. 1949–53; Vice-Pres., Hungarian Council of Publishing 1953–55; Chair. Hungarian Bd. of Publishing 1955; Head, Cultural Dept. Hungarian Socialist Workers' Party 1964–66; Prof. Univ. of Budapest 1964, Vice-Rector 1967; mem. Hungarian Acad. of Sciences, Deputy Gen. Sec. 1970–72, Gen. Sec. 1972–75, Deputy Sec.-Gen. 1975–82; Minister of Culture and Educ. 1982–88; Dr. h.c. (Paris) 1979, (Rome); State Prize 1980; Commdr. Palmes académiques (France). *Publications:* La France et la Hongrie au début du XVIIIe siècle 1971, Révolté ou révolutionnaire 1973, L'autobiographie d'un prince rebelle 1977, Staatsräson und christliche Solidarität 1983, Hongrois et Français de Louis XIV à la Révolution française 1983, A francia felvilágosodás (The Age of French Enlightenment) 1986, History of Transylvania (ed.) 1986, A bujdosó Rákóczi (Prince Rákóczi in exile) 1991, Histoire de la culture hongroise 1994, Nemzetképkutatás és XIX. századi román irodalom magyarság képe (The Search for National Identity and Hungarian Image in Romanian Literature of the 19th Century) 1995, Az emberisors és a XX szazadifrancia regény (The human condition and the French novel in the 20th century) 1997. *Leisure interests:* literature, music, travelling. *Address:* Tulipán-u. 5, 1022 Budapest, Hungary (Home).

KOPELSON, Arnold, B.S., J.D.; American film producer; b. 14 Feb. 1935, New York; m. Anne Kopelson; ed. New York Univ., New York Law School; with Anne Kopelson exec. producer, producer, packager, developer and distributor of over 100 films; Chair. Arnold Kopelson Productions; Co-Chair. Inter-Ocean Film Sales Ltd.; NATO/ShoWest Producer of the Year 1994. *Films produced:* Lost and Found (exec. producer) 1979, The Legacy (exec. producer) 1979, Night of the Juggler (exec. producer) 1980, Foolin' Around 1980, Final Assignment (exec. producer) 1980, Dirty Tricks (exec. producer) 1981, Model Behavior (exec. producer) 1984, Platoon 1986 (Acad. Award Best Picture), Warlock (exec. producer and int. distributor) 1989, Triumph of the Spirit 1989, Fire Birds (exec. producer) 1990, Out for Justice 1991, Falling Down 1993, The Fugitive 1993, Outbreak 1995, Seven 1995, Eraser 1996, Murder at 1600 1997, Mad City 1997, The Devil's Advocate 1997, U.S. Marshals 1998. *TV film:* Past Tense. *Address:* Kopelson Entertainment, 2121 Avenue of the Stars, Suite 1400, Los Angeles, CA 90067, U.S.A.

KOPPEL, Ted, M.A.: American journalist; b. 1940, Lancs., England; m. Grace A. Dorney; four c.; ed. Syracuse and Stanford Univs.; went to U.S.A. 1953; news corresp., writer, WMCA, New York 1963; with ABC News 1963, news corresp. Vietnam; Chief, Miami Bureau, ABC News; Chief, Hong Kong Bureau; diplomatic corresp. Hong Kong Bureau, ABC News, Washington; anchorman, ABC News Nightline 1980–; corresp. for TV specials including The People of People's China 1973, Kissinger: Action Biography 1974, Second to None 1979, The Koppel Reports 1988–90; co-author with Marvin Kalb, TV special: In the National Interest (Overseas Press Club Award), numerous awards. *Publications:* The Wit and Wisdom of Adlai Stevenson 1985, In The National Interest 1977, Nightline: History In the Making 1996. *Address:* c/o Nightline, 1717 De Sales Street, N.W., Washington, DC 20036, U.S.A.

KOPPER, Hilmar; German banker; b. 13 March 1935; C.E.O. Deutsche Bank AG –1997, Chair. Supervisory Bd. 1997–; Chair. of Supervisory Bd. Daimler-Benz AG, Stuttgart, Lincas GmbH, Hamburg; mem. Supervisory Bd. Akzo, Arnhem, Netherlands, Bayer AG, Leverkusen, Deutsche Lufthansa AG, Cologne, Deutsche Bank, Frankfurt, Mannesmann AG, Düsseldorf, Münchener Rückversicherungs-Gesellschaft, Munich, VEBA AG, Düsseldorf; Chair. Advisory Bd. Brauerei Beck & Co., Bremen, Frowein GmbH & Co. KG, Wuppertal, Leopold Kostal GmbH & Co. KG, Lüdenscheid; mem. Advisory Bd. Solvay & Cie. SA, Brussels; fmr. Deputy Chair. Bd. Morgan Grenfell Group PLC, London; mem. Bd. St. Helens. *Leisure interests:* reading, collecting the wrappings that encase citrus fruits in greengrocers' shops. *Address:* c/o Deutsche Bank AG, Taunusaulage 12, 60262 Frankfurt/Main, Germany.

KOPTEV, Yuri Nikolayevich, CAND. TECH. SC; Russian engineer and manager; b. 13 March 1940, Stavropol; m.; two s.; ed. Bauman Higher Tech. School; worked as engineer Lavochkin Science-Tech. Corpn. 1965–69; author of a number of space-rocket projects; Sr. Engineer, Head of Dept., then Deputy Minister, Ministry of Gen. Machine Construction 1969–91; Vice-Pres. Kosmos Corpn. 1991–92; Dir.-Gen. Russian Space Agency 1992–; Co-Chair. Space Cttee. Russian-American Comm. for Econ. and Tech. Co-operation 1993–; U.S.S.R. State Prize. *Address:* Russian Space Agency, Shchepkina str. 42, 129857 Moscow, Russia (Office). *Telephone:* (095) 971 8021, 288 9905 (Office).

KORALEK, Paul George, C.B.E., R.A., R.I.B.A.; British architect; b. 7 April 1933, Vienna, Austria; s. of the late Ernest Koralek and Alice (née Müller); m. (Audrey) Jennifer Koralek 1956; one s. two d.; ed. Aldenham, Architectural Asscn.; Partner and Dir. Ahrends, Burton & Koralek, Architects 1961–; maj. work includes: new British Embassy, Moscow; stations for extensions of Docklands Railway; Templeton Coll., Oxford 1969, Nebenzahl House, Jerusalem 1972, Warehouse and Showroom for Habitat, Wallingford 1974, residential bldg. for Keble Coll., Oxford 1976, Arts Faculty Bldg. Trinity Coll., Dublin 1979, factory for Cummins Engines, Shotts 1983, supermarket J. Sainsbury, Canterbury 1984, Retail HQ, W. H. Smith, Swindon 1985, dept. store John Lewis, Kingston 1990, St. Mary's Hosp., Newport, Isle of Wight 1990, White Cliffs Heritage Centre, Dover 1991, Dublin Dental Hosp. 1994–, Techniquest Science Discovery Centre, Cardiff 1995, Tralee Regional Tech. Coll. 1996–; Winner Int. Competition for New Library, Trinity Coll., Dublin 1961, Competition for Nat. Gallery Extension 1982–85, Int. Competition for Devt. Plan, Grenoble Univ. 1991, R.I.B.A. Architecture Award 1978, 1996,

R.I.B.A. Housing Award 1977, Structural Steel Design Award 1976, 1980, 1985, Financial Times Award 1976 (Commendation 1986, 1987), Civic Trust Award 1986, 1992. *Publication:* Ahrends, Burton & Koralek (Monograph) 1991. *Address:* Unit 1, 7 Chalcot Road, London, NW1 8LH, England. *Telephone:* 0171-586 3311. *Fax:* 0171-722 5445.

KORD, Kazimierz; Polish conductor; b. 18 Nov. 1930, Pogórza-Cieszyn; m.; ed. Acad. of Music in Leningrad (piano with Wladimir Nilsen) 1949–55; State Higher School of Music in Cracow (conducting with Artur Malawski) 1956–60; Artistic Man. Music Theatre, Cracow 1962–69; Man. and Music. Man. the Great Symphonic Orchestra of Polish Radio and TV in Katowice 1969–73; Gen. and Artistic Man. of State Philharmonic, Warsaw 1977–; Chief Conductor Südwestfunk Orchestra in Baden Baden 1980–86; six years' co-operation with Metropolitan Opera, New York; conducted in the most important music centres all over the world; Critics Award at Music Biennale in Berlin 1971; Gold Orpheus Prize of Polish Musicians Union 1972, Star of the Year, Munich 1975, Minister of Culture and Arts Prize (1st Class) 1977, 1998. *Leisure interest:* astronomy. *Address:* Filharmonia Narodowa, ul. Jasna 5, 00-950 Warsaw, Poland. *Telephone:* (22) 826 56 17. *Fax:* (22) 826 56 17.

KORDA, Michael Vincent, B.A.; American publishing executive; b. 8 Oct. 1933, London, England; s. of Vincent Korda and Gertrude (née Musgrove) Korda; m. Carolyn Keese 1958; one s.; ed. Magdalen Coll., Oxford; served R.A.F. 1952–54; joined Simon and Schuster, New York 1958–, firstly as Ed., then Sr. Ed., Man. Ed., Exec. Ed., now Sr. Vice-Pres. and Ed.-in-Chief; mem. Nat. Soc. of Film Critics, American Horse Shows Asscn. *Publications:* Male Chauvinism: How It Works 1973, Power: How to Get It, How to Use It 1975, Success! 1977, Charmed Lives 1979, Worldly Goods 1982, The Fortune 1989. *Address:* Simon and Schuster, 1230 Avenue of the Americas, New York, NY 10020, U.S.A.

KORDA, Petr; Czech tennis player; b. 23 Jan. 1968, Prague; s. of Petr Korda and Jana Korda; m. Regina Rajchrtova 1992; coached by his father until aged 18; coached by Tomas Petera 1991–; winner Wimbledon jr. doubles 1986; turned professional 1987; winner Stuttgart Open 1997, Australian Open 1998, Qatar Open 1998; mem. Czechoslovak Davis Cup Team 1988, 1996; runner-up French Open 1992; winner Grand Slam Cup 1993; lives in Monte Carlo.

KORHONEN, Keijo Tero, PH.D.; Finnish diplomatist; b. 23 Feb. 1934, Paltamo; s. of Hannes Korhonen and Anna née Laari; m. 1st Anneli (née Torkkila) 1958, three s.; m. 2nd Anita (née Uggeldahl) 1990; ed. Turku Univ.; Prof. of Int. Relations, Univ. of Arizona 1964–; Deputy Dir. for Political Affairs, Ministry of Foreign Affairs 1971–74; Prof. of Political History, Univ. of Helsinki 1974–77; Minister of Foreign Affairs 1976–77; Under-Sec. of State for Political Affairs, Ministry of Foreign Affairs 1977–83; Perm. Rep. to UN 1983–88; Special Adviser to Prime Minister 1988–89; Ed.-in-Chief Kainuun Sanomat 1989–94; Presidential cand. (independent) 1994. *Publications:* four books about Finnish-Soviet and Finnish-Russian relations since 1808; Finland in the Russian Political Thought of the 19th century 1966, An Ambassador's Journal, Urho Kekkonen, the Leader and the Man, The Reverse Side of the Coin 1989, This Country Is Not For Sale 1991. *Leisure interests:* reading, jogging, horse riding. *Address:* HC 1, Box 611, Tucson, AZ 85736, U.S.A. *Telephone:* (520) 822-2705. *Fax:* (520) 822-2706.

KOŘÍNKOVÁ, Květoslava, C.SC.; Czech politician; b. 10 July 1940, Český Brod, Dist. Kolín; m. Ant. Peltrám 1975; ed. Inst. of Transport, Žilina, Slovakia –1967; worked as railwaywoman, deputy head, Goods Depot, Station of Český Brod 1957–64; technician, research worker, Research Inst. of Transport, Prague 1964–71; specialist, Ministry for Technological Devt. and Investment of ČSSR 1971–72; mem. Presidium, Czech Council of the Czechoslovak Scientific-Technological Soc. 1972–87; Minister-Chair., Fed. People's Control and Auditing Cttee. 1989–90; Fed. Govt. Minister of Control and Auditing 1990–92; mem. Presidium, EUROSAI 1990–; Chair. Women's Comm., Czechoslovak Scientific-Technological Soc. 1970–89, Chair. Women's Club 1989–; mem. Govt. Comm. for Equal Rights for Women 1990–; teacher, Pardubice Univ. of Transport 1993–; mem. Czech Social Democratic Party 1994–, Deputy Chair. 1995–; mem. Municipal Metropolitan Council of Prague 1994–; mem. Parl. (Social Democratic Party) 1996–98, Vice-Pres. Foreign Cttee. of Parl. 1996–, mem. Standing Comm. of Parl. for banking –1998, Standing Del. for co-operation with European Parl. –1998; Insp.-Gen. of Railways 1998–. *Publications:* text-books for secondary schools of transport and numerous articles.

KORNAI, János, DR.SC.; Hungarian economist; b. 21 Jan. 1928, Budapest; m. Zsuzsa Dániel 1971; two s. one d.; ed. Univ. of Budapest; Econ. Ed. 1947–55; Research Assoc. Inst. of Econs., Hungarian Acad. of Sciences 1955–58, Inst. of Textile Industry 1958–63; Sr. Research Assoc., Computer Centre, Hungarian Acad. of Sciences 1963–67; Research Prof., Inst. of Econs., Hungarian Acad. of Sciences 1967–; Prof. of Econs., Harvard Univ. 1986–; Perm. Fellow, Collegium Budapest 1992–; Visiting Prof., L.S.E. 1964, Univ. of Sussex 1966, Stanford Univ. 1968, Yale 1970, Princeton and Stanford 1972–73, Stockholm 1976–77, Geneva 1981, Munich 1983, Princeton 1983–84, Harvard 1984–85; mem. Hungarian Acad. of Sciences; Corresp. mem. British Acad.; Foreign mem. Royal Swedish Acad., Finnish Acad., Russian Acad. of Sciences; Hon. mem. American Acad. of Arts and Sciences, American Econ. Asscn.; Hon. Dr. (Paris) 1978, (Poznań) 1978, (London) 1990, (Amsterdam), (Budapest) 1992, (Wrocław) 1993, (Turin) 1993; Seidman Award 1982, Hungarian State Prize 1983, Humboldt Prize 1983, Széchenyi Prize 1994. *Publications:* Overcentralization in Economic Administration 1959, Mathematical Planning of Structural Decisions 1967, Anti-Equilibrium 1971, Rush versus Harmonic Growth 1972, Economics of Shortage 1980, Non-Price Control 1981, Growth, Shortage and Efficiency 1982, Contradictions and Dilemmas 1985, The Road to a Free Economy 1990, Vision and Reality 1990, The Socialist System 1992, Highways and Byways 1994, Struggle and Hope 1997. *Address:* Collegium Budapest, Institute for Advanced Study, Szentháromság utca 2, 1014 Budapest (Office); Department of Economics, Harvard University, Littauer Center, Cambridge, MA 02138, U.S.A.; Dobsinai utca 13, 1124 Budapest, Hungary (Home). *Telephone:* (1) 457-7612 (Office, Hungary); (617) 495-1236 (U.S.A.). *Fax:* (1) 457-7628 (Hungary); (617) 495-7730 (U.S.A.).

KORNBERG, Arthur, M.D., D.SC., LL.D., L.H.D.; American biochemist; b. 3 March 1918, New York; s. of Joseph and Lena Katz Kornberg; m. 1st Sylvy R. Levy 1943 (died 1986); three s.; m. 2nd Charlene W. Levering 1988; ed. City Coll. of New York and Univ. of Rochester; commissioned Officer, U.S. Public Health Service 1941–42; Nat. Insts. of Health, Bethesda, Md. 1942–52; Prof. and Chair. Dept. of Microbiology, Washington Univ. School of Medicine 1953–59; Prof., Dept. of Biochemistry, Stanford Univ. School of Medicine 1959–88, Prof. Emer. 1988–, Head 1959–69; mem. N.A.S., American Philosophical Soc., American Acad. of Arts and Sciences, Foreign mem. Royal Soc. 1970; Hon. LL.D., City Coll. of New York 1960, D.Sc. (Notre Dame, Washington, Rochester and Pennsylvania), L.H.D. (Yeshiva Univ.) 1962, D.Sc. (Prince-ton) 1970, D.Sc. (Colby Coll.) 1970, M.D. (Univ. of Barcelona) 1970; Nobel Prize in Medicine and Physiology (with Prof. Ochoa) 1959 and many other awards. *Publications:* For the love of Enzymes: the odyssey and a biochemist (autobiog.) 1989, numerous original research papers and reviews on subjects in biochemistry, particularly enzymatic mechanisms of biosynthetic reactions. *Address:* Department of Biochemistry, Stanford University Medical Center, Stanford, CA 94305 (Office); 365 Golden Oak Drive, Portola Valley, CA 94025, U.S.A. (Home).

KORNBERG, Sir Hans (Leo), Kt., M.A., D.SC., SC.D., PH.D., F.R.S., F.R.S.A., F.I. BIOL.; British professor of biochemistry; b. 14 Jan. 1928, Herford, Germany; s. of Max and Margarete (née Silberbach) Kornberg; m. 1st Monica M. King 1956 (died 1989); twin s. two d.; m. 2nd Donna Haber 1991; ed. Queen Elizabeth Grammar School, Wakefield and Univ. of Sheffield; John Stokes Research Fellow, Univ. of Sheffield 1952–53; mem. Medical Research Council Cell Metabolism Research Unit, Univ. of Oxford 1955–61; Lecturer in Biochem., Worcester Coll., Oxford 1958–61; Prof. of Biochem., Univ. of Leicester 1961–75; Sir William Dunn Prof. of Biochem., Univ. Cambridge 1975–95; Univ. Prof. and Prof. of Biology, Boston Univ., Boston, Mass., U.S.A. 1995–; Fellow Christ's Coll., Cambridge 1975–, Master 1982–95; Chair. Science Bd., S.R.C. 1969–72, mem. 1967–72; Chair. Royal Comm. on Environmental Pollution 1976–81; mem. Agric. and Food Research Council 1980–84; mem. Priorities Bd. for Research and Devt. in Agric. 1984–90; Chair. Advisory Cttee. Genetic Modification 1986–95, Jt. Policy Group Agric. and Environment 1986–89; mem. of Bd. NIREX 1986–95; Pres. Int. Union of Biochem. and Molecular Biology 1991–94, The Biochemical Soc. 1990–95; mem. Advisory Council for Applied Research and Devt. 1982–85; Scientific Advisory Cttee. Inst. for Molecular Biology and Medicine, Monash Univ. 1987–; Commonwealth Fund Fellow (Yale Univ. and Public Health Research Inst., New York) 1953–55; Hon. mem. Soc. Biological Chem. (U.S.A.) 1972, Japanese Biochem. Soc. 1981; mem. German Acad. of Sciences Leopoldina 1982; Foreign Assoc. N.A.S. 1986; Foreign Hon. mem. American Acad. of Arts and Sciences 1987; mem. Acad. Europaea 1988; Fellow, American Acad. of Microbiology 1992; Foreign mem. American Philosophical Soc. 1993, Accad. Nazionale dei Lincei, Italy 1997; Hon. F.R.C.P. 1989; Vice-Pres. Inst. of Biology 1969–72; Vice-Chair. European Molecular Biological Org. 1978–81; Pres. British Asscn. for the Advancement of Science 1984–85; Pres. Asscn. for Science Educ. 1991–92; Leeuwenhoek Lecturer, Royal Soc. 1972; Man. Trustee, Nuffield Foundation 1973–93; Trustee, Wellcome Trust 1990–95; Hon. Fellow Worcester Coll. Oxford, Brasenose Coll. Oxford, Wolfson Coll. Cambridge; Hon. Sc.D. (Cincinnati) 1974, Hon. D.Sc. (Warwick) 1975, (Leicester) 1979, (Sheffield) 1979, (Bath) 1980, (Strathclyde) 1985, (South Bank) 1994, (Leeds) 1995, (La Trobe) 1997; Hon. D.Univ. (Essex) 1979, Hon. M.D. (Leipzig) 1984; Colworth Medal (Biochemical Soc.) 1963, Warburg Medal (Gesellschaft für biologische Chemie der Bundesrepublik, Fed. Repub. of Germany) 1973. *Publications:* numerous articles in scientific journals. *Leisure interests:* conversation, cooking. *Address:* The University Professors, Boston University, 745 Commonwealth Avenue, Boston, MA 02215, U.S.A.

KORNBLUM, John Christian, B.A.; American diplomatist; b. 6 Feb. 1943, Detroit, Mich.; s. of Samuel Christian Kornblum and Ethelyn Kornblum (née Tonkin); m. Helen Sen 1987; two s.; ed. Michigan State Univ., Georgetown Univ., D.C.; Officer-in-Charge of Berlin and Eastern Affairs, Bonn 1970–73; mem. policy planning staff Dept. of State 1973–75, Officer-in-Charge of European Regional Political Affairs 1977–79, Dir. of Cen. European Affairs 1981; political adviser to U.S. mission, Berlin 1979–81, Minister and Deputy Commdt. 1985; Deputy Rep. to NATO, Brussels 1987; Amb., Rep. to CSCE 1991; Sr. Deputy Asst. Sec. of State for European Affairs 1994; Asst. Sec. of State for European and Canadian Affairs 1996; Amb. to Germany 1997–; mem. U.S. Del. to Quadripartite Negotiations, Berlin 1970–72; co-ordinator meeting of 1977, Chair. U.S. Del. to Helsinki 1992, Head U.S. Del. to Vienna 1992; Kt.'s Cross, Germany 1991, Order of Merit, Austria 1994. *Leisure interests:* music, sports, gardening, travel. *Address:*

American Embassy, Deichmanns Aue 29, 53170 Bonn, Germany (Office). *Telephone:* (228) 3391. *Fax:* (228) 3392663.

KÖRNER, Stephan, JUR.DR., PH.D., F.B.A.; British philosopher; b. 26 Sept. 1913, Ostrava, Czechoslovakia; s. of Emil Körner and Erna Maier Körner; m. Edith Laner 1944; one s. one d.; ed. Classical Gymnasium, Charles Univ., Prague, and Trinity Hall, Cambridge; Army Service 1936–39, 1943–46; Lecturer in Philosophy, Univ. of Bristol 1946–52, Prof. 1952–79, Dean, Faculty of Arts 1965–66; Pro-Vice-Chancellor, Univ. of Bristol 1968–71; Prof. Yale Univ. 1970–83; Visiting Prof. of Philosophy, Brown Univ. 1957, Yale Univ. 1960, Texas Univ. 1964, Indiana Univ. 1967, Graz Univ. 1980–84; Ed. Ratio 1961–80; Pres. British Soc. for Philosophy of Science 1965, Aristotelian Soc. 1967, Int. Union of History and Philosophy of Science (Div. of Logic, Methodology and Phil. of Science) 1969–71, Mind Asscn. 1973; Fellow of British Acad. 1967; mem. Int. Inst. of Philosophy 1971; Hon. D.Litt. (Queen's Univ.) Belfast 1983, Dr. h.c. (Graz Univ.) 1984, Hon. Fellow, Bristol Univ. 1986, Trinity Hall, Cambridge 1991. *Publications:* Kant 1955, Conceptual Thinking 1955, The Philosophy of Mathematics 1960, Experience and Theory 1966, Kant's Conception of Freedom (British Acad. Lecture) 1967, What is Philosophy? 1969, Categorial Frameworks 1970, Abstraction in Science and Morals 1971, Experience and Conduct 1976; Ed. Observation and Interpretation 1957, Ed. Philosophy of Logic 1976, Metaphysics: Its Structure and Function 1984; contributor to philosophical periodicals. *Leisure interest:* walking. *Address:* 10 Belgrave Road, Bristol, BS8 2AB, England. *Telephone:* (0117) 9733036.

KORNILOV, Vladimir Nikolaevich; Russian writer and poet; b. 29 June 1928, Dnepropetrovsk; s. of Nikolai Kornilov and Elisaveta Manzon; m. 1st Galina Eremeeva 1952 (divorced 1963), 2nd Larisa Bespalova 1963; two d.; ed. Gorky Inst. of Literature; first works published 1953; expelled from Writers' Union 1977, membership restored 1988; mem. PEN 1975–. *Publications include:* Driver 1961, The Harbour 1964, The Age (lyrics) 1967, Without Arms, Without Legs 1975, Building a Prison 1984, Girls to the Front 1985, Hope 1988, Music for Oneself 1988, The Benefit of Impressions 1989, Demobilization 1990, Selected Poetry 1991, My Very Own Verses 1995, So Long As Verse Makes Us Cry (essays on poetry) 1997. *Leisure interests:* chess, carpentry. *Address:* Krasnoarmeiskaya str. 21, Apt. 76, 125319 Moscow, Russia. *Telephone:* 151-32-82.

KOROLEV, Mikhail Antonovich, DR.ECON.SC.; Russian statistician; b. 12 Sept. 1931, Alma-Ata; s. of A. I. Korolev and T. A. Ivanova; m. Letalina Koroleva 1957; one d.; ed. Moscow Plekhanov Inst. of Nat. Econ.; Asst. Dean, Dept. Head, Moscow Inst. of Econ. Statistics 1954–66, Rector 1966–72, Prof. 1967–; Deputy, First Deputy Dir. Cen. Statistics Board of U.S.S.R. 1972–85, Dir. 1985–87; Pres. U.S.S.R. State Cttee. on Statistics 1987–89; Adviser to Prime Minister of U.S.S.R. 1991; Pres. Interstate Statistical Cttee. of the C.I.S. 1992–; cand. mem. of CPSU Cen. Cttee. 1986–90; Deputy to U.S.S.R. Supreme Soviet 1986–89; Chair. Statistical Comm. of UN 1979–81, Vice-Chair. 1976–79, 1989–91; mem. Int. Statistical Inst.; mem. Int. Informatics Acad.; Hon. Scientist. *Publications:* 20 books, numerous articles. *Address:* Interstate Statistical Committee of the Commonwealth of Independent States, 39 Myasnitskaya Street, Moscow, Russia. *Telephone:* (095) 921-19-73. *Fax: (095)* 207-45-92.

KOROMA, Abdul G.; Sierra Leonean diplomatist and lawyer; ed. King's Coll., Univ. of London, Kiev State Univ.; barrister and Hon. Bencher (Lincoln's Inn) and legal practitioner, High Court of Sierra Leone; joined Sierra Leone govt. service 1964, Int. Div., Ministry of External Affairs 1969; del., UN Gen. Assembly; mem. Int. Law Comm. (Chair. 43rd Session); mem. of dels. to 3rd UN Conf. on the Law of the Sea, UN Conf. on Succession of States in Respect of Treaties, UN Comm. on Int. Trade Law, Special Cttee. on the Review of the UN Charter and on the Strengthening of the Role of the Org. Cttee. on the Peaceful Uses of Outer Space; Vice-Chair. UN Charter Cttee. 1978; Chair. UN Special Cttee. of 24; Deputy Perm. Rep. of Sierra Leone to the UN 1978–81, Perm. Rep. 1981–85; fmr. Amb. to EEC and Perm. Del. to UNESCO; Amb. to Ethiopia and OAU 1988; Perm. Rep. to UN –1993; Judge Int. Court of Justice 1994–; High Commr. in Zambia and Tanzania; Chair., UN 6th Cttee. (Legal); Vice-Pres. African Soc. of Int. and Comparative Law, African Soc. of Int. Law; del. to numerous int. confs.; lecturer at numerous univs.; mem. Int. Planning Council of Int. Ocean Inst.; mem. American Soc. of Int. Law; Hon. LL.D. (Kiev State Univ.); Insignia of Commdr. of Rokel 1991. *Publications:* articles on int. law. *Leisure interests:* reading, music, sports. *Address:* International Court of Justice, Peace Palace, Carnegieplein, 2517 KJ The Hague, The Netherlands. *Telephone:* (70) 302 2323. *Fax:* (70) 302 2409.

KOROMA, Sorie Ibrahim; Sierra Leonean politician; b. 30 Jan. 1930, Port Loko; m.; c.; ed. Govt. Model School, Freetown, Bo Govt. School and Co-operative Coll., Ibadan, Nigeria; worked in Co-operative Dept. 1951–58; in pvt. business 1958–62; First Sec.-Gen. Sierra Leone Motor Transport Union 1958; M.P. 1962–65, 1967; Councillor and Deputy Mayor of Freetown 1964; Minister of Trade and Industry 1968–69, of Agric. and Nat. Resources 1969–71; Vice-Pres. of Sierra Leone 1971–79, First Vice-Pres. 1981–86, Prime Minister 1971–75, Minister of the Interior 1971–73, 1981–82, of Finance 1975–78, of Devt. and Econ. Planning 1977–78, of State Enterprises 1978–79; Vice-Chair. FAO Conf., Rome 1971; Rep. of Sierra Leone to OAU Summit Conf., Addis Ababa 1971, Morocco 1972; Commdr. of the Republic of Sierra Leone; decorations from Lebanon, People's Repub. of China, Ethiopia, Liberia. *Leisure interests:* reading, football, sport. *Address:* c/o Office of the First Vice-President, Tower Hill, Freetown, Sierra Leone. *Telephone:* 2757.

KOROTCHENYA, Ivan Mikhailovich; Belarus politician; b. 1948, Minsk Region; ed. Minsk Agric. Acad.; worked as chief agronomist, Chair. collective farm, Chair. Regional Union of Collective Farms, Chair. Viley Dist. Soviet of People's Deputies; Deputy of Belarus Supreme Soviet, mem. Accord faction 1994–96; mem. Presidium; Chair. Comm. on Problems of Glasnost, Mass Media and Human Rights 1990–92; elected coordinator of Workgroup at Council of Leaders of States and Leaders of Govts. C.I.S. Countries after disintegration of U.S.S.R. 1992–98; Deputy Exec. Sec. C.I.S. Secr. 1998–. *Address:* Secretariat on Problems of C.I.S., Kirova str. 17, 220050 Minsk, Belarus (Office).

KOROTEYEV, Anatoly Sazonovich; Russian physicist; b. 22 July 1936, Moscow Region; s. of Sazon Z. Koroteyev and Maria P. Koroteyeva; m.; one s.; ed. Moscow Aviation Inst.; engineer, sr. engineer, head of div., First Deputy Dir. Research Inst. of Thermal Processes (now Keldysh Research Centre) 1959–88, Dir. 1988–; Corresp. mem. U.S.S.R. (now Russian) Acad. of Sciences 1990, mem. 1994; research in generation and diagnostics of low-temperature plasma; U.S.S.R. State Prize. *Publications:* Generator of low-temperature plasma 1966, Applied Dynamics of Thermal Plasma 1975, Plasmotrons: Structures, Characteristics, Calculation 1993; numerous articles. *Leisure interests:* history, skiing. *Address:* M. Keldysh Research Centre, Onezhskaya str. 8/10, 125438 Moscow, Russia. *Telephone:* (095) 456 4608. *Fax:* (095) 456-8228.

KOROTYCH, Vitaliy Alekseyevich; Ukrainian/Russian writer and poet; b. 26 May 1936, Kiev; s. of Alexy Korotych and Zoa Korotych; m. Linaida Korotych 1958; two s.; ed. Kiev Medical Inst.; physician 1959–66; ed. of Ukrainian literary journal Ranok 1966–77; Ed.-in-Chief Jesuit magazine 1978–86; Ed.-in-Chief Ogoniok weekly magazine 1986–91; Sec. of Ukrainian Writers' Union 1966–69; mem. U.S.S.R. Writers' Union 1981–90; U.S.S.R. People's Deputy 1989–91; two State Prizes, U.S.S.R. *Publications include:* Golden Hands 1961, The Smell of Heaven 1962, Cornflower Street 1963, O Canada! 1966, Poetry 1967, Metronome (novel) 1982, The Face of Enmity (novel) 1984, Memory, Bread and Love 1986, many translations from English into Ukrainian and other Slavonic languages. Lived in U.S.A. 1991–98, returned to Moscow.

KORS, Michael; American fashion designer; b. 9 Aug. 1959, Mineola, N.Y.; s. of William Kors and Joan L. Kors; ed. Fashion Inst. of Tech.; f., proprietor Kors Co. 1981, Pres. 1981–; Dupont American Original Prize. *Publications:* articles in Vogue, The New York Times and other newspapers and magazines. *Leisure interests:* theatre, film, travel. *Address:* 550 7th Ave, 7th Floor, New York, NY 10018, U.S.A.

KORTHALS, Robert W., B.SC., M.B.A.; Canadian banker; b. 7 June 1933, Maracaibo,Venezuela; ed. Univ. of Toronto, Harvard Business School; with Electric Reduction Co. of Canada Ltd. 1955–59; with Nesbitt, Thomson and Co. Ltd. 1961–67; with Toronto-Dominion Bank 1967–, Supt. Term Financing, Int. Div. 1967–68, Supt. Nat. Accounts Div. 1968–69, Asst. Gen. Man. 1969–72, then Gen. Man. Nat. Accounts Div. 1972, Vice-Pres. Admin. 1972–76, Sr. Vice-Pres. 1976–78, Exec. Vice-Pres. and Chief Gen. Man. 1978–81, Pres. 1981–95; Chair. N. American Life Assurance Co.; Dir. many other cos. including TD Mortgage Corpn., Hayes-Dana Inc., Toronto Dominion Bank, Jannock Ltd. and Co-Steel Inc.; Gov. Cen. Hospital, Toronto; mem. Ont. Business Advisory Council. *Leisure interests:* sailing, tennis, skiing. *Address:* 2525–121 King Street W., Toronto, Ontario, M5H 3T9, Canada.

KORTLANDT, Frederik H. H., PH.D.; Netherlands professor of linguistics; b. 19 June 1946, Utrecht; ed. Univ. of Amsterdam; Asst. Prof. of Slavic Linguistics, Univ. of Amsterdam 1969–72; Assoc. Prof. of Balto-Slavic Languages, Univ. of Leiden 1972–74, Prof. 1974–; Prof. of Descriptive and Comparative Linguistics 1985–; mem. Royal Netherlands Acad. 1986–; Spinoza Prize Laureate 1997. *Publications:* Modelling the phoneme 1972, Slavic accentuation 1975, numerous articles on linguistics and Slavic, Germanic, Celtic, Armenian, Japanese and other languages. *Leisure interest:* classical music. *Address:* Faculty of Letters, P.O. Box 9515, 2300 RA Leiden (Office); Cobetstraat 24, 2313 KC Leiden, Netherlands (Home). *Telephone:* (71) 527-2501.

KORTÜM, Franz-Josef; German business executive; b. 18 Aug. 1950, Billerbeck, Coesfeld; m.; three c.; ed. studies in Münster and Regensburg; employed in family car retailing co. Billerbeck 1975; car sales exec. Bielefeld subsidiary of Daimler-Benz AG 1976; Head, Passenger Car Field Sales, Used Vehicle Sales and Truck Sales, Berlin subisidiary of Daimler-Benz AG 1979; Asst. to Dir. of Sales Org. Germany, Daimler-Benz AG, Stuttgart-Untertürkheim 1985; Dir. Saarbrücken subsidiary of Daimler-Benz AG 1987; Dir. Cen. Admin. Daimler-Benz AG 1989; Man. Dir. Mercedes-Benz-owned co. Rheinische Kraftwagengesellschaft (RKW), Bonn 1990; mem. Man. Bd. AUDI AG 1992, Chair. 1993–95. *Address:* c/o AUDI AG, Postfach 10 02 20, 8070 Ingolstadt, Germany.

KORVALD, Lars; Norwegian politician; b. 29 April 1916, Nedre Eiker; s. of Engebret Korvald and Karen Wigen; m. Ruth Borgersen 1943; one s. four d.; ed. Coll. of Agriculture; Teacher, Tomb School of Agric. 1943–48; Chief Adviser, League of Norwegian Agricultural Clubs 1948–52; Headmaster, Tomb School of Agric. 1952–77; mem. Storting 1961–81; del. to UN Gen.

Assembly 1963, 1968; mem. Advisory Assembly, Council of Europe 1965–70; mem. Nordic Council 1966–81, Vice-Pres. 1979–81; Chair. Christian Dem. Party 1967–75, 1977–79; Pres. Lagting (Upper House of Storting) 1969–72; Prime Minister 1972–73; Gov. Østfold Dist. 1981–86; Commdr. St. Olav's Order (Norway) 1986. *Publication:* Politics and Christianity (memoirs, with Per Øyvind Heradstveit) 1982. *Leisure interests:* skiing, literature. *Address:* Vinkelgt. 6, 3050 Mjondalen, Norway.

KORZHAKOV, Lieut.-Gen. Aleksander Vasilyevich; Russian army officer; b. 31 Jan. 1950, Moscow; m.; two d.; ed. All-Union Inst. of Law; mem. Dept. 9 State Security Cttee. 1970–89; personal bodyguard of First Sec. Moscow CPSU Cttee. Boris Yeltsin (q.v.) 1986–87; f. and Chief Security Service of Russian Supreme Soviet 1990–91; Head Security Service of Pres. of Russia 1991–96, Deputy Chief Main Admin. of Bodyguards 1992–96 (discharged); participated in suppression of attempted coup of Aug. 1991 and confrontation of Oct. 1993; mem. State Duma (Parl.) 1997–. *Publication:* From Dawn to Decline (memoirs) 1997. *Leisure interest:* tennis. *Address:* State Duma, Okhotny Ryad 1, 103009 Moscow, Russia. *Telephone:* (095) 292 8000.

KORZHAVIN, Naum (pseudonym of Naum Moiseyevich Mandel); Russian author and poet; b. 14 Oct. 1925, Kiev; ed. Karaganda Mining Inst. and Gorky Inst. of Literature, Moscow 1959; first publication 1941; exiled to West (U.S.A.) 1974; revisited Moscow 1989; citizenship and membership of Writers' Union restored 1990. *Publications include:* The Years 1963, Where Are You? 1964, Bread, Children in Auschwitz, Autumn in Karaganda, Verse 1981, Selected Verse 1983, Interlacements 1987, Letter to Moscow 1991, The Time is Given 1992; contributor to émigré dissident journal Kontinent. *Address:* 28c Colborne Road, Apt. 2, Brighton, MA 02135, U.S.A.

KORZHEV-CHUVELYOV, Gely Mikhailovich; Russian artist; b. 7 July 1925, Moscow; ed. Surikov State Inst. of Arts, Moscow; professional artist 1950–; has participated in many Soviet and foreign exhbns. 1950–; Prof. Moscow Higher Artist-Tech. Inst. 1966–; mem. U.S.S.R. (now Russian) Acad. of Arts 1970; Chair. of Bd. of Artists' Union of R.S.F.S.R. (now Russia) 1968–75; Sec. Bd. of Dirs. of Artists' Union of U.S.S.R. (now Russia); Merited Worker of Arts of the R.S.F.S.R.; Repin State Prize of U.S.S.R.; People's Artist of the R.S.F.S.R. 1972. *Address:* Bolshoi Devyatinski per. 5, Apt. 45, Moscow, Russia. *Telephone:* 212-55-29.

KOSAI, Akio, B.A.; Japanese business executive; b. 19 April 1931, Okayama; ed. Univ. of Tokyo; joined Sumitomo Chemical Co., Ltd. 1954, Dir. and Gen. Man. Industrial Chemicals and Fertilizers Div. 1983; Pres. Petrochemical Corpn. of Singapore (Pte) Ltd. 1984–87; Man. Dir. Sumitomo Chemical Co., Ltd. 1987, Sr. Man. Dir. 1991, Pres. 1993–. *Address:* Sumitomo Chemical Co., Ltd., 27-1, Shinkawa 2-chome, Chuo-ku, Tokyo, 104, Japan. *Telephone:* 03-5543-5152. *Fax:* 03-5543-5908.

KOSÁRY, Domokos; Hungarian historian; b. 31 July 1913, Selmecbánya; m. Klára Huszti 1937; one d.; ed. Univ. of Budapest, Eötvös Coll., Budapest, Sorbonne Paris, Inst. of Historical Research, London; Prof. Eötvös Coll. 1937–50; Dir. Inst. of History, Teleki Inst. 1945–49; founder and Ed.-in-Chief Revue d'Histoire Comparée (Budapest) 1943–48; Prof. of Modern History Univ. of Budapest 1946–49; divested of functions by the authorities 1949; Pres. Revolutionary Council of Historians 1956; sentenced to four years imprisonment 1957, released 1960; archivist, later scientific researcher, then scientific counsellor Inst. of History Hungarian Acad. of Sciences, corresp. mem. 1982; mem. Hungarian Acad. of Sciences 1985–, Pres. 1990–96; mem. Academia Europaea, London, Académie Européenne, Paris, British Acad., London, Croatian Acad. of Sciences and Arts, Zagreb, Romanian Acad., Bucharest; Pres. Nat. Cttee. of Hungarian Historians 1985–90; Laureate of Hungarian State Prize 1988; Széchenyi Grand Prize (Hungary); Gold Medal, Slovak Acad. of Science 1997; Officier Ordre des Palmes académiques 1988, Officier Légion d'honneur 1996; Grand Cross (Hungary) 1993. *Publications:* numerous works include: Introduction to the Sources and Literature of Hungarian History (3 vols.) 1951–58, Culture in 18th Century Hungary 1980, Small States Facing Cultural, Political and Economic Changes, from 1750 to 1914 1985, History of the Görgey Problem 1994. *Leisure interest:* gardening. *Address:* Institute of History, Hungarian Academy of Sciences, Uri u. 53, 1014 Budapest, Hungary. *Telephone:* (1) 356-9539. *Fax:* (1) 356-9539.

KOSCHNICK, Hans Karl-Heinrich; German politician; b. 2 April 1929, Bremen; m. Christel Risse; ed. Mittelschule; Local Govt. Official, Bremen 1945–51, 1954–63; Trade Union Sec. of the Union of Public Employees, Transport and Communications (ÖTV) 1951–54; mem. Social Democratic Party (SPD) 1950–, Fed. Exec. Council 1970–, Party Bd. 1975–, Deputy Chair. SPD 1975–79; mem. Provincial Diet of Land Bremen (Landtag) and City Admin. 1955–63; Senator for the Interior 1963–67; Mayor of Bremen 1967–85; Pres. of the Senate, Bremen 1967–85; mem. Fed. Council (Bundesrat) 1965–, Pres. 1970–71, 1981–82; Nat. Vice-Chair. SPD 1975–79; Chair., German Union of Local Authorities (Deutscher Städtetag) 1971–77; mem. Bd. Städtetag (Assoc. of German Municipalities) 1970–, Pres. 1971–77; mem. Exec. Cttee. Int. Union of Local Authorities (IULA) 1972–77, 1980–85, Pres. 1981–85; M.P. 1987–. *Leisure interest:* chess. *Address:* Rudolstädterweg 9, 28329 Bremen, Germany. *Telephone:* 4673733.

KOSHIRO, Matsumoto, IX (b. Teruaki Fujima); Japanese actor; b. 1942; s. of the late Koshiro VIII; m.; one s.; debut in Kabuki (Japanese traditional theatre) when child; as child acted under name Kintaro, as young man Somegoro Ichikawa; became Koshiro IX 1980. *Plays acted in include:* Kanjincho (and many other Kabuki plays), Man of La Mancha (included 10-week run on Broadway), The King and I (including 6-month run in West End), Half a Sixpence, Sweeney Todd, Fiddler on the Roof, Amadeus (Salieri). *Address:* c/o Kabukiza Theatre, No. 12–15 Ginza 4 chome, Chuo-ku, Tokyo 104, Japan.

KOSHLAND, Daniel E., Jr., B.S., PH.D.; American professor of biochemistry; b. 30 March 1920, New York; s. of Daniel E. and Eleanor Haas Koshland; m. Marian Elizabeth Elliott 1945; two s. three d.; ed. Univs. of California and Chicago; Analytical Chemist, Shell Chemical Co. 1941–42; Research Assoc. and Group Leader, Manhattan District, Univ. of Chicago and Oak Ridge Nat. Lab. 1941–46; Post-doctoral Fellow, Harvard Univ. 1949–51; Assoc. Biochemist, Biochemist, Sr. Biochemist, Brookhaven Nat. Lab. 1951–65; Affiliate, Rockefeller Univ. 1958–65; Prof. of Biochem., Univ. of Calif., Berkeley 1965–97, Prof. of Molecular Biology 1997, Chair. Dept. Biochem. 1973–77; Visiting Prof. Cornell Univ. 1957–58; Pres. American Soc. of Biological Chemists 1973–74; Ed.-in-Chief, Science Magazine 1985–95; mem. N.A.S., American Acad. of Arts and Sciences, American Philosophical Soc.; Hon. mem. Japanese Biochem. Soc., Royal Swedish Acad. of Science; Guggenheim Fellow 1972, Visiting Fellow, All Souls Coll., Oxford 1971–72; Fellow, American Asscn. for Advancement of Science; Hon. Ph.D. (Weizmann Inst.) 1984; Hon. Sc.D. (Carnegie Mellon Univ.) 1985, Hon. LL.D. (Simon Fraser Univ.) 1986; Hon. L.H.D. (Mt. Sinai Univ.) 1981; J. Duckett Jones Award 1977, Pauling Award, American Chemical Soc. 1979, Edgar Fahs Smith Award, American Chemical Soc. 1979, Rosenstiel Award 1984, Waterford Prize 1984, Nat. Medal of Science 1990, Merck Award, American Soc. of Biochemistry and Molecular Biology 1991. *Publications:* articles on enzymes in scientific journals; Bacterial Chemotaxis as a Model Behavioural System 1980. *Leisure interests:* tennis, golf, sailing. *Address:* c/o Department of Molecular and Cell Biology, University of California, Berkeley, CA 94720 (Office); 3991 Happy Valley Road, Lafayette, CA 94549, U.S.A. (Home). *Telephone:* (415) 642-0416 (Office).

KOSICE, Gyula; Argentinian artist and poet; b. 26 April 1924, Košice, Czechoslovakia (now Slovakia); s. of Joseph F. Kosice and Eta Kosice (née Berger); m. Haydée Itaovit 1947; two d.; ed. Acad. of Arts, Buenos Aires; co-f. Arturo magazine 1944, Concrete Art Invention 1945; f. Madí Art Movement 1946, f., Ed. Universal Madí Art magazine 1947; first use of neon gas in art 1946; introduction of water as essential component of his work 1948; creator Hydrospatial City (concept) 1948–; works include sculptures, hydrospatial courses, hydromurals; over 30 solo and 400 jt. exhbns. including Madí Art exhbn. Salon des Réalités Nouvelles, Paris 1948, 50-year retrospective Museum of Fine Arts, Buenos Aires 1991; works included in museums and pvt. collections in Argentina, Latin America, U.S.A., Europe and Asia; Ordre des Arts et des Lettres 1989; numerous prizes. *Publications:* Invención 1945, Madí Manifesto 1946, Golse-Se (poems) 1952, Peso y Medida de Alberto Hidalgo 1953, Antología Madí 1955, Geocultura de la Europa de Hoy 1959, Poème hydraulique 1960, Arte Hidrocinético 1968, La Ciudad Hidroespacial 1972, Arte y Arquitectura del Agua 1974, Arte Madí 1982 (Best Art Book, Asscn. of Art Critics 1982), Obra Poética 1984, Entrevisiones 1984, Teoría sobre el Arte 1987, Arte y Filosofía Porvenirista 1996. *Leisure interests:* writing books on art, creating works of art. *Address:* Humahuaca 4662, Buenos Aires (Office); República de la India 3135 6° A, 1425 Buenos Aires, Argentina (Home). *Telephone:* (1) 867-1240 (Office); (1) 801-8615 (Home). *Fax:* (1) 807-0115 (Home).

KOSSACK, Georg, F.B.A.; German professor of pre- and early history; b. 25 June 1923, Neuruppin; s. of Fritz Kossack and Franziska (née v. Unruhe) Kossack; m. Ruth Kossack 1947; one s. one d.; Prof. Univ. of Kiel 1959–75, Univ. of Munich 1975–, now Prof. Emer.; mem. German Archaeological Inst., Bayerische Akademie der Wissenschaften; Fellow British Acad., mem. Slovenian Acad. Ljubljana. *Publications:* Studien zum Symbolgut Urnenfelder und Hallstallzeit 1954, Sübayern während Hallstallzeit 1959, Graeberfelder Hallstallzeit 1979, Archsum auf Sylt I 1980, II 1987, Ed. Siedlungen im deutschen Küstengebiet 1984, Skythika 1987, Maoqinggou (with T. Höllmann) 1992, Towards Translating the Past. Selected Studies in Archaeology 1998. *Leisure interest:* reading nineteenth century history. *Address:* Pietzenkirchen 56a, 83083 Riedering, Germany. *Telephone:* 08036-7342.

KOSTABI, Kalev Marki; American artist and composer; b. 27 Nov. 1960, Los Angeles; ed. Calif. State Univ., Fullerton; became involved in East Village art movement, New York 1984; f. Kostabi World (studio, gallery, offices) 1988; retrospective exhbns. Mitsukoshi Museum, Tokyo 1992, Art Museum of Estonia, Tallinn 1998; represented in various perm. collections including Museum of Modern Art, New York, Metropolitan Museum of Art, New York, Guggenheim Museum, New York, Brooklyn Museum, Corcoran Gallery of Art, Washington, D.C., Groninger Museum; has designed album covers including Guns 'n' Roses' Use Your Illusion, The Ramones' Adios Amigos; has also designed a Swatch watch, limited-edition vases, computer accessories; produces weekly cable TV show Inside Kostabi; lectures internationally. *Album:* I Did It Steinway 1998. *Publications include:* Sadness Because the Video Rental Store Was Closed, Kostabi: The Early Years, Conversations With Kostabi. *Address:* Kostabi World, 555 West 25th Street, New York, NY 10001, U.S.A. *Telephone:* (212) 645-1174. *Fax:* (212) 645-1314.

KOSTENKO, Lina Vasilievna; Ukrainian poet; b. 12 March 1930, Rzhischevo, Kiev Region; ed. Maxim Gorky Inst. of Literature, Moscow; Ukrainian

S.S.R. State Prize 1987. *Publications:* Lights of the Earth 1957, The Winds 1958, Particles of the Heart 1961, Bank of the Eternal River 1977, Inimitability 1980, Marusya Churay (novel in verse) 1979–82, Scythian Woman 1981, Garden of Unmelting Snow 1987, Selected Poetry 1990, numerous publs. in literary magazines. *Address:* Chkalova str. 52, Apt. 8, 252054 Kiev, Ukraine (Home). *Telephone:* (044) 224 70 38 (Home).

KOSTIĆ, Branko; Yugoslav (Montenegrin) politician; b. 1939, Rvaši, Montenegro; joined CP 1957; Pres. of Presidency of Montenegro 1989–90; mem. Yugoslav Collective Presidency, Vice-Pres. 1991–92; Prof. of Law Univ. of Montenegro 1992–. *Address:* University of Montenegro, 81000 Podgorica, Cetinjski, put b.b., Yugoslavia.

KOSTIKOV, Vyacheslav Vasilyevich; Russian politician, journalist and diplomatist; b. 24 Aug. 1940; Moscow; m. Marina Smirnova, one d.; ed. Moscow State Univ., All-Union Acad. of Foreign Trade, Sheffield Univ., U.K.; staff-mem., ed. Div. of Information UNESCO Secr. in Paris 1972–78, 1982–88; political reviewer Press Agency Novosti 1978–82; Press Sec. of Pres. Boris Yeltsin 1992–95; plenipotentiary rep. of Russia in Vatican City and Amb. to Malta 1995–96; Pres. Finance Group Moskovsky Delovoy Mir (MDM) 1996–97; Deputy Dir.-Gen. Media-Most Holding Oct. 1997–. *Publications:* numerous books including Romance with the President 1996; numerous articles in dailies Izvestia, Ogonyok, reviews in Times of India. *Address:* Most-Media, Maly Gnezdikovskiy per. 7, 103009 Moscow, Russia. *Telephone:* (095) 229-62-14.

KOSTOV, Ivan; Bulgarian politician; fmr. economist; Minister of Finance 1990–92; Chair. Union of Democratic Forces; Prime Minister of Bulgaria May 1997–. *Address:* Council of Ministers, 1000 Sofia, Blvd. Knjaz Dondukov 1, Bulgaria.

KOSTRZEWSKI, Jan Karol, M.D., M.P.H.; Polish scientist; b. 2 Dec. 1915, Cracow; s. of Jan Kostrzewski and Maria Sulikowska; m. Ewa Sobolewska 1948; one s. three d.; ed. Jagiellonian Univ., Cracow and Harvard School of Public Health, Boston; Health Service Doctor 1939–51; Head of Epidemiology Dept., State Hygiene Inst., Warsaw 1951–78; Prof. of Epidemiology Warsaw Medical Acad. 1954–60; Under-Sec. of State, Ministry of Health and Social Welfare and Chief Sanitary Inspector 1961–68; Minister of Health and Social Welfare 1968–72; Scientist State Hygiene Inst. 1973–78; fmr. Head of Epidemiology Dept.; Corresp. mem. Polish Acad. of Sciences (PAN) 1967–76, mem. 1976–, mem. Presidium 1971–89, Sec. Dept. of Medical Sciences 1972–80, Vice-Pres. 1981–83, Pres. 1984–89; Chair. Cttee. Nat. Health Protection Fund 1981–; Chair. Research Strengthening Group UNDP/World Bank/WHO Special Programme on Tropical Diseases Research; Vice-Chair. Nat. Council of Patriotic Movt. for Nat. Rebirth 1983–89; Deputy to Sejm (Parl.) 1985–89; Chair. Presidium of Ecological Social Movt. 1986–; fmr. mem. Consultative Council attached to Chair. of Council of State; mem. Exec. Bd. WHO 1973, Chair. 1975; mem. Council Int. Epidemiological Asscn. 1974, Pres. 1977–81; Hon. mem. Mechnikov Soc. Microbiologists and Epidemiologists 1956–, later Pres.; Sec. Int. Comm. for Assessment of Smallpox Eradication in India, Nepal, Ethiopia, Horn of Africa and Bhutan 1977–79; Corresp. mem. Acad. Nationale de Médecine (Paris) 1979, Global Advisory Comm. for Medical Research 1980, Foreign mem. Acad. of Medical Sciences, U.S.S.R. 1986, Foreign Fellow Indian Nat. Science Acad. 1986; Visiting Prof. of Centre Diseases Control, Atlanta, U.S.A. 1976; Heath Clark Lecturer Univ. of London 1986–87; Dr. h.c. (WAM, Łódź) 1979, (AM, Lublin) 1985; mem. External Review Team for Human Reproduction Research Program 1988–89; Order of Banner of Labour 1st and 2nd Class, Commdr. and Knight's Cross, Order of Polonia Restituta, Cross of Valour, Gold Cross of Merit, Warsaw Insurgent Cross and others. *Publications:* numerous works on epidemiology. *Leisure interests:* sport, photography, skiing, fishing. *Address:* al. Róż 10 m. 6, 00-556 Warsaw, Poland. (Home). *Telephone:* (22) 49 31 04 (Office).

KOSTYUK, Platon Grigorievich; Ukrainian neurophysiologist, physician and biologist; b. 20 Aug. 1924, Kiev; s. of G. S. Kostyuk and M. F. Kostyuk; m. Liudmila V. Kostyuk 1950; two d.; mem. CPSU 1947–91; ed. Kiev State Univ. and Kiev Medical Inst.; Head, Dept. of Gen. Physiology of Nervous System, A.A. Bogomoletz Inst. of Physiology 1958–, Dir. of Inst. 1966–; Head, Dept. of Membrane Biophysics, Moscow Physico-Tech. Inst. 1982–; mem. Ukrainian Acad. of Sciences, Russian, Czechoslovak and Hungarian Acads., Akad. Leopoldina; mem. Exec. Cttee. European Neurosciences Asscn. (ENA); Chair. United Scientific Council for Problems of Human and Animal Physiology; Pavlov Prize 1960; Sechenov Prize 1977; State Prize 1983; A.A. Bogomoletz Prize 1987. *Publications:* Intracellular Perfusion of Excitable Cells 1984, Role of Calcium Ions in Nerve Cell Function 1991. *Leisure interests:* tennis, downhill skiing. *Address:* A.A. Bogomoletz Institute of Physiology, 4 Bogomoletz Street, 252601 Kiev 24, Ukraine. *Telephone:* (044) 293-20-13 (Office); 224-20-71 (Home). *Fax:* (044) 293-64-58.

KOSUGI, Takashi; Japanese politician; mem. House of Reps.; fmr. Parl. Vice-Minister of Environment; Minister of Educ. 1996–97. *Address:* c/o Ministry of Education, Science and Culture, 3-2-2, Kasumigaseki, Chiyoda-ku, Tokyo 100, Japan (Office).

KOSUTH, Joseph; American artist; b. 31 Jan. 1945, Toledo, Ohio; Prof. School of Visual Arts, New York City 1967–, Hochschule für Bildende Kunst, Hamburg 1988–91, Kunstakademie, Stuttgart 1991–; Brandeis Univ. Creative Art Award 1991, Frederick R. Weisman Art Foundation Award 1991, Venice Biennale Menzione d'Onore 1; Chevalier Ordre des Arts et des Lettres. *Publication:* Art After Philosophy and After (collected writings) 1991. *Address:* 591 Broadway, New York, NY 10012, U.S.A.; Maagdestraat 6, 9000 Ghent, Belgium. *Telephone:* (212)-219-8984 (New York); (9) 233-4849 (Ghent).

KOSZAROWSKI, Tadeusz Tomasz; Polish surgeon and oncologist; b. 16 Sept. 1915, Bicas (Brazil); s. of Walery Koszarowski and Stanisława Koszarowska; m. 1st Alina Węgrowicz Koszarowska 1941 (died 1989); m. 2nd Bogna Schubert-Zborowska 1991; ed. Warsaw Univ.; Asst., Prof. 1954, Extraordinary Prof. 1961, Ordinary Prof. 1973; with Inst. of Tuberculosis, Wola Hospital, Warsaw: surgeon 1939–52, Head Oncological Surgery Ward 1948–52, Maria Skłodowska-Curie Radium Inst. (later Oncological Inst.) Warsaw, Chief Surgeon, Vice-Dir. 1952–72, Dir. 1972–86; Dir. Nat. Cancer Programme 1975–85; Pres. Polish Medical Soc. 1962–70, Pres. Main Council Asscn. of Polish Medical Socs. 1966–70; Deputy to Sejm (Parl.) 1980–85, mem. Consultative Council Presidium of Sejm 1986; mem. of Consulting Council attached to Chair. Council of State 1986–89; Chair. Social Health Council attached to Ministry of Health and Social Welfare 1982–86; mem. Science Council of Minister of Health and Social Welfare 1962–83; Pres. Nat. Council Polish YMCA 1990–91, Hon. Pres. 1991–; Pres. Council Ecumenical Foundation "Tolerance" 1993; Pres. Cttee. for bldg. New Cancer Centre in Warsaw 1990–; mem. New York Acad. of Science 1984; Hon. mem. Polish Acad. of Medicine 1991; Alfred Jurzykowski Foundation Award, New York 1969; numerous Polish decorations including Order of Builders of People's Poland, Order of Banner of Labour (First Class) 1984. *Publications:* over 200 scientific works in Polish and foreign journals on oncological surgery, combating cancer and epidemiology of cancer; major works: Onkologia praktyczna w klinice chirurgicznej 1965, Chirurgia onkologiczna 1972, Cancer in Poland, City of Warsaw and Selected Rural Areas 1977, Oncological Surgery 1980, Cancer Surgery 1982, Onkologia kliniczna 1984, Epidemiology of Cancer in Poland 1952–82 1985. *Leisure interests:* literature, art. *Address:* ul. Orłowicza 6 m. 22, 00-414 Warsaw, Poland. *Telephone:* (22) 628 58 75 (Office).

KOTAITE, Assad, LL.D.; Lebanese international aviation official and lawyer; b. 6 Nov. 1924, Hasbaya; s. of Adib Kotaite and Kamle Abousamra; m. Monique Ayoub 1983; ed. French Univ., Beirut, Univ. of Paris and Acad. of Int. Law, The Hague; Head of Legal and Int. Affairs, Directorate of Civil Aviation, Lebanon 1953–56; Rep. of Lebanon, Council of ICAO 1956–70; Sec.-Gen. ICAO, 1970–76, Pres. Council 1976–; Pres. Int. Court of Aviation and Space Arbitration, Paris 1995–. *Address:* c/o International Civil Aviation Organisation, 999 University Street, Suite 12.20, Montreal, Quebec, H3C 5H7 (Office); 5955 Wilderton Avenue, Apt. O4A, Montreal H3S 2V1, Canada. (Home). *Telephone:* (514) 954-8011 (Office).

KOTCHEFF, Ted; Canadian film and stage director; b. 7 April 1931, Toronto; with CBC Television 1952–57; joined ABC-TV, London 1957; plays include Play With A Tiger, Maggie May, The Au Pair Man, Have You Any Dirty Washing, Mother Dear? *Films include:* Life At The Top 1965, Two Gentlemen Sharing 1968, Wake In Fright 1971, The Apprenticeship of Duddy Kravitz (in Canada) 1973–74, Fun with Dick and Jane 1977, Who is Killing the Great Chefs of Europe? 1978, North Dallas Forty (dir. and wrote) 1979, First Blood, Split Image, 1982–83, Uncommon Valour 1984, Joshua, Then and Now 1985, Weekend at Bernie's 1989, Winter People (dir.) 1990, Folks! (actor), The Shooter 1996. *TV plays include:* The Human Voice 1966, Of Mice And Men 1968, Edna The Inebriate Woman 1971. *Address:* c/o ICM, 8942 Wilshire Boulevard, Beverly Hills, CA 90211, U.S.A.

KOTELKIN, Maj.-Gen. Aleksander Ivanovich; Russian politician; b. 19 Nov. 1954, Kiev; m.; one s.; ed. Kiev Higher School of Eng. and Aviation, Mil. Diplomatic Acad.; served in the army, engineer of aviation equipment Kiev Mil. command 1976–87; with U.S.S.R. Mission in U.N., New York 1988–90; on staff Ministry of External Econ. Relations 1991–94; Head Chief Dept. on mil.-tech. co-operation 1993–94; Dir.-Gen. State Co. Rosvooruzheniye 1994–97; First Deputy Minister of Foreign Econ. Relations and Trade 1997–98. *Address:* MVES, Smolenskaya-Sennaya 32/34, 121200 Moscow, Russia. *Telephone:* (095) 220-19-56 (Office).

KOTELNIKOV, Vladimir Aleksandrovich; Russian radio and electronics engineer; b. 6 Sept. 1908, Kazan; s. of Alexander Petrovich Kotelnikov and Varvara Petrovna Kotelnikova; m. Anna Ivanova Bogatskaya 1990 (deceased); one s. two d.; ed. Power Eng. Inst., Moscow; Prof. and Dean, Radio Eng. Faculty, Moscow Power Eng. Inst. 1931–47, Head, Chair. of Radio Eng. Principles, Moscow Power Eng. Inst. 1947–80; Deputy Dir. Inst. of Radio Eng. and Electronics, U.S.S.R. (now Russian) Acad. of Sciences 1953–54, Dir. 1954–87, Hon. Dir. 1987–; mem. U.S.S.R. (now Russian) Acad. of Sciences 1953–, Vice-Pres. 1970–88, Acting Pres. May–Nov. 1975, Counsellor 1988–; Chair. 'Intercosmos' Section of Council on Space, Russian Acad. of Sciences 1993–, Vice-Chair. Council on Space 1993–; Chair. Supreme Soviet of R.S.F.S.R. 1973–79; Vice-Pres. Int. Acad. of Astronautics; Life Fellow Int. Inst. of Electrical and Electronics Engineers; Foreign mem. Polish Acad. of Sciences, Czechoslovak Acad. of Sciences, Mongolian Acad. of Sciences, Bulgarian Acad. of Sciences; State Prize 1943, 1946, Lenin Prize 1964, Hero of Socialist Labour (twice), and other decorations. *Publications:* works on improvement of wireless communications, radio-location of planets. *Leisure interest:* books. *Address:* Russian Academy of Sciences, Leninsky Prospekt 14, 117901, GSP-I, Moscow V-71, Russia. *Telephone:* 954-38-28, 954-30-06. *Fax:* (7095) 954-10-74.

KOTENKOV, Maj.-Gen. Aleksander Alekseyevich; Russian politician; b. 23 Sept. 1952, Krasnodar Territory; m.; one s.; ed. Rostov-on-Don Inst. of Agric. Machine Construction, Mil.-Political Acad. by corresp.; engineer Rostov-Don Factory Rubin 1974–75; army service 1975–90; People's Deputy Russian Fed. 1990–93; Deputy Chair. Cttee. Supreme Soviet on Defence and Security 1991; Deputy Head, Head State Law Dept., Russian Presidency, 1992–93; Head Provincial Admin. Martial Law Zone N. Ossetia and Ingushetia 1993–95; Deputy Minister of Nat. Policy 1995–96; mem. State Duma (Parl.) 1993–96; Rep. of Russian Presidency in State Duma 1996–. *Address:* State Duma. Okhotny Ryad 1, 103265 Moscow, Russia (Office). *Telephone:* (095) 292 9123 (Office).

KOTLYAKOV, Vladimir Mikhailovich; Russian scientist; b. 6 Nov. 1931, Voldja, Tomsk Region; m.; two c.; ed. Moscow State Univ.; jr. researcher, sr. researcher, Head of Glaciology Dept., Inst. of Geography U.S.S.R. (now Russian) Acad. of Sciences 1956–91, Dir. 1991–; corresp. mem., Russian Acad. of Sciences 1976, mem. 1991–; Pres. Russian Geographical Soc.; mem. European Acad.; Hon. mem. American and Mexican Geographical Socs. *Publications include:* Snow Cover of Antarctica 1961, Snow Cover of the Earth and Glaciers 1968, Glaciology Dictionary 1977. *Leisure interests:* travelling. *Address:* Institute of Geography, Staromonetny per. 29, 109017 Moscow, Russia. *Telephone:* (095) 238 8277 (Office).

KOTT, Jan, PH.D.; American (b. Polish, naturalized 1978) literary critic and university professor; b. 27 Oct. 1914, Warsaw; s. of Maurycy Kott and Kazimiera Wertenstein; m. Lidia Steinhaus 1939; one s. one d.; served with Polish Army 1939, Polish Resistance Movt. 1943–45; Prof. of History of Polish Literature, Univ. of Warsaw; Visiting Prof. at Yale Univ. 1966–67, 1968–69, 1978–79, at Univ. of Calif. Berkeley 1967–68; Prof. of Comparative Drama, State Univ. N.Y. at Stony Brook 1969–74, of English and Comparative Literature 1974–85, Prof. Emer. 1985–; Visiting Prof. of Drama, Hebrew Univ. Jerusalem 1972; Visiting Prof. of English at Istituto Universitario Orientale, Naples 1983; Guggenheim Fellow 1972–73; Getty Scholar 1985–86; Herder Award, Vienna 1964, Alfred Jurzykowski Award, New York 1976, George G. Nathan Award, Best Dramatic Criticism 1985; Hon. mem. Modern Language Assn.; Officier, Ordre des Arts et des Lettres 1989. *Publications:* Mitologia i realizm (Mythology and Realism) 1946, Szkoła klasyków (The School of the Classics) 1949, Jak wam się podoba (As You Like It) 1955, Postęp i głupstwo (Progress and Folly) 1956, Szkice o Szekspirze (Essays on Shakespeare) 1961, Shakespeare, notre contemporain (French trans.) 1962, Miarka za miarkę (Measure for Measure) 1962, Shakespeare, Our Contemporary (English trans.) 1964, Szekspir Wspólczesny 1965, Aloes 1966, Theatre Notebook 1947–67 1968, The Eating of the Gods: An Interpretation of Greek Tragedy 1973, Arcadia amara 1978, The Publications of Jan Kott 1979, Kamienny Potok (essays) 1981, The Theater of the Essence 1984, Gledaliski Ejeji 1985, Zjadanie Bogow 1986, Pozorište Esencije i Drugi Esei (essays) 1986, Kamienny Potok (essays) 1986, Marlowe and Shakespeare and the Carnival Tradition 1987, Four decades of Polish Essays 1990, La vie en sursis: Esquisses pour une biographie 1991, Przyczynek do biografii 1990, Gott-Essen 1991, Pisma wybrane (selected works) 1991, The Gender of Rosalind: Interpretations—Shakespeare, Büchner, Gautier 1992, The Memory of the Body 1992, Nowy Jonasz i inne szice 1994, Przyczynek do biografii Zawal 1994, Still Alive: An autobiographical essay 1994, Bajki dla Lidusi 1994, Kadysz. Strony o Tadeuszu Kantorze 1997, Bajke za Lidusju 1997. *Leisure interest:* collecting kitsch postcards. *Address:* 2501 Beverly Avenue, Apt. 17, Santa Monica, CA 90405, U.S.A. *Telephone:* (310) 452-6225. *Fax:* (310) 452-6225.

KOTTO, Yaphet Fredrick; American actor; b. 15 Nov. 1944, Harlem, New York; s. of Yaphet Mangobell Kotto and Gladys M. Kotto; m. Antoinette Pettyjohn 1975; six c.; appeared in Off-Broadway and Broadway productions including Great White Hope, Blood Knot, Black Monday, In White America, A Good Place to Raise a Boy, Fences (London) 1990. TV appearances in Raid on Entebbe 1977, Rage 1980, Women of San Quentin 1983, In Self Defense 1987, Badge of the Assassin, Harem, Desperado, Perry Mason, Prime Target, After the Shock, Chrome Soldiers, It's Nothing Personal, Extreme Justice, The American Clock, Deadline For Murder. *Films include:* Nothing But a Man 1963, Liberation of Lord Byron Jones 1964, Across 110th Street 1973, Live and Let Die 1974, Report to the Commissioner 1974, Sharks Treasure 1974, Monkey Hustle 1975, Drum 1976, Blue Collar 1977, Alien 1978, Brubaker 1979, Hey Good Looking 1982, Fighting Back 1982, Star Chamber 1983, Eye of the Tiger, Prettykill, The Running Man, Midnight Run, Nightmare of the Devil (also dir.), Terminal Entry, Jigsaw, A Whisper to a Scream, Tripurie, Ministry of Vengeance, Hangfire, Freddy's Dead, Almost Blue, Intent to Kill, The Puppet Masters, Two If By Sea.

KOUANDÉTÉ, Lieut.-Col. Maurice; Benin politician and army officer; b. 1939; ed. Ecole de Guerre, Paris; Dir. of Cabinet of Head of State 1967–69; Head of State and Head Provisional Govt. Dec. 1967; Chief of Staff of Dahomey (now Benin) Army 1969–70; leader of coup which overthrew Pres. Zinsou Dec. 1969; mem. of Directory (three man body ruling Dahomey), Minister of the Economy, Finance and Co-operation 1969–70; arrested 1970; Deputy Sec. for Defence 1970–72; arrested Feb. 1972, sentenced to death May 1972, granted amnesty and released Dec. 1972; arrested Feb. 1996, detention overturned by constitutional court.

KOUASSI, Kwam, DR.RER.POL.; Togolese diplomatist; ed. Caen Univ. and the Sorbonne, Paris; Asst. in Public Law, Univ. of Benin 1975, then Lecturer at Ecole Supérieure d'Administration et des Carrières Juridiques, later Asst. Dir. of Univ. and Chair. of Univ.'s Comité de Lectures des Annales; served as Togo's Amb. to Cuba and to Costa Rica; Vice-Pres. UN's Conf. for the Announcement of Contributions to the Int. Year of Peace and Pres. of same to the World Disarmament Campaign, Perm. Rep. of Togo to UN 1985–88, Vice-Chair. UN Special Political Cttee. 1985, Chair. 1986–88. *Address:* c/o Ministry of Foreign Affairs and Co-operation, place du Monument aux Morts, Lomé, Togo.

KOUCHNER, Bernard, D. EN MED.; French politician and doctor; b. 1 Nov. 1939, Avignon; two s. one d. by Evelyne Pisier; one s. by Christine Ockrent (q.v.); gastro-enterologist, Hôpital Cochin; Founder, Dir. and Pres. Médecins sans Frontières 1971–79; founder, Médecins du Monde 1980; has organized and undertaken numerous humanitarian missions around the world since 1968; Sec. of State, Ministry of Social Affairs and Employment May 1988; Sec. of State responsible for Humanitarian Action, Office of Prime Minister 1988–91, Ministry of Foreign Affairs 1991–92; Minister of Health and Humanitarian Action 1992–93, 1997–; Founder Foundation for Humanitarian Action 1993–; mem. European Parl. 1994–; Deputy Pres. Radical Movt. 1996–; radio broadcaster RTL 2 1995; Dag Hammarskjold Prize 1979; Louis Weiss Prize (European Parl.) 1979; Athinai Prize (Alexander Onassis Foundation) 1981; Prix Europa 1984. *Publications:* La France Sauvage, Les Voraces, L'Ile de Lumière, Charité Business, Le Devoir d'Ingérence (jtly.) 1988, Les Nouvelles Solidarités 1989, Le Malheur des Autres 1991, Dieu et les Hommes (jtly.) 1993, Vingt idées pour l'an 2000 1995, Ce que je crois 1995; scripts for TV series under pseudonym Bernard Gridaine. *Address:* Secrétariat d'Etat à la Santé et à l'Action Sociale, 8 avenue de Ségur, 75350 Paris 07 SP; c/o Editions Robert Laffont, 24 avenue Marceau, 75008 Paris, France.

KOUDELKA, Josef; Czech photographer; b. 1938, Boskovice; ed. Univ. of Prague; specialized in photography 1967–; extensive travel throughout Europe documenting lives of gypsies; exhibited in Prague 1961, 1967, 1970, Bergamo 1970, U.K. 1973, Amsterdam 1978, Stockholm 1980, Harvard Univ. 1981, Hayward Gallery, London 1984; *solo exhbns.:* Museum of Modern Art, New York 1975, "Prague 1968", London 1998; mem. Magnum Photos Inc. 1971–. *Publications:* Gypsies 1975, Exiles 1988. *Address:* c/o Magnum Photos Ltd., Mooreland Buildings, 23 Old Street, London, EC1V 9HL, England.

KOULOUMBIS, Evangelos; Greek politician and engineer; b. 1929, Athens; s. of Athanasios Kouloumbis and Anastasia Kouloumbis; m. Dimitra Lambrou; one s. one d.; ed. Athens Polythechnic Univ.; founder mem. Civil Eng. Assn., mem. Gov. Council 1965–67, Pres. 1974–75; Pres. of Tech. Chamber 1974–81; Minister of Public Works in caretaker Govt. 1974; Pres. Greek Cttee. for Balkan Agreement and Co-operation 1975–; mem. Parl. 1981–89; Chair. Council of Energy Ministers of EEC 1983 and many Greek and int. conventions, Perm. Conf. of Engs. of S.E. Europe (COPISEE) 1978–80; hon. mem. League of Cypriot Engs. and Architects; mem. Greek Cttee. UNESCO 1982–83; Minister without Portfolio 1981–82, for Energy and Nat. Resources 1982–84, of Physical Planning, Housing and Environment 1984, for Physical Planning, Housing, Public Works, Transport 1985–88, for the Environment, Physical Planning and Public Works 1985–88; Gov. Nat. Mortgage Bank of Greece 1993–95; Pres. Jt. County Authorities of Athens and Piraeus 1995, Union of County Councils of Greece 1995. *Publications:* articles on economic, social and political matters. *Address:* 11 Kleomenous Street, 106 75 Athens, Greece. *Telephone:* 01-7250333.

KOULOURIANOS, Dimitri, PH.D.; Greek economist; b. 4 Dec. 1930, Koroni; m.; one s. one d.; ed. School of Econ. and Commercial Sciences, Athens and Univ. of Calif., Berkeley; Econ. Research Dept. Bank of Greece 1957–67; World Bank (IBRD) 1968–81, participated in many missions to Africa, Asia and Latin America and was seconded as econ. adviser to Govt. of Ethiopia; mem. European Parl. 1981; Gov. Hellenic Industrial Devt. Bank; Minister of Finance 1982–83; fmr. consultant to UNESCO; Perm. Rep. of Greece to OECD 1986–90; Alt. Dir. European Bank for Reconstruction and Devt. 1991–.

KOUMAKOYE, Kassiré Delwa; Chadian politician; fmr. Minister of Justice; Prime Minister of Chad 1993–95; mem. and Pres. Rassemblement nat. pour la démocratie et le progrès (RNDP); also Leader Convention de l'opposition démocratique (alliance of opposition parties); champion of Cen. Africa in 3,000 m. steeple chase 1965 (record unbroken); sentenced to three months imprisonment for possessing illegal weapons 1996. *Address:* c/o RNDP, N'Djamena, Chad.

KOUMI, Margaret (Maggie); British journalist; b. 15 July. 1942, d. of the late Yiasoumis Koumi and of Melexidia Paraskeva; m. Ramon Sola 1980; ed. Buckingham Gate, London; sec. Thomas Cook 1957–60; sub-ed., feature and fiction writer Visual Features Ltd. 1960–66; sub-ed. TV World 1966–67; Production Ed. 19 Magazine 1967–69, Ed. 1969–86, concurrently Ed. Hair Magazine; Man. Ed. Practical Parenting, Practical Health, Practical Hair and Beauty 1986–87; Jt. Ed. Hello! 1988–93, Ed. 1993–; Eds. of the Year Award 1991. *Publication:* Beauty Care 1981. *Address:* Hello!, Wellington House, 67–71 Upper Ground, London, SE1 9PQ, England. *Telephone:* 0171-667 8721. *Fax:* 0171-667 8722.

KOURGANOFF, Vladimir, D.SC.; French astronomer; b. 1912, Moscow, Russia; m. Ruth Moj 1935; one s. one d.; ed. Univ. of Paris; Research Assoc. Astrophysical Inst. of Paris (C.N.R.S.) 1938–52; Exchange Prof. Oslo Univ. 1946–48; Prof. Lille Univ. 1952–61; Visiting Prof. Berkeley Univ. 1959; Prof.

Univ. of Paris XI (Orsay) 1961–77, Prof. Emer. 1977. *Publications include:* Basic Methods in Transfer Problems 1952, La recherche scientifique (with J. C. Kourganoff) 1958, Astronomie fondamentale élémentaire 1961, Initiation à la théorie de la relativité 1964, Introduction à la théorie générale du transfert des particules 1967, Exercices d'initiation rapide au Russe scientifique (with Ruth Kourganoff) 1969, Introduction à la physique des intérieurs stellaires 1969, La face cachée de l'université 1972, Introduction to Advanced Astrophysics 1980, Quelle école? Pour un enseignement véritable 1984, Un Itinéraire insolite 1998; numerous contribs. to learned journals. *Leisure interests:* piano, general problems of research and of education. *Address:* 20 avenue Paul Appell, 75014 Paris, France.

KOUROS, Andreas Kyriakou, M.A., PH.D.; Cypriot educationist; b. 6 Nov. 1918, Vasilia; s. of Kyriacos Kouros and Eleni Sava; m. Sonia Koskarian 1946; two d.; ed. London and Oxford Univs., Int. Inst. of Educ. Planning, Paris; Teacher 1944–53; Inspector of Schools, Ministry of Educ. 1953–59, Sr. Inspector 1959–61; Head Dept. of Primary Educ. 1961–68; Head of Educ. Planning 1968–70; Dir. of Educ. 1970–72, Minister 1972–74; Educ. Specialist, World Bank 1975–80; Educ. Consultant 1981–. *Publications:* The Construction and Validation of a Group Test of Intelligence for Greek Cypriot Children 1956, Education in Cyprus under the British Administration 1959, Electra 1968. *Leisure interests:* swimming, walking. *Address:* The Kenwood, 5101 River Road, Apartment 610, Bethesda, MD 20816, U.S.A. *Telephone:* (301) 652-2894.

KOUTECKÝ, Josef, M.D., D.SC.; Czech oncologist and university professor; b. 31 Aug. 1930, Prague; s. of Josef Koutecký and Ludmila Koutecká; m. Jitka Popelková 1962; two s. one d.; ed. Charles Univ., Prague; physician Nový Bydžov 1955, Jánské Lázně 1955–57, Surgical Dept., Children's Hosp., Prague 1957–74; Head Centre for Child Cancer 1978–83; Head Inst. of Pediatric Oncology Teaching Hosp., Prague 1983–; Dean 2nd Medical Faculty, Charles Univ., Prague 1990–97; Vice-Rector for External Relations 1997–; Chair. Czech Oncological Soc. 1990–; Chair. 21st Meeting of Int. Soc. of Pediatric Oncology 1989; mem. Grants Agency, Acad. of Sciences 1993–; mem. several scientific socs.; Pres. XXI Meeting of Int. Soc. of Paediatric Oncology 1989; Medal for Merit 1996. *Publications:* 194 publs. including 9 monographs. *Leisure interests:* classical music, graphic art, literature, history of art, collecting antiques. *Address:* Faculty Hospital, V Úvalu 84, 151 12 Prague 5-Motol (Office); Janovského 19, 170 00 Prague 7, Czech Republic (Home). *Telephone:* 02-52 95 64 00 (Office); 02-87 87 90 (Home).

KOUYATÉ, Lansana; Malian international official and diplomatist; fmr. economist; fmr. Special Rep. of UN Sec.-Gen., including missions to Somalia and Rwanda; Exec. Sec. Econ. Community of W. African States (ECOWAS) 1997–. *Address:* ECOWAS, Secretariat Building, Asokoro, Abuja, Nigeria. *Telephone:* (9) 5231858.

KOVÁČ, Michal; Slovak politician, economist and banker; b. 5 Aug. 1930, Lubiša, E. Slovakia; m. Emília Kováčová; two s.; ed. Commercial Acad., Bratislava Univ. of Econs.; Asst. Lecturer Bratislava Univ. of Econs. 1954; joined staff State Bank of Czechoslvakia 1956; fmr. financial adviser to Nat. Bank of Cuba; Deputy Dir. Zivnostenska (trade bank), London 1967–69, recalled, expelled from CP and demoted to bank clerk 1969; researcher, lecturer 1970–78; elected to Fed. Ass. 1990; Minister of Finance, Slovak Repub. 1990, resgnd. 1991; re-elected to Fed. Ass., Chair. Czech Fed. Ass. of Czech and Slovak Fed. Rep. June–Dec. 1992; Pres. of Slovak Repub. 1993–98; C.-in-C. the Armed Forces 1993–98; fmr. mem. Movt. for a Democratic Slovakia, Deputy Chair. 1991–93; Grand Cross, Order of Merit (Poland) 1994, CEELIA Award, American Bar Asscn. 1995, Lions Club Award 1995, White Eagle Order (Poland) 1997, numerous Slovak awards including White Double Cross Order, Lúdovít Štúr Order; *Address:* c/o Office of the President, Hodžovo nám. 1, P.O. Box 128, 810 00 Bratislava, Slovakia.

KOVACEVICH, Stephen; American pianist; b. 17 Oct. 1940, San Francisco; s. of Nicholas and Loreta (née Zuban) Kovacevich; ed. Berkeley High School, Calif.; studied under Lev Shorr and Dame Myra Hess; London début 1961; subsequently appeared at int. music festivals in Edinburgh, Bath, Harrogate, Berlin, San Sebastián and Salzburg; a soloist at Henry Wood Promenade Concerts for fourteen seasons; tours frequently in Europe, America and Australasia; fmr. prin. guest conductor of Australian Chamber Orchestra; fmr. music dir. of Irish Chamber Orchestra; has conducted City of Birmingham Symphony, BBC Philharmonic, Bournemouth Symphony, Royal Liverpool Philharmonic orchestras, Chamber Orchestra of Europe, Nat. Youth Chamber Orchestra; numerous recordings; winner of Kimber Award, Calif. 1959, Mozart Prize, London 1962, Edison Award (for recording of Bartok's 2nd. Piano Concerto), Gramophone Award 1993 (for recording of Brahms 1st Piano Concerto). *Publication:* Schubert Anthology. *Leisure interests:* tennis, chess, cinema, Indian food. *Address:* c/o Van Walsum Management Ltd., 4 Addison Bridge Place, London, W14 8XP, England. *Telephone:* 0171-371 4343. *Fax:* 0171-371 4344.

KOVACIC, Ernst; Austrian violinist; b. 12 April 1943, Kapfenburg; m. A. Kovacic; four s.; ed. Acad. of Music, Vienna; prizewinner, int. competitions, Geneva 1970, Barcelona 1971, Munich 1972; appears throughout Europe, U.K. and U.S.A. with leading orchestras and has appeared at many festivals including Salzburg, Berlin, Vienna, Bath, Edin. and Aldeburgh; repertoire includes major works of baroque, classical and romantic periods and contemporary works. *Address:* c/o Ingpen & Williams, 14 Kensington Court, London, W8 5DN, England. *Telephone:* 0171-937 5158. *Fax:* 0171-938 4175.

KOVÁCS, András; Hungarian film director and script writer; b. 20 June 1925, Kide (now in Romania); ed. Győrffy Coll. and Acad. of Dramatic and Cinematic Arts; Drama reader, Hungarian Film Studio 1950, Drama Dept. Head 1951–57, Film Dir. 1960–; Chair. Parl. Curatorium of Public Foundation for Hungarian TV 1996–98; Pres. Fed. of Hungarian Film and TV Artists 1981–86; Balázs B. Prize, Kossuth Prize 1970; named Eminent Artist. *Author:* Egy film forrásvidéke 1972; *TV films:* Menekülés Magyarországra (Flight to Hungary) 1980, György Lukács Portray 1986. *Films:* Zápor (Summer Rain) 1960, Pesti háztetők (On the Roofs of Budapest) 1961, Isten őszi csillaga (Autumn Star) 1962, Nehéz emberek (Difficult People) 1964, Hideg napok (Cold Days) 1966, Falak (Walls) 1968, Ecstasy from 7 to 10 1969, Staféta (Relay Race) 1970, A magyar ugaron (Fallow Land) 1973, Bekötött szemmel (Blindfold) 1975, Labirintus (Labyrinth) 1976, A ménesgazda (The Stud Farm) 1978, Októberi vasárnap (A Sunday in October) 1979, Ideiglenes Paradicsom (Temporary Paradise) 1981, Szeretők (An Afternoon Affair) 1983, A vörös grófnö (The Red Countess) 1985, Valahol Magyarországon (Rearguard Struggle) 1987, Az álommenedzser (The Dream Manager) 1994, Volt egyszer egy egyetem (Once Upon a University) 1995, Utak Vásárhelyröl (Roads from Vásárhely) 1996. *Leisure interest:* gardening. *Address:* 1122 Budapest, Magyar Jakobinusok tere 2/3, Hungary. *Telephone:* 3567227.

KOVÁCS, Dénes; Hungarian violinist; b. 18 April 1930, Vác; s. of József Kovács and Margit Juhász; m.; one s. one d.; ed. Budapest Acad. of Music under Ede Zathureczky; First Violinist, Budapest State Opera 1951–60; leading Violin Prof. at Budapest Music Acad. 1957–, Dir. of Budapest Music Acad. 1967; Rector Ferenc Liszt Acad. of Music 1971–80, Dean of String Dept. 1980–; concert tours all over Europe, in U.S.A., U.S.S.R., Iran, India, China and Japan; mem. jury in int. competitions: Tchaikovsky, Moscow; Long-Thibaud, Paris; Jean Sibelius, Helsinki; Joseph Joachim, Vienna; Wieniawski, Warsaw; Tokyo; Kossuth Prize 1963, awarded Eminent Artist title 1970, Golden Medal of Labour 1974. *Address:* Music Academy, 1061 Budapest VI, Liszt Ferenc tér 8 (Office); Irányi utca 12, Budapest V, Hungary (Home). *Telephone:* 141-4788 (Office).

KOVÁCS, Pál, M.D.; Hungarian politician and physician; b. 14 July 1940, Gyón; m.; one s.; ed. Medical Univ. of Pécs; gen. practitioner City Hosp. of Dunaujváros 1965–68, Dunaujváros and Nagyvenying 1969–84, Dir. of Health Div., Dunaujváros 1985–90; mem. of Parl. 1990–94; vice-pres. Social, Health and Family Policy Cttee. 1992–94; Minister of Welfare 1994–98; mem. Hungarian Medical Chamber Scientific Asscn. of Hung. Gen. Practitioners.

KOVALEV, Anatoliy Gavrilovich; Russian fmr. diplomatist and poet; b. 18 May 1923, Rostov Dist.; m.; one s.; ed. Moscow Inst. of Int. Relations; entered diplomatic service 1948; mem. CPSU 1945–91; mem. Apparat U.S.S.R. Foreign Ministry 1957–65; Head of First European Dept. at Foreign Ministry 1965–71; U.S.S.R. Deputy Minister of Foreign Affairs and Head of Admin. for Foreign Planning 1971–85; First Deputy Minister of Foreign Affairs 1986–92, Adviser to Minister 1992–; Amb.-at-Large 1993–; mem. U.S.S.R. (now Russian) Union of Writers; U.S.S.R. State Prize 1976. *Publications:* Alphabet of Diplomacy 1965, poems in leading Russian periodicals. *Address:* Ministry of Foreign Relations, Smolenskaya-Sennaya pl. 32/34, Moscow (Office); B. Bronnaya Str. 2/6, Apt. 54, 103104 Moscow, Russia (Home). *Telephone:* 244-47-15 (Office).

KOVALEV, Col.-Gen. Nikolai Dmitriyevich; Russian security officer; b. 1949, Moscow; m.; one d.; ed. Moscow Inst. of Electronic Machine Construction; on staff system of state security KGB 1974–; for 2 years served in Afghanistan; staff mem. Dept. of Fed. Service of Counterespionage of Moscow and Moscow Region –1994; Deputy Dir. Fed. Security Service (FSB) 1994–96; Acting Dir, then Dir. 1996–98; mem. Security Council of Russia; mem. Comm. on Higher Mil. Titles and Posts, Council on Personnel Policy of Pres. of Russia. *Address:* c/o FSB, Bolshaya Lubyanka 1/3, 101000 Moscow, Russia.

KOVALEV, Sergey Adamovich, PH.D.; Russian politician; b. 2 March 1930, Seredina-Buda, Ukraine; s. of Adam Vasil'evich Kovalev and Valentina Vasilerna Kovaleva; m. 1st Elena Viktorovna Tokareva 1949, 2nd Luydmila Uyr'evna Boitsova 1967; one s. two d.; ed. Moscow Univ.; worked as researcher, Moscow Univ.; active participant in movt. for human rights since late 1960s; one of assocs. of Academician A. Sakharov, one of founders Initiative Group for Human Rights 1969; ed. Samizdat Bulletin Chronicles of Current Events, expelled from Moscow Univ. 1969; arrested on charge of anti-Soviet propaganda 1974, sentenced to seven years' imprisonment and three years in exile 1974; lived in Kalinin, returned to Moscow 1987; mem. Project Group for Human Rights of Int. Foundation for Survival and Devt. of Humanity, Engineer Inst. of Problems of Data Transmission U.S.S.R. Acad. of Sciences 1987–90; People's Deputy of Russian Fed. 1990–93; Chair. Cttee. for Human Rights of Supreme Soviet of Russia 1990–93; Co-Chair. Soviet Del. on Moscow Conf. on Human Rights 1991; Chief of Russian Del. to UN Comm. on Human Rights 1992–95; one of founders and leaders of Vybor Rossii; mem. State Duma (Parl.) 1993–; Chair. Pres.'s Cttee. on Human Rights 1994–96; Ombudsman of Russian Fed. 1994–95; Council of Europe Human Rights Prize 1995. *Leisure interests:* hunting, fishing. *Address:* State Duma, Okhotny Ryad 1, 103009 Moscow, Russia. *Telephone:* (095) 292-93-43.

KOVALEVSKY, Jean, D. ÈS SC.; French astronomer; b. 18 May 1929, Neuilly-sur-Seine; s. of Jean Kovalevsky and Helène Pavloff; m. Jeannine Reige 1956; two s. one d.; ed. Univ. of Paris and Ecole Normale Supérieure;

Research Asst. Paris Observatory 1955–59, Yale Univ. 1957–58; Head of Computing and Celestial Mechanics Service, Bureau des Longitudes 1960–71; Exec. Dir. Groupe de Recherches de Geodésie Spatiale 1971–78; founder and first Dir. Centre d'Etudes et de Recherches Géodynamiques et Astronomiques 1974–82, 1988–92; astronomer, Observatoire de la Côte d'Azur, Grasse 1986; Sec. Bureau Int. des Poids et Mesures 1991–97, Pres. 1997–; Pres. Bureau Nat. de Métrologie 1995–; mem. French Acad. of Sciences, Int. Acad. of Astronautics, Academia Europeae, Acad. of Sciences of Turin, Scientific Cttee. European Space Agency 1979–81. *Publications:* Introduction to Celestial Mechanics 1967, Traité de Géodésie (with J. Levallois), Vol 4. 1971, Astrométrie moderne 1990, Modern Astronomy 1995; about 250 scientific papers. *Leisure interests:* gardening, stamp collection. *Address:* CERGA, Observatoire de la Côte d'Azur, avenue Copernic, 06130 Grasse (Office); Villa La Padovane, 8 rue St. Michel, Saint-Antoine, 06130 Grasse, France (Home). *Telephone:* 04-93 40 53 53 (Office); 04-93 70 60 29 (Home). *Fax:* 04-93 40 53 33.

KOVANDA, Karel, M.B.A., PH.D.; Czech diplomatist; b. 5 Oct. 1944, Gilsland, U.K.; s. of Oldrich Kovanda and Ivy Norman; m. Noemi Berová 1993; one s. one d.; ed. Prague School of Agric., Massachusetts Inst. of Tech. and Pepperdine Univ.; leadership, Czech Nat. Student Union 1968–69; emigrated to U.S.A. 1970; lecturer in political science and freelance journalist 1975–80; man. positions in U.S. pvt. sector 1980–90; returned to Czechoslovakia 1990; Czech Ministry of Foreign Affairs 1991–93, Political Dir. 1993, Deputy Minister 1997–98; Perm. Rep. of Czech Repub. to UN 1993–97, to NATO 1998–; Pres. ECOSOC 1997. *Leisure interests:* literature, theatre, travel. *Address:* Czech Mission to NATO, NATO HQ, 1110 Brussels, Belgium. *Telephone:* (02) 707 1727. *Fax:* (02) 707 1703.

KOWALCZYK, H. E. Archbishop Józef, PH.D.; Polish ecclesiastic and diplomatist; b. 28 Aug. 1938, Jadowniki Mikre; ed. Hosianum Higher Ecclesiastic Seminary, Olsztyn, Catholic Univ. of Lublin, Pontifical Gregorian Univ., Rome, Roman Rota Studium; ordained Priest 1962; employee Roman Rota; employee Congregation for the Discipline of the Sacraments; organiser and head Polish Section, State Secr. 1978–89; titular Archbishop of Heraklea and Apostolic Nuncio in Poland 1989–. *Publications:* Dojrzewanie czasu 1998 and ed. of Karol Wojtyła's papers and Polish edition of papal teaching (14 vols.). *Address:* Nuncjatura Apostolska, al. J. Ch. Szucha 12, skr. poczt. 163, 00-582 Warsaw, Poland. *Telephone:* (22) 621 23 37, 628 84 88. *Fax:* (22) 628 45 56.

KOYAMBOUNOU, Gabriel; Central African Republic politician; fmr. civil servant; Prime Minister of Cen. African Repub. 1995–96. *Address:* c/o Office of the Prime Minister, Bangui, Central African Republic.

KOZAKOV, Mikhail Mikhailovich; Russian actor and theatre director; s. of Mikhail Kozakov; b. 14 Oct. 1934, Leningrad; m. 1st; three c.; m. 3rd Anna Yampolskaya; one s. one d.; ed. Moscow Art Theatre Studio School; actor Moscow Mayakovsky Theatre 1958–59, Sovremennik Theatre 1959–64, Moscow Art Theatre 1964–72; Theatre on Malaya Bronnaya 1972–81; worked in Israel as actor, Ghesher Theatre, Chamber Theatre Tel-Aviv 1991–96; returned to Russia 1996; actor, Moscow Mayakovsky Theatre 1996–; f. own theatre co.; gives poetic concerts; debut in film Murder on Dante Street 1956. *Films include:* The Year 1918, Nine Days of a Year, Eugene Grande, An Amphibian Man, A Straw Hat, A Comedy of Errors. *Films directed include:* Anonymous Star, Prokrovsky Gates, If to Believe Lopotukhin, Shadow, Faustus; Peoples' Artist of Russia 1980, U.S.S.R. and Russian State Prizes. *Publications:* Third Call, Sketches in the Sand. *Address:* Mayakovsky Theatre, B. Nikitskaya str. 17, 103009 Moscow, Russia. *Telephone:* (095) 277 0617 (Home).

KOŽENÁ, Magdalena; Czech singer (mezzo-soprano); b. 26 May 1973, Brno; ed. Conservatoire, Brno, Acad. of Music and Dramatic Art, Bratislava; guest of Janáček's Opera, Brno 1991–; soloist Volksoper, Vienna 1996–97; has toured in Europe, U.S.A., Japan, Venezuela, Taiwan, Hong Kong, S. Korea; First Place in Int. Mozart Competition, Salzburg 1995. *Opera roles include:* Dorabella in Così Fan Tutte, Isabella in The Italian Girl in Algiers, Mercedes in Carmen, Annius in La Clemenza di Tito. *Leisure interests:* philosophy, music, swimming, cycling. *Address:* c/o Agency Symfonieta, Beethovenova 4, 602 00 Brno (Office); Národní divadlo, Dvořákova 11, 600 00 Brno, Czech Republic (Home). *Telephone:* (42) 21.97.80, (42) 21.97.87 (Office); (42) 21.30.99, (42) 32.12.85 (Home).

KOZHOKIN, Yevgeny Mikhailovich, CAND. HIST; Russian politologist; b. 9 April 1954; m.; two d.; ed. Moscow State Univ.; on staff Inst. of Comprehensive History U.S.S.R. Acad. of Sciences 1979–92; People's Deputy of Russian Fed. 1990–93; f. and Dir. Russian Inst. of Strategic Studies (R.I.S.I.) 1994. *Address:* Russian Institute of Strategic Studies, Flotskaya str. 15, 125 413 Moscow, Russia (Office). *Telephone:* (095) 454 9254 (Office).

KOZLÍK, Sergej; Slovak politician; b. 27 July 1950, Bratislava; ed. Univ. of Econs.; clerk with Price Authority 1974–88; Head Dept. of Industrial Prices, Ministry of Finance 1988–90; Dir. Exec. Dept. of Antimonopoly Office 1990–92; Sec. Movt. for Democratic Slovakia 1992–; Vice-Premier, Govt. of Slovakia 1993–94; Minister of Finance of Slovak Repub. 1994–97; Deputy to Nat. Council 1994–; Gov. World Bank 1994–, Alt. Gov. IMF 1994–. *Address:* National Council of the Slovak Republic, Mudroňova 1, 812 80 Bratislava, Slovakia. *Telephone:* (07) 535 1111.

KOZLOV, Alexey Semenovich; Russian composer, saxophone player and band leader; b. 13 Oct. 1935, Moscow; m. Lyalya Adburakhmanovna Absalyamova; one s.; ed. Moscow Inst. of Architecture, Moscow Music Coll.; researcher Inst. of Design 1963–76; started playing saxophone in youth clubs 1955; founder and leader of jazz quintet 1959, jazz band of café Molodezhnoye 1961–66; arranger and soloist orchestra VIO-66; f. and music dir. jazz-rock ensemble Arsenal 1973– (awarded Ovation Prize as the best jazz band in Russia 1995); festivals and tours including Delhi and Bombay 1989, Woodstock 1990, Jazz Rally, Düsseldorf 1993, Carnegie Hall 1995, Bonn 1996, with Arsenal, Chamber Soloists of Moscow, the Shostakovich String Quartet, Ars Nova Trio; teacher Moscow Experimental Studio of Jazz Music 1967–76; master classes in towns of Russia and Oklahoma City Univ. 1994; Gen.-Man. Jaz Div., Goskoncert 1995–97; mem. musical cttee. under Pres. of Russia 1997–; author of TV programmes, All That Jazz, Improvisation; composer of jazz, film and theatre music; Merited Artist of Russia. *Publications:* Rock: Roots and Development 1989, Memoirs—My 20th Century; numerous articles in music journals. *Address:* Shchepkin str. 25, Apt. 28, 129090 Moscow, Russia. *Telephone:* (095) 288 3156 (Home). *Fax:* (095) 288 3156.

KOZŁOWIECKI, H.E. Cardinal Adam; Zambian (b. Polish) ecclesiastic; b. 1 April 1911, Huta Komorowska; s. of Adam Kozłowiecki and Maria Janocha; ed. Jesuit Faculty, Cracow, Jesuit Faculty, Lublin; entered Soc. of Jesus 1929; ordained priest 1937; arrested by Nazis 1939, in prison in Cracow and Wisnicz, then Auschwitz and Dachau Concentration Camps; Missionary, Kasisi Mission, Northern Rhodesia 1946–50; apptd. Apostolic Admin., Lusaka 1955, Titular Bishop of Lower Diospolis and Vicar Apostolic of Lusaka 1955; Archbishop of Lusaka 1959–69 (resgnd.); Missionary in Zambia 1969–; Commdr., Order of Freedom, Zambia, Cross Commdr., Order of Merit, Poland. *Publications:* Chester-Beatty Papyrus p. 45, p. 46, p. 47 and the Greek Translation of the Gospel of St. Luke by Fr. A. Merk, in Przegląd Biblijny 1938, Ucisk i Strapienie (memoirs of outbreak of war and life in the concentration camps) 1966, Moja Afryka — Moje Chingombe (Letters to Friends) 1997. *Leisure interests:* classical music, reading, especially history books, also P. G. Wodehouse. *Address:* P.O. Box 50003, 15101 Ridgeway, Zambia.

KOZOL, Jonathan, B.A.; American author; b. 5 Sept. 1936, Boston; s. of Dr. Harry L. Kozol and Ruth Massell Kozol; ed. Harvard Coll. and Magdalen Coll., Oxford; teacher in Boston area 1964–72; lecturer at numerous univs. 1973–85; Guggenheim Fellow 1972, 1984; Field Foundation Fellow 1973, 1974; Rockefeller Fellow 1978, Sr. Fellow 1983; Rhodes Scholar 1958; Nat. Book Award 1968, Robert F. Kennedy Book Award 1989, New England Book Award 1992, Anisfield-Wolf Book Award 1996. *Publications:* Death At An Early Age 1967, Free Schools 1972, The Night Is Dark 1975, Children of the Revolution 1978, On Being a Teacher 1979, Prisoners of Silence 1980, Illiterate America 1985, Rachel and Her Children: Homeless Families in America 1988, Savage Inequalities: Children in America's Schools 1991, Amazing Grace 1995. *Leisure interests:* reading history and religion. *Address:* P.O. Box 145, Byfield, MA 01922, U.S.A.

KOZYREV, Andrey Vladimirovich; Russian politician; b. 27 March 1951, Brussels, Belgium; m. 2nd; one d.; ed. Moscow State Inst. of Int. Relations; worker Kommunar factory, Moscow 1968–69; mem. staff U.S.S.R. Ministry of Foreign Affairs, various posts, to Head of Sector 1974–86, Head of Dept. of Int. Orgs. 1986–90; Foreign Minister of Russian Fed. 1990–95; mem. State Duma (Parl.) Dec. 1995–; Lecturer, Moscow Inst. of Int. Relations 1996–. *Publications:* Transfiguration 1995; numerous articles on foreign policy. *Address:* State Duma, Okhotny Ryad 1, 103009 Moscow, Russia. *Fax:* 292-32-94.

KRABBE, Jeroen; Netherlands actor and artist; b. 5 Dec. 1944; m. Herma van Geemert; three s.; ed. Acad. of Fine Arts and Toneel Drama School, Amsterdam; acted in repertory theatre and formed own acting co. within the Netherlands; two major exhbns. Francis Kyle Galleries, London 1993, 1995; Best Actor Award, Madrid, Sorrento, Oxford 1984, Anne Frank Medal 1985, Golden Heart of Rotterdam 1986, Golden Calf Award 1996. *Theatre includes:* The Diary of Anne Frank, Clouds, Relatively Speaking, How the Other Half Lives, Cyrano de Bergerac. *Films include:* Soldier of Orange 1977, A Flight of Rainbirds 1981, The Fourth Man 1984, The Shadow of Victory 1985, Turtle Diary, No Mercy 1987, The Living Daylights, A World Apart, Crossing Delancey, Melancholia 1989, The Prince of Tides 1991, Stalin 1991, Kafka 1991, King of the Hill 1991, The Fugitive 1993, Farinelli 1994, Immortal Beloved 1994, The Disappearance of Garcia Lorca 1995, Business for Pleasure 1996, The Honest Courtesan 1996, Cinderella 1997, Left Luggage (dir.) 1997. *Address:* Van Eeghenstraat 107, 1071 EZ Amsterdam, Netherlands.

KRABBE, Katrin; German athlete; b. 1970; m. Michael Zimmerman 1994; one s.; mem. Neubrandenburg team; winner of three gold medals in European Track and Field Championships 1990; World Champion 100m, 200m; winner 100m, World Championships, Tokyo 1991; failed drugs test 1992, banned from athletics by German Athletics Fed. until 1996; ban reduced to one year March 1993; ban reversed by Regional Court in Munich May 1995.

KRAFT, Christopher Columbus, Jr., B.S.; American space administrator; b. 28 Feb. 1924, Phoebus, Va.; s. of Christopher Columbus and Vanda Olivia (Suddreth) Kraft; m. Elizabeth Anne Turnbull 1950; one s. one d.; ed. Virginia Polytechnic Inst.; mem., Langley Aeronautical Lab., Nat. Advisory Cttee. for Aeronautics 1945; selected to join Space Task Group on Project Mercury 1958; Flight Dir. all Mercury Missions: Dir. of Flight Operations,

Manned Spacecraft Center 1963–69; Deputy Dir. Johnson Space Center 1970–72; Dir. NASA Johnson Space Center 1972–82; Fellow, American Inst. of Aeronautics and Astronautics 1966; Fellow, American Astronautical Soc; Hon. D.Eng. (Indiana Inst. of Tech.) 1966, (St. Louis Univ., Ill.) 1967, (Villanova) 1979; Arthur S. Fleming Award 1963, NASA Outstanding Leadership Award 1963, Spirit of St. Louis Medal, American Soc. of Mechanical Engineers 1967, NASA Distinguished Service Medal (twice) 1969, Chevalier, Légion d'honneur 1976, Nat. Civil Service League Career Service Award 1976, W. Randolph Lovelace Award (American Astronautical Soc.) 1977, Daniel and Florence Guggenheim Award (Int. Astronautics Fed.) 1978, AAIA von Karman Lectureship Award 1979, Goddard Memorial Trophy 1979, Roger W. Jones Award 1979, inducted into Virginia Aviation Hall of Fame 1979.

KRAFT, Robert Paul, PH.D.; American professor of astronomy and astrophysics; b. 16 June 1927, Seattle, Wash.; s. of Victor P. Kraft and Viola E. Ellis; m. Rosalie A. Reichmuth 1949; two s.; ed. Univ. of Washington and Univ. of California at Berkeley; Instructor in mathematics and astronomy, Whittier Coll. 1949–51; Asst. Prof. of Astronomy, Indiana Univ. 1956–58; Asst. Prof. of Astronomy, Univ. of Chicago 1958–59; mem. staff, Mt. Wilson and Palomar Observatories 1960–67; Astronomer and Prof., Lick Observatory 1967–92, Astronomer and Prof. Emer. 1993–, Acting Dir. Lick Observatory 1968–70, 1971–73, Dir. 1981–91; Dir. Univ. of California Observatories 1988–91; Visiting Fellow, Joint Inst. of Laboratory Astrophysics, Univ. of Colo. 1970; Pres. American Astronomical Soc. 1974–76; Vice-Pres. Int. Astronomical Union 1982–88, Pres. 1997–; mem. N.A.S., American Acad. of Arts and Sciences; Nat. Science Foundation Fellow 1953–55, Fairchild Scholar, California Inst. of Tech. 1980; Beatrice Tinsley Visiting Prof., Univ. of Texas 1991–92; Henry Norris Russell Lecturer 1995, Distinguished Alumnus Award, Univ. of Wash. 1995; D.Sc. h.c. (Ind. Univ.) 1995; Warner Prize, American Astronomical Soc. 1962. *Publications:* articles in professional journals. *Leisure interests:* music (classical and rock), oenology, duplicate bridge. *Address:* Lick Observatory, University of California, Santa Cruz, CA 95064, U.S.A. *Telephone:* (831) 459-3281. *Fax:* (831) 426-3115.

KRAGERUD, Alv; D.PHIL., D.THEOL.; Norwegian professor of comparative religion; b. 30 Aug. 1932, S. Höland; s. of John Kragerud and Borghild Kragerud; m. 1st Dagny Kaul 1959 (divorced 1977); one s.; m. 2nd Unni Larsen 1977; ed. Univs. of Oslo, Uppsala, Sweden and Hamburg, Fed. Repub. of Germany; Church of Sweden Minister, Sweden 1955–60; Prof. of Comparative Religion, Univ. of Bergen 1967–81; mem. Norwegian Acad. of Science. *Publications:* Der Lieblingsjünger im Johannesevangelium 1959, Die Hymnen der Pistis Sophia 1967. *Address:* Kirkeveien 47, 1480 Slattum, Norway. *Telephone:* 67 07 93 39.

KRAGGERUD, Egil, DR.PHIL.; Norwegian professor of classical philology; b. 7 July 1939, S. Höland; s. of John Kraggerud and Borghild Westeren; m. Beate Sinding-Larsen 1963; three s. one d.; ed Oslo Katedralskole and Oslo Univ.; Research Fellow, Oslo Univ. 1965–67, lecturer in Classics 1967–68, Prof. of Classical Philology 1969–; Ed. Symbolae Osloenses 1972–94; mem. Norwegian Acad. of Science and Letters, Royal Norwegian Soc. of Sciences and Letters, Acad. Europaea. *Publications:* Aeneisstudien 1968, Horaz und Actium 1984, Aeneiden (7 vols.) 1983–89. *Leisure interests:* skiing, concerts. *Address:* University of Oslo, P.O. Box 1007, Blindern, 0315 Oslo; Bygdöy allé 13, 0257 Oslo, Norway.

KRAGULY, Radovan; British artist; b. 10 Sept. 1935, Prijedor, Yugoslavia; s. of Dracoja Kraguly and Mileva Kraguly; ed. Acad. of Fine Arts, Belgrade, Cen. School of Arts and Crafts, London; lecturer Cambridge School of Art and Tech. –1965, Manchester Coll. of Art 1965–67, London Coll. of Printing and Design 1967–69, Ecole des Beaux Arts, Mons 1969–78, Parson School of Art and Design 1978–88; has exhibited in over 50 one-man shows, and over 200 group shows in Europe and U.S.A.; represented in perm. and maj. collections at Museum of Modern Art, Paris, British Museum, Victoria and Albert Museum, Museum of Modern Art, New York, Leicester Univ. Library, Library of Congress, Washington, City Art Gallery, Sarajevo, Art Council of Wales, Cardiff, Power Gallery, Sydney, Prenten Cabinet, Brussels; numerous prizes and awards including Printmaking Prize (Jazu-Zagreb) 1962, Yugoslav Trienale Prize 1967, Grafika Creative Prize (Helsinki) 1975, Int. Grand Prix Fondation Pierre Cornette de St. Cyr (Paris) 1978, Int. Grand Prix, Drawing Biennial (Rijeka) 1980. *Publications include:* La vache dans l'imaginaire 1989, The Imaginary Cow of Kraguly 1990, Kraguly—Gallery Vero Van Laer 1992, Hathor: Voies Cartees Kraguly 1995, Kraguly Hathor: VLK 1998. *Address:* 22 rue Quincampoix, 75004 Paris, France. *Telephone:* (1) 42.74.70.47 (Paris); (01597) 860340 (Wales). *Fax:* (1) 42.74.70.47 (Paris).

KRAIGHER, Sergej; Slovenian politician (retd.); b. 30 May 1914, Postojna, Slovenia; s. of Anton Kraigher and Marija Joške; m. Lidija Šentjurc 1939; two d.; ed. Zagreb Univ.; mem. CP Cttee., Ljubljana Univ.; imprisoned 1934–36; Sec. Regional Cttee. CP of Slovenia, Ljubljana, Instructor of Cen. Cttee. Trbovje, active in war 1941–45 as Sec. of provincial cttee. and Liberation Front for Styria; various regional posts after war; Pres. Planning Comm. of Slovenia 1946–50; Vice-Pres. of Govt. of Slovenia 1951; Gov. Nat. Bank 1951–53; Dir. Fed. Office for Econ. Planning 1953–58; Sec. for Industry 1958–59; Pres. Foreign Trade Cttee., Sec. of State for Foreign Trade 1959–63; Vice-Pres. Fed. Chamber, Pres. Comm. for Socio-Econ. Relations and for Econ. System of Fed. Assembly 1963–67; Pres. Assembly Socialist Repub. of Slovenia 1967–74; mem. Presidency of S.F.R. of Yugoslavia 1979–84; Pres. of Presidency of Slovenia 1974–79; fmr. mem. Cen. Cttee., League of Communists of Slovenia 1952–, of Yugoslavia 1969–73; mem. Collective Presidency of Yugoslavia 1979–84, Vice-Pres. 1980–81, Pres. 1981–82; Hon. Dr. Edvard Kardelj Univ., Maribor 1979; national decorations including partisan Memorial Badge and foreign decorations. *Publications:* numerous articles on socio-political and economic issues. *Leisure interests:* literature, fine arts, theatre, mountaineering, swimming.

KRAIJENHOFF, Jonkheer Gualtherus; Netherlands business executive; b. 11 July 1922; s. of Albertus Kraijenhoff and Gualthera Kraijenhoff; m. Yvonne Kessler; one s. two d.; ed. Switzerland; Royal Air Force (U.K.) pilot 1943–47; joined N.V. Organon, Oss 1947, Man. Dir. 1957; mem. Bd. of Man. N.V. Kon. Zwanenberg-Organon 1959, Pres. 1963; mem. Bd. of Man., Kon. Zout-Organon N.V. 1967, Pres. 1969; Vice-Pres. AKZO N.V., Arnhem 1969, Pres. 1971–78, mem. Supervisory Council May 1978– (fmr. Chair.); Dir. S. G. Warburg and Co. 1978–; Dir. APV Holdings 1983–; Pres. Netherlands. Red Cross 1966–86, Chair. Cen. Laboratories for Bloodtransfusion, Red Cross 1990–; Kt., Netherlands Lion, Order of St. John. *Address:* Zomerland, Louiseweg 15, Nijmegen, Netherlands (Home).

KRAINEV, Vladimir Vsevolodovich; Russian pianist; b. 1 April 1944, Krasnoyarsk; m. Tatyana Tarasova; ed. Moscow State Conservatory with Heinrich Neuhaus and Stanislav Neuhaus; début with orchestra as child prodigy in Kharkov 1953, in Moscow 1963; prize winner of several int. competitions; soloist with maj. orchestras in many European cultural centres and festivals; played with Carlo Maria Guilini, Pierre Boulez, John Pritchard, Dmitry Kitaenko; repertoire including most of classical concertos and all concertos by Mozart and Prokofiev; teacher in Moscow Conservatory 1987–91, Hochschule für Musik in Hanover 1991–; People's Artist of Russia 1984, U.S.S.R. State Prize 1986. *Address:* Staatliche Hochschule für Musik und Theater, Walderseestrasse 100, Hanover, Germany. *Telephone:* (095) 158-24-56 (Home, Moscow).

KRAIVICHIEN, Thanin, LL.B.; Thai politician and jurist; b. 5 April 1927; m. Karen Andersen; five c.; ed. Suan Kularp School, Thammasat Univ., Univ. of London, Gray's Inn; Sr. Judge, Civil Court 1969; Sr. Judge, Court of Appeal 1972; Judge, Supreme Court 1972–76, Sr. Judge 1976; mem. Nat. Assembly 1973–76; Prime Minister 1976–77 (deposed in coup); Chair. Investment Bd. of Thailand 1976–77; mem. of Privy Council. *Publications:* Democracy, Communist Ideology and Tactics, The Language of the Thai Law, The Use of Anti-Communist Law, Constitutional Monarchy, The Reform of the Legal and Judicial Systems during the Reign of King Chulalongkorn. *Address:* c/o Office of the Prime Minister, Government House, Bangkok, Thailand.

KRAJICEK, Richard; Netherlands tennis player; b. 6 Dec. 1972, Rotterdam; started playing tennis aged 3; reached semi-finals Australian Open 1992; Wimbledon men's singles champion 1996; won 16 titles to date.

KRALL, Hanna; Polish journalist, writer; b. 20 May 1935, Warsaw; m.; ed. Univ. of Warsaw; reporter Życie Warszawy 1955–66, Polityka 1966–, correspondent in Moscow 1966–69; corresp. Tygodnik Powszechny, Gazeta Wyborcza; Prize of Minister of Culture and Art 1989, J. Shocken Literary Prize (Germany), Solidarity Cultural Prize 1995, Kulture Foundation Award 1999. *Publications include:* Na wschód od Arbatu (To the East of Arbat) 1972, Zdążyć przed Panem Bogiem (To Outwit God) 1976, Sześć odcieni bieli (Six shades of White) 1978, Sublokatorka (The Sub-tenant) 1983, Trudności ze wstawaniem (Difficulties Getting Up) 1988, Hipnoza (Hypnosis) 1989, Taniec na cudzym weselu (Dance at a Stranger's Wedding) 1993, Co się stało z naszą bajką (What's happened to our Fairy Tale) 1994, Dowody na istnienie (Proofs of Existence) 1995, Tam jnż nie ma Żadnej rzeki (There isn't any river any more) 1998 (translated into over 10 languages). *Address:* Stowanynune Pisarzy Polskich, ul. Krakowskie Przedmieście 87/89, 00-079 Warsaw, Poland.

KRAMER, Larry, B.A.; American author; b. 25 June 1935, Bridgeport, Conn.; ed. Yale Univ.; Production Exec. Columbia Pictures Corpn. London 1961–65; Asst. to Pres. United Artists, New York; producer-screenwriter, Women in Love 1970; co-founder, Gay Men's Health Crisis Inc. New York 1981; founder, ACT UP-AIDS Coalition to Unleash Power, New York 1988. *Publications:* Faggots 1978, The Normal Heart (play) 1985, Just Say No 1988, The Furniture of Home 1989, The Destiny of Me 1993.

KRAMER, Dame Leonie (Judith), A.C., D.B.E., D.PHIL., F.A.H.A., F.A.C.E.; Australian emeritus professor of literature; b. 1 Oct. 1924; d. of the late A. L. Gibson and G. Gibson; m. Harold Kramer 1952 (deceased); two d.; ed. Presbyterian Ladies Coll., Melbourne and Univs. of Melbourne and Oxford; Tutor, St. Hugh's Coll., Oxford 1949–52; Assoc. Prof. Univ. of N.S.W. 1963–68; Prof. of Australian Literature, Univ. of Sydney, 1968–89, Prof Emer. 1989–; Deputy Chancellor, Univ. of Sydney 1988–91, Chancellor 1991–; Vice-Pres. Australian Asscn. for Teaching of English 1967–70; Vice-Pres. Australian Soc. of Authors 1969–71; mem. Nat. Literature Bd. of Review 1970–73; mem. Council, Nat. Library of Australia 1975–81; Pres., then Vice-Pres. Australian Council for Educ. Standards 1973–; mem. Univs. Council 1977–86; Commr. Australian Broadcasting Comm. (ABC) 1977–81, Chair. 1982–83, Dir. Australia and N.Z. Banking Group 1983–94, Western Mining Corpn. 1984–96, Quadrant Magazine Co. Ltd. 1987–, (Chair. 1988–); mem. Council Nat. Roads and Motorists' Asscn. 1984–95, Queen Elizabeth II Trust 1989–, Asia Soc. 1991–; Nat. Pres. Australia—Britain Soc. 1984–93;

mem. Council Australian Nat. Univ. 1984–87; Chair. Bd. of Dirs. Nat. Inst. of Dramatic Art (NIDA) 1987–92, Deputy Chair. 1992–95; Sr. Fellow Inst. of Public Affairs (IPA) 1988–96; Commr. Electricity Comm. (N.S.W.) 1988–95; mem. World Book Encyclopaedia Advisory Bd. 1989–, Int. Advisory Cttee. Encyclopaedia Britannica 1991, N.S.W. Council of Australian Inst. of Co. Dirs. 1992–; Chair. Operation Rainbow Australia Ltd. 1996–; Hon. Fellow St. Hugh's Coll. Oxford 1994; Hon. D.Litt. (Tasmania), 1977 (Queensland) 1991, (N.S.W.) 1992; Hon. LL.D. (Melbourne) 1983, (Australian Nat. Univ.) 1984; Hon. M.A. (Sydney) 1989; Britannica Award 1986. *Publications include:* (as L. J. Gibson): Henry Handel Richardson and Some of Her Sources 1954; (as Leonie Kramer): Australian Poetry (ed.) 1961, Companion to Australia Felix 1962, Myself When Laura 1966, A Guide to Language and Literature (with Robert D. Eagleson) 1977, A. D. Hope 1979, The Oxford History of Australian Literature (ed.) 1981, The Oxford Anthology of Australian Literature (Ed. with Adrian Mitchell) 1985, My Country: Australian Poetry and Short Stories—Two Hundred Years (2 vols.) 1985, James McAuley: Poetry, Essays etc. (Ed.) 1988, David Campbell: Collected Poems (Ed.) 1989, Collected Poems of James McAuley 1995. *Leisure interests:* gardening, music. *Address:* 12 Vaucluse Road, Vaucluse, N.S.W., 2030 Australia. *Telephone:* 93514164.

KRAMER, Stanley, B.SC.; American film producer and director; b. 29 Sept. 1913, New York; m. 1st Ann Pearce 1950; two s.; m. 2nd Karen Sharpe 1966; two d.; ed. New York Univ.; M.G.M. Research Dept.; film cutter for three years and film ed.; film and radio writer; served U.S. Signal Corps; formed own film production co. to produce This Side of Innocence; founder and Pres. Kramer Pictures 1949–. *Films include:* (assoc. producer) So Ends Our Night 1941, The Moon and Sixpence 1942; (producer) So This is New York 1948, Home of the Brave 1949, The Men 1950, Cyrano de Bergerac 1950, Death of a Salesman 1951, High Noon 1952, The Happy Time 1952, Eight Iron Men 1952, The Caine Mutiny; (producer-dir.) Not As a Stranger 1955, The Pride and the Passion 1957, The Defiant Ones 1958, On The Beach 1959, Inherit the Wind 1960, Judgment at Nuremberg 1961, It's a Mad, Mad, Mad, Mad World 1963, Ship of Fools 1965, Guess Who's Coming to Dinner 1967, The Secret of Santa Vittoria 1969, R.P.M. 1971, Bless the Beasts and Children 1971, Oklahoma Crude 1973, The Domino Principle 1977, The Runner Stumbles 1979.

KRÄMER, Werner, DR.PHIL.; German archaeologist; b. 8 March 1917, Wiesbaden; s. of Max and Martha Krämer; ed. Univs. of Munich, Frankfurt, Kiel, Marburg; Curator and Departmental Dir. Bavarian State Office for Preservation of Monuments 1947–56; First Dir. and Prof. Roman-German Comm. of German Archaeological Inst. Frankfurt 1956–72; Pres. German Archaeological Inst. 1972–79; mem. Royal Irish Acad., Soc. of Antiquaries, London, Istituto Italiano di Preistoria e Prostoria, British Acad., etc. *Address:* Klopstockstrasse 5, 65187 Wiesbaden, Germany. *Telephone:* (0611) 84 22 20.

KRANIDIOTIS, Nicos; Cypriot diplomatist, scholar and journalist; b. 25 Nov. 1911, Kyrenia; s. of John N. Kranidiotis and Polyxeni J. Kranidiotis; m. Chryssoula Vizakas 1946; one s. one d.; ed. Pan Cyprian Gymnasium, Cyprus, Athens Univ. and Harvard Univ. Center for Int. Affairs; worked as schoolmaster in Cyprus; Dir. of Hellenic Cyprus (official political organ of Cyprus Ethnarchy) 1949; Gen. Sec. Cyprus Ethnarchy 1953–57, Councillor 1957–60; Amb. to Greece 1960–79, concurrently Amb. to Yugoslavia 1963–79, to Italy 1964–79, to Bulgaria 1970–79, to Romania 1970–79; Sec. of 2nd and 3rd Cyprus Nat. Assemblies 1954, 1955; Founder, Dir. (with others) of Kypriaka Grammata (Cyprus Literature), a literary magazine 1934, Ed. 1946–56. *Publications include:* Chronicles (short stories) 1945, The Neohellenic Theatre (Essay) 1950, Studies (poems) 1951, Forms of Myth (short stories) 1954, The Poet G. Seferis (essay) 1955, The National Character of Cyprus Literature 1958, Cyprus in her Struggle for Freedom (history) 1958, Introduction to the Poetry of G. Seferis (essay) 1965, Cyprus-Greece (essay) 1966, Cypriot Poetry (essay) 1969, Kypriaka Grammata (essay) 1970, Epistrophi (poems) 1974, Poesie (poems) 1974, The Cyprus Problem (history) 1975, Archbishop Makarios (essay), Critical Years – Cyprus 1950–1960, The International Aspects of the Cyprus Problem, A Journey to the Southern Island (poetry), The Unfortified City, Cyprus 1960–1974 (2 vols.), Our Own Small World (poetry), Poetry 1951–1986, Short Stories, Poetry Vol. II 1987–1995. *Leisure interests:* reading, writing. *Address:* Dimokratias 44, P. Psychico, Athens, Greece; 16 Prometheus Street, Nicosia, Cyprus (Home). *Telephone:* 6712744 (Athens); 2907.

KRANTZ, Judith, B.A.; American author; b. 9 Jan. 1928, New York City; d. of Jack David Tarcher and Mary Brager; m. Stephen Krantz 1954; two s.; contrib. to Good Housekeeping 1948–54, McCalls 1954–59, Ladies Home Journal 1959–71; contributing ed. Cosmopolitan 1971–79. *Publications:* Scruples 1978, Princess Daisy 1980, Mistral's Daughter 1982, I'll Take Manhattan 1986, Till We Meet Again 1988, Dazzle 1990, Scruples Two 1992, Lovers 1994, Spring Collection 1996, The Jewels of Teresa Kant 1998.

KRĄPIEC, Mieczysław Albert; Polish ecclesiastic and professor of philosophy; b. 25 May 1921, Berezowica Mała n. Zbaraż (now Ukraine); ed. Dominican Friars' College, Kraków, St. Thomas Pontifical Univ., Rome, Catholic Univ. of Lublin: dominican friar; ordained Priest 1945, lecturer in Philosophy Dominican Friars' Coll., Kraków 1946–, teacher Catholic Univ. of Lublin 1951–, Prof. 1962, Dean Christian Philosophy Faculty 1959–62, 1969–70, Rector 1970–83, head Metaphysics Faculty; Corresp. mem. Polish Acad. of Sciences 1994–; mem. Polish Acad. of Art and Sciences, St. Thomas Aquinash Pontifical Univ., Rome, European Acad. of Sciences and Arts, Salzburg; fmr. Chair. and mem. Catholic Univ. of Lublin Scientific Soc.; Dr. h.c. (Pontifical Inst. of Medieval Studies, Toronto), (Catholic Univ. of Louvain, Belgium), (Tarnopol Univ. of Pedagogics, Ukraine); Commdr.'s Order of Polonia Restituta, Grand Officer's Cross of Order of Leopold II (Belgium), Order of Academic Insignia of the French Acad. *Publications:* Theory of the Analogy of Existence of Metaphysical Methodology (jtly.) 1964, Metaphysics 1966, Aristotelian Concept of Substance 1966, I: a man 1974, A Man and Natural Law 1975, Language and Real World 1985, About Understanding Philosophy 1991, At the Foundations of Understanding Culture 1991, Introduction to Philosophy (jtly.) 1992, 1996, About Human Policy 1993. *Leisure interests:* picking mushrooms, cooking. *Address:* ul. Złota 9, 20-112 Lublin, Poland. *Telephone:* (81) 532 87 27.

KRASHENINNIKOV, Pavel Vladimirovich, D.JUR; Russian lawyer; b. 21 June 1964, Polevskoye, Sverdlovsk Region; m.; one d.; ed. Sverdlovsk Inst. of Law; teacher, Sverdlovsk Inst. of Law 1991–93; Deputy Head, Chief Dept. of Housing Policy, State Cttee. on Construction of Russian Fed. 1993–; Head, Dept. of Civil and Econ. Law, Ministry of Justice 1993–96; Deputy Chair. State Cttee. on Antimonopoly Policy and Support of New Econ. Structures 1996–97; First Deputy Minister of Justice 1997–98, Acting Minister March 1998, Minister April 1998–; Co-ordinator, Pres., Comm. for Counteraction against Political Extremism in Russia July 1998–; lecturer Moscow State Univ. 1995–. *Publications:* over 70 articles on civil law. *Address:* Ministry of Justice, Yermolovoi str. 10A, 101434 Moscow, Russia. *Telephone:* (095) 206 0081 (Office). *Fax:* (095) 209 6098 (Office).

KRASIKOV, Anatoly Andreyevich, D.HIST.; Russian journalist; b. 1931; m.; two d.; ed. Moscow Inst. of Int. Relations; on staff U.S.S.R. Telegraph Agency TASS 1992; Deputy Dir.-Gen. ITAR-TASS 1978–92; on staff of Pres. Yeltsin, Head of Press, Exec. Sec., Council on Interaction with Religious Orgs. of Russian Presidency; Chair. Int. Christianity Cttee. 1992–96; Head, Centre for Studies of Problems of Religion and Soc.; chief researcher, Inst. of Europe, Russian Acad. of Sciences. *Leisure interests:* music, archives, tourism. *Address:* Institute of Europe, Mokhovaya str. 8, bldg. 3v, 103973 Moscow, Russia. *Telephone:* (095) 203 7343 (Office).

KRASIN, Yuri Andreyevich, D.PHIL.; Russian academic; b. 7 June 1929, Penza; ed. Leningrad State Univ.; lecturer, docent, Leningrad State Pedagogical Inst. 1952–60; docent, Inst. of Professional Skill Improvement, Moscow State Univ. 1960–63; sr. teacher, Inst. of Philosophy U.S.S.R. (now Russian) Acad. of Sciences 1963; consultant, Int. Div. CP Cen. Cttee., Prof., Moscow Inst. of Professional Skill Improvement at Moscow State Univ. 1963–75; Prof., Head of Dept., Prorector, Acad. of Social Sciences at CPSU Cent. Cttee. 1975–87; Rector, Inst. of Social Sciences at CPSU Cen. Cttee. 1987–91; Dir.-Gen. Foundation of Social and Political Studies 1991–92; Dir. Centre of Social Programmes, Int. Foundation of Social, Econ. and Political Studies 1992–97; Head Centre for Analysis of Social and Political Processes, Inst. of Sociology Russian Acad. of Sciences 1993–; mem. Presidium Acad. of Political Sciences; U.S.S.R. State Prize; Lomonosov Prize of Moscow State Univ. *Publications:* articles on social movts., democratic reform in Russia, civil, social and political matters. *Leisure interests:* classical music, skiing. *Address:* Institute of Sociology, Krzhizhanovskogo str. 24/35, korp. 5, 117218 Moscow, Russia. *Telephone:* (095) 128 8676 (Office).

KRASNOV, Mikhail Mikhailovich; Russian ophthalmologist; b. 31 May 1929, Ivanovo Region; ed. Second Moscow Inst. of Medicine; asst. researcher Golmholtz Inst. of Ophthalmology 1947–53, researcher 1953–60; lecturer, docent Cen. Medical Inst. of Advance Training 1960–64; Head of Chair, Prof. Second Moscow Inst. of Medicine 1964–73; concurrently Head of Chair First Moscow Inst. of Medicine 1966–73; f. and Dir. Research Inst. of Eye Diseases 1973–; mem. Russian Acad. of Medical Sciences; mem. Int. Ophthalmologic Acad.; Ed.-in-Chief journal Vestnik Oftalmologii, Annals of Ophthalmology (U.S.A.), Glaucoma (U.S.A.). Dr. h.c. (Karlov Univ., Prague); Hero of Socialist Labour, Prize of U.S.S.R. Council of Ministers, Lenin's Prize, Filatov Prize U.S.S.R. Acad. of Medical Sciences, U.S.S.R. State Prize, other decorations. *Address:* Rossolimo str. 11a, 119021 Moscow, Russia (Office). *Telephone:* (095) 248 0125 (Office).

KRASOVSKAYA, Vera Mikhailovna, D.F.A.; Russian ballet historian and critic; b. 11 Sept. 1915; d. of Mikhail Krasovskiy and Maria Krasovskaya; m. David Zolotnitskiy 1949; one s.; ed. Choreographical School, Leningrad and Inst. of Theatre, Music and Cinematography, Leningrad; Ballet Dancer, Kirov Ballet 1933–41; Sr. Scientific Worker Inst. of Theatre, Music and Cinematography 1953–96, Prof. 1975; Head, Chair of Choreographic Art, Acad. of Russian Ballet 1996–; Triumph Prize 1998. *Publications:* Vachtang Chabukiani 1956, 1960, Russian Ballet Theatre from the Beginning to the middle of the XIX Century 1958, Leningrad's Ballet 1961, Russian Ballet Theatre of the Second Half of the XIX Century 1963, Anna Pavlova 1964, 1965, Russian Ballet Theatre at the beginning of the XX Century, vol. I Choreographers 1971, vol. II Dancers 1972, Nijinsky 1974, The Ballet of Western Europe: Vol. I From the Beginning to the Middle of the 18th Century 1979, Vol. II The Era of Noverre 1981, Vol. III The Pre-Romantic Ballet 1983, Nikita Dolgushin 1985, Vaganova 1989, The Ballet of Western Europe: Vol. IV The Romantic Ballet 1996. *Leisure interest:* reading. *Address:* Sadovaya 14, apt. 14, 191011 St. Petersburg, Russia. *Telephone:* 311-72-50.

KRASOVSKIY, Nikolay Nikolayevich, DR. PHYS.MATH. SC.; Russian mathematician and mechanician; b. 7 Sept. 1924, Sverdlovsk; ed. Ural

Polytechnic Inst.; teaching and scientific work, Ural Polytechnic Inst. 1949–55, 1957–59; mem. CPSU 1954–91; Research worker, Inst. of Mechanics, U.S.S.R. (now Russian) Acad. of Sciences 1955–57, Prof. Ural Univ. 1959–70; scientific and admin. work, Inst. of Math. and Mechanics of Ural Scientific Centre, U.S.S.R. (now Russian) Acad. of Sciences 1970–, Dir. 1970–77, Chief Scientific Researcher 1977–; Corresp. mem. U.S.S.R. (now Russian) Acad. of Sciences 1964–68, mem. 1968–; Hero of Socialist Labour 1974, Lenin Prize 1976, U.S.S.R. State Prize 1984, Gold Medal of Liapunov, Russian Acad. of Sciences 1992; Order of Lenin, Order of the Red Banner and other decorations. *Publications:* works in field of stability of motion theory and theory of control systems, including Stability of Motion 1963, Game-Theoretical Control Problem (with A. I. Subbotin) 1988, Control under Lack of Information (with A. N. Kravoskii) 1995. *Address:* c/o Institute of Mathematics and Mechanics, 620219 GSP-384, S. Kovalevskaya Str. 16, Yekaterinburg, Russia. *Telephone:* (3432) 74-40-13 (Office), (3432) 59-41-73 (Home). *Fax:* (3432) 74-25-81.

KRASTS, Guntars; Latvian politician; b. 16 Oct. 1957, Riga, Latvia; ed. Latvian State Univ.; researcher Inst. of Agric. Econ. 1983–91; Chair. Exec. Bd. R.A.N.G. Ltd 1991–95; Minister of Econs. 1995–97; Prime Minister of Latvia 1997–98. *Address:* c/o Government House, Brīvības blvd. 36, 226170 Riga, Latvia (Office). *Telephone:* (371) 733-22-32.

KRASUCKI, Henri: French (b. Polish) trade union official and machine-fitter; b. 2 Sept. 1924, Wolomin, Poland; s. of Isaac Krasucki and Léa Krasucki; m. Jacqueline Delhaye 1987; one s. one d. from previous marriage; ed. Lycée Voltaire, Paris; Sec. Seine Dept. CGT 1949, mem. confederal bureau 1961, Gen. Sec. 1982–92; mem. Cen. Cttee. CP 1956, Politbureau 1964–94, Nat. Cttee. 1994–; mem. Admin. Council la Vie Ouvrière; Vice-Pres. Fed. World Trade Unions 1986–; Chevalier Légion d'honneur. *Publications:* Syndicats et luttes de classes 1969, Syndicats et socialisme 1972, Syndicats et unité 1980, Un Syndicat moderne? Oui! 1987. *Address:* Confédération générale du travail, 263 rue de Paris, 93516 Montreuil Cedex, France.

KRATOCHVÍLOVÁ, Jarmila; Czech athlete; b. 26 Jan. 1951, Golčův Jeníkov; ed. gymnasium, Čáslav 1966–70; accountant, Triola, Golčův Jeníkov 1970–71, mem. of the centre of top-level performance sports, Vysoké školy, Prague 1971–87 (retd.); now coach; *world records:* 400-metre track event, Helsinki, 1983, 800-metre track event, Munich 1983; *international competitions include:* Gold Medal, 400-metre track event, World Cup, Rome 1981; Silver Medal, Olympic Games, Moscow 1980; Silver Medal, 400-metre track event, European Championships, Athens 1982; Gold Medal, 400- and 800-metre track events, World Championships, Helsinki 1983; UNESCO Fair Play Prize 1988; Order of Labour (Czechoslovakia) 1983. *Publication:* Waiting (with M. Krač, her coach). *Address:* TJ Slavoj Čáslav, TSM-Voaranty, 286 01 Čáslav (Office); Pod Vyšehradem 207, 582 82 Golčův Jeníkov, Czech Republic (Home).

KRAUCH, Carl Heinrich, DR.RER.NAT.; German business executive and chemist; b. 14 Sept. 1931, Heidelberg; s. of Carl Krauch and Maria (Lüders) Krauch; m. Ursula Kneller 1958; three s. one d.; ed. Ruprecht-Karl Univ., Heidelberg, Georg-August Univ., Göttingen; Head of research group, radiochemical dept., Max-Planck Inst. für Kohlenforschung, Mülheim/Ruhr 1958–67; Lecturer, Univ. of Cologne 1965; Head of research group testing plastic materials, BASF, Ludwigshafen 1967; Prof. Johannes Gutenberg Univ., Mainz 1971; Head of Research and Devt., mem. Bd., Henkel & Cie. GmbH., Düsseldorf 1971–80, Head, Chemical Products Div. 1975–80; mem. Bd., Hüls AG, Marl Jan. 1980–, Chair. 1980–93; mem. Bd., VEBA AG, Düsseldorf July 1980–. *Publications:* over 40 in field of chemistry. *Leisure interests:* hunting and farming. *Address:* Hüls AG, Postfach 1320, 45743 Marl, Germany. *Telephone:* 02365/49 52 71.

KRAUCHANKA, Pyotr Kuzmich, C.HIS.SC.; Belarus politician; b. 1950; m.; one s. one d.; ed. State Univ. of Belarus; lecturer, State Univ. of Belarus 1975; posts in party admin. 1975–85; Sec. Minsk City CP Ctee. 1985–90; Deputy, Supreme Soviet of Repub. of Belarus 1990; Minister of Foreign Affairs 1990–94; mem. Supreme Soviet 1995–96. *Address:* K. Marksa str. 38, Dom Urada, 220016 Minsk, Belarus. *Telephone:* (3752) 29-33-13.

KRAUS, Andreas, D.PHIL.; German historian; b. 5 March 1922, Erding; s. of Karl Kraus and Katharina Mayer; m. Maria Kastner 1947; one d.; ed. Univ of Munich; teacher 1949–61; Extraordinary Prof. of History, Philosophical and Theological Hochschule, Regensburg 1961–67; Prof. Univ. of Regensburg 1967–77; Prof. of Bavarian History Univ. of Munich 1977–, Prof. Emer. 1989–; mem. Bayerischen Akad. der Wissenschaften 1971; Bayerischer Verdienstorden 1983, Bundesverdienstkreuz 1993, Komtur des St. Gregorius Ordens mit Stern 1995. *Publications:* Die historische Forschung an der bayerischen Akademie der Wissenschaften 1959, Vernunft und Geschichte 1963, Das päpstliche Staatssekretariat 1964, Civitas Regia 1972, Regensburg 1979, Die naturwissenschaftliche Forschung an der bayerischen Akademie der Wissenschaften 1979, Geschichte Bayerns 1983, Handbuch d. Bayerischen Geschichte Vol. II 1988, Maximilian I., Bayerns Grosser Kurfürst 1990, Handbuch d. Bayerischen Geschichte Vol. III 1-3, 1996–99, Erding. Stadt mit vielen Gesichtern 1997. *Address:* Nederlingerstrasse 30a, 80638 Munich 19; Landsbergerstr. 74, 86938 Schondorf, Germany. *Telephone:* 089-1575354 (Home); 081-921407 (Schondorf).

KRAUSE, Günther; German politician; b. 1953, Halle; m.; fmr. lecturer, Tech. Univ. Wismar; nat. service 1972–74; joined Christian Democratic Union (CDU) 1974; CDU Chair. Mecklenburg-Vorpommern 1989–90; State Sec. to fmr. G.D.R. Prime Minister Lothar de Maizière (q.v.) April 1990; Minister without Portfolio (responsible for structural changes to economy of fmr. East Germany) 1990–91, of Transport 1991–93. *Address:* Bundestag, 53113 Bonn, Germany.

KRAUSHAAR, William L., PH.D.; American professor of physics; b. 1 April 1920, Newark, N.J.; s. of Lester A. Kraushaar and Helen Ousterhoudt; m. 1st Margaret Freidinger 1943 (divorced 1980), two s. one d.; m. 2nd Elizabeth Rodgers 1980; ed. Lafayette Coll. and Cornell Univ.; with Nat. Bureau of Standards 1942–45; Pres. White Fellow Cornell Univ. 1946–49; Asst. Prof., Assoc. Prof. then Prof. of Physics M.I.T. 1949–65; Prof. of Physics Univ. of Wis. 1965–80, Max Mason Prof. of Physics 1980–; Fulbright Fellow, Japan 1953–54, Guggenheim Fellow, Harvard and Calif. Inst. of Tech. 1963, Leiden Observatory 1973, mem. Bd. of Trustees Coll. of the Atlantic 1970–74, Univs. Research Asscn. 1983–88; mem. N.A.S., American Acad. of Arts and Sciences, A.A.A.S.; Sr. Scientist Prize, Humboldt Foundation 1983. *Publications:* Introduction to Mechanics, Matter and Waves (with Uno Ingard) 1960; numerous publications on cosmic ray, x-ray and gamma ray astronomy. *Address:* Department of Physics, Chamberlin Hall, University of Wisconsin, Madison, WI 53711 (Office); 462 Togstad Glen, Madison, WI 53711, U.S.A. (Home). *Telephone:* (608) 262–5916 (Office); (608) 238-5945 (Home).

KRAUSKOPF, Konrad Bates, PH.D.; American geologist; b. 30 Nov. 1910, Madison, Wis.; s. of Francis C. and Maude Bates Krauskopf; m. Kathryn Isabel McCune 1936; one s. three d.; ed. Univ. of Wisconsin, Univ. of Calif. and Stanford Univ.; Instructor in Chem., Univ. of Calif. 1934–35; Asst. Prof. of Geology, Stanford Univ. 1939–42, Assoc. Prof. 1942–50, Prof. of Geochem. 1950–76, Assoc. Dean, School of Earth Sciences, Stanford Univ. 1963–76, Prof. Emer. 1976–; Chief, Geographical Section, G.2, U.S. Army, Far East Command 1947–48; Geologist, U.S. Geological Survey, various times 1942–; Pres. American Geological Inst. 1964, Geological Soc. of America 1967, Geochemical Soc. 1970; mem. N.A.S.; Hon. D.Sc. (Wisconsin) 1971, Day Medal, Geological Soc. of America 1961, Goldschmidt Medal, Geochemical Soc. 1982, Ian Campbell Medal, American Geological Inst. 1984. *Publications:* Fundamentals of Physical Science 1941, Introduction to Geochemistry 1967, The Third Planet 1974, The Physical Universe (with Arthur Beiser) 1986, Radioactive Waste Disposal and Geology 1988; articles in tech. scientific journals. *Address:* Geology Department, Stanford University, CA 94305 (Office); Pearce Mitchell Place, No. 13, Stanford University, CA 94305, U.S.A. (Home). *Telephone:* (650) 723-3325 (Office); (650) 324-1660 (Home). *Fax:* (650) 725-2199.

KRAUTHAMMER, Charles, M.D.; American journalist; b. 13 March 1950, New York; s. of Shulim Krauthammer and Thea Krauthammer; m. Robyn Trethewey; one s.; ed. McGill Univ., Balliol Coll. Oxford and Harvard Univ., Medical School; Resident in Psychiatry, Mass. Gen. Hosp. Boston 1975–78; Scientific Adviser, Dept. of Health and Human Services, Washington, D.C. 1978–80; speech writer to Vice-Pres. Walter Mondale (q.v.), Washington, D.C. 1980–81; Sr. Ed. The New Republic, Washington, D.C. 1981–88; essayist, Time Magazine 1983–; syndicated columnist, The Washington Post 1984–; mem. Bd. of Advisers, The Nat. Interest, Public Interest; Nat. Magazine Award (for essays), American Soc. of Magazine Eds. 1984, Pulitzer Prize (for commentary) 1987. *Publications:* Cutting Edges 1985; contributions to psychiatric journals. *Leisure interest:* chess. *Address:* c/o The Washington Post Writers Group, 1150 15th Street, N.W., Washington, DC 20071, U.S.A.

KRAVCHENKO, Adm. Victor Andreyevich; Russian naval officer; b. 5 Dec. 1943, Bogdanovich, Sverdlovsk Region; m.; one d.; ed. Higher Mil. Marine School, Mil. Marine Acad., Acad. of Gen. Staff; served as sr. asst., submarine commdr., Head of staff, submarine div. commdr., First Deputy Head of Staff, Black Sea Fleet 1968–91; First Deputy Commdr., Baltic Fleet 1991–96; Commdr., Black Sea Fleet 1996–; numerous orders and medals. *Address:* c/o Ministry of Defence, 103160 Moscow, ul. Myasnitskaya 37, Russia. *Telephone:* (095) 296-89-00.

KRAVCHUK, Leonid Makarovich, PH.D.; Ukrainian politician; b. 10 Jan. 1934, Velykyi Zhytyn; s. of Makar Olexiyovich and Khima Ivanivna Kravchuk; m. Antonina Mikhailivna 1957; one s.; ed. Kiev State Univ. and Acad. of Social Sciences, Moscow; teacher of Political Economy, Chernovitsky Tech. School; party work since 1960, on staff Ukrainian CP Cen. Cttee. 1970–; Head Propaganda Dept. 1980–88, Ideology Dept. 1988–89, Sec. Cen. Cttee., Cand. mem. Politburo 1990; Chair. Ukrainian Supreme Soviet 1990–91; Pres. of Ukraine 1991–94; C.-in-C. Armed Forces of Ukraine 1991–94; mem. Verkhovna Rada (Parl.) 1994–; f. Mutual Understanding Movt. 1994; Protector Kievo-Mogylianskaya Acad. Kiev 1991; Head Trusteeship Council, Children and Youth Activity Cen. of Ukraine 1992; Hon. Pres. East European Asscn. of Businessmen; Hon. Ph.D. (La Salle Univ., Philadelphia) 1992; Order of Red Banner of Labour (thrice). *Leisure interests:* chess, books, cinema. *Address:* Verkhovna Rada, M. Hruspevskoho 5, 252019 Kiev, Ukraine. *Telephone:* (044) 291-51-00.

KRAWCZUK, Aleksander, H.H.D.; Polish historian, writer and politician; b. 7 June 1922, Cracow; m.; two s.; ed. Jagiellonian Univ., Cracow; served with Home Army during Nazi occupation; scientific worker Jagiellonian Univ., Cracow, Asst., subsequently Sr. Asst. and lecturer 1949–64, Asst. Prof. 1964–74, Extraordinary Prof. 1974–85, Ordinary Prof. 1985–, Head Ancient History Research Centre, History Inst.; Minister of Culture and Art

1986–89; mem. Polish Writers' Union 1971–83, newly created Polish Writers' Union (ZLP) 1983–90, Pres. ZLP Cracow Br. 1986–87; mem. Nat. Culture Council 1986–90; Deputy to Sejm (Parl.) 1991–97; mem. Civic Cttee. for Rescue of Cracow Monuments; Pres. Gen. Bd. Soc. of Popular Knowledge, Soc. of Polish-Italian Friendship; Commdr.'s Cross of Polonia Restituta Order and other Polish awards and decorations. *Publications:* Kolonizacja Sullańska 1960, Gajusz Juliusz Cezar 1962, Virtutis ergo, nadania obywatelstwa rzymskiego przez wodzów republiki 1963, Cesarz August 1964, Herod król Judei 1965, Neron 1965, Perykles i Aspazja 1967, Siedmiu przeciw Tebom 1968, Sprawa Alkibiadesa 1968, Wojna trojańska 1969, Kleopatra 1969, Pan i jego filozof 1970, Konstantyn Wielki 1970, Ród Konstantyna 1972, Sennik Artemidora 1972, Tytus i Berenika 1972, Groby Cheronei 1972, Rzym i Jerozolima 1974, Julian Apostata 1974, Maraton 1976, Ostatnia Olimpiada 1976, Upadek Rzymu 1978, Starożytność odległa i bliska 1980, Mitologia starożytnej Italii 1982, Ród Argeadów 1982, Stąd do starożytności 1985, Poczet cesarzy rzymskich 1986, Poczet cesarzowych rzymskich 1998. *Leisure interest:* hiking. *Address:* ul. Radockiego 5 m. 1, 30-540 Cracow, Poland (Home). *Telephone:* (12) 66 09 94 (Home).

KRAYEVSKY, Aleksander Antonovich; Russian biologist; b. 7 Nov. 1932, Moscow; s. of Anton Pavlovich Krayevsky and Marilia Bernardovna Krayevskaya; m. Elena Krayevskaya 1955; one s. one d.; ed. Moscow Inst. of Fine Chem. Tech.; on staff as asst., docent 1962–66; sr. researcher V. Engelgart Inst. of Molecular Biol. U.S.S.R. Acad. of Sciences 1966–85, head of lab. 1985–; corresp. mem. U.S.S.R. (now Russian) Acad. of Sciences 1990, mem. 1994; research in lipid chem., chem. of nucleic acids, study of protein formation in cells, mechanisms of DNA biosynthesis, studies on AIDS by chemotherapy and molecular action mechanisms of anti-AIDS drugs; mem. Exec. Bd. European Soc. on chem. of nucleic acids. *Publications include:* Molecular bases of Protein Biosynthesis 1971, Mechanism of Formation of Peptide Bonds in Ribosomes 1979, DNA Replication in Eukaryotes 1985, Physical-Chemical aspects of DNA Polymerase Functioning 1990, numerous articles in scientific journals. *Leisure interests:* fiction and poetry. *Address:* V. Engelgart Institute of Molecular Biology, Russian Academy of Sciences, Vavilov str. 32, 117984 Moscow, Russia. *Telephone:* (095) 135 22 55 (Office). *Fax:* (095) 135 1405.

KREBS, Edwin Gerhard, M.D., D.SC.; American professor of biochemistry; b. 6 June 1918, Lansing, Iowa; s. of William Krebs and Louise Stegeman; m. Virginia French 1945; one s. two d.; ed. Univ. of Illinois and Washington Univ. St. Louis; intern, Barnes Hosp. St. Louis 1944–45; Research Fellow, Washington Univ. St. Louis 1946–48; Asst. Prof. of Biochem. Univ. of Washington, Seattle 1948–52, Assoc. Prof. 1952–57, Prof. 1957–66; Prof. and Chair. Dept. of Biological Chem., School of Medicine Univ. of Calif. Davis 1968–76; Prof. and Chair. Dept. of Pharmacology, Univ. of Washington, Seattle 1977–83, Prof. of Biochem. and Pharmacology 1984–91; Sr. Investigator, Howard Hughes Medical Inst. Seattle 1983–90, Sr. Investigator Emer. 1991–; mem. N.A.S., American Soc. of Biological Chemists, American Acad. of Arts and Sciences; numerous professional appts.; Nobel Prize for Medicine (with Edmond Fischer q.v.) 1992; Hon. D.Sc. (Birmingham) 1998; other awards and distinctions. *Address:* c/o Department of Pharmacology, University of Washington, Box 357370, Seattle, WA 98195, U.S.A.

KREBS, Sir John Richard, Kt., M.A., D.PHIL., F.R.S.; British zoologist and scientific administrator; b. 11 April 1945, Sheffield; s. of Prof. Sir Hans Krebs and Margaret Fieldhouse; m. Katharine A. Fullerton 1968; two d.; ed. city of Oxford High School and Pembroke Coll. Oxford; departmental demonstrator in Ornithology, Edward Grey Inst. and Oxford Lecturer in Zoology, Pembroke Coll. Oxford 1969–70; Asst. Prof. Inst. of Resource Ecology, Univ. of B.C. Vancouver 1970–73; lecturer in Zoology, Univ. of Coll. of N. Wales, Bangor 1973–74; SRC Research Officer, Animal Behaviour Research Group, Dept. of Zoology, Oxford 1975–76; lecturer in Zoology, Edward Grey Inst. of Field Ornithology, Oxford 1976–88, Fellow, Wolfson Coll. 1976–81, Fellow Pembroke Coll. 1981–; E. P. Abraham Fellow in Zoology, Pembroke Coll. 1981–88, Fellow 1988–; Royal Soc. Research Prof. Univ. of Oxford 1988–; Chief Exec. Natural Environment Research Council 1994–; Dir. AFRC Unit of Ecology and Behaviour and NERC Unit of Behavioural Ecology 1989–94; Sr. Scientific Consultant and Chair. Animals Research Cttee., Agricultural and Food Research Council 1991–94; External scientific mem. Max Planck Soc. 1985; Pres. Int. Soc. of Behavioural Ecology 1988–90, Asscn. for Study of Animal Behaviour 1992–94; mem. Agricultural and Food Research Council 1988–94; mem. Academia Europaea; Hon. mem. British Ecological Soc.; Hon. D.Sc. (Sheffield) 1993, (Wales) 1997, (Birmingham) 1997, (Exeter) 1998; Nuffield Foundation Science Fellowship 1981; Scientific Medal, Zoological Soc. 1981, Bicentenary Medal, Linnaean Soc. 1983, Frink Medal, Zoological Soc. 1996. *Publications:* Behavioural Ecology: An Evolutionary Aproach (ed. with N. B. Davies) 1978, 1984, 1991, 1997, An Introduction to Behavioural Ecology (with N. B. Davies) 1981, 1986, Foraging Theory. Princeton Monographs in Behaviour and Ecology, No. 4 (with D. W. Stephens) 1987, Foraging Behaviour (ed. with A. Kamil and H. R. Pulliam) 1987, Behavioural and Neural Studies of Learning and Memory (ed. with G. Horn) 1991. *Leisure interests:* gardening, violin, running, walking. *Address:* Natural Environment Research Council, Polaris House, Swindon, SN2 1EU (Office); 11 Brookside, Headington, Oxford, OX3 7PJ, England (Home). *Telephone:* (01793) 411653 (Office).

KREBS, Robert Duncan, M.B.A.; American transport executive; b. 2 May 1942, Sacramento; s. of Ward C. Krebs and Eleanor B. (née Duncan) Krebs; m. Anne Lindstrom 1971; two s. one d.; ed. Stanford Univ., Harvard Univ.; Asst. Gen. Man. S. Pacific Transportation Co., Houston 1974–75, Asst. Regional Operations Man. 1975–76, Asst. Vice-Pres. San Francisco 1967–77, Asst. to Pres. 1977–79, Gen. Man. 1979, Vice-Pres. Transportation 1979-80, Operations 1980–82, Pres. 1982–83; Dir. and Pres. Santa Fe S. Pacific Corpn. (now Santa Fe Pacific Corpn.) 1983–96, Pres., Chair. and C.E.O. 1988–96, Pres., C.E.O. Burlington Northern Santa Fe Corpn. 1995–, Chair. April 1997–; Dir. Phelps Dodge Corpn., Fort Worth Symphony Orchestra, several other orgs. *Address:* Burlington Northern Santa Fe Corporation, 1700 East Golf Rd., Schaumburg, IL 60173, U.S.A.

KREDEL, Elmar Maria, DR.THEOL.; German ecclesiastic; b. 24 Feb. 1922, Nuremberg; s. of Georg and Josephine (née Weirather) Kredel; ed. gymnasium in Nuremberg and studies in philosophy and theology in Bamberg and Innsbruck and Papal Inst., Rome; ordained in Bamberg 1950; chaplain, Pegnitz 1952–54; studies in Rome 1954–56; Asst., Exeget Seminar, Univ. of Munich 1958–62; parish admin. and parson, Freienfels and Hollfeld 1962–67; cathedral staff, Bamberg 1967; diocesan adviser in youth work, adult educ., Caritas, Pro-synodal judge, Deputy Vicar-Gen. and Canonicus theologus 1967–77; Hon. Papal Prelate 1975; Archbishop of Bamberg 1977–94, Archbishop Emer. 1994–; Pres. of the Episcopal Comm. for Social and Charitable Questions, Comm. VI of the German Bishop's Conf. 1977–86; Roman Catholic Mil. Bishop, Deutsche Bundeswehr 1978–90; Bayerische Verdienstorden; Grosses Bundesverdienstkreuz; Hon. Citizen, Bamberg 1987. *Publications:* various theological articles. *Leisure interest:* classical music. *Address:* Obere Karolinenstrasse 8, 96049 Bamberg, Germany. *Telephone:* 0951/56255.

KREISEL, Georg; F.R.S.; British professor of logic; b. 15 Sept. 1923, Graz, Austria; s. of Heinrich Kreisel and Bertha (née Wahrmann) Kreisel; Prof. of Logic and the Foundation of Math., Stanford Univ., Calif. *Address:* Institut für Wissenschaftstheorie Internationales Forschungszentrum Salzburg, Mönchsberg 2, A-5020 Salzburg, Austria. *Telephone:* (0662) 842521 (Salzburg).

KREJČA, Otomar: Czech actor and director; b. 23 Nov. 1921, Skrýšov; s. of František Krejča and Ludmila Pechová; m. Marie Tomasova 1986; one s.; ed. Charles Univ., Prague; Mem. Prague Nat. Theatre 1951–69, Art Chief, Nat. Theatre Drama Section 1956–61; Founder and Artistic Dir. of Divadlo za branou (Theatre Beyond the Gate) 1965–71, Dir. 1971–72 (theatre shut 1972); Dir. Theatre S.K.N. 1973–75; allowed to work only outside C.S.S.R. 1976–89; Artistic Dir. Schauspielhaus Düsseldorf 1976–78, Atelier Théâtral de Louvain-la-Neuve 1979–81; Founder and Dir. Divadlo za branou II, Prague 1990–94; Dir. Prague Nat. Theatre 1997–98. *Plays directed include:* all Chekhov's plays, Romeo and Juliet, Hamlet, Measure for Measure (Shakespeare), Antigone (Sophocles), Life Is A Dream (Calderon), Waiting for Godot (Beckett) and other classical and modern dramas; Guest Dir. for productions in Havana, Brussels, Cologne, Salzburg, Vienna, Stockholm, Paris, Avignon, Genoa, Berlin; State Prize 1951, 1968, Honoured Artist 1958, Kainz Medal (Austria) 1969, Int. Pirandello Prize (Italy) 1978, Distinction of Union of Soviet Asscns. for Cultural Links and Friendship with Overseas 1991, Medal for Merit 1998; Ordre des Arts et des Lettres (France) 1978, 1991. *Address:* Národní divadlo, Ostrovní 1, Prague 1, Czech Republic (Office). *Telephone:* 688 17 59.

KRELLE, Wilhelm Ernst, DR.RER.POL.; German professor of economics; b. 24 Dec. 1916, Magdeburg; s. of Dr. Willy Krelle and Elisabeth (née Dienemann) Krelle; m. Rose-Alix Scholz 1944 (died 1981); two s. (one deceased) two d.; ed. gymnasium in Magdeburg and Nordhausen and Univs. of Frankfurt, Tübingen and Freiburg; Officer, German Army 1937–45; Rockefeller Fellow, Harvard Univ. 1953–54; Assoc. Prof. Univ. of St. Gall, Switzerland 1956–58; Prof. of Econs. Univ. of Bonn 1958–; mem. Bd. of econ. advisers to Minister of Commerce; mem. Gesellschaft für Wirtschafts- und Sozialwissenschaften (Pres. 1974–78), Acad. of Sciences of North Rhine–Westphalia, American Econ. Asscn.; corresp. mem. Bavarian Acad. of Sciences; Fellow, Econometric Soc.; Dr. h.c. (St. Gall, Vienna, Karlsruhe, Münster, Mannheim, Humboldt-Univ., Berlin), Hon. Prof. Univ. of Vienna. *Publications:* Theorie wirtschaftl. Verhaltensweisen 1953, Lohnhöhe und Beschaftig. (with H. Haller) 1955, Beitrag z. Theorie d. Produktion u.d. Einkommensverteil (with K. Brandt and J. H. Müller) 1956, Lineare Programmierung (with H. P. Künzi) 1958, Volksw. Gesamtrechnung einschl. Input-Output-Analyse m. Zahlen f.d. BRD 1959, Preistheorie 1960, Verteilungstheorie 1962, Nichtlineare Programmierung (with Künzi) 1962, Präferenz- u. Entscheidungstheorie 1968, Übertriebliche Ertragsbeteiligung der Arbeitnehmer (with Schunck and Siebke) 1968, Produktionstheorie 1969, Einführung in d. math. Optimierung (with Künzi) 1969, Ein Prognosesystem f.d. wirtschaftl. Entwicklung d. BRD 1969, (with Beckerhoff, Langer and Fuss) 1969, Wachstumstheorie (with Gabisch) 1972, Erfahr. mit einem ökonometrischen Prognosemodell f.d. BRD 1974, Gesamtwirtschaftliche Auswirkungen einer Ausweitung des Bildungssystems (with Fleck and Quinke) 1975, Preistheorie II 1976, Nichtlineare Programmierung (with Künzi and von Randow) 1979, Theorie des Wirtschaftlichen Wachstums 1985, Der "Maschinenbeitrag" (with others) 1985, Gossen und seine Gesetze in unserer Zeit (with Recktenwald) 1987, Theorie des wirtschaftlichen Wachstums (2 vols.) 1988, The Future of the World Economy 1989, Heinrich von Stackelbergs Marktform und Gleichgewicht (co-author) 1993; many articles and contributions to books. *Leisure interests:* music, hiking, literature. *Address:* Institut für Gesellschafts- und Wirtschaftswissenschaften der Universität Bonn, Adenauerallee 24–42, 53113

Bonn (Office); Am Domblick 15, 53177 Bonn, Germany (Home). *Telephone:* 0228/73 79 57 (Office); 0228/32 31 35 (Home). *Fax:* 0228/73 91 00.

KREMENYUK, Victor Aleksandrovich, D. HIST.; Russian civil servant; b. 13 Dec. 1943; ed. Moscow Inst. of Int. Relations; army service 1963–68; with Mezdunarodnaya Zhizn magazine 1968–70; with Inst. of U.S.A. and Canada, U.S.S.R. (now Russian) Acad. of Sciences 1968–70; expert, Cttee. on Int. Problems, U.S.S.R. Supreme Soviet 1989–91; expert, State Duma 1993–; worked on project Process of Int. Negotiations in Int. Inst. of Applied System Analysis Austria, lectures and seminars in U.S.A., Germany, Austria; Deputy Dir. Inst. of U.S.A. and Canada 1989–; Chair. Expert Council of Political Sciences 1992–; mem. Council on Higher Policy at Ministry of Foreign Affairs 1991–96; mem. Scientific Council, Russian Inst. of Strategic Studies 1995–; mem. Council of Social Sciences, Presidium of Russian Acad. of Sciences 1991–; mem. Nat. Geographical Soc., U.S.A., Int. Asscn. of Conflictology; mem. Consultative and Observation Councils Salzburg Seminar, Austria, Centre of Applied Studies on Negotiations, Switzerland; mem. Ed. Bds., magazines Econ., Politics and Ideology, Journal of Negotiations, U.S.A., Journal of Peace Studies, U.S.A. *Publications:* over 100 articles and 12 scientific monographs, ed. over 50 scientific works in Russian and English. *Address:* Institute of U.S.A. and Canada, Khlebny per. 2/3, 121069 Moscow, Russia. *Telephone:* (095) 291 1166 (Office).

KREMER, Gidon; Russian/German (b. Latvian) violinist; b. 27 Feb. 1947, Riga; ed. Riga School of Music, Moscow Conservatory (with David Oistrakh); prizewinner at Queen Elizabeth Competition, Brussels, Montréal Competition and Fourth Int. Tchaikovsky Competition (First Prize) 1970, Paganini Prize, Genoa; recitalist and orchestral soloist worldwide; has played in most major int. festivals including Berlin, Dubrovnik, Helsinki, London, Moscow, Prague, Salzburg, Tokyo and Zürich; has played with most major int. orchestras including Berlin Philharmonic, Boston Symphony, Concertgebouw, L.A. Philharmonic, New York Philharmonic, Philadelphia, San Francisco Symphony, Vienna Philharmonic, London Philharmonic, Royal Philharmonic, Philharmonia, NHK Symphony of Japan and all main Soviet orchestras; has worked with Bernstein, von Karajan, Giulini, Jochum, Previn, Abbado, Levine, Maazel, Muti, Harnoncourt, Mehta and Marriner; has made more than 45 records and has won Grand Prix du Disque and Deutsche Schallplattenpreis; first performances include Henze, Stockhausen, Schnittke, Pärt, Astor Piazzola; f. Lockenhaus Chamber Music Festival 1981; plays a Stradivarius. *Address:* c/o ICM Artists, 40 West 57th Street, New York, NY 10023, U.S.A.

KREMNEV, Roald Savvovich; Russian mechanical engineer; b. 13 July 1929, Irkutsk; m. Galina Vasilyevna Golikova; ed. Kazan Aviation Inst.; mem. CPSU 1961–91; engineer, leading constructor, deputy chief constructor S.A. Lavochkine experimental design office 1954–85; Dir. and Chief Designer G.N. Babakin Centre, S.A. Lavochkine Scientific Industrial Asscn. 1985–; State Prize 1972; Lenin Prize 1986. *Address:* NPO S. Lavochkin, G.N. Babakin Centre, 125212 Khimki, Moscow oblast, Leningradskoye shosse 24a, Russia. *Telephone:* 5739191; 5738202 (Office).

KREMP, Herbert, DR.PHIL.; German journalist; b. 12 Aug. 1928, Munich; s. of Johann and Elisabeth Kremp; m. Brigitte Steffal 1956; two d. (one deceased); ed. Munich Univ.; Reporter, Frankfurter Neue Presse 1956–57; Political Ed. Rheinische Post 1957–59; Dir. Political Dept., Der Tag, Berlin 1959–61; Bonn Corresp. Rheinische Post 1961–63; Ed.-in-Chief, Rheinische Post 1963–68; Ed.-in-Chief, Die Welt 1969–77, Joint Ed. 1981–, Co-Publr. 1984–87; Chief Corresp. in Beijing 1977–81, Editor-in-Chief 1981–85, Chief Corresp. in Brussels 1987–, Jt. Ed., Springer Group newspapers 1984–87; Konrad Adenauer Prize 1984, Bundesverdienstkreuz 1988. *Publications:* Am Ufer der Rubikon: Eine politische Anthropologie, Die Bambusbrücke: Ein asiatisches Tagebuch 1979, Wir brauchen unsere Geschichte 1988. *Address:* c/o Die Welt, Kochstrasse 50, 10969 Berlin, Germany.

KRENS, Thomas; American museum director; b. 26 Dec. 1946, New York; ed. Williams Coll., Southern Univ. of New York (SUNY), Albany and Yale Univ.; Asst. Prof. of Art, Williams Coll., Williamstown, Mass. 1972–80, Asst. Prof. of History of Art, grad. program. 1977–80, Adjunct. Prof. of Art History 1988–; Dir. Williams Coll. Museum of Art 1980–88; consultant, Solomon R. Guggenheim Museum, New York 1986–88, Dir. 1988–; Dir. The Peggy Guggenheim Collection, Venice 1988–; Dir., Trustee Solomn R. Guggenheim Foundation 1988–; Hon. D.Hum.Litt. (SUNY). *Publications:* Jim Dine Prints: 1970–77 1977, The Prints of Helen Frankenthaler 1980, The Drawing of Robert Morris 1982, Robert Morris: The Mind/Body Problem 1994. *Address:* Solomon R. Guggenheim Museum, 1071 Fifth Avenue, New York, NY 10128, U.S.A.

KRENZ, Egon; German politician; b. 1937; ed. Teacher Training Inst. Putbus and Cen. Cttee. of CPSU Party Univ. Moscow; joined Freie Deutsche Jugend (FDJ) 1953, Socialist Unity Party (SED) and Confed. of Free German Trade Unions 1955; various functions within FDJ and SED 1957–64; Sec. Ernst Thälmann Pioneer Org. 1967–74, Chair. 1971–74; First Sec. FDJ Cen. Council 1974–83; mem. Nat. Council of Nat. Front 1969–; cand. mem. Cen. Cttee. of SED 1971–73, mem. 1973–90, Sec. 1989–90, cand. mem. Politburo 1976–83, mem. 1983–90, Gen. Sec. 1989–90; Deputy to Volkskammer 1971–90, mem. Presidium 1971–81, Chair. FDJ Faction 1971–76; mem. Council of State 1981–84, Deputy Chair. 1984–89, Chair. (Head of State) 1989–90; stripped of membership of C.P. (fmrly. SED); now property developer, Berlin; faced charges of manslaughter for killings of persons fleeing over Berlin Wall and other borders 1994; on trial Aug. 1995; sentenced to six and a half years' imprisonment for the deaths of those trying to cross the Berlin Wall Aug. 1997; decorations include Karl Marx Orden, Banner der Arbeit, Verdienstmedaille der DDR.

KRENZ, Jan; Polish conductor and composer; b. 14 July 1926, Włocławek; s. of Otton and Eleonora Krenz; m. Alina Krenz 1958; one s.; conducting début, Łódź Philharmonic Orch. 1946; Chief Conductor, State Poznań Philharmonic Orchestra 1947–49; Chief Conductor Polish Nat. Radio Symphony Orchestra of Katowice 1953–67; Chief Conductor Danish Radio Orchestra, Copenhagen 1960s; Leader, Grand Opera House Orchestra (Teatr Wielki), Warsaw 1968–73; conducted Berlin Philharmonic, Staatskapelle Dresden, Leningrad Philharmonic, and all the maj. London orchestras; Gen. Dir. of Music, Bonn Orchestra 1978–82; frequent collaboration with Yomiuri Nippon Symphony Orchestra; performing only as guest conductor 1983–; State Prize 1955, 1972; Prize of Union of Polish Composers 1968; Grand Prix du Disque, France 1972; Prize of Polish Artists' and Musicians' Asscn. (SPAM) "Orfeusz" 1974; Diploma of Ministry of Foreign Affairs 1980; numerous decorations. *Compositions include:* chamber, vocal and symphonic music, orchestral transcriptions of Polish classics, J. S. Bach and Szymanowski. *Leisure interest:* painting. *Address:* Filharmonia Narodowa, ul. Jasna 5, Warsaw, Poland.

KREPS, Juanita Morris, M.A., PH.D.; American politician, economist and teacher; b. 11 Jan. 1921, Lynch, Ky.; d. of the late Elmer and Cenia Blair Morris; m. Dr. Clifton H. Kreps, Jr. 1944; one s. two d.; ed. Berea Coll., Duke Univ.; Instructor in Econs., Denison Univ., Ohio 1945–46, Asst. Prof. 1947–50; Lecturer, Hofstra Univ., N.Y., 1952–54, Queens Coll., N.Y. 1954–55; Visiting Asst. Prof. Duke Univ., N.C., Asst. Prof. 1958–61, Assoc. Prof. 1962–67, Prof. 1967–77, Dean of Women's Coll., Asst. Provost 1969–72, James B. Duke Prof. 1972–77, Vice-Pres. of Univ. 1973–77; U.S. Sec. of Commerce 1977–79; Ford Faculty Research Fellow 1964–65; Dir. N.Y. Stock Exchange 1972–77, AT&T 1980–91, Armco Inc. 1980–91, UAL Inc. 1979–92, Eastman Kodak Co. 1975–77, 1979–91, J. C. Penney Co. 1972–77, 1979–91, Zurn Industries Inc. 1982–93, Deere & Co. 1982–92, Chrysler Corpn. 1983–91, Citicorp 1979–89, RJR Nabisco 1975–77, 1979–89; Trustee, Coll. Retirement Equities Fund 1972–77, 1985–92, Berea Coll., Duke Endowment; Chair. Bd. of Trustees, Educational Testing Service 1975–76; Pres. American Asscn. for Higher Educ. 1975–76; Pres. Bd. of Overseers, Teachers Insurance and Annuity Asscn. and Coll. Retirement Equities Fund 1992–96; mem. Comm. on Future of Worker-Man. Relations to advise Secs. of Commerce and Labor 1993–95; Trustee Berea Coll. 1972–78, 1980–98, Kenan Inst. of Pvt. Enterprise Univ. of N.C., Chapel Hill 1995–; 20 hon. degrees; Duke Endowment 1979–; N.C. Public Service Award 1976, Haskins Award 1984. *Publications:* ed.: Employment, Income and Retirement Problems of the Aged 1963, Technology, Manpower and Retirement Policy 1966; ed. and contrib.: Lifetime Allocation of Work and Income 1971, Sex in the Marketplace: American Women at Work 1971; co-author: Principles of Economics (with C. E. Ferguson) 1962, 1965, Contemporary Labor Economics 1974, Sex, Age and Work 1975, Women and the American Economy, a Look to the 1980s 1976; over 60 papers on ageing, retirement and econs. *Leisure interests:* music, art. *Address:* 115 East Duke Building, Duke University, Durham, NC 27708, U.S.A.

KRESS, Victor Melkhiorovich; Russian politician; b. 16 Nov. 1948, Kostroma Region; m.; two c.; ed. Novosibirsk Inst. of Agric.; agronomist, agric. enterprises Tomsk Region; Deputy Chair., Agric.-Industrial complex Tomsk Region 1971–87; First Sec. Dist. CP Cttee., Tomsk Region 1987–90; Chair. Tomsk Regional Soviet 1990–91; Head, Admin. of Tomsk Region 1991–96, Gov. 1996–; mem. Fed. Ass. of Russian Fed. 1993–; Chair. Interregional Asscn. Siberian Agreement. *Address:* Office of the Governor, Lenina square 6, 634050 Tomsk, Russia. *Telephone:* (3822) 22 36 86 (Office).

KRETZENBACHER, Leopold, DR. PHIL.; Austrian/German academic; b. 13 Nov. 1912, Leibnitz; s. of Michael Kretzenbacher and Franziska Kuder; m. Elfriede Jauker 1940; two s. four d.; ed. Univ. of Graz; Univ. of Zagreb 1943–44; Prof. Univ. of Kiel 1961–66, Univ. of Munich 1966–78; Prof. Emer. Inst. für Deutsche und Vergleichende Volkskunde, Univ. of Munich 1978–; has undertaken extensive travels in Europe for purpose of ethnological research; mem. Acads. of Munich, Uppsala, Vienna, Slovenia, New York; Dr.iur. h.c. (Graz). *Publications:* approximately 30 books and 400 studies. *Leisure interests:* mountain walking, cross-country skiing, swimming, listening to music. *Address:* 80803 Munich, Clemensstrasse 36/I, Germany. *Telephone:* 089-396284.

KRIANGSAK CHOMANAN, Gen.; Thai politician and army officer; b. 1917; ed. Thai Royal Mil. Acad. and U.S. Army Staff Coll.; served in Second World War and Korean War; Deputy Chief of Staff, Supreme Command Headquarters to 1974, Chief of Staff 1974–76; Deputy Supreme Commdr. of Royal Thai Armed Forces 1976–77, Supreme Commdr. 1978; participated in mil. coups Oct. 1976 and 1977–78; Gen. Sec. Nat. Admin. Reform Council Oct. 1976; Vice-Chair. Prime Minister's Advisory Council Oct. 1976–Oct. 1977; Sec.-Gen. Revolutionary Council, Nat. Dir. of Peacekeeping Oct.–Nov. 1977; Sec.-Gen. Nat. Policy Council 1977–79; Prime Minister 1977–80, Minister of Finance 1979–80, of the Interior 1977–78, of Defence 1978–79, of Agric. 1979–80; M.P. for Muang Roi Et Aug. 1981; ordained as monk Jan. 1983; Leader, Nat. Democratic Party; arrested Sept. 1985, granted bail Feb. 1986. *Address:* National Assembly, Bangkok, Thailand.

KRIEL, Hermanus Jacobus, B.A., LL.B.; South African politician and lawyer; b. 14 Nov. 1941, Kakamas; s. of Prof. Kriel and Mrs. Kriel; one s. two d.; ed. Hugenote Hoërskool, Univ. of Stellenbosch; conveyancer, notary 1968; Chair. Cape Div. Council 1976–77; mem. Cape Prov. Council 1977–84, Cape Exec. Cttee. 1981–84; M.P. 1984–89; Minister of Planning, Prov. Affairs and Nat. Housing 1989–91, of Law and Order 1991–94; Premier of Western Cape Provincial Parl. 1994–97; F.C. Erasmus Award, Stella Officii Egregii. *Leisure interests:* golf, reading. *Address:* c/o Private Bag 9043, Cape Town 8000, South Africa.

KRIELE, Martin, DR.JUR., LL.M.; German professor of law; b. 19 Jan. 1931, Opladen; s. of late Dr. Rudolf Kriele and Konstanze Henckels; m. 1st Christel Grothues 1960; one s. one d.; m. 2nd Alexa Michalsen; ed. Freiburg, Münster, Bonn and Yale Univs.; admitted to the Court 1961; Prof. of Philosophy of Law and Public Law, Univ. of Cologne 1967–; Dir. Inst. for Political Philosophy and Problems of Legislation 1967; Judge, Constitutional Court of North Rhine–Westphalia 1976–88; Ed. Zeitschrift für Rechtspolitik 1968–. *Publications:* Kriterien der Gerechtigkeit 1963, Theorie der Rechtsgewinnung 1967, Einführung in die Staatslehre 1975, Legitimitätsprobleme der Bundesrepublik 1977, Die Menschenrechte zwischen Ost und West 1977, Recht und praktische Vernunft 1979, Befreiung und politische Aufklärung 1980, Nicaragua, das blutende Herz Amerikas 1985, Die Demokratische Weltrevolution 1987, Recht, Vernunft, Wirklichkeit (essays) 1990. *Leisure interest:* music (piano). *Address:* University of Cologne, Seminar für Staatsphilosophie und Rechtspolitik, Albertus-Magnus-Platz 1, 50923 Cologne, Germany (Office); Dorf 11, 6900 Möggen, Austria (Home). *Telephone:* (0221) 4702230 (Office); (05573) 3772 (Home). *Fax:* (0221) 470 5010 (Office); (05573) 3772 (Home).

KRIER, Léon; Luxembourg architect; b. 7 April 1946, Luxembourg; ed. Univ. of Stuttgart; Asst. to James Stirling London 1968–70, 1973–74; project partner with J. P. Kleihues, Berlin 1971–72; in pvt. practice in London 1974–; lecturer Architectural Asscn. School, London 1973–76, Royal Coll. of Art, London 1977, Princeton Univ. 1977; Jefferson Prof. of Architecture, Univ. Va. Charlottesville 1982; works include numerous city centre and housing redevt. plans, schools, univs., public bldgs. etc. in U.K., Germany, Luxembourg, Spain, Italy, Greece, Sweden and U.S.A; numerous exhbns. including Triennale, Milan 1973, Léon Krier and Rita Wolff, Inst. for Architecture & Urban Studies, New York 1978, City Segments, Walker Art Center, Minn. and elsewhere in U.S.A. 1980, Léon Krier: la ricostruzione della città europea, Verona 1980, Drawings by Léon Krier, Max Protech Gallery, New York 1981, Model Futures, ICA, London 1983, Léon Krier, Max Protech Gallery, New York 1984; City of Berlin Architecture Prize (with Rob Krier) 1975. *Publications include:* Buildings and Projects of James Stirling (ed.) 1974, The Reconstruction of the European City 1978, The City within the City (ed.) 1979, Südliche Friedrichstadt (with M. Culot) 1981, Architecture and Urban Design (ed. by Richard Economakis) 1967–92; articles in journals. *Address:* 16 Belsize Park, London, N.W.3, England (Office).

KRIKALEV, Sergey Konstantinovich; Russian cosmonaut; b. 27 Aug. 1958, Leningrad; m.; ed. Leningrad Mechanical Inst.; worked in Research Production Co. Energia, took part in developing new samples of space tech.; Master of Sports in piloting; mem. Cosmonauts' team since 1985; took part in jt. space flights Soviet-French 1988–89, Soviet-British 1991, American Endeavor flight to new Int. Space Station Nov. 1998; spent 310 days in orbit on Soyuz TM-12 1991–92; third-rank cosmonaut; Hero of the Soviet Union 1989, Hero of the Russian Fed. 1992. *Address:* Yuriy Gagarin Centre for Cosmonauts Training, Zvezdny Gorodok, Moscow Region, Russia. *Telephone:* (095) 9718616.

KRINGS, Hermann, DR.PHIL.; German professor of philosophy; b. 25 Sept. 1913, Aachen; s. of Wilhelm Krings and Jenny Dechamps; m. Inge Birkmann 1949; one d.; Prof. of Philosophy, Univ. of Munich 1956–60; Prof. of Philosophy, Univ. of Saarland, Saarbrücken 1960–68, Univ. Rector 1965–67; Prof. of Philosophy, Univ. of Munich 1968–80, Prof. Emer. 1980–; mem. Bayerische Akad. der Wissenschaften. *Publications:* Ordo. Philosophisch-historische Grundlegung einer abendländischen Idee 1941, 1982, Fragen und Aufgaben der Ontologie 1954, Meditation des Denkens 1956, Transzendentale Logik 1964, System und Freiheit. Gesammelte Aufsätze 1980. *Address:* Zuccalistrasse 19a, 80639 Munich, Germany.

KRIPKE, Saul Aaron, B.A., L.H.D.; American professor of philosophy; b. 13 Nov. 1940, Bay Shore, New York; s. of Myer Samuel Kripke and Dorothy Kripke; m. Margaret P. Gilbert 1976; ed. Harvard Univ.; Soc. of Fellows, Harvard Univ. 1963–66, concurrently lecturer with rank of Asst. Prof. Princeton Univ. 1964–66; lecturer Harvard Univ. 1966–68; Assoc. Prof. Rockefeller Univ. 1968–72, Prof. 1972–76; McCosh Prof. of Philosophy, Princeton Univ. 1977–; Fellow, American Acad. of Arts and Sciences; corresp. Fellow, British Acad.; Fulbright Fellow 1962–63; Guggenheim Fellow 1968–69, 1977–78; Visiting Fellow, All Souls Coll. Oxford 1977–78, 1989–90; other visiting professorships etc.; Hon. D.Hum.Litt. (Univ. of Neb. at Omaha). *Publications:* Naming and Necessity 1980, Wittgenstein on Rules and Private Language 1982; numerous papers in professional journals and anthologies. *Address:* Department of Philosophy, Princeton University, Princeton, NJ 08544, U.S.A.

KRISHNAMURTY, G. V. G., B.A., B.SC., B.L.; Indian election commissioner and lawyer; b. 19 Nov. 1934, Chirala, Andhra Pradesh; s. of G. V. Subbarao and Mrs. G. Rajeswaramma; m. Mrs. G. Padma 1957; one s. one d.; ed. Andhra Univ.; anti-British student activist and mem. Azad Hindu Fauz Youth League 1945–47; advocate, Andhra Pradesh High Court 1958; lecturer, Law Coll. Osmania Univ. 1958, 1962; Sr. Research Officer, Indian Law Inst. 1962–63; advocate, Supreme Court; Deputy Legal Adviser, Comm. of Inquiry, Cabinet Secr. 1972–73; Additional Legal Adviser, Ministry of Law and ex-officio Govt. Counsel, Delhi High Court 1973–76, 1978–79; Govt. Arbitrator 1979–83; Jt. Sec. and Legal Adviser 1983–87; Additional Sec. Govt. of India 1987–88, Special Sec. 1988–89; Sec. Law Comm. of India 1989–92; Election Commr. of India Oct. 1993–; Hon. LL.D. (Jhansi Univ.) 1996; del. to various int. confs. etc.; numerous professional appts. and other distinctions. *Publications include:* Dynamics of Diplomacy 1968, Modern Diplomacy, Dialectics and Dimensions 1980; articles in legal journals. *Leisure interests:* reading, watching nature, cultural activities. *Address:* Election Commission of India, Nirvachan Sadan, Ashoka Road, New Delhi 110001 (Office); Bungalow No. 9, Janpath, New Delhi, India (Home). *Telephone:* 3720012 (Office); 3794131, 3018332 (Home). *Fax:* 3739933 (Office); 3018138 (Home).

KRISHNAN, Natarajan, B.A.ECONS.; Indian diplomatist; b. 6 Oct. 1928, Mayuram, Tamil Nadu; s. of the late V. Natarajan; m. Lalitha Krishnan; one s. two d.; ed. Univ. of Madras; joined Indian Foreign Service 1951; Third Sec., later Second Sec., Bangkok 1955–56; Second Sec., Chargé d'Affaires, Phnom-Penh 1956–57; Under Sec. Ministry of External Affairs 1957–58; First Sec., Chargé d'Affaires, Buenos Aires 1959–62; Deputy Sec., Dir. Ministry of External Affairs 1962–67; Consul-Gen. and Perm. Rep. to UN Offices, Geneva 1967–71; Joint Sec. Ministry of External Affairs 1971–76; Amb. to Yugoslavia 1976–79; Additional Sec. Ministry of External Affairs 1979–81; Amb. and Perm. Rep. to UN 1981–87; Dean, School of Int. Studies, Pondicherry Univ. 1988–90; Prime Minister's Special Envoy for Africa 1987–89; mem. Exec. Bd. UNESCO 1989–. *Address:* Flat 2C, King's Crest Apts., No. 8 Millers Road, Bangalore 560046, India.

KRISHNAN, Rappal Sangameswara, D.SC., PH.D., Indian physicist; b. 23 Sept. 1911, Chittur, Palghat Dist., Kerala; s. of R. P. Sangameswara Iyer and C. R. Ammini Ammal; m. Rajammal 1934; two s. three d. (one deceased); ed. Univ. of Madras, St. Joseph's Coll., Trichy, Indian Inst. of Science, and Trinity Coll., Cambridge; Research Asst. Indian Inst. of Science 1935–38; 1851 Exbn. Overseas Scholar, Univ. of Cambridge 1938–41; lecturer in Physics, Inst. of Science 1942–45, Asst. Prof. 1945–48, Prof. and Head of Dept. of Physics 1948–72, Emer. Prof. 1972–73; Vice-Chancellor Kerala Univ. 1973–77; Prin. Investigator, DST Project, Indian Inst. of Science, Bangalore 1977–82, Emer. Prof. 1983–87; Visiting Scientist and Investigator, CSIR Project, Nat. Aeronautical Lab., Bangalore 1987–90, CSIR Emer. Scientist 1990–; Fellow Inst. of Physics, London, American Physical Soc., Indian Acad. of Sciences, Indian Natural Sciences Acad.; Pres. Physics Section, Indian Science Congress 1949; Nat. Science Foundation Sr. Foreign Scientist, Fellow, Dept. of Physics, North Tex. State Univ. Denton, Tex. 1971–72; original contributions to colloid optics (Krishnan Effect), light-scattering, Raman effect, crystal physics, etc.; mem. Bd., Int. Bd., American Biographical Inst. Research Asscn.; mem. Int. Biographical Asscn.; recipient I.I.Sc. Golden Jubilee Distinguished Alumni Award 1986, Chandrasekhard Venkata Raman (Nobel Laureate) Centenary Medal 1988, MA of the Year, American Biographical Inst. Research Asscn. *Publications:* Progress in Crystal Physics, Vol. I 1958, Two Chapters in Raman Effect, Vol. I 1971, Thermal Expansion of Crystals 1979, Source Book on Raman Effect Vol. I (1928–1957) 1989, Vol II (1958–1970) 1991, and contribs. to other books. *Leisure interests:* tennis, walking, photography. *Address:* Material Science Division, National Aeronautical Laboratory, Bangalore 560017 (Office); 232, 18th Cross, Palace Upper Orchards, Sadasivanagar, Bangalore 560080, Karnataka, India (Home). *Telephone:* 570098 (Office); 3340703 (Home).

KRISTAN, Ivan, DR. JUR.; Slovenian politician and lawyer; b. 12 June 1930, Arnovo; ed. Ljubljana Univ.; worked in trade unions 1956–67; teacher, Faculty of Law, Ljubljana Univ. 1967–77, Prof. 1977–87, Dean 1983–85, Rector 1985–87; mem. Cttee. for Constitutional Reforms Slovenian Repub. 1970–74, 1987–90; mem. Constitutional Court of Yugoslavia 1987–91; Pres. Nat. Council of Slovenian Repub. 1992–98; author of over 200 books, articles and scientific papers on legal problems of human rights, federalism, self-determination and sovereignty of nations, including Constitutional law of SFR Yugoslavia (co-author); Pres. of Supervising Cttee., Int. Asscn. for Constitutional Law (IACL). *Address:* National Council, Subeceva 4, 61000 Ljubljana, Slovenia. *Telephone:* (386-61) 126 1221. *Fax:* (386-61) 212 251.

KRISTENSEN, Finn; Norwegian politician; b. 24 July 1936, Brevik, Telemark; s. of Bjarne Kristensen and Jenny Eikefjord; m. Bodil Lia 1957; three c.; ed. Oslo Elementary Tech. School; maritime electrician 1955–56; electrician, Dalen Portland Cement Plant 1958–62; Instructor, Norwegian Workers' Educational Asscn. 1963–66; Dir. T-Invest of Porsgrunn 1985–86; Sec. Telemark Co. Labour Party 1966–; mem. Storting 1969–; Minister of Industry Feb.–Oct. 1981, 1986–89; Minister of Petroleum and Energy 1990–93; mem. Labour Party Nat. Bd. 1977; Chair. Standing Cttee. on Industry 1979–81; Dir. Statoil 1990–. *Address:* c/o Ministry of Petroleum and Energy, Grubbegt 8, P.O. Box 8148 Dep., 0033 Oslo 1, Norway.

KRISTIANSEN, Erling (Engelbrecht); Danish diplomatist and government official; b. 31 Dec. 1912, Terndrup; s. of the late Kristian E. Kristiansen and Andrea née Madsen; m. 1st Annemarie Selinko 1938 (died 1986); m. 2nd Harriet (née Lund Jensen) Laursen 1996; ed. Herning Gymnasium,

Univs. of Copenhagen and Geneva, Paris and London; Danish Civil Service, Ministry of Labour 1941, with Free Danish Legations Stockholm 1943, Washington 1944, London 1945; Commercial Sec. Danish Legation, London 1945–47; Head, Del. to OEEC 1948–50; Sec., Econ. Cttee. of Cabinet 1950–51; Asst. Under-Sec. of State, Ministry of Foreign Affairs 1951–53, Deputy Under-Sec. 1954–64; Amb. to U.K. 1964–77, (Doyen of the Diplomatic Corps 1973–77); concurrently to Ireland 1964–73; Chair. Danish Dels. to major econ. confs. 1954–63; Chair. Nordic Investment Bank 1978–80, mem. 1980–86; mem. Bd., The East Asiatic Co.; mem. Int. Advisory Bd. S. G. Warburg & Co. (Mercury Int. Group); Dir. several cos.; Hon. Pres. Anglo-Danish Soc.; co-f. and mem. Bd. CARE Denmark; Knight Grand Cross, Order of Dannebrog, Royal Victorian Order, Order of Falcon of Iceland, Grand Officier Légion d'honneur and other decorations. *Publication:* Folkeforbundet (The League of Nations) 1938. *Leisure interests:* outdoor sports, languages. *Address:* Kratkrogen 8, 2920 Charlottenlund, Denmark.

KRISTOFFERSON, Kris, B.A.; American singer, song writer and actor; b. 22 June 1936, Brownsville, Texas; one s. one d. (by first marriage); m. 2nd Rita Coolidge 1973 (divorced 1980); one s.; m. 3rd Lisa Meyers 1983; four c.; ed. Pomona Coll. and Oxford Univ.; Capt. in U.S. Army 1960–65; performed at Newport Folk Festival 1969; recording artist 1970–. *Songs include:* Help Me Make It Through the Night, Me and Bobby McGee, For the Good Times, When I Loved Her, Original Intent, Night of the Cyclone, Sandino, No Place to Hide, Cheating Hearts; *albums include:* Kristofferson, The Silver-Tongued Devil and I, Border Lord, Jesus Was a Capricorn, Spooky Lady's Sideshow, Songs of Kristofferson, Who's to Bless and Who's to Blame, Easter Island, Shake Hands with the Devil (with Rita Coolidge) 1979, Third World War 1990, Highwayman II (with Highwaymen) 1990, Singer, Songwriter 1991. *Films include:* Cisco Pike 1972, Pat Garrett and Billy the Kid 1973, Blume in Love 1973, Bring Me the Head of Alfredo Garcia 1974, Alice Doesn't Live Here Anymore 1974, The Sailor Who Fell From Grace With The Sea 1976, A Star is Born 1976, Vigilante Force 1976, Semi-Tough 1977, Convoy 1978, Heaven's Gate 1981, Rollover 1981, Welcome Home 1989, Millenium 1989, A Soldier's Daughter Never Cries 1998, Come Dance with Me 1999; TV appearances include: Freedom Road (TV film) 1979, Amerika (series) 1987, Rip 1989, Sandino, Christmas in Connecticut 1992, Tad 1995. *Address:* c/o One Way, 1 Prospect Avenue, P.O. Box 6429, Albany, NY 12206, U.S.A.

KRISTOPANS, Vilis; Latvian politician; b. 13 June 1954; m.; ed. Riga State Tech. Univ.; basketball player, Latvian team 1972–81; sports instructor Sports Cttee., Daugava Cen. Council 1977–83; coach, Head coach, basketball team VEF 1983–89; Chair. co-operative soc. Noster 1990; Dir.-Gen. jt. Dardedze 1990–92; Vice-Pres. Interbaltija Ltd. 1992–93; Minister of State Revenue 1993–94; Chair. Deutsche-Lettische Bank 1994–95; Minister of Transport Latvian Repub. 1995–98; Prime Minister of Latvia, also Minister of Agric. 1998–; mem. Parl. (Seimas) 1993–; mem. Bd. Latvijas Cefs Party; Pres. Latvian Basketball League 1992–97; mem. Ventspils Free Ports Bd. 1994–. *Address:* Council of Ministers, Brīvības blvd. 36, 226170 Riga, Latvia. *Telephone:* (371) 708 7111 (Office).

KRIVINE, Alain; French journalist; b. 10 July 1941, Paris; m. Michèle Martinet 1960; two d.; ed. Lycée Condorcet and Faculté des Lettres de Paris; mem. Jeunesses communistes 1956, French Communist Party 1958; leader Union of Student Communists, Paris-Sorbonne Univ. 1964–65; f. Revolutionary Communist Youth 1966 (disbanded by the Govt. 1968), Communist League 1969 (dissolved 1973); Cand. Presidential Elections 1969, 1974; Journalist Rouge 1969–; mem. Political Bureau of Ligue Communiste Révolutionnaire 1974–. *Publications:* La farce électorale 1969, Questions sur la révolution 1973, Mai si, rebelles et repentis (with Daniel Bensaid) 1988. *Address:* 2 rue Richard-Lenoir, 93100 Montreuil, France. *Telephone:* 1 48 70 42 30. *Fax:* 1 48 59 23 28.

KRIWET, Heinz, DR.RER.POL.; German business executive; b. 2 Nov. 1931, Bochum; ed. Univs. of Cologne and Freiburg; trainee, German Iron & Steel Fed. 1960–61; Personal Asst. to Vice-Pres. Sales, Hüttenwerk Rheinhausen (Krupp) 1962–63, Man. Planning and Marketing Dept. 1964–67; Gen. Man. Sales, Friedrich Krupp Hüttenwerke AG, Bochum 1968, mem. Exec. Bd. in charge of Sales 1969–72; mem. Exec. Bd. in charge of Sales, Thyssen AG, Düsseldorf 1973–83; Chair. Exec. Bd. Thyssen Stahl AG, Duisburg 1983–91; Chair. Exec. Bd. Thyssen AG, Düsseldorf March 1991–; Chair. Supervisory Bd. Thyssen Industrie AG, Thyssen Handelsunion AG, Thyssen Edelstahlwerke AG, Thyssen Stahl AG, Thyssen Wohnbau GmbH, Rheinische Kalksteinwerke GmbH; mem. Supervisory Bd. Allianz Lebensversicherungs AG, Commerzbank AG, Mannesmann-Röhrenwerke AG, Pechiney Int. Paris, RWE Energie AG, Gerling Group, Hapag Lloyd, Leipziger Messe GmbH; mem. Bd. of Dirs. The Budd Co. Troy, Mich., U.S.A.; mem. Man. Bd. Inst. Int. du Fer et de l'Acier, Brussels; Chair. German Iron & Steel Fed. 1984–88. *Address:* Thyssen AG, August-Thyssen-Strasse 1, 40211 Düsseldorf, Germany.

KROGH, Desmond Charles, M.A., EC. DRS., D.PHIL.; South African banking and assurance executive; b. 19 July 1931, Windhoek, Namibia (S.W. Africa); s. of P. I. Krogh and B. Theron; m. Surine Groenewald 1956; two s.; ed. Swakopmund High School, Univs. of Cape Town, Amsterdam and Pretoria; lecturer in Econs., Univ. of Orange Free State 1956, Univ. of Pretoria 1957–61; Asst. Econ. Adviser to Prime Minister 1961; Prof. of Econs., Univ. of South Africa 1962–69; Expert Witness to Int. Court of Justice on Econ. Devt. of S.W. Africa 1966; mem. Prime Minister's Econ. Advisory council 1967–73; Full-time Adviser to Fiscal and Monetary Policy Comm. 1968–69; Exec. Dir. of South African Federated Chamber of Industries 1969–73; Adviser to Govt. negotiations with GATT 1971–72; Adviser to Reserve Bank of Zimbabwe (fmrly. Rhodesia) 1973–74, Deputy Gov. 1974–76, Gov. 1976–83; Alt. Gov. IMF and World Bank 1980–83; Pres. Zimbabwe Inst. of Bankers 1981–82; Exec. Deputy Chair. Lifegro Assurance Ltd. 1983–86; Dir. Devt. Bank of Southern Africa; Special Adviser to Ministry of Finance 1986–89; Adviser to Reserve Bank of S.A. 1989–96; Council mem. Univ. of Pretoria 1986, S.A. Inst. of Int. Affairs 1988, Africa Inst. of S.A. 1988; Prof. Extraordinaire in Econs., Univ. of S.A. 1987; Medal and Prize of S.A. Econ. Soc. 1953, Netherlands-S. African Scholarship 1954–55, Ebden Prize 1957, U.S.A. Carnegie Study Grant 1960, Official Visitor to U.K. 1971; Commdr. Order of Legion of Merit (Rhodesia) 1978. *Publications:* numerous articles on economic structure, development, inflation and finance in Southern Africa. *Leisure interests:* golf, history. *Address:* P.O. Box 11005, Maroelana 0161, South Africa.

KROGSGAARD-LARSEN, Povl, PH.D., D.SC.; Danish professor of medicinal chemistry; b. 17 May 1941, Frøslev Mors; s. of Niels Saaby and Marie Saaby (née Krogsgaard) Larsen; m. Tove Krogsgaard-Larsen 1964; one s. one d.; Asst. Prof. Royal Danish School of Pharmacy 1970–75, Assoc. Prof. 1975–86, Prof. 1986–; mem. Royal Danish Acad. of Sciences and Letters 1986, Danish Acad. of Natural Sciences 1987, Danish Acad. of Tech. Sciences 1987. *Publications:* 260 scientific articles, 70 scientific reviews, 6 science books (ed.), 1 textbook (ed.). *Leisure interests:* history, sport. *Address:* Department of Medicinal Chemistry, The Royal Danish School of Pharmacy, 2 Universitetsparken, DK-2100 Copenhagen (Office); Elmevej 25, Blovstrød DK-3450 Allerød, Denmark (Home). *Telephone:* 35370850, Ext. 247 (Office); 48171215 (Home).

KRÓL, Jan Władysław; Polish politician; b. 24 June 1950; Mielec; m.; two c.; ed. Higher School of Econs., Cracow, Jagiellonian Univ., Cracow; PAX Soc. 1974–81; mem. Solidarity Independent Self-governing Trade Union (NSZZ Solidarność) 1980–; assoc. Dziekania Political Thought Club 1984–88; deputy Govt. Plenipotentiary for Local Govt. Reform 1989–90; Deputy to the Sejm (Parl.) 1989–, Vice-Leader Trade and Services Comm. 1989–97, Sec. Democratic Union (UD) Parl. Club 1989–91, leader Extraordinary Cttee. for consideration of bills within the State Enterprise Pact 1991–93, Vice-Marshal of Sejm 1997–; co.-f. and mem. ROAD (Democratic Campaign Citizens' Movt.) 1990–91; Chair Polish-Canadian Econ. Council 1990; co.-f. and mem. Democratic Union 1991–94; mem. Nat. Polish Bd. of the Friends of Lithuania Club 1992; mem. Freedom Union (UW) 1994–. *Publications:* Świadectwo (Evidence) 1989, Przodem do przodu (Face forward) 1993 and numerous articles. *Address:* Kancelaria Sejmu RP, ul. Wiejska 4/6/8, 00-902 Warsaw, Poland. *Telephone:* (22) 621 32 86.

KROL, John A., M.SC.; American business executive; b. 16 Oct. 1936, Ware, Mass.; m. Janet Valley; two d.; ed. Tufts Univ., Bettis Nuclear Reactor Eng. School; commissioned into U.S. Navy 1959, worked as nuclear eng. Bureau of Ships Naval Reactors Branch; joined DuPont as chemist, Wilmington, Del. 1963; marketing and manufacturing positions with DuPont Fibers 1965–83, Vice-Pres. 1983, Sr. Vice-Pres. 1990; Group Vice-Pres., Sr. Vice-Pres. DuPont Agric. Products 1986; mem. Nat. Agricultural Chemists Asscn., Bd. of Dirs. 1987–; Vice-Chair. DuPont 1992, Chair. Oct. 1997–98, Pres. 1995–97, C.E.O. 1995–98; Dir. Mead Corp., J. P. Morgan & Co., Nat. Asscn. of Mfrs., Del. Art Museum, Wilmington 2000, Catalyst; Trustee Tufts Univ., Univ. of Del., Hagley Museum, U.S. Council for Int. Business; mem. American Chemical Soc. Corp. Liaison Bd., Business Roundtable, Business Council; mem. exec. cttee. Del. Business Roundtable, Business/Public Educ. Council. *Address:* E.I. DuPont De Nemours and Co., 1007 Market Street, Wilmington, DE 19898, U.S.A. *Telephone:* (302) 774-1000.

KROLL, Alexander, S., B.A.; American advertising executive; b. 1937; ed. Rutgers Univ.; fmr. player, N.Y. Titans., American Football League; with Young & Rubicam, Inc., New York 1962–, copywriter 1962–68, Vice-Pres. 1968–69, Sr. Vice-Pres. 1969–70, Exec. Vice-Pres. and Worldwide Creative Dir. 1970–75, Pres. and C.O.O. 1982, C.E.O. 1985, Chair. and C.E.O. 1986–, also Dir.; Man. Dir. Young & Rubicam U.S.A. 1975–77, Pres. 1977; Kodak Life Achievement Award 1985, Nat. Coll. Athletic Asscn. Silver Anniversary Award 1987. *Address:* Young & Rubicam Inc., 285 Madison Avenue, New York, NY 10017, U.S.A.

KROLL, Lucien; Belgian architect and town-planner; b. 17 March 1927, Brussels; m. Simone Marti; two d.; ed. Athénée Royal de Huy, Ecole Nat. Supérieure de la Cambre, Institut Supérieur de la Cambre, Institut Supérieur et International d'Urbanisme Appliqué, Brussels; numerous works in Belgium, France, Italy, Fed. Repub. of Germany and Italy 1953–; founder mem. Inst. d'Esthétique Industrielle 1956; own architectural practice 1952–; works include houses, churches, schools, exhbns., industrial design, monasteries Ottignies and Rwanda; town-planning in Brussels and Kigali, Rwanda, Brussels (housing, with participation of future inhabitants) 1967, ministries and Pres.'s Palace, Rwanda Medical Faculties Neighbourhood, Brussels, Froidmont Dominican house 1970, housing, Cergy-Pontoise (with participation of future inhabitants) 1977, housing rehabilitation, Alençon 1978, Alma underground station, Brussels 1979, housing, Marne-la-Vallée 1980, Utrecht Acad., computer-aided design and creation of "Landscape" program 1981, housing, Laroche-Clermault, France, Bordeaux, St-Germain, France,

Haarlem, Netherlands, Knokke, Pessac-Bordeaux, Bethoncourt, etc.; schools Saint-Germain, Cinais en Touraine, Candry, Faenza (Italy); tech. lycée Belfort; Maison de 3e âge, Ostend; extension Univ. of Saint-Etienne; environmental research, Ecolonia, Netherlands; exhbns. of work in Brussels, Hanover, Utrecht, Auvervilliers, Copenhagen, Aarhus, Luxembourg, Boston; organized confs. including Habiter?, Brussels 1972; visiting prof. and lecturer many univs. throughout Europe, U.S.A. and Japan; mem. Acad. française d'Architecture 1985–; Médaille J.-F. Delarue (Acad. française d'Architecture) 1980. *Publications:* CAD-Architektur 1985, Architecture of Complexity 1986, Buildings and Projects (also in German and French) 1987, Componenten 1995, Bien vieillir chez soi 1995, Enfin chez soi 1996, Eco, Bio, Psycho about Urban Ecology 1996; over 500 articles on industrial and urban architectural design and comparative architecture. *Address:* Atelier d'Urbanisme, d'Architecture et d'Informatique L. Kroll, Avenue Louis Berlaimont 20, Boîte 9, B-1160, Brussels, Belgium. *Telephone:* 673 35 39. *Fax:* 673 89 27.

KROLOW, Karl; German poet and essayist; b. 11 March 1915, Hannover; s. of Albert Krolow; m. Luzie Gaida 1941; one c.; ed. Univs. of Göttingen and Breslau; writer 1942–; mem. Deutsche Akad. für Sprache und Dichtung (Vice-Pres. 1966, 1975, Pres. 1972), Mainzer Akad. der Wissenschaften und der Literatur, Acad. of Fine Arts of Bavaria, PEN Club; Dr. h.c. (Darmstadt) 1976; Georg Büchner Prize 1956, Grosser Niedersächsischer Kunstpreis 1965, Rainer-Maria-Rilke-Preis 1975; Grosses Bundesverdienstkreuz 1975; Hessischer Kulturpreis 1983, Literatur Preis, Bayerische Akademie der Schönen Künste 1985, Friedrich Hölderlin Preis 1988. *Publications:* Poetry: Die Zeichen der Welt 1952, Wind und Zeit 1954, Tage und Nächte 1956, Fremde Körper 1959, Gedichte 1962, Unsichtbare Hände 1962, Gesammelte Gedichte 1965–85 (3 vols.), Landschaften für mich 1965, Alltägliche Gedichte 1968, Nichts weiter als leben 1970, Zeitvergehen 1972, Die Einfachheit halber 1977, Sterblich 1980, Herbstsonett mit Hegel 1981, Zwischen Null und Unendlich 1982, Herodot oder der Beginn von Geschichte 1983, Schönen Dank und vorüber 1984, Die andere Seite die Welt 1987, Als es soweit war 1988; Essays: Poetisches Tagebuch 1966, Minuten-Aufzeichnungen 1968, Ein Land, das es nicht gibt 1972, Ein Gedicht entsteht—Selbstdeutungen, Interpretationen, Aufsätze 1973, Die Geschichte eines Namens 1983; Trans.: Contemporary French Lyric Poetry 1957, Spanish Poems of the 20th Century 1962. *Address:* Park Rosenhöhe 5, 64287 Darmstadt, Germany. *Telephone:* 77380.

KROON, Ciro Dominico; Netherlands Antilles politician; b. 31 Jan. 1916, Curaçao, Netherlands Antilles; s. of Eduard Bernardus Kroon and Catrijn Zimmerman; m. Edna Huis 1936; three s. one d.; ed. Higher Grade School; in business until 1942; Admin., Social and Econ. Dept., Netherlands Antilles 1942–51; mem. Legis. Council of Netherlands Antilles 1949–51; Deputy for Social and Econ. Affairs and mem. Admin. Bd. of island territory of Curaçao 1951–57; on various occasions Acting Gov. of Curaçao; Minister for Social and Econ. Affairs and Public Health, Netherlands Antilles 1957–68; Prime Minister of Netherlands Antilles Feb. 1968–May 1969; mem. Island Council of Curaçao 1971–73; Minister of Econ. Affairs 1973–75; Pres. Banco Mercantil Venezolano N.V. 1976– (Chair. Supervisory Bd. 1994–); Commdr. Order of Orange-Nassau, Knight Order of Netherlands Lion, and Orders from Venezuela, Colombia and France. *Leisure interests:* sailing, fishing. *Address:* Banco Mercantil Venezolano N.V., Abraham de Veerstraat No. 1, P.O. Box 565, Willemstad, Curaçao, Netherlands Antilles.

KROPIWNICKI, Jerzy Janusz, D.ECON.; Polish politician and economist; b. 5 July 1945, Częstochowa; m.; one s.; ed. Warsaw School of Econs.; scientific worker, Łódź Univ. 1968–81 (dismissed); mem. Solidarity Independent Self-governing Trade Union 1980–, Deputy Chair. Solidarity Łódź Region Br., mem. Solidarity Nat. Comm., co-organizer demonstration against martial law, arrested 13 Dec. 1981, sentenced to 6 years' imprisonment, released under amnesty July 1984; illegal activity 1984–90, co-organizer, Solidarity Regional Exec. Comm., Łódź 1984–86, co-organizer and activist, Working Group of Solidarity Nat. Comm. 1986–90; co-organizer and activist of Pastoral Care of Working People 1985–; lay worker, St. Teresa's Roman Catholic Parish Church, Łódź 1986–89; scientific worker, Econ.-Sociological Faculty of Łódź Univ. 1989–; mem. Christian-Nat. Union (ZChN) 1989–, mem. Presidium of ZChN Gen. Bd. 1989–93, Vice-Pres. 1991–93; Deputy to Sejm (Parl.) 1991–93 and 1997–; Minister of Labour and Social Policy 1991–92; Minister-Head of Cen. Office of Planning 1992–93; Minister and Chair. Governmental Strategic Studies Centre 1997–. *Publications:* numerous articles on econ. and four books. *Leisure interests:* mountain hiking, reading (history and science-fiction). *Address:* Rządowe Centrum Studiów Strategicznych, ul. Wspólna 2/4, 00-926 Warsaw, Poland (Office). *Telephone:* (22) 661 86 00. *Fax:* (22) 621 25 50.

KROSS, Jaan; Estonian author and translator; b. 19 Nov. 1920, Tallinn; ed. Tartu Univ.; lecturer Tartu Univ. 1946–54; deported to Komi Autonomous Repub. by Soviet authorities 1946–54; fully exonerated 1960; Sec. Estonian Writers' Union 1976–81, Deputy Chair. 1981–; published prose and poetry 1970–; mem. Riigikogu (Estonian Parl.) 1992–93; Hon. D. Tartu Univ. 1989. *Publications:* historical novels about Estonian history including Tsar's Fool, some travel books, literary and cultural reviews, opera librettos; active as translator in 20 languages. *Address:* Harju Street 1, Apt. 6, 0001 Tallinn, Estonia (Home). *Telephone:* (3726) 44 16 97 (Home).

KROTO, Sir Harold Walter, Kt., PH.D., F.R.S.; British professor of chemistry; b. 7 Oct. 1939; s. of Heinz Kroto and Edith Kroto; m. Margaret Henrietta Hunter 1963; two s.; ed. Bolton School, Univ. of Sheffield; research student Univ. of Sheffield 1961–64; Postdoctoral Fellow NRCC 1964–66; Research Scientist Bell Telephone Labs., N.J., U.S.A. 1966–67; Tutorial Fellow Univ. of Sussex 1967–68, Lecturer 1968–77, Reader 1977–85, Prof. of Chem. 1985–91, Royal Soc. Research Prof. 1991–; Visiting Prof. Univ. of B.C. 1973, Univ. of S. Calif. 1981, Univ. of Calif. at L.A. 1988–92, Univ. of Calif., Santa Barbara, Distinguished Visiting Prof. 1997–; Chair. Vega Science Trust, Exec. Producer Science Programmes for Network TV; shared Nobel Prize for Chem. 1996; Dr. h.c. (Nottingham) 1997, Brussels, Stockholm, Helsinki and many others; Hon. D.Sc. (Leicester) 1998; numerous awards. *Publications:* Molecular Rotation Spectra 1975, 1983; 260 papers in chemistry, chemical physics and astronomy journals. *Leisure interests:* graphic design (winner Sunday Times Book Jacket Design Competition 1964, Moet Hennessy/Louis Vuitton Science pour l'Art Prize 1994), tennis. *Address:* School of Chemistry, Physics and Environmental Science, University of Sussex, Brighton, BN1 9QJ, England. *Telephone:* (01273) 678329.

KRÖYER, Haraldur, M.A.; Icelandic diplomatist; b. 9 Jan. 1921, Akureyri; m.; four c.; ed. Akureyri Coll. and Univ. of California (Berkeley); joined foreign service 1945; Sec. Stockholm 1947–49, Oslo 1949–52, Paris 1952–54; Counsellor, Paris and Perm. Rep. to Council of Europe 1954–56; Sec. to Pres. of Iceland 1956–62; Counsellor, Moscow 1962–66; Deputy Perm. Rep. to UN 1966–69; Amb. to Sweden, Finland and Austria 1970–72; Perm. Rep. to UN 1972–73; Amb. to U.S.A., Canada, Cuba, Mexico and Brazil 1973–76; Perm. Rep. to Int. Orgs., Geneva and Amb. to Egypt, Kenya and Tanzania 1976–80, to U.S.S.R., Bulgaria, G.D.R., Hungary, Mongolia and Romania 1980–85; Amb. to France, Spain, Portugal and Cape Verde and Perm. Rep. to OECD and UNESCO 1985–89. *Address:* c/o Ministry of Foreign Affairs, Reykjavík, Iceland.

KRUEGER, Alan Douglas; American business executive; b. 24 Dec. 1937, Little Rock, Ark.; s. of Herbert Krueger and Estelle Krueger; m. Betty Burns 1975; four s. by previous m.; ed. Univ. of Illinois and Wright Coll.; Project Eng. Motorola Inc. Chicago 1956–64; Service Man., Field Tech. Rep. Motorola Inc. Indianapolis 1964–67; Pres. Communications Maintenance Inc. Indianapolis 1967–68, Communications Unlimited Inc. Indianapolis 1968–. *Address:* Communications Unlimited Inc., 4032 Southeastern Avenue, Indianapolis, IN 46203 (Office); 6242N. 575 E. Franklin, Franklin, IN 46131, U.S.A. (Home).

KRUEGER, Anne O., PH.D.; American international official and economist; b. 12 Feb. 1934, Endicott, N.Y.; d. of Leslie A. Osborn and Dora W. Osborn; m. James Henderson 1981; one d.; ed. Oberlin Coll. and Univ. of Wisconsin; Asst. Prof. of Econs., Univ. of Minn. 1959–63, Assoc. Prof. 1963–66, Prof. 1966–82; Research Assoc., Nat. Bureau of Econ. Research 1969–82; Vice-Pres. Econs. and Research, IBRD Sept. 1982–86; Univ. Arts and Sciences Prof. of Econs., Duke Univ. 1987–92; Sr. Fellow (non-resident) Brookings Inst. 1988–94; Prof. of Econs., Stanford Univ. 1992–; visiting prof. at univs. in U.S.A., Denmark, Germany, France, Australia and Sweden; mem. editorial bds. of several int. econ. journals; fmr. Vice-Pres. American Econ. Asscn., Pres. 1996–97; Fellow, American Acad. of Arts and Sciences, Econometric Soc.; mem. N.A.S. *Publications:* Foreign Trade Regimes and Economic Development; Turkey 1974, The Benefits and Costs of Import Substitution in India: A Microeconomic Study 1975, Trade and Development in Korea 1975, Growth, Distortions and Patterns of Trade Among Many Countries 1977, Liberalization Attempts and Consequences 1977, The Development Role of the Foreign Sector and Aid: Korea 1979, Trade and Employment in Developing Countries 1981, Exchange Rate Determination 1983, The Political Economy of International Trade 1989, Aid and Development 1989, Perspectives on Trade and Development 1990, The Political Economy of Economic Policy Reform 1993, American Trade Policy 1995, The WTO as an International Organization. *Address:* Department of Economics, Stanford University, Stanford, CA 94305; 41 Linaria Way, Portola Valley, CA 94028, U.S.A.

KRUEGER, Hans-Joachim, DR.ING., M.B.A.; German businessman; b. 27 Feb. 1938, Berlin; mem. Exec. Bd. Krupp Hoesch Stahl AG -1994; Chair. Eko Stahl GmbH 1994–. *Address:* Eko Stahl GmbH, Postfach 7252, 15872 Eisenhuettenstadt, Germany.

KRÜGER, Hardy; German actor and writer; b. 12 April 1928, Berlin; s. of Max and Auguste (née Meier) Krüger; m. 1st Renate Damrow; one d.; m. 2nd Francesca Marazzi; one s. one d.; m. 3rd Anita Park 1978; German repertory theatre 1945–56, entered films in 1943; several awards and prizes. *Films include:* Der Rest ist Schweigen 1959, Blind Date 1959, Taxi pour Tobrouk 1961, Hatari 1961, Les Dimanches de Ville d'Avray 1962, Les Quatre Verités 1962, Le Gros Coup 1963, Le Chant du Monde 1964, Flight of the Phoenix 1965, The Defector 1966, La Grande Sauterelle 1966, The Battle of Neretva 1968, The Secret of Santa Vittoria 1969, Death of A Stranger 1972, Le Solitaire 1973, Barry Lyndon 1974, Paper Tiger 1974, Potato Fritz (Best Actor Award, Cannes) 1975, A Bridge Too Far 1976, L'Autopsie d'un Monster 1976, The Wild Geese 1978. *Publications:* Ein Farm in Afrika 1970, Sawimbulu 1971, Wer stehend stirbt, lebt länger 1973, Der Schallmauer 1978, Die Frau der Griechen 1980, Junge Unrast 1983, Sibirienfahrt, Tagebuch einer Reise 1985, Frühstück mit Theodore 1990. *Address:* Maximilianstrasse 23, 80539 Munich, Germany.

KRÜGER, Horst; German author; b. 17 Sept. 1919, Magdeburg; s. of Fritz and Margarethe Krüger; m. (divorced); ed. Grunewald Gymnasium, Berlin and philosophical studies in Berlin and Freiburg i. Br.; started as literary critic and essayist, Badische Zeitung, Freiburg im Breisgau after World War II; ed. of night programmes, Südwestfunk, Baden-Baden 1952–67; now freelance author; mem. Deutsche Akad. für Sprache und Dichtung, Darmstadt and German PEN Centre; several prizes inc. Goethe-Plakette (City of Frankfurt/Main) 1980 and Golden Camera for screenplay for film Der Kurfürstendamm 1982. *Publications:* Fremde Vaterländer 1971, Zeitgelächter 1973, Ostwest-Passagen 1975, Das zerbrochene Haus 1976, Poetische Erdkunde 1978, Ludwig lieber Ludwig 1979, Unterwegs 1980, Spötterdämmerung 1981, Der Kurfürstendamm 1982, Tiefer deutscher Traum 1983, Zeit ohne Wiederkehr: gesammelte Feuilletons 1985, Kennst du das Land: Reiseerzählungen 1987. *Address:* Mendelssohnstrasse 49, 60325 Frankfurt/Main, Germany. *Telephone:* 069-74 62 65.

KRÜGER, Manfred Paul, D.PHIL.; German writer, professor and editor; b. 23 Feb. 1938, Köslin; s. of Paul Krüger and Hildegard Krüger; m. Christine Petersen 1962; three s. four d.; ed. Oberrealschule Ansbach, Heidelberg Univ., Tübingen Univ.; Asst. Prof., Erlangen Univ. 1966–73; lecturer at Inst. for Spiritual Science and Arts, Nuremberg 1972–; Co-Ed. of the weekly Goetheanum 1984–96. *Publications:* Gérard de Nerval 1966, Wandlungen des Tragischen 1973, Nora Ruhtenberg 1976, Bilder und Gegenbilder 1978, Wortspuren 1980, Denkbilder 1981, Literatur und Geschichte 1982, Mondland 1982, Nah ist er 1983, Meditation 1983, Rosenroman 1985, Meditation und Karma 1988, Anthroposophie und Kunst 1988, Ästhetik der Freiheit 1992, Ichgeburt 1996, Das Ich und seine Masken 1997. *Address:* Ermreuther Strasse 25, 90411 Nuremberg, Germany. *Telephone:* (0911) 5298491.

KRUGMAN, Paul Robin, PH.D.; American professor of economics; b. 28 Feb. 1953, Albany, New York; s. of David Krugman and Anita Krugman; m. Robin Leslie Bergman 1983; ed. Yale Univ., Massachusetts Inst. of Tech.; Asst. Prof., Yale Univ. 1977–79; Asst. Prof. M.I.T. 1979–80, Assoc. Prof. 1980–82, Prof. 1983; Sr. Staff Economist, Council of Econ. Advisers 1982–83; John Bates Clark Medal 1991. *Publications:* Market Structure and Foreign Trade (with E. Helpman) 1985, International Economics, Theory and Policy (with M. Obsfeld) 1988, The Age of Diminished Expectations 1990, Rethinking International Trade 1990, Geography and Trade 1991, Currencies and Crises 1992, Peddling Prosperity 1994. *Leisure interest:* music. *Address:* Department of Economics, Massachusetts Institute of Technology, 77 Massachusetts Avenue, Cambridge, MA 02139; 1453 Kings Lane, Palo Alto, CA 94303, U.S.A. *Telephone:* (617) 253-2655.

KRUMMACHER, Hans-Henrik, DR.PHIL.; German academic; b. 24 Aug. 1931, Essen-Werden; m. Eva Wentscher 1956; one s. four d.; ed. Humboldt Univ. Berlin, Univs. of Heidelberg and Tübingen; Archivist, Schiller-Nationalmuseum, Marbach a.N. 1956–58; Asst. Prof., Univ. of Cologne 1958–67; Prof. of German Literature, Univ. of Mainz 1967–; mem. Akademie der Wissenschaften und der Literatur zu Mainz 1984; Corresp. mem. Österreichische Akad. der Wissenschaften 1993. *Publications:* Das 'als ob' in der Lyrik 1965, Der junge Gryphius und die Tradition 1976; Ed. Eduard Mörike, Werke und Briefe 1967–, Neudrucke deutscher Literaturwerke 1975–. *Address:* Am Mainzer Weg 10, D-55127 Mainz-Drais, Germany. *Telephone:* 06131-477550.

KRUPP, Georg; German banker; b. 15 July 1936; fmr. Deputy mem. Bd. of Man. Dirs. Deutsche Bank; Chair. Supervisory Bd. WMF Aktiengesellschaft, Geislingen; mem. Supervisory Bd. IVECO Magirus AG, Ulm, Strabag AG, Cologne, Gerling-Konzern Versicherungs-Beteiligungs AG, Cologne, Rheinmetall Berlin AG, Düsseldorf, VEW Vereinigte Elektrizitätswerke Westfalen AG, Dortmund, BHS Tabletop AG, Selb. *Address:* Deutsche Bank, Taunusanlage 12, 60325 Frankfurt/Main, Germany.

KRUSE, Martin, DR.THEOL.; German ecclesiastic; b. 21 April 1929, Lauenberg, Einbeck; s. of late Walter Kruse and of Gertrud Kruse (neé Oppermann); m. Marianne Kittel 1959; two s. two d.; ed. Mainz, Heidelberg, Bethel and Göttingen; Bishop of Evangelical Church in Berlin-Brandenburg 1977–94; mem. Council of Evangelical Church in Germany 1979–91, Chair. 1985–91; mem. Cen. Cttee. Ecumenical Council of Churches 1983–91. *Publications:* Die Kritik am Landesherrlichen Kirchenregiment bei Ph.J. Spener und ihre Vorgeschichte 1971, Verführung zur Güte 1977, Gruppierungen in der Kirche 1982, Hochwürden 10% 1984, Aufmerksamkeiten 1984. *Leisure interests:* walking, playing the piano, reading. *Address:* Prinz-Friedr.-Leopold-Strasse 14, 14129 Berlin, Germany. *Telephone:* 8035011. *Fax:* 2791155.

KRYLOV, Sergey Borisovich; Russian diplomatist; b. 26 Oct. 1949, Moscow; m.; two d.; ed. Moscow State Inst. of Int. Relations, Diplomatic Acad. of Ministry of Foreign Relations; diplomatic service 1971–; translator, attaché Embassy, Zaire 1971–76; attaché, Third, Second Sec. Second Africa Dept., U.S.S.R. Ministry of Foreign Affairs 1976–79; First Sec., Counsellor to Minister 1979–86, Asst. to Deputy Minister 1986–89; Minister-Counsellor U.S.S.R. Embassy, Portugal 1990–92; Dir. of Dept., Exec. Sec. Ministry of Foreign Affairs of Russia 1992–93; Deputy Minister of Foreign Affairs, Russia 1993–96; Perm Rep. to UN office and other int. orgs., Geneva 1997–98; Amb. to Germany 1998–. *Address:* Russische Botschaft, Waldstrasse 42, 53177 Bonn, Germany. *Telephone:* (0228) 312085. *Fax:* (0228) 311563.

KRYUCHKOV, Gen. Vladimir Aleksandrovich; Russian army officer and politician; b. 29 Feb. 1924, Volgograd; ed., Moscow All-Union Judicial Inst., Higher School for Diplomats, U.S.S.R. Foreign Ministry; mem. CPSU 1944–91; Third Sec. in Soviet Embassy, Hungary 1955–59; practised in public procurator service for many years; on staff of Party Cen. Cttee. 1959–67; has held posts in KGB (State Security Service) 1967–91, Deputy Chair. 1978–88, Chair. Oct. 1988–Aug. 1991; mem. Party Cen. Cttee. 1986–91; mem. Politburo 1989–90, mem. Pres. Council March–Dec. 1990; Gen. of Army 1988; Deputy to U.S.S.R. Supreme Soviet 1984–89; arrested 22 Aug. 1991 after participation as mem. of Emergency Cttee. in failed coup d'état; charged with conspiracy Jan. 1992; released on amnesty 1994.

KRZAKLEWSKI, Marian, D.ING.; Polish politician and trade union activist; b. 23 Aug. 1950, Kolbuszowa; m.; two s.; ed. Silesian Tech. Univ., Gliwice 1975; scientific worker Polish Acad. of Sciences (PAN) and Silesian Tech. Univ., Gliwice 1976–90; mem. Solidarity Trade Union (independent, self-governing union) 1980–; Chair. of Solidarity 1991–; mem. ICFTU 1991–; Co-founder and Leader Solidarity Election Action (AWS) 1996–; Deputy to Sejm (Parl.) 1997–; Chair. Solidarity Election Action Parl. Club 1997–; main negotiator and jt. architect of parl. and govt. coalition Solidarity Election Action—Freedom Union; Co-founder and Chair. Social Movt. of Solidarity Election Action (RS AWS) 1997–. *Leisure interests:* family life, tourism, sport, arts, literature. *Address:* ul. Wały Piastowskie 24, 80-855, Gdańsk, Poland. *Telephone:* (58) 35 90 44. *Fax:* (58) 35 90 44.

KU CHEN-FU; Chinese civil servant; Dir. Straits Communication Foundations; Adviser to Pres.; mem. Kuomintang (KMT) Cen. Standing Cttee. 1994–. *Address:* c/o Office of the President, Chieshou Hall, 122 Chungking South Road, Sec. 1, Taipei 100, Taiwan. *Telephone:* (2) 3113731. *Fax:* (2) 3140746.

KUBAISI, Tarrad Al-; Iraqi journalist; b. 1937, Hit; m. Widdad Al-Jourani 1962; one s. two d.; ed. Coll. of Literature, Univ. of Baghdad; Ed.-in-Chief, Al-Mawsu'a Al-Sagira (small encyclopaedia) 1976–77; Ed.-in-Chief, Al-Aqlam (magazine) 1978–81, Al-Maurid (magazine) 1984–87, 1989–90; Man. and Ed.-in-Chief, Afaq Arabia (magazine) 1991; Press Office and Iraq Cultural Centre, London 1982–84; Press Attaché, Morocco 1988–89; now Chair. Cultural Affairs Office. *Publications:* Introductions in Sumerian Sufi-African Poetry 1971, The New Iraqi Poetry 1972, The Stony Forest Trees 1975, The Forest and Seasons 1979, Al-Munzalat Book (Vol. I) 1992, (Vol. II) 1995, The Artistic Construction in Epic Literature 1994. *Leisure interests:* reading, swimming. *Address:* P.O. Box 4032, Adhamiya, Baghdad, Iraq. *Telephone:* 4436044, 4435446 (Office); 5544746 (Home).

KUBÁT, Milan, PROF.ING., DR.SC.; Czech business executive and technician; b. 20 Jan. 1927, Bratislava; s. of Miloslav Kubát and Blazena Kubátová; m. 1st Jitka Kubátová 1956 (divorced 1992), two s.; m. 2nd Hana Kubátová 1992; ed. Czech Tech. Coll., Prague; worker at Research Inst. of Heavy-Current Electrical Eng., Běchovice, later ČKD Prague 1951–62; Tech. Dir., ČKD Prague 1962–65; various posts in cen. authorities, Prague 1966–72; Deputy Minister for Tech. Devt. and Investments, Prague 1972–79; Prof., Electrical Eng. Faculty, Czech Tech. Univ., Prague 1972–90; Fed. Minister of the Electrical Eng. Industry 1979–88; leading scientist, Prognostics Inst. and corresp. mem., Czechoslovak Acad. of Sciences 1990–91; mem. of scientific councils at academic insts. of higher learning; in pvt. business 1992–; four State prizes and awards 1960, 1977, 1980, 1987. *Publications:* Power Semiconductors 1985; five books in Czech; numerous articles. *Leisure interests:* windsurfing, travel. *Address:* Seacom s.r.o., Nad Opatovem 2140/2, 149 00 Prague 4 (Office); Záhřebská 3, 12000 Prague 2, Czech Republic (Home). *Telephone:* 25 15 49 (Home).

KUBILIUS, Jonas, D.SC.; Lithuanian mathematician; b. 27 July 1921, Fermos, Jurbarkas Dist.; s. of Petras Kubilius and Petronėlė Giedraitytė; m. Valerija Pilypaitė 1950; one s. one d.; ed. Vilnius and Leningrad Univs. and Math. Inst. Moscow; Lab. Asst., Asst. Prof. Vilnius Univ. 1945–48, Assoc. Prof., Prof. 1951–, Rector 1958–91; mem. Lithuanian Acad. of Sciences 1962–, mem. Presidium 1962–92; People's Deputy of U.S.S.R. 1989–91; mem. Parl. of Lithuania 1992–96; State Prize in Science 1958, 1980; Dr. h.c. (Greifswald, Prague, Salzburg and Latvian Univs.) etc. *Publications:* Probability Methods in the Theory of Numbers 1959, Real Analysis 1970, Probability and Statistics 1980, Limit Theorems 1998; several hundred papers. *Leisure interests:* music, history, bibliophilism. *Address:* Vilniaus Universitetas, Universiteto 3, 2734 Vilnius (Office); Kuosų 14, 2055 Vilnius, Lithuania (Home). *Telephone:* (2) 632228 (Office).

KUBO, Ryogo; Japanese physicist and professor; b. 15 Feb. 1920, Tokyo; s. of Tokuji Kubo and Sei Terada; m. Chizuko Kamijo 1946, one s. two d.; ed. Tokyo Imperial Univ. and Tokyo Univ.; Asst. Prof., Dept. of Physics, Tokyo Univ. 1948–54, Prof. 1954–80, Dean, Faculty of Science 1968–71; Prof., Research Inst. of Fundamental Physics, Kyoto Univ. 1980–81; Prof. Faculty of Science and Tech., Keio Univ. 1981; mem. American Acad. of Arts and Sciences 1973–; Foreign Assoc. N.A.S. 1974–; Pres. Nishina Memorial Foundation 1979–; mem. Japan Acad. 1982–; Hon. D.Sc. (Chicago Univ.) 1978; Hon. Imperial Award, Japan Acad. 1969, Order of Culture, Japan 1973, Boltzmann Medal 1977. *Leisure interest:* reading. *Publications:* several articles in scientific periodicals. *Address:* 1-6-5 Komagome Toshimaku, Tokyo 170, Japan (Home). *Telephone:* 03 941 8748 (Home).

KUČAN, Milan; Slovenian politician and lawyer; b. 14 Jan. 1941, Krizevci, Slovenia; ed. Ljubljana Univ.; joined Fed. of Communists of Slovenia 1958; mem. Cen. Cttee. Fed. of Communists of Slovenia; Chair. Comm. on Educational Problems of Cen. Cttee., Youth Union of Slovenia 1963–65; Chair. Cen. Cttee. 1968–69; mem. Cen. Cttee. Communist Union of Slovenia 1973–78, Chair. 1986–89; Sec. Republican Conf. of Socialist Union of Slovenia

1973–78; Chair. Slovenian Skupščina (Parl.) 1978–86; Pres. of Slovenia April 1990–. *Address:* Office of the President, 61000 Ljubljana, Erjavčeva 17, Slovenia.

KUCHMA, Leonid Danilovich; Ukrainian politician and manager; b. 1938, Chernigov Region; ed. Dniepropetrovsk State Univ.; mem. CPSU 1960–91; constructor Research-Production Union Yuzhny Mashinostroitelny Zavod 1960–75, Sec. Party Cttee. 1975–82, Deputy Dir.-Gen. 1982–86, Dir.-Gen. 1986–92; mem. Cen. Cttee. CP Ukraine 1981–91; People's Deputy of Ukraine 1991–94; Prime Minister of Ukraine 1992–93; Chair. Ukrainian Union of Industrialists and Entrepreneurs 1993–94; Pres. of Ukraine July 1994–. *Address:* Office of the President, Bankova Str. 11, 252011 Kiev, Ukraine. *Telephone:* 291-51-52.

KUDELKA, James Alexander; Canadian ballet company artistic director, choreographer and dancer; b. 10 Sept. 1955, Newmarket, Ont.; s. of John Kudelka and Kathleen Mary Kudelka (née Kellington); ed. Nat. Ballet School of Canada; Dancer, Nat. Ballet of Canada 1972–81, Artist in Residence 1992–96, Artistic Dir. 1996–; Prin. Dancer, Grand Ballets Canadiens 1981–84, Resident Choreographer 1984–90; Isadora Duncan Dance Award 1988, Dora Mavor Moore Award (for Fifteen Heterosexual Duets) 1991–92, (for The Nutcracker) 1995–96, Jean A. Chalmers Choreographic Award 1993, numerous Canada Council Grants; major works: (for Nat. Ballet of Canada) Washington Square 1977, Pastorale 1990, Musings 1991, The Miraculous Mandarin 1993, Spring Awakening 1994, The Actress 1994, The Nutcracker 1995, The Four Seasons 1997; (for Grand Ballets Canadiens) In Paradisum 1983, Désir 1991; (for Toronto Dance Theatre) Fifteen Heterosexual Duets 1991; (for Birmingham Royal Ballet, U.K.) Le Baiser de la fée 1996; (for American Ballet Theatre) Cruel World 1994, States of Grace 1995; (for San Francisco Ballet) The Comfort Zone 1989, The End 1992, Terra Firma 1995; (for Joffrey Ballet) The Heart of the Matter 1986. *Address:* The National Ballet of Canada, 470 Queens Quay West, Toronto, Ont., M5V 3K4, Canada. *Telephone:* (416) 345-9686. *Fax:* (416) 345-8323.

KUDLOW, Lawrence A., B.A.; American economist and government official; b. 20 Aug. 1947, Englewood, N.J.; s. of Irving Howard and Ruth (née Grodnick) Kudlow; m. 1st Susan Cullman 1981, one d.; m. 2nd Judith Pond 1987; ed. Univ. of Rochester, Woodrow Wilson School of Public and Int. Affairs, Princeton Univ.; Economist, Fed. Reserve Bank of New York 1973–75; Chief Economist and Corporate Vice-Pres. Paine, Webber, Jackson, and Curtis, New York 1975–79; Chief Economist and Partner, Bear, Stearns and Co., New York 1979–81; Asst. Dir. for Econ. Policy, Office of Man. and Budget, Washington, D.C. 1981–82, Assoc. Dir. for Econs. and Planning 1982–83; Pres. and C.E.O. Lawrence Kudlow and Assocs., Washington D.C. 1983–84; Pres. and C.E.O. Rodman and Renshaw Economics Inc. 1984–86; Chief Economist and Man. Dir. Rodman and Renshaw Capital Group Inc. 1984–86; Chief Economist, Bear, Stearns and Co. 1986–94. *Leisure interests:* c/o tennis, golf. *Address:* c/o Bear, Stearns and Co. Inc., 245 Park Avenue, New York, NY 10041, U.S.A.

KUDRIN, Aleksey Leonidovich, CAND. ECON.; Russian politician; b. 12 Oct. 1960, Dobele, Latvia; m.; one d.; ed. Leningrad State Univ., Inst. of Econs. U.S.S.R. Acad. of Sciences; on staff Inst. of Social-Econ. Problems Acad. of Sciences 1983–90; Deputy Chair. Cttee. on Econ. Reform Leningrad City Exec. Bd. 1990–91; Chair. Cttee. on Finance St. Petersburg Mayor's Office 1992–94; First Deputy Mayor of St. Petersburg, Head Dept. of Finance Mayor's Office, St. Petersburg 1994–96; Deputy Head of Admin., Head Controlling Dept. at Russian Presidency 1996–97; First Deputy Minister of Finance Russian Fed. March 1997–, concurrently Deputy Man. BRD May 1997–. *Address:* Ministry of Finance, Ilyinka str. 9, 103097 Moscow, Russia (Office). *Telephone:* (095) 923 8114, 298 5188 (Office).

KUDRYAVTSEV, Vladimir Nikolaevich; Russian jurist; b. 10 April 1923, Moscow; m. Dodonova Yevgenia Nikolaevna 1945; two s.; served in Soviet Army 1941–45; mem. CPSU 1945–91; ed. Mil. Law. Acad.; on staff of Acad. 1950–56; teacher at Lenin Mil.-Political Acad. 1956–60; on staff of Mil. Coll. of U.S.S.R. Supreme Court 1960–63; Deputy Dir. of All-Union Inst. for Crime Prevention 1963–69, Dir. 1969–73; Dir. of U.S.S.R. Inst. of State and Law of Acad. of Sciences 1973–89, Hon. Dir. 1989–; corresp. mem. of U.S.S.R. (now Russian) Acad. of Sciences 1974–84, mem. 1984–, Vice-Pres. 1988–91; Foreign mem. Bulgarian, Hungarian Acads. of Science; Vice-Pres. Int. Assn. of Democratic Lawyers 1984–90; People's Deputy of the U.S.S.R. 1989–91; State Prize 1984. *Publications:* over 200 works on criminology and criminal law, including What Sort of State Are We Building? 1991, Social Deformations 1992, (ed.) The Manual of International Law (7 vols.) 1993–. *Leisure interests:* theatre, music, cinema, reading. *Address:* Leninski pr. 14, 17901 Moscow, Russia. *Telephone:* 237-68-08. *Fax:* 237-44-21.

KUENHEIM, Eberhard von; German motor executive; b. 2 Oct. 1928, Juditten, Kreis Bartenstein; ed. Technische Hochschule, Stuttgart; Chair. Exec. Bd. BMW AG, Munich 1970–93, of Supervisory Bd. 1993–; Deputy Chair. Exec. Bd. Industriewerke Karlsruhe Augsburg AG (IKWA); mem. Supervisory Bd. Bayerische Vereinsbank AG, Munich, Royal Dutch Petroleum Co. –1992, Münchner Rückversicherungsgesellschaft AG; Pres. Assn. of Bavarian Industry; Vice-Pres. German Motor Industry Assn.; mem. Senate, Max Planck Soc. for the Advancement of Sciences; hon. Senator Munich Technical Univ. *Leisure interests:* sciences, hockey, walking, books on politics and modern history. *Address:* c/o Bayerische Motorenwerke AG, Petuelring 130, 80788 Munich, Germany.

KUHARIĆ, H.E. Cardinal Franjo; Croatian ecclesiastic (retd.); b. 15 April 1919, Pribić, near Zagreb; ordained priest 1945; Bishop of titular church of Meta 1964–; Archbishop of Zagreb 1970–96; Pres. of Croatian Episcopal Conf.; cr. Cardinal 1983. *Address:* Kaptol 31, PP 553, 41000 Zagreb, Croatia. *Telephone:* (041) 275-132.

KUHLMANN, Kathleen Mary; American opera singer; b. 7 Dec. 1950, San Francisco; d. of Elvira L. and Hugo S. Kuhlmann; m. 1983 (divorced 1998); ed. Mercy High School, San Francisco and Univ. of San Francisco; student Chicago Lyric Opera School 1976–79; Resident Mezzo-soprano, Cologne Opera 1980–82; freelance 1982–; int. débuts: Teatro alla Scala, Milan 1980, San Francisco Opera 1982, Royal Opera House, Covent Garden 1982, Teatro Regio Parma 1983, Glyndebourne Festival Opera 1983, Wiener Staatsoper 1983, Teatro Communale Pisa 1983, Chicago Lyric Opera 1984, Salzburger Festspiele 1985, Stuttgart Opera 1985, Hamburg State Opera 1985, Lausanne/Geneva 1986, Australian Opera 1986, Napoli 1987, Tel Aviv 1988, Capitôle de Toulouse 1988, Metropolitan Opera, New York 1989, Théâtre Châtelet, Paris 1989, Semperoper Dresden 1992, Bayerische Staatsoper, Munich 1994, Staatsoper Unter den Linden, Berlin 1995, Deutsche Oper, Berlin 1995, Aix-en-Provence 1996, Opéra de Paris 1997, Opera di Roma 1998, Opéra de Bordeaux 1998; specializes in Rossini roles, also Monteverdi and Handel. *Address:* c/o IMG Paris (Vocal Division), 54 Avenue Marceau, 75008 Paris, France.

KUHN, Gustav, DR.PHIL.; Austrian conductor; b. 28 Aug. 1946, Salzburg; s. of Friedrich Kuhn and Hilde Kuhn; m. Andrea Kuhn 1971; one s. one d.; ed. Acads. of Salzburg and Vienna and Univs of Salzburg and Vienna; advanced conducting studies under Bruno Maderna and Herbert von Karajan; professional conductor in Istanbul (three years), Enschede (Netherlands), Dortmund (prin. conductor) and Vienna; début at Vienna State Opera (Elektra) 1977, Munich Nat. Theatre (Così fan tutte) 1978, Covent Garden, London 1979, Glyndebourne, Munich Opera Festival and Salzburg Festival 1980, Chicago (Fidelio) 1981, Paris Opéra 1982, La Scala, Milan 1984, Arena di Verona (Masked Ball) 1986, Rossini Opera Festival, Pesaro 1987; Gen. Music Dir. in Berne, Bonn and Rome; production début in Trieste (Fliegender Holländer) 1986; other projects include Parsifal, Naples 1988, Salome, Rome 1988, Don Carlos (French version) and Don Carlo (Italian) for 250th anniversary Teatro Reggio, Turin 1990; Artistic Dir. Macerata Festival, Italy (productions of Così fan tutte and Don Giovanni) 1990/91; Founder and Pres. Accademia di Montegal 1990, Tiroles Festspiele Erl festival, Austria 1997–; First Prize, Int. Conducting Contest of Austrian TV and Broadcasting Corpn. (ORF) 1969; Lilly Lehmann Medal (Mozarteum Foundation); Max Reinhardt Medal (Salzburg); Senator of Honour Award 'Lorenzo il Magnifico' (Florence) 1988. *Leisure interest:* sailing. *Address:* A-6343 Erl, Austria. *Telephone:* (05373) 8181.

KUHN, Michael, LL.B.; film company executive; ed. Cambridge Univ.; solicitor Supreme Court 1974; lawyer Denton, Hall and Burgin, London; legal advisor Polygram U.K., London 1974–78, Dir. 1978–83; gen. counsel Polygram Int., London 1983–87, Sr. Vice-Pres. 1987–93; Pres. Polygram Filmed Entertainment, Beverly Hills, Calif. 1991–93, Exec. Vice-Pres. Polygram Holding Inc., New York 1993–; mem. Man. Bd. Polygram N.V. 1993–; Pres. and C.E.O. Polygram Filmed Entertainment, Beverly Hills. *Address:* Polygram Filmed Entertainment, 9333 Wilshire Boulevard, Beverly Hills, CA 90210, U.S.A.

KÜHNE, Gunther Albert Hermann, DR.IUR., LL.M.; German professor of law; b. 25 Aug. 1939, Gelsenkirchen; s. of Friedrich and Gertrud (née Belgard) Kühne; m. Elvira Schulz 1992; ed. Univ. of Cologne and Columbia Univ., New York; part-time legal adviser to German mining cos. 1963–68; Research Asst. Bochum Univ. Law School 1967–70; Sr. Govt. official, Ministry of Econs., Bonn 1971–74; Sr. official German del. OECD, Paris 1972–73; Sr. Govt. official, Ministry of Justice, Bonn 1974–78; Lecturer Private Law, Private Int. and Comparative Law, Bochum Univ. 1971–79; Prof. of Mining and Energy Law, Dir. Inst. for German and Int. Mining and Energy Law, Tech. Univ. Clausthal 1978–; Hon. Prof. of Law, Univ. of Göttingen 1986–; Visiting Prof. Bergakademie Freiberg 1992, Tel Aviv Univ. 1993–; Ordinary mem. Braunschweig Soc. of Sciences 1994. *Publications:* numerous books and articles on aspects of law, including Die Parteiautonomie im internationalen Erbrecht 1973, IPR-Gesetz-Entwurf (Private Int. Law Reform Draft) 1980, Memorandum on the State and Reform of German International Family Law 1980, Wandel und Beharren im Bergrecht (jtly.) 1992, Rechtsfragen der Aufsuchung und Gewinnung von in Steinkohleflözen beisitzendem Methangas 1994, Gegenwartsprobleme des Bergrechts (jtly.) 1995, Wettbewerb, Bestandsschutz, Umweltschutz (jtly.) 1997, Bestandsschutz alten Bergwerkseigentums unter besonderer Berücksichtigung des Art. 14 Grundgesetz 1998. *Address:* Arnold-Sommerfeld-Strasse 6, 38678 Clausthal-Zellerfeld, Germany. *Telephone:* 05323-723025. *Fax:* 05323-722507.

KUHNT, Dietmar, PH.D.; German business executive; b. 16 Nov. 1937, Wrocław (Breslau); m. 1966; two c.; ed. Univs. of Cologne and Freiburg; Perm. legal adviser, Rheinisch-Westfälisches Elektrizitätswerk AG 1968; mem. Bd. Man. RWE Energie AG 1989, Chair. 1992; mem. Bd. Man. RWE AG 1992, Chair. 1995–. *Address:* RWE AG, Opernplatz 1, 45128 Essen, Germany.

KUI FULIN, Lieut.-Gen.; Chinese army officer; b. Feb. 1938, Xinbin Co., Liaoning Prov.; joined CCP 1961; joined PLA Infantry School, Qiqihar 1956; served in combat units of Shenyang Mil. Region, successively promoted from platoon commdr. to div. chief-of-staff; studied PLA Mil. Acad. 1982; served as div. commdr. then corps chief-of-staff; Deputy Dir. and Dir. Operation Dept., PLA Gen. Staff HQ 1985, Asst. to Chief of Gen. Staff 1992–95, Deputy Chief PLA Gen. Staff 1995–; mem. 15th CCP Cen. Cttee. 1997–. *Address:* c/o Ministry of National Defence, Jingshanqian Jie, Beijing, People's Republic of China.

KUIPERS, J. D., M.A., M.SC.ECON., D.SC.; Netherlands consultant; b. 9 July 1918, Timperley, England; s. of Johannes and Marion Kuipers-Sewell; m. Johanna Adriana de Roon 1940; three s.; ed. Univ. of Cambridge, L.S.E. and Univ. of Amsterdam; served British and Royal Netherlands Army 1940–45; Dir. Royal De Betuwe Co. 1945–65; Vice-Pres. Fed. of Netherlands Industry, Brussels 1970–75; Chair. Foreign Affairs Cttee., Council of Netherlands Industrial Feds., Brussels 1970–75; Prof., Strathclyde Univ. Business School 1974–80; mem. Econ. and Social Cttee. of EEC 1962–74, Pres. 1970–72; mem. Pres. Council, Union of Industrial Feds. of EEC 1964–75, Council of Business and Advisory Cttee. to OECD; Hon. LL.D. (Strathclyde) 1974; Kt. Order of Netherlands Lion, Officer Order of Orange Nassau, Commdr. Order Léopold II, Order of Merit (Italy), Order George I (Greece). *Publication:* Resale Price Maintenance in Great Britain 1951. *Leisure interests:* arts, history. *Address:* 7 avenue Paul Hymans, Brussels 1200, Belgium.

KUKAN, Eduard, LL.D.; Slovak politician and diplomatist; b. 26 Dec. 1939, Trnovec nad Vahom, West Slovakia; m.; one s. one d.; ed. Moscow Inst. of Int. Relations, Charles Univ., Prague; joined Czechoslovakian Foreign Service 1964, mem. Africa Dept. 1964–68, various posts at Embassy in Zambia 1968–73, mem. Secr. of Minister for Foreign Affairs 1973–77, Minister Counsellor, Embassy in U.S.A. 1977–81, Head Dept. of Sub-Saharan Africa 1981–85, Amb. to Ethiopia 1985–88, Perm. Rep. of Czechoslovakia to UN, New York 1990–93, of Slovakia 1993–94; Deputy to Nat. Council of Slovak Repub. (Parl.) 1994–, Minister of Foreign Affairs March–Dec. 1994, mem. Foreign Relations Cttee. 1994–; mem. Exec. Cttee. Democratic Union of Slovakia 1994–, Chair. 1997–98; Vice-Chair. Slovak Democratic Coalition (SDK) 1998–; Minister of Foreign Affairs 1998–. *Leisure interests:* tennis, theatre. *Address:* Ministry of Foreign Affairs, Hlboká cesta 2, 833 36 Bratislava, Slovakia. *Telephone:* (07) 5978 3001. *Fax:* (07) 5978 3009.

KULAKOV, Anatoly Vasilyevich; Russian scientist; b. 15 July 1938; m.; one s.; ed. Leningrad Polytech. Inst.; researcher, sr. engineer., Deputy Dean, Leningrad Polytech. Inst. 1962–79; Scientific Sec., Deputy Chair., First Deputy Chair., Council on Science and Tech., U.S.S.R. Council of Ministers 1979–90; Dir.-Gen. Russian Industrialists and Entrepreneurs Union 1991–; corresp. mem. U.S.S.R. (now Russian) Acad. of Sciences 1984; main research in theory of electromagnetic interactions in systems of charged particles, plasma and solids. *Address:* Russian Academy of Sciences, Leninsky prosp. 32A, 117995 Moscow, Russia. *Telephone:* (095) 938 1400 (Office).

KULCSÁR, Kálmán, D.IUR.; Hungarian professor of sociology of law; b. 27 June 1928, Erdőtelek; s. of Ödön Kulcsár and Margit Szücs; m. Dr. Erzsébet Balogh; one d.; ed. Eger and Pázmány Péter Univ. of Budapest; various Judical posts to mem. of the Supreme Court of Justice 1950–57; research worker, Hungarian Acad. of Sciences with Eötvös Loránd Univ. Budapest; sr. mem. Inst. of Political and Legal Sciences 1957–69; Ford Scholarship for study in USA 1965–66; Dir. Hungarian Acad. of Sciences Inst. of Sociology 1969–83; Prof. of Sociology of Law, Eötvös Loránd Univ., Budapest 1970–; Minister of Justice 1988–90; Amb. to Canada 1990–93; Dir. Inst. for Political Science 1994–; corresp. mem. Hungarian Acad. of Sciences 1973, mem. 1980–, Deputy Gen. Sec. 1983–88; Pres. Hungarian Sociological Soc. 1983–89; Pres. Bd. of European Inst. for Sociology in Law 1990–; mem. editorial bd. International Journal of the Sociology of Law 1982–; State Prize 1985, Thomas Dehler Gold Medal, Germany 1990. *Publications include:* A jogszociológia problémái (Problems of the sociology of law) 1960, A szociológiai gondolkodás fejlődése (Development of the Sociological Thought) 1966, Társadalom, politika, jog (Society, Politics, Law) 1974; A jogszociológia alapjai (Foundations of the Sociology of Law) 1976, Gazdaság, társadalom, jog (Economy, Society, Law) 1983, Rechts-soziologische Abhandlungen 1982, People's Assessors in the Court 1983, Contemporary Hungarian Society 1984, Modernization and Hungarian Society 1986, Politics and Sociology of Law 1987, Modernization and Law 1992, Between Two Worlds, Changes of Political System in Hungary 1888–1990 1994; numerous studies in Hungarian and foreign papers. *Leisure interest:* memoirs by statesmen before and after World War II.

KULIDZHANOV, Lev Aleksandrovich; Russian film producer; b. 19 March 1924, Tbilisi; m. Natalia Anatolievna Fokina 1948; two s.; ed. All-Union Film Inst. (VGIK); producer, later dir., Gorky Film Studio 1955–; mem. CPSU 1962–90; Chair. Organizing Cttee., U.S.S.R. Union of Film Workers 1964–65, First Sec. 1965–86; Prof. VGIK 1977–; Deputy to U.S.S.R. Supreme Soviet 1966–89; Chair. U.S.S.R.-Mexico Friendship Soc. 1966; mem. Cen. Auditing Comm. of CPSU 1966–76, cand. mem. Cen. Cttee. CPSU 1976–87; U.S.S.R. People's Artist 1976, Lenin Prize 1982, R.S.F.S.R. State Prize 1971; Order of Lenin, Hero of Socialist Labour 1984. *Films include:* It Happened So 1956, The House in which I Live 1957, My Father's House 1959, The Lost Photo 1959, When Trees Were Big 1961, The Blue Book 1963, Crime and Punishment 1969, Starry Minute 1975, Young Marx (TV) 1990, It is Not Terrifying to Die 1991, The Forgetmenots 1994. *Address:* Barvikha, House 92, Odintsovo Region, 143082 Moscow District, Russia. *Telephone:* (095) 418-54-98.

KULIEV, Avdy, C.PHIL.SC.; Turkmen politician; b. 1936, Ashkhabad; ed. Turkmen State Univ., U.S.S.R. Ministry of Foreign Affairs; researcher Inst. of Language and Literature Turkmenian Acad. of Sciences; mem. Inst. of Asian Peoples' Acad. of Sciences; Dir. Russian language courses in Soviet Cultural Centre in Yemen 1960–71; diplomatic posts in U.S.S.R embassies in Arabic countries 1971–87, Acting Chargé d'Affaires Embassy in Qatar, Oman 1987–89, Counsellor Dept. of Near East and North Africa U.S.S.R. Ministry of Foreign Affairs 1989–90; Minister of Foreign Affairs of Turkmenistan 1990–92; fmr. mem. Pres.'s Council; leader of opposition to Pres. Nijazov 1992–94; Pres. of Turkmenistan Fund; lives in Prague.

KULIK, Gennady Vasilyevich; Russian politician; b. 20 Jan. 1935; m.; one s.; ed. Leningrad State Univ.; researcher, Head of dept., Siberian Div. of All-Union Inst. of Agricultural Econ. 1957–65; First Deputy Head, Novosibirsk Regional Dept. of Agric. 1965; Deputy Head, Chief Dept. of Planning and Econs., Ministry of Agric. R.S.F.S.R. 1965–86; First Deputy Chair., R.S.F.S.R. State Cttee. of Agric. and Industry 1986–90; First Deputy Chair., R.S.F.S.R. Council of Ministers, Minister of Agric. and Food 1990–91; U.S.S.R. Peoples' Deputy 1990–92; advisor to Dir., Inex-Interexport (Moscow) 1993; mem. Exec. Bd. Russian Agrarian Party, Deputy Chair. Russian Agrarian Union; mem. State Duma; Deputy Chair. Cttee. on Budget, Taxes, Banks and Finance 1993–98; Deputy Chair. Govt. of Russian Fed. Sept. 1998–; Merited Economist of Russia. *Address:* Parliament Buildings, Krasnopresnenskaya nab. 2, 103274 Moscow, Russia. *Telephone:* (095) 205 4013 (Office).

KULIKOV, Army Gen. Anatoly Sergeyevich, DR. ECON.SC.; Russian politician and military officer; b. 4 Sept. 1946, Aigursky, Stavropol Region; m.; two s. one d.; ed. Ordzhonikidze Higher Mil. Commdg. School U.S.S.R. Ministry of Internal Affairs, M. Frunze Mil. Acad., Mil. Acad. of Gen. Staff; served on commdg. posts from commdr. co. to highest posts Ministry of Internal Affairs of Russia 1966–; Commdr. of Internal Troops 1992–95; Head United Grouping of Fed. Troops in Chechen Repub. Jan.–July 1995; Minister of Internal Affairs of Russian Fed. 1995–98; Deputy Chair of Russian Govt. March 1997–98; mem. Security Council of Russian Fed.; mem. Defence Council 1995–98; mem. Org. Bd. Otechestvo (Fatherland) movt. Nov. 1998–; Sr. Researcher, Inst. of Social and Political Studies (ISPIRAN), Acad. of Sciences 1998–. *Address:* ISPIRAN, Leninski prosp. 32A, 117334 Moscow, Russia. *Telephone:* (095) 938-19-10.

KULIKOV, Marshal Viktor Georgiyevich; Russian army officer (retd.); b. 5 July 1921; ed. Frunze Military Acad., Acad. of General Staff; joined Soviet Army 1938; Commdr. of Platoon 1940, Chief of Staff tank battalion, regt., brigade 1941–45; various command posts in tank detachments 1945–48; Frunze Mil. Acad. 1948–53; Commdr. tank regt., Chief of Staff tank div., Deputy Commdr. of Army, Commdr. of Army 1953–67; Commdr. Kiev Mil. Area 1967–69; C.-in-C. Soviet Forces in Germany 1969–71; mem. CPSU 1942–; mem. Cen. Cttee. of CPSU 1971–89; Chief of Gen. Staff and First Deputy Minister of Defence 1971–77; Marshal of the Soviet Union 1977; C.-in-C. of Armed Forces of Warsaw Pact 1977–89; Gen. Insp., Ministry of Defence Inspectorate 1989–91; State Mil. Adviser 1992; U.S.S.R. People's Deputy 1989–91; Deputy Prime Minister 1997–; also in charge of Tax, Police and Customs Service; Hero of the Soviet Union and other decorations. *Address:* Ministry of Defence, Myasnitskaya str. 37, 10100 Moscow, Russia. *Telephone:* (095) 293-31-76.

KULIYEV, Eldar Gulam ogly; Azerbaijani diplomatist; b. 29 Aug. 1939, Baku; m.; two c.; ed. Azerbaijani State Univ., Baku, Diplomatic Acad., Moscow; interpreter Project Aswan-Cairo, Egypt 1963–65; Second Sec., First Sec. Ministry of Foreign Affairs, Baku 1965–69; Vice-Consul, U.S.S.R. Consulate, Aswan 1969–71, Consul 1971–73; First Sec. Soviet Embassy, Cairo 1973–76; Consul, U.S.S.R. Consulate-Gen., Istanbul 1978–83; advanced studies at Diplomatic Acad., Moscow 1983–84; Counsellor Div. of Cultural Relations with Foreign Countries, Ministry of Foreign Affairs, Moscow 1983–85, Expert 1985–86; Expert Dept. of Humanitarian and Cultural Relations, Ministry of Foreign Affairs, Moscow 1986–88; Minister-Counsellor U.S.S.R. Embassy, Aden 1988–90; Deputy Consul-Gen. U.S.S.R. Consultate-Gen., Aden 1990–91; Expert Legal Dept., Ministry of Foreign Affairs, Moscow 1991-92; Sr. Counsellor Dept. of Int. Orgs. and Global Affairs, Ministry of Foreign Affairs, Moscow; Sr. Counsellor Analysis and Research Dept., Ministry of Foreign Affairs, Moscow 1993–94; Perm. Rep. of Azerbaijan to UN, Sept. 1994–. *Address:* Permanent Mission of Azerbaijan to the United Nations, 747 Third Avenue, 17th Floor, New York, NY 10017, U.S.A. *Telephone:* (212) 371-2559. *Fax:* (212) 371-2784.

KULKA, Konstanty Andrzej; Polish violinist; b. 5 March 1947, Gdańsk; m.; two d.; ed. Higher State School of Music, Gdańsk; Prof. Acad. of Music 1999–; participant in 2 music competitions: Paganini Competition, Genoa 1964, Diploma and Special Prize; Music Competition, Munich 1966 (1st Prize); since 1967 has given concerts all over the world and participates in many int. festivals including Lucerne, Prague, Bordeaux, Berlin, Granada, Barcelona, Brighton; many gramophone, radio and TV recordings; soloist with State Philharmonic Orchestra, Warsaw; Minister of Culture and Art Prize 1969, 1973, Minister of Foreign Affairs Prize 1977, Pres. of Radio and TV Cttee. Prize 1978, Prize Winner 33 Grand Prix du Disque Int. Sound Festival, Paris 1981; Gold Cross of Merit. *Leisure interests:* collecting gramophone records, bridge, collecting interesting kitchen recipes. *Address:* Filharmonia Narodowa, ul. Jasna 5, 00-007 Warsaw, Poland. *Telephone:* (22) 826 57 13; (22) 827 52 63.

KULUKUNDIS, Sir Eddie, Kt., O.B.E., F.R.S.A.; business executive and theatre director; b. 20 April 1932; s. of late George Elias Kulukundis and of Eugenie Diacakis; m. Susan Hampshire (q.v.) 1981; ed. Collegiate School, New York, Salisbury School, Conn. and Yale Univ.; mem. Baltic Exchange 1959–; mem. Lloyds 1964–95, mem. Council 1983–89; Dir. Rethymnis & Kulukundis Ltd. 1964–, London & Overseas Freighters 1980–85, 1989–; Chair. Knightsbridge Theatrical Productions Ltd. 1970–; part-owner, Duke of York's Theatre, Ambassadors Theatre; Chair. Sports Aid Foundation 1988–93; mem. Council of Man. Royal Shakespeare Theatre, Royal Shakespeare Theatre Trust (Vice-Chair. 1983–); Gov. Raymond Mander and Joe Mitchenson Theatre Collection Ltd., Royal Shakespeare Theatre; Vice-Pres. Greenwich Theatre Ltd., Traverse Theatre Club.; Dir. Hampstead Theatre Ltd.; mem. Exec. Council, SWET; *London productions include:* (some jtly.): Enemy 1969, The Happy Apple, Poor Horace, The Friends, How the Other Half Loves, Tea Party and the Basement (double bill), The Wild Duck 1970, After Haggerty, Hamlet, Charley's Aunt, Straight Up 1971, London Assurance, Journey's End 1972; Small Craft Warnings, A Private Matter, Dandy Dick 1973, The Waltz of the Toreadors, Life Class, Pygmalion, Play Mas, The Gentle Hook 1974, A Little Night Music, Entertaining Mr Sloane, The Gay Lord Quex, What the Butler Saw, Travesties, Lies, The Seagull, A Month in the Country, A Room with a View, Too True to be Good, The Bed Before Yesterday 1975, Dimetos, Banana Ridge, Wild Oats 1976, Candida, Man and Superman, Once a Catholic 1977, Privates on Parade, Gloo Joo 1978, Bent, Outside Edge, Last of the Red Hot Lovers 1979, Beecham, Born in the Gardens 1980, Tonight at 8.30, Steaming, Arms and the Man 1981, Steafel's Variations 1982, Messiah, Pack of Lies 1983, Of Mice and Men, The Secret Diary of Adrian Mole Aged 13¾ 1984, Camille 1985, The Cocktail Party 1986, Curtains 1987, Separation, South Pacific, Married Love, Over My Dead Body 1989, Never the Sinner 1990, The King and I, Carmen Jones 1991, Noel & Gertie, Slip of the Tongue, Shades, Annie Get Your Gun, Making it Better 1992, The Prime of Miss Jean Brodie 1994, Neville's Island 1994, The Killing of Sister George 1995. *New York productions include:* (jtly.): How the Other Half Loves 1971, Sherlock Holmes, London Assurance 1974, Travesties 1975, The Merchant 1977, Players 1978, Once a Catholic 1979. *Address:* c/o Rethymnis & Kulukundis Ltd., 21 New Fetter Lane, London, EC4A 1JJ; c/o Knightsbridge Theatrical Productions Ltd., 21 New Fetter Lane, London, EC4A 1JJ, England. *Telephone:* 0171-583 8687.

KUMAGAI, Hiroshi; Japanese politician; mem. House of Reps.; fmr. Deputy Sec.-Gen. Japanese Renewal Party (Shinseito) (JRP); fmr. mem. House of Councillors; Minister of Int. Trade and Industry 1993–94, Chief Cabinet Sec. May–June 1994. *Address:* House of Representatives, Tokyo, Japan.

KUMARATUNGA, Chandrika Bandaranaike, PH.D.; Sri Lankan politician; b. 29 June 1945, Colombo; d. of late S.W.R.D. Bandaranaike (f. Sri Lanka Freedom Party (SLFP) and fmr. Prime Minister 1956–59, assassinated 1959) and Sirima R.D. Bandaranaike (q.v.) (first elected woman Prime Minister in the world in 1960–65, 1970–77, 1994–); m. Vijaya Kumaratunga 1978 (assassinated 1988); one s. one d.; ed. St. Bridget's Convent, Colombo, Univ. of Paris; mem. Exec. Cttee. Women's League of SLFP 1974, Exec. Cttee. and Working Cttee. 1980, Cen. Cttee. 1992, (Deputy Leader of SLFP); Chair., Man. Dir. Dinakara Sinhala (daily newspaper) 1977–85; Vice-Pres. Sri Lanka Mahajana (People's) Party (SLMP) 1984, Pres. 1986; Leader SLMP and People's Alliance; Chief Minister, Minister of Law and Order, Finance and Planning, Educ., Employment and Cultural Affairs of the Western Prov. Council 1993–94; Prime Minister Aug.–Nov. 1994, Minister of Finance and Planning, Ethnic Affairs and Nat. Integration July 1994–, of Defence, of Buddha Sasana Nov. 1994–; Pres. of Sri Lanka Nov. 1994–; Additional Prin. Dir. Land Reform Comm. 1972–75; Chair. Janawasa Comm. 1975–77; Expert Consultant, FAO 1977–80; Research Fellow, London Univ. 1988–91; Guest Univ. Lecturer, Bradford Univ., U.K. 1989, Jawaharlal Nehru Univ., India 1991. *Publications:* several research papers on land reform and food policies. *Leisure interests:* playing piano and guitar, tennis, swimming, Kandyan (nat.) dance, music, reading, art and sculpture, drama, cinema. *Address:* Presidential Secretariat, Republic Square, Colombo 1, Sri Lanka. *Telephone:* (1) 24801.

KUMIN, Maxine Winokur, M.A.; American writer and poet; b. 6 June 1925, Philadelphia; d. of Peter Winokur and Doll Simon; m. Victor M. Kumin 1946; one s. two d.; ed. Radcliffe Coll; consultant in poetry, Library of Congress 1981–82; Fellow, Acad. of American Poets, Chancellor 1995–; Visiting Prof. M.I.T. 1984, Univ. of Miami 1995, Pitzer Coll. 1996; McGee Prof. of Writing Davidson Coll. 1997; mem. Poetry Soc. of America, PEN America, Authors' Guild, Writers' Union; Pulitzer Prize for Poetry 1973, The Poets' Prize 1994, Aiken Taylor Poetry Prize 1995, Harvard Grad. School of Arts and Sciences Centennial Award 1996; Levinson Award, Poetry magazine 1987, American Acad. and Inst. of Arts Award 1989, Centennial Award, Harvard Grad. School of Arts & Sciences 1996. *Publications:* poetry: Halfway 1961, The Privilege 1965, The Nightmare Factory 1970, Up Country 1972, House, Bridge, Fountain, Gate 1975, The Retrieval System 1978, Our Ground Time Here Will Be Brief 1982, The Long Approach 1985, Nurture 1989, Looking for Luck 1992, Connecting the Dots 1996, Selected Poems 1960–1990 1997; novels: Through Dooms of Love 1965, The Passions of Uxport 1968, The Abduction 1971, The Designated Heir 1974; essays, short stories, children's books and poetry contributions to nat. magazines. *Leisure interests:* breeding horses. *Address:* c/o Curtis Brown Associates, 10 Astor Place, New York, NY 10003, U.S.A.

KUMMER, Wolfgang, DR.TECH.; Austrian physicist; b. 15 Oct. 1935, Krems; s. of Dr Friedrich Kummer and Maria Kummer; m. Lore Pokorny 1960; ed. Gymnasium Krems and Technical Univ. Vienna; Asst. Tech. Univ. Vienna 1958–66; Dir. Inst. of High Energy Physics, Austrian Acad. of Sciences 1966–71; Prof. of Theoretical Physics, Technical Univ. Vienna 1968–; Pres. CERN Council 1985–87; Chair. High Energy Particle Physics Bd., European Physical Soc. 1997–; Visiting Prof. Univ. of Philadelphia 1973, Princeton Univ. 1975, Brookhaven Nat. Lab. 1977, 1980 etc.; mem. Austrian Acad. of Sciences; Culture Award, Fed. Province of Lower Austria 1971; Innitzer Award 1981, E. Schrodinger Award (Austrian Acad. of Science) 1988. *Publications:* more than 140 scientific publs. on the theory of elementary particle physics and of gravity. *Leisure interests:* music, tennis, skiing. *Address:* Institut für Theoretische Physik, Technische Universität Wien, Wiedner Hauptstrasse 8-10, 1040 Vienna (Office); Liebhartstalstrasse 31, 1160 Vienna, Austria (Home). *Telephone:* (1) 58801/13620 (Office); (1) 9146790 (Home). *Fax:* (1) 58801/13699 (Office).

KUMP, Ernest Joseph, M.A. (ARCH.); American architect; b. 29 Dec. 1911, Bakersfield, Calif.; s. of Ernest J. Kump, Sr. and Mary Petsche Kump; m. Josephine Miller Kump 1934; one s. one d.; ed. Univ .of Calif. (Berkeley) and Harvard Grad. School of Design; fmr. Prof. of Architecture, Columbia Univ. and has lectured at numerous univs.; founded own architectural firm 1934; Chair. Bd. of Dirs. Tekto Systems Research 1977–82; Sr. Partner, KUMP, Architecture Research Assocs. 1983; work has included college and univ. campuses, civic centres, performing arts centres and other public bldgs. and new residential communities; consultant and panel or cttee. mem. for numerous orgs. including British Bldg. Comm., Carnegie Foundation and U.S. Govt.; Consulting Architect to Ronald Reagan Pres. Library Foundation, Calif. 1987; mem. Task Force on Arts and Humanities 1981; Hon. Fellow, R.I.B.A.; mem. Berlin Akad. der Künste; Fellow American Inst. of Architects (Architectural Firm Award 1970), Life mem. R.S.A. London. *Publication:* A New Architecture for Man 1957. *Leisure interests:* inventing, philosophy, classical music, literature. *Address:* Villa Boecklin, Jupiterstrasse 15, 8032 Zürich, Switzerland.

KUNADZE, Georgy Fridrikhovich, C.HIS.SC.; Russian diplomatist; b. 21 Dec. 1948, Moscow; m.; one s.; ed. Moscow Inst. of Oriental Languages; researcher Inst. of Oriental Studies U.S.S.R. Acad. of Sciences 1971–83; diplomatic service 1983–, scientific attaché Embassy, Japan 1982–87, head of sector, Chief of Div. Inst. of World Econs. and Int. Relations 1987–91; Deputy Minister of Foreign Affairs of Russia 1991–93; Amb. to Repub. of Korea 1993–96, Amb.-at-large 1996–; Deputy Dir. Inst. of U.S.A. and Canada, Russian Acad. of Sciences 1998–. *Publications:* numerous articles. *Address:* ISCAN, Khlebny per. 2/3, 121069 Moscow, Russia. *Telephone:* (095) 291-11-66.

KUNDERA, Milan; Czech/French writer; b. 1 April 1929, Brno; s. of Dr. Ludvik Kundera and Milada Kunderová-Janosikova; m. Věra Hrabánková 1967; ed. Film Faculty, Acad. of Music and Dramatic Arts, Prague; Asst., later Asst. Prof., Film Faculty, Acad. of Music and Dramatic Arts, Prague 1958–69; Prof., Univ. of Rennes 1975–80; Prof. Ecole des hautes études en sciences sociales, Paris 1980–; mem. Union of Czechoslovak Writers 1963–69; mem. Editorial Bd. Literární noviny 1963–67, 1968; mem. Editorial Bd. Listy 1968–69; Klement Lukeš Prize 1963; Union of Czechoslovak Writers' Prize 1968, Czechoslovak Writers' Publishing House Prize 1969, Prix Médicis (for Life is Elsewhere) 1973, Premio letterario Mondello (for The Farewell Party) 1978, Commonwealth Award (for all his work) 1981, Prix Europa-Littérature 1982, Los Angeles Times Prize (for Unbearable Lightness of Being) 1984, Jerusalem Prize (for all his work) 1985, Nelly Sachs Preis (for all his work) 1987, Österreichische Staatspreis für Europäische Literatur 1988, The Independent (newspaper) Prize, London 1991, Aujourd'hui Prize (France) 1993, Medal of Merit (Czech Repub.) 1995, Andreas Gryphia Prize for Understanding between Nations in Middle Europe, Germany 1998, Hon. Citizen, Kunštát 1998; Officier, Légion d'honneur 1990. *Publications:* Drama: Jacques et son maître 1971–81; Short stories: Laughable Loves 1970; Novels: The Joke 1967, Life is Elsewhere 1973, La Valse aux adieux (The Farewell Party) 1976, Livre du rire et de l'oubli (The Book of Laughter and Forgetting) 1979, The Unbearable Lightness of Being 1984, The Art of the Novel 1987, Immortality 1990, Les testaments trahis, Slowness 1995, Testaments Betrayed: An Essay in Nine Parts 1995, L'Identità (Identity) 1997. *Address:* c/o Gallimard, 5 rue Sébastien-Bottin, 75007 Paris, France.

KUNENE, Mazisa, M.A.; South African poet, political activist and lecturer; m. Mabowe Mathabo Kunene; four c.; ed. Natal Univ., London Univ.; European and U.S. African Nat. Congress (ANC) Rep. 1959; co-f. Int. Anti-Apartheid Movt.; lecturer Stanford Univ., Univ. of Calif., L.A.; named Africa's Poet Laureate 1993. *Publications include:* Zulu Poems 1970, Emperor Shaka the Great (16,400 verses) 1979, Anthem of the Decades 1981, The Ancestor and the Sacred Mountain 1982.

KUNERT, Günter; German author; b. 6 March 1929, Berlin; s. of Adolf Kunert and Edith Warschauer; m. Marianne Todten 1951; Visiting Assoc. Prof. Univ. of Tex. (Austin) 1972; Writer-in-Residence Univ. of Warwick 1975; mem. Akad. der Künste, W. Berlin, Akad. für Sprache und Dichtung, Darmstadt; Pres. literaturgezellschaft, Schleswig-Holstein 1987–; Dr. h.c. (Allegheny Coll., Penn.) 1988; Heinrich Mann Prize, Akad. der Künste (E. Berlin) 1962, Becher Prize for Poetry 1973, Heinrich Heine Prize (City of Düsseldorf) 1985, Hölderlin Prize 1991, E.R. Curtius Prize 1991, Georg-

Trakl-Preis (Austria), Erwachsenespiele (autobiog.), etc. *TV screenplays:* King Arthur 1990, An Obituary of the Wall 1991, Endstation: Harembar 1991; radio plays. *Publications:* 55 volumes of poetry, prose, satire, essays, novels, short stories and lectures. *Leisure interests:* travel, collecting tin toys. *Address:* Schulstrasse 7, 25560 Kaisborstel, Germany. *Telephone:* 04892/1414. *Fax:* 04892/8403.

KÜNG, Hans, D.THEOL.; Swiss theologian and academic; b. 19 March 1928, Sursee, Lucerne; ed. Gregorian Univ., Rome, Inst. Catholique and Sorbonne, Paris; ordained priest 1954; mem. practical ministry, Lucerne Cathedral 1957–59; Scientific asst. for Dogmatic Catholic Theol., Univ. of Münster/Westfalen 1959–60; Prof. Fundamental Theol., Univ. of Tübingen 1960–63; Prof. of Dogmatic and Ecumenical Theology and Dir., Inst. Ecumenical Research 1963–80, Prof. of Ecumenical Theology, Dir. Inst. of Ecumenical Research (under direct responsibility of Pres. and Senate Univ. of Tübingen) 1980–96, Prof. Emer. 1996–; Guest Prof., Univ. of Chicago 1981, of Mich. 1983, of Toronto 1985, of Rice Univ., Houston 1987; numerous guest lectures at univs. worldwide; mem. PEN; Pres. Foundation Global Ethic, Germany 1995–, Switzerland 1997–; Co-Pres. World Conf. on Religion and Peace, New York; Founding mem. Int. Review of Theology, Concilium; Hon. D.D. (Univ. of Wales) 1998, numerous hon. degrees; Oskar Pfister Award, American Psychiatric Asscn. 1986, Karl Barth Prize, Evangelische Kirche der Union, Berlin 1992, Hirt Prize, Zürich 1993, Silver Medal, Univ. of Tübingen 1996, Theodor Heuss Prize, Stuttgart 1998, Bundesverdienstkreuz (First Class). *Publications:* The Council: Reform and Reunion 1961, That the World May Believe 1963, The Council in Action 1963, Justification: The Doctrine of Karl Barth and a Catholic Reflection 1964, (with new introductory chapter, and response of Karl Barth) 1981, Structures of the Church 1964, (with new preface) 1982, Freedom Today 1966, The Church 1967, Truthfulness 1968, Menschwerdung Gottes 1970, Infallible?—An Inquiry 1971, Why Priests? 1972, Fehlbar?—Eine Bilanz 1973, On being a Christian 1976, Signposts for the Future 1978, The Christian Challenge 1979, Freud and the Problem of God 1979, Does God Exist? 1980, The Church–Maintained in Truth 1980, Eternal Life? 1984, Christianity and the World Religions: Paths to Dialogue with Islam, Hinduism and Buddhism (with others) 1986, The Incarnation of God 1986, Church and Change: The Irish Experience 1986, Why I am still a Christian 1987, Theology for the Third Millennium: An Ecumenical View 1988, Christianity and Chinese Religions (with Julia Ching) 1989, Paradigm Change in Theology: A Symposium for the future 1989, Reforming the Church Today 1990, Global Responsibility: In Search of a New World Ethic 1991, Judaism 1992, Credo: The Apostles' Creed Explained for Today 1993, Great Christian Thinkers 1994, Christianity 1995, Islam, A Dignified Dying: a plea for personal responsibility (with Walter Jens) 1995, Yes to a Global Ethic (Ed.) 1996, A Global Ethic for Global Politics and Economics 1997; ed. Journal of Ecumenical Studies, Revue Internationale de Théologie Concilium, Theological Meditations, Ökumenische Theologie. *Leisure interests:* watersport, skiing, classical music. *Address:* 72076 Tübingen, Waldhäuserstrasse 23, Germany. *Telephone:* 62646. *Fax:* 610140.

KUNIN, Madeleine May, M.A., M.S.; American politician and diplomatist; b. 28 Sept. 1933, Zürich, Switzerland; d. of Ferdinand May and Renee Bloch; m. Arthur S. Kunin 1959 (divorced 1995); three s. one d.; ed. Univ. of Mass., Columbia Univ. and Univ. of Vermont; reporter, Burlington Free Press, Vermont 1957–58; Asst. Producer, WCAX-TV, Burlington 1960–61; freelance writer and instructor in English, Trinity Coll. Burlington 1969–70; mem. Vermont House of Reps. 1973–78; Lt.-Gov. of Vermont 1979–82, Gov. 1985–91; Deputy Sec. of Educ. 1993–96; Fellow, Inst. of Politics, Kennedy School of Govt. Harvard Univ. 1983–93; Amb. to Switzerland 1996–; Lecturer, Middlebury Coll., St. Michael's Coll. 1984; Fellow, Bunting Inst., Radcliffe Coll., Cambridge, Mass. 1991–92; several hon. degrees and other distinctions; Democrat. *Publications:* The Big Green Book (with M. Stout) 1976, Living a Political Life 1994; articles in professional journals, magazines and newspapers. *Address:* American Embassy, Jubiläumsstr. 93, 3005 Berne, Switzerland. *Telephone:* (31) 351 7011. *Fax:* (31) 351 7344.

KUNITZ, Stanley J., M.A.; American writer and educator; b. 29 July 1905, Worcester, Mass.; s. of Solomon Z. Kunitz and Yetta Helen Jasspon; m. 1st Helen Pearce 1930, 2nd Eleanor Evans 1939, 3rd Elise Asher 1958; one d. from 2nd m.; ed. Harvard Univ.; Ed. Wilson Library Bulletin 1928–42; service with U.S. Army, rising to rank of Staff Sergeant 1943–45; Prof. of Literature, Bennington Coll., Vt. 1946–49; Dir. of Seminar, Potsdam Summer Workshop in Creative Arts 1949–53; Lecturer and Dir. of Poetry Workshop, New School for Social Research, New York 1950–57; Dir. Poetry Workshop, The Poetry Center, New York, 1958–62; Lecturer, Columbia Univ. 1963–66; Adjunct Prof. School of the Arts (Columbia) 1967–85; Founding mem., mem. Bd. of Dirs. Fine Arts Work Center, Provincetown, Mass. 1968–; Sr. Fellow in the Humanities (Princeton) 1978; Montgomery Fellow, Dartmouth Univ. 1991; Ed., Yale Series of Younger Poets, Yale Univ. Press 1969–77; Poetry Consultant of the Library of Congress 1974–76, Hon. Consultant in American Letters 1976–82; mem. American Acad. of Arts and Letters 1963, Nat. Inst. of Arts and Letters; Founding Pres. Poets House, New York 1985–90; Fellow, Yale Univ. 1969; Chancellor, Acad. of American Poets 1970–95; Hon. Litt.D. (Clark Univ.) 1961, (Anna Maria College) 1977, (Worcester State Coll.) 1980, (St. Mary's Coll., Md.) 1994; Hon. D. Hum.Litt. (State Univ. of New York) 1987; awards include Garrison Medal for Poetry 1926, Blumenthal Prize 1941, Levinson Prize 1956, Harriet Monroe Award 1958, Pulitzer Prize for Poetry 1959, Brandeis Creative Arts Poetry Medal 1965, Fellowship Award, Acad. of American Poets 1968, Lenore Marshall Award for Poetry 1980, Bollingen Prize in Poetry 1987, designated New York State Poet, with Walt Whitman Citation of Merit 1987, Centennial Medal (Harvard Univ.) 1992, Nat. Medal of Arts 1993, Sr. Fellowship Award, Nat. Endowment for the Arts 1984, named Walt Whitman Birthplace Poet 1989, Shelley Memorial Award 1995, Nat. Book Award 1995. *Publications:* Intellectual Things 1930, Editions: Living Authors 1931, Authors Today and Yesterday 1933, Junior Book of Authors 1934, British Authors of the XIX Century 1936, American Authors 1600–1900 1938, XX Century Authors 1942, Passport to the War 1944, British Authors Before 1800 1952, XX Century Authors (First Supplement) 1955, Selected Poems 1958, Poems of John Keats 1964, European Authors 1000–1900 1967, The Testing-Tree (verse) 1971, Poems of Akhmatova (translations) 1973, The Terrible Threshold (verse) 1974, Story under Full Sail (trans. of A. Voznesensky) 1974, The Coat Without a Seam (verse) 1974, A Kind of Order, a Kind of Folly 1975, Orchard Lamps (trans. of Ivan Drach) 1978, The Poems of Stanley Kunitz 1928–1978, 1979, The Wellfleet Whale and Companion Poems 1983, Next-to-Last Things: New Poems and Essays 1985, Ed. The Essential Blake 1987, Interviews and Encounters 1993, Passing Through: The Later Poems 1995. *Address:* 37 West 12th Street, New York, NY 10011, U.S.A.

KUNITZSCH, Paul Horst Robert, D.PHIL.; German professor of Arabic Studies (retd.); b. 14 July 1930, Neu-Krüssow; ed. Free Univ. of West Berlin; lecturer in Arabic, Univ. of Göttingen 1956–57; taught German, Cairo 1957–60; lecturer, Goethe Inst., Fed. Repub. of Germany 1960–63; Special Adviser, Radio Deutsche Welle, Cologne 1963–68; Research Fellow, Deutsche Forschungsgemeinschaft 1969–75; Lecturer in Arabic, Univ. of Munich 1975–77, Prof. of Arabic Studies 1977–95; mem. Bavarian Acad. of Sciences, Acad. Int. d'Histoire des Sciences, Paris; corresp. mem. Acad. of Arabic Language, Cairo; Göttingen Acad. of Sciences Prize 1974. *Publications:* Arab. Sternnamen in Europa 1959, Der Almagest 1974, The Arabs and the Stars 1989; C. Ptolemäus, Der Sternkatalog (Ed.), 3 vols. 1986–91. *Address:* Davidstr. 17, 81927 Munich, Germany. *Telephone:* (089) 91 62 80.

KUNZE, Horst, DR. PHIL.; German librarian; b. 22 Sept. 1909, Dresden; s. of Max Kunze and Helene Gibson; m. Wilma Repp 1941; two s. two d.; ed. Sächsische Landesbibliothek, Dresden and Deutsche Bücherei,Leipzig; Research Librarian, Landesbibliothek, Darmstadt 1939–42; Dir. Universitäts- und Landesbibliothek Sachsen-Anhalt, Halle 1947–50; Gen. Dir. Deutsche Staatsbibliothek 1950–76; Dir. Inst. of Library Science and Scientific Information, Humboldt-Univ. Berlin 1955–68; Full Prof. of Library Science, Univ. of Berlin 1954–75; Dr. h.c. *Publications:* Lieblingsbücher von dazumal 1938 (reprint 1965), Über das Registermachen 1964 (4th edn. 1992), Schatzbehalter Vom Besten aus der älteren deutschen Kinderliteratur (6th edn. 1981), Werner Klemkes gesammelte Werke 1968 (3rd edn. 1977), Lexikon des Bibliothekwesens (ed. with G. Rückl) 1969 (2nd edn. 2 vols. 1974–75), Geschichte der Buchillustration in Deutschland: Das 15. Jahrhundert (2 vols.) 1975, Grundzüge der Bibliothekslehre (4th edn.) 1977, Das Grosse Buch vom Buch 1983, Spiegel proletarischer Kinder-und Jugend-Literatur 1870–1936 (with H. Wegehaupt) 1985, Von Bild im Buch (collected papers) 1988, Geschichte der Buchillustration in Deutschland: Das 16. und 17. Jahrhundert (2 vols.) 1993. *Leisure interest:* books. *Address:* Regattastrasse 246, 12527 Berlin, Germany. *Telephone:* 6744809.

KUNZE, Reiner; German author; b. 16 Aug. 1933, Oelsnitz/Erzgeb.; s. of Ernst Kunze and Martha (née Friedrich) Kunze; m. Dr Elisabeth Mifka 1961; one s. one d.; ed. Univ. of Leipzig; mem. Bavarian Acad. of Fine Arts, Acad. of Arts, West Berlin 1975–92, German Acad. for Languages and Literature, Darmstadt, Free Acad. of Arts Mannheim; Hon. mem. Collegium Europaeum Jenense of Friedrich-Schiller-Universität Jena; Dr. h.c.; numerous awards and prizes including Literary Prize of Bavarian Acad. of Fine Arts 1973, Georg Trakl Prize (Austria) 1977, Andreas Gryphius Prize 1977, Georg Büchner Prize 1977, Bavarian Film Prize 1979, Eichendorff Literature Prize 1984, Weilheimer Literaturpreis 1997, Europapreis für Poesie, Serbia 1998; Bayerischer Verdienstorden, Grosses Verdienstkreuz der BRD. 1984. *Publications:* Sensible Wege 1969, Der Löwe Leopold 1970, Zimmerlautstärke 1972, Brief mit blauem Siegel 1973, Die wunderbaren Jahre 1976, Auf eigene Hoffnung 1981, Eines jeden einziges Leben 1986, Das weisse Gedicht 1989, Deckname "Lyrik" 1990, Wohin der Schlaf sich schlafen legt 1991, Mensch ohne Macht 1991, Am Sonnenhang 1993, Wo Freiheit ist . . . 1994, Steine und Lieder 1996, Der Dichter Jan Skácel 1996, Bindewort "deutsch" 1997, Ein Tag auf dieser Erde 1998. *Address:* Am Sonnenhang 19, 94130 Obernzell, Germany.

KUOK, Robert; Malaysian business executive; b. 6 Oct. 1923, Johore Bahru; m. twice; eight c.; ed. Raffles Coll., Singapore; joined Mitsubishi, Johore Bahru 1941; worked for father's food distribution co. (supplying produce for Japanese P.O.W.s in British Malaya) 1945–48, f. (with other family mems.) Kuok Brothers co. 1948, moved business to Singapore and began sugar trade 1953, built first sugar refinery in Singapore, also trading in sugar futures, palm oil; built first of chain of Shangri-La hotels in Singapore early 1970s; acquired real estate in Malaysia, Singapore and China throughout the 1970s and 1980s; now Head Kerry Group (Hong Kong) with holdings in South-East Asia, People's Repub. of China, Australia and Canada; acquired holding in TV Broadcasts Ltd. (Hong Kong) 1988, majority shareholding in Coca-Cola plant in China 1993, controlling share of South China Morning Post newspaper 1993 (Chair. South China Morning Post Publrs. 1993–97); also owns significant shareholding in Citic Pacific, Chinese Govt.'s overseas conglomerate; est. several charitable foundations. *Address:* c/o Malayan Sugar Manufacturing Company, 18th Floor, Wisma Jerneh, 38 Jalan Sultan Ismail, 50250 Kuala Lumpur, Malaysia; c/o Kerry Group, 344 Bank of China Tower, 1st Garden Road, Hong Kong Special Administrative Region, People's Republic of China.

KUO WAN-RONG; Chinese politician; ed. Massachusetts Inst. of Tech.; fmrly. Minister of Finance; mem. Kuomintang Cen. Standing Cttee. 1994–. *Address:* c/o Ministry of Finance, 2 Ai Kuo West Road, Taipei, Taiwan.

KUO WEI-FAN, DR., M.ED.; Chinese politician and educationalist; b. 3 Sept. 1937, Tainan City; m. Mei-Ho L. Kuo 1969; one s. one d.; ed. Provincial Taiwan Normal Univ. and Univ. of Paris; Assoc. Prof. Grad. Inst. of Educ., Nat. Taiwan Normal Univ. 1967–70, Prof. 1970–72, 1977–78, Dir. 1978, Pres. Nat. Taiwan Normal Univ. 1978–84; Admin. Vice-Minister of Educ. 1972–77; Pres. Chinese Asscn. of Special Educ. 1973–75, 1979–81, Chinese Asscn. of Comparative Educ. 1981–82, 1993–; Minister of State 1984–88, 1993; Chair. Council of Cultural Planning and Devt. 1988–93; Pres. Chinese Educ. Soc. 1985–87. *Leisure interests:* table tennis, tennis, music.

KUPA, Mihály, PH.D.; Hungarian economist; b. 3 April 1941, Budapest; worker Chinoin Pharmaceutical Works 1959–69; on staff of Cen. Office of Statistics 1969–74; Dept. Dir. Finance Research Inst. 1976–84; Ministry of Finance dept. of tax and state budget reform 1984–90; Minister of Finance 1990–93. *Address:* c/o Ministry of Finance, 1051 Budapest, József Nádor tér 2/4 Hungary.

KUPISZEWSKI, Henryk; Polish diplomatist; b. 13 Jan. 1927, Książnice Wielkie; ed. Jagiellonian Univ., Cracow, Münster Univ.; Dir. Inst. of Greek and Roman Law and Papyrology, Warsaw Univ. 1974–80, deputy rector 1981–82; Prof. of Roman and Hellenic law, Acad. of Catholic Theology, Warsaw 1960–90; assoc. mem. of many scientific insts.; Amb. to the Vatican 1990; mem. many Polish and foreign academic socs. *Publications:* author of over 100 publs. in various languages. *Address:* c/o Ministry of Foreign Affairs, Al. Szucha 23, 00-580 Warsaw, Poland.

KUPTSOV, Valentin Aleksandrovich; Russian politician; b. 4 Dec. 1937, Vologda Dist.; ed. Northwestern Polytechnic Inst.; mem. CPSU 1966–91; army service 1956–58; truck driver, shop-master Cherepovets Metallurgical Factory (Vologda Dist.) 1958–68; Sec., shop party cttee. at same factory 1967–68; worked on installation of rolling mill in E. Czechoslovakia 1968; deputy sec. of shop party cttee. 1968–74; Second Sec. Cherepovets City Cttee. (Vologda Dist.) 1974–76, First Sec. 1976–79; First Sec. Vologda City Cttee. 1979–84; Second Sec. Vologda Dist. Cttee. (obkom) 1984–85, First Sec. –91; CPSU Cen. Cttee. Inspector 1985; First Sec. CP R.S.F.S.R. Cen. Cttee. July–Sept. 1991; mem. CPSU Cen. Cttee. 1986–91; U.S.S.R. Supreme Soviet Deputy 1986–89; U.S.S.R. People's Deputy 1989–91, Leader Russian CP 1991, Rep. Russian CP at Constitutional Court Trial 1992; mem. Bd., Deputy Chair. CP of Russian Fed. 1992–95, Head of Staff 1993–; mem State Duma (Parl.) 1995–. *Address:* Communist Party of Russian Federation, Bolshoi Zlatoustinsky per. 8/7, 10100 Moscow, Russia. *Telephone:* 206-87-89 (Party); 292-15-80 (Dama).

KURATA, Hiroyuki; Japanese politician; fmr. Parl. Vice-Minister of Int. Trade and Industry; Minister of Home Affairs Jan.–Oct. 1996; mem. House of Councillors; mem. LDP. *Address:* Ministry of Home Affairs, 2-1-2, Kasumigaseki, Chiyoda-ku, Tokyo 100, Japan. *Telephone:* (3) 3581-5311. *Fax:* (3) 3593-3758.

KUREISHI, Hanif; British author; b. 1954, Bromley; ed. King's Coll. London; worked as typist at Riverside Studios; Thames TV Playwright Award for first full-length play The Mother Country 1980; writer-in-residence, Royal Court Theatre, London 1981. *Stage plays include:* Birds of Passage (Hampstead), Outskirts (RSC), Borderline (Royal Court), adaptation of Brecht's Mother Courage (RSC). *Screenplays:* My Beautiful Laundrette 1986 (winner of Evening Standard Best Film Award 1986 and New York Critics' Best Screenplay Award 1987), Sammy and Rosie Get Laid 1988, London Kills Me (also directed) 1991. *Publications:* The Rainbow Sign (autobiography) 1986, The Buddha of Suburbia (novel) 1990, London Kills Me 1991, Eight Arms to Hold You (essay) 1991, The Black Album (novel) 1995, Love in a Blue Time (stories) 1997, My Son the Fanatic 1997, Intimacy (novel) 1998, Sleep with Me (play) 1998; ed. (jtly.) The Faber Book of Pop 1995; stories in Granta, Harpers (U.S.A.), London Review of Books and The Atlantic; regular contribs. to New Statesman and Society. *Leisure interests:* jazz, cricket. *Address:* c/o Deborah Rogers Ltd., 20 Powis Mews, London, W11 1SN, England.

KUROKAWA, Kisho, M.TECH.; Japanese architect; b. 8 April 1934, Aichi Prefecture; s. of Miki and Ineko Kurokawa; m. Ayako Wakao; one s. one d.; ed. Kyoto and Tokyo Univs.; Pres. Kisho Kurokawa Architect & Assocs.; Chair. Urban Design Consultants Inc.; Adviser, Int. Design Conf. in Aspen, U.S.A.; Prin. Inst. of Social Eng.; Adviser, Ministry of Construction; Analyst, Japan Broadcasting Corpn.; mem. numerous govt. cttees., Japan Inst. Architects, City Planning Inst. of Japan, Japan Architects' Asscn.; Life Fellow, Royal Soc. of Arts; Hon. Fellow, A.I.A., R.I.B.A.; Hon. Prof., Univ. of Buenos Aires; Visiting Prof. Tsinghua Univ., Beijing 1986; awarded The Madara, Bulgarian First Order 1979; Commandeur de l'Ordre de Lion de Finlande 1985; Gold Medal French Acad. of Architecture; Takamura Kotaro Design Prize and prizes in int. competitions in Peru, France, Fed. Repub. of Germany, Tanzania and Bulgaria, prize for conference city, Abu Dhabi, U.A.E. 1976, for Univ. New Town, Al Ain, U.A.E.; Chevalier de l'Ordre des Arts et Lettres, Ministry of Culture, France 1989, 1st Prize Osaka Pref. Govt. HQ (Nat. Competition) 1989, Prize of Japan Art Academy 1992; Grand Prix with Gold Medal for Hiroshima Museum at Sofia Biennale 1989, and numerous Japanese architectural awards. *Works include:* Nitto Food Co. 1963, Cen. Lodge in Nat. Childrens Land 1964, Hans Christian Andersen Memorial Lodge 1964, Sagae City Hall 1967, Odakyu Rest House 1969, Takara, Toshiba and Theme Pavilions, Expo 1970, Nakagin Capsule Tower 1972, Head Offices of Fukuoka Bank 1975, Sony Tower 1976, Sports Centre, Italy, Fujisawa New Town 1976, Ishikawa Cultural Centre 1977, Head Office, Japanese Red Cross Society 1977, Nat. Ethnology Museum 1977, Kumamoto Municipal Museum 1978, Daido Insurance Bldg., Tokyo 1978, Hotel Vitostia the New Otani, Sofia, Bulgaria 1979, Shoto Club, Tokyo 1980, Fukuoka Prefectural Governmental Headquarters 1981, Suginami Ward Cen. Library, Tokyo 1982, Saitama Pref. Museum of Modern Art 1982, Nat. Bunraku Theatre 1983, Kanagawa Citizens' Mutual Aid Asscn. Bldg., Yokohama 1983, Wacoal Kojimachi Bldg., Tokyo, Roppongi Prince Hotel, Tokyo, Pavilions of IBM Japan, Toshiba, Mitsui, Foreign Reps., Electric Power 1984, Yasuda Fire Insurance Bldg., Automobile Mfrs.' Asscn. at Tsukuba Int. Science Exposition 1985, Yoshiundo Bldg. 1985, Koshi Kaikan Centre 1986, Nagoya City Art Museum 1987, Central Plaza 1 and 2, Brisbane 1988, Hiroshima City Museum of Contemporary Art 1988, Japanese-German Centre of Berlin 1988, Lotte World, Seoul 1989, Chinese-Japanese Youth Centre, Beijing 1990, Melbourne Centre, Australia 1991, Nara City Museum of Photography 1992, Pacific Tower, Paris la Défense 1992. *Works in progress include:* Le Colisée, Nîmes, France, Repub. Plaza Singapore, Osaka Pref. Govt. HQ, Japan. *Publications include:* Prefabricated House, Metabolism 1960 1960, Urban Design 1964, Action Architecture 1967, Homo-Movens 1969, Architectural Creation 1969, The Work of Kisho Kurokawa 1970, Creating Contemporary Architecture 1971, Conception of Metabolism, In the Realm of the Future 1972, The Archipelago of Information: The Future Japan 1972, Introduction to Urbanism 1973, Metabolism in Architecture, 1977, A Culture of Grays 1977, Concept of Space 1977, Concept of Cities 1977, Architecture and Design 1982, Thesis on Architecture 1982, A Cross Section of Japan 1983, Architecture of the Street 1983, Landscapes under the Road 1984, Prospective Dialogues for the 21st Century, Vols. 1–3 1985, Philosophy of Symbiosis 1987, Rediscovering Japanese Space 1989, The Era of Nomad (Japanese) 1989, Intercultural Architecture 1991, Kisho Kurokawa—From Metabolism to Symbiosis 1992, The New Wave of Japanese Architecture 1993. *Leisure interest:* photography. *Address:* Aoyama Bldg. 11f., 1-2-3 Kita Aoyama, Minato-ku, Tokyo, Japan. *Telephone:* 81-3-3404-3481. *Fax:* 81-3-3404-6222.

KUROKAWA, Takeshi, B.A.; Japanese trade unionist; b. 1 April 1928, Gunma Pref.; one s. one d.; ed. Chuo Univ.; Pres. Gen. Fed. of Pvt. Railway Workers' Union (Shitetsu Soren) 1980–88, Adviser 1988–; Vice-Pres. SOHYO 1980–83, Pres. 1983–. *Leisure interest:* reading. *Address:* 3-2-11 Kanda Surugadai, Chiyoda-ku, Tokyo, Japan. *Telephone:* (03) 251-0311.

KUROŃ, Jacek Jan, M.A.; Polish politician, historian and publicist; b. 3 March 1934, Lvov; m.; one s.; ed. Warsaw Univ.; mem. Polish United Workers' Party (PZPR) March–Nov. 1953, 1956–64; mem. Chief Council of Polish Pathfinders' Union 1956; Assoc. workers' councils of Żerań and participant revival movt. at Warsaw Univ. 1956; teacher, Fine Arts Lycée, Warsaw 1957; Assoc. Na Przełaj (weekly) and Drużyna 1957–61; arrested 1964 and sentenced to three years' imprisonment for writing Open Letter to PZPR mems.; arrested March 1968 and sentenced to 3½ years; co-f. illegal Cttee. for Defence of Workers (KOR) 1976–81; lecturer, Scientific Courses Soc. 1978–89; mem. Solidarity Ind. Self-governing Trade Union 1980–91, adviser to Solidarity Interfactory Founding Cttee., Gdańsk, then to Nat. Understanding Comm. and Nat. Comm. of Solidarity Trade Union 1980–81; interned 1981–82, indicted on a charge of attempt of subverting a political system Sept. 1982, released under amnesty Aug. 1984; mem. Civic Cttee. attached to Lech Wałęsa, Chair. of Solidarity Trade Union 1988–90; participant Round Table plenary debates, mem. group for political reforms Feb.–April 1989; Deputy to Sejm (Parl.) 1989–, Chair. Sejm Comm. for Nat. and Ethnic Minorities 1993–97, Deputy Chair. Civic Parl. Club 1989–90; Democratic Union Parl. Club 1990–93, Freedom Union Parl. Club 1994–; Minister of Labour and Social Policy 1989–91, 1992–93; mem. Democratic Union 1991–94, Freedom Union 1994–; Chair. S.O.S. Foundation; Dr. h.c. (Emory Univ.) 1990. *Publications:* Uwaga Zespół 1961, Polityka i odpowiedzialność (Politics and Responsibility) 1984, Zło, które czynię (The Evil I Do) 1984, Zdobyć milczącą większość (To gain the Silent Majority) 1988, Wiara i wina (Faith and Fault, autobiography, part 1) 1990, Moja zupa 1991, Gwiezdny czas (autobiog., part 2) 1991. *Address:* ul. Mickiewicza 27 m. 64, 01-562 Warsaw, Poland. *Telephone:* (22) 694 21 35 (Office).

KUROSAWA, Yoh, LL.B.; Japanese banker; ed. Univ. of Tokyo and Harvard Business School; joined Industrial Bank of Japan (IBJ) 1950; seconded to Deutsche Bank 1961–63; Chief rep. of IBJ, Frankfurt am Main 1966–71; Gen. Man. Int. Dept. IBJ 1975; Pres. IBJ 1991–96, Chair. Bd. of Dirs. 1996–. *Address:* Industrial Bank of Japan, 3-3, Marunouchi 1-chome, Chiyoda-ku, Tokyo 100, Japan. *Telephone:* (03) 3214-1111.

KUROYANAGI, Tetsuko, B.A.; Japanese actress; b. 9 Aug. 1933, Tokyo; d. of Moritsuna Kuroyanagi and Cho Kuronyanagi; ed. Tokyo Coll. of Music; theatrical training at Bungakuza Theatre, Tokyo and Mary Tarcai Studio, New York; TV debut with Japan Broadcasting Corpn. (NHK) 1954; host,

Tetsuko's Room (TV chat show), Asahi Nat. Broadcasting Co. 1976–94; regular guest, Discover Wonders of the World (quiz show), Tokyo Broadcasting System 1987–; numerous stage appearances throughout Japan; founder and Pres. Totto Foundation (for training of deaf actors) 1981–; Trustee, World Wide Fund for Nature, Japan 1977–; UNICEF Goodwill Amb. 1984–; Dir. Chihiro Iwasaki Art, Music and Picture Books 1995–; Minister of Foreign Affairs Award, etc. *Publications:* From New York With Love 1972, Totto-Chan: The Little Girl at the Window 1981, Animal Theatre (photographic essay) 1983, Totto-channel 1984, My Friends 1986. *Leisure interests:* travel, calligraphy, study of giant pandas. *Address:* Yoshida Naomi Office, No. 2 Tanizawa Building, 4th Floor, 3-2-11 Nishi-Azabu, Minato-ku, Tokyo 106, Japan. *Telephone:* 3403-9296. *Fax:* 3403-5322.

KURSANOV, Andrey Lvovich, SC.D.; Russian plant physiologist; b. 8 Nov. 1902, Moscow; s. of Lev. I. Kursanov and Ljubov V. Kursanova; m. 1928; one d.; ed. Moscow Univ. Cen. Inst. of Sugar Industry 1929–34; A. N. Bakh Inst. of Biochem. 1934–54; Dir. K. A. Timiriazev Inst. of Plant Physiology and Head of Lab. of Translocation of Substances 1952–88, Hon. Dir. 1988–; mem. U.S.S.R. (now Russian) Acad. of Sciences 1953, Acad. of Agric. 1985, Leopoldina German Acad. of Natural Science 1958, Acad. of Agric. of France 1964; foreign mem. Polish Acad. of Sciences; Hon. mem. German Botanical Soc. 1961, American Acad. of Arts and Sciences 1962; M.V. Lomonosov Gold Medal, U.S.S.R. Acad. of Sciences 1984, Gold Medal of Czechoslovak Acad. of Science 1982; Hero of Socialist Labour 1969, Order of Lenin (four times), Red Banner of Labour (twice), Commdr. Ordre de Léopold II (Belgium). *Publications:* The Reversible Action of Enzymes in Living Plant Cells 1940, Synthesis and Transformation of the Tannins in Tea Leaves 1953, In France and W. Africa 1956, The Root System as an Organ of Metabolism 1957, The Interaction of Physiological Processes in Plants 1960, Metabolism and the Transport of Organic Substances in the Phloem 1963, Competition of Sugars for Penetrations into Cells 1964, Biochemical basis of transport and accumulation of Sucrose in the Sugarbeet plant, Translocations of Assimilates in the Plant (monograph) 1976, Scientist and Auditorium 1982, Assimilate Transport in Plants 1984. *Leisure interests:* fishing, boating. *Address:* K. A. Timiriazev Plant Physiology Institute, Academy of Sciences, 35 Botanicheskaya, 127276 Moscow, Russia. *Telephone:* 482-51-36 (Office), 237-27-67 (Home).

KURTÁG, György; Hungarian composer; b. 19 Feb. 1926, Lugos; ed. Franz Liszt Music Acad., Budapest and in Paris; Prof. of Chamber Music, Franz Liszt Acad. of Music, Budapest 1967–86; Composer in residence Wissenschaftskolleg zu Berlin 1993–95, Wiener Konzerthaus, Vienna 1995–96; mem. Bayerische Akademie der Schönen Künste, Munich 1987, Akademie der Künste, Berlin 1987; Herder Prize, Hamburg 1993, Feltrinelli Prize, Accademia dei Lincei, Italy 1993, Austrian State Award for European Composers 1994, Denis de Rougemont Prize 1994; Officier des Arts et des Lettres. *Compositions include:* Viola Concerto 1954, String Quartet 1959, Wind Quintet 1959, The Sayings of Péter Bornemissza 1963–68, Hommage à Mihály András 1977, Bagatelles 1981, Scenes from a Novel 1981–82, Three Old Inscriptions 1967–86, Kafka-Fragmente 1985–87, Requiem for the Beloved 1982–87, Officium breve in memoriam Andreae Szervánszky 1988–89, Ligatura—Message to Frances-Marie 1989, Hommage à R. Sch. 1990, Transcriptions from Machaut to Bach 1974–91, Attila József Fragments 1981, Three in memoriam 1988–90, Games, two series, Beads 1994, Omaggio a Luigi Nono 1979, eight Choruses 1981–82, Songs of Despondency and Grief 1980–94, Inscriptions on a grave in Cornwall 1994, Rückblick (Altes und Neues für vier Spieler, Hommage à Stockhausen) 1986, Three Songs to poems by János Pilinszky 1986, Mémoire de Laïka 1990, Curriculum Vitae 1992, Messages of the Late Miss R. V. Troussova, Grabstein für Stephan, . . . quasi una fantasia . . ., Double Concerto, Samuel Beckett: What is the Word Stele. *Address:* Lihegő v.3, H-2621 Verőce; Liszt Ferenc tér 9.I.6, H-1061 Budapest, Hungary. *Telephone:* 36-27-350-177; 36-1-121 3994.

KUSAKABE, Etsuji; Japanese business executive; b. 31 Oct. 1923, Hyogo Pref.; s. of Yasutaro and Hisae Kusakabe; m. Masako Yoshikawa 1949; two s.; ed. Kyoto Univ.; Dir. The Furukawa Electric Co. Ltd. 1972, Man. Dir. 1975, Sr. Man. Dir. 1977, Vice-Pres. 1982, Pres. 1983–89, Chair. June 1989–. *Leisure interest:* golf. *Address:* The Furukawa Electric Co. Ltd., 6-1, Marunouchi 2-chome, Chiyoda-ku, Tokyo 100, Japan. *Telephone:* 03 (286) 3011.

KUSAKIN, Oleg Grigoryevich; Russian zoologist and hydrobiologist; b. 12 July 1930, Leningrad; s. of Gregor P. Kussakin and Eugenia A. Kussakina; m. Alla P. Kassatkina 1960; one s.; ed. Leningrad State Univ., jr. researcher Zool Inst.; asst. of Chair, Leningrad State Univ., Prof. Far E. State Univ. in Vladivostok; head of lab. Inst. of Marine Biology, Far E. br. U.S.S.R. Acad. of Sciences; corresp. mem. U.S.S.R. (now Russian) Acad. of Sciences 1990, mem. 1994; mem. American Crustacean Soc. *Publications include:* books and numerous articles on isopod taxonomy, intertidal ecology, megataxonomy and biogeography of ocean in scientific journals. *Leisure interests:* poetry, ancient history, ethnology. *Address:* Institute of Biology of the Sea, Far East Branch of Russian Academy of Sciences, Palchevskogo str. 17, 690041 Vladivostok, Russia. *Telephone:* (4232) 31-09-21 (Office); (4232) 25-97-67 (Home). *Fax:* (4232) 31-09-00.

KUSHNER, Aleksandr Semyonovich; Russian poet; b. 14 Sept. 1936, Leningrad; s. of Semyon Semyonovich Kushner and Asya Aleksandrovna Kushner; m. Elena Vsevolodavna Nevzglyadova 1981; one s.; ed. Leningrad Pedagogical Inst.; lecturer in literature 1959–69. *Publications include:* First Impression 1962, Night Watch 1966, Omens 1969, Letter 1974, Direct Speech 1975, Voice 1978, Canvas 1981, The Tavrichesky Garden 1984, Daydreams 1986, Poems 1986 (Selected Poems), The Hedgerow 1988, A Night Melody 1991, Apollo in the Snow (selected essays on Russian literature of the nineteenth and twentieth centuries and personal memoirs) 1991, Apollo in the Snow (selected poems trans. into English) 1991, On the Gloomy Star 1994 (State Prize 1995), Selected Poetry 1997, essays in literary journals. *Leisure interests:* reading, world painting. *Address:* Kaluzhsky pereulok No. 9, Apt. 48, 193015 St. Petersburg, Russia. *Telephone:* (812) 271-98-45.

KUSHNER, Eva, O.C., PH.D., F.R.S.C.; Canadian professor of French; b. 18 June 1929, Prague, Czechoslovakia; d. of late Josef Dubsky and Anna Dubsky-Cahill (née Kafka); m. Donn J. Kushner 1949; three s.; ed. McGill Univ., Montreal; Prof. Carleton Univ. 1961–76; Prof. McGill Univ. 1976–87, Chair. French Dept. 1976–80; Prof., Pres. Vic. Univ. 1987–94; Dir., Comparative Literature, Univ. of Toronto 1994–95; Vice-Pres. Int. Fed. for Modern Languages and Literatures 1987–93, Pres. 1996–; Vice-Pres. R.S.C. 1980–82; Hon. Lit.D. (Acadia Univ.) 1988, Hon. D.D. (United Theological Coll., Montreal) 1992, Hon. D.Litt. (Univ. of St. Michael's Coll.) 1993, (Univ. of Western Ont.) 1996; *Publications:* Patrice de la Tour du Pin 1961, Le Mythe d'Orphée dans la littérature française contemporaine 1961, Chants de Bohême 1963, Rina Lasnier 1967, Saint-Denys Garneau 1967, François Mauriac 1972, Théorie littéraire: problèmes et perspectives (co-author) 1989, La problématique du sujet chez Montaigne (co-author) 1995, Histoire des poetiques 1997. *Leisure interests:* reading, swimming, travel, writing. *Address:* Victoria University, 73 Queen's Park, Toronto, Ont., M5S 1K7 (Office); 63 Albany Avenue, Toronto, Ont. M5R 3C2, Canada (Home). *Telephone:* (416) 585-4592 (Office); (416) 538-0173 (Home).

KUSHNER, Robert Ellis, B.A.; American artist; b. 19 Aug. 1949, Pasadena, Calif.; s. of Joseph Kushner and Dorothy Browdy; m. Ellen Saltonstall 1978; two s. one d.; ed. Univ. of Calif. San Diego; one-man shows include: Holly Solomon Gallery, New York 1976, 1979, 1980, 1982, 1985, 1987, 1989, Michael Lord Gallery, Milwaukee 1988, 1989, 1990, Gallery Rudolf Swirner, Cologne 1982, 1986, Univ. of Colo. Art Gallery, Boulder 1982, American Graffiti Gallery, Amsterdam 1982, Studio Marconi, Milan 1982, Castelli-Goodman-Solomon, East Hampton, New York, 1982, Whitney Museum 1985, ICA, Philadelphia 1987–88, J.B. Speed Art Museum, Louisville 1988, Aspen Art Museum, Colo. 1988, Wichita Art Museum 1989, Staller Art Center, State Univ. of N.Y. Stony Brook 1990, Irving Gallery, Palm Beach 1990, First Gallery, Moscow 1991, Sydney Art Museum 1992, Yoshiaki Inoue Gallery, Osaka 1992, 1994, David Floria Gallery, Aspen 1995, D. C. Moore Gallery, N.Y. 1997, 1998, Hiroshima Prefectural Museum 1997; has participated in numerous group shows at Whitney Museum and Museum of Modern Art, New York etc.; Venice Biennale 1980, 1984; works represented in maj. permanent collections in U.S.A., Tate Gallery, London etc. *Address:* D. C. Moore Gallery, 724 Fifth Avenue, New York, NY 10019, U.S.A.

KUSHNER, Tony; American playwright; b. New York; ed. Columbia Univ., New York Univ.; Tony Award, Critics' Circle Award, London Evening Standard Award, Pulitzer Prize for Angels in America (part one). *Publications:* Actors on Acting 1986, A Bright Room called Day 1990, Millennium Approaches (part one of Angels in America) 1992, Perestroika (part two) 1993, Slavs! 1994, Thinking about the Longstanding Problems of Virtue and Happiness 1995. *Address:* c/o Joyce Ketay, The Joyce Ketay Agency, 1501 Broadway, Suite 1910, New York, NY 10036, U.S.A.

KÜSS, René; French surgeon and academic; b. 3 May 1913, Paris; s. of the late Georges Küss and of Elise-Jeanne Amos; m. Josette Beneteau 1958, four d.; ed. Lycée Janson-de-Sailly and Univ. of Paris; surgeon in Paris hosps. 1950–; Prof. at Faculty of Medicine, Paris 1964–88; Prof. of Urology, La Pitié-la Salpêtrière Coll. of Educ. and Research; Chair. and Founder, Société française de transplantation 1972; Chair. Int. Urological Soc. 1979–88; mem. Académie de chirurgie 1964; mem. Académie nationale de médecine 1979; Commdr., Légion d'honneur, Commandeur, Ordre nat. du Mérite, Croix de guerre 1939–45. *Leisure interest:* painting. *Address:* 63 ave. Niel, 75017 Paris, France.

KUSTURICA, Emir; Bosnian film director; ed. FAMU School, Prague; teacher Columbia Univ. *Films:* Do You Remember Dolly Bell? (Golden Lion Award, Venice 1981), Time of the Gipsies (Best Dir., Cannes), When Father Was Away On Business (Palme d'Or, Cannes 1984), Arizona Dream (Special Jury Prize, Berlin 1993), Underground (Palme d'Or, Cannes 1995); lives abroad.

KUSUMAATMADJA, Mochtar, LL.D.; Indonesian politician; b. Feb. 1929, Jakarta; ed. Univ. of Indonesia, Yale and Harvard Law Schools and Univ. of Chicago Law School; Minister of Justice 1974–77; Acting Foreign Minister 1977–78, then Minister of Foreign Affairs 1978–88, fmr. Head of of UN Comm. responsible for the demarcation of the Iraq-Kuwait Border, resgnd. 1992; Indonesian rep. at Law of the Sea Conference, Geneva, and at Seabed Cttee. sessions, New York; involvement in numerous int. orgs. *Address:* c/o Ministry of Foreign Affairs, Jalan Taman Pejambon 6, Jakarta, Indonesia.

KUTAKOV, Leonid Nikolayevich, PH.D.; Russian diplomatist (retd.); b. 6 Nov. 1919, Moscow; m. Aza Tucanova 1960; one s. one d.; ed. Moscow Inst. of History, Philosophy and Literature; Soviet Army, Second World War;

Chief of Historical Diplomatic Div., Ministry of Foreign Affairs 1946–51; Pro-Rector Moscow State Inst. of Int. Relations 1952–55; Adviser to Dir. of Peking Inst. of Diplomacy, Chinese Ministry of Foreign Affairs 1955–57; Counsellor, Soviet Embassy, Japan 1957–59; Deputy Dir. Inst. of History of Acad. of Sciences of U.S.S.R. 1961–63; Rector, Moscow State Inst. of Int. Relations 1963–65; Sr. Counsellor for Political Questions, Perm. Soviet Mission to UN 1965–68; Under Sec.-Gen. for Political and Security Council Affairs, UN Secr. 1968–73; mem. Exec. Bd. UNESCO 1974–78. *Publications:* A New History of International Relations 1918–45 1958, History of Soviet-Japanese Diplomatic Relations 1962, The Portsmouth Peace Treaty 1905 1961, Foreign Policy and Diplomacy of Japan 1964, Japanese Foreign Policy on the Eve of the Pacific War 1972, History of International Relations and Foreign Policy 1917–73, 1975, View from the 35th Floor 1975, From Beijing to New York 1983, Russia and Japan 1988, Moscow and Tokyo: Outline of Diplomatic Relations 1988, Leaders and Diplomats 1995. *Address:* Frunzenskaya nab. 28, Apt. 96, 119146 Moscow, Russia. *Telephone:* 242-26-20.

KUTZ, Kazimierz; Polish film and theatrical director; b. 16 Feb. 1929, Szopienice; m.; two s. two d.; ed. Łódź Higher Film School 1953; Senator 1997–. *Films include:* Krzyż Walecznych 1959, Nikt nie woła 1960, Sól ziemi czarnej 1969, Perła w koronie 1970, Linię 1975, Paciorki jednego różańca 1976, Na straży swej stać będę 1983, Śmierć jak kromka chleba 1994, Pułkownik Kwiatkowski 1995. *Address:* ul. Marconich 5 m. 6, 02-954 Warsaw, Poland. *Telephone:* (22) 840 92 59.

KUWABARA, Takeo, B.A.; Japanese writer; b. 10 May 1904, Turuga; s. of Jitsuzo Kuwabara and Shin Uta; m. Tazu Tanaka 1933; one s. five d.; ed. Kyoto Univ.; Lecturer Kyoto Univ. 1931–42; Asst. Prof. Tohoku Univ. 1943–48; Prof. Kyoto Univ. 1948–68, Emer. Prof. 1968–; Dir. Univ. Inst. of Humanistic Studies 1959–63; mem. Science Council of Japan 1951–71, Vice-Pres. 1960–71; Vice-Pres. Japan PEN Club 1974–75, 1981–85; mem. Japanese Acad. of Arts 1977; Man of Cultural Merits (govt. award) 1979. *Publications:* Fiction and Reality 1943, Reflections on Contemporary Japanese Culture 1947, Some Aspects of Contemporary French Literature 1949, Introduction to Literature 1950, Conquest of Mount Chogolisa 1959, Studies on J.-J. Rousseau 1951, Studies on the Encyclopédie 1954, Studies on the French Revolution 1959, Studies on Chomin Nakae 1966, European Civilization and Japan 1974, Selected Works (in 10 vols.) 1980-81. *Leisure interest:* mountaineering. *Address:* 421, Tonodan-Yabunosita, Kamikyo-ku, Kyoto, 602 Japan. *Telephone:* 231-0261.

KUWAIT, H.H. The Ruler of (see Sabah, Sheikh Jaber al-Ahmad al-Jaber al-).

KUWAIZ, Abdullah Ibrahim el, M.A., M.B.A., PH.D.; Saudi politician and international official; b. 1939; two s. two d.; ed. Pacific Lutheran Univ., U.S.A., St. Louis Univ., U.S.A.; Accountant, Pensions Dept. 1959–67, Economist, Ministry of Finance and Nat. Economy 1967–81 (Adviser 1977–81); Exec. Dir. Arab Monetary Fund, Abu Dhabi 1977–83; Co-Chair. Financial Co-operation Cttee., Euro-Arab Dialogue 1978–83; Asst. Under-Sec. for Econ. Affairs 1981–87; Deputy Minister of Finance and Nat. Economy, Saudi Arabia 1987–; Dir.-Gen. 1987, Chair. of Bd. Arab Monetary Fund, Abu Dhabi 1987; Asst. Sec.-Gen. for Econ. Affairs, Co-operation Council for the Arab States of the Gulf 1981–; mem. of Bd. and mem. Exec. Cttee., Gulf Int. Bank, Bahrain 1977–; mem. of Bd. Gulf Co-operation Council's Org. for Measures and Standards 1984–, Oxford Energy Inst., Oxford, U.K. 1985–, Int. Maritime Bureau, London 1985–88. *Publications:* numerous papers relating to oil affairs and econ. devt. delivered at symposia in N. America, Europe and the Middle East. *Address:* Gulf Co-operation Council for Arab States, P.O. Box 7153, Riyadh 11462, Saudi Arabia. *Telephone:* 4827777.

KUZMIN, Aleksander Viktorovich; Russian architect; b. 12 July 1951, Moscow; s. of Victor Alexandrovich Kouzmine and Antonina Alexeevna Kouzmine; m. 1996; one s. one d.; ed. Moscow Inst. of Architecture; researcher Research and Project Inst. of the Gen. Plan of Moscow, Dir. 1987–; Deputy Head, Chief Moscow Dept. of Architecture 1991, First Deputy Chair. Moscow Cttee. of Architecture; elected Chief Architect of Moscow 1996, Chair. Chief Moscow Dept. of Architecture. *Leisure interest:* collecting old medals. *Address:* Moscow Committee of Architecture, Triumphalnaya pl.1, 125047 Moscow, Russia (Office). *Telephone:* (095) 250 5520 (Office). *Fax:* (095) 250 2051 (Office).

KUZMIN, Leonid Filippovich; Russian diplomatist (retd.); b. 28 March 1930, Kiev; m.; two s.; ed. Moscow Inst. of Int. Relations; fmr. mem. CPSU; on staff, Ministry of Foreign Relations 1952–; counsellor, U.S.S.R. Embassy to Brazil 1968–73; Deputy Chief Latin American Dept., U.S.S.R. Ministry of Foreign Affairs 1973–75; Amb. to Peru 1975–83; Head Second Latin American Dept. 1986–88; Amb. to Brazil 1988–93. *Address:* c/o Foreign Ministry, Sadovaya-Seunaya 32-34, Moscow, Russia.

KUZMUK, Col.-Gen. Aleksander Ivanovich; Ukrainian military officer; b. 17 April 1954, Dyagilevka, Khmelnitsk Region, Ukraine; m.; two c.; ed. Kharkov Guards' Higher Tank School; Moscow Mil. Acad. of Tank Troops; commdr. tank co., platoon, bn.; deputy commdr. regt., Group of Soviet Troops in Germany 1975–83; commdg. posts in Leningrad, Carpathian, Odessa Mil. commands 1983–95; Commdr. Nat. Guards of Ukraine 1995–96; Minister of Defence 1996–. *Address:* Ministry of Defence, Bankova str. 6, 252005 Kiev, Ukraine (Office). *Telephone:* (044) 226-26-56.

KUZNETSOV, Boris Avramovich; Russian barrister; b. 19 March 1944, Kirov; s. of Avram Mikhailovich Kuznetsov and Nina Aleksandrovna Ukhanova; m. 2nd Chernaya Nadezhda Georgiyevna, two c.; ed. Moscow Juridical Acad., Research Inst. U.S.S.R. Ministry of Internal Affairs; on staff Criminal Investigation Dept. St. Petersburg and Magadan Region 1962–82; mem. Magadan Regional Bd. of Lawyers 1982–85, twice expelled for disagreement with party officials; Head of Lab. Inst. of Biology Problems of the N. br. U.S.S.R. Acad. of Sciences, Magadan 1985–89; advisor to mems. Inter-regional people's deputy 1989–91; mem. St. Petersburg Bd. of Lawyers 1991–95; mem. Lawyers' Interrepub. Bd. 1995–; Head Boris Kuznetsov and Partners Lawyer's Agency. *Address:* Boris Kuznetsov and Partners, Vozdvizhenka 4/7, P.O. Box 10, 121205 Moscow, Russia (Office). *Telephone:* (095) 202 7515 (Office). *Fax:* (095) 202 9845 (Office).

KUZNETSOV, Fedor Andreyevich; Russian chemist; b. 12 July 1932; m.; two c.; ed. Leningrad State Univ.; army engineer 1955–58; researcher, head of lab., Deputy Dir., Inst. of Inorganic Chem., Siberian br. U.S.S.R. (now Russian) Acad. of Sciences 1961–83, Dir. 1983–; corresp. mem., U.S.S.R. (now Russian) Acad. of Sciences 1984, mem. 1987–; main research in synthesis and studies of inorganic materials; Foreign mem. American Electro-Chemical Soc.; U.S.S.R. State Prize 1981; N. Kurnakov Medal. *Address:* Institute of Inorganic Chemistry, Akademika Lavrentyev prosp. 3, 630090 Novosibirsk, Russia. *Telephone:* (3832) 135 5950 (Office).

KUZNETSOV, Ivan Andreyevich; Russian diplomatist (retd.); b. 27 July 1937; ed. Moscow State Inst. of Int. Relations; with U.S.S.R. Ministry of Foreign Affairs 1966; Embassy, London 1966–70; mem. Gen. Consulates San Franciso 1973–76, New York 1976–79; Gen. Consul of U.S.S.R. (later Russia) in New York 1990–96; Deputy Minister of Foreign Affairs 1996–97. *Address:* Ministry of Foreign Affairs, Smolenskaya-Sennaya 32/34, Moscow, Russia.

KUZNETSOV, Col.-Gen. Leonty Vasilievich; Russian army officer; b. 13 Aug. 1938, Arkadak, Sverdlovsk Region; m.; two d.; ed. Frunze Mil. Acad., U.S.S.R. Gen. Staff Acad.; commdr. of platoon, bn., Div., army; Head of Staff Moscow mil. command 1988–90, 1992–95, C.-in-C. 1995–; Chief Operations Dept. of Gen. Staff 1990–92. *Address:* Moscow Military Command, Sadovnicheskaya str. 53, 113035 Moscow, Russia. *Telephone:* (095) 271-7112.

KUZNETSOV, Nikolai Aleksandrovich; Russian cybernetician; b. 9 March 1939; m.; two c.; ed. Moscow Inst. of Physics and Tech.; jr., sr. researcher, Deputy Dir. Inst. of Problems of Man. 1965–88; Dir. Gen. of Research Production Union Moskva 1988–89; Dir. Inst. of Problems of Data Transfer 1989–; corresp. mem. U.S.S.R. (now Russian) Acad. of Sciences 1986; research in theory of automatic man. and informatics; U.S.S.R. State Prize. *Publications:* Management of Observations in Automatic Systems 1961, Synthesis of Algorithms at Variable Criterion of Optimality 1966, Methods of Study of Stability of Dissynchronized Pulse Systems 1991. *Leisure interests:* mountain skiing, singing. *Address:* Institute of Problems of Data Transfer, Russian Academy of Sciences, Bolshoi Karetny per. 19, 101447 Moscow, Russia. *Telephone:* (095) 209 4225 (Office). *Fax:* (095) 209 0579.

KUZNETSOV, Nikolai Vasilyevich; Russian mathematician; b. 24 June 1939, Hachmas, Azerbaijan; s. of Vasilii Kuznetsov and Evdokia Gureutieva; m. Galina Pavlovna Kuznetsova 1975; two c.; ed. Moscow Inst. of Physics and Tech.; jr. researcher Inst. of Math. U.S.S.R. Acad. of Sciences 1965–69; jr., sr. researcher Moscow V. Lenin Pedagogical Inst. 1969–70; head of div., head of dept. Cen. Research Inst. of Information and Tech.-Econ. Studies 1970–71; head of div. Research Inst. of Systems of Man. and Econs. 1972–73; sr. researcher, head of lab. Khabarovsk Research Inst. of Complex Studies 1973–81; Deputy Dir. Computer's Cen. Far E. br. U.S.S.R. Acad. of Sciences 1989–91; Deputy Dir. Inst. of Applied Math. 1991–92; corresp. mem. U.S.S.R. (now Russian) Acad. of Sciences 1987; research in spectral theory, theory of modular and automorphic functions in math. Physics. *Publications:* On Egenfunctions of one Integral Equation 1970, Poincaré Series and Extended Lemer Hypothesis 1985, numerous articles in scientific journals. *Leisure interest:* chess. *Address:* Institute of Applied Mathematics, Far East Branch of Russian Academy of Sciences, Radio str. 7, 690041 Vladivostock, Russia. *Telephone:* (4232) 311907 (Office, Vladivostok); (4212) 334676 (Office, Khabarovsk); (4212) 227636 (Home).

KUZNETSOV, Oleg Leonidovich, D.TECH.; Russian geophysicist; b. 1938; m.; two c.; ed. Moscow S. Ordzhonikidze Inst. of Geological Research, Moscow State Univ.; researcher, Inst. of Oil, U.S.S.R. (now Russian) Acad. of Sciences 1962–70; Head of lab., All-Union Inst. of Nuclear Geophysics and Geochemistry, U.S.S.R. Ministry of Geology (now State Scientific Centre of All-Russian Inst. of Geosystems) 1970–79, Dir. 1979–; Prof. Moscow State Univ. 1986–; a founder, Vice-Pres. Russian Acad. of Nat. Sciences 1990, Pres. 1994–; f. and Rector, Int. Univ. of Nature, Soc. and Man., Dubna 1994–; main research in geophysical processes, seismoacoustics, non-linear geophysics, geoinformatics and information tech.; mem. New York Acad. of Sciences 1994, Int. Acad. of Sciences on Nature and Soc. 1993, Int. Acad. of Higher Schooling 1995, Oriental Acad. of Oil and Gas 1994; Hon. mem. Hungarian Soc. of Geophysics, Euro-Asian Geophysical Soc.; U.S.S.R. State Prize 1982, Prize of German Econ. Club 1996, A. Chizhevsky Prize 1997. *Publications:* over 280 scientific works including 11 monographs, 4 reference books, 67 inventions, over 60 patents. *Address:* Russian Academy of Natural Sciences, Varshavskoye shosse 8, 113105 Moscow, Russia. *Telephone:* (095) 954 5350 (Office). *Fax:* (095) 958 3711 (Office).

KVAPIL, Radoslav; Czech pianist. b. 15 March 1934, Brno; s. of Karel Kvapil and Marie Kvapilová; m. Eva Mašlaňová 1960 (died 1993); one s.; ed. Gymnasium Dr. Kudely, Brno and Janáček Acad. of Musical Arts; first piano recital Brno 1954; 1st prize Janáček Competition 1958, Int. Competition, Czechoslovak Radio 1968; Prof. of Piano, Prague Conservatory 1963–73; concerts in countries throughout Europe, in U.S.A. and Japan 1963–; performed world premiere of Dvořák's Cypresses 1983; Dir. South Bohemia Music Festival 1991–; Hon. Vice-Pres. Dvořák Soc., London; Pres. Yehudi Menuhin Soc., Prague 1990–, Dvořák Soc., Prague 1997–; Janáček Medal (Cultural Ministry). *Recordings include:* complete piano works of Dvořák and Martinů, complete piano and chamber music of Janáček, complete piano works of Jan Hugo Voříšek 1973–74, complete polka cycles of Smetana, Czech contemporary piano music, Piano Concerto by A. Rejcha (first ever recording), Anthology of Czech piano music (for Unicorn-Kanchana label), 8 vols, works of Dvořák performed on the composer's piano 1999. *Leisure interest:* chess. *Address:* Hradecká 5, 13000 Prague 3, Czech Republic. *Telephone:* (2) 67312430.

KVASHA, Igor Vladimirovich; Russian actor and stage director; b. 4 Feb. 1933, Moscow; m. Tatyana Semenovna Putiyevskaya; one s.; ed. Moscow Art Theatre; with Moscow Art Theatre 1955–57; one of founders and leading actor Theatre Sovremennik 1956–; theatre roles in classical and contemporary plays, including Cyrano de Bergerac (Cyrano de Bergerac by Rostand), Jimmy Porter (Look Back in Anger by Osborne), Luka (On the Bottom by Gorky), Balalaikin (Balalaikin and Co. by Saltykov-Schedrin), Gayev (Cherry Orchard by Chekhov), Chebutykin (Three Sisters by Chekhov), Dr. Stockman (Dr. Stockman by Ibsen); staged productions include Days of the Turbins, The Hypocrites' Servitude by Bulgakov, The Average Downy Home Cat by Voinovich and G. Gorin, Cyrano de Bergerac (together with Yefremov); roles in over 50 films by dirs. Roshal, Room, Klimov, Bondarchuk, Daneliya and others 1960–; regularly appears on TV and radio, reciting prose and poems; People's Artist of Russia; prizes of many film and theatre festivals for performing Russian repertoire including plays by A. Chekhov. *Leisure interest:* painting. *Address:* Clinishchevsky per. 5/7, Apt. 90, 103009 Moscow, Russia. *Telephone:* (095) 209 6108 (Home).

KVASHNIN, Col.-Gen., Anatoly Vassilyevich; Russian politician; b. 15 Aug. 1946, Ufa; ed. Kurgan Machine Construction Inst., Acad. of Armoured Units, Acad. of Gen. Staff; army service, commdr. of regiment, div., army 1969–; Deputy, First Deputy Head Main Operation Dept. 1993–95; Commdr. Allied Group of armed forces in Chechnya 1994–95; Commdr. Armed Forces of N. Caucasian Command 1995–97; Acting Head, Head Gen. Staff of Armed Forces of Russian Fed. 1997–, concurrently First Deputy Minister of Defence Russian Fed. May 1997–. *Address:* Ministry of Defence, Znamenka str. 19, 103160 Moscow, Russia (Office). *Telephone:* (095) 293 2047 (Office).

KVITSINSKY, Yuliy Aleksandrovich; Russian diplomatist; b. 28 Sept. 1936, Rzev; s. of Alexander Kvitsinsky and Maria Orlova; m. Inga Kuznetsova 1955; two d.; ed. Moscow Inst. of Int. Relations; served in Embassy in G.D.R. 1959–65, in Fed. Repub. of Germany 1978–81; head of Soviet del., negotiations on medium-range nuclear weapons until latter broken off Nov. 1983; subsequently responsible for negotiations on Strategic Defence Initiative (SDI) Geneva talks 1985; Amb. to Fed. Repub. of Germany 1986–90; Deputy Foreign Minister 1990–91, First Deputy Foreign Minister May–Sept. 1991; Chief Adviser, Dept. of Planning 1991–92; Vice-Pres. Foreign Policy Assen. 1992–; Adviser to Pres., Council of Russian Fed. (Upper Chamber) 1996–; Amb. to Norway 1997–; cand. mem. CPSU Cen. Cttee 1986–89, mem. 1989–91. *Publications:* Vor dem Sturm 1993, Judas Ischariot 1996, General Wlassow 1997. *Leisure interest:* fishing. *Address:* Brammensveien 74, 0271 Oslo, Norway. *Telephone:* 22553278/79. *Fax:* 22550070.

KWAPONG, Prof. Alex. A., PH.D.; Ghanaian professor; b. 8 March 1927, Akropong, Akwapim; s. of E. A. and Theophilia Kwapong; m. Evelyn Teiko Caesar 1956; six d.; ed. Achimota Coll. and King's Coll., Cambridge; Visiting Prof., Princeton Univ. 1962; fmr. Pro Vice-Chancellor and Head of Classics Dept., Ghana Univ., Vice-Chancellor 1966–75; Vice-Rector for Institutional Planning and Resource Devt. UN Univ. 1976–88; Lester B. Pearson Chair. in Devt. Studies, Dalhousie Univ. 1988–91; Dir. of African Programmes, Teacher Educ., Research and Evaluation, The Commonwealth of Learning 1991–93; mem. Political and Educ. Cttees., Nat. Liberation Council 1966; mem. Bd. Aspen Inst. Berlin, Harold Macmillan Trust, Int. Council for Educ. Devt., Int. Foundation for Educ. and Self-help; Fellow, Ghana Acad. of Arts and Sciences; Hon. D.Litt. (Warwick, Ife, Ghana, Univ. of Ghana); Hon. LL.D. (Princeton); Order of Volta (Ghana). *Publications:* Higher Education and Development in Africa Today: A Reappraisal 1979; Under-development and the Challenges of the 1980s: The Role of Knowledge 1980, The Relevance of the African Universities to the Development Needs of Africa 1980, Medical Education and National Development 1987, Culture, Development and African Unity 1988, African Scientific and Technical Institution Building and the Role of International Co-operation 1988, The Challenge of Education in Africa 1988, Some Reflections on International Education in the 90s—in the Role of Service Learning in International Education 1989, Capacity Building and Human Resource Development in Africa (Ed. with B. Lesser) 1990, Meeting the Challenge, The African Capacity Building Initiative (Ed. with B. Lesser) 1992. *Address:* 19 Highfield Avenue, London, NW11 9EU, England. *Telephone:* 0181-209 0878.

KWAŚNIEWSKI, Aleksander; Polish politician; b. 15 Nov. 1954, Białogard, Koszalin Prov.; s. of Zdzisław Kwaśniewski and Aleksandra Kwaśniewska; m. Jolanta Konty 1979; one d.; ed. Gdańsk Univ.; former active leader of youth movt., including Chair. Univ. Council of Polish Socialist Students' Union (SZSP) at Gdańsk Univ., Head of Culture Dept. of SZSP Gen. Bd. 1979–80, mem. Exec. Cttee. of SZSP Chief Council 1980–81; Ed.-in-Chief of students' weekly Itd, Warsaw 1981–84; Ed.-in-Chief of daily Sztandar Młodych (Banner of Youth), Warsaw 1984–85; mem. Council of Ministers 1985–89; Head Socio-Political Cttee. 1988–89; Minister for Youth 1985–87; Chair. Cttee. for Youth and Physical Culture 1987–90; mem. Polish United Workers' Party (PZPR) 1977–90; mem. Social Democracy of Repub. of Poland Party (SdRP) 1990–95, Chair. 1990–95; participant Round Table plenary debates, Co-Chair. team for trade union pluralism, mem. team for political reforms and group for asscns. and territorial self-govt 1989; Chair. Polish Olympic Cttee. 1988–91; Deputy to Sejm (Parl.) 1991–95; Chair Constitutional Comm. 1993–95; Supreme Commdr. of Armed Forces 1995–; Pres. of Poland 1995–. *Leisure interests:* sport, literature, films. *Address:* Pałac Prezydencki; ul. Krakowskie Przedmieście 48-50, 00-021 Warsaw, Poland.

KWON YOUNG-HAE; Korean politician and fmr. army officer; b. 1937, Wolsong, N. Kyongsang Prov.; ed. Korea Mil. Acad.; commissioned 1959; Commdr. 6th Army Div. 1984–86; Chief of Staff of 3rd Army 1986–88; Commdr. Olympic Support Command 1988; rank of Gen., retd. 1988; Head, Planning and Man. Office, Ministry of Defence 1988; Vice-Minister of Defence 1990, Minister 1993. *Address:* c/o Ministry of Defence, 3-1 Yong San-dong, Yongsan-ku, Seoul, Republic of Korea.

KWONG, Most Rev. Peter K. K., M.TH., D.D.; Chinese ecclesiastic; b. 28 Feb. 1936, Hong Kong; s. of Kwok-Keun Kwong and Ching-lan Chan; m. Emily Ha; one s. two d.; ed. Chung Chi Coll., Kenyon Coll., and Bexley Hall, Colgate Rochester; ordained priest, Anglican Church in Hong Kong 1966; Clergy-in-charge, Crown of Thorns Church, Hong Kong 1956–66; Vicar, St. James' Church, Hong Kong 1967–70; Curate, St. Paul's Church, Hong Kong 1971–72; mem. teaching staff, Chinese Univ. of Hong Kong 1972–79; Diocesan Sec. Anglican Diocese of Hong Kong and Macao 1979–81; Bishop of Hong Kong and Macao 1981–98, Archbishop and Primate of Hong Kong Sheng Kung Hui 1998, Bishop of Hong Kong Island 1998–; mem. Exec. Cttee., Consultative Cttee. for Basic Law of Hong Kong 1985–90, Chair. Finance Cttee. 1987–90; Adviser on Hong Kong Affairs, State Dept. of People's Repub. of China 1992–97; mem. Preparatory Cttee. for Special Admin. Region 1996–97, Selection Cttee. 1996–97, CPPCC 1998–; Hon. Treas. Council of the Church in East Asia 1981–83; Dir. Chinese Christian Churches Union 1981–90; mem. Court, Hong Kong Univ. 1981–; Vice-Pres. Church Missionary Soc. 1995–; numerous appts. in health, educ., social welfare, youth orgs. etc. *Address:* Bishop's House, 1 Lower Albert Road, Hong Kong Special Administrative Region, People's Republic of China. *Telephone:* 2526-5355. *Fax:* 2521-2199.

KY, Air Vice-Marshal Nguyen Cao (see Nguyen Cao Ky, Air Vice-Marshal).

KYL, Jon Llewellyn, B.A., LL.B.; American politician; b. 25 April 1942, Oakland, Neb.; s. of John H. Kyl and Arlene Griffith; m. Caryll Collins 1964; one s. one d.; ed. Univ. of Arizona; practising lawyer, Jennings, Strouss & Salmon, Phoenix, Ariz.. 1966–86; legal counsel, Ariz. State Republican Party 1970–75; mem. U.S. House of Reps. 1986–94; Senator from Arizona Jan. 1995–. *Address:* U.S. Senate, 702 Senate Hart Building, Washington, DC 20515, U.S.A.

KYNASTON, Nicolas; British organist; b. 10 Dec. 1941; s. of late Roger Tewkesbury Kynaston and late Jessie Dearn Caecilia Kynaston (née Parkes); m. 1st Judith Felicity Heron 1961 (divorced 1989); two s. two d.; m. 2nd Susan Harwood Styles 1989; ed. Westminster Cathedral Choir School, Downside, Accademia Musicale Chigiana, Siena, Conservatorio Santa Cecilia, Rome, Royal Coll. of Music; Westminster Cathedral Organist 1961–71; début recital, Royal Festival Hall 1966; recording début 1968; concert career 1971–, travelling throughout Europe, North America, Asia and Africa; Artistic Dir. J. W. Walker & Sons Ltd. 1978–82, Consultant 1982–83; Organist Athens Concert Hall 1995–; Jury mem. Grand Prix de Chartres 1971, St. Albans Int. Organ Festival 1975; Pres. Inc. Asscn. of Organists 1983–85; Chair. Nat. Organ Teachers Encouragement Scheme 1993–96; consultant for various new organ projects; Hon. F.R.C.O. 1976; recordings include 6 nominated Critic's Choice, The Gramophone 1996 (also Ed.'s Choice); EMI/CFP Sales Award 1974; Deutscher Schallplattenpreis 1978. *Leisure interests:* walking, church architecture. *Address:* 28 High Park Road, Kew Gardens, Richmond-upon-Thames, Surrey, TW9 4BH, England. *Telephone:* 0181-878 4455. *Fax:* 0181-392 9314.

KYO, Machiko, Japanese actress; b. 1924; began her career as a dancer with the Shochiku Girls' Opera Co., Osaka; film début in Saigo ni Warau Otoko (Last Laughter) 1949; has appeared in over 80 films including Rashomon 1950, Ugetsu Monogatari 1953, Gate of Hell 1954, Story of Shunkin 1955, Akasen Chitai (Street of Shame), Teahouse of the August Moon 1956, Yoru no Cho (Night Butterflies) 1957, Odd Obsession 1959, Floating Weeds 1959, A Woman's Testament 1960, Ugetsu; Best Actress Award for Rashomon 1950; Jussie (Finland) Award 1957.

KYPRIANOU, Spyros; Cypriot politician and lawyer; b. 28 Oct. 1932, Limassol; s. of Achilleas and Maria (née Araouzou) Kyprianou; m. Mimi Papatheoklitou 1956; two s.; ed. City of London Coll. and Gray's Inn, London; called to the Bar 1954; f. Nat. Union of Cypriot Students in England

(EFEKA), elected its first Pres. 1952–54; London Sec. to Ethnarch Makarios 1952–54; London Sec. of Ethnarchy 1954–56; journalist 1952–56; New York rep. of Ethnarchy 1956–57, London rep. 1957–59; mem. Cen. Cttee. of Nat. Dem. Front for Reconstruction (EDMA) 1959; Minister of Foreign Affairs 1960–72 (resigned); Pres. Cttee. of Foreign Ministers of Council of Europe April-Dec. 1967; led numerous Dels. to UN Gen. Ass., Security Council, also led talks on the association of Cyprus to the EEC; legal practice 1972–; mem. Cyprus Del. to UN Gen. Ass. 1974, ad hoc mem. to UN Security Council 1975; Founder and Chair. Democratic Party 1976–; Pres. House of Reps. 1976–77, 1996–; Pres. of Cyprus 1977–88; Grand Star of the U.A.R. 1961, Grand Cross, Order of George I of Greece 1962, Grand Cross of Fed. Repub. of Germany 1962, Grand Cross, Order of Boyaca (Colombia) 1966, Grand Cross, Order of Merit (Chile) 1966, Order of St. Aikaterini of Sinai 1966, Grand Silver Cross of Austria 1973, Star of the Socialist Repub. of Romania 1979, Grand Cross of the Order of the Saviour (Greece) 1983, Collar of the Order of Isabel la Católica (Spain) 1987 etc. *Leisure interests:* literature, music, sports. *Address:* Antistaseos 1, Engomi, Nicosia, Cyprus. *Telephone:* 303451 (Office). *Fax:* 366611 (Office).

KYRIAKOU, Minos, B.A.; Greek shipowner and business executive; b. 1946, Athens; s. of Xenophon Kyriakou and Athina Revidies; m. (divorced); two s. one d.; ed. in France and Switzerland and Columbia Univ. New York; owner Athenian Tankers Inc. 1965–; formed Bacoil Int. and Athenian Oil Trading Inc. (oil trading corpns.) 1978; founder and Pres. Aegean Foundation 1985–; org. Antenna FM (pvt. radio station) 1987; Chair. and C.E.O. Antenna 1988–; started Antenna TV (TV network) 1989; through Antenna Satellite Inc. Antenna began broadcasting to whole American continent, Australia and Cyprus 1992; Hon. Consul-Gen. of Singapore in Greece 1988–; mem. Bd. Govs. Singapore Port Authority 1988; Chair. of UN org. for civil, linguistic and religious rights of nat. minorities 1989; founder, Mediterranean Affairs Inc. (non-profit org.) publishing Mediterranean Quarterly, Washington, D.C. 1990–; Hon. Consul of Poland in Thessaloniki 1994–; Gold Medal, Legion of Honour of Poland; First Prize for book The Aegean Crisis 1987. *Publications:* The Aegean Crisis 1986, Siesta on a Volcano 1988. *Leisure interests:* reading (especially of history); collecting paintings and sculpture. *Address:* 10–12 Kifisias Avenue, 15125 Marousi, Greece.

KYRIAZIDIS, Nicolas; Greek economist; b. 3 Sept. 1927, Athens; m. Ellie Kyrou 1960; one s. one d.; ed. Oxford, Illinois and Chicago Univs.; Head of Reports Section, Ministry of Co-ordination 1949; Dir. Monetary Policy Service 1950; Dir. Foreign and Trade Payments 1951–54; Asst. Econ. Adviser, Bank of Greece 1956–60, Alt. 1960–64; Deputy Dir.-Gen. Ministry of Co-ordination 1962–64; Econ. Adviser, Nat. Bank of Greece 1964–67; Senior Economist IMF 1968–70; Adviser to Govt. of Cyprus in negotiations for association with European Community 1971–73, 1978–82; Deputy Gov. Bank of Greece 1974–77; Amb. to U.K. 1982–86; Alt. Exec. Dir. IMF 1986–92; Deputy Minister of Finance 1994–96; took part in negotiations for EFTA 1957–58, for association between Greece and EEC 1959–61, led Greek Del. in accession negotiations 1976; mem. Board, Soc. for the Study of Greek Problems 1971–72; mem. Cttee. for Restoration of Democratic Legality 1973; Commdr. George I (Greece), Kt. Commdr. Léopold II (Belgium), Knight Commdr. Order of Merit of Italian Repub., Commdr. Order of Merit of Fed. Repub. of Germany. *Leisure interests:* reading, opera, collecting antiques. *Address:* Loukianou 28, Athens 10675, Greece (Home). *Telephone:* (1) 7245808 (Home). *Fax:* (1) 7252297 (Home).

KYRILL (GUNDYAEV, Vladimir Mikhailovich), Metropolitan of Smolensk and Kaliningrad; Russian ecclesiastic; b. 20 Nov. 1946, Leningrad; ed. Leningrad Theological Acad.; took monastic vows, deacon, celibate priest 1969; personal sec. of Metropolitan of Leningrad 1970–71; ordained as archimandrite 1971; Rep. of Moscow Patriarchate to WCC, Switzerland 1971–74; mem. Cen. and Exec. Cttees., WCC 1975–79; Rector Leningrad Theological Acad. 1974–84; consecrated Bishop of Vyborg, Vicar of Leningrad Diocese 1976; Archbishop of Vyborg 1977–84, of Smolensk and Vyazma 1984–89, of Smolensk and Kaliningrad 1989–91; Metropolitan of Smolensk and Kaliningrad 1991–; Chair. Dept. of External Church Relations of Moscow Patriarchate, mem. Holy Synod 1989–; Admin. Patriarchal parishes in Finland 1990–. *Address:* Moscow Patriarchate, Danilov Monastery, Danilovsky val. 22, 113191 Moscow, Russia. *Telephone:* 230-22-50. *Fax:* 230-26-19.

KYUMA, Fumio; Japanese politician; mem. House of Reps.; fmr. Parl. Vice-Minister of Transport; Dir. Gen. Defence Agency (State Minister) Nov. 1996–. *Address:* Defence Agency, 9-7-45, Akasaka, Minato-ku, Tokyo 107, Japan (Office). *Telephone:* 3-3408-5211 (Office).

KYUNG-WHA CHUNG (see Chung, Kyung-Wha).

L

LAAGE, Gerhart, DIPL. ING.; German architect and town planner; b. 19 April 1925, Hamburg; s. of Richard and Valerie (née Pitzner) Laage; m. Ursula Gebert 1959; one s. two d.; ed. Technische Hochschule, Brunswick; freelance architect 1954–; Prof. of Theory of Architectural Planning, Univ. of Hanover 1963–92, Pro-rector and Rector 1973–75, Dean 1983–84; Adviser to Fed. Govt. on planning for city of Bonn 1977–82; Pres. Fed. Architects Assen. 1990–92. *Publications:* Wohnungen von heute für Ansprüche von Morgen 1971, Planung und Mitbestimmung 1973, Planungstheorie für Architekten 1976, Wohnen beginnt auf der Strasse 1977, Handbuch für Architekturplanung 1978, Weder Traum noch Trauma 1978, Das Stadthaus—mehr als eine Bauform 1980, Kosten- und flächensparendes Bauen 1984, Warum wird nicht immer so gebaut 1985, Von Architecten, Bossen und Banausen 1989, Architektur ist Glücksache 1997. *Address:* Schulterblatt 36, 20357 Hamburg, Germany. *Telephone:* 040-43195-0.

LAAR, Mart; Estonian politician, historian and journalist; b. 22 April 1960, Viljandi; s. of Tõnis Laar and Aime Laar; m. Katrin Kask 1982; one s. one d.; ed. Tartu State Univ.; teacher schools of Tallinn 1983–87; Head of Dept. Ministry of Culture of Estonia 1987–90; Deputy of Christian Democratic Party, Supreme Soviet of Estonia 1989–92; mem. Constitutional Ass., mem. Estonian Parl. (Riigikogu) 1992–; Chair. Isamaa (Motherland) nat. coalition party 1992–; Prime Minister of Estonia 1992–94; Leader Isamaa Faction in Parl. 1996–; mem. Bd., City Council of Tallinn 1996–; Young Politician of the World (Jr. Chamber Int.) 1993. *Publications:* June 14 1941, Estonian History, War in the Woods; a number of scientific papers. *Address:* Estonian Parliament (Riigikogu), Lossi plats 1a, Tallinn EE 0100, Estonia (Office). *Telephone:* (6) 6316600. *Fax:* 6316604.

LABARDAKIS, Augoustinos; Greek ecclesiastic; b. 7 Feb. 1938, Voukoulies-Chania, Crete; s. of Emmanouil and Eurydike Labardakis; ed. theological schools in Chalki, Turkey, Salzburg, Münster, West Berlin; ordained as priest, Greek Orthodox Church, Fed. Repub. of Germany 1964, worked as priest, West Berlin 1964–72, ordained as Bishop 1972, as Greek Orthodox Metropolitan of the Fed. Repub. of Germany and Exarch of Cen. Europe Nov. 1980; Grosses Bundesverdienstkreuz, Verdienstorden des Landes Nordrhein-Westfalen, Höchste Stufe des Ehrenordens der Republik Griechenland. *Address:* Greek Orthodox Metropolis of Germany, Dietrich-Bonhoeffer-Strasse 2, 53227 Bonn; P.O. Box 300555, 53185 Bonn, Germany. *Telephone:* (0228) 462041. *Fax:* (0228) 464989.

LABARRÈRE-PAULÉ, André, D. ÈS L.; French politician and academic; b. 12 Jan. 1928, Pau; s. of Maximien Labarrère-Paulé and Catherine Bouilhat; ed. Ecole Henri-IV, Collège Beau-Frêne, Pau, Univ. of Paris; Teacher, Digne Lycée 1956–58; scholarship to Arts Council of Canada 1958–59; Prof. Faculty of Arts and of Admin. Sciences, Laval Univ., Québec 1959–66; Prof. of History of Art, Ecole des Beaux-arts, Québec 1964–66; Deputy (Pyrénées-Atlantiques) to Nat. Assembly 1967–68, 1973, 1978, 1981, Vice-Pres. Nat. Assembly 1973–74; Gen. Councillor, Pau-Ouest 1967–73, Jurançon 1973–88; teacher, Lycée Carnot, Paris 1968–70, Auch Lycée 1970; mem. Political Bureau and Steering Cttee., Parti Socialiste 1969–; Mayor of Pau 1971, re-elected 1977, 1983, 1989; mem. Regional Council for Aquitaine 1974–, Pres. of Council 1979–81; Minister-Del. for Relations with Parl., attached to Prime Minister 1981–86. *Publications:* Pierre-Joseph-Olivier Chauveau 1962, Les instituteurs laïques au Canada français 1836–1900, Les laïques et la presse pédagogique au Canada français au XIXe siècle 1965, Les secrets de l'écriture 1965, Monseigneur Laflèche 1970, Pau 1973, Pau, ville jardin, Votre écriture, Messieurs! Les politiques dévoilés par leur écriture 1987, L'écriture des stars 1991, Le Bal des célibataires (novel) 1992, Le Baron rouge 1997. *Leisure interests:* geography, swimming, graphology, dogs, flowers. *Address:* Assemblée Nationale, 75355 Paris; Mairie de Pau, Place Royale, 64036 Pau Cedex (Offices); 29 rue Carnot, 64000 Pau, France (Home). *Telephone:* 59.27.85.80 (Office). *Fax:* 59.27.26.18.

LABIS, Attilio; French ballet dancer and choreographer; b. 5 Sept. 1936, Vincennes; s. of Umberto and Renée (née Cousin) Labis; m. Christiane Vlassi 1959; two s.; ed. Ecole de danse académique de l'Opéra, Paris; mem. Corps de Ballet at the Paris Opera 1952, Premier Danseur 1959, Principal Premier Danseur 1960–65, Maître de ballet adjoint 1965–; Guest Dancer in London, Paris, Washington, Tokyo, Moscow, Kiev, Leningrad, Rome, Milan, Berlin, Munich, Stuttgart, Rio de Janeiro and Sydney; Chief Choreographer at the Paris Opera; World Amb. for l'Ecole Française; devised choreography for productions including Rencontre (TV) 1961, Arcades 1964, Iphigénie en Tauride 1965, Romeo and Juliet 1967, Spartacus 1973, Raymonda 1973; has created and interpreted numerous ballets including Giselle, Sleeping Beauty, Swan Lake, Don Quixote, Pièces Chorégraphiques (Peter Van Dijk), Pas de Dieux (Gene Kelly), Marines (Georges Skibine), Icare (Serge Lifar), Symphonie Concertante, Sarracenia (Michel Descombey), Renart, Pas de danse (music by Gluck), Schéhérazade, Coppélia, Sarrabande, Casse-Noisette; Chevalier des Arts et des Lettres. *Address:* Opéra de Paris, 120 rue Lyon, 75012 Paris; 36 rue du Chemin-de-fer, 78380 Bougival, France. *Telephone:* 01.30.82.64.92. *Fax:* 01.39.69.26.99.

LABRECQUE, Thomas G.; American banker; b. 17 Sept. 1938, Long Branch, N.J.; s. of Theodore Labrecque and Marjorie Uprichard; m. Sheila Cardone 1962; two s. two d.; ed. Villanova, American and New York Univs.; Chase Manhattan Corpn. New York 1964–; Exec. Vice-Pres. Treasury Dept. 1974–76; mem. Exec. Cttee. responsible for commercial banking, retail banking, trust and fiduciary investment, operations and systems functions 1976–80; Vice-Chair. Bd., Dir., C.O.O. 1980–81, Pres. 1981–90, Chair. Bd., C.E.O. 1990–96; Pres., C.O.O. Chase Manhattan Corpn. (following merger of Chemical Banking Corpn. and Chase Manhattan Corpn.) 1996–, Dir. Pfizer Inc. *Address:* Chase Manhattan Corporation, 1 Chase Manhattan Plaza, New York, N.Y. 10081, U.S.A.

LABUDA, Gerard, PH.D.; Polish historian; b. 28 Dec. 1916, Nowahuta, Kartuzy Dist.; s. of Stanisław Labuda and Anastazja Baranowska; m. Countess Alberta Wielopolska 1943; four s. one d.; ed. Clandestine Univ. of Western Lands, Warsaw; Docent 1945–50, Extraordinary Prof. 1950–56, Prof. 1956–; Rector, Adam Mickiewicz Univ., Poznań 1962–65; Sec.-Gen. Poznań Soc. of Friends of Learning 1961–72, Pres. 1972–75; Ed. Roczniki Historyczne (Annals of History) 1969–85; Corresp. mem. Polish Acad. of Sciences 1964–69, mem. 1969–, mem. Presidium 1972–94, Vice-Pres. 1984–86, 1987–89; mem. Consultative Council attached to Chair. of State Council 1986–89; Chair. Cttee. for Research on Poles Living Abroad, Polish Acad. of Sciences 1973–80; fmr. Chair. Poznań Br. of Polish Acad. of Sciences; Pres. Polish Acad. of Sciences and Letters, Cracow 1989–94; mem. European Soc. of Culture 1963–; Fellow Wissenschaftskoll. zu Berlin-Inst. for Advanced Studies 1981–82; mem. New York Acad. of Sciences 1995; Dr. h.c. (Gdańsk) 1986, (Toruń) 1993, (Jagiellon Univ. Cracow) 1995, (Warsaw) 1997; State Prizes (3rd class) 1949, 1951, (2nd class) 1970; Kt.'s Cross, Order of Polonia Restituta 1954, Officer's Cross 1960, Commdr.'s Cross with Star 1965 and others; Palacki Medal (Czechoslovakia) 1968. *Publications:* Pierwsze państwo słowiańskie—państwo Samona (First Slavonic State—Samon's State) 1949, Fragmenty dziejów Słowiańszczyzny Zachodniej (Fragments of History of the West Slavs) vols. I–III 1960–74, Polska granica zachodnia: Tysiąc lat dziejów politycznych (The Western Frontier of Poland: A Thousand Years of Political History) 1971–1974, co-author, Słownik Starożytności Słowiańskich (Dictionary of Slavonic Antiquities), Historia Pomorza (History of Pomerania), Historia dyplomacji polskiej (Średniowiecze) (History of Polish Medieval Diplomacy) 1981, Dzieje Zakonu Krzyżackiego w Prusach (History of the Order of the Teutonic Knights in Prussia) 1986, Studia nad początkami państwa polskiego (Studies of the Origin of the Polish State Vols. I and II) 1987–88, Mieszko II, King of Poland (1025–1034) 1992, Kaszubi and their History 1995, Polsko-niemieckie rozmowy opnenlości 1996; numerous articles. *Leisure interests:* sociology, linguistics. *Address:* ul. Kanclerska 8, 60-327 Poznań, Poland. *Telephone:* (61) 867 35 85.

LACALLE HERRERA, Luis Alberto; Uruguayan politician, farmer and lawyer; b. 13 July 1941, Montevideo; s. of Carlos Lacalle and María Hortensia de Herrera Uriarte; m. María Julia Pou Brito del Pino 1970; two s. one d.; Deputy to Legis. Ass. 1971; elected Senator 1984; cand. for Pres. for Blanco Party 1989; Pres. of Uruguay 1990–94. *Address:* c/o Oficina del Presidente, Casa de Gobierno, Edif. Libertad, Avda Luis Alberto de Herrera 3350 esq. Avda José Pedro Varela, Montevideo, Uruguay.

LACAMBRA MONTERO, Carmen; Spanish librarian; b. 3 Feb. 1947, Madrid; ed. Univ. Complutense, Madrid; various posts with Gen. Directorate of Books and Libraries, Ministry of Culture; Dir. Spanish Agency of Int. Standard Book Nos. (ISBN) 1987; Dir. Centro del Libro y de la Lectura 1988–91; Dir.-Gen. Organismo Autónomo Biblioteca Nacional 1991. *Address:* Biblioteca Nacional, Paseo de Recoletos 20, 28071 Madrid, Spain.

LACANT, Jacques, D. ÈS L.; French university professor and literary critic; b. 10 May 1915, Paris; s. of Jean and Edmée (née Pontarlier) Lacant; m. Germaine Le Houérou 1948; three s. one d.; ed. Lycée Louis-le-Grand, Paris, and Ecole normale supérieure; attached to Econ. Del. 1942–44; broadcaster to Germany and Austria, Radiodiffusion Française 1944–45; Admin. in French occupation zone, Germany 1945–52; Dir. French Inst., Cologne 1952–60; Asst. Instructor, Sorbonne 1960–66; Head of Educ. Arts Faculty, Dijon Univ. 1966–69, Nanterre Univ. 1969; Prof. Paris X Univ., Prof. Emer. 1984; Producer Langue française, joyau de notre patrimonie (radio broadcast) 1988–; mem. Higher Council of Univ. Bodies; Drama Critic; lecturer abroad; Vice-Pres. Défense de la Langue Française; Officier, Légion d'honneur; Officier des Palmes Académiques; Officier of Merit (Fed. Repub. of Germany); Laureate, Acad. Française 1976; Pierre Brisson Prize 1977; Grand Prix du Rayonnement Français, Acad. Française 1984; Daudet Prize 1997. *Publications:* La Correspondence Wagner-Liszt 1943, L'Université de Fribourg 1947, Marivaux en Allemagne 1975, numerous works of literary history. *Leisure interest:* books. *Address:* 10 square du Croisic, 75015 Paris, France (Home). *Telephone:* 47 34 16 14.

LACARTE-MURO, Julio; Uruguayan international civil servant; b. 29 March 1918, Montevideo; s. of Antonio Lacarte and Julieta Muró de Lacarte; m. Ivy E. O'Hara de Lacarte 1940; three c.; Deputy Exec. Sec. GATT 1947, Amb. to GATT, Chair. (Governing Council and the Contracting Parties), has participated in all eight GATT rounds 1947, 1949, 1951, 1956, 1960–61, 1964–67, 1973–79, 1986–93 (Uruguay round), as Chief Negotiator (for Uruguay); fmr. Minister of Industry and Trade; fmr. Amb. to numerous countries; mem. Appellate Body World Trade Org. 1995–; lecturer and int. consultant; decorations from Bolivia, Argentina and Germany. *Publications:* several books on int. trade. *Leisure interests:* tennis, golf, chess, history. *Address:* c/o GATT, Centre William Rappard, 154 rue de Lausanne, 1211 Geneva 21, Switzerland.

LACAZE, Gen. Jeannou; French politician and army officer; b. 11 Feb. 1924, Hué, Viet Nam; s. of Jean Joseph and Andrée (née Momert) Lacaze; m. 2nd Geneviève Agostini 1997; two s. two d. (from fmr. marriage), entered mil. acad., Saint-Cyr 1945; joined infantry; served Foreign Legion, Algeria, Tunisia and the Far East; Major 11th demi-brigade parachutiste de choc 1959–63; Commdr. 2nd Foreign Parachute Regt. (for a time in Chad) 1967; Dir. of Intelligence, Service de documentation extérieure et de contre-espionage (SDECE) 1971–76; first mem. secret service to be made Gen.; Commdr. 11th Parachute Div. 1976–79; Inspecteur de l'infanterie Aug. 1979; Lieut.-Gen. Feb. 1980; Commdr. 1st mil. region and 3rd army corps, Commanding Officer, Paris Sept. 1980; Armed Forces Chief of Staff Jan. 1981–85; Special Counsellor, military relations with African continent countries 1985–89; mem. European Parl. 1989–94; Founder and Pres. Union des Indépendants political party 1990; Pres. Asscn. for the Devt. of Relations between Europe and the Third World (Apretem), SEI (Int. Strategy and Expertise); Founder and Pres. Council Commerce et Industrie franco-irakien; Grand Officier, Légion d'honneur; Croix de guerre, Croix de la Valeur militaire. *Publication:* Le President et le champignon 1991. *Leisure interests:* riding, golf. *Address:* 1 bis quai aux Fleurs, 75004 Paris, France.

LACEY, Richard Westgarth, PH.D., M.D., F.R.C.P.; British professor of clinical microbiology; b. 11 Oct. 1940, London; s. of Jack Lacey and Sybil Lacey; m. Fionna Margaret Lacey 1972; two d.; ed. Felsted School, Essex, Jesus Coll., Cambridge, London Hosp.; house officer, London Hosp. 1964–66, St. Mary's Hosp., Eastbourne 1966; Sr. House Officer, Registrar in Pathology, Bristol Royal Infirmary 1966–68; lecturer, Reader in Clinical Microbiology, Univ. of Bristol 1968–74; Consultant in Chemical Pathology, Queen Elizabeth Hosp., King's Lynn 1975–83; Consultant in Infectious Diseases, East Anglian Regional Health Authority 1974–83, Leeds Health Authority 1983–; Prof. of Medical Microbiology, Leeds Univ. 1983–; Consultant, WHO 1983–; Dick Memorial Lecture, Edinburgh Veterinary School 1990; Evian Health Award Winner 1989, Caroline Walker Award 1989, Campaign for Freedom of Information Award 1990. *Publications:* Safe Shopping, Safe Cooking, Safe Eating 1989, Unfit for Human Consumption 1991, Hard to Swallow 1994, Mad Cow Disease: the History of B.S.E. in Britain 1994; numerous papers and articles for journals. *Leisure interests:* gardening, painting, antique restoration (intermittently). *Address:* Department of Microbiology, University of Leeds, Leeds, LS2 9JT, England. *Telephone:* 0113-233 5596.

LACHMANN, Peter Julius, SC.D., F.R.S., F.R.C.P., F.R.C.PATH., F.MED.SCI.; British immunologist; b. 23 Dec. 1931, Berlin, Germany; s. of Heinz Lachmann and Thea Heller; m. Sylvia Stephenson 1962; two s. one d.; ed. Trinity Coll., Univ. of Cambridge and Univ. Coll. Hospital, London; Research Student, Dept. of Pathology, Univ. of Cambridge 1958–60, Research Fellow, Empire Rheumatism Council 1962–64, Asst. Dir. of Research, Immunology Div. 1964–71; Prof. of Immunology, Royal Postgraduate Medical School, Univ. of London 1971–75; Hon. Consultant Pathologist, Hammersmith Hosp. 1971–75; Dir. MRC Research Group on serum complement 1971–75; Sheila Joan Smith Prof. of Immunology, Univ. of Cambridge 1977–; Hon. Dir., MRC Molecular Immunopathology Unit 1980–97; Hon. Consultant Clinical Immunologist, Cambridge Health Dist. 1976–; Pres. Royal Coll. of Pathologists 1990–93, Acad. of Medical Sciences 1998–; Biological Sec. and Vice-Pres. The Royal Soc. 1993–98; Visiting Investigator Rockefeller Univ., New York 1960–61, Scripps Clinic and Research Foundation, La Jolla, Calif. 1966, 1975, 1980, 1986, Basel Inst. for Immunology 1971; Meyerhof Visiting Prof., Weizmann Inst., Rehovot 1989; Visiting Prof., Coll. de France 1993; Fellow, Christ's Coll., Univ. of Cambridge 1962–71, 1976–, Royal Postgraduate Medical School 1995; Foreign Fellow Indian Nat. Acad. of Science 1997; mem. Medical Advisory Cttee., British Council 1983–97, Scientific Advisory Bd. SmithKline Beecham 1995–; Chair. Science Cttee. Asscn. Medical Research Charities 1988–92; Chair. Medical Research Cttee. Muscular Dystrophy Group 1986–90; Jt. Ed. Clinical Aspects of Immunology 1993–; Foundation Lecturer, Royal Coll. of Pathologists 1983; Langdon Brown Lecturer, Royal Coll. of Physicians 1986; Heberden Orator, British Soc. of Rheumatology 1986; Charnock Bradley Memorial Lecture 1992; Plenary Lecture, Vienna 1993; Congress Lecture, BSI 1993, Frank May Lecture, Leicester 1994; Vanguard Medical Lecture, Univ. of Surrey 1998. *Publications:* Jt. Ed. Clinical Aspects of Immunology, 1975, 1982, 1993. *Leisure interests:* keeping bees, walking in mountains. *Address:* Centre for Veterinary Science, Madingley Road, Cambridge, CB3 0ES (Office); 36 Conduit Head Road, Cambridge, CB3 0EY, England (Home). *Telephone:* (01223) 766245 (Office); (01223) 354433 (Home). *Fax:* (01223) 766244.

LACINA, Ferdinand; Austrian politician; b. 31 Dec. 1942, Vienna; s. of Anna and Ferdinand Lacina; m. Monika Lacina 1966; one s. one d.; ed. Hochschule für Welthandel, Vienna; various posts in Kammer für Arbeiter und Angestellte, Vienna 1964; Beirat für Wirtschafts- und Sozialfragen 1974; Dir. Dept. of Financial Planning, Österreichische Industrieverwaltungs-A.G. 1978; Dir. Pvt. Office of Fed. Chancellor Kreisky 1980; Sec. of State, Fed. Chancellery 1982; Fed. Minister of Transport Sept. 1984–Jan. 1985, of Public Economy and Transport 1985–86, of Finance 1986–95. *Publications:* Auslandskapital in Österreich (with O. Grünwald); articles in trade union newspapers and political and econ. journals. *Leisure interests:* literature, walking. *Address:* c/o Ministry of Finance, 1010 Vienna, Himmelpfortgasse 4-8B, Austria.

LACLOTTE, Michel René, L. ÈS L.; French museum director; b. 27 Oct. 1929, Saint-Malo; s. of Pierre Laclotte and Huguette de Kermabon; ed. Lycée Pasteur, Neuilly, Inst. d'art et d'archéologie de l'Univ. de Paris and Ecole du Louvre; Insp. Gen. Inspectorate of Provincial Museums 1955–66; Chief Curator of Paintings, Musée du Louvre 1966–, of collection of Musée d'Orsay 1978–; Insp.-Gen. of Museums 1980; Dir. Musée du Louvre 1987–92, Pres. de l'Etablissement Public (Musée du Louvre) 1992–94; Pres. Mission de préfiguration, Institut Nat. d'Histoire de L'Art 1994–; Officier, Légion d'honneur, Ordre nat. du Mérite, Commdr. des Arts et des Lettres; Grand prix nat. des Musées 1993; Hon. C.B.E. 1994. *Publications:* l'Histoire artistique de l'Europe, le Moyen Age 1995, various works on history of art, catalogues and articles in reviews. *Address:* 10 bis rue du Pré-aux-Clercs, 75007 Paris, France (Home).

LACOMBE, Henri; French oceanographer; b. 24 Dec. 1913, Nîmes; s. of Adrien Lacombe and Marguerite Llorens; m. Geneviève Geoffroy 1939; three s. four d.; ed. Lycée de Nice, Lycée Saint-Louis, Paris, and Ecole Polytechnique, Paris; Marine Hydrographical Engineer 1935–55; Dir. Lab. of Physical Oceanography, Muséum de Paris 1955–82, Hon. Prof. 1982–; Dir. of scientific expeditions at sea—in the Mediterranean and Strait of Gibraltar; fmr. Pres. Int. Asscn. for the Physical Sciences of the Ocean 1970–75; Chair. UNESCO Intergovernmental Oceanographic Comm. 1965–67; mem. French Acad. of Sciences 1973, Marine Acad. 1976, Acad. Europaea 1993; Commdr. Ordre nat. du Mérite, Officier, Légion d'honneur, Croix de guerre, Chevalier du Mérite Maritime, des Palmes académiques, Commdr. Etoile d'Anjouan, Médaille d'Or Prince Albert 1er de Monaco 1976, etc. *Publications:* Etudes d'acoustique sous-marine 1946, Ouvrage sur courants de marée 1953, Mission hydrographique Maroc 1959; various studies on the movement of the sea 1949–84; Cours d'océanographie physique 1965, Les énergies de la mer 1968, 1979, Les mouvements de la mer 1971. *Address:* 43 rue Cuvier, 75231 Paris Cedex 05; 20 bis avenue de Lattre-de-Tassigny, 92340 Bourg-La-Reine, France (Home). *Telephone:* 46-64-23-22 (Home).

LACOSTE, Paul, O.C., PH.D.; Canadian university administrator; b. 24 April 1923, Montréal; s. of Emile and Juliette (née Boucher) Lacoste; m. 1st Louise Mackay (divorced), 2nd Louise Marcil 1973 (died 1995); one s. two d.; ed. Montreal, Chicago, Paris Univs.; Vice-Pres., Montreal Univ. 1966–75; Prof. Dept. of Philosophy, Montreal Univ. 1948–86; lawyer 1960–; Pres. Asscn. des universités partiellement ou entièrement de langue francaise 1978–81, Fonds Int. de coopération universitaire 1978–81, Asscn. of Univs. and Colls. of Canada 1978-79, Conf. of Rectors and Principals of Québec Univs. 1977–80, mem. Bd. Asscn. of Commonwealth Univs. 1977–80, Ecole polytechnique Montreal 1975–85, Clinical Research Inst. of Montreal 1975–, Ecole des hautes commerciales de Montreal 1982–85; Pres. Univ. of Montreal 1975–85; Chair. Comm. and Cttees. of the Fed. Environmental Assessment Review to the Great-Whale Hydroelectric Project 1991–98; Chevalier, Légion d'honneur 1985; Hon. LL.D. (McGill Univ.) 1975, (Univ. of Toronto) 1978; Dr. h.c. (Laval Univ.). *Publications:* Justice et paix scolaire 1962, A Place of Liberty 1964, Le Canada au seuil du siècle de l'abondance 1969, Principes de gestion universitaire 1970, Education permanente et potentiel universitaire 1977. *Leisure interests:* reading, music, travel. *Address:* 356 Woodlea Avenue, Ville Mont-Royal, P.Q., H3P 1R5, Canada. *Telephone:* (514) 343-7727 (Office); (514) 342-6150 (Home).

LACOUTURE, Jean Marie-Gérard, D. EN SOCIOLOGIE; French author; b. 9 June 1921, Bordeaux; s. of Antoine-Joseph Lacouture and Anne-Marie Servantie; m. Simonne Grésillon; one d.; journalist 1946–72; Press Attaché, Résidence-Générale of France, Morocco 1947–49; Diplomatic Ed. Combat 1950–51; reporter, Le Monde 1951–72; corresp. France-Soir, Egypt 1954–56; Research Fellow, Harvard Univ. 1966; Dir. of collections, Editions du Seuil 1962–80; Officer, Légion d'honneur, Commdr. des Arts et des Lettres; Prix Sola Cabiati de la Ville de Paris 1996. *Publications include:* Cinq Hommes et la France 1961, De Gaulle 1965, Le Vietnam entre deux paix 1965, Hô Chi Minh 1967, Nasser 1971, André Malraux, une vie dans le siècle 1973, Un sang d'encre 1974, Léon Blum 1977, Survive le peuple cambodgien! 1978, Signes du Taureau 1979, François Mauriac (2 vols.) 1980, Pierre Mendès France 1981, Le Piéton de Bordeaux 1981, Profils perdus 1983, De Gaulle (3 vols.) 1984–86, Algérie: la guerre est finie 1985, Champollion: Une vie de lumières 1989, Enquête sur l'auteur 1989, Jésuites (2 vols.) 1991–92, Voyous et gentlemen: une histoire du rugby 1993, le Désempire (jtly.) 1993, Une adolescence du siècle 1994, Mes héros et nos monstres 1995, Montaigne à cheval 1996, Histoire de France en cent tableaux; several works in collaboration with Simonne Lacouture and others. *Leisure interests:* reading, music, sport. *Address:* 37 quai des Grands Augustins, 75006 Paris, France.

LACROIX, Christian Marie Marc; French fashion designer; b. 16 May 1951, Arles; s. of Maxime Lacroix and Jeannette Bergier; m. Françoise Roesenstiehl 1989; ed. Lycée Frédéric Mistral, Arles, Univ. Paul Valéry, Montpellier, Univ. Paris-Sorbonne and Ecole du Louvre; Asst. Hermès 1978–79, Guy Paulin 1980–81; Artistic Dir. Jean Patou 1981–87, Christian Lacroix Feb. 1987–; design for Carmen, Nimes, France 1988, for L'as-tu revue? 1991, for les Caprices de Marianne 1994, for Phèdre à la Comédie

Française 1995; Dés d'or 1986, 1988, Council of fashion designers of America; Chevalier, Arts et Lettres 1991; Prix Balzac 1989. *Publication:* Pieces of a Pattern 1992, illustrations for albums Styles d'aujourd'hui 1995, Journal d'une collection 1996. *Address:* 73 Faubourg Saint Honoré, 75008 Paris, France. *Telephone:* (1) 42 65 79 08.

ŁĄCZKOWSKI, Paweł Julian; Polish politician; b. 31 July 1942, Kielce; m. Maria Łączkowska; one s., three d.; ed. Adam Mickiewicz Univ., Poznań; fmr. scientific worker, Adam Mickiewicz Univ., Poznań 1966–90; mem. Solidarity Independent Self-governing Trade Union 1980–; Deputy to Sejm (Parl.) 1989–93, 1997–, Deputy Chair. Civic Parl. Club 1989–90, Chair. Sejm Circle of Christian Democrats 1990–91, Chair. Parl. Club of Christian Democrats' Party (PChD) 1991–93, Parl. Comm. for Regulations and Deputies 1997–; mem. Solidarity Election Action Parl. Club 1997–; co-founder and leader Christian Democrats' Party (PChD) 1991–; Deputy Chair. Council of Ministers 1992–93. *Leisure interest:* gardening. *Address:* Sejm RP, ul. Wiejska 4/6/8, 00-902 Warsaw, Poland (Office). *Telephone:* 694 21 45/691 16 99.

LADER, Malcolm Harold, O.B.E., PH.D., M.D., D.SC., F.R.C.PSYCH.; British professor of clinical psychopharmacology; b. 27 Feb. 1936, Liverpool; m. Susan Packer 1961; three d.; ed. Liverpool Inst. High School and Liverpool and London Univs.; Research Asst. in Pharmacology, Univ. Coll. and Inst. of Psychiatry, London 1960–63; training in psychiatry 1963–66; external mem. of scientific staff of MRC 1966–; Reader Univ. of London 1973–78, Prof. 1978–; Consultant Psychiatrist, Bethlem Royal and Maudsley Hospitals 1970–; mem. various U.K. govt. advisory bodies; Hon. Fellow American Coll. of Psychiatrists 1994, British Asscn. for Psychopharmacology 1994, Soc. for the Study of Addiction 1998; Heinz Karger Memorial Foundation Prize 1974, Taylor Manor Award 1989. *Publications:* Psychiatry on Trial 1977, Introduction to Psychopharmacology 1980, Dependence on Tranquillizers 1984, Biological Treatments in Psychiatry 1990; numerous articles on psychopharmacology. *Leisure interests:* antiques, paintings. *Address:* Addiction Sciences Bldg., Institute of Psychiatry, De Crespigny Park, Denmark Hill, London, SE5 8AF, England. *Telephone:* 0171-703 5411.

LADER, Philip, M.A., J.D.; American diplomatist and government official; b. 17 March 1946, Jackson Heights, N.Y.; ed. Duke Univ., Univ. of Michigan, Oxford and Harvard Univs.; practised at bar 1972–79; law clerk to circuit judge 1973; partner Hartzog, Lader and Richards, Washington and Hilton Head Island, S.C. 1974–89; Pres. Sea Pines Co. and other cos. in Hilton Head Island, S.C. 1979–91, Winthrop Univ., S.C. 1983–85, Bond Univ., Gold Coast, Australia 1991–93, Business Execs. for Nat. Security, Washington 1991; Deputy Dir. for Man., Office of Man. and Budget, Exec. Office of the Pres.; Chair. Pres.'s Council for Integrity and Efficiency 1993, Pres.'s Man. Council, Policy Cttee., Nat. Performance Review 1993; Deputy Chief of Staff, White House 1993–94; Amb. to U.K. 1997–; mem. Chief Execs. Org.; Hon. LL.D. (Limestone Coll.), Hon. S.J.D. (Univ. of S.C.), Hon. L.H.D. (Youngstown State Univ., Lander Univ.). *Address:* American Embassy, 24–32 Grosvenor Square, London, W1A 1AE, England. *Telephone:* 0171-499 9000. *Fax:* 0171-629 9124.

LADOUCETTE, Philippe de; French government official; b. March 1948; civil engineer; held appt. with DATAR 1983–86; Adviser to Minister of Industry 1986–88; Deputy Dir. Office of Minister for Trade and Econ. Devt., also assigned to Secr. of Channel Tunnel 1988–93; Pres. Admin Council, Houillères du Bassin du Centre et du Midi 1994–; Pres., Dir.-Gen. Charbonnages de France 1996– (Dir. 1995–). *Leisure interest:* tennis. *Address:* Charbonnages de France, 100 avenue Albert 1er, B.P. 220, 92503 Rueil-Malmaison Cedex (Office); 40 avenue Marceau, 75008 Paris, France.

LADREIT DE LACHARRIERE, Marc; French business executive; b. 6 Nov. 1940, Nice; m. Sibylle Lucet 1967; one s. three d.; ed. Ecole Nat. d'Admin.; Asst. Man. Banque de Suez et de l'Union des Mines 1970, Asst. Dir. 1971, Deputy Dir. 1973; Vice-Pres. Masson Belfond Armand Colin 1974–; Vice-Dir. Banque de l'Indochine et de Suez 1975, Corporate Affairs Dir. 1976; Financial Dir. L'Oreal 1976, Man. Dir. Admin. and Finance 1977, Vice-Pres. Man. Cttee. 1978, mem. Strategic Cttee., Dir. and Exec. Vice-Pres. 1984–91, Pres. of Finances 1987–91; Pres. la Revue des deux Mondes 1990–, Financière Marc de Lacharrière (Fimalac) 1991–, Council Banque de la Mutuelle industrielle 1988; Vice-Pres. Sofres 1992–, fmr. Vice-Pres. Centenaire Blanzy, Pres. 1994–; Pres. Financière Sofres 1992–, Lille Bonnières & Colombe et Alspi 1993–, Comptoir Lyon Allemand Louyot 1995; Chair. Geral, U.S.A.; Man. Dir. Regefi and Holdilux, Luxembourg; Vice-Chair. L'Oreal (G.B.), Editions Masson; Dir. Collection de l'Inst. de l'Entreprise, France Télécom 1995–, Air France 1996–; Lecturer, Inst. d'Etudes Politiques, Paris 1971, then Prof.; Adviser, Foreign Trade of France; numerous directorships; Officier, Légion d'honneur, Ordre Nat. du Mérite, Officier des Arts et des Lettres. *Leisure interests:* tennis, skiing. *Address:* Fimalac, 97 rue de Lille, 75007 Paris, France.

LAERMANN, Karl-Hans; German politician and university professor; b. 26 Dec. 1929, Kaulhausen; s.of Johann Laermann and Elisabeth Laermann; m. Hilde Woestemeyer 1955; three s. one d.; ed. Rhenish-Westphalian Coll. of Advanced Tech., Aachen; lecturer in Experimental Statics, Rhenish-Westphalian Coll. of Advanced Tech. 1966–74; Prof. of Statics, Bergische Univ. G.H. Wuppertal, Head Lab. for Experimental Stress Analysis and Measurement 1974–; mem. FDP 1968–, mem. Fed. Exec. Cttee. 1980–90, N. Rhine-Westphalian Exec. Cttee. 1978–94, Chair. Fed. Cttee. on Research and Tech. of FDP 1981–96; mem. Bundestag (Parl.) 1974–; Deputy Chair. working group of FDP Parl. Group on Educ. and Science, Research and Tech. 1980–94; Fed. Minister of Educ. and Science Feb.–Nov. 1994; mem. Bd. Trustees Volkswagen Foundation 1984–94, Friedrich Naumann Foundation 1984–, Anglo-German Foundation for the Study of Industrial Society 1989–; mem. Admin. Bd. Inter Nationes 1995–; Extraordinary mem. Goethe Institut 1995–; Hon. C.B.E. (U.K.) 1978, Commdr. Order of Orange-Nassau (Netherlands) 1982, Great Cross of Order of Fed. Repub. of Germany 1985. *Publications:* Konstruktiver Ingenieurbau (Ed.) 1967, Experimentelle Plattenuntersuchungen-Theoretische Grundlagen 1971, Experimentelle Spannungsanalyse I, II 1972, 1977, Perpektiven—Ein Wissenschaftler in der Politik 1984; about 210 publs. on science and politics in int. journals. *Leisure interests:* painting, sailing. *Address:* Am Tannenberg 19, 41189 Mönchengladbach, Germany. *Telephone:* 02166-58164. *Fax:* 02166-58164.

LAEYENDECKER, Leonardus, PH.D.; Netherlands sociologist and institute director; b. 18 June 1930, Utrecht; s. of Leonardus Laeyendecker and Jacoba Petronella Pot; m. Mary Anne Thung 1969; ed. Univ. of Amsterdam; lecturer in Sociology, Univ. of Amsterdam 1964–69, Reader 1969–73; Prof. of Gen. Sociology, Univ. of Leyden 1973–89; Dir. Multidisciplinary Inst. for Church and Soc. 1989–92; Fellow Netherlands Inst. for Advanced Study in the Humanities and Social Sciences; mem. Soc. of Sciences of Holland, Royal Netherlands Acad. of Arts and Sciences. *Publications:* Religion and Conflict 1967, Strategies of Social Change (with W. F. van Stegeren) 1978, Order, Change and Inequality 1981, Social Change, Problems and Theories 1984, Choice as a Necessity 1984, Does Progress Help Us? 1986, Exploring the New Religious Consciousness (with M. A. Thung, G. van Tillo and others) 1985, To Control Charisma. Salvation and Power in the Roman Catholic Church 1993, Culture in Danger: essays on modernity, science and religion 1994. *Leisure interests:* photography. *Address:* Marskramersbaan 16, 3981 TK Bunnik, The Netherlands. *Telephone:* (030) 6567803.

LAFFAN, Brigid, PH.D.; Irish professor of European politics; b. 6 Jan. 1955; d. of Con Burns and Aileen Burns; m. Michael Laffan 1979; one s. two d.; ed. Univ. of Limerick, Coll. of Europe, Bruges, Trinity Coll. Dublin; researcher, European Cultural Foundation 1977–78; lecturer, Coll. of Humanities, Univ. of Limerick 1979–86; lecturer, Inst. of Public Admin. 1986–89; Newman Scholar, Univ. Coll. Dublin 1989–90, lecturer, Dept. of Politics 1990–91, Jean Monnet Prof. of European Politics 1991–; Visiting Prof., Coll. of Europe, Bruges 1992–. *Publications:* Ireland and South Africa 1988, Integration and Co-operation in Europe 1992, The Finances of the European Union 1992, Constitution Building in the European Union (Ed.) 1996; numerous articles on Irish foreign policy, EC budgetary policy, insts., governance and political union. *Leisure interests:* theatre, reading, swimming. *Address:* Department of Politics, University College, Belfield, Dublin 4 (Office); 4 Willowbank, The Slopes, Monkstown, Co. Dublin, Ireland (Home). *Telephone:* (1) 706 8344 (Office); (1) 286 2617 (Home). *Fax:* (1) 706 1171 (Office); (1) 284 5331 (Home).

LAFFITTE, Pierre Paul; French engineer and politician; b. 1 Jan. 1925, Saint Paul, Alpes Maritimes; s. of Jean Laffitte and Lucie Fink; m. 1st Sophie Glikman-Toumarkine (deceased), 2nd Anita Garcia; ed. Lycée de Nice and Ecole Polytechnique; Dir. Office of Geological, Geophysical and Mining Research 1953; Asst. Dir.-Gen. Office of Geological and Mining Research 1959–62, Deputy Dir. 1963, Dir. 1973–84; Gen. Engineer Mines 1973–; Pres. Conseil de Perfectionnement, Ecole Nat. Supérieure des Mines, Paris 1984–91; Founder Pres. Sophia-Antipolis 1969; Pres. Franco-German Asscn. for Science and Tech., AFAST (German-French Asscn. for Science and Tech.); Senator from Alpes Maritimes 1985–; shared Adenauer—de Gaulle Prize 1995; Officier, Légion d'honneur; Officier, Ordre Nat. du Mérite; Commdr. Order of Polar Star (Sweden); Commdr. Order of Merit of Fed. Repub. of Germany. *Publications:* works on mining and geology, and science parks. *Leisure interest:* gardening. *Address:* Palais du Luxembourg, 75291 Paris Cedex 06; Ecole des Mines, 60 boulevard Saint Michel, 75006 Paris, France. *Telephone:* 01.40.51.90.30.

LAFFONT, Jean-Jacques Marcel, PH.D.; French economist; b. 13 April 1947, Toulouse; s. of Jean Laffont and Emilienne Perry; m. Colette Sonntag 1968; four d.; ed. Lycée Pierre de Fermat, Toulouse, Univ. of Toulouse, Univ. of Paris, Harvard Univ.; researcher Nat. Centre for Scientific Research (CNRS) 1975–77; Prof., Univ. of Amiens 1977–78, Univ. of Toulouse 1978–; Sr. Polytechnic Lecturer 1975–87; Dir. of Studies Ecole des hautes études en sciences sociales 1980–; Fairschild Fellow, Calif. Inst. of Tech. 1987; Taussig Research Prof., Harvard Univ. 1988; mem. Inst. Universitaire de France 1991; Fellow, then Pres. Econometric Soc. 1992; hon. mem. American Econ. Asscn., French Asscn. of Econ. Sciences; foreign mem. A.A.A.S.; Chevalier, Légion d'honneur; Wells Prize, Harvard Univ., CNRS Silver Medal. *Publications:* Externalités et théorie économique 1977, Incentives in Public Decision-Making 1979, Fondements de l'économie publique 1982, Economie de l'information et de l'incertain 1985, A Theory of Incentives in Procurement and Regulation 1993; numerous articles in econ. publs. *Leisure interests:* gardening, tennis, skiing. *Address:* Université des sciences sociales, place Anatole France, 31042 Toulouse (Office); 11 chemin des Tuileries, 31770 Colomiers, France (Home).

LAFFONT, Robert Raoul, L. EN D.; French publishing executive; b. 30 Nov. 1916, Marseille; s. of Raymond Laffont and Nathalie Périer; m. Hélène Furterer 1987; three s. two d. (from previous marriages); ed. Lycée Périer, Marseille and Ecole des Hautes Etudes Commerciales, Paris; Lieut. 94th

Regt. of Artillery, Montagne; f. Edns. Robert Laffont, Marseille 1941, transferred to Paris 1945, Pres. 1959–86; Fondateur du Pont-Royal; Chevalier, Légion d'honneur, Officier, Ordre nat. du Mérite. *Publication:* Robert Laffont, éditeur 1974, Léger étonnement avant le saut 1995. *Leisure interest:* football. *Address:* Editions Robert Laffont, 24 avenue Marceau, 75008 Paris (Office); 11 rue Pierre Nicole, Paris 75005, France (Home). *Telephone:* 43.29.12.33 (Office); 43.26.02.41 (Home).

LAFONTAINE, Oskar; German politician; b. 16 Sept. 1943, Saarlouis; m.; ed. Univs. of Bonn and Saarbrücken; Mayor of Saarbrücken 1976–85; mem. Saarland Landtag (Regional Parl.), Minister-Pres. 1985–98; Chair. SPD Regional Asscn., Saar 1977–96; mem. SPD Cen. Cttee.; Chair. SPD Regional Asscn., Saar 1977–96; Vice-Chair. SPD 1987–96; Cand. for Chancellorship 1990; Leader SPD 1995–99; Minister of Finance 1998–99; Social Democrat. *Publications:* Angst vor den Freunden 1983, Der andere Fortschritt 1985, Die Gesellschaft der Zukunft 1988, Das Lied vom Teilen 1989, Deutsche Wahrheiten 1990. *Address:* c/o Ministry of Finance, 53117 Bonn, Graurheindorfer Str. 108, Germany.

LA FOREST, Gerard V., B.C.L., M.A., LL.M., J.S.D., LL.D., D.U., D.C.L., F.R.S.C.; Canadian judge; b. 1 April 1926, Grand Falls, N.B.; s. of J. Alfred La Forest and Philomene Lajoie; m. Marie Warner 1952; five d.; ed. St. Francis Xavier Univ., Univ. of New Brunswick, St. John's Coll. Oxford and Yale Univ.; called to Bar, New Brunswick 1949; Q.C. 1968; practising lawyer, Grand Falls 1951–52; Advisory Counsel, Dept. of Justice, Ottawa 1952–55; Legal Adviser, Irving Oil and assoc. cos. 1955–56; Assoc. Prof. of Law, Univ. of New Brunswick 1956–63, Prof. 1963–68; Dean of Law, Univ. of Alberta 1968–70; Asst. Deputy Attorney-Gen. of Canada (Research and Planning) 1970–74; Commr. Law Reform Comm. of Canada 1974–79; Prof. and Dir. Legis. Drafting Program, Faculty of Law (Common Law Section), Univ. of Ottawa 1979–81; Judge, Court of Appeal of New Brunswick 1981; Judge, Supreme Court of Canada 1985–97; consultant to fed. and provincial govts.; mem. numerous cttees., public bodies etc.; Fellow, World Acad. of Art and Science; numerous hon. degrees and other distinctions. *Address:* c/o Supreme Court of Canada, Wellington Street, Ottawa, Ont. K1A 0J1, Canada.

LAFORTE, Conrad, D. ÈS L., F.R.S.C.; Canadian university professor; b. 10 Nov. 1921, Kenogami, P.Q.; s. of Philippe Laforte and Marie-Mathilda Dallaire; m. Hélène Gauthier 1957; one d.; ed. Montréal Univ. and Laval Univ.; librarian and archivist, Folklore Archives, Laval Univ. 1951–75; Instructor CELAT, Laval Univ. 1965–67, Asst. Prof. 1967–73, Assoc. Prof. 1973–77, Prof. 1977–81, Titular Prof. Dept. of History and CELAT 1981–88; mem. Royal Soc. of Canada 1982; Fellow Emer. CELAT, Laval Univ. 1984; several awards for folklore research etc., including Médaille Luc Lacourcière 1981; Distinguished Perm. mem. Folklore Studies Asscn. of Canada 1988. *Publications:* Le chanson folklorique et les écrivains du XIXe siècle 1973, Poétiques de la chanson traditionnelle française 1976, Catalogue de la chanson folklorique française (6 vols.) 1977–87, Menteries drôles et merveilleuses 1978, Survivances médiévales dans la chanson folklorique 1981, Chansons folkloriques à sujet religieux 1988, La chanson de tradition orale, une découverte des écrivains du XIXe siècle (en France et au Québec) 1995, Vision d'une société par les chausons de tradition orale à caractère épique et tragique 1997, Chansons de facture médiévale retrouvées dans la tradition orale (2 vols.) 1997. *Address:* 949 rue Gatineau, Sainte-Foy, P.Q., G1V 3A2, Canada.

LÅG, Jul, DR.AGR.; Norwegian professor of soil science; b. 13 Nov. 1915, Flesberg; s. of Torsten S. Buind Låg and Jøran Låg; m. Ingrid Brenner 1956 (died 1979); one s. one d.; ed. Agric. Univ. of Norway; Prof. of Soil Science, Agric. Univ. of Norway 1949–85, Rector 1968–71; Chair. Agric. Council of Norway 1972–73; mem. Council, Int. Soc. of Soil Science 1977–79, Chair. Working Group on Soils and Geomedicine 1986–; Pres. Norwegian Acad. of Science and Letters 1976–84; Vice-Chair. Norwegian Council of Parliaments and Scientists 1969–86; corresp. mem. Soil Science Soc. of Germany, Michelsens Inst. of Science and Intellectual Freedom; hon. mem. Dokuchaev Soil Science Soc. of Russia; mem. of Royal Norwegian Soc. of Science and Letters; mem. of Danish, Finnish, Polish and Swedish Acads.; mem. ed. bds. of Agrochimica (Italy), Geoderma (Netherlands), Ambio (Sweden), Soil Science (U.S.A.), Alexandria Science Exchange, Trends in Agricultural Sciences (India), Pedosphere (China); Commdr. Cross of Icelandic Order of the Falcon; Copernicus Medal (Polish Acad.). *Publications:* 18 books and more than 200 papers in soil science and related subjects. *Leisure interests:* skiing, literature. *Address:* Department of Soil and Water Sciences, Agricultural University of Norway, P.O. Box 5027, 1432 Ås, Norway. *Telephone:* 09-94 7500. *Fax:* 09-948211.

LAGARDE, Paul, D. EN D.; French professor of law; b. 3 March 1934, Rennes; s. of Gaston Lagarde and Charlotte Béquignon; m. Bernadette Lamberts 1962; two s. one d.; ed. Paris Univ.; Prof. Faculty of Law, Nancy 1961–69, Nanterre 1969–71; Prof. of Private Int. Law, Univ. of Paris I 1971–; Gen. Sec. Revue critique de droit international privé 1962, Ed.-in-Chief 1976, Dir 1990; Pres. Comité Français de droit int. privé 1987–90; Conseiller d'Etat enservice extraordinaire 1996–; Assoc. mem. Inst. of Int. Law; Dr. h.c. (Freiburg i.Br.). *Publications:* Recherches sur l'ordre public en droit international privé 1959, La réciprocité en droit international privé 1977, Le principe de proximité dans le droit international privé contemporain 1987, La nationalité française 1989, Traité de droit international privé (with Henri Batiffol, q.v.) 1993. *Address:* 32 bis boulevard Jean Jaurès, 92100 Boulogne-Billancourt, France. *Telephone:* (1) 48.25.69.03. *Fax:* (1) 41.10.84.80.

LAGARDÈRE, Jean-Luc; French business executive and engineer; b. 10 Feb. 1928, Aubiet, Gers; s. of André Lagardère and Marthe Fourcade; m. Elizabeth Pimenta Lucas 1993; one s. (from previous marriage); ed. Lycée Buffon, Auch, Lycée Saint-Louis, Paris, École supérieure d'électricité; eng. then Head of Dept. Marcel Dassault Gen. aéronautique 1951–62; Admin., Dir.-Gen. Soc. Matra 1963–76, Pres., Dir-Gen. 1977–92; Admin. Europe No. 1 Images et Son 1972, Vice-Pres., Del 1973, Pres., Del. 1979–81; Pres. Supervisory Bd. Europe No. 1 Télécie., Régie No. 1 1978–; Vice-Pres. Supervisory Bd. CERT 1978–; Admin. Manurhin 1978–; Pres., Dir.-Gen. Soc. Hachette, merged with Matra to form Lagardère Group Dec. 1992– (Matra Hachette) 1981–92, Pres. Matra Hachette 1992; Man. Partner, Gen. Man. Lagardère S.C.A. 1996–; fmr. Pres. Librairie Hachette, Chair. and C.E.O. 1991–; Pres. de la Société unifiée France galop 1995–; mem. Admin. Council Renault 1988–, mem. Bd. 1988–; mem. Bd. Crédit Lyonnais 1994–; Pres. Hachette Foundation 1989–; Man. of the Year, Nouvel Economiste 1979; Officier, Légion d'honneur, Commdr., Ordre nat. du Mérite. *Leisure interests:* football, tennis, skiing. *Address:* Matra Hachette, 4 rue de Presbourg, 75116 Paris, France (Office).

LAGAYETTE, Philippe Ernest Georges; French government official; b. 16 June 1943, Tulle (Corrèze); s. of Elie Lagayette and Renée Portier; m. Marie-Louise Antoni 1979; two s. two d.; ed. Ecole Polytechnique and Ecole Nat. d'Admin.; Eng. Génie Maritime 1965; Insp. des Finances 1970; Deputy Dir. Treasury Man., Ministry of Economy, Finance and Budget 1980; Dir. Cabt. of Minister of Economy, Finance and Budget 1981–84; Deputy Gov. Banque de France 1984, First Deputy Gov. 1990; Insp.-Gen. des Finances 1988–; Dir.-Gen. Caisse des Dépôts et Consignations 1992–97; Pres. JP Morgan and Cie SA 1998–; Chevalier, Légion d'honneur, Officier, Ordre nat. du Mérite. *Address:* JP Morgan, Place Vendôme, Paris (Office); 10 avenue d'Eylau, 75116 Paris, France (Home).

LAGERCRANTZ, Olof, PH.D.; Swedish journalist; b. 10 March 1911, Stockholm; s. of Carl and Agnes (née Hamilton) Lagercrantz; m. Martina Ruin 1939; three s. two d.; Cultural Ed., Dagens Nyheter 1951–60, Chief Ed. 1960–75; Prize of Nordic Council (jointly) 1965. *Publications:* Från helvetet till paradiset 1964, Den pågående skapelsen 1966, Att finnas till Joyce's Ulysses 1970, China-Report 1971, Tretton lyriker o fågeltruppen 1973, Enhörningen 1977, August Strindberg, a Biography 1979 (English and American edns. 1984), Min första krets (autobiog.) 1982, Om konsten att läsa och skriva 1985, Färd med Mörkrets Hjärta (on Joseph Conrad's Heart of Darkness) 1987, Ett år på sextiotalet 1990, Att Läsa Proust 1992, Gunnar Ekelöf: "Jag bor i en annan värld men du bor ju i samma", Dikten om livet på den andra sidan: en bok om Emanuel Swedenborg 1996, Tysk Övers 1997; biographies and collections of poems and essays. *Leisure interest:* writing. *Address:* Box 28, 17802 Drottingholm, Sweden. *Telephone:* 08-7590651.

LAGERFELD, Karl-Otto; German fashion designer; b. 1938, Hamburg; ed. privately and at art school, Hamburg; fashion apprentice with Balmain and Patou 1959; freelance designer associated with Fendi, Rome 1963–, Chloe, Paris 1964–83, Chanel, Paris 1982–, Isetan, Japan; designer Karl Lagerfeld's Women's Wear, Karl Lagerfeld France Inc. 1983–; first collection under his own name 1984; Hon. Teacher, Vienna 1983; costume design for film Comédie d'Amour 1989; awarded Golden Thimble 1986. *Publications:* Lagerfeld's Sketchbook (with Anna Piaggi), Helmut Newton 1990, Karl Lagerfeld Off the Record 1995.

LAGERGREN, Gunnar Karl Andreas; Swedish judge; b. 23 Aug. 1912, Stockholm; m. Nina von Dardel 1943; one s. three d.; ed. Stockholm Univ.; Arbitrator, Int. Chamber of Commerce, Paris 1949–81; Judge, Stockholm Court of Appeal 1957–66; Pres. Court of Appeal for Western Sweden, Göteborg 1966–77; Judge, European Court of Human Rights, Strasbourg 1977–88; Pres. Comm. on Int. Commercial Practice of Int. Chamber of Commerce 1951–67; Pres. Supreme Restitution Court, Fed. Repub. of Germany 1964–91; Chair. Italian-Somali Arbitration Tribunal in Mogadishu 1964; Chair. Indo-Pakistan Western Boundary Tribunal, Geneva 1965–69; Vice-Pres. Arbitration Comm. on Property Rights and Interests in Germany, Koblenz 1956–69; mem. Int. Court, Tangier 1953–56; mem. Permanent Court of Arbitration, The Hague 1966–90; sole Arbitrator of the BP/Libya Concession Tribunal, Copenhagen 1972–75; Deputy Chair. Appeals Bd. of the Council of Europe 1981–87, Chair. 1987–90 and 1994 (*ad hoc*); Pres. Iran-U.S.A. Claims Tribunal, The Hague 1981–84; Pres. Arbitral Tribunal for German External Debts, Koblenz 1982–; Pres. Egypt-Israel Taba Arbitration Tribunal, Geneva 1986–89; Marshal of the Realm (Excellency) 1976–82; Dr. h.c. (Uppsala Univ.) 1965. *Address:* Dahlbergsvägen 22, 182 62 Djursholm, Sweden. *Telephone:* 8/7555826.

LAGHI, H.E. Cardinal Pio, S.T.D., J.C.D.; Italian ecclesiastic; b. 21 May 1922, Castiglione (Fiorlì); ed. Pontifical Lateran Univ. Rome and Pontifical Ecclesiastical Acad.; Sec. Apostolic Nunciature, Managua 1952–54, Apostolic Del. Washington, D.C. 1954–61, Apostolic Nunciature, New Delhi 1961–64; served in Secr. of State of Vatican 1964–69; elevated to rank of Archbishop 1969; Apostolic Del. in Jerusalem and Palestine 1969–74, also assumed duties of Pro-Nuncio to Cyprus and Apostolic Visitor to Greece; Apostolic Nuncio, Argentina 1974–80; Apostolic Del. in U.S.A. 1980–84, Apostolic Pro-Nuncio 1984; Prefect, Congregation for Catholic Educ., Vatican 1990–; cr.

Cardinal 1991; Pres. Pontifical Oratory of St. Peter 1992; Cardinal Patron, Sovereign Mil. Order of Malta 1993. *Address:* Congregation for Catholic Education, Palazzo delle Congregazioni, Piazza Pio XII 3, 00193 Rome, Vatican City.

LAGRAVENESE, Richard, B.F.A.; American film screenplay writer, director and producer; b. 30 Oct. 1959, Brooklyn, New York; s. of Patrick LaGravenese and Lucille LaGravenese; m. Ann Weiss LaGravenese 1986; one d.; ed. Lafayette High School, Emerson Coll. and New York Univ. *Screenplays:* Rude Awakening, The Fisher King 1991, The Ref (also producer) 1994, A Little Princess 1995, The Bridges of Madison County 1995, The Horse Whisperer 1998, Living Out Loud (also dir.) 1998, Unstrung Heroes; Independent Film Project Writer of the Year. *Leisure interests:* theatre, books, family. *Address:* c/o Kirsten Bonelli, 8383 Wilshire Boulevard, Suite 340, Beverly Hills, CA 90211, U.S.A.

LAGU, Lieut.-Gen. Joseph; Sudanese politician, army officer and diplomatist; b. 21 Nov. 1931; s. of Yakobo Yanga and Marini Kaluma; ed. Rumbek Secondary School, Mil. Acad. Omdurman; served in Sudanese Army 1960–63; joined South Sudan Liberation Movt. 1963, Leader SSLM 1969; signed peace agreement with Govt. of Sudan March 1972; Second Vice-Pres. of Sudan 1978–80, 1982–85; Pres. Supreme Exec. Council for the South 1978–80; fmr. Perm. Rep. to U.N.; Order of the Two Niles 1972. *Publication:* The Anya-Nya—what we fight for 1972. *Address:* c/o Ministry of Foreign Affairs, Khartoum, Sudan.

LAGUNA, Frederica, PH.D.; American anthropologist; b. 3 Oct. 1906, Ann Arbor, Mich.; d. of Theodore and Grace Andrus de Laguna; ed. Phoebe Anna Thorne School, Bryn Mawr, Pa., Bryn Mawr Coll. and Columbia Univ.; on staff of Univ. of Pa. Museum 1931–34; U.S. Soil Conservation Service 1935–36; Lecturer, Bryn Mawr Coll. 1938–41, Asst. Prof. 1941–42, 1946–49, Assoc. Prof. 1949–55, Prof. of Anthropology 1955–75; U.S.N.R. 1942–45; Chair. Dept. of Sociology and Anthropology, Bryn Mawr Coll. 1950–67, Chair. Dept. of Anthropology 1967–72, R. Kenan Jr. Prof. 1974–75, Prof. Emer. 1975–; Bryn Mawr Coll. European Fellowship 1927; Columbia Univ. Fellowship 1930–31; Nat. Research Council Fellow 1936–37; Rockefeller Post-War Fellow 1945–46; Viking Fund Fellow 1949, Social Science Research Council Faculty Fellow 1962–63; Hon. Fellow Rochester (New York) Museum of Arts and Sciences 1941; Fellow A.A.A.S., American Anthropological Asscn. (Pres. 1966–67); Fellow and Hon. Life mem. Arctic Inst. of N. America; mem. N.A.S.; Hon. Life Mem. Alaska Anthropological Asscn. (Hon. Pres. 1991–), Asscn. for Northern Studies (Japan); Hon. D.Hum.Litt. (Alaska); Lindback Award for Distinguished Teaching 1975, Distinguished Service Award, American Anthropological Asscn. 1986, Fiftieth Anniversary Award, Soc. for American Archaeology 1988, Alaska Anthropology Asscn. Award for Lifetime Contributions 1993, American Book Award, Before Columbus Foundation 1995. *Publications:* The Archaeology of Cook Inlet, Alaska 1934, The Eyak Indians of the Copper River Delta, Alaska (with Kaj Birket-Smith) 1938, The Prehistory of Northern North America as Seen from the Yukon 1947, Chugach Prehistory: The Archaeology of Prince William Sound, Alaska 1956, The Story of a Tlingit Community 1960, Selected Papers from the American Anthropologist 1888–1920 (ed.) 1960, Archeology of the Yakutat Bay Area, Alaska (jtly.) 1964, Under Mount Saint Elias: The History and Culture of the Yakutat Tlingit 1972, Voyage to Greenland: A Personal Initiation into Anthropology 1977, The Tlingit Indians, by George Thornton Emmons (ed.) 1991, Tales from the Dena 1995; novels: The Thousand March: Adventures of an American Boy with Garibaldi 1930, The Arrow Points to Murder 1937, Fog on the Mountain 1938; contribs. to learned journals. *Address:* The Quadrangle, Apt. 1310, 3300 Darby Road, Haverford, PA 19041-1067, U.S.A. *Telephone:* (610) 658-2298.

LAHHAM, Duraid, B.SC.; Syrian actor and academic; b. 1934, Damascus; m. Hala Bitar; two s. one d.; ed. Damascus Univ.; lecturer, Univ. of Damascus 1955–60; stage roles 1960–; comedian, Pres. of the Syrian Assoc. of Artists 1967. *Films include:* The Pearl Necklace 1965, Dream Castle 1966, Love Affair in Istanbul 1967, As Saalik 1968, Khayyat As-Sayyidate 1969. *Publications:* author of several comedies. *Leisure interest:* accordionist. *Address:* Syrian Broadcasting Corporation, Omayya Square, Damascus, Syria.

LAHNSTEIN, Manfred; German politician and civil servant; b. 20 Dec. 1937, Rhineland; joined SPD 1959; at European Comm., Brussels, latterly as Chef de Cabinet to Commr. Wilhelm Haferkamp 1967–73; econ. adviser, Chancellery 1973; moved to Finance Ministry 1974, successively Div. Head and State Sec. in charge of Financial and Monetary Policy 1974–80; Chancellor's Chief Civil Servant 1980–82; Minister of Finance April–Oct. 1982; Pres. Electronic Media Group; mem. Bd. Dirs. Bertelsmann AG 1983–. *Address:* Carl-Bertelsmannstrasse 270, 33335 Gütersloh, Germany.

LAHOUD, Gen. Emile; Lebanese politician and army officer; b. 1936, Baabdate; s. of Gen. Jamil Lahoud and Adrenee Bajakian; m. Andrée Amadouni; two s. one d.; ed. Brumana High School, also attended various courses at Naval Acads. in U.K. and U.S.A. 1958–80; joined Mil. Acad. as cadet officer 1956, promoted to Ensign 1959, Sub.-Lieut. 1962, Lieut. 1968, Lieut.-Commdr. 1974, Commdr. 1976, Cap. 1980, Rear Adm. 1985, Gen. 1989; Commdr. of Second Fleet 1966–68, of First Fleet 1968–70; Staff of Army Fourth Bureau 1970–72; Chief of Personal Staff of Gen. and Commdr. of Armed Forces 1973–79; Dir. of Personnel, Army HQ 1980–83; Pres. of Mil. Office, Ministry of Defence 1983–89; Gen. and Commdr. of Armed Forces 1989–; Pres. of the Lebanon 1998–; Lebanese Medal of Merit Gen. Officer 1989, Medal of Merit and Honour, Haiti 1974, War Medals 1991, 1992, Dawn of the South Medal 1993, Nat. Unity Medal 1993, Medal of Esteem 1994; Grand Cordon Order of the Cedar 1993, Commdr. Légion d'Honneur, Grand Cross of Argentina 1998. *Address:* Office of the President, Baabda, Beirut, Lebanon. *Telephone:* 1-220000.

LAI SHAOQI; Chinese painter and calligrapher; b. 16 May 1915, Puning Co., Guangdong Prov.; m. Zeng Fei 1943; one s. two d.; ed. Guangzhou Inst. of Fine Arts; joined Nat. Resistance Woodcut Asscn. 1937; joined CP and New 4th Army 1939; Deputy Dir. Propaganda Dept. of Anhui Prov. CP 1960–66, 1977–82; Vice-Chair. Graphic Art Asscn. 1980, Chinese Graphic Artists' Asscn. 1991–; Pres. Anhui Prov. Br. of Writers' Union 1981–; mem. Nat. Cttee. of 6th CPPCC 1986–; Art Advisor Guangzhou and Guandong NPC; Advisor to Guandong Chinese Art Acad.; Hon. Chair. Guangzhou municipal asscn. of artists; Pres. Huang Binghong Research Soc.; Hon. Prof. Shantou Univ., Anhui Univ.; Chair. Anhui Prov. Fed. of Literary and Art Circles. *Address:* Room 302, No 7, Shui Yin Road No. 45, Huan Shi Dong Road, Guangzhou, People's Republic of China. *Telephone:* 755362, 76553.

LAI, Jimmy; Hong Kong business executive, journalist and publisher; Propr. Giordano (retail clothing chain) 1980–, Chair. 1980–94; Publr. Next Magazine 1990–, Apple Daily 1995–. *Address:* Apple Daily, 6/F Garment Centre, 576–586 Castle Peak Road, Cheung Sha Wan; Next Magazine, Westlands Centre, 10/F, 20 Westlands Road, Quarry Bay, Hong Kong. *Telephone:* 2990 8685 (Apple Daily); 2811 9686 (Next Magazine). *Fax:* 2370 8908 (Apple Daily); 2811 3862 (Next Magazine).

LAIDLAW, Sir Christophor Charles Fraser, Kt.; British business executive; b. 9 Aug. 1922; s. of late Hugh Alexander Lyon Laidlaw and Sarah Georgina Fraser; m. Nina Mary Prichard 1952; one s. three d.; ed. Rugby School and St. John's Coll. Cambridge; served War of 1939–45, Europe and Far East, Maj. on Gen. Staff; joined British Petroleum Co. Ltd. (BP) 1948, BP rep. in Hamburg 1959–61, Gen. Man. Marketing Dept. 1963–67, Dir. BP Trading 1967, Pres. BP Belgium 1967–71, Dir. (Operations) 1971–72, Chair. BP Germany 1972–83, Man. Dir. BP Co. Ltd. 1972–81, Deputy Chair. 1980–81; Chair. BP Oil 1977–81, BP Oil Int. 1981, ICL 1981–84; Pres. ICL France 1983; Dir. Dalgety 1984–92, Redland 1984–92, Commercial Union Assurance Co. 1978–83, Barclays Bank Int. Ltd. 1980–87, Barclays Bank 1981–88, Amerada Hess Corpn. 1983–94, Barclays Merchant Bank 1984–87, Mercedes-Benz (U.K.) 1986–93, Amerada Ltd. 1985–, Daimler Benz (U.K.) Ltd. 1994–; Chair. Boving & Co. 1984–85, Bridon PLC 1985–90; Dir. INSEAD 1987–94 (Chair. U.K. Advisory Bd. 1984–91); Master Tallow Chandlers Co. 1988–89; Pres. German Chamber of Industry and Commerce 1983–86; Vice-Pres. British-German Soc. 1996–; Hon. Fellow St. John's Coll., Cambridge 1996. *Leisure interests:* fishing, shooting. *Address:* 49 Chelsea Square, London, SW3 6LH, England.

LAIDLER, David Ernest William, PH.D., F.R.S.C.; Canadian/British economist; b. 12 Aug. 1938, Tynemouth, U.K.; s. of John Alphonse Laidler and Leonora Laidler (née Gosman); m. Antje Charlotte Breitwisch 1965; one d.; ed. Tynemouth School, London School of Econs., Univs. of Syracuse and Chicago, U.S.A.; Asst. Lecturer, L.S.E. 1961–62; Asst. Prof., Univ. of Calif., Berkeley 1963–66; lecturer, Univ., of Essex 1966–69; Prof., Univ. of Manchester 1969–75; Prof. of Econs., Univ. of Western Ont. 1975–, Dept. Chair. 1981–84; Special Advisor Bank of Canada 1998–99; Adjunct Scholar, C.D. Howe Inst., Toronto 1990–; Visiting Economist, Reserve Bank of Australia 1977; Assoc. Ed. Journal of Money, Credit and Banking 1979–; mem. Editorial Bd. Pakistan Devt. Review 1987–, Journal of Policy Modelling 1990–; fmr. mem. editorial bd. several other journals; co-founder and mem. Exec. Cttee. Money Study Group 1970–75; mem. Econs. Cttee., C.N.A.A., G.B. 1971–75, Econs. Cttee., S.S.R.C., G.B. 1972–75, Consortium on Macroeconomic Modelling and Forecasting, E.S.R.C., G.B. 1981–88, Econ. Advisory Panel to Minister of Finance, Canada 1982–84; Co-ordinator Research Advisory Group on Econ. Ideas and Social Issues, Royal Comm. on the Econ. Union and Devt. Prospects for Canada (Macdonald Comm.) 1984–85; Dir. Philip Allan Publrs. Ltd. 1972–; Pres. Canadian Econs. Asscn. 1987–88; BAAS Lister Lecturer 1972. *Publications:* The Demand for Money 1969, Essays on Money and Inflation 1975, Monetarist Perspectives 1982, Taking Money Seriously 1990, The Golden Age of the Quantity Theory 1991, The Great Canadian Disinflation (with W. P. B. Robson) 1993, Money and Macroeconomics: Selected Essays 1998, Fabricating the Keynesian Revolution 1999. *Leisure interests:* going to concerts, opera and theatre. *Address:* Department of Economics, University of Western Ontario, London, Ont., N6A 5C2 (Office); 345 Grangeover Avenue, London, Ont., N6G 4K8, Canada (Home). *Telephone:* (519) 661-3400 (Office); (519) 438-0527 (Home). *Fax:* (519) 661-3666 (Office)

LAINE, Dame Cleo (Mrs. Clementina Dinah Dankworth), D.B.E.; British singer; b. 28 Oct. 1927, Southall, Middx.; m. 1st George Langridge 1947 (dissolved 1957), one s.; m. 2nd John Philip William Dankworth (q.v.) 1958, one s. one d.; joined Dankworth Orchestra 1953; lead in Seven Deadly Sins, Edinburgh Festival and Sadler's Wells 1961; acting roles in Edinburgh Festival 1966, 1967; f. Wavendon Stables Performing Arts Centre (with John Dankworth) 1970; many appearances with symphony orchestras performing Façade (Walton) and other compositions; Julie in Show Boat, Adelphi Theatre 1971; title role in Colette, Comedy Theatre 1980; Desiree in A Little Night Music, Mich. Opera House, U.S.A. 1983; The Mystery of Edwin Drood (Broadway, N.Y.) 1986; Into the Woods (U.S. Nat. Tour) 1989; frequent tours and TV appearances, Europe, Australia and U.S.A.; Melody Maker and New Musical Express Top Girl Singer Awards 1956; Moscow Arts Theatre Award for acting role in Flesh to a Tiger 1958; top place in Int. Critics' Poll of American Jazz magazine Downbeat 1965; Woman of the Year (9th annual Golden Feather Awards) 1973; Edison Award 1974; Variety Club of G.B. Show Business Personality Award (with John Dankworth) 1977; TV Times Viewers' Award for Most Exciting Female Singer on TV 1978; Grammy Award for Best Jazz Vocalist-Female 1985; Best Actress in a Musical (Edwin Drood) 1986; Theatre World Award for Edwin Drood 1986, Nat. Asscn. of Recording Merchandisers (NARM) Presidential Lifetime Achievement Award 1990, Vocalist of the Year (British Jazz Awards) 1990; Hon. M.A. (Open Univ.) 1975, Hon. D.Mus. (Berklee School of Music) 1982, (York) 1993; Hon. D.A. (Luton) 1994; Lifetime Achievement Award (U.S.A.) 1991. *Publications:* Cleo: An Autobiography 1994, You Can Sing If You Want To 1997. *Leisure interest:* painting. *Address:* The Old Rectory, Wavendon, Milton Keynes, MK17 8LT, England. *Fax:* (01908) 584414.

LAINE, Jermu Tapani; Finnish politician; b. 1931, Turku; Functionary, Ministry of Trade and Industry 1955–65; Lecturer in Commercial Studies, Valkeakoski 1965–69; Rector, Commercial Inst., Mänttä 1969–; municipal positions in Valkeakoski and Mänttä 1968–; Political Sec. to Prime Minister Sorsa 1972–73; Minister for Foreign Trade 1973–75; M.P. 1975–; Minister, Ministry of Finance 1982–83; Minister for Foreign Trade 1983–87; Chair. Supervisory Bd. Valmet Og 1987–88; Dir.-Gen. Finnish Customs Bd. 1988–94; Social Democratic Party. *Address:* Haapaniemenkatu 20D 60, 00530 Helsinki, Finland.

LAING, Edward Arthur; Belizean judge; b. 27 Feb. 1942, Belize; s. of Edward A. Laing and Marjorie Laing (née Dunn); m. Margery Fairweather 1969; one s. one d.; ed. Wesley Coll., Queens' Coll., Cambridge, Columbia Univ.; Asst. Magistrate and Crown Counsel, Belize 1966–67; pvt. law practice, Baker and Mackenzie, Chicago and New York 1968–69 and Belize 1969–70; lecturer, Univ. of the West Indies, Barbados 1970–74, Sr. Lecturer 1975–76; Asst. Prof. Notre Dame Law School, Ind. 1974–76; Assoc. Prof. Univ. of Md. 1976–81; Prof., Dir. Grad. Programme Howard Univ. School of Law 1980–85; Amb. to U.S.A., Canada and OAS 1985–90; Special Counsel, Ministry of Foreign Affairs 1985–90; Prof. New York Law School 1990–93; Perm. Rep. to UN 1993–96; rep. UNDP Exec. Bd. 1995–96; Judge, Int. Tribunal for the Law of the Sea 1996–; Int. Legal Consultant, arbitrator and lecturer 1996–. *Publications:* numerous articles in professional journals. *Leisure interests:* camping, golf, outdoor activities. *Address:* International Tribunal for the Law of the Sea, Wexstrasse 4, 20355 Hamburg, Germany (Office); 80 Vaughn Avenue, New Rochelle, NY 10801, U.S.A. (Home). *Telephone:* 40-35-60-71-10 (Office); (914) 576-9206 (Home). *Fax:* 40-35-60-71-19 (Office).

LAING, Jennifer Charlina Ellsworth; British advertising executive; b. 1947, Southampton; d. of late James Ellsworth Laing and of Mary McKane (née Taylor); m. (divorced); joined Garland Compton 1969, firm subsequently taken over by Saatchi & Saatchi, Dir. Saatchi & Saatchi Garland Compton 1977; Dir. Leo Burnett 1978–80; rejoined Saatchi & Saatchi, Deputy Chair. 1981–87, Jt. Chair. 1987–88, Chair. Saatchi & Saatchi Advertising 1995–96, Chief Exec. N. American Operations, N.Y. 1996–; Chair. C.E.O. Aspect Hill Holliday 1988; formed Laing Henry Ltd. 1990, merged with Saatchi & Saatchi 1995; Dir. (non-exec.) Great Ormond Street Hosp. for Children NHS Trust; Fellow, Marketing Soc., Inst. of Practitioners in Advertising; mem. Exec. Bd. Saatchi & Saatchi Advertising Worldwide 1996–. *Leisure interests:* racing, ballet, opera. *Address:* Saatchi & Saatchi, 375 Hudson Street, New York, NY 10014, U.S.A. *Telephone:* (212) 463-2000.

LAING, Sir (John) Maurice, Kt.; British building and civil engineering contractor (retd.); b. 1 Feb. 1918, Carlisle; s. of late Sir John (William) Laing, C.B.E., and late Lady Laing; m. Hilda Violet Richards 1940; one s.; ed. St. Lawrence Coll., Ramsgate; served with R.A.F. 1941–45; Dir. Bank of England 1963–80; Chair. Fed. of Civil Eng. Contractors 1959–60, Vice-Pres. 1960–77, Pres. 1977–80; Pres. British Employers' Confed. 1964–65, CBI 1965–66; Chair. Export Group for the Constructional Industries 1957–59, Pres. 1976–79; Hon. Pres. John Laing PLC 1982– and fmr. Chair.; mem. U.K. trade missions to Middle East 1953, to Egypt, Sudan and Ethiopia 1955; mem. Export Credits Guarantees Advisory Council 1959–63, Econ. Planning Bd. 1961, Ministry of Transport Cttee. of Inquiry into major ports of Great Britain (Rochdale Cttee.) 1961–62, NEDC 1962–66; Visiting Fellow, Nuffield Coll., Oxford 1965–70; Gov. Admin. Staff Coll. 1966–72, Nat. Inst. of Econ. and Social Research 1964–82; Pres. London Bible Coll. 1993–; Hon. LL.D. (Strathclyde) 1967; Hon. D.Sc. (Exeter) 1996; Hon. F.C.G.I. 1991; Cdre., Royal Ocean Racing Club 1973–75, Adm. 1976–82; Pres. Royal Yachting Asscn. 1983–87; AIMS Award 1980. *Leisure interests:* keen interest in church activities at home and abroad, sailing and swimming. *Address:* John Laing PLC, Page Street, London, NW7 2ER, England.

LAING, R(obert) Stanley, B.S.MECH.ENG., M.B.A.; American business executive; b. 1 Nov. 1918, Seattle; s. of Robert Vardy Laing and Marie (Scott) Laing; m. 1st Janet Emmott Orr 1947 (died 1986), one s. four d.; m. 2nd Eva Nofke 1986 (died 1988); m. 3rd Mary Wilshire 1988; ed. Univ. of Washington and Harvard Business School; Nat. Cash Register Co., Dayton, Ohio 1947–72; Special Asst. in Exec. Office 1947–49; Asst. to Comptroller 1949; Gen. Auditor 1950–53; Asst. Comptroller 1953–54; Comptroller 1954–60; Vice-Pres. (Finance) 1960–62, Exec. Vice-Pres. 1962–64, Pres. 1964–72; Dir. and Chair. Business Equipment Mfg. Asscn. 1963–64; fmr. Chair. Denison Univ. Bd. of Trustees; fmr. Dir. Gen. Mills Inc., Mead Corpn., NCR Corpn., Cincinnati Milacron Inc., B. F. Goodrich Co., Armco Corpn., Amdahl Corpn., Sinclair Community Coll. Foundation; consultant to Fujitsu Ltd., Japan 1977–95; Order of Lateran Cross (Vatican). *Address:* 3430 South Dixie, Dayton, OH 45439 (Office); 650 West David Road, Dayton, OH 45429, U.S.A. (Home). *Telephone:* (513) 298-0884 (Office).

LAING, Stanley (see Laing, Robert Stanley).

LAING OF DUNPHAIL, Baron (Life Peer), cr. 1991, of Dunphail in the District of Moray; **Hector Laing**; British company executive; b. 12 May 1923, Edinburgh; s. of Hector Laing and Margaret Norris Grant; m. Marian Clare Laurie 1950; three s.; ed. Loretto School, Musselborough, and Jesus Coll., Cambridge; joined McVitie & Price Ltd. as a Dir. 1947, Chair. 1963–64; Dir. of United Biscuits Ltd. 1953, Man. Dir. 1964; Chair. United Biscuits (Holdings) PLC. 1972–90, Life Pres. May 1990–; Council mem. Inst. of Dirs. 1969–75; mem. Intervention Bd. for Agric. Produce 1972–75; Chair. Food & Drink Industries Council 1977–79; Dir. Court of Bank of England 1973–91, Royal Insurance Co. 1970–78, Allied-Lyons 1979–82, Exxon Corpn. (U.S.A.) 1984–94; mem. Advisory Council, London Enterprise Agency 1981; Jt. Treas. Conservative Party 1988–93; Dr. h.c. (Stirling) 1985, Hon. D. Litt. (Herriot Watt) 1986; Bronze Star (U.S.A.), Hambro Award 1979; Businessman of the Year 1979; Nat. Free Enterprise Award 1980. *Leisure interests:* gardening, walking, flying. *Address:* High Meadows, Windsor Road, Gerrards Cross, Bucks., England. *Telephone:* (01753) 882437 (Home).

LAINSON, Ralph, O.B.E., F.R.S.; British scientist; b. 21 Feb. 1927, Upper Beeding, Sussex; s. of Charles Harry Lainson and Anne Denyer; m. 1st Ann Patricia Russell (divorced 1976), one s. two d.; m. 2nd Zéa Constante Lins 1978; ed. Steyning Grammar School, Univ. of London; lecturer in Medical Protozoology London School of Hygiene and Tropical Medicine 1955–59, Attached Investigator, Dept. of Medical Protozoology 1962–65; Officer-in-Charge Dermal Leishmaniasis Unit, Baking-Pot, Cayo Dist., Belize 1959–62; Dir. Wellcome Parasitology Unit, Inst. Evandro Chagas, Fundação Serviços de Saúde Pública, Pará, Brazil 1965–92; Chalmers Medal 1971, Manson Medal 1983 Royal Soc. of Tropical Medicine and Hygiene, Oswaldo Cruz Medal, Conselho Estadual de Cultura do Pará (Brazil) 1973; Medalha Comemorativa do 10° Aniversario da Instalação do Conselho Estadual de Saúde do Pará (Brazil) 1983; Hon. Fellow, London School of Hygiene and Tropical Medicine 1982, Hon. Prof. Fed. Univ. of Pará 1982, Hon. mem. British Soc. of Parasitology 1984, Soc. of Protozoologists, Assoc. Fellow Third World Acad. of Sciences 1989. *Publications:* author or co-author of approx. 300 articles in scientific journals. *Leisure interests:* fishing, collecting S. American Lepidoptera, music, philately. *Address:* Avenida Visconde de Souza Franco 1237 (Edificio 'Visconti'), Apartamento 902, 66.053.000 Belém, Pará, Brazil. *Telephone:* (91) 211-4453 (Office); (91) 223-2382 (Home). *Fax:* (91) 226-1284 (Office).

LAIRD, Sir Gavin Harry, Kt., C.B.E.; British trade union official; b. 14 March 1933, Clydebank, Scotland; s. of James and Frances Laird; m. Catherine Gillies Campbell 1956; one d.; shop stewards' convener, Singer, Clydebank for seven years; Regional Officer, Amalgamated Eng. Union (fmrly. Amalgamated Union of Eng. Workers) 1972–75, Exec. Councillor for Scotland and N.W. England 1975–82, Gen. Sec. (AEU Section) 1992–95; Chair. Greater Manchester Buses North 1994–; mem. Scottish TUC Gen. Council 1973–75; mem. TUC Gen. Council 1979–82; part-time Dir. Highlands and Islands Devt. Bd. 1974–75; mem. Industrial Devt. Advisory Bd. 1979; Arts Council 1983–86; part-time Dir. BNOC 1976–86; Chair. The Foundries E.D.C. Oct. 1982–; Dir. Bank of England 1986–94; Dir. (non-exec.) Scottish TV PLC 1986–, Britannia Life 1988–, Britannia Investment Mans. Ltd., Britannia Fund Mans. Ltd. 1996–, GEC Scotland 1991–, Edin. Investment Trust 1994–; Forestry Comm. 1991–95; Trustee Anglo-German Foundation 1994–; mem. Editorial Bd. European Business Journal; mem. Advisory Bd. Know-How Fund for Poland –1995; mem. Armed Forces Pay Review Body 1995–98, Employment Appeal Tribunal 1996–. *Leisure interests:* music, hill-walking, reading. *Address:* 35 Southlands Grove, Bromley, BR1 2DA, England (Home). *Telephone:* 0181-464 2376. *Fax:* 0181-464 2376.

LAIRD, Melvin Robert, B.A.; American government official; b. 1 Sept. 1922, Omaha, Neb.; s. of Melvin and Helen (Connor) Laird; m. 1st Barbara Masters 1945 (died 1992); two s. one d.; m. 2nd Carole Fleischman 1993; ed. Carleton Coll., Northfield, Minn; served with Task Force 38 and 58, U.S. Navy Pacific Fleet 1942–46; mem. Wisconsin Senate 1946–52, Chair. Wisconsin Legis. Council; mem. U.S. House of Reps. 1952–69, served on Appropriations Cttee., Chair. House of Republican Minority, mem. Republican Coordinating Council, Vice-Chair. Republican Nat. Platform Council 1960, Chair. 1964; U.S. Sec. of Defense 1968–73; Counsellor to Pres. for Domestic Affairs 1973–74; Senior Counsellor for Nat. and Int. Affairs, Readers' Digest Asscn. 1974–, now Vice-Pres.; Chair. COMSAT Corpn. 1992–96; fmr. mem. Bd. the Kennedy Center, George Washington Univ., Airlie Foundation; mem. Bd. Nat. Defence and Energy Projects of American Enterprise Inst., Thomas Jefferson Center Foundation of Univ. of Virginia, World Rehabilitation Fund; fmr. Dir. The Reader's Digest Asscn., Inc., Metropolitan Life Insurance Co., Northwest Airlines, IDS Mutual Funds Group, Communications Satellite Corpn. (Chair. 1992–96), Martin Marietta Corpn., Science Application Int. Corpn., Dir. Public Oversight Bd.; Trustee, DeWitt and Lila Wallace-Reader's Digest Funds; over 300 awards and hon. degrees, including Albert

Lasker Public Service Award, Statesman in Medicine Award (Airlie Foundation), The Harry S. Truman Award for distinguished service in defense; Presidential Medal of Freedom (U.S.A.), Order of Merit (1st Class) (Fed. Repub. of Germany), Commdr. Légion d'honneur (France); Republican. *Publications include:* A House Divided: America's Strategy Gap 1962, The Conservative Papers (Ed.) 1964, Republican Papers (Ed.) 1968. *Address:* 1730 Rhode Island Avenue, N.W., Suite 212, Washington, DC 20036, U.S.A. (Office).

LAISTER, Peter, B.SC.TECH., F.INST.PET., F.INST.CHEM.ENG., C.ENG., C.B.I.M.; British business executive; b. 24 Jan. 1929, Birmingham; s. of late Horace Laister and Mrs I. L. Bates; m. 1st Barbara Cooke 1951, one s. one d.; m. 2nd Eileen A. Goodchild (née Town) 1958, one d.; ed. King Edward's School, Birmingham and Manchester Univ.; with Esso Petroleum Co. 1951–66; with British Oxygen Co. (now BOC Int.) 1966–75, Group Man. Dir. 1969–75, Chair. BOC Financial Corpn. (U.S.A.) 1974–75; Group Man. Dir. Ellerman Lines Ltd. 1976–79; Chair. Tollemache and Cobbold Breweries 1977–79, London and Hull Insurance 1976–79, Park Hotels PLC 1985–91, Tower Group PLC 1985–89, Premiere PLC 1985–89, Oceonics PLC 1986–88, Contec PLC 1986–87, Nimbus Records 1988–94, Maxwell Communications Corpn. PLC 1991–92; Group Man. Dir. Thorn Electrical Industries (later Thorn EMI PLC) 1979–85, Chair. 1984–85; Gov. BUPA 1982–93; non-exec. Dir. BMCL 1976–86, Chair. 1984–86; Dir. (non-exec.) Inchcape PLC 1982–93, Fluor Daniel Ltd. 1985–89, A. and P. Appledore 1986–87; Dir. British Printing and Communications Corpn. (BPCC) PLC 1985–88, SelecTV 1987–94 (Chair. March–April 1993); mem. B.I.M. Exec. Bd. 1983; Chair. MTV Europe 1988–91, NIMBUS Records Ltd. 1986–92, NIMBUS U.S.A. Inc. 1992–94, i Basc Ltd. 1996–; Vice-Chair. The Farnsworth Group 1996–; mem. Univ. Coll. Council 1978–88; Chair. Foundation for Age Research 1982–86; mem. Council, Industrial Soc. 1971–86; mem. Industrial Devt. Advisory Bd. 1981–83. *Leisure interests:* private flying, boating and angling, gardening, photography. *Address:* Thatches, 92 Staines Road, Wraysbury, Middx., England.

LAJOINIE, André; French politician; b. 26 Dec. 1929, Chasteaux, Corrèze; s. of Joseph Lajoinie and Maria Jauberty; m. Paulette Rouffiange 1960; one s.; mem. French Communist Party (PCF) 1948–, mem. Cen. Cttee. 1972–, mem. Politburo 1976–, in charge of agric. section 1976–; Dir. La Terre (weekly paper) 1977–; Deputy from l'Allier to Nat. Ass. 1978–93, 1997–; Pres. Communist group in Nat. Ass. 1981–93; mem. comm. de la production et des echanges 1978–86. *Publications:* A coeur ouvert 1987, L'Enjeu agricole et alimentaire 1988. *Address:* Assemblée nationale, 75355 Paris; 28 rue de la Ronde, 03500 Saint-Pourçain-sur-Sioule, France (Home).

LAKAS BAHAS, Demetrio Basilio; Panamanian politician and administrator; b. 29 Aug. 1925, Colón; s. of Basilio Demetrio Lakas and Zaharo Bahas de Lakas; m. Elizabeth Fannia Roger de Lakas 1959; two s. one d.; ed. Texas Wesleyan Coll. and Texas Tech. Coll.; fmr. Dir. of Social Security; Pres. of Provisional Govt. Council 1969–72; Pres. of Panama 1972–78. *Leisure interests:* sailing, fishing. *Address:* c/o Palacio de las Garzas, Panama City, Panama.

LAKE, N. Anthony, PH.D.; American public servant and academic; b. 1939, New York; m.; three c.; ed. Harvard Univ., Cambridge Univ., U.K., Woodrow Wilson School of Public and Int. Affairs, Princeton Univ.; joined Foreign Service 1962, Special Asst. to Amb. Henry Cabot Lodge, Viet Nam; an aide to Sec. of State Henry Kissinger 1969–70; Head State Dept.'s policy planning operation –1981; Prof., Amherst Coll., Mass. 1981–84, Mount Holyoke Coll. 1984–92; co-f. journal Foreign Policy; a foreign policy adviser to Gov. (now Pres.) Clinton (q.v.) during presidential campaign 1992; Nat. Security Adviser 1993–96; nominated Dir. C.I.A. Dec. 1996, nomination withdrawn March 1997. *Publications:* The 'Tar Baby' Option: American Policy Toward Southern Rhodesia 1976, Third World Radical Regimes: U.S. Policy under Carter and Reagan 1985, Somoza Falling: A Case Study of Washington at Work 1990. *Address:* c/o National Security Council, Executive Office Building, 1600 Pennsylvania Avenue, N.W., Washington, DC 20500, U.S.A.

LAKER, Sir Frederick Alfred, Kt.; British business executive; b. 6 Aug. 1922; m. 4th Jacqueline Harvey; ed. Simon Langton School, Canterbury; worked for Short Bros., Rochester 1938–40; Gen. Aircraft 1940–41; served with Air Transport Auxiliary 1941–46; with Aviation Traders 1946–60; British United Airways 1960–65; Chair. and Man. Dir. Laker Airways Ltd. 1966–82, Laker Airways (Bahamas) Ltd. 1992–; Dir. Skytrain Holidays 1982–83, Sir Freddie Laker Ltd. 1982–, Northeastern Int. Airlines Inc. (U.S.A.) 1984–; mem. Jockey Club 1979–; Chair. Guild of Air Pilots and Navigators Benevolent Fund; Hon. D.Sc. (City Univ.) 1979, (Cranfield Inst. of Tech.) 1980, Hon. LL.D. (Victoria Univ. of Manchester) 1981; Hon. Fellow (U.M.I.S.T.) 1978. *Address:* Princess Tower, West Sunrise, Box F-4207, Freeport, Grand Bahama, Bahamas.

LAKHOVA, Yekaterina Filippovna; Russian politician; b. 26 May 1948; m.; one d.; ed. Sverdlovsk State Medical Inst.; pediatrician, Deputy Head of Div., Sverdlovsk (now Yekaterinburg) City Dept. of Public Health, Deputy Head, Main Dept. of Public Health, Sverdlovsk Regional Exec. Cttee. 1972–90; R.S.F.S.R. Peoples' Deputy, mem. Council of Repub. R.S.F.S.R. Supreme Soviet, Chair. Cttee. on Problems of Women, Motherhood and Childhood 1990–93; State Adviser on Problems of Family, Protection of Motherhood and Childhood 1992–; adviser to Russian Pres. on Problems of Family, Protection of Motherhood and Childhood 1992–94; Chair. Cttee. on Problems of Women, Family and Demography of Russian Presidency 1992–; f. political movt. Women of Russia 1993; mem. State Duma 1993–; mem. Socialist Party of Russia 1996. *Address:* State Duma, Okhotny Ryad 1, 103265 Moscow, Russia. *Telephone:* (095) 292 1900 (Office).

LAKÓS, László, PH.D.; Hungarian politician; b. 31 Aug. 1945, Furta, Hajdú-Bihar County; m. Piroska Erdős; two c.; ed. Univ. of Budapest; Chair. Árpád Cooperative of Köröstetétlen 1992; mem. of Hungarian Socialist Party (HSP) 1989; mem. Presidium HSP 1989; mem. Parl. 1994–; Vice-Chair. Econ. Standing Cttee. 1992–94; mem. Hungarian-Australian Inter-Parl. Section of IPU; Vice-Chair. Hungarian-Arabian Inter-Parl. Section 1990; Minister of Agric. 1994–96; Golden Order of Labour. *Address:* Mezőgazdasági Minisztérium, 1055 Budapest, Kossuth Lajos tér 11, Hungary. *Telephone:* 153-3000.

LAL, Bansi, LL.B.; Indian politician; b. 26 Aug. 1927, Golagarh, Bhiwani District; s. of Chaudhary Mohar Singh; m. Smt. Vidya Devi 1945; two s. four d.; ed. Punjab Univ. and Law Coll., Jullundur; started practice at Bhiwani 1956; Sec. Loharu Praja Mandal 1943–44; Gen. Sec. Tosham Mandal Congress Cttee. 1955–58; Pres. Mandal Congress Cttee., Jural 1958–62; mem. Punjab PCC 1958–62, Rajya Sabha 1960–66, 1976–80, Haryana Assembly 1967; Chief Minister Haryana 1968–75, 1986–87; Minister without portfolio, Govt. of India Dec. 1975, Minister of Defence 1975–77; Minister of Railways 1984–85; Minister of Transport 1985–86; mem. 9th Lok Sabha 1989–; Chair. Cttee. on Public Undertakings 1980–82, Cttee. on Estimates 1982–84; Hon. LL.D. (Kurukshetra Univ., Haryana) 1972, Hon. D.Sc. (Haryana Agric. Univ.) 1972. *Leisure interest:* reading. *Address:* c/o B. N. Chakravarty Road, Hissr, Haryana State, India.

LAL, Deepak Kumar, M.A., B.PHIL.; British professor of political economy; b. 3 Jan. 1940, Lahore, India; s. of the late Nand Lal and of Shanti Devi; m. Barbara Ballis 1971; one s. one d.; ed. Doon School, Dehra Dun, St. Stephen's Coll., Delhi, Jesus Coll., Oxford; Indian Foreign Service 1963–65; Lecturer, Christ Church, Oxford 1966–68; Research Fellow, Nuffield Coll., Oxford 1968–70; lecturer, Univ. Coll. London 1970–79, Reader 1979–84, Prof. of Political Economy, Univ. of London 1984–93, Prof. Emer. 1993–; James S. Coleman Prof. of Int. Devt. Studies, Univ. of Calif. at Los Angeles 1991–; Consultant, Indian Planning Comm. 1973–74; Research Admin., World Bank, Washington, D.C. 1983–87; Dir. Trade Policy Unit, Centre for Policy Studies 1993–96, Trade and Devt. Unit, Inst. of Econ. Affairs 1997–; consultancy assignments ILO, UNCTAD, OECD, World Bank, Ministry of Planning, Sri Lanka, Repub. of Korea 1970–. *Publications:* Wells and Welfare 1972, Methods of Project Analysis 1974, Appraising Foreign Investment in Developing Countries 1975, Unemployment and Wage Inflation in Industrial Economies 1977, Men or Machines 1978, Prices for Planning 1980, The Poverty of "Development Eonomics" 1983, Labour and Poverty in Kenya (with P. Collier) 1986, Stagflation, Savings and the State (Ed. with M. Wolf) 1986, The Hindu Equilibrium, 2 vols. 1988, 1989, Public Policy and Economic Development (Ed. with M. Scott) 1990, Development Economics, 4 vols. (Ed.) 1991, The Repressed Economy 1993, Against Dirigisme 1994, The Political Economy of Poverty, Equity and Growth (with H. Myint) 1996, Unintended Consequences 1998, Unfinished Business 1999. *Leisure interests:* opera, theatre, tennis, bridge. *Address:* Department of Economics, 8369 Bunche Hall, University of California at Los Angeles, 405 Hilgard Avenue, Los Angeles, CA 90024, U.S.A.; A30 Nizamuddin West, New Delhi 110013, India; 2 Erskine Hill, London NW11 6HB, England. *Telephone:* (310) 825-4521, (310) 206-2382 (Los Angeles); 462 9465 (New Delhi); 0181-458 3713 (London).

LAL, Devendra, M.SC., PH.D., F.R.S.; Indian scientist; b. 14 Feb. 1929, Varanasi (Banaras); s. of the late Dr. Radhekrishna Lal and of Sita Devi; m. Aruna Damany 1955 (died 1993); ed. Harish Chandra High School, Banaras Hindu Univ., Varanasi, and Bombay Univ.; Assoc. Prof. Tata Inst. of Fundamental Research 1960–63, Prof. 1963–70, Sr. Prof. 1970–72, Visiting Prof., Univ. of Calif. 1965–66; Prof., Scripps Inst. of Oceanography, Univ. of Calif. 1967–; Dir. Physical Research Lab., Ahmedabad, 1972–83, Sr. Prof. 1983–89, Fellow 1989–; Chair. working group on River Inputs to Ocean System 1977–81; Vice-Pres. Indian Acad. of Sciences, Bangalore 1978–82; Pres. Int. Asscn. for Physical Sciences of the Ocean 1979–82, Int. Union of Geodesy and Geophysics 1983–87, Indian Geophysical Union 1980–82; Foreign Sec. Indian Nat. Science Acad., New Delhi 1981–84; mem. Scientific Advisory Cttee. to the Cabinet 1979–83; mem. Jt. Scientific Cttee. of WMO 1979–83; mem. Group of Experts on Scientific Aspects of Marine Pollution, UNESCO, 1979–81; mem. Advisory Cttee. on Environment, ICSU 1990–94; Foreign Assoc., N.A.S. (U.S.A.); Fellow, Indian Acad. of Sciences, Bangalore, Indian Nat. Science Acad., New Delhi, Centre of the Earth Sciences Studies, Cochin 1983, Nat. Acad. Sciences, Allahabad 1988, Physical Research Laboratory, Ahmedabad 1990, Tata Inst. of Fundamental Research, Bombay 1996, Geochemical Soc. (U.S.A.) 1997, A.A.A.S. 1997; Founding mem. Third World Acad. of Sciences, Italy 1983; Assoc. Royal Astronomical Soc. 1984; mem. Int. Acad. of Astronautics 1985; Hon. D.Sc. (Banaras Univ., Varanasi) 1981; Krishnan Medal for Geochemistry and Geophysics 1965; Shanti Swarup Bhatnagar Award for Physical Sciences, Council of Scientific and Industrial Research 1967; Repub. Day Nat. Award, Padma Shri 1971; Fed. of Indian Chambers of Commerce and Industry Award in Science and Tech. 1974, Jawaharlal Nehru Award for Science 1986, Goldschmidt Medal 1997. *Publications:* over 200 articles in scientific journals; Early Solar System Processes and the Present Solar System (Ed.), Biogeochemistry of the Arabian Sea (Ed.). *Leisure interests:* photography, painting, mathematical puzzles, chess. *Address:* Scripps Institution of Oceanography, GRD/0220, University of California, San Diego, La Jolla, CA 92093-0220, (Office); 4445 Via Precipicio, San Diego, CA 92122, U.S.A. (Home); No. 20, Jayantilal Park, Amli Bopal Road, Village Makarba, Ahmedabad 380054, India (Home). *Telephone:* (619) 534-2134 (Office); (619) 587 1535 (Home U.S.A.); 79-6741451 (Home India).

LAL, Devi; Indian politician; b. 1914; mem. Punjab legis. Ass. 1952–65; Chief Parl. Sec. of Punjab 1956; Chair. Haryana Khadi and Village Industries Bd. 1968–71; Chief Minister of Haryana 1977–79; mem. Parl. 1980–82; elected to Haryana Assembly 1982 (resgnd.), re-elected 1985; Deputy Prime Minister of India 1989–90, 1990–92; Minister of Agric. and Tourism 1990–92. *Address:* c/o Office of the Prime Minister, South Block, New Delhi 110 011, India.

LALIVE d'EPINAY, Pierre, B.A., PH.D. (brother of Jean-Flavien Lalive d'Epinay); Swiss lawyer; b. 8 Oct. 1923, La Chaux-de-Fonds; s. of Auguste Lalive and Mme. Lalive; m. Michèle-Hélène Villard 1957; ed. Geneva and Cambridge Univs.; Geneva Bar; Prof. of Law, Geneva Univ. 1955, Dir. Dept. of Pvt. Law, Dean of Law School 1967–69; Prof. of Int. Business Law, Graduate Inst. of Int. Studies 1962–86, Hon. Prof. 1986–; Sr. Partner Lalive, Budin and Partners; Pres. ICC Inst. of Int. Business Law and Practice, Swiss Arbitration Asscn.; Visiting Prof. Columbia, Brussels and Cambridge Univs.; Pres. Inst. of Int. Law, numerous Swiss Fed. Comms. and dels.; D.Jur. h.c. (Lyon, Paris, Brussels). *Publications:* more than 100 publs. on int. law (public, pvt.), arbitration, contracts and family law. *Address:* Geneva University, Faculty of Law, 24 rue Général-Dufour, 1211 Geneva 4; Senebier 20, Geneva (Office); Ermitage 47, Chene-Bougeries, Geneva, Switzerland (Home). *Telephone:* 29-46-66 (Office); 789-03-12 (Home).

LALLA AICHA, H.R.H. Princess; Moroccan diplomatist; eldest daughter of the late King Mohammed V.; Amb. to U.K. 1965–69, to Italy 1969–73 (also accred. to Greece); Pres. Moroccan Red Crescent; Grand Cordon of Order of the Throne. *Address:* c/o Ministry of Foreign Affairs, ave. Franklin Roosevelt, Rabat, Morocco.

LALONDE, Brice; French politician; b. 10 Feb. 1946, Neuilly; s. of Alain Lalonde and Fiona Forbes; m. Patricia Raynaud 1986; two s. (one deceased) two d.; one s. one d. from previous marriage; student leader 1968; Chair. Friends of the Earth 1972, French Branch 1978; Candidate for the Green Party, French Pres. Election 1981; Admin. European Environment Bureau 1983; Dir. Paris Office Inst. for European Environmental Policy 1987; Sec. of State for the Environment 1988–89, for the Environment and the Prevention of Tech. and Natural Disasters 1989–90, Minister del. 1990–91, Minister of the Environment 1991–92; Pres. Génération Ecologie (Political Movt.) 1990–; Chair. Cttee to free Alexandr Nikitin 1996–. *Address:* Génération Ecologie, 73 avenue Paul Doumer, 75116 Paris, France (Office). *Telephone:* (1) 45.03.82.82.

LALONDE, Marc, Q.C., P.C., O.C., LL.L., M.A.; Canadian fmr. politician and lawyer; b. 26 July 1929, Ile Perrot; s. of J. Albert and Nora (St. Aubin) Lalonde; m. Claire Tétreau 1955; two s. two d.; ed. St. Laurent Coll., Montréal and Univs. of Montréal, Ottawa and Oxford; called to the Bar, Québec 1955; Prof. of Commercial Law and Econs., Univ. of Montréal 1957–59; mem. Bd. of Dirs. Inst. of Public Law, Univ. of Montréal 1960–64; mem. Cttee. on Broadcasting 1964; Special Asst. to Minister of Justice, Ottawa 1959–60; Partner, Gélinas, Bourque, Lalonde & Benoit, Montréal 1960–68; Policy Adviser to Prime Minister 1967, Prin. Sec. to Prime Minister 1968–72; mem. Parl. 1972–84; Minister of Nat. Health and Welfare 1972–77, responsible for the Status of Women 1975–78, for Federal-Provincial Relations 1977–78, of Justice and Attorney-Gen. of Canada 1978–79, of Energy, Mines and Resources 1980–82, of Finance 1982–84; Chair. Hotel-Dieu de Montréal 1985–96; Dir. Citibank Canada, O&Y Properties, Inc., Orleans Ressources Inc.; partner, Stikeman Elliott 1984–; several directorships; Counsel before several Royal Comms., including Royal Comm. on Great Lakes Shipping; Liberal. *Publication:* The Changing Role of the Prime Minister's Office 1971. *Leisure interests:* jogging, skiing, swimming, reading. *Address:* Suite 3900, 1155 René-Levesque Boulevard, W., Montreal, Quebec, H3B 3V2 (Office); 5440 Légaré, Outremont, Quebec H3T 1Z4, Canada (Home).

LALOR, Patrick Joseph; Irish politician; b. 21 July 1926, Dublin; s. of Joseph and Frances Lalor; m. Myra Murphy 1952; one s. three d.; ed. in Abbeyleix and Knockbeg Coll., Carlow; fmr. mem. Laois County Council and fmr. exec. mem. Retail Grocery, Dairy and Allied Trades Asscn. (RGDATA); mem. Dáil Eireann Oct. 1961–81; Parl. Sec. to Minister of Agric. and Fisheries 1965–66, to Minister for Transport, Power, Posts and Telegraphs 1966–69; Minister of Posts and Telegraphs 1969–70, for Industry and Commerce 1970–73; mem. Fianna Fáil, Chief Whip Parl. Party 1973–77; Parl. Sec. to the Taoiseach (Prime Minister) and to Minister of Defence Jan.–Dec. 1977, Minister of State at Depts. of the Taoiseach and of Defence 1979 (resgnd.); mem. of European Parl. 1979–, Leader of Fianna Fail Party in European Parl. 1979, Vice-Pres. Group of European Progressive Democrats 1979–84; Quaestor 1979–82; Vice-Pres. of European Parl. 1982–87; Vice-Pres. European Democratic Alliance Group 1988–, European Renewal and Democratic Alliance Group 1986–; Quaestor of European Parl. 1989–; mem. European Parl. Cttees. on Transport and Tourism, Rules of Procedure, Political Affairs, Bureau and Enlarged Bureau 1989–; Grand Officier du Ouissam Alaouite (Morocco) 1981. *Leisure interests:* hurling, Gaelic football, golf, drama. *Address:* Main Street, Abbeyleix, Portlaoise, Co. Laois, Ireland. *Telephone:* 0502-31206.

LALUMIÈRE, Catherine; French politician; b. 3 Aug. 1935, Rennes; m. Pierre Lalumière; specialist in public law; lecturer, Univ. of Paris; mem. Steering Cttee., Parti Socialiste 1979; mem. Nat. Ass. for Gironde 1986–89; Adviser to Pres. on civil service; Sec. of State for the Civil Service and Admin. Reforms May-June 1981, Minister for Consumer Affairs 1981–83, Sec. of State 1983–84, Minister for European Affairs 1984–86; Sec.-Gen. Council of Europe 1989–94; Urban Community Councillor, Bordeaux 1989–; Municipal Councillor, Talence 1989–95; mem. European Parl. 1994–; Deputy Pres. Radical France 1996 (now Radical Socialist Party); Hon. D.C.L. (Durham) 1995. *Address:* European Parliament, 97–113 rue Wiertz, B-1047 Brussels, Belgium.

LAMB, Allan Joseph; South African cricketer; b. 20 June 1954, Langebaanweg, Cape Province; s. of Michael Lamb and Joan Lamb; m. Lindsay Lamb 1979; one s. one d.; ed. Wynberg Boys' High School and Abbotts Coll.; middle-order right-hand batsman; teams: Western Province 1972–82 and 1992–93, O.F.S. 1987–88, Northants. 1978–95 (Capt. 1989–95); qualified for England 1982 and played in 79 Tests 1982–92 (3 as Capt.), scoring 4,656 runs (average 36.0) including 14 hundreds; toured Australia 1982–83, 1986–87, 1990–91; scored 32,502 first-class runs (89 hundreds); 1,000 15 times; 122 limited-overs ints.; owner of incentive travel and corporate entertainment co. *Publication:* Silence of the Lamb (autobiog.) 1995. *Leisure interests:* tennis, golf, rugby, horse-racing, fly-fishing. *Address:* Lamb Associates, First Floor, 4 St. Giles Street, Northampton, NN1 1JB, England. *Fax:* (01604) 239930.

LAMB, Willis Eugene, Jr., PH.D., SC.D., L.H.D.; American physicist; b. 12 July 1913, Los Angeles, Calif.; s. of Willis Eugene and Marie Helen (Metcalf); m. 1st Ursula Schaefer 1939 (died 1996); m. 2nd Bruria Kaufman 1996; ed. Univ. of California; Instructor, Columbia Univ. 1938, Prof. of Physics 1948–52; Loeb Lecturer, Harvard 1953–54; Prof. of Physics, Stanford Univ. 1951–56; Wykeham Prof. of Physics and Fellow, New Coll., Univ. of Oxford 1956–62; Henry Ford II Prof. of Physics, Yale Univ. 1962–72, J. Willard Gibbs Prof. of Physics, Yale Univ. 1972–74; Prof. of Physics and Optical Sciences, Univ. of Arizona 1974–, Regents Prof. 1990–; Sr. Alexander von Humbert Fellow 1992–94; mem. N.A.S.; Hon. Fellow, Royal Soc. Edinburgh; awarded Rumford Premium (American Acad. of Arts and Sciences) 1953; Hon. Sc.D. (Pennsylvania) 1953, Hon. L.H.D. (Yeshiva) 1964, Hon. Sc.D. (Gustavus Adolphus Coll.) 1975, (Columbia) 1990; Nobel Prize in Physics (shared with Prof. P. Kusch) 1955; Research Corpn. Award 1955; Guggenheim Fellow 1960, Humboldt Fellowship 1992. *Address:* Optical Sciences Center, University of Arizona, Tucson, AZ 85721, U.S.A.

LAMBECK, Kurt, F.R.S., F.A.A., D. PHIL., D.SC.; Australian professor of geophysics; b. 20 Sept. 1941, Loosdrecht, The Netherlands; s. of J. Lambeck and J. Weber; m. Bridget Marguerite Nicholls 1967; one s. one d.; ed. Univ. of N.S.W., Tech. Univ. of Delft, Tech. Univ. of Athens and Oxford Univ.; Geodesist, Smithsonian Astrophysical Observatory 1967–70; Dir. of Research, Paris Observatory 1970–73; Prof. of Geophysics, Univ. of Paris 1973–77, A.N.U. 1977–, Dir. Research School of Earth Sciences 1984–93; Sec. (Physical Sciences), Australian Acad. of Science 1996–; Harold Jeffreys Lecturer Royal Astronomical Soc. 1989; Hon. mem. European Geophysics Soc. 1988–; Foreign mem. Royal Netherlands Acad. of Arts and Sciences 1993, Norwegian Acad. of Science and Letters 1994; Fellow American Geophysical Union 1976; Hon. D.Eng. (Nat. Tech. Univ. Greece); Macelwane Award, American Geophysical Union 1976, Whitten Medal 1993, Jaeger Medal, Australian Acad. of Science 1995, Alfred Wegener Medal, European Union of Geosciences 1996. *Publications:* The Earth's Variable Rotation 1980, Geophysical Geodesy 1988, numerous papers on geodesy and geophysics. *Address:* Research School of Earth Sciences, Australian National University, Canberra, A.C.T. 0200; 31 Brand Street, Hughes, A.C.T. 2605, Australia. *Telephone:* (02) 62495161.

LAMBERT, Christopher; American actor; b. 29 March 1957, New York; ed. L'Ecole Roche, Int. School, Lycée d'Annemasse, Coll. Floriment, Geneva, Florent School, Paris and Paris Conservatoire; mil. service with Alpine Corps, Grenoble; trainee, Barclay's Bank, London 1976; professional debut in TV film Douchka 1977. *Films include:* Greystoke: the Story of Tarzan, Lord of the Apes 1983, Paroles et Musiques 1984, Subway 1985, Highlander 1986, I Love You 1986, The Sicilian, To Kill A Priest, Knight Moves 1992, Fortress 1994, Gunmen 1994, Roadflower, Mortal Kombat 1994, North Star (also exec. producer), Nirvana 1997, exec. producer When Saturday Comes.

LAMBERT, Henry Uvedale Antrobus, M.A.; British banker; b. 9 Oct. 1925, London; s. of the late R. U. Lambert and M. F. Lambert; m. Diana Dumbell 1951; two s. one d.; ed. Winchester Coll., New Coll., Oxford; served R.N., war of 1939–45; joined Barclays Bank Ltd. (now Barclays Bank PLC) 1948, local Dir. Lombard Street 1957–59, Southampton 1959–69, Birmingham 1969–72, Vice-Chair. Barclays Bank Int. Ltd. 1972–79, Chair. 1979–83, Deputy Chair. Barclays Bank PLC 1979–85, Dir. 1966–91; Deputy Chair. Agricultural Mortgage Corpn. PLC 1977–85, Chair. 1985–93; Vice-Chair. Sun Alliance and London Insurance Group 1978–83, Deputy Chair. 1983–85, Chair. 1985–93; Dir. British Airways PLC 1985–90; Vice-Pres. Navy Records Soc. 1985–89, 1992–96; Trustee Nat. Maritime Museum 1990–95; Chair. White Ensign Asscn. 1992–96; Fellow, Winchester Coll.

1979–91. *Leisure interests:* fishing, gardening, golf, naval history. *Address:* c/o Barclays Bank PLC, Jewry Street, Winchester, Hants., SO23 8RG, England.

LAMBERT, Phyllis, B.A., M.S.ARCH., O.C., C.Q., O.A.L., F.R.A.I.C., O.A.Q., F.R.S.C., R.C.A.; Canadian architect; b. 24 Jan. 1927, Montreal, Quebec; d. of Samuel and Saidye (Rosner) Bronfman; ed. The Study, Montreal, Vassar Coll., New York, Illinois Inst. of Tech., Chicago; Auxiliary Prof., School of Architecture, McGill Univ.; Assoc. Prof., Faculty of Planning, Univ. of Montreal; Bd. Chair. and Prin., Ridgway Ltd., Architects/Developers, Los Angeles 1972–84; Founder and Dir. Centre Canadien d'Architecture, Montreal 1979–98; projects (as architect, consultant etc.) include: Seagram Bldg., New York (as Dir. of Planning) 1954–58, Toronto-Dominion Centre 1962, Saidye Bronfman Centre, YM-YWHA, Montreal 1963–68, Les Promenades St.-Bruno Shopping Centre, Quebec 1974, Jane Tate House renovation, Montreal 1974–76, Biltmore Hotel renovation, Los Angeles 1976, renovation of housing units, St.-Hubert St., Montreal 1979; instigated 700-unit co-operative housing renovation project, Milton Park, Montreal 1979–85; renovation Ben Ezra synagogue, Cairo, Egypt 1987–; jury mem. several cttees. for architectural and urban design projects; numerous exhbns.; mem. Bd. of Trustees Inst. of Fine Arts, New York Univ., Visiting Cttee. Princeton Univ., N.J., Advisory Cttee. on Architectural and Urban History, Harvard Univ.; Founding mem. Bd. Int. Confed. of Architectural Museums (Pres. 1985–89) and several other bodies; frequent guest lecturer; mem. Bd. of Overseers, Coll. of Architecture, Ill. Inst. of Tech., Advisory Council to School of Architecture, Princeton Univ.; numerous hon. degrees; numerous awards and prizes including American Inst. of Architects 25-Year Award of Excellence (Seagram Bldg.), New York Landmarks Conservancy Award, Massey Medal, Royal Architectural Inst. of Canada (Saidye Bronfman Centre), Médaille de l'Académie d'Architecture, Paris 1988, Gabrielle Léger Medal, Heritage Canada Foundation 1988, Medal of Honour, Société Historique de Montréal 1990, Prix d'excellence en architecture, Ordre des Architectes du Québec 1990, Royal Architectural Inst. of Canada Gold Medal Award 1991, 1992 Honor Award (A.I.A.), Lescarbot Award, Govt. of Canada 1992, Prix Gérard-Morisset, Gov. of Quebec 1994. *Address:* c/o Centre Canadien d'Architecture, 1920 rue Baile, Montreal, Quebec, H3H 2S6, Canada. *Telephone:* (514) 939-7020.

LAMBERT, Richard Peter, B.A.; British journalist; b. 23 Sept. 1944; s. of Peter Lambert and Mary Lambert; m. Harriet Murray-Browne 1973; one s. one d.; ed. Fettes Coll. and Balliol Coll. Oxford; mem. staff, Financial Times 1966–, Lex Column 1972, Financial Ed. 1978, New York Corresp. 1982, Deputy Ed. 1983, Ed. Financial Times 1991–. *Address:* Financial Times, 1 Southwark Bridge, London, SE1 9HL, England. *Telephone:* 0171-873 3000.

LAMBERT, Yves Maurice; French international official and engineer; b. 4 June 1936, Nancy, Meurthe-et-Moselle; s. of André Arthur Lambert and Paulette Franck; m. Odile Revillon 1959; three s. two d.; ed. Ecole Polytechnique, Paris, Nat. Civil Aviation School, Centre de Préparation à l'Admin. des Entreprises; Dir. Org. de Gestion et de Sécurité de l'Algérie (OGSA), Algeria 1965–68; Tech. Adviser to Minister of Transport, France 1969–72; Rep. of France to ICAO Council 1972–76; Sec.-Gen. ICAO Aug. 1976–88, Dir. of Air Navigation, Ministry of Equipment and Housing, Transport and the Sea 1989–93; Dir.-Gen. Eurocontrol 1994–; Fellow Royal Aeronautical Soc. (U.K.); mem. Acad. Nat. de l'Air et de l'Espace; Chevalier, Légion d'honneur, Ordre nat. du Mérite, Médaille de l'Aéronautique, Glen Gilbert Award, Air Traffic Control Asscn. 1997. *Address:* Eurocontrol, 96 rue de la Fusée, 1130 Brussels, Belgium.

LAMBO, (Thomas) Adeoye, O.B.E., M.B., CH.B., M.D., F.R.C.P.E., F.R.C.PSY.; Nigerian neuro-psychiatrist; b. 29 March 1923, Abeokuta; s. of the late Chief David Basil Lambo and Felicia Lambo; m. Dinah V. Adams 1945; three s.; ed. Baptist Boys' High School, Abeokuta, Birmingham Univ., England, London Univ. Inst. of Psychiatry; Medical Officer, Nigerian Medical Services 1950–56; Govt. Specialist-in-charge, Aro Hospital for Nervous Diseases; Consultant Physician, Univ. Coll., Ibadan 1956–63; Prof. and Head of Dept. of Psychiatry and Neurology, Univ. of Ibadan 1963–71, Dean of Medical Faculty 1966–68; Vice-Chancellor, 1968–71; Asst. Dir.-Gen. WHO 1971–73, Deputy Dir.-Gen. 1973–88; mem. Exec. Comm. World Fed. for Mental Health 1964–; Exec. Dir. Lambo Foundation 1988–; Chair. Scientific Council for Africa, UN Advisory Cttee. for Prevention of Crime and Treatment of Offenders, Co-ordinating Bd. African Chairs of Tech. in Food Processing, Biotechnology, Nutrition and Health; Vice-Pres. World Asscn. of Social Psychiatry; mem. of numerous asscns. including Advisory Cttee. for Mental Health, WHO, Exec. Cttee. Council for Int. Org. for Medical Sciences, UNESCO, Expert Advisory Panel on Mental Health, WHO, WHO Advisory Cttee. for Health Research (Geneva), Royal Medico-Psychological Asscn., U.K., Pontifical Acad. of Sciences Int. Epidemiological Asscn., Int. Hosp. Fed., Nigerian Medical Council; Founding mem. African Acad. of Sciences; Assoc. mem. Int. Asscn. For Child Psychiatry and Allied Professions; Hon. mem. Swiss Acad. of Medical Sciences, Third World Acad. of Sciences (founding mem.); numerous hon. degrees; Haile Selassie African Research Award 1970; Nigerian Nat. Order of Merit 1979, Commdr. Order of the Niger 1979. *Publications:* Psychiatric Disorder among the Yorubas (co-author) 1963 and numerous articles in various medical journals. *Leisure interests:* collection of ethnographic material on Africa, of art of traditional and tribal religions, and of ancient books on the history of medicine, on literature and philosophy. *Address:* Lambo Foundation, 15 Olatunbosun Street, Shonibare Estate, Maryland, P.O. Box 702, Ikeja, Lagos State, Nigeria. *Telephone:* 4976110/4976111; 961102 (Home). *Fax:* 962051; 4936667.

LAMBRAKIS, Christos; Greek newspaper proprietor and journalist; b. 24 Feb. 1934; ed. L.S.E.; Publr. and Ed. weekly Tachydromos (Courier) 1955–; succeeded father as propr. of dailies To Vima (Tribune), Ta Nea (News) and the weeklies Economicos Tachydromos (Economic Courier) 1957, Omada (The Team) 1958; Publr. monthly Epoches 1963; Pres. Greek Section, Int. Press Inst.; in prison (Folegandros Prison Island) Nov. 1967. *Address:* c/o Lambrakis Press, Odos Christou Lada 3, 102 37 Athens, Greece. *Telephone:* 3230-221; 3237-283.

LAMBRON, Marc; French journalist; b. 4 Feb. 1957, Lyon; s. of Paul Lambron and Jacqueline Lambron (née Denis); m. Sophie Missoffe 1983; one s. two d.; ed. Ecole normale supérieure, Institut d'etudes politiques, Ecole national d'administration; columnist Point 1986–, Madame Figaro; mem. Conseil d'Etat 1985–; Prix des Deux Magots 1989, Prix Colette 1991, Prix Femina 1993. *Publications:* L'Impromptu de Madrid 1988, La nuit des masques 1990, Carnet de bal 1992, L'oeil du silence 1993, 1941 1997. *Leisure interests:* music, cinema. *Address:* 17 rue Lagrange, 75005 Paris, France. *Telephone:* (01) 40-51-02-12. *Fax:* (01) 46-33-43-18.

LAMBSDORFF, Otto Graf Friedrich Wilhelm von der Wenge, D.IUR.; German politician, government official and fmr. company executive; b. 20 Dec. 1926, Aachen; ed. Univs. of Bonn and Cologne; Mil. service, prisoner of war, seriously wounded 1944–46; admitted to bar at local and dist. courts of Düsseldorf 1960; activities in credit business, rising to power of attorney for a private bank 1955–71; mem. board of dirs. of an insurance co. 1971–77; mem. Bundestag 1972–; Fed. Minister of Econs. 1977–84; Chair. Free Democratic Party (FDP) 1988–93, European Chair. Trilateral Comm. 1991–; Chair. Bd. Friedrich Naumann Foundation 1995–; Pres. Liberal Int. 1993–96; Dr. h.c. 1980. *Publications:* Zielsetzungen-Aufgaben und Chancen der Marktwirtschaft 1978, Bewährung-Wirtschaftspolitik in Krisenzeiten 1980. *Address:* Strässchensweg 7, 53113 Bonn, Germany. *Telephone:* 0228 236061. *Fax:* 0228 236069.

LAMBY, Werner, DR.JUR.; German business executive; b. 1 Oct. 1924, Oberwörresbach, Rheinland-Pfalz; s. of Peter and Anna Lamby; m. Gisela Bürfent 1956; three s.; ed. Univs. of Heidelberg and Mainz; Civil service 1952–73; Chair. Supervisory Bd. VIAG AG 1974–90, mem. 1990–; Chair. Supervisory Bd. Saarbergwerke 1983–, Berliner Kraft und Licht (BEWAG) AG 1989–. *Address:* Lyngsbergstrasse 19, 53177 Bonn, Germany (Home).

LAMFALUSSY, Alexandre, L. ÈS SC.ECON., D.PHIL.; Belgian banker; b. 26 April 1929, Kapuvar, Hungary; m. Anne-Marie Cochard 1957; two s. two d.; ed. Univ. of Louvain and Nuffield Coll. Oxford; economist, then econ. adviser, Banque de Bruxelles 1955–65; Visiting lecturer, Yale Univ. 1961–62; Exec. Dir. and Chair. Exec. Bd. Banque de Bruxelles 1965–75; Exec. Dir. Banque Bruxelles Lambert 1975; Econ. Adviser, Head of Monetary and Econ. Dept. BIS 1976–81, Asst. Gen. Man. 1981–85, Gen. Man. 1985–93; Pres. of the European Monetary Inst. 1994–97. *Publications:* Investment and Growth in Mature Economies: The Case of Belgium 1961, The U.K. and the Six: An Essay on Growth in Western Europe 1963, Les marchés financiers en Europe 1968. *Address:* Postfach 102031, 60020 Frankfurt, Germany. *Telephone:* (69) 27 227-0. *Fax:* (69) 27 227-227.

LAMINE LOUM, Mamadou; Senegalese politician; fmr. Minister of Econ., Finance and Planning; Prime Minister of Senegal July 1998–; mem. Parti Socialiste (PS). *Address:* Office of the Prime Minister, ave. Leopold Sedar Senghor, Dakar, Senegal. *Telephone:* 823-10-88. *Fax:* 822-55-78.

LAMIZANA, Lieut.-Gen. Aboubakar Sangoulé; Burkinabê politician and army officer; b. 1916, Dianra., Tougan; s. of Kafa and Diantoro Lamizana; m. Mouilo Kékélé Bintou 1947; six c.; served in French Army in Second World War, and later in N. Africa; joined Bataillon Autonome du Soudan Nigérien, Ségou 1947; with Centre d'Etudes Africaines et Asiatiques, Paris 1950; served in Indo-China; Jt. Chief of Mil. Cabinet, Côte d'Ivoire 1956–59; Capt. 1957; served N. Africa 1959–60; Chief of Staff, Army of Upper Volta (now Burkina Faso) 1961, Lt.-Col. 1964, Brig.-Gen. 1967, Maj.-Gen. 1970, Lieut.-Gen. 1973; led coup d'état in Jan. 1966; Pres. of Upper Volta 1966–80 (deposed in coup); Prime Minister 1966–71, 1974–78; Minister of Defence 1966–67, of Foreign Affairs 1966–67, of Information, Youth and Sports 1966–67, of Justice 1974–75; Grand Croix, Ordre nat. de Haute-Volta, Légion d'honneur, Croix de guerre, Croix de Valeur Militaire, other foreign decorations. *Leisure interest:* sport.

LAMJAV, Banzrachiin; Mongolian fmr. politician; b. 1920; ed. Higher School for Party Cadres, Ulaanbaatar and Higher Party School of the CPSU Cen. Cttee.; Instructor at Prov. Cttee. of the Mongolian Revolutionary Youth League; served in army as private, elected as Bureau secretary of the Youth League Cttee., worked as asst. and deputy chief of political dept. of regt., then a brigade; head of section Political Directorate, Mongolian People's Army (MPRP), then deputy chief of dept.; Deputy Chair. Party Cen. Cttee. of MPRP Cen. Cttee. 1954–56; First Sec. Party Cttee. of Zavkhan Aimak (Prov.) 1956–58; Instructor at the MPRP Cen. Cttee. 1958–62; Head of Personnel Dept. MPRP Cen. Cttee. 1962–86; concurrently First Deputy Chair. Party Control Cttee. of MPRP Cen. Cttee. 1979–86; Alt. mem. Political Bureau of MPRP Cen. Cttee. 1986–87, mem. 1987–90 and Chair. Party Control Cttee. MPRP Cen. Cttee. 1986–90 (resgnd.); fmr. Deputy to the Great People's Hural; mem. of Presidium of Great People's Hural 1976–86.

LAMM, Donald Stephen, B.A.; American publisher; b. 31 May 1931, New York; s. of Lawrence W. Lamm and Aleen A. Lassner; m. Jean S. Nicol 1958; two s. one d.; ed. Fieldston School, Yale and Oxford Univs.; Counter-intelligence Corps, U.S. Army 1953–55; joined W. W. Norton & Co. Inc. 1956, college rep. 1956–59, Ed. 1959–, Dir. 1964–, Vice-Pres. 1968–76, Chair. 1984–; Regents Lecturer, Univ. of Calif., Berkeley 1997; Pres. Yale Univ. Press; mem. Advisory Council Inst. of Early American History and Culture 1979–82; mem. Council on Foreign Relations 1978–; mem. Council, Woodrow Wilson Center, Int. advisory Bd., Logos; Guest Fellow, Yale Univ. 1980, 1985; Trustee, The Roper Center 1984–; Fellow, Branford Coll. Yale Univ. 1985–; Guest Fellow Woodrow Wilson Center 1996; Pres. Bd. of Govs. Yale Univ. 1986–; Ida H. Beam Distinguished Visiting Prof. Univ. of Iowa 1987–88; Fellow Center for Advanced Study in the Behavioral Sciences 1998–. *Publications:* Economics and the Common Reader 1989; Beyond Literacy 1990, Book Publishing in the United States Today 1997. *Leisure interests:* wilderness canoeing, skiing. *Address:* W. W. Norton & Co., Inc., 550 Fifth Avenue, New York, NY 10110 (Office); 741 Calle Picacho, Santa Fe, NM 87301, U.S.A. (Home).

LAMM, Richard D., LL.B., C.P.A.; American politician and lawyer; b. 8 Aug. 1935, Madison, Wis.; s. of A. E. Lamm; m. Dottie Lamm; one s. one d.; ed. Univs. of Wisconsin and California; Certified Public Accountant, Ernst & Ernst, Denver 1961–62; Lawyer, Colorado Anti-Discrimination Comm. 1962–63; Lawyer, Jones, Meiklejohn, Kilroy, Kehl & Lyons 1963–65; private practice 1965–74; mem. Colorado House of Reps. 1966–74; Assoc. Prof. of Law, Univ. of Denver 1969–74; Gov. of Colo. 1975–87; Dir. Center for Public Policy and Contemporary Issues, Univ. of Denver 1987–. *Publications:* The Angry West (with Michael McCarthy) 1982, 1988 (with Arnie Grossman) 1985, Megatraumas 1985, The Immigration Time Bomb 1985, A California Conspiracy (with Arnold Grossman) 1988. *Leisure interests:* mountain climbing, reading, bicycling. *Address:* Center for Public Policy and Contemporary Issues, University of Denver, 2050 East Iliff Avenue, Ste. 224, Denver, CO 80208, U.S.A. *Telephone:* (303) 871-3400. *Fax:* (303) 871-3066.

LAMO DE ESPINOSA Y MICHELS DE CHAMPOURCÍN, Jaime; Spanish politician and agronomic engineer; b. 4 April 1941, Madrid; s. of Emilio Lamo de Espinosa and Maria Luisa Michels de Champourcin; m. Carmen Rocamora 1965; four d.; ed. Colegio de Nuestra Señora del Pilar, Escuela Técnica Superior de Ingenieros Agrónomos, Univ. of Madrid; Asst. Engineer, Study Group, Servicio Nacional de Concentración Parcelaria 1964–69; Tech. Dir. Fondo de Ordenación y Regulación de Productos y Precios Agrarios (FORPPA) 1969–73; Sub-commissar for Devt. Plan 1973; Dir. of Tech. Cttee., Ministry of Agric. 1974; Dir.-Gen. Food Industries 1974–76; Under-Sec. of Agric. 1976; Asst. to Third Vice-Pres. of Govt. 1977–78; Minister of Agric. and Fisheries 1978–81; Minister Asst. to Pres. Council of Ministers 1981–82; mem. Congress of Deputies for Castellón 1979–; mem. Unión de Centro Democrático (UCD); Chief UCD spokesman in Congress 1981–82; Pres. 20th FAO World Conf. 1979–81; Pres. Conf. of OECD Ministers of Agric. 1980; Prof., Int. Centre for Advanced Mediterranean Agronomic Studies, Montpellier, France (OECD) 1980; Gran Cruz del Mérito Agrícola, Gran Cruz del Mérito Civil, Encomienda del Mérito Agrícola; Cross of Merit (Fed. Repub. of Germany); Croix du Mérite Civil (France). *Publications:* Agricultura a tiempo parcial y minifundios, Reflexiones sobre la política de precios y su armonización con la política general agraria, Los latifundios y el desarrollo agrario, Interrelación de las políticas de precio y de estructura en la agricultura, La agricultura en una sociedad democrática. *Leisure interests:* reading, music, painting. *Address:* José Abascal 46, Madrid, Spain. *Telephone:* 441 34 15.

LAMONICA, Roberto de; Brazilian artist; b. 27 Oct. 1933; ed. Escola de Belas Artes de São Paulo and Museu de Arte Moderna, Rio de Janeiro; Prof. School of Fine Arts, Lima 1961–62, Univ. de Chile and Univ. Católica de Chile 1962–63, School of Fine Arts, Viña del Mar 1963–64; Prof. of Printmaking, Museum of Modern Art, Rio de Janeiro 1964–; has exhibited in Graphic Art Exhbns. all over the world; illustrations and covers for several books; numerous prizes. *Address:* Rua Aníbal de Mendonça 180, A.P. 202, Rio de Janeiro ZC-37, RJ, Brazil.

LAMONT, Most Rev. Donal, M.A., S.T.L.; Irish ecclesiastic; b. 27 July 1911, Ballycastle, Co. Antrim; s. of Daniel Lamont and Margaret Tumelty; ed. Terenure Coll., Dublin, Univ. Coll., Dublin, Collegio Sant'Alberto, Rome; professed in Carmelite Order 1930; ordained priest, Rome 1937; Superior Carmelite Mission Rhodesia 1946; Prefect Apostolic, Umtali (now Mutare, Zimbabwe) 1953; Bishop of Umtali 1957–82; attended Second Vatican Council 1962–65; mem. Vatican Secr. for Promoting Christian Unity 1962–75; Pres. Rhodesia Catholic Bishop's Conf. 1970–72, rep. at Roman Synods 1969, 1971, 1974; sentenced to prison for opposition to regime and deported from Rhodesia March 1977; returned to Umtali Diocese after Independence 1980; resgnd. as Bishop of Diocese 1982, now Emer. Bishop of Mutare; Hon. LL.D. (Univs. of Notre Dame, Indiana, Seton Hall, N.J. Mount St. Mary's, Md., Marymount, N.Y.); postage stamp issued in his honour by Govt. of Kenya 1979; People of God Award, Washington Theological Union. *Publications:* Purchased People 1959, Speech from the Dock 1977. *Leisure interests:* reading, poetry, walking. *Address:* Terenure College, Dublin 6W, Ireland. *Telephone:* 4904621. *Fax:* 4902403.

LAMONT OF LERWICK, Baron (Life Peer), cr. 1998, of Lerwick in the Shetland Islands; **Rt. Hon. Norman Stewart Hughson Lamont,** P.C.; British politician; b. 8 May 1942, Lerwick, Shetland; s. of the late Daniel Lamont and of Helen Irene Hughson; m. Alice Rosemary White 1971; one s. one d.; ed. Loretto School, Fitzwilliam Coll., Cambridge; P.A. to Rt. Hon. Duncan Sandys M.P. 1965; mem. staff Conservative Research Dept. 1966–68; M.P. for Kingston upon Thames 1972–97; Merchant Banker with N.M. Rothschild & Sons 1968–79; Parl. Pvt. Sec. to Norman St. John Stevas (Lord St. John of Fawsley, q.v.) 1974; Opposition Spokesman on Prices and Consumer Affairs 1975–76, on Industry 1976–79; Parl. Under-Sec. of State, Dept. of Energy 1979–81; Minister of State, Dept. of Trade and Industry 1981–85, of Defence Procurement 1985–86; Financial Sec. to Treasury 1986–89, Chief Sec. 1989–90; Chancellor of the Exchequer 1990–93; Chair. Conservatives Against a Fed. Europe 1998; Dir. (non-exec.) N. M. Rothschild & Sons Ltd. 1993–95, First Philippine Investment Trust 1993–, Jupiter Asset Man. 1993–; Dir. Balli Group; Chair. Cambridge Univ. Conservative Asscn. 1963; Pres. Cambridge Union 1964; Conservative. *Publication:* Sovereign Britain 1995. *Leisure interests:* ornithology, reading. *Address:* c/o Balli Group PLC, 5 Stanhope Gate, London, W1Y 5LA, England.

LAMRANI, Mohammed Karim (see Karim-Lamrani, Mohammed).

LAMY, Pascal Lucien Fernand; French civil servant; b. 8 April 1947, Levallois-Perret; s. of Jacques Lamy and Denise Dujardin; m. Geneviève Luchaire 1972; three s.; ed. Lycée Carnot, Paris, Ecole des Hautes Etudes Commerciales, Paris, Inst. d'Etudes Politiques, Ecole National d'Admin., Paris; served Inspection Générale des Finances 1975–79; Deputy Sec.-Gen., then Sec. Gen. Interministerial Cttee. for the Remodelling of Industrial Structures (CIASI) Treasury Dept. 1979–81; Tech. Advisor, then Deputy Dir. Office of the Minister for Econ. and Financial Affairs 1981–82; Deputy Dir. Office of the Prime Minister (Mr Mauroy) 1983–84; Chef de Cabinet to Pres. of Comm. of EC (Jacques Delors) 1985–94; mem. Exec. Cttee. Crédit Lyonnais 1994–; Chevalier Légion d'honneur 1990, Kt. Commdr.'s Cross (Badge and Star) of the Order of Merit (Germany), Commdr. Order of Merit (Luxembourg). *Publications:* jt. author report on welfare assistance for children. *Leisure interests:* tennis, jogging, marathon running. *Address:* Crédit Lyonnais, 19 blvd. des Italiens, 75002 Paris, France (Office); 29 avenue Lequime, 1640 Rhode-Saint-Genèse, Belgium (Home).

LANC, Erwin; Austrian politician; b. 17 May 1930, Vienna; s. of Engelbert Johann Franz Lanc and Maria Amalie Lanc (née Rippar); m. 1st Melitta Fröhlich (died 1983); m. 2nd Christiane Karen Maria Krammer 1990; one s. one d.; mem. Socialist Party 1948–; with Fed. Ministry of Social Admin. 1949–55; Nat. Sec. Austrian Youth Hostels Asscn. 1955–59; mem. Diet and Municipal Council of Vienna 1960–66; mem. Special Cttee. for Examination of Vienna Public Transport Co. 1961, Chair. 1964; Man. Information Bureau for Communal Financing 1965; mem. Parl. 1966–83; Pres. Viennese Workers' Asscn. for Sport and Physical Culture (ASKO) 1968–82; Minister of Transport 1973–77, of Interior 1977–83, of Foreign Affairs 1983–84; Man. Zentralsparkasse und Kommerzialbank, Vienna; Man. Handelsbank A.G., Vienna 1985–93; Chair. Bd. of Advisers ICD-Austria 1985–96; mem. Exec. Cttee. Austrian Socialist Party 1977–91; Pres. Int. Handball Fed. Aug. 1984–; Pres. Int. Inst. for Peace 1988–; mem. Council, Asscn. of Summer Olympic Sport Feds. *Publications:* Volksaktie ohne make-up 1960, Gemeinden und Kapitalmarkt 1967, Sozialdemokratie i.d. Krise 1996. *Leisure interests:* skiing, swimming, handball. *Address:* c/o International Institute for Peace, Möllwaldplatz 5, 1040 Vienna (Office); Feldkellergasse 70, 1130 Vienna, Austria (Home). *Telephone:* (1) 504 64 37. *Fax:* (1) 505-32-36.

LANCASTER, (Christopher Ronald) Mark, B.A.; British artist; b. 14 May, 1938, Holmfirth; s. of Charles Ronald Lancaster and Muriel Roebuck; ed. Holme Valley Grammar School, Bootham School, York, Univ. of Newcastle upon Tyne; Lecturer Univ. of Newcastle 1965–66, Bath Acad. of Art 1966–68; Artist in Residence King's Coll., Cambridge 1968–70; Artistic Advisor Merce Cunningham Dance Co., N.Y. 1980–84; N.Y. Dance and Performance Award 1989.

LANCASTER, Henry Oliver, A.O., M.D., D.SC., F.A.A.; Australian statistician (retd.); b. 1 Feb. 1913, Sydney; s. of Llewellyn B. Lancaster and Edith H. (née Smith) Lancaster; m. Joyce Mellon 1940; five s.; ed. Univ. of Sydney; Resident Medical Officer, Sydney Hosp. 1937–39; pathologist Royal Australian Army Medical Corps 1940–46; lecturer, Sr. Lecturer, Assoc. Prof. School of Public Health and Tropical Medicine, Sydney 1946–59; Rockefeller Fellow in Medicine, London School of Hygiene 1948–49; Prof. of Math. Statistics, Univ. of Sydney 1959–78, Prof. Emer. 1978–; T. R. Lyle Medal 1961, E. J. G. Pitman Medal 1980; Hon. Life mem. Statistical Soc. of Australia 1972, Australian Math. Soc. 1981; Hon. Fellow Royal Statistical Soc. 1975; Fellow A.A.A.S. 1988. *Publications:* Bibliography of Statistical Bibliographies 1968, The Chi-squared Distribution 1969, An Introduction to Medical Statistics 1974, Expectations of Life 1990, Quantitative Methods in Biological and Medical Sciences: A Historical Essay 1994; over 140 articles on medical statistics and math. *Leisure interests:* reading. *Address:* The Garrison, 13 Spit Road, Spit Junction, N.S.W. 2088, Australia. *Telephone:* (02) 9969 9034.

LANCE, James Waldo, A.O., C.B.E., M.D., F.R.C.P., F.R.A.C.P., F.A.A.; Australian professor of neurology; b. 29 Oct. 1926, Wollongong, N.S.W.; s. of Waldo and Jessie (née Stewart) Lance; m. Judith L. Logan 1957; one s. four d.; ed. Geelong Grammar School, The King's School, Parramatta and Univ. of Sydney; Chair. Div. of Neurology, Prince Henry and Prince of Wales Hosps., Sydney 1961–91; Prof. of Neurology, Univ. of N.S.W. 1975–91, Prof. Emer. 1992–; Pres. Australian Asscn. of Neurologists 1978–81, Int. Headache Soc.

1987–89; Vice-Pres. Australian Acad. of Sciences 1984–85, World Fed. of Neurology 1991–93; Hon. D.Sc.; Harold G. Wolff Award of American Asscn. for Study of Headache 1967, 1983. *Publications:* Headache 1975, The Golden Trout 1978, A Physiological Approach to Clinical Neurology (with J. G. McLeod 1981), Migraine and other Headaches 1986, The Mechanism and Management of Headache 1993, Introductory Neurology (with J. G. McLeod) 1995. *Leisure interests:* swimming, trout fishing, skiing. *Address:* Institute of Neurological Sciences, The Prince of Wales Hospital, Randwick, N.S.W. 2031; 15 Coolong Road, Vaucluse, N.S.W. 2030, Australia (Home). *Telephone:* (2) 9398-7789 (Office); (2) 9337-5790 (Home). *Fax:* (2) 9398-7451 (Office).

LANCELOT, Alain, D. ÈS L. ET SC. HUM.; French university professor; b. 12 Jan. 1937, Chêne-Bougeries, Geneva, Switzerland; s. of Elisée Lancelot and Suzanne Perrin-Lancelot; m. Marie Thé Merlet Lancelot 1958; one s. one d.; ed. Inst. d'Etudes Politiques, Paris and Univ. of Paris-Sorbonne; Asst. French Political Science Asscn. 1959–62, Sec.-Gen. 1970–75; naval service 1962–63; Researcher, C.N.R.S. 1963–67; Prof. Inst. d'Etudes Politiques, Paris 1967–99; Dir. Centre for Study of French Political Life 1975–86; Dir. Inst. d'Etudes Politiques de Paris and Exec. Officer Fondation Nat. des Sciences Politiques 1987–96; mem. Conseil Constitutionnel 1996–; Officier, Légion d'Honneur, Ordre Nat. du Mérite, des Arts et des Lettres, des Palmes Académiques; decorations from Germany and Italy. *Publications:* L'abstentionnisme électoral en France 1968, La vie politique en France depuis 1940 1975, Les élections sous la cinquième république 1983, etc. *Leisure interest:* sailing. *Address:* Conseil Constitutionnel, 2 rue de Montpensier, 75001 Paris, France. *Telephone:* 33 1 40 15 30 07. *Fax:* 33 1 40 20 93 27.

LANCHBERY, John Arthur, O.B.E., A.R.A.M., F.R.A.M.; British conductor and composer; b. 15 May 1923, London; s. of William E. Lanchbery and Violet S. Mewett; m. Elaine Fifield 1951 (divorced 1960); one d.; ed. Alleyn's School, Dulwich and Royal Acad. of Music; served R.A.C. 1943–45; Musical Dir. Metropolitan Ballet 1948–50; Sadler's Wells Theatre Ballet 1951–57; Royal Ballet 1957–72, Prin. Conductor 1959–72; Musical Dir. Australian Ballet 1972–77, American Ballet Theatre 1978–80. *Arrangements and composition of ballets include:* Pleasuredrome 1949, Eve of St. Agnes 1950, House of Birds 1955, La Fille Mal Gardée 1960, The Dream 1964, Don Quixote 1966, Giselle 1968, La Sylphide 1970, Tales of Beatrix Potter 1971, Tales of Hoffman 1972, Merry Widow 1975, Month in the Country 1976, The Turning Point 1977, Mayerling 1978, Rosalinda 1978, Papillon 1979, La Bayadere 1980, Peer Gynt 1981, Evil Under the Sun 1982, The Sentimental Bloke 1985, Le Chat Botté 1985, A Midsummer Night's Dream 1985, Hunchback of Notre Dame 1988, Figaro 1992; Robinson Crusoe (opéra comique) 1986, Birth of a Nation 1992, The Iron Horse 1994, Madam Butterfly 1995, Dracula 1997, Snowmaiden 1998; Bolshoi Theatre Medal 1961, Queen Elizabeth II Coronation Award (Royal Acad. Dancing) 1989. *Leisure interests:* walking, reading. *Address:* 71 Park Street, St. Kilda West, Vic. 3182, Australia. *Telephone:* (3) 9537-0520. *Fax:* (3) 9537-0521.

LAND, Michael Francis, M.A., PH.D., F.R.S.; British professor of biology; b. 12 April 1942, Dartmouth; s. of late Prof. F. W. Land and of Mrs. N. B. Land; m. 1st Judith Drinkwater 1966 (divorced 1980), one s.; m. 2nd Rosemary Roper 1980, two d.; ed. Birkenhead School, Jesus Coll., Cambridge, Univ. Coll., London and Univ. of Calif., Berkeley (Miller Fellowship); Asst. Prof. Univ. of Calif., Berkeley 1969–71; Lecturer, School of Biological Sciences, Univ. of Sussex 1971–77, Reader 1977–84, Prof. of Neurobiology 1984–; Visiting Prof. Univ. of Ore. 1980; Sr. Visiting Fellow, A.N.U., Canberra 1982–84. *Publications:* 90 articles and papers on aspects of vision in animals from visual optics to behaviour. *Leisure interests:* gardening, music. *Address:* School of Biological Sciences, University of Sussex, Brighton, BN1 9QG (Office); White House, Cuilfail, Lewes, Sussex, BN7 2BE, England (Home). *Telephone:* (01273) 678505 (Office); (01273) 476780 (Home).

LANDABURU ILLARRAMENDI, Eneko; Spanish European public servant; b. 11 March 1948, Paris; s. of Francisco Javier Nicolas Landaburu and Prudencia Francisca Constantina Illarramendi; m. Dominique Rambaud 1971; two s. one d.; ed. Univ. of Paris, France; mem. staff Admin. and Financial Man. Dept., Société Labaz, Paris 1971–73, Asst. to Man. Belgian subsidiary SA Labaz NV, Brussels 1973–75; Head of Study and Lecture Programmes, Centre Européen d'Etudes et d'Information sur les Sociétés Multinationales (CEEIM), Brussels 1975–79; PSOE Deputy, Spanish Basque Regional Parl. 1980–81; Adviser to Latin American Dept., Nestlé, Vevey, Switzerland 1981–82; Dir. Institut de Recherche sur les Multinationales (IRM), Geneva, Switzerland 1983–86; Dir.-Gen. for Regional Politics, EC Comm., Brussels 1986–; Lecturer, Institut d'Etudes Européennes, Free Univ. of Brussels 1990–94; Alt. mem. Bd. of Dirs. of EIB 1993–; mem. Supervisory Bd. European Investment Fund FEI-EIF 1994–; mem. Bd. of Dirs. Fondation "Notre Europe" 1996–. *Address:* 200 rue de la Loi, 1049 Brussels (Office); Avenue du Grand Air 5A, 1640 Rhode St. Genèse, Belgium. *Telephone:* 295 1968 (Office). *Fax:* 295 0149.

LANDAIS, Hubert Léon; French museum administrator; b. 22 March 1921; s. of Pierre Landais and Odette Surmont; m. Madeleine Legris 1946; five s. one d.; ed. Ecole Nat. des Chartes, Ecole du Louvre; at the Louvre Museum 1946, Attendant 1946–48, Curator Middle Ages, Renaissance, Modern objects d'art 1948–62, Asst. Curator to the Dir. of Museums 1962–63, Chief Curator Nat. Museums 1963–65, Dir. objects d'art dept. 1965–68, Inspector-Gen. of Museums 1968, Dir. of the Museums 1977–87, Sec.-Gen. 1962–73, Pres. French Cttee. 1973–, mem. Int. Council 1974–77; Pres. Réunion des musées nationaux 1977; Vice-Pres., Conseil d'admin. du musée de l'Armée 1962–87; mem. Int. Council of Museums 1974–77, Pres. 1977–83, Pres. professional ethics cttee. 1990–97; Pres. Int. Council of Museums; Dir. l'Univers des Formes 1977–91, numerous other appointments; Commdr., Légion d'honneur, Ordre nat. du Mérite et des Arts et des Lettres. *Publications:* numerous articles on objects d'art, especially Renaissance works and porcelain. *Address:* 23 rue Bourdignon, 94100 Saint-Maur-des-Fossés, France (Home). *Telephone:* (1) 48 83 25 82.

LANDAU, Jean-Pierre; French economist; b. 7 Nov. 1946, Paris; s. of André Landau and Andrée Pestre; m. Evelyne Dova 1979; ed. Inst. d'études politiques de Paris, Ecole nat. d'admin.; served in Ministry of Health and Social Security 1978–79; Asst. Sec. for Trade Policy, Direction des Relations Économiques Extérieures 1986–89, various other positions in Ministry of Econ. and Finance; Exec. Dir. IMF 1989–93; Dir. Relations Economiques Extérieurs (DREE) 1993–96; fmr. teacher of econs., Inst. d'études politiques; fmr. mem. of Bd., Renault. *Address:* 13 rue de l'Odéon, 75006 Paris, France.

LANDAU, Moshe, LL.B.; Israeli judge (retd.); b. 29 April 1912, Danzig (now Gdańsk, Poland); s. of Dr. Isaac Landau and Betty (née Eisenstädt); m. Leah Doukhan 1937; three d.; ed. London Univ.; went to Israel 1933; called to Palestine Bar 1937; Magistrate of Haifa 1940, District Court Judge, Haifa 1948; Justice, Supreme Court, Jerusalem 1953–82, (Presiding Judge, Eichmann Trial), Deputy Pres. 1976–80, Pres. 1980–82; Israel Prize 1991. *Leisure interest:* piano. *Address:* 10 Alharizi Street, Jerusalem, Israel. *Telephone:* (2) 5632757.

LANDAU, Peter, DR.JUR.; German professor of law; b. 26 Feb. 1935, Berlin; m. Angelika Linnemann 1971; one s. one d.; ed. Univs. of Berlin, Freiburg, Bonn and Yale Univ.; Prof. Univ. of Regensburg 1968–87; Prof. of Law, Univ. of Munich 1987–; mem. Bayerische Akad. der Wissenschaften; mem. Inst. for Advanced Study, Princeton, U.S.A. 1990–91; Pres. Soc. for Medieval Canon Law (Zurich); Pres. Inst. of Medieval Canon Law. *Publications:* Die Entstehung des kanonischen Infamiebegriffs von Gratian bis zur Glossa ordinaria 1966, Ius patronatus 1975, Strafrecht, Strafprozess und Rezeption (Jt. Ed.) 1984, Officium und Libertas christiana 1991. *Leisure interest:* art. *Address:* Leopold-Wenger-Institut für Rechtsgeschichte, 80539 Munich, Professor-Huber-Platz 2 (Office); Sperberstr. 21c, 81827 Munich, Germany (Home). *Telephone:* 089/2180-3263 (Office); 089/4300121 (Home).

LANDÁZURI RICKETTS, H.E. Cardinal Juan, D.C.L.; Peruvian ecclesiastic; b. 19 Dec. 1913, Arequipa; ed. Univs. of Arequipa and Antonianum, Rome; Franciscan Friar; Teacher of Canon Law; Ordained Priest 1939; Titular Archbishop of Roina 1952; cr. Cardinal 1962; Archbishop of Lima 1955–90; cr. Kt., Commdr. of Order of Malta and many honours. *Address:* Luis Espejo, 1064, Urbanización Santa Catalina, La Victoria, Lima, Peru.

LANDER, Stephen, PH.D.; British public servant; m. Felicity Lander 1972; one s. one d.; ed. Bishop's Stortford Coll., Herts., Queens' Coll., Cambridge Univ.; with Inst. of Historical Research, London Univ.; joined MI5 1975–, Dir. 1992–96, Dir.-Gen. 1996–; fmrly. with Foreign Office, Nr. E. and N. Africa Dept. *Address:* P.O. Box 3255, London, SW1P 1AE, England.

LANDES, David S., PH.D.; American professor of history; b. 29 April 1924, New York; s. of Harry and Sylvia Landes; m. Sonia Tarnopol 1943; one s. two d.; ed. City Coll., New York, Harvard Univ.; Jr. Fellow, Soc. of Fellows, Harvard Univ. 1950–53; Asst. Prof. of Econs., Columbia Univ., New York 1952–55, Assoc. Prof. 1955–58; Fellow, Center for Advanced Study in Behavioral Sciences, Stanford, Calif. 1957–58; Prof. of History and Econs., Univ. of Calif., Berkeley 1958–64; Prof. of History, Harvard Univ. 1964–72, LeRoy B. Williams Prof. of History and Political Science 1972–75, Robert Walton Goelet Prof. of French History 1975–81, Prof. of Econs. 1977–98, Coolidge Prof. of History 1981–; Chair. Faculty Cttee. on Social Studies 1981–; Pres. Council on Research in Econ. History 1963–66; Dir. Center for Middle Eastern Studies, Harvard Univ. 1966–68; Acting Dir. Center for West European Studies, Harvard Univ. 1969–70; Pres. Econ. History Asscn. 1976–77; Ellen McArthur Lecturer, Univ. of Cambridge 1964; Visiting Prof., Univ. of Paris IV 1972–73, Univ. of Zürich and Eidgenössische Technisch Hochschule, Zürich 1978; Richards Lectures, Univ. of Va. 1978, Janeway Lectures, Princeton Univ. 1983; mem. Bd. of Eds., various journals of history; Fellow, N.A.S., American Acad. of Arts and Sciences, American Philosophical Soc., British Acad., Royal Historical Soc.; Overseas Fellow, Churchill Coll., Cambridge 1968–69; Visiting Fellow, All Souls, Oxford 1985; mem. American Historical Asscn., Econ. History Asscn. (also Trustee), Econ. History Soc., Soc. for French Historical Studies, Soc. d'Histoire Moderne and other socs.; Assoc. mem. Fondation Royaumont pour le Progrès des Sciences de l'Homme; Dr. h.c. (Lille) 1973. *Publications:* Bankers and Pashas 1958, The Unbound Prometheus 1968, Revolution in Time: Clocks and the Making of the Modern World 1983 and other books and articles on economic and social history. *Leisure interests:* antiquarian horology, squash, tennis. *Address:* Department of Economics, Harvard University, Cambridge, MA 02138 (Office); 24 Highland Street, Cambridge, MA 02138, U.S.A. (Home). *Telephone:* (617) 495-4849 (Office); (617) 354 6308 (Home).

LANDON, Howard Chandler Robbins, B.MUS.; American author and educator; b. 6 March 1926, Boston, Mass.; s. of William G. Landon and Dorothea LeB. Robbins; m. Else Radant 1957; ed. Lenox School, Mass., Swarthmore Coll. and Boston Univ.; corresp. The Times 1958–61; Hon. Professorial Fellow, Univ. Coll. Cardiff 1971–78, John Bird Prof. of Music

1978–; Prof. of the Humanities, Middlebury Coll., Vt. 1980–83; Verdienstkreuz für Kunst und Wissenschaft (Austria); Hon. D. Mus. (Boston) 1969, (Belfast) 1974, (Bristol) 1982, (Toulouse) 1991. *Publications:* The Symphonies of Joseph Haydn 1955, Beethoven 1970, Joseph Haydn: Chronicle and Works (5 vols.) 1976–80, Haydn: A Documentary Study 1982, Mozart & the Masons 1983, Handel and his World 1984, 1791: Mozart's Last Year 1987, Mozart: The Golden Years 1989, Mozart and Vienna 1991, Vivaldi 1992, Une journée particulière, 12 novembre 1791 1993; critical edns. of many of works of Haydn, Mozart and 18th century composers. *Leisure interests:* walking, swimming, cooking. *Address:* Château de Foncoussières, 81800 Rabastens (Tarn), France. *Telephone:* 63.40.61.45.

LANDRY, Monique; Canadian politician; b. 25 Dec. 1937, Montréal; m. Jean-Guy Landry; four s.; ed. Univ. of Montréal; M.P. 1984–; mem. of several inter-parl. asscns.; fmr. Parl. Sec. to the Sec. of State and the Minister of Int. Trade, Minister for External Relations 1986; Minister of State for External Relations and Int. Devt. 1991–93, of Science and Sec. of State of Canada Jan.–Nov. 1993; Consultant Dessau Int. 1994–; fmr. mem. Standing Cttee. on Communications and Culture, Jt. Cttee. on Official Languages Policy and Programs and the Standing Cttee. on Finance, Trade and Econ. Affairs, Canada-Europe Parl. Asscn., Canada-France Inter-Parl. Asscn., Canada-NATO Parl. Asscn.

LANDSBERGIS, Vytautas; Lithuanian politician and musicologist; b.18 Oct. 1932, Kaunas; s. of Vytautas Landsbergis-Žemkalnis and Ona Jablonskyte-Landsbergiene; m. Gražina Ručyte; one s. two d.; ed. J. Gruodis School of Music and Vilnius Conservatoire; teacher of piano and prof. of musicology, Vilnius Conservatoire, Vilnius Pedagogical Inst.; fmr. mem. Exec. Council and Secr. Composers' Union; Pres. M. K. Čiurlionis Soc.; mem. various arts and science bodies; elected to Initiative Group, Sajúdis Reform Movt., then to Sajūdis Seimas (Ass.) and Council 1988, Pres. Sajūdis Seimas Council 1988–90, Hon. Pres. Sajūdis Dec. 1991–; f. Lithuanian Conservative Party, Chair. 1993–; elected Deputy to U.S.S.R. Congress of People's Deputies 1989–90; elected to Supreme Council of Lithuania Feb. 1990, Pres. Supreme Council 1990–92, mem. Seimas (Parl.) and Leader of Parl. Opposition 1992–, Chair. Seimas 1996–; LL.D. h.c. (Loyola Univ., Chicago) 1991; Academician, Lithuanian Catholic Acad. 1997; Hon. Ph.D. (Vytautas the Great Univ., Kaunas) 1992; Klaipėda Univ. (Lithuania) 1997; Hon. H.D. (Weber Univ., U.S.A.) 1992; Lithuanian State Award (for monograph on M. K. Čiurlionis) 1975; Norwegian People's Peace Prize (for role in restoration of Lithuanian independence; has used prize to est. Landsbergis Foundation to help disabled children and young musicians) 1991, Award of France Fund of Future 1991, Hermann-Ehlers Prize 1992, Catalonian Ramon Llull IX Int. Prize 1994, Légion d'honneur 1997, Vibo Valentia Testimony Prize (Italy) 1998, Order of Grand Duke Vytautas, First Class (Lithuania) 1998, Grand Cross, Royal Norwegian Order of Merit 1998. *Publications:* fifteen books on musicology, art and music history (especially on artist and composer M. K. Čiurlionis) and politics. *Leisure interests:* history, poetry. *Address:* Seimas of Lithuania, Prosp. Gedimino 53, Vilnius, Lithuania. *Telephone:* (3702) 615680 (Office). *Fax:* (3702) 227875.

LANE, Baron (Life Peer), cr. 1979, of St. Ippollitts in the County of Hertfordshire; **Geoffrey Dawson Lane,** P.C., A.F.C.; British judge; b. 17 July 1918; s. of the late Percy Albert Lane; m. Jan Macdonald 1944; one s.; ed. Shrewsbury, Trinity Coll., Cambridge; served in R.A.F. 1939–45, Squadron Leader 1942; called to the Bar, Gray's Inn 1946, Bencher 1966; Q.C. 1962; Deputy Chair. Bedfordshire Quarter Sessions 1960–66, Recorder of Bedford 1963–66; mem. Parole Bd. 1970–72, Vice-Chair. 1972; a Judge, High Court of Justice, Queen's Bench Div. 1966–74; a Lord Justice of Appeal 1974–79; Lord of Appeal in Ordinary 1979; Lord Chief Justice of England 1980–92; Hon. Master of Bench, Inner Temple 1980; Hon. D.C.L. (Cambridge) 1984. *Address:* Royal Courts of Justice, Strand, London, WC2A 2LL, England.

LANE, Anthony Milner, PH.D., F.R.S.; British research physicist (retd.); b. 27 July 1928, Wilts.; s. of Herbert W. and Doris R. Lane; m. 1st Anne S. Zissman 1952 (died 1980); two s. one d.; m. 2nd Jill V. Parvin 1983; five step-d.; ed. Trowbridge Boys' Grammar School, Univ. of Cambridge; with UKAEA 1954–89, Deputy Chief Scientific Officer 1975–89. *Publications:* research articles in theoretical physics. *Leisure interests:* churches, birds. *Address:* 6 Walton Street, Oxford, OX1 2HG, England (Home). *Telephone:* (01865) 556565 (Home).

LANE, Neal Francis, M.A., PH.D.; American physicist; b. 22 Aug. 1938, Oklahoma; s. of Walter Lane and Harietta Hollander; m. Joni Williams 1960; one s. one d.; ed. Univ. of Oklahoma; Nat. Science Foundation (N.S.F.) Post-doctoral Fellow 1964–65; Asst. Prof. of Physics, Rice Univ. Houston 1966–69, Assoc. Prof. 1969–72, Prof. 1972–84, 1986–93, Prof. of Space Physics and Astronomy 1972–84, Chair. Dept. of Physics 1977–82, Provost 1986–93; Dir. Div. of Physics, N.S.F., Washington, D.C. 1979–80, Dir. N.S.F. 1993–; Chancellor, Univ. of Colo. Colorado Springs 1984–86; Visiting Fellow, Jt. Inst. for Lab. Astrophysics, Univ. of Colo. Boulder, Colo. 1965–66, 1975–76, non-resident Fellow 1984–93; Distinguished Visiting Scientist, Ky. Univ., Lexington 1980; mem. Comm. on Physics, Science, Math. and Applications, Nat. Research Council 1989–93, Bd. Overseers Superconducting Super Collider (SSC), Univs. Research Asscn. 1985–93, Advisory Cttee., Math. and Physical Sciences, N.S.F. 1992–93; other professional appts.; Fellow, American Physics Soc., A.A.A.S.; mem. American Inst. of Physics etc.; Alfred P. Sloan Foundation Fellow 1967–71; Hon. D.H.L. (Okla., Marymount Univs.) 1995, Hon. D.Sc. (Univ. of Ala.) 1994, (Mich. State Univ.) 1995, (Ohio State Univ.) 1996, (Washington Coll.) 1998. *Publications:* Quantum States of Atoms, Molecules and Solids, Understanding More Quantum Physics, articles in professional journals. *Leisure interests:* tennis, squash. *Address:* National Science Foundation, 4201 Wilson Boulevard, Arlington, VA 22230, U.S.A.

LANE, Ronald Anthony Stuart, C.M.G., M.C., F.I.B.; British banker; b. 8 Dec. 1917, Bushey, Herts.; s. of Wilmot Ernest Lane and Florence Blakey; m. Anne Brenda Walsh 1948; one s. one d.; ed. Lancing Coll.; served with Chartered Bank of India, Australia and China in the Far East 1939–60; 7th Light Cavalry, Indian Army 1940–45; Chief Gen. Man. the Chartered Bank 1972; mem. Export Guarantees Advisory Council 1972 (Deputy Chair. 1977–78); mem. Council, Inst. of Bankers 1975; Man. Dir. Standard Chartered Bank Ltd. 1975–77, Vice-Chair. 1977–83, Deputy Chair. Chartered Trust Ltd. 1979–83. *Leisure interest:* sailing. *Address:* West Hold, by the Church, West Mersea, Essex, England. *Telephone:* (01206) 2563.

LANG, Andrew Richard, PH.D., F.INST.P., F.R.S.; British professor of physics; b. 9 Sept. 1924, St. Annes-on-Sea. Lancs.; s. of late Ernest F. S. Lang and Susannah (Gueterbock) Lang; ed. Univ. Coll. of South-West, Exeter and Univ. of Cambridge; Research Dept. Lever Bros. Port Sunlight 1945–47; Research Asst. Cavendish Lab. 1947–48; North American Philips, Irvington-on-Hudson, New York 1952–53; Instr. Harvard Univ. 1953–54, Asst. Prof. 1954–59; Lecturer in Physics, Univ. of Bristol 1960–66, Reader 1966–79, Prof. 1979–87, Prof. Emer. 1987–, Sr. Research Fellow 1995–; Foreign Assoc. Royal Soc. of S.A.; Charles Vernon Boys Prize, Inst. of Physics 1964, Hughes Medal, Royal Soc. 1997. *Publications:* contributions to learned journals. *Address:* 1B Elton Road, Bristol, BS8 1SJ, England. *Telephone:* (0117) 973 9784.

LANG, Anton, DR.NAT.SC.; American (naturalized 1956) plant physiologist; b. 18 Jan. 1913, St. Petersburg, Russia; s. of Dr. George Lang and Vera Davidov; m. Lydia Kamendrovsky 1946; two s. one d.; ed. High School, Berlin and Labes, Pomerania, and Univ. of Berlin; Scientific Asst., Kaiser Wilhelm (later Max Planck) Inst. of Biology, Berlin, later Tübingen, Germany 1939–49; Research Assoc., Genetics Dept., McGill Univ., Montreal 1949; Visiting Prof. Agronomy and Genetics Depts., Texas Agric. and Mech. Coll. 1950; Research Fellow and Sr. Research Fellow, Div. of Biology, Calif. Inst. of Tech. Pasadena 1950–52; Asst. and Assoc. Prof., Dept. of Botany, Univ. of Calif., Los Angeles 1952–59; Prof. of Biology in charge of Earhart-Campbell Plant Research Labs., Calif. Inst. of Tech. 1959–65; Dir. MSU-DOE Plant Research Lab., Prof. Botany and Plant Pathology, Michigan State Univ., E. Lansing 1965–78, Prof. 1978–83, Prof. Emer. 1983–; Visiting Prof., Dept. of Botany and Plant Sciences, Univ. of Calif., Riverside 1984; Lady Davis Foundation Fellowship 1949; Lalor Foundation Fellowship 1950–52; Sr. Research Fellowship, Nat. Science Foundation 1948–49; mem. N.A.S. (Chair. Botany Section 1983–86, Sec. Class 2 1986–92), American Acad. of Arts and Sciences, Akademie Leopoldina; Chair. Nat. Research Council Cttee. on the Effects of Herbicides in Viet Nam 1971–74; mem. President's Cttee. on Nat. Medal of Science 1976–78; Hon. mem. German Botanical Soc. 1982; Hon. LL.D. (Glasgow) 1981; Distinguished Faculty Award, Mich. State Univ. 1976, Stephen Hales Price and Charles Reid Barnes Life Membership Awards, American Soc. Plant Physiologists 1976, Merit Award, Botanical Soc. of America 1979, Silver Medal (Mass. Horticultural Soc.) 1979. *Publications:* Over 100 publs. on plant physiology (physiology of flowering, hormone physiology). *Leisure interests:* reading, music. *Address:* MSU/DOE Plant Research Laboratory, Michigan State University, East Lansing, MI 48824-1312 (Office); 1538 Cahill Drive, East Lansing, MI 48823, U.S.A. (Home). *Telephone:* (517) 351-5431 (Home); (517) 355-5149 (Office).

LANG, Brian Andrew, PH.D.; British library executive; b. 2 Dec. 1945, Edin.; s. of Andrew Lang and Mary Lang; m. 1st 1975 (divorced), 2nd 1983; two s. one d.; ed. Royal High School, Edin. and Univ. of Edin.; social anthropological field research, Kenya 1969–70; lecturer in Social Anthropology, Aarhus Univ. Denmark 1971–75; scientific staff, Social Science Research Council 1976–79; Head, Historic Bldgs. Br., Scottish Office 1979–80; Dir. Nat. Heritage Memorial Fund 1980–87; Dir. of Public Affairs, Nat. Trust 1987–91; Chief Exec. and Dep. Chair. British Library 1991–. *Leisure interests:* reading, music, tennis. *Address:* The British Library, 96 Euston Road, London, NW1 2DB (Office); 42 Grandison Road, London, SW11 6LW, England (Home). *Telephone:* 0171-412 7262 (Office); 0171-228 0767 (Home). *Fax:* 0171-412 7268 (Office).

LANG, Helmut; Austrian fashion designer; b. 10 March 1956, Vienna; established own studio in Vienna 1977; made-to-measure shop opened in Vienna 1979; development of ready-to-wear collections 1984–86; presented Helmut Lang women's wear, Paris fashion week 1986–, menswear 1987–; began licence business 1988; Helmut Lang Underwear 1994; Helmut Lang Protective Eyewear 1995; Prof. of Masterclass of Fashion, Univ. of Applied Arts, Vienna 1993–; Council of American Fashion Designers of the Year yyAward 1996. *Address:* c/o Michele Montagne, 184 rue St Maur, 75010 Paris, France. *Telephone:* (1) 42 03 91 00. *Fax:* (1) 42 01 12 22.

LÁNG, István; Hungarian agrochemist; b. 26 Dec. 1931, Mohács; s. of József Láng and Anna Világi; m. Etelka Sorosinszki; one d.; ed. Agricultural Univ. of Ivanovo, U.S.S.R.; Fellow Research Inst. for Soil Sciences and Agricultural Chemistry, Budapest 1955–63; Exec. Sec. Section of Biological Sciences, Hungarian Acad. of Sciences 1963–70, Deputy Sec. Gen. 1970–85,

Sec.-Gen. 1985–93, Science Policy Adviser 1993–; Chair. Advisory Bd., Ministry of Environmental and Regional Policy 1994–96, Vice-Chair. 1998–; Chair. Hungarian Research Fund 1986–90; mem. World Comm. on Environment and Devt. (Brundtland Comm.), Advisory Cttee. on Environment, Int. Council for Science; exec. bd. mem. Int. Council of Scientific Unions (ICSU). *Leisure interests:* philately, bird watching. *Address:* c/o Hungarian Academy of Sciences, 1051 Budapest, Roosevelt tér 9, Hungary. *Telephone:* (1) 269 2656. *Fax:* (1) 269 2655.

LANG, Jack, D. EN D.; French politician; b. 2 Sept. 1939, Mirecourt; s. of Roger Lang and Marie-Luce Bouchet; m. Monique Buczynski 1961; two d.; ed. Lycée Henri-Poincaré, Nancy, Inst. of Political Studies, Paris; Founder and Dir. World Festival of Univ. Theatre, Nancy 1963–77; Dir. Théâtre du palais de Chaillot 1972–74; Prof. of Int. Law 1976–; Dir. Educ. and Research Unit for econ. and legal sciences, Nancy 1977; Councillor, Paris 1977–81; deputy Nat. Ass. 1986; Special Adviser to First Sec., Parti Socialiste (PS) 1978–81, PS Nat. Del. for Culture 1979–81; Minister of Culture and Communications 1981–83, 1984–86, May–June 1988, 1991–92, of Educ. and Culture 1992–93, also Minister for Major Public Works and Bicentenary 1988–89; Govt. spokesman 1991; Mayor of Blois 1989–; mem. European Parl. 1994–97; Socialist Deputy from Loir-et-Cher March–Dec. 1993, 1997–; Pres. Foreign Affairs Cttee., Nat. Ass.; Hon. D.Litt. (Nottingham) 1990, Dr. h.c. (Royal Coll. of Art) 1993; Chevalier, Légion d'honneur. *Publication:* Lettre A Malraux 1996, Demain les femmes 1995, François Premier 1997. *Address:* Mairie, 41000 Blois, France.

LANG, k.d. (Kathy Dawn); Canadian popular singer and songwriter; b. Consort, Alberta; d. of Adam Lang and Audrey L. Lang; began playing guitar aged 10; formed own band 'the reclines' in early 1980s; first single Friday Dance Promenade; other singles include Crying (duet with Roy Orbison), Constant Craving, Just Keep Me Moving, If I Were You; albums include: A Truly Western Experience, Angel With A Lariat 1987, Shadowland 1988, Absolute Torch And Twang 1989, Ingenue 1992, Even Cowgirls Get The Blues (film soundtrack) 1993, All You Can Eat 1995; performed with Sting, Bruce Springsteen, Peter Gabriel and Tracy Chapman in Amnesty Int. tour 1988; acting debut in film Salmonberries 1991; recipient of several awards including three Grammy awards. *Address:* c/o WEA Records, The Warner Building, 28 Kensington Church Street, London, W8 4SP, England; Sire Records, 75 Rockefeller Plaza, New York, NY 10019, U.S.A. *Telephone:* 0171-937 8844 (London). *Fax:* 0171-938 3563 (London).

LANG, Hon. Otto Emil, P.C., Q.C., B.A., LL.B., B.C.L., LL.D.; Canadian lawyer, politician and business executive; b. 14 May 1932, Handel, Sask.; s. of Otto T. Lang and Maria Theresa Wurm; m. 1st Adrian Ann Merchant 1963 (divorced 1988), three s. four d.; m. 2nd Deborah J. McCawley 1989, one step-s. one step-d.; ed. Univ. of Saskatchewan and Oxford Univ.; admitted to Sask. Bar 1956, to Ont., Yukon and N.W.T. Bars 1972, Manitoba Bar 1988; Asst. Prof., Univ. of Saskatchewan, Faculty of Law 1956, Assoc. Prof. 1957, Prof. 1961, Dean of Law School 1961–68; M.P. for Saskatoon-Humboldt 1968–79; Minister without Portfolio 1968, with responsibility for Energy and Water Resources 1969, with responsibility for Canadian Wheat Bd. 1969–79; Minister of Manpower & Immigration 1970–72, of Justice 1972–75, of Transport 1975–79, of Justice and Attorney-Gen. Aug.–Nov. 1978; Pres. Asscn. of Canadian Law Teachers 1962–63; Vice-Pres. Saskatchewan Liberal Asscn. 1956–63; Fed. Campaign Chair. Liberal Party 1963–64; Past Pres. Saskatoon Social Planning Council; Exec. Vice-Pres. Pioneer Grain Co. Ltd. 1979–88; Chair. Transport Inst., Univ. of Manitoba 1988–93; Pres. and C.E.O. Centra Gas Manitoba Inc. 1993–; Vice-Chair. of Bd., Winnipeg Airports Authority 1995–; Chair. of Bd. Humboldt Flour Mills Inc. 1996–98; Campaign Chair. Winnipeg United Way 1983; Rhodes Scholar 1953; Q.C. for Ont. 1972; Q.C. for Sask. 1972; Hon. Consul-Gen. of Japan 1992–97. *Publication:* Contemporary Problems of Public Law in Canada (Ed.) 1968. *Leisure interests:* curling, bridge, golf. *Address:* Twin Oaks, 292 River Road, St. Andrews, Man., R1A 2X2, Canada. *Telephone:* (204) 925 0722 (Office); (204) 334 9476 (Home).

LANG DAZHONG; Chinese state official; b. March 1933; alt. mem. 12th CCP Cen. Cttee. 1982, mem. 1983–87, mem. 13th Cen. Cttee. 1987–; Dir. Dehong Dai and Jingpo Autonomous Pref. Cttee. 1978–83, Party Sec. 1983–; Sec. Comm. for Discipline Inspection 1992–; Standing Cttee. mem. Cen. Comm. for Discipline Inspection Oct. 1992–; Vice-Chair. CPPCC 7th Yunnan Prov. Cttee. *Address:* Dehong Dai and Jingpo Autonomous Prefectural People's Government, Yunnan, People's Republic of China.

LANG OF MONKTON, Baron (Life Peer) Cr. 1997, of Merrick and the Rhinns of Kells in Dumfries and Galloway, **Ian (Bruce) Lang;** British politician; b. 27 June 1940; s. of late James F. Lang, D.S.C. and of Maude Stewart; m. Sandra Montgomerie 1971; two d.; ed. Lathallan School, Kincardineshire, Rugby School and Sidney Sussex Coll. Cambridge; Dir. Rose, Thomson, Young & Co. (Glasgow) Ltd. 1966–75, Hutchison & Craft Ltd. 1975–81, Hutchison & Craft (Underwriting Agents) Ltd. Lloyd's 1976–81, P. MacCallum & Sons Ltd. 1976–81, Glasgow Chamber of Commerce 1978–81, Marsh & McLennan 1997–, Second Scottish Nat. Trust 1997–, Lithgows 1997–; Trustee, Savings Bank of Glasgow 1969–74, West of Scotland Trustee Savings Bank 1974–83; mem. Queen's Bodyguard for Scotland (Royal Co. of Archers) 1974–; mem. Parl. for Galloway 1979–83, for Galloway and Upper Nithsdale 1983–97; Asst. Govt. Whip 1981–83; a Lord Commr. of H.M. Treasury 1983–86; Parl. Under-Sec. of State, Dept. of Employment 1986, Scottish Office 1986–87; Minister of State, Scottish Office 1987–90; Sec. of State for Scotland and Lord Keeper of the Great Seal of Scotland 1990–95; Pres. of Bd. of Trade 1995–97; D.L. Ayrshire and Arran 1998; Conservative. *Address:* House of Lords, London, SW1A 0AA, England.

LÅNGBACKA, Ralf Runar, M.A.; Finnish theatre director and professor of theatre science; b. 20 Nov. 1932, Närpes; s. of Runar Emanuel Långbacka and Hulda Emilia Långbacka (née Backlund); m. Runa Birgitta Danielsson 1961; two s. one d.; ed. Åbo Akademi, Munich Univ. and Freie Univ., Berlin; Ed. Finnish Radio literary programmes 1955–56; Asst. and Dir. Lilla Teatern, Helsinki 1958–60; Man. and Artistic Dir. Swedish Theatre, Turku 1960–63; Dir. Finnish Nat. Theatre 1963–65; Artistic Dir. Swedish Theatre, Helsinki 1965–67; free-lance Dir. in Finnish Nat. Opera, Helsinki, Municipal Theatre, Gothenburg, Sweden, Royal Dramatic Theatre, Stockholm, Sweden 1967–71; mem. Finnish State Comm. of Dramatic Art 1967–70; Artistic Dir. Municipal Theatre, Turku 1971–77; Head Finnish Dirs. Asscn. 1978–82; Artistic and Man. Dir. Municipal Theatre, Helsinki 1983–87, Artistic Prof. 1979–83, 1988–93; Prof. of Theatre Science, Åbo Akademi, Turku 1994–97; Pres. Finnish Centre, Int. Theatre Inst. (ITI) 1983–96, mem. Bd. (Excom) of ITI 1991–95; Corresp. mem. Akad. der Künste, Berlin 1979; The Critics Spurs 1963, Pro Finlandia 1973; Henrik-Steffens Award (Germany) 1994. *Publications:* Teatterikirja (The Theatre Book) (with Kalle Holmberg) 1977, Bland annat om Brecht (On Brecht and Others) 1981, Möten med Tjechov (Meetings with Chekhov) 1986, Denna långa dag, detta korta liv (This long day, this short life: poems) 1988, Krocketspelaren (The Croquet Player, play) 1990, Olga, Irina och jag (Olga, Irina and I, play) 1991, Brecht og det realistiske teaten (Brecht and the Realist Theatre) and articles. *Leisure interests:* music, mushrooms, sailing. *Address:* Hopeasalmenranta 1B, 00570 Helsinki 57, Finland. *Telephone:* (9) 6849508. *Fax:* (9) 6849508.

LANGBO, Arnold G.; Canadian business executive; b. 13 April 1937, Richmond, B.C.; s. of Osbjourn Langbo and Laura Marie (Hagen) Langbo; m. Martha Langbo; eight c.; ed. Univ. of British Columbia, Vancouver; Sales Rep. Kellogg Canada Inc. 1956–67, Int. Div. 1967–69, Admin. Asst. to Kellogg Co., Pres. 1969–70, Exec. Vice-Pres. 1970–71, Vice-Pres. of Kellogg Canada 1971–76, Salada Foods Ltd. 1971–76, Pres., C.E.O. Kellogg Salada Canada Ltd. Inc. 1976–78, Pres. U.S. Food Products Div. of Kellogg Co. 1978–79, Corp. Vice-Pres. 1979–81, Exec. Vice-Pres. 1981–83, Group Exec. Vice-Pres. Kellogg Co. 1983–86, Pres. Kellogg Int. 1986–90, Pres., C.O.O., Dir. Kellogg Co. 1990–91, Chair., C.E.O. 1992–98; Pres. Mrs Smith's Frozen Food Co. 1983–85, Chair./C.E.O. 1985–; mem. Bd. Dirs. Johnson and Johnson, Grocery Mfrs. of America, Advisory Bd. J. L. Kellogg Grad. School of Man. at Northwestern Univ. *Address:* Kellogg Company, One Kellogg Square, P.O. Box 3599, Battle Creek, MI 49017, U.S.A. *Telephone:* (616) 961-2000. *Fax:* (616) 961-6598.

LANGE, Rt. Hon. David Russell, C.H., LL.M., P.C.; New Zealand politician and fmr. lawyer; b. Sept. 1942, Otahuhu; m. 1st Naomi Lange 1968 (divorced); three c.; m. 2nd Margaret Forsyth Pope 1992; one d.; ed. Otahuhu Coll., Auckland Univ.; barrister and solicitor, sole practice at Kaikohe 1968, Auckland 1970–77; Labour Party M.P. for Mangere, Auckland 1977–; Opposition Spokesman on Justice 1978, on Foreign Affairs 1993–; Deputy Leader, Parl. Labour Party 1979–83, Leader 1983–89; fmr. Opposition Spokesman on Foreign Affairs, Overseas Trade, Justice, Pacific Islands Affairs and Regional Devt.; Prime Minister 1984–89; Minister in Charge of the Security Intelligence Service 1984–89, Minister of Foreign Affairs 1984–87, Minister of Educ. 1987–89; Attorney-Gen. 1989–90; Minister of State 1989–90; Minister in charge of SFO (Serious Fraud Office) 1989–90. *Publication:* Nuclear Free the New Zealand Way 1990. *Address:* 14 Ambury Road, Mangere Bridge, Auckland, New Zealand (Home).

LANGE, Hartmut; German author; b. 31 March 1937, Berlin; s. of Johanna Lange and Karl Lange; m. Ulrike Ritter 1971; ed. Babelsberg Film School; playwright at Deutsches Theater, Berlin 1961–65; freelance writer, West Berlin 1965–; Gerhart-Hauptmann-Preis 1968, Literatur Preis der Adenauer Stiftung 1998. *Publications:* Die Selbstverbrennung 1982, Deutsche Empfindungen 1983, Die Waldsteinsonate 1984, Das Konzert 1986, Die Ermüdung 1988, Vom Werden der Vernunft 1988, Die Wattwanderung 1990, Die Reise nach Triest 1991, Die Stechpalme 1993, Schnitzlers Würgeengel 1995, Der Herr im Café 1996. *Leisure interest:* chess. *Address:* Hohenzollerndamm 197, 10717 Berlin, Germany. *Telephone:* 86 1 72 58.

LANGE, Hermann, DR. JUR.; German professor of law; b. 24 Jan. 1922, Dresden; s. of Arno Lange and Käthe (née Braun) Lange; m. Ulrike Moser 1960; one s. one d.; ed. Kreuzgymnasium, Dresden and Univs. of Leipzig, Munich and Freiburg/Breisgau; Asst. Inst. of Legal History, Univ. of Freiburg/Breisgau 1949–53; Privatdozent, Freiburg/Breisgau 1953–55; Extraordinary Prof. Univ. of Innsbrück 1955–57; Prof. Univ. of Kiel 1957–62, Univ. of Mainz 1962–66, Univ. of Tübingen 1966– (now Emer.); mem. Akad. der Wissenschaften und Literatur, Mainz. *Publications:* Schadensersatz und Privatstrafe in der mittelalterlichen Rechtstheorie 1955, Familienrecht (Kommentar) 1962, Die Consilien des Baldus de Ubaldis 1974, Schadensersatz 1979, Wandlungen des Schadenersatzrechts 1987, Die Anfänge der modernen Rechtswissenschaft 1993, Römisches Recht im Mittelalter 1997. *Address:* Ferdinand-Christian-Baur-Strasse 3, 72076 Tübingen, Germany. *Telephone:* 07071/61216.

LANGE, Jessica; American actress; b. 20 April 1949, Cloquet, Minn.; d. of Al Lange and Dorothy Lange; m. Paco Grande 1970 (divorced 1982); one d.

(with Mikhail Baryshnikov); one s. one d. (with Sam Shepard); ed. Univ. of Minn.; student of mime with Etienne DeCroux, Paris; Dancer Opera Comique, Paris; model, Wilhelmina Agency, N.Y.; Acad. Award for Blue Sky 1995. *Films include:* King Kong 1976, All That Jazz 1979, How to Beat the High Cost of Living 1980, The Postman Always Rings Twice 1981, Frances 1982, Tootsie 1982 (Acad. award for best supporting actress 1982), Country 1984, Sweet Dreams 1985, Crimes of the Heart 1986, Everbody's All American 1989, Far North 1989, Music Box 1989, Men Don't Leave 1989, Blue Sky 1990, Cape Fear 1991, Far North 1991, Night and the City 1993, Losing Isaiah, Rob Roy 1994, Blue Sky 1994 (Acad. award for Best Actress 1995), A Thousand Acres 1997, Hush 1998, Cousin Bette 1998; Star Showtime TV production Cat On A Hot Tin Roof 1984; in Summer stock production Angel On My Shoulder, N.C. 1980; play: A Streetcar Named Desire (London) (Theatre World Award, Golden Globe (for TV performance) 1996) 1996. *Address:* c/o CAA, Ron Meyer, 9830 Wilshire Boulevard, Beverly Hills, CA 90212, U.S.A.

LANGE, Otto Ludwig, DR. RER. NAT.; German professor of botany; b. 21 Aug. 1927, Dortmund; s. of Otto Lange and Marie (née Pralle) Lange; m. Rose Wilhelm 1959; two d.; ed. Univs. of Göttingen and Freiburg; Asst. Prof. Univ. of Göttingen 1953–61; Dozent Technische Hochschule Darmstadt 1961–63; Prof. Forest Botany Univ. Göttingen 1963–67; Prof. Botany Univ. of Würzburg 1967–92, Emer. 1992–; Visiting Scientist Utah State Univ. 1973, 1985, Australian Nat. Univ., Canberra 1978–79; Dir. Botanical Garden, Univ. of Würzburg 1967–92; mem. Deutsche Akad. der Naturforscher Leopoldina, Bayerische Akad. der Wissenschaften, Acad. Europaea, Acad. Scientiarum et Artium Europaea; Corresp. mem. Akad. der Wissenschaften Göttingen; Foreign Hon. mem. American Acad. of Arts and Sciences 1994, Dr.h.c (Bayreuth) 1995, (Tech. Univ., Lisbon) 1996; Antarctic Service Medal, U.S. Govt. 1974, Gottfried-Wilhem-Leibniz Prize, Deutsche Forschungsgemeinschaft 1986, Balzan Prize for "Applied botany including ecology" 1988; Adalbert Seifriz Prize for transfer of technology 1990, Bayerische Maximiliansorden for Science and Art 1991, Acharius Medal, Int. Asscn. of Lichenology 1992; Bundesverdienstkreuz (1st Class) 1985. *Publications:* Ed. (with others) 4 vols. of Physiological Plant Ecology in Encyclopedia of Plant Physiology 1981–83; books on water and plant life, plant response to stress, forest decline, and air pollution; co-ed. of scientific journals Flora, Trees; book series Ecological Studies; 320 scientific papers. *Address:* Julius-von-Sachs-Institut für Biowissenschaften der Universität Würzburg, Julius-von-Sachs-Platz 3, 97082 Würzburg (Office); Leitengraben 37, 97084 Würzburg, Germany (Home). *Telephone:* 0931-888 6205 (Office); 0931-65249 (Home).

LANGELAND, Arne Lodvar; Norwegian diplomatist and international official; b. 24 Nov. 1928, Nötterö; m. Harriet Karen Lulla 1954; two s. three d.; ed. Univ. of Oslo; joined Foreign Service 1953; served in Del. to OEEC, NATO in Paris 1954–56, Embassy in Turkey 1957–59; Ministry of Foreign Affairs 1959–65; served in Del. to Geneva 1965–70; private business 1970–75; Deputy Sec.-Gen. EFTA 1976–78; Dir.-Gen., Ministry of Trade and Shipping, Oslo 1978–81, Sec.-Gen. 1981–82; Dir.-Gen. Norwegian Export Council 1983–88; Amb. to France 1988–94; Amb. to the Netherlands 1994–97. *Address:* c/o Ministry of Foreign Affairs, 7 juni pl. 1, P.O. Box 8114 Dep., 0032 Oslo, Norway.

LANGHOLM, Sivert; Norwegian professor of history; b. 19 May 1927, Haugesund; s. of Karl Johan Langholm and Anna Langholm; m. Eva Synnøve Bakkum 1959; one s. one d.; ed. Univ. of Oslo; lecturer in History, Univ. of Oslo 1961–71, research (project) leader 1971–74, Reader in History 1974–76, Prof. 1976–, Dean, Faculty of Humanities 1985–90; mem. Det Norske Videnskaps Akademi. *Publications:* Stillingsretten 1966, Historisk Rekonstruksjon og Begrunnelse 1967, Elitenes Valg 1984. *Leisure interests:* literature, sports (skiing, jogging). *Address:* Universitetet i Oslo, Avdeling for Historie, Postboks 1008, 0315 Blindern, Oslo 3 (Office); Parkgt. 12, 3500 Hønefoss, Norway (Home). *Telephone:* 22856809 (Office); 32121448 (Home). *Fax:* 22854828.

LANGLANDS, (Robert) Alan, S.C., B.Sc.; British healthcare administrator; b. 29 May 1952; s. of James Langlands and May (née Rankin) Langlands; m. Elizabeth McDonald 1977; one s. one d.; ed. Allan Glen's School, Univ. of Glasgow; grad. trainee Nat. Health Service Scotland 1974–76; with Argyll and Clyde Health Bd. 1976–78; with Simpson Memorial Maternity Pavilion, Elise Inglis Hosp. 1978–81; Unit Admin. Middx. and Univ. Coll. Hosps. and Hosp. for Women, Soho 1981–85; Dist. Gen. Man. Harrow Health Authority 1985–89; Practice Leader Health Care, Towers Perrin 1989–91; Gen. Man. N.W. Thames Regional Health Authority 1991–92; Deputy Chief Exec. Nat. Health Service 1993–94, Chief Exec. 1994–; mem. Central Research and Devt. Cttee. Nat. Health Service 1991–92; mem. Inst. of Health Services Man., Nat. Forum for Research and Devt. 1994–; mem. Advisory Bd. Centre for Corp. Strategy and Change, Univ. of Warwick; Hon. F.F.P.H.M. 1994; Hon. Prof. (Warwick) 1996. *Leisure interests:* walking in Yorkshire. *Address:* Department of Health, Richmond House, 79 Whitehall, London, SW1A 2NS, England.

LANGLANDS, Robert Phelan, M.A., PH.D., F.R.S.; Canadian mathematician; b. 6 Oct. 1936, New Westminster; s. of Robert Langlands and Kathleen J. Phelan; m. Charlotte Cheverie 1956; two s. two d.; ed. Univ. of British Columbia, Yale Univ.; Instructor, Assoc. Prof. Princeton Univ. 1960–67; Prof. Yale Univ. 1968–72; Prof. Inst. for Advanced Study, Princeton 1972–; several awards. *Publications:* Automorphic Forms on GL(2) (with H. Jacquet) 1970, Euler Products 1971, On the Functional Equations Satisfied by Eisenstein Series 1976, Base Change for GL (2) 1980, Les Débuts d'une Formule des Traces Stable 1983. *Leisure interests:* reading, travel. *Address:* School of Mathematics, Institute for Advanced Study, Princeton, NJ 08540 (Office); 60 Battle Road, Princeton, NJ 08540, U.S.A. (Home). *Telephone:* (609) 734–8106 (Office); (609) 921-7222 (Home).

LANGSLET, Lars Roar, M.A.; Norwegian author; b. 5 March 1936, Nesbyen; s. of Knut Langslet and Alma Langslet; ed. Univ. of Oslo; Assoc. Prof. 1969–89; M.P. 1969–89; Minister of Culture and Science 1981–86; writer Aftenposten newspaper 1990–97; Ed. Ordet 1997–; State Scholarship 1997–; Pres. of Norwegian Acad. 1995–. *Publications:* Karl Marx 1963, Conservatism 1965, biogs. of John Lyng 1989, King Olav V 1995, St. Olav 1995, King Christian IV 1997. *Address:* Rosenborggt. 5, 0356 Oslo, Norway. *Telephone:* 22-46-34-12. *Fax:* 22-55-37-43.

LANGUETIN, Pierre; Swiss diplomatist and central banker; b. 30 April 1923, Lausanne; m. Florentina Lobo 1951; one s. one d.; ed. Univ. de Lausanne and L.S.E.; diplomatic career 1949–; in Div. of Exchange, OEEC, Paris; in Div. of Commerce, Fed. Dept. of Public Economy 1955–57, Head of Secr. 1957–61, Chief of Section IA 1961–63; Chief of Subdiv. 1963; has been concerned with problems of European econ. co-operation; Asst. Head of Bureau of Integration, Fed. Political Dept. and Dept. of Public Economy 1961–; Swiss Del. to Trade Cttee., OECD, Paris 1961–76, Vice-Pres. 1963–76; mem. Swiss Del. to UNCTAD Geneva 1964; Swiss Rep. at various int. orgs. 1965–66; Del. of Fed. Council for Trade Negotiations, title of Minister Plenipotentiary 1966–68; Head of Swiss Del. to EFTA Geneva 1967–77, title of Amb. 1968–76; Head of Swiss Del. to Second UNCTAD New Delhi 1968; Head of Swiss Del., Trade and Devt. Bd. 1967–70; Deputy Head of Swiss Negotiating Team with EEC 1970–72; Head of Swiss Del. to Exec. Cttee. in special session OECD 1972–76; Head of Swiss Del. for accession negotiations to Int. Energy Agency 1974, Rep. for Switzerland to Governing Bd. 1974–76; mem. Governing Bd. of Swiss Nat. Bank 1976–81, Vice-Chair. 1981–84, Chair. 1985–88; Chair. Inst. for Public Admin. Studies, Lausanne 1988–97, Inst. for Bank and Financial Man., Lausanne 1990–96; Vice-Chair. Sandoz S.A. 1988–95; Chair. UNEXIM Bank (Switzerland) 1995–; mem. Bd. of Dirs. Swiss Reinsurance Co. 1988–93, Ludwig Inst. 1987–, Pargesa Holding SA 1988–, Paribas (Suisse) 1989–96 (Vice-Chair. 1992), Renault Finance 1989–; mem. Advisory Bd. American Int. Group 1989–97, Arthur Andersen (Switzerland) 1991–97; mem. Bd. of Dirs. Chase Manhattan Pvt. Bank (Switzerland) 1991–; mem. Int. Red Cross Cttee. 1988–93; Dr. h.c. (Lausanne) 1979. *Address:* 37 Muelinenstrasse, 3006 Berne, Switzerland. *Telephone:* (31) 3526613.

LANKESTER, Sir Timothy Patrick, K.C.B., M.A.; British government and university administrator; b. 15 April 1942, Cairo, Egypt; s. of Robin P. A. Lankester and Jean D. Gilliat; m. Patricia Cockcroft 1968; three d.; ed Monkton Combe School, St. John's Coll. Cambridge and Jonathan Edwards Coll., Yale; teacher St. Michael's Coll., Belize 1960–61; Fereday Fellow, St. John's Coll. Oxford 1965–66; Economist IBRD, Washington, D.C. 1966–69, New Delhi 1970–73; HM Treasury 1973–78, Under-Sec. 1983–85, Deputy Sec. 1988–89; Pvt. Sec. to Prime Minister Callaghan 1978–79, to Prime Minister Thatcher 1979–81; seconded to S. G. Warburg & Co. 1981–83; Perm. Sec. Overseas Devt. Admin., FCO 1989–93, Dept. for Educ. 1994–95; Dir. S.O.A.S., Univ. of London 1996–; Dir. European Investment Bank 1988–89, Commercial Union 1996–, Smith and Nephew 1996–, Simba Fund 1996–, London Metal Exchange 1997–; Gov. Asia-Europe Foundation 1997–; mem. Bd. Overseas Devt. Council 1996–, British Council 1994–; Econ. Minister, Washington, D.C. and U.K. Exec. Dir. IMF and IBRD 1985–88. *Address:* School of Oriental and African Studies, Thornhaugh Street, Russell Square, London WC1H 0XG, England. *Telephone:* 0171-323 6025. *Fax:* 0171-580 6769.

LANOVOY, Vasiliy Semenovich; Russian stage and film actor; b. 16 Jan. 1934, Moscow; s. of Semion Petrovitch Lanovoy and Agafia Ivanovna Yakubenko; m. Irina Petrovna Kupchenko 1972; two s.; ed. Shchukin Theatre School; actor with Vakhtangov Theatre 1957–; also works as narrator; Prof., Faculty of Artistic Speech, Schukin's Theatre School, Moscow 1995–; mem. CPSU 1968–90; Lenin Prize 1980, People's Artist of U.S.S.R. 1985. *Theatrical roles include:* Ognev in Korneichuk's Front, Prince Calaf in Gozzi's Princess Turandot, Caesar in Shaw's Antony and Cleopatra, Sagadeev in Abdullin's Thirteenth President, Don Juan in Pushkin's The Stone Guest, Trotsky in M. Shatrov's Peace of Brest, Oscar in La Bize's Murder at Lursin Street, Astrov in Uncle Vanya, J.B. Shaw in I. Kiltye's Dear Liar, King Henry in Lion in Winter; *films include:* War and Peace, Anna Karenina, The Strange Woman, Going in a Thunderstorm, The Picture, The Scarlet Sails, The Officers, Unknown War, The Colleges, Strategy for Victory, The Trifles of Life, Barin's Daughter. *Leisure interests:* volleyball, badminton, hunting, skiing, dogs. *Address:* Starokonyushenny per. 39, Apt. 18, 121002 Moscow, Russia. *Telephone:* (095) 203-94-03.

LANSBURY, Angela, C.B.E.; British actress; b. 1925, London; d. of Edgar Lansbury and of the late Moyna Macgill; m. 1st Richard Cromwell (divorced); m. 2nd Peter Shaw; one s. one d., one step-s.; ed. Webber Douglas School of Singing and Dramatic Art, Kensington; film debut in Gaslight 1944; numerous appearances on London and New York stage and on TV; Hon. D.Hum.Litt. (Boston) 1990, Silver Mask for Lifetime Achievement BAFTA

1991; Lifetime Achievement Award, Screen Actors' Guild 1997, numerous other awards. *Films include:* Manchurian Candidate, In the Cool of the Day, Harlow, Moll Flanders, Bedknobs and Broomsticks, Death on the Nile, The Lady Vanishes, The Mirror Cracked, The Pirates of Penzance, Company of Wolves, Beauty and the Beast; Murder She Wrote (TV series) 1984–96. *Publication:* Angela Lansbury's Positive Moves (with Mimi Avins) 1990. *Address:* Bldg. 426, 100 Universal City Plaza, Universal City, CA 91608, U.S.A.; c/o William Morris, 31 Soho Square, London, W.1, England.

LANSDOWNE, 8th Marquess of; **George John Charles Mercer Nairne Petty-Fitzmaurice,** P.C.; British politician; b. 27 Nov. 1912; s. of the late Major Lord Charles Mercer Nairne and of Lady Violet Elliot; m. 1st Barbara Chase 1938 (died 1965), two s. two d. (one deceased); m. 2nd Mrs. Polly Carnegie (d. of Viscount Eccles, q.v.) 1969 (divorced 1978); m. 3rd Gillian Morgan 1978 (died 1982); m. 4th Penelope Eve Astor 1995; ed. Eton Coll. and Christ Church, Oxford Univ.; Army service 1939–45, Major 1944, served with Free French Forces; Private Sec. to Rt. Hon. A. Duff Cooper, Amb. to France 1944–45; Lord-in-Waiting to H.M. The Queen 1957–58; Joint Parl. Under-Sec. of State, Foreign Office 1958–62; Chair. Intergovernmental Cttee. Malaysia Aug.–Dec. 1962; Minister of State for Colonial Affairs 1962–64; Pres. Franco-Scottish Soc.; Prime Warden Fishmongers' Co. 1967–68; Conservative. *Address:* Meikleour House, Meikleour, Perth PH2 6EA, Scotland.

LANSING, Sherry, B.S.; American business executive; b. 31 July 1944, Chicago, Ill.; d. of Norton and Margot Lansing; m. 2nd William Friedkin (q.v.) 1991; ed. Northwestern Univ., Evanston, Ill.; mathematics teacher, Public High Schools, Los Angeles, Calif. 1966–69; model, TV commercials, Max Factor Co. and Alberto-Culver 1969–70; appeared in films Loving and Rio Lobo 1970; Exec. Story Ed., Wagner Int. 1970–73; Vice-Pres. for Production, Heyday Productions 1973–75; Exec. Story Ed., then Vice-Pres. for Creative Affairs, MGM Studios 1975–77; Vice-Pres., then Sr. Vice-Pres. for Production, Columbia Pictures 1977–80; Pres. 20th Century-Fox Productions 1980–83; founder Jaffe-Lansing Productions, L.A. 1982–; Chair. Paramount Pictures 1992–; producer Racing with the Moon 1984, Firstborn 1984, Fatal Attraction 1987, The Accused 1989, Black Rain 1990, School Ties 1992, Indecent Proposal 1993. *Address:* Paramount Pictures Corporation, 5555 Melrose Avenue, Los Angeles, CA 90038, U.S.A.

LANXADE, Adm. Jacques; French naval officer; b. 8 Sept. 1934, Toulon; m. Loïse Rostan d'Ancezune 1959; one s. three d.; ed. Ecole Navale; Commdr. destroyers Le Champenois 1970–72, La Galissonnière 1976–77, frigate Duguay-Trouin 1980–81; rank of Rear-Adm. 1984; Commdr. Indian Ocean maritime zone 1984–86; Commdr. aircraft carrier Clemenceau in the Gulf 1986; rank of Vice-Adm. 1987; Chef du Cabinet Militaire to Minister of Defence 1988–89; Chief of Staff, Elysée Palace 1989; Chief of Staff of French Armed Forces 1991–95; Amb. to Tunisia 1995–; French Embassy, Place de l'Indépendence, Tunis, Tunisia; mem. Atomic Energy Cttee. 1991–95; Commdr. Légion d'honneur, Officier, Ordre nat. du Mérite, Croix de la Valeur Militaire. *Leisure interests:* tennis, skiing. *Address:* French Embassy, 2 place de l'Indépendance, B.P. 689, Tunis, Tunisia.

LAO CHONGPIN; Chinese artist; b. 3 Nov. 1936, Xinxing City., Guangdong; s. of Lao Xianguang and Chen Ermei; m. Luo Yuzing 1956; two s. one d.; ed. Fine Arts Dept., Cen. China Teachers' Coll.; has painted more than one thousand landscapes and human figures in Japan, Canada, France, Egypt, Yugoslavia, Democratic People's Repub. of Korea, Pakistan, Burma, Jordan, Hungary, U.S.S.R., Albania 1973–; Dir. Poetry Inst. 1987–; mem. staff Chinese Exhbn. Agency, Ministry of Culture; mem. Chinese Artists' Asscn., Advisory Cttee., Beijing Children's Fine Arts Research Acad., Chinese Poetry Asscn., Int. Biographical Asscn.; Hon. Dir. Hanlin Forest of Steles, Kaifeng, China Shaolin Research Inst. of Painting and Calligraphy 1989. *Major works:* Harvest Time, Spring Ploughing, Harbour, Riverside, Arashiyama in Rain, Mosque in Lahore, Golden Pagoda of Rangoon, Pyramid and Sphinx, Autumn in Amman, Morning Glory on Seine River, Niagara Falls; Group exhbns. include Seven Star Cliff, Japan 1979, Scenery on Xinghu Lake, Mexico 1980, Drum Beaters, Hong Kong 1982, Panda, Wulongtang Waterfall, Belgium 1982, Scenery on Huangshan Mountain, Jordan 1983, Light Boats on the Yangtze River (Nat. Arts Museum, Romania) 1986, Scenes of Petra (Sact City Museum, Jordan) 1987, Waterfall of Lushan Mountain (Zacheta Art Museum, Poland) 1987; one-man exhbns. in many Chinese cities and provs. 1979–, Hong Kong 1988, Philippines 1989, Jordan 1990, Singapore 1995, India 1996; Sixth Asian Art Biennale, Bangladesh 1993. *Publication:* An Album of Sketches of Life in Foreign Countries 1986. *Leisure interests:* travel, music. *Address:* 1-301 Building no. 43, Xidahe Dongli, Chaoyang Qu, Beijing 100028, People's Republic of China. *Telephone:* 64672946.

LAPESA MELGAR, Rafael; Spanish author and university professor; b. 1908, Valencia; s. of Prof. Rafael Lapesa and Ascensión Melgar de Lapesa; m. Pilar Lago Couceiro 1932; ed. Instituto Cardenal Cisneros and Madrid Univ.; research at Centro de Estudios Históricos, Madrid, under guidance of Ramón Menéndez Pidal 1927–39; Prof., Madrid Univ. 1947–78; has lectured as guest Prof. in Univs. of Princeton, Yale, Harvard, California, Pennsylvania, Wisconsin, La Plata, Puerto Rico, Colegio de México and Buenos Aires; mem. Real Acad. Española, Real Acad. de la Historia, Hispanic Soc. of America; corresp. mem. Acad. Argentina de Letras, Acad. Nac. de Letras del Uruguay, Acad. de Artes y Letras de Puerto Rico, etc.; hon. mem. Modern Language Asscn. of America, American Asscn. of Teachers of Spanish and Portuguese; Dr. h.c. (Toulouse, San Marcos, Lima, Valencia, Salamanca, Oviedo, UNED, Valladolid, Helsinki, Seville). *Publications:* Historia de la Lengua Española 1942, 1951, 1955, 1980, 1981, Asturiano y Provenzal en el Fuero de Avilés 1948, La trayectoria poética de Garcilaso 1948, 1968, La obra literaria del Marqués de Santillana 1957, De la Edad Media a nuestros días 1967, 1971, Poetas y prosistas de ayer y de hoy 1977, Estudios de Historia Linguística Española 1984, Garcilaso: Estudios completos 1985, De Ayala a Ayala 1988, El Español Moderno y Contemporáneo 1996, Crisis históricas y crisis de la lengua espaňda 1996, De Berceo a Jorge Guillén 1997. *Address:* Residencia de Profesores, Ministro Ibáñez Martín 3, 28015 Madrid, Spain. *Telephone:* 543-77-66.

ŁAPICKI, Andrzej; Polish actor and director; b. 11 Nov. 1924, Riga, Latvia; s. of Borys Łapicki and Zofia Łapicka; m. Zofia Chrząszczewska 1947; one s. one d.; ed. Underground Inst. of Theatrical Art, Warsaw; Actor in Łódź: Polish Army Theatre 1945–48, Kameralny (Chamber) Theatre 1948–49; in Warsaw: Współczesny (Contemporary) Theatre 1949–64, 1966–72, Dramatyczny (Dramatic) Theatre 1964–66, 1982–83, Narodowy (Nat.) Theatre 1972–81, Polski Theatre, Warsaw 1983–89; Artistic Dir. Polski Theatre 1995–98; Lecturer Higher State School of Drama, Warsaw 1953–, Asst. Prof. 1970–79, Extraordinary Prof. 1979–87, Ordinary Prof. 1987–, Dean Actors' Faculty 1971–81, Rector 1981–87, 1993–96; mem. SPATiF-ZASP (Asscn. of Polish Theatre and Film Actors) until 1982, 1989–96, (Vice-Pres. 1976–79), Pres. 1989–96; mem. Int. Theatre Inst. (ITI) 1983–, mem. Gen. Bd. 1983–91, Pres. 1989–96; Deputy to Sejm (Parl.) 1989–91 (Solidarity); Chair. Parl. Comm. of Culture and Mass Media 1989–91; Minister of Culture and Art Prize (1st Class), Pres. of Radio and TV Cttee. Prize (five times), Commdr.'s Cross with Star Order of Polonia Restituta, Gold Cross of Merit and other distinctions. *Stage appearances:* about 100 roles, including The Respectable Prostitute, The Night of the Iguana, L'Ecole des femmes, Ring Round the Moon, Biedermann und die Brandstifter, Way of Life. *Film appearances:* about 30 roles, including Everything for Sale, Pilatus und Andere, The Wedding, How Far from Here, How Near; also some 50 TV roles; dir. of about 30 TV and 20 theatre plays. *Address:* Jeatr Polski, ul. Karłowicza 1/7 m. 50, 02-501 Warsaw, Poland. *Telephone:* (22) 845 30 40.

LAPIDUS, Ted (Edmond); French fashion designer; b. 23 June 1929, Paris; m. 2nd Ursula Mai 1970; two s. (one s. from previous marriage) one d.; ed. Lycée Saint-Charles, Marseilles, Lycée Voltaire, Paris and medical studies at Univ. of Paris; mainly self-taught in fashion design; part-time fashion designer in Paris 1945–59; tailor, Club de Paris 1950; founder-man. Ted Lapidus Couture, Paris 1951–70, Pres.-Dir.-Gen. 1970–; Admin. Ted Lapidus Int. SA.; est. boutiques in Paris, London, New York etc.; instr. in cutting and clothing design, Tokyo 1961; mem. Chambre Syndicale de la Couture Parisienne. *Address:* 35 rue François 1er, 75008 Paris; 66 boulevard Maurice-Barrès, 92200 Neuilly-sur-Seine, France.

LAPIEDRA CIVERA, Ramón, DR.LIC.; Spanish professor of physics; b. 10 July 1940, Almenara, Castellón; s. of Rafael Lapiedra and Amparo Civera; Prof. of Theoretical Physics; Rector Univ. of Valencia 1984–95. *Address:* c/o Universitat de Valencia, C/. La Nave, 2, 46003 Valencia, Spain.

LAPIERRE, Dominique; French journalist, author and philanthropist; b. 30 July 1931, Châtelaillon, Charente-Maritime; s. of Jean Lapierre and Luce (Andreotti) Lapierre; m. 2nd Dominique Conchon 1980; one d. (by first m.); ed. Lycée Condorcet, Paris and LaFayette Univ., Easton, U.S.A.; journalist and reporter, Paris Match 1954–67; f. and Pres. Action Aid for Lepers' Children of Calcutta; Citizen of Honor of the City of Calcutta; Dr. h.c. (Lafayette Univ.) 1982; Christopher Book Award 1986; Commdr. Confrérie du Tastevin 1990; Gold Medal of Calcutta. *Publications:* Un dollar les mille kilomètres 1949, Honeymoon around the World 1953, En liberté sur les routes d'U.R.S.S. 1957, Russie portes ouvertes 1957, Les Caïds de New York 1958, Chessman m'a dit 1960, The City of Joy 1985, Beyond Love 1991, A Thousand Suns 1998; with Larry Collins: Is Paris Burning? 1964, . . . Or I'll Dress You In Mourning 1967, O Jerusalem 1971, Freedom at Midnight 1975, The Fifth Horseman 1980. *Leisure interests:* riding, tennis, collecting antiques. *Address:* 37 Rue Charles-Laffitte, 92200 Neuilly; Les Bignoles, 83350 Ramatuelle, France. *Telephone:* (1) 46-37-34-34 (Neuilly); (4) 94-97-17-31 (Ramatuelle). *Fax:* (4) 94-97-38-05.

LAPIS, Károly, D.SC.; Hungarian pathologist and clinical oncologist; b. 14 April 1926, Túrkeve; s. of Károly Lapis and Eszter Földesi; m. Ibolya Keresztes 1955; one s. one d.; ed. Lóránd Eötvös Univ. Budapest; Scientific worker Oncopathological Research Inst. 1954–63; Prof. Postgraduate Medical School, Budapest 1963–68; Prof. 1st Inst. of Pathology and Experimental Cancer Research, Semmelweis Medical Univ. 1968–96, Emer. Prof. 1998– (Dir. 1968–93); Gordon Jacob Fellow Chester Beatty Research Inst., London 1959–60; Eleanor Roosevelt Fellow, Paris 1963–64; Visiting Prof. Duke Univ. Medical School, Durham, N.C. 1972; Fogarty Scholar, Nat. Cancer Inst., Bethesda 1984–85; Corresp. mem. Hungarian Acad. of Sciences 1970, mem. 1979–; Foreign mem. Medical Acad. of the U.S.S.R. (now Acad. of Medical Sciences of Russia) 1987, Serbian Acad. of Sciences and Arts 1989; Pres. 14th Int. Cancer Congress of the UICC, Budapest 1986; Vice-Pres. European Assoc. for Cancer Research 1979–85; mem. Exec. Cttee. European Soc. of Pathology 1989–93, French Electron Microscope Soc., German Soc. of Pathology, Int. Gastro-Surgical Club, Hungarian Cancer Soc. (Pres. 1974–84), Hungarian Soc. of Gastroenterology, Hungarian Soc. of Pathologists, Int. Acad. of Pathology (Hungarian section); Corresp. mem. American Asscn. for Cancer Research; Dir. Metastasis Research Soc. 1986–90; Chief

Ed. Acta Morphologica Hungarica 1985–94; Hon. Citizen of Mezotur 1997; Széchényi Prize 1996; Labour Order of Merit 1978, 4 of April Order of Merit 1986, George Weber Foundation Prize 1997. *Publications:* Lymphknotengeschwülste (co-author) 1966, The Liver 1979, Mediastinal Tumors and Pseudotumors (co-author) 1984, Co-ed. Liver carcinogenesis 1979, Ultrastructure of Tumours in Man 1981, Regulation and Control of Cell Proliferation 1984, Tumour Progression and Markers 1982, Models, Mechanisms and Etiology of Tumour Promotion 1984, Biochemistry and molecular genetics of cancer metastasis 1985, Lectures and Symposia of the 14th International Cancer Congress 1987, Morphological Diagnosis of Liver Diseases (in Russian) 1989, Pathology (Textbook in Hungarian) 1989. *Leisure interests:* tennis, gardening. *Address:* First Institute of Pathology and Experimental Cancer Research, Semmelweis University of Medicine, Üllői út 26, Budapest 1085, Hungary. *Telephone:* (1) 266-1912, 266-1638. *Fax:* (1) 317-1074.

LA PLANTE, Lynda; British television dramatist; m. Richard La Plante; ed. Royal Coll. of Dramatic Art; fmr. actress; appeared in The Gentle Touch, Out, Minder etc.; TV dramas include Prime Suspect 1991, Civvies, Framed, Seekers, Widows (series), Comics (two-part drama) 1993, Cold Shoulder 2 1996, Cold Blood, Bella Mafia 1997. *Publications include:* Entwined, Cold Shoulder, The Governor, She's Out, Cold Heart.

LAPORTE, William F., A.B., M.B.A.; American business executive; b. 3 Sept. 1913, New York; m. Ruth W. Hillard 1946; one s. two d.; ed. Princeton Univ., and Harvard Coll. of Business Admin.; Pres. Whitehall Pharmacal Co. 1950–57; Vice-Pres. American Home Products Corpn. 1957–60, Dir. 1957–, Pres. 1960–73, Chair. of Bd. 1965–81, Chair. Exec. Cttee. 1981–; Dir. Mfrs. Hanover Trust Co. 1965–82, American Standard Inc. 1975–, B. F. Goodrich Co. 1978–; Trustee, Dime Savings Bank of New York 1966–. *Address:* American Home Products Corporation, 685 Third Avenue, New York, NY 10017 (Office); 435 East 52nd Street, New York, NY 10022, U.S.A. (Home).

LAPPAS, Alfons; German trade unionist; b. 3 June 1929, Wiesbaden; s. of Peter and Therese (née Klee) Lappas; m. Sigrid Albrecht 1954; one d.; ed. secondary school; Dist. Organizer of Horticulture, Agric. and Forestry Union, Fulda and Darmstadt 1951–57, Rheinland-Palatinate Organizer 1957–59, Head of Collective Bargaining Dept., Head Office 1959–61, mem. Exec. 1961–, Vice-Pres. 1966, Pres. 1968; mem. Exec., German Trade Union Confed. (Deutscher Gewerkschaftsbund—DGB) 1969; Dir. holding co. for enterprises of DGB 1977–, Chair. –1986; Pres. European Fed. of Agricultural Workers 1968–71; Alt. mem. European Confed. of Trade Unions 1969–77, Finance and Gen. Purpose Cttee., Int. Confed. of Trade Unions 1969–77; mem. Econ. and Social Cttee. of European Communities 1970–76, Pres. 1972–74, 1977. *Leisure interests:* modern literature, music, cross-country running. *Address:* Theaterplatz 2, 60311 Frankfurt/Main, Germany.

LAPPERT, Michael F., PH.D., D.SC., F.R.C.S., F.R.S.; British professor of chemistry; b. 31 Dec. 1928, Brno, Czechoslovakia; s. of Julius and Kornelie (née Beran) Lappert; m. Lorna McKenzie 1980; ed. Wilson's Grammar School and Northern Polytechnic, London; Asst. Lecturer, Northern Polytechnic, London 1952–53, Lecturer 1953–55, Sr. Lecturer 1955–59; Lecturer, Univ. of Manchester Inst. of Sciences and Tech. (UMIST) 1959–61, Sr. Lecturer 1961–64; Reader, Univ. of Sussex 1964–69, Prof. of Chem. 1969–97, Research Prof. 1997–; Science and Eng. Research Council Sr. Research Fellow 1980–85; Pres. Dalton Div. (Royal Soc. of Chemistry) 1989–91; Tilden Lecturer 1972–73; Nyholm Lecturer 1994; Hon. Dr. rer. nat., Munich 1989; Chem. Soc. Award in Main Group Metal Chem. 1970; Award in Organometallic Chem. 1978; F.S. Kipping Award, American Chem. Soc. 1976. *Publications:* Metal and Metalloid Amides (jointly) 1980, Chemistry of Organo-Zirconum and -Hafnium Compounds (jointly) 1986; more than 600 papers in scientific journals. *Leisure interests:* theatre, opera, art, travel, walking, tennis. *Address:* 4 Varndean Gardens, Brighton, BN1 6WL, England. *Telephone:* (01273) 503661. *Fax:* (01273) 677196.

LAPSHIN, Mikhail Ivanovich, C.ECON.SC.; Russian politician; b. 1 Sept. 1934, Setovka, Altai Territory; m.; three s.; ed. Moscow Timiryazev Agricultural Acad., Moscow Inst. of Foreign Languages; Dir. sovkhoz Zavety Ilyicha, Stupino, Moscow Region 1962–91; Pres. Jt.-Stock Co. Zavety Ilyicha 1991–; People's Deputy of Russia 1990–93; mem. Agrarian Union; Chair. Agrarian Party of Russia 1992–; mem. State Duma (Parl.) Dec. 1993–95. *Address:* Agrarian Party, Lesnaya str. 45A, Suite 401, Moscow, Russia. *Telephone:* (095) 978-8884, 978-7588.

LAPTEV, Ivan Dmitrievich, D.PHIL.SC.; Russian editor and journalist; b. 15 Oct. 1934, Sladkoye, Omsk Dist.; m. Tatyana Kareva 1966; one d.; ed. Siberian Road Transport Inst., Acad. of Social Sciences; worked for CPSU Cen. Cttee.; mem. CPSU 1960–91; worked at Omsk River Port 1952–60; teacher 1960–61; instructor, Soviet Army Sports Club 1961–64, literary collaborator and special corresp. Sovietskaya Rossiya 1964–67; Consultant on Kommunist 1967–73; work with CPSU Cen. Cttee. 1973–78; Section Ed. Pravda 1978–82, Deputy Ed. 1982–84; Chief Ed. Izvestiya 1984–90; mem. U.S.S.R. Supreme Soviet 1989–91; People's Deputy of the U.S.S.R. 1989–91; Chair. Council of Union 1990–91; Gen. Man. Isvestiya Publishers 1991–94; Deputy Chair. Fed. Press Cttee. 1994–95, Chair. 1995–; Head of Service Professional Acad. of State Service to Russian Presidency 1995–; mem. Int. Acad. of Information 1993; Pres. Asscn. of Chief Eds. and Publrs. 1993–95. *Publications:* Ecological Problems 1978, The World of People in the World of Nature 1986; over 100 scientific articles on ecological problems. *Leisure interests:* reading, automobile engineering, cycle racing. *Address:* Goskompetchat, Strastnoy blvd. 5, 101409 Moscow, Russia. *Telephone:* (095) 209-63-52. *Fax:* (095) 200-22-81.

LAPTEV, Vladimir Viktorovich, D.JUR.; Russian jurist; b. 28 April 1924, Moscow; s. of V. I. Laptev and V. A. Lapteva; m. 1950; two s.; ed. Law Dept., Moscow Inst. for Foreign Trade; mem. staff Inst. of State and Law, Moscow Int. Univ., Prof. 1966–, Chief Scientific Researcher 1989–; Prof., Head Centre of Enterprise Law, Moscow Int. Univ. 1992–; Visiting Prof. Emory Univ., Atlanta, Ga., U.S.A. 1992–93; Corresp. mem. U.S.S.R. (now Russian) Acad. of Science 1979–87, mem. 1987. *Publications:* more than 300 books and articles on econ. law, including Legal Status of Enterprises in Russia 1993, Introduction to Entrepreneurial Law 1994, Entrepreneurial Law: Notion and Subjects 1977, Joint Stock Company Law 1999. *Address:* Institute of State and Law, Znamenka Str. 10, 119841 GSP, Moscow G-19, Russia. *Telephone:* (095) 291-86-03 (Office); (095) 331-32-24 (Home). *Fax:* (095) 291-85-74.

LAQUEUR, Walter; American historian and political commentator; b. 26 May 1921, Breslau, Germany (now Wrocław, Poland); s. of Fritz Laqueur and Else Berliner; m. 1st Barbara Koch 1941 (deceased); m. 2nd C. S. Wichmann; two d.; Ed. Survey 1955–65; Dir. Inst. of Contemporary History and Wiener Library, London 1964–91; Ed. Journal of Contemporary History 1965–; Prof. of History Brandeis Univ. 1967–72; Prof. of History, Tel Aviv Univ. 1970–87; Prof. of Govt. Georgetown Univ. 1977–90; Chair. Int. Research Council, Center for Strategic and Int. Studies, Washington D.C. 1973–; Ed. Washington Papers 1973–; Washington Quarterly 1978–; Visiting Prof. of History, Harvard 1977; Rockefeller Fellow, Guggenheim Fellow; several hon. degrees. *Publications:* Young Germany 1962, The Road to War 1967 1968, Europe Since Hitler 1970, A History of Zionism 1972, Confrontation 1974, Weimar 1974, Guerrilla 1976, Terrorism 1977, A Continent Astray: Europe 1970–78 1979, The Missing Years (novel) 1980, The Terrible Secret 1981, Farewell to Europe (novel) 1981, Germany Today 1985, A World of Secrets 1985, Breaking the Silence 1986, The Age of Terrorism 1987, The Long Road to Freedom 1989, Stalin 1990, Thursday's Child has Far to Go (autobiog.) 1993, Black Hundred 1993, The Dream That Failed 1994, Fascism 1997. *Leisure interest:* swimming. *Address:* Center for Strategic and International Studies, 1800 K Street, N.W., Washington, DC, U.S.A.

LARA, Brian Charles; Trinidadian cricketer; b. 2 May 1969, Santa Cruz; started playing cricket aged 6; played football for Trinidad Under-14; played cricket for West Indies Under-19; captained a West Indies Youth XI against India, scoring 186; left-hand batsman; teams: Trinidad and Tobago 1987– (Capt. 1993–), Warwicks. 1994, 1998 (Capt.), making world record first-class score of 501 not out, including most runs in a day (390) and most boundaries in an innings (72) v. Durham, Edgbaston, 3 and 6 June 1994; 59 Tests for West Indies 1990–Feb. 1999 (12 as Capt.), scoring 4,860 runs (average 49.5) including 10 hundreds, highest score 375 (world record v. England, St. John's, Antigua 16–18 April 1994); has scored 12,676 first-class runs (34 hundreds) to 31 Oct. 1998, including 2,066 off 2,262 balls for Warwicks. 1994, with 6 hundreds in his first 7 innings; toured England 1991, 1995; 133 limited-overs ints. to 31 Dec. 1998 (10 as Capt.). *Publication:* Beating the Field (autobiog.) 1995. *Address:* c/o West Indies Cricket Board, P.O. Box 616, St. John's, Antigua.

LARA BUSTAMANTE, Fernando; Costa Rican politician and lawyer; b. 12 Jan. 1911, San José; s. of Ernesto Lara Iraeta and Angela Bustamante Castro; m. Ofelia Calvo; four s. four d.; ed. Liceo de Costa Rica and Escuela de Derecho; graduated in law 1934; Police Official, San José 1932–37; Official in Ministry of Educ. 1937–40; Dir. Jurisprudencia (law magazine) 1933–36; Deputy to Nat. Assembly 1942, re-elected 1946; mem. Editorial Comm. for Political Constitution 1948; Prof. Faculty of Law 1940–52; Deputy, First Sec., Legis. Assembly 1949; Minister of Foreign Affairs 1949–52, 1966–70; Pres. Colegio de Abogados de Costa Rica 1954–55; Deputy to Legis. Ass. 1958–62, 1966; Pres. 1960–61; Sec.-Gen. Partido Unión Nacional 1958–66; decorations from Mexico, El Salvador, Panama, France, Italy, Vatican, Ecuador, Taiwan and Cuba.

LARAKI, Azeddine, PH.D.; Moroccan politician; b. 1929, Fez; ed. Faculty of Medicine, Paris; Cabinet Dir., Ministry of Nat. Educ. 1958, of Public Health 1959; Dir. Avicenne Hosp., Head of Respiratory Surgery and Pneumology 1960–, Prof. of Medicine 1967–; fmr. mem. Exec. Cttee. Istiqlal –1984; Minister of Nat. Educ. 1977–86; Prime Minister of Morocco 1986–92; Sec.-Gen. Org. of the Islamic Conf. 1996–; mem. Royal Acad. of Morocco. *Address:* Organization of the Islamic Conference, Kilo 6, Mecca Road, P.O. Box 178, Jeddah 21411, Saudi Arabia.

LARAKI, Moulay Ahmed; Moroccan politician, physician and diplomatist; b. 15 Oct. 1931, Casablanca; ed. Univ. de Paris; with Ministry of Foreign Affairs 1956–57; Perm. Rep. to UN 1957–59; Head of Hosp. Services, Casablanca 1956–61; Amb. to Spain 1962–65, to Switzerland 1965–66, to U.S.A. and concurrently accred. to Mexico, Canada and Venezuela 1966–67; Minister of Foreign Affairs 1967–69; Prime Minister 1969–71; medical affairs 1971–74; Minister of State for Foreign Affairs 1974–77. *Address:* Office of the Prime Minister, Rabat, Morocco.

LARCO COX, Guillermo; Peruvian politician and engineer; b. 19 Feb. 1932; mem. Alianza Popular Revolucionaria Americana (APRA); Mayor of Trujillo 1964–66, 1967–68; civil engineer; Parl. Deputy for Dept. of La Libertad 1980–85; Senator 1985; Prime Minister of Peru 1987–88, 1990;

Minister for Presidency 1987–88; Minister of Foreign Affairs 1989–90. *Address:* c/o Ministry of Foreign Affairs, Ucayali 363, Lima, Peru. *Telephone:* 273860.

LARDY, Henry Arnold, PH.D.; American professor of biochemistry; b. 19 Aug. 1917, S. Dakota; s. of Nick and Elizabeth Lardy; m. Annrita Dresselhuys 1943; three s. one d.; ed. S. Dakota State Univ. and Univs. of Wis. and Toronto; Asst. Prof., Univ. of Wis. 1945–47, Assoc. Prof. 1947–50, Prof. 1950–66, Co-Dir. Inst. for Enzyme Research 1950–88, Vilas Prof. of Biological Sciences 1966–88, Prof. Emer. 1988–; Pres. Citizens vs. McCarthy 1952; mem. Nat. Acad. of Sciences, American Acad. of Arts and Sciences, American Philosophical Soc., American Soc. Biological Chemists (Pres. 1964), The Endocrine Soc., Harvey Soc.; Hon. mem. Japanese Biochemical Soc.; Hon. D.Sc. (S. Dakota State Univ.) 1978; Paul Lewis Award in Enzyme Chem., American Chemical Soc. 1949, Neuberg Medal, American Soc. of European Chemists 1956, Wolf Foundation Prize in Agric. 1981, Nat. Award for Agricultural Excellence 1981, Amory Award, American Acad. of Arts and Sciences 1984, Carl Hartman Award, Soc. for the Study of Reproduction 1984, W. C. Rose Award American Soc. of Biochem. and Molecular Biology 1988, Hilldale Award, Univ. of Wis. 1988. *Publications:* The Enzymes (Co-Editor), 8 vols 1958–63; and research papers in biochemistry in scientific journals. *Leisure interests;* tennis, riding, retriever field trials. *Address:* Thorstrand Road, Madison, WI 53705, U.S.A. (Home). *Telephone:* 608-233-1584 (Home).

LARGE, Sir Andrew Mcleod Brooks, Kt., M.A. (ECON.), M.B.A.; British banker and regulatory official; b. 7 Aug. 1942, Goudhurst, Kent; s. of late Maj.-Gen. Stanley Large and of Janet Brooks; m. Susan Melville 1967; two s. one d.; ed. Winchester Coll., Univ. of Cambridge and European Inst. of Business Admin. (INSEAD), Fontainebleau; British Petroleum 1964–71; Orion Bank Ltd. 1971–79; Swiss Bank Corpn. 1980–89, Man. Dir. SBCI London 1980–83, Chief Exec. and Deputy Chair. SBCI London 1983–87, Group Chief Exec. SBCI London 1987–88, mem. Bd. SBC 1988–90; Chair. Large, Smith & Walter 1990–92; Chair. Securities & Investments Bd. (SIB) 1992–97; Deputy Chair. Barclays Bank 1997–, Dir. 1998–; Chair. Euroclear 1998–; non-exec. Dir. English China Clays 1991–96; mem. Bd. on Banking Supervision, Bank of England 1996–97. *Leisure interests:* skiing, walking, gardening, apples, photography, music. *Address:* Barclays PLC, 54 Lombard Street, London, EC3P 3AH, England (Office); Cui Parc, Talybont-on-Usk, Brecon, Powys, LD3 7YW, Wales (Home).

LARGE, David Clay, PH.D.; American university professor and writer; b. 13 Aug. 1945, Scott Field, Ill.; s. of H. R. Large, Jr.; m. 1st Jacque Hambly 1968 (divorced 1977), one s.; m. 2nd Margaret Wheeler 1980; ed. Univ. of Washington Univ. of California at Berkeley; taught Modern European History, Smith Coll. 1973–78, Yale Univ. 1978–83, Dean, Pierson Coll., Yale Univ. 1981–83; Prof. of European History, Mont. State Univ. 1983–; Contributing Ed. Mil. History Quarterly 1989; Woodrow Wilson Fellowship, Morse Fellowship (Yale), Nat. Endowment for the Humanities Fellowship, German Marshall Fund Fellowship. *Publications:* The Politics of Law and Order: A History of the Bavarian Einwohnerwehr 1980, Wagnerism in European Culture and Politics 1984, Between Two Fires: Europe's Path in the 1930s 1990, Contending with Hitler: Varieties of German Resistance in the Third Reich 1991, Germans to the Front: West German Rearmament in the Adenauer Era 1996, Where Ghosts Walked: Munich's Road to the Third Reich 1997. *Leisure interests:* running, skiing, music, hiking. *Address:* 721 W. Koch, Bozeman, MT 59715, U.S.A. (Home). *Telephone:* (406) 587-5079 (Home).

LA RIVIÈRE, Jan Willem Maurits, PH.D.; Netherlands professor of environmental biology; b. 24 Dec. 1923, Rotterdam; m. Louise A. Kleijn 1958; one s. two d.; ed. Erasmus Gymnasium, Rotterdam and Delft Univ. of Tech.; Postdoctoral Rockefeller Fellowship, Stanford Univ.; mem. scientific staff, Microbiology Dept. Delft Univ. of Tech. 1953–63; Prof. of Environmental Microbiology and Deputy Dir. Int. Inst. for Infrastructural, Hydraulic and Environmental Eng., Delft 1963–88, now Prof. Emer., Hon. Fellow 1996; Visiting Prof. Harvard Univ. 1967–68; Sec.-Gen. ICSU 1988–93; mem. numerous int. and nat. cttees., del. to UN confs., adviser, lecturer etc.; Hon. mem. Council, Int. Cell Research Org.; Fellow, World Acad. of Art and Science; Kt. Order of Lion of Netherlands. *Publications:* Microbiology of Liquid Waste Treatment 1977, Biotechnology in Development Cooperation 1983, Water Quality: Present Status, Future Trends 1987, Threats to the World's Water 1989, Co-operation between Natural and Social Scientists in Global Change Research: Imperatives, Realities, Opportunities 1991, The Delft School of Microbiology in Historical Perspective 1996; some 80 publications in fields of microbiology, environment, water quality, and int. scientific cooperation. *Leisure interests:* gardening, travel. *Address:* International Institute for Infrastructural, Hydraulic and Environmental Engineering, P.O. Box 3015, 2601 DA Delft, Netherlands. *Telephone:* (015) 2151715. *Fax:* (015) 2122921.

LARKIN, Anatoly Ivanovich; Russian physicist; b. 14 Oct. 1932; m.; two c.; ed. Moscow Inst. of Physics and Eng.; worked as engineer 1955–57; jr. researcher, sr. researcher, Inst. of Nuclear Energy 1957–65; Head of sector, Landau Inst. of Theoretical Physics, Russian Acad. of Sciences 1965; corresp. mem. U.S.S.R. (now Russian) Acad. of Sciences 1979, mem. 1991–; mem. Ed. Bd. Uspekhi Fizicheskikh Nauk, mem. Bd. Scientific Council on Superlow-Temperature Physics; main research in superconductivity theory, phase transition theory. *Address:* L. D. Landau Institute for Theoretical Physics, Kosygina str. 2, 117334 Moscow, Russia. *Telephone:* (095) 137 3244 (Office).

LAROQUE, Michele; French actress; b. 15 June 1960, Nice; d. of Claude Laroque and Doïna Trandabur; m. Dominique Deschamps; one d.; ed. Univ. of Nice; f. own production co. Achetez Nos Films Merci (ANFM). *Films include:* The Hairdresser's Husband, Pédale Douce, Le Plus Beau Métier du Monde, Ma Vie En Rose. *Theatre:* Une jolie, silence en coulisses, Ils s'aiment; Chevalier des Arts et des Lettres. *Leisure interests:* tennis, skiing, riding. *Address:* c/o Agents associés, Joelle Bonnet, 201 rue du Faubourg Saint-Honoré, 75008 Paris, France (Office).

LAROSIÈRE DE CHAMPFEU, Jacques Martin Henri Marie de; French international civil servant; b. 12 Nov. 1929, Paris; s. of Robert and Hugayte (de Champfeu) de Larosière; m. France du Bos 1960; one s. one d.; ed. Lycée Louis-le-Grand, Paris Univ. and Ecole nat. d'admin.; Insp. adjoint 1958, Insp. des Finances 1960; Chargé de Mission in Inspectorate-Gen. of Finance 1961, External Finance Office 1963, Treasury 1965; Asst. Dir. Treasury 1967; Deputy Dir. then Head of Dept., Ministry of Econs. and Finance 1971; Principal Private Sec. to Valéry Giscard d'Estaing (then Minister of Econs. and Finance) 1974; Under-Sec. of Treas. 1974–78; Pres. Group of Ten 1976–78; Dir.-Gen. IMF 1978–87; Gov. Banque de France 1987–93, Hon. Gov. 1993–; Chair. Cttee. of Govs., Group of Ten 1990–93; Pres. EBRD 1993–98; Insp. Gen. des Finances 1981; Dir. Renault 1971–74, Banque nat. de Paris 1973–78, Air France and Soc. nat. de chemins de fer français (S.N.C.F.) 1974–78, Soc. nat. industrielle aérospatiale 1976–78; Censeur Banque de France 1974–78, Crédit nat. 1974–78, Comptoir des Entrepreneurs 1973–75, Crédit foncier de France 1975–78; Vice-Pres. Caisse nat. des Télécommunications 1974–78; mem. Acad. of Moral and Political Sciences 1993; Hon. mem. Soc. des Cincinnati de France; Officier, Légion d'honneur, Chevalier, Ordre nat. du Mérite, numerous other awards. *Address:* Banque de France, 1 rue La Vrillière, 75001 Paris, France (Office).

LARQUIÉ, André Olivier, L. EN D.; French civil servant; b. 26 June 1938, Nay; s. of Henri Larquié and Simone Tauziede; ed. Lycée Louis-le-Grand and Univ. of Paris; Deputy Dir. Musique Art lyrique et Danse, Ministry of Culture and Communications 1978–79, Official Rep. 1981–83, 1987; Govt. Commr. Centre nat. d'art et de Culture Georges Pompidou 1981–84; Pres. Paris Opera 1983–87; Tech. Adviser to the Prime Minister May 1988–89; Pres. Théâtre Contemporain de la Danse, Asscn. pour le Dialogue entre les Cultures 1985; Pres. Radio France Int. 1989–95; now rep. of recording industry to EU; Chevalier Légion d'honneur, Ordre nat. du Mérite, Palmes académiques, Commandeur des Arts et Lettres. *Publications:* official reports. *Leisure interests:* song and dance. *Address:* 9 rue Geoffroy l'Asnier, 75004 Paris (Office); 15 rue de Saint-Simon, 75007 Paris, France (Home).

LARRABEE, Martin Glover, PH.D.; American professor of biophysics; b. 25 Jan. 1910, Boston, Mass.; s. of Ralph Clinton Larrabee and Ada Perkins Miller; m. 1st Sylvia Kimball 1932 (divorced 1944), one s.; m. 2nd Barbara Belcher 1944, one s. (deceased); ed. Harvard Coll. and Univ. of Pennsylvania; Research Asst. and Fellow, Univ. of Pa. 1934–40, Assoc., Asst. Prof., Assoc. Prof. 1941–49; Asst. Prof. of Physiology, Cornell Medical Coll., New York City 1940–41; Assoc. Prof. of Biophysics, Johns Hopkins Univ. 1949–63, Prof. of Biophysics 1963–; mem. Nat. Acad. of Sciences, American Physiological Soc., Biophysical Soc., Int. Soc. for Neurochem., American Soc. for Neurochem., Soc. for Neuroscience; Foreign Assoc. Physiological Soc., England; Hon. M.D. (Lausanne) 1974. *Publications:* About 60 technical papers and 60 abstracts covering original research in the circulatory, respiratory and nervous systems of mammals, especially on synaptic and metabolic mechanisms in sympathetic ganglia. *Leisure interests:* hiking, trail construction and maintenance, skiing. *Address:* Department of Biophysics, Johns Hopkins University, Baltimore, MD 21218, U.S.A. *Telephone:* (410) 516-7256 or 7245. *Fax:* (410) 516-4118.

LARROCHA, Alicia de; Spanish concert pianist; b. 23 May 1923, Barcelona; d. of Eduardo and Teresa (de la Calle) de Larrocha; m. Juan Torra 1950; one s. one d.; ed. private school; first public recital, Barcelona 1928; first orchestral concert with Madrid Symphony Orchestra under Fernández Arbós, Madrid 1935; concert tours in Europe, South America, U.S.A., Canada, Japan, South Africa, New Zealand, Australia; Dir. Academia Marshall, Barcelona 1959; mem. Bd. Dirs. Musica en Compostela 1968; Hon. Pres. Int. Piano Archives, New York 1969; corresp. mem. Hispanic Soc. of America, New York 1972; Gold Medal, Academia Marshall 1943, Harriet Cohen Int. Music Award 1956, Grand Prix du Disque Académie Charles Cros, Paris 1960, 1974, Paderewski Memorial Medal 1961, Orders of Civil Merit 1962, Isabel la Católica 1972, Edison Award, Amsterdam 1968, first Gold Medal, Mérito a la Vocación 1973, Grammy Award, U.S.A. 1974, 1975, Musician of the Year (Musical America Magazine) 1978, Edison Award, Amsterdam 1978, Gold Medal, Spanish Int. (U.S.A.) 1980.

LARSEN, Kai, B.A., M.SC.; Danish professor of botany; b. 15 Nov. 1926, Hillerød; s. of Axel G. Larsen and Elisabeth Hansen; m. Supee Saksuwan 1971; one s. three d.; ed. Univ. of Copenhagen; Asst. Scientist, Botany Dept. Univ. of Copenhagen 1952–55; Asst. Prof. Royal Danish School of Pharmacy 1955–62, Assoc. Prof. 1962–63; Prof. of Botany, Aarhus Univ. 1963–; founder, Botanical Inst. and Herbarium Jutlandicum, Aarhus; Ed.-in-Chief Nordic Journal of Botany and Opera Botanica; Ed. Flora of Thailand; Danish Ed. Flora Nordica; mem. exec. cttee. Flora Malesiana Foundation (Leiden, Netherlands); adviser to Flora of China; led 13 botanical expeditions to

Thailand 1958–95; Consultant, Queen Sirikit Botanical Gardens, Thailand 1996–; botanical consultant, Danish Nat. Encyclopedia; Visiting lecturer, Russian Acad. of Sciences, Acad. Sinica; Pres. Int. Asscn. of Botanic Gardens 1981–87; mem. Royal Danish Acad. and Royal Norwegian Acad. of Science, and corresp. mem. of other int. socs.; Hon. D.Sc. (Prince of Songkla Univ., Thailand) 1994; Kt. Order of Dannebrog; Officer, Crown of Thailand. *Publications:* about 200 scientific books and articles on tropical botany, nature conservation. *Leisure interests:* classical music (playing piano). *Address:* Botanical Institute, Nordlandsvej 68, 8240 Risskov (Office); Graastenvej 6, Søften, 8382 Hinnerup, Denmark (Home). *Telephone:* (45) 8942 4700. *Fax:* (45) 8942 4747.

LARSEN, Ralph Stanley, B.A.; American business executive; b. 19 Nov. 1938, Brooklyn, N.Y.; s. of Andrew Larsen and Gurine (née Henningsen) Larsen; m. Dorothy M. Zeitfuss 1961; one s. two d.; ed. Hofstra Univ.; served in USN 1956–58; manufacturing trainee, then supervisor of Production and Dir. Marketing, Johnson & Johnson, New Brunswick, N.J. 1962–77, Vice-Pres. Operations and Marketing, McNeil Consumer Products Co. Div. 1977–81, Pres. Chicopee Div. 1982–83, Co. Group Chair. 1985–86, Vice-Chair. Exec. Cttee., Bd. of Dirs. 1986–89, Chair. and C.E.O. 1989–, also Pres.; Pres. Becton Dickenson Consumer Products, Paramus, N.J. 1981–83; mem. Bd. of Dirs. AT&T, Xerox, N.Y. Stock Exchange. *Leisure interests:* skiing, boating, art. *Address:* Johnson & Johnson, 1 Johnson & Johnson Plaza, New Brunswick, NJ 08933, U.S.A.

LARSON, Gary, B.A.; American cartoonist; b. 14 Aug. 1950, Tacoma, Washington; s. of Vern Larson and Doris Larson; m. Toni Carmichael 1988; ed. Washington State Univ.; performed in jazz duo 1972–75; worked in a music store; sold first cartoons to Pacific Search magazine; subsequently sold cartoons to Seattle Times, San Francisco Chronicle, Chronicle Features Syndicate; Exhibitions include: The Far Side of Science, Calif. Acad. of Sciences 1985, Smithsonian Nat. Museum of Nat. History, American Museum of Nat. History, New York, Los Angeles County Museum of Nat. History; Animated films: Gary Larson's Tales From the Far Side 1994 (Grand Prix, Annecy Film Festival 1995), Gary Larson's Tales From the Far Side II 1997; Nat. Cartoonists Soc. Award for best syndicated panel of 1985; Outstanding Cartoonist of the Year Award 1991, 1994; Max and Moritz Prize for Best Int. Cartoon 1993; announced retirement Oct. 1994; insect named after him: Strigiphilus garylarsoni (biting louse), also butterfly. *Publications:* The Far Side, Beyond The Far Side, In Search of the Far Side, Bride of the Far Side, Valley of the Far Side, It Came From the Far Side, Hound of the Far Side, The Far Side Observer, Night of the Crash-test Dummies, Wildlife Preserve, Wiener Dog Art, Unnatural Selections, Cows of Our Planet, Last Chapter and Worse 1996; Anthologies: The Far Side Gallery 1, 2, 3, 4 and 5, The PreHistory of the Far Side, The Chickens Are Restless, The Curse of Madame "C", Last Chapter and Worse, There's A Hair in my Dirt! A Worm's Story. *Leisure interests:* jazz guitar, pickup basketball. *Address:* c/o Universal Press Syndicate, 4520 Main Street, Kansas City, MO 64111, U.S.A.

LASDUN, Sir Denys (Louis), Kt., C.H., C.B.E., R.I.B.A.; British architect; b. 8 Sept. 1914; s. of Norman Lasdun and Julie Abrahams; m. Susan Bendit 1954; two s. one d.; ed. Rugby School, Architectural Asscn., London; served with Royal Engineers 1939–45 (M.B.E.); practised with Wells Coates, Tecton & Drake 1935–48; in pvt. practice 1960–; with Peter Softley and Assocs. 1986–; Hoffman Wood Prof. of Architecture, Univ. of Leeds 1962–63; Assessor, Competitions for Belgrade Opera House 1971, and new Parl. Bldg., London 1971–72. *Works include (in London):* housing and schools for Bethnal Green and Paddington, HQ of Govt. of N.S.W., flats at 26 St. James's Place, Royal Coll. of Physicians, work for the Univ. of London (S.O.A.S., Inst. of Educ., Law Inst., project for Courtauld Inst.), Nat. Theatre and IBM Cen. London Marketing Centre, office bldgs., 6–12 Fenchurch St. and Milton Gate. *Other works include:* Fitzwilliam Coll. and Christ's Coll. extensions, Cambridge, devt. plan and bldgs. for new Univ. of East Anglia, Univs. of Leicester and Liverpool redevts.; EEC HQ for EIB Luxembourg, design for new Hurva Synagogue (Old City of Jerusalem), Cannock Community Hosp., Genoa Opera House; Retrospective Exhbn., Royal Acad. 1997; Hon. Dip. Architectural Asscn. 1994; Trustee, British Museum 1975–85; mem. CIAM and MARS Group 1935–59, Jerusalem Town Planning Cttee. 1970, Victoria and Albert Advisory Council 1973–83, Slade Cttee. 1976–92, Arts Panel, Arts Council of G.B. 1980–84; mem. Acad. d'Architecture (Paris) 1984, Accad. Nazionale di San Luca (Rome) 1984, Int. Acad. of Architecture, Bulgaria 1986; Hon. Fellow, A.I.A. 1966; Hon. F.R.C.P. 1975; R.A. 1991; Hon. Fellow Royal Incorporation of Architects in Scotland 1995; Hon. D.Arch (Manchester) 1966; Hon. D.Litt. (E. Anglia) 1974, (Sheffield) 1978; Hon. Diploma Architects Asscn. 1994; R.I.B.A. London Architecture Bronze Medallist 1960, 1964; Civic Trust Awards, Class 1 1967, Group A 1969, Special Award, São Paulo Biennale, Brazil 1969, Concrete Soc. Award 1976, R.I.B.A. Royal Gold Medal 1977, R.I.B.A. Architectural Award for London Region 1978, shared Wolf Prize 1992, R.I.B.A. Trustees' Medal 1992, Architects Journal Centenary Medal 1995, IAA Bulgaria Gold Medal 1997. *Publications include:* An Architect's Approach to Architecture 1965, A Language and a Theme 1976, Architecture in an Age of Scepticism 1984; and contribs. to architectural and other papers. *Address:* 146 Grosvenor Road, London, SW1V 3JY, England. *Telephone:* 0171-630 8211.

LASKO, Peter Erik, C.B.E, B.A., F.S.A., F.B.A., F.R.HIST.S.; British professor emeritus, writer and lecturer (retd.); b. 5 March 1924, Berlin, Germany; s. of Leo Lasko and Wally Lasko; m. Gwendoline Joan Norman 1948; three d.; ed. St. Martin's School of Art and Univ. of London; Asst. Keeper, Dept. of British and Medieval Antiquities, British Museum 1950–65; Prof., School of Fine Arts, Univ. of E. Anglia, Norwich 1965–74; Dir. and Prof. Courtauld Inst., Univ. of London 1975–85; Trustee, British Museum 1980–95, Royal Armouries 1983–91; Commr., Cathedrals Advisory Comm. 1980–91, Royal Comm. on Historical Monuments of England 1984–90; Commr., Vice-Chair. Cathedrals Fabric Comm. for England 1991–96; Hon. D.Litt. *Publications:* Ars Sacra 800–1200 1972, 1994, The Kingdom of the Franks 1971, Studies on Metalwork, Ivories and Stone 1994. *Leisure interest:* walking. *Address:* The Green, 17 Lower Street, Hoveton, Norwich, NR12 8JG, England. *Telephone:* (01603) 782094.

LASLETT, Peter, F.B.A., C.B.E., D.LITT.; British historical sociologist, writer and innovator; b. 18 Dec. 1915, Bedford; s. of Rev. G. H. R. Laslett and Eveline E. Alden; m. Janet Crockett Clark 1947; two s.; ed. Watford Grammar School, St. John's Coll., Cambridge; Royal Navy, R.N.V.R. 1940–45; Producer BBC Talks, Third Programme 1946–late 1950s; Fellow St. John's Coll., Cambridge 1948–51; Reader in Politics and History of Social Structure, Cambridge Univ. 1966–84; Co-founder and Dir. Cambridge Gp. for the History of Population and Social Structure 1964–; Visiting Prof. Coll. de France 1976, Johns Hopkins Univ. 1980, Yale Univ. 1982: Fellow, Trinity Coll., Cambridge 1953–; mem. Working Party on Foundation of Open Univ. 1965; Dir. Unit on Ageing at the Cambridge Group; f. with Michael Young British Univs. of the Third Age (U3A) 1981; Dr. h.c. (Open Univ.) 1979, (Keele) 1993. *Publications:* a series of works on John Locke the philosopher, The World We Have Lost 1965, Household and Family in Past Time 1972, Family Life and Illicit Love in Earlier Generations 1977, Bastardy and its Comparative History (Co-author) 1980, A Fresh Map of Life: The emergence of the Third Age 1989, Justice between Age Groups and Generations (with J. Fishkin) 1992, Ageing in the Past (with D. Kertzer) 1995. *Leisure interests:* book collecting, gardening. *Address:* Trinity College, Cambridge, CB2 1TQ; Cambridge Group, 27 Trumpington Street, Cambridge, CB2 1QA, England. *Telephone:* (01223) 338455 (Coll.); (01223) 333181 (Cambridge Group). Fax: (01223) 338564.

LASSALLE, Jacques Louis Bernard; French theatre director, actor and writer; b. 6 July 1936, Clermont-Ferrand; s. of Antoine Lassalle and Louise Lassalle (née Courbouleix); m. Françoise Marty 1958; three s.; ed. Sorbonne, Paris, Conservatoire National Supérieur d'Art Dramatique de Paris; Asst. teacher, Institut d'Etudes Théâtrales 1969–77; f. Studio Théâtre de Vitry 1970; taught Conservatoire Nat. Supérieur de Paris 1981–83, 1994–98; Dir.-Gen. Théâtre Nat. de Strasbourg 1983–90; Administrateur Général, Comédie Française 1990–93; dir. about 80 plays, particularly by Molière, Corneille, Racine, Euripides, Marivaux, Goldoni, Shakespeare, Labiche, Pirandello, Chekhov, Ibsen, Svevo, Lessing, Büchner, Hofmannsthal, Kundera, Sarraute and Vinaver, also operas; Grand prix national du théâtre; Chevalier, Légion d'honneur 1992, Officier, Arts et Lettres; Chevalier, Ordre Nat. du Mérite. *Publications:* Jonathan des années 30, Un couple pour l'hiver, Pauses 1991, Conversations sur Don Juan 1994, Tout comme il faut et Dix Hamlet de plus 1997, Pour un oui, pour un non, le Misanthrope 1998; numerous articles. *Leisure interests:* walking, swimming, reading, music, pre-1970 American films. *Address:* 47 boulevard Voltaire, 75011 Paris, France (Home). *Telephone:* (1) 47-00-32-78 (Home).

LASSERRE, Bruno Marie André, M.P.L.; French public servant; b. 4 Jan. 1954, Talence, Gironde; s. of Jacques Lasserre and Marie Garrigou-Lagrange de David de Lastours; m. Marie-Laure Sergent 1988; two d.; ed. Bordeaux Faculty of Law, Inst. of Political Studies, Bordeaux, Ecole Nationale d'Administration, Paris; mem. Conseil d'Etat 1978–, Maître des Requêtes 1983–; Chair.-Del. Nat. Comm. on right of reply on radio and TV 1980–82, Nat. Comm. on Freedom of Information 1982–86; Commissaire du gouvernement, Litigation Section of Conseil d'Etat 1984–86; Legal Counsel, France Telecom 1986–89; Head Regulatory Directorate for Posts and Telecommunications 1989–93; Dir.-Gen. of Posts and Telecommunications 1993–97; consultant to Ministers for Industry and Foreign Affairs on Int. Telecommunications (1997–98); Pres. comité de sélection des inspecteurs des finances au tour extérieur 1998–; mem. Conseil de la concurrence 1998–; Chevalier, Légion d'honneur, Ordre Nat.du Mérite. *Publication:* Open Government 1987. *Address:* Conseil d'Etat, place du Palais royal, 75100 Paris (Office); 14 avenue de Breteuil, 75007 Paris, France (Home).

LATASI, Kamuta; Tuvalu politician; fmr. Minister of Health, Educ. and Community Services; Prime Minister of Tuvalu 1993–97, Minister of Foreign Affairs and Econ. Planning 1993–97. *Address:* c/o Office of the Prime Minister, Vaiaku, Funafuti, Tuvalu.

LATERZA, Vito; Italian publisher; b. 11 Dec. 1926, Bari; m. Antonella Chiarini 1955; two c.; ed. Univ. of Florence; joined family-owned publishing house Gius. Laterza & Figli 1949, Gen. Man. 1975–. *Address:* Gius Laterza & Figli S.p.A., Via Sparano 162, 70121 Bari, Italy. *Telephone:* (080) 5216713.

LATOUR-ADRIEN, Hon. Sir (Jean François) Maurice, Kt., LL.B.; Mauritian judge; b. 4 March 1915; s. of late Louis C. E. Adrien and Maria E. Latour; ed. Royal Coll., Mauritius, Univ. Coll., London and Middle Temple, London; called to the Bar, Middle Temple 1940, and in Mauritius 1946; District Magistrate 1947–48; Crown Counsel 1948–60; Asst. Attorney-Gen. 1960–61; Solicitor-Gen. 1961–64; Dir. of Public Prosecutions 1964–66; Puisne Judge 1966–70; Chief Justice of the Supreme Court of Mauritius 1970–77;

Acting Gov.-Gen. Feb. 1973, July-Aug. 1974, Jan.-Feb. 1975, June–Aug. 1975, July-Sept. 1976; Pres. Mauritius Red Cross 1978–; Vice-Pres. Mauritius Mental Health Asscn. 1978–85, Pres. 1986–; Dir. Mauritius Union Assurance Co. 1978–, Chair. 1982–; Dir. Mauritius Commercial Bank Ltd. 1980–83, 1984–87, 1988–91, 1992–95, 1996–; Legal Consultant 1983–, Dir. 1992–95, 1996–, Vice-Pres. 1993, Pres. 1994, Vice-Pres. 1996–97; Legal Consultant, Fincorp Investment Ltd. (fmrly. Mauritius Commercial Bank Finance Corpn.) 1991–, Caudan Devt. Co. Ltd. 1991–, Mauritius Commercial Bank Registry and Securities Ltd. 1991–, Promotion and Devt. Co. Ltd. 1985–; Dir. Union and Policy Investment Ltd. 1998–, Union and Policy Offshore Ltd. 1998–, MUA Leasing Ltd. 1998–; Co-Ed. Mauritius Law Reports 1970–77; mem. War Memorial Bd. of Trustees 1978–84, Vice-Pres. 1985–; Vice-Pres. Institut de Droit d'Expression Française; Kt. Order of St. Lazarus of Jerusalem 1969. *Address:* c/o Mauritius Union Assurance Co. Ltd., 4 Léoville l'Homme Street, Port Louis (Office); Vacoas, Mauritius (Home).

LA TOURETTE, John Ernest, PH.D.; American economist; b. 5 Nov. 1932, Perth Amboy, N.J.; s. of John C. La Tourette and Charlotte R. Jones; m. Lillie (Lili) M. Drum 1957; one s. one d.; ed. Rutgers Univ.; Service U.S.A.F., rank of capt. 1955–58; Instr. in Econs. Rutgers Univ. 1960–61; Asst. Prof., Assoc. Prof., Prof. State Univ. of New York, Binghamton 1961–76, Chair. Dept. of Econs. 1967–75; Vice-Provost for Research and Dean, Grad. School, Bowling Green State Univ., Ohio 1976–79; Vice-Pres. and Provost, Northern Ill. Univ. 1979–86, Pres. 1986–; Ford Foundation Fellowship 1963; Brookings Inst. Research Professorship 1966–67; Univ. Research Fellowship, State Univ. of N.Y. 1970. *Publications:* contributions to journals of econs. *Leisure interests:* fishing, collecting antiques. *Address:* Lowden Hall, Northern Illinois University, DeKalb, IL 60115 (Office); 3734 N. Pine Grove Avenue, Apt. 304, Chicago, IL 60613, U.S.A. (Home). *Telephone:* (815) 753-9500 (Office).

LATSIS, John; Greek shipowner and banker; b. 14 Sept. 1910, Katakolo Ilias; m. Erietta Tsoukala; one s. two d.; ed. Pyrgos Commercial School, Merchant Naval Acad.; fmr. worker, seaman and capt.; shipowner 1946–; contractor; f. of Petrola Oil Refinery, Greece, and Rabigh Oil Refinery, S. Arabia; f. of several banks in Geneva, Luxembourg, London, Guernsey, Monaco, Athens etc.; creator and sponsor Athens Latsis Foundation, and Fondation Latsis Internationale; Commr. Finix, Greece; Gold Medal Ecumenical Patriarchate of Constantinople; Athens Academy Award. *Address:* 4 Xenias Street, 145 62 Kefalari, Greece.

LATSIS, Otto Rudolfovich, DR.ECON.SC.; Russian economist and journalist; b. 22 June 1934, Moscow; m.; one s. one d.; ed. Moscow Univ.; mem. CPSU 1959; worked for newspapers, including Izvestiya 1956–71; joined staff of Problems of Peace and Socialism (journal), Prague 1971–75; worked on staff of Inst. of Econ. and World Socialist System, Moscow 1975–86; staff of journal Kommunist (renamed Free Thought 1991), Deputy Ed. 1986–91; mem. Cen. Cttee. CPSU 1990–91; Political Observer, Izvestiya 1990–97, mem. Editorial Bd. 1991–97; political observer, Noviye Izvestiya 1997–, Deputy Ed.-in-Chief 1998–; mem. Bd. Social and Political Research Fund; Journalist of the Year Prize 1997. *Publications:* ten books including Tireless Builder, What Happened to Us and What Will Happen 1995; numerous articles. *Address:* Dolgorukovskaya str. 19/8, 103006 Moscow, Russia. *Telephone:* 795-31-57. *Fax:* 795-31-38/39.

LATTÈS, Robert; French business executive; b. 13 Dec. 1927, Paris; s. of Sadi Lattès and Renée Levi; m. Monique Lang 1949; two d.; ed. Ecole Normale Supérieure; researcher in Pure Math., C.N.R.S. 1953–56; worked in math. physics and computers, French Atomic Energy Agency, Saclay 1956–59; joined Metra Group 1959, f. SIA (Société d'Informatique Appliquée) within Metra 1962, with SIA until 1974; Adviser to Chair. and Pres., then Exec. Vice-Pres. Paribas 1975–87; Pres. Pallas Venture 1988–, Parindev 1988–; Founding Chair., then Hon. Chair. Transgène 1980–87; Vice-Pres. Conseil supérieur du mercenat culturel; Dir. Expand S.A., European Venture Capital Asscn., Orchestre de Paris, Inst. des Vaisseaux et du Sang, Institut Pasteur, Lille; mem. Bd. of Dirs. L'Institut Lumière, mem. Conseil des applications de l'Académie des Sciences; winner, World Bridge Championship 1956; Officier, Légion d'honneur, Commandeur, Ordre Nat. du Mérite. *Publications:* Méthode de Quasi-Réversibilité et Applications (with J.-L. Lions; trans. in English and other languages) 1967, Quelques problèmes aux limites de la Physique Mathématique 1967, Mille Milliards de dollars 1969, Matière grise année zero 1970, Pour une autre croissance 1973, La Fortune des Français 1977, L'Apprenti et le Sorcier (Les défis de l'innovation) 1988, le Risque et le fortune 1990. *Leisure interests:* books, symphonic music, opera, art, cinema. *Address:* Electra Fleming, 31 rue de Lisbonne, 75008 Paris (Office); 74 rue Raynouard, 75016 Paris, France (Home). *Telephone:* (1) 53.83.79.10 (Office); (1) 42.88.17.05 (Home). *Fax:* (1) 53.83.79.20 (Office); (1) 42.88.85.55 (Home).

LATTEUR, Jean Pierre, D.JUR.; Belgian administrative official; b. 11 Feb. 1936, Charleroi; s. of Paul Latteur and Antoinette Haegeman; m. Marie Leytens 1961; one s. three d.; Admin. Sec. Sobeac S.A. 1960; Sec.-Gen. and Ed., Adic A.S.B.L. 1964; Consultant, Eurosurvey S.A. 1970; Asst. Gen. Man. Dechy S.A. 1971; Gen. Man. Portal S.A. 1975; Advisory Sec.-Gen., Fabrimetal A.S.B.L. 1985; Gen. Man. Fédération de l'Industrie Cimentière Belge 1986–; Pres. COBATY 1995–; Vice-Pres. Building Material Producers (BMP) 1995–. *Publications:* La participation aux responsabilités dans l'entreprise 1965, L'homme et la révolution urbaine 1968. *Leisure interests:* riding, skiing. *Address:* Rue César Franck 46, 1050 Brussels, Belgium. *Telephone:* (322) 645 52 11.

LATTRE, André Marie Joseph de; French banker; b. 26 April 1923, Paris; m. Colette Petit 1947; three s. two d.; ed. Univs. de Paris à la Sorbonne and Grenoble, and Ecole libre des sciences politiques; Insp. of Finance 1946; with Ministry of Finance 1948–; Dept. of External Finance 1949–54, Sub-Dir. 1955–58; Alt. Exec. Dir. IMF 1954; Prof. Inst. d'Etudes Politiques, Paris 1958–83; Financial Adviser to Pres. of the Repub. 1958–60; Perm. Sec. Ministry of Finance 1960–61; Dir. of External Finance 1961; Censor, Bank of France 1962, Vice-Gov. 1966–74; Mission to India for Pres. IBRD 1965; Alt. Dir. BIS 1973; Pres. Crédit National 1974–82; World Bank Special Rep. to IDA 1983; Man. Dir. Inst. of Int. Finance, Washington 1983–86; Chair. Banque Française Standard-Chartered 1987–89; Chair. Banque Française de Service et de Crédit 1990–97; Commandeur Légion d'honneur and foreign awards. *Publications:* Les finances extérieures de la France 1959, Politique économique de la France depuis 1945 1967. *Leisure interests:* skiing, tennis. *Address:* 69 rue Perronet, 92200 Neuilly, France. *Telephone:* (1) 46-24-79-00.

LATYPOV, Col. Ural Ramdrakovich, LL.D.; Belarus politician; b. 24 Feb. 1951, Katayevo, Bashkir A.S.S.R.; m.; one s. one d.; ed. Kazan State Univ., Higher KGB courses in Minsk; army service in KGB forces 1974–89; Head Inst. of Nat. Security, Repub. of Belarus 1989–94; asst. to Belarus Pres. 1994–98; Minister of Foreign Affairs 1998–. *Publications:* articles on int. law. *Address:* Ministry of Foreign Affairs, Lenina str. 19, 220030 Minsk, Belarus. *Telephone:* (375) 227 2922 (Office).

LAU SIU-KAI; Chinese academic and political adviser; Assoc. Dir. Hong Kong Inst. of Asia-Pacific Studies, Chinese Univ.; mem. professional section, Preparatory Cttee. for Hong Kong Special Admin. Region (SAR). *Address:* Hong Kong Institute of Asia-Pacific Studies, Chinese University of Hong Hong Shatin, Hong Kong Special Administrative Region, People's Republic of China.

LAUDA, Andreas-Nikolaus ("Niki"); Austrian racing driver; b. 22 Feb. 1949, Vienna; s. of Ernst Peter and Elisabeth Lauda; m. Marlene Knaus 1976; two s.; competed in hill climbs 1968, later in Formula 3, Formula 2 and sports car racing; winner 1972 John Player British Formula 2 Championship; started Formula 1 racing in 1971; World Champion 1975, 1977, 1984, runner-up 1976; *Grand Prix wins:* 1974 Spanish (Ferrari), 1974 Dutch (Ferrari), 1975 Monaco (Ferrari), 1975 Belgian (Ferrari), 1975 Swedish (Ferrari), 1975 French (Ferrari), 1975 United States (Ferrari), 1976 Brazilian (Ferrari), 1976 South African (Ferrari), 1976 Belgian (Ferrari), 1976 British (Ferrari), 1977 South African (Ferrari), 1977 German (Ferrari), 1977 Dutch (Ferrari), 1978 Swedish (Brabham-Alfa Romeo); 1978 Italian (Brabham-Alfa Romeo); retd. 1979; winner of Victoria Sporting Club's Int. Award for Valour in 1977, following recovery from near-fatal crash in 1976 German Grand Prix at Nürburgring; now runs own airline in Austria; returned to racing 1981, won U.S. Formula 1 Grand Prix, British Grand Prix 1982, Dutch Grand Prix 1985; retd. again 1985, Chair. Lauda Air. *Leisure interests:* music, skiing. *Address:* Hof, near Salzburg, Austria; Sta. Eulalia, Ibiza, Spain.

LAUDER, Estee; American business executive; b. New York; m. Joseph Lauder (deceased); two s.; Chair. Bd. Estee Lauder Inc. (cosmetics co.) 1946–; recipient of numerous awards inc. Neiman-Marcus Fashion Award 1962, 1992, Albert Einstein Coll. of Medicine Spirit of Achievement Award 1968, Harpers Bazaar Top Ten Outstanding Women in Business 1970, Médaille de Vermeil de la Ville de Paris 1979, Athena Award 1985, Golda Meir 90th Anniversary Tribute Award 1988, Pres.'s Award (Cosmetic Exec. Women) 1989; Chevalier, Legion d'honneur; Hon. LL.D. (Univ. of Pa.) 1986. *Publication:* Estee: A Success Story 1985. *Address:* Estee Lauder Inc., 767 Fifth Avenue, New York, NY 10153, U.S.A.

LAUDER, Leonard Alan; American business executive; b. 19 March 1933, New York; s. of Joseph Lauder and Estee Lauder (née Mentzer) (q.v.); m. Evelyn Hausner 1959; two s.; ed. Wharton School, Univ. of Pennsylvania; with Estee Lauder Inc. (cosmetics and fragrance co.) New York 1958–, Exec. Vice-Pres. 1962–72, Pres. 1972–82, Pres. and C.E.O. 1982–; Gov. Joseph H. Lauder Inst. of Man. and Int. Studies 1983–; Trustee Aspen Inst. for Humanistic Studies 1978–, Univ. of Pa. 1977–; Pres. Whitney Museum of American Art 1977–. *Address:* Estee Lauder Inc., 767 Fifth Avenue, New York, NY 10153, U.S.A.

LAUDER, Ronald Stephen, B.S.; American business executive and diplomatist; b. 26 Feb. 1944, New York; s. of Joseph Lauder and Estee Lauder (q.v.); m. Jo Carole Knopf 1967; two d.; ed. Univ. of Pennsylvania, Univ. of Paris (Sorbonne), Univ. of Brussels; Estee Lauder N.V. Belgium 1965–67, Estee Lauder S.A. France 1967, Estee Lauder Sales Promotion Dir. 1968–69, Vice-Pres. Sales Promotion, Clinique 1969–72, Exec. Vice-Pres., Gen. Man. Clinique, Inc. 1972–75, Exec. Vice-Pres. Estee Lauder Int. 1975–78, Exec. Vice-Pres. Estee Lauder Inc., Chair. Estee Lauder Int. 1978–83; Deputy Asst. Sec. of Defense for European and NATO Policy 1983–86; Amb. to Austria 1986–87, pvt. investment man. New York 1987–; Trustee, Museum of Modern Art 1975– (Chair. 1995–), Mt. Sinai Medical Center 1981–; Chair. and Pres. Lauder Investments; Chair. Cen. European Devt. Corpn.; Trustee Mount Sinai Medical Center 1981–; Ordre du Mérite (France), Great Cross of the Order of Aeronautical Merit with White Ribbon (Spain), Dept. of Defense Medal for Distinguished Public Service. *Address:* Lauder Investments Inc., 767 Fifth Avenue, Suite 4200, New York, NY 10153, U.S.A.

LAUER, Reinhard, DR.PHIL.; German professor of Slavonic Philology; b. 15 March 1935, Bad Frankenhausen; s. of Erich Lauer and Rose Fischer;

m. Stanka Ibler 1962; one d.; ed. Univs. of Marburg, Belgrade and Frankfurt and Freie Univ. Berlin; reader in German Language, Univ. of Zagreb 1960–62; Research Fellow, Univ. of Frankfurt 1962–69; Prof. of Slavonic Philology and Head of Dept. of Slavonic Philology, Univ. of Göttingen 1969–; mem. Göttingen Acad., Serbian Acad., Croatian Acad., Austrian Acad.; Hon. mem. Bulgarian Philology Soc.; Valjavec Prize 1961, Yugoslav Flag with Golden Garland 1989. *Publications:* Heine in Serbien 1961, Gedichtform zwischen Schema und Verfall 1975, Europäischer Realismus (ed.) 1980, M. Krleža und der deutsche Expressionismus 1984, Sprachen und Literaturen Jugoslaviens (ed.) 1985, Poetika i ideologija 1987, Sprache, Literatur und Folklore bei Vuk St. Karadžić (ed.) 1989, Kulturelle Traditionen in Bulgarien (co-ed.) 1989, Künstlerische Dialektik und Identitätssuche (ed.) 1990, Die Moderne in den Literaturen Sudosteuropas (ed.) 1991, Höfische Kultur in Südosteuropa (co-ed.) 1994, Serbokroatische Autoren in deutscher Übersetzung (ed.) 1995, Slavica Gottingensia (ed.) 1995, Die Kultur Griechenlands in Mittelalter und Neuzeit (co-ed.) 1996, Die russische Seele 1997. *Leisure interests:* music, painting, ornithology. *Address:* Seminar für Slavische Philologie der Universität, Humboldt-Allee 19, 3400 Göttingen (Office); Allensteiner Weg 32, 37120 Bovenden, Germany. *Telephone:* (0551) 394701 (Office); (0551) 81375 (Home).

LAUGERUD GARCÍA, Gen. Kjell Eugenio; Guatemalan politician and army officer; b. 24 Jan. 1930, Guatemala City; s. of Pedro E. Laugerud and Catalina García; m. Helen Losi 1951; three s, two d.; Minister of Defence, Chief of Gen. Staff of Army 1970–74; Presidential Cand. of Movimiento de Liberación Nacional/Partido Institucional Democrático (MLN/PID) March 1974; Pres. of Guatemala 1974–78; numerous awards, including Legion of Merit (U.S.A.) 1971, Gran Collar Orden del Quetzal (Guatemala) 1974, Gran Cruz Brillantes Orden de El Sol (Peru), Orden del Mérito (Chile) 1978, etc. *Leisure interests:* horseback riding, collecting small arms, military history. *Address:* c/o Oficina del Presidente, Guatemala City, Guatemala.

LAUGHTON, Sir Anthony Seymour, Kt., PH.D., F.R.S.; British oceanographic scientist; b. 29 April 1927; s. of Sydney T. Laughton and Dorothy (Chamberlain) Laughton; m. 1st Juliet A. Chapman 1957 (dissolved 1962), one s.; m. 2nd Barbara C. Bosanquet 1973, two d.; ed. Marlborough Coll. and King's Coll. Cambridge; RNVR 1945–48; John Murray Student, Columbia Univ. New York 1954–55; Nat. Inst. of Oceanography, later Inst. of Oceanographic Sciences 1955–88, fmr. Dir.; mem. Jt. IOC/IHO Guiding Cttee. GEBCO (ocean charts) 1974–, Chair. 1986–; mem. Council, Univ. Coll. London 1983–93; mem. Co-ordinating Cttee. for Marine Science and Tech. 1987–91; Pres. Challenger Soc. for Marine Science 1988–90; Trustee Natural History Museum 1990–95; Pres. Soc. Underwater Tech. 1995–97, Hydrographic Soc. 1997–; mem. Governing Body Charterhouse School 1981– (Chair. 1995–); Royal Soc. of Arts Silver Medal 1958; Prince Albert 1er Monaco Gold Medal 1980, Founders Medal, Royal Geographical Soc. 1987, Murchison Medal, Geological Soc. 1989. *Publications:* papers on marine geophysics. *Leisure interests:* music, gardening, sailing. *Address:* Okelands, Pickhurst Road, Chiddingfold, Surrey, England. *Telephone:* (01428) 683941.

LAUNDER, Brian Edward, D.SC., D.ENG., F.R.S., F.ENG.; British professor of engineering; b. 20 July 1939, London; s. of Harry Edward Launder and Elizabeth Ann Launder (née Ayers); m. Dagny Simonsen 1968; one s. one d.; ed. Enfield Grammar School, Imperial Coll., London, M.I.T.; lecturer, then reader Mechanical Eng. Dept., Imperial Coll., London 1964–76; Prof. of Mechanical Eng. Univ. of Calif. at Davis 1976; Prof. of Mechanical Eng. UMIST 1980–98, Research Prof. 1998–; Dir. Environmental Strategy Group 1998–; Ed.-in-Chief Int. Journal of Heat and Fluid Flow 1987–; assessor of French Research Labs. for Nat. Centre for Scientific Research (CNRS), Paris 1992–; assessor Center for Turbulence Research, Stanford Univ., Calif. 1996–; Hon. Prof. (Nanjing Aerospace Inst.) 1993; Busk Prize, Royal Aeronautical Soc. 1995, Computational Mechanics Award, Japan Soc. of Mechanical Engineers 1995. *Publications include:* Mathematical Models of Turbulence 1972, Turbulent Shear Flows, vols. 1–9 (ed.), over 200 papers on measurement and modelling of turbulent flow. *Address:* Mechanical Engineering Department, University of Manchester Institute of Science and Technology, P.O. Box 88, Manchester, M60 1QD (Office); 4 Velvet House, 60 Sackville Street, Manchester, M1 3WE, England (Home). *Telephone:* (0161) 200-3700 (Office). *Fax:* (0161) 200-3723 (Office).

LAURA, Ernesto Guido; Italian film festival director; b. 4 May 1932, Villafranca, Veronese; s. of the late Manuel Laura and of Pia Romei Laura; m. Anna Maria Vercellotti 1958; two s.; ed. Dept. of Law, Catholic Univ., Milan; Co-Nat. Sec. Centri Universitari Cinematografici 1953–54; Admin. Nat. Sec. Federazione Italiana Circoli del Cinema 1954–55; Chief Ed. Bianco e Nero 1956–58, Filmlexicon 1968; Film Critic, Il Veltro 1958–; mem. Editorial Bd. Rivista del Cinematografo 1967–; Pres. Immagine, Centro Studi Iconografici 1968–; Dir. Venice Film Festival 1969–; has directed various film documentaries including Diario di Una Dama Veneziana 1958, Riscoperta di un Maestro 1960, Alla Ricera di Franz Kafka 1964, Spielberg 1964, Don Minzoni (Special Award) 1967. *Publications:* Il Film Cecoslovacca 1960, La Censura Cinematografica 1961, Ladri di Biciclette 1969.

LAUREL, Salvador Hidalgo, A.B., LL.D., LL.B.; Philippine politician; b. 18 Nov. 1928, Manila; s. of José P. Laurel; m. Celia Franco Diaz Laurel; eight c.; ed. Univ. of the Philippines and Yale Univ.; Senator 1967–73 until imposition of martial law; Prof. of Law and Jurisprudence; founded Legal Aid Soc. of the Philippines; mem. interim Nat. Ass. 1978; active in opposition politics since 1982; leader, United Nationalist Democratic Org. (UNIDO) 1981–91, Union for Nat. Action 1988–91; Vice-Pres. of Philippines 1986; Prime Minister Feb.–March 1986; Minister of Foreign Affairs 1986–87, Pres. Nacionalista Party 1989.

LAUREN, Ralph; American couturier; b. 14 Oct. 1939, Bronx, N.Y.; s. of Frank Lifschitz and Frieda Lifschitz; m. Ricky L. Beer 1964; three s.; salesman, Bloomingdale's, New York, Brooks Bros. New York; Asst. Buyer, Allied Stores, New York; Rep. Rivetz Necktie Mfrs. New York; neckwear designer, Polo div. Beau Brummel, New York 1967–69; established Polo Menswear Co., New York 1968–, Ralph Lauren's Women's Wear, New York 1971–, Polo Leathergoods 1978–, Polo Ralph Lauren Luggage 1982–, Ralph Lauren Home Collection 1983–; Chair. Polo Ralph Lauren Corpn. (66 stores in U.S.A., over 140 worldwide); recipient of many fashion awards inc. American Fashion Award 1975, Council of Fashion Designers of America Award 1981. *Address:* Polo Ralph Lauren Corporation, 650 Madison Ave, New York, NY 10022, U.S.A.

LAURÉN, Reidunn, D.IUR.; Swedish lawyer and politician; m.; three c.; fmr. Judge Admin. Court of Appeal, Stockholm; fmr. Deputy Sec. Parl. Standing Cttee. on Social Affairs; Legal Adviser Ministry of Labour; Perm. Under-Sec. Ministry of Housing and Physical Planning; Justice of the Supreme Admin. Court; Chair. Labour Court; Chair. Equal Opportunities Tribunal; Minister for Constitutional and Civil Law 1991–93; Pres. Administrative Court of Appeal 1994–97. *Publications:* Equal Opportunities at Work for Women and Men, numerous articles on legal matters. *Address:* Administrative Court of Appeal, Box 2302, 103 17 Stockholm, Sweden. *Telephone:* 700 3801.

LAURENS, André Antoine; French journalist; b. 7 Dec. 1934, Montpellier (Hérault); s. of André Laurens and Mme née Raymonde Balle; unmarried; ed. Lycée de Montpellier; journalist, L'Eclaireur Meridional (fortnightly), Montpellier 1953–54, Agence centrale de Presse, Paris 1958–62; mem. political staff, Le Monde 1963–69, Asst. to head of political dept. 1969–82; Dir. Le Monde 1982–84, Leader writer 1986–, Ombudsman 1994–; Vice-Pres. Société des Rédacteurs. *Publications:* Les nouveaux communistes 1972, D'une France à l'autre 1974, Le Métier politique ou la conquête du pouvoir 1980. *Address:* le Monde, 15 rue Falguière, 75015 Paris (Office); 34 rue de Clichy, 75009 Paris, France (Home).

LAURENT, Jacques; French author and journalist; b. 5 Jan. 1919, Paris; s. of Jean Laurent-Cely and Louise Deloncle; m. 3rd Elisabeth Nilsonn 1969; ed. Lycées Condorcet, Carnot and Charlemagne, Paris and Faculté des Lettres, Paris; f. Literary review La Parisienne 1953; Pres. Dir.-Gen. Arts (weekly magazine) 1954–59; has written screenplay for several films; mem. Académie française; Prix Goncourt for Les Bêtises 1971, Grand Prix de Littérature, Acad. Française 1981, Prix Littéraire Prince Pierre de Monaco 1983. *Publications:* under pseudonym Cecil Saint-Laurent: Caroline chérie, Le fils de Caroline chérie, Lucrèce Borgia, Prénom Clotilde, Ici Clotilde, Les passagers pour Alger, Les agités d'Alger, Hortense 1914–18, A Simon l'honneur, L'histoire imprévue des dessous féminins, La Communarde, Demandez-moi n'importe quoi 1973, La Bourgeoise 1974, La Mutante 1978, Clarisse 1980, L'erreur 1986; as Jacques Laurent: Les corps tranquilles, Paul et Jean-Paul, Le petit canard, Mauriac sous de Gaulle 1964, Année 1940, Lettre ouverte aux étudiants, Les Bêtises 1971, Dix perles de culture 1972, Histoire Egoïste 1976, Roman du Roman 1977, Le Nu vêtu et dévêtu 1979, Les sous-ensembles flous 1981, Les dimanches de Mademoiselle Beaunon 1982, Stendhal comme Stendhal 1984, Clotilde Jolivet ou le hasard des rencontres 1985, Le dormeur debout 1986, Le français en cage 1988, Les années 50 1989, Le Miroir aux Tiroirs 1990, Du Mensonge 1994, L'Inconnu du temps qui passe 1994, La Fin de Lamiel 1995. *Leisure interest:* painting. *Address:* c/o Editions Grasset, 61 rue des Saints-Pères, 75006 Paris (Office); 11 bis rue Chomel, 75007 Paris, France (Home).

LAURENT, Torvard Claude, M.D.; Swedish biochemist; b. 5 Dec. 1930, Stockholm; s. of Torbern Laurent and Bertha Svensson; m. Ulla B. G. Hellsing 1953; one s. two d.; ed. Karolinska Inst., Stockholm; Instructor Karolinska Inst. 1949–52, 1954–58; Research Fellow and Research Assoc. Retina Foundation, Boston, Mass. 1953–54, 1959–61; Asst. Prof. in Medical Chem. Swedish Medical Research Council 1961–66; Prof. of Medical and Physiological Chem. Univ. of Uppsala 1966–96; mem. Swedish Natural Science Research Council 1968–70, Swedish Medical Research Council 1970–77; Chair. Swedish Biochemical Soc. 1973–76; Visiting Prof. Monash Univ. 1979–80; Pres. Swedish Royal Acad. of Sciences 1991–94; Science Sec., Wenner-Gren Foundation 1993–; Hon. M.D. (Turku Univ.) 1993; Hon. Pharm. D. (Bologna Univ.) 1994; Anders Jahre Prize (Univ. of Oslo) 1968, Pharmacia Award 1986, Eric Fernström Nordic Prize in Med. (Lund Univ.) 1989, Björkén Prize (Uppsala Univ.) 1990. *Publications:* approximately 200 scientific papers. *Address:* Department of Medical and Physiological Chemistry, University of Uppsala BMC, Box 575, 751 23 Uppsala (Office); Hävelvägen 9, 756 47 Uppsala, Sweden (Home). *Telephone:* (018) 471-41-55 (Office); (018) 30-96-12 (Home). *Fax:* (018) 515870.

LAURENTS, Arthur; American playwright; b. 14 July 1918, New York; s. of Irving Laurents and Ada Robbins; ed. Cornell Univ.; Radio Script-Writer 1939–40; mem. Screenwriters Guild, Acad. Motion Picture Arts and Sciences; Dir. La Cage aux Folles (Tony Award) 1983, Sydney (Best Dir. Award) 1985, London 1986, Birds of Paradise 1987; American Acad. of Arts and Letters Award (for play Home of the Brave) 1946; Writers Guild of America Award (for The Turning Point) 1977; Tony Award 1967, 1984; Drama Desk Award 1974, Screenwriters' Guild Award and Golden Globe Award (best screenplay) for Turning Point. *Publications:* (novels) The Way We Were 1972, The Turning Point 1977; screenplays: The Snake Pit 1948, Rope 1948, Caught 1948, Anna Lucasta 1949, Anastasia 1956, Bonjour Tristesse 1958, The Way We Were 1972, The Turning Point 1978; (plays) Home of the Brave 1946, The Bird Cage 1950, The Time of the Cuckoo 1952, A Clearing in the Woods 1956, Invitation to a March 1960, The Enclave 1973, Scream 1978, Jolson Sings Again 1995, The Radical Mystique 1995, My Good Name 1997; musical plays: West Side Story 1957, Gypsy 1959, Anyone Can Whistle 1964, Do I Hear a Waltz? 1964, Hallelulah Baby 1967, Nick and Nora 1991; screenwriter, co-producer film The Turning Point 1977; writer and dir. of several Broadway plays including The Enclave 1973, Gypsy 1974. *Address:* c/o William Morris Agency, 1325 Avenue of the Americas, New York, NY 10019, U.S.A.

LAURIE, Hugh; British actor and comedian; b. 1959; m. Jo Laurie; three c.; ed. Eton, Cambridge Univ.; fmrly. Pres. Footlights, Cambridge Univ. *Television appearances include:* (with Stephen Fry (q.v.)) A Bit of Fry and Laurie 1989–91, Jeeves and Wooster 1990–92. *Film appearances include:* Peter's Friends, Cousin Bette 1998. *Publications:* Fry and Laurie 4 (with Stephen Fry) 1994, The Gun Seller 1996.

LAURIE, Robert Stephen, B.A.; Australian diplomatist; b. 5 Nov. 1936, Sydney; s. of late W. R. Laurie; m. Diana V. M. Doyne 1969; one s. one d.; ed. Knox Grammar School and Univ. of Sydney; joined Dept. of External Affairs (now Dept. of Foreign Affairs and Trade) 1958; served Colombo 1960, Moscow 1960–63; First Sec. Washington 1965–68; Counsellor, Hong Kong 1968–69; Deputy High Commr. in India 1969–71; Amb. to Burma 1975–77, to Poland 1977–80; High Commr. in Canada 1985–89, in New Zealand 1989–92; First Asst. Sec., South Pacific, Middle East and Africa Divs., Dept. of Foreign Affairs and Trade 1993–97; High Commr. in India 1997–. *Leisure interests:* tennis, cricket, golf, music. *Address:* Department of Foreign Affairs and Trade, Canberra, A.C.T. 2600; 31 Arthur Circle, Manuka, A.C.T. 2603, Australia.

LAURISTIN, Marju; Estonian politician and sociologist; b. 7 April 1940, Tallinn; d. of Johannes Lauristin (fmr. Prime Minister of Estonia) and Olga Lauristin; m. Peeter Vihalemm 1978; two d.; ed. Tartu Univ.; sociologist and head of Dept. of Journalism, Tartu Univ. –1989, Prof. 1993–; mem. CPSU –1990; f. of Popular Front of Estonia 1988–92; mem. governing council 1988–; Chair. Estonia Social-Democratic Party 1990–94; U.S.S.R. People's Deputy 1989–90; Deputy Speaker of Estonian Supreme Soviet (now Parl.) 1990–92; mem. Estonian Parl. 1992–95; Minister of Social Affairs 1992–94; Prof. Tartu Univ. 1994–. *Publication:* Return to the Western World: Cultural and Political Perspectives on the Estonian Post-Communist Transition (ed., with P. Vihalemm). *Leisure interest:* literature. *Address:* Ropka 19-12, Tartu, Estonia. *Telephone:* (372 7) 471 532. *Fax:* (372 7) 375440.

LAUSTSEN, Agnete, LL.D.; Danish politician; b. 25 Sept. 1935, Copenhagen; m. Ole Tjellesen 1996; ed. Univ. of Copenhagen; mem. staff Ministry of Interior, subsequently Head of Office, Ombudsman for Consumer Affairs; mem. Folketing (Parl.) 1979–; alt. mem. European Parl. 1979–84; mem. Nordic Council 1983; Chair. Parl. Social Cttee. 1983–87; Minister of Health 1987–88, of Housing and Bldg. 1988–90; Conservative mem. Copenhagen City Council 1962–87; Danish Del. to UN Gen. Ass. 1991; Chair. Danish Section, European Union of Women; Vice-Chair. Danish Interparl. Union. *Leisure interests:* travels, ballet, art. *Address:* Christiansborg, 1240 Copenhagen, Denmark. *Telephone:* 33375500. *Fax:* 39637720.

LAUTENBERG, Frank R., B.S., D.H.L.; American politician and business executive; b. Jan. 1924, Paterson, N.J.; s. of Samuel and Mollie Lautenberg; m.; one s. three d.; ed. Columbia Univ.; f. Automatic Data Processing Inc., Clifton, N.J. 1953, Exec. Vice-Pres. Admin. 1961–69, Pres. 1969–75, Chair. and C.E.O. 1975–82; Senator from N.J. Jan. 1982–; Nat. Pres. American Friends of Hebrew Univ. 1973–74; Gen. Chair. and Pres. Nat. United Jewish Appeal 1975–77; Commr. Port Authority, New York; mem. Int. Bd. of Govs. Hebrew Univ., Jerusalem; mem. Pres.'s Comm. on the Holocaust; f. Lautenberg Center for Gen. and Tumor Immunology, Medical School, Hebrew Univ., Jerusalem 1971; fmr. Pres. Asscn. of Data Processing Service Orgs.; mem. Advisory Council, Columbia Univ. School of Business; Torch of Learning Award, American Friends of Hebrew Univ. 1971; Scopus Award 1975; Hon. D.H.L. (Hebrew Union Coll., Cincinnati and New York) 1977; Hon. Ph.D. (Hebrew Univ., Jerusalem) 1978; Democrat. *Address:* US Senate, 506 Hart Senate Office Building, Washington, DC 20510; 405 Route 3, Clifton, NJ 07015, U.S.A. (Home).

LAUTENSCHLAGER, Hans Werner; German diplomatist; b. 31 Jan. 1927, Tientsin, China; m. Renate Lautenschlager (née Rall) 1953; one s. one d.; ed. German School, Shanghai and studied law and political science at Heidelberg and Hamburg, Germany and Basle, Switzerland; joined diplomatic service of Fed. Repub. of Germany 1955; served in Ministry of Foreign Affairs, participating in negotiations to set up EEC and EURATOM 1956–57; attached to EURATOM 1958–64; Counsellor for Political Affairs, Embassy New Delhi 1964–68; Deputy Head, Soviet Affairs Div., Foreign Office 1968–69; Head of EEC Trade and Agricultural Policy Div. 1969–73; Dir. of Foreign Trade and European Econ. Integration 1973–75; Dir.-Gen. Ministry of Foreign Affairs 1975–79, State Sec., Ministry of Foreign Affairs 1979–84, 1987–93; Perm. Rep. to UN 1984–87. *Address:* Alte Hecke 5, D53343 Wachtberg-Pech, Germany.

LAUTI, Rt. Hon. Toaripi, P.C.; Tuvaluan politician; b. 28 Nov. 1928, Papua New Guinea; m.; three s. two d.; ed. Queen Victoria School, Fiji, Wesley Coll., Paerata, N.Z., St. Andrew's Coll., Christchurch, Christchurch Teachers' Coll.; teacher in Tarawa, Gilbert Is. (now Kiribati) 1953–62; Labour Relations and Training Officer for Nauru and Ocean Is. Phosphate Comm. 1962–74; returned to Ellice Is. (now Tuvalu) 1974; Chief Minister of Tuvalu 1975–78, Prime Minister 1978–81; Leader of the Opposition 1981–90; Gov. Gen. of Tuvalu 1990–95; also fmr. Minister of Finance and Foreign Affairs. *Address:* P.O. Box 84, Funafuti, Tuvalu.

LAUTMANN, Rüdiger, D.PHIL., D.JUR.; German professor of sociology; b. 22 Dec. 1935, Koblenz; s. of Kurt Lautmann and Sibylle Lautmann; Research Asst. Univ. of Bielefeld and Dortmund 1968–71; Prof. of Sociology Univ. of Bremen, Law School 1971–82, Dept. of Sociology 1982–. *Publications:* Wert und Norm 1969, Die Funktion des Rechts in der modernen Gesellschaft (co-Ed.) 1970, Die Polizei (co-Ed.) 1971, Soziologie vor den Toren der Jurisprudenz 1971, Justiz—die stille Gewalt 1972, Seminar Gesellschaft und Homosexualität 1977,Rechtssoziologie—Examinatorium (co-Ed.) 1980, Der Zwang zur Tugend 1984, Die Gleichheit der Geschlechter und die Wirklichkeit des Rechts 1990, Das pornographierte Begehren (co-author) 1990, Männerliebe im alten Deutschland (co-Ed.) 1992, Homosexualität (Ed.) 1993, Vom Guten, das noch stets das Böse schafft (co-Ed.) 1993, Die Lust am Kind 1994, Lexikon zur Soziologie (co-Ed.) 1994, Der Homosexuelle und sein Publikum 1997, Ausgrenzung macht krank (jtly.) 1999. *Address:* 20099 Hamburg, Holzdamm 41, Germany. *Telephone:* 040-2802503. *Fax:* 040-2802509.

LAUTNER, Georges Charles; French film director; b. 24 Jan. 1926, Nice; s. of Charles Lautner and Marie-Louise Vittoré; m. Caroline Ragon 1950; one s. one d.; ed. Lycée Janson-de-Sailly, Ecole Montcel, Paris, Ecole Libre des Sciences Politiques and Faculté de Droit, Paris; Commdr. des Arts et des Lettres, Chevalier, Légion d'honneur; Prix de l'Amicale des cadres de l'industrie cinématographique. *Films:* Marche ou crève 1959, Arrêtez les tambours 1960, Le Monocle noir, En plein cirage 1961, Le Septième Juré 1961, L'Oeil du Monocle 1962, Les Tontons Flinguers 1963, Les Pissenlits par la racine 1963, Le Monocle rit jaune 1964, Les Barbouzes 1964, Les Bons Vivants 1965, Ne nous fâchons pas, Galia 1965, La Grande Sauterelle 1966, Fleur d'oseille 1967, Le Pacha 1967, La Route de Salina 1969, Laisse aller . . . c'est une valse 1970, Il était une fois un flic . . . 1971, Quelques Messieurs trop tranquilles 1972, La Valise 1973, Les Seins de glace 1974, Pas de problème 1975, On aura tout vu 1976, Mort d'un pourri 1977, Ils sont fous ces sorciers 1978, Flic ou voyou 1978, Le Guingolo 1979, Est-ce bien raisonnable? 1980, Le Professionnel 1981, Attention, une femme peut en cacher une autre 1983, Joyeuses Pâques 1984, Le Cowboy 1985, La Cage aux folles III 1985, La Vie dissolue de Gérard Floque 1986, La Maison assassinée 1987, L'Invité surprise 1988, Présumé dangereux 1989, Triplex 1990, Room Service 1991, L'inconnu dans la maison 1992. *Address:* 9 chemin des Basses Ribes, 06130 Grasse, France. *Telephone:* (04) 93363006. *Fax:* (04) 93360010.

LAUVERGEON, Anne Alice Marie; French government official; b. 2 Aug. 1959, Dijon; d. of Gérard Lauvergeon and Solange Martellière; m. Jean-Eric Molinard 1986; ed. Lycées Lakanal, Sceaux, Lycée Voltaire, Orléans, Ecole Normale Supérieure and Ecole Nat. Supérieure des Mines, Paris; with Usinor 1983–84; Eng. Inst. for Protection and Nuclear Safety, Centre d'Energie Atomique and Head of Div. Direction Régionale de l'Industrie et de la Recherche, Ile-de-France 1985–88; Asst. to Head of Service of Conseil-Gén. des Mines 1988–89; Adviser on int. econ. and foreign trade, Presidency of Repub. 1990; Deputy Sec.-Gen. Presidency of Repub. 1990–95; Man. Lazard Frères & Cie 1995–97; Deputy Dir.-Gen. Alcatel Alsthom 1997–; mem. Bd. Pechiney 1996–. *Publication:* Sur les traces des dirigeants ou la vie du chef dans les grandes entreprises (co-author) 1988. *Address:* Alcatel Télécom, 33 rue Emeriau, 75015 Paris, France.

LAUZANNE, Bernard, L. ÈS L.; French journalist; b. 22 June 1916, Paris; s. of Gaston Lauzanne and Sylvia Scarognino; m. Lucie Gambini 1949; two d.; ed. Lycée Condorcet and Univ. of Paris; war service and prisoner of war in Germany 1939–45; joined Radiodiffusion Française (R.T.F.) and worked on programme "Paris vous parle" 1945–59; Chief Sub-Ed., Le Monde 1945–59, News Ed. 1959–69, Asst. Ed. 1969–74, Ed. 1974–78, Man. Ed. 1978–83; Directeur de Collection Éditions Denoël 1983–; Pres. France-Japan Asscn., Comité d'histoire de la radio; Lauréat de l'Acad. française; Chevalier, Légion d'honneur, Croix de guerre, Commdr. of Sacred Treasure, Japan. *Leisure interests:* music, theatre, painting. *Address:* Éditions Denoël, 9 rue du Cherche-Midi, 75278 Paris Cedex 06 (Office); 5 rue Jean-Bart, 75006 Paris, France (Home). *Telephone:* (1) 42-84-01-74.

LAVE, Lester B., PH.D.; American professor of economics; b. 5 Aug. 1939, Philadelphia, Pa.; m. Judith Rice 1965; one s. one d.; ed. Reed Coll., M.I.T. and Harvard Univ.; Prof., Carnegie-Mellon Univ. 1963–, James Higgins Prof. of Econs. 1984, Prof. 1992–; Sr. Fellow, Brookings Inst. 1978–82; Visiting Asst. Prof. Northwestern Univ. 1965–66; consultant, Gen. Motors Research Labs., U.S. Depts. of Justice, Defense, Transportation, Health and Welfare, Environmental Protection Agency, Nuclear Regulatory Comm., Nat. Science Foundation, Office of Tech. Assessment; Pres. Soc. for Risk Analysis 1985–86. *Publications:* Technological Change 1966, Air Pollution and Human Health 1977, The Strategy of Social Regulation 1981, Scientific

Basis of Health & Safety Regulation 1981, Clearing the Air 1981, Quantitative Risk Assessment 1982, Toxic Chemicals, Health and the Environment (with A. Upton) 1987; more than 200 scientific articles. *Leisure interests:* swimming, skiing. *Address:* Graduate School of Industrial Administration, Carnegie-Mellon University, Pittsburgh, PA 15213, U.S.A. *Telephone:* 412-268-8837.

LAVELLE, Roger Garnett, C.B., B.A., LL.B.; British financial executive; b. 23 Aug. 1932, Derby; s. of Henry Allman Lavelle and Evelyn Alice Garnett; m. Gunilla Odeberg 1956; three s. one d.; ed. Leighton Park, Trinity Hall Cambridge; Prin., H.M. Treasury 1961; Special Asst. to Lord Privy Seal (Edward Heath) 1961–63; Pvt. Sec. to Chancellor of Exchequer (James Callaghan) 1965–68; Under-Sec., Treasury 1975, Deputy Sec. 1985, Head, European Secr., Cabinet Office 1987; Vice-Pres. European Investment Bank 1989–93; Dir. EBRD 1993–. *Address:* European Bank for Reconstruction and Development, 1 Exchange Square, London, EC2A 2EH, England. *Telephone:* 0171-338 6427.

LAVELLI, Jorge; French theatre and opera director; b. Buenos Aires, Argentina; ed. Ecole Charles Dullin et Jacques Lecoq, Paris, Université du Théâtre des Nations; Dir. Théâtre Nat. de la Colline 1987–; Pres. Centre français de l'Inst. Int. du Théâtre (UNESCO) 1991–. *Plays include:* Le Mariage, Paris 1963, Berlin Festival 1964 (Grand Prix at Concours nat. des jeunes compagnies), Jeux de Massacre, Paris 1970 (Prix de la Critique), Le Roi se meurt, Paris 1976 (Prix Dominique de la mise en scène, Prix de la Critique), Doña Rosita La Soltera, Madrid, Jerusalem and Caracas Festivals, and Paris 1980; at Théâtre Nat. de la Colline: Une Visite inopportune by Copi 1988 (Prix de la meilleure création française, Syndicat de la Critique), Réveille-toi Philadelphie 1988 (Prix de la meilleure création d'une pièce française, Syndicat de la Critique), La Veillée 1989, Greek 1990 (Molière Prize for best production), La Nonna 1990, Heldenplatz 1991, 1992. *Operas include:* The Trial (by Von Einem), Vienna State Opera 1970, Idomeneo, Angers 1975, Faust, Opéra de Paris 1975, L'Heure Espagnole and L'Enfant et les Sortilèges, La Scala Milan 1975, La Traviata, Aix-en-Provence Festival 1976, Faust, Metropolitan Opera, New York, Kennedy Center, Washington 1976, Pelléas et Mélisande, Opéra de Paris 1977, Fidelio, Toulouse 1977, Madame Butterfly, La Scala, Milan and Opéra de Paris 1978, Alcina, Aix-en-Provence Festival 1978, Carmen, Strasbourg, Brussels 1978, Oedipus Rex, Opéra de Paris 1979, Le Nozze di Figaro, Aix-en-Provence Festival, Liège 1979, Dardanus (by Rameau), Opéra de Paris 1980, Les Arts Florissants (by Charpentier), Versailles 1982, Norma, Bonn 1983, Salome, Zürich 1986, La Clemenza di Tito, Hamburg 1986, The Makropoulos Affair, Buenos Aires 1986, Die Zauberflöte, Aix-en-Provence Festival 1989, Die Entführung aus dem Serail Aix-en-Provence Festival 1990; several opera productions for TV; Chevalier Légion d'honneur; Chevalier Ordre nat. due Mérite, Commdr. Ordre des arts et des lettres, Cross of Commdr. Order of Merit, Poland. *Address:* Théâtre National de la Colline, 15 rue Malte Brun, 75020 Paris, France. *Telephone:* (1) 44.62.52.00. *Fax:* (1) 44.62.52.90.

LAVENTHOL, David, M.A.; American publisher; b. 15 July 1933, Philadelphia; s. of Jesse Laventhol and Clare Horwald; m. Esther Coons 1957; one s. one d.; ed. Yale Univ. and Univ. of Minnesota; Reporter, later News Ed. St. Petersburg Times 1957–63; City Ed. New York Herald Tribune 1963–66; Asst. Man. Ed. The Washington Post 1966–69; Assoc. Ed. Newsday 1969, Exec. Ed. 1969–70, Ed. 1970–78, Publr. and C.E.O. 1978–86, Chair. 1986–87; Group Vice-Pres. Times Mirror 1981–86, Sr. Vice-Pres. 1986, Pres. 1987–93; C.E.O. and Publr. L.A. Times 1989–93; Ed.-at-large Times Mirror Co., L.A. 1994–; Chair. Pulitzer Prize Board 1988–89; Vice-Chair. Int. Press Inst. 1985–92, Chair. 1992–95; Chair. Museum of Contemporary Art, L.A. 1993–97; Dir. Newspaper Advertising Bureau, American Press Inst. 1988–, L.A. Times Washington Post/News Service, Times Mirror Foundation, United Negro Coll. Fund mem. Bd. Dirs Assoc. Press 1993–96, Columbia Journalism School 1995–, Nat. Parkinson Foundation 1995–, Saratoga Performing Arts Center 1993–96; mem. American Soc. of Newspaper Eds. Writing Awards Bd., American Newspaper Publr. Asscn., Century Asscn., Council on Foreign Relations. *Address:* LA Times, Times Mirror Square, Los Angeles, CA 90053; 800 West First Street, Los Angeles, CA 90012, U.S.A. (Home). *Telephone:* (213) 617 2541 (Home).

LAVER, Rod(ney) George, M.B.E.; Australian tennis player; b. 9 Aug. 1938, Rockhampton, Queensland; s. of R. S. Laver; m. Mary Benson 1966; one s.; ed. Rockhampton Grammar School and High School; Professional player since 1963; Australian Champion 1960, 1962, 1969; Wimbledon Champion 1961, 1962, 1968, 1969; U.S.A. Champion 1962, 1969; French Champion 1962, 1969; first player to win double Grand Slam 1962, 1969; first player to win over U.S. $1 million in total prize money 1972; played Davis Cup for Australia 1958, 1959, 1960, 1961, 1962 and 1973 (first open Davis Cup). *Publications:* How to Play Winning Tennis 1964, Education of a Tennis Player 1971. *Leisure interests:* golf, fishing, skiing.

LAVEROV, Nikolai Pavlovich; Russian geologist; b. 12 Jan. 1930, Pozharishche, Archangel Region; m.; two d.; ed. Moscow Inst. of Nonferrous Metals; mem. CPSU 1959–91; participated in geological expeditions, jr. researcher, scientific sec. on geological stations of Inst. of Geology, Ore Deposits, Mineralogy and Chemistry 1958–66; Deputy Chief Dept. of research orgs., U.S.S.R. Ministry of Geology 1966–68, Chief 1968–72; Scientific Leader on research of Resources of Urals Project 1972–87; Corresp. mem. U.S.S.R. (now Russian) Acad. of Sciences 1979, mem. 1987; Vice-Pres. 1988–; Prof., Prorector, Head of Chair of Ecology and rational use of natural resources, Acad. of Nat. Econs., U.S.S.R. Council of Ministers 1983–87; Pres. Acad. of Sciences of Kirgiz S.S.R. 1987–89; Vice-Chair. U.S.S.R. Council of Ministers, Chair. Ctte. on Science and Tech. 1989–91; mem. Cen. CPSU Cttee. 1990–91; Head of Comms. of Acad. of Sciences investigating consequences of earthquake in Armenia 1988–; Chair. U.S.S.R. Nat. Cttee. of Geologists 1990–91; Head Comm. on problem of safe burial of radioactive waste; Ed.-in-C. Geology of Ore Deposits. *Publications:* works on geology of uranium deposits, continental volcanism, econs. of mineral products. *Address:* Presidium of Russian Academy of Sciences, Leninsky prospekt 12, 117901 Moscow, Russia. *Telephone:* 954-2968.

LAVIER, Bertrand; French artist; b. 14 June 1949, Châtillon-sur-Seine; s. of Jean Lavier and Geneviève Duteil; m. Gloria Friedmann 1989; ed. Ecole Nat. Supérieure d' Horticulture; landscape artist and town planner, Marne Lavallée New Town 1971–72; at Centre de Recherches et d'Etudes sur le Paysage, Paris 1973–75; artist 1974–; first one-man exhbn., Centre Nat. d'Art contemporain, Paris 1975; subsequent exhbns. at Biennale, Venice 1976, 1997, Europa 79, Stuttgart 1979, Musée d'Art Moderne, Paris 1980, 1985, Galerie Massimo Minini, Milan 1982, Dokumenta 7, Kassel 1982, Noveau Musée, Lyon Villeurbanne 1983, Lisson Gallery, London 1984, Galerie Durand–Dessert, Paris 1984, Kunsthalle, Bern 1984, Museum of Modern Art, New York 1984, Biennales, Paris, São Paulo 1985, I.C.A., London 1986, Museum of Modern Art, Tokyo 1986, Musée des Beaux-Arts, Dijon 1986, Gallery Buchmann, Basel 1986, Biennale of Sydney 1986, John Gibson Gallery, New York 1986, Museé des Beaux Arts, Grenoble 1986, Stedjelik van Abbemuseum, Eindhoven 1987, Galerie Durand-Dessert, Paris 1987, Dokumenta 8, Kassel 1987, Kröller-Müller Museum, Netherlands 1987, Univ. Art Museum, Berkeley, U.S.A. 1988, Nat. Museum of Modern Art, Vienna 1992, Museum of African and Oceanian Art, Paris 1995, Castello di Rivoli Museum of Contemporary Art, Turin 1996, Martin Gropius Museum, Berlin 1997; First Prize (Sculpture), Biennale, Budapest 1984, Grand prix nat. de la sculpture 1994. *Publication:* Bertrand Lavier présente la peinture des Martin de 1603 à 1984 1984. *Leisure interests:* hunting, motor-racing, tennis. *Address:* Galerie Durand-Dessert, 28 rue de Lappe, 75011 Paris (Office); rue La Demoiselle, 21510 Aignay-le-Duc, France (Home).

LAVROV, Kyrill Yuriyevich; Russian actor; b. 15 Sept. 1925, Kiev; army service 1943–50; actor Kiev Lesya Ukrainka Drama Theatre 1950–55; with Leningrad Big Drama Theatre 1955–; Artistic Dir. 1989–; acted in numerous classical and contemporary plays including Cabal and Lourc (Schiller), Macbeth, Wit Works Woe (Griboyedov), Three Sisters (Chekhov). *Films include:* Alive and Dead 1964, Retribution 1969, The Taming of the Fire 1974, The Brothers Karamasov 1970, Tchaikovsky 1970; Chair. Exec. Bd. U.S.S.R. Union of Theatre Workers 1986–92; Pres. Int. Confed. of Theatre Unions 1992–; Deputy to U.S.S.R. Supreme Soviet 1979–89; U.S.S.R. People's Deputy 1989–91; Hero of Socialist Labour 1985, U.S.S.R. People's Artist 1972, U.S.S.R. State Prize 1978, 1982. *Address:* Michurinskaya 1, Apt. 36, 197046 St. Petersburg, Russia (Home). *Telephone:* 233 5235 (Home).

LAVROV, Sergey Viktorovich; Russian diplomatist; b. 21 March 1950, Moscow; m.; one d.; ed. Moscow Inst. of Int. Relations; diplomatic service 1972–; attache U.S.S.R. Embassy in Sri Lanka 1972–76, Sec. Dept. of Int. Econ. Organizations Ministry of Foreign Affairs 1976–81, Sec., Counsellor U.S.S.R. Mission, UN, New York 1981–88; Deputy Chief, then Chief Dept. of Int. Econ. Relations Ministry of Foreign Affairs 1988–90; Dir. Dept. of Int. Organizations and Global Problems, Ministry of Foreign Affairs of Russia 1990–92, Deputy Minister 1992–94; Perm. Rep. to UN 1994–. *Address:* Permanent Mission of Russia, 136 East 67th Street, New York, NY 10021, U.S.A. *Telephone:* (212) 861-4900 (Office). *Fax:* (212) 628-0252.

LAVROVSKY, Mikhail Leonidovich; Russian ballet dancer; b. 29 Oct. 1941, Tbilisi; s. of Yelena Chikvaidze and Leonid Ivanov Lavrovsky; m. Dolores Carcía Ordonyez 1987; one s.; ed. Moscow School of Choreography, Moscow State Inst. of Theatre Art; soloist Bolshoi Theatre 1961–88; coach Bolshoi Theatre 1992–; f. and Head Choreographic School of M. Lavrovsky in Moscow 1993; prize winner Int. Competition in Varna, Bulgaria; Lenin's Prize 1970, Nizhinsky Prize Paris Acad. of Dance 1972; U.S.S.R. State Prize 1977; U.S.S.R. People's Artist 1976. *Repertoire includes:* Giselle, Flames of Paris, Cinderella, Legend about Love, Don Quixote, Romeo and Juliet, Nutcracker, Angara, Paganini, Ivan the Terrible, Anyuta. *Choreography:* Jazz Ballet (Porgy and Bess), Blues (Gershwin), Film Ballet Prometheus (Scriabin), Novella (Bach and Liszt), Plastic Ballet Revelations (Kikta), Fantasia Ballet Casanova (Mozart), Bolshoi Theatre 1993. *Leisure interests:* sport, fencing. *Address:* Voznesensky per. 16/4, Apt. 7, 103009 Moscow, Russia (Home). *Telephone:* (095) 229 6549 (Home).

LAW, H. E. Cardinal Bernard F.; American ecclesiastic; b. 4 Nov. 1931, Torreón; s. of Bernard A. Law and Helen Stubblefield; ordained 1961; Bishop of Springfield-Cape Girardeau 1973; Archbishop of Boston 1984–; cr. Cardinal by Pope John Paul II 1985. *Address:* 2101 Commonwealth Avenue, Brighton, MA 02135, U.S.A. *Telephone:* (617) 782-2544.

LAW, Bob; British artist; b. 22 Jan. 1934, Brentford, Middx.; m. Georgina Cann 1965; one s. one d.; works include paintings and sculptures; exhibited in public collections including (in London) Tate Gallery, Victoria & Albert Museum, Arts Council of G.B., British Council; Southampton Art Gallery, City Art Gallery, Peterborough, Stedelijk Museum, Amsterdam, Museum of

Modern Art, New York, Guggenheim Museum, New York, the Panza Collection, Milan, City Art Gallery, Johannesburg, Art Gallery of N.S.W., Sydney; French Govt. Scholarship 1961–62; Arts Council of G.B. Award 1967, 1975, 1981. *Leisure interests:* architecture, prehistory. *Address:* Lisson Gallery Ltd., 67 Lisson Street, London, NW1 5DP; 60 St. John's Street, Folkestone, Kent, CT20 1JB, England. *Telephone:* (01303) 246161.

LAW, Admiral Sir Horace Rochfort, G.C.B., O.B.E., D.S.C.; British naval officer; b. 23 June 1911, Dublin, Ireland; s. of Samuel Horace Law and Mary Clay; m. Heather Valerie Coryton 1941; two s. two d.; ed. Sherborne School; Capt., Royal Naval Coll., Dartmouth 1960; Flag Officer, Sea Training, Portland 1961; Flag Officer, Submarines 1963; Controller of the Navy 1965; C.-in-C. Naval Home Command 1970–72; First and Prin. Naval A.D.C. to H.M. The Queen 1970–72; fmr. mem. Security Comm.; Chair. R. & W. Hawthorn Leslie 1973–81; Pres. Royal Inst. of Naval Architects 1975–77; Chair. Church Army 1980–87. *Leisure interests:* walking, gardening. *Address:* West Harting, near Petersfield, Hants., GU31 5NT, England. *Telephone:* (01730) 825511.

LAW, Jude; British actor; b. London; partner Sadie Frost; two s.; fmrly. with Nat. Youth Music Theatre; co-f. Natural Nylon (production co.). *Stage appearances include:* Joseph and the Amazing Technicolour Dreamcoat, Les Parents Terribles. *Film appearances include:* Shopping, Wilde, Gattaca, Midnight in the Garden of Good and Evil, Bent, Music From Another Room, The Wisdom of Crocodiles, Existenz. *Address:* Jonathan Altaras Associates, 27 Floral Street, London, WC2E 9DP, England.

LAW, Phillip Garth, A.C., C.B.E., M.SC., F.T.S.E., F.A.A., F.A.I.P., F.A.N.Z.A.A.S., F.R.G.S.; Australian scientist, Antarctic explorer and educationist; b. 21 April 1912, Tallangatta, Victoria; s. of the late Arthur James Law and Lillie Law; m. Nel Allan 1941; ed. Ballarat Teachers' Coll. and Univ. of Melbourne; Science master in secondary schools 1933–38; Tutor in Physics Newman Coll., Melbourne Univ. 1940–45 and Lecturer in Physics 1943–47; Research Physicist and Asst. Sec. Scientific Instrument and Optical Panel, Ministry of Munitions 1940–45; Scientific Mission to New Guinea battle areas for the Australian Army 1944; Sr. Scientific Officer Aust. Nat. Antarctic Research Expeditions 1947–48, Leader 1949–66; Dir. Antarctic Div., Dept. of External Affairs 1949–66; Australian Observer Norwegian-British-Swedish Antarctic Expedition 1950; led expeditions to establ. first perm. Australian research station at Mawson, MacRobertson Land 1954 and at Davis, Princess Elizabeth Land 1957; exploration of coast of Australian Antarctica 1954–66; mem. gov. council Melbourne Univ. 1959–78, La Trobe Univ. 1964–74; Exec. Vice-Pres. Victoria Inst. of Colls. 1966–77; Chair. Australian Nat. Cttee. on Antarctic Research 1966–80, Royal Melbourne Inst. of Tech. Foundation 1994–; mem. Council of Science Museum of Victoria 1968–83; Pres. Royal Soc. of Victoria 1967, 1968, Graduate Union, Univ. of Melbourne 1972–77, Victorian Inst. of Marine Sciences 1978–80, Australia and N.Z. Scientific Exploring Soc. 1976–81, Patron 1982–; Fellow Royal Soc. of Vic.; Hon. Fellow Royal Melbourne Inst. of Tech.; several hon. degrees including D.App.Sci. (Melbourne), D.Sc. (La Trobe), D.Ed. (Vic. Inst. of Colls.); Award of Merit Commonwealth Professional Officers Asscn. 1957, Clive Lord Memorial Medal Royal Soc. of Tasmania 1958, Founder's Medal Royal Geographical Soc. 1960, John Lewis Gold Medal Royal Geographical Soc. of Australia 1962, Vocational Service Award Melbourne Rotary Club 1970, James Cook Medal of the Royal Soc. of N.S.W. 1988, Gold Medal Australian Geographic Soc. 1988. *Publications:* ANARE (with Bechervaise) 1957, Antarctic Odyssey 1983, The Antarctic Voyage of H.M.A.S. Wyatt Earp 1995, You Have to be Lucky 1995, also numerous articles on Antarctic exploration and research and papers on cosmic rays, thermal conductivity, optics and education. *Leisure interests:* music, tennis, skiing, swimming. *Address:* 16 Stanley Grove, Canterbury, Vic. 3126, Australia. *Telephone:* (03) 9882-5575.

LAWLER, James Ronald, M.A., D.U.P.; Australian academic; b. 15 Aug. 1929, Melbourne; m. Christiane Labossière 1954; one s. one d.; ed. Univs. of Melbourne and Paris; lecturer in French, Univ. of Queensland 1955–56; Sr. Lecturer, Univ. of Melbourne 1956–62; Prof. of French, Head of Dept., Univ. of Western Australia 1963–71; Prof. of French, Chair., Univ. of Calif., Los Angeles 1971–74; McCulloch Prof. of French, Dalhousie Univ. 1974–79; Prof. of Romance Languages, Univ. of Chicago 1979–; Edward Carson Waller Distinguished Service Prof., Univ. of Chicago 1983–97, Prof. Emer. 1997–; Visiting Prof. Collège de France 1985; Pres. Asscn. Int. des Etudes Françaises 1998–; Carnegie Fellowship 1961–62; Commonwealth Interchange Visitor 1967; Guggenheim Fellowship 1974; Nat. Endowment of Humanities Fellowship 1984–85; Foundation Fellow, Australian Acad. of the Humanities; Officier, Palmes académiques; Prix Int. des Amitiés Françaises 1986. *Publications:* Form and Meaning in Valéry's Le Cimetière Marin 1959, An Anthology of French Poetry 1960, Lecture de Valéry: Une Etude de Charmes 1963, The Language of French Symbolism 1969, The Poet as Analyst: Essays on Paul Valéry 1974, Paul Valéry: An Anthology 1976, René Char: The Myth and the Poem 1978, Edgar Poe et les Poètes français 1989, Paul Valéry (ed.) 1991, Rimbaud's Theatre of the Self 1992, Poetry and Moral Dialectic: Baudelaire's Les Fleurs du Mal 1997; Founding Ed.: Essays in French Literature 1964–, Dalhousie French Studies 1979–. *Address:* Wieboldt 205, 1050 East 59th Street, Chicago, IL, U.S.A. *Telephone:* (312) 702 8481.

LAWRENCE, Carmen Mary, PH.D.; Australian politician and fmr. psychologist; b. 2 March 1948, Western Australia; d. of Ern Lawrence and Mary Lawrence; m. 1979; one s.; ed. Santa Maria Coll., Perth; Sr. Tutor, Dept. of Psychiatry and Behavioural Science, Univ. of W.A. 1979, lecturer, and Course Controller in Behavioural Science applied to Medicine 1980–83; Research Psychologist in Research and Evaluation Unit, Psychiatric Services, Health Dept. of W.A. 1983–86; mem. House of Reps. 1986–, apptd. Minister for Educ. 1988, fmr. Minister for Educ. and Aboriginal Affairs, Premier of W.A. 1990–93, also Treasurer, Minister for the Family and for Women's Interests; Leader of the Opposition, Shadow Treasurer, Shadow Minister for Employment, for Fed. Affairs 1993–94; Fed. Shadow Minister of Health 1994–96, on Status of Women and on Environment and the Arts 1996–97; mem. Fed. Parl. for Fremantle 1994–; Benjamin Rosenstamm Prize in Econs., British Psychological Soc. Prize for Psychology, Australian Psychological Soc. Prize for Psychology, H.I. Fowler Prize for Research in Psychology, J.A. Wood Memorial Prize and other awards and prizes. *Publications:* several academic papers on psychology. *Leisure interests:* reading, theatre, music. *Address:* Unit 7, Queensgate Mall, William Street, Fremantle WA 6160, Australia.

LAWRENCE, Henry Sherwood, M.D.; American physician and immunologist; b. 22 Sept. 1916, New York; s. of Victor J. and Agnes B. (Whalen) Lawrence; m. Dorothea W. Wetherbee 1943; two s. one d.; ed. New York Univ.; Instructor in Medicine, New York Univ. School of Medicine 1949–52, Asst. Prof. 1952–55, Assoc. Prof. 1955–61, Prof. of Medicine 1961–, Jeffrey Bergstein Prof. of Medicine 1979–, Head Infectious Disease and Immunology Div. 1959–; Co-Dir. New York Univ. Medical Services 1964–; Dir. Cancer Center 1974–79; Dir. Center for AIDS research 1989–94; Commonwealth Fund Fellow, Univ. Coll., London 1959; f. and Ed.-in-Chief Cellular Immunology 1970–96; mem. N.A.S.; Hon. Fellow American Acad. of Allergy, Soc. Française d'Allergie, Royal Coll. Physicians and Surgeons (Glasgow); Harvey Soc. Lecturer 1973, Councillor 1974–77; Von Pirquet Award, American Coll. of Physicians Award, New York Acad. of Medicine Science Medal, American Coll. of Allergy Scientific Achievement Award, Infectious Diseases Soc. of America Bristol Award, Chapin Medal, City of Providence, Lila Gruber Award for Cancer Research, American Acad. of Dermatology, Dowling Lectureship Award, Alpha Omega Alpha Award, New York Univ. School of Medicine Alumni Scientific Achievement Award and Distinguished Teachers Award, New York Univ. Washington Square Coll. Alumni Achievement Award. *Publications:* Cellular and Humoral Aspects of Hypersensitivity (Ed.) 1959, Mediators of Cellular Immunity (Ed. with M. Landy) 1969, Immunobiology of Transfer Factor (Ed. with C. H. Kirkpatrick, D. Burger) 1983; articles in professional journals. *Leisure interests:* landscape painting, medieval English history. *Address:* Department of Medicine, New York University School of Medicine, 550 First Avenue, New York, NY 10016 (Office); 343 East 30th Street, New York, NY 10016, U.S.A. (Home). *Telephone:* (212) 263-6400 (Office); (212) 684-0997 (Home). *Fax:* (212) 263-7369.

LAWRENCE, Peter Anthony, PH.D., F.R.S.; British biologist; b. 23 June 1941, Longridge; s. of Ivor D. Lawrence and Joy Liebert; m. Birgitta Haraldson 1971; ed. Univ. of Cambridge; Commonwealth Fellowship, U.S.A. 1965–67; Dept. of Genetics, Univ. of Cambridge 1967–69; Staff, MRC Lab. of Molecular Biology, Cambridge 1969–, Jt. Head, Cell Biology Div., 1984–87; Medal of Zoological Soc. of London 1977, Darwin Medal (Royal Soc.) 1994. *Publications:* The Making of a Fly 1992, numerous scientific papers. *Leisure interests:* garden, golf, trees, fungi, ascalaphidae, theatre. *Address:* 9 Temple End, Great Wilbraham, Cambridge, CB1 5JF, England. *Telephone:* (01223) 880505.

LAWRENCE, Robert Swan; American physician; b. 6 Feb. 1938, Philadelphia; s. of Thomas George Lawrence and Catherine Swan Lawrence; m. Cynthia Starr Cole 1960; three s. two d.; ed. Harvard Coll. and Medical School; Medical Epidemiologist, Center for Disease Control, U.S. Public Health Service, Atlanta 1966–69; Asst. to Assoc. Prof. of Medicine, Dir. Div. of Community Medicine, N.C. Univ. School of Medicine 1970–74; Dir. Div. of Primary Care, Asst. to Assoc. Prof. of Medicine, Harvard Medical School 1974–91, Charles Davidson Assoc. Prof. of Medicine 1981–91; Assoc. Chief of Medicine, Cambridge Hosp. 1974–77, Chief of Medicine, Dir. Dept. of Medicine 1980–91; Dir. Health Sciences, Rockefeller Foundation 1991–95; Adjunct Prof. of Medicine, New York Univ. 1991–95; Prof. of Health Policy, Assoc. Dean of Professional Educ. and Dir. Center for a Livable Future, Johns Hopkins School of Hygiene and Public Health 1995–, Prof. of Medicine and Dir. Center for a Livable Future, Johns Hopkins School of Medicine 1996–; Chair. U.S. Preventive Services Task Force, Dept. of Health and Human Services, U.S. Govt. 1984–89, mem. 1990–95; Ed. American Journal of Preventive Medicine 1990–92; Maimonides Prize 1964; mem. Inst. of Medicine, N.A.S 1978; Special Recognition Award (American Coll. of Preventive Medicine) 1988; Duncan Clark Lecture (Asscn. of Teachers of Preventive Medicine) 1993, John Atkinson Ferrell Prize, U.N.C. 1998. *Publications:* Co-ed. Preventing Disease: Beyond the Rhetoric 1990, Health Promotion and Disease Prevention in Clinical Practice 1996, International Perspectives on Environment, Development and Health 1997; 60 articles in scientific journals. *Address:* Johns Hopkins School of Hygiene and Public Health, 615 N. Wolfe Street, Baltimore, MD 21205 (Office); Highfield House 1112, 4000 N. Charles Street, Baltimore, MD 21218-1737, U.S.A. (Home). *Telephone:* (410) 614-4590 (Office); (410) 235-5474 (Home). *Fax:* (410) 614-8126.

LAWRENCE, Walter Nicholas Murray, M.A.; British underwriting agent; b. 8 Feb. 1935, London; s. of Henry Walter Neville Lawrence and Sarah Schuyler Lawrence (née Butler); m. Sally Louise O'Dwyer 1961; two d.; ed. Winchester Coll., Trinity Coll., Oxford; with C. T. Bowring and Co. Ltd.

1957–62, 1976–84, Treaty Dept. 1957–62, Dir. 1976–84; with Harvey Bowring and Others 1962–84, Asst. Underwriter 1962–70, Underwriter 1970–84; Dir. C. T. Bowring (Underwriting Agencies) Ltd. 1973–84; Chair. Fairway Underwriting Agencies Ltd. 1979–85; mem. Lloyd's Underwriter's Non-Marine Assen., Deputy Chair. 1977, Chair. 1978; served Cttee. of Lloyd's 1979–82, 1991, Deputy Chair. 1982, mem. Council of Lloyd's 1984–, Deputy Chair. 1984–87, Chair. 1988–90; Dir., Chair. Murray Lawrence Holdings Ltd. 1988–94, Murray Lawrence Mems. Agency Ltd. 1988–92, Murray Lawrence & Partners Ltd. 1989–93. *Leisure interests:* golf, opera, travel. *Address:* Lloyd's of London, Lime Street, London, E.C.3, England. *Telephone:* 0171-327 1000.

LAWRENSON, Peter John, D.SC., F.I.E.E.E., F.ENG., F.R.S.; British electrical engineer and business executive; b. 12 March 1933, Prescot; s. of John Lawrenson and Emily Houghton; m. Shirley H. Foster 1958; one s. three d.; ed. Prescot Grammar School and Manchester Univ.; research eng. General Electric Co., Ltd. 1956–61; Lecturer, Univ. of Leeds 1961–65, Reader 1965–66, Prof. of Electrical Eng. 1966–91, Head, Dept. of Electrical and Electronic Eng. 1974–84, Chair. Faculty of Science and Applied Science 1978–80; Chair. Switched Reluctance Drives Ltd. 1981–97, Dir. 1997–; Pres. I.E.E. 1992–93; James Alfred Ewing Medal 1983, Royal Soc. Esso Medal 1985, Faraday Medal (I.E.E.) 1990 and other awards. *Publications:* The Analytical and Numerical Solution of Electromagnetic Field Problems 1992; other books and over 150 articles in the field of electrical eng., particularly electromagnetics and electromechanics. *Leisure interests:* squash, lawn tennis, bridge, chess, jewellery making. *Address:* Switched Reluctance Drives Ltd., East Park House, Otley Road, Harrogate, HG3 1PR, England (Office). *Telephone:* (01423) 845200 (Office); (0113) 2755849 (Home). *Fax:* (01423) 845201 (Office).

LAWS, Richard Maitland, SC.D., F.R.S., C.B.E.; British scientist; b. 23 April 1926, Whitley Bay; s. of Percy Malcolm Laws and Florence May Heslop; m. Maureen Isobel Holmes 1954; three s.; ed. Dame Allan's School, Newcastle, and St. Catharine's Coll., Cambridge; Biologist and Base Leader, Falkland Islands Dependencies Survey 1947–53; Whaling Insp., F/F Balaena 1953–54; Prin. Scientific Officer, Nat. Inst. of Oceanography, Godalming 1954–61; Dir., Nuffield Unit of Tropical Animal Ecology, Uganda 1961–67; Dir., Tsavo Research Project, Kenya 1967–68; Head, Life Sciences Div., British Antarctic Survey 1969–73; Dir., British Antarctic Survey, Cambridge 1973–87; Dir. Sea Mammal Research Unit, Cambridge 1977–87; Master, St. Edmund's Coll., Cambridge 1985–96; Sec. Zoological Soc. of London 1984–88; mem. Council of the Senate, Univ. of Cambridge 1989–92, Financial Bd. 1988–91; Pres. Scientific Cttee. for Antarctic Research 1990–94, Hon. mem. 1996; Hon. mem. Soc. for Marine Mammalogy 1994; Hon. Fellow St. Catharine's Coll. 1982, St. Edmund's Coll. 1996; Hon. Warden, Uganda Nat. Parks 1996; Foreign mem. Norwegian Acad. of Science and Letters 1998; Hon. D.Sc. (Bath) 1991. *Publications:* Elephants and Their Habitats (co-author) 1975, Scientific Research in Antarctica (Ed.) 1977, Antarctic Ecology (Ed.) 1984, Antarctic Nutrient Cycles and Food Webs (co-ed.) 1985, Antarctica: The Last Frontier 1989, Life at Low Temperatures (co-ed.) 1990, Antarctica and Environmental Change (co-ed.) 1992, Antarctic Seals: Research Methods and Techniques (ed.) 1993, Elephant Seals: Population Ecology, Behavior and Physiology (co-ed.) 1994. *Leisure interests:* gardening, photography, painting. *Address:* 3 The Footpath, Coton, Cambs., CB3 7PX, England. *Telephone:* (01954) 210567.

LAWSON, Hon. Dominic Ralph Campden, B.A., F.R.S.A.; British journalist and editor; b. 17 Dec. 1956, London; s. of Nigel Lawson, now Lord Lawson of Blaby, (q.v.) and late Lady (Vanessa) Ayer; m. 1st Jane Fiona Wastell Whytenead 1982 (divorced 1991); m. 2nd Hon. Rosamond Monckton 1991; two d.; ed. Westminster School, Christchurch, Oxford; with World Tonight and The Financial World Tonight, BBC 1979–81; mem. staff Financial Times (Energy Corresp. and Lex column) 1981–87; Deputy Ed. The Spectator 1987–90, Ed. 1990–95; Ed. The Sunday Telegraph Oct. 1995–; Ed. The Spectator Cartoon Book; Columnist, Sunday Corresp. 1990, The Financial Times 1991–94, Daily Telegraph 1994–95; Ed. of the Year, Soc. of Magazine Eds. 1990. *Publications:* Korchnoi, Kasparov 1983, Britain in the Eighties (jtly.) 1989, ed. The Spectator Annual 1992, 1993, 1994, The Inner Game 1993. *Leisure interests:* chess, cricket. *Address:* The Sunday Telegraph, 1 Canada Square, Canary Wharf, London, E14 5AR, England.

LAWSON, John David, SC.D., F.INST.P., F.R.S.; British research physicist; b. 4 April 1923, Coventry; s. of Ronald and Ruth (née Houseman) Lawson; m. Kathleen Wyllie 1949; two s. one d.; ed. Wolverhampton Grammar School, St. John's Coll., Cambridge; TRE (now Royal Signals and Radar Establishment) Malvern, Aerials Group 1943–47; A.E.R.E. Malvern, Accelerator Group 1947–51; A.E.R.E. Harwell, Gen. Physics Div. 1951–62; Microwave Lab., Stanford, U.S.A. 1959–60; Rutherford Lab. (now Rutherford Appleton Lab.) 1962–, fmrly. Deputy Chief Scientific Officer, now retd., Hon. Scientist; Visiting Prof., Dept. of Physics and Astronomy, Univ. of Md. 1971; Technology Div., Culham Lab. 1975–76. *Publications:* The Physics of Charged Particle Beams 1977, 1988; numerous papers on applied physics. *Leisure interests:* travel, walking, book collecting (especially science books including historical studies). *Address:* 7 Clifton Drive, Abingdon, Oxon., OX14 1ET, England. *Telephone:* (01235) 521516.

LAWSON, Lesley (Twiggy), British model, singer and actress; b. 19 Sept. 1949, London; d. of William and Helen (née Reeman) Hornby; m. 1st Michael Whitney Armstrong 1977 (died 1983); one d.; m. 2nd Leigh Lawson 1988; ed. Brondesbury and Kilburn Grammar School; model 1966–76; Man. and Dir. Twiggy Enterprises Ltd. 1966–; f. Twiggy & Co. 1998–; own British TV series; has made several LP records. *Films include:* The Boy Friend 1971, W, There Goes the Bride 1979, Blues Brothers 1981, The Doctor and the Devils 1986, Club Paradise 1986, Harem Hotel, Istanbul 1988, Young Charlie Chaplin (TV) 1989, Madame Sousatzka 1989, Woundings 1998. *Plays:* Cinderella 1976, Captain Beaky 1982, My One and Only 1983–84, Blithe Spirit, Chichester 1997, Noel and Gertie, U.S.A. 1998. *Publications:* Twiggy: An Autobiography 1975, An Open Look 1985, Twiggy in Black and White (with Penelope Dening) 1997. *Leisure interests:* daughter Carly, music, design. *Address:* c/o Paul Lyon-Maris, I.C.M., Oxford House, 76 Oxford Street, London, W1R 1RB, England. *Telephone:* 0171-636 6565. *Fax:* 0171-323 0101.

LAWSON, Gen. Sir Richard George, K.C.B., D.S.O., O.B.E.; British army officer; b. 24 Nov. 1927, Hatfield; s. of John Lawson and Rebecca (née White) Lawson; m. Ingrid Montelin 1956; one s.; ed. St. Albans School, Birmingham Univ., Royal Mil. Acad., Sandhurst, Staff Coll., Camberley, U.S. Armed Forces Staff Coll., Royal Coll. of Defence Studies; Asst. Mil. Attaché, Baghdad 1957–61; Brigade Major, Royal Nigerian Army 1961–63; C.O. Independent Squadron (Berlin), Royal Tank Regiment 1963–64; Chief of Staff, South Arabian Army 1967; C.O. 5th Royal Tank Regiment 1968–69; Commdr. 20th Armoured Brigade 1972–73; G.O.C. 1st Armoured Div. 1977–79; G.O.C. Northern Ireland 1980–82; C.-in-C. Allied Forces, N. Europe 1982–86; Kt. Commdr., Order of St. Sylvester (Vatican), Leopold Cross (Belgium). *Publications:* Strange Soldiering 1963, All the Queen's Men 1967, Strictly Personal 1972. *Leisure interest:* sailing. *Address:* c/o Drummonds, 49 Charing Cross Road, London, WC2 2DX, England.

LAWSON, Sonia, M.A., R.A., R.W.S.; British artist; b. 2 June 1934, Darlington; d. of late Frederick Lawson and Muriel Metcalfe; m. Charles William Congo 1969; one d.; ed. Royal Coll. of Art, London; Visiting Lecturer, Royal Acad. Schools 1985–; solo exhbns. include London 1960, 1963, 1967, 1989, 1995, 1998, Leeds 1964, Billingham/Middlesbrough 1973, Harrogate 1979, retrospective touring exhbn. 1982–83, Milton Keynes 1982, Sheffield 1982, Bradford 1982, 1989, Leicester and Hull 1983, 1987, Wakefield 1988, Birmingham 1994, Halifax (retrospective) 1996; numerous group exhbns.; works in collections including Imperial War Museum, London, Arts Council of England, Sheffield Graves, Belfast Art Gallery, Leeds Univ., Middlesbrough Art Gallery, Miny Works, Royal Acad. and Royal Coll. of Art Collections, Wakefield, Carlisle, Bolton and Rochdale Galleries, Univ. of Birmingham, St. Peter's Oxford, Chatsworth House, The Vatican, Rome, and pvt. collections in Europe, U.S.A., Canada and Australia; works commissioned by Imperial War Museum, B.A.O.R. 1984, Lambeth Palace and The Vatican 1989, Univ. Centre Birmingham 1994; Rowney Drawing Prize 1984, Eastern Arts Drawing Prize 1984, 1989, Lorne Award 1987. *Publications:* drawings for collection of poems by James Kirkup 1993, short story by Fay Weldon 1995. *Address:* c/o Royal Academy of Arts, Burlington House, Piccadilly, London, W1A 0DS, England. *Telephone:* 0171-300 5680 (Royal Acad.); (01525) 850687 (Studio). *Fax:* 0171-300 5812.

LAWSON OF BLABY, Baron (Life Peer), cr. 1992, of Newnham in the County of Northamptonshire; **Nigel Lawson,** M.A., P.C.; British politician; b. 11 March 1932, London; s. of Ralph and Joan (née Davis) Lawson; m. 1st Vanessa Salmon (dissolved 1980); m. 2nd Thérèse Mary Maclear 1980; two s. four d. (one deceased); ed. Westminster School and Christ Church, Oxford; Sub Lieut., R.N.V.R. 1954–56; mem. editorial staff, Financial Times 1956–60; City Ed. Sunday Telegraph 1961–63; Special Asst. to Prime Minister 1963–64; Financial Times columnist and BBC broadcaster 1965; Ed. The Spectator 1966–70; regular contributor to Sunday Times and Evening Standard 1970–71, The Times 1971–72; Fellow, Nuffield Coll., Oxford 1972–73; Special Political Adviser, Conservative Party HQ 1973–74; M.P. for Blaby, Leics. 1974–92; Opposition Whip 1976–77; Opposition spokesman on Treasury and Econ. Affairs 1977–79; Financial Sec. to the Treasury 1979–81; Sec. of State for Energy 1981–83, Chancellor of the Exchequer 1983–89; Dir. (non-exec.) Barclays Bank 1990–98; Chair. Cen. Europe Trust 1990–, CAIB Emerging Russia Fund 1997–; Adviser BZW 1990–91; Dir. (non-exec.) and Consultant Guinness Peat Aviation (GPA) 1990–93; Dir. Inst. for Int. Econs., Wash. 1991–; mem. Int. Advisory Bd. Creditanstalt Bankverein 1991–, TOTAL S.A. 1994–, Advisory Council Prince's Youth Business Trust 1994–; Pres. British Inst. of Energy Econs. 1995–; Finance Minister of the Year, Euromoney Magazine 1988; Hon. Student Christ Church, Oxford 1996. *Publications:* The Power Game (with Jock Bruce-Gardyne) 1976, The View from No. 11: Memoirs of a Tory Radical 1992, The Nigel Lawson Diet Book (with Thérèse Lawson) 1996, and various pamphlets. *Address:* House of Lords, London, SW1A 0PW, England.

LAWZI, Ahmed Abdel Kareem al–; Jordanian politician; b. 1925, Jubeiha, nr. Amman; m.; ed. Teachers' Training Coll., Baghdad, Iraq.; Teacher, 1950–53; Asst. to Chief of Royal Protocol 1953–56; Head of Ceremonies, Ministry of Foreign Affairs 1957; mem. Parl. 1961-62, 1962-63; Asst. to Chief of Royal Court 1963–64; Minister of State, Prime Minister's Office 1964–65; mem. Senate 1965, 1967; Minister of the Interior for Municipal and Rural Affairs April-Oct. 1967; Minister of Finance 1970–71; Prime Minister 1971–73; Pres. Nat. Consultative Council 1978–79; various Jordanian and foreign decorations. *Address:* c/o Ministry of Foreign Affairs, Amman, Jordan.

LAX, Melvin, PH.D.; American physicist; b. 8 March 1922, New York; s. of Morris Lax and Rose Hutterer; m. Judith Heckelman 1949; two s. two d.; ed. New York Univ. and Mass. Inst. of Tech.; Research Physicist M.I.T. 1942–45, Research Assoc. 1947; Prof. of Physics, Syracuse Univ. 1947–55; Consultant Naval Research Lab. 1951–55; lecturer in Physics Princeton Univ. 1961, Oxford Univ. 1961–62; mem. Tech. Staff Bell Labs. 1955–72, Head Theoretical Physics Dept. 1962–64, Consultant 1972–; Consultant Army Research Office 1972–, Los Alamos Science Lab. 1975–; Distinguished Prof. City Coll. of New York 1971–; Ed. Advanced Series in Applied Physics 1988–; mem. Publs. Tech. Cttee. of Optical Soc. of America 1992–94; Charles Hayden Scholar New York Univ.; Fellow American Physical Soc.; mem. N.A.S. 1989–92, 1995–98. *Publications:* Scattering and Radiation from Circular Cylinders and Spheres (with M. Morse, A. N. Lowan and H. Feshbach) 1946, Elementary Nuclear Theory (contrib.) 1947, Fluctuations and Coherence Phenomena in Classical and Quantum Physics (in Statistical Physics, Vol. 2) 1968, Symmetry Principles in Solid State and Molecular Physics 1974, and articles in journals. *Leisure interest:* tennis. *Address:* Department of Physics, City College, 138th Street and Convent Avenue, New York, NY 10031 (Office); 12 High Street, Summit, NJ 07901, U.S.A. (Home). *Telephone:* (212) 650-6864 (Office); (201) 273-6188 (Home). *Fax:* (212) 650-6940.

LAX, Peter D., PH.D.; American mathematician; b. 1 May 1926, Budapest, Hungary; s. of Henry Lax and Klara Kornfeld; m. Anneli Cahn 1948; two s.; ed. New York Univ.; with Los Alamos Scientific Lab., Manhattan Project 1945–46; Asst. Prof., New York Univ. 1951, Prof. 1957–, Dir. AEC Computing and Applied Math. Center 1964–72, Courant Inst. of Math. Sciences 1972–80, Courant Math. and Computing Lab. 1980–; Fulbright Lecturer in Germany 1958; Visiting Lecturer, Oxford Univ. 1969; Pres. American Math. Soc. 1969–71, 1978–80; mem. American Acad. of Arts and Sciences, N.A.S., American Philosophical Soc.; Foreign Assoc. French Acad. of Sciences, Academia Sinica, Hungarian Acad. of Sciences; mem. Nat. Science Bd. 1980–86; Foreign mem. Soviet (now Russian) Acad. of Sciences 1989; 8 hon. degrees; Chauvenet Prize, Math. Asscn. of America 1974, Norbert Wiener Prize, American Math. Soc. and Soc. of Industrial and Applied Math. 1975, Nat. Medal of Science 1986, Wolf Prize 1987, Steele Prize, American Math. Soc. *Publications:* papers in learned journals. *Address:* Courant Institute of Mathematics, New York University, 251 Mercer Street, New York, NY 10012, U.S.A.

LAY, Kenneth L., M.A., PH.D.; American business executive; b. 1942, Missouri; s. of Omer Lay and Ruth Lay; m. Linda Lay; five c.; ed. Univs. of Missouri and Houston; corp. economist, Exxon Co. 1965; subsequent man. positions; Pres. Continental Resources Co. (fmrly. Florida Gas Co.) and Exec. Vice-Pres. Continental Group 1974–79; Pres. and C.O.O. Transco Energy Co. 1981–84; Chair. and C.E.O. Houston Natural Gas Corpn. 1984–85; Chair. and C.E.O. Enron Corpn. 1985–; mem. Bd. Dirs Eli Lilly & Co., Trust Co. West, Compaq Computer Corpn.; mem. Bd. Trustees The John Heinz III Center for Science, Econs. and the Environment, The Business Council, American Enterprise Inst.; Guggenheim Fellow; Pvt. Sector Council Leadership Award 1997, Horatio Alger Award 1998. *Publications:* articles in books and journals. *Leisure interests:* skiing, running, golf. *Address:* Enron Corporation, P.O. Box 1188, Houston, TX 77002, U.S.A. *Telephone:* (713) 853-3129.

LAYARD, Peter Richard Grenville, B.A., M.SC.; British economist; b. 15 March 1934, Welwyn Garden City; s. of John Willoughby Layard and Doris Layard; m. Molly Meacher 1991; ed. Cambridge Univ., London School of Economics; school teacher, London County Council 1959–61; Sr. Research Officer, Robbins Cttee. on Higher Educ. 1961–64; Deputy Dir. Higher Educ. Research Unit, L.S.E. 1964–74, lecturer, L.S.E. 1968–75, Reader 1975–80, Prof. of Econ. 1980–, Dir. Centre for Econ. Performance 1990–, Head, Centre for Labour Econ. 1974–90; Consultant, Centre for European Policy Studies, Brussels 1982–86; mem. Univ. Grants Cttee. 1985–89; Chair. Employment Inst. 1987–92; Co-Chair., World Economy Group of the World Inst. for Devt. Econs. Research 1989–; Econ. Adviser to Russian Govt. 1991–97; Fellow Econometric Soc. *Publications:* Cost Benefit Analysis 1973, Causes of Poverty (with D. Piachaud and M. Stewart) 1978, Microeconomic Theory (with A. A. Walters) 1978, More Jobs, Less Inflation 1982, The Causes of Unemployment (Ed. with C. Greenhalgh and A. Oswald) 1984, The Rise in Unemployment (Ed. with C. Bean and S. Nickell) 1986, How to Beat Unemployment 1986, Handbook of Labor Economics (Ed. with Orley C. Ashenfelter) 1987, The Performance of the British Economy (jtly.) 1988, Unemployment: Macroeconomic Performance and the Labour Market (jtly.) 1991, East-West Migration: the alternatives (jtly.) 1992, Post-Communist Reform: pain and progress 1993 (jtly.), Macroeconomics: a text for Russia 1994, The Coming Russian Boom 1996 (jtly.), What Labour Can Do 1997. *Leisure interests:* walking, tennis. *Address:* Centre for Economic Performance, London School of Economics, Houghton Street, London, WC2A 2AE (Office); 45 Cholmeley Park, London, N6 5EL, England (Home). *Telephone:* 0171-955 7281 (Office).

LAYNE, Kingsley, B.A.; Saint Vincent and Grenadines civil servant and diplomatist; b. 1949; ed. Univ. of the West Indies, Univ. of British Columbia, Inst. for Applied Behavioural Sciences; economist, Ministry of Trade, Agric. and Tourism 1973–74; Sr. Official, Econ. Affairs Secr., Org. of Eastern Caribbean States, St. John's, Antigua 1982–86; Perm. Sec., Ministry of Trade, Agric. and Industry 1986–87, Tourism, Aviation and Culture 1987–89, Trade and Tourism 1989–90; Perm. Rep. of Saint Vincent and Grenadines to UN, New York 1990–94. *Publications:* several publs. on staff devt. and man. training. *Address:* c/o Ministry of Foreign Affairs, Kingstown, Saint Vincent and the Grenadines.

LAYNIE, Tamrat; Ethiopian politician; mem. Ethiopian People's Revolutionary Democratic Front (EPRDF); Prime Minister of Ethiopia 1991–95. *Address:* c/o Office of the Prime Minister, P.O. Box 1013, Addis Ababa, Ethiopia.

LAZAR, Philippe; French scientist and administrator; b. 21 April 1936, Paris; s. of Maximilien Lazar and Françoise Lazar; m. Monique Lazar 1960; one s. one d.; ed. Ecole Polytechnique, Paris; researcher, Nat. Inst. of Hygiene 1960, Dir. of Research INSERM (French Nat. Inst. of Health and Medical Research) 1964, Dir. Environmental Health Research Unit 1977, Chair. Scientific Council 1981, Dir.-Gen. INSERM 1982–96; Chair. European Medical Research Councils (EMRC) 1994–96; Visiting Prof. Harvard School of Public Health 1975; Officier de l'Ordre Nat. du Mérite; Officier, Légion d'honneur; Chevalier, Ordre des Arts et des Lettres. *Publications:* Eléments de probabilités et statistiques 1967, Méthodes statistiques en expérimentation biologique 1974, Les explorateurs de la santé 1989, L'éthique biomédicale en question 1995. *Leisure interests:* arts, literature. *Address:* INSERM, U155 Château de Longchamp, Bois de Boulogne, 75016 Paris, France. *Telephone:* (1) 44-23-60-60.

LAZARENKO, Pavel Ivanovich; Ukrainian politician; b. 23 Jan. 1953, Karpovka, Dniepropetrovsk Region, Ukraine; m.; one s. two d.; ed. Dniepropetrovsk Inst. of Agric.; worked as agronomist, chair. of kolkhoz, Head Dist. Dept. of Agric. Man.; First Deputy Chair. Dist. Exec. Cttee.; Chair. Council of Agro-Industrial Complex Dniepropetrovsk Region, First Deputy Chair. Regional Exec. Cttee; Rep. Pres. of Ukraine in Dniepropetrovsk Region 1992–95; concurrently Chair. Dniepropetrovsk Regional State Admin.; First Vice-Prime Minister of Ukraine 1995–96; Prime Minister of Ukraine 1996–97; mem. Verkhovna Rada 1997–; charged with corruption 1999. *Address:* Verkhovna Rada, Hrushevskogo str. 5, 252012 Riiv, Ukraine.

LAZAREV, Alexander Nikolayevich; Russian conductor; b. 5 July 1945; m. Tamara Lazarev; one d.; ed. Leningrad and Moscow Conservatoires; conducting debut at Bolshoi Theatre 1973, conducted numerous ballets and operas of the Bolshoi Theatre's European and Russian repertoires, f. and conductor, Ensemble of Soloists of the Bolshoi Theatre 1978–89, Chief Conductor, Artistic Dir. Bolshoi Theatre 1987–95; Chief Conductor Duisburg Symphony Orchestra 1988–93; has conducted with numerous orchestras including Berlin Philharmonic, Munich Philharmonic, Orchestra Sinfonica del Teatro alla Scala di Milano, Orchestre Nat. de France and others; UK debut with Royal Liverpool Philharmonic Orchestra 1987; subsequently performed with the City of Birmingham Symphony Orchestra, the Royal Scottish Nat. Orchestra, etc.; Prin. Guest Conductor BBC Symphony Orchestra, 1992–95, Royal Scottish Nat. Orchestra 1994–97, Prin. Conductor 1997–; First Prize U.S.S.R. Nat. Competition 1971, First Prize and Gold Medal Karajan Competition (Berlin) 1972. *Address:* c/o Tennant Artists, Unit 2, 39 Tadema Road, London, SW10 0PY, England. *Telephone:* 0171-376 3758 (London); 095-203-2636 (Moscow). *Fax:* 0171-351 0679.

LAZENBY, Alec, A.O., SC.D., F.T.S.E., F.I.BIOL., F.A.I.A.S.T.; Australian agronomist and university administrator; b. 4 March 1927, U.K.; s. of G. and E. Lazenby; m. Ann J. Hayward 1957; one s. two d.; ed. Univ. Coll. of Wales and Univ. of Cambridge; Scientific Officer, Welsh Plant Breeding Station 1949–53; Demonstrator, Agricultural Botany, Univ. of Cambridge 1953–58, Lecturer in Agricultural Botany 1958–65, Fellow and Asst. Tutor, Fitzwilliam Coll. 1962–65; Foundation Prof. of Agronomy, Univ. of New England, N.S.W. 1965–70, Vice-Chancellor 1970–77; Dir. Grassland Research Inst. 1977–82; Visiting Prof. Reading Univ. 1978–82; Hon. Professorial Fellow, Univ. of Wales 1979–82; Vice-Chancellor, Univ. of Tasmania 1982–91; Prin. Consultant Int. Devt. Programme of Australian Univs. (IDP) 1991–; Hon. D.Rur. Sci. (New England) 1981; Hon. Prof. (Vic. Univ. of Tech.) 1992; Hon. LL.D. (Univ. of Tasmania) 1992. *Publications:* Intensive Pasture Production (Jt. Ed.) 1972, Australian Field Crops (Jt. Ed.), Vol I 1975, Vol. II 1979, Australia's Plant Breeding Needs 1986, The Grass Crop (Jt. Ed.) 1988; papers on pasture plant breeding, agronomy and weed ecology in various scientific journals. *Leisure interests:* golf, gardening and current affairs. *Address:* International Development Program, GPO Box 2006, Canberra, A.C.T. 2601, Australia.

LAZUTKIN, Valentin Valentinovich, CAND. PHIL.; Russian politician and journalist; b. 10 Jan. 1945, Kraskovo, Moscow Region; m.; one s. one d.; ed. Moscow State Univ., Acad. of Social Sciences Cen. Cttee. CPSU; Head Div. of Press and Information Cttee. of Youth Orgs. 1967–73; Deputy Head, Head Dept. of Int. Relations, mem. Exec. Bd., Deputy Chair. U.S.S.R. State Cttee. on Radio and TV 1974–91; First Deputy Chair. 1991, Deputy Chair., Dir.-Gen. on int. relations Russian State TV-Radio Broadcasting Co. Ostankino 1991–93; First Deputy Chair. Feb.–Dec. 1993, First Deputy Head Russian Fed. Service on TV and Radio Broadcasting, concurrently Dir.-Gen. Russian State TV-Radio Broadcasting Co. Ostankino 1993–95; Head Russian Fed. Service on TV and Radio Broadcasting 1995-98. *Address:* Federal Service on TV and Radio, Pyatnitskaya str. 25, 113326 Moscow, Russia (Office). *Telephone:* (095) 233 6181 (Office).

LEA, Ruth Jane, B.A., M.SC., F.R.S.A., F.S.S.; British economist; b. 22 Sept. 1947; d. of Thomas Lea and Jane Lea (née Brown); ed. Lymm Grammar School, Univs. of York and Bristol; asst. statistician, Sr. Econ. Asst. H.M.

Treasury 1970–73, statistician 1977–78; lecturer in Econs. Thames Polytechnic 1973–74; statistician Civil Service Coll. 1974–77, Cen. Statistics Office 1978–84; briefing and policy posts Dept. of Trade and Industry 1984–88; with Mitsubishi Bank 1988–93, Chief Economist 1990–93; Chief UK Economist Lehman Brothers 1993–94; Econs. Ed. Ind. TV News 1994–95; Head of Policy Unit Inst. of Dirs. 1995–; mem. Retail Prices Advisory Cttee. 1992–94, Nat. Consumer Council 1993–96, Rowntree Foundation Income and Wealth Inquiry Group 1993–94, Nurses' Pay Review Body 1994–, Research Centres Bd. ESRC 1996, Research Priorities Bd. 1996–97, Statistics Advisory Cttee. Office of Nat. Statistics 1996–97; Hon. D.B.A. (Greenwich) 1997. *Leisure interests:* music (singing), philately, cat worship. *Publications:* various publs. for the Inst. of Dirs. on business and econ. topics. *Address:* Policy Unit, The Institute of Directors, 116 Pall Mall, London, SW1Y 5ED (Office); 25 Redbourne Avenue, Finchley, London, N3 2BP, England (Home). *Telephone:* 0171-451 3291 (Office); 0181-346 3482 (Home). *Fax:* 0171-839 2337 (Office); 0181-346 3482 (Home).

LEACH, Admiral of the Fleet Sir Henry (Conyers), G.C.B., D.L.; British naval officer; b. 18 Nov. 1923; s. of Capt. John Catterall Leach and Evelyn Burrell Lee; m. Mary Jean McCall 1958 (died 1991); two d.; ed. St. Peter's Court, Broadstairs, Royal Naval Coll., Dartmouth; served cruiser Mauritius, S. Atlantic and Indian Ocean 1941–42; battleship Duke of York (involved in Scharnhorst action) 1943–45, destroyers, Mediterranean 1945–46, gunnery 1947; gunnery appointments 1948–51; Gunnery Officer, cruiser Newcastle, Far East 1953–55; staff appointments 1955–59; commanded destroyer Dunkirk 1959–61; frigate Galatea (Capt. 27th Squadron and Mediterranean) 1965–67; Dir. of Naval Plans 1968–70; commanded Commando Ship Albion 1970; Asst. Chief of Naval Staff (Policy) 1971–73; Flag Officer First Flotilla 1974–75; Vice-Chief of Defence Staff 1976–77; C.-in-C. Fleet and Allied C.-in-C., Channel and Eastern Atlantic 1977–79; Chief of Naval Staff and First Sea Lord 1979–82; First and Prin. Naval ADC to the Queen 1979–82; Pres. R.N. Benevolent Soc., Sea Cadet Asscn. 1984–93; Vice-Pres. Royal Bath & West of England Soc.; Chair. St. Dunstan's 1983–98, Council, King Edward VII Hosp. 1987–98, Hon. Vice-Pres. 1998–; Gov. Cranleigh School 1983–93, St. Catherine's 1987–93; Patron Meridian Trust Asscn., Hampshire Royal British Legion 1994–; Hon. Freeman Merchant Taylors, Shipwrights, City of London. *Leisure interests:* fishing, gardening, antique furniture repair. *Address:* Wonston Lea, Wonston, Winchester, Hants., SO21 3LS, England.

LEAF, Alexander, M.D.; American physician; b. 10 April 1920, Yokohama, Japan; s. of Dr. Aaron L. and Dora Hural Leaf; m. Barbara L. Kincaid 1943; three d.; ed. Univs. of Washington and Michigan; Intern, Mass. Gen. Hosp. 1943–44, mem. staff 1949–, Physician-in-Chief 1966–81, Physician 1981–; Resident, Mayo Foundation, Rochester, Minn. 1944–45; Research Fellow, Univ. of Mich. 1947–49; mem. Faculty, Medical School, Harvard Univ. 1949–, Jackson Prof. of Clinical Medicine 1966–81, Ridley Watts Prof. of Preventive Medicine 1980–90, Jackson Prof. of Clinical Medicine Emer., 1990–; Visiting Fellow, Balliol Coll., Oxford 1971–72; Distinguished Physician, Brockton/West Roxbury Medical Center, Va. 1992–97; mem. N.A.S., A.A.A.S., American Acad. of Arts and Sciences, American Coll. of Physicians, The Biochemical Soc. (U.K.), Inst. of Medicine 1978 etc.; Kober Medal, Asscn. of American Physicians 1995, A. M. Richards Award, Int. Soc. of Nephrology 1997. *Publications:* 300 articles in professional journals; Significance of the Body Fluids in Clinical Medicine, Youth in Old Age, Renal Pathophysiology. *Leisure interests:* music (flautist), jogging. *Address:* One Curtis Circle, Winchester, MA 01890, U.S.A. (Home). *Telephone:* (617) 729-5852.

LEAHY, Sir John H. G., K.C.M.G., M.A.; British diplomatist (retd); b. 7 Feb. 1928, Worthing, Sussex; s. of the late William H. G. Leahy and Ethel Leahy; m. Elizabeth Anne Pitchford 1954; two s. two d.; ed. Tonbridge School, Clare Coll., Cambridge, Yale Univ.; joined diplomatic service 1951, Third Sec., Singapore 1955–57; Second Sec., then First Sec., Paris 1958–62; First Sec., Teheran 1965–68; Counsellor, Paris 1973–75; attached to Northern Ireland Office, Belfast 1975–76; Amb. to South Africa 1979–82; Deputy Under-Sec. (Africa and the Middle East), FCO 1982–84; High Commr. to Australia 1984–88; Dir. Observer newspaper 1989–92; Dir. (non-exec.) Lonrho PLC 1993–98, Chair. 1994–97; Master, Skinners' Co. 1993–94; Chair. Britain-Australia Soc. 1994–97; mem. Franco-British Council (Chair. 1989–93); Chair. Govs.' Cttee. Tonbridge School; Pro-Chancellor City Univ. 1991–97; Hon. D.C.L. (City Univ.) 1997; Officier, Légion d'honneur. *Address:* Manor Stables, Bishopstone, Near Seaford, E. Sussex, BN25 2UD, England.

LEAHY, Patrick Joseph, J.D.; American politician and lawyer; b. 31 March, 1940, Montpelier, Vt.; s. of Howard and Alba (Zambon) Leahy; m. Marcelle Pomerleau 1962; two s. one d.; ed. St. Michael's Coll., Winooski, Vt., and Georgetown Univ. Law Center, Washington, D.C.; admitted to practise law, State of Vermont 1964, U.S. Supreme Court, Second Circuit Court of Appeals, New York, U.S. Fed. Dist. Court of Vt.; Senator from Vermont 1975–; Vice-Chair. Senate Intelligence Cttee. 1985–86; mem. Vt. Bar Asscn. 1964–; Vice-Pres. Nat. Dist. Attorneys' Asscn. 1971–74; Distinguished Service Award of Nat. Dist. Attorneys' Asscn. 1974. *Leisure interests:* photography, reading, hiking, cross country skiing. *Address:* 433 Russell Senate Office Building, Washington, DC 20510, U.S.A. (Office).

LEAKEY, Richard Erskine Frere, F.R.A.I.; Kenyan palaeontologist; b. 19 Dec. 1944, Nairobi; s. of the late Louis Leakey and of Mary Leakey (q.v.); m. Meave Gillian Epps 1970; three d.; ed. the Duke of York School, Nairobi; leader of expeditions to West Natron, Tanzania 1963, 1964, Baringo, Kenya 1966, Omo River, Ethiopia 1967 and East Rudolf, Kenya 1968–70; researcher on Origin of Man, Lake Turkana 1971–76, Bulok 1980, Rusinga Island 1983–84, W. Turkana 1984–85; Admin. Dir. Nat. Museums of Kenya 1968–74, Dir. 1974–89; mem. Museum Bd. of Govs.; Trustee, Nat. Fund for the Disabled; Chair. East African Wildlife Soc. 1985–; Dir. Wildlife and Conservation Man. Service 1989–90; Chair. Wildlife Clubs of Kenya 1969–84, Kenya Exploration Soc. 1969–72, Foundation for Research into Origin of Man (U.S.A.), Trustee Foundation for Social Habilitation, Rockford Coll., Callman Memorial Foundation; Dir. and Exec. Chair. Kenya Wildlife Service 1990–94 (Chair. 1989–93, 1998–); co.-f., Sec.-Gen. Safina Party 1995–; M.P. –1999; Man. Dir. Richard Leakey & Assocs. wildlife consultancy 1994–; Franklin Burr Prize 1965, 1973; Hon. D.Sc. (Wooster Coll.) 1978, (Rockford Coll.) 1984, (Bristol) 1996, Hon. D.Litt. (Kent) 1987; Golden Ark Medal for Conservation 1989. *Publications:* numerous articles on finds in the field of palaeontology in scientific journals, including Nature, Journal of World History, Science, American Journal of Physics and Anthropology, etc.; contrib. to General History of Africa (vol. I), Perspective on Human Evolution, and Fossil Vertebrates of Africa; Origins (book, with Roger Lewin), People of the Lake: Man, His Origins, Nature and Future (book, with Roger Lewin) 1979, The Making of Mankind (also TV Series) 1981, Human Origins 1982, One Life 1984, Origins Reconsidered (with R. Lewin) 1992, The Origin of Humankind 1994, The Sixth Extinction (with Roger Leuni) 1996. *Leisure interests:* sailing and cooking. *Address:* P.O. Box 24926, Nairobi, Kenya (Home).

LEALOFI IV, Chief Tupua Tamasese; Samoan politician and doctor; b. 8 May 1922, Apia; m. Lita 1953; five c.; ed. Fiji School of Medicine and postgraduate studies at Suva; Medical practitioner 1945–69; succeeded to Paramount Chief (Tama-a-Aiga) of Tupua Tamasese 1965; mem. Council of Deputies 1968–69; mem. Legis. Ass. 1970; Prime Minister of Western Samoa 1970–73, 1975–76; Minister of Internal and External Dist. Affairs, Labour and Audit, Police and Prisons 1975–76. *Leisure interests:* reading, golf. *Address:* Legislative Assembly, Apia, Samoa.

LEAR, Evelyn, American soprano; b. 8 Jan. 1926, Brooklyn, New York; d. of Nina Quartin; m. 2nd Thomas Stewart (q.v.); one s. one d. by previous marriage; ed. New York Univ., Hunter Coll., Juilliard Opera Workshop; Fulbright Scholarship for study in Germany 1957; joined Berlin Opera, début in Ariadne auf Naxos 1959; début in U.K. in Four Last Songs with London Symphony Orchestra 1957; début at Metropolitan Opera in Mourning Becomes Electra 1967; début at La Scala, Milan, in Wozzeck 1971; regular performances with leading opera cos. and orchestras in Europe and U.S.A.; guest appearances with Berlin Opera and Vienna State Opera; soloist with the leading American orchestras including New York Philharmonic, Chicago Symphony, Philadelphia Orchestra, Boston Symphony, San Francisco Symphony and Los Angeles Philharmonic, has given many recitals and orchestral concerts and operatic performances with Thomas Stewart; Concert Artists Guild Award 1955. *Major roles include:* Marie in Wozzeck, Marschallin in Der Rosenkavalier, Countess in The Marriage of Figaro, Fiordiligi in Così fan tutti, Desdemona, Mimi, Dido in The Trojans, Donna Elvira in Don Giovanni, Marina in Boris Godunov, Tatiana in Eugene Onegin, Lavinia in Mourning Becomes Electra, title role in Lulu; appeared in film Buffalo Bill 1976. *Recordings include:* Wozzeck, Lulu, The Flying Dutchman, The Magic Flute, Boris Godunov, Eugene Onegin, Bach's St. John Passion, Pergolesi's Stabat Mater, Der Rosenkavalier. *Leisure interests:* reading, teaching, golf. *Address:* 414 Sailboat Circle, Lauderdale, FL 33326, U.S.A.

LEATHER, Sir Edwin Hartley Cameron, LL.D., K.C.M.G., K.C.V.O.; British politician and administrator; b. 22 May 1919, Toronto, Canada; s. of Harold H. Leather and Grace C. Leather; m. Sheila A. A. Greenlees 1940 (died 1994); two d.; ed. Trinity Coll. School, Royal Mil. Coll., Kingston, Canada; M.P. for N. Somerset 1950–64; mem. Exec. Cttee. British Commonwealth Producers' Asscn. 1960–63, British Caribbean Asscn.; Chair. Horder Centres for Arthritics 1962–65, Nat. Union of Conservative and Unionist Asscns. 1970–71; Canadian Rep. Exec. Cttee., British Commonwealth Ex-servicemen's League 1954–63; Chair. Bath Festivals Soc. 1960–65; with Yehudi Menuhin School and Orchestra 1965–, mem. Bd. of Dirs. 1967–, Deputy Chair. 1967–73; Gov. of Bermuda 1973–77; Chair. United World Colls. Cttee. of Bermuda; Nat. Gov. Shaw Festival of Canada 1990–; Trustee Canadian Gurkha Welfare Asscn. 1990–, Menuhin Foundation of Bermuda 1975–; Dir. N. M. Rothschild (Bermuda), and other cos.; Past Grand Warden, Grand Lodge of England, Past Grand Registrar, Grand Lodge of Canada (Ont.); Hon. Fellow, Royal Soc. of Arts 1968; Hon. Bachelor of Mil. Science (R.M.C. of Canada) 1974; Hon. LL.D. (Bath) 1975; Nat. Inst. Social Sciences Gold Medal 1977; K.St.J. 1974. *Publications:* The Vienna Elephant, The Mozart Score, The Duveen Letter. *Leisure interests:* music, travel, reading. *Address:* 23 Inwood Drive, Paget, Bermuda. *Telephone:* (441) 236-0240.

LÉAUD, Jean-Pierre; French film actor; b. 5 May 1944, Paris; s. of Pierre Léaud and Jacqueline Pierreux; début as Antoine Doinel in Truffaut's The 400 Blows 1959, first of a series of Doinel films dir. by Truffaut over 20 years. *Films include:* The 400 Blows 1959, Le Chinoise, Weekend, Stolen Kisses, Le Gai Savoir, Last Tango in Paris, Masculin Féminin, Love on the Run 1978, Detective 1984, Virgin 1987, The Color of the Wind, Femme de Papier, Bunker Palace Hotel, I Hired a Contract Killer 1991, Paris at Dawn, The Birth of Love.

LEAVER, Sir Christopher, G.B.E., K.ST.J., J.P.; British business executive; b. 3 Nov. 1937, London; s. of Dr Robert Leaver and Audrey Kerpen; m.

Helen Mireille Molyneux Benton 1975; one s. two d.; ed. Eastbourne Coll.; commissioned Royal Army Ordnance Corps 1956–58; mem. Retail Food Trades Wages Council 1963–64; J.P., Inner London 1970–83, City 1974–93; mem. Council, Royal Borough of Kensington and Chelsea 1970–73; Court of Common Council (Ward of Dowgate), City of London 1973, Sheriff, City of London 1979–80; Lord Mayor of London 1981–82; Chair. London Tourist Bd. Ltd. 1983–89; Deputy Chair. Thames Water PLC 1989–93, Chair. 1993–94, Vice-Chair. 1994–; Bd. of Brixton Prison 1975–78; Adviser to Sec. of State on Royal Parks 1993–96; Bd. of Govs., City Univ. 1978–; Gov. Christ's Hospital School 1975, City of London Girls' School 1975–78; Chair. Young Musicians' Symphony Orchestra Trust 1979–81, Eastbourne Coll.; Trustee, London Symphony Orchestra 1983–91; Chancellor, City Univ. 1981–82; Vice-Pres. Nat. Playing Fields Asscn.; Church Commr. 1982–93, 1996–; Hon. Col. 151 Regt. RCT(V) 1983–89, Hon. Col. Commdt. RCT 1988–91; Dir. (non-exec.) Unionamerica Holdings 1994–97; Trustee, Chichester Festival Theatre 1982–97; Hon. Liveryman, Farmers' Co.; Hon. Freeman Co. of Water Conservators; Freeman Co. of Watermen and Lightermen; Fellow, Chartered Inst. of Transport; Order of Oman. *Leisure interests:* gardening, music, travel. *Address:* Thames Water PLC, 14 Cavendish Place, London, W1M 0NU, England. *Telephone:* 0171-636 8686.

LEAVER, Christopher John, B.SC., M.A., PH.D., D.I.C., A.R.C.S., F.R.S.E., F.R.S.; British professor of plant sciences; b. 31 May 1942, Bristol; s. of Douglas P. Leaver and Elizabeth C. Leaver; m. Anne Huggins 1971; one s. one d.; ed. Imperial Coll. of Science, London; Fulbright Scholar, Purdue Univ., Ind., U.S.A. 1966–68; Scientific Officer, ARC Unit of Plant Physiology, Imperial Coll. London 1968–69; Lecturer, Univ. of Edinburgh 1969–80, Reader 1980–86, Science and Engineering Research Council Sr. Research Fellow, 1985–89, Prof. of Plant Molecular Biology 1986–89; Sibthorpian Prof. of Plant Sciences 1990–, Head of Dept., Univ. of Oxford 1991–; Nuffield Commonwealth Bursary, Sr. Visiting Fellowship (S.E.R.C), CSIRO Div. of Plant Industry, Canberra 1975; EMBO Long-term Fellowship, Biozentrum, Basle 1980; Trustee, John Innes Foundation, Norwich 1984–, Nat. History Museum, London 1997–; mem. Council, Agric. and Food Research Council 1990–93; mem. Ministry of Agric., Fisheries and Food Priorities Bd. 1990–93; mem. editorial bd. of several int. scientific journals.; mem. Royal Soc. Council 1992–94; mem. European Molecular Biology Org. (Council mem. 1992–97, Chair. 1996–97), Advisory Council on Science and Tech. 1992–93, Council Biochemical Soc. (Chair. N.A. & M.B. Group); Chair. Advisory Bd. IACR, Rothamsted; mem. Acad. Europaea; Fellow, St. John's Coll., Oxford; Huxley Gold Medal, Imperial Coll. 1970; Tate & Lyle Award, Phytochemical Soc. of Europe 1984, Humboldt Prize 1997. *Publications:* Ed. several books; numerous papers in int. scientific journals. *Leisure interests:* walking and talking in Upper Coquetdale. *Address:* Department of Plant Sciences, University of Oxford, South Parks Road, Oxford, OX1 3RB, England. *Telephone:* (01865) 275143. *Fax:* (01865) 275144.

LEAVER, Peter Lawrence Oppenheim, Q.C.; British lawyer and football executive; b. 28 Nov. 1944; s. of Marcus Isaac Leaver and Lena (née Oppenheim) Leaver; m. Jane Rachel Pearl 1969; three s. one d.; ed. Aldenham School, Elstree, Trinity Coll., Dublin; called to Bar Lincoln's Inn 1967, Recorder 1994–, Bencher 1995; Chief Exec. Football Asscn. Premier League 1997–; Chair. Bar Cttee. 1989; Chair. Int. Practice Cttee. 1990; mem. Cttee. on Future of the Legal Profession 1986–88, Council of Legal Ed. 1986–91, Gen. Council of the Bar 1987–90; Dir. Investment Man. Regulatory Org. 1994–. *Leisure interests:* sport, theatre, wine. *Address:* 1 Essex Court, Temple, London, EC4Y 9AR (Office); 5 Hamilton Terrace, London, NW8 9RE, England (Home). *Telephone:* 0171-583 2000 (Office); 0171-286 0208 (Home).

LEAVEY, Thomas Edward, M.A., PH.D.; American international postal official; b. 10 Nov. 1934, Kansas City, Mo.; m. Anne Roland 1968; ed. Josephinum Coll. Columbus, Ohio, Inst. Catholique, Paris and Princeton Univ.; Prof. Farleigh Dickinson Univ. Teaneck, N.J. and George Washington Univ. Washington, D.C. 1968–70; various man. and exec. positions in U.S. Postal Services, Los Angeles, Chicago and Washington D.C. 1970–87; Asst. Postmaster-Gen. Int. Postal Affairs, USPS H.Q. 1987–94; Chair. Exec. Council, Universal Postal Union (UPU) 1989–94; Dir.-Gen. Int. Bureau of UPU 1995–; John Wanamaker Award 1991, Heinrich von Stephan Medal. *Leisure interests:* golf, tennis. *Address:* Universal Postal Union, International Bureau, Postfach, 3000 Berne 15, Switzerland (Office).

LEAVITT, Michael Okerlund; American politician and insurance executive; b. 11 Feb. 1951, Cedar City, Utah; s. of Dixie Leavitt and Anne Okerlund; m. Jacalyn Smith; four s. one d.; ed. S. Utah Univ.; Sales rep. Leavitt Group, Cedar City 1972–74, Account Exec. 1974–76; Man. Underwriting, Salt Lake City 1976–82, C.O.O. 1982–84, Pres. and C.E.O. 1984–; mem. Bd. Dirs. Pacificorp, Portland, Ore., Utah Power and Light Co. Salt Lake City, Great Western Thrift & Loan, Salt Lake City; mem. staff, Reagan-Bush '84; Gov. of Utah 1993–; Republican. *Leisure interest:* golf. *Address:* Office of the Governor, 210 State Capitol Building, Salt Lake City, UT 84114, U.S.A.

LEBED, Lieut.-Gen. Aleksander Ivanovich; Russian army officer; b. 20 April 1950, Novocherkassk; m.; two s. one d.; ed. Ryazan Higher School of Airborne Troops, M. Frunze Mil. Acad.; platoon, then Co. Commdr. Ryazan Higher Airborne Troops Commanding School 1973–81; Bn. Commdr. in Afghanistan 1981–82; Regimental Commdr. 1985–86; Deputy Commdr. Airborne Troops Formation 1986–88; Commdr. Tula Airborne Troops Div. 1989–92; stood guard with bn. of paratroopers at bldg. of Supreme Soviet during attempted coup of Aug. 1991; Deputy Commdr. Airborne Troops and Mil. Educ. Inst. 1991–92; Commdr. 14 Russian Army in self-proclaimed "Pridniestr Repub." 1992–94; Deputy Chair. Nat. Council, Congress of Russian Communities 1995–96; mem. State Duma (Parl.) 1995–96; cand. Pres. election 1996; Sec. Security Council of Russia June–Oct. 1996; started negotiations with Chechen separatist leaders; discharged by Pres. Yeltsin; founder Russian People's Republican Party; Gov. Krasnoyarsk Territory; mem. Council of Fed. 1998–; awarded several mil. orders. *Publication:* It is a Pity for the Power 1995, My Life and My Country 1997, Ideology of Common Sense 1997. *Address:* House of Administration, Mira prospect 110, 660009 Krasnoyarsk, Russia. *Telephone:* (3912) 22-22-63. *Fax:* (3912) 22-11-75.

LEBED, Aleksey Ivanovich; Russian politician; b. 14 April 1955, Novocherkassk, Rostov Region; m.; one s. one d.; ed. Ryazan Higher School of Airborne Troops; mil. service in Afghanistan 1982; took part in mil. operations in different parts of U.S.S.R. 1980–92; regt. commdr., 14th Army in Chişinău 1992, resgnd. 1995; mem. State Duma 1995–96; Head of Govt. Repub. of Khakassia 1996–; mem. Council of Feds. of Russia 1996–; mem. Congress of Russian Communities. *Address:* House of Government, Lenina str. 67, 662600 Abakan, Russia. *Telephone:* (39022) 991 02 (Office). *Fax:* (39022) 650 96 (Office).

LEBEDEV, Aleksander Yevgenyevich; Russian banker; b. 16 Dec. 1959; m.; one s.; ed. Moscow Inst. of Int. Relations; on staff Inst. of Econs. of World Socialist System U.S.S.R. Acad. of Sciences 1984–91; Chair. of Bd. Russian Investment Finance Co. 1993–; Chair. of Bd. Nat. Reserve Bank 1995–. *Address:* National Reserve Bank, 1st Breskaya str. 29, 125047 Moscow, Russia (Office). *Telephone:* (095) 250 8612 (Office).

LEBEGUE, Daniel Simon Georges, B.L.; French banker; b. 4 May 1943, Lyon; s. of Robert Lebegue and Denise (née Flachet) Lebegue; m. Chantal Biron 1970; one s. one d.; ed. Univ. of Lyons, Inst. for Political Sciences and Nat. School for Admin., Paris; civil servant, Ministry of Economy and Finance 1969–73; Financial Adviser, Embassy in Japan 1974–76; Head of Balance of Payments Section, Treasury 1976–79, Head of Monetary Funds Section 1979–80; Deputy Dir. of Savings and Financial Market 1980–81; Counsellor in charge of Economy and Finance, Prime Minister's Office 1981–83; Head of Dept. of Financial and Monetary Affairs at Treasury 1983–84, Head of Treasury 1984–87; Pres. and C.O.O. Banque Nat. de Paris 1987–96, Vice-Chair. 1996–97; C.O.O. Caisse des dépôts et consignations 1997–; Prof., Inst. for Political Sciences, Paris; Pres. Finance Comm., Asscn. française des banques (AFB) 1988–, BNPI 1997–; Dir. CDC Marchés, CDC Participations, CDC Projets, Dexia France, Dexia Belgique, Crédit local de France, Crédit communal de Belgique, Thomson CSF; Chevalier Légion d'honneur, Chevalier Ordre Nat. du Mérite. *Publications:* Le Trésor et la politique financière 1988, La fiscalité de l'épargne dans le marché unique européen 1988. *Leisure interests:* opera, cinema, hiking. *Address:* Caisse des dépôts et consignations, 56 rue de Lille, 75356 Paris (Office); 25 rue de Bourgogne, 75007 Paris, France (Home).

LEBER, Georg; German politician and trade unionist; b. 7 Oct. 1920, Obertiefebach; s. of Jakob Leber and Elisabeth (née Geis) Leber; m. Erna Maria Wilfing 1942 (died 1984); one s.; m. 2nd Katja Grüttner; ed. primary and commercial schools in Limburg (Lahn); soldier 1939–45; joined trade union and Social Democrat Party (SPD) 1947; trade union leader, Limburg 1949; Chair. of local branch of SPD 1951; Ed. Der Grundstein (trade union paper) 1952; mem. Man. Cttee. Bau-Steine-Erden Trade Union 1953–57, Chair. 1957; mem. Man. Cttee. Fed. of German Trade Unions 1957; mem. Man. Cttee. of Int. Federation of Building and Timber Workers and Pres. Jt. Cttee. of Trade Unions of Building and Timber Trade in European Common Market 1957; mem. Bundestag 1957–82; mem. European Parl. 1958–59; mem. Man. Cttee. SPD Faction in Bundestag 1961, mem. Presidium 1968; Fed. Minister of Transport 1966–69, of Transport, Posts and Telecommunications 1969–72, of Defence 1972–78; Vice-Pres. German Bundestag 1979–82; Dr. h.c. (Tübingen) 1980; Grosses Bundesverdienstkreuz mit Stern und Schulterband; Ludger-Westrick Preis 1983, Theodor-Heuss-Preis 1985, Freiherr von Stein-Preis 1987. *Address:* Krennstrasse 41, 83471 Schönau, Germany.

LE BLANC, Bart, PH.D.; Netherlands banker; b. 4 Nov. 1946, 's Hertogenbosch; s. of Christian Le Blanc and Johanna Bogaerts; m. Gérardine van Lanschot; one s. two d.; ed. Leiden and Tilburg Univs.; Special Adviser, Prime Minister's Office, Deputy Sec. to Cabinet 1973–79; Deputy Dir.-Gen. for Civil Service at Home Office 1979–80; Dir.-Gen. for Budget at Treasury 1980–83; Deputy Chair. Man. Bd. F. van Lanschot Bankiers NV, 's Hertogenbosch 1983–91; Sec.-Gen. EBRD 1991–94, Vice-Pres., Finance 1994–98; Dir. Int. Finance, Caisse des Dépôts et Consignations, Paris 1998–; Hon. Prof. Tilburg Univ. 1991–; Kt., Order of Netherlands Lion. *Publications:* books and contribs. on econ. and fiscal policy to nat. and int. journals. *Leisure interest:* farming in France. *Address:* 56 Rue de Lille, Paris (Office); La Feuillaie, 62170 Wailly Beaucamp, France (Home). *Telephone:* (3) 21.86.82.47.

LEBLANC, Rt. Hon. Roméo A., P.C., C.C., C.M.M., C.D.; Canadian Governor General; b. 18 Dec. 1927, L'Anse-aux-Cormier, Memramcook, N.B.; s. of Philias and Lucie LeBlanc; m. Diana Fowler; four c.; ed. St-Joseph and Paris Univs.; teacher, Drummond High School, N.B. 1951–53, N.B. Teachers'

Coll., Fredericton 1955–59; corresp., Radio-Canada, Ottawa 1960–62, U.K. 1962–65, U.S.A. 1965–67; Press Sec. to Prime Minister Lester Pearson 1967–68, to Prime Minister Pierre Trudeau 1968–71; Asst. to Pres. and Dir. of Public Relations, Université de Moncton 1971–72; M.P. for Westmorland-Kent 1972–84; Minister of Fisheries 1974–76, of Fisheries and the Environment 1976–79, of Fisheries and Oceans 1980–82, of Public Works 1982–84; Senator, Beauséjour, New Brunswick 1984–95, Speaker 1993–95; Gov. Gen. of Canada and C.-in-C. Feb. 1995–; Visiting Scholar, Inst. of Canadian Studies, Carleton Univ., Ottawa 1985–86; Founding Pres. CBC/Radio-Canada Corresps.' Asscn. 1965; mem. Canada-France Parl. Asscn.; 5 hon. degrees 1979. *Address:* Rideau Hall, 1 Sussex Drive, Ottawa, Ont., K1A 0A1, Canada. *Telephone:* (613) 993-8200.

LEBLOND, Charles Philippe, O.C., L. ÈS S., M.D., PH.D., D.SC., F.R.S.C., F.R.S.; Canadian professor of anatomy; b. 5 Feb. 1910, Lille, France; s. of Oscar Leblond and Jeanne Desmarchelier; m. Gertrude Elinor Sternschuss 1936; three s. one d.; ed. Univs. of Lille, Paris, Montreal and the Sorbonne; Asst. in Histology, Medical School, Univ. of Paris 1934–35; Rockefeller Fellow, School of Medicine, Yale Univ. 1936–37; Asst. Laboratoire de Synthèse Atomique, Paris 1938–40; lecturer in Histology and Embryology, McGill Univ. 1942–43, Asst. Prof. of Anatomy 1943–46, Assoc. Prof. 1946–48, Prof. of Anatomy 1948–, Chair. Dept. of Anatomy 1957–75; Fellow Royal Soc. of Canada, Royal Soc. (London); mem. American Asscn. of Anatomists, Canadian Asscn. of Anatomists, American Soc. for Cell Biology, Histochemical Soc., Soc. for Experimental Biology and Medicine, and others; Hon. D.Sc. (Acadia, McGill, Montreal, York, Sherbrooke Univs.); Prix Saintour, French Acad. 1935; Flavelle Medal, Royal Soc. of Canada 1961, Gairdner Fed. Award 1965, American Coll. of Physicians Award 1966, Province of Quebec Biology Prize 1968, American Soc. for Cell Biology, E. B. Wilson Award 1982, Marie-Victorin Prize 1992. *Publications:* The Use of Radioautography in Investigating Protein Synthesis (with K. B. Warren) 1965, and over 300 articles in scientific journals. *Leisure interests:* history, gardening. *Address:* 68 Chesterfield Avenue, Westmount, Quebec, H3Y 2M5, Canada. *Telephone:* (514) 398-6340.

LEBOUDER, Jean-Pierre; Central African Republic politician; b. 1944; ed. Ecole nationale supérieure agronomique, Toulouse, France; Dir. Research Centre, Union cotonnière centrafricaine 1971–72, Dir.-Gen. 1974–76; Minister of Rural Devt. 1976, of Planning, Statistics and Int. Co-operation 1978–80; Prime Minister 1980–81. *Address:* c/o Office du Premier Ministre, Bangui, Central African Republic.

LEBOWITZ, Joel L., M.S., PH.D.; American professor of mathematics and physics; b. 10 May 1930, Taceva, Czechoslovakia; m. Estelle Mandelbaum 1953 (died 1996); ed. Brooklyn Coll. and Syracuse Univ.; Nat. Science Foundation Postdoctoral Fellow, Yale Univ. 1956–57; Asst. Prof. Stevens Inst. of Tech. 1957–59; Asst. Prof. Belfer Grad. School of Science, Yeshiva Univ. 1959–60, Assoc. Prof. 1960–65, Prof. of Physics 1965–77, Chair. Dept. of Physics 1968–76; Dir. Center for Mathematical Sciences Research and Prof. of Math. and Physics, Rutgers Univ. 1977–; mem. N.A.S., A.A.A.S., New York Acad. of Sciences, American Physical Soc., IUPAP; Dr. h.c. (Ecole Polytechnique Fédérale, Lausanne); Boltzmann Medal 1992, Max Planck Research Award 1993, Delmar S. Fahrney Medal, Franklin Inst. 1994, A.A.A.S. Scientific Freedom and Responsibility Award 1999 and other distinctions. *Publications:* 350 scientific papers. *Address:* Centre for Mathematical and Scientific Research, Busch Campus-Hill Center, Rutgers University, New Brunswick, NJ 08903, U.S.A. *Telephone:* (201) 932-3117.

LEBRANCHU, Marylise; French university lecturer and politician; b. 25 April 1947, Loudéac (Côtes d'Armor); d. of Adolphe Perrault Lebranchu and Marie Epert; m.; three c.; responsible for research, Nord-Finistère Semi-public Co. 1973–78; joined Parti Socialiste Unifié (PSU) 1972, Parti Socialiste (PS) 1977; Parl. Asst. to Marie Jacq 1978–93; municipal councillor, Morlaix (Finistère) 1983, Mayor 1995–97; regional councillor 1986–; Nat. Ass. Deputy for Morlaix Constituency 1997–; Minister of State attached to Minister for the Economy, Finance and Industry, with responsibility for small and medium-sized enterprises, trade and artisan activities 1997–; Jr. Lecturer in Econs. applied to town and country planning, Univ. of Brest 1990–. *Leisure interest:* music. *Address:* Secrétariat d'Etat aux Petites et Moyennes enterprises, au Commerce et à l'Artisanat, 80 rue de Lille, 75700 Paris, France.

LEBRAT, Jean Marcel Hubert; French engineer; b. 21 Jan. 1933, Levallois/Seine; s. of Marcel Lebrat and Simone Landré; m. Andrée Blaize 1956; two s.; ed. Coll. de Mirecourt, Lycée Henri Poincaré, Nancy and Ecole spéciale des travaux publics; head of office of studies of navigation service of Saint-Quentin 1956–59; head of office of studies of construction service of canal from the North to Compiègne 1959–63; eng. Etablissement Public pour l'Aménagement de La Défense (Epad) 1963–68, asst. to head of highway div. Epad 1968–70; divisional eng. 1970; Asst. Tech. Dir. Soc. d'Aménagement des Halles (Semah) 1970–79, Tech. Dir. 1979–83, Dir. 1984–89; Pres. Etablissement public du Grand Louvre 1989–; Engineer of bridges and roads 1995, Engineer-Gen. 1995–; Chevalier, Légion d'honneur, Officier, Ordre Nat. du Mérite. *Leisure interests:* drawing, tennis, water sports. *Address:* Etablissement public du Grand Louvre, 153 rue Saint-Honoré, 75001 Paris (Office); 23 rue de Bourgogne, 75007 Paris, France (Home).

LE BROCQUY, Louis, D.LITT., LL.D., H.R.H.A., F.S.I.A.D.; Irish artist; b. 10 Nov. 1916, Dublin; s. of the late Albert le Brocquy and Sybil de Lacy Staunton; m. 1st Jean Atkinson Stoney 1938, one d.; m. 2nd Anne Madden-Simpson 1958, two s.; ed. St. Gerard's School, Wicklow; founder mem., Irish Exhbn. of Living Art 1943; Visiting Instructor, Cen. School of Arts and Crafts, London 1947–54; Visiting Tutor, R.C.A., London 1955–58; mem. Irish Council of Design 1963–65; Dir. Kilkenny Design Workshops 1965–77; Dir. Irish Museum of Modern Art 1989–94; exhibits in Albright Knox Museum, Buffalo, Carnegie Inst., Pittsburgh, Detroit Inst., Hirshhorn Museum, Washington, Kunsthaus, Zürich, Guggenheim Museum, New York, Musée Picasso, Antibes, Uffizi Gallery, Florence, Columbus Museum, Ohio, San Diego Museum, Tate Gallery, London; retrospective exhbns.: Fondation Maeght, 1973, Musée d'Art Moderne, Paris 1976, New York State Museum 1981, Boston Coll. 1982, Palais des Beaux Arts, Charleroi 1982, Arts Council, Dublin 1987, Ulster Museum 1987, aegis Nat. Gallery of Victoria, Melbourne, Festival Centre, Adelaide, Museum of Contemporary Art, Brisbane 1988, Musée Picasso, Antibes 1989, Museum of Modern Art, Kamakura, City Museum of Art, Osaka, City Museum of Contemporary Art, Hiroshima 1990, Irish Museum of Modern Art, Dublin 1996, Espace Ricard 1996, Galerie Maeght, Paris 1996, Château Musée de Tours 1997; illustrated The Tain (trans. Kinsella) 1969, The Playboy of the Western World (Synge) 1970, The Gododdin (trans. O'Grady) 1978, Dubliners (Joyce) 1986, Stirrings Still (Samuel Beckett) 1988; Premio Prealpina, Venice Biennale 1956; Commdr. du Bontemps de Médoc et des Graves 1969; Chevalier, Légion d'honneur; Officier, Ordre des Arts et des Lettres. *Address:* c/o Gimpel Fils, 30 Davies Street, London, W1Y 1LG, England.

LE BRUN, Christopher Mark, M.A., D.F.A., R.A.; British artist; b. 20 Dec. 1951, Portsmouth; s. of John Le Brun and Eileen B. Le Brun (née Miles); m. Charlotte Verity 1979; two s. one d.; ed. Portsmouth Southern Grammar School, Slade School of Fine Art and Chelsea School of Art; Visiting Lecturer, Brighton Polytechnic 1975–82, Slade School of Fine Art 1978–83, Wimbledon School of Art 1981–83; one-man exhbns. Nigel Greenwood Inc., London 1980, 1982, 1985, 1989, Gillespie-Laage-Salomon, Paris 1981, Sperone Westwater, New York 1983, 1986, 1988, Fruitmarket Gallery, Edinburgh 1985, Arnolfini Gallery, Bristol 1985, Kunsthalle Basel 1986, D.A.A.D. Gallery, Berlin 1988, Rudolf Zwirner, Cologne 1988, Marlborough Fine Art, London 1994, 1998, Astrup Fearnley Museum of Modern Art, Oslo 1995, Fitzwilliam Museum, Cambridge 1995, Art Center, Pasadena 1992; has participated in group exhbns. in U.K., Europe, Japan and U.S.A. including Venice Biennale 1982, 1984, Zeitgeist Berlin 1982; work in several public collections including Tate Gallery, London and Museum of Modern Art, New York; Trustee Tate Gallery 1990–95, Nat. Gallery 1996–; maj. comms. include Liverpool Anglican Cathedral 1996; Gulbenkian Printmakers Award 1983, D.A.A.D. Award, W. Berlin 1987–88 and other prizes. *Address:* c/o Marlborough Fine Art, 6 Albemarle Street, London, W1X 4BY, England.

LEBRUN MORATINOS, H.E. Cardinal José Alí; Venezuelan ecclesiastic; b. 19 March 1919, Puerto Cabella, Valencia, Venezuela; ordained priest 1943; Titular Bishop of Arado 1956, Bishop of Maracay 1958–62, of Valencia 1962–80; given title of Archbishop 1972; Archbishop of Caracas 1980; cr. Cardinal 1983. *Address:* c/o Arzobispado, Plaza Bolívar, Apartado 954, Caracas 1010-A, Venezuela.

Le CARRÉ, John (see Cornwell, David John Moore).

LECAT, Jean-Philippe; French politician; b. 29 July 1935, Dijon; s. of Jean Lecat and Madeleine Bouchard; m. Nadine Irène Romm 1965; two d.; ed. Ecole Nationale d'Administration; mem. Council of State 1963–66, 1974, Auditor 1963–; Chargé de Mission, Prime Minister's Office 1966–68; Deputy to the Nat. Ass., Beaune 1968–72, 1973, 1978–81; Nat. Del. for Cultural Affairs, Union des Démocrates pour la République 1970–71, Asst. Sec.-Gen. for Cultural Affairs and Information 1971–72; Spokesman of the Govt. 1972–73; Sec. of State for Econ. 1973–74; Minister of Information 1973–74, of Culture and Communication 1978–81; mem. Bourgogne Regional Council 1973–; Del. to Natural Resources Conservation Conf. 1975; Chargé de Mission, Pres. of Repub. 1976–78, and Spokesman of the Pres. 1976–81, Conseiller d'Etat 1988; Pres. Amis de Mozart Asscn. 1987, Admin Council Ecole Nat. du Patrimoine 1990–, Admin. Council Acad. of France in Rome (Villa Medici) 1996; Special Adviser to Pres. Thomson Consumer Electronics 1991 (later Thomson Multimedia 1994–97); Pres. Acad. de France, Rome 1996–; Chevalier, Légion d'honneur, Officier, Order nat. du Mérite, Commdr., Arts et Lettres; Grand Prix Nat. awarded by Minister of Culture 1996. *Publications:* Quand flamboyait la Toison d'or 1982, Beaune 1983, La Bourgogne 1985, Le siècle de la Toison d'or 1986, Bourgogne 1989, l'Ardeur et le tourment 1989. *Address:* Conseil d'Etat, 1 place du Palais-Royal, 75100 Paris (Office); 131 boulevard du Général Koenig, 92200 Neuilly-sur-Seine, France (Home).

LECERF, Olivier Maurice Marie; French industrialist; b. 2 Aug. 1929, Merville-Franceville; s. of Maurice and Colette (Lainé) Lecerf; m. Annie Bazin de Jessey 1958; two s. two d.; ed. Univ. of Paris, Centre d'Etudes Industrielles, Geneva; joined Ciments Lafarge 1956, marketing and man. responsibilities in Brazil and Canada 1956–65; Vice-Pres. Canada Cement Lafarge 1965–71; Vice-Chair. and Gen. Man. Ciments Lafarge 1973–74, Chair. and C.E.O. 1974–82; Vice-Chair. and C.O.O. Lafarge S.A. 1983, Chair. and C.E.O. 1984–89, Hon. Chair. 1989–; Dir. Compagnie de Saint-Gobain, L'Oreal; Officier, Légion d'honneur, Commandeur, Ordre nat. du Mérite. *Publication:* Au risque de gagner (jtly.) 1991. *Leisure interest:* tennis. *Address:* 61–63 rue des Belles Feuilles, 75116 Paris (Office); 8 rue Guy de Maupassant, 75116 Paris, France (Home). *Telephone:* (01) 44-34-11-03 (Office).

LECHÍN OQUENDO, Juan; Bolivian politician and diplomatist; b. 1915; fmr. professional footballer; fmr. Minister of Mines; Pres. Bolivian Mine Workers' Confed.; fmr. Pres. of Senate; Vice-Pres. of Repub. 1960–64; Amb. to Italy 1962–63; exiled May 1965; fmr. Leader, Left Sector of Movimiento Nacionalista Revolucionario (MNR); sought asylum in Chile June 1967; Exec. Sec. Cen. Obrera Boliviana 1952–65, 1970, 1982–86; re-elected Exec. Sec. Fed. Sindical de Trabajadores Mineros de Bolivia 1970.

LECHÍN SUÁREZ, Gen. Juan; Bolivian army officer; b. 8 March 1921, Cochabamba; s. of Juan Alfredo Lechín and Julia Suárez de Lechín; m. Ruth Varela de Lechín 1947; one s. three d.; ed. Bolivian Military Acad., General Staff Coll. (Fort Leavenworth), U.S.A.; Chief of Operations, Bolivian Army H.Q.; Mil. and Air Attaché Bolivian Embassy Fed. Repub. of Germany; Commdr. 5th Infantry Div. (Bolivian); Pres. Bolivian Mining Corpn. and Minister of State; Commdr. 3rd Infantry Div. (Bolivian); Amb. to U.K., also accred. to Netherlands 1969–74; Minister for Planning and Co-ordination to the Pres. 1974–78; Chair. Nat. Advisory and Legis. Council 1980; mem. Bolivian Acad. of History 1990–, Bolivian Acad. of Mil. History 1991–; Cóndor de los Andes (Bolivia), Grosses Verdienstkreuz (Fed. Repub. of Germany), Guerrillero José M. Lanza, Mérito Aeronáutico, Mérito Naval (Bolivia). *Publications:* La Batalla de Villamontes - Ensayo crítico, Estrategia del Altiplano Boliviano and essays on military history and geo-politics. *Address:* Casilla 4405, La Paz, Bolivia.

LECLANT, Jean, D. ÈS L.; French professor of Egyptology; b. 8 Aug. 1920, Paris; s. of René Leclant and Laure Pannier; m. Marie-Françoise Alexandre-Hatvany 1988; ed. Ecole Normale Supérieure, Paris and Inst. Français d'Archéologie Orientale, Cairo; Prof. Univ. of Strasbourg 1953–63, Sorbonne 1963–79, Coll. de France (Chair. of Egyptology) 1979–90 (Hon. Prof. 1990–); Dir. of Studies, Ecole Pratique des Hautes Etudes (Vème Section) 1963–90; Perm. Sec. Acad. des Inscriptions et Belles Lettres (Inst. de France) 1983–; annual excavations Egypt, especially Karnak 1948–, Saqqarah 1963–; mem. Inst. Français in Cairo 1948–52; led archaeological expedition, Ethiopia 1952–56; Pres. Soc. Française d'Egyptologie; mem. Acad. des Sciences d'Outre-Mer and many other learned socs. in France and abroad; Dr. h.c. (Leuven, Bologna); Commdr., Légion d'honneur; Commdr. Ordre du Mérite; Commdr. Ordre des Palmes Académiques; Commdr. Ordre des Arts et Lettres; Chevalier du Mérite Militaire; Imperial Order of Menelik (Ethiopia), Grand Officier ordre de la Répub. d'Egypte. *Publications:* Karnak-Nord IV (jtly.) 1954, Dans les Pas des Pharaons 1958, Montouemhat, Prince de la Ville 1963, Soleb I, Soleb II (Jt. Ed.) 1966, 1971, Kition II (jtly.) 1976, La culture des chasseurs du Nil et du Sahara, 2 vols. (with P. Huard) 1980, and about 1,000 articles, etc. *Address:* 77 rue Georges Lardennois, Paris 75019; 23 quai de Conti, Paris 75006, France. *Telephone:* (01) 43.26.96.75; (01) 44.41.43.10. *Fax:* (01) 44.41.43.11.

LECLERC, Edouard; French business executive; b. 20 Nov. 1926, Landerneau; s. of Eugène Leclerc and Marie Kerouanton; m. Hélène Diquélou 1950; one s. two d.; ed. seminaries in Paris, Uriage-les-Bains and Saint-Cirgues; pioneer of Leclerc supermarket chain (first opened Landerneau) 1949–, more than 600 branches; Pres. Asscn. nat. des centres Leclerc 1960–; Chevalier, Ordre Nat. du Mérite. *Publications:* Ma vie pour un combat, la Part du bonheur 1976, Combat pour la distribution, Le soleil de l'Ouest. *Leisure interests:* archaelogy, writing. *Address:* 11 rue Bélerit, 29800 Landernau (Office); La Haye-Saint-Divy, P.O. Box 733, 29207 Landerneau, France (Home).

Le CLÉZIO, Jean Marie Gustave; French/British writer; b. 13 April 1940, Nice; m. 1st Rosalie Piquemal 1961; one d.; m. 2nd Jemia Jean 1975; ed. Lycée and Univ. de Nice; travelled in Nigeria 1948, England (studied at Bristol and London Univs.), U.S.A. 1965; Chevalier des Arts et des Lettres, Légion d'honneur; Prix Renaudot 1963, Grand Prix Paul Morand (Acad. française) 1980, Grand Prix Jean Giono 1997, Prix Prince de Monaco 1998. *Publications:* Le procès-verbal (The Interrogation) 1963, La fièvre (Fever) (short stories) 1965, Le procès 1965, Le déluge 1966, L'extase matérielle (essay) 1967, Terra amata (novel) 1967, Le livre des fuites 1969, La guerre 1970, Haï 1971, Conversations 1971, Les géants 1973, Mydriase 1973, Voyages de l'autre côté 1975, Les prophéties du Chylam Balam 1976, Mondo et autres histoires, L'inconnu sur la terre 1978, Désert 1980, Trois villes saintes 1980, La ronde et autres faits divers 1982, Journal du chercheur d'or 1985, Voyage à Rodrigues 1986, Le rêve mexicain (essay) 1988, Printemps et autres saisons 1989, Sirandanes, Suivi de Petit lexique de la langue créole et des oiseaux (jtly.) 1990, Onitsha 1991, Etoile errante 1992, Diego et Frida 1993, La Quarantaine 1995, Le Poisson d'or 1997, La Fête chantée 1997. *Address:* c/o Editions Gallimard, 5 rue Sébastien-Bottin, 75007 Paris, France.

LECONTE, Patrice; French film director; b. Tours; ed. Inst. des Hautes Etudes Cinématographiques; directing debut with Les Vécés Etaient Fermés de l'Intérieur; other films include: Monsieur Hire, Le Mari de la Coiffeuse 1990, Tango 1993, Ridicule 1996; also some 20 film advertisements a year including commercials for cos. such as Peugeot and Carlsberg beer.

LECOURT, Robert, D. EN D.; French politician and lawyer; b. 19 Sept. 1908, Pavilly; s. of Léon and Angèle (née Lépron) Lecourt; m. Marguerite Chabrerie 1932; one d.; ed. Coll. Saint-Jean-Baptiste-de-la-Salle, Rouen, and Law Faculty, Caen; Lawyer, Court of Appeal, Rouen 1928–32, Paris 1932–73; mem. Comité directeur du mouvement Résistance 1942–45, L'Assemblée consultative provisoire 1944–45; mem. two Constituent Assemblies 1945–46, Nat. Assembly 1946–58; Minister of Justice 1948–49, 1957–58; concerned with Constitutional Reform 1957–58; Minister of State for Overseas Relations 1959–61; Judge, European Court of Justice 1962–76, Pres. 1967–76; mem. Constitutional Council 1979–89; Hon. Bencher, Gray's Inn; Hon. Dr. (Exeter); Commdr., Légion d'honneur, Croix de guerre, Grand Cross of Belgium, Luxembourg, Fed. Repub. of Germany, Italy, Yugoslavia, Gabon, Madagascar and others. *Publications:* Le juge devant le Marché commun 1970, L'Europe des juges 1976, Concorde sans concordat 1978. *Address:* 11 boulevard Suchet, 75016 Paris, France (Home).

LE COUTEUR, Kenneth James, M.A., PH.D. (CANTAB.), F.A.A.; British academic; b. 16 Sept. 1920, Jersey, C.I.; s. of the late P. Le Couteur and E. Le Couteur; m. Enid Domville 1950; three d.; ed. Victoria Coll., Jersey and Cambridge Univ.; Scientific Officer Ministry of Aircraft Production 1941–45; Fellow St. John's Coll., Cambridge 1945–48; Turner and Newall Fellow, Manchester Univ. 1947–49; Sr. Lecturer and Reader Univ. of Liverpool 1949–56; Prof. of Theoretical Physics, Inst. of Advanced Studies, Australian Nat. Univ. 1956–85, Prof. Emer. 1985–. *Publications:* scientific articles. *Leisure interests:* fishing, sailing. *Address:* Unit 3, Ginnindera Gardens, 23 Burkitt Street, Page, A.C.T. 2614, Australia. *Telephone:* (02) 6254 1221.

LEDERBERG, Joshua, PH.D.; American geneticist; b. 23 May 1925, Montclair, N.J.; s. of Zwi H. and Esther Goldenbaum Lederberg; m. Marguerite Stein Kirsch 1968; one s. one d.; ed. Columbia and Yale Univs.; U.S.N. 1943–45; Research Fellow Yale Univ. 1946–47; Prof. of Genetics Univ. of Wis. 1947–59; Prof. of Genetics, Biology and Computer Science Stanford Univ. School of Medicine 1959–78; Pres. Rockefeller Univ., New York City 1978–90, Sackler F. Scholar 1990–; Sr. Fellow Center for Int. Security, Stanford Univ. 1998–; Visiting Prof. Univ. of Calif. at Berkeley 1950; Fulbright Visiting Prof. Univ. of Melbourne 1957; Trustee and mem. numerous bds. and cttees.; mem. bd. Council on Foreign Relations, New York City; scientific adviser to several cos. especially in biotech.; mem. N.A.S.; Hon. Life Gov. New York Acad. of Sciences; Hon. mem. A.O.A.; Foreign mem. Royal Soc., London; Hon. Fellow New York Acad. of Medicine; Fellow A.A.A.S., American Philosophical Soc., American Acad. of Arts and Sciences; Founder-mem. Acad. Univ. des Cultures; numerous hon. degrees; Nobel Prize in Medicine (for studies on org. of the genetic material in bacteria) (with Beadle and Tatum) 1958; U.S. Nat. Medal of Science 1989; Commdr. Ordre des Arts et des Lettres. *Publications:* Emerging Infections 1992; numerous papers and articles in various scientific and lay publications. *Address:* Rockefeller University, 1230 York Avenue, Suite 400, New York, NY 10021, U.S.A. *Telephone:* (212) 327-7809.

LEDGER, Philip Stevens, C.B.E., M.A., MUS.B., LL.D., F.R.C.M., F.R.N.C.M., F.R.S.E., F.R.C.O.; British musician; b. 12 Dec. 1937, Bexhill-on-Sea, Sussex; s. of late Walter Stephen and of Winifred Kathleen Ledger (née Stevens); m. Mary Erryl Wells 1963; one s. one d.; ed. Bexhill Grammar School, King's Coll., Cambridge; Master of the Music, Chelmsford Cathedral 1962–65; Dir. of Music, Univ. of East Anglia 1965–73, Dean of School of Fine Arts and Music 1968–71; an Artistic Dir. Aldeburgh Festival of Music and Arts 1968–89, Vice-Pres. 1989–; Conductor, Cambridge Univ. Musical Soc. 1973–82; Dir. of Music and Organist, King's Coll., Cambridge 1974–82; Prin. Royal Scottish Acad. of Music and Drama 1982–; John Stewart of Rannoch Scholar in Sacred Music; Hon. mem. Royal Acad. of Music, Guildhall School of Music; Pres. Royal Coll. of Organists 1992–94; Pres. Inc. Soc. of Musicians 1994–95; Chair. Cttee. of Principals of Conservatoires 1994–98; Hon. Prof. Univ. of Glasgow 1993–98; Silver Medal of Worshipful Company of Musicians. *Publications:* (ed.) Anthems for Choirs 2 and 3 1973, Oxford Book of English Madrigals 1978, editions of Byrd, Handel and Purcell and carol arrangements. *Leisure interests:* swimming, theatre, membership of Sette of Odd Volumes. *Address:* The Royal Scottish Academy of Music and Drama, 100 Renfrew Street, Glasgow, G2 3DB, Scotland. *Telephone:* (0141) 332-4101. *Fax:* (0141) 332-8901.

LEDINGHAM, John Gerard Garvin; British professor of medicine; b. 19 Oct. 1929, London; s. of John Ledingham and Una C. Garvin; m. Dr Elaine Maliphant 1962; four d.; ed. Rugby School, New Coll. Oxford and Middx. Hosp. London; Registrar, Middx. Hosp. 1960–62; Sr. Registrar in Medicine, Westminster Hosp. 1962–64; Visiting Fellow, Col. Univ. New York 1965–66; Consultant Physician, United Oxford Hosps. 1966–74; May Reader in Medicine, Univ. of Oxford 1974–95, Prof. of Clinical Medicine 1989–95, Prof. Emer. 1995–, Dir. of Clinical Studies 1977–81, 1990–95; Fellow, New Coll. Oxford 1974–95, Emer. Fellow 1995–, Sub-Warden 1994–95, Hon. Clinical Dir. Biochemical and Clinical NMR Unit, Medical Research Council 1988–. *Publications:* Oxford Textbook of Medicine (co-ed.) 1983; contribs. to medical journals. *Leisure interests:* music, reading, golf. *Address:* 22 Hid's Copse Road, Cumnor Hill, Oxford, OX2 9JJ, England. *Telephone:* (01865) 862023.

LE DUC ANH, Gen; Vietnamese politician and army officer; b. 1 Dec. 1920, Thua Thien-Hue; mem. Dang Cong Sang Viet Nam (CP); led Viet Cong combat units during Viet Nam War; mem. CP Politburo, Secr.; fmr. Minister of Nat. Defence; Pres. of Viet Nam 1992–97. *Address:* c/o Office of the President, Hanoi, Viet Nam.

LEE, Allen Peng-Fei, O.B.E., B.S., J.P.; Chinese business executive; b. 24 April 1940, Chefoo; m. Maria Choi Yuen Ha; two s. one d.; ed. Univ. of Mich.; joined Lockheed Aircraft Ltd. 1966, Test Eng. Supervisor 1966–67, Test

Eng. Man. 1968–70; Eng. Operations Man. Fabri-Teck Ltd. 1967; Test Man. Ampex Ferrotec Ltd. 1970–72, Man. Dir. 1974–79; Gen. Man. Dataproducts Hong Kong Ltd. 1972–74; Man. Dir. Ampex World Operations SA 1979–83, Ampex Far East Operations 1983–; Dir., consultant Elec & Eltek Co. Ltd. 1984; Chair. Hong Kong Productivity Council 1982, Hong Kong Liberal Party; mem. Industry Devt. Bd. 1983, Hong Kong Gen. Chamber of Commerce (cttee. and council mem.), Fed. of Hong Kong Industries, Broadcasting Review Bd. 1984, Political Section of Preparatory Cttee. for Hong Kong Special Admin. Region (S.A.R.); Outstanding Young Persons of Hong Kong Award 1977. *Leisure interests:* fishing, swimming, tennis. *Address:* Liberal Party, Shun Ho Tower, 2/F, 24–30 Ice House Street, Central; Energy Plaza, Tsimshatsui East, Kowloon, Hong Kong Special Administrative Area, People's Republic of China. *Telephone:* 2869 6833 (Liberal Party). *Fax:* 2845 3671 (Liberal Party).

LEE, Christopher Frank Carandini; British actor, author and singer; b. 27 May 1922, London; s. of late Lieut.-Col. Geoffrey Trollope Lee and of Estelle Marie Carandini; m. Birgit Kroenke 1961; one d.; ed. Summer Fields Preparatory School, Wellington Coll.; served R.A.F. 1941–46; mentioned in despatches 1944; film industry 1947–; appeared in over 200 motion pictures; Officier, Ordre des Arts et des Lettres 1973; Commdr. St. John of Jerusalem 1997. *Films include:* Moulin Rouge 1953, The Curse of Frankenstein 1956, Tale of Two Cities 1957, Dracula 1958, The Hound of the Baskervilles 1959, The Mummy 1959, Rasputin the Mad Monk 1965, The Wicker Man 1973, The Three Musketeers 1973, The Private Life of Sherlock Holmes 1973, The Four Musketeers 1975, The Man With the Golden Gun 1975, To the Devil a Daughter 1976, Airport 77 1977, Return from Witch Mountain, 1977, How the West Was Won 1977, Caravans 1977, The Silent Flute 1977, The Passage 1978, 1941 1978, Bear Island 1978, The Serial 1979, The Salamander 1980, An Eye for an Eye, Goliath Awaits, Charles and Diana, The Last Unicorn, The Far Pavilions, The House of the Long Shadows, The Return of Captain Invincible, The Howling Z, Behind the Mask, Roadstrip, Shaka Zulu, Mio my Mio, The Girl, Un Métier du Seigneur, Casanova, The Disputation (TV), Murder Story, Round The World in 80 Days (TV), For Better, For Worse, Return of the Musketeers, Outlaws, Gremlins II 1989, Sherlock Holmes (U.S. TV), Rainbow Thief, L'Avaro (Italy), Wahre Wunde (German TV) 1990, Young Indy (TV) 1991, Cybereden 1991, Death Train 1992, The Funny Man 1993, Police Academy–Mission to Moscow 1993, A Feast at Midnight 1994, The Stupids 1995, Moses (TV) 1995, Jinnah 1997. *Publications:* Christopher Lee's Treasury of Terror, Christopher Lee's Archives of Evil 1975, Christopher Lee's The Great Villains 1977, Tall, Dark and Gruesome (autobiog.) 1977. *Leisure interests:* music, travel, golf. *Address:* c/o London Management, 2–4 Noel Street, London, W1V 3RB, England.

LEE, David Morris, PH.D.; American professor of physics; b. 20 Jan. 1931, Rye, N.Y.; s. of Marvin Lee and Annette (Franks) Lee; m. Dana Thorangkul 1960; two s.; ed. Harvard Univ., Univ. of Connecticut, Yale Univ.; served U.S. Army 1952–54; Instructor of Physics, Cornell Univ., Ithaca, N.Y. 1959–60, Asst. Prof. 1960–63, Assoc. Prof. 1963–68, Prof. 1968–97; James Gilbert White Distinguished Prof. of Physical Sciences 1997–; Visiting Scientist Brookhaven Nat. Lab., Upton, N.Y. 1966–67; Visiting Prof. Univ. of Fla., Gainesville 1974–75, 1994, Univ. of Calif. San Diego, La Jolla 1988; Visiting Lecturer, Peking Univ., Beijing, China 1981; Chair. Joseph Fourier Univ., Grenoble, France 1994; co-discoverer superfluid 3He, tricritical point of 3He-4He mixtures; co-observation of spin waves in spin polarized hydrogen gas; Fellow A.A.A.S.; mem. American Acad. of Arts and Sciences, N.A.S.; John Simon Guggenheim Fellow 1966–67, 1974–75; Japan Soc. for Promotion of Sciences Fellow 1977; Sir Francis Simon Memorial Prize, British Inst. of Physics 1976, Oliver Buckley Prize, American Physical Soc. 1981, shared Nobel Prize for Physics 1996. *Address:* Physics Department, Cornell University, Clark Hall, Ithaca, NY 14853, U.S.A.

LEE, David Tawei, PH.D.; Taiwanese government official; b. 15 Oct. 1949, Taipei; m.; one s. one d.; ed. Nat. Taiwan Univ., Univ. of Virginia; Man. Ed. Asia and the World Forum 1976–77; Staff Consultant Co-ordination Council for North American Affairs, Washington, D.C. 1982–88; Prin. Asst. to Minister of Foreign Affairs 1988–89; Adjunct Assoc. Prof. of Int. Politics, Grad. School of Social Science, Nat. Taiwan Normal Univ. 1988–93; Deputy Dir. Dept. of Int. Information Services, Govt. Information Office 1989–90; Deputy Dir. Dept. of N. American Affairs, Ministry of Foreign Affairs 1990–93; Assoc. in Research, Fairbank Center for E. Asian Research, Harvard Univ. 1993–96; Dir.-Gen. Taipei Econ. and Cultural Office, Boston 1993–96; Dir. Dept. of N. American Affairs, Ministry of Foreign Affairs March–Aug. 1996; Deputy Dir.-Gen. Govt. Information Office, Exec. Yuan 1996–97; Dir.-Gen. Govt. Information Office, Exec. Yuan and Govt. Spokesman May 1997–. *Address:* Government Information Office, 2 Tientsin Street, Taipei, Taiwan. *Telephone:* (2) 3228888. *Fax:* (2) 3568733.

LEE, Dong Chan; South Korean business executive; b. 5 Aug. 1922, Seoul; s. of Won Man Lee and Oui Mun Lee; m. Duck-Jin Shin 1944; one s. five d.; ed. Waseda Univ., Tokyo; Pres. Kyemyung Commercial Co., Ltd. 1960, Samkyung Corpn. 1964, Kolon Nylon Co. 1970, Kolon Polyeser Inc. 1971; Chair. Kolon Group 1977, Hanyang Investment and Finance Corpn. 1981, Council, Korean Employers' Orgs. 1989–, Beram Bank 1991; Pres. Korea Employers' Fed. 1982–, Korea Golf Asscn. 1985–; Order of Industrial Service Merit Goldtower; Dr. Econ. h.c. (Chung-Ang Univ.) 1988. *Leisure interests:* fishing, mountain-climbing, golf, oriental chess, drawing, calligraphy. *Address:* Korea Employers' Federation, Sungjee Building, 16th Floor, 538 Dohwa-dong, Mapo-ku, Seoul 121-743 (Office); 45 Mugyo-Dong, Jung-Gil, Seoul, Republic of South Korea (Home). *Telephone:* (02) 702-0614 (Office); (02) 778-8588 (Home). *Fax:* (02) 706-1059.

LEE, Edward Graham, Q.C., LL.M.; Canadian diplomatist and lawyer; b. 21 Nov. 1931, Vancouver, B.C.; s. of William C. Lee and Dorothy F. Graham; m. Beverly J. Saul 1955; three d.; ed. Univ. of British Columbia and Harvard Univ.; joined Canadian Dept. of External Affairs 1956; Second Sec. Djakarta 1959–61; Counsellor, London 1965–69; Dir. of Personnel, Dept. of External Affairs 1969–72, Legal Adviser 1973–75; Amb. to Israel 1975–79, to S. Africa 1982–86; Asst. Under-Sec. for U.S.A. Affairs 1979–82; Legal Adviser and Asst. Deputy Minister for Legal, Consular and Immigration, Dept. of External Affairs 1986–90; Amb. to Austria and Perm. Rep. to UN, Vienna 1990–93; Gov. IAEA 1990–93; Adjunct Prof. of Int. Law, Univ. of Ottawa 1993–; UN Observer, S.A. Elections 1994; lecturer, S.A. Ministry of Foreign Affairs 1994; Pres. Canadian Council on Int. Law 1994–96. *Publications:* numerous articles in Canadian legal journals. *Leisure interests:* golf, walking, reading, gardening. *Address:* 703 Chapman Boulevard, Ottawa, Ont., K1G 1T5, Canada.

LEE, Hermione, M.A., M.PHIL., F.R.S.L.; British academic; b. 29 Feb. 1948, Winchester; d. of Dr. Benjamin Lee and Josephine Lee; m. John Barnard 1991; ed. Univ. of Oxford; Instructor, Coll. of William and Mary, Williamsburg, Va. 1970–71; Lecturer, Dept. of English, Univ. of Liverpool 1971–77; Lecturer Dept. of English, Univ. of York 1977–87, Senior Lecturer 1987–90, Reader 1990–93, Prof. 1993–98; Goldsmiths' Chair of English Literature and Fellow New College, Oxford 1998–; Presenter of Book Four on Channel Four TV 1982–86; reviewer, broadcaster. *Publications:* The Novels of Virginia Woolf 1977, Elizabeth Bowen 1981, Philip Roth 1982, The Secret Self I 1985, and II 1987, The Mulberry Tree: Writings of Elizabeth Bowen 1986, Willa Cather: A Life Saved Up 1989, Virginia Woolf 1996. *Leisure interests:* reading, music, countryside. *Address:* New College, Oxford, OX1 3BN, England. *Telephone:* (01865) 79555.

LEE, Gen. Honkon; Korean diplomatist and army officer; b. 11 Dec. 1920, Kongjoo, Choong Chung Nam-Do, Korea; s. of Kidong Lee and Jinsil Ahn; m. Kwiran Lee 1946; two s. four d.; ed. Japanese Imperial Mil. Acad., Japanese Field Artillery School and U.S. Infantry School; Supt. Korean Mil. Acad. 1946–48; Mil. Attaché, Washington 1949; Commdg. Gen., Eighth Repub. of Korea Army Div. 1949–50, Third Army Corps 1950–51, First Army Corps 1952–54; UN Command Del. to Korean Armistice 1951–52; Chair. Jt. Chiefs of Staff 1954–56, Chief of Staff 1956–58; Nat. Pres. Korean Veterans Asscn. 1958–61; Amb. to Philippines 1961–62, to U.K. 1962–67 (also to Scandinavian countries, Iceland, Malta and African countries concurrently); Amb. at large 1967–69; Chair. President's Advisory Comm. on Govt. Admin. 1969; Chair. Korea Anti-Communist League 1976–; Chair. Korea-British Soc. 1978–; decorations from Republic of Korea, U.S.A., France, U.K., Greece and Vatican. *Publications:* Nation's Destination 1950, Free Opinion (monthly publ.) 1976–. *Leisure interests:* horse riding, reading, music appreciation.

LEE, Hyung-Koo; South Korean banker; b. 30 Aug. 1940; m. 1969; ed. Seoul Nat. Univ.; Deputy Dir. Planning and Man. Office, Budget Bureau, Econ. Planning Bd. (EPB) 1964; Sec. for Econ. Affairs, Presidential Secr. 1969–70; Dir. and Dir.-Gen. EPB 1971–81; Parvin Fellow, Woodrow Wilson School of Public Admin. Princeton Univ. 1978–79; Asst. Minister, Ministry of Finance 1982; Vice-Minister, Ministry of Construction 1986, Ministry of Finance 1988, EPB 1988; Gov. Korea Devt. Bank 1990–96. *Publications:* Economic Development in Korea, The Korean Economy, The Korean Economy Looks to the 21st Century. *Leisure interests:* golf, tennis. *Address:* 10-2, Kwanchol-dong, Chongro-ku, C.P.O. Box 28, Seoul, 110-111, Republic of Korea. *Telephone:* (02) 398-6114.

LEE, John Joseph, M.R.I.A.; Irish historian; b. 9 July 1942, Tralee; s. of Thomas P. Lee and Catherine Burke; m. Anne Marie Mitchell 1969; one s. two d.; ed. Franciscan Coll., Gormanston, Univ. Coll. Dublin, Inst. for European History, Mainz, Peterhouse, Cambridge; Admin. Officer, Dept. of Finance, Dublin 1963; Asst. in History, Univ. Coll. Dublin 1963–68; Research Fellow, Peterhouse, Cambridge Univ. 1968–70, Official Fellow, lecturer, Tutor 1970–74; Prof. of Modern History, Univ. Coll. Cork 1974–93, Prof. of History 1993–, Dean Faculty of Arts 1976–79, Vice-Pres. Univ. Coll. Cork 1982–85; Visiting Mellon Prof., Univ. of Pittsburgh, U.S.A. 1979, European Univ. Inst., Florence, Italy 1981; Guest Fellow, Austrian Acad. 1989; Eisenhower Fellow, U.S.A. 1989, Distinguished Visiting Prof. of World Peace, L.B.J. School, Univ. of Texas 1989–90; Visiting Sr. Parnell Fellow, Magdalene Coll., Cambridge 1992–93, Visiting Arbuthnot Fellow, Univ. of Edin. 1997; Visiting Prof. Glucksman Ireland House, New York Univ. 1996; Columnist Sunday Tribune 1996–; Chair. Irish Scholarships Exchange Bd. 1980–92, Irish Fulbright Comm. 1992–; mem. Irish Senate 1993–97; mem. British-Irish Parl. Body 1993–97; Donnelly Prize, American Conf. for Irish Studies 1990, Irish Life/Sunday Independent Arts Award 1990, Aer Lingus/Irish Times Prize for Literature 1991. *Publications:* The Modernization of Irish Society 1848–1918 1973, 1989, Labour in German Industrialisation, in Cambridge Economic History of Europe, VII 1978, Ireland 1912–1985: Politics and Society 1989, Europe and America in the 1990s (Jt. Ed.) 1991. *Leisure interests:* sport, reading. *Address:* Department of History, University College, Cork, Ireland. *Telephone:* 021-902685.

LEE, Kun Hee, M.B.A.; Korean business executive; b. 9 Jan. 1942, Utryung, Kyongnam; s. of Byung-Chull Lee and Doo Eul Park; m. Ra Hee-ong 1967;

four c.; ed. Waseda Univ. Tokyo and George Washington Univ.; Exec. Dir. Joong-Ang Daily News, Seoul 1968–78, Tong-Yang Broadcasting Corpn. Seoul 1968–78; Vice-Chair. Samsung Group, Seoul 1978–87, Chair. 1987–; Vice-Chair. Korea-Japan Econ. Comm. Seoul 1981–, Fed. of Korean Industries 1987; Pres. Korean Amateur Wrestling Fed. 1982–; Dir. Korean Youth Asscn. 1982–; Vice-Pres. Korean Olympic Cttee. 1993–; found guilty of bribery and sentenced to two years' imprisonment suspended for three years Aug. 1996. *Leisure interests:* horse-riding, golf. *Address:* Samsung Group, 250, 2-Ga Taepyung-ro, Chung-ku, Seoul, 100-102 (Office); 740-10 Hannam-Dong, Yongsan-ku, Seoul 100-102, Republic of Korea (Home).

LEE, Martin, Q.C., J.P.; Chinese politician and lawyer; b. 8 June 1938; m. Amelia Lee 1969; one s.; mem. Hong Kong Legis. Council 1985–95, Hong Kong Law Reform Comm. 1985–91, Basic Law Drafting Cttee. 1985–90; formed United Democrats of Hong Kong, groups opposed to Chinese crackdown on Tiananmen Square demonstrators in 1989, Leader 1990– (joined with Meeting Point Party to form Democratic Party 1994); expelled from Beijing-appointed Basic Law Drafting Cttee. for criticism of People's Repub. of China 1990 (mem. 1985–90); mem. Legis. 1998–; Int. Human Rights Award (American Bar Asscn.) 1995. *Publication:* The Basic Law: some basic flaws (with Szeto Wah) 1988. *Address:* Democratic Party of Hong Kong, Rooms 401/413, Central Government Offices, West Wing, 11 Ice House Street, Central, Hong Kong Special Administrative Region; Admiralty Centre, Room 704A, Tower I, 18 Harcourt Road, Hong Kong Special Administrative Region, People's Republic of China. *Telephone:* 2537-2471 (Democratic Party); 2529-0864. *Fax:* 2397-8998 (Democratic Party).

LEE, Shau-kee; Chinese business executive; Founder and Chair, Henderson Investment Ltd. *Address:* Henderson Land Development Co. Ltd., 6th Floor, World-Wide House, 19 Des Voeux Road, Central, Hong Kong Special Administrative Region, People's Republic of China. *Telephone:* 2525-1033.

LEE, Spike (pseudonym of Shelton Jackson Lee); American film maker and actor; b. 20 March 1957, Atlanta, Ga.; s. of Bill Lee and Jacquelyn Shelton; m. Tonya Lewis 1993; one d.; ed. Morehouse Coll., Atlanta and New York Univ. Inst. of Film and Television; Dr. h.c. (New York Univ.) 1998; wrote scripts for Black Coll.: The Talented Tenth, Last Hustle in Brooklyn; produced, wrote, dir. Joe's Bed-Stuy Barbershop: We Cut Heads; has directed music videos, TV commercials, and other short projects. *Films include:* She's Gotta Have It 1985 (Cannes Film Festival Prize for Best New Film), School Daze 1988, Do the Right Thing 1989, Love Supreme 1990, Mo' Better Blues 1990, Jungle Fever 1991, Malcolm X 1992, Crooklyn, Girl 6, Clockers 1995, Girl 6, Get on the Bus, 4 Little Girls, He Got Game 1998. *Publications:* Spike Lee's Gotta Have It: Inside Guerilla Filmmaking 1987, Uplift the Race 1988, The Trials and Tribulations of the Making of Malcolm X 1992, Girl 6 1996, Get on the Bus 1996. *Leisure interest:* basketball. *Address:* Forty Acres and a Mule Filmworks, 124 De Kalb Avenue, Brooklyn, New York, NY 11217, U.S.A.

LEE, Yeh Kwong Charles, LL.M., F.C.C.A., A.C.I.S.; Chinese lawyer; b. 16 July 1936, Shanghai, China; m. Nancy Lee 1960; one s. one d.; ed. London School of Econs. and Political Science; Audit Asst., Li Kwan Hung 1954–57, Peat Marwick Mitchell & Co., Hong Kong 1957–60; Asst. Registrar, Registrar-Gen.'s Dept. 1960–65; Articled Clerk, Nigel, Wallis & Apfel, Solicitors, U.K. 1965–68; Solicitor, Registrar-Gen.'s Dept. 1968–70, Johnson Stokes & Master 1970–72, partner 1972–73; partner Charles Lee & Stephen Lo 1973, Woo Kwan Lee & Lo 1973–; mem. Council, Stock Exchange of Hong Kong Ltd. 1988–, Chair. 1991; Dir. several listed cos. *Leisure interests:* boating, scuba diving. *Address:* Woo Kwan Lee & Lo, 26/Fl. Jardine House, 1 Connaught Place, Hong Kong Special Administrative Region, People's Republic of China. *Telephone:* 847 7823. *Fax:* 845 0239.

LEE, Yuan Tseh, PH.D.; American professor of chemistry; b. 29 Nov. 1936, Hsinchu, Taiwan; s. of Tse Fan Lee and Pei Tsai; m. Bernice W. Lee 1963; two s. one d.; ed. Nat. Taiwan Univ., Nat. Tsinghua Univ., Taiwan and Univ. of Calif., Berkeley; Asst. Prof. James Franck Inst. and Dept. of Chemistry, Univ. of Chicago 1968–71, Assoc. Prof. 1971–72, Prof. of Chem. 1973–74; Prof. of Chem. Univ. of Calif., Berkeley 1974–94; Head Academia Sinica 1994; Sloan Fellow 1969; Guggenheim Fellow 1976; Miller Professorship 1981; mem. American Acad. of Arts and Sciences; shared Nobel Prize for Chemistry 1986; E. O. Lawrence Award (U.S. Dept. of Environment), 1981, and many other awards and prizes. *Publications:* articles in professional journals. *Address:* Department of Chemistry, University of California (Berkeley), CA 94720, U.S.A. *Telephone:* (510) 486-6154.

LEE HAE-KOO; Korean politician; b. 1937, Ansong, Kyonggi Prov.; ed. Korea Univ. Law Coll.; various posts in police dept., Nat. Chief of Police 1983; Gov. Kyonggi Prov. and First Vice-Dir. Agency for Nat. Security Planning 1986–87; Minister for Home Affairs 1993. *Address:* c/o Ministry of Home Affairs, 77 Sejong-no, Chongno-ku, Seoul, Republic of Korea.

LEE HONG-KOO, PH.D.; South Korean politician and political scientist; b. 9 May 1934, Seoul; m.; one s. two d.; ed. Seoul Nat. Univ., Emory and Yale Univs., U.S.A.; Asst. Prof. Emory Univ. 1963–64, Case Western Reserve Univ. 1964–67; Asst. Prof., Assoc. Prof., Prof. of Political Science, Seoul Nat. Univ. 1968–88, Dir. Inst. of Social Sciences 1979–82; Fellow Woodrow Wilson Int. Center for Scholars, Smithsonian Inst. 1973–74, Harvard Law School 1974–75; Minister of Nat. Unification 1988–90; Special Asst. to Pres. 1990–91; Amb. to U.K. 1991–93; Sr. Vice-Chair. Advisory Council for Unification, Chair. Seoul 21st Century Cttee., The World Cup 2002 Bidding Cttee. 1993–94; Deputy Prime Minister and Minister of Nat. Unification April–Dec. 1994, Prime Minister 1994–95; mem. Comm. on Global Governance 1991–; Chair. New Korea Party May 1996. *Publications:* An Introduction to Political Science, One Hundred Years of Marxism, Modernization.

LEE HSIEN LOONG, Brig.-Gen.; Singaporean politician; b. 1952; s. of Lee Kuan Yew (q.v.) and Kwa Geok Choo; m. 1st (deceased 1982), one s. one d.; m. 2nd Ho Ching 1985; one s.; ed. Nanyang Girls High School, Catholic High School, Nat. Jr. Coll., Cambridge, Harvard Univ.; nat. service 1971; Sr. Army course at Fort Leavenworth, U.S.A.; Asst. Chief of Gen. Staff (Operations) 1981–82, Chief of Staff (Gen. Staff) Singapore army 1982–84; resgnd. as Brig.-Gen. Aug. 1984; Political Sec. to Minister of Defence; M.P. for Teck Ghee Dec. 1984–; Minister of State for Defence and for Trade and Industry 1985–86, for Trade and Industry 1986–93; Deputy Prime Minister 1990–, Minister of Defence 1993–95, Second Minister of Defence (Services); Second Asst. Sec.-Gen. People's Action Party 1989–. *Leisure interests:* swimming, reading, jogging, computers. *Address:* Office of the Prime Minister, Istana Annexe, Istana, Singapore 238823.

LEE HUAN, M.A.; Taiwanese politician; b. 8 Feb. 1917, Hankow City; m.; two s. two d.; ed. Nat. Chengchi Univ. and Columbia Univ.; Dir. Shenyang Daily News 1946–48; Chief Sec., Deputy Dir.-Gen. and Dir.-Gen. China Youth Corps 1952–77; Prof. Nat. Chengchi Univ. 1962–79; Chair. Comm. for Youth Assistance and Guidance, Exec. Yuan 1967–72; Exec. Officer, Alumni Asscn. of Nat. Chengchi Univ. 1977–80; Pres. Nat. Sun Yat-sen Univ. 1979–84; Minister of Educ. 1984–87; Prime Minister of Taiwan 1989–90; Sec.-Gen. Cen. Cttee. Kuo-Min-Ta-Hui 1987–; Hon. Ph.D. (Tan Kok) 1978; Hon. LL.D. (Sun Kyun Kwan) 1981.

LEE KI-TAEK, B.SC.; South Korean politician; b. 25 July 1937, Pohang; s. of late Lee Dong-Sup and Kim Nam-Chool; m. Lee Kyung-Ui 1968; one s. three d.; ed. Korea Univ., Seoul, Univ. of Pennsylvania; involved in politics as student; mem. Korean Nat. Ass. 1967–; Chair. Special Cttee. on Investigation of Political Corruption of the 5th Repub. 1988, and of Special Investigation Cttee. of the 5th Repub. 1990; Chair. Pusan City Charter, New Democratic Party 1972, Sec. Gen. 1976, Vice-Pres. 1979; Chair. Inst. of Democratic Thoughts 1979; Vice-Pres. New Korea Democratic Party 1984, 1986; Vice-Pres. Reunification Democratic Party 1988–89, Floor Leader 1989; Chair. Democratic Party of Korea 1990, 1993, Co-Chair. 1991, Adviser 1995–96, Pres. 1995, 1996–; Hon. Prof. Yonbyun Univ., China 1995; Nat. Foundation Medal, 1963. *Publications:* The Bridge of No Return 1978, History of Minority Parties in Korea 1987. *Leisure interest:* calligraphy. *Address:* 51-5, Yong Kang-dong, Mapo-ku, Seoul (Office); 187-12, Ahyun-dong, Seodeamooh-ku, Seoul, Republic of Korea (Home). *Telephone:* 02-711-3301 (Office); 02-313-8551 (Home). *Fax:* 02-711-3326 (Office); 02-313-5219 (Home).

LEE KUAN YEW, M.A.; Singaporean politician and barrister; b. 16 Sept. 1923, Singapore; s. of the late Lee Chin Koon and Chua Jim Neo; m. Kwa Geok Choo 1950; two s. one d.; ed. Raffles Coll., Singapore, Fitzwilliam Coll., Cambridge; called to Bar, Middle Temple, London 1950, Hon. Bencher 1969; Advocate and Solicitor, Singapore 1951; one of founders of People's Action Party 1954, Sec.-Gen. 1954–92; mem. Legis. Assembly 1955–; first Prime Minister Repub. of Singapore 1959, re-elected 1963, 1968, 1972, 1976, 1980, 1984, 1988; resgnd. as Prime Minister Nov. 1990; Sr. Minister in the Prime Minister's Office 1990–; mem. Singapore Internal Security Council 1959–; M.P. Fed. Parl. of Malaysia 1963–65; Chair. Singapore Investment Corpn. 1981–; Fellow, Inst. of Politics, Harvard Univ. 1968; Hoyt Fellow, Berkeley Coll., Yale Univ. 1970; Hon. Fellow, Fitzwilliam Coll., Cambridge 1969, Royal Australasian Coll. of Surgeons 1973, R.A.C.P. 1974; Hon. LL.D. (Royal Univ. of Cambodia) 1965, (Hong Kong) 1970, (Liverpool) 1971, (Sheffield) 1971; Hon. C.H. 1970; Hon. G.C.M.G. 1972; Bintang Republik Indonesia Adi Pradana 1973, Order of Sikatuna (Philippines) 1974, Most Hon. Order of Crown of Johore (First Class), 1984, Hon. Freeman, City of London 1982, numerous other distinctions. *Leisure interests:* jogging, swimming, golf. *Address:* Prime Minister's Office, Istana Annexe, Singapore 238823, Republic of Singapore.

LEE KYUNG-SHIK; Korean politician and banker; ed. Korea Univ.; joined Bank of Korea; Econ. Planning Bd. 1961–72; served in Office of Pres. 1972–74; later Vice-Minister of Communications and mem. Monetary Bd. of Korea; Pres. Daewoo Motor Co. 1988–93, Korea Gas Corpn. until 1993; Deputy Prime Minister and Minister of Econ. Planning 1993; Gov. Bank of Korea 1995–98. *Address:* Bank of Korea, 110, 3-Ka, Namdaemun-no, Chung-ku, Seoul 100-794, Republic of Korea.

LEE SOO SUNG; Korean politician and academic; fmr. Pres. Seoul Nat. Univ.; Prime Minister of Repub. of Korea 1995–97. *Address:* c/o Office of the Prime Minister, 77 Sejong-no, Chongno-ku, Seoul, Republic of Korea.

LEE TENG-HUI, PH.D.; Taiwanese politician; b. 15 Jan. 1923, Taiwan; m. Tseng Wen-fui; two d.; ed. Kyoto Imperial Univ., Japan, Nat. Taiwan Univ., Iowa State Univ. and Cornell Univ.; Asst. Prof. Nat. Taiwan Univ. 1948–55, Assoc. Prof. 1956–58; Prof. Nat. Chengchi Univ. 1958–78; Research Fellow, Taiwan Provincial Co-operative Bank 1955–57; Specialist, Joint Comm. on Rural Reconstruction (JCRR) 1957–61, Sr. Specialist and Consultant 1961–70, Chief, Rural Economy Div. 1970–72; Minister of State 1972–78; Mayor of Taipei City 1978–81; Gov. Taiwan Province 1981–84; Vice-Pres. of

Repub. of China (Taiwan) 1984–88, Pres. 1988–. *Publications:* several works on agricultural development in Taiwan. *Leisure interests:* art, music and sport. *Address:* Office of the President, 122 Chungking South Road, Sec. 1, Taipei 100, Taiwan.

LEE TSUNG-DAO, PH.D.; Chinese physicist; b. 25 Nov. 1926, Shanghai; m. Jeanette H. C. Chin 1950; two s.; ed. National Chekiang Univ., National Southwest Univ. (China) and Univ. of Chicago; Research Assoc. in Astronomy, Univ. of Chicago 1950; Research Assoc. and lecturer in Physics. Univ of California 1950–51; mem. Inst. for Advanced Study, Princeton, N.J. 1951–53; Asst. Prof. of Physics, Columbia Univ., New York 1953–55, Assoc. Prof. 1955–56, Prof. 1956–60, 1963; Enrico Fermi Prof. of Physics 1964–, Univ. Prof. 1984; Prof. Princeton Inst. for Advanced Study 1960–63; mem. N.A.S.; shared Nobel Prize for Physics 1957 with Prof. Yang Chen-ning for work on elementary particles; Albert Einstein Award in Science 1957. *Publications:* articles in physical journals. *Address:* Department of Physics, Columbia University, Bldg. 538, Morningside Heights, W. 120th Street, New York, NY 10027 (Office); 25 Claremont Avenue, New York, NY 10027, U.S.A. (Home).

LEE WON KYUNG; Korean politician; b. 15 Jan. 1922; ed. Tokyo Univ., Japan, Seoul Nat. Univ.; joined foreign service 1957, Chief Protocol Officer and Counsellor, Korean Embassy, Tokyo 1957–60, Vice-Minister of Foreign Affairs 1961–62, Minister of Culture and Information 1974–75, of Sports 1982–83, of Foreign Affairs 1983–86; Pres. Hapdong News Agency 1966–74; Chair. Doosan Industrial Co. 1976, Korean Foreign Service Asscn. 1980–82, Hapdong Inc. 1981; Vice-Chair. Korean Amateur Sports Asscn. 1971–74; mem. Korean Olympic Cttee. 1968–74, Vice-Chair. and Hon. Sec. 1971–74, Standing Adviser 1976–, Hon. Chair. 1978–; Vice-Chair. and Sec.-Gen. Seoul Olympic Organizing Cttee. 1981–88, mem. Exec. Cttee. 1982–88; Amb. to Japan 1988; mem. Legis. Ass. 1981–. *Address:* c/o Ministry of Foreign Affairs, 77 Sejong-no, Chongno-ku, Seoul, Republic of Korea.

LEE YOCK SUAN, B.SC.; Singaporean politician; b. 1946; m.; one s. one d.; ed. Queenstown Secondary Technical School, Raffles Institution, Imperial Coll., Univ. of London, U.K., Univ. of Singapore; Div. Dir (Projects), Econ. Devt. Bd. 1969–80; elected M.P. for Cheng San 1980; Deputy Man. Dir. Petrochemical Corpn. of Singapore (Pte.) Ltd. Jan.–Sept. 1981; Minister of State (Nat. Devt.) 1981–83, (Finance) 1983–84, Sr. Minister of State and Acting Minister for Labour 1985–86, Minister for Labour 1987–92, Second Minister of Educ. 1991–92, Minister of Educ. 1992; Deputy Chair. People's Asscn. 1984–; Minister of Trade and Industry 1998–. *Leisure interest:* badminton. *Address:* Ministry of Trade and Industry, 100 High Street, 09-01 The Treasury, Singapore 179434. *Telephone:* 2259911. *Fax:* 3327260.

LEE YUAN-TSEH, PH.D.; Taiwanese professor of chemistry; b. 19 Nov. 1936, Hsinchu; ed. Nat. Taiwan Univ., Univ. of California, Berkeley; Asst. Prof., then Prof. Dept. of Chemistry, Univ. of Chicago 1968–74, Prof. Univ. of Calif. at Berkeley 1974–, also prin. investigator, Lawrence Berkeley Lab.; Hon. Prof., Inst. of Chemistry, Chinese Acad. of Sciences, Beijing 1980–; Nobel Prize for Chemistry 1986. *Address:* Department of Chemistry, Lawrence Berkeley Laboratory, Building 70A, Room 4414, University of California, CA 94072, U.S.A. *Telephone:* (415) 486-6154.

LEENHARDT, Jacques; French sociologist; b. 17 April 1942, Geneva, Switzerland; s. of Franz J. Leenhardt and Antoinette Cheneviѐre; m. Françoise Warnod 1964 (divorced 1970); one s.; contrib. to Le Journal de Genève 1963–98, to Le Temps 1998–; Fellow Inst. for Advanced Study, Princeton Univ., N.J. 1979–80; Visiting Prof. to univs. in Brazil, Chile, Germany, Mexico, Portugal, Puerto Rico, U.S.A. 1974–; now Dir. of Studies, School of Advanced Studies in Social Sciences, Paris; Pres. French Art Critics Asscn. 1981–90, Crestet Centre d'Art 1987–, Int. Art Critics Asscn. 1990–96, Art in Nature 1991–; mem. European Acad. of Arts and Sciences 1992–; Chevalier Ordre nat. des Arts et des Lettres 1983, Ordre nat. du Mérite 1987. *Publications include:* Lecture politique du roman 1973, Lire la lecture 1982, La force des mots 1982, Au Jardin des Malentendus 1990, Les Amériques latines en France 1992, Dans les jardins de Roberto Burle Marx 1994, Villette-Amazone 1996. *Address:* École des Hautes Études en Sciences Sociales, 10 rue Monsieur le Prince, 75006 Paris, France. *Telephone:* (1) 44-41-46-74. *Fax:* (1) 44-41-46-76.

LEES, Sir David (Bryan), Kt., C.B.I.M., F.C.A., F.R.S.A.; British business executive; b. 23 Nov. 1936, Aberdeen; s. of late Rear-Admiral D. M. Lees, C.B., D.S.O., and of C. D. M. Lees; m. Edith M. Bernard 1961; two s. one d.; ed. Charterhouse; articled clerk, Binder Hamlyn & Co. (Chartered Accountants) 1957–62, Sr. Audit Clerk 1962–63; Chief Accountant, Handley Page Ltd. 1964–68; Financial Dir. Handley Page Aircraft Ltd. 1969; Chief Accountant, GKN Sankey Ltd. 1970–72, Deputy Controller 1972–73, Dir., Sec., Controller 1973–76; Group Finance Exec. GKN Ltd. 1976–77, Gen. Man. Finance 1977–82; Finance Dir. GKN PLC 1982–87, Group Man. Dir. 1987–88, Chair. 1988–, C.E.O. 1988–97; Chair. Courtaulds 1996–98 (Dir. 1991–), Dir. Bank of England 1991–, Royal Opera House 1998–; now Chair. Tate & Lyle PLC; Pres. Eng. Employers' Fed. (EEF) 1990–92, Soc. of Business Economists 1994–; mem. CBI Council 1988–, Chair. CBI Econ. Affairs Cttee. 1988–94, mem. CBI Pres.'s Cttee.; Commr., Audit Comm. 1983–90; Gov. Shrewsbury School 1986–; mem. Midlands Industrial Council 1988–, Listed Cos. Advisory Cttee. 1990–, Nat. Defence Industries Council 1995–, European Round Table 1995–, and other bodies; Officer's Cross, Order of Merit (Germany) 1996. *Leisure interests:* walking, golf, opera, music. *Address:* Tate & Lyle PLC, Sugar Quay, Lower Thames Street, London, EC3R 6DQ, England.

LE FLOCH-PRIGENT, Loïk; French business executive; b. 21 Sept. 1943, Brest; s. of Gérard Le Floch and Gabrielle Julienne; m.; one s. two d.; ed. Inst. Nat. Polytechnique, Grenoble and Univ. of Missouri; scientific and tech. research, D.G.R.S.T. 1969–81; Dir. of Cabinet of Industry Minister, Pierre Dreyfus 1981–82; Chair. and C.E.O. Rhône-Poulenc 1982–86, Elf Aquitaine 1989–93, SNCF 1995–96; Chair. Gaz de France 1993–95, Asscn. Europe et Entreprises 1994–, Club des présidents d'université et entreprise, Ecole Nat. Supérieure de Création Industrielle 1992–95; Dir. Crédit Nat. 1985–97, Compagnie Gén. des Eaux 1990–96, Banco Cen. Hispano Americano 1990–94, Pallas 1991–, Pinault Printemps Redoute 1992–, Entrepose-Montalev 1994–; Officier, Légion d'honneur, Ordre nat. du Mérite. *Address:* Energy and Transport Consulting, 7 Square Gabriel Fauré, 75017 Paris, France (Office).

LEFRANÇOIS, Jacques Roger; Belgian accountant; b. 1 March 1929, Seine Maritime, France; s. of Roger Lefrançois and Simone Boussy; m. R. Van Laer Londerzeel 1952; one s. one d.; ed. Coll. of EU; second accountant (Sogeco mar) 1948–52; Publicity Agent (Publi-Buro) 1952–66; confidential employee 1966–78; mem. Congress of European People (EFB-MFE) 1961–65; World Citizen for Peace through Human Rights 1965; proposed UN Day for World Peace and the Environment 1970; mem. Professional Union of Int. School of Detective Experts 1950–75, Belgium Comm. World Political Union, The Hague 1978–; First Sec. Universal Charter for Survival (UFOS) 1975; Pres. Group 'L'Homme Planétaire' 1970–98, f. and Sec. Gén. Conseil mondial de crise 1998–; mem. Flemish Asscn. of Journalists of Periodical Press 1970–97; Ed. L'Indépendant Schaerbeek 1964–, Het Watervlietje 1975–97; Sec. Flemish Regions, Parti Progressiste Belge 1989–93, Pres. 1985–89; Belgian Ombudsman/Médiateur Belge 1986–88; Pres. Flemish Progressive Party, European Flemish Programme 1989–92; Vice-Pres. European Progressive Party; Hon. Pres. and Public Relations Ombudsman Parti Mondial du Coeur 1993–97; Prize for Action to Promote European Federalism 1967. *Address:* 9 rue Leo Baekelandstr., 2030 Antwerp, Belgium.

LE GENDRE, Bertrand; French journalist; b. 25 Feb. 1948, Neuilly-sur-Seine; s. of Bernard Le Gendre and Catherine Chassaing de Borredon; m. 1st Jacqueline de Linares 1987 (divorced 1995); one s.; m. 2nd Nadia du Luc-Baccouche 1995; one s.; ed. Collège Sainte-Croix-de-Neuilly, Univ. of Paris X, Inst. d'études politiques, Paris, Inst. des hautes études de défense nationale; joined Le Monde as journalist 1974, in charge of judicial desk 1983, Reporter 1987, Ed.-in-Chief 1993; Sub-Ed. Gallimard 1986–89; Prix de la Fondation Mumm pour la presse écrite 1986. *Address:* 16 rue de la Glacière, 75013 Paris, France (Home).

LEGHARI, Farooq Ahmed; Pakistani politician; b. 2 May 1940, Dera Ghazi Khan; s. of Nawabzada Sardar and Mohammad Khan Leghari; m. 1965; two s. two d.; ed. Punjab and Oxford Univs.; mem. Pakistan People's Party; Chief Baluchi Leghari Tribe; Pakistan Civil Service 1964–73; elected to Senate 1975, to Nat. Ass. 1977; Minister for Production 1977; periods of imprisonment for opposition to govt. 1977–88; Sec. Gen. Pakistan People's Party and mem. Exec. Cttee. 1978; elected mem. Nat. Ass. and Provincial Ass. 1988–, Leader of Opposition, Prov. Ass. 1988, Minister for Water and Power 1988–90, Deputy Leader of Opposition 1990–93, Minister of Finance 1993, Minister of Foreign Affairs Oct.–Nov. 1993; Pres. of Pakistan Nov. 1993–97. *Leisure interests:* hunting, horseriding. *Address:* c/o Office of the President, Constitution Avenue, Islamabad, Pakistan. *Telephone:* 816061-9. *Fax:* 51-211018.

LE GOFF, Jacques Louis; French professor of history; b. 1 Jan. 1924, Toulon; s. of Jean Le Goff and Germaine Ansaldi; m. Anna Dunin-Wasowicz 1962; one s. one d.; ed. Lycées, Toulon, Marseilles and Louis-le-Grand, Paris, Ecole normale supérieure, Paris; history teacher 1950; Fellow of Lincoln Coll., Oxford 1951–52; mem. Ecole française de Rome 1953–54; Asst. at Univ. of Lille 1954–59; Prof., then Dir. of Studies, 6th Section, Ecole des hautes études (EHE) 1960, Pres. Ecole des hautes études en sciences sociales (fmr. 6th Section of EHE) 1972–77; mem. Comité nat. de la recherche scientifique 1962–70, Comité des travaux historiques 1972, Conseil supérieur de la Recherche 1985–87; Co-Dir. reviews Annales-Economies, sociétés, civilisations and Ethnologie Française 1972; Pres. Univ. Scientific Research Cttee. 1993–; Grand Prix nat. 1987, Gold Medal, C.N.R.S. 1991, Grand Prix Gobert 1996, Grand Prix d'histoire 1997. *Publications:* Les Intellectuels au Moyen Age 1957, Le Moyen Age 1962, La Civilisation de l'occident médiéval 1964, Das Hochmittelalter 1965, Pour un autre Moyen Age 1978 (English trans. Time, Work and Culture in the Middle Ages 1980), La naissance du purgatoire 1981, L'apogée de la chrétienté 1982, L'imaginaire médiéval 1985, La bourse et la vie 1986, Histoire de la France religieuse (jtly.) 1988, l'Homme médiéval 1989, L'Etat et les pouvoirs 1989, History and Memory 1993, Saint Louis 1996, Une vie pour l'histoire 1996, l'Europe racontée aux jeunes 1996. *Leisure interests:* gastronomy and swimming. *Address:* 11 rue Monticelli, 75014 Paris, France (Home).

LEGORRETA VILCHIS, Ricardo; Mexican architect; b. 7 May 1931, México, D.F.; s. of Luis Legorreta and Guadalupe Vilchis; m. María Luisa Hernández 1956; three s. three d.; ed. Univ. of Mexico; Draughtsman and Chief Designer with José Villagran García 1948–55, Partner 1955–60; Prof. of Design, Univ. of Mexico 1959–62, Head of Experimental Group 1962–64; private practice 1961–63; f. Legorreta Arquitectos (LA) with Noe Castro and

Carlos Vargas 1963, Dir. 1963–; f. LA Diseños 1977, Pres. 1977–; main works: Camino Real Hotel, Mexico City, Hotel Regina, Cancun, Solana Project, Dallas, U.S.A., Cathedral in Managua, Nicaragua; mem. Int. Cttee., Museum of Modern Art, New York 1970; mem. Bd. of Judges, A.I.A. 1977; Emer. Fellow, Colegio de Arquitectos de México 1978, mem. Bd. of Judges 1980; mem. Pritzker Prize Jury 1984; mem. IAA (Sofia) 1989; Hon. mem. North American Inst. of Architects. *Publication:* Los muros de México (with Celanese Mexicana). *Leisure interests:* tennis, music. *Address:* Palacio de Versalles 285-A, Col. Lomas Reforma, Código Postal 11020, México 10, D.F. (Office); Palacio de Versalles 285-A, Col. Lomas Reforma, Código Postal 11020, México 10, D.F., Mexico (Home). *Telephone:* 596-04-11 (Office); 596-21-88 (Home).

Le GOY, Raymond Edgar Michel, M.A.; British civil servant; b. 1919, London; s. of J. A. S. M. N. Goy and May Callan; m. Silvia Ernestine Burnett 1960; two s.; ed. William Ellis School, London, Gonville and Caius Coll., Cambridge; British Army 1940–46; entered Civil Service 1947, Road Transport and Establishments Divs., Ministry of Transport 1947–48; U.K. Shipping Adviser in Japan, Far East and S.E. Asia 1948–52; various posts in shipping and highway divs., Ministry of Transport and Civil Aviation 1952–57; Dir. Goeland Co. 1953; Asst. Sec. Railways and Inland Waterways Div., Ministry of Transport and Civil Aviation 1958; Asst. Sec. Finance and Supply Ground Services and Aerodrome Management, Ministry of Aviation 1959–61, Dir. of Admin. Navigational Services 1961–62; Asst. Sec. Aviation Overseas Policy, Ministry of Aviation and Bd. of Trade 1962–67; Under-Sec. of Civil Aviation 1968–73; Head Del. to European Civil Aviation Conf.; Dir.-Gen. of Transport Comm. of EEC 1973–81, of Comm. of EU 1981. *Publication:* The Victorian Burletta 1953. *Leisure interests:* theatre, music, race relations. *Address:* c/o Société Générale de Banque, Agence Européenne, Rond Point Schuman 10, 1040 Brussels, Belgium.

LEGRAS, Guy; French European Community official; b. 19 July 1938, Angers; s. of René Legras and Pauline Legras; m. Borka Oreb 1971; one s. one d.; ed. Faculté de Droit, Paris, Inst. d'Etudes Politiques, Paris and Ecole Nat. d'Admin.; joined Ministry of Foreign Affairs 1967; Cabinet of Sec. of State for Foreign Affairs 1968–71; Secr.-Gen. of Interministerial Cttee. (SGCI) for European Affairs (Prime Minister) 1971–74; Cabinet of Sec.-Gen. of OECD 1974–77; Counsellor, Perm. Rep. of France at European Communities, Brussels 1977–80; Asst. Sec.-Gen. SGCI 1980-82; Head, Dept. of Econ. Affairs, Ministry of Foreign Affairs 1982–85; Dir.-Gen. for Agric. Comm. of European Communities (now European Comm.), Brussels 1985–; Minister Plenipotentiary 1988; Officier, Ordre nat. du Mérite, Chevalier, Légion d'honneur. *Address:* 200 rue de la Loi, 1000 Brussels, Belgium (Office); 111 rue de Rennes, 75006 Paris, France.

LE GREW, Daryl John, M.ARCH.; Australian university vice-chancellor and professor of architecture; b. 17 Sept. 1945, Melbourne; s. of A. J. Le Grew; m. Josephine Le Grew 1971; one s. two d.; ed. Trinity Grammar School, Kew and Univ. of Melbourne; lecturer Dept. of Town and Regional Planning, Univ. of Melbourne 1969–73, lecturer and sr. lecturer Dept. of Architecture and Building 1973–85; Prof. of Architecture, Deakin Univ. 1986–98, Dean Faculty of Design and Tech. 1992–93, Chair. Academic Bd. 1992–98, Pro-Vice-Chancellor (Academic) 1993–94, Deputy Vice-Chancellor and Vice-Pres. (Academic) 1994–98; Vice-Chancellor Univ. of Canterbury, N.Z. July 1998–; Visiting Fellow Bartlett School of Architecture and Planning, Univ. Coll., London Univ.; consultant U.K. Science Research Council Training Programme; architectural consultant and Adviser to Dir. and Trustees of Nat. Gallery of Vic., Melbourne for redevt. of gallery site, to Dir. and Council Museum of Vic., Melbourne for its redevt., mem. Council; several sr. appts. in business and higher educ.; Life Fellow Museum of Vic. 1997. *Leisure interests:* swimming, music, poetry, philosophy. *Address:* University of Canterbury, Private Bag 4800, Christchurch 1, New Zealand.

LEGRIS, Manuel Christophe; French ballet dancer; b. 19 Oct. 1964, Paris; s. of Michel Legris and Raymonde Gazave; ed. Paris Opera School of Dancing; mem. corps de ballet, Paris Opéra 1980, 'Danseur Etoile' 1986–; maj. roles at Paris Opéra include Arepo (Béjart) 1986, In the Middle Somewhat Elevated (Forsythe) 1987, Magnificat (Neumeier) 1987, Rules of the Game (Twyla Tharp) 1989, La Belle au Bois Dormant (Nureyev) 1989, Manon (MacMillan) 1990, Dances at the Gathering (Robbins) 1992; in Hamburg created Cinderella Story and Spring and Fall (Neumeier); has also appeared at Bolshoi Ballet, Moscow, La Scala, Milan, Royal Ballet, London, New York City Ballet, Tokyo Ballet, Stuttgart Ballet, etc.; Gold Medal, Osaka Competition 1984; Prix du Cercle Corpeaux 1986, Nijinsky Prize 1988; Chevalier des Arts et des Lettres. *Address:* Théâtre national de l'Opéra de Paris, 8 rue Scribe, 75009 Paris, France.

LE GUIN, Ursula Kroeber, M.A.; American writer; b. 1929, Berkeley, Calif.; d. of Alfred L. and Theodora K. Kroeber; m. Charles A. Le Guin 1953; one s. two d.; ed. Radcliffe Coll., Columbia Univ.; taught French, Mercer Univ., Univ. of Ida. 1954-56; teacher, resident writer or visiting lecturer at numerous univs., including Univ. of Washington, Portland State Univ., Pacific Univ., Reading Univ., Univ. of Calif. at San Diego, Indiana Writers' Conf., Kenyon Coll., etc. 1971–; Mellon Prof. Tulane Univ. 1986; mem. Science Fiction Research Asscn., Authors' League, Writers' Guild W., PEN; Hubbub annual poetry award 1995, Asimov's Reader's award 1995, Nebula Award 1996, James Tiptree Jr. Retrospective Award 1995, 1997, Locus Readers Award 1995, 1996; Hon. D.Litt (Bucknell Univ., Lawrence Univ.), Hon. D.Hum.Litt. (Lewis and Clark Coll., Occidental Coll. Emory Univ.), Distinguished Service Award (Univ. of Oregon). *Publications include: novels:* Rocannon's World 1966, Planet of Exiles 1966, City of Illusions 1966, A Wizard of Earthsea 1968, The Left Hand of Darkness (Nebula Award, Hugo Award) 1969, The Lathe of Heaven 1971, The Tombs of Atuan 1971, The Farthest Shore (Nat. Book Award) 1972, The Dispossessed (Hugo Award) 1974, The Word for World is Forest 1976, Malafrena 1979, The Beginning Place 1980, The Eye of the Heron 1983, Always Coming Home (Kafka Award 1986) 1985, Dancing at the Edge of the World 1988, Tehanu 1990, Searoad 1991, Four Ways to Forgiveness 1995, Unlocking the Air 1996, The Twins, The Dream 1997, Lao Tzu: Tao Te Ching: A Book about The Way and the Power of The Way 1997, Jane on her Own 1998, Steering the Craft 1998; *screenplays:* King Dog 1985; *short stories:* The Wind's Twelve Quarters 1975, Orsinian Tales 1975, The Compass Rose 1982, Buffalo Gals 1987, Searoad 1991, A Fisherman of the Inland Sea 1994; *poetry:* Wild Angels 1974, Hard Words 1981, In the Red Zone (with H. Pander) 1983, Wild Oats and Fireweed 1987, Going Out with Peacocks 1994; *for children:* A Visit from Dr. Katz 1988, Catwings 1988, Solomon Leviathan 1988, Catwings Return 1989, Fire and Stone 1989, Fish Soup 1991, Wonderful Alexander 1994; Ed. Nebula Award Stories XI 1977, Interfaces 1980, Edges 1980. *Address:* c/o Virginia Kidd, Box 278, Milford, PA 18337; c/o Matthew Bialer, William Morris Agency, 1350 Avenue of the Americas, New York, NY 10019, U.S.A. *Telephone:* (212) 903-1355 (New York).

LEGWAILA, Legwaila Joseph, M.A.; Botswana diplomatist; b. 2 Feb. 1937, Mathathane; s. of Madume and Morongwa Legwaila; m. Pholile Matsebula 1975; three d.; ed. Bobonong School, Brussels School, S.A., Serowe Teacher Training Coll., Univ. of Calgary and Univ. of Alberta; Asst. Prin. External Affairs, Govt. of Botswana 1973–74, Sr. Pvt. Sec. to Pres. of Botswana 1974–80; Perm. Rep. to UN 1980–, High Commr. in Guyana 1981–, in Jamaica 1982–, Amb. to Cuba 1983, Deputy Special Rep. of the UN Sec.-Gen. for Namibia 1989–90. *Publication:* Safari to Serowe (co-author) 1970. *Leisure interests:* music, cycling. *Address:* Botswana Mission to the United Nations, 103 East 37th Street, New York, NY 10016, U.S.A. *Telephone:* (212) 889-2277 (Office); (914) 636-4858 (Home). *Fax:* (212) 725-5061.

LEHMAN, Ronald Frank, II, PH.D.; American government official; b. 25 March 1946, Napa, Calif.; s. of Ronald Lehman and Esther Suhr; m. Susan Young 1979; no c.; ed. Claremont Men's Coll. and Claremont Grad. School; army service, Vietnam 1969–71; Legis. Asst. U.S. Senate 1976–78; mem. professional staff, U.S. Senate Armed Services Cttee. 1978–82; Deputy Asst. Sec. of Defense, Office of Int. Security Policy 1982–83; Sr. Dir. Defense Programs and Arms Control, Nat. Security Council 1983–86; Deputy U.S. Negotiator for Strategic Nuclear Arms, Dept. of State, Washington, D.C. 1985–86, Chief U.S. Negotiator Geneva 1986–88; Deputy Asst. to Pres. for Nat. Security Affairs 1986; Asst. Sec. Dept. of Defense 1988–89; Dir. Arms Control and Disarmament Agency, Washington, D.C. 1989–93; Asst. to Dir. Lawrence Livermore Nat. Lab. 1993–, Dir. Center for Global Security 1996–; mem. Presl. Advisory Bd. on Arms Proliferation Policy 1995–96; Adjunct Prof. Georgetown Univ. 1982–89; mem. Bd. Dirs. U.S. Inst. of Peace 1988–93, Keck Center for Int. and Strategic Studies (now Chair.), Claremont McKenna Coll.; mem. Int. Advisory Bd. Inst. of Global Conflict and Cooperation, Univ. of Calif. San Diego 1994–; mem. Int. Inst. for Strategic Studies, Council on Foreign Relations, Atlantic Council. *Address:* Lawrence Livermore National Laboratory, P.O. Box 808, L-1, Livermore, CA 94551 (Office); 693 Encina Grande Drive, Palo Alto, CA 94306, U.S.A. (Home). *Telephone:* (510) 423-3711 (Office); (415) 856-8046 (Home).

LEHMANN, Erich Leo, PH.D.; American professor of statistics; b. 20 Nov. 1917, Strasbourg, France; s. of Julius Lehmann and Alma Schuster; m. Juliet Popper Shaffer; one s. two d.; ed. High School, Zurich, Switzerland, Univ. of Cambridge, Univ. of Calif., Berkeley; mem. Dept. of Math. Univ. of Calif., Berkeley 1946–55, Dept. of Statistics 1955–88, Prof. Emer. 1988–, Chair. Dept. of Statistics 1973–76; Visiting Assoc. Prof. Columbia Univ. 1950, Stanford Univ. 1951–52, Visiting Lecturer Princeton Univ. 1951, Guggenheim Fellow 1955, 1966, 1979, Miller Research Prof. 1967, 1972; Sr. Scholar, Educ. Testing Service 1995–; mem. N.A.S., American Acad. of Art and Sciences; fmr. Pres. Inst. Math. Statistics; American Statistical Asscn. Samuel S. Wilks Memorial Award 1996; Dr. h.c. (Leiden) 1985, (Chicago) 1991. *Publications:* Testing Statistical Hypotheses 1959, 1986, Basic Concepts of Probability and Statistics (with J. L. Hodges, Jr.) 1964, Nonparametrics: Statistical Methods based on Ranks 1975, Theory of Point Estimation 1983, Ed. Annals of Mathematical Statistics 1953–55. *Leisure interests:* music, reading, hiking. *Address:* Research Statistics Group, Education Testing Service, Mail Stop 15-T, Princeton, NJ 08541, U.S.A. *Telephone:* (609) 734-5151.

LEHMBERG, Stanford Eugene, PH.D.; American professor of history; b. 23 Sept. 1931, McPherson, Kan.; s. of W.E. Lehmberg and Helen Lehmberg; m. Phyllis Barton 1962; one s.; ed. Univ. of Kansas, Cambridge Univ., U.K.; mem. History Faculty, Univ. of Tex. at Austin 1956–69; Prof. of History, Univ. of Minn. 1967–98; Organist and Choirmaster, St. Clement's Episcopal Church, St. Paul, Minn. 1970–98; Fulbright Scholarship 1954–56; Guggenheim Fellow 1955–56, 1985–86, Fellow Royal Historical Soc., Soc. of Antiquaries; Hon. Litt. D. (Cambridge) 1990. *Publications:* Sir Thomas Elyot, Tudor Humanist 1960, Sir Walter Mildmay and Tudor Government 1966, The Reformation Parliament, 1529–1536 1970, The Later Parliaments of Henry VIII 1977, The Reformation of Cathedrals 1988, The Peoples of the

British Isles from Prehistoric Times to 1688 1991, Cathedrals Under Siege 1996; Ed. Sir Thomas Elyot, The Book Named the Governor 1962; articles, reviews. *Leisure interests:* music, the arts. *Address:* 1005 Calle Largo, Santa Fe, NM 87501, U.S.A. (Home). *Telephone:* (505) 486-5074.

LEHN, Jacques André, L. ÈS L.; French business executive; b. 15 July 1944, Lausanne, Switzerland; s. of Françoise-Xavier Lehn and Geneviève Jaeger; ed. lycées in Rabat (Morocco) and Sceaux, Sorbonne, Paris, Inst. d'Etudes Politiques, Paris and Ecole des Hautes Etudes Commerciales; man. consultant, Arthur Andersen 1969–76; Finance Dir. Warner Lambert France 1976–79; Dir.-Gen. Adams' France 1979–80; Dir. Matra, Médias Br. 1980–81; Dir. Hachette Group 1981–84, Deputy Dir.-Gen. 1984–90, Dir.-Gen. 1990; Dir.-Gen. Matra-Hachette 1993–; Vice-Pres. Europe I Communication 1986–94, Deputy Pres. 1994–; Pres., Dir.-Gen. Europe développement int. 1996–; Pres. Supervisory Bd. Europa Plus, France 1996–, Holpa 1996–; numerous other business affiliations; Chevalier, Ordre Nat. du Mérite. *Leisure interests:* squash, windsurfing, yachting. *Address:* Hachette, 4 rue de Presbourg, 75116 Paris; 47 blvd. Lannes, 75116 Paris, France.

LEHN, Jean-Marie Pierre, D. ÈS SC.; French professor of chemistry; b. 30 Sept, 1939, Rosheim, Bas-Rhin; s. of Pierre and Marie (née Salomon) Lehn; m. Sylvie Lederer 1965; two s.; ed. Univ. of Strasbourg; various posts, C.N.R.S. 1960–66; post-doctoral research assoc. with Prof. R. B. Woodward, Harvard Univ. 1963–64; Asst. Prof., Univ. of Strasbourg 1966–70, Assoc. Prof. 1970, Prof. 1970–79; Visiting Prof. of Chem., Harvard Univ. 1972, 1974, E.T.H., Zurich 1977, Cambridge Univ. 1984, Barcelona Univ. 1985; Prof Coll. de France, Paris 1979–; Pres. Scientific Council of Rhône-Poulenc 1992–, of Ministry of Nat. Educ., Youth and Sport 1989–93; mem. Research Strategy Cttee. 1995, Inst. de France, Deutsche Akad. der Naturforscher Leopoldina, Accad. Nazionale dei Lincei; Foreign assoc. N.A.S.; foreign hon. mem. American Acad. of Arts and Sciences; Foreign mem. Royal Netherlands Acad. of Arts and Sciences, Royal Soc. and many others; shared Nobel Prize in Chemistry 1987; Gold, Silver and Bronze Medals of C.N.R.S.; Gold Medal, Pontifical Acad. of Sciences 1981; Paracelsus Prize, Swiss Chem. Soc. 1982, von Humboldt Prize 1983, Karl Ziegler Prize (German Chem. Soc.) 1989, Davy Medal (Royal Soc.) 1997; Commdr. Légion d'honneur, Officier Ordre nat. du Mérite; mem. Order "Pour le Mérite" 1990. *Publications:* about 500 scientific publications. *Leisure interest:* music. *Address:* Collège de France, 11 place Marcellin Berthelot, 75005 Paris; 21 rue d'Oslo, 67000 Strasbourg, France (Home). *Telephone:* (1) 44-27-13-60 (Coll. de France); (88) 37-06-42 (Home). *Fax:* 44-27-13-56 (Coll. de France).

LEHR, Ursula M., PH.D.; German politician and psychologist; b. 5 June 1930, Frankfurt-am-Main; d. of Georg-Josef Leipold and Gertrud Jendorff; m. Helmut Lehr 1950 (died 1994); two s.; Research Asst., Univ. of Bonn 1955–60, Research and Teaching Asst., Inst. of Psychology 1960–68, mem. perm. staff. 1968–69, Additional Prof. and Head Dept. of Developmental Psychology 1969–72, Chair. Dept. of Psychology and Dir. Inst. of Psychology 1976–86, Hon. Prof. 1987–; Chair. of Pedagogics and Pedagogical Psychology, Albertus Magnus Univ., Cologne 1972; Dir. Inst. of Gerontology, Ruprecht Karls Univ., Heidelberg 1986–88, 1991–96; Head German Centre for Research on Aging, Heidelberg 1996–; Fed. Minister of Youth, Families, Women and Health 1988–91; mem. Families Advisory Bd., Fed. Ministry of Youth, Families and Health 1972–80, WHO Expert Advisory Panel on Health of Elderly Persons 1983–87; mem. Parl. 1990–94; Vice-Pres. German Gerontological Soc. 1973–78, 1980–84, Pres. 1997–; Founder mem. Acad. of Sciences, Berlin 1987–91; Hon. Ph.D. (Fribourg, Switzerland). *Publications:* more than 700 scientific texts. *Leisure interests:* art (paintings of the Middle Ages), history of art. *Address:* Am Büchel 53B, 53173 Bonn, Germany. *Telephone:* 0228-352849.

LEHTO, Olli Erkki, PH.D.; Finnish professor of mathematics; b. 30 May 1925, Helsinki; s. of Paul V. L. Lehto and Hilma Autio; m. Eva G. Ekholm 1954; one s. two d.; ed. Univ. of Helsinki; Docent, Univ. of Helsinki 1951–56, Assoc. Prof. 1956–61, Prof. of Math. 1961–88, Dean, Faculty of Science 1978–83, Rector 1983–88, Chancellor 1988–93; Pres. Finnish Math. Soc. 1962–85, Finnish Acads. of Science and Letters 1979–; mem. Exec. Cttee. Int. Math. Union 1975–90, Sec.-Gen. 1982–90; mem. Gen. Cttee. Int. Council of Scientific Unions 1982–90; mem. Admin. Bd. Int. Asscn. of Univs. 1985–95, Vice-Pres. 1990–95; Visiting Prof. at numerous univs. in Europe, N. America and Asia; Ph.d. h.c. (Turku) 1980, (Moscow) 1989, (Åbo) 1993, (Bucharest) 1996. *Publications:* four monographs and 60 papers in mathematical journals. *Leisure interest:* butterflies. *Address:* Office of the Academies, Mariankatu 5, 00170 Helsinki (Office); Ritarikatu 3 A 7, 00170 Helsinki, Finland (Home). *Telephone:* (3589) 633005 (Office); (3589) 662526 (Home). *Fax:* (3589) 19123213.

LEHTO, Sakari Tapani, B.LL., B.SC.(ECON).; Finnish business executive and writer; b. 26 Dec. 1923, Turku; s. of Reino and Hildi Lehto; m. Karin Hildén 1950; three d.; ed. Helsinki School of Econs. and Business Admin., Helsinki Univ., and M.I.T. Sloan School; Chief Legal Counsellor and Dir. Foreign Activities, United Paper Mills Ltd. 1952–64; Man. Dir. and Pres. Fed. of Finnish Industries 1964–71; Pres. and C.E.O. Partek Corpn. 1972–87, Vice-Chair. 1987–95; Chair. Insurance Ltd. Sampo 1976–89, Insurance Co. Kaleva 1978–91, Tamfelt Oy Ab 1982–94, Keskus-Sato Oy 1984–91, Pensions Sampo 1985–90; Kuratorium Pro Baltica Forum 1993–; Minister of Foreign Trade 1975–76; mem. Finland Defence Bd. 1976–92; Tech. Dr. h.c.; Econ. Dr. h.c. *Publications:* Managing Change—Strategies and Thoughts, Experiences Within Industry; numerous articles in the areas of commercial law, trade and industrial policy. *Leisure interests:* golf, boating, skiing. *Address:* Puistokatu 9A5, 00140 Helsinki, Finland (Office/Home). *Telephone:* (09) 660349 (Office/Home). *Fax:* (09) 653447.

LEI JIEQIONG, M.A.; Chinese politician and jurist; b. 1905, Guangzhou, Guangdong Prov.; d. of Lei Zichang and Li Peizhi; m. Yan Jingyao 1941; ed. in U.S.A.; Prof. Yenching Univ., 1931–52; Vice-Dean Inst. of Politics and Law 1953–73; mem. Cttee. for Implementation Campaign of Marriage Laws 1953; Deputy Dir., Bureau of Foreign Experts Admin. under State Council 1956–66, Prof. Beijing Univ. 1973–; Vice-Mayor of Beijing 1979–83; Chair. China Asscn. for Promoting Democracy 1987–97; Hon. Pres. China Asscn. of Women Judges, Asscn. for Int. Understanding of China, Western Returned Students' Asscn., China Social Workers' Asscn.; mem., Standing Cttee. 5th CPPCC 1978–83; mem. Standing Cttee. 6th NPC and Vice-Chair. of Law Cttee. 1983–88; Vice-Chair. 6th NPC 1986–88; Vice-Chair. 7th NPC 1988–93; Vice-Chair. Standing Cttee. 8th NPC 1994–98; numerous other appointments and hon. positions. *Address:* c/o 19 Xi Jiaomen Xiang, Xicheng District, Beijing, People's Republic of China.

LEI MINGQUI, Lieut.-Gen.; Chinese army officer; b. March 1942, Jiangjiaqiao, Qidong Co., Hengyang City, Hunan Prov.; ed. Zhuzhou Aeronautical Acad. Hunan and PLA Political Acad.; entered armed services 1962; Dir. Political Dept. Guangzhou Mil. Region 1992–95; Deputy Political Commissar, Nanjing Mil. Region 1995–; mem. 14th and 15th CCP Cen. Cttee. *Address:* Office of the Deputy Political Commissar, Nanjing Military Region, People's Republic of China.

LEI ZUHUA; Chinese bank official; fmr. Vice-Pres. Bank of China, Vice-Chair. Bd. of Dirs. 1993–; Pres. Import and Export Bank of China 1994–. *Address:* Import and Export Bank of China, 1 Dingandongli, Yongdingmenwai, Beijing, People's Republic of China. *Telephone:* (10) 67626688. *Fax:* (10) 67638940.

LEIBINGER, Berthold; German business executive; joined TRUMPF as engineer 1950, now owner and Chief Exec.; mem. Advisory Bd. Deutsche Bank, BMW, BASF. *Address:* TRUMPF, GmbH. and Co., Johann-Maus-Strasse 2, 71254 Ditzingen, Germany. *Telephone:* (07156) 3030.

LEIBLER, Kenneth Robert, B.A.; American business executive; b. 21 Feb. 1949, New York; s. of Max and Martha (née Dales) Leibler; m. Marcia Kate Reiss 1973; one s. one d.; ed. Syracuse Univ. and Univ. of Pennsylvania; Options Man. Lehman Bros. 1972–75; Vice-Pres. Options American Stock Exchange, N.Y. 1975–79, Sr. Vice-Pres. Admin. and Finance 1979–81, Exec. Vice-Pres. Admin. and Finance 1981–85, Sr. Exec. Vice-Pres. 1985–86, Pres. 1986–90; Pres. Liberty Financial Cos. 1990–; Instructor N.Y. Inst. of Finance; Dir. Securities Industry Automation Corpn.; mem. Finance Execs. Inst. of Securities Industry Asscn. American Stock Exchange Clearing Corpn. *Publication:* (contrib.) Handbook of Financial Markets: Securities, Options, Futures 1981. *Address:* Liberty Financial Companies, 600 Atlanta Avenue, Boston, MA 02110, U.S.A.

LEIBOVITZ, Annie; American photographer; b. 2 Oct. 1949, Conn.; ed. San Francisco Art Inst.; photographed rock 'n' roll stars and other celebrities for Rolling Stone magazine in 1970s; chief photographer, Vanity Fair 1983–; proprietor Annie Leibovitz Studio, New York; celebrity portraits include studies of John Lennon, Mick Jagger, Bette Midler, Louis Armstrong, Ella Fitzgerald, Jessye Norman, Mikhail Baryshnikov, Arnold Schwarzenegger and Tom Wolfe; retrospective exhbn. Smithsonian Nat. Portrait Gallery, Washington, D.C. 1991; Innovation in Photography Award (American Soc. of Magazine Photographers) 1987. *Publication:* Photographs 1970–90 1992. *Address:* Annie Leibovitz Studio, 55 Vandam Street, New York, NY 10013; Annie Leibovitz Studio, 101 W. 18th Street, New York, NY 10013, U.S.A.

LEIFERKUS, Sergey Petrovich; Russian baritone; b. 4 April 1946, Leningrad; ed. Leningrad Conservatory; stage debut in Leningrad Theatre of Musical Comedy 1972; soloist Maly Theatre of Opera and Ballet 1972–78; Kirov (now Mariinsky) Theatre of Opera and Ballet 1978–85; winner of int. competitions Belgrade 1973, Zwickau 1974, Paris 1976, Ostend 1979; sings in various opera houses of Europe and America; repertoire includes leading parts in Don Giovanni, Eugene Onegin, Queen of Spades, Otello (Verdi), Carmen, Lohengrin, Faust, Traviata, Aida, Die Königskinder (Humperdinck), Les Pêcheurs des Perles (Bizet), War and Peace, The Flaming Angel (S. Prokofiev), Dead Souls (R. Shchedrin), etc.; wide concert repertoire includes oratorios and cycles by Bach, Handel, Mozart, Schumann, Mahler, Mussorgsky. *Address:* 5 The Paddocks, Abberbury Road, Iffley, Oxford, OX4 4ET, England.

LEIFLAND, Leif, LL.B.; Swedish diplomatist; b. 30 Dec. 1925, Stockholm; s. of Sigfrid and Elna Leifland; m. Karin Abard 1954; one s. two d.; ed. Univ. of Lund; joined Ministry of Foreign Affairs 1952; served Athens 1953, Bonn 1955, Washington 1961, 1970; Sec. Foreign Relations Cttee., Swedish Parl. 1966–70; Under-Sec. for Political Affairs 1975–77; Perm. Under-Sec. of State for Foreign Affairs 1977–82; Amb. to U.K. 1982–91; Chair. Bd., Swedish Inst. of Int. Affairs 1991–; Hon. G.C.V.O. *Publications:* The Blacklisting of Axel Wenner-Gren 1989, General Böhme's Choice 1992, The Year of the Frost 1997; various articles on foreign policy and national security questions. *Address:* Nybrogatan 77, 114 40 Stockholm, Sweden. *Telephone:* 661 46 12. *Fax:* 663 16 13.

LEIGH, Jennifer Jason; American actress; b. 5 Feb. 1962, Los Angeles, Calif.; d. of late Vic Morrow and of Barbara Turner; ed. Palisades High School; appeared in Walt Disney TV movie The Young Runaways aged 15; other TV films include The Killing of Randy Webster 1981, The Best Little Girl in the World 1981; stage appearances include Sunshine, Off-Broadway 1989. *Films include:* Eyes of a Stranger 1981, Fast Times at Ridgemont High 1982, Grandview, U.S.A. 1984, Flesh and Blood 1985, The Hitcher 1986, The Men's Club 1986, Heart of Midnight 1989, The Big Picture 1989, Miami Blues 1990, Last Exit to Brooklyn 1990, Crooked Hearts 1991, Backdraft 1991, Rush 1992, Single White Female 1992, Short Cuts 1993, The Hudsucker Proxy 1994, Mrs Parker and the Vicious Circle 1994, Georgia 1995, Kansas City 1996, Washington Square 1997, eXistenZ 1999. *Address:* c/o Elaine Rich, 2400 Whitman Place, Los Angeles, CA 90211, U.S.A.

LEIGH, Mike, O.B.E.; British dramatist and film and theatre director; b. 20 Feb. 1943, Salford, Lancs.; s. of the late A. A. Leigh and of P. P. (née Cousin) Leigh; m. Alison Steadman 1973; two s.; ed. R.A.D.A., Camberwell School of Arts and Crafts, Cen. School of Art and Design, London Film School; Officier, Ordre des Arts et des Lettres; Golden Leopard (Locarno Film Festival) and Golden Hugo (Chicago Film Festival) 1972 for Bleak Moments, George Devine Award 1973, London "Evening Standard" and "Drama" London Critics' Choice best comedy awards 1981 for Goose-Pimples, Int. Critic's Prize, Venice Film Festival 1988 for High Hopes, Best Film Coup de Coeur Geneva 1989, London Evening Standard Peter Sellers Best Comedy Film Award (for High Hopes) 1990, (Alexander Korda Award; B.A.F.T.A. 1997). *Plays:* The Box Play 1965, My Parents Have Gone to Carlisle, The Last Crusade of the Five Little Nuns 1966, Nenaa 1967, Individual Fruit Pies, Down Here and Up There, Big Basil 1968, Epilogue, Glum Victoria and the Lad with Specs 1969, Bleak Moments 1970, A Rancid Pong 1971, Wholesome Glory. The Jaws of Death, Dick Whittington and His Cat 1973, Babies Grow Old, The Silent Majority 1974, Abigail's Party 1977 (also television play), Ecstasy 1979, Goose-Pimples 1981, Smelling A Rat 1988, Greek Tragedy 1989 (in Australia), 1990 (in U.K.), It's a Great Big Shame 1993. *Television films:* A Mug's Game 1972, Hard Labour 1973, The Permissive Society, The Birth of the 2001 F.A. Cup Final Goalie, Old Chums, Probation, A Light Snack, Afternoon 1975, Nuts in May, Knock for Knock 1976, The Kiss of Death 1977, Who's Who 1978, Grown Ups 1980, Home Sweet Home 1981, Meantime 1983, Four Days in July 1984, The Short and Curlies 1987. *Feature films:* Bleak Moments 1971, Abigail's Party 1977, High Hopes 1989, Life is Sweet 1991, Naked (Best Dir. Cannes Film Festival 1993) 1993, Secrets and Lies (winner Palme d'Or) 1996, (Alexander Korda Award; B.A.F.T.A. 1997), Career Girls 1997. *Radio play:* Too Much of a Good Thing 1979; Hon. M.A. (Salford) 1991. *Publication:* Career Girls 1997. *Address:* c/o Peters, Fraser & Dunlop, 503 The Chambers, Chelsea Harbour, Lots Road, London, SW10 0XF, England. *Telephone:* 0171-376 7676.

LEIGH GUZMÁN, Gen. Gustavo; Chilean air force officer; b. 19 Sept. 1920; m. Gabriela García Powdich; three s. one d.; ed. Liceo José Victorino Lastarria, Mil. Acad., Nat. Defence Acad.; postgraduate studies specializing in Supply and Maintenance, Command and Staff; Academic Instructor of Operations and Logistics; Deputy Commdr. Group 11 1953; Commdr. Group 10 1961; Commdr. of Supply Wing 1963; Air Attaché to U.S.A. 1964; Sec.-Gen. Chilean Air Force 1966; Dir. Aviation School 1968; Chief of Gen. Staff 1971–78; fmr. C.-in-C. of Chilean Air Force; mem. Mil. Junta 1973–78; many mil. decorations including Grand Mil. Merit Cross, Mil. Star, and Nat. Order of Merit (Paraguay), Legion of Merit (U.S.A.), Grand Cross for Aeronautical Merit (Spain), and others.

LEIGH-PEMBERTON, Rt. Hon. Robert (Robin) (see Kingsdown, Baron).

LEIJONHUFVUD, Axel Stig Bengt, PH.D.; Swedish professor of economics; b. 9 June 1933, Stockholm; s. of Erik G. Leijonhufvud and Helene A. Neovius; m. 1st Marta E. Ising 1955 (divorced 1977), 2nd Earlene J. Craver 1977; one s. two d.; ed. Univs. of Lund, Pittsburgh and Northwestern Univ.; Acting Asst. Prof. of Econs., Univ. of Calif. at Los Angeles (UCLA) 1964–67, Assoc. Prof. 1967–71, Prof. of Econs. 1971–, Chair. Dept. of Econs. 1980–83, 1990; Visiting Prof. Stockholm School of Econ. and Commerce 1979–80, 1986, 1987, Inst. for Advanced Studies, Vienna 1976, 1987, Inst. for Advanced Studies, Jerusalem 1987, Nihon Univ. Tokyo 1980, European Univ. Inst., Florence 1982, 1986–87, 1989, Istituto Tocuato di Tella, Buenos Aires 1989; Ständiger Gastprof. Univ. of Konstanz 1982–85; mem. Econ. Export Cttee. of Pres. of Kazakhstan 1991; other professional appts., cttee. memberships etc.; Brookings Inst. Fellow 1963–64; Marshall Lecturer, Univ. of Cambridge 1974; Overseas Fellow, Churchill Coll. Cambridge 1974; Inst. for Advanced Study Fellow 1983–84; Hon. Ph.D. *Publications:* On Keynesian Economics and the Economics of Keynes: A Study in Monetary Theory 1968, Keynes and the Classicals: Two Lectures 1969, Information and Coordination: Essays in Macroeconomic Theory 1981; contribs. to professional journals. *Address:* Department of Economics, University of California, Los Angeles, 405 Hilgard Avenue, Los Angeles, CA 90024-1477, U.S.A. *Telephone:* (213)-206-1412; (213)-825-4126.

LEINONEN, Tatu Einari, D.TECH.; Finnish professor of machine design; b. 21 Sept. 1938, Kajaani; m. Tuula Tuovinen 1968; one s. two d.; lecturer, Tech. Inst. of Helsinki 1963; researcher, Tech. Research Centre of Finland 1965; Design Engineer State Railway Co. 1966; Prof. of Machine Design, Univ. of Oulu 1968–; Visiting Prof. Univ. of Vt., U.S.A. 1976, Mich. Tech. Univ., U.S.A. 1977, 1981–82, 1991, Univ. of Fla., U.S.A. 1991, Lakehead Univ., Canada 1991, Toin Univ. of Yokohama, Japan 1994. *Publications:* more than 200 papers and books 1966–. *Leisure interests:* cross-country skiing, golf. *Address:* University of Oulu, Department of Mechanical Engineering, P.O. Box 444, 90571 Oulu, Finland. *Telephone:* (8) 5532050. *Fax:* (8) 5532026.

LEIRNER, Sheila; Brazilian art critic and curator; b. 25 Sept. 1948, São Paulo; d. of Abraham L. Klinger and Giselda Leirner Klinger; m. 1st Décio Tozzi 1970 (divorced 1972), 2nd Gustavo Halbreich 1974 (divorced 1988); two s.; ed. Univ. of Vincennes and Ecole Pratique des Hautes Etudes, Sorbonne, Paris; production asst. to Luis S. Person and film critic 1970; visual arts columnist, Ultima Hora, São Paulo 1971–74; art critic, O Estado de São Paulo 1975–90, now independent curator and art critic; mem. Brazilian Asscn. of Art Critics 1976; mem. Cen. Advisory Bd. Fantastic Art in Latin America, Indianapolis Museum 1984; Exec. Dir. Latin American Asscn. of Visual Arts, Buenos Aires 1984; corresp. Colombia magazine and D'Ars, Milan 1984–90; mem. arts and culture comm. São Paulo Biennial Foundation 1982–87; Gen. Curator, 18th and 19th São Paulo Biennial 1984–88; Curator, Painterly/Pictorico, Los Angeles Municipal Art Gallery and Museu de Arte de São Paulo 1989–90; other profesional memberships, appts. and honours. *Publications:* selected works of art criticism. *Leisure interests:* literature, music, collecting dolls houses.

LEITH, Prudence Margaret (Prue), O.B.E., F.R.S.A.; British caterer and author; b. 18 Feb. 1940, Cape Town, South Africa; d. of late Stewart Leith and of Margaret Inglis; m. Rayne Kruger; one s. one d.; ed. Haywards Heath, Sussex, St. Mary's, Johannesburg, Cape Town Univ., Sorbonne, Paris and Cordon Bleu School, London; started Leith's Good Food (commercial catering co.) 1965, Leith's restaurant 1969; cookery corresp. Daily Mail 1969–73; Man. Dir. Prudence Leith Ltd. 1972–94, Chair. Leith's Ltd. 1994–96; opened Leith's School of Food and Wine 1975; added Leith's Farm 1976; cookery corresp. Daily Express 1976–80; cookery Ed. The Guardian 1980–85, columnist 1986–90; subject of TV documentaries by BBC and Channel 4; presented series Tricks of the Trade, BBC 1; Vice-Pres. Restaurateurs' Asscn. of G.B.; Gov. Nat. Inst. of Econ. and Social Research; Vice-Patron Women in Finance and Banking; Chair. UK Cttee. New Era Schools' Trust 1994–, Royal Soc. of Arts 1995–97 (Deputy Chair. 1998–), The British Food Heritage Trust 1997–; Dir. (non-exec.) Halifax PLC 1995–. Whitbread PLC 1995–, Argyll Group 1989–96; Hon. Fellow Univ. Salford 1992; Visiting Prof., Univ. of N. London 1993–; mem. Nat. Council for Vocational Qualifications and U.K. Skills, Stamp Cttee. 1997–; Gov. Kingsmead City Tech. Coll., Ashridge Man. Coll.; Reader for Queen's Anniversary Prizes; Patron Prue Leith Coll. of Food and Wine, Johannesburg 1997–; Fellow Salford Univ.; Business Woman of the Year 1990; Freeman City of London 1994; Dr. h.c. (Open Univ.) 1997. *Publications include:* Leith's All-Party Cook Book 1969, Parkinson's Pie 1972, Cooking for Friends 1978, The Best of Prue Leith 1979, Leith's Cookery Course (with J. B. Reynaud) 1979–80, The Cook's Handbook 1981, Prue Leith's Pocket Book of Dinner Parties 1983, Dinner Parties 1984, Leith's Cookery School (with C. Waldegrave) 1985, Entertaining with Style (with P. Tyrer) 1986, Confident Cooking (part-work) 1989–90, Leith's Cookery Bible 1991, Leith's Complete Christmas 1992, Leith's Book of Baking 1993, Leith's Vegetarian Cookery 1993, Leith's Step by Step Cookery 1993. *Leisure interests:* walking, fishing, gardening, tennis, old cookbooks, kitchen antiques, Trollope. *Address:* 94 Kensington Park Road, London, W11 2PN, England. *Telephone:* 0171-221 5282.

LEJEUNE, Michael L.; American international finance official; b. 22 March 1918, Manchester, England; s. of F. Arnold and Gladys (née Brown) Lejeune; m. Margaret Werden Wilson 1947; two s. one d.; ed. Cate School, Carpinteria, Calif., Yale Univ., and Yale Univ. Graduate School; Teacher St. Paul's School, Concord, New Hampshire 1941; Volunteer in King's Royal Rifle Corps in British Army 1942–46; joined staff of IBRD (World Bank) 1946, Personnel Officer 1948–50, Asst. to Loan Dir. and Sec. Staff Loan Cttee., Loan Dept. 1950–52, Chief of Div., Europe, Africa and Australasia Dept. 1952–57, Asst. Dir. of Operations, Europe, Africa and Australasia 1957–63, Asst. Dir. of Operations, Far East 1963–64; Dir. of Admin., IBRD, IDA and IFC 1964–67, Dir. Middle East and North Africa Dept. 1967–68, Dir. Europe, Middle East and North Africa Dept. 1968–69, Dir. Eastern Africa Dept. 1970–74, Exec. Sec. Consultative Group on Int. Agric. Research 1974–83, Sr. Adviser to Vice-Pres. Operations Policy 1983; Consultant 1983–; Trustee, Santa Barbara Foundation 1991–, Vice-Pres. 1999–. *Publication:* Partners Against Hunger: The Consultative Group on International Agricultural Research (with Warren C. Baum) 1986. *Address:* 80 Conejo Road, Santa Barbara, CA 93103, U.S.A. *Telephone:* (805) 963-6598.

LEKHANYA, Maj.-Gen. Justin; Lesotho politician and army officer; Commdr. of Lesotho Army; Head Mil. Council and Council of Ministers 1986–91, Minister of Defence and Internal Security 1986–91, also Minister of Public Service, Youth and Women's Affairs, Food Man. Units and Cabinet Office; ousted in coup.

LE K HA PHIEU, Gen.; Vietnamese army officer and politician; fmrly. Chief of Army Political Dept.; Sec.-Gen. CP of Viet Nam Dec. 1997–; mem. Politburo, Politburo Standing Bd. *Address:* Communist Party of Viet Nam, 1 Hoang Van Thu, Hanoi, Viet Nam.

LEKISHVILI, Niko Mikhailovich; Georgian politician; b. 20 April 1947, Tbilisi; m.; two d.; ed. Tbilisi Polytech. Inst., Moscow Acad. of Nat. Econ.; sr. lab. asst. Georgian Polytech. Inst. 1971–72; Komsomol functionary 1972–77;

Second Sec., Chair. Dist. Exec. Cttee., First Sec. Pervomay Dist. CP Cttee., Tbilisi 1977–89; Second Sec., First Sec. Tbilisi City CP Cttee. 1989–90; Chair. Tbilisi City Soviet 1990; Deputy Supreme Soviet Georgian S.S.R. 1990–91; Chief State Counsellor Georgian Cabinet of Ministers Jan.–Nov. 1992; mem. Parl. Repub. of Georgia 1992–95; Deputy Prime Minister Sept.–Oct. 1993; Mayor Tbilisi 1993–95; State Minister of Georgia 1995–98. *Address:* Ingorokva str. 7, 380034, Tbilisi, Georgia. *Telephone:* 93-62-40.

LEKOTA, Mosiuoa Patrick (Terror); South African politician; b. 13 Aug. 1948, Senekal, Free State; s. of the late Mapiloko Lekota and Mamosiuoa Lekota; m. Cynthia Lekota 1975; two s. two d. (deceased); ed. Univ. of the North (Turfloop); perm. organizer, South African Students' Org. (SASO) 1972–74; charged under Terrorism Act 1974; tried and imprisoned on Robben Island 1976–82; Nat. Publicity Sec. United Democratic Front (UDF) 1983–91; fmrly. with ANC org. in Natal; Organiser for ANC in Northern Free States 1990; mem. ANC Working Cttee. 1991–, Nat. Chair. ANC Nat. Exec. Cttee. 1991–, Chair. Southern O.F.S. of Nat. Exec. Comm. 1991, Sec. Elections Comm. 1992–94; Nat. Chair. ANC 1997–, detained 1983, 1984, 1985; on trial with 21 others charged with treason and murder in Delmas case 1986, convicted 1988, sentenced to 12 years' imprisonment after being held in custody for 4 years; conviction overturned by Appeal Court 1989; in exile, returned to S. Africa 1990; Premier Free State Prov. Legislature 1994; Chair. Nat. Council of Provinces 1997–. *Leisure interests:* cycling, reading, soccer, rugby and studying wildlife. *Address:* P.O. Box 15, National Council of Provinces, Cape Town 8000, South Africa (Office). *Telephone:* 021-403 2115. *Fax:* 021-461 9460.

LELONG, Pierre Alexandre; French politician and administrative official; b. 22 May 1931, Paris; s. of Prof. Marcel Lelong; m. Catherine Demargne 1958; four s. one d.; ed. Coll. Stanislas, Paris, Univ. of Paris and Ecole Nat. d'Administration; Ministry of Finance and Econ. Affairs 1958–62; Econ. Adviser to Prime Minister Pompidou 1962–67; Gen. Man. Fonds d'Orientation et de Régularisation des Marchés Agricoles (FORMA) 1967–68; M.P. for Finistère 1968–74; Sec. of State for Posts and Telecommunications 1974–75; Judge, Court of Accounts 1975–77; mem. European Court of Auditors 1977–, Pres. 1981–84; Pres. of Section (Defence) at Court of Accounts 1990–94, Pres. of Chamber (European Affairs) 1994–; Pres. UNAPEC (Union des Asscns. pour la Promotion Pédagogique dans l'Enseignement Catholique); Officier, Légion d'honneur, Officier, Ordre du Mérite; Grand Cross, Order Couronne de Chêne (Luxembourg). *Leisure interests:* sea fishing, hunting. *Address:* 13 rue Cambon, 75001 Paris (Office); 130 rue de Rennes, 75006 Paris; Keremma, 29255 Tréflez, Finistère, France (Home). *Telephone:* (1) 42-98-95-52 (Office); (1) 45-44-12-49 (Home). *Fax:* (1) 42-98-59-73.

LELONG, Pierre Jacques, D. ÈS SC.; French academic; b. 14 March 1912, Paris; s. of Charles Lelong and Marguerite (née Bronner) Lelong; m. 1st Jacqueline Ferrand 1947, two s. two d.; m. 2nd France Fages 1976; ed. Ecole Normale Supérieure and Ecole des Sciences Politiques; Prof. Science Faculty, Grenoble 1942–44; Prof. Science Faculty, Lille 1944–54, Université de Paris VI 1954–81; Research Counsellor for Pres. De Gaulle 1959–62; Pres. du Comité Consultatif de la Recherche et de la Comm. du Plan 1961–63; Pres. Comm. mathématique C.N.R.S. 1962–66; mem. Acad. des Sciences 1986–; Officier Légion d'honneur. *Publications:* Fonctions plurisousharmoniques 1942, Entire functions of several complex variables 1986; numerous research papers on complex analysis and articles on the org. of research. *Address:* 9 place de Rungis, 75013 Paris, France. *Telephone:* 45-81-51-45 (Home).

LELOUCH, Claude; French film director; b. 30 Oct. 1937, Paris; s. of Simon Lelouch and Charlotte Abeilard; m. Christine Cochet 1968 (divorced); m. 2nd Marie-Sophie Pochat; three c., three c. from previous relationships; m. 3rd Alessandra Martines 1995; Pres. and Dir.-Gen. Société Les Films 13, 1966–; Chevalier, Ordre nat. du Mérite, Officier des Arts et des Lettres, Grand Prix Nationaux 1993; Golden Globe, Ephèbe d'or (for Les Misérables) 1996; Dr. h.c. (UMIST) 1996; *films directed include:* l'amour des si..., La femme-spectacle, Une fille et des fusils, Les grands moments, Pour un maillot jaune, Un homme et une femme, (Palme d'or, Cannes 1966, Acad. Award 1966), Vivre pour vivre, Treize jours en France, La vie, l'amour, la mort, Un homme qui me plaît, Le Voyou, Smic, Smac, Smoc, co-dir. Visions of Eight 1973, L'Aventure c'est l'aventure, La bonne année 1973, (producer, dir., author) Toute une vie 1974, Mariage 1974, Le chat et la souris 1975, Le bon et les méchants 1975, Rendez-vous 1976, Si c'était à refaire 1976, Un autre homme, une autre chance 1977, Robert et Robert 1978, A nous deux 1979, Les uns et les autres 1981, Edith et Marcel 1983, Viva la vie 1984, Partir, revenir 1985, Un homme et une femme . . . 20 ans après 1986, Attention bandits 1987, Itinéraire d'un enfant gâté 1988, Il y a des jours . . . et de lunes 1990, La Belle Histoire 1992, Tout Ça Pour Ça 1993, Hommes, Femmes, Mode d'Emploi 1995, Les Misérables 1995. *Address:* 15 avenue Hoche, 75008 Paris, France. *Telephone:* 42-25-00-89.

LELYVELD, Joseph Salem; American journalist; b. 5 April 1937, Cincinnati; s. of Arthur Joseph Lelyveld and Toby Bookholz; m. Carolyn Fox 1958; two d.; ed. Columbia Univ.; Reporter, Ed. New York Times 1963–, Foreign Correspondent Johannesburg, New Delhi, Hong Kong, London 1965–86, columnist, staff writer 1977, 1984–85, Foreign Ed. 1987–89, Deputy Man. Ed. 1989–90, Man. Ed. 1990–94, Exec. Ed. April 1994–; George Polk Memorial Award 1972, 1984. *Publication:* Move Your Shadow (Pulitzer Prize) 1985. *Address:* The New York Times, 229 W. 43rd Street, New York, NY 10036, U.S.A.

LEM, Stanisław; Polish writer and essayist; b. 12 Sept. 1921, Lvov; s. of Samuel and Sabina Lem; m. Barbara Leśniak 1953; one s.; ed. Lvov Med. Inst., Jagellonian Univ., Cracow; literary début with novel Człowiek z Marsa (Man from Mars) in weekly Nowy Świat Przygód, Katowice 1946; mem. Poland 2000 Comm. of Polish Acad. of Sciences 1972–, Polish Acad. of Skills 1994; mem. Science Fiction Writers of America, Polish PEN Club, Asscn. of Polish Authors; Dr. h.c. (Jagellonian Univ., Cracow) 1998; several literary awards. *Major works:* science-fiction novels include Astronauci (The Astronauts) 1951, Obłok Magellana (Magellan's Cloud) 1955, Eden 1959, Śledztwo (The Investigation—detective story) 1959, Powrót z gwiazd (Return from the Stars) 1961, Solaris 1961, Pamiętnik znaleziony w wannie (Memoirs Founded in a Bathtub) 1963, Niezwyciężony (The Invincible) 1964, Głos Pana (Master's Voice) 1968, Doskonała próżnia (A Perfect Vacuum) 1971, Bezsenność. Opowiadania 1971, Transfer 1975, Katar (The Chain of Chance, thriller) 1976, Maska (The Mask) 1976, Wizja lokalna 1982, Kongres Futurologiczny (Futurological Congress) 1983, Prowokacja 1984; *science fiction stories include:* Dzienniki gwiazdowe (The Star Diaries) 1957, Księga robotów (Book of Robots) 1961, Bajki robotów (Robots' Fairy-Tales) 1964, Cyberiada (Cyberiad) 1965, Opowieści o pilocie Pirxie (The Tales of Pirx the Pilot) 1967, Fiasko 1987; *essays include:* Dialogi (The Dialogues) 1957, Fantastyka i futurologia 1970, 1972, 1984, Golem XIV 1981, Summa technologiae 1964, 1967, 1974, 1984; series of novels; Czas nieutracony Part I–III 1955, autobiographical novel: Wysoki Zamek (High Castle) 1966; books translated into 36 languages. *Address:* ul. Narwik 66, 30-437 Cracow, Poland. *Telephone:* (12) 262-00-42. *Fax:* (12) 262-00-32.

LEMAN, Alexander B., F.R.A.I.C., F.R.S.A.; Canadian urban analyst and planner; b. 5 May 1926, Belgrade, Yugoslavia; s. of Boris E. and Nataly Leman; m. 1st Catherine B. Leman 1950 (deceased), 2nd N. Bella Leman 1968; two s. two d.; ed. Univ. of Belgrade; Prin. Partner, The Leman Partnership, Architects 1956–; Pres. Leman Group Inc., Consultants on Human Settlements and Devt. 1971–; Chair. and C.E.O. Urbanitas, Inc., Planners and Builders of Urban Communities; Chair. of Bd. Royal Architectural Inst. of Canada Research Corpn. 1982–86; Co-Chair. UNESCO Int. Conf. on Culture and Devt. 1985; Chair. World Congress on Conservation of Natural and Built Environments 1989; Dir. Devt. of Bangkok Regional Plan 1992–95; Advisor to Ont. Ministry of Housing on New Town Devt. 1994–95; Founding mem. and Dir. Shelter for the Homeless Foundation; Progressive Architecture Award 1973, UN Habitat Award 1990. *Publications:* Great Lakes Megalopolis: from Civilization to Ecumenization 1976; articles on human settlements, environment and urban planning and analysis in professional journals. *Leisure interests:* travel, community activities. *Address:* Leman Group Inc., The Hudson's Bay Centre, 2 Bloor Street East, 28th Floor, Toronto, Ont., M4W 1A8 (Office); 44 Charles Street W., Suite 4203, Toronto, Ont., M4Y 1R8, Canada (Home). *Telephone:* (416) 964-1865 (Office). *Fax:* (416) 964-6065 (Office).

LEMIEUX, Joseph Henry, B.S.; American business executive; b. 2 March 1931, Providence, R.I.; s. of Joseph C. Lemieux and Mildred L. Lemieux; m. Frances J. Schmidt 1956; two s. two d.; ed. Stonehill Coll., Univ. of Rhode Island, Bryant Coll., Providence; joined Glass Container Div., Owens-Ill. as trainee 1957, numerous posts include Plant Comptroller 1961, Admin. Man. 1964, Plant Man. 1965–72, Vice-Pres. 1972–78, Group Vice-Pres. 1979–84, Exec. Vice-Pres. and Pres. Packaging Operations 1984–86, Pres and C.O.O. 1986–90, Pres., C.E.O. 1990–91, Chair., C.E.O. 1991–, also Sr. Vice-Pres. and Chief Financial Officer; Chair. Bd. of Dirs. Health Care and Retirement Corpn. of America 1986, C.E.O. and Chair. 1991–; mem. Bd. Dirs Nat. City Bank Northwest, Toledo, Nat. City Corpn., Cleveland; Outstanding Young Man of America, U.S. Jr. Chamber of Commerce 1965. *Leisure interests:* golf, tennis. *Address:* Owens-Illinois, Inc., One Sea Gate, Toledo, OH 43666, U.S.A. *Telephone:* 419-247 5800.

LEMIEUX, Raymond Urgel, C.C., PH.D., F.R.S. ; Canadian chemist; b. 16 June 1920, Lac La Biche, Alberta; s. of Octave Lemieux; m. Virginia Marie McConaghie 1948; one s. five d.; ed. Univ. of Alberta, Edmonton, and McGill Univ., Montreal; Research Fellow, Ohio State Univ. 1947; Asst. Prof., Univ. of Saskatchewan 1948–49; Sr. Research Officer, Nat. Research Council 1949–54; Prof. and Chair. Univ. of Ottawa 1954–61; Prof. of Organic Chem., Univ. of Alberta 1961–81, Univ. Prof. 1980, Prof. Emer. 1985–; Pres. Chemical Inst. of Canada 1984–85; Fellow, Chemical Inst. of Canada 1954, Royal Society of Canada 1955, Royal Soc. (London) 1967; Hon. D.Sc. (New Brunswick) 1967, (Laval) 1970, (Provence, France) 1972, (Ottawa) 1975, (Waterloo) 1980, (Newfoundland) 1981, (Quebec) 1982, (Queen's, Ont.) 1983, (McGill) 1984, (Sherbrooke) 1986, (McMaster) 1986, (Alberta) 1991; Hon. D. Jur. (Calgary) 1979, (Saskatchewan) 1993; Hon. Ph.D. (Stockholm) 1988; Hon. Fellow, Chemical Inst. of Canada 1992; Chemical Inst. of Canada Palladium Medal 1964, C. S. Hudson Award, American Chemical Soc. 1966, Officer Order of Canada 1968, Haworth Medal, Chemical Soc. of England 1978, Award of Achievement, Province of Alberta 1979, Diplôme d'honneur, Groupe Français des Glucides, Lyons 1981, Killam Memorial Prize, The Canada Council 1981, Univ. of Alberta Research Prize 1982, Sir Frederick Haultain Prize 1982, Tishler Prize (Harvard Univ.) 1983, Medal of Honour, Canadian Medical Asscn. 1985, Gairdner Foundation Int. Award 1985, Rhône-Poulenc Award, Royal Soc. of Chem., England 1989, King Faisal Int. Prize in Science 1990, Alberta Order of Excellence 1990, Gold Medal (Natural Sciences and Eng. Research Council) 1991, E.C. Manning Nat. Award of Distinction 1992, PMAC Health Research Foundation Medal of Honor 1992,

Albert Einstein World Award of Science 1992, Great Canadian Award 1993, Alberta Pioneer (Special Alberta Science and Tech. Foundation Award) 1993. *Publications:* over 200 research papers mostly appearing in Canadian Journal of Chemistry. *Leisure interests:* golf, curling, fishing. *Address:* Department of Chemistry, University of Alberta, Edmonton, Alberta T6G 2G2 (Office); 7602 119th Street, Edmonton, Alberta T6G 1W3, Canada (Home).

LEMMON, Jack; American actor; b. (as John Uhler Lemmon III) 8 Feb. 1925, Boston; s. of John Uhler Lemmon II and Mildred LaRue Noel; m. 1st Cynthia Boyd Stone 1950, one s.; m. 2nd Felicia Farr 1962, one d.; ed. Phillips Andover Acad., Harvard Univ.; actor, stage, radio and television 1948–; numerous Broadway appearances; Acad. Award 1956, 1974; Best Actor, Cannes Film Festival 1979, American Film Inst.'s Life Achievement Award 1988. *Films include:* It Should Happen to You 1953, Three for the Show 1953, Phffft 1954, My Sister Eileen 1955, Mister Roberts 1955, You Can't Run Away From It 1956, Fire Down Below 1957, Bell, Book and Candle 1958, It Happened to Jane 1958, Some Like it Hot 1959, The Apartment 1960, The Notorious Landlady 1962, Days of Wine and Roses 1962, Irma La Douce 1963, Under the Yum Yum Tree 1964, Good Neighbour Sam 1964, How to Murder Your Wife 1965, The Great Race 1965, The Fortune Cookie (British title Meet Whiplash Willie) 1966, Luv 1967, The Odd Couple 1968, The April Fools 1969, The Out-of-Towners 1969, Kotch (Dir. only) 1971, The War Between Men and Women 1972, Avanti 1972, Save The Tiger 1973, The Prisoner of Second Avenue 1974, The Front Page yy1975, The Entertainer 1975, Alex and the Gypsy 1976, Airport 77 1977, The China Syndrome 1979, Tribute 1980, Buddy Buddy 1981, Missing 1982, Mass Appeal 1984, Macaroni 1986, Film Crisis 1986, That's Life 1986, Long Day's Journey Into Night 1986, Dad 1989, Glengarry Glen Ross 1989, JFK 1991, The Player, Grumpy Old Men 1993, Short Cuts 1994, Getting Away with Murder 1995, The Grass Harp 1995, Grumpier Old Men 1995, A Weekend in the Country, Hamlet 1996, My Fellow Americans 1996, Out to Sea. *Plays include:* Veterans Day 1989. *Address:* CAA, 9830 Wilshire Boulevard, Beverly Hills, CA 90212, U.S.A.

LEMOS, Nikolas Spyridon; Greek business executive; b. 8 Sept. 1933, Oinoussai, Chios; s. of Spyros A. Lemos and Irene N. Pateras; m. Irini Doxiadis 1976; three s. three d.; ed. Univ. School of Navigation, Southampton, Edin. Univ.; officer, Capt. on various types of merchant ships; port capt. several shipyards in numerous countries; Man. Dir. Lemos & Pateras 1966–83; founder, Man. Dir. N.S. Lemos & Co. Ltd. (shipbrokers) 1983–; Pres. Maritime Museum Oinoussai; Deputy Perm. Rep. of Cyprus to IMO; mem. Bd. of Greek Shipowners Union 1974–78, 1997–; mem. council Det Norske Veritas; Trustee Thyateira and St. Nicholas Trust; Actuarius of Ecumenical Patriarche Constantinopoulos. *Leisure interests:* fishing, sailing, scuba diving, skiing, swimming. *Address:* N.S. Lemos & Co. Ltd., St. Clare House, 30/33 Minories, London, EC3N 1DP (Office); "Xasteria", 35 Ingram Avenue, London, NW11 6TG, England (Home). *Telephone:* 0171-481 8921; 0181-458 9377. *Fax:* 0171–481 4177.

LEMOS SIMMONDS, Carlos, DR. IUR.; Colombian politician; b. Popayán, Cauca; m. Martha Blanco Guake; four c.; ed. Lycée of Cauca Univ. and Cauca Univ.; Prof. of Colombian Political History, Universidad Javeriana; Prof. of Colombian Econ. History, Free Univ. of Colombia; Dir. of Consigna magazine 1982–87; mem. of Bogotá Council 1972–74, 1986–88; mem. House of Reps 1974–78; Gov. of Cauca Prov. 1976–77; Sec.-Gen. of the Presidency 1978–79; Senator 1978–81; Minister of Foreign Affairs 1981–82; Amb. to the OAS 1987–89; Minister of Communications Feb.-Oct. 1989; Minister of Government (Interior) 1989–90; del. to Nat. Constitutional Ass. 1990–91; Chair of Bogotá Council 1992; cand. for Pres. of Colombia 1992; Amb. to Austria 1995, to U.K. 1995; Vice-Pres. of Colombia 1996; Orders of Boyacá, San Carlos, Civil Merit (Spain), Independence (Equatorial Guinea), Merit (Italy, Chile and Ecuador), Sol (Peru) and Balboa (Panama), Commdr. Order of Isabel la Católica. *Publications include:* Francisco de Paula Santander, An Iconography; The Pre-Columbian Economy. *Address:* Palacio de Nariño, Carrera 8A, 7–26, Santafé de Bogotá, DC, Colombia.

LEMPER, Ute; German singer, dancer and actress; b. 4 July 1963, Münster; ed. Max-Reinhardt-Seminar, Vienna; leading role in Viennese production of Cats 1983; appeared in Peter Pan, Berlin, Cabaret, Düsseldorf and Paris (recipient of Molière Award 1987), Chicago (Laurence Olivier Award) 1997–98; French Culture Prize 1993. *Albums include:* Ute Lemper Sings Kurt Weill 1988, (Vol. 2) 1993, Threepenny Opera 1988, Mahoganny Songspiel 1989, Illusions 1992, Espace Indécent 1993, City of Strangers 1995, Berlin Cabaret Songs 1996. *Film appearances include:* L'Autrichienne 1989, Moscou Parade 1992, Coupable d'Innocence 1993, Prêt à Porter 1995, Bogus 1996. *Address:* c/o Oliver Gluzman, 40 rue de la Folie Régnault, 75011 Paris, France. *Telephone:* 44-93-02-02. *Fax:* 44-93-04-40.

LENAERTS, Koen, LL.M., M.P.A., PH.D.; Belgian judge; b. 20 Dec. 1954, Mortsel; m. Kris Grimonprez; six d.; ed. Univs. of Namur and Leuven and Harvard Univ.; Asst. Prof. Leuven Univ. 1979–82, Assoc. Prof. 1982–83, Prof. of EC Law 1983–; Prof. of European Insts., Coll. of Europe, Bruges 1984–89; law clerk to Judge R. Joliet, Court of Justice of European Communities 1984–85; mem. Brussels bar 1986–89; Judge, Court of First Instance of European Communities, Luxembourg 1989–; Visiting Prof. Univ. of Burundi 1983, 1986, Univ. of Strasbourg 1986–89, Harvard Univ. 1988–89; various academic distinctions, fellowships and prizes. *Publications:* "The Negative Implications" of the Commerce Clause and "Preemption" Doctrines as Federalism Related Limitations on State Power: a Historical Review 1978, Constitutie en rechter 1983, International privaatrecht (with G. Van Hecke) 1986, Le juge et la constitution aux Etats-Unis d'Amérique et dans l'ordre juridique européen 1988, Two Hundred Years of U.S. Constitution and Thirty Years of EEC Treaty: Outlook for a Comparison 1988; articles and contribs. to reviews etc. *Address:* Court of the First Instance of the European Communities, Palais de la Cour de Justice, 2925 Luxembourg. *Telephone:* (00352) 4303-3553. *Fax:* (00352) 4303-2900.

LENDL, Ivan; American professional tennis player (retd.); b. 7 March 1960, Ostrava, Czechoslovakia; m. Samantha Frankel 1989; winner, Italian Jr. Singles 1978, French Jr. Singles 1978, Wimbledon Jr. Singles 1978, Spanish Open Singles 1980, 1981, S. American Open Singles 1981, Canadian Open Singles 1980, 1981, WCT Tournament of Champion Singles 1982, WCT Masters Singles 1982, WCT Finals Singles 1982, Masters Champion 1985, 1986, French Open Champion 1984, 1986, 1987, U.S. Open Champion 1985, 1986, 1987, U.S. Clay Court Champion 1985, Italian Open Champion 1986, Australian Open Champion 1989, 1990; finalist Wimbledon 1986; held world no. 1 ranking for a record 270 weeks; named World Champion (Int. Tennis Fed.) 1985, 1986, 1990; retd. Dec. 1994; granted American citizenship 1992. *Leisure interests:* golf, collecting art.

LENICA, Jan; Polish graphic artist, painter and animator; b. 4 Jan. 1928, Poznań; s. of Alfred Lenica and Janina Lenica; m. Merja Alanen; two d.; ed. Faculty of Arch. Warsaw Univ. of Tech.; satirical drawings 1945–60, book illustrations 1945–, posters 1950–, author of experimental animated cartoons 1957–, stage design 1963–, costume design for opera; contribs. to many journals including Szpilki; mem. Jury Theatrical Poster Biennale, Rzeszów 1995; individual exhbns. Paris 1980, Berlin 1990, Hamburg 1991, Warsaw 1996; many children's books; Prof. Hochschule der Künste, Berlin, Harvard Univ., Hught Film School, Kassel; Int. Poster Biennale (1st Prize), Oberhausen 1968, Toulouse-Lautrec Prize, Paris, Max Ernst Prize for animated cartoon 1966, St. Marcus' Lion, Venice 1957, Emil Cohl Prize and about 20 prizes at film festivals worldwide. *Major works:* book illustrations: Lokomotywa by J. Tuwim 1956, Population Explosion by Sauvy 1962, Jan Lenica Noiret Blanc 1988; *posters: c.* 200 designs including Wages of Fear 1954, Phèdre 1957, Il bidone 1957, Wozzeck 1964, Faust 1964, Othello 1968, Olympic Games 1969; *animated cartoons:* Once Upon a Time 1957, House (with W. Borowczyk) 1958 (Grand Prix, World Cartoon Exhbn., Brussels), Monsieur Tête 1959, Labyrinth 1960, Rhinoceros 1963, A 1964, Adam 2 1968, Martwa natura (Still Life) 1969, Fantorro 1972, Pejzaz (Landscape) 1974, Ubu 1980, cartoon series for Austrian television. *Address:* Passauerstr. 34, 10789 Berlin, Germany. *Telephone:* 211 99 33.

LENK, Hans Albert Paul, PH.D.; German professor of philosophy; b. 23 March 1935, Berlin; s. of Albert and Annemarie Lenk; m. Ulrike Reincke; two s. one d.; ed. Lauenburgische Gelehrtenschule, Ratzeburg, Freiburg and Kiel Univs., Tech. Univ. of Berlin; Asst. Prof. Tech. Univ. of Berlin 1962, Assoc. Prof. 1966, Prof. (Wissenschaftlicher Rat und Professor) 1969; Chair. and Prof. of Philosophy, Karlsruhe Univ. 1969–, Dean, Coll. of Humanities and Social Sciences 1973–75; Dean and Prof. Philosophy of Social Sciences and Theory of Planning, European Faculty of Land Use and Devt., Strasbourg 1983–; Visiting Prof. numerous foreign univs.; Hon. Prof. Tech. Univ., Budapest 1992; Green Honors Chair. Tex. Christian Univ., Fort Worth 1987; Pres. Int. Philosophic Soc. for Study of Sport 1980–81, Int. Olympic Union 1980–90, European Forum, Baden 1980–; Vice-Pres. European Acad. of Sciences and Philosophy of Law 1986–; Pres. Gen. Soc. for Philosophy in Germany 1991–93; Pres. Argentine-German Soc. of Philosophy 1992–, German-Hungarian Soc. of Philosophy 1993, Chilean-German Soc. of Philosophy 1995–; Vice-Pres. Féd. Int. des Socs. de Philosophie 1998–; mem. American Acad. of Kinesiology and Physical Educ., Nat. Olympic Cttee. for Germany –1992, German UNESCO Comm. –1992, Inst. Int. de Philosophie 1994 (mem. Bd. 1996–), Int. Acad. of Philosophy of Science 1995; Amateur Coach World Champion Eight Oar Crew 1966; Dr. h.c. (Deutsche Sporthochschule, Cologne) 1986, (Córdoba) 1992, (Tech. Univ. Budapest) 1993, (Univ. Pécs) 1994, Moscow (Univ. of Humanistic Studies) 1995; Hon. mem. Int. Olympic Acad.; four German, two European, one Olympic titles for rowing, Silver Leaf of Fed. Pres. 1959, 1960, Scientific Diem Plaque 1962, Sievert Award (Olympian International) 1973, Noel Baker Prize (UNESCO) 1978, Outstanding Academic Book Award 1979. *Publications:* more than 80 books, including Kritik der logischen Konstanten 1968, Team Dynamics 1977, Pragmatische Vernunft 1979, Social Philosophy of Athletics 1979, Zur Sozialphilosophie der Technik 1982, Zwischen Wissenschaftstheorie und Sozialwissenschaft 1985, Zwischen Sozialpsychologie und Sozialphilosophie 1987, Kritik der kleinen Vernunft 1987, Das Prinzip Fairness 1989, Tagebuch einer Rückreise 1991, Prometheisches Philosophieren zwischen Praxis und Paradox 1991, Zwischen Wissenschaft und Ethik 1992, Philosophie und Interpretation 1993, Interpretationskonstrukte 1993, Macht u. Machbarkeit der Technik 1994, Schemaspiele 1995, Interpretation u. Realität 1995, Einführung in die angewandte Ethik 1997, Einführung in die Erkenntnistheorie 1998, Konkrete Humanität 1998; more than 1,000 articles. *Address:* Universität (TH) Karlsruhe, Institut für Philosophie, Kollegium am Schloss, Bau 11, 76128 Karlsruhe (Office); Neubrunnenschlag 15, 76337 Waldbronn, Germany (Home). *Telephone:* (0721) 608-21 49 (Office); (07243) 6 79 71 (Home). *Fax:* (0721) 6083084.

LENK, Thomas; German sculptor and graphic artist; b. 15 June 1933, Berlin; s. of Franz and Anneliese (née Hoernecke) Lenk; m. Maria Bendig 1959; two d.; one-man shows in Wiesbaden 1958, Stuttgart 1962, 1965, 1968, 1970, 1974, 1977, 1981, Wuppertal 1963, 1994, Ulm 1964, 1970, Zürich 1966, 1969, Kassel 1966, New York, London, Milan 1967, Münster 1968, 1980, Darmstadt 1968, Detroit 1969, Bochum 1971, Essen 1971, 1973, Düsseldorf 1971, 1974, 1980, Saarbrücken 1971, 1982, Cologne 1976, Alexandria 1978, Tübingen 1980, Nürnberg, Munich 1983, Mannheim, Leverkusen, Linz 1985, Staatsgaleri, Stuttgart 1986, Cottbus, Dessau, Ingoldstadt, Munich 1995, Badisches Landesmuseum, Karlsruhe 1998; has participated in numerous group exhbns. in Europe, Canada, U.S.A. and Japan; exhibited at XXXV Venice Biennale 1970, IV Documenta, Kassel 1968; Guest Prof., Heluwan Univ., Cairo 1978; mem. Humboldt-Gesellschaft 1992; Carnegie Int. Purchase Award 1967; Third Prize, Socha Piestanskych Parkov, Bratislava 1969, Prize of 2nd Norwegian Graphics Biennale 1974, Hon. Life mem., Art Gallery of Ont., Toronto 1988, Verleihung des Professorentitels 1989. *Address:* 74542 Schloss Tierberg, Gemeinde Braunsbach, Schloss Tierberg, Germany. *Telephone:* (07905) 362. *Fax:* (07905) 362.

LENNINGS, Manfred, DR.ING.; German industrialist; b. 23 Feb. 1934, Oberhausen; s. of Wilhelm Lennings and Amanda Albert; m. Renate Stelbrink 1961; one s. one d.; ed. Gymnasium Geislingen/Steige, Univ. of Munich and Bergakademie Clausthal; Chair. German Student Org. 1959–60; Asst. of Man. Bd., Gutehoffnungshütte Aktienverein 1964–67, Deputy mem. 1968, Chair. 1975–83; mem. Man. Bd., Deutsche Werft AG 1968–69; Chair. Man. Bd. Howaldtswerke-Deutsche Werft AG 1970–74; Chair. Supervisory Bd., Fried. Krupp AG Hoesch-Krupp, Gildemeister AG, E. Heitkamp GmbH and IVG AG; Dir. several cos.; Consultant Westdeutsche Landesbank 1984–. *Leisure interests:* modern painting and literature, swimming, horse riding. *Address:* c/o Westdeutsche Landesbank, Herzogstr. 15, 40217 Düsseldorf, Germany. *Telephone:* (0211) 8264800. *Fax:* (0211) 8263503.

LENNKH, Georg, LL.D.; Austrian diplomatist; b. 8 Dec. 1939, Graz; s. of Friedrich and Elisabeth Lennkh; m. Annie Lechevalier 1966; one s. one d.; ed. Univ. of Graz, Johns Hopkins School of Advanced Informational Studies, Bologna and Univ. of Chapel Hill, N.C., U.S.A.; entered Fed. Ministry for Foreign Affairs 1965; served Tokyo 1968–72, Austrian Mission to UN, New York 1972–76, Dept. for Int. Orgs., Ministry of Foreign Affairs 1976–78; served Cabinet Office of Fed. Chancellor Kreisky, with responsibility for foreign relations 1978–82; Perm. Rep. to OECD 1982–93; Dir. Gen. Dept. for Devt. Cooperation, Fed. Ministry for Foreign Affairs 1997–. *Leisure interest:* skiing. *Address:* Ministry for Foreign Affairs, 1014 Vienna, Minoritenplatz 9, Austria. *Telephone:* 531 15-4432. *Fax:* 531 85-270.

LENNOX, Annie, A.R.A.M.; British rock singer; b. 25 Dec. 1954; d. of late Thomas A. Lennox and of Dorothy Lennox (née Ferguson); m. Uri Fruchtmann 1988; two d.; ed. Aberdeen High School for Girls, Royal Acad. of Music; founder mem. (with Dave Stewart, q.v.) The Tourists 1978–80, Eurythmics 1982–90; Eurythmics tours U.K., Europe, U.S.A., 1983, 1984, world tours 1986–87, 1989–90; solo albums: Diva 1992, Medusa 1995; numerous singles and album sales awards; other awards include Best U.K. Video (for Love is a Stranger) 1982, Grammy Awards for Best Video Album and for Best Female Performance (for Sweet Dreams), Ivor Novello Award for Best Pop Song (Sweet Dreams), American Soc. of Composers Award, BPI Award for Best Female Vocalist 1982/83, 1987/88, 1989/90, 1992/93, BPI for Best Album (for Diva) 1992/93, Ivor Novello Award for Best Song (for Why), Brit Award for Best Female Vocalist 1996, Grammy Award for Best Female Pop Vocals (for No More I Love You) 1996. *Address:* c/o 19 Management Ltd., Unit 32, Ransomes Dock, 35–37 Parkgate Road, London, SW11 4NP, England. *Telephone:* 0171-228 4000. *Fax:* 0171-924 1608.

LENNOX-BOYD, Simon Ronald Rupert (see Boyd of Merton, 2nd Viscount).

LENZ, Carl Otto, DR. JUR.; German lawyer; b. 5 June 1930, Berlin; s. of late Dr. Otto Lenz and of Marieliese Pohl; m. Ursula Heinrich 1960; two s. three d.; ed.in Germany, Switzerland and Harvard and Cornell Univs.; Sec.-Gen. Christian Democratic Group, European Parl. 1956–66; mem. Bundestag 1965–84; Advocate-Gen. European Court of Justice 1984–97; Hon. Prof. of European Law, Saarland Univ. 1990–. *Publications:* Die Notverstandsverfassung des GG 1971, EG Handbuch Recht im Binnenmarkt 1994, EG-Vortrag Kommentar 1994. *Address:* Rodensteinstrasse 22, 64625 Bensheim, Germany.

LENZ, Siegfried; German writer; b. 17 March 1926, Lyck, East Prussia; m. Liselotte Lenz; ed. High School, Samter, and Univ. of Hamburg; Cultural Ed. Die Welt 1949–51; freelance writer 1952–; Gerhart Hauptmann Prize 1961, Bremer Literaturpreis 1962, German Freemasons' Literary Prize 1970, Kulturpreis, Goslar 1978 and numerous other prizes. *Publications* include novels: Es waren Habichte in der Luft 1951, Duell mit dem Schatten 1953, Der Mann im Strom 1957, 1958, Brot und Spiele 1959, Stadtgespräche 1963, Deutschstunde 1968, Das Vorbild 1973, Heimatmuseum 1978, Der Verlust 1981, Ein Kriegsende 1984, Die Auflehnung 1994; stories: So zärtlich war Suleyken 1955, Jäger des Spotts 1958, Das Feuerschiff 1960, Der Spielverderber 1965, Einstein überquert die Elbe bei Hamburg 1975; plays: Zeit der Schuldlosen 1961, Das Gesicht 1963, Haussuchung (radio plays) 1967. *Address:* Preusserstrasse 4, 22605 Hamburg, Germany. *Telephone:* 880-83-09.

LEÓN PORTILLA, Miguel, PH.D.; Mexican anthropologist and historian; b. 22 Feb. 1926, Mexico City; s. of Miguel León Ortiz and Luisa Portilla Nájera; m. Ascensión Hernández Triviño 1965; one d.; ed. Loyola Univ. of Los Angeles and Nat. Univ. of Mexico; Sec.-Gen. Inter-American Indian Inst. 1955–59, Asst. Dir. 1959–60, Dir. 1960–66; Asst. Dir. Seminar for Náhuatl Culture, Nat. Univ. of Mexico 1956, Dir. Inst. of Historical Research 1963–78, Prof. Emer. 1988–; Dir. América Indígena 1960; Adviser, Int. Inst. of Different Civilisations 1960; Perm. Rep. of Mexico to UNESCO, Paris 1987; mem. Bd. Govs. Nat. Univ. Mexico 1976; mem. American Anthropological Asscn. 1960–, Mexican Acad. of Language 1962–, Société des Américanistes de Paris 1966–, Mexican Acad. of History 1969–, Nat. Coll. of Mexico 1971–; Corresp. mem. Royal Spanish Acad. of History 1969–; Hon. mem. American Historical Asscn. 1991, N.A.S. 1995; Guggenheim Fellow 1969; American Anthropological Asscn. Fifth Distinguished Lecturer 1974; Hon. Ph.D. (Southern Methodist Univ., Dallas, Tex.) 1980, (California) 1986, (Tel Aviv) 1987, (Toulouse) 1990, (Colima) 1993, (San Andrés, Bolivia) 1994, (Brown Univ.) 1996; Commendatore Repub. Italiana 1977, Serra Award 1978, Nat. Prize in the Social Sciences (Mexico) 1981, Manuel Gamio Anthropological Award 1983, Nat. Univ. of Mexico Prize 1994. *Publications:* La Filosofía Náhuatl 1956, Visión des los Vencidos 1959, Los Antiguos Mexicanos 1961, The Broken Spears, Aztec Account of the Conquest of Mexico 1962, Rückkehr der Götter 1962, Aztec Thought and Culture 1963, Literaturas Precolombinas de México 1964, Imagen del México Antiguo 1964, Le Crépuscule des Aztèques 1965, Trece Poetas del Mundo Azteca 1967, Pre-Columbian Literatures of Mexico 1968, Tiempo y Realidad en el Pensamiento Maya 1968, Testimonios Sudcalifornianos 1970, De Teotihuacan a los Aztecas 1971, The Norteño Variety of Mexican Culture 1972, The Voyages of Francisco de Ortega to California 1632-1636 1972, Time and Reality in the Thought of the Maya 1973, Historia Natural y Crónica de la Antigua California 1973, Il Rovescio della Conquista, Testimonianze Asteche, Maya e Inca 1974, Aztecs and Navajos 1975, Endangered Cultures: The Indian in Latin America 1975, Indian Place Names of Baja California 1977, L'Envers de la conquête 1977, Los Manifestos en Náhuatl de Emiliano Zapata 1978, Toltecayotl, Aspectos de la Cultura Náhuatl 1980, Mesoamerican Spirituality 1980, Middle America 1981, Literaturas de Anahuac y del Imcario 1982, Mesoamerica before 1519 1984, Codex Fejeŕváry-Mayer, a Book of the Merchants, 1985, La Pensée Aztèque 1985, Libro de los Coloquios 1986, Das Alte Mexiko: Religion 1986, Huehuehtlahtolli, Testimonies of the Ancient Word 1988, Mesoamerica in 1492 and on the eve of 1992, 1988, Poésie Náhuatl d'amour et d'amitié 1991, Fifteen Poets of the Aztec World 1992, Raíces indígenas, presencia hispánica 1993, La flecha en el blanco 1995. *Leisure interests:* scouting and gardening. *Address:* Calle de Alberto Zamora 131, Coyoacán, 04000 México, D.F., Mexico. *Telephone:* (5) 554 0802. *Fax:* (5) 665-00-70.

LEONARD, Brian E., PH.D., D.SC., M.R.I.A.; Irish professor of pharmacology; b. 30 May 1936, Winchester; s. of Harold E. Leonard and Dorothy Coley; m. Helga F. Mühlpfordt 1959; two d.; ed. Univ. of Birmingham; Dept. of Medical Biochem. Univ. of Birmingham 1956–62; lecturer in Pharmacology, Univ. of Nottingham 1962–68; Tech. Officer, CNS Research, ICI Pharmaceuticals Div. Alderley Park, Cheshire 1968–71; Group Leader, CNS Pharmaology, Organon International BV, Oss, Netherlands 1971–74; Prof. of Pharmacology, Univ. Coll. Galway 1974–; Councillor C.I.N.P. 1996–, Treas. 1992–96; Pres. British Asscn. Psychopharmacology 1988–90; mem. Royal Irish Acad.; assoc. mem. Royal Coll. of Psychiatrists; foreign corresp. mem. American Coll. Neuropsychopharmacology. *Publications:* Fundamentals of Psychopharmacology 1992, over 300 articles. *Leisure interests:* entomology, classical music, political science. *Address:* Department of Pharmacology, University College, Galway, Ireland. *Telephone:* (091) 524411 (Ext. 2246). *Fax:* (091) 525300.

LEONARD, Elmore, PH.B.; American novelist and screenwriter; b. 11 Oct. 1925, New Orleans; s. of Elmore John and Flora Amelia (Rivé) Leonard; m. 1st Beverly Claire Cline 1949 (divorced 1977), three s. two d.; m. 2nd Joan Leanne Lancaster 1979 (died 1993); m. 3rd Christine Kent 1993; ed. Univ. of Detroit; mem. Writers' Guild of America, Authors' Guild, Mystery Writers of America, Western Writers of America. *Publications:* 31 novels including: Hombre 1961, City Primeval 1980, Split Images 1982, Cat Chaser 1982, La Brava 1983, Stick 1983, Glitz 1985, Bandits 1987, Touch 1987, Freaky Deaky 1988, Killshot 1989, Get Shorty 1990, Maximum Bob 1991, Rum Punch 1992, Pronto 1993, Riding the Rap 1995, Out of Sight 1996. *Address:* c/o Michael Siegel, 9150 Wilshire Blvd., Suite 350, Beverly Hills, CA 90212, U.S.A.

LEONARD, Rev. and Rt. Hon. Father Graham Douglas, K.C.V.O., P.C., M.A., D.D., S.T.D.; British ecclesiastic; b. 8 May 1921, Greenwich; s. of the late Rev. Douglas Leonard; m. Vivien Priscilla Swann 1943; two s.; ed. Monkton Combe School, Balliol Coll., Oxford, Westcott House, Cambridge; Capt. Oxon. and Bucks. Light Infantry 1941–45, Army Operational Research Group 1944–45; ordained Deacon 1947, Priest 1948; Curacies 1948–52; Vicar of Ardleigh 1952–55; Dir. Religious Educ., Diocese of St. Albans, Canon, St. Albans Cathedral 1955–58; Gen. Sec. Nat. Soc. and Gen. Sec. Church of England Schools Council 1958–62; Archdeacon of Hampstead, Rector of St. Andrew Undershaft and St. Mary Axe 1962–64; Bishop of Willesden 1964–73, of Truro 1973–81, of London 1981–91; received into Roman Catholic Church and ordained conditionally as a priest April 1994; mem. Anglican/Orthodox Joint Doctrinal Comm. 1974–81; Superior Gen. Soc. of Mary 1973–94 (Vice-

Pres. 1994–); Chair. Church of England Bd. for Social Responsibility 1976–83, Churches Main Cttee. 1981–91, BBC and IBA Cen. Religious Advisory Cttee. 1984–89, Bd. of Educ. 1983–88; Pres. Path to Rome Int. Convention 1998–; mem. Polytechnics and Colls. Funding Council 1989–93; Dean of H.M. Chapels Royal 1981–91, Prelate of Order of British Empire 1981–91, Prelate Imperial Soc. of Kts. Bachelor 1986–91; Episcopal Canon of Jerusalem 1981–91; Hon. Fellow, Balliol Coll., Oxford 1986; Hon. Bencher, Middle Temple 1981; Hon. D.D. (Episcopal Theological Seminary, Kentucky) 1974; Hon. D.Cn.L. (Nashotah House) 1983; Hon. S.T.D. (Siena Coll.) 1994; Hon. LL.D. (Simon Greenleaf School of Law) 1987; Hon. D.D. (Westminster Coll., Fulton) 1987; Hon. D.Litt. (C.N.A.A.) 1989; John Findlay Green Foundation Lecture, Fulton 1987; Hensley Henson Lecturer, Oxford Univ. 1991–92. *Publications:* The Gospel is for Everyone 1971, God Alive: Priorities in Pastoral Theology 1981, Firmly I Believe and Truly 1985, Life in Christ 1986, contribs. to several theological works. *Leisure interests:* music, reading. *Address:* 25 Woodlands Road, Witney, Oxon., OX8 6DR, England.

LEONARD, Hugh (John Keyes Byrne); Irish playwright; b. 9 Nov. 1926, Dublin; m. Paule Jacquet 1955; one d.; ed. Presentation Coll., Dún Laoghaire; worked as Civil Servant 1945–49; Script Ed. Granada TV, England 1961–63; Literary Ed., Abbey Theatre, Dublin 1976–77; Programme Dir., Dublin Theatre Festival 1978–; Hon. D.H.L. (R.I.); Hon. D.Litt. (Trinity Coll., Dublin); Writers' Guild Award 1966, Tony Award, Critics Circle Award, Drama Desk Award, Outer Critics Award 1978. *Stage plays include:* The Big Birthday 1957, A Leap in the Dark 1957, Madigan's Lock 1958, A Walk on the Water 1960, The Passion of Peter Ginty 1961, Stephen D 1962, The Poker Session 1963, Dublin 1 1963, The Saints Go Cycling In 1965, Mick and Mick 1966, The Quick and the Dead 1967, The Au Pair Man 1968, The Barracks 1969, The Patrick Pearse Motel 1971, Da 1973, Thieves 1973, Summer 1974, Times of Wolves and Tigers 1974, Irishmen 1975, Time Was 1976, A Life 1977, Moving Days 1981, The Mask of Moriarty 1984, Moving 1991, Senna for Sonny 1994, The Lily Lally Show 1994, Chamber Music (2 plays) 1994, Magic 1997. *Writing for television includes:* Silent Song 1967, Nicholas Nickleby 1977, London Belongs to Me 1977, The Last Campaign 1978, The Ring and the Rose 1978, Strumpet City 1979, The Little World of Don Camillo 1980, Kill 1982, Good Behaviour 1982, O'Neill 1983, Beyond the Pale 1984, The Irish RM 1985, A Life 1986, Troubles 1987, Parnell and the Englishwoman 1988. *Films:* Herself Surprised 1977, Da 1984, Widows' Peak 1984, Troubles 1984, Banjaxed 1995. *Adaptations:* Great Expectations 1995, A Tale of Two Cities 1996. *Publications:* Home Before Night (autobiog.) 1979, Out After Dark (autobiog.) 1988, Parnell and the Englishwoman 1989, I, Orla! 1990, Rover and other Cats (a memoir) 1992, The Off-Shore Island (novel) 1993, The Mogs (for children) 1995, Magic 1997. *Leisure interests:* river cruising, conversation, travel, gastronomy, vintage movies, travel in France. *Address:* 6 Rossaun, Pilot View, Dalkey, Co. Dublin, Ireland. *Telephone:* (01) 280 9590.

LEONARD, Hugh Terence; New Zealand broadcasting executive; b. 20 July 1938, Greymouth; s. of Michael James Leonard and Elizabeth Leonard (née Storey); m. Pauline Lobendahn 1965; one s. two d.; joined N.Z. Broadcasting Service 1956, Fiji Broadcasting Comm. 1960, Gen. Man. 1973–85; Sec.-Gen. Asia-Pacific Broadcasting Union (ABU) 1985–; Fiji Independence Medal 1970. *Leisure interests:* classic motorcycles, remote-controlled model aircraft, computers. *Address:* Asia-Pacific Broadcasting Union, P.O. Box 1164, 59700 Kuala Lumpur, Malaysia. *Telephone:* (3) 282 3592. *Fax:* (3) 282 5292.

LEONARD, Nelson Jordan, B.S., D.SC., PH.D.; American professor of chemistry; b. 1 Sept. 1916, Newark, N.J.; s. of Harvey Nelson Leonard and Olga Pauline Jordan; m. 1st Louise Cornelie Vermey 1947 (died 1987); three s. one d.; m. 2nd Peggy Phelps 1992; ed. Lehigh, Oxford and Columbia Univs.; Research Asst., Univ. of Ill. 1942–43, Instructor 1943–44, Assoc. 1944–45, 1946–47, Asst. Prof. 1947–49, Assoc. Prof. 1949–52, Prof. of Chem. 1952–, Head of Div. of Organic Chem. 1954–63, and Prof. of Biochem. 1973–86; mem. Center for Advanced Study, Univ. of Ill. 1968–86, Reynold C. Fuson Prof. of Chem. 1981–86, R.C. Fuson Prof., Emer. 1986–; Fogarty Scholar-in-Residence, N.I.H., Bethesda 1989–90; Sherman Fairchild Distinguished Scholar, Calif. Inst. of Tech. 1991, Faculty Assoc. 1992–; Scientific Consultant and Special Investigator, Field Intelligence Agency Technical, U.S. Army and U.S. Dept. of Commerce, European Theater 1945–46; Ed. Organic Syntheses 1951–58, mem. Advisory Bd. 1959–, Bd. of Dirs. 1969–, Vice-Pres. 1976–80, Pres. 1980–88; mem. Exec. Cttee. Journal of Organic Chemistry 1951–54, mem. Editorial Bd. 1957–61; mem. Editorial Bd. Journal of A.C.S. 1960–72; mem. Advisory Bd. Biochemistry 1973–78; Sec., Div. of Organic Chem., A.C.S. 1949–54, Chair. 1956; mem. Advisory Panel for Chem. of Nat. Science Foundation 1958–61, Program Cttee. in the Basic Physical Sciences of Alfred P. Sloan Foundation 1961–66, Study Section in Medicinal Chem. of N.I.H. 1963–67, Educational Advisory Bd. of John Simon Guggenheim Memorial Foundation 1969–88, Cttee. of Selection 1977–88, Advisory Cttee., Searle Scholars Program, Chicago Community Trust 1982–85; Visiting Prof. Univ. of Calif. at Los Angeles 1953; mem. N.A.S. 1955–; titular mem. Organic Chem. Div., Int. Union of Pure and Applied Chem. 1981–85, co-opted mem. 1985–87, Sec. 1987–89, Vice-Pres. 1989–91, Pres. 1991–93; Fellow, American Acad. of Arts and Sciences 1961– (Vice-Pres. 1990–93), American Philosophical Soc. 1996–; Foreign mem. Polish Acad. of Sciences; Swiss American Foundation Lecturer 1953, 1970, Julius Stieglitz Memorial Lecturer (A.C.S.) 1962, Backer Lecturer, Univ. of Groningen 1972 and other lectureships; Hon. Sc.D. (Lehigh, Ill., Adam Mickiewicz Univ., Poland); A.C.S. Award for Creative Work in Synthetic Organic Chem. 1963, Synthetic Organic Chemical Mfrs. Asscn. Medal 1970, Edgar Fahs Smith Award and Memorial Lecturer of A.C.S. and Univ. of Pa. 1975, Roger Adams Award in Organic Chemistry, A.C.S. 1981, Wheland Award, Univ. of Chicago 1991, Creativity Award (Univ. of Oregon) 1994, Paul G. Gassman Distinguished Service Award (A.C.S.) 1994, Arthur C. Cope Scholar Award (A.C.S.) 1995. *Publications:* numerous research articles in scientific journals. *Leisure interests:* skiing, swimming. *Address:* Division of Chemistry and Chemical Engineering, Mail Code 164-30, Pasadena, CA 91125; 389 California Terrace, Pasadena, CA 91105, U.S.A. *Telephone:* (626) 395-6541; (626) 792-7745. *Fax:* (626) 568-3749.

LEONARD, Ray Charles ("Sugar Ray"); American boxer; b. 17 May 1956, Wilmington, N.C.; s. of Cicero Leonard and Getha Leonard; m. Juanita Wilkinson 1980 (divorced 1990); two s.; amateur boxer 1970–77; won 140 of 145 amateur fights; world amateur champion 1974, U.S. Amateur Athletic Union champion 1974, Pan-American Games gold medallist 1975, Olympic gold medallist 1976; guaranteed record purse of $25,000 for first professional fight Feb. 1977; won North American welterweight title from Pete Ranzany August 1979; won World Boxing Council version of world welterweight title from Wilfred Benitez Nov. 1979; retained title against Dave Green March 1980, lost it to Roberto Durán (q.v.), Montreal, June 1980, regained it from Durán, New Orleans, Nov. 1980; world junior middleweight title, World Boxing Asscn. (W.B.A.) June 1981; won W.B.A. world welterweight title from Tommy Hearns to become undisputed World Champion Sept. 1981, drew rematch June 1989; 36 professional fights, 33 wins, lost 2, drawn 1; retd. from boxing Nov. 1982; returned to the ring April 1987; won World middleweight title, lost to Terry Norris 1991, retd. from boxing 1991, 1997; returned to ring March 1997; lost Int. Boxing Council middleweight title fight to Hector Camacho 1997; commentator for Home Box Office TV Co. *Address:* Suite 303, 4401 East West Highway, Bethesda, MD 20814, U.S.A.

LEONE, Giovanni; Italian politician and professor; b. 3 Nov. 1908, Naples; s. of Mauro and Maria (Gioffrida) Leone; m. Vittoria Michitto 1946; four s. (one deceased); ed. Univ. of Naples; Prof. of Law, Univ. of Naples; elected to Constituent Assembly 1946, to Chamber of Deputies 1948 and 1953; Vice-Pres., Chamber of Deputies 1948–49, Pres. 1955–63; Prime Minister June–Nov. 1963, June-Dec. 1968; made life Senator 1967; Pres. of Italian Repub. 1971–78; Christian Democrat. *Address:* c/o Senato, Piazza Madama, Rome, Italy.

LEONG, Lampo, M.F.A.; Chinese artist and educator; b. 3 July 1961, Guangzhou; ed. Guangzhou Fine Arts Inst., California Coll. of Arts & Craft, Oakland, U.S.A.; Instructor, Calif. Coll. of Arts & Crafts 1986–87; lecturer, San Francisco State Univ., Calif. 1988–96, Asst. Prof. 1996–; Instructor, Univ. of Calif., Berkeley 1989, Art Studio 1990–; Instructor Chabot Coll., Hayward, Calif. 1989–94, Diablo Valley Coll., Pleasant Hill, Calif. 1998–; 30 solo exhbns. China, U.S.A., Canada 1986–; numerous group exhbns. China, Taiwan, Macao, Hong Kong, U.S.A. 1981–; works in many collections in China, Macao, U.S.A., Japan, Indonesia; Vice-Pres. Oriental Art Asscn., U.S.A.; Co-founder, Dir. Chinese American Culture Exchange Asscn., U.S.A.; mem. Nat. Modern Meticulous Painting Soc., China, Macao Soc. of Social Sciences. *Leisure interests:* photography, film, travel, ballroom dancing. *Address:* Brushwork Gallery, 166 Palisades Drive, Daly City, CA 94015, U.S.A. *Telephone:* (650) 994-5018. *Fax:* (650) 994-5018.

LEONHARD, Kurt Ernst Albert; German author, translator and editor; b. 5 Feb. 1910, Berlin; s. of Paul Leonhard and Erna Leonhard; m. Ilse Bliedner 1943; two d.; ed. Reformrealgymnasium, Berlin-Karlshorst and Univ. of Berlin; bookseller, author, art critic and publisher's reader 1937–41; mil. service 1941–46; freelance author, translator and lecturer 1946–; publisher's reader, Esslingen 1950–59; Prof. h.c. 1976; Verdienstmedaille, Baden-Württemberg 1984; Hon. mem. Stuttgart Acad. 1985. *Publications:* Die heilige Fläche 1947, Augenschein und Inbegriff 1953, Gegenwelt (poems) 1956, Cézanne (monograph) 1966, Picasso, Graphik 1966, Dante Alighieri (monograph) 1970, Wort wider Wort (poems) 1974, Das zehnte Loch (poems) 1983, Gegenbilder (poetry and prose) 1986, Zirkelschlüsse 1988, Texte aus sechs Jahrzehnten 1995. *Leisure interests:* travel, art, nature. *Address:* Auchtweg 24, 73734 Esslingen, Germany. *Telephone:* 0711-384688.

LEONHARDT, Rudolf Walter, DR.PHIL.; German journalist; b. 9 Feb. 1921, Altenburg; s. of Rudolf and Paula (née Zeiger) Leonhardt; m. Ulrike (née Zoerb) Leonhardt; two s. one d.; ed. Berlin, Leipzig, Bonn, Cambridge and London; Lecturer in German, Cambridge Univ. 1948–50; Foreign Corresp. Die Zeit, London 1953–55, Cultural Ed. Die Zeit, Hamburg 1957–73, Deputy Editor-in-Chief 1974–. *Publications:* The Structure of a Novel 1950, Notes on German Literature 1955, 77 x England 1957 (trans. into Spanish 1964), Der Sündenfall der deutschen Germanistik 1959, Leben ohne Literatur? 1961, x-mal Deutschland 1961 (trans. into English, Italian, Spanish 1964), Zeitnotizen 1963, Junge deutsche Dichter für Anfänger 1964, Reise in ein fernes Land (with Marion Gräfin Dönhoff and Theo Sommer) 1964 (trans. into Japanese 1965); Kästner für Erwachsene 1966, Wer wirft den ersten Stein? 1969, Sylt für Anfänger 1969, Haschisch-Report 1970, Drei Wochen und drei Tage—Japan-Tagebuch 1970, Deutschland 1972, Argumente Pro und Contra 1974, Das Weib, das ich geliebet hab—Heines Mädchen und Frauen 1975, Journalismus und Wahrheit 1976, Lieder aus dem Krieg 1979, Sylt 1870–1920 1980, Hamburg 1985, Deutschland 1990.

Leisure interest: people. *Address:* Leuchtturmweg 42A, 22559 Hamburg, Germany.

LEONI, Tea; American actress; m. David Duchovny (q.v.). *Films:* Switch 1991, A League of Their Own 1992, Wyatt Earp 1994, Bad Boys 1995, Flirting with Disaster 1996. *TV:* (sitcoms) Naked Truth, Flying Blind 1995. *Address:* c/o ICM, 8942 Wilshire Boulevard, Beverly Hills, CA 90211, U.S.A.

LEONOV, Maj.-Gen. Aleksey Arkhipovich; Russian cosmonaut; b. 30 May 1934, Listianka, Kamerovo Region; s. of Arkhip and Yevdokia Leonov; m. Svetlana Leonova; two d.; ed. Chuguevsky Air Force School for Pilots and Zhukovsky Air Force Engineering Academy; Pilot 1956–59; mem. CPSU 1957–91; cosmonaut training 1960; first man to walk in space 1965: took part in flight of space-ship Voskhod 2, and moved 5 metres into space outside space-ship; Pilot-Cosmonaut of U.S.S.R.; Deputy Commdr. Gagarin Cosmonauts Training Center 1971; took part in joint flight Soyuz 19-Apollo 1975; Maj.-Gen. 1975; Chair. Council of Founders of Novosti Press Agency 1969–90; Deputy Head, Centre of Cosmonaut Training 1975–92; Dir. Cheteck-Cosmos Co. 1992–, Vice-Pres. Investment Fund Alfa-Capital 1997–; Co-Chair. Bd. Int. Asscn. of Cosmonauts; Hon. Dr. Sc.Eng.; Hero of the Soviet Union 1965, 1975, Hero of Bulgaria, Hero of Vietnam, Order of Lenin (twice), U.S.S.R. State Prize 1981. *Leisure interests:* painting, shooting movies. *Address:* Alfa-Capital, Acad. Sakharov Prospect 12, 107078 Moscow, Russia. *Telephone:* 208-87-15.

LÉONTIEFF, Alexandre, D. EN SC. ECON.; French Polynesian politician; b. 20 Oct. 1948, Teahupoo, Tahiti; s. of Maxime Léontieff and Louise Teahu; m. Demecia Jurd 1972; two s.; mem. of Territorial Ass. French Polynesia 1977–; Vice-Pres. Govt. of Polynesia 1984–86; Minister of Economy, of the Sea and Tourism 1986–87; Pres. Govt. of Polynesia 1987–91; Deputy to French Nat. Ass. 1986. *Address:* Résidence Taina, B.P. No. 2737, Papeete, French Polynesia.

LEONTYEV, Mikhail Vladimirovich; Russian journalist; b. 12 Oct. 1958, Moscow; ed. Moscow Plekhanov Inst. of Nat. Econs.; political reviewer Kommersant (newspaper) 1987–90; on staff newspaper Atmoda (Riga) and Experimental Creative Cen. in Moscow 1989–91; Ed. Div. of Politics Nezavisimaya Gazeta (newspaper) 1990–92; First Deputy Ed.-in-Chief daily Business MN 1992–93; First Deputy Ed.-in-Chief Segodnya (newspaper) 1993–97; political reviewer TV-Cen. Channel 1997–. *Address:* TV-Centre, Akademika Koroleva str. 12, 127000 Moscow, Russia (Office). *Telephone:* (095) 217 9248 (Office).

LEOPHAIRATANA, Prachai, M.S.EE.; Thai business executive; b. 28 Aug. 1944; s. of Phorn Leophairatana and Boonsri Leophairatana; m. Orapin Leophairatana 1974; ed. Canterbury Univ., New Zealand, Univ. of Calif., Berkeley; C.E.O. Thai Petrochemical Industry PCL 1988–, TPI Polene PCL, TPI Group of Cos. 1988–; Man. Dir. Hong Yiah Seng Co. Ltd. 1986–; mem. Senate; Chair. Bd. of Dirs. United Grain Industry Co. Ltd. 1986–, Bangkok Union Insurance PCL 1986–, Thai Industrial Estate Corp. Ltd. 1988–, Exec. Bd. Thai Caprolactam PCL 1989–, Uhde (Thailand) Co. Ltd. 1990–, Thai Int. Tankers Co. Ltd. 1994–; Vice-Chair. Bd. of Dirs. Thai Alliance Textile Co. Ltd. 1986–; Dir. Rice Export Asscns., Thai–Chinese Friendship Asscn., Thai–Chinese Promotion of Investment and Trade Asscn., Bd. of Trade of Thailand; Sec.-Gen. Environment for Better Life Foundation; Kt. Grand Cross Most Noble Order of the Crown of Thailand; Kt. Grand Cross (1st Class) Exalted Order of the White Elephant; Kt. Grand Cordon (Special Class) Most Noble Order of the Crown of Thailand; Companion (4th Class) Most Admirable Order of the Direkgunabhom. *Address:* Thai Petrochemical Industry PCL, TPI Tower, 29th Floor, 26/56 Chan Tat Mai Road, Kwang Thungmahamek, Khet Sathorn, Bangkok 10210, Thailand. *Telephone:* 6785000. *Fax:* 6785001.

LEOPOLD, Luna Bergere, PH.D.; American geologist and engineer; b. 8 Oct. 1915, New Mexico; s. of Aldo Leopold and Estella Bergere; m. 1st Carolyn Clugston 1940; m. 2nd Barbara Beck Nelson 1973; one s. one d.; ed. Harvard Univ. and Univs. of California and Wisconsin; U.S. Army 1941–46; Head Meteorologist, Pineapple Research Inst. of Hawaii 1946–50; Hydraulic Engineer, U.S. Geological Survey, Washington, D.C. 1950–66, Chief Hydrologist 1956–66, Sr. Research Hydrologist 1966–71; Prof. of Geology, Univ. of Calif. 1973–; mem. N.A.S.; Hon. D.Sc. (St. Andrews) 1981, (Murcia); Kirk Bryan Award, Geological Soc. of America, Cullum Geographical Medal, American Geographical Soc., Distinguished Service Award, U.S. Dept. of Interior, Veth Medal, Royal Netherlands Geographical Soc., Rockefeller Public Service Award, Warren Prize, N.A.S., Busk Medal, Royal Geographical Soc., R. K. Linsley Award, American Inst. of Hydrology, Nat. Medal of Science and other awards. *Publications:* The Flood Control Controversy (with Thomas Maddock, Jr.) 1954, Fluvial Processes in Geomorphology 1964, Water 1974, Water in Environmental Planning (with Thomas Dunne) 1978, A View of the River 1994, Water, Rivers and Creeks 1997 and over 100 scientific papers on water, hydrology and rivers. *Address:* Department of Geology, University of California, Berkeley, CA 94720; 400 Vermont Avenue, Berkeley, CA 94707, U.S.A. (Home).

LÉOTARD, François Gérard Marie; French politician; b. 26 March 1942, Cannes; s. of André Léotard and Antoinette Tomasi; m. 1st France Reynier 1976; m. 2nd Isabelle Duret 1992; one s. one d.; ed. Lycées Charlemagne and Henri IV, Paris, Faculté de Droit and Inst. d'Etudes Politiques, Paris, and Ecole Nationale d'Administration; Sec. of Chancellery, Ministry of Foreign Affairs 1968–71; Admin. Town Planning 1973–75; Sous-préfet 1974–77; Mayor of Fréjus 1977–92, 1993–97, Municipal Councillor 1992; Deputy to Nat. Ass. (UDF-PR) 1978–86, 1988–92; Conseiller-General, Var 1980–88; Sec.-Gen. Parti Républicain 1982–88, Pres. 1988–90, 1995–97, Hon. Pres. 1990–95; Vice-Pres. Union pour la Démocratie Française (UDF) 1983–84, Pres. March 1996–; Minister of Culture and Communications 1986–88, of Nat. Defence 1993–95; Deputy for Var 1988–92, 1995–; Chevalier, Ordre nat. du Mérite. *Publications:* A Mots Decouverts 1987, Culture: Les Chemins de Printemps 1988, La Ville aimée: mes chemins de Fréjus 1989, Pendant la Crise, le spectacle Continue 1989, Adresse au Président des Républiques françaises 1991, Place de la République 1992, Ma Liberté 1995, Pour l'honneur 1997. *Address:* UDF, 25 avenue Charles Floquet, 75007 Paris; Assemblée Nationale, 75355 Paris, France. *Telephone:* (1) 44381001. *Fax:* (1) 44381021.

LEPAGE, Corinne Dominique Marguerite; French politician and lawyer; b. 11 May 1951, Boulogne-Billancourt; d. of Philippe Lepage and Jacqueline Schulmann; m. 1st Christian Jessua, one d.; m. 2nd Christian Huglo, one s.; ed. Lycée Molière, Univ. of Paris II and Inst. d'Etudes Politiques, Paris; in legal partnership 1971–76; barrister, Paris 1978–; Dir. of Studies, Univ. of Paris II 1974–77; Dir. of Educ. Univ. of Metz 1978–80; Maître de conférences, Inst. d'Etudes Politiques, Paris 1979–87; Course Dir. Univ. of Paris II 1982–86, Univ. of Paris XII 1984–; mem. Bar Council 1987–89; Vice-Pres., Pres. Asscn. of Admin. Law Advocates 1989–95; Minister of the Environment 1995–97. *Publications:* Code annoté des procédures administratives contentieuses 1990, Les audits de l'environnement 1992, On ne peut rien faire, Madame le ministre 1998; numerous articles in La Gazette du Palais. *Leisure interests:* cinema, reading, tennis, skiing, swimming. *Address:* 30 rue La Boétie, 75008 Paris, France.

LEPAGE, Robert; French-Canadian actor and television and theatre director; b. 1957, Quebec City; ed. Conservatoire d'Art Dramatique Quebec, Canada; Artistic Dir. Nat. Arts Centre Ottawa, Canada 1990–92. *Productions include:* TV, Needles and Opium, Tectonic Plates 1990, A Midsummer Night's Dream (Nat. Theatre) 1992, Coriolanus 1993, Elsinore 1996, Seven Streams of the River Ota 1998; staged Duke Bluebeard's Castle for Canadian Opera Co.; TV series: The Dragon's Trilogy; Film No (dir. and writer) 1999.

LE PEN, Jean-Marie, L. EN D.; French politician; b. 20 June 1928, La Trinité-sur-Mer, Morbihan; s. of Jean Le Pen and Anne-Marie Hervé; m. 1st Pierrette Lalanne, 1960 (divorced); three d.; m. 2nd Jeanne-Marie Paschos 1991; ed. Coll. des jésuites Saint-François-Xavier, Vannes, Lycée de Lorient, Univ. de Paris; Pres. Corpn. des étudiants en droit de Paris 1949–51; Sub-Lieut. 1st foreign bn. of paratroopers, Indochina 1954; Political Ed. Caravelle 1955, Nat. Del. for Union de défense de la jeunesse française, then Deputy 1st Sector, La Seine; mem. Groupe d'union et de fraternité at Nat. Ass., independent Deputy for la Seine 1958–62; Gen. Sec. Front nat. combattant 1956, of Tixier Vignacour Cttee. 1964–65; Dir. Soc. d'études et de relations publiques 1963–; Pres. Front nat. 1972–, Front Nat. Provence-Alpes-Côte d'Azur 1992–; mem. Nat. Ass. 1986–88; mem. European Parl. 1984, Pres. groupe des droites européennes 1984–; Presidential cand. 1988; guilty of physical assault and banned from holding or seeking public office for 2 years, given 3 month suspended prison sentence April 1998; Sentence on appeal: immunity removed by European Parl. Oct. 1998. Croix de la Valeur militaire. *Publications:* Les Français d'abord 1984, La France est de retour 1985, L'Espoir 1986, J'ai vu juste 1998. *Address:* 6 rue de Beaune, 75007 Paris (Office); 8 parc de Montretout, 92210 Saint-Cloud, France (Home).

LE PENSEC, Louis; French politician; b. 8 Jan. 1937, Mellac; s. of Jean Le Pensec and Marie-Anne Hervé; m. Colette Le Guilcher 1963; one s.; Personnel Officer, Société nationale d'étude et de construction de moteurs d'aviation 1963–66, Société anonyme de véhicules industriels et d'équipements mécaniques 1966–69; Teacher of Personnel Man., Legal Sciences Teaching and Research Unit, Univ. of Rennes 1970–73; Mayor of Mellac 1971–97; Deputy (Finistère) to Nat. Assembly 1973–81, 1983–88, 1993–; Councillor for Finistère 1976–; mem. Steering Cttee., Parti Socialiste 1977, Exec. Bureau 1979; Minister for the Sea 1981–83, 1988, of Overseas Depts. and Territories 1988–93; Govt. Spokesperson 1989–91; Vice-Pres. for Europe, Council of European Communities 1983–; Minister of Agric. and Fisheries 1997–; Vice-Pres. Regional Council (Finistère) 1998–; Head ASEAN Mission for External Trade. *Leisure interests:* reading, tennis, the sea. *Address:* Ministry of Agriculture and Fisheries, 78 rue de Varenne, 75700 Paris (Office); Assemblée Nationale, 75355 Paris (Office); Kerviguennou, 29300 Mellac, France (Home). *Telephone:* (02) 98.96.15.60 (Office).

LE PICHON, Xavier; French geologist; b. 18 June 1937, Quinhon, Viet Nam; s. of Jean-Louis Le Pichon and Hélène Tyl; m. Brigitte Barthélemy 1962; five c.; Research Asst. Columbia Univ., New York 1963; Scientific Adviser, Centre Nat. pour l'Exploitation des Océans 1968, 1973; Head, Dept. of Oceanography, Centre Océanologique de Bretagne, Brest 1969; Prof. Univ. P. & M. Curie, Paris 1978; Dir. Dept. of Geology, Ecole Normale Supérieure, Paris 1984–91, Dir. Lab. of Geology 1984–; Prof. Collège de France (Chair. of Geodynamics) 1987–; Pres. Ifremer Scientific Council 1991–, Sr. Jury Inst. Universitaire de France 1997; Visiting Prof. Oxford Univ. 1994, Univ. of Tokyo 1995; mem. Acad. des Sciences; f. mem. Acad. Europaea 1988, N.A.S., U.S.A. 1995; Dr. h.c. (Dalhousie Univ.) 1989, (E.T.H., Zürich) 1992; Maurice Ewing Medal, American Geophysical Union 1984, Huntsman Award (Canada) 1987, Japan Prize 1990; Wollaston Medal (Geological Soc. of

London) 1991. *Publications:* Plate Tectonics (with others) 1973, Expédition Famous, à 3000m sous l'Atlantique (with C. Riffaud) 1976, Kaiko, voyage aux extrémités de la mer 1986, Aux racines de l'homme, De la Mort à l'Amour, Presses de la Renaissance 1997. *Address:* Département de Géologie, Ecole Normale Supérieure, 24 rue Lhomond, 75005 Paris Cedex 05, France. *Telephone:* (1) 44-32-22-50. *Fax:* 44-32-20-00.

LE PORS, Anicet; French politician and economist; b. 28 April 1931, Paris; s. of François Le Pors and Gabrielle Croguennec; m. Claudine Carteret 1959; one s. two d.; ed. Collège Arago, Paris, Ecole de la Météorologie, Univ. of Paris, Centre d'étude des programmes économiques; Meteorological Eng., Marrakesh, Morocco 1953, Paris 1957–65; trade union official (CGT) 1955–77; Consultant, World Meteorological Org., Léopoldville, Congo (now Kinshasa, Zaire) 1960; Sec. Communist section of Met. Office 1962; Head of Dept., Ministry of Economy and Finance 1965; Sec. Cttee. of Cen. Admin., Parti Communiste Français (PCF) 1976–77, Head of Nationalizations, Industrial Policy and Insts. Dept., then of Int. Dept., PCF 1978, mem. Cen. Cttee. 1979; Head of Interministerial Comm., Univ. of Paris XIII 1976–77, and Ecole supérieure des Sciences Economiques et Commerciales 1978; Senator (Hauts-de-Seine) 1977–81; Minister-Del. for the Civil Service and Admin. Reforms, attached to Prime Minister 1981–83; Sec. of State in charge of Public and Admin. Reform 1983–84; Sr. mem. Council of State 1985; mem. Higher Council for Integration; Councillor-Gen. from Hauts-de-Seine 1985–98; Officier, Légion d'honneur; Officier, Ordre nat. du Mérite. *Publications:* Les transferts Etats-industries en France et dans les pays occidentaux 1976, Les béquilles du capital 1977, Marianne à l'encan 1980, Contradictions 1984, L'état efficace 1985, Pendant la mue, le serpent est aveugle 1993, Le Nouvel Age de la estoyenneté 1997, La Citoyenneté 1999. *Leisure interests:* swimming, sailing. *Address:* Conseil d'Etat, place du Palais-Royal, 75001 Paris (Office); 189 boulevard de la République, 92210 Saint-Cloud, France (Home).

Le PORTZ, Yves; French financial executive; b. 30 Aug. 1920, Hennebont; m. Bernadette Champetier de Ribes 1946; five c.; ed. Univ. de Paris à la Sorbonne, Ecole des Hautes Etudes Commerciales, and Ecole Libre des Sciences Politiques; attached to Gen. Inspectorate of Finances 1943, Dir. Adjoint du Cabinet, Président du Conseil 1948–49, Sous-Dir., Chef de Service, Ministry of Finance and Econ. Affairs 1951; Chief of Staff to Sec. of State for Finance and Econ. Affairs 1951–52; Chief of Staff to Minister for Posts, Telegraphs and Telephones 1952–55; Chief of Staff to Minister for Reconstruction and Housing 1955–57; French Del. to Econ. and Social Council of UN 1957–58; Dir.-Gen. of Finance for Algeria 1958–62; Dir.-Gen. Bank for Devt. of Algeria 1959–62; Vice-Pres. and Vice-Chair. Bd. Dirs. European Investment Bank (EIB) 1962–70, Pres. and Chair. 1970–84, Hon. Pres. 1984; Pres. Supervisory Cttee., Bourse (Stock Exchange) Aug. 1984–88; Pres. Supervisory Cttee. Investment Cos. and Funds, Principality of Monaco 1988–; Insp.-Gen. of Finances 1971–84; Commdr., Légion d'honneur 1978, Grand Officier, Ordre nationale de Mérite. *Address:* 127 avenue de Wagram, 75017 Paris, France (Home). *Telephone:* (1) 42-27-76-88.

LEPPARD, Raymond John, C.B.E., M.A.; British conductor and composer; b. 11 Aug. 1927, London; s. of A. V. Leppard and B. M. Beck; ed. Trinity Coll., Cambridge; Fellow of Trinity Coll., Univ. Lecturer in Music 1958–68; Music Dir., BBC Philharmonic (fmrly. BBC Northern Symphony) Orchestra 1973–80; Prin. Guest Conductor, St. Louis Symphony Orchestra 1984–93; Music Dir. Indianapolis Symphony Orchestra 1987–; has conducted New York Philharmonic, Chicago Symphony, Philadelphia and Pittsburgh Symphony Orchestras, and Royal Opera, Covent Garden, English Nat. Opera, Metropolitan Opera, New York, New York City Opera and San Francisco Opera; realizations of Monteverdi's L'Incoronazione di Poppea, Il Ritorno d'Ulisse and L'Orfeo, and Cavalli's L'Ormindo, L'Egisto, La Calisto and L'Orione. *Publication:* Authenticity in Music 1989. *Leisure interests:*friends, theatre, reading. *Address:* c/o Colbert Artists Management, 111 West 57th Street, New York, NY 10019; Indianapolis Symphony Orchestra, 45 Monument Circus, Indianapolis, IN 46204, U.S.A.

LEPPING, Sir George, G.C.M.G., M.B.E.; Solomon Islands politician and government official; b. 22 Nov. 1947; s. of Chief Dionisio Tanutanu and Regina Suluki; m. Margaret Kwalea Teioli 1972; two s. five d.; ed. King George VI Secondary School, Agric. Coll., Vudal, Reading Univ.; Field Officer, Dept. of Agric. and Rural Econ. 1968, Pres. Solomon Is. Amateur Athletics Union 1970–73, 1981–82; Sr. Field Officer then Under-Sec. (Agric.), Ministry of Agric. 1979–80; Perm. Sec. Ministry of Home Affairs and Nat. Devt. 1981–84; Project Dir. Rural Services Project 1984–87; Minister of Finance 1988; Leader, People's Alliance Party 1996–; fmr. mem., Dir. or Chair., various govt. bodies. *Leisure interests:* reading, swimming, lawn tennis, snooker, snorkelling, high-speed boat driving, fishing; first Solomon Islands athlete to win int. sports medals, K.St.J. 1991. *Address:* P.O. Box 1431, Honiara; People's Alliance Party, P.O. Box 722, Honiara, Solomon Islands.

LEPRETTE, Jacques; French diplomatist; b. 22 Jan. 1920; m. Carina Leprette; one s. two d.; ed. Univ. of Paris and Ecole Nationale d'Administration; Ministry of Foreign Affairs (European Div.) 1947–49, Counsellor, Council of Europe 1949–52; Head Political Div., French Mil. Govt., Berlin 1952–55; Counsellor, French Embassy, U.S.A. 1955–59; Ministry of Foreign Affairs (African Div.) 1959–61; Amb. to Mauritania 1961–64; Dir. Int. Liaison Service for Information 1964–65; Minister-Counsellor, Washington 1966–71; Dir. of UN and int. org. affairs at the Foreign Office 1971–74; Asst. Dir. of Political Affairs 1975–76; Amb. and Perm. Rep. to UN 1976–81; Amb. and Perm. Rep. to EEC 1982–85; Ambassadeur de France; Commdr., Légion d'honneur, Croix de guerre, Bronze Star Medal. *Publications:* Le statut international de Trieste 1949, Une clef pour l'Europe 1994 (Prix des Ambassadeurs). *Address:* 36 rue Miollis, 75015 Paris, France (Home). *Telephone:* (01) 45-66-77-47.

LEPRINCE-RINGUET, Louis; French scientist; b. 27 March 1901, Alès-Gard; s. of Félix Leprince-Ringuet and Renée Stourm; m. 2nd Jeanne Motte 1929 (deceased); three s. four d.; ed. Lycée Louis-le-Grand, Ecole Polytechnique and Ecole Supérieure d'Electricité et des P.T.T.; worked as engineer and did research on cosmic rays and fundamental particles physics; Prof. at Ecole Polytechnique 1936–69; Dir. of Lab. at Ecole des Hautes Etudes Pratiques; mem. Atomic Energy Comm. 1951–71; Prof. of Nuclear Physics at Collège de France 1959–72; Pres. CERN Scientific Council 1964–66; Pres. Union Catholique des Scientifiques Français 1948–63; Pres., Soc. Française de Physique 1956; mem. Acad. des Sciences (Physics) 1949–, Acad. Pontificale des Sciences 1956–, Acad. Française 1966–; Pres. Jeunesses Musicales de France 1971–83, Vice-Pres. 1983–; Pres. Mouvement Européen (France) 1974–90; Grand Officier, Légion d'honneur, Grand Croix Ordre nat. du mérite, Commdr. des Palmes académiques. *Publications:* Rayons cosmiques, Les inventeurs célèbres, Les grandes découvertes du XXe siècle, Des atomes et des hommes, La science contemporaine, Science et bonheur des hommes, L'aventure de l'électricité, Le grand merdier ou l'espoir pour demain, La potion magique, Les pieds dans le plat, Noces de diamant avec l'atome 1991, Foi de physicien 1996. *Leisure interests:* painting, tennis, skiing. *Address:* 86 rue de Grenelle, 75007 Paris, France. *Telephone:* (1) 45-49-12-06.

LE QUESNE, Sir (John) Godfray, Kt., Q.C., M.A.; British lawyer; b. 1924, London; s. of the late C. T. Le Quesne; brother of Sir (Charles) Martin Le Quesne (q.v.); m. Susan Mary Gill 1963; two s. one d.; ed. Shrewsbury School, Exeter Coll., Oxford; Pres. Oxford Union 1943; called to Bar, Inner Temple 1947; Q.C. 1962; Deputy Chair. Lincolnshire (Parts of Kesteven) Quarter Sessions 1963–71; Judge, Court of Appeal, Jersey 1964–97, Guernsey 1964–95; Recorder 1972–97; Chair. Monopolies and Mergers Comm. 1975–87; Chair. Council, Regent's Park Coll., Oxford 1958–87; Master of the Bench, Inner Temple 1969, Reader 1988, Treasurer 1989. *Publication:* Jersey and Whitehall in the Mid-Nineteenth Century 1992. *Leisure interests:* music, railways. *Address:* 1 Crown Office Row, Temple, London, EC4Y 7HH, England. *Telephone:* 0171-583 9292.

LERAY, Jean, D. ÈS SC., F.R.S.; French mathematician; b. 7 Nov. 1906, Nantes; m. Marguerite Trumier 1932; two s. one d.; ed. Ecole Normale Supérieure; Prof. Faculty of Sciences, Nancy 1936–41, Paris 1941–47; Prof. of Differential and Functional Equations, Collège de France 1947–78; mem. Inst. de France; Foreign Assoc. N.A.S.; Foreign mem. U.S.S.R. (now Russian) Acad. of Sciences, Accad. Naz. dei Quaranta, Accad. Naz. dei Lincei and Acads. of Sciences of Belgium, Boston, Göttingen, Milan, Palermo, Poland, Romania and Turin; Commdr. Légion d'honneur; Prix Feltrinelli 1971, Wolf Prize 1979, Médaille Lomonosov 1989. *Publications:* papers on math. and mechanics. *Address:* Quietus, App. 39, B.P. 191, 44505 La Baule-Escoublac cedex, France.

LERCHE, Peter Fritz Franz, DR.JUR.; German professor of law; b. 12 Jan. 1928, Leitmeritz; s. of Dr. Fritz and Karoline (née Artmann) Lerche; m. Dr. Ilse Lerche (Peschek) 1955; two s.; ed. Univ. of Munich; Prof. Freie Universität Berlin 1960; Prof. of Public Law, Univ. of Munich 1965; mem. Bavarian Acad. of Sciences; fmr. mem. Council of Science; First Pres. Union of German Lecturers in Public Law 1982; fmr. mem. numerous govt. comms. and attorney in governmental lawsuits, etc.; Bavarian Order of Merit, Maximiliansorden. *Publications:* Ordentlicher Rechtsweg und Verwaltungsrechtsweg 1953, Übermass und Verfassungsrecht 1961, Werbung und Verfassung 1967, Rundfunkmonopol 1970, Verfassungsrechtliche Fragen zur Pressekonzentration 1971, Verfassungsrechtliche Aspekte der 'inneren Pressefreiheit' 1974, Kernkraft und rechtlicher Wandel 1981, Städte und Kabelkommunikation 1982, Mitarbeit an Maunz/Dürig, Kommentar zum Grundgesetz. *Leisure interest:* study of the hippopotamus. *Address:* Junkerstrasse 13, 82131 Gauting, Germany. *Telephone:* 089/850 20 88.

LE RIVEREND, Julio; Cuban historian and philosopher; b. 4 Jan. 1959, Santiago de Cuba; s. of Ibis Le Riverend and Elíades Le Riverend; m. Marcia Medina Cruzata 1992; three c.; ed. Rostov del Don Univ., Russia; fmr. adviser Banco Nacional; Deputy Minister of Educ. and Amb. of Cuba to UNESCO 1973–76; fmr. Vice-Pres. Acad. of Sciences and Pres. and Cultural Dir. of Ateneo, Santiago de Cuba; now Dir. Biblioteca Nacional José Martí de Habana. *Publications:* works on Cuban economic history and the sugar cane industry, articles on cultural devt., problems of post modernity and social sciences: 1898–1998, Cien respuestas para un siglo de dudas 1998, El 98: La guerra que no cesa 1999. *Leisure interests:* literature, cinema. *Address:* Biblioteca Nacional José Martí, Avenida Independencia y 20 de Mayo, Plaza de la Revolución, Apdo. Postal 6881, Havana; Edificio Alamar No. 20, Apto. 19, Zona 1 Alamar, Havana, Cuba. *Telephone:* 81-8876. *Fax:* 81-6224.

LE ROY LADURIE, Emmanuel, D. ÈS L.; French historian; b. 19 July 1929, Les Moutiers en Cinglais; s. of Jacques Le Roy Ladurie and Léontine Dauger; m. Madeleine Pupponi 1955; one s. one d.; taught Lycée de Montpellier 1955–57, C.N.R.S. 1957–60, Faculté de Montpellier 1960–63, the Sorbonne 1970–71, University of Paris VII 1971–73; Titular Prof. Collège de

France 1973–; Gen. Admin. Bibliothèque Nat. 1987–94, Pres. Scientific Council 1994–; Dir. d'études, Ecole pratique des hautes études 1965–; mem. Conseil scientifique de l'Ecole normale Supérieure 1998–; Dr. h.c. (Univ. of Geneva); Hon. D.Litt. (Leeds) 1982, Hon. L.H.D. (East Anglia) 1985, Hon. D.Litt. (Durham) 1987, Commdr. Légion d'honneur. *Publications:* Les paysans de Languedoc 1966, Histoire du climat depuis l'an mil 1967, Le territoire de l'historien 1973, Montaillou, village occitan de 1294 à 1324 1975, Le carnaval de Romans 1579–80 1979, L'argent, l'amour et la mort en pays d'oc 1980, Parmi les historiens 1983, The French Peasantry 1450–1680, Pierre Prion, scribe 1987, Monarchies 1987, l'Histoire de France de: l'Etat Royal 1460–1610 (jtly.) 1987, l'Ancien Régime 1610–1770 (jtly.) 1991, The Royal French State 1460–1610 1994, The Ancien Régime: A History of France 1610–1774 1996, Mémoires 1902–1945 1997. *Leisure interests:* cycling, swimming. *Address:* Collège de France, 11 Place Marcelin-Berthelot, 75005 Paris; 88 rue d'Alleray, 75015 Paris, France (Home). *Telephone:* 4842 01 27.

LESCHLY, Jan; business executive; b. Denmark; m. Lotte Enngelbred 1963; four s.; ed. Coll. of Pharmacy, School of Econ. and Business Administration Copenhagen, Princeton Univ.; Novo Industries A/S 1972–1979; Vice-Pres. Commercial Devt., Squibb Corpn. 1979, US Pres. 1981, Group Vice-Pres. and Dir. 1984, Exec. Vice-Pres. 1986; Pres. and C.O.O. 1988; Chair. SmithKline Beecham Pharmaceuticals 1990, C.E.O. 1994–; Chair. British Pharma Group; mem. pharmaceutical assocs and educational bodies. *Address:* SmithKline Beecham, One New Horizons Court, Brentford, Middx. TW8 9EP, England. *Telephone:* 0181-975-2000.

LESHER, Richard Lee, M.S.; American administrator; b. 28 Oct. 1933, Doylesburg, Pa.; s. of Richard E. Lesher and Rosalie Orabelle (Meredith) Lesher Ehrhart; m. Agnes Marie Plocki 1981; two s. two d. by previous m.; ed. Univ. of Pittsburgh, Pennsylvania State Univ., Indiana Univ.; served with U.S. Army 1954–56; Asst. Prof., Coll. Commerce and Admin., Ohio State Univ. 1963–64; consultant with NASA, Washington, D.C. 1964–65, Deputy Asst. Admin. 1965–66, Asst. Admin. 1966–69; business and man. consultant, Washington 1969–71; Pres. Nat. Center for Resource Recovery, Washington 1971–75, U.S. Chamber of Commerce, Washington 1975–97; mem. Bd. Dirs. G&L Realty Corpn., Accugraph Corpn., World Heart Corpn., Iridium; appointments with other orgs. *Publications:* Economic Progress . . . It's Everybody's Business 1980, Meltdown on Main Street 1996; author syndicated newspaper column. *Leisure interests:* golf, fishing, riding, tennis. *Address:* 1126 Cider Press Road, Chambersburg, PA 17201, U.S.A. (Home).

LESLIE, Frank Matthews, PH.D., F.R.S., F.R.S.E.; Scottish professor of mathematics; b. 8 March 1935, Dundee; s. of William Ogilvy Leslie and Catherine Pitkethly Matthews; m. Ellen Leitch Reoch 1965; one s. one d.; ed. Harris Acad., Dundee, Queen's Coll., Dundee, Univ. of Manchester; asst. lecturer Univ. of Manchester 1959–61; Research Assoc. M.I.T. 1961–62; lecturer Univ. of Newcastle 1962–68; Asst. Prof. Johns Hopkins Univ., Baltimore (sabbatical) 1966–67; sr. lecturer Strathclyde Univ. 1968–71, reader 1971–79, Personal Prof. of Mathematics 1979–82; consultant Dera Malvern 1977–; Chair. British Liquid Crystal Soc. 1987–91; Hon. D.Sc. (St. Andrews) 1995; Sykes Gold Medal, St. Andrews 1996, G. W. Gray Medal, British Liquid Crystal Soc. 1997. *Publications:* c. 70 papers in scientific journals, predominantly on mathematical models of liquid crystals. *Leisure interests:* golf, walking. *Address:* Department of Mathematics, University of Strathclyde, Livingstone Tower, Richmond Street, Glasgow, G1 1XH, Scotland. *Telephone:* (0141) 548-3655. *Fax:* (0141) 552-8657.

LESLIE, Sir Peter Evelyn, Kt., M.A., F.I.B., F.L.S.; British banker; b. 24 March 1931, Oxford; s. of Patrick Holt Leslie and Evelyn (née de Berry); m. Charlotte Chapman-Andrews 1975; two step-s. two step-d.; ed. Stowe School and New Coll. Oxford; joined Barclays Bank DCO 1955, served in Sudan, Algeria, Zaire, Kenya and the Bahamas; Gen. Man. Barclays Bank Ltd. 1973–76, Dir. 1979–91; Sr. Gen. Man. Barclays Bank Int. 1980–83; Chief Gen. Man. Barclays Bank PLC 1985–87, Man. Dir. 1987–88, Deputy Chair. 1987–91; Deputy Chair. Midland Group 1991–92; Chair. British Bankers' Asscn. Exec. Cttee. 1978–79, mem. Export Guarantees Advisory Council 1978–81, Chair. 1987–92; Chair. Cttee. London and Scottish Clearing Bankers 1986–88; mem. Bd. of Banking Supervision, Bank of England 1989–94; Chair. NCM UK 1995–98, mem. Supervisory Bd. NCM Holding NV Amsterdam 1995–; Chair. Overseas Devt. Inst. 1988–95, Commonwealth Devt. Corpn. 1989–95; Gov. Stowe School 1983– (Chair. 1994–); mem. Council for Ind. and Higher Educ. 1987–91; Chair. Queen's Coll., London 1989–94; Oxford Univ. Audit Cttee. 1992–; Curator Univ. Chest, Oxford 1990–95; mem. Council, Ranfurly Library Service 1991–94, Royal Inst. of Int. Affairs, Chatham House 1991–97; mem. Bd. Int. Inst. for Environment and Devt. 1992–95. *Leisure interests:* natural history, historical research. *Address:* 153 Sutherland Avenue, London, W9 1ES, England. *Telephone:* 0171-289 4920.

LESOTHO, King of (see Letsie III).

LESOURNE, Jacques François; French newspaper editor and academic; b. 26 Dec. 1928, La Rochelle; s. of André Lesourne and Simone Lesourne (née Guille); m. Odile Melin, 1961; one s. two d.; ed. Lycée Montaigne, Bordeaux, École Nationale Supérieure des Mines de Paris; Head Econ. Service of French Collieries 1954–57; Dir. Gen., later Pres. METRA Int. and SEMA 1958–75; Prof. of Econs. École des Mines de Saint-Étienne 1958–61; Prof. of Industrial Econs. École Nationale Supérieure de la Statistique 1960–63; Pres. Asscn. Française d'Informatique et de Recherche Operationnelle 1966–67; mem. Council Int. Inst. of Applied Systems Analysis, Vienna 1973–79, Inst. of Man. Science 1976–79; Prof. Conservatoire Nat. des Arts et Métiers 1974–; Dir. Projet Interfuturs OECD 1976–79; Dir. of Studies, Inst. Auguste Comte 1979–81; Pres. Comm. on Employment and Social Relations of 8th Plan 1979–81; mem. Comm. du Bilan 1981, Council European Econ. Asscn. 1984–89; Pres. Asscn. Française de Science Économique 1981–83, Int. Federation of Operational Research Socs. 1986–89; Dir. and Man. Ed. Le Monde 1991–94; Pres. Futuribles Int. 1993–, Centre for Study and Research on Qualifications 1996–; Officier, Légion d'honneur, Commdr., Ordre nat. du Mérite, Chevalier des Palmes Académiques. *Publications:* Economic Technique and Industrial Management 1958, Du bon usage de l'étude économique dans l'entreprise 1966, Les systèmes du destin 1976, L'entreprise et ses futurs 1985, Éducation et société, L'après-Communisme, de l'Atlantique à l'Oural 1990, The Economics of Order and Disorder 1991, Vérités et mensonges sur le chômage 1995, Le Modèle Français: Grandeur et Décadence 1998. *Leisure interest:* piano. *Address:* 52 rue de Vaugirard, 75006 Paris, France (Home). *Telephone:* (1) 43-25-66-05 (Home). *Fax:* (1) 56-24-47-98.

LESSARD, Claude; Canadian business executive; b. 29 July 1949, Notre Dame du Portage; s. of Carmen Cerat and Jean-Luc Lessard; m. Marie Lessard (née Lortie) 1971; three s.; ed. Univ. Laval, Québec; Pres. and C.E.O. Cossette Communication-Marketing 1980–; Dir. Canam-Manac, Inst. de Cardiologie de Québec, Opéra de Québec, Fac. des Sciences de l'Admin., Univ. Laval, Fondation Communautaire du Grand Québec, DiagnoCure Inc.; Co.-Chair. Canadian Congress of Advertising 1995; Hermes Prize (Univ. of Laval) 1984, Dimensions Prize 1987, 'Spiess' Bessies Award 1993, ACA Gold Medal 1994. *Leisure interests:* golf, skiing, riding. *Address:* Cossette Communication-Marketing, 437 Grande-Allée Est, Québec, Qué. G1R 2J5, Canada. *Telephone:* (418) 647-2727. *Fax:* (418) 523 1689.

LESSELS, Norman, C.B.E., C.A.; British chartered accountant; b. 2 Sept. 1938, Edinburgh; s. of John Clark Lessels and Gertrude Margaret Ellen Lessels (née Jack); m. 1st Gillian Durward Clark 1960 (died 1979); one s. (and one s. one d. deceased); m. 2nd Christine Stevenson Hitchman 1981; ed. Melville Coll., Edin., Edinburgh Acad.; apprentice with Graham Smart & Annan, Edin. 1955–60, with Thomson McLintock & Co., London 1960–61; partner, Wallace & Somerville, Edin., subsequently merged with Whinney Murray & Co., latterly Ernst & Whinney 1962–80; partner, Chiene & Tait, C.A. 1980–93, Sr. Partner 1993–; Dir. (non-exec.) The Scottish Eastern Investment Trust PLC 1980–, The Standard Life Assurance Co. 1978– (Chair. 1988–98), Cairn Energy PLC 1988–, Bank of Scotland 1988–97, General Surety & Guarantee Co. Ltd. 1988–97, Havelock Europa PLC –1998 (Chair. 1993–98), NWS Bank PLC 1989–97, Robert Wiseman Dairies PLC 1994–; Pres. Inst. of Chartered Accountants of Scotland 1987–88; Chair. Tilney & Co. 1993–. *Leisure interests:* golf, bridge, music. *Address:* 3 Albyn Place, Edinburgh, EH2 4NQ (Office); 11 Forres Street, Edinburgh, EH3 6BJ, Scotland (Home). *Telephone:* (0131) 225 7515 (Office); (0131) 225 5596 (Home). *Fax:* (0131) 220-1083 (Office).

LESSING, Doris May; British writer; b. 22 Oct. 1919, Kermanshah, Persia; d. of Alfred Cook Taylor and Emily Maude (McVeagh) Taylor; m. 1st F. A. C. Wisdom 1939–43, 2nd Gottfried Anton Nicolai Lessing 1944–49; two s. (one deceased) one d.; ed. Roman Catholic Convent, and Girls' High School, Salisbury, Southern Rhodesia; Assoc. mem. American Acad. of Arts and Letters 1974; Nat. Inst. of Arts and Letters (U.S.A.) 1974; mem. Inst. for Cultural Research 1974; Hon. Fellow M.L.A. (U.S.) 1974; Pres. Book Trust 1996–; D. Fellow in Literature (East Anglia) 1991; Hon. D.Litt (Princeton) 1989, Durham (1990), (Warwick) 1994; Hon. D.Litt. (Bard Coll. New York State) 1994, (Harvard) 1995, (Oxford) 1996; five Somerset Maugham Awards, Soc. of Authors 1954–, Austrian State Prize for European Literature 1981, Shakespeare Prize, Hamburg 1982, Grinzane Cavour Award, Italy 1989, Woman of the Year, Norway 1995. *Publications:* (novels): The Grass is Singing 1950 (made into film), Children of Violence (Martha Quest 1952, A Proper Marriage 1954, A Ripple from the Storm 1965, The Four-Gated City 1969), Retreat to Innocence 1956, The Golden Notebook 1962 (Prix Médicis for French trans., Carnet d'or 1976), Briefing for a Descent into Hell 1971 (shortlisted for Booker Prize 1971), The Summer Before the Dark 1973, The Memoirs of a Survivor 1974 (made into film), Canopus in Argos series (Re: Colonised Planet 5, Shikasta 1979, The Marriages between Zones Three, Four and Five 1980, The Sirian Experiments 1981, The Making of the Representative for Planet 8 1982, The Sentimental Agents in the Volyen Empire 1983), The Diary of a Good Neighbour (under pseudonym Jane Somers) 1983, If the Old Could (under pseudonym Jane Somers) 1984, The Diaries of Jane Somers 1984, The Good Terrorist 1985 (W. H. Smith Literary Award 1986, Palermo Prize and Premio Internazionale Mondello 1987), The Fifth Child 1988, Love, Again 1996, Mara and Dann 1999; (short stories): Collected African Stories: Vol. 1, This Was the Old Chief's Country 1951, Vol. 2, The Sun Between Their Feet 1973, Five 1953, The Habit of Loving 1957, A Man and Two Women 1963, African Stories 1964, Winter in July 1966, The Black Madonna 1966, The Story of a Non-Marrying Man and Other Stories 1972, A Sunrise on the Veld 1975, A Mild Attack of the Locusts 1977, Collected Stories: Vol. 1, To Room Nineteen 1978, Vol. 2, The Temptation of Jack Orkney 1978, London Observed: Stories and Sketches 1992; (non-fiction includes): Going Home 1957 (revised edn. 1968), Particularly Cats 1967, Particularly Cats and More Cats 1989, African Laughter: Four Visits to Zimbabwe 1992, Under My Skin 1994 (Los Angeles Times Book Prize 1995, James Tait Memorial Prize 1995), Walking in the Shade

1997, Mara and Dann 1999; (plays): Each His Own Wilderness 1958, Play with a Tiger 1962, The Singing Door 1973; (other publs. include): Fourteen Poems 1959, A Small Personal Voice 1974, Doris Lessing Reader 1990. *Address:* c/o Jonathan Clowes Ltd., 10 Iron Bridge House, Bridge Approach, London, NW1 8BD, England.

LESTER, Richard; American film director; b. 19 Jan. 1932, Philadelphia; s. of Elliott Lester and Ella Young; m. Deirdre V. Smith 1956; one s. one d.; ed. William Penn Charter School, Univ. of Pennsylvania; TV Dir., CBS 1952–54, ITV 1955–59; Composer 1954–57; Film Dir. 1959–; Acad. Award Nomination 1960; Grand Prix, Cannes Festival 1965; Best Dir. Rio de Janeiro Festival 1966; Gandhi Peace Prize, Berlin Festival 1969; Best Dir. Teheran Festival 1974. *Films directed:* The Running, Jumping and Standing Still Film 1959, It's Trad, Dad 1962, The Mouse on the Moon 1963, A Hard Day's Night 1963, The Knack 1965, Help! 1965, A Funny Thing Happened on the Way to the Forum 1966, How I Won the War 1967, Petulia 1969, The Bed Sitting Room 1969, The Three Musketeers 1973, Juggernaut 1974, The Four Musketeers 1974, Royal Flash 1975, Robin and Marian 1976, The Ritz 1976, Butch and Sundance: The Early Days 1979, Cuba 1979, Superman II 1980, Superman III 1983, Finders Keepers 1984, The Return of the Musketeers 1989, Get Back 1990. *Leisure interests:* tennis, music. *Address:* c/o Creative Artists Agency, 9830 Wilshire Boulevard, Beverly Hills, CA 90212, U.S.A.

LESTER OF HERNE HILL, Baron (Life Peer) cr. 1993, of Herne Hill in the London Borough of Southwark; **Anthony Paul Lester,** Q.C., B.A., LL.M.; British lawyer; b. 3 July 1936, London; s. of Harry and Kate Lester; m. Catherine Elizabeth Debora Wassey 1971; one s. one d.; ed. City of London School, Trinity Coll., Cambridge, Harvard Law School; called to Bar, Lincoln's Inn 1963, Bencher 1985; Special Adviser to Home Sec. 1974–76; Q.C. 1975; Special Adviser to Northern Ireland Standing Advisory Comm. on Human Rights 1975–77; Recorder, South-Eastern Circuit 1987–93; Hon. Visiting Prof., Univ. Coll. London 1983–; mem. Bd. of Dirs. Salzburg Seminar; mem. Bd. of Overseers, Univ. of Pa. Law School 1977–90, Council of Justice; mem. Court of Govs., L.S.E. 1980–94; Pres. Interights 1983–; Gov. British Inst. of Human Rights; Chair. Bd. of Govs., James Allen's Girls' School 1987–93, Gov. Westminster School 1998–; Chair. Runnymede Trust 1990–93; hon. degrees/fellowships from Open Univ., Univ. Coll., London Univ., Ulster Univ., South Bank Univ.; Liberty Human Rights Lawyer of the Year 1997. *Publications:* Justice in the American South (Amnesty Int.) 1964, Race and Law (co-author) 1972; Ed.-in-Chief Butterworths Human Rights Cases; Consultant Ed. and Contrib. Halsbury's Laws of England Title Constitutional Law and Human Rights (4th edn. 1996); articles on race relations, public affairs and international law. *Address:* Blackstone Chambers, Blackstone House, Temple, London, EC4Y 9BW, England. *Telephone:* 0171-583 1770.

LETOKHOV, Vladilen Stepanovich, PH.D.; Russian physicist; b. 10 Nov. 1939, Irkutsk; s. of Stepan G. Letokhov and Anna V. (Sevastianova) Letokhova; m. 1st Maria Letokhova 1965 (divorced 1973), 2nd Tina Karu 1979; one d.; ed. Moscow Physical Tech. Inst., P.N. Lebedev Physical Inst.; researcher, P.N. Lebedev Physical Inst. 1966–70; Head Laser Spectroscopy Dept., Inst. of Spectroscopy, U.S.S.R. (now Russian) Acad. of Sciences 1970–, Vice-Dir. for Research 1970–89; Prof., Moscow Physical-Tech. Inst. 1973–; Dir. Laser Lab., Soviet (now Russian) Branch of World Lab. 1990–; Fellow American Optical Soc.; mem. New York Acad. of Sciences, Max Planck Soc., Germany; Lenin Prize for Science and Tech. 1978. *Publications:* Nonlinear Laser Spectroscopy 1977, Nonlinear Laser Chemistry 1987, Photoionization Laser Spectroscopy 1987, and 10 other scientific books; about 600 publs. in scientific journals. *Leisure interests:* music, swimming, house construction. *Address:* Institute of Spectroscopy, Troitzk, 142092 Moscow (Office); Puchkovo-66, Troitzk, Moscow, Russia (Home). *Telephone:* (095) 3340578 (Office); (095) 3340230 (Home). *Fax:* (095) 3340886.

ŁĘTOWSKA, Ewa Anna, LL.D.; Polish politician and lawyer; b. 22 March 1940, Warsaw; m.; ed. Warsaw Univ.; Asst. Prof. 1975, Extraordinary Prof. 1985; scientific worker, Inst. of State and Law, Polish Acad. of Sciences, Warsaw 1961–87, Head of Team for civil law 1975–87, Prof. 1992–; lecturer Warsaw Univ. and Postgraduate Training Centre of Admin. Personnel 1961–87; Civic Rights' Intercessor (Ombudsman) 1988–92; mem. of Bd., Int. Ombudsman Inst.; scientific awards; Kt.'s Cross of Polonia Restituta Order. *Publications:* Wzorce umowne—ogólne warunki, wzory, regulaminy 1975, Obywatel—przedsiębiorstwo. Zagadnienia prawne świadczeń na rzecz konsumenta (ed. and co-author) 1982, Tendencje rozwojowe prawa cywilnego 1983 (ed. and co-author), Komentarz do ogólnych warunków umów konsumenckich (co-author) 1985, Przygoda z operą (with J. Łętowski) 1991. *Leisure interests:* serious music, vocalism. *Address:* Instytut Państwa i Prawa PAN, ul. Nowy Świat 72, 00-930 Warsaw, Poland. *Telephone:* (22) 826 78 53.

LETSIE III, B.LL.; King of Lesotho; b. 17 July 1963, Morija; s. of the late King Moshoeshoe II and Queen Mamohato Berenc Seeiso; ed. Nat. Univ. of Lesotho, Univs. of Bristol, Cambridge and London; Prin. Chief of Matsieng 1989; installed as King Nov. 1990, abdicated Jan. 1995, reinstated following his father's death Feb. 1996–; Patron of Prince Mohato Award (Khau Ea Khosana Mohato). *Leisure interests:* classical and traditional music, horse riding, rugby, squash, tennis. *Address:* Royal Palace, Maseru, Lesotho.

LETTE, Kathy; Australian author; b. 11 Nov. 1958, Sydney; d. of Mervyn Lette and Val Lette; m. Geoffrey Robertson (q.v.) 1990; one s. one d.; ed. Sylvania High School, Sydney. *Publications:* HIT and MS 1984, Girls' Night Out 1987, The Llama Parlour 1991, Foetal Attraction 1993, Mad Cows 1996, Puberty Blues (with G. Carey) 1997; (plays) Grommitts 1988, I'm So Sorry For You, I Really Am 1994, Perfect Mismatch 1995, Wet Dreams 1995; (essays) She Done Him Wrong, The Constant Sinner in Introduction to Mae West 1995, Altar Ego 1998. *Address:* c/o Ed Victor, 6 Bayley Street, London, WC1B 3HB, England. *Telephone:* 0171-304 4100. *Fax:* 0171-304 4111.

LETTERMAN, David; American broadcaster; b. 12 April 1947, Indianapolis; m. Michelle Cook 1969 (divorced 1977); ed. Ball State Univ.; radio and TV announcer, Indianapolis; performer, The Comedy Store, Los Angeles 1975–; TV appearances include: Rock Concert, Gong Show; frequent guest host, The Tonight Show; host, David Letterman Show 1980, Late Night with David Letterman 1982; The Late Show with David Letterman, (also writer) CBS 1993–; TV scriptwriter including Bob Hope Special, Good Times, Paul Lynde Comedy Hour, John Denver Special; recipient of six Emmy Awards. *Publications include:* David Letterman's Book of Top Ten Lists 1996. *Address:* Late Show with David Letterman, Ed Sullivan Theater, 1697 Broadway, New York, NY 10019, U.S.A.

LEUENBERGER, Moritz; Swiss politician and lawyer; b. 21 Sept. 1946, Biel/Bienne; s. of Robert Leuenberger and Ruth Leuenberger; two s.; ed. Univ. of Zürich; pvt. practice as lawyer 1972–91; joined Social Democratic Party (SP) 1969, Leader Zürich SP 1972–80; mem. Zürich City Council 1974–83; Pres. Swiss Tenants' Asscn. 1986–91; elected to Nat. Council 1979; elected to Zürich Cantonal Council 1991, Dir. of Justice and Internal Affairs 1991–95; Fed. Councillor 1995–; Minister, Fed. Dept. of Transport, Communications and Energy Nov. 1995–. *Address:* Federal Department of Transport, Communications and Energy, Bundeshaus-Nord, 3003 Berne, Switzerland. *Telephone:* (31) 3225511. *Fax:* (31) 3119576.

LEUNG, Oi Sie (Elsie), LL.M., J.P.; Chinese legal official; b. 24 April 1939, Hong Kong; ed. Univ. of Hong Kong; admitted as Solicitor, Supreme Court of Hong Kong 1968, as overseas solicitor, U.K. Supreme Court 1976; Notary Public 1978; admitted as barrister and solicitor of Vic., Australia 1982; founding mem. and Hon. Sec. Hong Kong Fed. of Women Lawyers 1976; Country Vice-Pres. Int. Fed. of Women Lawyers 1978, First Vice-Pres. 1992, Pres. 1994–; del. 7th People's Congress, Guangdong, People's Repub. of China 1989, 8th Nat. People's Congress 1993; founding mem. and mem. Exec. Cttee. Hong Kong Fed. of Women 1993; Sec. for Justice of Hong Kong Special Admin. Region 1997–; Fellow Int. Acad. of Matrimonial Lawyers 1994. *Address:* Department of Justice, Secretary for Justice's Office, 4th Floor, High Block, Queensway Government Offices, 66 Queensway, Hong Kong Special Administrative Region, People's Republic of China. *Telephone:* (852) 2869 2001. *Fax:* (852) 2877 3978.

LEUNG CHUN-YING; Chinese civil servant; b. 1954, Hong Kong; m. Regina Tong Ching Yee; three c.; ed. Bristol Polytechnic; fmr. Sec. Gen. Basic Law Consultative Cttee.; Vice-Chair. Preparatory Cttee., Hong Kong Special Admin. Region; mem. Exec. Council. *Address:* Government Secretariat, Central Government Offices, Lower Albert Road, Hong Kong Special Administrative Region, People's Republic of China.

LEUNG KAM CHUNG, Antony, B.SC.; Chinese banker and official; b. 29 Jan. 1952, Hong Kong; m. Sophie Leung; ed. Univ. of Hong Kong, Harvard Business School; Man. Dir. and Regional Man. for Greater China and the Philippines, Chase Manhattan Bank; Chair. Univ. Grants Cttee. 1993–; Dir. Hong Kong Futures Exchange 1987–90, Hong Kong Policy Research Inst. 1996–; Trustee Queen Mary Hosp. Charitable Trust 1993–, Hong Kong Centre for Econ. Research 1995–; Hong Kong Affairs Adviser 1994–; Arbitrator China Int. Econ. and Trade Arbitration Comm. 1994–; mem. Industrial Devt. Bd. 1985, Univ. and Polytechnic Grants Cttee. 1990–93, Bd. Provisional Airport Authority 1990–95, Airport Authority 1995–, Cen. Policy Unit 1992–93, Bd. Hong Kong Community Chest 1992–94, Educ. Comm. 1993–, Standing Council Chinese Soc. of Macroeconomics, State Planning Comm. 1994–, Exchange Fund Advisory Cttee. 1995–, Prep. Cttee. of Hong Kong Special Admin. Region 1996–97, Exec. Council Hong Kong Special Admin. Region July 1997–. *Address:* Executive Council Secretariat, 1st Floor, Main Wing, Central Government Offices, Central, Hong Kong Special Administrative Region, People's Republic of China.

LEUTHEUSSER-SCHNARRENBERGER, Sabine; German politician; b. 26 July 1951, Minden, Westphalia; m.; ed. Univs. of Göttingen and Bielefeld; with German Patent Office 1979–90; Head Admin., Personnel and Budget Dept. 1990; Fed. Minister of Justice 1992–96; mem. Free Democratic Party (FDP), Chair (Dist. Asscn., Starnberg) 1984–; mem. Bundestag 1990–, mem. FDP Nat. Exec. 1991–96, of numerous cttees. *Address:* Bundeshaus, 53113 Bonn, Germany. *Telephone:* (228) 16-85162. *Fax:* (228) 16-86402.

LEVELT, Willem J. M., PH.D.; Netherlands psychologist and psycholinguist; b. 17 May 1938, Amsterdam; s. of Dr. W. H. Levelt and J. Levelt-Berger; m. Elisabeth C. M. Jacobs 1963; two s. one d.; ed. Leiden Univ.; Staff. mem. Inst. for Perception, Soesterberg 1962–65; Research Fellow Center for Cognitive Studies, Harvard Univ. 1965–66; Visiting Asst. Prof. Univ. of Illinois 1966–67; Prof. of Experimental Psychology, Groningen Univ. 1967–70, Nijmegen Univ. 1971–79, Hon. Prof. of Psycholinguistics 1980–; Leader Max-Planck Project Group for Psycholinguistics, Nijmegen 1976–79; Dir. Max-Planck-Inst. for Psycholinguistics, Nijmegen 1980–; Visiting Prof. Louvain Univ. 1967–70; mem. Inst. for Advanced Study, Princeton 1971–72; mem. Royal Netherlands Acad. of Sciences, Academia Europaea. *Publica-*

tions: On binocular rivalry 1968, Formal grammars in linguistics and psycholinguistics, 3 Vols. 1974, Speaking: From intention to articulation 1989. *Leisure interest:* playing the traverso. *Address:* Max-Planck-Institute for Psycholinguistics, Wundtlaan 1, 6525 XD Nijmegen, Netherlands. *Telephone:* (24) 3521-911. *Fax:* (24) 3521-213.

LEVENE, Ben, R.A.; British artist; b. 23 Dec. 1938, London; s. of Charlotte Levene and Mark Levene; m. Susan Margaret Williams 1978; one s. two d.; ed. Slade School of Fine Art; teaches painting at the R.A. Schools; Boise Scholarship 1961–62; elected Assoc. of Royal Acad. 1975; Royal Academician 1988; one-man shows at Thackeray Gallery 1973–81, at Browse and Darby 1986–; Curator Royal Acad. Schools 1995–. *Leisure interest:* gardening. *Address:* c/o Browse & Darby, 19 Cork Street, London, W1X 2LP; c/o The Royal Academy of Arts, Piccadilly, London, W1V 0DS, England. *Telephone:* 0171-734 7984 (Gallery); 0171-439 7438 (Royal Academy).

LEVENE OF PORTSOKEN, Baron (Life Peer), cr. 1997, of Portsoken in the City of London; **Peter Keith Levene,** K.B.E., B.A., J.P., F.C.I.T., C.I.MGT.; British business executive; b. 8 Dec. 1941, Pinner, Middx.; s. of the late Maurice Levene and Rose Levene; m. Wendy Ann Levene 1966; two s. one d.; ed. City of London School and Univ. of Manchester; joined United Scientific Holdings 1963, Man. Dir. 1968, Chair. 1982; Personal Adviser to Sec. of State for Defence 1984; Chief of Defence Procurement, Ministry of Defence 1985–91; mem. S.E. Asia Trade Advisory Group 1979–83, Council, Defence Mfrs. Asscn. 1982–85, Vice-Chair. 1983–84, Chair. 1984–85; Chair. European NATO Nat. Armaments Dirs. 1990–91, Docklands Light Railway Ltd. 1991–94; Special Adviser to Sec. of State for the Environment 1991–92; Adviser to Prime Minister on Efficiency 1992–97; Special Adviser to Pres. of the Bd. of Trade 1992–95; Chair. Public Competition and Purchasing Unit, H.M. Treasury 1991–92; Deputy Chair. Wasserstein Perella & Co. Ltd. 1991–94; Chair. and C.E.O. Canary Wharf Ltd. 1993–96; Sr. Adviser Morgan Stanley & Co. Ltd. 1996–98; Chair. Bankers Trust Int. 1998–; Alderman, City of London 1984–, Sheriff 1995–96, Lord Mayor of London 1998–; Hon. Col. Commdt. Royal Corps of Transport 1991–93, Royal Logistics Corps 1993–; Master Worshipful Co. of Carmen 1992–93; Fellow Queen Mary and Westfield Coll., London Univ. 1995; Commdr. Ordre Nat. du Mérite 1996. *Leisure interests:* skiing, travel, watching Association football. *Address:* Bankers Trust International PLC, 1 Appold Street, London, EC2A 2HE, England.

LEVENTAL, Valery Yakovlevich; Russian artist and stage designer for opera and ballet; b. 17 Aug. 1942, Moscow; ed. All-Union State Cinematography Inst.; with Bolshoi Theatre 1965–95, Chief designer 1988–95; corresp. mem. U.S.S.R. (now Russian) Acad. of Arts 1988; People's Artist of the U.S.S.R. 1989; designs and sets for Cinderella, Romeo and Juliet, Anna Karenina, Khovanshchina, Prince Igor (Vilnius and Sofia), Tosca, Così fan tutte, Madam Butterfly, Otello, Till Eulenspiegel, Icarus, décor for experimental ballets of Maiya Plisetskaya (q.v.) and Vladimir V. Vasiliyev (q.v.); also for Love for Three Oranges (Berlin), War and Peace, Dead Souls (Bolshoi). *Theatrical designs:* Woe from Wit, The Bedbug, The Wedding (Gogol), The Marriage of Figaro, The Duenna, Macbeth (1979), The Seagull (1979), Boris Godunov. *Address:* Sadovaya-Spasskaya Street 19, Apartment 88, 107078 Moscow, Russia. *Telephone:* (095) 975-14-94.

LÉVÊQUE, Jean André Eugène; French aeronautical engineer; b. 30 April 1929, Béthune; s. of André and Elise (Forêt) Lévêque; m. Geneviève Cauwet 1953; two s.; ed. Ecole Polytechnique, Paris; with Air Navigation Directorate of Ministry of Public Works and Transport 1954–60, Eng. in Air Traffic Bureau 1954, Head of Airports Bureau 1956–60; Civil Aviation Tech. Adviser to Minister of Public Works and Transport 1960–63; Head of Div. in European Org. for the Safety of Air Navigation (EUROCONTROL), Brussels 1964–67; with Secretariat-General for Civil Aviation, Paris 1968–78, Tech. Adviser to Sec.-Gen. 1968–70, Acting Sec.-Gen., then Dir. of Air Navigation 1971–78; Dir.-Gen. EUROCONTROL 1978–83; Head of Gen. Inspection for Civil Aviation 1983; Chair. Conseil Superieur Infrastructure and Air Navigation 1989–94; Pres. Admin. Council Ecole Nationale de l'Aviation Civile; Vice-Pres. Admin. Bd. Météo-France; Officier, Légion d'honneur, Commdr. de l'Ordre national du Mérite, Médaille de l'Aéronautique. *Leisure interests:* skiing, table tennis. *Address:* 13 rue Gambetta, 92100 Boulogne-Billancourt, France (Home). *Telephone:* (1) 48-25-50-66.

LÉVÊQUE, Jean-Maxime; French banker; b. 9 Sept. 1923, Paris; s. of Pierre Lévêque and Marthe Tisserand; m. Anne Charles-Laurent 1947; one s. two d. (one d. deceased); ed. Lycée Buffon, Faculté de Droit, Paris, Ecole libre des sciences politiques and Ecole nat. d'admin.; Inspector of Finances 1950; external finance official 1950–56; temporary appt. IMF and IBRD 1956–58; Dir. European Investment Bank 1958–60; Adviser, Sec.-Gen. of Presidency of Repub. 1960–64; Sec.-Gen. Conseil Nat. du Crédit 1960–64; Dir.-Gen. Crédit Commercial de France 1964, Chief Exec. 1966, Vice-Pres. 1971, Pres. 1976, then Hon. Pres.; Pres. Union des Banques pour l'Equipement 1965, Vice-Pres. 1976–82; Pres., Dir.-Gen. Crédit Lyonnais 1986–88, Hon. Pres. 1988; Pres. Banque de l'Union Maritime et Financière 1989–97, Euro-Clinvest 1988–94, Financière Galliéra 1990–94; numerous other directorships and professional appts.; Officier, Légion d'honneur, Commdr. Ordre Nat. du Mérite; Croix de Guerre; Prix Renaissance 1983. *Publications:* Dénationalisations: mode d'emploi 1985, En première ligne 1986. *Address:* 91 Quai d'Orsay, 75007 Paris, France.

LÉVÊQUE, Michel, L. EN D.; French diplomatist; b. 19 July 1933, Algiers; s. of Raymond Lévèque and Suzanne (née Lucchini) Lévèque; m. Georgette Vandekerchove 1956; one s. two d.; ed. Lycée Henri-IV, Faculté de Droit, Paris Univ.; Adviser to Minister of Finance and Planning, Abidjan 1960–63; Adviser on Atomic Affairs Ministry of Foreign Affairs, Paris 1963–64, First Sec. American Section 1968–69, Second Adviser Personnel Dept. 1972–73, Asst. Dir. of African and Malagasy Affairs 1982–85, Dir. 1989–91; First Embassy Sec. Moscow 1965–67, Second Adviser Sofia 1970–71, Cultural and Co-operation Adviser Tunis 1974–78; Political Adviser NATO Int. Secr. 1978–82; Amb. to Libya 1985–89, to Morocco 1991–93, to Brazil 1993–94, to Algeria 1995–97, Minister of State for the Principality of Monaco 1997–; Officier, Légion d'honneur, Officier Ordre Nat. du Mérite, Croix de la Valeur Militaire. *Address:* Hôtel du Gouvernement, Place de la Visitation, Monaco; 57 rue de l'Université, 75007 Paris, France. *Telephone:* 37793 158215. *Fax:* 37793 158012.

LEVER, Jeremy Frederick, M.A., Q.C.; British lawyer; b. 23 June 1933, London; s. of late Arnold Lever and of Elizabeth (née Nathan) Cramer; ed. Bradfield Coll., Berks., University Coll., Oxford, Nuffield Coll., Oxford; Fellow All Souls Coll., Oxford 1957, Subwarden 1982–84, Sr. Dean 1988–; Q.C. (England and Wales) 1972, (Northern Ireland) 1988; Bencher, Gray's Inn 1986–; Dir. (non-exec.) Dunlop Holdings Ltd. 1973–80, The Wellcome Foundation 1983–94; mem. arbitral tribunal, U.S.A./U.K. arbitration concerning Heathrow Airport user charges 1989–94, Univ. of Portsmouth Ind. Inquiry 1995; Chair. Oftel Advisory Body on Fair Trading in Telecommunications 1996–, Performing Rights Soc. Appeals Panel 1997–; Visiting Prof. Wissenschafts-Zentrum, Berlin, für Sozialforschung Jan.–March 1999; Pres. Oxford Union Soc. 1957; mem. Council British Inst. of Int. and Comparative Law 1987. *Publications:* The Law of Restrictive Trading Agreements 1964, Mergers and Take-overs (European co-ed.) and other legal works. *Leisure interests:* porcelain, music. *Address:* 26 John Street, London, WC1N 2BL; All Souls College, Oxford, OX1 4AL, England. *Telephone:* 0171-831 0351 (London); (01865) 279379 (Oxford). *Fax:* 0171-405 1675 (London); (01865) 279299 (Oxford).

LEVER, Sir Paul, K.C.M.G., M.A.; British diplomatist; b. 31 March 1944; s. of John Morrison Lever and Doris Grace (née Battey); m. Patricia Anne Lever 1990; ed. St. Paul's School, Queen's Coll., Oxford; Third Sec. FCO 1966–67; Third then Second Sec., Embassy Helsinki 1967–71; Second then First Sec., U.K. Del. to NATO 1971–73; with FCO, London 1973–81; Asst. Pvt. Sec. to Sec. of State for Foreign and Commonwealth Affairs 1978–81; Chef de Cabinet to Vice-Pres. of EEC 1981–85; Head UN Dept., FCO 1985–86, Head Defence Dept. 1986–87, Security Policy Dept. 1987–90; Amb. and Head U.K. Del. to Conventional Arms Control Negotiations, Vienna 1990–92; Asst. Under-Sec. of State, FCO 1992–94, Deputy Sec. Cabinet Office and Chair. Jt. Intelligence Cttee. 1994–96; Deputy Under-Sec. of State (Dir. for EU and Econ. Affairs), FCO 1996–97; Amb. to Germany 1997–. *Leisure interests:* walking, art deco pottery. *Address:* British Embassy, 53113 Bonn, Friedrich-Ebert-Allee 77, Germany. *Telephone:* (228) 91670. *Fax:* (228) 9162700.

LEVERHULME, 3rd Viscount, cr. 1922, of the Western Isles; **Philip William Bryce Lever,** K.G., T.D.; British university chancellor; b. 1 July 1915; s. of 2nd Viscount and Marion Lever; m. Margaret Ann Moon 1937 (died 1973); three d.; ed. Eton Coll. and Trinity Coll., Cambridge; Lord Lieut. of City and County of Chester 1949–90; Maj. Cheshire Yeomanry, now Hon. Col.; Pres. Council Liverpool Univ. 1957–63, Sr. Pro-Chancellor 1963–66, Chancellor 1980–93; Advisory Dir. Unilever Ltd.; mem. Nat. Hunt Cttee. 1961 (Steward 1965–68); Deputy Sr. Steward Jockey Club 1970–73, Sr. Steward 1973–76; Council of King George's Jubilee Trust; Chair. Exec. Cttee. Animal Health Trust 1964; Hon. F.R.C.S. 1970, Hon. Assoc. Royal Coll. of Veterinary Surgeons 1975; Hon. LL.D. (Liverpool) 1967; Kt. of Order of St. John of Jerusalem. *Leisure interests:* shooting, fishing. *Address:* Badanloch, Kinbrace, Sutherland, KW11 6UE, Scotland; Thornton Manor, Thornton Hough, Wirral, Merseyside, L63 1JB; Flat 6, Kingston House East, Prince's Gate, Kensington, London, SW7 1LJ, England.

LEVETT, Michael John (Mike), B.COMM., F.I.A., F.F.A.; South African insurance executive; b. 6 June 1939, Cape Town; m. Mary Gillian Aston 1966; two s. one d.; ed. Christian Brothers Coll., Cape Town, Univ. of Cape Town; joined Old Mutual Life Assurance Soc. 1959, Gen. Man. 1981–85, Man. Dir. 1985–, Chair. 1990–; Chair. Mutual & Federal; Dir. Barlows, Cen. Africa Bldg. Soc., S. African Breweries, Nedcor, Sasol Ltd., Hon. D.Econ.Sc.; *Leisure interests:* skiing, tennis. *Address:* South African Mutual Life Assurance Society, P.O. Box 66, Cape Town 8000, South Africa. *Telephone:* (21) 509-2005. *Fax:* (21) 509-3899.

LEVEY, Sir Michael (Vincent), Kt., L.V.O., F.B.A., F.R.S.L.; British art historian; b. 8 June 1927, London; s. of the late O. L. H. Levey and Gladys Mary Milestone; m. Brigid Brophy 1954 (died 1995); one d.; ed. Oratory School and Exeter Coll., Oxford; officer, British Army 1945–48; Asst. Keeper Nat. Gallery 1951–66, Deputy Keeper 1966–68, Keeper 1968–73. Deputy Dir. 1970–73, Dir. 1973–86; Slade Prof. of Art Cambridge Univ. and Fellow of King's Coll. Cambridge 1963–64; Slade Prof. of Art, Oxford Univ. 1994–95; fmr. Chair. Nat. Dirs. Conf.; Hon. Fellow, Exeter Coll., Oxford; Hon. Litt. D. (Manchester); Foreign mem. Ateneo Veneto, Italy. *Publications:* Edited Nat. Gallery Catalogues: 18th Cent. Italian Schools 1956, The German School 1959, Painting in XVIIIth c. Venice 1959; From Giotto to Cézanne

1962, Later Italian Pictures in the Royal Collection 1964, Dürer 1964, A Room-to-room Guide to the National Gallery 1964, Rococo to Revolution 1966, Fifty Works of English and American Literature We Could do Without (with Brigid Brophy and Charles Osborne) 1967, Bronzino 1967, Early Renaissance 1967 (awarded Hawthornden Prize 1968), A History of Western Art 1968, Holbein's Christina of Denmark, Duchess of Milan 1968, 17th and 18th Cent. Italian Schools (Nat. Gallery Catalogue) 1971, Painting at Court 1971, The Life and Death of Mozart 1971, Art and Architecture in 18th Cent. France (co-author) 1972, High Renaissance 1975, The World of Ottoman Art 1976, The Case of Walter Pater 1978, Sir Thomas Lawrence (exhbn. catalogue) 1979, The Painter Depicted (Neurath Lecture) 1982, Tempting Fate (fiction) 1982, An Affair on the Appian Way (fiction) 1984, Giambattista Tiepolo 1986 (Banister Fletcher Prize), The National Gallery Collection 1987, Men At Work (fiction) 1989, The Soul of the Eye (anthology) 1990, Painting and Sculpture in France 1700–1789 1993, Florence: A Portrait 1996. *Address:* 36 Little Lane, Louth, Lincs., LN11 9DU, England.

LEVI, Arrigo, PH.D.; Italian journalist and political writer; b. 17 July 1926, Modena; s. of Enzo and Ida (Donati) Levi; m. Carmela Lenci 1952; one d.; ed. Univs. of Buenos Aires and Bologna; refugee in Argentina 1942–46; Negev Brigade, Israeli Army 1948–49; BBC European Services 1951–53; London Corresp. Gazzetta del Popolo and Corriere d'Informazione 1952–59; Moscow Corresp. Corriere della Sera 1960–62; news anchor man on Italian State Television 1966–68; special corresp. La Stampa 1969–73, Ed. in Chief 1973–78, special corresp. 1978–; columnist on int. affairs, The Times 1979–83; Leader Writer C. Della Sera 1988–; Premio Marconi, Premio Saint Vincent. *Publications:* Il potere in Russia 1965, Journey among the Economists 1972. *Address:* c/o Piazza S. Carlo 206, 10121 Turin, Italy.

LEVI, Edward Hirsch; American lawyer and university professor; b. 26 June 1911, Chicago; s. of Gerson B. and Elsa B. Hirsch; m. Kate Sulzberger 1946; three s.; ed. Univ. of Chicago and Yale; Asst. Prof. Univ. of Chicago Law School 1936–40, Prof. of Law 1945–75, Dean of Law Faculty 1950–62, Provost 1962–68, Pres. 1968–75, Pres. Emer. 1975–; Karl Llewellyn Distinguished Service Prof. in Jurisprudence (on leave) 1975–77; Glen A. Lloyd Distinguished Service Prof. in Law School and Coll. 1977–85, Prof. Emer. 1985–; Special Asst. to U.S. Attorney-Gen., Washington 1940–45; mem. Research Advisory Bd., Cttee. for Econ. Devt. 1951–54, Citizens' Comm. on Graduate Medical Educ. 1963–66; mem. White House Council on Domestic Affairs 1964, several comms. on internal affairs 1966–71, Council on Legal Educ. and Professional Responsibility 1968–74 (Chair. 1969–73), Nat. Comm. on Productivity and Work Quality 1970–74; Attorney-Gen. 1975–77; Trustee, Aspen Inst. for Humanistic Studies 1970–75, 1977–79, Council of Nat. Endowment for the Humanities 1974–75; mem. Bd. of Overseers Univ. of Pa. Law School 1978–80, Bd. of Trustees Nat. Humanities Center 1978–90 (Chair. 1979–83), Bd. of Trustees Aerospace Corpn. 1978–80, Bd. of The William Benton Foundation 1980–; Dir. MacArthur Foundation 1979–84, Foundation of Liberty 1979–, Inst. for Civil Justice 1979–81; lecturer, Salzburg Seminar in American Studies 1980, mem. Bd. 1986–90; mem. Bd. of Govs., Univ. of Calif. Humanities Research Inst. 1988–91; Fellow, American Acad. of Arts and Sciences, (Pres. 1986–89), American Philosophical Soc. (Vice-Pres. 1991–94), American Bar Foundation; mem. Council of American Law Inst.; Hon. Trustee, Int. Inst. of Educ.; Learned Hand Medal (Fed. Bar Council, New York) 1976, Fordham-Stein Prize (Fordham Law School) 1977, Louis Dembitz Brandeis Medal (Brandeis Univ.) 1979, Constitutional Rights Award 1992; Légion d'honneur. *Publications:* Introduction to Legal Reasoning 1949, Four Talks on Legal Education 1952, Ed. Gilbert's Collier on Bankruptcy (with J. W. Moore) 1937, Elements of the Law (with R. S. Steffen) 1950, Points of View 1969, The Crisis in the Nature of Law 1969, The Place of Professional Education in the Life of the University 1971, The Collective Morality of a Maturing Society 1973. *Address:* The University of Chicago, 1116 East 59th Street, Harper Library, Chicago, IL 60637; 4950 Chicago Beach Drive, Chicago, IL 60615, U.S.A. (Home). *Telephone:* (312) 702-8588.

LEVI, Isaac, PH.D.; American professor of philosophy; b. 30 June 1930, New York; m. Judith R. Levi 1951; two s.; ed. New York and Columbia Univs.; Asst. Prof. of Philosophy, Case Western Reserve Univ. 1957–62, The City Coll. of New York 1962–64; Assoc. Prof. then Full Prof. of Philosophy, Case Western Reserve Univ. 1964–67, Chair. Dept. 1968–70; Prof. of Philosophy, Columbia Univ. 1970–, Chair. Dept. 1973–76, 1989–91, John Dewey Prof. of Philosophy 1992–; Visiting Fellow Corpus Christi Coll., Cambridge, U.K. 1973, Darwin Coll. 1989, All Souls Coll., Oxford 1988, Inst. of Advanced Study, Hebrew Univ. of Jerusalem 1994, Wolfson Coll., Cambridge 1997; Guggenheim Fellow, Fulbright Scholar and other awards; mem. American Acad. of Arts and Sciences; Dr. h.c. (Lund) 1988; Univ. of Helsinki Medal. *Publications:* For the Sake of the Argument 1966, Gambling with Truth 1967, Enterprise of Knowledge 1980, Decisions and Revisions 1984, Hard Choices 1986, The Fixation of Belief and its Undoing 1991, For the Sake of the Argument 1996, The Covenant of Reason 1997. *Address:* 718 Philosophy Hall, Columbia University, New York, NY 10027 (Office); 25 Claremont Avenue, New York, NY 10027, U.S.A. (Home). *Telephone:* (212) 854 6946; 854 5197 (Office); (212) 864 3615 (Home).

LEVI, Wasangula Noel, C.B.E., B.A.; Papua New Guinea politician and diplomatist; b. 6 June 1942, Nonopai; m. Josepha Muna 1971; two s. two d.; ed. Univ. of Papua New Guinea; joined Public Service 1961; Sec. for Defence 1974–77; M.P. for New Ireland 1977–87; Minister for Foreign Affairs and Trade 1980–82; Amb. to People's Repub. of China 1987–90, High Commr. to U.K. (also accred. to Israel, Egypt and Zimbabwe) 1991–95; Sec. Dept. of the Prime Minister and Cabinet 1995–97; Sec.-Gen. Forum Secr. 1998–. *Leisure interests:* reading, walking, watching rugby. *Address:* Forum Secretariat, Private Mail Bag, Suva, Fiji. *Telephone:* 302375. *Fax:* 300747.

LEVI, Yoel, M.A.; Romanian/American conductor; b. 16 Aug. 1950, Romania; m.; ed. Tel Aviv and Jerusalem Acads. of Music, Guildhall School of Music, London; studied under Mendi Rodan, Franco Ferrara, Kiril Kondrashin; won First Prize Conductors' Int. Competition Besançon, France 1978; asst. to Lorin Maazel Cleveland Orchestra for six years, Resident Conductor 1980–84; Music Dir. Atlanta Symphony Orchestra (ASO) 1988–, extensive European tour 1991; frequent guest conductor of orchestras throughout N. America, Europe and the Far East; conducted Stockholm Philharmonic at Nobel Prize Ceremony 1991; performed at Opening Ceremonies of Centennial Olympic Games 1996; apptd. first Music Adviser to Israel Festival for 1997/98 seasons; opera conducting debut La Fanciulla del West at Teatro Comunale, Florence 1997; Best Orchestra of the Year (awarded to ASO), Int. Classical Music Awards 1991–92; Distinguished Visiting Prof., Univ. of Ga. School of Music; Hon. D.F.A. (Oglethorpe Univ., Atlanta) 1997. *Address:* Askonas Holt Ltd., Lonsdale Chambers, 27 Chancery Lane, London, WC2A 1PF, England. *Telephone:* 0171-400 1700. *Fax:* 0171-400 1799.

LEVI-MONTALCINI, Rita; Italian research scientist; b. 22 April 1909, Turin; d. of Adamo Levi and Adele Montalcini; ed. Turin Univ. Medical School; engaged in neurological research in Turin and Brussels 1936–41, in a country-cottage in Piemonte 1941–43; in hiding in Florence during German occupation 1943–44; medical doctor working among war refugees in Florence 1944–45; resumed academic positions at Univ. of Turin 1945; worked in St. Louis, U.S.A. with Prof. Viktor Hamburger from 1947, Assoc. Prof. 1956, Prof. 1958–77; Dir. Inst. of Cell Biology of Italian Nat. Council of Research, Rome 1969–78, Guest Prof. 1979–89, Guest Prof. Inst. of Neurobiology 1989–; Pres. Inst. della Enciclopedia Italiana Treccani; Nobel Prize for Medicine 1986 (with Stanley Cohen q.v.) for work on chemicalgrowth factors which control growth and devt. in humans and animals. *Publication:* In Praise of Imperfection: My Life and Work 1988. *Address:* Institute of Neurobiology, C.N.R., Viale Marx 15, 00137, Rome, Italy. *Telephone:* (39-6) 86 090 510 (Office). *Fax:* (39-6) 86 090 269 (Office).

LÉVI-STRAUSS, Claude; French anthropologist, university professor and writer; b. 28 Nov. 1908, Brussels, Belgium; s. of Raymond Lévi-Strauss and Emma Lévy; m. 1st Dina Dreyfus 1932; m. 2nd Rose Marie Ullmo 1946, one s.; m. 3rd Monique Roman 1954, one s.; ed. Lycée Janson de Sailly, Paris, and Univ. de Paris à la Sorbonne; Prof. Univ. of São Paulo, Brazil 1935–39; Visiting Prof. New School for Social Research, New York 1942–45; Cultural Counsellor, French Embassy to U.S.A. 1946–47; Assoc. Dir. Musée de l'Homme, Paris 1949–50; Dir. of Studies, Ecole Pratique des Hautes Etudes, Paris 1950–74; Prof. Collège de France 1959–82, Hon. Prof. 1983–; mem. Acad. Française; Foreign mem. Royal Acad. of the Netherlands, Norwegian Acad. of Sciences and Letters, American Acad. of Arts and Sciences, American Acad. and Inst. of Arts and Letters, British Acad.; Foreign Assoc. U.S. N.A.S.; Hon. mem. Royal Anthropological Inst., American Philosophical Soc., and London School of Oriental and African Studies; Dr. h.c. (Brussels, Harvard, Yale, Chicago, Columbia, Oxford, Stirling, Zaire, Mexico, Uppsala, Johns Hopkins, Montreal, Quebec, Visva-Bharati Univ., India); Prix Paul Pelliot 1949; Huxley Memorial Medal 1965, Viking Fund Gold Medal 1966, Gold Medal Centre National de la Recherche Scientifique 1967; Erasmus Prize 1973, Aby M. Warburg Prize 1996; Grand Croix, Légion d'honneur, Commdr. Ordre Nat. du Mérite, des Palmes académiques, des Arts et des Lettres. *Publications:* La vie familiale et sociale des indiens Nambikwara 1948, Les structures élémentaires de la parenté 1949, Tristes tropiques 1955, Anthropologie structurale 1958, Le totémisme aujourd'hui 1962, La pensée sauvage 1962, Le cru et le cuit 1964, Du miel aux cendres 1967, L'origine des manières de table 1968, L'homme nu 1971, Anthropologie structurale deux 1973, La voie des masques 1975, 1979, Le regard éloigné 1983, Paroles données 1984, La potière jalouse 1985, De près et de loin (with Didier Eribon) 1988, Histoire de Lynx 1991, Regarder, écouter, lire 1993, Saudades do Brasil 1994. *Leisure interest:* country life. *Address:* Laboratoire d'Anthropologie Sociale, Collège de France, 52 rue du Cardinal Lemoine, 75005 Paris (Office); 2 rue des Marronniers, 75016 Paris, France (Home). *Telephone:* (1) 44-27-17-31 (Office); (1) 42-88-34-71 (Home). *Fax:* (1) 44-27-17-66.

LEVIE, Simon Hijman; Netherlands art historian (retd.); b. 17 Jan. 1925, Rheden; m. Mary Levie-Lion 1955; one s. two d.; ed. Univ. of Basel, Switzerland; Keeper, Central Museum, Utrecht; Dir., Historical Museum, Amsterdam; Dir.-Gen. Rijksmuseum Amsterdam; Chair. Council Thyssen-Bornemisza Foundation, Lugano; Dir. Simart Art Consultancy, Amsterdam. *Address:* Chopinstraat 29, 1077 GM Amsterdam, Netherlands. *Telephone:* (020) 671-88-95. *Fax:* (020) 673-80-88.

LEVIN, Bernard (see Levin, Henry Bernard).

LEVIN, Carl, J.D.; American politician; b. 28 June 1934, Detroit, Mich.; s. of Saul R. and Bess (née Levinson) Levin; m. Barbara Halpern 1961; three d.; ed. Central High School, Detroit, Swarthmore Coll., Pa., and Harvard Law School; Asst. Mich. Attorney Gen. and Gen. Counsel for Mich. Civil Rights Comm. 1964–67; Special Asst. Attorney Gen. and Chief Appellate Attorney for Defender's Office of Legal Aid and Defender Assoc. of Detroit

1968–69; elected to Detroit City Council 1969, re-elected as City Council Pres. 1973; U.S. Senator from Michigan 1979–; mem. Governmental Affairs Cttee.; Democrat. *Address:* U.S. Senate, 459 Russell Senate Office Building, Washington, DC 20510, U.S.A. *Telephone:* (202) 224-6221.

LEVIN, Gerald Manuel, B.A., LL.B; American publishing executive; b. 6 May 1939, Philadelphia; s. of David Levin and Pauline Schantzer; m. 1st Carol S. Needlemam 1959 (divorced 1970), two s. (one s. deceased), one d.; m. 2nd Barbara Riley 1970, one s. one d.; ed. Haverford Coll. and Univ. of Pa.; Assoc. Simpson, Thatcher & Bartlett, New York 1963–67; Gen. Man., C.O.O. Devt. and Resources Corpn. New York 1967–71; Rep. Int. Basic Economy Corpn. Teheran 1971–72; Vice-Pres. Programming, Home Box Office, New York 1972–73, Pres., C.E.O. 1973–76, Chair., C.E.O. 1976–79; Group Vice-Pres. (Video), Time Inc. New York 1979–84, Exec. Vice-Pres. 1984–88, Vice-Chair., Dir. 1988–90; Vice-Chair., Dir. Time-Warner Inc. (to merge with Turner Broadcasting Systems) New York 1990–92, C.O.O. 1991, Chair. 1990–95; Pres. 1992–95, Jt. C.E.O. 1992–93, C.E.O. Jan 1992–; Dir. N.Y. Stock Exchange; Treas. N.Y. Philharmonic Orchestra; mem. Bd. of Dirs. Whittle Communications Partnership, New York, Ronald H. Brown Foundation, Living Memorial to the Holocaust (Museum of Jewish Heritage); Hon. LL.D. (Texas Coll.) 1985. *Leisure interests:* reading, jogging. *Address:* Time Warner Inc., 75 Rockefeller Plaza, New York, NY 10019, U.S.A.

LEVIN, (Henry) Bernard, C.B.E., B.SC.(ECON.); British journalist and author; b. 19 Aug. 1928; s. of late Phillip Levin and Rose Levin (née Racklin); ed. Christ's Hosp., L.S.E., Univ. of London; writer, regular and occasional, many newspapers and magazines, U.K. and abroad, including The Times, London, Sunday Times, Observer, Manchester Guardian, Truth, Spectator, Daily Express, Daily Mail, Newsweek, Int. Herald Tribune 1953–; writer and broadcaster for radio and TV 1952–; Pres. English Asscn. 1984–85, Vice-Pres. 1985–88; numerous awards for journalism; Hon. Fellow (L.S.E.) 1977–; mem. Order of Polonia Restituta (by Polish Govt.-in-Exile) 1976, Chairman's Award, British Press Awards 1997. *Publications:* The Pendulum Years 1971, Taking Sides 1979, The Conducted Tour 1981, Speaking Up 1982, Enthusiasms 1983, The Way We Live Now 1984, Hannibal's Footsteps 1985, In These Times 1986, To the End of the Rhine 1987, All Things Considered 1988, A Walk up Fifth Avenue 1989, Now Read On 1990, If You Want My Opinion 1992, A World Elsewhere 1994, I Should Say So 1995, Enough Said 1998. *Address:* c/o The Times, 1 Pennington Street, London, E1 9XN, England. *Telephone:* 0171-782 5859. *Fax:* 0171-782 5229.

LEVIN, Ira, A.B.; American writer; b. 27 Aug. 1929, New York; s. of Charles Levin and Beatrice (née Schlansky); m. 1st Gabrielle Aronsohn 1960 (divorced 1968); three s.; m. 2nd Phyllis Finkel 1979 (divorced 1982); ed. Horace Mann School, Drake Univ., Iowa, New York Univ.; U.S. Army 1953–55, wrote training films for the troops and a service comedy No Time for Sergeants (film version released 1958); *Plays include:* Interlock 1958, Critic's Choice 1960, General Seeger 1962, Drat! The Cat! 1965, Doctor Cook's Garden 1967, Veronica's Room 1973, Deathtrap 1978, Cantorial 1982, Sliver 1991; Novels include: A Kiss Before Dying 1953, Rosemary's Baby 1967, This Perfect Day 1970, The Stepford Wives 1972, Boys from Brazil 1976, Sliver 1991, Son of Rosemary 1997; mem. Authors' Guild, American Soc. of Composers, Authors and Publishers, Dramatists Guild (mem. Council 1980–). *Address:* c/o Harold Ober Associates, 425 Madison Avenue, New York, NY 10017, U.S.A.

LEVIN, Richard Charles, PH.D.; American professor of economics; b. 7 April 1947, San Francisco; s. of Derek Levin and Phylys Goldstein; m. Jane Aries 1968; two s. two d.; ed. Stanford and Yale Univs. and Merton Coll. Oxford; Asst. Prof. of Econs. Yale Univ. 1974–79, Assoc. Prof. 1979–82, Prof. of Econs. and Man. 1982–92, Dir. Grad. Studies in Econs. 1984–86, Chair. Dept. of Econs. 1987–92, Frederick William Beinecke Prof. of Econs. 1992–, Dean, Grad. School 1992–93, Pres. Yale Univ. 1993–; Trustee Yale-New Haven Hosp. 1993–, Univs. Research Asscn. 1994–; Fellow Merton Coll., Oxford 1996; Fellow American Acad. of Arts and Sciences; mem. Yale-New Haven Hosp. Bd. of Trustees 1993–, Yale-New Haven Health Services Corpn. Inc. 1993–; mem. American Econ. Asscn., Econometric Soc.; numerous professional and consulting activities; Hon. LL.D. (Princeton) 1993, (Harvard) 1994. *Address:* Office of the President, Yale University, 105 Wall Street, New Haven, CT 06511, U.S.A.

LEVINE, Alan J., J.D.; American entertainment company executive; b. 8 March 1947, Los Angeles; s. of Phil Levine and Shirley Lauber; m. Judy Birnbaum 1973; two c.; ed. Univ. of Southern Calif.; called to bar, Calif. 1972, U.S. Dist. Court (South Dist.), Calif. 1972; partner, Pacht, Ross, Warne, Bernhard & Sears, Los Angeles 1971–78, Schiff, Hirsch & Schreiber, Beverly Hills, Calif. 1978–80, Armstrong, Hirsch & Levine, Los Angeles 1980–89; Pres., C.O.O. SONY Pictures Entertainment Inc., Culver, Calif. 1989–, Chair. 1994–96; entertainment and media consultant 1997–. *Address:* c/o SONY Pictures Entertainment Inc., 9601 Wilshire Boulevard, Suite 630, Beverly Hills, CA 90210, U.S.A. *Telephone:* (310) 275-2611. *Fax:* (310) 275-7305.

LEVINE, David, B.F.A., B.S.; American artist; b. 20 Dec. 1926, Brooklyn; s. of Harry Levine and Lena Levine; one s. one d.; ed. Temple Univ. and Hans Hoffman School of Painting; served U.S. Army 1945–46; one-man shows Forum Gallery, New York 1966–, Georgia Museum of Art 1968, Calif. Palace Legion of Honor 1968–69, 1971–72, 1983, Wesleyan Univ. 1970, Brooklyn Museum 1971, Princeton Univ. 1972, Galerie Yves Lambert, Paris 1972, Yale Univ. 1973, Hirshhorn Museum and Sculpture Garden, Washington 1976, Galerie Claude Bernard 1979, Philips Gallery 1980, Pierpont Morgan Library 1981, Santa Fe East Gallery 1983, Meredith Long, Houston 1984, Ashmolean Museum 1987–88; mem. American Acad. of Arts and Letters; Guggenheim Fellow 1967; recipient of several awards. *Address:* c/o Forum Gallery, 745 5th Avenue, New York, NY 10151, U.S.A.

LEVINE, Jack; American artist; b. 3 Jan. 1915, Boston, Mass.; s. of Samuel and Mary (née Grinker) Levine; m. Ruth Gikow 1946 (died 1982); one d.; studied with Dr. Denman W. Ross, and H. K. Zimmerman; one-man exhibition Downtown Gallery, New York 1938; Artists 1942 Exhbn., Museum of Modern Art, New York 1943; exhibited at Jeu de Paume, Paris 1938; Carnegie Int. Exhbn. 1938, 1939, 1940; Retrospective Exhbns. Inst. of Contemporary Art, Boston 1953, Whitney Museum of American Art, New York 1955, Palacio de Bellas Artes, Mexico 1960; Dunn Int. Exhbn., Tate Gallery, London 1963; one-man exhbn. The Jewish Museum, New York 1978–79; pictures in Museum of Modern Art, William Hayes Fogg Museum (Harvard), Addison Gallery, Andover, Mass., Vatican Museum, etc.; mem. fmr. Pres., fmr. Chancellor American Acad. of Arts and Letters; fmr. Pres. Inst. of Arts and Letters; D.F.A. Colby Coll., Maine. *Address:* 68 Morton Street, New York, NY 10014, U.S.A.

LEVINE, James; American musician, conductor and pianist; b. 23 June 1943, Cincinnati, Ohio; s. of Lawrence M. Levine and Helen (Goldstein) Levine; ed. Walnut Hills High School, Juilliard School, New York; Asst. Conductor, Cleveland Orchestra 1964–70; Prin. Conductor, Metropolitan Opera, New York 1973–, Music Dir. 1976–, Artistic Dir. 1986–; Music Dir. Ravinia Festival 1973–93, Cincinnati May Festival 1974–78; Chief Conductor (desig.), Munich Philharmonic 1999; regular appearances as conductor and pianist in Europe and the U.S.A. with orchestras including Vienna Philharmonic, Berlin Philharmonic, Chicago Symphony, Philadelphia Orchestra, Philharmonia, Dresden Staatskapelle, Boston Symphony, New York Philharmonic, Israel Philharmonic, Salzburg and Bayreuth Festivals; conducted Metropolitan Opera premieres of I Vespri Siciliani, Stiffelio, I Lombardi (Verdi), The Rise and Fall of the City of Mahagonny (Weill), Lulu (Berg), Porgy and Bess (Gershwin), Oedipus Rex (Stravinsky), Idomeneo, La Clemenza di Tito (Mozart), Erwartung, Moses und Aron (Schönberg), La Cenerentola (Rossini), The Ghosts of Versailles (Corigliano) (world premiere); conductor Salzburg Festival premieres of Offenbach's Les contes d'Hoffmann 1980 and Schönberg's Moses und Aron 1987; Grammy awards for recordings of Orff's Carmina Burana, Mahler's Symphony No. 7, Brahms' A German Requiem, Verdi's La Traviata, Wagner's Das Rheingold, Die Walküre, Götterdämmerung, Strauss' Ariadne auf Naxos; Dr. h.c. (Univ. of Cincinnati, New England Conservatory, Northwestern Univ., State Univ. of New York); Cultural Award of New York City 1980, St. Nicholas Soc. Medallion of Merit, Smetana Medal 1987, Gold Medal, Nat. Inst. of Social Sciences 1996, Nat. Medal of Arts 1997. *Address:* Metropolitan Opera, Lincoln Center, New York, NY 10023, U.S.A.

LEVINE, Seymour, PH.D.; American university professor; b. 23 Jan. 1925, Brooklyn, New York; s. of Joseph Levine and Rose Reines; m. Barbara Lou McWilliams 1950; one s. two d.; ed. Univ. of Denver, New York Univ.; Asst. Prof., Div. of Research, Boston Univ. 1952–53; Postdoctoral Fellow, Michael Reese Hosp., Chicago 1953–55, Research Assoc. 1955–56; Asst. Prof., Dept. of Psychiatry, Ohio State Univ. 1956–60; Postdoctoral Fellow, Maudsley Hosp., London, England 1960–62; Assoc. Prof., Dept. of Psychiatry, Stanford Univ. 1962–69, Prof. 1969–96, Dir. Stanford Primate Facility 1976–; Dir. Biological Sciences Research Training Program 1971–; Consultant, Foundation of Human Devt., Univ. Coll. Dublin, Ireland 1973–; Pres. Int. Soc. of Developmental Psychobiology 1975–76; Pres. Elect Int. Soc. of Psychoneuroendocrinology; Hoffheimer Research Award 1961, Research Career Devt. Award 1962, Research Scientist Award 1967. *Publications:* (Co-author) Stress, arousal and the pituitary-adrenal system 1979, chapters and articles on stress in animals and humans. *Leisure interests:* music, art, sports. *Address:* Department of Psychiatry and Behavioral Sciences, Stanford University School of Medicine, Stanford, CA 94305, U.S.A. *Telephone:* (415) 723-5781 (Office).

LEVINGSTON, Gen. Roberto Marcelo; Argentinian politician and army officer; b. 10 Jan. 1920, San Luis; s. of Guillermo Levingston and Carmen Laborda; m. Betty Nelly Andrés 1943; two s. (one deceased) one d.; ed. Pius IX Coll., Nat. Mil. Coll., Army Intelligence School, Escuela Superior de Guerra and Center for High Mil. Studies; entered army as cadet, Nat. Mil. Coll. 1938, Sub-Lieut. 1941, Brig.-Gen. 1966; Army Information Officer 1947–50; mem. Gen. Staff 1951–57; Prof., Escuela Superior de Guerra 1958–62; Head of Army Information Services 1963–64; Dir.-Gen. Lemos School of Logistics 1965–66; Head of Intelligence of Jt. Chiefs of Staff 1967–68; Mil. Attaché Army del. to Interamerican Defense Bd. and Pres. Special Comm. on Acquisitions in U.S.A. 1969–70; Pres. and Prime Minister of Argentina 1970–71; Pres. Circle of Studies of Nat. Argentine Movement. *Publications:* political and military works. *Leisure interests:* reading of all kinds, particularly on politics, economics and military subjects, music and sport. *Address:* 11 de Septiembre 1735-17 A, Buenos Aires, Argentina. *Telephone:* 782-4433 (Home).

LEVINSON, Barry; American screenwriter and director; b. 6 April 1942, Baltimore, Md.; m. Diana Levinson; ed. American Univ.; fmrly. wrote and acted on TV comedy show in Los Angeles; later worked on network TV;

wrote and appeared, The Carol Burnett Show; worked on film scripts for Silent Movie and High Anxiety (with Mel Brooks q.v.). *TV work includes:* writer for Tim Conway Comedy Hour, The Marty Feldman Comedy Machine, The Carol Burnett Show (Emmy Awards 1974, 1975); exec. producer, Harry, 30 Minutes of Investigative Ticking, Diner, Homicide: Life on the Street. *Films directed:* Diner, The Natural, Young Sherlock Holmes, Tin Men, Good Morning Vietnam, Rain Man (Acad. Award 1988), Disclosure 1995; directed and produced Avalon, Bugsy, Toys; Jimmy Hollywood (dir., writer) 1994, Sleepers 1996, Wag the Dog 1997, Sphere 1998; *writer:* Diner, Tin Men, Avalon; co-wrote screenplays with Valerie Curtin for And Justice for All, Inside Moves, Best Friends, Unfaithfully Yours, Toys; *actor:* Quiz Show 1994. *Address:* c/o Baltimore Pictures, Bldg. 133-208, 4000 Warner Boulevard, Burbank, CA 91522, U.S.A.

LEVITIS, Yefim Zavelyevich; Russian religious leader; b. 29 Nov. 1930; m.; one s.; ed. Moscow Inst. of Aviation, Jewish seminary at Moscow Choral Synagogue, Higher Rabbis' School, Budapest; Scientific Sec. Moscow Jewish community 1975–80; rabbi, St. Petersburg 1980–91; Chief Rabbi, Great Choral Synagogue; Deputy Chief Rabbi of Russia responsible for co-operation with non-Jewish orgs.; mem. Jewish Conf. of Rabbis; mem. Working Group, Consultative Council of Confession Heads, St. Petersburg. *Address:* Great Choral Synagogue, 2nd Lermontovsky pr., St. Petersburg, Russia. *Telephone:* (812) 114 0078 (Office).

LEVITT, Arthur, Jr.; American business executive; b. 3 Feb. 1931, Brooklyn; s. of Arthur Levitt and Dorothy Wolff; m. Marylin Blauner 1955; one s. one d.; ed. Williams Coll.; Asst. Promotion Dir. Time Inc. New York 1954–59; Exec. Vice-Pres., Dir. Oppenheimer Industries Inc. Kansas City 1959–62; with Shearson Hayden Stone Inc. (now Shearson Lehman Bros. Inc.), New York 1962–78, Pres. 1969–78; Chair., C.E.O., Dir. American Stock Exchange, New York 1978–89; Chair. Levitt Media Co. New York 1989–93, New York City Econ. Devt. Corpn. 1990–93; Chair. Securities and Exchange Comm. 1993–; various directorships and other business and public appts.; Hon. LL.D. (Williams Coll.) 1980, (Pace) 1980, (Hamilton Coll.) 1981, (Long Island) 1984, (Hofstra) 1985. *Address:* Securities and Exchange Commission, 450 Fifth Street, N.W., Washington, DC 20001, U.S.A.

LEVITT, Brian Michael, B.A.SC., L.L.B.; Canadian businessman; b. 26 July 1947, Montreal; s. of Eric Levitt and Rya Levitt; m. Claire Gohier 1992; two d.; ed. Univ. of Toronto; special Asst. to Provost, Univ. of Toronto 1969–73; called to Bar, Ontario 1974; Dir. Interpretation, Prices and Profits Branch, Anti-Inflation Bd., Govt. of Canada 1975–76; Assoc. Osler, Hoskin & Harcourt, Toronto 1976–79, partner 1979–91; Pres. IMASCO Ltd., Montreal 1991–, also C.O.O., C.E.O. 1995–. *Publications:* various articles on business law. *Leisure interests:* skiing, riding, sailing. *Address:* IMASCO Ltd., 600 de Maisonneuve Blvd. West, 20th floor, Montreal, Quebec, H3A 3K7, Canada. *Telephone:* (514) 982 9111.

LEVY, Alain M., M.B.A.; record company executive: b. 19 Dec. 1946, France; ed. Ecole des Mines, France, Univ. of Pennsylvania; Asst. to the Pres. CBS Int., New York 1972–73, Vice-Pres. Marketing for Europe, Paris 1973, Vice-Pres. of Creative Operations for Europe, also Man. CBS Italy 1978; Man. Dir. CBS Disques, France 1979, C.E.O. PolyGram France 1984, Exec. Vice-Pres. PolyGram Group, France and Fed. Repub. of Germany 1988, Man. U.S. Operations PolyGram Group 1990–, Pres., C.E.O., mem. Bd. Man. PolyGram U.S.A. 1991–; mem. Group Man. Cttee. Phillips Electronics, majority shareholder PolyGram U.S.A. 1991–. *Address:* PolyGram Records Inc., 825 8th Avenue, New York, NY 10019, U.S.A.; 8 St. James's Square, London, SW1Y 4JU, England.

LEVY, Bernard-Henri; French writer; b. 5 Nov. 1948, Beni-Saf, Algeria; s. of André Levy and Ginette Levy; m. 1st Sylvie Bouscasse 1980; one s. one d.; m. 2nd Arielle Sonnery 1993; ed. Ecole Normale Supérieure (rue d'Ulm), Paris; War Correspondent for Daily Combat 1971–72; lecturer in Epistemology, Univ. of Strasbourg, in Philosophy, Ecole Normale Supérieure 1973; mem. François Mitterrand's Group of Experts 1973–76; joined Editions Grasset as Ed. "nouvelle philosophie" series 1973; Ed. Idées section, Quotidien de Paris; Contrib. to Nouvel Observateur and Temps Modernes 1974; Co-founder Action Int. contre la Faim 1980; f. and Dir. Règle du jeu 1990–; Pres. Supervisory Council Sept-Arte 1993–. *Publications:* Les Indes Rouges 1973, La Barbarie à Visage Humain 1977, Le Testament de Dieu 1979, L'Idéologie Française 1981, Questions de Principe 1983, Le Diable en tête (Prix Médicis) 1984, Impressions d'Asie 1985, Questions de Principe Deux 1986, Eloge des Intellectuels 1987, Les Dernier jours de Charles Baudelaire (Prix Interallié) 1988, Questions de Principe Trois 1990, Les Années 80 "de stella" 1990, Les Bronzes de César 1991, Les Aventures de la Liberté 1991, Piet Mondrian 1992, Piero Della Francesca 1992, Le Jugement Dernier (play) 1992, Questions de principe IV 1992, Les Hommes et les Femmes (jtly.) 1993, Un Jour dans la mort de Sarajevo (screenplay, jtly.) 1993, Bosna! (screenplay, jtly.) 1994, La pureté dangereuse 1995, Questions de principe V 1995, Le lys et la cendre 1996; dir. film Le Jour de la Nuit 1997, Comédie 1997. *Leisure interests:* skiing, judo, water-skiing. *Address:* 61 rue des Saint-Pères, 75006 Paris, France. *Telephone:* (01) 44-39-22-00. *Fax:* (01) 42-22-64-18.

LEVY, David; Israeli politician; b. 1938, Morocco; emigrated to Israel 1957; construction worker; joined Histadrut; elected to Knesset, representing Herut (Freedom) group of Gahal 1969– (subsequently of Likud Bloc); Likud cand. for Sec.-Gen. of Histadrut 1977, 1981; Minister of Immigrant Absorption 1977–78, of Construction and Housing 1978–90, of Foreign Affairs 1990–92, 1996–97, Deputy Prime Minister 1981–84, 1988–92; f. Gesher Party 1996. *Address:* c/o Gesher, Jerusalem, Israel.

LEVY, Jacques Bernard, D. ÈS SC.; French metallurgist; b. Jan. 1937, Constantine, Algeria; s. of Gilbert Levy and Renée Cassin; m. Marianne Neuburger 1964; two s. one d.; ed. Ecole Polytechnique, Ecole des Mines de Paris, Univ. de Paris VI; Prof. of Metallurgy, Ecole des Mines de Saint-Etienne 1962, Dir. Dept. of Metallurgy 1974; Post-doctoral Fellow, Univ. of Waterloo, Ont., Canada 1968; Scientific Dir. Ecole des Mines de Paris 1976, Dir. 1984–; Ingénieur général du corps des mines 1983; Chair. (Research Comm.) Conf. des Grandes Ecoles 1984; mem. Royal Swedish Acad. of Eng. Sciences 1989; Pres. Conf. of European Schools for Advanced Eng. Educ. and Research 1990; Pres. Conf. des Grandes Ecoles 1993; Dr. h.c. (Catholic Univ. of Louvain) 1996; Prix RIST (Soc. Française de Métallurgie); Officier, Légion d'honneur, Officier, Ordre nat. du mérite, Commdr., Palmes académiques. *Publications:* about 30 publs. on physical metallurgy (grain boundaries and interfaces, structure and properties of metals and alloys), official reports on materials science and eng. higher educ. *Leisure interests:* skiing, tennis. *Address:* Ecole nat. supérieure des mines, 60 boulevard Saint-Michel, 75272 Paris Cedex 06, France. *Telephone:* (01) 40-51-90-18. *Fax:* (1) 43-25-94-95.

LEVY, Raymond Haïm, M.S.; French company executive (retd.); b. 28 June 1927, Paris; s. of Sam and Rachel Levy; m. Jacqueline Schwartz 1955; three s. one d.; ed. Ecole Polytechnique, Ecole des Mines de Paris, M.I.T.; engineer in coal mines in north of France 1952–53, in Public Mines Service 1953–57; Chief Eng., Régie Autonome des Pétroles (RAP) 1957–65; Gen. Man. of Exploration and Production, ERAP-ELF 1966–72, Dir.-Gen., Refining and Distribution 1973–80; Gen. Man. ELF Union 1972–75; Vice-Pres. ERAP (Enterprise de recherches et d'activités pétrolières) 1976–89; Chair. and Pres. ELF Union and SOCANTAR 1976–80; Chair. and Pres. ELF France 1975–80; Vice-Pres. and Gen. Man. SNEA (Soc. Nat. Elf Aquitaine) 1976–80; Pres., Dir.-Gen. USINOR 1982–84; Chair. Cockerill-Sambre 1985–86; Chair. Renault Inc. 1986–92, Hon. Pres. 1992–; Vice-Pres. Conseil général des Mines 1987–92; Dir. Renault Vehicles Ltd. 1987–92, 1994–, Crédit Lyonnais 1988–, Société nationale Elf-Aquitaine 1987, Volvo AB 1990–93 (Hon. Pres. 1993–94); Pres. Strategic Cttee. Renault-Volvo 1990–92, EFQM 1991–92, Banque Paribas 1994–; Pres. Supervisory Council Lagardère Groupe 1993–; Pres. Consortium de réalisation (CDR) 1998–; Commdr., Légion d'honneur, Commdr. Ordre nat. du Mérite. *Address:* Lagardère Groupe, 4 rue de Presbourg, 75116 Paris, France.

LEVY, Robert Isaac, M.D.; American professor of medicine; b. 3 May 1937, New York; s. of George Gerson Levy and Sarah Levinson; m. Ellen Marie Feis 1958; one s. three d.; ed. Cornell and Yale Univs.; Intern, Asst. Resident in Medicine, Yale-New Haven Medical Center 1961–63; Clinical Assoc., Molecular Diseases, Nat. Heart Inst. 1963–66, Chief Resident 1965–66, Attending Physician, Molecular Disease Branch 1965–81, Head, Section on Lipoproteins 1966–78, Deputy Clinical Dir. 1968–69, Chief, Clinical Service 1969–73, Chief Lipid Metabolism Branch 1970–74, Dir. Div. of Heart and Vascular Diseases 1973–75, Dir. of Nat. Heart, Lung and Blood Inst. 1975–81; Prof. of Medicine, Dean of School of Medicine and Vice-Pres. for Health Sciences, Tufts Univ. 1981–83; Prof. of Medicine, Columbia Univ. 1983, Vice-Pres. for Health Sciences 1983–84, Sr. Advisor to Univ. 1984–86, Sr. Assoc. Vice-Pres. for Health Sciences 1985–87; Pres. Sandoz Research Inst. 1988–92; Pres. Wyeth-Ayerst Research, Wyeth-Ayerst Lab. Div., American Home Products, Pa. 1992–98, Sr. Vice-Pres. Science and Tech., American Home Products Corpn. 1998–; Arthur S. Flemming Award 1975, Asscn. Health Foundation Humanitarian Award 1976, American Asscn. for Clinical Chemistry Award 1979, Donald D. Van Slyke Award in Clinical Chemistry 1980, Roger J. Williams Award in Preventive Nutrition 1985, Humana Heart Foundation Award 1988, Special Recognition Award, American Heart Asscn. Council on Arteriosclerosis 1995. *Publications:* over 300 scientific papers. *Address:* American Home Products Corporation, 5 Giralda Farms, Madison, NJ 07940, U.S.A. *Telephone:* (973) 660-5021. *Fax:* (973) 660-7529.

LEVY, Yitzhak; politician and rabbi; b. 1947, Morocco; m.; five c.; ed. Kerem B'Yavne and Yeshivat Hakotel; immigated to Israel in 1957; ordained rabbi; served in Israeli Defence Forces, to rank of Maj.; Nat. Religious Party mem. Knesset (Parl.) 1988–, mem. Knesset House Cttee., Cttees. on Finance, on Constitution, Law and Justice, on Labour and Social Welfare 1988–92, on Knesset House Cttee. and Cttee. on Constitution, Law and Justice 1992–96; Minister of Transport 1996–98; mem. Bnei Akiva Exec. and World Secr.; Gen. Sec. Nat. Religious Party; Chair. Israel–Argentina Parl. Friendship League. *Address:* c/o Ministry of Transport, Klal Building, 97 Rehov Jaffa, Jerusalem 91000, Israel.

LEWANDO, Sir Jan Alfred, Kt., C.B.E.; British business executive; b. 31 May 1909; s. of Maurice and Eugénie (née Goldsmid) Lewando; m. Nora Slavouski 1948; three d.; ed. Manchester Grammar School and Manchester Univ.; served British Army in Europe, Middle East and Far East 1939–45, British Army Staff in Washington D.C. and British Ministry of Supply Mission 1941–45 (Lieut.-Col. 1943); with Marks & Spencer Ltd. 1929–70, Dir. 1954–70; mem. Export Council for Europe 1965–69, British Nat. Export Council 1969–71, Council of CBI 1971–75, European Steering Cttee. CBI 1968–71, British Overseas Trade Bd. 1972–77, British Overseas Trade Advisory Council 1975–77, European Trade Cttee. 1973–83; Vice-Chair.

Clothing Export Council 1966–70; Pres. British Textile Confed. 1972–73; Vice-Chair. Comitextil, Brussels 1972–73; Chair. Carrington Viyella Ltd. 1970–75, Consolidated Textile Mills Ltd., Canada 1972–75, Gelvenor Textiles Ltd., South Africa 1973–75; Dir. Carrington Tesit, Italy 1971–75, Heal & Son Holdings Ltd. 1975–81 (Deputy Chair. 1977–81), Bunzl PLC 1975–85, W. A. Baxter & Sons Ltd. 1976–98, Johnston Industries Inc., U.S.A. 1976–84, Royal Worcester Spode Ltd. 1978–79, Edgars Stores Ltd., South Africa 1976–82, Bunzl and Biach AG (Austria) 1979–80, Johnston Industries Ltd. 1980–84; Vice-Pres. Transport Trust 1975–89, 1992–, Pres. 1989–91; Chair. Appeal Cttee., British Inst. of Radiology 1979–84; Companion Textile Inst. 1972–; Legion of Merit (U.S.A.) 1946. *Address:* Langham House, Drews Park, Beaconsfield, Bucks., HP9 2TT, England.

LEWANDOWSKI, Janusz Antoni, PH.D.; Polish politician and economist; b. 13 June 1951, Lublin; s. of Karol Lewandowski and Halina Lewandowska; m. Lidia Talenska Lewandowska 1997; one d.; ed. Gdańsk Univ.; on staff Gdańsk Univ. 1974–84 (dismissed); econ. adviser Solidarity Trade Union, Gdańsk 1980–81; lecturer Harvard Univ., U.S.A.; with Polish Ocean Lines, then consulting firm 1984–85; assoc. journal Przegląd Polityczny (pen-name Jędrzej Branecki) 1985–; co-founder pvt. Gdańsk Inst. of Market Research; Minister of Proprietary Transformations 1991–93; co-founder and Pres. Liberal-Democratic Congress 1990–94; Deputy to Sejm (Parl.) 1991–93, 1997–; Vice-Chair. Parl. Comm. for Treasury, Affranchisement and Privatization 1997–; mem. Freedom Union (UW) 1994–; mem. Presidium Freedom Union Parl. Club. *Publication:* Neoliberalizm wobec współczesności 1989. *Leisure interests:* arts, football. *Address:* Sejm RP, ul. Wiejska 4/6/8, 00-902 Warsaw, Poland. *Telephone:* (22) 694 15 43. *Fax:* (22) 628 11 09.

LEWIN, Benjamin, M.A., PH.D.; British scientist; s. of Dr. S. Lewin and A. Lewin; m. Ann Lewin 1972; two s.; ed. City of London School and Univ. of Cambridge; Tutorial Fellow, Univ. of Sussex 1969–70; Ed. Nature New Biology 1970–71; Visiting Scientist, Nat. Cancer Inst.; Ed. Cell 1974–. *Publications:* Gene Expression, Prokaryotic Genomes 1974, Gene Expression, Eukaryotic Chromosomes 1976, Gene Expression, Plasmids and Phages 1977, Genes 1994. *Leisure interests:* theatre, books, wine. *Address:* Cell Press, 50 Church Street, Cambridge, MA 02138, U.S.A. *Telephone:* (617) 661-7057. *Fax:* (617) 661-7061.

LEWIS, Baron (Life Peer) cr. 1989, of Newnham; **Jack Lewis,** Kt., PH.D., F.R.S.C., F.R.S.; British professor of chemistry; b. 13 Feb. 1928, Barrow; m. Elfreida M. Lamb 1951; one s. one d.; ed. Barrow Grammar School and Univs. of London and Nottingham; Lecturer, Univ. of Sheffield 1954–56, Imperial Coll. London 1956–57; Lecturer-Reader, Univ. Coll. London 1957–61; Prof. of Chem. Univ. of Manchester 1961–67, Univ. Coll. London 1967–70, Univ. of Cambridge 1970–95; Hon. Fellow, Sidney Sussex Coll. Cambridge (Fellow 1970–77); Warden, Robinson Coll. Cambridge 1975–; mem. numerous cttees. etc.; Foreign Assoc. N.A.S.; Foreign mem. American Philosophical Soc. 1994, Accademia Naz. dei Lincei 1995; 20 hon. degrees; Davy Medal, Royal Soc. 1985; Chevalier, Ordre des Palmes Académiques, Commdr. Cross of the Order of Merit (Poland) and other distinctions and awards. *Publications:* papers in scientific journals. *Address:* Robinson College, Grange Road, Cambridge, CB3 9AN, England. *Telephone:* (01223) 339120. *Fax:* (01223) 339962.

LEWIS, Andrew Lindsay, Jr., B.S., M.B.A.; American business executive; b. 3 Nov. 1931, Philadelphia, Pa.; s. of Andrew Lindsay and Lucille (Bricker) Lewis; m. Marilyn S. Stoughton 1950; two s. one d.; ed. Haverford Coll., Pa., Harvard Univ.; foreman, job supt., production man. and Dir. Henkels & McCoy, Inc., Blue Bell, Pa. 1955–60; Dir. of Marketing, Vice-Pres. (Sales) and Dir. American Olean Tile Co. Inc., Lansdale, Pa. 1960–68; Vice-Pres. and Asst. to Chair. Nat. Gypsum Co., Buffalo, N.Y. 1969–70; Chair. Simplex Wire and Cable Co., Boston, Mass. 1970–72; Pres. and C.E.O. Snelling and Snelling Inc. 1970–74; Lewis and Assocs. (Financial and Man. Consultants), Plymouth Meeting, Pa. 1974–81; U.S. Sec. of Transportation 1981–83; Dir. Campbell Soup Co. 1983; Chair. Warner Amex Satellite Entertainment Co. 1983–86; Chair., Pres. and C.E.O. Union Pacific Corpn., New York City 1987–98; mem. Bd. Dirs. American Express, Ford Motor Co. and numerous others; Trustee Reading Co., operating freight and mass transit railroad network (now, with five other railroad lines, Consolidated Rail Corpn.) 1971–81; fmr. Dir. numerous cos.; Deputy Chair. Republican Nat. Cttee. Aug. 1980. *Address:* c/o Union Pacific Corporation, 1717 Main Street, #5900, Dallas, TX 75201, U.S.A.

LEWIS, Bernard, B.A., PH.D., F.B.A., F.R.HIST.S.; American (naturalized 1982) university professor; b. 31 May 1916, London, England; m. Ruth Hélène Oppenhejm 1947 (divorced 1974); one s. one d.; ed. Univs. of London and Paris; Lecturer in Islamic History, School of Oriental Studies, Univ. of London 1938; served R.A.C. and Intelligence Corps 1940–41; attached to Foreign Office 1941–45; Prof. of History of the Near and Middle East, Univ. of London 1949–74; Cleveland E. Dodge Prof. of Near Eastern Studies, Princeton Univ. 1974–86, Prof. Emer. 1986–; Dir. Annenberg Research Inst., Philadelphia 1986–90; Visiting Prof. of History, Univ. of Calif. at Los Angeles 1955–56, Columbia Univ. 1960, Ind. Univ. 1963, Princeton Univ. 1964, Univ. of Calif. at Berkeley 1965, Coll. de France 1980, École des Hautes Études en Sciences Sociales, Paris 1983, 1988, Univ. of Chicago 1985; Visiting mem. Inst. for Advanced Study, Princeton 1969, mem. 1974–86; A.D. White Prof.-at-Large, Cornell Univ. 1984; Jefferson Lecturer in the Humanities, U.S. Nat. Endowment for the Humanities 1990; Tanner Lecturer, Brasenose Coll., Oxford 1990; Henry M. Jackson Memorial Lecturer (Seattle) 1992; mem. American Acad. of Arts and Sciences 1983, Council, American Historical Assen. 1984; Corresp. mem. Inst. d'Egypte, Cairo, American Philosophical Soc., Inst. de France; Hon. mem. Société Asiatique, Paris, Ataturk Acad. of History, Language and Culture, Ankara, Turkish Acad. of Sciences; Fellow Univ. Coll., London 1976; Hon. Fellow S.O.A.S., London 1986; Hon. Dr. (Hebrew Univ., Jerusalem) 1974, (Tel-Aviv) 1979, (State Univ. of N.Y. Binghamton, Univ. of Penn., Hebrew Union Coll., Cincinnati) 1987, (Univ. of Haifa, Yeshiva Univ., New York) 1991, (Bar-Ilan Univ.) 1992, (Brandeis) 1993, (Ben-Gurion, Ankara) 1996; Harvey Prize 1978, Ataturk Peace Prize 1998. *Publications:* The Origins of Ismā'ilism 1940, Turkey Today 1940, British Contributions to Arabic Studies 1941, Handbook of Diplomatic and Political Arabic 1947, 1956, Land of Enchanters (Ed.) 1948, The Arabs in History 1950, 1993, Notes and Documents from the Turkish Archives 1952, The Emergence of Modern Turkey 1961, 1968, The Kingly Crown 1961, Historians of the Middle East (co-editor with P.M. Holt) 1962, Istanbul and the Civilization of the Ottoman Empire 1963, The Middle East and the West 1964, The Assassins 1967, Race and Colour in Islam 1971, Islam in History 1973, Ed. Islamic Civilization 1974, Islam from the Prophet Muhammad to the Capture of Constantinople (2 vols.) 1974, History— Remembered, Recovered, Invented 1975, The World of Islam (Ed.) 1976, Population and Revenue in the Towns of Palestine in the Sixteenth Century (with Amnon Cohen) 1978, The Muslim Discovery of Europe 1982, The Jews of Islam 1984, Semites and Anti-Semites 1986, As Others See Us (co.-ed.) 1986, The Political Language of Islam 1988, Race and Slavery in the Middle East 1990, Islam and the West 1993, The Shaping of the Modern Middle East 1994, Cultures in Conflict: Christians, Muslims, and Jews in the Age of Discovery 1995, The Middle East: Two Thousand Years of History from the Rise of Christianity to the Present Day 1995, Semites and Anti-Semites 1997, The Future of the Middle East 1997, The Multiple Identities of the Middle East 1998. *Address:* Department of Near Eastern Studies, Princeton University, Princeton, NJ 08544, U.S.A. *Telephone:* (609) 258-4280.

LEWIS, Carl; American athlete; b. 1 July 1961; Birmingham, Ala.; s. of William Lewis and Evelyn Lawler Lewis; ed. Univ. of Houston; Bronze Medal for long jump, Pan-American Games 1979; won World Cup competition 1981, first World Championships (with 8.55 metres); achieved world record 8.79 metre jump 1983; Gold medals at Olympic Games 1984 for 100 metres, 200m, long jump and 4×100m; 65 consecutive wins in long jump since 1985; Silver Medal for 200 metres, Gold Medal for 100 metres (following disqualification of Ben Johnson), Olympic Games 1988; jumped 8.64m New York 1991; World Record for 100 metres 9.86 seconds Aug. 1991 (surpassed 1994); Gold Medal, long jump Olympic Games 1992; Gold Medal for long jump (27ft. 10.75in.), Olympic Games 1996; retd. Aug. 1997; attached to Trialtir 1997; Track and Field News Athlete of the Decade 1980–1989. *Address:* c/o Carl Lewis International Fan Club, P.O. Box 57–1990, Houston, TX 77257–1990, U.S.A.

LEWIS, Charles Edwin; American professor of medicine; b. 28 Dec. 1928, Kansas City, Mo.; s. of Claude Herbert Lewis and Maudie Friels (Holaday); m. Mary Ann Gurera 1963; three s. one d.; ed. Univs. of Kansas and Cincinatti and Harvard Medical School; U.S.A.F. 1955–56; Fellow, The Kettering Lab. 1956–59; Asst. Prof. Epidemiology, Baylor Univ. 1959–61; Assoc. Prof. of Medicine, Univ. of Kansas 1962–64, Prof. and Chair. Dept. of Community Medicine 1964–69; Prof. and Head of Div. of Health Services and Prof. of Medicine, Univ. of Calif. Los Angeles (UCLA) 1970–72, Chief, Div. of Gen. Internal Medicine 1972–90, Prof. of Nursing, School of Nursing 1973–, Dir. UCLA Center for Health Promotion and Disease Prevention 1991–, Head Div. of Preventive and Occupational Medicine 1991–93, Dir. Health Services Research Center 1991–93, Chair. Academic Senate 1995–96; Regent, A.C.P. 1989; mem. Inst. of Medicine (N.A.S.); Rosenthal Award (A.C.P.) 1980. *Publications:* more than 120 research publs. in journals and 15 chapters in books. *Leisure interests:* music, travel. *Address:* 221 Burlingame Avenue, Los Angeles, CA 90049, U.S.A. (Home). *Telephone:* (310) 825-6709. *Fax:* (310) 206-5717.

LEWIS, Dan, PH.D., D.SC., F.R.S.; British geneticist; b. 30 Dec. 1910, Stoke-on-Trent; s. of Ernest Albert and Edith Jane Lewis; m. Mary P. E. Burry 1933; one d.; ed. High School, Newcastle under Lyme, and Univs. of Reading and London; plant breeder, John Innes Inst. 1935, Head Dept. of Genetics 1947; Quain Prof. of Botany, Univ. Coll. London 1957–78, Prof. Emer. 1978–; Hon. Research Fellow, Univ. Coll. London 1978–; Visiting Prof. of Genetics, Univ. of Calif., Berkeley 1961, Delhi 1965, Singapore 1970; Visiting Prof., Queen Mary Coll., London 1978–; Pres. Genetical Soc. 1968–71; mem. Univ. Grants Cttee. 1968–74. *Publications:* Sexual Incompatibility in Plants, and articles on genetics; Ed. Science Progress. *Leisure interests:* swimming, music. *Address:* Flat 2, 56/57 Myddelton Square, London, EC1R 1YA, England. *Telephone:* 0171-278 6948.

LEWIS, David Kellogg, PH.D.; American professor of philosophy; b. 28 Sept. 1941, Oberlin, Ohio; s. of John D. Lewis and Ewart Lewis; m. Stephanie Robinson 1965; ed. Swartmore Coll. and Harvard Univ.; Asst. Prof. of Philosophy, Univ. of Calif., Los Angeles 1966–70; Assoc. Prof. of Philosophy, Princeton Univ. 1970–73, Prof. 1973–; Corresp. Fellow British Acad.; mem. American Acad. of Arts and Sciences; Hon. Fellow, Australian Acad. of the Humanities; Hon. D.Litt. (Melbourne) 1995; Matchette Prize 1972. *Publications:* Convention 1969, Counterfactuals 1973, On the Plurality of Worlds 1986, Philosophical Papers, (Vol. I) 1983, (Vol. II) 1986, Parts of

Classes 1991, Papers in Philosophical Logic 1998, Papers in Metaphysics and Epistemology 1999. *Leisure interests:* railway modelling, folk music. *Address:* Department of Philosophy, Princeton University, Princeton, NJ 08544, U.S.A.

LEWIS, Denise, M.B.E.; British athlete; b. 27 Aug. 1972, W. Bromwich; specializes in heptathlon; Commonwealth heptathlon record-holder (6,736 points) 1997; fifth European Jr. Championships 1991; Gold Medal Commonwealth Games 1994; Gold Medal European Cup 1995; Bronze Medal Olympic Games 1996; Silver Medal World Championships 1997; Gold Medal European Championships 1998; Gold Medal Commonwealth Championships 1998; British Athletics Writers Female Athlete of the Year 1998.

LEWIS, Douglas Grinslade, P.C., LL.B., F.C.A., Q.C.; Canadian politician; b. 17 April 1938, Toronto, Ont.; s. of Horace Grinslade and Brenda Hazeldine (Reynolds) Lewis; m. Linda Diane Haggans 1962; two s. three d.; ed. Univ. of Toronto, Osgoode Hall Law School; Progressive Conservative M.P. for Simcoe N. 1979–93; Parl. Sec. to Minister of Supply and Services 1979; Deputy Opposition House Leader 1981, Opposition House Leader 1983; Parl. Sec. to Pres. of Treasury Bd. 1984, to Pres. of Privy Council 1985, to Deputy Prime Minister and Pres. of Queen's Privy Council for Canada 1986–87; Minister of State (Deputy House Leader) and Minister of State (Treasury Bd.) 1987–88; Acting Pres. Treasury Bd. 1988; Minister of Justice, Attorney-Gen. and Govt. House Leader 1989–90; Minister of Transport 1990–91; Solicitor-Gen. 1991–93. *Address:* Box 535, Orillia, Ont., L3V 6K2, Canada.

LEWIS, Edward B., PH.D.; American professor of biology; b. May 20 1918, Wilkes-Barre; s. of Edward B. Lewis and Laura Histed Lewis; m. Pamela Harrah 1946; three s. (one deceased); ed. Minnesota Univ. and Calif. Inst. of Tech.; Instructor, Calif. Inst. of Tech. 1946–48, Asst. Prof. 1948–49, Assoc. Prof. 1949–56, Prof. 1956–88, Thomas Hunt Morgan Prof. of Biology Emer. 1988–; Rockefeller Foundation Fellow, Cambridge Univ. 1947–48; Sec. Genetics Soc. of America 1962–64, Vice-Pres. 1966–67, Pres. 1967; Guest Prof., Inst. of Genetics, Copenhagen Univ. 1975–76; mem. N.A.S., American Acad. of Arts and Sciences, Genetics Soc. of America, American Philosophical Soc.; Foreign mem. Royal Soc. 1989; Hon. mem. Genetical Soc. of Great Britain 1990; Hon. PH.D. (Umeå, Sweden) 1981; Hon. D.Sc. (Minn. Univ.) 1993; Thomas Hunt Morgan Medal, Gairdner Foundation Int. Award 1987, Wolf Prize for Medicine (jtly. with John B. Gurdon, q.v.) 1989, Rosenstiel Medical Research Award 1990, Nat. Medal of Science (U.S.A.) 1990, Albert Lasker Basic Medical Research Award (jtly.) 1991, Louisa Gross Horwitz Prize 1992, shared Nobel Prize for Medicine 1995. *Leisure interest:* playing the flute. *Address:* Biology Division 156–29, California Institute of Technology, 1201 E. California Boulevard, Pasadena, CA 91125; 805 Winthrop Road, San Marino, CA 91108, U.S.A. *Telephone:* (626) 395-4941. *Fax:* (626) 564-9685.

LEWIS, Geoffrey David, M.A., F.S.A.; British museologist; b. 13 April 1933, Brighton, Sussex; s. of David and Esther Lewis; m. Frances May Wilderspin 1956; three d.; ed. Varndean Grammar School, Brighton, Univ. of Liverpool; Asst. Curator, Worthing Museum and Art Gallery 1950–60; Deputy Dir. (and Keeper of Antiquities) Sheffield City Museum 1960–65; Dir. Sheffield City Museums 1966–72, Liverpool City Museums 1972–74, Merseyside Co. Museums 1974–77; Dir. of Museum Studies, Univ. of Leicester 1977–89, Assoc. Teacher 1989–92; Hon. Lecturer in British Prehistory, Univ. of Sheffield 1965–72; Pres. Int. Council of Museums 1983–89, Chair. Advisory Cttee. 1974–80, Chair. Ethics Cttee. 1996–; mem. Bd. of Trustees Royal Armouries 1990–, Chair. Design Cttee. 1995–; Chair. Printing Matters (Bude) Ltd. 1991–96; Deputy Chair. The Genesis Agendum 1996–; Gov. Wolvey School 1993–, Chair. of Govs. 1998–; Hon. Fellow Museums Asscn., London, Pres. 1980–81. *Publications:* The South Yorkshire Glass Industry 1964, Prehistoric and Roman Times in the Sheffield Area (Co-author) 1968, For Instruction and Recreation 1989, Manuel of Curatorship (Co-Ed.) 1992; many articles relating to archaeology and museums. *Leisure interests:* walking, computing. *Address:* 4 Orchard Close, Wolvey, Hinckley, Leics., LE10 3LR, England. *Telephone:* (01455) 220708. *Fax:* (01455) 220708.

LEWIS, Jerry (Joseph Levitch), American comedian; b. 16 March 1926; s. of Danny and Rachael Lewis; m. 1st Patti Palmer 1944 (divorced); six s.; m. 2nd Sandra Pitnick 1983; one d; performed in nightclubs as a comedian before teaming with Dean Martin in 1946 at the 500 Club, Atlantic City, N.J.; made film début with Martin in My Friend Irma 1949; other films include: My Friend Irma Goes West 1950, That's My Boy 1951, Sailor Beware 1952, Jumping Jack 1952, The Stooge 1953, Scared Stiff 1953, The Caddy 1953, Living it Up 1954, Three Ring Circus 1954, You're Never Too Young 1954, Pardners 1956, Hollywood or Bust 1956, The Delicate Delinquent 1957, The Sad Sack 1958, Rock a Bye Baby 1958, The Geisha Boy 1958, Visit to a Small Planet 1960, The Bellboy 1960, Cinderfella 1960, The Errand Boy 1961, It's Only Money? 1964, The Patsy 1964, The Disorderly Orderly 1964, The Family Jewels 1965, Boeing-Boeing 1965, Three On a Couch 1966, Way Way Out 1966, The Big Mouth 1967, Don't Raise the Bridge, Lower the River 1968, Hook, Line and Sinker 1969, Which Way to the Front? 1970, One More Time 1971, The Day the Clown Cried 1971, Hardly Working 1981, King of Comedy 1981, Slapstick 1982, Smorgasbord 1982, Retenez-moi . . . ou je fais un malheur!, How Did You Get In 1985, Arrowtooth Waltz 1991, Mr. Saturday Night 1992, Funny Bones 1995; Television appearances include: Startime, The Ed Sullivan Show and the Jazz Singer; play Damn Yankees 1995, on tour 1995–; Nat. Chair. Muscular Dystrophy Asscn. of America; Prof. of Cinema at Univ. of Southern Calif.; mem. Screen Directors Guild; Commdr. des Arts et Lettres 1984. *Leisure interests:* golf, sailing. *Publications:* The Total Film-Maker 1971, Jerry Lewis in Person 1982. *Address:* Jerry Lewis Films Inc., 3160 W. Sahara Avenue, C-16, Las Vegas, NV 89102, U.S.A.

LEWIS, Joseph C. (Joe); British business executive; b. London; s. of late Charles Lewis; m.; one d.; joined father's small catering business; with father ran Hanover Grand chain of banqueting suites, London 1970s; moved to New Providence, Bahamas 1979; founder and owner Tavistock Group of financial services, property and retail businesses; shareholder Rapallo Ltd., London, English Nat. Investment Corpn. (ENIC), Tamarind Int., Hong Kong, auction house Christie's, London. *Address:* P.O. Box N7776, Lyford Cay, New Providence, Bahamas.

LEWIS, Juliette; American film actress; b. 21 June 1973, Fernando Valley, Calif.; d. of Geoffrey Lewis and Glenis Batley Lewis; TV appearances include Homefires (mini-series), I Married Dora 1988, Too Young To Die (movie) 1989, A Family For Joe 1990. *Films include:* My Stepmother is an Alien 1988, Meet the Hollowheads 1989, National Lampoons Christmas Vacation 1989, Cape Fear 1991, Crooked Hearts 1991, Husbands and Wives 1992, Kalifornia 1993, One Hot Summer, That Night 1993, What's Eating Gilbert Grape 1993, Romeo is Bleeding 1994, Natural Born Killers 1994, Mixed Nuts 1994, The Basketball Diaries 1995, Strange Days 1995, From Dusk Till Dawn 1996, The Evening Star 1996, The Audition, Full Tilt Boogie 1997. *Address:* c/o William Morris Agency, 151 El Camino Boulevard, Beverly Hills, CA 80212, U.S.A.

LEWIS, Lennox, M.B.E.; British heavyweight boxer; b. 2 Sept. 1965; defeated Jean Chanet to win European Heavyweight Title, Crystal Palace 1990; defeated Gary Mason to win British Heavyweight Title, Wembley 1991; Commonwealth Heavyweight; WBC Heavyweight 1992; WBC World Champion 1993–94, 1997–; defended WBC title, and challenged for World Boxing Asscn. (WBA) and Int. Boxing Fed. (IBF) titles, against Evander Holyfield (q.v.) March 1999, bout declared a draw; defeated Frank Bruno (q.v.) Oct. 1993. *Address:* c/o Frank Maloney, Panix Promotions, 99 Middlesex Street, London, E1 7DA, England.

LEWIS, Neville Brice, M.P.; Jamaican politician; b. 19 May 1936, Middle Quarters, St. Elizabeth; s. of Neville C. and Marie Lewis; m. Jasmin Lewis; one s. one d.; ed. Munro Coll., St. Elizabeth and Lincoln's Inn, London; accounting clerk, McCaulay's Motor Service, Kingston 1959–61; legal studies in London 1961; later worked in property management in London; returned to Jamaica 1976; M.P. for N.W. St. Elizabeth 1976–; Minister of Social Security 1980–83, of Local Govt. 1983–89; Jamaica Labour Party (Deputy Leader 1983). *Address:* c/o Jamaica Labour Party, 20 Belmont Road, Kingston 5, Jamaica.

LEWIS, Samuel Winfield, M.A.; American diplomatist; b. 1 Oct. 1930, Houston; s. of Samuel W. Lewis and Sue Roselle Hurley Lewis; m. Sallie S. Smoot 1953; one s. one d.; ed. Yale and Johns Hopkins Univs.; Exec. Asst. American Trucking Asscn., Washington 1953–54; entered Foreign Service 1954; with Consulate, Naples 1954–55; Consul, Florence 1955–59; Officer-in-Charge Italian Affairs, Dept. of State 1959–61; Special Asst. to Under-Sec. of State 1961–63; Deputy Asst. Dir. U.S. AID Mission to Brazil 1964–66; Deputy Dir. Office for Brazil Affairs, Dept. of State 1967–68; senior staff mem. for Latin American Affairs, Nat. Security Council, White House 1968–69; Special Asst. for Policy Planning, Bureau of Inter-American Affairs 1969, to Dir.-Gen. Foreign Service 1969–71; Deputy Chief of Mission and Counsellor, U.S. Embassy, Kabul 1971–74; Deputy Dir. Policy Planning Staff, Dept. of State 1974–75, Asst. Sec. of State for Int. Organization 1975–77; Amb. to Israel 1977–85; Pres. U.S. Inst. of Peace 1987–93; Dir. Policy Planning Staff, Dept. of State 1993–94; Visiting Fellow, Princeton Univ. 1963–64; Diplomat-in-Residence, Johns Hopkins Foreign Policy Inst. 1985–87; Guest Scholar, The Brookings Institution, Washington, D.C. 1987; Visiting Prof., Hamilton Coll. 1995, 1997; Counselor, Washington Inst. for Near East Policy 1995–98; Adjunct Prof. Georgetown Univ. 1996; mem. Council on Foreign Relations, Vice-Chair. Center for Preventive Action 1995–97; Vice-Chair. American Acad. of Diplomacy 1995–; mem. The Middle East Inst., Cousteau Soc.; mem. Bd. of Dirs. Inst. for the Study of Diplomacy, Georgetown Univ. 1994–, Inst. of World Affairs 1996–; Chair. Bd. of Overseers, The Harry S. Truman Inst. for Advancement of Peace, Hebrew Univ. of Jerusalem 1986–91; Sr. Int. Fellow, Dayan Centre for Middle Eastern and African Affairs, Tel Aviv Univ. 1986–87; Hon. Ph.D.; Hon. D.Hum.Litt.; William A. Jump Award 1967, Meritorious Honor Award (Dept. of State, AID) 1967, Presidential Man. Improvement Award 1970, Distinguished Honor Awards 1977, 1985, Wilbur J. Carr Award 1985. *Publications:* Soviet and American Attitudes toward the Arab-Israeli Peace Process, in Super Power Rivalry in the Middle East 1987, The United States and Israel 1977–1988, in The Middle East: Ten Years after Camp David 1988, Making Peace among Arabs and Israelis 1991; numerous articles. *Leisure interests:* tennis, scuba diving, nature photography, travel, painting. *Address:* 6232 Nelway Drive, McLean, VA 22101, U.S.A.

LEWIS, Stephen; Canadian international civil servant, politician and lecturer; b. 11 Nov. 1937, Ottawa; s. of David and Sophie Lewis; m. Michele Landsberg 1963; three c.; ed. Univ. of Toronto, Univ. of British Columbia; spent two years teaching and travelling in Africa; fmr. Dir. of Org., New Democratic Party (NDP), Prov. Leader 1970–77; M.P.P. for Scarborough W., Ont. Legis. 1963–78; Amb. and Perm Rep. of Canadian Mission to UN

1984–88; Special Adviser to UN Sec.-Gen. on African Econ. Recovery 1986–91; Special Rep. to UNICEF 1990; Hon. LL.D from 12 univs.; Gordon Sinclair ACTRA Award 1982; B'nai B'rith Human Rights Award 1983. *Publication:* Art Out of Agony 1983. *Address:* 6 Montclair Avenue, Toronto, Ont., M4V 1W1, Canada.

LEWIS, Trevor, C.B.E., M.A., PH.D., D.SC.; British entomologist; b. 8 July 1933, Derbyshire; s. of Harold Lewis and Maggie Lewis; m. Margaret E. Wells 1959; one s. one d.; ed. Univs. of Nottingham, Cambridge and London; Head, Dept. of Entomology, Rothamsted 1976–87, Head of Crop Protection Div. 1983–89, Head, Rothamsted Experimental Station 1987–93, Dir. of Research, AFRC Inst. of Arable Crops Research 1989–93, Lawes Trust Senior Fellow 1994–. *Publications:* Thrips: Their Biology, Ecology and Economic Importance 1973, Insect Communication (ed.) 1984, Thrips as Crop Pests (ed.) 1997. *Leisure interests:* gardening, music. *Address:* Institute of Arable Crops Research, Rothamsted Experimental Station, Harpenden, Herts., AL5 2JQ (Office); 41 Tennyson Road, Harpenden, Herts., AL5 4BD, England (Home). *Telephone:* (01582) 763133 (Office); (01582) 715861 (Home). *Fax:* (01582) 760981 (Office).

LEWIS, Vaughan Allen, PH.D.; Saint Lucia politician and academic; b. 17 May 1940; ed. Univ. of Manchester, U.K.; temporary Asst. Lecturer, Dept. of Political Theory, Univ. Coll. Swansea, Wales 1963–64; Asst. Lecturer, Dept. of Politics, Univ. of Liverpool 1964–66; Research Fellow Dept. of Govt., Univ. of Manchester 1966–68; Lecturer, Dept. of Govt., Univ. of W.I. (UWI), Mona, Jamaica 1968–72, Part-time Lecturer, Inst. of Int. Relations, UWI, St. Augustine, Trinidad 1974–80, Acting Dir. Inst. of Social and Econ. Research, UWI 1974, Dir. (rank of full Prof.) 1977–82; Dir.-Gen. Org. of Eastern Caribbean States, Castries, St. Lucia 1982–95; Prime Minister of St. Lucia 1995–97; Visiting Prof. Fla. Int. Univ. 1980, Ford Foundation Visiting Fellow Yale Univ. 1981. *Publications:* numerous books, papers and articles on int. relations, particularly concerning the Caribbean. *Address:* c/o United Workers Party, 1 Riverside Road, Castries, Saint Lucia.

LEWITT, Sol, B.F.A.; American artist; b. 1928, Hartford, Conn.; ed. Syracuse Univ.; Instructor Museum of Modern Art School 1964–67, Cooper Union 1967, School of Visual Arts, N.Y. 1969–70, New York Univ. 1970; one-man shows include: Guggenheim Museum 1971, Museum of Modern Art, N.Y. 1971, Walker Art Center 1972, Museum of Modern Art, Oxford 1973, Stedelijk Museum, Amsterdam 1974, Visual Arts Museum, N.Y. 1976, San Francisco Museum of Art 1975, Wadsworth Atheneum, Hartford 1981, Musée d'Art Contemporain, Bordeaux 1983, Stedelijk Museum, Amsterdam 1984, Stedelijk Van Abbemuseum, Eindhoven 1984, Tate Gallery 1986, Hirshhorn Museum 1987, Walker Art Center, Minn. 1988, Kunsthalle, Berne 1989, Tokyo Museum of Contemporary Art 1990; group exhbns. include Sculpture Annual, Whitney Museum of American Art, N.Y. 1967, Minimal Art, The Hague 1968, Stadtische Kunsthalle, Düsseldorf 1969, La Jolla Museum of Contemporary Art 1970, Tokyo Biennale 1970, Guggenheim Int., N.Y. 1971, Whitney Biennial N.Y. 1979, Hayward Gallery, London 1980, Int. Sculpture Exhbn. Basle 1980, Musée Nat. d'Art Moderne, Paris 1981, Art Inst. Chicago 1982, Museum of Modern Art, N.Y. 1983, Museum of Contemporary Art, Los Angeles 1986, Venice Biennale 1988; numerous retrospective exhbns. including retrospective travelling exhbn. 1990–95; also represented in a number of perm. collections. *Publications:* numerous articles for specialist magazines on sculpture, drawing and conceptual art. *Address:* c/o Susanna Singer, 50 Riverside Drive, New York, NY 10024, U.S.A.

LEYE, Jean-Marie; Ni-Vanuatu politician; Pres. of Vanuatu March 1994–. *Address:* Office of the President, Port Vila, Vanuatu.

LHEUREUX-DUBÉ, Claire, LL.L.; Canadian judge; b. 7 Sept. 1927, Quebec City; m. Arthur Dubé 1957 (died 1978); one s. (died 1994) one d.; ed. Coll. Notre-Dame and Laval Univ.; called to Quebec Bar 1952; practised with Bard, L'Heureux & Philippon (known as L'Heureux, Philippon, Garneau, Tourigny, St. Arnaud & Assocs. from 1969) 1952–73; Q.C. 1969; Judge, Superior Court of Quebec 1973, Quebec Court of Appeal 1979; Judge, Supreme Court of Canada 1987–; Vice-Pres. Canadian Consumers' Council 1970–73, Vanier Inst. of the Family 1972–73; mem. Canadian Bar Assen., Canadian Inst. for Admin. of Justice; Pres. Int. Comm. of Jurists (Canadian Section) 1981–83; mem. Nat. Council, Canadian Human Rights Foundation 1980–84; numerous other professional appts. and affiliations; six hon. degrees. *Address:* Supreme Court of Canada, Supreme Court Building, Wellington Street, Ottawa, K1A 0J1, Canada.

LHO SHIN-YONG; Korean politician and diplomatist; b. 28 Feb. 1930, S. Pyongyang Prov.; ed. Law Coll. of Seoul Nat. Univ., Kentucky State Univ.; joined diplomatic service 1956, Dir. Planning and Man. Office, Ministry of Foreign Affairs 1967; Consul-Gen., Los Angeles, U.S.A. 1969–72; Amb. to India 1973, to Geneva 1976; Vice-Foreign Minister 1974, Foreign Minister 1980–82, Prime Minister 1985–87; Head, Agency of Nat. Security Planning 1982–85; Democratic Justice Party (now New Korea Party).

LI BAOTIAN; Chinese actor; b. Dec. 1946, Xuzhou, Jiangsu Prov.; ed. Cen. Acad. of Drama; teacher Cen. Acad. of Drama 1981–; acted in Judou, Shanghai Triad, Prime Minister Hunchback Liu (TV series). *Address:* Central Academy of Drama, Beijing, People's Republic of China.

LI BOYONG; Chinese state official and engineer; b. 1932, Tianjin City; ed. Air Force Inst. of Mil. Eng., fmr. U.S.S.R.; Vice-Minister, Labour and Personnel 1986–93; mem. 14th CCP Cen. Cttee. 1992–97; Minister of Labour 1993–98; Vice-Chair. Legal Affairs Cttee. of 9th NPC 1998–. *Address:* c/o Standing Committee of National People's Congress, Beijing 100716, People's Republic of China.

LI CHANG; Chinese party official (retd.); b. (as Lei Junshui) 12 Dec. 1914, Hunan Province; s. of Lei Chengwu and Tian Yangying; m. Feng Lanrui 1946; two s. three d.; ed. Qinghua Univ.; joined CCP 1936; mem. CCP Cttee., Qinghua Univ. 1936; Gen. Chief Pioneers of Nat. Liberation Vanguard Corps 1936–38; Dir. Org. Bureau, Cttee. for Youth Work, CCP Cen. Cttee. 1938–42; Sec. CCP Cttee., Xing Xian Co. and Lishan Co. 1943–45; Dir. Political Dept., 64th Army, PLA 1946–49; mem. E. China Mil. Admin. Council 1951; posts in New Democratic Youth League 1949–53; Pres. Harbin Polytech. Univ. 1953–64; Deputy for Harbin, 1st NPC 1954; Alt. mem. CCP 8th Cen. Cttee. 1956–66; Vice-Chair. Comm. for Cultural Relations with Foreign Countries, State Council 1964–75; Deputy for Shanghai and mem. Standing Cttee. 5th NPC 1978–83; Vice-Pres. and Deputy Sec., CCP Cttee., Acad. of Sciences (CAS) July–Nov. 1975, Vice-Pres., Exec. Chair. of Presidium and Sec. CAS CCP Cttee. 1975–82; mem. CCP 11th Cen. Cttee. 1979–82; Sec. CCP Cen. Comm. for Discipline Inspection 1982–85; mem. CCP Cen. Advisory Comm. 1985–92; Chair. Bd. of Dirs. Experimental Univ. of Beijing, Wuling Univ.; Vice-Chair. Bd. of Dirs. Research Inst. of Dialectics of Nature 1983–91; Dir. Research and Consulting Centre for Regional Devt. 1986–90; Dir. Social Devt. Research Inst. of China Research Inst. of Dialectics of Nature 1994–; Hon. Prof., Harbin Polytech. Univ. and Tongji Univ. 1986. *Publications:* Three Great Revolutions in Modern History 1993, and several articles on socialist spiritual civilization, scientific research and tech. devt. *Leisure interests:* art, literature. *Address:* 34 Dong Zongbu Hutong, Beijing 100005, People's Republic of China. *Telephone:* (010) 5257465.

LI CHANG'AN; Chinese party and state official; b. 1935, Tai'an Co., Liaoning Prov.; ed. Shandong Tech. Coll.; joined CCP 1961; alt. mem. 12th CCP Cen. Cttee. 1982, mem. 1985; Deputy Sec. CCP Cttee., Shandong Prov. 1983–88; Gov. of Shandong 1985–88; Deputy Sec.-Gen. CCP State Council 1987; Deputy Head State Flood Control Headquarters 1988, Central Forest Fire Prevention 1987; Deputy Head Leading Group for Comprehensive Agricultural Devt. 1990–; Vice-Chair. State Tourism Cttee. 1988. *Address:* State Council, Zhong Nan Hai, Beijing, People's Republic of China.

LI CHANGCHUN; Chinese party and government official; b. 1944, Jilin City; m. Zhang Shurong; ed. Harbin Polytechnic Univ.; joined CCP 1965; Mayor, Shenyang Municipality 1983–86; Sec. Shenyang Mun. CCP Cttee. 1985; Deputy Sec. Liaoning Prov. CCP Cttee. 1985–86; Dir. Foreign Affairs Office 1988–; Gov. of Liaoning Prov. 1986–90; Gov. of Henan Prov. 1991–93; Sec. CCP 5th Henan Prov. Cttee. 1992–98; Chair. Standing Cttee. Henan Provincial People's Congress 1993–98; alt. mem. 12th CCP Cen. Cttee. 1985; Dir. Foreign Affairs Office 1988–; mem. 13th CCP Cen. Cttee. 1987–92, 14th CCP Cen. Cttee. 1992–97, 15th CCP Cen. Cttee. 1997–, CCP Politburo 1997–, Sec. CCP Guangdong Prov. Cttee. 1998–. *Address:* Chinese Communist Party Guangdong Provincial Committee, Guangzhou, People's Republic of China.

LI CHUNTING; Chinese provincial governor; b. Oct. 1936, Luotang village, Zhaili, Qixia Co., Shandong Prov.; joined CCP 1958; worked as farmer; assumed leading posts at village, township, co., prefectural and city level; fmr. Deputy Sec. CCP Qixia Co. Cttee., Deputy Sec. CCP Yantai Prefectural Cttee., Head Prov. Metallurgical Dept.; Vice-Gov. Shandong Prov. 1988–95, Gov. 1995–; Deputy Sec. CCP Shandong Prov. Cttee. 1992–; Alt. mem. 14th CCPCC; mem. 15th CCP Cen. Cttee. 1997–. *Address:* Shandong Provincial Committee of the CCP, Jinan, Shandong Province, People's Republic of China.

LI DAOYU; Chinese diplomatist; b. 7 Aug. 1932, Shanghai; m. Ye Zhao Lie 1956; two s.; ed. Univ. of Shanghai; joined Foreign Service 1952; held various posts Dept. of Int. Orgs. and Confs.; Deputy Perm. Rep. to UN at Geneva 1983–84; Dir. Dept. of Int. Orgs., Foreign Ministry 1984–88; Asst. Foreign Minister 1988–90; Perm. Rep. to UN, New York 1990–93, Amb. to U.S.A. 1993–98; led China's del. to ESCAP session 1989; fmr. Vice-Chair. Chinese Nat. Comm., UNESCO, Nat. Cttee. for Pacific Econ. Co-operation, Preparatory Cttee. of China for Int. Space Year 1992, Nat. Cttee. for Int. Decade for Natural Disaster Reduction; fmr. rep. of China on Comm. on Human Rights, ECOSOC and UNCTAD; Vice-Chair. Overseas Chinese Affairs Cttee. of 9th NPC 1998. *Address:* c/o Standing Committee of National People's Congress, Beijing, People's Republic of China.

LI DELUN; Chinese orchestral conductor; b. 6 June 1917, Beijing; s. of Li Yuxiang and Tie Jingou; m. Li Jue 1947; one s. two d.; Adviser to China Nat. Symphony Orchestra; Vice-Chair. China Musicians' Assen. 1985–; Hon. Dir. Beijing Symphony Orchestra. *Leisure interests:* photography, calligraphy. *Address:* China National Symphony Orchestra, 11-1 Heping St., 100013 Beijing, People's Republic of China. *Telephone:* 6421-1504. *Fax:* 6421-6848.

LI DESHENG, Gen.; Chinese army officer (retd.); b. 1916, Xinxian Co., Henan Prov.; joined Red Army 1930, CCP 1932; Commdr., Red 4th Front Army on Long March 1934–36; Div. Commdr. 2nd Field Army, People's Liberation Army 1949; Maj.-Gen. PLA 1955, Gen. 1988; Commdr. Anhui Mil. Dist., PLA 1967; Chair. Anhui Revolutionary Cttee. 1968; Alt. mem. Politburo, 9th Cen. Cttee. of CCP 1969; Dir., Gen. Political Dept., PLA 1969–74; First Sec. CCP Anhui 1971–73; mem. Standing Cttee. of Politburo and Vice-Chair. 10th Cen. Cttee. of CCP 1973–75; mem. Politburo 11th Cen.

Cttee. of CCP 1977; mem. Politburo 12th Cen. Cttee. of CCP 1982–85; Commdr. Shenyang Mil. Region, PLA 1974–85, Head, Leading Group for the Prevention and Treatment of Endemic Disease in N. China, Cen. Cttee. 1977; First Sec. CCP Cttee., PLA Shenyang Mil. Region 1978–85; mem. Standing Cttee., Cen. Advisory Comm. 1985–92; Political Commissar, Leading Group of All-Army Financial and Econ. Discipline Inspection 1985–, PLA Nat. Defence Univ.; mem. Standing Comm. CCP Cen. Advisory Comm. 1985, 1987; Hon. Pres. Beijing Inst. of Modernization Admin. Aug. 1986–; Sr. Adviser China Soc. of Mil. Sciences 1991–; Pres. Chinese Patriotic Programs Fed. 1995–; Hon. Pres. Wushi (Martial Arts) Asscn. 1988–; mem. Presidium 14th CCP Nat. Congress Oct. 1992. *Address:* c/o Shenyang Military Region, People's Republic of China.

LI DEZHU; Chinese party and government official; b. 1943, Wangqing Co., Jilin Prov.; ed. Yanbian Univ.; joined CCP 1965; Vice-Gov. of Jilin Prov. 1988–93; Deputy Head United Front Work Dept. 1992–; Pres. Chinese Asscn. of Ethnic Minorities for External Exchanges 1992–; Minister State Comm. of Ethnic Affairs 1998–; mem. 14th CCP Cen. Cttee. 1992–97, 15th CCP Cen. Cttee 1997–. *Address:* c/o State Council, Xi Chang'an Jie, Beijing, People's Republic of China.

LI FANG; Chinese political scientist; b. 7 March 1925, Changde City, Hunan Prov.; s. of Li Xin Zhai and Wang Fu Ying; m. Zhang Cun Li 1954; one s. one d.; ed. Nanjing Univ.; Prof. and Research Fellow, Beijing Inst. of Political Science, Chinese Acad. of Social Sciences 1980–; Dir. Research Dept. of Public Admin. Inst. of Political Science; Prof. Beijing Univ., Nanjing Univ., Lanzhou Univ.; Perm. Council mem. Chinese Soc. of Public Admin.; council mem. Asscn. Political Reform of China; Visiting Prof. Erasmus Univ. (Holland), Newcastle Univ. (G.B.), Tokyo Univ., City Coll. of New York, Col. Univ.; Visiting Research Fellow, Albert Einstein Inst. (U.S.A.); Deputy Ed.-in-Chief The Volume of Public Administration of the Encyclopedia of China. *Publications:* Outline of Public Administration, numerous articles on science and literature. *Leisure interest:* carpentry. *Address:* Department of Public Administration, Institute of Political Science, 5 Jianguomennei Dajie, Beijing; 9th Building, 905 Furongli, Wanquanhelu, Haidian, Beijing 100080, People's Republic of China. *Telephone:* 256-9305. *Fax:* 256-2721.

LI FENG; Chinese state and party official; b. Jan. 1921, Xushui, Hebei; s. of Gao Dong and Gao Lishi; m. Zhang Wenying 1950; one s. three d.; county, then municipal dir.; Deputy Sec.-Gen., Hebei Prov. CCP Cttee. 1958; Deputy Gov., Hebei Prov. 1978–86; alt. mem. CCP 12th Cen. Cttee.; Adviser, Hebei Prov. People's Govt. 1986; Vice-Pres. China Nat. Packaging Import and Export Corpn. 1983. *Address:* Hebei Provincial People's Government, Hebei, People's Republic of China.

LI FOOK-SEAN, Simon, LL.B.; Chinese judge; b. 19 April 1922, Hong Kong; m. Marie Veronica Lillian 1946; four s. one d.; ed. King's Coll. London, Univ. of Hong Kong, Nat. Kwangsi Univ., Univ. Coll. London and Lincoln's Inn, London; Crown Counsel, Attorney-Gen.'s Chambers 1953–65; Hong Kong Govt. Magistrate 1957; Dist. Judge 1966–71; High Court Judge 1971–80; now Vice-Chair. Preparatory Cttee. for Hong Kong Special Admin. Region (SAR). *Address:* New Supreme Court Building, Queensway, Hong Kong Special Administrative Region, People's Republic of China.

LI FURONG; Chinese sports administrator; b. 1942, Shanghai City; Deputy, 5th NPC 1978–83; Deputy Dir. Training Bureau under the Comm. for Physical Culture and Sports 1983, Dir. 1986–; Vice-Chair. Youth Fed. 1983; Vice-Minister of the Physical Culture and Sports Comm. 1987; Sec.-Gen. Chinese Olympic Team, Seoul 1988; Vice-Pres. Chinese Olympic Cttee. 1989–. *Address:* The Ministry of Physical Culture and Sports Commission, Beijing, People's Republic of China.

LI FUSHAN; Chinese artist and engraver; b. June 1940, Quinhuangdao, Hebei; s. of Li Yinchang and Wang Lihui; m. Lei Suoxia 1961; one s. two d.; worked at Quinhuangdao Cultural Centre 1959–62, at Shanhaiguan Cultural Centre 1962–, deputy researcher 1994–; his works are in pvt. collections in Canada, U.S.A., Italy, N.Z. and countries in S.E. Asia; Dir. Quinhuangdao Arts Asscn.; mem. Hebei br. China Arts Asscn., Hebei Prov. Research Asscn. of Etched Plates. *Leisure interests:* classical literature, photography. *Address:* Shanhaiguan Cultural Centre, Quinhuangdao, Hebei Province, People's Republic of China. *Telephone:* Quinhuangdao 5051418; 3069987.

LI GANG; Chinese state official; b. 1926, Fuzhou Co., Fujian Prov.; ed. Qinghua Univ.; joined CCP 1949; Gen. Man. China Automotive Industry Corpn. 1982, Chair. of Bd. 1985–87; Deputy Gen. Man. China Investment Corpn. for Machinery, Electric Equipment, Light and Textile Industries 1988; Vice-Chair. Econ. Cttee.; alt. mem. 12th CCP Cen. Cttee. 1982–87; mem. Standing Cttee. CPPCC 8th Nat. Cttee. 1993–; Acting Dir. Bureau of Cultural Relations with Foreign Countries 1994–. *Address:* Chinese Investment Corporation, Beijing, People's Republic of China.

LI GENSHEN; Chinese party official and engineer; b. 1 July 1930, Huzhou City, Zhejiang Prov.; s. of Li Xin-pei and Zhang Zhu-bao; m. Xu Ying; one s. two d.; ed. Jiaotong Univ., Shanghai, and in U.S.S.R.; Dir. and Chief Engineer, No. 3 Research Inst., No. 7 Research Acad., China Shipbldg. Industrial Corpn.; mem. Standing Cttee. Heilongjiang Prov. CCP Cttee. 1983–92, Sec.-Gen. 1984, Deputy Sec. 1985–86; Vice-Chair. Heilongjiang Prov. 8th People's Congress 1993–96; Sec. Harbin Mun. CCP Cttee. 1985, Chair. 1983–; Standing Cttee. CCP Heilongjiang Prov. Cttee. 1988; mem. CCP Cen. Cttee. 1987; mem. Standing Cttee. 1988. *Publication:* Principles, Design and Testing of Marine Steam and Turbines. *Leisure interest:* reading. *Address:* No. 1 Guomin Street, Nangang District, Harbin 150001, Heilongjiang Province, People's Republic of China. *Telephone:* 451-3624054. *Fax:* 451-2135700.

LI GUIXIAN; Chinese party official; b. 23 Aug. 1937, Yingkou Co., Liaoning Prov.; ed. Mendeleyev Chemical Tech. Inst., Moscow; joined CCP 1962; Vice-Gov., Liaoning 1982–83; Sec. CCP Cttee., Liaoning 1983–86; Sec. CCP Cttee., Anhui Prov. 1986–88; State Councillor and Gov. PRC Cen. Bank 1988–93; mem. 14th CCP Cen. Cttee. 1992–97; State Councillor 1993–98; Pres. State Administrative Coll. 1994–; Head State Council Leading Group on Boundary Delimitation 1995–; mem. 15th CCP Cen. Cttee. 1997–; Vice-Chair. Nat. Cttee. of 9th CPPCC 1998–. *Address:* National Committee of Chinese People's Political Consultative Conference, 23 Taipingqiao Street, Beijing, People's Republic of China.

LI GUOGUANG; Chinese judge; Vice-Pres., mem. judicial Cttee. Supreme People's Court 1995–. *Address:* Supreme People's Court, Beijing, People's Republic of China.

LI GUOHAO, ENG.D.; Chinese bridge engineer; b. 13 April 1913, Meixian Co., Guangdong Prov.; ed. Shanghai Tongji Univ., Darmstadt Polytech. Inst., Germany; Chair. Nanjing Changjiang River Bridge Tech. Advisory Cttee. 1958–66; council mem. Shanghai People's Govt. 1955–; Vice-Pres. Shanghai Tongji Univ. 1962–66; in disgrace during Cultural Revolution 1966–76; Pres. Shanghai Tongji Univ. 1979–84, Hon. Pres. 1984–; Vice-Pres. Soc. of Civil Eng. of China 1984; Chair. Shanghai CPPCC 1983–88; Sr. Fellow Chinese Acad. of Sciences, Chinese Acad. of Eng. 1998–; Goethe Medal (Fed. Repub. of Germany) 1982. *Publications:* The Torsion Theory of Truss Girders-Torsion, Stability and Vibration of Truss Bridges 1977, Analysis of Box Girder and Truss Bridges 1987 and 7 other monographs and 50 papers. *Address:* Fuxing Xilu 34, 3C, Shanghai, People's Republic of China. *Telephone:* 337833.

LI HAO; Chinese politician; b. Dec. 1926, Dianbai Co., Guangdong Prov.; s. of Li Hansan and Cheng Li; m. Cheng Huizheng 1943; one s. two d.; ed. Zhongshan Univ., Guangzhou; joined CCP 1949; Deputy Sec.-Gen. of State Council, Beijing 1983–85; Vice-Gov. Guangdong Prov. 1985–88; Mayor, Shenzhen City, Sec. of CCP Shenzhen Cttee. 1985–93; mem. and Vice-Chair. Financial and Econ. Cttee. 8th NPC 1993–; part-time Prof. Beijing Univ. and People's Univ. of China. *Address:* Shenzhen People's Government, Guangdong, People's Republic of China. *Telephone:* 86-755-2239440.

LI HUAJI; Chinese artist; b. 16 Feb. 1931, Beijing; s. of Li Jue-Tian and Zhang Yun-Zheng; m. Quan Zhenghuan 1959; two d.; mem. Acad. Cttee. and Dir. Mural Painting Dept., Cen. Acad. of Fine Arts; Vice-Dir. Mural Painting Cttee., Artists' Asscn. of China; mem. Oil Painting Research Asscn. 1988–; important murals include Hunting (Harbin Swan Hotel), 5,000 Years of Culture (Beijing Nat. Library). *Leisure interests:* classical music, Beijing opera. *Address:* 6/F Hongmiao Beili, 100025 Beijing 3-601, People's Republic of China. *Telephone:* (01) 552213.

LI JIANGUO; Chinese politician; b. April 1946, Juanchen Co., Shandong Prov.; ed. Shandong Univ., joined CCP 1971; Dir. Gen. Office of CCP Tianjin Mun. Party Cttee. 1983; Vice-Sec.-Gen., Dir. Gen. Office of CCP Tianjin Mun. Party Cttee. 1988, Sec.-Gen. 1989, Sec. CCP Heping Dist. Cttee. 1991; Vice-Sec. CCP Tianjin Mun. Cttee. 1992; alt. mem. 14th CCP Cen. Cttee. 1992; Sec. CCP Shaanxi Provincial Cttee. 1997–; mem. 15th CCP Cen. Cttee. 1997–. *Address:* Chinese Communist Party Shaanxi Provincial Committee, Xi'an City, Shaanxi Province, People's Republic of China.

LI JIATING; Chinese politician; b. April 1944, Shiping, Yunnan Prov.; ed. Tsinghua Univ.; joined CCP 1964; cadre CCP Heilongjiang Prov. Cttee.; Vice-Dir. Office of Heilongjiang Prov. Econ. Comm. then Vice-Dir. of Comm.; Vice-Mayor then Mayor of Harbin; Asst. Gov. of Heilongjiang Prov. 1968–93; Vice-Gov. Yunnan Prov. 1993–98, Gov. 1998–; alt. mem. CCP 14th and 15th Cen. Cttee. 1992–. *Address:* Yunnan Provincial People's Government, Kunming, People's Republic of China.

LI JIJUN, Lieut.-Gen.; Chinese army officer and academic; b. May 1934, Harbin, Heilongjiang Prov.; s. of Li Dianshu and Zhou Jixing; m. Dong Wenfang 1960; one s.; joined PLA 1950, CCP 1953; Staff Officer, Chinese People's Volunteers, Korean War; Dir. Dept. of Academic Investigation and Research, PLA's Acad. of Mil. Science (AMS) 1978–82; Div. Commdr. 1982–85; Group Army Commdr. 1985–87; Deputy Dir. Gen. Office, CCP Cen. Mil. Comm. 1987–91, Dir. 1991–92; Vice-Pres. AMS 1992–97; alt. mem. 12th CCP Cen. Cttee. 1982–85, mem. 1985–87; mem. 13th CCP Cen. Cttee. 1987–92, 14th CCP Cen. Cttee. 1992–97; mem. 9th CPPCC; Vice-Pres. China Mil. Science Asscn.; Adviser to China Inst. for Int. Strategic Studies; Pres. China Inst. of Sun Zi Studies; mem. Academic Degree Cttee. of PLA; Guest Prof. Beijing Univ. of China, Renmin Univ. of China; tutor to doctorate cands. *Publications:* Military Theory and Practice 1994, Military Strategic Thinking 1996; numerous articles on mil. affairs; Ed. History of the Second World War 1995, History of Chinese Military 1998, World Military Yearbook. *Leisure interest:* swimming. *Address:* Academy of Military Science, Beijing, People's Republic of China.

LI JINAI; Chinese military official; b. July 1942, Tengzhou City, Shandong Prov.; joined CCP 1965; ed. Harbin Acad. of Mil. Eng.; joined PLA 1967; various posts 2nd Artillery; Dir. Cadre Dept. PLA Gen. Political Dept.

1987–90, Deputy Dir. 1990–92; Deputy Political Commissar, State Comm. of Science, Tech. and Industry for Nat. Defence 1992–95, Political Commissar 1995, PLA Gen. Equipment Dept. 1998–; rank of Maj.-Gen. 1988, Lieut.-Gen. 1993; Alt. mem. 14th CCP Cen. Cttee; mem. 15th CCP Cen. Cttee. 1997–. *Address:* State Commission of Science, Technology and Industry for National Defence, Jingshanqian Jie, Beijing, People's Republic of China. *Telephone:* (1) 6370000.

LI JING, Gen.; Chinese army officer and party official; b. 1930; ed. Air Force Aviation Acad. of China; joined PLA 1946, CCP 1949; Deputy Commdr. PLA Navy and concurrently Commdr. Naval Air Force 1983–91; Deputy Chief of PLA Gen. Staff HQ 1992–95; rank of Vice-Adm. 1988, Gen. 1994; mem. 14th CCP Cen. Cttee. 1992–97; Vice-Chair. Foreign Affairs Cttee., 9th Nat. Cttee. of CPPCC 1998–. *Address:* c/o National Committee of Chinese People's Political Consultative Conference, 23 Taipingqiao Street, Beijing, People's Republic of China.

LI JINHUA; Chinese politician; b. 1943, Rudong Co., Jiangsu Prov.; joined CCP 1965; ed. Cen. Inst. of Public Finance and Banking; Dir. Econ. and Trade Dept. of Shaanxi Prov. 1985; Deputy Auditor Gen. Nat. Audit Office1985–98, Auditor Gen. 1998–; mem. CCP Cen. Cttee. for Discipline Inspection 1992; mem. 15th CCP Cen. Cttee. 1997–. *Address:* National Audit Office, 1 Bei Lu Yuan, Zhanlan Road, Xicheng District, Beijing 100830, Beijing, People's Republic of China. *Fax:* 86 10 68330958.

LI JIULONG, Gen.; Chinese army officer; b. 1929, Fengrun Co., Hebei Prov.; joined Red Army and CCP 1945; took part in Jinzheng Campaign of Korean War 1953; Commdr., 160th Div., 54th Army 1972; Commdr., 54th Army 1980; Commdr. Jinan Mil. Region, PLA 1985, Chengdu Mil. Region 1991–94; Vice-Chair. Internal Affairs and Judicial Cttee. of 9th NPC 1998–; mem. 12th CCP Cen. Cttee. 1985–87, 13th CCP Cen. Cttee. 1987–92, 14th CCP Cen. Cttee. 1992–97; rank of Lieut.-Gen. 1988, Gen. 1994. *Address:* Jinan Military Region Headquarters, Jinan, Shandong, People's Republic of China.

LI KA-SHING; Chinese industrialist, financier and property developer; b. 1928; m. Chong Yuet-ming; two s.; moved with family from mainland to Hong Kong 1940; salesman for toy mfg. co. 1942–1950; est. Cheung Kong plastics factory 1950; acquired Hutchison Whampoa trading and industrial conglomerate 1979, now Chair.; Chair., Man. Dir. Cheung Kong Holdings; owner or shareholder numerous cos. Hong Kong and Canada; local Adviser for People's Repub. of China 1992; mem. Preliminary Working Cttee. of the Preparatory Cttee. of the Hong Kong Special Admin. Region. *Address:* Hutchison Whampoa Ltd, Hutchison House, 22nd Floor, 10 Harcourt Road, Hong Kong Special Administrative Region, People's Republic of China. *Telephone:* 2523-0161. *Fax:* 2810-0705.

LI KEQIANG; Chinese politician; b. 1955, Dingyuan Co., Anhui Prov.; joined CCP 1976; ed. Peking Univ.; Sec. Communist Youth League, Beijing Univ. Cttee.; Vice-Dir. Dept. of Schools and Colls. of Communist Youth League Cen. Cttee.; Sec. Secr. of Communist Youth League Cen. Cttee. 1982–93, First Sec. Communist Youth League 1993–98; Acting Gov. He'nan Prov.; mem. 15th CCP Cen. Cttee. 1997–. *Address:* He'nan Provincial People's Government, Zhengzhou, He'nan Province, People's Republic of China.

LI KEYU; Chinese fashion and costume designer; b. 15 May 1929, Shanghai; m. Yuan Mao 1955; ed. Cen. Acad. of Fine Arts; Chief Costume Designer of Cen. Ballet; Deputy Dir. Chinese Soc. of Stage Design; mem. Bd. All-China Artists' Asscn., Chinese Dancers' Asscn.; Deputy Dir. China Export Garments Research Centre; Sr. consultant, Beijing Inst. of Fashion Tech.; has designed costumes for many works, including Swan Lake, Le Corsaire, The Maid of the Sea, The Fountain of Bakhchisarai, La Esmeralda, The Red Detachment of Women, The East is Red, The New Year Sacrifice (Ministry of Culture costume design prize), Zigeunerweisen (Ministry of Culture costume design prize), Othello (for Peking Opera, Beijing's costume design prize), Tang Music and Dance, Zheng Ban Qiao (Houston Ballet), Fu (Hongkong Ballet), La Péri (Houston Ballet); winner sole costume design prize, 4th Japan World Ballet Competition, Osaka 1984. *Publications:* two vols. of sketches. *Address:* 21 Gong-jian Hutong, Di An-Men, Beijing 100009, People's Republic of China. *Telephone:* 4035474.

LI KWOH-TING, B.S.; Taiwanese government official; b. 28 Jan. 1910, Nanking; s. of P. L. Li and Jean Liu; m. Pearl Sung 1937; one s.; ed. Nat. Central Univ., China, and Cambridge Univ., England; Supt. Tze Yu Iron Works, Chungking 1942–45; Pres. Taiwan Shipbuilding Corpn. 1951–53; mem. Industrial Devt. Comm., Econ. Stabilisation Bd. 1953–58; Publisher of The Industry of Free China (monthly) 1954–71; Sec.-Gen. Council for U.S. Aid 1958–63; Convener of Industrial Planning and Co-ordination Group of Ministry of Econ. Affairs 1958–63; Head of Industrial Devt. and Investment Center 1958–63; Vice-Chair. Council for Int. Econ. Cooperation and Devt. 1963–73; Minister of Econ. Affairs 1965–69, of Finance 1969–76, of State 1976–88; Sr. Adviser to the Pres. 1988–; mem. Nat. Security Council 1967–90; Vice-Chair. Nat. Reconstruction Planning Cttee. 1967–72; mem. Council of Academia Sinica 1981–; Gov. Int. Bank for Reconstruction and Devt. 1969–76; mem. Council for Econ. Planning and Devt., Nat. Taiwan Univ. 1977–; Hon. Fellow (Emmanuel Coll., Cambridge) 1991; Hon. D.Sc. (Nat. Cen. Univ.) 1983, (Univ. of Md.) 1989, Hon. D. Econ. (Sung Kyun Kwan Univ.) 1978, Hon. D.Eng. (Nat. Chiao-Tung Univ.) 1989; Hon. Ph.D. (Chung Yuan Univ.) 1990; Hon. D.Law (Boston Univ.) 1990, (Chinese Univ. of Hong Kong) 1991, Hon. D.Man.Sc. (Nat. Cheng Kung Univ.) 1995, Hon. D.Sc. (Providence) 1995, Hon. D.Hum.Litt. (State Univ. of N.Y.) 1996; Distinguished Service Award, New York Chinese Inst. of Engineers; Ramon Magsaysay Award for Govt. Service 1968, President's Medal Award (Johns Hopkins Univ.) 1989, (Catholic Univ.) 1995, and decorations from Repub. of Korea, Spain, Repub. of Viet Nam, Jordan, Madagascar, Paraguay, Thailand, South Africa and Gabon. *Publications:* Symposium on Nuclear Physics, British Industries, Japanese Shipbuilding Industry, The Growth of Private Industry in Free China, Economic Policy and Economic Development, The Experience of Dynamic Economic Growth in Taiwan, My Views on Taiwan Economic Development: A Collection of Essays 1975–80, Prospects for Taiwan's Economic Development—a Collection of Essays from 1980–1984 1985, The Economic Transformation of Taiwan 1976–88, Vision and Devotion 1987, The Evolution of Policy Behind Taiwan's Development Success 1988, Experience and Belief 1991. *Leisure interest:* golf. *Address:* 3 Lane 2, Tai-an Street, Taipei, Taiwan. *Telephone:* 737-7711, 737-7717 (Office); 351 5595 (Home). *Fax:* 737-7737.

LI LAIZHU, Gen.; Chinese army officer and party official; b. 1932, Shen Co., Shandong Prov.; ed. PLA Mil. and Political Acad.; joined PLA 1947, CCP 1948; Deputy Commdr. of Beijing Mil. Area Command 1985; rank of Lieut.-Gen. PLA 1988; Commdr. Beijing Mil. Region 1994–97; Gen. mem. 14th CCP Cen. Cttee. 1992–97; rank of Gen. 1994. *Address:* Beijing Military Area Command, People's Liberation Army, Beijing, People's Republic of China.

LI LANQING; Chinese government and party official; b. May 1932, Zhengjiang Co., Jiangsu Prov.; ed. Shanghai Fudan Univ.; joined CCP 1952; Vice-Mayor Tianjin 1983–85; Vice-Minister Foreign Econ. Relations and Trade 1986–90, Minister 1990–93; mem. 8th NPC 1993–; alt. mem. 13th CCP Cen. Cttee. 1987–92; mem. 14th CCP Cen. Cttee. 1992–97, 15th CCP Cen. Cttee. 1997–; mem. CCP Politburo 1992–, Standing Cttee., CCP Politburo 1997–; Vice-Premier 1993–; Head Nat. Leading Group for Foreign Investments (State Council) 1994–; Chair. Academic Degrees Cttee. 1995–; Deputy Head Cen. Leading Group for Party Bldg. Work 1994–. *Address:* Central Committee of the Chinese Communist Party, Zhong Nan Hai, Beijing, People's Republic of China.

LI LI'AN; Chinese party official; b. 19 July 1920, Wutai Co., Shanxi Prov.; s. of Zhoa Xu Cheng and Wang Yong Di; joined CCP 1935; Deputy Dir., Office of Personnel Admin. Dept., Cen. Govt. 1952–54; Deputy Dir., a section, Org. Dept., Cen. Cttee. CCP 1954–55, Dir., a section, Finance and Commerce Dept. 1956–60, Dir., a section, and Deputy Dir. Org. Dept. 1961–64; Sec. CCP Cttee., Heilongjiang 1964–66, 1973–81; Deputy for Heilongjiang, 5th NPC 1978–81; Second Sec. CCP Cttee., Heilongjiang 1981–83; First Sec. 1983–87; First Sec., CCP Cttee., Harbin City 1981–83; mem. Cen. Cttee. CCP 1982–87; Sec.-Gen., mem. Cen. Advisory Comm. 1987–92; Vice-Pres. Prov. Party School, Heilongjiang 1978–83; mem. Presidium 14th CCP Nat. Congress Oct. 1992; Pres. Soc. for study on Party Mems. 1991–. *Address:* Office of the CCP Committee, Harbin, Heilongjiang, People's Republic of China.

LI LIANGHUI, Maj.-Gen.; Chinese army officer; b. 1940, Shenxian Co., Hebei Prov.; joined PLA 1961; joined CCP 1963; Vice-Army Commdr. and Chief of Staff, Army Commdr., Vice-Commdr. then Commdr. Ningxia Provincial Mil. Command 1990; Commdr. Xinjiang Mil. Command; mem. 15th CCP Cen. Cttee. *Address:* Xinjiang Military Command, Urumqi, Xinjiang Uygur Autonomous Region, People's Republic of China.

LI LIGONG; Chinese party official; b. 20 Feb. 1925, Jiaocheng, Shanxi; s. of Li Zhengliang and Li Shi; m. Xie Bin; two s. three d.; Sec. CCP County Cttee., Sec. CCP Pref. Cttee., Sec. Communist Youth League of Shanxi Prov., mem. Cen. Cttee. Communist Youth League 1953–65; Sec. Communist Youth League, Beijing Municipal Cttee. 1966; Vice-Dir. Beijing Municipal Revolutionary Cttee. 1977; Sec. CCP Beijing Municipal Cttee. 1978–81; Exec. Sec. CCP Shanxi Prov. Cttee. 1981–83, Sec. 1983–91; Dir. CCP Shanxi Advisory Cttee. 1991–92; mem. CCP Cen. Comm. for Inspecting Discipline 1979–82; mem. 12th Cen. Cttee. CCP 1982, 13th Cen. Cttee. 1987; mem. Standing Cttee. 8th NPC 1992–98; mem. 9th NPC. *Publication:* Shanxi in Contemporary China (Chief Ed.). *Leisure interests:* swimming, fencing, tennis, hiking. *Address:* General Office of the Chinese Communist Party Shanxi Provincial Committee, 369 Yingze Street, Taiyuan, Shanxi, People's Republic of China. *Telephone:* 4045093.

LI LIN; Chinese physicist; b. 31 Oct. 1923, Beijing; d. of J.S. Lee and Lin Hsu; m. C. L. Tsou 1949; one d.; ed. Birmingham Univ., Cambridge Univ.; returned to China 1951; researcher, Mechanics Lab., Academia Sinica 1951–57; Research Fellow, Beijing Atomic Energy Inst. 1958–; Research Fellow, Inst. of Physics, Academia Sinica 1978–; mem. Dept. of Math. and Physics, Academia Sinica 1980–; mem. Chinese Acad. of Sciences; First Prize Nat. Science and Tech. Awards; winner of several collective prizes. *Leisure interest:* music. *Address:* Institute of Physics, Chinese Acad. of Sciences, P.O. Box 603, Beijing 100080, People's Republic of China. *Telephone:* 62852175. *Fax:* 62562605.

LI LING; Chinese musician; b. 28 Dec. 1913, Taishan Co., Guangdong Prov.; s. of Li Daoxi and Wu Lianzhu; m. Chen Yunfeng; one s. three d.; ed. Yan'an Lu Xun Art Coll.; joined CCP 1941; Art Dir., Cen. Song and Dance Ensemble 1952–56; Dir. Cen. Philharmonic Soc. 1956–66; in disgrace during Cultural

Revolution 1966–77; Vice-Chair. Chinese Musicians' Asscn. 1979–; Sec. Fed. Literary and Art Circles of China 1981–; Dir. China Musical Coll. 1980–86; Vice-Chair. Standing Cttee, 8th Guizhou Provincial Peoples' Congress 1994–. *Leisure interest:* painting. *Address:* Chinese Musicians Association, Beijing, People's Republic of China. *Telephone:* 861 5029308.

LI LINGWEI; Chinese badminton player; b. 1964; won women's single title at 3rd World Badminton Championships, Copenhagen 1982; elected 7th in list of ten best Chinese athletes 1984; won Women's Singles and Women's Doubles (co-player Wu Dixi) at 5th ALBA World Cup, Jakarta 1985; won Women's Singles, at World Badminton Grand Prix finals. Tokyo 1985, at Dunhill China Open Badminton Championship, Nanjing 1987, at Malaysian Badminton Open, Kuala Lumpur 1987, at World Grand Prix, Hong Kong 1988, at China Badminton Open 1988, at Danish Badminton Open, Odense 1988, at All-England Badminton Championships 1989, at 6th World Badminton Championships, Jakarta. *Address:* China Sports Federation, Beijing, People's Republic of China.

LI LUN, Lieut.-Gen.; Chinese army officer; b. 1927, Wuhu, Anhui Prov.; ed. Yanan Inst. of Natural Sciences, Chinese People's Anti-Japanese Mil. and Political Coll. and Artillery Acad.; joined 8th Route Army 1939; mem. CCP 1945–; Staff Officer, Shanxi-Suiyuan Mil. Command H.Q., Deputy Bn. Commdr. E. China Field Army, Bn. Commdr. 3rd Field Army 1946–49; Deputy Chief of Staff of a regt. 1950; Section Chief, Transportation H.Q. under Cen. Mil. Comm. 1951; Head, Scientific Research Office of Ministry of Mil. Transport Dept. under H.Q. of Gen. Staff 1959; Deputy Chief, Training Div. Mil. Transport Dept. 1962; Div. Chief, Transport Dept. of PLA Gen. Logistics Dept. (GLD) 1969; Deputy Dir. Mil. Communication Dept. of PLA GLD 1978, Dir. 1982; Pres. PLA Logistics Acad. 1986; Deputy Dir. PLA GLD 1989–; Deputy Head, Leading Group for Traffic readiness for War under State Council and Cen. Mil. Comm. 1990–; mem. NPC Financial and Econ. Cttee.; mem. 8th NPC Standing Cttee. *Address:* c/o Ministry of National Defence, Jingshanqian Jie, Beijing, People's Republic of China.

LI LUYE; Chinese diplomatist; b. 1925, Beijing; Dir. Dept. of Int. Orgs. of Foreign Ministry 1980–; Pres. of Chinese People's Asscn. for Friendship with Foreign Countries 1990–, Dir. Chinese Int. Studies Centre 1990–, Vice-Chair. Foreign Affairs Cttee.; Pres. China Nat. Cttee. for Pacific Econ. Co-operation 1991; mem. Standing Cttee. of 8th NPC. *Address:* Chinese People's Association for Friendship with Foreign Countries, Taijichang, Beijing 100002, People's Republic of China.

LI MING; Chinese state official; b. (as Zheng Yuxiang) Nov. 1927, Tienjin; m. 1954; two s. one d.; Deputy, Chief of Production Office, Anshan Iron and Steel Corpn. 1949–68; Chief Engineer, Pres. Panzhihua Iron and Steel Complex 1968–82; Gen. Dir., Leading Office, Shanghai Baoshan Steel Complex Project, Pres. Baoshan Steel Complex 1983; Chair. Baoshan Iron and Steel Complex Corpn. (Group) 1988–; Vice-Minister of Metallurgical Industry 1982; alt. mem. 12th CCP Cen. Cttee. 1982–85, mem. 1985–87; alt. mem. 13th CCP Cen. Cttee. 1987–92, 14th CCP Cen. Cttee. 1992–; Dir. Radio and TV Dept. Hubei Provincial People's Govt. 1994–. *Leisure interest:* swimming. *Address:* 2 Mundangjiang Lu, Shanghai 201900, People's Republic of China. *Telephone:* (21) 5646944. *Fax:* (21) 56600260.

LI PENG; Chinese politician; b. Oct. 1928, Shanghai City; s. of the late Li Shuoxun and Zhao Juntao; m. Zhu Lin 1958; two s. one d.; ed. Moscow Power Inst.; Vice-Minister of Electric Power Industry 1980–81, Minister 1981–82; Vice-Minister of Water Conservancy and Electric Power 1982–83; Vice-Premier of State Council 1983–87; Minister in Charge of State Educ. Comm. 1985–88; Acting Premier 1987–88; Premier of People's Repub. of China 1988–98; Chair. Standing Cttee. 9th NPC 1998–; mem. 12th Cen. Cttee. of CCP 1982–87, 13th CCP Cen. Cttee. 1987–92, 14th CCP Cen. Cttee. 1992–97, 15th CCP Cen. Cttee. 1997–; mem. Political Bureau 1985–, Standing Cttee. 1987–; mem. Secr. CCP Cen. Cttee. 1985–87. *Address:* Standing Committee of National People's Congress, Beijing, People's Republic of China.

LI QI; Chinese artist; b. Sept. 1928, Pingyao, Shanxi Prov.; ed. North China United Univ.; lecturer then Prof. of Chinese Painting, Cen. Acad. of Fine Art 1950–; several portraits of Chinese leaders. *Publication:* Portraits by Li Qui. *Address:* Central Academy of Fine Art, Beijing, People's Republic of China.

LI QINGKUI, PH.D.; Chinese biologist and administrator; b. 1912, Ningpo Co., Zhejiang Prov.; ed. Univ. of Illinois, U.S.A.; Chair. Soc. of Pedology 1962; Deputy Dir. Nanjing Inst. of Pedology 1965; Pres. Soc. of Pedology 1978; Vice-Chair. Jiangsu Prov. CP 1983; mem. Dept. of Biology, Academia Sinica 1985–. *Address:* Nanjing Institute of Pedology, Nanjing City, Jiangsu Province, People's Republic of China.

LI QIYAN; Chinese politician; b. 15 Oct. 1938, Qihe Co., Shandong Prov.; s. of late Li Detie and of Liu Shuliang; m. Wu Yuhuan; one s. one d.; ed. Beijing Teachers Coll.; joined CCP 1961; Deputy Sec. CCP Beijing Municipality Cttee. 1987–96; mem. 14th CCP Cen. Cttee. 1992–97; Mayor of Beijing Municipality 1993–96; Vice-Minister of Labour 1996–98, of Labour and Social Security 1998–. *Leisure interests:* history books, biographies. *Address:* Ministry of Labour and Social Security, 12 Hepingli Zhongjie, Beijing 106716, People's Republic of China. *Telephone:* (10) 64277640. *Fax:* (10) 64213056.

LI RENCHEN; Chinese journalist; b. Oct. 1941, Changyi County, Shandong Prov.; ed. Fudan Univ.; mem. CCP 1975–; ed. Features and Photos Service, Comm. for Cultural Relations with Foreign Countries 1965–68; Ed. Huizhou Bao, Anhui Prov., Ed. People's Daily and Deputy Dir. Commentary Dept. People's Daily 1983–86; Deputy Ed.-in-Chief, Renmin Ribao (People's Daily) 1986–; writes under pen name Chen Ping. *Address:* Renmin Ribao, 2 Jin Tai Xi Jie, Beijing, People's Republic of China. *Telephone:* (1) 5092121. *Fax:* (1) 50919820.

LI RENJUN; Chinese business executive; b. 1929; joined CCP 1964; Chair. of Bd. China Petro-Chemical Corpn. 1990–. *Address:* China Petro-Chemical Corporation. 24 Xiaoguan Street, Chaoyang District, Beijing 100013, People's Republic of China.

LI RUI; Chinese party official; b. 1917, Pingjiang Co., Hunan Prov.; ed. Wuhan Univ.; joined CCP 1937; cadre in Hunan 1950; Asst. Minister of Water Conservancy and Electrical Power 1955–58; in political disgrace 1967–79; Vice-Minister, 4th Ministry of Machine Building 1979–82; Vice-Minister, Power Industry 1979–82; Dir. State Bureau of Computers 1980–; mem. 12th Cen. Cttee. CCP 1982–85; mem. Cen. Advisory Comm. 1987–; Deputy Dir. State Bureau of Tech. Supervision 1991–; Deputy Head Org. Dept. CCP 1983. *Publications:* The Early Revolutionary Activities of Comrade Mao Zedong, Some Fundamental Problems Concerning the Total Utilization Plan for the Yellow River. *Address:* Central Committee of the Chinese Communist Party, Beijing, People's Republic of China.

LI RUIHUAN; Chinese party and government official; b. Sept. 1934, Baodi Co., Tianjing; Vice-Chair. Beijing Trade Union 1973; Dir.-Gen. Work Site for Mao Zedong Memorial Hall, Beijing 1977; Deputy for Beijing, 5th NPC 1978; Sec. Communist Youth League 1979–81; mem. Standing Cttee., 5th NPC 1978–; Deputy Mayor Tianjin 1981, Acting Mayor 1982, Mayor Tianjin 1982–89; Sec. CCP Cttee., Tianjin 1982–89; Vice-Pres. All-China Youth Fed. 1980; mem. 12th CCP Cen. Cttee. 1982–87, 13th CCP Cen. Cttee. 1987–92, 14th CCP Cen. Cttee. 1992–97, 15th CCP Cen. Cttee. 1997–; mem. Politburo 1987–, Standing Cttee. Politburo 1989, Perm. mem. Politburo 1992–; Chair. 8th Nat. Cttee. CPPCC 1993–98; Chair. 9th Nat. Cttee. CPPCC 1998–; named Nat. Model Worker 1979; Hon. Pres. Chinese Fed. for the Disabled 1993–; Hon Pres. Chinese Table Tennis Asscn. 1990–. *Address:* National Committee of Chinese People's Political Consultative Conference, 23 Taipingqiao Street, Beijing, People's Republic of China.

LI SHENGLIN; Chinese politician; b. Nov. 1946, Nantong Co., Jiangsu Prov.; ed. Zhejiang Coll. of Agricultural Machinery 1970; joined CCP 1973; Vice-Mayor of Tianjin 1991–93, Mayor 1993–; Vice-Sec. CCP Tianjin Mun. Cttee. 1993–; mem. 15th CCP Cen. Cttee. 1997–. *Address:* Chinese Communist Party Tianjin Municipal Committee, Tianjin, People's Republic of China.

LI SHIJI; Chinese opera singer; b. May 1933, Suzhou Co., Jiangsu Prov.; Head First Troupe, Beijing Opera Theatre 1989–; mem. 7th CPPCC 1987–92, 8th 1993–. *Address:* Beijing Opera Theatre, 11 Hufang Road, Xuanwu District, Beijing 100052, People's Republic of China.

LI SHOUSHAN; Chinese party official; b. 1929, Inner Mongolia; joined CCP 1948; alt. mem. 12th CCP Cen. Cttee. 1982, 13th Cen. Cttee. 1987–; Sec. CCP Cttee., Tacheng Pref., Xinjiang Autonomous Region 1982; mem. CCP Standing Cttee., Xinjiang 1983–85, 1987–; Deputy Sec. CCP 4th Xinjiang Uygur Autonomous Regional Cttee. 1985–. *Address:* Xinjiang Autonomous Regional Chinese Communist Party, Urumqi, Xinjiang, People's Republic of China.

LI TIEYING; Chinese state official; b. Sept. 1936, Yan'an, Shaanxi Prov.; s. of late Li Weihan; m. Qin Xinhua; ed. Charles Univ., Czechoslovakia; fmr. deputy dir. of an electronics research inst.; Sec. CCP Cttee., Shenyang Municipality 1981–85; alt. mem. 12th CCP Cen. Cttee. 1982, mem. 1985; mem. 13th CCP Cen. Cttee. 1987–92, 14th CCP Cen. Cttee. 1992–97, 15th CCP Cen. Cttee. 1997–; Sec. CCP Cttee., Liaoning Prov. 1983–86; Minister of Electronics Industry 1985–88; Minister in charge of State Educ. Comm. 1988–93, of State Comm. for Econ. Reconstruction 1987–88; Chair. Cen. Patriotic Public Health Campaign Cttee.; State Councillor 1988–98; Minister of State Ed. Comm. 1988–93, of State Comm. for Econ. Restructuring 1993–; Head Leading Group for the Reform of the Housing System 1993–; Deputy Head Nat. Leading Group for Anti-Disaster and Relief Work 1991–; mem. Politburo of CCP 1992–; Del., World Conf. on Educ., Bangkok 1990, visited India, Laos 1992; Hon. Pres. Athletics Asscn., Soc. of Nat. Conditions. *Address:* State Commission for Economic Restructuring, Beijing, People's Republic of China.

LI TINXIANG; Chinese business executive; b. Dec. 1928, Beijing; ed. Beiyang Univ., Tianjin; Gen. Man. China Nat. Oil and Gas Corpn. 1993–. *Address:* China National Oil and Gas Corporation, 18A Ganjiakou Street, Beijing 100037, People's Republic of China.

LI XIMING; Chinese party and government official; b. 1926, Shulu Co., Hebei Prov.; ed. Qinghua Univ.; Sec. CCP Cttee., Shijingshan Power Plant; identified as govt. cadre 1975; Vice-Minister of Water Conservancy and Electric Power 1976–79; Vice-Minister of Electric Power Industry 1979–82; Minister of Urban and Rural Construction and Environmental Protection 1982–84; mem. 12th Cen. Cttee., CCP 1982–87; mem. Politburo 13th Cen. Cttee. CCP 1987–92; First Political Commissar PLA Garrison, Beijing

1984–92; CCP First Sec. Beijing 1984–92; mem. Political Bureau CCP; Vice-Chair. Cen. Patriotic Public Health Campaign Cttee., CCP Cen. Cttee. 1983; Vice-Chair. Environmental Protection Cttee., State Council 1984; Pres. Urban Devt. Scientific Research Soc. 1984; Vice-Chair. Cen. Greening Cttee. 1983; Vice-Chair. Standing Cttee. of 8th NPC 1993–98. *Address:* Standing Committee of National People's Congress, Beijing, People's Republic of China.

LI XINLIANG, Gen.; Chinese army officer and party official; b. 1936, Laiyang Co., Shandong Prov.; joined PLA 1953, CCP 1956; Commdr. Autonomous Region Mil. Dist., Guangxi Prov. 1983–88; Party Cttee. Sec. PLA Guangxi Mil. Area Command 1986–89; mem. 13th CCP Cen. Cttee. 1987–92; Deputy Commdr. Guangzhou Mil. Region 1989–94; Political Commissar Shenyang Mil. Region 1994–95, Commdr. Shenyang Mil. Area Command 1995–97; rank of Lieut.-Gen. 1993; Commdr. Beijing Mil. Area Command 1997–; rank of Gen. 1998; mem. 15th CCP Cen. Cttee. 1997–. *Address:* Commander's Office, Beijing Military Area Command, Beijing, People's Republic of China.

LI XIPU; Chinese party official; b. 1923, Yexian Co., Shandong Prov.; joined CCP 1939; Gen. Man. Xi'an Aircraft Mfrs. 1975–81; mem. Shaanxi Prov. CCP Cttee., Dir. Industry-Transportation Dept. 1981; mem. 12th CCP Cen. Cttee. 1982; Sec. CCP Cttee. Shaanxi 1983; Deputy Dir. Advisory Cttee. Shaanxi 1986–; Chair. Shaanxi Prov. 7th People's Congress Standing Cttee. May 1988–. *Address:* Shaanxi Provincial Chinese Communist Party, Xian, Shaanxi, People's Republic of China.

LI XU'E; Chinese state and aerospace official; b. 1928, Hanyang, Hubei Prov.; joined CCP 1955; ed. Qinghua Univ.; Vice-Minister of Space Industry 1982–85; Minister of Astronautics (Space) Industry 1985–88; Vice-Minister State Science and Tech. Comm. 1988–93; Chair. Bd. of Dirs. China Science and Tech. Consultant Corpn. 1983–; Vice-Chair. Environmental Protection Cttee. 1988–; a Deputy Head Co-ordination Group for Weather Change 1990–; a Vice-Chair. China Cttee. of Int. Decade for Nat. Disaster Reduction 1991–; Pres. Soc. of Social Devt. Science 1992–, of China Soc. of Geographic Information System 1994–; mem. 12th CCP Cen. Cttee. 1982–87, 8th NPC 1993–98, 9th NPC 1998–; Vice-Chair. Educ., Science, Culture and Public Health Cttee.; Head Dels. to Poland, Finland, India. *Address:* Standing Committee of National People's Congress, Beijing, People's Republic of China.

LI XUEZHI; Chinese politician; b. 1923, Linqing Co., Shandong Prov.; s. of Li Wencai and Li Zhangshi; m. 1945; two s. two d.; with guerrilla forces 1937; joined CCP 1938; CCP Sec. of Chinhua Admin. Dist., Zhejiang prior to Cultural Revolution; Sec. Ningxia Hui Autonomous Regional Cttee. 1977–79; alt. mem. CCP 11th Cen. Cttee. 1979; First Sec., CCP Ningxia Hui Autonomous Regional Cttee. 1979–; First Political Commissar, Ningxia PLA Mil. Dist. 1981–86; mem. 12th Cen. Cttee. CCP 1982–87, 7th NPC Standing Cttee. 1988–, 8th NPC Standing Cttee.; mem. Credentials Cttee. 1988– (Vice-Chair. 1993–); Vice-Chair. Nationalities Affairs Cttee. 1988–. *Address:* Nationalities Committee, National People's Congress, Great Hall of the People, Beijing 100805, People's Republic of China. *Telephone:* (861) 821-6348. *Fax:* (861) 309-8936.

LI YAN (Zhuang bei); Chinese painter; b. Nov. 1943, Beijing; s. of Li Ku Chan and Li Hui Wen; m. Sun Yan Hua 1972; one d.; Prof. Cen. Inst. of Arts and Crafts and of Shandong; fmr. Vice-Pres. Li Ku Chan Museum; mem. Chinese Artists' Asscn.; Assoc. Prof. Cen. Acad. of Art and Design; Deputy Dir. of Li Kuchan Memorial; Vice-Pres. Int. Soc. Yi Jing, Research Fellow Research Soc. Yi Jing; Specialist, Appraising Cttee. of Chinese Arts of Calligraphy and Painting; specializes in painting figures, animals and mountains and water scenes, and in calligraphy; over 10,000 sketches and paintings from life, 3,000 exercises in Chinese painting 1956–; mem. 9th CPPCC; mem. Beijing PCCC; works have been exhibited in Sweden, U.S.A., Canada, Japan, Singapore, Philippines, Hong Kong, Tanzania; gave lectures at Hong Kong Univ. 1980; held lectures and exhbn. in India 1989, in Malaysia 1991, in Indonesia 1993; subject of TV films by Shen Zhen TV 1986 and Swedish TV 1986, presenter of CCTV's The Wind of China 1995; important works include Chinese Emperor, Zhou Wen Emperor, Lao Zi, Confucian Worry about Taoism, Lao Zi and Einstein, Five-Colour Earth, Start Sailing, A Swarm of Monkeys, Cat and Chrysanthemum, Tiger Cub. *Publications:* Yi Jing Album 1993; several magazine articles on art. *Leisure interests:* writing poetry, Qigong, The Book of Changes. *Address:* No. 2-1, Building 15, Nan sha Go, San Li He, Xi Cheng District, Beijing, People's Republic of China. *Telephone:* 68523844.

LI YAOWEN, Adm.; Chinese military officer and diplomatist; b. (as Zhang Xishen) 1918, Rongcheng Co., Shandong Prov.; joined CCP 1937; Political Commissar, 26th Corps, 3rd Field Army 1949; served in Korea 1950; Dir. Political Dept., Jinan Mil. Region 1955; Deputy Political Commissar, Jinan Mil. Region 1965; Deputy Dir. Standing Cttee., Revolutionary Cttee., Shandong Prov. 1969; Deputy Minister of Foreign Affairs 1970; Amb. to Tanzania 1972–76, concurrently to Madagascar 1973–74; alt. mem. 11th CCP Cen. Cttee. 1977–82; Political Commissar, Nat. Defence Scientific and Technological Comm. 1977–80, PLA Navy 1980–90; mem. 12th CCP Cen. Cttee. 1982–87, Cen. Advisory Comm. 1987–; Gen. PLA 1988–; Head PLA Del. to North Korea 1990–. *Address:* PLA Navy Headquarters, Beijing, People's Republic of China.

LI YINING; Chinese economist; b. Nov. 1930, Yizheng Co., Jiangsu Prov.; ed. Peking Univ.; Prof., Dean Economy Admin. Dept., Peking Univ.; joined CCP 1984; Vice-Chair. 8th Chinese Democratic League Cen. Cttee. 1997–; mem. Standing Cttee. 7th NPC, 8th NPC; Vice-Chair. Finance and Econ. Cttee. of 9th NPC 1998–; now Dean Guanhua School of Man. *Address:* Guanhua School of Management, Peking University, 1 Loudouqiao, Hai Diau, Beijing 100871, People's Republic of China.

LI YUANCHAO; Chinese politician; b. 1950, Lianshui Co., Jiangsu Prov.; ed. Shanghai Fudan Univ.; joined CCP 1978; Sec. Communist Youth League 1983; Sec. Shanghai Branch of the Communist Youth League 1983; Dir. Nat. Cttee. for Young Pioneer's work under the Communist Youth League 1984; Vice-Chair. Youth Fed. 1986–; Deputy Dir. First Bureau, Information Office 1993–, Cen. Office for Overseas Publicity 1994–; Vice-Minister of Information Office, State Council 1993–96, of Culture 1996–; Vice-Chair. Women and Youth Cttee.; mem. CPPCC 7th Nat. Cttee. 1988–. *Address:* Central Committee, Communist Youth League of China, Beijing; 22 An Yuan Bei Li Asian Games Village, Beijing, People's Republic of China. *Telephone:* 00861-4912919.

LI YUMIN; Chinese business executive; b. May 1930, Dunhua Co., Jilin Prov.; Gen. Man. People's Insurance Corpn. of China 1992–94, Pres. 1994–; mem. 8th CPPCC 1993–94. *Address:* People's Insurance Corporation of China, 22 Xi-jiaomin Xiang Street, Xicheng District, Beijing 100031, People's Republic of China.

LI ZEMIN; Chinese party official; b. 1934, Cangxi Co., Sichuan Prov.; Deputy Sec. Shenyang Mun. CCP Cttee. Liaoning Prov. 1985; Deputy Sec. Liaoning Prov. CCP Cttee. 1985–86; mem. CCP Cen. Cttee. 1987–; Sec. CPC Zhejiang Prov. Cttee. 1988–98; Chair. Standing Cttee. of People's Congress 1993–; mem. 15th CCP Cen. Cttee. 1997–. *Address:* Standing Committee of Zhejiang Provincial People's Congress, Hangzhou, Zhejiang Province, People's Republic of China.

LI ZHAOJI; Chinese administrator and engineer; b. 1934; ed. Shanghai Datong Univ.; Council mem. of Electronics Soc. 1976–; Dir. Communications Eng. Research Inst. 1978–; Vice-Mayor Shanghai Municipality 1983–. *Address:* People's Government of Shanghai Municipality, Shanghai, People's Republic of China.

LI ZHENGWU; Chinese academic; Pres. Soc. of Nuclear Fusion and Plasma 1980–; mem. Nat. Cttee. 7th CPPCC 1988–. *Address:* Chinese Academy of Sciences, 52 San Li He Road, Beijing 100864, People's Republic of China.

LI ZHENGYOU; Chinese politician and agronomist; b. 1936, Sichuan Prov.; ed. Xinan Agric. Inst.; lecturer, Kunming Inst. of Agric. and Forestry 1961, Deputy Dir. of Rice Research Office 1979; Vice-Gov. Yunnan Prov. 1983–. *Address:* Yunnan Provincial People's Government, Kunming City, Yunnan, People's Republic of China.

LI ZHUN; Chinese writer; b. 17 May 1928, Luo Yang, Henan; s. of Li Jun-Ren and Yang Fen; m. Dong Bing; four s. two d.; Cttee. mem., Presidium of Writers' Union of China and of Film Specialists' Union of China 1984–; Vice-Pres. Soc. of Film Literary Inst. 1980–; mem. Presidium Writers' Asscn. 1985–; Vice-Chair., Membership Sec. 5th Nat. Cttee. Chinese Writers' Asscn. 1996; Deputy-Dir. Literature and Art Bureau, Propaganda Dept., CCP Cen. Cttee. 1989–91, Dir. 1991–. *Publications:* five collections of short stories, including The Biography of Li Shuang-Shuang; novels, including The Yellow River Flows to the East (Mao Dun Literature Prize); over 20 film scripts, including The Herdsmen (Hundred Flowers Award) and The Wreath at the Foot of the Mountain (Golden Rooster Award). *Leisure interests:* calligraphy, painting, drama. *Address:* 2-401A, No. 15 Hu Fang Road, Beijing, People's Republic of China. *Telephone:* 336700.

LIANG CHENGYE; Chinese state official; b. April 1924, Chongzuo Co., Guangxi Prov.; s. of Liang Chaoji and Ye Shi; m. Li Pianqun 1949; two s. one d.; CCP local leader, Wuzhou, Beihai, and Nanning cities, Guangxi, before 1978; Deputy to NPC and Mayor of Guilin City 1978; Vice-Chair. Guangxi People's Govt. 1980–84; alt. mem. 12th CPC Cen. Cttee. 1980–84; Adviser to Guangxi People's Govt. 1985–. *Leisure interest:* swimming. *Address:* 1 Minle Road, Nanning, Guangxi, People's Republic of China. *Telephone:* 205648. *Fax:* 209270.

LIANG DONG-CAI (D. C. LIANG); Chinese molecular biophysicist and protein crystallographer; b. 29 May 1932, Guangzhou; Prof., Inst. of Biophysics, Chinese Acad. of Sciences (Dir. 1983–86); mem. Chinese Acad. of Sciences 1980–; Fellow Third World Acad. of Sciences 1985–; Vice-Chair. Nat. Natural Science Foundation of China 1986–95, adviser 1995–; mem. Cttee. on Biomacromolecule Crystallography of Int. Soc. of Crystallography 1981–84; mem. Council of Int. Soc. of Biophysics 1993–; Pres. Chinese Biophysics Soc. 1983–86, 1991–98; Vice-Pres. Chinese Biochemistry Soc. 1987–90. *Address:* Institute of Biophysics, Chinese Academy of Sciences, Beijing 100101, People's Republic of China. *Telephone:* (01) 64888506. *Fax:* (01) 64889867.

LIANG GUANGLIE; Chinese army officer; b. Dec. 1940, Santai Co., Sichuan Prov.; joined PLA 1958; joined CCP 1959; ed. Xinyang Infantry Acad. 1963, PLA Mil. Acad. 1982; Vice-Div. Commdr. and then Div. Commdr. 1979–82; Vice-Army Commdr. then Army Commdr., Vice-Commdr. PLA Beijing Mil. Area Command 1983–97; alt. mem. 13th CCP Cen. Cttee. 1987, 14th CCP Cen. Cttee. 1992; Commdr. PLA Shenyang Mil. Area Command

1997–; mem. 15th CCP Cen. Cttee. 1997. *Address:* Shenyang Military Area Command Headquarters, Shenyang City, Liaoning Province, People's Republic of China.

LIANG LINGGUANG; Chinese politician and government official (retd.); b. 31 Oct. 1916, Yongchun Co., Fujian Prov.; m. Zhu Han-Zhang 1939; two d.; fmr. administrator in Fujian; Minister of Light Industry 1977–80; First Sec. CPC Cttee., Guangzhou Municipality 1980–83; Sec. CCP Cttee. Guangdong Prov. 1980–85; Mayor of Guangzhou 1981–86; Gov. Guangdong Prov. 1983–85; mem. 12th CCP Cen. Cttee. 1982–85; Chair. Hong Kong China Travel Service Group 1986–93; Pres. Jinan Univ. 1983–85; mem. Preparatory Cttee. for 6th Nat. Games 1985–93; Chair. Prov. Advisory Cttee., Guangdong 1985–93, NPC Standing Comm.; mem. 7th NPC 1988–93; Vice-Chair. Overseas Chinese Affairs Cttee. 1988–93; mem. Standing Cttee. 7th NPC 1988–93. *Leisure interest:* Chinese and foreign literature. *Address:* c/o Office of the Governor, Guangdong, People's Republic of China.

LIANG SHOUPAN, M.S.; Chinese rocket engineer; b. 13 April 1916, Fujien; s. of Ching Tung Liang and Yun Jiao Lin; m. He Fu 1942; one s.; ed. Tsinghua Univ., Massachusetts Inst. of Tech., U.S.A.; Deputy Dir. Rocket Research Inst. 1965–81; Deputy Dir. of Science and Tech., Ministry of Astronautics 1982–88; Sr. Technical Adviser, Ministry of Aeronautics and Astronautics Industry 1989–; Chief designer 'Silkworm' and other anti-ship missile projects; mem. Dept. of Tech. Sciences, Academia Sinica 1981–; Hon. Special Prize of Nat. Tech. 1988. *Leisure interests:* Chinese history, novels, Chinese chess. *Address:* Ministry of Aeronautics and Astronautics Industry, P.O. Box 849, Beijing, People's Republic of China. *Telephone:* (01) 68371539. *Fax:* (01) 68370849.

LIANG XIAOSHENG; Chinese writer; b. Sept. 1949, Harbin; worker on land reclamation project; local newspaper reporter; Chinese language student, Fudan Univ. 1975; mem. Chinese Writers' Asscn., Chinese Film-makers' Asscn.; mem. and official of Chinese Film Script-writers' Asscn.; Film Script Ed., Beijing Film Studio. *Publications:* four anthologies of short stories, an anthology of medium-length novels and two novels, most of which have been adapted as films or TV plays; works include: This is a Strange Land, Literary Accomplishments, Blizzard at Midnight (all of which have won All-China Short Novel Prizes), For the Harvest, TV play based on Blizzard at Midnight (awarded All-China TV Playscript Grand Prize). *Address:* Editorial Department, "Creative Cinema", 19 Bei-huan Xilu Street, Beijing, People's Republic of China.

LIAO BINGXIONG; Chinese cartoonist; b. 21 Oct. 1915, Canton; one s. three d.; Vice-Chair. Guangdong branch, Chinese Artists' Asscn. *Exhibitions include:* Spring and Autumn in Cats' Kingdom 1945, A 50 Years' Retrospective 1982. *Publication:* Bingxiong's Cartoons 1932–82. *Address:* RM 302, Block 2, 871 Renmin Road, Guangzhou 510180, People's Republic of China. *Telephone:* 6661480.

LIAO HANSHENG, Lieut.-Gen.; Chinese government official; b. 1911, Sangzhi Co., Hunan Prov.; Political Commissar 6th Div., 2nd Front Army 1934; Political Commissar, Div. 2nd Front, Red Army 1936; Political Comm. 716 Regiment, 120th Div., 8th Route Army; Political Commissar 1st Column, N.W. Liberation Army 1947; Political Commissar 2nd Army Group, CCP Red Army 1949; Chair. Qinghai Mil. & Admin. Cttee. 1949; Political Commissar, Qinghai Mil. Area 1949; Vice-Chair., Qinghai People's Provincial Govt. 1949–56; Deputy Commdr. Qinghai Mil. Area 1950; mem. N.W. Mil. and Admin. Cttee. 1950; mem. N.W. Admin. Cttee. 1953; Deputy Political Commissar N.W. Mil. Area 1954; Deputy for PLA to 1st NPC 1954; mem. Nat. Defence Council 1954; rank of Lieut.-Gen. 1955; Alt. mem. CCP 8th Cen. Cttee. 1956; Pres. Mil. Acad. of PLA 1957; responsible person PLA Units, Nanjing 1957, Beijing 1962; Deputy for Beijing PLA Units to 3rd NPC 1964; mem. Presidium 3rd NPC 1964; Sec. CCP N. China Bureau 1965; detained in Beijing Garrison HQ, 1967; Branded a 3-Anti Element 1967; resumed activities 1972; Vice-Pres. Acad. of Mil. Science 1974; First Political Commissar PLA Nanjing Mil. Region 1978–80, PLA Shenyang Units 1980–85; mem. 12th CCP Cen. Cttee. 1982–85; Vice-Chair. Standing Cttee. 6th Nat. People's Congress 1983–87, 7th 1988–93; Chair. Cen. Patriotic Public Health Campaign Cttee. 1983–; Chair. Foreign Affairs Cttee. 1988; mem. Presidium 6th NPC 1986, 7th NPC 1988; Vice-Chair. 7th NPC 1988; Chair. Credentials Cttee., NPC 1986–; Hon. Pres. Sports Aviation Asscn. 1988–; Adviser Soc. for the Promotion of Chinese Cultural Exchanges and Co-operation 1992–. *Address:* c/o Standing Committee, National People's Congress, Tian An Men Square, Beijing, People's Republic of China.

LIAO HUI; Chinese government official; b. 1941, Huiyang Co., Guangdong Prov.; s. of late Liao Chengzhi and Jing Puchum; joined CCP 1965; mem. 12th CCP Cen. Cttee. 1985, 13th CCP Cen. Cttee. 1987–92, 14th CCP Cen. Cttee. 1992–97, 15th CCP Cen. Cttee. 1997–; Dir. Overseas Chinese Affairs Office, State Council 1984–; Dir. Hong Kong and Macau Affairs Office 1997–; mem. 21st Century Comm. for China-Japan Friendship 1985–; Hon. Vice-Chair. Zhonghai Inst. of Agricultural Tech. 1987–. *Address:* c/o State Council, Zhong Nan Hai, Beijing, People's Republic of China.

LIAO SHANTAO, PH.D.; Chinese professor of mathematics; b. 4 Jan. 1920, Hunan Prov.; m. Wang Hongyi 1943; three s.; ed. South-West United Univ., Univ. of Chicago; Prof. of Math., Beijing Univ. 1961–; Nat. Scientific Prize of China 1982; TWAS Award in Math. 1986. *Address:* Department of Mathematics, Beijing University, Beijing, People's Republic of China. *Telephone:* (01) 2552471.

LIAO XILONG, Lieut.-Gen.; Chinese army officer; b. June 1940, Sinan Co., Guizhou Prov.; joined PLA 1959, CCP 1963; served as Platoon Commdr. 1966–67, Co. Commdr. 1969–71, Deputy Chief of a regt. combat training section 1971–73, Deputy Chief of a div. mil. affairs section 1973–78, Deputy Regt. Commdr. 1978–79, Regt. Commdr. 1979–80, Deputy Div. Commdr. 1981–83, Div. Commdr. 1983, Corps Commdr. 1984–85, Deputy Commdr. Chengdu Mil. Region 1985–95, Commdr. 1995–. *Address:* Chengdu Military Region, Sichuan Province, People's Republic of China.

LIBAI, David, LL.D.; Israeli politician and lawyer; b. 1934, Tel Aviv; ed. Chicago Univ.; Head Israel Bar Asscn.; Deputy Attorney-Gen.; Dir. Inst. of Criminology and Criminal Law, Tel Aviv Univ., Dean of Students; Chair. Labour Party Constitution Cttee.; Chair. Israel-Britain Parl. Friendship Asscn.; Chair. Public Audit (Control) Cttee. 1984–92; Spokesman Ministry of Justice, Minister of Justice 1992–96; fmr. mem. Nat. Comm. of Inquiry on Prison Conditions, Press Council, Knesset 1984–, served on various cttees.; Labour. *Publications:* numerous articles on legal issues. *Address:* Knesset, Jerusalem, Israel.

LIBANIO CHRISTO, Carlos Alberto (Frei Betto); Brazilian Dominican brother and writer; b. 25 Aug. 1944, Belo Horizonte; s. of Antônio Carlos Vieira Christo and Maria Stella Libanio Christo; ed. Univ. of Brazil, Escola Dominicana de Teologia and Seminário São Leopoldo; Nat. leader, Catholic Young Students 1962–64; political prisoner 1964; newspaper and magazine ed. 1966–69; political prisoner 1969–73; organizer of basic Church communities 1973–79; teacher, popular educ. 1977–; writer and teacher with Workers' Pastoral 1979–; Dir. América Libre (magazine) 1993–; mem. Council Swedish Foundation for Human Rights 1991–96; Consultant, Movimento dos Trabalhadores Rurais Sem Terra (MST); mem. Inst. for Critical Research, Amsterdam; Intellectual of the Year Prize, Brazilian Writers' Union 1986, Human Rights Prize, Bruno Kreisky Foundation, Vienna 1987, Paolo E. Borsellino Award (Italy) for work in human rights 1998. *Publications include:* Batismo de Sangue (Jabuti Prize, Brazilian Book Asscn., 1985); Oração na Ação, Letters from a Prisoner of Conscience, Les Frères de Tito, Against Principalities and Powers, Fidel and Religion, Fome de Pão e de Beleza 1990, A Menina e o Elefante 1990, Uala, o Amor 1991, Alucinado Som de Tuba 1992, O Paraíso Perdido-Nos bastidores do socialismo 1993, A Obra do Artista-Uma Visão Holística do Universo 1995, Comer como um frade . . . O Vencedor, Entre todos os homens, Cotidiano e Mistério, O Vencedor, Talita abre a porta dos Evangelhos, A noite em que Jesus nasceu (Best Young Readers' Book, Art Critics Asscn. of S. Paulo 1998). *Leisure interests:* cooking, swimming. *Address:* Rua Atibaia 420, 01235-010 São Paulo, S.P., Brazil. *Telephone:* (011) 864-0844; (011) 38651473. *Fax:* (011) 38656941.

LIBERADZKI, Bogusław Marian, Polish politician and economist; b. 12 Sept. 1948, Sochaczew; m.; two s.; ed. Main School of Planning and Statistics, Warsaw and Univ. of Illinois; Scientific worker, Main School of Planning and Statistics 1970–87; Dir. Transport Econs. Research Centre, Warsaw 1986–89; Deputy Minister of Transport 1989–93; fmr. mem. Transport Comm. Polish Acad. of Science, European Rail Congress Council, Brussels; Chair. Supervisory Bd. Polish LOT Airways –1993; Minister of Transport and Maritime Economy 1993–97; Deputy to Sejm (Parl.) 1997–; mem. Democratic Left Alliance (SLD) Parl. Club. *Address:* Sejm RP, ul. Wiejska 4/6/8, 00-902 Warsaw, Poland. *Telephone:* (22) 694-25-00.

LIBERAKI, Margarita; Greek novelist and dramatist; b. 1919, Athens; d. of Themistuclis and Sapho Liberaki; m. Georges Karapanos 1941 (divorced); one d.; ed. Athens Univ.; lives in Paris and Greece, writes in Greek and French; plays performed at Festival d'Avignon, Festival of Athens, Nat. Theatre, Athens. *Publications:* The Trees 1947, The Straw Hats 1950, Trois étés 1950, The Other Alexander 1952, The Mystery 1976; plays: Kandaules' Wife 1955, The Danaids 1956, L'autre Alexandre 1957, Le saint prince 1959, La lune a faim 1961, Sparagmos 1965, Le bain de mer 1967, Erotica 1970, Zoe 1985; film scripts: Magic City 1953, Phaedra 1961, Three Summers (TV series) 1996. *Leisure interest:* painting. *Address:* 7 rue de L'Eperon, 75006 Paris, France; 2 Strat. Sindesmou, 106 73 Athens, Greece. *Telephone:* (1) 46-33-05-92 (Paris).

LIBERIA-PETERS, Maria; Netherlands Antilles politician; m.; leader Nat. Volkspartij (Nat. People's Party); Prime Minister of Netherlands Antilles 1984–85, 1988–93. *Address:* c/o Partido Nashonal di Pueblo, Willemstad, Curaçao, Netherlands Antilles.

LIBERMAN, Alexander; American publisher; b. 4 Sept. 1912, Kiev, Russia; s. of Simon Liberman and Henriette (Pascar) Liberman; m. 1st Tatiana Yacovleff du Plessix 1942 (died 1991); one step-d.; m. 2nd Melinda Pechangco 1992; ed. Ecole des Roches, France, Ecole des Beaux Arts, Paris; Art Dir., Man. Dir. VU, Paris 1931–36; joined Vogue Magazine, Condé Nast Publs., New York 1941, Art Dir. 1943–62, Editorial Dir. Condé Nast Publs. 1962–94; Deputy Chair. (Editorial) 1994–; Henry Johnson Fisher Award 1995; Chevalier Légion d'honneur. *Publications:* The Artist in his Studio 1960, 1988, Greece, Gods and Art 1968, Marlene: An Intimate Photographic Memoir 1992, Campidoglio: Michelangelo's Roman Capitol 1994, Alexander Liberman Photographs 1925–1995 1995, Prayers in Stone 1997. *Address:* Condé Nast Publications Inc., 350 Madison Avenue, New York, NY 10017 (Office); Andre Emmerich Gallery, 41 East 57th Street, New York, NY 10022, U.S.A.

LIBESKIND, Daniel; American architect; b. 1946, Poland; ed. Cooper Union for the Advancement of Science and Art, New York, Univ. of Essex;

fmr. Head Dept. of Architecture Cranbrook Acad. of Art; fmr. Sr. Scholar John Paul Getty Centre; fmr. Visiting Prof. Harvard Univ.; fmr. Bannister Fletcher Prof. Univ. of London; fmr. holder Davenport Chair Yale Univ.; architectural practice Berlin 1989–; projects include extension to Berlin Museum with Jewish Museum, Ouzu Mountain Observatory, Japan, Musicon: Philharmonic Hall, Bremen, Germany, extension to Victoria & Albert Museum, London, Polderland Garden, Almere, Netherlands, Landsberger Allee, Berlin. *Publication:* Radix–Matrix: Architecture and Writings 1997.

LICHFIELD, 5th Earl of, cr. 1831; **Thomas Patrick John Anson,** F.R.P.S.; British photographer; b. 25 April 1939; s. of the late Viscount Anson and Princess Anne of Denmark; m. Lady Leonora Grosvenor 1975 (divorced 1986); one s. two d.; ed. Harrow School, Sandhurst; army service, Grenadier Guards 1957–62; now works as photographer; Fellow British Inst. of Professional Photographers, Fellow Royal Photographic Soc.; Hon. D.L. (Stafford) 1996. *Publications:* The Most Beautiful Women 1981, Lichfield on Photography 1981, A Royal Album 1982, Patrick Lichfield's Unipart Calendar Book 1982, Patrick Lichfield Creating the Unipart Calendar 1983, Hot Foot to Zabriskie Point 1985, Lichfield on Travel Photography 1986, Not the Whole Truth (autobiog.) 1986, Lichfield in Retrospect 1988, Queen Mother: the Lichfield Selection 1990, Elizabeth R.: a photographic celebration of 40 years 1991. *Address:* Shugborough Hall, Stafford; Lichfield Studios, 133 Oxford Gardens, London, W10 6NE, England (Studio). *Telephone:* (01889) 881-454 (Stafford); 0181-969 6161 (London). *Fax:* 0181-960 6994 (London).

LICHNEROWICZ, André, D. ÈS SC.; French mathematician; b. 21 Jan. 1915, Bourbon; s. of Jean Lichnerowicz and Antoinette Gressin; m. Suzanne Magdelain 1942; three s.; ed. Lycée Louis-le-Grand, Paris, Ecole Normale Supérieure, Paris, and Univ. de Paris; research assignments, Centre National de Recherche Scientifique 1938–41; mem. staff, Univ. of Strasbourg 1941–46, Full Prof. 1946–49; Full Prof. Univ. de Paris 1949–52, Prof. of Math. Physics, Collège de France 1952–; mem. Acad. des Sciences, Accad. Naz. dei Lincei, Rome, Acad. Real de Ciencias, Madrid, Acad. Royale de Belgique, Pontifical Acad. of Sciences; Dr. h.c. (Waterloo) 1977, (Liège) 1982, (Coimbra) 1984; Médaille Copernic de l'Acad. Polonaise des Sciences 1973; Prix int. Fubini 1955; Commdr. Légion d'honneur; Grand Officier Ordre nat. du Mérite, Commdr. Ordre des Palmes académiques. *Publications:* Algèbre et analyse linéaire 1946, Eléments de calcul tensoriel 1949, Théories relativistes de la gravitation 1954, Théorie globale des connexions 1955, Géométrie des groupes de transformation 1958, Relativistic hydrodynamics and magnetohydrodynamics 1967, Waves and Shock Waves on a Curved Space-Time 1994. *Leisure interests:* philosophy, gardening, tennis. *Address:* 6 avenue Paul Appell, 75014 Paris, France. *Telephone:* (01) 45-40-51-66.

LICK, Dale Wesley, PH.D.; American professor of educational leadership; b. 7 Jan. 1938, Marlette, Mich.; s. of John R. Lick and Florence May (Baxter) Lick; m. Marilyn Kay Foster 1956; one s. three d.; ed. Michigan State Univ., Univ. of California, Riverside; Instructor and Chair. Dept. of Math., Port Huron Jr. Coll. (later St. Clair Co. Community Coll.), Port Huron, Mich. 1959–60; Asst. to Comptroller, Line and Staff Man., Michigan Bell Telephone Co., Detroit, Mich. 1961; Instructor of Math., Univ. of Redlands, Calif. 1961–63; Teaching Asst. in Math., Univ. of Calif., Riverside, Calif., 1964–65; Asst. Prof. of Math., Univ. of Tenn. 1965–67, Assoc. Prof. 1968–69; textbook and manuscript reviewer for several publrs. 1966–; Visiting Research Mathematician, Applied Math. Dept., Brookhaven Nat. Lab., Upton, New York 1967–68; Consultant, Computing Tech. Center, Union Carbide Corpn., Oak Ridge, Tenn., under auspices of U.S. Atomic Energy Comm. 1966–71; Adjunct Assoc. Prof., Dept. of Pharmacology (Biomathematics), Temple Medical School, Temple Univ. 1969–72; Head and Assoc. Prof., Dept. of Math., Drexel Univ., Philadelphia, Pa. 1969–72; Vice-Pres. for Academic Affairs, Russell Sage Coll., Troy, New York 1972–74; Dean, School of Sciences and Health Professions, and Prof. of Math. and Computing Sciences, Old Dominion Univ., Norfolk, Va. 1974–78; Pres. and Prof. of Math. and Computer Sciences, Georgia Southern Coll, Statesboro, Ga. 1978–86; Pres. Univ. and Prof. of Math., Univ. of Maine 1986–91, Fla. State Univ., Tallahassee 1991–93; Univ. Prof., Fla. State Univ. 1993–; mem. American Asscn. of Univ. Admins., American Asscn. of Univ. Profs., American Math. Soc., Math. Asscn. of America. *Publications:* Fundamentals of Algebra 1970, Whole-Faculty Study Groups: A Powerful Way to Change School and Enhance Learning (jtly.) 1998, New Directions in Mentoring: Creating a Culture of Synergy (jtly.) 1999; numerous book chapters, and papers and articles in learned journals. *Leisure interests:* sports, reading, writing, the arts, church work. *Address:* C-3508 University Center, Florida State University, Tallahassee, FL 32306-2540, U.S.A. *Telephone:* (850) 644-0013. *Fax:* (850) 644-4952.

LIDMAN, Sara; Swedish writer; b. 30 Dec. 1923; d. of Andreas and Jenny (née Lundman) Lidman; ed. Uppsala Univ.; first four books deal with life in sparsely populated N. Sweden; in S. Africa 1960, in Kenya 1962–64, in N. Viet Nam 1965. *Publications include:* Tjärdalen 1953, Hjortronlandet 1955, Aina 1956, Regnspiran 1958, Bära mistel 1960, Jag o min son 1961, Med fem diamanter 1964, Samtal i Hanoi 1966, Gruva 1968, Vänner o uvänner 1969, Marta, Marta 1970, Fåglarna i Nam Dinh 1973, Libretto till två baletter, Inga träd skall väcka dig 1974, Balansen 1975, Din tjänare hör 1977.

LIEBENBERG, Christo Ferro, M.P.A., P.M.D.; South African politician and retd. banker; b. 2 Oct. 1934, Touwsriver; s. of Christiaan Liebenberg and Helene Griessel; m. Elly Liebenberg 1959; two s.; ed. Worcester Boys' High School, Harvard Univ., INSEAD and Cranfield; joined Nedbank, Cape Town 1952; Man. Dir. Nedbank, Johannesburg 1988–90; C.E.O. Nedcor 1990–94; fmr. Chair. Credit Guarantee Insurance Corpn. of Africa Ltd., Syfrets Ltd., Cape Town; fmr. Deputy Chair. NedPerm Bank; Pres. Inst. of Bankers in S. Africa 1991; Minister of Finance 1994–96; Dir. various financial insts. *Leisure interests:* music, photography, theatre, ballet, reading, golf. *Address:* c/o Ministry of Finance, 240 Vermeulen Street, Pretoria 0002, South Africa.

LIEBERMAN, Joseph I., B.A., J.D.; American politician; b. 24 Feb. 1942, Stamford, Conn.; s. of Henry and Marcia (née Manger) Lieberman; m. Hadassah Freilich 1983; two s. two d.; ed. Yale Univ.; called to Bar, Conn. 1967; mem. Conn. Senate 1971–81, Senate Majority Leader 1975–81; Partner Lieberman, Segaloff & Wolfson, New Haven 1972–83; Attorney Gen. State of Conn., Hartford 1983–88, Senator for Conn. 1989–; Chair. Democratic Leadership Council; mem. Governmental Affairs Cttee., Small Business Cttee., Trustee Wadsworth Atheneum, Univ. of Bridgeport; Democrat. *Publications:* The Power Broker 1966, The Scorpion and the Tarantula 1970, The Legacy 1981, Child Support in America 1986. *Address:* U.S. Senate, 706 Hart Senate Office Building, Washington, DC 20510, U.S.A.

LIEBERMAN, Seymour, PH.D.; American professor of biochemistry; b. 1 Dec. 1916, New York; s. of Samuel D. Lieberman and Sadie Levin; m. Sandra Spar 1944; one s.; ed. Brooklyn Coll., New York, Univ. of Illinois and Stanford Univ., Calif.; Prof. of Biochemistry, Coll. of Physicians and Surgeons, Columbia Univ. 1962–87, Prof. Emer. 1987–, Assoc. Dean 1984–90, Vice-Provost 1988–89, Assoc. Dir. Office of Science and Tech. 1991–; Program Officer The Ford Foundation 1974–75; Pres. St. Luke's-Roosevelt Inst. for Health Sciences 1981–97; mem. N.A.S. 1977–; Ciba Award 1952, Koch Award 1970, Roussel Prize (France) 1984, Dale Medal 1986, Dist. Service Award (Columbia Univ.) 1991. *Publications:* A Heuristic Proposal for Understanding Steroidogenic Processes 1984, Detection in Bovine Brain of Sulfate Esters of Cholesterol and Sitosterol 1985 and more than 150 other publs. *Leisure interest:* tennis. *Address:* 515 E. 72nd Street, New York, NY 10021, U.S.A.

LIEM SIOE LIONG; Indonesian business executive; b. 1917, Fuqing District, Fujan, S. China; m.; three s. one d.; emigrated to Central Java 1938; began own coffee powder business during World War II, establishing himself as provisions supplier for rebel army fighting for independence from the Dutch; began to build own business empire in late 1940s, now has substantial shareholdings in 192 cos. involved in trade, finance, food, chemicals, pharmaceuticals, textiles; majority shareholder in First Pacific Group (Hong Kong-based banking, trading and property co.); major shareholdings in Bank Cen. Asia (Indonesia's largest pvt. bank), Indocement and Bogasari Flour Mills. *Address:* PT Perkasa Indonesia Cement Enterprise, Level 13, Wisma Indocement Kav. 70–71, Jalan Jenderal Sudirman, Jakarta, Indonesia.

LIEN CHAN, M.SC., PH.D.; Taiwanese politician; b. 27 Aug. 1936, Sian, Shansi; s. of Chen Tung Lien and Chao Lan-Kun Lien; m. Yui Fang; two s. two d.; ed. Nat. Taiwan Univ. and Univ. of Chicago; Assoc. Prof. Nat. Taiwan Univ. 1968–69, Prof. and Chair. Dept. of Political Science and Dir. Graduate Inst. of Political Science 1969–75; Amb. to El Salvador 1975–76; Dir. Dept. of Youth Affairs, Cen. Cttee. Kuomintang 1976–78; Deputy Sec.-Gen. Cen. Cttee. Kuomintang 1978, mem. Cen. Standing Cttee. 1983–; Chair. Nat. Youth Comm., Exec. Yuan 1978–81; Minister of Communications 1981–87; Vice-Premier 1987–88; Minister of Foreign Affairs 1989–90; Gov. Taiwan Provincial Govt. 1990–93; Premier of Taiwan 1993–97; Vice-Pres. of Taiwan 1997–; Pres. The Chinese Asscn. of Political Science 1979–82. *Publications:* The Foundation of Democracy, Taiwan in China's External Relations, Western Political Thought. *Leisure interests:* golf, swimming, music. *Address:* c/o Office of the President, Chiehshou Hall, 122 Chungking South Road, Sector 1, Taipei 100, Taiwan.

LIENDO, Maj.-Gen. Horacio Tomás; Argentinian politician and army officer; b. 17 Dec. 1924, Córdoba; ed. Mil. Coll.; first post with 4th Bn., Communications; with 6th Motorized Bn., Communications; as Capt., entered Army War Coll. 1954, later Gen. Staff Officer; served in Communications Inspection, Army Gen. Staff, and, as Second-in-Command, 4th Bn., Communications; rank of Major 1959; 61st Communications Command; under orders of Mil. Attaché, U.S.A. 1962; rank of Lieut.-Col. 1965, Col. 1970, Gen. 1980; Minister of Labour 1976–79; Chief of Staff, Armed Forces 1979–81; Minister of the Interior March-Nov. 1981; Pres. of Argentina (a.i.) Nov.–Dec. 1981.

LIEPA, Andris; Russian/Latvian ballet dancer and choreographer; b. 6 Jan. 1962, Moscow; s. of the late Marius Liepa and of Margarita Zhigunova; ed. Moscow Choreographic School of Bolshoi Theatre; with Bolshoi Ballet 1980–87; prize-winner int. competitions Moscow 1985, Jackson, U.S.A. (Grand Prix) 1986; lived in the West 1987–; appeared with New York City Ballet, subsequently with American Ballet Theater; danced in Raymonda Variations, Swan Lake (Baryshnikov), Romeo and Juliet (Macmillan), Violin Concerto (Balanchine); worked with Nina Ananiashvili, Carla Fracci and other partners; choreographer 1993–; has adapted Fokine ballets for film, including Return to the Firebird; guest artist with Kirov (now Mariinsky) Ballet, London tour 1990; works in U.S.A., Russia and Latvia. *Address:* Bryusov per. 17, Apt. 12, 103009 Moscow, Russia. *Telephone:* 229-2388.

LIEPA, Ilza; Russian/Latvian ballerina; b. 22 Nov. 1963; d. of Maris Liepa; m. Sergey Valentinovich Stadler (divorced); ed. Moscow Choreographic School of Bolshoi Theatre; with Bolshoi ballet 1982–; danced on various stages of Europe and America performing parts of classic repertoire, including Legend about Love, Romeo and Juliet, Firebird, Don Quixote, Corsair, Raimonda, Prince Igor; début in England concert Stars of World Ballet, Covent Garden (Firebird), tours with Bolshoi Theatre in most countries of Europe and America, independently toured in Argentina, Greece, Taiwan, Japan; Artistic Dir. Golden Age Asscn. 1994–; Prize of Russian Trade Unions. *Address:* Bryusov per. 17, Apt. 12, 103009 Moscow, Russia. *Telephone:* 229-2388.

LIEQUE; Chinese politician; b. Oct. 1944, Gyangze, Tibet; joined CCP 1972; Sec. CCP Lhasa City Cttee. 1991–98; Chair. Tibetan Autonomous Region 1998–; mem. CCP 15th Cen. Cttee. 1997–. *Address:* People's Government of Tibetan Autonomous Region, Lhasa, Tibet, People's Republic of China.

LIESEN, Klaus, DR. JUR.; German business executive; b. 15 April 1931; fmr. Chair. Exec. Bd. Ruhrgas AG, Chair. Supervisory Bd. 1996–; Chair. Supervisory Bd. Volkswagen AG; other directorships in steel, energy, banking and insurance cos.; Dr. rer. pol. h.c. *Address:* Ruhrgas AG, Huttropstrasse 60, 45138 Essen, Germany. *Telephone:* 20118400.

LIESNER, Hans Hubertus, C.B., M.A.; British civil servant and economist; b. 30 March 1929, Naumburg, Germany; s. of Curt Liesner and Edith Liesner (née Neumann); m. Thelma Seward 1968; one s. one d.; ed. Univ. of Bristol, Nuffield Coll., Oxford; Asst. Lecturer, later Lecturer in Econs., London School of Econs. and Political Science 1955–59; Lecturer in Econs., Univ. of Cambridge, Fellow, Dir. of Studies in Econs., also Asst. Bursar of Emmanuel Coll. 1959–70; Under-Sec. (Econ.), H.M. Treasury 1970–76; Chief Econ. Adviser, Dept. of Trade and Industry (fmrly. Depts. of Trade, Industry and Prices and Consumer Protection) 1976–89; Deputy Chair. Monopolies and Mergers Comm. 1989–95, mem. 1995–97; Chair. Advisory Group, ESRC Centre for Econ. Learning and Social Evolution 1996–; standing mem. Advisory Body on Fair Trading in Telecommunications 1997–. *Publications:* The Import Dependence of Britain and Western Germany 1957, Case Studies in European Economic Union: the Mechanics of Integration (with J. E. Meade and S. J. Wells) 1962, Atlantic Harmonisation: Making Free Trade Work 1968, Britain and the Common Market: the effect of entry on the pattern of manufacturing production (with S. S. Han) 1971. *Leisure interests:* skiing, video recording, gardening, walking. *Address:* 32 The Grove, Brookmans Park, Herts, AL9 7RN, England. *Telephone:* (01707) 653269.

LIFVON GUO; Taiwanese singer; m.; cowherd aged ten; performs folk songs and folk chants mixed with modern dance beats; with wife and some 30 indigenous singers toured Switzerland, France, Germany, Netherlands and Italy 1987; albums include Return to Innocence (more than 5 million copies sold) and Cross of Changes. *Address:* Taitung, Taiwan.

LIGACHEV, Yegor Kuzmich; Russian politician (retd.); b. 29 Sept. 1920; m.; one s.; ed. Moscow Inst. of Aviation and CPSU Higher Party School; Engineer 1943–49; joined CPSU 1944; Party and Local Govt. Official Novosibirsk 1949–55; Vice-Chair. Novosibirsk Regional Soviet of Working People's Deputies 1955–58; Sec. Novosibirsk Regional Cttee. CPSU 1959–61, mem. Cen. Cttee. CPSU 1961–65; First Sec. Tomsk Regional Cttee. CPSU 1965–83; Cand. mem. Cen. Cttee. CPSU 1966–76, mem. 1976–90, mem. Politburo 1985–90; Deputy to Supreme Soviet 1966–89; Sec. Cen. Cttee. in Charge of Personnel and Ideology 1983–88; in Charge of Agric. 1988–90; People's Deputy of the U.S.S.R. 1989–91; active in Russian nat. and communist movt.; Vice-Chair. Union of Communist Parties of fmr. U.S.S.R. 1995–. *Publication:* Inside Gorbachev's Kremlin 1993. *Address:* Communist Party of Russia, Bolshoy Zlatoustinsky per. 8/7, 101000 Moscow, Russia. *Telephone:* 206-87-89.

LIGETI, György Sándor; Austrian composer; b. 28 May 1923, Dicsöszentmárton, Hungary; s. of Dr. Sándor Ligeti and Dr. Ilona Somogyi; m. Dr. Vera Spitz 1957; one s.; ed. Budapest Acad. of Music; studied with Ferenc Farkas and Sándor Veress, Budapest Acad. of Music; taught Budapest Acad. of Music 1950–56; left Hungary 1956; Guest Prof., Stockholm Acad. of Music 1961–71; Composer-in-Residence, Stanford Univ., Calif. 1972; worked in Electronic Studios, Cologne, Fed. Repub. of Germany; active in music composition, Cologne, Vienna, Stockholm, Berlin and Darmstadt; Prof. of Composition, Hamburg Music Acad. 1973–89; mem. Swedish Royal Acad. of Music 1964, Acad. of Arts, Berlin 1968, Free Acad. of Arts, Hamburg 1972, Bavarian Acad. of Fine Arts, Munich 1978, American Acad. and Inst. of Arts and Letters 1984; Orden pour le mérite, Bonn 1975, Grawemeyer Award 1986; Commdr., Ordre Nat. des Arts et Lettres, France 1988; Praemium Imperiale Prize (Japan) 1991, Balzan Award 1991; shared Wolf Prize 1996. *Works include:* Artikulation (tape piece) 1958, Apparitions (orchestral) 1958–59, Atmosphères (orchestral) 1960, Volumina (organ) 1961–62, Poème Symphonique for 100 metronomes 1962, Aventures for three singers and seven instrumentalists 1962, Requiem for soprano, mezzo-soprano, two choirs and orchestra 1963–65, Lux Aeterna for 16-part chorus 1966, Concerto for 'cello and orchestra 1966, Lontano (orchestral) 1967, Continuum (harpsichord), Ten pieces for wind quintet 1968, Ramifications for string orchestra or 12 solo strings 1968–69, String Quartet No. 2 1968, Melodien (orchestral) 1971, Monument, Selfportrait, Movement (for two pianos) 1976, Le Grand Macabre (opera) 1974–77, Trio (violin, horn, piano) 1982, 3 Phantasien nach Hölderlin (chorus) 1982, Hungarian Etudes (chorus) 1983, 9 Piano Etudes 1985–89, Piano Concerto 1985–88, Nonsense Madrigals for 6 Singers 1988, Violin Concerto 1991, Viola Sonata 1996. *Address:* Himmelhofgasse 34, 1130 Vienna, Austria; Mövenstrasse 3, D-2000 Hamburg 60, Germany.

LIGGINS, Sir Graham Collingwood, Kt., C.B.E., M.B., CH.B., PH.D., F.R.S., F.R.C.S.(E.), F.R.A.C.S.; New Zealand professor of obstetrics and gynaecology; b. 24 June 1926, Thames; s. of James Bull Liggins and Isabella Graham Liggins (née Mandeno); m. Cecilia Ward 1954; two s. two d.; ed. Auckland Grammar School and Univs. of Auckland and Otago; Registrar in Obstetrics, Gen. Hosp., Newcastle upon Tyne, England 1954–58; Consultant Obstetrician and Gynaecologist, Nat. Women's Hosp., Auckland, N.Z. 1960–86; Prof. (fmrly. Assoc. Prof.) of Obstetrics and Gynaecology, Univ. of Auckland 1968–86, Prof. Emer. 1986–, Dir. Research Centre in Reproductive Medicine; mem. Royal Coll. of Gynaecologists, London; Fellow Royal N.Z. Coll. of Gynaecologists; Hon. M.D. (Lund) 1983, Hon. D.Sc. (Edin.); Hector Medal, Royal Soc. of N.Z. 1980. *Publications:* 200 papers. *Leisure interests:* sailing, fishing, forestry. *Address:* University of Auckland, Private Bag, Auckland 1 (Office); 3/38 Awatea Road, Auckland 1, New Zealand (Home). *Telephone:* (09) 630-9856 (Office); (09) 377-5127 (Home). *Fax:* (09) 630-9858 (Office).

LIIKANEN, Erkki Antero, M. POL. SC.; Finnish politician; b. 19 Sept. 1950, Mikkeli; m. Hanna-Liisa Issakainen 1971; mem. Parl. 1972–; Minister of Finance 1987–90; mem. Social Democratic Party (SDP) Cttee. 1978–, Gen. Sec. 1981–87; Amb. to EU 1990–95; EC Commr. for Budget, Personnel and Admin. 1995–. *Address:* Commissioner for Budget, Personnel and Administration, avenue d'Auderghem 45, B-1040 Brussels, Belgium.

LIKHACHEV, Dmitriy Sergeyevich, D.SC.; Russian professor of literature; b. 28 Nov. 1906, St. Petersburg; s. of Sergey Likhachev and Vera Likhacheva; m. Zinaida Makarova 1936; two d.; ed. Leningrad State Univ.; in concentration camps 1928–32; ed. in a publishing house 1932–38; Assoc. Inst. of Russian Literature (Pushkin House) of U.S.S.R. (now Russian) Acad. of Sciences 1938–, Head of Section of Early Russian Literature 1954–, mem., Acad. of Sciences 1970–, mem. Acad. of Sciences Council for Russian Cultural Problems 1987–; lecturer, Kazan State Univ. 1942–43; Prof. Leningrad State Univ. 1946–53; Pres. Soviet (now Russian) Cultural Fund 1986–93; mem. Directorate, Int. Foundation of Human Survival 1988–; U.S.S.R. People's Deputy 1989–91; Hon. mem. Bulgarian Acad. of Sciences, Hungarian Acad. of Sciences, Serbian Acad. of Sciences and Arts, Accad. dei Lincei (Italy); corresp. foreign mem. Austrian Acad. of Sciences; corresp. mem. British Acad., Göttingen Acad. (Germany), American Acad. of Arts and Sciences; mem. Philosophical Soc. of U.S.A.; Dr. h.c. (Oxford, Edinburgh, Budapest, Sofia, Toruń, Siena, Karlov, Zürich and St. Petersburg Hum. Univs.); State Prize 1952, 1969, 1993. *Publications include:* National Self-Awareness in Ancient Russia 1945, The Culture of Old Russia at the Time of the Formation of the Centralised State 1946, Russian Chronicles 1947, The Image of Man in the Literature of Old Russia 1958; The Culture of the Russian People from the 10th to the 17th Centuries 1961, Russian Culture of the Time of Andrei Rublev 1962, Textology 1962, The Poetics of Old Russian Literature 1967, The Artistic Heritage of Old Russia 1971, The Evolution of Russian Literature from the 10th to the 17th Centuries 1973, A Great Heritage: The Classical Works of Old Russian Literature 1975, The 'Laughing World' of Old Russia 1976, Russische Literatur und europäische Kultur des 10-17 Jahrhunderts 1977, The Slovo and the Culture of the Time 1978, Studies on Russian Literature 1981, The Garden Party 1982, Selected Works (3 vols.) 1987, Poétique historique de la Littérature russe (Xe-XXe siècle) 1988, Notes and Reflections: from the Notebooks of Bygone Days 1989, Reflections on Russia 1991, Le radici dell'arte: Russia dal Medioevo alle Avanguardié 1991, Russian Art from Ancient Times to Vanguard 1992. *Leisure interests:* Problems of town-buildings (theory) and the history of Petersburg-Leningrad. *Address:* Russian Academy of Sciences, Institute of Russian Literature, 4 Makarov Embankment, St. Petersburg V-34 (Office); 34 Prospekt Shvernika, Apartment 16, 194021 St. Petersburg, Russia (Home). *Telephone:* (812) 218-12-74 (Office). *Fax:* (812) 218-12-74.

LIKHACHEV, Vasily Nikolayevich, D.JUR.; Russian politician; b. 5 Jan. 1952, Gorky; s. of Nina F. Likhacheva; m. Nailya Imatovna Taktasheva; two d.; ed. Kazan State Univ.; asst., then docent Chair of State Law, Kazan State Univ. 1978–82, 1983–87; teacher Nat. School of Law Guinea-Bissau 1982–83; Prof. Univ. of Madagascar 1987–88; Head Div. of State Law Tatar Regional CPSU Cttee. 1988–90; Chair. Cttee. of Constitutional Control Tatar S.S.R. 1990–91; elected Vice-Pres. Repub. of Tatarstan 1991–95, Chair. State Council of Tatarstan 1995–; Deputy Chair. Council of Fed. of Russian Parl. 1996–98; Amb. and Perm. Rep. of Russian Fed. to EU 1998–. *Leisure interests:* music, art, sailing. *Address:* Av. Louis Lepoutre 56, 1050 Brussels, Belgium. *Telephone:* (32) 343-03-39. *Fax:* (32) 346-24-53.

LILIĆ, Zoran; Yugoslav politician; b. 27 Aug. 1953, Brza Palanka, Serbia; s. of Sokol Lilić and Dobrila Lilić; m. Ljubica Brković-Lilić 1980; one s.; ed. Belgrade Univ.; several posts as grad. engineer, then man., with state-owned Rekord enterprise, Belgrade; fmr. Pres. Exec. Bd. Yugoslav Tyre Makers Business Asscn., mem. Presidency of Belgrade Chamber of Economy, Pres. Man. Bd. of Belgrade Airport, mem. Council of Faculty of Tech.; mem. Serbian League of Communists, subsequently Socialist Party of Serbia (SPS); Deputy to Nat. Ass. of Repub. of Serbia 1990, Chair. Cttee. on Industry, Energy, Mining and Construction, Chief of Group of SPS Deputies; re-elected Deputy and also Pres. of Nat. Ass. 1992; Pres. of Fed. Repub. of Yugoslavia 1993–97; Vice-Prime Minister of Yugoslavia 1997–; Vice-Pres. SPS 1995–. *Leisure interests:* fishing, football, chess. *Address:* Office of the Federal Government, Lenjina 2, 11070 Belgrade, Yugoslavia. *Telephone:* (11) 334-281.

LILL, John Richard, O.B.E., F.R.C.M.; British pianist; b. 17 March 1944, London; s. of George Lill and the late Margery (née Young) Lill; ed. Leyton County High School and Royal Coll. of Music; London début at Royal Festival Hall 1962; plays regularly in European capitals, the U.S.A. and the Far East, as recitalist and as soloist with most prin. orchestras; recognized as leading interpreter of Beethoven; Prof., Royal Coll. of Music; Fellow, Trinity Coll. of Music, London, London Coll. of Music; Hon. D.Sc. (Univ. of Aston), Hon. D.Mus. (Exeter Univ.); numerous prizes include First Prize, Int. Tchaikovsky Competition, Moscow 1970; recordings include complete Beethoven piano sonatas and concertos, complete piano music of Rachmaninov, Brahms piano concertos and Prokofiev sonatas. *Leisure interests:* chess, amateur radio, walking. *Address:* c/o Harold Holt Ltd., 31 Sinclair Road, London, W14 0NS, England. *Telephone:* 0171-603 4600.

LILLEE, Dennis Keith, M.B.E.; Australian cricketer; b. 18 July 1949, Perth; m. Helen Lillee 1970; two s.; ed. Belmay State School, Belmont High School; right-arm fast bowler, lower order right-hand batsman; played for W.A. 1969–84, Tasmania 1987–88, Northants 1988; 70 tests for Australia 1970–84, taking then world record 355 wickets (average 23.9), including record 167 wickets in 29 Tests against England; toured England 1972, 1975, 1980, 1981, 1983 (World Cup), took 882 first-class wickets. *Publications:* Back to the Mark 1974, The Art of Fast Bowling 1977, Dennis Lillee's Book of Family Fitness 1980, My Life in Cricket 1982, Over and Out 1984. *Address:* c/o Swan Sport, PO Box 158, Byron Bay, NSW 2481, Australia.

LILLEY, James Roderick, M.A.; American diplomatist; b. 15 Jan. 1928, Tsingtao, China; s. of late Frank W. Lilley and Inez Bush; m. Sally Booth 1954; three s.; ed. Phillips Exeter Acad., Yale Univ. and George Washington Univ.; Adjunct Prof. School of Advanced Int. Studies, Johns Hopkins Univ. 1978–80; Consultant, Hunt Oil, Dallas, Tex. 1979–81; East Asian Dir. Nat. Security Council, White House, Washington, D.C. Jan.–Nov. 1981; Dir. American Inst. in Taiwan, Taipei 1982–84; Consultant, Otis Elevator Co., Farmington, Conn. 1984–85; Deputy Asst. Sec. of State, East Asian and Pacific Affairs, Dept. of State 1985–86; Amb. to Republic of Korea 1986–89, to China 1989–91; Asst. Sec. Defense Dept., Wash. 1991–93; Resident Fellow American Enterprise Inst., Washington 1993–; Distinguished Intelligence Medal. *Publication:* Beyond MFN 1994. *Leisure interests:* swimming, bicycling. *Address:* 11th Floor, 1150 17th Street, N.W., Washington, DC 20036 (Office); 7301 Maple Avenue, Bethesda, MD 20815, U.S.A. (Home)

LILLEY, Rt. Hon. Peter Bruce, M.A.; British politician; b. 23 Aug. 1943, Kent; s. of S. Arnold Lilley and Lillian (Elliot) Lilley; m. Gail Ansell 1979; ed. Dulwich Coll., Clare Coll. Cambridge; Chair. Bow Group 1973; M.P. for St. Albans 1983–97, for Hitchin and Harpenden 1997–; Econ. Sec. to Treasury 1987–89, Financial Sec. 1989–90; Sec. of State for Trade and Industry 1990–92, for Social Security 1992–97; Opposition Front Bench Spokesman for Treasury 1997–98; Deputy Leader of the Opposition 1998–; fmr. Dir. Greenwell Montague (Oil Analysts). *Publications:* The Delusion of Incomes Policy (with Samuel Brittan) 1977, The End of the Keynesian Era 1980, Thatcherism: The Next Generation 1990. *Leisure interest:* France (and most things French). *Address:* House of Commons, London, SW1A 0AA, England.

LILOV, Alexander Vassilev, PH.D.; Bulgarian politician and scientist; b. 31 Aug. 1933, Granichak, Vidin; s. of Vassil Lilov and Kamenka Petrovski; m. Anna Lilova 1962; one s. two d.; ed. Sofia Univ.; leading mem. Young Communist League (YCL) 1951–63; Deputy Head Propaganda Dept., Head Arts and Culture Dept., BCP Cen. Cttee.; mem. BCP Cen. Cttee. 1971–, Sec. 1972–83, 1989–, mem. Politburo 1974–83, 1989–; Dir. Inst. for Contemporary Sciences 1983–90; Chair. Higher Council Bulgarian Socialist Party 1990–91, mem. 1991–; Dir. Inst. for Strategic Investigations 1991–; fmr. mem. State Council; M.P. Nat. Ass. 1990–; corresp. mem. Bulgarian Acad. of Sciences. *Publications:* The Nature of Works of Art 1979, Imagination and Creative Work 1986, Europe: To Be or Not to Be 1988 (co-author), Europe: Dialogue and Co-operation 1989. *Leisure interests:* art, skiing. *Address:* Higher Council of the Bulgarian Socialist Party, P.O. Box 382, 20 Positano Street, Sofia (Office); 12 Veliko Tirnovo Str., 1504 Sofia, Bulgaria (Home). *Telephone:* 87-34-64 (Office); 44-60-33 (Home).

LIM KENG YAIK, Dato' M.B., B.CH.; Malaysian politician; b. 8 April 1939, Tapah, Perak; m. Wong Yoon Chuan; three c.; ed. Queen's Univ., Belfast; Senator 1972–78; Minister with Special Functions 1972–73, of Primary Industries 1986–; mem. State Exec. Council, Perak 1978–86; mem. Parl. 1986–; Pres. Gerakan 1980–. *Address:* Ministry of Primary Industries, 6th-8th Floors, Menara Daya Bumi, Jalan Sultan Hishamuddin, 50654 Kuala Lumpur, Malaysia.

LIM KIM SAN; Singaporean politician; b. 30 Nov. 1916, Singapore; s. of Choon Huat and Wee Geok Khuan Lim; m. Pang Gek Kim 1939; two s. four d.; ed. Anglo-Chinese School, Raffles Coll., Singapore; Dir. United Chinese Bank Ltd., Chair. Batu Pahat Bank Ltd., and Pacific Bank Ltd. 1940–; mem. and Deputy Chair. Public Service Comm., Singapore 1959–63; Chair. Housing Devt. Bd. 1960–63; Deputy Chair. Econ. Devt. Bd. 1961–63; Minister for Nat. Devt. 1963–65, for Finance 1965–67, for the Interior and Defence 1967–70, for Educ. 1970–72, for the Environment 1972–75, 1979–81, of Nat. Devt. 1975–79, for Communications 1975–78; Acting Pres. March 1989; Chair. Council of Presidential Advisers 1992–; Chair. Port of Singapore Authority 1979–94; Chair. Public Utilities Bd. 1971–78, Bd. Trustees, Consumers' Co-operative Ltd. 1973; Man. Dir. Monetary Authority of Singapore 1981–82; mem. of Dewan Ra'ayat; Exec. Chair. Singapore Press Holdings Ltd. 1988–; Chair. Times Publication Ltd.; Darjah Utama Temasek (Order of Temasek) 1962, Ramon Magsaysay Award for community leadership 1965 and others. *Leisure interest:* golf. *Address:* Singapore Press Holdings Ltd., News Centre, 82 Genting Lane, Singapore 349567 (Office).

LIM PIN, M.A., M.D., F.R.C.P., F.R.C.P.E., F.R.A.C.P., F.A.C.P.; Singaporean university vice-chancellor; b. 12 Jan. 1936, Penang, Malaysia; m. Shirley Loo Ngai Seong 1964; two s. one d.; ed. Raffles Inst., Singapore and Cambridge Univ.; Registrar, King's Coll. Hosp., London 1965; Medical Officer, Ministry of Health, Singapore 1965–66; Lecturer in Medicine, Nat. Univ. of Singapore 1966–70, Sr. lecturer 1971–73, Assoc. Prof. of Medicine 1974–77, Prof. and Head of Dept. 1978–81, Deputy Vice-Chancellor 1979–81, Vice-Chancellor 1981–; Commonwealth Medical Fellow, The Royal Infirmary, Edinburgh 1970; Chair. Nat. Biotech. Cttee. 1995–, NUS Tech. Holdings Pty. Ltd. 1995–; Deputy Chair. Econ. Devt. Bd. 1995–; Dir. Neptune Orient Lines, Singapore 1981–, Nat. Univ. Hosp., Singapore, Lee Kuan Yew Exchange Fellowship; mem. Nat. Productivity Council, Cttee. on Nat. Computerisation, Econ. Devt. Bd.; mem. Bd. of Govs., Inst. of East Asian Philosophies, Inst. of Policy Studies, Singapore Inst. of Labour Studies, Singapore Int. Foundation, Chinese Heritage Centre 1995–, Nat. Science and Tech. Council 1996–; mem. Bd. of Dirs. Overseas Union Bank; Chair. Applied Research Corpn. 1982–; Eisenhower Fellow 1982; Hon. Fellow, Coll. of General Practitioners, Singapore; Hon. Fellow, Royal Australian Coll. of Obstetricians and Gynaecologists 1992; Rep. of Singapore Public Admin. Medal (Gold) 1984, Meritorious Service Medal 1990; Officier, Ordre des Palmes Académiques 1988. *Publications:* numerous articles in medical journals. *Address:* National University of Singapore, 10 Kent Ridge Crescent, 0511 Singapore. *Telephone:* 7756666.

LIMERICK, 6th Earl of, cr. 1803 (Ireland); **Patrick Edmund Pery,** K.B.E., M.A., C.A.; British business executive; b. 12 April 1930, London; s. of 5th Earl of Limerick (Edmund Colquhoun Pery) and Angela Olivia Trotter; m. Sylvia Rosalind Lush 1961; two s. one d.; ed. Eton Coll. and New Coll., Oxford; Nat. Service Comm. with 2nd Dragoon Guards 1948–50; Territorial Army Comm. with City of London Yeomanry 1950–61; qualified as Chartered Accountant with Peat, Marwick, Mitchell & Co. 1953–58; joined Kleinwort Sons & Co. 1958; Dir. Kleinwort Benson Ltd. 1967–87, Vice-Chair. 1983–85, Deputy Chair. 1985–87; Dir. Kleinwort, Benson Group PLC 1982–90, Kleinwort Benson Australian Income Fund, Inc. 1986–; mem. Council, London Chamber of Commerce and Industry 1968–79; London Dir. Commercial Bank of Australia Ltd. 1969–72; Parl. Under-Sec. of State for Trade 1972–74; Pres. Assn. of British Chambers of Commerce 1974–77, Vice-Pres. 1977–; mem. British Overseas Trade Bd. 1975–91 (Chair. 1979–83); Chair. Cttee. for Middle East Trade 1975–79, Mallinson-Denny Ltd. 1979–81, Chair. British Invisibles 1984–91, Polymeters Response Int. 1988–93; Dir. Brooke Bond Group PLC 1981–84; Dir. De La Rue PLC 1983–97, Chair. 1993–97; Dir. T. R. Pacific Investment Trust PLC 1987–92; Chair. Pirelli U.K. PLC 1989–; Chair. of Court of Govs., London Guildhall Univ. (fmrly. City of London Polytechnic) 1984–; AMP Asset Man. 1992–98; Master, Co. of World Traders 1991; Chair. of Trustees, City Parochial Foundation 1992–96; Pres. Canning House 1994–97; Chair. Cttee. of Univ. Chairs. 1995–98; Deputy Chair. Henderson PLC 1998–; Pres. Ski Club of Great Britain 1974–81, Inst. of Export 1983–95; Vice-Pres. Alpine Ski Club 1975–77, Pres. 1985–87; Pres. Anglo-Swiss Soc. 1984–, Vice-Pres. Alpine Club 1989–91; Chair. Britain-Australia Soc. 1997–; mem. Council, Royal Inst. of Int. Affairs 1980–85; Hon. Col. 71st (Yeomanry) Signal Regt. (Volunteers) 1993–98; D.L. County of W. Sussex 1988–. *Publications:* numerous specialist articles. *Leisure interests:* mountaineering, skiing, boating. *Address:* Chiddinglye, West Hoathly, East Grinstead, West Sussex, RH19 4QT; 30 Victoria Road, London, W8 5RG, England. *Telephone:* (01342) 810214 (Sussex); 0171-937 0573 (London).

LIMONOV, Eduard (pseudonym of Eduard Veniaminovich Savenko); Russian poet and writer; b. 1952, Dzerzhinsk, Gorky Dist.; m. 1st Yelena Limonova Shchapova 1971 (divorced); m. 2nd Natalia Medvedeva; first wrote poetry at age of 15; in Kharkov 1965–67, moved to Moscow in 1967, where acquired reputation of "unofficial" poet; left U.S.S.R. 1974; settled in New York 1975; participant in Russian nationalist movt. 1990–; Chair. Nat. Bolshevik Party 1994–. *Publications include:* verse and prose in Kontinent, Ekho, Kovcheg, Apollon -1977 (in trans. in England, U.S.A., Austria and Switzerland), It's Me—Eddie (novel) 1979 and Russian (Russkoye) (verse) 1979, Diary of a Failure 1982, Teenager Savenko 1983, The Young Scoundrel 1986, The Death of Contemporary Heroes 1993, The Murder of the Sentry 1993; articles in Soviet Communist newspapers 1989–.

LIN, Chia-Chiao, M.A., PH.D., LL.D.; American applied mathematician; b. 7 July 1916, Fukien, China; s. of Kai and Y. T. Lin; m. Shou-Ying Liang 1946; one d.; ed. Nat. Tsing Hua Univ., Univ. of Toronto, Calif. Inst. of Technology; Asst. Prof. of Applied Math., Brown Univ. 1945–46, Assoc. Prof. 1946–47; Assoc. Prof. of Math., M.I.T. 1947–53, Prof. 1953–66, Inst. Prof. of Applied Math. 1966–87; Prof. Emer. of Math., Mass. Inst. of Tech. 1987–; Guggenheim Fellow 1954–55, 1960; Pres. Soc. for Industrial and Applied Maths. 1973; mem. N.A.S.; John von Neumann Lecturer, Soc. for Industrial and Applied Math. 1967. *Publications:* The Theory of Hydrodynamic Stability 1955, Turbulent Flow, Theoretical Aspects 1963. *Leisure interest:* astronomy. *Address:* c/o Department of Mathematics, Massachusetts Institute of Technology, Cambridge, MA 02139, U.S.A.

LIN, Cho-Liang, B.MUS.; American concert violinist; b. 29 Jan. 1960, Taiwan; s. of Kuon-Jing Lin and Kuo-Ling Yu; ed. Juilliard School, New York; concert tours worldwide; over 100 performances a year; soloist with leading orchestras including London Symphony Orchestra, Philharmonia, Concertgebouw, Orchestre de Paris, Chicago Symphony Orchestra, Philadelphia Orchestra and Boston Symphony Orchestra; 10 solo albums; mem. Faculty Juilliard School 1991–. *Address:* Juilliard School, 60 Lincoln Center Plaza, New York, NY 10023, U.S.A.

LIN CHING-HSIA; Taiwanese film actress; b. 1955, Taiwan; lived in Calif. 1979–81; now lives mainly in Hong Kong; has appeared in 82 films including: Outside the Window, Dream Lovers, Police Story, Starry, Starry Night. *Address:* c/o Taiwan Cinema and Drama Association, 10/F, 196 Chunghua Road, Sec. 1, Taipei, Taiwan.

LIN CHIN-SHENG, B.L.; Taiwanese government official; b. 4 Aug. 1916; ed. Law Coll., Tokyo Imperial Univ.; Magistrate, Chiayi Co. Govt. 1951–54; Chair. Yunlin Co. HQ, Kuomintang (Nationalist Party of China) 1954–57; Magistrate, Yunlin Co. Govt. 1957–64; Dir. Cheng-Ching Lake Industrial Waterworks 1964–67; Commr. Taiwan Prov. Govt. 1966–70; Sec.-Gen. Taiwan Provincial HQ, Kuomintang 1967–68, Chair. Taipei Municipal HQ 1969–70, Deputy Sec.-Gen. Cen. Cttee. 1970–72, mem. Standing Cttee. of Cen. Cttee. 1976–; Minister of the Interior 1972–76, of Communications 1976–81, without Portfolio 1981–84; Vice-Pres. Examination Yuan 1984–93; Sr. Adviser to Pres. of Taiwan 1993–; mem. Standing Cttee. of Kuomintang Cen. Cttee. 1976–; Order of the Brilliant Star. *Address:* c/o Kuomintang, 53 Jen Ai Road, Sec. 3, Taipei, Taiwan.

LIN HANXIONG; Chinese administrator and engineer; b. 1929, Huanggang Co., Hubei Prov.; ed. Moscow Power Industry Inst.; joined CCP 1946; Pres. Energy Research Soc. 1981–85; mem. State Econ. Comm. 1984–; Dir. of State Admin. for Bldg. Materials Industry 1986–; Minister of Construction 1988; a Vice-Chair. All-China Greening Cttee. 1989–, Beijing Planning and Construction Cttee. 1991–. *Address:* c/o State Economic and Trade Commission, 26 Xuanwumenxidajie, Xuanwumen District, Beijing, People's Republic of China.

LIN LANYING, PH.D.; Chinese scientist; b. 7 Feb. 1918, Putian Co., Fujian Prov.; ed. Fujian Xiehe Univ., Pennsylvania Univ., U.S.A.; returned to China 1957; Research Fellow, Semiconductors Inst. Academia Sinica 1959–; Vice-Chair., Youth Fed. of China 1962–66; mem. Standing Cttee. 3rd NPC 1964–66; Deputy, 4th NPC 1974–78; Deputy Dir., Semiconductors Inst. 1977; Vice-Chair. Nat. Cttee. China Science and Tech Asscn. 1980–; mem. Standing Cttee. 5th NPC 1978–83, 6th NPC 1983–88, 7th NPC 1988–; mem. Dept. of Tech. Sciences, Academia Sinica 1985–; mem. Presidium, 5th, 6th, 7th NPC; Vice-Pres. Asscn. for Science and Tech. 1980–; mem. 7th NPC 1988–93; mem. Educ., Science, Culture and Public Health Cttee. 7th NPC 1988–93; mem. Standing Cttee. 8th NPC 1993, mem. Educ., Science, Culture and Public Health Cttee.; numerous prizes. *Publications:* CZ-Silicon and FZ Silicon Crystal Growth and its Property Studies 1957–78, Vapour and Liquid Phase Epitaxy Growth of the High Purity GaAs and its Property Studies 1978–1982, A Study on New Donors in CZ-Si 1984–1988, GaAs Grown in Space 1986, High Electron Mobility Materials MBE Growth and Property Studies 1993. *Address:* Room 401, Building 809, Haidian Huang Zhuang, Beijing 100080, People's Republic of China. *Telephone:* (861) 2554942. *Fax:* (861) 2562389.

LIN LIN; Chinese writer; b. 27 Sept. 1910, Zhao'an Co., Fujian Prov.; s. of the late Lin Hede and Zhen Yilian; m. 1st Wu Lanjiao 1930 (deceased); m. 2nd Chen Ling 1950; two s. two d.; ed. Zhao'an middle school, Chinese Univ., Beijing, Waseda Univ. Tokyo, Japan; joined Left-Wing Movt. in Literature, 1934–36; returned to Shanghai 1936; Ed., Jiuwang Daily, Shanghai 1937, Guangzhou 1938, Guilin 1939–41; Chief Ed. of Huaqiao Guide, Manila, Philippines 1941–47; Prof., Dept. of Chinese Literature, Dade Coll., Hongkong 1947–49; Cultural Counsellor, Embassy, New Delhi, India 1955–58; Vice-Pres. of the China-Japan Friendship Asscn. 1965–; Vice-Pres. Chinese People's Asscn. for Friendship with Foreign Countries 1973–86; Pres. China Soc. for Study of Japanese Literature 1980–94, Hon. Pres. 1994–; Adviser, Soc. for Study of Sino-Japanese Relations 1984–; Adviser, Chinese Writers' Asscn. 1996–; mem. 5th, 6th and 8th Nat. Cttees. CPPCC 1978–93; Yakushi Inoue Cultural Exchange Award 1996. *Publications:* Poems of India 1958, Essays about Japan 1982, A Selection of Japanese Classical Haiku 1983, The Sea and the Ship (essays) 1987, A Selection of Japanese Modern Haiku 1990, Amaranthus (poems) 1991, Cutting Clouds (Chinese haiku) 1994, Continued Essays About Japan 1994. *Address:* Room 402, Bldg. 22, Congwenmen Dongdajie Street, 100062 Beijing, People's Republic of China.

LIN LIYUN; Chinese state official; b. 1933, Taizhong, Taiwan; ed. Kobe, Japan, Beijing Univ.; council mem. Sino-Japanese Friendship Asscn. 1973–; mem. 10th CCP Cen. Cttee. 1973; mem. Standing Cttee. 4th NPC 1975; Deputy for Taiwan to 5th NPC 1978, 6th NPC 1983; Vice-Pres. Women's Fed. 1978–, mem. Exec. Council 1988–; Pres. Fed. of Taiwan Compatriots 1981–; mem. 12th CCP Cen. Cttee. 1982–87; mem. Presidium 6th NPC 1986–; Standing Cttee. NPC 1984–88; mem. Credentials Cttee. NPC 1984–88; mem. Overseas Chinese Cttee. NPC 1986– (now Vice-Chair.); mem. 13th CCP Cen. Cttee. 1987–92, 14th CCP Cen. Cttee. 1992–97, 15th CCP Cen. Cttee. 1997–; Vice-Chair. 14th N.P.C. Overseas Chinese Affairs Cttee.; adviser Asscn. for the Promotion of the Peaceful Reunification of China 1988–; mem. Working Group for Unification of the Motherland 1984–; Vice-Pres. China Int. Cultural Exchange Centre 1984–; Vice-Pres. All China Fed. of Returned Overseas Chinese 1994–; Vice-Pres. All-China Sports Fed. 1979–; Adviser Asscn. for Relations Across the Taiwan Straits. *Address:* Chinese Communist Party Central Committee, Beijing, People's Republic of China.

LIN RUO; Chinese party official; b. 1924, Chaoan, Guangdong Prov.; ed. Zhonshan Univ.; joined CCP 1945; First Deputy Sec. Zhanjiang Pref. 1966–, Deputy Dir. Nanfang Daily 1971–, Sec. CCP Cttee. Zhanjiang Pref. 1977–; Dir. Nanfang ribao 1980; mem. 12th CCP Cen. Cttee. 1982–; Sec. CCP Cttee., Guangdong Prov. 1983–93; mem. 13th CCP Cen. Cttee. 1987–92; Del. 7th NPCC 1988–92; Chair. People's Congress of Guangdong Prov. 1990–96. *Address:* c/o Guangdong Provincial Chinese Communist Party, Guangzhou, Guangdong, People's Republic of China.

LIN, See-Yan, M.A., M.P.A., PH.D., F.I.B., F.I.S.; Malaysian banker; b. 3 Nov. 1939, Ipoh, Malaysia; ed. Univ. of Malaya in Singapore, Harvard Univ.; Tutor in econs., Univ. of Malaya 1961–63, Harvard Univ. 1970–72, 1976–77; Statistician, Dept. of Statistics 1961–63; Econ. Adviser, Minister of Finance 1966–69; Dir. Malaysian Rubber Exchange and Licensing Bd. (MRELB) 1974–85; mem. Council on Malaysian Invisible Trade (COMIT) 1981–85, Econ. Panel of the Prime Minister 1982–87, Capital Issues Cttee. (CIC) 1985–86; Chief Economist, Bank Negara Malaysia (Cen. Bank of Malaysia) 1973–77, Econ. Adviser 1977–80, Deputy Gov. 1980; Chair. Credit Guarantee Corpn. Malaysia Berhad (CGC), Malaysian Insurance Inst. (MII); Deputy Chair. Industrial Bank of Malaysia Berhad (Bank Industri); Dir. Malaysia Export Credit Insurance Berhad (MECIB), Govt. Officers Housing Corpn., Seacen Research and Training Centre, Malaysian Wildlife Conservation Foundation; mem. Malaysia Program Advisory Council, US-ASIAN Centre for Tech. Exchange, Commonwealth Group of Experts on the Debt Crisis 1984, IMF Working Party on Statistical Discrepancy in World Currency Imbalances 1985–87, IMF Cttee. of Balance of Payments Compilers 1987; Pres. Malaysian Econ. Asscn.; Eisenhower Fellow 1986. *Publications:* numerous articles in academic, banking and business journals. *Address:* Bank Negara Malaysia, Jalan Kuching, POB 10922, 50929 Kuala Lumpur, Malaysia.

LIN SHENGZHONG, PH.D.; Chinese politician and scientist; b. 1942, Taiwan Prov.; ed. Brown Univ., U.S.A.; Vice-Chair. of Taiwan Democratic Self-Govt. League 1983, mem. of Presidium 1987–; Research Fellow of Geology and Mineral Resources Inst. 1985–; mem. Nat. Cttee. 7th CPPCC 1982–88, 7th CPPCC 1988–. *Address:* Geology and Mineral Resources Institute, Ministry of Coal Industry, Beijing, People's Republic of China.

LIN SHUILONG; Chinese administrator; b. 1931, Indonesia; returned to China 1952; served in Embassies in Indonesia and Philippines 1956–84; Deputy Dir. of State Overseas Chinese Office 1985–96; a Vice-Chair. Overseas Chinese Cttee.; Vice-Pres. All-China Fed. of Returned Overseas Chinese 1989–96. *Address:* Overseas Chinese Office, State Council, Zhong Nan Hai, Beijing, People's Republic of China.

LIN YANG-KANG, B.A.; Taiwanese politician; b. 10 June 1927, Nantou Co.; s. of Lin Chih-Chang and Lin Chen Ruan; m. Chen Ho 1945; one s. three d.; ed. Nat. Taiwan Univ.; Chair. Yunlin Co. H.Q., Kuomintang 1964–67; Magistrate, Nantou Co. 1967–72; Commr. Dept. of Reconstruction, Taiwan Provincial Govt. 1972–76; Mayor of Taipei 1976–78; Gov. Taiwan Prov. 1978–81; Minister of Interior 1981–84; Vice-Premier of Taiwan 1984–87; Pres. Judicial Yuan 1987–94; Sr. Advisor to Pres. 1994–95 (party membership suspended 1995); stood as independent Presidential cand. March 1996. *Leisure interests:* hiking, reading and studying, music, films. *Address:* 124 Chungking South Road, Sec. 1, Taipei, Taiwan.

LIN YINCAI; Chinese politician; b. 1930, Zhenghai Co., Zhejiang Prov.; ed. U.S.S.R.; joined CCP 1955; Vice-Minister of Chemical Industry 1982–96; alt. mem. 12th CCP Cen. Cttee. 1982–87, mem. 13th Cen. Cttee. 1987–92, 14th Cen. Cttee. 1992–. *Address:* c/o Ministry of Chemical Industry, Beijing, People's Republic of China.

LIN ZHAOHUA; Chinese theatre director; b. 1 July 1936, Tianjin; s. of Lin Baogui and Zhang Shuzhen; m. Binzhu He 1964; one s. one d.; Vice-Pres. and Dir. Beijing People's Art Theatre 1984–; mem. Standing Cttee., China Theatre Asscn. 1984–. *Productions include:* The Red Heart 1978, Just Opinion 1980, Warning Signal 1982, Bus Stop 1983, Marriage and Funerals 1984, Wild Man 1985, Amadeus Schweyk in the Second World War; A Grandfather's Nirvana 1986, Peace Lake 1988, Farmland is Greenspread Again 1989, Chinese Orphan 1989, Hamlet 1989, Countryside Anecdote 1990, A Report from Hu-tuo River 1991, Mountain Flower (Beijing Opera) 1991, Bird and Man: Romulus the Great 1993, Ruan Lingyu 1994, Faust 1994, Chess and Man 1996, Fisherman 1997, Three Sisters Waiting For Godot (adapted from Chekhov's Three Sisters and Beckett's Waiting for Godot) 1998. *Publications:* Stage Art of Warning Signal (ed.) 1985, Stage Art of Marriages and Funerals. *Leisure interest:* Chinese yoga. *Address:* Beijing People's Art Theatre, Beijing, People's Republic of China. *Telephone:* 65135801 (Office); 64214081 (Home).

LINACRE, Sir (John) Gordon (Seymour), Kt., C.B.E., A.F.C., D.F.M., C.B.I.M.; British newspaper executive; b. 23 Sept. 1920; s. of John J. Linacre and Beatrice B. Linacre; m. Irene A. Gordon 1943; two d.; ed. Firth Park Grammar School, Sheffield; served R.A.F., rank of Squadron Leader 1939–46; journalistic appts. Sheffield Telegraph/Star 1937–47; Kemsley News Service

1947–50; Deputy Ed. Newcastle Journal 1950–56, Newcastle Evening Chronicle 1956–57; Ed. Sheffield Star 1958–61; Asst. Gen. Man. Sheffield Newspapers Ltd. 1961–63; Exec. Dir. Thomson Regional Newspapers Ltd., London 1963–65; Man. Dir. Yorkshire Post Newspapers Ltd. 1965–83, Deputy Chair. 1981–83, Chair. 1983–90, Pres. 1990–; Dir. United Newspapers PLC 1969–91, Deputy Chair. 1981–91, Chief Exec. 1983–88; Deputy Chair. Express Newspapers PLC 1985–88; also fmr. Chair. United Provincial Newspapers Ltd., Sheffield Newspapers Ltd., Lancashire Evening Post Ltd., Northampton Mercury Co. Ltd., East Yorkshire Printers Ltd. etc.; Dir. Yorkshire TV 1969–90; Chair. Leeds Univ. Foundation 1989–; Chair. Chameleon TV Ltd. 1994–; Chair. Opera N. Ltd. 1978–98, Pres. 1998–; many other professional and public appts.; Hon. LL.D. (Leeds) 1991; Grand Ufficiale, Ordine al Merito della Repubblica Italiana. *Address:* White Windows, Staircase Lane, Bramhope, Leeds, LS16 9JD, England. *Telephone:* (0113) 284-2751.

LINAKER, Lawrence Edward (Paddy); British business executive; b. 22 July 1934, Hants.; s. of late Lawrence Wignall and Rose Linaker; m. Elizabeth Susan Elam 1963; one s.; ed. Malvern Coll.; with Esso Petroleum 1957–63; joined M & G Group 1963, Deputy Chair. and Chief Exec. 1987–94; Chair. M & G Investment Man. 1987–94; Dir. Securities Inst. 1992–94; Chair. Fleming Geared Growth Investment Trust PLC 1997–, Fleming Geared Income and Investment Trust PLC 1997–; fmr. Chair. Marling Industries PLC, Fisons; mem. Bd. Lloyds TSB Group PLC, Fleming Mercantile Investment Trust, Wolverhampton & Dudley Breweries PLC; mem. Council, Royal Postgrad. Medical School 1977–88, Gov. Body, Soc. for the Promotion of Christian Knowledge 1976–94, Council, Malvern Coll. 1989–; Chair. Institutional Fund Man.'s Asscn. 1992–94, YMCA Nat. Coll. 1992; Trustee TSB Foundation for England and Wales. *Leisure interests:* music, wine, gardening. *Address:* Swyre Farm, Aldsworth, Nr. Cheltenham, Glos., England.

LINCOLN, Blanche Lambert; American politician; fmrly. mem. of U.S. House of Reps. from Ark.; senator from Arkansas Jan. 1999–; Democrat. *Address:* U.S. Senate, Washington, DC 20510, U.S.A.

LINDAUER, Martin, DR.RER.NAT.; German professor of zoology; b. 19 Dec. 1918, Wäldle; s. of Matthias and Katharina Lindauer; m. 1st. Franziska Fleck 1943; two s. one d.; m. 2nd Rosemarie Angerbauer; ed. Univ. of Munich; Prof. Univ. of Munich 1961, Univ. of Frankfurt 1963, Univ. of Würzburg 1973–87; Vice-Pres. Univ. of Würzburg 1976–82; Fellow Rockefeller Foundation; Prather Lecturer Harvard Univ., Prof.-at-large Cornell Univ.; mem. Akad. der Wissenschaften und Literatur, Mainz, Deutsche Akad. der Naturforscher Leopoldina, Halle, American Acad. of Arts and Sciences, Nat. Acad. of Sciences, American Philosophical Soc., Accad. Nazionale dei Lincei, Rome; Dr. h.c. (Zurich, Umeå and Saarbrücken). *Publication:* Communication among Social Bees 1961. *Leisure interests:* mountain climbing, music. *Address:* Biozentrum, Am Hubland, 97074 Würzburg, Germany. *Telephone:* 0931-31695.

LINDBECK, Assar, PH.D.; Swedish professor of international economics; b. 26 Jan. 1930, Umeå; s. of Karl Lindbeck and Eugenia (Sundelin) Lindbeck; m. Dorothy Nordlund 1953; one s. one d.; ed. Univs. of Uppsala and Stockholm; Asst. Prof., Univ. of Mich., U.S.A. 1958; with Swedish Treasury 1958–62; Asst. Prof. of Econs., Univ. of Stockholm 1962–63, Prof. 1964–71, Prof. of Int. Econs., Dir. Inst. of Int. Econs. 1971–; Visiting Prof. Columbia Univ., U.S.A. 1968–69, Univ. of Calif. Berkeley 1969, Nat. Univ. Australia 1970, Yale Univ. 1976, Stanford Univ. 1977; Consultant World Bank 1986–87; Dir. Nobel Prize Cttee. on Econs.; several prizes. *Publications:* A Study in Monetary Analysis, Swedish Economic Policy, Economics of the Agricultural Sector, The Political Economy of the New Left, The Insider-Outsider Theory (with Dennis Snower). *Leisure interest:* painting. *Address:* Institute of International Economics, Stockholm University, 10691 Stockholm (Office); 50 Östermalmsgatan, 11426 Stockholm, Sweden (Home).

LINDBLOM, Seppo Olavi, LIC.POL.SC.; Finnish bank executive and politician; b. 9 Aug. 1935, Helsinki; s. of Olavi and Aura (née Sammal) Lindblom; m. Anneli Johanson 1958; four d.; ed. Univ. of Helsinki; Man. branch office, Finnish Workers' Savings Bank 1958–60; economist, Bank of Finland 1960–68; Sec. to Prime Minister 1968–70; Head, Labour Inst. for Econ. Research 1970–72; Minister in Ministry of Trade and Industry 1972; Head, Dept. of Nat. Econ. Ministry of Finance 1973–74; Nat. Conciliator for Incomes Policy 1973–74; Dir. Bank of Finland 1974–82, mem. Bd. of Man. 1982–87; Minister of Trade and Industry 1983–87; Chair. and Chief Exec. Postipankki Ltd. 1988–96. *Leisure interests:* music, chess.

LINDEMAN, Fredrik Otto, D.PHIL.; Norwegian professor of linguistics; b. 3 March 1936, Oslo; s. of Carl Fredrik Lindeman and Agnes Augusta Lindeman; m. Bente Konow Taranger 1960; one s. one d.; ed. Univ. of Oslo; Prof. of Indo-European Linguistics, Univ. of Copenhagen 1970, Univ. of Oslo 1976–. *Publications:* Les Origines Indo-Européennes de la 'Verschärfung' Germanique 1964, Einführung in die Laryngaltheorie 1970, The Triple Representation of Schwa in Greek and some related problems of Indo-European Phonology 1982, Studies in Comparative Indo-European Linguistics 1996, Introduction to the 'Laryngeal Theory' 1997. *Leisure interest:* music. *Address:* P.O. Box 1102, Blindern, 0317 Oslo (Office); Abbedikollen 13, 0280 Oslo 2, Norway (Home). *Telephone:* 22-85-67-87 (Office); 22-50-92-78 (Home).

LINDENSTRAUSS, Joram, PH.D.; Israeli professor of mathematics; b. 28 Oct. 1936, Tel-Aviv; m. Naomi Salinger 1962; one s. three d.; ed. Hebrew Univ., Jerusalem; Sr. Lecturer in Math., Hebrew Univ. 1965, Assoc. Prof. 1967, Prof. 1970–; Visiting Prof. Univs. Yale, Washington, California, Texas, Inst. Mittag Leffler, Inst. for Advanced Study, Princeton; mem. Israel Acad. of Science and Humanities; Israeli Prize in Math. 1981. *Publications:* Absolutely summing operators in Lp spaces and their applications (with A. Pelczynski) 1968, The dimension of almost spherical sections of convex bodies 1977, Classical Banach spaces, Vols. I–II, 1977, 1979. *Address:* Hebrew University of Jerusalem, Mount Scopus, 91 905 Jerusalem; 36 Habanai Str., Jerusalem, Israel. *Telephone:* (02) 522-762.

LINDERBERG, Jan Erik, F.D.; Danish professor of theoretical chemistry; b. 27 Oct. 1934, Karlskoga, Sweden; s. of David Linderberg and Sara Bäckström; m. Gunnel Björstam 1957; two s.; ed. Uppsala Univ.; Docent, Uppsala Univ. 1964–68; Prof. of Theoretical Chem. Aarhus Univ. 1968–; Adjunct Prof. of Chem., Univ. Fla. Gainesville, Univ. Utah; mem. Royal Danish Soc. of Sciences and Letters, Int. Acad. of Quantum Molecular Science, Royal Soc. of Science (Uppsala). *Publications:* Role of Correlation in Electronic Systems 1964, Propagators in Quantum Chemistry (co-author), Quantum Science (with others) 1976. *Leisure interest:* orienteering. *Address:* Janus la Cours gade 20, 8000 Aarhus C, Denmark. *Telephone:* 89 42 38 29 (Office); 86 12 02 41 (Home).

LINDEROTH, Karl-Axel, M.B.A.; Swedish insurance executive; b. 7 Aug. 1927, Jönköping; m. Gun Ryberg 1955; one s. one d.; ed. Gothenburg School of Econs.; Finance Dir. Co-operative Co. 1952–54; Man. Consultant Volvo 1955; Man. Consultant Swedish Council of Personnel Admin. 1956–59; Exec. Vice-Pres. Finance and Personnel COOP Sweden 1959–76; Man. Dir. Svenska Personal—Pensionskassan (insurance co. owned by Swedish labour orgs.) 1976–; mem. Cen. Cttee. of Int. Co-operative Alliance 1972–76; mem. Bd. Int. Co-operative Bank 1972–80, Sydkraft AB 1972–76, Swedish Pension Fund 1972–77, Uddeholm AB 1977–, Incentive AB 1976–, AB Diligentia 1977–82, Swedish Insurance Orgs. 1976–; Chair. Bd. Statsföretag AB (Swedish State Co.) 1978–82; Chair. Bd. of Swedish Man. Inst. 1978–. *Leisure interests:* sailing, skiing, tennis, YMCA (mem. YMCA President's Cttee. 1965–73). *Address:* c/o Svenska Personal—Pensionskassan, Regeringsgatan 107, 103 73 Stockholm, Sweden.

LINDH, Ylva Anna Maria, B.L.; Swedish politician; b. 19 June 1957, Stockholm; d. of Staffan Lindh and Nancy Lindh; m. Bo Holmberg 1991; two s.; ed. Sanobro School, Enkoping, Univ. of Uppsala; Pres. of the Nat Council of Swedish Youth 1981–83; M.P. and mem. Standing Cttee. on Taxation 1982–85; Pres. of the Social Democratic Youth League 1984–90; Pres. Govt. Council of Alcohol and Drug Politics 1986–90; Vice-Pres. Int. Union of Socialist Youth 1987–89; mem. Exec. Cttee. Social Democratic Party 1991–; Pres. Cttee. for Home Affairs, Party of European Socialists 1992–94; Minister of the Environment 1994–98; M.P. 1998–; Minister for Foreign Affairs 1998–; mem. Stockholm City Council; Vice-Mayor, Stockholm 1991–94, mem. Central (Exec.) Cttee., Pres. Culture Cttee., Leisure Cttee.; Pres. Bd. Stockholm City Theatre. *Leisure interests:* theatre, music, novels. *Address:* Ministry for Foreign Affairs, SE-10339 Stockholm, Sweden. *Telephone:* (8) 405 1000. *Fax:* (8) 723 1176.

LINDNER, Carl Henry; American business executive; b. 22 April 1919, Dayton, Ohio; s. of Carl Henry and Clara (née Serrer) Lindner; m. Edith Bailey 1953; three s.; co-founder United Dairy Farmers 1940; Pres. American Finance Corpn., Cincinnati 1959–84, Chair. 1959–, C.E.O. 1984–; Chair., C.E.O., Chair. Exec. Cttee. United Brands Co. (now Chiquita Brands Int. Inc.), N.Y. 1984–; Chair. Penn Cen. Corpn. (now American Premier Underwriters), Greenwich, Conn. 1983–, C.E.O. 1987–94; Chair. and C.E.O. Great American Communications Co. 1987–; now Chair. and C.E.O. American Finance Group, Cincinnati; mem. bd. of Dirs. Mission Inst., bd. of Advisers Business Admin. Coll., Univ. of Cincinnati. *Address:* Charter Co., 1 W. Charter Plaza, Jacksonville, FL 32202, U.S.A.

LINDON, Jérôme; French publisher; b. 9 June 1925, Paris; s. of Raymond Lindon and Thérèse Baur; m. Annette Rosenfeld 1947; two s. one d.; ed. Lycée Pasteur, Neuilly-sur-Seine, Lycée Mignet, Aix-en-Provence; Pres., Dir. Gen. Editions de Minuit 1948–, has published novels of the "nouveau roman" (Beckett—Nobel Prizewinner 1969, Robbe-Grillet, Butor, Nathalie Sarraute, Simon—Nobel Prizewinner 1985, Pinget, Marguerite Duras, etc.); mem. Supreme Council of the French Language. *Address:* Editions de Minuit, 7 rue Bernard Palissy, 75006 Paris, France. *Telephone:* (1) 44-39-39-20.

LINDSAY, John Vliet; American politician (retd.) and lawyer; b. 24 Nov. 1921, New York City; s. of George and Eleanor (Vliet) Lindsay; brother of Robert V. Lindsay (q.v.); m. Mary Harrison 1949; one s. three d.; ed. The Buckley School, St. Paul's School, Concord, Yale Univ., and Yale Law School; admitted to New York Bar 1949, D.C. Bar 1957; mem. Webster and Sheffield, New York 1948–55, 1974–91, Presiding Partner 1989–91; Exec. Asst. to U.S. Attorney-Gen. 1955–57; mem. U.S. House of Reps. 1959–65; Mayor of New York 1965–73; fmr. Commentator on ABC-TV programmes; New York Int. Trade Rep. 1981–; Int. Rep. of Mayor's Cttee. for New York 1983–; Chair. Vivian Beaumont Theater, New York 1984–; Counsel Mudge Rose Guthie Alexander and Ferdon 1991–94; mem. Asscn. of Bar of City of NY, mem. American Bar Asscn., mem. State Bar Asscn.; Hon. LL.D. (Williams Coll.) 1968, (Harvard) 1969. *Publications:* Journey into Politics 1966, The City 1970, The Edge 1976.

LINDSAY, Orland Ugham, O.J., B.D.; Jamaican/Antiguan ecclesiastic (retd.); b. 24 March 1928, Jamaica; s. of Hubert Lindsay and Ida Lindsay; m. Olga Daphne Wright 1959; three s.; ed. Mayfield Govt. School, Southfield, Jamaica, Culham Coll., Oxford, England, St. Peter's Theological Coll., Jamaica, Montreal Diocesan Theological Coll. at McGill Univ., Canada; served in R.A.F. 1944–49; teacher Franklin Town Govt. School 1949–52; Asst. Master Kingston Coll. 1952–53, 1958–63; ordained deacon, Jamaica 1956; asst. curate St. Peter's Vere Cure 1956–57; ordained priest 1957; Chaplain Kingston Coll. 1958–63; asst. curate in charge of Manchioneal Cure 1960–63; Sec. Jamaica Diocesan Synod 1962–70; Chaplain Jamaica Defence Force 1963–67; Prin. Church Teachers' Coll., Mandeville, Jamaica 1967–70; Bishop of Antigua, latterly of N.E. Caribbean and Aruba 1970–98; Archbishop of the W. Indies 1986–98; Order of Distinction (Antigua) 1996; Hon. D.D. (Berkeley Divinity School, Yale Univ.) 1978, (St. Paul's Coll., S. Va.) 1998; Hon. S.T.D. (Diocesan Theological Coll., Montreal) 1997. *Leisure interests:* swimming, listening to music. *Address:* Flagstaff, Crosbies, P.O. Box 3456, Antigua. *Telephone:* 268 560 1724. *Fax:* c/o 268 462 2090.

LINDSAY, Robert; British actor; b. 1951, Ilkeston, Derbys.; m. Cheryl Hall (divorced); one d. by actress Diana Weston; ed. Royal Acad. of Dramatic Art (RADA); stage career commenced at Manchester Royal Exchange; appeared in Me and My Girl, London, Broadway and Los Angeles 1985–87 (recipient Olivier, Tony and Fred Astaire awards); appeared as Henry II in Anouilh's Beckett, London 1991, Cyrano de Bergerac, London 1992–; TV appearances include Edmund in King Lear (Granada), Wolfie in comedy series Citizen Smith, Michael Murray in serial GBH (Channel 4) 1991; Genghis Cohn, Jake's Progress, Goodbye My Love 1996, Oliver (Olivier Award for Best Actor in a Musical), Richard III 1998. *Films:* Bert Rigby, You're a Fool, Loser Takes All, Strike It Rich, Fierce Creatures 1996.

LINDSAY, Robert V.; American banker; b. 1 Jan. 1926, New York City; s. of George and Eleanor (Vliet) Lindsay; brother of John V. Lindsay (q.v.); m. Nancy A. Dalley 1950; two s. one d.; ed. Yale Univ.; joined Morgan Guaranty Trust Co. 1949, Asst. Treas. 1954, Asst. Vice-Pres. 1955, Vice-Pres. 1960, Sr. Vice-Pres. 1969, Exec. Vice-Pres. 1976, Chair. 1979–80, Pres. 1980–87, Chair. Int. Council 1987–89; Chair. of Exec. Cttee. and Dir. J. P. Morgan & Co. Inc. 1979–86; Dir. St. Joe Minerals Corpn., Chubb Corpn., Russell Reynolds Assocs. 1983–; mem. Bd. of Dirs. Philharmonic Symphony Soc. of New York, Inc. 1977–85; Trustee Guggenheim Memorial Foundation 1983–, Chair. 1991; Chair. Foreign Policy Asscn. 1986–90. *Address:* Morgan Guaranty Trust Company, 15 Broad Street, New York, NY 10005 (Office); Rural Route 3, Box 219 Altamont Road, Millbrook, New York, NY 12545, U.S.A. (Home).

LINDSLEY, Donald Benjamin, A.B., M.A., PH.D.; American professor of psychology and physiology; b. 23 Dec. 1907, Brownhelm, Ohio; s. of Benjamin Kent Lindsley and Martha Elizabeth Jenne; m. Ellen Ford 1933; two s. two d.; ed. Wittenberg Univ. and Univ. of Iowa; Instructor in Psychology, Univ. of Ill. 1932–33; Nat. Research Council Fellow, Harvard Medical School 1933–35; Research Assoc., W. Reserve Univ. Medical School 1935–38; Asst. Prof. Brown Univ. and Dir. Psychology and Neurophysiology Lab., Bradley Hosp. 1938–46; Dir. Radar Research Project, Office of Scientific Research and Devt., Yale Univ., Camp Murphy and Boca Raton Air Force Base, Fla. 1943–45; Prof. of Psychology, Northwestern Univ. 1946–51; Prof. of Psychology, Physiology and Psychiatry, Univ. of Calif., Los Angeles 1951–77, Prof. Emer. 1977–, mem. Brain Research Inst., Univ. of Calif., Los Angeles 1961–, Chair. Dept. of Psychology 1959–62; Phillips Visiting Lecturer, Haverford Coll. 1961; Pillsbury Visiting Lecturer, Cornell Univ. 1963; Special Visiting Lecturer, Mich. State Univ. 1964; mem. Amazon Neurobiological Expedition on Research Vessel Alpha Helix 1967; Visiting Lecturer, Univ. of Sydney, Australia 1972 and 10 South African univs. 1969; Lashley Lecturer, Queens Coll., N.Y. 1979; mem. N.A.S., American Acad. of Arts and Sciences, Soc. of Experimental Psychologists, Int. Brain Research Org., American Physiological Soc., Soc. for Neuroscience (Annual Donald B. Lindsley Prize in Behavioral Neuroscience est. in his name 1978); Hon. mem. American Electroencephalographic Soc. 1980; Hon. mem. of Great Distinction, Western Electroencephalography Soc.; Foreign mem. Finnish Acad. of Science and Letters 1987; William James Lecturer, Harvard 1958; Guggenheim Fellow 1959; Hon. Fellow Univ. of Calif. at Los Angeles School of Medicine 1986; Hon. D.Sc. (Brown Univ.) 1958, (Wittenberg Univ.) 1959, (Trinity Coll.) 1965, (Loyola Univ.) 1969; Ph.D. h.c. (Johannes Gutenberg Univ., Mainz) 1977; Presidential Certificate of Merit for Second World War Research Work, Distinguished Scientific Contribution Award, American Psychological Asscn., Distinguished Scientific Achievement Award, Soc. Psychophysiological Research 1984, Ralph Gerard Prize (jtly.), Soc. for Neuroscience 1988, American Psychological Foundation Gold Award 1989, Herbert Jasper Award (American Electro-encephalographic Soc.) 1994, Wilder Penfield Award (Western Electroencephalographic Soc.) 1996, Century Award, Int. Org. of Psychophysiology 1998. *Publications:* 250 publs., including scientific works in journals and 40 chapters in books; subjects: emotion, electro-encephalography, neurophysiology, perception, attention, brain function, developmental neurology, autonomic function, sleep and wakefulness, conditioning and learning, etc. *Leisure interests:* music, photography, gardening, golf, travel. *Address:* 471 23rd Street, Santa Monica, CA 90402-3125, U.S.A. (Home). *Telephone:* (310) 395-8026 (Home).

LINDSTEN, Jan Eric, PH.D., M.D.; Swedish professor of clinical genetics; b. 23 Jan. 1935, Stockholm; s. of Carl-Eric Lindsten and Lisa M. Hallberg; m. Marianne E. Östling 1960; two s. one d.; ed. Uppsala Univ. and Karolinska Inst. Stockholm; Prof. of Human Genetics, Aarhus 1968–70; Prof. of Medical Genetics, Karolinska Inst. 1969–, Head, Dept. of Clinical Genetics 1970–90; Chief Medical Officer, Karolinska Hosp. 1987–90, Man. Dir. 1990–94; Man. Dir. Nat. Univ. Hosp. Copenhagen 1994–96; Dean Medical Faculty, Karolinska Inst. 1996–98; Sec. Nobel Ass. and Medical Nobel Cttee. Karolinska Inst. 1979–90; mem. Royal Swedish Acad. of Sciences. *Publications:* 300 publs. in the field of medical genetics, especially clinical genetics. *Address:* CMM, Karolinska Hospital, S-17176 Stockholm, Sweden. *Telephone:* (8) 51776353. *Fax:* (8) 51776480.

LINDSTROM, Torsten L., M.SC.; Swedish company executive; b. 21 Sept. 1921, Kiruna; s. of Sigurd and Henny (Andersson) Lindstrom; m. Else Maj Mortberg 1945; one d.; ed. Royal Inst. of Tech., Stockholm; Asst. Prof. Electrical Eng., Royal Inst. of Tech. 1946–60; joined ASEA AB 1961, Man. Low-Voltage Switchgear and Controlgear Design Dept. 1961–63, Gen. Man. Low-Voltage Switchgear and Controlgear Div. 1964–66, Exec. Vice-Pres. in charge of Research and Product Devt. 1967–75, Pres. of ASEA AB 1976–80, Group Exec. Officer 1980–81; Bd. mem. ASEA AB, and several other cos. and insts. 1989–; Hon. D.Tech. 1979; Kt. of Royal Order of Vasa; H.M. the King's Gold Medal 1994. *Publications:* articles on electrotechnical subjects. *Leisure interests:* outdoor life, music. *Address:* ASEA Stockholm Office, P.O. Box 7373, 103 91 Stockholm (Office); Sankt Johannesgatan 23 F, 75312 Uppsala, Sweden (Home). *Telephone:* 018/6136500 (Office); 018/14 28 23 (Home). *Fax:* 018-150044.

LINEKER, Gary Winston, O.B.E.; British footballer (retd.); b. 30 Nov. 1960, Leicester; s. of Barry Lineker and Margaret Patricia Morris Lineker (née Abbs); m. Michelle Denise Cockayne 1986; three s.; ed. City of Leicester Boys' Grammar School; debut as professional footballer, Leicester City 1978; transferred to Everton 1985; rep. England 1986 World Cup, Mexico, 1990 World Cup, Italy, Capt. of England 1991–92; F.C. Barcelona 1986–89; transferred to Tottenham Hotspur 1989–92; 80 caps, 48 goals June 1992; with Grampus Eight Team, Japan 1994; presenter Football Focus, BBC TV; Hon. M.A. (Leicester) 1992, (Loughborough) 1992. *Leisure interests:* cricket, golf. *Address:* c/o Markee U.K., 6 George Street, Nottingham, NG1 3BE, England. *Telephone:* (0115) 948 3206.

LING JIEFANG (pseudomyn of Er Yuehe); Chinese writer; b. Oct. 1945, Xiyang, Shanxi Prov.; Chair. Nanyang Fed. of Literary and Art Circles 1985–. *Publications:* The Great Emperor Kangxi (4 vols.), Emperor Yongzheng (3 vols.), Emperor Qianlong (5 vols.). *Address:* Wolonggang, Nanyang, He'nan Province, People's Republic of China.

LING LIONG SIK, Dato', M.B., B.S.; Malaysian politician; b. 18 Sept. 1943, Kuala Kangsar, Perak; m. Datin Ee Nah Ong 1968; two c.; ed. King Edward VII School, Royal Mil. Coll. and Univ. of Singapore; Parl. Sec. Ministry of Local Govt. and Fed. Territory 1976–77; Deputy Minister of Information 1978–82, of Finance 1982–84, of Educ. 1985–86; Minister of Transport 1986–; Deputy Pres. Malaysian Chinese Asscn. 1985–87, Pres. 1987–. *Leisure interests:* reading, golf. *Address:* Ministry of Transport, 5th–7th Floors, Wisma Perdana, Jalan Dungun Bukit Damansara, 50616 Kuala Lumpur, Malaysia.

LING, Sergey Stepanovich; Belarus politician and agronomist; b. 7 May 1937; m.; three c.; ed. Belarus Agricultural Acad., Higher CPSU School, CPSU Cen. Cttee.; agronomist sovkhoz, Lesnoye Kopylsk Dist., chief agronomist sovkhoz, Krynitsa Kopylsk Dist., chief agronomist, Deputy Dir. Lyuban Production Co., Chief Soligorsk Production Agric. Admin.; Deputy Chair. then Chair. Slutsk Dist. Exec. Cttee., Sec. Smolevichi Dist. CPSU Cttee. 1960–72; Chief Agric. Div., Sec. Minsk Regional Belarus CP Cttee. 1972–82; First Deputy Chair. then Chair. Exec. Cttee. Minsk Regional Soviet 1982–86; Chair. Belarus State Cttee. on Prices, Deputy Chair. State Planning Cttee. 1986–90; Head Agric. Div., Sec. Cen. Cttee. Belarus CP 1990–91; Deputy Chair. Belarus Council of Ministers; Chair. State Cttee. on Econs. and Planning 1991–; Deputy Prime Minister of Belarus 1994–96, Acting Prime Minister 1996–97, Prime Minister Feb. 1997–. *Address:* Council of Ministers, 220010, pl. Nezavisimosti, Minsk, Belarus. *Telephone:* (2) 296043.

LINGHU AN; Chinese politician; b. Oct. 1946, Pinglu Co., Shanxi Prov.; joined CCP 1965; ed. Beijing Eng. Inst.; Exec. Vice-Mayor Dalian City 1988; Vice-Minister of Labour 1989; Vice-Sec. CCP Yunnan Provincial Cttee. 1993, Sec. 1997–; mem. 15th CCP Cen. Cttee. 1997–; Chair. Yunnan Prov. People's Political Consultative Conf. 1998–. *Address:* Chinese Communist Party Yunnan Provincial Committee, Kunming, Yunnan Province, People's Republic of China.

LINK, Christoph, D.JUR.; German/Austrian professor of law; b. 13 June 1933, Dresden; s. of late Hellmuth Link and of Gerda Link; m. 1st Eva Link 1957; m. 2nd Sibylle Obermayer 1991; two s. one d.; ed. Kreuzschule, Dresden and Univs. of Marburg, Cologne and Munich; Prof. Vienna 1971–77, Salzburg 1977–79, Hon. Prof. 1979–, Göttingen 1979–86; Prof. of State Admin. and Church Law, Univ. of Erlangen and Dir. Hans-Liermann-Inst. für Kirchenrecht 1986–; mem. Akad. der Wissenschaften, Göttingen. *Publications:* Die Grundlagen der Kirchenverfassung im lutherischen Konfessionalismus des 19. Jahrhunderts 1966, Herrschaftsordnung und bürgerliche Freiheit 1979, Kirchen und privater Rundfunk (with A. Pahlke) 1985. *Address:* Hans-Liermann-Institut für Kirchenrecht, 91054 Erlangen, Hindenburgstrasse 34 (Office); Staffelweg 4, 91054 Erlangen, Germany (Home). *Telephone:* 09131-852242 (Office); 09131-209335 (Home).

LINKEVIČIUS, Linas Antanas; Lithuanian politician and diplomatist; b. 6 Jan. 1961, Vilnius; m. 1982; two d.; ed. Kaunas Polytechnical Inst.; worked in technical insts. 1983–92; reviewer newspaper Tiesa 1992–93; mem. Democratic Labour Party 1990–95; elected to Seimas (Parl.) 1992; mem. Parl. delegation to N. Atlantic Asscn. 1992–93; Deputy Chair. Parl. Comm. on Foreign Affairs 1992–93; Minister of Nat. Defence 1993–96; Amb. to NATO and to WEU 1997–. *Address:* Mission of the Republic of Lithuania, c/o NATO, blvd. Leopold III, 1110 Brussels, Belgium. *Telephone:* (2) 707 2849. *Fax:* (2) 707 2850.

LINKLATER, Richard; American film director; b. 1962; f. own film co. Detour Films, Austin, Tex.; Founder, Artistic Dir. Austin Film Soc.; Silver Bear, Berlin Film Festival 1995 for Before Sunrise. *Films:* Slacker 1991, Dazed and Confused 1993, Before Sunrise 1995, Suburbia 1997, The Newton Boys 1998. *Address:* Detour Films, Austin, TX, U.S.A.

LINNANE, Anthony William, A.M., D.SC., PH.D., F.R.S., F.A.A.; Australian biochemist; b. 17 July 1930, Sydney; s. of late W. P. Linnane; m. 1st Judith Neil 1956 (dissolved 1979); one s. one d.; m. 2nd Daryl Woods 1980; one s. one d.; ed. Sydney Univ., Univ. of Wisconsin; Postdoctoral Fellow, Univ. of Wis. 1956–58; Lecturer, then Sr. Lecturer, Sydney Univ. 1958–62; Reader, Monash Univ. 1962, Prof. of Biochem. 1965–94, Emer. Prof. 1996–; Dir. Centre of Molecular Biology and Medicine 1984–; Ed.-in-Chief Biochemistry and Molecular Biology Int. 1980–98; Visiting Prof., Univ. of Wis. 1967–68; Hon. Prof., Melbourne Univ. 1996–; Pres. Australian Biochemical Soc. 1974–76, Fed. of Asian and Oceanic Biochemical Socs. 1975–77, 12th Int. Congress of Biochem., Perth 1982; Treas., Int. Union of Biochemistry and Molecular Biology 1988–97. *Publications:* over 300 scientific publs. *Leisure interests:* golf, reading, horseracing. *Address:* Centre for Molecular Biology and Medicine, 185–187 Hoddle Street, Richmond, Vic. 3121, Australia. *Telephone:* (3) 9426 4200. *Fax:* (3) 9426 4201.

LINNEMANN, Hans, D.ECON.; Netherlands economist; b. 7 May 1931, Rotterdam; s. of Philippus Linnemann and Johanna Verkaik; m. Alida J. van Noort 1956; three s. one d.; ed. Netherlands School of Econs.; Staff mem. Netherlands Econ. Inst. 1951–58; UN Expert, Ecuador 1959–60, Egypt 1962–63; Staff mem. Netherlands School of Econs. 1960–62, 1964–66; Asst. Prof. American Univ. of Cairo 1963–64; Prof. of Devt. Econs., Inst. of Social Studies, The Hague 1966–70, Free Univ. of Amsterdam 1970–96; mem. Royal Netherlands Acad. of Sciences; Hon. Fellow, Inst. of Social Studies, The Hague. *Publications:* An Analysis and Projection of the Exports of Ecuador 1960, An Econometric Study of International Trade Flows 1966, MOIRA-Model of International Relations in Agriculture (with others) 1979, Export-Oriented Industrialization in Developing Countries (ed.) 1987, South-South Trade Preferences (ed.) 1992, Economic Reforms and Poverty Alleviation in India (ed.) 1996. *Leisure interests:* chess, coin collecting, jogging. *Address:* Patryslaan 70, 2261 EG Leidschendam, Netherlands. *Telephone:* 70-327 64 88.

LINNER, Carl Sture, M.A., PH.D.; Swedish international civil servant; b. 15 June 1917, Stockholm; s. of Carl W. Linner and Hanna Hellstedt; m. Clio Tambakopoulou 1944; two s.; ed. Stockholm and Uppsala Univs.; Assoc. Prof. of Greek, Uppsala Univ. 1943; Del. to Int. Red Cross, Greece 1943–45; Dir. A.B. Electrolux, Stockholm 1945–50; Dir. Swedish Employers' Confed. 1950–51; Exec. Vice-Pres. A.B. Bahco, Stockholm 1951–57; Pres. Swedish Lamco Syndicate 1957; Exec. Vice.-Pres. and Gen. Man. Liberian-American-Swedish Minerals Co., Monrovia 1958–60; Chief UN Civilian Operations, later UN Mission, in the Congo 1960–61; Special Rep. of UN Sec.-Gen. in Brussels and London 1962; UN Rep. in Greece, Israel and Cyprus 1962–65, in London 1965–68, in Tunis 1968–71, UNDP, New York 1971–73; Resident Rep. UNDP in Egypt 1973-77; Sr. Consultant, FAO 1977–87; mem. Royal Swedish Acad. of Letters, History and Antiquities, Royal Acad. of Arts and Sciences, Uppsala, Societas Litterarum Humaniorum Regiae Upsaliensis; Hon. Prof. (Uppsala) 1992; Dr. Phil. h.c. (Cyprus) 1998; Prince Carl Medal, Royal Award, Swedish Acad., Letterstedts Award, Royal Acad. of Science, Cultural Award, Natur & Kultur, Bonniers Award, City of Athens Award; Star of Africa, Commdr. Order of Phoenix, Commdr. Order of Honour (Greece). *Publications:* Syntaktische und lexikalische Studien zur Historia Lausiaca des Palladios 1943, Giorgos Seferis 1963, Roms Konungahävder 1964, Fredrika Bremer i Grekland 1965, W. H. Humphreys' First Journal of the Greek War of Independence 1967, Thucydides 1978, Min odyssé 1982, Bysantinska porträtt 1984, Homeros 1985, Bistånd till Afrika 1985, Disaster Relief for Development 1986, Hellenika 1986, En värld utan gränser 1988, Den gyllene lyran: Archilochos, Sapfo, Pindaros 1989, Europas födelse 1991, Lans och bage. Aischylos Perserna 1992, Anna Komnenas värld 1993, Bysantinsk Kulturhistoria 1994, Ensamhet och gemenskap 1995, Mulåsnan på Akropolis 1996, Pol Pot och Kambodja 1997, Ökenfäderna 1998, Hellenskt och romerskt 1998. *Leisure interests:* poetry, sports. *Address:* 24 Phokylidou, 10673 Athens, Greece. *Telephone:* 3611780.

LINOWITZ, Sol Myron, LL.B.; American diplomatist and lawyer; b. 7 Dec. 1913, Trenton, N.J.; s. of Joseph and Rose (née Oglenskye) Linowitz; m. Evelyn Zimmerman 1939; four d.; ed. Hamilton Coll., and Cornell Univ. Law School; Asst. Gen. Counsel, Office of Price Admin., Washington 1942–44; Officer, Office of Gen. Counsel, Navy Dept. 1944–46; fmr. Partner, Harris, Beach, Wilcox, Dale & Linowitz; Gen. Counsel, Chair. Bd. and Chair. Exec. Cttee. Xerox Corpn. 1958–66; Chair. Bd. Xerox Int. 1966; Chair. Nat. Urban Coalition 1970–75; Pres. Fed. City Council 1974–78; Pres. NY State, American Asscn. for UN; mem. Council on Foreign Relations, American Jewish Cttee., American Bar Asscn., NY Bar Asscn., American Asscn. UN; U.S.A. Amb. to OAS and U.S. Rep. on the Inter-American Cttee. of the Alliance for Progress 1966–69; Sr. Partner Coudert Brothers (Int. Law firm) 1969–84, Sr. Counsel 1984–94; co-negotiator, Panama Canal Treaties 1977; personal Amb. of Pres. Carter to Middle East negotiations 1979–81; Chair. Presidential Cttee. on World Hunger 1978–79; Head of Comm. for U.S.-Latin American Relations; Co-Chair. Inter-American Dialogue 1981–92; Fellow, American Acad. of Arts and Sciences; Chair. American Acad. of Diplomacy 1984–89; Hon. Chair. Acad. for Educ. Devt. 1986–; Trustee, Cornell Univ., Hamilton Coll., Johns Hopkins Univ., American Assembly; hon. degrees (LL.D. and L.H.D.) from more than 40 colls. and univs. *Publications:* This Troubled Urban World 1974, The Making of a Public Man (a memoir) 1985, The Betrayed Profession: Lawyering in the Twentieth Century 1994. *Leisure interest:* violin. *Address:* Academy for Educational Development, 1875 Connecticut Avenue, Washington, DC 20009 (Office); 2325 Wyoming Ave., Washington, DC 20008, U.S.A. *Telephone:* (202) 884-8156. *Fax:* (202) 884-8401.

LINSKENS, Hansferdinand, DR.PHIL.; German professor of botany; b. 22 May 1921, Lahr; s. of late Albert W. Linskens and Maria E. Bayer; m. Ingrid M. Rast 1954; two s. two d.; ed. Univs. of Berlin, Cologne and Bonn, Eidgenössische Tech. Hochschule, Zürich; Battelle Memorial Fellow, ETH, Zürich 1952–53; Privat Dozent, Univ. of Cologne 1954–56; Prof. of Botany, Univ. of Nijmegen, Netherlands 1957–86, Dean, Faculty of Science 1980–85; Prof. of Geobotany, Univ. of Eichstätt 1986–; Adjunct Prof. Univ. of Mass. 1988–; Prof. a Contratto, Univ. of Siena 1987–; mem. Royal Dutch Acad., Deutsche Akad. der Naturforscher Leopoldina, Linnean Soc. of London, Royal Belgian Acad., New York Acad. of Science etc.; NATO stipendiary, Lisbon 1960; Visiting Prof. Marine Biological Lab. Woods Hole, Mass. 1966, 1968; Dr. h.c. (Lille) 1982, (Siena) 1985; K. Heyer Prize for Allergy Research 1984; Man. Ed. Sexual Plant Reproduction 1988–93, Theoretical and Applied Genetics 1975–85. *Publications:* Papierchromatographie in der Botanik 1958, Pollen Physiology and Fertilization 1964, Fertilization in Higher Plants 1974, Pollen Biology Biochemistry 1974, Cellular Interaction (with J. Heslop-Harrison) 1985; Modern Methods in Plant Analysis (series) 1966–, Monographs in Theoretical and Applied Genetics (series) 1975–. *Leisure interests:* history of science, collecting autographs. *Address:* Oosterbergweg 5, 6573 EE Beek, Netherlands; Goldberglein 7, 91056 Erlangen, Germany. *Telephone:* 024-6841652 (Beek); 09131-440517 (Erlangen). *Fax:* 24-652409 (Nijmegen).

LIONAES, Aase; Norwegian politician; b. 10 April 1907, Oslo; d. of Erling and Anna Lionaes; m. Kurt Jonas 1938; one d.; ed. Univ. of Oslo and L.S.E.; mem. Storting (Parl.) 1953; Vice-Pres. of the Lagting (Upper House) 1965–69, of the Odelsting (Lower House) 1969–77; mem. Govt. del. to UN 1946–65; mem. Nobel Peace Prize Cttee. 1948, Pres. 1968–79; Hon. LL.D. (Oxford Coll., Ohio); Labour. *Address:* Pans Vei nr. 8, Ulvøya, N. Oslo, Norway. *Telephone:* 282408.

LIONS, Jacques L.; French scientist; b. 2 May 1928, Grasse; s. of Honoré and Anne (née Muller) Lions; m. Andrée Olivier 1950; one s.; ed. Ecole normale supérieure, Paris; Centre Nat. de la Recherche Scientifique (CNRS) 1950–54; Prof. Univ. of Nancy 1954–62, Univ. of Paris 1962–, Coll. de France 1973–98; Pres. INRIA, Paris 1980–84, Centre Nat. d'Etudes Spatiales (CNES), Paris 1984–92, Scientific Council of Electricité de France 1986, Scientific Cttee. of Nat. Meteorology 1990–, Scientific Council of Péchiney 1991–, of ELF Argenteuil 1993–, of Gaz de France 1994–, of France Télécom 1998–, Dassault Aviation's Scientific and Space Council 1993–; Dir. Saint-Gobain 1994–, Péchiney 1996–, Dassault Systèmes; Hon. Prof. Ecole Polytechnique; Dr. h.c. (Madrid, Liège, Academia Sinica, Edin., Göteborg, Santiago de Compostela, Fudan, Wuhan, Santiago (Chile), Málaga Univs., Hebrew Univ. of Jerusalem, Universidad Nacional Autónoma, Mexico); mem. Acad. of Sciences, Paris 1973 (Vice-Pres. 1995–96, Pres. 1997, 1998), Brazilian Acad. of Sciences, Soc. Royale de Science, Liège; Foreign mem. Inst. Lombardo, U.S.S.R. Acad. of Sciences, Acad. of Arts, Sciences and Letters, Boston, Int. Acad. of Astronautics, Acad. Europaea, Chilean Acad. of Sciences, Argentinian Acad. of Sciences, Ukrainian Acad. of Sciences, Pontifical Acad. of Sciences, Royal Society (U.K.), N.A.S. (U.S.A.), Third World Acad. of Sciences, Acad. of Sciences of Spain, of Portugal, Accademia Nazionale dei Lincei, Italy; Hon. Fellow Tate Inst. of Fundamental Research 1996–; Commdr., Légion d'honneur, Grand Officier, Ordre nat. du Mérite, Order of the Rising Sun; Cognacq-Jay Prize (Acad. of Sciences) 1972, John von Neumann Prize 1986, Japan Prize 1991, Harvey Prize 1991. *Publications:* 20 books on analysis, optimal control, partial differential equations and numerical analysis. *Address:* Collège de France, 3 rue d'Ulm, 75231 Paris Cedex 05 (Office); 7 rue Paul Barruel, 75015 Paris, France (Home).

LIOTTA, Ray, B.F.A.; American film actor; b. 18 Dec. 1955, Newark, N.J.; s. of Alfred Liotta and Mary Liotta; ed. Univ. of Miami; TV appearances include: Another World, NBC 1978–80, Hardhat & Legs (CBS movie) 1980, Crazy Times (ABC pilot) 1981, Casablanca, NBC 1983, Our Family Honour, NBC 1985–86, Women Men = In Love There Are No Rules 1991. *Films:* The Lonely Lady 1983, Something Wild 1986, Arena Brains 1987, Dominick and Eugene 1988, Field of Dreams 1989, Goodfellas 1990, Article 99 1992, Unlawful Entry 1992, No Escape 1994, Corrina, Corrina 1994, Operation Dumbo Drop 1995, Unforgettable 1996, Turbulence 1997, Phoenix 1997,

Copland 1997. *Address:* Creative Artists Agency Inc., 9830 Wilshire Boulevard, Beverly Hills, CA 90212, U.S.A.

LIPKIN, Semen Izrailevich; Russian writer, poet and translator; b. 19 Sept. 1911, Odessa; s. of Israel Lipkin and Rosalia Lipkin; m. Inna L'vovna Lisnyanskaya (q.v.) 1967; two s. three d.; ed. Moscow Econ. Inst.; served in Soviet Army 1941–45; Rudaki State Prize 1967, People's Poet of Kalmyk A.S.S.R. 1968; resgnd. from Union of Writers 1980 (membership restored 1989). *Translations include:* Dzangar (Kalmyk epic) 1940, Geser (Buryat epic) 1968, Mahabharata (Indian epic) 1969, also from classical Tadzhik, Uzbek and Kirghiz writers; *poetry:* Eyewitness 1967, A Notebook of Being 1977, Freewill 1981, A Nomadic Flame 1984, Lire 1989; *novels:* Ten-day Period 1983, Life and Destiny of Vasilii Grossman 1990, The Flaming Coal 1991, The Characters 1991, Moonlight 1991, The Notes of the Lodger 1992, April 1993, Before the Sunset 1995, The Second Road (memoirs) 1995; Tukai Prize 1991, Sakharov Prize, Pushkin Prize (Germany) 1995, Quadriga (memoirs) 1997. *Address:* Usievicha Street 8, Apt. 4b, 125315 Moscow, Russia. *Telephone:* 155-75-98.

LIPOVSEK, Marjana; Austrian singer; b. Yugoslavia; after studies in Ljubljana, went to Music Acad., Graz, Austria; joined Vienna State Opera, then Hamburg State Opera, Fed. Repub. of Germany; operatic roles include Oktavian, Dorabella, Ulrica, Mistress Quickly, Orfeo, Azucena, Amneris, Brangäne, Fricka, Marfa (in Khovanshina) and Marie (in Wozzeck); has sung in the leading European opera houses including Berlin, Madrid, Frankfurt, La Scala, Vienna State Opera and Bavarian State Opera, Munich; int. debut as recitalist, Salzburg Festival 1985; recordings include the Bach Passions, Gluck's Orfeo, Handel's Messiah, Beethoven's Choral Symphony, Wagner's Das Rheingold, Johann Strauss' Die Fledermaus and Frank Martin's Cornet (Grand Prix du Disque). *Address:* c/o Artists Management Zürich, Rütistr. 52, 8044 Zürich-Gockhausen, Switzerland.

LIPPOLD, Richard, B.F.A.; American sculptor; b. 3 May 1915, Milwaukee; s. of Adolph Lippold and Elsa (Schmidt) Lippold; m. Louise Greuel 1940; one s. two d.; ed. Univ. of Chicago, Art Inst. of Chicago; taught Layton School of Art, Milwaukee 1940–41, Univ. of Mich., 1941–44, Goddard Coll. 1945–47, Trenton (N.J.) Jr. Coll. 1948–52; Prof., Hunter Coll., New York 1952–67; works in several collections including Museum of Modern Art, Whitney Museum, Metropolitan Museum of Art, New York; comms. for Inland Steel Bldg., Chicago, Portsmouth (R.I.) Priory Church, Pan Am Bldg., New York, Avery Fisher Hall, Lincoln Center, New York, St. Mary's Cathedral, San Francisco, Air and Space Museum, Washington, D.C., King's Retiring Room, Riyadh, Saudi Arabia, Kish Island, Iran, Hyatt Regency, Milwaukee, Shiga Sacred Garden, Kyoto, Japan, Park Ave. Atrium Bldg., New York, One Financial Center, Boston, Deutsche Bank, Frankfurt, First Interstate Bank, Seattle, Seoul, S. Korea, atrium Crystal City, Va., Marina Square, Singapore, Orange Co. Center for Performing Arts, Calif., Emerald-Shapery Center, San Diego, Calif.; mem. Nat. Inst. of Arts and Letters (Vice-Pres. 1966); Third Prize Int. Sculpture Competition, ICA, London 1953, Silver Medal, Architectural League, New York 1960, Fine Arts Medal, American Inst. of Architecture 1970. *Address:* P.O. Box 248, Locust Valley, NY 11560, U.S.A.

LIPPONEN PAAVO, Tapio; Finnish politician; b. 23 April 1941, Turtola; journalist 1963–67; Research and Int. Affairs Sec. and Head Political Section Finnish Social Democratic Party (SDP) 1967–79; Pvt. Sec. (Special Political Adviser) to Prime Minister 1979–82; Man. Dir. Viestintä Teema Oy 1988–95; Head Finnish Inst. of Int. Affairs 1989–91; Chair. Supervisory Bd. Outokumpu Oy 1989–90; mem. Helsinki City Council 1985–94; M.P. 1983–87, 1991–; mem. SDP Party Cttee. 1987–90, Chair. SDP Helsinki Dist. 1985–92, Chair. of SDP 1993–; Prime Minister of Finland April 1995–; Speaker of Parl. March–April 1995. *Address:* Office of the Prime Minister, Snellmaninkatu 1, 00170 Helsinki, Finland.

LIPSCOMB, William Nunn Jr., PH.D.; American professor of chemistry; b. 9 Dec. 1919, Cleveland, Ohio; s. of Dr. William Lipscomb and Edna Porter Lipscomb; m. 1st Mary Adele Sargent 1944; one s. one d.; m. 2nd Jean Craig Evans 1983; one d.; ed. Univ. of Kentucky and Calif. Inst. of Tech.; Asst. Prof. of Physical Chem., Univ. of Minn. 1946–50, Assoc. Prof. 1950–54, Acting Chief, Physical Chem. Div. 1952–54, Prof. and Chief, Physical Chem. Div. 1954–59; Prof. of Chem., Harvard Univ. 1959–71, Chair. Dept. of Chem. 1962–65, Abbott and James Lawrence Prof. of Chem. 1971–90, Prof. Emer. 1990–; Dir. Midland Dow Chemical Co., Mich. 1982–90; Overseas Fellow of Churchill Coll., Cambridge 1966; mem. N.A.S., American Acad. of Arts and Sciences, Acad. Européenne des Sciences, des Arts et des Lettres, Paris 1980; Foreign mem. Royal Netherlands Acad. of Arts and Sciences 1976–; Hon. mem. The Chemical Soc., London 1972, Int. Asscn. of Bioinorganic Scientists 1979, Int. Acad. Quantum Molecular Science 1980; Pres. American Crystallographic Soc. 1955; Hon. Fellow, Royal Soc. of Chemistry; Dr. h.c. Munich 1976, Hon. D.Sc. (Long Island Univ.) 1977, (Rutgers Univ.) 1979, (Gustavus Adolphus Coll.) 1980, (Marietta Coll.) 1981, (Ohio State Univ.) 1991; Harrison Howe Award in Chem. 1958, Award for Distinguished Service in the Advancement of Inorganic Chem. 1968, Ledlie Prize, Harvard Univ. 1971, Peter Debye Award in Physical Chem., A.C.S. 1973, Nobel Prize in Chem. 1976, Distinguished Alumni Award, Calif. Inst. of Technology 1977, Senior U.S. Scientist Award, Alexander von Humboldt-Stiftung 1979. *Publications:* Boron Hydrides 1963, Nuclear Magnetic Resonance Studies of Boron and Related Compounds (with G. R. Eaton) 1969, Crystallography in North America 1983; and papers on structure and function of enzymes and natural products in inorganic chem. and theoretical chem. *Leisure interests:* chamber music, tennis. *Address:* Department of Chemistry, Harvard University, 12 Oxford Street, Cambridge, MA 02138, U.S.A. *Telephone:* (617) 495-4098.

LIPSET, Seymour Martin, PH.D.; American professor of political science and sociology; b. 18 March 1922, New York; s. of Max Lipset and Lena Lippman; m. 1st Elsie Braun 1944 (died 1987); two s. one d.; m. 2nd Sydnee Guyer 1990; ed. City Coll. of New York and Columbia Univ.; Asst. Prof. Univ. of Calif., Berkeley 1948–50; Asst. then Assoc. Prof. and Asst. Dir. Bureau of Applied Social Research, Columbia Univ. 1950–56; Prof. of Sociology, Univ. of Calif. (Berkeley) 1956–66; George D. Markham Prof. of Govt. and Sociology, Harvard Univ. 1966–75; Sr. Fellow, The Hoover Inst., Stanford Univ. 1975–, Caroline S.G. Munro Prof. of Political Science and Sociology 1975–92; Hazel Prof. of Public Policy, George Mason Univ., Fairfax, Va. 1990–; Pres. American Political Science Asscn. 1981–82, American Sociological Asscn. 1992–93; Fellow, N.A.S., American Acad. of Arts and Sciences; Dir. Aurora Foundation 1985–, U.S. Inst. of Peace 1996–; MacIver Award 1962; Gunnar Myrdal Award 1970; Fellow Guggenheim Foundation 1971–72; Rawson Award 1986; numerous hon. degrees. *Publications:* Agrarian Socialism 1950, Political Man: The Social Bases of Politics 1960, The First New Nation 1963, Revolution and Counterrevolution 1968, Rebellion in the University (with W. Schneider) 1972, The Confidence Gap: Business, Labor and Government in the Public Eye 1983, Unions in Transition (ed.) 1986, Consensus and Conflict 1987, Continental Divide: The Institutions and Values of the United States and Canada 1990, The Educational Background of American Jews 1994, Jews and the New American Scene 1995 (with Earl Raab), American Exceptionalism 1996, Who's Who in Democracy 1997, Democracy in Asia and Africa 1998, Democracy in Europe and the Americas 1998. *Leisure interests:* swimming, reading, walking, politics. *Address:* Institute of Policy Studies, George Mason University, Pohick Module, Fairfax, VA 22030; 213 Hoover Memorial Bldg., Stanford University, Stanford, CA 94305, U.S.A. *Telephone:* (703) 993-2283 (Fairfax).

LIPTON, Stuart; British property developer; b. 9 Nov. 1942; s. of Bertram Green and Jeannette Lipton; m. Ruth Marks 1966; two s. one d.; Dir. Sterling Land Co. 1971–73, First Palace Securities Ltd. 1973–76; Man. Dir. Greycoat PLC 1976–83; Chief Exec. Stanhope Properties PLC 1983–95, Stanhope PLC 1995–; Dir. Royal Opera House 1998–; mem. Royal Fine Art Comm. 1988–. *Address:* 26 Mount Row, London, W1Y 5DA, England (Office). *Telephone:* 0171-495 7575.

LIPWORTH, Sir (Maurice) Sydney, Kt., B.COM., LL.B.; British barrister and businessman; b. 13 May 1931, Johannesburg, South Africa; m. Rosa Liwarek 1957; two s.; ed. King Edward VII School, Johannesburg, Univ. of Witwatersrand; practising barrister, Johannesburg 1956–64; non-exec. Dir. Liberty Life Asscn. of Africa Ltd. 1956–64; Exec. Private Trading Cos. 1964–67; Exec. Dir. Abbey Life Assurance PLC 1968–70; Vice-Pres. and Dir. Abbey Int. Corpn. Inc. 1968–70; one of co-founders and Dir. Allied Dunbar Assurance PLC 1970–88, Deputy Man. Dir. 1977–79, Jt. Man. Dir. 1979–84, Deputy Chair. 1984–88; Dir. J. Rothschild Holdings PLC 1984–87, BAT Industries PLC 1985–88; Deputy Chair., Dir. (non-exec.) Nat. Westminster Bank 1993–; Chair., Dir. (non-exec.) Zeneca Group PLC 1995–99 (Dir. 1994–99); Dir. (non-exec.) Carlton Communications PLC 1993–; Chair. Monopolies and Mergers Comm. 1988–92, Bar Asscn. for Commerce, Finance and Industry 1991–92, Financial Reporting Council 1993–; mem. Senior Salaries Review Body 1994–; Deputy Chair. of Trustees Philharmonia Orchestra 1986–93, Chair. 1993–; Trustee South Bank Ltd. 1996–; mem. European Policy Forum; Hon. Q.C. 1993. *Leisure interests:* music, theatre, tennis. *Address:* 41 Lothbury, London, EC2P 2BP, England (Office). *Telephone:* 0171-726 1000. *Fax:* 0171-726 1038.

LIŠČÁK, Jozef, LL.D.; Slovak politician; b. 18 Jan. 1947, Svrčinovec, Čadca Dist.; ed. Komenský Univ. Bratislava; worked as notary in Čadca; judge in Bánská Bystrica; Chair. Bench, Bánská Bystrica 1990–94; Minister of Justice, Govt. of Slovakia 1994–98; Deputy Chair. Govt. Council to Combat Subversive Activities against the State 1995–98. *Address:* SNR-Slovak National Council, Mudroňova 1, Bratislava 812 80, Slovakia. *Telephone:* (7) 534 1111 (Office).

LISITSYN, Anatoly Ivanovich; Russian politician; b. 26 June 1947, Bolshiye Smenki, Kalinin Region; m.; one c.; ed. Leningrad Acad. of Forest Tech.; Rybinsk furniture factory 1987, also Chair., Rybinsk City Dist. Exec. Cttee. 1987–90; Chair. Rybinsk City Exec. Cttee 1990–91; Deputy Head, Head, Yaroslavl Regional Admin. 1991–92; mem. Council of Fed. 1993–; mem. movt. Our Home is Russia; mem. People's Democratic Party 1995; Gov. of Yaroslavl Region 1995–; mem. Council of Feds. of Russia 1996–. *Address:* Office of the Governor, Sovetskaya pl. 3, 150000 Yaroslavl, Russia. *Telephone:* (3022) 23 34 93 (Office). *Fax:* (3022) 23 02 22 (Office).

LISITZYN, Aleksander Petrovich; Russian marine geologist and geophysicist; b. 3 July 1923; m.; two c.; ed. Moscow Geological Prospecting Inst.; jr., sr. researcher, head of lab., head of div. Inst. of Oceanology U.S.S.R. Acad. of Sciences 1953–81, head of dept. 1981–; corresp. mem. U.S.S.R. (now Russian) Acad. of Sciences 1974, mem. 1994; research in geochem. of seas and oceans; U.S.S.R. State Prize, F. Shepard Award. *Publications include:* Sedimentation in the World Ocean 1972, Geological History of Oceans,

1980, Biogeochemistry of Oceans 1983, Marine Glacial and Marine Ice Sedimentation 1994, Oceanic Sedimentation, Lithography and Geochemistry 1996. *Address:* Institute of Oceanology, Russian Academy of Sciences, Krasikova str. 23, 117218 Moscow, Russia. *Telephone:* (095) 124 8528 (Office).

LISNYANSKAYA, Inna L'vovna; Russian writer; b. 24 June 1928, Baku; m. Semen I. Lipkin (q.v.); first works published 1949; resigned from Union of Writers 1980 (membership restored 1989). *Publications include:* This Happened to Me 1957, Faithfulness 1958, Not Simply Love 1963, The Light of Grape 1978; contributed to the literary almanack Metropole 1979; Verse 1970–83, 1984, On the Edge of Sleep 1984, The Circle 1985, Airy Layer 1990, Poetry 1991, About Music of the Poem without Hero by Akhmatova 1991, After All 1994, The Lonely Gift 1995, The Box with a Triple Bottom (Study on Akhmatova's Poem Without the Hero) 1995. *Address:* Usievicha Street 8, Apt. 16, 125315 Moscow, Russia. *Telephone:* (095) 155-75-98.

LISOV, Yevgeny Kuzmich; Russian politician and lawyer; b. 1940, Ivanovo Region; ed. Saratov State Univ.; investigator, Dist. Prosecutor's Office Kursk Region, sr. investigator, Head of Div., Deputy Head, Investigation Dept., R.S.F.S.R. Prosecutor's Office; Deputy Gen. Prosecutor of Russian Fed. 1991–93; investigated coup d'état 1991; Deputy Prosecutor of Moscow 1993–95; attorney, Moscow Regional Coll. of Barristers; expert, magazine Ogonyok 1995–98; Deputy Head, Admin. of Russian Presidency, Head, Main Control Dept., Admin. of Russian Presidency 1998–. *Publications:* Kremlin Conspiracy (with V. Stepankov, q.v.), articles in magazines and newspapers. *Address:* Security Council, Ipatyevsky per. 4/10, entr. 6, Moscow, Russia. *Telephone:* (095) 206 6596 (Office).

LISSAKERS, Karin Margareta, M.A.; American international civil servant; b. 16 Aug. 1944; m.; two c.; ed. Ohio State Univ. and Johns Hopkins Univ.; mem. staff, Cttee. on Foreign Relations, U.S. Senate, Washington, D.C. 1972–78; Deputy Dir. Econ. Policy Planning Staff, U.S. Dept. of State 1978–80; Sr. Assoc. Carnegie Endowment for Int. Peace, New York 1981–83; lecturer in int. banking, Dir. int. business and banking programme, School of Int. Public Affairs, Columbia Univ. New York 1985–93; U.S. Exec. Dir. IMF 1993–. *Publications:* Banks, Borrowers and the Establishment 1991; articles in professional journals. *Address:* International Monetary Fund, 700 19th Street, N.W., Room 13-320 Washington, DC 20431, U.S.A.

LISSNER, Stéphane Michel; French theatre director; b. 23 Jan. 1953, Paris; s. of Georges Lissner and Elisabeth Landenbaum; two s. one d.; ed. Coll. Stanislas and Lycée Henri IV, Paris; Sec.-Gen. Centre dramatique, Aubervilliers 1977–78; Co-Dir. Centre dramatique, Nice 1978–83; Dir.-Gen. Orchestre de Paris 1994–96; Artistic Dir. Teatro Real de Paris 1996–97; Dir. Aix-en-Provence Festival 1996–, Théâtre des Bouffes du Nord 1998–. *Address:* CICT, 13 blvd. Rouchechouart, 75009 Paris, France (Office).

LISSOUBA, Pascal, D. ÈS SC.; Republic of the Congo politician; b. 15 Nov. 1931, Tsinguidi, Congo (Brazzaville); s. of Albert Lissouba and Marie Bouanga; m. 2nd Jocelyne Pierrot 1967; one s. six d.; ed. secondary education in Nice, France, and Ecole Supérieure d'Agriculture, Tunis; fmr. agricultural specialist; Prime Minister of Congo (Brazzaville) 1963–66, concurrently Minister of Trade and Industry and Agric.; Prof. of Genetics, Brazzaville 1966–71, concurrently Minister of Planning 1968, Minister of Agric., Waterways and Forests 1969; Dir. Ecole Supérieure des Sciences, Brazzaville 1970; sentenced to life imprisonment for complicity in assassination of Pres. Ngouabi 1977, subsequently released and exiled; Dir. African Bureau for Science and Tech., Nairobi 1981–; Leader Union panafricaine pour la Démocratie sociale (UPADS); Pres. of Congo People's Repub. 1992–97; in exile, Burkina Faso. *Leisure interests:* geology, music.

LIST, Roland, DR.SC.NAT., F.R.S.C.; Canadian international official and meteorologist; b. 21 Feb. 1929, Frauenfeld, Thurgau, Switzerland; s. of August Joseph List and Anna Kaufmann; m. Gertrud K. Egli 1956 (died 1996); two c.; ed. Swiss Fed. Inst. of Tech., Zürich; Head, Hail Section, Swiss Fed. Inst. for Snow and Avalanche Research, Davos 1952–63; Prof. of Physics (Meteorology), Dept. of Physics, Univ. of Toronto 1963–82, 1984–94, Prof. Emer. 1994–, Assoc. Chair. Dept. of Physics 1969–73; Deputy Sec.-Gen. WMO 1982–84; Chair. Exec. Cttee. Panel of Experts on Weather Modification, WMO, Geneva 1969–82; Dir. Corpn. for Atmospheric Research, Boulder, Colo. 1974–77; mem. Science Council, Space Shuttle Program (NASA) 1978–80; Chair. Italian Scientific Cttee. for Rain Enhancement 1990–; Sec.-Gen. Int. Assn. Meteorology and Atmospheric Sciences 1995–; mem. Exec. Cttee. Int. Union for Geodesy and Geophysics 1995–; mem. or chair. many int., Canadian and Swiss cttees.; consultant to UN, UNEP, World Bank and many other orgs.; Visiting Prof. Swiss Fed. Inst. of Tech., Zürich 1974, 1998; Pres. Rotary Club of Toronto–Don Mills 1995–96; mem.Canadian Acad. of Sciences, Canadian Meteorological and Oceanic Soc., American Meteorological Soc., American Geophysical Union, Royal Meteorological Soc., European Geophysical Soc., etc.; Sesquicentennial Medal, Univ. of Leningrad 1970; Patterson Medal, Canadian Meteorological Service. *Publications:* over 220 papers and many reports in the field of cloud physics, weather modification and classical physics. *Address:* Department of Physics, University of Toronto, Toronto, Ont., M5S 1A7; 58 Olsen Drive, Toronto, Ont. M3A 3J3, Canada. *Telephone:* (416) 978-2982 (Office); (416) 445-2947 (Home). *Fax:* (416) 978-8905.

LISULO, Daniel Muchiwa, S.C., B.A., LL.B.; Zambian politician and lawyer; b. 6 Dec. 1930, Mongu; s. of Musialela Lisulo and Wamusheke Lisulo; m. Mary Mambo 1968 (died 1976); three s. two d.; ed. Loyola Coll. of Madras Univ., Law Faculty of Delhi Univ., India; active in independence struggle 1953–63; with Anglo-American Corpn. (Cen. Africa) 1963–64; Asst. Solicitor, Ellis & Co., Lusaka 1964–67; Sr. Partner Lisulo & Co. 1968–; Dir. Bank of Zambia 1964–77; mem. and Chair. Local Govt. Service Comm. 1964–72; mem. Nat. Comm. on One Party System in Zambia; Dir. various cos.; mem. Cen. Cttee. United Nat. Independence Party (UNIP) 1972–88, Legal Counsel of UNIP 1972–76; mem. Nat. Assembly 1977–83; Minister of Legal Affairs and Attorney-Gen. 1977–78, Prime Minister of Zambia 1978–81; Vice-Pres. Nat. Party (NP) 1995; Chair. Social and Cultural Sub-Cttee., UNIP 1981–82, Appointments and Disciplinary Cttee., UNIP 1982–83, Political and Legal Cttee. of UNIP 1983–88; Chair. ZIMCO (Zambia Industrial and Mining Corpn. Ltd.) 1979–81; Vice-Pres. World Peace Council 1986–89; mem. Inter-Action Council 1988–. *Leisure interests:* swimming, hunting, boating, soccer. *Address:* Lisulo and Co., 6th Floor, Kulima Tower, Katunjila Road, P.O. Box 32259, Lusaka 10101, Zambia. *Telephone:* 228627/28. *Fax:* 225777.

LITAVRIN, Gennady Grigoryevich; Russian historian; b. 6 Oct. 1925; m.; two c.; ed. Moscow State Univ.; teacher Moscow State Univ. 1954–55; sr. ed. Ministry of Public Educ. 1955; jr., sr. researcher Inst. of History U.S.S.R. Acad. of Sciences 1955–68; sr., leading researcher Inst. of Slavonic Studies U.S.S.R. Acad. of Sciences 1968–87, head of div. 1987–; corresp. mem. U.S.S.R. (now Russian) Acad. of Sciences 1987, mem. 1994; research in history of Bulgaria, processes of formation of feudal regime, agrarian relations and social struggle in Byzantium, of Russian-Byzantine relations, problems of Balkan ethnogenesis; mem. Comm. on Studies and Promotion of Slavic Cultures. *Publications include:* Byzantine Society and State in the X–XI Centuries 1977; mem. Comm. on studies of Treasures of Aphone Monasteries. *Address:* Institute of Slavonic Studies, Russian Academy of Sciences, Leninsky pr. 32, 117334 Moscow, Russia. *Telephone:* (095) 938-57-85, 938-17-80 (Office); (095) 211-88-87 (Home).

LITHERLAND, Albert Edward, PH.D., F.R.S., F.R.S.C.; Canadian professor of physics; b. 12 March 1928, Wallasey, England; s. of Albert Litherland and Ethel Clement; m. Anne Allen 1956; two d.; ed. Wallasey Grammar School and Liverpool Univ.; Scientific Officer, Atomic Energy of Canada 1955–66; Prof. of Physics, Toronto Univ. 1966–79, Univ. Prof. 1979–93, Univ. Prof. Emer. 1993–, Dir. Isotrace Lab. 1982–; Hon. D.Sc. (Toronto) 1998; Gold Medal, Canadian Assn. of Physicists 1971, Rutherford Medal and Prize, Inst. of Physics 1974, Henry Marshall Tory Gold Medal 1993; Guggenheim Fellow 1986. *Publications:* numerous scientific papers. *Leisure interests:* reading, travel. *Address:* Apartment 801, 120 Rosedale Valley Road, Toronto, Ont., M4W 1P8, Canada. *Telephone:* (416) 923-5616.

LITTLE, Ian Malcolm David, A.F.C., C.B.E., D.PHIL., F.B.A.; British economist; b. 18 Dec. 1918, Rugby; s. of Brig.-Gen. M. O. Little and Iris H. Little (née Brassey); m. 1st Doreen Hennessey 1946 (died 1984); one s. one d.; m. 2nd Lydia Segrave 1991; ed. Eton Coll. and New Coll., Oxford; R.A.F. officer 1939–46; Fellow, All Souls Coll., Oxford 1948–50, Trinity Coll., Oxford 1950–52, Nuffield Coll., Oxford 1952–76, Prof. Econs. of Underdeveloped Countries 1971–76, Fellow Emer. 1976–; Deputy Dir. Econ. Section, H.M. Treasury 1953–55; mem. M.I.T. Center for Int. Studies, India 1958–59, 1965; Vice-Pres. OECD Devt. Centre, Paris 1965–67; mem. Bd. British Airports Authority 1969–74; Special Adviser, IBRD, Washington, D.C. 1976–78, Consultant 1984–85; Project Dir. Twentieth Century Fund, New York 1978–81; Hon. D.Sc. (Edinburgh). *Publications:* A Critique of Welfare Economics 1950, The Price of Fuel 1952, Aid to Africa 1964, Economic Development, Theory, Policy and International Relations 1982; jt. author of several other books. *Address:* Nuffield College, Oxford, OX1 1NF (Office); 43 Blandford Avenue, Oxford, OX2 8EB, England (Home). *Telephone:* (01865) 278539 (Office); (01865) 557626. *Fax:* (01865) 278621.

LITTLE, Robert Alastair, M.A.; British restaurateur and chef; b. 25 June 1950, Colne, Lancs; s. of R. G. Little and M. I. Little; m. Kirsten Pedersen 1981; one s. one d.; ed. Downing Coll., Cambridge; Chef Old Compton Wine Bar 1974–77, L'Escargot 1981–82, 192 Kensington Park Road 1982–83; Chef, Propr. Le Routier 1977–79, Simpsons 1979–81, Alastair Little 1985–; food columnist Daily Mail 1993–. *Publications:* Keep it Simple 1993, Mediterranean Redefined (with Richard Whittington) 1995, Alastair Little's Italian Kitchen 1996. *Leisure interests:* jigsaws, trashy novels, travel, wine. *Address:* 49 Frith Street, London, W1V 5TE, England. *Telephone:* 0171-437 6733.

LITTLE, Tasmin E., A.R.C.M.; British concert violinist; b. 13 May 1965, London; d. of George Little and Gillian Little; m. Michael Hatch 1993; ed. Yehudi Menuhin School, Guildhall School of Music; studied pvtly. with Lorand Fenyves in Canada; performed with Leipzig Gewandhaus, Berlin Symphony, London Symphony, Philharmonia, Royal Philharmonic, Royal Liverpool Philharmonic, European Community Chamber, Royal Danish and Stavanger Symphony orchestras; has played in orchestras conducted by Kurt Masur, Vladimir Ashkenazy, Leonard Slatkin, Tadaaki Otaka, Sir Charles Groves, Andrew Davis, Jerzy Maksymiuk, Vernon Handley, Yan Pascal Tortelier, Sir Edward Downes, Yehudi Menuhin; played at the Proms since 1990; concerto and recital performances in U.K., Europe, Scandinavia, South America, Hong Kong, Oman, Zimbabwe, Australia, N.Z.; several TV appearances including BBC Last Night of the Proms 1995; Hon. D.Litt. (Bradford) 1996. *Recordings include:* concertos of Bruch, Dvořák, Brahms, Sibelius, Delius, Rubbra, Saxton; George Lloyd, Ravel, Debussy, Poulenc violin sonatas, Bruch Scottish Fantasy, Lalo Symphonie Espagnole. *Publica-*

tion: paper on Delius' violin concerto. *Leisure interests:* theatre, cinema, swimming, languages. *Address:* c/o Harold Holt, 31 Sinclair Road, London, W14 0NS, England. *Telephone:* 0171-603 4600. *Fax:* 0171-603 0019.

LITTLECHILD, Stephen Charles, PH.D.; British economist and public servant; b. 27 Aug. 1943, Wisbech; s. of Sidney F. Littlechild and Joyce M. Littlechild; m. Kate Crombie 1974 (died 1982); two s. one d.; ed. Wisbech Grammar School, Univ. of Birmingham, Univ. of Texas, U.S.A.; Sr. Research Lecturer in Econs., Graduate Centre for Man. Studies, Univ. of Birmingham 1970–72, Prof. of Commerce, Head Dept. of Industrial Econs. and Business Studies 1975–89; Prof. of Applied Econs. and Head of Econs., Econometrics, Statistics and Marketing Subject Group, Aston Man. Centre, Birmingham 1972–75; Visiting Scholar, Dept. of Econs., Univ. of Calif., L.A., U.S.A. 1975; Visiting Prof., New York, Stanford and Chicago Univs. and Va. Polytechnic 1979–80; mem. Monopolies and Mergers Comm. 1983–89, Sec. of State for Energy's Advisory Council on Research and Devt. 1987–89; Dir.-Gen. of Electricity Supply 1989–98; Harkness Fellow 1965–66. *Publications:* Operational Research for Managers 1977, (with M. F. Shutler) 1991, The Fallacy of the Mixed Economy 1978, 1986, Elements of Telecommunications Economics 1979, Energy Strategies for the UK (with K. G. Vaidya) 1982, Regulation of British Telecommunications' Profitability 1983, Economic Regulation of Privatised Water Authorities 1986. *Address:* c/o Office of Electricity Regulation, Hagley House, Hagley Road, Birmingham, B16 8QG, England.

LITTLEWOOD, Joan; British theatre director and artist; b. 6 Oct. 1914, London; Dir. Theatre of Action, street theatre co., Manchester 1931–37; Founder, Theatre Union, Manchester, introducing the Individual Work System 1937–39; freelance writer, banned from BBC and Entertainments Nat. Service Asscn. for political opinions 1939–45; founded Theatre Workshop with Gerry Raffles 1945, Artistic Dir. 1945–75, tours in U.K. and Europe with original works 1945–53, Theatre Royal, Stratford, London, E.15 1953–75; invited to Theatre of the Nations, Paris yearly from 1955; transfers to West End, London and Broadway, New York 1960–61; Centre Culturel, Hammamet, Tunisia 1965–67; Image India, Calcutta 1968; created children's entertainments outside Theatre Royal Stratford 1968–75; working in France 1975–; Seminar, Relais Culturel, Aix-en-Provence 1976; mem. French Acad. of Writers 1964–; Dr. h.c. (Open Univ.) 1977, (Open Univ. Brussels) 1995; Gold Medal for production of Lysistrata, Berlin, German Democratic Repub. 1958, Olympic Award, Taormina 1959, Best Production of the Year (three times), Theatre of the Nations, Paris, Soc. of West End Theatre Award 1983, The Vildrosen Award, Folkkulturcentrum, Stockholm 1995, Lifetime's Achievement Award, Dirs.' Guild 1995. *Productions include:* The Quare Fellow 1956, A Taste of Honey 1958, The Hostage 1958, Fings Ain't Wot They Used T'Be 1959, Oh, What a Lovely War! (with Gerry Raffles and co.) 1963; film Sparrers Can't Sing 1962. *Publications:* Milady Vine: Biography of Philippe de Rothschild 1984, Joan's Book (autobiog.) 1994. *Address:* c/o Theatre Royal Stratford East, Gerry Raffles Square, Newham, E15 1BN, England; 1 place Louis Revol, 38200 Vienne, France.

LITTMAN, Mark, Q.C.; British barrister-at-law and business executive; b. 4 Sept. 1920, London; s. of Jack and Lilian Littman; m. Marguerite Lamkin 1965; ed. Owen's School, L.S.E. and Queens Coll., Oxford; Lieut. R.N.V.R. 1941–46; called to Bar, Middle Temple 1947; Dir. Rio Tinto-Zinc Corpn. 1968–91; Pres. Bar Asscn. for Commerce, Finance and Industry 1974–80; mem. Bar Council 1973–75, mem. of Senate of the Inns of Court and the Bar 1974–75; Deputy Chair. British Steel Corpn. 1970–79; Dir. Commercial Union Assurance Co. Ltd. 1970–81, Granada Group Ltd. 1977–93, British Enkalon Ltd. 1972–80; Amerada Hess Corpn. 1973–86, Envirotech Corpn. 1974–78, Burton Group PLC 1983–93; Treas. Middle Temple 1988; Bencher of the Middle Temple 1970; mem. Royal Comm. on Legal Services 1976; mem. Int. Council for Commercial Arbitration 1978–; mem. Court of Govs., L.S.E. 1980–; Vice-Chair. London Int. Arbitration Trust 1980–. *Address:* 79 Chester Square, London, SW1W 9DU, England. *Telephone:* 0171-730 2973.

LITTON, Andrew, M.M.; American orchestral conductor and pianist; b. 16 May 1959, New York; ed. Fieldston High School, Mozarteum, Juilliard School; Asst. Conductor, La Scala, Milan 1980–81; Exxon/Arts Endowment Asst. Conductor, then Assoc. Conductor, Nat. Symphony Orchestra, Washington, D.C. 1982–86; Prin. Guest Conductor, Bournemouth Symphony Orchestra 1986–88, Prin. Conductor and Artistic Adviser 1988–94, Conductor Laureate 1994–; Music Dir. Dallas Symphony Orchestra 1994–; guest conductor many leading orchestras world-wide, including Chicago Symphony, Philadelphia, Los Angeles Philharmonic, Pittsburgh Symphony, Toronto Symphony, Montreal Symphony, Vancouver Symphony, London Philharmonic, Royal Philharmonic, London Symphony, English Chamber, Leipzig Gewandhaus, Moscow State Symphony, Stockholm Philharmonic, RSO Berlin, RAI Milan, Orchestre Nat. de France, Suisse Romande, Tokyo Philharmonic, Melbourne Symphony and Sydney Symphony orchestras; début at Metropolitan Opera, New York with Eugene Onegin 1989; conducted Leoncavallo, La Bohème and Falstaff, St. Louis Opera, Hansel and Gretel, Los Angeles Opera 1992, Porgy and Bess, Royal Opera House, Covent Garden 1992, Salome, English Nat. Opera 1996; recordings include Mahler Symphony No. 1 and Songs of a Wayfarer, Elgar Enigma Variations, complete Tchaikovsky symphony cycle, complete Rachmaninov symphony cycle, Shostakovich Symphony No. 10, Gershwin Rhapsody in Blue, Concerto in F and Ravel Concerto in G (as piano soloist and conductor), Bernstein Symphony No. 2, Brahms Symphony No. 1; music consultant to film The Chosen; Hon. D.Mus. (Bournemouth) 1992; winner William Kapell Memorial U.S. Nat. Piano Competition 1978; winner Bruno Walter Conducting Fellowship 1981, BBC/Rupert Foundation Int. Conductors Competition 1982. *Address:* c/o IMG Artists Europe, Media House, 3 Burlington Lane, London, W4 2TH, England.

LITVAK KING, Jaime, M.A., PH.D.; Mexican archaeologist; b. 10 Dec. 1933, Mexico City; s. of Abraham Litvak and Eugenia King; m. 1st Elena Kaminski 1954 (divorced 1968); one d.; m. 2nd Carmen Aguilera 1972 (divorced 1978); ed. Univ. Nacional Autónoma de México; Asst. Dept. of Prehistory, Inst. Nacional de Antropología e Historia 1960–63, Researcher 1963–66; Lecturer Escuela Nacional de Antropología e Historia 1963–74; Head Sección de Máquinas Electrónicas, Museo Nacional de Antropología 1966–68; Asst. Research Fellow, Anthropological Section, Univ. Nacional Autónoma de México 1968–72, Full Research Fellow 1972–74, Head of Section 1973; Dir. Inst. for Anthropological Research, Univ. Nacional Autónoma de México 1973–85, Dir.-Gen. for Academic Projects 1985–86; Chair. Anthropology, Univ. of the Americas 1987–89; Joint Chair. Archaeology, Escuela Nacional de Antropología 1966–67, Chair. 1969–71; Co-Ed. Antropología Matemática 1968–74; Research Ed. American Antiquity 1971–74; Advisory Ed. Mesoamerican Archaeology, Abstracts in Anthropology 1973–74; Visiting Prof., Univ. of Minn. 1981, Univ. of New Mexico 1985–86; Mellon Prof. of Humanities, Tulane Univ. 1988; Prof. Emer., Univ. of Mexico 1998–; Coordinator Library of the Inst. of Anthropological Research 1993–; Gen. Sec. Mexican Anthropological Soc. 1970–76, 1981–83; mem. Mexican Scientific Research Acad. 1972–, Nat. Researcher, Class III, Mexico; mem. Bd. of Dirs. Museum Computer Network 1982–88; Fray Bernardino de Sahagún (Mexican Nat. Award for Anthropology) 1970, Nat. Researcher, Mexican Scientific Research Acad. 1984. *Publications:* El Valle de Xochicalco 1970, Cihuatlán y Tepecoacuilco 1971, Xochicalco: Un Asentamiento Urbano Prehispánico 1974, Ancient Mexico 1985, Todas las piedras tienen 2000 años 1985, etc. *Address:* Instituto de Investigaciones Antropológicas, Universidad Nacional Autónoma de México, Ciudad Universitaria, 04510 México, D.F., Mexico.

LITVINOV, Boris Vasilyevich; Russian physicist and engineer; b. 12 Nov. 1929, m.; three c.; ed. Moscow Inst. of Mech.; lab., engineer, sr. engineer, sr. researcher, Deputy Head of Div., Research Inst. of Experimental Physics 1952–61; Chief constructor, All-Union Inst. of Tech. Physics, U.S.S.R. (now Russian) Acad. of Sciences, Constructor-Gen., First Deputy Scientific Dir. 1961–78; corresp. mem. U.S.S.R. (now Russian) Acad. of Sciences 1991, mem. 1997–; Hero of Socialist Labour, Lenin's Prize 1966; main research in applied physics, devt. of new constructions of exploding devices. *Address:* Institute of Technical Physics, P.O. Box 245, 454070 Chelyabinsk, Russia. *Telephone:* (651) 725 5216 (Office).

LITVINOV, Pavel Mikhailovich; Russian dissident activist and physicist; b. 1940, Moscow; (grandson of fmr. People's Commissar for Foreign Affairs M. M. Litvinov); m. M. Rusakovskaya; two c.; employed in Lomonosov Inst. of Chemical-Tech., Moscow 1968; author of various samizdat documents protesting at trials of dissidents; sentenced to 5 years exile 1968–73; released 1973; expelled from U.S.S.R. 1974; returned in 1992. *Publications include:* The Demonstration on Pushkin Square 1967, Letters and Telegrams to Pavel Litvinov Dec. 1967–May 1968, 1969, Self-Awareness 1976.

LIU, Ts'un-yan, A.O., PH.D., D.LIT.; Australian professor of Chinese; b. 11 Aug. 1917, Peking, China; s. of Tsung-ch'üan Liu (deceased) and Huang Yü-shu Liu (deceased); m. Chiang Szuyung 1940; one s. one d.; ed. Univs. of Peking, London and Hong Kong; Chair. Chinese Panel, Queen's Coll., Hong Kong 1952–59; lecturer Northcote Training Coll., Hong Kong 1959–62; Sr. Lecturer Govt. Evening School, Hong Kong 1959–62; Sr. Lecturer, Reader in Chinese, A.N.U. 1962–66, Prof. and Head of Dept. of Chinese 1966–82, Dean Faculty of Asian Studies 1970–72, 1973–75, Prof. Emer. 1983–, Univ. Fellow 1983–; Visiting Prof. Columbia Univ. 1966, Harvard-Yenching Inst. 1969, Hawaii Univ. 1969, Univ. of Paris (Vincennes) 1973, Univ. of Malaya 1976, Chinese Univ. of Hong Kong 1976–77, Waseda Univ. 1981, Nat. Univ. of Singapore 1984–85; Fellow, Royal Asiatic Soc. 1957; Foundation Fellow, Australian Acad. of the Humanities 1969; Hon. D. Litt. (Yeungnam Univ., South Korea) 1972, (Hong Kong) 1988, (Murdoch) 1989, (A.N.U.) 1997. *Publications:* Buddhist and Taoist Influences on Chinese Novels 1962, Chinese Popular Fiction in Two London Libraries 1967, Selected Papers from the Hall of Harmonious Wind 1976, Chinese Middlebrow Fiction from the Ch'ing and Early Republican Era 1984, New Excursions from the Hall of Harmonious Wind 1984, Hofengtang Wenji (selected papers in Chinese) 1992, Ta Tu, The Grand Capital 1996) Hofentang Xinwenji 1997. *Leisure interests:* singing, Beijing opera. *Address:* China Centre, Australian National University, A.C.T. 2601, Australia.

LIU ANYUAN, Lieut.-Gen.; Chinese army officer and party official; b. 1927, Gaoqing, Shandong; joined CCP 1943, Red Army 1945; Political Cttee., Canton Mil. Region 1985–86; Political Commissar of PLA Gen. Logistics Dept. 1987–; mem. 13th CCP Cen. Cttee. 1987–92, 14th CCP Cen. Cttee. 1992–; Lieut.-Gen., PLA 1988; Political Commissar Nanjing Mil. Region 1992–96. *Address:* Central Committee of the Chinese Communist Party, Zhong Nan Hai, Beijing, People's Republic of China.

LIU BINYAN; Chinese writer and journalist; b. 7 Feb. 1925, Changchun City, Jilin Prov.; journalist, Renmin Ribao, Beijing 1980–88; Vice-Pres. Writer's Union of China 1985–87; charged with "bourgeois liberalization" and expelled from CCP 1987; visiting Prof. in U.S.A. 1988–. *Publications:* On Literature and Life 1985, Selected Works of Liu Binyan 1988. *Address:*

Room 204, Gate 7, Building Min 20, Jintai Xi Road, Beijing, People's Republic of China.

LIU BOSU; Chinese professor of fine art; b. Nov. 1935, Nanchang City, Jiangxi Prov.; ed. Cen. Inst. of Fine Arts 1955; Assoc. Prof. 1981–83, Prof. 1983–, Vice Dir. Cen. Inst. of Fine Art 1986–; Dir. Chinese Painting Acad. 1993–; mem. 7th CPPCC 1987–92, 8th 1993–. *Address:* 5 Jiaowei Hutong Lane, Dongcheng District, Beijing 100005, People's Republic of China.

LIU DANIAN; Chinese historian; b. 1 Aug. 1915, Huarong, Hunan Prov.; two s. one d.; ed. Chinese People's Anti-Japanese Mil. and Political Coll., Yan'an; joined CCP 1938; Deputy Ed. Historical Research 1954–60; Deputy Dir. Inst. of Modern Chinese History, Chinese Acad. of Sciences (later Social Sciences) 1954–66, Dir. 1978–82, Hon. Dir. 1982–; mem. Chinese Asscn. of History, Exec. Chair. 1982–88; Vice-Pres. Sun Yatsen Soc. 1984–; Pres. Anti-Japanese War History Soc. 1991–; Del. to 3rd NPC and mem. 4th, 5th, 6th and 7th Standing Cttee. of NPC; mem. Acad. Sinica 1955. *Publications:* The History of America's Invasion of China, General Descriptions on the History of Taiwan, Problems of Modern History in China, Speech on History at the University of Tokyo, Chinese Modern History (Ed.-in-Chief of Vols. 1, 2 and 3), Liu Danian's Historical Research Selection 1988, Various Issues of History Science 1992, The Era of the Anti-Japanese War 1996, The Pivot of China's Revival (Ed.-in-Chief) 1997. *Leisure interest:* reading classical literature. *Address:* Institute of Modern History, Chinese Academy of Social Sciences, 1 Dongchang Hutong, Wangfu Dajie, Beijing, People's Republic of China.

LIU DANZHAI; Chinese traditional artist; b. 4 March 1931, Wenzhou, Zhejiang; s. of Liu Xiuqing and Liu Chenshi; m. Wang Weilin 1953; one s. one d.; also known as Liu Xiaosu, Liu Hun and Hai Yun Sheng; noted for "ren wu hua" (figure painting); teacher Wenzhou Westlake Elementary School 1949–51; Painter, Shanghai Books Publs. 1951–56; Art Ed. Shanghai Educational Publishing House 1956–72; Painter, Shanghai People's Fine Arts Publishing House 1972–83; Prof. Shanghai Teachers' Univ. 1985–; Visiting Prof. Wenzhou Univ. 1985–; Artist, Shanghai Acad. of Chinese Arts 1956–; Art Counsellor, Shanghai Jiaotong Univ. 1981–; Head of Fine Arts Faculty, Shanghai Teacher's Univ. 1987–; mem. Chinese Artists' Asscn. 1953–, mem. Bd. of Dirs., Shanghai Br. 1953–; exhbns. (Liu Xiaosu) Wenzhou 1941, 1946; (Liu Danzhai) Shanghai 1979, Hongzhou 1984, Ishimaki, Japan 1985, Hong Kong 1988, Taiwan 1989, 1991, South-east Asia 1993, Taiwan 1996, Hong Kong 1996, travelling exhbn. Paris, Rome, Amsterdam, Heidelberg 1996; jt. exhbn., Four Contemporary Chinese Ink Painting Masters from Shanghai, Taiwan 1994; works in Nat. Museum of Fine Arts, Nat. Museum of History, Beijing and in many pvt. collections in Asia, Europe and N. America; Nat. First Award for Prints 1981; First Award for Chinese Prints (Japan) 1981; Hon. Prize for Chinese Sport Art (Chinese Olympic Cttee.) 1985. *Publications:* Images of a Dream of Red Mansions 1979, The 12 Beauties of Jinling from A Dream of Red Mansions (prints) 1981, Album of Chinese Poets 1983, Liu Danzhai: One Hundred Illustrations for 'Strange Studio' 1985, A Dream of Red Mansions 1985, Liu Danzhai (monograph) 1987, Liu Danzhai: Selections from Picture-Story Book 1987, Album of Liu Danzhai's Paintings 1988, Calendar of Paintings 1993; monographs on paintings and calligraphy by Liu Danzhai Shanghai, Hong Kong, Taiwan 1996. *Leisure interests:* poetry, travel, stone collecting. *Address:* 43 An Ting Road, Apt. 6, Shanghai, 200031, People's Republic of China. *Telephone:* 6472-0332.

LIU DEHAI; Chinese musician and university professor; b. May 1937, Cangxian Co., Hebei Prov.; ed. Centre Music Inst.; Prof. Centre Music Inst. 1984–; mem. 7th CPPCC 1987–92, 8th 1993–.

LIU FANGREN; Chinese party official; b. 1936, Wugong, Shaanxi; joined CCP 1954; Deputy Sec. Jiangxi Prov. CCP Cttee. 1985; alt. mem. CCP Cen. Cttee. 1987–92; Sec. CCP 7th Guizhou Prov. Cttee. 1993–; Chair. Standing Cttee. Guizhou Prov. People's Congress 1998–; mem. 15th CCP Cen. Cttee. 1997–. *Address:* Standing Committee of Guizhou Provincial People's Congress, Guiyang, Guizhou Province, People's Republic of China.

LIU GANG; Chinese dissident; leader of Tiananmen Square pro-democracy demonstrations 1989; imprisoned 1989–95; fled China; granted temporary asylum in U.S.A. 1996.

LIU GUOFAN; Chinese party official; b. 1929, Kaiyuan, Liaoning; joined CCP 1954; mem. Standing Cttee. Ningxia Autonomous Region CCP Cttee. 1983, Deputy Sec. 1985; Chair. CPPCC 6th Ningxian Hui Autonomous Regional Cttee. 1993–; alt. mem. CCP Cen. Cttee. 1985. *Address:* Central Committee of the Chinese Communist Party, Zhong Nan Hai, Beijing, People's Republic of China.

LIU GUOGUANG; Chinese party official and economist; b. 16 Oct. 1923, Nanjing; s. of Liu Zhihe and Zhiang Shulang; m. Liu Guoshiang 1948; two s. one d.; ed. South-West Univ., Kunming, and Moscow, U.S.S.R.; joined CCP 1961; Vice-Pres. Chinese Acad. of Social Sciences 1982–93, Special Adviser 1993–; Prof. Beijing Univ.; Alt. mem. 12th Cen. Cttee., CCP 1982–87, 13th Cen. Cttee. 1987–92; mem. 8th Nat. People's Congress Standing Cttee. 1993–98, mem. Financial and Econ. Cttee.; mem. State Academic Degree Comm. 1988–95; mem. State Council Project Review Cttee. for Three Gorges Project 1990–93. *Publications include:* The Problem Concerning the Reform of the Management System of the National Economy, Problems Concerning China's Strategy of Economic Readjustment, Economic Reform and Economic Readjustment, Developing Marxist Theory in the Practice of Reform, Reform, Stability and Development: Macroeconomic Management under the Dual-Track System, New Stage of China's Economic Reform and Development. *Leisure interest:* music. *Address:* Chinese Academy of Social Sciences, Beijing, People's Republic of China. *Telephone:* 65137435. *Fax:* 65138154.

LIU HONGRU; Chinese banker; b. 1930, Yushu, Jilin; ed. Northeast Mil. Coll., Chinese People's Univ., Moscow Univ., Moscow Financial Coll.; joined CCP 1948; Deputy Gov. Agricultural Bank of China 1979; Deputy Gov. People's Bank of China 1980–, Vice-Chair. Council People's Bank of China 1983–, Distribution System Reform Cttee. 1991–; Alt. Gov. IMF Sept. 1986; Vice-Minister State Comm. for Restructuring the Economy May 1988; Vice-Chair. Securities Comm. of the State Council 1992; Part-time Prof., Beijing, Qinghua and Nankai Univs.; Pres. Financial and Banking Inst. of China, China Monetary Coll. 1989–, China Finance and Economies Univ.; Deputy Head Leading Group for the Reform of the Housing System 1991–; Chair. China Securities Control Comm. 1992–95; alt. mem. 13th CCP Cen. Cttee. 1987–92; Vice-Chair. Econ. Cttee., 9th Nat. Cttee. of CPPCC 1998–. *Address:* National Committee of Chinese People's Political Consultative Conference, 23 Taipingqiao Street, Beijing, People's Republic of China.

LIU HUAN; Chinese singer; b. Aug. 1963, Tianjin; ed. Beijing Int. Relations Inst.; numerous albums; songs include theme from The Water Margin (TV). *Address:* Department of French, Beijing International Relations Institute, Beijing, People's Republic of China.

LIU HUANZHANG; Chinese sculptor; b. 30 Dec. 1930, Balihan, Inner Mongolia; m. Shen Chaohui 1968; one d.; ed. Beijing Yuying Pvt. School, Beijing Cen. Acad. of Fine Arts; Assoc. Prof., Sculpture Studio, Beijing Cen. Acad. of Fine Arts 1956–; exhbns. at China Art Gallery 1958, 1961, 1981, 1989, Paris Salon (France) 1981, West Africa 1981, Hong Kong 1985, U.S.A., Hungary; works at Tangshan No. 1 Middle School, Chen Jinlun Middle School, Beijing, Meixian, Guangdong Prov., Lanzhou Inst., Gansu Prov. *Publications:* Liu Huanzhang Carre Works Selection 1984, Sculpture Works Selection 1985, Seals Selection 1988. *Leisure interests:* sports, growing flowers. *Address:* Building No. 3, 1-102, Hong Miao Beili Chao Yang, Beijing, People's Republic of China.

LIU HUAQING, Gen.; Chinese naval officer; b. Oct. 1916, Dawu Co., Hubei Prov.; m. Xu Hongxin; joined Red Army 1931, CCP 1935; Head, Political Dept., 11th Corps, 2nd Field Army 1949; transferred to Navy 1950; Maj.-Gen. PLA 1955; Rear-Admiral, PLA, Luda (Port Arthur and Dairen) 1958; Vice-Chair. Scientific and Technological Comm. for Nat. Defence 1967, First Vice-Chair. 1968; mem. Cultural Revolution Group, PLA 1967; disappeared during Cultural Revolution; Vice-Minister, State Scientific and Technological Comm., State Council 1978–80; Asst. to Chief of PLA Gen. Staff 1979–80; Deputy Chief of Staff, PLA 1980–88, Commdr. PLA Navy 1982–88; Vice-Chair. CPC Cen. Mil. Comm. 1990–; mem. 12th CCP Cen. Cttee. 1982–85, 14th CCP Cen. Cttee. 1992–; mem. Cen. Advisory Cttee. 1985–92; Gen., PLA 1988–; Vice-Chair. Cen. Mil. Comm. 1989–97; standing mem. CCP Politburo 1992–97; Vice-Chair. Cen. Mil. Comm. of PRC 1994; Hon. Pres. Chinese Soc. of Mil. Sciences 1991–, Yachting Asscn. *Address:* c/o People's Liberation Army, Central Military Commission of the People's Republic of China, Beijing, People's Republic of China.

LIU HUAQIU; Chinese diplomatist; b. Nov. 1939, Wuchuan Co., Guangdong Prov.; ed. Foreign Affairs Inst.; joined CCP 1965; Second Sec. Embassy, Ghana 1973; Clerk Gen. Office of State Council 1981; Counsellor then Minister Embassy, Australia 1984; Dir. Dept. of Affairs of the Americas and Oceania, Ministry of Foreign Affairs 1986; Asst. to Minister of Foreign Affairs 1988; Vice-Minister of Foreign Affairs 1989; alt. mem. 14th CCP Cen. Cttee. 1992; Dir. Foreign Affairs Office, State Council 1995–; mem. 15th CCP Cen. Cttee. 1997–. *Address:* Foreign Affairs Office, State Council, Beijing, People's Republic of China.

LIU JIANFENG; Chinese provincial administrator; b. 1936, Ninghe Co., Hebei Prov.; ed. in U.S.S.R.; joined CCP 1956; Vice-Minister of Electronics Industry 1984–88; Deputy Sec. Hainan Prov. 1988; Gov. Hainan Prov. 1989–93; mem. 14th CCP Cen. Cttee. 1992–97, 15th CCP Cen. Cttee. 1997–; Vice-Minister of Electronics Industry 1993–98; Vice-Minister of Information Industry 1998; Dir. Civil Aviation Admin. of China 1998–. *Address:* Civil Aviation Administration of China, Beijing, People's Republic of China.

LIU JIANG; Chinese government official; b. 1940, Beijing; joined CCP 1978; Vice-Minister of Agric., Animal Husbandry and Fishery 1986–90; Vice-Minister State Planning Comm. 1986–93; Minister of Agric. 1993–98; Vice-Minister State Devt. and Planning Comm. 1998–; Deputy Head State Working Group for Comprehensive Agricultural Devt.; mem. 15th CCP Cen. Cttee. 1997–. *Address:* State Development and Planning Commission, 38 Yuetan Nan Jie, Xicheng Qu, Beijing, People's Republic of China.

LIU JIBIN; Chinese politician; b. Dec. 1938, Longkou, Shandong Prov.; ed. Beijing Aeronautics Inst.; joined CCP 1966; engineer, Section Dir. then Vice-Man. Shenyang Songling Machinery Factory, Vice-Chief Engineer Ministry of Aeronautics Industry then Vice Minister, Dir. State Admin. for State-Owned Assets 1962–88; Vice-Minister of Finance 1988–98; Minister of Science, Tech. and Industry Comm. for Nat. Defence 1998–. *Address:* Science, Technology and Industry Commission for National Defence, 1 Aimin Dajie, Xicheng Qu, Beijing 100035, People's Republic of China.

LIU JINGSONG, Gen.; Chinese army officer; b. 1933, Shishou, Hubei; ed. Mil. Coll., PLA; joined CCP 1954; Commdr., Shenyang Mil. Region, PLA 1985–; mem. 12th CCP Cen. Cttee. 1985–87, 13th CCP Cen. Cttee. 1987–92, 14th CCP Cen. Cttee. 1992–97, 15th CCP Cen. Cttee. 1997–; rank of Lieut.-Gen., PLA 1988, Gen. 1994; Commdr. Lanzhou Mil. Region 1992–; Pres. Acad. of Mil. Sciences 1997–. *Address:* Office of the President, PLA Academy of Military Sciences, Beijing, People's Republic of China.

LIU JIYUAN; Chinese aeronautical engineer; b. 1933, Xing Co., Shanxi Prov; ed. higher industrial inst. Moscow; mem. CCP 1952–; technician, No. 5 Research Acad. Ministry of Nat. Defence 1960–64; Dir. and Sr. Engineer No. 12 Research Inst. of No. 1 Research Acad. under 7th Ministry of Machine-Bldg. Industry 1980–83; Deputy Dir. No. 1 Research Acad. under Ministry of Astronautics Industry 1983–84; Vice-Minister of Astronautics Industry 1984; Vice-Minister, Ministry of Aeronautics and Astronautics Industry 1988–93; Pres. China Aerospace Industry Corpn. (State Aerospace Bureau) 1993–; mem. 14th CCP Cen. Cttee. 1992–97, 15th CCP Cen. Cttee. 1997–. *Address:* China Aerospace Industry Corporation, Beijing, People's Republic of China.

LIU KEMING; Chinese academic; b. 28 July 1919, Liaoning; Prof., Beijing Univ. 1979–; Dir. Soviet Research Inst. 1976–80; Dir. Inst. of Soviet and East European Studies 1980–82; Prof., Coll. of Foreign Affairs 1985–; Vice-Pres. Chinese Soc. of E. European, Russian and Cen. Asian Studies 1982–. *Address:* Chinese Academy of Social Sciences, Institute of East European, Russian and Central Asian Studies, P.O. Box 1103, Beijing, People's Republic of China.

LIU MINGZU; Chinese political official; Chair. Guangxi Regional People's Congress 1993–94; Deputy Sec., Standing Cttee. mem. and mem. CCP Guangxi Regional Cttee. –1994; mem., Standing Cttee., mem. and Sec. CCP Inner Mongolia Regional Cttee 1994–; Chair. Inner Mongolia Regional People's Congress; mem. 15th CCP Cen. Cttee. 1997–. *Address:* Inner Mongolia Regional Committee of the CCP, Hohhot, Nei Menggu, People's Republic of China.

LIU NIANQU; Chinese composer; b. 24 Nov. 1945, Shanghai; s. of Liu Jin Chuang and Wang Yun Cong; m. Cai Lu 1973; one d.; Art Inspector Gen. Shanghai Int. Arts Festival 1987; Art Dir. Shanghai Creation Center; Vice Sec.-Gen. Org. Cttee. 1990, Shanghai Art Festival; Vice-Chair. Exec. Cttee. 1991, Shanghai Spring Art Festival; Vice-Chair. Shanghai Musicians Asscn.; Councillor China Musicians Asscn. *Compositions include:* Phoenix Singing at Qi San Mountain (dance drama) 1983, 1989, Spring of Life and Universe (oratorio) 1989 (1st Prize Shanghai Art Festival. *Leisure interests:* table tennis, football. *Address:* Shanghai Municipal Bureau of Culture, 709 Ju Lu Road, Shanghai, People's Republic of China.

LIU QI; Chinese government official; b. 1936; joined CCP 1960; alt. mem. CCP Cen. Cttee. 1992–; Minister of Metallurgical Industry 1993–98; mem. 15th CCP Cen. Cttee. 1997–; Vice-Sec. CCP Beijing Municipal Cttee. and Vice-Mayor of Beijing 1998–. *Address:* Beijing Municipal People's Government, Beijing, People's Republic of China.

LIU SHAHE; Chinese poet; b. 11 Nov. 1931, Chengdu, Sichuan Prov.; m. 1966; one s. one d.; ed. Sichuan Univ.; mem. editorial staff The Stars (poetry magazine) –1957 and 1979–; satirical poem Verses of Plants (1957) led to condemnation as 'bourgeois rightist'; in labour camp during Cultural Revolution 1966–77, rehabilitated 1979. *Publications include:* Night on the Farm 1956, Farewell to Mars 1957, Liu Shahe Poetic Works 1982, Travelling Trace 1983, Farewell to my Home 1983, Sing Alone 1989, Selected Poems of Seven Chinese Poets 1993. *Leisure interest:* UFOs. *Address:* 87 Hongxinglu Erduan Road, Chengdu City, Sichuan Province, People's Republic of China.

LIU SHAOHUI; Chinese artist; b. 27 Aug. 1940, Szechuan; s. of Liu Veizheng and Xiong Wenying; m. Yang Yijing 1968; one s. one d.; ed. Cen. Inst. of Applied Arts, Beijing; fmr. Dir. Art Layout Office, Yunnan People's Publishing House; Assoc. Prof. Pedagogical Inst., Guilin Pref.; mem. Chinese Artists Asscn.; Assoc. Pres. Guilin Chinese Painting Acad. 1995–; engaged in design and research; exhbns. in U.S.A., Japan, Bulgaria, Hong Kong, Italy, Taiwan; works at Guilin Arts Garden; Prize of Nat. Art Works of Excellence 1981 and 1983; main designer for film Fire Boy (1st Prize, Int. Animated Film Festival, Japan 1984). *Works include:* Zhaoshutun—Legend of a Dai Prince, An Elementary Theory on Binding and Layout of Books, The Candlewick Fairy 1985, Cowrie and a Little Girl 1986, Fine Arts Collection 1989; Japanese Int. Fine Arts Exhbn. Prize of the Highest Honour. *Publications:* Yunnan School—A Renaissance in Chinese Painting 1988, Selected Paintings by Liu Shaohui 1989, The Third Sister Liu 1993, Selected Paintings of Guilin Chinese Painting Academy 1995. *Leisure interests:* music, travel, table-tennis. *Address:* Pedagogical Institute, Guilin Prefecture, 45 Xing Yi Road, Guilin, People's Republic of China. *Telephone:* 2822672-2567.

LIU SHUNYAO, Commdr.; Chinese air force officer; ed. PLA Nat. Defence Univ.; fmrly. Deputy Commdr., then Commdr. Air Force, Lanzhou Mil. Region; Deputy Commdr. of Air Force, rank of Lieut.-Gen. 1994, Commdr. 1996–; mem. 15th CCP Cen. Cttee. 1997–. *Address:* c/o Ministry of National Defence, Jingshangian Jie, Beijing, People's Republic of China. *Telephone:* (10) 6637-0000.

LIU SHUQING; Chinese diplomatist; b. 1925, Jiangying Co., Jiangsu Prov.; joined New Fourth Army 1942, CCP 1943; Counsellor for Political Affairs, Embassy, U.S.S.R. 1970–71; Amb. to Poland 1972–77, to Norway 1977–80, to Bangladesh 1980–82; Asst. Foreign Minister, Dir. of Asian Dept. Foreign Ministry 1982–84; Vice Foreign Minister 1984–89; Sec.-Gen. Foreign Affairs Leading Group and Dir. Foreign Affairs Office, State Council 1989–91; Head Chinese del. to 6th, 7th and 8th Round of Sino-Indian Negotiations 1985, to 2nd, 3rd and 4th China-Bhutan Boundary Talks; Pres. Chinese People's Inst. of Foreign Affairs 1991–; mem. 8th CPPCC 1991–. *Address:* 71 Nan Chizi, Beijing, People's Republic of China. *Telephone:* (01) 65131832. *Fax:* (01) 65131831.

LIU SHUSHENG; Chinese party official; b. 1926, Mengcun, Hebei; joined CCP 1946; alt. mem. 12th CCP Cen. Cttee. 1982–87; Deputy Sec. CCP Cttee., Yunnan Prov. 1981, 1983–, Chair. 1988–98; rep. to CCP 13th Nat. Congress. *Address:* Yunnan Provincial Committee of Chinese Communist Party, Kunming, Yunnan, People's Republic of China.

LIU SHUTIAN, Lieut.-Gen.; Chinese army officer; b. 1940, Tengzhou Co., Shandong Prov.; joined PLA 1958; joined CCP 1960; Dir. Army Political Dept. 1986, Army Political Commissar, Deputy Political Commissar Guangzhou Mil. Area Command; mem. 15th CCP Cen. Cttee. 1997–. *Address:* Guangzhou Military Area Command Headquarters, Guangzhou, People's Republic of China.

LIU WEIMING; Chinese party official and fmr. youth leader; b. 25 Oct. 1938, Ningxiang Co., Hunan Prov.; s. of Liu Ziyi and Zhou Shuzhen; m. Wang Aiping 1961; two s.; Vice-Chair. Revolutionary Cttee., Guangdong Prov. 1975–78; alt. mem. 11th CCP Cen. Cttee. 1977–82, and 12th Cen. Cttee. 1982–87; Sec. Communist Youth League 1978–83; Vice-Chair. All China Youth Fed. 1979–81, Acting Chair. 1981–83; mem. Standing Cttee. CCP Prov. Cttee., Guangdong 1985–88, Vice-Gov. 1988–. *Publication:* The Historical Choice—A Study on Guangdong's Implementation of the Reform and Opening to the Outside World. *Leisure interest:* snooker. *Address:* The People's Government of Guangdong Province, 305 Dongfengzhong Road, Guangzhou, People's Republic of China. *Telephone:* (20) 83132176. *Fax:* (20) 83331606.

LIU XIAOQING; Chinese actress; b. 30 Oct. 1955, Chengdu City, Sichuan Prov.; d. of Ran Changru and Liu Huihua; m. Chen Guojun (divorced 1991); ed. Sichuan Music School; 10th Hundred Flowers Best Actress Award for Furong Zhen (Lotus Town) 1986; 7th Golden Cock Best Actress Award for Furong Zhen 1986; 11th Hundred Flowers Best Actress Award for Yuanye 1988, 12th Hundred Flowers Best Actress Award for Chuntao 1989. *Publication:* My Way, My Eight Years, From a Movie Star to Billionaire. *Address:* P.O. Box 38, Asia Sport Village, Beijing, People's Republic of China. *Telephone:* (01) 4915988. *Fax:* (01) 4915899.

LIU XINWU; Chinese writer; b. 4 June 1942, Chengdu, Sichuan; s. of Liu Tianyan and Wang Yuntao; m. Lu Xiaoge 1970; one s.; lived in Beijing since 1950; ed. Beijing Teachers' Coll.; school teacher 1961–76; ed. Beijing Publishing House 1976–80; Ed.-in-Chief People's Literature 1987–89; professional writer since 1980; mem. Standing Cttee., China All Nation Youth Fed. –1992; mem. Council, Chinese Writers' Asscn. *Publications:* short stories: Class Counsellor (Nationwide Short Story Prize 1977), The Position of Love 1978, I Love Every Piece of Green Leaves (Nationwide Short Story Prize 1979), Black Walls 1982, A Scanning over the May 19th Accident 1985; novels: Ruyi (As You Wish) 1980, Overpass 1981; novel: Drum Tower (Mao Dun Literature Prize 1984); Liu Xinwu Collected Works (8 vols.) 1993. *Leisure interests:* reading, travelling, painting, stamp collecting, music, gardening. *Address:* 8 Bldg. No. 1404, Anding Menwai Dongheyan, Beijing 100011, People's Republic of China. *Telephone:* 4213965 (Home).

LIU YANDONG; Chinese politician; b. 1944, Nantong City, Jiangsu Prov.; joined CCP 1964; Sec. of Secr. of Cen. Cttee. of Communist Youth League of China 1982–; mem Standing Cttee. CPPCC 8th Nat Cttee.; Deputy Head United Front Work Dept. 1991–; alt. mem. 15th CCP Cen. Cttee. 1997–99. *Address:* All-China Youth Federation, Bldg. 10, Qianmen Dong Dajie Street, Beijing 100051, People's Republic of China.

LIU YI; Chinese party and government official; b. 24 Nov. 1930, Rushan City, Shandong Prov.; s. of Liu Ting Jia and Jiang Xi; m. Zeng Hua 1952; one s. one d; joined CCP 1947; mem. Cttee. to Examine Proposals at 2nd Session of 5th NPC 1979; Pres. Soc. of Refrigeration 1980–; Minister of Commerce 1982–88; Pres. Cttee. China-Hungary Econ. Trade, Science and Tech. 1986–87; Pres. Cttee. China-Iran Econ. Trade, Science and Tech. 1987; Dir. Nat. Tourism Admin. May 1988–; Vice-Chair. State Tourism Cttee. 1988; Alt. mem. 12th Cen. Cttee., CCP 1982, 13th Cen. Cttee. 1987–92, 14th Cen. Cttee. 1992–; Standing mem. CPPCC 1996–. *Leisure interests:* golf, calligraphy. *Address:* National Tourism Administration, No. 9 A Jian Guo Mennei, Avenue 100740, Beijing (Office); Room 603, Bldg. 38, Xinghua Apt., Zhongfang Li, Chaoyang District, 100020 Beijing, People's Republic of China (Home). *Telephone:* (10) 65138866. *Fax:* (10) 65122096.

LIU YOUFA, Vice-Adm.; Chinese naval officer; b. 1922, Guanyun, Jingsu; joined CCP 1941; cadre of United Front Work Dept. under CCP Cen. Cttee. 1973–77; Sec. CCP Cttee. for Discipline Inspection of PLA Navy 1985; Vice-Adm., PLA Navy 1988–; mem. Cen. Discipline Inspections Comm., CCP Cen. Cttee. 1987–, Internal and Judicial Affairs Cttee.; alt. mem. 12th CCP Cen. Cttee. 1982–87. *Address:* c/o Chinese Communist Party Central Committee, Beijing, People's Republic of China.

LIU YUAN; Chinese government official; b. 1951, Beijing; s. of the late Liu Shaoqi, fmr. Chair. of PRC and Wang Guangmei (q.v.); joined CCP 1982; Vice-Mayor of Zhengzhou City 1988; Second Political Commissar PRC Police Force 1993–. *Address:* Headquarters of Chinese People's Armed Police Force, Beijing, People's Republic of China.

LIU YUNSHAN; Chinese politician; b. July 1947, Tumed, Inner Mongolia; ed. Jining Normal School, Inner Mongolia 1968; joined CCP 1971; Vice-Sec. Communist Youth League Inner Mongolia Autonomous Regional Cttee., Dir. Propaganda Dept, then Vice-Sec. CCP, Sec. CCP Chifeng City Cttee.; Sec. CCP Inner Mongolia Autonomous Regional Cttee.; Vice-Dir. Propaganda Dept. of CCP Cen. Cttee. 1993–; alt. mem. 12th, 14th CCP Cen. Cttee., mem. 15th CCP Cen. Cttee. 1997–. *Address:* Propaganda Department of Chinese Communist Party Central Committee, Beijing, People's Republic of China.

LIU ZHENG; Chinese government official; b. 1929, Changsha City, Hunan Prov.; ed. Hunan Univ., Changsha; joined CCP 1949; Gov. of Hunan Prov. 1983–85; Deputy Sec. CCP Provincial Cttee. 1983–88, Chair. 1988–; Deputy Sec.-Gen. 8th NPC 1993–. *Address:* Office of the Governor, Hunan Province, People's Republic of China.

LIU ZHENGWEI; Chinese party official; b. 1930, Xinzheng, Henan; joined CCP 1952; mem. 12th CCP Cen. Cttee. 1982; Sec. CCP Cttee., Nanyang Pref., Henan 1982–83; Sec. CCP Cttee., Henan Prov. 1983, Deputy Sec. 1983; Deputy Sec. CCP Guizhou Provincial Cttee. 1987, Sec. 1988–93; mem. 13th CCP Cen. Cttee. 1987–92, 14th CCP Cen. Cttee. 1992–; Chair. Standing Cttee. of People's Congress, Guizhou 1993; Deputy Sec. Work Cttee for Cen. Govt. Organs 1993–94, Sec. 1994–. *Address:* c/o Guizhou Provincial Chinese Communist Party, Guiyang, Guizhou, People's Republic of China.

LIU ZHENHUA, Gen.; Chinese army officer; b. 1921, Tai'an Co., Shandong Prov.; m. Liu Junxiao; joined Red Army 1938, CCP 1938; Amb. to Albania 1971–76; Vice-Minister Foreign Affairs 1976–79; Deputy Political Commissar, Shenyang Mil. Region 1980–82; mem. 12th Cen. Cttee. CCP 1982; mem. 13th Cen. Cttee. 1987, alt. mem. 14th Cen. Cttee. 1992–; CCP Cttee. Sec. Fushun City 1987–; Sec. Political Science and Law Comm. 1994–; Chair. Cttee. for Comprehensive Man. of Social Security 1994–; Political Commissar, Shenyang Mil. Region 1982–88, Beijing Mil. Region 1988–90; NPC Deputy PLA; Vice-Chair. Overseas Chinese Affairs Cttee. *Address:* People's Liberation Army, Beijing Units, Beijing, People's Republic of China.

LIU ZHENWU, Maj.-Gen.; Chinese army officer; Commdr. PLA Hong Kong Garrison 1997; alt. mem. 15th CCP Cen. Cttee. 1997–. *Address:* Ministry of National Defence, Jingshanqian Jie, Beijing, People's Republic of China.

LIU ZHONGDE; Chinese administrator; b. 1933, Ji'an Co., Jilin Prov.; Deputy Sec.-Gen. of State Council 1988–92; Deputy Head Propaganda Dept. 1990–; mem. Cen. Group for Propaganda and Thought; Vice-Minister of Culture 1992–93, Minister 1993–98; Chair. Science, Educational Culture, Public Health and Physical Culture Cttee., 9th Nat. Cttee. of CPPCC 1998–; Pres. Asscn. for Artists of Ministry of Culture 1993–; Vice-Pres. Party Bldg. Research Soc.; mem. 14th CCP Cen. Cttee. 1992–97, 15th CCP Cen. Cttee. 1997–. *Address:* A 83 Beiheyan Street, Beijing 100722, People's Republic of China.

LIU ZHONGLI; Chinese state official; b. 1934, Ningbo City, Zhejiang Prov.; joined CCP 1954; Deputy Div. Chief, Vice-Chair., Chair. Heilongjiang Prov. Planning Comm. 1973–84, Chair. Planning and Econ. Comm. 1984–95; Vice-Gov. Heilongjiang Prov. 1985–88; Vice-Chair. State Cttee. for Enterprise Man. 1988; Vice-Minister of Finance 1988–93, Minister 1993–98; Dir. State Gen. Admin. of Taxation 1994–; Deputy Head Cen. Financial and Econ. Leading Group; mem. 14th CCP Cen. Cttee. 1992–97, mem. 15th CCP Cen. Cttee. 1997–. *Address:* Ministry of Finance, 3, Nansanxiang, Sanlihe Road, Xicheng District, Beijing 100820, People's Republic of China. *Telephone:* (01) 868731.

LIU ZHONGYI; Chinese administrator; b. 1930, Wuchang City, Hubei Prov.; joined CCP 1954; Vice-Minister State Planning Comm. 1985–89; Minister of Agric. 1990–93; mem. 14th CCP Cen. Cttee. 1992–97; Deputy Dir.-Gen. Devt. Research Centre 1993–; State Leading Group for Comprehensive Agricultural Devt. 1990–; Vice-Chair. Agric. and Rural Affairs Cttee., 9th NPC 1998–; *Address:* c/o Standing Committee of National People's Congress, Beijing, People's Republic of China.

LIVADIOTTI, Massimo; Italian painter; b. 20 Nov. 1959, Zavia, Libya; s. of Mario Livadiotti and Giovanna Mattera; ed. Accad. di Belle Arti, Rome; maj. shows; Rome 1987, 1989, 1994, Milan 1990, 1992, Bologna 1994, retrospective Petőfi Museum, Budapest 1997; numerous group exhbns.; work inspired by San Filippo Neri acquired by the Vatican 1995. *Publications:* Monograph 1987, Anthology Monograph to accompany exhbn. at Petőfi Museum, Budapest. *Leisure interests:* gardening and light exercise. *Address:* Piazza Vittorio Emanuele II, N. 31, 00185 Rome, Italy. *Telephone:* (06) 4468302. *Fax:* (0765) 423234.

LIVELY, Penelope Margaret, O.B.E., F.R.S.L.; British author; b. 17 March 1933, Cairo, Egypt; d. of Roger Low and Vera Greer; m. Jack Lively 1957; one s. one d.; ed. St. Anne's Coll., Oxford; mem. British Council 1998–; mem. Soc. of Authors, PEN. *Publications:* Astercote 1970, The Whispering Knights 1971, The Wild Hunt of Hagworthy 1971, The Driftway 1972, The Ghost of Thomas Kempe 1973 (Carnegie Medal), The House in Norham Gardens 1974, Going Back 1975, Boy Without a Name 1975, A Stitch in Time 1976 (Whitbread Award), The Stained Glass Window 1976, Fanny's Sister 1976, The Presence of the Past (non-fiction) 1976, The Road to Lichfield 1977, The Voyage of QV66 1978, Nothing Missing but the Samovar and other stories 1978 (Southern Arts Literature Prize), Treasures of Time 1979 (Nat. Book Award), Fanny and the Monsters 1979, Judgement Day 1980, Fanny and the Battle of Potter's Piece 1980, The Revenge of Samuel Stokes 1981, Next to Nature, Art 1982, Perfect Happiness 1983, Corruption 1984, According to Mark 1984, Uninvited Ghosts and other stories 1984, Pack of Cards (short stories) 1986, Debbie and the Little Devil 1987, A House Inside Out 1987, Moon Tiger 1987 (Booker-McConnell Prize), Passing On 1989, Going Back 1991, City of the Mind 1991, Cleopatra's Sister 1993, The Cat, The Crow and the Banyan Tree 1994, Oleander, Jacaranda (autobiog.) 1994, Beyond the Blue Mountains 1997, Spiderweb 1998; television and radio scripts. *Leisure interests:* gardening, landscape history, talking, listening. *Address:* c/o David Higham Associates, 5–8 Lower John Street, Golden Square, London, W1R 4HA, England. *Telephone:* 0171-437 7888. *Fax:* 0171-437 1072.

LIVINGSTONE, Ken(neth) Robert; British politician; b. 17 June 1945, London; s. of Robert Moffat Livingstone and Ethel Ada Kennard; m. Christine Pamela Chapman 1973 (divorced 1982); ed. Tulse Hill Comprehensive School, Phillipa Fawcett Coll. of Educ.; Technician, Cancer Research Unit, Royal Marsden Hospital 1962–70; Councillor, Borough of Lambeth 1971–78, of Camden 1978–82, of Greater London Council 1973–86 (Leader 1981–86); M.P. for Brent East June 1987–; joined Labour Party 1969, mem. Regional Exec. 1974–86, Nat. Exec. Council 1987–89, 1997–, Northern Ireland Select Cttee. 1997–; mem. Council, Zoological Soc. of London 1994– (Vice-Pres. 1996–). *Publications:* If Voting Changed Anything They Would Abolish It 1987, Livingstone's Labour 1989. *Leisure interests:* science fiction, cinema, natural history. *Address:* House of Commons, Westminster, London, SW1A 0AA, England.

LIVINGSTONE, Marco Eduardo, M.A.; American art historian; b. 17 March 1952, Detroit; s. of Leon Livingstone and Alicia Arce Fernández; ed. Univ. of Toronto, Courtauld Inst. of Fine Art, Univ. of London; asst. keeper of British Art Walker Art Gallery, Liverpool 1976–82; Deputy Dir. Museum of Modern Art, Oxford 1982–86; Area Ed. for 20th Century The Dictionary of Art 1986–91, Deputy Ed. for 19th and 20th Centuries 1987–91; U.K. adviser to Art Life, Tokyo 1989–98; freelance writer and exhbn. organizer 1991–. *Publications include:* Sheer Magic by Allen Jones 1979, David Hockney 1981, Patrick Caulfield 1981, Peter Phillips Retrovision 1982, R. B. Kitaj 1985, Pop Art: A Continuing History 1990, Tom Wesselmann 1993, Duane Hanson 1994, David Hockney in California 1994, Jim Dine: Flowers and Plants 1994, Allen Jones Prints 1995, George Segal 1997, The Essential Duane Michals 1997, R. B. Kitaj: An American in Europe 1998, Jim Dine: The Alchemy of Images 1998. *Leisure interests:* music, languages, travel, collecting art. *Address:* 36 St. George's Avenue, London, N7 0HD, England; 27 rue des Ecouffes, 75004 Paris, France. *Telephone:* 0171-607 0282 (London); (1) 48.87.60.65 (Paris). *Fax:* 0171-607 8694 (London).

LIVNAT, Limor, B.A.; Israeli politician; b. 1950, Haifa; m.; two c.; ed. Tel-Aviv Univ.; worked in advertising and public relations; mem. Knesset (Parl.) 1992–, mem. Knesset Educ. and Culture Cttee., Labour and Social Affairs Cttee. 1991–96, Chair. Knesset Cttee. for Advancement of Status of Women 1993–94, Sub-Cttee. on Women's Representation, Parl. Comm. of Inquiry into domestic violence 1995; Chair. of Likud and of Benjamin Netanyahu's election campaign 1996; Minister of Communications 1996–; fmr. Vice-Chair. World Likud Movt., fmr. mem. Educ. and Cultural Cttee., Labour and Social Affairs Cttee., Comm. for Commercial TV. *Address:* Ministry of Communications, 23 Jaffa Street, Jerusalem 91999, Israel. *Telephone:* 2-6706301. *Fax:* 2-6240029.

LIVSHITZ, Aleksander Yakovlevich, DR. ECON.; Russian economist; b. 6 Sept. 1946, Berlin, Germany; s. of Yakov Livshitz and Liya Livshitz; m. Galina Markina 1966; two d.; ed. G. Plekhanov Inst. of Nat. Econ.; teacher, Chair, Prof. Moscow Machine Tool Instrumentation Inst. 1974–; Deputy Chief Analytical Centre, Admin. of Pres. 1992–94; Head of Pres.'s Advisers 1994; Asst. to Pres. on problems of economy Nov. 1994–96; Deputy Prime Minister and Minister of Finance 1996–97; Deputy Head of Pres.'s Admin. March 1997–98; Head Econ. Policy Fund 1998–. *Publications:* Introduction to Market Economy 1991, Economic Reform in Russia and its Price 1994, more than 150 works on econ. problems of Russia, econ. situation in U.S.A. in 1980s.

LJUNGGREN, Olof, LL.B.; Swedish publisher and business executive; b. 5 Jan. 1933, Eskilstuna; s. of Lars and Elisabeth Ljunggren; m. 1st Lena Carlsöö; m. 2nd Margreth Bäcklund; three s.; ed. Univ. of Stockholm; Sec. Tidningarnas Arbetsgivareförening (Swedish Newspaper Employers' Asscn.) 1959–62, Pres. and C.E.O. 1962–66; Deputy Pres. and C.E.O. Allers Förlag AB 1967–72, Pres. and C.E.O. 1972–74; Pres. and C.E.O. Svenska Dagbladet 1974–78; Pres. and C.E.O. Svenska Arbetsgivareföreningen (Swedish Employers' Confed.) 1978–89; Chair. of Bd. Askild & Kärnekull Förlag AB 1971–74, Nord Artel AB 1971–78, Centralförbundet Folk och Försvar (Vice-Chair. 1978–83) 1983–86, Richard Hägglöf Fondkommission AB 1984–87, Svenska Dagbladel 1989–91, Liber AB 1990–, Intentia AB 1994–, AMF 1995–, Addum AB 1996–; mem. Bd., SPP 1978–93, Investor 1989–92, Providentia 1989–92, Alfa Laval 1989–92, Trygg Hansa 1990–95, and numerous other bds.; Kt. Commdr. Order of the White Rose of Finland 1982, The King's Medal of the 12th Dimension with the Ribbon of the Order of the

Seraphim 1987, Kommendörskorset av Den Kgl. Norske Fortjenstorden. *Leisure interests:* shooting, golf. *Address:* Skeppargatan 7, 114 52 Stockholm, Sweden. *Telephone:* (08) 667 87 85.

LJUNGQVIST, Bengt, B.A.; Swedish business executive and lawyer; b. 13 Aug. 1937, Stockholm; s. of Gunnar Ljungqvist and Solveig Ljungqvist; m. 1st Sylvia Elmstedt 1961 (divorced 1977); m. 2nd Christina (née Hedén) Ljungqvist 1978; two s. two d.; ed. Stockholm Univ.; joined Malmström and Malmenfelt Advokatbyrå, Stockholm 1967, Partner 1971–; Solicitor-Royal 1995–; Pres. Bd. of City Planning, Danderyd 1976–85, Chair. City Council, Danderyd 1986–; mem. Council, Swedish Bar Assn. 1983–, Vice-Pres. 1985–; Pres. Swedish Bar Assn. 1989–92; mem. Council Int. Bar Assn. 1984–90; Pres. JP-Bank Stockholm, Swedish Real Property Owners Assn. 1991–96; Vice-Pres. Union Int. de la Propriété Immobilière 1993–96; mem. Bd., Länsförsäkringar-Stockholm 1993–, Pres. 1995–. *Address:* Malmström and Malmenfelt Advokatbyrå, Box 1665, 111 96 Stockholm (Office); Midgårdsvägen 1, 182 61 Djursholm, Sweden (Home). *Telephone:* (08) 679-69-50 (Office); (08) 755 31 96 (Home).

LLESHI, Maj.-Gen. Haxhi; Albanian politician; b. 1913; fought with Resistance against Italian and German occupations 1939–45; mem. provisional Govt. 1944; Minister of the Interior 1944–46; Maj.-Gen. Albanian Army; Pres. Presidium of the People's Assembly (Head of State) 1953–82; mem. Cen. Cttee. Albanian Workers' Party 1953. *Address:* Abdyl Frasheri Str., Tirana, Albania.

LLEWELLYN, John; American scientist; b. 22 April 1933, Cardiff, U.K.; s. of John and Morella (Roberts) Llewellyn; m. Valerie Davies-Jones; one s. two d.; ed. Univ. Coll., Cardiff, Wales; Research Fellow, Nat. Research Council of Canada 1958–60; Assoc. Prof. School of Eng. Science, Florida State Univ. 1964–72; selected by NASA as scientist-astronaut 1967; Dean, School of Eng. Science, Florida State Univ. 1970–72; Prof. Depts. of Chemical and Mechanical Eng., Coll. of Eng., Univ. of South Fla., Tampa 1973–, Dir. Eng. Computing 1986–, Dir. Academic Computing 1993–; Co-ordinator, Scientist in the Sea Project 1973; aquanaut Nat. Oceanographic Atmospheric Admin.; Scientific consultant on marine environment, energy and industrial computer applications; Pres. J. Vector Inc., K. Vector Inc.; mem. Royal Inst. of Chem., A.I.A.A., Radiation Research Soc. *Publications:* Principles and Applications of Digital Devices 1983, Basic Elements of Digital Systems 1983. *Leisure interests:* sailing, underwater exploration. *Address:* Academic Computing, University of South Florida, 4202 E. Fowler Avenue, L1B 618, Tampa, FL 33620 (Office); 3010 St. Charles Drive, Tampa, FL 33618, U.S.A. (Home). *Telephone:* (813) 974 1780 (Office). *Fax:* (813) 974 1799.

LLEWELLYN SMITH, Christopher Hubert, D.PHIL., F.R.S.; British theoretical physicist; b. 19 Nov. 1942; s. of the late John Clare Llewellyn Smith and of Margaret Emily Frances Crawford; m. Virginia Grey 1966; one s. one d.; ed. Wellington Coll. and New Coll., Oxford; Royal Soc. Exchange Fellow, Lebedev Inst., Moscow 1967–68; Fellow, Centre Européen pour la Recherche Nucléaire (C.E.R.N.), Geneva 1968–70, Staff mem. 1972–74, Chair. Scientific Policy Cttee. 1990–92, Dir.-Gen. C.E.R.N. 1994–98; Dir. Gen. European Lab. for Particle Physics 1998–; Research Assoc., Stanford Linear Accelerator Center (SLAC), Calif., U.S.A. 1970–72; Univ. Lecturer in Theoretical Physics, Oxford Univ. and Fellow St. John's Coll. 1974–98, Reader in Theoretical Physics 1980–87, Prof. 1987–98 (on leave of absence, 1994–98), Chair. of Physics 1987–92; mem. various advisory bodies for SLAC, C.E.R.N., DESY (Deutsches Elektronen-Synchrotron, Hamburg) and SERC (Science and Eng. Research Council) 1972–92; mem. Advisory Council on Science and Tech. 1989–92; Fellow American Physical Soc.; Foreign Fellow Nat. Science Acad.; mem. Academia Europaea; Hon. D.Sc. (Bristol, Shandong); Hon. D.Cien. (Granada); Gold Medal, Slovak Acad. of Science, Glazebrook Medal, Inst. of Physics 1998. *Publications:* numerous articles in scientific journals including Nuclear Physics, Physics Letters, Physics Review. *Leisure interests:* books, travel, opera. *Address:* University College of London, Gower Street, WC1E 6BT, England.

LLEWELLYN-SMITH, Elizabeth, C.B., M.A.; British university administrator; b. 17 Aug. 1934, Upshire; d. of the late J.C. Llewellyn-Smith and of Margaret E.F. Crawford; ed. Christ's Hospital, Univ. of Cambridge and Royal Coll. of Defence Studies; fmr. civil servant; Deputy Dir.-Gen. of Fair Trading 1982–87; Deputy Sec. Dept. of Trade and Industry 1987–90; Dir. European Investment Bank 1987–90; Prin. St. Hilda's Coll. Oxford 1990–; mem. Business Appointments Panel, DTI 1996–. *Leisure interests:* travel, books, entertaining. *Address:* St. Hilda's College, Oxford, OX4 1DY, England. *Telephone:* (01865) 276814.

LLEWELLYN-SMITH, Sir Michael John, K.C.V.O., C.M.G., D.PHIL.; British diplomatist (retd.); b. 25 April 1939; s. of the late J.C. Llewellyn-Smith and of Margaret E.F. Crawford; m. Colette Gaulier 1967; one s. one d.; ed. New Coll., Oxford, St. Antony's Coll., Oxford; at Embassy, Moscow 1973–75, at Embassy, Paris 1976–78; at Royal Coll. of Defence Studies 1979; at Embassy, Athens 1980–83; Head W. European Dept. FCO 1984–85, Head Soviet Dept. 1985–88; Minister Embassy, Paris 1988–91; British Amb. to Poland 1991–96, to Greece 1996–99. *Publications:* The Great Island: A Study of Crete 1965, Ionian Vision: Greece in Asia Minor 1919–22 1973. *Address:* c/o United Oxford and Cambridge University Club, 71 Pall Mall, London, SW1Y 5HD, England.

LLOREDA CAICEDO, Rodrigo; Colombian politician; b. 2 Sept. 1942, Cali; s. of Alvaro Lloreda and Mercedes Caicedo; m. María E. Piedrahita 1974; two s. three d.; ed. Pontificia Univ. Javeriana; Gov. Valle del Cauca 1968–70; Dir. El País, Cali 1970–78, 1991–95; Senator 1978–; Minister of Educ. 1978–80, of Foreign Affairs 1982–84; Vice-Pres. of Colombia 1984–86; Amb. to U.S.A. 1984–86; Presidential Cand. 1990; mem. Constitutional Congress 1991; del. to several int. confs.; Dir. El País newspaper, Cali; Gran Cruz de la Orden de Boyacá and decorations from Venezuela, Mexico, Panama, Chile, Honduras and Spain. *Publications:* El Sistema Presidencial de Gobierno, La Juventud en el Gobierno, Reforma de la Educación Superior, La Nueva Política Internal de Colombia 1984, Una Gestión por Colombia 1986, Frente a la Crisie 1990. *Leisure interests:* reading, music, tennis. *Address:* Cra 2 No. 24-46, Cali, Colombia. *Telephone:* 8835018. *Fax:* 8890999.

LLOWARCH, Martin Edge, C.B.I.M., F.C.A., F.I.C.A.; British business executive; b. 28 Dec. 1935; s. of Wilfred Llowarch and Olga Llowarch; m. Ann Marion Buchanan 1965; one s. two d.; ed. Stowe School; with Buckingham, Coopers & Lybrand 1962–68; with British Steel PLC (fmrly. British Steel Corpn.) 1968–, Head of Special Projects 1968, Man. Dir. (S.A.) 1971, Dir. Finance and Admin. (Int.) 1973, Finance Dir. Tubes Div. 1975, Financial Controller Strip Products Group 1980, Man. Dir. for Finance 1983, Dir. 1984–91, Deputy C.E.O. 1986, C.E.O. 1986–91; Chair. (part-time) Transport Devt. Group PLC 1992–; Deputy Chair. (non-exec.) Firth Rixson (fmrly. Johnson and Firth Brown PLC) 1992–93, Chair. 1993–; Dir. (non-exec.) Abbey Nat. PLC 1989– (Deputy Chair. 1994–), Hickson Int. PLC 1992–; mem. Accounting Standards Cttee. 1985–87. *Leisure interests:* sport, music, gardening, reading. *Address:* Abbey National PLC, 215 Baker Street, London, N.W.1, England. *Telephone:* 0171-612 4000.

LLOYD, Chris(tine) Marie Evert (see Evert, Chris(tine) Marie).

LLOYD, Christopher; American actor; b. 22 Oct. 1938, Stamford, Conn.; m. Carol Lloyd; ed. Neighbourhood Playhouse, New York; film debut One Flew over the Cuckoo's Nest 1975; *films include:* Butch and Sundance: The Early Days, The Onion Field, The Black Marble, The Legend of the Lone Ranger, Mr. Mom, To Be or Not To Be, Star Trek III: The Search for Spock, Adventures of Buckaroo Banzai, Back to the Future, Clue, Who Framed Roger Rabbit?, Track 29, Walk Like a Man, Eight Men Out, The Dream Team, Why Me?, Back to the Future, Part II, Back to the Future, Part III, The Addams Family, Twenty Bucks, Dennis the Menace, Addams Family Values, The Pagemaster, Camp Nowhere, The Radioland Murders, Things To Do in Denver When You're Dead, Cadillac Ranch, Changing Habits; *TV includes:* Taxi, Best of the West, The Dictator, Tales from Hollywood Hills: Pat Hobby—Teamed with Genius, September Gun, Avonlea; winner Drama Desk and Obie Awards (Kaspar) 1973. *Address:* c/o Guild Management Corporation, Penthouse A, Los Angeles, CA 90035, U.S.A.

LLOYD, Clive Hubert, C.B.E.; Guyanese cricketer; b. 31 Aug. 1944, Georgetown, British Guiana (now Guyana); left-hand batsman, right-arm medium-paced bowler; played for British Guiana/Guyana 1963–83, Lancashire 1968–86 (Capt. 1981–83, 1986); 110 Tests for W. Indies 1966–1985, record 74 as Capt., scoring 7,515 runs (average 46.6) including 19 hundreds; toured England 1969, 1973, 1975 (World Cup), 1976, 1979 (World Cup), 1980, 1983 (World Cup), 1984; scored 31,232 first-class runs including 79 hundreds; W. Indies team man. 1988–89 and 1996–; Int. Cricket Council referee 1992–95; Exec. Promotions Officer, Project Fullemploy 1987–; Dir. Red Rose Radio PLC 1981–. *Publications:* Living for Cricket (with Tony Cozier) 1980, Winning Captaincy (with Mihir Bose) 1995. *Address:* c/o Harefield, Harefield Drive, Wilmslow, Cheshire, SK9 1NJ, England.

LLOYD, David Robert, SC.D., F.INST.P.; British professor of chemistry; b. 19 May 1937, Derby; s. of George Lloyd and Effie Lloyd; m. Heidi Hoffman 1964; one s. one d.; ed. Halesowen Grammar School, Worcs. and Selwyn Coll., Cambridge; temporary lecturer, Chem. Dept., Northwestern Univ., Evanston, U.S.A. 1963–65; lecturer in Chem., Univ. of Birmingham 1965–78; Prof. of Chem., Trinity Coll., Dublin, Ireland 1978–, Head Chem. Dept. 1978–85, 1992–94; A. von Humboldt Fellowship 1962–63; mem. Royal Irish Acad.; Fellow, Trinity Coll., Dublin. *Publications:* approx. 100 papers on science. *Leisure interests:* music, hill walking, domestic chores, theology. *Address:* Trinity College, Dublin 2, Ireland. *Telephone:* (01) 608-1306.

LLOYD, Sir Geoffrey Ernest Richard, Kt., PH.D., F.B.A.; British professor of philosophy; b. 25 Jan. 1933, London; s. of William Ernest Lloyd and Olive Irene Neville Lloyd; m. Janet Elizabeth Lloyd 1956; three s.; ed. Charterhouse and King's Coll., Cambridge; Univ. Asst. Lecturer in Classics, Cambridge 1965–67, Univ. Lecturer 1967–74, Reader in Ancient Philosophy and Science 1974–83, Prof. 1983–; Master, Darwin Coll., Cambridge 1989–; Fellow King's Coll. 1957–89, Hon. Fellow 1990–; A. D. White Prof.-at-Large, Cornell Univ. 1990–96; Chair. East Asian History of Science Trust 1992–; mem. Japan Soc. for the Promotion of Science, Int. Acad. of the History of Science; Foreign Hon. mem. American Acad. of Arts and Sciences 1995; Sarton Medal 1987. *Publications:* Polarity and Analogy 1966, Aristotle, the Growth and Structure of his Thought 1968, Early Greek Science: Thales to Aristotle 1970, Greek Science after Aristotle 1973, Hippocratic Writings (Ed.) 1978, Aristotle on Mind and the Senses (Ed.) 1978, Magic, Reason and Experience 1979, Science, Folklore and Ideology 1983, Science and Morality in Greco-Roman Antiquity 1985, The Revolutions of Wisdom 1987, Demystifying Mentalities 1990, Methods and Problems in Greek Science 1991, Adversaries and Authorities 1996, Aristotelian Explorations 1996, Le Savoir Grec (Ed.) 1996. *Leisure interest:* travel. *Address:* 2 Prospect Row, Cambridge, CB1 1DU, England. *Telephone:* (01223) 355970.

LLOYD, John Nicol Fortune, M.A.; British journalist; b. 15 April 1946; s. of Christopher Lloyd and Joan A. Fortune; m. 1st Judith Ferguson 1974 (divorced 1979); m. 2nd Marcia Levy 1983; one s.; ed. Waid Comprehensive School and Univ. of Edinburgh; Ed. Time Out 1972–73; reporter, London Programme 1974–76; Producer, Weekend World 1976–77; industrial reporter, labour corresp., industrial and labour ed. Financial Times 1977–86; Ed. New Statesman 1986–87, Assoc. Ed. 1996–; with Financial Times 1987– (Moscow Corresp. 1991–95); columnist The Times 1997–; Journalist of the Year, Granada Awards 1984, Specialist Writer of the Year, IPC Awards 1985; Rio Tinto David Watt Memorial Prize 1997. *Publications:* The Politics of Industrial Change (with Ian Benson) 1982, The Miners' Strike: Loss without Limit (with Martin Adeney) 1986, In Search of Work (with Charles Leadbeater) 1987, Counterblasts (contrib.) 1989, Rebirth of a Nation: an Anatomy of Russia 1998. *Leisure interests:* opera, hill walking, squash. *Address:* c/o New Statesman and Society, 38 Kingsland Road, London, E2 8DQ, England.

LLOYD, Robert Andrew, C.B.E.; British opera singer; b. 2 March 1940, Southend; s. of William Edward Lloyd and May (née Waples) Lloyd; m. 1st Sandra D. Watkins 1964 (divorced 1990); one s. three d.; m. 2nd Lynda A. Hazell (née Powell) 1992; ed. Southend High School for Boys, Keble Coll., Oxford, London Opera Centre; served as Lieut. in Royal Navy 1963–66; lecturer, Bramshill Police Coll. 1966–68; Prin. Bass, Sadlers Wells Opera 1969–72, Royal Opera House 1972–83; freelance singer with all maj. opera houses and orchestras world-wide, frequent broadcasts as presenter, BBC radio and TV 1983–; film appearances: Parsifal, Bluebeard's Castle; performed title role in Tarkovsky production of 'Boris Godunov' at Kirov Opera, Leningrad 1990; Visiting Prof. Royal Coll. of Music, London 1996–; Pres. British Youth Opera 1988–94, Southend Choral Soc. 1996–; mem. Exec. Cttee. Musicians' Benevolent Fund 1989–92; mem. Conservatoires Advisory Group 1993–; Patron Carl Rosa Trust 1994–; Hon. Fellow Keble Coll. 1990; Artist of the Year, Teatro Colón, Buenos Aires 1996; Charles Santley Award 1997; Chaliapin Commemoration Medal (St. Petersburg) 1998. *Publications:* numerous contribs. to magazines. *Leisure interests:* sailing, hill walking, history. *Address:* c/o Lies Askonas Ltd., 6 Henrietta Street, London, WC2E 8LA, England. *Telephone:* 0181-883 0664.

LLOYD-JONES, David Mathias, B.A.; Welsh musician; b. 19 Nov. 1934, London; s. of the late Sir Vincent Lloyd-Jones and Margaret Alwena Mathias; m. Anne Carolyn Whitehead 1964; two s. one d.; ed. Westminster School, Magdalen Coll., Oxford; Chorus Master, New Opera Co. 1961–64; conducted at Bath Festival 1966, City of London Festival 1966, Wexford Festival 1967–70, Scottish Opera 1968, Welsh Nat. Opera 1968, Royal Opera, Covent Garden 1971, Sadler's Wells Opera Co. (now English Nat. Opera) 1969; Artistic Dir. Opera North 1978–90; also conductor for TV operas (Eugene Onegin, The Flying Dutchman, Hansel and Gretel), for operas in Amsterdam and Paris, and has appeared with most British symphony orchestras; Chair. Delius Trust 1997–; Hon. D.Mus. (Leeds) 1986. *Publications:* Boris Godunov—Translation, Vocal Score, Eugene Onegin—Translation, Vocal Score, Boris Godunov—Critical Edition of Original Full Score, numerous contributions to publs. including Grove's Dictionary of Music and Musicians, Musik in Geschichte und Gegenwart, Music and Letters, The Listener. *Leisure interests:* theatre, French cuisine, rose growing. *Address:* 94 Whitelands House, Cheltenham Terrace, London, SW3 4RA, England (Home). *Telephone:* 0171-730 8695.

LLOYD-JONES, Sir (Peter) Hugh (Jefferd), Kt., M.A., F.B.A.; British classical scholar; b. 21 Sept. 1922, St. Peter Port, Guernsey; s. of Brevet-Major W. Lloyd-Jones, D.S.O., and Norah Leila Jefferd; m. 1st Frances Elisabeth Hedley 1953 (dissolved 1981); two s. one d.; m. 2nd Mary R. Lefkowitz 1982; ed. Lycée Français du Royaume-Uni (London), Westminster School, and Christ Church, Oxford; Fellow, Jesus Coll., Cambridge 1948–54; Fellow and E.P. Warren Praelector in Classics, Corpus Christi Coll., Oxford 1954–60; Regius Prof. of Greek and Student of Christ Church 1960–89, Prof. Emer. 1989–; Chancellor's Prize for Latin Prose, Ireland and Craven Scholarships 1947; J. H. Gray Lecturer, Cambridge 1961; Visiting Prof. Yale Univ. 1964–65, 1967–68; Sather Prof. of Classical Literature, Univ. of Calif. at Berkeley 1969–70; Alexander White Visiting Prof. Univ. of Chicago 1972; Visiting Prof., Harvard Univ. 1976–77; Corresp. mem. Acad. of Athens, American Acad. of Arts and Sciences, Nordrhein-Westfälische Akad. der Wissenschaften, Accad. di Archeologia Lettere e belle Arti di Napoli, Bayerische Akad. der Wissenschaften, American Philosophical Soc.; Hon. D.Hum.-Litt. (Chicago) 1970, Hon. D.Phil. (Tel Aviv) 1984. *Publications:* Appendix to Aeschylus (Loeb Classical Library) 1957, Menandri Dyscolus (Oxford Classical Texts) 1960; The Justice of Zeus 1971, (ed.) Maurice Bowra: a Celebration 1974, Females of the Species 1975, Myths of the Zodiac 1978, Mythical Beasts 1980, Blood for the Ghosts 1982, Classical Survivals 1982, Supplementum Hellenisticum (with P. J. Parsons) 1983; translated Paul Maas, Greek Metre 1962, Aeschylus Agamemnon, The Libation-Bearers and The Eumenides 1970, Sophoclea (with N. G. Wilson) 1990, Academic Papers (2 vols.) 1990, Sophoclis Fabulae (ed. with N. G. Wilson) 1990, Greek in a Cold Climate 1991, Sophocles (Loeb Classical Library, 3 vols.) 1994–96, Sophocles: Second Thoughts (with N. G. Wilson) 1997; edited The Greeks 1962, Tacitus 1964; articles and reviews in classical periodicals. *Address:* 15 West Riding, Wellesley, MA 02181, U.S.A. *Telephone:* (781) 237-2212. *Fax:* (781) 237-2246.

LLOYD WEBBER, Baron (cr. Life Peer 1997) of Sydmonton in the County of Hampshire; **Andrew Lloyd Webber**, Kt.; British composer; b. 22 March 1948; s. of the late William Southcombe Lloyd Webber and Jean Hermione Johnstone; (brother of Julian Lloyd Webber, q.v.); m. 1st Sarah Jane Tudor (née Hugill) 1971 (divorced 1983); one s. one d.; m. 2nd Sarah Brightman 1984 (divorced 1990); m. 3rd Madeleine Astrid Gurdon 1991; two s. one d.; ed. Westminster School, Magdalen Coll., Oxford, Royal Coll. of Music; awards include 6 Tony Awards, 4 Drama Desk Awards, 5 Laurence Olivier Awards, Triple Play Awards ASCAP 1988, Praemium Imperiale Award 1995, 3 Grammy Awards, Richard Rodgers Award 1996. *Works:* (musicals): Joseph and the Amazing Technicolor Dreamcoat (lyrics by Tim Rice) 1968, Jesus Christ Superstar (lyrics by Tim Rice) 1970, Jeeves (lyrics by Alan Ayckbourn) 1975, Evita (lyrics by Tim Rice) 1976 (stage version 1978), Variations 1977 (symphonic version 1986), Tell me on a Sunday (lyrics by Don Black) 1980, Cats (based on T. S. Eliot's Old Possum's Book of Practical Cats) (Tony Awards for Best Score and Best Musical 1983) 1981, Song and Dance (lyrics by Don Black) 1982, Starlight Express (lyrics by Richard Stilgoe) 1984, The Phantom of the Opera (Tony Award for Best Musical 1988) (lyrics by Richard Stilgoe and Charles Hart) 1986, Aspects of Love (lyrics by Don Black and Charles Hart) 1989, Sunset Boulevard (Tony Awards for Best Score and Best Musical 1995) (lyrics by Christopher Hampton and Don Black) 1993, By Jeeves 1996 (lyrics by Alan Ayckbourn), Whistle Down the Wind (lyrics by Jim Steinman) 1996; (other compositions): Variations 1978, Requiem Mass 1985, Amigos Para Siempre (official theme for 1992 Olympic Games); (film scores): Gumshoe 1971, The Odessa File 1974, Jesus Christ Superstar 1974. *Producer:* Cats 1981, Song and Dance 1982, Daisy Pulls It Off 1983, The Hired Man 1984, Starlight Express 1984, On Your Toes 1984, The Phantom of the Opera 1986, Lend Me a Tenor 1988, Aspects of Love 1989, Shirley Valentine 1989, Joseph and the Amazing Technicolor Dreamcoat 1991, La Bête 1992, Sunset Boulevard 1993, By Jeeves 1996, Whistle Down the Wind 1996, Jesus Christ Superstar 1996, 1998, and others. *Publications:* Evita (with Tim Rice) 1978, Cats: the book of the musical 1981, Joseph and the Amazing Technicolor Dreamcoat (with Tim Rice) 1982, The Complete Phantom of the Opera 1987, The Complete Aspects of Love 1989, Sunset Boulevard: from movie to musical 1993; food critic Daily Telegraph. *Leisure interests:* architecture, art. *Address:* 22 Tower Street, London, WC2H 9NS, England.

LLOYD WEBBER, Julian, F.R.C.M.; British cellist; b. 14 April 1951, London; s. of the late Dr. William S. Lloyd Webber and Jean H. Johnstone; (brother of Lord Lloyd Webber, q.v.); m. 1st Celia M. Ballantyne 1974 (divorced 1989); m. 2nd Zohra Mahmoud Ghazi 1989; one s.; ed. Univ. Coll. School and Royal Coll. of Music; debut at Queen Elizabeth Hall 1972; debut with Berlin Philharmonic Orchestra 1984; appears at major int. concert halls and has undertaken concert tours throughout Europe, North and South America, Australasia, Singapore, Japan, Hong Kong and Korea; numerous television appearances and broadcasts in U.K., Netherlands, Africa, Germany, Scandinavia, France, Belgium, Spain, Australasia and U.S.A.; recordings include world premieres of Britten's 3rd Suite for Solo Cello, Bridge's Oration, Rodrigo's Cello Concerto, Holst's Invocation, Gavin Bryar's Cello Concerto, James MacMillan's Kiss on Wood, Sullivan's Cello Concerto, Vaughan Williams' Fantasia on Sussex Folk Tunes, Andrew Lloyd Webber's Variations; recordings also include Elgar's Cello Concerto (British Phonographic Industry Award for Best Classical Recording 1986), Dvořák Concerto, Saint-Saëns Concerto, Lalo Concerto, Walton Concerto, Britten Cello Symphony, etc.; Crystal Award, World Economic Forum (Switzerland) 1998. *Publications:* Frank Bridge, Six Pieces 1982, Young Cellist's Repertoire (3 vols.) 1984, Travels with my Cello 1984, Song of the Birds 1985, Recital Repertoire for Cellists 1986, Short Sharp Shocks 1990, The Great Cello Solos 1992, The Essential Cello 1997. *Leisure interests:* reading horror stories, topography (especially British). *Address:* c/o IMG Artists Europe, Media House, 3 Burlington Lane, London, W4 2TH, England. *Telephone:* 0181-233 5800. *Fax:* 0181-233 5801.

LO, K. S.; Chinese business executive; b. 1909, Guangdong Prov., China; m.; ed. Univ. of Hong Kong; lived in Malaysia aged 10 to 20; set up Vitasoy soy milk factory in Causeway Bay dist. of Hong Kong 1940–42; resumed business after World War II; Vitasoy (now run by his son Winston Lo) listed on Hong Kong Stock Exchange 1994; maj. benefactor of Hong Kong Museum of Tea Ware. *Leisure interest:* collecting teapots. *Address:* c/o Vitasoy, Whole Building 1, Kinwong Street, Tuen Mun, New Territory, Hong Kong Special Administrative Region, People's Republic of China. *Telephone:* 2466 0333. *Fax:* 2456 3441.

LO, Vincent; Chinese business executive; b. 18 April 1948, Hong Kong; m. Jean Lo 1981; one s. one d.; f. Shui On Group 1971, now Chair.; Chair. Hong Kong Gen. Chamber of Commerce 1991–92; mem. Exec. Cttee. Basic Law Consultative Cttee. 1985–90; mem. Bd. Land Devt. Corpn. 1988–90; mem. Hong Kong Trade Devt. Council 1991–92, Hong Kong/Japan Business Co-operation Cttee. 1991–92; mem. Gen. Cttee. Fed. of Hong Kong Industries 1991–92; mem. Council Hong Kong Univ. of Science and Tech. 1988–90, Hong Kong Baptist Coll. 1987–89; mem. Standing Cttee. on Judicial Salaries & Conditions of Service 1988–94, Standing Cttee. on Directorate Salaries & Conditions of Service 1988–94; mem. Council, Exec. Cttee. Hong Kong Man. Asscn. 1984–94; Pres. Business and Professionals Fed. of Hong Kong; mem. Preparatory Cttee. for the Hong Kong Special Admin. Region; Hong Kong Affairs Adviser, PRC State Council's Office of Hong Kong & Macao Affairs/

Xinhua News Agency, Hong Kong Br.; Adviser China's Nat. Macroeconomic Asscn.; mem. Gov.'s Business Council, Airport Authority, Hong Kong/United States Econ. Co-operation Cttee.; Dir. The Real Estate Developers Asscn. of Hong Kong, The Community Chest of Hong Kong; Court mem. Univ. of Science and Tech. *Address:* 34/F Shui On Centre, 6–8 Harbour Rd, Hong Kong Special Administrative Region, People's Republic of China.

LOACH, Kenneth, B.A.; British film director; b. 17 June 1936, Nuneaton; s. of the late John Loach and of Vivien Loach (née Hamlin); m. Lesley Ashton 1962; three s. (one deceased) two d.; ed. King Edward VI School, Nuneaton, St. Peter's Hall (now Coll.), Oxford; BBC trainee, Drama Dept. 1963; freelance film dir. 1963–; Hon. D.Litt. (St. Andrews), (Staffs. Univ., Bristol); Dr. h.c. (Royal Coll. of Art) 1998; Hon. Fellow, St. Peter's Coll. Oxford. *Films:* Poor Cow 1967, Kes 1969, In Black and White 1970, Family Life 1971, Black Jack 1979, Looks and Smiles 1981, Fatherland 1986, Hidden Agenda 1990, Riff-Raff 1991, Raining Stones 1993, Ladybird, Ladybird 1994, Land and Freedom 1995, Carla's Song 1996, My Name is Joe 1998. *Television:* Diary of a Young Man 1964, Three Clear Sundays 1965, The End of Arthur's Marriage 1965, Up the Junction 1965, Coming Out Party 1965, Cathy Come Home 1966, In Two Minds 1966, The Golden Vision 1969, The Big Flame 1970, After a Lifetime 1971, The Rank and File 1972, Days of Hope (four films) 1975, The Price of Coal 1977, The Gamekeeper 1979, Auditions 1980, A Question of Leadership 1980, The Red and the Blue 1983, Questions of Leadership 1983, Which Side are You on? 1984, The View from the Woodpile 1988, Time to Go 1989, Dispatches: Arthur Scargill 1991, The Flickering Flame 1996, Another City 1998. *Address:* c/o Parallax Pictures, 7 Denmark Street, London, WC2H 8LS, England.

LOBASHEV, Vladimir Mikhailovich; Russian nuclear physicist; b. 29 July 1934, Leningrad; s. of Mikhail Yefimovich Lobashev and Nina Vladimirovna Yevropeitseva; m. Muza Romanovna Lobasheva; two s. two d.; ed. Leningrad Univ.; mem. CPSU 1970–91; mem. of staff of Physical-Tech. Inst. 1957–72; Scientific Leader, Moscow Meson Factory Programme; Head, Experimental Physics Div. of Inst. for Nuclear Research at U.S.S.R. (now Russian) Acad. of Sciences 1972–; Leader, Lab. for Weak Interaction Study, Leningrad (now St. Petersburg) Inst. for Nuclear Physics 1972–; Corresp. mem. U.S.S.R. (now Russian) Acad. of Sciences 1970–. *Leisure interest:* tennis. *Address:* Institute for Nuclear Research, Academy of Sciences, Prospect 60 Let Oktyabrya 7a, 117312 Troitsk, Moscow Region, Russia. *Telephone:* (095) 334-01-90 (Office); 334-03-18 (Home).

LOBKOWICZ, Michal; Czech politician; b. 20 July 1964, Prague; m.; one s.; ed. Charles Univ., Prague; M.P. for O.D.S./Civic Democratic Party 1996–98; mem. for Freedom Union (F.U.) 1998; fmr. Head of Foreign Minister's Office; Minister of Defence Jan.–July 1998; mem. Cttee. for European Integration 1998–, mem. Cttee. for Defence and Security 1998–. *Address:* Parliament of the Czech Republic, Sněmovní 4, 118 26 Prague 1, Czech Republic. *Telephone:* 57-17-11-11.

LOBKOWICZ, Nicholas, DR.PHIL.; American political philosopher; b. 9 July 1931, Prague, Czechoslovakia; s. of Prince Jan Lobkowicz and Countess Marie Czernin; m. Countess Josephine Waldburg-Zeil 1953; three s. two d.; ed. Collegium Maria Hilf, Switzerland, Univs. of Erlangen and Fribourg; Assoc. Prof. of Philosophy, Univ. of Notre Dame, Ind. 1960–67; Prof. of Political Theory and Philosophy, Univ. of Munich 1967–90, Dean School of Arts and Letters 1970–71, Rector Magnificus 1971–76, Pres. Univ. of Munich 1976–82; Pres. Catholic Univ. of Eichstätt 1984–96, Dir. Inst. of Cen. and E. European Studies 1994–; mem. Bd. of Dirs. Fed. Inst. of Int. and E. European Studies, Cologne 1972–75, Senate, W. German Rectors' Conf. 1976–82, Perm. Cttee. European Rectors' Conf. 1979–84, Council Int. Fed. of Catholic Univs. 1984–91; founding mem. Int. Metaphysical Asscn.; mem. Cen. Cttee. of German Catholics 1980–84; mem. Ukrainian Acad. of Arts and Science (U.S.A.) 1979–; mem. W. Europe Advisory Cttee. to Radio Free Europe/Radio Liberty 1980–, Chair. 1994–; Pres. Freier Deutscher Autorenverband 1985–91; mem. Pontifical Council for Culture 1982–93; Pres. Czechoslovak Christian Acad. in Rome 1983–90; Hon. D.H.L. (Wayne State Univ.); Hon. D.LL. (Univ. of Notre Dame); Dr.phil. h.c. (Seoul and Ukrainian Univ., Munich, Catholic Univ. of America); Hon. Citizen Dallas, Tex. *Publications:* Theory and Practice 1967, Ende aller Religion? 1976, Marxismus und Machtergreifung 1978, Wortmeldung zu Staat, Kirche, Universität 1981, Irrwege der Angst 1983, Das europäische Erbe 1984, Das Konzil 1986, Zeitwende 1993, Czas przelomu 1996. *Address:* Katholische Universität, 85071 Eichstätt, Germany. *Telephone:* (08421) 931717. *Fax:* (08421) 931780.

LOBO, José Carlos; Mozambican politician and fmr. teacher; b. 14 Sept. 1942, Quelimane; s. of Carlos Lobo Chibaia and Catarina Carlos Ernesto; m. Iveth Venichand Lobo 1978; two c.; ed. California State Univ., U.S.A.; joined Mozambique Liberation Front (FRELIMO) in Tanzania 1964; Teacher and Dean of Students at Mozambique Inst., Dar es Salaam 1965–66; studied at Calif. State Univ., U.S.A. until 1973; Headmaster, FRELIMO Secondary School, Bagamoyo, Tanzania 1974–75; Headmaster, FRELIMO Secondary School, Ribaue, Mozambique 1975; Dir. of Int. Orgs. and Confs. Dept., Ministry of Foreign Affairs 1975–76; Perm. Rep. to UN 1976–83; mem. Cen. Cttee. FRELIMO 1983–; Minister of Mineral Resources 1983–84; mem. of People's Ass. 1983–; Vice-Minister of Foreign Affairs 1984–; FRELIMO 20th Anniversary Medallion. *Address:* c/o Ministry of Foreign Affairs, Maputo, Mozambique.

LOBO ANTUNES, António, M.D.; Portuguese novelist; b. 1 Sept. 1942, Lisbon; three d.; higher educ. in Portugal; fmr. doctor and psychiatrist; now full-time writer (his experience of the Portuguese colonial war in Africa being a major influence); French Culture Prize, Prix du Meilleur Livre Etranger, awards for novels, etc. *Publications:* thirteen novels. *Address:* Avenida Afonso III 23, 3°c, 1900 Lisbon, Portugal. *Telephone:* 8155566.

LOBOV, Oleg Ivanovich; Russian politician; b. 7 Sept. 1937, Kiev; m. Valentina Pavlovna; one s. two d.; ed. Rostov Eng. Inst. of Railway Transport; construction engineer 1960–70; Head of Dept. Sverdlovsk Dist. Cttee. CPSU 1972–76; Head Construction Directorate for Middle Ural 1976–82; Second Sec. Sverdlovsk Regional Cttee. 1982–85; Chair. Sverdlovsk Dist. Exec. Cttee. 1985–87; Deputy Chair. R.S.F.S.R. Council of Ministers 1987–89, 1990–91; Second Sec. of Armenian CP 1989–90; U.S.S.R. People's Deputy 1989–91; First Deputy Chair. Russian Council of Ministers July–Nov. 1991; Chair. Council of Experts of Russian Govt. 1991–92, of Russian Pres. 1992–93; First Deputy Chair. Govt. of Russia, Minister of the Economy Jan.–Aug. 1993; Sec. of Security Council 1993–96; Plenipotentiary Rep. of Pres. Yeltsin in Chechen Repub. Nov. 1995–96; First Deputy Prime Minister June–Aug. 1996, Deputy Prime Minister 1996–97.

LØCHEN, Yngvar Formo, D.PHIL.; Norwegian professor of sociology; b. 31 May 1931, Oslo; s. of Arne and Valgjerd Løchen; m. Vivi Poulsen 1956; ed. Univ. of Oslo; Researcher, Norwegian Research Council 1956–60; Research Fellow, Univ. of Oslo 1960–65, Assoc. Prof., Inst. of Social Medicine 1965–71; Prof. of Sociology, Univ. of Tromsø 1971–, Chair. Cen. Cttee. of Research 1975–77, Rector Univ. of Tromsø 1977–81; Chair. Social Science, Norwegian Research Council 1986–89; mem. Norwegian Acad. of Science. *Publications:* Ideals and Realities in a Mental Hospital 1965, The Dilemma of the Sociologist 1970, The Treatment Society 1971, Rely on Your Own Forces 1976, A Common Purpose and Communality (Ed.) 1990, Commitment and Imagination 1993. *Leisure interest:* music.

LOCK, Thomas Graham, C.B.I.M.; British business executive; b. 19 Oct. 1931, Cardiff; s. of Robert H. and Morfydd (née Thomas) Lock; m. Janice O. B. Jones 1954 (divorced 1992, died 1995); two d.; ed. Whitchurch Grammar School, Univ. Coll. of S. Wales and Monmouthshire Coll. of Advanced Tech. (Aston) and Harvard Business School; Instructor Lieut. R.N. 1953–56; joined Lucas Industries Ltd. 1956; Production Foreman, Lucas Electrical Ltd. 1957–59, Factory Man. 1959–61; Dir. Girling Bremsen GmbH 1961–66; Overseas Operations Dir. Girling Ltd. 1966–73; Gen. Man. and Dir. Lucas Service Overseas Ltd. 1973–79; Man. Dir. Industrial Div. Amalgamated Metal Corpn. PLC 1979–83, Chief Exec. 1983–91; Dir. (non-exec.) Evode Group PLC 1985–91, Marshalls Universal PLC 1983–86; Liveryman Co. of Gold and Silver Wyre Drawers 1988–; Fellow Inst. of Metals; Chartered Engineer; Freeman, City of London. *Leisure interests:* sailing, music, skiing. *Address:* Parolas Villa, Pareklisia, Nr. Limassol, Cyprus. *Telephone:* 5314965.

LOCKE, Edwin Allen, Jr., A.B.; American business executive; b. 8 June 1910, Boston, Mass.; s. of Edwin A. and Elizabeth Ferguson Locke; m. 1st Dorothy Q. Clark 1934 (divorced); two s. one d.; m. 2nd Karin Marsh 1952; one s.; ed. Harvard Univ.; with Paris Branch, Chase Nat. Bank, N.Y. 1933–35, London Branch 1935–36, New York 1936–40; served in Office of Co-ordinator of Purchases, Advisory Comm. to Council of Nat. Defense 1940–41; Asst. Deputy Dir. Priorities Div., Office of Production Man. 1941; Deputy Chief Staff Officer Supply Priorities and Allocation Bd. 1941–42; Asst. to Chair. War Production Bd. 1942–44; Exec. Asst. to Personal Rep. of the Pres. 1944–45; Personal Rep. of the Pres., Washington and China 1945–46, Special Asst. to the Pres. March–Dec. 1946; Vice-Pres. of the Chase Nat. Bank, New York 1947–51; Trustee, China Medical Bd. Inc. 1947–80; apptd. Special Rep. of Sec. of State, with personal rank of Amb. to co-ordinate econ. and tech. assistance programmes in the Near East 1951–53; Pres. and Dir. Union Tank Car Co. 1953–63; Dir. Harris Trust and Savings Bank 1955–63; Dir. Federal Home Loan Bank of Chicago 1956–63, Chair. 1961–63; mem. special Presidential mission to Liberia and Tunisia; Pres. and Dir. Modern Homes Construction Co. 1963–67, Coastal Products Corpn. 1963–67; Dir. Manpower Inc. 1961–75, Warner Nat. Corpn. 1969–77, Nat. American Life Insurance Co. of Pa. 1968–85, Bankers Nat. Life Insurance Co. 1982–85, Nat. American Insurance Co. of New York 1981–85; financial consultant and investment banker 1985–; Pres. and C.E.O. American Paper Inst. 1968–77; Dir. Alusit Holdings L.P. 1993–; Pres. Econ. Club of New York 1977–85. *Address:* 935 N. Halifax Avenue, Apt. 1009, Daytona Beach, FL 32118, U.S.A.

LOCKHART, James, B.MUS., F.R.C.O.(CHM), F.R.C.M.; British conductor and music director; b. 16 Oct. 1930, Edinburgh; s. of Archibald C. Lockhart and Mary B. Lawrence; m. Sheila Grogan 1954; two s. one d.; ed. George Watson's Coll., Edin., Univ. of Edinburgh and Royal Coll. of Music; Asst. Conductor, Yorkshire Symphony Orchestra 1954–55; Repetiteur and Asst. Conductor, Städtische Bühnen Münster 1955–56, Bayerische Staatsoper, Munich 1956–57, Glyndebourne Festival Opera 1957–59; Dir. Opera Workshop, Univ. of Texas 1957–59; Repetiteur and Asst. Conductor, Royal Opera House, Covent Garden 1959–60, Conductor 1962–68; Asst. Conductor, BBC Scottish Orchestra 1960–61; Conductor, Sadler's Wells Opera 1961–62; Prof. Royal Coll. of Music 1962–72; Musical Dir. Welsh Nat. Opera 1968–73; Generalmusikdirektor, Staatstheater Kassel 1972–80, Koblenz and Theater der Stadt Koblenz 1981–88, Rheinische Philharmonie 1981–91; Prin. Guest Conductor,

BBC Concert Orchestra 1982–87; Dir. of Opera, Royal Coll. of Music 1986–92, London Royal Schools' Vocal Faculty 1992–96, Opera Consultant 1996–98; Guest Prof. of Conducting, Tokyo Nat. Univ. of Fine Arts and Music (Tokyo Geidai) 1998–; Hon. R.A.M. *Leisure interests:* travel, swimming, hill-walking. *Address:* 105 Woodcock Hill, Harrow, Middx., HA3 0JJ, England. *Telephone:* 0181-907 2112. *Fax:* 0181-907 2112.

LOCKWOOD, David, C.B.E., PH.D., F.B.A., F.R.S.A.; British university professor; b. 9 April 1929, Holmfirth, Yorks.; s. of Herbert Lockwood and Edith Annie Lockwood, née Lockwood; m. Leonore Davidoff 1954; three s.; ed. Honley Grammar School, L.S.E.; Trainee, Victoria Textiles, Honley, Yorks. 1944–47; Nat. Service, Intelligence Corps, Austria 1947–49; Univ. of London Postgraduate Studentship in Econs. 1952–53; Asst. Lecturer and Lecturer in Sociology, L.S.E. 1953–60; Rockefeller Fellow, Univ. of Calif. (Berkeley), U.S.A. 1958–59; Univ. Lecturer, Faculty of Econs. and Fellow of St. John's Coll. Cambridge 1960–68; Visiting Prof., Dept. of Sociology, Columbia Univ., U.S.A. 1966–67; Prof., Dept. of Sociology, Univ. of Essex 1968–, Pro-Vice-Chancellor 1989–92; Visiting Prof., Delhi School of Econs. 1975, Stockholm Univ. 1989; Visiting Fellow, A.N.U. 1993; mem. Social Science Research Council (Chair. Sociology and Social Admin. Cttee. 1973–76), Academia Europaea 1990; Chair. Econ. and Social Research Council 1994–. *Publications:* The Affluent Worker in the Class Structure, 3 vols. (jtly.) 1968–69, The Blackcoated Worker 1989, Solidarity and Schism 1992; numerous articles in journals and symposia. *Address:* University of Essex, Wivenhoe Park, Colchester, CO4 3SQ; 82 High Street, Wivenhoe, Essex, England. *Telephone:* (01206) 87333 (Office); (01206) 823530 (Home). *Fax:* (01206) 873598.

LODDER, Celsius Antonio, M.SC.; Brazilian international administrator and economist; b. 28 May 1944, Nova Lima, Minas Gerais; s. of Ary Lodder and Maria van Krimpen Lodder; three d.; ed. Fed. Univ. of Minas Gerais, Belo Horizonte, Getúlio Vargas Foundation, Rio de Janeiro and Inst. of Social Studies, The Hague; researcher, Applied Econs. Research Inst. Ministry of Econ., Finance and Planning 1970–80; subsequently held appts. with State of Minas Gerais and Fed. Govt. of Brazil; Sec. for Commercial Policy, Ministry of Finance, later at Ministry of Industry, Commerce and Tourism; Supt. Nat. Supply Authority, Ministry of Finance; Chief Adviser, State Bank of Minas Gerais 1983–84; Co-ordinator, Intergovernmental Relations Office, Civil Cabinet of Pres. of Brazil; lecturer in econs. at various Brazilian univs.; Exec. Dir. Int. Coffee Org. 1994–. *Publications:* books and reports on matters related to regional planning and devt. *Leisure interests:* reading, walking. *Address:* International Coffee Organization, 22 Berners Street, London, W1P 4DD, England. *Telephone:* 0171-580 8591. *Fax:* 0171-580 6129.

LODGE, David John, C.B.E., PH.D., F.R.S.L.; British novelist and fmr. professor of modern English literature; b. 28 Jan. 1935; s. of William F. and Rosalie M. (née Murphy) Lodge; m. Mary F. Jacob 1959; two s. one d.; ed. St. Joseph's Acad., Blackheath and Univ. Coll., London; British Council, London 1959–60; Asst. Lecturer in English, Univ. of Birmingham 1960–62, Lecturer 1963–71, Sr. Lecturer 1971–73, Reader 1973–76, Prof. of Modern English Literature 1976–87, Hon. Prof. 1987–; Chair. Booker Prize Cttee. 1989; Harkness Commonwealth Fellow, 1964–65; Visiting Assoc. Prof. Univ. of Calif. (Berkeley) 1969; Chevalier, Ordre des Arts et des Lettres (France) 1997; Henfield Writing Fellow, Univ. of E. Anglia 1977; Hon. Prof. (Goldsmith's Coll.) 1992; Fellow, Univ. Coll. London 1982; Yorkshire Post Fiction Prize 1975; Hawthornden Prize 1976. *Publications:* The Picturegoers 1960, Ginger, You're Barmy 1962, The British Museum is Falling Down 1965, Out of the Shelter 1970, Changing Places 1975, How Far Can You Go? 1980 (Whitbread Book of Year Award), Small World 1984, Nice Work 1988 (Sunday Express Book of the Year Award), The Writing Game (play) 1991, Paradise News 1991, Therapy 1995, Home Truths (play) 1999; eight vols. of criticism. *Leisure interests:* tennis, television, cinema. *Address:* c/o Department of English, University of Birmingham, Birmingham, B15 2TT, England.

LOEHNIS, Anthony David, C.M.G., M.A.; British banker; b. 12 March 1936, London; s. of Sir Clive and Rosemary (née Ryder) Loehnis; m. Jennifer Forsyth Anderson 1965; three s.; ed. Eton Coll., New Coll., Oxford, Harvard School of Public Admin.; in Diplomatic Service 1960–66; with J. Henry Schroder Wagg and Co. Ltd. 1967–80 (seconded to Bank of England 1977–79); Assoc. Dir. Bank of England 1980–81, Exec. Dir. (Overseas Affairs) 1981–89; Group Exec. Dir., Vice-Chair. S. G. Warburg and Co. 1989–92; Non-exec. Dir. J. Rothschild Int. Assurance Holdings PLC 1992–, J. Rothschild Assurance Holdings PLC 1993–, St. James's Place Capital PLC 1993–, Alpha Bank London PLC 1994–, Tokyo-Mitsubishi Int. PLC 1996–, AGCO Corpn. (U.S.A.) 1997–; Chair. Henderson Japanese Smaller Cos. Trust PLC 1993–, Centre for Econ. Policy Research 1990–, The Knox D'Arcy Trust PLC 1996–, Public Works Loan Bd. 1997–. *Address:* c/o 27 St. James's Place, London, SW1A 1NR, England.

LOEPFE, Otto, M.SC.; Swiss airline executive; b. 23 June 1936, Zürich; m.; three d.; ed. Fed. Inst. of Tech. Zürich and Stanford Univ. Grad. School of Business; joined Swissair 1969; Gen. Man. Planning and Quality Assurance 1974–79, Vice-Pres. Tech. 1979–84, Vice-Pres. EDP Services 1984–87, Deputy Pres. 1987–88; Pres. Swissair 1988–96. *Leisure interest:* flying.

LÖFGREN, Lars, PH.D.; Swedish theatre, film and television director, playwright and poet; b. 6 Sept. 1935, The Arctic Circle; m. Anna-Karin Gillberg 1963; one s. two d.; ed. Gustavus Adolphus Coll., U.S.A., Stanford Univ., U.S.A., Sorbonne, France, Üppsala Univ., Sweden; Dir. Royal Dramatic Theatre of Sweden 1985–. *Publications:* various plays, filmscripts, TV-scripts, poetry, novels. *Address:* Lagman Linds Vag 14, 18275 Stocksund, Sweden.

LOFSTAD, Knut; Norwegian business executive and mechanical engineer; b. 27 April 1927, Oslo; s. of Nils Lofstad and Margit Iversen; m. Anne-Lise Ravnsborg-Gjertsen 1960; one s. one d.; ed. Univ. of Wisconsin; Sales Engineer, A/S G. Hartmann 1950–61; Sales Man., Man. Dir. Eureka 1962–; Man. Dir. Thune Eureka 1969–81; Dir.-Gen. Fed. of Norwegian Industries 1982–88; Deputy Dir. Gen. Confed. Norwegian Business and Industry 1989–92. *Leisure interests:* skiing, hunting. *Address:* Ankerveien 18, 0390 Oslo 3, Norway (Home). *Telephone:* 02-14 18 32 (Home).

LOGACHEV, Nikolay Alekseyevich, D.GEOL.MIN.SCI.; Russian geologist and academic; b. 7 Oct. 1929, Novoshipunovo Village, Altai; s. of Aleksey and Marina Logachev; m. Tamara Kashkina 1949; one s. one d.; ed. Irkutsk Univ.; research at Inst. of Geology, East Siberian Br. of Acad. of Sciences 1952–59; mem. CPSU 1959–91; sr. researcher, head of lab. at Inst. of the Earth's Crust, Siberian Div. of Acad. of Sciences 1959–73; Deputy Chair. of Presidium of East Siberian Branch, Siberian Div. of Acad. of Sciences 1973–76; Dir. of Inst. of Earth's Crust 1976–; simultaneously Chair. of Presidium of Irkutsk Scientific Centre, Siberian Div. of Acad. of Sciences 1977–92; mem. Supreme Soviet of U.S.S.R. 1979–89; corresp. mem. of U.S.S.R. (now Russian) Acad. of Sciences 1979–84, mem. 1984–; State Prize 1978; U.S.S.R. Council of Ministers Prize 1988. *Publications:* works on the sedimentary fill, volcanism and geodynamics of Cainozoic continental rift zones. *Leisure interests:* carpentry, literature. *Address:* Institute of the Earth's Crust, Lermontov Street 128, Irkutsk 664033, Russia. *Telephone:* (3952) 46-40-00 (Office); (3952) 24-61-63 (Home).

LOGAN, Malcolm Ian, A.C., DIP.ED., PH.D.; Australian university vice-chancellor; b. 3 June 1931, Inverell, N.S.W.; s. of the late A. J. Logan; m. Antoinette Lalich 1954; one d.; ed. Tamworth High School, New England Univ. Coll., Sydney Teachers' Coll., Sydney Univ.; lecturer in Geography, Sydney Teachers' Coll. 1956–58, Univ. of Sydney 1959–64, Sr. Lecturer 1965–67; Prof. of Geography and Urban and Regional Planning, Univ. of Wis., Madison, U.S.A. 1967–71; Prof. of Geography, Monash Univ. 1971–86, Pro-Vice-Chancellor 1982–85, Deputy Vice-Chancellor 1986, Vice-Chancellor 1987–96, also fmr. Pres.; Deputy Chair. Int. Devt. Program of Australian Univs. 1991–93; Chair. Australian Centre for Contemporary Art 1990, Open Learning Agency of Australia 1993–, Monash Int. Pty. Ltd. 1994–; mem. Comm. for the Future 1995–; Visiting Prof. Univ. of Ibadan, Nigeria 1970–71, L.S.E., London, U.K. 1973; Nanyang Univ., Singapore 1979. *Publications:* (Co-Author) Studies in Australian Geography 1968, New Viewpoints in Urban and Industrial Geography 1971, Urban and Regional Australia 1975, Urbanisation, The Australian Experience 1980, The Brittle Rim 1989. *Leisure interests:* golf, reading. *Address:* c/o Monash University, Wellington Road, Clayton, Vic. 3168, Australia.

LOGUE, Christopher John; British writer; b. 23 Nov. 1926, Southsea; s. of John Logue and Molly Logue (née Chapman); m. Rosemary Hill 1985; ed. Prior Park Coll., Bath and Portsmouth Grammar School. *Screenplays:* Savage Messiah (dir. Ken. Russell 1972), Crusoe (based on Defoe's novel, with Walon Green) 1989. *Recordings:* Red Bird (poetry and jazz, with Tony Kinsey and Bill Le Sage) 1960, Songs from the Establishment 1962, The Death of Patroclus 1963. *Film roles:* Swinburne in Ken Russell's Dante's Inferno 1966, John Ball in John Irvin's The Peasant's Revolt 1969, Cardinal Richelieu in Ken Russell's The Devils 1970; also TV and stage roles. *Publications:* (verse) Wand & Quadrant 1953, Devil, Maggot & Son 1956, Songs 1959, Patrocleia 1962, Pax 1967, New Numbers 1969, War Music 1981, Ode to the Dodo 1981, Kings 1991, The Husbands 1995, Selected Poems 1996; (plays) The Trial of Cob & Leach 1959, The Lilywhite Boys (with Harry Cookson) 1959, trans. Brecht and Weill, The Seven Deadly Sins 1986; (anthologies) The Children's Book of Comic Verse 1979, Sweet and Sour 1983, The Oxford Book of Pseuds 1983, The Children's Book of Children's Rhymes 1986; contrib. Private Eye, The Times, Sunday Times. *Address:* 41 Camberwell Grove, London, SE5 8JA, England.

LOGUNOV, Anatoly Alekseyevich; Russian theoretical physicist; b. 30 Dec. 1926, Obsharovka, Samara Region; s. of Aleksei Ivanovich Logunov and Agrippina Kuzminichna Logunova; m. Anna Nikolayevna Eshliman 1951 (died 1997); one s. (deceased) one d.; ed. Moscow State Univ.; mem. CPSU 1960–91; mem. faculty staff Moscow State Univ. 1951–56; Deputy Dir. for Research, Theoretical Physics Lab., Jt. Inst. for Nuclear Research, Dubna 1956–63, Prof. 1961; Dir. of Serpukhov Inst. for High Energy Physics (IHEP), Protvino, Moscow 1963–74, IHEP Research Leader 1974–, Dir. State Research Centre IHEP 1993–; Rector Moscow State Univ. 1977–92; mem. U.S.S.R. (now Russian) Acad. of Sciences 1972–, Vice-Pres. 1974–91; Head, State Scientific-Tech. Programme of High Energy Physics 1987–90; Vice-Pres. Acad. of Creative Endeavours 1992–; mem. Int. Acad. of Sciences; Full Prof. Inst. of Fundamental Research, Molise, Italy; mem. Editorial Bd. Asia-Pacific Peace Forum 1992–; Chief Ed. annual publ. Science and Humankind 1977–92, journal Theoretical and Math. Physics 1989–; main research on quantum field theory, elementary particle physics, gravitation and relativity theory; Cand. mem. Cen. Cttee. CPSU 1981–86, mem. 1986–90; Deputy, U.S.S.R. Supreme Soviet 1978–89; numerous hon. degrees; Lenin Prize 1970, U.S.S.R. State Prizes 1973, 1984, Lyapunov Medal, Gibbs Medal and many others; Hero of Socialist Labour 1980, four Orders of Lenin, Order of Honour,

Order of Merit III degree, Order of Pole Star (Mongolia), Order of Yugoslavian Banner with Ribbon, Commdr. Cross of Order of Merit (Poland) and other honours. *Publications include:* Lectures on Relativity and Gravitation Theory, The Updated Analysis of the Problem 1987, On Henrie Poincaret's work "On the Dynamics of Electron" 1988, The Third Irisated Bridge 1988, Relativistic Theory of Gravitation 1989, Principles of Quantum Field Theory 1990, etc.; more than 350 contribs. to scientific journals on high energy and elementary particle physics, and on latest ideas about space-time and gravitation. *Address:* State Research Centre Institute for High Energy Physics, 142284 Protvino, Moscow Region, Russia. *Telephone:* (095) 924-67-52. *Fax:* (095) 230-23-27.

LOHIA, Renagi Renagi, M.A.; Papua New Guinea broadcasting executive and fmr. diplomatist; b. 15 Oct. 1945, Tubesereia; s. of Lohia and Koborei Lohia; m. 1969; three s. two d.; ed. Univ. of Papua New Guinea and London Univ.; Research Asst. Univ. of Papua New Guinea 1970–73; Sr. Tutor 1973, Lecturer in Educ. 1974–82, Pro-Vice-Chancellor 1976, Deputy Vice-Chancellor 1977, Vice-Chancellor 1977–82, Chair. Educational Planning Cttee. 1974–75, Educ. Faculty Rep. Jt. Cttee. on Teacher Educ. 1975–76; Chair. Public Services Comm. 1982–83; Amb. to U.S.A. and Mexico, and High Commr. in Canada 1983–89; Perm. Rep. to UN 1983–94; Chair. UN Decolonization Cttee.; Special Asst. Dept. of Foreign Affairs 1986–87; Chief of Staff, Office of Prime Minister 1994–95; Chair. and Chief Exec. Nat. Broadcasting Comm. 1995–. *Leisure interest:* sports. *Address:* National Broadcasting Commission, P.O. Box 1359, Boroko, Papua New Guinea. *Telephone:* 257175. *Fax:* 256296.

LOHR, Helmut H. W., DR.OEC, DIPL. ING.; German business executive and engineer; b. 7 April 1931, Munich; s. of Eduard and Gertrud (Schnitzler) Lohr; m. Franziska Wiedemann 1959; two d.; ed. Munich Tech. Univ., Harvard Business School, U.S.A.; worked for Int. Switching Systems Dept. (FTZ), Deutsche Bundespost 1959; joined Standard Elektrik Lorenz AG 1965, Dir. 1974, Man. Dir. 1976–89; Sr. Vice-Pres. Alcatel NV 1989–91; ind. industrial business strategy consultant. *Address:* Gerokstrasse 68, 71665 Vaihingen, Germany.

LOHSE, Eduard, D.THEOL.; German ecclesiastic; b. 19 Feb. 1924, Hamburg; s. of Dr. Walther Lohse and Dr. Wilhelmine Lohse (née Barrelet); m. Roswitha Flitner 1952; two s. one d.; ed. Bethel/Bielefeld and Göttingen; Pastor, Hamburg 1952; Privatdozent, Faculty of Protestant Theology, Mainz 1953; Prof. of New Testament, Kiel 1956, Göttingen 1964; Bishop of Hanover 1971–88; Pres. of the Council of the Evangelical Church in Germany 1979–85; mem. Göttingen Akad. der Wissenschaften; Hon. D.Theol. (Mainz) 1961, (Glasgow) 1983. *Publications:* Märtyrer und Gottesknecht 1955, Die Offenbarung des Johannes 1960, Die Texte aus Qumran 1964, Die Geschichte des Leidens und Sterbens Jesu Christi 1964, Die Briefe an die Kolosser und an Philemon 1968, Umwelt des Neuen Testaments 1971, Entstehung des Neuen Testaments 1972, Die Einheit des Neuen Testaments 1973, Grundriss der neutestamentlichen Theologie 1974, Die Urkunde der Christen 1979, Die Vielfalt des Neuen Testaments 1982, Die Ethik der Bergpredigt 1984, Kleine Evangelische Pastoralethik 1985, Theologische Ethik des Neuen Testaments 1988, Erneuern und Bewahren Evangelische Kirche 1970–90 1993, Paulus—eine Biographie 1996. *Leisure interest:* music. *Address:* Ernst-Curtius-Weg 7, 37075 Göttingen, Germany. *Telephone:* (0551) 42424.

LOISEAU, Bernard; French chef; b. 13 Jan. 1951, Chamalières; s. of Pierre Loiseau and Edith Rullière; m. 1st Chantal Le Bras (divorced); m. 2nd Dominique Brunet 1989; two s. one d.; apprentice chef Troisgros, Roanne 1968–71; chef La Barrière de Clichy 1973–74; chef Hôtel de la Côte d'Or, Saulieu 1975–, propr. 1982–; Chevalier Ordre nat. du mérite, Ordre nat. des arts et des lettres, Ordre du mérite agricole; Guide Hachette Best Chef under 40 1984; Gault-Millau Cook of the Year 1986; Le Chef magazine Chef of the Year 1991. *Publications:* Envolée des Saveurs, Les dimanches de B. Loiseau, Trucs et Astuces, Le Monde des saveurs, B. Loiseau: Cuisine en famille. *Leisure interests:* fishing, hunting. *Address:* Hôtel de la Côte d'Or, 2 rue d'Argentine, 21210 Saulieu, France. *Telephone:* (3) 80-90-53-53. *Fax:* (3) 80-64-08-92.

LOISELLE, Gilles, P.C.; Canadian politician and fmr. diplomatist; b. 1929; m. Lorraine Benoît; one s. one d.; ed. Laval Univ.; teacher and admin., Ethiopia 1951–53, 1956–61; Co-ordinator 1986 Francophonie Summit; Progressive Conservative M.P. for Quebec 1988–93; Minister of State (Finance) 1989–93; Pres. Treasury Bd. 1990–93; Minister of Finance 1993; Adviser to Chair. Power Corpn. of Canada 1994–; fmr. Prov. Rep. for Quebec in G.B., France and Italy; Founder-mem. Quebec-France Asscn. *Address:* 3460-404 Simpson Street, Montreal, Que. H3G 2J4, Canada.

LOKOLOKO, Sir Tore, G.C.M.G., O.B.E.; Papua New Guinea politician; b. 21 Sept. 1930, Iokea, Gulf Province; s. of Paramount Chief Lokoloko Tore and Kevau-Sarufa; m. Lalahaia Meakoro 1950; four s. six d.; elected to House of Assembly (now Nat. Parl.) as Opposition mem. for Kerema (Gulf Province); Gov.-Gen. of Papua New Guinea 1977–83; Chair. Indosuez Niugine Bank 1983–89; K.St.J. *Leisure interests:* golf, fishing. *Address:* P.O. Box 5622, Port Moresby, Papua New Guinea.

LOLLOBRIGIDA, Gina; Italian actress; b. 4 July 1927, Sibiaco; d. of Giovanni and Giuseppina Mercuri; m. Milko Skofic 1949; one s.; ed. Liceo Artistico, Rome; first screen role in Pagliacci 1947; has since appeared in numerous films including Campane a Martello 1948, Cuori senza Frontiere 1949, Achtung, banditi! 1951, Enrico Caruso 1951, Fanfan la Tulipe 1951, Altri Tempi 1952, The Wayward Wife 1952, Les belles de la nuit 1952, Pane, amore e fantasia 1953, La Provinciale 1953, Pane, amore e gelosia, La Romana 1954, Il Grande Gioco 1954, La Donna più Bella del Mondo 1955, Trapeze 1956, Notre Dame de Paris 1956, Solomon and Sheba 1959, Never So Few 1960, Go Naked in the World 1961, She Got What She Asked For 1963, Woman of Straw 1964, Le Bambole 1965, Hotel Paradiso 1966, Buona Sera Mrs. Campbell 1968, King, Queen, Knave 1972, The Bocce Showdown 1990, Plucked, Bad Man's River, The Lonely Woman, Bambole. *Publications:* Italia Mia (photography) 1974, The Philippines. *Leisure interest:* photography. *Address:* Via Appia Antica 223, 00178 Rome, Italy.

LOM, Herbert; British actor; b. 11 Sept. 1917, Prague, Czechoslovakia; s. of Charles and Olga Lom; m. (divorced); two s. one d.; ed. Prague Univ., Old Vic., Westminster School; theatre work in Prague before coming to England in 1939; joined the Old Vic theatre co.; entered films 1940; worked with BBC European Section 1940–46. *Films include:* Tomorrow We Live 1941, The Young Mr. Pitt 1942, The Dark Tower 1943, Night Boat to Dublin 1945, Appointment With Crime 1946, Good Time Girl 1947, Cage of Gold 1950, Star of India 1953, The Ladykillers 1955, War and Peace 1955, Passport to Shame 1958, North-West Frontier 1959, El Cid 1961, The Phantom of the Opera 1962, A Shot in the Dark 1963, Marrakesh 1965, Gambit 1966, Doppelganger 1968, The Picture of Dorian Gray 1970, Return of the Pink Panther 1974, The Pink Panther Strikes Again 1976, Charleston 1976, Revenge of the Pink Panther 1977, Trail of the Pink Panther 1981, Curse of the Pink Panther 1983, Dead Zone 1984, Memed My Hawk 1984, King Solomon's Mines 1985, Whoops Apocalypse, Going Bananas 1986, Scoop 1987, Coast of Skeletons, Master of Dragonard Hill 1987, Ten Little Indians 1989, The Masque of the Red Death 1990, The Pope Must Die 1991, The Sect 1991, Son of the Pink Panther 1992. *Television appearances include:* The Human Jungle 1963, Hawaii Five-O 1971, The Acts of Peter and Paul 1980, Lace 1985. *Publications:* Enter a Spy, the Double Life of Christopher Marlowe 1978, Dr. Guillotine 1992. *Leisure interest:* books. *Address:* c/o London Management, 2–4 Noel Street, London W1V 3RB, England.

LOMAX, Alan, B.A.; American collector of folk songs, radio, television and film producer/director, and musical anthropologist; b. 31 Jan. 1915, Austin, Texas; s. of John A. and Bess B. Lomax; m. 1st Elizabeth Harold 1937; m. 2nd Antoinette Marchand 1962; one d.; ed. Univ. of Texas, Harvard and Columbia Univs.; Archive of American Folk Song, Library of Congress 1937–42; CBS 1939–44; Decca 1947–49; Research at Univ. of W. Indies 1962, Columbia 1963–; Dir. Cantometrics Project, Dept of Anthropology, Columbia Univ. 1963–, American Patchwork Project, Choreometrics Project; Research Fellow, Smithsonian Inst. 1991–; Fellow, American Folklore Soc., A.A.A.S. (1979); Pres. Asscn. for Anthropological Film Research 1980–86, Asscn. for Cultural Equity 1982–; Pres. American Film Research Inst., American Anthropological Asscn.; Dir. The Global Jukebox Project; many lectures, radio programmes and over 100 recordings of folk and primitive music; Ed., World Library Folk and Primitive Music, Columbia Records (19 vols.) 1951–57 and other series; Nat. Medal of Arts 1986. *Publications:* Co-ed. with John A. Lomax: American Ballads and Folk Songs 1934, Negro Folk Songs as Sung by Leadbelly 1936, Cowboy Songs 1937, Our Singing Country 1938, Folk Song U.S.A. 1946; Mister Jelly Roll 1949, The Rainbow Sign 1959, Harriett and her Harmonium, Folk Songs of North America 1960, Penguin Book of American Folk Songs 1961, Folk Song Style and Culture 1968, 3,000 Years of Black Poetry (with R. Abdul) 1969, The Land Where the Blues Began 1993 (NBCC Award for Gen. Non-Fiction); Cantometrics: A Method in Musical Anthropology (audio-cassettes and handbook) 1977, World Dance and Movement Style (with Forrestine Paulay); many articles. *Films:* Dance and Human History, Step Style, Palm Play (with Forrestine Paulay), The Longest Trail (Dir. and Ed.) 1984, American Patchwork (TV series; winner PBS Award) 1997. *Recordings:* The Alan Lomax collection (more than 100 CDs) 1997–. *Leisure interests:* travel, the sea, reading (literature and science), cinema, television. *Address:* 450 West 41st Street, 6th Floor, New York, NY 10036, U.S.A.

LOMEYKO, Vladimir Borisovich; Russian diplomatist; b. 27 Nov. 1935, Novorossiisk; m.; ed. Moscow Inst. of Int. Relations; fmr. mem. CPSU; Official, Embassy to G.D.R. 1960–62; komsomol work 1962–66; at CPSU Cen. Cttee. 1966–68; Novosti Press Agency 1968–78; on staff of Literaturnaya gazeta 1974–78; Head Press Dept., U.S.S.R. Ministry of Foreign Affairs 1984–86; Amb. Extraordinary 1986–88; mem. Collegium of Foreign Affairs Ministry 1986; U.S.S.R. Rep. UN Conference on Rights of Man, Geneva 1986–89, U.S.S.R. (now Russian) Perm. Rep. to UNESCO 1989–93, adviser to Dir. Gen. of UNESCO 1995–. *Publications:* books and articles on int. relations, including New Thinking in Nuclear Age 1984 (Vorovsky Prize), Right and Left Radicalism in the Federal Republic of Germany. *Address:* UNESCO, 7 place de Fontenoy, 75352 Paris, France. *Telephone:* (1) 45-68-1000.

LOMU, Jonah; New Zealand rugby football player and athlete; b. 1975, Mangere; m. Tanya Rutter 1996; bank officer ASB Bank of N.Z.; youngest ever capped All Black; wing; int. debut N.Z. versus France 1994–; semi-finalist at World Cup, S. Africa 1995; affil. to Rugby Union; ran 100m. in 10.7 seconds.

LONDOÑO PAREDES, Julio; Colombian politician; b. 10 June 1938, Bogotá; m.; ed. San Isidro Hermanos Maristas School, El Carmen Inst. and

Mil. Cadet School, Bogotá; Prof. of Int. Politics at Univ. of Jorge Tadeo Lozano, Bogotá; Prof. of Int. Public Law at Univ. of El Rosario, Bogotá; served in Army, retd. 1981 with rank of Lieut.-Col.; Head of Frontier Div. at Ministry of Foreign Affairs 1968–79, Sec.-Gen. 1979–82, Vice.-Minister 1982–83, Minister 1986–90; Amb. to Panama 1983–86; Perm. Rep. to U.N. 1994–. *Publications:* History of the Colombo-Peruvian Conflict of 1932; Colombian Territorial Law; Colombian Border Issues. *Address:* Permanent Mission of Columbia to UN, 140 East 57th Street, 5th Floor, New York, NY 10022, U.S.A.

LONG, Malcolm William, LL.B; Australian broadcasting executive; b. 13 April 1948, Fremantle, W. Australia; s. of William Long and Dorothy Long; m. Helen Maxwell 1973; two d.; ed. Univ. of W. Australia; Dir. Radio Talks and Documentaries, ABC 1978–82; Man. (Radio) Victorian ABC 1982–84; Dir. ABC Radio 1985–92; Deputy Man. Dir. Australian Broadcasting Corpn. 1992–93; Dir. PANTU Party 1996–; Man. Dir. SBS Corpn. 1993–97; Pres. Australian Museum Trust 1995–; Chair. Exec. Cttee. Int. Inst. of Communications; Dir. Nat. Inst. of Dramatic Art. *Publications:* Marx & Beyond 1973, Beyond the Mechanical Mind (with P. Fry) 1977; numerous articles on broadcasting policy and culture. *Leisure interests:* music, reading, running. *Address:* c/o Communications Strategies and Management Party Ltd., 36 Dettman Avenue, Longueville, NSW 2066, Australia.

LONG, Marceau, L. ÈS L., L. EN D.; French civil servant; b. 22 April 1926, Aix-en-Provence, Bouches-du-Rhône; s. of Lucien Long and Marcelle Seymard; m. Josette Niel 1949; two s. three d.; ed. Lycée Mignet, Univ. of Aix-en-Provence. École nat. d'administration; lecturer, Ecole Nationale d'Admin. 1953–56, Inst. d'Etudes Politiques 1953–56; seminars Ecole Nationale d'Admin. 1963–68; at Council of State 1952–57, 1975–, Vice-Pres. 1987–95, apptd. auditor 1952, master of petitions 1957, Sec.Gen. to Govt. 1975–82, Counsellor of State on long-term secondment 1976; apptd. Govt. Comm. 1957, Tech. Counsellor to Cabinet, Sec. of State on Tunisian and Moroccan Affairs, then Foreign Affairs, then Judicial Counsellor to French Embassy, Morocco 1958, Dir.-Gen. Admin. and Public Offices 1961–67, Sec. Gen. Admin. Ministry of Armies 1967–73, mem. Atomic Energy Cttee. 1975–82; Chair. Organisation de la radio et de la télévision françaises (O.R.T.F.) 1973–74; Chair. Cie. Air-Inter 1982–84; Chair. Cie. Air France 1984–87; Chair. Cttee. Inquiry on Law of Nationality 1987, Council of Admin. Tribunals and courts of Appeal 1988–; lecturer Inst. d'études politiques de Paris, École nat. d'admin. 1963–68 (Chair. Bd. of Govs. 1987); Dir. Crédit industriel et commercial bank 1982–87, Soc. de Gestion de participations aéronautiques 1985; Pres. Admin Council Ecole Nationale d'Admin., Institut Int. d'Admin. Publique 1987–; Pres. Franco-American Foundation 1989–92, Hon. Pres. 1993–; Pres. Haut Conseil à L'Intégration 1989–93, 1994–95, Inst. des hautes études de la justice 1995–97, Inst. de la gestion déléguée 1996–; mem. Court of Arbitration, The Hague 1991–; mem. numerous admin. councils and cttees.; Grand Officier, Légion d'honneur, Commdr. Ordre nat. du Mérite. *Publications:* L'Economie de la Fonction Publique 1967, Les Services de Premier Ministre 1981, Les Grands Arrêts de la Jurisprudence Administrative (co-author) 1984, Etre Français aujourd'hui et demain, Rapport de la Commission de la Nationalité 1988, l'Esprit de justice: Portalis 1997, and numerous contribs. to magazines and books on public office and law. *Address:* Ecole nationale d'administration, 13 rue de l'Université, 75007 Paris, France.

LONG, Richard; British artist; b. 2 June 1945, Bristol; s. of Maurice Long and Frances Carpenter; m. Denise Johnston 1969; two d.; ed. West of England Coll. of Art, Bristol and St. Martin's School of Art, London; has exhibited widely since mid-1960s; work exhibited Venice Biennale 1976, Tate Gallery 1990, Hayward Gallery, London (retrospective) 1991, A.R.C., Paris 1993; Hon. D.Lit. (Bristol) 1995; Chevalier, Ordre des Arts et des Lettres 1990; Turner Prize 1989. *Publications include:* South America 1972, Twelve Works 1981, Countless Stones 1983, Stone Water Miles 1987, Old World New World 1988, Nile 1990, Walking in Circles 1991, Mountains and Waters 1992, River to River 1993. *Address:* c/o Anthony D'Offay, 20 Dering Street, London, W.1, England.

LONG, Russell B.; American politician and lawyer; b. 3 Nov. 1918, Shreveport, La.; s. of Huey Pierce Long and Rose McConnell; m. 2nd Carolyn Bason 1969; two d. by previous m.; ed. Fortier High School and Louisiana State Univ.; served U.S. Navy 1942–45; in pvt. legal practice 1945–48, Exec. Counsel to Gov. of Louisiana 1948; U.S. Senator from Louisiana 1948–86, Senate Majority Whip 1965–69; Chair. Finance Cttee. 1966–81; partner Long Law Firm, Washington and Baton Rouge 1987–; Democrat.

LONGFORD, Countess of; **Elizabeth Pakenham,** C.B.E., F.R.S.L.; British writer; b. 30 Aug. 1906, London; d. of the late N. B. Harman, F.R.C.S., and of Katherine Chamberlain; m. Francis A. Pakenham (now Earl of Longford, q.v.) 1931; four s. four d. (one deceased); ed. Headington School, Oxford, and Lady Margaret Hall, Oxford; Parliamentary Candidate (Labour) Cheltenham 1935, Oxford 1950; Trustee Nat. Portrait Gallery 1967–78; mem. Advisory Bd., Victoria and Albert Museum 1969–75, Advisory Bd., British Library 1976–80; Hon. D.Litt. (Sussex) 1970; James Tait Black Prize for Victoria R.I. 1964; Yorkshire Post Book of the Year Prize for Wellington: The Years of the Sword 1969. *Publications:* Jameson's Raid 1959, Victoria R.I. 1964, Wellington: The Years of the Sword 1969, Wellington: Pillar of State 1972, Winston Churchill 1974, The Royal House of Windsor 1974, Byron's Greece (with photographer Jorge Lewinski) 1975, Byron 1976, Wilfrid Scawen Blunt 1978, Louisa, Lady in Waiting to Queen Victoria and Queen Alexandra 1980, The Queen Mother 1981, Eminent Victorian Women 1981, Elizabeth R 1983, The Pebbled Shore: The Memoirs of Elizabeth Longford 1986, The Oxford Book of Royal Anecdotes (ed.) 1989, Darling Loosy, The Correspondents of Princess Louise 1856–1939, 1991, Wellington (abridged) 1992, Poets' Corner: an anthology 1992, Royal Throne: The Future of the Monarchy 1993. *Leisure interests:* Victoriana, gardening. *Address:* 18 Chesil Court, Chelsea Manor Street, London, SW3 5QP; Bernhurst, Hurst Green, East Sussex, TN19 7QN, England. *Telephone:* 0171-352 7794 (London); (01580) 86248.

LONGFORD, 7th Earl of (cr. 1785); **Francis Aungier Pakenham** (cr. Baron 1945), K.G., P.C., M.A.; British writer and politician; b. 5 Dec. 1905; s. of the late 5th Earl of Longford and Lady Mary Julia Child-Villiers; m. Elizabeth Harman (now Countess of Longford, q.v.) 1931; four s. four d. (one deceased); ed. Eton Coll. and New Coll., Oxford; Tutor, Univ. Tutorial Courses, Stoke-on-Trent 1929–31; with Conservative Party Econ. Research Dept. 1930–32; Lecturer in Politics, Christ Church, Oxford 1932; Student in Politics, Christ Church 1934–46 and 1952–64; Prospective Parl. Labour Candidate for Oxford City 1938; served Bucks. Light Infantry 1939–40; personal asst. to Sir William Beveridge 1941–44; Lord-in-Waiting 1945–46; Parl. Under-Sec. to War Office 1946–47; Chancellor of the Duchy of Lancaster 1947–48; Minister of Civil Aviation 1948–51; First Lord of the Admiralty May-Oct. 1951; Lord Privy Seal and Leader of House of Lords 1964–65, 1966–68; Sec. of State for Colonies 1965–66; Chair. Nat. Youth Employment Council 1968–71; fmr. Chair. Matthew Trust, Chair. Nat. Bank Ltd. 1955–62; Chair. Sidgwick and Jackson Ltd. (Publishers) 1970–80, Dir. 1980–85; Jt. Founder and Dir. The Help Charitable Trust 1986. *Publications:* Peace by Ordeal (The Anglo-Irish Treaty of 1921), Born to Believe 1953, The Causes of Crime 1958, Five Lives 1963, Humility 1969, De Valéra (with T. P. O'Neill) 1970, The Grain of Wheat 1974, The Life of Jesus Christ 1974, Abraham Lincoln 1974, Kennedy 1976, Francis of Assisi: A Life for All Seasons 1978, Nixon 1980, Ulster 1981, Pope John Paul II (biog.) 1982, Diary of a Year 1982, Eleven at No. 10: A Personal View of Prime Ministers 1931–84, 1984, One Man's Faith 1984, The Search for Peace 1985, The Bishops: A Study of Leaders in the Church today 1986, Saints 1987, A History of the House of Lords 1989, Suffering and Hope 1990, Punishment and the Punished 1991, Prisoner or Patient 1992, Young Offenders 1993, Avowed Intent (autobiog.) 1994. *Address:* 18 Chesil Court, Chelsea Manor Street, London, SW3 5QP; Bernhurst, Hurst Green, East Sussex, TN19 7QN, England. *Telephone:* (01580) 86248.

LONGO, Jeannie Michèle Alice; French cyclist; b. 31 Oct. 1958, Annecy; d. of Jean Longo and Yvette Longo; m. Patrice Ciprelli 1985; ed. Inst. d'Etudes Commerciales (Grenoble) and Univ. of Limoges; French Cycling Champion 1979–86; winner of 13 world titles including World Champion (road) 1985, 1987, World Champion 1988, 1989, World Champion (against the clock) Spain 1997; winner Tour of Colorado 1986, 1987, Tour of Colombia 1987, 1988, Tour of Norway 1987, Tour de France 1987; Silver Medal World Track Race 1987; holder of several world records including World Record for 3 km., Covered Track, Grenoble 1992; winner French Cycle Racing Championship 1992; Silver Medallist Olympic Games, Barcelona 1992, Gold Medallist Road Race, Olympic Games, Atlanta 1996; Médaille d'Or, La Jeunesse et les Sports, Médaille d'Or, Acad. des Sports. *Address:* Fédération Française de Cyclisme, 5 rue de Rome, 93561 Rosny-sous-Bois, France.

LONGUET, Gérard Edmond Jacques; French politician; b. 24 Feb. 1946, Neuilly-sur-Seine; s. of Jacques Longuet and Marie-Antoinette Laurent; m. Brigitte Fossorier 1967; four d.; ed. Paris Univ.; Pvt. Sec. to Prefect of Eure's Office 1973–74, to Prefect of Somme's Office 1974–76, to Sec. of State (attached to Prime Minister's Office) 1977–78; Deputy of Meuse 1978–81, 1988–93, Vice-Pres. Gen. Councillor's Office 1982–92; Gen. Councillor Seuil d'Argonne 1979–92, Town Councillor 1983; mem. European Parl. 1984–86; Sec. of State March–Aug. 1986, then Minister at Ministry of Industry 1986–88, Minister of Industry, Posts and Telecommunications and Foreign Trade 1993–94; Sec.-Gen. Union pour la Démocratie Française (UDF) 1989; Pres. Republican Party 1990–95, Regional Council of Lorraine 1992–; Gen. Councillor Fresne-en-Woëvre 1998–; Collection Dir. France Empire publrs. *Publications:* L'Epreuve de vérité 1995, L'Espoir industriel 1995. *Address:* Conseil Regional de Lorraine, Place Gabriel Hocquard, BP 1004, 57036 Metz cedex 1, France.

LONGUET-HIGGINS, Hugh Christopher, M.A., D.PHIL., F.R.S., F.R.S.E.; British university professor; b. 11 April 1923, Lenham, Kent; s. of the late Henry H. L. Longuet-Higgins and Albinia Cecil Bazeley; brother of Michael Selwyn Longuet-Higgins (q.v.); ed. Winchester Coll., Balliol Coll., Oxford; Research Fellow Balliol Coll. 1947–48; Research Assoc. Univ. of Chicago 1948–49; Lecturer and Reader in Theoretical Chem., Victoria Univ. of Manchester 1949–52; Prof. of Theoretical Physics King's Coll., London Univ. 1952–54; Fellow, Corpus Christi Coll. and Prof. of Theoretical Chem., Univ. of Cambridge 1954–67; Royal Soc. Research Prof., Univ. of Edin. 1968–74, Univ. of Sussex 1974–89, Prof. Emer. 1989–, Harrison Memorial Prize 1950; Gov. of BBC 1979–84; Foreign mem. American Acad. of Arts and Sciences 1961; Foreign Assoc. N.A.S. 1968–; Life Fellow, Corpus Christi Coll., Cambridge, Hon. Fellow, Balliol Coll., Oxford 1969, Wolfson Coll., Cambridge 1977; Dr. h.c. (York) 1973, (Essex) 1981, (Bristol) 1983, (Sussex) 1989, (Sheffield) 1995. *Publications include:* The Nature of Mind (Gifford Lectures) 1972, Mental Processes 1987, and about 200 papers in scientific journals. *Leisure interest:* music. *Address:* Centre for Research on Perception and

Cognition, Laboratory of Experimental Psychology, University of Sussex, Falmer, Brighton, BN1 9QG, England. *Telephone:* (01273) 678341.

LONGUET-HIGGINS, Michael Selwyn, M.A., PH.D., F.R.S.; British research scientist; b. 8 Dec. 1925, Lenham, Kent; s. of the late Henry H. L. Longuet-Higgins and Albinia Cecil Bazeley; brother of Hugh Christopher Longuet-Higgins (q.v.); m. Joan R. Tattersall 1958; two s. two d.; ed. Winchester Coll., Trinity Coll., Cambridge Univ.; Research Fellow, Trinity Coll., Cambridge 1951–55, Commonwealth Fund Fellow, Scripps Inst., La Jolla, 1951–52; Research Scientist, Nat. Inst. of Oceanography 1954–67; Visiting Prof. M.I.T. 1958; Visiting Prof. Inst. of Geophysics, Univ. of Calif. 1961–62; Visiting Prof. Univ. of Adelaide 1963–64; Prof. of Oceanography, Oregon State Univ., Corvallis 1967–69; Royal Soc. Research Prof., Cambridge Univ. (joint appointment with Inst. of Oceanographic Sciences) 1969–89; Sr. Research Physicist, La Jolla Inst. 1989–; Fellow Trinity Coll., Cambridge 1969–; Foreign Assoc. N.A.S. 1979; Hon. LL.D. (Glasgow) 1979; Hon. D.Tech. (Tech. Univ. of Denmark) 1979; Fellow, Royal Soc. 1963, Sverdrup Gold Medal of American Meteorological Soc. 1983; Int. Coastal Eng. Award, American Soc. of Civil Engineers 1984. *Publications:* Contributions to scientific journals on physics and math. of the sea, especially ocean waves and currents. *Leisure interests:* music, gardening, mathematical toys. *Address:* Gage Farm, Comberton, Cambridge, CB3 7DH, England (Home). *Telephone:* (619) 456 5451 (U.S.A.); (0122 026) 2346 (Home).

LØNNING, Inge Johan, DR.THEOL.; Norwegian theologian, politician and fmr. university rector; b. 20 Feb. 1938, Bergen; s. of late Per Lønning and Anna (née Strømø) Lønning; m. Kari Andersen 1962; two s. two d.; ed. Univs. of Bergen and Oslo and Pastoral Seminary of Church of Norway; Naval Chaplain 1964–65; Asst. Prof. Univ. of Oslo 1965–70; Research Fellow, Univ. of Tübingen 1967; Prof. of Systematic Theology, Univ. of Oslo 1971–, Dean, Faculty of Theology 1977–81, Rector, Univ. of Oslo 1985–92; ed. journal Kirke og Kultur 1968–; mem. Oslo City Council 1972–76; Chair. Bd. Norwegian Research Council for Science and Humanities 1980–84; Pres. Norsemen's Fed. 1989–, Nat. Rectors' Conf. 1989–92; Leader, European Movt. in Norway 1993–95; mem. Parl. 1997–; Vice-Pres. Hóyre 1997–; Ed. Journal Kirke g. Kültür 1968–; mem. Norwegian Acad. of Science and Letters, Royal Norwegian Soc., Royal Soc. of Letters, Sweden; Commdr. Royal Norwegian Order of St. Olav; Commdr. with Star, Order of Merit of Fed. Repub. of Germany; Hon. D.D. (Luther Coll. Decorah U.S.A., Åbo Acad., Finland). *Publications:* Kanon im Kanon. Zum Dogmatischen Grundlagenproblem des Neutestamentlichen Kanons 1972, Martin Luther: Selected Writings (6 vols), (Ed.) 1978–83, Fellesskap og frihet. Tid for idepolitikk 1997. *Leisure interests:* fishing, skiing. *Address:* Skullerudstubben 22, 1188 Oslo, Norway (Home). *Telephone:* 22-850324 (Office); 22-289512 (Home). *Fax:* 22-850301.

LONSDALE, Anne M., B.A. LIT. HUM.; British university administrator; b. 16 Feb. 1941, Huddersfield, Yorks.; d. of Dr A. C. G. Menzies and Molly Menzies; m. 1st Geoffrey Griffin 1962 (died 1962); m. 2nd Roger Lonsdale 1964 (divorced 1994); one s. one d.; ed. St Anne's Coll. Oxford; lecturer in Classical Chinese, St. Anne's Coll. Oxford 1965–73; Univ. Admin. 1973–86; Dir. External Relations Office, Univ. of Oxford 1986–93; Sec.-Gen. Cen. European Univ. 1993–96; Pres. New Hall, Cambridge Univ. 1996–, Pro-Vice-Chancellor Cambridge Univ. 1998–; Council of Senate, Cambridge Univ. 1997–; Advisory Bd. BBC East 1997–; mem. Commonwealth Scholarship Comm. 1996–; Cavaliere Ordine al Merito della Repubblica Italiana. *Publications:* publs. on Chinese literature and univ. admin. *Leisure interests:* travel, conversation, film. *Address:* New Hall, Cambridge, CB3 0DF, England. *Telephone:* (01223) 762201. *Fax:* (01223) 762217.

LOOMIS, Henry, A.B.; American broadcasting executive and fmr. government official; b. 19 April 1919, Tuxedo Park, N.Y.; s. of Alfred Lee Loomis and Ellen Holman Farnsworth Loomis; m. 1st Mary Paul Macleod 1946 (divorced 1974); two s. two d.; m. 2nd Jacqueline C. Williams 1974; four step-s.; ed. Harvard Univ. and Univ. of California; U.S. Navy 1940–45; Asst. to the Pres., M.I.T. 1947–50; Asst. to Chair. of Research and Devt. Bd., Dept. of Defense, Washington, D.C. 1950–51; Consultant, Psychological Strategy Bd., Washington, D.C. 1951–52; mem. Staff, Pres. Cttee. on Int. Information 1953; Chief, Office of Research and Intelligence, U.S. Information Agency, Washington, D.C. 1954–57; Staff Dir. to Special Asst. to Pres. for Science and Tech., White House 1957–58; Dir. Broadcasting Service (Voice of America), U.S. Information Agency, Washington, D.C. 1958–65; Deputy U.S. Commr. of Educ., Dept. of Health, Educ. and Welfare, Washington, D.C. 1965–66; Partner, St. Vincent's Island Co., New York 1966–69; Deputy Dir. U.S. Information Agency, Washington, D.C. 1969–72; Pres. Corpn. for Public Broadcasting 1972–78; mem. Bd. of Trustees, Mitre Corpn. 1979–91, Bd., Nat. History Museum 1990– (Vice-Chair. 1991–92), Bd., Jacksonville Zoological Soc. 1991–96; Trustee Museum of Science and History Jacksonville 1991–96; Rockefeller Public Service Award in Foreign Affairs 1963; Distinguished Service Award, U.S. Information Agency 1963. *Leisure interests:* sailing, hunting, fishing, skiing. *Address:* 4661 Ortega Island Drive, Jacksonville, FL 32210, U.S.A.

LOONE, Eero; Estonian philosopher; b. 26 May 1935, Tartu; s. of Nikolai Loone and Leida (née Rebane) Loone; m. 1st Halliki Uibo 1965; m. 2nd Leiki Sikk 1971; two d.; ed. Moscow Univ. and Acad. of Sciences, Moscow; mem. CPSU 1965–90; teacher, Univ. Tartu 1963–, Prof. 1985–, Head Dept. of Philosophy 1986–89, 1993–94, Head Dept. of Philosophy and Political Science 1989–93; Visiting Prof. British Acad. 1993, Ashby Lecturer 1994; Founding mem. independent Estonian Union of Scientists 1989–, Estonia Foreign Policy Inst. 1991, Estonian Political Science Asscn. 1993–; mem. Int. Political Science Asscn. 1994–; NATO Democratic Insts. Fellow 1993–94; Life mem. Clare Hall (Cambridge) 1990–. *Publications include:* Contemporary Philosophy of History 1980 (in English trans. as Soviet Marxism and Analytical Philosophies of History 1990). *Leisure interest:* science fiction. *Address:* Department of Philosophy, University of Tartu, Estonia. *Telephone:* (7) 465314. *Fax:* (7) 465345.

LOPARDO, Frank; American opera singer; b. 23 Dec. 1957; m. Carolyn J. Montalbano 1982; two s.; ed. Queen's Coll. New York and Juilliard School of Music; studied with Dr. Robert White Jr.; professional debut as Tamino in The Magic Flute, St. Louis 1984; debut at La Scala, Milan 1987, Glyndebourne Festival 1987, Metropolitan Opera as Almaviva in Il Barbiere di Siviglia 1989–90; now appears regularly at leading opera houses and music festivals around the world; roles include Alfredo in La Traviata, Lenksy in Eugene Onegin, Edgardo in Lucia di Lammermoor, The Duke in Rigoletto, Ferrando in Cosi Fan Tutte, Don Giovanni; also appears as soloist with leading orchestras and in recordings of such works as Mozart's Requiem, Berlioz' Requiem, Rossini's Stabat Mater, Handel's Messiah and Beethoven's Symphony No. 9; Hon. D.Mus. (Aaron Copland School of Music). *Leisure interest:* golf. *Address:* 167 Shaw Avenue, Valley Stream, New York, NY 11580, U.S.A. *Telephone:* (516) 568-0355. *Fax:* (516) 568-0355.

LOPATKIN, Nikolai Alekseyevich, D.MED.; Russian urologist; b. 18 Feb. 1924; ed. Second Moscow Medical Inst.; intern, docent Second Moscow Medical Inst. 1950–62; Prof., Head of Chair of Urology and Operative Nephrology 1963; Main Urologist of U.S.S.R. Ministry of Public Health 1978–83; Dir. Research Inst. of Urology 1983–; Chair. All-Union Soc. of Urologists 1972–91; mem. Russian Acad. of Medical Sciences; Chair. Scientific Council on Urology and Operative Nephrology, Russian Acad. of Sciences 1991; Ed.-in-C. Urology and Nephrology; U.S.S.R. State Prize (three times), Hero of Socialist Labour and other decorations. *Publications:* more than 250 works on urology. *Address:* Research Institute of Urology, 3 Parkovaya ul. 51, 105483 Moscow, Russia. *Telephone:* 164-66-20.

LOPATKINA, Ulyana Vyacheslavovna; Russian ballerina; b. 23 Oct. 1973, Kerch; ed. Vaganova Acad. of Russian Ballet; soloist Mariinsky Theatre 1991; *repertoire includes:* leading roles in Giselle, Sleeping Beauty, Anna Karenina, Fountain of Bakhchisarai, Raimonda, Chekherezada, Swan Lake, Bayadera, (Corsair), performs in Goya-Divertissement; tours with Mariinsky Theatre in Europe, N. and S. America. Several prizes. *Address:* Mariinsky Theatre, Teatralnaya pl. 1, St. Petersburg, Russia (Office). *Telephone:* (812) 315 5724 (Office).

LOPES, António Simões, PH.D.; Portuguese university professor; b. 3 Feb. 1934, Colmeal, Góis; s. of António Lopes de Oliveira and Emília Simões; m. Maria Helena Simões 1960; ed. Instituto Superior de Ciências Económicas e Financeiras, Universidade Técnica de Lisboa, Brasenose Coll., Oxford Univ., U.K.; Asst. Prof. 1962–68; researcher, Gulbenkian Inst. for Science 1964–72; Consultant, Gulbenkian Foundation 1972–74; Prof., Tech. Univ. of Lisbon 1973, Vice-Rector 1982–85, Acting Rector 1985–87, Rector 1987; mem. Bd., Univ. of Evora 1974–77; Prof., Portuguese Catholic Univ. 1979–81; mem. Scientific Bd., Faculty of Econs., Univ. of Coimbra 1979–; Chair. Portuguese Council of Rectors 1985–87, Portuguese Asscn. for Regional Devt. 1985–90, Asscn. of Univs. of Portuguese-Speaking Countries 1986–89; Hon. Prof. Univ. of Maranhão, Brazil; Hon. D.C.L. (Kent) 1992; Chevalier, Ordre Nat. du Mérite, France, Grã-Cruz, Ordem da Instrucção Pública, Portugal. *Publications:* Estrutura da População Activa Portuguesa 1967, As Funções Económicas dos Pequenos Centros 1971, Desenvolvimento Regional (3rd edn.) 1989, and other books; various articles. *Address:* R. Abade Baçal 21, Mercês, 2725 Mem Martins; Alameda St.o António Capuchos 1, 1100 Lisbon, Portugal. *Telephone:* 521061; 521227.

LOPES, Henri; Republic of the Congo author and politician; b. 12 Sept. 1937, Léopoldville, Belgian Congo (now Kinshasa, Democratic Republic of the Congo); s. of Jean-Marie Lopes and Micheline Vulturi; m. Nirva Pasbeau 1961; one s. three d.; ed. France; Minister of Nat. Educ. 1968–71, of Foreign Affairs 1971–73; mem. Political Bureau, Congolese Labour Party 1973; Prime Minister and Minister of Planning 1973–75, of Finance 1977–80; UNESCO Asst. Dir.-Gen. for Programme Support 1982–86, UNESCO Asst. Dir.-Gen. for Culture and Communication 1986–90, for Culture 1990–94, for Foreign Affairs 1994–95, Deputy Dir.-Gen. 1996–98; Repub. of the Congo Amb. to France 1998–; mem. du Haut Conseil de la Francophonie; Chevalier, Légion d'Honneur, Commdr. du Mérite Congolais, etc.; Prix littéraire de l'Afrique noire 1972, Prix SIMBA de littérature 1978, Prix de littérature du Président (Congo), Prix de l'Acad. de Bretagne et des Pays de la Loire 1990, Grand Prix de la Francophonie de l'Académie Française 1993. *Publications:* Tribaliques (short stories), La Nouvelle Romance (novel), Learning to be (with others), Sans tam-tam (novel) 1977, Le Pleurer Rire (novel) 1982, Le Chercheur d'Afriques (novel) 1990, Sur l'autre Rive (novel) 1992, Le Lys et le flamboyant (novel) 1997. *Address:* UNESCO, 7 place de Fontenoy, 75700 Paris, France.

LOPEZ, Jennifer; American actress and dancer; b. 24 July 1970, Bronx, N.Y. *Film appearances include:* My Little Girl, My Family – Mi Familia, Money Train 1995, Jack 1996, Blood and Wine 1996, Anaconda 1997, Selena 1997, U-Turn 1997, Out of Sight 1998. *Television appearances include:*

Second Chances, Hotel Malibu, Nurses on the Line: The Crash of Flight 7. *Address:* United Talent Agency, 9560 Wilshire Boulevard, 5th Floor, Beverly Hills, CA 90212, U.S.A.

LÓPEZ ARELLANO, Gen. Oswaldo; Honduran politician and air force officer; b. 30 June 1921; ed. School of Mil. Aviation and Flight Training, U.S.A.; joined armed forces 1939, Lieut. 1947, Col. 1958; Chief of Armed Forces 1956–75; mem. Mil. Junta, Chief of Mil. Govt. of Honduras, Minister of Nat. Defence, Minister of Public Security 1963–66; Pres. of Honduras 1966–71, 1972–75; now Pres. Servicio Aéreo de Honduras; several decorations. *Address:* Servicio Aéreo de Honduras, Apdo 129, Tegucigalpa, D.C., Honduras.

LÓPEZ-COBOS, Jesús, D.PHIL.; Spanish orchestral conductor; b. 25 Feb. 1940, Toro; s. of Lorenzo López and Gregoria Cobos; ed. Madrid Univ. (philosophy), Madrid Conservatory (composition) and Vienna Acad. (conducting); worked with major orchestras including London Symphony, Royal Philharmonic, Philharmonia, Concertgebouw, Vienna Philharmonic, Vienna Symphony, Berlin Philharmonic, Hamburg NDR, Munich Philharmonic, Cleveland, Chicago Symphony, New York Philharmonic, Philadelphia, Pittsburgh Symphony; conducted new opera productions at La Scala, Milan, Covent Garden, London and Metropolitan Opera, New York; recordings include Bruckner symphonies, Haydn symphonies, Donizetti's Lucia di Lammermoor, Rossini's Otello and recital discs with José Carreras; Gen. Musikdirektor, Deutsche Oper, Berlin 1981–90; Prin. Guest Conductor London Philharmonic Orchestra 1981–86; Prin. Conductor and Artistic Dir., Spanish Nat. Orchestra 1984–89; Music Dir., Cincinnati Symphony Orchestra 1986–, Music Dir. Lausanne Chamber Orchestra 1990–99; First Prize, Besançon Int. Conductors' Competition 1969; Prince of Asturias Award (Spanish Govt.) 1981, Founders Award, American Soc. of Composers, Authors and Publrs. 1988; Cross of Merit (1st Class) (Fed. Repub. of Germany) 1989. *Address:* c/o Terry Harrison Artists, The Orchard, Market Street, Charlbury, Oxon., OX7 3PJ, England. *Telephone:* (01608) 810330. *Fax:* (01608) 811331.

LÓPEZ-GARCÍA, Antonio; Spanish artist; b. 1936, Tomelloso; m. María Moreno; ed. Escuela de Bellas Artes de San Fernando, Madrid; travelled in Italy and Greece 1955, 1958; one-man exhbns. in Madrid 1957, 1961, Staempfli Gallery, New York 1965, 1968–69, Paris, Turin 1972; group exhbns. in Madrid 1955, 1964, World Fair Exhbn., New York 1964, Carnegie Int., Pittsburgh 1965, 1967, European tour of Contemporary Spanish Art exhbn. 1968, 1969; Prize of Diputación de Jaén 1957, Prize of Fundación Rodríguez Acosta 1958, Molino de Oro Prize of Exposición Regional de Valdepeñas 1959. *Address:* c/o Marlborough Fine Art Ltd., 6 Albemarle Street, London, W.1, England.

LÓPEZ-IBOR, Juan José, M.D.; Spanish professor of psychiatry; b. 17 Dec. 1941, Madrid; s. of Juan J. López-Ibor Sr. and Socorro Alino; m. Cristina Alcocer 1967; four c.; ed. Madrid and Frankfurt Univs. and St. Bartholomew's Hosp., London; Asst. Prof. of Psychiatry, Madrid Univ. 1962–72; Head Prof. of Psychiatry, Oviedo Univ. 1972–73, Salamanca Univ. 1973–77, Alcalá de Henares Univ. 1982–; Head, Psychiatric Unit, Ramón y Cajal Hosp. 1977–; Pres. Spanish Psychiatry Soc. 1978–80; Pres. Int. Coll. of Psychosomatic Medicine 1985; Temporary Adviser WHO 1984; hon. mem. World Psychiatric Asscn. *Publications:* Los Equivalentes Depresivos 1972, 1978, El Cuerpo y la Corporalidad 1974, Las Depresiones 1976, Tratado de Psiquiatría 1982, 1984. *Leisure interests:* skiing, water skiing. *Address:* Avenida Nueva Zelanda 44, 28035 Madrid, Spain. *Telephone:* (91) 3739199.

LÓPEZ MICHELSEN, Alfonso; Colombian politician and lawyer; b. 30 June 1913, Bogotá; s. of Alfonso López Pumarejo (Pres. of Colombia 1934–38, 1942–45) and María Michelsen; m. Cecilia Caballero de López; ed. London, Brussels, Colegio Mayor de Nuestra Señora del Rosario, Bogotá, Santiago (Chile) and Georgetown Univ., Washington, D.C., U.S.A.; fmr. teacher at Univ. Nacional de Colombia, Univ. Libre de Bogotá and Colegio Mayor de Nuestra Señora del Rosario; legal practice; spent seven years as emigré in Mexico 1952–58; later an Ed. of El Liberal (weekly); mem. Chamber of Deputies 1960–62, 1962–66; Founder, Leader of moderate wing of Movimiento Revolucionario Liberal 1958–67; joined Partido Liberal 1967, Leader 1982; Gov. of César Dept. 1967–68; Minister of Foreign Affairs 1968–70; Pres. of Colombia 1974–78. *Publications:* Introduction to the Study of the Colombian Constitution 1942, Benjamín Constant or the Father of Bourgeois Liberalism 1946, Colombian Inquiries, The Elected (novel). *Address:* c/o Partido Liberal, Avda. Caracas 36-01, Santa Fe de Bogotá, Colombia.

LÓPEZ-PORTILLO Y PACHECO, José; Mexican politician and lawyer; b. 16 June 1920, Mexico City; s. of José López-Portillo y Weber; m. Carmen Romano; one s. two d.; ed. Law Nat. Faculty, Univ. Nacional Autónoma de México, Univ. de Chile; Prof. of Gen. Theory on the State, Univ. Nacional Autónoma de México 1954, Assoc. Prof. of Political Sciences 1956–58; Founder Prof. in Admin. Sciences Doctorate, Comm. School of the Nat. Polytechnical Inst. 1961; with Partido Revolucionario Institucional (PRI) 1959–64; Technical Assoc., Head Office of Ministry of Patrimony 1960; Coordinator Border Urban Devt. Cttee. 1962; mem. Intersecretarial Comm. for Nat. Devt. 1966; Under-Sec. of the Presidency 1968; Under-Sec. Ministry of Patrimony 1970; Gen. Dir. Electricity Fed. Comm. 1972–73; Sec. for Finances and Public Credit 1973–75; Pres. of Mexico 1976–82; fmr. Gov. for Mexico, IMF; Ordem Nacional do Cruzeiro do Sul (Brazil) 1978. *Publications:* Valoración de la Estatal, Génesis y Teoría del Estado Moderno, Quetzalcoatl, Don Q. *Address:* c/o Palacio de Gobierno, México, D.F., Mexico.

LÓPEZ TRUJILLO, H.E. Cardinal Alfonso; Colombian ecclesiastic; b. 8 Nov. 1935, Villahermosa, Ibagué; ordained priest 1960; Titular Bishop of Boseta with personal title of Archbishop 1971–; Archbishop of Medellín 1979–90; Pres. Pontifical Council for the Family 1990–; Pres. Latin American Conf. of Bishops; Pontifical Comm. for Latin America (CELAM); mem. Sacred Congregation for the Doctrine of the Faith, Congregation for Bishops, for Evangelisation of Peoples, Secr. for Non-believers; cr. Cardinal 1983. *Address:* Arzobispado, Calle 57, N. 48-28, Medellín, Colombia. *Telephone:* 317980.

LORD, Alan, C.B., B.A.; British business executive; b. 12 April 1929, Rochdale, s. of Frederick and Ann (née Whitworth) Lord; m. Joan Ogden 1953; two d.; ed. Rochdale Grammar School and St. John's Coll., Cambridge; Admin. Civil Servant, Inland Revenue 1950–59; H.M. Treasury 1959–62; Principal Private Sec. to First Sec. of State 1962–63; Commr. Inland Revenue 1969, Deputy Chair. Bd. 1971–73; Prin. Finance Officer, Depts. of Industry, Trade and Prices 1973–75; Second Perm. Sec. H.M. Treasury 1975–77; Man. Dir. Dunlop Int. Ltd. 1978–79; Exec. Dir. Dunlop Holdings PLC 1978–79, Man. Dir. and C.E.O. 1980–84, Deputy Chair. and C.E.O. of Lloyds 1986–92; Non-Exec. Dir. Allied-Lyons PLC 1979–86; Dir. Bank of England 1983–86, Dunlop Olympic, Australia; Gov. Nat. Inst. of Econ. and Social Research (NIESR) 1978; Fellow, Plastics and Rubber Inst. *Publications:* A Strategy for Industry (Sir Ellis Hunter Memorial Lecture, Univ. of York 1976), Earning an Industrial Living (Johnian Soc. Lecture 1985). *Leisure interest:* gardening. *Address:* Mardens, Hildenborough, Tonbridge, Kent, TN11 8PA, England. *Telephone:* (01732) 832268.

LORD, Winston, B.A.; American civil servant and diplomatist; b. 14 Aug. 1937, New York; s. of Oswald Bates and Mary (Pillsbury) Lord; m. Bette Bao 1963; one s. one d.; ed. Yale Univ., Fletcher School of Law and Diplomacy; mem. Staff Congressional Relations, Politico-mil. and Econ. Affairs, U.S. Dept. of State, Washington 1961–65, Geneva 1965–67; mem. staff Int. Affairs, U.S. Dept. of Defense, Washington 1967–69; mem. staff Nat. Security Council, Washington 1969–73, Special Asst. to Asst. to Pres. on Security Affairs 1970–73; Dir. Policy Planning Staff, U.S. Dept. of State, Washington 1973–77; Pres. Council on Foreign Relations 1977–85; Amb. to People's Repub. of China 1985–89; freelance lecturer, writer New York 1989–93; Asst. Sec. of State for East Asian and Pacific Affairs 1993–; Chair. Carnegie Endowment Nat. Comm. on America and the New World 1991–92, Nat. Endowment for Democracy 1992–93; Vice-Chair. Int. Rescue Cttee. 1991–93; fmr. mem. Bd. of Dirs. Fletcher School of Law and Diplomacy, Int. Rescue Cttee., Nat. Cttee. on U.S.-China Relations, Nat. Endowment for Democracy, U.S.-Japan Foundation; several hon. degrees. *Leisure interests:* sports, literature, arts. *Address:* Bureau of East Asian and Pacific Affairs, Department of State, Room 6205, Washington, DC 20520, U.S.A. *Telephone:* (202) 647-9596.

LORDKIPANIDZE, Vazha Grigoriyevich, DR. ECON.; Georgian politician and sociologist; b. 28 Nov. 1949, Tbilisi; ed. Tbilisi State Univ.; teacher Tbilisi State Univ. 1975–; Sec., Second, First Secr. Cen. Comsomol Cttee. of Georgia 1980–86; First Sec. Tbilisi Dist. CP Cttee. 1986–88; head Dept. of Culture and Ideology Cen. Cttee. CP of Georgia 1988–90; sr. researcher Inst. of Demography and Sociology Georgian Acad. of Sciences 1991–92; Chief State Counsellor State Council of Georgia 1992; Head of Personnel Ed. Shevarnadze Admin. 1992–95; Amb. to Russia 1995–98; Minister of State 1998–. *Address:* House of Government, Ingorokva Street 7, 380034, Tbilisi, Georgia. *Telephone:* (32) 93-62-40.

LOREN, Sophia; Italian actress; b. 20 Sept. 1934, Rome; d. of Riccardo Scicolone and Romilda Villani; m. Carlo Ponti (q.v.) 1957 (marriage annulled 1962, m. 1966); two s.; ed. Scuole Magistrali Superiori; first screen appearance as an extra in Quo Vadis; has appeared in many Italian and other films including E Arrivato l'Accordatore 1951, Africa sotto i Mari (first leading role), La Tratta delle Bianche, La Favorita 1952, Aida 1953, Il Paese dei Campanelli, Miseria e Nobiltà, Il Segno di Venere 1953, Tempi Nostri 1953, Carosello Napoletano 1953, L'Oro di Napoli 1954, Attila 1954, Peccato che sia una canaglia, La Bella Mugnaia, La Donna del Fiume 1955, Boccaccio 1970, Matrimonio All'Italiana; and in the following American films: The Pride and the Passion 1955, Boy on a Dolphin, Legend of the Lost 1956, Desire Under the Elms 1957, That Kind of Woman 1958, Houseboat 1958, The Key 1958, The Black Orchid 1959, It Started in Naples, Heller in Pink Tights 1960, The Millionairess 1961, Two Women 1961, El Cid 1961, Madame Sans Gêne 1962, Yesterday, Today and Tomorrow 1963, The Fall of the Roman Empire 1964, Lady L 1965, Operation Crossbow 1965, Judith 1965, A Countess from Hong Kong 1965, Arabesque 1966, More than a Miracle 1967, The Priest's Wife 1970, Sunflower 1970, Hot Autumn 1971, Man of La Mancha 1972, Brief Encounter (TV) 1974, The Verdict 1974, The Voyage 1974, The Cassandra Crossing 1977, A Special Day 1977, Firepower 1978, Brass Target 1979, Blood Feud 1981, Mother Courage 1986, Two Women 1989, Prêt à Porter 1995, Grumpier Old Men; Chair. Nat. Alliance for Prevention and Treatment of Child Abuse and Maltreatment; Venice Festival Award for The Black Orchid 1958, Cannes Film Festival Award for best actress (Two Women) 1961, Hon. Acad. Award 1991; Chevalier Légion d'honneur; Goodwill Amb. for Refugees 1992. *Publications:* Eat with Me 1972, Sophia Loren on Women and Beauty 1984. *Address:* Chalet Daniel Burgenstock, Luzern, Switzerland.

LORENTZ, Francis; French business executive; b. 22 May 1942, Mulhouse; s. of Paul Lorentz and Lucienne Lorentz (née Biechy); ed. Lycée Kléber,

Strasbourg, Ecole des Hautes Etudes Commerciales, Ecole Nationale de l'Admin.; with Ministry of Economy 1970–78; Exec. Vice-Pres. Société Lyonnaise des Eaux 1978–80; joined Honeywell-Bull 1982, Chair. and C.E.O. Groupe Bull S.A. 1987–92; Chair. Dir.-Gen. Régie autonome des transports parisiens (RATP) 1992–94; Prof., Univ. of Paris-Dauphine 1994–; Chair. Etablissement public de financement et de restructuration (EPFR) 1996–. *Publications:* several publs. on devt. admin., state-owned cos. and industrial policy. *Leisure interests:* skiing, mountaineering, contemporary art, diving. *Address:* 49 rue St. Roch, 75001 Paris, France.

LORENZ, Hans-Walter, DR.RER.POL.; German economist; b. 3 Aug. 1951, Bielefeld; s. of Walter Lorenz and Lieselotte Lorenz; m. Karin Hottmann 1987; ed. Univ. of Göttingen; Research Asst. Univ. of Göttingen 1977–82, Asst. Prof. 1984–91, Privatdozent 1991–94; Prof., Univ. of Jena 1994–; Visiting Scholar, Univ. of Calif. Berkeley 1982–83. *Publications:* Business Cycle Theory (with G. Gabisch) 1987, Nonlinear Dynamical Economics and Chaotic Motion 1989, Determinismus, nicht-lineare Dynamik und wirtschafliche Evolution 1991. *Address:* Hermann-Föge-Weg 1a, 37073 Göttingen, Germany. *Telephone:* (49) 551-44317. *Fax:* (49) 551-44974.

LORENZO, Francisco A., B.A., M.B.A.; American airline executive; b. 19 May 1940, New York; s. of Olegario and Ana (née Mateos) Lorenzo; m. Sharon Neill Murray 1972; ed. Columbia Univ. and Harvard Univ.; Financial Analyst TransWorld Airlines 1963–65; Man. Financial Analysis Eastern Airlines 1965–66; Founder, Chair. of Bd. Lorenzo, Carney & Co., N.Y. 1966–; Chair. of Bd. Jet Capital Corpn., Houston 1969–; Pres. Texas Int. Airlines Inc. 1972–80, Chair. Exec. Cttee. 1980–; Pres. Texas Air Corpn. 1980–85, Chair., C.E.O. 1986–; Chair. N.Y. Airlines 1980–87, Continental Airlines Corpn., Houston 1982–88, C.E.O. 1989–91, Eastern Air Lines Inc., Miami 1987–; Chair. Bd. of Dirs. Eastern Airlines (in receivership April 1989). *Address:* Eastern Airlines Inc., Miami International Airport, Miami, FL 33148, U.S.A.

LORIMER, George Huntly, PH.D., F.R.S.; British scientist; b. 14 Oct. 1942; s. of the late Gordon Lorimer and Ellen Lorimer; m. Freia Schulz-Baldes 1970; one s. one d.; ed. George Watson's Coll. Edinburgh and Univ. of St. Andrews, Univ. of Illinois, Michigan State Univ.; scientist, Max-Planck Society, Berlin, 1972–74; Research Fellow, Inst. for Advanced Studies, Canberra 1974–77; Prin. Investigator, then Research Leader Cen. Research Dept., E.I. Du Pont de Nemours & Co. 1978–91, Dupont Fellow 1991–97; scientist, Soc. for Environmental Research, Munich 1977; mem. N.A.S. 1997, Editorial Bd. Journal of Biological Chem. 1998; Research Award, Alexander von Humboldt Foundation 1997. *Leisure interests:* philately, music. *Address:* 7705 Lake Glen Drive, Glen Dale, MD 20769, U.S.A.

LORING, John Robbins, B.A.; American artist; b. 23 Nov. 1939, Chicago; s. of Edward D'Arcy and China Robbins (Logeman) Loring; ed. Yale Univ., Ecole des Beaux Arts, Paris; Distinguished Visiting Prof., Univ. of Calif. (Davis) 1977; Bureau Chief Architectural Digest magazine, New York 1977–78; Assoc. Dir. Tiffany and Co., New York 1979–, Exec. Vice-Pres., Design Dir. 1981–84, Sr. Vice-Pres. Design and Merchandising 1984–; mem. acquisitions comm. dept. of prints and illustrated books, Museum of Modern Art, New York 1990–; Contributing Ed. Arts magazine 1973–; one-man exhbns. Baltimore, New York, Long Beach, San Francisco 1972–76; group exhbns. include Phila., New York, Chicago, Ljubljana, Cracow 1971–76; work in perm. collections Museum of Modern Art, New York, Whitney Museum of American Art, Chicago Art Inst., Boston Museum of Fine Arts, R.I. School of Design, Baltimore Museum of Art, Yale Univ. Art Gallery; works commissioned by U.S. Customhouse, New York, Prudential Insurance Co., Woodbridge, N.J., City of Scranton, Pa.; Hon. Dr. Arts (Pratt Inst.) 1996; Edith Wharton award, Design and Art Soc. 1988. *Publications:* The New Tiffany Table Settings 1981, Tiffany Taste 1986, Tiffany's 150 Years 1987, The Tiffany Wedding 1988, Tiffany Parties 1989, The Tiffany Gourmet 1992, A Tiffany Christman 1996, Tiffany's 20th Century 1997. *Leisure interests:* collecting 20th-century decorative arts, writing on design and lifestyle. *Address:* Tiffany & Co., 727 Fifth Avenue, New York, NY 10022 (Office); 860 Fifth Avenue, New York, NY 10021, U.S.A. (Home). *Telephone:* (212) 605-4473 (Office).

LORIOD, Yvonne; French pianist; b. 20 Jan. 1924, Houilles; d. of Gaston and Simone (née Bilhaut) Loriod; m. Olivier Messiaen 1961 (died 1992); Prof. of Piano, Conservatoire National de Musique, Paris; specializes in interpretation of complete works including Bach's Well-Tempered Klavier, Beethoven sonatas, Mozart piano concertos, works of Chopin and Debussy and complete works of Olivier Messiaen; first performances in Paris of Bartok's 1st and 2nd concertos, Schoenberg concerto and works by Messiaen, Jolivet, Boulez and other contemporary composers; 7 Grand Prix du Disque, Grand Prix de la Sacem 1986; Commdr. Légion d'honneur, Officier des Arts et Lettres, Grand Officier du Mérite. *Address:* c/o Bureau de Concerts Maurice Werner, 7 rue Richepance, 75008 Paris, France.

LORSCHEIDER H.E. Cardinal Aloisio; Brazilian ecclesiastic; b. 8 Oct. 1924, Linha Geraldo, Porto Alegre; ordained priest 1948; Bishop of Santo Angelo 1962–73; Archbishop of Fortaleza 1973–95, of Aparecida July 1995–; cr. Cardinal 1976; mem. Sacred Congregation for the Clergy, for Religious Orders and Secular Insts., Secr. for Non-Christians; entitled S. Pietro in Montorio. *Address:* Gúna Metropolitana, CP 05, Tone de Basilica 48 andar, 12570-000 Aparecida, SP, Brazil. *Telephone:* (0125) 362418.

LÖSCHNAK, Franz, DR.JUR.; Austrian politician; b. 4 March 1940, Vienna; m.; one s.; ed. Univ. of Vienna; employed with Vienna City Council 1959–77, Dir. of Personnel Affairs and Admin. Org. 1977; Under-Sec. Fed. Chancellery 1977; Minister, Fed. Chancellery 1985–87; Minister of Health and the Civil Service 1987–89; Minister of the Interior 1989–95.

LOTHE, Jens, DR.PHIL.; Norwegian professor of physics; b. 25 Nov. 1931, Oslo; s. of Jakob Lothe and Borghild Lothe; m. Solveig E. Seeberg 1960; two s. one d.; ed. Univ. of Oslo; lecturer, Univ. of Oslo 1959–63, Assoc. Prof. 1963–72, Prof. of Physics 1972–; mem. Norwegian Acad. of Science and Letters. *Publications:* The Theory of Dislocations (with J. P. Hirth) 1967; numerous papers on elastic waves. *Address:* Sverrestien 7, 1300 Sandvika, Norway. *Telephone:* 67-543670.

LOTON, Brian Thorley, A.C., B.MET.E.; Australian business executive; b. 17 May 1929, Perth; s. of late Sir Thorley Loton; m. Joan Kemelfield 1956; two s. two d.; ed. Hale School, Perth, Trinity Coll., Melbourne Univ.; started as Cadet, Broken Hill Pty. Co. Ltd. 1954, Tech. Asst. to Production Superintendent 1959, Asst. Chief Engineer 1961, Gen. Man. Planning and Devt. 1969, Man. Dir. 1982–91, C.E.O. 1985–91, Deputy Chair. 1991–92, Chair. 1992–97; Gen. Man., Newcastle Steelworks 1970, Exec. Gen. Man. Steel Div. 1973, Dir. 1976, Chief Gen. Man. 1977; Chair. Business Council of Australia 1989–90, Pres. 1990–92; Pres. Australian Mining Industry Council 1983–84; Chair. Int. Iron and Steel Inst. 1991–92; Jt. Vice-Chair. Nat. Australia Bank 1992–99 (Dir. 1988–99); Dir. Amcor 1992–; mem. Faculty of Eng., Melbourne Univ. 1980–83; Int. Counsellor, The Conf. Bd. 1984–96, Int. Counsellor Emer. 1996–; Dept. of Immigration and Ethnic Affairs Advisory Cttee. 1980–82; Australasian Inst. of Mining and Metallurgy, Australian Science and Tech. Council 1977–80; Fellow, Australian Inst. of Co. Dirs., Australian Acad. of Tech. Sciences and Eng., Trinity Coll. (Univ. of Melbourne) 1990; Hon. Fellow, Inst. of Engineers Australia. *Address:* c/o P.O. Box 86A, Melbourne, Victoria, Australia 3001. *Telephone:* (03) 609 3919. *Fax:* (03) 609 3626.

LOTT, (Chester) Trent, B.P.A., J.D.; American politician; b. 9 Oct. 1941, Grenada, Miss.; s. of Chester P. and Iona (née Watson) Lott; m. Patricia E. Thompson 1964; one s. one d.; ed. Univ. of Mississippi; called to Miss. Bar 1967; Assoc. Bryan & Gordon, Pascagoula, Miss. 1967; Admin. Asst. to Congressman Colmer 1968–73; mem. 93rd–100th Congresses from 5th Dist. Miss., Repub. Whip 97th and 98th Congresses; Senator from Miss. 1989–; Senate Majority Leader 1996–; named as observer from House to Geneva Arms Control talks; mem. Senate Republican Policy Cttee.; mem. American Bar Asscn.; recipient Golden Bulldog award, Guardian of Small Business Award; Republican. *Address:* U.S. Senate, 487 Russell Senate Building, Washington, DC 20510, U.S.A.

LOTT, Dame Felicity Ann, D.B.E., B.A., F.R.A.M.; British singer; b. 8 May 1947, Cheltenham; d. of John A. Lott and Whyla Lott (née Williams); m. 1st Robin Golding 1973 (divorced); m. 2nd Gabriel Woolf 1984; one d.; ed. Pate's Grammar School for Girls, Cheltenham, Royal Holloway Coll., Univ. of London and Royal Acad. of Music; début English Nat. Opera 1975, Glyndebourne 1977; has sung prin. roles Covent Garden, Glyndebourne, English Nat. Opera, Metropolitan Opera, New York, Vienna, La Scala, Milan, Paris Opera, Brussels, Hamburg, Munich, Chicago; wide recital repertoire; founder mem. Songmakers' Almanac; many recordings; Hon. Fellow Royal Holloway Coll.; Dr. h.c. (Sussex) 1990, D.Litt. (Loughborough) 1996; Hon. D.Mus. (London) 1997; Hon. D.Mus. Royal Scottish Acad. of Music and Drama 1998; Chevalier des Arts et des Lettres. *Leisure interests:* reading, gardening. *Address:* c/o Askonas Holt Ltd., Lonsdale Chambers, 27 Chancery Lane, London, WC2A 1PF, England. *Telephone:* 0171-405 1808. *Fax:* 0171-242 1831.

LOTZ, Károly, PH.D.; Hungarian politician and economist; b. 30 April 1937, Budapest; m.; two s. one d.; ed. Budapest Univ. of Econs.; lecturing in UNIDO Workshop with special emphasis on the Agro Industrial Sector, Havana, Cuba 1983; lecturing at the congresses and confs. Int. Assoc. of Packing Research Inst. (IAPRI); M.P. 1990–94; mem. Perm. Cttee. of Econ. Affairs and Devt. of Nat. Ass. 1990–94; Deputy Chair. Hungarian Atlantic-Council 1992–; Minister of Transport, Communications and Water Man., 1994–98. *Publications:* Economics of Packing (Textbook) and numerous articles on packing. *Address:* 1077 Budapest, Dob u. 75–81, Hungary (Home). *Telephone:* 351-0409 (Office).

LOUCKS, Vernon R., Jr., M.B.A.; American business executive; b. 24 Oct. 1934, Evanston, Ill.; m. Linda Olson; six c.; ed. Yale Univ. and Harvard Graduate School of Business Admin.; served as First Lieut. U.S. Marine Corps; fmr. sr. man. consultant, George Fry & Assocs.; joined Baxter Int. Inc. 1966, mem. Bd. of Dirs. 1975, Pres. and C.O.O. 1976, C.E.O. 1987–98, Chair. 1987–; Dir. The Dun & Bradstreet Corpn., Emerson Electric Co., Inc., Quaker Oats Co., Anheuser-Busch Cos.; numerous civic and educational appts. etc.; Yale Medal 1997; several awards inc. Chicago Inst. of Medicine Citizen Fellowship Award 1982. *Address:* c/o Baxter Healthcare Corporation, 1450 Waukegan Road, Waukegan, IL 60085, U.S.A.

LOUDON, Aarnout Alexander, LL.M.; Netherlands business executive; b. 10 Dec. 1936, The Hague; m. Talitha Adine Charlotte Boon 1962; two s.; ed. Univ. of Utrecht; joined Bank Mees & Hope 1964, Head, New Issues Dept. 1967; joined Akzo Group 1969, Dir. cen. staff dept. Finance 1971; Finance Dir. Astral (subsidiary of Akzo Coatings), France 1972; Pres. Akzo, Brazil

1975–77; mem. Man. Bd. Akzo N.V. 1977, Deputy Pres. 1978, mem. Exec. Cttee. 1979, Pres. 1982–93; Chair. Akzo Nobel (formed by merger of Akzo NV and Nobel Industriet AB) 1993; Chair. Supervisory Bd. ABN Amro Holding NV 1996–. *Leisure interests:* horseback riding, skiing. *Address:* Kluizenaarsweg 6, 6881 BS Velp, Netherlands (Home). *Telephone:* 085-646606 (Home).

LOUDON, Rodney, D.PHIL., F.R.S.; British theoretical physicist; b. 25 July 1934, Manchester; s. of Albert Loudon and Doris Helen (née Blane) Loudon; m. Mary A. Philips 1960; one s. one d.; ed. Bury Grammar School, Oxford Univ., Univ. of California at Berkeley, U.S.A.; Scientific Civil Servant, RRE, Malvern 1960–65; mem. Tech. Staff, Bell Laboratories, Murray Hill, N.J., U.S.A. 1965–66, 1970, RCA, Zürich, Switzerland 1975, British Telecom Research Labs. 1984, 1989–95; Prof. of Physics, Essex Univ. 1967–; Visiting Prof. Yale 1975, Univ. of Calif. Irvine 1980, Ecole Polytechnique, Lausanne 1985, Univ. of Rome 1987, 1996; Fellow Optical Soc. of America 1994; Thomas Young Medal and Prize (Inst. of Physics) 1987, Max Born Award (Optical Soc. of America) 1992, Humboldt Award 1998. *Publications:* The Quantum Theory of Light 1973, 1983, Scattering of Light by Crystals (with W. Hayes) 1978, Surface Excitations (Ed. with Agranovich) 1984, An Introduction to the Properties of Condensed Matter (with D. Barber) 1989. *Leisure interests:* classical music, choral singing, musical instrument making. *Address:* 3 Gaston Street, East Bergholt, Colchester, Essex, CO7 6SD, England. *Telephone:* (01206) 298 550.

LOUEKOSKI, Matti Kalevi; Finnish politician; b. 14 April 1941, Oulu; m. Pirjo Hiltunen 1969; one s. one d.; Sec.-Gen. Union of Finnish Student Corpns. 1967–69; official at Ministry of Finance and Ministry of Interior 1969–70; Counsellor of Higher Educ. 1970–72; Special Adviser, Office of the Council of State 1975–76; established own law firm 1978; Dir. Finnish Workers' Savings Bank 1979–83; mem. Parl. 1976–79, 1983–; Minister of Educ. 1971–72; Minister without Portfolio Feb.–Sept. 1972; Minister of Justice 1972–75, of Justice and Nordic Co-operation 1987–90, of Finance 1990–91; Vice-Speaker of Parl. 1985–87, 1995–96; mem. Bd. Bank of Finland 1996–; Social Democratic Party. *Address:* Bank of Finland, P.O. Box 160, 00101 Helsinki, Finland. *Telephone:* 1831. *Fax:* 661676.

LOUET, Philippe Marie Alexandre Gabriel, L. EN D.; French diplomatist; b. 7 July 1933, Paris; s. of Michel Louet and Marguerite Louet (née Perrin); m. 1st Hélène Delorme; one s.; m. 2nd Penelope Wilkinson 1974; two s. one step-s.; ed. Coll. Saint-Martin, Pontoise, Lycée Janson-de-Sailly, Inst. d'études politiques de Paris, Ecole nat. d'admin.; with Dept. of Political Affairs, Ministry of Foreign Affairs 1962–66; second, later First Sec. to Perm. Rep. of France to the EEC 1966–71; Tech. Adviser, Ministry of Industrial and Scientific Devt. 1971–74, Ministry of Foreign Affairs 1974, Deputy Dir. for Scientific Affairs and Dir. for Spatial and Atomic Matters 1976–81; Deputy Perm. Rep. to the UN 1981–86; Amb. to Turkey 1986–88; Perm. Rep. to the EEC, Brussels 1988–89; Amb. to Sweden 1989–92; Diplomatic Adviser to the Govt. 1992–; Officier, Légion d'honneur, Officier, Ordre nat. du Mérite, Grand Officier Ordre de l'Etoile Polaire (Sweden). *Leisure interest:* sailing. *Address:* Conseiller diplomatique du gouvernement, 19 ave Kléber, 75116 Paris (Office); 2 avenue de Camoëns, 75116 Paris (Home); 4-6 rue Jean Chavoix, 24160 Excideuil, France (Home). *Telephone:* (1) 43.17.77.66. (Office). *Fax:* (1) 43.17.77.73.

LOUF, Jacques (religious name: André); Belgian Trappist monk; ed. Gregorian Univ., Rome and Inst. Biblique, Rome; Ed. Collectanea Cisterciensia 1959–63; Abbot of Mont-des-Cats 1963–89; Dr. h.c. (Univ. Louvain-la-Neuve). *Publications:* Seigneur, Apprends-Nous à Prier 1972, La Voie Cistercienne 1979, Seul l'Amour Suffirait (3 vols.) 1982–84, Au Gré de Sa Grâce 1989, La Grâce Peut Davantage 1992; translations into French of works of Ruusbroec 1990–93. *Address:* Abbaye du Mont-des-Cats, 59270 Godewaersvelde, France. *Telephone:* 28.42.52.50. *Fax:* 28.49.49.29.

LOUGH, John, M.A., PH.D., F.B.A.; British professor of French; b. 19 Feb. 1913, Newcastle upon Tyne; s. of the late Wilfred Gordon Lough and Mary Turnbull Lough; m. Muriel Alice Barker 1939; one d.; ed. Royal Grammar School, Newcastle upon Tyne, St. John's Coll., Cambridge, Sorbonne, Paris; Asst., later Lecturer in French, Univ. of Aberdeen 1937–46, Univ. of Cambridge 1946–52; Prof. of French, Univ. of Durham 1952–78, Emer. 1978–; Hon. Dr. (Clermont), Hon. D.Litt. (Newcastle upon Tyne). *Publications:* Locke's Travels in France 1953, Paris Theatre Audiences in the 17th and 18th Centuries 1957, Essays on the Encyclopédie 1968, Writer and Public in France 1978, The Philosophes and Post-Revolutionary France 1982, France Observed in the Seventeenth Century by British Travellers 1985, France on the Eve of Revolution: observations by British Travellers 1763–1788 1987, John Graham Lough (1798–1876), a Northumbrian Sculptor (with E. Merson) 1987. *Leisure interest:* gardening. *Address:* Hallgarth Nursing Home, Hallgarth Street, Durham City, DH1 3AY, England. *Telephone:* (0191) 383 2244. *Fax:* (0191) 382-2266.

LOUGHRAN, James; British conductor; b. 30 June 1931, Glasgow; s. of James and Agnes (née Fox) Loughran; m. 1st Nancy Coggon 1961 (divorced 1983, died 1996); two s.; m. 2nd Ludmila Navratil 1985; ed. Glasgow, Bonn, Amsterdam and Milan; Assoc. Conductor, Bournemouth Symphony Orchestra 1962–65; debut Royal Opera House, Covent Garden 1964; Principal Conductor BBC Scottish Symphony Orchestra 1965–71; Prin. Conductor and Musical Adviser, Hallé Orchestra 1971–83, Conductor Laureate 1983–91; debut New York Philharmonic with Westminster Choir 1972; Prin. Conductor Bamberg Symphony Orchestra 1979–83; Chief Guest Conductor BBC Welsh Symphony Orchestra 1987–90; Guest Conductor of prin. orchestras of Europe, America, Australia and Japan, Guest Perm. Conductor, Japan Philharmonic Symphony Orchestra 1993; Chief Conductor Aarhus Symphony Orchestra, Denmark 1996–; recorded complete Beethoven Symphonies with London Symphony Orchestra as contribution to Beethoven Bicentenary Celebrations 1969–70; recordings with Hallé, London Philharmonic, Philharmonia, BBC Symphony and Scottish Chamber Orchestras; Fellow Royal Northern Coll. of Music 1976, Royal Scottish Acad. of Music and Drama 1983; Hon. D.Mus. (Sheffield) 1983; Liveryman, Worshipful Co. of Musicians 1992; First Prize, Philharmonia Orchestra Conducting Competition 1961, Gold Disc EMI 1983. *Leisure interest:* unwinding. *Address:* 34 Cleveden Drive, Glasgow G12 0RX, England.

LOUIS, Jean-Victor, D. EN D.; Belgian lawyer and university professor; b. 10 Jan. 1938, Uccle; m. Maria Rosa Moya Benavent 1963; three s.; ed. Univ. Libre de Bruxelles; Sec. Inst. d'Etudes Européennes, Univ. Libre de Bruxelles 1967–71, Dir. 1971–72, Dir. of Research 1977–80, Pres. 1980–92; lecturer, Univ. Libre de Bruxelles 1970–73, Prof. 1973–; Adviser, Nat. Bank of Belgium 1972–80, Head, Legal Dept. 1980–97, Adviser to Bd. of Dirs. 1990–97; Pres. Belgian Asscn. for European Law 1983–85; legal expert, Institutional Cttee. European Parl. 1992–94; Pres. Initiative Cttee. 96, European Movt. 1995–; mem. Bd. Inst. de l'Euro, Lyons, Groupe d'Etudes Politiques Européennes (TEPSA), Monetary Cttee. of Int. Law Asscn.; Dir. Cahiers de Droit Européen 1977–; Emile Bernheim Prize 1969; P. H. Spaak Prize 1979; Commdr. Order of Belgian Crown. *Publications:* Les règlements de la Communauté économique européenne 1969, Le Droit de la Communauté économique européenne (dir. and co-author), 15 vols. 1970–, The European Community Legal Order 1979, Implementing the Tokyo Round (with J. Jackson and M. Matsushita) 1984, Vers un Système européen de banques centrales (ed.) 1989, From the EMS to the Monetary Union 1990, Banking Supervision in the EC (ed.), l'Union européenne et l'avenir de ses institutions 1996; many articles on EC law, especially in field of monetary cooperation and integration. *Address:* avenue Louise 524, Boîte 9, 1050 Brussels, Belgium (Home).

LOUIS-DREYFUS, Robert Louis Maurice, M.B.A.; French business executive; b. 14 June 1946, Paris; s. of Jean Louis-Dreyfus and Jeanne Depierre; m. 1st Sarah Oberholzer; m. 2nd Margarita Bogdanova; three s.; ed. Lycée Marcel Roby, Saint-Germain-en-Laye and Harvard Business School, U.S.A.; Dir. Louis-Dreyfus, S.A. 1973–81, Sr. Exec. Vice-Pres. and C.O.O. 1982–83; Pres. and C.E.O. I.M.S. Int. 1984–89; Gen. Man. Saatchi & Saatchi 1989–93, C.E.O. 1990–93, Dir. (non-exec.) 1993; Pres. Adidas AG 1993–, Directorate of Adidas AG 1993–; Pres. L'Olympique de Marseille 1996–; Chair. Bd. Dirs Tag Heuer à Mariu 1997–. *Address:* adidas AG, Adi Dassler Strasse 2, 91072 Herzogenaurach, Germany.

LOUISY, Rt. Hon. Allan (Fitzgerald Laurent), P.C., C.B.E.; Saint Lucia politician; fmr. Judge Supreme Court of Grenada; Leader of St. Lucia Labour Party 1974–82; Prime Minister of Saint Lucia, Minister of Finance, Home Affairs, Information and Tourism 1979–81, Minister without Portfolio May 1981–Jan. 1982, Minister of Legal Affairs Jan.–May 1982. *Address:* Laborie, Castries, Saint Lucia.

LOUISY, Calliopa Pearlette, PH.D.; Saint Lucia politician and educator; b. 8 June 1946; d. of Rita Louisy; ed. St. Joseph's Convent Secondary School, Univ. of the West Indies, Université Laval, Univ. of Bristol, U.K.; grad. teacher St. Joseph's Convent 1969–72, 1975–76; tutor Saint Lucia 'A' Level Coll. 1976–1981, Prin. 1981–86; Dean Sir Arthur Lewis Community Coll. 1986–94, Vice-Prin. 1994–95, Prin. 1996–97; Gov.-Gen. of Saint Lucia 1997–; Commonwealth Scholar 1972; Int. Woman of the Year 1998. *Publications:* A Guide to the Writing of Creole 1981, The Changing Role of the Small State in Higher Education 1994, Dilemmas of Insider Research in a Small Country Setting 1997. *Leisure interests:* the performing arts, culture, gardening. *Address:* Government House, Morne Fortune, Castries, Saint Lucia, West Indies. *Telephone:* (758) 452 2481. *Fax:* (758) 453 2731.

LOULY, Lieut.-Col. Mohamed Mahmoud Ould Ahmed; Mauritanian politician and army officer; Minister for Control and Investigation July 1978–Jan 1979, in charge of the Perm. Secr. of the Mil. Cttee. for Nat. Recovery (CMRN) Jan.–March 1979, for the Civil Service and Higher, Technical and Vocational Training March-May 1979; Pres. of Mauritania 1979–80. *Address:* c/o Office du Président, Comité de Redressement National, Nouakchott, Mauritania.

LOUNASMAA, Olli Viktor, M.S., D.PHIL.; Finnish physicist; b. 20 Aug. 1930, Turku; s. of Aarno and Inki (née von Hellens) Lounasmaa; m. Inkeri Kupiainen 1951; two d.; ed. Univs. of Helsinki, Turku and Oxford; Resident Research Assoc., Argonne Nat. Lab., Chicago 1960–65; Prof. of Tech. Physics, Helsinki Univ. of Technology 1965–70; Prof., Acad. of Finland 1970–95; Dir. Low Temperature Lab., Helsinki Univ. of Tech. 1968–95; Visiting Prof. in U.S.A., Japan, India, Germany; Chair. Ministry of Educ. Working Groups on basic research 1980, 1984; Assessor of Math. Sciences for Ministry of Educ. 1995; mem. Comité Int. des Poids et Mesures; fmr. Pres. Comm. on Cryophysics, Int. Inst. of Refrigeration; fmr. Chair. Very Low Temperature Physics Comm., Int. Union of Pure and Applied Physics; fmr. mem. Int Cryogenic Engineering Comm., Exec. Cttee. European Physical Soc.; mem. Finnish Acad. of Tech. Sciences 1965, Finnish Acad. of Sciences and Letters 1969 (Pres. 1992), Royal Swedish Acad. of Sciences 1974, Societas Scientiarum Fennica 1976, Acad. Europaea 1990; Academician (Finland) 1997; Foreign mem. N.A.S. (U.S.A.) 1998; Hon. mem. Finnish Physical Soc. (Chair. 1967); Hon. Fellow Indian Cryogenics Council 1976; Fellow American Physical Soc. 1986; Dr h.c. (Helsinki) 1990, (Tampere Univ. of Tech.) 1992, (Helsinki Univ. of Tech.) 1998; Homén Prize 1969, Emil Aaltonen Foundation Prize 1973, Finnish Cultural Foundation Prize 1978, Fritz London Memorial Award (U.S.A.) 1984, Körber-Stiftung Prize for the Advancement of European Science (Germany) 1987, Finnish Govt. Inventor's Prize 1990, Prof. of the Year Award 1991, Forschungspreise of the Alexander von Humboldt Stiftung (Germany), Wihuri Int. Prize (Finland) 1994, P.L. Kapitza Gold Medal (Russia) 1995, Italgas Prize for Physics (Italy) 1995, Mendelssohn Prize (U.K.) 1996; Commdr., First Class, Order of White Rose of Finland, Commdr. Order of the Lion of Finland. *Publications:* Experimental Principles and Methods Below 1K; 220 scientific papers. *Leisure interests:* gardening, fishing. *Address:* Low Temperature Laboratory, Helsinki University of Technology, 02150 Espoo (Office); Ritokalliontie 21 B, 00330 Helsinki, Finland (Home). *Telephone:* (9) 4512952 (Office); (9) 481541; (9) 2215178 (Home). *Fax:* (9) 4512969 (Office).

LOURDUSAMY, H.E. Cardinal Simon; Indian ecclesiastic; b. 5 Feb. 1924, Kalleri, Pondicherry; ordained 1951; consecrated Bishop (Titular Church of Sozusa, Libya) 1962; Titular Archbishop of Philippi 1964; Archbishop of Bangalore 1968–71; cr. Cardinal 1985; Sec. Congregation for the Evangelization of Peoples 1973–85; Pres. Pontifical Missionary Work. *Address:* Congregation for the Eastern Churches, Palazzo dei Convertendi, Via della Conciliazione 34, 00193 Rome (Office); Palazzo dei Convertendi, Via dei Corridori 64, 00193 Rome, Italy (Home).

LOUTFY, Aly, PH.D.; Egyptian fmr. politician and professor of economics; b. 6 Oct. 1935, Cairo; s. of Mahmoud Loutfy; m. Eglal Mabrouk 1966; one s.; ed. Ain Shams and Louzan Univs.; joined staff, Faculty of Commerce Ain Shams Univ. 1957, Prof. and Chair. Dept. of Econs. 1980; Prof. High Inst. of Co-operative and Admin. Studies; Part-time Prof. Inst. of Arab Research and Studies, Cairo; mem. Bd. of Dirs. Bank of Alexandria 1977–78, Bank of Commerce and Devt. (Cairo) 1981–; mem. Legis., Political Science and Econ. Asscn. 1977, Delta Sugar Co. 1978, Bank of Commerce and Devt. 1980; Minister of Finance 1978–80; Prime Minister of Egypt 1985–86; Speaker of the Shoura Council 1985–89; Ideal Prof. Award, Egyptian Univs. 1974, Gold Mercury Int. Award 1979. *Publications:* Economic Evolution, Economic Development, Economic Planning, Studies on Mathematical Economics and Econometrics, Financing Problems in Developing Countries, Industrialization Problems in Under-Developed Countries; 30 research papers in economics in Arabic, French and English. *Leisure interests:* tennis, reading, travel. *Address:* 29 Ahmed Heshmat Street, Zamalek, Cairo, Egypt (Home). *Telephone:* 3416068.

LOUVIER, Alain; French composer and conductor; b. 13 Sept. 1945, Paris, France; s. of René Louvier and Marthe (née Fournier) Louvier; m. 2nd Anne Le Forestier 1990; one s. one d. from previous marriage; ed. Centre Nat. de Télé-Enseignement, Conservatoire Nat. Supérieur de Musique, Paris; Dir. Conservatoire Nat. de Région, Boulogne-Billancourt 1972–86; Dir. Conservatoire Nat. Supérieur de Musique, Paris 1986–91, Prof. of Musical Analysis 1991–; Rome Prize 1968, Arthur Honegger Award 1975, Paul Gilson Award 1981. *Works include:* Chant des limbes (for orchestra) 1969, 3 Atmosphères (for clarinet and orchestra) 1974, le Clavecin non tempéré 1978, Messe des Apôtres 1978, Casta Diva (with Maurice Béjart) 1980, Poèmes de Ronsard (for voice ensemble and chamber orchestra) 1984, Envol d'écailles (for flute, viola and harp) 1986, Chant des aires (for 25 flutes) 1988, l'Isola dei Numeri 1992, Itinéraires d'outre-rêve 1994, Un gamelan à Paris 1995, Concerto for alto 1996. *Publication:* l'Orchestre 1997. *Leisure interests:* botany and entomology. *Address:* CNSMP, 14 rue de Madrid, 75008 Paris (Office); 53 avenue Victor Hugo, 92100 Boulogne-Billancourt, France (Home).

LOUW, Eugene, B.A., LL.B.; South African politician and lawyer; b. 15 July 1931, Cape Town; s. of Anath Louw and Johanna de Jager; m. Hantie Phyfer 1964; three s. one d.; ed. Bellville High School and Univ. of Stellenbosch; Chair. Students' Council, Univ. of Stellenbosch 1957; attorney, pvt. practice, Durbanville 1964–79, 1993–; Mayor of Durbanville 1967–72; mem. Parl. for Durbanville 1974–79, Malmesbury 1972–74, Paarl 1989–94; Admin. of Cape Prov. 1979–89; Minister of Home Affairs 1989–92, of Defence and Public Works 1992–93; Chair. Nat. Huguenot Tercentenary Festival Cttee. 1988, Capab 1982–88, Nat. Dias Quincentenary Festival Cttee. 1988, Constitutional Investigation Cttee. into Regional Local Govt.; Patron, W. Prov. Rugby Union 1979–89; Abe Bailey Travel Bursary Holder; Alumnus of the Year Award (Stellenbosch Univ.) 1993; recipient of 7 hon. citizenships. *Address:* P.O. Box 15432, Panorama 7506, South Africa. *Telephone:* (021) 930 5620. *Fax:* (021) 964288.

LOUW, Michael James Minnaar, B.A.; South African civil servant; b. 9 Nov. 1939; m.; three c.; ed. Orange Free State Univ.; with Dept. of Labour; with Directorate for Mil. Intelligence, South African Defence Force (SADF) 1964–69; joined Bureau for State Security (became Nat. Intelligence Service) 1969, Special Adviser to Dir.-Gen., Deputy Dir.-Gen. 1988–92, Dir.-Gen. 1992–94, Chief 1994–. *Address:* Private Bag X3, Hatfield 0028, South Africa.

LOUW, Raymond; South African publisher and editor; b. 13 Oct. 1926, Cape Town; s. of George K. E. and Helen K. Louw (née Finlay); m. Jean Ramsay Byres 1950; two s. one d.; ed. Parktown High School, Johannesburg; reporter on Rand Daily Mail 1946–50, Worthing Herald 1951–52, North-Western Evening Mail 1953–54, Westminster Press Provincial Newspapers (London) 1955–56; Night News Ed. Rand Daily Mail 1958–59, News Ed. 1960–65, Ed. 1966–77; News Ed. Sunday Times 1959–60; Chair. S.A. Morning Newspaper Group 1975–77; Gen. Man. S.A. Associated Newspapers 1977–82; Ed. Southern Africa Report; Chair. Media Defence Fund 1989–, Campaign for Open Media 1985–94 (now merged as Freedom of Expression Inst., Deputy Chair. 1994–); New Era Schools Trust; mem. Task Group on Govt. Communications 1996–; mem. Exec. Bd., Int. Press Inst., London, 1979–87, Fellow 1994; mem. Independent Media Comm. 1994; Pringle Medal for services to journalism 1976, 1992. *Publications:* Four Days in Lusaka—Whites from 'Home' in talks with the ANC 1989, Report on the media situation in South Africa (for UNESCO) 1994; narrative for Nelson Mandela Pictorial Biography by Peter Magubane; numerous papers and articles on the media and press freedom. *Leisure interests:* sailing, walking, travel, wildlife. *Address:* Southern Africa Report, P.O. Box 261579, Excom, Johannesburg 2023; 23 Duncombe Road, Forest Town, Johannesburg 2193, South Africa (Home). *Telephone:* (011) 646-8790, 646-6085 (Office). *Fax:* (011) 646-2596.

LOVE, Andrew Henry Garmany, C.B.E., M.D., F.R.C.P., F.R.C.P.I., F.MED.SCI.; British professor of medicine; b. 28 Sept. 1934, Bangor, Northern Ireland; s. of Andrew Love and Martha Love; m. Margaret Jean Lennox 1963; one s.; ed. Queen's Univ. of Belfast; Lecturer in Physiology, Queen's Univ. Belfast 1960–63, in Medicine 1963–65; Physician and Guest Investigator U.S. Naval Medical Research Unit, Taipei, Taiwan 1965–66; Hon. Consultant SEATO Cholera Research Labs., Dacca 1967–73; Prof. of Gastroenterology, Queen's Univ. Belfast 1973–83, of Medicine 1983–, Dean of Faculty of Medicine 1981–86, Head Div. of Medicine 1996–; Dir. Educ., Research and Devt., Royal Hosps. Trust 1998–; mem. Gen. Medical Council (GMC) 1981–87, Exec. Cttee. Asscn. of Medical Deans of Europe 1985 (Pres. 1988–91), Research Cttee. Ulster Cancer Foundation 1983– (Pres. Desig. 1999–); Chair. Northern Ireland Council for Postgrad. Medical and Dental Educ. 1995–, Review Bd. for Overseas Practitioners, GMC 1994–; Censor Royal Coll. of Physicians; Hans Sloane Trustee 1981–; Irish Amateur Golf Champion 1956. *Publications:* various contributions to medical literature. *Leisure interests:* golf, sailing, horse riding, gardening. *Address:* Department of Medicine, Queen's University Institute of Clinical Science, Grosvenor Road, Belfast, BT12 6BJ (Office); The Glen Farm, Carrowdore Road, Greyabbey, Co. Down, BT22 2LU, Northern Ireland (Home). *Telephone:* (01232) 240503, Ext. 2519 (Office); (01247) 788414 (Home). *Fax:* (01232) 329899.

LOVE, Courtney; American rock musician; b. 1967; m. Kurt Cobain (deceased); one d.; mem. rock band Hole (f. in Los Angeles 1989); recordings: Retard Girl 1990, Pretty on the Inside 1991, Beautiful Son (single) 1993, Live Through This 1994; *films:* The People vs. Larry Flynt 1996, Basquiat 1996, Life 1997. *Address:* c/o David Geffen Co., 9130 W. Sunset Boulevard, Los Angeles, CA 90069, U.S.A.

LØVEID, Cecilie Meyer; Norwegian playwright and poet; b. 21 Aug. 1951, Mysen; d. of Erik Løveid and Ingrid Meyer; m. Bjørn H. Ianke 1978; one s. two d.; ed. arts and crafts school in Bergen and studies in graphic design, theatre history and drama; mem. editorial staff, Profil (magazine) 1969; Sec. Norsk Forfattersentrum, Vestlandsardelingen 1974; teacher, Writing Arts Centre, Bergen 1986; mem. Literary Council, Den norske Fordatterforening 1987; Prix Italia 1982; Aschehons Prize; Donblans Prize. *Publications:* Most (novel) 1972, Sug (novel) 1979, Måkespisere (radio play) 1982, Balansedame (play) 1986, Maria Q. (play) 1991, Rhindøtrene (play) 1996. *Leisure interests:* old wooden toys, walking in the mountains, swimming. *Address:* Huitfeldtsgt. 36, 0253 Oslo, Norway. *Telephone:* 22 83 05 63. *Fax:* 22 83 43 73.

LOVEJOY, Derek Alfred Walter, M.A., F.R.I.B.A., F.R.S.A.; British architect and town planner; b. 16 Sept. 1925, London; s. of Jonah Lovejoy and Mabel A. Stoner; m. June Dorris Hotz 1952; one s. two d.; ed. St. Olave's Grammar School, London and Harvard Univ.; architect/planner, London Co. Council 1952–54; Chief Asst. Planner, West Ham Borough Council 1954–56; Architect/Chief Landscape Architect, Crawley Devt. Corpn. 1956–58; founding partner, Derek Lovejoy & Assocs. 1958–68; Sr. Partner, Derek Lovejoy and Partners 1968–88; Sr. Consultant, Derek Lovejoy Partnership 1988–; teaching appts. at Polytechnic of the South Bank 1957–62, Univ. of Aberdeen 1976, Oxford Polytechnic 1977–80; Visiting Prof. of Landscape Architecture, Univ. of Sheffield 1986–; contrib. to radio and TV; mem. numerous cttees. etc.; Fellow Royal TV Soc., Royal Town Planning Inst., Inst. of Highways and Transportation, Faculty of Bldg.; Past Pres. Inst. of Landscape Architecture; Fulbright Fellowship 1949. *Publications include:* Land Use and Landscape Planning. *Leisure interests:* travelling, music. *Address:* c/o Derek Lovejoy Partnership, 8-11 Denbigh Mews, Denbigh Street, London, SW1V 2HQ (Office); Hobtye, Church Lane, Godstone, Surrey, RH9 8BW, England (Home). *Telephone:* 0171-828 6392 (Office); (01883) 743331 (Home).

LOVELL, Sir (Alfred Charles) Bernard, Kt., F.R.S., O.B.E., PH.D., M.SC.; British radio astronomer; b. 31 Aug. 1913, Oldland Common, Glos.; s. of Gilbert and Emily Laura Lovell (née Adams); m. Mary Joyce Chesterman 1937 (died 1993); two s. three d.; ed. Bristol Univ.; Asst. Lecturer in Physics, Univ. of Manchester 1936–39, Lecturer 1945–47, Sr. Lecturer 1947–49, Reader 1949–51, Prof. of Radio Astronomy 1951–81, Emer. Prof. 1981–; with Telecommunications Research Est. 1939–45; Founder and Dir. Nuffield Radio Astronomy Labs., Jodrell Bank 1945–81; Fellow, Royal Soc. 1955; Hon. Foreign mem. American Acad. of Arts and Sciences 1955, Hon. mem.

New York Acad. of Sciences 1960; Pres. Royal Astronomical Soc. 1969–71, British Assen. 1974–75; Vice-Pres. Int. Astronomical Union 1970–76; mem. Aeronautical Research Council 1955–58, Science Research Council 1965–70; Pres. Guild of Church Musicians 1976–89; Master Worshipful Co. of Musicians 1986–87; Hon. mem. Royal Northern Coll. of Music; Hon. Fellow, Royal Swedish Acad. 1962, Inst. of Electrical Engineers 1967, Inst. of Physics 1975; Hon. Freeman City of Manchester 1977, Hon. LL.D. (Edinburgh) 1961, (Calgary) 1966, Hon. D.Sc. (Leicester) 1961, (Leeds) 1966, (Bath, London) 1967, (Bristol) 1970, Hon. D.Univ. (Stirling) 1974, (Surrey) 1975; Royal Medal of Royal Soc. 1960; Daniel and Florence Guggenheim Int. Astronautics Award 1961; Maitland Silver Medal, Inst. of Structural Engineers 1964; Churchill Gold Medal, Soc. of Engineers 1964, Benjamin Franklin Medal, Royal Soc. of Arts 1980, Gold Medal, Royal Astronomical Soc. 1981; Ordre du Mérite pour la Recherche et l'Invention 1962; Polish Order of Merit 1975. *Publications:* Science and Civilisation 1939, World Power Resources and Social Development 1945, Radio Astronomy 1952, Meteor Astronomy 1954, The Exploration of Space by Radio 1957, The Individual and the Universe (The Reith Lectures 1958), The Exploration of Outer Space 1962, Discovering the Universe 1963, Our Present Knowledge of the Universe 1967; Ed. (with Tom Margerison) The Explosion of Science: The Physical Universe 1967, The Story of Jodrell Bank 1968, The Origins and International Economics of Space Exploration 1973, Out of the Zenith: Jodrell Bank 1957–1970 1973, Man's Relation to the Universe 1975, P. M. S. Blackett—a Biographical Memoir 1976, In the Centre of Immensities 1978, Emerging Cosmology 1981, The Jodrell Bank Telescopes 1985, Voice of the Universe 1987, Pathways to the Universe (with Sir Francis Graham-Smith) 1988, Astronomer by Chance 1990, Echoes of War 1991. *Leisure interests:* music, gardening, cricket. *Address:* The Quinta, Swettenham, Nr. Congleton, Cheshire, England (Home). *Telephone:* (01477) 571254. *Fax:* (01477) 571254.

LOVELOCK, James Ephraim, C.B.E., PH.D., F.R.S.; British scientist; b. 26 July 1919; s. of Tom Arthur Lovelock and Nellie Ann Elizabeth (March) Lovelock; m. 1st Helen Mary Hyslop 1942 (died 1989); two s. two d.; m. 2nd Sandra Jean Orchard 1991; ed. Manchester Univ., London Univ.; staff scientist, Nat. Inst. for Medical Research 1941–61; Prof. of Chem. Baylor Univ. Coll. of Medicine, Tex., U.S.A. 1961–64; independent scientist 1964–; Fellow Harvard Univ. 1954–55, Yale Univ. 1958–59; Visiting Prof., Reading Univ. 1967–90; Hon. Visiting Fellow Green Coll. Oxford; Pres. Marine Biology Assen. 1986–90; Amsterdam Environment Prize 1990, Volvo Environment Prize 1996, The Blue Planet Prize 1997. *Publications:* Gaia 1979, The Great Extinction (co-author) 1983, The Ages of Gaia 1988, Gaia: The Practical Science of Planetary Medicine 1991. *Address:* Coombe Mill, St. Giles on the Heath, Launceston, PL15 9RY, England.

LOWE, Douglas Ackley; Australian fmr. politician and administrator; b. 15 May 1942, Hobart; s. of Ackley Reginald and Dulcie Mary Lowe; m. Pamela June Grant 1963; two s. two d.; ed. St. Virgil's Coll.; worked as electrical fitter, Electrolytic Co.; State Sec. Tasmanian Section, Australian Labour Party 1965–69, State Pres. 1974–75; mem. Tasmania House of Ass. for Franklin 1969–81, Independent 1981–86; Minister for Housing 1972–74; Chief Sec. 1974–76; Deputy Premier 1975–77; Minister for Planning and Reorganization 1975–76, for Industrial Relations 1976–79, for Planning and Environment 1976, for Health 1976–77; Premier of Tasmania 1977–81; Minister for Manpower Planning 1977–79, for Econ. Planning and Devt. 1979–80, for Energy 1979, Treas. 1980–81; mem. Tasmanian Legis. Council 1986–92; Deputy Govt. Leader Tasmanian Legis. Council 1989–92; Exec. Officer, Tasmanian Br., Australian Medical Assen. 1992–; del. to Australian Constitutional Convention; Queen's Silver Jubilee Medal 1977; State Pres., Tasmanian Swimming Inc. 1991–. *Publication:* The Price of Power 1984. *Leisure interests:* swimming, tennis, fishing, football. *Address:* Australian Medical Association (Tasmanian Branch), 2 Gore Street, South Hobart, Tasmania 7004 (Office); 1 Michele Court, Berriedale, Tasmania 7010, Australia (Home). *Telephone:* (0362) 23 2047 (Office). *Fax:* (0362) 23 6469.

LOWE, Frank Budge; British business executive; b. 23 Aug. 1941; s. of Stephen Lowe and Marion Lowe; m. Dawn Lowe 1991; two s. one d.; ed. Westminster School; Man. Dir. Collett Dickenson Pearce 1972–79; founder and Chair. Lowe Group 1981; founder and Chair. Octagon 1997; Dir. Interpublic 1990–. *Leisure interests:* tennis, skiing, shooting. *Address:* The Lowe Group, 4 Eaton Gate, London, SW1 9BJ, England.

LOWRY, Bates, PH.B., M.A., PH.D.; American art historian and museum director; b. 21 June 1923, Cincinnati, Ohio; m. Isabel Barrett 1946; two d.; ed. Univ. of Chicago; Asst. Prof. Univ. of Calif. 1954–57; Asst. Prof. New York Univ., Inst. of Fine Arts 1957–59; Prof., Chair. Art Dept. Pomona Coll. 1959–63, Prof. Brown Univ. 1963–68, Chair. Dept. of Art 1965–68; Dir. Museum of Modern Art, New York 1968–69; mem. Inst. for Advanced Study 1971; Prof., Chair. Art Dept., Univ. of Mass., Boston 1971–80; Dir. Nat. Bldg. Museum, Washington, D.C. 1980–87; mem. Bds. of Dirs. Soc. of Architectural Historians 1959–61, 1963–65, College Art Assen. 1962–65; Ed.-in-Chief, Art Bulletin 1965–68; Ed. College Art Assen. Monographs Series 1957–59, 1965–68; mem. Bd. of Consultants, NEH 1975–81; mem. Editorial Bd. Smithsonian Inst. Press 1981–87; Consultant, Getty Museum (Calif.) 1992; Chair. Nat. Exec. Cttee., Cttee. to Rescue Italian Art (CRIA) 1966–76; Pres. The Dunlap Soc. 1974–92; Distinguished Visiting Prof., Univ. of Delaware 1988–89; Hon. mem. Accademia del Disegno (Florence); Trustee, American Fed. of Arts; Guggenheim Fellowship 1972; Govs. award for Fine Arts, Rhode Island 1967; Grand Officer Star of Solidarity of Italy 1968. *Publications:* The Visual Experience 1961, Renaissance Architecture 1962, Muse or Ego 1963, The Architecture of Washington, D.C. 1977–80, Building a National Image 1985, Looking for Leonardo 1993, The Silver Canvas: Daguerreotype Masterpieces from the J. Paul Getty Museum 1998. *Address:* 255 Massachusetts Avenue, Boston, MA 02115, U.S.A.

LOWRY, Sir (John) Patrick, (Pat), Kt., C.B.E, F.R.S.A., B.COM.; British administrator; b. 31 March 1920; s. of John McArdle and Edith Mary Lowry; m. Sheilagh Mary Davies 1952; one s. one d.; ed. Wyggeston Grammar School, Leicester, London School of Econs.; Statistical Clerk, Eng. Employers' Fed. 1938; served Army 1939–46; various posts in Eng. Employers' Fed. 1946–70, Dir. 1965–70; Dir. of Industrial Relations, British Leyland Motor Corpn. 1970, Bd. Dir. 1972; Dir., Personnel, British Leyland Ltd. 1975–77, Personnel and Admin. 1977–78, Personnel and External Affairs 1978–81; Chair. Advisory, Conciliation and Arbitration Service (ACAS) 1981–87; Pres. Inst. of Personnel Man. 1987–89; mem. U.K. Employers' Del., ILO 1962, 1963, 1967, Court of Inquiry, Barbican and Horseferry Road Bldg. Disputes 1967, Grunwick Dispute 1977; Pres. Inst. of Supervisory Man. 1972–74; Chair. Univ. Academics' Salary Cttee. 1987–; Chair. Nat. Joint Council for Eng. Construction Industry 1987–; Hon. LL.D. (Leicester) 1984, Dr. h.c. (Middx.) 1994. *Publication:* Employment Disputes and the Third Party 1990. *Leisure interest:* theatre. *Address:* 31 Seaton Close, Lynden Gate, London, SW15 3TJ, England. *Telephone:* 0181-785 6199.

LOYN, Henry Royston, D.LITT., F.S.A., F.R.HIST.S., F.B.A.; British professor of history; b. 16 June 1922, Cardiff, Wales; s. of the late Henry George Loyn and Violet Monica Loyn; m. Patricia Beatrice Haskew 1950; three s.; ed. Cardiff High School, Univ. Coll., Cardiff; Asst. Lecturer, Dept. of History, Univ. Coll., Cardiff 1946, Lecturer 1949, Sr. Lecturer 1961, Reader 1966, Prof. of Medieval History 1969–77, Dean of Students 1968–70, 1975–76, Fellow 1981; Prof. of History, Westfield Coll., Univ. of London 1977–87, Vice-Prin. 1980–86, Fellow 1989, Prof. Emer., Univ. of London 1987–; Hon. Prof. Univ. of Wales, Cardiff 1996–; Pres. Historical Assen. 1976–79, Glamorgan Historical Assen. 1975–77, Cardiff Naturalists' Soc. 1975–76, Soc. for Medieval Archaeology 1983–86, St. Albans Architectural and Archaeological Soc. 1990–93; Vice-Pres. Soc. for Medieval Archaeology 1971–74, Soc. of Antiquaries 1983–87, Royal Historical Soc. 1983–86; mem. Ancient Monuments Bd. for England 1982–84, Chair. St. Albans Abbey Fabric Advisory Comm. 1991; W.N. Medlicott Medal for service to History, Historical Assen. 1986. *Publications:* Anglo-Saxon England and the Norman Conquest 1962, Norman Conquest 1965, Norman Britain 1966, Alfred the Great 1967, A Wulfstan MS, Cotton, Nero Ai 1971, British Government and Administration (Ed. with H. Hearder) 1974, The Reign of Charlemagne (with J. Percival) 1975, Medieval Britain (with Alan and Richard Sorrell) 1977, The Governance of England (Vol. 1) 1984; introduction, facsimile ed. Domesday Book 1987, The Middle Ages: A Concise Encyclopedia (ed.) 1989, The Making of the English Nation 1991, Societies and Peoples: studies in the history of England and Wales c 600–1200 1992, The Vikings in Britain 1994; contribs. to English Historical Review, Antiquaries Journal and Medieval Archaeology. *Leisure interest:* natural history. *Address:* 4 Clinton Road, Penarth, S. Glamorgan, CF64 3JB, Wales. *Telephone:* (01222) 707584.

LOZOYA-SOLIS, Jesús; Mexican paediatric surgeon; b. 3 March 1910, Parral, Chihuahua; s. of late Leodegario Lozoya and late Josefa Solis; m. 1st Susana Thalmann 1937 (divorced 1958); 2nd Margarita Prieto de Lozoya 1959; four s. one d.; ed. Mil. Medical School of Mexico, Western Reserve Univ. Hosp., Cleveland, Ohio, Harvard Univ. Children's Hosp.; founder of pediatric surgery in Mexico 1940–52; Hosp. Infantil of Mexico 1940–52; Asst. Prof. Pediatrics and Surgical Pediatrics 1940; Pres. Mexican Soc. of Paediatrics 1948–50; Pres. Mexican branch American Acad. of Pediatrics 1944–46; Pres. Laboratorios Infan of Mexico 1949–; Pres. Mexican Soc. Pediatric Surgery 1958–60; founder and first Pres. Pan-American Pediatric Surgery Assen. 1966–68, World Symposium Pediatric Surgery 1965–68, World Fed. Pediatric Surgeons 1974; founder of Dept. of Pediatrics of Armed Forces of Mexico 1940 (Prof. Emer. Mexico Mil. Medical School), Nat. Inst. for the Protection of Children 1958; Senator of the Repub. 1952–55; Gov. of Chihuahua 1955–56; Gen. of Mexican Army 1949 (retd. 1977); Guest Prof. of Pediatric Surgery at numerous Univs.; mem. American Acad. of Paediatrics 1944, American Coll. of Surgeons 1945, American Mil. Surgeons Assen., Mediterranean Acad.; hon. mem. American Pediatric Surgical Assen., Pacific Assen. of Paediatric Surgeons, and many pediatric surgery assens.; Pres. organizing cttee. World Fed. of Pediatric Surgery Assens. 1972–74; Pediatric Surgery Adviser to Int. Paediatric Assen. 1980–83; Chevalier, Hospitalare of Malta 1976, Medical Benefactor 1976. *Publications:* Paedriatría Quirúrgica 1959, México ayer y hoy, visto por un pedíatra mexicano 1965, La escuela médico militar de México 1977, and numerous articles. *Leisure interests:* history, philosophy, anthropology, writing, lecturing, gardening, travelling, riding. *Address:* Calzada Tlalpan 4515, México 22, D.F., Mexico. *Telephones:* 5730094, 5732200/01/02/03.

LU GONGXUN; Chinese party official; b. 1933, Shuoxian Co., Shanxi Prov.; joined CCP 1950; alt. mem. 12th CCP Cen. Cttee. 1982, 13th Cen. Cttee. 1987; Sec. CCP Cttee., Zuoyun Co., Shanxi Prov. 1982–83, Chair. Standing Cttee. of People's Congress, Shanxi Prov. 1993; alt. mem. Cen. Cttee. 1987; mem. CCP Cttee., Shanxi 1983–, Deputy Sec. 1988–. *Address:* Shanxi Provincial Chinese Communist Party, Taiyuan, Shanxi, People's Republic of China.

LÜ JI; Chinese musician; b. 23 April 1909, Hunan; s. of Lü Xing and Yi Zong-Ying; m. Guan Li-Ren 1942; two s. two d.; Chair. Chinese Musicians'

Asscn. 1949–85, Hon. Chair. 1985–; Vice-Dir. Cen. Conservatory 1949–57; mem. Standing Cttee. NPC 1978–; mem. Educ., Science, Culture and Public Health Cttee. NPC 1983–88; Hon. Chair. Chinese Musicians' Asscn. 1985–; Hon. mem. Int. Music Council 1985; mem. Presidium 6th NPC 1986. *Leisure interest:* visual arts appreciation. *Address:* Chinese Musicians' Association, 10 Nong Zhan Quan Nan Li, Beijing 100026, People's Republic of China.

LU JIAXI, PH.D.; Chinese scientist; b. 26 Oct. 1915, Xiamen, Fujian; s. of Lu Dongqi and Guo Wanqing; m. Wu Xunyu; five s. two d.; ed. Xiamen Univ. and London Univ.; Prof. Xiamen Univ. 1946–60, Fuzhou Univ. 1960–81; Vice-Pres. Fuzhou Univ. 1960-81, Hon. Pres. 1981–; Research Prof. Fujian Inst. of Research on Structure of Matter, Chinese Acad. of Sciences 1960–, Dir. 1960–83, Hon. Dir. 1983–; Vice-Chair. 7th Nat. Cttee. of CPPCC 1988–93, 9th Nat. Cttee. 1998–; mem. Chinese Peasants' and Workers' Democratic Party, Vice-Chair. 9th Cen. Cttee. 1983–88, Chair. 10th Cen. Cttee. 1988–92, 11th Cen. Cttee. 1992–97, Hon. Chair. 12th Cen. Cttee. 1997–; Vice-Chair. Standing Cttee. of 8th NPC 1993–98; mem. Chinese Acad. of Sciences 1955–, Pres. 1981–87, Exec. Chair. Presidium, 1984, Special Adviser 1987–; mem. Chinese Chemical Soc. 1944 (Vice-Chair. 1978–82, Exec. Chair. 1982–86); Vice-Chair. China Asscn. for Science and Tech. 1986–; a Pres. Chinese Council for Promoting Peaceful Reunification 1988–; Hon. Pres. Soc. of Gerontology 1986–; Vice-Pres. Asscn. for Cultural Exchange with Foreign Countries 1987–. *Address:* Chinese Academy of Sciences, Beijing 100864, People's Republic of China. *Telephone:* 8012794.

LU LIANGSHU; Chinese agronomist; b. 3 Nov. 1924, Shanghai; s. of Lu Zezhi and Hu Lian; m. Yin Xueli 1950; three s.; deputy to 3rd NPC 1965, 5th NPC 1978; Deputy to 13th CCP 1988; Deputy Dir. Science and Tech. Committee, Ministry of Agric. 1983; Pres. Chinese Acad. of Agricultural Sciences 1982–87; Pres. of Chinese Asscn. of Agricultural Science Soc's. 1982–92; a Vice-Pres. Chinese Acad. of Eng. (CAE) 1994–. *Publications:* Food Composition and Development Strategy in China, Compilation on China's Agricultural Devt. Strategy and the Progress of Science and Tech. *Leisure interests:* swimming, music. *Address:* Nong Zhan Guan nan Li 11, Beijing, People's Republic of China. *Telephone:* 5002124, 898024.

LU MAOZENG; Chinese politician and agronomist; b. Dec. 1928, Zhenjiang City, Jiangsu Prov.; ed. Nanjing Univ.; mem. CCP 1953–; leader, Wheat Group of Research Inst., Deputy Dir. Academic Office, Dir. Crops Research Inst., Sr. Agronomist, Vice-Pres. Shandong Provincial Acad. of Agricultural Science 1952–83; Vice-Chair. Shandong Provincial Asscn. for Science and Tech. 1983; Deputy Sec. CCP Shandong Provincial Cttee. 1983–88, 1995–; Vice-Chair. CPPCC 6th Shandong Provincial Cttee.; Chair. CPPCC 7th Shandong Provincial Cttee. 1993–; mem. CPPCC 8th Nat. Cttee. 1993; alt. mem. 12th CCP Cen. Cttee.; mem. 13th CCP Cen. Cttee. *Publications:* Wheat, Wheat Breeding and Breeding of Improved Varieties, The Record of Varieties of China's Wheat. *Address:* Shandong Provincial Committee of Chinese Communist Party, Shandong, People's Republic of China.

LU PEIJIAN; Chinese adminstrator; b. Aug. 1928, Hongze Co., Jiangsu Prov.; m. Sheng Lixia 1985; three c.; joined CCP 1944; Pres. People's Bank of China 1982–85; Auditor-Gen. of Nat. Audit Office of China 1985–94; Chair. Governing Bd. of ASOSAI 1991–94, Bd. of Supervisors, Nat. Devt. Bank 1994–; mem. 12th, 13th and 14th CCP Cen. Cttee. 1982–96, *Address:* The State Development Bank of China, No. 29 Fuchengmenwai Street, Xicheng District, Beijing 100037, People's Republic of China. *Telephone:* (10) 68306532.

LU PING; Chinese civil servant; b. 7 Oct. 1927, Shanghai; m. Xi Liang 1949; one s. one d.; ed. St. John's Univ., Shanghai; Deputy Dir. of Hong Kong and Macao Affairs Office, State Council 1987–90, Dir. 1990–97; mem. 14th CCP Cen. Cttee. 1992–97; Vice-Chair. Preparatory Working Cttee. for the Hong Kong Special Admin. Region 1993–95, Sec.-Gen. 1995–; Dir. Hong Kong Govt. Admin. Dept. 1994–97. *Address:* State Council, Zhong Nan Hai, Beijing, People's Republic of China.

LU QIHUI; Chinese sculptor; b. 8 April 1936, Shanghai; d. of Ren Jin; m. Fang Zen-Xian 1960; one s. one d.; ed. Sculpture Dept., Cen. Art Acad., E. China Branch 1955–61; teacher, Shanghai Art College 1961–65; professional sculptor, Shanghai Oil Painting and Sculpture Inst. 1965–, Prof. 1988–; mem. Chinese Artists' Asscn. *Works include:* Transplanting rice seedlings, workers group statues, Nat. Industrial Exhibition 1960, Statue of Child Labourers 1974, Sculpture for Chairman Mao Memorial Hall 1977, Statue of Lu Xun 1979, Angrily seeking Verses against Reign of Terror 1980, Plateau in the Morning Sun 1986, Bada, an ancient Chinese Artist 1987 (exhibited New York in Contemporary Oil Painting from the P.R.C.), Sampan (bronze), for Shanghai Stadium 1987, the Emotion at Plateau 1989, Zhang Zhong-Jingi a Pioneer of Chinese Medical Science 1990 (bronze), Song Jie-Cai Rang of a Tibetan 1990 (stone), Hawk-dancing 1991 (statue), Wang Ge-Ji memorial (bronze) 1992, Magic painter Mar-Lang (bronze) 1993, Wu Chan-Shu memorial (bronze), one for Shanghai Memorial Hall 1994, one for Japanese Fakuoka 1995, Xia-Qiu-Son (bronze) 1995, Balzac Memorial (bronze), Garden of Famous People, Shanghai 1996, Wu Fu-Zhi memorial (bronze) 1998. *Leisure interests:* Chinese painting, sport. *Address:* 100-301, 398 Xin-Pei Road, Xin-Zuan, Shanghai, People's Republic of China. *Telephone:* (021) 64987283.

LU QIKENG; Chinese mathematician; b. 17 May 1927, Fushan City, Guangdong Prov.; m. Mulan Zhang 1962; one s. one d.; ed. Zhongshan Univ.; research fellow, Math. Inst. Academia Sinica 1978–; Deputy Dir. of Math. Inst. 1981–83; Research Prof. Shantou Univ. 1994–; mem. Dept. Math. and Physics, Academia Sinica 1980–92, Chinese Math. Soc. 1952–, Chinese Acad. of Sciences 1980–, American Math Soc. 1992–, A.A.A.S. (U.S.A.) 1996–, New York Acad. of Sciences 1997–; Hua Loo Keng Prize 1992. *Publication:* The Classical Manifolds and Classical Domains 1994, New Results of Classical Manifolds and Classical Domains 1997. *Leisure interest:* classical music. *Address:* Institute of Mathematics, Shantou University, Beijing 515063, People's Republic of China. *Telephone:* (10) 6254-1841 (Office); (10) 6255-5142 (Home). *Fax:* (10) 6256-8356.

LU RONGJING; Chinese adminstrator; b. 1933, Lujiang Co., Anhui Prov.; joined CCP 1954; Gov. Anhui Prov. 1987–93; Sec. CCP Anhui Prov. Cttee. 1988–; mem. 14th CCP Cen. Cttee. 1992–97, 15th CCP Cen. Cttee. 1997–. *Address:* Anhui Provincial Government, 1 Changjang Road, Hefei City, Anhui Province, People's Republic of China.

LU RUIHUA, M.A.; Chinese politician; b. Nov. 1938, Chaozhou City, Guangdong Prov.; ed. Zhongshan Univ.; joined CCP 1972; fmrly. engineer, Deputy Dir., Dir. Foshan Analytical Instrument Factory; fmrly. Mayor of Foshan, Vice-Chair. Foshan City Econ. Cttee., mem. Standing Cttee. CCP Guangdong Prov. Cttee., mem. then Deputy Sec. Standing Cttee. CCP Foshan City Cttee., Deputy 7th NPC 1988, 8th NPC 1996; Vice-Gov. Guangdong Prov. 1991–96, Gov. 1996–; alt. mem. 14th CCP Cen. Cttee. 1992–97, mem. 15th CCP Cen. Cttee. 1997–. *Address:* People's Government of Guangdong, Guangzhou, Guangdong Province, People's Republic of China.

LU SHENGRONG; Chinese sports official; b. 1940, Beijing; ed. Beijing Foreign Languages Inst.; Vice-Pres. Int. Badminton Fed. 1984–93, Pres. 1993–; mem. IOC 1996–. *Address:* c/o State General Bureau for Physical Culture and Sports, 9 Tiyuguan Road, Chongwen District, Beijing, People's Republic of China.

LU SHENGZHONG M.A.; Chinese artist; b. 4 Jan. 1952, Pingdu Co., Shandong Prov.; s. of Lu Wanjin and Jiang Yongzhen; m. Liu Guangjun 1980; one s.; ed. Cen. Acad. of Fine Arts; specializes in Chinese folk arts; instructor at Cen. Acad. of Fine Arts; Deputy Sec.-Gen. Chinese Asscn. of Fine Artists; Rep. works: When Heaven and Earth are in Harmony, All Living Things, Thrive, Life, Solitary Walking, Magic and Acrobatics. *Exhibitions include:* China Avant Garde, Asia and Pacific Museum, U.S.A., Paper Cut Art: Exhibition of Calling the Souls. *Publications include:* Chinese Folk Papercut, Chinese Folk New Year Paintings, Arts from My Mother, Solitary Walk on the Holy Road, Outline of Chinese Folk Woodcut Print, Words of Calling the Souls. *Address:* Central Academy of Fine Arts, 5 Xiaowei Hutong, Beijing, People's Republic of China. *Telephone:* 554731-303.

LU SHIH-PENG, B.A.; Taiwanese professor of history; b. 16 Sept. 1928, Kao-yu, Chiang Su; s. of late Lu Chun-tai and Lu Chia Chu-yin; m. Julia Wei-chun; one s. one d.; ed. Nat. Taiwan Univ., Taipei, Harvard Univ., U.S.A.; Teaching Asst., Nat. Taiwan Univ., Taipei 1953–55; Research Asst., Academica Sinica, Taipei 1955–58; lecturer, Tunghai Univ., Taichung 1958–63, Assoc. Prof. 1963–67, Prof. of History 1967–, Dir. Evening School 1972–81, Chair. Dept. of History 1981–87, Dean Coll. of Arts 1988–94; Visiting Scholar, Harvard Univ. 1961–63; Outstanding Youth, China Youth Corps 1952; Outstanding Prof., Ministry of Educ. 1992. *Publications:* Vietnam during the period of Chinese Rule 1964, The Modern History of China 1979, The Contemporary History of China 1992. *Address:* 19-8A Tunghai Road, Taichung, Taiwan. *Telephone:* (04) 3590209 (Office); (04) 3596556 (Home). *Fax:* (04) 3596556.

LU WENFU; Chinese writer; b. 1928, Taixing Co., Jiangsu Prov.; ed. Huazhong Univ.; Vice-Chair. of Chinese Writers' Asscn. 1985–; joined Int. PEN in New York 1986. *Publications:* Hidden Deep in the Lane, Dedication (Nat. Prize 1978), The Pedlar's Family (Nat. Prize 1980), Fence (Nat. Prize 1983), The Gourmet (Nat. Prize 1984). *Address:* Suzhou Branch of the Federation of Literary and Art Circles, Suzhou City, Jiangsu Province, People's Republic of China.

LU XUEJIAN; Chinese business executive; b. 15 Nov. 1928, Rongcheng Co., Shandong Prov.; m. Liu Yi-ting 1953; one s. two d.; Vice-Chair. China Int. Trust and Investment Corp. 1990–; mem. 8th Nat. Cttee. CPPCC 1993–. *Leisure interests:* reading, swimming. *Address:* China International Trust and Investment Corporation, Capital Mansion, 6 Xinyuan Nanlu Street, Chaoyang District, Beijing 100004, People's Republic of China. *Telephone:* 64660088. *Fax:* 64661186.

LU XUEYI; Chinese economist; b. 1933, Wuxi, Jiangsu Prov.; ed. Beijing Univ. Inst. of Philosophy, Chinese Acad. of Social Sciences; Vice-Dir. Rural Devt. Research Inst., Vice-Dir. then Dir. Inst. of Sociology, Chinese Acad. of Social Sciences 1985–. *Publications:* A Golden Time for Agricultural Development, Contemporary Chinese Countryside, Contemporary Chinese Peasants. *Address:* Institute of Sociology, Chinese Academy of Social Sciences, Beijing, People's Republic of China.

LU YANSHAO; Chinese artist; b. 26 June 1909, Jiading Cty., Shanghai, Subei Yancheng; s. of Lu Yunbo and Zhu Xuan; m. Zhu Yanyin 1929; three s. two d.; Prof. Zhejiang Acad. of Fine Arts 1982–; Deputy 6th NPC 1983–; Bd. Dir. All-China Artists' Asscn.; Pres. Zhejiang Landscape Soc.; mem. NPC. *Publications:* Some Opinions on Landscape Painting 1980, Manual of Lu Yanshao's Studio Drawings 1985, Lu Yanshao's Autobiography 1985.

LU YONG XIANG; Chinese university professor and government official; b. 28 April 1942, Ningbo City, Zhejiang Prov.; s. of Lu Zhau and Lee Feng; m. Diao Linlin 1966; one s. one d.; ed. Zhejiang Univ., Tech. Univ. of Aachen, Germany; Asst. Lecturer, Dept. of Mechanical Eng., Zhejiang Univ. 1964–79, Assoc. Prof. 1981–83, Full Prof., Dir. Inst. of Fluid Power Transmission and Control 1983–, Vice-Pres. Univ. 1985–88, Pres. 1988–; Pres. Zhejiang Univ. 1989–95; Vice-Pres. Chinese Acad. of Sciences 1993–97, Pres. 1997–, Academician 1991; Vice-Chair. China Asscn. for Science and Tech. 1986–96; mem. Chinese Acad. of Eng. 1993, Academic Degrees Comm. of State Council 1986–, TWAS 1990; Vice-Pres. the Third World Acad. of Sciences 1999–; Del. NPC 1983–91; alt. mem. 14th CCP Cen. Cttee., mem. 15th CCP Cen. Cttee. 1997–; Second Prize for Nat. Invention 1988, Third Prize 1989, Higher Eng. Educ. Prize of Nation 1989, Gao Hua Super Prize 1993, Rudolf Diesel Gold Medal (Germany) 1997, and many other awards and prizes. *Publications:* Electrohydraulic Proportional Technique 1988; more than 160 published papers; more than 20 patents. *Leisure interests:* model aeroplanes, playing football. *Address:* China Academy of Sciences, 52 San Li He Road, Beijing 100864, People's Republic of China. *Telephone:* (10) 68597289. *Fax:* (10) 68512458.

LU YOUMEI; Chinese engineer; b. 1934, Taicang Co., Jiangsu Prov.; ed. Dept. of River Structure and Hydropower Station Construction of E. China Inst. of Water Conservancy; mem. CCP 1956–; engineer Bureau for Construction of Liujia Gorge Hydropower Station of Yellow River until 1970; posts in various bureaux of Ministry of Water Conservancy and Electric Power 1978–84; Vice-Minister of Water Conservancy and Electric Power 1984–88; Vice-Minister, Ministry of Energy Resources 1988–93; Pres. China Yangtze Three Gorges Project Construction; Vice Chair. Three Gorges Project Construction Cttee. 1993–.

LUBACHIVSKY, H.E. Myroslav Ivan; Ukrainian ecclesiastic; b. 24 June 1914, Dolyna; ordained 1938; consecrated Archbishop Metropolitan of Philadelphia of the Ukrainians 1979; Coadjutor to Archbishop Major of Lviv of the Ukrainians 1980, Major Archbishop 1984; cr. Cardinal by Pope John Paul II 1985. *Address:* Piazza Madonna dei Monti 3, 00184 Rome, Italy. *Telephone:* (06) 47.44.068.

LUBBERS, Ruud (Rudolphus) Frans Marie; Netherlands politician; b. 7 May 1939, Rotterdam; s. of Paulus J. Lubbers and Wilhelmine K. Van Laack; m. Maria E. J. Hoogeweegen 1962; two s. one d.; ed. Erasmus Univ., Rotterdam; Sec. to Man. Bd., Lubbers Hollandia Eng. Works 1963–65, Co-Dir. 1965; mem. Bd. Netherlands Christian Employers' Fed., Fed. of Mechanical and Electrical Eng. Industries; mem. Programmes Advisory Council of Catholic Broadcasting Asscn.; Minister of Econ. Affairs 1973–77; mem. Second Chamber of States-Gen. (Parl.) May 1977–; Prime Minister of the Netherlands 1982–94; Hon. Minister of State; mem. Christian Democratic Appeal 1977, Parl. Leader 1978. *Address:* c/o Office of the Prime Minister, Binnenhof 20, P.O. Box 20001, 2500 EA The Hague, Netherlands.

LUBICH, Chiara; Italian religious movement leader; b. 22 Jan. 1920; d. of Luigi and Luigia Lubich; ed. Teachers' Training Inst. and Faculty of Philosophy, Univ. of Venice; Founder and Pres. Focolare Movt., a worldwide spiritual movt. based on the Gospel currently active in 184 countries 1943–; participated in extraordinary Synod of Bishops 1985, Synod on the Vocation and Mission of the Laity 1987; consultant, Pontifical Council for the Laity; Hon. Pres. World Conf. on Religion and Peace; Templeton Prize for Progress in Religion and Peace 1977, Cross of Order of St. Augustine of Canterbury 1981, Byzantine Cross, Phanar, Istanbul 1984, Plaque of St. Catherine of Siena 1987, Ecumenical Augustan Peace Prize, Augsburg, Germany 1988; First Int. Prize Franciscan Int. Centre of Studies for Dialogue among Peoples 1993; Ardent Eagle of St. Wenceslaus, Seal of City of Trent 1995; UNESCO Prize for Peace Educ. 1996; Cross of the South (Brazil) 1997, Human Rights Prize, Council of Europe 1998; numerous hon. doctorates and other decorations. *Publications include:* 4 vols. of Spiritual Writings, Diary 1964/65 1967, It's A Whole New Scene 1969, Conversations with the Gen 1974, To the Gen 3, I 1974, II 1976, Why Have You Forsaken Me, the Key to Unity 1984, Encounters with the Orient 1986, On the Holy Journey 1987, From Scripture to Life 1991, Into the Light 1996, Journey to Heaven 1997, And Christmas Comes Back 1997, Where Life Lights Up 1998, Love Wins 1998. *Address:* 306 via di Frascati, 00040 Rocca di Papa, RM, Italy. *Telephone:* (06) 947989.

LUBIN, Steven, B.A., M.S., PH.D.; American pianist; b. 22 Feb. 1942, New York; m. Wendy Lubin 1974; two s.; ed. Harvard Univ., Juilliard School, New York Univ.; piano studies with Lisa Grad, Nadia Reisenberg, Seymour Lipkin, Rosina Lhevinne, Beveridge Webster; recital and concert tours N. America and Europe; f. The Mozartean Players 1978–; mem. Faculty Juilliard School 1964–65, Aspen Music School 1967, Cornell Univ. 1971–75, Vassar Coll. 1971–75; Adjunct. Prof., School of the Arts, State Univ. of N.Y.-Purchase 1975–. *Recordings:* complete Beethoven Piano Concertos, Mozart and Schubert Trios, Six Mozart Concertos as soloist and conductor, and other solo and chamber music. *Publications:* articles in The New York Times, Keynote, Ovation, Keyboard Classics and Historical Performance. *Leisure interests:* reading about relativity and quantum mechanics. *Address:* Music Division, School of the Arts, SUNY, Purchase, NY 10577, U.S.A.

LUBIS, Mochtar; Indonesian journalist; b. 7 March 1922, Padang, Sumatra; s. of Raja Pandapotan and Siti Madinah; m. Siti Halimah 1945; two s. one d.; joined Indonesian Antara News Agency 1945; publisher daily Indonesian Raya 1949–61, Ed. 1956–51, 1966; published and edited The Times of Indonesia 1952; now Dir.-Gen. Press Foundation of Asia, Manila, Philippines; Chair. The Jakarta Acad.; Chair. Yayasan Obor Indonesia (books); Ass. Ed. Worldpaper, Boston, U.S.A.; Chair. Editorial Bd., Solidarity Magazine, Manila; Nat. Literary Award 1953; Pres. Magsaysay Award for the Press 1958 returned award 1995; Golden Pen of Freedom, Int. Fed. of Publishers 1967, Press Foundation of Asia; mem. Bd. Int. Press Inst.; mem. UNESCO Comm. for Communication Problems; Dir.-Gen. Press Foundation of Asia; Chair. Obor Indonesia Foundation. *Publications:* Pers and Wartawan, Tak Ada Esok, Si Djamal (short stories), Djalan Tak Ada Udjung, Korean Notebook, Perkenalan Di Asia Tenggara, Melawat Ke Amerika, Stories from Europe, Indonesia Dimata Dunia, Stories from China, A Road with No End (novel) 1952, Twilight in Djakarta 1963, Tiger! Tiger!, Subversive Notes, Love and Death 1976, Indonesia, Land under the Rainbow (history), Land under the Sun (a report on Indonesia Today) 1983, Bromocorah (short stories) 1987, Termites. *Leisure interests:* gardening, sailing, nature study. *Address:* Jalan Bonang No. 17, Jakarta 10320, Indonesia. *Telephone:* 331128.

LUBOVITCH, Lar; American choreographer; b. 9 April 1943, Chicago, Ill.; ed. Univ. of Iowa, Juilliard School; danced in numerous modern, ballet and jazz cos.; Founder and Artistic Dir. Lar Lubovitch Dance Co. 1968–; has choreographed more than 50 dances for the co.; his works are included in repertoires of several major int. dance cos. including New York City Ballet, American Ballet Theater, Paris Opera Ballet, Royal Danish Ballet, Stuttgart Ballet, White Oak Dance Project and Netherlands Dance Theatre; has created dances for ice-skaters including John Curry; *dances created include:* Whirligogs (music by Luciano Berio) 1969, The Time Before the Time After (After the Time Before) (Stravinsky) 1971, Les Noces (Stravinsky) 1976, Marimba (Steve Reich) 1976, Exultate, Jubilate (Mozart) 1977, Scriabin Dances (Scriabin) 1977, North Star (Philip Glass) 1978, Cavalcade (Reich) 1980, Beau Danube (Strauss) 1981, Big Shoulders (no music) 1983, A Brahms Symphony 1985, Concerto Six Twenty-Two (Mozart) 1986, Sleeping Beauty (Tchaikovsky; full-length televised ice-dancing version starring Robin Cousins and Rosalynn Sumners) 1987, Into the Woods (Sondheim) 1987, Musette (Poulenc) 1988, Rhapsody in Blue (Gershwin) 1988, Fandango (Ravel) 1989, Waiting for the Sunrise (Les Paul and Mary Ford) 1991, American Gesture (Charles Ives) 1992, The Red Shoes (Jule Styne; Astaire Award, Theater Devt. Fund) 1993, The Planets (Holst) 1994, Oklahoma! (Rodgers and Hammerstein) 1994, The King and I (Rodgers and Hammerstein) 1996, Adagio (Bach) 1996, Othello (Goldenthal) 1997. *Address:* Lar Lubovitch Dance Company, 625 Broadway, Suite 11-H, New York, NY 10012, U.S.A. *Telephone:* (212) 673-4477. *Fax:* (212) 533-1663.

LUBRANI, Uri; Israeli diplomatist; b. 7 Oct. 1926, Haifa; s. of Ahron and Rose Lubrani; m. Sarah Levi 1953; four d.; ed. Univ. of London; fmr. Head of Chancery, Office of Foreign Minister, Office of Prime Minister, Adviser to Prime Minister on Arab Affairs; later Amb. to Uganda, Rwanda, Burundi, Ethiopia and Iran; now Govt. Co-ordinator for Lebanese Affairs; in charge of airlift of 18,000 Ethiopian Jews (Falashas) to Israel 1991; head Israeli team, negotiations on release of Israeli hostages in Lebanon and Shia Muslim prisoners in Israel; head Israeli del. to bilateral peace talks with Lebanon, Washington, D.C. 1992. *Address:* Office of the Government Co-ordinator for Lebanese Affairs, Ministry of Defence, Hakirya, Tel-Aviv, Israel. *Telephone:* 03-697 5157/88. *Fax:* 02-697 7358.

LUCAS, Colin Renshaw, D.PHIL., F.R.HIST.S.; British academic; b. 25 Aug. 1940; s. of Frank Renshaw Lucas and Janine Charpentier; m. 1st Christiane Berchon de Fontaine Goubert 1964 (divorced 1975); one s.; m. 2nd Mary Louise Hume 1990; ed. Sherborne School, Lincoln Coll. Oxford; Asst. Lecturer, then Lecturer Sheffield Univ. 1965–69; Visiting Asst. Prof. Indiana Univ., U.S.A. 1969–70; Lecturer Manchester Univ. 1970–73; Fellow Balliol Coll. Oxford, Lecturer in Modern History, Oxford Univ. 1973–90; Prof. Chicago Univ., U.S.A. 1990–94, Dean Div. of Social Sciences 1993–94; Master Balliol Coll. 1994–; Pro-Vice-Chancellor Oxford Univ. 1995–97, Vice-Chancellor 1997–(2001); Hon. D.Litt (Lyon) 1989; Officier Ordre des Arts et des Lettres, Chevalier Ordre du Mérite (France). *Publications:* The Structure of the Terror 1973, Beyond the Terror (with G. Lewis) 1983, The Political Culture of the French Revolution (Ed.) 1988; contribs. to academic journals. *Address:* University Offices, Wellington Square, Oxford, OX1 2JD, England. *Telephone:* (01865) 270243.

LUCAS, Cornel, F.R.P.S., F.B.I.P.P.; British photographer; b. 12 Sept. 1923, London; s. of the late John Thomas Lucas and Mary Elizabeth Lucas; m. Jennifer Susan Linden Travers 1960; three s. one d.; ed. Northern Poly., Regent Street Poly.; R.A.F. Photographic School 1941–46; mem. staff Two Cities Films, Denham, Pinewood Studios, Columbia Pictures, Universal Int. Films 1947–59; opened own studios No. 2, Chelsea Manor Studios, London 1959, Man. Dir. 1959–; work in perm. collections of Nat. Portrait Gallery, Nat. Museum of Photography, Museum of Photography, Bradford, Royal Photographic Soc., Bath, Jersey Museum of Photography; mem. B.A.F.T.A. *Publication:* Heads and Tales 1988. *Leisure interests:* painting, music, gardening, tennis. *Address:* 57 Addison Road, London, W14 8JJ, England.

LUCAS, Craig, B.F.A.; American playwright and screenwriter; b. 30 April 1951, Atlanta, Ga.; s. of Charles Samuel Lucas and Eleanore Alltmont Lucas; ed. Boston Univ.; Rockefeller and Guggenheim Fellowships. *Plays:* Missing Persons 1980, Reckless 1983, Blue Window 1984, Prelude to a Kiss 1987, The Scare 1989, God's Heart 1994, The Dying Gaul 1996, Savage

Light (with David Schulner) 1996. *Musicals:* Marry Me a Little (anthology of songs by Stephen Sondheim) 1981, Three Postcards (music and lyrics by Craig Carnelia) 1987. *Films:* Blue Window 1987, Longtime Companion 1990, Prelude to a Kiss 1991, Reckless 1995. *Publications:* Anti-Naturalism 1989, Reckless and Blue Window 1989, Prelude to a Kiss 1991. several plays. *Address:* c/o Peter Franklin, William Morris Agency, 151 South El Camino Drive, Beverly Hills, CA 90212, U.S.A.

LUCAS, Sir Cyril (Edward), Kt., C.M.G., D.SC., F.R.S.E., F.R.S.; British marine scientist; b. 30 July 1909, Hull, Yorks.; s. of the late Archibald Lucas and Edith Lucas; m. Sarah A. Rose 1934 (died 1974); two s. one d.; ed. Hull Grammar School and Univ. Coll. Hull; Research Biologist, Univ. Coll. Hull 1931, Head, Dept. of Oceanography 1942; Dir. of Fisheries Research, Scotland (Dept. of Agric. and Fisheries for Scotland) and Dir. Marine Lab. Aberdeen 1948–70; U.K. expert or del. to various int. confs. on marine fisheries and conservation 1948–; Hon. D.Sc. (Hull) 1975, Hon. LL.D. (Aberdeen) 1977. *Publications:* papers in scientific journals. *Address:* 16 Albert Terrace, Aberdeen, AB18 1XY, Scotland. *Telephone:* (01224) 645568.

LUCAS, George, B.A.; American film director; b. 14 May 1944, Modesto, Calif.; ed. Univ. Southern Calif.; with Warner Bros. Studio; Asst. to Francis Ford Coppola on The Rain People, also dir. documentary on making of that film; f. Lucasfilm Ltd.; dir., co-author screenplay films THX-1138 1970, American Graffiti 1973; dir., author screenplay Star Wars 1977, also novel of same title 1977 dir., author screenplay to prequel The Phantom Menace 1999; Exec. Producer More American Graffiti 1979, The Empire Strikes Back 1980, Raiders of the Lost Ark 1981, Return of the Jedi 1982, Indiana Jones and the Temple of Doom 1984, Howard the Duck 1986, Labyrinth 1988, Willow 1988, Tucker: The Man and His Dream 1988; co. exec. producer Mishima 1985, Indiana Jones and the Last Crusade 1989; Exec. Producer The Young Indiana Jones Chronicles (TV Series) 1992–93, Radioland Murders 1994; Dr. h.c. (Univ. of S. Calif.) 1994; Irving Thalberg Award 1992. *Address:* Lucasfilm Ltd., P.O. Box 2009, San Rafael, CA 94912, U.S.A.

LUCAS, Georges, L. EN D.; French publisher; b. 29 Aug. 1915, Rennes; s. of René and Madeleine (Bazin) Lucas; m. Evelyne Torres 1941; one s.; Man. Dir. and Pres. Livraria Bertrand-Amadora, Lisbon 1948–75; Pres. Franco-Portuguese Chamber of Commerce, Lisbon 1963–72; mem. Bd. Editions Robert Laffont 1967–75, Man. Dir. 1976–79; Vice-Pres. and Man. Dir. Banque Franco-Portuguaise d'Outre-Mer 1966–73; Chair. and Man.-Dir. Librairie Larousse 1979–83, Adviser 1984–86; Conseiller Nat. du Commerce Extérieur 1973–86; Chevalier, Légion d'honneur, Croix de Guerre. *Address:* 5 avenue Emile Deschanel, 75007 Paris, France.

LUCAS, Peter Charles; Australian businessman; b. 9 July 1934; s. of P. W. Lucas; m. Norma McBrien 1958; two s. three d.; ed. Univ. Law School., N.S.W.; Dir. Endeavour Resources Ltd. 1978, Petro Energy Ltd,, N. Kalgurli Mines Ltd., Metals Exploration Ltd. 1984; Chair. Waltons Bond Ltd. 1986; Man. Dir. Bond Corpn. Int. Ltd. Hong Kong 1987; Exec. Dir. Bond Corpn. Holdings Ltd. 1985, Chair. 1990–92; Chair. First Pacific Davies Australia 1993; Chair., C.E.O. St Malo, Australia Ltd. 1994–; Deputy Chair. Sunbase China Ltd 1995–; Trustee CEDA; mem. Council HKABA. *Leisure interests:* tennis, golf.

LUCAS, Robert; American economist; b. 1937, Yakima, Wash.; Prof. Univ. of Chicago 1975–80, John Dewey Distinguished Service Prof. 1980–; Fellow A.A.A.S.; mem. N.A.S.; Nobel Prize for Econs. 1995. *Address:* Department of Economics, University of Chicago, 5801 S. Ellis Avenue, Chicago, IL 60637, U.S.A.

LUCAS GARCÍA, Gen. Fernando Romeo; Guatemalan politician; Minister of Nat. Defence 1975–76; Pres. of Guatemala 1978–82; Cand. for Partido Revolucionario and Partido Institucional Democrático.

LUCE, Charles F., LL.B.; American lawyer and business executive; b. 29 Aug. 1917, Platteville, Wis.; s. of James O. Luce and Wilma Grindell; m. Helen G. Oden 1942; two s. two d.; ed. Univ. of Wisconsin Law School and Yale Law School; admitted to Wis. Bar 1941, Ore. Bar 1945, Wash. Bar 1946, New York Bar 1981; Law clerk to late Mr. Justice Hugo Black, Supreme Court 1943–44; Attorney, Bonneville Power Admin., Portland, Ore. 1944–46; in private law practice, Walla Walla, Wash. 1946–61; Bonneville Power Administrator 1961–66; Under-Sec. of the Interior 1966–67; Chair. Bd. of Trustees, Consolidated Edison Co. of New York Inc. 1967–82, C.E.O. 1967–81, Chair. Emer. 1982–; partner Preston, Ellis and Holman, Portland 1982–86; Special Counsel Metropolitan Life Insurance Co. 1987–94; Dir. Emer. Metropolitan Life Insurance Co.; Trustee Henry M. Jackson Foundation; Trustee Emer. Columbia Univ.; mem. various advisory cttees., etc. *Address:* Consol Edison, 4 Irving Place, New York, NY 10003, U.S.A.

LUCE, Henry, III; American publisher, journalist and foundation administrator; b. 28 April 1925, New York; s. of Henry R. Luce and Lila Hotz Tyng; m. 1st Patricia Potter 1947 (divorced 1954); one s. one d.; m. 2nd Claire McGill 1960 (died 1971); three step-s.; m. 3rd Nancy Bryan Cassiday 1975 (died 1987); two step-s. (one deceased); m. 4th Leila Eliott Burton Hadley 1990; two step.-s. two step-d.; ed. Brooks School and Yale Univ.; served U.S.N.R. 1943–46; Commr.'s Asst., Hoover Comm. on Org. Exec. Branch of Govt. 1948–49; Reporter, Cleveland Press 1949–51; Washington Corresp. Time Inc. 1951–53, Time writer 1953–55, Head New Bldg. Dept. 1956–60, Asst. to Publr. 1960–61, Circulation Dir. Fortune and Architectural Forum 1961–64, House and Home 1962–64, Vice-Pres. 1964–80, Chief London Bureau 1966–68, Publr. Fortune 1968–69, Publr. Time 1969–72; Pres. Asscn. of American Corresps. in London 1968; Vice-Pres. for Corporate Planning, Time Inc. 1972–80; Dir. Time Warner Inc. 1967–89; Pres. and C.E.O. Henry Luce Foundation 1958–90, Chair. and C.E.O. 1990–; Pres. The New Museum of Contemporary Art 1977–98; Chair. American Security Systems Inc.; mem. American Council for UN Univ., Foreign Policy Asscn. (Gov., Medal 1997); Trustee, Eisenhower Exchange Fellowships, Princeton Theological Seminary, Center of Theological Inquiry, Coll. of Wooster, China Inst. in America, A Christian Ministry in the Nat. Parks, New-York Historical Soc.; Pres. The New Museum of Contemporary Art; Acting Pres. The Pilgrims; Chair. American Russian Youth Orchestra; Dir. Nat. Cttee. on U.S.-China Relations, Fishers Island Devt. Co.; Hon. L.H.D. (St. Michael's Coll., Long Island Univ., Pratt Inst.); Hon. LL.D. (Coll. of Wooster); American Asscn. of Museums Medal for Distinguished Philanthropy 1994, Cen. Park Conservancy Frederick Law Olmstead Award 1996. *Leisure interest:* art collecting. *Address:* Suite 1500, 720 Fifth Avenue, New York, NY 10019 (Office); Mill Hill Road, Mill Neck, NY 11765, U.S.A. (Home).

LUCE, Rt. Hon. Sir Richard Napier, Kt., P.C.; British politician; b. 14 Oct. 1936, London; s. of late Sir William Luce, G.B.E., K.C.M.G. and of Lady Luce (née Margaret Napier); m. Rose Helen Nicholson 1961; two s.; ed. Wellington Coll. and Christ's Coll., Cambridge; Dist. Officer, Kenya 1960–62; Brand Man. Gallaher Ltd. 1963–65; Marketing Man. Spirella Co. of G.B.; Dir. Nat. Innovations Centre 1968–71; Chair. IFA Consultants Ltd. 1972–79, Selanex Ltd. 1973–79, Courtenay Stewart Int. Ltd. 1975–79; mem. European Advisory Bd. Corning Glass Int. 1975–79; Dir. (non-exec.) Booker Tate 1991–96, Meridian Broadcasting 1991–97; M.P. for Arundel and Shoreham 1971–74, for Shoreham 1974–92; Parl. Under-Sec. of State 1979–81; Minister of State, FCO 1981–82, 1983–85; Minister of State (Minister for the Arts) and Minister of State for Civil Service, Privy Council Office 1985–90; Gov. and C.-in-C. Gibraltar 1997–; Vice-Chancellor Univ. of Buckingham 1992–96; Chair. Commonwealth Foundation 1992–96, Atlantic Council of U.K. 1993–96; Conservative. *Leisure interests:* walking, swimming, painting, sailing, tennis. *Address:* The Convent, Gibraltar. *Telephone:* 47828. *Fax:* 47823.

LUCE, R(obert) Duncan, PH.D.; American mathematical psychologist; b. 16 May 1925, Scranton, Pa.; s. of Robert R. and Ruth Downer Luce; m. 1st Gay Gaer 1950; m. 2nd Cynthia Newby 1967; one d.; m. 3rd Carolyn A. Scheer 1988; ed. M.I.T.; Member of Staff, Research Lab. of Electronics M.I.T. 1950–53; Asst. Prof. of Sociology and Mathematical Statistics, Columbia Univ. 1954–57; Fellow Center for Advanced Study in the Behavioral Sciences 1954–55, 1966–67, 1987–88; Lecturer in Social Relations, Harvard Univ. 1957–59, Prof. of Psychology 1976–83, Victor S. Thomas Prof. of Psychology 1984–88, Emer. 1988–; Distinguished Prof. of Cognitive Sciences, Dir. Irvine Research Unit in Math. Behavioral Science, Univ. of Calif. at Irvine 1988–92, Dir. Inst. for Math. Behavioral Sciences 1992–98, Distinguished Research Prof. of Cognitive Sciences and Research Prof. of Econs. 1994–; Prof. of Psychology, Univ. of Pa. 1959–68, Benjamin Franklin Prof. 1968–69; Visiting Prof. Inst. for Advanced Study, Princeton, N.J. 1969–72; Prof. of Social Science, Univ. of Calif., Irvine 1972–75; mem. N.A.S., American Acad. of Arts and Sciences, American Philosophical Soc., Soc. of Experimental Psychologists; American Psychological Asscn. Distinguished Scientific Contribution Award. *Publications:* Games and Decisions (with H. Raiffa), Individual Choice Behavior, Handbook of Mathematical Psychology (Jt. Ed.), Contemporary Developments in Mathematical Psychology (Jt. Ed.), Foundations of Measurement Vols. I, II, III (with D. H. Krantz, P. Suppes and A. Tversky) 1971–90, Response Times, Stevens' Handbook of Experimental Psychology (Jt. Ed.), Sound & Hearing, and over 190 articles in scientific journals. *Address:* Social Science Plaza, University of Calif. at Irvine, CA 92697-5100; 20 Whitman Court, Irvine, CA 92612-4057, U.S.A. (Home). *Telephone:* (949) 824-6239 (Office); (949) 854 8203 (Home).

LUCEBERT (pseudonym of L. J. Swaanswijk); Netherlands painter and poet; b. 15 Sept. 1924; ed. School of Applied Arts, Amsterdam; mem. Experimental COBRA group; has lived and worked in Berlin (with Bertolt Brecht) 1954, Bulgaria 1955, France 1964 and Spain 1965; first one-man exhbn., Galerie Espace, Haarlem 1958, also Stedelijk Museum, Amsterdam 1959, and Marlborough New London Gallery 1963; retrospective exhbn. Stedelijk Museum, Amsterdam 1969, 1987; Amsterdam Poetry Prize 1954, Premio Marzotto 1962, Graphic Art Prize, Biennale Carrara 1962, Del Naviglio Prize, Venice Biennale 64, P.C. Hooft Prize 1967, Combined Belgian–Dutch Prize for Literature 1983. *Publications:* Collected Poems 1974, Harvest in a Labyrinth 1981, Swamprider from Paradise 1982; trans.: Wir sind Gesichter 1972, Die Silbenuhr 1981, Antologia 1978, Skola Amsterdamska 1986. *Address:* Boendermakerhof 10, 1861 TB BergenN-H, Netherlands. *Telephone:* 02208-13551.

LUCHKO, Klara Stepanovna; Russian cinema and stage actress; b. 1 July 1925, Poltava, Ukraine; m. 1st Sergey Lukianov 1959 (died 1963); m. 2nd Dmitriy Mamleev; one d.; ed. VGIK; actress, Cinema Actors' Theatre-Studio 1948–; People's Artist of U.S.S.R., Badge of Honour; mem. Nika Cinema Acad. *Roles include:* Dasha Shelest in Cossacks by Kuban (U.S.S.R. State Prize 1951), Viola and Sebastian in Twelfth Night, Lisa in Big Family (Prize at Cannes Film Festival 1955), Jadwiga in Red Lives 1958, Natasha in Under the Seven Winds 1962, Claudia Pushlakova in The Gypsies (TV serial), Madlen in Cascet, Mother in Another's Child 1982, Nuikina in We, the Undersigned (TV) 1982, Dgozephina in Carnival 1983, Golovina in The

Alarming Sunday 1983, Claudia in Budulai's Return 1986, Marianna in Play in Death 1991, doctor in Eyes 1993, Nastya in Parable 1995; narrator in weekly TV programme Films of our Memory 1993–96 and Movie Star 1997–99. *Publication:* Am I Guilty? (screenplay). *Leisure interests:* travelling, music, the arts. *Address:* Kotelnicheskaya Nab. 1/15, Korp. B, Apt. 308, 109240 Moscow, Russia. *Telephone:* (095) 915 43 67.

LUCIE-SMITH, (John) Edward (McKenzie), M.A., F.R.S.L.; British art critic and poet; b 27 Feb. 1933, Kingston, Jamaica; s. of John Dudley Lucie-Smith and Mary Lushington; ed. King's School, Canterbury, Merton Coll., Oxford; officer R.A.F. 1954–56; fmrly. worked in advertising and as freelance journalist and broadcaster; contributes to The Times, Sunday Times, Independent, Mail-on-Sunday, Spectator, New Statesman, Evening Standard, Encounter, London Magazine, Illustrated London News. *Publications as sole author include:* A Tropical Childhood and Other Poems 1961, Confessions and Histories 1964, What is a Painting? 1966, Thinking About Art 1968, Towards Silence 1968, Movements in Art Since 1945 1969, Art in Britain 69–70 1970, A Concise History of French Painting 1971, Symbolist Art 1972, Eroticism in Western Art 1972, The First London Catalogue 1974, The Well Wishers 1974, The Burnt Child (autobiog.) 1975, The Invented Eye (early photography) 1975, World of the Makers 1975, Joan of Arc 1976, Fantin-Latour 1977, The Dark Pageant (novel) 1977, Art Today 1977, A Concise History of Furniture 1979, Super Realism 1979, Cultural Calendar of the Twentieth Century 1979, Art in the Seventies 1980, The Story of Craft 1981, The Body 1981, A History of Industrial Design 1983, Art Terms: An Illustrated Dictionary 1984, Art in the Thirties 1985, American Art Now 1985, Lives of the Great Twentieth Century Artists 1986, Sculpture Since 1945 1987, Art in the Eighties 1990, Art Deco Painting 1990, Fletcher Benton 1990, Jean Rustin 1991, Harry Holland 1992, Art and Civilisation 1992, Andres Nagel 1992, Wendy Taylor 1992, Alexander 1992, British Art Now 1993, Race, Sex and Gender: Issues in Contemporary Art 1994, American Realism 1994, Art Today 1995, Visual Arts in the Twentieth Century 1996; has edited numerous anthologies. *Leisure interest:* the Internet. *Address:* c/o Rogers, Coleridge and White, 20 Powis Mews, London, W11 1JN, England.

LUCINSCHI, Petru, CAND.PHIL.SC.; Moldovan politician; b. 27 Jan. 1940, Floresti; s. of Chiril Lucinschi and Parascovia Lucinschi; m. Antonina Georgievna Lucinschi 1965; two s.; ed. Kishinev Univ. and CPSU Cen. Cttee. Higher Party School; served in Soviet Army 1962–63; Komsomol work for Cen. Cttee. of Moldavian CP 1963–71; mem. CPSU 1964–91; First Sec. of Bălti City Komsomol Cttee. 1964–65; Head of Section, Second Sec., First Sec. of Cen. Cttee. of Moldavian Komsomol 1965–71; Sec. of Cen. Cttee. of Moldavian CP 1971–76, First Sec. Nov. 1989–91; First Sec. of Kishinev City Cttee. 1976–78; Deputy Head, Propaganda Dept. of CPSU Cen. Cttee. 1978–86; Second Sec. of Cen. Cttee. of Tadzhik CP 1986–89; Cand. mem. of CPSU Cen. Cttee. 1986–89, mem. 1989–91, Sec. 1990–91; Deputy to U.S.S.R. Supreme Soviet 1986–89; U.S.S.R. People's Deputy 1989–91; mem. CPSU Politburo, 1990–91; Moldovan Amb. to Russia 1992–93; Leader Agrarian Democratic Party; Chair. Moldovan Parl. 1993–; Pres. of Moldova Nov. 1996; numerous awards. *Leisure interests:* sports, travelling, reading, theatre. *Address:* Office of the President, 23 Nicolae Jorga str., 277033 Chişinău, Moldova. *Telephone:* (2) 23-72-17, 23-36-83.

LUCIUS, Wulf D. von, DR.RER.POL.; German scientific publisher; b. 29 Nov. 1938, Jena; s. of late Tankred R. von Lucius and of Annelise Fischer; m. Akka Achelis 1967; three s.; ed. Heidelberg, Berlin and Freiburg; mil. service 1958–60; Asst. Inst. of Econometrics, Freiburg 1965–66; worked in several publishing houses and as public accountant 1966–69; partner and Man. Dir. Gustav Fischer Verlag 1969–95; mem. Bd. of Exec. Officers, German Publrs. Asscn. (Börsenverein) 1976–86; Publr. and Pres. Lucius & Lucius Verlag, Stuttgart 1996–; Chair. Int. Publishers Copyright Council, Asscn. of Scientific Publrs. in Germany 1994–. *Publications:* numerous articles on publishing, copyright and book history. *Leisure interests:* collecting fine print and art books. *Address:* Gerokstr. 51, 70184 Stuttgart (Office); Ameisenbergstrasse 22, 7000 Stuttgart 1, Germany. *Telephone:* 0711-242060 (Office); 0711-264386 (Home).

ŁUCZAK, Aleksander Piotr, PH.D.; Polish politician and historian; b. 10 Sept. 1943, Legionowo; m. Janina Zakrzewska; one d.; ed. Warsaw Univ. and Adam Mickiewicz Univ. Poznań; mem. Polish Peasants' Party (PSL); lecturer, Dept. of History of the Peasant Movt. Cen. Cttee. PSL until 1976; mem. Faculty, Univ. of Warsaw 1976–, Asst. Prof. 1983–91, Prof. 1991–; Adviser to Pres. of Cen. Cttee. PSL 1976–79; Head, Dept. of Ideology, Press and Propaganda, Cen. Cttee. PSL 1986, Vice-Chair., Head Council PSL 1992–97; Head, Office of Council of Ministers June–Oct. 1992; Deputy Prime Minister and Minister of Educ. 1993–94; Deputy Prime Minister, Minister and Head of Scientific Research Cttee. 1994–96; Minister and Head of Scientific Research Cttee. 1996–97; Deputy to Sejm (Parl.) 1989–. *Publications:* more than 30 publs. on recent history of Poland and the peasant movt. *Address:* Sejm RP, ul. Wiejska 4/6/8, 00-902 Warsaw, Poland. *Telephone:* (22) 694 25 00.

LUDER, Owen (Harold), C.B.E., F.R.S.A.; British architect, planner and environmentalist; b. 7 Aug. 1928, London; s. of late Edward Charles Luder and of Ellen Clara Luder; m. 1st Rose Dorothy (Doris) Broadstock 1951 (dissolved 1988); one s. (deceased) four d.; m. 2nd Jacqueline Ollerton 1989; ed. Brixton School of Building, Regent St. Polytechnic Evening School of Architecture, Brixton School of Architecture; f. Owen Luder Partnership 1957, Sr. Partner until 1978 (when partnership became an unlimited co.), Chair. and Man. Dir. 1978–87; f. Owen Luder Consultancy Communication in Construction 1988; Dir. (non-exec.) Jarvis PLC 1995–; Council mem. R.I.B.A. 1967–, Hon. Treas. 1975–78, Pres. 1981–83, Sr. Vice-Pres. 1994–95, Pres. 1995–97, Architect mem. Architects' Registration Bd. and Vice-Chair. 1997–; Pres. Norwood Soc. 1982–92; Sec./Treas. Commonwealth Asscn. of Architects 1985–87; Pres. VIA Congress 1986; Vice-Pres. Membership Communications 1989–90; Dir. Communication in Construction Ltd. 1990, Jarvis 1995–; Consultant to Nat. Coal Bd. for environmental, architectural and planning issues on Vale of Belvoir Coal Mining Project, U.K. 1975–87; Architect/Planner for Revitalisation schemes for British Rail Eng. Works at Shildon Co. Durham and Swindon; Consultant for many commercial devt. schemes; mem. British Acad. of Experts 1992–, Vice-Chair. 1997–; R.I.B.A. Architecture Bronze Medal 1963, Town Planning and Housing Council Silver Jubilee Award 'Housing in the 80s' and various other architectural, design and civic trust awards and commendations. *Publications:* Promotion and Marketing for Building Professionals 1988, Sports Stadia After Hillsborough 1990; frequent contributions to nat. and tech. publications. *Leisure interests:* golf, photography, writing, Arsenal Football Club. *Address:* Communication in Construction Ltd., 2 Smith Square, London, SW1P 3HS, England. *Telephone:* 0171-222 4737. *Fax:* 0171-233 0428.

LUDEWIG, Johannes, PH.D.; German civil servant and business executive; b. 6 July 1945, Hamburg; m.; three c.; ed. Univ. of Hamburg, Stanford Univ., Ecole Nationale d'Administration, Paris; worked on energy, econ. and business policy Fed. Ministry of Econs. 1975–83; joined Office of the Fed. Chancellor 1983, Ministerial Dir. Dept. of Econ. and Financial Policy 1991–94; fmr. State Sec. Fed. Ministry of Econs.; fmr. Commr. of Fed. Govt. for New German Fed. States; mem. Exec. Bd. Deutsche Bahn AG May 1997–, Chair. July 1997–. *Address:* Deutsche Bahn AG, Stephensonstrasse 1, 60326 Frankfurt-am-Main, Germany. *Telephone:* (69) 97-33-64-04.

LUDLUM, Robert, B.A.; American author; b. 25 May 1927, New York; s. of George Hartford Ludlum and Margaret Wadsworth; m. Mary Ryducha 1951; two s. one d.; ed. Wesleyan Univ.; actor and theatrical producer, New York 1952–69; novelist 1969–. *Publications:* The Scarlatti Inheritance 1971, The Osterman Weekend 1972, The Matlock Paper 1973, The Rhinemann Exchange 1974, The Gemini Contenders 1976, The Chancellor Manuscript 1977, The Holcroft Covenant 1978, The Matarese Circle 1979, The Bourne Identity 1980, The Parsifal Mosaic 1982, The Aquitaine Progression 1983, The Icarus Agenda 1988, Trevayne 1989, The Bourne Ultimatum 1990, The Road to Omaha 1992, The Scorpio Illusion 1993, The Apocalypse Watch 1995, The Matarese Countdown 1997. *Address:* c/o Henry Morrison Inc., P.O. Box 235, Bedford Hills, NY 10507, U.S.A.

LUDWIG, Christa; Austrian mezzo-soprano; b. 16 March 1928, Berlin, Germany; d. of Anton Ludwig and Eugenie Besalla-Ludwig; m. 1st Walter Berry (q.v.) 1957 (divorced 1970); one s.; m. 2nd Paul-Emile Deiber 1972; opera debut at 18, guest appearance at the Athens Festival in Epidauros 1965; joined Vienna State Opera 1955, Hon. mem. 1981; Hon. mem. Vienna Konzerthaus; appearances at Festivals in Salzburg, Bayreuth, Lucerne, Holland, Prague, Saratoga, Stockholm; guest appearances in season in Vienna, New York, Chicago, Buenos Aires, Scala Milano, Berlin, Munich; numerous recitals and soloist in concerts; recordings of Lieder and complete operas including Norma (with Maria Callas), Lohengrin, Cosí fan tutte, Der Rosenkavalier, Carmen, Götterdämmerung, Die Walküre, Herzog Blaubarts Burg, Don Giovanni, Die Zauberflöte, Le Nozze di Figaro, Capriccio, Fidelio; winner of Bach-Concours, record award for Fricka in Walküre, and Des Knaben Wunderhorn; awarded title of Kammersängerin by Austrian Govt. 1962; Prix des Affaires Culturelles, for recording of Venus in Tannhäuser, Paris 1972; Silver Rose (Vienna Philharmonic) 1980; Golden Ring (Staatsoper, Vienna) 1980; Golden Gustav Mahler Medal 1980, Hugo Wolf Medal 1980, Gold Medal (City of Vienna) 1988, Commdr. des Arts et des Lettres 1989, Chevalier, Légion d'honneur 1989, Grosses Ehrenreichen 1994. *Leisure interests:* music, archaeology, reading, home movie making, cooking, sewing, fashion, shopping, weaving, rug knitting and travelling. *Address:* Calliopie, 162 Chemin du Santon, 06250 Mougins, France.

LUEDERITZ, Alexander, DR.IUR. ; German professor of law; b. 19 March 1932, Göttingen; s. of Heinrich and Gertrud Luederitz; m. Renate (née Wessling) Luederitz 1960; one s. one d.; ed. Cologne and Lausanne Schools of Law; mem. of the Bar 1961–65; Prof. of Law, Frankfurt Univ. 1966–70, Dean, Faculty of Law 1969–70; Prof. of Law and Dir. Inst. for Int. and Foreign Private Law, Univ. of Cologne 1971–, Dean, Faculty of Law 1979–80; Visiting Prof. Univ. of Calif., Berkeley 1982, Univ. d'Auvergne 1989, 1991, Univ. of Ill., Urbana 1995, Univ. of Toulouse 1995, 1996; Fellow, American Council of Learned Socs. *Publications:* Auslegung von Rechtsgeschäften 1966, International Sales 1991, International Privatrecht 1992, Commentary on German Conflicts Law (Corporation, Agency, Torts) 1996, Family Law 1997; articles in learned journals. *Leisure interests:* hiking, stamp collecting. *Address:* Kellerhardtsweg 12, 51503 Roesrath, Germany. *Telephone:* (221) 470-2288; (02205) 3124. *Fax:* (221) 470 5129; (02205) 3124.

LUERS, William Henry, M.A.; American diplomatist and art museum president; b. 15 May 1929, Springfield, Ill.; s. of Carl U. and Ann L. Luers; m. Wendy Woods Turnbull 1979; three s. one d. by previous marriage; ed. Hamilton Coll., Columbia and Northwestern Univs.; Foreign Service Officer

Dept. of State 1957; Vice-Consul, Naples, Italy 1957–60; Second Sec. Embassy, Moscow 1963–65; Political Counsellor, Caracas, Venezuela 1969–73; Deputy Exec. Sec., Dept. of State 1973–75; Deputy Asst. Sec. for Inter-American Affairs, Washington 1975–77, Deputy Asst. Sec. 1977–78; Amb. to Venezuela 1978–82, to Czechoslovakia 1983–86; Pres. Metropolitan Museum of Art, New York 1986–99; Head. UN Asscn. of U.S.A. 1999–; bd. mem., Transco Energy Co., Tex., 1986; mem. Council on Foreign Relations, Int. Inst. for Strategic Studies, London; Fellow A.A.A.S. *Address:* Metropolitan Museum of Art, 1000 Fifth Avenue, New York, NY 10028, U.S.A. *Telephone:* (212) 570 3900 (Office).

LUGAR, Richard Green, M.A.: American politician; b. 4 April 1932, Indianapolis, Ind.; s. of Marvin L. Lugar and Bertha Green Lugar; m. Charlene Smeltzer 1956; four s.; ed. Shortridge High School, Denison Univ., Ohio, Pembroke Coll., Oxford Univ.; Rhodes Scholar, Pembroke Coll., Oxford 1956; served U.S.N. 1957–60; Vice-Pres. and Treas. Thomas Green & Co. Inc. 1960–67, Sec.-Treas. 1968; Treas. Lugar Stock Farms Inc. 1960; mem. Bd. of Trustees, Denison Univ. 1966, Advisory Bd., Ind. Univ., Purdue Univ. at Indianapolis 1969–75, Bd. of Trustees of Ind. Cen. Univ. 1970; Vice-Chair. 1975, Visiting Prof. of Political Science, Dir. of Public Affairs 1975–76; mem. Visiting Cttee. of Harvard—M.I.T. Joint Centre for Urban Studies 1973–; mem. Bd. of Dirs., Indianapolis Centre for Advanced Research 1973–76; mem. Indianapolis Bd. of School Commrs. 1964–67, Vice-Pres. 1965; Mayor of Indianapolis 1968–75; del. and keynote speaker, Ind. Republican Convention 1968, del. 1972; del. mem. Platform Cttee., Repub. Nat. Convention 1968, del., keynote speaker and mem. Platform Cttee. 1972; Candidate for U.S. Senate 1974, Senator from Indiana 1977–; mem. Advisory Comm. on Intergovernmental Relations 1969–75, Vice-Chair. 1970–75; mem. Advisory Bd. of U.S. Conf. of Mayors 1969–75; mem. Pres. Model Cities Advisory Task Force 1969–70, State and Local Govt. Advisory Cttee. of Office of Econ. Opportunity 1969–73, Nat. Advisory Comm. on Criminal Justice Standards and Goals 1971–73; Pres. of Advisory Council, Nat. League of Cities 1971, mem. Council 1972–75; Chair. Nat. Republican Senatorial Cttee. 1983–84; Chair. Foreign Relations Cttee. 1985–87, Cttee. on Agric. 1995–; mem. Bd. of Dirs. of Westview Osteopathic Hosp. 1969–76, Indianapolis Symphony Orch., Nat. Endowment for Democracy; mem. Nat. Acad. of Public Admin., Rotary Club of Indianapolis and other civic orgs.; Trustee Denison Univ., Indianapolis Univ.; Hon. Doctorates from 20 colls. and univs. in U.S.A. 1970–78; Exceptional Service Award, Office of Econ., Opportunity 1972, Fiorello La Guardia Award, New School of Social Research 1975. *Publication:* Letters to the Next President 1988. *Leisure interests:* music, reading, running, golf, tennis. *Address:* U.S. Senate, 306 Hart Senate Office Building, Washington, DC 20510, U.S.A. *Telephone:* (202) 224-4814.

LUI, Frank Fakaotimanava; Niuean politician; Premier of Niue 1993–, also Minister for External Relations, Niueans Overseas, Police and Immigration, Civil Aviation and Public Service Comm. *Address:* Office of the Premier, Alofi, Niue.

LUIK, Juri; Estonian diplomatist, politician and journalist; b. 17 Aug. 1966, Tallinn; ed. Tartu Univ.; Political Ed. Vikerkaar (monthly) 1988–90; specialist on Anglo-Saxon Countries Estonian Inst. 1990; Head Political Dept., Ministry of Foreign Affairs 1991–92; mem. Riigikogu (Parl.) 1992–95; Minister without portfolio responsible for Estonian-Russian Negotiations 1992–93; Minister of Defence 1993–94; Minister of Foreign Affairs 1994–95; Amb. to NATO, Brussels 1996–; mem. Pro Patria (Isamaa) Party 1989–; works as lecturer in U.S.A. *Leisure interests:* theatre, films, tennis.

LUKASHENKA, Aleksandar Rygorovich; Belarus politician and economist; b. 30 Aug. 1954, Kopys, Belarus; m. Galina Rodionovna Lukashenko; two s.; ed. Mogilev Pedagogical Inst., Belarus Agric. Acad.; Sec. Komsomol Cttee., Shklov, instructor Political Div. Komsomol Cttee. W. Border Dist. 1975–77; Sec. Komsomol Cttee. Mogilev City Food Dept.; instructor regional Exec. Cttee. 1977–80; Deputy Commdr. of Co. 1980–82; Deputy Chair. Udarnik collective farm 1982–83; Deputy Dir. Enterprise of Construction Materials 1983–85; Sec. CP cttee. Collective Farm of V. I. Lenin, Shklov Dist. 1985–87; Dir. Gorodets state farm 1987–94; elected Deputy of Supreme Council of Belarus S.S.R. 1990–94; Chair. Parl. Comm. on Struggle against Corruption 1993–94; elected Pres. of Belarus 1994–; Chair. Higher Council of Belarus and Russia Union 1997–. *Address:* Office of the President, J.K. Marks Street 38, 220016 Minsk, Belarus. *Telephone:* (17) 22-32-84 (Office).

LUKEŠ, Milan, PH.D.; Czech academic; b. 14 Dec. 1933, Prague; s. of Miloš Lukeš and Bohumila Topičová; m. Ilona Milatová; one d.; ed. Acad. of Performing Arts; Ed. Orbis Publishing House, Prague 1956–60; Ed. then Ed.-in-chief, Theatre (journal) 1960–69; Reader, then Lecturer, Prof. Faculty of Arts, Charles Univ., Prague 1960–; Dir. Nat. Theatre, Prague 1985–89, Chair. Council 1994–; Co-Ed. Svět a divadlo (World and Theatre journal) 1996–; Chair. Int. Theatre Festival, Pilsen 1996–98; Minister of Culture, Czech Repub. 1989–90; Vice-Premier, Govt. of Czech Repub. 1990–92; Deputy to Czech Nat. Council (Parl.) 1990–92. *Publications:* Eugene O'Neill, Principles of Shakespearean Text Theory, The Art of Drama; critical reviews and essays, translations of dramas. *Address:* Svět a divadlo, Celetná 17, Prague 1, 11000, Czech Republic. *Telephone:* 248 17 180. *Fax:* 248 18 184.

LUKIANENKO, Levko (Hryhorovych); Ukrainian politician; b. 24 Aug. 1928, Chrypivka, Chernigiv Region; s. of Hryzko Lukianenko and Natalka Lukianenko; m.; ed. Moscow Univ.; mem. CPSU 1953–61; served in Soviet Army 1944–53; legal adviser, Lvov CPSU Regional Cttee. 1958–61; sentenced to death 1961 for formation of Ukrainian Workers' and Peasants' League, but sentence commuted to 15 years' imprisonment, released 1976; co-founder, on release, of Ukrainian Helsinki Group 1976, again arrested, sentenced to 10 years' imprisonment and 5 years' exile, returned to Ukraine 1989; mem. Verkhovna Rada (Parl.) 1990–92, 1994–98; Chair. Ukrainian Republican Party 1990–92, Hon. Chair. 1992–; Presidential Cand. Ukrainian elections 1991; Amb. to Canada 1992–93; Hon. LL.D. (Alberta); Merit of Honour of Ukrainian Pres. *Publications:* 5 books 1990–. *Leisure interests:* music, gardening. *Address:* 20 Sadova Street, Kyivo-Sviatosh District, 255206 Kiev, Ukraine. *Telephone:* (44) 489-0527. *Fax:* (44) 489-0527.

LUKIN, Vladimir Petrovich, D.HIST.; Russian politician and diplomatist; b. 13 July 1937, Omsk; m.; two s.; ed. Moscow State Pedagogical Inst.; researcher, Museum of Revolution, Inst. of World Econs. and Int. Relations, U.S.S.R. Acad. of Sciences 1959–65; on staff of journal Problems of Peace and Socialism, Prague until Aug. 1968 after Soviet invasion; staff-mem. of the Inst. of USA, Canada 1968–87; deputy dir. Dept. of Assessment and Planning of the U.S.S.R. Ministry of Foreign Affairs 1987–90; People's Deputy of R.S.F.S.R. (now Russia) 1990–93; Chair. Foreign Affairs Cttee. of the Russian Supreme Soviet 1990–92; Amb. to USA 1992–94; leader of pre-election bloc Yabloko (with G. Javlinsky); mem. State Duma (Parl.) Dec. 1993–, Chair. Cttee. for Foreign Affairs 1994–. *Leisure interests:* Russian literature, soccer. *Address:* State Duma, Okhotny Ryad 1, 103009 Moscow, Russia. *Telephone:* 292-57-47. *Fax:* 292-67-27.

LUKINOV, Ivan Illarionovich, D.ECON.SC.; Ukrainian economist; b. 5 Oct. 1927, Belgorod Region; s. of Illarion Ivanovich Lukinov and Praskovya Alexeyevna Lukinova; m. Tatyana Borisovna Kozminskaya 1956; one s. one d.; ed. Kharkov Agric. Inst.; mem. CPSU 1953–91; worked for Ukrainian Acad. of Sciences Inst. of Econ. 1951–56; head of a section of Cen. Cttee. of Ukrainian CP 1956–67; head of section at Ukrainian Inst. of Econs. 1965–67; Dir. of Schlichter Ukrainian Inst. of Econ. and Org. of Agric. Production 1967–76; Prof. 1968; Dir. Inst. of Econs., Ukrainian Acad. of Sciences 1976–, Acad. Sec. 1976–77; Vice-Pres. Ukrainian Nat. Acad. of Sciences 1979–93; mem. of U.S.S.R. (now Russian) Acad. of Sciences 1984–, Lenin All-Union (now Russian) Acad. of Agric. Science 1973–, European Assoc. of Agric. Economists (EAAE) 1977–; Vice-Pres. EAAE 1990–93; Hon. mem. Royal Swedish Acad. of Agric. and Forestry 1975. *Publications:* author of 420 research works on econ. theory, price policy and reproduction; cooperation and integration in agro-industrial complexes. *Leisure interests:* tennis, skiing. *Address:* National Academy of Sciences, Volodimirskaya 54, 252601 Kiev 30, Ukraine. *Telephone:* (44) 224-77-16, 290-84-44 (Office); 229-64-50 (Home).

LUKMAN, Rilwanu, B.SC., C.ENG.; Nigerian international civil servant, business executive and engineer; b. 26 Aug. 1938, Zaria, Kaduna State; s. of Qadi Lukman and Hajia Ramatu Lukman; m. 1966; two s. one d.; ed. Govt. Coll. Zaria (now Barewa), Nigerian Coll. of Arts, Science and Tech. (now Ahmadu Bello Univ.), Royal School of Mines, Imperial Coll. of Science and Tech., Univ. of London, Inst. of Prospecting and Mineral Deposits, Univ. of Mining and Metallurgy, Leoben, Austria, McGill Univ., Montreal, Canada; Asst. Mining Engineer, A.G. Statagruvor, Sweden 1962–64; Inspector of Mines and Sr. Inspector of Mines, Ministry of Mines and Power, Jos 1964–67, Acting Asst. Chief Inspector of Mines 1968–70; Gen. Man. Cement Co. of Northern Nigeria Ltd., Sokoto 1970–74; Gen. Man. and Chief Exec. Nigerian Mining Corpn., Jos 1974–84; Fed. Minister of Mines, Power and Steel, Lagos 1984–85, of Petroleum Resources, Lagos 1986–89, of Foreign Affairs 1989–90; Pres. OPEC Conf. 1986–89, Sec.-Gen. OPEC 1995–; Fellow and Hon. Fellow Inst. of Mining and Metallurgy; Fellow Imperial Coll. London, Nigerian Mining and Geoscience Soc.; Past Vice-Pres. Asscn. of Geoscientists for Int. Devt.; mem. Soc. of Mining Engineers of AIME; Ph.D. h.c. (Bologna) 1988, Hon. D.Sc. (Maiduguri) 1989, (Ahmadu Bello) 1991; Dr. h.c. (Moore House Coll. Atlanta) 1989; Hon. K.B.E. 1989, Officier Légion d'honneur 1990, Order of Liberator, First Class, Venezuela 1990. *Leisure interests:* reading, walking. *Address:* OPEC, Obere Donaustrasse 93, 1020 Vienna, Austria. *Telephone:* (1) 211120. *Fax:* (1) 2164320.

LUKOJI, Mulumba; Democratic Republic of the Congo politician; university professor; First State Commr. March–July 1991.

LUKYANOV, Anatoliy Ivanovich, D.JUR.SC.; Russian politician and poet; b. 7 May 1930; m.; one d.; ed. Moscow Univ.; mem. CPSU 1955–91; mem. CP of Russian Fed. 1992–; Chief Consultant on Legal Comm. of U.S.S.R. Council of Ministers 1956–61; Deputy Head of Dept. of Presidium of U.S.S.R. Supreme Soviet 1969–76, Head of Secr. 1977–83; mem. of editorial staff of Sovietskoe gosudarstvo i pravo 1978; mem. Cen. Auditing Comm. CPSU 1981–86, 1986–89; Deputy of R.S.F.S.R. Supreme Soviet 1984–91; Head of Gen. Dept. of Cen. Cttee. CPSU 1985–87, Sec. of Cen. Cttee. 1987–88; Cand. mem. Political Bureau 1988–90; First Vice-Chair. of Presidium, U.S.S.R. Supreme Soviet 1988–90, Chair. 1990–91; Chief Adviser on Legal Reform in U.S.S.R. 1986–89; mem. Cen. Cttee. CPSU 1986–91; People's Deputy of U.S.S.R. 1989–91; arrested 1991 following failed coup d'état; charged with conspiracy Jan. 1992; released on bail Dec. 1992, on trial 1993–94; mem. State Duma (Parl.) Dec. 1993–, mem. Cttee. for legis. and judicial reform 1994, Chair. 1996; mem. Presidium, Cen. Exec. Cttee. CP of Russian Fed. *Publications include:* many articles and books on Soviet legal system and Soviet constitution, three vols. of poetry (under pseudonym A. Osenev). *Address:* State Duma, Okhotny Ryad 1, 103009 Moscow, Russia. *Telephone:* 292-37-30. *Fax:* 292-32-65.

LULA DA SILVA, Luis Inácio; Brazilian politician and trade unionist; b. 27 Oct. 1945, Garanhuns, Pernambuco; s. of Euridice Ferreira de Mello; m. Marisa Leticia 1974; qualified as mechanic; started working at Indústrias Villares steelworks 1966; Assoc. mem. Exec. Cttee., São Bernardo do Campo and Diadema Metalworkers' Union 1969–72, First Sec. (responsible for social security) 1972–75, Pres. 1975–80; led steelworkers' strikes 1978, 1979; Pres. Partido dos Trabalhadores (Workers' Party) 1980–87, 1993; a leader of the 'Elections Now' campaign for direct presidential elections 1984, of campaign to impeach Pres. Collor de Mello 1992; Fed. Deputy 1986–; presidential cand. 1989, 1994; f. a "Parallel Govt." (to prepare an alternative set of policies for the country) 1990. *Address:* Partido dos Trabalhadores (PT), Brasília, DF, Brazil.

LUMET, Sidney; American film director; b. 25 June 1924, Philadelphia; s. of Baruch Lumet and Eugenia Wemus; m. 1st Rita Gam (divorced); m. 2nd Gloria Vanderbilt 1956 (divorced 1963); m. 3rd Gail Jones 1963 (divorced 1978); m. 4th Mary Gimbel 1980; two d.; ed. Columbia Univ.; started as a child actor, later theatrical dir. and teacher; Assoc. Dir. CBS 1950, Dir. 1951–57; Hon. Life mem. Directors Guild of America; D. W. Griffith Award. *Films include:* Twelve Angry Men 1957, Stage Struck 1958, That Kind of Woman 1959, The Fugitive Kind 1960, A View from the Bridge 1961, A Long Day's Journey into Night 1962, The Pawnbroker 1963, Fail Safe 1964, The Hill 1965, The Group 1965, The Deadly Affair 1966, Bye, Bye Braverman 1968, The Seagull 1968, The Appointment 1969, Blood Kin 1969, The Offence, The Anderson Tapes 1972, Child's Play 1973, Serpico 1973, Lovin' Molly 1974, Murder on the Orient Express 1974, Dog Day Afternoon 1975, Network 1976, Equus 1977, The Wiz 1978, Just Tell Me What You Want 1980, Prince of the City 1981, Deathtrap 1982, The Verdict 1982, Daniel 1983, Garbo Talks 1984, Power 1986, The Morning After 1987, Running on Empty 1988, Family Business 1989, Q & A 1989, Close to Eden 1992, A Stranger Among Us 1992, Guilty as Sin 1993, Making Movies 1995, Night Falls on Manhattan 1997, Critical Care 1997, Gloria 1998. *Play:* Caligula 1960. *Publication:* Making Moses 1995. *Address:* Amjen Entertainment Inc., 259 W. 54 Street, New York, NY 10019, U.S.A.

LUMLEY, Joanna, O.B.E.; British actress; b. 1 May 1946, Kashmir; m. 1st Jeremy Lloyd (divorced); m. 2nd Stephen Barlow 1986; one s.; Hon. D.Litt. (Kent) 1994; TV appearances include: Release, Mark II Wife, Comedy Playhouse, It's Awfully Bad for Your Eyes Darling, Satanic Rites of Dracula 1973, Coronation Street, The Protectors, General Hospital 1974–75, The New Avengers 1976–77, Steptoe & Son, Are You Being Served?, The Cuckoo Waltz, Up The Workers, Sapphire and Steel 1978, Absolutely Fabulous (TV series) 1992–94, Class Act 1994, Joanna Lumley in the Kingdom of the Dragon (documentary) 1997, Coming Home 1998; stage appearances in London in Noël Coward's Blithe Spirit 1986, Vanilla 1990, Revengers Comedies 1991, The Letter 1995. *Films include:* Some Girls Do, Tam Lin, The Breaking of Bumbo, Games That Lovers Play, Don't Just Lie There Say Something, On Her Majesty's Secret Service, Trail of the Pink Panther, Curse of the Pink Panther, That Was Tory, Mistral's Daughter, A Ghost in Monte Carlo, Shirley Valentine, Forces Sweetheart, Innocent Lies 1995, James and the Giant Peach 1996, Cold Comfort Farm 1996, Prince Valiant 1997, Parting Shots 1998. *Publications:* Stare Back and Smile (memoirs) 1989, Girl Friday 1994, Joanna Lumley in the Kingdom of the Thunder Dragon 1997. *Address:* c/o Caroline Renton, 23 Crescent Lane, London, S.W.4, England.

LUMSDEN, Sir David (James), Kt., M.A., D.PHIL., MUS.B., F.R.C.M., F.R.S.A.M.D., F.R.N.C.M., F.R.S.C.M.; British musician; b. 19 March 1928, Newcastle upon Tyne; s. of Albert Lumsden and Vera May Lumsden (née Tate); m. Sheila Daniels 1951; two s. two d.; ed. Dame Allan's School, Newcastle upon Tyne, Selwyn Coll. Cambridge (organ scholar); Asst. Organist, St. John's Coll. Cambridge 1951–53; Organist and Choirmaster St. Mary's, Nottingham 1954–56; Founder and Conductor Nottingham Bach Soc. 1954–59; Rector Chori Southwell Minster 1956–59; Dir. of Music, Keele 1958–59; Prof. of Harmony, R.A.M. 1959–61; Fellow and Organist New Coll. Oxford and Lecturer, Faculty of Music, Oxford Univ. 1959–76; Principal RSAMD Glasgow 1976–82; Prin. R.A.M. 1982–93; Conductor Oxford Harmonic Soc. 1961–63; Organist Sheldonian Theatre 1964–76; Harpsichordist to the London Virtuosi 1972–75; Pres. Inc. Asscn. of Organists 1966–68; Visiting Prof. Yale Univ., U.S.A. 1974–75; Conductor Oxford Sinfonia 1967–70; Choragus Oxford Univ. 1968–72; Pres. Inc. Soc. of Musicians 1984–85, Royal Coll. of Organists 1986–88; Chair. Nat. Youth Orchestra 1985–94, Nat. Early Music Asscn. 1986–89; mem. Bd. Scottish Opera 1978–83, English Nat. Opera 1984–88; Fellow, King's Coll. London; Hon. Fellow, Selwyn Coll., Cambridge, New Coll. Oxford, Trinity Coll. London, London Coll. of Music; Hon. R.A.M.; Hon. F.R.C.O.; Hon. G.S.M.D.; Hon. F.T.C.L.; Hon. F.L.C.M.; Hon. D.Litt. (Reading) 1989. *Publications:* An Anthology of English Lute Music 1954, Thomas Robinson's Schoole of Musicke 1603 1971, Music for the Lute (Gen. Ed.) 1965–. *Leisure interests:* reading, walking, theatre, photography, travel. *Address:* Melton House, Soham, Cambridgeshire, CB7 5DB, England. *Telephone:* (01353) 720100. *Fax:* (01353) 720918.

LUMSDEN, Lynne Ann; American publishing executive; b. 30 July 1947, Battle Creek, Mich.; d. of Arthur Lumsden and Ruth Pandy; m. Jon Harden 1986; one d.; ed. Univ. of Paris, Sarah Lawrence Coll., City Grad. Center and New York Univ.; copy ed. Harcourt, Brace, Jovanvich, New York 1970–71; ed. Appleton-Century Crofts, New York 1971–73; Coll. Div. Prentice Hall 1974–78, Sr. Ed. Coll. Div. 1978–81; Asst. Vice-Pres. and Ed.-in-Chief, Spectrum Books 1981–82, Vice-Pres. and Editorial Dir., Gen. Publishing Div. 1982–85; Exec. Vice-Pres., Publr. and Co-owner, Dodd, Mead & Co., Inc. New York 1985–89; Owner, Chair. JBH Communications Inc. Hartford, Conn. 1989–; Publr. Hartford News and Southside Media 1989–. *Address:* 191 Franklin Ave, Hartford, CT 06114; 16 Oak Ridge Lane West, Hartford, CT 06114, U.S.A.

LUNA, Bigas; Spanish film director; m. *Films:* Jamoń, Jamoń, Huevos de Oro (Golden Balls) 1994, The Tit and the Moon.

LUNA, Ricardo V., A.B., M.I.A.; Peruvian diplomatist; b. 19 Nov. 1940, Lima; s. of Ricardo Luna and Victoria Mendoza de Luna; m. Margarita Proaño 1969; one d.; ed. Princeton Univ., N.J. and Columbia Univ., U.S.A., Diplomatic Acad. of Peru; joined Diplomatic Service 1967, posts held include Third Sec., Div. of Econ. Affairs, Foreign Ministry 1967, Third Sec., Embassy in U.K. 1968–70, Second Sec., Embassy in Israel 1970–71, First Sec., Perm. Mission of Peru to UN Office at Geneva; Head UN Dept., Foreign Ministry 1975–77; Counsellor, Embassy in U.S.A. 1978; Chef du Cabinet of Minister for Foreign Affairs 1979; Minister Counsellor, Mission of Peru to UNESCO 1980, Embassy in Ecuador 1987; Fellow Center for Int. Affairs, Harvard Univ., U.S.A. 1980–81; Minister, Perm. Mission to UN 1984; Under-Sec. for Multilateral Policy, Ministry of Foreign Affairs 1987–89; Perm. Rep. of Peru to UN 1989–92; Amb. to U.S.A. 1992–; Founding mem. Peruvian Centre for Int. Studies; mem. Peruvian Soc. of Int. Law. *Leisure interests:* art, art history, jazz, cinema, mountain climbing, hiking. *Address:* Embassy of Peru, 1700 Massachusetts Avenue, N.W., Washington, DC 20036, U.S.A. *Telephone:* (202) 833-9860. *Fax:* (202) 659-8124.

LUND, Henning, D.PHIL.; Danish professor of chemistry; b. 15 Sept. 1929, Copenhagen; s. of Prof. Hakon Lund and Bergljot I. G. (née Dahl) Lund; m. Else Margrethe (née Thorup) Lund 1953; one s. three d.; ed. Aarhus Katedralskole and Tech. Univ. of Copenhagen; Research Chemist Leo Pharmaceutical Products 1952–60; Research Fellow Harvard Univ. 1954–55; Asst. Prof. of Chemistry 1960, Prof. 1964–; Visiting Prof. Japan 1976, France 1981; Chair. UNESCO workshop for European Co-operation in Organic Electro-chemistry 1976–81; Section Co-Chair. Int. Soc. of Electrochemistry 1973–78, 1986–90, Nat. Sec. 1986–90; Pres. Learned Soc., Univ. of Aarhus 1973–79; mem. Danish Research Council for Tech. Sciences 1977–82, Vice-Chair. 1980–82; mem. Royal Danish Acad. of Sciences and Letters 1979; Dr. h.c. (Rennes) 1998; Bjerrums Gold Medal 1969, M. M. Baizer Award (Electrochemical Soc.) 1996. *Publications:* Elektrodereaktioner i Organisk Polarografi og Voltammetri 1961, Encyclopaedia of Electrochemistry of the Elements, Vols. 11-15 1978–84, Organic Electrochemistry (Co-Ed.) 1983, 1991. *Leisure interests:* music, literature, jogging. *Address:* Department of Chemistry, University of Aarhus, 8000 Aarhus (Univ.); Vinkelvej 8A, 8240 Risskov, Denmark (Home). *Telephone:* 89 42 39 07 (Univ.); 86 17 90 27 (Home).

LUND, Peter Anthony; American broadcasting executive; b. 12 Jan. 1941, Minneapolis; s. of Arthur H. Lund and Elizabeth Rohan; m. Theresa M. Kessel 1960; two s.; ed. St. Thomas Coll.; announcer, sales rep. Station KCCR, Pierce, S.Dak. 1961–62; sales rep. Station KELO TV, Sioux Falls, S. Dak. 1962–64; sales rep., sales man. Station WTTC, Minneapolis 1964–66; Gen. Sales Man. Westinghouse Broadcasting Co. 1966–71; Vice-Pres., Man. Station KSDO, San Diego, Calif. 1972–75, Station WTOP, Washington, D.C. 1976–77; Vice-Pres. CBS-owned AM Stations, New York 1977–80; Vice-Pres., Gen. Man. WBBM-TV, Chicago 1980–83, WCBS-TV, New York 1983–84; Exec. Vice-Pres. CBS Sports, New York 1984–85, Pres. 1985–87; Pres. Multimedia Entertainment 1987–90; Exec. Vice-Pres., Pres. Marketing, CBS 1990–94; CBS Broadcast Group Pres. CBS Pres. 1995–97, Exec. Vice-Pres. CBS TV Network 1994–95, C.E.O. CBS 1995–97, Pres. C.E.O. CBS TV and Cable 1997–. *Address:* CBS, 51 W 52nd Street, New York, NY 10019, U.S.A.

LUNDBERG, Bo Klas Oskar, Dr. in Aeronautics; Swedish aeronautical scientist; b. 1 Dec. 1907, Karlskoga; s. of Ehrenfried and Fanny Lundberg; m. Svea Maria Johansson 1935; two s. two d.; ed. Hudiksvalls Läroverk and Royal Inst. of Tech., Stockholm; Designer Test Pilot, AB Svenska Järnvägsverkstäderna, Aeroplanavdelningen, Linköping 1931–35, Sparmanns flygplanverkstad, Stockholm 1935–37; Asst. Insp. at the Bd. of Civil Aviation, Stockholm 1937–38; Chief, Aeronautical Dept., Götaverken, Gothenburg 1939; Chief Designer, J-22 Fighter, Royal Air Bd. 1940–44; Chief, Structures Dept., Aeronautical Research Inst. of Sweden 1944–47, Dir.-Gen. 1947–67, Aviation Consultant 1967–; F.R.Ae.S., Hon. Fellow A.I.A.A., Fellow Canadian Aeronautics and Space Inst., Socio Onorario, Instituto Internazionale delle Comunicazioni; mem. A.A.A.S., Fellow Royal Swedish Acad. of Eng. Sciences; Thulin Medal, Silver 1948, Gold 1955, Flight Safety Foundation Air Safety Award 1960, Sherman Fairchild Certificate of Merit 1963, Monsanto Aviation Safety Award 1963, Carl August Wicander Gold Medal 1966. *Publications include:* Fatigue Life of Airplane Structures (18th Wright Brothers Lecture) 1954, Should Supersonic Airliners be Permitted? 1961, Some Special Problems Connected with Supersonic Transport 1961, Speed and Safety in Civil Aviation (3rd Daniel and Florence Guggenheim Memorial Lecture) 1962, The Allotment of Probability Shares (APS) Method, A Guidance for Flight Safety Measures 1966, Economic and Social Aspects of Commercial Aviation at Supersonic Speeds 1972, Why the SST Should Be Stopped Once and For All 1973; numerous articles and papers mainly on the problems of aircraft safety and supersonic transport. *Leisure interests:* golf, tennis.

LUNDBERG, Henry; Swedish business executive and chemical engineer; b. 11 July 1931, Boliden; s. of Karl and Dagmar Lundberg; m. 2nd. Tua Forsström 1981; one s. six d.; Mining Div. Boliden AB 1952, Gen. Man. Smelting Div. 1967, Man. Dir. Boliden Metall AB 1975; Exec. Vice-Pres. SSAB Swedish Steel Corpn. 1980, Pres. and C.E.O. 1981–87; mem. Bd. Fed. of Swedish Industries, Swedish Employees' Confed. (SFO), Swedish Iron Masters' Asscn.; mem. Exec. Cttee. Int. Iron and Steel Inst. (IISI); mem. Advisory Council, Royal Swedish Acad. of Eng. Sciences; Chair. Audit Cttee. IISI, Swedish Iron and Steel Works' Asscn., Swedish Inst. of Steel Construction 1981–87, Expolaris, Nordisk Industrifysik, Aura, Inpipe Sweden, Voith Nordic n. veg. *Leisure interests:* hunting, orienteering, skiing. *Address:* Stavgårdsgatan 5, 16756 Bromma, Sweden. *Telephone:* (08) 803736. *Fax:* (08) 805615.

LUNDGREEN-NIELSEN, Flemming Torkild Jacob, D.PHIL; Danish university professor; b. 24 Jan. 1937, Hellerup; s. of Otto Nielsen and Edith Mortensen; ed. Frederiksborg Statsskole and Univ. of Copenhagen; teaching posts at Univ. of Copenhagen 1965–, Lektor 1972–88, Prof. DIS Study Div. 1970–90, Docent 1988–; mem. Danish Soc. of Language and Literature, Royal Acad. of Sciences and Letters. *Publications:* Grundtvig. Skaebne og forsyn 1965, Den nordiske fortaelling i det 18. årh. 1968, Det handlende ord I-II 1980, C.C. Lyschanders digtning I-II 1989, Jens Bielke: Relation om Grønland 1990, Grundtvig og danskhed, in Dansk identitetshistorie 3 1992, På sporet af dansk identitet 1992, København laest og påskrevet 1997; articles on Danish and Scandinavian literary subjects. *Address:* Institute of Nordic Philology, University of Copenhagen, Njalsgade 80, 2300 Copenhagen S (Office); Upsalagade 22, 2100 Copenhagen Ø, Denmark (Home). *Telephone:* 35 32 83 11; 35 32 83 37 (Office); 35 43 46 68 (Home). *Fax:* 35 32 83 77.

LUNDGREN, Dolph, M.A.; American actor; b. 1959, Stockholm, Sweden; ed. Washington State Univ., Mass. Inst. of Tech. and Royal Inst. of Tech. Stockholm; fmr. doorman at Limelight disco, New York. *Films include:* A View to a Kill, Rocky IV, Masters of the Universe, Red Scorpion, The Punisher, I Come in Peace, The Eleventh Station, Dark Angel, Showdown in Little Tokyo, Universal Soldier, The Joshua Tree, Meltdown, Army of One, Johnny Mnemonic, The Shooter, The Algonquin Goodbye.

LUNDSTROM, Hans Olof; Swedish economist and civil servant; b. 29 April 1927, Ystad; m. 1st Eva Lundquist 1959; one s. one d.; m. 2nd Marianne Svennilson 1982; ed. Stockholm School of Economics, Institut d'Etudes Politiques, Paris and College of Europe, Bruges; Bank of Sweden 1952–61; Head of Section for Devt. Assistance, Ministry of Finance 1962–64, Head of Int. Secr. 1965–66; Under-Sec. of State for Econ. Affairs 1967–68; Under-Sec. of State, Ministry of Industry 1969–72; Deputy Gov. Bank of Sweden 1973–79; Exec. Dir. IBRD 1980–82; Chair. Review Comm. on the Swedish Concessional Credit System, Ministry of Foreign Affairs 1983; Exec. Dir. IMF 1985–87; Consultant Ministry of Foreign Affairs and Swedish Int. Devt. Authority 1987–89; Chair. Parl. Cttee. on Multilateral Devt. Assistance 1989–91, Review Comm. on Devt. Co-operation with Mozambique 1992–93. *Publications:* Capital Movements and Economic Integration 1960, Policy-Related Assistance 1988; numerous articles on Swedish econ. policy and int. affairs. *Address:* Seglarvägen 13, 13333 Saltsjöbaden, Sweden. *Telephone:* 08-7170763.

LUNDY, Victor Alfred, M.ARCH., F.A.I.A.; American architect; b. 1 Feb. 1923, New York; s. of Alfred Henry Lundy and Rachel Lundy; m. 1st Shirley Corwin 1947 (divorced 1959); one s. one d.; m. 2nd Anstis Manton Burwell 1960; one s.; ed. New York Univ. Coll. of Architecture, Harvard Univ.; mil. service 1943–46; pvt. practice, Sarasota, Fla. 1951–59, New York 1960–75, projects include U.S. Tax Court Bldg. and Plaza, Washington, D.C., U.S. Embassy in Colombo, Sri Lanka, Recreation Shelters for Smithsonian Inst., travelling air-supported exhbn. bldg. and exhibit for U.S. Atomic Energy Comm., and commercial, religious and govt. bldgs. throughout the U.S.A. and overseas; pvt. practice, Houston, Tex. 1976–87, Design Prin. and Vice-Pres. HKS Inc., Dallas, Tex. 1984–, projects include GTE Telephone Operations World HQ, Irving, Tex., Greyhound Corp. (now Dial Corp.) Center, Phoenix, Ariz., Mack Center II, Tampa, Fla., Walnut Glen Tower (now Dr. Pepper Bldg.), Dallas, Tex., Austin Centre-Radisson Hotel and One Congress Plaza, Austin, Tex.; visiting professorships and lectureships, Harvard, Yale, Columbia, Calif. (Berkeley) and Houston Univs., and Rome Univ., Italy; work included in many exhbns. including São Paulo Int. Biennial Exhbn. of Architecture 1957, America Builds, Berlin 1957, Fifth Congress Union Internationale des Architectes, Moscow 1958, Expo '70, Osaka, Japan 1970; Fellow A.I.A.; numerous prizes and awards; Purple Heart Medal and U.S. Combat Infantry Badge. *Address:* HKS Inc., 1111 Plaza of the Americas North, Suite LB 307, Dallas, TX 75201 (Office); 701 Mulberry Lane, Bellaire, TX 77401, U.S.A. (Home). *Telephone:* (214) 969-3396.

LUNENFELD, Bruno, M.D., F.R.C.O.G.; Israeli endocrinologist; b. 11 Feb. 1927, Vienna, Austria; s. of David Lunenfeld and Ernestine Lunenfeld; m. Pnina Buxanover 1996; two s.; ed. British Inst. of Eng. Tech., Medical School, Univ. of Geneva, Switzerland; Acting Chief, Endocrine Research and Devt., Tel-Hashomer 1962–64; Scientist, Weizman Inst. of Science 1961–66; Assoc. Prof. and Head Dept. of Biology, Bar-Ilan Univ. 1964–69, Prof. Ordinarius and Head Dept. of Life Sciences 1969–71, Prof. of Life Sciences 1971; Dir. Inst. of Endocrinology, Sheba Medical Centre 1964–92, Chair. Div. of Labs. 1977–81, Chair. Research and Ethical Cttee. 1977–81; mem. Expert Cttee. on Biological Standardization, WHO 1967–87; Counsellor External Relations to Minister of Health and Head Dept. of Int. Relations, Ministry of Health 1981–85; Acting Chief Scientist, Ministry of Health 1984–86; mem. Nat. Council for Research and Devt. 1985–87; Visiting Prof., Yale School of Medicine, U.S.A. 1986–87; mem. Nat. Council for Health and Social Affairs 1985–87; Pres. Israel Fertility Asscn. 1979–83, Israel Endocrine Soc. 1992–95; Pres. Int. Soc. for the Study of the Aging Male 1997–; Medical Dir. Int. Fertility Inst., Ranana 1996–; Vice-Pres. Scientific Council of Israel Medical Asscn.; mem. Exec. Bd. Scientific Council, Exec. Council of Int. Cttee. for Research in Reproduction, Exec. Council Medical Examination Bd., Exec. Council of Int. Andrology Soc., Exec. Council of Int. Soc. of Gynaecological Endocrinology (and Treas. 1992–96); Hon. Fellow American Coll. of Obstetricians and Gynaecologists; Pliskin Prize, Israel Trade Union Sick Fund 1962, Yaffeh Prize, Ministry of Health 1963, U.S. Public Health Service Special Recognition Award 1983, Jacob Henle Medal (Georg Augustus Univ., Göttingen) 1993, Verdienstkreuz First Class (Germany) 1995. *Publications:* 21 books including, Infertility, Diagnosis and Treatment of Functional Infertility 1978, Ovulation Induction 1982, Diagnosis and Management of Male Infertility 1984, Ovulation Induction and In Vitro Fertilization 1986, Infertility in Male and Female 1986, 1993; 25 chapters in books; 420 papers in scientific journals; 112 published lectures and abstracts. *Leisure interest:* sailing. *Address:* 7 Rav Ashist, 69395 Tel Aviv, Israel (Home). *Telephone:* (3) 6425 434 (Home). *Fax:* (3) 6424 454 (Home).

LUNS, Joseph Marie Antoine Hubert, G.C.M.G., C.H., D.C.L., LL.D.; Netherlands diplomatist and politician; b. 28 Aug. 1911, Rotterdam; m. Baroness Elisabeth Van Heemstra; one s. one d.; ed. Amsterdam and Brussels, Univs. of Leiden, Amsterdam, London and Berlin; Ministry of Foreign Affairs 1938–40; Attaché, Dutch Legation, Berne 1940–41, Lisbon 1941–42, Second Sec. 1942–43; Second Sec. Netherlands Ministry for Foreign Affairs, London 1943–44; Second, then First Sec. Dutch Embassy, London 1944–49; Perm. Del. to UN 1949–52; Co-Minister for Foreign Affairs 1952–56; Minister of Foreign Affairs 1956–71; Pres. NATO Council 1958–59; Sec.-Gen. NATO 1971–83; Hon. Fellow, L.S.E.; Kt. Grand Cross of the Order of the Netherlands Lion, Officer Order of Orange-Nassau, Charlemagne Prize 1967, Hon. C.H. (U.K.) 1971, Ataturk Int. Peace Prize, and foreign awards. *Publications:* Several studies on Netherlands Navy in British and Portuguese magazines and articles about current political problems in various magazines, incl. International Affairs and Atlantic Review. *Leisure interests:* swimming, walking, reading. *Address:* 117 Avenue Franklin Roosevelt, 1050 Brussels, Belgium.

LUO GAN, DIP.ENG.; Chinese state and party official; b. 14 July 1935, Jinan, Shandong; m. He Zuozhi 1965; one s. one d.; ed. Leipzig Univ.; joined CCP 1960; metallurgical and casting engineer; Vice-Gov. Henan Prov. 1981–83; alt. mem. 12th CCP Cen. Cttee. 1982–87, mem. 13th Cen. Cttee. 1987–92, 14th Cen. Cttee. 1992–97, 15th CCP Cen. Cttee. 1997–; Sec. CCP Cttee., Henan 1983–85; mem. CCP Politburo, Sec. Secr. CCP Cen. Cttee. 1997–; Vice-Pres. All-China Fed. of Trade Unions 1983–88; Sec. Gen. of State Council 1988–98; State Councillor 1993–; Sec. Work Cttee. for Cen. Govt. Organs 1989–; Vice-Premier of State Council 1998–. *Address:* State Council, Zhong Nan Hai, Beijing, People's Republic of China.

LUO HAOCAI; Chinese judge and politician; b. March 1934, Anxi Co., Fujian Prov. ed. Beijing Univ.; teaching asst., lecturer, Assoc. Prof., Prof. Dept. of Law, Beijing Univ. 1960–86; Vice-Pres. Beijing Univ. 1986–95; Chair. Beijing Fed. of Returned Overseas Chinese; Vice-Chair. China Law Soc.; mem. Standing Cttee. China Admin. Man. Asscn.; Vice-Pres. and mem. Judicial Cttee. Supreme People's Court 1995–98; Vice-Chair. China Zhi Gong Dang (Party for Public Interests) 1992–97, Chair. 1997–; mem. Standing Cttee. and Deputy Sec.-Gen. CPPCC 8th Nat. Cttee. 1993–98, Vice-Chair. 9th Nat. Cttee. 1998–. *Address:* National Committee of Chinese People's Political Consultative Conference, 23 Taipingqiao Street, Beijing, People's Republic of China.

LUO PINGAN; Chinese artist; b. 12 April 1945, Xian; s. of Luo Deyu and Tian Cuilan; m. Qi Juyan 1969; two s.; mem. China Artists' Asscn., Shaanxi Br.; Artist of Shaanxi Imperial Art Gallery (traditional Chinese painting); Vice-Pres. Changan Imperial Art Acad.; 2nd exhbn. of paintings, sponsored by China Art Gallery and Research Inst. of Traditional Chinese Painting, Beijing, Feb. 1988; third exhbn. Hubei Prov. 1991; 4th exhbn. Tabei City, Taiwan; Dir. Artistic Cttee. of China Artistic Asscn., Shaanxi Br.; Excellent Works Prize, Beijing 1988, Copper Medal of 7th Nat. Artistic Works-Exhbn. 1989. *Publication:* The Collection of Luo Pingan's Painting. *Leisure interests:* literature, fork art, countryside and music. *Address:* 32 North Street, Xian, Shaanxi Province, People's Republic of China. *Telephone:* 2-5333.

LUO SHANGCAI; Chinese state and party official; b. 1929, Zhengning Co., Guizhou Prov.; joined CCP 1954; alt. mem. 12th CCP Cen. Cttee. 1982, 13th Cen. Cttee. 1987; First Sec. CCP Cttee., South Guizhou Buyi and Miao Autonomous Pref. 1982–; Vice-Gov., Guizhou Prov. 1983–88; Vice-Chair. Guizhou Prov. People's Congress 1988–93; mem. Nationalities Cttee.; Deputy for Guizhou to 6th NPC 1983; mem. 8th NPC 1993–. *Address:* Guizhou Provincial People's Government, Guiyang, Guizhou, People's Republic of China.

LUO YUANZHENG, PH.D.; Chinese university professor; b. 14 Feb. 1924, Chengdu, Sichuan Prov.; s. of Zhungi Luo and Suqing You; m. Lida Feng

1947; one s. one d.; ed. West Union Univ. Chengdu, Univ. of Calif., St. Olife Coll. (U.S.A.) and Univ. of Leningrad; Sec. Econ. Dept. Scientific Planning Cttee. State Council 1956–57; Dir. Co-ordination Office for Econ. Affairs, State Planning Comm. 1978–80; Deputy Dir. and Research Fellow, Inst. of World Econs. and Politics, Chinese Acad. of Social Sciences 1978–83; mem. Econ. Research Centre, State Council 1980–84; Exec. Chair. Sec. and Founder, All-China Union of Asscns. for Econ. Studies 1981–84; Visiting Prof. Australian Nat. Univ. 1981; Prof. Beijing Univ. (and a dozen other Chinese univs.) 1981–; sr. adviser to several provs. and municipalities 1981–; Pres. Chinese Correspondence Univ. of Econ. Sciences 1984–88; Prof. European Man. School, Paris 1988; other professional appts., editorships etc.; Vice-Pres. Int. Econ. Asscn. 1989–92; Pres. China Int. Cultural Educ. Inst. 1992–; Chair. Econ. Forum of Hong Kong 1992; mem. Academic Advisory Bd. Int. Centre for Econ. Growth (ICEG) 1992–; mem. CPPCC 1986–, mem. Econ. Cttee. 1986–; Gen. Adviser to China Chamber of Commerce; Dir. Asia Pacific Bd. of Lucas; recipient of awards of State Council, Ministry of Higher Educ. etc. *Publications include:* On an Economic Community in the Pacific Region 1981, Impact of Socio-Economic Model on Education, Science and Culture 1983, Internationalization of Economic Life and China's Policy of Opening to the Outside World 1984, World Economy and China, On the Developmental Strategy Problems of an Economic Society 1986, Structural Reform and Economic Development in China 1989, Selected Works of Luo Yuangheng, The New Phase of China's Economic Development and Prospects for the New Century; papers on China's economy, world econ. devt. etc. *Leisure interests:* music, Chinese classical poetry and verse. *Address:* 10-7-41 Xibianmenwai Dajei, 100045, Beijing, People's Republic of China. *Telephone:* 8523152 (Office); 8312308 (Home). *Fax:* 8534865 (Office); 8312308 (Home).

LUPERTZ, Markus; German artist and professor; b. 25 April 1941, Liberec, Bohemia; ed. Werkkunstschule, Krefeld, Kunstakademie, Dusseldorf, Villa Romana, Florence; Prof. State Acad. of Fine Arts, Karlsruhe 1976, Prof. and Dir. Acad. of Art, Düsseldorf 1986–; numerous exhbns.; Villa Romana Prize 1970, Prize of Deutschen Kritikerverband, Esslingen Artists' Guild 1990. *Publications:* Selected Poems 1961–83. *Address:* c/o Galerie Michael Werner, Gertrudenstrasse 24-28, 5000 Cologne 1, Germany. *Telephone:* (02 21) 92 54 62.

LUPU, Radu, M.A.; Romanian pianist; b. 30 Nov. 1945, Galaţi; s. of Meyer Lupu and Ana Gabor; ed. High School, Braşov, Moscow Conservatoire, U.S.S.R.; first piano lessons 1951; won scholarship to Moscow 1961; entered Moscow Conservatoire 1963, graduated 1969; First Prize, Van Cliburn Competition 1966; First Prize, Enescu Int. Competition, Bucharest 1967; First Prize, Leeds Int. Competition 1969; a leading interpreter of the German classical composers; appears frequently with all the major orchestras; has toured Eastern Europe with London Symphony Orchestra; American debut 1972; gave world première of André Tchaikowsky Piano Concerto, London 1975; Grammy Award for Best Instrumental Record of Year (for Schubert record) 1995, Edison Award for Best Instrumental Record of Year (for Schumann record) 1995. *Recordings include:* complete Beethoven cycle (with Israel Philharmonic and Zubin Mehta), complete Mozart sonatas for violin and piano with Szymon Goldberg), Brahms piano concerto No. 1 (with Edo de Waart and London Philharmonic Orchestra), Mozart piano concerto K467 (with Uri Segal and English Chamber Orchestra), various Beethoven and Schubert sonatas, Mozart and Beethoven wind quintets in E flat, Mozart concerto for 2 pianos and concerto for 3 pianos transcribed for 2 pianos (with Murray Perahia and English Chamber Orchestra), Schubert Fantasie in F minor and Mozart sonata in D for 2 pianos (with Murray Perahia), Schubert Lieder (with Barbara Hendricks), Schubert Piano Duets (with Daniel Barenboim). *Leisure interests:* history, chess, bridge. *Address:* c/o Terry Harrison Artists, The Orchard, Market Street, Charlbury, Oxon., OX7 3PJ, England. *Telephone:* (01608) 810330. *Fax:* (01608) 811331.

LURAGHI, Giuseppe; Italian business executive; b. 12 June 1905, Milan; s. of Felice Luraghi and Giuditta Talamona; m. Maria Magdalena Poli 1927; two s. three d.; ed. Univ. Commerciale Luigi Bocconi, Milan; started career in textile industry; with Pirelli Group 1930–50; Gen. Man. Finmeccanica Group 1951–56, and Dir. several subsid. and affiliated cos.; Chair. and Man. Dir. Lanerossi S.p.A. 1956–60; Chair. Bd. of Dirs. Alfa Romeo S.p.A., Milan 1960–74, COGIS (Compagnia Generale Interscambi 1960–73, SICA 1967–74, Alfa Romeo-ALFASUD 1968–74, Necchi S.p.A. 1974–79, SOFIST (Società Finanziazia Sviluppo Tessile) 1975–80, Mondadori Editore S.p.A. 1977–83, Finservizi S.p.A. 1980; Dir. Club degli Editori 1980–82. *Publications:* Le macchine della libertà, Capi si diventa, Due Milanesi alle piramidi, Miracolo a Porta Ticinese, Castelli di Carte. *Address:* Via Revere 2, 20123 Milan, Italy. *Telephone:* 02-436984.

LURIE, Alison, A.B.; American novelist; b. 3 Sept. 1926, Chicago; d. of Harry Lawrence and Bernice Stewart Lurie; m. Jonathon Peale Bishop 1948 (divorced 1985); three s.; ed. Radcliffe Coll.; lecturer in English, Cornell Univ. 1969–73, Adjunct Assoc. Prof. 1973–76, Assoc. Prof. 1976–79, Prof. 1979–; Yaddo Foundation Fellow 1963, 1964, 1966, 1984, Guggenheim Fellow 1965, Rockefeller Foundation Fellow 1967; Literature Award, American Acad. of Arts and Letters 1978, Pulitzer Prize in Fiction 1985. *Publications:* V. R. Lang: a Memoir 1959, Love and Friendship 1962, The Nowhere City 1965, Imaginary Friends 1967, Real People 1969, The War Between the Tates 1974, Only Children 1979, The Language of Clothes 1981, Foreign Affairs 1985, The Man with a Shattered World 1987, The Truth about Lorin Jones 1988, Don't Tell the Grown Ups; Subversive Children's Literature (essays) 1990, Women and Ghosts 1994, The Last Resort 1998. *Address:* Department of English, Cornell University, Ithaca, New York, NY 14853, U.S.A.

LURIE, Ranan Raymond; American political cartoonist; b. 26 May 1932, Port Said, Egypt; s. of Joseph and Rose (Sam) Lurie (parents Israeli citizens); m. Tamar Fletcher 1958; two s. two d.; ed. Herzelia Coll., Tel-Aviv, and Jerusalem Art Coll.; Corresp. Maariv Daily 1950–52; Features Ed. Hador Daily 1953–54; Ed.-in-Chief Tavel (weekly magazine) 1954–55; staff political cartoonist Yedioth Aharonot Daily 1955–66, Honolulu Advertiser 1979; went to U.S.A. (invited by Life Magazine) 1968, naturalized 1974; political cartoonist, Life Magazine, New York 1968–73; political cartoonist interviewer Die Welt, Bonn 1980–81; Contrib. New York Times 1970–; Contrib. Ed. and political cartoonist, Newsweek Int. 1974–76; Ed., political cartoonist, Vision Magazine of S. America 1974–76; syndicated United Features Syndicate 1971–73; syndicated nationally by Los Angeles Times and internationally by New York Times to over 260 newspapers 1973–75; syndicated nationally by King Features Syndicate, internationally by Editors Press Syndicate (345 newspapers) 1975–83, in U.S.A. by Universal Press Syndicate 1982–86; lecturer, Univ. of Hawaii, American Program Bureau, Boston; political cartoonist, The Times, London 1981–83; Sr. Political Analyst and cartoonist, The Asahi Shimbun, Tokyo 1983–84; Sr. Analyst and political cartoonist, U.S. News and World Report, Washington 1984–85; political cartoonist Time Magazine 1994–97; Ed.-in-Chief Cartoon News 1996–; Chief Editorial Dir. Editors' Press Service 1985; inventor of first animated electronic television news cartoon; joined MacNeil/Lehrer News Hour as daily political cartoonist/analyst, appearing on 275 TV stations; Nightline (ABC TV network programme), and ZDF (German nat. TV); launched TV cartoon nationally; creator of Taiwan's official new nat. cartoon symbol "Cousin Lee"; cr. Japan's nat. cartoon symbol "Taro San"; TV Cartoon launched by ABC (USA) and ZDF (Germany); fine arts shows in Israel, Canada, U.S.A. 1960–75, including Expo 1967, Canada, Dominion Gallery, Montreal, Canada, Lim Gallery, Tel Aviv 1965, Overseas Press Club, New York 1962, 1964, 1975, U.S. Senate, Washington, Honolulu Acad. Fine Arts 1979; exhibited in numerous group shows including Smithsonian Inst. 1972; trained as Parachute Officer, French Foreign Legion 1955, served as Combat Paratroop Maj., Israeli Army Reserve 1950–67; Sr. Adjunct Fellow with The Center for Strategic and Int. Studies, Washington, D.C.; mem. Asscn. of Editorial Cartoonists, Nat. Cartoonists' Soc. of America; Hon. Assoc. mem. Asahi Shimbun; mem. MENSA, Nat. Cartoonist Soc. of America; Nat. Fed. of Hispanic-owned Papers est. Ranan R. Lurie Political Cartoon Award 1994; syndicated internationally to 1,098 papers in 104 countries; listed in Guinness Book of World Records as most widely syndicated political cartoonist in the world (Certificate of Merit for 10 years as Consecutive title holder); Chief Judge Seoul Int. Cartoon Competition 1996; recipient highest Israeli journalism award 1954; U.S. Headliners Award 1972; named Outstanding Editorial Cartoonist of Nat. Cartoonist Soc. 1972–78; Salon Award, Montreal Cartoon 1971; New York Front Page Award 1972, 1974, 1977, certificate of Merit of U.S. Publication Designers 1974, Hon. mention Overseas Press Club 1979, winner of John Fischetti Political Cartoon Award 1982, Toastmasters' Int. and Leadership Award 1985, UN Soc. of Writers Award for Excellence 1995, Hubert H. Humphrey First Amendment Freedoms Prize 1996. *Publications:* Among the Suns 1952, Lurie's Best Cartoons (Israel) 1961, Nixon Rated Cartoons (New York Times) 1973, Pardon Me, Mr. President (New York Times) 1974, Lurie's Worlds (U.S.A.) 1980, So sieht es Lurie (Germany) 1981, Lurie's Almanac (U.K.) 1982, (U.S.A.) 1983, Taro's International Politics, Taro-San No Kokusai Seijigaku (Japan) 1984, Lurie's Middle East 1986, Lurie's Mideast Almanac (Israel) 1986, Lurie's Fareast Views (China) 1987; creator The Expandable Painting 1969. *Address:* Cartoonews Inc., 9 Mountain Laurel Drive, Greenwich, CT 06831, U.S.A. *Telephone:* (203) 622-1994.

LUSCOMBE, David Edward, LITT.D., F.B.A., F.S.A., F.R.HIST.S.; British historian; b. 22 July 1938, London; s. of Edward Dominic Luscombe and Nora Luscombe; m. Megan Phillips 1960; three s. one d.; ed. St. Michael's Convent School, Finchley Catholic Grammar School, London and King's Coll., Cambridge; Fellow, King's Coll. 1962–64, Churchill Coll., Cambridge 1964–72; Prof. of Medieval History, Univ. of Sheffield 1972–95, Leverhulme Personal Research Prof. of Medieval History 1995–, Dean of Faculty of Arts 1985–87, Pro-Vice-Chancellor 1990–94, Chair. Humanities Research Inst. 1992–, Dir. for Research in the Humanities Div. of Grad. School 1994–; mem. Governing Body, later the Asscn. of St. Edmund's House, Cambridge 1971–84; Dir. Historical Asscn. Summer School 1976, 1992; Visiting Prof. Royal Soc. of Canada 1991, Univ. of Conn. at Storrs 1993; Visiting Fellow All Souls Coll. Oxford 1994; Raleigh Lecturer, at British Acad. 1988; British Acad. Exchange Visitor to Japan Acad. 1996; mem. Council, British Acad. 1989–97, Publs. Sec. 1990–97, Chair. Medieval Texts Editorial Cttee. 1991–; mem. Publs. Cttee. (Chair. 1990–97), mem. Humanities Research Bd. 1994–96; mem. Cttee., Soc. for Study of Medieval Languages and Literature 1991–96, Council, Royal Historical Soc. 1981–85, Cttee., Ecclesiastical History Soc. 1976–79, Supervisory Cttee. British Acad./Oxford Univ. Press for New Dictionary of Nat. Biography 1992–, Assoc. Ed. 1993–; Vice-Pres. Société int. pour l'étude de la philosophie médiévale 1987–97, Pres. 1997–; mem. Commonwealth Scholarships Comm. in U.K. 1994–; Auditor, Higher Educ. Quality Council, Div. of Quality Audit 1994–97; mem. Council Worksop Coll. and Ranby House; Hon. Sec. Cambridge Univ. Catholic Asscn. 1968–70.

Publications: The School of Peter Abelard, Peter Abelard's Ethics, Church and Government in the Middle Ages (Jt. Ed.) 1976, Petrus Abaelardus (1079–1142): Person, Werk, und Wirkung (Jt. Ed.) 1980, The Evolution of Medieval Thought by David Knowles (Ed. revised edn. with C. Brooke) 1988, David Knowles Remembered (Co-author) 1991, Anselm, Aosta, Bec and Canterbury (Jt. Ed.) 1996, Medieval Thought 1997; Cambridge Studies in Medieval Life and Thought, 4th series (Advisory Ed.) 1983–88, (Gen. Ed.) 1988–; articles in learned journals. *Leisure interests:* swimming, walking a spaniel, using libraries. *Address:* Department of History, The University, Sheffield, S10 2TN; 4 Caxton Road, Sheffield, S10 3DE, England (Home). *Telephone:* (01142) 222559 (Office); (01142) 686355 (Home). *Fax:* (01142) 788304.

LUSINCHI, Jaime; Venezuelan politician and paediatrician; b. 27 May 1924, Clarines, Anzoátegui; m. Gladys Castillo (divorced 1988); five c.; ed. Univ. del Oriente, Univ. Central; active mem. Acción Democrática (AD) Party 1941–; Pres. Legis. Ass. for Anzoátegui and regional Gen. Sec. 1948–52; arrested during presidency of Gen. Marcos Pérez Jiménez; in exile in Argentina, Chile and U.S.A. 1952–58; returned to Venezuela 1958; mem Rómulo Betancourt's electoral comm. 1958, mem. Nat. Exec. Ctte. of AD 1958, Dir. Int. Affairs 1958–61, Deputy for Anzoátegui 1959–67, Pres. Parl. Gp. 1968–78, Senator for Anzoátegui 1979–83, Presidential Cand. 1977, Sec.-Gen. AD 1980–83, Party Leader 1980–84; Pres. of Venezuela 1984–89; Senator 1989; Paediatrician, Lincoln Hosp., Bellevue Medical Centre, New York 1958; mem. American Acad. of Pediatrics. *Address:* c/o Palacio de Miraflores, Avenida Urdaneta, Caracas 1010, Venezuela.

LUSSER, Markus, D.IUR.; Swiss central banker (retd.); b. 8 April 1931, Altdorf, Uri; m. Elisabeth Degen 1965; one s.; ed. Univs. of Berne and Paris; Sec. (later Dir.) Swiss Bankers' Asscn., Basel 1958–75, Dir. 1976–78, Del., Admin. Bd. 1979–80; mem. Governing Bd., Swiss Nat. Bank, Zürich 1981–84; mem. and Vice-Chair. Gov. Bd. Swiss Nat. Bank, Berne 1985–88; Chair. Governing Bd. Swiss Nat. Bank, Zürich 1988–96; mem. Bd. of Dirs. BIS 1988–96; Gov., IMF, Washington, DC 1992–96. *Address:* c/o Schweizerische Nationalbank, Börsenstrasse 15, 8022 Zürich, Switzerland.

LÜST, Reimar, DR.RER.NAT.; German physicist; b. 25 March 1923, Barmen; s. of Hero and Grete (née Strunck) Lüst; m. 1st Dr. Rhea Kulka 1953; two s.; 2nd Nina Grunenberg 1986; ed. Univs. of Frankfurt/M and Göttingen; Research Physicist, Max Planck Insts. Göttingen and Munich 1950–60, Enrico Fermi Inst., Univ. of Chicago 1955–56, Princeton Univ. 1956; Head, Dept. for Extraterrestrial Physics, Max Planck Inst. for Physics and Astrophysics 1960, Dir. Inst. of Extraterrestrial Physics 1963–72; Visiting Prof., Univ. of New York 1959, M.I.T. 1961, Calif. Inst. of Tech. 1962, 1966; Chair. German Research Council 1969–72, Deutsche Gesellschaft für Luft- und Raumfahrt 1968–72; Pres. Max-Planck-Gesellschaft 1972–84; Dir. Gen. European Space Agency 1984–90; Prof. Univ. of Hamburg 1992–; Pres. Alexander Von Humboldt Foundation 1989–; Hon. Prof. Inst. for Theoretical Physics, Chinese Acad. of Sciences, Beijing 1997, Beijing Univ. 1997; mem. Int. Acad. of Astronautics, Royal Astronomical Soc., Bavarian Acad. Sciences; Hon. Foreign mem. American Acad. of Arts and Sciences, Austrian Acad. of Sciences; Hon. mem. Heidelberg Acad. of Sciences, Senat Max-Planck-Gesellschaft, Deutsche Gesellschaft für Luft- und Raumfahrt; Corresp. mem. Real Acad. de Ciencias Exactas, Físicas y Naturales de Madrid; Fellow Imperial Coll. of Science and Tech.; Hon. Dr. (Sofia) 1991, (Birmingham) 1993, (Slovak Acad. of Sciences) 1995, and several other hon. degrees from int. univs.; Planet 4386 named Lüst 1991; Daniel and Florence Guggenheim Int. Astronautics Award, Personality of the Year 1986, Tsiolkowsky Medal (U.S.S.R. Fed. of Cosmonauts) 1987, Harnack Medal of Max Planck Soc. 1993; and numerous other awards; shared Adenauer-de Gaulle Prize 1994; Officier Ordre des Palmes Académiques; Officier, Légion d'honneur; Bayerischer Maximiliansorden für Wissenschaft und Kunst; Grosses Verdienstkreuz mit Stern und Schulterband des Verdienstordens der Bundesrepublik Deutschland; Distinguished Service Cross (Poland) 1997. *Publications:* articles on space research, astrophysics and plasmaphysics. *Leisure interests:* history, tennis, skiing. *Address:* Max-Planck-Institut für Meteorologie, Bundesstrasse 55, 20146 Hamburg, Germany. *Telephone:* (040) 41173-300. *Fax:* (040) 41173-390.

LUSTIG, Arnošt; Czech writer; b. 21 Dec. 1926, Prague; s. of Emil and Terezie Lustig (née Löwy); m. Věra Weislitz 1949; one s. one d.; ed. Coll. of Political and Social Sciences, Prague; in concentration camps at Terezín, Auschwitz and Buchenwald, Second World War; Radio Prague corresp. in Arab-Israeli war 1948, 1949; Radio Prague reporter 1948–58; Ed. Mladý svět (weekly) 1958–59, screenplay writer for Studio Barandov 1960–68, for Jadran-Film Yugoslavia 1969–70; naturalized American citizen 1979; mem. Cen. Cttee. Union of Czechoslovak Writers 1963–69, mem. Presidium 1963–69; mem. Int. Writing Program 1970–71; Visiting Lecturer Univ. of Iowa 1971–72; Visiting Prof. Drake Univ., Iowa 1972–73; Prof. of Literature and Film, American Univ., Washington, D.C. 1973–; Hon. Pres. Franz Kafka Soc., Prague 1990–; Hon. Dr. Hebrew Letters, Spertus Coll. of Judaica, Chicago 1986; Klement Gottwald State Prize 1967, B'nai B'rith Prize 1974, Nat. Jewish Book Award 1980, 1986, Emmy, The Nat. Acad. of Television Arts and Sciences 1986, Publrs.' Weekly Literary Prize, U.S.A. 1991, Karel Čapek Literary Prize, Prague PEN Club Int. 1996. *Publications:* Démanty noci (Diamonds of the Night—short stories, two of which were filmed 1961, 1964) 1958, Blue Day (story, filmed for TV) 1960, remade 1995, Night and Hope (short stories) 1958, filmed as Transport z ráje (Transport from Paradise) 1962, Modlitba za Kateřinu Horovitzovou (A Prayer for Katerina Horovitzova—novel, filmed for TV) 1965, Dita Saxova (novel) 1962 (filmed 1968, republished 1994), The Street of Lost Brothers (short stories) 1962, Prague Crossroads 1964, The Man the Size of a Stamp 1965 (radio plays), Nobody will be Humiliated (long stories) 1965, The White Birches in Autumn (novel) 1966, Bitter Smell of Almonds (novel) 1968, Darling (novel) 1969, Darkness Casts No Shadow (novel) 1976, Children of Holocaust (3 vols., collected stories) 1977–78, 1986, 1995, 1996, The Holocaust and the Film Arts (essay with Josef Lustig) 1980, The Precious Legacy (screenplay for documentary) 1984, The Unloved (from the diary of 17-year-old Pearl Sch.—novel) 1985, 1996, Indecent Dreams (collection of short novels) 1988, Street of Lost Brothers (collection of stories) 1990, Colette, Girl from Antwerp (novel, in Czech) 1993, Tanga, Girl from Hamburg (novel, in Czech) 1993, Porges (novel, in Czech) 1995, Friends (novel, in Czech) 1995, House of the Echo Returned (novel) 1995, Chasm (novel, in Czech) 1996, Beautiful Green Eyes (in Czech), in Jewish Yearbook 1997–1998, Fire on the Water (3 novellas) 1998; text for symphonic poem Night and Hope (with Otmar Macha) 1963, The Beadle of Prague (text for a cantata) 1983. *TV documentaries:* Names for which there are no people (Prague) 1960, Theresienstadt (Prague) 1965, Stolen Childhood (Italy) 1966, Triumph of Memory (PBS) 1984. *Film:* Europa (co-author; autobiographical documentary) 1998. *Leisure interests:* swimming, travelling, skiing, soccer. *Address:* 4000 Tunlaw Road N. W., Apartment 825, Washington, DC 20007, U.S.A. *Telephone:* (202) 338-5357. *Fax:* (202) 885-2938 (Office).

LUSTIGER, H.E. Cardinal Jean-Marie, M.PH., L. EN. THEOL.; French ecclesiastic; b. 17 Sept. 1926, Paris; s. of Charles and Gisèle Lustiger; ed. Carmelite Seminary, Inst. Catholique de Paris and Université de Paris (Sorbonne); ordained priest 1954; Chaplain to the students, Sorbonne 1954–69; Dir. Centre Richelieu, Paris 1959–69; Pastor, Sainte-Jeanne-de-Chantal parish, Paris 1969–79; Bishop of Orléans 1979–81; Archbishop of Paris Jan. 1981, cr. Cardinal Feb. 1983; mem. Académie Française. *Publications:* Sermons d'un curé de Paris 1978, Pain de vie, Peuple de Dieu 1981, Habt Vertrauen 1982, Osez vivre, Osez croire 1985, Premiers pas dans la prière 1986, Six sermons aux élus de la Nation 1986, The Mass 1987, Le choix de Dieu 1987, The Lord's Prayer 1988, La Messe 1988, Le Sacrement de l'Onction des malades 1990, Dieu merci, les droits de l'homme 1990, Nons avons rendez-vous avec l'Europe 1991, Petites paroles de nuit de Noël 1992, Devenez dignes de la condition humaine 1995, Le Baptême de votre enfant 1997, Soyez heureux 1997. *Address:* Maison diocésaine, 8 rue de la Ville-l'Evêque, 75384 Paris cedex 08, France.

LUSZTIG, George, M.A., PH.D., F.R.S.; American professor of mathematics; b. 20 May 1946, Timisoara, Romania; m. Michal-Nina Abraham 1972; two d.; ed. Univ. of Bucharest and Princeton Univ.; Visiting mem. Inst. for Advanced Study, Princeton, N.J. 1969–71; Research Fellow, Dept. of Math., Univ. of Warwick 1971–72, Lecturer 1972-74, Prof. 1974-78; Prof. of Math. M.I.T. 1978–; mem. N.A.S.; Guggenheim Fellowship 1982; Cole Prize in Algebra (American Math. Soc.) 1985. *Publications:* The Discrete Series of GLn over a Finite Field, 1974, Characters of Reductive Groups over a Finite Field 1984, Introduction to Quantum Groups 1993. *Address:* Department of Mathematics, Massachusetts Institute of Technology, Room 2276, 77 Massachusetts Avenue, Cambridge, MA 02139 (Office); 106 Grant Avenue, Newton, MA 02159, U.S.A.

LUTON, Jean-Marie; French engineer; b. 4 Aug. 1942, Chamalières; s. of Pierre Luton and Marie Luton; m. Cécile Robine 1967; three s.; ed. Lycée Blaise Pascal, Clermont-Ferrand, Lycée Saint Louis, Paris, Faculté des Sciences, Paris and Ecole Polytechnique; Centre National de la Recherche Scientifique (CNRS) 1964–71; Ministry of Industrial and Scientific Devt. 1971–73; Head of Research, Centre Nat. d'Etudes Spatiales (CNES) 1974–75, Head of Planning 1975–78, Dir. of Programmes and Planning 1978–84, Deputy Dir.-Gen. 1984–87; Dir. of Space Programmes, Aérospatiale 1987–89; Dir.-Gen. CNES 1989–90; Dir.-Gen. European Space Agency 1990–97; Pres., Dir.-Gen. Arianespace 1997–; Chevalier, Légion d'honneur, Officier, Ordre nat. du Mérite; Prix de l'Astronautique; Prix de l'Innovateur industriel, Society of Satellite Professionals (U.S.A.) 1998. *Leisure interests:* tennis, sailing. *Address:* Arianespace, boulevard de l'Europe, B.P. 177, 91006 Evry cedex, France.

LUTTER, Marcus Michael, PH.D.; German professor of law; b. 11 Dec. 1930, Munich; s. of Michael Lutter; m. Rebecca Garbe 1957; one s. two d.; ed. Univs. of Munich, Paris and Freiburg-i-Br.; notary, Rockenhausen 1957–60; research scholarship, Deutsche Forschungsgesellschaft, Brussels, Strasbourg, Paris, Rome, Utrecht 1961–63; notary, Rockenhausen and external lecturer, Univ. of Mainz 1964–65; Prof. Inst. for Civil Law, German and European Trade and Econ. Law, Univ. of Bochum 1966–79; now Prof. and Dir. Inst. for Trade and Econ. Law, Univ. of Bonn; Visiting Prof. Univ. of Calif. Berkeley 1972, Oxford Univ. 1997; Pres. German Lawyers' Asscn. 1982–88; Hon. Ph.D. (Vienna). *Publications:* The Letter of Intent 1983, Information and Confidentiality in the Supervisory Board 1984, Duties and Rights of Board Members 1993, European Company Law 1995; various monographs and treatises especially on participation, jt.-stock cos. and supervisory bds; Publr. Zeitschrift für Unternehmens-und Gesellschaftsrecht. *Address:* Institut für Handels- und Wirtschaftsrecht der Universität Bonn, Adenauerallee 24-42, 53113 Bonn (Office); Auf der Steige 6, 53129 Bonn, Germany (Home). *Telephone:* 0228-739112 (Office); 0228-73 95 59 (Home). *Fax:* 0228-739111.

LUTTWAK, Edward Nicolae, PH.D.; American academic, international consultant and writer; b. 4 Nov. 1942, Arad, Romania; s. of Joseph Luttwak and Clara Baruch; m. Dalya Iaari 1970; one s. one d.; ed. elementary schools in Palermo and Milan, Carmel Coll., Wallingford, U.K., London School of Econs. and Johns Hopkins Univ.; Lecturer, Univ. of Bath, U.K. 1965–67; Consultant, Walter J. Levy S.A. (London) 1967–68; Visiting Prof. Johns Hopkins Univ. 1974–76; Sr. Fellow, Georgetown Univ. Center for Strategic and Int. Studies 1977–87; Burke Chair. of Strategy, at Center for Strategic and Int. Studies, Washington D.C. 1987–; Consultant to Office of Sec. of Defense 1975, to Policy Planning Council, Dept. of State 1981, Nat. Security Council 1987, Dept. of Defense 1987, to Govts. of Italy, Korea, Spain; Prin., Edward N. Luttwak Inc. Int. Consultants 1981–; Int. Assoc. Inst. of Fiscal and Monetary Policy, Japan Ministry of Finance (Okurasho); mem. editorial Bd. of The American Scholar, Journal of Strategic Studies, The National Interest, Géopolitique, The Washington Quarterly, Orbis. *Publications:* Coup d'Etat 1968, Dictionary of Modern War 1972, The Israeli Army 1975, The Political Uses of Sea Power 1976, The Grand Strategy of the Roman Empire 1978, Strategy and Politics: Collected Essays 1979, The Grand Strategy of the Soviet Union 1983, The Pentagon and the Art of War 1985, Strategy and History: collected essays 1985, International Security Yearbook 1984/85 (with Barry M. Brechman) 1985, On the Meaning of Victory 1986, Strategy: The Logic of War and Peace 1987, The Dictionary of Modern War (with Stuart Koehl) 1991, The Endangered American Dream 1993, Il Fantasma della Povertà (co-author) 1996, Cose è davvero la Democrazia 1996, La Renaissance de la puissance aérienne stratégique 1998, Turbo-Capitalism 1999; books have been translated into 14 languages. *Leisure interests:* hunting, fishing. *Address:* CSIS, 1800 K Street, N.W., Washington, DC 20006, U.S.A. *Telephone:* (202) 775-3145. *Fax:* (202) 775-3199.

LUTZ, Robert A., M.B.A.; American business executive; b. 1932, Zürich, Switzerland; s. of Robert H. and Marguerite Lutz; m. 1st Betty D. Lutz 1956 (divorced 1979); m. 2nd Heide-Marie Schmid 1980 (divorced 1993); m. 3rd Denise Ford 1994; four d. from 1st marriage; ed. Univ. of Calif. (Berkeley); Capt. U.S. Marine Corps 1954–59; Research Assoc. IMEDE, Lausanne 1962–63; Senior Analyst, Forward Planning, Gen. Motors, New York 1963–65; Staff Asst., Man. Dir.'s Staff, Adam Opel AG (GM) 1965–66; various man. positions, GM (France) 1966–69; Asst. Domestic Gen. Sales Man., Merchandising, Adam Opel AG 1969, Dir. of Sales and mem. Management Bd. 1969–70; Vice-Pres. (Sales) and mem. Management Bd., BMW AG 1970–74; Gen. Man. Ford of Germany 1974–76; Vice-Pres. (Truck Operations), Ford of Europe 1976-77; Pres. Ford of Europe 1977–79; Vice-Pres. Ford Motor Co. and Chair. of Bd., Ford of Europe 1979–82; Exec. Vice-Pres. Ford Int. Automotive Operations 1982–86, Exec. Vice-Pres. N. American Truck Operations 1986; Head, Int. Operations Chrysler 1986–91, Chrysler Corpn. 1991–96, (now) Corpn. Vice-Chair. 1997–, Exec. Vice-Pres. 1986–88, Pres., Chrysler Motors Corpn. 1988–96, also C.O.O.; Bd. Divs. Silicon Graphics, ASCOM, Switzerland. *Address:* Chrysler Corporation, 1000 Chrysler Drive East, Auburn Hills, MI 48326, U.S.A.

LUX, Josef; Czech politician; b. 1 Feb. 1956, Usti nad Orlici; m.; six c.; ed. Agricultural Coll. Brno; Vice-Chair. for Environment of Parl. of Nations of Fed. Parl. of Czechoslovakia 1990–92; Chair. Czechoslovak Populist Party 1990; Chair. Christian and Democratic Union/Czechoslovak Populist Party 1992–98; Vice-Premier and Minister of Agriculture 1992–98; Chair. Presidium of the Land Fund 1993–; mem. Parl. 1996–. *Address:* KDU-ČSL, Karlovo nám. 5, 120 00 Prague 2, Czech Republic. *Telephone:* 24 91 47 93.

LUXEMBOURG, Grand Duke of (see Jean).

LUXON, Benjamin Matthew, C.B.E., F.G.S.M.; British musician; b. 24 March 1937, Redruth, Cornwall; s. of Maxwell Luxon and Lucille Grigg; m. Sheila Amit 1969; two s. one d.; ed. Truro School, Westminster Training Coll., Guildhall School of Music and Drama; always a freelance artist; sang with English Opera Group 1963–70; has sung with Royal Opera House, Covent Garden, and Glyndebourne Festival Opera 1971–, Boston Symphony Orchestra 1975–, Netherlands Opera 1976–, Frankfurt Opera House 1977–; performs as recitalist with piano accompanist David Willison; folk-singing partnership with Bill Grofut 1976–; has recorded for all major record cos.; Hon. mem. R.A.M.; Hon. D.Mus. (Exeter Univ.), (R.S.A. of Music and Drama) 1996, (Canterbury Christ Church Coll.) 1997; Bard of Cornish Gorseth. *Leisure interests:* most sports, English watercolours of 18th and 19th centuries. *Address:* The Mazet, Relubbus Lane, St. Hilary, Penzance, Cornwall TR20 9DS, England.

LUXTON, John, B.SC.; New Zealand politician; m.; three c.; ed. Massey Univ.; fmr. businessman, farmer and agricultural consultant; Nat. Party M.P. for Karapiro 1987–; Minister of Housing and Energy, Assoc. Minister of Educ. 1990–93, Minister of Police and Maori Affairs., Assoc. Minister of Educ. 1993–96, Minister of Commerce and for Industry 1996–98, Minister of Fisheries, of Lands, for Biosecurity, for Industry, Assoc. Minister of Trade, of Border Control, of Agric., Forestry, Fisheries, Land and Customs 1998–; fmr. Chair. Tatua Dairy Co., Deputy Chair. Wallford Meats Ltd. *Address:* House of Representatives, Wellington, New Zealand.

LUZHKOV, Yuri Mikhailovich; Russian politician; b. 21 Sept. 1936, Moscow; m.; two s. two d.; ed. Gubkin Inst. of Oil and Gas, Moscow; researcher, Research Inst. of Plastic Materials 1958–64; Head of Div. Ministry of Chemical Industry 1964–87; First Deputy Chair. Exec. Cttee., Moscow City Council and Chair. Moscow Agric. Industry Dept. 1987–90; Chair. Exec. Cttee., Moscow City Council 1990–91; Vice-Mayor of Moscow and Premier Moscow City Govt. 1991–92, Mayor and Head of City Govt. 1992–; mem. Russian Council of Fed. 1996–; Head Otechestvo (Fatherland) Movt. 1998–. *Publications:* 72 Hours of Agony 1991, The Quietist Negotiations 1994, We Are Your Children, Moscow 1996. *Leisure interests:* football, tennis. *Address:* Government of Moscow, Tverskaya str. 13, 103032 Moscow, Russia. *Telephone:* 200-54-45; 229-48-87. *Fax:* 299-70-90; 200-53-22.

LUZÓN LÓPEZ, Francisco; Spanish banker; b. 1 Jan. 1948, Cañavate (Cuenca); trainee, Banco de Vizcaya 1972, Regional Man. Seville 1974, Man. of Planning and Man. Control, Bilbão 1975–78, Int. Div. Madrid 1978–80, Man. London 1980–81; mem. Bd. and Gen. Man. Banco de Crédito Comercial 1981–82; mem. Bd. and Gen. Man. Banco Occidental 1982–85; Gen. Man. Commercial Banking Network 1985–87; mem. Bd. and Gen. Man. Banco de Vizcaya 1987–88, Banco Bilbão-Vizcaya 1988; Chair. Banco Exterior de España 1988–; Vice-Pres. Banco Atlántico and mem. Bd. Teneo 1991–94; Chair. Argentaria 1991, Caja Postal S.A. 1991–, Banco de Crédito Local 1994–, Banco Hipotecario de España 1994–, Corporación Bancaria de España S.A. *Address:* Paseo de Recoletos 10, 28001 Madrid, Spain. *Telephone:* 91/5377000. *Fax:* 91/5378034.

LUZZATTO, Lucio, F.R.C.PATH., F.R.C.P.; Italian geneticist and haematologist; b. 28 Sept. 1936, Genoa; s. of late Aldo Luzzatto and Anna Luzzatto Gabrielli; m. Paola Caboara 1963; one s. one d.; ed. Liceo D'Oria, Genoa, Univ. of Genoa Medical School, Univ. of Pavia; Sr. Lecturer in charge of Sub-Dept. of Haematology, Univ. of Ibadan, Nigeria 1967–68, Prof. of Haematology 1968–74, Consultant Haematologist, Univ. Coll. Hosp. Ibadan, Nigeria 1967–68; Dir. Int. Inst. of Genetics and Biophysics, CNR, Naples 1974–81; Prof. of Haematology (Univ. of London) and Dir. of Haematology Dept. Royal Postgrad. Medical School, Consultant Haematologist Hammersmith Hosp., London, U.K. 1981–94, Hon. Dir. MRC/LRF Leukaemia Unit, London 1987–93; Chair. Dept. of Human Genetics, Courtney Steel Chair., Attending Physician in Genetics and Haematology, mem. Cell Biology Program, Memorial Sloan-Kettering Cancer Center, New York, Prof. of Medicine and Human Genetics, Cornell Univ. Medical Coll., New York 1994–; Dr. h.c. of Pharmacy (Urbino) 1990; Pius XI Medal 1967, Sanremo Int. Prize for Human Genetics 1982, Int. Chiron Award for Biomedical Research 1995, Premio Napoli 1995. *Publications:* 260 articles in scientific journals; scientific and medical textbooks. *Address:* Department of Human Genetics, Memorial Sloan-Kettering Cancer Center, 1275 York Avenue, New York, NY 10021, U.S.A. *Telephone:* (212) 639-6165. *Fax:* (212) 717-3374.

LVOV, Dmitry Semenovich; Russian economist; b. 2 Feb, 1930; m.; two c.; ed. Moscow S. Ordzhonikidze Inst. of Eng. and Econ.; sr. researcher, head of lab., head of div. Moscow Inst. of Eng. and Econ., later Inst. of Econ. U.S.S.R. Acad. of Sciences; Deputy Dir. Cen. Inst. of Math. and Econ.; corresp. mem. U.S.S.R. (now Russian) Acad. of Sciences 1987, mem. 1994, Acad.-Sec. Dept. of Econs. 1996–; author of alternative econ. reform project Oct. 1998–; works on econ. efficiency of capital investments and new tech., pricing, prognosis of tech. processes; Pres. Int. Cen. for studies of econ. reforms. *Publications include:* Effective Management of Technical Development 1990. *Leisure interests:* poetry. *Address:* Central Institute of Mathematics and Economics, Krasikov str. 32, 117418 Moscow, Russia. *Telephone:* (095) 129-0822; (095) 129 1644 (Office).

LWIN, U; Myanma politician and diplomatist; b. 10 Dec. 1912; m.; two s. two d; fmr. officer, Burma army; Mil. Adviser, Burma Del. to UN Gen. Assembly 1953; Amb. to Fed. Germany 1966–71, also to Netherlands 1969–71; Perm. Rep. to UN 1971–72; Minister for Planning and Finance 1972–75, for Information 1975–77; Deputy Prime Minister 1974–77; withdrew from Cen. Cttee. of Burma Socialist Programme Party 1977; Gen. Sec. Nat. League for Democracy (NLD). *Address:* 97B West Shwegondine Road, Bahan Township, Yangon, Myanmar.

LYAKHOV, Vladimir Afanasyevich; Russian cosmonaut (retd.); b. 20 July 1941, Antratsit; ed. Kharkov Aviation School for Pilots, Gagarin Mil. Acad.; mem. CPSU 1963–91; served in fmr. Soviet Air Force 1964–; Cosmonaut 1967–; Commdr. of space-ship Soyuz-32, 1979, and Soyuz T-9 which connected up with orbital station Salyut-7; Commdr. Soyuz TM5-6 1988; space-walked 1983; Hero of Soviet Union (twice). *Address:* Yuriy Gagarin Centre, Zvezdny Gorodok, Moscow Region, Russia. *Telephone:* (095) 971-86-16.

LYAKISHEV, Nikolai Pavlovich; Russian metallurgist; b. 5 Oct. 1929; m.; two d.; ed. Moscow Inst. of Steel; researcher, then Head of Lab., Deputy Dir., Dir. Bardin Cen. Research Inst. of Black Metals; Dir. Baikov Inst. of Metallurgy, U.S.S.R. (now Russian) Acad. of Sciences; Corresp. mem. U.S.S.R. (now Russian) Acad. of Sciences 1981, mem. 1987, mem. Presidium 1991; Lenin Prize, U.S.S.R. State Prize. *Publications include:* main works in the field of metallurgy of steel and ferric alloys, construction materials, including Niobium in Black Metallurgy 1971, Aluminiumthermia 1978, Problems of Contemporary Metallurgy 1983, Physical and Chemical Studies of Low Waste Materials 1985. *Leisure interest:* chess. *Address:* Institute of Metallurgy, Leninsky prospect 49, 117911 Moscow, Russia (Office). *Telephone:* 135 2080 (Office).

LYELL, Sir Nicholas (Walter), Kt., P.C., Q.C.; British politician; b. 6 Dec. 1938; s. of late Sir Maurice Legat Lyell and Veronica Mary Lyell; m. Susanna Mary Fletcher 1967; two s. two d.; ed. Stowe School, Christ Church, Oxford;

nat. service R.A. 1957–59; Walter Runciman & Co. 1962–64; called to the Bar, Inner Temple 1965, Bencher 1986; pvt. practice London (Commercial and Industrial Law) 1965–86; a Recorder 1985–; Jt. Sec. Constitutional Cttee. 1979; M.P. for Hemel Hempstead 1979–83, for Mid Bedfordshire 1983–97, for Bedfordshire North East 1997–; Parl. Pvt. Sec. to Attorney Gen. 1979–86; Parl. Under-Sec. of State (Social Security) DHSS 1986–87; Solicitor Gen. 1987–92, Attorney Gen. 1992–97; Shadow Law Officer July 1997–; Chair. Soc. of Conservative Lawyers 1985–86 (Vice-Chair. 1982–85); Vice-Chair. British Field Sports Soc. 1983–86; Gov. Stowe School 1990–. *Leisure interests:* gardening, shooting, drawing. *Address:* House of Commons, London, SW1A 0AA, England.

LYGO, Adm. Sir Raymond Derek, K.C.B., F.R.AE.S., F.R.S.A., C.B.I.M.; British business executive; b. 15 March 1924, Ilford, Essex; s. of the late Edwin and of Ada E. Lygo; m. Pepper van Osten 1950; two s. one d.; ed. Ilford County High School and Clarkes Coll., Bromley; The Times 1940; naval airman, Royal Navy 1942; served V.S.N. 1949–51; C.O. 759 Squadron 1951–53, 800 Squadron 1954–56, H.M.S. Lowestoft 1959–61, H.M.S. Juno 1967–69, C.O. H.M.S. Ark Royal 1969–71; Vice-Chief of Naval Staff 1975–77, Chief of Naval Staff 1977–78; joined British Aerospace 1978, Man. Dir. Hatfield/Lostock Div. 1978–80, Chair. and Chief Exec. Dynamics Group 1980–82; Man. Dir. British Aerospace PLC 1983–86, mem. Bd. 1980–89, Chief Exec. 1985–89; Chair. British Aerospace Enterprises Ltd., British Aerospace (space systems) Ltd. and British Aerospace Holdings Inc. 1988–89, Rutland Trust PLC 1992–, TNT Express (U.K.) 1992–, TNT Europe Ltd. 1992–, River and Mercantile First UK Investment Trust 1997–; Dir. James Capel Corporate Finance 1990–92; Chair. Royal Ordnance PLC 1987; Pres. Soc. of British Aerospace Cos. 1984–85, Vice-Pres. 1985–; Patron Youth Sports Trust 1996–; Freeman City of London, Liveryman Coachmakers. *Leisure interests:* building, gardening, joinery. *Address:* c/o Barclays Premier Banking, 54 Lombard Street, London, EC3 9EX, England.

LYKKETOFT, Mogens; Danish politician; b. 9 Jan. 1946, Copenhagen; ed. Univ. of Copenhagen; worked at Econ. Council of the Labour Movt. 1966–81, Head of Dept. 1975–81; mem. Folketing 1981–, Political Spokesman for Social Democratic Party 1991–93; Minister for Inland Revenue 1981; Minister of Finance 1993–. *Publications:* ed. of several books and numerous articles in magazines, periodicals and newspapers. *Address:* Ministry of Finance, Christiansborg Slotspladi 1, 1218 Copenhagen K, Denmark.

LYMAN, Princeton, PH.D.; American diplomatist; b. 20 Nov. 1935, San Francisco; s. of Arthur Lyman and Gertrude Lyman; m. Helen Ermann 1957; three d.; ed. Univ. of Calif. Berkeley and Harvard Univ.; joined U.S. govt. service 1961; Agency for Int. Devt. 1961–80; Dir USAID, Addis Ababa 1976–78; Dept. of State 1980–; Deputy Asst. Sec. for Africa 1981–86; Amb. to Nigeria 1986–89, to South Africa 1992–95; Dir. Bureau of Refugee Programs 1989–92; Asst. Sec. of State for Int. Org. Affairs Dec. 1995–; Bd. Divs. American Foreign Service Asscn.; Dept. of State Superior Honor Award; Pres.'s Distinguished Service Award. *Publications include:* Korean Development: The Interplay of Politics and Economics 1971. *Leisure interests:* tennis, photography, piano. *Address:* Bureau of International Organizations, 2201 C Street, N.W., Washington, DC 20520, U.S.A.

LYMPANY, Dame Moura, D.B.E., F.R.A.M.; British concert pianist; b. 18 Aug. 1916, Saltash, Cornwall; d. of John Johnstone and Beatrice Lympany; m. 1st Colin Defries 1944 (divorced 1950); m. 2nd Bennet H. Korn 1951 (divorced 1961); one s. (deceased); ed. Belgium, Austria, England; first performance, Harrogate 1929; has played in U.S.A., Canada, South America, Australia, New Zealand, India and most European countries including the U.S.S.R.; started Festival de la Musique et du Vin, (Rasiguères France) 1981, Le Festival des Sept Chapelles (Brittany), 1986; Medal of Cultural Merit (Portugal) 1989, Charles Heidsieck Prize (Royal Philharmonic Soc.) 1989; Commdr. Order of Crown (Belgium) 1980, Chevalier des Arts et des Lettres (France) 1992. *Publication:* Autobiography 1991. *Leisure interests:* gardening, reading, tapestry. *Address:* c/o Transart, 8 Bristol Gardens, London, W9 2JG, England.

LYNAM, Desmond Michael, A.C.I.I.; British sports broadcaster; b. 17 Sept. 1942; s. of Edward Lynam and Gertrude Veronica Malone; m. Susan Eleanor Skinner (dissolved 1974); one s.; ed. Varndean Grammar School, Brighton, Brighton Business Coll.; career in insurance –1967; freelance journalist and reporter local radio 1967–69; reporter, presenter and commentator BBC Radio 1969–78; presenter and commentator BBC TV Sport 1978– (including Grandstand, Sportsnight, Match of the Day, Commonwealth and Olympic Games and World Cup coverage); presenter Holiday (BBC) 1988–, How Do They Do That? (BBC) 1994–; TV Sports Presenter of the Year, TRIC 1985, 1987, 1988, 1992, 1997; Radio Times Male TV Personality 1989, RTS Sports Presenter of the Year 1994, Richard Dimbleby Award, B.A.F.T.A. 1995. *Publications:* Guide to the Commonwealth Games 1986, The 1988 Olympics 1988, The 1992 Olympics 1992. *Leisure interests:* golf, tennis, Brighton and Hove Albion, reading, theatre. *Address:* c/o BBC Television Centre, Wood Lane, London, W12 7RJ, England.

LYNCH, David; American film director; b. 20 Jan. 1946, Missoula, Mont.; m. 1st Peggy Reavey 1967 (divorced); one d.; m. 2nd Mary Fisk 1977 (divorced); one s.; ed. Hammond High School, Alexandria, Corcoran School of Art, Washington, D.C., School of Museum of Fine Arts, Boston and Pennsylvania Acad. of Fine Arts, Philadelphia; Fellow, Center for Advanced Film Studies, American Film Inst., Los Angeles 1970; Dr. h.c. (Royal Coll. of Art) 1991. *Films include:* The Grandmother 1970, Eraserhead 1977, The Elephant Man 1980, Dune 1984, Blue Velvet 1986 (Golden Palm, Cannes), Wild at Heart 1990 (Golden Palm, Cannes 1990), Storyville 1991, Twin Peaks: Fire Walk With Me 1992, Lost Highway 1997, Crumb (presenter); *TV includes:* Twin Peaks 1990. *Address:* c/o CAA, 9830 Wilshire Boulevard, Beverly Hills, CA 90212, U.S.A.

LYNCH, John Mary, B.L.; Irish politician and lawyer; b. 15 Aug. 1917, Cork; s. of Daniel Lynch and Norah O'Donoghue; m. Mairin O'Connor 1946; ed. North Monastery, Cork, Univ. Coll., Cork, and King's Inns, Dublin; mem. Civil Service (Dept. of Justice) 1936–45; called to Bar 1945; mem. of Dáil Éireann (Parl.) 1948–81; Alderman, Cork Corpn. 1950–57; Parl. Sec. to Govt. and to Minister for Lands 1951–54; Minister for Educ. 1957–59; Minister for Industry and Commerce 1959–65, for Finance 1965–66; Vice-Pres. Council of Europe 1958, Pres. European Council (EEC) July-Dec. 1979; Pres. Int. Labour Conf. 1962; Taoiseach (Prime Minister) 1966–73, 1977–79; Pres. Fianna Fáil (Republican Party) 1966–79; Leader of the Opposition 1973–77; Dir. Irish Distillers Group 1980–86, Jefferson Smurfit Group PLC 1980–92, Algemene Bank Nederland (Ireland) Ltd. 1980–87, Hibernian Insurance PLC 1980–89; Chair. Galway Irish Crystal 1984; Hon. LL.D. (Dublin Univ.) 1967, (Nat. Univ. of Ireland) 1969, Hon. D.C.L. (Belmont Abbey, Univ. Coll., N. Carolina, U.S.A.) 1971, (Rhode Island Coll.) 1981, (Limerick) 1995; Freeman City of Cork 1980; Grand Cross of Belgian Order of the Crown 1968, Robert Schumann Gold Medal 1973, Mérite Européen Gold Medal 1981. *Leisure interests:* reading, music (operatic and folk), swimming, boating, inshore sea fishing. *Address:* 21 Garville Avenue, Rathgar, Dublin 6, Ireland (Home).

LYNCH, Patrick, M.A., M.R.I.A.; Irish public administrator (retd.) and university professor; b. 1917, Dublin; s. of Daniel and Brigid Lynch; m. 1st Mrs. Mary Crotty 1965 (died 1982); m. 2nd Mary Moloney 1991; ed. Univ. Coll., Dublin; joined Irish Civil Service 1941; served Finance Dept. 1941–48; Asst. Sec. Dept. of Prime Minister 1950–52; Lecturer, Nat. Univ. of Ireland 1952–66; Chair. Aer Lingus 1954–75, Capital Investment Advisory Cttee.; Dir. Provincial Bank of Ireland 1959–66; Chair. Inst. of Public Admin. 1973–76, Medico-Social Research Bd. 1966–72; Dir. Allied Irish Banks 1966–84; Dir. OECD Govt. Surveys on Investment in Educ. and Research and Devt. 1962–66; mem. Governing Body, Univ. Coll., Dublin 1964–76; mem. Senate Nat. Univ. of Ireland 1972–77; Fellow Commoner, Peterhouse, Cambridge; Assoc. Prof. of Political Econ. (Applied Econs.) 1966–75, Prof. 1975–80, Prof. Emer.; Treas. Royal Irish Academy 1971–80; mem. Nat. Science Council 1967–77, Higher Educ. Authority 1968–72, Club of Rome 1973, Patron British-Irish Asscn. 1973, EEC Group EMU 1980 1974–75, Exec. Council, European Science Foundation 1975–77; Chair. Econ. and Social Research Inst. 1983–88; Deputy Chair. Allied Irish Banks 1976–84; Dir. Allied Irish Finance Co. 1976–82; Jt. Deputy Chair. Co-operation North 1981–84; Hon. Fellow Trinity Coll. Dublin 1995; Dr. h.c. (Brunel) 1976; LL.D. h.c. (Dublin) 1979; Dr. Econ. Sc. h.c. (Nat. Univ.) 1985, (Limerick) 1994. *Publications:* The Economics of Independence 1959, Planning for Economic Development (with C. F. Carter) 1959, Guinness's Brewery in the Irish Economy (with J. Vaizey) 1960, The Role of Public Enterprises in Ireland 1961, essay on The Irish Economy in Conor Cruise O'Brien Introduces Ireland 1969, Ireland in the War Years and After (ed. Nowlan and Williams) 1969, Ireland in the International Labour Organization (with B. Hillery) 1970, Economics of Educational Costing (with J. Vaizey) 1971, Readings in Public Administration (ed. with B. Chubb) 1971, essay in Travel and Transport in Ireland (ed. K. B. Nowlan) 1973, Whither Science Policy 1979, Essays in Memory of Alexis Fitzgerald (ed. with J. Meenan) 1987, (recorded contrib. to) Culture of Ireland 1991, Essay in Memory of Dáithí ó hUaithe ed Proinsias MacAonghasa and Tomás de Bhláldraithe 1994, Thomas Davis Lecture, in Centenary Vol. of Irish Congress of Trade Unions 1994, James Larkin 1997. *Address:* 79 Wellington Road, Dublin 4, Ireland. *Telephone:* 6680041.

LYNCH, Peter; American stock investor; b. 1944; m. Carolyn Lynch; three d.; Man. Fidelity Magellan Fund, Boston 1977–90; Trustee Fidelity Investments 1990–. *Publication:* One Up on Wall Street. *Address:* 27 State Street, Boston, MA 02109, U.S.A.

LYNCH, Philip; business executive; fmr. Man. Dir. Lehman Brothers; fmr. Chair. Int. Petroleum Exchange; Chief Exec. Exchange Clearing House (ECHO) 1996–.

LYNDEN-BELL, Donald, M.A., PH.D., F.R.S.; British professor of astrophysics; b. 5 April 1935, Dover; s. of late Lieut.-Col. L. A. Lynden-Bell and of M. R. Lynden-Bell; m. Ruth M. Truscott 1961; one s. one d.; ed. Marlborough Coll. and Clare Coll. Cambridge; Harkness Fellow, Calif. Inst. of Tech. and Hale Observatories 1960–62, Visiting Assoc. 1969–70, Research Fellow, then Fellow and Dir. of Studies in Math. Clare Coll., Cambridge 1960–65; Asst. Lecturer in Applied Math. Univ. of Cambridge 1962–65; Prin. Scientific Officer, later Sr. Prin. Scientific Officer, Royal Greenwich Observatory, Herstmonceux 1965–72; Prof. of Astrophysics, Univ. of Cambridge 1972–; Dir. Inst. of Astronomy, Cambridge 1972–77, 1982–87, 1992–94; Visiting Professorial Fellow, Queen's Univ., Belfast 1996–; Pres. Royal Astronomical Soc. 1985–87; Foreign Assoc., N.A.S. 1993; Hon. D.Sc. (Sussex) 1987; Eddington Medal 1984; Gold Medal (Royal Astronomical Soc.) 1993, (Royal Soc. of S.A.); Catherine Wolf George Medal 1998. *Publications:* contributions to Monthly Notices of Royal Astronomical Soc. *Leisure interest:* hill-walking.

Address: Institute of Astronomy, The Observatories, Madingley Road, Cambridge, CB3 0HA, England. *Telephone:* (01223) 337526.

LYNE, Adrian; British film director; b. Peterborough; m. Samantha Lyne; one d.; ed. Highgate School; joined J. Walter Thompson (advertising agency) in post room, later became asst. producer of commercials; with two partners set up own co. Jennie & Lyne 1971; dir. commercials including advertisements for Calvin Klein clothes and Pepsi Cola; Palme d'Or, Cannes Commercial Film Festival 1976, 1978. *Films include:* Foxes, Flashdance 1983, 9½ Weeks 1984, Fatal Attraction, Jacob's Ladder (also co-writer), Indecent Proposal, Lolita; two short films: The Table, Mr Smith.

LYNN, Dame Vera, D.B.E.; British singer; b. 20 March 1917; d. of Bertram Welch and Ann Welch; m. Harry Lewis 1941; one d.; ed. Brampton Road School, East Ham; joined singing troupe 1928; ran dancing school 1932; broadcast with Joe Loss and joined Charlie Kunz band 1935; singer with Ambrose Orchestra 1937–40, then went solo; voted most popular singer in Daily Express competition 1939; own radio show Sincerely Yours 1941–47; sang to troops abroad during Second World War, named "Forces' Sweetheart"; appeared in Applesauce, London 1941; post-war radio and TV shows and numerous appearances abroad including Denmark, Canada, South Africa and Australia; most successful record Auf Wiederseh'n; Pres. Printers' Charitable Corpn. 1980; Hon. Citizen Winnipeg 1974; Freedom of City of London 1978, Commdr. Order of Orange-Nassau (Holland), Burma Star Medal and War Medal 1985, Variety Club Int. Humanitarian Award, European Woman of Achievement Award 1994. *Publications:* Vocal Refrain (autobiog.) 1975, We'll Meet Again (with Robin Cross) 1989, The Woman Who Won the War (with Robin Cross and Jenny de Gex) 1990, Unsung Heroines 1990. *Leisure interests:* gardening, painting, sewing, swimming.

LYNTON, Michael; American publisher; b. 1 Jan. 1960, London, U.K.; s. of Mark O. L. Lynton and Marion Sonnenberg; m. Elizabeth Jane Alter; two d.; ed. Harvard Coll., Harvard Business School; Assoc., The First Boston Corpn. 1982–85; Sr. Vice-Pres. Disney Publishing Group 1987–93, Pres. Hollywood Pictures, The Walt Disney Co. 1993–96; Chair. and C.E.O. The Penguin Group 1996–. *Address:* c/o The Penguin Group, 375 Hudson Street, New York, NY 10014, U.S.A. *Telephone:* (212) 366-2900. *Fax:* (212) 366-2910.

LYON, John David Richard, M.A.; British business executive; b. 4 June 1936, London; s. of F. A. Lyon and E. G. Lyon; m. 1st Nicola M. E. Bland 1960 (marriage dissolved 1986); three s. (one deceased); m. 2nd Lillis Lanphier 1987; ed. Wellington Coll., Magdalen Coll. Oxford and Harvard Business School; 1st Bn. The Rifle Brigade 1954–56; Courtaulds PLC 1959–70; Rank Org. PLC 1970–71; Man. Dir. Redland Roof Tiles, Redland PLC 1971–76, Dir. Redland PLC 1976–80, Deputy Man. Dir. 1980–82, Group Man. Dir. 1982–87; C.E.O. Bowater Industries (now Rexam PLC) 1987–96; Chair. Stocks Austin Sice 1997–; mentioned in despatches, Kenya 1954. *Leisure interests:* deer stalking and gardening. *Address:* P.O. Box 12, Arundel, West Sussex, BN18 9ND, England.

LYON, Mary Frances, B.A., PH.D., SC.D., F.R.S., F.I.BIOL.; British geneticist; b. 15 May 1925, Norwich; d. of Clifford James and Louise Frances (née Kirby) Lyon; ed. Woking Grammar School, Girton Coll., Cambridge; on Medical Research Council (MRC) Scientific Staff, Inst. of Animal Genetics Edinburgh 1950–55; Scientific Staff MRC Radiobiology Unit, Harwell 1955–90, Head of Genetics Section 1962–87; Clothworkers Visiting Research Fellow, Girton Coll., Cambridge 1970–71; Foreign Assoc. Nat. Acad. of Sciences 1979; Foreign Hon. mem. American Acad. of Arts and Sciences 1980; Francis Amory Prize, American Acad. of Arts and Sciences 1977, Royal Medal, Royal Soc. 1984, San Remo Int. Prize for Genetics 1985, Gairdner Int. Award 1985, William Allan Award, American Soc. of Human Genetics 1986, Wolf Prize in Medicine 1997. *Publications:* papers on genetics in scientific journals. *Address:* Medical Research Council Mammalian Genetics Unit, Harwell, Didcot, Oxon. OX11 0RD, England. *Telephone:* (01235) 834393. *Fax:* (01235) 834776.

LYON, Hon. Mr. Justice Sterling Rufus Webster, P.C., B.A., LL.B.; Canadian politician and judge of appeal; b. 30 Jan. 1927, Windsor, Ont.; s. of late David Rufus Lyon and Ella Mae (Cuthbert) Lyon; m. Barbara Mayers 1953; two s. three d.; ed. Portage la Prairie public and high schools, Univs. of Manitoba and Winnipeg; Univ. Officers Training R.C.A.F. Reserve 1950–53; Pres. Man. Law Students Asscn. 1952–53; Counsel, Bracken Liquor Enquiry 1954–56; called to the Bar 1953, Q.C. 1960; Crown Attorney, Manitoba Dept. of Attorney-Gen. and legal practice 1953–57; mem. Man. Legis. Ass. 1958–69, 1976–86; Attorney-Gen. 1958–63, 1966-69; Minister of Municipal Affairs 1960–61, of Public Utilities 1961–63, of Mines and Natural Resources 1963–66, of Tourism and Recreation 1966–67; Chair. Canadian Council of Resource Ministers 1965–66; legal practice 1969–75; Govt. House Leader 1966–69; Leader, Man. Progressive Conservative Party 1975–83; Leader of Opposition, Man. 1976–77, 1981–83; Premier of Man. 1977–81; Chair. Canadian Premiers' Conf. 1980–81; Minister of Dominion-Provincial Affairs 1977–81; Judge Manitoba Court of Appeal 1986–. *Leisure interests:* reading, wildlife conservation, hunting, fishing, gardening. *Address:* The Law Courts, Winnipeg, Man., OP9 R3C, Canada.

LYONS, Sir John, Kt., LITT.D., PH.D., F.B.A.; British professor of linguistics; b. 23 May 1932, Manchester; s. of Michael Austin Lyons and Mary Bridget O'Sullivan; m. Danielle Jacqueline Simonet 1959; two d.; ed. St. Bede's Coll. Manchester and Christ's Coll. Cambridge; Lecturer in Comparative Linguistics, S.O.A.S., Univ. of London 1957–61; Lecturer in Linguistics and Fellow of Christ's Coll., Univ. of Cambridge 1961; Prof. of Gen. Linguistics, Univ. of Edin. 1964–76; Prof. of Linguistics, Univ. of Sussex 1976–84, Dean, School of Social Sciences 1979–81, Pro-Vice-Chancellor 1981–84, Visiting Prof. of Linguistics 1984–; Master of Trinity Hall, Cambridge 1984–; Hon. Fellow Christ's Coll. Cambridge 1985; Hon. mem. Linguistic Soc. of America; Dr. h.c. (Univ. Catholique, Louvain) 1980, Hon. D.Litt. (Reading) 1986, (Edin.) 1988, (Sussex) 1990, (Antwerp) 1992. *Publications:* Structural Semantics 1963, Introduction to Theoretical Linguistics 1968, Chomsky 1970, 1977, 1991, New Horizons in Linguistics 1970, Semantics 1 and 2 1977, Language and Linguistics 1980, Language, Meaning and Context 1981, Natural Language and Universal Grammar 1991, Linguistic Semantics 1995. *Address:* Master's Lodge, Trinity Hall, Cambridge, CB2 1TJ, England. *Telephone:* (01223) 332540. *Fax:* (01223) 462116.

LYONS, Lawrence Ernest, PH.D., F.R.A.C.I., F.A.A.; Australian professor of physical chemistry; b. 26 May 1922, Sydney; s. of Ernest Lyons and Doris Lyons; m. Alison Hargreaves 1956; two s.; ed. Sydney Boys' High School and Univs. of Sydney and London; R.A.A.F. 1944–45; Lecturer, then Reader in Chem. Univ. of Sydney 1945–63; Prof. of Physical Chem. Univ. of Queensland 1963–87, Prof. Emer. 1987–; Dir. New Univ. Colls. Council 1960–87; Liversidge Lecturer, Royal Soc., N.S.W. 1966, 1976; Visiting Prof. Univ. of British Columbia 1967, Waterloo Univ. 1986; Leverhulme Sr. Fellow, Tokyo Univ. 1971; Pres., Chem. Section of Australian and N.Z. Asscn. for Advancement of Science 1967; Founder Inst. for the Study of Christianity in the Age of Science 1988; mem. Science and Industry Forum 1978–82, Nat. Energy Research, Devt. and Demonstration Council 1978–81, Australian Nat. Comm. for UNESCO 1982–84; mem. Ed. Bd. Chemical Physics Letters 1967–77, Molecular Crystals 1966–83; Visiting Fellow Clare Hall Cambridge 1986, Ramsay Fellow 1952–53; Debye Lecturer, Cornell Univ., Ithaca 1979; Burfitt Prize 1968; Smith Medal 1968. *Publications:* co-author of Organic Semiconductors, (Part A) 1967, (Part B) 1983. *Leisure interest:* reading. *Address:* 2172 Moggill Road, Kenmore, Queensland 4069, Australia. *Telephone:* 07-33781614.

LYSSARIDES, Vassos, M.D.; Cypriot politician; b. 13 May 1920, Lefkara; s. of Michael Lyssarides and Eleni Lyssanides; m. Barbara Cornwall 1963; ed. Univ. of Athens; mem. House of Reps. 1960–, Pres. 1985–91; Pres. Socialist Party of Cyprus (EDEK) 1969–; Sec.-Gen. Int. Cttee. of Solidarity with the Struggle of the Peoples of Southern Africa; Vice-Pres. Presidium, Afro-Asian Peoples' Solidarity Org.; Hon. Pres. Nicosia Medical Asscn. Hippocrates. *Leisure interests:* poetry, painting. *Address:* EDEK Socialist Party of Cyprus, P.O. Box 1064, 40 Byron Avenue, Nicosia, Cyprus. *Telephone:* (2) 458617. *Fax:* (2) 458894.

LYTH, Ragnar Vilhelm, B.A.; Swedish theatre director; b. 2 April 1944, Karlstad; s. of Arne Lyth and Reidunn Eleonore; m. 1st Karin Falk 1967; m. 2nd Kerstin Österlin 1996; two s.; ed. Nat. Film School, Swedish Dramatic Inst.; theatre and TV director in Sweden, Norway and Denmark; represented Sweden at int. TV festival 'INPUT', Philadelphia, Banff, Montreal 1985, 1989, 1993; Head of Stage Dirs. Swedish Dramatic Inst. 1984–86; Chair. Swedish Dirs's Union; Head Vestmanlands Theatre; recipient of Sweden Art Award. *Leisure interest:* nature. *Address:* Sjöbjörnsvägen 25, 11767 Stockholm, Sweden. *Telephone:* (8) 198893.

LYTHGOE, Basil, F.R.S.; British professor of organic chemistry; b. 18 Aug. 1913; s. of Peter W. Lythgoe and Agnes Lythgoe; m. Kathleen C. Hallum 1946; two s.; ed. Leigh Grammar School and Manchester Univ.; Asst. Lecturer, Manchester Univ. 1938; Univ. Lecturer, Cambridge 1946; Fellow, King's Coll. Cambridge 1950; Prof. of Organic Chem. Univ. of Leeds 1953–78, now Emer. *Publications:* papers in Journal of Chemical Soc. *Leisure interest:* mountaineering. *Address:* 113 Cookridge Lane, Leeds, LS16 7NB, England. *Telephone:* (0113) 267 8837.

LYTTELTON, Humphrey Richard Adeane; British bandleader and journalist; b. 23 May 1921, Eton, Bucks.; s. of the late Hon. George William Lyttelton; m. 1st Patricia Mary Braithwaite 1948 (divorced 1952); one d.; m. 2nd Elizabeth Jill Richardson 1952; two s. one d.; ed. Sunningdale School, Eton Coll.; Grenadier Guards 1941–46; Camberwell Art School 1947–48; formed own band 1948; cartoonist for London Daily Mail 1949–53; freelance journalist and leader of Humphrey Lyttelton's Band 1953–; recorded Parlophone 1950–60, Columbia 1960–63, Black Lion 1973–83, Calligraph Records (own label) 1984–, contrib. Melody Maker 1954–61, Reynolds News 1955–62, Sunday Citizen 1962–67, Harpers and Queen (Restaurant column) 1968–76, Punch; Compère BBC jazz programmes: Jazz Scene, Jazz Club, Jazz 625 (TV); frequent television appearances; Chair. "I'm Sorry I Haven't a Clue" BBC Radio 4 1972–; Pres. Soc. for Italic Handwriting 1991–; Hon. Prof. of Music, Keele Univ. 1993–; Hon. D.Litt. (Warwick) 1987, (Loughborough) 1988, Hon. D. Mus. (Durham) 1989, (Keele) 1992. *Publications:* I Play as I Please 1954, Second Chorus 1958, Take it from the Top 1975, The Best of Jazz—Basin Street to Harlem 1978, Humphrey Lyttelton's Jazz and Big Band Quiz 1979, The Best of Jazz 2—Enter the Giants 1981, Why No Beethoven? the diary of a vagrant musician 1984, The Best of Jazz 1998. *Leisure interests:* birdwatching, calligraphy. *Address:* BBC, Broadcasting House, Portland Place, London, W1A 4WW; Alyn Close, Barnet Road, Arkley, Herts., EN5 3LS, England. *Telephone:* 0171-580 4468 (London).

LYUBIMOV, Alexey Borisovich; Russian pianist; b. 16 Sept. 1944, Moscow; m. Ada Lubimova; one d.; ed. Moscow State Conservatory; winner int. competitions in Rio de Janeiro 1965 (1st prize) and Montreal 1968; soloist, chamber musician, pianist, harpsichordist, organist; organizer and artistic dir. of chamber ensembles of experimental character; teacher Moscow Conservatory 1968–75. *Address:* Klimentovskiy per. 9, Apt. 12, Moscow, Russia (Home). *Telephone:* 231-62-51. *Fax:* 152-28-29.

LYUBIMOV, Yuriy Petrovich; Russian actor and theatrical director; b. 30 Sept. 1917, Yaroslavl'; m. seven times; ed. Vakhtangov Theatre Studio; served in Soviet Army 1940–47; mem. CPSU 1947–84; teacher and producer Shchukin Drama School (Vakhtangov Theatre) 1953–63; Dir. Moscow Theatre of Drama and Comedy (Taganka) 1964–84, 1989–93; left the Soviet Union 1984, acquired Israeli citizenship, returned 1987, citizenship restored 1989; awards include State Prizes 1952, People's Artist of Russia 1992. *Roles include:* Oleg Koshevoy (The Young Guard by Fadeyev), Shubin (On the Eve by Turgenev), Chris (All My Sons by A. Miller), Benedict (Much Ado About Nothing), Mozart (The Little Tragedies by Pushkin); prominent in Soviet films 1947–, including Robinson Crusoe. *Theatre productions include:* The Good Woman of Szechuan 1963, Ten Days that Shook the World 1965, Mother (Gorky) 1969, Hamlet 1972, Crime and Punishment (London) 1983, The Devils (London, Paris) 1985, Boris Godunov (Moscow) 1987, Hamlet (London) 1989, Self-Murderer (Moscow) 1990, Electra (Moscow) 1992. *Opera productions include:* Al gran sole d'amore (La Scala) 1975, Boris Godunov (La Scala) 1981, The Queen of Spades (Grand Opera), Eugene Onegin (Bonn), Lady Macbeth of Mtsensk (Munich). *Address:* Taganka Theatre, Chkalova str. 76, Moscow, Russia. *Telephone:* 272-63-00.

LYUBSHIN, Stanislav Andreyevich; Russian actor; b. 6 April 1933; m.; two s.; ed. Shchepkin Theatre School; worked with various Moscow theatres: Sovremenvik, Taganka, Yermolova, Malaya Bronnaya 1959–80; one of prin. actors with Moscow Arts Theatre 1980–, A. Chekhov Arts Theatre 1987–; film debut 1959; R.S.F.S.R. People's Artist 1981. *Roles in:* No Sackings Today 1959, I am Twenty Today 1965, Sword and Shield 1968, Red Square 1970, Defence Counsel 1977, Call Me into the Faraway 1978, Five Evenings 1979, Three Years 1980 (dir. with D. A. Dolinin), Encounter 1981, Tartuffe 1984, Phantoms among us 1985, Ivanov 1989, and many other film and stage roles. *Address:* Vernadskogo prosp. 123, Apt. 171, 117571 Moscow, Russia. *Telephone:* 433-35-14.

M

NOTE: All names beginning Mc and Mac are treated as if they began Mac.

MA, Yo Yo, B.A.; American cellist; b. 7 Oct. 1955, Paris; of Chinese parentage; m. Jill A. Hornor 1978; one s. one d.; ed. Harvard Univ. and 'cello studies with his father, with Janos Scholz and at Juilliard School of Music, New York; first public recital at age of five; winner Avery Fisher Prize 1978 since when he has performed under many distinguished conductors with all the major orchestras of the world including Berlin Philharmonic, Boston Symphony, Chicago Symphony, Israel Philharmonic, London Symphony Orchestra and New York Philharmonic; regularly participates in festivals of Tanglewood, Ravinia, Blossom, Salzburg and Edinburgh; also appears in chamber music ensembles with artists such as Emanuel Ax, Leonard Rose, Pinchas Zukerman, Gidon Kremer and Yehudi Menuhin; Glenn Gould Prize 1999; received 1984 Grammy Award for his recording of the six Bach Suites for Unaccompanied 'Cello; second Grammy Award 1985; records for CBS Masterworks; Dr. h.c. (Northeastern) 1985. *Address:* c/o I.C.M. Artists, 40 W. 57th Street, New York, NY 10019, U.S.A.

MA CHUNG-CH'EN (see Ma Zhongchen).

MA DAYOU (DAH-YOU MAA), PH.D.; Chinese acoustician; b. 1 March 1915, Chaoyang Co., Guangdong Prov.; s. of Ma Youlue and Gao Qi; m. Wang Ronghe 1947; one s. one d.; ed. Beijing Univ., Harvard Univ., U.S.A.; Prof., Qinghua Univ. and Nat. S.W. Univ., Kunming 1940–45; Prof. and Dean Beijing Univ. 1946–52; Prof. and Dean Harbin Polytechnic Univ. 1952–55; successively Research Prof. and later Deputy Dir., Inst. of Physics, Electronics and Acoustics, Academia Sinica 1955–86; Research Prof., Inst. of Acoustics 1986–; Ed.-in-Chief Acta Acustica and Chinese J. Acoustics 1964–; Chair. Nat. Acoustics Standardization Tech. Cttee. 1981–; mem. Academia Sinica 1955–, Chinese Oral and Written Language Cttee., Beijing 1980–; Vice-Chair. China Democratic League 1987–97, Hon. Vice-Chair. 1997–; Deputy Head, Graduate School, Univ. of Science and Tech., Beijing 1981–86; mem. and Hon. Pres. Acoustic Soc. China; mem. A.A.A.S.; Fellow Electronics Soc. China, Acoustic Soc. America. *Publications:* Handbook of Acoustics, Environmental Acoustics, Information and Processing of Speech, Noise Control Engineering, Study of Modern Acoustics, and selections of scientific works containing 70 papers in journals. *Leisure interest:* bridge. *Address:* Room 403, Bldg. 810, Zhongguancun Haidian, Beijing 100080, People's Republic of China. *Telephone:* (010) 6255 1957. *Fax:* (010) 6255 3898.

MA FENG (MA SHUMING); Chinese writer; b. 1922, Xiaoyi Co., Shanxi Prov.; ed. Lu Xun Acad. of Literature and Art, Yanan; joined 8th Route Army and CCP 1938; first short story (First Reconnaissance) published 1942; mem. China-Britain Friendship Asscn. 1983–; Vice-Chair. CPPCC Provincial Cttee., Shanxi 1986–; Pres. Soc. of Chinese Folk Literature May 1987–; Exec. Vice-Chair. Nat. Cttee. China Fed. of Literary and Art Circles 1988–; Vice-Chair. Chinese Writers' Asscn. 1990–; mem. Foreign Affairs Cttee. *Publications include:* Heroes of Lüliang (with Xi Rong), Liu Hulan (novel), The Young People of One Village (film script), and numerous short stories, including The Marriage Ceremony (Nat. Short Story Award Winner 1980). *Address:* China Federation of Literary and Art Circles, 10 Nong Zhan Guan Nanli, Beijing 100026, People's Republic of China. *Telephone:* 5005588.

MA HONG; Chinese economist; b. 1920, Dingxiang Co., Shanxi Prov.; ed. Marxism-Leninism Coll., Yan'an; joined CCP 1937; Vice-Pres. Chinese Acad. of Social Sciences 1979–82, Pres. 1982–85; Adviser to State Planning Comm. and State Comm. for Restructuring Econ. System 1982–85; Deputy Sec.-Gen. State Council, Dir.-Gen. Research Centre for Econ., Tech. and Social Devt. of State Council 1982–85, Pres. Devt. Research Centre, State Council 1985, Hon. Dir.-Gen. Devt. Research Center 1993–; Pres. China Comprehensive Devt. Research Inst. 1991–; Pres. China Scientific Research Soc. for Policy Study 1994–; mem. NPC Standing Cttee.; Chief Ed. Contemporary China Series, China in the Year 2000 Series. *Address:* Development Research Centre of the State Council, 22 Xianmen Street, Beijing, People's Republic of China. *Telephone:* 6013530.

MA QIZHI; Chinese politician; b. Nov. 1943, Jingyuan, Ningxia; ed. Cen. Inst. of Nationalities; joined CCP 1972; high school teacher in Anshan and Yinchuan; cadre of Communist Youth League Ningxia Hui Autonomous Region Cttee.; Vice-Sec. CCP Guyuan Pref. Cttee.; Vice-Sec. CCP Yinnan Pref. Cttee.; Dir. Propaganda Dept. of CCP Ningxia Hui Autonomous Region Cttee. 1969–93, Vice-Sec. 1993–98; Chair. Ningxia Hui Autonomous Region 1998–; alt. mem. CCP 14th and 15th Cen. Cttee. 1992–. *Address:* People's Government of Ningxia Hui Autonomous Region, Yinchuan, Ningxia, People's Republic of China.

MA SIZHONG; Chinese party and state official; b. 1931, Xiji, Ningxia; joined CCP 1947; Deputy for Ningxia Autonomous Region to 3rd NPC 1964, 7th NPC 1988–92; 8th NPC 1993–, mem. Nationalities Cttee.; alt. mem. 11th CCP Cen. Cttee. 1977, 12th Cen. Cttee. 1982, mem. 13th CCP Cen. Cttee. 1987–92; Vice-Chair. Revolutionary Cttee., Ningxia 1977–79; mem. CCP Cttee., Ningxia 1979; Vice-Chair. Ningxia Hui Autonomous Region 1980–88, Chair. 1998–; Chair. People's Political Consultative Conf. of Ningxia Hui Autonomous Region 1998–. *Address:* People's Political Consultative Conference of Ningxia Autonomous Hui Region, Yinchuan, Ningxia, People's Republic of China.

MA SZU-CHUNG (see Ma Sizhong).

MA WANFAN (MAYI); Chinese business executive; b. 1930, Longkou Co., Shandong Prov.; Chair. China Nat. Chemicals Corpn. 1989–; mem. 7th CPPCC 1987–92, 8th 1993–. *Address:* China National Chemicals Corporation, 16 Hepingli 7 District, Beijing 100013, People's Republic of China.

MA WANQI; Chinese politician; b. 1919, Nanhai Co., Guandong Prov.; mem. 5th Nat. Cttee. CPPCC 1978–82; Perm. mem. 6th Nat. Cttee. CPPCC 1983–88; mem. 6th Standing Cttee. NPC 1986–88; 7th Standing Cttee. NPC 1988–92; Vice-Chair. 8th Nat. Cttee. CPPCC 1993–98, 9th Nat. Cttee. 1998–; Vice-Pres. All-China Sports Fed. *Address:* National Committee of Chinese People's Political Consultative Conference, 23 Taiping Qiao Street, Beijing, People's Republic of China.

MA YONGWEI; Chinese banker; b. 1942; ed. Qinghua Univ.; joined CCP 1965; Chair., Pres. People's Insurance Co. of China, now China Insurance Group; fmr. Pres. Agric. Bank of China. *Address:* China Insurance Group, 410 Fu Cheng Men Nei Dajie, Beijing, People's Republic of China. *Telephone:* (10) 66016688. *Fax:* (10) 66011689.

MA YUAN; Chinese judge; b. 30 June 1930, Xinmin Co., Liaoning Prov.; two s.; ed. Chinese People's Univ., Beijing; joined CCP 1953; teacher Dept. of Law, Beijing Univ., and part-time lawyer 1955–62, part-time Prof. 1990–; Asst. Judge, Judge Supreme People's Court 1963–82, Deputy Dir. Civil Dept. 1982–85, Vice-Pres. Supreme People's Court 1985–; mem. Standing Cttee. All China Women's Fed.; Vice-Pres. China Marriage and Family Research Inst. 1983–; Pres. Chinese Asscn. of Women Judges 1994–; Asst. Sec.-Gen. Civil and Econ. Law Cttee., China Law Soc. 1983–. *Address:* Supreme People's Court, 27 Dong Jiaomin Xiang, Beijing 1000745, People's Republic of China.

MA YUZHEN; Chinese diplomatist; b. 26 Sept. 1934, Beijing; s. of Ma Zhiqiang and Li Jinhui; m. Zou Jichun 1961; one s. one d.; ed. Beijing Inst. of Foreign Languages; served in Information Dept. of the Ministry of Foreign Affairs 1954–63, Deputy Div. Chief, then Div. Chief 1969–80, Dir. 1984–88; Attaché, Third Sec. Embassy, Burma 1963–69, First Sec., Counsellor Embassy, Ghana 1980–84, Consul-Gen. (ambassadorial rank) L.A. 1988–91, Amb. to the U.K. 1991–95; Deputy Dir. State Council's Information Office 1995–97; Foreign Ministry Commr. for China, Hong Kong 1997–; *Leisure interests:* reading, music. *Address:* c/o Ministry of Foreign Affairs, Beijing, People's Republic of China.

MA ZHENGANG; Chinese diplomatist; b. 9 Nov. 1940, Shandong; m. Chen Xiaodong; one s.; ed. Beijing Foreign Languages Univ., Ealing Tech. Coll., London, L.S.E.; staff mem., Attaché, Embassy in Yugoslavia 1970–74; Attaché N. American and Oceanic Affairs Dept., Ministry of Foreign Affairs, Beijing 1974–81, Deputy Dir., Dir. N. American and Oceanian Affairs Dept. 1985–90, Deputy Dir.-Gen., Dir.-Gen. N. American and Oceanian Affairs Dept. 1991–95; Vice-Consul, Consul Consulate-Gen., Vancouver 1981–85; Counsellor, Embassy in Washington, D.C. 1990–91; Vice-Minister of Foreign Affairs 1995–97; Amb. to U.K. March 1997–. *Leisure interests:* literature, bridge, table tennis. *Address:* Embassy of the People's Republic of China, 49–51 Portland Place, London, W1N 4JL, England. *Telephone:* 0171-636 5726. *Fax:* 0171-636 2981.

MA ZHONGCHEN; Chinese party official; b. 1936, Tai'an, Shandong; joined CCP 1956; alt. mem. 12th CCP Cen. Cttee. 1982, 13th Cen. Cttee. 1987; Sec. CCP Cttee., Tai'an Municipality, Shandong Prov. 1982–88; Vice-Gov. Shandong 1988–89; Deputy Sec. Shandong Prov. CP 1988–92, Henan Prov. CCP Cttee.; NPC Deputy; alt. mem. 14th Cen. Cttee. CCP 1992–97, mem. 15th CCP Cen. Cttee. 1997–; Gov. Henan Prov. 1993–98. *Address:* c/o Office of the Governor, Zhengzhou City, Henan Province, People's Republic of China.

MAAG, Peter; Swiss conductor; b. 10 May 1919, St. Gall; s. of Otto and Nelly Maag; m. Marica Franchi 1980, one d.; one s. from previous marriage; ed. theology and philosophy studies at Zürich and Basel Univs.; studied piano with Alfred Cortot; began conducting in small theatre; Asst. to Wilhelm Furtwängler; Asst. to Ernest Ansermet, Orchestre de la Suisse Romande; Düsseldorf Opera 1952–55; Chief Conductor Bonn Opera 1956–59, Volksoper, Vienna 1962, Teatro Regio, Turin 1974, Berne Symphony Orchestra 1984–91; Musical Dir. Treviso Opera, Italy 1990–; fmr. Prin. Guest Conductor Radiotelevisione Italiana (RAI), Orquesta Nacional, Madrid; regular guest conductor at La Scala, Milan, Metropolitan Opera, New York, Teatro Colón, Buenos Aires, Venice, Royal Opera House, Covent Garden; First Guest Conductor, Orchestra da Camera di Padova e del Veneto (ex Solisti Veneti), Teatro le Fenice, Venice; also at various festivals incl. Aix-en-Provence, Zürich, Netherlands, Vienna, Salzburg; Toscanini Medal, Parma

1969, Verdi Medal 1973. *Leisure interest:* theology. *Address:* I.C.M. Artists Ltd., 40 W. 57th Street, New York, NY 10019, U.S.A.; Orchestra Camera Padova Veneto, Via Marsilio da Padova 19, I-35139, Padua, Italy.

MAATHAI, Wangari, PH.D.; Kenyan ecologist and biologist; b. 1 April 1940, Nyeri; d. of Muta Njugi and Wanjiru Kibicho; m. Mwangi Maathai 1969 (divorced 1980); two s. one d.; fmr. Head, Veterinary Anatomy, Nairobi Univ.; f. Kenya Green Belt Movt. 1977; fmr. mem. Forum for Restoration of Democracy; arrested 1992; shared Hunger Project Prize 1991; Right Livelihood Award 1984, Edin. Medal 1993, Goldman Environment Prize 1994 and others. *Leisure interests:* swimming, reading. *Address:* Green Belt Movement, P.O. Box 67545, Nairobi, Kenya. *Telephone:* 504264. *Fax:* 504264.

MAAZEL, Lorin, F.R.C.M.; American conductor and musician; b. 6 March 1930, Neuilly, France; s. of Lincoln and Marie Varencove Maazel; m. 1st Israela Margalit; four c.; m. 2nd Dietlinde Turban 1986; one s.; ed. under Vladimir Bakaleinikoff and at Univ. of Pittsburgh; début as conductor 1938; Conductor, American Symphony Orchestras 1939–; violin recitalist; European début 1953; festivals include Bayreuth, Salzburg, Edinburgh; tours include South America, Australia, U.S.S.R. and Japan; Artistic Dir., Deutsche Oper Berlin 1965–71; Musical Dir. Radio Symphony Orchestra, Berlin 1965–75; Assoc. Prin. Conductor, New Philharmonia Orchestra, London 1970–72; Dir. Cleveland Orchestra 1971–82, Conductor Emer. 1982–86; Prin. Guest Conductor London Philharmonia 1976–80; Dir. Vienna State Opera 1982–84, Music Dir. Pittsburgh Symphony Orchestra 1988–96; Music Dir. Bavarian Radio Symphony Orchestra 1993–; Music Dir. Orchestre Nat. de France 1988–90; Hon. D.Mus. (Pittsburgh) 1968, (Royal Coll. of Music) 1984; D.Hum.Litt. (Beaver Coll.) 1973; Hon. DCL (Univ. of South Sewanee) 1988; Hon. Dr. (Ind.) 1988; Officier, Légion d'honneur 1981; Finnish Commdr. of the Lion; Portuguese Commdr.; Bundesverdienstkreuz (Germany). *Leisure interests:* swimming, tennis, reading. *Address:* c/o Marcel de Valmalète, 11 avenue Delcassé, 75008 Paris, France.

MABILANGAN, Felipe H., M.A.; Philippine diplomatist; m. Ada Kalaw Ledesma; three c.; ed. Univs. of Oxford and Geneva; various positions, Dept. of Foreign Affairs 1971–79, Dir.-Gen. for European Affairs 1988; Amb. to France (also accred. to Portugal) 1979–87, to China (also accred. to Mongolia) 1989–95; Perm. Rep. to UN 1995–; del. to numerous int. confs.; Nat. Order of Merit. *Address:* Permanent Mission of the Philippines to the United Nations, 556 Fifth Avenue, New York, NY 10036, U.S.A. *Telephone:* (212) 764-1300.

MABROUK, Ezzidin Ali, LL.M.; Libyan politician; b. 28 May 1932; ed. Cairo Univ. and Univ. Coll., London; Public Prosecutor, Tripoli 1956; subsequently Judge, Summary Court, Tripoli, Pres. Tripoli Court and Counsellor of Supreme Appeal Court; Sr. Legal Adviser, Org. of Petroleum Exporting Countries (OPEC); Minister of Petroleum, Libya 1970–77; Sec. for Petroleum, Gen. People's Cttee. 1977–80; Chair. Org. of Arab Petroleum Exporting Countries 1979; under house arrest 1980.

MABUS, Raymond Edwin, Jr., M.A., J.D.; American politician and lawyer; b. 11 Oct. 1948, Starkville, Miss.; s. of Raymond Edwin Mabus, Sr. and Lucille C. Mabus; m. Julia Hines Mabus 1987; two d.; ed. Univ. of Mississippi, Johns Hopkins Univ., Harvard Univ.; called to Texas Bar 1976, Washington, D.C. 1978, Mississippi 1982; Law Clerk U.S. Circuit Court of Appeals, Montgomery, Ala. 1976–77; Legal Counsel to House of Reps., D.C. 1977–78; Assoc. Fried, Frank et al., Washington, D.C. 1979–80; Gov.'s Legislative Aide, State of Miss., Jackson 1980–83; State Auditor, State of Miss. 1984–88; Gov. of Miss. 1988–92; Amb. to Saudi Arabia 1994–96; Counsel, Baker Donaldson Bearman & Caldwell 1996–; Pres. Int. Man. & Devt. Group Ltd. 1998–; Chair. Southern Govs'. Asscn., Southern Regional Educ. Bd.; Woodrow Wilson Scholarship, Johns Hopkins Univ. 1969; King Abdul Aziz Award, Saudi Arabia 1996, Distinguished Public Service Award, U.S. Dept. of Defense; Democrat. *Leisure interests:* spectator sports, walking, reading, photography, scuba diving. *Address:* P.O. Box 2000, Jackson, MS 39215, U.S.A. (Home). *Telephone:* (601) 351-2400 (Office); (601) 362-7400 (Home). *Fax:* (601) 351-2424 (Office); (601) 713-0800 (Home).

McALEESE, Mary Patricia, LL.B., M.A., M.I.L.L.; Irish university administrator; b. 27 June 1951; d. of Patrick J. Leneghan and Claire McManus; m. Martin McAleese 1976; one s. two d.; ed. Queen's Univ. Belfast, Inn of Court of N. Ireland, King's Inns, Dublin and Trinity Coll., Dublin; Reid Prof. Trinity Coll., Dublin 1975–79, 1979–87; Dir. Inst. of Professional Legal Studies 1987–97; Pro-Vice-Chancellor, Queen's Univ., Belfast 1994–97; Dir. (non-exec). N. Ireland Electricity 1992–97, Channel 4 TV 1993–97, fmr. Dir. Royal Group of Hosps. Trust; Pres. of Ireland Oct. 1997–; Hon. LL.D. (Queen's, Belfast), (Nottingham) 1998. *Publications:* The Irish Martyrs 1995, Reconciled Beings 1997. *Leisure interests:* hillwalking, theology. *Address:* Áras an Uachtaráin, Phoenix Park, Dublin 8, Ireland. *Telephone:* (1) 6772815. *Fax:* (1) 6710529.

MACAPAGAL ARROYO, Gloria, PH.D.; Philippine politician, economist, educator and journalist; b. 4 May 1948, Lubao, Pampanga; d. of late Diosdado Macapagal and Evangelina Macaraeg Macapagal; two s. one d.; ed. Assumption Coll., Georgetown Univ., Ateneo de Manila Univ., Univ. of the Philippines; Under-Sec. Dept. of Trade and Industry 1986–92; Senator 1992–98; Sec. Dept. of Social Welfare and Devt., Vice-Pres. of Repub. 1998–; named Outstanding Senator by Asiaweek, Woman of the Year by Catholic Educ. Asscn. of Philippines. *Address:* Office of the Vice-President, PICC Building, CCP Complex, Roxas Boulevard, Pasay City, Philippines. *Telephone:* 832-7554; 832-7559. *Fax:* 832-7548.

MACARA, Sir Alexander Wiseman, Kt., PH.D., D.SC.; British physician; b. 4 May 1932, Irving, Scotland; s. of the Rev. Alexander Macara and Marion Macara; m. Sylvia May Williams 1964; one s. one d.; ed. Irvine Royal Acad., Univ. of Glasgow, London School of Hygiene and Tropical Medicine; lecturer, then consultant sr. lecturer in Social Medicine, Univ. of Bristol 1964–97; Sec.-Gen. Asscn. of Schools of Public Health in Europe 1975–89, World Fed. for Educ. and Research in Public Health 1988–97; Dir. WHO Collaborating Centre in Environmental Health 1988–97; Chair. B.M.A. 1993–98; Visiting Prof. of Health Studies, Univ. of York 1998–; Hon. F.R.C.P. (U.K.); Hecht Prize, London School of Hygiene and Tropical Medicine. *Publications:* has published extensively on public health, ethics in medicine, health care and epidemiology. *Leisure interests:* music, gardening, human rights activities. *Address:* Elgon, 10 Cheyne Road, Stoke Bishop, Bristol, BS9 2DH, England. *Telephone:* (0117) 9682838. *Fax:* (0117) 9684602.

MACARRÓN JAIME, Ricardo; Spanish painter; b. 9 April 1926, Madrid; m. Alicia Macarrón Jaime 1951; two d.; ed. Escuela Superior de Bellas Artes de San Fernando, Madrid and scholarship in Paris; Prof. of Drawing and Painting, Escuela Superior de Bellas Artes, Madrid; has painted many portraits of royalty and nobility; mem. Royal Soc. of Portrait Painters 1962; numerous one-man exhbns. in Spain and abroad including two in London and one in New York; represented at Museo de Arte Contemporáneo, Madrid, Univ. of Oslo and Fundación Güell, Barcelona, portraits at the Royal Soc. of Portrait Painters; numerous awards. *Leisure interests:* walking in the country, hunting, playing chess. *Address:* Agustín de Bethencourt No. 7, Madrid 3, Spain.

McBAIN, Ed (see Hunter, Evan).

McBRIDE, William Griffith, A.O., C.B.E., M.D., F.R.C.O.G., F.R.A.C.O.G., F.R.S.M., M.A.C.T.; Australian molecular biologist and medical practitioner; b. 25 May 1927, Sydney; s. of John McBride and Myrine Griffith; m. Patricia Glover 1957; two s. two d.; ed. Canterbury Boys' High School, Sydney, Conservatorium of Music, Sydney, Univ. of London, Univ. of Sydney; Medical Officer, St. George Hosp. 1950, Consultant Obstetrician and Gynaecologist 1958–; Medical Officer, Launceston Gen. Hosp. 1951; Medical Officer, Women's Hosp., Sydney 1952–53, Medical Supt. 1955–57, Consultant Obstetrician 1966–83; Consultant Gynaecologist, Bankstown Hosp., Sydney 1957–66; Consultant Obstetrician and Gynaecologist, Royal Hosp. for Women 1983–88; Consultant, L.B. Johnson Tropical Medicine Center, American Samoa 1998–, Govt. of Solomon Is. Medical Services (for AUSAID) 1999–; examiner in Obstetrics and Gynaecology Univs. of Sydney and N.S.W.; Fellow of the Senate Univ. of Sydney 1974–90; mem. Faculty of Medicine Univ. of Sydney 1966–90; mem. WHO Cttee. on Safety of Contraceptives 1971; Dir., Foundation 41 Research Lab. 1972–93; discovered that thalidomide caused birth defects (Lancet 1961), that thalidomide is a mutagen (B.M.J. 1994); showed that radioactive labelled thalidomide binds with DNA in rats 1997; Dir. Australian Opera 1979–82; mem. Australian Opera Council 1984–; Hereford cattle judge, W. Midlands Show 1988; mem. A.A.A.S. American Coll. of Toxicologists, Soc. for Risk Analysis, New York Acad. of Sciences; Gold Medal and B.P. Prize (L'Institut de la Vie) 1971. *Publications:* Killing the Messenger 1994; over 100 papers in medical and scientific journals. *Leisure interests:* surfing, tennis, riding, golf, breeder of Hereford cattle. *Address:* Foundation 41, 211 Bourke Street, E. Sydney, N.S.W. 2011; 95 Elizabeth Bay Road, Elizabeth Bay, N.S.W. 2011, Australia. *Telephone:* (2) 9368 7808. *Fax:* (2) 9368 7807.

McBRIDE, William James, M.B.E.; Irish rugby football player and business executive (retd.); b. 6 June 1940, Toomebridge, Northern Ireland; s. of William James McBride and Irene Patterson; m. Penny Michael 1966; one s. one d.; ed. Ballymena Acad.; first played rugby for Ireland against England 1962; six Lions tours, S. Africa 1962, N.Z. 1966, S. Africa 1968, N.Z. 1971, S. Africa 1974, Capt. unbeaten Lions 1974, Man. Lions 1983 N.Z.; holder of 63 int. caps; 17 Test appearances for Lions (record); toured Australia 1967 and Argentina 1970 for Ireland; fmr. Asst. Bank Man.; Pres. Ballymena R.F.C., Northern Ireland Riding for Disabled; Freeman Borough of Newtownabbey. *Leisure interests:* golf, gardening, after-dinner speaking. *Address:* Gorse Lodge, 105 Ballycorr Road, Ballyclare, Co. Antrim, BT39 9DE, Northern Ireland. *Telephone:* (01960) 352710. *Fax:* (01960) 352710.

McBRIEN, Rev. Richard Peter, M.A., S.T.D.; American professor of theology and ecclesiastic; b. 19 Aug. 1936, Hartford, Conn.; s. of late Thomas H. McBrien and Catherine Botticelli; ed. St. Thomas Seminary, Bloomfield, St. John Seminary, Brighton, Mass. and Pontifical Gregorian Univ., Rome; Prof. of Theology and Dean of Studies Pope John XXIII Nat. Seminary, Weston, Mass. 1965–70; Prof. Boston Coll., Newton, Mass. 1970–80; Chair. Dept. of Theology, Univ. of Notre Dame, Ind. 1980–91, Prof. 1980–; John Courtney Murray Award, Catholic Theology Soc. of America 1976, Christopher Award for Catholicism (book) 1981. *Publications:* Do We Need the Church? 1969, Church: The Continuing Quest 1970, The Remaking of the Church 1973, Catholicism (2 vols.) 1980, Caesar's Coin: Religion and Politics in America 1987, Report on the Church: Catholicism since Vatican II 1992, Catholicism (new edn.) 1994, The Harper Collins Encyclopedia of Catholicism (Gen. Ed.) 1995, Responses to 101 Questions on the Church 1996, Lives of the Popes: The Pontiffs from St. Peter to John Paul II 1997. *Leisure interests:* reading, films. *Address:* Department of Theology, University of Notre Dame, Notre Dame, IN 46556, U.S.A. *Telephone:* (219) 631-5151.

McCABE, Eamonn Patrick; British photographer; b. 28 July 1948; s. of James McCabe and Celia McCabe; m. 1st Ruth Calvert 1972 (divorced 1993); one s.; m. 2nd Rebecca Smithers 1997; one d.; ed. Challoner School, Finchley and San Francisco State Coll.; fmr. freelance photographer for local papers and The Guardian for one year; staff photographer, The Observer 1977–86, 1987–88; Official Photographer, Pope's Visit to Britain 1982; Picture Ed. Sportsweek 1986–87, The Guardian 1988–; Fellow in Photography, Nat. Museum of Photography and TV, Bradford 1988; Hon. Prof. Thames Valley Univ. 1994; Sports Photographer of the Year, Royal Photographic Soc. and Sports Council 1978, 1979, 1981, 1984, News Photographer of the Year, British Press Awards 1985, Picture Ed. of the Year (Nikon Press Awards) 1992, 1993, 1995, 1997. *Publications:* Sports Photographer 1981, Eamonn McCabe, Photographer 1987. *Leisure interest:* playing tennis. *Address:* c/o The Guardian, 119 Farringdon Road, London EC1R 3ER, England. *Telephone:* 0171-278 2332.

McCABE, John, C.B.E., MUS.B., F.R.M.C.M., F.L.C.M., F.R.C.M., R.A.M., F.T.C.L.; British musician; b. 21 April 1939, Huyton, Lancs. (now Merseyside); s. of Frank and Elisabeth (Herlitzius) McCabe; m. 1st Hilary Tann 1968 (divorced 1974); m. 2nd Monica Smith 1974; ed. Liverpool Inst. High School for Boys, Manchester Univ., Royal Manchester Coll. of Music, Staatliche Hochschule für Musik, Munich; Pianist-in-residence, University Coll., Cardiff 1965–68; Pres. Inc. Soc. of Musicians 1983–84; Dir. London Coll. of Music 1983–90; Chair. Asscn. of Professional Composers 1985–86; travels world-wide as pianist-composer; Royal Manchester Inst. Medal 1962, Royal Philharmonic Prize 1962, Special Citation, Koussevitsky Recording Foundation 1974, Award for service to British music, Composers Guild 1975. *Publications:* Rachmaninov, Bartok's Orchestral Music, Haydn's Piano Sonatas, Alan Rawsthorne: Portrait of a Composer, and numerous articles on music. *Compositions include:* The Chagall Windows, Variations on a theme of Hartmann, Notturni ed Alba, Concerto for Orchestra, Cloudcatcher Fells, Fire at Durilgai, Canyons, Edward II (ballet), plus other stage works, symphonies, concertos, much orchestral and chamber music, vocal works and keyboard music; numerous piano recordings including complete piano works of Haydn and Nielsen. *Leisure interests:* books, films, cricket, snooker. *Address:* c/o Novello and Co. Ltd., Music Sales, 8/9 Frith Street, London, W1V 5TZ, England.

McCABE, Patrick; Irish writer; b. Co. Monaghan, 1955; m.; two d.; fmr. teacher of disabled children; has written plays for BBC Radio, and stage play Frank Pig Says Hello, based on novel The Butcher Boy; awards include Hennessy Award. *Publications:* Music on Clinton Street 1986, Carn 1989, The Butcher Boy 1992 (Irish Times/Aer Lingus Fiction Prize 1992, shortlisted for Booker Prize 1992), The Dead School 1996. *Address:* c/o Picador, Macmillan General Books, 25 Eccleston Place, London, SW1W 9NF, England. *Telephone:* 0171-881 8000. *Fax:* 0171-881 8001.

McCAFFREY, Gen. Barry R; American government official and fmr. army officer; b. 17 Nov. 1942, Taunton, Mass., s. of William Joseph McCaffrey and Mary Veronica Curtin; m. Jill Ann Faulkner 1964; one s. two d.; ed. US Military Acad., American Univ., Command and General Staff Coll., Army War Coll.; commissioned into US Army 1964, Co. Commdr. 1st Cavalry Div., Viet Nam 1968–69, Asst. Prof. of Social Sciences, Dept. of Social Sciences, U.S. Mil. Acad. 1972–75; Bn. Commdr. 3rd Infantry Div., Germany 1979–83; Div. Chief of Staff, Brigade Commdr. 9th Infantry Div. 1983–86; Asst. Commandant U.S. Army Infantry School 1986–88; U.S. Deputy Military Rep. to NATO 1988–89; Prin. Staff Asst. to Chair. of Jt. Chiefs of Staff, Chief of Strategic Planning 1989–90; Div. Commdr. 24th Infantry Div. 1990–95, led. div. into Iraq in Operation Desert Storm 1991; fmr. Cmmdr.-in-Chief U.S. Armed Forces Southern Command; at retirement youngest four-star Gen. in Army; Dir. White House Office of Nat. Drug Control Policy Feb. 1996–; fmr. mem. prin. negotiation team START II Nuclear Arms Control Treaty; mem. Nat. Security Council, Council on Foreign Relations, Nat. Asscn. for Advancement of Coloured People; most highly decorated combat officer on retirement; Distinguished Service Cross (twice), Silver Star (twice), Distinguished Service Medal, Combat and Infantry Badge. *Publications:* Proceedings of the Twenty-Fifth Student Conference on United States Affairs 1973, We Are Soldiers All: An Analysis of Possible Roles for Women in the Army 1973, numerous articles on mil. subjects. *Address:* Office of National Drug Control Policy, 750 17th Street, N.W., Washington, DC 20006, U.S.A. *Telephone:* (202) 395-6792.

McCAIN, G. Wallace, F.B.A.; Canadian business executive; b. 9 April 1930, Florenceville, N.B.; s. of late A.D. McCain and Laura B. McCain; m. Hon. Margaret L.A. Norrie; two s. two d.; ed. Mount Allison Univ.; Chair. Bd. Maple Leaf Foods Inc. and Dir. of other assoc. cos.; Vice-Chair. McCain Foods Ltd. Florenceville, N.B. and Dir. of other assoc. cos.; Dir. Royal Bank of Canada, Alliance for a Drug-Free Canada; Hon. LL.D. (Mt. Allison) 1973; Hon. D.C.L. (Univ. of King's Coll.) 1987. *Leisure interests:* skiing, swimming, tennis. *Address:* Maple Leaf Foods Inc., 30 St. Clair Avenue West, Toronto, Ont. M4V 3A2, Canada.

McCAIN, John Sidney III, D.F.C.; American politician; b. 29 Aug. 1936, Panama Canal Zone, Panama; s. of John Sidney McCain and Roberta Wright; m. Cindy Hensley 1980; five s. one d.; ed. U.S. Naval Acad. and Nat. War Coll.; Ensign, U.S. Navy 1958, Capt. 1977; Dir. Navy Senate Liaison Office, Washington 1977–81; Bd. Dirs. Community Assistance League, Phoenix 1981–82; mem. 99th Congress from 1st Ariz. Dist.; Senator from Arizona Jan. 1987–; mem. Armed Services Cttee., Science and Transport Cttee., Indian Affairs Cttee.; various decorations including Legion of Merit, Silver Star, Purple Heart Vietnamese Legion of Honour; Republican. *Address:* U.S. Senate, 111 Russell Senate Office Building, Washington, DC 20510, U.S.A.

McCANDLESS, Bruce, II; American astronaut; b. 8 June 1937, Boston, Mass.; s. of late Rear-Adm. Bruce McCandless and Sue W.B. McCandless Inman; m. Alfreda Bernice Doyle 1960; one s. one d.; ed. U.S. Naval Acad., Stanford Univ. and Univ. of Houston; flight training, Pensacola, Fla. and Kingsville, Tex.; weapons system and carrier landing training, Key West, Fla. 1960; carrier duty, Fighter Squadron 102 1960–64; instrument flight instructor, Attack Squadron 43, Naval Air Station, Apollo Soucek Field, Oceana, Va.; graduate studies in electrical eng., Stanford Univ. until 1966; selected by NASA as astronaut April 1966; Co-investigator Astronaut Manoeuvring Unit Experiment on Skylab 1968–74; back-up crew for first Skylab Mission 1973; Mission Specialist on STS-11, first flight of manned manoeuvring unit; Mission Specialist on STS-31, Hubble Space Telescope deployment; retd. from Navy as Capt. Aug. 1990; Man. Payload Systems and Tech., Lockheed Martin Astronautics Group and Vice-Pres. Lockheed Martin Overseas Corpn. 1990–; Prin. Staff Engineer Lockheed Martin Astronautics 1990–97; Chief. Scientist Reusable Launch Systems 1997–. *Leisure interests:* electronics, scuba diving, sailing, photography. *Address:* Mail Stop S8000, Lockheed Martin Astronautics, P.O. Box 179, Denver, CO 80201, U.S.A. *Telephone:* (303) 971-6308. *Fax:* (303) 971-2390.

McCANN, Norman, A.R.A.M., F.R.S.A., F.I.D.; British concert agent; b. 24 April 1920, London; s. of Bert McCann and Violetta McCann; m. Lucille Graham 1945; one s; ed. Royal Acad. of Music; has appeared in opera, concerts, musical shows, Shakespearean productions and on radio and television; lecturer at the Comenius Univ. and Trinity Coll. of Music; Admin. and Artistic Dir. British Opera Co.; Curator, Int. Music Museum; Dir. of Production, Hintlesham Festival; Artistic Adviser, Battle Festival; Exec. Dir. Children's Opera Group; Concerts Organizer, Int. Eisteddfod; Concert Man. Goldsmith's Choral Union; Chair. Minerva Ballet Trust; Concerts Man. and Artistic Adviser, S. and N. Wales Asscn. of Choirs; Pres. and Chair. English Singers and Speakers Asscn. of G.B.; Past Pres. British Asscn. of Concert Agents; Pres. Lewisham Chamber of Commerce; Chair. Lewisham Conservative Asscn.; manager and business adviser to many distinguished artists; Hon. Assoc. Royal Acad. of Music; mem. British Inst. of Man.; Order of Kyril & Methodius (Bulgaria). *Leisure interests:* gardening, music, food. *Address:* c/o International Artists Ltd., The Coach House, 56 Lawrie Park Gardens, London, SE26 6XJ, England. *Telephone:* 0181-778 6474.

McCARTHY, Callum, PH.D.; British civil servant and economist; b. 29 Feb. 1944, Brentwood, Essex; s. of Ralph McCarthy and Agnes Graham; m. Penelope Ann Gee 1966; two s. one d.; ed. Univs. of Oxford and Stirling, Business School, Stanford Univ.; econ. and operations researcher ICI 1965; Prin. Pvt. Sec. to Roy Hattersley (q.v.) and Norman Tebbit (q.v.), Dept. of Trade and Industry 1972–85, also Under-Sec.; Dir. of Corp. Finance, Kleinwort Benson 1985–89; Man. Dir., Head of Corp. Finance, BZW 1989–93; C.E.O. BZW Japan and N. America 1993–98; Dir.-Gen. of UK Gas Supply 1998–; Dir.-Gen. of UK Electricity Supply 1999–. *Publication:* Introduction to Technological Economics (with D. S. Davies) 1967. *Leisure interests:* walking, reading, bee-keeping. *Address:* Stockley House, 130 Wilton Road, London, SW1V 1LQ, England. *Telephone:* 0171-932 1661. *Fax:* 0171-932 1662.

McCARTHY, Cormac; American author; b. 1933, Rhode Island; m. 1st Lee Holleman 1961 (divorced); one s.; m. 2nd Annie DeLisle (divorced); ed. Univ. of Tennessee; U.S.A.F. 1953–57; MacArthur Fellowship 1981. *Publications:* novels: The Orchard Keeper 1965, Outer Dark 1968, Child of God 1973, Suttree 1979, Blood Meridian 1985, All the Pretty Horses (Vol. 1 of trilogy) 1992, The Crossing (Vol. 2 of trilogy) 1994, Cities of the Plain (Vol. 3 of trilogy) 1998; play: The Stonemason 1994. *Address:* 1011 N. Mesa, El Paso, TX 79902, U.S.A.

McCARTHY, Eugene Joseph, M.A.; American politician and writer; b. 29 March 1916, Watkins, Minn.; s. of late Michael J. McCarthy and Anna Baden McCarthy; m. Abigail Quigley 1945; one s. three d.; ed. St. John's Univ., Collegeville, Minn. and Minnesota Univ.; successively Prof. of Econs. and Educ., St. John's Univ., Collegeville, Minn.; Civilian Tech. Asst., War Dept. Mil. Intelligence Division; Acting Chair. Sociology Dept., St. Thomas Coll., St. Paul, Minn.; mem. U.S. House of Reps. (Fourth Minn. district) 1949–58; Senator from Minnesota 1959–70; Liberal Independent cand. for Presidency 1976; Adlai Stevenson Prof. of Political Science, New School for Social Research 1973–74; syndicated columnist 1977–; Dir. Harcourt Brace Jovanovich Inc.; Hon. LL.D. (St. Louis) 1955; Cardinal Newman Award 1955. *Publications:* Frontiers in American Democracy 1960, Dictionary of American Politics 1962, A Liberal Answer to the Conservative Challenge 1964, The Limits of Power: America's Role in the World 1967, The Year of the People 1969, Other Things and the Aardvark (poems) 1970, The Hard Years 1975, Mr. Raccoon and his friends (children's stories) 1977, America Revisited 1978, Ground Fog and Night (poetry) 1979, A Political Bestiary (co-author) 1979, The Ultimate Tyranny 1979, Gene McCarthy's Minnesota 1982, The View from Rappahanock 1984, Up 'Til Now: A Memoir of the

Decline of American Politics 1987, The View from Rappahannock II 1989, Required Reading—Book of Essays (jtly.) 1989, Colony of the World 1993. *Address:* 271 Hawlin Road, Woodville, VA 22749, U.S.A.

McCARTHY, Rt. Hon. Sir Thaddeus (Pearcey), O.N.Z., K.B.E., Kt., P.C.; New Zealand judge (retd.); b. 24 Aug. 1907, Napier; s. of Walter McCarthy and Isabella Pearcey; m. Joan Margaret Miller 1938; one s. three d.; ed. St. Bede's Coll., Christchurch and Victoria Univ. Coll., Wellington, N.Z.; war service 1939–45; barrister and solicitor 1930–57; Judge of Supreme Court 1957–62; Judge of the Court of Appeal of New Zealand, 1963–76, Pres. 1973–76; mem. Judicial Cttee. Privy Council 1968–76; Chair. N.Z. Press Council 1978–87; Chair. Royal Comm. on Horse Racing 1970; Chair. Royal Comm. on State Services 1961–62, on Salary and Wage Fixing Procedures in the State Services, 1968, on Social Security 1969, on Salaries and Wages in the State Services 1972, on Nuclear Power Generation 1976–78, on Maori Land Courts 1979–; Chair. Security Review Authority and Commr. of Security Appeals 1977–94; Chair. Advisory Cttee., N.Z. Computer Centre 1977–86; Chair., Winston Churchill Memorial Trust 1966–76, Queen Elizabeth Nat. Trust 1978–84; Fellow N.Z. Inst. of Public Admin. 1984; Hon. LL.D. (Vic. Univ. of Wellington) 1978; Hon. Bencher, Middle Temple. *Leisure interests:* golf, sailing, walking. *Address:* 6B, 274 Oriental Parade, Wellington, New Zealand. *Telephone:* (04) 382-9706.

McCARTNEY, Sir (James) Paul, Kt., M.B.E., F.R.C.M.; British songwriter and performer; b. 18 June 1942, Liverpool; s. of James McCartney; m. Linda Eastman 1969 (died 1998); one s. two d. one step-d.; ed. Stockton Wood Road Primary School, Speke, Joseph Williams Primary School, Gateacre, and Liverpool Inst.; plays guitar, piano and organ; taught himself to play trumpet at age of 13; wrote first song 1956, wrote numerous songs with John Lennon; joined pop group The Quarrymen 1956; appeared under various titles until formation of The Beatles 1960; appeared with The Beatles in the following activities: performances in Hamburg 1960, 1961, 1962, The Cavern, Liverpool 1960, 1961; worldwide tours 1963–66; attended Transcendental Meditation Course at Maharishi's Acad., Rishikesh, India Feb. 1968; formed Apple Ltd., parent org. of The Beatles Group of Cos. 1968; left The Beatles after collapse of Apple Corps. Ltd. 1970; formed MPL group of cos. 1970; first solo album McCartney 1970; formed own pop group Wings 1971 (disbanded 1981); tours of Britain and Europe 1972–73, U.K. and Australia 1975, Europe and U.S.A. 1976, U.K. 1979, World Tour 1989–90; albums with the Beatles: Please Please Me 1963, With the Beatles 1963, A Hard Day's Night 1964, Beatles for Sale 1965, Help! 1965, Rubber Soul 1966, Revolver 1966, Sgt. Pepper's Lonely Hearts Club Band 1967, Magical Mystery Tour 1967, The Beatles (White Album) 1968, Yellow Submarine 1969, Abbey Road 1969, Let it Be 1970, Anthology I 1995, Anthology II 1996; other albums: Ram 1971, Wildlife 1971, Red Rose Speedway 1973, Band on the Run 1973, Venus and Mars 1975, Wings at the Speed of Sound 1976, Wings Over America 1976, London Town 1978, Wings Greatest 1978, Back to the Egg 1979, McCartney II 1980, Tug of War 1982, Pipes of Peace 1983, Give My Regards to Broad Street 1984, Press to Play 1986, All the Best 1987, Flowers in the Dirt 1989, Jet 1989, Tripping the Live Fantastic 1990, Unplugged: The Official Bootleg 1991, Paul McCartney's Liverpool Oratorio 1991, Off the Ground 1993, Flaming Pie 1997; composed Liverpool Oratorio (with Carl Davis q.v.) 1991; Symphony: Standing Stone 1997; two Grammy Awards for Band on the Run (incl. Best Pop Vocal Performance) 1975, Ivor Novello Award for Best Selling British Record 1977–78 for single Mull of Kintyre, for Int. Hit of the Year 1982 for single Ebony and Ivory, for Outstanding Services to British Music 1989; Guinness Book of Records "Triple Superlative Award" (43 songs each selling more than 1 million copies, holder of 60 gold discs, estimated sales of 100 million albums and 100 million singles) 1979; Lifetime Achievement Award 1990; Freeman of Liverpool 1984; Lifetime Achievement Award People for the Ethical Treatment of Animals (with Linda McCartney) 1996; Hon. Dr. (Sussex) 1988; Hon. Fellow (Liverpool John Moores Univ.) 1998; composed soundtrack music for The Family Way 1966, James Paul McCartney 1973, Live and Let Die 1973, The Zoo Gang (TV series) 1973; Films by The Beatles: A Hard Day's Night 1964, Help! 1965, Yellow Submarine (animated colour cartoon film) 1968, Let it Be 1970; TV film Magical Mystery Tour 1967; Wings over the World (TV) 1979, Rockshow 1981; Give My Regards to Broad Street (wrote and dir.) 1984, Rupert and the Frog Song (wrote and produced) 1985 (BAFTA Award Best Animated Film), Press to Play 1986; concert film Get Back 1991; Polar Music Prize 1992. *Address:* c/o MPL Communications Ltd., 1 Soho Square, London, W1V 6BQ, England.

McCARTNEY, Stella, B.A.; British fashion designer; b. 1972; d. of Paul McCartney and the late Linda McCartney; ed. Cen. St. Martins Coll. of Art and Design; work with Christian Lacroix at age 15 and later with Betty Jackson; work experience in Fashion Dept., Vogue magazine; after graduating set up own design co. in London; now Chief Designer for Chloe, Paris. *Address:* Chloe, Faubourg St. Honoré, Paris, France.

McCARTY, Maclyn, A.B., M.D.; American medical research scientist; b. 9 June 1911, South Bend. Ind.; s. of Earl Hauser and Hazel Beagle McCarty; m. 1st Anita Davies 1934 (divorced 1966), 2nd Marjorie Steiner 1966; three s. one d.; ed. Kenosha High School, Wis., Stanford and Johns Hopkins Univs.; Intern and Asst. Resident in Paediatrics, Johns Hopkins Hosp. 1937–40; Fellow in Medicine, New York Univ. 1940–41; Fellow in Medical Sciences of Nat. Research Council (with O. T. Avery), Rockefeller Inst. for Medical Research (now Rockefeller Univ.) 1941–42, Active Duty (U.S.N.R.) Naval Research Unit 1942–46, Assoc. and Assoc. Physician 1946–48, Assoc. mem. and Assoc. Physician 1948–50, mem. (Prof.) 1950–81, Physician in Chief to the Hosp. 1960–74, Vice-Pres. 1965–78, John D. Rockefeller, Jr. Prof. 1977–81, Prof. Emer. 1981–; Vice-Pres. Helen Hay Whitney Foundation, Chair. Scientific Advisory Cttee. 1963–96; Ed. Journal of Experimental Medicine 1963–; 1st Waterford Biomedical Award 1977; Robert Koch Gold Medal (Fed. Repub. of Germany) 1981, Kovalenko Medal, N.A.S. 1988, Wolf Prize, Israel 1990, Albert Lasker Special Public Health Award 1994; Order of Repub., First Degree (Egypt) 1982; Commdr.'s Cross of the Order of Merit (Fed. Repub. of Germany) 1984. *Publications:* The Transforming Principle: Discovering that Genes are made of DNA 1985, numerous scientific papers, mainly in Journal of Experimental Medicine. *Leisure interests:* travel, reading. *Address:* The Rockefeller University, 66th Street and York Avenue, New York, NY 10021, U.S.A. *Telephone:* (212) 327-8158. *Fax:* (212) 327-8960.

McCLURE, Donald S., PH.D.; American professor of chemistry; b. 27 Aug. 1920, Yonkers, New York; s. of Robert H. McClure and Helen Campbell; m. Laura Lee Thompson 1949; two s. one d.; ed. Yonkers High School and Univs. of Minnesota and Calif. (Berkeley); War Research Div. Columbia Univ. 1942–46; Instructor in Chem. Univ. of Calif. (Berkeley) 1948–50, Asst. Prof. 1950–55; RCA Labs. Princeton, N.J. 1955–62; Prof. of Chem. Univ. of Chicago 1962–67, Princeton Univ. 1967–91; Prof. Emer. Princeton Univ. 1991–; mem. N.A.S., American Acad. of Arts and Sciences; Guggenheim Fellow, Univ. of Oxford 1972–73; Humboldt Fellow 1982; Irving Langmuir Award 1979. *Publications:* numerous articles in professional journals. *Address:* 23 Hemlock Circle, Princeton, NJ 08540, U.S.A. (Home).

McCOLGAN, Elizabeth (Liz), M.B.E.; British athlete; b. 24 May 1964, Dundee, Scotland; m. Peter McColgan; one d.; coached by Grete Waitz; Gold Medal Commonwealth Games 10,000m. 1986, 1990; Silver Medal World Cross Country Championships 1987, Bronze Medal 1991; Silver Medal Olympic Games 10,000m. 1988; Silver Medal World Indoor Championships 3,000m. 1989; Bronze Medal Commonwealth Games 3,000m. 1990; Gold Medal World Championships 10,000m. 1991; Gold Medal World Half-Marathon Championships 1992; first in New York City Marathon 1991; first in Tokyo Marathon 1992, third in 1996; third in London Marathon 1993, fifth in 1995, first in 1996, second in 1997, 1998.

McCOLL OF DULWICH, Baron (Life Peer) cr. 1989, of Bermondsey in the London Borough of Southwark, **Ian McColl,** C.B.E., M.S., F.R.C.S., F.A.C.S.; British professor of surgery; b. 6 Jan. 1933; s. of the late Frederick George McColl and Winifred Edith McColl; m. Jean Lennox McNair 1960; one s. two d.; ed. Hutchesons' Grammar School, Glasgow, St. Paul's School, London, Guy's Hosp. Medical School, Univ. of London; Moynihan Fellowship, Asscn. of Surgeons 1967; Reader in Surgery, St. Bartholomew's Hosp., London 1967–71, Sub-Dean, St. Bartholomew's Hosp. Medical Coll. 1969–71; Prof. of Surgery, Guy's Hosp., London 1971–, Consultant Surgeon 1971–, Dir. of Surgery 1985–; Chair. Dept. of Surgery, United Medical and Dental Schools, St. Thomas' Hosps. 1985–92; Hon. Consultant to British Army 1976, Hon. Consultant 1982–98; Parl. Pvt. Sec. (Lords) to Prime Minister 1994–97; Deputy Speaker House of Lords 1994–97; Chair. Bd. of Govs. Mildmay Mission Hosp. 1984–; Vice-Chair. Disablement Services Authority for England 1987–91; mem. Council, Royal Coll. of Surgeons 1986–94, Council, Imperial Cancer Research Fund 1986–94; Pres. Nat. Asscn. of Limbless Disabled, Soc. of Minimally Invasive Surgery; Vice-Pres. John Grooms Asscn. for the Disabled; mem. Bd. of Govs. American Coll. of Surgeons 1982–88. *Publications:* Intestinal Absorption in Man 1976, NHS Data Book 1984, Govt. Report on supply of artificial legs and wheelchairs for England; articles on colonic diseases, medical audit and amputations. *Leisure interest:* forestry. *Address:* House of Lords, London, S.W.1, England.

McCONAUGHEY, Matthew; American actor; b. 4 Nov. 1969, Ulvade, Tex.; ed. Univ. of Texas at Austin. *Film appearances include:* Dazed and Confused, The Return of the Texas Chainsaw Massacre, Boys on the Side, My Boyfriend's Back 1993, Angels in the Outfield 1994, Scorpion Spring, Submission 1995, Glory Daze, Lone Star, A Time to Kill 1996, Larger Than Life 1997, Amistad, Contact, Making Sandwiches, Last Flight of the Raven, Newton Boys, South Beach. *Address:* c/o William Morris Agency, 151 El Camino Drive, Beverly Hills, CA 90212; c/o Warner Brothers Incorporated, 4000 Warner Boulevard, Suite 1101, Burbank, CA 91522, U.S.A.

McCONNELL, David John, PH.D., M.R.I.A.; Irish professor of molecular genetics; b. 15 May 1944, Dublin; s. of John J. McConnell and Joan Warwick; m. Janet Overend 1966; two s.; ed. Zion Nat. Schools, Rathgar, Dublin, Sandford Park School, Ranelagh, Dublin, Trinity Coll. Dublin and Calif. Inst. of Tech.; lecturer in Genetics, Trinity Coll. Dublin 1970–85, Fellow 1978, Assoc. Prof. of Genetics 1985–90, Head, Dept. of Genetics 1987–, Prof. of Genetics 1990–; Eleanor Roosevelt Fellow, Int. Union Against Cancer, Lab. of Prof. Wally Gilbert, Dept. of Biochem. and Molecular Biology Harvard Univ. 1976–77; Visiting Prof. Univ. of Calif. (Davis) 1979; EMBO Fellowship, Lab. of Prof. Pierre Chambon, Univ. of Strasbourg 1980; consultant in genetic eng. and biotech. UNIDO 1982–; UNDP Star consultant, Beijing Agric. Univ. 1987; Chair. Adelaide Hosp. 1988–94; Vice-Pres. Royal Zoological Soc. of Ireland 1990–92, Pres. 1992–; other professional appts.; mem. European Molecular Biological Org. (EMBO); Vice-Provost for Quatercentenary Affairs, Trinity Coll., Dublin 1991–92. *Publications:* more than 100 papers in scientific journals. *Leisure interests:* windsurfing, Kerry, gardening. *Address:* Department of Genetics, Trinity College, Dublin 2, Ireland. *Telephone:* (01) 702 2008, 702 1140. *Fax:* (01) 671 4968.

McCONNELL, Harden M., PH.D.; American professor of chemistry; b. 18 July 1927, Richmond, Va.; s. of Harry R. McConnell and Frances (née Coffee) McConnell; m. Sofia Glogovac 1956; two s. one d.; ed. George Washington Univ., California Inst. of Tech. and Univ. of Chicago; with Dept. of Physics, Univ. of Chicago, Nat. Research Fellow 1950–52; Shell Devt. Co., Emeryville, Calif. 1952–56; Asst. Prof. of Chem., Calif. Inst. of Tech. 1956–58, Assoc. Prof. of Chem. 1958–59, Prof. of Chem. 1959–63, Prof. of Chem. and Physics 1963–64; Prof. of Chem. Stanford Univ. 1964–79, Robert Eckles Swain Prof. of Chemistry 1979–, Chair. Dept. of Chem. 1989–; mem. several bds., Neuroscience Research Program, M.I.T.; f. Molecular Devices Corpn. 1983; Pres. Foundation for Basic Research in Chemistry 1990–96; Fellow, American Physical Soc., Biophysical Soc., American Soc. of Biological Chemists, American Asscn. for the Advancement of Science 1982; mem. A.C.S., N.A.S., Int. Acad. of Quantum Molecular Science, A.A.A.S.; Foreign mem. Serbian Acad. of Sciences and Arts; Harkins Lecturer, Univ. of Chicago 1967, Falk-Plaut Lecturer, Columbia Univ. 1967, Renaud Foundation Lecturer 1971, Peter Debye Lecturer, Cornell Univ. 1973, Harvey Lecturer, Rockefeller Univ. 1977, A. L. Patterson Lecturer, Inst. for Cancer Research, Phil. 1978, Pauling Lecturer, Stanford Univ. 1981, Remsen Memorial Lecturer, Maryland Section A.C.S. 1982, Prof. du Collège de France 1986, Le Bel Lecturer, Strasbourg 1986, Swift Lecturer, Calif. Inst. of Tech. 1986, Venable Lecturer, Univ. of N. Carolina 1987, Linus Pauling Distinguished Lecturer, Oregon State Univ. 1987, Davis Lecturer, Univ. of New Orleans 1994; Calif. Section Award of A.C.S. 1961, Nat. A.C.S. Award in Pure Chem. 1962, Harrison Howe Award 1968, Irving Langmuir Award in Chemical Physics 1971, Alumni Achievement Award (George Washington Univ.) 1971, Dickson Prize for Science (Carnegie-Mellon Univ.) 1982, Distinguished Alumni Award (Calif. Inst. of Tech.) 1982, Wolf Prize in Chemistry 1983–84, ISCO Award 1984, Pauling Medal, Puget Sound and Oregon A.C.S. Sections 1987, Wheland Medal, Univ. of Chicago 1988, N.A.S. Award in Chemical Sciences 1988, Sherman Fairchild Distinguished Scholar, Calif. Inst. of Tech. 1988, Nat. Medal of Science 1989, Peter Debeye Award, Physical Chemistry, American Chemistry Society 1990, Bruker Prize, Royal Soc. of Chem. 1995, A.C.S. Award in Surface Science 1997, Gold Medal of Int. ESR Soc. 1997. *Publications:* over 400 scientific publs. in the field of chem., chemical physics, biophysics and immunology. *Leisure interest:* mathematics. *Address:* Department of Chemistry, Stanford University, Stanford, CA 94305, U.S.A. (Office). *Telephone:* (415) 723 4571.

McCONNELL, James Desmond Caldwell, PH.D., F.R.S.; British professor of the physics and chemistry of minerals; b. 3 July 1930; s. of Samuel D. McConnell and Cathleen McConnell; m. Jean Elspeth Ironside 1956; one s. two d.; ed. Queen's Univ. of Belfast and Univ. of Cambridge; demonstrator, Univ. of Cambridge 1955, lecturer 1960, Reader 1972–82; Fellow, Churchill Coll., Cambridge 1962–82, Extraordinary Fellow 1983–88; Head of Dept. of Rock Physics, Schlumberger Cambridge Research 1983–86; Prof. of the Physics and Chemistry of Minerals, Dept. of Earth Sciences, Univ. of Oxford 1986–95, Head of Dept. 1991–95, now Emer.; Fellow St. Hugh's Coll., Oxford 1986–95, Hon. Fellow 1995–; Humboldt Prize 1996. *Publications:* Principles of Mineral Behaviour (with A. Putnis) 1980, numerous papers in physics and mineralogical journals. *Leisure interests:* local history, hill walking, singing, sailing. *Address:* 8 The Croft, Old Headington, Oxford, OX3 9BU, England.

MacCORMAC, Richard Cornelius, C.B.E., P.P.R.I.B.A., F.R.S.A., R.A.; British architect; b. 3 Sept. 1938; s. of Henry MacCormac and Marion Maud Broomhall; m. Susan Karin Landen 1964; two s. (one deceased); ed. Westminster School, Trinity Coll. Cambridge, Univ. Coll. London; served R.N. 1957–59; Project Architect, London Borough of Merton 1967–69; est. pvt. practice 1969; partner MacCormac, Jamieson, Prichard Architects 1972–; taught in Dept. of Architecture, Cambridge Univ. 1969–75, 1979–81, Univ. Lecturer 1976–79; Visiting Prof. Univ. of Edin. 1982–85; Dir. Spitalfields Workspace 1981–; mem. Royal Fine Art Comm. 1983–93; Pres. R.I.B.A. 1991–93; Adviser British Council 1993–. *Major works include:* Cable & Wireles Coll., Coventry (Royal Fine Art Comm./Sunday Times Bldg. of the Year Award 1994); Garden Quadrangle, St. John's Coll., Oxford (Independent on Sunday Bldg. of the Year Award 1994); Bowra Bldg., Wadham Coll., Oxford; Burrell's Fields, Trinity Coll., Cambridge; Ruskin Library, Lancaster Univ. (Independent on Sunday Bldg. of the Year Award 1996). *Leisure interests:* sailing, music, reading. *Address:* 9 Heneage Street, London, E1 5LJ, England. *Telephone:* 0171-377 9262.

McCORMACK, Mark Hume, LL.B.; American business executive and lawyer; b. 6 Nov. 1930; s. of Ned H. and Grace W. McCormack; m. 1st Nancy Breckenridge McCormack 1954 (divorced); two s. one d.; m. 2nd Betsy Nagelsen 1986; ed. Princeton and Yale Univs. and William and Mary Coll.; admitted to Ohio Bar 1957; Assoc. Arter, Hadden, Wykoff & Van Duzer 1957–63, Partner 1963–; started Int. Management Group 1962, Pres.. and C.E.O. 1964–; commentator for televised golf, B.B.C.; mem. Cleveland Bar Assoc. *Publications:* The World of Professional Golf 1967, Arnie: The Evolution of a Legend 1967, The Wonderful World of Professional Golf 1973, What They Did Not Teach You At Harvard Business School 1984, The Terrible Truth about Lawyers 1987, What They Still Don't Teach You At Harvard Business School 1989, Success Secrets 1989, The 110% Solution 1990, On Negotiating 1995, McCormack on Communications 1996. *Leisure interest:* golf. *Address:* International Management Group, No. 1300, One Erieview Plaza, Cleveland, OH 44114 (Office); 2830 Lander Road, Pepperpike, Cleveland, OH 44124, U.S.A. (Home).

MacCORMICK, (Donald) Neil, M.A., LL.D., F.B.A., F.R.S.E.; British professor of law; b. 27 May 1941, Glasgow; s. of John MacDonald MacCormick and Margaret Isobel Miller; m. 1st Caroline Rona Barr 1965 (divorced 1991); three d.; m. 2nd Flora Margaret Britain (née Milne) 1992; ed. High School of Glasgow, Univ. of Glasgow, Balliol Coll., Oxford; Lecturer in Jurisprudence, Queen's Coll., Dundee, St. Andrews Univ. 1965–67; Fellow and Tutor in Jurisprudence, Balliol Coll., Oxford 1967–72; Regius Prof. of Public Law and the Law of Nature and Nations, Univ. of Edin. 1972–, Dean of the Faculty of Law 1973–76, 1985–88; Vice Principal (Int.) Univ. of Edin. 1997–, Leverhulme Personal Research Prof. 1997–; Pres. Soc. of Public Teachers of Law 1983–84; mem. Nat. Council of Scottish Nat. Party 1978–84, 1985–86, 1989–; Dr. h.c. (Uppsala Univ.) 1986. *Publications:* Legal Reasoning and Legal Theory 1978, H. L. A. Hart 1981, Legal Right and Social Democracy 1982, An Institutional Theory of Law 1986, The Scottish Debate (ed.) 1970, The Legal Mind (ed.) 1986, Enlightenment Rights and Revolution (ed.) 1989, Interpreting Statutes (ed.) 1991, Essays on Legal Reasoning (2 vols., ed.) 1991, Controversies About the Ontology of Law (ed.) 1991. *Leisure interests:* gardening, hill-walking, dinghy sailing, politics (Scottish Nat. Party), piping. *Address:* Faculty of Law, University of Edinburgh, The Old College, South Bridge, Edinburgh, EH8 9YL (Office); 19 Pentland Terrace, Edin., EH10 6HA, Scotland (Home). *Telephone:* 0131-650 2029 (Office); 0131-447 7945 (Home). *Fax:* 0131-662 4902.

McCOWEN, Alec, C.B.E.; British actor; b. 26 May 1925, Tunbridge Wells; s. of Duncan McCowen and Mary Walkden; ed. Skinners School, Tunbridge Wells, and Royal Acad. of Dramatic Art; mem. Nat. Theatre; Evening Standard (now The Standard) Best Actor 1968, 1973, 1982; Variety Club Stage Actor 1970; Old Vic Theatre: played Touchstone, Ford, Richard II, Mercutio, Malvolio, Oberon 1959–60; with R.S.C.: played Fool in King Lear 1964, Hadrian VII 1968, The Philanthropist 1970, The Misanthrope 1972, Dr. Dysart in Equus 1972, Henry Higgins in Pygmalion 1974, Ben in The Family Dance 1976; with Prospect Co.: Antony in Antony and Cleopatra 1977; solo performance of St. Mark's Gospel 1978, 1981; Frank in Tishoo 1979; Malvolio in Twelfth Night (TV) 1980; with Nat. Theatre: Crocker-Harris in The Browning Version, Arthur in Harlequinade, Capt. Corcoran in H.M.S. Pinafore 1981, Adolf Hitler in The Portage to San Cristobal of AH 1982, solo performance in Kipling 1983, Reilly in The Cocktail Party 1986, Nicolai in Fathers and Sons 1987, Vladimir in Waiting for Godot 1987, Modern Love 1988, Dr. Scoper in The Heiress 1989, Harry in Exclusive 1989, George in A Single Man 1990, Father Jack in Dancing at Lughnasa 1990, Caesar in Caesar and Cleopatra, Michael in Someone Who'll Watch Over Me 1992, Prospero in The Tempest 1993, Elgar in Elgar's Rondo, Gaev in The Cherry Orchard 1995, Clem in Tom and Clem 1997, Narrator in Peter Pan 1998; Dir.: Definitely the Bahamas 1987. *Films:* Frenzy 1971, Travels with my Aunt 1973, Stevie 1978, The Assam Garden 1985, Personal Services 1986, Henry V 1989, Age of Innocence 1992. *Television:* Private Lives 1976, Mr. Palfrey of Westminster 1984, Hunted Down 1989. *Publications:* Young Gemini 1979, Double Bill 1980 and Personal Mark 1984. *Leisure interests:* music and gardening. *Address:* c/o Jeremy Conway, Eagle House, 18–21 Jermyn Street, London, SW1Y 6HP, England.

McCRACKEN, Paul Winston, PH.D.; American economist; b. 29 Dec. 1915, Richland, Ia.; s. of late C. Sumner McCracken and Mary (Coffin) McCracken; m. E. Ruth Siler 1942; two d.; ed. William Penn Coll. and Harvard Univ.; mem. Faculty, Foundation School, Berea Coll., Kentucky 1937–40; economist, Dept. of Commerce, Washington 1942–43; Financial Economist, Dir. of Research, Fed. Reserve Bank of Minneapolis 1943–48; Assoc. Prof. School of Business Admin., Univ. of Mich. 1948–50, Prof. 1950–66, Edmund Ezra Day Univ. Prof. of Business Admin. 1966–86, Prof. Emer. 1986–; mem. Council of Econ. Advisers, Washington 1956–59, Chair. 1969–72; mem. Pres.'s Advisory Bd. on Econ. Policy 1980–89; Fellow American Statistics Asscn. ; mem. American Econs. Asscn., American Finance Asscn. *Publications:* Hypothetical Projection of Commodity Expenditures, Northwest in Two Wars, Future of Northwest Bank Deposits, Rising Tide of Bank Lending, Balance of Payments and Domestic Prosperity, Economic Progress and the Utility Industry. *Address:* 2564 Hawthorn Road, Ann Arbor, MI 48104, U.S.A.

McCREA, Sir William Hunter, Kt., PH.D., SC.D., F.R.S.; British astronomer and mathematician; b. 13 Dec. 1904, Dublin; s. of the late Robert Hunter McCrea and the late Margaret Hutton; m. Marian Nicol Core Webster 1933 (died 1995); one s. two d.; ed. Chesterfield Grammar School, Cambridge and Göttingen Univs.; Lecturer in Math., Edin. Univ. 1930–32; Reader in Math., Univ. of London and Asst. Prof. Imperial Coll. of Science 1932–36; Prof. of Math., Queen's Univ. of Belfast 1936–44; Temporary Prin. Experimental Officer, Admiralty 1943–45; Prof. of Math., Univ. of London (Royal Holloway Coll.) 1944–66; Comyns Berkeley Bye-Fellow, Caius Coll., Cambridge 1952–53; Visiting Prof. of Astronomy, Univ. of Calif. 1956, 1967, Case Inst. of Tech. 1964; Research Prof. of Theoretical Astronomy, Univ. of Sussex 1966–72, Emer. 1972–; Fellow Imperial Coll. of Science and Tech., London 1967–; Georges Lemaître Prof., Univ. of Louvain 1969; Royal Soc. Leverhulme Visiting Prof. Cairo 1973; Visiting Prof. of Astronomy, Univ. of B.C. Vancouver 1975–76; Visiting Prof. Univ. of Istanbul 1977–78; William Evans Visiting Prof. Univ. of Otago, N.Z. 1979; Pres. Royal Astronomical Soc. 1961–63, Treas. 1976–79; Pres. Math. Asscn. 1973–74, Hon. mem. 1985;

mem. Akad. Leopoldina, Halle; Foreign mem. Turin Acad. of Sciences 1990; Hon. Fellow Royal Holloway Coll. 1984–; Hon. D.Sc. (Nat. Univ. of Ireland, Queen's Univ. Belfast, Univ. of Sussex), Sc.D. (Dublin), Dr. h.c. (Nat. Univ. of Córdoba, Argentina); Keith Prize, Royal Soc. of Edinburgh, Gold Medal, Royal Astronomical Soc. 1976; Freeman of City of London 1988. *Publications:* Relativity Physics 1935, Analytical Geometry of Three Dimensions 1942, Physics of the Sun and Stars 1950, trans. of A. Unsöld's The New Cosmos 1969, Cosmology 1969, The Royal Greenwich Observatory 1975, and numerous papers in mathematical and astronomical journals. *Address:* Astronomy Centre, University of Sussex, Falmer, Brighton BN1 9QH (Office); 87 Houndean Rise, Lewes, Sussex BN7 1EJ, England (Home). *Telephone:* (01273) 606755 (Office); (01273) 473296 (Home).

McCREDIE, Andrew Dalgarno, A.C., A.M., M.A., D.PHIL., F.A.H.; Australian professor of musicology; b. 3 Sept. 1930, Sydney; s. of Harold A. McCredie and Marjorie C. (née Dalgarno) McCredie; m. Xenia Rosner 1965; one d.; ed. Univ. of Sydney, Royal Acad. of Music, London, Univs. of Copenhagen, Stockholm, Hamburg; Sr. Research Fellow, Univ. of Adelaide 1965–69, Sr. Lecturer in Musicology 1970–73, Reader in Musicology 1974–77, Prof. 1978–; Visiting Lecturer Univs. of Amsterdam, Utrecht 1964, Western Australia 1970, City Univ. of New York 1974, Yale, Pennsylvania 1977, Ljubljana, Bologna, Marburg, Frankfurt, Cracow, Warsaw 1978, Copenhagen, Belfast (Queen's Univ.), Hamburg, Munich, Zentral Inst. für Musikforschung (Berlin), Berne, Basle, Zurich 1983, Melbourne, Stockholm, Tübingen 1986, Heidelberg, Saarbrücken, Queen's Univ., Kingston, Ont., Brandeis (Boston), City Univ. of New York, N.S.W. (Sydney) 1987, Munich, Braunschweig 1988, Wolfenbüttel, Mainz, Edmonton, Calgary, Saskatoon, London (Ont.), Toronto 1989; mem. Council Int. Musicological Soc. 1977–87; Mem. Inst. for Advanced Musical Studies, King's Coll. Univ., London 1993; Adviser Musica Antiqua Europae Orientalis 1977–; advisory, corresp., ed. appts. Int. Review of Aesthetics and Sociology of Music 1981–, Current Musicology 1987–, Studies in Music 1980; Edward J. Dent Medal 1974, Paderewski Medal-Bydgoszcz Philharmonia 1982. *Publications:* Musical Composition in Australia (3 vols.) 1969, Karl Amadeus Hartmann: Catalogue of all his works with biography 1981 (trans. German), Miscellanea Musicologica, Adelaide (Ed.) 1966–, Paperbacks on Musicology (Gen. Ed.) 1978–, From Colonel Light into the Footlights; The Performing Arts in South Australia from 1836 to the Present 1988, Clemens von Franckenstein 1991, Ludwig Thuille 1993. *Leisure interests:* travel, books, art, antiques, walking and sailing. *Address:* Department of Music Studies, University of Adelaide, G.P.O. Box 498, Adelaide, S.A. 5001 (Office); 8 Hawker Avenue, Belair, S.A. 5052, Australia (Home). *Telephone:* 228.5138, 228.5286 (Office); 278.3950 (Home).

McCREEVY, Charlie, B.COMM., F.C.A.; Irish politician; b. Sept. 1949; m. (separated); three s. three d.; ed. Univ. Coll. Dublin; partner, Tynan Dillon & Co. (chartered accountants), Dublin, Naas and Ballyhaunis; mem. Kildare Co. Council 1979–85; mem. Dáil 1977–; Minister for Social Welfare 1992–93, for Tourism and Trade 1993–94, for Finance July 1997–; fmr. Fianna Fáil Spokesperson on Finance. *Address:* Dáil Éireann, Dublin; Department of Finance, Government Buildings, Upper Merrion Street, Dublin 2; Hillview House, Kilcullen Ross, Naas, Co. Kildare, Ireland.

McCRUM, (John) Robert, M.A.; British writer and newspaper editor; b. 7 July 1953; s. of Michael William McCrum and Christine Mary Kathleen fforde; m. 1st Olivia Timbs (divorced 1984); m. 2nd Sarah Lyall 1995; one d.; ed. Sherborne School, Corpus Christi Coll., Cambridge and Univ. of Pennsylvania; house reader Chatto & Windus 1977–79; Editorial Dir. Faber and Faber Ltd. 1979–89, Ed.-in-Chief 1990–96; Literary Ed. Observer newspaper 1996–; scriptwriter and co-producer The Story of English TV series 1980–86; Tony Godwin Prize 1979, Peabody Award 1986, Emmy Award 1987. *Publications:* In the Secret State 1980, A Loss of Heart 1982, The Fabulous Englishman 1984, The Story of English 1986, The World is a Banana 1988, Mainland 1991, The Psychological Moment 1993, Suspicion 1996, My Year Off 1998. *Leisure interest:* gardening. *Address:* The Observer, 119 Farringdon Road, London, EC1R 3ER, England.

McCRUM, Michael William, C.B.E., M.A.: British university administrator and headmaster; b. 23 May 1924, Alverstoke, Gosport, Hants.; s. of late Capt. C. R. McCrum, R.N. and Ivy H. C. (née Nicholson) McCrum; m. Christine M. K. fforde 1952; three s. one d.; ed. Sherborne School and Corpus Christi Coll., Cambridge; Asst. Master, Rugby School 1948–50; Fellow, Corpus Christi Coll., Cambridge 1949–80, Second Tutor 1950–51, Tutor 1951–62, Master 1980–94; Headmaster of Tonbridge School 1962–70; Head Master of Eton Coll. 1970–80; Gov. Sherborne School 1980–94, King's School, Canterbury 1980–94, Rugby School 1982–94; Vice-Chancellor Cambridge Univ. 1987–89; Pres. Cambridge Soc. 1989–96, Chair. Faculty Bd. of Educ. 1990–93; Chair. Cathedrals Fabric Comm. for England 1991–, Governing Bodies Asscn. 1989–94, Independent Schools Jt. Council 1992–94; Hon. Fellow Corpus Christi Coll. 1994–; Trustee Henry Fund 1994–95; Hon. D.Ed. (Univ. of Vic.); Hon. Freeman, Skinners Co. 1980; Comendador de la Orden de Isabel la Católica (Spain) 1988. *Publications:* Select Documents of the Principates of the Flavian Emperors AD 68-96 1961, Thomas Arnold, Head Master 1989. *Address:* 32 Clarendon Street, Cambridge, CB1 1JX, England. *Telephone:* (01223) 353303.

McCULLIN, Donald, C.B.E.; British photographer; b. 9 Oct. 1935, London; s. of Frederick and Jessica McCullin; m. Christine Dent 1959 (marriage dissolved 1987); two s. one d. and one s. by Laraine Ashton; m. Marilyn Bridges 1995; ed. Tollington Park Secondary Modern, Hammersmith Art and Crafts School; R.A.F. Nat. Service; photographer with Observer for four years; photographer with Sunday Times, London for eighteen years; freelance 1980–; has covered eight wars—Viet Nam, Cambodia, Biafra, Congo, Israel, Cyprus, Chad, Lebanon—and many famine areas; has travelled to 64 countries; World Press Photographer 1964, Warsaw Gold Medal 1964, Granada TV Award 1967, 1969, Two Gold, One Silver Art Director Awards, U.K. *Publications:* The Destruction Business 1971, The Concerned Photographer II 1972, Is Anyone Taking Notice? 1973, Hearts of Darkness 1980, Battle Beirut—A City in Crisis 1983, Perspectives 1987, Skulduggery 1987, Open Skies 1989, Unreasonable Behaviour (autobiog.) 1990, Sleeping with Ghosts; A Life's Work in Photography 1995. *Leisure interests:* walking in countries, collecting Victorian children's books, looking at things and people. *Address:* Holly Hill House, Batcombe, Shepton Mallet, Somerset, BA4 6BL, England.

McCULLOUGH, Colleen; Australian author; b. 1 June 1937, Wellington, N.S.W.; m. Ric Robinson 1984; ed. Holy Cross Coll., Woollahra, Sydney Univ., Inst. of Child Health, London Univ.; career as neurophysiologist in Sydney, London and at Yale Univ. Medical School, U.S.A.; moved to Norfolk Island, S. Pacific 1979; Hon. D.Litt. (Macquarie) 1993. *Publications:* novels: Tim 1974, The Thorn Birds 1977, An Indecent Obsession 1981, A Creed for the Third Millennium 1985, The Ladies of Missalonghi 1987, The First Man in Rome 1990, The Grass Crown 1991, Fortune's Favorites 1993, Caesar's Women 1996, Caesar 1997, The Song of Troy 1998; Cooking with Colleen McCullough and Jean Easthope 1982; Roden Cutler, V.C. The Biography 1998. *Address:* "Out Yenna", Norfolk Island, Oceania (via Australia). *Fax:* (6723) 23313.

McDAID, James, M.B., B.CH.; Irish politician; b. 3 Oct. 1949, Termon, Co. Donegal; m. Marguerite McLoughlin; three s. one d.; ed. St. Eunan's Coll., Letterkenny, Univ. Coll., Galway; Sr. Surgical House Officer, Letterkenny Gen. Hosp. 1974–79; Gen. Practitioner, Letterkenny 1979; f., Chair. Donegal Hospice Movt. 1988; mem. Dáil Éireann for Donegal N.E. 1988–; mem. Dáil Cttee. on Women's Rights 1992, Cttee. of Public Accounts 1993, Cttee. on Foreign Affairs and N. Ireland Sub-Cttee. 1995; Spokesperson on North/South Devts. Jan. 1995, for Equality and Law Reform 1996–97; Minister for Tourism, Sport and Recreation June 1997–. *Address:* Department of Tourism, Sport and Recreation, Kildare Street, Dublin 2 (Office); Pearse Road, Letterkenny, Co. Donegal, Ireland (Home). *Telephone:* (1) 6621444 (Office); (74) 25132 (Home). *Fax:* (1) 6612727 (Office).

MacDERMOTT, Rt. Hon. Sir John Clarke, Kt.; British judge (retd.); b. 1927; s. of Baron MacDermott and Louise Palmer Johnston; m. Margaret H. Dales; four d.; ed. Campbell Coll. Belfast, Trinity Hall, Cambridge and Queen's Univ. Belfast; called to Bar, Inner Temple and N. Ireland 1949; Q.C. (N. Ireland) 1964; Judge, High Court of N. Ireland 1973–87; a Lord Justice of Appeal, Supreme Court of Judicature, N. Ireland 1987–98. *Address:* c/o Royal Courts of Justice, Belfast; 6 Tarawood, Holywood, Co. Down, Northern Ireland.

MCDONAGH, Enda; Irish professor of moral theology; b. 27 June 1930, Co. Mayo; s. of Patrick McDonagh and Mary Kelly; ed. St. Jarlath's Coll., Tuam, St. Patrick's Coll., Maynooth, Gregorianum Univ., Rome and Univ. of Munich; Prof. of Moral Theology (and Canon Law), St. Patrick's Coll. 1958–, Dir. Postgraduate Studies in Theology 1970–76, Dean of Faculty of Theology 1973–79; lecturer in Irish School of Ecumenics, Dublin 1970–; Husking Prof. of Theology, Univ. of Notre Dame, U.S.A. 1979–81; Ferguson Lecturer, Univ. of Manchester March 1978; Leverhulme Research Fellow, Univ. of Cambridge 1978. *Publications:* Roman Catholics and Unity 1963, Religious Freedom 1967, Invitation and Response 1972, Gift and Call 1975, Social Ethics and the Christian 1979, Doing the Truth 1979, Church and Politics: The Case History of Zimbabwe 1980, The Making of Disciples 1982, Between Chaos and New Creation 1987, ed. and contrib. The Meaning of Christian Marriage 1963, Moral Theology Renewed 1965, Truth and Life 1968. *Leisure interests:* poetry and music. *Address:* St. Patrick's College, Maynooth, Co. Kildare, Ireland. *Telephone:* 285222.

MACDONALD, Hon. Donald Stovel, P.C., C.C., LL.M.; Canadian politician and lawyer; b. 1 March 1932, Ottawa, Ont.; s. of Donald A. Macdonald and Marjorie I. Stovel; m. 1st Ruth Hutchison 1961 (died 1987); four d.; m. 2nd Adrian Merchant Lang 1988; three step-s. three step-d.; ed. Ottawa public schools, Ashbury Coll., Ottawa, Univs. of Toronto and Cambridge, and Osgoode Hall and Harvard Law Schools; with McCarthy and McCarthy, Barristers, Toronto 1957–62; M.P. 1962–78; Parl. Sec. to Minister of Justice 1963–65, to Minister of Finance 1965, to Sec. of State for External Affairs 1966–68, to Minister of Industry 1968; Minister without Portfolio 1968; Pres. Privy Council and Govt. House Leader 1968; Minister of Nat. Defence 1970–72, of Energy, Mines and Resources 1972–75, of Finance 1975–77; partner, firm McCarthy & McCarthy, Toronto 1977–88; Counsel, McCarthy Tétrault, Toronto 1991–; High Commr. in the U.K. 1988–91; Chair. Royal Comm. on the Econ. Union and Devt. Prospects for Canada 1982–85, Inst. for Research and Public Policy, Montreal 1991–97; Chair. and Dir. Siemens Canada Ltd., Celanese Canada Inc.; Dir. Alberta Energy Co. Ltd., Slough Estates Ltd., Sun Life Assurance Co. of Canada, Trans-Canada Pipelines Ltd., BFC Construction Corpn., CanEnerco Inc., Boise Cascade Corpn. 1996–, Inst. of Corp. Dirs. (Chair. 1995–96); Chair. Special Advisory Cttee. to determine the effectiveness of Ont.'s electricity system 1995–96, Design

Exchange, Toronto 1993–96, Canadian Friends of Cambridge Univ. 1995–97; Rowell Fellowship, Canadian Inst. of Int. Affairs 1956; Hon. Fellow Trinity Hall, Cambridge Univ. 1994; Hon. LL.D. (St. Lawrence Univ., Univ. of New Brunswick), Hon. D.Eng. (Colorado School of Mines); Freeman City of London. *Leisure interests:* cross-country skiing, tennis. *Address:* McCarthy Tétrault, Suite 4700, Toronto Dominion Tower, P.O. Box 48, Toronto Dominion Centre, Toronto, Ont., M5K 1E6 (Office); 27 Marlborough Avenue, Toronto, Ont., M5R 1X5, Canada (Home). *Telephone:* (416) 601-7932 (Office); (416) 964-6757 (Home). *Fax:* (416) 868-0673.

McDONALD, Edward Lawson, M.A., M.D., F.R.C.P., F.A.C.C.; British cardiologist; b. 8 Feb. 1918; s. of Charles S. McDonald and Mabel D. McDonald; m. (divorced); one s.; ed. Felsted School, Clare Coll. Cambridge, Middlesex Hosp., Univ. of London and Harvard Univ.; served on H.M.S. Glasgow, World War II, Temporary Surgeon-Lieut. R.N.V.R. 1943–46; Consultant Cardiologist, Nat. Heart Hosp., London 1961–83 (Hon. Consultant 1983–), King Edward VII Hosp. for Officers, London 1968–83, King Edward VII Hosp. Midhurst 1970–92, Consultant Emer. 1992–; Asst. Dir. Inst. of Cardiology 1955–61; mem. Scientific Council Revista Portuguesa de Cardiologia; mem. Cardiology Cttee. Royal Coll. of Physicians 1963–76, Bd. of Govs. Nat. Heart and Chest Hosps. 1975–82, Council, British Heart Foundation 1975–83; Adviser to Malaysian Govt.; visiting lecturer univs. and cardiac socs. Europe, N. and S. America, China and fmr. U.S.S.R.; Emer. Fellow American Heart Asscn.; Int. Fellow Council on Clinical Cardiology; Fellow American Coll. of Cardiology; Hon. Fellow Turkish Medical Soc.; mem. British Cardiac Soc. (Chair. 1979), Asscn. of Physicians of G.B. and Ireland, Italian Soc. of Cardiology, Pakistan Cardiac Soc. and other medical socs.; mem. Most Honourable Order of Crown of Johore. *Publications:* Medical and Surgical Cardiology 1969, Very Early Recognition of Coronary Heart Disease (Ed.) 1978; contributions to learned journals. *Leisure interests:* art, skiing, mountain walking, sailing. *Address:* 9 Bentinck Mansions, Bentinck Street, London, W1M 5RJ, England. *Telephone:* 0171-935 7101.

MACDONALD, Rev. Fergus, M.A., B.D.; British ecclesiastic; b. 2 March 1936, Evanton, Scotland; s. of Rev. John A. Macdonald and Dr. May F. (née Urquhart) Macdonald; m. Dolina M. Mackay 1961; one s. four d.; ed. Univ. of Edinburgh, Free Church Coll., Edinburgh; Asst. Minister Hope Street Free Church, Glasgow 1960–62; Minister St. Andrew's Evangelical Presbyterian Church, Lima, Peru 1962–67; Minister Cumbernauld Free Church of Scotland 1968–81; Gen. Sec. Nat. Bible Soc. of Scotland 1981–; Moderator of Gen. Ass. of Free Church of Scotland 1987–88; Ed. The Instructor 1973–81. *Publications:* Prospects for Scotland 2000 (with Peter Brierley) 1985, Word Evangelism 1990. *Leisure interests:* gardening, D.I.Y. *Address:* The National Bible Society of Scotland, 7 Hampton Terrace, Edinburgh, EH12 5XU (Office); 113 St. Albans Road, Edinburgh, EH9 2PQ, Scotland (Home). *Telephone:* 0131-337 9701 (Office). *Fax:* 0131-337 0641.

MACDONALD, Hon. Flora Isabel, C.C., P.C., F.R.S.A.; Canadian politician; b. 3 June 1926, North Sydney, N.S.; d. of George Frederick and Mary Isabel (née Royle) MacDonald; ed. North Sydney High School, Empire Business Coll. and National Defence Coll., Kingston; Exec. Dir. Progressive Conservative Headquarters 1957–66; admin. officer and tutor Dept. of Political Studies Queen's Univ. 1966–72; Nat. Sec. Progressive Conservative Asscn. of Canada 1966–69; M.P. for Kingston and the Islands, Ont. 1972–88; Sec. of State for External Affairs 1979–80; Minister for Employment and Immigration 1984–86, of Communications 1986–88; Host, weekly TV series North/South 1990–94; Chair. Int. Devt. Research Centre 1992–97, Shastri Indo-Canada Advisory Council; Co-Chair. Canadian Co-ordinating Cttee. UN Year of Older Persons 1999; Patron, Commonwealth Human Rights Initiative; Dir. Care Canada, Refugee Policy Group (Washington), Future Generations, Franklin, Help Age Int., London, U.K.; Dir. or Adviser Partnership Africa-Canada, C.O.D.E., Mines Action Canada; mem. Carnegie Comm. on Preventing Deadly Conflict; Hon. Patron for Canada of Nat. Museums of Scotland; Visiting Fellow, Centre for Canadian Studies, Edin. Univ. 1989; Progressive Conservative. *Leisure interests:* travel, reading, speedskating. *Address:* 1103-350 Driveway, Ottawa, Ont., K1S 3N1, Canada (Home). *Telephone:* (613) 238-1098.

McDONALD, Forrest, PH.D.; American professor of history; b. 7 Jan. 1927, Orange, Tex.; s. of Forrest McDonald and Myra M. McGill; m. Ellen Shapiro 1963; five c.; ed. Orange High School and Univ. of Tex. (Austin); State Historical Soc. of Wis. 1953–58; Assoc. Prof. Brown Univ. 1959–64, Prof. 1964–67; Prof. Wayne State Univ. 1967–76; Prof. Univ. of Ala. 1976–87, Distinguished Research Prof. 1976, 1987–; J.P. Harrison Visiting Prof. Coll. of William and Mary 1986–87; Guggenheim Fellow 1962–63; George Washington Medal (Freedom's Foundation) 1980, Fraunces Tavern Book Award 1980, American Revolution Round Table Book Award 1986, 16th Jefferson Lecturer in the Humanities (Nat. Endowment for the Humanities) 1987, Ingersoll Prize, Richard M. Weaver Award 1990, Salvatori Award for Academic Excellence 1992. *Publications:* We The People: The Economic Origins of the Constitution 1958, Insull 1962, E Pluribus Unum: The Formation of the American Republic 1965, Presidency of George Washington 1974, Presidency of Thomas Jefferson 1976, Alexander Hamilton: A Biography 1980, A Constitutional History of the United States 1982, Novus Ordo Seclorum: The Intellectual Origins of the Constitution 1985, Requiem: Variations on Eighteenth-Century Themes 1988, The American Presidency: An Intellectual History 1994. *Leisure interests:* gardening, tennis. *Address:* P.O. Box 155, Coker, AL 35452, U.S.A. *Telephone:* (205) 339-0317.

McDONALD, Gabrielle Kirk; American judge; fmr. law professor; fed. judge, Houston, Tex.; serving on UN int. tribunal on war crimes in fmr. Yugoslavia, the Hague 1993–, Pres. Nov. 1997–. *Address:* United Nations International Criminal Tribunal for Former Yugoslavia, P.O. Box 15833, Churchillplein, The Hague 2501 EU, The Netherlands.

MACDONALD, Ian Grant, M.A., F.R.S.; British professor of mathematics; b. 11 Oct. 1928, London; s. of Douglas G. and Irene A. (née Stokes) Macdonald; m. Margaretha Van Goethem 1954; two s. three d.; ed. Winchester Coll, and Trinity Coll., Cambridge; Asst. Prin., Prin., Ministry of Supply 1952–57; Asst. Lecturer, Manchester Univ. 1957–60; Lecturer, Exeter Univ. 1960–63; Fellow and Tutor in Math., Magdalen Coll., Oxford 1963–72; Fielden Prof. of Pure Math. Manchester Univ. 1972–76; Prof. of Pure Math., Queen Mary (now Queen Mary and Westfield) Coll., London 1976–90. *Publications:* various monographs and papers in mathematical journals. *Address:* 8 Blandford Avenue, Oxford, OX2 8DY, England.

McDONALD, John W., DR. JUR.; American diplomatist, international official and lawyer; b. 18 Feb. 1922, Koblenz, Germany; s. of John Warlick McDonald and Ethel Mae Raynor; m. 1st Barbara Jane Stewart 1943 (divorced); one s. three d.; m. 2nd Christel Meyer 1970; ed. Univ. of Illinois, Nat. War Coll., Washington, D.C.; admitted to Ill. Supreme Court Bar 1946, to U.S. Supreme Court 1951; Legal Div., U.S. Office of Mil. Govt., Berlin 1947; Asst. District Attorney, U.S. Mil. Govt. Courts, Frankfurt 1947–50; Sec. Law Cttee., Allied High Comm. 1950–52; mem. Mission to NATO and OECD, Paris 1952–54; Office of Exec. Sec. Dept. of State 1954–55; Exec. Sec. to Dir. of Int. Co-operation Admin. 1955–59; U.S. Econ. Co-ordinator for CENTO Affairs, Ankara 1959–63; Chief, Econ. and Commercial Sections, Cairo 1963–66; Deputy Dir. Office of Econ. and Social Affairs, Dept. of State 1967–68, Dir. 1968–71; Co-ordinator, UN Multilateral Devt. Programmes, Dept. of State 1971–74, Acting Deputy Asst. Sec. for Econ. and Social Affairs 1971, 1973; Deputy Dir.-Gen. Int. Labour Org. (ILO) 1974–78; Pres. Int. Telecommunications Satellite Org. (INTELSAT) Conf. on Privileges and Immunities 1978; Amb. to UN Conf. on TCDC 1978; Sec.-Gen. 27th Colombo Plan Ministerial Meeting 1978; U.S Co-ordinator for UN Decade on Drinking Water and Sanitation 1979; rep. to UN Confs. with rank of Amb. 1978–; Amb. to UNIDO III 1979–80; Chair. Fed. Cttee. for UN Int. Year of Disabled Persons; Amb. to UN World Assembly on Ageing 1981–82; Co-ordinator for Multilateral Affairs, Center for the Study of Foreign Affairs, U.S. Dept. of State 1983–87; Pres. Iowa Peace Inst. 1988–92, People-to-People Cttee. for the Handicapped, Countdown 2001, World Cttee.: UN Decade of Disabled Persons; del. to many int. confs.; Bd. of Dirs. Global Water; Chair. American Asscn. for Int. Ageing 1983–; Professorial Lecturer in Law, The George Washington Univ. Nat. Law Center 1987–89; Adjunct Prof. Political Science, Grinnell Coll. 1989–92; Distinguished Visiting Prof., George Mason Univ., Fairfax, Va. 1992–93; Chair. and C.E.O. Inst. for Multi-Track Diplomacy, Washington 1992–; mem. Cosmos Club, American Foreign Service Asscn., U.S. Asscn. for the Club of Rome; Hon. Ph.D. (Mt. Mercy Coll.) 1989, (Teiko Mary Crest Univ.) 1991, (Salisbury State Univ.) 1993; Superior Honour Award, Dept. of State 1972, Presidential Meritorial Service Award 1984. *Publications:* The North-South Dialogue and the United Nations 1982, How To Be a Delegate 1984, International Negotiations 1985, Perspectives on Negotiation: Four Case Studies 1986, Conflict Resolution: Track Two Diplomacy 1987, U.S.-Soviet Summitry 1987, U.S. Base Rights Negotiations 1989, Multi-Track Diplomacy 1996, Defining a U.S. Negotiating Style 1996. *Leisure interests:* reading, tennis, fencing, skiing. *Address:* IMTD, 1819 H Street N.W., Suite 1200, Washington, DC 20006, U.S.A.

MACDONALD, Julien, M.A.; Welsh fashion designer; ed. Royal Coll. of Art; worked for Alexander McQueen and Koji Tatsuno as a student; knitwear designer for Chanel Ready-to-Wear, Chanel Couture and Karl Lagerfeld; has had four shows in his own right; Art Dir. Max Factor Spring/Summer 1999 advertising campaign (including TV commercial). *Address:* First Floor Studio, 135–139 Curtain Road, London, EC2A 3BX, England. *Telephone:* (0973) 886 779.

McDONALD, Trevor, O.B.E.; broadcasting journalist; b. 16 Aug. 1939, Trinidad; m.; two s. one d.; worked on newspapers, radio and TV, Trinidad 1960–69; Producer BBC Caribbean Service and World Service, London 1969–73; reporter Ind. TV News 1973–78, sports corresp. 1978–80, diplomatic corresp. 1980–87, newscaster 1982–87, Diplomatic Ed. Channel Four News 1987–89, newscaster News at 5.40 1989–90, News at Ten 1990–99, ITV Evening News 1999–; Hon. D. Litt. (Nottingham) 1997; Dr. h.c. (Open Univ.) 1997; Hon. Fellow Liverpool John Moores Univ. 1998; Newscaster of the Year TV and Radio Industries Club 1993, 1997; Gold Medal, Royal TV Society 1998. *Publications:* Clive Lloyd: a biography 1985, Vivian Richards: a biography 1987, Queen and Commonwealth 1989, Fortunate Circumstances (autobiography) 1993, Favourite Poems 1997. *Address:* c/o ITN, 200 Gray's Inn Road, London, WC1 8XZ, England.

McDONNELL, Sanford N., M.S.; American business executive; b. 12 Oct. 1922, Little Rock, Ark.; s. of William A. and Carolyn C. McDonnell; nephew of James S. McDonnell; m. Priscilla Robb 1946; one s. one d.; ed. Princeton Univ., Univ. of Colorado and Washington Univ.; joined McDonnell Aircraft Co. 1948, Vice-Pres. (Project Man.) 1959, F4H Vice-Pres. and Gen. Man. 1961, mem. Bd. of Dirs. 1962–67, mem. Finance Cttee. 1962, Exec. Cttee. 1963; Vice-Pres. Aircraft Gen. Man. 1965, Pres. 1966; Dir. McDonnell Douglas Corpn. 1967, Vice-Pres. March 1971; Exec. Vice-Pres. McDonnell

Aircraft Co. March 1971; Pres. McDonnell Douglas Corpn. 1971–72, Pres. 1972–80, C.E.O. 1972–88, Chair. 1980–88, Chair. Emer. 1988–; mem. Bd. of Govs. Aerospace Industries Asscn. Nov. 1974–; Fellow, American Inst. of Aeronautics and Astronautics and mem. many other professional orgs.; mem. Bd. of Dirs. First Union Bankcorpn. in St. Louis; mem. Nat. Exec. Bd., Boy Scouts of America. *Address:* McDonnell Douglas Corporation, P.O. Box 516, St. Louis, MO 63166, U.S.A.

McDONOUGH, William J., B.S., M.A.; American banker; b. 21 April 1934, Chicago, Ill.; m. Suzanne Clarke 1985; three s. three d.; ed. Holy Cross Coll., Worcester, Mass. and Georgetown Univ.; U.S. Navy 1956–61; U.S. State Dept. 1961–67; First Nat. Bank of Chicago 1967–89, Vice-Chair. Bd. and Dir. holding co. 1986–89; subsequently served as adviser to IBRD and IFC; special adviser to Pres. of IDB; Chair. Ill. Comm. on Future of Public Service; Exec. Vice-Pres. and Head, Markets Group, Fed. Reserve Bank of New York and Man. Open Market Operations for Fed. Open Market Cttee. 1992–93; Vice-Chair. Fed. Open Market Cttee.; Pres. and C.E.O. Fed. Reserve Bank of New York 1993–; mem. Bd. of Dirs. B.I.S. and Chair. Basle Cttee. on Banking Supervision; mem. Council on Foreign Relations, Trilateral Comm., New York Philharmonic Orchestra; Bd. of Govs. N.Y. Acad of Sciences; Chair. Bd. of Trustees Econ. Club of N.Y. *Address:* 33 Liberty Street, New York, NY 10045, U.S.A. *Telephone:* (212) 720-5000.

McDORMAND, Frances; American actress; b. 1957, Ill.; ed. Yale Univ. School of Drama; stage appearances include: Awake and Sing 1984, Painting Churches 1984, The Three Sisters 1985, All My Sons 1986, A Streetcar Named Desire 1988, Moon for the Misbegotten 1992, Sisters Rosensweig 1993, The Swan 1993; *films include:* Blood Simple 1984, Raising Arizona 1987, Mississippi Burning 1988, Chattahoochee 1990, Darkman 1990, Miller's Crossing 1990, Hidden Agenda 1990, The Butcher's Wife 1991, Passed Away 1992, Short Cuts 1993, Beyond Rangoon 1995, Fargo 1996 (Acad. Award for Best Actress), Paradise Road 1997, Johnny Skidmarks 1997; has appeared in several TV series. *Address:* c/o William Morris Agency, 1325 Avenue of the Americas, New York, NY 10019, U.S.A.

MacDOUGALL, Sir (George) Donald (Alastair), C.B.E., D.SC., LL.D., LITT.D., F.B.A.; British economist; b. 26 Oct. 1912, Glasgow, Scotland; s. of Daniel MacDougall and Beatrice Miller; m. 1st Bridget Christabel Bartrum 1937 (divorced 1977); one s. one d.; m. 2nd Laura Margaret, Lady Hall 1977 (died 1995); ed. Balliol Coll., Oxford; Asst. Lecturer, Leeds Univ. 1936–39; mem. Sir Winston Churchill's Statistical Branch 1939–45 and 1951–53; Fellow Wadham Coll., Oxford 1945–50, Nuffield Coll. 1947–64; Hon. Fellow, Wadham Coll. 1964–, Nuffield Coll. 1967–, Balliol Coll. 1992–; Reader in Int. Econs., Oxford 1951–52; Econ. Dir. OEEC, Paris 1948–49; Econ. Dir. Nat. Econ. Devt. Office 1962–64; Dir.-Gen. Dept. of Econ. Affairs 1964–68; Head of Govt. Econ. Service and Chief Econ. Adviser to Treasury 1969–73; Chief Econ. Adviser CBI 1973–84; Pres. Royal Econ. Soc. 1972–74; Chair. EEC Study Group on Role of Public Finance in European Integration 1975–77. *Publications:* The World Dollar Problem 1957, Studies in Political Economy (2 vols.) 1975, Don and Mandarin: Memoirs of an Economist 1987, and other books and articles on economic matters. *Leisure interest:* fishing. *Address:* 19 Warwick Square, London, SW1V 2AB, England. *Telephone:* 0171-821 1998.

MACDOUGALL, Patrick Lorn, M.A., F.C.A., F.R.S.A.; British banker; b. 21 June 1939, Edinburgh; s. of the late J. A. Macdougall; m. 1st Alison Offer 1967 (divorced 1982); two s.; m. 2nd Bridget Young 1983; three d.; ed. Millfield School and Univ. Coll. Oxford; called to the Bar, Inner Temple 1962; Hambros Bank Ltd. 1962–63; Arthur Andersen & Co. 1963–67; N. M. Rothschild & Sons 1967–70; Dir. Rothschild Intercontinental Bank (renamed Amex Bank 1975) 1970–72, Deputy Man. Dir. 1972–75, Man. Dir. 1975–77, Chief Exec. 1977–78; Exec. Dir. Jardine Matheson & Co. Hong Kong 1978–85, Standard Chartered PLC 1988–89; Chief Exec. West Merchant Bank, London (fmrly. Standard Chartered Merchant Bank Ltd.) 1985–97, Chair. 1989–98; Chair. Scimitar Asset Man. 1989–90; Dir. Global Natural Resources Inc. 1994–96, Nuclear Electric PLC 1994–96, Nat. Provident Inst. 1997–; mem. Int. Advisory Bd. Creditanstalt-Bankverein, Vienna 1982–85, Advisory Council Seagull Energy Corpn. 1996–99. *Leisure interests:* skiing, golf, bridge. *Address:* 40 Stevenage Road, London, SW6 6ET, England (Home). *Telephone:* 0171-736 3506. *Fax:* 0171-731 8912.

MacDOWELL, Andie; American film actress; b. 21 April 1958, S. Carolina; m. Paul Qualley; two c. *TV appearances include:* Women and Men 2, In Love There Are No Rules 1991, Sahara's Secret. *Films include:* Greystoke 1984, St. Elmo's Fire 1985, Sex, Lies and Videotape 1989, Green Card 1990, Hudson Hawk 1991, The Object of Beauty 1991, The Player 1992, Ruby 1992, Groundhog Day 1993, Short Cuts 1993, Bad Girls 1994, Four Weddings and a Funeral 1994, Unstrung Heroes 1995, My Life and Me 1996, Multiplicity 1996, The End of Violence 1997, Town and Country 1998, Shadrack 1998, The Scalper 1998, Just the Ticket 1998. *Address:* c/o I.C.M., 8942 Wilshire Blvd., Beverly Hills, CA 90211, U.S.A.

McDOWELL, David Keith, M.A.; New Zealand diplomatist and conservationist; b. 30 April 1937, Palmerston North; s. of Arthur McDowell and Gwen McDowell; m. Jan Ingram 1960; one s. three d.; ed. Victoria Univ. of Wellington; joined Ministry of Foreign Affairs 1959, Head, UN and African and Middle East Divs. 1973, Dir. of External Aid 1973–76, Head, Econ. Div. 1980–81, Special Asst. to Sec. Gen., Commonwealth Secr., London 1969–72; High Commr. in Fiji 1977–80, in India, Nepal and Bangladesh 1983–85; Asst. Sec. of Foreign Affairs for Asia, Australia and the Americas 1981–85; First Sec., Perm. Mission to UN 1964–68, Perm. Rep. 1985–88; Dir.-Gen. Dept. of Conservation 1988–89; C.E.O. Dept. of Prime Minister and Cabinet 1989–91; Amb. to Japan 1992–94; Dir.-Gen. World Conservation Union, Switzerland 1994–99. *Leisure interests:* fishing, boating, tennis, conservation, gardening, music. *Address:* 86 Waegrenga Road, Otaki, New Zealand.

McDOWELL, John Henry, M.A., F.B.A., F.A.A.A.S.; British professor of philosophy; b. 7 March 1942, Boksburg, South Africa; s. of Sir Henry McDowell and Norah (née Douthwaite) McDowell; m. Andrea Lehrke 1977; ed. St. John's Coll. Johannesburg, Univ. Coll. of Rhodesia and Nyasaland, New Coll. Oxford; Fellow, Praelector in Philosophy, Univ. Coll. Oxford 1966–86; Prof. of Philosophy, Univ. of Pittsburgh 1986–88, Univ. Prof. 1988–. *Publications:* Ed. (with Gareth Evans) Truth and Meaning, Ed. (with Philip Pettit) Subject, Thought and Context, Mind and World, Mind, Value and Reality, Meaning, Knowledge and Reality; trans. of Plato, Theaetetus. *Leisure interests:* gardening, reading. *Address:* Department of Philosophy, University of Pittsburgh, Pittsburgh, PA 15260, U.S.A. *Telephone:* (412) 624-5792.

McDOWELL, Malcolm (Malcolm Taylor); British actor; b. 13 June 1943, Leeds; m. 1st Mary Steenburgen 1980; one s. one d.; m. 2nd Kelley Kuhr 1992; began career with the R.S.C. at Stratford 1965–66; early television appearances in such series as Dixon of Dock Green, Z Cars. *Stage appearances:* RSC, Stratford 1965–66, Entertaining Mr. Sloane, Royal Court 1975, Look Back in Anger, New York 1980, In Celebration, New York 1984, Holiday Old Vic 1987, Another Time, Old Vic 1993. *Films include:* If. . . . 1969, Figures in a Landscape 1970, The Raging Moon 1971, A Clockwork Orange 1971, O Lucky Man 1973, Royal Flash 1975, Aces High 1976, Voyage of the Damned 1977, Caligula 1977, The Passage 1978, Time After Time 1979, Cat People 1981, Blue Thunder 1983, Get Crazy 1983, Britannia Hospital 1984, Gulag 1985, The Caller 1987, Sunset 1987, Sunrise 1988, Class of 1999, Il Maestro 1989, Moon 44, Double Game, Class of 1999, Snake Eyes, Schweitzer, Assassin of the Tsar 1991, The Player, Chain of Desire, East Wind, Night Train to Venice, Star Trek: Generations 1995, Tank Girl 1995, Kids of the Round Table, Where Truth Lies. *TV includes:* Our Friends in the North. *Address:* c/o Markham and Froggatt, 4 Windmill Street, London, W1P 1HF, England.

MacEACHEN, Hon. Allan J., P.C., M.A.; Canadian politician; b. 6 July 1921, Inverness, N.S.; s. of Angus MacEachen and Annie Gillies; ed. St. Francis Xavier Univ., Univs. of Toronto and Chicago, and M.I.T.; Prof. of Econs., St. Francis Xavier Univ. 1946–48, later Head, Dept. of Econs. and Social Sciences; mem. House of Commons 1953–58, 1962–84; M.P. for Cape Breton Highlands-Cans., N.S. 1953–84; Special Asst. and Consultant on Econ. Affairs to Lester Pearson 1958; Minister of Labour 1963–65; Minister of Nat. Health and Welfare 1965–68, of Manpower and Immigration 1968–70, of Finance 1980–82; Pres. Privy Council and Govt. House Leader 1970–74; Sec. of State for External Affairs 1974–76; Pres. Privy Council 1976–77, and Deputy Prime Minister 1977–79; Deputy Leader of Opposition and Opposition House Leader 1979; Deputy Prime Minister and Minister of Finance 1980–82; Deputy Prime Minister and Sec. of State for External Affairs 1982–84; mem. Senate 1984–96, Leader of Govt. in Senate June-Oct. 1984, Leader of Opposition in Senate 1984–91; Chair. Int. IMF Group of Ten 1980–81, Interim Cttee. of IMF, Conf. on Int. Econ. Co-operation, 1982 Ministerial Meeting of the GATT, Int. Advisory Council of Bank of Montreal 1986–91; Canadian Chair. Atlantik-Brücke Annual Symposium (Canada-Germany Conf.) 1984–; Chair. Advisory Council Int. Ocean Inst. 1996–; Bd. Dirs. North-South Inst. 1996–; Trustee Royal Ottawa Health Care Group 1987–95; mem. Bd. of Govs. St. Francis Xavier Univ.; Order of Merit, Germany; Liberal. *Address:* 140 Wellington Street, Room 804, Ottawa, K1A 0A4, Ont.; R.R.1, Whycocomagh, B0E 3M0, Nova Scotia, Canada (Home).

MACEDO, Air Marshal Joelmir Campos de Araripe; Brazilian air force officer; b. Rio de Janeiro; joined Brazilian Army 1928, transferred to Air Force 1941; a pioneer of the Govt. air service linking the remote areas of Brazil to prov. capitals, Correio Aéreo Nacional (CAN); has held posts of Dir. Galvão Air Factory, Pres. Nat. Engines Plant, Dir. of Air Routes, Pres. Co-ordinating Cttee. for Rio de Janeiro Int. Airport; Minister of Aeronautics 1974–79. *Address:* c/o Ministério da Aeronáutica, Brasília, Brazil.

McELHINNEY, Robert Stanley, PH.D., F.R.S.C., M.R.I.A.; Irish organic chemist; b. 24 Sept. 1933, Milford, Co. Donegal; s. of Robert McElhinney and Gertrude McMahon; m. Margaret Thompson 1957; two s. two d.; ed. Coleraine Academical Inst. and Queen's Univ. Belfast; U.S. Public Health Service Post-doctoral Fellowship, Univ. of Mich. Ann Arbor 1958–59; Research Fellow, Medical Research Council of Ireland Labs., Trinity Coll. Dublin 1960–76, Deputy Dir. of Labs. 1976–84, Co-ordinator of Labs. 1985–90, Research Assoc. in cancer chemotherapy, Chem. Dept. 1991–; mem. Royal Irish Acad. (Sr. Vice-Pres. 1985). *Publications:* numerous research papers in chemical and pharmacological literature. *Leisure interests:* Bible study, playing piano, golf. *Address:* University Chemical Laboratory, Trinity College, Dublin 2 (Office); Lantaur, Delgany, Co. Wicklow, Ireland (Home). *Telephone:* 01-7021602 (Office); 01-2875204 (Home). *Fax:* 01-353.1.671.2826.

McELROY, William David, PH.D.; American scientist; b. 22 Jan. 1917, Rogers, Tex.; s. of William D. McElroy and Ora Shipley McElroy; m. 1st Nella Winch 1940 (divorced); two s. two d.; m. 2nd Marlene Anderegg DeLuca 1967; two s.; ed. Reed Coll. and Stanford and Princeton Univs.; Instructor in Biology, Johns Hopkins Univ. 1946, Asst. Prof. 1946–48, Assoc. Prof.

1948–51, Dir. McCollum-Pratt Inst. 1949–64, Prof. of Biology 1951–69, Chair. Dept. of Biology 1956–69; Harvey Lecturer, New York Acad. of Sciences 1957; Exec. Ed. Archives of Biochemistry and Biophysics 1958–69; Ed. Biochemical and Biophysical Research Communications 1959–; Chair. AIBS Microbiology Advisory Cttee., Office of Naval Research 1952–57; mem. President's Science Advisory Cttee. 1962–67, Bd. of Dirs. of Nat. Insts. of Health 1966–; Dir. U.S. Nat. Science Foundation 1969–72; Chancellor, Univ. of Calif., San Diego 1972–80, Prof. 1980–, now Emer.; mem. Soc. of Biological Chemists (Pres. 1963–64), American Acad. of Arts and Sciences, A.A.A.S., Pres. 1975, Chair. Bd. of Dirs. 1977, American Inst. of Biological Sciences (Pres. 1968), N.A.S., etc.; numerous hon. degrees; Barnett Cohen Award, American Soc. of Bacteriology 1958, Rumford Prize, American Acad. of Arts and Sciences 1964. *Publications:* Cell Physiology and Biochemistry 1961; Ed. with B. Glass: Copper Metabolism 1950, Phosphorus Metabolism (2 vols.) 1951–52, Mechanism of Enzyme Action 1954, Amino Acid Metabolism 1955, Inorganic Nitrogen Metabolism 1956, The Chemical Basis of Heredity 1957, The Chemical Basis of Development 1958, Light and Life 1961; Ed. with C. P. Swanson: Foundations of Modern Biology (series) 1961–64; co-editor: Analytical Biochemistry. *Leisure interests:* golf, music, tennis. *Address:* Department of Biology, University of California, San Diego, La Jolla, CA 92067, U.S.A.

McENERY, Peter Robert; British actor; b. 21 Feb. 1940; s. of the late Charles McEnery and of Ada Mary Brinson; m. 1978; one d.; founder mem. and assoc. artist with the R.S.C. *Theatre roles include:* Eugene in Look Homeward Angel 1962, Rudge in Next Time I'll Sing to You 1963, Konstantin in The Seagull 1964, Edward Gover in Made in Bangkok 1986, Trigorin in The Seagull 1975, Fredrick in A Little Night Music 1990, Torvald in A Doll's House 1994, Hector in Heartbreak House 1997; Dir. plays Richard III 1971, The Wound 1972. *TV:* Clayhanger 1976, The Aphrodite Inheritance 1979, The Jail Diary of Albie Sachs 1980, Japanese Style 1982, The Collectors 1986, The Mistress 1986, Witchcraft 1991. *Films:* Tunes of Glory 1961, Victim 1961, The Moonspinners 1963, Entertaining Mr Sloane 1970. *Leisure interests:* steam railway preservation, skiing, American football. *Address:* Dennis Selinger, ICM Ltd., Oxford House, 76 Oxford Street, London, W1N 0AX, England. *Telephone:* 0171-636 6565. *Fax:* 0171-323 0101.

McENROE, John Patrick; American lawn tennis player; b. 16 Feb. 1959, Wiesbaden, Fed. Repub. of Germany; s. of John P. McEnroe I and Katy McEnroe; m. Tatum O'Neal (q.v.) 1986; two s. one d.; ed. Trinity High School, N.J., and Stanford Univ., Calif.; amateur player 1976–78, professional 1978–93; U.S.A. singles Champion 1979, 1980, 1981, 1984; U.S.A. doubles Champion 1979, 1981, 1989; Wimbledon Champion (doubles) 1979, 1981, 1983, 1984, 1992 (singles) 1981, 1983, 1984; WCT Champion 1979, 1981, 1983, 1984, 1989; Grand Prix Champion 1979, 1983, 1984; played Davis Cup for U.S.A. 1978, 1979, 1980, 1981, 1982, 1983, 1984, 1985; only player to have reached the Wimbledon semi-finals (1977) as pre-tournament qualifier, semi-finalist 1989; tennis sportscaster USA Network 1993; mem. Men's Sr.'s. Tours Circuits 1994. *Leisure interest:* music. *Address:* c/o John P. McEnroe Sr., Paul Weiss Rifkind Wharton & Garrison, 1285 Avenue of the Americas, New York, NY 10019, U.S.A.

McEWAN, Angus David, B.E., M.ENG.SC., PH.D., F.A.A., F.T.S.; Australian oceanographer; b. 20 July 1937, Alloa, Scotland; s. of David R. McEwan and Anne Marion McEwan; m. Juliana R. Britten 1961 (divorced 1982); two d.; ed. Melbourne High School, Caulfield Tech. Coll., Melbourne Univ., Cambridge Univ.; engineer, Aeronautical Research Labs., Melbourne 1956–58, Research Scientist 1961–62, 1966–69; Research Scientist, Program Leader, Chief Research Scientist, Div. of Atmospheric Research, CSIRO, Aspendale, Vic. 1972–81, Foundation Chief, Div. of Oceanography, Hobart 1981–95; Sr. Scientific Adviser (Oceanographer) to CSIRO and Bureau of Meteorology 1995–; Hon. Research Prof. Univ. of Tasmania 1988–; Chief Australian Nat. Del., Inter-governmental Oceanographic Comm. (IOC) 1995–; Chair. Intergovernmental Cttee. for the Global Ocean Observing System 1997–, for the Global Climate Observing System 1997–; Nat. Del., ASEAN, IOC, Scientific Cttee. Oceanic Research (SCOR); mem. numerous other nat. bodies and cttees. concerning marine science; Queen Elizabeth Fellow 1969–71; Rossby Fellow (Woods Hole Oceanographic Inst.) 1975. *Publications:* scientific articles on geophysical fluid dynamics. *Leisure interests:* sailing, sketching, woodwork. *Address:* Bureau of Meteorology, Box 727 G, Hobart, Tasmania 7001; 300 Sandy Bay Road, Sandy Bay, Tasmania 7005, Australia. *Telephone:* (03) 6221 2090. *Fax:* (03) 6221 2089.

McEWAN, Geraldine; British actress; b. 9 May 1932, Old Windsor, Berks.; d. of Donald and Norah McKeown; m. Hugh Cruttwell 1953; one s. one d.; ed. Windsor County Girls' School; first engagement with Theatre Royal, Windsor 1949; London appearances in Who Goes There? 1951, Sweet Madness, For Better, For Worse, Summertime; Shakespeare Memorial Theatre, Stratford on Avon 1956, 1958, 1961 playing Princess of France (Love's Labours Lost), Olivia (Twelfth Night), Ophelia (Hamlet), Marina (Pericles), Beatrice (Much Ado about Nothing); played in School for Scandal, U.S.A. 1962, The Private Ear and The Public Eye, U.S.A. 1963; appearances as mem. Nat. Theatre 1965–71: Armstrong's Last Goodnight, Love for Love, A Flea in Her Ear, The Dance of Death, Edward II, Home and Beauty, Rites, The Way of the World, The White Devil, Amphitryon 38; other theatre appearances include: Dear Love 1973, Chez Nous 1974, The Little Hut 1974, Oh Coward! (musical) 1975, On Approval 1975, Look After Lulu 1978; with Nat. Theatre: The Browning Version 1980, Harlequinade 1980, The Provoked Wife 1980–81, The Rivals (Evening Standard Drama Award for Best Actress), You Can't Take It With You 1983–84; A Lie of the Mind (Royal Court) 1987, Lettice and Lovage (Globe Theatre) 1988–89, Hamlet (Riverside Studios) 1992, The Bird Sanctuary (Abbey Theatre) 1994, The Way of the World (Nat. Theatre; Evening Standard Drama Award for Best Actress) 1995, Grace Note (Old Vic) 1997, The Chairs (Royal Court) 1997, (Golden Theatre, New York) 1998. *Television:* The Prime of Miss Jean Brodie (TV Critics Best Actress Award) 1978, L'Elégance 1982, The Barchester Chronicles 1982, Come Into the Garden, Maude 1982, Mapp and Lucia 1985–86, Oranges Are Not The Only Fruit 1990 (B.A.F.T.A. Best Actress Award), Mulberry 1992–93, The Red Dwarf 1999. *Films:* The Adventures of Tom Jones 1975, Escape from the Dark 1978, Foreign Body 1986, Henry V 1989, Robin Hood: Prince of Thieves 1991, Moses 1995, The Love Letter 1999, Titus 1999. *Directed:* As You Like It 1988, Treats 1989, Waiting for Sir Larry 1990, Four Door Saloon 1991, Keyboard Skills 1993. *Address:* c/o Marmont Management Ltd., 303–308 Regent Street, London, W.1, England.

McEWAN, Ian, M.A.; British author; b. 21 June 1948, Aldershot, Hants.; s. of the late David McEwan and of Rose Moore; m. Penny Allen 1982 (divorced 1995); two s. two step-d.; ed. Woolverstone Hall, Univs. of Sussex and E. Anglia; Hon. D.Phil. (Sussex) 1989, (E. Anglia) 1993; Somerset Maugham Prize 1975; Primo Letterario, Prato 1982; Whitbread Fiction Prize 1987, Prix Femina 1993; Booker Prize 1998, Shakespeare Prize 1999. *Publications:* First Love, Last Rites 1975, In Between the Sheets 1978, The Cement Garden 1978, The Imitation Game 1980, The Comfort of Strangers 1981, Or Shall we Die? 1983, The Ploughman's Lunch 1983, The Child in Time 1987, Soursweet (screenplay) 1987, A Move Abroad 1989, The Innocent 1990, Black Dogs 1992, The Daydreamer 1994, The Short Stories 1995, Enduring Love 1997, Amsterdam (novel) 1998. *Address:* 15 Park Town, Oxford, OX2 6SN, England.

McFADDEN, Mary; American fashion designer; b. 1 Oct. 1938, New York; d. of Alexander Bloomfield McFadden and Mary Josephine Cutting; m. 1st Philip Harari 1964 (divorced); one d.; m. 2nd Frank McEwan 1968 (divorced); ed. École Lubec, Paris, Sorbonne, Paris, Traphagen School of Design, New York and Columbia Univ., New York; Dir. of Public Relations, Christian Dior, New York 1962–64; merchandising ed. Vogue, S.A. 1964–65; political and travel columnist, Rand Daily Mail, S.A. 1965–68; founder Vukutu Sculpture Workshop, Rhodesia 1968–70; freelance ed. My Fair Lady, Cape Town and French Vogue 1968–70; Special Projects Ed. American Vogue 1970–73; fashion and jewellery designer (noted for tunics made from African and Chinese silks), New York 1973–; Chair. Mary McFadden Inc. 1976–; partner MMcF Collection by Mary McFadden 1991–; adviser Nat. Endowment for Arts; numerous awards include Neiman Marcus Award 1979, Coty American Fashion Critics' Hall of Fame Award 1979, Woman of the Year, Police Athletic League 1990, New York Landmarks Conservancy 1994, Designer of the Decade and Beyond, Fashion Group Int. and Phila. Breast Health Inst. 1997. *Publications:* contribs. to Vogue and House & Garden. *Leisure interest:* tennis. *Address:* Mary McFadden Inc., 240 West 35th Street, Floor 17, New York, NY 10001, U.S.A.

McFADYEN, Jock, M.A.; British artist; b. 18 Sept. 1950, Paisley, Scotland; s. of James Lachlan McFadyen and Margaret McFadyen; m. 1st Carol Hambleton 1972 (divorced 1987); one s.; m. 2nd Susie Honeyman 1991; one s. one d.; ed. Chelsea School of Art; has made works about London, New York, Belfast and Berlin; has held 36 solo exhbns. including Nat. Gallery 1982, Camden Arts Centre 1988, Imperial War Museum 1991, Talbot Rice Gallery, Edin. 1998; has also exhibited in numerous maj. mixed exhbns. and int. touring shows, including a jt. exhbn. with his brother, Donald McFadyen, at St. Magnus Festival, The Pier Arts Centre, Orkney and in Chicago 1999; represented in 30 public collections, and in numerous pvt. and corp. collections; artist in residence Nat. Gallery, London 1981; tutor Slade School of Fine Art 1985–; designed sets and costumes for The Judas Tree, Royal Opera House, Covent Garden 1992; Arts Council Major Award 1979; Prize-winner John Moores Liverpool Exhbn. 1991. *Leisure interests:* cycling, motor-cycling, walking, swimming, children. *Address:* 284 Globe Road, London, E2 0NS, England; 73 Montgomery Street, Edinburgh, Scotland; Petite Maison, Orthe, Bais, France. *Telephone:* 0181-983 3825 (London).

McFALL, Richard Graham; British commodity merchant; b. 31 Jan. 1920, Blundellsands, Lancs.; s. of Henry Joseph Marshall McFall and Sarah Gertrude McFall; m. Louise Mitford 1945; one s. one d.; ed. Clifton Coll., Bristol; joined Pacol Ltd. 1938; served Hon. Artillery Co. 1939–40; Asst. Sec., then Sec. W. African Produce Control Bd. 1941–45; Motor and Air Products Ltd. 1946–48; rejoined Pacol Ltd. 1949, Dir. 1951–79; Chair. London Cocoa Terminal Market Asscn. 1954–55, Cocoa Asscn. of London Ltd. 1958–59; Dir. Gill & Duffus Group Ltd. 1962–82, Man. Dir. 1965–71, Chair. 1970–76, Vice-Chair. 1976–78; Chair. Fleming Enterprise Investment Trust PLC 1980–86. *Leisure interest:* golf. *Address:* Springfold Cottage, Green Dene, East Horsley, Surrey, KT24 5RG, England (Home). *Telephone:* (01483) 283282 (Home).

MACFARLANE, Alan Donald James, D.PHIL., PH.D., M.A., F.B.A.; British academic; b. 20 Dec. 1941, Assam, India; s. of Donald Macfarlane and Iris Macfarlane; m. 1st Gillian Ions 1965, 2nd Sarah Harrison 1981; one d.; ed. Sedbergh School, Worcester Coll., Oxford, London School of Econs. and School of Oriental & African Studies, London Univ.; Sr. Research Fellow, in History, King's Coll. Cambridge 1971–75; Lecturer in Social Anthropology,

Univ. of Cambridge 1975–81, Reader in Historical Anthropology 1981–91; Prof. of Anthropological Science 1991–; Fellow, King's Coll., Cambridge 1981–; Radcliffe-Brown Memorial Lecture (British Acad.) 1992; Rivers Memorial Medal 1984. *Publications:* Witchcraft in Tudor and Stuart England 1970, Family Life of Ralph Josselin 1970, The Diary of Ralph Josselin (Ed.) 1976, Resources and Population 1976, The Origins of English Individualism 1977, The Justice and the Mare's Ale 1981, Marriage and Love in England 1986, The Culture of Capitalism 1987, The Nagas: Hill Peoples of North India (Co-author) 1990, The Cambridge Database System Manual 1990, The Savage Wars of Peace 1997; Ed. and trans. (with Sarah Harrison) of Bernard Pignède, The Gurungs of Nepal 1993. *Leisure interests:* gardening, walking, music. *Address:* King's College, Cambridge, CB2 1ST; 25 Lode Road, Lode, nr. Cambridge, CB5 9ER, England. *Telephone:* (01223) 811976.

MacFARLANE, Alistair George James, C.B.E., D.SC., PH.D., SC.D., F.R.S., F.ENG., F.R.S.E.; British professor of engineering and vice-chancellor; b. 9 May 1931, Edinburgh; s. of George R. MacFarlane and Mary MacFarlane; m. Nora Williams 1954; one s.; ed. Hamilton Acad., Univ. of Glasgow, Univ. of London, Univ. of Manchester; with Metropolitan-Vickers, Manchester 1953–58; Lecturer Queen Mary Coll., Univ. of London 1959–65, Reader 1965–66; Reader in Control Eng. UMIST 1966–69, Prof. 1969–74; Prof. of Eng. Univ. of Cambridge 1974–89; Fellow Selwyn Coll., Cambridge 1974–89, Vice-Master 1980–88; Prin. and Vice-Chancellor Heriot-Watt Univ., Edin. 1989–96, Emer. Research Fellow 1997–; Chair. Cambridge Control Ltd. 1985–89; mem. Council SERC 1981–85, Computer Bd. 1983–88; Chair. Scottish Council for Research in Educ. 1992–98, Scottish Library and Information Council 1994–98, Advisory Body on High Performance Computing 1994–, BT Advisory Forum 1997–; Academic Advisor Univ. of Highlands and Islands Project 1997–; Trustee Scottish Library and Information System Council 1994–; Hon. Fellow, Selwyn Coll. 1989–; Hon. D.Eng. (Glasgow) 1995; Hon. D.Univ. (Heriot-Watt) 1997, (Paisley) 1997; Hon. D.Sc. (Abertay Dundee) 1998. *Publications:* Engineering Systems Analysis 1964, Dynamical System Models 1970, (with I. Postlethwaite) A Complex Variable Approach to the Analysis of Linear Multivariable Feedback Systems 1979, (Ed.) Frequency-Response Methods in Control Systems 1979, (Ed.) Complex Variable Methods for Linear Multivariable Feedback Systems 1980, (with S. Hung) Multivariable Feedback: a quasi-classical approach 1982, (with G. K. H. Pang) An Expert Systems Approach to Computer-Aided Design of Multivariable Systems 1987. *Address:* Flat 4, 13 Spylaw Road, Edin., EH10 5BH, Scotland.

MACFARLANE, Ian J., M.ECONS.; Australian banker; b. 22 June 1946, Sydney; ed. Monash Univ.; taught at Monash Univ.; with Inst. for Econs. and Statistics, Oxford Univ., then in economic forecasting and surveys at OECD, Paris 1971–79; joined Reserve Bank of Australia (Research Dept.) 1979, held sr. positions in econ. and financial markets areas then money, bond and foreign exchange market areas, Head Econ. Area 1988, Asst. Gov. (Econ.) 1990–92, Deputy Gov. 1992–96, Gov. 1996–. *Address:* Reserve Bank of Australia, GPOB 3947, Sydney, N.S.W. 2001, Australia. *Telephone:* (02) 9551-8111. *Fax:* (02) 9551 8030.

MCFARLANE, Robert Carl, M.S.; American government official; b. 12 July 1937, Washington, D.C.; s. of William McFarlane and Alma Carl; m. Jonda Riley 1959; one s. two d.; ed. U.S. Naval Acad. and Inst. des Hautes Etudes, Geneva; U.S. Marine Corps, Second Lieut. rising to Lieut.-Col. 1959–79; White House Fellow, Exec. Asst. Council to Pres. for Legis. Affairs 1971–72; Mil. Asst. to Henry Kissinger (q.v.) 1973–75; Exec. Asst. to Asst. to Pres. for Nat. Security Affairs 1975–76; Special Asst. to Pres. 1976–77; Research Fellow Nat. Defence Univ., Washington, D.C. 1977–78; mem. Professional Staff Senate Comm. on Armed Services 1979–81; Counsellor Dept. of State 1981–82; Deputy Asst. to Pres., Nat. Security Affairs 1982–83; Personal Rep. of U.S. Pres. in Middle East July–Oct. 1983; Asst. to Pres. for Nat. Security Affairs 1983–85; Chair. and C.E.O. McFarlane Asscn. 1986–; lobbyist for Macedonia 1992; Distinguished Service Medal and other medals and awards. *Publications:* At Sea Where We Belong 1971, Crisis Resolution (co-author) 1978, The Political Potential of Parity 1979.

MACFARLANE OF BEARSDEN, Baron (Life Peer) cr. 1991, in the District of the City of Glasgow, **Norman Somerville Macfarlane,** K.T., F.R.S.E.; British business executive; s. of Daniel Robertson Macfarlane and Jessie Lindsay Somerville; m. Marguerite Mary Campbell 1953; one s. four d.; ed. Glasgow High School; f. N. S. Macfarlane and Co. Ltd. 1949, Chair. Macfarlane Group PLC 1973–98, Man. Dir. 1973–90; Chair. Scottish Industrialists Council 1975–; Dir. Glasgow Chamber of Commerce 1976–79; Chair. The Fine Art Soc. PLC 1976–; Underwriting mem. of Lloyds 1978–97; Dir. American Trust PLC 1980–, Chair. 1984–97; Dir. Clydesdale Bank PLC 1980–96, Deputy Chair. 1993–96; Dir. Edin. Fund Mans. PLC 1980–; Dir. Gen. Accident Fire and Life Assurance Corpn. PLC 1984–96; Chair. Guinness Co. 1987–89, Jt. Deputy Chair. 1989–92; Chair. United Distillers PLC 1987–96, Hon. Life Pres. 1996–; Chair. Arthur Bell Distillers 1989; mem. Bd. Scottish Devt. Agency 1979–87; Chair. Glasgow Devt. Agency 1985–92; Dir. Scottish Ballet 1975–, Vice-Chair. 1983–87; Pres. Royal Glasgow Inst. of the Fine Arts 1976–87; Dir. Scottish Nat. Orchestra 1977–82; Gov. Glasgow School of Art 1976–87; Scottish Patron, Nat. Art Collection Fund 1978–; Chair. Govs., High School of Glasgow 1979–92; mem. Royal Fine Art Comm. for Scotland 1980–82; Lord High Commr. Gen. Ass., Church of Scotland 1992, 1993, 1997; mem. Court, Glasgow Univ. 1979–87; Trustee, Nat. Heritage Memorial Fund 1984–97, Nat. Galleries of Scotland 1986–97; D. L. Dunbartonshire 1993; five hon. degrees. *Leisure interests:* golf, cricket, theatre, art. *Address:* 50 Manse Road, Bearsden, Glasgow, G61 3PN, Scotland.

McGAHERN, John; Irish writer; b. 12 Nov. 1934, Dublin; s. of Francis McGahern and Susan McManus; m. Madeline Green 1973; ed. Presentation Coll., Carrick-on-Shannon, St. Patrick's Coll. and Univ. Coll. Dublin; primary school teacher 1955–64; Research Fellow, Univ. of Reading, England 1968–71; Northern Arts Fellow, Univs. of Durham and Newcastle upon Tyne, England 1974–76; Visiting Prof., Colgate Univ., New York, U.S.A. 1969, 1972, 1977, 1980, 1983, 1991, 1996; Literary Fellow, Trinity Coll., Dublin 1988; mem. Irish Acad. of Letters; Fellow Royal Literary Soc.; mem. Aosdana; AE Memorial Award; Macauley Fellowship, Arts Council of G.B. Award; Soc. of Authors Travelling Fellowship; American Irish Award; Hon. D.Litt. (Trinity Coll. Dublin) 1992, (Galway) 1994; Irish Times—Aer Lingus Literature Prize 1990, GPA Award 1992, Prix Etrangère Ecureuil 1994; Chevalier Ordre des Arts et des Lettres 1989. *Publications:* The Barracks 1963, The Dark 1965, Nightlines 1970, The Leavetaking 1975, Getting Through 1978, The Pornographer 1979, High Ground 1985, The Rockingham Shoot 1987, Amongst Women 1990, The Power of Darkness 1991, The Collected Stories 1992. *Address:* c/o Faber & Faber, 3 Queen Square, London, WC1N 3AU, England.

McGHEE, George C., D.PHIL.; American government official and business executive; b. 10 March 1912, Waco, Tex.; s. of George Summers McGhee and Magnolia Spruce; m. Cecilia DeGolyer 1938; two s. four d.; ed. Southern Methodist Univ., Dallas, Univ. of Oklahoma, Oxford Univ. and Univ. of London; Subsurface Geologist, The Atlantic Refining Co. 1930–31; Geophysicist, Continental Oil Co. 1933–34; Vice-Pres. Nat. Geophysical Co., Dallas 1937–39; Partner DeGolyer, MacNaughton and McGhee 1940–41; independent explorer for and producer of oil 1940–; Sr. Liaison Officer OPM and WPB 1941–43; U.S. Deputy Exec. Sec. Combined Raw Materials Bd. 1942–43; Special Asst. to the Under-Sec. of State for Econ. Affairs 1946–47; Co-ordinator for Aid to Greece and Turkey, Dept. of State 1947–49; Special Rep. of Sec. of State to Near East on Palestine Refugee problem with personal rank of Minister 1949; Special Asst. to Sec. of State 1949; Asst. Sec. Near East, South Asian and African Affairs 1949–51; Amb. to Turkey 1951–53; Adviser NATO Council, Ottawa 1951; Dir. Inst. of Inter-American Affairs, Inter-American Educ. Foundation 1946–51; Dir. U.S. Commercial Co. 1946; Dir. Foreign Service Educ. Foundation 1947–; Consultant, Nat. Security Council 1958–59; Counsellor, Dept. of State and Chair. Policy Planning Council Jan.-Nov. 1961; Under-Sec. of State for Political Affairs 1961–63; Amb. to Fed. Repub. of Germany 1963–68; Amb.-at-Large 1968–69; Dir. Panama Canal Co. 1962–63, Mobil Oil Co. 1969–82, Procter & Gamble Co. 1969–82, American Security & Trust Co. 1969–82, Trans World Airlines 1976–82; Chair. of Bd. Saturday Review/World 1973–76; Chair. Smithsonian Assocs. 1976–78; Owner McGhee Production Co.; Dir. of Trustees, Robert Coll., Istanbul 1953–61, Brookings Inst. 1954–61, Cttee. for Econ. Devt. 1957–, Aspen Inst. Humanistic Studies 1958–, Vassar Coll. 1959–61, Duke Univ. 1962–78; Chair. Business Council for Int. Understanding 1969–74; Chair. English Speaking Union, U.S.A. 1970–74, Deputy Chair. Int. Council of the English Speaking Union 1974; Chair. Nat. Trust for Historic Preservation 1971–75, Int. Man. and Devt. Inst. 1972–, Fed. City Housing Corpn. 1972–, Piedmont Environmental Council; Trustee, George C. Marshall Research Foundation, American Council on Germany, The American Univ., The Asia Foundation 1974–; Dir. Atlantic Council 1975–, Atlantic Inst. for Int. Affairs 1977–, Cordier Fellow, Advisory Council, Columbia Univ. 1977–; Pres. Fed. City Council 1970–74, etc.; mem. Bd. Nat. Civil Service League 1967–71, Salzburg Seminar 1969–71; mem. Japan-U.S. Econ. Advisory Council 1970–74, American Petroleum Inst., American Asscn. Petroleum Geologists, Soc. of Exploring Geophysicists, American Inst. Mining and Metallurgical Engineers, Council on Foreign Relations (New York), American Foreign Service Asscn., Acad. of Political Science, Washington Inst. of Foreign Affairs, Dept. of Conservation and Econ. Devt., Club of Rome, American Philosophical Soc.; mem. Bd. of Trustees, American Univ. 1981–, Council of American Ambs. 1984–, Visiting Cttee. for Arthur M. Sackler Gallery at Smithsonian Inst. 1986–; Vice-Chair. Bd. of Dirs. Inst. for the Study of Diplomacy, Georgetown Univ.; served in U.S.N.R. 1943–46; Lieut.-Col. U.S.A.F. Reserve 1949–; Hon. Fellow, Queen's Coll., Oxford 1968; Hon. LL.D. (Tulane Univ.) 1957, (Maryland Univ.) 1965; Hon. D.C.L. (Southern Methodist Univ.) 1953; Hon. D.Sc. (Univ. of Tampa) 1969; Legion of Merit; Asiatic Ribbon with three battle stars; mem. Order Hospital St. John of Jerusalem 1972–, numerous other awards. *Publications:* Envoy to the Middle World 1983, At the Creation of a New Germany 1989, The US-Turkish-NATO Middle East Connection 1990, Ed. Diplomacy for the Future 1987, Ed. National Interest and Global Goals 1989, Life in Alanya: Turkish Delight 1992, International Community, A Goal for a New World Order 1992, On the Frontline in the Cold War 1997. *Address:* Farmer's Delight, 36276 Mountville Road, Middleburg, VA 20117, U.S.A. *Telephone:* (540) 687-3451. *Fax:* (540) 687-3451.

McGILLIS, Kelly; American actress; b. 9 July 1957, Newport Beach, Calif.; m. Fred Tillman 1988; three c.; ed. Pacific School of Performing Arts and Juilliard School of Music, New York. *Films include:* Witness, Reuben, Reuben, Private Sessions, Top Gun, The Accused, The House on Carroll Street, Dreamers, Made in Heaven, Promised Land, Winter People, Lie Down With Lions, Cat Chaser, Before and After Death, Grand Isle, The

Babe, North, Painted Angels, Ground Control; several TV movies and stage appearances.

McGINN, Colin, M.A., B.PHIL.; British professor of philosophy; b. 10 March 1950; s. of Joseph McGinn and June McGinn; one s.; ed. Manchester and Oxford Univs.; lecturer, Univ. Coll. London 1974–85; Wilde Reader in Mental Philosophy, Oxford Univ. 1985–90; Prof., Rutgers Univ., U.S.A. 1990–; John Locke Prize 1973. *Publications:* The Character of Mind 1981, The Subjective View 1982, Wittgenstein on Meaning 1984, Mental Content 1989, The Problem of Consciousness 1991, The Space Trap 1992, Moral Literacy 1992, Problems in Philosophy 1993. *Leisure interest:* fitness. *Address:* 270 West End Avenue, Apt. 9E, New York, NY 10023, U.S.A.

McGOUGH, Roger, O.B.E., B.A.; British poet; b. 9 Nov. 1937, Liverpool; s. of Roger McGough and Mary McGarry; m. 1st Thelma Monaghan 1970 (divorced 1980); m. 2nd Hilary Clough 1986; three s. one d.; ed. St. Mary's Coll., Liverpool, Hull Univ.; Poetry Fellow Univ. of Loughborough 1973–75; writer-in-residence Western Australia Coll. of Educ., Perth 1986, Univ. of Hamburg 1994; Vice-Pres. The Poetry Society 1996– (mem. Exec. Council 1989–93); Trustee Chelsea Arts Club 1987–, fmr. Chair.; Hon. Prof. Thames Valley Univ.; Hon. M.A. (Nene Coll.) 1998. *Publications:* poetry: Summer with Monika 1978, Holiday on Death Row 1979, Blazing Fruit 1990, Defying Gravity 1992; for children: An Imaginary Menagerie 1988, The Magic Fountain 1995, Bad, Bad Cats 1997. *Address:* c/o Peters Fraser and Dunlop, 5th Floor, The Chambers, Chelsea Harbour, London, SW10 0XF, England. *Telephone:* 0171-344 1000. *Fax:* 0171-352 7356.

McGOVERN, George Stanley, PH.D.; American politician; b. 19 July 1922, Avon, S. Dakota; s. of Rev. J. C. McGovern and Frances McLean McGovern; m. Eleanor Faye Stegeberg 1943; one s. four d.; ed. Dakota Wesleyan Univ. and Northwestern Univ.; served U.S.A.F., Second World War; Teacher, Northwestern Univ. 1948–50; Prof. of History and Political Science, Dakota Wesleyan Univ. 1950–53; Exec. Sec. S. Dak. Democratic Party 1953–56; mem. U.S. House of Reps. 1957–61, served Agricultural Cttee.; Dir. "Food for Peace" Programme 1961–62; Senator from South Dakota 1963–81; partner John Kornmeier Assocs., Washington 1981; lecturer, North-Western Univ., Chicago 1981; Democratic cand. for U.S. Presidency 1972, 1984; Chair. Americans for Common Sense 1981–82; Perm. Rep. FAO, Rome 1998–; fmr. Pres. Middle East Policy Council; fmr. jt. owner roadside inn, Stratford, Conn. *Publications:* The Colorado Coal Strike 1913–14 1953, War Against Want 1964, Agricultural Thought in the Twentieth Century 1967, A Time of War, a Time of Peace 1968, The Great Coalfield War (with Leonard Guttridge) 1972, An American Journey 1974, Grassroots (autobiog.) 1978, Terry My Daughter's Life-and-Death Struggle with Alcoholism 1996. *Address:* FAO, Viale delle Terme di Caracalla, 00100 Rome, Italy; P.O. Box 5591, Friendship Station, Washington, DC 20016, U.S.A. (Home)

McGRATH, James A., P.C.; Canadian politician and administrator; b. 11 Jan. 1932, Buchans, Newfoundland; m. Margaret Smart; one s. five d.; Service R.C.A.F. 1950–53; radio and TV post 1953–56; Prov. Sec. Conservative Party 1955–57; M.P. for St. John's East 1957–65, 1968–84; Parl. Sec. to Minister of Mines and Tech. Surveys 1962–63; Exec. Asst. to Leader of the Opposition, Senate 1963–65; Pres. Progressive Conservative Asscn., Newfoundland 1965–67; mem. successive Shadow Cabinets 1968–79, 1980–84; Minister of Fisheries and Oceans 1979–80; Chair. Special Cttee. on Reform of House of Commons 1984; Vice-Chair. Canadian Br. Commonwealth Parl. Asscn. 1984; Gov. of Newfoundland 1986–91; mem. Canadian Transportation Agency 1992–95; Dir. Dr. Chas. A. Janeway Foundation, St. John's Newfoundland; Hon. LL.D. (St. Francis Xavier, Memorial Univ. of Newfoundland); Queen's Jubilee Medal; Kt. Sovereign Order of Malta, Kt. St. J., Officer of the Order of the Red Cross. *Leisure interests:* travel, reading. *Address:* 6 Riverview Avenue, St. John's, Newfoundland, A1C 2S5, Canada.

McGRATH, John Brian, B.SC.; British business executive; b. 20 June 1938; m. Sandy Watson 1964; one s. one d.; ed. Brunel Univ.; worked at UKAEA 1962–65; with NCB 1965–67; with Ford Motor Co. 1967–71; with Jaguar Cars 1971–75; with Stone-Platt 1976–82; Man. Dir. Construction and Mining Div. and Chief Exec. Compair 1982–83; joined Grand Metropolitan PLC 1985, Group Dir. Watney Mann & Truman Brewers Ltd. 1985, Chair. and Man. Dir. Grand Metropolitan Brewing 1986–88, Jt. Man. Dir. Int. Distillers & Vintners 1988–91, Man. Dir. and C.O.O. 1991–92, Chief Exec. 1992–93, Chair. and Chief Exec. 1993–96, Group Chief Exec. Grand Metropolitan PLC 1996–97; Dir. (non-exec.) Cookson Group 1993–; Chair. Scotch Whisky Asscn. 1995–; Chair. Guinness Ltd. 1997–. *Address:* 8 Henrietta Place, London, W1M 9AG, England (Office). *Telephone:* 0171-518 5443.

McGRATH, Most Rev. Archbishop Marcos Gregorio, S.T.D.; Panamanian ecclesiastic; b. 10 Feb. 1924, Panama; ed. La Salle Mil. Acad., Catholic Univ., Chile, Univ. Notre Dame, Holy Cross Theology Coll. and Catholic Inst., Paris; Dean Theological Coll., Catholic Univ., Santiago 1959–61, Auxiliary Bishop, Panama 1961–64, Bishop 1964–69; Archbishop of Panama 1969–94, Archbishop Emer. 1994–; mem. Doctrinal Comm., 2nd Vatican Council 1962–65; Vice-Pres. Council of Latin America Bishops 1967–72; Hon Dr. (Notre Dame), (Georgetown), (Louvain). *Publications:* articles in theological journals and others on int. affairs. *Address:* Arzobispado, Calle 20 y Avenida México 24–25, Apartado 386, Panamá 5, Panama. *Telephone:* 62-7284.

McGREGOR, Ewan; British actor; b. 31st March 1971, Perth; ed. Guildhall School of Music and Drama; fmrly. with Perth Repertory Theatre; *theatre includes:* What the Butler Saw, Little Malcolm and his Struggle against the Eunuchs (Hampstead Theatre Club) 1999; *TV includes:* Lipstick on Your Collar, Scarlet and Black, Kavanagh Q.C., Doggin' Around, Tales From the Crypt, ER; *films include:* Being Human, Family Style, Shallow Grave (Best Actor Dinard Film Festival 1994), Blue Juice, The Pillow Book, Trainspotting, Emma, Brassed Off, Nightwatch, The Serpent's Kiss, A Life Less Ordinary, Velvet Goldmine, Star Wars Prequel: The Phantom Menace, Little Voice, Rogue Trader, Eye of the Beholder, Nora. *Address:* c/o Peters, Fraser and Dunlop, 503/4 The Chambers, Chelsea Harbour, London, SW10 0XF, England. *Telephone:* 0171-344 1010. *Fax:* 0171-352 8135.

McGREGOR, Harvey, Q.C., M.A., D.C.L., S.J.D.; British barrister and academic lawyer; b. 25 Feb. 1926, Aberdeen; s. of late William G. R. McGregor and Agnes Reid; ed. Inverurie Acad., Scarborough Boys' High School, Queen's Coll. Oxford and Harvard Univ.; Bigelow Teaching Fellow, Univ. of Chicago 1950–51; called to the Bar, Inner Temple, London 1955, Bencher 1985; Fellow, New Coll. Oxford 1972–96, Warden 1985–96, Hon. Fellow 1996; consultant to Law Comm. 1966–73; Deputy Ind. Chair. London and Provincial Theatre Councils 1971–92, Ind. Chair. 1992–; Visiting Prof. New York Univ. and Rutgers Univ. 1963–69; Fellow, Winchester Coll. 1985–96; mem. Editorial Bd. Modern Law Review 1986–; mem. Acad. of European Pvt. Lawyers 1994–96; Trustee Oxford Union 1977–. *Publication:* McGregor on Damages (15th edn.) 1988. *Leisure interests:* music, theatre, travel, sailing. *Address:* 4 Paper Buildings, Temple, London, EC4Y 7EX (Chambers); Gray's Inn Chambers, Gray's Inn, London, WC1R 5JA, England (Residence). *Telephone:* 0171-353 3366 (Chambers); 0171-242 4942 (Residence).

McGREGOR, Sir Ian Alexander, Kt., C.B.E., F.R.C.P., D.T.M. & H., F.R.S., F.R.S.E.; British medical scientist; b. 26 Aug. 1922, Cambuslang, Lanarks.; s. of John McGregor and Isabella Taylor; m. Nancy J. Small 1954; one s. one d.; ed. Rutherglen Acad. and St. Mungo's Coll., Glasgow; mem. scientific staff, MRC Human Nutrition Unit 1949–53; Dir. MRC Labs., The Gambia 1954–74, 1978–80; Head, Lab. of Tropical Community Studies, Nat. Inst. for Medical Research (MRC), Mill Hill, London 1974–77; Liverpool Univ. Professorial Fellow, Liverpool School of Tropical Medicine 1981–87, Visiting Prof. 1981–94; mem. scientific staff MRC at Liverpool School of Tropical Medicine 1981–84; Pres. Royal Soc. of Tropical Medicine and Hygiene 1983–85; mem. various advisory cttees. etc. including WHO Advisory Panel on Malaria 1961; Chair. WHO Expert Cttee. on Malaria 1985–89; several awards and hon. degrees. *Publications:* Ed. (with W. H. Wernsdorfer) Malaria, 2 vols. 1988; some 170 papers on malaria and other aspects of health in the tropics. *Leisure interests:* ornithology, fishing, gardening. *Address:* Greenlooms House, Homington, Salisbury, Wilts., SP5 4NL, England. *Telephone:* (01722) 718452.

MacGREGOR, Joanna Clare, B.A., F.R.A.M.; British concert pianist; b. London; d. of Angela MacGregor and Alfred MacGregor; m. Richard Williams 1986; one d. (deceased); ed. South Hampstead High School for Girls, New Hall Coll. Cambridge, Royal Acad. of Music; Young Concert Artists Trust concerts and recitals, U.K. 1985–88; recitals and concerts U.K. and many other countries; has performed with all leading U.K. orchestras including London Symphony, Royal Philharmonic, Halle, City of Birmingham Symphony, Royal Scottish and Philharmonia and with Berlin, Oslo, Singapore, Sydney and Munich Symphony Orchestras; Artistic Dir. Platform Contemporary Music Festival 1991–93, Sound Circus, Bridgewater Hall, Manchester 1996–; numerous radio and TV appearances including Last Night of the Proms 1997; Fellow Trinity Coll. of Music; European Encouragement Prize for Music. *Publication:* Music Tuition Book. *Leisure interests:* cinema, horse riding. *Address:* c/o Ingpen & Williams Ltd., 14 Kensington Court, London, W8 5DN, England.

MacGREGOR, Rt. Hon. John Roddick Russell, O.B.E., P.C., M.A., LL.B.; British politician; b. 14 Feb. 1937; s. of the late Dr. N. S. R. MacGregor; m. Jean Mary Elizabeth Dungey 1962; one s. two d.; ed. Merchiston Castle School, Edin., St. Andrews Univ., King's Coll., London; Univ. Admin. 1961–62; Editorial Staff, New Society 1962–63; Special Asst. to Prime Minister, Sir Alec Douglas-Home 1963–64; Conservative Research Dept. 1964–65; Head of Pvt. Office of Rt. Hon. Edward Heath (Leader of Opposition) 1965–68; Conservative M.P. for South Norfolk 1974–; an Opposition Whip 1977–79; a Lord Commr. of H.M. Treasury 1979–81, Parl. Under-Sec. of State, Dept. of Industry 1981–83; Minister of State, Minister of Agric., Fisheries and Food 1983–85, 1987–89; Chief Sec. to H.M. Treasury 1985–87; Sec. of State for Educ. and Science 1989–90; Lord Pres. of the Council and Leader of the House of Commons 1990–92; Sec. of State for Transport 1992–94; with Hill Samuel & Co. Ltd. 1968–79, Dir. 1973–79, Deputy Chair. Hill Samuel Bank 1994–96, also Dir.; Dir. Slough Estates 1995–, Associated British Foods 1994–, Unigate 1996–, London and Manchester Group 1997–; Vice-Pres. Local Govt. Asscn. 1997–; mem. Neil Cttee. (Cttee. on Standards in Public Life) 1998–; Chair. Fed. of Univ. Conservative and Unionist Asscns. 1959, Bow Group 1963–64; First Pres. Conservative and Christian Democratic Youth Community 1963–65. *Leisure interests:* music, reading, travelling, gardening, conjuring. *Address:* House of Commons, London, SW1A 0AA, England.

MacGREGOR, (Robert) Neil; British editor and gallery director; b. 16 June 1946; s. of Alexander and Anna (née Neil) MacGregor; ed. Glasgow Acad., New Coll., Oxford, Ecole Normale Supérieure, Paris, Univ. of Edinburgh, Courtauld Inst. of Art; lecturer, Univ. of Reading 1976; Ed. The

Burlington Magazine 1981–86; Dir. Nat. Gallery 1987–; Trustee Pilgrim Trust 1990–; Chair. Conf. of U.K. Nat. Museum Dirs. 1991–97; mem. Faculty of Advocates, Edinburgh 1972; Hon. D.Litt. (Oxford) 1998. *Publications:* numerous articles in Apollo, The Burlington Magazine, Connoisseur, etc. *Address:* National Gallery, Trafalgar Square, London, W.C.2, England.

MacGREGOR, Susan (Sue) Katriona, O.B.E.; British broadcaster; b. 30 Aug. 1941, South Africa; d. of late James and Margaret MacGregor; ed. Herschel School, Cape, S.A.; announcer/producer South African Broadcasting Corpn. 1962–67; BBC Radio reporter World at One, World This Weekend, PM 1967–72; Presenter (BBC Radio 4) Woman's Hour 1972–87, Tuesday Call, Conversation Piece, Today 1984–, (BBC TV) Around Westminster, Dateline London; Visiting Prof. of Journalism Nottingham Trent Univ. 1995–; mem. Royal Coll. of Physicians Cttee. on Ethical Issues in Medicine 1985–; Hon. M.R.C.P. 1995; Hon. D.Litt. (Nottingham) 1996; Hon. LL.D. (Dundee) 1997. *Leisure interests:* theatre, cinema, skiing. *Address:* c/o British Broadcasting Corporation, Stage 6, Television Centre, Wood Lane, London, W12 8QT, England. *Telephone:* 0181-624 9644.

McGUFFIN, Peter, M.B., CH.B, PH.D., F.R.C.P., F.R.C.PSYCH.; British professor of psychological medicine; b. 4 Feb. 1949, Belfast; s. of Capt. William McGuffin and Melba M. Burnison; m. Dr Anne Farmer 1972; one s. two d.; ed. Univs. of Leeds and London; MRC Fellow and lecturer, Inst. of Psychiatry, London 1979–81; Visiting MRC Fellow, Washington Univ. Medical School, St. Louis, Mo. 1981–82; MRC Sr. Fellow, Hon. consultant and Sr. lecturer, Inst. of Psychiatry, King's Coll. Hosp. London 1982–86; Prof. of Psychological Medicine, Univ. of Wales Coll. of Medicine 1987–98; Prof. of Psychiatric Genetics and Dir. Social, Genetic and Developmental Psychiatry Research Centre, Inst. of Psychiatry, London 1998–. *Publications include:* Scientific Principles of Psychopathology, The New Genetics of Mental Illness, Seminars on Psychiatric Genetics, Essentials of Postgraduate Psychiatry; many scientific papers and articles. *Leisure interests:* music (especially classical guitar), horse riding. *Address:* Institute of Psychiatry, de Crespigny Park, London, SE5 8AF, England; 68 Heol-y-Delyn, Lisvane, Cardiff, CF4 5SR, Wales.

McGUINNESS, Frank, M.PHIL.; Irish playwright and university lecturer; b. 29 July 1953, Buncrana, Donegal; s. of Patrick McGuinness and Celine McGuinness; ed. University Coll. Dublin; Lecturer in English, Univ. of Ulster, Coleraine 1977–79, Univ. Coll. Dublin 1979–80, St. Patrick's Coll., Maynooth 1984–97, Univ. Coll. Dublin 1997–; Dir. Abbey Theatre, Dublin 1992–96; Harvey's Award, Evening Standard Drama Award, Ewart-Biggs Peace Prize, Cheltenham Literary Prize, Fringe First, Irish American Literary Prize 1992, Independent on Sunday Best Play 1992, New York Drama Critics' Award 1993, Writers' Guild Award 1993, Tony Award for Best Revival 1997; Officier des Arts et des Lettres. *Publications:* The Factory Girls 1982, Observe the Sons of Ulster Marching towards the Somme 1985, Baglady 1985, Innocence 1986, Rosmersholm, A Version 1987, Scout 1987, Yerma: A Version 1987, Carthaginians 1988, The Hen House 1989, Peer Gynt, A Version 1989, Mary and Lizzie 1989, Three Sisters, A Version 1990, The Bread Man 1990, The Threepenny Opera, A Version 1991, Someone Who'll Watch Over Me 1992, The Bird Sanctuary 1994, Hedda Gabler, A Version 1994, Uncle Vanya, A Version 1995, Booterstown: Poems 1995, Selected Plays: Vol. I 1996, The Dazzling Dark: Introduction 1996, A Doll's House: A Version 1996, The Caucasian Chalk Circle: A Version 1997, Electra: A Version 1997, Mutabilitie 1997, Dancing at Lughnasa: A Screenplay 1998, The Storm: A Version 1998, Dolly West's Kitchen 1999, The Sea With No Ships: Poems 1999. *Leisure interests:* walking, painting, botany. *Address:* 32 Booterstown Avenue, Dublin, Ireland.

McGUINNESS, Martin; Irish politician; b. Derry; m.; four c.; took part in secret London talks between Sec. of State for Northern Ireland and Irish Republican Army (IRA) July 1972; imprisoned for six months during 1973 in Irish Repub. after conviction for IRA membership; elected to Northern Ireland Ass., refused seat; stood against John Hume (q.v.) in gen. elections of 1982, 1987, 1992; M.P. for Mid-Ulster, House of Commons 1997–; mem. Ulster-Mid, N.I. Ass. 1998–; spokesperson for Sinn Fein, also mem. Nat. Exec.; involved in peace negotiations with British Govt. *Leisure interest:* fly-fishing. *Address:* Sinn Fein, 170 Falls Road, Belfast, Northern Ireland.

McGWIRE, Mark David; American professional baseball player; b. 1 Oct. 1963, Pomona, Calif.; s. of John McGwire and Ginger McGwire; m. Kathy McGwire; one s.; ed. Univ. of South California; with Oaklands Athletics 1984–97; St. Louis Cardinals 1997–; mem U.S. Olympic baseball team 1984; player World Series 1988–90; on All-Star team 1987–92, 1995–96; scored record 70 home runs during 1997–98 season; f. Mark McGwire Foundation for Children 1987; American League Rookie of the Year, Baseball Writers' Asscn. of America 1987; Golden Glove Award 1990; Silver Slugger Award 1992; Sportsman of the Year (jtly. with Sammy Sosa (q.v.)), Sports Illustrated 1998. *Address:* c/o St. Louis Cardinals, St. Louis, MO, U.S.A.

MACH, David Stefan, M.A., R.A.; British sculptor; b. 18 March 1956; s. of Joseph Mach and Martha Cassidy; m. Lesley June White 1979; ed. Buckhaven High School, Duncan of Jordanstone and Royal Colls. of Art; full-time sculptor 1982–; also occasional visiting lecturer; sculptures exhibited at galleries in England, Scotland, N.Y., São Paolo Biennale, Venice Biennale; City of Glasgow Lord Provost Prize 1992. *Leisure interests:* gardening, tennis, travelling, driving, films, television. *Address:* 64 Canonbie Road, Forest Hill, London, SE23 3AG, England. *Telephone:* 0181-699 1668.

McHARG, Ian Lennox, F.R.S.A., M.L.A., M.C.P.; American landscape architect and regional planner; b. 20 Nov. 1920, Scotland; s. of John Lennox McHarg and Harriet Bain; m. 1st 1947; m. 2nd Carol Smyster 1977; four s; ed. Harvard Univ.; Prof. Dept. of Landscape Architecture and Regional Planning Univ. of Pa., Philadelphia 1954–86; Prof. Emer. 1986–; f. Prof. Univ. of Auckland 1986; Sr. Visiting Prof. Univ. of Calif., Berkeley 1986–87; Visiting Prof. Pa. State Univ., Harvard Univ. 1994; inventor of ecological planning and environmental impact analysis; ecological researcher into river basins, metropolitan regions; designer Woodlands New Town, Tex., Pardisan, Teheran, Iran; Fellow Royal Soc. Art, American Soc. Landscape Architects, Inst. Landscape Architects, Royal Inst. British Architects; mem. N.A.S., A.I.A.; Hon. degree Coll. of the Atlantic 1998; AIA Medal, Nat. Medal of Art, American Soc. of Landscape Architects Medal; Environmentalist Award Sierra Club Film Festival 1998. *Publications:* Design with Nature 1969, Metropolitan Open Space from Natural Process, Pardisan, Quest for Life 1996. *Address:* Department of Landscape Architecture and Regional Planning, Pennsylvania University, Philadelphia, PA 19104; Box 778, Unionville, PA 19375, U.S.A. *Telephone:* (215) 898-2480.

MACHARSKI, H.E. Cardinal Franciszek, D.THEOL.; Polish ecclesiastic; b. 20 May 1927, Cracow; ed. Jagiellonian Univ., Cracow, Fribourg Univ., Switzerland; ordained priest 1950; engaged in pastoral work 1950–56; taught pastoral theology Pontifical Faculty of Theology, Cracow 1962–68; Rector, Cracow Seminary 1970–78; Archbishop Metropolitan of Cracow, 1979–; High Chancellor, Pontifical Acad. of Theology, Cracow; cr. Cardinal 1979, entitled S. Giovanni a Porta Latina; mem. Sacred Congregation for the Clergy 1979–, Sacred Congregation for Catholic Educ. 1981–, Sacred Congregation for Bishops 1983–, Sacred Congregation for Insts. of Consecrated Life and Socs. of Apostolic Life 1989–, Council for Public Affairs 1984–88; mem. Council of Cardinals and Bishops 1988–; Vice-Pres. of Polish Bishops' Conf. 1979–94; mem. Main Council of Polish Episcopate, Episcopate Cttee. for Gen. Ministry 1979–; Vice-Chair. Scientific Council of Polish Episcopate 1981–, Episcopate Cttee. for Ministry of Working People 1981–; Chair. Episcopate Cttee. for Laity 1981–91, Episcopate Cttee. for Catholic Science 1983–; mem. Episcopate Cttee. for Emigration Ministry 1988–; Dr. h.c. (Fu Jen Catholic Univ., Taipei, Adamson Univ., Manila) 1989, (Acad. of Catholic Theology, Warsaw) 1992. *Publications:* more than 250 articles, sermons, speeches and pastoral letters. *Address:* ul. Franciszkańska 3, 31-004 Cracow, Poland. *Telephone:* (12) 421 15 33.

MÂCHE, François-Bernard, D. ÈS L.; French composer and professor of musicology; b. 4 April 1935, Clermont-Ferrand; s. of Henry Mâche and Marie-Antoinette Bédabourg; m. Marie-Luce Staib 1973; one d.; ed. Ecole Normale Supérieure and Conservatoire nat. supérieur de Paris; teacher of classical philology 1962–83; Prof. of Musicology, Univ. of Strasbourg 1983–93, Dir. Inst. of Musicology 1983–87; Dir. of Studies School of Higher Educ. in the Social Sciences 1994–97; Prix Italia 1977; Grand Prix national de la Musique 1988; Commdr. Ordre des Arts et Lettres. *Major works:* Volumes 1960, La Peau du Silence 1962–66, Rituel d'oubli 1969, Danaé 1970, Korwar 1972, Naluan 1974, Kassandra 1977, Uncas 1986, Eridan 1987, Aliunde 1988, Tempora 1989, Cassiopée 1989, L'estuaire du temps 1993. *Publications:* Les mal entendus 1978, Musique, mythe, nature 1983, Entre l'observatoire et l'atelier 1998. *Leisure interests:* skin-diving, translations from modern Greek. *Address:* 83 rue Vieille du Temple, 75003 Paris, France (Home). *Telephone:* (1) 42.78.46.57 (Home).

McHENRY, Donald F., M.SC.; American diplomatist; b. 13 Oct. 1936, St. Louis, Mo.; m. Mary Williamson (divorced 1978); one s. two d.; ed. Illinois State Univ., Southern Illinois and Georgetown Univs.; taught Howard Univ., Washington 1959–62; joined dept. of State 1963, Head Dependent Areas Section, Office of UN Political Affairs 1965–68; Asst. to U.S. Sec. of State 1969; Special Asst. to Dept. Counsellor 1969–71; lecturer, School of Foreign Service, Georgetown Univ., Guest Scholar, Brookings Inst. and Int. Affairs Fellow, Council on Foreign Relations (on leave from State Dept.) 1971–73; resigned from State Dept. 1973; Project Dir. Humanitarian Policy Studies, Carnegie Endowment for Int. Peace, Washington 1973–76; served Pres. Carter's transition team 1976–77; Amb. and Deputy Perm. Rep. to UN 1977–79, Perm. Rep. 1979–81; Univ. Research Prof., School of Foreign Service, Georgetown Univ. 1981–; Dir. Int. Paper Co., Coca Cola Co., The First Nat. Bank of Boston, Bank of Boston Corpn., Inst. for Int. Econs., The American Ditchley Foundation, AT&T, SmithKline Beecham PLC, mem. Council on Foreign Relations (fmr. Dir.); mem. Editorial Bd. Foreign Policy Magazine, Foreign Affairs; Trustee The Brookings Inst., Mayo Foundation; fmr. Trustee Johnson Foundation; Chair. Bd. Africare; fmr. Gov. American Stock Exchange; Fellow American Acad. of Arts and Sciences; Superior Honor Award, Dept. of State 1966. *Publication:* Micronesia: Trust Betrayed 1975. *Address:* c/o The School of Foreign Service, Georgetown University, ICC 301, Washington, DC 20057, U.S.A.

MACHI, Sueo, PH.D.; Japanese atomic energy scientist; b. 15 Jan. 1934; s. of Yosaku Machi and Kichi Machi; m. 1964; one s. one d.; ed. Univs. of Shizuoka and Kyoto; employed in Japanese petrochemical industry 1959–63; joined Takasaki Radiation Chem. Research Establishment (TRCRE) of Japan Atomic Energy Research Inst. (JAERI) 1963; Gen. Man. Process Lab. II, TRCRE 1972–78; Gen. Man. Radiation Eng. Section, TRCRE 1978–80; Section Head, Industrial Applications and Chem. Section and Co-ordinator of Regional Co-operative Agreement for Asia and Pacific, IAEA; Deputy Dir. Office of Planning, JAERI, Tokyo; Dir. Dept. of Research, TRCRE 1986, later Dir. Dept. of Devt.; Dir.-Gen. TRCRE 1989–91; Deputy Dir.-Gen. and Head of Dept. of Research and Isotopes, IAEA 1991–; Dr. h.c. (Bucharest) 1995; Japan Chemical Soc. Prize 1969, The Iwatani Prize 1990, Minister of Science and Tech. Prize 1990. *Address:* International Atomic Energy Agency, Wagramerstrasse 5, P.O. Box 100, 1400 Vienna, Austria. *Telephone:* (1) 2360-1600. *Fax:* (1) 234564.

MACHULSKI, Juliusz; Polish film director, screenwriter and producer; b. 10 March 1955, Olsztyn; s. of Jan Machulski and Halina Machulski; m. 1995; two c.; ed. Film School Łódź, California Inst. of Arts, Valencia, U.S.A.; films: Direct Connection (TV) 1979, Vabank 1981, Seksmisja 1983, Vabank II 1984, Kingsajz 1987, Déjà vu 1989, V.I.P. 1991, Squadron 199, Girl Guide 1995, Mothers, Wives and Mistresses (TV series) 1995–98, Kiler 1997, Two Kilers 1998; numerous Polish and foreign film awards. *Leisure interest:* reading. *Address:* Studio Filmowe Zebra, ul. Puławska 61, 02-595 Warsaw, Poland. *Telephone:* (22) 845 54 84.

MACHUNGO, Mário Fernandes da Graça; Mozambican politician; b. 1 Dec. 1940, Chicuque-Maxixe, Inhambane Prov.; m. Maria Eugénia Paiva Cruz; two d.; ed. Inst. for Higher Learning in Econ. and Financial Sciences (ISCEF), Portugal; became underground mem. Mozambique Liberation Front (FRELIMO) 1962; Pres. Students' Union, ISCEF 1964–65; subsequently expelled from ISCEF; completed studies 1969; returned to Mozambique, worked as economist with Nat. Devt. Bank; apptd. Minister for Econ. Co-operation in transitional govt. 1974; Minister for Trade and Industry 1975–76, for Industry and Energy 1976–78, for Agric. 1978–80, for Agric. and Planning 1980–83, for Planning 1983–94, Prime Minister of Mozambique 1986–94; elected to Cen. Cttee. and Political Bureau of FRELIMO Party 1977, re-elected 1983, elected to Secr. and fmr. Sec. for Econ. Policy 1986. *Address:* c/o Office of the Prime Minister, Maputo, Mozambique.

McINERNEY, Jay; American writer; ed. Williams Univ.; m. 1st Linda Rossiter; m. 2nd Merry Raymond; m. 3rd Helen Bransford 1991; one s. one d. *Publications include:* Bright Lights, Big City 1984, Ransom 1986, Story of My Life 1988, Brightness Falls 1992, The Last of the Savages 1996, Model Behavior 1998.

MACINNIS, Joseph Beverley, C.M., M.D.; Canadian marine research scientist; b. 2 March 1937, Barrie, Ont.; s. of Allistair MacInnis and Beverly Saunders; m. Deborah J. Ferris 1971; one s. three d.; ed. Univs. of Toronto and Pennsylvania; Pres. Undersea Research Ltd. and has held consulting contracts for U.S. Navy, Smithsonian Inst., IBM, Canadian Ministry of State for Science and Tech. and Canadian Dept. of Environment; est. SUBLIMNOS, Canada's first underwater manned station programme 1969; led 14 scientific expeditions into Arctic 1970–79, and during third expedition, SUB-IGLOO, world's first polar dive station established under ice; co-ordinated diving programme for ICE Station LOREX 1979; led team which discovered remains of English barque Breadalbane, sunk in 1853, 700 miles north of Artic Circle in 340 feet of water, world's most noteworthy shipwreck discovered to date 1980; host, The New Wave (CBC television series) 1975–76, The Newfoundlanders: Voices from the Sea 1978; scientific consultant, Mysteries of the Sea (ABC) 1979; co-ordinator, Shot Point 260 (Texaco Canada film), Breakthrough (Dome Petroleum film) 1979; consultant Titanic Project 1985; first Canadian to dive to the Titanic 1987; Co-leader IMAX-Titanic Expedition 1991; has lectured and shown his films in all parts of world including Israel, Germany, Australia, the Philippines, U.S.S.R. and Singapore; Pres. Undersea Research Ltd.; mem. Canadian Environmental Advisory Council, Canadian Council of Fitness and Health; Fellow, Royal Canadian Geographical Soc.; Hon. LL.D.; Hon. F.R.C.P., Dr. h.c. (Queen's) 1990. *Publications:* Underwater Images 1971,Underwater Man 1974, Coastline Canada 1982, Shipwreck Shores 1982, The Land that Devours Ships 1984, Titanic: In a New Light 1992, Saving the Oceans 1992 (Gen. Ed.), more than 30 scientific papers and articles in Scientific American, National Geographic Magazine etc. *Address:* 14 Dale Avenue, Toronto, Ont. M4W 1K4, Canada.

McINTOSH, Genista Mary, B.A., F.R.S.A.; British theatrical administrator; b. 23 Sept. 1946, London; d. of Geoffrey and Maire Tandy; m. Neil S.W. McIntosh 1971 (marriage dissolved); one s., one d.; ed. Hemel Hempstead Grammar School, Univ. of York; Casting Dir., R.S.C. 1972–77, Planning Controller 1977–84, Sr. Admin. 1986–90, Assoc. Producer 1990; Exec. Dir. Royal Nat. Theatre 1990–96, 1997–; Chief Exec. Royal Opera House Jan.–May 1997; Dir. Marmont Man. Ltd. 1984–86; Chair. S.E. London Common Purpose. *Address:* Royal National Theatre, London, SE1 9PX, England.

McINTOSH, Sir Malcolm Kenneth, A.C., Kt., PH.D.; British/Australian civil servant; b. 14 Dec. 1945, Melbourne; s. of Kenneth Stuart McIntosh and Valerie (née MacKenzie) McIntosh; m. Margaret Beatrice Stevens 1971; three s. one d.; ed. Australian Nat. Univ.; research scientist Australian Weapons Research Establishment 1970–72; Maj. Australian Army 1972–74; with Australian Econ. Ministries 1974–82; with Dept. of Defence 1982–90; Chief of Defence Production 1987; Deputy Sec. Acquisition and Logistics 1988; Sec. Australian Dept. of Industry, Technology and Commerce 1990; Chief of Defence Procurement Ministry of Defence (U.K.) 1991–95; C.E.O. CSIRO Jan. 1996–. *Address:* Commonwealth Scientific and Industrial Research Organization, P.O. Box 225, Dickson, A.C.T. 2602, Australia.

McINTYRE, Sir Donald Conroy, Kt., C.B.E., O.B.E.; British bass opera singer; b. 22 Oct. 1934, Auckland, N.Z.; s. of George Douglas and Hermyn McIntyre; m. Jill Redington 1961; three d.; ed. Mt. Albert Grammar School, Auckland, Auckland Teachers' Training Coll. and Guildhall School of Music, London; Prin. Bass, Sadler's Wells Opera 1960–67; with Royal Opera House, Covent Garden 1967–; Hon. D.Mus. (Auckland) 1992; Fidelio Medal A.I.D.O. 1989, N.Z. Award for outstanding contribs., Festival of the Arts 1990; annual appearances at Bayreuth Festival 1967–81; frequent int. guest appearances. *Roles include:* Wotan and Wanderer (Der Ring), Dutchman (Der Fliegende Holländer), Telramund (Lohengrin), Barak (Die Frau ohne Schatten), Pizzaro (Fidelio), Golaud (Pelléas et Mélisande), Kurwenal (Tristan and Isolde), Gurnemanz, Klingsor and Amfortas (Parsifal), Heyst (Victory), Jochanaan (Salome), Macbeth, Scarpia (Tosca), the Count (Marriage of Figaro), Nick Shadow (The Rake's Progress), Hans Sachs (Die Meistersinger), Dr. Schöne (Woyzeck), Cardillac (Cardillac Hindemith), Rocco (Fidelio), The Doctor (Der Freischütz), Prospero (Un Re In Asloto), Sarastro (Magic Flute), Balstrode (Peter Grimes); The Ring (video); recordings include Pelléas et Mélisande, Oedipus Rex, Il Trovatore, etc. *Leisure interests:* farm, tennis, walking. *Address:* c/o Ingpen & Williams, 26 Wadham Road, London, SW15 2LR (Agent); Fox Hill Farm, Jackass Lane, Keston, Bromley, Kent, BR2 6AN, England (Home). *Telephone:* (01689) 855368 (Home). *Fax:* (01689) 860724 (Home).

MacINTYRE, Duncan, C.M.G., P.C., D.S.O., O.B.E., E.D.; New Zealand politician and farmer; b. 10 Nov. 1915, Hastings; s. of Archibald MacIntyre and Esther Mary Bell; m. Diana Hunter; two s. three d.; ed. Larchfield School, Scotland, Christ's Coll., Christchurch; farming 1933–39, 1947–; served Second World War in Middle East, Italy and Japan as mem. N.Z. Cavalry Regt. 1939–46; after war commanded 1st Battalion Hawke's Bay Regt.; the N.Z. Scottish Regt., 2nd Infantry Brigade and 4th Armoured Brigade in Territorial Army 1949–60; Territorial mem. of N.Z. Army Bd. 1960; M.P. for Hastings 1960–72, for Bay of Plenty 1975–78, for East Cape 1978–84; Minister of Lands, Minister of Forests, Minister in Charge of the Valuation Dept. 1966–72, of Maori and Island Affairs 1969–72, of the Environment Feb.-Dec. 1972, of Maori Affairs 1975–79, of Agric. and in Charge of the Rural Banking and Finance Corpn. 1975–84, of Fisheries 1978–84; Deputy Prime Minister 1981–84; Deputy Leader Nat. Party 1981; mem. Parl. Select Cttee. on Privileges; fmr. Chair. Soil Conservation Cttee., Hawkes Bay Catchment Bd.; fmr. Area Del. Hawkes Bay Branch of Federated Farmers, N.Z. 150 Year Commemoration Medal. *Address:* Taikura, RD4, Waipukurau, New Zealand.

MacINTYRE, Iain, M.B., CH.B., PH.D., D.SC., F.R.C.PATH., F.R.C.P., F.R.S.; British professor of chemical pathology; b. 30 Aug. 1924, Glasgow; s. of John MacIntyre and Margaret Fraser Shaw; m. Mabel Wilson Jamieson 1947; one d.; ed. Jordanhill Coll. School, Univs. of Glasgow and London; Asst. Clinical Pathologist, United Sheffield Hosps. and Hon. Demonstrator in Biochemistry, Univ. of Sheffield 1948–52; Registrar in Chemical Pathology, Royal Postgraduate Medical School, Hammersmith Hosp., London 1952–54, Sir Jack Drummond Memorial Fellow 1954–56, Asst. Lecturer in Chemical Pathology 1956–59, Lecturer 1959–63, Reader 1963–67, Prof. of Endocrine Chem. 1967–82, Dir. Endocrine Unit 1967–89, Chair. Academic Bd. 1986–89; Prof. of Chemical Pathology, Univ. of London 1982–89, now Research Dir. William Harvey Research Inst., St. Bartholomew's and the Royal London School of Medicine and Dentistry, Queen Mary and Westfield Coll., London; Visiting Scientist, N.I.H., Bethesda, Md., U.S.A. 1960–61; Visiting Prof. of Medicine, Univ. of Calif., San Francisco 1964, Univ. of Melbourne 1980; Visiting Lecturer, U.S.S.R. Acad. of Sciences, Moscow 1978; Visiting Prof. St. George's Hosp. Medical School 1989–; A. J. S. McFadzean Lecture, Univ. of Hong Kong 1981; Transatlantic Lecture, American Endocrine Soc. 1987; Per Edman Memorial Lecturer, Melbourne 1990; Hon. Consultant Chemical Pathologist, Hammersmith and Queen Charlotte's Hosps.; Vice-Pres. English Chess Asscn. 1989–; Founder Fellow Acad. of Medical Sciences 1998; Hon. mem. Asscn. of American Physicians 1998; Hon. M.D. (Turin); Gairdner Int. Award, Toronto 1967, Elsevier Int. Award 1992, Paget Foundation John B. Johnson Award 1995. *Publications:* numerous articles on endocrinology. *Leisure interests:* tennis, chess, music. *Address:* William Harvey Research Institute, St. Bartholomew's and the Royal London School of Medicine and Dentistry (Queen Mary and Westfield College), Charterhouse Square, London, EC1M 6BQ (Office); Great Broadhurst Farm, Broad Oak, Nr. Heathfield, East Sussex, TN21 8UX, England (Home). *Telephone:* 0171-982 6168 (Office); (01435) 883 515 (Home). *Fax:* 0171-982 6162 (Office); (01435) 883611 (Home).

McINTYRE, Very Rev. John, C.V.O., M.A., B.D., D.LITT., D.D., D.H.L., F.R.S.E.; British ecclesiastic and university professor; b. 20 May 1916, Glasgow; s. of John C. McIntyre and Annie Summers; m. Jessie B. Buick 1945; two s. one d.; ed. Bathgate Acad. and Univ. of Edinburgh; Minister, Church of Scotland, Fenwick Parish Church 1943-45; Hunter Baillie Prof. of Theology St. Andrew's Coll. Univ. of Sydney 1946–56, Prin. 1950–56; Prof. of Divinity, Univ. of Edin. 1956–86, Dean Faculty of Divinity and Prin. New Coll. 1968–74, Acting Prin. and Vice-Chancellor 1973–74, 1979; Chaplain to H.M. The Queen in Scotland 1974–86, Chaplain Extraordinary 1974, 1986–; Dean, Order of the Thistle 1974–89; Moderator, Gen. Ass. of Church of Scotland 1982; Vice-Pres. Royal Soc. of Edin. 1983–86; Fulbright Visiting Prof. Union Theological Seminary, New York 1953; Warfield Lecturer, Princeton Theol. Seminary 1966; Laidlaw Lecturer, Knox Coll. Toronto 1987; Sprunt Lecturer, Union Theological Seminary, Richmond, Va. 1988; Hon. Fellow St. Andrew's Coll., Univ. of Sydney 1991–; Dr. h.c. (Edin.) 1987. *Publications:* St Anselm and his Critics 1954, The Christian Doctrine of History 1957, On the Love of God 1962, Faith, Theology and Imagination 1987, The Shape of Soteriology 1992, Theology After the Storm 1997, The Shape of Pneumatology 1997, The Shape of Christology 1998. *Leisure interest:* travel. *Address:* 22/4 Minto Street, Edinburgh, EH9 1RQ, Scotland. *Telephone:* 0131-667 1203.

MACK, Connie (Cornelius McGillicuddy), III; American politician; b. 29 Oct. 1940, Philadelphia; s. of Cornelius M. and Susan (née Sheppard) McGillicuddy; m. Ludie Priscilla 1960; one s. one d.; ed. Univ. of Florida, Sun Bank, Ft. Myers, Fla.; Vice-Pres. Business Devt. First Nat. Bank, Ft. Myers 1968–71; Sr. Vice-Pres., Dir. Sun Bank, Cape Coral, Fla. 1971–75; Pres., Dir. Florida Nat. Bank, Cape Coral 1972–82; mem. U.S. House of Reps. from Fla. 1983–89, Senator from Florida 1989–(2000); Republican Conf. Chair. 105th Congress 1996; Dir. Fed. Reserve Bd., Miami 1981–82; mem. Bd. of Dirs., Chair. Palmer Drug Abuse Program, Cape Coral; mem. Bd. of Dirs. Cape Coral Hosp.; Republican. *Address:* U.S. Senate, 517 Senate Hart Building, Washington, DC 20515, U.S.A.

MACK SMITH, Denis, C.B.E., F.B.A., M.A.; British author and fmr. professor of history; b. 3 March 1920, London; s. of Wilfrid Mack Smith and Altiora Gauntlett; m. Catharine Stevenson; two d.; ed. St. Paul's Cathedral Choir School, Haileybury Coll., Peterhouse, Cambridge; Fellow, Tutor, Peterhouse, Cambridge 1947, now Hon. Fellow; Sr. Research Fellow, All Souls Coll., Oxford 1962, Emer. Fellow 1987–; Extraordinary Fellow, Wolfson Coll. 1987–; Chair. Asscn. for the Study of Modern Italy 1988–; Grande Ufficiale, Italian Order of Merit. *Publications:* Cavour and Garibaldi in 1860 1954, Garibaldi 1957, Medieval and Modern Sicily 1968, The Making of Italy 1796–1866 1968, Italy: a modern history 1969, Victor Emanuel, Cavour and the Risorgimento 1971, Mussolini's Roman Empire 1976, Cento Anni di Vita Italiana attraverso il Corriere della Sera 1978, Mussolini 1981, Cavour 1985, Italy and its Monarchy 1989, Mazzini 1993, Modern Italy 1997, La Storia Manipolata 1998. *Leisure interests:* music, travel. *Address:* White Lodge, Osler Road, Headington, Oxford, OX3 9BJ, England. *Telephone:* (01865) 762878.

McKANE, William, M.A., PH.D., D.LITT., D.D., F.B.A., F.R.S.E.; British academic; b. 18 Feb. 1921, Dundee; s. of Thomas and Jemima S. McKane; m. Agnes M. Howie 1952; three s. two d.; ed. Univs. of St. Andrews and Glasgow; R.A.F. 1941–45; Lecturer in Hebrew, Univ. of Glasgow 1953, Sr. Lecturer 1956; Prof. of Hebrew and Oriental Languages, Univ. of St. Andrews 1968–90, Emer. Prof. 1990–, Dean, Faculty of Divinity 1973–77; Prin. St. Mary's Coll., St. Andrews 1982–86; Fellow Nat. Humanities Centre, N.C., U.S.A. 1987–88; Corresp. mem. Akademie der Wissenschaft zu Göttingen; Hon. D.D. (Edin.) 1984; Burkitt Medal (British Acad.) 1985. *Publications:* Prophets and Wise Men 1965, Proverbs, A New Approach 1970, Studies in the Patriarchal Narratives 1979, Jeremiah 1–25 (introduction and critical commentary) 1986, Selected Christian Hebraists 1989, A Late Harvest 1995, Jeremiah 26–52 (introduction and critical commentary) 1996, Micah: Introduction and commentary 1998; articles in British and European journals. *Leisure interest:* walking. *Address:* 51 Irvine Crescent, St. Andrews, Fife, KY16 8LG, Scotland. *Telephone:* (01334) 473797.

MACKAY, Charles Dorsey, M.A., M.B.A.; British businessman; b. 14 April 1940, Congleton; s. of late Brig. Kenneth Mackay and Evelyn Ingram; m. Annmarie Joder-Pfeiffer 1964; two s. (one deceased) one d.; ed. Cheltenham Coll., Queens' Coll. Cambridge and European Inst. of Business Admin. (INSEAD), Fontainebleau; with BP Co. 1957–69, McKinsey & Co. 1969–76, Pakhoed Holding N.V. Rotterdam 1976–81; Dir. Chloride Group PLC 1981–86, Chair. Overseas Div. 1981–85, Power Electronics Div. 1985–86; Chair. Inchcape (Hong Kong) Ltd. and Dodwell & Co. Ltd. 1986–87; Chair. and Chief Exec. Inchcape Pacific Ltd. 1987–91; Deputy Chair. Thistle Hotels PLC 1996–; Dir. Inchcape PLC 1986–96, Chief Exec. 1991–96, Deputy Chair. 1995–96; Dir. (non-exec.) Hongkong and Shanghai Banking Corpn. Ltd. 1986–92, HSBC Holdings 1992–98, Midland Bank 1992–93, British Airways 1993–96, Gucci Group NV 1997–, Eurotunnel 1997–. *Leisure interests:* travel, tennis, skiing, classical music, opera, chess.

MacKAY, Sir Donald Iain, Kt., M.A., F.R.S.E., F.R.S.G.S.; British economist; b. 27 Feb. 1937, Kobe, Japan; s. of William MacKay and Rhona MacKay; m. Diana Marjory Raffan 1961; one s. two d.; ed. Dollar Acad., Aberdeen Univ.; with English Electric Co. 1959–62; lecturer Aberdeen Univ. 1962–65, Prof. 1971–76; lecturer Glasgow Univ. 1965–68, Sr. lecturer 1968–71; Consultant to Sec. of State for Scotland 1971–; Chair. Pieda PLC 1974–97; lecturer B.A.A.S. 1974; Lister Prof. Heriot-Watt Univ. 1976–82, Hon. Prof. 1990–; Chair. Scottish Enterprise 1993–97, Chair. DTZ Pieda Consulting 1997–, Scottish Science Trust 1997–, Edin. Business School 1997–; Dir. Grampian Holdings 1987–, Highland Distilleries 1997–; mem. Scottish Econ. Council 1985–; Dr h.c. (Stirling) 1994. *Publications:* Geographical Mobility and the Brain Drain 1969, Local Labour Markets and Wage Structures 1970, Labour Markets under Different Employment Conditions 1971, The Political Economy of North Sea Oil 1975, The Economics of Self-Government 1977, numerous articles in econ. and political journals. *Leisure interests:* bridge, golf, tennis. *Address:* Newfield, 14 Gamekeeper's Road, Edinburgh, EH4 6LU, Scotland. *Telephone:* 0131-336 1936.

MacKAY, Elmer MacIntosh, P.C., Q.C., B.A., LL.B.; Canadian politician, lumberman and lawyer; b. 5 Aug. 1936, Hopewell, N.S.; s. of Gordon MacKay and Laura MacIntosh; ed. Acadia Univ., Wolfville, Nova Scotia, Dalhousie Univ., Halifax; called to Bar of N.S. 1960; practised law in Pictou Co., N.S.; f. firm MacKay, White, Stroud and Langley, New Glasgow, N.S.; mem. House of Commons 1971–93; Minister of Regional Econ. Expansion and Minister responsible for Canada Mortgage and Housing Corpn. 1979–80; Sr. Adviser to Leader of Opposition 1983; Solicitor-Gen. of Canada 1984–85; Minister of Natural Revenue 1985–88, for Public Works 1989–93, for Atlantic Canada Opportunity Agency 1989–91; Minister responsible for Canada Mortgage and Housing Corpn. 1991–93; Progressive Conservative Party. *Address:* R.R.1, Hopewell, Pictou Co., Nova Scotia, B0K 1C0, Canada (Home).

McKAY, Rt. Hon. Sir Ian Lloyd, K.N.Z.M., P.C., B.A., LL.B.; New Zealand judge (retd.); b. 7 March 1929, Waipawa; s. of Neville McKay and Kathleen McGrath; m. Ruth Younger 1958; four s. two d.; ed. St. Patrick's Coll. Silverstream, Waipawa Dist. High School and Victoria Coll., N.Z. Univ.; barrister and solicitor 1952; partner, Swan Davies & McKay, Wellington (later Young Swan McKay & Co., Young Swan Morison McKay and from 1986 Kensington Swan) 1953, Sr. Partner 1967–91; mem. numerous legal cttees., etc.; dir. numerous public and pvt. cos. 1970–91; Judge, Court of Appeal of N.Z. 1991–97; mem. Judicial Cttee. Privy Council 1992–; Pres. Arbitrators Inst. of N.Z. 1994–96; Pres. The Electoral Comm.; Fellow Chartered Inst. of Arbitrators, Int. Acad. of Trial Lawyers; Hon. mem. American Bar Asscn.; mem. Int. Bar Asscn.; Wellington City Civic Award 1988. *Leisure interests:* Highland bagpipe music, tennis. *Address:* 3 Aylesbury Way, Karori, Wellington, New Zealand. *Telephone:* (04) 476-8950. *Fax:* (04) 476-7950.

MACKAY OF CLASHFERN, Baron (Life Peer), cr. 1979, of Eddrachillis in the District of Sutherland; **James Peter Hymers Mackay,** K.T., P.C., Q.C., M.A., LL.B., F.R.S.E.; British advocate; b. 2 July 1927, Scotland; s. of James Mackay and Janet Hymers; m. Elizabeth Gunn Hymers 1958; one s. two d.; ed. George Heriot's School, Edinburgh, Univ. of Edinburgh; Lecturer in Math., Univ. of St. Andrews 1948–50; Major Scholar, Trinity Coll., Cambridge 1947, Sr. Scholar 1951; admitted to Faculty of Advocates 1955, Vice-Dean 1973–76, Dean 1976–79, Lord Advocate 1979–84; Sheriff Prin., Renfrew and Argyll 1972–74; Commr. Northern Lighthouses 1972–84; Dir. Stenhouse Holdings Ltd. 1976–78; Senator of Coll. of Justice in Scotland 1984–85; Lord of Appeal in Ordinary 1985–87; Lord Chancellor 1987–97; Chancellor Heriot-Watt Univ. 1991–; Ed.-in-Chief Halsbury's Laws of England 1998–; Part-time mem. Scottish Law Comm. 1976–79; mem. Insurance Brokers' Registration Council 1978–79; Hon. Church Commr.; Fellow, Inst. of Taxation, Birmingham Univ., Newcastle Univ., American Coll. of Trial Lawyers, Int. Acad. of Trial Lawyers; Hon. Fellow, Inst. of Civil Engineers, Trinity Coll., Cambridge, Girton Coll., Cambridge; Hon. F.R.C.P.E.; Hon. F.R.C.S.(E.), Hon. F.R.C.P.; Hon. LL.D. (Edinburgh, Dundee, Strathclyde, Aberdeen, St. Andrews, Birmingham, Newcastle, Cambridge); Hon. D.C.L. (Newcastle), (Oxford) 1998. *Publication:* Armour on Valuation for Rating (Sr. Ed.) 1961, 1971. *Leisure interests:* walking, travel, country pursuits. *Address:* House of Lords, Westminster, London, SW1A 0PW, England.

McKECHNIE, Sheila, O.B.E.; British civil servant; b. 3 May 1948, Falkirk; ed. Falkirk High School, Edinburgh and Warwick Univs.; Research Asst. Oxford Univ. 1971–72; Asst. Gen. Sec. Wall Paper Workers Union Staff Section 1972–74; Workers' Educ. Assoc. Tutor Manchester 1974–76; Health and Safety Officer ASTMS 1976–85; Dir. Shelter 1985–94, Consumers' Assoc. 1995–; Dir. (non-exec.) Bank of England 1998–; Hon. D.Univ. (Open) 1994; Hon. D.Sc. (Edin.) 1994. *Address:* c/o Bank of England, Threadneedle Street, London, E.C.2, England.

McKEE, John Angus; Canadian business executive; b. 31 Aug. 1935, Toronto, Ont.; s. of John W. McKee and Margaret E. Phippen; m. Susan E. Harley 1970; one s. one d.; ed. Trinity Coll. School, Port Hope, Ont. and Univ. of Toronto; joined the Patiño Mining Corpn. 1962, Asst. to Pres. 1963, Vice-Pres. (Corporate Devt.) 1966; Man. Dir. Consolidated Tin Smelters Ltd. 1968–71; owner J. A. McKee and Assocs. Ltd. 1971–83; Pres. and C.E.O. Canadian Occidental Petroleum Ltd. 1983–93; Chair., Pres., C.E.O. Gulfstream Resources Canada 1993–; Dir. Stone and Webster Canada Ltd., Stone and Webster Inc. (U.S.A.), Teradyne Canada Ltd., CVI Ltd. and others; mem. Bd. of Govs., Trinity Coll. School, Port Hope. *Leisure interests:* skiing, shooting. *Address:* 1500, 635-8th Avenue, S.W., Calgary, Alta. T2P 3Z1, Canada.

MacKELLAR, Michael John Randal, B.SCI.AGR., M.A.; Australian politician; b. 27 Oct. 1938, Sydney; s. of Geoffrey Neil and Colleen Randal MacKellar; m. Robin Morey Smith 1969; two s. one d.; ed. Sydney Church of England Grammar School, Sydney Univ., Balliol Coll., Oxford; New South Wales Dept. of Agric. 1961–69; mem. for Warringah, N.S.W., House of Reps. 1969–94; Parl. Sec. to Leader of Opposition 1973–74; Shadow Minister for Immigration 1974–75; Minister for Immigration and Ethnic Affairs 1975–79, Minister Assisting the Treas. 1978–79, Minister for Health 1979–82, Minister Assisting the Prime Minister 1979–80, Minister for Home Affairs and Environment Feb.–March 1981; Shadow Minister for Foreign Affairs 1983–84, for Science and Special Minister of State 1984–85; Deputy Opposition Leader of the House 1985; Opposition Whip 1989; mem. numerous House of Reps. Cttees. 1970–90; Chair. House of Reps. Standing Cttee. on Environment and Conservation 1982–83; mem. first Australian Parl. del. to People's Repub. of China 1973, Leader del. to UN Habitat Conf. 1976; mem. N.S.W. Advisory Cttee. for Australian Broadcasting Comm. 1973–75, Advisory Council of CSIRO 1984, Council of Australian Nat. Univ. 1970–76; C.E.O. Plastics and Chemicals Industries Asscn. 1994–97; C.O.O. Baker Medical Research Inst. 1997–; Bd. mem. Sydney Paralympic Games Organising Cttee. 1997–; Chair. Australia/N.Z. Food Authority 1998–, Franchising Policy Council of Australia 1998–; Liberal Party. *Leisure interests:* tennis, cricket, golf, reading, photography. *Address:* 2a West Street, Balgowlah Heights, Sydney, N.S.W. 2093, Australia.

McKELLEN, Sir Ian Murray, Kt., C.B.E., B.A.; British actor; b. 25 May 1939, Burnley, Lancs.; s. of Denis Murray McKellen and Margery (Sutcliffe) McKellen; ed. Bolton School, St. Catharine's Coll., Cambridge; first stage appearance as Roper (A Man for All Seasons), Belgrade Theatre, Coventry 1961; numerous other parts include title-roles in Henry V, Luther, Ipswich 1962–63; Aufidius (Coriolanus), Arthur Seaton (Saturday Night and Sunday Morning), title-role in Sir Thomas More, Nottingham Playhouse 1963–64; London début as Godfrey (A Scent of Flowers), Duke of York's Theatre 1964; Claudio (Much Ado About Nothing), Protestant Evangelist (Last Goodnight), Capt. de Foenix (Trelawny of the Wells), Nat. Theatre Co. 1965; Alvin (A Lily in Little India), Hampstead and St. Martin's 1965–66; Andrew Cobham (Their Very Own and Golden City), Royal Court 1966; title-part in O'Flaherty, V.C. and Bonaparte (The Man of Destiny), Mermaid 1966; Leonidik (The Promise), Oxford Playhouse, Fortune, and Henry Miller (Broadway début) 1966–67; Tom (The White Liars), Harold Gorringe (Black Comedy), Lyric 1968; Richard II (Edinburgh Festival 1969), Edward II, Hamlet, Prospect Theatre Co. 1968–71, British tour, Mermaid and Piccadilly Theatres; Darkly (Billy's Last Stand), Theatre Upstairs 1970; Capt. Plume (The Recruiting Officer), Corporal Hill (Chips With Everything), Cambridge Theatre Co. 1970; Svetlovidov (Swan Song), Crucible, Sheffield 1971; founder-mem. Actors' Co., Edinburgh Festival 1972 and touring as Giovanni ('Tis Pity She's A Whore), Page-Boy (Ruling the Roost), Prince Yoremitsu (The Three Arrows), title-role in Michael, the Wood Demon, Footman (The Way of The World), then Knots, Shaw Theatre, Edgar (King Lear), Brooklyn Acad., and Giovanni, Wimbledon 1973–74; début with R.S.C. as Dr. Faustus (Edinburgh Festival) 1974; title-role in The Marquis of Keith, Philip the Bastard (King John), Aldwych 1974–75; Colin (Ashes), Young Vic. 1975; Aubrey Bagot (Too True to Be Good), also at Globe, Romeo, Macbeth, Bernick (Pillars of the Community), Face (The Alchemist) Stratford season 1976; Langevin (Days of the Commune) 1976–78; organized R.S.C. British tour of Twelfth Night (Toby Belch) and Three Sisters (Andrei); Max (Bent), Royal Court and Criterion 1979, Amadeus (New York) 1980, Short List (Hampstead Theatre Club), Cowardice (Ambassadors) 1983; int. tour of one-man show Acting Shakespeare (L.A. and Ritz Theatre, New York) 1984, (London) 1987; Assoc. Dir. Nat. Theatre of Great Britain (also actor) 1984–86; Venice Preserv'd (Pierre), Coriolanus; Wild Honey (Platonov); McKellen/Petherbridge Nat. Theatre Group: Duchess of Malfi (Bosola), Real Inspector Hound (Hound), The Critic (Mr Puff), The Cherry Orchard (Lopakhin); Wild Honey (Va. Theatre, New York), U.S.A. Shakespeare tour 1987; Henceforward (Vaudeville Theatre) 1988–89; Othello (Iago) R.S.C. 1989; Royal Nat. Theatre: Bent (Max), King Lear (Kent), Richard III 1990–92 (World Tour then U.S. Tour), Napoli Milionaria 1991, Uncle Vanya 1992, An Enemy of the People 1997, Peter Pan 1997; The Seagull, Present Laughter, The Tempest (W. Yorks. Playhouse) 1998–99. *Films include:* Alfred the Great 1969, The Promise 1969, A Touch of Love 1969, Priest of Love 1981, The Keep 1982, Plenty, Zina 1985, Scandal 1988, The Ballad of Little Jo 1992, I'll Do Anything 1992, Last Action Hero 1993, Six Degrees of Separation 1993, The Shadow 1994, Jack and Sarah 1994, Restoration 1994, Richard III 1995, Bent 1996, Swept from the Sea 1996, Apt Pupil 1997, Gods and Monsters 1998. *TV appearances include:* David Copperfield 1965, Ross 1969, Richard II, Edward II and Hamlet 1970, Hedda Gabler 1974, Macbeth, Every Good Boy Deserves Favour, Dying Day 1979, Acting Shakespeare 1981, Walter, The Scarlet Pimpernel 1982, Walter and June 1983, Countdown to War 1989, Othello 1990, Tales of the City 1993, Cold Comfort Farm 1995; Cameron Mackintosh Prof. of Contemporary Theatre, Oxford Univ. 1991; Clarence Derwent Award 1964; Hon. D.Litt. (Nottingham) 1989, (Oxford) 1991; Variety and Plays and Players awards 1966; Actor of the Year (Plays and Players) 1976; Soc. of W. End Theatres Award for Best Actor in Revival 1977, for Best Comedy Performance 1978, for Best Actor in a New Play 1979, Tony Award 1981, Drama Desk 1981, Outer Critics Circle Award 1981; Royal TV Soc. Performer of the Year 1983; Laurence Olivier Award 1984, 1991; Evening Standard Best Actor Award 1984, 1989; council mem. British Actors' Equity 1970–71. *Publication:* William Shakespeare's Richard III (jtly.) 1996. *Address:* c/o ICM, 76 Oxford Street, London, W1N 0AX, England. *Telephone:* 0171-636 6565. *Fax:* 0171-323 0101.

McKENNA, Frank Joseph, LL.B.; Canadian politician and lawyer; b. 19 Jan. 1948, Apohaqui, Kings Co., N.B.; s. of Joseph McKenna and Olive Moody; m. Julie Friel 1972; two s. one d.; ed. St. Francis Xavier Univ., Queen's Univ. and Univ. of N.B.; Special Asst. to Pres., Privy Council 1971; Research Asst. Constitutional Law Unit, PMO 1973; partner, Martin, Lordon, McKenna, Martin & Bowes; Counsel, McInnes, Cooper & Robertson; mem. N.B. Bar Asscn., Canadian Bar Asscn.; mem. Legis. Ass. 1982–97; Leader, N.B. Liberal Party 1985–97; Premier, Prov. of N.B. 1987–97; Dir. Bruncor Ltd., Major Drilling Ltd., Bank of Montreal, Alphanet Telecom Inc., Acier Leroux Inc.; Hon. LL.D. (Univ. of N.B.) 1988; Vanier Award 1988, Econ. Developer of the Year, Econ. Developers' Asscn. of Canada 1993, Distinction Award, Canadian Advanced Tech. Asscn. 1994. *Leisure interests:* reading, sports and current affairs. *Address:* Moncton Place, 655 Main Street, P.O. Box 1368, Moncton, N.B., E1C 8T6, Canada. *Telephone:* (506) 857-8970. *Fax:* (506) 857-4095.

McKENNA, Stephen Francis, D.F.A.; British/Irish painter; b. 20 March 1939, Ashford, Middx.; s. of the late Maj. James McKenna and Violet (née Kinnear) McKenna; one s.; ed. Cardinal Vaughan Memorial School, London, De La Salle Coll., Hong Kong, Andover Grammar School, St. Illtyd's Coll., Cardiff, Welbeck Coll., Royal Mil. Acad., Sandhurst, Slade School of Fine Art; Sr. Lecturer in Painting, Canterbury Coll. of Art 1965–68; Visiting Lecturer, Goldsmiths Coll., Univ. of London 1968–72; lived in Bonn 1971–79, Brussels 1979–84; invited to Berlin by Kunstler Programm DAAD 1984; in London, Donegal and Umbria 1985–; Guest Prof. of Painting, Hochschule für Bildende Künste, Braunschweig, Germany, 1995–. *One-man exhbns. include:* Barry Barker Gallery, London, 1978, 1979, Edward Totah Gallery, London 1985, 1986, 1988, Gallery Seno, Milan, Kunsthalle, Düsseldorf 1986, Raab Gallery, Berlin, ICA, London, Sander Gallery, N.Y. 1985, Van Abbemuseum Eindhoven, Gallery Springer, Berlin 1984, Museum of Modern Art, Oxford, Gallery Isy Brachot, Brussels, Gallery Swajcer, Antwerp 1983, Orchard Gallery, Derry 1981, 1988, Kerlin Gallery, Dublin 1988–90, 1993, 1995, Galeria Manuela Boscolo, Busto Arsizio 1990, Galería Estampa, Madrid 1990, 1992, Galeria Inge Baecker, Cologne 1990, Sala Uno, Rome 1991, Casa Masaccio, Valdarno 1991, Kerlin Gallery, Dublin 1992, Galerie des Beaux Arts, Brussels 1992, Galerie Nikolaus Fischer, Frankfurt/Main 1993, Irish Museum of Modern Art, Dublin 1993, Fruitmarket Gallery, Edin. 1994, Arts Council Gallery, Belfast 1994, Reeds Wharf Gallery, London 1995; works in numerous public collections. *Publications:* numerous catalogues; texts: 'On Landscape' 1984, Parables of Painting 1980. *Leisure interest:* conversation. *Address:* Crocknafeola, Killybegs, County Donegal, Ireland.

McKENNA, Thomas Patrick (T.P.); Irish actor; b. 7 Sept. 1931, Cavan; s. of Ralph and Mary McKenna; m. May White 1956; four s. one d.; joined Abbey Theatre Co., Dublin 1954, Hon. Life Mem. 1966. *Films include:* Siege of Sidney Street, Girl with Green Eyes, Ferry Cross the Mersey, Young Cassidy, Ulysses, Charge of the Light Brigade, Anne of the Thousand Days, Perfect Friday, Villain, Straw Dogs, Portrait of the Artist as a Young Man, A Child's Voice, Exposure, The Outsider, Silver Dream Racer, The Scarlet and the Black, To the Lighthouse, Mehmed my Hawk, Doctor and the Devils, Honour, Profit and Pleasure, Cat's Eyes, Anything Legal Considered, O.S.S., Strong Medicine, Pascali's Island, Red Scorpion, Valmont, Monarch, Kings in Grass Castles, The American 1998. *Television includes:* Jack the Ripper, Dr. Who, Miss Marple, Shoot to Kill (TV film), Parnell and the Englishwoman, The Chief (series 2, 3, 4), Rumpole of the Bailey, Events at Drimaghleen (TV film), The Law Lords (TV film), Lovejoy, Casualty, Heartbeat, Stendhal's Scarlet and Black, Kavanagh Q.C., The Ambassadors. *Stage:* Molly Sweeney by Brian Friel, world premiere, Gate Theatre, Dublin 1994 and Almeida Theatre, London, Hirst in No Man's Land, Pinter Festival at Gate Theatre 1997, Brian Friel's version of Uncle Vanya, world premiere, Gate Theatre 1998, The Weir, Royal Court, London 1999. *Leisure interests:* reading, sport, music. *Address:* 28 Claverley Grove, London, N3 2DH, England (Home). *Telephone:* 0181-346 4118 (Home).

McKENNA, Virginia; British actress; b. 7 June 1931, London; m. Bill Travers (died 1994); three s. one d.; f. Zoo Check Charitable Trust (now The Born Free Foundation) 1984; film debut in The Second Mrs Tanqueray; stage appearances have included The King And I 1983, Hamlet (R.S.C.) 1985, Winnie 1988, A Little Night Music, The Devils (R.S.C.), The Beggar's Opera (R.S.C.). *TV appearances include:* Lovejoy 1991, The Camomile Lawn, Ruth Rendell Mysteries 1992, September (mini-series) 1995, and documentary The Lion at World's End 1971, The Scold's Bridle 1998. *Films include:* Father's Doing Fine, The Cruel Sea, Simba, The Ship that Died of Shame, A Town Like Alice, The Smallest Show on Earth, The Barretts of Wimpole Street, Carve Her Name With Pride, The Passionate Summer, Wreck of the Mary Deare, Two Living, One Dead, Born Free, Ring of Bright Water, An Elephant Called Slowly, Waterloo, Swallows and Amazons, The Disappearance, Holocaust-2000, Staggered. *Publications:* On Playing with Lions (with Bill Travers), Some Of My Friends Have Tails, Into the Blue 1992, Journey to Freedom 1997; Co-Ed. and Contrib. Beyond the Bars, Headlines from the Jungle (verse) 1990, Back to the Blue 1997. *Address:* c/o Derek Webster, A.I.M., 5 Denmark Street, London, W.C.2; Born Free Foundation, 3 Grove House, Foundry Lane, Horsham, West Sussex, RH13 5PL, England.

McKENNON, Keith Robert, B.S.; American business executive; b. 25 Dec. 1933, Condon, Ore.; s. of Russell McKennon and Lois Edgerton; m. Patricia Dragon 1961; three s.; ed. Pendleton High School, Golden Gate Coll. and Oregon State Univ.; joined Dow Chemical U.S.A. 1955; Dir. Public Affairs, The Dow Chemical Co. 1978, Vice-Pres. 1980, Vice-Pres. Agricultural Products 1982; Vice-Pres. Product Dept. Man. Dow Chemical U.S.A. Jan. 1983; Group Vice-Pres. Global Agricultural Products, Legal, Employee Relations and Public Affairs, The Dow Chemical Co. April 1983; mem. Bd. of Dirs. The Dow Chemical Co. 1983–, Group Vice-Pres. and Dir. of Research and Devt. 1985, Exec. Vice-Pres. 1987–92; Pres. Dow Chemical U.S.A. 1987–90; Chair., C.E.O. Dow Corning Corpn. 1992–94; Chair. Pacific Corpn. 1994–; Dir. Chemical Bank and Trust Co., Chemical Financial Corpn., Dowell Schlumberger Inc., Dow Corning Corpn., Marion Merrill Dow, Pacific Corpn., Nat. Legal Center for the Public Interests etc. *Leisure interests:* tennis, fishing, reading. *Address:* Pacific Corporation, Suite 1600, 700 N.E. Multomah, Portland, OR 97202 (Office); P.O. Box 5542, Stateline, NV 89449, U.S.A.

McKENZIE, Dan Peter, M.A., PH.D., F.R.S.; British geologist; b. 21 Feb. 1942, Cheltenham; s. of W. S. and N. M. (née Fairbrother) McKenzie; m. Indira M. Misra 1971; one s.; ed. Westminster School and King's Coll., Cambridge; Fellow, King's Coll. 1965–73, 1977–, Sr. Asst. in Research, Dept. of Earth Sciences, Univ. of Cambridge 1969–73, Asst. Dir. of Research 1973–79, Reader in Tectonics 1979–85, Prof. of Earth Sciences 1985–96, Royal Soc. Research Prof. 1996–; Foreign Assoc. N.A.S.; Balzan Prize 1981, Japan Prize 1990. *Publications:* papers in professional journals. *Leisure interest:* gardening. *Address:* Bullard Laboratories, Madingley Rise, Madingley Road, Cambridge, CB3 0EZ, England.

MACKENZIE, Ian, D.S.O., M.A., LL.D., C.A.; South African business executive; b. 7 Sept. 1914, Johannesburg; s. of late George Mackenzie and Vera Mackenzie; m. Anne McNab Lindsay 1944; two s. two d.; ed. Glenalmond, Scotland, Pembroke Coll., Oxford; service in Royal Scots Fusiliers 1939–46, rank of Lieut.-Col.; Pres. Johannesburg Chamber of Commerce and Industry 1995; mem. 1820 Foundation, Bd. of Govs. Rhodes Univ.; Kt. of the Mil. and Hospitalier Order of St. Lazarus of Jerusalem. *Leisure interests:* fishing, nature conservation, travel. *Address:* P.O. Box 2105, Johannesburg 2000 (Office); 11 Duncombe Road, Forest Town, 2193, South Africa (Home). *Telephone:* 484 3950 (Office); 646 5369 (Home).

MACKENZIE, Gen. Sir Jeremy John George, G.C.B., O.B.E.; British army officer; b. 11 Feb. 1941, Nairobi, Kenya; s. of late Lieut.-Col. John William Elliot Mackenzie and of Valerie Mackenzie (née Dawes); m. Elizabeth Lyon (née Wertenbaker) 1969; one s. one d.; ed. Duke of York School, Nairobi, Kenya, Staff Coll.; commissioned Queen's Own Highlanders 1961; Canadian Forces Staff Coll. 1974; Brigade Maj. 24 Airportable Brigade 1975–76; C.O. 1 Queen's Own Highlanders, N. Ireland and Hong Kong 1979–82; Instructor Staff Coll. 1982–83; Col. Army Staff Duties 2 1983–84; Commdr. 12th Armoured Brigade 1984–86; Service Fellowship King's Coll., Univ. of London 1987; Deputy Commdt. 1987–89; Commdt. 1989, Staff Coll.; GOC 4th Armoured Div. BAOR 1989–91; Col. Commdt. WRAC 1990–92, AG Corps 1992–98, APTC 1997–; Col. Highlanders Regt. 1994–; Commdr. 1st (British) Corps 1991–92, NATO's ACE Rapid Reaction Corps (ARRC) 1992–94, Deputy Supreme Allied Commdr., Europe 1994–98; ADC (Gen.) 1997–99; Gov. Royal Hosp. Chelsea 1999–; mem. Queen's Bodyguard of Scotland (RCA); Commdr. U.S. Legion of Merit 1997; Hungarian Presidential Order of Merit (1st Class) 1998, Czech Defence Minister's Order of Merit (1st Class) 1998. *Publication:* The British Army and the Operational Level of War 1989. *Leisure interests:* shooting, fishing, painting. *Address:* Royal Hospital, Chelsea, London, SW3 4SR, England.

MacKENZIE, Kelvin; British journalist; b. 22 Oct. 1946; m. Jacqueline M. Holland 1969; two s. one d.; joined The Sun as sub-editor 1972, subsequently Night Ed.; apptd. Man. Ed. New York Post 1978; rejoined The Sun as Night Ed. 1980; Night Ed. Daily Express Feb. 1981; rejoined The Sun, Ed. 1981–94; Man. Dir. BSkyB Jan.–Oct. 1994 (resgnd.); Dir. Mirror Group PLC 1994–, Deputy Chief Exec. and Group Man. Dir. 1997–98; Man. Dir. UK Talk Radio 1998–. *Address:* Talk Co. Ltd., Suite 205, 10 Stratton Street, London, W1X 5FD, England.

McKENZIE, Kevin; American ballet dancer, choreographer and director; b. 29 April 1954, Burlington, Vt.; ed. Acad. of Washington School of Ballet; Prin. dancer, Joffrey Ballet 1977–78; Prin. dancer, American Ballet Theater 1979–91, Artistic Dir. 1992–; Perm. guest artist, Washington Ballet 1990–91, Artistic Assoc. 1991–92; Assoc. Dir. New Amsterdam Ballet 1984–; Hon. Ph.D. (St. Michael's Coll.). *Address:* American Ballet Theatre, 890 Broadway, New York, NY 10003, U.S.A. *Telephone:* (212) 477-3030. *Fax:* (212) 254-5938.

MACKENZIE-STUART, Baron (Life Peer) cr. 1988, of Dean in the District of the City of Edinburgh; **Alexander John Mackenzie Stuart;** LL.D., F.C.I.ARB., F.R.S.E.; British judge (retd.); b. 18 Nov. 1924, Aberdeen; s. of Prof. A. Mackenzie Stuart, K.C. and Amy Margaret Dean; m. Anne Burtholme Millar 1952; four d.; ed. Fettes Coll. Edinburgh, Cambridge and Edinburgh Univs.; Royal Engineers 1942–47; admitted to Faculty of Advocates 1951; Standing Jr. Counsel, Scottish Home Dept. 1956–57, Inland Revenue, Scotland 1957–63; Q.C. 1963; Keeper of Advocates Library 1970–72; Sheriff-Prin. of Aberdeen, Kincardine and Banff 1971–72; Senator, Coll. of Justice, Scotland 1972; Judge, Court of Justice of European Communities 1973–88, Pres. 1984–88; fmr. Pres. Acad. of Experts; Hon. Bencher Middle Temple and King's Inn, Dublin; Dr. h.c. (Stirling), Hon LL.D. (Exeter, Edinburgh, Glasgow, Aberdeen, Cambridge, Birmingham), Prix Bech for Services to Europe 1989. *Publications:* The European Communities and the Rule of Law 1977, A French King at Holyrood 1995. *Address:* 7 Randolph Cliff, Edinburgh, EH3 7TZ, Scotland; Le Garidel, Gravières, 07140 Les Vans, Ardèche, France.

McKERN, Leo Reginald, A.O.; Australian actor; b. 16 March 1920, Sydney; s. of Norman W. McKern and Vera Martin; m. Jane Holland 1946; two d.; ed. Sydney Tech. High School; eng. apprentice 1935–37; artist 1937–40; army service 1940–42; actor since 1944; came to England 1946; Combined Services Entertainment Unit (C.S.E.U.) tour, Germany; Arts Council tours 1947; Old Vic 1949–52; Shakespeare Memorial Theatre 1952–54; Old Vic last season 1962–63; New Nottingham Playhouse 1963–64; has since appeared regularly on London stage, including Boswell for the Defence 1989, Hobson's Choice (Lyric Theatre) 1995, When We Are Married (Savoy) 1996. *Films:* The French Lieutenant's Woman 1983, Ladyhawke 1984, The Chain 1985, Travelling North 1986, On Our Selection 1995, Dad and Dave on Our Selection 1995. *Television:* Rumpole of the Bailey 1977, 1991, 1992, Reilly–Ace of Spies 1983, Monsieur Quixote, Murder with Mirrors 1985, 1992, The Master Builder 1987, The Last Romantics 1992, A Foreign Field 1993, The Good King 1994. *Publication:* Just Resting (memoir) 1983. *Leisure interests:* photography, sailing, environment. *Address:* c/o Richard Hatton Ltd., 29 Roehampton Lane, London, SW15 5JR, England.

McKERNAN, John Rettie, J.D.; American politician; b. 20 May 1948, Bangor, Maine; s. of John Rettie McKernan Sr. and Barbara Guild; one s.; m. 2nd Olympia Snowe 1989; one s.; ed. Dartmouth Coll. and Southern Maine Univ.; Attorney, Sterns and Finnegan, Bangor, Maine 1974–76, Verrill and Dana, Portland, Maine 1976–82; mem. 98th–99th Congresses from 1st Dist. Maine 1982; Gov. of Maine 1987–95; mem. Pres. Comm. on Presidential Scholars 1981; Republican. *Address:* c/o Office of the Governor, State House, Station 1, Augusta, ME 04333, U.S.A.

MACKERRAS, Sir Charles, Kt., A.C., C.B.E.; British conductor; b. 17 Nov. 1925, Schenectady, U.S.A. of Australian parentage; s. of Alan and Catherine Mackerras; m. Judith Wilkins 1947; two d.; ed. Sydney Grammar School, N.S.W. Conservatoire, and Prague Acad. of Music; Prin. Oboist Sydney Symphony Orchestra 1943–46; Conductor Sadler's Wells 1948–53, BBC Concert Orchestra 1954–56; guest opera conductor at Covent Garden, English Nat. Opera, Berlin State Opera, Hamburg State Opera, Vienna State Opera, etc. 1956–66; First Conductor, Hamburg State Opera 1966–69; Musical Dir., English Nat. Opera 1970–77, Chief Guest Conductor 1978–80, Assoc. Artist 1980–; Chief Guest Conductor, BBC Symphony Orchestra 1976–79; Chief Conductor Sydney Symphony Orchestra 1982–85; Prin. Guest Conductor Royal Liverpool Philharmonic Orchestra 1986–88; Musical Dir. Welsh Nat. Opera 1987–92, Conductor Emer. 1993–; Prin. Guest Conductor Scottish Chamber Orchestra 1992–95, Conductor Laureate 1995–; Prin. Guest Conductor San Francisco Opera 1993–96, Royal Philharmonic Orchestra 1993–96, Czech Philharmonic Orchestra 1997–; Music Dir. Orchestra of St. Luke's 1998–; guest conductor in Europe, U.S.A., Canada and Australia; Hon. R.A.M., Hon. F.R.C.M.; Hon. D.Mus. (Hull) 1990, (Nottingham) 1991, (York, Masaryk, Brno, and Griffith, Brisbane) 1994, (Oxford) 1997; Evening Standard Award for Most Outstanding Achievement in Opera 1977, Janáček Medal 1978, Gramophone awards 1977, 1980, 1983, 1984, 1994, Gramophone Record of the Year 1977, 1980, Grammy Award for Best Opera 1981. *Arrangements:* Ballets: Pineapple Poll 1951, Lady and the Fool 1954, Melbourne Cup 1965. *Recordings:* numerous, notably Janáček, Mozart and Handel series. *Publications:* musical articles in various magazines. *Leisure interests:* languages, yachting. *Address:* 10 Hamilton Terrace, London, NW8 9UG, England. *Telephone:* 0171-286 4047. *Fax:* 0171-289 5893.

MACKEY, James Patrick, B.A., L.PH., B.D., S.T.L., D.D., PH.D.; Irish professor of theology and ecclesiastic; b. 9 Feb. 1934, Ireland; s. of Peter Mackey and Esther Morrissey; m. Noelle Quinlan 1973; one s. one d.; ed. Mount St. Joseph Coll., Nat. Univ. of Ireland, Pontifical Univ., Maynooth and Queen's Univ., Belfast; ordained priest 1958; lecturer in Philosophy Queen's Univ. 1960–66, Philosophy and Theology St. John's Coll., Waterford 1966–69; Assoc. Prof. of Philosophical and Systematic Theology Univ. of San Francisco 1969–73, Prof. 1973–79; Visiting Prof. Univ. of Calif. Berkeley 1974–75; Thomas Chalmers Prof. of Theology Univ. of Edin. 1979–, Dean of Faculty of Divinity 1984–88, Dir. Grad. School and Assoc. Dean 1995–98; Visiting Prof. Dartmouth Coll., N.H. 1989, Univ. of San Francisco 1990; British Acad. Research Scholarship 1964–65; scripted and presented TV series The Hall of Mirrors 1984, The Gods of War 1986, Dir. Derry City Int. Conf. on the Cultures of Europe 1992; Ed. Studies in World Christianity 1995–. *Publications:* Life and Grace 1966, Morals, Law and Authority (Ed.) 1969, The Problems of Religious Faith 1974, Jesus, The Man and the Myth 1979, The Christian Experience of God as Trinity 1983, Religious Imagination (Ed.) 1986, Modern Theology 1987, An Introduction to Celtic Christianity 1989, Power and Christian Ethics 1994, The Cultures of Europe (Ed.) 1994, etc. *Leisure interest:* sailing. *Address:* New College, Mound Place, Edinburgh, EH1 2LX (Office); 10 Randolph Crescent, Edinburgh, EH3 7TT, Scotland (Home). *Telephone:* (0131) 650-7994 (Office); (0131) 225-9408 (Home). *Fax:* (0131) 650-6579.

MACKIE, Robert Gordon; American costume and fashion designer; b. 24 March 1940, Monterey Park, Calif.; s. of Charles Robert Smith and Mildred Agnes (Smith) Mackie; m. Marianne Wolford 1960 (divorced); one s.; ed. Chouinard Art Inst.; mem. staff Edith Head 1962–63; designed costumes for film Divorce, American Style 1966; Co-Designer for films Lady Sings the Blues 1972, Funny Lady 1975; designer for numerous TV shows including: Brigadoon 1966, Alice Through the Looking Glass 1967, Carousel 1967, Kismet 1967, Fred Astair Show 1968, Diana Ross and The Supremes 1969, Carol Burnett Show 1967–77, Sonny and Cher Comedy Hour 1971, Cher 1976, Sonny and Cher Show 1976–77, Diahann Carroll Summer Show 1976; Co-Designer theatrical productions On The Town 1971, Lorelei 1972, The Best Little Whorehouse Goes Public 1994; ; Emmy Award (co-recipient) 1967, Emmy Award 1969, 1976, 1983, Costume Designers' Guild Award 1968. *Publication:* Dressing for Glamour 1969. *Address:* Bob Mackie Ltd., 530 7th Avenue, New York, NY 10018, U.S.A.

MACKIN, Martin, M.A.; Irish politician; b. 23 Dec. 1963, Drogheda, Co. Louth; s. of Thomas Mackin and Josephine Mackin; ed. Univ. Coll. Dublin, Coll. of Commerce, Dublin, Nat. Univ. of Ireland; press officer, Fianna Fáil 1992–95, Dir. Fianna Fáil European Office 1995–98, Gen. Sec. Fianna Fáil 1998–. *Leisure interests:* music, current affairs, reading. *Address:* c/o Áras

De Valera, 13 Upper Mount Street, Dublin 2, Ireland. *Telephone:* 01-676 1551. *Fax:* 01-678 5960.

McKINNEY, Robert Moody, B.A.; American diplomatist and newspaper publisher; b. 28 Aug. 1910, Shattuck, Okla.; s. of Edwin McKinney and Eva Moody; m. 1st Louise Trigg 1943; one d.; m. 2nd Marie-Louise de Montmollin 1970; ed. Univ. of Oklahoma; War Service, U.S. Navy 1942–45; Ed. and Publr., The New Mexican 1949–, Chair. The New Mexican Inc. 1949–; Chair. New Mexico Econ. Devt. Comm. 1949–51; Asst. Sec. U.S. Dept. of Interior 1951–52; Chair. Panel to report to Congress on impact of Peaceful Uses of Atomic Energy 1955–56; Perm. U.S. Rep. to Int. Atomic Energy Agency, Vienna 1957–58; U.S. Rep. to 2nd Int. Conf. on Peaceful Uses of Atomic Energy 1958; rapporteur, Cttee. on Scientific and Tech. Co-operation, Atlantic Congress, London 1959; apptd. by Joint Cttee. of U.S. Congress to review int. atomic policies and programmes of U.S.A. 1959–60; Amb. to Switzerland 1961–63; Exec. Officer, Presidential Task Force on Int. Investments 1963–64; Vice-Chair. Advisory Cttee. on Financial Investments 1966; U.S. Rep. Int. Centre for Settlement of Investment Disputes, Washington 1967–73; Chair. Presidential Industry-Gov. Special Task Force on Travel 1968; Chair. Robert Moody Foundation 1986–; mem. Foreign Policy Asscn.; Chair. Bd. of Visitors and Governors, Oklahoma Univ.; mem. American Soc. of Newspaper Eds., Council on Foreign Relations, Council of American Ambs., Newspaper Asscn. of America; Distinguished Service Citation 1965; Hon. LL.D. (New Mexico); Democrat. *Publications:* Hymn to Wreckage: A Picaresque Interpretation of History 1947, The Scientific Foundation for European Integration, Reappraising the European Energy Problem, On Increasing the Effectiveness of Western Science and Technology, all 1959, The Red Challenge to Technological Renewal 1960, Review of the International Atomic Policies and Programs of the United States 1960, The Bolshoi Ballet's Last Tour 1983, The Toad and the Water Witch 1985, Variations on a Marxist Interpretation of Culture 1986, The Bolshoi Ballet's Last Tour 1986. *Leisure interest:* farming. *Address:* P.O. Box 1705, Santa Fe, NM 87504 (Office); Wind Fields, 39850 Snickersville Turnpike, Middleburg, VA 20117, U.S.A. (Home).

McKINNON, Don; New Zealand politician; s. of Gen. Walter McKinnon and Anna McKinnon; m. 2nd Clare de Love 1995; one s.; three s. one d. from a previous marriage; fmr. estate agent and farm man. consultant; Nat. Party M.P. for Albany 1978–; fmr. Jr. and Sr. Govt. Whip, Spokesperson for Health; Sr. Opposition Whip 1984–87; Leader of the House 1993–96; Minister of Foreign Affairs and Trade, of Pacific Island Affairs, of Foreign Affairs 1991–, for Disarmament and Arms Control 1996–, of Trade 1998–. *Leisure interests:* rugby, cricket, jogging, tennis. *Address:* Ministry of Foreign Affairs and Trade, Private Bag 18901, Wellington, New Zealand.

McKINNON, Sir James, Kt., C.A., F.C.M.A.; British public servant; b. 1929; ed. Camphill School; Co. Sec. Macfarlane Lang & Co. Ltd., Glasgow 1955–65; Business Consultant, McLintock, Moores & Murray, Glasgow 1965–67; Finance Dir. Imperial Group PLC, London 1967–86; Dir.-Gen. Office of Gas Supply 1986–93; Chair. Ionica 1993–98; Chair. (non-exec.) Cowie Group 1994–; Pres. Inst. of Chartered Accountants of Scotland 1985–86. *Publications:* articles in professional publs. *Leisure interest:* skiing. *Address:* Ionica PLC, Cowley Road, Cambridge, CB4 4AS, England.

MACKINTOSH, Sir Cameron Anthony, Kt.; British theatre producer; b. 17 Oct. 1946, Enfield; s. of Ian Mackintosh and Diana Mackintosh; ed. Prior Park Coll. Bath; stage hand then Asst. Stage Man. Theatre Royal, Drury Lane; worked with Emile Littler 1966, with Robin Alexander 1967; producer 1969–; Chair. Cameron Mackintosh 1981–; Dir. Delfont Mackintosh 1991–; Observer Award for Outstanding Achievement, Laurence Olivier Award 1991. *Productions:* Little Women 1967, Anything Goes 1969, Trelawney 1972, The Card 1973, Winnie the Pooh 1974, Owl and the Pussycat Went to See 1975, Godspell 1975, Side by Side by Sondheim 1976, Oliver! 1977, Diary of a Madam 1977, After Shave 1977, Gingerbread Man 1978, Out on a Limb 1978, My Fair Lady 1979, Oklahoma! 1980, Tomfoolery 1980, Jeeves Takes Charge 1981, Cats 1981, Song and Dance 1982, Blondel 1983, Little Shop of Horrors 1983, Abbacadabra 1983, The Boyfriend 1984, Les Misérables 1985, Café Puccini 1985, Phantom of the Opera 1986, Follies 1987, Miss Saigon 1989, Just So 1990, Five Guys Named Moe 1990, Moby Dick 1992, Putting it Together 1992, The Card 1992, Carousel 1993, Oliver! 1994, Martin Guerre 1996. *Leisure interests:* cooking, taking holidays. *Address:* Cameron Mackintosh Ltd., 1 Bedford Square, London, WC1B 3RA, England. *Telephone:* 0171-637 8866. *Fax:* 0171-436 2683.

MACKINTOSH, Nicholas John, D.PHIL., F.R.S.; British professor of experimental psychology; b. 9 July 1935; s. of Dr. Ian Mackintosh and Daphne Mackintosh; m. 1st Janet Ann Scott 1960 (divorced 1978); one s. one d.; m. 2nd Bundy Wilson 1978 (divorced 1989); two s.; m. 3rd Leonora Caroline Brosan 1992; one s.; ed. Winchester and Magdalen Coll., Oxford; lecturer, Univ. of Oxford 1964–67; Resident Prof., Dalhousie Univ. 1967–73; Prof., Univ. of Sussex 1973–81; Prof. of Experimental Psychology and Professorial Fellow of King's Coll., Cambridge 1981–; Resident Fellow, Lincoln Coll., Oxford 1966–67; Visiting Prof., Univ. of Pennsylvania 1965–66, Univ. of Hawaii 1972–73, Bryn Mawr Coll. 1977; Ed. Quality Journal of Experimental Psychology 1977–84. *Publications:* Fundamental Issues in Associative Learning (ed. with W. K. Honig) 1969, Mechanisms of Animal Discrimination Learning (with N. S. Sutherland) 1971, the Psychology of Animal Learning 1974, Conditioning and Associative Learning 1983, Animal Learning and Cognition 1994, Cyril Burt: fraud or framed? 1995, IQ and Human Intelligence 1998, papers in psychological journals. *Address:* King's College, Cambridge, CB2 1ST, England. *Telephone:* (01223) 351386.

McKNIGHT, Hon. William Hunter; Canadian politician; b. 12 July 1940, Elrose, Sask.; m. Beverley Ogden; two s.; ed. Wartime and Elrose, Sask.; fmr. farmer and business exec.; M.P. 1979–93, fmr. Chair. House Standing Cttee. on Agric., fmr. mem. Transport Cttee., Man. and mem's. Services Cttee., Finance, Trade and Econ. Affairs Cttee., fmr. Progressive Conservative Party spokesperson on Canadian Wheat Bd., on Int. Trade, fmr. Deputy Opposition House Leader; Progressive Conservative Party Minister of Labour 1984–86, of Indian Affairs and Northern Devt. 1986–89, of Defence 1989–91, of Agric. 1991–93, of Energy, Mines and Resources 1993; Chair. NAFTA Trade Consultants Inc. 1993; f. Dir., Chair., Anvil Range Mining Corp. 1994–; Dir. Gamblers Restaurant Inc. 1995–, Marvas Devts. Ltd. 1995–, Mid-North Resources Ltd. 1995–, R.E.S. Int. Inc. 1995, Sci-Tec Instruments Inc. 1995–; Hon. Consul, Ecuador 1995. *Address:* c/o Progressive Conservative Party of Canada, 275 Slater Street, Suite 501, Ottawa, Ont. K1P 5H9, Canada.

McKUEN, Rod; American author and composer; b. 29 April 1933, Oakland, Calif; has appeared in numerous films, concerts and on TV, composer of film scores and background music for TV shows; composer-lyricist of many songs; Pres. of numerous record and book cos.; mem. Bd. of Dirs. American Nat. Theatre of Ballet, Animal Concern; mem. Bd. of Govs. Nat. Acad. of Recording Arts and Sciences; mem. A.S.C.A.P., Writers Guild, A.F.T.R.A., M.P.A., NARAS; Pres. of American Guild of Variety Artists (AGVA); mem. Bd. of Dirs. Calif. Music Theater; Grand Prix du Disque 1966, 1974, 1975, 1982, Golden Globe 1969, Motion Picture Daily Award 1969; Los Angeles Shrine Club Award 1975, Freedoms Foundation 1975, Horatio Alger Award 1976; Brandeis Univ. Literary Trust Award 1981, Freedoms Foundation Patriot Medal 1981, Salvation Army Man of the Year 1983, Rose d'Ore, Cannes 1986, Myastenia Gravis Community Service Award 1986. *Works include:* Symphony Number One, Concerto for Guitar and Orchestra, Concerto for Four Harpsichords, Seascapes for Piano and Orchestra, Adagio for Harp and Strings, Piano Variations, Concerto Number Three for Piano and Orchestra 1972, The Plains of My Country (ballet) 1972, The City (orchestral suite) 1973, Ballad of Distances (orchestral suite) 1973, Bicentennial Ballet 1975, Symphony Number Three 1975, over 200 record albums. *Film scores:* Joanna 1968, The Prime of Miss Jean Brodie 1969, Me, Natalie 1969, A Boy Named Charlie Brown 1970, Come to Your Senses 1971, Scandalous John 1971, Wildflowers 1971, The Borrowers 1973, Lisa Bright and Dark 1973, Awareness of Emily 1976, The Unknown War 1979, Man to Himself 1980, Portrait of Rod McKuen 1982, Death Rides this Trail 1983, The Living End 1983, The Beach 1984. *Publications:* And Autumn Came 1954, Stanyan Street and Other Sorrows 1966, Listen to the Warm 1967, Twelve Years of Christmas 1968, In Someone's Shadow 1969, With Love 1970, Caught in the Quiet 1970, Fields of Wonder 1971, The Carols of Christmas 1971, And to Each Season 1972, Beyond the Boardwalk 1972, Come to Me in Silence 1973, America—An Affirmation 1974, Seasons in the Sun 1974, Alone, Moment to Moment 1974, The McKuen Omnibus 1975, Celebrations of the Heart 1975, My Country 200 1975, I'm Strong but I Like Roses, Sleep Warm, Beyond the Boardwalk 1976, The Sea Around Me ... The Hills Above 1976, Finding My Father (biographical) 1977, Coming Close to Earth 1977, Hand in Hand . . . 1977, Love's Been Good to Me 1979, We Touch the Sky 1979, Looking for a Friend 1980, An Outstretched Hand 1980, The Power Bright and Shining 1980, Too Many Midnights 1981, Rod McKuen's Book of Days 1981, The Beautiful Strangers 1981, The Works of Rod McKuen, Vol. 1, Poetry 1982, Watch for the Wind . . . 1982, Rod McKuen—1984 Book of Days 1983, The Sound of Solitude 1983, Suspension Bridge 1984, Another Beautiful Day 1985, Valentines 1985, Intervals 1986. *Address:* P.O. Box 2783, Los Angeles, CA 90028, U.S.A.

McLACHLAN, Ian Murray, A.O., M.A.; Australian politician; b. 2 Oct. 1936; s. of I. McLachlan; m. Janet Lee 1964; two s. one d.; ed. Collegiate School, St. Peters, S. Australia, Cambridge Univ., U.K.; mem. House of Reps. (Liberal) for Barker, S. Australia 1990–; Shadow Minister for Infrastructure and Nat. Devt. 1993–94, for Environment and Heritage 1994–95; Minister of Defence 1996–98; Man. Dir. Nangwarry Pastoral Co. Pty. Ltd. 1983–90; Deputy Chair. S. Australia Brewing 1983–90 (Dir. 1978–); Dir. Elders IXL Ltd. 1980–90; Pres. Nat. Farmers' Fed. 1984–88. *Leisure interests:* golf, photography. *Address:* Parliament House, Canberra, A.C.T. 2600, Australia.

MacLACHLAN, Kyle, B.F.A.; American film actor; b. 22 Feb. 1959, Yakima, Wash.; ed. Univ. of Washington, Seattle; stage appearances in regional Shakespeare productions and off-Broadway in Palace of Amateurs; TV roles in Northwest Passage, The O'Conners, Twin Peaks 1990–91. *Films include:* Dune 1984, Blue Velvet 1986, The Hidden 1988, Don't Tell Her It's Me 1990, The Doors 1991, Where the Day Takes You 1992, The Trial 1993, Twin Peaks: Fire Walk With Me 1992, Rich in Love 1993, Against the Wall 1994, The Flintstones 1994, Roswell 1994, Showgirls 1995, Trigger Effect 1996, Mad Dog Time 1996. *Address:* U.T.A., 9560 Wilshire Boulevard, 5th Floor, Beverly Hills, CA 90212, U.S.A.

McLAGLEN, Andrew V.; British film director; b. 28 July 1920, London; s. of Victor McLaglen; ed. Univ. of Va. *TV includes:* Gunsmoke, Have Gun—Will Travel, Perry Mason, Rawhide, The Lineup, The Lieutenant, The Dirty Dozen, The Next Mission, On Wings of Eagles, The Blue and the Gray, The

Shadow Riders, Travis McGee. *Films include:* Gun the Man Down 1956, Man in the Vault 1956, The Abductors 1957, Freckles 1960, The Little Shepherd of Kingdom Come 1961, McLintock 1963, Shenandoah 1965, The Rare Breed 1966, Monkeys, Go Home! 1967, The Way West 1967, The Ballad of Josie 1968, The Devil's Brigade 1968, Bandoleroi 1968, Hellfighters 1969, The Undefeated 1969, Chisum 1970, One More Train to Rob 1971, Fool's Parade 1971, Something Big 1971, Cahill, U.S. Marshal 1973, Mitchell 1975, The Log of the Black Pearl 1975, Stowaway to the Moon 1975, Banjo Hackett: Roamin' Free 1976, The Last Hard Men 1976, Murder at the World Series 1977, Breakthrough Sergeant Steiner 1978, The Wild Geese 1979, North Sea Hijack 1980, The Sea Wolves 1981, Deprisa, Deprisa 1981, Sweet Hours 1982, Antonieta 1982, The Shadow Riders 1982, The Blue and the Gray 1982, Carmen 1983, Travis McGee 1983, Sahara 1983, Return to the River Kwai, Eye of the Widow 1989.

MacLAINE, Shirley; American film actress, writer and film director; b. 24 April 1934, Richmond, Va.; d. of Ira Beaty and Kathlyn MacLean; m. Steve Parker 1954; one d.; ed. grammar school and Lee High School, Washington; fmr. chorus girl and dancer; Star of the Year Award (Theater Owners of America) 1967; Best Actress Award for role in Desperate Characters, Berlin Film Festival 1971; Lifetime Achievement Award, Berlin Film Festival 1999. *Films include:* The Trouble With Harry, Artists and Models, Around The World in 80 Days, Hot Spell, The Matchmaker, Can-Can, Career, The Apartment, Two For The Seesaw, The Children's Hour, Irma La Douce, What A Way To Go, The Yellow Rolls-Royce, Gambit, Woman Times Seven, The Bliss of Mrs. Blossom, Sweet Charity, Two Mules For Sister Sara, Desperate Characters, The Possessions of Joel Delaney, The Turning Point 1977, Being There 1979, Loving Couples 1980, The Change of Seasons 1981, Slapstick 1981, Terms of Endearment (Acad. Award for Best Actress) 1984, Out on a Limb 1987, Madame Sousatzka (Golden Globe Award for Best Actress) 1989, Steel Magnolias 1989, Waiting for the Light 1990, Postcards from the Edge 1990, Used People 1993, Wrestling Ernest Hemingway 1994, Guarding Tess 1994, Mrs Westbourne 1995, The Evening Star 1995, Mrs. Winterbourne 1996; *Revues:* If My Friends Could See Me Now 1974, To London With Love 1976, London 1982, Out There Tonight 1990; *TV film:* The West Side Waltz 1994; *Video:* Shirley MacLaine's Inner Workout 1989; *Produced and Co-directed:* The Other Half of the Sky—A China Memoir 1973. *Publications:* Don't Fall Off the Mountain 1971, The New Celebrity Cookbook 1973, You Can Get There From Here 1975 (Vols. 1 and 2 of autobiog.), Out on a Limb (Vol. 3) 1983, Dancing in the Light 1985 (Vol. 4), It's All in the Playing (Vol. 5) 1987, Going Within (Vol. 6) 1989, Dance While You Can (Vol. 7) 1991, My Lucky Stars (Vol. 8) 1995. *Address:* MacLaine Enterprises Inc., 25200 Malibu Road, Suite 101, Santa Monica, CA 90265, U.S.A.

MacLANE, Saunders, PH.D.; American mathematician; b. 4 Aug. 1909, Norwich, Conn.; s. of Donald B. MacLane and Winifred A. Saunders; m. 1st Dorothy M. Jones 1933 (died 1985); two d.; m. 2nd Osa Skotting Segal 1986; ed. Yale Coll., Univ. of Chicago, Göttingen Univ.; Benjamin Peirce Instructor in Math., Harvard Univ. 1934–36; Instructor Cornell Univ. 1936–37, Chicago Univ. 1937–38; Asst. Prof., Harvard Univ. 1938–41, Assoc. Prof. 1941–46, Prof. 1946–47; Prof. Univ. of Chicago 1947–62, Max Mason Distinguished Service Prof. in Math., Univ. of Chicago 1963–82, Prof. Emer. 1982–; mem. Nat. Acad. of Sciences, Vice-Pres. 1973–81; Vice-Pres. American Philosophical Soc. 1968–71; mem. Nat. Science Bd. 1974–80; Pres. American Math. Soc. 1973–74; Hon. Sc.D., Hon. LL.D.; Nat. Medal of Science 1989. *Publications:* Survey of Modern Algebra (with G. Birkhoff) 1941, Homology 1963, Algebra (with G. Birkhoff) 1967, Categories for the Working Mathematician 1972, Mathematics: Form and Function 1985, Sheaves in Geometry and Logic, A First Introduction to Topos Theory (with Ieke Moerdijk) 1992. *Leisure interests:* sailing, skiing, photography, hiking. *Address:* Department of Mathematics, The University of Chicago, 5734 University Avenue, Chicago, IL 60637 (Office); 5712 South Dorchester Avenue, Chicago, IL 60637, U.S.A. (Home). *Telephone:* (773) 702-7330 (Office); (773) 363-0099 (Home). *Fax:* (773) 702-9787.

McLAREN, Dame Anne, D.B.E., M.A., D.PHIL., F.R.S., F.R.C.O.G.; British biologist; b. 26 April 1927; d. of 2nd Baron Aberconway; m. Donald Michie (divorced); one s. two d.; ed. Univ. of Oxford; mem. scientific staff of Agric. Research Council's Unit of Animal Genetics, Edin. 1959–74; Dir. MRC's Mammalian Devt. Unit, London 1974–92; Prin. Research Assoc., Wellcome/Cancer Research Campaign Inst. 1992–; Foreign Sec. Royal Soc. 1991–96, Vice-Pres. 1992–96; Pres. B.A.A.S. 1993–94; Research Fellow, King's Coll., Cambridge 1992–96, Hon. Fellow 1996–; Chair. Governing Body, Lister Inst. of Preventative Medicine 1994–; Gold Medal (Royal Soc.); Hon. Fellow Univ. Coll. London 1993; Trustee Nat. History Museum 1994–; author of many scientific publications. *Address:* Wellcome/CRC Institute, Tennis Court Road, Cambridge, CB2 1QR; 40 Ainger Road, London, NW3 3AT, England.

McLAREN, Digby Johns, O.C., M.A., PH.D., F.R.S., F.R.S.C.; Canadian geologist; b. 11 Dec. 1919, N. Ireland; s. of James and Louie (née Kinsey) McLaren; m. Phyllis Matkin 1942; two s. one d.; ed. Sedbergh School, Yorks., Queens' Coll., Cambridge, and Univ. of Michigan; Capt. Royal Artillery 1940–46; geologist, Geol. Survey of Canada 1948–80, Dir.-Gen. 1973–80; Dir. Inst. of Sedimentary and Petroleum Geology 1967–73; Asst. Deputy Minister, Science and Tech., Dept. of Energy, Mines and Resources 1980–81, Sr. Scientific Adviser 1980–84; Prof. Dept. of Geology, Univ. of Ottawa 1981–88; Chair. Int. Geological Correlation Prog., UNESCO/IUGS 1976–80, adviser in earth science to Dir.-Gen. of UNESCO 1980; Chair. and Organiser of two Dahlem Confs. (Berlin) on Resources and World Devt. 1986; Pres. Geological Soc. of America 1982, Royal Soc. of Canada 1987–90; Foreign Assoc., U.S. Nat. Acad. of Sciences; Corresp. mem. Société géologique de France; Foreign Hon. Fellow European Union of Geoscientists; Foreign mem. American Philosophical Soc.; Hon.D.Sc. (Ottawa) 1980, (Carleton) 1993, (Waterloo) 1996; Gold Medal (Science), Professional Inst. 1979, Leopold von Buch Medal, Geological Soc. of Germany 1983, Edward Coke Medal, Geological Soc. of London 1985, Logan Medal, Geological Asscn. of Canada 1987, Hollis Hedberg Award in Energy, Southern Methodist Univ. 1994. *Publications:* Resources and World Development (ed.) 1987, Planet Under Stress (ed.) 1990; papers, bulletins, memoirs and maps on regional geology, western and Arctic Canada, palæontology, time, historical geology, evolution, extinction, global change, population etc. *Leisure interests:* skiing, music. *Address:* No. 607, 420 Mackay Street, Ottawa, Ont. K1M 2C4, Canada. *Telephone:* (613) 742-3067.

MacLAREN, Rt. Hon. Roy, P.C., F.R.S.; Canadian politician; b. 26 Oct. 1934, Vancouver; s. of Wilbur MacLaren and Anne Bailey MacLaren; m. Alethea Mitchell 1959; two s. one d.; ed. Univ. of British Columbia, Cambridge Univ., U.K., Harvard Univ., U.S.A., Univ. of Toronto; joined Dept of External Affairs 1957; served in Hanoi, Prague, Geneva, Ottawa, New York; Dir. Public Affairs, Massey Ferguson Ltd. 1969–73; Pres. Ogilvy and Mather (Canada) Ltd. 1974–76; Chair. CB Media Ltd. 1977–83, 1984–93; Dir. Deutsche Bank (Canada), Royal LePage Ltd., London Insurance Group Inc.; elected Liberal M.P. for Etobicoke North 1979–96; Parl. Sec. to Minister of Energy, Mines & Resources 1980–82; Co-chair. Special Jt. Cttee. on Senate Reform 1983; Minister of State (Finance) 1983, Minister of Nat. Revenue 1984, for Int. Trade 1993–96; High Commr. in U.K. 1996–; Chair. Fed. Task Force on Business/Govt. Relations 1975–77; Special Lecturer in Econ. Geography, Univ. of Toronto 1971–75; fmr. Dir. Canadian Opera Co., Cambridge Canadian Trust.; Gov. Etobicoke Gen. Hosp., Canadian Journalism Foundation, Toronto School of Theology; Dr. Sacred Letters h.c. (Toronto). *Publications:* Canadians in Russia, 1918–1919 1976, Canadians on the Nile, 1882–1898 1978, Canadians Behind Enemy Lines, 1939–1945 1981, Honourable Mentions 1986, African Exploits: The Diaries of William Grant Stairs 1997. *Address:* Canadian High Commission, 1 Grosvenor Square, London, W1X 0AB, England. *Telephone:* 0171-258 6328. *Fax:* 0171-258 6303.

McLARTY, Thomas F. "Mack"; American politician and businessman; b. 1946; m. Donna K. Cochran 1969; two s.; ed. Univ. of Arkansas; worked in family automobile and transport business; elected to Ark. House of Reps. 1969; apptd. mem. Bd. Arkla Inc., La., subsequently joined staff, apptd. Chair. 1985; fmr. Chair. and Treasurer Ark. Democratic Party; Chief of Staff to Pres.-elect Bill Clinton 1993–94, Presidential Counsellor 1994–. *Address:* c/o Office of the President, The White House, 1600 Pennsylvania Avenue, Washington, DC 20500, U.S.A.

McLAUGHLIN, Rt. Hon. Audrey, P.C.; Canadian politician; one s. one d.; ed. Univ. of Western Ont., Univ. of Toronto; ran small business and consulting business, Whitehorse; fmr. Exec. Dir. Metro Toronto Br. of Canadian Mental Asscn., caseworker with Children's Aid Soc. of Toronto; taught at Adisadel Coll., Ghana; M.P. for Yukon 1987–; Fed. Leader New Democratic Party 1989–94. *Publication:* A Woman's Place: My Life and Politics 1992. *Address:* House of Commons, 649-D Center Block, 11 Wellington Street, Ottawa, Ont. K1A 0A6, Canada.

McLAUGHLIN, William Earle, O.C.; Canadian banker; b. 16 Sept. 1915, Oshawa, Ont.; s. of Frank McLaughlin and Frankie L. Houldon; m. Ethel Wattie 1940; one s. one d.; ed. Queen's Univ.; joined Royal Bank of Canada 1936, Asst. Man., London, Ont. 1942, Head Office 1945, Man. Montreal Branch 1951, Asst. Gen. Man. 1953, Asst. to Pres. 1959, Gen. Man. 1960, Pres. and Dir. 1960; Chair. The Royal Bank of Canada 1962–80, fmr. Pres., fmr. C.E.O. 1979; Dir. and Trustee of numerous cos. and orgs.; Chancellor, Concordia Univ.; Kt. of Grace, Venerable Order of the Hosp. of St. John of Jerusalem. *Leisure interest:* reading. *Address:* 67 Sunnyside Avenue, Westmount, Quebec, H3Y 1C3, Canada (Home).

MacLAURIN, OF KNEBWORTH, Baron (Life Peer) cr. 1996, of Knebworth in the County of Hertfordshire; **Ian Charter MacLaurin,** Kt., F.R.S.A.; British retailing company executive; b. 30 March 1937, Blackheath; s. of Arthur and Evelina MacLaurin; m. Ann Margaret Collar 1962; one s. two d.; ed. Malvern Coll., Worcs.; joined Tesco as a Trainee Man. 1959; Dir. Tesco Stores (Holdings) Ltd. 1970, Man. Dir. 1974–83, Deputy Chair. 1983–85, Chair. 1985–97; Chancellor, Univ. of Herts. 1996–; Chair. England and Wales Cricket Bd. 1996–; non-exec. Dir. Enterprise Oil 1984–91, Gleneagles Hotels PLC 1992–, Guinness PLC 1986–95, Nat. Westminster Bank PLC 1990–97, Vodafone 1997–, Whitbread PLC 1997–; Pres. Inst. of Grocery Distribution 1989–92; Fellow Inst. of Marketing 1987; Freeman of City of London 1981; mem. MCC; mem. Lords Taverners and Worshipful Co. of Carmen; Hon. D.Univ. (Stirling) 1986. *Leisure interests:* cricket, golf. *Address:* House of Lords, London, SW1A 0PW; c/o Tesco PLC, Tesco House, Delamare Road, Cheshunt, Herts., EN8 9SL, England. (Office). *Telephone:* (01992) 632222 (Office).

MACLAVERTY, Bernard, B.A.; Irish writer; b. 14 Sept. 1942, Belfast; s. of John MacLaverty and Mary MacLaverty; m. Madeline McGuckin 1967; four c.; fmrly. medical lab. technician, English teacher; fmr. writer-in-residence Univ. of Aberdeen; mem. Aosdana; has received numerous awards.

Publications: novels: Lamb, Cal, Grace Notes; short stories: Secrets and Other Stories, A Time to Dance and Other Stories, The Great Profundo and Other Stories, Walking the Dog and Other Stories. *Address:* 26 Roxburgh Street, Glasgow, G12 9AP, Scotland.

McLAY, James Kenneth, LL.B.; New Zealand politician, lawyer and business consultant; b. 21 Feb. 1945, Auckland; s. of late Robert McLay and Joyce Evelyn Dee; m. Marcy Farden 1983; one s.; ed. King's Coll. and Univ. of Auckland; Officer, Territorial Force 1967–70; began practice as solicitor 1971, practised solely as barrister from 1974; Man. Ed. Recent Law 1969–70; mem. Parl. for Birkenhead 1975–87; Attorney-Gen. and Minister of Justice 1978–84; Deputy Prime Minister 1984; Deputy Leader of Opposition 1984; Leader of Opposition 1984–86; Man. Dir. and Prin. J. K. McLay Ltd. 1986–; Chair. Macquarie New Zealand Ltd. (Subsidiary of Macquarie Bank, Australia); Dir. numerous cos.; mem. Comm. and Ministerial Working Party on Accident Compensation 1990; Chair. Review of Defence Funding and Financial Man., Wholesale Electricity Market Study 1992, Wholesale Electricity Market Devt. Group 1993; N.Z. Commr. to Int. Whaling Comm. 1993–; mem. Eminent Persons Panel on Accident Compensation 1994–95; Chair. Roading Advisory Group 1997; Convenor Project Manukau Audit Group 1998–; Nat. Party. *Leisure interest:* trout fishing. *Address:* P.O. Box 8885, Auckland 1, New Zealand. *Telephone:* 377-0633. *Fax:* 309-6220.

McLEAN, Don; American singer, instrumentalist and composer; b. 2 Oct. 1945, New Rochelle, N.Y.; s. of Donald McLean and Elizabeth Bucci; m. Patrisha Shnier 1987; one s. one d.; ed. Villanova Univ. and Iona Coll.; Pres. Benny Bird Corpn., Inc.; mem. Hudson River Sloop Singers 1969; solo concert tours throughout U.S.A., Canada, Australia, Europe, Far East etc.; numerous TV appearances; composer of film scores for Fraternity Row, Flight of Dragons; composer of over 200 songs including Prime Time, American Pie, Tapestry, Vincent (Starry, Starry Night), And I Love You So, Castles In the Air, etc.; recordings include Tapestry 1970, American Pie 1971, Don McLean 1972, Playin' Favorites 1973, Homeless Brother 1974, Solo 1976, Prime Time 1977, Chain Lightning 1979, Believers 1982, For the Memories Vol. I and II 1986, Love Tracks 1988, Headroom 1991, Don McLean Christmas 1992, Favourites and Rarities (Box Set) 1993, The River of Love 1995, numerous compiliation packages, etc.; recipient of many gold discs in U.S.A., Australia, U.K. and Ireland; Israel Cultural Award 1981. *Publications:* Songs of Don McLean 1972, The Songs of Don McLean (Vol. II) 1974. *Leisure interests:* antique furniture, film history, western horsemanship (trail riding). *Address:* Benny Bird Co., 1838 Black Rock Turnpike, Fairfield, CT 06432, U.S.A.

McLEAN, Hon. Rev. Walter Franklin, P.C., LL.D.; Canadian politician, clergyman and international consultant; b. 26 April 1936, Leamington, Ont.; m. Barbara Scott 1961; four s.; ed. Victoria Coll., Univ. of British Columbia, Knox Coll., Univ. of Toronto, Univ. of Edinburgh; co-founder CUSO (fmrly. first Nigerian Co-ordinator); fmr. Exec. Dir. Man. Centennial Corpn.; fmr. Minister of Knox Presbyterian Church, Waterloo; Alderman for City of Waterloo 1976–79; M.P. 1979–93; fmr. mem. Standing Cttee. on Communications and Culture, on External Affairs, on Nat. Defence; fmr. mem. Special Sub-Cttee. on Latin America and Caribbean; Sec. of State of Canada 1984–85, Minister of State (Immigration) and Minister Responsible for the Status of Women 1984–86; mem. Canadian Del. to UN 1986–93; Special Rep. to UN on Southern Africa and Commonwealth Affairs 1989–93; Canadian Rep. at Southern Africa Devt. Co-ordination Conf. (SADCC) 1987–93, at Commonwealth Foreign Ministers' Confs. 1987, 1988, 1989, 1991; Chair. Parl. Sub-Cttee. on Devt. and Human Rights, 1990–93; Chair. Malaysian Canadian Investments; Prin. Franklin Consulting Services Ltd.; fmr. Pres. Int. Council of Parliamentarians for Global Action; Hon. Consul of Namibia; Chair. Canadian UNA Human Rights Cttee.; Convenor Millennium Celebration, Presbyterian Church in Canada; Progressive Conservative Party. *Leisure interests:* golf, curling, music. *Address:* 122 Avondale Avenue, S., Waterloo, Ont., N2L 2C3, Canada. *Fax:* (519) 578-7799.

MACLENNAN, Rt. Hon. Robert Adam Ross, P.C., M.A., LL.B.; British politician and barrister-at-law; b. 26 June 1936, Glasgow; s. of Sir Hector Maclennan and Lady Maclennan; m. Helen Cutter Noyes 1968; one s. one d. one step-s.; ed. Glasgow Academy, Balliol Coll., Oxford, Trinity Coll., Cambridge, Columbia Univ., New York; M.P. for Caithness and Sutherland 1966–97, Caithness, Sutherland and Easter Ross 1997–; Parl. Pvt. Sec. to Sec. of State for Commonwealth Affairs and Minister without portfolio 1967–70, Parl. Under-Sec. of State for Prices and Consumer Protection 1974–79; Opposition Spokesman on Scottish Affairs 1970–71, on Defence 1971–72, on Foreign Affairs 1980–81; resigned from Labour Party 1981; founder mem. SDP 1981; SDP Spokesman on Agriculture 1981–87, on Home and Legal Affairs 1983–87, on Econ. Affairs 1987; Leader SDP 1987–88; Jt. Leader SLD 1988; Liberal Democrat convenor on Home Affairs 1988–94, Legal Affairs 1988–94, Nat. Heritage 1992–94; mem. Public Accounts Cttee. 1979–; Liberal Democrat 1994–98, Spokesperson on Constitutional Affairs, Culture and Media 1994–. *Leisure interests:* music, theatre, and visual arts. *Address:* House of Commons, London, SW1A 0AA; 74 Abingdon Villas, London, W8 6XB, England. *Telephone:* 0171-219 4133 (Office).

MACLEOD, Hugh Angus Macintosh, B.SC., D.TECH.; British professor of optical sciences; b. 20 June 1933, Glasgow; s. of Dr. John Macleod and Agnes Donaldson Macleod; m. Ann Turner 1957; four s. one d.; ed. Lenzie Acad., Univ. of Glasgow; engineer Sperry Gyroscope Co. Ltd. 1954–60; Chief Engineer Williamson Mfg. Co. Ltd. 1960–62; Sr. Physicist Mervyn Instruments Ltd. 1963; Tech. Man. Sir Howard Grubb, Parsons and Co. Ltd. 1963–70; Reader in Thin Film Physics, Newcastle upon Tyne Poly. 1971–79; Assoc. Prof. Univ. of Aix-Marseille III 1976, 1979; Prof. of Optical Sciences, Univ. of Arizona, U.S.A. 1979–95; Dir.-at-large, Optical Soc. of America 1987–89; Pres. Thin Film Center Inc. 1986–; Fellow SPIE, Optical Soc. of America, Inst. of Physics (London); Gold Medal SPIE 1987. *Publications:* Thin-Film Optical Filters 1969; over 100 articles, papers and book chapters on optics of thin films. *Leisure interests:* piano, computing. *Address:* 2745 E via Rotonda, Tucson, AZ 85716, U.S.A. (Home); 18 Black Swan Close, Pease Pottage, RH11 9BB, England. *Telephone:* (520) 795-5019 (Home); (01293) 518788 (England).

McLEOD, James Graham, A.O., M.B., D.PHIL., D.SC., F.R.A.C.P., F.R.C.P., F.A.A., F.T.S.E.; Australian professor of neurology and medicine; b. 18 Jan. 1932, Sydney; s. of Hector R. McLeod and Dorothy S. (née Craig) McLeod; m. Robyn E. Rule 1962; two s. two d.; ed. Univ. of Sydney, Oxford Univ., Univ. of London, Harvard Univ.; Sr. Lecturer, Univ. of Sydney 1967–69, Assoc. Prof. 1970–72, Bosch Prof. of Medicine 1972–, Bushell Prof. of Neurology 1978–; Visiting Medical Officer, Royal Prince Alfred Hosp., Sydney 1965–, Head, Dept. of Neurology 1978–; mem. Bd. of Dirs. Royal North Shore Hosp., Sydney (Vice-Chair.) 1978–86; Pres. Australian Assn. of Neurologists 1980–83; Rhodes Scholar 1953–56; Nuffield Travelling Fellow 1964–65; Sir Arthur Sims Travelling Prof. 1983–84; Commonwealth Sr. Medical Fellowship 1989; mem. Australian Science and Tech. Council 1987–93; Fellow Australian Acad. of Tech. Science and Eng., Australian Acad. of Science (Vice-Pres. 1987–88, Treas. 1993–). *Publications:* A Physiological Approach to Clinical Neurology (with J. W. Lance, q.v.), Introductory Neurology (with J. W. Lance, q.v.) 1989, Peripheral Neuropathy in Childhood (with R.A. Ouvrier and J.D. Pollard) 1990, Inflammatory Neuropathies (Ed.) 1984. *Leisure interests:* swimming, boating. *Address:* Department of Medicine, University of Sydney, Sydney, N.S.W. 2006 (Office); 2 James Street, Woollahra, N.S.W. 2025, Australia (Home). *Telephone:* 9351 3385 (Office); (612) 9362-8362 (Home). *Fax:* 9351 4018.

MACLEOD, Sir (Nathaniel William) Hamish, K.B.E., M.A.; British civil servant (retd.); b. 6 Jan. 1940; s. of George Henry Torquil Macleod and Ruth Natalie Wade; m. Fionna Mary Campbell 1970; one s. one d.; ed. Strathallan School, Perthshire, St. Andrews Univ., Univ. of Bristol; commercial trainee Stewarts and Lloyds, Birmingham 1958–62; Admin. Officer Hong Kong Govt. 1966, Dir. of Trade and Chief Trade Negotiator 1983–87, Sec. for Trade and Industry 1987–89, Sec. for the Treasury 1989–91, Financial Sec. 1991–95; J.P. (Hong Kong) 1979–95; mem. Bd. of Dirs. Fleming Asian Trust (Chair.), Highland Distillers, Scottish Community Foundation, Scottish Oriental Smaller Cos. Trust 1995–. *Leisure interests:* walking, golf. *Address:* 20 York Road, Edinburgh, EH5 3EH, Scotland. *Telephone:* 0131-552 5058. *Fax:* 0131-551 4996.

McMAHON, Sir Christopher William "Kit", Kt., M.A.; British banker; b. 10 July 1927, Melbourne, Australia; s. of late Dr. J.J. and Margaret McMahon; m. 1st Marion E. Kelso 1956; two s.; m. 2nd Alison Braimbridge 1982; ed. Melbourne Grammar School, Univ. of Melbourne and Magdalen Coll., Oxford; Econ. Asst., H.M. Treasury 1953–57; Econ. Adviser, British Embassy, Washington, D.C. 1957–60; Fellow and Tutor in Econs., Magdalen Coll., Oxford 1960–64; Adviser, Bank of England 1964–66, Adviser to Govs. 1966–70, Exec. Dir. 1970–80, Deputy Gov. March 1980–85; Deputy Chair. and Chair. (desig.) Midland Bank PLC 1986–87, Dir. 1986–, Chair. 1987–91; Dir. Eurotunnel 1987–91, Midland Montagu Holdings 1987–, Hong Kong and Shanghai Banking Corpn. 1987–91, (non-exec. Deputy Chair. 1993–), Thomas Cook 1989–91, Pentos 1991–95, Taylor Woodrow PLC 1991–, Angela Flowers 1992–, Aegis 1993–, FI Group 1994–; Chair. OECD Working Party Three, Japan Festival Fund 1992; Chair. (non-exec.) Coutts Consulting Group PLC 1992–96; Deputy Chair. Taylor Woodrow 1997–; mem. Steering Cttee., Consultative Group on Int. Econ. and Monetary Affairs (Group of Thirty) 1978–84; mem. Court London Univ. 1984–86; Trustee, Whitechapel Art Gallery 1984–; Trustee Royal Opera House Trust 1984–86, Bd. Royal Opera House 1989–97; Gov. Birkbeck Coll. 1991–; Chevalier, Légion d'honneur. *Publications:* Sterling in the Sixties 1964, Techniques of Economic Forecasting 1965. *Leisure interests:* gardening, walking. *Address:* The Old House, Burleigh, Stroud, Glos., GL5 2PQ, England.

McMANNERS, John, D.LITT., F.B.A.; British professor of ecclesiastical history; b. 25 Dec. 1916, Ferryhill, Co. Durham; s. of Rev. Canon Joseph McManners and Ann McManners; m. Sarah Carruthers Errington 1951; two s. two d.; ed. Oxford and Durham Univs.; mil. service in Royal Northumberland Fusiliers (rank of Maj.) 1939–45; Fellow St. Edmund Hall, Oxford 1948–56, Hon. Fellow 1983; Prof. of History, Univ. of Tasmania 1956–59, Univ. of Sydney, Australia 1959–66, Univ. of Leicester 1967–72; Regius Prof. of Ecclesiastical History, Univ. of Oxford 1972–84; Fellow and Chaplain, All Souls Coll., Oxford 1984–; Dir. d'études associé, Ecole Pratique des Hautes Etudes, Sec. IV, Paris 1980–81; Trustee Nat. Portrait Gallery 1970–78; mem. Doctrine Comm. Church of England 1978–81; Fellow Australian Acad. of the Humanities 1970; Hon. D.Litt. (Durham) 1984; Wolfson Literary Award 1982; Officer of the Order of King George I of The Hellenes 1945, Commdr., Ordre des Palmes Académiques 1990. *Publications:* French Ecclesiastical Society under the Ancien Régime–Angers 1960, Men, Machines and Freedom 1966, The French Revolution and the Church 1969, Church and State in France 1870–1914 1972, Death and the Enlightenment

1981, Church and Society in 18th-Century France (2 vols.) 1998; contrib. to New Cambridge Modern History Vols. VI and VIII, Ed. Oxford Illustrated History of Christianity 1990. *Leisure interest:* tennis. *Address:* All Souls College, Oxford, OX1 4AL; 71 Cunliffe Close, Oxford, OX1 4AL, England (Home). *Telephone:* (01865) 279368; (01865) 57589 (Home).

McMANUS, Jason Donald, B.A., M.P.A.; American journalist; b. 3 March 1934, Mission, Kan.; s. of John A. McManus and Stella F. Gosney; m. 1st Patricia A. Paulson 1958 (divorced 1966); one s.; m. 2nd Deborah H. Murphy 1973; two d.; ed. Davidson Coll., Princeton Univ. and Univ. of Oxford (Rhodes Scholar); Common Market Bureau Chief, Time Magazine, Paris 1962–64; Assoc. Ed. Time Magazine, New York 1964–68, Sr. Ed. 1968–75, Asst. Man. Ed. 1975–78, Exec. Ed. 1978–83; Corporate Ed. Time Inc. 1983–85; Man. Ed. Time Magazine 1985–87; Ed.-in-Chief, Time Inc. 1987–95; Hon. Litt.D. (Davidson Coll.) 1979. *Address:* c/o Time Warner Inc., Time & Life Building, Rockefeller Center, New York, NY 10020, U.S.A. *Telephone:* (212) 522-3753.

McMASTER, Brian John, C.B.E., LL.B.; British arts administrator; b. 9 May 1943; ed. Wellington Coll., Bristol Univ.; with Int. Artists' Dept., EMI Ltd. 1968–73; Controller of Opera Planning, English Nat. Opera 1973–76; Gen. Admin., subsequently Man. Dir. Welsh Nat. Opera 1976–91; Dir. Edin. Int. Festival 1991–; Artistic Dir. Vancouver Opera 1984–89. *Address:* Edinburgh International Festival, 21 Market Street, Edinburgh, EH1 1BW, Scotland. *Telephone:* (0131) 473 2001.

MACMILLAN, Jake, PH.D., D.SC., F.R.S.; British professor of organic chemistry; b. 13 Sept. 1924, Scotland; s. of John MacMillan and Barbara Lindsay; m. Anne Levy 1952; one s. two d.; ed. Lanark Grammar School and Glasgow Univ.; Assoc. Research Man., ICI 1962–63; Lecturer in Organic Chem., Bristol Univ. 1963–68, Reader 1968–78, Personal Chair. 1978–83, Head of Dept. and Alfred Capper Pass Prof. of Organic Chem. 1983–90, Prof. Emer. 1990–, Sr. Resident Fellow 1996–; Foreign Assoc. N.A.S. (U.S.A.) 1991–; Flintoff Medal 1978 and Hugo Muller Medal 1989, Royal Soc. of Chem., Research Medal, Int. Plant Growth Substance Asscn. 1982, Charles Reid Barnes Award, American Soc. of Plant Physiology 1988, Pergamon Phytochem. Prize 1995. *Publications:* over 290 papers and 3 books on organic chemistry and plant hormones. *Leisure interests:* gardening, theatre, golf. *Address:* IACR-Long Ashton Research Station, Department of Agricultural Sciences, University of Bristol, Long Ashton, Bristol, BS18 9AF (Office); 1 Rylestone Grove, Bristol, BS9 3UT, England (Home). *Telephone:* (01275) 392181 (Office); (0117) 9620535 (Home). *Fax:* (01275) 394281.

McMURTRY, Larry; American writer; b. 3 June 1936, Wichita Falls, Tex.; s. of William Jefferson McMurtry and Hazel McIver; m. Josephine Ballard 1959 (divorced 1966); one s.; co-writer and co-producer with Diana Ossana of CBS mini-series Streets of Laredo and ABC mini-series Dead Man's Walk 1996. *Publications:* Horseman Pass By (published in U.K. as Hud) 1961, Leaving Cheyenne 1963, The Last Picture Show 1966 (screenplay with Peter Bogdanovich 1971), In a Narrow Grave (essays) 1968, Moving On 1970, All My Friends Are Going to be Strangers 1972, It's Always We Rambled (essay) 1974, Terms of Endearment 1975, Somebody's Darling 1978, Cadillac Jack 1982, The Desert Rose 1983, Lonesome Dove 1985, Texasville 1987, Film Flam: Essay on Hollywood 1987, Anything for Billy 1988, Some Can Whistle 1989, Buffalo Girls 1990, The Evening Star 1992, Streets of Laredo 1993, Pretty Boy Floyd (with Diana Ossana) 1993, The Late Child 1995, Dead Man's Walk 1995, Zeke and Ned (novel, with Diana Ossana) 1996, Comanche Moon 1997, Duane Depressed 1998. *Leisure interest:* antiquarian bookselling. *Address:* Simon & Schuster, 1230 6th Avenue, New York, NY 10020; c/o Saria Co. Inc., 2509 North Campbell Avenue, Suite 95, Tucson, AZ 85719, U.S.A. *Fax:* (520) 690-1454.

McNALLY, Derek, PH.D.; British lecturer in astronomy; b. 28 Oct. 1934, Belfast; s. of David McNally and Sarah (née Long) McNally; m. Shirley Allen 1959; one s. one d.; ed. Royal Belfast Acad. Inst., Queen's Univ., Belfast and Royal Holloway Coll., London; Sec. Royal Astronomical Soc. 1966–72, Vice-Pres. 1972–73, Treas. 1996–; Asst. Dir. Univ. of London Observatory 1966–88, Dir. 1988–97; Sr. Lecturer in Astronomy, Univ. Coll., London 1970–; Asst. Gen. Sec. Int. Astronomical Union 1985–88, Gen. Sec. 1988–91; Chair. ICSU Working Group on Adverse Environmental Impacts on Astronomy 1993–96. *Publications:* Positional Astronomy 1974, The Vanishing Universe (Ed.) 1994; numerous articles in astronomical journals. *Leisure interests:* natural history, music, travel. *Address:* University of London Observatory, Mill Hill Park, London, NW7 2QS, England. *Telephone:* 0181-238 8855. *Fax:* 0181-906 4161.

McNAMARA, Robert Strange, LL.D.; American politician, international civil servant and business executive; b. 9 June 1916, San Francisco; s. of Robert James McNamara and Clara Nell Strange; m. Margaret Craig McNamara 1940 (died 1981); one s. two d.; ed. Univ. of California and Harvard Univ.; Asst. Prof. in Business Admin., Harvard Univ. 1940–43; served Army, Air Force 1943–46; Exec. Ford Motor Co. 1946–61, Vice-Pres. 1955–60, Pres. 1960–61; U.S. Sec. of Defense 1961–68; Pres. IBRD (World Bank) 1968–81; Dir. Royal Dutch Shell 1981; Dir. The Washington Post Co. 1981, Bank of America 1981, Corning Glass Works 1981, TWA 1981, Caspian Holdings 1995–; Chair. Overseas Devt. Council 1982; Adviser Robeco Group 1982; mem. Steering Cttee. on IBRD Reorganisation 1987; mem. Ford Foundation, Brookings Inst., Calif. Inst. of Tech., Urban Inst.; mem. American Acad. of Arts and Sciences, Advisory Council, Int. Reporting Systems 1981–83, Barbara Ward Fund 1982; Hon. LL.D. (St. Andrews) 1981; Hon. D.C.L. (Oxford) 1987, (Harvard) 1997; U.S. Medal of Freedom (with distinction) 1968, Albert Einstein Peace Prize 1983, Franklin D. Roosevelt Freedom Medal 1983, Onassis Award 1988; Legion of Merit. *Publications:* The Essence of Security: Reflections in Office 1968, One Hundred Countries—Two Billion People 1973, The McNamara Years at the World Bank 1981, Blundering into Disaster, Out of the Cold: New Thinking for American Foreign and Defence Policy in the 21st Century 1990, In Retrospect: The Tragedy and Lessons of Vietnam 1995, Argument Without End: The Search for Answers to the Vietnam Tragedy 1999. *Address:* 1350 I Street, N.W., Suite 500, Washington, DC, 20005, U.S.A. *Telephone:* (202) 682-3132. *Fax:* (202) 682-3130.

MACNAUGHTON, Sir Malcolm Campbell, Kt., M.D., L.L.D., F.R.C.O.G., F.R.C.P., F.R.S.E.; British professor of obstetrics and gynaecology; b. 4 April 1925, Glasgow; s. of James Hay Macnaughton and Mary Robieson Hogarth; m. Margaret-Ann Galt 1955; two s. three d.; ed. Glasgow Acad. and Glasgow Univ.; Sr. Lecturer, Obstetrics and Gynaecology, Dundee and St. Andrews Univs. 1961–70; Muirhead Prof. of Obstetrics and Gynaecology, Glasgow Univ. 1970–90; British Emer. Prof. of Obstetrics and Gynaecology; Pres. Royal Coll. of Obstetricians and Gynaecologists, London 1984–87; Chair. Working Party on Accident and Emergency Services in Scotland (Scotmeg); Vice-Pres. Royal Coll. of Midwives 1992–; mem. Academic Bd. St. George's Univ. Medical School, Grenada, W.I.; Hon. Fellow Sri Lanka Coll. of Obstetricians and Gynaecologists, Royal Australian Coll. of Obstetricians and Gynaecologists, American Coll. of Obstetricians and Gynaecologists, Royal Coll. of Anaesthetists. *Publications:* Combined Textbook of Obstetrics and Gynaecology 1976, The Ovary 1976, Medical Gynaecology 1985. *Leisure interests:* walking, fishing, curling. *Address:* Beechwood, 15 Boclair Road, Bearsden, Glasgow, G61 2AF, Scotland. *Telephone:* 0141-942-1909.

McNEALY, Scott, B.A., M.B.A.; American computer company executive; b. 1954; ed. Harvard and Stanford Univs.; Sales Engineer Rockwell Int. Corpn., Troy, Mich. 1976–78; Staff Engineer FMC Corpn., Chicago 1980–81; Dir. Operations, Onyx Systems, San José, Calif. 1981–82; joined Sun Microsystems Inc., Mountain View, Calif. 1982–, now Chair., Pres. C.E.O. and Dir. *Address:* Sun Microsystems Inc., 2550 Garcia Avenue, Mountain View, CA 94043, U.S.A.

McNEE, Sir David Blackstock, Kt., F.B.I.M., F.R.S.A.; British fmr. police officer; b. 23 March 1925, Glasgow; s. of John McNee and late Mary McNee (née Blackstock); m. Isabella Clayton Hopkins 1952 (died 1997); one d.; ed. Woodside Sr. Secondary School, Glasgow; Deputy Chief Constable, Dunbartonshire Constabulary 1968–71; Chief Constable, City of Glasgow Police 1971–75; Chief Constable, Strathclyde Police 1975–77; Commr., Metropolitan Police 1977–82; Dir. Fleet Holdings 1983–86; Chair. (non-exec.) Scottish Express Newspapers 1983–; Orr Pollock & Co. Ltd. (Greenock Telegraph), Craig M. Jeffrey Ltd. (Helensburgh Advertiser), Integrated Security Services Ltd.; Adviser Bd. British Airways 1982–87; Dir. (non-exec.) Clydesdale Bank PLC; Pres. Royal Life Saving Soc. 1982–90, Nat. Bible Soc. of Scotland 1983–96, Glasgow City Cttee., Cancer Relief 1987–93; Freeman, City of London 1977; C.B.I.M. 1980; Order of St. John 1974, Commdr. 1977; Hon. Col. 32 (Scottish) Signal Regt. (Volunteers) 1988–92; Queen's Police Medal 1975. *Publication:* McNee's Law 1983. *Leisure interests:* fishing, golf, music.

MacNEIL, Cornell Hill; American opera singer; b. 24 Sept. 1922, Minneapolis, Minn.; s. of Walter Hill and Harriette Belle (Cornell) MacNeil; m. 1st Margaret Gavan 1947 (divorced 1972); two s. three d.; m. 2nd Tania Rudensky 1972; ed. Julius Hartt School of Music, Univ. of Hartford, West Hartford, Conn. *Appeared on Broadway in:* Sweethearts 1947, Where's Charley 1949; operatic début as John Sorel in world premiere of The Consul (Menotti) 1950; début with New York City Opera as Germont in La Traviata 1953, at La Scala, Milan, as Charles V in Ernani 1959, at Metropolitan Opera, New York in title-role of Rigoletto 1959; has appeared in leading opera houses of Europe, U.S.A., S. America; Pres. American Guild of Musical Artists 1971–77; Alumnus of Year, Hartt School of Music 1976; Grammy Award for best opera recording (La Traviata) 1984; Medal of Achievement, Acad. of Vocal Arts 1985. *Leisure interests:* cooking, woodwork, gardening.

MACNEISH, Richard Stockton, M.A., PH.D., F.B.A.; American archaeologist; b. 29 April 1918, New York; s. of Harris Franklin MacNeish and Elizabeth Stockton; m. Phyllis Diana Walter 1963; two s.; ed. Colgate Univ., Univ. of Chicago, Harvard; Sr. Archaeologist, Nat. Museum of Canada 1949–63; Head, Dept. of Archaeology, Univ. of Calgary 1963–69; Dir., Peabody Foundation for Archaeology 1969–83; Sr. Research Prof., Boston Univ. 1983–86; Dir. Andover Foundation for Archaeological Research 1986–; participated in and supervised archaeological digs in Mexico, Canada, Honduras, Guatemala, Peru, Belize, China, etc.; Fellow, American Anthropological Asscn., Arctic Inst. for N. America, American Acad. of Arts and Sciences –1971; mem. U.S.. Presidental Advisory Comm. on Cultural Properties 1992–; mem. A.A.A.S., Int. Congress of Americanists, N.A.S.; Fellow Soc. for American Archaeology; numerous awards and honours, including Hon. LL.D (Simon Fraser Univ.) 1980, Spinden Medal for Archaeology 1964, Alfred Vincent Kidder Award 1971, Cornplanter Medal for Iroquois Research 1977. *Publications:* numerous articles and reports; The Origins of Agriculture and Settled Life, Macroblades and Megablades in Ancient Belize, Classic and Post-Classic States in Prehistoric Mexico, The Science of Archaeology 1976. *Leisure interest:* sports. *Address:* Andover Foundation for Archaeology Research, PO Box 83, Andover, MA 01810 (Office); 3 Longwood Drive, Unit 1, Andover, MA 01810, U.S.A. (Home). *Telephone:* (508) 475-1326 (Home).

McNICOL, Donald, PH.D., F.R.S.A.; Australian university vice-chancellor; b. 18 April 1939, Adelaide; s. of Ian Robertson McNicol and Sadie Isabelle Williams; m. Kathleen Margaret Wells 1963; one s. two d.; ed. Unley High School, Univ. of Adelaide, Cambridge Univ., U.K.; lecturer in Psychology, Univ. of Adelaide 1967–71; Sr. Lecturer in Psychology, Univ. of N.S.W. 1971–74, Assoc. Prof. 1975–81; Prof. of Psychology, Univ. of Tasmania 1981–86; Commr. for Univs. and Chair. Univs. Advisory Council of Commonwealth Tertiary Educ. Comm. 1986–88; Vice-Chancellor Univ. of New England 1988–90, Univ. of Sydney 1990–96, Univ. of Tasmania 1996–; Deputy Pres. Australian Vice-Chancellors' Cttee. 1993–94, Pres. 1994–96, Asscn. of Univs. of S. Asia and the Pacific (AUAP) 1998–; Fellow Australian Psychological Soc. *Publication:* A Primer of Signal Detection Theory 1972. *Leisure interests:* walking, music, reading. *Address:* Office of the Vice-Chancellor, University of Tasmania, G.P.O. Box 252C, Hobart, Tasmania, 2001, Australia. *Telephone:* (002) 202002. *Fax:* (002) 232026.

McNICOL, George Paul, C.B.E., F.R.S.E., M.D., PH.D., F.R.C.P., F.R.C.P.G., F.R.C.PATH.; British university vice-chancellor (retd.); b. 24 Sept. 1929, Glasgow; s. of M. W. McNicol and Elizabeth (Harper) McNicol; m. Dr. Susan Ritchie 1959; one s. two d.; ed. Hillhead High School, Glasgow and Univ. of Glasgow; Regimental Medical Officer, R.A.M.C. 1953–55; Registrar, Univ. Medical Unit, Stobhill Gen. Hospital 1955–57; Registrar, Univ. Dept. of Medicine, Royal Infirmary, Glasgow 1957–59, Hon. Sr. Registrar 1961–65, Lecturer in Medicine 1963–65, Hon. Consultant Physician 1966–71, Sr. Lecturer in Medicine 1966–70, Reader in Medicine 1970–71; Prof. of Medicine and Hon. Consultant Physician, Leeds Gen. Infirmary 1971–81; Chair. Bd. of Faculty of Medicine, Univ. of Leeds 1978–81; Prin. and Vice-Chancellor, Univ. of Aberdeen 1981–91; Vice-Chair. Raigmore Hosp. N.H.S. Trust 1993–95; mem. Aberdeen Local Bd. Bank of Scotland 1983–92; Harkness Fellow, Washington Univ. 1959–61; other professional appts.; foreign corresp. mem. Belgian Royal Acad. of Medicine; Hon. F.A.C.P.; Hon. D.Sc. (Wabash Coll.); Hon. LL.D. (Aberdeen) 1992. *Publications:* approximately 200 publications in biomedical literature in the field of haemostasis and thrombosis. *Leisure interests:* skiing, water-colour painting. *Address:* 17 Barton Farm, Cerne Abbas, Dorset, DT2 7LF, England. *Telephone:* (01300) 341758.

McPEAK, Merrill Anthony, D.S.M., D.F.C., M.S.; American air force officer; b. 9 Jan. 1936, Santa Rosa, Calif.; s. of Merrill Addison McPeak and Winifred Alice (Stewart) McPeak Bendall; m. Elynor Fay Moskowitz 1956; two s.; ed. San Diego State Coll., Calif., George Washington Univ., Washington; commissioned officer U.S.A.F. 1957, progressed through ranks to Gen. 1988; Commdr.-in-Chief Pacific Air Forces, Hickam, Hawaii 1988–90; Chief of Staff U.S.A.F. 1990–94; now Chair. ECC Int. Corpn. *Address:* 17360 S.W. Grandview, Lake Oswego, OR 97034, U.S.A.

MACPHERSON, Elle; Australian fashion model and business executive; b. 29 March 1963, Killara, Sydney; d. of Peter Gow and Frances Macpherson; m. Gilles Bensimon (divorced 1989); one s. by Arpad Busson; Chief Exec. Elle Macpherson Inc.; designs and promotes own lingerie for Brendon; promotes Elle Macpherson sportswear; co-owner Fashion Cafe, New York. *Films:* Sirens 1994, Jane Eyre 1994, If Lucy Fell 1996; video: Stretch and Strengthen, The Body Workout 1995. *Address:* c/o Women Model Management, 107 Greene Street, Floor 2, New York, NY 10012, U.S.A.

McPHERSON, Harry Cummings, Jr., B.A., LL.B.; American government official and lawyer; b. 22 Aug. 1929, Tyler, Tex.; s. of Harry Cummings and Nan (née Hight) McPherson; m. 1st Clayton Read 1952 (divorced 1981); two s.; m. 2nd Patricia DeGroot 1981; one s.; ed. Tyler High School, Texas, Southern Methodist Univ., Dallas, Univ. of the South, Tennessee, Columbia Univ. and Univ. of Texas Law School; U.S. Air Force 1950–53; admitted to Texas Bar 1955; Asst. Gen. Counsel, Dem. Policy Cttee., U.S. Senate 1956–59, Assoc. Counsel 1959–61, Gen. Counsel 1961–63; Deputy Under Sec. for Int. Affairs, Dept. of Army 1963–64; Asst. Sec. of State for Educational and Cultural Affairs 1964–65; Special Asst. and Counsel to Pres. Johnson 1965–69; Special Counsel to the Pres. 1966–69; Vice-Chair. John F. Kennedy Center for Performing Arts 1969–76, Gen. Counsel 1977–91; pvt. law practice, Washington, D.C. 1969–; Chair. Task Force on Domestic Policy, Democratic Advisory Council of Elected Officials 1974; mem. Pres.'s Comm. on the Accident at Three Mile Island 1979; Pres. Federal City Council, Washington, D.C. 1983–88; Vice-Chair. U.S. Int. Cultural and Trade Center Comm. 1988–93; Pres. Econ. Club of Washington 1992–; mem. Defense Base Closure and Realignment Comm. 1993. *Publication:* A Political Education 1972. *Address:* 901 15th Street, N.W., Washington, DC 20005 (Office); 10213 Montgomery Avenue, Kensington, MD 20895, U.S.A. (Home).

McPHERSON, James M., PH.D.; American historian; b. 11 Oct. 1936, Valley City, N.D.; s. of James M. McPherson and Miriam O. McPherson; m. Patricia Rasche 1958; one d.; ed. Gustavus Adolphus Coll. and Johns Hopkins Univ.; Instructor Princeton Univ. 1962–65, Asst. Prof. 1965–66, Assoc. Prof. 1966–72, Prof. of History 1972–82, Edwards Prof. of American History 1982–91, George Henry Davis Prof. of American History 1991; Anisfield-Wolf Award in Race Relations 1965; Guggenheim Fellow 1967–68; Huntington Seaver Fellow 1987–88; Pulitzer Prize in History 1989. *Publications:* The Struggle for Equality: Abolitionists and the Negro in the Civil War and Reconstruction 1964, The Negro's Civil War 1965, The Abolitionist Legacy 1975, Ordeal by Fire: The Civil War and Reconstruction 1982, Battle Cry of Freedom: The Civil War Era 1988, Abraham Lincoln and the Second American Revolution 1991, Images of the Civil War 1992, Gettysburg 1993, What They Fought For 1861–1865 1994, The Atlas of the Civil War 1994, Drawn With the Sword: Reflections on the American Civil War 1996, For Cause and Comrades: Why Men Fought in the Civil War 1997, Lamson of the Gettysburg: The Civil War Letters of Lieut. Roswell H. Lamson, US Navy, 1997. *Leisure interests:* tennis, bicycling, sailing. *Address:* 15 Randall Road, Princeton, NJ 08540, U.S.A. (Home). *Telephone:* (609) 924-9226 (Home).

McPHERSON, Melville Peter, B.A., M.B.A.; American government official and lawyer; b. 27 Oct. 1940, Grand Rapids, Mich.; s. of Donald McPherson and Ellura E. (Frost) McPherson; m. Joanne Paddock McPherson 1989; one s. one step s.; Peace Corps volunteer, Peru 1964–66; with Internal Revenue Service, Washington 1969–75; Special Asst. to Pres. and Deputy Dir. Presidential Personnel White House, Washington 1975–77; partner Vorys, Sater, Seymour & Pease, Washington 1977–81; Acting Counsel to Pres., White House 1981; Admin. Agency for Int. Devt., Washington 1981–87; Dep. Sec., Dept. of Treasury 1987–89; Group Exec. Vice-Pres. Bank of America 1989–93; Pres. Mich. State Univ. 1993–; Exec. Vice-Pres. Bank of America 1988–; mem. Bd. for Int. Food and Agric. Devt. 1977–80; mem. Michigan and D.C. Bar Asscn. *Address:* Office of the President, Michigan State University, 450 Administration Bldg., Lansing, MI 48824, U.S.A.

MACQUARRIE, Rev. John, T.D., PH.D., D.LITT., D.D., F.B.A.; British professor of theology and priest; b. 27 June 1919, Renfrew, Scotland; s. of John Macquarrie and Robina Macquarrie (née McInnes); m. Jenny Fallow Welsh 1949; two s. one d.; ed. Renfrew High School, Paisley Grammar School and Univ. of Glasgow; British Army Chaplain 1945–48; Incumbent, St. Ninian's Church, Brechin 1948–53; Lecturer in Systematic Theology, Univ. of Glasgow 1953–62; Prof. of Systematic Theology, Union Theological Seminary, New York, U.S.A. 1962–70; Hon. Curate, St. Mary's, Manhattanville, New York 1965–70; Lady Margaret Prof. of Divinity, Oxford Univ. and Canon of Christ Church Oxford 1970–86; Gifford Lecturer, Univ. of St. Andrews 1983–84; Consultant, Lambeth Conferences 1968, 1978. *Publications:* An Existentialist Theology 1955, Twentieth Century Religious Thought 1963, Principles of Christian Theology 1966, God-Talk 1967, Existentialism 1972, In Search of Humanity 1982, In Search of Deity 1984, Theology, Church and Ministry 1986, Jesus Christ in Modern Thought 1990, Mary for All Christians 1991, Heidegger and Christianity 1994, Invitation to Faith 1995, The Mediators 1995, A Guide to the Sacrament 1997, Christology Revisited 1998. *Leisure interests:* hill walking, the language and literature of Scottish Gaelic. *Address:* 206 Headley Way, Oxford, OX3 7TA, England. *Telephone:* (01865) 761889.

McQUEEN, Alexander, M.A.; British fashion designer; b. London; ed. St. Martin's School of Art, London; left school aged 16, worked for London tailors Anderson & Shepherd, Gieves & Hawkes and theatrical costumiers Bermans & Nathans, designer Koji Tatsuno, and Romeo Gigli in Rome; his final collection at St. Martin's 1992 est. his reputation; subsequent shows include The Birds, Highland Rape, The Hunger, Dante, La Poupee, It's a Jungle Out There, Untitled; acquired Italian mfg. co. Onward Kashiyama; Chief Designer, Givenchy, Paris 1996–; Designer of the Year, London Fashion Awards 1996, jt. winner (with John Galliano, q.v.) 1997, Special Achievement Award, London Fashion Awards 1998. *Address:* Givenchy, 3 avenue George V, 75008 Paris, France. *Telephone:* 44 31 50 00. *Fax:* 47 23 04 67.

MacRAE, Sir (Alastair) Christopher (Donald Summerhayes), K.C.M.G.; British diplomatist (retd.); b. 3 May 1937, Burleigh, Glos.; s. of Dr. Alastair MacRae and Dr Grace Summerhayes MacRae; m. Mette Willert 1963; two d.; ed. Rugby School, Lincoln Coll., Oxford and Harvard Univ.; Royal Navy 1956–58; joined Commonwealth Relations Office 1962; Third, later Second Sec. Dar es Salaam 1963; Middle East Centre for Arab Studies 1965; Beirut 1967; Foreign Office 1968; First Sec. and Head of Chancery, Baghdad 1970, Brussels 1972; Amb. to Gabon 1978, also to São Tomé & Príncipe 1979; FCO 1980, also Amb. to Chad (non-resident) 1982; Political Counsellor and Head of Chancery, Paris 1983; Minister and Head of British Interests Section, Tehran 1987; Cabinet Office 1988; High Commr. in Nigeria 1991–94 (concurrently Amb. to Benin); High Commr. in Pakistan 1994–97; Sec.-Gen. Order of St. John 1997–; K. St. J. *Leisure interests:* walking in hills and mountains, exploring Provence. *Address:* 4 Church Street, Wye, Kent, TN25 5BJ, England.

McSHARRY, Deirdre Mary; Irish journalist; b. 4 April 1932, London, England; d. of the late Dr. John McSharry and of Mary O'Brien; ed. Trinity Coll., Dublin Univ.; actress at Gate Theatre, Dublin 1953–55; freelance with The Irish Times 1953; mem. staff Evening Herald, Dublin 1955–56; with book shop Metropolitan Museum of Art, New York 1956; Reporter Women's Wear Daily, New York 1957–59; mem. staff Woman's Own 1959–62; Fashion Ed. Evening News 1962; Woman's Ed. Daily Express 1963–67; Fashion Ed. The Sun 1967–71; Fashion Ed. Cosmopolitan 1972, Ed. 1973–85; Ed.-in-Chief Country Living 1986–89; Consultant Nat. Magazine Co. and Magazine Div. The Hearst Corpn. 1990–92; Ed. Countryside magazine 1991–92; Chair. Bath Friends of The American Museum in Britain, Bath; Ed. of the Year (Periodical Publrs. Asscn.) 1981, 1987, Mark Boxer Award: Editor's Ed. 1991. *Leisure interests:* architecture, arts and crafts, gardens. *Address:* Southfield House, 16 High Street, Rode, BA3 6NZ, England.

MacSHARRY, Ray; Irish politician; b. 29 April 1938, Sligo; s. of Patrick McSharry and Annie Clarke; m. Elaine Neilan 1960; three s. three d.; ed. Summerhill Coll., Sligo; fmr. haulier, auctioneer, farm-owner; mem. Sligo

County Council and Sligo Corpn. 1967–78; mem. Dáil 1969–89; Minister of State, Dept. of Finance and Public Service 1977–79; Minister for Agriculture 1979–81; Tanaiste and Minister for Finance March-Nov. 1982; mem. European Parl. 1984–87; Minister for Finance 1987–88; EC Commr. with responsibility for Agric. and Rural Devt. 1989–93; pvt. business 1993–; Dir. (non-exec.) Jefferson Smurfit 1993–, Green Property 1994–; Dir. Bank of Ireland 1993–; Gov. E.I.B. 1982; Fianna Fáil. *Leisure interest:* sport. *Address:* Alcantara, Pearse Road, Sligo, Ireland. *Telephone:* (071) 69902. *Fax:* (071) 69902.

MACTAGGART, Sandy A., A.B., M.B.A., LL.D.; Canadian university chancellor and business executive; b. 11 March 1928, Glasgow, Scotland; s. of Sir John Mactaggart, 2nd Bt.; m. Cecile Macy Erickson 1959; one s. two d.; ed. Belmont Hill School, Glasgow, Lakefield School, Canada, Choate School, U.S.A., Harvard Coll., Harvard Business School; served Lieut. Calgary Squadron Fleet Air Arm, Royal Canadian Naval Reserve 1955–58; f. Maclab Enterprises (with Jean La Bruyere) 1954, Pres. 1954–80, Chair. 1980–; Chair. Tempo School, Chair. Finance Cttee. American Univ. of Beirut; Gov. Univ. of Alberta 1984–90, Chancellor 1990–97; Hon. LL.D. (Univ. of Alberta). *Leisure interests:* flying, sailing, skiing, collecting books and oriental art. *Address:* P.O. Box 3160, Edmonton, Alberta, Canada, T5J 2G7. *Telephone:* (403) 420 6666.

McTEER, Janet; British actress; b. 5 August 1961; d. of Alan McTeer; ed. Royal Acad. of Dramatic Arts, London; Olivier Award, Evening Standard Award, Tony Award; Bancroft Gold Medal 1983. *Theatre includes:* Much Ado About Nothing, Uncle Vanya, Simpatico, Vivat! Vivat Regina, London 1995, A Doll's House, London, N.Y., 1996–97. *TV appearances include:* The Governor, A Masculine Ending, Don't Leave Me This Way, A Portrait of a Marriage, Precious Bane. *Address:* c/o Michael Foster, ICM Ltd., Oxford House, 76 Oxford Street, London, W1N 0AX, England. *Telephone:* 0171-636 6565. *Fax:* 0171-323 0101.

McTIERNAN, John; American film director; b. 8 Jan. 1951, New York; m. Donna Dubrow; ed. Juilliard School of Drama, State Univ. of New York, Old Westbury Filmmaking Coll. *Films:* Nomads (also screenplay), Predator, Die Hard, The Hunt for Red October, Medicine Man, Last Action Hero (also co-producer), Die Hard with a Vengeance. *Address:* c/o Creative Artists Agency, 9830 Wilshire Boulevard, Beverly Hills, CA 90212, U.S.A.

McVIE, John Gordon, M.D., F.R.C.P., F.R.C.P.S.; British cancer research director; b. 13 Jan. 1945, Glasgow; s. of John McVie and Lindsaye Mair; m. Evelyn Strang 1966 (divorced 1996); three s.; ed. Royal High School, Edinburgh and Univ. of Edinburgh; MRC Fellow, Univ. of Edinburgh 1970–71, lecturer in Therapeutics 1971–76; Sr. lecturer in Clinical Oncology, Univ. of Glasgow 1976–80; Head, Clinical Research Unit, Netherlands Cancer Inst. Amsterdam 1980–84, Clinical Research Dir. 1984–89; Scientific Dir. Cancer Research Campaign 1989–96, Dir. Gen. 1996–; Visiting Prof. British Postgrad. Medical Fed. Univ. of London 1990–; Pres. European Org. for Research and Treatment of Cancer 1994; mem. numerous advisory cttees. etc. *Publications:* Cancer Assessment and Monitoring 1979, Autologous Bone Marrow Transplantation and Solid Tumours 1984, Microspheres and Drug Therapy 1984, Clinical and Experimental Pathology and Biology of Lung Cancer 1985; 35 chapters in books; 159 articles in books and journals. *Leisure interests:* opera, theatre, cooking, Italian wine-tasting. *Address:* 10 Cambridge Terrace, London, NW1 4JL, England. *Telephone:* 0171-224 1333. *Fax:* 0171-224 2399.

McWHERTER, Ned R.; American politician; b. 15 Oct. 1930, Palmersville, Tenn.; s. of Harmon R. McWherter and Lucille Smith; m. Bette Jean Beck (deceased); one s. one d.; mem. Tenn. House of Reps. 1968–87, Speaker 1973–87; Gov. of Tennessee 1987–95; Chair. Bd. Eagle Distributors Inc., Weakley Gas and Oil Co.; Dir. Weakley Co. Bank, People's Bank; Democrat. *Address:* 22 Bypass Building, Dresden, TN 38225, U.S.A.

McWHIRTER, Norris Dewar, C.B.E., M.A.; British publisher and broadcaster; b. 12 Aug. 1925, London; s. of William Allan McWhirter and Margaret Williamson; m. 1st Carole Eckert 1957 (died 1987); one s. one d.; m. 2nd Tessa Mary Pocock 1991; ed. Marlborough Coll. and Trinity Coll., Oxford; Sub-Lieut. R.N.V.R. 1943–46; Dir. McWhirter Twins Ltd. (facts and figures agency) 1950–; Chair. William McWhirter & Son Ltd. (electrical eng.) 1955–86; Athletics Corresp. The Star 1951–60, The Observer 1951–67, Ed., Athletics World 1952–56; Dir. Guinness Publs. (fmrly. Guinness Superlatives) Ltd. 1954–96, Man. Dir. 1954–76; BBC TV commentator Olympic Games 1960–72; contested gen. elections, Orpington, Kent (Conservative) 1964, 1966; co-founder, Chair. Redwood Press Ltd. 1966–72; mem. Sports Council 1970–73; Dir. Gieves Group Ltd. 1972–95; Presenter BBC TV series "The Record Breakers" 1972–88; co-founder and Vice-Chair. The Freedom Asscn. 1975–83, Chair. 1983–. *Publications:* Get To Your Marks 1951, Guinness Book of World Records (Ed. and Compiler of approx. 340 editions in 38 languages to 1996, Advisory Ed. 1986–96) 1955–86; Dunlop Book of Facts 1964, 1966, Guinness Book of Answers, 10th edn. 1996, Ross, Story of a Shared Life 1976, Treason at Maastricht (jtly.) 1994. *Leisure interests:* family tennis, exploring islands. *Address:* c/o 35 Westminster Bridge Road, London, SE1 7JB, England.

McWILLIAM, Candia Frances Juliet, B.A.; British writer; b. 1 July 1955, Edinburgh; d. of Colin McWilliam and Margaret McWilliam; m. 1st Quentin Gerard Carew Wallop (now Earl of Portsmouth) 1981; one s. one d.; m. 2nd Fram Dinshaw; one s.; ed. Sherborne School, Dorset and Girton Coll., Cambridge. *Publications:* (novels) A Cast of Knives 1988, A Little Stranger 1989, Debatable Land 1994; (short stories) Wait till I Tell You 1997. *Address:* 21 Beaumont Buildings, Oxford, OX1 2LL, England. *Telephone:* (01865) 511931.

McWILLIAMS, Sir Francis, G.B.E., B.SC., F.ENG., F.C.I.A., F.C.G.I.; British arbitrator, civil engineer and company director; b. 8 Feb. 1926, Edinburgh; s. of John and Mary McWilliams; m. Winifred Segger 1950; two s.; ed. Holy Cross Acad., Edinburgh, Edinburgh Univ.; engineer with various local authorities and contractors in U.K. 1945–53; Town Engineer, Petaling Jaya Devt. Corpn., Malaysia 1954–64; Consulting Engineer, F. McWilliams & Assoc., Kuala Lumpur 1964–76; full-time student 1976–78; called to English bar at Lincoln's Inn 1978; pupil barrister 1978–79; Int. Arbitrator 1979–; Chair. Centre for Econs. and Business Research 1992–; Chair. British/Malaysian Soc. 1994–; Chair. 3 A's 1996–; Dir (non-exec.) Hongkong Bank Malaysia 1993–; mem. Panel of Arbitrators of Inst. of Civil Engineers, Panel of Int. Arbitrators of Chartered Inst. of Arbitrators and other bodies; Hon. Fellow Inst. of Civil Engineers; Sheriff City of London 1988–89, Lord Mayor of London 1992–93, fmr. mem. Court of Aldermen, City of London; several honours. *Publication:* Urban Regeneration and Environmental Challenge. *Leisure interests:* golf, skiing. *Address:* C.E.B.R., Bartlett House, 9–12 Basinghall Street, London, EC2V 5NS (Office); 85 North Road, Hythe, Kent, CT21 5ET, England (Home). *Telephone:* 0171-600 6661 (Office); (01303) 261800 (Home). *Fax:* 0171-600 6671 (Office); (01303) 261800 (Home).

MACY, William H.; American actor; b. 13 March 1950, Miami, Fla.; ed. Goddard Coll., Vermont; co-f. St. Nicholas Theatre Co., Atlantic Theatre Co. *Stage appearances include:* The Man in 605 1980, Twelfth Night, Beaurecrat, A Call From the East, The Dining Room, Speakeasy, Wild Life, Flirtations, Baby With the Bathwater, The Nice and the Nasty, Bodies Rest and Motion, Oh Hell!, Prairie du Chien, The Shawl, An Evening With Dorothy Parker, The Dining Room, A Call From the Sea, The Beaver Coat, Life During Wartime, Mr. Gogol and Mr. Preen, Oleanna, Our Town. *Play directed:* Boy's Life. *Film appearances include:* Without a Trace, The Last Dragon, Radio Days, Somewhere in Time, Hello Again, House of Games, Things Change, Homicide, Shadows and Fog, Benny and Joon, Searching for Bobby Fischer, The Client, Oleanna, The Silence of the Lambs, Murder in the First, Mr. Holland's Opus, Down Periscope, Fargo, Ghosts of Mississippi, Air Force One. *Film directed:* Lip Service. *Television appearances include:* Chicago Hope (series), The Murder of Mary Phagan (mini-series), Texan, A Murderous Affair, The Water Engine, Heart of Justice, A Private Matter.

MADDEN, (Albert) Frederick (McCulloch), D.PHIL.; British academic; b. 27 Feb. 1917, Tavistock; s. of A. E. Madden and G. McC. Madden; m. Margaret Gifford 1941; one s. one d.; ed. Bishop Vesey's Grammar School, Christ Church, Oxford; Deputy Supt. Rhodes House Library 1946–48; Beit Lecturer 1947–57, sr. tutor to Overseas Service Courses 1950–, co-dir. Foreign Service Course 1959–72; Dir. Inst. of Commonwealth Studies 1961–68; Reader in Commonwealth Govt., Oxford 1957–84; Professorial Fellow of Nuffield Coll. 1958–84, Emer. Fellow 1984–, Pro-Proctor 1988–89; Dir. Prospect Theatre 1963–66. *Publications include:* British Colonial Developments 1774–1834 (with V. Harlow) 1953, Essays in Imperial Government (with K. Robinson) 1963, Oxford and the Idea of Commonwealth 1982, Select Documents on the Constitutional History of the British Empire Vol. I 1985, Vol. II 1986, Vol. III 1987, Vol. IV 1989, Vol. V 1991, Vol. VI 1993, Vol. VII 1994, Vol. VIII 1997. *Leisure interests:* music, acting, country houses. *Address:* 1 Penstones Court, Marlborough Lane, Stanford-in-the-Vale, Oxon., SN7 8SW, England.

MADDEN, John; British film director; b. 8 April 1949, Portsmouth. *Television includes:* Inspector Morse (episodes), Prime Suspect IV, Ethan Frome. *Films:* Mrs. Brown 1997, Shakespeare in Love (Acad. Award for Best Film, BAFTA Award for Best Film) 1998.

MADDY, Penelope Jo, PH.D.; American professor of philosophy; b. 4 July 1950, Tulsa, Okla.; ed. Univ. of California, Berkeley, Princeton Univ.; lecturer then Asst. Prof. of Philosophy, Univ. of Notre Dame 1978–83; Assoc. Prof. of Philosophy, Univ. of Ill. at Chicago 1983–87; Assoc. Prof. of Philosophy and Math., Univ., of Calif. at Irvine 1987–89, Prof. 1989–, Chair. Philosophy Dept. 1991–95; Westinghouse Science Scholarship 1968–72, Marshall Scholarship 1972–73, AAUW Fellowship 1982–83, NSF Fellowships 1986, 1988–89, 1990–91, 1994–95. *Publications:* Realism in Mathematics 1990, Naturalism in Mathematics 1997. *Address:* Logic and Philosophy of Science, School of Social Sciences, University of California at Irvine, Irvine, CA 92697, U.S.A. *Telephone:* (949) 824-4133.

MADELIN, Alain, L. EN D.; French politician and lawyer; b. 26 March 1946, Paris; three c.; lawyer, Paris office, Fed. Nat. des Républicains Indépendents (FNRI) 1968–; mem. Nat. Secr. FNRI 1977; Deputy to Nat. Ass. (UDF-PR) 1978–86; co-organizer UDF 1989–; Minister of Industry, Posts and Telecommunications and Tourism 1986–88, of Enterprise and Econ. Devt. 1993–95, of Finance May-Aug. 1995; Sec.-Gen. Republican Party 1988–89, Vice-Pres. 1990–; Pres. France-Corée Asscn. 1991–; Vice-Pres. Regional Council of Brittany 1992–; Mayor of Redon 1995–; mem. European Parl. June 1989; Pres. Inst. Euro 92 1988–, f., Pres, Idées Action 1993–; Minister of Enterprise and Econ. Devt. with responsibility for small and medium-sized firms, commerce and craft industries 1993–95, Minister of Econ. and Finance 1995; Pres. Republican Party 1997– (now Liberal Democrats, Ind. Republicans and Republicans). *Address:* Démocratie libérale, 113 rue de l'Université, 75007 Paris; Euro 92 et Idées Action, 31 boulevard Latour Maubourg, 75007 Paris; Assemblée nationale, 75355 Paris; Mairie, 35600 Redon, France.

MADFAI, Husham H. Fahmi Al-, B.SC.; Iraqi engineering consultant and government official; b. 28 Oct. 1928, Baghdad; s. of Hassan Fahmi Al-Madfai and Wajiha Nouri Al-Madfai; m. 1st Suad A. Mohloom (died 1984); one s. one d.; m. 2nd Suha M. A. Bakri 1993; ed. Cen. High School, Baghdad, Eng. Coll., Univ. of Baghdad, Hammersmith School of Art & Design, London, Inst. of Structural Engineers, London; civil engineer, Basrah Petroleum Co. 1953–55; with Dept. of Housing and Tourism Design and Policies, Devt. Bd. 1957–63; Head. Tech. Dept., Municipality of Baghdad 1963–68; own consulting firm (architects, planners and designers) 1968–80; Deputy Mayor (responsible for planning and man.), City of Baghdad 1980–88; own consulting firm (studies and eng.) 1988–; Regional Consultant (feasibility, studies and design), Amman, Jordan 1994–; mem. Iraqi Asscn. of Philosophers and Scientists 1994. *Publications include:* Health Aspects in Town Planning 1968, Low-cost Prefabricated Housing 1975, Housing Programme for Iraq until the year 2000 1976, Environmental Problems in Arab Cities 1995. *Leisure interests:* archaeology, studying ancient cities, music, paintings, reading biographies, swimming, long walks. *Address:* Maghrib Street, Adhamiya 22/14/302, Baghdad, Iraq; P.O. Box 941021, Shmesan 1, Amman 11194, Jordan. *Telephone:* (1) 422 5021/2 (Iraq); (6) 5688 470 (Jordan). *Fax:* (6) 5688 498 (Jordan).

MADFAI, Kahtan al, B.ARCH., PH.D.; Iraqi architect, town planner and author; b. 15 April 1926, Baghdad; s. of late Hassan Fahmi al Madfai and of Wajiha Shaikh Noori Shirwai; m. Lily Vassiliki Vorré 1957; one d.; ed. Univ. of Wales Inst. of Science and Tech., Cardiff, U.K.; practised as architect in public housing sector 1957, planning and design 1961; co-f. Architectural School of Baghdad 1961; lecturer on theory of design 1955–69; f. architectural firm Dar al Imara 1954–79; Asst. Man. Gen. Housing Iraq Project 1973–(2000); designer and consultant architect; Chair. Pan-Arab Jury for awarding prizes for Arab Town Projects 1985–87; delivered papers and seminars Istanbul 1985, Oxford 1986, Tunis 1987, 1989, Bahrain 1994, Baghdad 1994, Univ. of S. Ga., U.S.A. 1996, A.I.A., Atlanta, U.S.A. 1996, Amman 1996; co-f. Soc. of Iraqi Artists; mem. S.P. Group of Artists, Baghdad; works in Baghdad include Ministry of Finance 1968, Bunniyd Mosque 1972, Museum of Natural History 1973, several first prizes in architectural competitions including Rohoon Bank Bldg., Baghdad 1955, Baghdad Cen. Commercial Zone 1970, Cen. P.O. 1975, Mohammedia Touristic Project, Basra 1977, Great Mosque Competition 1984. *Publications:* several books on architecture and town planning including Development of the Iraqi House 1956, Criteria for Baghdad's New Master Plan 1965, Architecture and Language 1987, Allah and the Architect 1997; poetry: Fulool 1965, Zem Zem Zeman 1972. *Leisure interests:* painting, poetry, philosophy. *Address:* 22 Vassileos Constantinou, 11635 Athens, Greece. *Telephone:* 7232836 (Office); 7217189 (Home). *Fax:* 7249920.

MADIGAN, Sir Russel Tullie, Kt., O.B.E., M.E., LL.B., F.S.A.S.M., F.AUS.I.M.M., F.T.S.; Australian business executive; b. 22 Nov. 1920, Adelaide; s. of the late C. T. Madigan; m. 1st Margaret Symons 1942 (deceased); four s. one d.; m. 2nd Satsuko Tamura 1981 (deceased); ed. Univ. of Adelaide; joined Zinc Corpn. 1946; Gowrie scholarship in Canada and U.S.A. 1947–49; Underground Man. Zinc Corpn. Ltd., NBHC Ltd. 1956–59; Gen. Man., Gen. Mining Div., CRA Ltd., (Conzinc Rio Tinto Australia Ltd.) 1960–64, Dir. 1968–87; Deputy Chair. 1978–87; Man. Dir. Hamersley Iron 1965–71, Chair. 1971–81; Chair. Blair Athol Coal Pty. Ltd. 1971–80, Interstate Oil Ltd. 1972–81, Hamersley Holdings Ltd., 1971–81; Dir. Rio Tinto Zinc Corpn., Ltd. 1971–85, Comalco Ltd. 1976–82, Nat. Commercial Union Ltd. 1969–90; Dir. APV Holdings 1983–87, Aluminium Smelters of Victoria Pty. Ltd. 1993–; Chair. APV Asia Pacific Ltd. 1983–87, Australian Mineral Foundation 1984–88, Australia-Japan Foundation 1977–81, Muswellbrook Energy and Minerals Ltd. 1987–90, Remproc Ltd. 1989–, Australian United Steel Industry Pty. Ltd. 1994–97; mem. Export Devt. Council 1970–76, Consultative Cttee. on Relations with Japan 1977–82, Australian Pacific Econ. Co-operation Cttee. 1986– (Chair. 1986–92); Life mem. of Pacific Basin Econ. Council; Councillor Australasian Inst. Mining and Metallurgy 1969–85, Pres. 1980; Councillor Australian Acad. of Tech. Sciences and Eng. 1978–89, Treas. 1985–89; Pres. Australian Inst. of Int. Affairs 1984–89; Chair. Australian Business Aircraft Asscn. 1986–89, Antarctic Names and Medal Cttee. 1981–94. *Leisure interests:* flying, farming. *Address:* 135 Collins Street, Melbourne, Vic. (Office); 99 Spring Street, Melbourne, Vic. 3000, Australia (Home). *Telephone:* 654 4277 (Office); 654 3854 (Home).

MADKOUR, Mohamed Abdel-Khalek, PH.D.; Egyptian business executive, university professor and consultant; b. 8 Jan. 1948, Giza; s. of Ibrahim Bayoumi Madkour and Bahia Abdel-Khalek Madkour; m. Afkar el Kharadly 1970; two d.; ed. Ecole des Hautes Etudes en Sciences Sociales, Univ. de la Sorbonne, Paris and Univ. of Cairo; Attache, Industrial Devt. Center for Arab Studies, League of Arab States, Cairo 1969–78; Dir.-Gen. Al-Ahram Org. 1978–85; mem. Bd. Al-Ahram Investment Co. 1981–85; Sr. Research Scientist, School of Information and Computer Sciences, Ga. Inst. of Tech. Atlanta, Ga., U.S.A. 1980–83; Dir. Egyptian Nat. Scientific and Tech. Information Network 1980–82; Prof. Faculty of Mass Communications, Univ. of Cairo 1982; Pres. Phoenix Int.-Madkour Assocs. Inc., McLean, Va., U.S.A. 1986; Chair. and C.E.O. Egyptian Co. for Tourism and Services, Cairo 1987; Chair. Cairo-Systems, S.A.R.L., Cairo 1990–, Multinat. Multimedia Computing Inc. Cairo 1992–; Chair. and C.E.O. Marketing Via Internet, Cairo 1997–. *Publications:* Information Services of Egypt 1981, Towards a National Information Policy for Egypt 1982, Information Systems in Egypt: New Trends, Latent Challenges 1984. *Leisure interests:* bridge, snooker, tennis, soccer. *Address:* 4 Gamal el Din Abu el Mahassen Square, Garden City, Cairo (Office); 8 Nile Street, Giza, Cairo, Egypt (Home). *Telephone:* (202) 3546833; 3560581 (Office); (202) 5703012 (Home). *Fax:* (202) 3562407 (Office); (202) 5703014 (Home).

MADKOUR, Nazli, M.A.; Egyptian artist; b. 25 April 1949, Cairo; d. of Mokhtar Madkour and Malak Salem; m. Mohamed Salmawy 1970; one s. one d.; ed. Cairo Univ., American Univ., Cairo; fmrly. econ. expert for Industrial Devt. Centre for Arab States; professional artist 1981–; numerous solo and collective exhbns.; represented in public and pvt. collections in Egypt and internationally. *Publication:* Egyptian Women and Artistic Creativity 1989. *Leisure interests:* travel, reading, music. *Address:* 9 Street 216 Digla, Maadi, Cairo 11742, Egypt. *Telephone:* (2) 352-2531. *Fax:* (2) 578-2631.

MÁDL, Ferenc, PH.D.; Hungarian politician and lawyer; b. 29 Jan. 1931, Bánd Co. Veszprém; s. of A. Mádl; m. 1955; one s.; ed. Univs. of Pécs and Eötvös Loránd Univ.; mem. Hungarian Acad. of Sciences, inst. for legal sciences and state admin. 1973; Dir. Inst. of Civil Law Disciplines, Eötvös Univ., Budapest 1978; head Dept. of the Law of Conflicts and Int. Economic Relations 1985; mem. Hungarian Acad. of Sciences 1987–; mem. Governing Council UNIDROIT 1989–; mem. European Acad. of Sciences and Art 1989–, European Acad., of Sciences 1990–, Int. Acad. of Commercial Law, Inst. of Int. Law 1991–; Minister Without Portfolio 1990–92, of Culture and Educ. 1992–94; cand. for Presidency June 1995. *Publications:* author of 14 books on law of int. econ. relations, int. investment law, EEC law, etc. *Address:* 1364 Budapest, Egyetem tér 1-3, Hungary. *Telephone:* 36 (1) 266-6486.

MADONNA (Madonna Louise Veronica Ciccone); American singer and actress; b. 16 Aug. 1958, Detroit; d. of Sylvio Ciccone and Madonna Ciccone; m. Sean Penn 1985 (divorced 1989); one d. by Carlos Leon; ed. Alvin Ailey Dance School; has sold over 55 million records worldwide (20 million albums, 35 million singles); toured U.K. 1983, 1987, France 1987, Fed. Germany 1987; appeared in play Speed-the-Plow 1988; Commercial for Pepsi Cola 1989; Vice-Pres. ICA, London; *Albums:* Madonna—the First Album, Like a Virgin, True Blue, You Can Dance, I'm Breathless 1990, The Immaculate Collection 1990, Erotica 1992, Bedtime Stories 1994, Something to Remember 1995, A Ray of Light. *Singles include:* Everybody, Burning Up, Holiday, Borderline, Like a Virgin, Material Girl, Into the Groove, Dress You Up, Crazy for You, Papa Don't Preach, La Isla Bonita, Who's That Girl?, True Blue, Like a Prayer, Justify My Love 1990, Erotica 1992, Bedtime Stories 1994, Frozen 1998; *Films include:* Desperately Seeking Susan, Shanghai Surprise, Who's That Girl?, Bloodhounds of Broadway, Dick Tracy 1989, Soap-dish 1990, Shadows and Fog 1991, A League of Their Own, In Bed with Madonna 1991, Body of Evidence 1992, Snake Eyes 1994, Dangerous Game 1994, Evita 1996, Four Rooms 1996; The Girlie Show 1994. *Publication:* Sex 1992. *Address:* Maverick Records, 800 Beverly Hills Boulevard, Los Angeles, CA 90048, U.S.A..

MADRID HURTADO, Miguel de la (see De La Madrid Hurtado, Miguel).

MADSEN, Ib Henning, PH.D.; Danish professor of mathematics; b. 12 April 1942, Copenhagen; s. of Henning Madsen and Gudrun (née Davids-Thomsen) Madsen; m. 1st Benedicte Rechnitzer 1963 (divorced 1982); m. 2nd Ulla Lykke Jorgensen 1984; two s.; ed. Univ. of Copenhagen and Univ. of Chicago; Research Stipend Aarhus Univ. 1965–70; Research Instructor Univ. of Chicago 1971–72; Assoc. Prof. Aarhus Univ. 1971–83, Prof. of Math. 1983–; ed. Acta Mathematica 1988–; mem. Royal Danish Acad. of Sciences 1978, Inst. for Advanced Study, Princeton 1986–87; Rigmor and Carl Holst-Knudsen Science Prize 1982, Humboldt Research Award 1992. *Address:* Department of Mathematics, Aarhus University, 8000 Aarhus C. (Univ.); Vestervang 2, 222, 8000 Aarhus C, Denmark (Home). *Telephone:* 45-8942-3451 (Univ.); 4586-133905 (Home).

MADSEN, Mette; Danish fmr. politician and writer; b. 3 July 1924, Pandrup, north Jutland; d. of Holger Fruensgaard; a professional writer, including collections of poetry; Liberal M.P. 1971–87; mem. of Presidium Folketing 1981–84; Minister for Ecclesiastical Affairs 1984–88; Chair. Supervisory Cttee. Royal Theatre 1978–84, Cttee. for Culture and Information, N. Atlantic Council 1982–84. *Publications:* Og så er der Kaffe (political memoirs) 1992, I Anledning Af. (songs and poetry) 1994, Husk Nu at Neje (memoirs) 1997. *Address:* Blegdalsparken 53, 9000 Ålborg, Denmark.

MADSEN, Michael; American actor; b. 25 Sept. 1958, Chicago, Ill.; m. Jeannine Bisignano; one s.; began acting career at Steppenwolf Theatre, Chicago, appearing in plays including Of Mice and Men, A Streetcar Named Desire; appeared in Broadway production of A Streetcar Named Desire 1992. *Films:* Wargames (debut) 1983, The Natural, Racing with the Moon 1984, The Killing Time 1987, Shadows in the Storm, Iguana 1988, Blood Red 1989, Kill Me Again 1990, The Doors 1991, The End of Innocence 1991, Thelma and Louise 1991, Fatal Instinct 1992, Inside Edge 1992, Reservoir Dogs 1992, Straight Talk 1992, Almost Blue 1992, Free Willy 1993, A House in the Hills 1993, Money for Nothing 1993, Trouble Bound 1993, Wyatt Earp 1993, The Getaway 1994, Dead Connection 1994, Species, Free Willy II: The Adventure Home 1995, The Winner 1996, Red Line 1996, Mulholland Falls 1996, Man With A Gun 1996, The Last Days of Frankie the Fly 1996, Rough

Draft 1997, The Maker 1997, Donnie Brasco 1997, Catherine's Grove 1997, Papertrail 1997, The Girl Gets Moe 1997, Executive Target 1997, The Thief and the Stripper 1998, Supreme Sanction 1998, The Florentine 1998, Species II 1998. *TV:* (series) Our Family Honor 1985–86; (films) Special Bulletin 1983, War and Remembrance 1988, Montana 1990, Baby Snatcher 1992, Beyond the Law 1994. *Address:* c/o Grant and Tane, 9100 Wilshire Boulevard, Beverly Hills, CA 90212; c/o Michael Manchal, 9830 Wilshire Boulevard, Beverly Hills, CA 90212, U.S.A.

MADUNA, Penuell Mpapa, LL.D.; South African politician and lawyer; b. 29 Dec. 1952; m. Nompumelelo Cheryl Maduna; three c.; ed. Univ. of Zimbabwe, Univ. of Witwatersrand; worked in underground structures of ANC in 1970s, twice incarcerated and prosecuted; left S.A. 1980; fmr. Regional Admin. Sec. Tanzania, Office of Treasurer-Gen. of ANC; fmr. staff mem. and Legal Adviser, ANC HQ Lusaka, est. Dept. of Legal and Constitutional Affairs 1985, founder mem. Constitutional Cttee., participated in meetings with S.A. govt. and officials in 1980s and early 1990s leading to est. of Convention for a Democratic South Africa, mem. Negotiating Comm., now mem. Nat. Exec. Cttee.; M.P. Nat. Ass.; Minister of Mineral and Energy Affairs 1996–; Bd. mem. Faculty of Law, Univ. of Witwatersrand. *Publication:* Fundamental Rights in the New Constitution 1994 (co-author). *Leisure interests:* soccer, reading, debating. Bd. mem. Faculty of Law, University of Witwatersrand. 1996–. *Address:* Ministry of Mineral and Energy Affairs, Dutch Reformed Church Synod Centre, Cnr. Andries and Visagie Streets, Pretoria 0002; Private Bag X646, Pretoria 0001, South Africa (Office). *Telephone:* 12-322-8695. *Fax:* 12-322-8699.

MAEGAARD, Jan Carl Christian, DR.PHIL; Danish musicologist and composer; b. 14 April 1926, Copenhagen; s. of late Johannes H. Maegaard and Gerda Glahnson; m. Kirsten Offer Andersen 1973; two d.; ed. Royal Danish Conservatory and Univ. of Copenhagen; freelance musician 1949–56; music critic for various newspapers 1952–60; teacher of theory and music history, Royal Danish Conservatory 1953–58; Asst. Prof. Univ. of Copenhagen 1959, Assoc. Prof. 1961–71, Prof. 1971–96; Visiting Prof. State Univ. of New York at Stony Brook 1974; Prof. of Music. U.C.L.A. 1978–81; consultant to music dept. Danish State Radio 1962–78, Chief Consultant 1982–; Chair. Music Cttee. State Endowment for the Arts 1968–71; mem. Bd. Danish State Radio and Television 1970–74; mem. Danish and Norwegian Acads. *Compositions include:* Elegy of Equinox (for voice, cello and organ), Five Preludes (solo violin), Trio Serenade (piano trio), Chamber Concerto No. 2, Due tempi (for orchestra), Musica riservata I (string quartet), Musica riservata II (for reed quartet), Canon for three flutes, Labirinto I (for viola), Labirinto II (for guitar), Triptykon (for violin, string orchestra), Partita (for organ), Concerto for cello and orchestra, Partita for cello, Orchestration of Arnold Shoenberg's Variations on a Recitative for organ, Completion of J. S. Bach's Die Kunst der Fuge (for organ). *Publications:* Musikalsk Modernisme 1964, Studien zur Entwicklung des dodekaphonen Statzes bei Arnold Schönberg 1972, Praeludier til Musik af Schönberg 1976, Indføring i Romantisk Harmonik I-II 1980, 1986, Kuhlaus Kanons (with Gorm Busk) 1996; numerous articles. *Leisure interest:* playing the double bass. *Address:* Duevej 14, 6, 2000 Frederiksberg, Denmark. *Telephone:* 3888 0780.

MAEHLER, Herwig Gustav Theodor, PH.D., F.B.A.; German papyrologist; b. 29 April 1935, Berlin; s. of Ludwig Maehler and Lisa Maehler; m. Margaret Anderson 1963; two d.; ed. Katharineum, Lübeck and Univs. of Hamburg, Tübingen and Basle; British Council Scholarship, Oxford 1961–62; Research Asst. Dept. of Classics, Univ. of Hamburg 1962–63, Dept. of Manuscripts, Hamburg Univ. Library 1963–64; Keeper of Greek Papyri, Egyptian Museum, West Berlin 1964–79; Lecturer in Classics, Freie Universität Berlin 1975–79; Reader in Papyrology, Univ. Coll. London 1979–81, Prof. 1981–; Visiting Fellow, Inst. for Advanced Studies in the Humanities, Edinburgh 1977; Visiting Prof., Univs. of Urbino 1984, Bologna 1986, Bari 1988, Basle 1990, Budapest 1998; corresp. mem. German Archaeological Inst. *Publications:* Die Auffassung des Dichterberufs im frühen Griechentum bis zur Zeit Pindars 1963, Die Handschriften der S. Jacobi-Kirche Hamburg 1967, Urkunden römischer Zeit 1968, Papyri aus Hermupolis 1974, Die Lieder des Bakchylides (2 vols.) 1982, 1997; Greek Bookhands of the Early Byzantine Period (with G. Cavallo) 1987; editions of Bacchylides and Pindar. *Leisure interests:* chamber music (viola), horse riding (dressage). *Address:* Department of Greek and Latin, University College London, Gower Street, London, WC1E 6BT (Office); 2 Oswald Road, St. Albans, Herts., AL1 3AQ, England. *Fax:* 0171-209 2324 (Office).

MAFATLAL, Arvind N.; Indian industrialist; b. 27 Oct. 1923, Ahmedabad; s. of late Navinchandra Mafatlal and of Vijayalaxmi N.; m. Sushila A. Mafatlal; two s. one d.; ed. St. Xavier's High School and Sydenham Coll. of Commerce and Econs., Bombay; joined Mafatlal Group of Cos. 1941, Chair. 1955–; Dir. Tata Eng. and Locomotive Co. Ltd., and others; Chair. Nat. Organic Chem. Industries Ltd., Shri Sadguru Seva Sangh Trust; Trustee Bharatiya Agro-Industries Foundation, Uruli Kanchan, Employers' Del. to 43rd Session, ILO Conf.; mem. Durga Prasad Khaitan Memorial Gold Medal 1966, Business Leadership Award (Madras Man. Asscn.) 1971, Sir Jehangir Ghandy Medal for Industrial Peace (Xavier Labour Relations Inst.) 1979. *Leisure interest:* golf. *Address:* Mafatlal House, Backbay Reclamation, Bombay 400 020 (Office); 10 Altamount Road, Bombay 400 026, India (Home). *Telephone:* 202-6944 (Office); 386-8350 (Home). *Fax:* (22) 202-7750.

MAGA, Hubert Coutoucou; Benin politician; b. 10 Aug. 1916; ed. Ecole Normale de Gorée; headmaster of school at Nabitingou until 1951; Gen. Counsellor of Dahomey 1947; Grand Counsellor of Art 1948–57; Deputy for Dahomey to French Nat. Assembly 1951–58; Under-Sec. for Labour, Gaillard Cabinet; Minister of Labour in Dahomey 1958–59, Premier 1959–63, Pres. 1960–63; under restriction 1963–65; Head of State, also Minister of Interior and of Defence 1970–72; under house arrest 1972; released April 1981; mem. Dahomeyan Democrat Group; awards incl. Grand-Croix, Légion d'honneur, Mérite Social and Etoile Noire de Bénin. *Address:* Cotonou, Benin.

MAGAÑA BORJA, Alvaro; Salvadorean politician; b. 1926; fmr. lawyer and economist; Dir. state mortgage bank for 17 years; worked abroad for OAS; Sec. of State for Housing 1960s; Pres. of El Salvador 1982–84.

MAGARIÑOS, Carlos Alfredo, M.B.A.; Argentinian international civil servant; b. 1962; ed. Nat. Univ. of Buenos Aires; analyst, Office of Strategic Planning and Foreign Trade, Banco Ciudad de Buenos Aires 1984–86; joined Ministry of Economy 1992, Under-Sec. of State for Industry 1992–93, Sec. of State for Mining and Industry 1993–96; Econ. and Trade Rep. of Argentina, Washington, D.C., U.S.A. 1996–97; rank of Amb. 1996; Dir.-Gen. UNIDO 1997–. *Publications:* El Rol del Estado en la Política Industrial de los 90; articles on econ. and industrial issues. *Address:* United Nations Industrial Development Organization, Vienna International Centre, P.O. Box 300, 1400 Vienna, Austria.

MAGAZINER, Henry J., F.A.I.A.; American architect and architectural historian; b. 13 Sept. 1911, Philadelphia; s. of Louis Magaziner and Selma Magaziner; m. Reba Henken 1938; one s. one d.; ed. Univ. of Pennsylvania, Stevens Inst. of Tech.; fmrly. in practice with Day and Zimmermann Inc., Albert Kahn, Wright Aeronautical Corpn., Louis Magaziner; has worked on own account for numerous public, institutional and commercial orgs.; Nat. Park Service Regional Historical Architect 1972–87; pvt. practice 1956–72, 1987–; responsible for historic buildings' preservation clauses in the standard building codes; mem. A.I.A. Coll. of Fellows and Comm. on Historic Resources; Founder, Past Pres. Ebenezer Maxwell Mansion (Victorian Museum); mem. Editorial Bd. Soc. of Architectural Historians 55-vol. Buildings of the United States; Presidential Award for Good Design for the Govt.. *Address:* 1504 South Street, Philadelphia, PA 19146, U.S.A. *Telephone:* (215) 545-1076. *Fax:* (215) 545-8397.

MAGEE, Bryan, M.A.; British author and broadcaster; b. 12 April 1930, London; s. of Frederick Magee and Sheila Lynch; m. Ingrid Söderlund 1954 (deceased); one d.; ed. Christ's Hosp., Lycée Hôche, Versailles, Keble Coll. Oxford and Yale Univ.; lecturer in Philosophy, Balliol Coll. Oxford 1970–71; Visiting Fellow, All Souls Coll. Oxford 1973–74; mem. Parl. for Leyton 1974–83; Pres. Critics Circle of G.B. 1983–84; Hon. Sr. Research Fellow, King's Coll. London 1984–94, Visiting Prof. 1994–; Hon. Fellow, Queen Mary Coll. London 1988–; Fellow, Queen Mary and Westfield Coll. London 1989–; Visiting Fellow Wolfson Coll. Oxford 1991–94, New Coll. Oxford 1995, Merton Coll. Oxford 1998; Hon. Fellow Keble Coll. Oxford 1994–; mem. Arts Council of G.B., and Chair. Music Panel 1993–94; Silver Medal, Royal TV Soc. *Publications:* The New Radicalism 1962, The Democratic Revolution 1964, Aspects of Wagner 1968 (revised edn. 1988), Modern British Philosophy 1971, Popper 1973, Facing Death 1977, Men of Ideas 1978, The Philosophy of Schopenhauer 1983, 1997, The Great Philosophers 1987, On Blindness 1995 (re-issued as Sight Unseen 1998), Confessions of a Philosopher 1997, The Story of Philosophy 1998. *Leisure interests:* music, theatre. *Address:* 12 Falkland House, Marloes Road, London, W8 5LF, England. *Telephone:* 0171-937 1210.

MAGISTRETTI, Vico; Italian architect, industrial designer and interior decorator; b. 6 Oct. 1920, Milan; s. of Piergiulio and Luisa Tosi Magistretti; one s. one d.; ed. Ginnasio Liceo Parini and Politecnico di Milano; industrial design for Artemide, Cassina S.p.A., Habitat-Conran, Knoll Int., Azucena, La Rinascente, De Padova I.C.F., Montina Fratelli, Oca Brazil, Asko Finlandia, Poggi, Carrara & Matta, Spalding (U.S.A.), Rosenthal-Selb (G.D.R.), Fiat Auto S.p.A. etc.; lectures at Venice architectural school, Barcelona Coll. of Architecture, Vienna, Toronto, Frankfurt, London, Belfast etc.; has participated in numerous exhbns. *Publications:* articles in journals, magazines and newspapers. *Leisure interest:* golf. *Address:* Via Conservatorio 20, Milan, Italy. *Telephone:* 702.964.

MAGLOIRE, Gen. Paul; Haitian politician and police officer; b. 1907; ed. Cap Haiti High School; taught at Lycée National Philippe Guerrier, Cap Haiti 1929–30; entered army as cadet 1931; Lieut. 1931; Head of Mil. School 1934; Asst. District Commdr., Cap Haiti 1935–37; Maj. 1938; District Commdr. 1938–41; Chief of Police, Port-au-Prince, and Commdr. of Palace Guard 1944; mem. provisional Mil. Govt. and Minister of Interior 1946 and 1950; Pres. of Haiti 1950–56; Orders of Honneur et Mérite, Brevet de Mérite, etc. *Address:* living in U.S.A.

MAGNÉLI, Arne, FIL.DR.; Swedish chemist; b. 6 Dec. 1914, Stockholm; s. of Agge and Valborg (née Hultman) Magnéli; m. Barbro Wigh 1946 (died 1989); two s. one d.; ed. Univs. of Stockholm and Uppsala; Research Asst., Univ. of Uppsala 1941–50; Docent in Chemistry 1950–53; Assoc. Prof. of Inorganic and Physical Chemistry 1953–61, Univ. of Stockholm, Prof. of Inorganic Chemistry 1961–80, Prof. Emer. 1981–; mem. Exec. Cttee., Int. Union of Crystallography 1972–81, Pres. 1975–78; Sec. Nobel Cttee. for Physics 1966–73, for Chemistry 1966–86, mem. Swedish Natural Science

Research Council 1965–71; mem. Bd. of Dirs., Nobel Foundation 1973–85; Chair. Swedish Nat. Cttee. for Chemistry 1984–95; mem. Royal Swedish Acad. of Sciences, Royal Soc. of Sciences, Uppsala (Pres. 1990–91); Foreign mem. French Acad. of Sciences 1989; Dr. h.c. (Univ. Pierre et Marie Curie, Paris) 1988; Bergstedt Prize 1947, Bjurzon Prize 1950, Norblad-Ekstrand Medal 1954, Bror Holmberg Medal 1980, Gregori Aminoff Prize 1989, Gold Medal of French Soc. for High Temperature and Ceramics Research (Soc. des Hautes Températures et des Refractaires) 1990, co-recipient 1992 Ettore Majorana-Erice Science for Peace Prize 1994; Commdr. Ordre nat. du Mérite; Officier des Palmes Académiques. *Publications:* research articles in chemical crystallography and solid state inorganic chemistry. *Address:* Arrhenius Laboratory, University of Stockholm, 106 91 Stockholm; Royal Academy of Sciences, 104 05 Stockholm; Öregrundsgatan 14, 115 28 Sweden (Home). *Telephone:* (08) 16 12 55; 673 95 00 (Univ.); (018) 51 86 50 (Home). *Fax:* (08) 15 26 99.

MAGNUSSON, Magnus, M.A., F.R.S.E., F.R.S.A., F.S.A.; Icelandic writer and broadcaster; b. 12 Oct. 1929; s. of the late Sigursteinn Magnusson and Ingibjorg Sigurdardottir; m. Mamie Baird 1954; one s. three d. (and one s. deceased); ed. Edinburgh Acad. and Jesus Coll., Oxford; Asst. Ed. Scottish Daily Express then The Scotsman; presenter various TV and radio programmes including: Chronicle, Mastermind, Pebble Mill at One, BC, The Archaeology of the Bible Lands, Tonight, Cause for Concern, All Things Considered, Living Legends, Vikings!, Birds for All Seasons; Ed. The Bodley Head Archaeologies, Popular Archaeology 1979–80; Chair. Ancient Monuments Bd. for Scotland 1981–89, Cairngorms Working Party 1991–93, N.C.C. for Scotland 1991–92, Scottish Nat. Heritage 1992–99; Rector Edin. Univ. 1975–78; mem. U.K. Cttee. for European Year of the Environment 1987, Bd. of Trustees Nat. Museums of Scotland 1985–89; Pres. R.S.P.B. 1985–90; Hon. Vice-Pres. Age Concern Scotland, R.S.S.P.C.C.; F.S.A. Scot. 1974; Hon. Fellow (Oxford) 1990; Hon. F.R.I.A.S. 1987; F.R.S.G.S. 1991; Dr. h.c. (Edin.) 1978; Hon. D.Univ. (York) 1981, (Paisley) 1993, Hon. D.Litt. (Strathclyde) 1993, (Napier) 1994; Iceland Media Award 1985, Silver Jubilee Medal 1977, Medlicott Medal 1989; Kt. of Order of the Falcon (Iceland) 1975, Commdr. 1986; Hon. K.B.E. *Publications:* Introducing Archaeology 1972, Viking Expansion Westwards 1973, The Clacken and the Slate 1974, Hammer of the North (Norse mythology) 1976, BC, The Archaeology of the Bible Lands 1977, Landlord or Tenant?: A View of Irish History 1978, Iceland 1979, Vikings! Magnus on the Move 1980, Treasures of Scotland 1981, Lindisfarne: The Cradle Island 1984, Iceland Saga 1987. *Translations:* Icelandic sagas (with Hermann Pálsson) and works by Halldor Laxness and Samivel; contribs. to various historical and novelty books; introductions to numerous books on historical, geographical and cultural themes. *Edited* Echoes in Stone 1983, Reader's Digest Book of Facts 1985, Chambers Biographical Dictionary 1990, The Nature of Scotland 1991. *Leisure interests:* digging and delving. *Address:* Blairskaith House, Balmore-Torrance, Glasgow, G64 4AX, Scotland. *Telephone:* (01360) 620226.

MAGNUSSON, Thor Eyfeld; Icelandic state antiquary; b. 18 Nov. 1937, Hvammstangi; s. of Magnus Richardson and Sigridur Thordardottir; m. Maria V. Heiddal 1964; two s. one d.; ed. Univ. of Uppsala; Asst. Curator, Nat. Museum 1964, State Antiquary 1968–. *Address:* National Museum, Sudurgata 41, 101 Reykjavík (Office); Bauganes 26, 101 Reykjavík, Iceland (Home). *Telephone:* 530 2200. *Fax:* 530 2201.

MAGOMEDOV, Magomedali Magomedovich; Russian/Dagestan politician; b. 1930, Levashi, Dagestan Autonomous Repub.; m.; two c.; ed. Dagestan State Pedagogical Inst., Dagestan Inst. of Agric.; teacher, Dir. Levashi secondary school, then Head Levashi Dept. of Nat. Educ. 1949–57; Chair. Levashi Kolkhoz 1957–66; Head Agric. Production unit Levashi Dist. 1966–69; Chair. Levashi Dist. Exec. Cttee. 1969–70; First Sec. Levashi Dist. CP Cttee. 1970–75; Head Div. of Agric. Dagestan Regional CP Cttee. 1975–79; Deputy Chair., Chair. Council of Ministers Dagestan Autonomous Repub. 1979–87; Chair. Presidium Supreme Soviet Dagestan Autonomous Repub. 1987–94; Chair. State Council (Head Repub. of Dagestan) 1994–; mem. Russian Council of Fed. 1993–. *Address:* House of Government, Lenina pl., 167005 Makhachkala, Dagestan, Russia (Office). *Telephone:* (8722) 67 30 59, 67 30 60 (Office).

MAGOWAN, Peter Alden, M.A.; American business executive; b. 5 April 1942, New York; s. of Robert Anderson and Doris Merrill Magowan; m. 1st Jill Tarlau (divorced 1982); m. 2nd Deborah Johnston 1982; three d. from 1st marriage; ed. Stanford Univ., Oxford Univ., Johns Hopkins School of Advanced Int. Studies; Store Man., Washington, D.C., Safeway Stores, 1968–70, Dist. Man., Houston, Tex. 1970, Retail Operations Man., Phoenix, Ariz. 1971–72, Div. Man., Tulsa, Okla. 1973–76, Man., Int. Div., Toronto, Canada 1976–78, Western Regional Man., San Francisco, Calif. 1978–79, Dir., Safeway Stores, Inc. 1979, Chair. of the Bd. 1980–, C.E.O. 1980–93, Pres. and C.O.O. 1988, also Chair. Exec. Cttee.; Pres., Man. Gen. Partner, San Francisco Giants Baseball Team 1993–; fmr. Dir. of U.S. Chamber of Commerce, The Hudson Inst., Pacific Gas and Electric Co., Food Marketing Inst.; Dir. Caterpillar, Chrysler Corpn.; mem. Advisory Council, Johns Hopkins School of Advanced Int. Studies; Trustee, Johns Hopkins Univ.. *Address:* San Francisco Giants, 3 Com Park, San Francisco, CA 94124; Safeway Stores Inc., 201 4th Street, Oakland, CA 94660, U.S.A. *Telephone:* (415) 891-3300.

MAGRI, Charles George; British boxer; b. 20 July 1956, Tunisia; s. of André and Rose (née Tonna) Magri; m. Jacqueline Britton 1979; one d.; ed. Cardinal Griffin Secondary School, Stepney, London; Amateur Boxing Asscn. (A.B.A.) light-flyweight champion 1974, A.B.A. flyweight champion 1975, 1976, 1977; rep. England and Great Britain; boxed in Olympic Games, 1976; professional boxer 1977–84; won vacant British flyweight title in third professional fight Dec. 1977 (new British record); won European title from Franco Udella May 1979, retained it v. Manuel Carrasco Dec. 1979, Giovanni Camputaro June 1980, Rodriguez Cal 1981 and 1982; world flyweight champion 1983; 29 professional fights, 27 wins. *Leisure interest:* helping schoolboy and junior boxers.

MAGRIS, Claudio; Italian journalist, writer and university professor; b. 10 April 1939, Trieste; s. of Duilio Magris and Pia de Grisogono Magris; m. Marisa Madieri 1964; two s.; ed. Univ. of Turin; lecturer in German Language and Literature, Univ. of Trieste 1968–70, Turin 1970–78, Trieste 1978–; mem. Deutsche Akademie für Sprache und Dichtung (Darmstadt), Österreichische Akademie der Wissenschaften, Accademia delle Scienze di Torino, Ateneo Veneto, Akademie der Wissenschaften (Göttingen); prizes and awards include: Debenedetti 1972, Val di Comino 1978, Goethe Medaille 1980, Aquileia 1983, Premiolino 1983, San Giusto d'Oro 1984, Musil Medaille der Stadt Klagenfurt 1984, Bagutta 1987, Accademia dei Lincei 1987, Marotta 1987, Città di Modena 1987, Antico Fattore 1988, Juan Carlos I 1989; Osterreichisches Ehrenkreuz für Wissenschaft und Kunst (First Class). *Publications:* Il Mito absburgico nella letteratura austriaca moderna 1963, 1988, Wilhelm Heinse 1968, Lontano da dove. Joseph Roth e la tradizione ebraico-orientale 1971, Dietro le parole 1978, Itaca e oltre 1982, Trieste. Un'identità di frontiera 1982, 1987, L'anello di Clarisse 1984, Illazioni su una sciabola 1984, Danubio 1986 (trans. in numerous languages), Stadelmann 1988; numerous essays and book reviews in Corriere della Sera and other European newspapers and periodicals; trans. Ibsen, Kleist, Schnitzler, Büchner. *Address:* Via Carpaccio 2, Trieste, Italy. *Telephone:* (040) 305428.

MAGUIRE, Adrian Edward, B.PHIL., M.A., F.S.A.; Irish jockey; b. 29 April 1971; s. of Joseph Maguire and of the late Philomena Maguire; m. Sabrina Maguire 1995; one d.; ed. Kilmessan Nat. School, Trim Vocational School; champion pony race rider 1986, champion point-to-point rider 1990–91, champion conditional jockey 1991–92. *Winner of following races:* Cheltenham Gold Cup, Irish Grand Nat. (youngest ever winning jockey), Galway Plate, Imperial Cup, Greenalls Gold Cup, Queen Mother Champion Chase, King George VI Chase, Triumph Hurdle and Cathcort Chase; holds records for most point-to-point winners in a season, most winners in a season for a conditional jockey (71) 1991–92. *Leisure interests:* squash, watching television. *Address:* c/o The Jockey Club (Jockey Section), 42 Portman Square, London, W1H 0EM, England.

MAGYAR, Balint, PH.D.; Hungarian sociologist and politician; b. 1952, Budapest; m. Róza Hodosán; one d.; ed. Eötvös Loránd Univ. of Budapest; Research Fellow Inst. of World Econ., Hungarian Acad. of Sciences, Financial Research Ltd. 1988–90; involved in dissident political activities from 1979; founding mem. Alliance of Free Democrats (SZDSZ); M.P. 1990–, mem. Parl. Cttee. on Local Govt. Issues 1990–92, on European Integration Issues 1992–, Vice-Chair. Parl. Cttee. on Nat. Security 1994–; Minister of Culture and Educ. 1996–; dir. Hungarian Stories (documentary film); mem. Alliance of Free Democrats Exec. Bd., Coalition Council; awarded Ferenc Erdei Prize 1986 (for Dunaapát), Special Prize, Critics' Prize Budapest Film Festival 1988 (for Hungarian Stories). *Publication:* Dunaapát 1944–58 (sociography of a Hungarian village). *Address:* Múvelődési és Közoktatási Minisztérium, Budapest 1055, Szalay u. 10–14, Hungary. *Telephone:* 312-6417.

MAHACHI, Moven Enock, M.P.; Zimbabwean politician and farmer; b. 13 June 1948, Rusape; s. of Prisca Mahachi and Enock Mahachi; m. Rashiwe Mahachi 1970; one s. three d.; ed. Univ. of London, Univ. of South Africa; Vice-Chair. Cold Comfort Farm Soc. 1970–71; Man. Dir. Nyafonu Devt. Co. 1971–74; serving 15-year sentence as political prisoner 1974–79; Z.A.N.U. (PF) Prov. Admin. Manicaland Prov. 1979–80; Deputy Minister of Land Resettlement and Rural Devt. 1980–82, Minister 1982–85; M.P. for Manicaland Prov. 1980–85, for Makoni West and mem. Cen. Cttee. 1985–; Minister of Land, Agriculture and Rural Resettlement 1985–88, of Home Affairs 1988, of Defence 1992–; Deputy Sec. for Production, Z.A.N.U. (PF) Politburo. *Leisure interests:* soccer, farming, squash, hunting, fishing. *Address:* Ministry of Defence, Munhumutapa Building, Samora Machel Avenue, Private Bag 7713, Causeway, Harare, Zimbabwe.

MAHARAJ, Mac, (Sathyandranath Ragunanan) B.ADMIN.; South African politician; b. 22 April 1935, Newcastle; m. Zarina Maharaj; two c.; ed. St. Oswald's High School; Ed. New Age 1956; lived in U.K. 1957–61, founding mem. British Anti-Apartheid Movement; mem. Umkhonto Wesizwe (ANC's armed wing) 1961, underwent mil. training in G.D.R. 1961–62; returned to S.A. 1962; sentenced to 12 years' imprisonment Dec. 1964, served prison sentence on Robben Island 1965–76; left S.A. 1976; with ANC H.Q., Lusaka, Zambia, Sec. Underground Section 1977; mem. Revolutionary Council 1978, Politico-Mil. Council 1985; mem. ANC Negotiation Cttee., Political Cttee. 1984, Nat. Exec. Council 1985–90, 1991–, Nat. Working Cttee.; Commdr. Operation Vula, S.A. 1988–90; mem. Political Bureau and Cen. Cttee. 1990; with Codesa Secr.; Jt. Sec. Transitional Exec. Council 1994; Minister of Transport, Govt. of Nat. Unity 1994–99. *Address:* c/o Private Bag X193 Pretoria 0001, South Africa.

MAHAT, Ram S., M.A., PH.D.; Nepalese politician; b. 1 Jan. 1951, Nuwakot; s. of Tol Kumari Mahat; m. Roshana Mahat; one s. one d.; ed. Tribhuban Univ., Gokhale Inst. of Politics and Econs., Poona, India, School of Int. Service, American Univ.; Asst. Resident Rep. UNDP, Islamabad 1989–90; econ. adviser to Prime Minister of Nepal 1991–92; Vice-Chair. Nat. Planning Comm. 1991–94; M.P. from Nuwakot Dist. 1994–; Minister of Finance 1995–. *Publications:* Industrial Financing in Nepal, numerous articles on nat. and int. econ. issues. *Leisure interests:* social service, reading books. *Address:* Ministry of Finance, Bagdurbar, Kathmandu (Office); Bansbari, Kathmandu, Nepal (Home). *Telephone:* (1) 259809 (Office); (1) 373132 (Home). *Fax:* (1) 259831 (Office); (1) 372356 (Home).

MAHATHIR BIN MOHAMED, Dr.; Malaysian politician; b. 20 Dec. 1925, Alur Setar, Kedah; m. Dr. Siti Hasmah binti Haji Mohd Ali 1956; three s. two d.; ed. Sultan Abdul Hamid Coll. and Univ. of Malaya in Singapore; Medical Officer, Kedah, Langkawi and Perlis 1953–57; private practice 1957–64; mem. UMNO (now Umno Baru) Supreme Council 1965–69, 1972– (Pres. 1981–), mem. Supreme Council 1972–; mem. House of Reps. for Kota Setar Selatan 1964–69, for Kubang Pasu 1974–; mem. Senate 1973; Chair. Food Industries of Malaysia Sdn. Bhd. 1973; Minister of Educ. 1974–77, of Trade and Industry 1977–81, of Defence 1981–86, of Home Affairs Oct. 1986–, of Justice 1987, of Natural and Rural Devt.; Deputy Prime Minister 1976–81, Prime Minister of Malaysia July 1981–. *Publication:* The Malay Dilemma 1969, The Way Forward 1998. *Address:* Prime Minister's Department, Kuala Lumpur, Malaysia. *Telephone:* (3) 2321957. *Fax:* (3) 2329227.

MAHAYNI, Mohammad Khaled al-; PH.D.; Syrian politician and economist; b. 30 May 1943, Damascus; s. of Salim al-Mahayni; m. Falak Sakkal 1966; two s. two d.; ed. Damascus Univ.; various public financial and econ. appts. 1961–70; auditor 1970–77; Dir. of Public Debt, Ministry of Finance 1977–79, of Computerized Data Processing 1979–80, of Public Enterprises 1981–84; Deputy Minister of Finance 1984–87, Minister 1987–; Govt. of IBRD 1987–; Prof. Damascus Univ. 1992–. *Publications:* Methodology of the General Budget of the State in the Syrian Arab Republic 1984, Supplementary Policies for Financial Planning 1985, Government Accounting 1996, Public Finance and Tax Legislation 1999. *Leisure interests:* reading and computing. *Address:* Ministry of Finance, P.O. Box 13136, Jule Jammal Street, Damascus, Syria. *Telephone:* (11) 2239624. *Fax:* (11) 2224701.

MAHBUBANI, Kishore; Singaporean diplomatist; b. 24 Oct. 1948, Singapore; s. of Mohandas Mahbubani; m. Anne King Markey 1985; two s. one d.; ed. Univ. of Singapore and Dalhousie Univ., Canada; joined Ministry of Foreign Affairs 1971, Deputy Dir. 1979–82, Deputy Sec. 1989–93, Perm. Sec. 1993–; Chargé d'affaires to Cambodia 1973–74; Counsellor at Singapore Embassy in Malaysia 1976–79; mem. of Singapore dels. to several sessions of UN Gen. Ass. and int. confs. 1979–83; Deputy Chief at Washington D.C. Embassy 1982–84; Perm. Rep. of Singapore to UN, New York (concurrently High Commr. in Canada and Amb. to Mexico) 1984–89; Dean, Civil Service Coll. 1993–96; Perm. Rep. to UN 1998–. *Leisure interests:* golf, jogging. *Address:* 231 East 51st Street, New York, NY 10022, U.S.A. *Telephone:* (212) 826-0840. *Fax:* (212) 826-2964.

MAHDI, Sadiq Al (since 1978 known as **Sadiq Abdul Rahman);** Sudanese politician; b. 1936; great grandson of Imam Abdul-Rahman El Mahdi, s. of late Siddik El Mahdi; ed. Comboni Coll., Khartoum and St. John's Coll., Oxford; Leader, Umma Mahdist (now New Nat. Umma) Party 1961–; Prime Minister 1966–67, 1986–89; overthrown in coup June 1989, arrested July 1989, released and put under house arrest Nov. 1989; Minister of Defence 1986–89; arrested on a charge of high treason 1969; exiled April 1970; returned to Sudan and arrested Feb. 1972, released April 1974; exiled 1974–77; led unsuccessful coup against fmr. Pres. Nimeri July 1976, returned to Sudan Sept 1977; reconciliation with Pres. Nimeri 1977; mem. Cttee. Sudanese Socialist Union (SSU) 1978–79; mem. Nat. Ass. 1986–89; led mediation mission in U.S. hostages in Iran Crisis Jan. 1980; Visiting Fellow St. Antony's Coll., Oxford 1983; returned to prison Sept. 1983, released Dec. 1984; granted amnesty May 1991; arrested on charges of conspiring against mil. govt. June 1994; rearrested May 1995; escaped from house arrest Dec. 1996; in Eritrea 1996–. *Publication:* Problems of the South Sudan.

MAHDI, Salah el-, PH.D.; Tunisian flautist and composer; b. 9 Feb. 1925, Tunis; ed. Rashidia Inst., Zituna Univ., Inst. of Admin. Tunis and Univ. of Poitiers; teacher of music, Rashidia Inst. 1943; Dir. Rashidia Inst. 1949; Judge, Law Courts of Tunis 1951; fmr. Dir. Dept. of Fine Arts, Ministry of Educ.; participated in setting-up of Nat. Acad. of Music, Dance and Dramatic Art; Head of Direction of Music and Folk Art, Ministry of Culture 1961; later Pres. Nat. Cultural Cttee. and Pres. Nat. Cttee. of Music; f. Nat. Troup of Popular Arts 1962; set up Tunisian Symphony Orchestra 1962, Nat. Soc. for Presrvation of Koran, Nat. School of Koranic Intoned Psalms; participant at numerous UNESCO and other int. congresses; founding mem. Int. Inst. of Comparative Music, Berlin; Pres. World Org. of Folk Arts and Traditions, Vienna; has held many other int. musical and cultural appts.; mem. Soc. des Auteurs, Compositeurs et Editions de Musique (SACEM) now Hon. mem.; more than 600 compositions including classical and folk songs, oriental and Western instrumental music, four nubas, several muwashahs, bashrafs, symphonic poems, chamber music and pieces for piano, flute, violin and harp. *Publications:* many musical, historical and literary works on Arab music including a compilation of Tunisian musical heritage; radio and stage plays. *Address:* 22 rue Brasil, Tunis, Tunisia.

MAHDI AL TAJIR, Mohamed; Dubai diplomatist and administrator; b. 26 Dec. 1931, Bahrain; m. Zohra Al-Tajir 1956; five s. one d.; ed. Bahrain Govt. School and Preston Grammar School, Lancs., England; Department of Port and Customs, Govt. of Bahrain, Dir. 1955–63; Dir. Dept. of His Highness the Ruler's Affairs and Petroleum Affairs March 1963–; Dir. Nat. Bank of Dubai Ltd. 1963–; Dir. Dubai Petroleum Co. April 1963–; Dir. Dubai Nat. Air Travel Agency Jan. 1966–; Dir. Qatar-Dubai Currency Bd. Oct 1965–73; Chair. South Eastern Dubai Drilling Co. April 1968–; Dir. Dubai Dry Dock Co. 1973–; Amb. of the United Arab Emirates to U.K. 1972–82, 1983–86, also accred. to France 1972–77; Hon. Citizen of State of Texas, U.S.A. 1963. *Address:* P.O. Box 207, Dubai, United Arab Emirates.

MAHELE BOKOUNGO LIEKO, Gen.; Democratic Republic of the Congo army officer; joined Zairean army, involved in numerous conflicts in Zaire, also in Zairean action in Rwanda 1990; fmr. Chief of Staff, Zaire Armed Forces (F.A.Z.), reappointed Dec. 1996; removed when Mobutu Govt. overthrown May 1997.

MAHER, Terence Anthony; British bookseller and publisher; b. 5 Dec. 1935, Manchester; s. of late Herbert Maher and Lillian Maher; m. Barbara Grunbaum 1960; three s.; ed. Xaverian Coll., Manchester; Controller, Carborundum Co. Ltd. 1961–69; Dir. Corp. Finance, First Nat. Finance Corpn. 1969–72; f. Pentos PLC 1972, Chair., C.E.O. –1993; Chair. and C.E.O. Dillons Bookstores 1977–93; Athena Int. 1980–93, Ryman 1987–93; Chair. The Chalford Publishing Co. Ltd. 1994–98, Maher Booksellers Ltd. 1995–, Race Dynamics Ltd. 1998–; Founder Trustee of Liberal Democrats 1988; mem. Advisory Council on Libraries 1997–98; Fellow of the Chartered Asscn. of Certified Accountants. *Publications:* (jointly) Counterblast 1965, Effective Politics 1966, Against My Better Judgement (autobiog.) 1994. *Leisure interests:* skiing, tennis, walking, reading, bridge. *Address:* 33 Clarence Terrace, Regent's Park, London, NW1 4RD; The Old House, Whichford, nr. Shipston on Stour, Warwicks., CV36 5PG, England. *Telephone:* 0171-723 4254 (London); (01608) 684 614 (Whichford).

MAHER ALI, Abdel Moneim; Egyptian biologist and business executive; b. 9 March 1922, Dammanhour; s. of Ali Elsayed Shehata and Nagia M. Manaā; m. Fardous Abbas Abdelal 1948; two s.; ed. Cairo Univ., Univ. Coll. London, Ein Shams Univ.; Founder, Gen. Sec. Egyptian Youth Hostel Assoc. 1955–1970; Dir Cen. Agric. Pesticide Lab. UNDP Project 1963–69; Head Plant Protection Dept. Assiut Univ. 1970, now Emer. Prof.; Gen. Sec. Egyptian Zoological Soc., Egyptian Asscn. for Conservation of Nature and Natural Resources, Egyptian Asscn. for Environment Care, Egyptian Asscn. for Medicinal Plants 1975–; Founder then Consultant, Wady Elassiuty Protected Area 1980–94; Pres. ARADIS Co. S.A.E., Arab. Co. Environment Disinfection S.A.E. Co. 1983–; now Chief Ed. Egyptian Journal for Natural Resources and Wildlife. Awards include: Conservation Merit Award, World Wildlife Fund, Science and Arts 1st Class, Order of the Repub. 5th, 3rd and 2nd. *Publications include:* textbook on pest control, articles in scientific periodicals. *Leisure interests:* travel, sight-seeing, archaeological tours. *Address:* 45 Jule Gamal Street, Agouza; P.O. Box 318, Dokki, Gizah (Office); 50 Wizaret El Ziraā Street, 12th Floor, Dokki, Gizah, Egypt. *Telephone:* 202-346-2029 (Office). *Fax:* 202-346-2029.

MAHFUZ, Nagib; Egyptian author; b. 11 Dec. 1911, Gamaliya, Cairo; m. Attiyah-Allah; c.; ed. Univ. of Cairo; civil servant 1934; successively with Univ. of Cairo, Ministry of Waqfs, Dept. of Arts and Censorship Bd.; fmr Dir.-Gen., then Adviser, Cinema Org. of Egypt; contrib. to Al Ahram; State Prize for 1st vol. Bain al-Kasrain 1957, Nobel Prize for Literature 1988. *Publications:* novels: Khan al Khalili 1946, Midaq Alley 1947, The Castle of Desire (Vol. I) 1956, Between the Two Castles (Vol. II) 1957, The Sugar Bowl (Vol. III) 1957 (trilogy Bain al-Kasrain), The Thief and the Dogs 1961, Quails in Autumn 1962, The Road 1964, The Beggar 1965, Gossip by the Nile 1966, Miramar 1967, Children of Gebelani (novel) 1980, High Mile Ribbon 1988, Sons of our District 1989, Palace Walk 1990, Palace of Desire 1992, Sugar Street 1992, The Journey of Ibn Fattouma 1992, Adrift on the Nile 1993, The Harafish 1993, Arabian Nights and Days 1995, The Day The Leader was Killed 1997, Akhenaton: Dweller in Truth 1998; Short story collections: The Whisper of Madness 1938, God's World 1963, At the Sign of the Black Cat 1969, Under the Umbrella 1969, A Story Without Beginning or End 1971, Mirrors (Contemporary History) 1972. *Address:* American University in Cairo Press, 113 Sharia Kasr El Aini, Cairo; 172 Nile Street, Agouza, Cairo, Egypt.

MAHGOUB, Mohammed Ahmed; Sudanese politician and lawyer; b. 1908; ed. Gordon Coll. and Khartoum School of Law; practising lawyer; fmr. mem. Legis. Assembly; accompanied Umma Party Del. to UN 1947; mem. Constitution Amendment Comm.; non-party candidate in Gen. Election 1954; Leader of the Opposition 1954–56; Minister of Foreign Affairs 1956–58, 1964–65, Prime Minister 1965–66, 1967–69; practising solicitor 1958–64. *Publications:* Democracy on Trial 1974, and several vols. of poetry (in Arabic). *Address:* 60C Prince's Gate, Exhibition Road, London, S.W.7, England.

MAHINDRA, Keshub, B.SC.; Indian business executive; b. 9 Oct. 1923, Simla; s. of late Kailash Chandra Mahindra and Savitri Mahindra; m. Sudha Y. Varde 1956; three d.; ed. Univ. of Pennsylvania, U.S.A.; Chair. Mahindra and Mahindra Ltd., Mahindra Ford India Ltd., Otis Elevator Co. (India) Ltd., Kema Services (Int.) Pvt. Ltd.; Dir. Bombay Dyeing and Mfg. Co. Ltd., Bombay Burmah Trading Corpn. Ltd., Tata Iron and Steel Co. Ltd., Tata Chemicals Ltd., Housing Devt. Finance Corpn. Ltd. (now Vice-Chair.), The

Atul Products Ltd., Mahindra Ugine Steel Co. Ltd., Baring Peacock Fund Ltd., Guernsey, Infrastructure Leasing & Financial Services Ltd., Tata Trustee Co. Ltd. etc.; Pres. Asscn. of Indian Automobile Mfrs. 1964–65, Bombay Chamber of Commerce and Industry 1966–67, Assoc. Chamber of Commerce and Industry 1969–70, Maharashtra Econ. Devt. Council 1969–70; Chair. Indian Council of Trade Fairs and Exhbns. 1964–69, Indian Soc. of Advertisers 1968–71; mem. Apex Advisory Council of Assoc. Chambers of Commerce and Industry of India, Bd. of Govs. Mahindra United World Coll. of India, Asia Soc. 1983–97; Vice-Pres. Nat. Soc. for Clean Cities; Chair. Nat. Asscn. for the Blind; Trustee Urban Design Research Inst.; Hon. Fellow All India Man. Asscn. 1990; Modi Enterprises Man of the Year Award 1980, Giants Int. Business Leadership Award 1972–82, Madras Man. Asscn. Business Leadership Award 1983, Companion of the British Inst. of Management, Indian Businessman of the Year 1989, Rotary Award 1992, Rashtra Bhushan Award 1993, Sri Ghandy Medal for Industrial Peace 1994, Rotary Vocational Excellence Award in the Field of Industry 1996; Chevalier Légion d'honneur 1987. *Leisure interests:* golf, tennis, photography, reading. *Address:* Mahindra & Mahindra Ltd., Gateway Building, Apollo Bunder, Bombay 400 001 (Office); St. Helen's Court, Pedder Road, Bombay 400 026, India (Home). *Telephone:* 2021031 (Office); 3804106 (Home). *Fax:* 2875489.

MAHLER, Halfdan, M.D.; Danish health official; b. 21 April 1923, Vivild; m. Dr. Ebba Fischer-Simonsen; two s.; ed. Univ. of Copenhagen; Planning Officer, Mass Tuberculosis Campaign, Ecuador 1950–51; joined WHO 1951; Sr. WHO Officer attached to Nat. TB Programme, India 1951–61; Visiting Prof., postgraduate medical schools, Rome and Prague 1961–; Chief Medical Officer, Tuberculosis Unit, WHO HQ, Geneva 1962–69, also Sec. to WHO Expert Panel on TB; Dir. Project Systems Analysis 1969; Asst. Dir.-Gen. WHO, responsible for Div. of Family Health, Div. of Org. of Health Services, Div. of Research in Epidemiology and Communication Science 1970–73, Dir.-Gen. 1973–88, Dir.-Gen. Emer. 1988–; Sec.-Gen. Int. Planned Parenthood Fed. (IPPF) 1989–95; Fellow, Royal Coll. of Physicians, London 1981; various hon. fellowships and memberships; Hon. LL.D. (Nottingham) 1975, (McMaster Univ., Hamilton, Canada) 1989, (Exeter) 1990, (Toronto) 1990; Hon. Dr. (Univ. des Sciences Sociales, Toulouse) 1977, Hon. Dr. of Public Health (Seoul Nat. Univ.) 1979, Hon. D.Sc. (Lagos) 1979, (Emory Univ., Atlanta, U.S.A.) 1989, (State Univ. of New York) 1990; Hon. M.D. (Karolinska Inst., Stockholm) 1977, (Warsaw Medical Acad.) 1980, (Charles Univ., Prague) 1982, (Mahidol Univ., Bangkok) 1982, (Aarhus Univ., Denmark) 1988, (Univ. of Copenhagen, Denmark) 1988, (Aga Khan Univ., Pakistan) 1989, (Newcastle upon Tyne) 1990; Dr. h.c. (Gand Univ., Belgium) 1983, (Nat. Univ. of Nicaragua) 1983, (Semmelweis Univ. of Medicine, Budapest, Hungary) 1987, D. Hum. Litt. h.c. (Mount Sinai School of Medicine, City Univ. of New York) 1989; numerous awards and decorations. *Publications:* several publications relating to the epidemiology and control of TB and to the utilization of operational research in health care delivery systems. *Leisure interests:* sailing, skiing. *Address:* 12 chemin du Pont-Céard, 1290 Versoix, Switzerland. *Telephone:* (022) 755 13 01. *Fax:* (022) 755 26 10.

MAHMAH, Mustapha el-, B.A.; Moroccan administrator and fmr. journalist; b. 1943, Asilah; s. of Abdeslam el-Mahmah and Fatima el-Mahmah; m. 1982; two s. one d.; ed. Univ. Mohamad V, Rabat; fmr. Ed.-in-Chief Revue al-Irchad; admin. Asscn. for Devt. of Assilah and various cultural asscns.; mem. Union of Moroccan Writers, Asscn. of Moroccan Sociologists; fmr. Gen. Sec. Moroccan Journalists' Asscn. *Publications:* La Femme Marocaine et le Souffisme au 17ème siècle 1975, L'historie du théâtre enfantine au Maroc 1986, Asila: Etude historique et social, Liaison du détroit de Gibraltar; several stories and sociological articles. *Leisure interests:* football, reading, writing, scientific research. *Address:* B.P. 4044, Hassan, Rabat, Morocco. *Telephone:* (07) 668-01.

MAHMUD, Air Vice-Marshal Sultan; Bangladeshi politician and army officer; b. Noakhali Dist.; s. of Nurul Huda; m.; two s.; ed. Armanitola Govt. High School, Dhaka, Pakistan Air Force Public School, Sargodha, U.S.A.F. Air Command and Staff Coll. and Academic Instructors' School, also Iran, U.S.S.R.; joined Pakistan Air Force 1960, served Liberation war, then Pioneer Commdr. First Bangladeshi air force Contingent, then engaged in reconstruction of Air Force, then Commdr. Air Force bases at Basher, Matiur Rahman, Air Force Acad., then at Air HQ, Dir. of Operations, then Asst. Chief-of-Staff; Chief of Air Staff 1981–87; apptd. Deputy Chief Martial Law Admin. 1981–86; Minister for Energy and Mineral Resources 1981–85, Minister for Industry, Commerce, Jute and Textiles –July 1985, for Industry 1985–86; Bir Uttam. *Leisure interest:* football. *Address:* c/o Ministry of Commerce and Industries, Shilpa Bhaban, Motijheel C/A, Dhaka, Bangladesh.

MAHOMED, Ismail, B.A., LL.B.; South African judge; b. 25 July 1931, Pretoria; s. of Hajee Mahomed and Khatoon Mahomed; m. Hawa Bava 1956; ed. Univ. of Witwatersrand; began career as barrister 1957; Sr. Counsel 1974; conducted defence of anti-apartheid activists during about 35 years at the Bar; apptd. Judge of Appeal, Swaziland 1979, Lesotho 1982; Pres. Court of Appeal, Lesotho 1990; Judge of Supreme Court of S.A. 1991–96; Chief Justice Oct. 1996–; Chief Justice of Namibia 1992–97; Judge, Constitutional Court of S.A. 1994–97, Deputy Pres. 1995–97; Co-Chair. Convention for Democratic S.A. 1991–92; Chair. S.A. Law Comm. 1996–; mem. Council of Univ. of Witwatersrand 1993–95, Bd. of Faculty of Law 1990–97; mem. Editorial Bd. S.A. Journal of Human Rights and Annual Survey of S.A. Law; invited lecturer on law and human rights in India, U.S.A., U.K., Canada, Phillipines, Australia and Pakistan; Post-grad. Research Fellow Univ. of Columbia 1993; Hon. Prof. of Law, Univ. of Witwatersrand 1992–; Hon. LL.D. (Pennsylvania) 1992, (Delhi) 1993, (Natal) 1995, (Pretoria, Witwatersrand, Bangalore) 1997; Indicator Human Rights Award 1990, Black Lawyers' Asscn. Award 1994, Duma Nokwe Award for Human Rights 1997. *Leisure interests:* music, reading, political science, philosophy, history. *Address:* Supreme Court, P.O. Box 258, Bloemfontein 9300 (Office); 247, 3rd Avenue, Laudium 0037, South Africa (Home). *Telephone:* (12) 374-3863, (11) 403-8032, (11) 403-6524.

MAHON, Sir (John) Denis, Kt., C.B.E., M.A., F.B.A.; British art historian; b. 8 Nov. 1910; s. of the late John FitzGerald Mahon and Lady Alice Evelyn Browne; ed. Eton and Christ Church, Oxford; Trustee of the Nat. Gallery 1957–64, 1966–73; mem. Advisory Panel, Nat. Art Collections Fund 1975–; specialist in 17th Century Italian paintings; mem. Cttee. of the Biennial Exhbns., Bologna, Italy; Corresp. Fellow Accad. Raffaello, Urbino 1968, Ateneo Veneto 1987; Hon. D. Litt. (Newcastle) 1969, (Oxford) 1994; Medal for Benemeriti della Cultura for services to criticism and history of Italian art 1957, Archiginnasio d'Oro, City of Bologna 1968, Serena Medal for Italian Studies, British Acad. 1972, Hon. Citizen, Cento 1982. *Publications:* Studies in Seicento Art and Theory 1947, The Drawings of Guercino in the collection of H.M. The Queen at Windsor Castle (with N. Turner) 1989; various contribs. to catalogues of art exhbns. and numerous articles in publs. on history of art. *Address:* 33 Cadogan Square, London, SW1X 0HU, England. *Telephone:* 0171-235 7311; 0171-235 2530.

MAHONEY, Rev. John Aloysius (Jack), S.J., M.A., D.THEOL., F.R.S.A., C.I.MGT.; British university professor; b. 14 Jan. 1931, Coatbridge, Scotland; s. of Patrick Mahoney and Margaret Doris; unmarried; ed. Our Lady's High School, Motherwell, St. Aloysius Coll. Glasgow, Univ. of Glasgow and Gregorian Univ. Rome; lecturer in Moral and Pastoral Theology, Heythrop Coll. Oxon. 1967–70; lecturer in Moral and Pastoral Theology, Heythrop Coll. Univ. of London 1970–86, Prin. 1976–81; F.D. Maurice Prof. of Moral and Social Theology, King's Coll. London 1986–93, founding Dir. King's Coll. Business Ethics Research Centre 1987–93; Mercers' School Memorial Prof. of Commerce, Gresham Coll. City of London 1987–93; now Dixons Prof. of Business Ethics and Social Responsibility, London Business School; Hon. Fellow Faculty of Divinity, Edin. Univ. 1998–. *Publications:* Seeking the Spirit: Essays in Moral and Pastoral Theology 1981, Bioethics and Belief: Religion and Medicine in Dialogue 1984, The Making of Moral Theology: A Study of the Roman Catholic Tradition 1987, Teaching Business Ethics in the U.K., Europe and the U.S.A. 1990, Business Ethics in a New Europe (ed.) 1992. *Leisure interests:* piano, sketching, unrequited golf. *Address:* 114 Mount Street, London, W1Y 6AH, England. *Telephone:* 0171-493 7811. *Fax:* 0171-499 0549.

MAHUAD WITTS, Jamil, LL.D.; Ecuadorean politician and lawyer; b. 29 July 1949, Loja; ed. Pontificia Universidad Católica del Ecuador; legal assessor and Dir. of pvt. credit banks 1973–78; Pres. Federación de estudiantes Universitarios Católicos del Ecuador 1974–75; Regional Sec. Federación de Estudiantes de las Universidades Católicas de América Latina 1975–81; mem. Democracia Popular 1981; Dir. Empresa Nacional de Productos Vitales 1981–83; Minister of Labour 1981–83; Pres. Democracia Popular 1987–88, 1991–93; Vice-Pres. Demócrata Cristiano de América (ODCA), Andina Region 1991–97; Governor of Quito 1992, re-elected 1996; Pres. of Ecuador 1998–. *Address:* Palacio Nacional, García Moreno 1043, Quito, Ecuador. *Telephone:* (2) 216-300.

MAHUTA, Sir Robert Te Kotahi, K.N.Z.M., M.A.; New Zealand professor of Maori studies; b. 26 April 1939, Te Kuiti; s. of Koroki Te Rata Mahuta and Te Atairangikaahu Mahuta (née Herangi); m. Eliza Irimana Edmonds 1963; one s. two d.; ed. Mount Albert Grammar School, Univ. of Auckland and Wolfson Coll., Univ. of Oxford; Dir. Centre for Maori Studies and Research, Univ. of Waikato 1972–, Raupatu Research Prof., mem. Ngarimu V.C. and 28th Maori Bn. Scholarship Bd. 1984–; Prin. Negotiator Waikato Raupatu Claim 1989–; Chair. Maori Devt. Corpn. 1992–; Commr. Treaty of Waitangi Fisheries Comm. 1993–. *Publications:* Te Whenua, Te Iwi (contrib. to Te Whenua Te Iwi: The Land and the People, ed. by Jock Phillips) 1987, The Kiingitanga (contrib. to Te Ao Huirihuri, ed. by Michael King) 1991 and articles on Maori culture in learned journals. *Leisure interests:* reading, fishing, rugby league. *Address:* Awhina House, Waahi Pa, Huntly, New Zealand. *Telephone:* (07) 824 7688. *Fax:* (07) 824 7553.

MAIDEN, Sir Colin James, Kt., M.E. (N.Z.), D.PHIL.; New Zealand university vice-chancellor (retd.) and company director; b. 5 May 1933, Auckland; s. of Henry A. Maiden and Lorna Richardson; m. Jenefor Mary Rowe 1957; one s. three d.; ed. Univs. of Auckland and Oxford; Head, Hypersonic Physics Section, Canadian Armament Research and Devt. Establishment, Quebec City, Canada 1958–60; Sr. lecturer in Mechanical Eng. Univ. of Auckland 1960–61; Head, Material Sciences Lab. Gen. Motors Corpn. Defence Research Labs. Santa Barbara, Calif. 1961–66; Man. of Process Eng. Gen. Motors Corpn. Tech. Centre, Warren, Mich. 1966–70; Vice-Chancellor, Univ. of Auckland 1971–94; Chair. N.Z. Energy Research and Devt. Cttee. 1974–81, N.Z. Vice-Chancellor's Cttee. 1977–78, 1991, Liquid Fuels Trust Bd. 1978–86, NZ Synthetic Fuels Corpn. Ltd. 1980–90, Nat. Insurance Co. of N.Z. Ltd. 1988–, Fisher & Paykel Ltd. 1978–, Independent Newspapers Ltd. 1989–; Dir. Mason Industries Ltd. 1971–78, Farmers Trading Co. Ltd., 1973–86, Winstone Ltd. 1978–88, Wilkins & Davies Ltd. 1986–89, New Zealand Steel

Ltd. 1988–92, ANZ Banking Group (NZ) Ltd. 1990–93, The N.Z. Refining Co. Ltd. 1991–, Progressive Enterprises Ltd. 1992–, DB Group Ltd. 1994–, Sedgwick (NZ) Ltd. 1994–98, Transpower New Zealand Ltd. 1994–, Tower Corpn. 1995–; various professional appts.; Hon. Treas. Asscn. of Commonwealth Univs. 1988–98; Hon. LL.D. (Auckland); Queen Elizabeth Silver Jubilee Medal 1977, Medal of Univ. of Bonn 1983, Thomson Medal, Royal Soc. of N.Z. 1986, Symons Award, Asscn. of Commonwealth Univs. 1999. *Publications:* numerous scientific and tech. papers. *Leisure interest:* tennis. *Address:* 7 Chatfield Place, Remuera, Auckland 5, New Zealand. *Telephone:* (09) 529 0380. *Fax:* (09) 522 4374.

MAIDOU, Henri; Central African Republic politician and banker; b. 14 Feb. 1936, Bangui; fmr. Pres. Banque Centrale des Etats de l'Afrique de l'Ouest; Minister of Nat. Educ., Youth, Sports and Arts 1970–1973, of Nat. Health and Social Affairs 1973–74; Minister of State charged with Town Planning and Territorial Devt. 1974–76, with Nat. Educ. and Educational Reform April–Sept. 1976; Second Deputy Prime Minister, charged with Nat. Educ. and Admin. Reform Sept.–Dec. 1976, with Nat. Educ., Youth, Sports, Arts and Culture 1976–78; Prime Minister 1978–79; Vice-Pres. of Central African Repub. 1979–80; imprisoned Aug.–Oct. 1980; Leader, Parti Républicain du Progrès 1981 (political parties banned Sept. 1981); Pres. Union Bancaire en Afrique Centrale 1988–91. *Address:* c/o Union Bancaire en Afrique Centrale, rue de Brazza, B.P. 59, Bangui, Central African Republic.

MAIJ-WEGGEN, Hanja; Netherlands politician; b. 29 Dec. 1943; trained as nurse; subsequently became lecturer in health care; mem. European Parl. 1979–, Vice-Chair. European People's Party (Christian Democratic Group) 1987; Minister of Transport 1989–94, also of Public Works and Water Man.; mem. Christian Democratic Appeal. *Address:* c/o Ministry of Transport, Public Works and Water Management, Plesmanweg 1, P.O.B. 20901, 2500 EX The Hague, Netherlands.

MAILER, Norman Kingsley, B.S.; American writer; b. 31 Jan. 1923, Long Branch, N.J.; s. of Isaac Barnett Mailer and Fanny Schneider; m. 1st Beatrice Silverman 1944 (divorced 1952); one d.; m. 2nd Adele Morales 1954 (divorced 1962); two d.; m. 3rd Lady Jeanne Campbell 1962 (divorced 1963); one d.; m. 4th Beverly Rentz Bentley 1963 (divorced 1980); two s. one d.; m. 5th Carol Stevens (divorced); one d.; m. 6th Norris Church 1980; one s.; ed. Harvard Univ.; served in U.S. Army 1944–46; Co-founder New York weekly Village Voice 1955; mem. Editorial Bd. of Dissent magazine 1953–69, American Acad. of Arts and Letters 1984–; Pres. of PEN (U.S. Chapter) 1984–86; Dir. films: Wild 90 1967, Beyond the Law 1967, Maidstone 1968, Tough Guys Don't Dance 1987; Nat. Book Award for Arts and Letters 1969; Pulitzer Prize for Non-Fiction 1969, for Fiction 1980; 14th Annual Award for outstanding service to the arts, McDowell Colony 1973; acted in film Ragtime 1981. *Publications:* The Naked and The Dead 1948, Barbary Shore 1951, The Deer Park 1955 (dramatized 1967), Advertisements for Myself 1959, Deaths for the Ladies (poems) 1962, The Presidential Papers 1963, An American Dream 1964, Cannibals and Christians 1966, Why are we in Vietnam? (novel) 1967, The Armies of the Night 1968, Miami and the Siege of Chicago 1968, Moonshot 1969, A Fire on the Moon 1970, The Prisoner of Sex 1971, Existential Errands 1972, St. George and the Godfather 1972, Marilyn 1973, The Faith of Graffiti 1974, The Fight 1975, Some Honourable Men 1976, Genius and Lust—A Journey Through the Writings of Henry Miller 1976, A Transit to Narcissus 1978, The Executioner's Song 1979, Of Women and Their Elegance 1980, The Essential Mailer (selections) 1982, Pieces and Pontifications 1982, Ancient Evenings (novel) 1983, Tough Guys Don't Dance (novel) 1984, Harlot's Ghost (novel) 1991, Oswald's Tale 1995, Portrait of Picasso as a Young Man 1995, The Gospel According to the Song 1997, The Time of Our Time 1998, contributions to numerous magazines. *Address:* c/o Random House Inc., Authors' Mail, 201E. 50th Street, New York, NY 10022, U.S.A.

MAILLET, Pierre Paul Georges; French professor of economics; b. 7 July 1923, Paris; s. of Marcel Maillet and Madeleine Cuvinot; m. Monique Chassagne 1956; two s. one d.; ed. Ecole Polytechnique, Paris; Budget Forecasting Dept., Ministry of Finance 1954–60; Dir. of Econ. Studies, ECSC 1960–67; Dir. of Scientific Policy, EEC 1967–71, Dir. of Budget 1971–73, Hon. Dir.-Gen. of EEC 1973–; Prof. of Econ. Sciences, Univ. of Lille 1973–92, Prof. Emer. 1992 (European Chair. Jean Monnet); fmr. Pres. French Asscn. for Econ. Science; fmr. mem. Exec. Cttee., Int. Econ. Asscn.; Hon. Pres. Confed. of European Econ. Asscns.; Chevalier des Palmes Académiques. *Publications:* Intégration économique européenne 1988, La politique économique dans l'Europe d'après 1993 (trans. into Italian and Spanish) 1992, Trois défis de Maastricht 1993, L'Europe à géometrie variable 1994, Une Europe plus favorable à l'emploi 1996; Gen. Ed. Jean Monnet series on econs.; numerous articles on econs., Europe, etc. *Leisure interest:* travel. *Address:* 8 rue Richepanse, 75001 Paris, France (Home).

MAIORESCU, Mircea, PH.D.; Romanian professor of medicine and politician; b. 23 May 1926, Bucharest; s. of Octav Maiorescu and Elena Maiorescu; m.; one s. one d.; ed. Paediatrics Coll. of Bucharest, taught at Inst. of Medicine and Pharmacy, Bucharest 1956, Prof. 1974; div. Prof., Marie Curie Paediatrics Clinic of the Medical and Pharmaceutical Inst., Bucharest; mem. European Asscn. of Cardiologist Paediatricians 1983, of Acad. of Medical Sciences 1991; Minister of Health 1991; Vice-Pres. WHO Gen. Ass. 1992; Visiting Prof. Louisville Univ., Ky., U.S.A. 1995. *Leisure interests:* classical music, essays., philosophy, poetry. *Publications:* over 300 works. *Address:* Marie Curie University Hospital for Children, Bulevard Brâncoveanu 20, 75544 Bucharest, Romania.

MAIRE, Edmond; French trades union official; b. 24 Jan. 1931, Epinay-sur-Seine; m. Raymonde Le Goff 1954; three c.; ed. Conservatoire Nat. des Arts et Métiers; technician, chemical industry; Perm. Sec. Fed. of Chemical Industries of Conféd. Française Démocratique du Travail (C.F.D.T.) 1958–70; mem. Exec. Cttee. of C.F.D.T., in charge of professional and social action; Sec.-Gen. of C.F.D.T. 1971–88; Pres. Villages-Vacances-Familles (VVF) 1989–; Pres. de la Section Affaires Sociales du Conseil Nat. du Tourisme 1989–; mem. Conseil Economique et Social 1969–74. *Publications:* Demain l'autogestion 1976, Nouvelles frontières pour le syndicalisme 1987. *Address:* Villages Vacances Familles, 172 boulevard de la Villette, 75918 Paris Cédex 19, France.

MAISEL, Sherman Joseph, PH.D.; American economist; b. 8 July 1918, Buffalo, N.Y.; s. of Louis Maisel and Sophia (née Beck) Maisel; m. Lucy Cowdin 1942; one s. one d.; ed. The Nichols School, Harvard Coll. and Harvard Univ.; Economist, Fed. Reserve Bd. 1939–41; U.S. Army 1941–45; mem. staff, U.S. del. to Interallied Reparations Agency 1945–46; Prof. of Business Admin. Univ. of Calif. (Berkeley) 1948–65, 1972–86, Econ. Consultant 1973–; mem. Bd. of Govs. Fed. Reserve System 1965–72; Co-Dir. Nat. Bureau of Econ. Research-West 1973–77; Chair. Bd. of Dirs. Farmers Savings and Loan 1986–88; Pres. Sherman J. Maisel and Assocs. Inc. 1986–; Fellow, Inst. for Advanced Study in the Behavioral Sciences, Stanford 1972–73; Pres. American Finance Asscn. 1973. *Publications:* Housebuilding in Transition 1953, Fluctuations, Growth and Forecasting 1957, Financing Real Estate 1965, Managing the Dollar 1973, Real Estate Investment and Finance 1976, Risk and Capital Adequacy in Commercial Banks 1981, Macroeconomics: Theories and Policies 1982, Real Estate Finance 1987, 1992 and various pamphlets. *Address:* Haas School of Business, University of California, Berkeley, CA 94720 (Office); 2164 Hyde Street, San Francisco, CA 94109, U.S.A. (Home). *Telephone:* (415) 771-9650 (Home).

MAISENBERG, Oleg; Austrian pianist; b. 29 April 1945, Odessa, U.S.S.R. (now Ukraine), s. of Adel and Josef Maisenberg; two c.; ed. Moscow Gnessin Inst. of Music (pupil of A. Yokheles); winner Franz Schubert Competition in Vienna 1967, 20th Century Music Competition, Vienna 1967; performed Rachmaninov's 1st Piano Concerto with Nat. Orchestra of Moldavia; emigrated to Austria 1981; concert performances worldwide as soloist and chamber musician; recordings of Schubert, Schuman, Liszt, Scriabin, Berg, Stravinsky, R. Strauss, Dvořák, Milhand, Weber, Schönberg, Bartok, Rachmaninov and Prokofiev; Prof. Stuttgart Conservatory and Vienna Acad. of Music. *Address:* In Der Gugl 9, Klosterneuburg, Austria. *Telephone:* (022) 432 6485. *Fax:* (022) 432 6485.

MAISKY, Mischa (Michael); Israeli concert cellist; b. 10 Jan. 1948, Riga, U.S.S.R.; m. Maryanne Kay Lipman 1983; ed. Moscow Conservatory (with Mstislav Rostropovich), Univ. of Southern California; début with Leningrad Philharmonic Orchestra 1965; emigrated to Israel 1972; début with Pittsburg Symphony Orchestra at Carnegie Hall 1973; début at Royal Festival Hall 1976; début at Berlin Philharmonic Hall 1978; numerous TV, film and video appearances all over the world; All-Soviet prize-winner 1965, Int. Tchaikovsky Competition 1966; also winner of Cassada Competition, Florence 1973 and Rostropovich Competition, Paris 1981; Grand Prix du Disque, Paris 1985; Record Acad. Prize, Tokyo 1985; recordings include Six Suites for Solo Cello (Bach), Three Sonatas for Cello and Piano (Bach), Concerto in A minor Op. 102 for Violin, Cello and Orchestra (Brahms), Concerto for Cello and Orchestra in A Minor (Schumann). *Leisure interests:* music, chess, computing.

MAITLAND, Sir Donald James Dundas, G.C.M.G., O.B.E., M.A.; British diplomatist and civil servant (retd.); b. 16 Aug. 1922, Edinburgh; s. of Thomas D. Maitland and Wilhelmina S. Dundas; m. Jean Marie Young 1950; one s. one d.; ed. George Watson's Coll. and Edinburgh Univ.; Army Service 1941–47; joined Diplomatic Service 1947; Consul, Amara 1950; British Embassy, Baghdad 1950–53; Private Sec. to Minister of State, Foreign Office 1954–56; Dir. Middle East Centre for Arab Studies, Lebanon 1956–60; Foreign Office 1960–63; Counsellor, British Embassy, Cairo 1963–65; Head, News Dept., Foreign Office 1965–67; Prin. Private Sec. to Foreign and Commonwealth Sec. 1967–69; Amb. to Libya 1969–70; Chief Press Sec. to Prime Minister 1970–73; Perm. Rep. to UN 1973–74; Deputy Under-Sec., FCO 1974–75; mem. British Overseas Trade Bd. 1974–75; U.K. mem. Commonwealth Group on Trade, Aid and Devt. 1975; U.K. Perm. Rep. to European Communities 1975–79; Deputy Perm. Under-Sec. FCO 1979–80; Perm. Under-Sec. of State, Dept. of Energy 1980–82; Chair. Ind. Comm. World-wide Telecommunications Devt. 1983–85; Govt. Dir. Britoil 1983–85; Dir. Slough Estates 1983–92, Northern Eng. Industries 1986–89; Adviser, British Telecom 1985–86; Deputy Chair. Independent Broadcasting Authority (IBA) 1986–89; Chair. Health Educ. Authority 1989–94; Pro-Chancellor, Bath Univ. 1996–; Chair. U.K. Cttee. World Communications Year 1983; mem. Commonwealth War Graves Comm. 1983–87; Chair. Christians for Europe (later Charlemagne Inst.) 1984–93; Pres. Federal Trust for Educ. and Research 1987–; Chair. Govs. Westminster Coll., Oxford 1994–97; Chair. Thinknet Comm. 1989–95; Hon. LL.D. (Bath). *Publications:* Diverse Times, Sundry Places (autobiog.) 1996, Spring Blossom, Autumn Leaves (miscellany) 1998; articles on foreign affairs, Europe, telecommunications. *Leisure interests:* music, hill-walking. *Address:* Murhill Farm House, Limpley Stoke, Bath, BA3 6HH, England. *Telephone:* (01225) 723157.

MAITLAND SMITH, Geoffrey; British business executive and accountant; b. 27 Feb. 1933, London; s. of late Philip John Maitland Smith and of Kathleen Goff; m. 3rd Lucinda Enid Whyte 1986; four s. two d.; ed. Univ. Coll. School, London; Partner, Thornton Baker & Co., Chartered Accountants 1960–70; Dir. Sears PLC (fmrly. Sears Holdings PLC) 1971–95, Chief Exec. 1978–88, Jt. Chair. 1984–85, Chair. 1985–95; Chair. British Shoe Corpn. 1984–92, Mallet PLC 1986–89, Selfridges Ltd. 1985–93, Garrard & Co. 1985–90, Mappin & Webb Ltd. 1985–90, Hammerson PLC 1993– (Dir. 1990–), W. and F. C. Bonham and Sons Ltd. 1996–; Pres. Intercontinental Group of Dept. Stores 1990–95; Deputy Chair. Midland Bank 1992–96 (Dir. 1986–96); Dir. Asprey PLC 1980–93, Cen. Ind. Television 1983–85, Courtaulds PLC 1983–90, Imperial Group PLC 1984–86, HSBC Holdings PLC 1992–96; Hon. Vice-Pres. Inst. of Marketing 1987–94; mem. Bd. Financial Reporting Council 1990–98; Chair. Council, Univ. Coll. School 1987–96. *Address:* 100 Park Lane, London, W1Y 4AR, England. *Telephone:* 0171-887 1000.

MAITLIS, Peter M., B.SC., PH.D., D.SC., F.R.S., F.R.S.C., F.C.I.C.; British professor of chemistry; b. 15 Jan. 1933, Berlin; s. of Jacob Maitlis and Judith Maitlis; m. Marion Basco 1959; three d.; ed. Univ. of Birmingham and Univ. of London; Asst. Lecturer, Univ. of London 1956–60; Fulbright Fellow and Research Assoc., Harvard and Cornell Univs., U.S.A., 1960–62; Asst. Prof., Assoc. Prof. and Prof., McMaster Univ., Canada 1962–72; Prof. of Inorganic Chem., Sheffield Univ. 1972–94, Research Prof. 1994–; Chair. Science and Eng. Research Council, Chem. Cttee. 1985–88; Pres. Dalton Div., Royal Soc. of Chem. 1985–87, Ludwig Mond Lecturer 1997; mem. Council The Royal Soc. 1991–93; Sir Edward Frankland Lecturer, Royal Soc. of Chem. 1985; Tilden Lecturer 1979; Fellow, Alfred P. Sloan Foundation 1967–69; Steacie Prize in Natural Sciences 1970, Royal Soc. of Chem. Medal 1981, Kurnakov Medal of Russian Acad. of Sciences 1998. *Publications:* The Organic Chemistry of Palladium, 2 vols. 1971; numerous research publs. in scientific journals. *Leisure interests:* music, travel, reading. *Address:* Department of Chemistry, The University, Sheffield, S3 7HF, England. *Telephone:* (0114) 222 9320.

MAJALI, Abdel Salam al-, M.D., D.L.C., F.A.C.S., DH.C.; Jordanian university president; b. 1925, Karak; s. of Attallah Majali and Khadeejeh Serougi; m. Joan M. Lachlan 1956; two s. one d.; ed. Medical Coll., Syrian Univ., Damascus; Dir.-Gen. and Ear, Nose and Throat Consultant, The Royal Medical Services, Jordanian Armed Forces, Amman 1960–69; Minister of Health 1969–71; Pres. Univ. of Jordan, Amman 1971–76, 1980–90; Minister of Educ. and Minister of State for Prime Ministry Affairs 1976–79; Prime Minister of Jordan 1993–95, 1997–99, Minister of Defence and Foreign Affairs 1993–95, Minister of Defence 1997–99; Chair. and mem. UN Univ. Council, Tokyo 1977–83; Fellow, American Coll. of Surgeons; Dr.h.c. (Hacettepe Univ., Ankara) 1974; Jordan Independence Medal; Medal of St. John of Jerusalem and other decorations.

MAJEKODUNMI, Chief The Hon. Moses Adekoyejo, C.M.G., C.F.R., LL.D., M.A., M.D., F.R.C.P.I., F.M.C.O.G., F.R.C.O.G., M.A.O., D.C.H., L.M.; Nigerian administrator and physician; Chief Otun of Egbaland, Chief Maiyegun of Lagos, Chief Bashegun of Ede, Chief Agba-Akin of Oshogbo, Chief Kaiyero of Akure, Chief Maiyegun of Iwo, Chief Asipa of Iragbiji; b. 17 Aug. 1916, Abeokuta; s. of Chief J. B. Majekodun, Chief Otun of Egbaland and Alice Oladunni (Soetan); m. 1st Nola C. Maclaughlin 1943 (divorced 1963), five s. three d.; m. 2nd Katsina Saratu Atta 1964; ed. Abeokuta Grammar School, St. Gregory's Coll., Lagos, Trinity Coll., Dublin; House Physician, Nat. Children's Hosp., Dublin 1941–43; Medical Officer, Nigeria 1943–49; Consulting Obstetrician, Massey Street Maternity Hosp., General Hosp. and Creek Hosp., Lagos 1949–60; Sr. Specialist Obstetrician, Nigerian Federal Gov. Medical Services 1949–60; Senator and Leader of Senate 1960; Minister of State for the Army 1960–61, Fed. Minister of Health 1961–66; Fed. Minister of Health and Information 1965; Admin. for W. Nigeria 1962; Pres. 16th World Health Assembly 1963; Int. Vice-Pres., 3rd World Conf. on Medical Educ., New Delhi 1966; Chancellor Ogun State Univ. 1986–; Chair. Merchant Banking Corpn. Nigeria Ltd., Westminster Dredging (Nigeria) Ltd. 1990–; mem. Bd. of Govs., St. Gregory's Coll., Lagos; Chair. Bd. of Govs., St. Nicholas Hosp., Lagos 1967–; Chair. Bd. Dirs. Lion Bldgs. Ltd.; Dir. Abbott Labs. (Nigeria) Ltd., Swiss Nigeria Chemical Co., Johnson and Johnson (Nigeria) Ltd.; Trustee, J. K. Randle Memorial Hall, Lagos; mem. Soc. Gynaecology and Obstetrics, Nigeria; Hon. LL.D. (Trinity Coll., Dublin), Hon. D.Sc. (Lagos), (Ogun State Univ.). *Publications:* Premature Infants: Management and Prognosis 1943, Behold the Key (play) 1944, Partial Atresia of the Cervix Complicating Pregnancy 1946, Sub-Acute Intussusception in Adolescents 1948, Thiopentone Sodium in Operative Obstetrics 1954, Rupture of the Uterus involving the Bladder 1955, Effects of Malnutrition in Pregnancy and Lactation 1957, Medical Education and the Health Services: A Critical Review of Priorities in a Developing Country 1966. *Leisure interests:* riding, squash, swimming. *Address:* PMB 2002, Ago-Iwoye, Ogun State (Office); 3 Kingsway, Ikoyi, Lagos, Nigeria (Home). *Telephone:* (037) 390149 (Office); 681660 (Home).

MAJKO, Pandeli Sotir; Albanian politician; b. 15 Nov. 1967; m.; one c.; ed. Univ. of Tirana; Rep. Dec. 1990 Movt. 1990; co-f. Democratic Party 1990, left party 1991; joined Socialist Party of Albania 1991, Sec. of Public Relations 1996–97, Sec. 1997, also leader of Parl. Group, head of del. to Org. for Security and Co-operation in Europe; Prime Minister of Albania 1998–; f. Forum of Euro-Socialist Youth 1991; Chair. Euro-Socialist Forum 1992–95; M.P. 1992–; Torch of Democracy Award. *Address:* Këshilli i Ministrave, Tirana, Albania.

MAJOR, Clarence, PH.D.; American novelist and poet; b. 31 Dec. 1936, Atlanta, Ga.; m. Pamela Ritter 1980; ed. Union Graduate School, Yellow Springs and Cincinnati, Ohio Univ. of the State of New York, Albany; Prof., Dept. of English, Univ. of California, Davis 1989–; has given lectures in U.S.A., Europe, and in N. and W. Africa; Western States Book Award for Fiction (for My Amputations); The Pushcart Prize; Fulbright Fellowship; Nat. Council on the Arts Award. *Publications:* (novels) All-Night Visitors 1969, NO 1973, Reflex and Bone Structure 1975, Emergency Exit 1979, My Amputations 1986, Such was the Season 1987, Painted Turtle: Woman with Guitar 1988; (short stories) Fun and Games 1990, Calling the Wind: Twentieth Century African-American Short Stories 1993, Dirty Bird Blues 1996, All-Night Visitors (new version) 1998; (poetry) Swallow the Lake 1970, Symptoms and Madness 1971, Private Line 1971, The Cotton Club 1972, The Syncopated Cakewalk 1974, Inside Diameter: The France Poems 1985, Surfaces and Masks 1987, Some Observations of a Stranger at Zuni in the Latter Part of the Century 1989, The Garden Thrives, Twentieth Century African-American Poetry 1995, Configurations: New and Selected Poems 1958–98, 1998; (non-fiction) Dictionary of Afro-American Slang 1970, The Dark and Feeling: Black American Writers and their Work 1974, Juba to Jive: A Dictionary of African-American Slang 1994; numerous works in anthologies and periodicals. *Address:* Department of English, 281 Voorhies Hall, University of California, Davis, CA 95616, U.S.A. *Telephone:* (916) 752-5677.

MAJOR, Jean-Louis, L.PH., M.A., PH.D., F.R.S.C.; Canadian author and academic; b. 16 July 1937, Cornwall, Canada; s. of Joseph Major and Noella Daoust; m. Bibiane Landry 1960; one d.; ed. Univ. of Ottawa and Ecole Pratique des Hautes Etudes; Lecturer, Dept. of Philosophy, Univ. of Ottawa 1961–65, Prof. Dept. de Lettres Françaises 1965, Titular Prof. 1971–, Assoc. Dean (Research), Faculty of Arts 1991–97; Visiting Prof. Dept. of French, Univ. of Toronto 1970–71; Dir. Corpus d'editions critiques and Bibliothèque du nouveau monde 1981–; Chair. Academic Advisory Cttee. of Ont. Council on Univ. Affairs 1991–93; mem. Acad. des Lettres et Sciences Humaines. *Publications include:* Saint-Exupéry, l'écriture et la pensée 1968, Le jeu en étoile 1978, Entre l'écriture et la parole 1984, a critical edn. of Cocteau's Léone, Journal d'Henriette Dessaules 1989, Trente arpent de Ringuet 1991. *Address:* Département des Lettres Françaises, University of Ottawa, Ottawa, Ont., K1N 6N5 (Office); P.O. Box 357, St. Isidore, Ont., K0C 2B0, Canada (Home). *Telephone:* (613) 562-5798. *Fax:* (613) 562-5207.

MAJOR, Rt. Hon. John, C.H., P.C., A.I.B.; British politician and banker; b. 29 March 1943, Merton; s. of late Thomas Major and Gwendolyn Major; m. Norma Christina Elizabeth Johnson 1970; one s. one d.; ed. Rutlish School, Merton; mem. Lambeth Borough Council 1968–71; sr. exec. Standard Chartered Bank PLC 1965–79; M.P. for Huntingdon 1983– (Huntingdonshire 1979–83); Parl. Pvt. Sec. to Home Office Minister 1981–83; Asst. Govt. Whip 1983–84; Lord Commr. of Treasury 1984–85; Under-Sec. of State for Social Security 1985–86; Minister for Social Security and the Disabled 1986–87; Chief Sec. to Treasury 1987–89; Sec. of State for Foreign and Commonwealth Affairs July–Oct. 1989; Chancellor of the Exchequer 1989–90; Prime Minister, First Lord of the Treasury and Minister for the Civil Service 1990–97; Leader of the Conservative Party 1990–97; Parl. Consultant to Guild of Glass Engravers 1979–83; Pres. Eastern Area Young Conservatives 1983–85, Nat. Asthma Campaign 1998–; Hon. Master of the Bench of the Middle Temple 1992. *Leisure interests:* football, cricket and opera. *Address:* House of Commons, London, SW1A 0AA.

MAJOR, Kathleen, M.A., F.B.A.; British academic (retd.); b. 10 April 1906, London; d. of George Major and Gertrude Blow; ed. St. Hilda's Coll., Oxford; Librarian, St. Hilda's Coll., Oxford 1931–35; Archivist to Bishop of Lincoln 1936–45; Lecturer, and subsequently Reader in Diplomatic, Univ. of Oxford 1945–55; Prin., St. Hilda's Coll., Oxford 1955–65; Part-time Prof. of History, Univ. of Nottingham 1966–71; Hon. Vice-Pres. Royal Historical Soc. 1981–; Hon. D.Litt. (Nottingham) 1961. *Publications:* Registrum Antiquissimum of the Cathedral Church of Lincoln Vol. IV (jt. Ed.), V–X (sole Ed.) 1938–73; Acta Stephani Langton 1950, Fascicule IV, The Bail of Lincoln 1996. *Leisure interest:* reading. *Address:* 21 Queensway, Lincoln, LN2 4AJ, England. *Telephone:* (01522) 525370.

MAJOR, Dame Malvina Lorraine, D.B.E.; New Zealand operatic soprano; b. 28 Jan. 1943, Hamilton; d. of Vincent Major and Eva Major; m. Winston William Richard Fleming 1965; one s. two d.; ed. Hamilton Tech. Coll. and London Opera Centre; debut as Rosina in The Barber of Seville, Salzburg Festival 1968; performances in Europe, U.K., U.S.A., Australia, Japan, Jordan, Egypt and N.Z.; concerts in N.Z. with N.Z. Symphony Orchestra, regional opera cos. and for N.Z. TV and radio; Founder Dame Malvina Major Foundation (for excellence in the performing arts) 1991; Amb. for the N.Z. Year of the Family 1994; N.Z. winner Mobil Song Quest 1963, Kathleen Ferrier Competition winner 1966, Outstanding Achievements in Music Award 1988, N.Z. Medal 1990, Entertainer and Int. Performer of the Year 1992, N.Z. Music Award—Classical Disc 1993, 1994 and numerous other awards for services to music. *Address:* P.O. Box 11-175, Manners Street, Wellington, New Zealand. *Telephone:* (64) 4 495 7483.

MAKANIN, Vladimir Semenovich; Russian writer; b. 13 March 1937, Orsk, Orenburg Region; ed. Moscow Univ., Higher Workshop for Scenario

Writers and Film Dirs.; started writing 1965; Russian Booker Prize 1993, Pushkin Prize 1998. *Publications include:* Straight Line 1965, Air-Vent, Portrait and Around (novel) 1976, Story about an Old Settlement (collection of short stories) 1974, Voices 1982, River with a Fast Current 1983, Where the Skies Meet the Hills 1987, One and One 1987, Subject of Averaging 1992, A Baize-Covered Table with a Decanter in the Middle 1993, Quasi 1993, Caucasian Captive 1995, Underground, or a Hero of Our Time 1998. *Address:* Novinski blvd. 16, Apt. 14, 121069 Moscow, Russia. *Telephone:* (095) 291-92-53.

MAKARCZYK, Jerzy, LL.D.; Polish judge and professor of law; b. 24 July 1938; s. of Zbigniew Makarczyk and Hanna Olszowska; ed. Warsaw Univ. and Inst. of Legal Sciences, Polish Acad. of Sciences; Assoc. Prof. of Int. Public Law 1975, Prof. 1988; Deputy Dir. Inst. of Legal Sciences, Polish Acad. of Sciences 1981–88; Deputy Minister of Foreign Affairs 1989–90; Sec. of State, Ministry of Foreign Affairs 1990–92; in charge of negotiations with U.S.S.R. and then Russia on withdrawal of troops from Polish Territory 1990–92; Judge, European Court of Human Rights 1992–; Pres. Int. Law Asscn. 1988–90; Assoc. Inst. de Droit Int. 1993; Manfred Lachs Foundation Award 1998; Commdr. Légion d'honneur. *Publications:* Financing of Economic Development in the United Nations System 1974, Principles of a New International Economic Order 1988, ed. Collection of Essays in Honour of Judge Manfred Lachs 1984, Theory of International Law at the Threshold of the XXIst Century (ed.) 1996. *Leisure interests:* tennis, sailing. *Address:* ul. Bernardyńska 30 m. 5, 02-904 Warsaw, Poland. *Telephone:* (22) 642 95 40. *Fax:* (22) 642 95 40.

MAKAROV, Andrey Mikhailovich, C.JUR.; Russian barrister; b. 22 July 1954, Moscow; ed. Moscow State Univ.; worked in Research Inst., U.S.S.R. Ministry of Internal Affairs 1976–83; mem. Moscow City Bd. of Lawyers 1983–, acted as the defence lawyer in numerous maj. trials, including trial of fmr. Deputy Minister of Internal Affairs V. Churbanov; Chief of Dept. supervising activities of Comm. of Security Council in struggle against crime and corruption July–Oct. 1993; mem. State Duma (Parl.) 1993–; Exec. Dir. Russian br. of SOROS Foundation; Pres. Chess Fed. of Russia 1994–97; mem. Exec. Cttee. Int. Chess Fed. (FIDE). *Address:* Russian Chess Federation, Gogolevski blvd. 14, 121019 Moscow, Russia. *Telephone:* (095) 291-97-55.

MAKAROV, Askold Anatolyevich; Russian ballet dancer and teacher; b. 3 May 1925; s. of Olga Anatolyevna Makarova; m. Petrova Ninel Alexandrovna 1959; one s.; ed. Leningrad Ballet School (under V. I. Ponomarev); dancer with Kirov Ballet 1942–70; main roles include: Spartacus, Ziegfried (Swan Lake), Jean (Raymonda), Vazlav and Gyrey (Bachchisaray Fountain), Prince (Cinderella), Ostap (Taras Bulba), Basil (Don Quixote), Danila (Stone Flower), Otello, Mayakovsky (The Bug) etc.; Prof., Leningrad (now St. Petersburg) Conservatoire 1970–; Artistic Dir. and Man. of Leningrad (now St. Petersburg) State Academic Ballet 'Choreographic Miniatures' 1976–; Artistic Dir. and Man. St. Petersburg State Academic Ballet Theatre 1997–; mem. Int. Ballet competition jury; Chair. St. Petersburg Union of Performers; Hon. Academician, Ukrainian Acad. of Dance; People's Artist of the U.S.S.R., U.S.S.R. State Prize. *Address:* Plutalova str. 18-4, 197136 St. Petersburg, Russia. *Telephone:* 233-80-32.

MAKAROV, Igor Mikhailovich, D.SC.; Russian scientist; b. 22 Oct. 1927, Saratov; s. of Mikhail Ilyich Makarov and Yelena Ivanovna Makarova; m. Praskovia Alexandrovna Makarova 1953; one s.; ed. S. Ordzhonikidze Moscow Aviation Inst.; scientific worker and deputy chief of lab. 1949–62; Instructor, Deputy Chief, Dept. of Science and Educ., C.P.S.U. 1962–75; Deputy Minister for Higher and Specialized Secondary Educ. of U.S.S.R. 1975–88; Corresp. mem. U.S.S.R. (now Russian) Acad. of Sciences 1974–87, mem. 1987–; Chief Scientific Sec. Presidium of U.S.S.R. (now Russian) Acad. of Sciences 1988–92, Chief Scientific Sec. Russian Acad. of Sciences 1992–96, Adviser to Pres. 1996–; Chair. Dept. of Cybernetics, Moscow Inst. of Radio-electronics and Automation 1978–; Russian Rep. to Int. Council of Scientific Unions; Chair. Scientific Council on Robotics and Flexible Mfg., Russian Acad. of Sciences; Deputy Chief Ed. Automatic Control; mem. Editorial Bd. Future of Science, Science and Humanity; Chief Ed. Herald of the Russian Acad. of Sciences; Chief Ed. Series Cybernetics; Deputy Chief Ed. Automation and Telemechanics; U.S.S.R. State Prize 1984, Russian State Prize 1995; Order of Red Banner of Labour. *Publications:* Linear Automatic Systems 1975, Theory of Automatic Control (2 vols.) 1977, Objective-oriented Complex Programs 1980, Theory of Choice and Decision-making 1982, Cybernetics Today: Achievements, Challenges, Prospects 1984, Cybernetics and Informatics 1986, Informatics and Progress in Science and Technology 1987, Time-Impulse Automatic Control System 1998; numerous scientific papers on man. and control, artificial intelligence, robotics, mfg. tech., educ. *Leisure interests:* tennis, skiing, hunting. *Address:* Presidium of the Russian Academy of Sciences, 32A Leninsky Prospect, 117993 Moscow GSP-1, Russia. *Telephone:* (095) 938-19-06. *Fax:* 938-53-58.

MAKAROV, Valery Leonidovich, PH.D.; Russian economist; b. 25 May 1937, Novosibirsk; s. of Leonid Makarov and Dina Yershov; m. Irena Nikolaev 1961; one s. one d.; ed. Moscow Econ. Inst.; scientific worker, Inst. of Math., Siberian Div. U.S.S.R. Acad. of Sciences 1961–67, Lab. Chief 1967–73, Deputy Dir. 1973–80, Gen. Sec. Siberian Div. 1980–83; Prof. of Mathematical Econs. Novosibirsk Univ. 1970–83; Dir. Nat. Inst. of Industrial Man., Moscow 1983–85; Dir. Central Econs. and Math. Inst. 1985–; Prof. at Moscow Univ.; Founder and Rector, New Econ. School, Moscow 1992–; Ed.-in-Chief, Journal of Math. and Econ. Methods.; mem. Ed. Bd. Econs. of Planning, Econs. of Transition, Econ. Systems Research; mem. Exec. Cttee., Int. Econ. Asscn. 1995–; mem. several govt. comms.; Corresp. mem. U.S.S.R. (now Russian) Acad. of Science 1979, mem. 1990; Fellow Econometric Soc.; Kantorovich Award (for conbrib. to econ. theory) 1995. *Publications:* Mathematical Theory of Economic Dynamics and Equilibria (with A. Rubinov) 1977, Models and Computers in Economics 1979, Computer Simulation in Analysis of Regional Problems 1987, Mathematical Economic Theory: Pure and Mixed Types of Economic Mechanisms (with A. Rubinov and M. Levin) 1994. *Leisure interests:* tennis, skiing. *Address:* Central Economics and Mathematics Institute, Russian Academy of Sciences, Nakhimouski Prospect 47, 117418 Moscow, Russia. *Telephone:* (095) 129-10-11 (Office); (095) 229-01-50 (Home). *Fax:* (095) 310-70-15.

MAKAROVA, Inna Vladimirovna; Russian actress; b. 28 July 1926, Taiga, Kemerovo district; d. of Vladimir Makarov and Anna German; m. 1st S. Bondarchuk 1947, 2nd M. Perelman; one d.; ed. All-Union Film Inst.; U.S.S.R. State Prize 1949; Order of Red Banner of Labour, People's Artist of U.S.S.R. 1985, Order of Merit R.S.F.S.R. 1967. *Roles include:* Luba Shevtsova (Young Guard) 1948, Katya (Vysota) 1957, Varya (My Dear Man) 1958, Nadya (Girls) 1962, Dusya (Women) 1966, Nonna (The Rumyantsev Affair) 1956, Anfisa (Balsaminov's Wedding) 1965, Maria (Russian Field) 1972, Anna Pavlovna (Poshechonsk Old Times) 1977, Larissa (The Meek Love) 1980, The Governess (Dead Souls) 1983, Netla (Childhood and Youth of Bembi) 1988, Actress (A Loan for Marriage) 1990. *Leisure interest:* gardening. *Address:* Ukrainian Blvd. 11, Apt. 14, 121059 Moscow, Russia. *Telephone:* (095) 243-00-93.

MAKAROVA, Natalia Romanovna; Russian ballerina; b. 1940, Leningrad; m. 3rd Edward Karkar 1976; one s.; ed. Vagonova Ballet School, Leningrad; mem. Kirov Ballet 1959–70; sought political asylum, London 1970; Prin. Dancer, American Ballet Theatre 1970–92; appeared with Kirov Co. in London 1988, U.S.S.R. 1989; f. Makarova and Co. 1980; Guest Artist, Royal Ballet 1972; Guest Artist, London Festival Ballet 1984; retd. from dancing 1992; acted in St. Petersburg theatres 1991–; Honoured Artist of R.S.F.S.R. *Publications:* A Dance Autobiography 1979, On Your Toes 1984.

MAKEYEV, Evgeny Nikolaevich; Russian diplomatist (retd.); b. 28 April 1928, Kirov; m. Leniana Makeyeva 1950; two d.; ed. Moscow Inst. of Int. Relations; entered diplomatic service 1950; served in People's Republic of China 1950–53; Official Ministry of Foreign Affairs 1953–60, Deputy Head European Dept. 1967–68, Head 1968–71, Head Dept. of Int. Econ. Org. 1980–86; first Sec., counsellor Perm. Mission to the UN, New York 1960–64, Deputy Perm. Rep. 1964–67, with rank of Amb. 1971–80; Perm. Rep. to UN Office, Geneva 1986–94; Amb.-at-large 1994–98; numerous decorations. *Address:* Ministry of Foreign Affairs, Smolenskaya Sennaya 32/34, Moscow, Russia.

MAKHULU, Most Rev. Walter Paul Khotso; British ecclesiastic; b. 2 July 1935, Johannesburg, S.A.; s. of Paul Makhulu; m. Rosemary Makhulu 1966; one s. one d.; ed. Pimville Govt. School, Johannesburg, Khaiso Secondary School, Coll. of the Resurrection and St. Peter, S.A., St. Andrew's Coll., Birmingham; Area Sec. for Eastern Africa and African Refugees, Comm. on Inter-Church Aid Refugee and World Service, World Council of Churches 1975–79; Bishop of Botswana 1979–; Archbishop of Cen. Africa 1980–; Pres. All Africa Conf. of Churches 1981–86; Pres. World Council of Churches 1983–91; Hon. Curate Holy Trinity, Geneva; Hon. D.D. (Kent) 1988, (Gen. Theol. Seminary, New York) 1990; Officier, l'Ordre des Palmes Académiques 1981. *Leisure interests:* music, international affairs. *Address:* P.O. Box 769, Gaborone, Botswana. *Telephone:* 353779 (Office).

MAKI, Fumihiko, M.ARCH.; Japanese architect; b. 6 Sept. 1928, Tokyo; m. Misao 1960; two d.; ed. Univ. of Tokyo, Cranbrook School of Art, Michigan and Harvard Univ.; Assoc. Prof. Washington Univ. 1956–62, Harvard Univ. 1962–66; lecturer, Dept. of Urban Eng., Univ. of Tokyo 1964–, Prof. of Architecture 1979; Prin. Partner, Maki and Assocs. 1964–; mem. of Trilateral Comm. 1975–; Visiting Prof. at Berkeley, Univ. of Calif. 1970, Los Angeles, Univ. of Calif. 1977, Colombia Univ. 1977, Tech. Univ. of Vienna 1978; mem. Japan Inst. of Architecture; Hon. Fellow, American Inst. of Architects 1980; awards include Gold Medal of Japan Inst. of Architects 1964, 1st prize in Low Cost Housing Int. Competition, Lima 1969, art award from Mainichi Press 1969. *Major works include:* Toyoda Memorial Hall, Nagoya Univ. 1960, Rissho Univ. Campus 1966, Nat. Aquarium, Okinawa 1975, Tsukuba Univ. Complex 1976, Hillside Terrace Housing Complex 1978, The Royal Danish Embassy in Tokyo 1979, Nippon Center 1989, Tokyo Municipal Gymnasium 1990. *Publications:* Investigations in Collective Form 1964, Movement Systems in the City 1965, Metabolism 1960, Structure in Art and Science (contrib.) 1965. *Leisure interests:* reading, chess. *Address:* 16-22, 5-chome Higashi-Gotanda, Shinagawa-ku, Tokyo, Japan.

MAKIHARA, Minoru; Japanese business executive; b. 1930, Hampstead, England; m. Kikuko Makihara; ed. in England, Japan, Harvard Univ.; joined Mitsubishi Corpn. Marine Products Dept. 1956–59, London Br. 1959–70, Rep. Mitsubishi Int. Seattle and Washington 1970–80, Gen. Man. Marine Products Dept., Tokyo 1980–87, Pres. Mitsubishi Int. New York 1987–90, Sr. Man. Dir. Mitsubishi Corpn., also Chair. Mitsubishi Int. 1990–92, Pres. Mitsubishi Corpn. 1992–98. *Address:* Office of the Chairman, Mitsubishi Corporation, 2-6-3 Marunouchi, Chiyoda-ku, Tokyo 100-8086, Japan.

MAKIN, Andre (Andrei); French/Russian writer; b. 1957; s. of Maria Stepanovna Dolina; worked as teacher of literature in Novgorod; emigrated from U.S.S.R. to France 1987, wrote in French, awarded Goncourt Prix and Medici Prize for The French Testament 1995. *Publications include:* (novel) Daughter of the Hero of the Soviet Union, Time of the River of Amur, The French Testament. Lives in Paris.

MAKK, Károly; Hungarian film director; b. 22 Dec. 1925; s. of Kálmán Makk and Emma Szmolka; m. Andrea Zsiga-Kiss; one s. one d.; ed. Budapest Univ. of Sciences, Univ. of Dramatic and Cinematic Arts; asst. lecturer 1953, lecturer 1959–; mem. Univ. Council; worked as assistant dir. MAFILM Studio 1946–53, dir. 1954–; Guest lecturer Istituto Centro Sperimentale per Film, Rome 1976 and German Film Acad., Munich 1973–74; mem. Hungarian Acad. of Art 1992–; Merited Artist and Eminent Artist titles, Balázs Béla prize, Kossuth prize 1973. *Productions:* Liliomfi 1955, Ház a sziklák alatt (House under the Rocks) (San Francisco Grand Prix 1959), 39-es dandár (The Brigade No. 39) 1959, Megszállottak (The Fanatics) 1962, Elveszett paradicsom (The Lost Paradise) 1963, Az utolsó előtti ember (The Last but One) 1963, Isten és ember előtti (Before God and Man) 1968, Szerelem (Love) (1971 International Journalist Fed. Award and Jury's Special Award of Cannes), Macskajáték (Catsplay) 1973, Egy erkölcsös éjszaka (A very moral night) 1977, Két történet a félmúltból (Two stories from the Recent Past), A téglafal mögött (Behind the Brickwall), Philemon and Baucis, 1981, Egymásra nézve (Another Way) (1984 Int. Critiques Award and Best Female Performance of Cannes), Játszani kell (Playing for Keeps) 1984, Az utolsó kézirat (The last Manuscript) 1987, Magyar rekviem (Hungarian Requiem) 1990. *Address:* 1022 Budapest, Hankóczy Jenő utca 15, Hungary. *Telephone:* 135-1010.

MAKKAWI, Khalil, PH.D.; Lebanese diplomatist; b. 15 Jan. 1930, Beirut; s. of Abdel Basset Makkawi and Rosa Makkawi; m. Zahira Sibaei 1958; one s. one d.; ed. American Univ. of Beirut, Cairo Univ., Columbia Univ., New York; joined Foreign Ministry 1957, served in UN Section 1957–59, Deputy Perm. Rep. to UN, New York 1961–64, First Sec., Embassy in Washington 1964–67, Chief of Int. Relations Dept., Foreign Ministry, Beirut 1967–70, Counsellor, Embassy in London 1970–71, Minister Plenipotentiary, London 1971–73, Amb. to G.D.R. 1973–78, to U.K. and Repub. of Ireland 1978–83; Dir. Political Dept., Foreign Ministry, Beirut, Chair. Preparatory Cttee. of Lebanese Nat. Dialogue, mem. Lebanese Security Arrangement Cttee. for South of Lebanon 1983–85, Amb. to Italy and Perm. Rep. to FAO 1985–90, Perm. Rep. to UN, New York 1990–94; Vice-Chair. Exec. Bd. UNICEF 1993–95, Pres. 1995–. *Address:* P.O. Box 113, 5897 Beirut, Lebanon. *Telephone:* (961-1) 362662. *Fax:* (961-1) 738 749.

MAKKI, Mohammed Hassan, D.ECON.; Yemeni politician and diplomatist; b. 22 Dec. 1933; ed. Univs. of Bologna and Rome; Adviser, Ministry of Econ. 1960–62, Deputy Minister 1962, Minister 1963–64; Minister of Foreign Affairs April-Sept. 1966, 1967–68; Amb. to Italy 1968–70, 1977–79, to Fed. Repub. of Germany 1970–72; Deputy Prime Minister 1972–74; Prime Minister March-June 1974; Deputy Prime Minister for Econ. Affairs June–Oct. 1974, 1980–84; Deputy Prime Minister of Yemen Arab Repub. 1985–90; First Deputy Prime Minister of Republic of Yemen 1990–93; Perm. Rep. to UN 1974–76, Amb. to U.S.A. (also accred. to Canada) 1975–76. *Address:* c/o Office of the Deputy Prime Minister, San'a, Republic of Yemen.

MAKOGON, Yuri Feodorovich, DR.TECH.SC.; Russian physicist and engineer; b. 15 May 1930; s. of Feodor Ivanovich Makogon and Efrosinia Shevchenko; m. Inna Aleksandrovna Makogon 1961; one s. one d.; ed. Krasnodar Petroleum Inst., Moscow Gubkin Petroleum Inst.; worked at Shebelinka Gas Field 1956–58; Asst. then Asst. Prof. Moscow Petroleum Inst. 1961–74; Head of Lab. All-Union Gas Research Inst. 1974–88; Head of Lab. Oil and Gas Research Inst. 1988–; Head Natural Gas Hydrates Lab., Russian Sciences Acad.; Dir. Hydrocarbons and Environment Inst., Russian Acad. of Natural Sciences 1991–; Deputy Chair. Earth Sciences Section, Natural Sciences of Russia Acad.; mem. U.S. Soc. of Petroleum Engineers (SPE), Chair. SPE Moscow section, Chair. Oil and Gas Scientific Council, Presidium of Russian Acad. of Natural Sciences, mem. Russian Oil and Gas Industry, Scientific-Tech. Soc., mem. Earth Sciences Section Bureau; Gubkin State Prize 1989. *Publications:* more than 200 publs.; author of 8 monographs, 217 papers, 33 patents. *Address:* Vernadskogo prosp. 9, Apt. 509, Moscow 117311, Russia; Offshore Technology Research Center, 1200 Mariner Drive, Texas A-M University, College Station, TX 77845, U.S.A. *Telephone:* (095) 131-02-09 (Russia); (409) 847 9011 (Office); (409) 846 4608 (Home) (U.S.A.).

MAKOVECZ, Imre; Hungarian architect; b. 20 Nov. 1935, Budapest; m. Marianne Szabó; two s. one d.; ed. Budapest Tech. Univ.; with Buváti (architectural planning inst.) 1959–62; held various positions at planning and architectural insts. Szövterv 1971–77, Váti 1977–81; planning architect Pilis Forest Park State Farm 1981–; projects include Hungarian Pavilion, Int. Fair, Seville 1992, hotel and cultural bldgs. in Hungary, churches at Paks 1987, Siófok 1989, Százhamlombatta 1997; Head MAKONA (architectural planning co-operative); Prof. Budapest Tech. Univ., Applied Arts School; mem. editorial bd. Magyar Nemzet (newspaper) 1996–; mem. Int. Architectural Acad. 1992–; Hon. Fellowship American Architectural Assen., German and Scottish Architectural Asscns.; Dr. h.c. (Dundee); Ybl Miklós Prize 1969, Kossuth Prize 1990; Grand Gold Medal of French Architectural Acad. 1997. *Address:* Magyar Művészeti Akadémia, 1034 Budapest, Kecske u. 25, Hungary. *Telephone:* (1) 367-2480.

MAKSIMOVA, Yekaterina Sergeyevna; Russian ballet dancer; b. 1 Feb. 1939, Moscow; m. Vladimir Vasilyev; ed. Bolshoi Theatre Ballet School; with Bolshoi Theatre Ballet Co. 1958–88; toured widely; coach, Kremlin Ballet 1995–; Honoured Artist of R.S.F.S.R., Gold Medal, Varna (int. competition) 1964, Pavlova Prize of Paris Acad. of Dance 1969; People's Artist of U.S.S.R. 1973; U.S.S.R. State Prize 1981. *Main roles:* Masha (Nutcracker), Katerina (Stone Flower), Seventh Waltz, Prelude (Chopiniana), Maria (Fountain of Bakhchisarai), Giselle (Giselle), Mavka (Song of the Forest by Zhukovsky), Jeanne (Flames of Paris), the Muse (Paganini by Rachmaninov), Lizzie (The Path of Thunder by Karayev), Cinderella (Cinderella), Aurora (Sleeping Beauty), Kitri (Don Quixote), Frigia (Spartacus by Khachaturyan), leading role in Hussars' Ballad by Khrennikov, Juliet (Romeo and Juliet by Béjart). *Films:* Galatea, The Old Tango, Anyuta, Fouette. *Address:* c/o State Academic Bolshoi Theatre, Teatralnaya pl. 1, Moscow, Russia. *Telephone:* 244-02-27 (Home).

MAKSYMIUK, Jerzy; Polish conductor, composer and pianist; b. 9 April 1936, Grodno, Byelorussia; s. of Roman Maksymiuk and Bronisława Maksymiuk; m. Irena Kirjacka; ed. Warsaw Conservatory; fmr. Conductor, Polish Nat. Radio Symphony Orchestra, Katowice; Conductor, Teatr Wielki, Warsaw 1970–72; f. Polish Chamber Orchestra 1972; Prin. Conductor BBC Scottish Symphony Orchestra, Glasgow 1983–; (tours of Greece, Canada and Fed. Repub. of Germany); guest conductor Calgary Symphony, Nat. Arts Centre (Ottawa), English Chamber, Scottish Chamber, City of Birmingham Symphony, London Symphony, London Philharmonic, Tokyo Metropolitan, Staatskapelle and other orchestras; has toured Europe, U.S.A., Canada, Japan, Israel and Australia with Polish Chamber Orchestra; collaborated with English Nat. Opera (Mozart's Don Giovanni) 1991. *Address:* c/o Natalie Cruse, IMG Artists Europe, Media House, 3 Burlington Lane, London, W4 2TH, England; Hoża 5A, m. 13, 00-528 Warsaw, Poland. *Telephone:* (22) 621 39 43.

MAKTOUM, Sheikh Hamdan bin Rashid al-; United Arab Emirates politician; b. 1945; s. of Rashid bin Said al-Maktoum; Deputy Prime Minister U.A.E. 1971–73, Minister of Finance and Industry 1973–97; Pres. Dubai Municipal Council. *Address:* c/o Ministry of Finance and Industry, P.O. Box 433, Abu Dhabi, United Arab Emirates.

MAKTOUM, H.H. Sheikh Maktoum bin Rashid al-; Ruler of Dubai; b. 1941; s. of the late Rashid bin Said al-Maktoum; m. 1971; succeeded his father Sheikh Rashid bin Said al Maktoum, as 5th Sheikh 1990; Prime Minister, U.A.E. 1971–79, 1991–; Deputy Prime Minister 1979–90; Vice-Pres. 1990–. *Address:* Ruler's Palace, Dubai, United Arab Emirates.

MAKTOUM, Sheikh Mohammed bin Rashid al-; Crown Prince of Dubai and race-horse owner; b. 1948; s. of late Sheikh Rashid al-Maktoum; trained in British army and R.A.F.; Minister of Defence of Dubai; with brothers Sheikh Maktoum al-Maktoum, Sheikh Hamdan al-Maktoum and Sheikh Ahmed al-Maktoum has had racing interests in U.K. 1976–; first winner, Hatta, Goodwood 1977; with brothers now owns studs, stables, country houses and sporting estates in Newmarket and elsewhere in U.K.; worldwide racing interests based at Dalham Hall Stud, Newmarket; horses trained in England, Ireland and France; Dir. Godolphin Racing, Dubai; f. Racing Post (daily) 1986; owner, Balanchine, winner, Irish Derby 1994; winner, numerous classic races; leading owner 1985–89, 1991–93. *Address:* Ministry of Defence, P.O. Box 2838, Dubai, United Arab Emirates; c/o Warren Towers, Newmarket, Suffolk, England.

MAKWETU, Clarence Mlamli; South African politician; b. 6 Dec. 1928, Cofimvaba, Transkei; s. of Minah Makwetu and late Gqongo Makwetu; ed. Hoyita Primary School, Keilands Mission School, Nkwanca Sr. Secondary School and Lovedale School; joined ANC Youth League 1954; instrumental in formation of ANC 1959; detained several times 1960–63; then served five years on Robben Island; subsequently returned to Transkei, working in construction and insurance; detained again 1977, 1979; banished by Chief Kaiser Matanzima (q.v.) to Libido Dist. 1979–84; returned home and continued farming 1984; detained 1986; First Pres. Pan Africanist Movt. 1989–90; Deputy Pres. Pan Africanist Congress of Azania (PAC) March–Dec. 1990; Pres. PAC 1990; M.P. Nat. Ass. 1994–. *Address:* c/o P.A.C., P.O. Box 25245, Ferreirastown 2048, South Africa.

MALABO, Capt. Cristino Seriche Bioke (see Bioke Malabo, Capt. Cristino Seriche).

MAŁACHOWSKI, Aleksander; Polish politician and journalist; b. 23 Nov. 1924, Lvov; m.; three s.; ed. Wrocław Univ., during Nazi occupation soldier of Resistance 1942–45; Asst., Wrocław Univ. 1946; journalist on many periodicals and Polish Radio and TV 1953–88; Deputy to Sejm (Parl.) 1989–97; mem. Cttee. Mass Media and Cttee. Econ. Politics and Finance; mem. Labour Union Parl. Club; Vice-Marshal of Sejm 1995–97; mem. Polish del. to Parl. Ass., Council of Europe; mem. Solidarity Trade Union (NSZZ Solidarność) 1980–91; co-f. and mem. Labour Union 1992–; Chair. Polish Red Cross; numerous TV films, documentaries and articles. *Address:* Polski Czerwony Krzyż, ul. Mokotowska 14, 00-561 Warsaw, Poland. *Telephone:* (022) 628 55 75; 628 43 38. *Fax:* (022) 628 41 68.

MALAN, Gen. Magnus André de Merindol, B.SC.; South African politician and fmr. army officer; b. 30 Jan. 1930, Pretoria; m. Magrietha Johanna Van der Walt 1962; two s. one d.; ed. Univ. of Pretoria; rank of Gen., S. African Defence Force; Chief of the Army 1973–76; Chief of Defence Staff 1976–80;

Minister of Defence 1980–91, of Housing and Works, Water Affairs and Forestry 1991–93; Chair. Ministers Council House of Ass. 1991–93; arrested, charged with murder Nov. 1995, acquitted Oct. 1996; medals include Star of South Africa 1975, Southern Cross Decoration 1977, Pro Patria Medal 1977.

MALAN, Pedro, PH.D.; Brazilian economist; b. 19 Feb. 1943, Rio de Janeiro; s. of Elysio S. Malan and Regina S. Malan; m. 1st Ana María Toledo Piza Rudge; m. 2nd Catarina Gontijo Souza Lima 1980; one s. one d.; ed. St. Ignatius School, Rio de Janeiro, Polytechnic School of Catholic Univ. of Rio de Janeiro, School of Econs. and Univ. of California, Berkeley; with Inst. of Applied Research, Brazilian Ministry of Planning 1967–69, 1973–79, 1981–83; Faculty of Econs., Catholic Univ. of Rio de Janeiro Jan.–Dec. 1979; Head Int. Trade and Finance Section, Inst. of Applied Econ. Research 1980–83; Dir. Policy Analysis and Research Div. Centre of Transnat. Corpns, UN, New York 1983–84, Dept. of Int. Econs. and Social Affairs 1985–86; Exec. Dir. World Bank, Washington, D.C. 1986–89; Pres. Cen. Bank of Brazil 1993–94; Fed. of São Paulo Industries Prize for book External Economic Policy and Industrialization in Brazil. *Publications:* The Structure of Protection in Brazil (with J. Bergsman) 1971, The Brazilian Economy in the 1970s: Old and New Developments (with R. Bonelli) 1977, Brazilian External Debt and its Implications 1978, Structural Models of Inflation and Balance of Payments Disequilibria in Semi-Industrialized Economies (with John R. Wells) 1984, Financial Integration with the World Economy, The Brazilian Case 1982, Relações Internacionais do Brasil no Periodo 1946–64 1984, Debt, Trade and Development: the crucial years ahead 1985. *Leisure interests:* literature, classical music, diplomatic and financial history, swimming, tennis. *Address:* c/o Banco Central do Brasil, SBS Q 03, Bloco B, 70-074, Brasília, DF, Brazil.

MALAN, Wynand Charl, L.L.B.; South African politician, attorney and consultant; b. 25 May 1943, Port Elizabeth; s. of Dawid Johannes Malan and Annie (née de Swardt) Malan; m. Judith Rousseau 1967; two s. one d.; ed. Linden Hoerskool, Johannesburg and Univ. of Pretoria; attorney and partner, van Wyk de Vries, Malan & Steyn, Johannesburg 1966–67, Leader Nat. Jeugbond, Transvaal 1972–74; mem. Rapportraad 1971–73, Nat. Chair. 1974–76; Randburg Town Councillor and Chair. Man. Cttee. 1977; Nat. Party M.P. for Randburg 1977–87, Independent M.P. for Randburg 1987–88, Democratic Party M.P. for Randburg 1989–90; fmr. Leader Nat. Democratic Movt.; fmr. Co-Leader Democratic Party; mem. The Truth and Reconciliation Comm. 1995–; Eisenhower Fellowship 1980, ASPU Newsmaker of the Year Award 1987. *Leisure interests:* golf, chess, numismatics. *Address:* P.O. Box 2075, Randburg 2125, South Africa.

MALASHENKO, Igor Yevgenyevich, CAND.PHIL.SC.; Russian journalist; b. 2 Oct. 1954, Moscow; m.; one d.; ed. Moscow State Univ.; jr., sr. researcher Inst. of U.S.A. and Canada U.S.S.R. Acad. of Sciences 1980–89, research in problems of the concept of nuclear deterrence and public opinion; staff-mem. Int. Div. Cen. Cttee. CPSU, admin. of Pres. Gorbachev March-Dec. 1991; political dir. TV & Radio Co. Ostankino 1992–93; Pres. and Dir.-Gen. Ind. TV Co. NTV 1993–; adviser to Pres. of Russia on public relations problems, mem. election campaign staff of B. Yeltsin 1996; Prize of Russian Union of Journalists 1994. *Leisure interests:* golf, photography. *Address:* NTV, Novy Arbat 36, 121021 Moscow, Russia. *Telephone:* (095) 290 7093 (Office).

MALATESTA, Lamberto; Italian chemist; b. 20 June 1912, Milan; s. of Dr. Giuseppe Malatesta and Clara Tombolan Fava; m. Rachele Pizzotti 1947; one s. two d.; ed. Milan Univ.; Asst. to the Chair of Industrial Chem., Milan Univ. 1937, Reader 1940, Lecturer 1942, Chair. Prof. of Analytical Chem. 1948–51, of Gen. and Inorganic Chem. 1951–87, Dir. Istituto di Chimica Generale 1951–82, Dir. Dept. Inorganic Chem. 1982–87, Prof. Emer. 1987–; Dir. of a Centre of Consiglio Nazionale delle Ricerche 1970–82; Dir. Gazzetta Chimica Italiana 1971–84; Pres. Società Chimica Italiana 1971–73, 1981–83; Pres. of Div. of Inorganic Chem., IUPAC 1975–77, Pres. Chemical Sciences Cttee., Nat. Research Council (CNR) 1976–81; Fellow, Accad. Nazionale dei Lincei, Istituto Lombardo Accad. di Scienze e Lettere; Hon. Fellow, Chemical Soc. (London); Prize of the Pres. of Italian Repub. 1963; Gold Medal for Educ., Culture and Art 1974. *Publications:* General Chemistry (in Italian) 1965, Inorganic Chemistry (in Italian) 1968; co-author: Isocyanide Compounds of Metals 1968, Zerovalent Compounds of Metals 1974; about 140 original papers in scientific journals. *Leisure interests:* swimming, playing bridge. *Address:* Via Carpaccio 2, 20133 Milan, Italy. *Telephone:* 236-0350.

MALAUD, Philippe, L. EN D.; French politician and diplomatist; b. 2 Oct. 1925, Paris; s. of Jaques Malaud and Odette Malaud (née Desruol du Tronçay); m. Chantal de Gorguette d'Argoeuves 1951; one d.; ed. Lycée Lamartine, Mâcon, Lycée Janson-de-Sailly, Paris Univ., Ecole Libre des Sciences Politiques; joined cen. admin. of Foreign Office 1947; Embassy Attaché, Warsaw 1949; 2nd Sec., Cairo 1952; studied Ecole Nat. d'Admin. 1954–56; Personnel Dept. Foreign Office 1957; Deputy Chief 1958–61, then Chief of Cabinet of Foreign Ministry under Couve de Murville 1961–67; Dir. Cabinet A. Bettencourt, Sec. of State for Foreign Affairs 1967–68; elected Deputy for Saône-et-Loire, Nat. Ass. 1968, 1973, 1978; Sec. of State for the Civil Service and Information 1968–73; Minister of Information 1973, of Civil Service 1973–74; Ministere Plenipotentiaire, Foreign Office 1975; Mayor of Dompierre-les-Ormes 1965, 1971, 1972, 1978; Gen. Councillor for Canton of Matour 1967, 1973, 1979, 1985; Pres. of Gen. Council of Saône-et-Loire 1970–79; European Pres. World Fed. of Twin Towns 1973–; Political Dir. Nouveaux Jours 1975; Pres. of Nat. Centre of the Self Employed and Agricultural Workers 1980–87 (Hon. Pres. 1992–), Pres. Nat. Fed. of the Self-Employed 1988–; Vice-Pres. R.D.E. Group, European Parl., Strasbourg; mem. European Parl. 1984–89, Pres. Confed. of European Conservative Movements 1989–, Union for Enterprise in Europe (U.E.E.); Officer, Légion d'honneur, Ordre du Mérite; Commdr., American Legion. *Publications:* La Révolution Libérale 1976, La Renaissance Conservatrice 1992. *Leisure interest:* history. *Address:* 8 rue du Commandant Schloesing, 75116 Paris; Bois du Lin, 71970 Dompierre-les-Ormes, France. *Telephone:* (6) 80.33.35.15.

MALAURIE, Jean, D. ÈS L.; French anthropogeographer and writer; b. 22 Dec. 1922, Mainz, Germany; s. of Albert Malaurie and Isabelle (Regnault) Malaurie; m. Monique Laporte 1951; one s. one d.; ed. Lycée Condorcet and Faculté des Lettres de Paris; Attaché then Research Fellow C.N.R.S. 1948–56; mem. Nat. Comm. on Geography 1955–67, 1980–82; Prof. of Arctic Geomorphology and Anthropogeography, Ecole des Hautes Etudes en Sciences Sociales (E.H.E.S.S.), Paris 1957–; Founder and Dir. Centre for Arctic Studies, C.N.R.S.-E.H.E.S.S. 1957–; Dir. Arctic Research, C.N.R.S. 1979–91, Dir. Emer. 1992–; Pres. Fondation Française d'études nordiques 1964–75, Société Arctique Française 1981–90; Hon. Dean Northern People's State Univ. Herzen, St. Petersburg 1992 (and Gold Medal); Founder and Dir. Terre Humaine anthropological book series 1955–; Founder Inter-Nord int. journal of Arctic studies 1961; Chair. and organizer 14 int. Arctic confs. and seminars; has made 9 documentary films on the Inuit, including The Last Kings of Thule 1970, Inuit, from Siberia to Greenland 1980, Hainak-Inuit 1993; has led 31 Arctic scientific expeditions; the first European explorer to reach North geomagnetic pole 29 May 1951; Pres. State Polar Acad. St. Petersburg 1994–; Chair. Cttee. for the Defence of Arctic Minorities in Russia; Foundation for Culture, Moscow 1990–; Special Adviser to Dir.-Gen. UNESCO on problems of traditional ethnic groups 1995; mem. Acad. of Human Sciences of Russia 1997–; Award of Acad. française 1968, Polar Medal, Société de Géographie, Paris 1953, 1961, Académie des sciences Award 1967, Gold Medal Société arctique française 1990, C.N.R.S. Medal 1992, Gold Medal, Société de Géographie Paris 1996; Officier Légion d'honneur, Ordre nat. du mérite, des Arts et Lettres. *Publications include:* Hoggar 1954, Les Derniers Rois de Thulé (trans. into 22 languages) 1955, Thèmes de recherche géomorphologique dans le nord-ouest du Groenland 1968, Ultima Thulé 1990, Hummocks 1999. *Address:* Centre d'études arctiques (E.H.E.S.S.), 105 boulevard Raspail, 75006 Paris, France. *Telephone:* (1) 45.49.76.45. *Fax:* (1) 45.49.76.01.

MALAVOLTA, Euripedes, D.SC.; Brazilian agricultural biochemist; b. 13 Aug. 1926, Araraquara, São Paulo; s. of Antônio Malavolta and Lucia Canassa Malavolta; m. Leila M. B. Malavolta 1953 (divorced 1988); two s. three d.; ed. Escola Superior de Agricultura, Luiz de Queiroz (Univ. de São Paulo) and Univ. of California (Berkeley), U.S.A.; Instructor in Agricultural Chem., Univ. de São Paulo 1949, Private Docent 1951, Prof. of Agricultural Biochem. 1958–84; Research Assoc. Univ. of Calif. 1952–53, Visiting Prof. 1959–60; Dean, Escola Superior de Agricultura, Luiz de Queiroz, Univ. de São Paulo 1964–70, Dean Inst. of Physics and Chem. (São Carlos) 1972–76; State Council of Educ. 1980–84; mem. Brazilian Acad. of Sciences, São Paulo Acad. of Sciences, Int. Cttee. of Plant Analysis and Fertilizer Problems, Int. Cttee. of Plant Nutrition, Int. Soc. Soil Science, Third World Acad. of Sciences; Hon. mem. Brazilian Soil Science Soc., Colombian Soil Science Soc.; Fellow Rockefeller Foundation, U.S.A.; Moinho Santista Prize (Agric. Sciences) 1982, Fernando Costa Medal 1991, Prudente de Moraes Medal 1991. *Publications:* Elements of Agricultural Chemistry 1954, Manual of Agricultural Chemistry 1959, On the Mineral Nutrition of Some Tropical Crops 1962, Manual of Agricultural Chemistry-Soil Fertility and Plant Nutrition 1976, ABC of Fertilization 1954, Elements of Plant Nutrition 1981, Evaluation of the Nutritional Status of Plants 1989, Nutritional Disorders in Cerrado Soils 1985, Nutrition and Fertilization of Citrus 1990, Nutrition and Fertilization of Coffee 1992, Fertilizers and Their Impact on the Environment: Myths and Facts 1994, Nutrient and Fertilizer Management in Sugarcane 1994. *Leisure interests:* reading, music, stamp-collecting. *Address:* Centro de Energia Nuclear na Agricultura, Universidade de São Paulo, Piracicaba, 13416-000 São Paulo, SP (Office); Travessa Portugal, 146 Piracicaba, 13416-470 São Paulo, SP, Brazil (Home). *Telephone:* (19) 429-4695 (Office); (19) 422-3948 (Home). *Fax:* (19) 429-4610.

MALAYSIA, The Yang di Pertuan Agung (Supreme Head of State) of (see Selangor, H.R.H. the Sultan of).

MALCOLM, Wilfred Gordon, PH.D.; New Zealand university administrator; b. 29 Nov. 1933, Feilding; s. of Norman A. Malcolm and Doris A. Soole; m. Edmee R. Prebensen 1959; two s. four d.; ed. Feilding Agricultural High School, Wellington Teachers' Coll., Victoria Univ. of Wellington and Univ. of Cambridge; Travelling Sec. Crusader Movt. 1957–58; lecturer in Math. Victoria Univ. of Wellington 1960–63, 1967–75, Prof. of Pure Math. 1975–84; Gen. Sec. Inter-Varsity Fellowship 1963–67; Vice-Chancellor, Univ. of Waikato 1985–94; Chair. N.Z. Vice-Chancellors' Cttee. 1987–88. *Publications:* Number and Structure 1975; papers on mathematical and educational topics. *Leisure interests:* tennis, yachting. *Address:* 76 Hamurana Road, Omokoroa, Bay of Plenty, New Zealand.

MALCOMSON, James Martin, PH.D.; British professor of economics; b. 23 June 1946, Staunton-on-Wye; s. of E. Watlock Malcomson and Madeline (Stuart) Malcomson; m. Sally Claire Richards 1979; one d. (deceased);

ed. Gonville and Caius Coll., Univ. of Cambridge, Harvard Univ., U.S.A.; Research Fellow, lecturer, Sr. Lecturer, Univ. of York 1971–85; Prof. of Econs. Univ. of Southampton 1985–99, Univ. of Oxford 1999–; Fellow All Souls Coll. Oxford 1999–. *Publications:* contrib. to Efficiency Wage Models of the Labour Market 1986; numerous articles in scientific journals. *Leisure interests:* walking, music, film, theatre. *Address:* All Souls College, Oxford, OX1 4AL, England. *Telephone:* (01865) 279379. *Fax:* (01865) 279299.

MALECELA, Cigwiyemisi John Samwel; Tanzanian politician and diplomatist; b. 1934, Dodoma; m. Ezerina Mwaipopo; one s. three d.; ed. Bombay Univ. and Cambridge Univ.; Admin. Officer, Civil Service 1960–61; Consul in U.S.A. and Third Sec. to the UN 1962; Regional Commr., Mwanza Region 1963; Perm. Rep. to the UN 1964–68; Amb. to Ethiopia 1968; E. African Minister for Communications, Research and Social Services, E. African Community 1969–72; Minister of Foreign Affairs 1972–75, of Agric. 1975–80, of Mines 1980–81, of Transport and Communications 1982–85; Regional Commr., Iringa 1987–89; High Commr. in U.K. 1989–90; Prime Minister and First Vice-Pres. of Tanzania 1990–95; Minister without Portfolio 1995; Vice-Chair. Chama Cha Mapinduzi Party 1992–95; Vice-Chair. Desert Locust Control Org. for East Africa; mem. Commonwealth Group on S. Africa 1985; Order of Merit of First Degree, Egypt; First Order of Independence, Equatorial Guinea. *Leisure interests:* reading, sports. *Address:* P.O. Box 2324, Dodoma, Tanzania.

MALEK, Redha; Algerian politician and diplomatist; b. 1931, Batna; s. of Malek Ahmed and Ladjouze Zoulikha; m. Rafida Cheriet 1963; two s. one d.; ed. in Algiers and Paris; Editor-in-Chief El-Moudjahid (weekly newspaper of F.L.N.); mem. Algerian delegation to negotiations of Evian 1961–62, Drafting Cttee. of Program of Tripoli setting out F.L.N. political programme 1962, mem. Central Cttee. FLN 1979–; Drafting Cttee. of Nat. Charter 1976; Amb. to Yugoslavia 1963–65, to France 1965–70, to U.S.S.R. 1970–77, to U.S.A. 1979–82, to U.K. 1982–84; Minister of Information and Culture 1978–79; Pres. Conseil Nat. Consultatif 1992; Minister of Foreign Affairs 1992–93; mem. High Council of State 1992–94; Prime Minister of Algeria 1993–94; Pres. Alliance Nat. Républicaine (A.N.R.) 1995; involved in negotiations for release of 52 American hostages in Iran 1980–81; Harold Weill Medal (New York Univ.). *Publications:* Tradition et Révolution 1993, L'Algérie à Evian 1995. *Address:* 2 Rue Ahmed Bey, Algiers, Algeria.

MALEKOU, Paul, L. EN D.; Gabonese politician; b. 17 Nov. 1938, Fougamou; m. Odette Maroundou 1965; ten c.; ed. Univs. of Lille and Paris, Inst. des Hautes Etudes d'Outre-Mer, and admin. course, Strasbourg; Head, Interregional Service for Labour, Centre-Gabon, Port-Gentil 1963–64; Minister of Labour and Social Affairs 1964–65, of Nat. Educ., Youth and Sports, subsequently of Co-ordination in charge of Nat. Educ. 1965–68; Minister Del. at the Presidency, in charge of Co-ordination and Foreign Affairs Jan.-July 1968, for State Controls 1984; Minister of Public Works and Transport 1968–69, of Public Works and charged with Special Functions at the Presidency 1969–70, of Public Works, Housing and Urbanism 1970; Minister of State in charge of Public Works, Housing and Urbanism 1970–74, concurrently of Land Registry 1972–74; Dir.-Gen. Agence pour la Sécurité de la Navigation Aérienne en Afrique et au Madagascar 1974–; Pres. Coll. des Hauts Conseillers de l'Etat 1983–; Minister of State for State Control 1984–87; Man. Dir. Soc. Nat. des Bois du Gabon 1987–96; Chair. Bd. of Dirs. Société d'Energie et d'Eau du Gabon 1988–; Special Adviser to Pres. of Repub. 1988–; Grand Croix de l'Ordre nat. de l'Etoile equatoriale, Palmes académiques, Ordre nat. Guinéen, Légion d'honneur, Grand Officier, Ordre nat. du Lion (Senegal), Ordre nat. de l'Etoile equatoriale (Gabon), Ordre nat. de la République Italienne, Ordre de Malte and numerous other decorations. *Leisure interests:* hunting, fishing, flying. *Address:* B.P. 2825, Libreville, Gabon. *Telephone:* 72.55.97; 76.63.25.

MALENCHENKO, Col. Yuri Ivanovich; Russian/Ukrainian cosmonaut; b. 22 Dec. 1961, Svetlovodsk, Ukraine; ed. Khar'kov Higher Mil. Aviation School, Zukovsky Mil. Aviation Eng. Acad.; army service 1979–; mil. pilot of 3rd class, flew more than 800 hours in fighters; mem. staff Cen. of Cosmonauts' Training 1987–; participant of flight to space station Mir Aug.–Sept. 1994; achieved manual docking with the cargo spaceship Progress after two failures of automatic docking. *Address:* Yuri Gagarin Cosmonauts' Training Centre, Zvezdny gorodok, Moscow Region, Russia.

MALER, Leopoldo Mario, LL.B.; Argentinian artist and art foundation executive; b. 2 April 1937, Buenos Aires; s. of Abraham Maler and Esther Kraiselburd; m. 1st Silvia Oclander 1967, 2nd Joyce Pieck 1973, 3rd María Rosa Baquero 1988; one s.; ed. Univ. of Buenos Aires; journalist, BBC World Service (Latin American Service) 1961–64, 1967–74, UN Radio, New York 1980–82; Dean Parsons School of Design, Dominican Repub. 1983–85; Dir. Napa Contemporary Arts Foundation 1988–91; Examiner Prof., Leeds Polytechnic and Middlesex Polytechnic Depts. of Art, U.K. 1976–78; group exhbns. include Silence, Camden Arts Centre, London 1972, Mortal Issues, Whitechapel Gallery 1975, Hayward Gallery, London 1978, Venice Biennale 1981, 1985, Int. Sculpture Conf., Washington, DC 1990; one-man show Otros Diluvios, Centro Cultural, Buenos Aires 1987; monuments at Olympic Park, Korea, Parque de las Naciones, Madrid, Lamentin, Guadaloupe (Madonna and Child); Ed. NACA Journal 1992–; Guggenheim Fellow 1977; First Grand Prix, 14th Int. Biennale, São Paulo 1977, Gen. Motors Prize, Biennale of Sports in the Arts, Montevideo 1982, Gandhi Prize for Social Communication, Buenos Aires 1984, City of Madrid Medal for Artistic Merit 1991. *Film:* Man in Silence 1964 (Best Short Film, London Film Festival 1964). *Ballet:* X IT, The Place, London 1969. *Leisure interests:* scuba-diving, psychology, sailing, music. *Address:* Apdo. Postal 25320, Santo Domingo, Dominican Republic. *Telephone:* (809) 696-0072.

MALERBA, Luigi; Italian author and scriptwriter; b. 11 Nov. 1927, Berceto (Parma); s. of Pietro and Maria Olari; m. Anna Lapenna 1962; two s.; ed. Liceo Classico Romagnosi di Parma, and Faculty of Law, Univ. of Parma; Dir. of review Sequenze 1948–51; Advertising Man. of review Discoteca 1956–60, Ed. 1960–65; Premio Selezione Campiello for Il Serpente 1966; Golden Nymph Award for best TV film, Int. TV Festival, Monte Carlo for Ai poeti non si spara; Premio Sila for Salto mortale 1969; Prix Médicis (France) for best non-French novel for Salto mortale 1970. *Publications:* La scoperta dell'alfabeto 1963, Il serpente 1966, Salto mortale 1968, Storie dell'Anno Mille (with Tonino Guerra, illustrations by Adriano Zannino) 1969–71, Il protagonista 1973, Le rose imperiali 1974, Mozziconi 1975, Storiette 1977, Le parole abbandonate 1977, Pinocchio con gli stivali 1977, Il pataffio 1978, C'era una volta la città di Luni 1978, La storia e la gloria 1979, Dopo il pescecane 1979, Le galline pensierose 1980, Diario di un sognatore 1981, Storiette tascabili 1984, Cina Cina 1985, Il pianeta azzurro 1986, Testa d'argento 1988, Il fuoco greco 1990, Le pietre volanti 1992, Il cavaliere e la sua ombra 1992, Il viaggiatore sedentario 1993, Le maschere 1995, Che vergogna scrivere 1996, Interviste impossibili 1997, Avventure 1997. *Leisure interests:* agriculture and protection of nature. *Address:* Via Tor Millina 31, 00186 Rome, Italy.

MALESKI, Denko, PH.D.; Macedonian diplomatist; b. 14 Nov. 1946, Skopje; s. of Vlado Maleski and Maria Alivantova; m. Miriana Ivanskova 1970; three d.; ed. Univs. of London, Skopje and Ljubljana; Prof. of Int. Politics, Univ. Cyric & Methodius, Skopje 1981–91; Visiting Prof. (Fulbright Scholar), Bowling Green (Ohio) State Univ. 1990; Minister of Foreign Affairs 1991–93; Amb. and Perm. Rep. of Macedonia to UN 1993–97. *Publications:* Contemporary Political Systems 1985; numerous articles on democracy, political systems and int. relations. *Leisure interests:* reading, jogging. *Address:* c/o Ministry of Foreign Affairs, 91000 Skopje, Dame Gruev 4, Macedonia.

MALFATTI DI MONTETRETTO, Baron Francesco; Italian diplomatist (retd.); b. 13 Jan. 1920, Vienna; s. of Giuseppe Malfatti di Montetretto and Felicita Newickluf; m. Adonella Brenciaglia 1945 (died 1995); two s.; ed. Lycée Janson-de-Sailly, Paris, and Univ. of Rome; Army Officer 1939–43; Resistance Movement 1943–45; on mission to London 1945; Sec. to Deputy Prime Minister 1946; Vice-Chef de Cabinet Ministry of Foreign Affairs 1946; Sec. Italian Mission for Econ. Negotiations with U.S. 1947; entered Diplomatic Service 1947; Consul in Geneva 1948; Consul-Gen., Munich 1949, also on mission to Berlin 1949; then Ministry of Foreign Affairs posts; Counsellor, Italian Embassy, Paris 1956, Minister-Counsellor 1958–63; later Chef de Cabinet, Ministry of Foreign Affairs; Diplomatic Counsellor to Pres. of Repub. 1965–69; Amb. to France 1969–77; Sec.-Gen. Ministry of Foreign Affairs 1977–85; Grand Cross, Légion d'honneur, mil. awards for bravery in the war and in the Resistance. *Leisure interests:* painting, history, tennis, antiques, politics. *Address:* Piazza del Popolo 3, Rome, Italy. *Telephone:* 3611-788.

MALFITANO, Catherine; American opera singer (soprano); d. of Maria Maslova and Joseph Malfitano; one d.; has appeared at Lyric Opera, Chicago, Metropolitan Opera, N.Y., La Scala, Milan, Deutsche Opera, Berlin, Salzburg Festival, Royal Opera House, Covent Garden, London, Paris, Geneva, Vienna, Rome, Marseilles, Los Angeles, Florence, Hamburg, Barcelona, Israel. *Operas:* 60 roles in operas including: Madame Butterfly 1995, 1997, Il Trittico, Salome, Wozzeck, Eugene Onegin, Tosca, Don Giovanni, Fidelio, McTeague (world première), Antony and Cleopatra, The Makropulos Case; received Emmy for Tosca.

MALHERBE, René Cornelis; Netherlands publisher; b. 22 Aug. 1942, 's-Hertogenbosch; s. of G. Malherbe and R. Algra; m. Renate Emma van de Venne 1966; two s. one d.; qualified as electro-tech. engineer; with Philips Medical Equipment 1960–62, with Smeets Printing Weert 1964–66, Cargill Marketing, London and Eindhoven 1966–68, Marketing & Promotion, Eindhoven 1968–74, M & P Publishing Weert 1974–86; Dir. Malherbe Group Publishing Weert 1986–. *Leisure interests:* hockey, tennis, golf.

MALHOTRA, R. N.; Indian financial official; b. 1926; ed. Punjab and Lucknow Univs.; mem. Indian Admin. Service 1951; Head Depts. of Taxes, Finance, and Planning, Govt. of Madhya Pradesh; Fiscal Adviser IMF 1970–75; in charge of External Finance, Dept. of Econ. Affairs, Govt. of India; fmr. Sec. Dept. of Econ. Affairs, Ministry of Finance; fmr. Alt. Sec. World Bank, ADB, African Devt. Fund; Exec. Dir. IMF 1982–85; Gov. Reserve Bank of India –1990. *Address:* c/o Ministry of Foreign Affairs, New Delhi, India.

MALHOUTRA, Manmohan; Indian international official and consultant; b. 15 Sept. 1937, Izatnagar; s. of Col. Gopal Das Malhoutra and Shukla Malhoutra; m. Leela Nath 1963; two d.; ed. Delhi Univ., Balliol Coll., Oxford; entered Indian Admin. Service 1961; mem. Prime Minister's Secr. 1966–73; joined Commonwealth Secr. 1974; Dir. Sec.-Gen.'s Office and Int. Affairs Div. 1977–82, Asst. Commonwealth Sec.-Gen. 1982–93; Conf. Sec. to Commonwealth Heads of Govt. Meetings, London 1977, Lusaka 1979, Melbourne 1981, also at Asia-Pacific Regional Heads of Govt. Meetings; led Commonwealth Secr. team in Observer Group at pre-independence elections in

Zimbabwe 1980; elections in Uganda 1980; Sec. Commonwealth Southern Africa Cttee.; Head of Secr. of Commonwealth Group of Eminent Persons on Southern Africa 1986; Chef de Cabinet, Commonwealth Sec.-Gen.'s Office 1982–90, Head Commonwealth Secr. Human Resource Devt. Group 1983–93; mem. Bd. of Dirs. Int. Inst. for Democracy and Electoral Assistance, Stockholm 1996–; mem. Editorial Bd. of the Round Table, Commonwealth Journal of Int. Affairs; Rhodes Scholar 1958. *Leisure interests:* reading, music, tennis. *Address:* 118 Golf Links, New Delhi 110 003, India; 10 Oakeshott Avenue, Highgate, London, N6 6NS, England. *Telephone:* (11) 463-3475 (India); 0181-340 3189 (England).

MALICK, Terrence; American film director; b. Ottawa, Ill.; ed. Centre for Advanced Film Studies, American Film Inst. *Films:* Badlands, Days of Heaven 1978 (New York Film Critics Award, Nat. Soc. of Film Critics Award, Cannes Film Festival Award), The Thin Red Line 1998.

MALIELEGAOI, Tuila'epa Sa'ilele; Samoan politician; fmr. Deputy Prime Minister and Minister of Finance, Trade, Industry and Commerce and Tourism; Prime Minister of Samoa Nov. 1998–; mem. Human Rights Protection Party (HRPP). *Address:* Prime Minister's Department, P.O. Box L 1861, Apia, Samoa. *Telephone:* 21500. *Fax:* 21504.

MALIETOA TANUMAFILI II, H.H., C.B.E.; Samoan Head of State; b. 4 Jan. 1913; ed. Wesley Coll., Auckland, New Zealand; Adviser, Samoan Govt. 1940; mem. N.Z. del. to UN 1958; fmr. mem. Council of State; Joint Head of State of Western Samoa (now Samoa) 1962–63, Sole Head (O le Ao o le Malo) April 1963–; Fautua of Maliena. *Address:* Government House, Vailima, Apia, Samoa, South Pacific.

MALIK, Art; British actor; m.; two d. *Television:* The Jewel in the Crown, Chessgame, The Far Pavilions, The Black Tower, Death is Part of the Process, After the War, Shadow of the Cobra, Stolen. *Films:* Richard's Things, A Passage to India, Underworld, Living Daylights, Side Streets. *Theatre:* Othello (R.S.C.), Cymbeline, and Great Expectations (Royal Exchange, Manchester).

MALIK, Gunwantsingh Jaswantsingh, M.A.; Indian diplomatist; b. 29 May 1921, Karachi; s. of late Jaswant Singh Malik and Balwant Kaur (Bhagat) Malik; m. Gurkirat Kaur 1948 (dissolved 1982); two s.; R.A.F. 1943–46; Indian Foreign Service 1947–79, Second Sec., Indian Embassy, Brussels 1948–50, Addis Ababa 1950; Under-Sec. Ministry of External Affairs 1950–52; First Sec. and Chargé d'affaires Argentina 1952–56; in Japan 1956–59; Counsellor (Commercial) and Asst. Commr. Singapore 1959–63; Dir. Ministry of Commerce 1963–64; Jt.-Sec. Ministry of External Affairs 1964–65; Amb. to Philippines 1965–68, to Senegal, concurrently to the Ivory Coast, Mauritania, The Gambia and Upper Volta 1968–70, to Chile (also accred. to Peru, Ecuador and Colombia) 1970–74, to Thailand 1974–77, to Spain 1977–79; Leader trade del. to S. America 1964; mem. del. to ECAFE 1965, to Group of 77 in Lima 1971, to Gov. Body of UNDP 1971, to UNCTAD III 1972, to ESCAP 1975; Chair. Tech. and Drafting Cttee., ESCAP 1976; Deputy Chair. Cttee. of the Whole 1977; Dir. Indian Shaving Products 1986–88; Sec. Asscn. Indian Diplomats 1983–84, 1989–91, Vice-Pres. 1985–86, Pres. 1986–87; Vice-Chair. Delhi Chapter Soc. for Int. Devt. 1985–89; Chair. Aluwalia Baradi Trusts 1988–93; Vice-Pres. Alliance Française de Delhi 1990–98; Chair. Maharani Voyages Pvt. Ltd. 1995–. *Publications:* numerous literary, political and economic articles. *Leisure interests:* photography, writing, touring. *Address:* C224 Defence Colony, New Delhi, India. *Telephone:* 461 9785. *Fax:* 464 5819.

MALINVAUD, Edmond, L. EN D.; French economist; b. 25 April 1923, Limoges; s. of Auguste Malinvaud and Andrée Ballet; m. Elizabeth Compagnon 1952; two d.; ed. Lycée Gay-Lussac, Limoges, Lycée du Parc, Paris, Univ. of Paris, Ecole polytechnique; Dir. Inst. nat. de statistique et des études économiques 1948–66, Insp. Gen. 1966–74, Man. Dir. 1974–87; Prof. Collège de France 1987–93; Researcher, Cowles Foundation for Research in Econs., Chicago 1951; Dir. of Studies, Ecole pratique des hautes études 1957–93; Prof., Univ. of Calif. at Berkeley 1961, 1967; Dir. Ecole nat. de la statistique et de l'admin. économique 1962–66; Chair. Int. Econometric Soc. 1963; Assoc. Prof., Law Faculty, Univ. of Paris 1969–71; Vice-Chair. Soc. de Statistique de Paris 1971–73, Chair. 1974; Dir. of Econ. Projections, Ministry of Econ. and Finance 1972–74; mem. Bd. Banque de France 1972–88; Dir. Banque nat. de Paris 1973–81; Vice-Pres. Asscn. française des sciences économiques 1985–87; Chair. Int. Econ. Asscn. 1974–77; Chair. Int. Statistical Inst. 1979–81; Admin. Groupe des assurances nationales 1981–89; Prof. Coll. de France 1987–93, Hon. Prof. 1993–; Pres. l'Academie pontificale des sciences sociales 1994–; Dr. h.c. (Univs. of Basle, Louvain, Helsinki, Geneva, Lausanne, Montreal, Rome, Frankfurt, Milan, Lisbon, Athens, Santiago de Compostela, Bonn); Médaille d'argent, C.N.R.S., Paolo Baffi Prize for Economics, Recktenwald Prize for Econs.; Commdr., Légion d'honneur, Commdr., Palmes académiques, Grand Officier, Ordre nat. du mérite. *Publications:* Initiation à la compatibilité nationale 1957, 1961, 1964, Méthodes statistiques de l'économétrie 1964, 1969, Leçons de théorie micro-économique 1968–71, La croissance française 1972, Réexamen de la théorie du chômage 1980, Théorie macroéconomique 1981, Essais sur la théorie du chômage 1983, Voies de la recherche macroéconomique 1991, Equilibre général dans les économies de marché 1993, Diagnosing Unemployment 1994. *Address:* 42 avenue de Saxe, 75007 Paris, France (Home).

MALJERS, Floris; Netherlands business executive; b. 12 Aug. 1933, Middelburg; m. J. H. de Jongh 1958; two s. one d. (deceased); ed. Univ. of Amsterdam; joined Unilever 1959; Man. Dir. Unilever, Colombia 1964, Unilever, Turkey 1966; Man. Dir. Vdberg & Jurgens, Netherlands 1970; mem. Parent Bd. of Unilever and Head of Man. Edible Fats Group 1974; Chair. Unilever N.V. 1984–94, Vice-Chair. Unilever PLC 1984; Chair. Supervisory Bd. Philips, Electronics NV, 1994–; Dir. Amoco 1994–, ABN/Amro Bank, KLM, Royal Dutch Airlines, Philips Electronics, Guinness; Gov. European Policy Forum 1993–; Hon. K.B.E. 1992. *Address:* Phillips Electronics N.V., Groenewoudseweg 1, 5621 BA, Eindhoven, Netherlands. *Telephone:* (40) 279-1111. *Fax:* (40) 278-5486.

MÄLK, Raul; Estonian diplomatist; b. 14 May 1952, Parnu, Estonia; ed. Tartu Univ., Leningrad Inst. of Political Studies; economist and researcher Inst. of Econs, Estonian Acad. of Sciences 1975–77; sr. editor, Deputy Ed.-in-Chief, Ed.-in-Chief Estonian Radio 1977–90; Deputy Head Office of Chair. Supreme Soviet of Estonia 1990–92; adviser to Minister of Foreign Affairs 1992–93; Head Office of Minister of Foreign Affairs 1993–94; Deputy Perm. Under-Sec. Ministry of Foreign Affairs 1994–96; Amb. to U.K. 1996–98; Head Estonian dels. for negotiations with Russia, Finland, Latvia 1994–96. *Address:* Ministry of Foreign Affairs, Rävala-pst. 9, EE0001 Tallinn, Estonia. *Telephone:* (06) 31-70-91.

MALKOVICH, John; American actor; b. 9 Dec. 1953, Christopher, Ill.; m. Glenne Headley 1982 (divorced); one d.; one s. by Nicoletta Peyran; ed. Eastern Illinois and Illinois State Univs.; co-founder Steppenwolf Theatre, Chicago 1976. *Theatre appearances include:* True West 1982, Death of a Salesman 1984, Burn This 1987; Dir. Balm in Gilead 1984–85, Arms and the Man 1985, Coyote Ugly 1985, The Caretaker 1986, Burn This 1990, A Slip of the Tongue 1992, Libra 1994, Steppenwolf 1994. *Film appearances include:* Places in the Heart 1984, The Killing Fields 1984, Eleni 1985, Making Mr. Right 1987, The Glass Menagerie 1987, Empire of the Sun 1987, Miles from Home 1988, Dangerous Liaisons 1989, Jane, La Putaine du roi 1989, Queen's Logic 1989, The Sheltering Sky 1989, The Object of Beauty 1991, Shadows and Fog 1992, Of Mice and Men 1992, Jennifer Eight, Alive, In the Line of Fire, Mary Reilly 1994, The Ogre 1995, Mulholland Falls 1996, Portrait of a Lady 1996, Con Air, The Man in the Iron Mask 1997, Rounders 1998; Exec. Prod. The Accidental Tourist.

MALLABY, Sir Christopher Leslie George, G.C.M.G., G.C.V.O., B.A.; British diplomatist and business executive; b. 7 July 1936, Camberley, Surrey; s. of Brig. A. W. S. Mallaby and M. C. Mallaby (née Jones); m. Pascale Thierry-Mieg 1961; one s. three d.; ed. Eton Coll., King's Coll., Cambridge; diplomatic postings in Moscow 1961–63, Berlin 1966–69, New York 1970–74, Moscow 1974–77, Bonn 1982–85; Head of Arms Control, Soviet and E. European and Planning Depts., FCO 1977–82; Deputy Sec. to Cabinet 1985–88; Amb. to Fed. Repub. of Germany (now Germany) 1988–92, to France 1993–96; Chair. Primary Immunodeficiency Asscn. 1996–; Dir. Charter European Investment 1996–, Sun Life and Provincial Holdings PLC 1996–; Adviser to UBS 1996–, Herbert Smith 1997–; Trustee Tate Gallery 1996–, Reuters 1998–; Grand Cross, Order of Merit, (Germany), Grand Officier, Légion d'honneur. *Leisure interests:* looking at pictures, reading, travel, fishing. *Address:* c/o UBS, 2 Finsbury Avenue, London, EC2M 2PP, England.

MALLET, Robert Albert Marie Georges, D. ÈS L., D.EN D.; French university rector and author; b. 15 March 1915, Paris; m. 1st Francine Leullier 1944 (divorced); two s.; m. 2nd Yvonne Noviant 1985; ed. Faculté des Lettres and Faculté de Droit, Paris; Dir., Ecole Nat. des Lettres, Antananarivo, Malagasy Repub. 1959, subsequently Dean, Faculty of Letters, Madagascar; Rector, Acad. d'Amiens 1964–68, Univ. of Paris 1969–80; Pres. Asscn. des universités partiellement ou entièrement de langue française 1972–75, Hon. Pres. 1975–; Pres. Comité perm. des mondialistes de France 1978–; Pres. Jury du Prix Apollinaire; mem. Universal Movement for Scientific Responsibility (Pres. 1974), Acad. royale de Belgique; Silver Medal, City of Paris 1952; Prix de la Critique 1955; Grand prix de poésie, Acad. française 1977, Prix des libraires 1987, Grand Prix de la Société des poètes français 1989, Prix mondial Cino del Duca 1993; Grand Officier, Légion d'honneur, Commdr. des Arts et Lettres, Croix de guerre, Commdr., Palmes académiques, Ordre nat. Malagasy. *Publications:* poems: Le poème du sablier, La rose en ses remous, Quand le miroir s'étonne, Silex éclaté, l'Espace d'une fenêtre 1978, l'Ombre chaude 1984, Presqu'îles, presqu'amours 1986, Cette plume qui tournoie 1988, Semer l'arbre 1991; plays: Le filandier, Satire en trois temps cinq mouvements, Le train de nuit, L'équipage au complet; novels: Région inhabitée, Ellynn, Les rives incertaines; numerous other publications. *Address:* 18 rue de la Glacière, 75013 Paris, France.

MALLET, W. George, C.B.E.; Saint Lucia politician; b. 24 July 1923; m. Beryl Bernadine; ed. R.C. Boys' School, Castries Intermediate Secondary School; worked in a Castries commercial firm; mem. Castries City Council 1952–64; elected to Legis. Council 1958; Minister for Trade, Industry, Agric. and Tourism 1964–79; mem. Opposition 1979–82; Minister for Trade, Industry and Tourism 1982–92, for Caricom (Caribbean Community) Affairs and Deputy Prime Minister 1992–; mem. House of Ass. –1996; Gov.-Gen. of St. Lucia 1996–97. *Address:* Government House, Castries, St. Lucia.

MALLINCKRODT, Georg Wilhelm von; German banker; b. 19 Aug. 1930, Eichholz; s. of Arnold von Mallinckrodt and Valentine von Mallinckrodt (née von Joest); m. Charmaine Brenda Schroder 1958; two s. two d.; ed. Schule Schloss Salem; with Afga AG, Munich 1948–51; with Munchmeyer & Co., 1951–53; with Kleinwort & Co., London 1953–54; with J. Henry Schroder Bank Corp., N.Y. 1954–55, 1957–, with J. Henry Schroder & Co. Ltd. 1960,

Dir. Schroders PLC 1977, Chair. 1984–97, Pres. 1995–; Chair. J. Henry Schroder Bank AG, Zurich 1984–, Schroder Inc., N.Y. 1984–; Dir. Shroders Australia Holdings Ltd., Sydney 1984–, Schroder & Co. Inc., N.Y. 1986–, Schroder Int. Merchant Bankers Ltd., Singapore 1988–, Siemens PLC 1989–; with Union Bank of Switzerland, Geneva 1956–57; Cross of the Order of Merit (Fed. Repub. of Germany) 1990; Hon. K.B.E.; Hon. D.C.L. (Bishop's Univ., Quebec) 1994. *Leisure interests:* opera, shooting. *Address:* Schroders PLC, 120 Cheapside, London, EC2V 6DS, England. *Telephone:* 0171-658 6370. *Fax:* 0171-658 2211.

MALLOUM, Brig.-Gen. Félix; Chadian army officer; b. 1932, Fort-Archambault (now Sarh); ed. Mil. Schools, Brazzaville, Fréjus, Saint-Maixent; served in French Army, Indo-China 1953–55, Algeria; joined Chad Nat. Army; Lieut.-Col. 1961, Capt. 1962, Col. 1968; fmr. Head of Mil. Corps at the Presidency; Chief of Staff of the Army Dec. 1972–Sept. 1972; C.-in-C. of the Armed Forces 1972–73; under house arrest June 1973, released April 1975 after coup deposed Pres. Tombalbaye; Head of State, Chair. Supreme Mil. Council 1975–79, Pres. Council of Ministers, Minister of Defence and Ex-Servicemen 1975–79; resigned March 1979 after signing Kano Peace Agreement with Front Nat. du Tchad.

MALOFEEV, Anatoly Aleksandrovich; Belarus politician; b. 14 May 1933, Gomel; one d.; ed. Gomel Railway Coll., Belarus State Inst. of Nat. Econ.; worked as locksmith, Minsk, then Gomel and Minsk carriage repair plants 1949–62; mil. service; mem. CPSU 1954–91; various posts on CP cttees. Gomel, at Dept. of Chemical and Light Industries of Cen. Cttee. of CP of Belarus, Chair. Gomel Regional Exec. Cttee. of CP of Belarus, mem. Cen. CPSU Cttee. 1986–91, Politburo 1990–91; U.S.S.R. People's Deputy 1989–92; Deputy Supreme Soviet of Belorussia 1982–92; First Sec. Cen. Cttee. of CP of Belorussia 1990–93; Chair. Chamber of Reps. 1996–; Chair. Parl. Comm. for Econ. Policies and Reforms 1996; Order Red Banner of Labour (twice). *Address:* Parliament House, Dom Urada, Karl Marx prospekt. 36, 220016 Minsk; Sovetskaya Str. 11, 220010 Minsk, Belarus (Home). *Telephone:* (17) 29 33 13 (Office); (17) 222 35 14 (Home).

MALONE, John C.; American telecommunications executive; b. 1941; m. Leslie Malone; ed. Yale, Johns Hopkins Univs.; fmr. Pres. Jerrold Electronics Corpn.; Pres., C.E.O. Tele-Communications Inc. Denver, then Chair., C.E.O. 1996–; Chair., Dir. Liberty Media Corpn. Denver. *Address:* Tele-Comm Inc., 5619 DTC Parkway, Englewood, CO 80111, U.S.A.

MALONE, Thomas Francis, SC.D.; American geophysicist; b. 3 May 1917, Sioux City, Iowa; s. of John and Mary (Hourigan) Malone; m. Rosalie A. Doran 1942; six c.; ed. S. Dakota State School of Mines and Tech. and M.I.T.; mem. of Staff M.I.T. 1941–43, Asst. Prof. 1943–51, Assoc. Prof. 1951–54; Dir. Travelers Weather Service and Travelers Weather Research Center for Travelers Insurance Co., Hartford, Conn. 1954–56, Dir. of Research 1956–69, Second Vice-Pres. 1964–66, Vice-Pres. 1966–68, Sr. Vice-Pres. 1968–70; Dean of Graduate School, Univ. of Connecticut 1970–73; Dir. Holcomb Research Inst., Butler Univ. 1973–83, Dir. Emer. 1983–; Sec.-Gen. Scientific Cttee. on Problems of Environment 1970–72; Pres. Inst. of Ecology 1978–81; Vice-Pres. Int. Council of Scientific Unions 1970–72, Treas. 1978–84; Foreign Sec. Nat. Acad. of Sciences 1978–82, Chair. Bd. on Atmospheric Sciences and Climate 1981–84; Scholar in Residence St. Joseph Coll., Conn. 1983; Distinguished Scholar, N.C. State Univ. 1990–; Dir. Sigma Xi Center 1992–95, Chief Scientist 1996–98; mem. Scientific Advisory Cttee. on Climate Impact Assessment and Response, UNEP 1992–; Fellow, Nat. Sciences Resources for the Future 1983–84; Exec. Scientist, Connecticut Acad. of Science and Eng. 1987–91; mem. N.A.S., A.A.A.S., American Geophysical Union; Hon. D.Eng., Hon. L.H.D.; Hon. Sc.D. (Bates Coll.) 1988; Losey Award, Inst. of Aerospace Sciences 1960; Charles Franklin Brooks Award 1964 and Cleveland Abbe Award 1968 (American Meteorological Soc.), Int. Meteorological Soc. Prize 1984, World Meteorological Org. Gold Medal 1984, St. Francis of Assisi Prize for Environment 1991, A.A.A.S. Award for Int. Scientific Co-operation. *Publications:* numerous articles in scientific journals. *Address:* 5 Bishop Road, Apartment 203, West Hartford, CT 06119 (Office); 5 Bishop Road, Apt. 203, W. Hartford, CT 06119, U.S.A. (Home).

MALOTT, Robert H., M.B.A.; American business executive; b. 6 Oct. 1926, Boston; s. of Deane W. Malott and Eleanor (Thrum) Malott; m. Elizabeth Harwood Hubert 1960; one s. two d.; ed. Kansas Univ., Harvard Graduate School of Business Admin., New York Univ. Law School; Asst. to Dean, Harvard Graduate School of Business Admin. 1950–52; joined FMC Corpn. 1952, Controller Niagara Chemical Div. 1955–59, Controller Organic Chemicals Div. 1959–62, Div. Man. 1963–65, Vice-Pres. Film Operations American Viscose Div. 1966–67, Exec. Vice-Pres., mem. Pres.'s Office 1967–70, Man. Machinery Divs., Chicago 1970–72, Pres. FMC Corpn. 1972–93, C.E.O. 1972–91, Chair. 1973–91, Chair. Exec. Cttee. 1991; Dir. FMC Corpn., Amoco Corpn., United Technologies Corpn.; Trustee Univ. of Chicago; mem. Bd. of Govs. Argnonne Labs.; mem. Bd. of Overseers Hoover Inst.; mem. Nat. Bd. of Nat. Museum of Natural History, Smithsonian Inst., Bd. of Dirs. Nat. Park Foundation; mem. Business Council; served with U.S.N.R. 1944–46. *Address:* c/o FMC Corporation, 200 East Randolph Drive, Chicago, IL 60601-6401, U.S.A.

MALOUF, David George Joseph, A.O., B.A.; Australian writer; b. 20 March 1934, Brisbane; ed. Brisbane Grammar School and Univ. of Queensland; Hon. Fellow, Australian Acad. of the Humanities; Gold Medal, Australian Literature Soc. 1962, 1974, Age Book of the Year, N.S.W. Premier's Award for Fiction, Vance Palmer Award, Pascal Prize, Commonwealth Writers' Prize and Prix Femina Etranger, for The Great World 1991, inaugural IMPAC Dublin Literary Award 1993; many other awards. *Publications include:* poetry: Bicycle and other poems 1970, Neighbours in a Thicket 1974, First Things Last 1981, Selected Poems 1991, Poems 1959–89 1992; novels: Johnno 1975, An Imaginary Life 1978, Child's Play 1982, Fly Away Peter 1982, Harland's Half Acre 1984, Antipodes (stories), 12 Edmonstone Street 1985, The Great World 1990, Remembering Babylon 1993, The Conversations at Curlow Creek 1996; play, Blood Relations 1987; opera librettos: Voss 1986, Mer de Glace 1991, Baa Baa Black Sheep 1993. *Address:* c/o Barbara Mobbs, 35A Sutherland Crescent, Darling Point, Sydney, N.S.W. 2027, Australia.

MALPAS, Sir Robert, Kt., C.B.E., B.SC., F.ENG., F.I.MECH.E., F.I.CHEM.E.; British business executive; b. 9 Aug. 1927; s. of the late Cheshyre Malpas and of Louise Marie Marcelle Malpas; m. Josephine Dickenson 1956; ed. Taunton School, St. George's Coll., Buenos Aires, Argentina, Durham Univ.; joined ICI Ltd. 1948; C.E.O. ICI Europa Ltd. 1973; Dir. ICI 1975; Pres. Halcon Int. Inc., New York 1978–82; Chair. Power Gen PLC 1988–90, Cookson Group PLC 1991–97; Man. Dir. British Petroleum (BP) 1983–89; Dir. (non-exec.) Bd. BOC Group 1981–96, Eurotunnel 1987– (Chair. 1996–), Barings PLC 1989–95, Repsol S.A. (Spain) 1989–; mem. Eng. Council 1983–88; (Vice-Chair. 1984–88); Sr. Vice-Pres. Royal Acad. of Eng. 1989–92; Chair. LINK 1987–93; Chair. Natural Environment Research Council 1993–96; Hon. Fellow Royal Soc. of Chem.; Hon. degrees from Loughborough, Newcastle, Surrey, Bath, Durham Univs.; Order of Civil Merit, Spain 1968. *Leisure interests:* theatre, opera, reading, music, sports. *Address:* 2 Spencer Park, London, SW18 2SX, England.

MALTBY, Per Eugen, D.PHIL.; Norwegian astrophysicist; b. 3 Nov. 1933, Oslo; s. of Olaf K. Maltby and Else M. (née Raastad) Maltby; m. Elisabet Ruud 1956; two c.; ed. Univ. of Oslo; Research Asst., Univ. of Oslo 1955–60, lecturer 1963–66, Assoc. Prof. 1967–82, Prof. 1983–, Chair., Astronomy Dept. 1975–77; Research Fellow, Calif. Inst. of Tech. 1960–61, Sr. Research Fellow 1964–65; worked at Univ. of Bergen 1961–63; Visiting Scientist CSIRO, Sydney 1974–75; Chair. Norwegian Council for Natural Science Research 1978–80; mem. Norwegian Acad. of Sciences, Int. Astronomical Union, American Astronomical Soc., European Physics Soc., Norwegian Physics Soc. *Address:* Postboks 1029, Blindern, 0315 Oslo 3 (Office); Vaekerøvn 126A, 0383 Oslo, Norway (Home).

MAMALONI, Solomon Sunaone; Solomon Islands politician; b. 1943, Macedonia Village, Arosi, West Makira; ed. King George VI School, Malaita, Te Aute Coll., N.Z.; joined British Colonial Admin. Service, Honiara 1966; Exec. Officer in Civil Service, then clerk to Legis. Council 1970; Governing Council mem. for Makira 1970–76; M.P. for W. Makira 1976–77, 1980–; Chief Minister, (British) Solomon Islands 1974–76; Prime Minister of Solomon Islands 1981–84, 1989–93, 1994–98, Acting Prime Minister Oct.–Nov. 1994, f. and Leader People's Progress Party (merged with Rural Alliance Party to form People's Alliance Party 1979), Parl. Leader People's Alliance Party 1980; Man. Dir. Patosha Co. 1977; Grand Gwanghwa Medal, Order of Diplomatic Service Merit (Repub. of Korea). *Publications:* AEDO, Census Day (radio plays) 1978. *Address:* Office of the Prime Minister, P.O. Box G1, Honiara, Guadalcanal, Solomon Islands.

MAMBA, George Mbikwakhe; Swazi diplomatist; b. 5 July 1932; s. of Ndabazebelungu Mamba and Getrude Mthwalose Thwala; m. Sophie Sidzandza Sibande 1960; three s. two d.; ed. Franson Christian High School, Swazi Nat. High School, Morija Teacher Training Coll., Cambridge Inst. of Educ., Nairobi Univ., Kenya; Head Teacher Makhonza Mission School 1956–60; Teacher Kwaluseni Cen. School 1961–65; Head Teacher Enkamheni Cen. School 1966–67; Insp. of Schools, Manzini Dist. 1969–70; Welfare and Aftercare Officer, Prison Dept. 1971–72; Counsellor, Swaziland High Comm., Nairobi 1972–77; High Commr. in U.K. 1978–88, concurrently High Commr. to Malta, Amb. to Denmark, Norway and Sweden and Perm. Del. to UNESCO; Vice-Pres. Swaziland Nat. Union of Teachers 1966–67; Minister of Foreign Affairs 1988–94; Field Commr. Swaziland Boy Scouts Asscn. 1967–68, Chief Commr. 1971–72; Hon. Q.C.V.O. 1987. *Publication:* Children's Play 1966. *Leisure interests:* scouting, reading. *Address:* c/o Ministry of Foreign Affairs, P.O. Box. 518, Mbabane, Swaziland.

MAMEDOV, Georgy Enverovich, C.HIS.SC.; Russian diplomatist; b. 9 Sept. 1947, Moscow; m.; one s. one d.; ed. Moscow Inst. of Int. Relations; researcher Inst. of U.S.A. and Canada 1970–77, mem. staff U.S.S.R. Embassy in U.S.A. 1977–81, Sec., Counsellor, Deputy Chief, then Chief Dept. of U.S.A. and Canada U.S.S.R. Ministry of Foreign Affairs 1981–91, Deputy Minister of Foreign Affairs of Russia 1991–. *Address:* Ministry of Foreign Affairs, Smolenskaya-Sennaya 32/34, Moscow, Russia. *Telephone:* (095) 244-92-55.

MAMERT, Jean Albert; French public servant; b. 26 March 1928; m. Monique Petit 1966; one s. one d.; ed. Lycée et Faculté de Droit, Montpellier, Inst. d'Études Politiques, Paris, Ecole Nat. d'Admin., Paris; Auditor 1955, later Master of Requests, Council of State 1962–; Tech. Counsellor of Govt. for Constitutional Problems, 1958–59, Sec.-Gen. Constitutional Consultative Cttee. 1958; Chief of Prime Minister's Office Jan.-July 1959; Sec.-Gen. Econ. and Social Council 1959–72; Dir.-Gen. Cino del Duca 1978; mem. EEC Econ. and Social Cttee. 1970–74; with Michelin Group 1972–78, Pres. Pneumatiques Michelin S.A., Spain 1974–78; Dir.-Gen. Editions Mondiales 1978–80; Pres. Société Lorraine de matériel minier et métallurgique (S.L.M.M.) 1980;

Dir. France-Soir 1983–84; Dir. Avenir-Publicité 1984–89; Gen. Del. Asscn. Nat. des Sociétés par Action 1986–89, Pres. 1989–97; Vice Prin. SICOVAM 1986–; Dir. 1996–; mem. Operations Comm. of the Bourse (Paris Stock Exchange); Hon. Pres., Dir. Nat. Asscn. of Jt. Stock Cos. (ANSA) 1997–. *Address:* 15 place du Général Catroux, 75017 Paris (Office); 89 rue de l'Assomption, 75016 Paris, France.

MAMET, David Alan, B.A.; American playwright and director; b. 30 Nov. 1947, Chicago; s. of Bernard Morris Mamet and Lenore June (née Silver) Mamet; m. 1st Lindsay Crouse 1977 (divorced); m. 2nd Rebecca Pidgeon 1991; ed. Goddard Coll., Plainfield, Vermont; Artist-in-residence Goddard Coll. 1971–73; Artistic Dir., St. Nicholas Theatre Co., Chicago 1973–75; Guest Lecturer, Univ. of Chicago 1975, 1979, N.Y. Univ. 1981; Assoc. Artistic Dir. Goodman Theatre, Chicago 1978; Assoc. Prof. of Film, Columbia Univ. 1988; Dir. (films) House of Games 1986, Things Change 1987, Homicide 1991; (play) A Life in the Theatre 1989; recipient Outer Critics Circle Award for contrib. to American theatre 1978; Hon.D.Litt. (Dartmouth Coll.) 1996. *Publications:* The Duck Variations 1971, Sexual Perversity in Chicago 1973 (Village Voice Obie Award 1976), The Reunion 1973, Squirrels 1974, American Buffalo (Village Voice Obie Award 1976) 1976, (N.Y. Drama Critics Circle Award 1977), A Life in the Theatre 1976, The Water Engine 1976, The Woods 1977, Lone Canoe 1978, Prairie du Chien 1978, Lakeboat 1980, Donny March 1981, Edmond 1982 (Village Voice Obie Award 1983), The Disappearance of the Jews 1983, The Shawl 1985, Glengarry Glen Ross (Pulitzer prize for Drama, N.Y. Drama Critics Circle award) 1984, Speed-the-Plow 1987, Bobby, Gould in Hell 1989, The Old Neighborhood 1991, Oleanna 1992, Ricky Jay and his 52 Assistants 1994, Death Defying Acts 1996; (screenplays) The Postman Always Rings Twice 1979, The Verdict 1980, The Untouchables 1986, House of Games 1986, Things Change (with Shel Silverstein) 1987, We're No Angels 1987, Oh Hell! 1991, Homicide 1991, Hoffa 1991, Glengarry Glen Ross 1992, The Rising Sun 1992, Oleanna 1994, The Edge 1996, The Spanish Prisoner 1996, Wag the Dog 1997; (childrens' books) Mr. Warm and Cold 1985, The Owl (with Lindsay Crouse) 1987; (essays) Writing in Restaurants 1986, Some Freaks 1989, On Directing Film 1990, The Hero Pony 1990, The Cabin 1992, A Whore's Profession 1993 (also screenplay adaptation), The Cryptogram 1994, The Village (novel) 1994, Passover 1995, Make-Believe Town: Essays and Remembrances 1996, Plays 1996, Plays 2 1996, The Duck and the Goat 1996, The Old Religion 1996, True and False 1996, The Old Neighborhood 1998.

MAMIAKA, Gen. Raphaël; Gabonese politician; b. 12 Nov. 1936, Lambaréné; ed. Inst. d'Enseignement Secondaire, Paris, Ecole d'Officiers de Gendarmerie Nat., Melun, France, Univ. of Paris; Sub-Lieut. of Gendarmerie 1964, Lieut. 1966, Capt. 1968, Commdt. 1970; served French Army in Cen. Congo, Oubangui-Chari, Far East and Algeria; fmr. Commdr. Gendarmerie of Ndeu-N'Tem, Moanda and N'Gounie; Sec. of State for the Interior in charge of the Prison Service Feb.-Dec. 1969; Sec. of State at the Presidency in charge of the Interior 1969–70; Minister of the Interior 1970–73, of Public Health and Population 1973–75, 1978–81, of Public Works and Buildings 1975–76, of Justice 1976–78, of Social Affairs, Veterans, War Victims and Women's Promotion 1978–80; Commdr., Légion d'honneur and other nat. and foreign decorations. *Address:* c/o Ministry of Public Health, Libreville, Gabon.

MAMLIN, Gennadiy Semenovich; Russian author; b. 7 Nov. 1925, Simferopol; m. Diana Karakhanova; studied piano; worked as accompanist, wrote music, served in Soviet Army 1942–44, was wounded; first works published 1950. *Plays include:* Nikita Snegiryov 1956, But with Alyoshka We Are Friends 1961, Miracle at Noon 1964, Fireworks 1965, Hey there, Hello! 1970, Let's speak about the Strangeness of Love 1975, Salute to Dinosaurs 1979, The Bells 1985, Two Steps from the End of the World 1988, Life 1989, Magic Shoes 1992, On the Last Turn 1997, The Diamond Grief 1998. *Address:* Krasnoarmeiskaya Str. 27, Apt. 104, 125319 Moscow, Russia. *Telephone:* 151-88-20.

MAMO, Sir Anthony Joseph, K.ST.J., O.B.E., Q.C., LL.D., B.A.; Maltese former Head of State and judge; b. 8 Jan. 1909, Birkirkara; s. of late Joseph and Carola (née Brincat) Mamo; m. Margaret Agius 1939; one s. two d.; ed. Archbishop's Seminary, Malta and Royal Univ. of Malta; mem. Statute Law Revision Comm. 1936–42; Crown Counsel 1942–51; Prof. of Criminal Law, Royal Univ. of Malta 1943–57; Deputy Attorney-Gen. 1952–54; Attorney-Gen. 1955; Chief Justice and Pres. of H.M. Court of Appeal 1957; Pres. H.M. Constitutional Court 1964; Pres. H.M. Court of Criminal Appeal 1967; Gov.-Gen. of Malta 1971–74; Pres. of the Repub. 1974–76; Hon. LL.D. (Libya) 1971; Hon. D.Litt. (Malta) 1969; Companion of Honour, Nat. Order of Merit of Malta 1990, Xirka Gieh ir-Repubblika 1992. *Publications:* lectures on criminal law and criminal procedure delivered at the Royal Univ. of Malta. *Leisure interest:* reading. *Address:* c/o Casa Arkati, Constitution Street, Mosta, Malta. *Telephone:* 434342.

MANABE, Kenji; Japanese politician; mem. for Kagawa, House of Councillors; Sec. to Prime Minister 1958–77; fmr. Parl. Vice-Minister for Int. Trade and Industry; Chair. Educ. Cttee. and Policy Research Council; Dir.-Gen. Environment Agency 1998–. *Address:* Environment Agency, 1-2-2, Kasumigaseki, Chiyoda-ku, Tokyo 100, Japan. *Telephone:* (03) 3581-3351. *Fax:* (03) 3504-1634.

MANABE, Syukuro, D.SC.; American (b. Japanese) meteorologist; b. 21 Sept. 1931; s. of Seiichi Manabe and Sueko (Akashi) Manabe; m. Nobuko Nakamura 1962; two d.; ed. Tokyo Univ.; research meteorologist, Gen. Circulation Research Section, U.S. Weather Bureau, Washington, D.C. 1958–63; Sr. Research Meteorologist, Geophysical Fluid Dynamics Lab., Environmental Science Services Admin., Washington, D.C. 1963–68, Nat. Oceanic and Atmospheric Admin., Princeton, N.J. 1968–, mem. Sr. Exec. Service, U.S.A. 1979–96, Sr. Scientist 1996–97; lecturer with rank of Prof., Atmospheric and Oceanic Sciences Program, Princeton Univ. 1968–; mem. U.S. Nat. Research Council Comm. on Geosciences, Environment and Resources 1990–93; mem. N.A.S.; Foreign mem. Academia Europaea, Royal Soc. of Canada; Hon. mem. American Meteorological Soc. (AMS); Fellow American Geophysical Union (AGU), American Asscn. for the Advancement of Science; Rossby Research Medal (AMS) 1992, Blue Planet Prize (Asahi Glass Foundation) 1992, Revelle Medal (AGU) 1993, Asahi Prize (Asahi Shimbun Foundation), Volvo Environmental Prize (Volvo Foundation) 1997, Milankovitch Medal (European Geophysical Soc.) 1998, and many other awards. *Publications:* more than 100 papers in scientific journals. *Leisure interests:* swimming, running. *Address:* Institute for Global Change Research, Frontier Research System for Global Change, 7F Seavans-N bldg., Shibaura 1-2-1, Minato-ku, Tokyo 105-6791, Japan. *Telephone:* (3) 5765-7100. *Fax:* (3) 5765-7103.

MANAGADZE, Nodar Shotayevich; Georgian film director; b. 19 March 1943, Tbilisi, Georgia; s. of Shota Managadze and Gabilaia Ketevan; m. Jarnelidze Manana 1966; one s.; ed. Rustaveli Theatre Inst., Tbilisi. *Films include:* Expectation 1970, The Warmth of Your Hands 1972 (1st Prize Tbilisi Film Festival 1972, A Common Wall 1973, The Silver Siren 1973 (1st Prize Naples Film Festival 1973), How the Fine Fellow was Married 1974, Living Legends 1979 (participant of Cannes Film Festival, Best Film, Sitges Film Festival 1988), The Dam in the Mountains 1980, Spring is on the Wane 1984, Eh! Maestro 1987 (Special Prize, San Remo Film Festival 1988, First Prize, Baku Film Festival 1988), Noah 1990, Epiphany 1994 (Grand Prix, Tbilisi Film Festival 1994, Special Prize, Sochi Int. Film Festival 1994). *Leisure interests:* mountains, music, sports. *Address:* Bakradze Str. 11, 380009, Tbilisi, Georgia. *Telephone:* 93-27-17; 99-99-71. *Fax:* (8832) 510910.

MANASSEH, Leonard Sulla, O.B.E., R.A., F.R.I.B.A., F.C.S.D.; British architect; b. 21 May 1916; s. of the late Alan Manasseh and Esther Manasseh (née Elias); m. 1st 1947 (divorced 1956), two s.; m. 2nd Sarah Delaforce 1957, two s. one d. (deceased); ed. Cheltenham Coll., The Architectural Asscn. School of Architecture; Asst. Architect, CREN London and Guy Morgan & Partners; teaching staff, Architectural Asscn. and Kingston School of Art 1941–43; served Fleet Air Arm 1943–46; Asst. Architect, Herts. County Council 1946–48; Sr. Architect, Stevenage New Town Devt. Corpn. 1948–50; partner, Leonard Manasseh Partnership 1950–; teaching staff, Architectural Asscn. 1951–59; opened office in Singapore and Malaysia with James Cubitt & Partners 1953–54; mem. Council, Architectural Asscn. 1959–66, Pres. 1964–65, Council of Industrial Design 1965–68, Council R.I.B.A. 1968–70, 1976–82 (Hon. Sec. 1979–81), Council, Nat. Trust 1977–91, Ancient Monuments Bd. 1978–84, Bd., Chatham Historic Dockyard Trust 1984–97; Pres. Franco-British Union of Architects 1978–79; R.A. Rep. Bd. of Govs. Dulwich Schools Foundation 1987–95; Surveyor to Dulwich Picture Gallery 1987–94, Chair. 1988–93; Pres. Royal West of England Acad. 1989–94. *Work includes:* houses, housing and schools, industrial work, power stations, research centres, municipal offices, conservation plan for Beaulieu Estate, Nat. Motor Museum, Beaulieu, Wellington Country Park, Stratfield Saye, Pumping Station, Weymouth, British Museum refurbishment, additions to Old Royal Observatory, Greenwich, Service Yard, Hampstead Heath, for City of London 1992. *Publications:* Office Buildings (with 3rd Baron Cunliffe) 1962, Snowdon Summit Report (Countryside Comm.) 1974, Eastbourne Harbour Study (Trustees, Chatsworth Settlement) 1976; planning reports and studies. *Leisure interests:* photography, travel, painting, watching aeroplanes, being optimistic. *Address:* 6 Bacon's Lane, Highgate, London, N6 6BL, England. *Telephone:* 0181-340 5528.

MANATT, Charles Taylor, B.S., J.D.; American politician and lawyer; b. 9 June 1936, Chicago, Ill.; s. of William Price Manatt and Lucille (Taylor) Manatt; m. Margaret K. Klinkefus 1957; two s. one d.; ed. Ia. State and George Washington Univs.; legis. asst. to congressman, Washington, D.C. 1959–60; admitted to Calif. Bar 1962; practised Los Angeles 1962–63, Beverly Hills, Calif. 1963–64, Van Nuys, Calif., and Los Angeles 1964; mem. firm Manatt, Phelps, Rothenburg and Tunney, Los Angeles; Chair. Democratic Cttee., Calif. 1971–73, 1975–77; mem. Democratic Exec. Cttee. 1976; mem. Democratic Nat. Cttee. 1976, Chair. 1981–85, Chair. Nat. Finance Council 1978; Pres. Calif. Bankers Asscn.; Chair. Nat. Democratic Inst. *Address:* Manatt Phelps & Phillips, Trident Centre, E. Tower, 11355 W. Olympic Boulevard, Los Angeles, CA 90064, U.S.A.

MANCEL, Jean-François; French politician; b. 1948; s. of Michel Mancel and Renée Baque; six c.; ed. Faculté de droit et Inst. d'etudes politiques, Paris; Pres. Conseil Général, Oise; Pres. Oise Departmental Ass. 1985; Deputy to Nat. Ass. 1978–; Conseiller Général 1979; Sec.-Gen. Rassemblement pour la République (RPR) 1995–97. *Leisure interests:* skiing, tennis. *Address:* Conseil Général, 1 rue Cambry, 60000 Beauvais; Rassemblement pour la République, 123 rue de Lille, 75007 Paris, France.

MANCERA, Miguel; Mexican central bank governor; b. 18 Dec. 1932, Mexico City; m.; ed. Instituto Tecnológico Autónomo de México (ITAM), Yale Univ., U.S.A.; employee, officer, Banco de Comercio S.A. 1953–56; economist, Public Investments Comm. under Presidency of Repub. 1957–58; economist,

Banco de México (cen. bank) 1958–62, Admin. FOMEX, Export Finance and Export Credit Guarantee Fund 1962–67, Man. Int. Affairs, Banco de México 1967–71, Deputy Dir. 1971–73, Deputy Gen. Dir. 1973–82, Dir.-Gen. 1982–94 (except Sept.-Nov. 1982), Gov. 1994–98; lecturer, Free School of Law 1957, ITAM 1958–64, Latin American Center of Econ. Studies 1962–64; mem. Colegio Nacional de Economistas A.C., Bd. of Govs. ITAM; Rey Juan Carlos Prize for Econs., Madrid 1992, Ciudad de México Medal 1994; Gran Oficial, Orden de Río Branco, Brazil, Officier Légion d'honneur. *Address:* c/o Banco de México, Avenida 5 de Mayo No. 2, Centro, 06059, Mexico D.F., Mexico. *Telephone:* 237-2030. *Fax:* 237-2070.

MANCHAM, Sir James Richard Marie, Kt., F.R.S.A.; British politician, lawyer and int. consultant; b. 11 Aug. 1939, Victoria, Mahé, Seychelles; s. of the late Richard and Evelyne (née Tirant) Mancham; m. 1st Heather Jean Evans 1963 (divorced 1974); one s. one d.; m. 2nd Catherine Olsen 1985; one s.; ed. Univ. of Paris and Middle Temple, London; Called to the Bar, Middle Temple 1961; mem. Legis. Council of the Seychelles 1961; mem. Govt. Council 1967; founder and leader, Social Dem. Party 1964, revived 1992–; mem. Legis. Ass. 1970–76, of Nat. Ass. 1976–77; Chief Minister 1970–75, Prime Minister 1975–76; Pres. of the Republic of Seychelles 1976–77 (deposed by coup); int. trade consultant 1981–; Chair. Airominor Ltd. 1987–; Pres. Berlin-European Airways 1988–90; Founder and Chair. Crusade for the Restoration of Democracy in Seychelles 1990–; Leader of the Opposition, Pres. Democratic Party 1992–; lecturer in Geopolitics of the Indian Ocean, Int. Univ. of Japan 1996; Hon. K.B.E. 1976; Officier, Légion d'honneur, Grand Chevalier La Chaire de Rotisseur and numerous medals and decorations. *Publications:* Reflections and Echoes from the Seychelles, Paradise Raped 1983, Galloo: The Undiscovered Paradise 1984, New York's Robin Island 1985, Peace of Mind 1989, Adages of An Exile 1991. *Leisure interests:* travel, water sports, tennis, writing. *Address:* c/o Lloyds Bank Ltd., 195 Edgware Road, London, W2 1EY, England.

MANCHESTER, William, B.A., A.M.; American writer; b. 1 April 1922, Attleboro, Mass.; s. of William Raymond Manchester and Sallie Thompson Manchester; m. Julia Brown Marshall 1948; one s. two d.; ed. Univ. of Massachusetts, Dartmouth Coll., and Univ. of Missouri; Reporter Daily Oklahoman 1945–46; Reporter, Foreign Corresp., War Corresp. Baltimore Sun 1947–55; Man. Ed. Wesleyan Univ. publs. 1955–64; Fellow, Wesleyan Univ. Center for Advanced Studies 1959–60, Wesleyan Univ. E. Coll. 1968–86; mem. faculty, Wesleyan Univ. 1968–69, Writer-in-Residence 1975–, Adjunct Prof. of History 1979–92, Prof. Emer. 1992–; Fellow Pierson Coll., Yale Univ. 1991; Hon. Fellow Yale Univ. 1988; Pres. Bd. of Trustees, Univ. of Mass. Library 1970–72; mem. bd. dirs. Winston Churchill Travelling Fellowship 1990–; mem. PEN, Soc. of American Historians, American History Asscn.; Hon. L.H.D. (Univ. of Mass.) 1965, (Univ. of New Haven) 1979, (Russell Sage Coll.) 1990; Hon.Litt.D. (Skidmore Coll.) 1987, (Univ. of Richmond) 1988; Purple Heart 1945; Guggenheim Fellow 1959; Dag Hammarskjöld Int. Prize in Literature 1967, Overseas Press Club Award 1968, Univ. of Missouri Award 1969, President's Cabinet Award (Univ. of Detroit) 1980, McConaughty Award (Wesleyan Univ.) 1980, Troy Medal (Univ. of Mass.) 1980, Lincoln Literary Award 1983, Distinguished Public Service Award, Conn. Bar Assen. 1985, Blenheim Award 1986, Washington Irving Award 1988, Sarah Josepha Hale Award 1994. *Publications:* Disturber of the Peace 1951, The City of Anger 1953, Shadow of the Monsoon 1956, Beard the Lion 1958, A Rockefeller Family Portrait 1959, The Long Gainer 1961, Portrait of a President 1962, The Death of a President 1967, The Arms of Krupp 1968, The Glory and the Dream 1974, Controversy and Other Essays in Journalism 1976, American Caesar 1978, Goodbye Darkness 1980, The Last Lion: Winston Spencer Churchill 1874–1932, (vol. 1), Visions of Glory (vol. 2), Alone 1983, One Brief Shining Moment 1983, In Our Time 1989, A World Lit Only by Fire: The Medieval Mind and the Renaissance, Portrait of an Age 1992. *Leisure interest:* photography. *Address:* Wesleyan University, Middletown, CT 06459, U.S.A. *Telephone:* (860) 685-3884.

MANCINI, Giuseppe Federico, LL.D.; Italian professor of law and advocate; b. 23 Dec. 1927, Perugia; s. of Ettore Mancini and Fulvia Lina Valigi; m. Vittoria Ghigi 1956; two d.; ed. Bologna, Bordeaux, Paris and Chicago Univs.; Lecturer (Libero docente) in Labour Law 1956; Lecturer Univ. of Urbino 1956–62; Visiting Prof. of Italian Politics, Johns Hopkins Bologna Center 1957–76; Supply Lecturer in Labour Law, Univ. of Bologna 1962; taught a course at Univ. of N. Carolina and gave seminars in Dept. of Govt. Harvard Univ. 1965, 1990; Prof. of Labour Law Univ. of Bologna 1965–79; Prof. Faculty of Pol. Science, Rome Univ. 1979–82; Prof. of Pvt. Comparative Law, Univ. of Bologna 1982; mem. Consiglio Superiore della Magistratura (Gen. Council of the Judiciary) 1976–81; Advocate-Gen., Court of Justice of the European Communities, Luxembourg 1982–, First Advocate-Gen. 1985–86, Judge 1988–, Pres. 6th Chamber 1990–93; Dr. h.c. (Univ. of Cordoba, Spain) 1984. *Publications:* La responsabilità contrattuale del prestatore di lavoro 1958, Il recesso unilaterale e i rapporti di lavoro 1962, Giuffrè (Vol. I) 1962, (Vol. II) 1965, Lo Statuto dei diritti dei lavoratori, Commentario (with G. Ghezzi, L. Montuschi and U. Romagnoli), Costituzione e movimento operaio 1976, Terroristi e riformisti 1981. *Leisure interests:* swimming, science fiction. *Address:* Court of Justice of the European Communities, Palais de la Cour de Justice, 2925 Luxembourg. *Telephone:* 43 03 22 24.

MANCINO, Nicola; Italian politician and lawyer; b. 15 Oct. 1931, Montefalcione, Avellino; fmr. communal, prov. and regional councillor, Chair. Campania Regional Exec. Council (twice), Christian Democrat (DC) Prov. Sec., Avellino, Regional Sec. Campania; elected Senator from Avellino 1976, 1979, 1983, 1987; Chairman DC Parl. Group 1984; Minister of Interior 1992–94, Speaker of Senate May 1996–. *Address:* The Senate, Rome, Italy.

MANCUSO, Frank G.; American film industry executive; b. 25 July 1933, Buffalo; m. Fay Mancuso; one s. one d.; ed. State Univ., N.Y.; joined Paramount Pictures Corpn., Buffalo, N.Y. 1962; Vice-Pres. and Gen. Sales Man. Paramount Pictures Corpn. of Canada Ltd., Toronto 1970–72, Pres. and subsequently head of Paramount's Western Div., Los Angeles, U.S.A. 1972-76; Vice-Pres., Gen. Sales Man. Paramount's Motion Picture Div., New York 1976–78, Sr. Vice-Pres. 1978–79, Exec. Vice-Pres. in charge of Distribution and Marketing 1979–80; Pres. Paramount Distribution 1980–83; Pres. Motion Picture Group of Paramount Pictures Corpn. 1983–84; Chair. and C.E.O. Paramount Pictures Corpn. 1984–91; Chair., C.E.O. MGM 1993–; Vice-Pres. Variety Clubs Int. and of Motion Picture Pioneers; Chair. of Bd. of Will Rogers Memorial Fund; Dir. Will Rogers Memorial Fund, N.Y.-Cornell Medical Centre, Burke Rehabilitation Centre, UCLA Medical Centre, Museum of Broadcasting, Acad. of Motion Picture Arts and Sciences, Motion Picture Asscn. and other orgs.; Sherrill G. Corwin Human Relations Award, American Jewish Cttee. 1985. *Address:* MGM Inc., 1350 Avenue of the Americas, New York, NY 10019, U.S.A.

MANDABA, Jean-Luc; Central African Republic politician and medical practitioner; Minister of Health 1981; imprisoned for political opinions 1982, case against him subsequently dismissed; Vice-Chair. Mouvement de Libération du Peuple Centrafricain (MPLC); Prime Minister of Cen. African Repub. 1993–95. *Address:* c/o Office of the Prime Minister, Bangui, Central African Republic.

MANDELA, Nelson Rolihlahla; South African politician and lawyer; b. 1918, Umtata, Transkei; s. of Chief of Tembu tribe; m. 1st Evelyn Mandela 1944 (divorced 1957); four c. (two deceased); m. 2nd Winnie Mandela (q.v.) 1958 (divorced 1996); two d.; m. 3rd Graca Machel (widow of the late Pres. Machel of Mozambique) 1998; ed. Univ. Coll. of Fort Hare, Univ. of the Witwatersrand; legal practice, Johannesburg 1952; Nat. organizer African Nat. Congress (ANC); on trial for treason 1956–61 (acquitted 1961); arrested 1962, sentenced to five years' imprisonment Nov. 1962; on trial for further charges 1963–64, sentenced to life imprisonment June 1964; released Feb. 1990; Deputy Pres. ANC 1990–91, Pres. 1991–97, mem. Nat. Exec. Cttee. 1991–; elected Pres. of South Africa May 1994–(99); Chancellor Univ. of the North 1992–; Jt. Pres. United World Colls. 1995–; Hon. LL.D. (Nat. Univ. of Lesotho) 1979, (City Coll. of City Univ. of New York) 1983, (Lancaster) 1984, (Strathclyde) 1985, (Calcutta) 1986, (Harare) 1987, (Kent) 1992, Hon. D.Litt. (Texas Southern Univ.) 1991; Dr. h.c. (Complutense) 1991; Hon. D.C.L. (Oxford) 1996, Cambridge (1996), Hon. LL.D. (London) 1996, Bristol (1996), (Nottingham) 1996, (Warwick) 1996, (De Montfort) 1996, (Glasgow Caledonian) 1996; Hon. Freeman of London; Jawaharlal Nehru Award (India) 1979, Bruno Kreisky Prize for Human Rights 1981, Freedom of City of Glasgow 1981, Hon. Citizen of Rome 1983, Simon Bolivar Int. Prize (UNESCO) 1983; Third World Prize 1985, Sakharov Prize 1988, Gaddafi Human Rights Prize 1989, Freeman of Dublin 1988, Bharat Ratna (India) 1990, Order of the Niger 1990, jt. winner Houphouët Prize (UNESCO) 1991, Nishan-e-Pakistan 1992, Asturias Prize 1992, Liberty Medal (U.S.A.) 1993; shared Nobel Prize for Peace 1993; Mandela-Fulbright Prize 1993; Hon. Bencher Lincoln's Inn 1994; Tun Abdul Razak Award 1994; Anne Frank Medal 1994. *Publications:* No Easy Walk to Freedom 1965, How Far We Slaves Have Come: South Africa and Cuba in Today's World (with Fidel Castro) 1991, Nelson Mandela Speaks: Forging a non-racial democratic South Africa 1993, Long Walk to Freedom 1994. *Address:* c/o Office of the President, Private Bag X1000, Pretoria 0001, South Africa.

MANDELA, (Nomzano) Winnie; South African politician; b. 1934, Bizana, Pondoland, Transkei; m. Nelson Mandela (q.v.) 1958 (divorced 1996); two d.; active mem. of African Nat. Congress (ANC) until its banning in 1960; campaigned constantly on behalf of her husband gaoled for life for political activities 1964–90; held in solitary confinement 1969–70; named a 'banned person' by S. African authorities 1976, Head ANC Social Welfare Operations 1990–92; suspended from Nat. Cttee. of League of ANC Women 1992; sentenced to six years' imprisonment on four counts of kidnapping and of being an accessory to assault May 1991; sentence upheld on appeal, except charge of being an accessory to assault; prison term waived to suspended two-year term, fine imposed June 1993; suspended from ANC Women's League 1993, Head April 1997–; mem. ANC Nat. Exec. Cttee. 1994, Deputy Minister for Arts, Culture, Science and Tech., Govt. of Nat. Unity 1994–95; Third World Prize 1985. *Publication:* Part of My Soul Went with Him 1985. *Address:* Orlando West, Soweto, Transvaal, South Africa.

MANDELBROT, Benoit B., PH.D.; French mathematician, scientist and university professor; b. 20 Nov. 1924, Warsaw, Poland; s. of Charles M. Mandelbrot and Belle Lurie Mandelbrot; m. Aliette Kagan 1955; two s.; ed. Ecole Polytechnique, Paris, California Inst. of Technology, Pasadena, Faculté des Sciences, Paris; jr. mem. and Rockefeller Scholar Inst. for Advanced Study, Princeton, N.J. 1953–54; jr. Prof. of Maths. Univ. Geneva 1955–57, Univ. Lille and Ecole Polytechnique, Paris 1957–58; Research Staff mem. IBM Thomas J. Watson Research Center, New York 1958–74, IBM Fellow 1974–93; Abraham Robinson Adjunct Prof. of Math. Sciences, Yale Univ. 1987–; Prof. Acad. of Sciences of Paris 1995–; Visiting Prof. Harvard Univ.

1962–64, 1979–80, 1984–87; Einstein Coll. of Medicine 1970; Visitor M.I.T. 1953, Univ. Paris 1966, Coll. de France 1973, etc.; Fellow American Acad. of Arts and Sciences, American Physical Soc., American Geophysical Union, Inst. of Math. Statistics, Econometric Soc., A.A.A.S.; mem. European Acad. of Arts, Sciences and Humanities (Paris), Int. Statistical Inst., Société Mathématique de France, American Math. Soc., Soc. for Industrial and Applied Math.; Foreign Assoc. N.A.S.; Hon. D.Sc. (Syracuse) 1986, (Laurentian) 1986, (Boston) 1987, (State Univ. of N.Y.) 1988, (Bremen) 1988, (Guelph) 1989, (Dallas) 1992, (Union) 1993, (Buenos Aires) 1993, (Tel Aviv) 1995, (Open Univ.) 1998; Hon. D.H.L. (Pace) 1989; Humboldt Prize 1988, Wolf Prize for Physics 1993 and numerous other awards; Chevalier, Légion d'honneur. *Publications include:* Les objets fractals: forme, hasard et dimension 1975, Fractals: Form, Chance and Dimension 1977, The Fractal Geometry of Nature 1982, Fractals and Scaling in Finance: Discontinuity, Concentration, Risk 1997, Fractales, hasard et finance 1997, Multifractals and Low-Frequency Noise: Wild Self-Affinity in Physics 1998. *Leisure interest:* music. *Address:* Mathematics Department, Yale University, New Haven, CT 06520-8283 (Office); 21 Overhill Road, Scarsdale, NY 10583, U.S.A. (Home). *Telephone:* (203) 432-6471 (Yale).

MANDELSON, Rt. Hon. Peter Benjamin; British politician; b. 21 Oct. 1953; s. of the late George Mandelson and of Mary (née Morrison) Mandelson; ed. St. Catherine's Coll., Oxford; joined TUC, with Econ. Dept. 1977–78; Chair. British Youth Council 1978–80; producer London Weekend TV 1982–85; Dir. of Campaigns and Communications, Labour Party 1985–90; M.P. for Hartlepool 1992–; an Opposition Whip 1994–97, Shadow Frontbench Spokesman on Civil Service 1995–96, on Election Planning 1996–97; Chair. Gen. Election Planning Group 1995–97; Minister without Portfolio 1997–98; Sec. of State for Trade and Industry July–Dec. 1998; mem. council London Borough of Lambeth 1979–82; industrial consultant SRU Group 1990–92; mem. Int. Advisory Cttee. Centre for European Policy Studies 1993–; Trustee Whitechapel Art Gallery 1994–; mem. Panel 2000 1998–. *Publications:* Youth Unemployment: causes and cures 1977, Broadcasting and Youth 1980, The Blair Revolution: Can New Labour Deliver? 1996. *Leisure interests:* country walking, swimming. *Address:* House of Commons, London, SW1A 0AA; 30 Hutton Avenue, Hartlepool, Cleveland, TS26 9PN, England.

MANDELSTAM, Stanley, PH.D., F.R.S.; British professor of physics; b. 12 Dec. 1928, Johannesburg, S. Africa; s. of Boris Mandelstam and Beatrice née Liknaitzky; ed. Univs. of Witwatersrand, Cambridge and Birmingham; Boese Postdoctoral Fellow, Columbia Univ., U.S.A. 1957–58; Asst. Research Physicist, Univ. of Calif. (Berkeley) 1958–60; Prof. of Math. Physics, Univ. of Birmingham 1960–63; Prof. of Physics, Univ. of Calif. (Berkeley) 1963–, now Prof. Emer.; Prof. Associé. Univ. de Paris Sud 1979–80, 1984–85. *Publications:* papers on theoretical particle physics. *Leisure interests:* reading, music. *Address:* Department of Physics, University of California, Berkeley, CA 94720 (Office); 1800 Spruce Street, Berkeley, CA 94720, U.S.A. (Home). *Telephone:* (415) 642-5237 (Office); (415) 540-5318 (Home).

MANDIL, Claude; French administrative official, engineer and business executive; b. 9 Jan. 1942, Lyons; s. of Léon Mandil and Renée née Mizraki; m. Annick Goubelle 1966; four s. one d.; ed. Lycée Pasteur de Neuilly and Ecole Polytechnique; Mining Engineer, Metz 1967–71, Rennes 1971–74; Délégation à l'Aménagement du Territoire et à l'Action régionale (DATAR) 1974–77; Inter-dept. Dir. and Regional Del. Agence nat. de Valorisation de la Recherche, Anvar 1978–81; Tech. Adviser to Prime Minister 1981–82; Dir.-Gen. Inst. of Industrial Devt. (IDI) 1983, Pres. 1984–88; Dir.-Gen. Bureau des recherches géologiques et minières (BRGM) 1988; Dir.-Gen. Energies et Matières Premières, Ministry of Industry and Land Devt. 1990–; Dir. Cie. Boussac-Saint-Frères, Régie nat. des Usines Renault 1983; Deputy Man. Dir. Gaz de France 1998–; Officier, Ordre nat. du Mérite, Chevalier, Légion d'honneur. *Leisure interest:* music. *Address:* GDF, 23 rue Philibert Delorme, 75840, Paris, Cedex 17 (Office); 21 rue du Colonel de Bange, 78150 Le Chesnay, France (Home).

MANEKSHAW, Field-Marshal Sam Hormuzji Framji Jamshedji, M.C.; Indian army officer; b. 3 April 1914, Amritsar; s. of Dr. H. F. J. Manekshaw and Mrs. H. F. J. Manekshaw; m. Silloo Manekshaw 1939; two d.; ed. Sherwood Coll., Nainital, Indian Mil. Acad., Dehra Dun; commissioned 1934; active service in Waziristan, N.W. Frontier Provs. 1940–41; W.W.II Burma 1942 wounded in action, awarded immediate Mil. Cross; graduated Staff Coll., Quetta 1943; served as Brigade Maj. Razmak Brigade, Waziristan 1943–44; Instructor Staff Coll., Quetta 1944; active service in Burma and French Indo-China 1945–46; Gen. Staff Officer Grade I, Mil. Operations Directorate, Army H.Q. 1946–47, Brig. 1947; Dir. Mil. Operations 1948–52; Commdr. 167 Infantry Brigade 1952–54; Col. 8th Gurkha Rifles 1953–; Dir. Mil. Training 1954–55; Commdr. Infantry School, Mhow 1955–56; attended Imperial Defence Coll., London 1957; promoted Maj.-Gen. and appointed G.O.C. 26 Infantry Div. in Jammu and Kashmir 1957; Commdt. Defence Services Staff Coll., Wellington 1958–62; G.O.C. IV Corps. 1962–63; G.O.C.-in-C. Western Command 1963–64, Eastern Command 1964–69; Chief of the Army Staff 1969–73; promoted Field-Marshal Jan. 1973; Gen. of Nepalese Army 1970; Chair. of six cos.; dir. of ten cos.; awarded Padma Bhushan 1967, Padma Vibhushan 1971, U.S. Order of Merit 1970. *Leisure interests:* fishing, gardening, music. *Address:* Stavka, Springfield, Coonor, The Nilgiris, South India.

MĂNESCU, Corneliu; Romanian politician and diplomatist (retd.); b. 6 Feb. 1916, Ploieşti; s. of Constantin and Elena Mănescu; m. Dana Dobrescu 1950; one d.; ed. Law Coll., Bucharest; mem. Democratic Students Front, mem. Romanian CP 1936–89; Deputy Minister of Armed Forces 1948–55; Deputy Chair. State Planning Cttee. 1955–60; Chief of Political Dept. Ministry of Foreign Affairs 1960; Amb. to Hungary 1960–61; Minister of Foreign Affairs 1961–72; mem. Cen. Cttee. of the Romanian CP 1965–84; Deputy to Grand Nat. Ass. 1965–80; Head of Romanian Del. to UN Gen. Ass. 1961–72; Pres. 22nd Session of UN Gen. Ass. 1967–68; Pres. Romanian Interparl. Group 1973–77; Vice-Pres. Nat. Council of Socialist Unity Front 1973–77; Chair. Grand Nat. Ass. Comm. on Foreign Policy and Int. Co-operation 1973–77; Amb. to France 1977–82; Romanian Perm. Del. to UNESCO 1979–82; excluded from Romanian C.P. and confined to house arrest for anti-Ceauşescu activities until Dec. 1989 revolution; mem. Exec. Bd. Provisional Council for Nat. Unity 1990; Chair. Comm. on Foreign Policy 1990–92; mem. Romanian del. to 46th Session of UN Gen. Ass. 1991–92, 50th Session 1995–96; Pres. Asscn. for Int. Law and Int. Relations of Romania; mem. French League of Human Rights 1977–; Star of Romania (1st Class), Grand Officier, Légion d'honneur, Romanian Cross of World War II (awarded 1995), Slovakian 50 Years Commemorative Medal, and other Romanian and foreign decorations. *Address:* Şoseaua Kiseleff 24, Bucharest, Romania. *Telephone:* (1) 222-6303. *Fax:* (1) 222-4422.

MANESSIS, Aristovoulos; Greek professor of law; b. 23 March 1922, Argostoli; s. of Ioannis Manessis and Eustathia Vlysma; m. Mary Manoledaki 1961; ed. Univs. of Thessaloniki, Paris and Heidelberg; lecturer in Constitutional Law, Univ. of Thessaloniki 1957, Prof. 1961–68 (dismissed by mil. regime); Prof. of Public Law, Univ. of Amiens 1970–74; Prof. and Dean, Faculty of Law, Univ. of Thessaloniki 1974–80; mem. Special Supreme Court 1976–77, 1987–88; Prof. of Constitutional Law, Univ. of Athens 1980, Dean, Faculty of Law 1982–83, 1987–88, Prof. Emer. 1988–; Pres. Union of Greek Constitutionalists 1984–89; Pres. Council of Studies of Greek Parl. 1987–; mem. Acad. of Athens 1992–; Dr. h.c. (Amiens) 1980, (Thrace) 1990. *Publications:* The Law of Necessity 1953, The Guarantees of the Observance of the Constitution (Vol. 1) 1956, (Vol. 2) 1965, The Legal and Political Status of the President of the Republic 1975, Constitutional Law 1980, Constitutional Theory and Practice 1980, Civil Liberties 1982, Law, Politics, Constitution 1984, The Constitutional Revision of 1986 1989, The Constitution in the 21st Century 1993, Problems Regarding the Protection of Human Rights 1995; in French: Deux Etats nés en 1830, Ressemblances et dissemblances constitutionnelles entre la Belgique et la Grèce 1959, L'évolution des institutions politiques de la Grèce 1986, La protection constitutionnelle des droits de l'homme en Grèce et dans les autres Etats membres de l'Union Européenne 1993. *Leisure interest:* listening to classical music. *Address:* 14A, J. Gennadiou Street, 11521 Athens, Greece. *Telephone:* (01) 7210644. *Fax:* (01) 3234064.

MANGAKIS, Georgios Alexandros; Greek politician and lawyer; b. 25 June 1922; m. Angeliki St. Gonata; ed. Univs. of Athens and Munich; Lecturer in Penal Law, Univ. of Athens 1955–69; political prisoner 1969–72; lecturer in Criminal Law, Univ. of Heidelberg 1972–74; Minister of Public Works 1974; Deputy for Athens, EKND Party 1974–77; supporter of Pasok 1978–; Minister of Justice 1982–85, 1985–86, of Health and Welfare July–Sept. 1987. *Address:* 54 Solonos Street, 106 72 Athens, Greece. *Telephone:* 01-3634.750.

MANGANYI, Noel Chabani, D.LITT., D.PHIL.; South African civil servant and psychologist; b. 13 March 1940; s. of Frans Manganyi and Sophie Manganyi; m. 1st Esmé Kakana (divorced); m. 2nd Dr. Peggy Sekele 1990; two d.; Post Doctoral Fellow School of Medicine, Yale Univ. 1973–75; Prof. of Psychology Univ. of Transkei 1976–80; Prof., Sr. Research Fellow Witwatersrand Univ. 1981–90; in active forensic practice of psychology as expert witness for defence of anti-apartheid activists at Supreme Court, S.A.—1991; Vice-Chancellor Univ. of the N., Pietersburg 1991–92; Exec. Dir. PSI Jt. Educ. Trust 1993–94; Dir.-Gen. of Nat. Educ. 1994–; Founder, Violence and Health Resources Project, Witwatersrand Univ. 1986; mem. several psychology orgs. *Publications:* Treachery and Innocence: Psychology and Racial Difference in South Africa 1991, A Black Man Called Sekoto, 7 other books and 12 articles in scientific and professional journals. *Address:* Private Bag X212, Pretoria 0001, South Africa.

MANGLA, P. B.; Indian professor of library and information science; b. 5 July 1936, India; s. of Radha Krishan; m. Raj Mangla 1961; one s. one d.; ed. Univ. of Delhi, Columbia Univ., New York, London; Prof. and Head of Dept. of Library Sciences, Univ. of Tabriz, Iran 1970–72, Visiting Prof. 1974–75; UNESCO expert, Guyana 1978–79; Prof. and Head of Dept. of Library and Information Sciences, Univ. of Delhi 1972–, Dean Faculty of Arts 1976–78, 1984–88, Chair. Bd. of Research Studies 1979–85; Library Consultant, Reserve Bank of India, Bombay 1992–93; Library Adviser, YMCA New Delhi 1992–; various other admin. posts in Delhi and numerous other univs. 1972–; Chair. Manpower Devt. Cttee. of Nat. Information System in Science and Tech. 1977–; Sr. Vice-Pres. and founder-mem. Indian Asscn. of Academic Librarians 1981–83; mem. Bd. Int. Fed. of Library Asscns. and Insts. 1983– (Vice-Pres. 1987–89, 1989–91), Inst. of Information Scientists; Nat. Prof. of the U.G.C. 1984–86; Chair. Bd. of Eds. Univ. of Delhi Annual Reports 1989–; mem. Ed. Bd. Third World Libraries (U.S.A.) 1989–, Journal of Library and Information Science, Education for Information, Amsterdam, Review in Library and Information Science, U.S.A., LIBRI (Copenhagen), Third World Libraries (Chicago), Int. Journal of Information and Library Research (U.K.) 1989–; Special Adviser IFLA Regional Section for Asia and Oceania 1991–; Chair. Programme Implementation Cttee., Nat. Service Scheme, Delhi Univ. 1989–, Gov. Body Deshbandhu Coll. (Delhi Univ.) 1990–, Univ. Grants Cttee. (UGC) Panel of Library and Information Science 1992–; mem. Steering Cttee. Inflibnet (UGC) 1990–; mem. Planning Comm. (Govt. of India) Working Group on Modernization of Libraries and Informatics for 8th and 9th Five-Year Plans; Hon. Fellow Indian Library Asscn.; several memorial lectures; Rockefeller Foundation (New York) Merit Scholarship 1961–62; Int. Library Movt. Award (India) 1984, Shiromani Award for Human Excellence 1991, IFLA Gold Medal 1991; received British Council sponsorship 1979, 1980, 1987, 1989. *Publications:* author/ed. of numerous books and specialist reviews in India and overseas. *Leisure interests:* travel. *Address:* 19/4 Cavalry Lines, Delhi University Campus, Delhi 110007, India. *Telephone:* 725 7725, Ext. 317 (Office); 725-7652 (Home).

MANGLAPUS, Raul S.; Philippine politician and lawyer; b. 20 Oct. 1918, Manila; s. of Valentin Manglapus and Justina Sevilla; m. Pacita Lao 1948; five c.; ed. Ateneo de Manila, Univ. of Santo Tomas and Georgetown Univ.; wartime broadcaster; prisoner-of-war 1942–44; Chief Broadcasting Div. Office of Pres. Sergio Osmena 1945–46; Prof. of Constitutional Law, Ateneo de Manila 1948–54; Under-Sec. of Foreign Affairs 1954–57; Sec. for Foreign Affairs 1957; f. Party for Philippine Progress (with M. P. Manahan) 1957, Grand Alliance Party 1959; coalesced with Liberal Party 1961; elected Senator 1961–67; founded Christian Social Movt. 1968; elected Del. to Constitutional Convention 1970, leader of progressive opposition in Convention 1971–72; granted political asylum in U.S.A. 1973; f. Movt. for a Free Philippines 1973; Ford Foundation Fellowship, Visiting Prof. and Sr. Research Assoc. Cornell Univ. 1973–74; Sr. Assoc. Carnegie Endowment for Int. Peace, Washington, D.C. 1974–75; Adjunct Prof. for Int. Relations, School of Int. Service, American Univ. 1977–80; lecturer in Int. Relations, Labour Studies Program, D.C. Consortium of Univs. 1978; Vice-Pres. Christian Democrats Int. 1980; Pres. Democracy Int. (org. of exiles in U.S.A.) 1983; Fellow, Harvard Univ. 1985; returned to Philippines 1986; fmr. Vice-Pres. Int. Center for Devt. Policy, Washington D.C.; Sec. for Foreign Affairs 1987–90; Senator of the Philippines 1987–90; sentenced to life imprisonment Feb. 1990; recipient of several grants, awards and decorations. *Publications:* five books and numerous articles in major U.S. newspapers and magazines.

MANGOLD, Robert Peter, M.F.A.; American artist; b. 12 Oct. 1937, N. Tonawanda, N.Y.; ed. Cleveland Inst. of Art and Yale Univ.; Instructor School of Visual Arts, New York 1963–, Hunter Coll. 1964–65, Cornell Univ. Skowhegan Summer Art School 1968; one-man exhbns. Daniel Weinberg Gallery, Los Angeles 1984, Akron Art Museum 1984, Pace Gallery 1992, Le Consortium Dijon, France 1992; retrospective exhbn. Stedelijk Museum, Amsterdam 1982; has participated in numerous exhbns. notably at Whitney Museum, New York 1968, 1973, 1979, 1983, Solomon R. Guggenheim Museum, New York 1971, Documenta, Kassel, W. Germany 1972, 1977, 1982, Museum of Contemporary Art, Chicago 1974, Ritter Klagenfurt, Austria 1992–93; work represented in numerous public collections in U.S.A., U.K. and Europe including Whitney Museum, Solomon R. Guggenheim Museum, Museum of Fine Arts, Houston, Tate Gallery, London, Kunsthaus Zürich and Stedelijk Museum Amsterdam; Nat. Council on Arts Award 1966; Guggenheim Grant 1969.

MANGOPE, Chief Lucas Manyane: South African politician and tribal chief; b. 27 Dec. 1923, Motswedi, Zweerust; s. of Manyane and Semakaleng Mangope; m. Leah Tscholofelo Dolo 1951; four s. three d.; ed. St. Peter's Coll. and Bethel Coll.; worked in the Dept. of Bantu Admin. and Devt., later taught at Motswedi; succeeded his father as Chief of the Bahurutshe-Boo-Manyane Sept. 1959; Vice-Chair. Tswana Territorial Authority 1961–68, Chief Councillor, Exec. Council 1968–72; Chief Minister of Bophuthatswana Homeland 1972–77; fmr. Prime Minister, Minister of Finance, Minister of Law and Order; Pres. 1977–94. *Leisure interests:* soccer, tennis, choral music. *Address:* PO Box 245, Buhrmannsdrif 2867, South Africa.

MANHIRE, William (Bill), M.PHIL.; New Zealand poet and academic; b. 27 Dec. 1946, Invercargill; s. of Jack Manhire and Madeline Mary Manhire; m. Barbara Marion McLeod 1970; one s. one d.; ed. S. Otago Dist. High School, Otago Boys' High School, Univ. of Otago, Univ. Coll., London; Lecturer in English, Vic. Univ., Wellington 1973, f. influential creative writing programme 1976, Prof. of Creative Writing and English Literature 1997–; Fiction Ed. Victoria Univ. Press 1976–96; Fulbright Visiting Prof. in N.Z. Studies, Georgetown Univ., U.S.A. Jan.–June 1999; inaugural Poet Laureate of N.Z. 1997–; N.Z. Book Award 1977, 1984, 1992, 1996; Montana Book Award 1994; Nuffield Fellowship 1981. *Publications:* The Elaboration 1972, How to Take Off Your Clothes at the Picnic 1977, Good Looks 1982, Some Other Country (ed.) 1984, Zoetropes 1984, Maurice Gee 1986, Six By Six (ed.) 1989, Milky Way Bar 1991, Soho Square (ed.) 1991, South Pacific 1994, 100 New Zealand Poems 1994 (ed.), Sheet Music 1996, My Sunshine 1996, Mutes and Earthquakes 1997. *Leisure interest:* swimming. *Address:* School of English, Film and Theatre, Victoria University, P.O. Box 600, Wellington, New Zealand. *Telephone:* (04) 472-1000. *Fax:* (04) 495-5148.

MANIATOPOULOS, Constantinos S.; Greek European Union official and business executive; b. 1941; m.; one s.; ed. Athens and Paris; fmrly. employed in energy and industry sectors; Chair. and Man. Dir. EKO Petroleum Co., Greece; Special Adviser to Minister of Energy; mem. Bd. various nat. advisory bodies; Gen. Sec. Tech. Chamber of Greece; Dir.-Gen. for Energy, EC (now EU) Comm. 1986–95. *Address:* 13 Makedonias Street, Kifissia, Athens, Greece.

MANIGAT, Leslie; Haitian politician and academic; b. 16 Aug. 1930, Port-au-Prince; m. 2nd Mirlande Manigat 1970; f. School of Int. Studies at Univ. of Haiti, first Dir.; fmr. Research Assoc. Johns Hopkins Univ., Washington; fmr. Prof. Inst. of Political Studies, Paris; then with Univ. of West Indies, Trinidad and Tobago; with Simón Bolívar Univ., Caracas 1978; returned from 23 years in exile 1986; Pres. of Haiti Jan. 1988, overthrown June 1988.

MANIKFAN, Hussein; Maldivian politician; b. 16 June 1936; s. of Ali Manikfan and Khadheeja Manike'; m. 1st Aminath Shareefa 1959; m. 2nd Haseena Ali 1971; six c.; served in civil service, Ministry of Educ., Dept. of Information, Ministry of Finance and Office of the Pres. of the Repub. 1953–58; Sec. Ministry of Trust and Public Endowment 1958; teacher, Ministry of Educ. 1959; served in Ministry of Home Affairs, Dept. of Posts and Telecommunications and at Pres.'s Official Residence 1959–74; Sec. Dept. of Electricity 1974; mem. Maldives Parl. 1970–; Under-Sec. Ministry of Transport 1978; Dir. Unit, Malé Int. Airport 1978; Man. Dir. Govt. Fishing Corpn. 1982; Deputy Minister of Trade and Industries 1982–88; Perm. Rep. to UN 1988–91; Minister of State in charge of Customs 1991–. *Leisure interests:* reading, tennis, T.T.

MANILOV, Col.-Gen. Valery Leonidovich; Russian civil servant and army officer; b. 10 Jan. 1939, Tulchin, Ukraine; ed. Odessa Higher Infantry School, Mil.-Political Acad., Gen. Staff Mil. Acad.; service in Odessa, Baikal mil. commands, S. Group of armed forces, service in Afghanistan; on staff U.S.S.R. Ministry of Defence 1988–; Head Information Service of Jt. Armed Forces of C.I.S. 1992–93; Asst. to Sec. Russian Security Council July-Oct. 1993, Deputy Sec. 1993–96; First Deputy Head of Gen. Staff. 1998–. *Address:* c/o Ministry of Defence, Myasnitskaya 37, 101000 Moscow, Russia.

MANILOW, Barry; American singer and composer; b. 17 June 1946, New York; s. of Harold Manilow and Edna Manilow; ed. New York Coll. Music; worked in mailroom, CBS; film ed. WCBS-TV; Dir. Music Ed Sullivan's Pilots; Dir. Music, Conductor and Producer for Bette Midler; singer and composer; appeared in TV film Copacabana 1985; Amb. for Prince's Trust 1996. *Songs include:* Mandy, I Write the Songs, At the Copa, Looks Like We Made It, Can't Smile Without You, Even Now, Could it be Magic, and others; Broadway production, Barry Manilow at the Gershwin 1989; Producer of Year 1975; Ruby Award, After Dark magazine 1976; Photoplay Gold Medal Award 1976; Tony Award (jt.) 1977, named Humanitarian of the Year (Starlight Foundation) 1991. *Publication:* Sweet Life: Adventures on the Way to Paradise 1987. *Address:* Arista Records, 6 W. 57th Street, New York, NY 10019, U.S.A.

MANKIEWICZ, Frank, M.S., A.B., LL.B.; American public affairs executive; b. 16 May 1924, New York; s. of Herman J. and Sara Mankiewicz; m. Holly Jolley 1952 (divorced); two s.; m. 2nd Patricia O'Brien 1988; ed. Columbia Univ., Univ. of Calif., Berkeley and Los Angeles; mem. Calif. and D.C. Bars; practised as lawyer, Los Angeles 1955–61; served with Peace Corps as Country Dir., Lima, Peru and later as Regional Dir. for Latin America; Press Sec. to late Senator Robert F. Kennedy 1966–68; syndicated columnist (with Tom Braden), Washington and co-presenter, nightly newscast on CBS television affiliate 1968–71; Campaign Dir. presidential campaign of George McGovern 1972; Pres. Nat. Public Radio 1977–83; Vice-Chair. Gray and Co. (now Hill and Knowlton) 1983–; Univ. of Calif. (L.A.) Public Service Award; Hon. D.H.L. (Lincoln Univ.). *Publications:* Perfectly Clear: Nixon from Whittier to Watergate 1973, U.S. *v.* Richard Nixon: The Final Crisis 1975, With Fidel: A Portrait of Castro and Cuba 1975, Remote Control: Television and the Manipulation of American Life 1977. *Leisure interests:* baseball, literature, U.S. political history. *Address:* Hill and Knowlton, 600 New Hampshire Avenue, N.W., Washington, DC 20037, U.S.A. *Telephone:* (202) 333-7400.

MANLEY, Albert Leslie; South African diplomatist; b. 1945, Cape Town; s. of Albert George Rowan Manley and Mary Leslie Manley; m. Charlene Manley 1988; three s.; ed. Univ. of Orange Free State; entered Dept. of Foreign Affairs 1969, Desk Officer for Middle E. 1974–76, Planning Section of Ministry, Pretoria and Cape Town 1981–82, other posts 1982–86; Vice-Consul in Lourenço Marques (now Maputo) 1970–74; Counsellor for Political Affairs at Embassy, London 1977–81; Perm. Rep. to UN, New York 1987–88, Geneva 1988–92; Head Int. Econs., Foreign Ministry 1992–94, Head Int. Devt. and Econ. Affairs 1995–; Fellow Center for Int. Affairs, Harvard Univ. 1994–95. *Leisure interests:* golf, music, books. *Address:* Department of Foreign Affairs, Private Bag X152, Pretoria 0001, South Africa. *Telephone:* (12) 351-1920. *Fax:* (12) 351-1628.

MANLEY, John; Canadian politician and lawyer; m. Judith Manley; one s. two d.; fmrly. practitioner in business and income tax law, Ottawa; mem. Parl. 1988–; Minister of Industry 1993–, also Minister responsible for Atlantic Canada Opportunities Agency, Canada Econ. Devt. and Western Econ. Diversification 1996–97; holds responsibility for numerous govt. agencies including Canadian Space Agency, Nat. Research Council, Business Devt. Bank of Canada, Canadian Tourism Comm. etc. *Address:* Department of Industry, C.D. Howe Bldg., 235 Queen Street, Ottawa, Ont., K1A 0H5, Canada. *Telephone:* (613) 995-9001. *Fax:* (613) 992-0302.

MANN, Michael K.; American producer, director and writer; b. Chicago; ed. Univ. of Wisconsin, London Film School; Exec. Producer (TV) Miami Vice, Crime Story, Drug Wars: Camarena Story, Drug Wars: Cocaine Cartel, Police Story, Starsky and Hutch; mem. Writers Guild, Dirs. Guild; Best Dir.

Award (for The Jericho Mile), Dirs. Guild; two Emmy Awards. *Films directed include:* The Jericho Mile (TV film, also scriptwriter, 1979), Thief (also exec. producer and scriptwriter) 1981, The Keep (also scriptwriter) 1981, Manhunter (also scriptwriter) 1986, Last of the Mohicans (also co-producer, scriptwriter) 1992, Heat (also co-producer, scriptwriter) 1995. *Address:* c/o Creative Artists Agency, 9830 Wilshire Boulevard, Beverly Hills, CA 90212, U.S.A.

MANN, Robert Wellesley, S.B., S.M., SC.D.; American professor of engineering design and biomedical research; b. 6 Oct. 1924, Brooklyn, New York; s. of Arthur Wellesley Mann and Helen Rieger Mann; m. Margaret Florencourt Mann 1950; one s. one d.; ed. M.I.T.; Draftsman Bell Telephone Labs. 1942–43, 1946–47; Technician (3rd) U.S. Army Signal Corps 1943–46; Research Engineer and Supervisor Design Div. Dynamic Analysis and Control Lab., M.I.T. 1951–56, Asst. Prof. of Mechanical Eng. 1953–58, Head Eng. Design Div. Dept. of Mechanical Eng. 1957–66, 1982–83, Assoc. Prof. of Mechanical Eng. 1958–63, Prof. 1963–70, Germeshausen Prof. 1970–72, Prof. of Eng. 1972–74, Whitaker Prof. of Biomedical Eng. 1974–92, Whitaker Prof. Emer. 1992–; Prof. Harvard-M.I.T. Div. of Health Sciences and Tech. 1973–; Dir. Newman Lab. for Biomechanics and Human Rehabilitation 1975–92; Dir. Bioeng. Programmes, Whitaker Coll., M.I.T. 1986–89; Dir. Harvard-MIT Rehabilitation Eng. Centre 1988–92; mem. N.A.S., Nat. Acad. of Eng., Inst. of Medicine; Fellow American Acad. of Arts and Sciences, Inst. of Electrical and Electronics Engineers, American Soc. of Mechanical Engineers, A.A.A.S., American Inst. of Medical and Biological Engineers; Gold Medal, American Soc. of Mechanical Engineers, Lissner Award for Outstanding Bioeng., New England Award, Goldenson Award for Outstanding Scientific Research for the Physically Handicapped, James R. Killian Jr. Faculty Achievement Award, M.I.T., Inaugural Recipient, Dr. Martin Luther King, Jr. Leadership Award, M.I.T. *Publications:* over 360 professional publs. and four patents on missile research, eng. design, computer-aided design, biomedical eng., human rehabilitation, synovial joint biomechanics and the etiology of osteoarthritis. *Leisure interests:* gardening, crafts, sailing. *Address:* Massachusetts Institute of Technology, Room 3-137D, 77 Massachusetts Avenue, Cambridge, MA 02139 (Office); 5 Pelham Road, Lexington, MA 02173, U.S.A. (Home). *Telephone:* (617) 253-2220 (Office); (617) 862-6953 (Home). *Fax:* (617) 862 6953.

MANN, Yuri Vladimirovich, DR.PHIL.SC.; Russian literary scholar and historian; b. 9 June 1929, Moscow; s. of Vladimir Mann and Sonja Mann; m. Galina Mann 1956; two s.; ed. Moscow Univ.; Prof. of Russian Literature, Gorky Inst. of World Literature –1992; Prof. Russian State Humanitarian Univ. 1992–; mem. CPSU 1952–90, Russian PEN Centre 1995, Acad. of Natural Sciences 1996. *Publications include:* Russian Philosophical Aesthetics 1820s–1830s 1969, The Poetics of Russian Romanticism 1976, The Poetics of Gogol 1978, In Search of a Live Soul—Gogol's Dead Souls 1984, The Dialectics of Image 1987, The Aksakov Family 1992, Beyond the Mask of Laughter: The Life of Nikolai Gogol 1994, The Dynamics of Russian Romanticism 1995. *Address:* Astrakhansky pereulok, 5, Apt. 99, Moscow 129010, Russia. *Telephone:* 280-16-71.

MANNING, David Geoffrey, C.M.G., M.A.; British diplomatist; b. 5 Dec. 1949, Portsmouth; s. of John Robert Manning and Joan Barbara Manning; m. Catherine Marjory Parkinson 1973; ed. Ardingly Coll., Oriel Coll. Oxford, Johns Hopkins Univ., U.S.A.; Third Sec., FCO (Mexico, Cen. America Dept.) 1972; Third, later Second Sec., Warsaw 1974–76; Second, later First Sec., New Delhi 1977–80; E. European and Soviet Dept. FCO 1980–82; Policy Planning Staff, FCO 1982–84; First Sec. (Political Internal), Paris 1984–88; Counsellor on loan to Cabinet Office 1988–90; Counsellor, Head of Political Section, Moscow 1990–93; Head, Eastern Dept. (fmrly. Soviet Dept.), FCO 1993–94; British mem. of ICFY Contact Group on Bosnia April–Nov. 1994; Head of Planning Staff 1994–95; Amb. to Israel 1995–98. *Address:* c/o Foreign and Commonwealth Office (Tel Aviv), King Charles Street, London, SW1A 2AH, England.

MANNING, Jane, O.B.E., F.R.A.M., F.R.C.M., G.R.S.M.; British concert and opera singer; b. 20 Sept. 1938, Norwich; d. of Gerald Manning and Lily Thompson; m. Anthony Payne 1966; ed. Norwich High School for Girls, R.A.M., London and Scuola di Canto, Cureglia, Switzerland; London début concert 1964; since then active world-wide as freelance soprano soloist with special expertise in contemporary music; more than 350 BBC broadcasts; regular tours of U.S.A. since 1981, and of Australia since 1978; appearances at all leading European festivals and concert halls; New York début 1983; more than 300 world premières including several operas; Founder/Artistic Dir. Jane's Minstrels (ensemble) 1988; also active as lecturer; Visiting Artist, Univ. of Manitoba, Canada 1992; many recordings including complete vocal works of Messiaen and Satie; Vice-Pres. Soc. for Promotion of New Music 1996–; Visiting Prof., Mills Coll., Oakland, Calif. 1981, 1982, 1983, 1986, Royal Coll. of Music 1995–; Hon. Prof. Keele Univ. 1996–(99); visiting lecturer, univs. in U.K., U.S.A., Australia, N.Z. and Scandinavia; mem. Exec. Cttee. Musicians' Benevolent Fund; Hon. D. Univ. (York) 1988; Special Award for Services to British Music, Composers' Guild of G.B. 1973. *Publications:* New Vocal Repertory (Vol. I) 1986, (Vol. II) 1998, A Messiaen Companion 1995. *Leisure interests:* cooking, ornithology, cinema, philosophy, reading. *Address:* 2 Wilton Square, London, N.1, England. *Telephone:* 0171-359 1593. *Fax:* 0171-226 4369.

MANNING, Patrick Augustus Mervyn, B.SC.; Trinidad and Tobago politician; b. 17 August 1946, Trinidad; s. of Arnold Manning and Elaine Manning; m. Hazel Anne-Marie Kinsale 1972; two s.; ed. Presentation Coll., San Fernando and Univ. of the West Indies; refinery operator Texaco, Trinidad 1965–66; Parl. Sec. 1971–78, Minister 1978–86; Minister of Information, and of Industry and Commerce 1981, of Energy 1981–86; Leader of the Opposition 1986–90; Prime Minister 1991–95, also fmr. Minister of Nat. Security; Leader People's Nat. Movt. 1987–. *Leisure interests:* table tennis, chess, reading. *Address:* Prime Minister's Residence, La Fantaisie Road, St. Ann's, Trinidad (Home). *Telephone:* 658-5838 (Home).

MANNING, Robert Joseph; American journalist; b. 25 Dec. 1919, Binghamton, N.Y.; s. of Joseph James Manning and Agnes Pauline Brown; m. 1st Margaret Marinda Raymond 1944 (died 1984); three s.; m. 2nd Theresa Slomkouski 1987; U.S. Army service 1942–43; Nieman Fellow, Harvard Univ. 1945–46; State Dept. and White House Corresp. United Press. 1944–46, Chief UN Corresp. United Press. 1946–49; Writer, Time magazine 1949–55, Senior Ed. 1955–58, Chief, London Bureau, Time, Life, Fortune, Sports Illustrated magazines 1958–61; Sunday Ed., New York Herald Tribune 1961–62; Asst. Sec. of State for Public Affairs, U.S. Dept. of State 1962–64; Exec. Ed. Atlantic Monthly 1964–66, Ed.-in-Chief 1966–80; Vice-Pres. Atlantic Monthly Co. 1966–80; Ed.-in-Chief Boston Publishing Co. 1981–87; Pres., Ed.-in-Chief Bobcat Books Inc., Boston 1987–; Fellow, Kennedy Inst. of Politics, Harvard Univ. 1980; mem. A.A.A.S. *Address:* 191 Commonwealth Avenue, Boston, MA 02116, U.S.A. (Office and Home).

MANOLIČ, Josip; Croatian politician and lawyer; b. 22 March 1920, Kalinovac; m. Maria Manolic; three d.; ed. Zagreb Univ.; youth orgs. and trade union activist 1938–; mem. anti-fascist movt.; Sec. Dist. Cttee. League of Communist Youth of Croatia; Chief Dept. of Nat. Security in Bjelovar 1945–46 (dismissed); worked in Ministry of Internal Affairs of Croatia 1948–60; Interior Affairs Secr. in Zagreb 1960–65; mem. of Parl. Repub. of Croatia, Pres. Legis. Body of Constitutional Comm. 1965–71; mandate suspended because of nationalist activities; co-founder Croatian Democratic Union (HDZ); first Chair. Exec. Cttee. 1989; Vice-Pres. 1990–; mem. of Croatian Parl. 1990–; Vice-Pres. Presidency of Repub. Croatia 1990–; Pres. Croatian Govt. 1990–91; Pres. House of Counties of Croatian Parl. 1992–94; Pres. Emergency Bd. of Croatia; Dir. Bureau of Constitutional Order 1991–93; an organizer of Croatian army. *Leisure interest:* chess. *Address:* Nazorova str. 57, 41000 Zagreb, Croatia (Office).

MANSELL, Nigel, O.B.E.; British racing driver; b. 8 Aug. 1953, Upton-on-Severn; m. Rosanne Perry; two s. one d.; began in Kart-racing, then Formula Ford (won Brush Fusegear 1977), Formula 3 1978–79, first Grand Prix, Austria 1980; winner S. African Grand Prix 1992; mem. Lotus Grand Prix team 1980–84, Williams team 1985–88, 1991–92, Ferrari team 1989–90, Newman-Haas IndyCar team 1992–95, McLaren team 1995–; winner of 31 Grands Prix (Nov. 1994); surpassed Jackie Stewart's (q.v.) British record of 27 wins, winner of 31 Grand Prix 1995; World Champion 1992; PPG IndyCar World Series Champion 1993; Hon. D.Eng. (Birmingham) 1993; BBC Sports Personality of the Year 1986, 1992; special constable Isle of Man. *Publications:* Mansell and Williams (with Derick Allsop) 1992, Nigel Mansell's IndyCar Racing (with Jeremy Shaw) 1993, My Autobiography (with James Allen) 1995. *Leisure interests:* golf, fishing. *Address:* c/o Nicki Dance, Woodbury Park Golf and Country Club, Woodbury Castle, Woodbury, Exeter, Devon, EX5 1JJ, England.

MANSER, Michael John, C.B.E., R.A., DIPL. ARCH., P.R.I.B.A.; British architect; b. 23 March 1929, London; s. of the late Edmund G. and Augusta M. Manser; m. Dolores Josephine Bernini 1953; one s. one d.; ed. School of Architecture, The Polytechnic of Cen. London; Chair. Manser Assocs. Ltd. (architects) 1961–; architectural corresp. The Observer 1964–66; engaged on wide variety of architectural projects including private housing, industrial buildings, research labs., schools, swimming pools, commercial and domestic renovation and refurbishment, hotel alterations in Paris and factory extensions in Netherlands; Pres. R.I.B.A. 1983–85; Academician Royal Acad. 1994; R.I.B.A. Rep. R.S.A. 1987–93 (Chair. Art for Architecture Award Scheme 1990–); mem. Council Nat. Trust 1991–93; Assessor Art in the Workplace Awards 1988–, Chair. Art and Work Awards 1996–; mem. Royal Acad. Council 1998–; Architectural Cttee. 1998–; Hon. F.R.A.I.C.; Royal W. of England Academician 1993–; Civic Trust Award 1967, Civic Trust Commendation 1973, European Architectural Heritage Award 1975, Dept. of Environment Good Design in Housing Award 1975, Structural Steel Design Award 1976, 1995, R.I.B.A. Award Commendation 1977; R.I.B.A. Award, R.I.B.A. Regional Award 1991, Royal Fine Art Comm. and Sunday Times Building of the Year Finalist 1991, Quarternario Int. Award for Innovative Tech. in Architecture Finalist 1993, Civic Trust Award 1993, R.I.B.A. Regional Award 1995. *Publications:* Planning Your Kitchen (co-author); contributions to nat. and tech. press. *Leisure interests:* architecture, music, gardening, boats, books. *Address:* Manser Associates Ltd., Bridge Studios, Hammersmith Bridge, London, W6 9DA; Morton House, Chiswick Mall, London, W4 2PS, England. *Telephone:* 0181-741 4381 (Office).

MANSFIELD, Eric Harold, M.A., SC.D., F.I.M.A., F.ENG., F.R.AE.S., F.R.S.; British structural research scientist; b. 24 May 1923, Croydon, Surrey; s. of Harold G. and Grace Pfundt Mansfield; m. 1st 1947 (divorced 1973), 2nd Eunice Shuttleworth-Parker 1974; two s. one d.; ed. St. Lawrence Coll., Ramsgate, Trinity Hall, Cambridge; various grades, Structures Dept., Royal Aircraft Est., Farnborough 1943–83, Chief Scientific Officer 1980–83; Visiting Prof. Univ. of Surrey 1984–90; mem. British Nat. Cttee. for Theoretical and Applied Mechanics 1973–79, Gen. Ass. Int. Union of Theoretical and Applied Mechanics 1976–80; originator of Neutral Hole Theory, The Inextensional Theory for thin plates, Wrinkled Membrane Theory (modern version), Theory of Gravity-induced Wrinkles in Vertical Membranes, Theory for Objects Supported by Surface Tension; Bronze Medal, Royal Aeronautical Soc. 1967, James Alfred Ewing Gold Medal for Eng. Research 1991, Royal Medal, Royal Soc. 1994. *Publications:* Bending and Stretching of Plates 1964, 1989, Bridge: the Ultimate Limits 1986, articles in professional journals. *Leisure interests:* bridge, palaeontology, snorkelling. *Address:* Manatoba, Dene Close, Lower Bourne, Farnham, Surrey, GU10 3PP, England. *Telephone:* (01252) 713558.

MANSFIELD, Michael, Q.C., B.A.; British barrister; b. 12 Oct. 1941, London; s. of Frank Mansfield and Marjorie Sayers; m. 1st Melian Mansfield 1967 (divorced 1992); three s. two d.; m. 2nd Yvette Mansfield 1992; one s.; ed. Highgate School and Keele Univ.; began practising 1967; est. Tooks Court chambers 1984; specialist in civil liberties work; Prof. of Law, Westminster Univ. 1996; films for BBC TV: Inside Story 1991, Presumed Guilty; Patron Acre Lane Neighbourhood Chambers, Brixton 1997–; Hon. Fellow, Kent Univ.; Hon. LL.D. (South Bank Univ.) 1994, (Univ. of Herts.) 1995, (Keele Univ.) 1995. *Publication:* Presumed Guilty. *Leisure interests:* my children, drumming. *Address:* Tooks Court Chambers, 14 Tooks Court, Cursitor Street, London, EC4Y 1JY, England. *Telephone:* 0171-405 8828. *Fax:* 0171-405 6680.

MANSFIELD, Michael Joseph, A.M.; American politician and diplomatist; b. 16 March 1903, New York; s. of Patrick and Josephine O'Brien Mansfield; m. Maureen Hayes 1932; one d.; ed. Univ. of Montana; fmr. mining engineer; Prof. of History and Political Science, Univ. of Montana 1933–42; mem. House of Reps. 1943–52, Senator from Montana 1952–76; Majority Whip 1957–61; Leader of Senate 1961–76; Amb. to Japan 1977–89; Dr. h.c. (Soka) 1986; Nelson Rockefeller Public Service Award 1988; Democrat. *Address:* 1101 Pennsylvania Avenue, N.W., Suite 900, Washington, DC 20004, U.S.A.

MANSFIELD, Sir Peter, Kt., PH.D., F.R.S.; British professor of physics; b. 9 Oct. 1933, London; s. of late S. G. Mansfield and R. L. Mansfield; m. Jean M. Kibble 1962; two d.; ed. William Penn School, Peckham and Queen Mary Coll., London; Research Assoc. Dept. of Physics, Univ. of Ill. 1962; lecturer, Univ. of Nottingham 1964, Sr. Lecturer 1967, Reader 1970, Prof. of Physics 1979–94, Prof. Emer. 1994–; MRC Professorial Fellow 1983–88; Sr. Visitor, Max Planck Inst. for Medical Research, Heidelberg 1972–73; Fellow, Queen Mary Coll. 1985; Pres. Soc. of Magnetic Resonance in Medicine 1987–88; Hon. F.R.C.R. 1992; Hon. Fellow Inst. of Physics 1996; Hon. mem. British Inst. of Radiology (BIR) 1993; Hon. Dr. Med. (Strasbourg) 1995; Hon. D.Sc. (Univ. of Kent at Canterbury) 1996; Royal Soc. Wellcome Foundation Gold Medal and Prize 1985, Duddell Medal, Inst. of Physics 1988, Royal Soc. Mullard Medal 1990, ISMAR Prize 1992, Barclay Medal, BJR 1993, Gold Medal, European Asscn. of Radiology 1995, Garmisch-Partenkirchen Prize for MRI 1995, Rank Prize 1997 and other awards. *Publications:* NMR Imaging in Biomedicine 1982, NMR Imaging (co-ed.) 1990, MRI in Medicine 1995; some 200 scientific publs. in learned journals. *Leisure interests:* reading, languages, flying. *Address:* Magnetic Resonance Centre, Department of Physics, University of Nottingham, NG7 2RD, England. *Telephone:* (0115) 9514740. *Fax:* (0115) 9515166.

MANSFIELD, Terence Arthur, PH.D., F.R.S.; British professor of biology; b. 18 Jan. 1937, Ashby-de-la-Zouch; s. of Sydney W. Mansfield and Rose (née Sinfield) Mansfield; m. Margaret M. James 1963; two s.; ed. Univ. of Nottingham, Univ. of Reading; Research Fellow Reading Univ. 1961–65; lecturer and Prof. Univ. of Lancaster 1965–87, Dir. Inst. of Environmental and Biological Sciences 1987–94, Prov. of Science and Eng. 1994–; mem. Agric. and Food Research Council 1989–93. *Publications:* Physiology of Stomata (co-author) 1968, Stomatal Physiology (co-Ed.) 1981, Plant Adaptation to Environmental Stress (co-Ed.) 1993, Disturbance of the Nitrogen Cycle (co-Ed.) 1998; numerous chapters and journal articles on aspects of botanical science. *Address:* Institute of Environmental and Biological Sciences, University of Lancaster, Bailrigg, Lancaster, LA1 4YQ, England. *Telephone:* (01524) 65201 (Office). *Fax:* (01524) 843854.

MANSHARD, Walther, DR. RER. NAT.; German international civil servant and university professor; b. 17 Nov. 1923, Hamburg; s. of Otto and Ida Manshard; m. Helga Koch 1951; one d.; ed. Univ. of Hamburg; Asst. lecturer, Univ. of Southampton, U.K. 1950–52; lecturer, Univ. of Ghana 1952–60; Dozent, Univ. of Cologne 1960–63; Prof. Univ. of Giessen 1963–70; Prin. Dir. UNESCO Dept. of Environmental Sciences 1970–73; Prof., Head of Dept. Univ. of Freiburg 1973–77, 1980–; Vice-Rector, UN Univ., Tokyo 1977–80; Sec.-Gen. and Treas. Int. Geographical Union 1976–84; Sr. Adviser UN Univ. 1990–93; Hon. D.Litt. 1991. *Publications:* Die geographischen Grundlagen der Wirtschaft Ghanas 1961, Tropisches Afrika 1963, Agrargeographie der Tropen 1968, Afrika—Südlich der Sahara 1970, Tropical Agriculture 1974, Die Städte des tropischen Afrika 1977, Renewable Natural Resources and the Environment 1981, Entwicklungprobleme in Agrarräumen Tropen-Afrikas 1988, Umwelt v. Entwicklung in den Tropen 1995. *Address:* Geographisches Institut, University of Freiburg, Werderring 4, 79085 Freiburg i. Br.; Schwarzwaldstrasse 24, 79189 Bad Krozingen, Germany.

MANSINGH, Lalit, M.A.; Indian diplomatist; b. 29 April 1941, Cuttack; s. of the late Mayadhar Mansingh and of Hemalata (Behura) Mansingh; m. Indira Singh 1976; one s. one d.; ed. Stewart and C. S. Zila Schools, Utkal Univ., Indian School of Int. Studies, New Delhi; lecturer in political science 1961–63; joined diplomatic service 1963, Deputy Chief of Mission to Kabul 1971–74, to Brussels 1976–80, to Washington 1989–92, Amb. to U.A.E. 1980–83; High Commr. to Nigeria 1993–95, to London 1998–; Jt. Sec. Dept. of Econ. Affairs, Ministry of Finance 1984–85; Dir. Gen. Indian Council for Cultural Relations 1985–89; Dean Foreign Service Inst., New Delhi 1995–96; Perm. Sec. Ministry of External Affairs 1997–98. *Publication:* Indian Foreign Policy: Agenda for the 21st Century (Ed.-in-Chief) 1998. *Leisure interests:* classical music, dance, fine arts, theatre. *Address:* Indian High Commission, India House, Aldwych, London, WC2B 4NA, England. *Telephone:* 0171-836 8484; 0171-836 2556. *Fax:* 0171-240 4688.

MANSUR, Mallikarjun; Indian classical singer; b. 31 Dec. 1910, Mansur; s. of Bheemraiappa Mansur and Neelamma Mansur; m. Gangambika Mansur; one s. seven d.; ed. elementary educ.; joined drama co. 1919; started sangeet lessons with Neela Kanth Bua 1922; first gramophone record 1933; mem. Legis. Council, Karnataka State 1985–; Padmashri Award 1970; Padmabhusan award 1975 and many other awards. *Publications:* Sangeet Ratna, Ananna Rasayatre. *Leisure interests:* shivapooja, sangeet, reading. *Address:* Mruthunjaya Nilava, A.I.R. Road, Dharwar, 580008, India. *Telephone:* 8906.

MANSUROV, Tair Aimukhametovich, DR. POLIT. SC.: Kazakhstan diplomatist; b. 1 Jan. 1948, Sarkand, Taldyorgan Region, Kazakhstan; m.; three c.; ed. Kazakh Polytech. Inst., Higher CP School at Cen. CPSU Cttee.; worked in construction orgs. Alma-Ata, chief engineer Almaatacentrostroi 1965–79; CP Functionary 1979–88; Second Sec. Karaganda Region CP Cttee., Head of Sector Cen. CPSU Cttee. 1989–91; deputy to Kazakhstan Supreme Soviet, co-ordinator Interparl. Comm. of Russia and Kazakhstan 1990–93; Pres. Foundation of Devt. Kazakhstan (Moscow) 1991–93; rank of Amb.; Amb. to Russian Fed. Jan. 1994–, concurrently Amb. to Finland Aug. 1996–; mem. Acad. of Creativity, Int. Acad. of High School, Acad. of Social Sciences. *Publications:* Faces of Sovereignty: Sovereignty in Terms of Social History, Kazakhstan and Russia: Sovereignization, Integration, Experience of Strategic Partnership. *Leisure interests:* literature, philosophy, history, memoirs. *Address:* Embassy of Republic of Kazakhstan, Chistoprudny blvd. 3a, 101000 Moscow, Russia (Office). *Telephone:* (095) 208 9852 (Office).

MANT, Arthur Keith, M.D., B.S., M.R.C.S., F.R.C.P., F.R.C. PATH., D.M.J. PATH.; British professor of forensic medicine; b. 11 Sept. 1919, Purley, Surrey; s. of George A. Mant and Elsie M. Slark; m. Emma O. H. Smith 1947; two s. one d.; ed. Denstone Coll. Staffs. and Univ. of London; rank of Maj., R.A.M.C. 1945–48; Research Fellow, Dept. of Forensic Medicine, Guy's Hosp. London 1949–55, lecturer 1955–66, Head of Dept. 1972–74; Reader in Forensic Medicine, Univ. of London 1966–74, Prof. 1974–84, Prof. Emer. 1984–; Sr. Lecturer in Forensic Med. King's Coll. Hosp. 1965–67, Hon. Consultant 1967–84; Visiting Lecturer, St. Mary's Hosp. 1955–84; Visiting Prof. Univ. of Jordan and Nihon Univ. Tokyo; Gerin Medal 1978; H. Ward Smith Memorial Award 1984. *Publications:* Forensic Medicine 1960, Modern Trends in Forensic Medicine 1973, Taylor's Principles and Practice of Medical Jurisprudence (13th Edn.) 1984; over 100 scientific papers. *Leisure interests:* orchidology, fly fishing. *Address:* 29 Ashley Drive, Walton-on-Thames, Surrey, KT12 1JT, England. *Telephone:* (01932) 225005.

MANTEL, Hilary Mary, B.JUR., F.R.S.L.; British writer; b. 6 July 1952, Hadfield, Derbyshire; m. Gerald McEwen 1972; ed. Hanytown Convent, Cheshire, London School of Econs., Sheffield Univ. *Publications:* Every Day is Mother's Day 1985, Vacant Possession 1986, Eight Months on Ghazzah Street 1988, Fludd 1989 (Winifred Holtby Memorial Award, Southern Arts Literature Prize, Cheltenham Festival Prize), A Place of Greater Safety 1992 (Sunday Express Book of the Year Award 1993), A Change of Climate 1994, An Experiment in Love 1995 (Hawthornden Prize 1996), The Giant, O'Brien 1998. *Address:* c/o A.M. Heath & Co., 79 St. Martin's Lane, London, WC2N 4AA, England.

MANUEL, Trevor Andrew; South African politician; b. 31 Jan. 1956, Cape Town; s. of Abraham J. Manuel and Philma van Söhnen; m. Lynn Matthews; three s.; ed. Harold Cressy High School; mem. Labour Party Youth 1969–71, Policy Man. on Devt. 1989–; construction technician 1974–81; Sec. Kensington Civic Asscn. 1977–82; founding mem. W. Cape United Democratic Front (UDF) 1980s, Sec. Regional Exec. UDF 1983–90, mem. UDF Nat. Exec. Cttee. 1983–86, 1989–90; Organizer CAHAC 1981–82; field worker Educational Resource and Information Centre 1982–84; in detention 1985, 1987–88, 1989, restricted 1985–86, 1986–90 (when not in detention); Publicity Sec. ANC W. Cape; mem. ANC Nat. Exec. Cttee. 1991–; Minister of Trade and Industry, Govt. of Nat. Unity 1994–96, Minister of Finance April 1996–. *Address:* Private Bag X115, Pretoria 0001, South Africa.

MANUKYAN, Vazgen Mikayelovich; Armenian politician and mathematician; b. 13 Feb. 1946, Leninakan (now Kuimayri); s. of Mikael Manukyan and Astkhik Manukyan; m. Vardui Rafaelovna Ishkhanyan; three d.; ed. Yerevan State Univ.; jr. researcher Computation Cen. Armenian Acad. of Sciences 1969–72; teacher, sr. researcher Yerevan State Univ. 1972–90; political activities since 1960s, one of founders and leaders Club of Armenian Culture 1967, mem. and co-ordinator Cttee. Karabakh 1988–; mem. of Bd., co-ordinator Armenian Pan-Nat. Movt. 1989–90, leader Nat. Democratic Union 1991–; deputy Armenian Supreme Soviet 1990–93; Chair. Armenian Council of Ministers 1990–91; State Minister of Armenia Sept.–Oct. 1992; mem. Council of Nat. Security at Pres. 1992–93; Minister of Defence 1992–93;

Chair. Cttee. on Econ. Reform, State Comm. on Land Reform and Privatization; mem. Parl. 1996–; one of leaders of opposition; Cand. for Presidency 1996. *Address:* National Assembly, Marshal Bagramian Prosp. 26, 375019 Yerevan, Armenia.

MANZ, Wolfgang; German pianist; b. 6 Aug. 1960, Düsseldorf; m. Julia Goldstein 1985; two s. one d.; studied with Drahomir Toman, Prague and Karlheinz Kämmerling, Hanover; teacher, High School of Music, Karlsruhe 1994–; concert tours U.K., Germany, Belgium and Japan; performed Promenade Concerts, London 1984, Gilels Memorial Concert, Düsseldorf 1986, Karajan Foundation, Paris 1987; recordings: Chopin Studies, Beethoven Triple Concerto, with English Chamber Orchestra, solo recital Liszt, Schumann and Debussy, Dohnanyi Piano Quintet; First Prize Mendelssohn Competition, Berlin 1981, Second Prize, Leeds Piano Competition 1981, Second Prize Brussels Queen Elizabeth Competition 1983. *Leisure interests:* composing, swimming, gardening. *Address:* Pasteurallee 55, 30655 Hanover, Germany. *Telephone:* (0511) 5476025. *Fax:* (0511) 5497432.

MANZONI, Giacomo, MUS.M.; Italian composer; b. 26 Sept. 1932, Milan; m. Eugenia Tretti 1960; one s.; ed. Bocconi Univ., Milan, Univ. of Tübingen and Conservatorio Verdi, Milan; Ed. Il Diapason (music review) 1956; music critic, l'Unità 1958–66; music ed. Prisma 1968; mem. editorial staff, Musica/Realtà 1980–; Prof. Conservatorio Verdi 1962–64, 1974–91, Conservatorio Martini, Bologna 1965–68, 1969–74, Scuola di Musica Fiesole 1988–, Accademia Musicale Pescarese 1993–; mem. Accad. Nazionale di Santa Cecilia, Rome 1994–. *Compositions include:* Atomtod 1965, Per M. Robespierre 1975, Parole da Beckett 1971, Masse: omaggio a E. Varèse 1977, Ode 1982, Scene Sinfoniche per il Dr. Faustus 1984, Dedica (su testi di Maderna) 1985, Dr. Faustus: Scene dal romanzo di T. Mann 1989, 10 versi di E. Dickinson 1989, Malinamusik 1991, Finale e aria 1991, Il deserto cresce (F. Nietzsche) 1992, Moi, Antonin A. (testi di Artaud) 1997; Musica notturna 1966, and other chamber music; Una voce chiama 1994, Quanto oscura selva trovai (Dante), for trombone, chorus and live electronics; film and incidental music. *Publications:* A. Schoenberg 1975, Scritti 1991, Tradizione e Utopia 1994 (translations Adorno, Schönberg). *Address:* Viale Papiniano 31, 20123 Milan, Italy. *Telephone:* 02/4817955.

MAO RUBO; Chinese politician; b. 1938, Yangzhou City, Jiangsu Prov.; joined CCP 1959; ed. Nanjing Univ.; Vice-Dir. then Dir. Meteorological Office of Tibet; Vice-Sec. CCP Tibet Autonomous Regional Cttee., Vice-Chair. Tibet Autonomous Region; Sec. CCP Ningxia Hui Autonomous Regional Cttee.; mem. 15th CCP Cen. Cttee. 1997–; Chair. People's Congress of Ningxia Hui Autonomous Region 1998–. *Address:* Standing Committee, People's Congress of Ningxia Hui Autonomous Region, Yinchuan City, Ningxia Hui Autonomous Region, People's Republic of China.

MAO ZHIYONG; Chinese party official; b. 1929, Yueyang Co., Hunan Prov.; joined CCP 1952; Chair. Yueyang Co. Revolutionary Cttee. 1968–70, Sec. 1970–; Vice-Chair. Hunan Peasants Asscn. 1973–77; Sec. Hunan Prov. CCP Cttee. 1973–77; mem. 11th CCP Cen. Cttee. 1977; Chair. Hunan Prov. CPPCC Cttee. 1977–79; Chair. Hunan Prov. Revolutionary Cttee. 1977–79; First Sec. Political Cttee. of Mil. Dist., Hunan; mem. 5th NPC 1978–80; Head of CCP party workers del. to Romania Aug. 1979; Goodwill del. to Japan April 1980; mem. 12th CCP Cen. Cttee. Sept. 1982; Presidium of 12th CCP Nat. Congress Sept. 1982; Head of Party Group for Party Rectification, Hunan Prov. CCP Cttee. 1983; mem. 13th Cen. Cttee. CCP 1987–92; mem. 14th Cen. Cttee. CCP 1992–97; Sec. Jiangxi Prov. Cttee. 1988–95; Chair. Jiangxi Provincial 8th People's Congress Feb. 1993–. *Address:* National Committee of Chinese People's Political Consultative Committee, 23 Taipingqiao Street, Beijing, People's Republic of China.

MAOR, Galia, M.B.A.; Israeli banker; m.; three c.; joined Bank of Israel, supervisor of banks 1982–89; with Bank Leumi 1991–, Man. Dir. and CEO 1995–; mem. various cttees. *Address:* Bank Leumi le-Israel BM, P.O. Box 2, 24-32 Yehuda Halevi Street, Tel-Aviv 65546, Israel. *Telephone:* 3-5148111. *Fax:* 3-5661872.

MAPONYA, Richard John; South African business executive; b. 24 Dec. 1926, Pietersburg; s. of late Godfrey Kgabane Maponya and Mary Machichane (née Mogashoa) Maponya; m. Marina Nompinti Sondlo (died 1992); two s. four d.; ed. Kagiso Teacher's Training Coll., Pietersburg; proprietor Maponya's Supply Stores 1952–; Dir. Maponya's Bus Services 1965, Maponya's Funeral Parlour (Pty) Ltd. 1976, Afro Shopping Construction Enterprises (Pty) Ltd., Maponya's Discount Supermarket 1983–, Maponya's Bottle Store, Maponya's Motors (Pty) Ltd, Maponya Motors Property Holdings (Pty) Ltd., Maponya's Orlando Restaurant (Pty) Ltd., Maponya's Stud Farm, Lebowa Devt. Corpn., numerous other cos.; Man. Dir. M.A. Africa (Pty) Ltd., Mountain Motors, Soweto 1978–; propr. BMW Agency, Soweto; race horse owner; f. and Pres. NAFCOC 1965; Chair. Trade and Transport Cttee., Soweto Council; mem. Urban Bantu Council 1965–76; Pres. Black Proprietors Garage Owners' Asscn. *Leisure interests:* racing, music. *Address:* P.O. Box 783045, Sandton 2146, South Africa.

MARA, Rt. Hon. Ratu Sir Kamisese Kapaiwai Tuimacilai, P.C., G.C.M.G., K.B.E., M.A.; Fijian politician; b. 13 May 1920; s. of the late Tui Nayau and Adi Lusiana Qolikoro; m. Adi Lala Mara 1951; three s. five d.; ed. Queen Victoria School and Cen. Medical School, Suva, Fiji, Sacred Heart Coll., Otago Univ., Oxford Univ., and London School of Econs.; joined British Colonial Service 1950; Admin. Officer, Dist. Officer and Commr., Fiji 1951–61; mem. Legis. Council, Fiji 1953–89; mem. Exec. Council, Fiji 1959–61; mem. for Natural Resources 1964–66; f. Alliance Party 1960; Leader, Fiji Del. Constitutional Conf., London 1965; Chief Minister 1967–70; Prime Minister 1970–87, Prime Minister and Minister of Foreign Affairs 1977–87, 1987–92, and of Foreign Affairs and the Public Service Dec. 1987–89, of Foreign Affairs and Home Affairs 1989; Leader of Opposition April–May 1987; Pres. of Fiji Jan. 1994–; Adviser on Foreign Affairs Gov. Gen.'s Interim Govt. May-Sept. 1987; Hon. Fellow Wadham Coll. 1971; Hon. LL.D. (Guam, Otago, New Delhi, Papua New Guinea); Hon. Dr. Political Science (Yonsei Univ., Korea) 1978; Hon. Dr. Univ. (Univ. of S. Pacific) 1980; Pacific Man of the Year 1984; K. St. J., Grand Master, Order of the National Lion (Senegal) 1975, Order of Diplomatic Service Merit (Repub. of Korea) 1978; Meritorious Service Decoration (Fiji). *Leisure interests:* fishing, golf. *Address:* Office of the President, Government Buildings, POB 2513, Suva, Fiji. *Telephone:* 314244. *Fax:* 301645.

MARADONA, Diego Armando; Argentinian footballer; b. Lanus, 1960; m. Claudia Villafane; two d.; with Boca Juniors, Argentina –1982; then with Barcelona Football Club; with Naples Football Club 1984–91, Sevilla (Spain) 1992, Boca Jrs. 1997, Badajoz 1998–; founded Maradona Producciones; fmr. Amb. for UNICEF; banned from football for 15 months after drugs test; convicted by Naples Court on charges of possession of cocaine, 14 month suspended sentence and fine of 4 million lire, Sept. 1991; Fed. Court in Buenos Aires ruled he had complied with the treatment; suspended for 15 months for taking performance-enhancing drugs in World Cup Finals June 1994; indicted for shooting an air rifle at journalists Aug. 1994; resgnd. as coach of Deporto Mandiyu 1994; Capt. of Argentina 1993; Pres. Int. Asscn. of Professional Footballers 1995–.

MARAFINO, Vincent Norman, M.B.A.; American business executive; b. 8 June 1930, Boston; m. Doris M. Vernall 1958; three d.; ed. San Jose State Coll. and Santa Clara Univ.; served with U.S.A.F. 1953–55; Chief Accountant, American Standard Advance Tech. Lab., Mountain View, Calif. 1956–59; with Lockheed Missiles & Space Co., Sunnyvale, Calif. 1959–70; Asst. Controller, Lockheed Corpn. Burbank, Calif. 1970–71, Vice Pres., Controller 1971–77, Sr. Vice-Pres. Finance 1977–83, Exec. Vice-Pres., Chief Financial and Admin. Officer 1983–88, Vice-Chair. of Bd. and Chief Financial and Admin. Officer 1988–; mem. Bd. of Dirs. Lockheed Missiles and Space Co., Inc.; Chair. Bd. of Dirs. Lockheed Finance Corpn.; mem. Bd. of Trustees Holy Cross Medical Center, Mission Hills; mem. Financial Execs. Inst., American Inst. of CPAS. *Address:* Lockheed Corporation, 6801 Rockledge Drive, Bethesda, MD 20817, U.S.A.

MARAGALL, Pasqual; Spanish civil servant and academic; ed. Barcelona Univ., New School for Social Research, New York; lecturer in econs. Barcelona Univ.; Oficina Mayor of Barcelona 1982–, organizer of 1992 Olympic Games in Barcelona. *Address:* Oficina del Alcalde, Barcelona, Spain.

MARAINI, Dacia; Italian author; b. 13 Nov. 1936; d. of Fosco Maraini and Alliata Topazia; ed. Collegio S.S. Annunziata, Florence and Rome; Prix Formentor for L'Età del Malessere (The Age of Discontent) 1962. *Publications:* La Vacanza 1962, L'Età del Malessere 1962, Crudeltà All' Aria Aperta (poems) 1966, A Memoria (novel) 1967, La famiglia normale (one-act play) 1967, Il ricatto a teatro (play) 1968, Memoirs of a Female Thief 1973, Donna in Guerra (novel) 1975, Mangiami Pure (poems) 1980, I Sogni di Clitennestra (5 plays) 1981, Lettere a Marina (novel) 1981, Lezioni d'Amore (6 plays) 1982, Dimenticato di Dimenticare (poems) 1983, Isolina (novel) 1985, Devour me too (short stories) 1987, La Bionda, la bruna e l'asino (essays) 1987. *Address:* Via Beccaria 18, 00196 Rome, Italy. *Telephone:* 3611795.

MARAK, Salseng Chada, B.A.; Indian politician; b. 16 Jan. 1941, Baghmara; s. of late M. Rongmuthu; m. Truitline K. Sangma 1968; two s. four d.; teacher and headmaster 1965–71; mem. Meghalaya Legis. Ass. 1972–76; joined Indian Nat. Congress 1976–78, re-elected to Ass. 1978–; Chief Minister of Meghalaya 1993–97. *Leisure interests:* reading, music, farming. *Address:* Meghalaya Secretariat, Main Bldg., Shillong, Meghalaya, India (Office); Gajingpara, P.O. Mundipathar, East Garo Hills, India (Home). *Telephone:* 224282 (Office); 223922 (Home).

MARANDA, Pierre Jean, M.A., L.PH., PH.D., F.R.S.C.; Canadian professor of anthropology; b. 27 March 1930, Quebec; s. of Lucien Maranda and Marie-Alma Rochette; m. Elli-Kaija Köngäs 1962 (deceased); two s.; ed. Laval Univ., Quebec, Univ. of Montreal and Harvard Univ.; Asst. Prof. of Classics, Univ. Laval 1955–58; Research Fellow, Harvard Univ. 1966–70; Dir. of Research Ecole Pratique des Hautes Etudes, Paris 1968–69; Assoc. Prof. of Anthropology Univ. of B.C. 1969–71, Prof. 1971–75; Prof. Collège de France, Paris 1975; Research Prof. Laval Univ. 1976–96, Prof. Emer. 1996–; Pres. Steering Cttee. of Cultural Hypermedia Encyclopedia of Oceania 1996–; Visiting Prof., Fed. Univ. of Rio de Janeiro 1983, Univ. of Toronto, ISISSS 1985, 1987, Univ. of B.C. 1986, Université Omar Bongo, Libreville, Gabon 1991, 1992, Ecole des hautes études en sciences sociales, Paris 1994; Dr. h.c. (Memorial Univ., Newfoundland) 1985; Médaille du Collège de France 1975, Canada Council Molson Prize in the Social Sciences and Humanities 1997. *Publications:* Structural Models in Folklore and Transformational Essays (with E.K. Köngäs) 1963, French Kinship: Structure and History 1974, Mythology 1974, Soviet Structural Folkloristics 1974, Dialogue conjugal 1985, DISCAN: A Computer Programme for Discourse Analysis 1989, L'unité dans la diversité culturelle: Une geste bantu, Vol. 1: Le sens des symboles fang, mbede, eshira 1993; plus over 60 articles in scientific journals.

Leisure interests: skiing, swimming, tennis, bridge, music, art. *Address:* Département d'Anthropologie, Université Laval, Quebec, G1K 7P4, Canada. *Telephone:* (418) 656-2131, ext. 2168, 8124. *Fax:* (418) 656-2831.

MARAVALL HERRERO, José María; Spanish politician and university professor; b. 7 April 1942, Madrid; s. of José Antonio and María Teresa Maravall Herrero; m. Maria Jesús 1966; two c.; ed. Univ. of Madrid, Univ. of Oxford; fmr. mem. Frente de Liberación Popular and Federación Universitaria de Estudiantes; Research Fellow, St. Antony's Coll. 1973–74; Prof. Sociology Dept., Univ. of Warwick 1974–78; joined Partido Socialista Obrero Español 1974, Sec. of Educ., Fed. Exec. 1979; Chair. of Political Sociology, Universidad Complutense de Madrid 1978; Minister of Educ. and Science 1982–88; mem. Parl. 1986–. *Publications:* Trabajo y Conflicto Social 1967, El Desarrollo Económico y la Clase Obrera 1970, Sociología de lo Posible, Dictadura y Disentimiento Político (Dictatorship and Political Dissent) 1978, La Política de la Transición (The Transition to Democracy in Spain) 1982, La Reforma de la Enseñanza 1985. *Leisure interests:* travelling, cinema, walking, swimming. *Address:* c/o PSOE, Ferraz 68y 70, 28008, Madrid, Spain. *Telephone:* (1) 582 0444. *Fax:* (1) 582 0422.

MARBER, Patrick; British writer and director; b. 19 Sept. 1964, London; s. of Brian Marber and Angela Benjamin; ed. Wadham Coll., Oxford; Evening Standard Award for Best Comedy (for Dealer's Choice) 1995; Writers' Guild Award for Best West End Play 1995; Evening Standard Best Comedy Award (for Closer) 1997; Olivier Award (for Closer) 1998. *Plays directed and/or written include:* Dealer's Choice 1995, Blue Remembered Hills, Closer 1997. *Television work includes:* The Day Today, Paul Calf Video Diary, Knowing Me Knowing You, 3 Fights 2 Weddings and a Funeral, The Curator, After Miss Julie. *Publications include:* Dealer's Choice 1995, After Miss Julie 1996, Closer 1997. *Address:* c/o Judy Daish Associates Ltd., 2 St. Charles Place, London, W10 6EG, England. *Telephone:* 0181-964 8811. *Fax:* 0181-964 8966.

MARCEAU, Félicien (pseudonym of Louis Carette); French writer; b. 16 Sept. 1913, Cortenberg, Belgium; s. of Louis Carette and Marie Lefèvre; m. 2nd Bianca Licenziati 1953; ed. Coll. de la Sainte Trinité à Louvain and Univ. de Louvain; Prix Interallié for Les élans du coeur 1955; Prix Goncourt for Creezy 1969; Prix Prince Pierre de Monaco 1974; Grand Prix du Théâtre 1975; mem. Acad. Française 1975. *Publications:* Novels: Chasseneuil 1948, L'Homme du Roi 1952, Bergère Légère 1953, Creezy 1969, Le corps de mon ennemi 1975, Appelez-moi Mademoiselle 1984, la Carriole du Père Juniet 1985, Les passions partagées 1987, Un Oiseau dans le Ciel 1989, Les ingénus 1992, La Terrasse de Lucrezia 1993, Le Voyage de noce de Figaro 1994, La grande fille 1997, La Fille du Pharaon 1998; plays: L'oeuf 1956, La bonne soupe 1958, La preuve par quatre 1965, Un jour j'ai rencontré la vérité 1967, Le babour 1969, L'ouvre-boîte 1972, L'homme en question 1973, A nous de jouer 1979; essays: Balzac et son monde 1955, Le roman en liberté 1977, Une insolente liberté: Les aventures de Casanova 1983, L'Imagination est une science exacte 1998; memoirs: Les années courtes 1968. *Leisure interest:* painting. *Address:* c/o Les Editions Gallimard, 5 rue Sébastien-Bottin, 75007 Paris, France. *Telephone:* 49.54.42.00.

MARCEAU, Marcel; French mime; b. 22 March 1923, Strasbourg; s. of Charles and Anne (née Werzberg) Mangel; m. 1st Huguette Mallet (divorced); two s.; m. 2nd Ella Jaroszewicz 1966 (divorced); m. 3rd Anne Sicco 1975 (divorced); two d.; ed. Lille and Strasbourg Lycées; Dir. Compagnie de Mime Marcel Marceau 1948–64, Int. School of Mime, Paris 1978–; annual world tours, and numerous television appearances throughout the world; created Don Juan (mime drama) 1964, Candide (ballet), Hamburg 1971; creator of the character "Bip"; Dir. Ecole de Mimodrame Marcel Marceau Aug. 1978–; mem. Académie des Beaux Arts 1991; Officier, Légion d'honneur, Commdr., Ordre nat. du Mérite, Commdr. des Arts et des Lettres; Hon. degrees from Princeton and Oregon Univs., Colombia 1987. *Mimes include:* Le manteau, Exercices de style (both filmed), Mort avant l'aube, Le joueur de flûte, Moriana et Galvau, Pierrot de Montmartre, Les trois perruques, etc.; other films: Pantomime, Un jardin public, Le fabricant de masques, Paris qui rit, Paris qui pleure, Barbarella, Silent Movies 1976, Shanks, Scrooge de Dickens. *Publications:* Les sept péchés capitaux, Les rêveries de Bip, Alphabet Book, Counting Book, L'histoire de Bip, The Third Eye, Pimporello 1987. *Leisure interests:* painting, poetry, fencing. *Address:* c/o Compagnie de Mime Marcel Marceau, 32 rue de Londres, 75009 Paris, France. *Telephone:* (01) 42.80.48.32.

MARCEAU, Sophie (pseudonym of Sophie Danièle Sylvie Maupu); French actress; b. 17 Nov. 1966, Paris; d. of Benoît Maupu and Simone Morisset; one s.; stage appearances include: Eurydice 1991, Pygmalion 1993. *Films:* La Boum 1981, La Boum 2 1982, Fort Saganne 1984, Joyeuses Pâques 1985, L'Amour Braque 1985, Police 1985, Descente aux Enfers 1986, Chouans! 1987, L'Etudiante 1988, Mes Nuits Sont Plus Belles Que Vos Jours 1989, Pacific Palisades 1989, Pour Sacha 1991, La Note Bleue 1991, Fanfan 1993, La Fille de D'Artagnan 1994, Braveheart 1995, Beyond the Clouds 1995, Firelight 1998, The World is not Enough 1998. *Leisure interests:* countryside, music, reading, travel. *Publication:* Menteuse 1996. *Address:* c/o Artmédia, 10 avenue George V, 75008 Paris, France.

MARCELLIN, Raymond, D. EN D.; French politician and lawyer; b. 19 Aug. 1914, Sézanne; s. of Gustave and Anaïs (née Gominard) Marcellin; ed. Meaux Coll., Paris and Strasbourg Univs.; Barrister, Cour d'Appel, Paris 1945–; elected Deputy for Morbihan, Nat. Ass. 1946, 1951, 1956, 1958, 1962, 1967, 1968, 1973, 1981; Under-Sec. of State of the Interior 1948–49; Sec. of State of Industry and Commerce 1949–50, of the Pres. of the Council 1952, of Information 1952–57, of Public Functions and Admin. Reform 1957–62; Minister of Public Health and Population 1962–66, of Industry 1966–67; Minister under Prime Minister, Responsible for Planning 1967–68; Minister of Interior 1968–74, of Agric. and Rural Devt. March–May 1974; Vice-Pres. Fed. nat. des républicains indépendants 1962–, Pres. Fed. bretonne des républicains indépendants 1968–; Pres. Conseil général du Morbihan 1964–98, Conseil régional de Bretagne; Mayor of Vannes 1965–77; Senator for Morbihan 1974–81; Vice-Pres. Conseil régional de Bretagne 1986–88, Hon. Pres. 1989; Deputy for Morbihan 1981–97; Croix de guerre, Médaille des Evadés, etc. *Publications:* L'ordre public et les groupes révolutionnaires 1969, L'importune vérité 1978, La guerre politique 1985, L'expérience du pouvoir 1990. *Address:* Hôtel du Département, 2 rue Saint-Tropez, 56009 Vannes, France (Home).

MARCHAND, Philippe, L. EN D.; French politician and lawyer; b. 1 Sept. 1939, Angoulême, Charente; s. of Guy Marchand and Madeleine Bonat; m. Marie-Odile Filliau 1965; three s.; ed. Collège de Parthenay, Univ. of Poitiers; lawyer at Saintes bar 1965; local councillor, Charente-Maritime 1976–, Saintes 1982–; Socialist Deputy for Charente-Maritime 1978–90, Vice-Pres. Assemblée Nationale 1985–86; Vice-Pres. Socialist Group in Parl. 1990–91; Titular Judge, High Court 1987; mem. Nat Comm. on Information Tech. and Freedom 1982–86, 1988–; Minister-del. in Ministry of the Interior 1990–91, Minister of the Interior 1991–92; regional councillor, Poitou-Charentes 1992–; Chevalier Légion d'honneur, Grand Cross of the Orden Isabel la Católica (Spain). *Address:* Conseil d'Etat, Palais Royal, 75100 Paris; 17 rue de la Tour, 75016 Paris (Offices); 19 rue de la Fauvette, 17100 Saintes, France (Home).

MARCHANDISE-FRANQUET, Jacques; French company executive and lawyer; b. 6 July 1918, Paris; s. of Paul Marchandise and Mme Franquet; m. Jacqueline Feuillette 1940; three s. (one s. deceased) two d.; ed. Ecole Libre des Sciences Politiques; training as barrister 1939; sous-préfet, Dir. of office of Commissaire of the Repub., Laon 1944; auditeur, Council of State 1946; head of office of Minister for War Veterans 1948; legal adviser, Caisse Cen. de la France d'Outre-mer 1948; Chargé de mission for Minister of France Overseas 1952, head of office 1953–54; Maître des Requêtes, Council of State 1954, Maître des Requêtes Honoraire 1962; legal adviser, office of Pres. of Council of Ministers 1954–55; Asst. Dir. to Dir.-Gen., Bureau of Mines of France Overseas 1955; Sec.-Gen. Fria (int. aluminium production corpn.) 1956–60, Vice-Pres. 1967, Pres. 1969, Vice-Pres. Friguia (part-nationalized successor to Fria) 1976–; Dir. Pechiney 1960, Asst. Dir.-Gen. 1970, Dir. délégué to Pechiney Ugine Kuhlmann 1971–75; Dir. Aluminium de Grèce 1961, Pres. 1968–75; Vice-Pres. and Dir.-Gen. Librairie Hachette 1975, Pres. and Dir.-Gen. 1976–81; Pres. and Dir.-Gen. Soc. Frialco 1982–84; Pres. Groupement de l'Industrie chimique 1981–93; Pres. Franco-American Foundation 1982–90 (Hon. Pres. 1990–), Institut pour l'histoire de l'Aluminium 1986–97, Hon. Pres. 1997–; Dir. Banque de Paris et des Pays-Bas 1978–92, S.A. Philips Industrielle 1982–90, Cie. Générale des Eaux 1984–93; Commdr., Légion d'honneur, Ordre des Palmes académiques, Officier, Ordre nat. du Mérite, Croix de guerre. *Address:* Immeuble Pechiney Balzac, 10 place des Vosges – la Défense 5, 92048 Paris-La-Défense Cedex (Office); 25 ter boulevard de La Saussaye, 92200 Neuilly, France (Home). *Telephone:* (1) 46.91.50.01 (Office).

MARCHUK, Guriy Ivanovich; Russian mathematician; b. 8 June 1925, Petro-Khersonets Village, Orenburg Region; m.; three c.; ed. Leningrad State Univ.; Sr. Research Assoc., Head of Dept., Inst. of Physics and Energetics, Obninsk 1953–62; Inst. of Maths. of Siberian Br. of U.S.S.R. Acad. of Sciences 1962–64; Prof., Novosibirsk Univ. 1962–80; Deputy Chair., Chair. of Presidium, Siberian Br. of U.S.S.R. Acad. of Sciences 1964–79; Dir. Computing Centre of Siberian Br. of U.S.S.R. Acad. of Sciences 1964–79; Deputy Chair. U.S.S.R. Council of Ministers and Chair. State Cttee. for Science and Tech. 1980–86; Dir. Dept. of Computing Math. (now Inst.), Acad. of Sciences 1980–; Corresp. mem. U.S.S.R. (now Russian) Acad. of Sciences 1962–68, mem. 1968–, Vice-Pres. 1975–78, Pres. 1986–91, Chair. Scientific Council on Medicine 1987–; Deputy to U.S.S.R. Supreme Soviet 1979–89; Lenin Prize 1961, A. Karpinski Prize, Hamburg 1988; Order of Lenin (four times), Keldysh Gold Medal 1981, Chebyshev Gold Medal 1996 and other decorations. *Publications:* works on problems of computational math. and physics of atmosphere. *Address:* Institute of Numerical Mathematics, Gubkin Str. 8, 117333, Moscow, Russia. *Telephone:* (095) 938-17-69. *Fax:* (095) 938-18-21.

MARCHUK, Yevgeny Kirillovich; Ukrainian politician; b. 1941; ed. Kirovograd Pedagogical Inst.; with Ukrainian KGB (State Security Cttee.) 1963–91; Chair. Nat. Security Service of Ukraine 1991; State Minister of Defence, Nat. Security and Emergencies 1991–94; Deputy Prime Minister July 1994, First Deputy Prime Minister 1994–95; Prime Minister of Ukraine 1995–96; mem. Verkhovna Rada 1996–; Head, Social Market Choice faction 1996–. *Address:* Verkhovna Rada, M. Hrushevskoho Str. 5, 252008, Kiev, Ukraine.

MARCINKEVIČIUS, Justinas; Lithuanian poet, playwright and translator; b. 10 March 1930, Vazhatkiemis, Lithuania; s. of Motiejus Marcinkevičius and Ieva Marcinkevičius; m. Genovaite Kalvaityte 1955; two d.; ed. Univ. of Vilnius; began literary career 1953; mem. CPSU 1957–90;

U.S.S.R. People's Deputy 1989–91; mem. Lithuanian Acad. of Science 1990, Lithuanian Council of Culture and Art 1991; awards include State Prizes (twice), People's Poet of Lithuania, J. G. Horder Award 1997, Polish PEN Centre Award 1997, Santarvė Award 1999; Grand Duke Gediminas Order. *Publications include:* I Ask to Speak 1955, The Twentieth Spring 1955, The Pine that Laughed 1961, Blood and Ashes 1961, Hands that Share out the Bread 1963, The Wall 1965, Mindaugas 1968, The Cathedral 1971, Mazhvidas 1977, The Tender Touch of Life 1978, The Only Land 1984, For the Living and the Dead 1988, Lullaby to the Homeland and the Mother 1992, By the Rye and by the Hearth 1993, Poems from the Diary 1993, The Harmony of the Flowing River 1995. *Address:* Mildos gve. 33, Apt. 6, 2055 Vilnius, Lithuania. *Telephone:* (02) 740162.

MARCINKUS, Most Rev. Paul Casimir; American ecclesiastic; b. 15 Jan. 1922; ordained as a Roman Catholic priest 1947; Asst. Pastor, St. Cristina's Parish, Chicago 1947–52; joined Vatican State Secr. 1952; served as papal diplomatist in Canada and Bolivia; Gen. Man. Istituto per le Opere di Religione (Vatican Bank) 1969–71, Chair. 1971–89; Pro-Pres. Pontifical Comm. for the Vatican City State 1981–90; Titular Archbishop of Orta 1981–. *Address:* living in Chicago, U.S.A.

MARCKER, Kjeld Adrian, PH.D.; Danish molecular biologist; b. 27 Dec. 1932, Nyborg; s. of Kjeld A. C. Marcker and Minna C. Callesen; m. Anne Birgit Hansen 1964; three d.; ed. Nyborg Gymnasium and Univ. of Copenhagen; Dept. of Physical Chem., Univ. of Copenhagen 1958; Carlsberg-Wellcome Fellow, MRC Lab. of Molecular Biol., Cambridge 1962, mem. staff 1964; Fellow, King's Coll. Cambridge 1968; Prof. in Molecular Biology, Aarhus Univ. 1970–; mem. Royal Danish Acad., Danish Acad. of Tech. Science, Academiae Europaeae; Novo Medical Prize 1971; Anders Jahre Medical Prize 1973. *Publications:* articles in scientific journals. *Leisure interests:* soccer, bird-watching, history. *Address:* Laboratory of Gene Expression, Department of Molecular Biology, University of Aarhus, Gustav Wieds Vej 10, 8000 Aarhus C; Toftevej 1, 8250 Egå, Denmark (Home). *Telephone:* 89425017. *Fax:* 86 201222.

MARCOPOULOS, Christos, D.SC.; Greek politician and nuclear chemist; b. 25 Dec. 1925, Athens; s. of Antony Marcopoulos and Paraskevi Vergopoulou; m. 1st Sapfo Mazaraki 1954 (divorced 1960); one s.; m. 2nd Kleopatra Papadopoulou 1974; two s.; ed. Varvakios High School, Teachers' Acad., Athens, Univ. of Athens, Leicester Coll. of Tech., U.K.; Nat. State Chem. Lab. 1956–59; Group Leader, Greek Atomic Energy Comm. 1962–69, Dir. Radio-immunochem. 1977–81; Asst. Prof., Nat. Tech. Univ. of Athens 1965; Sr. Researcher, Imperial Coll., London 1968; Visiting Scientist, Tech. Hochschule, Darmstadt, Fed. Repub. of Germany; Visiting Prof., Univ. of Bologna 1973; Pres. Hellenic Nuclear Soc. 1975–81; mem. Steering Cttee., European Nuclear Soc. 1979–81; mem. Cen. Cttee., Panhellenic Socialistic Movement (PASOK) 1975–; mem. European Parl. 1981–84 (mem. Energy, Research and Tech. Comm.); Amb.-at-Large for West European Countries 1984–85; mem. Nat. Parl. of Greece 1985– (Pres. Foreign Affairs Cttee. 1986–87); Head of Greek Parl. Del. in Council of Europe 1986–88 (Vice-Pres. Parl. Ass. 1987–88); Minister in charge of Int. Orgs. 1988–89; Pres. Panhellenic Movt. for Nat. Independence, World Peace and Disarmament 1981–90; Founder Int. Peace Olympiad Bureau, Co-ordinator First Peace Olympiad 1989; Founder and Pres. Movt. for Peace, Human Rights and Nat. Independence 1991–, Fed. of Balkan Non-Governmental Orgs. for Peace and Co-operation 1993–; Pres. Int. Organizing Cttee., 2nd European Conf. on Peace, Democracy and Co-operation in Balkans 1996. *Publications:* Organic Chemistry (2 vols.) 1963 and 1971, Inorganic Chemistry (2 vols.) 1968 and 1971, Introduction to Modern Chemistry 1973, The Dominance of Prota and the Theory of Enforced Randomness 1991, Order and Anarchy 1996, Chance and Order 1997, and numerous articles on nuclear disarmament, peace, int. affairs, European relations and human rights. *Leisure interests:* swimming, classical music. *Address:* 34 Eratous Street, Holargos, Athens, Greece (Home). *Telephone:* 36 41 230 (Office), 65 24 687 (Home). *Fax:* 3617047.

MARCOS, Imelda Romualdez; Philippine politician and social leader; b. c. 1930; m. Ferdinand E. Marcos (died 1989); one s. two d.; Gov. of Metro Manila 1975–86; Roving Amb.; visited Beijing 1976; took part in negotiations in Libya over self-govt. for southern provinces 1977; leader Kilusan Bagong Lipunan (New Society Movement) 1978–81; mem. Batasang Pambansa (Interim Legis. Assembly) 1978–83; Minister of Human Settlements 1978–79, 1984–86, of Human Settlements and Ecology 1979–83; mem. Cabinet Exec. Cttee. 1982–84; Chair. Southern Philippines Devt. Authority 1980–86; indicted for embezzlement 1988, acquitted 1990; returned to Philippines Nov. 1991; sentenced to 18 to 24 years' imprisonment for criminal graft Sept. 1993; convicted of two charges of corruption, sentenced to 9–12 years on each Sept. 1993; sentenced on appeal to Supreme Court; facing four charges of graft Sept. 1995; Presidential Cand. 1992; mem. Senate 1995–. *Records include:* Imelda Papin featuring songs with Mrs. Imelda Romualdez Marcos 1989.

MARCUS, Claude, D.ECON.; French advertising executive; b. 28 Aug. 1924, Paris; s. of Jack Marcus and Louise Bleustein; m. Claudine Pohl 1948; one s. three d.; ed. Faculté des Lettres, Aix and Faculté de Droit, Paris; Vice-Chair. Supervisory Bd. Publicis; Légion d'honneur; Officier, Ordre nat. du Mérite, Médaille des Evadés, Chevalier, Palmes académiques et de l'Economie nationale. *Leisure interests:* antiques, tennis. *Address:* 133 avenue des Champs-Elysées, 75008 Paris, France. *Telephone:* 44.43.70.04.

MARCUS, Rudolph Arthur; American professor of chemistry; b. 21 July 1923, Montreal, Canada; s. of Myer and Esther Marcus; m. Laura Hearne 1949; three s.; ed. McGill Univ.; worked for Nat. Research Council of Canada 1946–49; Univ. of N. Carolina 1949–51; Asst. Prof. Polytech. Inst. of Brooklyn 1951–54, Assoc. Prof. 1954–58, Prof. 1958–64; Prof. Univ. of Ill. 1964–68; Arthur Amos Noyes Prof. of Chem., Calif. Inst. of Tech. 1978–; Visiting Prof. of Theoretical Chem., Oxford Univ. 1975–76; Visiting Linnett Prof. of Chemistry, Univ. of Cambridge 1996; Hon. Prof. Fudan Univ., Shanghai 1994–; Hon. Prof. Inst. of Chem., Chinese Acad. of Sciences, Beijing 1995; mem. Courant Inst. of Mathematical Sciences, New York Univ. 1960–61, Council, Gordon Research Confs. 1965–68, Chair. Bd. of Trustees and mem. Bd. 1966–69; Chair. Div. of Physical Chem., American Chemical Soc. 1964–65; mem. Exec. Cttee. American Physical Soc. Div. of Chemical Physics 1970–72, Advisory Bd. American Chemical Soc. Petroleum Research Fund 1970–72, Review Cttee. Argonne Nat. Laboratory Chem. Dept. 1966–72 (Chair. 1968–69), Brookhaven Nat. Lab. 1971–73, Radiation Lab., Univ. of Notre Dame 1976–78, External Advisory Bd., NSF Center for Photoinduced Charge Transfer 1990–, Nat. Research Council/N.A.S., Cttee. on Climatic Impact; Chair. Cttee. on Kinetics of Chemical Reactions 1975–77, Panel on Atmospheric Chem. 1975–78, Cttee. on Chemical Sciences 1977–79, Cttee. Survey Opportunities in Chem. 1982–86, Math. Panel, Int. Benchmarking of U.S. Research Fields 1996–, Advisory Cttee. for Chem. Nat. Science Foundation 1977–80, Review Cttee. Chem. Depts. Princeton Univ. 1972–78, Polytech. Inst. of N.Y. 1977–80, Calif. Inst. of Tech. 1977–78; Adviser, State Key Lab. for Structural Chem. of Unstable and Stable Species, Beijing 1995, Center for Molecular Sciences, Chinese Acad. of Sciences, Beijing 1995–; mem. editorial bds., Laser Chem. 1982–, Advances in Chemical Physics 1984–, World Scientific Publishing 1987–, Int. Reviews in Physical Chem. 1988–, Progress in Physics, Chem. and Mechanics (China) 1989–, Journal of the Chemical Soc. Perkin Transactions 2 1992–, Chemical Physics Research (India) 1992–, Trends in Chemical Physical Research (India) 1992–; Hon. Ed. Int. Journal of Quantum Chem. 1996–; mem. N.A.S., American Philosophical Soc.; Fellow, American Acad. of Arts and Sciences, Co-Chair. Exec. Cttee. Western Section; Foreign mem. Royal Society, London; Hon. Fellow Royal Soc. of Chem.; Foreign Fellow, Royal Soc. of Canada; Foreign mem. Chinese Acad. of Sciences; mem. Int. Acad. Quantum Molecular Science; Assoc. mem. Center for Advanced Studies, Univ. of Ill. 1968–69; Hon. mem. Int. Soc. of Electrochemistry, Korean Chem. Soc.; numerous lectureships; Hon. D.Sc. (Chicago) 1983, (Polytechnic Univ.) 1986, (Gothenborg) 1987, (McGill) 1988, (New Brunswick) 1993, (Queen's) 1993, (Oxford) 1995, (Yokohama Nat. Univ.) 1996, (Univ. of N.C.) 1996, (Univ. of Ill.) 1997, (Technion—Israel Inst. of Tech.) 1998; Anne Molson Prize for Chem. 1943; Nat. Science Foundation Sr. Post-Doctoral Fellowship 1960–61; Alfred P. Sloan Fellowship 1960–63; Fulbright-Hays Sr. Scholar 1971–72; Alexander von Humboldt Foundation Sr. U.S. Scientist Award 1976, Irving Langmuir Award in Chem. Physics (American Chemical Soc.) 1978, R. A. Robinson Medal, Faraday Div., Royal Soc. of Chem. 1982, C. F. Chandler Medal (Univ. of Columbia) 1983, Wolf Prize 1985, Peter Debye Award in Physical Chem. (American Chemical Soc.) 1988, Willard Gibbs Medal (American Chemical Soc.) 1988, Centenary Medal, Faraday Div., Royal Soc. Chem. 1988, Nat. Medal of Science 1989, Theodore William Richards Medal (American Chem. Soc.) 1990, Evans Award (Ohio State Univ.) 1990, Edgar Fahs Smith Award, Remsen Award, Pauling Medal (all American Chemical Soc.) 1991, Nobel Prize for Chemistry 1992, Hirschfelder Prize in Theoretical Chem. (Univ. of Wisconsin) 1993, American Acad. of Achievement Golden Plate Award 1993, Lavoisier Medal (Soc. Française de Chimie) 1994, Hon. Citizen of Winnipeg 1995, Auburn-Kosolapoff Award (American Chem. Soc.) 1996, Award in Theoretical Chem., Oesper Award (both American Chem. Soc.) 1997, Top 75 Award, Chemical and Eng. News, American Chemical Soc. 1998. *Publications:* numerous articles in scientific journals, especially Journal of Chemical Physics and Journal of Physical Chem. *Leisure interests:* music, history, tennis and skiing. *Address:* Noyes Laboratory, 127-72, California Institute of Technology, Pasadena, CA 91125, U.S.A. *Telephone:* (626) 395-6566 (Office). *Fax:* (626) 792-8485.

MARCUS, Ruth Barcan, PH.D.; American professor of philosophy; b. 2 Aug. 1921, New York; d. of Samuel Barcan and Rose Post; m. Jules A. Marcus 1942 (divorced 1976); two s. two d.; ed. New York and Yale Univs.; Research Assoc. Inst. for Human Relations, Yale Univ. 1945–47; Assoc. Prof. Roosevelt Univ. 1959–64; Prof. and Chair. Dept. of Philosophy, Univ. of Ill. 1964–70; Prof. Northwestern Univ. 1970–73; Reuben Post Halleck Prof. of Philosophy, Yale Univ. 1973–93, Sr. Research Scholar 1994–; Visiting Distinguished Prof., Univ. of Calif., Irvine 1994–99; Adviser, Oxford Univ. Press New York 1980–90; Guggenheim Fellow 1953–54; N.S.F. Fellow 1963–64; Fellow, Center for Advanced Studies, Stanford Univ. 1979, Inst. for Advanced Study in the Humanities, Univ. of Edin. 1983, Wolfson Coll. Oxford 1985, 1986, Clare Hall, Cambridge 1988 (Perm. mem. Common Room); Fellow, American Acad. of Arts and Sciences; mem. and Pres. Inst. Int. de Philosophie, Paris 1990–93, Hon. Pres. 1993–; Chair. Nat. Bd. of Officers, American Philosophical Asscn. 1977–83; Pres. Asscn. for Symbolic Logic 1983–86; Pres. Elizabethan Club 1988–90; mem. Council on Philosophical Studies (Pres. 1988–), Steering Cttee., Fed. Int. Soc. de Philosophie 1985– (Pres. 1990–93, Hon. Pres. 1994–); mem. numerous editorial bds.; Hon. D.Hum.Litt. (Ill.) 1995; Medal, Coll. de France 1986. *Publications:* The Logical Enterprise (ed. with A. Anderson and R. Martin) 1975, Logic Methodology and Philosophy of Science (ed.) 1986, Modalities 1993, 1995;

articles in professional journals. *Address:* Department of Philosophy, Box 208306, Yale University, New Haven, CT 06525 (Office); 311 St. Ronan Street, New Haven, CT 06511, U.S.A. (Home). *Telephone:* (203) 432-1665 (Office). *Fax:* (203) 432-7950.

MÅRDH, Per-Anders, M.D., PH.D.; Swedish university professor and physician; b. 9 April 1941, Stockholm; s. of Gustav-Adolf Mårdh and Inga-Greta (née Bodin) Mårdh; m. 1st Ingrid Ekstrand 1967; one s. one d.; m. 2nd Nina Ulvelius 1997; ed. Univ. of Lund; Assoc. Prof. Univ. of Lund 1973; Dir. WHO Collaboration Centre for Sexually Transmitted Diseases, Univ. of Lund 1980–85, then Uppsala Univ. 1985–; Prof. Clinical Bacteriology, Univ. of Uppsala 1984–; founder Scand. Asscn. for Travel Medicine and Health 1990; mem. Bd. Int. Tourist Health Org.; Fernström's Award for young prominent research workers 1982. *Publications:* as Ed.: Genital Infections and Their Complications 1975, Chlamydia trachomatis in Genital and Related Infections 1982, Chlamydial Infections 1982, International Perspectives on Neglected Sexually Transmitted Diseases 1983, Gas Chromatography/Mass Spectrometry in Applications in Microbiology 1984, Sexually Transmitted Diseases 1984, Bacterial Vaginosis 1984, Coagulase—negative Staphylococci 1986, Infections in Primary Health Care 1986, Genital Candida-infection 1990, Vaginitis/Vaginosis 1991, Travel and Migration Medicine 1997; Author: Chlamydia 1988, Swedish Red Houses 1991, Travel Well Travel Healthy 1992, Travel Medicine 1994. *Leisure interests:* art, skiing. *Address:* Centre for STD Research, Uppsala, University Box 552, 751 22 Uppsala, Sweden. *Telephone:* (18) 4710000.

MAREE, John B., B.COMM., A.M.P.; South African business executive; b. 13 Aug. 1924, Middelburg, Cape; s. of Dr. John Maree; m. Joy du Plessis 1950; one s.; ed. Univ. of the Witwatersrand and Harvard Business School; Chair. Eskom Electricity Council 1985–97, Nedcor Group of Cos. 1990–97, Denel Ltd. 1992–95; Dir. Devt. Bank of S.A., Old Mutual; Fellow Inst. of Marketing Man. 1991–; Hon. D. Com.; Star of S.A. 1985; Order for Meritorious Service (Gold) 1989; one of top 5 Businessmen of the Year 1981; Chevalier, Legion d'honneur. *Leisure interests:* golf, gardening. *Address:* 52 4th Road, Hyde Park, Sandton 2146, South Africa (Home). *Telephone:* (11) 881-4363 (Office); (1) 788-8812 (Home). *Fax:* (11) 881-4555.

MARGALEF, Ramon, D.SC.; Spanish professor of ecology; b. 16 May 1919, Barcelona; s. of Ramon Margalef and Vicenta López; m. Maria Mir 1952; two s. two d.; ed. Univ. of Barcelona; research worker, Instituto Investigaciones Pesqueras, Barcelona 1952–70; Prof. of Ecology, Univ. of Barcelona 1967–86, Prof. Emer. 1987–; Dr. h.c. (Aix-Marseille, Laval); Huntsman, Ramón and ITALGAS prizes. *Publications:* over 400 books and papers including: Perspectives in Ecological Theory 1968, Ecología 1974, La Biosfera entre la termodinámica y el juego 1980, Limnología 1983. *Leisure interest:* hiking. *Address:* Department of Ecology, University of Barcelona, Diagonal 645, 08028 Barcelona, Spain. *Telephone:* (343) 4021516.

MARGARET ROSE, H.R.H. The Princess, Countess of Snowdon, C.I., G.C.V.O., G.C.St.J.; b. 21 Aug. 1930, Glamis Castle, Angus, Scotland; d. of the late H.R.H. Prince Albert, Duke of York (later H.M. King George VI) and Duchess of York (now H.M. Queen Elizabeth The Queen Mother, q.v.); sister of H.M. Queen Elizabeth II (q.v.); m. Antony Armstrong-Jones (cr. Earl of Snowdon, q.v.) 1960 (divorced 1978); one s. (Viscount Linley, David Albert Charles Armstrong-Jones, b. 1961) one d. (Lady Sarah Frances Elizabeth Chatto, b. 1964); awarded the Royal Victorian Chain 1990; Pres. English Folk Dance and Song Soc., Friends of the Elderly and Gentlefolk's Help, The Guide Asscn., Horder Centre for Arthritis, Nat. Soc. for the Prevention of Cruelty to Children, The Royal Ballet, Royal Scottish Soc. for Prevention of Cruelty to Children, Birmingham Royal Ballet, Scottish Children's League, Victoria League for Commonwealth Friendship, Commonwealth Trust; Grand Pres. St. John Ambulance Asscn. and Brigade; Jt. Pres. Lowland Brigade Club; Pres. and Chair. of Council Invalid Children's Aid Nationwide; Patron Architects' Benevolent Soc., Asscn. of Anaesthetists of G.B. and Ireland, Barristers' Benevolent Asscn., Bristol Royal Soc. for the Blind, Ladies' Guild of the British and Int. Sailors' Soc., Combined Theatrical Charities Appeals Council, Friends of the Iveagh Bequest, Kenwood, Friends of St. John's Smith Square, Friends of Southwark Cathedral, Friends of the London Hosp. (Whitechapel), Hallé Concerts Soc., Heart Disease and Diabetes Research Trust, Light Infantry Club, London Lighthouse, Mary Hare Grammar School for the Deaf, Mathilda and Terence Kennedy Inst. of Rheumatology, Migraine Trust, Mustique Educational Trust, Nat. Pony Soc., Northern Ballet Theatre, Olave Baden-Powell Soc., Pottery and Glass Trades' Benevolent Inst., Queen Alexandra's Royal Army Nursing Corps. Asscn., Royal Coll. of Nursing and Nat. Council of Nurses of the U.K., St. Margaret's Chapel Guild, Edinburgh Castle, St. Pancras Housing Asscn. in Camden, Services Sound and Vision Corpn., Suffolk Regimental Asscn., Tenovus and Tenovus Scotland, Union of Schools for Social Service, Youth Clubs Scotland, Zebra Trust, Clarence House Restoration Trust, Purine Research Laboratory; Hon. Life Fellow Zoological Soc. of London; Hon. Life mem. Century House Asscn. (British Columbia); Hon. mem. Automobile Asscn., Order of the Road, Royal Automobile Club, Sealyham Terrier Breeders' Asscn.; Patron and Hon. mem. Grand Antiquity Soc. of Glasgow; Hon. Patron Winnipeg Art Gallery; Life mem. British Legion Women's Section; mem. Court of Assistants, Worshipful Co. of Haberdashers; Master of the Bench The Hon. Soc. of Lincoln's Inn; Patron-in-Chief English Harbour Repair Fund; Hon. Fellow Royal Inst. of British Architects, Royal. Coll. of Obstetricians and Gynaecologists, Royal Coll. of Surgeons of England, Royal Photographic Soc. of G.B., Royal Soc. of Medicine; Hon. Pres. British Museum Devt. Trust; Vice-Patron Royal Anglian Regt. Asscn.; Visitor King George VI and Queen Elizabeth Foundation of St. Catherine's; Col-in-Chief The Bermuda Regt., Highland Fusiliers of Canada (Militia), Queen Alexandra's Royal Army Nursing Corps, Royal Highland Fusiliers (Princess Margaret's Own Glasgow and Ayrshire Regt.), The Princess Louise Fusiliers (Royal Canadian Infantry Corps-Militia), The Light Dragoons; Deputy Col.-in-Chief The Royal Anglian Regt.; Hon. Air Cdre. R.A.F. Coningsby; Freeman of the City of London; Hon. Life mem. R.A.F. Club; Sponsor H.M.S. Illustrious, H.M.S. Norfolk. *Address:* Kensington Palace, London, W8 4PU, England.

MARGÉOT, H.E. Cardinal Jean; Mauritian ecclesiastic; b. 3 Feb. 1916, Port-Louis; ordained 1938, elected bishop of Port-Louis 1969, consecrated 1969; cr. Cardinal 1988. *Address:* Bonne Terre, Vacoas, Mauritius. *Telephone:* 424-5716. *Fax:* 426-5190.

MARGOLIASH, Emanuel, M.D.; American biochemist; b. 10 Feb. 1920, Cairo, Egypt; s. of Wolf Margoliash and Bertha Margoliash (née Kotler); m. Sima Beshkin 1944; two s.; ed. Mission Laïque Française, Cairo, American Univ. of Beirut, Lebanon; Research Fellow, Dept. of Experimental Pathology, Hebrew Univ., Jerusalem 1945–48; served as Medical Officer in the Israel Army 1948–49; Sr. Asst. in Experimental Pathology, Cancer Research Labs., Hadassah Medical School, Hebrew Univ., Jerusalem 1951; worked under Prof. D. Keilin, Molteno Inst., Univ. of Cambridge, England 1951–53; Acting Head, Cancer Research Labs., Hadassah Medical School, Hebrew Univ., Jerusalem 1954–58, Lecturer in Experimental Pathology, 1955; worked at Nobel Inst., Dept. of Biochem. under a fellowship of the Dazian Foundation for Medical Research 1958; Research Assoc., Dept. of Biochem., Univ. of Utah Coll. of Medicine, Salt Lake City, Utah, U.S.A. 1958–60; Research Assoc., McGill-Montreal Gen. Hospital Research Inst., Montreal, Canada 1960–62; Research Fellow and Head, Protein Section, Dept. of Molecular Biology, Abbott Labs., North Chicago, Ill. 1962–71; Professorial Lecturer, Dept. of Biochem., Univ. of Chicago, Ill. 1964–71; Prof. of Biochem. and Molecular Biology, Northwestern Univ., Evanston, Ill. 1971–90, Chair. Dept. of Biochem., Molecular Biology and Cell Biology 1979–82, Owen L. Coon Prof. of Molecular Biology 1988–90, Prof. Emer. 1990–; Prof., Lab. of Molecular Biology, Dept. of Biological Sciences, Univ. of Ill., at Chicago 1989–, Co-ordinator 1989–93; mem. Nat. Acad. of Sciences and numerous scientific socs.; Fellow, American Acad. of Arts and Sciences, American Acad. of Microbiology; mem. Editorial Bd. of Journal of Biological Chem. 1966–72, Biochemical Genetics 1966–80, Journal of Molecular Evolution 1971–82, Biochem. and Molecular Biology Int. 1981–; mem. Int. Union of Biochem. Cttee. on Nomenclature 1962–, Advisory Cttee., Mich. State Univ. Atomic Energy Comm. Plant Research Lab. 1967–72; Co-Chair. Gordon Research Conf. on Proteins 1967; Keilin Memorial Lectureship of the Biochemical Soc. 1970; Harvey Soc. Lectureship 1970–71; mem. Publs. Cttee., American Soc. of Biological Chemists Inc. 1973–76; mem. of Exec. Cttee. of U.S. Bioenergetics Group of the Biophysical Soc. 1980–; Rudi Lemberg Fellow, Australian Acad. of Science 1981; Guggenheim Fellow 1983. *Publications:* more than 275 scientific papers and volumes. *Address:* Department of Biological Sciences, (M/C 066), The University of Illinois at Chicago, 845 W. Taylor Street, Chicago, IL 60607-7060, U.S.A. *Telephone:* (312) 996-8268. *Fax:* (312) 996-2805.

MARGRAVE, John, B.S., PH.D.; American professor of chemistry; b. 13 April 1924, Kansas City; s. of Orville Frank Margrave and Bernice J. Hamilton Margrave; m. Mary Lou Davis 1950; one s. one d.; ed. Univ. of Kansas, Lawrence; AEC Postdoctoral Fellow, Univ. of Calif., Berkeley 1951–52; Instructor, Assoc. Prof. then Prof. of Chem., Univ. of Wis. 1952–63; Prof. of Chem., Rice Univ. 1963–, Chair. Dept. of Chem. 1967–72, E. D. Butcher Prof. 1986–, Dean of Advanced Studies and Research, Rice Univ. 1972–80, Vice-Pres. 1980–86; consultant to govt. agencies and pvt. industry; Pres. MarChem Inc. 1970–, High Temperature Science Inc. 1976–; Vice-Pres. for Research, Houston Area Research Center (HARC) 1986–89, Chief Scientific Officer 1989–; Dir. Materials Science Center 1986–94; Chair. Cttee. on Chemical Processes in Severe Nuclear Accidents, Nat. Research Council 1987–88; Chair. Cttee. on Remediation of Molten Salt Reactor, Nat. Research Council 1996–97; Fellow A.A.A.S., American Physical Soc.; mem. Chemical Soc. (U.K.) and other socs.; Fellow American Inst. of Chemists; mem. N.A.S.; Alfred P. Sloan Research Fellow 1956–57, 1957–58; Guggenheim Research Fellow 1961; numerous awards include American Chemical Soc. Award in Inorganic Chem. 1967, Award in Fluorine Chem. 1980, Distinguished Alumnus Award 1981, two IR-100 Awards; mem. numerous advisory cttees. and editorial bds. *Publications:* over 670 scientific publs., including 4 books and 19 patents. *Address:* Rice University, P.O. Box 1892, 6100 South Main, Houston, TX 77005 (Office); 4511 Verone, Bellaire, TX 77401, U.S.A. (Home), U.S.A. *Telephone:* (713) 527-4813 (Office). *Fax:* (713) 523-8236 (Office).

MARGRETHE II, H.M. Queen of Denmark; b. 16 April 1940; d. of late King Frederik IX and of Queen Ingrid; m. Count Henri de Laborde de Monpezat (now Prince Henrik of Denmark) 1967; two s.; ed. Univs. of Copenhagen, Aarhus and Cambridge, The Sorbonne, Paris, and London School of Econs.; succeeded to the throne 14 Jan. 1972; has undertaken many official visits abroad with her husband, travelling extensively in Europe, the Far East, North and South America; illustrated The Lord of the Rings 1977; Norse Legends as told by Jorgen Stegelmann 1979, Bjarkemaal 1982; Hon. LL.D. (Cambridge) 1975, (London) 1980; Hon. Dr. (Univ. of Iceland) 1986; Dr. of Civil Law by Diploma Oxford Univ. 1992; Hon. Fellow

Lucy Cavendish Coll. Cambridge 1989, Hon. Bencher of the Middle Temple 1992, Hon. Fellow Girton Coll. Cambridge 1992, Medal of the Headmastership, Univ. of Paris 1987; Hon. K.G. 1979. *Publications:* (Trans.) All Men are Mortal (with Prince Henrik) 1981, The Valley 1988, The Fields 1989, The Forest (trans.) 1989. *Address:* Amalienborg Palace, 1257 Copenhagen K, Denmark.

MARGULIS, Lynn, PH.D.; American biologist; b. 5 March 1938, Chicago; d. of Morris and Leone Wise Alexander; m. 1st Carl Sagan 1957; m. 2nd T. N. Margulis 1967; three s. one d.; ed. Univs. of Chicago, Wisconsin and Calif. at Berkeley; Research Assoc. Dept. of Biology, Brandeis Univ. 1963–64, Lecturer 1963–65, Biology Co-ordinator, Peace Corps, Colombia Project 1965–66; Consultant and Staff mem. The Elementary Science Study, Educational Services 1963–67; Adjunct Asst. Prof. Dept. of Biology, Boston Univ. 1966–67, Asst. Prof. 1967–71, Assoc. Prof. 1971–77, Prof. 1977–88, Univ. Prof. 1986–88; Distinguished Prof. Univ. of Mass., Amherst 1988–; Visiting Prof. Dept. of Marine Biology, Scripps Inst. of Oceanography Jan.-March 1980, Dept. of Geology and Planetary Science Calif. Inst. of Tech. 1980, Dept. of Microbiology, Universidad Autónoma de Barcelona, Spain 1986; NASA-Ames Planetary Biology and Microbial Ecology Summer Research Programme 1980, 1982, 1984; Guggenheim Foundation Fellow 1979; Sherman Fairchild Distinguished Scholar, Calif. Inst. of Tech. 1977; mem. N.A.S.; Fellow A.A.A.S.; NASA Public Service Award 1981. *Publications:* Origin of Eukaryotic Cells 1970, Origins of Life I (Ed.) 1970, Origins of Life II (Ed.) 1971, Origins of Life: Planetary Astronomy (Ed.) 1973, Origins of Life: Chemistry and Radioastronomy (Ed.) 1973, Limits of Life (Ed. with C. Ponnamperuma) 1980, Symbiosis in Cell Evolution 1981, Early Life 1982, Five Kingdoms: An Illustrated Guide to the Phyla of Life on Earth (with K. V. Schwartz) 1982, Origins of Sex (with D. Sagan) 1986, Microcosmos: Four billion years of evolution from our bacterial ancestors (with D. Sagan) 1986, 1991, Garden of Microbial Delights 1988, Biospheres From Earth to Space (with Dorion Sagan) 1988, Global Ecology (with René Fester) 1989, Handbook Protoctista (Ed.) 1990, Mystery Dance (with D. Sagan) 1991, Symbiosis as a Source of Evolutionary Innovation: Speciation and Morphogenesis (Ed. with R. Fester) 1991, Environmental Evolution: the Effect of the Origin and Evolution of Life on Planet Earth (Ed. with L. Olendzenski) 1992, Concepts of Symbiogenesis (Ed.) 1992, Diversity of Life: The Five Kingdoms 1992, Symbiosis in Cell Evolution: Microbial Communities in the Archean and Proterozoic Eons 1993, Illustrated Glossary of the Protoctista (with H. McKhann and L. Olendzenski) 1993, The Illustrated Five Kingdoms. A Guide to the Diversity of Life on Earth (with K. V. Schwartz and M. Dolan) 1993, What is Life? (with D. Sagan) 1995, Slanted Truths (with D. Sagan) 1997, What Is Sex? (with D. Sagan) 1998. *Leisure interests:* fiction, Spain, pre-Columbian Mexican culture. *Address:* Department of Geosciences, Morrill Science Center, University of Massachusetts, Amherst, MA 01003, U.S.A. *Telephone:* (413) 545-3244. *Fax:* (413) 545-1200.

MARIAM, Lt.-Col. Mengistu Haile; Ethiopian politician and army officer; b. 26 May 1937, Addis Ababa; m. Wubanchi Bishaw 1968; one s. two d.; ed. Holeta Mil. Acad.; served in Army's Third Div., attaining rank of Maj.; mem. Armed Forces Co-ordinating Cttee. (Derg) June 1974–; took leading part in overthrow of Emperor Haile Selassie Sept. 1974, Head of Derg Exec. Cttee. Nov. 1974; First Vice-Chair. Provisional Mil. Admin. Council (PMAC) 1974–77, Chair. (Head of State) 1977–91; Pres. of Democratic Repub. of Ethiopia 1987–91 (overthrown in coup); Chair. PMAC Standing Cttee.; Chair. Council of Ministers 1976–91, OAU 1983–84; Sec.-Gen. Workers' Party of Ethiopia 1984–91; accused of genocide in absentia; now living in Zimbabwe as political refugee. *Leisure interests:* swimming, tennis, chess, reading, watching films. *Address:* PO Box 1536, Gunhill Enclave, Harare, Zimbabwe. *Telephone:* 745254.

MARIANI, Carlo Maria; Italian artist; b. 25 July 1935, Rome; s. of Anastasio Mariani and Anita de Angelis; m. 1st B. Brantsen 1959 (divorced 1983), 2nd Carol Lane 1990; one s. one d.; ed. Acad. of Fine Arts, Rome; lives and works in Rome and New York; one-man shows include: Galerie Paul Maenz, Cologne 1977, Sperone Westwater Fischer, New York 1981, Sperone Westwater, New York 1984, 1987, Galerie Séroussi, Paris 1985, Galerie Tanit, Munich 1986, Michael Kohn Gallery, Los Angeles 1988, 1992, Studio d'Arte Cannaviello, Milan 1988, Drammen Kunstforening, Norway 1990, Hirschl & Adler Modern, New York 1990, 1993, Mathildenhöhe, Darmstadt 1991–92, L.A. Co. Museum of Art 1992; participated in Documenta 7, Kassel 1982, Venice Biennale 1982, 1984, 1990, Sydney Biennial 1986 and numerous other group exhbns. in U.S.A., Canada, U.K., U.S.S.R. and Europe. *Address:* Box 494, Bridgehampton, NY 11932, U.S.A.

MARIÁTEGUI, Sandro; Peruvian politician; b. 5 Dec. 1922; s. of José Carlos Mariátegui; m. Matilde de Zela; one d.; Deputy for Lima 1963–68; Minister of Finance and Trade 1965–67; Founder Acción Popular (AP) Party, Sec.-Gen. 1985–87; Senator 1980–; Pres. of Senate 1982–83; Prime Minister and Minister of Foreign Affairs April-Oct. 1984. *Address:* Av. Ramírez Gaston 375, Miraflores, Lima, Peru.

MARIE, Aurelius John Baptiste Lamothe, M.B.E.; Dominican politician and lawyer; b. 23 Dec. 1904, Portsmouth, Dominica; s. of Bright Percival Marie and Lily Marie; m. Bernadette Dubois 1964; fmr. magistrate; Pres. of Dominica Feb. 1980–83. *Leisure interests:* gardening, reading, hiking. *Address:* Zicack, Portsmouth, Dominica.

MARIN, Maguy; French choreographer and artistic director; b. 2 June 1951, Toulouse; s. of Antonio Marin and Luisa Calle; ed. Conservatoire de Toulouse; joined Maurice Béjart's Ballet du XXème siècle; joined Ballet Théâtre de l'Arche (subsequently Compagnie Maguy Marin) 1979; choreographic works include: May B 1981, Babel Babel 1982, Jaleo 1983, Hymen 1984, Calambre 1985, Cinderella 1985, Eden 1986, Leçons de Ténèbres 1987, Coups d'états 1988, Groosland 1989, Cortex 1991, Made in France 1992, Ay Dios 1993, Waterzooï 1993, Ramdam 1995, Aujourd'hui peut-être 1996; Grand Prix Nat. de la chorégraphie 1983; Chevalier, Ordre des Arts et des Lettres. *Address:* Compagnie Maguy Marin, Maison des Arts et de la Culture, Place Salvador Allende, 94000 Creteil, France. *Telephone:* 49.80.55.80. *Fax:* 43.99.21.58.

MARIN GONZALEZ, Manuel, M.A.; Spanish international official; b. 21 Oct. 1949, Ciudad Real; m. Carmen Ortiz; two c.; ed. Madrid Univ., Coll. of Europe, Bruges and Univ. of Nancy; joined Spanish Socialist Party 1975; M.P. for Ciudad Real, La Mancha 1977; Sec. of State for Relations with the EEC 1982–85; EEC (now European Commission) Commr. for Social Affairs, Employment, Educ. and Training 1986–89, for Co-operation and Devt. 1989–94, for External Relations with the Mediterranean (South), Near and Middle East, Latin America and Asia (except Japan, People's Repub. of China, Repub. of Korea, Hong Kong, Macau, Taiwan) 1995–, a Vice-Pres. of Comm. March 1993–; Grand Cross, Order of Isabel la Católica. *Address:* avenue d'Auderghem 45, bureau 11/32, B-1040 Brussels, Belgium. *Telephone:* 295-3716.

MARINOS, Yannis, B.A.; Greek journalist; b. 20 July 1930, Hermoupolis; unmarried; ed. Univ. of Athens; journalist, To Vima (daily) 1953–65; journalist, Economicos Tachydromos, Ed.-in-Chief 1956, Ed. and Dir. 1964–96, consultant/columnist 1996–; political commentator in Ta Nea (daily) 1972–75; columnist, To Vima (weekly political journal) 1992–; commentator for many radio and TV stations in Greece; mem. Bd. Lambrakis Research Foundation, Org. of Music Hall of Athens; mem. Advisory Council of Users of European Comm.; Hon. Ph.D (Aristotelian Univ. Salonika) 1998; more than 30 awards including Best European Journalist of 1989 (EC Comm. and Asscn. of European Journalists) and awards from UN and Athens Acad. *Publications:* The Palestinian Problem and Cyprus 1975, For a Change Towards Better 1983, Greece in Crisis 1987, Common Sense 1993. *Leisure interests:* literature, history, classical music, fishing. *Address:* 3 Christou Lada Street, Athens 102 37 (Office); 2 Kontziadon Street, Piraeus 185 37, Greece (Home). *Telephone:* 3333630 (Office); 4526823 (Home). *Fax:* 3238740.

MARIO, Ernest, P.H.D.; American company director and pharmacist; b. 12 June 1938, Clifton, N.J.; s. of Jerry Mario and Edith Mario; m. Mildred Martha Daume 1961; three s.; ed. Rutgers Coll. of Pharmacy, New Brunswick, N.J., Univ. of Rhode Island; Vice-Pres. Mfg. Operations, Smith Kline 1974–77; joined E. R. Squibb & Sons 1977, Vice Pres. Mfg. for U.S. Pharmaceuticals Div. 1977–79, Vice-Pres. Gen. Man., Chemical Div. 1979–81, Pres. Chemical Eng. Div. and Sr. Vice-Pres. 1981–83, Pres. and C.E.O. Squibb Medical Products 1983–86, mem. Bd. 1984–85; Pres. Glaxo Inc. 1986–89, Chair. 1989–91, apptd. to Bd. of Glaxo Holdings PLC 1988, Chief Exec. 1989–93, Deputy Chair. 1992–93; Chair. and C.E.O. ALZA Corpn. 1993–; Chair. American Foundation for Pharmaceutical Educ.; Trustee Duke Univ., Rockefeller Univ., Univ. of R.I. Foundation. *Leisure interests:* golf, swimming. *Address:* ALZA Corporation, 950 Page Mill Road, Palo Alto, CA 94304, U.S.A. *Telephone:* (650) 494-5668. *Fax:* (650) 496-8819.

MARION, Jean-Luc; French professor of history of classical philosophy; b. 3 July 1946, Meudon; s. of late Jean E. Marion and of Suzanne Roussey; m. Corinne Nicolas 1970; two s.; ed. Lycée Int. de Sèvres, Ecole Normale Supérieure, Ulm and Univ. of Paris Sorbonne; Asst. Prof., Univ. of Paris, Sorbonne 1973–81; Prof. Univ. of Poitiers 1981–88, Univ. of Paris X (Nanterre) 1988–95, Univ. of Paris IV (Sorbonne) 1995–; Ed.-in-Chief, Communio (review), Paris 1975–85; Dir. Epiméthée, Presses Universitaires de France, Paris 1981–; Visiting Prof. Loyola Univ. Chicago, Washington Univ., St. Louis and Laval Univ., Quebec; Prof. at Univ. of Chicago; Titular, Cardinal Mercier Chair. Catholic Univ., Leuven 1987; Prix Charles Lambert, Acad. des Sciences Morales et Politiques 1978; Grand Prix de Philosophie, Acad. Française 1992. *Publications:* Sur l'ontologie grise de Descartes 1975, L'idole et la distance 1977, Sur la théologie blanche de Descartes 1981, Dieu sans l'être 1982, Sur le prisme métaphysique de Descartes 1986, Réduction et Donation 1989, La croisée du visible 1991, Questions cartésiennes 1991, Questions cartésiennes X 1996, Etant donné 1997. *Address:* 28 rue d'Auteuil, 75016 Paris; 1 rue V. Cousin, 75230 Paris, France. *Telephone:* 40.46.22.11.

MARJANOVIĆ, Mirko; Yugoslav (Serbian) politician and economist; b. 27 July 1937, Knin, Croatia; s. of Disan Marjanović and Marija Marjanović; m. Borjana Marjanović, one s. one d.; ed. Belgrade Univ.; Man., Deputy Gen. Dir. TVIK 1970–72; Dir. Rep. in Moscow 1973–77; Dir. Chelik Co. 1977–79; Gen. Dir., Foreign Trade Co. Progres 1979–94; Prime Minister of Repub. of Serbia 1993–. *Address:* Vlada Republike Srbije, Nemanjiná 11, 11000 Belgrade, Yugoslavia. *Telephone:* (11) 685 872. *Fax:* (11) 659 682.

MARJORIBANKS, Kevin, B.SC., M.A., PH.D., F.A.S.S.A., F.A.C.E., F.R.S.S.; Australian academic; b. 25 July 1940; s. of Hugh Marjoribanks and Irene Marjoribanks; m. Janice Lily 1962; one s. one d.; ed. Univ. of N.S.W., Univ. of New England, Harvard Univ., U.S.A., Univ. of Toronto, Canada; Teaching Fellow Harvard Univ. 1967–69, Asst. Prof. Univ. of Toronto 1969–70, lecturer in Sociology, Univ. of Oxford 1970–75; Prof. of Educ. Univ. of Adelaide

1974–, Pro-Vice-Chancellor 1986–87, Vice-Chancellor 1987–93; Visiting Prof., Oxford Univ. 1994–. *Publications:* Environments for Learning 1974, Families and Their Learning Environments 1979, Ethnic Families and Children's Achievements 1980, The Foundations of Students' Learning 1991, Families, Schools and Children's Learning 1994. *Leisure interests:* writing, music, reading. *Address:* University of Adelaide, Adelaide (Office); 81 Molesworth Street, North Adelaide, S.A. 5006, Australia (Home).

MARK, Alan Francis, C.B.E., PH.D., F.R.S.N.Z.; New Zealand professor of botany; b. 19 June 1932, Dunedin; s. of Cyril L. Mark and Frances E. Marshall; m. Patricia K. Davie 1957; two s. two d.; ed. Mosgiel District High School, Univ. of Otago and Duke Univ., N. Carolina; Otago Catchment Bd., Dunedin 1959–61; Sr. Research Fellow, Hellaby Indigenous Grasslands Research Trust 1961–65, Adviser in Research 1965–; Lecturer, Univ. of Otago 1960, Sr. Lecturer 1966, Assoc. Prof. 1969, Prof. of Botany 1975–98, Prof. Emer. 1998–; Visiting Asst. Prof. Duke Univ. 1966; Fulbright Travel Award 1955; James B. Duke Fellowship 1957; Loder Cup 1975, N.Z. 1990 Commemoration Medal, The Awards of N.Z. (Conservation/Environment) 1994, Hutton Medal (Botanical/Conservation Research), Royal Soc. of N.Z. 1997. *Publications:* New Zealand Alpine Plants (with N. M. Adams) 1973, about 140 scientific papers. *Leisure interests:* nature conservation, enjoying the outdoors. *Address:* Department of Botany, University of Otago, Box 56, Dunedin (Office); 205 Wakari Road, Helensburgh, Dunedin, New Zealand (Home). *Telephone:* (3) 4797573 (Office); (3) 4763229 (Home). *Fax:* (3) 479-7583.

MARK, Reuben, A.B., M.B.A.; American business executive; b. 21 Jan. 1939, Jersey City, N.J.; s. of Edward Mark and Libbie (née Berman) Mark; m. Arlene Slobzian 1964; two s. one d.; ed. Middlebury Coll. and Harvard Univ.; with Colgate-Palmolive Co., New York 1963–, Pres., Gen. Man. Venezuela 1972–73, Canada 1973–74, Vice-Pres., Gen. Man. Far East Div. 1974–75, Household Products Div. 1975–79, Group Vice-Pres. Domestic Operations 1979–81, Exec. Vice-Pres. 1981–83, C.O.O. 1983–84, Pres. 1983–86, C.E.O. 1984–, Chair. 1986–; lecturer in Business Admin., Univ. of Conn. 1977; mem. Bd. of Dirs. Soap and Detergent Asscn. *Address:* Colgate-Palmolive Co., 300 Park Avenue, New York, NY 10022, U.S.A.

MARK, Sir Robert, Kt., G.B.E., M.A.; British fmr. police official; b. 13 March 1917, Manchester; s. of the late John and Louisa Hobson Mark; m. Kathleen Mary Leahy 1941 (died 1997); one s. one d.; ed. William Hulme's Grammar School, Manchester; Constable to Chief Supt., Manchester Police 1937–42, 1947–56; Chief Constable of Leicester 1957–67; Asst. Commr., Metropolitan Police (London) 1967–68, Deputy Commr. 1968–72, Commr. 1972–77; Royal Armoured Corps 1942–47, Lieut. Phantom (GHQ Liaison Regt.) N.W. Europe 1944–45, Maj. Control Comm. for Germany 1945–47; mem. Standing Advisory Council on Penal System 1966; Assessor to Lord Mountbatten's Inquiry into Prison Security 1966; mem. Advisory Cttee. on Police in N. Ireland 1969; Dir. Automobile Asscn. 1977–87, Control Risks Ltd. 1981–87; Visiting Fellow Nuffield Coll., Oxford 1970–78; Lecture tour of N. America for World Affairs Council and FCO Oct. 1971; Dimbleby Memorial Lecturer, BBC TV 1973; Queen's Police Medal 1965; Hon. LL.M. (Leicester) 1966, Hon. D.Litt. (Loughborough) 1976, Hon. LL.D. (Liverpool) 1978, (Manchester) 1978; K.St.J.; Hon. Freeman City of Westminster 1977. *Publications:* numerous articles in the national press and in legal and police journals; Edwin Stevens Lecture to the Laity at the Royal Society of Medicine 1972, Policing a Perplexed Society 1977, In the Office of Constable (autobiog.) 1978. *Address:* Esher, Surrey, KT10 8LU, England.

MARKERT, Clement L., PH.D.; American biologist; b. 11 April 1917, Las Animas, Colo.; s. of Edwin John Markert and Sarah Esther Norman; m. Margaret Rempfer 1940; two s. one d.; ed. Univ. of Colo., Univ. of Calif. at Los Angeles, Johns Hopkins Univ. and Calif. Inst. of Tech.; Asst. Prof. of Zoology, Univ. of Mich. 1950–56, Assoc. Prof. 1956–57; Prof. of Biology, Johns Hopkins Univ. 1957–65; Prof. of Biology, Yale Univ. 1965–86, Chair. Dept. of Biology 1965–71; Dir. Yale Center for Research in Reproductive Biology 1974–86; Distinguished Univ. Research Prof. North Carolina State Univ. 1986–93, Distinguished Univ. Prof. Emer. 1993–96; Visiting Prof. Kyoto Univ., Japan 1996–97; mem. N.A.S. 1967–, Nat. Inst. of Medicine 1974–; American Acad. of Arts and Sciences; mem. Bd. Scientific Advisors, La Jolla Cancer Research Foundation 1977–86; mem. Bd. Scientific Advisors, Jane Coffin Childs Memorial Fund for Medical Research 1979–86; Trustee Bermuda Biological Station for Research 1959–83, Life Trustee 1983–, Trustee BIOSIS 1976–81, Chair. of Bd. 1981; numerous editorial posts on biological journals. *Publications:* Over 100 articles, several books. *Leisure interests:* skin diving, ranching. *Address:* 4005 Wakefield Drive, Colorado Springs, CO 80906, U.S.A. *Telephone:* (719) 540-8848.

MARKESINIS, Spyros; Greek politician, lawyer and historian; b. 1909, Athens; s. of Basil Markesinis and Helen Flora Markesinis; m. Ieta Xydis 1943; one s. one d.; ed. Univ. of Athens; Legal Adviser to late King George II of the Hellenes 1936–46; served in Greek Nat. Resistance 1941–44; M.P. for the Cyclades 1946, for Athens 1952–67; f. New Party 1947 (dissolved 1951); Minister without Portfolio 1949; Minister for Co-ordination and Econ. Planning until 1954; formed Progressive Party 1955, re-formed 1977; Prime Minister Oct.-Nov. 1973; Kt., Gold Cross George I, D.S.M., Kt. Commdr. St. Saba; Grand Cross of the following orders: Phoenix (Greece), Al Merito della Repubblica Italiana, Order of Merit (First Class) of the Fed. Repub. of Germany; Légion d'honneur; Order of St. Mark of the Patriarchate of Alexandria and of Constantinople. *Publications:* The Supreme Ruler in Contemporary Democracies, The King, the Royal Family in Private Law 1936, The King as International Representative 1937, The Divorce, From War to Peace 1949, Political History of Modern Greece (1828-1936) (8 vols.), Contemporary Political History of Greece (1936–1975), 3 Vols. 1994. *Leisure interests:* books, chess. *Address:* 26 Isiodou Street, 106 74 Athens, Greece. *Telephone:* 724-56-56/57/58.

MARKHAM, Kenneth Ronald, PH.D., F.R.S.N.Z.; New Zealand research chemist; b. 19 June 1937, Christchurch; s. of Harold W. Markham and Alicia B. Markham; m. E. P. Eddy 1966; two d.; ed. Victoria Univ. of Wellington, Melbourne Univ.; Tech. Trainee, Dominion Lab., Wellington 1955–62; Scientist Chem. Div., DSIR, Lower Hutt 1962–65; Post-Doctoral Fellow, Botany Dept., Univ. of Texas 1965–66, Asst. Prof. 1967; Scientist, Organic Chem. Section, Chem. Div., DSIR 1968–75, Section Leader, Natural Products Section 1976–92, Group Leader Chem. Div. 1980–87; Distinguished Scientist, Industrial Research Ltd. 1992–; Monsanto Chemicals Research Fellow 1960, Easterfield Award (Royal Inst. of Chem.) 1971, Sr. Research Fellow (Chem. Div. DSIR) 1987; mem. Ed. Advisory Bd. int. journal Phytochemical Analysis 1990–, Int. Journal of Flavonoid Research 1998–; Int. Corresp., Groupe Polyphenols 1992–; N.Z. Govt. Ministerial Award for Excellence in Science 1990, Science and Tech. Medal, Royal Soc. of N.Z. 1997. *Publications:* The Systematic Identification of Flavonoids (with Mabry and Thomas) 1970, Techniques of Flavonoid Chemistry 1982; 17 invited chapters on flavonoids and spectroscopy, 220 scientific papers on phytochem. and its interpretation in int. journals 1960–; two provisional patents on flower colour modification and one on UV screens. *Leisure interests:* philately, swimming, stock market, photography, table tennis, world news. *Address:* N.Z. Institute for Industrial Research and Development, P.O. Box 31310, Lower Hutt (Office); 2/48 Whitemans Road, Silverstream, New Zealand (Home). *Telephone:* 5690 577 (Office); 5285 991 (Home). *Fax:* (4) 5690055 (Office).

MARKIEWICZ, Władysław; Polish sociologist; b. 2 Jan. 1920, Ostrów Wielkopolski; s. of Józef and Bronisława Markiewicz; m. Ludgarda Trzybińska 1949; one s. one d.; ed. Poznań Univ.; Doctor 1959–61, Docent 1961–66, Assoc. Prof. 1966–72, Prof. 1972–; imprisoned in Mauthausen-Gusen concentration camp 1941–45; active mem. youth orgs. 1947–50; mem. Polish United Workers' Party (PZPR) 1948–90, mem. Comm. for investigation into social conflicts, PZPR Cen. Cttee. 1981–84; mem. Voivodship Nat. Council, Poznań 1949–54; Dir. Inst. of Sociology, Poznań Univ. 1957–71; Vice-Dir. Western Inst., Poznań 1962–66, Dir. 1966–72; Head, Dept. of Sociology of Labour and Org., Warsaw Univ. 1972–76; fmr. Ed.-in-Chief Studia Socjologiczne (quarterly) and Polish Western Affairs; Vice-Chair. Polish Cttee. of UNESCO; Pres. Polish Sociological Soc. 1968–72; Corresp. mem. Polish Acad. of Sciences (PAN) 1971–76, Ordinary mem. 1976–, mem. Presidium 1972–89, Sec., Dept. of Social Sciences 1972–83, Vice-Pres. 1984–89; mem. Polish Cttee. of Pugwash confs.; Chair. Poland-Fed. Repub. of Germany Soc. 1989–; Gold Cross of Merit, Kt.'s and Officer's Cross, Order of Polonia Restituta, Medals of 10th and 30th Anniversaries of People's Poland, Order of Banner of Labour (2nd Class 1976, 1st Class 1986), Gold Award of Polish Teachers' Asscn., Grosse Verdienstkreuz (F.R.G.) 1989. *Publications:* Przeobrażenia świadomości narodowej reemigrantów polskich z Francji 1960, Społeczeństwo i socjologia w Niemieckiej Republice Federalnej 1966, Sociology in People's Poland 1970, Propedeutyka nauki o społeczeństwie 1971, Socjologia a służba społeczna 1972, Konflikt społeczny w PRL 1983, Spraw polskich splątanie 1987; numerous articles. *Address:* ul. Wiejska 18 m. 13, 00-490 Warsaw, Poland. *Telephone:* 629 80 30 (Home).

MARKING, Sir Henry Ernest, K.C.V.O., C.B.E., M.C., F.B.I.M.; British fmr. company director and lawyer; b. 11 March 1920, Saffron Walden, Essex; s. of Isaac and Hilda Jane Marking; ed. Saffron Walden Grammar School, Univ. Coll., London, Middle East Centre for Arab Studies, Jerusalem; army service, The Sherwood Foresters 1940–45, Adjutant 1944–45; admitted Solicitor 1948; Asst. Solicitor Cripps, Harries, Hall & Co., Tunbridge Wells 1948–49; Asst. Solicitor British European Airways (BEA) 1949, Sec. BEA 1950, C.E.O. 1964–71, Chair. and C.E.O. 1971–72; mem. Bd. of British Overseas Airways Corpn. (BOAC) 1971–72; Group Man. Dir. British Airways 1972–74, Deputy Chair. and Man. Dir. 1974–77, mem. Bd. 1977–81; mem. Bd. British Tourist Authority 1969–77, Chair. 1977–84; Chair. Rothmans (U.K.) Ltd. 1979–86, Holiday Care Service 1981–86; Dir. Barclays Bank Int. 1977–86, Rothmans Int. Ltd. 1979–86; Gov. Bell Educational Trust 1984–90; Trustee, London City Ballet 1978–87; Trustee Leonard Cheshire Foundation 1962–95. *Address:* 6A Montagu Mews North, London, W1H 1AH, England. *Telephone:* 0171-935 3305.

MARKOVA, Dame Alicia, D.B.E. (Lilian Alicia Marks); British prima ballerina; b. 1 Dec. 1910, London; d. of Arthur Tristman Marks and Eileen Barry; ed. privately; first appeared in Dick Whittington at the Kennington Theatre 1920; studied under Astafieva and appeared with Legat Ballet Group 1923; taken into Russian Ballet by Serge Diaghilev 1924, studied under Enrico Cecchetti and toured with the co. until Diaghilev's death in 1929 (Song of a Nightingale created for her); Prima Ballerina, Rambert Club 1931–34; first Prima Ballerina of Vic-Wells (now the Royal Ballet) 1933–35; formed Markova-Dolin Ballet Co 1935 and toured U.K. till 1938; with Ballet Russe de Monte Carlo 1938–41; and Ballet Theatre 1941–44; toured North and Cen. America with Markova-Dolin group 1944–45; many guest appearances 1946–47; concerts with Dolin in U.S.A., Far East and South Africa 1947–49; formed Festival Ballet company with Dolin 1950–52; guest artist with Teatro Colón in Buenos Aires 1952, Sadler's Wells, Ballet Theatre, Marquis de Cuevas Ballet and Metropolitan Opera 1953; Royal Winnipeg Ballet 1953; with de Cuevas Ballet in London 1954; with Royal Danish Ballet 1955; Scala Milan, Municipal Theatre Rio de Janeiro 1956; Royal Ballet Covent Garden 1957; Italian Opera Season, Drury Lane, Festival Ballet Tour 1958, and Season 1959; appearances with Royal Ballet and Festival Ballet 1960; with the Metropolitan Opera Co. 1954–58; British Prima Ballerina Assoluta; Dir. Metropolitan Opera Ballet of New York 1963–69; Distinguished Lecturer on Ballet at Cincinnati Univ. 1970, Prof. of Ballet and Performing Arts 1970–; produced Les Sylphides, Australian Ballet 1976, London Festival Ballet 1977, Northern Ballet Theatre 1978, Royal Ballet School 1978, Royal Winnipeg Ballet 1979; "Masterclass" BBC TV series 1980; Pres. London Ballet Circle 1981–, All England Dance Competition 1983–, Arts Educational Trust Schools 1984–, London Festival Ballet 1986–, English Nat. Ballet 1989–; A.N.C.E.C. (Italy) 1990–; Vice-Pres. Royal Acad. of Dancing 1958–; Guest Prof., Royal Ballet School 1972–; Gov. Royal Ballet 1973–; Prof. Yorkshire Ballet Seminars 1973–; int. consultant 1990–; London Studio Centre consultant 1990–; Guest Prof. de Danse, Paris Opera Ballet 1975; Guest Prof., Australian Ballet 1976; Pres. Int. Dance Competition, Paris 1986; Patron Abingdon Ballet Seminars 1990–; Hon. Dr. Music (Leicester) 1966, Hon. Mus.D. (E. Anglia Univ.) 1982. *Publications:* Giselle and I 1960, Markova Remembers 1986. *Leisure interest:* music. *Address:* c/o Barclays Bank, P.O. Box 4599, London, SW3 1XE, England.

MARKOVÍC, Ante; Croatian politician (retd.); b. 25 Nov. 1924, Konjic; ed. Zagreb Univ.; Sec. League of Communist Youth; Engineer, Designer and Head Test Dept., Rade Koncar factory, Dir.-Gen. 1961–86; Pres. Exec. Council of Croatia 1982–86; Pres. Presidency of Croatia May 1986–88; Pres. Federal Exec. Council 1989–91.

MARKOWITZ, Harry M., PH.D.; American professor of finance; b. 24 Aug. 1927, Chicago; s. of Morris Markowitz and Mildred Gruber; m. Barbara Gay; research staff, Rand Corpn. Santa Monica, Calif. 1952–60, 1961–63; Tech. Dir. Consolidated Analysis Centers, Ltd., Santa Monica 1963–68; Prof. Univ. of Calif. Los Angeles, Westwood 1968–69; Pres. Arbitrage Man. Co., New York 1969–72; in pvt. practice as consultant, New York 1972–74; research staff, T. J. Watson Research Center, IBM, Yorktown Hills, N.Y. 1974–83; Speiser Prof. of Finance, Baruch Coll. City Univ. of New York 1982–90, Vice-Pres. Inst. of Man. Science 1960–62; Dir. Research Daiwa Securities Trust Co. 1990–; Fellow, Econometric Soc., American Acad. of Arts and Sciences; Pres. American Finance Asscn. 1982; Nobel Prize in Econs. (with W. F. Sharpe and M. H. Miller (qq.v.)), 1990. *Publications:* Portfolio Selection: Efficient Diversification of Investments 1959, Mean-Variance Analysis in Portfolio Choice 1987; co-author, SIMSCRIPT Simulation Programming Language 1963; co-ed. Process Analysis of Economic Capabilities 1963. *Address:* 1010 Turquoise Street, Suite 245, San Diego, CA 92109; Daiwa Securities, 1 Evertrust Plaza, Jersey City, NJ 07302, U.S.A.

MARKS, Dennis Michael, B.A.; British music and arts executive and programme maker; b. 2 July 1948, London; s. of Samuel Marks and Kitty Ostrovsky; m. Sally Groves 1992; one s. one d.; ed. Haberdashers Askes School, Elstree, Trinity Coll., Cambridge; Dir. and Producer BBC TV Music and Arts 1972–78; co-f. Bristol Arts Unit 1978–81; f. Third Eye Productions 1981–85; Ed. Music Features BBC TV 1985–88, Asst. Head of Music and Arts 1988–91, Head of Music BBC TV 1991–93; Gen. Dir. English Nat. Opera 1993–97; Pres. Int. Music Centre, Vienna 1989–92; Italia Prize 1989, Royal Philharmonic Soc. Award 1990. *Publications:* Great Railway Journeys 1981, Repercussions (Afro-American Music) 1985. *Leisure interests:* cookery, travel. *Address:* 17 Dalmeny Road, London, N7 0HG, England.

MARKS, Leonard Harold, B.A., LL.B.; American government official and lawyer; b. 5 March 1916; m. Dorothy L. Ames 1948; two s.; ed. Univ. of Pittsburgh, and Univ. of Pittsburgh Law School; Faculty Fellow, Univ. of Pittsburgh Law School 1938–39, Asst. Prof. 1939–42; Asst. Prof. Nat. Univ. Law School, Washington, D.C. 1943–50; Asst. to Gen. Counsel, Fed. Communications Comm., Washington, D.C. 1943–46, Operations Counsel 1986–; Partner, Cohn and Marks (law firm), Washington, D.C. 1946–65, 1969–86; Dir. Communications Satellite Corpn. 1963–65; Dir. U.S. Information Agency 1965–69; Pres. Broadcasters' Club of Washington, Nat. Home Library Foundation, Int. Rescue Cttee. 1973–79; Chair. Int. Telecommunications Satellite Conf., U.S. Del., Washington, D.C. 1969, U.S. Advisory Comm. on Int. Educational and Cultural Affairs 1974–78, Nat. Savings and Trust Co. 1977–; Pres. Honor America Cttee. 1977–83; Vice-Chair. Foreign Policy Asscn. 1979–81, Chair. 1981–85; mem. A.B.A., Bar Asscn. D.C., World Affairs Council, Washington (also Chair). *Address:* 1920 Street North, N.W., Washington, DC 20036 (Office); Shoreham West, Apt. 714, 2700 Calvert Street, N.W., Washington, DC 20008, U.S.A. (Home). *Telephone:* (202) 293-3860 (Office); (202) 232-7214 (Home).

MARKS, Paul Alan, M.D.; American oncologist and cell biologist; b. 16 Aug. 1926, New York; s. of Robert R. Marks and Sarah (Bohorad) Marks; m. Joan Harriet Rosen 1953; two s. one d.; ed. Columbia Coll. and Columbia Univ.; Fellow, Columbia Coll. of Physicians and Surgeons 1952–53, Assoc. 1955–56, mem. of Faculty 1956–82, Dir. Haematology Training 1961–74, Prof. of Medicine 1967–82, Dean Faculty of Medicine and Vice-Pres. Medical Affairs 1970–73, Dir. Comprehensive Cancer Center 1972–80, Vice-Pres. Health Sciences 1973–80, Prof. of Human Genetics and Devt. 1969–82, Frode Jensen Prof. of Medicine 1974–80; Prof. of Medicine and Genetics, Cornell Univ. Coll. of Medicine, New York 1982–; Prof. Cornell Univ. Grad. School in Medical Sciences 1983–; Attending Physician Presbyterian Hosp., New York 1967–83; Pres. and C.E.O. Memorial Sloan-Kettering Cancer Center 1980–; Attending Physician Memorial Hosp. for Cancer and Allied Diseases 1980–; mem. Sloan-Kettering Inst. for Cancer Research 1980–; Adj. Prof. Rockefeller Univ. 1980–; Visiting Physician, Rockefeller Univ. Hosp. 1980–; Trustee Hadassah Medical Centre, Jerusalem 1996; mem. Advisory Cttee. to Dir., N.I.H. 1993–, N.I.H. External Advisory Cttee.-Intramural Research Program Review 1993–; mem. editorial bds. of several scientific journals; Gov. Weizmann Inst. 1976–; Dir. Revson Foundation 1976–91; Master American Coll. of Physicians; mem. Inst. of Medicine, N.A.S.; Fellow Royal Soc. of Medicine, London; Dr. h.c. (Urbino), (Tel Aviv) 1993; Hon. Ph.D. (Hebrew Univ., Jerusalem) 1987; Recognition for Acad. Accomplishments, Chinese Acad. of Medical Sciences 1982, Centenary Medal, Institut Pasteur 1987, Pres.'s Nat. Medal of Science 1991, Gold Medal for Distinguished Academic Accomplishments, Coll. of Physicians and Surgeons of Columbia Univ., New York, Japan Foundation for Cancer Research Award 1995, John Jay Award for Distinguished Professional Achievement, Columbia Coll. 1996, Lifetime Achievement Award Greater N.Y. Hosp. Asscn. 1997; and other awards. *Publications:* over 350 articles in scientific journals. *Address:* Memorial Sloan-Kettering Cancer Center, 1275 York Avenue, New York, NY 10021 (Office); P.O. Box 1485, Washington, CT 06793, U.S.A. (Home).

MARLER, Peter Robert, PH.D.; American biologist; b. 24 Feb. 1928, London, England; s. of Robert A. and Gertrude Hunt Marler; m. Judith G. Gallen 1954; one s. two d.; ed. Univ. Coll. London and Univ. of Cambridge; Research Fellow, Jesus Coll., Cambridge 1954–56; Asst. Prof., later Prof., Univ. of Calif., Berkeley 1957–66; Prof. The Rockefeller Univ. 1966; Sr. Research Zoologist, New York Zoological Soc. 1966–72; Dir. Inst. for Research in Animal Behaviour 1969–72; Dir. Rockefeller Univ. Field Research Center 1972–81; mem. N.A.S.; mem. Council Smithsonian Inst. 1979–; Fellow, American Acad. of Arts and Sciences, A.A.A.S. 1965, New York Zoological Soc., American Psychological Asscn. 1975; Guggenheim Fellow 1964–65; mem. American Philosophical Soc. 1983. *Publications:* Mechanisms of Animal Behaviour (with W. J. Hamilton) 1966, Handbook of Behavioral Neurobiology 3: Social Behavior and Communication (with J. G. Vandenbergh) 1979, The Biology of Learning (ed. with H. S. Terrace), (Eds. J. P. Rauschecker and P. Marler) Imprinting and Cortical Plasticity 1987. *Leisure interests:* gardening, natural history. *Address:* Rockefeller University, New York, NY 10021, U.S.A.

MARMOT, Michael Gideon, M.B.B.S., M.F.C.M., PH.D., F.F.P.H.M.; British professor of cardiovascular epidemiology and director of health research; b. 26 Jan. 1945; s. of Nathan Marmot and Alice Marmot (née Weiner); m. Alexandra Naomi Ferster 1971; two s. one d.; ed. Univ. of Sydney and Univ. of California at Berkeley; Resident Medical Officer Royal Prince Alfred Hosp. 1969–70; Fellowship in Thoracic Medicine 1970–71; Resident Fellow and Lecturer Univ. of Calif. at Berkeley 1971–76 (fellowships from Berkeley and American Heart Asscn.); lecturer then Sr. Lecturer in Epidemiology London School of Hygiene and Tropical Medicine 1976–85, Prof. of Epidemiology and Public Health Medicine 1985–; Dir. Int. Centre for Health and Society, Univ. Coll., London Univ. 1994–; Hon. Consultant in Public Health Medicine, Bloomsbury and Islington Dist. Health Authority 1985–; Visiting Prof. Royal Soc. of Medicine 1987; M.R.C. Research Professorship 1995. *Publications:* numerous articles in learned journals. *Address:* Royal Free and University College Medical School, Department of Epidemiology and Public Health, 1–19 Torrington Place, London, WC1E 6BT, England. *Telephone:* 0171-391 1717. *Fax:* 0171-813 0242.

MARONI, Roberto; Italian politician; b. 15 March 1955, Varese; m.; two s.; graduated in law; worked in banks for ten years, then head of legal office of a U.S. multinational for eight years; entered politics 1979; co-f. Lega Lombarda party (subsequently Lega Nord); elected Councillor, Varese; apptd. mem. Lega Lombarda Nat. Council; Deputy 1992–; became Leader of party in Chamber of Deputies; elected Lega Nord Deputy in Gen. Elections March 1994; Minister for the Interior 1994–95. *Leisure interests:* football, playing saxophone. *Address:* c/o Ministero dell'Interno, Piazzale del Viminale, 00184 Rome, Italy. *Telephone:* (6) 46671. *Fax:* (6) 482 5792.

MAROSI, Ernö, PH.D.; Hungarian art historian; b. 18 April, 1940, Miskolc; s. of Ferenc Marosi and Magdolna Kecskés; m. Julia Szabó; ed. Budapest University of Arts and Sciences; lecturer at the Dept. of Art History (Budapest Acad. of Arts and Sciences) 1963, Prof. 1991; mem. Research Group Hungarian Acad. of Sciences, then Deputy Dir. of Research Inst. 1974–91, Head of Dept. 1974–91, Dir. 1991–; mem. Int. Cttee. of UNESCO on the History of Art 1991–; Sec. of TMB (Nat. Postgrad. Degree Granting Board), Special Cttee. on the History of Art, Architecture and Archaeology; corresp. mem. of Hungarian Acad. of Sciences 1993–. *Publications:* A középkori müvészet világa (The World of Arts of the Middle Ages) 1969, A román kor müvészete (The Arts of the Romanesque Age) 1972, Bevezetés a müvészettörténetbe (Introduction to the History of Arts) 1973, Magyar falusi templomok (Village Churches in Hungary) 1975, Emlék márványból vagy homokkőből (Relics from Marble or Sandstone) 1976, Die Änfange der Gotik in Ungarn 1984, Magyarországi müvészet 1300–1470 körül (Arts in Hungary 1300–1470) 1984, A budavári szoborlelet (jtly.) 1989. *Address:* MTA, Müvészettörténeti Intézete, 1014 Budapest, Úri utca 49, Hungary. *Telephone:* (1) 175-9011.

MAROUF, Taha Muhyiddin, LL.B.; Iraqi politician and diplomatist; b. 1924, Sulaimaniyah; s. of Muhyiddin and Fatima Marouf; ed. Coll. of Law, Univ. of Baghdad; worked as lawyer; joined Diplomatic Service 1949; Minister of State 1968–70; Minister of Works and Housing 1968; Amb. to Italy, concurrently non-resident Amb. to Malta and Albania 1970–74; Vice-Pres. of Iraq April 1974–; mem. Higher Cttee. of Nat. Progressive Front 1975–; Chair. African Affairs Bureau of Revolutionary Command Council 1976–. *Address:* Office of the Vice-President of the Republic, National Assembly Building, Baghdad, Iraq.

MAROVIĆ, Svetozor; Yugoslav (Montenegrin) politician; b. 21 March 1955, Kotor, Montenegro; s. of Jovo Marović and Ivana Marović; m. Djina Marović; two c.; ed. Univ. of Podgorico; Dir. Municipal Public Accounting Dept. in Budva; mem. Presidency of Cen. Cttee. of League of Communists of Montenegro; Sec.-Gen. of Democratic Socialist Party of Montenegro; mem. Parl. of Montenegro, Speaker 1993–; mem. Chamber of Citizens Parl. of Yugoslavia 1997, Chair. 1997–. *Address:* Jaovana Tomaševića bb., 81000 Podgorica, Yugoslavia (Office).

MARQUAND, David Ian, F.B.A., F.R.HIST.S., F.R.S.A.; British professor of politics; b. 20 Sept. 1934, Cardiff; s. of Rt. Hon. Hilary Marquand and Rachel Marquand; m. Judith M. Reed 1959; one s. one d.; ed. Emanuel School, Magdalen Coll. Oxford; Sr. scholar, St. Antony's Coll. Oxford 1957–58; teaching asst. Univ. of Calif. 1958–59; editorial writer, The Guardian 1959–61; Research Fellow, St. Antony's Coll. Oxford 1962–64; lecturer in politics, Univ. of Sussex 1964–66; mem. Parl. (Labour) for Ashfield, Notts. 1966–77; del. to Council of Europe and W.E.U. assemblies 1970–73; Opposition spokesman on treasury affairs 1971–72; Chief Adviser, Sec. Gen. European Comm. 1977–78; Prof. of Contemporary History and Politics, Salford Univ. 1978–91; Prof. of Politics, Univ. of Sheffield 1991–96, Dir. Political Economy Research Centre 1993–96; Prin. Mansfield Coll., Univ. of Oxford 1996–; Jt. Ed. The Political Quarterly 1987–96; George Orwell Memorial Prize 1979. *Publications:* Ramsay Macdonald 1973, Parliament for Europe 1979, The Unprincipled Society 1988, The Progressive Dilemma 1991, The New Reckoning 1997. *Leisure interest:* walking. *Address:* Mansfield College, Oxford, OX1 3TF, England. *Telephone:* (01865) 270980.

MARQUARDT, Klaus Max, DR.RER.POL.; German business executive; b. 18 Dec. 1926, Berlin; s. of Dr. Arno Marquardt and Ruth Marquardt; m. Brigitte Weber; three d.; ed. Realgymnasium Berlin, Univ. Berlin and Tech. Univ. Berlin; mem. Bd. ARAL AG –1971, Chair. 1971–86; Pres. Petroleum Econ. Asscn. 1979–86; Chair. Supervisory Bd., Westfalenbank AG, Bochum; mem. Supervisory Bd. Energieversorgung Sachsen Ost AG, Dresden; Grosses Bundesverdienstkreuz. *Address:* Roggenkamp 14, 44797 Bochum, Germany (Office). *Telephone:* 0234-791091 (Office). *Fax:* 0234-791091.

MÁRQUEZ, Gabriel García (see García Márquez, Gabriel).

MÁRQUEZ DE LA PLATA IRARRAZAVAL, Alfonso; Chilean politician; b. 19 July 1933, Santiago; s. of Fernando Márquez de la Plata Echenique and Rosa Yrarrazaval Fernández; m. María de la Luz Cortes Heyermann 1957; one s. one d.; ed. Universidad Católica de Chile; Vice-Chair. Sociedad Nacional de Agricultura 1969–73, Chair. 1973–77; Chair. Banco de Santiago 1977–78; Minister of Agric. 1978–80; mem. Govt. Legislative Comm. 1981–83; Dir. A.F.P. Provida 1981–83, Compañía de Cervecerías Unidas 1981–83, Banco de Crédito e Inversiones 1981–83; Co-Proprietor and Admin. Sociedad Agrícola Caren Ltda.; Govt. Minister-Sec.-Gen. 1983–84, Minister of Labour and Social Security 1984–88; Chair. Nat. Television Council 1989–92. *Publications:* El Salto al Futuro 1992, El Gobierno Ideal 1993, Mirando al Futuro 1998. *Address:* Av. Presidente Kennedy 4150, Dp. 901, Santiago, Chile. *Telephone:* (02) 2084229. *Fax:* (02) 2061731.

MARR, Andrew William Stevenson, B.A.; British journalist; b. 31 July 1959, Glasgow; s. of Donald Marr and Valerie Marr; m. Jackie Ashley 1987; one s. two d.; ed. Dundee High School, Craigflower School, Loretto School, Trinity Hall, Cambridge; gen. reporter, business reporter The Scotsman 1982–84, Parliamentary Corresp. 1984–86, Political Ed. 1988; Political Ed. The Economist 1988–92; Political Corresp. The Independent 1986–88, Chief Commentator 1992–96, Ed. 1996–98, ed.-in-Chief 1998; columnist The Observer and The Express 1998–; Commentator of the Year 1995. *Leisure interests:* reading, whining and dining. *Publications:* The Battle for Scotland 1992, Ruling Britannia 1995. *Address:* c/o United News & Media, Ludgate House, 245 Blackfriars Road, London, SE1 9UX, England.

MARR, Geoffrey Vickers, D.SC., PH.D., F.INST.P., F.R.S.E.; British professor of natural philosophy; b. 30 Jan. 1930, Darlington; s. of John Marr and Florrie (Vickers) Marr; m. Jean Tebb 1954; two s. one d.; ed. Darlington Queen Elizabeth Grammar School and Univs. of Manchester and Reading; Postdoctoral Fellow, Dept. of Physics, Univ. of Western Ont. 1954–57; Assoc. Inst. of Physics 1956; Lecturer, Eaton Electronics Lab. Dept. of Physics, McGill Univ. 1957–59; Physicist, English Electric, Nuclear Power Div. Whetstone, Leicester 1959–61; Fellow, J. J. Thomson Lab. Dept. of Physics, Univ. of Reading 1961–63, Lecturer, Dept. of Physics 1963–68, Reader 1968–81; Prof. of Natural Philosophy, Aberdeen Univ. 1981–90, Prof. Emer. 1990–; Head, Dept. of Physics 1981–89; current research at Aberdeen Univ. and Daresbury Synchrotron Radiation Source; mem. numerous cttees. etc.; Chartered Physicist; mem. Cttee. Two Dales Gardening Club. *Publications:* Photoionization Processes in Gases 1967, Plasma Spectroscopy 1968, An Introduction to the Theory of Photoelectron Spectroscopy for Experimentalists 1975, Feasibility Study European Synchrotron Radiation Facility III Instrumentation 1979, Handbook of Synchrotron Radiation, Vol. 2 1987. *Leisure interests:* walking, painting, bee-keeping, gardening. *Address:* Rose Warren. Arkengarthdale Road, Reeth, Nr. Richmond, N. Yorks, DL11 6QX, England. *Telephone:* (01748) 884281.

MARRINER, Sir Neville, Kt., C.B.E., F.R.C.M., F.R.A.M.; British music director and conductor; b. 15 April 1924, Lincoln; s. of Herbert H. Marriner and Ethel M. Marriner; m. Elizabeth M. Sims 1955; one s. one d.; ed. Lincoln School, Royal Coll. of Music; f. and Dir. Acad. of St. Martin in the Fields 1956–; Musical Dir. L.A. Chamber Orchestra 1969–78; Dir. S. Bank Festival of Music 1975–78, Dir. Meadowbrook Festival Detroit 1979; Music Dir. Minn. Orchestra 1979–86, Stuttgart Radio Symphony Orchestra 1984–89, Barbican Summer Festival 1985–87; Fellow Trinity Coll. of Music, Hong Kong Acad. for Performing Arts; Hon. D.Mus. (Hull); Tagore Gold Medal, six Edison Awards (Netherlands), two Mozart Gemeinde Awards (Austria), Grand Prix du Disque (France) (three times); Kt. of the Polar Star 1984, Officier, Ordre des Arts et des Lettres 1995. *Address:* c/o Academy of St. Martin-in-the-Fields, Raine House, Raine Street, London, E1 9RG, England.

MARRIS, Stephen Nicholson, M.A., PH.D.; British international economist; b. 7 Jan. 1930, London; s. of Eric Denyer Marris and Phyllis May Marris; m. Margaret Swindells 1955; two s. one d.; ed. Bryanston School and King's Coll., Cambridge; Parker of Waddington Research Student, Cambridge Univ. 1952–53; Nat. Inst. of Econ. and Social Research, London 1953–54; with Org. for European Econ. Co-operation, later named Org. for Econ. Co-operation and Devt. (OECD) 1956–83, Econ. Adviser to the Sec.-Gen. 1975–83; Sr. Fellow, Inst. for Int. Econs., Washington, D.C. 1983–88; Visiting Research Prof., Int. Econs., Brookings Inst., Washington, D.C. 1969–70; Hon. Dr. (Stockholm Univ.) 1979. *Publications:* Managing the World Economy: Will We Ever Learn? 1984, Deficits and the Dollar: The World Economy at Risk 1985. *Leisure interest:* sailing. *Address:* 8 Sentier des Pierres Blanches, 92190 Meudon, France.

MARSALIS, Wynton; American trumpeter; b. 18 Oct. 1961, New Orleans; s. of Ellis Marsalis and Dolores Marsalis; ed. Berks. Music Centre, Tanglewood, Juilliard School, New York; joined Art Blakey's big band; in addition to regular appearances in many countries with his own jazz quintet, he follows a classical career and has performed with the world's top orchestras; numerous int. awards, including the Grand Prix du Disque and Grammy Award in both jazz and classical categories in 1983; Pulitzer Prize for Music 1997, Algur H. Meadows Award, Southern Methodist Univ. 1997. *Albums include:* The Majesty of the Blues 1989, Crescent City Christmas Card 1989, Tune in Tomorrow 1991, Baroque Duet 1992, Blue Interlude 1992, Citi Movement 1993, In This House, On This Morning 1994, Wynton Marsalis 1995, The All-American Hero 1996 (jtly.) Live at Bubba's 1996. *Publications:* Sweet Swing Blues on the Road 1994, Marsalis on Music 1995. *Address:* Agency for the Performing Arts, 9200 Sunset Boulevard, Suite 1200, West Hollywood, CA 90069, U.S.A.

MARSH, Baron (Life Peer), cr. 1981; of Mannington in the County of Wiltshire; **Richard William Marsh,** Kt., P.C.; British public servant and politician; b. 14 March 1928; m. 1st Evelyn Mary Andrews 1950 (divorced 1973); two s.; m. 2nd Caroline Dutton 1973 (died 1975); m. 3rd Felicity McFadzean 1979; ed. Jennings School, Swindon, Woolwich Polytechnic and Ruskin Coll., Oxford; Health Services Officer, Nat. Union of Public Employees 1951–59; mem. Clerical and Admin. Whitley Council for Health Service 1953–59; M.P. for Greenwich 1959–71; Parl. Sec. Ministry of Labour 1964–65; Jt. Parl. Sec. Ministry of Tech. 1965–66; Minister of Power 1966–68, of Transport 1968–69; Dir. Michael Saunders Man. Services 1970–71, Nat. Carbonising Ltd. 1970–71, Concord Rotaflex 1970–71; Chair. British Railways Bd. 1971–76, Newspaper Publishers Asscn. Ltd. 1976–89, Allied Investments Ltd. 1977–82, British Iron & Steel Consumers' Council 1977–82, Lee Cooper Licensing Services 1980–83, Dual Fuel Systems 1981, Lee Cooper Group 1983, TV-am 1983–84 (Deputy Chair. 1981–83), Lopex PLC 1986–97, Laurentian Financial Group PLC 1986–; Dir. Imperial Life of Canada UK 1983–90; Chair. British Industry Cttee. on S.A. Ltd. 1989–, Mannington Man. Services 1989–; Chair. and Chief. Exec. Laurentian Holdings Co. 1989; Chair. China and Eastern Investments Trust, Hong Kong 1990–98 (Dir. 1987–98); Adviser Nissan Motor Co. 1981–, Fujitec 1982–. *Publication:* Off the Rails (memoirs) 1978. *Address:* House of Lords, London, SW1A 0PW, England.

MARSHALL, Alexander Badenoch, M.A.; British business executive; b. 31 Dec. 1924, Dunfermline, Fife, Scotland; s. of David Marshall; m. Mona K. D. Kirk 1961; two s. one d.; ed. Glenalmond and Worcester Coll., Oxford; served R.N. 1943–46; with the P & O Group 1947–79, C.E.O. 1972–79; Chair. Bestobell PLC 1979–85; Dir. Commercial Union Assurance Co. PLC 1970–90, Chair. 1983–90; Dir. The Maersk Co. Ltd. 1980–95, Vice-Chair. 1983–87, Chair. 1987–93; Dir. Royal Bank of Canada 1985–95; Chair. RBC (UK) Holdings Ltd. 1988–95; Vice-Chair. The Boots Co. PLC 1985–91; Chair. U.K.-S. Africa Trade Asscn. 1982–85; Co-Chair. British N. American Cttee. 1985–90; Pres. U.K. Chamber of Shipping 1994–95; Dir. Seascope Shipping Holdings PLC 1997–. *Leisure interests:* gardening, hill-walking, sheep. *Address:* Crest House, Woldingham, Surrey, CR3 7DH, England.

MARSHALL, Cedric Russell, B.A.; New Zealand politician. b. 15 Feb. 1936, Nelson; s. of Cedric Thomas Marshall and Gladys Margaret (née Hopley) Marshall; m. Barbara May Watson 1961; two s. one d.; ed. Nelson

Coll., Christchurch Teachers' Coll., Trinity Theological Coll., Auckland; teacher at various schools 1955–58; Methodist Minister in Christchurch 1960–66, Masterton 1967–71; M.P. for Wanganui 1972–90; Minister of Educ. and for the Environment 1984–86, of Educ. and of Conservation 1986–87, of Foreign Affairs 1987–90, Disarmament and Arms Control 1987–89, Pacific Island Affairs 1989–90; Chief Opposition Whip 1978–79; Chair. N.Z. Comm. for UNESCO 1990–99, Africa Information Centre Trustees 1991–95, Commonwealth Observer Group, Seychelles 1993, Commonwealth Observer Mission to S. Africa 1994, Cambodia Trust (Aotearoa-N.Z.) 1994–, Polytechnics Int. N.Z. 1994–, Educ. N.Z. 1998–; mem. Commonwealth Observer Group, Lesotho 1993, Victoria Univ. (Wellington) Council 1994–, UNESCO Exec. Bd. 1995– (Chair. Finance and Admin. Comm. 1997-), Nelson Mandela Trustees 1995–, Advisory Cttee. for Int. Global Change Inst., Waikato 1998–; Labour. *Leisure interests:* classical music, genealogy. *Address:* 26 Mana Esplanade, Paremata, Porirua 6006, New Zealand. *Telephone:* (04) 233-9178. *Fax:* (04) 233-9178.

MARSHALL, (C.) Penny; American actress and director; b. 15 Oct. 1943, New York; d. of Anthony Marshall and Marjorie Ward; m. 1st Michael Henry (divorced), one d.; m. 2nd Robert Reiner 1971 (divorced 1979); ed. Univ. of New Mexico; numerous TV appearances including: The Odd Couple 1972–74, Friends and Lovers 1974, Let's Switch 1974, Chico and the Man 1975, Mary Tyler Moore 1975, Heaven Help Us 1975, Saturday Night Live 1975–77, Battle of Network Stars 1976, Barry Manilow Special 1976, The Tonight Show 1976–77, Mike Douglas Show 1975–77, Merv Griffin Show 1976–77, $20,000 Pyramid 1976–77, Laverne and Shirley 1976–83, More Than Friends (TV film) 1978, Love Thy Neighbour (TV film) 1984. *Films:* appeared in: How Sweet It Is 1967, The Savage Seven 1968, The Grasshopper 1979, '1941' 1979, Movers and Shakers 1985, She's Having a Baby 1988, The Hard Way 1991, Hocus Pocus 1993, Get Shorty 1995; directed: Jumpin' Jack Flash 1986, Big 1988, Awakenings 1990, A League of their Own 1992, Renaissance Man 1994, The Preacher's Wife 1996, The Time Tunnel: The Movie 1999; produced: Getting Away With Murder 1995, With Friends Like These 1998, Saving Grace 1998. *Address:* Parkway Productions, 10202 Washington Blvd., Culver City, CA 90232, U.S.A.

MARSHALL, Geoffrey, PH.D., F.B.A.; British academic; b. 22 April 1929, Chesterfield; s. of Leonard William and Kate Marshall; m. Patricia Anne Woodcock 1957; two s.; ed. Arnold School, Blackpool, Univs. of Manchester and Glasgow; Research Fellow, Nuffield Coll., Oxford 1955–57; Fellow and Praelector in Politics, Queen's Coll. Oxford 1957–93, Provost 1993–99; Visiting Prof.-at-large, Cornell Univ. 1985–91; mem. Oxford City Council 1964–74; Sheriff of City of Oxford 1970; del. Oxford Univ. Press 1987–. *Publications:* Parliamentary Sovereignty and the Commonwealth 1957, Some Problems of the Constitution (with G. C. Moodie) 1959, Police and Government 1965, Constitutional Theory 1971, Constitutional Conventions 1984, Ministerial Responsibility 1989. *Address:* 33 The Villas, Rutherway, Oxford, OX2 6QY, England. *Telephone:* (01865) 310828.

MARSHALL, Malcolm Denzil; Barbadian cricketer; b. 18 April 1958, Bridgetown, Barbados; s. of Eleanor James; one c.; ed. St. Giles Boys' School and Parkinson Comprehensive School, Barbados; middle-order right-hand batsman, right-arm fast bowler; played for Barbados 1977–78 to 1990–91 (cap. 1987–88), Hampshire 1979 to 1993, Natal 1992–93 to 1995–96; played in 81 Tests for West Indies 1978–79 to 1991, scoring 1,810 runs (average 18.8) and taking 376 wickets (West Indies record); scored 11,004 first-class runs (7 hundreds) and took 1,651 wickets; toured England 1980, 1983 (World Cup), 1984, 1988 and 1991; played in 136 limited-overs internationals; West Indies team coach 1996–97 to date. *Publication:* Marshall Arts (autobiog.). *Leisure interests:* tennis, golf, soul music, reggae. *Address:* c/o West Indies Cricket Board, P.O. Box 616, St. John's, Antigua.

MARSHALL, Margaret Anne, O.B.E.; British concert and opera singer; b. 4 Jan. 1949, Stirling; d. of Robert and Margaret Marshall; m. Dr Graeme G. K. Davidson 1970; two d.; ed. High School of Stirling and Royal Scottish Acad. of Music and Drama; first opera appearance in Orfeo ed Euridice, Florence 1977; has since sung at La Scala, Covent Garden, Glyndebourne, Scottish Opera, Barcelona, Hamburg, Cologne and Salzburg; concert performances in major European and U.S. cities and festivals with major orchestras; First Prize, Munich Int. Competition 1974; numerous recordings. *Leisure interests:* squash, golf, cooking. *Address:* Woodside, Main Street, Gargunnock, Stirling, FK8 3BP, Scotland.

MARSHALL, Sir Peter, K.C.M.G.; British diplomatist; b. 30 July 1924, Reading; s. of late R. H. Marshall and Winifred Marshall; m. 1st Patricia R. Stoddart 1957 (died 1981); one s. one d.; m. 2nd Judith (née Miller) Tomlin 1989; ed. Tonbridge School and Corpus Christi Coll., Cambridge; R.A.F.V.R. 1943–46; served H.M. Foreign (later Diplomatic) Service 1949–83; Aide to British Amb., Washington, D.C. 1952–56; Head of Chancery, Baghdad 1961, Bangkok 1962–64, Paris 1969–71; Deputy Dir. Treasury Centre for Admin. Studies 1965–66; Counsellor, U.K. Mission, Geneva 1966–69; Head, Financial Relations Dept., FCO 1971–73, Asst. Under-Sec. of State 1973–75; Minister, U.K. Mission to UN, New York 1975–79; Perm. Rep. U.K. Mission, Geneva 1979–83; Commonwealth Deputy Sec.-Gen. (Econ.) 1983–88; Chair. Royal Commonwealth Soc. 1988–92, Commonwealth Trust 1989–92; Chair. Jt. Commonwealth Socs. Council 1993–; Hon. Fellow, Corpus Christi Coll., Cambridge 1989, Univ. of Westminster 1992; Pres. Queen Elizabeth House, Oxford 1990–94; Visiting Lecturer, Diplomatic Acad. of London 1989–. *Publications:* The Dynamics of Diplomacy 1989, The United Kingdom—the United Nations (contrib.) 1990, Diplomacy Beyond 2000 (ed.) 1996, Positive Diplomacy 1997. *Leisure interests:* music, golf. *Address:* 26 Queensdale Road, London, W11 4QB, England. *Telephone:* 0171-229 1921.

MARSHALL, Ray, PH.D.; American economist and government official; b. 22 Aug. 1928, Oak Grove, La.; m. Patricia Williams 1946; one s. three d.; ed. Millsaps Coll., Miss., Louisiana State Univ., Univ. of Calif. at Berkeley; Fulbright Research Scholar, Finland; post-doctoral research, Harvard Univ.; Instructor San Francisco State Coll.; Assoc. Prof. and Prof. Univs. of Miss., Ky., La.; Prof. of Econs., Texas Univ. 1962–67, Prof. of Econs. 1969, and fmrly. Dir. Center for Study of Human Resources, Chair. Dept. 1970–72, Prof. of Econs. and Public Affairs, Lyndon B. Johnson School of Public Affairs 1981; Rapoport Prof. Econs. and Public Affairs, Univ. of Tex. at Austin; Co-Chair. Comm. on the Skills of the American Workforce; Pres. Int. Labor Rights Research & Educ. Fund; Chair. Quality Educ. for Minorities Project; mem. Comm. on Future of Labor/Man. Relations; U.S. Sec. of Labor 1977–81. *Publications:* The Negro Worker 1967, The Negro and Apprenticeship 1967, Cooperatives and Rural Poverty in the South 1971, Human Resources and Labor Markets 1972, Anthology of Labor Economics 1972, Human Resources and Labor Markets 1975, Labor Economics: Wages, Employment and Trade Unionism 1976, The Role of Unions in the American Economy 1976, An Economic Strategy for the 1980s, 1981, Work and Women in the Eighties 1983, Unheard Voices: Labor and Economic Policy in a Competitive World 1987, Economics of Education 1988, Losing Direction: Families, Human Resource Development, and Economic Performance 1991, Thinking for a Living (with Marc Tucker). *Address:* c/o University of Texas at Austin, L.B.J. School of Public Affairs, Drawer Y, University Station, Austin, TX 78713, U.S.A.

MARSHALL, Robin, PH.D., F.R.S.; British professor of physics; b. 5 Jan. 1940, Skipton, Yorks.; s. of late Robert Marshall and of Grace Eileen Marshall; m. 1963; two s. one d.; ed. Ermysted's Grammar School, Skipton; research scientist, DESY, M.I.T., Daresbury Lab., Rutherford Appleton Lab. 1965–92; Sr. Prin. Scientific Officer (Individual Merit) Rutherford Appleton Lab. 1985–92; Prof. of Experimental Physics, Univ. of Manchester 1992–; Dir. and Co. Sec. Frontiers Science and TV Ltd.; Max Born Medal and Prize, German Physical Soc. 1997. *Publications:* over 200 scientific papers. *Leisure interests:* painting and drawing, movies. *Address:* Department of Physics and Astronomy, University of Manchester, Manchester, M13 9PL, England. *Telephone:* 0161-275 4170. *Fax:* 0161-275 4246.

MARSHALL OF KNIGHTSBRIDGE, Baron (Life Peer), cr. 1998, of Knightsbridge in the City of Westminster, **Colin (Marsh) Marshall,** Kt.; British airline executive; b. 16 Nov. 1933; s. of Marsh Marshall and Florence M. Marshall; m. Janet Cracknell 1958; one d.; ed. Univ. Coll. School, Hampstead; cadet purser, later Deputy Purser, Orient Steam Navigation Co. 1958–64; with Hertz Corpn. 1958–64; with Avis Inc. 1964–79, Exec. Vice-Pres. and C.O.O. New York 1971–75, Pres. and C.O.O., New York 1975–76, Pres. and C.E.O., New York 1976–79; Exec. Vice-Pres. and Sector Exec. Norton Simon Inc., 1979–81; Dir. and Deputy Chief. Exec. Dir. Sears Holdings PLC 1981–83; Chief Exec. British Airways 1983–95, Deputy Chair. 1989–93, Exec. Chair. 1993–95, Chair. (non-exec.) 1996–; Chair. Inchcape 1996–, Siebe PLC 1996–; Deputy Chair. British Telecommunications 1996–; Deputy Pres. CBI 1995–96, Pres. 1996–98; Dir. Grand Metropolitan PLC 1988–, Midland Group 1989–, HSBC Holdings 1992–, US Air 1993–96, Qantas 1993–96, British Telecommunications 1995–; Chair. Int. Advisory Bd. British American Business Council 1994–; mem. Bd. IBM U.K. Ltd 1990–, Panel 2000 1998–. *Leisure interests:* tennis, skiing. *Address:* c/o British Airways Head Office, P.O. Box 10, Heathrow Airport London, Hounslow, Middx., TW6 2JA, England. *Telephone:* 0181-562 5474.

MARS-JONES, Adam; British author; b. 1954; s. of the late Sir William Mars-Jones; ed. Westminster School, Trinity Hall, Cambridge and Univ. of Va.; film critic, The Independent 1989–97. *Publications:* Lantern Lecture (short stories) 1981, Mae West is Dead 1983, The Darker Proof (with Edmund White) 1987, Monopolies of Loss 1992, The Waters of Thirst (novel) 1993, Blind Bitter Happiness (essays) 1997. *Address:* 42B Calabria Road, Highbury, London, N5 1HU, England.

MARSTON, Robert Quarles, B.S., M.D.; American science administrator; b. 12 Feb. 1923, Toano, Va.; s. of Warren and Helen Smith Marston; m. Ann Carter Garnett 1946; two s. one d.; ed. Virginia Mil. Inst., Medical Coll. of Virginia and Oxford Univ.; Intern, Johns Hopkins Univ. 1949–50; Asst. Resident, Vanderbilt Univ. Hospital, Nashville, Tenn. 1950–51; Asst. Resident, Medical Coll. of Va., Richmond 1953–54, Asst. Prof. of Medicine 1954–57, Dean in Charge of Student Affairs 1959–61; Asst. Prof. of Bacteriology and Immunology, Univ. of Minn. 1958–59; Dir. of Univ. of Miss. Medical Center and Dean of School of Medicine, Jackson, Miss. 1961–65; Vice-Chancellor, Univ. of Miss. and Dean of School of Medicine 1965–66; Assoc. Dir. Nat. Insts. of Health, Bethesda, Md., and Dir. of Regional Medical Programs 1966–68, Dir. Nat. Insts. of Health 1968–73; Scholar-in-Residence Univ. of Va. 1973–74; Pres. Univ. of Fla. 1974–84, Pres. Emer., Prof. Emer. of Medicine 1984; Jt. Prof. of Fish and Aquaculture 1986; Dir., Johnson and Johnson; Rhodes Scholar 1947–49, Markle Scholar 1954–59; Chair. Fla. Marine Fisheries Comm. 1995–; mem. Exec. Cttee. Nat. Asscn. of State Univs. and Land Grant Colls., Council Inst. of Medicine, Asscn. of American Physicians; Chair. Bd. of Dirs. Cordis Corpn., Chair. Safety Advisory Bd.

Three Mile Island, Chair. Comm. on Medical Educ., Robert Wood Johnson Foundation; Hon. mem. Nat. Medical Asscn. 1969, American Hospital Asscn. 1969; Distinguished Fellow Inst. of Medicine, N.A.S. 1973; Distinguished mem. Asscn. of American Medical Colls.; Hon. Fellow, Lincoln Coll.; five hon. degrees; Swedish Kt. of the North Star. *Publications:* Numerous articles in the field of infectious diseases, medical educ., and admin. of health programmes. *Leisure interests:* sailing, camping, music, reading. *Address:* 19813 Old Bellamy Road, Alachua, FL 32615, U.S.A. (Home). *Telephone:* (904) 462-1008. *Fax:* (904) 462-0158.

MÁRTA, Ferenc, D.CHEM.; Hungarian chemist; b. 12 Jan. 1929, Kiskundorozsma; s. of Ferenc Márta and Matild Forrai; m. 1954; one d.; Head of Dept. of Physical Chem., Attila József Univ., Szeged 1962–75, Rector 1967–73; Corresp. mem. Hungarian Acad. of Sciences 1970, mem. 1976–, Gen. Sec. 1975–80, mem. Presidium, Vice-Pres. 1985–90, Gen. Dir. of Acad.'s Cen. Research Inst. for Chem.; mem. Council of Asscn. of Hungarian Chemists; Foreign mem. Russian and Czechoslovakian Acad. of Sciences; Hon. Dr. Odessa State Univ. 1975; Order of Labour (Silver 1964, Gold 1973), State Prize 1985. *Address:* Chemical Research Centre, Hungarian Academy of Sciences, 1025 Budapest, Pusztaszeri ut 59/67, Hungary. *Telephone:* (1) 325-7748. *Fax:* (1) 325-7554.

MARTELLI, Claudio; Italian politician; b. 1944; Deputy Leader of Socialist Party (PSI) 1978; Deputy Prime Minister 1989–92, Minister of Justice 1991–93. *Address:* c/o Socialisti Italiani, Via del Corso 476, 00186 Rome, Italy.

MARTENS, Wilfried, D. EN D.; Belgian politician; b. 19 April 1936, Sleidinge; ed. Louvain Univ.; lawyer Court of Appeal, Ghent 1960; fmr. Leader Vlaamse Volksbeweging; Adviser to Harmel Cabinet 1965, to Vanden Boeynants Cabinet 1966; Head of Mission. to Tindemans Cabinet (Community Affairs) 1968; Pres. Christelijke Volkspartij-Jongeren (CVP Youth Org. 1967–71), Pres. CVP 1972–79; mem. Parl. for Ghent-Eeklo 1974–91, mem. Senate for Brussels-Halle-Vilvoorde 1991–94; co-founder European People's Party (EPP) 1976, Pres. Working Cttee. on Policy 1976–77, Pres. 1990–99, Pres. EPP Group, European Parl. 1994–99; Prime Minister 1979–81, 1981–92; Minister of State 1992–; Pres. European Union of Christian Democrats 1993–96. *Address:* European Parliament, 47–53 rue Wiertz, 1047 Brussels, Belgium. *Telephone:* (2) 284.57.69. *Fax:* (2) 284.97.69.

MÅRTENSON, Jan; Swedish diplomatist; b. 14 Feb. 1933, Uppsala; m.; two s. two d.; ed. Univ. of Uppsala; held various Foreign Ministry and diplomatic posts until 1966; Head Section UN Dept. Ministry for Foreign Affairs, Stockholm 1966–67, Head Information Dept. 1973–75; Deputy Dir. Stockholm Int. Peace Research Inst. 1968–69; Sec.-Gen. Swedish Prep. Cttee. for UN Conf. on Human Environment 1970–72; Chef de Cabinet for King of Sweden 1975–79; Asst. Sec.-Gen. Centre for Disarmament UN Dept. of Political and Security Council Affairs 1979–82, Under-Sec.-Gen. for Disarmament Affairs 1983–87; Chair. UN Appointments and Promotions Bd. 1984–86; Sec.-Gen. Int. Conf. on Relationship between Disarmament and Devt. 1987; Dir.-Gen. UN Office, Geneva 1987–92, Under-Sec.-Gen. and Head UN Centre for Human Rights, Geneva 1987–92, Co-ordinator UN Second Decade Against Racism 1987; Amb. to Switzerland and Liechtenstein 1993–95; Amb.-at-Large, Ministry of Foreign Affairs 1996–98; Chair. Int. Club., Stockholm. *Publications:* some 40 books, articles on disarmament and human rights. *Address:* Karlaplan 14, 115 20 Stockholm, Sweden. *Telephone:* (08) 660 98 39.

MÅRTENSSON, Arne, M.B.A.; Swedish banker; b. 10 Oct. 1951, Vänersborg; s. of Aldo Mårtensson and Ingrid Mårtensson; m. 2nd Heléne Melin-Mårtensson 1996; ed. Stockholm School of Econs., Harvard Business School, U.S.A.; Industrial Devt. Dept., Svenska Handelsbanken 1972–75, Vice-Pres. and Head Credit Dept., Regional Unit, Western Sweden 1975–77, Sr. Vice-Pres. Admin., Cen. Sweden 1977–80, Sr. Vice-Pres. and Area Man. Stockholm City 1980–84, Exec. Vice-Pres. and Gen. Man., Western Sweden, 1984–89, Pres. Stockholm 1989–90, Pres. and C.E.O. Svenska Handelsbanken 1991–; mem. Bd. Mo och Domsjö AB, V & S, Vin & Sprit AB, OM Gruppen AB, ICC Sweden, Teleoptimering AB, Swedish Industry and Commerce Stock Exchange Cttee.; Vice-Chair. Svenska Bankföreningen (Swedish Bankers' Asscn.). *Leisure interests:* sailing, jogging, skiing. *Address:* Svenska Handelsbanken, 106 70 Stockholm (Office); Stenbocksvägen 3, 182 62 Djursholm, Sweden (Home). *Telephone:* (8) 229220 (Office). *Fax:* (8) 701 1195 (Office).

MARTIN, Agnes; American artist; b. 22 March 1912, Maklin, Sask., Canada; d. of Malcolm I. Martin and Margaret Kinnon; first showing in Betty Parsons Gallery, New York 1958; retrospective exhbns. ICA Philadelphia 1955, Pasadena 1956, Hayward Gallery, London 1977, Stedelijk Museum, Amsterdam 1977, 1990, Whitney Museum, New York 1991; represented in perm. collections Museum of Modern Art, New York, Albright-Knox Gallery, Solomon R. Guggenheim Museum, Tate Gallery, London, and many others. *Address:* Pace Gallery, 32 E. 57th Street, New York, NY 10022; 414 Placitas Road, Taos, NM 97571, U.S.A. *Telephone:* (212) 421-3292; (505) 758-9636.

MARTIN, Archer John Porter, C.B.E., M.A., PH.D., F.R.S.; British chemist (retd.); b. 1 March 1910, London; s. of Dr. William A. P. and Lillian K. Martin; m. Judith Bagenal 1943; two s. three d.; ed. Bedford School, and Peterhouse, Cambridge; Research, Cambridge, Physical Chemical Lab., Nutritional Lab. 1933–38; Wool Industries Research Asscn., Leeds 1938–46; Boots' Pure Drug Co. Research Dept., Nottingham 1946–48; mem. staff Medical Research Council 1948–52; Head of Physical Chem. Div., Nat. Inst. for Medical Research, Mill Hill, London, 1952–56; Chemical Consultant 1956–59; Dir. Abbotsbury Laboratories Ltd. 1959–70; Consultant to Wellcome Foundation Ltd. 1970–73; Extraordinary Prof. Eindhoven Technological Univ., Holland 1964–74; MRC Professorial Fellowship of Chem., Univ. of Sussex 1973–78; Robert A. Welch Prof. of Chem., Univ. of Houston, Tex. 1974–79; Visiting Prof. Ecole Polytechnique Fédérale de Lausanne 1980–83; Hon. D.Sc. (Leeds) 1968, (Glasgow) 1972, (Urbino) 1985; Berzelius Gold Medal of Swedish Medical Soc. 1951, shared Nobel Prize in Chem. 1952, Hon. Fellow (Cambridge) 1974, John Scott Award 1958, John Price Wetherill Medal 1959, Franklin Inst. Medal 1959, Leverhulme Medal 1963, Kolthoff Medal 1969, Callendar Medal 1971, Randolf Major Medal (Conn. Univ.) 1979, Fritz Pregl Medal (Austria) 1985, Order of the Rising Sun, 2nd Class (Japan).

MARTIN, G. Steven, PH.D., F.R.S.; American/British biochemist and biologist; b. 19 Sept. 1943, Oxford, England; s. of Kurt Martin and Hannah Martin; m. Gail Zuckerman 1969; one s.; ed. Manchester Grammar School, Univ. of Cambridge; Postdoctoral Fellow, Virus Lab., Univ. of Calif. at Berkeley 1968–71; mem. of staff Imperial Cancer Research Fund, London 1971–75; Asst. Prof. Dept. of Zoology, Univ. of Calif. at Berkeley 1975–79, Assoc. Prof. 1979–83, Prof. 1983–89, also Asst. Research Virologist Cancer Research Lab. 1975–79, Assoc. Research Virologist 1979–83, Research Virologist 1983–, Prof. Dept. of Molecular and Cell Biology 1989–; American Coll. of Surgeons Scholar Award in Cancer Research 1991–92. *Publications:* articles in various learned journals including Nature, Science, Cell. *Leisure interests:* hiking, bicycling, reading. *Address:* University of California at Berkeley, 401 Barker Hall #3204, Berkeley, CA 94720, U.S.A. *Telephone:* (510) 642-1508. *Fax:* (510) 643-1729.

MARTIN, Sir George (Henry), Kt., C.B.E.; British music industry executive, producer and composer (retd.); b. 3 Jan. 1926; s. of Henry Martin and Bertha Beatrice Martin; m. 1st Sheena Rose Chisholm 1948; one s. one d.; m. 2nd Judy Lockhart Smith 1966; one s. one d.; ed. Bromley Co. School, Kent, Guildhall School of Music and Drama; Sub-Lieut. R.N.V.R. 1944–47; worked at BBC 1950; with EMI Records Ltd. 1950–65, produced all records featuring The Beatles and numerous other artists; formed AIR Group of cos. 1965, Chair. 1965–; built AIR Studios 1969; built AIR Studios, Montserrat 1979; completed new AIR Studios, Lyndhurst Hall, Hampstead 1992; co. merged with Chrysalis Group 1974, Dir. 1978–; Chair. Heart of London Radio 1994-; scored the music for 15 films; Hon. D.Mus. (Berklee Coll. of Music, Boston) 1989, M.A. (Salford) 1992; Grammy Awards 1964, 1967 (two), 1973, 1993, 1996; Ivor Novello Awards 1963, 1979. *Publications:* All You Need Is Ears 1979, Making Music 1983, Summer of Love 1994. *Leisure interests:* boats, sculpture, tennis, snooker. *Address:* c/o AIR Studios, Lyndhurst Hall, Hampstead, London, NW3 5NG, England.

MARTIN, Henri-Jean, D. ÈS L.; French professor of bibliographic studies; b. 16 Jan. 1924, Paris; s. of Gabriel Martin and Louise Desbazeille; m. Odile Lorber 1955; one s. three d.; ed. Sorbonne, Ecole Nationale des Chartes; librarian, then Conservator, Bibliothèque Nationale 1947–58; seconded to C.N.R.S. 1958–62; Chief Conservator City Libraries, Lyon 1962–70; Dir. of Studies, Ecole Pratique des Hautes Etudes 1960–; Emer. Prof., Ecole Nationale des Chartes; Visiting Fellow All Souls Coll. 1993; Corresp. Fellow British Acad.; Médaille d'Argent (C.N.R.S.) 1970, Grand Prix d'Histoire de la Ville de Paris 1985, Prix Louise Weiss (Bibliothèque Nationale), 1st Grand Prix Gobert (Académie française) 1989, Gutenberg-Preis 1998; Chevalier Légion d'honneur. *Publications:* L'Apparition du livre (with Lucien Febvre) 1958, Livre, pouvoirs et société à Paris au XVIIe siècle (2 vols.) 1969, Histoire et pouvoirs de l'écrit 1988; Co-Ed. Histoire de l'édition française with Roger Chartier (4 vols.) 1983–86. *Leisure interest:* travelling. *Address:* Ecole Nationale des Chartes, 19 rue de la Sorbonne, 75005 Paris, France. *Telephone:* (1) 55.42.75.00.

MARTIN, James Grubbs, PH.D.; American politician; b. 11 Dec. 1935, Savannah, Ga.; s. of Arthur M. and Mary J. (Grubbs) Martin; m. Dorothy A. McAulay 1957; two s. one d.; ed. Davidson (N.C.) Coll. and Princeton Univ.; Assoc. Prof. of Chem. Davidson Coll. 1960–72; mem. 93rd–98th Congresses from N.C.; Gov. of North Carolina 1985–93; Dir. James G. Cannon Medical Research Center 1993–, J. A. Jones Construction 1993–, Family Dollar Stores Inc. 1997–; Trustee Davidson Coll. 1998–; Republican. *Leisure interests:* golf, sailing. *Address:* Carolinas Medical Center, P.O. Box 32861, Charlotte, NC 28232, U.S.A. *Telephone:* (704) 355-3959. *Fax:* (704) 355-7648.

MARTIN, John Joseph Charles; British public relations executive; b. 25 Nov. 1940, Hove, Sussex; s. of Benjamin Martin and Lucille Martin; m. Frances Oster 1979; one s. one d.; ed. Latymer Upper School; Dir. Welbeck Public Relations 1972, Chief Exec. 1984, Chair. Welbeck Golin/Harris Communications Ltd. 1988–; Founder John Martin Communications 1997. *Leisure interests:* painting, tennis. *Address:* Welbeck Golin/Harris Communications, 43 King Street, Covent Garden, London, WC2E 8RJ (Office); 53 Hampstead Way, Hampstead Garden Suburb, London, N.W.11, England (Home). *Telephone:* 0171-836 6677 (Office); 0181-455 8482 (Home). *Fax:* 0171-836 5820 (Office).

MARTIN, Sir (John) Leslie, Kt., R.A., F.R.I.B.A.; British architect; b. 17 Aug. 1908; s. of the late Robert Martin; m. Sadie Speight (died 1992); one

s. one d.; ed. Manchester Univ. School of Architecture; Asst. Lecturer, Manchester Univ. 1930–34; Dir. Hull School of Architecture 1934–39; Prin. Asst. Architect L.M.S. Railway 1939–48; Deputy Architect, London County Council 1948–53, Architect 1953–56; Prof. of Architecture, Cambridge Univ. 1956–72, Prof. Emer. 1973; Fellow, Jesus Coll., Cambridge 1956–72, Hon. Fellow 1976; Council mem. R.I.B.A. 1952–58, Vice-Pres. 1955–57; Slade Prof. Oxford 1965–66; Ferens Prof. Hull 1966–67; Visiting Prof. of Architecture, Yale Univ. 1973–74; Lethaby Prof. Royal Coll. of Art, London 1981–82; mem. Royal Fine Art Comm. 1958–72; *Work includes:* scheme design, Royal Festival Hall, buildings designed for the Univs. of Cambridge, Oxford, Leicester and Hull; RSAMD Glasgow, Gallery of Modern Art, Gulbenkian Foundation, Lisbon, scheme design, Royal Concert Hall, Glasgow; Hon. mem. Asscn. of Finnish Architects; Corresp. mem. Nat. Acad. S. Luca, Rome; Hon. Litt.D. (Cambridge); Hon. LL.D. (Leicester, Manchester, Hull and Essex); awards include Soane Medal 1930 and London Bronze Architectural Medal 1954, R.I.B.A. Distinction in Town Planning, Royal Gold Medal (Arch.) 1973, R.I.B.A. Trustees Medal 1991, Architects Journal Centenary Award 1995, Order of Santiago da Espada (Portugal). *Publications:* Joint Ed. Cambridge Architectural and Urban Studies; Buildings and Ideas from the Studio of Leslie Martin 1933–83, Architecture, Education and Research: The Work of Leslie Martin 1997 (ed. by Peter Carolin and Trevor Dannatt). *Address:* The Barns, Church Street, Great Shelford, Cambridge, CB2 5EL, England.

MARTIN, Sir Laurence Woodward, Kt., M.A., PH.D., D.L.; British professor; b. 30 July 1928, St. Austell; s. of Leonard Martin and Florence Mary Woodward; m. Betty Parnall 1951; one s. one d.; ed. St. Austell Grammar School, Christ's Coll., Cambridge, Yale Univ.; R.A.F. Flying Officer 1948–51; Asst. Prof. M.I.T. 1956–61; Assoc. Prof. Johns Hopkins Univ. 1961–64; Prof. Univ. of Wales 1964–68, King's Coll. London 1968–78; Vice-Chancellor Univ. of Newcastle 1978–90, Emer. Prof. 1991–; Visiting Prof. Univ. of Wales 1985–; Dir. Royal Inst. of Int. Affairs 1991–96; Hon. Prof. Univ. of Wales; Fellow, King's Coll., London; Lees Knowles Lecturer, Cambridge; Reith Lecturer BBC; Hon. D.C.L. (Newcastle) 1991. *Publications:* Peace Without Victory 1958, The Sea in Modern Strategy 1967, Arms and Strategy 1973, The Two Edged Sword 1982, The Changing Face of Nuclear War 1987, British Foreign Policy (jtly.) 1997. *Leisure interests:* travel, walking, fishing. *Address:* c/o The Royal Institute of International Affairs, Chatham House, 10 St. James's Square, London, SW1Y 4LE, England.

MARTIN, Sir Leslie (see Martin, Sir (John) Leslie).

MARTIN, Lynn; American politician; b. 26 Dec. 1939, Chicago, Ill.; m. Harry Leinenweber; two d.; ed. Univ. of Ill.; mem. Winnebago Co. Bd. 1972–76; mem. Ill. House of Reps. 1977–79, Senate 1979–81; mem. House of Reps. 1981–91; Sec. of Labor 1991–93; Vice-Chair. House Repub. Conf. 1982–86; Co-Chair. Bi-partisan Ethics Task Force; mem. House Rules Cttee, House Budget Cttee., Cttee. on Public Works and Transportation, Cttee. on Dist. of Columbia; Prof. of Govt., Harvard Univ. 1993–. *Address:* Department of Government, Harvard University, Cambridge, MA 02138, U.S.A.

MARTIN, Micheál, M.A.; Irish politician; b. 16 Aug. 1960, Cork; s. of Paddy Martin; m. Mary O'Shea; one s.; ed. Colaiste Chriost Ri, Univ. Coll., Cork; fmr. secondary school teacher; elected to Cork Corpn. 1985, Alderman 1991; former. Chair. Arts Cttee.; Lord Mayor of Cork 1992–93; mem. Dáil Éireann 1989–; fmr. Chair. Oireachtas All Party Cttee. on the Irish Language; fmr. mem. Dail Cttee. on Crime, Dail Cttee. on Finance and Gen. Affairs; Minister for Educ. June 1997–; Nat. Chair. Fianna Fail Nat. Exec. 1988–; Nat. Chair. Ogra Fianna Fail; mem. Bd. Cork Opera House, Graffiti Theatre Co., Nat. Sculpture Factory, Everyman Palace Theatre, Crawford Gallery, College of Commerce and several school bds.; fmr. mem. Governing Body Univ. Coll., Cork; won Cork Examiner Political Speaker of the Year Award 1987. *Address:* Department of Education, Marlborough Street, Dublin 1, Ireland (Office); 16 Silver Manor, Ballinlough, Cork, Ireland (Home). *Telephone:* (1) 8734700 (Office); (1) 295218 (Home). *Fax:* (1) 8729553.

MARTIN, Paul; Canadian politician; b. 1938, Ontario; m. Sheila Cowan; three s.; ed. Univs. of Ottawa and Toronto; worked in legal branch of ECSC; called to Bar, Ontario 1966; with Power Corpn. of Canada, Montreal; Chair. and C.E.O. Canada Steamship Lines; Dir. of seven maj. Canadian cos.; mem. Parl. 1988–; cand. for leadership of Liberal Party 1990; Minister of Finance 1993–, also Minister Responsible for Fed. Office of Regional Devt. 1993–95. *Address:* Finance Canada, Esplanade Laurier, 140 O'Connor Street, Ottawa, Ont., K1A 0G5, Canada. *Telephone:* (613) 992-1573. *Fax:* (613) 996-8404.

MARTIN, R(obert) Bruce, PH.D.; American professor of chemistry; b. 29 April 1929, Chicago; s. of Robert Frank Martin and Helen Woelffer Martin; m. Frances Young 1953; ed. Northwestern Univ., Univ. of Rochester, New York; Asst. Prof. of Chem. American Univ. of Beirut, Lebanon 1953–56; Research Fellow, Calif. Inst. of Tech., Pasadena, Calif. 1956–57, Harvard Univ. 1957–59; Asst. Prof. of Chem. Univ. of Va. 1959–61, Assoc. Prof. 1961–65, Prof. 1965–; Program Dir., Molecular Biology, Nat. Science Foundation 1965–66; Fellow A.A.A.S. *Publications:* Introduction to Biophysical Chemistry 1964; over 200 scientific papers. *Address:* Chemistry Department, University of Virginia, McCormick Road, Charlottesville, VA 22901, U.S.A. *Telephone:* (804) 924-3640.

MARTIN, Roger Léon René; French businessman; b. 8 April 1915, Asnières; s. of Gilbert Martin and Andrée Eugénie (Portemer); m., two s. one d.; m. 2nd Renée Guernier, one s. two d. (previous marriage); ed. Ecole Polytechnique and Ecole Nat. Supérieure des Mines; Ingénieur des Mines, Nancy 1941–42; Asst. to Steel Industry Dir., Dept. of Industry (French Govt.) 1942–46; Lecturer Ecole Nat. des Mines 1945–53; joined Compagnie de Pont-à-Mousson 1948, Asst. Gen. Man. 1953, Gen. Man. 1959–64, Pres. and Gen. Man. 1964–70; Pres. Cie. de Saint-Gobain Pont-à-Mousson 1970–80, Hon. Pres. 1980–82; Dir. Saint-Gobain Corpn.; Commdr. Légion d'honneur, Officier Ordre nat. du Mérite. *Publication:* Patron de droit divin 1984. *Address:* Compagnie de Saint-Gobain, "Les Miroirs", 18 avenue d'Alsace, 92400 Courbevoie (Office); 86 rue d'Assas, 75006 Paris, France (Home). *Telephone:* (1) 47 62 30 00 (Office).

MARTIN, Steve; American actor and comedian; b. 1945, Waco, Texas; s. of Glenn Martin and Mary Lee Martin; m. Victoria Tennant 1986 (divorced 1994); ed. Long Beach State Coll., Univ. of California, Los Angeles; TV writer for several shows; nightclub comedian; TV special Steve Martin: a Wild and Crazy Guy 1978; Georgie Award, American Guild of Variety Artists 1977, 1978. *Recordings:* Let's Get Small 1977 (Grammy Award), A Wild and Crazy Guy 1978 (Grammy Award), Comedy is not Pretty 1979, The Steve Martin Bros. *Film appearances include:* The Absent Minded Waiter, Sgt. Pepper's Lonely Hearts Club Band 1978, The Muppet Movie 1979, The Jerk 1979 (also screenwriter), Pennies from Heaven 1981, Dead Men Don't Wear Plaid 1982, The Man With Two Brains 1983, The Lonely Guy 1984, All of Me 1984 (Nat. Soc. of Film Critics Actor's Award), Three Amigos 1986, Little Shop of Horrors 1986, Roxanne 1987 (also screenwriter and Exec. Producer), Planes, Trains and Automobiles 1987, Parenthood 1989, My Blue Heaven, L.A. Story, Grand Canyon, Father of the Bride, Housesitter 1992, Leap of Faith 1992, Twist of Fate 1994, Mixed Nuts 1994, Father of the Bride 2, Sgt. Bilko 1995. *Address:* ICM, 8942 Wilshire Blvd, Beverly Hills, CA 90211, U.S.A.

MARTIN, Todd; American tennis player; b. 8 July 1970, Hinsdale, Ill.; s. of Dale Martin and Lynn Martin; ed. Northwestern Coll.; winner, New Haven Challenger 1989; turned professional 1990; semi-finalist Stella Artois Grass Court Championships, London 1993, Champion 1994, Champion (doubles with Pete Sampras, q.v.) 1995; finalist, Australian Open 1994, Grand Slam Cup, Munich 1995; semi-finalist, U.S. Open 1994, Wimbledon 1994, 1996, Paris Open 1998; Champion, Scania Stockholm Open 1998; mem. U.S. Davis Cup Team 1994–99; Pres. ATP Players' Council 1996–97; Adidas/ATP Tour Sportsmanship Award 1993, 1994, ATP Tour Most Improved Player 1993 and other awards. *Address:* c/o Advantage International, 1751 Pinnacle Drive, Suite 1500, McLean, VA 22102, U.S.A.

MARTIN DELGADO, José María, D. EN. D.; Spanish university rector; b. 26 June 1947, Málaga; s. of Rafael Martın Delgado and María Jesús Martín Delgado; m. Irene Martín Delgado 1973; one s. two d.; ed. Univs. of Granada and Bologna; Prof. of Fiscal and Tax Law, Univ. of Granada, Univ. Autónoma de Madrid, Univ. Autónoma de Barcelona, Univ. La Laguna, and Univ. of Málaga (fmr. Dean Faculty of Law) 1969–; Rector, Univ. of Málaga 1984–; mem. Spanish Asscn. of Fiscal Law, Int. Fiscal Asscn.; Dr. h.c. (Dickinson Coll., Pa.). *Publications:* Análisas Jurídico del Fondo de Previsiones para Inversiones, Ordenamiento Tributario Español 1977, Sistema Democrático y Derecho Tributario. *Leisure interests:* reading, music, fishing, tennis. *Address:* Plaza El Ejidio, s/n. Edificio Rectorado, 29071 Málaga (Office); C/. Mariano de Cavia, No. 9, 29016, Málaga, Spain (Home). *Telephone:* 253200, 253208 (Office); 296063 (Home).

MARTÍN FERNÁNDEZ, Miguel; Spanish banker; b. 9 Nov. 1943, Jerez de la Frontera; m. Anne Catherine Cleary 1972; one s. two d.; ed. Univ. Complutense, Madrid; Head Budget and Finance Sections, Ministry of Finance 1969–72, Deputy Dir. 1972–76; Economist, World Bank, Latin American Region 1976–77, Alt. Exec. Dir. for Spain, Italy and Portugal, World Bank 1977–78; Dir.-Gen. Treasury, Ministry of Finance 1978–79; Under-Sec. for Budget and Public Expenditure 1979–81; Pres. Inst. for Official Credit 1982; Head Annual Accounts Centre, Banco de España 1983–84; Under-Sec. Economy and Finance 1984–86; Dir.-Gen. Banco de España 1986–92, Deputy Gov. 1992–; Gran Placa de la Orden del Mérito Postal, Encomienda del Mérito Agrícola. *Address:* Banco de España, Calle Alcalá 50, 28014 Madrid, Spain. *Telephone:* 338.52.44.

MARTIN MATEO, Ramón; Spanish professor of administrative law; b. 31 Aug. 1928, Valladolid; s. of Andrés Martín Mateo and Julia Martín Mateo; m. Clara Abad Lobejón 1966; four c.; Prof. of Admin. Law, Univs. of País Vasco, Madrid, Valladolid and Alicante; Rector Univ. of Alicante 1986; Order Mérito Civil; Order of Andrés Bello (Venezuela). *Publications:* Dº Administrativo Económico 1974, Manual de Derecho Administrativo, Bioética y Derecho 1987, Liberalización de la Economía: Más Estado, menos Administración, La eficacia social de la jurisdicción contencioso-administrativa 1989. *Leisure interests:* mountaineering, music. *Address:* c/o Rectorado de la Universidad de Alicante, Carretera de S. Vicente del Raspeig, 03690 Alicante, Spain.

MARTÍN VILLA, Rodolfo; Spanish politician; b. 3 Oct. 1934, Santa María del Páramo, León; m. María Pilar Pena Medina; two c.; ed. Escuela Superior de Ingenieros Industriales, Madrid; Leader of Madrid Section, Sindicato Español Universitario, Nat. Leader 1962–64; Sec.-Gen. Syndical Org. 1969–74; mem. Council of the Realm; Nat. Econ. Adviser, Nat. Inst. of Industry; Nat. Econ. Adviser, Banco de Crédito Industrial, later Pres.; Civil Gov. of Barcelona and Prov. Head of Falangist Movement 1974–75; Minister for Relations with Trade Unions 1975–76, of the Interior 1976–79, of Territorial Admin. 1980–82; mem. Parl. (for Unión de Centro Democrático) 1977–83; First Deputy Prime Minister 1981–82; mem. Parl. (for Partido Popular) 1989–; mem. Exec. Cttee., Partido Popular 1989–; mem. Sr. Corps of Inspectors of State Finance; fmr. mem. special group of industrial engineers assisting Treasury. *Address:* c/o Partido Popular, Génova 13, 28004 Madrid, Spain.

MARTINA, Dominico (Don) F.; Netherlands Antilles politician; fmr. finance officer, Govt. of Curaçao; head, govt. social affairs dept.; f. Movimentu Antiyas Nobo 1979, Leader 1979–; M.P. 1979–; Prime Minister of Netherlands Antilles 1979–84, 1985–88. *Address:* Movimentu Antiyas Nobo, Landhuis Morgenster, Willemstad, Curaçao, Netherlands Antilles.

MARTINEAU, Rt. Hon. Paul, P.C., Q.C.; Canadian, lawyer and judge politician; b. 10 April 1921, Bryson, Quebec; s. of Alphonse Martineau and Lucienne Lemieux; m. Hélène Neclaw 1946; two d.; legal practice at Campbells Bay, Que. 1950–, at Hull, Que. 1966–; fmr. Crown Attorney for District of Pontiac, Quebec; M.P. 1958–65; Parl. Asst. to Prime Minister 1959–61; Deputy Speaker of House of Commons 1961–62; Minister of Mines and Tech. Surveys 1962–63; mem. Royal Comm. on Admin. of Justice 1967–70; Puisne Judge Superior Court Prov. of Quebec 1980–96; Progressive Conservative. *Leisure interests:* painting, writing, travelling, hiking. *Address:* 1204 Mountain Road, Aylmer, Quebec J9H 5E1, Canada (Home). *Telephone:* (819) 827-2065 (Home). *Fax:* (819) 827-9169.

MARTINEZ, Arthur C., M.B.A.; American business executive; b. 25 Sept. 1939, N.Y.; son of Arthur F. Martinez and Agnes (Caulfield) Martinez; m. Elizabeth Rusch 1966; two c.; ed. Polytechnic Univ., Harvard Univ., joined Exxon Chemical Co. 1960; Int. Paper Co. 1967–69; Talley Industries 1969–70; exec. positions in int. finance, RCA Corpn. New York 1970–80; Sr. Vice-Pres. and Chief Financial Officer, Saks 1980–84, Exec. Vice-Pres. for Admin. 1984-87; Sr. Vice-Pres. and Group Chief Exec. Retail Div. BATUS Inc. 1987–90; Chair. and C.E.O. Sears Merchandise Group, Sears, Roebuck & Co. 1992–95; fmr. Vice-Chair. and mem Bd. Dirs. Saks Fifth Avenue, New York; Chair., C.E.O. and mem. Bd. Dirs. Sears, Roebuck & Co., 1995–; Chair. Bd. Dirs. Nat. Retail Fed.; mem. Bd. Dirs. Ameritech Corpn., Amoco Corpn., Fed. Reserve Bank of Chicago; Trustee Chicago Symphony Orchestra. *Address:* 3333 Beverly Road, Hoffman Estates, IL 60192, U.S.A.

MARTINEZ, Conchita; Spanish tennis player; b. 16 April 1972, Monzon; d. of Cecilio Martinez and Conchita Martinez; turned professional 1988; reached last 16 French Open 1988, quarter-finals French Open 1989, 1990, 1991, 1992, 1993, semi-finals Italian Open 1991, French Open 1994, Australian, French, and U.S. Opens and Wimbledon 1995, French and U.S. Opens 1996, quarter-finals Olympic Games 1992; with Arantxa Sanchez-Vicario (q.v.) won Olympic doubles silver medal 1992; won Italian Open 1993, Hilton Head (S.C.), Italian Open, Stratton (Vt.) 1994, Wimbledon Singles Champion 1994.

MARTINEZ, Victor Hipolito; Argentinian politician, lawyer and law professor; b. 24 Nov. 1924, Córdoba; m. Fanny Munte; three s.; ed. Univ. of Córdoba; Rep. to the Prov. Ass. of Córdoba 1967; Mayor of Córdoba 1963–66; Dir. of newspaper Los Principios 1970–72; Vice-Pres. of Argentina 1983–89. *Address:* Senado de la Nación Argentina, Hipolito Yrigoyen 1849, C.P. 1089, Buenos Aires, Argentina.

MARTÍNEZ DE PERÓN, María Estela (Isabelita); Argentinian politician and fmr. dancer; b. 6 Feb. 1931, La Rioja Province; m. Gen. Juan Domingo Perón (Pres. of Argentina 1946–55, 1973–74) 1961 (died 1974); joined troupe of travelling folk dancers; danced in cabaret in several S. American countries; lived in Spain 1960–73; returned to Argentina with Juan Perón, became Vice-Pres. of Argentina 1973–74, Pres. 1974–76 (deposed by mil. coup); Chair. Peronist Party 1974–85; detained 1976–81; settled in Madrid, Spain.

MARTÍNEZ SOMALO, H.E. Cardinal Eduardo; Spanish ecclesiastic; b. 31 March 1927, Baños de Río Tobía; ordained 1950; elected Bishop of Tagora 1975, consecrated 1975, then Archbishop; cr. Cardinal 1988; mem., fmr. Prefect of the Congregation for Divine Worship and the Discipline of the Sacraments; Prefect of Congregation for Insts. of Consecrated Life and for Socs. of Apostolic Life 1992–; mem. Pontifical Comm. for Latin America, Congregations for Evangelization of Peoples, for the Clergy, for Catholic Educ. *Address:* Palazzo delle Congregazioni, Piazza Pio XII 3, 00193 Rome, Italy.

MARTINI, H.E. Cardinal Carlo Maria; Italian ecclesiastic; b. 15 Feb. 1927, Turin; ordained priest 1952; Archbishop of Milan 1980–; Consultant to Sacred Congregations for the Bishops, Doctrine of Faith, Religions and Catholic Educ.; mem. Pontifical Council for Culture; cr. Cardinal 1983; Pres. CCEE (Consilium Conferentiarum Episcopalium Europae) 1987–. *Address:* Palazzo Arcivescovile, Piazza Fontana 2, 20122 Milan, Italy. *Telephone:* (02) 85561.

MARTINI-URDANETA, Alberto, DR.RER.POL., D.SC.S.; Venezuelan politician, lawyer and diplomatist; b. 2 April 1930, Trujillo; m.; five c.; ed. Cen. Univ. of Venezuela; Clerk at Third Court of First Instance, Fed. Dist. 1949–51, Sec. Labour Third Court of First Instance 1954–62; Substitute Judge, Labour Court of First Instance 1956, Judge 1957; Legal Counsellor to Ministry for Foreign Relations 1958; f. mem. (1956) and Sec.-Gen. Venezuelan Inst. of Social Legislation 1960–69; Pres. Venezuelan Industrial Bank 1971; Minister of Labour 1972–74; Dir.-Gen. Venezuelan Inst. for Social Legis. 1978–79; Perm. Rep. to UN and other int. orgs., Geneva 1979–81, Perm. Rep. to UN, New York 1981–84; Chair. numerous int. cttees. and orgs., including several ILO cttees. and confs. *Publications:* numerous articles on labour and social matters. *Address:* c/o Ministerio de Relaciones Exteriores, Caracas, Venezuela.

MARTIN-LÖF, Per Erik Rutger, PH.D.; Swedish mathematician and philosopher; b. 8 May 1942, Stockholm; s. of Sverker Emil Bernhard Martin-Löf and Gertrud Cecilia Benedicks; m. Kerstin Maria Birgitta Forsell; one s. two d.; ed. Stockholm Univ.; Asst., Math. Statistics, Stockholm Univ. 1961–64, Doctoral Scholar, Faculty of Science 1965–66, 1967–68, Docent, Math. Statistics 1969–70; State Scholar of Swedish Inst., Moscow Univ. 1964–65; Amanuensis, Math. Inst., Aarhus Univ., Denmark 1966–67; Asst. Prof., Dept. of Math., Univ. of Ill., Chicago, U.S.A. 1968–69; researcher in Math. Logic, Swedish Natural Science Research Council 1970–81, in Logic 1981–83, Prof. of Logic 1983–; mem. Academia Europaea, Royal Swedish Acad. of Sciences. *Publications:* Notes on Constructive Mathematics 1970, Intuitionistic Type Theory 1984. *Leisure interest:* ornithology. *Address:* Department of Mathematics, Stockholm University, 106 91 Stockholm (Office); Barnhusgatan 4, 111 23 Stockholm, Sweden (Home). *Telephone:* (08) 16 45 32 (Office); (08) 20 05 83 (Home).

MARTINO, Antonio; Italian politician and university lecturer; b. 22 Dec. 1944, Messina, Sicily; s. of Gaetano Martino; lecturer in Monetary History and Politics, Chair. Faculty of Political Science, mem. Bd. of Dirs. Libera Università Internazionale degli Studi Sociali (LUISS), Rome; fmr. mem. Liberal Party (PLI); joined Forza Italia party Jan. 1994; Parl. Deputy March 1994–; Minister for Foreign Affairs 1994–95. *Address:* c/o Ministero degli Affari Esteri, Piazzale della Farnesina, 00194 Rome, Italy.

MARTINS, António Gentil da Silva; Portuguese paediatric and plastic surgeon; b. 10 July 1930, Lisbon; s. of António Augusto da Silva Martins and Maria Madalena Gentil da Silva Martins; m. Maria Guilhermina Ivens Ferraz Jardim da Silva Martins 1963; three s. five d.; ed. Univ. of Lisbon; Medical Faculty, Univ. of Lisbon 1953–; intern, Hospitais Civis, Lisbon; Registrar, Alder Hey Children's Hosp., Liverpool; founder and Head, Paediatric Dept. Instituto Português de Oncologia de F. Gentil 1960–85, consultant paediatric surgeon 1985–; paediatric surgeon, Hosp. D. Estefania (Children's Hosp.), Lisbon 1965, Dir. of Paediatric Surgery 1987–; Assoc. Prof. of Paediatric Surgery, Faculty of Medical Sciences, Lisbon 1984–(2002); Temporary Consultant Paediatric Cancer, WHO 1977, EEC 1991; Pres. Portuguese Soc. of Plastic and Reconstructive Surgery 1968–74, Ordem dos Médicos (Portuguese Medical Asscn.) 1978–86, Portuguese Asscn. of Paediatric Surgeons 1975–84, 1991–94, World Medical Asscn. 1981–83, Southern Branch Portuguese League Against Cancer 1988–94; Pres. Portuguese League Against Cancer 1995–97; mem. Exec. Council World Fed. of Asscns. of Paediatric Surgeons 1983–89; Council, Int. Conf. of Childhood Cancer Parent Asscns. 1994–95; mem. numerous other professional socs. etc.; awarded Silver Plate for film on separation of Siamese twins; Grande Oficial da Ordem do Infante D. Henrique and other awards. *Publication:* textbook on Plastic Surgery of the Ibero-Latin-American Foundation of Plastic Surgery (co-author) 1986, textbook on Intersexual States (co-author). *Leisure interests:* target-shooting, volleyball, tennis, collecting stamps and coins, music, photography. *Address:* Av. António Augusto Aguiar 22 1 Dto, 1000 Lisbon (Office); Rua D. Francisco Manuel de Melo 1 3°, Lisbon 1070, Portugal (Home). *Telephone:* 3560807 (Office); 3851436 (Home).

MARTINS, Peter; American ballet director, choreographer, and former dancer; b. 27 Oct. 1946, Copenhagen, Denmark; m. 1st Lise la Cour (divorced 1973); one c.; m. 2nd Darci Kistler (q.v.) 1991; one d.; pupil of Vera Volkova and Stanley Williams with Royal Danish Ballet; Dir. N.Y. City Ballet; Teacher, School of American Ballet 1975, N.Y. Ballet 1975, Ballet Master 1981–83, Co-Ballet Master-in-Chief 1983–89, Master-in-Chief 1989; Artistic Adviser, Pa. Ballet 1982–; mem. Royal Danish Ballet 1965–67, Prin. Dancer (including Bournonville repertory) 1967; Guest Artist, N.Y. Ballet 1967–70, Prin. Dancer 1970–83; Guest Artist Regional Ballet Cos. U.S., also Nat. Ballet, Canada, Royal Ballet, London, Grand Theatre, Geneva, Paris Opera, Vienna State Opera, Munich State Opera, London Festival Ballet, Ballet Int., Royal Danish Ballet; *choreographed Broadway musicals include:* Dream of the Twins (co-choreographer) 1982, On your Toes 1982, Song and Dance 1985; *works choreographed include:* Calcium Light Night 1977, Tricolore (Pas de Basque Section) 1978, Rossini Pas de Deux 1978, Tango-Tango (ice ballet) 1978, Dido and Aeneas 1979, Sonate di Scarlatti 1979, Eight Easy Pieces 1980, Lille Suite 1980, Suite from Histoire de Soldat 1981, Capriccio Italien 1981, The Magic Flute 1981, Symphony No. 1 1981, Delibes Divertissement 1982, Piano-Rag-Music 1982, Concerto for Two Solo Pianos 1982, Waltzes 1983, Rossini Quartets 1983, Tango 1983, A Schubertiad 1984, Mozart Violin Concerto 1984, Poulenc Sonata 1985, La Sylphide 1985, Valse Triste 1985, Eight More 1985, We Are the World 1985, Eight Miniatures 1985, Ecstatic Orange, Tanzspiel 1988, Jazz 1993, Symphonic Dances 1994, Barber Violin Concerto 1994, Mozart Piano Concerto (No. 17) 1994, X-Ray 1995; Dance magazine award 1977; Cue's Golden Apple award 1977, Award of Merit, Phila. Art Alliance 1985. *Publication:* Far From Denmark (autobiog.) 1982. *Address:* New York City Ballet, New York State Theater, Lincoln Center Plaza, New York, NY 10023, U.S.A.

MARTINS, Rudolf, LL.D.; Austrian diplomatist (retd.); b. 9 Feb. 1915, Zürich; s. of Martin Martins and Carola (née Dobolschek) Martins; ed.

Humanistisches Gymnasium (Vienna XIII), and Univ. of Vienna; with Fed. Chamber of Commerce, Vienna 1946–47; Austrian Trade Commr. for Switzerland and Liechtenstein and Sec. of Austrian Chamber of Commerce for Switzerland, Zürich 1947–49; with Fed. Chamber of Commerce, Vienna 1949–59; Counsellor, Adviser on Multilateral Trade and Commerce, Ministry of Foreign Affairs 1959–63; Counsellor, Head of Dept. for Multilateral Trade and Commerce Questions, Ministry of Trade and Reconstruction 1963–65; Amb. and Perm. Austrian Rep. to Office of UN and UN Specialized Agencies, Geneva, and Leader of Austrian Del. to European Free Trade Asscn. (EFTA) 1965–68, 1972–76; Envoy Extraordinary and Minister Plenipotentiary, Head of Dept. for Multilateral Trade and Commerce Questions, Ministry of Foreign Affairs 1968–72; Office of the Sec.-Gen. Ministry of Foreign Affairs 1977; Consul-Gen. of Austria at Zagreb 1978–80; Hon. Amb. for Life 1980; Goldenes Ehrenzeichen für Verdienste um die Republik Österreich. *Publications:* Statesmanship in Civil War (Spain's President Azana) 1982, Medieval Bosnia 1987, enlarged edn. 1995, Von der Souveränität zur Globalisierung im Erlebnis eines Diplomaten 1998; numerous articles; Ed. Der Arlberg und seine Strasse (by Martin Martins) 1992. *Leisure interests:* music, linguistics. *Address:* Schloss Schönbrunn 39, A-1130 Vienna, Austria (Home). *Telephone:* 813 15 77.

MARTINSON, Ida Marie, PH.D.; American professor of nursing; b. 8 Nov. 1936, Mentor, Minn.; m. Paul Martinson 1962; one s. one d.; ed. St. Luke's Hosp. School of Nursing, Duluth, Minn. and Univs. of Minnesota and Illinois; Instructor in Tuberculosis Nursing, St Luke's Hosp., Duluth 1957–58; Instructor in Nursing, Thornton Jr. Coll., Harvey, Ill. 1967–69; Asst. Prof. and Chair. of Research, Univ. of Minn. School of Nursing 1972–74, Assoc. Prof. and Dir. of Research 1974–77, Prof. and Dir. of Research 1977–82; Prof. Dept. of Family Health Care Nursing, Univ. of Calif., San Francisco 1982–, Chair. 1982–89; Carl Walter and Margaret Davis Walter Visiting Prof. at Payne Bolton School of Nursing, Case Western Reserve Univ., Cleveland, Ohio 1994–; Chair., Prof., Dept. of Health Sciences, Hong Kong Polytechnic Univ. 1996–; Fellow American Acad. of Nursing; mem. Inst. of Medicine, N.A.S. 1981–, mem. Governing Council 1984–86; Pres. Children's Hospice Int. 1986–88; Co-founder of Children's Cancer Foundation, Taiwan. *Publications:* Home Care: A manual for implementation of home care for children dying of cancer 1978, Home Care: A manual for parents (with D. Moldow) 1979, Family Nursing 1989, Home Care Health Nursing 1989; more than 100 articles in journals, 56 book chapters (1994) and one film; ed. of several books on home and family nursing. *Leisure interests:* skiing, walking, reading. *Address:* Room N411Y, Department of Family Health Care Nursing, University of California, San Francisco, CA 94143, U.S.A. *Telephone:* (415) 476-4558.

MARTIROSSIAN, Radick M., PH.D.; Armenian scientist; b. 1 May 1936, Madagis, Nagorno Karabakh; s. of Martiros A. Martirossian and Astkhik G. Harutunian; m. Rena A. Kasparova 1965, two s.; ed. Yerevan State Univ. and Lebedev Physics Inst. of Acad. of Sciences, Moscow; Dir. Inst. of Radiophysics and Electronics, Nat. Acad. of Sciences of Armenia 1980–; Rector, Yerevan State Univ. Oct. 1993–; mem. Armenian Acad. of Sciences, 'Intercosmos' and 'Radioastronomy' scientific councils, Russian Acad. of Sciences; research areas: microwave quantum amplifiers, remote sensing, microwave telecommunications, radioastronomy; Armenian State Prize in Science and Eng. 1988, Ukrainian State Prize 1989; Gagarin Medal for Space Research. *Leisure interest:* chess. *Address:* Yerevan State University, 1 Alex Manoogian Street, 375049 Yerevan, Armenia. *Telephone:* (02) 554629. *Fax:* (02) 151087.

MARTONYI, János, PH.D.; Hungarian politician and lawyer; b. 5 April 1944, Kolozsvár (now Cluj-Napoca, Romania); m.; one s. one d.; ed. József Attila Univ., Szeged, City of London Coll., Hague Acad. of Int. Law; Trade Sec., Brussels 1979–84; Head of Dept., Ministry of Foreign Trade 1984–89; Commr. for Privatization 1989–90; Deputy Chair. Bd. of Dirs., Nat. Property Agency 1990–92; State Sec. Ministry of Int. Econ. Relations 1990–91, Ministry of Foreign Affairs 1991–94, Minister of Foreign Affairs 1998–; Prof. Loránd Eötvös Univ., Budapest 1990; Head Inst. of Private Int. Law, József Attila Univ., Szeged 1997; Visiting Prof. Colls. of Europe, Bruges and Natolin, Poland; man. partner Baker and McKenzie (law firm), Budapest office 1994–98. *Publications:* numerous papers in various languages. *Address:* Ministry of Foreign Affairs, 1027 Budapest, Bem rkp. 47, Hungary. *Telephone:* (1) 458-1000. *Fax:* (1) 212-5918.

MARTRE, Henri Jean François; French telecommunications and space engineer; b. 6 Feb. 1928, Bélesta; s. of Marius Martre and Paule Maugard; m. Odette Coppier 1953; three d.; ed. Ecole Polytechnique; telecommunications eng. 1952–59; Deputy Head of telecommunications service in the production of armaments 1961–64, Head of Bureau Département Electronique, then Head Industrial Bureau of the Cen. Service of Telecommunications to the Ministeriel Del. for Armaments 1964–66, Deputy Dir. Industrial Affairs 1966, Dir. of Programmes and Industrial Aspects of Armaments 1971–74, Gen. Eng. First Class for Armaments 1974, Gen. Del. for Armaments 1977–83, State Admin. Société Nat. Industrielle Aérospatiale 1974–77, also SNECMA, Société Française d'Equipements pour la Navigation Aérienne; mem. Atomic Energy Cttee. 1977–83; Pres. and Dir.-Gen. Société Aérospatiale 1983–92; Vice-Pres. Surveillance Council for the Airbus Industry 1986–92; Pres. Club d'information et de reflexion sur l'economie mondiale (Cirem) 1987–, Asscn. européenne des constructeurs de matériel aérospatial 1988 (Hon. Pres. 1988), Groupement des industries françaises aéronautiques et spatiales (Gifas) 1990–93, France-Japan Cttee. 1991–, Edifrance 1992–94, Asscn. Française de Normalisation (Afnor) 1993–, Supervisory Bd. ESL Network 1996–; Vice-Pres. Supervisory Bd. Bertin & Cie. 1996–; State rep. Renault Bd. of Dirs. 1996–; Dir. Bertin and Cie Coll. of Science and Tech. 1995–, now Pres.; Vice-Pres. Conseil de Surveillance de Bertin & Cie 1996, Pres. 1997–; mem. Conseil supérieur de l'aviation marchande 1998–; Trustee d'Aérospatiale, d'Eurocopter, de Sopega, Siemens France; Grand Officier Légion d'honneur, Commdr., Ordre nat. du Mérite, Médaille de l'Aéronautique, Grand Officer Order of Merit (Germany), Order of the Crown (Belgium), Order of the Pole Star (Sweden), Commdr. Legion of Merit (U.S.A.), Commdr. White Rose (Finland), Order of Mil. Merit (Brazil). *Leisure interests:* skiing, sailing. *Address:* 115 rue de Bellevue, 92100 Boulonge-Billancourt, France (Office).

MARTY, Martin E., M.DIV., PH.D., S.T.M.; American professor of religious history and ecclesiastic; b. 5 Feb. 1928, West Point, N.E.; s. of Emil A. Marty and Anne Louise Wuerdemann Marty; m. 1st Elsa Schumacher 1952 (died 1981); seven c.; m. 2nd Harriet Lindemann 1982; ed. Concordia Seminary, St. Louis, Lutheran School of Theology, Chicago and Univ. of Chicago; Lutheran Minister 1952–63; Prof. of History of Modern Christianity Univ. of Chicago 1963–, Fairfax M. Cone Distinguished Service Prof. 1978–98; Assoc. Ed. The Christian Century 1956–85, Sr. Ed. 1985–98; Sr. Scholar in Residence, Park Ridge Center 1985, Pres. 1985–89; Pres. American Soc. of Church History 1971, American Catholic History Asscn. 1981, American Acad. of Religion 1988; Dir. Fundamentalism project American Acad. of Arts and Sciences 1988–, The Public Religion Project 1996–; Fellow A.A.A.S., Soc. of American Historians; Nat. Book Award for Righteous Empire 1972; Nat. Medal Humanities 1997. *Publications:* many books and numerous articles on religious history, theology and cultural criticism. *Leisure interests:* good eating, baroque music, calligraphy. *Address:* Christian Century Magazine, 407 S. Dearborn Street, Suite 1405, Chicago, IL 60605; 919 N. Michigan Avenue, Suite 540, Chicago, IL 60611, U.S.A. *Telephone:* 708-442-9453.

MARTYNOV, Vladlen Arkadyevich, DR.ECON.SC.; Russian economist; b. 14 Dec. 1929, Saratov; s. of Arkady Martynov and Evdokiya Martynova; m. Liya Romanova 1955; m.; one s.; ed. Leningrad Univ.; mem. CPSU 1952–91; lecturer, Leningrad Eng. Inst. 1955–57; sr. researcher, Head of Sector, Deputy Dir. Inst. of World Economy and Int. Relations (IMEMO) 1957–89, Dir. 1989–; Corresp. mem. U.S.S.R. (now Russian) Acad. of Sciences 1987–, mem. 1994–; U.S.S.R. State Prize 1977; mem. CPSU Cen. Cttee. 1990–91. *Publications:* articles on agriculture of industrially developed countries and capitalist economies. *Leisure interests:* classical music, swimming. *Address:* Institute of World Economy and International Relations (IMEMO), Profsoyuznaya Str. 23, GSP-7, 117859 Moscow, Russia. *Telephone:* 120-43-32 (Office); 429-66-41 (Home).

MARUSIN, Yury Mikhailovich; Russian tenor; b. 8 Dec. 1945, Kizel, Perm Region; ed. Leningrad State Conservatory; soloist Maly Opera and Ballet Theatre Leningrad 1972–77; soloist Mariinsky Theatre 1980–; guest soloist Wiener Staatsoper 1986–91; *repertoire includes:* over 50 parts in operas; U.S.S.R. State Prize, People's Artist of Russia; Diploma Best Singer in Italy 1982. *Address:* Mariinsky Theatre, Teatralnaya pl. 1, St. Petersburg, Russia (Office).

MARUSTE, Rait; Estonian judge; b. 27 Sept. 1953, Pärnu; s. of Albert Maruste and Mare Maruste; m. Mare Maruste (née Nurk) 1976; one s. one d.; ed. Pärnu Jaagupi Secondary School, Tartu Univ.; lecturer, Tartu Univ. 1977–85, Sr. Lecturer 1985–87, Asst. Prof. 1987–, Head of Dept. of Criminal Law and Procedure 1991; cand. for doctorate 1991–93; cand. for doctorate 1991–93; Chief Justice of Supreme Court 1992–. *Publications:* Human Rights and Principles of Fair Trial 1993. *Leisure Interests:* sailing, skiing. *Address:* Lossi 17, EE 2400 Tartu, Estonia; Pikk 94–27; EE 2400 Tartu, Estonia (Home). *Telephone:* 372–744–1411; 372–743–6696 (Home). *Fax:* 372–744–1433.

MARX, György, PH.D.; Hungarian physicist; b. 25 May 1927, Budapest, s. of Dr. István Marx and Julia László; m. Edit Koczkás 1952; two s. one d.; ed. Eötvös Univ., Budapest; started as staff member, Univ. Inst. for Theoretical Physics, Eötvös Univ., Univ. Prof. 1964–; Prof., Dept. of Atomic Physics 1970–92, Prof. Emer. 1997–; Pres. Hungarian Physical Soc. 1996–; Fellow Hungarian Acad. of Sciences 1970–, Int. Astronautical Acad., Paris 1976–, Academia Europaea, London 1988–, American Physical Soc. 1998–, Inst. of Physics, London 1998–; Hon. mem. Group for Int. Research in Educ. of Physics 1998–; Hon. Prof. Univ. of Vienna 1970–; fmr. Vice-Pres. Int. Union for Pure and Applied Physics, Int. Astronautical Fed.; fmr. Chair. High Energy Div. of European Physical Soc., Bioastronomy Comm. of Int. Astronomical Union; Pres. Roland Eötvös Physical Soc.; Visiting Prof. Univs. of Stanford 1965–66, Vienna 1970, Lahore 1973, Nanjing 1987, Kyoto 1988; initiator Int. Neutrino Conf. series; principal fields: particle, nuclear and astrophysics; discoverer of lepton charge conservation; Kossuth Prize 1956; Labour Order of Merit; Golden Degree 1968; Golden Comenius Medal, Bratislava 1996, Medal of Simón Bolívar Univ., Caracas 1996, Medal of IUPAP's Int. Comm. on Physics Educ. 1997. *Leisure interests:* education, space, archaeology. *Publications:* Életrevaló atomok (Atoms in Action) 1978, Jövőidőben (Future Tense) 1979, Atomközelben (Atom at Close Range) 1981, Atommag-közelben 1996, The Voice of the Martians 1997, and other books; 400 papers in Hungarian and 200 in foreign scientific journals. *Address:* Department of Atomic Physics, Eötvös University, Pázmány sétány 2, 1117 Budapest (Office); Fehérvári út 119, 1119 Budapest, Hungary (Home). *Telephone:* (1) 3722751 (Office); (1) 2055139 (Home). *Fax:* (1) 3722753.

MASÁR, Vladimír; Slovak banker; b. 2 May 1958, Partizánske; s. of Vladimír Masár and Jolana Masárová; m. Dagmar Glasová 1983; one s. one d.; ed. Univ. of Econs. Bratislava; State Bank of Czechoslovakia 1981–90; Deputy Dir. City Br., Gen. Credit Bank 1990–91; Dir. Credit Dept. Tatra Bank-Slovakia 1992; State Sec. Ministry of Finance of Slovakia 1992; Gov. Nat. Bank of Slovakia 1993–. *Leisure interests:* swimming, tennis. *Address:* National Bank of Slovakia, Štúrova 2, 818 54 Bratislava, Slovakia. *Telephone:* (7) 368 897. *Fax:* (7) 364 721.

MASARSKY, Mark Veniaminovich, CAND. PHIL. SC.; Russian business executive and journalist; b. 19 June 1940, Muryinskoye, Novgorod Region; m. Olga Yevgen'yevna Fedosova; one s. one d.; ed. Rostov Univ.; teacher, Taganrog Radio-Tech. Inst. 1965–67, Rostov Univ. 1967–70, Khabarovsk Polytechnical Inst. 1970–75; Corresp. Young Communist 1977–82; f. and mem. Gold-diggers of Petchora co-operative 1982–87; f. and Chair. Volkhov jt.-stock co. (now Russian Gold co.) 1987–; one of founders of Moscow Stock Exchange; Pres. Int. Asscn. of Factory Leaders 1992–; Chair. Entrepreneurs Council, Moscow Govt.; mem. Bd. of Dirs. Russian Bank of Reconstruction and Devt., Novobank Volkhov-Presnaya Investment Co., ITAR-TASS Co.; mem. Expert-Analytical Council to Pres. Yeltsin; mem. Conciliatory Comm. on Public Accord Agreement; mem. Bd. Public Chamber, Pres.'s Admin. *Address:* Association of Factory Leaders, Varvarka str. 11, bldg. 1, 103012 Moscow, Russia. *Telephone:* (095) 206-21-29.

MASCARENHAS MONTEIRO, Antonio; Cape Verde politician and lawyer; m. Maria Monteiro 1967; one s. two d.; ed. Univ. of Lisbon, Univ. of Coimbra, Catholic Univ. Louvain, Belgium; asst. and researcher, Inter-university Centre Public Law, Belgium 1974–77; Sec.-Gen. Nat. Ass. 1977–80; Judge of Supreme Court 1980–90; Pres. of Cape Verde 1991–; f. Asscns. of Magistrates of Cape Verde 1977; Pres. Third Conference on Regional System of Human Rights Protection in Africa, America and Europe, Strasbourg 1992; mem. OAU good-office mission to Angola 1992; Pres. Colloquium on Constitutional Transition in Africa at Catholic Univ. Louvain 1993; Presidential Medal of Freedom 1991. *Publications:* Reflexions sur compétence d'un gouvernement démissionnaire 1977, La notion de l'expédition des affaires courrantes 1977, La Charte Africaine des Droits de l'Homme et des Peuples 1991. *Address:* Presidência da República, C.P. 100, Praia, Santiago, Cape Verde. *Telephone:* 612669.

MASCHLER, Thomas Michael; British publisher; b. 16 Aug. 1933; s. of Kurt Leo Maschler and Rita Masseron; m. 1st Fay Coventry 1970 (divorced 1987); one s. two d.; m. 2nd Regina Kulinicz 1988; ed. Leighton Park School; Production Asst., André Deutsch 1955–56; Editor, MacGibbon and Kee 1956–58; Fiction Editor, Penguin Books 1958–60; Editorial Dir., Jonathan Cape Ltd. 1960–70, Dir. 1960–, Chair. 1970–91, Publr. 1991–; Dir. Random House 1987; Assoc. Producer The French Lieutenant's Woman (film) 1981. *Publications:* Ed. Declarations 1957, New English Dramatists Series 1959–63. *Address:* c/o Random Century House, 20 Vauxhall Bridge Road, London, SW1V 2SA, England.

MASEFIELD, John Thorold, C.M.G., M.A.; British diplomatist; b. 1 Oct 1939, Kampala, Uganda; s. of Dr. Geoffrey Bussell Masefield and Mildred Joy Thorold Rogers; m. Jennifer Mary Trowell 1962; two s., one d. (and one d. deceased); ed. Repton School, Derbyshire, St. John's Coll. Cambridge; joined Commonwealth Relations Office 1962, Pvt. Sec. to Perm. Under-Sec. 1963–64, Second Sec. Kuala Lumpur 1964–65, Warsaw 1966–67, FCO 1967–69, First Sec. U.K. Del. to Disarmament Conf., Geneva 1970–74, Deputy Head Planning Staff. FCO 1974–77, Far Eastern Dept. 1977–79, Counsellor, Head of Chancery, Consul-Gen. Islamabad 1979–82, Head Personnel Services Dept. FCO 1982–85, Head Far Eastern Dept. 1985–87, Fellow Center for Int. Affairs, Harvard Univ. 1987–88, mem. Civil Service Selection Bd. 1988–89; High Commr. in Tanzania 1989–92; Asst. Under-Sec. of State for S. and S. E. Asia and the Pacific, FCO 1992–94; High Commr. in Nigeria 1994–97 (also accred. to Benin and Chad); Gov. of Bermuda 1997–. *Leisure interest:* fruit and vegetables. *Address:* Government House, 11 Langton Hill, Pembroke, HM13, Bermuda.

MASEFIELD, Sir Peter Gordon, Kt., M.A., C.ENG., F.R.AE.S., F.C.INST.T., F.B.I.M., C.I.MECH.E.; British administrator and engineer; b. 19 March 1914, Trentham, Staffordshire; s. of late Dr. W. Gordon Masefield, C.B.E., M.R.C.S., L.R.C.P. and Marian Ada Lloyd-Owen; m. Patricia Doreen Rooney 1936; three s. one d.; ed. Westminster School, Chillon Coll., Switzerland and Jesus Coll., Cambridge; on Design Staff, Fairey Aviation Co. Ltd. 1935–37; Asst. Tech. Ed. The Aeroplane 1937–39, Tech. Ed. 1939–43; war corresp. and air corresp. The Sunday Times 1940–43; Personal Adviser on Civil Air Transport to Lord Privy Seal and Sec. of Civil Aviation Cttee. of War Cabinet 1943–45; British Civil Air Attaché, British Embassy, Washington, D.C. 1945–46; Dir.-Gen. of Long-Term Planning and Projects, Ministry of Civil Aviation 1947–48; Chief Exec. and mem. of Bd. British European Airways 1949–56; Man. Dir. Bristol Aircraft Ltd. 1956–60, British Executive and General Aviation Ltd., Beagle Aircraft Ltd. 1960–67 (Chair. 1968–70); Chair. London Transport Exec. 1980–82; Dir. Pressed Steel Co. Ltd. 1960–67; Pres. Inst. of Transport 1955–56; mem. Aeronautical Research Council 1956–60, Pres. Royal Aeronautical Soc. 1959–60; Chair. Air Transport Section, London Chamber of Commerce 1962–65; Chair. British Airports Authority 1965–71; Chair. Royal Aero Club of the U.K. 1968–70; Vice-Chair. United Service and Royal Aero Club 1970–71; Chair. Imperial War Museum 1977–78; Chair. British Asscn. of Aviation Consultants 1972–, Project Man. Ltd. 1972–88; Pres. Nigerian-British Chamber of Commerce 1977–81; Chair., C.E.O. London Transport 1980–82; Dir. Nationwide Building Soc. 1973–86, London Transport Exec. 1973–82, Worldwide Estates Ltd. 1972–88, Worldwide Properties Ltd.; Deputy Chair. Caledonian Airways Ltd. 1978–87; Chair. Royal Soc. of Arts 1977–79, Vice-Pres. 1980; Chair. Brooklands Museum Trust 1987–93, Pres. 1993–; mem. CAA Flight Time Limitations Bd., Bd. of London Transport Exec.; Hon. Fellow, Inst. Aeronautics and Astronautics (U.S.A.), Canadian Aeronautics and Space Inst.; Hon. D.Sc. (Cranfield), D.Tech. (Loughborough). *Publication:* To Ride the Storm 1982. *Leisure interests:* reading, writing, gardening, photography, flying. *Address:* Rosehill, Doods Way, Reigate, Surrey, RH2 0JT, England. *Telephone:* (01737) 242396.

MASEKELA, Hugh; South African trumpeter; b. near Johannesburg 1939; fmrly. in voluntary exile since early 1960s, in U.K., U.S.A., Ghana, Nigeria, Guinea and Botswana; f. Botswana Int. School of Music 1986. *Recordings include:* Home is Where the Music Is (with Dudu Pukwana, in London) 1972, I Am Not Afraid (with Hedzoleh Soundz) Technobush 1985, Beatin' Aroun De Bush 1992; wrote Broadway musical Sarafina; Musical Dir. Graceland.

MASERA, Rainer Stefano, D.PHIL.; Italian banker; b. 6 May 1944, Como; s. of Francesco Masera; m. Giovanna Aveta; two c.; ed. La Sapienza Univ., Rome, Oxford Univ., U.K.; Economist, Bank for Int. Settlements, Basle 1971–75; mem. staff, then Head Int. Dept., Research Dept., Bank of Italy 1975–77, Head Research Dept. 1982–84, Cen. Dir. for Econs. Research 1985–88; Alt. mem. EEC Monetary Cttee. 1977–81; Dir.-Gen. Istituto Mobiliare Italiano (IMI) 1988–; fmr. Minister of the Budget. *Publications:* L'Unificazione Monetaria e lo SME 1980, A European Central Bank 1989, International Monetary and Financial Integration 1988, Prospects for the European Monetary System 1990, Intermediari, Mercati e Finanza d'Impresa 1991. *Leisure interests:* tennis, skiing. *Address:* Istituto Mobiliare Italiano, Viale dell'Arte 25, 00144 Rome, Italy (Office).

MASERI, Attilio, M.D., F.R.C.P.; Italian physician; b. 12 Nov. 1935; s. of Adriano Maseri and Antonietta Albini; m. Countess Francesca Maseri Florio di Santo Stefano 1960; one s.; ed. Classical Lycée Cividale, Padua Univ. Medical School; Research Fellow Univ. of Pisa 1960–65, Columbia Univ., New York, U.S.A. 1965–66, Johns Hopkins Univ., Baltimore, U.S.A. 1966–67; Asst. Prof., Univ. of Pisa 1967–70, Prof. of Internal Medicine 1970, Prof. of Cardiovascular Pathophysiology, Prof. of Medicine (Locum) 1972–79, Sir John McMichael Prof. of Cardiovascular Medicine, Royal Postgraduate Medical School, Hammersmith Hosp., Univ. of London 1979–91; Prof. of Cardiology and Dir. Inst. of Cardiology, Catholic Univ. of Rome 1991–; Fellow American Coll. of Cardiology; Life mem. The Johns Hopkins Soc. of Scholars; King Faisal Int. Prize 1992; Distinguished Scientist Award, American Coll. of Cardiology 1996. *Publications:* Myocardial Blood Flow in Man 1972, Primary and Secondary Angina 1977, Perspectives on Coronary Care 1979, Ischemic Heart Disease 1995; articles in major int. cardiological and medical journals. *Leisure interests:* skiing, tennis, sailing. *Address:* Via Zandonai 9-11, 00194 Rome, Italy.

MASHEKE, Gen. Malimba; Zambian politician and army officer; fmr. Army Commdr.; Minister of Defence 1985–88, of Home Affairs 1988–89; Prime Minister of Zambia 1989–91. *Address:* c/o Office of the Prime Minister, P.O. Box 30208, Lusaka, Zambia.

MASHKOV, Vladimir Lvovich; Russian actor; b. 27 Nov. 1963, Tula; s. of Lev Petrovich Mashkov and Natalya Ivanovna Nikiforova; m. Tatyana Lvovna Mashkova; one d.; ed. Theatre-Studio of Moscow Art Theatre; actor and stage dir. Oleg Tabakov Theatre-Studio 1988–; main roles in most productions; staged 4 productions including Deadly Number (K. Stanislavsky Prize, Crystal Turandot Prize). *Film roles include:* Moscow Nights (dir. V. Todorovsky), American Daughter (dir. K. Shakhnazarov), Thief (dir. P. Chukhrai), Limita (dir. D. Yevstigneyev). *Address:* Oleg Tabakov Theatre-Studio, Chaplygina str. 12A, Moscow, Russia. *Telephone:* (095) 916 2121 (Theatre); 915 3301 (Yelena Chukhrai Art Agency).

MASHOLOGU, Mothusi Thamsanga; Lesotho diplomatist; b. 7 March 1939, Morija; s. of Bennie and Sarah Mashologu; m. Debrah Mokhitli 1968; one s. two d.; ed. Univ. Coll. of Fort Hare, S.A., Univ. of Rhodesia and Nyasaland, Queen's Univ., Belfast, and L.S.E.; Teacher at Basutoland Training Coll. and at Basutoland High School 1960–64; Asst. Sec., Ministry of External Affairs and Asst. Sec. in Cabinet Office 1965–66; Counsellor, Perm. Mission of Lesotho to UN 1966–68; Prin. Asst. Sec. and Acting Perm. Sec., Ministry of Foreign Affairs 1968–69; Amb. to U.S.A. 1969–73, also Perm. Rep. to UN 1969–71; Sec. to Cabinet 1974–75; Pro-Vice-Chancellor, Nat. Univ. of Lesotho Oct. 1975–76, Vice-Chancellor 1976–80; High Commr. to Canada 1980–85; Prin. Sec. for Foreign Affairs 1985–86; Govt. Sec. 1986–88; Dir. Red Cross Inst. 1988–91; Publr. and Consultant 1991–. *Publications:* A Long, Long Way 1991, Oh, Independence 1992. *Leisure interests:* music, theatre, tennis. *Address:* 3 Allan Wilson Avenue, Harare, Zimbabwe; Maloti Publishers, P.O. Box 1109, Maseru, Lesotho.

MASIRE, Quett Ketumile Joni, LL.D., J.P.; Botswana politician; b. 23 July 1925, Kanye; s. of Joni Masire and Gabaipone Masire; m. Gladys Olebile Molefi 1957; three s. three d.; ed. Kanye and Tiger Kloof; founded Seepapitso Secondary School 1950; reporter, later dir., African Echo 1958; mem. Bangwaketse Tribal Council, Legis. Council; fmr. mem. Exec. Council; founder mem. Botswana Democratic Party (BDP); mem. Legis. (now Nat.) Ass. March

1965; Deputy Prime Minister 1965–66; attended Independence Conf., London Feb. 1966; Vice-Pres. and Minister of Finance 1966–80, and of Devt. Planning 1967–80, Pres. of Botswana 1980–; Chair. SADCC; Hon. LL.D. (Williams Coll.) 1980, (Sussex) 1986, (St. John); Naledi Ya Botswana (Star of the Nation) 1986; Hon. G.C.M.G. *Leisure interest:* watching football. *Address:* State House, Private Bag 001, Gaborone (Office); P.O. Box 70, Gaborone, Botswana (Home). *Telephone:* 350850 (Office); 353391 (Home). *Fax:* 357800.

MASKHADOV (MASKADOV), Gen. Aslan; Chechen politician and army officer; b. 1951, Kazakhstan, returned to Chechnya 1957; m.; one s. one d.; ed. Tbilisi Higher Artillery School, M. Kalinin Moscow Higher Artillery Acad; army service since 1969; commdr. platoon Far E., Cen. Group of Troops (Hungary), commdr. artillery regt., Head of staff rocket forces and artillery of Vilnius Garrison, took part in attack on Vilnius TV Jan. 1991; commdr. div. Baltic Mil. Command 1969–91; retd. as Col. 1992; rank of Gen. Nov. 1992–; Head of Counterespionage, Head of Staff of Armed Forces 1993–, concurrently Minister of Defence Chechen Repub. Ichkeria 1995–96; took part in negotiations with Russian authorities, signed peace agreement with Gen. A. Lebed 1996; Prime Minister and Minister of Defence Coalition Govt. Chechen Repub. Ichkeria 1996–97; elected Pres. of Ichkeria Jan. 1997. *Address:* Office of the President, Grozny, Chechen Republic Ichkeria.

MASLOV, Col.-Gen., Pavel Tikhonovich; Russian army officer; b. 10 Oct. 1946, Shakhty, Rostov Region; m.; two d.; ed. Ulyanovsk Higher Tank School, Gen. Staff Mil. Acad.; army service 1968–; Deputy Commdr., armed forces N. Caucasian Command, Deputy Commdr. United Grouping of Fed. Armed Forces in Chechnya 1995; First Deputy Minister of Internal Affairs, Head of Gen. Staff; Ministry of Internal Affairs 1997–98, Acting Minister March 1998; Deputy Minister, C.-in C., internal forces of Russian Fed. May 1998–; several decorations. *Address:* Ministry of Internal Affairs, Zhitnaya str. 19, 119049 Moscow, Russia. *Telephone:* (095) 239 6500 (Office).

MASLOV, Viktor Pavlovich, D.PHYS.MATH.SC.; Russian mathematician; b. 15 June 1930, Moscow; m. Le Vu Ann 1977 (deceased); one s. two d.; ed. Moscow Univ.; post-graduate 1953–56; asst. 1956–64, dean 1964–67, Sr. research asst. 1967–73 at Moscow Univ.; concurrently teacher at Moscow Inst. of Electronic Machine Construction 1968–73, Head of Dept. 1973–; mem. of U.S.S.R. (now Russian) Acad. of Sciences 1984–; specializes in theory of differential equation; Ed.-in-Chief Mathematicheskiye Zametki 1988–; U.S.S.R. State Prize 1978; Lenin Prize 1986;. Lyapunov Gold Medal (U.S.S.R. Acad. of Sciences) 1983. *Publications:* works on electronic machine construction; Unarmed Love (autobiog.) 1989. *Address:* Institute of Electronic Machine Construction, Bolshoy Vuzovsky per. 3/12, 109028 Moscow, Russia. *Telephone:* 297-20-52 ext. 276; 433-75-44 (Office); 137-79-09 (Home).

MASOL, Vitaliy Andreyevich, CAND. TECH. SC.; Ukrainian politician; b. 14 Nov. 1928, Chernigov Oblast; s. of Andrei Dmitrievich Masol and Lidiya Grigorievna Masol; m. Nina Vasilievna 1978; one s.; ed. Kiev Polytechnic Coll.; senior engineer 1951–63; mem. CPSU 1956–91; Dir. of machine-construction plant 1963–71; General Dir. of production unit of heavy machine-construction factories in Kramatov (Ukraine) 1971–72; First Deputy Pres. of Gosplan for Ukrainian SSR 1972–79; Deputy Chair. Ukrainian Council of Ministers 1979–87, Chair. (Prime Minister) 1987–90, 1994–95; mem. of CPSU Cen. Auditing Cttee. 1981–86; mem. Cen. Cttee. CPSU 1989–91; Deputy to U.S.S.R. Supreme Soviet 1979–89, U.S.S.R. People's Deputy 1989–91; mem. Parl. of Ukraine 1990–94; numerous orders and awards including Order of Lenin (twice). *Leisure interest:* tourism. *Address:* Desyatinnaya str. 8, Apt. 8, Kiev 252025, Ukraine.

MASON, The Hon. Sir Anthony Frank, A.C., K.B.E., B.A., LL.B., F.A.S.S.A.; Australian judge (retd.); b. 21 April 1925; s. of F. M. Mason; m. Patricia Mary McQueen 1950; two s.; ed. Sydney Grammar School, Univ. of Sydney; Flying Officer, R.A.A.F. 1944–45; admitted to the Bar, N.S.W. 1951–; Q.C. 1964; Commonwealth Solicitor-Gen. 1964–69, Judge, Court of Appeal of the Supreme Court, N.S.W. 1969–72, Justice of the High Court 1972–87, Chief Justice 1987–95; Chancellor Univ. of N.S.W. 1994–; Arthur Goodhart Prof. of Law, Cambridge Univ. 1996–97; Chair. Nat. Library of Australia 1994–98; Vice-Chair. UN Comm. of Int. Trade Law 1968; Pro-Chancellor, A.N.U. 1972–75; Nat. Fellow Research School of Social Sciences (R.S.S.S.), A.N.U. 1995–; Justice, Supreme Court of Fiji 1995–, Hong Kong Court of Final Appeal 1997; Pres. Solomon Islands Court of Appeal 1997–; Arthur Goodhart Prof. of Legal Science, Cambridge Univ. 1996–97; Visiting Fellow Gonville and Caius Coll., Cambridge 1996–97; Hon. LL.D. (A.N.U.) 1980, (Sydney) 1988, (Melbourne) 1992, (Monash, Griffith, Deakin) 1995; Hon. D.C.L. (Oxford) 1993. *Leisure interests:* gardening, tennis. *Address:* c/o Chief Justice's Chambers, High Court, P.O. Box E435, Queen Victoria Terrace, A.C.T. 2600, Australia.

MASON, Sir (Basil) John, Kt., C.B., D.SC., F.R.S.; British meteorologist; b. 18 Aug. 1923, Docking, Norfolk; s. of late John Robert and Olive Mason; m. Doreen Sheila Jones 1948; two s.; ed. Fakenham Grammar School and Univ. Coll., Nottingham; Commissioned, Radar Branch, R.A.F. 1944–46; Shirley Research Fellow, Univ. of Nottingham 1947; Asst. lecturer in Meteorology, Imperial Coll., London 1948–49, lecturer 1949; Warren Research Fellow, Royal Soc. 1957; Visiting Prof. of Meteorology, Univ. of Calif. 1959–60; Prof. of Cloud Physics, Imperial Coll. of Science and Tech., Univ. of London 1961–65; Dir.-Gen. Meteorological Office 1965–83, Pres. Royal Meteorological Soc. 1968–70; mem. Exec. Cttee. World Meteorological Org. 1965–75, 1977–83; Chair. Council, Univ. of Surrey 1971–75; Pro-Chancellor Univ. of Surrey Sept. 1979–85; Pres. Inst. of Physics 1976–78; Treas. and Sr. Vice-Pres. Royal Soc. 1976–86; Dir. Fulmer Research Inst. 1976–78; Pres. B.A.A.S. 1982–83; Dir. Royal Soc. Project on Acidification of Surface Waters 1983–90; mem. Advisory Bd. Research Councils 1983–86; Pres. UMIST 1986–94, Chancellor 1994–96; Chair. Grad. School for Environment, Imperial Coll., London 1995–; Chair. ICSU/WMO Scientific Cttee. for World Climate Research Prog., Co-ordinating Cttee. for Marine Science and Tech. 1987–89; Pres. Nat. Soc. for Clean Air 1989–91, Asscn. for Science Educ. 1992–93; Foreign mem. Norwegian Acad. of Science 1993; Hon. Fellow Imperial Coll. of Science and Tech. 1974, UMIST 1979; Bakerian Lecture, Royal Soc. 1971; Halley Lecture, Oxford Univ. 1977; Lecturer, Linacre Coll., Oxford 1990; Rutherford Lecture, Royal Soc. 1990; Hon. D.Sc. (Nottingham) 1966, (Durham) 1970, (Strathclyde) 1975, (City Univ.) 1980, (Sussex) 1983, (E. Anglia) 1988, (Plymouth Polytechnic) 1990, (Heriot-Watt) 1991, (UMIST) 1994, (Reading) 1998; Hugh Robert Mill Medal, Royal Meteorological Soc. 1959, Charles Chree Medal and Prize, Physical Soc. 1965, Rumford Medal, Royal Soc. 1972, Glazebrook Medal and Prize, Inst. of Physics 1974, Symons Memorial Gold Medal, Royal Meteorological Soc. 1975, Naylor Prize and Lectureship 1979, Royal Medal, Royal Soc. 1991. *Publications:* The Physics of Clouds 1957, Clouds, Rain and Rain-making 1962, Acid Rain 1992. *Leisure interests:* music, foreign travel. *Address:* Centre for Environmental Technology, Imperial College, London, S.W.7; 64 Christchurch Road, East Sheen, London, S.W.14, England (Home). *Telephone:* 0171-594 9287 (Office); 0181-876 2557 (Home). *Fax:* 0171-581 0245 (Office).

MASON, Sir John (see Mason, Sir (Basil) John).

MASON, Sir John (Charles Moir), K.C.M.G.; British fmr. diplomatist and business executive; b. 13 May 1927, Manchester; s. of late Charles M. Mason and Madeline Mason; m. Margaret Newton 1954; one s. one d.; ed. Manchester Grammar School and Peterhouse, Cambridge; army service 1944–48, Korea 1950–51; joined diplomatic service 1952; Second Sec., Rome 1954–56, Warsaw 1956–59; Foreign Office 1959–61; First Sec. (Commercial), Damascus 1961–65; Foreign Office 1965–68; Dir. of Trade Devt. and Deputy Consul-Gen., New York 1968–71; Head, European Integration Dept., FCO 1971–72; seconded as Under-Sec. Export Credits Guarantee Dept. 1972–75; Asst. Under-Sec. of State, FCO 1975–76; Amb. to Israel 1976–80; High Commr. in Australia 1980–84; Chair. Lloyds Bank NZA Ltd., Sydney 1985–90, Lloyds Int. Ltd. 1987–90, Thorn-EMI (Australia) Ltd. 1985–94, Vickers Shipbuilders (Australia) Ltd. 1985–91, Multicon Ltd. 1987–90, Prudential (Australia) Ltd. 1987–92, Prudential Finance Ltd. 1987–90, Prudential Funds Man. Ltd. 1987–92, Bequests Cttee., R.A.C.P. 1992–95; Bd. of Advisers Spencer Stuart and Assocs., Sydney 1985–96; Pres. Heart Foundation N. Shore Hosp., Sydney 1985–92; Dir. Wellcome (Australia) Ltd. 1985–90, Nat. Bank of New Zealand 1985–90, Churchill Memorial Trust 1985–, Fluor (Australia) Ltd., Melbourne 1985–92; Chair. Pirelli (Australia) Ltd. 1986–, Cttee. Magna Carta Park, Canberra 1996–; Public mem. Australian Press Council 1992–; lay mem. Professional Conduct Cttees., Bar Council and Law Soc. of N.S.W. 1992–; mem. Commonwealth Trust 1993–, Duke of Edin.'s Award Scheme in Australia 1996–. *Publication:* Diplomatic Despatches, From a Son to His Mother 1998. *Address:* 147 Dover Road, Dover Heights, Sydney, N.S.W. 2030, Australia; c/o Lloyds Bank PLC, Cox's & King's Branch, P.O. Box 1190, London, SW1Y 5NA, England. *Telephone:* (2) 9371-7863 (Sydney). *Fax:* (2) 9371-7863 (Sydney).

MASON, Sir Ronald, K.C.B., F.R.S., PH.D.; British professor of chemical physics and industrialist; b. 22 July 1930, Wales; s. of David John Mason and Olwen Mason (née James); m. 1st E. Pauline Pattinson 1953; m. 2nd E. Rosemary Grey-Edwards 1979; three d.; ed. Quaker's Yard Grammar School and Univs. of Wales and London; Research Assoc., Univ. Coll. London 1953–60; Lecturer, Imperial Coll. London 1960–63; Prof., Univ. of Sheffield 1963–70; Prof., Univ. of Sussex 1970–88; Chief Scientific Adviser, Ministry of Defence 1977–83; Pro-Vice-Chancellor, Univ. of Sussex 1977–78; many visiting professorships in Australia, Canada, France, Israel, New Zealand and U.S.A. 1965–83, Int. Relations, Univ. Coll. of Wales; Chair. Hunting Ltd. 1986–87, British Ceramics Research Ltd. 1990–96, Univ. Coll. London Hosps. 1992–, Science Applications Int. Corpn. (U.K.) Ltd. 1993–96; Pres. British Hydromechanics Research Asscn. 1986–95, Inst. of Materials 1995–96; Chair. Council for Arms Control, London 1986–91; mem. UN Disarmament Studies Comm. 1983–91; Fellow Univ. Coll., London 1995; Hon. Fellow Polytechnic of Wales 1987; Hon. D.Sc. (Wales) 1986, (Keele) 1993; medals of various learned societies. *Publications:* many scientific research publs. on structural chem. and chemical physics of surfaces, author/ed. of 10 monographs, papers on defence policies and technology. *Leisure interest:* gardening. *Address:* Chestnuts Farm, Weedon, Bucks, HP22 4NH, England.

MASON, Stephen Finney, F.R.S., D.PHIL., D.SC.; British professor of chemistry; b. 6 July 1923, Leicester; s. of Leonard Stephen and Christine Harriet Mason (née Finney); m. Joan Banus 1955; three s.; ed. Wyggeston School, Leicester and Wadham Coll., Oxford; Demonstrator, Museum of History of Science, Oxford 1947–53; Research Fellow in Medical Chem. Australian Nat. Univ. 1953–56; Reader in Chemical Spectroscopy Exeter Univ. 1956–64; Prof. of Chem. Univ. of East Anglia 1964–70; Prof. of Chem. King's Coll., Univ. of London 1970–87, Prof. Emer. 1987–. *Publications:* A History of the Sciences: main currents of scientific thought 1953, Molecular Optical Activity and the Chiral Discriminations 1982, Chemical Evolution: origins of the elements, molecules and living systems 1991. *Leisure interest:* history and philosophy of science. *Address:* 12 Hills Avenue, Cambridge, CB1 7XA, England. *Telephone:* (01223) 247827.

MASON OF BARNSLEY, Baron (Life Peer), cr. 1987, of Barnsley in South Yorkshire; **Roy Mason,** P.C.; British politician; b. 18 April 1924, Barnsley, Yorks; s. of Joseph and Mary Mason; m. Marjorie Sowden 1945; two d.; ed. Carlton Junior School, Royston Sr. School, and London School of Econs. (T.U.C. Course); mine worker 1938–53; branch official, Nat. Union of Mineworkers 1947–53; mem. Yorkshire Miners' Council 1949–53; M.P. for Barnsley (now Barnsley Cen.) 1953–87; Minister of State (Shipping), Bd. of Trade 1964–67; Minister of Defence (Equipment) 1967–68; Postmaster-Gen. April-June 1968; Minister of Power 1968–69; Pres. Bd. of Trade 1969–70; Sec. of State for Defence 1974–76, for Northern Ireland 1976–79; Opposition Spokesman for Agric., Fisheries and Food 1979–81; Labour. *Address:* House of Lords, Westminster, London, SW1A 0PW; 12 Victoria Avenue, Barnsley, S. Yorks., S70 2BH, England (Home).

MASRI, Taher Nashat, B.B.A.; Jordanian diplomatist; b. 5 March 1942, Nablus; s. of Nashat Masri and Hadiyah Solh; m. Samar Bitar 1968; one s. one d.; ed. North Texas State Univ., with Cen. Bank of Jordan 1965–73; M.P., Nablus Dist. 1973–74, 1984–97; Minister of State for Occupied Territories Affairs 1973–74; Amb. to Spain 1975–78, to France 1978–83, also accred. to Belgium 1978–80, Rep. to E.E.C. 1978–80; Perm. Del. to UNESCO 1978–83; Amb. to U.K. 1983–84; Minister of Foreign Affairs 1984–88, Jan.–June 1991; Deputy Prime Minister, Minister of State for Econ. Affairs April–Sept. 1989; Chair. Foreign Relations Cttee. 1989–91, 1992–93; Prime Minister and Minister of Defence June–Nov. 1991; Speaker Nat. Ass. 1993; Rapporteur Royal Comm. for Drafting of the Nat. Charter; numerous decorations and awards, including The Jewelled Al-Nahda (Jordan), Order of Al-Kawkab (Jordan) 1974, Gran Cruz de Mérito (Spain) 1977, Order of Isabela la Católica (Spain) 1978, Commdr., Légion d'honneur 1981; Grand Officier Order Nat. du Mérite, Grand Officier Légion d'honneur, Order of Merit (Fed. Repub. of Germany, Grand Cross, First Class), Hon. G.B.E.. *Address:* P.O. Box 5550, Amman 11183, Jordan. *Telephone:* (6) 642227 (Office); (6) 810600 (Home). *Fax:* (6) 642226.

MASSÉ, Hon. Marcel, P.C., M.P., O.C., Q.C., B.A., LL.B., B.PHIL.ECON.; Canadian politician and civil servant; b. 23 June 1940, Montreal; m. Josée M'Baye 1965; three s. one d.; ed. Univ. of Montreal, McGill Univ., Montreal, Univ. of Warsaw, Poland, Oxford Univ., England; called to Bar, Quebec 1963; Admin. and Econs Div., World Bank, Washington, D.C. 1967–71; Econ. Adviser, Privy Council Office, Ottawa 1971–73; Deputy Minister of Finance, Prov. of N.B. 1973–74, Chair. Cabinet Secr. 1974–77; Deputy Sec. Cabinet for Fed. Prov. Relations, Ottawa 1977–79, Deputy Sec. Cabinet (Operations), Privy Council Office 1979, Sec. to the Cabinet and Clerk of the Privy Council Office 1979–80; Pres. Canadian Int. Devt. Agency, Ottawa 1980–82; Under-Sec. of State for External Affairs, Ottawa 1982–85; Canadian Exec. Dir. IMF, Washington 1985–89; Pres. Canadian Int. Devt. Agency (CIDA) 1989–93; Sec. to Cabinet for Intergovernmental Affairs March–June 1993; M.P. for Hull-Aylmer 1993–; Pres. of the Privy Council and Minister of Intergovernmental Affairs and responsible for Public Service Renewal 1993–96; Pres. of Treasury Bd. Jan. 1996–; Hon. D.C.L. (Acadia Univ.) 1983; Hon. LL.D. (New Brunswick) 1984; Dr. h.c. (Univ. du Québec) 1992, (Ottawa Univ.) 1996. *Publication:* An Evaluation of Investment Appraisal Methods. *Leisure interests:* reading, computing. *Address:* Room 315, West Block, House of Commons, Ottawa, Ont. K1A 0A6, Canada.

MASSE, Marcel; Canadian politician; b. 27 May 1936, Saint-Jean-De-Matha, Quebec; s. of Rosaire Masse and Angeline Clermont; m. Cecile Martin 1960; one s. one d.; ed. Ecole normale Jacques-Cartier, Univ. of Montreal, Sorbonne, City of London Coll., European Inst. of Business Admin.; fmr. teacher of Ancient History, Lanaudière Regional School Bd.; Dir. Lavalin (Eng. Co.) 1974–84 (also Project Dir. for UNDP, Vice-Pres., Vice-Pres. of Marketing and Commercial Devt.); mem. Quebec Nat. Ass. 1966–73 (held portfolios of Minister of State for Educ., Minister Responsible for Public Service, for Inter-Governmental Affairs, Minister of Planning and Devt.); Minister of Communications 1984–85, 1985–86, of Energy, Mines and Resources 1986–89, of Communications 1989–90, responsible for La Francophonie 1990, of Defence 1991–93; Chief Consultant CFC 1994–95; Del.–Gen. of Québec to France 1996–; fmr. Pres. Wilfrid Pelletier Foundation; Dir. numerous orgs. including Montreal Symphony Orchestra, Canadian Writers' Foundation, Canadian Refugee Foundation, Lanaudière Summer Festival, Club de Dakar, Jeunesses Musicales du Canada; Progressive Conservative. *Leisure interests:* reading, music, fishing, skiing.

MASSENGALE, Martin Andrew, M.S., PH.D.; American university administrator and agronomist; b. 25 Oct. 1933, Monticello, Ky.; s. of late Elbert G. Massengale and Orpha Massengale; m. Ruth A. Klingelhofer 1959; one s. one d.; ed. W. Kentucky Univ. and Univ. of Wis.; Asst. Agronomist and Asst. Prof. Univ. of Ariz., Tucson 1958–62, Assoc. Agronomist and Assoc. Prof. 1962–65, Agronomist and Prof. 1965–66, Agronomist, Prof. and Head of Dept. 1966–74, Assoc. Dean, Coll. of Agric. and Assoc. Dir. Agricultural Experiment Station 1974–76; Vice-Chancellor for Agric. and Natural Resources, Univ. of Neb., Lincoln 1976–81, Chancellor 1981–90, Pres. 1991–94, Pres. Emer., Dir. Center for Grassland Studies, and Foundation Prof. 1994–; Pres. Grazing Lands Forum 1997–; Fellow, A.A.A.S., American Soc. of Agronomy, Crop Science Soc. of America and other professional socs.; mem. numerous cttees., nat. panels, advisory bds., etc.; Dr. h.c. (Neb. Wesleyan Univ., Senshu Univ., Tokyo); many other honours and awards. *Leisure interests:* reading, travel, golf, photography. *Address:* 220 Keim Hall, University of Nebraska, Lincoln, NE 68583-0953 (Office); 3436 West Cape Charles Road, Lincoln, NE 68516, U.S.A. (Home). *Telephone:* (402) 472-4101 (Office); (402) 420-5350 (Home). *Fax:* (402) 472-4104.

MASSERET, Jean-Pierre; French politician; b. 23 Aug. 1944, Cusset (Alliers); s. of Lucien Masseret and Claudia Rollet; m. Marie-Hélène Roddier 1967; three c.; ed. Inst. des Hautes Etudes de Défense Nat.; fmr. Chief Insp., Inland Revenue; mem. staff of Minister for War Veterans 1981–86; Senator for Moselle 1983–, Vice-Chair. Senate Finance Cttee.; Minister of State attached to Minister of Defence, with responsibility for War Veterans 1997–; Mayor of Hayange (Moselle); Lorraine regional councillor; mem. Parti Socialiste political cttee.; mem. Parl. Ass. of WEU, of Council of Europe, Socialist Party Nat. Office; fmr. Chair. Lorraine Athletics League; fmr. regional champion runner. *Address:* Palais du Luxembourg, 75291 Paris; Secrétariat d'Etat aux Anciens combattants, 37 rue de Bellechasse, 75700 Paris; Hôtel de Ville, place de la Résistance et de la Déportation, 57700 Hayange, France.

MASSEVITCH, Alla Genrikhovna, D.SC.; Russian astronomer; b. 9 Oct. 1918, Tbilisi; d. of Genrik Massevitch and Natalie Zhgenti; m. Joseph Friedlander 1942; one d.; ed. Moscow Industrial Pedagogical Inst., Moscow Univ.; Assistant Prof. of Astrophysics Moscow Univ. 1946–48, Prof. 1948–; Vice-Pres. Astronomical Council, U.S.S.R. (now Russian) Acad. of Sciences 1952–88, Chief Scientific Researcher; in charge of optical (visual, photographic and laser ranging) tracking of Soviet (now Russian) space vehicles 1958–89; mem. Nat. Cttee. for the Int. Space Year 1989–93; Chair. Working Group I, Cttee. for Space Research (COSPAR) 1961–66; Vice-Pres. Comm. 44 JAU (Extraterrestrial Astronomy) 1961–67; Pres. Comm. 35 JAU (Internal Structure of Stars) 1967–70; Deputy Sec.-Gen. UNISPACE –1982, Pres. of Section Satellite Tracking for Geodesy, Inter-Cosmos Co-operation 1968–89; Assoc. Ed. Astrophysics and Space Science 1986–94; mem. Editorial Bd. Astrophysica 1987–; Vice-Pres. Inst. for Soviet-American (now Russian-American) Relations 1967; Vice-Pres. Bd. Soviet Peace Cttee. 1967–92; Foreign mem. Royal Astronomical Soc. 1963, Indian Nat. Acad. of Sciences 1980, Austrian Acad. of Sciences 1985; mem. Int. Acad. of Astronautics 1964; Hon. mem. Russian Acad. of Cosmonautics 1997; U.S.S.R. State Prize 1975. *Publications:* three books on stellar evolution, one on satellite geodesy, several popular books on astronomy; 161 papers on internal structure of stars, stellar evolution and optical tracking of satellites, mainly in Astronomical Journal of the U.S.S.R., Publications of the Sternberg Astronomical Inst. and Scientific Information of the Astronomical Council 1945–. *Leisure interests:* collecting coffee machines and cookery books. *Address:* Astronomical Institute of the Russian Acad. of Sciences, 48 Pjatnitskaja Street, Moscow 109017; 6 Pushkurev per., Apt. 4, Moscow 103045, Russia. *Telephone:* 231-3980. *Fax:* 230-2081.

MASSEY, Anna; British actress; b. Sussex; d. of Raymond Massey and Adrienne Allen; m. 1st Jeremy Huggins 1958 (divorced 1963); one s.; m. 2nd Uri Andres 1988; ed. in London, New York, France, Switzerland and Italy; debut in The Reluctant Debutante aged 17; subsequent appearances in School for Scandal, The Doctor's Dilemma, The Right Honourable Gentleman, The Miracle Worker, The Glass Menagerie, The Prime of Miss Jean Brodie; appeared with Nat. Theatre in 1970s and 1980s in Heartbreak House, Close of Play, Summer, The Importance of Being Earnest, Alaska, Family Voices, King Lear, Mary Stuart; also appeared at The Royal Court in Spoiled, The Seagull; TV appearances include Mrs Danvers in Rebecca, Lady Nelson in I Remember Nelson, The Cherry Orchard, Mansfield Park; BAFTA Award for Best Actress for role in TV film Hotel du Lac 1987, The Respectable Trade 1998. *Films include:* Frenzy, David Copperfield, The Looking Glass War, The Corn is Green, Sweet William, Another Country, Five Days One Summer, Sakharov, The Chain, Mountains of the Moon, Killing Dad, Journey into the Shadows, Season's Greetings, The Day After the Fair, The Christmas Tree, Sunchild, A Tale of Two Cities, Haunted 1995, The Grotesque 1995, The Slab Boys 1997, Déjà Vu 1997, Captain Jack 1998, Mad Cows 1998. *Address:* c/o Markham and Froggatt Ltd., 4 Windmill Street, London, W1P 1HF, England.

MASSEY, Vincent, PH.D., F.R.S.; American (Australian born) professor of biochemistry; b. 28 Nov. 1926, Berkeley; s. of Walter and Mary A. Massey; m. Margot E. Grünewald 1950; one s. two d.; ed. Univs. of Sydney and Cambridge; Research Officer, McMaster Animal Health Lab., CSIRO, Sydney 1946–50; Ian McMaster Fellow, Univ. of Cambridge 1950–53, ICI Fellow 1953–55; Research Officer, Henry Ford Hosp., Detroit 1955–57; Lecturer, then Sr. Lecturer, Univ. of Sheffield 1957–63; Prof. of Biological Chem. Univ. of Michigan, Ann Arbor 1963, J. Lawrence Oncley Distinguished Univ. Prof. 1995–; Visiting Prof. Univ. of Ill. 1960, Univ. of Konstanz 1973–74, Guest Prof. 1975–; Guest Prof. Inst. of Applied Biochem., Mitake 1985, Yokohama City Univ. 1988; mem. N.A.S., Biochemistry Soc., American Soc. of Biochemistry and Molecular Biology, American Chem. Soc.; naturalized U.S. citizen 1986. *Publications:* over 450 research papers and reviews in scientific journals and books. *Leisure interests:* walking, sailing, gardening. *Address:* c/o Department of Biological Chemistry, University of Michigan, Ann Arbor, MI 48109, U.S.A.

MASSON, Jacques, L. EN D.; French banker; b. 17 April 1924, Paris; s. of Georges Masson and Yvonne née Poutot; m. Annie Bedhet 1946; one s. two d. (one deceased); ed. Faculté de Droit, Paris, Ecole Nat. d'Organisation

Economique et Sociale and Centre de Perfectionnement dans l'Administration des Affaires; joined Banque Nat. de Paris (BNP) 1950, Asst. Dir. 1963, Dir. in charge of Paris branches 1964, Dir. 1972, Asst. Dir.-Gen. 1978, Dir.-Gen. 1982–87, Hon. Dir.-Gen. 1987; Prof. Inst. Technique de banque du Conservatoire nat. des arts et métiers 1971–; Dir. Basaltes 1988–; mem. Banking Comm.; Pres. BNP Bail; Chair. Bd. of Dirs. Groupement des Cartes Bancaires CB 1988–93; Dir. SILEC, Nouvelles Galeries, Devanlay, Soc. Nouvelle des Basaltes, Econoler France, Soc. Cheddito France S.A.; mem. supervisory bd., SOVAC; Chevalier, Légion d'honneur, Officier, Ordre Nat. du Mérite. *Address:* 34 rue du Docteur Blanche, 75016 Paris, France (Home).

MASSONDE, Majidine Ben Said; Comoran politician; Prime Minister 1996–97; Interim Pres. of Comoros Nov. 1998–; mem. Parti Udzima. *Address:* c/o Office of the President, Moroni, The Comoros.

MASSOUD, Gen. Ahmed Shah; Afghanistan guerrilla commander; b. 1953; ed. Engineering Dept., Kabul Polytechnic; became a guerrilla 1975; guerrilla commdr. in Panjshir Valley against Soviet-backed regime of fmr. Pres. Najibullah 1979–92; Minister of Defence 1992; guerrilla commdr. against Taliban Islamic regime 1996–; fmr. mem. Muslim Youth League; mem. Jamiat-i-Islami. *Address:* c/o Ministry of Defence, Darulaman Wat, Kabul, Afghanistan.

MASSU, Gen. Jacques; French army officer (retd.); b. 5 May 1908, Châlons/Marne; s. of Charles and Marie (née Lefèvre) Massu; m. 1st Suzanne Rosambert 1948 (died 1977); one d. (deceased), one adopted s. one adopted d.; m. 2nd Catherine Drouin 1978; ed. Ecole Spéciale Mil. de St. Cyr; joined Free French Forces Aug. 1940; took part in all the campaigns of Gen. Leclerc's 2nd Armoured Div.; Commdr., Hanoi, Indochina 1945–47, 1st Demibrigade, Colonial Parachute Commandos, 4th A.O.F. Brigade 1951–54; Gen. of Brigade 1955; as Commdr. 10th Parachute Div., directed airborne operation and landing at Port Said, Nov. 1956; Mil. Commdr. Dept. of Algiers Jan. 1957–60; headed the first Cttee. of Public Safety set up in Algiers and called upon Gen. de Gaulle to assume power May 1958; Commdr. Algiers Army Corps 1958–60; retd. 1960; Mil. Gov. of Metz 1961–66; C.-in-C. French Troops in Germany 1966–69; Grand-Croix, Légion d'honneur, Compagnon de la Libération, Croix de guerre, D.S.O., etc. *Publications:* memoirs: La vraie bataille d'Alger (Vol. 1) 1971, Le torrent et la digue (Vol. 11) 1973, Sept ans avec Leclerc (Vol. III) 1974, Verité sur Suez 1956 (Vol. IV) 1978, L'aventure Viet Minh (Vol. V) 1980, Baden 68 1983, Massu, le soldat méconnu 1993, Avec de Gaulle 1998. *Leisure interests:* riding, hunting, shooting. *Address:* Le Prieuré, 45700 Conflans sur Loing, France. *Telephone:* (38) 94-71-46.

MASSY-GREENE, Sir (John) Brian, Kt., A.C., M.A., F.A.I.M.; Australian business executive; b. 20 April 1916, Tenterfield, N.S.W.; s. of late Sir Walter Massy-Greene, K.C.M.G., and Lula May Lomax; m. Margaret E. R. Sharp 1942; two s. two d.; ed. Sydney C. of E. Grammar School, Geelong Grammar School and Clare Coll., Cambridge; joined Metal Mfrs. Ltd. 1939; Lieut., AIF, New Guinea 1942–45; transferred to Austral Bronze Co. Pty. Ltd. (subsidiary of Metal Mfrs.) Gen. Man. 1953–62; Gen. Man. Dir. Consolidated Gold Fields Australia Ltd. 1962–66, Chair. and Man. Dir. 1966–76, Dir. Consolidated Gold Fields Ltd., London 1963–76; Chair. The Bellambi Coal Co. Ltd. 1964–72, Goldsworthy Mining Ltd. 1965–76, The Mount Lyell Mining & Railway Co. Ltd. 1969–76, Lawrenson Alumsac Holdings Ltd. 1964–73; Dir. Assoc. Minerals Consolidated Ltd. 1962–76, Commonwealth Mining Investments (Australia) Ltd. 1962–72, 1978–86, Dalgety Australia Ltd. 1968–78, Zip Holdings Ltd. 1964–73, Nat. Mutual Life Asscn. Ltd. 1977–85; Chair. Santos Ltd. 1985–89 (Dir. 1984–89), Hazelton Air Services Pty. Ltd. 1984–, Chair. (and Dir.) Hazelton Airlines Ltd. 1984–97, Pacific Dunlop Ltd. 1979–86 (Dir. 1968–86), Commonwealth Banking Corpn. 1985–88 (Dir. 1968–88); mem. Exec. Cttee. Australian Mining Industry Council 1967–76 (Pres. 1971), Mfg. Industries Advisory Council 1968–75, N.S.W. Advisory Cttee., C.S.I.R.O. 1968–75; Fellow Inst. of Engineers of Australia, Australian Inst. of Mining and Metallurgy. *Leisure interests:* farming, fishing, flying. *Address:* Nandillyan Heights, Molong, N.S.W. 2866, Australia. *Telephone:* (63) 668028. *Fax:* (63) 668028.

MASTER, Simon Harcourt; British publisher; b. 10 April 1944, Caterham; s. of Humphrey R. Master and Rachel B. Plumbly; m. Georgina M. C. Batsford 1969; two s.; ed. Ardingly Coll. Sussex; Publishing Dir. Pan Books Ltd. 1973–80, Man. Dir. 1980–87; Chief Exec. Random House U.K. and Exec. Vice-Pres. Random House Int. Group 1987–89, Group Man. Dir. Random Century Group 1989–90, Group Deputy Chair. 1989–, Chair., C.E.O. Gen. Books Div., Random House U.K. 1992–; Chair., Arrow Books 1990–92; Dir. (non-exec.) H.M.S.O. 1990–95; mem. Council Publrs. Asscn. 1989–95 (Vice-Pres. 1995–96, Pres. 1996–97). *Leisure interests:* gardening, golf, classic cars, scuba diving. *Address:* Random House, 20 Vauxhall Bridge Road, London, SW1V 2SA (Office); 13 Patten Road, London, SW18 3RH (Home); Brooklands, Ebbesbourne Wake, Nr. Salisbury, Wiltshire, England (Home). *Telephone:* 0181-874 2204 (Home, London).

MASTERKOVA, Svetlana Aleksandrovna; Russian track and field athlete; b. 1 Jan. 1968, Achinsk; m. Asyat Saitov; one d.; works with coaches Yakov Yelyanov and Svetlana Styrkina; 1996 Atlanta Olympic Games Champion (800m and 1500m), Silver Medal winner World Winter Championship 1993, Bronze Medal winner European Winter Championship 1996; twice World Record holder; Best Woman Athlete of the Year, Monte Carlo 1996; Merited Master of Sports; Best Woman Athlete of Russia 1996, 1997; Order For Service to Motherland; lives in France, Italy, Russia. *Address:* All-Russian Athletic Federation, Luzhnetskaya nab. 8, 119871 Moscow, Russia (Office). *Telephone:* (095) 201 0150 (Office).

MASTERSON, Patrick, PH.D., M.R.I.A.; Irish university professor; b. 19 Oct. 1936, Dublin; s. of Laurence Masterson and Violet Masterson; m. Frances Lenehan; one s. three d.; ed. Belvedere Coll., Castlenock Coll., Univ. Coll., Dublin, Univ. of Louvain; mem. staff Dept. of Metaphysics, Univ. Coll., Dublin 1963–72, Prof. Faculties of Arts, Philosophy and Sociology 1972–80, Dean of the Faculty of Philosophy and Sociology 1980–83, Registrar 1983–86, Pres. 1986–93; Pres. European Univ. Inst., Florence 1994–; Vice-Chancellor Nat. Univ. of Ireland 1987, 1988, 1993; Dr. h.c. (Caen), (Trinity Coll. Dublin). *Publications:* Atheism and Alienation: A Study of the Philosophical Sources of Contemporary Atheism 1971, Images of Man in Ancient and Medieval Thought: (Studia Gerardo Verbeke ab amicis et collegis dictata) 1976. *Leisure interests:* modern art, reading, theatre, fishing. *Address:* Office of the President, European University Institute, Badia Fiesolana, Via dei Roccettini 9, 50016 S. Domenico di Fiesole (FI), Italy. *Telephone:* (55) 4685310. *Fax:* (55) 4685312.

MASTERSON, Valerie, C.B.E., F.R.C.M.; British opera and concert singer; b. Birkenhead; d. of Edward Masterson and Rita McGrath; m. Andrew March; one s. one d.; Prof. of Singing, Royal Acad. of Music, London 1992–; Pres. British Youth Opera 1994–; has sung with D'Oyly Carte Opera, Glyndebourne, Royal Opera House, Covent Garden and English Nat. Opera, and on TV and radio; also in major opera houses abroad including Paris, Aix-en-Provence, Toulouse, Munich, Geneva, San Francisco and Chicago; title roles include La Traviata, Manon, Semele, Merry Widow, Louise, Lucia di Lammermoor, Mireille; other leading roles in Faust, Alcina, Die Entführung aus dem Serail, Nozze di Figaro, Così fan Tutte, La Bohème, Magic Flute, Julius Caesar, Rigoletto, Orlando, Der Rosenkavalier, Xerxes, Pearl Fishers, Die Fledermaus etc.; recordings include Julius Caesar, La Traviata, Elisabetta Regina d'Inghilterra, Bitter Sweet, Ring Cycle, recitals and various Gilbert and Sullivan discs; Hon. R.A.M. 1994. *Leisure interests:* tennis, swimming. *Address:* c/o Music International, 13 Ardilaun Road, London, N5 2QR, England.

MASUR, Kurt; German conductor; b. 18 July 1927, Silesia, Poland; ed. Hochschule für Musik, Leipzig; theatre conductor in Erfurt and Leipzig 1948–55, conductor, Dresden Philharmonic 1955–58, Chief Conductor 1967–72; Gen. Musical Dir., Mecklenburg State Theatre 1958–60; Prin. Musical Dir., Komische Oper in East Berlin 1960–64; Conductor, Leipzig Gewandhaus Orchestra 1970, Music Dir. 1996–; Music Dir. Conductor New York Philharmonic 1991–; Prin. Conductor London Philharmonic Orchestra 1991–; has toured extensively in Europe and the U.S.A.; début in U.S.A. with Cleveland Orchestra 1974; Freeman of City of Leipzig; Hon. Pres. Kulturstiftung, Leipzig; Hon. degrees from seven American univs. and Univ. of Leipzig; Officier, Légion d'honneur. *Address:* Leipzig Gewandhausorchester, Augustusplatz 8, 04109 Leipzig, Germany.

MASUREL, Jean-Louis Antoine Nicolas, M.B.A.; French industrialist; b. 18 Sept. 1940, Cannes; s. of Antoine and Anne-Marie (née Gallant) Masurel; m. 1st 1964; two d.; m. 2nd Martine Fabrega 1987; ed. Hautes Etudes Commerciales, Graduate School of Business Admin., Harvard Univ.; with Morgan Guaranty Trust Co., New York, last position Sr. Vice-Pres. New York 1964–80; Sr. Exec. Vice-Pres. Banque de Paris & des Pays Bas 1980–82; Deputy Pres. Banque Paribas Aug. 1982–83; Man. Dir. Moët-Hennessy 1983–89, Vice-Chair. 1987; Man. Dir. LVMH Moët-Hennessy Louis Vuitton 1987–89; Pres. Arcos Investissement SA 1989–, Hediard S.A. 1991–95; Hon. Pres. Harvard Business School Club de France 1993–; Dir. Peugeot S.A., Soc. des Bains de Mer (SBM), Monaco, Banco del Gottardo S.A.M., Monaco; Sr. Int. Adviser, BBL Investment Banking 1997–; Gov. American Hosp. in Paris. *Leisure interests:* hunting, skiing. *Address:* Arcos Investissement, 31 rue Raynouard, 75016 Paris, France. *Telephone:* (1) 42.30.86.41. *Fax:* (1) 42.15.16.30.

MATANE, Sir Paulias Nguna, Kt., C.M.G., O.B.E.; Papua New Guinea diplomatist; b. 21 Sept. 1931, Viviran, Rabaul; s. of Ilias and Elta (Toto) Matane; m. Kaludia Peril 1957; two s. two d.; senior positions in Dept. of Educ. 1957–69; mem. Public Service Bd. 1969; Head, Dept. of Lands, Surveys and Mines 1969, of Business Devt. 1970–75; Amb. to U.S.A. and Mexico 1975–80, Perm. Rep. to UN 1975–81, High Commr. in Canada 1977–81; Sec., Dept. of Foreign Affairs and Trade 1980–85; Chair. Cttee. on the Philosophy of Educ. for Papua New Guinea 1986–88, Cocoa Industry Investigating Cttee. of Cocoa Quality in Papua New Guinea 1986–88, Ocean Trading Co. Pty. Ltd. 1989–, Newton Pacific (PNG) Pty Ltd. 1989–; Censorship Bd. of PNG 1990–; Dir. Triad Pacific (PNG) Pty. Ltd. 1987– (Chair. 1987–91); mem. Nat. Investment and Devt. Authority, Nat. Tourism Authority, Nat. Citizenship Advisory Cttee., Univ. of Papua New Guinea Council; Hon. D.Tech. (Papua New Guinea) 1985; Hon. D.Phil. (Papua New Guinea) 1985; 10th Independence Anniversary Medal 1985, UN 40th Anniversary Medal. *Publications:* My Childhood in New Guinea, A New Guinean Travels through Africa, Two New Guineans Travel through South East Asia, What Good is Business?, Aimbe the Magician, Aimbe the Challenger, Aimbe the School Dropout, Aimbe the Pastor, Kum Tumun of Minj, Two Papua New Guineans Discover the Bible Lands (later retitled Travels Through the Bible Lands) 1987, To Serve with Love 1989, Chit-Chats 1991, East to West—The Longest Train Trip in the World 1991, Let's Do It PNG, Trekking through the New

Worlds, Voyage to Antarctica 1996, Laughter Made in PNG 1996, Amazing Discoveries in 40 Years of Marriage 1996, The Word Power 1998, The Other Side of Port Moresby . . . In Pictures 1998, A Trip of a Lifetime 1998, Waliling Community United Church Then and Now 1998, Coach Adventures Down Under 1999, Some Answers to our Management Problems in the Public and Private Sectors 1999, More Answers to Our Management Problems 1999. *Leisure interests:* reading, squash, writing, travel. *Address:* P.O. Box 680, Rabaul, ENBP, Papua New Guinea. *Telephone:* 9829152. *Fax:* 9829151.

MATANZIMA, Chief Kaiser; South African politician and lawyer; b. 1915, St. Mark's Dist.; s. of the late Mhlobo Matanzima; m. Nozuko Jayinja 1954; four s. five d.; ed. Lovedale Missionary Institution and Fort Hare Univ. Coll.; Chief, Amahale Clan of Tembus, St. Mark's District 1940; mem. United Transkeian Gen. Council 1942–56; Perm. Head Emigrant Tembuland Regional Authority and mem. Exec. Cttee. Transkeian Territorial Authority 1956–58; Regional Chief of Emigrant Tembuland 1958–61; Presiding Chief Transkeian Territorial Authority 1961–63; Chief Minister of Transkei 1963–76, Prime Minister 1976–79; Pres. Repub. of Transkei 1979–85; Leader, Transkei Nat. Party 1987–88; Chancellor, Univ. of Transkei 1977–88; Freeman of Umtata 1982; Hon. LL.D. (Fort Hare). *Publications:* Independence My Way 1977. *Address:* Qamata, Bizana District, Transkei, South Africa.

MATEŠA, Zlatko; Croatian politician; b. 7 June 1949, Zagreb; m.; two c.; ed. Zagreb Univ., Henley Man. College, U.K.; asst. judge, judge Zagreb Mun. Court 1978–; asst. man., Man. Legal Dept. INA-Trade (Industrija Nafte Asscn.) 1978–82, Dir. Legal and Personnel Dept. 1982–85, Dir. Joint Admin. Services 1985–89, mem. Man. Bd., Vice-Pres. 1989–90; asst. to Gen.-Man. INA-HQ 1990–92; mem. Croatian Democratic Union (HDZ); Dir. Agency for Reconstruction and Devt. of Govt. of Croatia 1992–93; Minister without Portfolio 1993–95; Minister of Econ. Sept.-Nov. 1995; Prime Minister of Croatia Nov. 1995–. *Address:* Office of the Prime Minister, Radićev trg 7, 41000 Zagreb, Croatia. *Telephone:* (041) 444 000 (Office). *Fax:* (041) 432 041.

MATHÉ, Georges, M.D.; French professor of medicine; b. 9 July 1922, Sermages; s. of Adrien and Francine (née Doridot) Mathé; m. Marie-Louise Servier 1954; one d.; ed. Lycée Banville, Moulins, and Univ. de Paris; Head of Clinic, Medical Faculty, Paris Univ. 1952–53, Assoc. Prof. of Cancer Research Fac. Medicine, Paris 1956–67; Head, Dept. of Haematology, Inst. Gustave-Roussy 1961; Tech. Counsellor, Ministry of Health 1964–66; Dir. Inst. de Cancérologie et d'Immunogénétique 1965; Prof. of Experimental Cancerology, Faculté de Médecine, Univ. de Paris-Sud, Villejuif 1966;Ed.-in-Chief Biomedicine and Pharmacotherapy; Co-ed. Medical Oncology & Tumor Pharmacotherapy; consultant Swiss Hospital of Paris 1991–, Hosp. of Oncology, Sofia; mem. Cen. Cttee. Rassemblement pour la Répub.; Prés. Comité Consultatif de la Recherche Scientifique et Tech. 1972–75, Medical Oncology Soc., Comité cancer, European Hospital of Rome; mem. Royal Soc. of Medicine, New York Acad. of Sciences; Médaille d'or des hôpitaux de Paris; Officier, Légion d'honneur; Ordre nat. du Mérite. *Publications:* Le métabolisme de l'eau (with J. Hamburger) 1952, La greffe (with J. L. Amiel) 1962, Aspects histologiques et cytologiques des leucémies et hématosarcomes (with G. Séman) 1963, L'aplasie myélolymphoide de l'irradiation totale (with J. L. Amiel) 1965, Sémiologie médicale (with G. Richet) 1965 (3rd edn. 1977), La chimiothérapie des cancers 1966 (3rd edn. 1974), Le cancer 1967, Bone Marrow Transplantation and White Cells Transfusions (with J. L. Amiel and L. Schwarzenberg) 1971, La santé: est-elle au dessus de nos moyens? (with Catherine Mathé) 1970, Natural History and Modern Treatment of Hodgkin's Disease (with M. Tubianan) 1973, Histocytological typing of the neoplastic diseases of the haematopoietic and lymphoid tissues (with H. Rappaport) 1973, Cancérologie générale et clinique (with A. Cattan) 1974, Le temps d'y penser 1974, Immunothérapie active des cancers: immunoprévention et immunorestauration 1976, Cancer Active Immunotherapy; Immunoporphylaxis and Immunorestoration: An Introduction 1976, Cancer Chemotherapy: Its Role in the Treatment Strategy of Hematologic Malignancies and Solid Tumors (with A. Clarysse and Y. Kenis) 1976, Dossier Cancer 1977, L'homme qui voulait être guéri 1985 (novel), Nagasaki (play), Le Sexe des Dieux et des Diables 1992 (play), Le Sida sidère la science, le sexe et les sceaux 1995. *Leisure interests:* novel writing, theatre. *Address:* ICI, 6 rue Minard, BP 60, 92133 Issy-les-Moulineaux; Hôpital Suisse de Paris, 10 rue Minard, 92130 Issy-les-Moulineaux; Le Fonbois, 10 Rue du Bon Puits, Arpajon, 91290 La Norville, France (Home). *Telephone:* 64.90.03.58 (Home).

MATHER, Graham Christopher Spencer, M.A.; British politician, solicitor and administrator; b. 23 Oct. 1954, Preston, Lancs.; s. of Thomas Mather and Doreen Mather; m. 1st Fiona Marion McMillan Bell 1981 (divorced 1995); two s.; m. 2nd Geneviève Elizabeth Fairhurst 1997; ed. Hutton Grammar School, New Coll., Oxford (Burnet Law Scholar); Asst. to Dir.-Gen. Inst. of Dirs. 1980, est. Policy Unit 1983, Head of Policy Unit 1983–86; Deputy Dir. Inst. of Econ. Affairs 1987, Gen. Dir. 1987–92; Pres. European Policy Forum 1992–; M.E.P. for Hampshire North and Oxford 1994–; Visiting Fellow, Nuffield Coll. Oxford 1992–; mem. Monopolies and Mergers Comm. 1989–94, Westminster City Council 1982–86; Conservative parl. cand. for Blackburn 1983; Vice-Pres. Strategic Planning Soc. 1993–, Asscn. of Dist. Councils 1994–97; mem. Public Policy Advisory Bd. Queen Mary and Westfield Coll. London 1993–; Consultant Tudor Investment Corpn., Primesquawk LLC; Patron Govt. Affairs Group, Inst. of Public Relations 1996–. *Publications:* Striking out Strikes (with C. G. Hanson) 1988; Europe's Constitutional Future (contrib.) 1990; papers and contribs. to journals. *Address:* 125 Pall Mall, London, SW1Y 5EA, England. *Telephone:* 0171-839 7557. *Fax:* 0171-839 7339.

MATHESON, Sir (James Adam) Louis, K.B.E., C.M.G., PH.D., F.T.S., F. ENG.; Australian university professor, engineer and administrator; b. 11 Feb. 1912, Huddersfield, Yorks., England; s. of William and Lily Edith Matheson; m. Audrey Elizabeth Wood 1937; three s.; ed. Bootham School, York and Manchester Univ.; Lecturer, Birmingham Univ. 1938–46; Prof. Civil Eng., Univ. of Melbourne 1946–50; Beyer Prof. of Eng., Manchester Univ. 1951–59; Vice-Chancellor, Monash Univ., Victoria, Australia 1959–76; mem. Mission on Tech. Educ. to the W. Indies 1957, Ramsay Cttee. on Devt. of Tertiary Educ. in Victoria 1961–63, Commonwealth Scientific and Industrial Research Org. Advisory Council 1962–67, Royal Comm. into Failure of Kings Bridge 1962–63; Trustee Inst. of Applied Science of Victoria, now Science Museum of Victoria 1964–83; mem. Council Inst. of Engineers, Australia 1965–81, Pres. 1975–76; mem. Council Inst. of Civil Engineers 1966–68; Vice-Pres. Inst. Structural Engineers 1967–68; mem. Interim Council Univ. of Papua New Guinea 1965–68; Chair. Papua New Guinea Inst. of Tech. Council 1966–73, now Papua New Guinea Univ. of Tech., Chancellor 1973–75; Chair. Australian Science and Tech. Council 1975–76, mem. 1977–78; Chair. Australian Vice-Chancellors Cttee. 1967–68, Asscn. of Commonwealth Univs. 1967–69, Buildings Cttee. Commonwealth Schools Comm. 1976–81, Newport Power Station Review 1977, Victorian Planning and Finance Cttee. Commonwealth Schools Comm. 1979–83, Sorrento Harbour Inquiry 1984, 1987, St. Kilda Harbour Inquiry 1986; mem. Enquiry Post-Secondary Educ., Victoria 1976–78; Nauru Phosphate Corpn. 1977–80; Fellow Australian Acad. of Tech. Sciences, Hon. Fellow Inst. Civil Engineers, Inst. of Engineers, Australia; Hon. D.Sc. (Hong Kong), Hon. LL.D. (Manchester, Melbourne and Monash Univs.); Kernot Medal 1970, Peter Nicol Russell Medal 1976. *Publications:* Hyperstatic Structures (2 vols.) 1959, Still Learning 1980, papers on technical and educational subjects. *Leisure interests:* music, woodcraft. *Address:* 26/166 West Toorak Road, South Yarra, Victoria 3141, Australia. *Telephone:* (03) 9866 4957.

MATHEWS, (Forrest) David, PH.D.; American educationalist; b. 6 Dec. 1935, Grove Hill, Ala.; s. of Forrest Lee and Doris Mathews; m. Mary Chapman 1960; two d.; ed. Univ. of Alabama and Columbia Univ.; Infantry Officer U.S. Army Reserves 1959–67; Pres. Univ. of Ala. 1969–80, Lecturer and Prof. of History 1969–80; Sec. of Health, Educ. and Welfare 1975–77; Chair. Nat. Council for Public Policy Educ. 1980–; Dir. Acad. Educ. Devt. 1975–; mem. numerous advisory bds., etc.; Trustee Nat. March of Dimes 1977–85, John F. Kennedy Center for Performing Arts 1975–77, Woodrow Wilson Int. Center for Scholars 1975–77, Miles Coll. 1978–, Teachers Coll., Columbia Univ. 1977–, Gerald R. Ford Foundation 1988–; Pres. and C.E.O. Charles F. Kettering Foundation 1981–; numerous awards and hon. degrees. *Publications:* works on history of Southern U.S.A., higher educ. in public policy, including The Changing Agenda for American Higher Education, The Promise of Democracy. *Leisure interest:* gardening. *Address:* Charles F. Kettering Foundation, 200 Commons Road, Dayton, OH 45429; 6050 Mad River Road, Dayton, OH 45459, U.S.A. *Telephone:* (513) 434-7300.

MATHIAS, Charles McC.; American politician and lawyer; b. 24 July 1922, Frederick, Md.; s. of Charles McC. Mathias, Sr., and Theresa Trail Mathias; m. Ann Hickling Bradford 1958; two s.; ed. public schools, Frederick, Md., Haverford Coll., Yale Univ. and Univ. of Maryland; apprentice seaman 1942, commissioned Ensign 1944, sea duty, Pacific 1944–46; Capt. U.S. Naval Reserve retd.; admitted to Maryland Bar 1949, to U.S. Supreme Court Bar 1954; Asst. Attorney-Gen. of Maryland 1953, 1954; City Attorney, Frederick, Md. 1954–59; mem. Md. House of Dels. 1958; mem. U.S. House of Reps. 1960–68; U.S. Senator from Maryland 1969–87; Milton S. Eisenhower Distinguished Professor in Public Policy, Johns Hopkins School for Advanced Int. Studies 1987–; Chair. Senate Rules and Admin. Cttee. 1981–87; Chair. of Bd. First American Bankshares 1993–; Légion d'honneur (France), Order of Orange-Nassau (Netherlands), Order of Merit (F.R.G.), Hon. K.B.E. (U.K.); Republican. *Address:* c/o Jones, Day, Reavis & Pogue, 1450 G. Street, N.W., Washington, D.C. 20005 (Office); 3808 Leland Street, Chevy Chase, MD 20815, U.S.A. (Home).

MATHIAS, Peter, C.B.E., M.A., D.LITT., LITT.D., F.B.A., F.R.HIST.S.; British professor of economic history; b. 10 Jan. 1928, Somerset; s. of John Samuel Mathias and Marian Helen Love; m. Elizabeth Ann Blackmore 1958; two s. one d.; ed. Colstons Hosp., Bristol, Jesus Coll. Cambridge and Harvard Univ., U.S.A.; Research Fellow, Jesus Coll. 1953–55; Lecturer, History Faculty, Cambridge Univ. 1955–68, Tutor and Dir. of Studies, Queens' Coll., Sr. Proctor, Cambridge Univ. 1965–66; Chichele Prof. of Econ. History, Oxford Univ. and Fellow of All Souls Coll. 1969–87; Master of Downing Coll., Cambridge 1987–95; Pres. Int. Econ. History Asscn. 1974–78, Hon. Pres. 1978–; Pres. Business Archive Council 1984–95, Vice-Pres. 1995–; Chair. British Library Advisory Council 1994–; Vice-Pres. Royal Historical Soc. 1975–80, Int. Inst. of Econ. History Francesco Datini Prato 1987–; Hon. Treas. British Acad. 1979–88, Econ. History Soc. 1967–88 (Pres. 1989–92, Vice-Pres. 1992–); mem. Advisory Bd. of the Research Councils 1983–88; Chair. History of Medicine Panel, Wellcome Trust 1980–88; Syndic Fitzwilliam Museum 1987–98; Chair. Fitzwilliam Museum Enterprises Ltd. 1990–, Friends of Kettle's Yard 1989–95, Bd. of Continuing Educ., Cambridge Univ. 1991–95; Curator Bodleian Library, Oxford 1972–87; mem. Academia Europaea, Beirat Wissenschaftskolleg, Berlin 1992–98; Foreign mem. Royal Danish Acad., Royal Belgian Acad.; Trustee GB-Sasakawa Foundation

1994–, Chair. 1997–; Hon. Litt.D. (Buckingham, Birmingham, Hull, Warwick, de Montfort). *Publications:* Brewing Industry in England 1700–1830 1959, Retailing Revolution 1967, Tradesmen's Tokens 1962, The First Industrial Nation 1969, 1983, The Transformation of England 1979, L'economia britannica dal 1815 al 1914 1994; Gen. Ed. Cambridge Economic History of Europe 1968–90. *Leisure interests:* travel, New Hall porcelain. *Address:* Bassingbourn Mill, Bassingbourn, Royston, Herts., SG8 5PP, England. *Telephone:* (01223) 334800.

MATHIESEN, Matthias (Árnason), CAND. JURIS; Icelandic politician and lawyer; b. 6 Aug. 1931, Hafnarfjörður; s. of Árni M. and Svava E. Mathiesen; m. Sigrún Thorgilsdóttir 1956; two s. one d.; ed. Univ. of Iceland; Chief Exec. Hafnarfjörður Savings Bank 1958–67, Chair. 1967; Advocate, Supreme Court 1967–74; mem. Althing (Parl.) 1959–, Speaker Lower Chamber 1970–71; Rep. of Althing to Nordic Council 1965–74, mem. Presidium 1970–71, 1973–74, Pres. 1970–71, 1980–81; Del. North Atlantic Ass., NATO 1963–69, 1972, Chair. Icelandic Del. 1964–67, Pres. of Ass. 1967–68; mem. Bd. E. Thorgilsson & Co. Ltd, Hafnarfjörður 1973–, Chair. 1982–; Dir. Nat. Bank of Iceland 1961–74, 1980–83; Icelandic mem. of Bd. of Govs. World Bank Group (IBRD, IDA, IFC) 1983–85; Minister of Finance 1974–78, Minister of Commerce (including Banking), and of Nordic Co-operation 1983–85, for Foreign Affairs 1985–87, of Communications 1987–88; mem. Cen. Cttee., Independence Party 1965–. *Address:* Hringbraut 59, Hafnarfjörður, Iceland (Home). *Telephone:* (91) 5-02-76 (Home).

MATHIEU, Georges Victor Adolphe, L. ÈS L.; French artist; b. 27 Jan. 1921, Boulogne; s. of Adolphe Mathieu d'Escaudoeuvres and Madeleine Dupré d'Ausque; ed. Facultés de droit et des lettres, Lille; Teacher of English; Public Relations Man., United States Lines; exhibited at Paris 1950, New York 1952, Japan 1957, Scandinavia 1958, England, Spain, Italy, Switzerland, Germany, Austria and South America 1959, Middle East 1961–62, Canada 1963; special exhbn. of work held at Musée Municipal d'Art Moderne, Paris 1963; exhbn. of 100 paintings, Galerie Charpentier, Paris 1965; designed gardens and buildings for B.C. transformer factory, Fontenay-le-comte 1966; 16 posters for Air France exhibited at Musée Nat. d'Art Moderne, Paris 1967; exhbn. of 10 tapestries at Musée de la Manufacture Nat. des Gobelins 1969; designed 18 medals for Paris Mint 1971, new 10F coin 1974; works exhibited in numerous countries including shows in Antibes 1976, Ostend 1977, Grand Palais, Paris 1978, Wildenstein Gallery, New York, Dominion Gallery, Montreal 1979, Musée de la Poste, Paris 1980, Galerie Kasper, Morges, Switzerland 1983, Théâtre municipal de Brives 1984; retrospective show, Palais des Papes, Avignon 1985; Galerie Calvin, Geneva 1985, Wally Findlay Galleries 1986, Galerie Schindler, Berne 1986, Galerie du Luxembourg 1986, Galerie Protée, Paris, Stockholm 1990, Boulogne sur Mer 1992, Museum of Modern Art, Toulouse 1995; creator of "Tachism"; mem. Acad. of Fine Arts; Officier, Légion d'honneur, des Arts et des Lettres; Ordre de la Couronne de Belgique. *Principal works:* Hommage à la Mort 1950, Hommage au Maréchal de Turenne 1952, Les Capétiens Partout 1954, La Victoire de Denain 1963, Hommage à Jean Cocteau 1963, Paris, Capitale des Arts 1965, Hommages aux Frères Boisserée 1967, Hommage à Condillac 1968, La prise de Berg op Zoom 1969, Election de Charles Quint 1971, Matta-Salums 1978, La Libération de Paris 1980, La libération d'Orléans par Jeanne d'Arc 1982, Monumental sculpture in Neuilly 1982, in Chareton 1982, Ceiling-painting in Boulogne-Billancourt town hall 1983, Massacre des 269 1985, le Paradis des orages 1988, l'Immortalité ruinée 1989, La Complainte silencieuse des enfants de Bogota 1989, Rumeur de paradis 1991. *Publications:* Au-delà du Tachisme, Le privilège d'Etre, De la Révolte à la Renaissance, La Réponse de l'Abstraction lyrique, L'abstraction prophétique, Le massacre de la sensibilité 1996, Désormais seul en face de Dieu 1998. *Address:* Institut de France, 23 quai Conti, 75006 Paris (Office); 125 Avenue de Malakoff, 75116 Paris, France.

MATHIS, Edith; Swiss soprano; b. 11 Feb. 1938, Lucerne; ed. Lucerne Conservatoire; début Lucerne 1956; sang with Cologne Opera 1959–62; appeared Salzburg Festival 1960, Deutsche Oper, W. Berlin 1963; début Glyndebourne (Cherubino in Nozze di Figaro) 1962, Covent Garden (Susanna in Nozze di Figaro) 1970, Metropolitan Opera House, New York (Pamina in The Magic Flute) 1970; mem. Hamburg State Opera 1960–75. *Address:* c/o Bueker-Management, Postfach 1169, 3000 Hannover, Germany; c/o Ingpen & Williams Ltd., 14 Kensington Court, London, W8 5DN, England. *Telephone:* 0171-937 5158 (London).

MATHIS-EDDY, Darlene, PH.D.; American poet and professor of English; b. 19 March 1937, Elkhart, Ind.; d. of the late William Eugene Mathis and Fern Roose Paulmer Mathis; m. Spencer Livingston Eddy, Jr. 1964 (died 1971); ed. Goshen Coll. and Rutgers Univ.; Instructor in English, Douglass Coll. 1962–64; Instructor in English, Rutgers Univ. 1964, 1965, Rutgers Univ. Coll. (Adult Educ.) 1967; Asst. Prof. in English, Ball State Univ. 1967–71, Assoc. Prof. 1971–75, Prof. 1975–, Poet-in-Residence 1989–93; Consulting Ed. Blue Unicorn 1995–; Founding Ed. The Hedge Row Press 1995–; mem. Comm. on Women for the Nat. Council of Teachers of English 1976–79; Poetry Ed. BSU Forum; Woodrow Wilson Nat. Fellow 1959–62, Notable Woodrow Nat. Fellow 1991, and numerous other fellowships. *Publications:* Leaf Threads, Wind Rhymes 1986, The Worlds of King Lear 1971, Weathering 1992; Contributing Ed. Snowy Egret 1988–90; numerous poems in literary reviews; articles in American Literature, English Language Notes, etc. *Leisure interests:* gardening, music, antiques, reading, sketching, photography, bird watching, cooking. *Address:* Department of English, Robert Bell Building, Office No. 248, Ball State University, Muncie, IN 47306; 1409 West Cardinal Street, Muncie, IN 47303, U.S.A. (Home).

MATHUR, Murari Lal, PH.D.; Indian professor of mechanical engineering; b. 10 July 1931, Masuda; s. of late Dr. S. D. Mathur and Lalti Devi; m. Vimla Mathur 1961; one s. three d.; ed. Govt. Coll., Ajmer, Birla Engineering Coll., Pilani, Glasgow Univ., U.K.; Asst. Prof., M.B.M. Eng. Coll., Govt. of Rajasthan 1952–57; Deputy Dir. of Tech. Educ. and Sec. Bd. of Tech. Educ., Govt. of Rajasthan 1957–58; Prof. and Head Mechanical Eng. Dept., Univ. of Jodhpur 1963–85, Prof., Dean Faculty of Eng. 1966–68, 1974, 1977–80, Vice-Chancellor 1985–90; Prof. Emer. 1991–; Chair. Automotive Prime-Movers Sectional Cttee., Indian Bureau of Standards; Co-ordinator "Solar Passive House Project; design consultant heat exchanger and heat recovery equipment; has produced two educational films; Sri Chandra Prakash Memorial Award, Pres. of India's Prize. *Publications:* books on thermal eng., internal combustion engines, gas turbines and jet propulsion, thermodynamics, fluid mechanics and machines, machine drawing and heat transfer; 75 research papers. *Leisure interests:* reading, writing, lecturing on educational topics and topics concerning energy and environment. *Address:* Alok Villa, 17-A, Shastri Nagar, Jodhpur 342 003, Rajasthan, India (Home). *Telephone:* 433207 (Home).

MATIBA, Kenneth; Kenyan politician; Chair. Kenya Breweries 1968–79; founder, Kenya Football League; fmr. Chair. Kenya Football Fed.; entered Parl. 1979; resigned from Govt. over election-rigging 1988; imprisoned for 10 months for leading multi-party democracy movt. July 1990; Chair. FORD-Asili Party; contested presidential election Dec. 1992. *Leisure interest:* mountain climbing. *Address:* Ford-Asili Party, Nairobi, Kenya.

MATIN, Abdul, M.A., PH.D.; Pakistani politician and economist; b. 1 March 1932, Sawabi; s. of Dur Jamil Khan; m. Azra Matin 1959; three s.; ed. Univs. of Peshawar and Bonn; Chair. Dept. of Econs., Univ. of Peshawar and Dir. Bd. of Econs., North-West Frontier Prov. (N.W.F.P.) 1959–70; Chief Economist, Govt. of N.W.F.P. 1970–72; Minister and Deputy Perm. Rep., Pakistan Mission at UN, New York 1973–76; Exec. Dir. ADBP, Islamabad 1977–85; Vice-Chancellor, Univ. of Peshawar 1987–89; Vice-Pres. and mem. of Cen. Cttee., Pakistan Tehrik-e-Insaf (PTI) 1996–; mem. Nat. Comm. on Manpower, Govt. of Pakistan; mem. Educ. Inquiry Cttee. N.W.F.P.; Chair. Govt. Working Group on Transport Policy 1991–92, Universities Services Reforms and Man. Cttee., Govt. of N.W.F.P. 1998; engaged in research project: "Revival and Reconstruction of Muslim World"; Hamdard Foundation Award for Outstanding Services 1992. *Publications:* Industrialization of N.W.F.P. 1970; 80 articles on the problems, policies and pattern of econ. devt. in professional journals. *Leisure interests:* extension lectures, public speeches. *Address:* House No. 27, Street No. 9, Sector D-3, Phase I, Hayat-ABAD, Peshawar, N.W.F.P., Pakistan. *Telephone:* 817144.

MATIN, M. A., F.R.C.S.; Bangladeshi politician; b. 1 Dec. 1937, Pabna; ed. Dhaka Medical Coll.; worked in Royal Eye Hosp. and King's Coll. Hosp., London 1964–67; Assoc. Prof. of Ophthalmology, Inst. of Postgraduate Medicine and Research, Dhaka 1967–72, Prof., then Head of Dept. 1972–; Hon. Col. and Consultant Ophthalmologist, Combined Mil. Hosp., Dhaka 1976; M.P. 1979–; Minister of Civil Aviation and Tourism 1979, Minister of Youth Devt. and of Health and Population Control 1981, Minister of Home Affairs 1981–82, Minister of Commerce 1984, Minister of Works 1985, Deputy Prime Minister in charge of Ministry of Home Affairs 1986–88; Deputy Prime Minister 1988–89; Minister of Health and Family Planning 1988, 1989, of Home Affairs 1988–89; fmr. Sec.-Gen. and Pres. Bangladesh Ophthalmological Soc. and Pres. Bangladesh Medical Services Asscn.; Vice-Chair. Bangladesh Medical Research Council and Vice-Pres. Bangladesh Coll. of Physicians and Surgeons; Alim Memorial Gold Medal; Int. Award, Asian Pacific Acad. of Ophthalmology 1981. *Address:* c/o Ministry of Health and Family Planning, 3rd Floor, Bangladesh Secretariat, Dhaka, Bangladesh.

MATLOCK, Jack Foust Jr., M.A.; American diplomatist; b. 1 Oct. 1929, Greensboro; s. of Jack Foust Matlock and Nellie McSwain; m. Rebecca Burrum 1949; four s. one d.; ed. Duke and Columbia Univs. and Russian Inst.; Instructor, Dartmouth 1953–56; joined foreign service, State Dept. 1956, Official in Washington 1956–58, Embassy Official, Vienna 1958–60, Consul Gen., Munich 1960–61, Embassy Official, Moscow 1961–63, Accra, Ghana 1963–66, Zanzibar 1967–69, Dar es Salaam 1969–70, Country Dir. for U.S.S.R., State Dept. 1971–74, Deputy Chief of Mission, Embassy in Moscow 1974–78, Diplomat-in-Residence, Vanderbilt Univ. 1978–79, Deputy Dir., Foreign Service Inst., Washington 1979–80, Amb. to Czechoslovakia 1981–83, to U.S.S.R., 1987–91; Special Asst. to Pres. and Sr. Dir. European and Soviet Affairs, Nat. Security Council 1983–87; Sr. Research Fellow Columbia Univ. 1991–93, Kathryn and Shelby Collum Davis Prof. 1993–96; Kennan Prof., Inst. for Advanced Study, Princeton, N.J. 1996–; mem. American Acad. of Diplomacy, Council on Foreign Relations, American Philosophical Soc. *Publications:* Ed. Index to J.V. Stalin's Works 1971, Autopsy on an Empire: The American Ambassador's Account of the Collapse of the Soviet Union 1995. *Address:* Institute for Advanced Study, Olden Lane, Princeton, NJ 08540 (Office); 2913 P Street, N.W., Washington, D.C. 20007; 63 Battle Road, Princeton, N.J. 08540, U.S.A. *Telephone:* (609) 734-8328. *Fax:* (609) 924-8399.

MATOKA, Peter Wilfred, PH.D.; Zambian politician, international civil servant and diplomatist; b. 8 April 1930, Mwinilunga, N.W. Prov.; m. Grace J. Mukahlera 1957; two s. one d.; ed. Univ. of Rhodes, S. Africa, American

Univ., Washington, DC, Univ. of Zambia, Univ. of Warwick, England; civil servant, N. Rhodesia Govt. 1954–64; mem. of Parl. of Zambia 1964–78; Minister of Information and Postal Services 1964–65, of Health 1965–66, of Works and Housing 1967, of Power, Transport and Works 1968; mem. Cen. Cttee., United Nat. Independence Party (UNIP) 1967, 1971–78; Minister for Luapula Prov. 1969; High Commr. of Zambia in U.K. 1969–70, concurrently accredited to the Vatican; Minister for the S. Prov. 1970, of Health 1971–72, of Local Govt. and Housing 1972–77, of Devt. Planning 1977, of Econ. and Tech. Co-operation 1977–78; Chief Whip, Nat. Ass. 1973–78; Sr. Regional Adviser UN Econ. Comm. for Africa, Addis Ababa 1979–83; Zambian High Commr. in Zimbabwe 1984–88; Chair. Social and Cultural Sub-Cttee. of Cen. Cttee. of UNIP 1988–90, of Science and Tech. Sub-Cttee. 1990–91; Sr. Lecturer, Social Devt. Studies Dept., Univ. of Zambia 1995–; Chair. WHO Africa Region 1966; Pres. Africa, Caribbean and Pacific Group of States 1977; Chair. Nat. Inst. of Scientific Research 1977; Chair. Zambia-Kenya and Zambia-Yugoslavia Perm. Comms. 1977; Chair. Lusaka MULPOC 1977; Chair. and Man. Dir. FilZam Projects and Investments Services Centre Ltd. 1992–; Vice-Chair. Nat. Tender Bd. 1977; Life mem. CPA; Kt. of St. Gregory (Vatican) 1964; Kt., Egypt and Ethiopia. *Leisure interests:* gardening, television, walking. *Address:* Ibex Hill, P.O. Box 50101, Lusaka, Zambia (Home). *Telephone:* (1) 260221 (Home).

MATOMÄKI, Tauno, M.SC.(ENG.); Finnish business executive; b. 14 April 1937, Nakkila; s. of Niilo Matomäki and Martta Matomäki; m. Leena (née Nilsson) Matomäki 1963; one s. three d.; ed. Tech. Univ., Helsinki; joined Rauma-Repola 1967, various positions, Pres. and C.E.O. 1987–, Pres. and C.E.O. Repola Ltd. 1991–; Chair. Bd. of Dirs. Rauma Ltd., United Paper Mills Ltd., Pohjolan Voima Ltd., Finnyards Ltd., Confed. of Finnish Industries, Finnish Employers' Confed.; mem. Bd. of Dirs. Effjohn AB; mem. Supervisory Bd. Teollisuuden Voima Oy (Chair.), Kansallis-Osake-Pankki, Pohjola Insurance Co., Ilmarinen Pension Insurance Co., Polar Rakennusosakeyhtiö, Uusi Suomi Oy; Kt., Order of the White Rose of Finland (First Class).

MATORIN, Vladimir Anatolievich; Russian singer (basso); b. 2 May 1948, Moscow; s. of Anatoly Ivanovich Matorin and Maria Tarasovna Matorina; m. Svetlana Sergeyevna Matorina; one s.; ed. Gnessin Pedagogical Inst. (now Acad.) of Music; soloist Moscow Stanislavky and Nemirovich-Danchenko Music Theatre 1974–92, Bolshoi Theatre 1991–; winner All-Union Glinka Competition of vocalists and Int. Competition of singers in Geneva, leading solo parts include Boris Godunov, Ivan Sysanin, King Rene (Iolanthe), Gremin (Eugene Onegin), Dosifei (Khovanshchina), Count Galitsky (Prince Igor), Don Basillo (Barber of Seville), Count (Tale about Invisible Town of Kitezh) and others; numerous int. tours; Merited Artist of Russia, People's Artist of Russia. *Leisure interests:* poetry, sacred music, travelling by car. *Address:* Bolshoi Theatre of Russia, Teatralnaya pl. 1, 103009 Moscow; Ulansky per. 21, korp. 1 Apt. 53, 103045 Moscow, Russia (Home). *Telephone:* (095) 292-38-86 (Bolshoi Opera), 292-06-58 (Manager, Opera); (095) 280-4417 (Home).

MATSEPE-CASABURRI, Ivy F., PH.D.; South African civil servant; d. of late Dorrington Matsepe and Violet Matsepe; m. (divorced); ed. Rutgers Univ., N.J. and Fort Hare Univ.; Academic Registrar and Sr. lecturer, UN Inst. for Namibia, Lusaka, Zambia 1985–90; Exec. Dir. Educ. Devt. Trust 1990–93; Chair. S.A.B.C. 1993; Pres. Asscn. of African Women for Research and Devt. 1988–. *Publications:* articles in African Journal of Political Economy. *Leisure interests:* music, reading, sports. *Address:* P.O. Box 91123, Auckland Park 2006, South Africa. *Telephone:* 011-714 3900/1/2. *Fax:* 011-714 3569.

MATSUMOTO, Ken, M.A.; Japanese business executive; b. 2 Feb. 1935, Shanghai, China; s. of Shigeharu and Hanako Matsumoto; m. Junko Masuda 1969; one s.; ed. Gakushuin High School, Swarthmore Coll., U.S.A., Univ. of Tokyo; mem. Bd. of Dirs., Auburn Steel Co. Inc., Auburn, N.Y. 1973–77; Sr. Man. Export Dept.-I, Nippon Steel Corpn. 1977–84; Dir. Research Div., The Fair Trade Center 1984–90, Man. Dir. 1990–; awarded Bancroft Scholarship. *Leisure interests:* tennis, skiing. *Address:* 5-11-38, Miyazaki, Miyamae-ku, Kawasaki-shi, Kanagawa-ken, 216 Japan. *Telephone:* 044-854-0693.

MATSUSHITA, Masaharu, B.IUR.; Japanese businessman; b. 17 Sept. 1912, Tokyo; s. of Eiji Matsushita and Shizuko Hirata; m. Sachiko Matsushita; two s. one d.; ed. Tokyo Imperial Univ.; Mitsui Bank 1935–40; Matsushita Electric Industrial Co. Ltd. 1940–, Auditor 1944–47, Dir., mem. Bd., 1947–49, Exec. Vice-Pres. 1949–61, Pres. 1961–77, Chair. Bd. 1977–; Dir. Matsushita Electronics Corpn. 1952–72, 1985–, Chair. 1972–85; Auditor, Matsushita Real Estate Co. Ltd. 1952–68, Dir. 1968–; Dir. Matsushita Communication Industrial Co. Ltd. 1958–70, Chair. 1970–86; Dir. Matsushita Seiko Co. Ltd. 1956–87, Kyushu Matsushita Electric Co. Ltd. 1955–87, Matsushita Reiki Co. Ltd. (formerly Nakagawa Electric Inc.) 1961–87, Matsushita Electric Corpn. of America 1959–74 (Chair. 1974–); Pres. Electronics Industries Asscn. of Japan 1968–70; Rep. Dir., Kansai Cttee. for Econ. Devt. 1962–, Dir. 1975–; mem. Standing Cttee., Osaka Chamber of Commerce 1966–; Standing Dir., Kansai Econ. Fed. 1970–, Vice-Pres. 1977–; Blue Ribbon Medal 1972; Commdr. of Order of Orange-Nassau (Netherlands) 1975. *Address:* Matsushita Electric Industrial Co. Ltd., 1006 Kadoma, Osaka 571, Japan.

MATSUSHITA, Yasuo; Japanese banker; Vice-Chair. Tokyo Chamber of Commerce –1994; Adviser Sakura Bank Ltd. 1994; Gov. Bank of Japan 1994–98. *Address:* c/o Bank of Japan, 2-1-1, Nihonbashi-Hongokucho, Chuo-ku, Tokyo 100-8630, Japan.

MATSUYAMA, Akira, B.ENG.; Japanese business executive; b. 24 Jan. 1912, Nagasaki Pref.; m.; one s. two d.; ed. Tokyo Univ.; Dir. East Japan Oil Devt. Co. Ltd. 1972–, Cen. Kagaku K.K. 1974–, Arctic Oil Co. Ltd. 1981–; Chair. Tonen Petrochemical Co. Ltd. 1975–, Nippon Unicar Co. Ltd. 1980–; Pres. Toa Nenryo Kogyo K.K. 1976–86, Chair. 1986, Tonen Tanker K.K. 1978–. *Leisure interest:* golf.

MATSUYAMA, Yoshinori, LL.D.; Japanese professor of psychology; b. 5 Dec. 1923, Kyoto; m. Michiko Kinugasa 1949; one s. two d.; ed. Doshisha and Osaka Univs.; Prof. of Psychology, Doshisha Univ. 1959–93, Pres. 1973–79, 1980–83, Chancellor 1985– (Chair. Bd. of Trustees 1985–93); Hon. LL.D. (Wesleyan Univ., Conn. and Amherst Coll., Mass.). *Publications:* A Study on Behaviour Disorders 1957, A Study on Anxiety 1961, Psychology of Motivation 1967, Human Motivation 1981. *Address:* 90 Matsubaracho Ichijoji Sakyoku, Kyoto 606, Japan. *Telephone:* (075) 701-8625.

MATSUZAWA, Takuji; Japanese banker; b. 17 July 1913, Tokyo; s. of Takanori and Tameko Matsuzawa; m. Toshiko Yoshioka 1942; one s. one d.; ed. Tokyo Imperial Univ.; joined The Yasuda Bank Ltd. 1938 (name changed to The Fuji Bank Ltd. 1948), Chief Man. Planning and Co-ordination Div. 1959–61, Dir. and Chief Man. Planning and Co-ordination Div. 1961–63, Man. Dir. 1963–71, Deputy Pres. 1971–75, Chair. of Bd. 1975–91, Pres. The Fuji Bank Ltd. 1975–81, Chair. 1981–87; Chair. of Research and Policy Cttee., Japan Cttee. for Econ. Devt. (Keizai Doyukai) 1973–75; Exec. mem. Bd. Japan Fed. of Econ. Orgs. (Keidanren) 1975–, Chair. Cttee. on Fiscal and Monetary Policies 1980–86; mem. Japanese Govt. Econ. Council Cttee. 1977–; Pres. Fed. of Bankers Asscns. 1978–79; Chair. Inquiry and Audit Bd. Japanese Nat. Railways 1983–, Cttee. on Admin. Reform 1986–, Cttee. on Int. Coordination of Econ. Policies 1986–; Vice-Chair. Japan Federation of Econ. Orgs. 1986–; Order of Sacred Treasure (First Class) 1983. *Leisure interests:* playing golf, reading, theatre-going. *Address:* 8-7, 2-chome Shoto, Shibuya-ku, Tokyo, Japan (Home).

MATTHAU, Walter; American actor; b. 1 Oct. 1920, New York; s. of Milton and Rose Matthau; m. Carol Marcus 1959; two s. one d.; ed. New York; New York Drama Critics Award 1951, 1958; Antoinette Perry Award 1961, 1964; Acad. Award for The Fortune Cookie; British Soc. of Film and TV Arts Award for Pete 'n' Tillie and Charley Varrick. *Stage appearances in:* Anne of a Thousand Days 1948, The Liar 1949, Season in the Sun 1950, Fancy Meeting You Again 1951, Twilight Walk 1951, One Bright Day 1951, In Any Language 1952, The Grey-Eyed People 1952, The Ladies of the Corridor 1953, Will Success Spoil Rock Hunter 1955, Once More with Feeling 1958, Once There Was a Russian 1960, A Shot in the Dark 1961, My Mother, My Father and Me 1963, The Odd Couple 1964. *Films include:* The Kentuckian 1955, Bigger than Life 1956, A Face in the Crowd 1957, Slaughter on Tenth Avenue 1957, Ride a Crooked Trail 1958, Lonely are the Brave 1962, Charade 1963, Fail Safe 1964, Mirage 1965, The Fortune Cookie (British title Meet Whiplash Willie) 1966, A Guide for the Married Man 1967, The Odd Couple 1968, The Secret Life of an American Wife 1968, Candy 1968, Hello Dolly 1969, Cactus Flower 1969, A New Leaf 1971, Plaza Suite 1971, Kotch 1971, Pete 'n' Tillie 1972, Charley Varrick 1973, The Laughing Policeman 1973, Earthquake 1974, The Taking of Pelham One Two Three 1974, The Front Page 1975, The Sunshine Boys 1975, The Bad News Bears 1976, Casey's Shadow 1978, House Calls 1978, California Suite 1979, Hopscotch 1980, Little Miss Marker 1980, First Monday in October 1980, Buddy Buddy 1981, I Ought to be in Pictures 1981, Movers and Shakers 1984, Pirates 1986, The Couch Trip 1987, JFK 1991, Dennis The Menace 1993, Grumpy Old Men 1993, Incident in a Small Town 1995, I.Q. 1995, The Grass Harp 1995, I'm Not Rappaport 1996, Grumpier Old Men, Out to Sea 1997. *Address:* c/o The Matthau Co., 1999 Avenue of the Stars, Suite 1200, Los Angeles, CA 90067, U.S.A.

MATTHÄUS-MAIER, Ingrid; German politician; b. 9 Sept. 1945, Werlte; d. of Heinz-Günther Matthäus and Helmtraud (née Hagen) Matthäus; m. Robert Maier 1974; one s. one d.; ed. law studies in Giessen and Münster; Academic Asst. Higher Admin. Court, later Judge, Admin. Court, Münster; mem. Bundestag (Free Democratic Party) 1976–82, Chair. Finance Cttee. 1979–82; mem. Bundestag (Social Democratic Party) 1983–; Deputy Chair. and Financial Policy Spokeswoman of SPD Parl. Group 1988–; mem. Mediation Cttee. *Address:* 53113 Bonn, Bundeshaus (Office); Am Paddenofen 4, 53757 Sankt Augustin, Germany (Home). *Telephone:* 0228/1685097 (Office).

MATTHES, Ulrich; German actor; b. 9 May 1959, Berlin; s. of Günter Matthes and Else Matthes; with Düsseldorfer Schauspielhaus 1986–87, Bayerisches Staatstheater, Munich 1987–89, Kammerspiele, Munich 1989–92, Schaubühne, Berlin 1992–; Förderpreis, Kunstpreis Berlin 1991, O.E. Hasse-Preis 1992. *Address:* Kuno-Fischer-str. 14, 14057 Berlin, Germany.

MATTHEW, (Henry) Colin Gray, D.PHIL., F.B.A.; British historian; b. 15 Jan. 1941, Inverness, Scotland; s. of Henry Johnson Scott and Joyce Mary Matthew; m. Sue Ann Curry 1966; two s. one d.; ed. Edinburgh Acad., Sedbergh School, Oxford Univ., Univ. of East Africa; Educ. Officer, Tanzania Civil Service 1963–66; Ed. The Gladstone Diaries 1972–94; Student, Christ Church, Oxford 1976–78; Fellow and Tutor, St. Hugh's Coll. Oxford 1978–; Prof. of Modern History, Oxford Univ. 1992–; Ed. The New Dictionary of

Nat. Biography 1992–; Literary Dir. Royal Historical Soc. 1985–89; mem. Council British Acad. 1997– (Vice-Pres. 1998–), Royal Comm. on Historical Manuscripts 1998–; Trustee Nat. Portrait Gallery 1998–; Wolfson Prize for History 1995. *Publications:* The Liberal Imperialists 1973, The Gladstone Diaries, vols 3–14 1974–94, Gladstone 1809–74 1986, Gladstone 1875–1898 1995; articles in books and learned journals. *Leisure interests:* fishing, book-buying. *Address:* St. Hugh's College, Oxford, OX2 6RE, England. *Telephone:* (01865) 267808.

MATTHEWS, Sir Peter Alec, Kt., A.O., C.B.I.M.; British business executive; b. 21 Sept. 1922, Duncan, Vancouver Island, B.C., Canada; s. of Major Alec B. Matthews and Elsie Lazarus Barlow; m. Sheila D. Bunting 1946; four s. one d., ed. Shawnigan Lake School, Vancouver Island, and Oundle School; army service 1940–46; joined Stewarts and Lloyds Ltd. 1946, Dir. of Research and Tech. Devt. 1962–68, mem. Research and Devt., British Steel Corpn. 1968–70; Man. Dir. Vickers PLC 1970–79, Chair. 1980–84; Dir. British Aircraft Corpn. (Holdings) 1971–77; Vice-Pres. Eng. Employers' Fed. 1971–82, Pres. 1982–84; Council mem. CBI 1971–77; Deputy Chair. British Steel Corpn. 1973–76; mem. British Overseas Trade Bd. 1973–77; mem. Export Credits Advisory Council 1973–77; Dir. Lloyds Bank PLC 1974–91, Chair. Cen. London Regional Bd. 1978–91; mem. Nat. Research Devt. Corpn. 1974–80; Dir. British Electric Traction Co. PLC 1976–87; mem. Advisory Council on Applied Research and Devt. 1977–80; Dir. Pegler-Hattersley PLC 1977–87 (Chair. 1979–86); Dir. Lloyds Bank U.K. Man. 1979–85, Lloyds and Scottish 1983–86, Sun Alliance and London Insurance PLC 1979–89, Lead Industries Group (renamed Cookson Group 1982) 1980–90, Hamilton Oil G.B., PLC 1981–90; Pres. Sino-British Trade Council 1983–86; Chair. Univ. Coll. London Council 1980–89; Chair. Export Credits Guarantee Dept. Review Cttee. 1983; Hon. Fellow Univ. Coll. London 1982. *Leisure interests:* sailing, gardening. *Address:* Chalkwell, Nether Wallop, Stockbridge, Hants., SO20 8HE, England. *Telephone:* (01264) 782136.

MATTHEWS, Peter Bryan Conrad, M.D., D.SC., F.R.S.; British professor of physiology; b. 23 Dec. 1928, Cambridge; s. of the late Sir Bryan Matthews; m. Margaret Rosemary Blears 1956; one s. one d.; ed. Marlborough Coll., King's Coll. Cambridge and Oxford Univ. Clinical School; Lecturer in Physiology Univ. of Oxford 1961–77, Reader 1978–87, Prof. of Sensorimotor Physiology 1987–96, Emer. Prof. 1996–; Tutor of Christ Church, Univ. of Oxford 1958–87, Student 1958–96; Sir Lionel Whitby Medal, Cambridge Univ. 1959; Robert Bing Prize, Swiss Acad. of Medical Science 1971. *Publications:* Mammalian Muscle Receptors and their Central Actions 1972 and papers on neurophysiology in various scientific journals. *Address:* University Laboratory of Physiology, Parks Road, Oxford, OX1 3PT, England. *Telephone:* (01865) 272500.

MATTHEWS, Peter Hugoe, LITT.D., F.B.A.; British academic; b. 10 March 1934, Oswestry; s. of John Hugo Matthews and Cecily Eileen Elmsley Hagarty; m. Lucienne Marie Jeanne Schleich 1984; one step-s. one step-d.; ed. Montpellier School, Paignton, Clifton Coll., St. John's Coll., Cambridge; lecturer, Univ. Coll. of N. Wales, Bangor 1960–65, at Ind. Univ., Bloomington 1963–64; Lecturer, Reader and Prof., Univ. of Reading 1965–80; Visiting Prof. Deccan Coll., Poona 1969–70; Sr. Research Fellow King's Coll., Cambridge 1970–71; Fellow, Nias Wassenaar, Holland 1977–78; Prof. and Head of Dept. of Linguistics, Univ. of Cambridge, and Fellow of St. John's Coll. 1980–, Praelector 1987–; Pres. Philological Soc. 1992–96, Vice-Pres. 1996–; Hon. mem. Linguistics Soc. of America 1994–. *Publications:* Inflectional Morphology 1972, Morphology 1974, Generative Grammar and Linguistic Competence 1979, Syntax 1981, Grammatical Theory in the United States from Bloomfield to Chomsky 1993, The Concise Oxford Dictionary of Linguistics 1997. *Leisure interests:* cycling, gardening. *Address:* St. John's College, Cambridge, CB2 1TP (Office); 10 Fendon Close, Cambridge, CB1 4RU, England (Home); 22 Rue Nina et Julien Lefevre, 1952 Luxembourg. *Telephone:* (01223) 335010 (Office); (01223) 247553 (Home); 224146 (Luxembourg).

MATTHEWS, Robert Charles Oliver, C.B.E., M.A., F.B.A.; British economist; b. 16 June 1927, Edinburgh; s. of Oliver Harwood Matthews and Ida Finlay; m. Joyce Lloyds 1948; one d.; ed. Edinburgh Acad. and Corpus Christi and Nuffield Colls., Oxford; Asst. Univ. Lecturer, then Lecturer, Cambridge 1949–65; Drummond Prof. of Political Economy 1965–75, All Souls Coll., Oxford; Master of Clare Coll., Cambridge 1975–93, Fellow 1993–; Prof. of Political Economy, Cambridge 1980–91, Prof. Emer.; Chair. Social Science Research Council 1972–75; Fellow, St. John's Coll., Cambridge 1950–65, All Souls Coll., Oxford 1965–75; Hon. Fellow, Corpus Christi Coll., Oxford; Hon. D.Litt. (Warwick Univ.) 1981, (Abertay) 1996. *Publications:* A Study in Trade Cycle History 1954, The Trade Cycle 1958, Economic Growth: A Survey (with F. H. Hahn) 1964, Economic Growth: Trends and Factors (ed.) 1981, British Economic Growth 1856–1973 (with C. H. Feinstein and J. Odling-Smee) 1982, Slower Growth in the Western World (ed.) 1982, Contemporary Problems of Economic Policy (ed., with J. R. Sargent) 1983, Economy and Democracy (ed.) 1985, Mostly Three-Movers; collected chess problems 1995, and articles in learned journals. *Leisure interest:* chess problems. *Address:* Clare College, Cambridge, CB2 1TL, England. *Telephone:* (01223) 333200.

MATTHEWS, Sir Stanley, Kt., C.B.E.; British football official; b. 1 Feb. 1915, Hanley, Stoke-on-Trent; s. of late Jack Matthews; m. 1st Elizabeth H. Vallance 1935 (divorced 1975); one s. one d.; m. 2nd Gertrud (Mila) Winterova 1975; ed. Wellington School, Hanley; Stoke City Football Club 1932–46, 1961–65, Pres. 1990–; as professional footballer first played for England 1934 and 55 times thereafter; Blackpool Football Club (FA Cup winners 1953) 1947–61. *Publication:* The Stanley Matthews Story 1960. *Leisure interests:* golf, tennis. *Address:* Stoke City Football Club, Britannia Stadium, Stoke-on-Trent, ST4 4EG, England.

MATTHIESSEN, Peter, B.A.; American writer; b. 22 May 1927, New York; s. of Erard A. Matthiessen and Elizabeth (née Carey) Matthiessen; m. 1st Patricia Southgate 1951 (divorced); m. 2nd Deborah Love 1963 (deceased); three s. one d.; m. 3rd Maria Eckhart 1980; ed. The Sorbonne, Paris, Yale Univ.; f. Paris Review (with Patricia Southgate); ordained a Zen Monk 1981; fmr. correspondent, New Yorker; Trustee New York Zoological Soc. 1965–78; mem. Nat. Inst. of Arts and Letters. *Publications:* Race Rock 1954, Partisans 1955, Raditzer 1960, Wildlife in America 1959, The Cloud Forest 1961, Under the Mountain Wall 1963, At Play in the Fields of the Lord 1965, The Shore Birds of North America 1967, Oomingmak: The Expedition to the Musk Ox Island in the Bering Sea 1967, Sal si Puedes 1969, Blue Meridian 1971, The Tree Where Man Was Born 1972, The Wind Birds 1973, Far Tortuga 1975, The Snow Leopard 1978, Sand Rivers 1981, In the Spirit of the Crazy Horse 1983, Indian Country 1984, Midnight Turning Grey 1984, Nine-Headed Dragon River 1986, Men's Lives 1986, Partisans 1987, On the River Styx 1989, Killing Mr Watson 1990, African Silences 1991, Baikal 1992, African Silences 1992, Shadows of Africa 1992, East of Lo Monthang: In the Land of Mustang 1995.

MATTHIESSEN, Poul Christian, M.A., D.SC.(ECON.); Danish professor of demography; b. 1 Feb. 1933, Odense; s. of Jens P. E. Matthiessen and Laura C. Nielsen; m. Ulla Bay 1986; two d.; research asst. Copenhagen Telephone Co. 1958–63; Lecturer in Statistics and Demography, Univ. of Copenhagen 1963–70, Prof. of Demography 1971–; Chair. Bd. of Dirs. Carlsberg Memorial Foundation 1993–; mem. Bd. of Dirs. Museum of Nat. History at Frederiksborg Castle 1993–; mem. European Population Cttee., Royal Danish Acad. of Science and Letters, Academia Europaea; mem. Bd. of Dirs. Carlsberg Ltd. 1989–, Chair. Supervisory Bd. Carlsberg Brewery Ltd. 1993–; mem. Bd. of Dirs. Royal Scandinavia 1993–, Fredericia Bryggerier 1993–97, Falcon Bryggerier AB 1998–. *Publications:* Infant Mortality in Denmark 1931–60 1964, Growth of Population: Causes and Implications 1965, Demographic Methods (Vol. I-III) 1970, Some Aspects of the Demographic Transition in Denmark 1970, The Limitation of Family Size in Denmark (Vol. I-II) 1985, Population and Society 1998. *Leisure interests:* literature, history, architecture. *Address:* Carlsbergfondet/The Carlsberg Foundation, H. C. Andersens Boulevard 35, 1553 Copenhagen V (Office); Prs. Alexandrines Allé 14, 2920 Charlottenlund, Denmark (Home). *Telephone:* 33 43 53 63 (Office). *Fax:* 33 43 53 64.

MATTHÖFER, Hans; German politician; b. 25 Sept. 1925, Bochum; m. Traute Mecklenburg 1951; ed. Univs. of Frankfurt/Main and Madison, Wis., U.S.A.; Mem. of Social Democratic Party (SPD) 1950–; mem. Econ. Dept. IG Metall 1953, Head of Educ. and Training Dept. 1961; mem. OECD Washington and Paris 1957–61; mem. Bundestag (Parl.) 1961–87; mem. Bundestag Cttees. for Econ., Econ. Co-operation, Law, Foreign Affairs; Parl. Sec. of State, Ministry of Econ. Co-operation 1972–74; mem. Exec. Cttee. SPD 1973–85, mem. Presidency and Treas. 1985–87; Minister for Research and Tech. 1974–78, of Finance 1978–82, of Posts and Telecommunications April-Oct. 1982; Chair. BG-AG Holding Co. 1987–97; Adviser to Bulgarian Govt. 1997–; Vice-Pres. Latin America Parliamentarians' Group 1961, 1983; mem. hon. Presidium of German Section, Amnesty Int. 1961; Pres. Deutsche Stiftung für Entwicklungsländer (Foundation for Overseas Devt.) 1971–73; Vice-Chair. Enquiry Comm. on Tech. Assessment of Bundestag 1984–86; Publisher of Vorwärts 1985–88; Pres. German Supporting Cttee. for ORT 1989–. *Publications:* Der Unterschied zwischen den Tariflöhnen und den Effektivverdiensten in der Metallindustrie der Bundesrepublik 1956, Technological Change in the Metal Industries 1961/62, Der Beitrag politischer Bildung zur Emanzipation der Arbeitnehmer—Materialien zur Frage des Bildungsurlaubs 1970, Streiks und streikähnliche Formen des Kampfes der Arbeitnehmer im Kapitalismus 1971, Für eine menschliche Zukunft—Sozialdemokratische Forschungs- und Technologiepolitik 1976, Humanisierung der Arbeit und Produktivität in der Industriegesellschaft 1977, 1978, 1980, Agenda 2000-Vorschläge zur Wirtschafts- und Gesellschaftspolitik 1992, numerous articles on trades unions, research, technology, development, politics, economics and finance. *Leisure interests:* chess, reading. *Address:* Schreyerstrasse 38, 61476 Kronberg/Taunus, Germany. *Telephone:* (6173) 79334 (Kronberg).

MATTHUS, Siegfried; German composer; b. 13 April 1934, Mallenuppen, E. Prussia; s. of late Franz Matthus and of Luise Perrey; m. Helga Spitzer 1958; one s.; ed. Hochschule für Musik, Berlin, Acad. of Arts and Music, Berlin (masterclass with Hanns Eisler); composer and consultant, Komische Oper, Berlin 1964–; Prof. 1985–; Artistic Dir. Chamber Opera Festival, Rheinsberg; mem. Acad. of Arts of G.D.R., Acad. of Arts of W. Berlin, Acad. of Arts, Munich; Nat. Prize 1972, 1984. *Compositions include:* nine operas, one oratorio, concertos, orchestral and chamber music etc. *Leisure interests:* swimming, jogging, carpentry. *Address:* Elisabethweg 10, 13187 Berlin; Seepromenade 15, 16348 Stolzenhagen, Germany. *Telephone:* (030) 485 7362 (Berlin); (033397) 21736 (Stolzenhagen). *Fax:* (030) 485 7362 (Berlin); (033397) 71400 (Stolzenhagen).

MATTILA, Karita Marjatta; Finnish opera singer; b. 5 Sept. 1960, Somero; d. of Arja Mattila and Erkki Mattila; m. Tapio Kuneinen 1992; ed. Sibelius Acad., Finland and with teachers Liisa Linko-Malmio and Vera Rozsa; operatic début at Finnish Nat. Opera as the Countess (Marriage of Figaro) 1983; appeared with Brussels Opera as Countess, Eva, Rosalinde 1984–85; début at Royal Opera House, Covent Garden as Fiordiligi 1986, subsequent appearances as Pamina, Countess and Agathe 1986–89, Donna Elvira 1992, Musetta 1994, Elizabeth de Valois 1996, Elsa 1997, Chrysothemis 1997; appeared at Barenboim-Ponnelle Festival, Paris 1986, Tel Aviv 1987, 1990; début at Metropolitan Opera as Donna Elvira 1990, Eva (Meistersinger) 1993, Lisa 1995, Musetta 1996; début at Opéra National de Paris as Elsa 1996, Hanna Glawari 1997; has also appeared in Washington, Houston, Chicago and San Francisco; recitals throughout Europe; has worked under major conductors including Sir Colin Davis, Claudio Abbado, von Dohnanyi, Giulini, Sinopoli; records for Philips, Deutsche Grammophon, EMI, Decca, Ondine and Sony; First Prize, Finnish Nat. Singing Competition 1981, First Prize, BBC Singer of the World, Cardiff 1983. *Leisure interests:* languages, sailing, sport. *Address:* c/o IMG Artists Europe, Media House, 3 Burlington Lane, London, W4 2TH, England.

MATTINGLY, Mack Francis, B.S.; American government official and business executive; b. 7 Jan. 1931, Anderson, Ind.; s. of Joseph Hilbert and Beatrice Wayts Mattingly; m. 1st Carolyn Longcamp 1957 (deceased); two d.; m. 2nd Leslie Ann Davisson 1998; ed. Indiana Univ.; served U.S.A.F. 1951–55; Account Supervisor, Arvin Industries, Ind. 1957–59; Marketing Man. IBM Corpn. Ga. 1959–79; Republican U.S. Senator from Georgia 1981–87; Asst. Sec.-Gen. for Defence Support, NATO, Brussels 1987–90; speaker and author on defence and foreign policy matters 1990–92, U.S. Amb. to Seychelles 1992–93; Chair. Southeastern Legal Foundation; mem. Bd. of Dirs. Marshall Leqacq Inst., Cumberland Preservation Soc., Novecon Tech.; Sec. of Defense Distinguished Service Medal for Outstanding Public Service 1988 and other awards. *Publications:* numerous articles, speeches and book chapters. *Address:* 4315 10th Street, East Beach, St. Simons Island, GA 31522, U.S.A. (Home). *Telephone:* (912) 638-5430.

MATUBRAIMOV, Almambet Matubraimovich; Kyrgyz politician; b. 1952, Osh Region, Kyrgyzstan; ed. Tashkent Inst. of Light and Textile Industry; worker in sovkhoz Kursheb Osh Region; master, sr. master textile factory KKSK 1977–80; army service 1980–82; head of workshop, head of production textile factory KKSK (later Bishkek) 1982–84, Dir. 1984–90; Chair. Exec. Cttee. Sverdlov Region, Frunze (later Bishkek) 1990–91; First Deputy Minister of Industry Repub. of Kyrgyzstan 1991–93; First Deputy Prime Minister 1991–93; Chair. People's Council of Repub. of Kyrgyzstan (Uluk Kenesh) 1995–. *Address:* Uluk Kenesh, 720003 Bishkek, Kyrgyzstan.

MATUSCHKA, Mario, Graf von, D.JUR.; German diplomatist; b. 27 Feb. 1931, Oppeln, Silesia; s. of Michael, Graf von Matuschka and Pia, Gräfin Stillfried-Rattonitz; m. Eleonore, Gräfin von Waldburg-Wolfegg 1962; two s. two d.; ed. St Matthias Gymnasium, Breslau, Domgymnasium, Fulda and Univs. of Fribourg, Paris and Munich; entered foreign service 1961; Attaché, German Observer's Mission at UN, New York 1961–62; Vice-Consul, Consul, Salzburg 1963–66; Second Sec. Islamabad 1966–68; First Sec. Tokyo 1968–71; Foreign Office, Bonn 1971–75, 1978–80, 1982–88, 1990–93; Economic Counsellor, London 1975–78; Deputy Chief of Protocol, UN, New York 1980–82; State Sec., Chief of Protocol, Land Berlin 1988–90; Amb. and Perm. Rep. of Germany to OECD 1993–96; Diplomatic Advisor to Commr. Gen., Expo 2000, Hanover 1996–97; Sec. Gen. Internationaler Club La Redoute e.V. 1997–; Order of Merit (Germany); decorations from Japan, Portugal and Sovereign Mil. Order of Malta. *Address:* Kurfürstenallee 1, 53177 Bonn (Office); Drachenfelsstr. 45, 53757 St. Augustin, Germany (Home). *Telephone:* (228) 353858 (Office); (2241) 337707 (Home). *Fax:* (228) 359189 (Office); (2241) 337707 (Home).

MATUTE AUSEJO, Ana María; Spanish writer; b. 26 July 1925, Barcelona; d. of Facundo Matute and Mary Ausejo; m. 1952 (dissolved 1963); one s.; ed. "Damas Negras" French Nuns Coll.; collaborated on literary magazine Destino; Visiting lecturer, Indiana Univ. 1965–66, Oklahoma Univ. 1969–; Writer-in-Residence, Univ. of Virginia 1978–79; mem. Hispanic Soc. of America; "Highly Commended Author", Hans Christian Andersen Jury, Lisbon 1972. *Publications:* Los Abel 1947, Fiesta Al Noroeste (Café Gijón Prize) 1952, Pequeño Teatro (Planeta Prize) 1954, Los niños tontos 1956, Los Hijos Muertos (Nat. Literary Prize and Critics Prize) 1959, Primera Memoria (Nadal Prize) 1959, Tres y un sueño 1961, Historias de la Artamila 1961, El Río 1963, El Tiempo 1963, Los Soldados lloran de noche 1964 (Fastenrath Prize 1969), El Arrepentido y otras Narraciones 1967, Algunos Muchachos 1968, La Trampa 1969, La Torre Vigia 1971, Olvidado Rey Gudu 1974; *Children's books:* El País de la Pizarra 1956, Paulina 1961, El Sal Tamontes Verde 1961, Caballito Loco 1961, El Aprendiz 1961, Carnavalito 1961, El Polizón del "Ulises" (Lazarillo Prize) 1965. *Leisure interests:* painting, drawing, the cinema.

MATUTES JUAN, Abel; Spanish international official; b. 31 Oct. 1941, Ibiza; s. of Antonio and Carmen Matutes; m. Nieves Prats; one s. three d.; ed. Univ. of Barcelona; studies in law and economics; fmr. entrepreneur in tourism and property in island of Ibiza; fmr. lecturer in Econs. and Public Finance, Univ. of Barcelona; Deputy Chair. Ibiza & Formentera Tourist Bd. 1964–69; Deputy Alianza Popular 1982–; Deputy Nat. Chair. Alianza Popular; Mayor of Ibiza 1970–71; EC Commr. for Credits and Investments, Small and Medium Sized Enterprises and Financial Eng. 1986–89, for American Policy, Latin American Relations 1989–93, for Energy and Euratom Supply Agency, Transport 1993–95; Nat. Vice-Pres. political party Partido Popular; mem. European Parl. 1994–96; Minister of Foreign Affairs May 1996–. *Leisure interests:* tennis, sailing. *Address:* c/o Ministerio de Asuntos Exteriores, Plaza de la Provincia 1, 28071 Madrid, Spain.

MATVEYEVA, Novella Nikolaevna; Russian poet and chansonnier; b. 7 Oct. 1934, Pushkin, nr. Leningrad; d. of Nikolai Nikolaevitch Matveye-Bodryi and Nadejda Timofeevna Matveyeva (Orleneva); m. Ivan Semjonovitch Kiuru 1963. *Publications:* Lirika 1961, Little Ship 1963, Selected Lyrics 1964, The Soul of Things 1966, Reflection of a Sunbeam 1966, School for Swallows 1973, River 1978, The Song's Law 1983, The Land of the Surf 1983, Rabbit's Village 1984, Selected Works 1986, Praising the Labour 1987, An Indissoluble Circle 1988, Poems 1988; (play) The Foretelling of an Eagle (in Theatre magazine) 1988. *Recordings:* A Gipsy Girl 1966, What a Strong Wind! 1966, Poems and Songs 1973, A Princess on a Peascorn 1980, A Trail is my Home 1982, (with Ivan Kiuru) The Music of Light 1984, My Small Raven 1985, Ballads 1985, A Red-haired Girl 1986, The Inseverable Circle 1991, (with I. Kiuru) The Poetic Dialogue 1993, (with I. Kiuru) Hosanna to Skhodnya 1993, Sonnets to Dashkova 1994, Minuet 1994. *Leisure interests:* listening to the radio (plays, classical music), reading. *Address:* Kammergerski per. 2, Apt. 42, 103009 Moscow, Russia. *Telephone:* 292-33-61.

MATVIYENKO, Valentina Ivanovna; Russian politician; b. 7 April 1949, Shepetovka, U.S.S.R. (now Ukraine); m. Vladimir Vasilyevich Matviyenko; one s.; ed. Leningrad Inst. of Chem. and Pharmaceuticals, Acad. of Social Sciences at CPSU Cen. Cttee.; Comsomol work 1972–84; First Sec. Krasnogvardeysk Dist. CP Cttee., Leningrad 1984–86; Deputy Chair. Exec. Cttee. Leningrad City Soviet on Problems of Culture and Educ. 1988–89; U.S.S.R. Peoples' Deputy, mem. Supreme Soviet 1989–92; mem. of Presidium, Chair. Cttee. on Problems of Family, Motherhood and Childhood Protection 1989–91; Russian Amb. to Malta 1991–95, to Greece 1997–98; Dir. Dept. on Relations with Subjects of Russian Fed., Parl. and Public Orgs. Ministry of Foreign Affairs 1995–97, Deputy Prime Minister of Russian Fed. Sept. 1998. Address: Parliament Buildings, Krasnopresnenskaya nab. 2, 103274 Moscow, Russia. *Telephone:* (095) 205 5143 (Office).

MAUCHER, Helmut; German business executive; b. 9 Dec. 1927, Eisenharz/Allgäu; joined Nestlé AG 1948, Chair. Bd. Nestlé SA 1990– and C.E.O. 1990–(97); Vice-Chair. CS Holding, Crédit Suisse; mem. Bd. ABB Asea Brown Boveri AG, BBC Brown Boveri AG, Zürich Insurance Co., L'Oréal Paris—Gesparal; mem. Int. Council, Morgan Bank; Fortune Magazine Gold Medal 1984; Grosses Bundesverdienstkreuz, Grosses Goldenes Ehrenzeichen mit dem Stern für Verdienste um die Republik Oesterreich. *Address:* Nestlé AG, Avenue Nestlé 55, 1800 Vevey, Switzerland.

MAUD, Hon. Sir Humphrey John Hamilton, K.C.M.G., M.A.; British diplomatist; b. 17 April 1934, Oxford; s. of Lord and Lady Redcliffe-Maud; m. Maria Eugenia Gazitua 1963; three s.; ed. Eton Coll., King's Coll., Cambridge; Instructor in Classics, Univ. of Minn., U.S.A. 1958–59; joined Diplomatic Service 1959, Third Sec. Madrid 1961–63, Third, later Second Sec. Havana 1963–65, at FCO 1966–68, Cabinet Office 1968–69, First Sec. Paris 1970–74, Sabbatical at Nuffield Coll., Oxford (Econs.) 1974–75, Head Financial Relations Dept., FCO 1975–79, Minister, Madrid 1979–82, Amb. to Luxembourg 1982–84; Asst. Under-Sec. of State (Econ. and Commercial) 1985–86; High Commr. in Cyprus 1988–89; Amb. to Argentina 1990–93; Commonwealth Deputy Sec.-Gen. 1993–99; mem. Nat. Youth Orchestra 1949–52. *Leisure interests:* music, sport, bird-watching. *Address:* c/o Commonwealth Secretariat, Marlborough House, Pall Mall, London, SW1Y 5HX; 31 Queen Anne's Grove, London, W4 1HW, England.

MAUDE, Rt. Hon. Francis (Anthony Aylmer), P.C., M.A.; British politician; b. 4 July 1953; s. of Baron Maude of Stratford-upon-Avon; m. Christina Jane Hadfield 1984; two s. three d.; ed. Abingdon School, Corpus Christi Coll., Cambridge; called to Bar 1977 (Forster Boulton Prize); Councillor Westminster City Council 1978–84; M.P. for Warwicks. N. 1983–92, for Horsham 1997–; Parl. Pvt. Sec. to Minister of State for Employment 1984–85; an Asst. Govt. Whip 1985–87; Parl. Under-Sec. of State Dept. of Trade and Industry 1987–89; Minister of State, FCO 1989–90; Financial Sec. to H.M. Treasury 1990–92; Chair. Govt.'s Deregulation Task Force 1994–97; Shadow Chancellor 1998–; Dir. Salomon Brothers 1992–93, Asda Group 1992–; Advisory Dir. Morgan Stanley and Co.; Conservative. *Leisure interests:* skiing, cricket, reading, music. *Address:* House of Commons, London, SW1A 0AA, England.

MAULDE, Bruno Guy André Jean de, L. EN D.; French banker; b. 27 March 1934, Toulouse; s. of Guy de Maulde and Suzanne Mazars; m. Dominique Le Henaff 1958; three d.; ed. Inst. of Political Studies, Toulouse, Nat. Coll. of Admin.; Insp. des Finances 1962; Adviser, External Econ. Relations Dept., Finance Ministry 1967–68; Alt. Exec. Dir. IMF for France 1968–70; Financial attaché, Embassy, U.S.A. 1968–70, in New York 1970–71; French Treasury Adviser 1971–74, Asst. Dir. 1974–77, Deputy Dir. 1977–78; Deputy Man. Dir. Caisse Nat. de Crédit Agricole 1979–81; Financial Minister, Embassy of France, and Exec. Dir. IMF and IBRD, Washington 1981–85; Chair. and C.E.O. Crédit du Nord 1986–93; Chair. Conseil des Bourses de Valeurs (CBV) 1990–94; Dir. Compagnie Financière de Paribas 1993–94; Dir of various other corpns. and public insts.; mem. Council of Monetary Policy, Banque de France 1994–97; Chevalier, Légion d'honneur, l'Ordre nat. du Mérite, Croix de la Valeur Militaire, Officier du Mérite Agricole. *Leisure interest:* yachting. *Address:* Rozareu, 29930 Pont-Aven, France.

MAUNG MAUNG GYEE, U, B.A.; Myanma diplomatist; b. 15 Feb. 1921; m.; four c.; ed. Univ. of Rangoon; officer, Burma Defence Army in the Burmese independence movt.; Ministry of Foreign Affairs 1948; served in embassies in Paris, Washington, D.C., Tokyo, Peking, Rome and Kathmandu as Third, Second and First Sec. and Counsellor; Dir.-Gen. Int. Orgs. and Econ. Dept., Ministry of Foreign Affairs; Perm. Rep. of Myanmar to UN 1977–81, 1985–90; fmr. Amb. to Sri Lanka. *Address:* c/o Ministry of Foreign Affairs, Prome Court, Prome Road, Yangon, Myanmar.

MAUNG MAUNG KHA, U; Myanma politician; mem. Cen. Exec. Cttee. Burma Socialist Programme Party (BSPP); Minister for Industry and Labour 1973–74, for Industry 1974–75, for Mines 1975–77, Prime Minister of Burma (now Myanmar) 1977–88; mem. State Council 1977–88. *Address:* c/o Office of the Prime Minister, Yangon, Myanmar.

MAUPIN, Armistead Jones, Jr.; American writer; b. 13 May 1944; s. of Armistead Jones Maupin and the late Diana Jane (Barton) Maupin; ed. Univ. of North Carolina; reporter News and Courier, Charleston, S.C. 1970–71; AP, San Francisco 1971–72; Account Exec. Lowry Russom and Leeper Public Relations 1973; columnist Pacific Sun Magazine 1974; publicist San Francisco Opera 1975; serialist San Francisco Chronicle 1976–77, 1981, 1983; Commentator K.R.O.N.-TV San Francisco 1979; serialist San Francisco Examiner 1986; Exec. Producer Armistead Maupin's Tales of the City 1993; contrib. to New York Times, Los Angeles Times and others; numerous awards, including: Freedom Leadership Award, Freedoms Foundation 1972, Communications Award, Metropolitan Elections Comm., Los Angeles 1989, Exceptional Achievement Award, American Libraries Asscn. 1990, Outstanding Miniseries Award, Gay and Lesbian Alliance Against Defamation 1994. *Publications:* Tales of the City 1978, More Tales of the City 1980, Further Tales of the City 1982, Babycakes 1984, Significant Others 1987, Sure of You 1989, 28 Barbary Lane 1990, Back to Barbary Lane 1991, Maybe the Moon 1992; Librettist: Heart's Desire 1990. *Address:* 584 Castro Street, # 528, San Francisco, CA 94114, U.S.A.

MAURA, Carmen; Spanish film actress; b. 15 Sept. 1945, Madrid; Best Actress, European Film Awards for roles in Pedro Almodóvar's Women on the Verge of a Nervous Breakdown 1989 and Carlos Saura's Ay, Carmela! 1991. *Other films include:* Law of Desire, Dark Habits, Le Saut Périlleux, Be Unfaithful and Don't Look With Whom, Matador, In Heaven as on Earth, The Anonymous Queen, How to be a Woman and Not Die in the Attempt, Shadows in a Conflict, Louis the Child King, How to be Miserable and Enjoy It, The Flower of My Secret.

MAURER, Ion Gheorghe, LL.D., D.JUR.; Romanian politician and jurist (retd.); b. 23 Sept. 1902, Bucharest; s. of Josef and Jeane Maurer; m. Elena Stanescu 1949; one s.; ed. Craiova Military School and Bucharest Univ.; joined Romanian Communist Party 1936; imprisoned in concentration camp for political activities; Under Sec. of State for Transport 1944–46, Ministry of Nat. Economy 1946–47; mem. Cen. Cttee. Romanian Workers' Party (now Romanian CP) 1945–74, Political Bureau of Cen. Cttee. 1960–65, Exec. Political Cttee. of Cen. Cttee. 1965–74, Perm. Presidium 1965–74; Deputy Minister of Industry and Trade 1948; Minister for Foreign Affairs 1957–58; mem. Grand Nat. Ass. 1948–75; Chair. Presidium Grand Nat. Ass. (Head of State) 1958–61; Chair. Council of Ministers 1961–74; mem. Defence Council of Romania 1969–74; mem. Romanian Acad. 1955–, Acad. of Social and Political Sciences 1970–90; fmr. Dir. Inst. of Juridical Research 1954–58; Hero of Socialist Labour 1962, Order "Victoria Socialismului" 1971, Hero of Socialist Republic of Romania 1972, Chevalier Légion d'honneur, etc. *Leisure interests:* tennis, hunting. *Address:* Str. Herăstrău 15, Bucharest 1, Romania.

MAUROY, Pierre; French politician; b. 5 July 1928, Cartignies; s. of Henri Mauroy and Adrienne Bronne; m. Gilberte Deboudt 1951; one s.; ed. Lycée de Cambrai, Ecole normale nationale d'apprentissage, Cachan; Nat. Sec. Jeunesses socialistes 1950–58; Tech. Teacher, Colombes 1952; Sec.-Gen. Syndicat des collèges d'enseignement tech. section, Féd. de l'Educ. Nationale 1955–59; Fed. Sec. for the North, Section Française de l'Internationale Ouvrière 1961, mem. Political Bureau 1963, Deputy Sec.-Gen. 1966; mem. Exec. Cttee., Féd. de la gauche démocratique et socialiste 1965–68; Gen. Councillor, Cateau 1967–73; Vice-Pres. Gen. Council, Nord Département 1967–73; Municipal Councillor, Lille 1971, First Deputy Mayor 1971, Mayor 1973–; First Sec. and Nat. Co-ordinating Sec., Northern Fed., Parti Socialiste 1971–79; Deputy (Nord) to Nat. Ass. 1973–81, 1986, Senator 1992–; First Sec. Parti Socialiste 1989–92; Pres. Socialist Int. 1992–, Regional Council, Nord-Pas-de-Calais 1974; Pres. Nat. Fed. Léo Lagrange youth centres 1972–81, Hon. Pres. 1981–84; mem. European Parl. 1979–81, Vice-Pres. Political Cttee.; Political Dir. Action socialiste Hebdo newspaper 1979–81; Prime Minister of France 1981–84; Pres. World Fed. of Twinned Towns 1984–; Pres. Communauté urbaine de Lille 1989–; founder, Pres. Jean Jaurès Foundation 1993–; Grand-croix, Ordre nat. du Mérite, Grand cordon de l'ordre de la Répub. de Tunisie. *Publications:* Héritiers de l'avenir 1977, C'est ici le chemin 1982, A gauche 1985, Parole de Lillois 1994, Léo Lagrange (biog.) 1997. *Address:* Sénat, 75291 Paris Cedex 06; 17–19 rue Voltaire, 59000 Lille, France (Home).

MAURSTAD, Toralv; Norwegian actor and theatre director; b. 24 Nov. 1926, Oslo; s. of Alfred and Tordis Maurstad; m. Eva Henning 1956; one s.; ed. Universitet i Uppsala and Royal Acad. of Dramatic Art, London; début in Trondheim 1947; Oslo Nye Teater 1951; Oslo Nat. Theatre 1954; Man. Dir. Oslo Nye Teater (Oslo Municipal Theatre) 1967–78; Man. Dir. Nat. Theatre 1978–86; Oslo Critics Award. *Plays acted in or directed include:* Young Woodley 1949, Pal Joey 1952, Peer Gynt 1954, Long Day's Journey 1962, Teenage Love 1963, Hamlet 1964, Arturo Ui (in Bremen, Germany) 1965, Brand (Ibsen) 1966, Of Love Remembered (New York) 1967, Cabaret 1968, Scapino 1975, Two Gentlemen of Verona 1976, The Moon for Misbegotten 1976, Same Time Next Year 1977, Twigs 1977 (also TV production), Sly Fox 1978, Whose Life is it Anyway? 1979, Masquerade 1980, Amadeus 1980, Much Ado about Nothing 1981, Kennen Sie die Milchstrasse? 1982, Duet for One 1982, Hamlet 1983. *Films:* Line 1960, Kalde Spor 1962, Song of Norway 1970, After Rubicon 1987. *Leisure interests:* skiing, hunting, fishing. *Address:* Nationaltheatret, Stortingsgt. 15, Oslo 1, Norway.

MAVROMMATIS, Andreas V.; Cypriot diplomatist and barrister; b. 9 June 1932, Larnaca; s. of Vladimiros and Marthe (Andreou) Mavrommatis; m. Mary Cahalane 1955; one s. three d.; ed. Greek Gymnasium, Limassol, Lincoln's Inn, London; practising advocate 1954–58; Magistrate 1958–60; Dist. Judge 1960–70; Minister of Labour and Social Insurance 1970–72; Special Adviser on Foreign and Legal Affairs to Pres. of Cyprus 1972–75; Perm. Rep. to UN Office at Geneva 1975–78, to UN, New York 1979–82; Greek Cypriot Interlocutor in Intercommunal Talks 1982–89; Perm. Rep. to UN, New York 1989–92; Adviser to the Pres. of the Republic, mem. of Working Group on the Cyprus Question July–Dec. 1992; Govt. Spokesman Dec. 1992–; Chair. UN Cttee. on Human Rights; fmr. Pres. ECOSOC; Chair. UN Cttee. on Relations with the Host Country. *Publication:* Treaties in Force in Cyprus. *Leisure interests:* reading, walking. *Address:* 10 Platon Street, Engomi, Nicosia, Cyprus. *Telephone:* 351878. *Fax:* 357111.

MAWHINNEY, Rt. Hon. Sir Brian Stanley, Kt., PH.D.; British politician; b. 26 July 1940; s. of Frederick Stanley Arnot Mawhinney and Coralie Jean Mawhinney; m. Betty Louise Oja 1965; two s. one d.; ed. Royal Belfast Academical Inst., Queen's Univ. Belfast, Univ. of Michigan, U.S.A., Univ. of London; Asst. Prof. of Radiation Research, Univ. of Iowa, U.S.A. 1968–70; lecturer, subsequently Sr. Lecturer, Royal Free Hosp. School of Medicine 1970–84; mem. MRC 1980–83; M.P. for Peterborough 1979–97, for Cambridgeshire N.W. 1997–; Parl. Under-Sec. of State for Northern Ireland 1986–90; Minister of State, Northern Ireland Office 1990–92, Dept. of Health 1992–94; Sec. of State for Transport 1994–95; Chair. Conservative Party 1995–97; Opposition Front Bench Spokesman on Home Affairs 1997–98; Pres. Conservative Trade Unionists 1987–90; mem. Gen. Synod of Church of England 1985–90. *Publication:* Conflict and Christianity in Northern Ireland (co-author) 1976. *Leisure interests:* sport, reading. *Address:* House of Commons, London, SW1A 0AA, England.

MAXIMOS V HAKIM (fmrly. **Archbishop George S. Hakim**), D.D.; Lebanese ecclesiastic; b. 18 May 1908, Tanta, Egypt; s. of Salim Hakim and Eugenie Gazaleh; ed. St. Louis School, Tanta, Holy Family Jesuit School, Cairo and St. Anne Seminary, Jerusalem; Teacher Patriarchal School, Beirut 1930–31; Rector and Prin. Patriarchal School, Cairo 1931–43; Archbishop of Acre, Haifa, Nazareth and all Galilee 1943–67; elected Greek Catholic Patriarch of Antioch and all the East, Alexandria and Jerusalem Nov. 1967; founded Le Lien (French) Cairo 1936, Ar-Rabita (Arabic) Haifa 1943; Grand Croix Légion d'honneur; Dr. h.c. (Laval Univ., Canada, Algiers Univ. and many U.S. univs.). *Publications:* Pages d'Evangile lues en Galilée (trans. into English, Dutch and Spanish) 1954, Life of Jesus (Arabic) 1980, Paroissien Byzantin (Arabic and French) 1980. *Address:* Greek Catholic Patriarchate, P.O. Box 50076, Beirut, Lebanon; P.O. Box 22249, Damascus, Syrian Arab Republic; Daher 16, Cairo, Arab Republic of Egypt. *Telephone:* (Beirut) 413111; (Damascus) 5443129; (Cairo) 5904697. *Fax:* 407 388 (Beirut); (11) 431 266 (Damascus).

MAXWELL, Ian, M.A.; British/French publisher; b. 15 June 1956, Maisons Laffitte, France; s. of the late (Ian) Robert Maxwell and of Elisabeth Meynard; brother of Kevin Maxwell (q.v.); m. Laura Plumb 1991 (divorced); ed. Marlborough Coll. and Balliol Coll., Oxford; Man. Dir. Pergamon Press France 1980–81; Jt. Man. Dir. Pergamon Pres. GmbH 1980; Marketing Dir. Pergamon Press Inc. 1982–83; Dir. Sales Devt. BPCC PLC 1985–86; Dir. Group Marketing BPCC PLC (now Maxwell Communication Corpn. PLC) 1986; Chair. Agence Centrale de Presse, Paris 1986–89; Dir. TFI TV station, Paris 1987–89; C.E.O. Maxwell Pergamon Publrs. 1988–89; Jt. Man. Dir. Maxwell Communication Corpn. 1988–91; Acting Chair. Mirror Group Newspapers 1991; Dir. New York Daily News –1991, Telemonde Holdings 1997–; publishing consultant Westbourne Communications Ltd. 1993; Publr. Maximor Publs. 1995–; Chair. Derby Co. Football Club 1984–87, Vice-Chair. 1987–91; mem. Nat. Theatre Devt. Council 1986; Pres. Club d'Investissement Media 1988. *Leisure interests:* skiing, water skiing, watching football.

MAXWELL, Kevin Francis Herbert, M.A.; British businessman; b. 20 Feb. 1959, Maisons Laffitte, France; s. of the late (Ian) Robert Maxwell and of Elisabeth Maxwell; brother of Ian Maxwell (q.v.); m. Pandora Deborah Karen Warnford-Davis 1984; two s. four d.; ed. Marlborough Coll., Balliol Coll. Oxford; Chair. Oxford United Football Club 1987–92; Vice-Chair. MacMillan Inc. 1988–91; Jt. Man. Dir. Maxwell Communication Corpn. 1988–91, Chair. 1991; Publr. and Chair. New York Daily News –1991; Chief Exec. Equitel Communications 1998–; Dir. Telemonde Holdings 1997–; Trustee New School N.Y. 1988–92. *Leisure interests:* football, watercolour painting. *Address:* Moulsford Manor, Moulsford, Oxon. OX10 9HO, England.

MAXWELL DAVIES, Sir Peter (see Davies, Sir Peter Maxwell).

MAY, Elaine; American actress, film director and entertainer; b. 1932, Philadelphia; d. of Jack Berlin; m. 1st Marvin May (divorced); one d.; m. 2nd Sheldon Harnick 1962 (divorced 1963); appeared on radio and stage as child; performed Playwright's Theatre, Chicago; appeared in student production Miss Julie, Univ. of Chicago; with Mike Nichols (q.v.) and others in improvisatory theatre group, The Compass (nightclub), Chicago 1954–57; improvised nightclub double-act with Mike Nichols, appeared New York Town Hall 1959; An Evening with Mike Nichols and Elaine May, Golden Theatre, New York 1960–61; numerous TV and radio appearances; weekly appearance NBC radio show Nightline. *Films:* Luv 1967, A New Leaf (also dir.) 1972, The Heartbreak Kid (dir.) 1973, Mikey and Nicky (dir.) 1976 (writer, dir. remake 1985), California Suite 1978, Heaven Can Wait (co-author screenplay) 1978, In The Spirit 1990, The Birdcage 1996 (co-author screenplay), Primary Colors (co-author screenplay). *Publications:* Better Part of Valour (play) 1983, Hotline 1983, Mr. Gogol and Mr. Preen 1991, Death Defying Acts 1995. *Address:* c/o Julian Schlossberg, Castle Hill Productions, 1414 Avenue of the Americas, New York, NY 10019, U.S.A.

MAY, Georges, PH.D., D.H.L.; American/French university professor; b. 7 Oct. 1920, Paris; s. of Lucien and Germaine May; m. Martha Corkery 1949; two d.; ed. Univs. of Paris, Montpellier and Illinois; mem. Faculty of Dept. of French, Yale Univ. 1946–; Instructor, Asst. Prof., Assoc. Prof., Prof. 1946–; Chair. Dept. of French 1978–79; Dean of Yale Coll. 1963–71; Sterling Prof. of French 1971–91, Sterling Prof. Emer. of French 1991–; Provost of Yale Univ. 1979–81; mem. bd. American Council of Learned Socs. 1979–89, Chair. 1982–89; Vice-Pres. Conseil Int. de la Philosophie et des Sciences Humaines 1982–84; mem. bd. Union Académique Internationale 1983–95, Vice-Pres. 1985–89, Pres. 1989–92; Guggenheim Foundation Fellow 1950, 1984; Chevalier Légion d'honneur 1971. *Publications:* Tragédie cornélienne, tragédie racinienne 1948, D'Ovide à Racine 1949, Quatre Visages de D. Diderot 1951, Diderot et la Religieuse 1954, J.-J. Rousseau par Lui-même 1961, Le dilemme du roman au XVIIIe siècle 1963, L'Autobiographie 1979, Les Mille et une nuits d'Antoine Galland, ou le Chef-d'oeuvre invisible 1986, La Perruque de Dom Juan, on du bon usage des énigmes 1995, Jean-Jacques Rousseau et Madame de la Tour: Correspondance 1998. *Leisure interests:* reading, drawing. *Address:* 177 Everit Street, New Haven, CT 06511, U.S.A. *Telephone:* (203) 562 5535.

MAY, Gerald William, M.S., PH.D.; American university president and professor of engineering; b. 2 Jan. 1941, Kenya; s. of late Wilhelm May and Ruth Koch May; m. Mary J. Pool 1963; one s. two d.; ed. Bradley Univ. Peoria, Ill. and Univ. of Colo.; civil engineer, Ill. Highway Dept. summers 1959–63; Teaching Asst. Univ. of Colo. 1962–65, Instructor 1965–67; Asst. Prof., Assoc. Prof., Prof. Univ. of N.M. 1967–79, Assoc. Dean of Eng. 1979–80, Dean 1980–86, Pres. 1986–90; eng. consultant 1967–; staff mem. Sandia Nat. Lab. Albuquerque, N.M. 1968–69; Dir. Accident Study Program 1971–75; Engineer of the Year Award, Nat. Soc. of Professional Engineers 1984 and other awards. *Publications:* numerous scientific research articles on structure analysis, safety, earthquake resistant low cost housing, engineering education, bldg. materials. *Address:* Civil Engineering Dept., University of New Mexico, Albuquerque, N.M. 87131 (Office); 1058 Red Oaks N.E., Albuquerque, NM 87122, U.S.A. *Telephone:* (505) 277-2473.

MAY, Sir Robert McCredie, A.C., Kt., PH.D., F.R.S., F.A.A.S.; Australian professor of biology; b. 1 Aug. 1936, Sydney; s. of Henry W. May and Kathleen M. McCredie; m. Judith Feiner 1962; one d.; ed. Sydney Boys' High School, Univ. of Sydney; Gordon Mackay Lecturer in Applied Math., Harvard Univ. 1959–61; at Univ. of Sydney 1962–73, Sr. Lecturer in Theoretical Physics 1962–64, Reader 1964–69, Personal Chair 1969–73; Prof. of Biology, Princeton Univ. 1973–88; Royal Soc. Research Prof., Dept. of Zoology, Oxford Univ. and Imperial Coll., London 1988–; Chief Scientific Advisor to U.K. Govt. and Head, Office of Science and Tech. 1995–; Visiting Prof. of Biology, Imperial Coll., Univ. of London 1975–88; Visiting appointments at Harvard Univ. 1966, Calif. Inst. of Tech. 1967, UKAEA Culham Lab., U.K. 1971, Magdalen Coll., Univ. of Oxford 1971, Inst. for Advanced Study, Princeton Univ. 1972, King's Coll., Univ. of Cambridge 1976; Fellow, Merton Coll., Oxford 1988–; Foreign Assoc. N.A.S.; Trustee British Museum 1989–, Royal Botanic Gardens 1991–95, Kew, WWF (U.K.) 1990–94, Nuffield Foundation 1993–; Croonian Lecturer, MacArthur Award, Weldon Memorial Prize, Hitchcock Lecturer, John M. Prather Lecturer, Edgeworth David Medal. *Publications:* Stability and Complexity in Model Systems 1973, Exploitation of Marine Communities (ed.) 1974, ed. Theoretical Ecology: Principles and Applications 1981 (2nd edition), Population Biology of Infectious Diseases 1982, Perspectives in Ecological Theory 1989, Ed. Exploitation of Marine Communities 1984, Infectious Diseases of Humans: Dynamics and Control (with R. M. Anderson) 1991, Extinction Rates 1995. *Leisure interests:* tennis, running, hiking. *Address:* Office of Science and Technology, Albany House, 84–86 Petty France, London, SW1H 9ST, England.

MAYAKI, Ibrahim Assane; Niger politician; b. 24 Sept. 1951, Niamey; s. of Assane Adamou Mayaki and Marie Mosconi; m. Marly Perez Marin 1976; one s. one d.; fmr. Minister of Foreign Affairs and Co-operation; Prime Minister of Niger Nov. 1997–. *Leisure interest:* taekwondo. *Address:* B.P. 353, Niamey, Niger. *Telephone:* 753782. *Fax:* 725059.

MAYALL, Richard Michael (Rik); British comedian, actor and writer; b. 7 March 1958; s. of John Mayall and Gillian Mayall; m. Barbara Robbin; one s. two d.; ed. Univ. of Manchester. *Theatre includes:* The Common Pursuit 1988, Waiting for Godot 1991–92, The Government Inspector, Cell Mates 1995. *Television includes:* The Young Ones (also creator and co-writer, two series, BBC) 1982, 1984, The Comic Strip Presents (Channel Four) 1983–84, 1992, George's Marvellous Medicine (five episodes, Jackanory, BBC) 1985, The New Statesman (four series, YTV) 1987–88, 1990, 1994 (Int. Emmy Award 1989, BAFTA Best New Comedy 1990, Special Craft Gold Medal Best Performer/Narrator), Grim Tales (two series 1990, Bottom (three series, BBC) 1990, 1992, 1994 (British Comedy Awards Best New Comedy 1992), Rik Mayall Presents (two trilogies of films, Granada TV) 1992–94 (British Comedy Awards Best Comedy Actor 1993), Wham Bham Strawberry Jam! (BBC) 1995, The Alan B'Stard Interview with Brian Walden 1995. *Films include:* Whoops Apocalypse 1982, Drop Dead Fred 1990, Horse Opera 1992, Remember Me 1996, Bring Me the Head of Mavis Davis 1996; provided voices for animations including Tom Thumb in The World of Peter Rabbit and Friends—The Tale of Two Bad Mice 1994, Toad in Willows in Winter 1995 (Emmy Award 1997), The Robber King in The Snow Queen 1995, Prince Froglip in The Princess and the Goblin, Hero Baby in How to be a Little Sod 1995, Young William Tell in Oscar's Orchestra 1996. *Live Stand Up includes:* Comic Strip 1982, Kevin Turvey and Bastard Squad 1983, Rik Mayall, Ben Elton, Andy De La Tour (UK tour & Edin. Fringe) 1983, Rik Mayall and Ben Elton 1984–85, (Australian tour) 1986, 1992, Rik Mayall and Andy De La Tour 1989–90, Rik Mayall and Adrian Edmondson (UK tours) 1993, 1995, 1997. *Address:* c/o The Brunskill Management Limited, Suite 8A, 169 Queen's Gate, London, SW7 5HE, England. *Telephone:* 0171-581 3388; (01768) 881430. *Fax:* (01768) 881850.

MAYCOCK, Ernest Besley, B.A.; Barbadian diplomatist and public servant; b. 5 Jan. 1935; m.; two c.; ed. Grad. Inst. of Int. Relations, Geneva, Switzerland; served at Barbados Perm. Mission to UN, New York 1979–86, Deputy Perm. Rep., and Deputy Perm. Sec., Ministry of Foreign Affairs 1986, Perm. Sec., Ministry of Educ. and Culture 1986–90, Perm. Rep. to UN 1990–96, Chair. Fifth Cttee. (Admin. and Budget) 1984, 1990. *Address:* c/o Permanent Mission of Barbados to United Nations, 800 Second Avenue, 18th Floor, New York, NY 10017, U.S.A. *Telephone:* (212) 867-8431.

MAYER, Christian (pseudonym Carl Amery); German author; b. 9 April 1922, Munich; s. of Dr. Anton Mayer and Anna (née Schneller); m. Marijane Gerth 1950; three s. two d.; ed. Humanistisches Gymnasium, Freising and Passau, Univ. of Munich and Catholic Univ. of America, Washington, D.C.; freelance author 1949–; Dir. of City Libraries, Munich 1976–77; mem., fmr. Chair. German Writers' Asscn.; co-founder, German Literary Fund 1980; Chair. E. F. Schumachergesellschaft 1980; Pres. PEN Centre of Fed. Repub. of Germany 1989–91. *Publications:* novels: Der Wettbewerb 1954, Die Grosse Deutsche Tour 1958, Das Königsprojekt 1974, Der Untergang der Stadt Passau 1975, An den Feuern der Leyermark 1979, Die Wallfahrer 1986; essays: Die Kapitulation 1963, Fragen an Welt und Kirche 1967, Das Ende der Vorsehung 1972, Natur als Politik 1976, Leb Wohl Geliebtes Volk der Bayern 1980, G. K. Chesterton oder Der Kampf gegen die Kälte 1981, Das Geheimnis der Krypta 1990, Die Botschaft des Jahrtausends 1994; various radio essays, radio plays, translations, etc. *Leisure interests:* gardening, cooking. *Address:* Dräschlstrasse 7, 81541 Munich, Germany. *Telephone:* 45 14 97.

MAYER, Hans; German university professor; b. 19 March 1907; ed. Univs. of Cologne, Bonn, Berlin, and Graduate Inst. of Int. Studies, Geneva; emigrated from Germany 1933; research at Int. Inst. of Social Research, New York, and Graduate Inst. of Int. Studies, Geneva 1933–40; literary and dramatic critic in Switzerland 1939–45; Chief Ed. Frankfurt Radio 1945–47; lecturer in Sociology and the History of Culture, Akad. der Arbeit, Frankfurt 1947–48; Prof. of History of Culture, Univ. of Leipzig 1948–50, Prof. of the History of German Literature 1950–64; Prof. of German Literature and Language Tech. University, Hanover 1965–73, Prof. Emer. 1975–; Prof. and Dir. of Inst. for the History of German Literature 1955; mem. Exec. Deutsche Goethe-Gesellschaft, Deutsche Schiller-Gesellschaft, Deutsche Schiller-Stiftung, PEN Club; Hon. Prof. Univ. of Tübingen 1975; mem. Acad. of Arts, Berlin 1964– (Dir. of Literature 1971); Hon. mem. Modern Languages Asscn. of America 1975; Humane Letters Dr. h.c., (Wisconsin) 1972, D. Phil. h.c. (Brussels) 1969; German Nat. Prize for Science 1955; Literaturpreis der deutschen Kritiker 1965, Medal of Collège de France 1974, Grosser Literaturpreis der Stadt Köln 1980. *Publications:* Von der dritten zur vierten Republik: Geistige Strömungen in Frankreich 1939–1945 1945, Georg Büchner und seine Zeit 1946, Thomas Mann, Werk und Entwicklung 1950, Studien zur deutschen Literaturgeschichte 1954, Schiller und die Nation 1954, Deutsche Literatur und Weltliteratur: Reden und Aufsätze 1957, Richard Wagner 1959, Von Lessing bis Thomas Mann 1959, Bertolt Brecht und die Tradition 1961, Aragon, Die Karwoche (trans. from the French), Heinrich von Kleist, Der geschichtliche Augenblick 1962, Meisterwerke deutscher Literaturkritik (Ed.) (four vols.) 1962–76, Ansichten zur Literatur der Zeit 1962, Dürrenmatt und Frisch, Anmerkungen 1963, Zur deutschen Klassik und Romantik 1963, Anmerkungen zu Brecht 1965, Anmerkungen zu Richard Wagner 1966, Grosse deutsche Verrisse (Ed.) 1967, Zur deutschen Literatur der Zeit: Zusammenhänge, Schriftsteller, Bücher 1967, Das Geschehen und das Schweigen, Aspekte der Literatur 1969, Der Repräsentant und der Märtyrer, Konstellationen der Literatur 1971, Brecht in der Geschichte 1971, Goethe, ein Versuch über den Erfolg 1974, Aussenseiter 1975, Richard Wagner in Bayreuth 1976, Richard Wagner, Mitwelt und Nachwelt 1978, Doktor Faust und Don Juan 1979, Thomas Mann 1980, Versuche über die Oper 1981, Ein Deutscher auf Widerruf (memoirs, two vols.) 1982–84, Reisen nach Jerusalem 1997, Zeitgenossen 1998. *Address:* Neckarhalde 41, 72070 Tübingen, Germany.

MAYER, H.E. Cardinal Paul Augustin, O.S.B.; German ecclesiastic; b. 23 May 1911, Altoetting; ordained 1935; consecrated Bishop (Titular See of Satrianum) 1972, then Archbishop; cr. Cardinal 1985. *Address:* Città del Vaticano, Rome; via Rusticucci 13, 00193 Rome, Italy (Home).

MAYER, Peter, M.A.; American publisher; b. Hampstead, London; ed. Columbia Univ., Christ Church, Oxford; graduate Fellow, Indiana Univ.; Fulbright Fellow, Freie Universität Berlin 1959; worked with Orion Press before joining Avon books for 14 years; Publr. and Pres. Pocketbooks 1976–78; Chief. Exec. Penguin Books Ltd., London 1978–96; with Overlook Press 1996–; now Chair. Penguin U.S.A.; Fellow Ind. Univ. *Publication:* The Pacifist Conscience (ed) 1966. *Address:* Penguin U.S.A., 375 Hudson Street, New York, NY 10014, U.S.A.

MAYER, Thomas; German conductor; ed. State Acad. of Music, Berlin; worked in opera houses of Beuthen, Leipzig, Teplitz and Aussig, subsequently asst. to Erich Kleiber, Fritz Busch and Arturo Toscanini, Teatro Colon, Buenos Aires; directed German opera season, Santiago, Chile, and State Symphony Orchestra of Montevideo, Uruguay; conducted at Metropolitan Opera, New York 1974, subsequently Dir. Venezuelan Symphony Orchestra, Halifax and Ottawa orchestras, Canada; guest conductor with many orchestras in Europe, N. America and Australia; a regular conductor of Sinfonie Orchestra Berlin (West) and Berlin Symphony Orchestra (East) 1974–. *Address:* c/o Norman McCann Ltd, Suite 620, Grand Buildings, Trafalgar Square, London, W.C.2, England. *Telephone:* 0171-930 5240.

MAYER-KUCKUK, Theo, DR.RER.NAT.; German nuclear physicist; b. 10 May 1927, Rastatt; m. Irmgard Meyer 1965; two s.; ed. Univ. of Heidelberg; Research Fellow, Max Planck Institut für Kernphysik, Heidelberg 1953–59, Scientific mem. 1964; Research Fellow, Calif. Inst. of Tech., Pasadena 1960–61; Dozent, Univ. of Heidelberg 1962, Tech. Univ. Munich 1963; Prof. of Physics, Univ. of Bonn 1965–92, Dir. Inst. of Nuclear and Radiation Physics 1965–92; Vice-Pres. Int. Union of Pure and Applied Physics (IUPAP) 1984–90; Pres. German Physical Soc. 1990–92, Vice-Pres. 1992–96; Scientific Dir. Magnus-Haus Berlin 1994–; mem. Acad. of Sciences of Nordrhein-Westfalen 1982; Röntgenpreis, Univ. of Giessen 1964. *Publications:* Kernphysik, Atomphysik, Der gebrochene Spiegel 1989, research papers and review articles in physics journals. *Leisure interest:* sailing. *Address:* Institut für Strahlen- und Kernphysik der Universität Bonn, Nussallee 14, 53113 Bonn (Office); Hardtweg 51, 53639 Königswinter, Germany (Home). *Telephone:* (0228) 732201 (Office); (02223) 22380 (Home).

MAYFIELD, Rt. Rev. Christopher John, M.A.; British ecclesiastic; b. 18 Dec. 1935; s. of Dr. Roger Mayfield and Muriel Mayfield; m. Caroline Roberts 1962; two s. one d.; ed. Sedbergh School, Gonville & Caius Coll. Cambridge and Linacre House, Oxford; ordained deacon 1963, priest 1964; curate, St. Martin-in-the-Bull Ring, Birmingham 1963–67; lecturer, St. Martin's, Birmingham 1967–71; Vicar of Luton 1971–80; Archdeacon of Bedford 1979–85; Bishop Suffragan of Wolverhampton 1985–93; Bishop of Manchester 1993–; Hon. M.Sc. (Cranfield) 1984. *Leisure interests:* marriage, evangelism, walking. *Address:* Bishopscourt, Bury New Road, Manchester, M7 4LE, England. *Telephone:* 0161-792 2096. *Fax:* 0161-792 6826.

MAYHEW OF TWYSDEN, Baron (Life Peer) cr. 1997, of Kilndown in the County of Kent, **Patrick Barnabas Burke Mayhew,** Kt., P.C., Q.C.; British politician and barrister; b. 11 Sept. 1929, Cookham, Berks.; s. of the late A. G. H. Mayhew and Sheila M. B. Roche; m. Jean Elizabeth Gurney 1963; four s.; ed. Tonbridge School and Balliol Coll., Oxford; Pres. Oxford Union Soc. 1952; called to Bar (Middle Temple) 1955; apptd. Q.C. 1972; M.P. (Conservative) for Tunbridge Wells (now Royal Tunbridge Wells) 1974–97; Parl. Sec., Dept. of Employment 1979–81; Minister of State, Home Office 1981–83; Solicitor-Gen. 1983–87; Attorney-Gen. 1987–92; Sec. of State for Northern Ireland 1992–97. *Leisure interests:* country pursuits, sailing. *Address:* House of Lords, Westminster, London, SW1A 0PW, England.

MAYNARD SMITH, John, B.A., B.SC., F.R.S.; British professor; b. 6 Jan. 1920, London; s. of Sidney Maynard Smith and Isobel Mary Pitman; m. Sheila Matthew 1941; two s. one d.; ed. Eton Coll., Trinity Coll., Cambridge, Univ. Coll., London; aircraft engineer 1941–47; lecturer in Zoology, Univ. Coll. London 1952–65; School of Biological Sciences, Univ. of Sussex, (Dean 1965–72), Prof. of Biology 1965–85, Emer. Prof. 1985–; Foreign Assoc. N.A.S.; Hon. D.Sc. (Kent, Sussex, Simon Fraser, Oxford, Chicago); Darwin Medal, Royal Soc. 1986, Royal Medal 1997, Balzan Prize 1991. *Publications:* The Theory of Evolution 1958, The Evolution of Sex 1978, Evolution and the Theory of Games 1983, Evolutionary Genetics 1989, The Major Transitions in Evolution (with E. Szathmáry) 1995. *Leisure interest:* gardening. *Address:* The White House, Kingston Ridge, Lewes, Sussex, BN7 3JX, England. *Telephone:* (01273) 474659.

MAYNE, David Quinn, PH.D., F.R.S., F.ENG.; British university professor; b. 23 April 1930, Germiston, South Africa; s. of Leslie Harper Mayne and Jane Quin; m. Josephine Mary Hess 1954; three d.; ed. Christian Brothers' Coll., Boksburg, Univ. of The Witwatersrand, South Africa; lecturer, Univ. of The Witwatersrand 1951–54, 1957–59; Research Engineer, British Thomson Houston Co. 1955–56; lecturer, Imperial Coll. of Science, Tech. and Medicine 1959–66, Reader 1967–70, Prof. 1970–89; Prof. of Electrical and Computer Eng., Univ. of Calif., Davis 1989–96, Prof. Emer. 1997–, Head Dept. of Electrical Eng. 1984–88, Sr. Research Fellow 1979; Sr. Research Fellow Dept. of Electrical and Electronic Eng., Imperial Coll., Univ. of London 1996–; Visiting Research Fellow, Harvard Univ., U.S.A. 1970; Visiting Prof. Univ. of Calif., Berkeley, Univ. of Newcastle, Australia, IIT, Delhi, Academia Sinica, China, Univ. of Calif., Davis; Hon. D.Sc. (Edin.) 1995. *Publications:* Differential Dynamic Programming 1970; more than 200 papers in professional journals on optimization, optimal control, adaptive control and optimization-based design. *Leisure interests:* walking, cross-country skiing, music. *Address:* 123 Elgin Crescent, London, W11 2JH, England.

MAYNE, (David) Roger, B.A.; British photographer and artist; b. 5 May 1929, Cambridge; s. of A. B. Mayne and D. (née Watson) Mayne; m. Ann Jellicoe 1962; one s. one d.; ed. Rugby School, Balliol Coll., Oxford; self-taught in photography; photographs of London and other city street scenes 1955–61; taught at Bath Acad. of Art, Corsham 1966–69; main solo exhbns.: ICA, London 1956, AIA Gallery, London 1959, Portraits, Royal Court Foyer 1960, Arnolfini Gallery, Bristol 1965, Daughter and Son, Half Moon, London 1972, then Arnolfini 1974 and Diaframma, Milan 1977, Landscape Photographs, ICA 1978, Retrospective, V & A Museum, London 1986, Parco, Tokyo 1986, Prakapas Gallery, New York 1989, Street Photographs 1956–61, South Bank Centre Tour 1987–91, Zelda Cheatle Gallery, London 1992; mixed exhbns. include: Art for Society, Whitechapel Art Gallery, London 1978, Objects the V & A Collects, V & A 1978, Personal Choice, V & A 1983, Subjective Fotografie, Folkwang Museum, Essen and tour 1984–85, Through the Looking Glass, British Photography 1945–89, Barbican Art Gallery, London and Manchester City Art Gallery 1989, The Sixties London Art Scene, Barbican Art Gallery, London 1993, Three Masters, Laurence Miller Gallery, New York 1993, Young Meteors, British Photojournalism 1957–65, Nat. Museum of Photography, Film and TV, Bradford 1998; works in Museum of Modern Art, New York, Metropolitan Museum of Art, New York, Art Inst. of Chicago, Bibliothèque Nationale, Paris, Nat. Gallery of Australia, Canberra, V & A Museum, London, Arts Council of G.B. *Publications:* Things Being Various (with others) 1967, The Shell Guide to Devon (with Ann Jellicoe) 1975, The Street Photographs of Roger Mayne 1986, 1993. *Leisure interests:* listening to music, gardening, looking at art exhbns., watching sport. *Address:* Colway Manor, Colway Lane, Lyme Regis, Dorset, DT7 3HD, England. *Telephone:* (01297) 442821.

MAYOR ZARAGOZA, Federico, DR.PHAR.; Spanish politician, biologist and university official; b. 27 Jan. 1934, Barcelona; s. of Federico Mayor and Juana Zaragoza; m. María Angeles Menéndez 1956; two s. one d.; ed. Univ. Complutense of Madrid; Prof. of Biochemistry, Faculty of Pharmacy, Granada Univ. 1963–73; Rector, Granada Univ. 1968–72; Prof. of Biochemistry, Autonomous Univ., Madrid 1973, Chair. Severo Ochoa Molecular Biology Centre (Higher Council of Scientific Research) 1974–78; Under-Sec. Ministry of Educ. and Science 1974–75; mem. Cortes (Parl.) for Granada 1977–78; Chair. Advisory Cttee. for Scientific and Tech. Research 1974–78; Deputy Dir.-Gen. UNESCO 1978–81, Dir.-Gen. Nov. 1987–; Minister for Educ. and Science 1981–82; Dir. Inst. of the Sciences of Man, Madrid 1983–87; mem. European Parl. 1987; mem. Club of Rome 1981–; Academician, Royal Acad. of Pharmacy; mem. European Acad. of Arts, Sciences and Humanities, Int. Cell Research Org. (ICRO), A.A.A.S., The Biochemical Soc. (U.K.), French Soc. of Biological Chem., American Chemical Soc., Academia de Bellas Artes and numerous other orgs.; Dr. h.c. (Westminster) 1995; Grand Cross, Alfonso X El Sabio, Orden Civil de la Sanidad, Carlos III, Caro y Cuervo (Colombia); Commdr. Placa del Libertador (Venezuela); Grand Officier, Ordre Nat. du Mérite (France). *Publications:* A contraviento (poems) 1987, Mañana siempre es tarde 1987 (English version: Tomorrow Is Always Too Late 1992), Aguafuertes (poems) 1991 (English version: Patterns 1994), La nueva página 1994, La mémoire de l'avenir 1994; numerous specialized works, transls., articles. *Leisure interests:* reading, writing, music. *Address:* Office of the Director-General, UNESCO, 7 place de Fontenoy, 75352 Paris 07 SP, France.

MAYOROV, Col.-Gen., Leonid Sergeyevich; Russian army officer; b. 22 July 1941, Georgiyevsk, Stavropol Territory; m.; two d.; ed. Mil. Automobile Commanding School, Mil. Acad. of Home Front and Transport, Mil. Gen. Staff Acad.; army service 1966-; Head of staff, Deputy Commdr. of Div. 1976–79; Commdr. of Div., Head of Staff of army, Commdr. of army Baikal Command 1979–91; Head of staff, First Deputy Commdr. Volga-Urals Command 1991–92; Commdr. N.-W. Group of Armed Forces 1992–94; First Deputy C.-in-C. United Armed Forces C.I.S. 1994–96; Deputy Sec. Security Council of Russian Fed. 1996–. *Address:* Security Council, Ipatyevsky per. 4/10, entrance 6, Moscow, Russia (Office). *Telephone:* (095) 206 7367 (Office).

MAYOUX, Jacques Georges Maurice Sylvain; French banker and businessman; b. 18 July 1924, Paris; s. of Georges Mayoux and Madeleine de Busscher; one s. one d.; ed. Ecole des Hautes Etudes Commerciales, Ecole Libre des Sciences Politiques, Faculté de Droit et des Lettres de Paris; studied at Ecole Nat. d'Admin. 1949–51; Personal adviser to Minister of Finance 1958, Asst. Gen. Sec. Comité Interministeriel pour les Questions de Coopération Economique Européenne 1958–63; mem. Gen. Council, Banque de France 1963–73; Gen. Man. Caisse Nat. de Crédit Agricole 1963–75; Prof., Inst. d'Etudes Politiques 1964–72; Chair., Gen. Man. Agritel 1972–75, SACILOR (Aciéries et laminoirs de Lorraine) 1978–82, SOLLAC (Soc. Lorraine de laminage continu) 1980–82; Pres. SOLMER 1980–81, Soc.

Générale S.A. 1982–86 (Hon. Pres. 1986), Cen. Cttee. for Rural Renovation 1971, Fondation H.E.C. 1978–90; Pres. French-Canadian Chamber of Commerce 1986–90; Vice-Chair. Goldman Sachs Europe 1989; Insp. Général des Finances 1976–87; Vice-Pres. Admin. Council Euris 1990–; mem. Supervisory Bd. Harpener Gesellschaft 1980–86, Conseil Ordre de la Légion d'honneur 1993–; Commdr., Légion d'honneur, Commdr. Ordre nat. du Mérite, Officier des Arts et des Lettres; Commdr., Phoenix (Greece). *Address:* Société Générale, 38 rue de Bassano, 75008 Paris (Office); Goldman Sachs (Europe), 2 rue de Thann, 75017 Paris, France (Office). *Telephone:* 42.12.11.30.

MAYR, Ernst, PH.D.; American professor of biology; b. 5 July 1904, Kempten, Germany; s. of Otto Mayr and Helene Pusinelli; m. Margarete Simon 1935; two d.; ed. Univs. of Greifswald and Berlin; Asst. Curator, Univ. of Berlin 1926–32; Assoc. Curator, Whitney-Rothschild Collection of American Museum of Natural History 1932–44, Curator 1944–53; Alexander Agassiz Prof. of Zoology, Harvard Univ. 1953–75, Emer. 1975–; Dir. Museum of Comparative Zoology 1961–70; Visiting Prof., Univ. of Minn. 1949, 1974, Univs. of Pavia and Wash. 1951–52; lecturer, Columbia Univ. 1941, 1950, Philadelphia Acad. of Sciences 1947, Univ. of Calif. at Davis 1967; expeditions to Dutch New Guinea, Mandated Territory of New Guinea and Solomon Islands 1928–30; 15 U.S. and foreign Hon. doctorates; Fellow, American Acad. of Arts and Sciences; mem. N.A.S., American Philosophical Soc.; Corresp. Fellow, Zoological Soc. of India; Foreign mem. Royal Soc., Acad. des Sciences 1989; Hon., Foreign and Corresp. mem. of 19 foreign socs.; numerous awards including Leidy Medal of Acad. of Natural Sciences, Philadelphia 1946, Wallace Darwin Medal of Linnean Soc., London 1958, Daniel Giraud Eliot Medal of N.A.S. 1967, Centennial Medal of American Museum of Natural History 1969, Nat. Medal of Science 1970, Linnean Medal 1977, Balzan Prize 1983, Darwin Medal, Royal Soc. 1984, Sarton Medal 1986, Japan Prize 1994, Benjamin Franklin Medal 1995, Lewis Thomas Prize 1998. *Publications:* List of New Guinea Birds 1941, Systematics and the Origin of Species 1942, Birds of the Southwest Pacific 1945, Birds of the Philippines 1946, Methods and Principles of Systematic Zoology 1953, The Species Problem (Editor, American Asscn. for the Advancement of Science Publication No. 50) 1957, Animal Species and Evolution 1963, Principles of Systematic Zoology 1969, 1991, Populations, Species and Evolution 1970, Evolution and the Diversity of Life 1976, The Evolutionary Synthesis (ed.) 1980, The Growth of Biological Thought 1982, Toward a New Philosophy of Biology 1988, One Long Argument 1991, This Is Biology 1997, and 600 articles in journals. *Leisure interests:* natural history, history of biology. *Address:* Museum of Comparative Zoology, Harvard University, 26 Oxford Street, Cambridge, MA 02138 (Office); 207 Badger Terrace, Bedford, MA 01730, U.S.A. (Home). *Telephone:* 495-2476 (Office); (781) 275-9777 (Home).

MAYRHOFER, Manfred, DR. PHIL.; Austrian professor of linguistics; b. 26 Sept. 1926, Linz; s. of late Josef Mayrhofer and Irma Fischer; m. Ingrid Gaissmayer 1984; ed. Univ. of Graz; Dozent 1951; Prof. Univ. of Würzburg 1958, Univ. of the Saar 1962; Prof. of Indo-European Linguistics, Univ. of Vienna 1966–88, now Prof. Emer.; mem. 16 acads. of sciences; Hon. D. Lit. (Illinois) 1985. *Publications:* twelve books including The Old Iranian Names 1979, Etymological Dictionary of Old Indo-Aryan 1992, 1996. *Address:* 1190 Vienna, Bauernfeldgasse 9/2/6, Austria. *Telephone:* 36 825 00.

MAYSTADT, Philippe, L. EN D.; Belgian politician; b. 14 March 1948, Petit-Rechain; m.; three c.; Adviser, Office of Minister for Regional Affairs 1974; Deputy for Charleroi 1977–; Sec. of State for Regional Economy 1979–80; Minister of Civil Service and Scientific Policy 1980–81, for the Budget, Scientific Policy and Planning 1981–85, of Econ. Affairs 1985–88; Minister of Finance 1988–, of Foreign Trade 1995–, also Deputy Prime Minister; Chair. IMF Interim Cttee. 1993–98. *Address:* Ministry of Finance, 12 rue de la Loi, 1000 Brussels, Belgium. *Telephone:* (02) 233-81-11. *Fax:* (02) 233-80-03.

MAZANKOWSKI, Hon. Donald Frank, P.C., M.P.; Canadian politician; b. 27 July 1935, Viking, Alta.; s. of the late Frank Mazankowski and Dora Lonowski; m. Lorraine E. Poleschuk 1958; three s.; ed. High School; mem. Parl. 1968–93; Minister of Transport and Minister responsible for Canadian Wheat Board 1979; Minister of Transport 1984–86; Pres. Treasury Bd. 1987–88; Minister responsible for Privatization, Regulatory Affairs and Operations 1988, of Agric. 1989–91, of Finance 1991–93; Deputy Prime Minister 1989–93, Pres. of the Queens Privy Council for Canada 1989–91; Gov. Univ. of Alta.; Dir numerous cos.; Progressive Conservative Party; Hon. D.Eng. (Tech. Univ. of Nova Scotia) 1987. *Leisure interests:* fishing, golf. *Address:* P.O. Box 1350, Vegreville, Alta., T9C 1S5, Canada (Home).

MAZEAUD, Pierre; French politician; b. 24 Aug. 1929, Lyon; m. 1st Marie Prohom 1953 (divorced 1960); two d.; m. 2nd Sophie Hamel 1967; one s. one d.; Judge of Tribunal of Instance, Lamentin, Martinique 1961; in charge of Conf., Faculty of Law, Paris 1955; Tech. Adviser to Prime Minister 1961; Judge of Tribunal of Great Instance, Versailles 1962; Tech. Adviser to Minister of Justice 1962; Tech. Adviser to Minister of Youth and Sports 1967–68; Deputy for Hauts-de-Seine 1968–73, for Haute-Savoie 1988–98, Vice.-Pres. Nat. Ass. 1992–93, 1997–98, Vice-Pres. Groupe des députés sportifs 1968; Minister responsible for Youth and Sport 1973–76; Counsellor of State 1976; Pres. Law Comm. of Assemblée Nationale 1987–88, 1993–98; Titular Judge, High Court 1987–; Mayor, Saint-Julien-en-Genevois 1979–89; regional counsellor, Rhône-Alpes 1992–98; mem. Constitutional Council 1998–; climbed Everest 1978 (oldest man to climb Everest); mem. Conseil Constitutionnel; Chevalier, Légion d'honneur; R.P.R. *Publications:* Montagne pour un homme nu 1971, Everest 1978, Sport et Liberté 1980, Nanga Parbat—montagne cruelle 1982, Des cailloux et des mouches ou l'échec à l'Himalaya 1985, Rappel au Règlement 1995. *Address:* Conseil constitutionnel, 2 rue de Montpensier, 75001 Paris (Office); 8 rue Charlemagne, 75004 Paris, France (Home).

MAZOWIECKI, Tadeusz; Polish politician and journalist; b. 18 April 1927, Płock; s. of Bronisław Mazowiecki and Jadwiga Mazowiecka; widower; three s.; Chair. Acad. Publishing Co-operative, Warsaw 1947–48; mem. Catholic Asscn. PAX; contrib. to daily and weekly PAX publs., dismissed 1955; co-f., mem. of Bd., Vice-Pres. Warsaw Catholic Intelligentsia Club (KIK) 1956; co-f. and Chief Ed. Catholic monthly Więź (Bond) 1958–81; Deputy to Sejm (Parl.) PRL (Polish People's Repub.) 1961–72; mem. of various opposition groups and protest movts. 1968–89; co-f. and mem. Council Soc. for Acad. Courses (Flying Univ.) 1977–89; Head, Team of Experts, Lenin Shipyard, Gdańsk 1980; co-Ed. Solidarity Trades Union Statutes; adviser to Solidarity Nat. Consultative Comm.; organiser and First Chief Ed. of Solidarity weekly 1981–89; interned 1981–82; participant Round Table plenary debates, Co-Chair. group for union pluralism, mem. group for political reforms, team for mass-media, co-ordinator negotiation teams from opposition 1989; Prime Minister of Poland 1989–90; Deputy to Sejm (Parl.) 1991–; Chair. Democratic Union 1990–94; Chair. (merged with Liberal Democratic Congress to form Freedom Union) Freedom Union 1994–95; Chair. Parl. Comm. for European Integration 1997–; UN Special Rapporteur of Comm. on Human Rights investigating human rights sitation in fmr. Yugoslavia 1992–95; mem. PEN Club; Dr. h.c. (Louvain) 1990, (Genoa) 1991, (Giessen) 1993, (Poitiers) 1994; Peace Prize (Anglican Church, New York) 1990, Premio Napoli 1992; Hon. LL.D. (Exeter) 1997; Andrzej Strug Award 1990, Freedom Award (American Jewish Congress) 1990, Giorgio La Pira Award of Peace and Culture 1991, Polish-German Award 1994, St. Adalbert Award 1995, Order of White Eagle 1995, European Human Rights Award 1996, Officier Légion d'honneur 1998. *Publications include:* Cross-roads and Values 1971, The Second Face of Europe 1979, Internment 1984. *Address:* Sejm RP, ul. Wiejska 4/6/8, 00-902 Warsaw, Poland. *Telephone:* (22) 694 21 35.

MAZRUI, Ali A., M.A., D.PHIL.; Kenyan professor of political science; b. 24 Feb. 1933, Mombasa; s. of Al'Amin Ali Mazrui and Safia Suleiman Mazrui; m. 1st Molly Vickerman 1962 (divorced 1982); three s.; m. 2nd Pauline Ejima Uti-Mazrui 1991; two s.; ed. Columbia Univ., New York, Univs. of Manchester and Oxford; Lecturer in Political Science, Makerere Univ., Uganda 1963–65, Prof. of Political Science 1965–72, Dean of Social Sciences 1967–69; Assoc. Ed. Transition Magazine 1964–73, Co-Ed. Mawazo Journal 1967–73; Visiting Prof. Univ. of Chicago 1965; Research Assoc. Harvard Univ. 1965–66; Dir. African Section, World Order Models Project 1968–73; Visiting Prof. Northwestern Univ., U.S.A. 1969, McGill and Denver Univs. 1969, London and Manchester Univs. 1971, Dyason Lecture Tour of Australia 1972; Vice-Pres. Int. Political Science Asscn. 1970–73, Int. Congress of Africanists 1967–73, Int. Congress of African Studies 1978–, Int. African Inst. 1987–, World Congress of Black Intellectuals 1988–; Fellow, Center for Advanced Study in the Behavioral Sciences, Stanford 1972–73; Prof. of Political Science, Univ. of Michigan 1973–91; Sr. Visiting Fellow, Hoover Inst. on War, Revolution and Peace, Stanford 1973–74; Dir. Centre for Afro-American and African Studies 1979–81; Research Prof. Univ. of Jos, Nigeria 1981–86; Andrew D. White Prof.-at-Large, Cornell Univ. 1986–92; Albert Schweitzer Prof. in the Humanities, State Univ. of New York, Binghamton 1989–; Reith Lecturer 1979; Presenter BBC TV series The Africans 1986; mem. World Bank's Council of African Advisers; Int. Org. Essay Prize 1964, Northwestern Univ. Book Prize 1969. *Publications:* Towards a Pax Africana 1967, On Heroes and Uhuru-Worship 1967, The Anglo-African Commonwealth 1967, Violence and Thought 1969, Co-Ed. Protest and Power in Black Africa 1970, The Trial of Christopher Okigbo 1971, Cultural Engineering and Nation Building in East Africa 1972, Co-Ed. Africa in World Affairs: The Next Thirty Years 1973, A World Federation of Cultures: An African Perspective 1976, Political Values and the Educated Class in Africa 1978, Africa's International Relations 1978, The African Condition (Reith Lectures) 1980, Nationalism and New States in Africa (Co-author) 1984, The Africans: A Triple Heritage 1986, Cultural Forces in World Politics 1989, Ed. Africa Since 1935 (Vol. VIII of UNESCO General History of Africa) 1993. *Leisure interests:* travel, dining out, swimming, reading thrillers and mystery novels.

MAZUROK, Yuri Antonovich; Ukrainian opera singer (baritone); b. 18 July 1931, Krasnik, Poland (now Ukraine); one s.; ed. Lvov Inst. and Moscow Conservatoire; awards include Prague Spring Vocal Competition 1960, Int. Enesco Singing Competition, Bucharest, 1961, First Prize at World Fair, Montreal, 1967; début with Bolshoi Opera 1963, Prin. of the co. 1964–; has performed world-wide; *roles include:* Eugene (Eugene Onegin), Prince Yeletsky (The Queen of Spades), Andrei (War and Peace), Figaro (The Barber of Seville), Scarpia (Tosca) and Escamillo (Carmen) and especially Verdi repertoire, including René (Un Ballo in Maschera), Rodrigo (Don Carlos), George Germont (La Traviata); U.S.S.R. People's Artist 1976. *Address:* Teatralnaya Pl. 1, Bolshoi Theatre, 103009 Moscow, Russia. *Telephone:* 201-24-85 (Home).

MAZURSKY, Paul, B.A.; American film writer and director; b. 25 April 1930, Brooklyn, N.Y.; s. of David Mazursky and Jean Gerson; m. Betsy

Purdy 1953; two d.; ed. Brooklyn Coll.; stage, TV and film actor 1951–; night club comedian 1954–60; writer, Danny Kaye Show 1963–67; co-writer, I Love You, Alice B. Toklas (film) 1968. *Films include:* as writer and dir., Bob & Carol & Ted & Alice 1969, Alex in Wonderland 1970, Blume in Love 1972, Harry & Tonto 1973, Next Stop, Greenwich Village 1976, An Unmarried Woman 1977–78, Willie & Phil 1979–80, Tempest 1982, Moscow on the Hudson 1984; as writer, producer and dir., Down and Out in Beverly Hills 1986, Moon Over Parador 1988, Enemies A Love Story, Scenes From a Mall, The Pickle 1992, Faithful 1995; as actor films include: A Star is Born, Scenes from the Class Struggle in Beverly Hills, Man Trouble, Deathwatch, Miami Rhapsody, Two Days in the Valley. *Address:* c/o Ken Kamins, 8942 Wilshire Boulevard, Beverly Hills, CA 92011, U.S.A.

MAZZAG, István; Hungarian artist; b. 14 April 1958, Györ; ed. Hungarian Acad. of Arts Faculty of Painting, Budapest; major one-man exhbns. Tatgalerie, Vienna (jtly. with Ákos Birkás) 1986, Dorottya Street Gallery, Budapest 1987, Landhaus Gallery, Solothurn 1988, Iparterv Gallery, Budapest 1988, Downtown Gallery, Prague 1988, Gallery of Miscolc, Miskolc 1988, Academia Ungheria, Rome 1989, Ujlak Gallery, Budapest 1990, Árkád Gallery, Budapest 1991, House of Free Culture, Székesfehérvár 1991, Eve Art Gallery, Budapest, Galerie Synthese, Linz 1992; has participated in some 50 group exhbns. around the world; Smohay Prize 1984; Derkovits Scholarship 1985; First Prize, Sibelius 2000, Rome 1989. *Leisure interest:* skiing.

MAZZARELLA, David; American newspaper editor; b. 1938; with Assoc. Press, Lisbon, New York, Rome 1962–70; with Daily American, Rome 1971–75, Gannett News, Washington, D.C. 1976–77, The Bridgewater, Bridgewater, N.J. 1977–83; now Ed. U.S.A. Today. *Address:* U.S.A. Today, 1000 Wilson Boulevard, Arlington, Va. 22209, U.S.A.

MAZZONI DELLA STELLA, Vittorio; Italian banker; b. 21 May 1941, Siena; ed. Univ. of Florence; joined Monte dei Paschi di Siena bank, Naples 1966, worked in Rome, then Siena brs., then in Market and Econ. Research Dept., apptd. Man. 1976, mem. Bd. of Dirs. 1990, Deputy Chair. 1991–, Deputy Chair. Monte dei Paschi Banque, Paris 1991; mem. Bd. of Dirs. Sindibank, Barcelona 1991; Chair. ICLE (MPS banking group), Rome 1991; mem. Bd. of Dirs. Centro Finanziaria S.p.A., Rome 1987–; mem. Bd. of Dirs. and Exec. Cttee. Deposit Protection Fund, Rome 1991–; mem. Bd. Asscn. of Italian Bankers (ABI) 1991–; elected Prov. Councillor, Siena 1980, Deputy Chair. Prov. Council 1980–82, Mayor 1983–90; Chair. Chigiana Foundation (music acad.), Siena 1991–. *Address:* Monte dei Paschi di Siena, Siena, Italy.

MBASOGO, Lieut.-Col. Teodoro Obiang Nguema; Equatorial Guinean politician and army officer; ed. in Spain; fmr. Deputy Minister of Defence; overthrew fmr. Pres. Macias Nguema in coup; Pres. of Equatorial Guinea Aug. 1979–; Supreme Commdr. of the Armed Forces 1979–; Minister of Defence 1986. *Address:* Oficina del Presidente, Malabo, Equatorial Guinea.

M'BAYE, Kéba; Senegalese judge; b. 5 Aug. 1924, Kaolack; s. of Abdoul M'baye and Coura M'bengue; m. Mariette Diarra 1951; three s. five d.; ed. Ecole Nat. de la France d'Outre-mer; Judge of Appeal, Supreme Court of Senegal, First Pres. 1964; fmr. Chair. Int. Comm. of Jurists, Chair. Comm. on Codification of Law of Civil and Commercial Liabilities; Vice-Chair. Exec. Cttee., Int. Inst. of Human Rights (René Cassin Foundation); mem. Supreme Council of Magistrature, Int. Penal Law Asscn. (and Admin. Council), Int. Criminology Asscn., Société de Législation comparée, Int. Olympic Cttee. (mem. Exec. Bd. 1985–); Judge, Int. Court of Justice, The Hague 1982–91 (Vice-Pres. 1987–91); fmr. mem. various UN bodies, fmr. mem. or Chair. Comm. on Human Rights and other such cttees. and in various symposia organized by Int. Asscn. of Legal Sciences, Red Cross, Unidroit and UNESCO; fmr. Pres. and mem. Int. Cttee. on Comparative Law, Int. African Law Asscn., Int. Cttee. for Social Science Documentation; Hon. Pres. World Fed. of UN Asscns. *Publications:* numerous publs. on Senegalese law, the law of black Africa and human rights. *Leisure interest:* golf. *Address:* Rue "G" angle rue Léon Gontran Damas, Boîte postale 5865, Dakar, Senegal. *Telephone:* (221) 25 55 01.

MBEKI, Thabo Mvuyelwa, M.A.; South African politician; b. 18 June 1942, Idutywa; s. of Govan Mbeki; m. Zanele Mbeki; ed. Lovedale, Alice, St. John's Umtata, Univ. of London and Sussex Univ.; Leader African Students Org. 1961; Youth Organiser for African Nat. Congress (ANC), Johannesburg 1961–62; 6 weeks detention, Byo 1962; left S.A. 1962; official, ANC offices, London, England 1967–70; mil. training, U.S.S.R. 1970; Asst. Sec. ANC Revolutionary Council 1971–72; Acting ANC Rep., Swaziland 1975–76; ANC Rep., Nigeria 1976–78; mem. ANC, N.E.C. 1975, re-elected 1985; Dir. Information and Publicity, ANC 1984–89, Head, Dept. of Int. Affairs 1989–93, Chair. ANC 1993; First Deputy Pres. of S.A. May 1994–(99); Pres. (desig.) of South Africa 1999–; mem. Nat. Exec. Cttee., A.N.C., A.N.C. Del. on Talks about Talks, with S.A. Govt. 1990; mem. Bd. IOC 1993–. *Address:* Office of the President, Private Bag X1000, Pretoria 0001, South Africa.

M'BOW, Amadou-Mahtar, L. ÈS L.; Senegalese educationist; b. 20 March 1921, Dakar; m. Raymonde Sylvain 1951; one s. two d.; ed. Faculté des Lettres, Univ. de Paris; Prof., Coll. de Rosso, Mauritania 1951–53; Dir. Service of Fundamental Educ. 1953–57; Minister of Educ. and Culture 1957–58; Prof. Lycée Faidherbe, St. Louis 1958–64; Ecole Normale Supérieure, Dakar 1964–66; Minister of Educ. 1966–68; Minister of Culture, Youth and Sports 1968–70; Asst. Dir.-Gen. for Educ., UNESCO 1970–74; Dir.-Gen. UNESCO 1974–87; Hon. Prof., Faculty of Humanities, Ind. Univ. of Santo Domingo (Dominican Repub.), Ecole Normale Supérieure, Dakar 1979, Nat. Independent Univ. of Mexico 1979, Escuela Superior de Administración y Dirección de Empresas, Barcelona 1984; mem. Acad. du Royaume du Maroc; Assoc. mem. Acad. of Athens; 46 hon. doctorates, 35 decorations, freedom of 11 cities (1987) including Dr. h.c. (Univ. of the Andes, State Univ. of Mongolia, State Univ. of Haiti, Khartoum, Sri Lanka, Tribhuvan Univ. Nepal, Pontifical Catholic Univ. of Peru, Buenos Aires, Granada, Sherbrooke, W. Indies, Open Univ. U.K., Belfast, Sofia, Nairobi, Philippines, Malaya, Venice, Uppsala, Moscow, Paris); Grand Cross of the Order of the Liberator (Venezuela), Grand Cross of the Order of the Sun (Peru), Commdr. and Grand Officier Ordre National (Ivory Coast), Commdr. des Palmes académiques (France), Officier, Ordre du Mérite (Senegal), Commdr. de l'Ordre national de Haute Volta, Bintang Jasa Utama (Order of Merit, Indonesia), Kawkab Star (Jordan), Order of Merit (Syria) and numerous other decorations; Prix "Terre des Hommes", Canada. *Publications:* numerous monographs, articles in educational journals, textbooks, etc. *Address:* B.P. 5276, Dakar-Fann, Senegal; B.P. 434, Rabat, Morocco.

MBOWENI, Tito, M.A.; South African politician; b. 1959; ed. Univ. of E. Anglia; mem. ANC 1980 (ANC Mil. Council, Zambia 1988), fmr. Deputy Head Dept. of Econ. Planning, Co-ordinator for Trade and Industry; Minister of Labour, Govt. of Nat. Unity 1994–99; Gov. (desig.) SA Reserve Bank 1999–. *Address:* South African Reserve Bank, 370 Church Street, P.O. Box 427, Pretoria 0001, South Africa. *Telephone:* (12) 3133911. *Fax:* (12) 3133197.

MDLALOSE, Frank Themba, B.SC., U.E.D., M.B., CH.B.; South African politician; b. 29 Nov. 1931, Nqutu Dist. KwaZulu; s. of Jaconiah Zwelabo Mdlalose and Thabitha Mthembu; m. Eunice Nokuthula 1956; three s. two d.; ed. Univ. of Fort Hare, Rhodes Univ. and Univ. of Natal; Intern, King Edward VII Hosp. Durban 1959; pvt. medical practice, Pretoria 1960–62, Steadville, Ladysmith, Natal, Atteridgeville 1962–70; medical practitioner, Madadeni 1970–78; Nat. Chair. Inkatha 1977; Minister of Health, KwaZulu 1983–90, Acting Minister of Educ. 1990, Minister without Portfolio 1991–94; Premier, KwaZulu-Natal 1994. *Address:* Private Bag X01, Ulundi 3838, KwaZulu, South Africa. *Telephone:* (0358) 202432. *Fax:* (0358) 202470.

MEACHER, Rt. Hon. Michael Hugh, P.C., M.P.; British politician; b. 4 Nov. 1939, Hemel Hempstead, Herts.; s. of late George H. and Doris M. (née Foxell) Meacher; m. 1st Molly C. (née Reid) 1962 (divorced 1985); two s. two d.; m. 2nd Lucianne Craven 1988; ed. Berkhamsted School, New Coll., Oxford and London School of Econs.; Lecturer in Social Admin., Univ. of York and L.S.E. 1966–70; M.P. for Oldham West 1970–97, for Oldham West and Royton 1997–; Jr. Minister, Dept. of Industry 1974–75, Dept. of Health and Social Security 1975–76, Dept. of Trade 1976–79; mem. Nat. Exec. Cttee. of Labour Party 1983–88, Shadow Cabinet 1983–97, Shadow Spokesman for Health and Social Security 1983–87, for Employment 1987–89, for Social Security 1989–92, for Overseas Devt. 1992–93, for Citizens' Rights 1993–94, for Transport 1994–95, for Employment 1995–96, for Environmental Protection 1996–97; Minister of State for the Environment May 1997–; mem. Treasury Select Cttee. 1980–83; cand. for deputy leadership of Labour Party 1983; mem. Child Poverty Action Group and other voluntary orgs. *Publications:* Taken for a Ride: Special Residential Homes for the Elderly Mentally Infirm: A Study of Separatism in Social Policy 1972, Socialism with a Human Face 1982, Diffusing Power 1992; over 1,000 articles on econ., industrial and social policy, regional devt., defence issues, the Welfare State, media reform, civil service reform, the police, etc. *Leisure interests:* sport, music, reading. *Address:* House of Commons, Westminster, London, S.W.1; 34 Kingscliffe Gardens, London, S.W.19, England.

MEADOWS, Bernard William; British sculptor; b. 19 Feb. 1915, Norwich; s. of W. A. F. Meadows and E. M. Meadows; m. Marjorie Winifred Payne 1939; two d.; ed. City of Norwich School, Norwich School of Art and Royal Coll. of Art; exhibited Venice Biennale 1952, 1964, British Council exhbns., N. and S. America, Germany, Canada, New Zealand, Australia, Scandinavia, Finland and France; open-air exhbns. of Sculpture, Battersea Park, London 1952, 1960, 1963, 1966, Paris 1956, Holland Park 1957, Antwerp 1953, 1959, Arnhem 1958, British Pavilion, Brussels 1958, São Paulo Bienal 1958, Carnegie Inst., Pittsburgh 1959–61; one-man exhibitions London and New York 1957–; works in Tate Gallery, Victoria and Albert Museum and collections in Europe, America and Australia; mem. Royal Fine Art Comm. 1971–76; Prof. of Sculpture, Royal Coll. of Art, London 1960–80. *Publication:* 34 etchings and box (for Molloy by Samuel Beckett) 1967. *Address:* 34 Belsize Grove, London, NW3 4TR, England. *Telephone:* 0171-722 0772.

MÉBIAME, Léon; Gabonese politician; b. 1 Sept. 1934, Libreville; ed. Coll. Moderne, Libreville, Centre de Préparation aux Carrières Administratives, Brazzaville, Ecole Fédérale de Police, Ecole Nat. de Police, Lyon, France; posted to Chad 1957–59; Police Supt. 1960; further studies at Sûreté Nat. Française, Paris; Deputy Dir. Sûreté Nat., Gabon 1962–63, Dir. 1963–67; successively Under-Sec. of State for the Interior, Minister Del. for the Interior and Minister of State in charge of Labour, Social Affairs and the Nat. Org. of Gabonese Women 1967; Vice-Pres. of the Govt., Keeper of the Seals and Minister of Justice Jan.–July 1968; Vice-Pres. of the Govt. in charge of Co-ordination 1968–75, Pres. Nat. Consultative Council 1972; Prime Minister 1975–90; Minister of Co-ordination, Housing and Town Planning 1975–76, of Land Registry 1976–78, of Co-ordination, Agric., Rural Devt., Waters and Forests 1978–79, in Charge of State Corpns. 1980–82, for Merchant Marine and Civil Service 1982–83, of Transport and Civil and

Commercial Aviation 1989–90; Presidential Cand. Dec. 1993; Commdr. Etoile Equatoriale; Grand Officier, Order nat. de Côte d'Ivoire, du Mérite Centrafricain; Chevalier, Etoile Noire du Bénin. *Address:* c/o Office du Premier Ministre, B.P. 546, Libreville, Gabon.

MECHANIC, David, M.A., PH.D.; American professor of behavioural sciences; b. 21 Feb. 1936, New York; s. of Louis Mechanic and Tillie (Penn) Mechanic; two s.; ed. City Coll. of N.Y. and Stanford Univ.; mem. Faculty, Univ. of Wis. 1960–79, Prof. of Sociology 1965–73, John Bascom Prof. 1973–79, Dir. Center for Medical Sociology and Health Services Research 1971–79, Chair. Dept. of Sociology 1968–70; Prof. of Social Work and Sociology, Rutgers Univ. 1979–, Univ. Prof. and Dean Faculty of Arts and Sciences 1981–84, Univ. Prof. and Rene Dubos Prof. of Behavioral Sciences 1984–, Dir. Inst. for Health, Health Care Policy and Aging Research 1985–; mem. various advisory panels etc.; mem. N.A.S.; mem. Inst. of Medicine of N.A.S., American Acad. of Arts and Sciences; Guggenheim Fellowship 1977–78; numerous awards. *Publications:* author of twelve books and about 300 papers and chapters and ed. of nine books on sociological and health care subjects. *Address:* Institute for Health Policy and Aging Research, Rutgers University, 30 College Avenue, New Brunswick, NJ 08901, U.S.A. *Telephone:* (732) 932-8415. *Fax:* (732) 932-1253.

MECHANIC, William M. (Bill), PH.D.; American business executive; b. Detroit, Mich.; ed. Michigan State Univ., Univ. of Southern California; Dir. of Programming SelecTV 1978–80, Vice-Pres. Programming 1980–82; Vice-Pres. Pay TV, Paramount Pictures Corpn. 1982–84; Vice-Pres. Pay TV Sales, Walt Disney Pictures and TV 1984–85, Sr. Vice-Pres. Video 1985–87, Pres. Int. Theatrical Distribution and Worldwide Video 1987–93; Pres. and C.O.O. 20th Century Fox Film Entertainment 1993–96, Chair. and C.E.O. 1996–; Pres. Fox Inc., Beverly Hills, Calif. *Address:* c/o Fox Filmed Entertainment, 20th Century Fox, 1020 West Pico Boulevard, Los Angeles, CA 90035, U.S.A.

MEČIAR, Vladimír, DR.IUR.; Slovak politician; b. 26 July 1942, Zvolen; s. of Jozef Mečiar and Anna (née Tomková) Mečiarová; m. Margita (née Bencková) Mečiarová; two s. two d.; ed. Komenský Univ., Bratislava; clerk 1959–69; various posts in Czechoslovak Union of Youth 1967–68; expelled from all posts and CP; employed as manual worker because of his attitude to Soviet occupation of C.S.S.R., Heavy Eng. Works, Dubnica nad Váhom 1970–73; clerk, later commercial lawyer for Skloobal Nemšová 1973–90; politically active again after collapse of communist system 1989; Minister of Interior and Environment, Govt. of Slovak (Fed.) Repub. 1990, Deputy to House of Nations, Fed. Ass. 1990–92; Chair. Movt. for Democratic Slovakia 1991–; Premier, Govt. of Slovak Repub. 1990–91, 1992, of Slovakia 1993–98; Hon. Citizen Ladomerská Vieska 1993; Dr. h.c. (Lomonosov Univ., Moscow) 1995, (Brača Karič Univ., Yugoslavia) 1996; Order of Maltese Cross 1995, Peutinger Award (Germany) 1995. *Leisure interests:* sport, music, literature, hiking. *Address:* Movement for Democratic Slovakia, Tomášikova 32/a, Bratislava, Slovakia. *Telephone:* (7) 23 01 44; 23 47 42.

MECKSEPER, Friedrich; German painter and printmaker; b. 8 June 1936, Bremen; s. of Gustav Meckseper and Lily Ringel-Debatin; m. Barbara Müller 1962; one s. two d.; ed. State Art Acad., Stuttgart, State Univ. for the Visual Arts, Berlin; numerous one-man and group exhbns. in Europe, U.S.A., Australia and Japan; represented in many major museums of contemporary art and at print biennials world-wide; Prof. of Art, Int. Summer Acad., Salzburg 1977–79; Guest lecturer, London 1968; German-Rome Prize 1963, Prize of the 7th Bienniale, Tokyo 1970, of the 6th Bienniale, Fredrikstad 1982. *Leisure interests:* locomotives, steamboats, ballooning, paintings, etchings, books. *Address:* Landhausstrasse 13, 10717 Berlin, Germany.

MEDAK, Peter; British film director; b. 23 Dec. 1940, Budapest, Hungary; worked with AB-Pathe, London 1956–63; Dir. Universal Pictures 1963–, Paramount Pictures 1967–. *Films directed include:* Negatives 1968, A Day in the Death of Joe Egg 1970, The Ruling Class 1973, Third Girl From the Left 1973, Ghost in the Noonday Sun 1975, The Odd Job 1978, The Changeling 1979, Zorro, Zorro, The Gay Blade 1981, Breaking Through 1984, The Men's Club, The Krays 1990, The Love You Make 1991, Let Him Have It 1991, Romeo is Bleeding 1994, Pontiac Moon; has also dir. several operas, plays and series for U.S. TV. *Address:* c/o Fred Actman & Co., 9255 W. Sunset Boulevard, Suite 901, Los Angeles, CA 90069, U.S.A.

MEDGYESSY, Péter, PH.D.; Hungarian politician and economist; b. 1942, Budapest; ed. Univ. of Budapest; held several positions in Ministry of Finance, Dept. of Finance, Dept. of Prices, Dept. of Int. Finances; fmr. Dir.-Gen. Dept. of State Budget; Minister of Finance 1987–88; Deputy Prime Minister in interim govt. of Miklós Németh (q.v.) 1988–89; Pres., Chief Exec. Magyar Paribas 1990–94; Pres., Chief Exec. Hungarian Bank for Investment and Devt. Ltd. 1994–96; Minister of Finance 1996–98; Pres. Inter-Europa Bank 1998–; Prof. Coll. of Finance and Accounting, Budapest; Vice-Pres. Hungarian Econ. Soc.; Dir. Int. Inst. of Public Finance, Saarbrücken; mem. Presidium Hungarian Bank Asscn. 1996–, Council of World Econ. Forum. *Publications:* several articles on budgetary and exchange rate policies and monetary system in financial and econ. publs. *Address:* Inter-Europa Bank, 1054 Budapest, Szabadság tér 15, Hungary. *Telephone:* 373-6208. *Fax:* (1) 373-6230.

MEDICI, Giuseppe; Italian politician and agricultural economist; b. 24 Oct. 1907; ed. Univs. of Milan and Bologna; Prof. of Agricultural Econs., Univ. of Perugia 1935, of Turin 1936–47; Pres. Istituto Nazionale di Economia Agraria, Rome 1947–62; mem. Italian dels. to ECA international confs.; Pres. Ente Maremma (Land Reform Agency) 1951–53; Prof. Univ. of Naples 1952, Univ. of Rome 1960; mem. of the Senate (Christian Democrat); Minister of Agric. 1954–55, of the Treasury 1956–58, of the Budget 1958–59, of Educ. 1959–60; Minister without Portfolio (with responsibilities for Admin. Reform) 1962–63, Minister of the Budget June–Nov. 1963, Minister of Industry and Commerce 1963–65; Minister of Foreign Affairs June–Dec. 1968, 1972–73; Chair. Montedison 1977; Gov. EIB 1958; Pres. Senate Comm. for Foreign Affairs 1960–62; Pres. World Food Conf., Rome 1974. *Publications include:* Principii di Estimo 1948 (abridged edn. in English Principles of Appraisal 1953), Italy: Agricultural Aspects 1949, I Tipi d'Impresa dell' Agricoltura 1951, Agricoltura e Disoccupazione Vol. I 1952, Land Property and Land Tenure in Italy 1952, Lezioni di Politica Economica 1967. *Address:* c/o Montedison, Foro Bonaparte 31, Milan, Italy.

MEDINA ESTÉVEZ, H.E. Cardinal Jorge Arturo; Chilean ecclesiastic; b. 23 Dec. 1926, Santiago de Chile; ordained priest 1954; Bishop 1985, of Rancagua 1987, of Valparaíso 1993; Archbishop Emer., See of Valparaíso and Pro-Prefect Congregation for Divine Worship and the Discipline of the Sacraments 1996; cr. Cardinal Feb. 1998. *Address:* Congregation for Divine Worship and the Discipline of the Sacraments, Piazza Pio XII 10, 00193 Rome, Italy. *Telephone:* (6) 69884316. *Fax:* (6) 69883499.

MEDVED', Aleksandr Vasilyevich; Ukrainian wrestler; b. 16 Sept. 1937, Belaya Tserkov', Kiev Dist.; Honoured Master of Sports 1964; dean at Minsk Radio Eng. Inst.; mem. CPSU 1965–91; Olympic champion 1964, 1968, 1972; champion of Europe (1966, 1968, 1971–72), champion of U.S.S.R. (eight times 1961–70) many times world champion in free-style middle-weight and heavy-weight wrestling; Order of Lenin; merited coach of U.S.S.R. 1984.

MEDVEDEV, Nikolai Pavlovich; Russian politician; b. 26 Nov. 1952, Anayevo, Mordovia; m.; one s. one d.; ed. Mordovian State Pedagogical Inst., Higher Comsomol School, Central Comsomol Cttee; with Saransk Professional Tech. School; worked in Comsomol orgs. 1975–83; instructor, Saransk City CP Cttee., Sec. CP Cttee. Saransk Machine-construction Factory 1983–90; Deputy Chair. Saransk City Soviet 1990–; R.S.F.S.R. Peoples' Deputy; mem. Presidium, Supreme Soviet; mem. Comm. on Int. Relations at Soviet of Nationalities 1990–93; Head of Dept., Admin. of Russian Presidency 1993–94; Dir. Inst. of Regional Policy 1995–; Deputy Minister on Co-operation with C.I.S. countries 1994–95; mem. State Duma 1996–. *Publications:* several books including Establishment of Federalism in Russia, National Policy in Russia: From Unitarism to Federalism, International Conflicts and Political Stability. *Address:* State Duma, Okhotny ryad 1, 103265 Moscow, Russia. *Telephone:* (095) 292 8000 (Office).

MEDVEDEV, Roy Aleksandrovich, PH.D.; Russian historian and sociologist; b. 14 Nov. 1925, Tbilisi; s. of Aleksandr Romanovich Medvedev and Yulia Medvedeva; twin brother of Zhores Medvedev (q.v.); m. Galina A. Gaidina 1956; one s.; ed. Leningrad State Univ., Acad. of Pedagogical Sciences of U.S.S.R.; mem. CPSU –1969, 1989–91; worker at mil. factory 1943–46; teacher of history, Ural Secondary School 1951–53; Dir. of Secondary School in Leningrad region 1954–56; Deputy to Ed.-in-Chief of Publ. House of Pedagogical Literature, Moscow 1957–59; Head of Dept., Research Inst. of Vocational Educ., Acad. of Pedagogical Sciences of U.S.S.R. 1960–70, Senior Scientist 1970–71; freelance author 1972–; People's Deputy of U.S.S.R., mem. Supreme Soviet of U.S.S.R. 1989–91; mem. Cen. Cttee. CPSU 1990–91; Co-Chair. Socialist Party of Labour 1991–. *Publications:* Vocational Education in Secondary School 1960, Faut-il réhabiliter Staline? 1969, A Question of Madness (with Zhores Medvedev) 1971, Let History Judge 1972, On Socialist Democracy 1975, Qui a écrit le "Don Paisible"? 1975, La Révolution d'octobre était-elle inéluctable 1975, Solschenizyn und die Sowjetische Linke 1976, Khrushchev—The Years in Power (with Zhores Medvedev) 1976, Political Essays 1976, Problems in the Literary Biography of Mikhail Sholokhov 1977, Samizdat Register 1978, Philip Mironov and the Russian Civil War (with S. Starikov) 1978, The October Revolution 1979, On Stalin and Stalinism 1979, On Soviet Dissent 1980, Nikolai Bukharin—The Last Years 1980, Leninism and Western Socialism 1981, An End to Silence 1982, Khrushchev 1983, All Stalin's Men 1984, China and Superpowers 1986, L'URSS che cambia (with G. Chiesa) 1987, Time of Change (with G. Chiesa) 1990, Brezhnev: A Political Biography 1991, Gensek s Lybianki: A Political Portrait of Andropov 1993, 1917. The Russian Revolution 1997, Capitalism in Russia? 1998, and over 300 professional and general articles. *Leisure interest:* allotment gardening. *Address:* c/o Z. A. Medvedev, 4 Osborn Gardens, London, NW7 1DY, England; Abonement Post Box 258, 125475 Moscow A-475, Russia. *Telephone:* (095) 451 1284 (Moscow).

MEDVEDEV, Zhores Aleksandrovich, PH.D.; British biologist; b. 14 Nov. 1925, Tbilisi, U.S.S.R.; s. of Aleksandr Romanovich Medvedev and Yulia Medvedeva; twin brother of Roy Medvedev (q.v.); m. Margarita Nikolayevna Buzina 1951; two s.; ed. Timiriazev Acad. of Agricultural Sciences, Moscow, Inst. of Plant Physiology, U.S.S.R. Acad. of Sciences; joined Soviet Army 1943, served at front as a pvt.; Scientist, later Sr. Scientist, Dept. of Agrochemistry and Biochemistry, Timiriazev Acad. 1951–62; Head of Lab., Molecular Radiobiology, Inst. of Medical Radiology, Obninsk 1963–69; Sr. Scientist All-Union Scientific Research Inst. of Physiology and Biochemistry of Farm Animals, Borovsk 1970–72; Sr. Scientist, Nat. Inst. for Medical Research, London 1973–92; mem. New York Acad. of Sciences, American Gerontological Soc., Biochemical Soc., Genetic Soc.; Soviet citizenship restored 1990; Book award of the Moscow Naturalist Soc. 1965, Aging Research Award of U.S. Aging Asscn. 1984, René Schubert Preis in Gerontology 1985. *Publications:* Protein Biosynthesis and Problems of Heredity, Development and Ageing 1963, Molecular-Genetic Mechanisms of Development 1968, The Rise and Fall of T. D. Lysenko 1969, The Medvedev Papers 1970, A Question of Madness (with Roy Medvedev) 1971, Ten Years After 1973, Khrushchev—The Years in Power (with Roy Medvedev) 1976, Soviet Science 1978, The Nuclear Disaster in the Urals 1979, Andropov 1983, Gorbachev 1986, Soviet Agriculture 1987, The Legacy of Chernobyl 1990, and over 400 papers and articles on gerontology, genetics, biochemistry, environment, history and other topics. *Leisure interests:* social research and writing, gardening. *Address:* 4 Osborn Gardens, London, NW7 1DY, England; Abonement Post Box 5063, Obninsk, Kaluga Region, Russia. *Telephone:* 0181-346 4158 (London); (8439) 40520 (Obninsk).

MEEK, Paul Derald, B.S.; American business executive; b. 15 Aug. 1930, McAllen, Tex.; s. of William Van Meek and Martha Mary (née Sharp) Meek; m. Betty Catherine Robertson 1954; four d.; ed. Univ. of Texas, Austin; with Tech. Dept. Humble Oil & Refining Co., Baytown, Tex. 1953–55; Cosden Oil & Chem. Co. 1955–76, Pres. 1968–76; Dir. American Petrofina Inc. (now FINA), Dallas 1968–, Vice-Pres., C.O.O. 1976–83, Pres., C.E.O. 1983–86, Chair. Bd., Pres., C.E.O. 1984–86, Chair. Bd. 1986–98; mem. Advisory Council Coll. Eng. Foundation, Univ. of Texas 1979–; Co-Chair. Industrial Div. United Way of Metropolitan Dallas 1981–82; Chair. Public Utilities Comm. of Tex. 1989–92; Trustee Southwest Research Inst.; mem. American Petroleum Inst., Dallas Wildcat Comm. (Chair. 1987–88). *Publication:* (contrib.) Advances in Petroleum Chemistry and Refining 1957. *Address:* c/o FINA Inc., P.O. Box 2159, 8350 N. Central Expressway, Dallas, TX 75221, U.S.A.

MEESE, Edwin III, LL.B.; American government official, lawyer and academic; b. 1931; s. of Edwin Meese Jr. and Leone Meese; m. Ursula Meese; one s. one d.; ed. Yale Univ. and Univ. of Calif. at Berkeley; taught law, Univ. of San Diego Law School, Dir. Center for Criminal Justice Policy and Man.; sr. position under Gov. Reagan, State House, Sacramento, Calif.; Reagan's Campaign Chief of Staff, presidential elections 1980, Dir. Transition Org. 1980–81; Counsellor to Pres. Reagan and Man. Nat. Security Council, Domestic Policy and Cabinet Staffs 1981–85; Attorney Gen. of U.S.A. 1985–88; Distinguished Fellow, Heritage Foundation, Washington 1988–; Distinguished Visiting Fellow, Hoover Inst., Stanford Univ., Calif. 1988–; Distinguished Sr. Fellow, Inst. for United States Studies, Univ. of London 1996–; Harvard Univ. John F. Kennedy School of Govt. Medal 1986. *Publication:* With Reagan: The Inside Story 1992. *Leisure interest:* collecting models of police patrol cars. *Address:* The Heritage Foundation, 214 Massachusetts Avenue, N.E., Washington, DC 20002, U.S.A. *Telephone:* (202) 546-4400. *Fax:* (202) 546-8328.

MEGARRY, Rt. Hon. Sir Robert (Edgar), M.A., LL.D., F.B.A.; British judge (retd.); b. 1 June 1910, Croydon, Surrey; s. of the late Robert Lindsay Megarry and Irene Clark; m. Iris Davies 1936; three d.; ed. Lancing Coll., Trinity Hall, Cambridge; Solicitor 1935–41, certificate of honour and called to the Bar, Lincoln's Inn 1944, in practice 1946–67, Q.C. 1956–67, Asst. Reader in Equity in the Inns of Court 1946–51, Reader 1951–71, judge, Chancery Div. of High Court 1967–76, Vice-Chancellor 1976–82, Vice-Chancellor of the Supreme Court 1982–85; Prin., Ministry of Supply 1940–44, Asst. Sec. 1944–46; Bencher, Lincoln's Inn 1962, Treas. 1981; Dir. of Law Soc.'s Refresher Courses 1944–47; Book Review Ed. and Asst. Ed., Law Quarterly Review 1944–67; Visiting Prof. New York Univ. School of Law 1960–61, Osgoode Hall Law School, Toronto 1964; Regents' Prof., U.C.L.A. 1983; mem. Gen. Council of the Bar 1948–52, Lord Chancellor's Law Reform Cttee. 1952–73, Senate of the Inns of Court and the Bar 1966–70, 1980–82, Advisory Council on Public Records 1980–85; Chair. Notting Hill Housing Trust 1967–68, Friends of Lancing Chapel 1969–93, Inc. Council of Law Reporting 1972–87; Pres. Soc. of Public Teachers of Law 1965–66, Selden Soc. 1976–79, Lancing Club 1974–98; Hon. Life mem., Canadian Bar Asscn., American Law Inst.; the Visitor, Essex Univ. 1983–90, Clare Hall, Cambridge 1984–88; Hon. LL.D. (Hull) 1963, (Nottingham) 1979, (Law Soc. of Upper Canada) 1982, (London) 1988; Hon. D.U. (Essex) 1991. *Publications:* The Rent Acts 1939, A Manual of the Law of Real Property 1946, Miscellany-at-Law 1955, The Law of Real Property (with Prof. H. W. R. Wade) 1957, Lawyer and Litigant in England 1962, Arabinesque-at-Law 1969, A Second Miscellany-at-Law 1973. *Leisure interests:* heterogeneous. *Address:* Institute of Advanced Legal Studies, 17 Russell Square, London, WC1B 5DR; 5 Stone Buildings, Lincoln's Inn, London, WC2A 3XT, England. *Telephone:* 0171-637 1731 (Russell Square); 0171-242 8607 (Lincoln's Inn).

MEGRET, Bruno André Alexandre, M.SC.; French politician and engineer; b. 4 April 1949, Paris; s. of Jacques Megret and Colette Constantinides; m. Catherine Rascovsky 1992; one s.; ed. Lycée Louis-le-Grand, Paris, Univ. of California at Berkeley, l'Ecole Polytechnique; Head of Dept. Nat. Devt. Programme 1975–76; Dist. Engineer, Eng. Dept., Essonne Département 1977–79; Tech. Adviser Office of Minister for Overseas Service 1979–81; Deputy Dir. Infrastructure and Transport Ile-de-France Region 1981–86; Deputy Front nat. d'Isère 1986–88, Vice-Pres. Front nat. parl. group 1987–98, expelled from Front nat. Dec. 1998; Leader Front nat.—Mouvement nat. (FN-MN) 1999–; M.E.P. 1989–; Regional Councillor Provence-Côte d'Azur 1992–, Special Adviser to Mayor of Vitrolles 1997; mem. and Hon. Pres. Comités d'action républicaine. *Publications:* Demain le chêne 1982, l'Impératif du renouveau 1986, la Flamme 1990, l'Alternative nationale 1996. *Address:* European Parliament, 97–113 rue Belliard, B-1047 Brussels, Belgium.

MÉHAIGNERIE, Pierre; French politician and engineer; b. 4 May 1939, Balazé; s. of Alexis and Pauline (Boursier) Méhaignerie; m. Julie Harding 1965; one s. one d.; ed. Lycée Saint-Louis, Paris, Ecole nationale supérieure agronomique, Rennes; engineer, Génie Rural des Eaux et Forêts, Tunisia 1965–67; technical counsellor, Ministry of Agric. 1969–71, Ministry of Cultural Affairs 1971–73; mem. Nat. Ass. for Ille-et-Vilaine 1973–76, 1981–86, 1988–93, 1995–; County Councillor for Vitré-Est 1976–, elected Mayor of Vitré April 1977–; Sec. of State to Minister of Agric. 1976–77; Minister of Agric. 1977–81, of Housing, Transport and Urban Affairs 1986–88, of Justice 1993–95; Pres. Finance Comm., Nat. Ass. 1995–97; mem. European Parl. 1979; Vice-Pres. Union pour la démocratie française 1988–; Pres. Conseil Gen. d'Ille et Vilaine 1982–, Pres. Centre des démocrates sociaux 1982–94; Commdr. du Mérite agricole. *Address:* 76 rue du Rachapt, 35500 Vitré, France (Home).

MEHDI, Mohammad T., PH.D.; American politician; m. 1953; three d.; ed. High School of Commerce, Baghdad, Iraq, Univ. of California at Berkeley; Sec.-Gen. Nat. Council on Islamic Affairs; Pres. American Arab Relations Cttee.; cand. for U.S. Senate 1992. *Publications include:* Constitutionalism: Western and Middle Eastern, A Nation of Lions, Kennedy and Sirhan . . . Why? 1968, Peace in the Middle East 1973, Peace in Palestine 1982, Palestine and the Bible (ed.) 1983, Terrorism: Why America is the Target 1989, Islam and Intolerance . . . A Reply to Salman Rushdie 1990; many articles and pamphlets. *Address:* American-Arab Relations Committee, National Council on Islamic Affairs, 230 East 44th Street, Suite 3F, New York, NY 10017, U.S.A. *Telephone:* (212) 972-0460. *Fax:* (212) 682-1405.

MEHROTRA, Ram Charan, D.PHIL., D.SC., PH.D.; Indian professor of chemistry; b. 16 Feb. 1922, Kanpur, Uttar Pradesh; s. of the late R. B. Mehrotra and Mrs. Chameli Mehrotra; m. Suman Mehrotra 1944; one s. two d.; ed. Allahabad Univ., London Univ.; lecturer Allahabad Univ. 1944–54; Reader Lucknow Univ. 1954–58; Prof. Gorakhpur Univ. 1958–62, Dean Faculty of Science 1959–62; Prof. Rajasthan Univ. 1962–82, Prof. Emer. 1982–, Dean Faculty of Science 1962–65, Vice-Chancellor 1968–69, 1972, 1973, Dir., Special Assistance Programme 1979; Vice-Chancellor Delhi Univ. 1974–79; Vice-Chancellor Allahabad Univ. 1991–; Pres. Chem. Section, Indian Science Congress 1967, Indian Chemical Soc. 1976–77, Indian Science Congress Asscn. 1979, Vigyan Parishad, Allahabad 1979–83; Vice-Pres. Indian Nat. Science Acad. 1977–78; mem. Bd. and Governing Body CSIR 1963–66, 1976–80, Chem. Advisory Cttee. Atomic Energy Establishment 1963–67, Univ. Grants Review Cttee. 1974–77, Inorganic Chem. Div., Int. Union of Pure and Applied Chem. 1977–81, Univ. Grants Comm. 1982–85, Comm. on Status of Teachers 1983–84; Inorg. Nomenclature Comm. 1981–; Fellow, Nat. Acad. of Sciences, Allahabad, Royal Inst. of Chem., U.K., Indian Nat. Science Acad., Indian Acad. of Sciences; D.Sc. h.c. (Meerut Univ.); E. G. Hill Memorial Prize, Allahabad Univ. 1949, Sir S. S. Bhatnagar Award 1965, Fed. of FICCI Award for Science and Tech. 1975, Seshadri Award of Indian Nat. Science Acad. 1976, P. C. Ray Memorial Award, Indian Chemical Soc. 1977, J. C. Ghosh Medal, Indian Chemical Soc. 1986, 1st Fed. of Asian Chemical Soc. Award 1987, Platinum Jubilee Award of the Indian Science Congress by the Prime Minister of India 1988, Atma Ram Award for popularization of Science (Silver Jubilee of Cen. Hindi Org.), N. R. Dhar Memorial Award (Diamond Jubilee Nat. Acad. Sciences) 1991, G. P. Chatterjee Award of ISCA 1991, and numerous other awards and distinctions. *Publications:* jt. ed. Bombay to Munbai 1998, textbooks, research papers and three treatises in chemistry. *Leisure interests:* photography and writing popular articles on science and technology. *Address:* Allahabad University, Allahabad 211002, India.

MEHTA, A. D. "Sonny"; publishing company executive; b. 1943, India; ed. Univ. of Cambridge; fmrly. with Pan and Picador Publs., U.K.; Pres. Alfred A. Knopf Div. of Random House, New York 1987–, now also Ed.-in-Chief. *Address:* Alfred A. Knopf Inc., 201 E. 50th Street, New York, NY 10022, U.S.A.

MEHTA, Zubin; Indian conductor; b. 29 April 1936, Bombay; s. of Mehli Nowrowji and Tehmina Daruvala Mehta; m. 1st Carmen Lasky 1958 (divorced); one s. one d.; m. 2nd Nancy Diane Kovack 1969; ed. Vienna Acad. of Music, studied under Hans Swarowsky; first professional conducting in Belgium, Yugoslavia and U.K. (Liverpool); Music Dir. Montreal Symphony 1961–67, Los Angeles Philharmonic Orchestra 1962–78; Music Dir. New York Philharmonic Orchestra 1978–91; Music Dir. Israel Philharmonic 1969–, appointed Dir. for Life 1981; Dir. Bavarian State Opera 1998–; conductor at festivals of Holland, Prague, Vienna, Salzburg and Spoleto; debut at La Scala, Milan 1969; conducts regularly with the Vienna and Berlin Orchestras; winner of Liverpool Int. Conductors' Competition 1958; Music Dir. Maggio Musicale, Florence 1969, 1986–; Dr. h.c. Tel Aviv Univ., Weizmann Inst. of Science, The Hebrew Univ. of Jerusalem, Jewish Theological Seminary, Westminster Choir Coll., Princeton, Brooklyn Coll., Colgate Univ.; shared Wolf Prize 1996; Padma Bhushan (India), Commendatore (Italy), Médaille d'Or Vermeil (City of Paris), Commdr. des Arts et des Lettres (France), Great Silver Medal of Service (Austria) 1997. *Address:* Israel Philharmonic Orchestra, 1 Huberman Street, Box 11292, 61112 Tel Aviv, Israel; Orchestra Maggio Musicale, Teatro Communale, Via Solferino 15, I-50123 Florence, Italy.

MEI YI; Chinese government official and translator; b. 1913, Shantou, Guangdong Prov.; Dir. State Broadcasting Admin. Bureau 1952–66; Deputy, 1st NPC 1954–58, 2nd NPC 1958–64; Vice-Pres. Journalists' Asscn. 1954–66; Dir. Planning Bureau of the Acad. of Social Sciences 1979–; Vice-Pres. Acad. of Social Sciences 1980–; Vice-Pres. Overseas Chinese History Soc. 1981–; mem. Standing Cttee. 6th NPC 1983–87; mem. Cen. Advisory Comm. CCP Cen. Cttee. 1985–93; Ed-in-Chief Encyclopaedia of China Publishing House; Pres. Gerontological Soc. of China 1986–. *Address:* The Academy of Social Sciences, Jianguomenwai Street, Beijing, People's Republic of China.

MEIER, Richard Alan, B.ARCH.; American architect; b. 12 Oct. 1934, Newark, N.J.; s. of Jerome and Carolyn (née Kaltenbacher) Meier; m. Katherine Gormley 1978 (divorced); one s. one d.; ed. Cornell Univ.; with Frank Grad & Sons, N.J. 1957, Davis, Brody & Wisniewski, New York 1958–59, Skidmore, Owings & Merrill 1959–60, Marcel Breuer & Assocs. 1960–63; Prof. Architectural Design Cooper Union 1962–73; Prin. Architect, Richard Meier & Assocs., New York 1963–80, Richard Meier & Partners 1980–; Visiting Critic Pratt Inst. 1960–62, 1965, Princeton 1963, Syracuse Univ. 1964; Architect American Acad. in Rome 1973–74; Visiting Prof. of Architecture Yale Univ. 1975, 1977, Harvard 1977; Eliot Noyes Visiting Critic in Architecture 1980–81; mem. Advisory Council Cornell Univ.; mem. Jerusalem Comm.; exhbns.: XV Triennale, Italy 1973, Princeton Univ., Biennale Italy 1976, Cooper Union, Cooper Hewitt Museum, New York 1976–77, Leo Castelli Gallery, New York 1977, Museum of Modern Art, New York 1981, Nat. Gallery, Athens 1982–83 and others; *major works:* Smith House, Darien, Conn. 1967, Bronx Devt. Center 1977, Renault Head., France 1981, High Museum of Art, Atlanta, Ga. 1983, Museum fur Kunsthandwerk, Germany 1984, Museum of Contemporary Art, Barcelona 1995, City Hall and Cen. Library, The Hague 1995, Aichi Prefectural Museum of Art, Nagoya 1996, J. Paul Getty Center 1997, and others; Fellow, American Acad. of Arts and Sciences; A.I.A. Awards: 1968–71, 1974, 1976, 1977, 1983, 1984 Award of Merit 1965, 1970, 1973, New York Chapel Dist. Architects Award 1982, 1984; Pritzker Architect Prize 1984, R.I.B.A. Gold Medal 1988, Progressive Architecture Gold Medal 1997; Officier, Ordre des Arts et lettres (France) 1984. *Address:* 475 10th Avenue, New York, NY 10018, U.S.A.

MEIJLER, Frits Louis, M.D., PH.D.; Netherlands cardiologist; b. 29 April 1925, Den Ham; s. of Gerzon S. Meijler and Anna Content; m. Annemarie P. Schendstok 1953; one s. two d.; ed. Almelo High School and Univ. of Amsterdam; served in Royal Dutch Army 1947–49; staff mem. Wilhelmina Gasthuis, Amsterdam 1962–68; Head, Dept. of Cardiology, Utrecht Univ. Hosp. 1968–83; Chair. Scientific Council and Dir. Interuniv. Cardiology Inst. of the Netherlands, Utrecht 1983–; mem. Royal Netherlands Acad. of Sciences, British Cardiac Soc., European Soc. of Cardiology, Dutch Cardiac Soc. (Hon.); Fellow American Coll. of Cardiology, American Heart Asscn., Int. Group Research in Cardiac Metabolism; House Order of Orange 1976, Order of the Dutch Lion 1986, Morawitz Prize 1987. *Publications:* numerous articles and 4 books on cardiology and related subjects. *Leisure interests:* photography, swimming, hiking. *Address:* ICIN, P.O.B. 19258, 3501 DG Utrecht (Office); De Meijlpaal, Ravelijn 1, 4351 TB Veere, Netherlands (Home). *Telephone:* 31 30 333600 (Office); 31 1181 1747 (Home).

MEINER, Richard; German publisher; b. 8 April 1918, Dresden; s. of Felix Meiner and Elisabeth (née Gensel) Meiner; m. Ursula Ehlert 1947; one s. one d.; mil. service 1937–45; f. Richard Meiner Verlages, Hamburg 1948–64; Dir. Verlage Felix Meiner 1964–81, Felix Meiner Verlag GmbH, Hamburg 1981–; Mil. Medal; Gold Medal of Union of German Booksellers 1983; Medal of Honour of German Bücherei Leipzig 1987, Hon. Fellow German Soc. for Philosophy in Germany 1988, Bundesverdienst kreuz I. Klasse 1989. *Publications:* Verlegerische Betreuung der Philosophischen Bibliothek, Corpus Philosophorum Teutonicorum Medii Aevi, G.W.F. Hegel, Gesammelte Werke. Krit. Ausgabe, G.W.F. Hegel, Vorlesungen, Kant-Forschungen, Nicolai de Cusa Opera omnia. Krit. Ausgabe, Handbuch PRAGMATIK, Studien zum achtzehnten Jahrhundert und weitere philosophische Reihen und Einzelmonographien. *Leisure interests:* tennis, skiing. *Address:* Felix Meiner Verlag GmbH, Richardstrasse 47, 22081 Hamburg, Germany. *Telephone:* (040) 29 48 70.

MEINWALD, Jerrold, M.A., PH.D.; American professor of chemistry; b. 16 Jan. 1927, New York, N.Y.; s. of Dr. Herman Meinwald and Sophie Baskind; m. 1st Dr. Yvonne Chu 1955 (divorced 1979); two d.; m. 2nd Dr. Charlotte Greenspan 1980; one d.; ed. Brooklyn and Queen's Colls., Univ. of Chicago and Harvard Univ.; Instructor in Chem. Cornell Univ. 1952–54, Asst. Prof. 1954–58, Assoc. Prof. 1958–61, Prof. 1961–72, Acting Chair. of Chem. 1968; Prof. of Chem. Univ. of Calif., San Diego 1972–73; Prof. of Chem. Cornell Univ. 1973–80, Goldwin Smith Prof. of Chem. 1980–, Andrew Mellon Foundation Prof. 1993–95; Visiting Prof. Harvard Medical School 1997; Pres. Int. Soc. of Chemical Ecology 1988–89; Chemical Consultant, Schering-Plough Corpn. 1957–, Procter & Gamble Pharmaceuticals 1958–96, Cambridge Neuroscience Research Inc. 1987–93; Consultant on Chemical Ecology, Max-Planck Soc. 1995–97; mem. of Visiting Cttee. for Chem., Brookhaven Nat. Lab. 1969–73; numerous lectureships U.S.A., Canada, U.K., Australia, N.Z., France, Czechoslovakia, Switzerland, Belgium, China, Taiwan, Brazil, Japan 1964–; mem. Medicinal Chem. Study Section "A" of Nat. Insts. of Health 1964–66, Chair. 1966–68; Editorial Bd. of Organic Reactions 1967–78, Journal of Chemical Ecology 1974–, Insect Science and its Application 1979–91; Chair. Div. of Organic Chem., American Chemical Soc. 1968; Alfred P. Sloan Foundation Fellow 1958–62, Guggenheim Fellow 1960–61, 1976–77, Nat. Insts. of Health Special Postdoctoral Fellow 1967–68, Fogarty Int. Scholar 1983–84; Distinguished Scholar-in-Residence, Hope Coll., Holland, Mich. 1984; N.A.S. Exchange Scholar to Czechoslovakia 1987; Fellow, Center for Advanced Study in the Behavioral Sciences (Stanford) 1990–91; Research Dir. Int. Centre of Insect Physiology and Ecology, Nairobi 1970–77; Advisory Bd., Petroleum Research Fund 1970–73, Advisory Bd., Research Corpn. 1978–83, Advisory Council Dept. of Chem. Princeton Univ. 1978–82, Advisory Bd. Chem. Section, Nat. Science Foundation 1979–82, Scientific Advisory Bd., Native Plants Inc. 1987–93; Organizing Chair. Sino-American Symposium on the Chemistry of Natural Products, Shanghai 1980, UNESCO's Working Group on Co-operation in the Field of Natural Products Chemistry 1982–87, Chemistry Program Cttee., Alfred P. Sloan Foundation 1985–91; mem. Bd. of Dirs. Xerces Soc. 1994–, Scientific Cttee. Probem/Amazonia 1996–; mem. N.A.S., American Philosophical Soc.; Fellow, American Acad. of Arts and Sciences, A.A.A.S., Japan Soc. for the Promotion of Science; Hon. Ph.D. (Göteborg) 1989; Edgar Fah Smith Award (American Chemical Soc.) 1977, E. Guenther Award, American Chem. Soc. 1984, Distinguished Scientist-Lecturer Award, Kalamazoo Section of American Chem. Soc. 1985, A. C. Cope Scholar Award, American Chem. Soc. 1989, Tyler Prize in Environmental Science 1990, Gustavus John Esselen Award for Chemistry in the Public Interest (American Chem. Soc.) 1991, Silver Medal (Int. Soc. of Chemical Ecology) 1991, J. Heyrovsky Medal (Czech Acad. of Sciences) 1996. *Publications:* Advances in Alicyclic Chemistry Vol. I (Co-Author) 1966, Co-Ed. Explorations in Chemical Ecology 1987, Co-Author Pheromone Biochemistry 1987; over 350 research articles in major chem. journals. *Leisure interests:* playing flute, baroque flute and recorder. *Address:* Department of Chemistry, Cornell University, Ithaca, NY 14853, U.S.A. *Telephone:* 607-255-3301. *Fax:* (607) 255-3407.

MEIRING, Gen. Georg Lodewyk, M.SC.; South African army officer; b. 18 Oct. 1939, Ladybrand; m. Anna Maria G. Brink; three s. two d.; ed. Univ. of Orange Free State; Officer Commdg. Witswatersrand Command, Johannesburg 1981–82; Chief of Army Staff, Logistics, S.A. Defence Force (SADF), Pretoria 1982–83; Gen. Officer Commdg. S.W. Africa Territory Defence Forces, Windhoek 1987–89; Gen. Officer Commdg. Far North, Pietersburg 1989–90; Deputy Chief, S.A. Army, SADF, Pretoria 1983–87, 1990–93, Chief 1993–94; Chief S. Africa Nat. Defence Force (SANDF) 1994–98; several mil. decorations. *Leisure interests:* hunting, gardening, reading, walking. *Address:* Private Bag X414, Pretoria 0001, South Africa.

MEISER, Richard Johannes, M.D.; German professor of internal medicine; b. 10 Aug. 1931, Cottbus; s. of Richard W. Meiser and Hasmig Bunyadian; ed. gymnasium and studies in philosophy and medicine; Univ. Prof. in Internal Medicine (Haematology), Univ. of Saarland 1971–; Pres. Univ. of Saarland 1983–97; Vice-Pres. for Int. Affairs, West German Rectors' Conf. (WRK) 1987; Officier, Ordre Nat. du Mérite (France); Officier, Ordre de Mérite (Luxembourg). *Publications:* studies on macroglobulinemia in tropical splenomegaly (1966/67), on the metabolism of mycloma cells (1970), on tropical parasites, on combination chemotherapy (1981); Aktuelle Probleme und Perspektiven des Arztrechts (co-ed.) 1989. *Leisure interests:* literature, souvenirs. *Address:* Domagkstrasse 2, 6650 Homburg-Saar, Germany (Home). *Telephone:* 06841/58 68 (Home).

MEISNER, Cardinal Joachim; German ecclesiastic; b. 25 Dec. 1933, Breslau; s. of Walter and Hedwig Meisner; ed. Univ. of Erfurt, Pastoral Seminary at Neuzelle; ordained as priest 1962, Chaplain of St. Ägidien, Heiligenstadt 1963–66, St. Crucis, Erfurt 1966, Rector of the Diocese of Erfurt 1966–75, Suffragan Bishop, Erfurt 1975–80, Bishop of Berlin April 1980–89; cr. Cardinal Feb. 1983; Archbishop of Cologne and Primate of Germany Feb. 1989–. *Publications:* Das Auditorium Coelicum am Dom zu Erfurt 1960, Nachreformatorische katholische Frömmigkeitsformen in Erfurt 1971, various articles in magazines. *Leisure interest:* Christian art. *Address:* Kard.-Frings-Str. 10, 50668 Cologne, Germany. *Telephone:* 1642-1.

MEJDANI, Rexhep; Albanian politician; fmr. Sec.-Gen. Socialist Party of Albania; Pres. of Albania July 1997–. *Address:* Office of the President, Tirana, Albania.

MEKSI, Aleksandr; Albanian politician and engineer; fmr. construction engineer and restorer of medieval architecture; mem. Democratic Party (DP); Prime Minister of Albania 1992–97. *Address:* c/o Council of Ministers, Tirana, Albania.

MELAMID, Aleksandr; Russian artist; b. 14 July 1945, Moscow; initial artistic training at Moscow Art School; originator (with Vitaliy Komar (q.v.)) of 'Sots-art'; mem. of U.S.S.R. Union of Artists, expelled for "distortion of Soviet reality and non-conformity with the principles of Socialist realism" 1972; emigrated to U.S.A. 1979. *Principal works include:* Young Marx 1976, Colour Writing 1972, Quotation 1972, Post Art 1973, Factory for Producing Blue Smoke 1975, Poster Series 1980; some work shown at Ronald Feldman Gallery, New York 1976; two-man exhbn. (with Vitaliy Komar (q.v.)) at same gallery 1985, and at museums in U.S.A., Australia, Europe.

MELANDRI, Giovanna, B.ECON.; Italian politician; b. 28 Jan. 1962, New York, U.S.A.; Co-ordinator Industrial and Tech. Policy Unit, Montedison 1983–87; Head Int. Office Legambiente (Environmental League) and Chair. Scientific Cttee. 1988–94; mem. Italian Del. to Conf. on Sustainable Devt., Bergen 1990, to UN Conf. on Environment and Devt., Rio de Janeiro 1992; mem. Exec. Cttee. Legambiente 1982–89, Nat. Secr. 1989–; mem. Nat. Exec.

Cttee. Partito Democratico Socialista (PDS) 1991–, Democratici di Sinistra 1998–; mem. Exec. with responsibility for Communications Policy 1996–; mem. Camera dei Deputati 1994–; Minister of Culture Oct. 1998–; fmr. mem. Progressisti-federativo Group, in charge of work on bioethics and assisted reproduction, External Cttee. to Special Comm. on Child Welfare, fmr. Pres. Cttee. on Human Rights, fmr. mem. Comm. on Culture and Comm. to regulate RAI (Italian TV); del. to first UN World Forum on TV 1997; Pres. Madre Provetta 1995–; f. Italian Emily's List 1998; mem. editorial cttee. Madre Provetta News 1997–, Tomorrow and La Nuova Ecologia environmental periodicals 1986–91. *Publications:* (Ed.): Ambiente Italia (annual environmental report of Legambiente) 1989–94, Italian World Watch Magazine 1986–91, Digitalia, l'ultima rivoluzione 1998. *Address:* c/o Ministero per i beni e le attività culturali, Via del Collegio Romano 27, Rome, Italy. *Telephone:* (06) 6723261. *Fax:* (06) 6789250.

MELEŞCANU, Teodor Viorel, PH.D.; Romanian jurist and politician; b. 10 March 1941, Brad, Hunedoara Co.; m.; one d.; ed. Bucharest Univ., Univ. Inst. for Higher Int. Studies, Geneva; with Ministry of Foreign Affairs 1966; mem. numerous dels. to UNO confs.; First Sec. UN, Geneva; Secretary, Ministry of Foreign Affairs; Minister of Foreign Affairs 1992–96, also Deputy Prime Minister; Senator (for Prahova constituency) 1996–; Assoc. Prof. of Int. Law, Univ. of Bucharest 1996–; researcher, Romanian Inst. for Int. Studies 1996–; Pres. Alliance for Romania socio-democratic party 1997–; mem. Asscn. of Int. Law and Int. Relations (ADIRI), Int. Law Comm. (UN). *Publications:* Responsibility of States for the Peaceful Use of Nuclear Energy 1973, International Labour Organization Functioning and Activity, numerous studies and articles. *Address:* Şoseaua Cotroceni nr. 31, Sector VI, Romania.

MELETINSKY, Yeleazar Moiseyevich, D.LIT.; Russian philologist; b. 1918, Kharkov, Ukraine; ed. Moscow Inst. of History, Philosophy and Literature; army service World War II 1941–46; Head of Chair. Petrozavodsk Univ. 1946–49; arrested, imprisoned in Gulag 1949–54; sr. researcher Inst.of World Literature U.S.S.R. Acad. of Sciences 1956–92; Dir. Inst. of Higher Humanitarian Studies 1992–; U.S.S.R. State Prize 1990. *Publications:* Poetics of Myth 1976 and works on problems of semiotics, history of folklore, mythology. *Address:* Institute of Higher Humanitarian Studies, Miusskaya str. 6, 125267 Moscow, Russia (Office). *Telephone:* (095) 250 6668 (Office).

MELIKISHVILI, Giorgi; Georgian historian; b. 30 Dec. 1918, Tbilisi; s. of Aleksandr and Yekaterina Melikishvili; m. Yelena Iosifovna Dochanashvili 1942; one s. two d.; ed. Tbilisi Univ.; works deal with the ancient history of the Near East and Transcaucasia; Prof. Tbilisi Univ.; Dir. of Historical Inst. of Georgian Acad. of Sciences 1965–; mem. Acad. of Sciences of Georgia 1960–; Lenin Prize 1957. *Publications:* Nairi-Urartu 1954, Urartian Inscriptions in Cuneiform Characters 1960, History of Ancient Georgia 1959, The Most Ancient Settlers of the Caucasus and Near East 1965, Die urartäische Sprache 1971, Sketches of Georgian History, Vol. I (ed.) 1989. *Address:* Rizhskaya ulitsa 3, kv. 37, Tbilisi 380079, Georgia. *Telephone:* 22-10-06.

MELLERS, Wilfrid Howard, O.B.E., M.A., D.MUS., D.PHIL.; British composer, author and university professor; b. 26 April 1914, Leamington; s. of Percy Wilfrid Mellers and Hilda Maria Lawrence; m. 1st Vera Hobbs 1940; m. 2nd Peggy Pauline Lewis 1950 (divorced 1975); two d.; m. 3rd Robin Hildyard 1987; ed. Leamington Coll. and Downing Coll. Cambridge; Supervisor in English Studies and Lecturer in Music, Downing Coll. 1945–48; Staff Tutor in Music, Extramural Dept., Univ. of Birmingham 1948–60; Distinguished Andrew Mellon Visiting Prof. of Music, Univ. of Pittsburgh, U.S.A. 1960–63; Prof. and Head of Dept. of Music, Univ. of York 1964–81, now Emer.; Part-time Prof., Guildhall School of Music, London, City Univ., London and Keele Univ. 1981–; Hon. D. Phil. (City) 1981; many compositions published. *Publications:* François Couperin and the French Classical Tradition 1950, Man and his Music 1957, Music in a New Found Land (themes and developments in American music) 1964, Harmonious Meetings 1964, Twilight of the Gods: The Beatles in Retrospect 1973, Bach and the Dance of God 1981, Beethoven and the Voice of God 1984, A Darker Shade of Pale: a backdrop to Bob Dylan 1984, Angels of the Night: Women Jazz and Pop Singers in the Twentieth Century 1986, The Masks of Orpheus 1986, Vaughan Williams and the Vision of Albion 1988, Le Jardin Retrouvé: Homage to Federic Mompou 1989, The Music of Percy Grainger 1992, The Music of Francis Poulenc 1993, Between Old Worlds and New 1997. *Address:* Oliver Sheldon House, 17 Aldwark, York, YO1 2BX, England. *Telephone:* (01904) 638686.

MELLES, Carl; Austrian conductor; b. 15 July 1926, Budapest; s. of György Melles and Maria Lazar; m. Gertrude Dertnig 1963; one s. one d.; ed. Gymnasium and Acad. of Music, Budapest; conducts all the major orchestras of Europe including Vienna and Berlin Philharmonic, New Philharmonia London, Scala Milan; guest appearances at Flanders, Salzburg and Bayreuth Festivals and Vienna State Opera; concert tours in Europe, Japan, S. Africa; Hon. Conductor Brunswick State Orchestra 1996–; Hon. mem. Vienna Singakademie 1978; Franz Liszt Prize, Budapest 1954, Prize of Italian Record Critic Asscn. for Dallapiccola's Il Prigioniera 1974; Brahms Medal, Vienna Singverein 1983, Hon. Gold Medal, city of Vienna 1986, Great Silver Badge of Honour, Austria. *Recordings:* Classical Excellence, Hollywood, Florida with the Austria Broadcast Symphony Orchestra, Beethoven Symphonies I-IX. *Leisure interest:* literature. *Address:* Grünbergstrasse 4, 1130 Vienna, Austria. *Telephone:* (1) 8135206. *Fax:* (1) 8135206.

MELLINK, Machteld Johanna, PH.D.; Netherlands archaeologist; b. 26 Oct. 1917, Amsterdam; d. of Johan Mellink and Machteld Kruyff; ed. Amsterdam and Utrecht Univs.; Field Asst. Tarsus excavations 1947–49; Asst. Prof. of Classical Archaeology Bryn Mawr Coll. 1949–53, Assoc. Prof., Chair. Dept. of Classical and Near Eastern Archaeology 1953–62, Prof. 1962–88; staff mem. Gordion excavations organized by Pennsylvania Univ. Museum 1950, during which the putative tomb of King Midas was discovered 1957; Field Dir. excavations at Karataş-Semayük in Lycia 1963–; excavator archaic and Graeco-Persian painted tombs near Elmali 1969–; advisory staff mem., Troy excavations, Univs. of Tübingen and Cincinnati 1988–; Pres. Archaeological Inst. of America 1981–84; Vice-Pres. American Research Inst. in Turkey 1980–, Pres. 1988–92; Hon. LL.D. (Pennsylvania) 1987; Hon. D.Hist. (Eskişehir, Turkey) 1990; L. Wharton Drexel Medal 1994. *Publications:* Hyakinthos 1943, A Hittite Cemetery at Gordion 1956, Kizilbel: an archaic painted tomb chamber in northern Lycia 1998; Archaeology in Anatolia (reports in American Journal of Archaeology) 1955–93; Co-author Frühe Stufen der Kunst 1974; Ed. Dark Ages and Nomads 1964, Ed. Troy and the Trojan War 1986, Ed. series Elmali-Karataş, Vol. I 1992, Vol. II 1994. *Address:* Bryn Mawr College, Bryn Mawr, PA 19010-2899, U.S.A. *Telephone:* (610) 526-5339. *Fax:* (610) 526-7480.

MELLOR, Rt. Hon. David, Q.C., F.Z.S.; British politician; b. 1949; m. Judith Hall 1974 (divorced 1996); two s.; ed. Swanage Grammar School, Christ's Coll. Cambridge; called to Bar (Inner Temple) 1972; apptd. Q.C. 1987; Chair. Cambridge Univ. Conservative Asscn. 1970; fmr. Vice-Chair. Chelsea Conservative Asscn.; M.P. for Putney 1979–97; Parl. Under-Sec. of State, Dept. of Energy 1981–83, Home Office 1983–86, Minister of State, Home Office 1986–87, FCO 1987–88; Minister for Health 1988–89; Minister of State, Home Office 1989–90; Minister for the Arts July–Nov. 1990; Chief Sec. to Treasury 1990–92; Sec. of State for Nat. Heritage April–Sept. 1992; Consultant Middle East Broadcasting Centre, Middle East Economic Digest, Abela Holdings, RACAL Tacticom, British Aerospace, Ernst & Young, G.K.N.; mem. Bd. ENO 1993–95; Chair. Sports Aid Foundation 1993–97, Football Task Force 1997–; Deputy Chair. Trustees London Philharmonic Orchestra 1989–; presenter 6.06 BBC Radio 5 1993–, The Midnight Hour, BBC 2 1997–, Across the Threshold (series), Classic FM 1998–; sports columnist, Evening Standard 1997–; fmr. mem. Council Nat. Youth Orchestra; Special Trustee Westminster Hosp. 1979–86; elected Hon. Assoc. British Veterinary Asscn., for work for animal welfare 1986; Variety Club Award for BBC Radio Personality of the Year 1994. *Leisure interest:* classical music. *Address:* c/o House of Commons, London, SW1A 0AA, England.

MELLOR, David Hugh, M.A., PH.D., SC.D., M.ENG., M.S., F.B.A.; British professor of philosophy; b. 10 July 1938, London; s. of S. D. and E. N. (née Hughes) Mellor; ed. Newcastle Royal Grammar School, Manchester Grammar School and Pembroke Coll., Cambridge; Harkness Fellowship in Chem. Eng., Univ. of Minnesota 1960–62, M.I.T. School of Chem. Eng. Practise 1962; Tech. Officer, Imperial Chemical Industries (ICI) 1962–63; research student in philosophy 1963–68; Fellow, Pembroke Coll., Cambridge 1964–70; Fellow, Darwin Coll., Cambridge 1971–, Vice-Master 1983–87; Asst. Lecturer in Philosophy, Univ. of Cambridge 1965–70, Lecturer 1970–83, Reader in Metaphysics 1983–86, Prof. of Philosophy 1986–; Hon. Prof. in Philosophy, Keele Univ. 1989–92; Visiting Fellow in Philosophy, Australian Nat. Univ. 1975; Radcliffe Fellow in Philosophy 1978–80, Visiting Prof. Auckland Univ. 1985; Pres. British Soc. for the Philosophy of Science 1985–87, Pres. Aristotelian Soc. 1992–93; Hon. Ph.D. (Lund Univ.) 1997. *Publications:* The Matter of Chance 1971, Real Time 1981, Matters of Metaphysics 1991, The Facts of Causation 1995, Real Time II 1998; numerous articles on philosophy of science, metaphysics and philosophy of mind. *Leisure interest:* theatre. *Address:* 25 Orchard Street, Cambridge, CB1 1JS, England. *Telephone:* (01223) 740017. *Fax:* (01223) 740017.

MELMON, Kenneth; American professor of medicine and pharmacology; b. 20 July 1934, San Francisco; s. of Abe Melmon and Jean Kahn; m. Elyce Ester Edelman 1957; one s. one d.; ed. Stanford Univ. and California Medical School, San Francisco; Clinical Assoc., Nat. Heart and Lung Inst. 1961–64; Chief Resident in Medicine, Washington Univ. 1964–65; Chief of Section of Clinical Pharmacology, Calif. Univ. (San Francisco) 1965–68, Chief of Div. 1968–78; Chair., Dept. of Medicine, Stanford Univ. 1978–84, Prof. of Medicine and Pharmacology 1978–; Chair. Academic Senate, School of Medicine 1996–, Steering Cttee. Academic Senate 1996–98; Dir. Technical Transfer Program, Stanford Univ. Hospital 1986–93, Assoc. Dean for Postgrad. Medical Educ. 1994–; mem. Nat. Bd. of Medical Examiners 1987–97; Burroughs Wellcome Clinical Pharmacology Scholar; Guggenheim Fellow 1971. *Publications:* Ed. Cardiovascular Therapeutics 1974, Clinical Pharmacology 1978; Assoc. Ed. The Pharmacological Basis of Therapeutics 1980; over 300 scientific papers. *Leisure interests:* backpacking, swimming, business, photography, bicycling, woodworking, fishing. *Address:* Stanford University Medical Center, Room S 025, Stanford, CA 94305; 51 Cragmont Way, Woodside, CA 94062, U.S.A. *Telephone:* (415) 723-5187.

MELNIKOV, Vitaly Vyacheslavovich; Russian film director; b. 1 May 1928; m. Tamara Aleksandrovna Melnikova; ed. All-Union State Inst. of Cinema (VGIK) under S. I. Yutkevich and M. I. Romm; series of documentary films 1953–64; Artistic Dir. Golos studio 1989–; People's Artist of Russia 1986. *Films include:* Barbos Visits Bobik, 1965, Chukotka's Boss 1967, Mum's got Married 1970, Hello and Goodbye! 1973, Xenia, Fyodor's Favourite Wife 1974, The Elder Son 1975, Marriage 1978, September Holiday 1979,

Two Lines in Small Handwriting 1981 (Venice Film Festival Prize), Unicum 1984, First Meeting—Last Meeting 1986, To Marry the Captain 1987, The Royal Hunting 1989, Chicha 1991, The Vareny's Case 1994. *Address:* Svetlanovsky proyezd 105, Apt. 20, 195269 St. Petersburg, Russia. *Telephone:* (812) 532-51-88.

MELNIZKY, Walter, DR. JUR.; Austrian judge; b. 1 Nov. 1928, Vienna; s. of Ernst Melnizky and Maria Melnizky; m. Gertrude Melnizky 1953; one s.; ed. Univ. of Vienna; Judge 1954–57, 1962–69; Public Prosecutor 1957–62; Gen. Prosecutor 1969–86; Pres. Supreme Court 1987–93; Pres. Automobilclub Austria 1980–93; consultant Syndicus Asscn. of Public Experts 1988–; Komturkreuz des Burgenlandes, Grosses Goldenes Ehrenzeichen am Bande, Grosse Verdienstkreuz mit Stern und Schulterband. *Publications:* numerous juridical essays, especially on traffic law and criminal law. *Leisure interests:* classical music, opera. *Address:* 1190 Vienna, Hannplatz 4/14, Austria (Home). *Telephone:* 36-73-74 (Home).

MELROSE, Donald Blair, D. PHIL., F.A.A.; Australian professor of physics; b. 13 Sept. 1940, Hobart, Tasmania; s. of late Andrew B. Melrose and of Isla L. Luff; m. Sara C. Knabe 1969; one s. one d.; ed. N. Sydney Boys' High School, John Curtin High School, Fremantle and Univs. of W. Australia, Tasmania and Oxford; Research Fellow, Univ. of Sussex 1965–66; Research Assoc. Belfer Grad. School of Science, Yeshiva Univ., New York 1966–68; Research Fellow, Center for Theoretical Physics, Univ. of Md. 1968–69; Sr. Lecturer in Theoretical Physics, Australian Nat. Univ. 1969–72, Reader 1972–79; Prof. of Theoretical Physics, Univ. of Sydney 1979–, Dir. Research Centre for Theoretical Astrophysics 1991–; Rhodes Scholar 1962; Pawsey Medal (Australian Acad. of Science) 1974, Walter Boas Medal (Australian Inst. of Physics) 1986, Thomas Ranken Lyle Medal (Australian Acad. of Science) 1987, Harrie Massey Medal and Prize (Inst. of Physics) 1998. *Publications:* Plasma Physics (2 vols.) 1980, Instabilities in Space and Laboratory Plasmas 1986, Electromagnetic Processes in Dispersive Media (with R. C. McPhedran) 1991, Plasma Astrophysics (with J. G. Kirk and E. R. Priest) 1994; over 200 papers in scientific publs. *Leisure interests:* rugby union, surfing, jogging, squash. *Address:* School of Physics, University of Sydney, N.S.W. 2006 (Office); 10 Balfour Street, Wollstonecraft, N.S.W. 2065, Australia (Home). *Telephone:* (02) 93514234 (Office); (02) 94383635 (Home). *Fax:* (02) 9351 7726.(Office).

MELVILL JONES, Geoffrey, M.A., M.B., B.CH., F.R.S., F.R.S.C., F.R.AE.S., F.C.A.S.I.; British/Canadian professor of clinical neuroscience; b. 14 Jan. 1923, Cambridge, England; s. of Benett Melvill Jones and Dorothy Laxton Jotham; m. Jenny Marigold Burnaby; two s. two d.; ed. King's Coll. Choir School, Cambridge, Dauntsey's School, Wilts., Cambridge Univ. and Middx. Hosp.; House Surgeon Middx. Hosp., London 1950; House Surgeon in Otolaryngology, Addenbrooke's Hosp., Cambridge 1950–51; Medical Scientist R.A.F. 1951–55; Scientific Officer Medical Research Council 1955–61; Assoc. Prof. Dept. of Physiology, McGill Univ., Montreal 1961–68, Prof. 1968–92, Hosmer Research Prof., Faculty of Medicine 1978–92, Dir. Aero-space Medical Research Unit 1961–88, Emer. Prof. 1992–; Adjunct Prof., Dept. of Clinical Neurosciences, Univ. of Calgary 1992–; Visiting Prof. Stanford Univ. 1971–72, Coll. de France 1979, 1995; Fellow Canadian Aeronautics and Space Inst., Aerospace Medical Asscn.; Harry G. Armstrong Lecture Award 1968; Arnold D. Tuttle Award 1971, Quinquennial Gold Medal, Bárány Soc. 1988, Wilbur Franks Award, Canadian Soc. for Aerospace Medicine 1988, Royal Aeronautical Soc. Stewart Memorial Lectureship Award 1989, Royal Aeronautical Soc. Buchanan Barbour Award 1990, McLaughlin Medal (Royal Soc. of Canada) 1991, Emeritus Award, McGill Univ. 1992. *Publications:* Mammalian Vestibular Physiology (with V. J. Wilson) 1979, Adaptive Mechanisms in Gaze Control (Co-Ed. with A. Berthoz) 1985, over 150 scientific publications. *Leisure interests:* outdoor activities, tennis, piano music and composition, sailing, reading, mountain skiing. *Address:* 1419 8th Street N.W., Calgary, Alta., T2M 3K4, Canada (Home).

MELVILLE, Sir Harry (Work), K.C.B., PH.D., D.SC., LL.D., D.C.L., D.TECH., F.R.I.C., F.R.S.; British chemist; b. 27 April 1908, Edinburgh; s. of Thomas Melville and Esther Burnett Melville; m. Janet Marian Cameron 1942; two d.; ed. George Heriot's School, Edinburgh, Edinburgh Univ. and Trinity Coll., Cambridge; Fellow Trinity Coll., Cambridge 1933–43; Asst. Dir. Colloid Science Laboratory, Cambridge Univ. 1938–40; Prof. of Chemistry, Aberdeen Univ. 1940–48; Scientific Adviser to Chief Supt. Chemical Defence, Min. of Supply 1940–43; Supt. Radar Research Station 1943–45; Mason Prof. and Dir. of Chemistry Dept., Birmingham Univ. 1948–56; mem. Advisory Council for Scientific and Industrial Research 1946–51; mem. Scientific Advisory Council, Ministry of Supply 1949–51, 1953–56; Advisory Council on Scientific Research and Development 1953–56; mem. Scientific Advisory Council, British Electricity Authority 1949–56; mem. Scientific Advisory Council, Ministry of Power 1954–60; mem. Advisory Council on Research and Devt., Ministry of Power (now Dept. of Trade and Industry) 1960–, Chair. 1970–74; mem. Nuclear Safety Advisory Cttee. DTI 1972–; Sec. Dept. of Scientific and Industrial Research 1956–65; Chair. Science Research Council 1965–67; Prin. Queen Mary Coll., London 1967–76; Cttee. of Managers, Royal Inst. of G.B. 1976–; Hon. degrees from Univs. of Aberdeen, Bradford, Exeter, Birmingham, Essex, Liverpool, Leeds, Kent, Heriot-Watt. *Publication:* Experimental Methods in Gas Reactions 1938. *Address:* Norwood, Dodds Lane, Chalfont St. Giles, Bucks., HP8 4EL, England. *Telephone:* (01494) 872222.

MELVILLE, Sir Leslie Galfreid, K.B.E., B.EC.; Australian economist; b. 26 March 1902, Marsfield; m. Mary Maud Scales 1925; two s.; ed. Church of England Grammar School, Sydney, and Univ. of Sydney; Public Actuary of South Australia 1924–28; Prof. of Econs., Univ. of Adelaide 1929–31; mem. of Cttees. on S. Australian Finances 1927–30; mem. of Cttees. on Australian Finances and Unemployment 1931 and 1932; Financial Adviser to Australian Dels. at Imperial Econ. Conf. 1932, and to Australian Del. at World Econ. Conf. 1933; mem. Australian Financial and Econ. Advisory Cttee. 1939; Chair. Australian Del. to UN Monetary Conf., Bretton Woods 1944; mem. Advisory Council of Commonwealth Bank 1945–50; Chair. UN Sub-Comm. on Employment and Econ. Stability 1947–50; Asst. Gov. (Central Banking) Commonwealth Bank of Australia; Exec. Dir. IMF and World Bank Nov. 1950–53; Vice-Chancellor, A.N.U. Canberra 1953–60; mem. Bd., Reserve Bank 1959–63, 1965–75; Chair. Commonwealth Grants Comm. 1966–74, mem. 1979–82; Chair. Tariff Bd. 1960–63; Devt. Advisory Service, Int. Bank for Reconstruction and Devt. 1963–65; Hon. LL.D. (Toronto) 1958, (A.N.U.) 1978; Hon. D.Sc.Econ. (Sydney) 1980. *Address:* Unit 61, The Grange, 67 Macgregor Street, Deakin, A.C.T. 2600, Australia. *Telephone:* (02) 62811838.

MELVILLE-ROSS, Timothy David; British business executive; b. 3 Oct. 1944, Westward Ho, Devon; s. of late Antony Melville-Ross and Anne Fane; m. Camilla Probert 1967; two s. one d.; ed. Uppingham School and Portsmouth Coll. of Tech.; BP 1963–73; Rowe Swann & Co. (stockbrokers) 1973–74; Nationwide Bldg. Soc. 1974, Dir. and Chief Exec. 1985–94; Dir. Monument Oil & Gas PLC 1992–; Dir.-Gen. Inst. of Dirs. 1994–99; Chair. Collectable Cards Ltd. 1998–; Deputy Chair. Monument Oil and Gas PLC 1997–99; Dir. Bovis Homes Ltd. 1997–. *Leisure interests:* reading, music, bridge, sport, the countryside. *Address:* Institute of Directors, 116 Pall Mall, London, SW1Y 5ED, England. *Telephone:* 0171-839 1233. *Fax:* 0171-930 1949.

MEMMI, Albert; Tunisian writer; b. 15 Dec. 1920, Tunis; s. of François Memmi and Marguerite née Sarfati; m. Germaine Dubach 1946; two s. one d.; ed. Lycée Carnot, Tunis, Univ. of Algiers and Univ. de Paris à la Sorbonne; Teacher of Philosophy, Tunis 1955; Dir. Psychological Centre, Tunis 1956; Researcher, C.N.R.S., Paris 1959–; Asst. Prof. Ecole pratique des hautes études 1959–66, Prof. 1966–70; Prof., Inst. de Psychanalise, Paris 1968–; Prof. Univ. of Paris 1970–, Dir. Social Sciences Dept. 1973–76, Dir. Anthropological Lab.; Vice-Pres. Fed. Int. des Ecrivains francophones 1985; mem. Acad. des Sciences d'Outre-mer; Vice-Pres. Pen Club 1977-80, Comité nat. Laïcité-République 1991; Officier Légion d'honneur; Commdr. Ordre de Nichan Iftikhar; Officier Palmes académiques, Officier Arts et Lettres, Officier Ordre République Tunisienne, Prix de Carthage 1953, Prix Fénéon 1953, Prix Simba 1978, Prix de l'Union Rationnaliste, Grand Prix Littéraire de l'Afrique du Nord. *Publications include:* The Pillar of Salt 1953, Strangers 1955, Colonizer, Colonized 1957, Portrait of a Jew 1962, Anthologie des écrivains nord-africains 1965, Les français et le racisme 1965, The Liberation of the Jew 1966, Dominated Man 1968, Decolonisation 1970, The Scorpion 1970, Jews and Arabs 1974, Entretien 1975, La terre intérieure 1976, Le désert 1977, The Dependence 1979, Le racisme 1982, Ce que je crois 1985, L'Écriture colorée 1986, Les écrivains francophones du Maghreb 1987, Le Pharaon 1988, Le Mirliton du Ciel 1990, Bonheurs 1992, A contre-courants 1993, Ah, quel bonheur 1995, Le Juif et l'autre 1995, Le Buveur et l'amoureux 1998. *Address:* 5 rue Saint Merri, 75004 Paris, France. *Telephone:* 40-29-08-31. *Fax:* 42-74-25-22.

MENAGARISHVILI, Irakly; Georgian politician; b. 18 May 1951, Tbilisi; s. of Afinogen Menagarishvili and Ekaterine Jorbenadze; m. Manana Mikaberidze 1975; two s.; ed. Tbilisi State Inst. of Medicine; leader Comsomol Orgs. 1976–80; head of City Public Health Dept. 1980–82; First Deputy Minister of Public Health 1982–86, Minister 1986–91, 1992–93; Dir. Georgian Cen. of Strategic Studies; Co-ordinator of Humanitarian Aid of State Council of Georgia 1991–92; Deputy Prime Minister 1993–95; Minister of Foreign Affairs, Repub. of Georgia Dec. 1995–. *Address:* Ministry of Foreign Affairs, 4 Chitadze Street, 380008 Tbilisi, Georgia. *Telephone:* (32) 98 93 77. *Fax:* (32) 98 93 80.

MÉNAGE, Gilles Marie Marcel; French government official; b. 5 July 1943, Bourg-la-Reine (Hauts-de-Seine); s. of Georges Ménage and Jeanne Paillotet; m. 1st Marie-France Beaussier (divorced); two d.; m. 2nd Doris Lenz; one s. one d.; ed. Lycée Lakanal, Sceaux, Lycée Berthollet, Annecy, Inst. d'Études Politiques, Paris and Ecole Nat. d'Admin.; civil admin., Ministry of Interior 1969; Deputy Prefect, Head of Staff for Prefect of Tarn-et-Garonne 1969–70, then for Prefect of Haute-Vienne and Limousin 1970–74; Tech. Adviser to Sec. of State for Posts and Telecommunications (PTT) 1974; Head of Staff for Pierre Lelong, Sec. for PTT 1974–76; Deputy Prefect and Special Adviser to Prefect of Paris 1976–77; Head of Staff for Prefect/Sec.-Gen. of Préfecture de Paris 1977–81; Sr. lecturer, Inst. d'Etudes Politiques, Paris 1976–77, Inst. Int. d'Admin. Publique 1980–81; Tech. Adviser, then Deputy Head of Staff for Pres. of France 1982–88, Chief of Staff 1988–92; Chair. Electricité de France 1992–95; working on energy project for Ministry of Industry 1996–97; Prefect 1997–; Chair. Int. Consortiums Consultants 1998–; Chevalier, Ordre Nat. du Mérite, Chevalier, Légion d'honneur. *Publication:* La France face aux dangers de guerre 1981. *Address:* EDF, 38 rue Jacques Ibert, 92300 Levallois-Perret; International Consortiums, 4/6 avenue Emile Acollas, 75007 Paris, France.

MENCHU, Rigoberta; Guatemalan human rights activist; d. of late Vicente Menchu and Juana Menchu; m. Angel Canil 1995; as a teenager began campaigning for rights for Indians; fled to Mexico after parents and brother were murdered by security forces 1980; co-ordinated protests in San Marcos against 500th anniversary of arrival of Columbus in Americas 1992; Int. Goodwill Amb. UNESCO 1996–; awarded Nobel Peace Prize 1992. *Publication:* I, Rigoberta (trans. in 12 languages) 1983. *Address:* c/o Vicente Menchú Foundation, P.O. Box 5274, Berkeley, CA 94705, U.S.A.

MENDES, Sam; British theatre director; b. 1 Aug. 1965; s. of Valerie Mendes and Peter Mendes; ed. Magdalen Coll. School, Oxford and Peterhouse, Cambridge Univ.; fmr. artistic dir. Minerva Studio Theatre, Chichester; artistic dir. Donmar Warehouse 1992–; plays directed include: London Assurance (Chichester), The Cherry Orchard (London), Kean (Old Vic, London), The Plough and the Stars (Young Vic, London) 1991, Troilus and Cressida (RSC) 1991, The Alchemist (RSC) 1991, Richard III (RSC) 1992, The Tempest (RSC) 1993; Nat. Theatre debut with The Sea 1991, The Rise and Fall of Little Voice (Nat. and Aldwych) 1992, The Birthday Party 1994, Othello (also world tour); Assassins, Translations, Cabaret, Glengarry Glen Ross, The Glass Menagerie, Company, Habeas Corpus, The Front Page, The Blue Room (all at Donmar Warehouse) 1992–; Oliver! (London Palladium); Cabaret, The Blue Room (Broadway, N.Y.); Critics' Circle Award 1989, 1993, 1996, Olivier Award for Best Dir. 1996, Tony Award 1998. *Leisure interest:* cricket. *Address:* Donmar Warehouse, 41 Earlham Street, London, WC2H 9LD, England. *Telephone:* 0171-240 4882. *Fax:* 0171-240 4878.

MÉNDEZ MONTENEGRO, Dr. Julio César; Guatemalan politician and law professor; b. 23 Nov. 1915, Guatemala City; s. of Marcial Méndez Mendoza and Mélida Montenegro de Méndez; m. Sara de la Hoz de León 1950; two s. one d.; Prof. of Law, fmr. Dean of Faculty of Law, Univ. de San Carlos de Guatemala; Pres. Colegio de Abogados; fmr. Under-Sec. of Admin. and of Foreign Affairs; fmr. Gen. Sec. to the Presidency of the Repub.; Pres. of Guatemala 1966–70; Amb. to Mexico; mem. Partido Revolucionario; author of numerous works on law. *Address:* Guatemalan Embassy, Esplanada 1025, Col. Lomas de Chapultepec, 1100 México, D.F., Mexico.

MENDOZA, June, A.O., R.P.; British portrait painter; b. Melbourne; d. of John Morton and Dot Mendoza; m. Keith Mackrell; one s. three d.; ed. Lauriston School for Girls, Melbourne, St. Martin's School of Art, London; portraits include H.M. Queen Elizabeth II, H.M. Queen Elizabeth, the Queen Mother, H.R.H. The Prince of Wales, Diana, Princess of Wales, Baroness Thatcher, Prime Ministers of Fiji, Australia, Philippines, Singapore, Pres. of Iceland, Philippines, and many other govt., academic, industrial, regimental, theatrical and sporting personalities, series of internationally-known musicians, large boardroom and family groups; large canvas for the House of Commons (440 portraits) of the House in session, for Australian House of Reps. (170 portraits) for Parl., Canberra; has made numerous TV appearances and lectures regularly in U.K. and overseas; mem. Royal Soc. of Portrait Painters, Royal Inst. of Oil Painters; Hon. mem. Soc. of Women Artists; Hon. D.Litt (Bath, Loughborough); Freedom of City of London 1997. *Address:* 34 Inner Park Road, London, SW19 6DD, England.

MENEM, Carlos Saul, D.JUR.; Argentinian politician; b. 2 July 1935, Anillaco, La Rioja; s. of Saul Menem and Muhibe Akil; m. Zulema Fátima Yoma 1966; one s. one d.; ed. Córdoba Univ.; f. Juventud Peronista (Peron Youth Group), La Rioja Prov. 1955; defended political prisoners following Sept. 1955 coup; Legal Adviser, Confederación General del Trabajo, La Rioja Prov. 1955–70; cand. Prov. Deputy 1958; Pres. Partido Justicialista, La Rioja Prov. 1963–; elected Gov. La Rioja 1973, re-elected 1983, 1987; imprisoned following mil. coup 1976–81; cand. for Pres. Argentine Repub. for Partido Justicialista 1989; Pres. of Argentina July 1989–; Vice-Pres. Conf. of Latin American Popular Parties (COPPAL) 1990–. *Publications:* Argentine, Now or Never, Argentina Year 2000, The Productive Revolution (with Eduardo Duhalde). *Address:* Casa de Gobierno, Balcarce 50, 1064 Buenos Aires, Argentina.

MENG LIANKUN; Chinese politician; b. 1925, Lixian Co., Hebei Prov.; joined CCP 1939; Deputy Dir., Org. Dept. of Cen. Cttee. CCP 1987–, Sec.-Gen. 1988–; mem. 7th Standing Cttee. NPC 1988–92, mem. 8th NPC 1993–; Chair. Credentials Cttee., Internal and Judicial Affairs Cttee. N.P.C. *Address:* Standing Committee, National People's Congress, Tiananmen Square, Beijing 100001, People's Republic of China.

MENGES, Chris; British cinematographer and film director; b. 15 Sept. 1940, Kingston; m. 2nd Judy Freeman 1978; five c. from 1st marriage; TV cameraman on documentaries filmed in Africa, Asia, S. America; cinematographer: Kes, The Empire Strikes Back, Local Hero, Comfort and Joy, The Killing Fields (Acad. Award 1984), Marie, The Mission (Acad. Award 1986), Singing the Blues in Red, Shy People, High Season, Michael Collins (LA Film Critics Award 1997); Dir. A World Apart, Crisscross, The Life and Death of Chico Mendes, Second Best.

MENGISTU HAILE MARIAM (see Mariam, Mengistu Haile).

MENK, Louis W.; American railroad executive; b. 8 April 1918, Englewood, Colo.; s. of Louis Albert Menk and Daisy Deane Frantz; m. Martha Jane Swan 1942; one s. one d.; ed. S. Denver High School, Denver and Harvard; messenger, telegrapher, Union Pacific Railroad 1937–40; from telegrapher to Chair. and Pres. St. Louis-San Francisco Railroad 1940–65; Pres. and Dir. Burlington Lines 1965–66; Pres. and Dir. Northern Pacific Railway Co. 1966–70; Pres. and Dir. Burlington Inc. March 1970–71, Chair. of Bd., C.E.O. and Dir. 1971–78, Chair. of Bd. and Dir. June 1978; Chair. Int. Harvester Co. 1982–84 (C.E.O. May–Nov. 1982); Dir. numerous other companies; mem. Bd. of Trustees, Univ. of Denver, Business Roundtable, New York; mem. Business Council, Washington D.C., Bd. of Trustees, Conference Board; Seley Award 1970; Hon. LL.D., Drury Coll. 1965, Univ. Denver 1966, Monmouth Coll. 1967. *Address:* 34815 North Arroyo, Carefree, AZ 85377, U.S.A. (Home).

MENKEN, Alan; American composer; b. 22 July 1949, New York; ed. New York Univ.; began composing and performing Lehman Engel Musical Theatre Workshop, BMI. *Theatre music includes:* God Bless You Mr Rosewater 1979 (Off-Broadway debut), Little Shop of Horrors (with Howard Ashman), Kicks, The Apprenticeship of Duddy Kravitz, Diamonds, Personals, Let Freedom Sing, Weird Romance, Beauty and the Beast, A Christmas Carol. *Film music includes:* Little Shop of Horrors 1986, The Little Mermaid 1988 (two Acad. Awards 1989), Beauty and the Beast 1990 (two Acad. Awards 1991), Lincoln 1992, Newsies 1992, Aladdin 1992 (two Acad. Awards 1993), Life with Mikey 1993, Pocahontas (with Stephen Schwartz) 1995 (Golden Globe Award 1996, two Acad. Awards 1996). *Address:* The Shukat Company, 340 West 55th Street, Apt. 1A, New York, NY 10019, U.S.A.

MENKERIOS, Haile, M.A.; Eritrean diplomatist and economist; b. 1 Oct. 1946, Adi Felesti; s. of Drar Menkerios and Negusse Giorgis; m. Tesfamariam Ghennet 1979; one s. one d.; ed. Addis Ababa, Brandeis and Harvard Univs.; teaching asst. Harvard Univ. 1971–73; combatant in Eritrean People's Liberation Army (EPLA) 1973–74; Head of Tigrigna Section, Dept. of Information and Propaganda, Eritrean People's Liberation Front (EPLF) 1974–75, mem. Foreign Relations Cttee. 1976–77, mem. Cen. Council 1977–, asst. to Head of Dept. of Foreign Relations 1977–79, Head of African Relations 1977–79, Research Div., Dept. of Conscientization, Educ. and Culture 1979–86, Research and Information Centre of Eritrea 1986–87, Research and Policy Div., Dept. of Foreign Relations 1987–90, Gov. of East and South Zone 1990–91; mem. Eritrean Nat. Council 1991–; Rep. of Provisional Govt. of Eritrea to Ethiopia 1991–93; Special Envoy of Pres. to Somalia 1991–96, to the Greater Lakes Region 1996–97; mem. High Level Horn of Africa Cttee. on Somalia 1993–95; Amb. of State of Eritrea to Ethiopia and OAU 1993–96; Amb., Perm. Rep. of State of Eritrea to UN 1997–; has also worked in different mediation efforts in conflicts within Horn of Africa and been Special Envoy of Pres. of Eritrea to numerous African countries and forums 1992–97. *Publications:* various articles on African politics. *Leisure interests:* reading, sports. *Address:* 800 Second Avenue, 18th Floor, New York, NY 10017, U.S.A. *Telephone:* 212-687 3390. *Fax:* 212-687 3138.

MENON, Mambillikalathil Govind Kumar, M.SC., PH.D., F.R.S.; Indian physicist; b. 28 Aug. 1928, Mangalore; s. of Kizhekepat Sankara Menon and Mambillikalathil Narayaniamma; m. Indumati Patel 1955; one s. one d.; ed. Jaswant Coll., Jodhpur, Royal Inst. of Science, Bombay, Univ. of Bristol; Research Assoc., Univ. of Bristol 1952–53; Sr. Award of Royal Comm. for Exhbn. of 1851, Univ. of Bristol 1953–55; Reader, Tata Inst. of Fundamental Research, Bombay 1955–58; Assoc. Prof. 1958–60, Prof. and Dean of Physics Faculty 1960–64, Sr. Prof. and Deputy Dir. (Physics) 1964–66, Dir. Tata Inst. of Fundamental Research 1966–75; Chair. Electronics Comm. and Sec. to Govt. of India Dept. of Electronics 1971–78; Scientific Adviser to Minister of Defence, Dir.-Gen. Defence Research and Devt. Org. and Sec. for Defence Research 1974–78; Dir.-Gen. Council of Scientific and Industrial Research 1978–81; Sec. to Govt. of India, Dept. of Science and Tech. 1978–82; Chair. Comm. for Additional Sources of Energy 1981–82; Chair. Science Advisory Cttee. to Cabinet 1982–85; C.V. Raman Prof., Indian Nat. Science Acad. 1986–91; Scientific Adviser to P.M. 1986–89, and mem. Govt. Planning Comm. (with rank of Minister of State) 1982–89; Minister of State for Science and Tech. and for Human Resource Devt. 1989–90; M.P. 1990–96; Chair. Cosmic Ray Comm. 1973–75; Chair. Bd. of Govs. IIT (Bombay) 1997–; Pres. Asia Electronics Union 1973–75, Indian Science Congress Asscn. 1981–82, India Int. Centre, New Delhi 1983–88, Int. Council of Scientific Unions 1988–93, Indian Statistical Inst. 1990–; Vice-Pres. Int. Union of Pure & Applied Physics (IUPAP), Third World Acad. of Sciences 1983–88; mem. Pontifical Acad. of Sciences, Rome; Fellow, Indian Acad. of Sciences (Pres. 1974–76), Indian Nat. Science Acad. (Pres. 1981–82); M.N. Saha Distinguished Fellow and Hon. Fellow Nat. Acad. of Sciences, India (Pres. 1987–88); Hon. Fellow Tata Inst. of Fundamental Research, Inst. of Electronics and Telecommunications Eng. of India, Indian Inst. of Science, Bangalore, Nat. Inst. of Educ., Inst. of Physics (U.K.) 1997; Hon. mem. Inst. of Electrical and Electronic Engineers Inc.; Foreign Hon. mem. American Acad. of Arts and Sciences, Russian Acad. of Sciences; Hon. Pres. Asia Electronic Union; Hon. Dr. Eng. (Stevens Inst. of Tech., U.S.A.); Hon. D.Sc. (Jodhpur, Delhi, Sardar Patel, Roorkee, Banaras Hindu, Jadavpur, Sri Venkateswara, Allahabad, Andhra, Utkal, North Bengal, Aligarh Muslim, Guru Nanak Dev and Bristol Univs., and I.I.T., Madras and Kharagpur); Shanti Swarup Bhatnagar Award for Physical Sciences, Council of Scientific and Industrial Research 1960; Repub. Day (Nat.) Awards, Govt. of India; Padma Shri 1961, Padma Bhushan 1968, Padma Vibhushan 1985, Khaitan Medal, Royal Asiatic Soc. 1973; G. P. Chatterjee Award of Indian Science Congress Asscn. 1984, Award for Professional Excellence 1984, Pandit Jawaharlal Nehru Award for Sciences 1983, Om Prakash Bhasin Award for Science and Tech. 1985, C. V. Raman Medal of Indian Nat. Science Acad. 1985, Fourth J. C. Bose Triennial Gold Medal of Bose Inst.; Sri Ashutosh Mukherjee Award of Indian Science Congress Asscn.; Abdus Salam Medal,

Third World Acad. of Sciences 1997. *Publications:* 140 papers on cosmic ray and elementary particle physics. *Leisure interests:* bird-watching, photography. *Address:* C-63, Tarang Apts., 19 I. P. Ext., Mother Dairy Road, Patparganj, Delhi 110092, India. *Telephone:* (11) 272-5010. *Fax:* (11) 695-9456.

MENOTTI, Gian Carlo; Italian composer; b. 7 July 1911, Cadegliano; ed. Curtis Inst. of Music, Philadelphia, Pa.; went to U.S.A. 1928; mem. teaching staff Curtis Inst. of Music 1941–45; Hon. B.M. (Curtis Inst. of Music); Guggenheim Award 1946, 1947; Pulitzer Prize 1950, 1955; Kennedy Center Award 1984; Hon. Assoc. Nat. Inst. of Arts and Letters 1953; Founder and Pres. Festival of Two Worlds, Spoleto, Italy. *Compositions include:* Operas: Amelia Goes to the Ball, The Old Maid and the Thief, The Island God, The Telephone, The Medium, The Consul, Amahl and the Night Visitors, The Labyrinth (own libretti), The Saint of Bleecker Street 1954, The Last Savage 1963, Martin's Lie 1964, Help, Help, The Glotolinks (space opera for children) 1968, The Most Important Man in the World 1971, Tamu Tamu 1973, Arrival 1973, La Loca 1979, St. Teresa 1982, The Boy Who Grew Too Fast 1982, Goya 1986, Giorno di Nozze 1988; Song of Hope (cantata) 1980; Ballet: Sebastian; Film: The Medium (producer); Vanessa (libretto) 1958, The Unicorn, The Gorgon and the Manticore—a Madrigal Fable, Maria Golovin 1959, The Last Superman 1961, The Death of a Bishop of Brindisi (cantata) 1963; chamber music, songs, etc. *Address:* Yester House, Gifford, E. Lothian, EH41 4JF, Scotland.

MENSAH, Joseph Henry, M.SC.; Ghanaian politician; b. 31 Oct. 1928; ed. Achimota Coll., Univ. Coll. of Gold Coast (now Univ. of Ghana), L.S.E. and Stanford Univ.; Asst. Insp. of Taxes 1953; Research Fellow, Univ. Coll. of Gold Coast 1953–57; lecturer in Econs., Univ. of Ghana 1957–58; Economist, UN H.Q., New York 1958–61; Chief Economist, Prin. Sec. and Exec. Sec. of Nat. Planning Comm. Ghana 1961–65; Economist, UN Dir., Div. of Trade and Econ. Co-operation and Econ. Comm. for Africa (ECA) 1965–69; Commr. of Finance April–July 1969; M.P. for Sunyani (Progress Party) 1969–72; Minister of Finance 1969–72, and of Econ. Planning 1969–71; arrested Jan. 1972, released July 1973; re-arrested 1975; sentenced to eight years' imprisonment with hard labour Oct. 1975, released June 1978, in exile in London; returned to Ghana Feb. 1995.

MENSCHING, Horst Georg, DR. RER. NAT.; German professor of geography; b. 5 June 1921, Porta Westfalica; s. of Georg Mensching and Christine (née Kahre) Mensching; m. 1st Anne Würdemann 1949 (divorced); m. 2nd Ute Esselborn 1983 (deceased); m. 3rd Renate Heilig 1989; ed. Universität Göttingen; Asst. Inst. of Geography, Univ. of Göttingen 1949–52; Prof. of Geography, Univ. of Würzburg 1952–62; Full Prof. of Geography, Technische Universität Hannover 1962–74, Univ. of Hamburg 1974–85, Prof. Emer. 1985–; Consultant for Third World devt. projects (govt. and NGO); mem. Acad. of Sciences, Göttingen 1974, Acad. Leopoldina, Halle, Vienna 1974, Hon. mem. Acad. of Hungary 1985; hon. mem. five geographical socs.; Nachtigal Medal for Studies in Africa, Rüppell Medal, Geographical Soc. of Frankfurt. *Publications:* Geography of Morocco 1957, Geography of Tunisia 1968, Sahel-Zone 1985, North Africa and Middle East 1989, Desertification 1990, The Sahelian Countries 1992; over 200 scientific articles. *Address:* Pulverhofsweg 46, 22159 Hamburg, Germany. *Telephone:* (040) 643 16 80.

MENSHIKOV, Oleg Yevgenyevich; Russian actor; b. 8 Nov. 1960, Sierpoukhov; ed. Shchepkin Higher School of Theatre Art, Maly Theatre. *Major roles in films:* Kinsfolk, Flights in Dreams and When Awake, Kiss, Pokrovskye Gates, M. Lomonosov, Staircase, Moozund, Duba-Duba, Burnt by the Sun, Caucasian Prisoner, My Favourite Clown, Barber of Siberia; in films of dirs. N. Mikhalkov, A. Proshkin, A. Muratov, D. Khvan, S. Bodrov, R. Balayan, V. Kozakov, A. Sakharov. *Theatre roles include:* Ganya Ivolgin (Idiot after Dostoyevsky) 1981, Sergey (Sports Scenes of 1981) 1986, Caligula (Caligula) 1989, Yesenin (When She Danced) London 1991 (L. Olivier Prize), Ikharev (Gamblers) London 1992, Nizhinsky (N. Nizhinsky) 1993; Film Critics Prize for Best actor of 1994, prizes for best men's role at Festivals Kinotaurus 1996, Baltic Pearl 1996, other awards. *Address:* Maly Kozykhinsky per. 8/18, Apt. 3, Moscow, Russia. *Telephone:* (095) 299 0217 (Home).

MENSHOV, Vladimir Valentinovich; Russian film director and actor; b. 17 Sept. 1939, Baku; m. Vera Alentova 1963; one d.; ed. Moscow Arts Theatre Studio School, All-Union State Inst. of Cinema (VGIK) 1970; R.S.F.S.R. State Prize 1978, U.S.S.R. State Prize 1981, R.S.F.S.R. Artist of Merit 1984. *Leading roles in* A Man in his Place 1973, Last Meeting 1974, Personal Opinions 1977, Time for Reflection 1983, The Intercept 1986, Where is Nofelet? 1987, The Town Zero 1988, Red Mob 1993, Russian Ragtime 1993; *Films include:* Loss (Rozygrysh) 1977, Moscow Does Not Believe in Tears 1980 (Oscar Prize), Love and Doves 1984, Shirly-Myrly 1995. *Address:* 3-d Tverskaya-Yamskaya 52, Apt. 29, 125047 Moscow, Russia. *Telephone:* 250-85-43.

MENTER, Sir James Woodham, Kt., M.A., PH.D., SC.D., F.R.S.; British physicist and fmr. university principal; b. 22 Aug. 1921; s. of late Horace Menter and Jane Anne Lackenby; m. Marjorie Jean Whyte-Smith 1947; two s. one d.; ed. Dover Grammar School and Peterhouse, Cambridge; Experimental Officer, Admiralty 1942–45; Researcher, Univ. of Cambridge 1946–54; Tube Investments Research Labs., Dir. of Research and Devt. 1965–76; Dir. Tube Investments Research Labs. 1961–68, Tube Investments PLC 1965–86, Round Oak Steelworks Ltd. 1967–76, British Petroleum PLC 1976–87, Steetley PLC 1981–85; mem. SRC 1967–72; Vice-Pres. Royal Soc. 1971–76, Treas. 1972–76; Deputy Chair. Advisory Council Applied Research and Devt. 1976-79; mem. Cttee. of Inquiry into Eng. Profession 1977–80; Man. Royal Inst. 1981–84, Vice-Pres. 1983–85, Chair. Council 1984–85; Fellow, Churchill Coll., Cambridge 1966–86; Pres. Inst. of Physics 1970–72, Metals Soc. 1976; Prin. Queen Mary Coll., Univ. of London 1976–86, Fellow 1986–; mem. Court Univ. of Stirling 1988–94; Hon. F.R.S.E. 1992; Hon. D. Tech. (Brunel) 1974; Hon. D.Univ. (Stirling) 1996; Bessemer Medal, Iron and Steel Inst. 1973, Glazebrook Medal and Prize, Inst. of Physics 1977. *Publications:* scientific papers, proceedings of Royal Society, Advances in Physics, Inst. Iron and Steel, and others. *Leisure interest:* fishing. *Address:* Carie, Kinloch Rannoch, Pitlochry, Perthshire, PH17 2QJ, Scotland. *Telephone:* 01882632-341.

MENTES, Cevdet; Turkish politician and judge; b. 1915, Bitlis; ed. Istanbul Univ.; fmr. public prosecutor and judge, mem. Supreme Court of Appeal 1958, Pres. 1972; Minister of Justice 1980–82. *Address:* c/o Ministry of Justice, Adalet Bakanlığı, Bakanlıklar, Ankara, Turkey.

MENTEŞE, Nahit; Turkish politician and lawyer; b. 1932, Milas; m.; two c.; ed. Istanbul Univ.; ind. lawyer; joined Adalet Partisi (AP), then Doğru Yol Partisi (DYP); parl. deputy 1991–; fmr. Minister of Customs and Monopolies, of Transport, of Energy and Natural Resources, of Tourism, of Educ., of the Interior 1993–95. *Address:* c/o Ministry of the Interior, İçişleri Bakanlığı, Bakanlıklar, Ankara, Turkey.

MENTRÉ, Paul; French civil servant and diplomatist; b. 28 June 1935, Nancy; s. of Paul Mentré and Cécile de Loye; m. 1st Sabine Brundsaux 1958 (divorced 1975); two d.; m. 2nd Gaëlle Bretillot 1975; two s.; m. 3rd Jehanne Collard 1992; ed. Ecole Polytechnique, Ecole Nat. d'Admin.; Insp. of Finance 1960; Special Asst., French Treas. 1965–70; Deputy Dir. of the Cabinet of the Minister of Finance (M. Giscard d'Estaing) 1971–73; Under-Sec. Ministry of Economy and Finance 1971–72; Dir. Crédit National 1973–75, Crédit lyonnais 1973–75; Gen. Del. for Energy 1975–78; Financial Minister, French Embassy in Washington, D.C. 1978–82; Exec. Dir. IMF and World Bank 1978–81; Insp.-Gen. of Finance 1981; Man. Dir. Banque Nationale de Paris 1986–87, Dir.-Gen. 1987–90; Pres. Dir.-Gen. Crédit National 1987–90; Pres. Crédit sucrier 1990, technopole de Caen Synergia 1991–94, Valréal 1992–, Trouville-Deauville dist. 1995–; mem. Supervisory Council Crédit local de France 1987–; Dir. European Investment Bank 1987–91; Chevalier, Ordre nat. du Mérite, des Arts et des Lettres; Saudi Royal Order. *Publications:* Imaginer l'Avenir, Gulliver Enchaîné 1982, L'Amerique et nous, L'insoutenable légèreté du fort 1989, articles on economic issues in Le Figaro, Le Monde and Les Echos. *Leisure interests:* tennis, skiing. *Address:* Banque CSIA, 22 rue de la Trémoille, 75700 Paris; 19 rue Casimir Perier, 75007 Paris, France.

MENUDIN, Ibrahim, B.COMM.; Malaysian business executive; b. 17 May 1948, Labuan; m. Jamilah Ibrahim; four s.; ed. Univ. of Western Australia; fmrly. Accountant-Gen. of Sabay, Chief Exec., Bumputra Investment Fund, Sabah; fmr. C.E.O. Malaysia Mining Corpn. *Leisure interests:* badminton, squash. *Address:* c/o Malaysia Mining Corporation Berhad, 38th Floor, Menara PNB, 201A Jalan Tun Razak, 50400 Kuala Lumpur, Malaysia.

MENZE, Clemens, DR.PHIL.; German professor of pedagogy; b. 20 Sept. 1928, Tietelsen, Höxter; s. of Clemens Menze and Elisabeth Menke; m. Dr. med. Sigrun Schütz 1968; one d.; ed. Univ. of Cologne; research asst. 1957–63; Asst. Prof. of Pedagogy 1963–65; Adviser in govt. service 1965–67; Prof. and Head, Pedagogical Seminar, Univ. of Cologne 1967–, Rector 1975–77. *Publications:* Wilhelm von Humboldts Lehre und Bild vom Menschen 1965, Die Bildungsreform Wilhelm von Humboldts 1975, Bildung und Bildungswesen (essays) 1980. *Address:* Pädagogisches Seminar, Universität Köln, Albertus-Magnus-Platz, 5000 Köln 1 (Office); Paul-Gerhardt-Strasse 8, 53332 Bornheim-Walberberg, Germany (Home). *Telephone:* 16 23.

MENZEL, Jiří; Czech film and theatre director and actor; b. 23 Feb. 1938; s. of Josef Menzel and Božena Jindřichová; ed. Film Acad. of Performing Arts, specialized in film directing, 1957–61; film dir. and actor 1962–89; Head of Dept. of Film Directing, Film Acad. of Performing Arts, Prague 1990–92; Producer of Studio 89 1991–; Dir. Vinohradské divadlo (theatre) 1997, 1998–; Oscar Prize, Santa Monica 1968 for Closely Observed Trains, Akira Kurosawa Prize for Lifelong Merits in Cinematography, San Francisco 1990, Ennio Flaiano, Prize for Lifetime Achievement in Cinematography, Pescara, Italy 1996; End of the Old Times awarded Grand Prize of the Int. Film Producers' Meeting, Cannes 1990, Officier, Ordre des Arts et des Lettres (France) 1990, Medal of Merit 1996, Czech Lion Prize, Czech Film and TV Acad. (for lifetime career) 1997, Golden Seal Prize (Yugoslavia) 1997. *Films directed include:* Closely Observed Trains, Skylarks on the String, Oh, My Village, End of the Old Times, The Beggar's Opera 1991, The Life and Extraordinary Adventures of Private Ivan Chonkin 1994. *Publication:* Tak nevím (novel) 1998. *Leisure interest:* literature. *Address:* Studio 89, Krátký film Praha a.s., Jindřišská 34, 112 07 Prague 1, Czech Republic (Office). *Telephone:* (02) 242-10-767 (Office). *Fax:* (02) 242-10-767.

MER, Francis Paul, L. ÈS SC. ECON.; French business executive; b. 25 May 1939, Pau, Basses Pyrénées; s. of René Mer and Yvonne Casalta; m. Catherine Bonfils 1964; three d.; ed. Lycée Montesquieu, Bordeaux, Ecole Nationale Supérieure des Mines, Paris and Ecole Polytechnique; mining engineer, Ministry of Industry 1966; tech. adviser, Abidjan 1967–68; Chair. Inter-ministerial Cttee. on European Econ. Co-operation 1969–70; Head of

Planning, Saint-Gobain Industries 1971; Dir. of Planning, Compagnie Saint-Gobain-Pont-à-Mousson 1973; Dir. of Planning, later Dir.-Gen. Saint-Gobain Industries 1973; Dir. Société des Maisons Phénix 1976–78; Asst. Dir.-Gen. Saint-Gobain-Pont-à-Mousson 1978–82, Pres.-Dir.-Gen. de Pont-à-Mousson SA 1982–86; Pres.-Dir.-Gen. Usinor-Sacilor 1986–; Pres. Chambre syndicale de la sidérurgie française 1988–, Conservatoire Nat. des Arts et Métiers 1989–, Eurofer 1990–, Asscn. nat. de Recherche Technique 1991–, Centre d'études prospectives et d'informations internationales 1995–; Pres. Int. Iron and Steel Inst. (INSI) 1997–; Dir. Crédit lyonnais 1997–, Electricité de France 1997–, Air France 1997–; Officier, Légion d'honneur, Ordre nat. du Mérite. *Address:* Usinor, immeuble Pacific, TSA 10001, 92070 La Défense (Office); 9 rue Bobierre-de-Vallière, 92340 Bourg-la-Reine, France (Home).

MERCADO JARRIN, Gen. Luis Edgardo; Peruvian politician and army officer; b. 19 Sept. 1919, Barranco, Lima; s. of Dr. Alejandro Mercado Ballón and Florinda Jarrín de Mercado; m. Gladys Neumann Terán de Mercado 1951; one s. four d.; ed. primary and secondary school, Colegio la Libertad de Moquegua, Escuela Militar de Chorrillos; commissioned 1940, Gen. of Div. Jan. 1970–; Prof. Escuela Militar, Escuela de Artillería, Escuela Superior de Guerra, Centro de Altos Estudios Militares, etc.; Dir. of Army Intelligence; del. of Peruvian Army to several inter-American army confs.; guest lecturer to U.S. Army, Fort Holabird and Fort Bragg; Commdt.-Gen. Centro de Instrucción Militar del Perú 1968; Minister of Foreign Affairs 1968–71; Army Chief of Staff Jan.-Dec. 1972; Prime Minister and Minister of War 1973–75; awards include Grand Cross of Orden Militar de Ayacucho and Orden al Mérito Militar, Orden del Sol and orders from Colombia, Portugal, Argentina, Bolivia, Brazil and Venezuela. *Publications:* La Política y la Estrategia Militar en la Guerra Contrasubversiva en América Latina, El Ejército de Hoy en Nuestra Sociedad en Período de Transición y en el Campo Internacional, El Ejército y la Empresa; contributor to magazine of Interamerican Defence Coll., U.S.A., Revista Militar del Perú, Brazilian Military Journal. *Leisure interests:* tennis, riding, classical music, reading (contemporary military philosophy, sociology and economics). *Address:* Avenida Velasco Astete 1140, Chacarrilla del Estanque, Lima, Peru. *Telephone:* 256823.

MERCHANT, Ismail, B.A., M.B.A.; Indian film producer; b. 25 Dec. 1936, Bombay; s. of Noormohamed Haji Abdul Rehman and Hazra Memon; ed. St. Xavier's Coll., Bombay, New York Univ.; f. Merchant Ivory Productions (with James Ivory q.v.) 1961. *Films:* (as producer) The Creation of Woman 1960, The Householder 1963, Shakespeare Wallah 1965, The Guru 1969, Bombay Talkie 1970, Adventures of a Brown Man in Search of Civilization, Savages 1972, Helen, Queen of the Nautch Girls 1973, Autobiography of a Princess, The Wild Party 1975, Sweet Sounds 1976, Roseland 1977, Hullabaloo Over Georgie and Bonnie's Pictures 1978, The Europeans 1979, Jane Austen in Manhattan 1980, Quartet 1981, Heat and Dust 1982, The Bostonians, A Room with a View 1986, Maurice 1987, The Deceivers 1988, Slaves of New York 1989, Mr and Mrs Bridge 1990, The Ballad of the Sad Cafe 1991, Howards End 1992, The Remains of the Day 1993, Jefferson in Paris 1994, Feast of July 1995, Surviving Picasso 1996, The Proprietor (as Dir.) 1996, A Soldier's Daughter Never Cries 1997; (as Dir.) Mahatma and the Mad Boy 1973, The Courtesans of Bombay 1983, In Custody 1994, Cotton Masy 1999. *Publications:* Ismail Merchant's Indian Cuisine 1986, Hullaballo in Old Jaypoore 1988, Ismail Merchant's Vegetarian Cooking 1992, Ismail Merchant's Florence 1994, Ismail Merchant's Passionate Meals 1994, Once Upon a Time, The Proprietor 1996. *Leisure interests:* cooking, music, cycling. *Address:* 400 East 52nd Street, New York, NY 10022, U.S.A. (Home); 32 Motlabai Street, Bombay, India. *Telephone:* (212) 759-3694 (U.S.A.); 378-376 (India).

MERCIECA, Mgr. Joseph, B.A., S.TH.D., J.U.D.; Maltese ecclesiastic; b. 11 Nov. 1928, Victoria, Gozo; s. of Saverio Mercieca and Giovanna Vassallo; ed. Gozo Seminary, Gregorian Univ. and Lateran Univ., Rome; ordained priest 1952; Rector Gozo Seminary 1952–69; Judge of Roman Rota 1969–74; ordained Titular Bishop of Gemelle in Numidia, apptd. Auxiliary Bishop of Malta 1974; Vicar-Gen. 1975–76; Consultor, Congregation of the Sacraments and Congregation for the Doctrine of Faith, Vatican City 1976; Archbishop of Malta, Pres. Maltese Episcopal Conf. 1976–; mem. Apostolic Segnatura, Rome 1991. *Address:* Archbishop's Curia, Floriana (Office); Archbishop's Palace, Mdina, Malta (Home). *Telephone:* 234317.

MEREDITH, William (Morris Meredith), A.B.; American poet and educationalist; b. 9 Jan. 1919, New York; s. of William Morris and Nelley (née Keyser) Meredith; ed. Princeton Univ.; reporter New York Times 1940–41; Instructor in English and Creative Writing Princeton Univ. 1946–50; Asst. Prof. in English Univ. of Hawaii 1950–51; mem. Faculty Conn. Coll. 1955, Prof. of English 1965–83; Dir. Conn. Coll. Humanities-Upward Bound Program 1964–68; Poetry Conservator Library of Congress 1978–80; Chancellor Acad. of American Poets 1964; mem. Nat. Inst. of Arts and Letters; Air Medal with Oak Leaf Cluster; awarded Loines Prize Nat. Inst. of Arts and Letters 1966, Van Wyck Brooks Award 1971, Int. Nicola Vaptsarov Prize in Literature, Sofia 1979, Pulitzer Prize for Poetry 1988. *Publications include:* poems: Love Letter from an Impossible Land 1944, Ships and Other Figures 1948, The Open Sea and Other Poems 1958, Shelley 1962, The Wreck of the Thresher and Other Poems 1964, Winter Verse 1964, Alcools (trans.) 1964, Earth Walk: New and Selected Poems 1970, Hazard, The Painter 1975, The Cheer 1980, Partial Accounts: New and Selected Poems 1987. *Address:* c/o Connecticut College, P.O. Box 1498, New London, CT 06320, U.S.A.

MEREZHKO, Viktor Ivanovich; Russian scriptwriter; b. 28 July 1937, Olginfeld, Rostov-on Don Region; m. (wife deceased); one s. one d.; ed. Ukrainian Inst. of Polygraphy, Lvov, All-Union Inst. of Cinematography; engineer Molot Publrs. Roston on Don 1961–64; freelance 1968–; wrote scripts for over 45 films. *Films include:* Hello and Goodbye 1971, The Quagmire 1979, The Kin 1981, Dream and Walking Flights 1983, Under the Blue Sky (Fipressi Prize. Venice Festival, 1987), Ryba: My Chicken 1993, The Two from Big Road 1996, Caucasus Roulette 1998; State Prize 1986. *Leisure interest:* collecting side-arms. *Address:* Usiyevicha str 8, Apt. 133, 125319 Moscow, Russia (Home). *Telephone:* (095) 155 7459 (Home).

MERI, Lennart; Estonian politician; b. 29 March 1929, Tallinn; s. of Georg-Peter Meri and Alice-Brigitta Meri; m. Helle Pihlak; two s. one d.; ed. Tartu Univ.; deported to Siberia with family 1941–46; forbidden to practise history, took part in scientific expeditions to Middle Asia; Head of Manuscript Section Vanemuine Theatre; worked for Estonian Radio; Scriptwriter and Dir. Tallinnfilm; Sec. Estonian Writers' Asscn.; founder, Dir. Estonian Inst. 1989–90; active in Movt. for Independence 1980s; Minister of Foreign Affairs 1990–92; Amb. to Finland April–Oct. 1992; Pres. of Estonia 1992–; Dr. h.c. (Helsinki Univ.) 1976; several decorations including from Mexico, Sweden, Finland, Denmark, Jordan, Latvia. *Publications:* numerous travel stories, literary essays, translations; several films depicting the history of Finno-Ugric people and the nations living by the Baltic Sea. *Leisure interests:* history, literature, maps. *Address:* Office of the President, Weizenbergi 39, 0100 Tallinn, Estonia. *Telephone:* (372) 631 62 02. *Fax:* (372) 631 62 50.

MERIDOR, Dan; Israeli politician and lawyer; b. 1947, Jerusalem; m.; three c.; ed. Hebrew Univ.; fmr. mem. Likud Party; Sec. of Govt. 1982–84; mem. Knesset 1984–; Minister of Justice 1988–92, of Finance 1996–97. *Address:* c/o Ministry of Finance, P.O. Box 883, 1 Rehov Kaplan, Kiryat Ben-Gurion, Jerusalem 91008, Israel.

MERIKAS, George, M.D.; Greek politician and professor of medicine; b. 5 May 1911, Agios Andreas; s. of Emmanuel Merikas and Helen (née Kritikou) Merikas; m. Irene (née Koutsogianni) Merikas 1945 (died 1971); two s. one d.; ed. Medical School, Univ. of Athens; Assoc. Prof. of Medicine, Univ. of Athens 1953, Prof. 1970–78; Dir. Dept. of Medicine, Evangelismos Hosp., Athens 1960–70; Fulbright Grant, Univ. of Cincinnati Medical School 1964–65; mem. Acad of Athens 1978–, Pres. 1988–89; Minister of Health, Welfare and Social Services 1989–90; Pres. Nat. Aids Cttee. in Greece 1988–; mem. Accad. Tiberina, New York Acad. of Sciences, Asscn. for the Advancement of Sciences. *Publications:* Hepatitis Associated Antigen in Chronic Liver Disease 1970, Australia Antigen in the Liver 1972, Hepatitis B Core Antigen and Antibody in Primary Liver Cancer 1975, Internal Medicine, 2 Vols. 1976, Cholesterol Gall-Stone Dissolution by CDC 1976. *Leisure interests:* literature, history. *Address:* 6 Vasileos Irakliou Str., 10682 Athens, Greece. *Telephone:* (01) 8210719.

MERILLON, Jean-Marie; French diplomatist; b. 12 Feb. 1926; s. of Robert Mérillon and Marguerite Dubourg; m. Jacqueline Plasschaert 1961; one s.; ed. Ecole Nat. d'Admin.; served at Ministry of Foreign Affairs 1952–68; Amb. to Jordan 1968–73, to S. Vietnam 1973–75, to Greece 1975–77; Dir. of Political Affairs 1977–79; Amb. to Algeria 1979–81, to NATO 1982–85, to Switzerland 1985–89, to U.S.S.R. 1989–91; Adviser to Pres. of Crédit Lyonnais 1991–95; Pres. Crédit Lyonnais Russie 1992–95; Pres. Banque Franco-Hellénique 1993; Officier Légion d'honneur, Ordre nat. du Mérite; numerous other decorations. *Address:* 80 boulevard de Courcelles, 75017 Paris, France (Home).

MERINO CASTRO, Admiral José Toribio; Chilean naval officer; b. 14 Dec. 1915; m. Gabriela Margarita Riofrío Bustos 1952; three d.; ed. Naval Acad.; specialized as Gunnery Officer, Naval Acad.; naval service on Maipo 1936, Rancagua 1939; Instructor Blanco Encalada 1940; Div. Officer Almirante Latorre 1943; Asst. F.C. Officer U.S.S. Raleigh, Pacific Theater 1944; Artillery Officer, Serrano 1945; Commdr. of Corvette Papudo 1952; Staff Coll. Course 1954; Tech. Adviser of Armaments 1955; Commdr. of destroyer Williams 1962, Riveros 1963; Vice-Chief of Gen. Staff 1964; C.-in-C. of the Fleet 1970–71; C.-in-C. of First Naval Zone 1972–73; C.-in-C. of the Navy 1973; mem. of the Govt. Junta 1973–90; Armed Forces Medal III, II, I, Grand Star of Merit, Cross for Naval Merit, Decoration of Pres. of Repub. (Chile).

MERKEL, Angela, DR.RER.NAT.; German politician; b. 17 July 1954, Hamburg; ed. Univ. of Leipzig; Research Assoc. Zentralinstitut für physikalische Chemie, East Berlin 1978–90; joined Demokratischer Aufruch (DA) 1989, Press Officer 1990; Deputy Spokesman for Govt. of Lothar de la Maizière March-Oct. 1990; joined CDU Aug. 1990; mem. Bundestag Dec. 1990–; Minister for Women and Young People 1991–94, for Family Women, Youth and Sr. Citizens 1994–98. *Address:* c/o Bundesministerin für Frauen und Jugend, Kennedyallee 5, 53175 Bonn, Germany.

MERKELBACH, Reinhold, D.PHIL.; German professor of classics; b. 7 June 1918, Grenzhausen; s. of Paul Merkelbach and Gertrud Stade; m. Lotte Dorn 1941; one s. two d.; ed. Schondorf Gymnasium, Univs. of Munich and Hamburg; Asst. at Classics Inst. Univ. of Cologne 1950–57, Prof. 1961–83, Prof. Emer. 1983–; Prof. Erlangen Univ. 1957–61; mem. Rheinisch-Westfälisch Akad. der Wissenschaften 1979–; Corresp. mem. British Acad. 1986–; Dr. h.c. Univ. of Besançon, France 1978. *Publications:* Untersuchungen zur Odyssee 1951, Die Quellen des griechischen Alexanderromans 1954, Roman und Mysterium im Altertum 1961, Isisfeste 1962, (with M. West) Fragmenta

Hesiodea 1968, (with F. Solmsen and M. West) Hesiodi Opera 1970, 1989, Mithras 1984, Die Hirten des Dionysos 1988, Platons Menon 1988, (with M. Totti) Abrasax I–IV 1990–96, Die Bedeutung des Geldes für die Geschichte der greichisch-römischen Welt 1992, Isis regina—Zeus Sarapis 1995, Hestia und Erigone 1996, Philologica 1997, (with J. Stauber) Steinepigramme aus dem griechischen Osten 1998; many edns. of Greek inscriptions, Ed. of Zeitschrift für Papyrologie und Epigraphik, Epigraphica anatolica, Beiträge zur klassischen Philologie. *Address:* Im Haferkamp 17, 51427 Bergisch-Gladbach, Germany. *Telephone:* (2204) 60727. *Fax:* (2204) 60727.

MERLINI, Cesare; Italian international affairs scholar and fmr. professor of nuclear technologies; b. 29 April 1933, Rome; m.; two s. two d.; lecturer in Nuclear Technologies 1967–76; Prof. of Nuclear Technologies, Turin Polytechnic 1976–85; Dir. Istituto Affari Internazionali, Rome 1970–79, Pres. 1979–; Pres. Exec. Cttee. Council for the U.S. and Italy 1983–; mem. Trilateral Comm. 1973–, Council, Int. Inst. for Strategic Studies, London 1983–, Gen. Council, Aspen Inst. Italia, Rome; mem. Bd. of Dirs., Assen. Jean Monnet, Paris, ISPI, Milan; mem. Bd. of Dirs. and Exec. Cttee. UTET SpA, Turin. *Publications:* Fine dell'atomo? Passato e futuro delle applicazioni civili e militari dell'energia nucleare 1987, L'Europa degli Anni Novanta; Scenari per un futuro imprevisto (Co-author and Ed.) 1991; co-author and ed. of numerous books on nuclear energy and int. strategy, author of numerous articles on European and int. affairs and of scientific publs. on nuclear reactors and related technological and eng. problems. *Address:* Istituto Affari Internazionali, Palazzo Rondinini, Via A. Brunetti 9, 00186 Rome, Italy. *Telephone:* (06) 322 4360. *Fax:* (06) 322 4363.

MERLONI, Vittorio; Italian industrialist; b. 30 April 1933, Fabriano, Ancona; Pres. Merloni Elettrodomestici S.p.A. 1970–; mem. Confederazione Generale dell'Industria Italiana (Confindustria) 1976–, Pres. 1980–84; Dir. Harvard Business School 1981; mem. two dels. to China; mem. Consiglio Nazionale dell'Economia e del Lavoro (Nat. Council of Economy and Labour); Cavaliere di Gran Croce al merito della Repubblica. *Address:* Confindustria, Viale dell'Astronomia 30, 00144 Rome (Office); Via Aristide Merloni 45, 60044 Fabriano, Ancona, Italy (Home). *Telephone:* 06-59031 (Office).

MERLYN-REES, Baron (Life Peer), cr. 1992, of Morley and South Leeds in the County of West Yorkshire and of Cilfynydd in the County of Mid Glamorgan, **Merlyn Merlyn-Rees,** P.C., M.SC.(ECON.); British politician and lecturer; b. 18 Dec. 1920, Cilfynydd; s. of late Levi Daniel Rees and Edith May Rees; name changed to Merlyn-Rees by deed poll 1992; m. Colleen Faith Cleveley 1949; three s.; ed. Harrow Weald Grammar School, Goldsmiths' Coll., London and London School of Econs.; served R.A.F. 1941–46, rank of Squadron Leader; Teacher, Harrow Weald Grammar School 1949–60; Labour Party Head Office 1960–62; Lecturer Luton Coll. of Tech. 1962–63; M.P. for Leeds South 1963–83, for Morley and Leeds South 1983–92; Parl. Private Sec. to Chancellor of Exchequer 1964–65; Under-Sec. Ministry of Defence 1965–68, Home Office 1968–70; Opposition Spokesman for N. Ireland 1970–74; mem. Departmental Cttee. Investigating Official Secrets Act; Sec. of State for N. Ireland 1974–76; Home Sec. 1976–79, Opposition Spokesman for Home Affairs 1979–80, for Energy 1980–83, Co-ordinator of Econ. Planning; mem. Cttee. of Inquiry into events leading to Argentine invasion of the Falklands 1982; Chancellor Univ. of Glamorgan 1994–; Chair. South Leeds Groundwork Trust 1987–97, Vice-Chair. 1997–; Pres. Video Standards Council 1990; Hon. Fellow, Goldsmiths' Coll., London; Hon. LL.D. (Wales) 1987, (Leeds) 1992. *Publications:* The Public Sector in the Mixed Economy 1973, Northern Ireland: A Personal Perspective 1985. *Leisure interest:* reading. *Address:* House of Lords, London, SW1A 0PW, England. *Telephone:* 0171-219 3000.

MERMAZ, Louis; French politician; b. 20 Aug. 1931, Paris; teacher lycée le Mans, lycée Lakanal, Sceaux; junior lecturer in contemporary history, Univ. of Clermont-Ferrand; Sec.-Gen. Convention des institutions républicaines 1965–69; mem. Socialist Party Nat. Secr. 1974–79, 1987–; mem. Nat. Assembly for Isère 1967–68, 1973–90, 1997–; Mayor of Vienne 1971–; Conseiller Gén. Canton of Vienne-Nord 1973–79, Vienne-Sud 1979–88; Pres. Conseil gén. of Isère 1976–85; Chair. Socialist Party Exec. Cttee. 1979; Minister of Transport May–June 1981, May–June 1988, of Agric. and Forests 1990–92, for Relations with Parl. and Govt. Spokesman 1992–93; Pres. Nat. Ass. 1981–86, Socialist Group in Nat. Ass. 1988–90, Asscn. Mer du Nord-Méditerranée 1989–94; Chevalier Légion d'honneur. *Publications:* Madame Sabatier, les Hohenzollern, l'Autre volonté 1984, Madame de Maintenon 1985. *Address:* Cabinet du Maire, Hôtel de Ville, 38209 Vienne Cédex, France. *Telephone:* (4) 74 78 31 48.

MERRICK, David; American theatrical producer; b. 27 Nov. 1912, St. Louis; s. of Samuel and Celia Margulios; m. Etan Aronson; ed. St. Louis Univ.; producer of numerous plays on Broadway, including Fanny 1954, The Matchmaker 1955, Look Back in Anger, Romanoff and Juliet, Jamaica 1957, The Entertainer, The World of Suzie Wong, La plume de ma tante, Epitaph for George Dillon, Maria Golovin 1958, Destry Rides Again, Gypsy, Take Me Along 1959, The Good Soup, Vintage '60', Irma la Douce, A Taste of Honey, Becket, Do Re Me 1960, Carnival 1961, Sunday in New York 1961, Ross 1961, I Can Get it for You Wholesale 1962, Stop the World, I Want to Get Off 1962, Tchin Tchin 1962, Oliver! 1962, Rehearsal 1963, Hello Dolly 1964, Pickwick 1965, Inadmissible Evidence 1965, Cactus Flower 1965, Marat/Sade 1965, Don't Drink the Water 1966, I do! I do! 1966, Philadelphia, Here I Come 1966, Rosencrantz and Guildenstern Are Dead 1967, How Now, Dow Jones 1967, The Happy Time 1967, Promises Promises 1968, 40 Carats 1968, Play It Again Sam 1969, Private Lives 1969, Child's Play 1970, A Midsummer Night's Dream, Four on a Garden, The Philanthropist 1971, There's One in Every Marriage, Vivat, Vivat Regina!, Moonchildren, Sugar 1972, Child's Play 1972, Out Cry 1973, Mack and Mabel 1974, Dreyfus in Rehearsal 1974, Travesties, The Red Devil Battery Sign, Very Good Eddie 1975, 42nd Street 1985, Oh Kay!; produced films The Great Gatsby 1974, Semi-Tough 1977, Rough Cut 1980.

MERRIFIELD, (Robert) Bruce; American biochemist; b. 15 July 1921, Texas; s. of George and Lorene Merrifield; m. Elizabeth Furlong 1949; one s. five d.; ed. Univ. of California, Los Angeles (U.C.L.A.); Chemist, Park Research Foundation 1943–44; Teaching Asst., Chem. Dept. U.C.L.A. 1944–47, Research Asst., Medical School 1948–49; Asst. to Assoc. Prof. Rockefeller Inst. 1949–66, Prof. of Biochem. 1966–92, John D. Rockefeller Jr. Prof. 1984–92, Prof. Emer. 1992–; developed solid phase peptide synthesis; mem. Nat. Acad. of Sciences; Nobel Guest Prof. 1968; Lasker Award 1969, Gairdner Award 1970, Intra-Science Award 1970, A.C.S. Award 1972, Nichols Award 1973, Pierce Award 1979, Nobel Prize for Chem. 1984 for devt. of method of synthesising peptides and proteins, Rudiger Award, European Peptide Soc. 1990, Chemistry Pioneer Award, American Inst. of Chemists 1993; Order of San Carlos (Columbia). *Publications:* 150 articles in various scientific journals. *Leisure interests:* tennis, camping, hiking. *Address:* Rockefeller University, 1230 York Avenue, New York, NY 10021; 43 Mezzine Drive, Cresskill, NJ 07626, U.S.A. (Home). *Telephone:* (212) 570-8244 (Office); (201) 567-0329 (Home).

MERRILL, Robert; American baritone; b. 4 June 1919, Brooklyn, New York; s. of Abraham Miller and Lillian (née Balaban) Merrill; m. Marion Machno 1954; one s. one d.; debut at Metropolitan Opera as Germont (La Traviata) 1945; has since appeared throughout U.S.A. and Europe in most of the baritone repertoire including: Gérard (André Chénier), Renato (A Masked Ball), Figaro (The Barber of Seville), Rodrigo (Don Carlos), Scarpia (Tosca), Amonasro (Aida) and Rigoletto; many concert and television appearances; frequent recordings; Nat. Medal of Arts 1993. *Publications:* Once More from the Beginning 1965, Between Acts 1976, The Divas 1978. *Leisure interests:* art and golf. *Address:* c/o RMAI, 79 Oxford Road, New Rochelle, NY 10804, U.S.A.

MERSON, Michael; American international civil servant; b. 7 June 1945, New York; ed. Johns Hopkins Univ.; joined Centre for Disease Control, Atlanta 1972; worked in several countries including Brazil and Bangladesh; joined WHO 1978; Dir. WHO Diarrhoeal Diseases Control Prog. and Acute Respiratory Infections Control Programme; Dir. Global Programme on AIDS 1990–. *Address:* World Health Organization, Avenue Appia, 1211 Geneva 27, Switzerland.

MERTENS DE WILMARS, Josse Marie Honoré Charles, Baron, D.L., D.POL.SC.; Belgian lawyer; b. 12 June 1912, St. Niklaas; s. of Albert Mertens and Jeanne Meert; m. Betty van Ormelingen 1939; eight c.; ed. Abbey School St. Andries, Bruges, Univ. of Louvain; mem. Bar 1935–67; Assessor, Conseil d'Etat 1948–51; M.P. 1951–61; Prof. of Law, Univ. of Leuven 1967–81; Judge, Court of Justice of European Communities 1967–84, Pres. 1980–84; Kt., Order of Léopold, Grand Croix Ordre de la Couronne, Grosskreuz Deutsche Verdienstorde, Grootkruis Orde Oranje Nassau, Grand Croix Ordre Couronne de Chêne. *Address:* Jan Van Ryswycklaan 192, 2020 Antwerp, Belgium. *Telephone:* 0032-3-238.07.68 (Home).

MERTIN, Klaus, DR.RER.POL.; German banker; b. 9 March 1922; Chair. of Supervisory Bd. Deutsche Bank Berlin AG, Berlin, Dierig Holding AG, Augsburg; Deputy Chair. of Supervisory Bd. Deutsche Centralbodenkredit A.G., Berlin, Cologne; mem. of Supervisory Bd. A.G. für Industrie und Verkehrswesen, Frankfurt, Badenwerk AG, Karlsruhe, Daimler-Benz AG, Stuttgart, Gerling-Konzern-Versicherungs-Beteiligungs AG, Cologne, Heidelberger Druckmaschinen AG, Heidelberg, Karstadt AG, Essen, Rheinmetall Berlin AG, Düsseldorf, Salamander AG, Kornwestheim, Schindler Aufzügefabrik GmbH, Berlin; mem. of Advisory Bd. Barmenia Versicherungen, Wuppertal; mem. of Admin. Council Deutsche Bank Compagnie Financière Luxembourg, Luxembourg; mem. of Exec. Council Schott Glaswerke, Mainz. *Address:* Deutsche Bank AG, Taunusanlage 12, 60325 Frankfurt am Main, Germany.

MERTON, John Ralph, M.B.E.(MIL.); British artist; b. 7 May 1913, London; s. of Sir Thomas Ralph Merton, K.B.E. and Violet Margery Harcourt Sawyer; m. Viola Penelope von Bernd 1938; three d. (one deceased); ed. Eton. Coll., Balliol Coll., Oxford; served W.W.II, Lieut. Col. Air Photo Reconnaissance Research Unit 1944; *portraits include:* Jane Dalkeith (now Duchess of Buccleuch) (Royal Acad. 'A' Award) 1958, Triple Portrait of H.R.H. The Princess of Wales 1988, drawing of H.M. The Queen as Head of the Order of Merit 1989, James Meade (winner Nobel Prize for Economics) 1987, Paul Nitze 1991, Lord and Lady Romsey with a mirror reflecting Broadlands 1997; Legion of Merit, U.S.A. 1944. *Publication:* A Journey through an Artist's Life (limited edn.) 1994. *Leisure interests:* music, making things, underwater photography. *Address:* Pound House, Oare, Nr. Marlborough, Wiltshire, SN8 4JA, England. *Telephone:* (01672) 563539.

MERTON, Patrick Anthony, M.D., F.R.S.; British professor of human physiology; b. 8 Oct. 1920, Kent; s. of the late Gerald Merton; m. Anna Gabriel Howe 1951; one s. three d.; ed. Beaumont, Trinity Coll., Cambridge, St.

Thomas's Hosp.; MRC Neurological Research Unit, London 1946–57; lecturer Physiological Lab., Cambridge 1957–77, Reader 1977–84; Fellow Trinity Coll., Cambridge 1962–; Prof. of Human Physiology, Cambridge Univ. 1984–88; Hon. Consultant Nat. Hosp., London 1979–. *Publications:* scientific papers in Journal of Physiology and Brain. *Address:* Trinity College, Cambridge, CB2 1TQ; 12 Lansdowne Road, Cambridge, CB3 0EU, England. *Telephone:* (01223) 359991.

MERTON, Robert C., PH.D.; American economist; b. 31 July 1944, New York; s. of Robert K. Merton and Suzanne Merton; m. June Rose 1966 (separated 1996); two s. one d.; ed. Columbia Univ., Calif. Inst. of Tech., Mass. Inst. of Tech.; instructor in econs. M.I.T. 1969–70; Asst. Prof. of Finance Alfred P. Sloan School of Man. 1970–73, Assoc. Prof. 1973–74, Prof. 1974–80, J.C. Penney Prof. of Man. 1980–88; Visiting Prof. of Finance, Harvard Univ. 1987–88, George Fisher Baker Prof. of Business Admin. 1988–98; John and Natty McArthur Univ. Prof. 1998–; Research Assoc. Nat. Bureau of Econ. Research 1979–; Prin., co-f. Long-Term Capital Man. Greenwich, Conn.; Sr. Fellow Int. Asscn. of Financial Engineers; Fellow Econometric Soc., American Acad. of Arts and Sciences; Hon. Prof. H.E.C. School of Man., Paris 1995–; mem. N.A.S., American Financial Asscn. (Dir. 1982–84, Pres. 1986); numerous editorial bds.; awarded Leo Melamed Prize, Univ. of Chicago Business School 1983, Financial Engineer of the Year Award, Int. Asscn. of Financial Engineers 1993, shared Nobel Prize for Econs. 1997 for devising Black-Scholes Model for determining value of derivatives, Michael Pupin Medal for Service to the Nation, Columbia Univ. 1998, Distinguished Alumni Award, Calif. Inst. of Tech. 1999, numerous other awards; Hon. M.A. (Harvard) 1989, Hon. LL.D. (Chicago) 1991; Hon. Dr. Econ. Sc. (Lausanne) 1996; Dir. h.c. (Paris-Dauphine) 1997; Hon. Dr. Man. Sc. (Nat. Sun Yat-Sen Univ., Taiwan). *Publications:* The Collected Scientific Papers of Paul A. Samuelson, Vol. III (Ed.) 1972, Continuous-Time Finance 1990, Casebook in Financial Engineering: Applied Studies in Financial Innovation (jtly.) 1995, The Global Financial System: A Functional Perspective (jtly.) 1995, Finance (jtly.) 1999, numerous articles in professional journals. *Address:* Graduate School of Business, Harvard University, 397 Morgan, Soldiers Field, Boston, MA 02163, U.S.A. *Telephone:* (617) 495-6678 (Office). *Fax:* (617) 495-8863 (Office).

MERTON, Robert K., PH.D.; American professor of sociology; b. 4 July 1910, Philadelphia, Pa.; ed. Temple Univ. and Harvard Univ.; Tutor and Instructor in Sociology, Harvard Univ. 1936–39; Assoc. Prof. and Prof. Tulane Univ. 1939–41; Asst. Prof. to Prof., Columbia Univ. 1941–63, Giddings Prof. of Sociology 1963–74, Univ. Prof. 1974–79; Emer. and Special Service Prof. 1979–85; Assoc. Dir., Bureau of Applied Social Research, Columbia Univ. 1942–70; Chair. Centre for the Social Sciences, Columbia Univ. 1976–84; Adjunct mem. Rockefeller Univ. 1979–; Foundation Scholar, Russell Sage Foundation 1979–; George Sarton Prof. of History of Science, Univ. of Ghent, Belgium 1986–88; mem. N.A.S., American Philosophical Soc., American Acad. of Arts and Sciences, Nat. Acad. of Educ., World Acad. of Arts and Sciences, Acad. Europaea; Foreign mem. British Acad.; Pres. American Sociological Asscn. 1957, Sociological Research Asscn. 1968, Eastern Sociological Soc. 1969, Soc. for Social Studies of Science 1975–76; Foreign mem., Royal Swedish Acad. of Sciences 1977; mem. John Simon Guggenheim Memorial Foundation Educ. Advisory Bd. 1964–79, Chair. 1971–79; numerous hon. degrees; Prize for Dist. Scholarship in Humanities, American Council of Learned Socs.; Lectureship in Recognition of Outstanding Scientific Achievement, Nat. Insts. of Health; Talcott Parsons Prize in Social Sciences, American Acad. of Arts and Sciences 1979, Sutherland Prize, American Soc. of Criminology 1996; Common Wealth Trust Award of Distinguished Service in Sociology 1979, American Sociological Asscn. Career of Distinguished Scholarship Award 1980, Memorial Sloan-Kettering Cancer Centre Award for outstanding support of biomedical science 1981, J. D. Bernal Award for Social Studies of Science 1982, MacArthur Prize Fellow 1983–88, first Who's Who in America Achievement Award in Social Science 1984, Nat. Medal of Science 1994. *Publications:* Science, Technology and Society in 17th-Century England 1938, Mass Persuasion 1946, Social Theory & Social Structure 1949, Continuities in Social Research 1950, Reader in Bureaucracy 1952, Focused Interview 1956, Student-Physician 1957, Freedom to Read 1957, Sociology Today 1959, Contemporary Social Problems 1961, On the Shoulders of Giants 1965, On Theoretical Sociology 1968, Social Theory and Functional Analysis 1969, Sociology of Science 1973, Sociological Ambivalence 1976, Toward a Metric of Science (co-ed.) 1978, The Sociology of Science in Europe 1977, (ed. with James Coleman and Peter Rossi) Qualitative and Quantitative Social Research: Papers in Honor of Paul Lazarsfeld 1979, The Sociology of Science: An Episodic Memoir 1979, Sociological Traditions from Generation to Generation 1980 (ed. with M. W. Riley), Continuities in Structural Inquiry 1981 (ed. with Peter Blau), Social Research and the Practicing Professions 1982, Social Science Quotations (co-ed.) 1991, Social Science Quotations 1992, On Social Structure and Science 1996, I Viaggi e le Avventure della Serendipity 1999. *Address:* East Gallery, Low Memorial Library, Columbia University, New York, NY 10027, U.S.A. *Telephone:* (212) 662-4040. *Fax:* (212) 864-2128.

MERTZ, Edwin Theodore, PH.D.; American consultant in biochemistry and nutrition; b. 6 Dec. 1909, Missoula, Mont.; s. of Gustav Henry and Louise (Sain) Mertz; m. 1st Mary Ellen Ruskamp 1936; one s. one d.; m. 2nd Virginia T. Henry 1987; ed. Univs. of Montana and Illinois; Research Biochemist, Armour and Co., Chicago 1935–37; Instructor in Biochemistry, Univ. of Ill., Urbana 1937–38; Research Assoc. in Pathology, Univ. of Iowa 1938–40; Instructor in Agricultural Chem., Univ. of Mo. 1940–43; Research Chemist, Hercules Powder Co. 1943–46; Prof. of Biochemistry, Purdue Univ., W. Lafayette, Ind. 1946–76, Emer. 1976–, Consultant in Biochemistry and Nutrition, INTSORMIL Project, Dept. of Agronomy, Purdue Univ. 1977–94; Affiliate Prof. of Crops and Soils, Montana State Univ. 1995–; Ed. Purdue Press, West Lafayette, Ind. 1997; co-discoverer of High Lysine Corn; mem. N.A.S., A.A.A.S.; Hon. D.Agr. (Purdue) 1977, Hon. D.Sc. (Montana) 1979; several awards. *Publications:* Quality Protein Maize 1964–94, Elementary Biochemistry 1979, and over 100 scientific articles in field of biochemistry and nutrition. *Leisure interest:* playing jazz piano music. *Address:* Department of Plant and Soils, Montana State University, Bozeman, MT 59717; 2088 Grizzly Gulch Drive, Helena, MT 59601, U.S.A. (Home). *Telephone:* (406) 442-6440 (Home).

MESAKI, Hachiro, B.A. (ECONS.); Japanese government official; b. 8 Feb. 1943, Niigate; m. Meaki Mitsuko 1967; two s.; ed. Univ. of Tokyo; Ministry of Finance 1967–94; Dir. Devt. Insts. Div. Int. Finance Bureau 1986–88; Dir. Budget Div. Nat. Defence Agency 1988–90; Dir. Budget Div. Minister's Secr. 1990–91; Dir.-Gen. Osaka Customs House 1991–93; Deputy Dir.-Gen. Int. Finance Bureau 1993–94; Exec. Dir. IMF 1994–97. *Leisure interest:* golf. *Address:* c/o Ministry of Finance, 3–1–1 Kasumigaseki, Chiyoda-ku, Tokyo 100, Japan.

MESELSON, Matthew Stanley, PH.B., PH.D., F.A.A.A.S.; American professor of biochemistry; b. 24 May 1930, Denver, Colo.; s. of Hymen Avram and Ann Swedlow Meselson; m. 1st Sarah Leah Page 1969; two d.; m. 2nd Jeanne Guillemin 1986; ed. Univ. of Chicago, Univ. of California (Berkeley) and California Inst. of Tech.; Research Fellow, Calif. Inst. of Tech. 1957–58, Asst. Prof. of Physical Chem. 1958–59, Sr. Research Fellow in Chemical Biology 1959–60; Assoc. Prof. of Biology, Harvard Univ. 1960–64, Prof. of Biology 1964–76, Thomas Dudley Cabot Prof. of Nat. Sciences 1976–; Chair. Fed. of American Scientists 1986–88; mem. Inst. of Medicine, N.A.S., American Acad. of Arts and Sciences, Acad. Santa Chiara, American Philosophical Soc., mem. Council on Foreign Relations; foreign mem. Royal Soc., Acad. des Sciences; Hon. D.Sc. (Oakland Coll.) 1966, (Columbia) 1971, (Chicago) 1975; Prize for Molecular Biology, N.A.S. 1963, Eli Lilly Award in Microbiology and Immunology 1964; Hon. Sc.D. (Yale) 1987; Dr h.c. (Princeton) 1988; Public Service Award, Fed. of American Scientists 1972 Alumni Medal, Univ. of Chicago Alumni Asscn. 1971, Alumni Distinguished Service Award, Calif. Inst. of Tech. 1975, Lehman Award of N.Y. Acad. of Sciences 1975, Leo Szilard Award, American Physical Soc. 1978, Presidential Award of N.Y. Acad. of Sciences 1983, MacArthur Fellow 1984–89, Scientific Freedom and Responsibility Award, A.A.A.S. 1990, Thomas Hunt Morgan Medal (Genetics Soc. of America) 1995. *Publications:* numerous papers on the biochemistry and molecular biology of nucleic acids, and on arms control of biological and chemical weapons, in various numbers of Proceedings of N.A.S. and of Scientific American, etc. *Address:* Sherman Fairchild Building, 7 Divinity Avenue, Harvard University, Cambridge, MA 02138, U.S.A. *Telephone:* (617) 495-2264.

MESGUICH, Daniel Elie Emile; French actor and theatre and opera director; b. 15 July 1952, Algiers; s. of William Mesguich and Jacqueline Boukabza; m. Danielle Barthélémy 1971; one s. three d.; ed. Lycée Thiers, Marseilles, Sorbonne, Paris and Conservatoire Nat. Supérieure d'Art Dramatique; actor 1969–; stage dir. 1972–; founded Théâtre du Miroir 1974; Prof. Conservatoire Nat. Supérieure d'Art Dramatique 1983–; Dir. Théâtre Gérard Philippe, Saint-Denis 1986–88, Théâtre de la Métaphore, Lille 1991–; numerous appearances on stage, film and TV and dir. of numerous stage plays and operas; Chevalier, Ordre Nat. du Mérite, Officier des Arts et des Lettres. *Films:* Molière 1977, La Fille de Prague avec un sac très lourd 1978, Dossier 51 1978, L'Amour en fuite 1978, Clair de femme 1979, La Banquière 1980, Allon-z'enfants 1981, La Chanson du mal-aimé 1981, Les Iles 1982, La Belle captive 1982, L'Araignée de satin 1982, Contes clandestins 1983, Les Mots pour le dire 1983, Paris vu par. 20 ans après 1984, Le Radeau de la Méduse 1988, L'Autrichienne 1989, Toussaint Louverture 1989, La Femme fardée 1990, Jefferson in Paris 1994, Tiré à part 1997. *Publication:* L'Eternel éphémère 1991. *Address:* Agence Monita Derrieux, 17-21 rue Duret, 75116 Paris; Théâtre National Nord-Pas-de-Calais, 4 place Charles de Gaulle, 59000 Lille, France.

MESHBERG, Lev; Ukrainian artist; b. 1933, Odessa; ed. Odessa Art College; mem. of Union of Soviet Artists 1960; participated in more than forty one-man and group exhbns. in U.S.S.R.; first prizes at All-Union Art Exhbns. 1965, 1967; work represented in Tretyakov Gallery, Moscow and Russian Museum, Leningrad; emigrated to U.S.A. 1973.

MESKILL, Thomas Joseph, B.S.; American politician and lawyer; b. 30 Jan. 1928, New Britain, Conn.; s. of late Thomas Joseph Meskill and of Laura Warren Meskill; m. Mary T. Grady; three s. two d.; ed. New Britain Senior High School, Trinity Coll., Hartford, Univ. of Connecticut Law School and New York Univ. School of Law; Asst. Corpn. Counsel, New Britain 1960–62; Mayor of New Britain 1962–64; Corpn. Counsel 1965–66; elected to Congress 1966, 1968; Gov. of Connecticut 1970–75; Judge U.S. Circuit Court 1975–, Chief Judge 1992–93; mem. American Bar Asscn.; Republican. *Address:* U.S. Court of Appeals, Old Post Office Plaza, Suite 204, 114 W Main Street, New Britain, CT 06051; 218 Stony Mill Lane, East Berlin, CT 06023, U.S.A. (Home). *Telephone:* (860) 828-1301. (Home).

MESSAGER, Annette; French artist; b. 30 Nov. 1943, Berck-sur-Mer; d. of André and Marie L. (née Chalessin) Messager; ed. Ecole Nationale Supérieure des Arts Décoratifs; one-man exhbns. include Munich and Grenoble 1973, Musée d'Art Moderne, Paris 1974, 1984, Rheinisches Landesmuseum, Bonn 1976, 1978, Galerie Seriaal, Amsterdam 1977, Holly Solomon Gallery, New York 1978, Galérie Gillespie-Laage, Paris 1979, 1980, Fine Arts Gallery, Univ. of Calif. and Irvine, San Franciso Museum of Modern Art 1981, PS 1, New York, Galerie Hans Mayer, Düsseldorf 1981, Artist's Space, New York 1982, Musée des Beaux-Arts, Calais, Galérie Gillespie-Laage-Salomon, Paris 1983, Vienna and Zurich 1984, Riverside Studio, London 1985, Galerie Gillespie-Laage-Salomon, Sydney 1985, Galerie Laage Salomon, Paris 1988, Consortium Dijon 1988, Centre d'Art Contemporain, Castres 1988, Musée de Grenoble 1989, Musée de la Roche sur Yon, Musée de Rochechouart, Bonner Kunstverein, Düsseldorf Kunstverein, Galerie Crousel-Robelin, Paris 1990, Galerie Elisabette Kaufmann, Basle, Mercer Union, Cold City Gallery, Toronto 1991, Arnolfini, Bristol, Douglas Hyde Gallery, Dublin, Camden Arts Centre, London, Univ. of Iowa Museum of Art 1992, Josh Baer Gallery, New York 1993, Monika Sprüth Gallery, Cologne 1994, Musée d'Art Moderne, Paris, Los Angeles Co. Museum of Art, Pace Roberts Foundation, San Antonio, U.S.A., Museum of Modern Art, New York 1995, Art Inst. of Chicago 1996, Larry Gagosian Gallery, New York 1997, Musée des Arts d'Afrique et d'Océanie, Paris 1998; Prix National de Sculpture 1996; Chevalier, Ordre des Arts et des Lettres. *Address:* 146 boulevard Camelinat, 92240 Malakoff, France. *Telephone:* 42.53.45.77.

MESSAGIER, Jean; French artist and sculptor; b. 13 July 1920, Paris; s. of Louis Messagier and Thérèse Winne; m. Marcelle Baumann 1944; three s.; ed. Ecole Nat. Supérieure des Arts Décoratifs, Paris and Coll. de France, Paris; more than 100 one-man exhbns. worldwide since 1950; retrospective exhbns. Galerie Nat. du Grand Palais, Paris 1981, Musée Toulouse-Lautrec, Albi 1990; represented France at XXVI Venice Biennale, VIII São Paulo Biennale, etc.; Commdr. Ordre des Arts et des Lettres, Chevalier, Légion d'honneur; other awards and prizes. *Address:* 8 rue Pierre et Marie Curie, 75005 Paris; Le Moulin, 25260 Colombier-Fontaine, France. *Telephone:* 81.93.61.27.

MESSAS, David, L.PH.; rabbi; b. 15 July 1934, Meknès, Morocco; s. of Shalom Messas; Dir. Edmond-Fleg Univ. Centre, Ecole Maimonde de Boulogne-Billancourt 1968, Tout Familial (student's forum) 1973; Rabbi for Algerons community, Synagogue du Brith Shalom 1984; Chief Rabbi of Geneva 1989–94, of Paris Jan. 1995–. *Address:* c/o Consistoire Israélite de Paris, 17 rue Saint Georges, 75009 Paris, France.

MESSER, Thomas M., M.A.; American museum director; b. 9 Feb. 1920, Bratislava, Czechoslovakia; s. of Richard and Agatha (Albrecht) Messer; m. Remedios Garcia Villa 1948; ed. Thiel Coll. (Greenville, Pa.), Boston, Paris and Harvard Univs.; Dir., Roswell Museum, New Mexico 1949–52; Asst. Dir. in charge of Nat. Exhibitions Programme, American Fed. of Arts 1952–53, Dir. of Exhbns. 1953–55, Dir. 1955–56, Trustee and First Vice-Pres. 1972–75; Dir., Boston Inst. of Contemporary Art 1956–61; Dir. Solomon R. Guggenheim Museum, New York 1961–88; Pres. Asscn. of Art Museum Dirs. 1974–75 (Hon. mem. 1988–); Chair. Int. Cttee. for Museums and Collections of Modern Art, Int. Council of Museums 1974–77, Hon. Chair. 1977–; Chair. Int. Exhbns. Cttee. 1976–78, US/ICOM (Nat. Cttee. of Int. Council of Museums) 1979–81; Adjunct Prof. of Art History, Harvard Univ. 1960; Barnard Coll. 1965, 1971; Sr. Fellow, Center for Advanced Studies, Wesleyan Univ. 1966; Trustee Center for Inter-American Relations (now Americas Soc.) 1974–, Exec. Council Int. Council of Museums 1983–85; Vice-Chair. U.S. Int. Council of Museums Cttee. of American Asscn. of Museums, Washington, D.C. 1979–81; Pres. MacDowell Colony Inc. 1977–80; Dir. Solomon R. Guggenheim Foundation 1980–88, Trustee 1988–91, Dir. Emer. 1990–; mem. Advisory Bd., Palazzo Grassi Venice 1986–97; Trustee Fontana Foundation, Milan 1988–; Chair. Arts Int., Inst. of Int. Educ. 1988–90; Trustee, Inst. of Int. Educ. 1991–, Fontana Foundation 1996–; Curatorial Adviser, Schirn Kunsthalle, Frankfurt 1988–94, Chief Curator 1994–; Sr. Adviser La Caixa Foundation, Barcelona 1990–94; Visiting Prof., Frankfurt Goethe Univ. 1991–92, 1993–96; Trustee, Nat. Gallery, Prague 1994–; fmr. mem. Museum Advisory Panel of Nat. Endowment for the Arts, Art Advisory Panel to Commr. of Internal Revenue Service 1974–77; mem. Council Nat. Gallery of the Czech Repub. 1994–; Dr. Fine Arts h.c., (Univ. of Mass.), (Univ. of Arts, Philadelphia); Kt., Royal Order of St. Olav (Norway); Officer's Cross of Order of Merit (Federal Repub. of Germany) 1975; Officer of Order of Leopold II (Belgium) 1978, Officier Légion d'honneur 1980, Austrian Cross of Honour for Science and Art 1981, Goethe Medal 1990, Officier, Légion d'honneur 1990. *Publications:* The Emergent Decade: Latin American Painters and Paintings in the 1960's 1966, Edvard Munch 1973, Vasily Kandinsky 1997; Museum Catalogues on: Vasily Kandinsky, Paul Klee, Edvard Munch, Egon Schiele, etc.; articles and contributions to numerous art journals. *Leisure interests:* music and literature, cultural pursuits. *Address:* Americas Society, 205 E. 77th Street, New York, NY 10021, U.S.A.

MESSMER, Pierre Auguste Joseph, LL.D.; French politician and overseas administrator; b. 20 March 1916, Vincennes; s. of Joseph Messmer and Marthe (née Farcy) Messmer; m. Gilberte Duprez 1947 (deceased); ed. Faculté de droit de Paris; mil. service 1937–45, with "Free French" forces 1940–45; Sec.-Gen. Interministerial Cttee. for Indochina 1946; Dir. of Cabinet High Comm. in Indochina 1947–48; Gov. Mauritania 1952, Ivory Coast 1954–56; High Commr. Cameroon 1956–58; High Commr.-Gen. French Equatorial Africa 1958, French West Africa 1958–59; Minister for the Armed Forces 1960–69; elected Deputy for Moselle, Nat. Assembly 1968, 1969, 1973, 1978, 1981, 1986; Minister of State for Overseas Depts. and Territories 1971–72; Prime Minister 1972–74; mem. European Parl. 1979–84; Pres. R.P.R. Group in Nat. Ass. 1986–88, Charles de Gaulle Inst. 1992–95, Fondation Charles de Gaulle 1992–97; Sec. in Perpetuity, Acad. des sciences Morales et Politiques 1995–98; mem. Institut de France (Académie des sciences morales et politiques) 1988– (Chancellor 1999–); Grand Croix, Légion d'honneur, Compagnon de la Libération, Croix de guerre, Médaille de la Résistance. *Address:* 24 rue de Penthièvre, 75008 Paris; Institut de France, 23 quai Conti, 75006 Paris; 1 rue de Général-Delanne, 92200 Neuilly-sur-Seine, France.

MESSNER, Reinhold; mountaineer, lecturer and author; b. 17 Sept. 1944; one s. two d.; began climbing aged four with his father; joined expedition to Nanga Parbat (8,000 m), N. Pakistan 1970; with partner Peter Habeler became first person to climb Everest without supplementary oxygen; later climbed Everest alone by North Col route without oxygen; the first person to climb all the world's 8,000m peaks in Himalayas and adjoining ranges; made first crossing of Antarctica on foot since Shackleton 1989; collaborated with dir. Werner Herzog in filming his story Schrei aus Stein 1991; f. int. org. Mountain Wilderness; f. Sulden Museum, Juval Museum (collections of Asiatica). *Publications:* Free Spirit: A Climber's Life, Antarctica 1998. *Address:* Europaallee 2, 39012 Merano (Office); Castle Juval, 39020 Kastelbell, Italy (Home). *Telephone:* (473) 221852 (Office). *Fax:* (473) 221852 (Office).

MESTEL, Leon, B.A., PH.D., F.R.S.; British professor of astronomy; b. 5 Aug. 1927, Melbourne, Australia; s. of Rabbi Solomon Mestel and Rachel née Brodetsky; m. Sylvia L. Cole 1951; two s. two d.; ed. West Ham Secondary School, London and Trinity Coll., Cambridge; ICI Research Fellow, Univ. of Leeds, 1951–54; Commonwealth Fund Fellow, Princeton Univ. Observatory 1954–55; Univ. Asst. Lecturer in Math., Cambridge 1955–58, Univ. Lecturer 1958–66; Fellow, St John's Coll., Cambridge 1957–66; Visiting mem. Inst. for Advanced Study, Princeton 1961–62; J. F. Kennedy Fellow, Weizmann Inst. for Science, Israel 1966–67; Prof. of Applied Math., Univ. of Manchester 1967–73; Prof. of Astronomy, Univ. of Sussex 1973–93, Prof. Emer. 1993–. *Publications:* Stellar Magnetism 1999; papers, reviews, conf. reports on different branches of theoretical astrophysics. *Leisure interests:* reading, music. *Address:* Astronomy Centre, CPES, University of Sussex, Falmer, Brighton, BN1 9QJ; 13 Prince Edward's Road, Lewes, E. Sussex, BN7 1BJ, England. *Telephone:* (01273) 673060 (Office); (01273) 472731 (Home). *Fax:* (01273) 678097 (Office).

MESTIRI, Mohamed Said; Tunisian professor of medicine; b. 22 June 1919, Tunis; s. of Tahar Mestiri and Khedija Kassar; m. Zohra Chenik (d. of fmr. Prime Minister Mohamed Chenik) 1950; four s. one d.; ed. Lycée Carnot, Tunis, Faculty of Medicine, Algiers; Intern and Resident Algiers Hosp. and Sadiki Hosp. Tunis 1947–51; Asst. Surgeon, Sadiki Hosp. 1951–57; Chief Surgeon, H. Thameur Hosp. Tunis 1957–64; Chief, Dept. of Gen. Surgery, La Rabta Hosp. 1965–85; Prof. of Surgery, Faculty of Medicine Tunis 1970–85, Hon. Prof. 1985–; Founder and Pres. Tunisian Soc. of Surgery 1973–85; Foreign mem. French Acad. of Surgery; Foreign corresp. mem. Nat. Acad. of Medicine (France), Royal Belgian Acad. of Medicine; Hon. mem. Soc. Belge de Chirurgie; mem. Int. Soc. of Surgery; Commdr. of Beylical Order Nichan Iftikhar 1957, Medal of Bizerta 1962, Chevalier of Tunisian Ind., Commdr. Order of Tunisian Repub. *Publications include:* Moncef Bey: Le Règne 1988, Moncef Bey: L'Exil 1990, Le Ministère Chenik 1991, Le Métier et la Passion (memoirs) 1995, Abulcasis, grand Maître de la Chirurgie arabe 1997, La Chirurgie arabe ancienne et son Impact en Occident 1998. *Leisure interests:* swimming, bridge. *Address:* 5 avenue Ferhat Hached-Gammarth, 2070 La Marsa, Tunisia. *Telephone:* (1) 746 965. *Fax:* (1) 775 663.

MESTRE, Phillipe, LL.B; French politician and civil servant; b. 23 Aug. 1927, Talmont, Vendee; s. of Raoul Mestre and Anne Lapie; m. Janine Joseph 1951; one s. two d.; ed. Paris Univ.; Admin. Overseas France 1951; Pvt. Sec. to High Commr., Congo 1957–60, to Indre-et-Loir Prefect 1967, to Prime Minister Raymond Barre 1978–81; Tech. Adviser to Pierre Messmer (Minister of Defence) 1964–69, to Prime Minister Jacques Chaban-Delmas 1969–70, 1971–72; Pres. Inter-ministerial Mission of Repatriation from Overseas Territories 1969–70; Prefect of Gers 1970–71, of Calvados 1973–76, of Loire-Atlantique 1976–78; Pres. Serpo 1981–; Deputy of Vendée 1981–86, 1986–93; Vice-Pres. Nat. Ass. 1986–88; Minister of War Veterans 1993–95; Officier, Légion d'honneur, Ordre nat. du Mérite, du Mérite agricole, Croix de la Valeur militaire. *Address:* 95 rue de Rennes, 75006 Paris, France (Home).

MESTVIRISHVILI, Mirian Alekseyevich, DR. PHYS. SC.; Georgian/Russian theoretical physicist; b. 15 June 1934, Telavi; s. of Aleksey Mestirishvili and Anna Mestirishvili; m. Inga Nikolaevna 1966; one s.; ed. Tbilisi Univ.; Postgraduate, Junior Research Asst., Georgian Acad. of Sciences Cybernetics Inst. 1958–63; Junior, Senior Researcher with United Inst. for Nuclear Research, Dubna 1963–70; Head of Laboratory of Acad. of Sciences Inst. of High Energy Physics 1970–86; Prof. 1983; Head of Laboratory of Faculty of Nuclear Physics, Moscow Univ., 1986–92; Inst. of Theoretical Problems of Micro-World, Moscow Univ. 1992–; Lenin Prize 1986; *Address:* Moscow State University, Leninskie Gory, 147294 Moscow (Office); Balaklavsky pr. 3, fl. 45, Moscow, Russia (Home). *Telephone:* (095) 230-23-37 (Office); (095) 316-48-74 (Home).

MESYATS, Gennady Andreyevich, D.SC.; Russian physicist; b. 28 Feb. 1936, Kemerovo; s. of Andrei Mesyats and Anna Mesyats; m. Nina Alexandrovna (née Mashukova) Mesyats 1959; one s.; ed. Tomsk Polytechnical Inst.; Sr. Research Physicist, Research Inst. for Nuclear Physics, Tomsk Polytechnical Inst. 1961–64, Head of Lab. 1966–71; Deputy Dir. Inst. of Atmospheric Optics, Tomsk 1971–76; Dir. Inst. of High Current Electronics, Tomsk 1976–86; Dir. Inst. of Electrophysics 1987–; mem. U.S.S.R. (now Russian) Acad. of Sciences 1984–, Pres. Ural Div. 1986–, Vice-Pres. of Acad. 1987–; Pres. Demidov Foundation; Vice-Pres. Int. Unit of Science and Eng. Fellowships; mem. Russian Electrical Eng. Acad.; Hon. Prof. Tomsk Polytechnic Univ. 1996; Dr. h.c. (Urals State Technical Univ.) 1996; Int. Dyke's Award in Electronics, E. Marx Award in Pulsed Power, State Prize of U.S.S.R., U.S.S.R. Council of Ministers Prize, A. G. Stoletov Prize, Order of Lenin, Order of the Red Banner of Labour, Badge of Honour, Order for Services to the Motherland. *Publications:* Techniques for the Production of High-Voltage Nanosecond Pulses 1963, Generation of High-Power Nanosecond Pulses 1974, Field Emission and Explosive Processes in Gas Discharges 1982, High-Power Nanosecond X-Ray Pulses 1983, Pulsed Electrical Discharge in Vacuum 1989, Ectons 1994, About Our Science 1995, Pulsed Electrical Discharge in Gas 1998, Explosive Electron Emission 1998. *Leisure interests:* reading fiction, studying Russian history, writing articles. *Address:* Russian Academy of Science, Ural Division, 91 Pervomaiskaya Street, Yekaterinburg 620219 (Office); Apt. 132, 11 Marshal Zhukov Street, Yekaterinburg 620077, Russia (Home). *Telephone:* (3432) 74-02-23 (Office); (095) 938-18-58 (Moscow).

MÉSZÁROS, Márta; Hungarian film director; b. 19 Sept. 1931, Budapest; d. of László Mészáros; m. 2nd Jan Nowicki; ed. Moscow Film School; emigrated with family to U.S.S.R. 1936; now lives in Hungary; Golden Bear Award OCIC 1975, Béla Balázs Prize 1977; Artist of Merit 1989. *Films include:* End of September 1973, Free Breath 1973, Adopted Child 1975, Nine Months 1976, The Two of Them 1977, En Route 1979, Heritage 1980, Diary for my Children 1982, Fata Morgana Land 1983, Diary for my Loves 1986, Diary III 1989. *Address:* c/o MAFILM Studio, Lumumba utca 174, 1149 Budapest, Hungary. *Telephone:* 36 1 183-1750.

MÉSZÖLY, Miklós; Hungarian novelist and playwright; b. 19 Jan. 1921, Szekszárd; s. of Sándor Molnár Mészöly and Jolán Szászi; m. Dr. Alaine Polcz; ed. Budapest Univ.; Ed. local periodicals of Szekszárd 1947–48; dramatic adviser, Puppet Theatre, Budapest 1951–53; full-time writer 1953–; Déry literary prize. *Publications:* Hétalvó puttonyocska (Slug-a-bed butt) 1955, Vadvizek (Wild waters) 1957, Fekete gólya (Black stork) 1960, The Bunker, (play) 1964, Sutting ezredes tündöklése (Colonel Sutting's brilliance) 1988. *Leisure interests:* hunting, sport. *Address:* 1026 Budapest, Guyon köz 3, Hungary. *Telephone:* 36 (1) 176-3184.

METCALF, John, B.A.; Canadian author; b. 12 Nov. 1938, Carlisle, U.K.; s. of Thomas Metcalf and Gladys Moore; m. Myrna Teitelbaum 1975; three s. three d.; ed. Beckenham and Penge Grammar School and Univ. of Bristol; emigrated to Canada 1962; writer-in-residence, Univs. of N.B. 1972–73, Loyola of Montreal 1976, Ottawa 1977, Concordia Univ. Montreal 1980–81, Univ. of Bologna 1985; Ed. Canadian Notes and Queries (literary magazine) 1997–. *Publications:* The Lady Who Sold Furniture 1970, Girl in Gingham 1978, Selected Stories 1982, Kicking Against the Pricks 1982, Adult Entertainment 1986, What is a Canadian Literature? 1988, Volleys 1990, How Stories Mean 1992, Shooting the Stars 1992, Freedom from Culture: Selected Essays 1982–1992 1994. *Leisure interest:* collecting modern first editions. *Address:* 128 Lewis Street, Ottawa, Ont. K2P 0S7, Canada. *Telephone:* (613) 233-3200.

METZ, Johann Baptist, DR. PHIL., DR. THEOL.; German professor of theology; b. 5 Aug. 1928, Auerbach; s. of Karl M. Metz and Sibylle Müller; ed. Univs. of Bamberg, Innsbrück and Munich; Prof. of Fundamental Theology, Univ. of Münster 1963–; Prof. of Philosophy of Religion, Univ. of Vienna, Austria 1993–; mem. founding comm. of Univ. of Bielefeld 1966; consultant to Papal Secr. Pro Non Credendibus 1968–73; Adviser to German Diocesan Synod 1971–75; mem. Advisory Council, Inst. für die Wissenschaften vom Menschen (Vienna) 1982–; mem. Advisory Council Wissenschaftszentrum Nordrhein-Westfalen/Kulturwissenschaftliches Inst. 1989–; Dr. h.c. (Univ. of Vienna); awards from Univ. of Innsbrück and Boston Coll., Mass. *Publications:* books on theological and political themes in several languages. *Address:* Katholisch-Theologische Fakultät, Seminar für Fundamentaltheologie, Johannisstrasse 8–10, 4400 Münster (Office); Kapitelstrasse 14, 48145 Münster, Germany. *Telephone:* 0251/83-2631 (Office); 0251/36662 (Home).

METZENBAUM, Howard Morton, LL.B.; American politician, lawyer and company executive; b. 4 June 1917, Cleveland; s. of Charles I. and Anna (Klafter) Morton; m. Shirley Turoff 1946; four d.; ed. Ohio State Univ.; mem. War Labour Bd. 1942–45, Ohio Bureau for Code Revision 1949–50; mem. Ohio House of Reps. 1943–46, Ohio Senate 1947–50; alt. del. to Democratic Nat. Convention 1964, del. 1968; mem. Ohio Democratic Exec. Cttee. 1966, Finance Cttee. 1969; U.S. Senator from Ohio 1977–95; Chair. Bd. Airport Parking Co. of America 1958–66, ITT Consumer Services Corpn. 1966–68; Chair. Exec. Cttee. ComCorp 1969–74, 1975–; Trustee, Mount Sinai Hosp., Cleveland 1961–73, Treas. 1966–73; mem. Bd. of Dirs., Council of Human Relations; mem. United Cerebral Palsy Asscn., Nat. Council on Hunger and Malnutrition, American, Ohio, Cuyahoga and Cleveland Bar Asscns., American Asscn. of Trial Lawyers. *Address:* Consumer Federation of America, 1424 16th Street, NW, Suite 504, Washington, DC 20036, U.S.A.

METZGER, Henry, A.B., M.D.; American (b. German) scientific researcher; b. 23 March 1932, Mainz, Germany; s. of Paul Alfred Metzger and Anne (Daniel) Metzger; m. Deborah Stashower 1957; two s. one d.; ed. Univ. of Rochester, Columbia Univ.; emigrated to U.S.A. 1938; Intern, then Asst. Resident, Col.-Presbyterian Medical Center 1957–59; Research Assoc., NIAMD, Nat. Insts. of Health (N.I.H.) 1959–61, Medical Officer, Arthritis and Rheumatism Branch, Bethesda, Md. 1963–73, Chief, Section on Chemical Immunology 1973–, Chief, Arthritis and Rheumatism Branch, Nat. Inst. of Arthritis and Musculoskeletal and Skin Diseases 1983–94, Dir. Intramural Research Program 1987–98; Fellow Helen Hay Whitney Foundation, Dept. of Biology, Univ. of Calif., San Diego 1961–63; Pres. American Asscn. of Immunologists 1991–92; Pres. Int. Union of Immunological Socs. 1992–95; mem. Health Research Council BMFT, German Govt. 1994-97; mem. N.A.S.; Fellow A.A.A.S.; Hon. mem. Chilean and French Socs. of Immunology; several awards. *Publications:* over 200 scientific papers and contribs. to scientific journals. *Address:* 3410 Taylor Street, Chevy Chase, MD 20815, U.S.A. (Home).

MEXANDEAU, Louis Jean; French politician and teacher; b. 6 July 1931, Wanquetin; s. of Hilaire Mexandeau and Jeanne Canel; m. Michèle Cusin 1960; one s. two d.; ed. Lycée d'Arras, Univs. of Lille and Paris, Inst. d'Etudes Politiques, Paris; mem. Nat. Bureau, Syndicat Nat. de l'Enseignement Secondaire 1955–57; History and Geography Teacher, Lycée Malherbe, Caen 1961–73; Founder and Sec. for Calvados, Convention des Institutions Républicaines 1966–71, mem. Perm. Cttee. and Nat. Political Bureau 1969–71; First Fed. Sec. Calvados section, Parti Socialiste (PS) 1971–73; Regional Councillor 1974–; Deputy (Calvados) to Nat. Assembly 1973–81, 1986–88, 1988–91, 1993–; PS Nat. Del. for Educ. 1975–81; Minister of Posts and Telecommunications 1981–83; Minister Del. attached to the Minister of Industrial Redeployment in charge of Posts and Telecommunications 1983–85, Minister 1985–86, Sec. of State for War Veterans 1991–92, for War Veterans and Victims of War 1992–93; Nat. Sec. Socialist Party 1988, Pres. Comm. d'histoire 1990–. *Publications:* Les Capétiens 1972, Plan socialiste pour l'éducation nationale 1977, Petite histoire du parti socialiste 1990. *Address:* Assemblée Nationale, 75355 Paris; 17 rue Paul Toutain, 14000 Caen; 38 rue de Bretagne, 14000 Caen, France (Home).

MEYER, Armin Henry; American diplomatist; b. 19 Jan. 1914, Fort Wayne, Ind.; s. of Rev. Armin Paul Meyer and Leona Buss Meyer; m. Helen Alice James 1949; one d.; ed. Lincoln Junior Coll., Capital Univ., Columbus, Ohio, Capital Univ. Theological Seminary and Ohio State Univ., Columbus, Ohio; Asst. Prof. and Dean of Men, Capital Univ. 1935–41; Radio Technician, Douglas Aircraft Co., Eritrea 1942–43; News Ed., Office of War Information, Cairo 1943–44; Public Affairs Officer, American Embassy, Baghdad 1944–48; Public Affairs Adviser, Dept. of State 1948–52; First Sec., Beirut 1952–55, Counsellor, Kabul 1955–57; Deputy Dir. Office of South Asian Affairs, Dept. of State 1957–58, Dir. Office of Near Eastern Affairs 1959–61, Deputy Asst. Sec. of State for Near Eastern and South Asian Affairs 1961; Amb. to Lebanon 1961–65, to Iran 1965–69, to Japan 1969–72; Special Asst. to Sec. of State 1972–73; Chair. of Cabinet Cttee. to Combat Terrorism 1972–73; Visiting Prof. American Univ. 1974–75; Dir. of Ferdowsi Project, Georgetown Univ. Washington D.C. 1975–79; Woodrow Wilson Visiting Fellow, Adjunct Prof. Georgetown Univ. 1975–86; Middle East consultant 1975–; Dir. of Int. Affairs, Ecology and Environment, Inc. 1978–; mem. Bd. of Dirs. Washington Inst. of Foreign Affairs 1978–, Pres. 1988–; hon. degrees (Capital Univ.) 1957, (Lincoln Coll.) 1969, (S. Dakota Tech.) 1972, (Wartburg Coll.) 1972, (Ohio State Univ.) 1972; Order of the Rising Sun (First Class), Japan 1982; Hall of Excellence, Ohio Fed. of Independent Colls. 1989. *Publication:* Assignment Tokyo 1974, Education in Diplomacy (Co-author) 1987. *Leisure interests:* amateur radio, sports, computer world. *Address:* 4610 Reno Road, N.W., Washington, DC 20008, U.S.A. *Telephone:* (202) 244-7737. *Fax:* (202) 237-7721.

MEYER, Sir Christopher John Rome, K.C.M.G., M.A.; British diplomatist; b. 22 Feb. 1944; s. of late Flight Lieut. R. H. R. Meyer and of E. P. L. Meyer (now Landells); m. Françoise Hedges 1976; two s. one step-s.; ed. Lancing Coll., Peterhouse, Cambridge and Johns Hopkins School of Advanced Int. Studies, Bologna; Foreign Office 1966–67; Army School of Educ. 1967–68; Third Sec., later Second Sec. Moscow 1968–70; Second Sec. Madrid 1970–73; FCO 1973–78; First Sec. Perm. Representation of UK at EC 1978–82; Counsellor and Head of Chancery, Moscow 1982–84; Head of News Dept. FCO 1984–88; Fellow, Center for Int. Affairs, Harvard 1988–89; Minister (Commercial), Washington, D.C. 1989–92, Minister and Deputy Head of Mission 1992–93; Press Sec. to Prime Minister 1994–96; Amb. to Fed. Repub. of Germany 1997, to U.S.A. 1997–. *Address:* c/o Foreign and Commonwealth Office, King Charles Street, London, S.W.1, England.

MEYER, Jean Léon André; French actor and director; b. 11 June 1914, Paris; s. of Léon Meyer and Mathilde Magnin; m. Pierrette-Martine de Kerpezdron-Laveissière 1942; two s.; ed. Conservatoire Nat. d'Art Dramatique; worked at Comédie Française as actor, director, pensionnaire from 1937, Sociétaire 1942–59, Hon. Sociétaire 1959–; Prof. Conservatoire Nat. d'Art Dramatique; Artistic Dir. Ecole Nat. Supérieure des arts et technique du théâtre; Artistic Dir. Théâtre du Palais-Royal 1960; Dir. Théâtre Michel 1964–71; Co-Dir. Théâtre des Célestins, Lyons 1968; mem. Acad. de Neuilly;

Officier, Légion d'honneur; Commdr. des Arts et des Lettres. *Directed* (Plays): Port-Royal, Les caves du Vatican, Le dindon, La Célestine, Don Giovanni, Donogoo, Cycle Molière, Les contes d'Hoffman, La ville dont le prince est enfant, l'Ecole des maris 1975, Topaze, Noix de coco 1984, Gigi 1985, La prise de Berg op Zoom 1986; (films): Le bourgeois gentilhomme, Le mariage de Figaro, Tartuffe, Les femmes savantes, La ville dont le prince est enfant; Les affaires sont les affaires (television) 1974. *Publications:* Molière, Gilles Shakespeare ou les aventures de Jean Perrin, Etudes des oeuvres complètes de Molière, Place au Théâtre 1991; (plays): Mic-Mac 1962, L'âge idiot 1963, Le vice dans la peau 1965, La courte paille 1967. *Address:* 3 boulevard des Sablons, 92000 Neuilly-sur-Seine, France (Home).

MEYER, Robert; Norwegian photohistorian; b. 2 Oct. 1945, Oslo; m. Ingebjørg Ydstie 1985; one s. one. d.; ed. Fotoskolan, Univ. of Stockholm; photographer, Norwegian State Police 1963–64; advertising photographer 1964–; freelance photographer 1964–71; debut exhbn. LYS, Oslo 1970; photojournalist, Norwegian Broadcasting, Oslo 1971–77; Ed. and Publr. Ikaros 1976–80; full-time photohistorian engaged in research work 1977–; Prof. Inst. of Photography (SHDK) Bergen 1990–; Munch stipend 1981; art stipend 1988–90; two book prizes. *Publications:* Norsk fotohistorisk Journal 1976–78, Jim Bengston i Photographs 1981, Slow Motion 1985, Simulo 1987, Norsk Landskapsfotografi 1988, Den glemte tradisjonen 1989, Splint 1991. *Address:* Institute of Photography Strømgt. 1, 5015 Bergen (Office); Professor Hansteens gate 68, 5006 Bergen, Norway (Home). *Telephone:* 55 31 2214 (Office); 55 31 0793 (Home). *Fax:* 55 32 6756.

MEYER, Robert Kenneth, PH.D., F.A.H.A.; American/Australian logician; b. 27 May 1932, Sharon Hill, Pa.; s. of the late Frank A. Meyer and Helen M. Mooney; m. 1st Bette Jane Gottschalk 1954 (divorced 1963); m. 2nd Barbara Lee Edwards 1963 (divorced 1973); four s. seven d.; ed. Sharon Hill High School, Lehigh Univ., Princeton Theological Seminary, Kyoto School of Japanese Language, Univ. of Pittsburgh; Asst. Minister Union Congregational Church, N.J. 1956–57; Missionary United Church of Christ 1957–62; Asst. Prof. of Philosophy and Math., West Virginia Univ. 1965–66; Asst. Prof. of Philosophy, Rice Univ. 1966–67, Bryn Mawr Coll. 1967–69, Assoc. Prof. Indiana Univ. 1969–72, Visiting Assoc. Prof. Univ. of Toronto 1972–73, Univ. of Pittsburgh 1973–74; Postdoctoral Fellow in Philosophy, A.N.U. 1974–76, Sr. Research Fellow 1976–81, Sr. Fellow 1981–92, Prof. 1992–97, Emer. Prof. 1998–, Visiting Fellow 1998–, Co-ordinator Automated Reasoning Project 1986–91; Visiting Fellow, Fujitsu Research Labs. (Numazu) 1991–92; mem. Australian Labor Party. *Publications:* Class Church and Labor Evangelism 1961, E, R, and Gamma (with J. M. Dunn) 1969, Semantics of Entailment (with R. Routley) 1973, Intuitionism, entailment, negation 1974, Solution to the P-W problem (with E. P. Martin) 1982, Relevant logics and their rivals (with R. Routley, V. Plumwood, R. T. Brady) 1983, Automated theorem-proving in non-classical Logics (with P. B. Thistlewaite, M. A. McRobbie) 1988; numerous articles in philosophy, especially logic. *Leisure interests:* chess, astronomy, personal computing. *Address:* Automated Reasoning Project, RSISE, Australian National University, Canberra, A.C.T. 0200 (Univ.); 3 Rawlings Place, Fadden, A.C.T. 2904, Australia (Home). *Telephone:* (2) 6279-8605 (Univ.); (2) 6291-4348 (Home). *Fax:* (2) 6279-8651 (Office).

MEYER, Roelof Petrus (Roelf), B.COMM., LL.B.; South African politician; b. 16 July 1947, Port Elizabeth; m. Carené Lubbe 1971; two s. two d.; ed. Fickburg High School, Univ. of Orange Free State; practised as attorney, Pretoria and Johannesburg –1980; M.P. for Johannesburg West 1979–97; Deputy Minister of Law and Order 1986–88, of Constitutional Devt. 1988–91, and of Information Services 1990–91; Minister of Defence and of Communication 1991–92, of Constitutional Devt. and of Communication 1992–96, of Provincial Affairs and Constitutional Devt. 1994–96; Sec.-Gen. Nat. Party 1996–97; Co-Leader United Democratic Movt. 1997, Deputy Pres. June 1998–; Chief Govt. Negotiator at Multi-Party Negotiating Forum for new S.A. Constitution; National Party, fmr. Chair. Standing Cttee. on Nat. Educ., fmr. Chair. Standing Cttee. on Constitutional Devt., fmr. Parl. Whip. *Leisure interests:* reading, outdoor life, jogging. *Address:* United Democratic Movement, P.O. Box 26290, Arcadia, Pretoria 0007, South Africa. *Telephone:* (12) 321 0010. *Fax:* (12) 321 0014.

MEYER, Ron; American theatrical agent; b. 1944; m. Kelly Chapman; one s. two d.; fmrly. served with U.S. Marine Corps; with Paul Kohner Agency 1965–70; agent William Morris Agency 1970–75; co-f., Pres. Creative Artists Agency 1975–95; Pres., C.E.O. Universal City Studios Inc. 1995–; now Pres., C.O.O. M.C.A. Inc. *Address:* Universal Studios Incorporated, 100 Universal City Plaza, Universal City, CA 91608, U.S.A.

MEYER, Wilhelm Olaf, M.ARCH., A.R.I.B.A., M.I.A., M.B.A.; South African architect; b. 14 May 1935, Pretoria; s. of Dr. F. Meyer; m. Angela Winsome 1961; one s. one d.; ed. Univs. of Witwatersrand and Pennsylvania; partner, Moerdyk & Watson, Pretoria 1961; founded own practice, Wilhelm O. Meyer & Partners, Johannesburg 1966, consultant 1993–; founder mem. Urban Action Group, Johannesburg 1971; mem. Council S.A. Council of Architects 1973–, Pres. 1983, 1985; co-founder, COPLAN jt. architectural practice with P.S.I. Hong Hong 1983; Pres.-in-Chief, Interbou 84 1984; opened architectural practice jtly in London 1986; mem. Bd. Faculty, School of Architecture, Univ. of Witwatersrand 1988–93; gen. consultant for Standard Bank Bldgs. nationwide 1993; Dir. Pancom Devt. Co. 1993–; many other appts.; work includes urban design, apt. bldgs., univ. bldgs., churches, Marine Parade Hotel, Durban, Johannesburg Civic Centre and Johannesburg Art Gallery; Medal of Honour for Architecture, S.A. Akad. vir Wetenskap en Kuns 1980; numerous other awards and competition prizes. *Publications:* contribs. to architectural journals. *Leisure interests:* music, windsurfing. *Address:* 64 Galway Road, Parkview 2193, Johannesburg, South Africa.

MEYER-CORDING, Dr. Ulrich; German economist; b. 22 May 1911, Dresden; s. of Dr. Waldemar Meyer and Klara Meyer; m. Dr. Gisela Cording 1950; one s.; ed. high school, Dresden and Univs. of Grenoble, Berlin, Kiel, Exeter and Leipzig; Lawyer, Stuttgart 1948–50; Ministerial Adviser, Ministry of Justice, Bonn 1950–57; Ministerial Man. in Ministry of Atomic Affairs 1957–58; Ministerial Dir. and Head of European Dept., Ministry of Commerce 1958–64; Prof. of Commercial and Business Law, Univ. of Cologne 1958–; Vice-Chair. European Investment Bank, Brussels 1964–72; Dir. Rheinische Hypothekenbank, Cologne 1972–77, Bundesverdienstkreuz mit Stern 1990. *Publications:* Das Recht der Banküberweisung 1951, Monopol und Marktbeherrschung als Rechtsbegriffe 1954, Die Vereinsstrafe 1957, Die Rechtsnormen 1971, Lehrbuch Wertpapierrecht 1995. *Leisure interests:* literature, theatre, sport. *Address:* Hinter Hoben 6, 53129 Bonn, Germany. *Telephone:* (0228) 23 28 10.

MEYER-LANDRUT, Andreas, PH.D.; German diplomatist; b. 31 May 1929, Tallinn, Estonia; s. of Bruno and Käthe (née Winter) Meyer-Landrut; m. Hanna Karatsony von Hodos 1960; one s. one d.; ed. Univs. of Göttingen and Zagreb; entered foreign service 1955, in Moscow, Brussels and Tokyo 1956–68, Amb. to Congo (Brazzaville) 1969; in Foreign Office, Bonn 1971–80, Head of Sub-Dept. for Policy towards E. Europe and G.D.R. 1974–78, Dir. Dept. of Relations to Asia, Near and Middle East, Africa and Latin America 1978–80, Amb. to U.S.S.R. 1980–83, 1987–89; State Sec. to Foreign Office 1983–87; Head of Fed. Pres.'s Office and State Sec. 1989–94; Man. Daimler Benz AG in Moscow. *Address:* DIHT, An der Kolonnade 10, 10117 Berlin; Europa Strasse 12, 5300 Bonn 2, Germany (Home).

MEYEROWITZ, Joel; American photographer; b. 1938, Bronx, New York; former art dir. in an advertising firm; began photography career in 1962; one-man exhbn. My European Trip: Photographs from a Moving Car, Museum of Modern Art, New York 1968; selection of photographs from unpublished work Going Places shown at Expo 70, Japan; gave lessons in colour photography at Cooper Union, New York 1971; commissioned by St. Louis Art Museum, Missouri to photograph Eero Saarinen's Gateway Arch 1977; photographed Empire State Building 1978; participant in Mirrors and Windows: American Photography since 1960, Museum of Modern Art, New York 1978; images from Cape Light exhibited at Museum of Fine Art, Boston 1979. *Publication:* Cape Light 1979.

MEYERS, Gerald Carl, M.S.; American management consultant; b. 5 Dec. 1928, Buffalo, N.Y.; s. of Meyer and Berenice Meyers; m. Barbara Jacob 1958; one s. two d.; ed. Carnegie Inst. of Tech. (now Carnegie-Mellon Univ.), Pittsburgh, Pa.; with Ford Motor Co., Detroit 1950–51, Chrysler Corpn., Detroit and Geneva 1954–62; with American Motors Corpn., Detroit 1962–, Vice-Pres. 1967–72, Group Vice-Pres. (Product) 1972–75, Exec. Vice-Pres. 1975–77, Pres. 1977–, C.O.O. 1977, C.E.O. 1977–, Chair. 1978–82; Pres. Gerald C. Meyers Assocs. Inc.; Ford Distinguished Prof., Carnegie-Mellon Univ. Graduate School of Industrial Admin.; Chevalier, Légion d'honneur 1981. *Leisure interests:* jogging, sailing. *Address:* 5600 West Maple Road, Suite 216-B, West Bloomfield, MI 48322, U.S.A.

MEYERSON, Martin, SC.D.; American fmr. university president; b. 14 Nov. 1922, New York; s. of S. Z. and Etta (née Berger) Martin; m. Margy Ellin Lazarus 1945; two s. one d. (deceased); ed. Columbia Univ., Harvard Univ.; Asst. Prof. of Social Sciences, Univ. of Chicago 1948; successively Research Dir., Exec. Dir., Vice-Pres., Vice-Chair., American Council to Improve Our Neighbourhoods; Assoc. Prof., Prof., Univ. of Pa. Inst. for Urban Studies and Dept. of City and Regional Planning 1952–57; Adviser on urban problems for UN in Indonesia, Japan and Yugoslavia 1958–66; Frank Backus Williams Prof. of City Planning and Urban Research, Harvard Univ. 1957–63; Dir. Joint Center for Urban Studies of M.I.T. and Harvard Univ. 1957–63; Dean Coll. of Environmental Design, Univ. of Calif. (Berkeley), Acting Chancellor 1963–66; Pres. State Univ. of New York at Buffalo, Prof. of Policy Sciences 1966–70; Prof. of Public Policy, Univ. of Pa. Foundation 1970–77, Chair. 1981–, Univ. Prof. 1977–81, Pres. Univ. of Pa. 1970–81, Pres. Emer. 1981–; Chair. Monell Chem. Senses Center 1993–, Bd. Marconi Int. Fellowship Foundation; mem. Int. Council for Educ. Devt. 1971–; Pres. Int. Asscn. Univs. 1975–85, Hon. Pres. 1985–; fmr. Gov. Centre for Environmental Studies, London, Gov. American Inst. of Planners; Fellow A.A.A.S., American Acad. of Arts and Sciences; mem. American Philosophical Soc., Council on Foreign Relations, Nat. Acad. of Educ.; Hon. LL.D. (Queens Univ., Canada, D'Youville Coll., Alfred Univ., Rutgers Univ., Univ. of Pa., Stonehill Coll.), Hon. D.Sc. (Chattanooga); Hon. Prof. Nat. Univ. of Paraguay; numerous hon. degrees and other decorations. *Publications:* Politics, Planning and the Public Interest (co-author) 1955, Housing, People and Cities 1962, Face of the Metropolis 1963, Boston 1966, Conscience of the City (Editor) 1970, Gladly Learn and Gladly Teach 1978. *Address:* Room 225, Van Pelt Library, University of Pennsylvania, Philadelphia, PA 19104 (Office); 2016 Spruce Street, Philadelphia, PA 19103, U.S.A. (Home). *Telephone:* (215) 898-5577 (Office). *Fax:* (215) 898-2379.

MEZHIROV, Aleksandr Petrovich; Russian poet; b. 26 Sept. 1923, Moscow; s. of Pyotr Izraelevich Mezhirov and Yelizaveta Semyonovna Mezhirova; m. Yelena Yaschenko; one d.; ed. Moscow Univ.; served in Soviet Army 1941–45; work first publ. 1947; Prof. in Literary Inst., Moscow 1966–91; State Prize for Poetry 1986, Georgian State Prize 1989. *Publications:* more than 50 books of poetry, including Long is the Road 1947, Returns 1955, Poems and Translations 1962, Ladoga Ice 1965, Selected Works (2 vols.) 1981, The Blind Turning 1983, The Outline of Things 1984, Prose in Poetry 1985, Bormotucha 1990, The What That Has No Name 1995, Ground Wind 1997, Apologia of a Circus 1997; trans. Georgian and Lithuanian poetry, articles, critical reviews, essays on history of Russian econs. *Leisure interest:* billiards. *Address:* 146–148 West 68 Street, Apt. 3B, New York, NY 10023, U.S.A. *Telephone:* (212) 873-0390.

MHLABA, Raymond; South African politician and civil servant; b. 12 Feb. 1920, Fort Beaufort; s. of Mxokozeli Mhlaba and Dinah (née Mnyazi) Mhlaba; m. 1st Joyce Meke 1943 (died 1960); m. 2nd Dideka Heliso 1986; three s. five d.; ed. Healdtown Missionary Inst.; mem. ANC Nat. Exec. Cttee. 1960–63, 1990–, Regional Exec. Cttee. E. Cape Br.; ANC Regional Head E. Cape Region; Deputy Chair. Cen. Cttee. and Politburo S.A. Communist Party 1990–; Vice-Chair. Mzingisi Devt. Trust, Port Elizabeth 1991–; Chair. E. Cape Regional Econ. Devt. Forum 1992–; Premier E. Cape Prov. Legislature 1994–97; High Commr. in Uganda July 1997–. *Address:* 5 Millard Crescent, Summerstrand, Port Elizabeth, South Africa. *Telephone:* (41) 533558. *Fax:* (41) 531056.

MI GUOJUN; Chinese business executive; b. 1933; joined CCP 1960; Amb. to Fiji 1977–80; Gen. Man. of China Int. Trust and Investment Corpn. 1993–. *Address:* China International Trust and Investment Corporation, 19 Jianguo Menwai Dajie Street, Beijing 100020, People's Republic of China.

MICHAEL, George; British singer, composer and producer; b. 25 June 1963, Finchley; s. of Jack Kyriacus Panayiotou and the late Lesley Panayiotou; ed. Bushey Meads School; has sold millions of records; creating promotional video for Coca-Cola 1989; Ivor Novello Award for Best Songwriter 1985, 1989, British Rock Industry Award for Best Male Artist 1988; Grammy Award for Best Album (Faith) 1989; debut in group The Executive 1979; formed (with Andrew Ridgeley) Wham, numerous consecutive hits; toured U.K., France, U.S.A., China, etc.; launched solo career 1986; *Singles include:* with Wham: Wham Rap, Young Guns Go For It, Bad Boys, Club Tropicana, Wake Me Up before You Go Go; duet: I Knew You Were Waiting (for me) (with Aretha Franklin, q.v.); solo: Careless Whisper, A Different Corner, I Want Your Sex, Faith, Father Figure, Jesus to a Child 1995, Fastlove 1996; *Albums include:* Fantastic, Make It Big, Music From The Edge of Heaven, Final, Faith (solo), Listen without Prejudice 1990; contrib. to albums: Two Rooms; Celebrating the Songs of Elton John and Bernie Taupin 1991, Red, Hot and Dance 1992, A Very Special Christmas II 1992, Older 1996. *Publication:* George Michael: Bare (with Tony Parsons) 1990.

MICHAEL, H.M. King; fmr. King of Romania; b. 25 Oct. 1921; s. of late King Carol II and Princess Helen of Greece; m. Princess Anne of Bourbon-Parma 1948; five d.; declared heir apparent, ratified by Parl. 4 Jan. 1926; proclaimed King 1927, deposed by his father 1930; succeeded to the throne of Romania following his father's abdication 1940; led coup d'etat against pro-Nazi dictator Ion Antonescu 1944; forced to abdicate following communist takeover of Romania 30 Dec. 1947; subsequently ran chicken farm in Herts., U.K.; went to Switzerland as test pilot 1956; has also worked for Lear Inc. started electronics co. and worked as stockbroker; deported from Romania on first visit since exile Dec. 1990; Order of Victory (U.S.S.R.) 1945; Chief Commdr. Legion of Merit (U.S.A.) 1946; Hon. K.C.V.O. *Leisure interest:* restoring Second World War jeeps. *Address:* Villa Serena, Versoix, Geneva, Switzerland.

MICHAEL, Alun Edward, B.A.; British politician; b. 22 Aug. 1943; m.; five c.; ed. Keele Univ.; journalist South Wales Echo 1966–71; Youth and Community Worker, Cardiff 1972–84; Area Community Education Officer, Grangetown and Butetown 1984–87; mem. Cardiff City Council 1973–89 (fmr. Chair. Finance, Planning, Performance Review and Econ. Devt., Chief Whip, Labour Group); mem. House of Commons (Labour and Co-op) for Cardiff S. and Penarth 1987–; an Opposition Whip 1987–88; Opposition frontbench spokesman on Welsh Affairs 1988–92, on Home Affairs and the Voluntary Sector 1992–97; Minister of State, Home Office 1997–98; Sec. of State for Wales 1998–(99); First Sec. of Nat. Ass. for Wales May 1999–; mem. Nat. Ass. for Wales for Mid and West Wales May 1999–; mem. numerous parl. groups and cttees.; Vice-Pres. YHA. *Leisure interests:* opera, reading, long-distance running. *Address:* National Assembly for Wales, Cardiff Bay, Cardiff, CF99 1NA, Wales.

MICHAEL, James Henry, PH.D., F.A.A.; Australian mathematician; b. 3 April 1920, Port Augusta, S. Australia; s. of Charles Michael and Susan V. M. Willoughby; m. Patricia Hartley 1952; one s. one d.; ed. Univ. of Adelaide; Lecturer, Sr. Lecturer, Univ. of Adelaide 1958–65, Reader 1965–67, Prof. 1968–69, Reader in Pure Math. 1970–83; Visiting Assoc. Prof. Purdue Univ. 1960–61, 1964–65; Nuffield Fellow 1956; Fulbright Fellow 1960. *Publications:* articles in mathematical journals. *Leisure interests:* rifle shooting, golf, skiing. *Address:* 31 Shakespeare Avenue, Tranmere, South Australia 5073, Australia. *Telephone:* (08) 8331 9748.

MICHAUD, Jean-Claude Georges; French broadcasting executive; b. 28 Oct. 1933; s. of Maurice Michaud and Suzanne Michaud; m. 2nd Heide Bakszies 1991; one s. one d. (from fmr. marriage); ed. Lycée Louis-le-Grand, Paris and Ecole Normale Supérieure, Paris; Counsellor, Ministry of Educ. 1961–62, Ministry of Information 1962–64; Asst. Dir. Television ORTF 1964–68, Counsellor to Dir.-Gen. 1968–70; man. position, Librairie Hachette 1970–73; Deputy Dir. for External Affairs and Co-operation, ORTF 1973–74; Dir. of Int. Affairs and Co-operation, Télédiffusion France 1975–80, Dir. of Commercial Affairs 1982–83, Overseas Dir. 1983–85; Pres.-Dir.-Gen. Soc. Française Radio-Télévision d'Outre-Mer (RFO) 1986–89; Pres. Dir.-Gen. Sofratev 1989–. *Publication:* Teoria e Storia nel Capitale di Marx 1960. *Leisure interests:* walking, skiing, reading. *Address:* Sofratev, 21–23 rue de la Vanne, 92120 Montrouge (Office); 55 boulevard du Montparnasse, 75006 Paris, France. *Telephone:* 46-12-47-39 (Office). *Fax:* 46-12-47-47 (Office).

MICHAUX-CHEVRY, Lucette; French politician; b. 5 March 1929, Sainte-Claude, Guadeloupe; m. Émile Michaux (deceased); two c.; Municipal Councillor, Sainte-Claude 1959–65; mem. Departmental Council of Guadeloupe 1976, Chair. 1982–85; founded Political Party for Guadeloupe (L.P.G.) 1984; mem. Regional Council 1984; Deputy to Nat. Ass. 4th Constituency of Guadeloupe 1986; Mayor of Gourbeyre 1987; State Sec. for French-speaking World, Govt. of France 1986–88; Chair. Regional Council of Guadeloupe 1992; Deputy to Nat. Ass. 1993; Nat. Minister with special responsibility for Humanitarian Measures and Human Rights 1993–95; Senator from Guadeloupe (R.P.R.) 1995–; mem. Comm. of Foreign Affairs and Nat. Defence. *Address:* Conseil Régional de la Guadeloupe, Place du Champ d'Arbaud, 97100 Basse-Terre, France.

MICHEL, François Claude, B.L.; French diplomatist; b. 30 July 1928, Saint-Denis, Réunion; s. of Claude Michel and Emilie Cabanne de Laprade; m. Jeanine Maurice 1953; three s. one d.; ed. Faculté de Droit, Paris, Ecole nat. de la France d'Outre-Mer; Colonial Officer, Cameroon 1951–57; attached to the Pvt. Staff, Ministry of Foreign Affairs 1959–60; Sec. French Embassy, Yaoundé 1960, Ankara 1963, Addis Ababa 1966–68; Liaison Officer to OAU and ECA in Ethiopia 1966–68; French spokesman for links with EEC 1968–71; Counsellor, Tananarive 1971–72, Dublin 1972–75; Dir. Dept. of Cultural Affairs 1978–82; Amb. to Haiti 1983–86; Dir. of Cabinet for Sec. of State for Foreign Affairs 1986–87; Amb. to Ethiopia 1987–90; seconded to U.G.A.P. (state-owned corpn.) as int. adviser 1990–; Officier Légion d'honneur, Officier de l'ordre national du Mérite. *Address:* UGAP, 1 Boulevard Archimède, 77420 Champs sur Marne; 57 rue du Docteur Blanche, 75016 Paris, France (Home).

MICHEL, Louis, PH.D.; French physicist; b. 4 May 1923, Roanne; s. of Alfred Michel and Camille Nugue; m. Thérèse Vallet 1947; two s. four d.; ed. Ecole Polytechnique, Paris and Univ. of Paris/Sorbonne; explosives engineer 1946–58; research, Univ. of Manchester 1948–50, Inst. for Teoretisk Fysik, Copenhagen 1950–53, mem. Inst. for Advanced Study, Princeton 1953–55; Prof. Univ. of Lille 1955–58, Univ. of Paris 1958–62; Prof. Inst. des Hautes Etudes Scientifiques, Bures-sur-Yvette 1962–; mem. French Acad. des Sciences; Officier Légion d'honneur; Prize Robin (Soc. Française de Physique) 1975; Leigh Page Prize Lecturer (Yale Univ.) 1976; Wigner Medal 1984; Dr. h.c. (Louvain, Barcelona). *Publications:* one book and 120 publs. in scientific journals. *Leisure interest:* music. *Address:* Champ Secret, 91440 Bures-sur-Yvette, France. *Telephone:* 01 69 07 69 49.

MICHEL, Robert Henry, B.S., L.H.D.; American politician; b. 2 March 1923, Peoria, Ill.; s. of Charles Michel and Anna (née Baer) Michel; m. Corinne Woodruff 1948; four s.; ed. Bradley Univ., Lincoln Coll.; Admin. Asst. to mem. of Congress 1949–56; mem. 85th–99th Congresses, 18th Dist. Ill. 1957–94; House Minority Leader 97th and 100th Congresses 1981–94; Del. Republican Nat. Convention 1964–; Chair. Nat. Republican Congressional Cttee. 1973–74.

MICHEL, Smarck; Haitian politician and businessman; petrol retailer; owns rice-importing business; fmr. Commerce Sec. in first Aristide Govt. 1991; Prime Minister of Haiti 1994–96. *Address:* c/o Office of the Prime Minister, Port-au-Prince, Haiti.

MICHELBERGER, Pál; Hungarian engineer; b. 4 Feb. 1930, Vecsés; s. of Pál Michelberger and Mária Komáromy; m. Ilona Torma; one s. one d.; ed. Technical Univ., Budapest; Assoc. Prof. Tech. Univ., Budapest 1963–68, Prof. 1968–, Rector 1990–94; mem. Bd. of Mans. IKARUS Motor Coach Factory 1991–95, HUNGAROCAMION Transport Co. 1992–94; Corresp. mem. Hungarian Acad. of Sciences 1982, mem. 1990 (Vice-Pres. 1993); Chair. Cttee. for Machine Design, Scientific Soc. for Mechanical Eng., Co-Pres. 1976–90, Vice-Pres. 1990–93; Councillor Fed. Int. des Techniques de l'Automobile 1974, Vice-Pres. 1978, Pres. 1992–94; Pres. (elect) Hungarian Rectors' Conf. 1994–95; mem. Perm. Cttee. European Rectors' Conf. 1991–94; Corresp. mem. Verein Deutscher Ingenieure 1983–; mem. Russian Acad. of Transportation 1992, Acad. Europaea 1993. *Publications:* seven books and numerous articles on vehicle dynamics. *Leisure interest:* music. *Address:* c/o Technical University, Budapest 1521, Műegyetem rakpart 3-9, Hungary. *Telephone:* (36 1) 463-1728. *Fax:* (36 1) 463-1783.

MICHELIN, François; French industrialist; b. 15 June 1926, Clermont-Ferrand; s. of Etienne Michelin and Madeleine (née Calliès) Michelin; m. Bernadette Montagne 1951; Man. Dir. Compagnie Générale des Etablissements Michelin, "Michelin & Cie." 1959–66, Jt. Man. Dir. 1966–99; Man. Dir. Cie. Financière Michelin, Manufacture française des pneumatiques Michelin; dir. Peugeot SA; Conseiller d'Etat en service extraordinaire 1989.

Address: Michelin, 12 cours Sablon, 63000 Clermont-Ferrand, France (Office).

MICHELL, Keith; actor; b. 1 Dec. 1928, Adelaide, Australia; s. of Joseph and Maud (née Aslat) Michell; m. Jeanette Sterk 1957; one s. one d.; ed. Port Pirie High School, Adelaide Univ., Old Vic. Theatre School; started career as art teacher; first stage appearance Playbox, Adelaide 1947; with Young Vic. Theatre Co. 1950–51, first London appearance in And So To Bed 1951; Artistic Dir., Chichester Festival Theatre 1974–77; Top Actor Award 1971, British Film Award 1973, Logie Award 1974, and numerous others. *Stage appearances include:* Troilus and Cressida 1954, Romeo and Juliet 1954, Macbeth 1955, Don Juan 1956, Irma La Douce 1958, The Art of Seduction 1962, The Rehearsal 1963, Robert and Elizabeth 1964, The King's Mare 1966, Man of La Mancha 1968–69, Abelard and Heloise 1970, Hamlet 1972, Dear Love 1973, The Crucifer of Blood 1979, Captain Beaky Christmas Show 1981–82, The Tempest 1982, On the Rocks 1982, Amadeus 1983, La Cage aux Folles 1984–85, Jane Eyre 1986, Portraits 1987, The Royal Baccarat Scandal 1988, Henry VIII 1991, Aspects of Love 1992, Scrooge 1993–94, Monsieur Amilcar 1995, Brazilian Blue 1995. *Television includes:* The Six Wives of Henry VIII 1972, Keith Michell in Concert at Chichester 1974, Captain Beaky and His Band, Captain Beaky, Vol. 2, The Story of the Marlboroughs, Jacob and Joseph, The Story of David, The Tenth Month, The Day Christ Died, My Brother Tom 1987, Capt. James Cook 1988, Murder She Wrote (series) 1988, The Prince and the Pauper 1996. *Television/Video:* The Gondoliers, The Pirates of Penzance, Ruddigore. *Films include:* Dangerous Exile, The Hell Fire Club, Seven Seas to Calais, The Executioner, House of Cards, Prudence and the Pill, Henry VIII and his Six Wives, Moments, The Deceivers. *One-Man Art Shows:* Jamaica paintings 1960, New York 1962, Portugal 1963, Outback in Australia 1965, Don Quixote series, New York 1969, Abelard and Héloise 1972, Hamlet 1972. *Publications:* Shakespeare Sonnet series of lithographs 1974, Captain Beaky (illustrated poems) 1975, Captain Beaky Vol. 2 1982, Alice in Wonderland 1982, Keith Michell's Practically Macrobiotic Cookbook 1987. *Address:* c/o Chatto and Linnit, 123A King's Road, London, SW3 4PL, England. *Telephone:* 0171-352 7722.

MICHELL, Robert H., PH.D., F.R.S.; British university professor; b. 16 April 1941, Yeovil; s. of Rowland C. Michell and Elsie L. (Hall) Michell; m. 1st June Evans 1967 (divorced 1971); m. 2nd Esther Margaret Oppenheim 1992; two s. one d.; ed. Crewkerne School and Univ. of Birmingham; Research Fellow, Birmingham Univ. 1965–66, 1969–70, Harvard Medical School 1966–68; Lecturer, Birmingham Univ. 1970–81, Sr. Lecturer 1981–84, Reader 1984–86, Prof. of Biochemistry 1986–87, Royal Soc. Research Prof. 1987–; other professional appts.; mem. Council, Royal Soc. 1996–97; Royal Soc. U.K.-Canada Rutherford Lecturer 1994; CIBA Medal, Biochemical Soc. 1988. *Publications:* Membranes and their Cellular Functions (with J. B. Finean and R. Coleman) 1974, 1978, 1984, Membrane Structure (ed. with J. B. Finean) 1981, Inositol Lipids and Transmembrane Signalling (ed. with M. J. Berridge) 1988, Inositol Lipids in Cell Signalling (ed. with A. H. Drummond and C. P. Downes) 1989. *Leisure interests:* birdwatching, photography, modern literature, wildernesses. *Address:* Centre for Clinical Research in Immunology and Signalling, The Medical School, University of Birmingham, Birmingham, B15 2TT (Office); 59 Weoley Park Road, Selly Oak, Birmingham, B29 6QZ, England (Home). *Telephone:* (0121) 414 5413 (Office); (0121) 472 1356 (Home). *Fax:* (0121) 414 6840.

MICHELSEN, Axel, DR. PHIL.; Danish professor of biology; b. 1 March 1940, Haderslev; s. of Erik Michelsen and Vibeke Michelsen; m. Ulla West-Nielsen 1980; two s. one d.; ed. Univ. of Copenhagen; Asst. Prof. of Zoophysiology and Zoology, Univ. of Copenhagen 1963–72; Prof. of Biology Odense Univ. 1973–; Chair. Danish Science Research Council 1975–78, Danish Nat. Cttee. for Biophysics 1980–90, Danish Nat. Cttee. for ICSU 1986–, Max-Planck Gesellschaft Fachbeirat 1978–82; Dir. Carlsberg Foundation 1986–, Centre for Sound Communication 1994–; mem. Royal Danish Acad. of Sciences and Letters, Akad. der Naturforscher Leopoldina, Academia Europaea; Corresp. mem. Akademie der Wissenschaften und der Literatur (Mainz), Bayerische Akad. der Wissenschaften; Alexander von Humboldt Prize 1990. *Publications:* The Physiology of the Locust Ear 1971, Sound and Life 1975, Time Resolution in Auditory Systems 1985, The Dance Language of Honeybees 1992. *Leisure interests:* wines, beekeeping, gardening. *Address:* Institute of Biology, Odense University, 5230 Odense M (Office); The Carlsberg Foundation, 35 H.C. Andersens Boulevard, 1553 Copenhagen V (Office); Laessøegade 204, 5230 Odense M, Denmark (Home). *Telephone:* 66-158600; 33-435363 (Office); 66-117568 (Home). *Fax:* 65-930457 (Office); 66-141603 (Home).

MICHELSEN, Hans Günter; German playwright; b. 1920, Hamburg; mil. service and P.O.W. 1939–49; began to write 1949; now freelance writer in Augsburg; Förderpreis des Niedersächsischen Kunstpreises, Hanover 1963, Förderpreis des Gerhart-Haupt-mann-Preises, Berlin 1963, Gerhart-Hauptmann-Preis, Berlin 1965, Literaturpreis der Freien Hansestadt Bremen 1967. *Publications:* plays: Stienz 1963, Feierabend 1 and 2 1963, Lappschiess 1964, Drei Akte 1965, Helm 1965, Frau L 1966, Planspiel 1969, Sein Leben 1975, Alltag 1978, Terror 1979; radio plays: Episode 1958, Kein schönes Land 1966, Ein Ende 1969, Himmelfahrt 1972. *Address:* Suhrkamp-Verlag, Postfach 2446, 6000 Frankfurt am Main, Germany. *Telephone:* (069) 726744.

MICHENER, Charles Duncan, B.S., PH.D.; American biologist (entomology); b. 22 Sept. 1918, Pasadena, Calif.; s. of Harold and Josephine Rigden Michener; m. Mary Hastings 1940; three s. one d.; ed. Univ. of California, Berkeley; Technical asst. in Entomology, Univ. of Calif. 1939–42; Asst. Curator, Lepidoptera and Hymenoptera, American Museum of Natural History, New York 1942–46, Assoc. Curator 1946–48, Research Assoc. 1949–; Curator, Snow Entomological Museum, Univ. of Kansas 1949–89, Dir. 1974–83; Assoc. Prof. Entomology, Univ. of Kansas 1948–49, Prof. 1949–89, Prof. Emer. 1989–; Chair. Dept. of Entomology 1949–61, 1972–75, Watkins Dist. Prof. of Entomology 1959–89, of Systematics and Ecology 1969–89; State Entomologist, S. Div. of Kansas 1949–61; Ed. Evolution 1962–64; American Ed. Insectes Sociaux (Paris), 1954–55, 1962–90; Assoc. Ed. Annual Review of Ecology and Systematics 1970–90; Pres. Soc. for the Study of Evolution 1967, Soc. of Systematic Zoology 1969, American Soc. of Naturalists 1978, Int. Union for the Study of Social Insects 1977–82 (Vice-Pres. Western Hemisphere Section 1979–80); mem. N.A.S., American Acad. of Arts and Sciences, Corresp. mem. Acad. Brasileira de Ciências; Foreign hon. mem. Russian Entomological Soc.; Hon. mem. Soc. of Systematic Biology; Guggenheim Fellow to Brazil 1955–56, Africa 1966–67; Fellow Royal Entomological Soc. of London, American Assen. for the Advancement of Sciences; Fulbright Scholar, Australia 1957–58; Morrison Prize, N.Y. Acad. of Sciences 1943; Founder's Award, American Entomological Soc. 1981, Thomas Say Award, Entomological Soc. of America 1997. *Publications:* Comparative external morphology, phylogeny and a classification of the bees (Hymenoptera) 1944, American social insects (with M. H. Michener) 1951, The nest architecture of the sweat bees (with S. F. Sakagami) 1962, A classification of the bees of the Australian and S. Pacific regions 1965, The social behaviour of the bees 1974, Kin Recognition in Animals (with D. Fletcher) 1987, The bee genera of North and Central America (with R. J. McGinley and B. N. Danforth) 1994. *Leisure interests:* travel, field work. *Address:* Snow Entomological Museum, Snow Hall, University of Kansas, Lawrence, KS 66045; 1706 West 2nd Street, Lawrence, KS 66044, U.S.A. (Home). *Telephone:* (785) 864-4610 (Office); (913) 843-4598 (Home). *Fax:* (785) 864-5260.

MICHIE, David Alan Redpath, O.B.E., F.R.S.A.; British painter and professor of art; b. 30 Nov. 1928, St. Raphael, France; s. of James Beattie Michie and Anne Redpath; m. Eileen Michie 1951; two d.; ed. Hawick High School, Edinburgh Coll. of Art; lecturer in Drawing and Painting, Gray's School of Art, Aberdeen 1957–61; Vice-Prin. Edin. Coll. of Art 1974–77, Head of School of Drawing and Painting 1982–90, Prof. of Painting 1988–90; Emer. Prof., Heriot Watt Univ. 1991–; Visiting Artist to Acad. of Fine Art, Belgrade 1979, to Art Studio Dept., Univ. of Calif. at Santa Barbara 1992; mem. Edin. Festival Soc. 1976–; solo exhbns.: Mercury Gallery, London 1966, 1969, 1971, 1974, 1980, 1983, 1992, 1996, Mercury Gallery, Edin. 1986, The Scottish Gallery, Edin. 1980, 1994, 1998, The Lothian and Region Chambers 1977, The Loomshop Gallery, Lower Largo 1981, 1987, De Kasteel de Hooge Vursche and Mia Joosten Gallery, Amsterdam 1991; mem. Royal Scottish Acad. 1972, Royal Glasgow Inst. of Fine Art 1983, Royal West of England Acad. 1991, Museums and Galleries Comm. 1991–96; Guthrie Award, R.S.A. 1964, David Cargill Award, R.G.I. 1977, Lothian Region Award 1977, Sir William Gillies Award, R.S.A. 1980, Glasgow City of Culture Award, R.G.I. 1990, Cornelissen Prize, R.W.A. 1992. *Leisure interest:* music. *Address:* 17 Gilmour Road, Edinburgh, EH16 5NS, Scotland (Home). *Telephone:* (0131) 667 2684 (Home).

MICHIE, Donald, D.PHIL., PH.D.; British scientist; b. 11 Nov. 1923; s. of late James Kilgour Michie and late Marjorie Crain Michie; m. 1st Zena Margaret Davies 1949 (divorced); one s.; m. 2nd Anne McLaren 1952 (divorced); one s. two d.; m. 3rd Jean Elizabeth Hayes (née Crouch) 1971; ed. Rugby School, Balliol Coll., Oxford; war service in F.O. Bletchley 1942–45; Research Assoc. Univ. of London 1952–58, Sr. Lecturer in Surgical Science 1958, Reader 1962, Dir. of Experimental Programming Unit 1965, Chair. Dept. of Machine Intelligence and Perception 1966, Prof. of Machine Intelligence 1967–84, Prof. Emer. 1984–; Dir. Machine Intelligence Research Unit 1974–84; Royal Soc. Lecturer in U.S.S.R. 1965; numerous visiting lectureships and professorships; Chief Ed. Machine Intelligence series 1967–; Founder, Dir. Turing Inst., Glasgow 1975–86, Chief Scientist 1986–92; Sr. Fellow 1992–94; Tech. Dir. Intelligent Terminals Ltd. (Knowledgelink) 1984–92; Fellow Royal Soc. of Edin. 1969, British Computer Soc. 1971; Hon. D.Sc. (CNAA) 1991, (Salford) 1992; Hon. D.Univ. (Stirling) 1996; Pioneer Award (jtly.) Int. Embryo Transfer Soc. 1988, I.E.E. Achievement Award 1995, Feigenbaum Medal, World Congress on Expert Systems 1996. *Publications:* An Introduction to Molecular Biology (jtly.) 1964, On Machine Intelligence 1974, Machine Intelligence and Related Topics 1982, The Creative Computer (jtly.) 1984; papers in scientific journals. *Leisure interests:* writing. *Address:* 6 Inveralmond Grove, Cramond, Edinburgh, EH4 6RA, Scotland. *Telephone:* (0131) 336 3826. *Fax:* (0131) 336 4603.

MICHON, John Albertus, PH.D.; Netherlands research director and university professor; b. 29 Oct. 1935, Utrecht; s. of late J. J. Michon and of S. Ch. A. de Ruyter; m. Hetty Sommer 1960; one s. one d.; ed. Utrecht Mun. Gymnasium and Univs. of Utrecht and Leiden; Research Assoc. Inst. for Perception, Soesterberg 1960–73, Head, Dept. of Road User Studies 1969–73; Co-founder, Netherlands Psychonomics Foundation 1968, Sec. 1968–72, Pres. 1975–80; Prof. of Experimental Psychology and Traffic Science, Univ. of Groningen 1971–92, Dir. Inst. for Experimental Psychology 1971–86, Chair. Traffic Research Center 1977–92, Chair. Dept. of Psychology 1978,

1983–86, Assoc. Dean, Faculty of Social Sciences 1983–86; mem. Bd. Center for Behavioral, Cognitive and Neurosciences 1990–92; Dir. Netherlands Inst. for the Study of Criminality and Law Enforcement 1992–; Prof. of Criminal Research, Univ. of Leiden 1992–; Pres. Int. Soc. for the Study of Time 1983–86; Co-founder, mem. Bd. European Soc. for Cognitive Psychology 1984–90; Vice-Chair. Nat. Council for Road Safety 1977–86; Ed.-in-Chief, Acta Psychologica 1971–74; Visiting Prof. Carnegie Mellon Univ., Pittsburgh, Pa. 1986–87; Co-ordinator EEC DRIVE Project Generic Intelligent Driver Support 1988–92; mem. Royal Netherlands Acad. of Arts and Sciences (Chair. Behavioral and Social Sciences Section); mem. Acad. Europaea, Acad. Scientiarum et Artium Europaea, Social Sciences Council (S.W.R.) 1994–; NATO Science Fellowship, NIAS Fellowship; Dr. h.c. (Liège) 1995. *Publications:* Timing in Temporal Tracking 1967, Sociale Verkeerskunde 1976, Handboek der Psychonomie 1976, 1979, Beïnvloeding van Mobiliteit 1981, Time, Mind and Behavior 1985, Guyau and the Idea of Time 1988, Handboek der Sociale Verkeerskunde 1989, Soar: A Cognitive Architecture in Perspective 1992, Generic Intelligent Driver Behaviour 1993; approx. 250 articles and chapters in scientific journals and books. *Leisure interests:* visual arts (painting, graphics), music (bassoon playing). *Address:* Netherlands Institute for the Study of Criminality and Law Enforcement, Wassenaarseweg 72, 2333 AL Leiden, Netherlands. *Telephone:* 71-5278527. *Fax:* 71-5278537 (Office).

MICHOT, Yves Raoul; French aviation executive; b. 4 Nov. 1941, Nantes; s. of Raoul Michot and Lucienne Ruffel; m. Michèle Gouth 1964; two s. one d.; Brétigny Flight Test Centre 1965–73; Govt. Concorde Project Man. 1973–75; Tech. Adviser to Nat. Armament Dir. 1975–78, to Minister of Defence 1978–80; Mirage 2000 Program Man. Ministry of Defence 1980–84; Mil. Programs Gen. Man. Aérospatiale 1984, Programs Gen. Man. 1985; Exec. Vice-Pres. Aérospatiale 1987, Exec. Vice-Pres. and C.O.O. 1989, Sr. Exec. Vice-Pres. and C.O.O. and Pres. Aérospatiale 1995–, Pres., Dir.-Gen. 1996–; Pres. European Asscn. of Aerospace Industries (AECMA) 1997–; Officier, Légion d'Honneur, Officier, Ordre Nat. du Mérite, Médaille de l'Aéronautique. *Address:* Aérospatiale, 37 boulevard de Montmorency, 75781 Paris, Cedex 16 (Office); 3 rue Chabrier, 78370 Plaisir, France (Home). *Telephone:* 42-24-24-24 (Office.).

MICOSSI, Stefano; Italian economist and international official; b. 27 Oct. 1946, Bologna; m. Daniela Zanotto; one s. one d.; ed. Università Statale di Milano, Yale Univ.; economist Bank of Italy Research Dept. 1974–78, Head 1980–84, Asst. Dir. 1984–86, Dir. Int. Div. 1986–88; seconded to IMF as Asst. to Italy's Exec. Dir. 1978–80; Dir. of Econ. Research Confindustria (Confed. of Italian Industries) 1988–94; Prof. of Macroeconomic Policy Int. Free Univ. of Social Sciences 1989–94, Prof. of Monetary Theory and Policy 1993–94; Prof. of Int. Monetary Econs. 1990–94; Dir.-Gen. for Industry Nov. 1994–. *Publications:* jt. Ed. Adjustment and Integration in the World Economy 1992, The Italian Economy 1993, Inflation in Europe 1997, and books on the European Monetary System 1988, numerous articles in professional journals. *Address:* Directorate-General III Industry, European Commission, 200 rue de la Loi (SC15 6/146), 1049 Brussels, Belgium. *Telephone:* (2) 2954022. *Fax:* (2) 2950126.

MIDDELHOEK, André, PH.D.; Netherlands civil servant; b. 13 Dec. 1931, Voorburg; s. of J. Middelhoek; m. Trudy van den Broek 1982; two d.; ed. Univ. of Amsterdam; Cen. Planning Office, Govt. of Netherlands 1958–69, Deputy Dir. 1966–69; lecturer, Int. Inst. for Social Studies, The Hague 1960–69; Dir.-Gen. of the Budget, Ministry of Finance 1969–77; mem. Court of Auditors of European Communities 1977–93; Pres. European Court of Auditors 1993–96; Commdr., Order of Netherlands Lion, Grand Croix, Gouronne de Chêne (Luxembourg). *Publications:* publs. in econs., econ. planning, public finance, policy analysis, EU finance and audit. *Leisure interests:* swimming, tennis, genealogy, hiking. *Address:* Marnixlaan 108, 3090 Overijse, Belgium. *Telephone:* (2) 6875553. *Fax:* (2) 6875553.

MIDDELHOFF, Thomas; German business executive; m.; five c.; fmr. lecturer in marketing, Munster Univ.; now Bd. mem. responsible for multimedia, Bertelsmann publishing; Vernon A. Walters Prize. *Address:* Bertelsmann AG, Carl-Bertelsmann-Str. 270, 33311 Gütersloh, Germany (Office). *Telephone:* 05241 80-0.

MIDDENDORF, J. William, II, B.S., M.B.A.; American fmr. government official, diplomatist and business executive; b. 22 Sept. 1924, Baltimore, Md.; s. of the late Henry Stump and Sarah Boone Middendorf; m. Isabelle J. Paine 1953; two s. two d.; ed. Holy Cross Coll., Harvard Univ. and New York Graduate School of Business Admin.; U.S. Navy service during Second World War; in Credit Dept. of Bank of Manhattan Co. (now Chase Manhattan Bank) 1947–52; Analyst, brokerage firm of Wood Struthers and Co. Inc., New York 1952–58, Partner 1958–62; Sr. Partner investment firm of Middendorf, Colgate and Co., New York 1962–69; U.S. Amb. to the Netherlands 1969–73; Under-Sec. of the Navy 1973–74, Sec. 1974–76; Pres. and C.E.O. of First American Bankshares, Washington, D.C. 1977–81; Pres. and C.E.O. Middendorf & Co., Inc. 1990–; Chair. Middendorf S.A. 1989–; U.S. Amb. to O.A.S. 1981–85, to EC 1985–87; Chair. Presidential Task Force on Project Econ. Justice 1985–86; numerous hon. degrees; State Dept. Superior Honor Award 1974, Dept. of Defense Distinguished Public Service Award 1975, 1976, U.S. Navy Public Service Award 1976, numerous other awards, Grand Master of Order of Naval Merit (Brazil) 1974, Distinguished Service Medal (Brazil) 1976, Order of Arab Repub. of Egypt (Class A) 1979, Grand Officer of the Order of Orange Nassau Netherlands 1985, Ludwig Von Mises Inst. Free Market Award 1985; U.S. Nat. Sculling Champion in Masters Div. 1979, won a world masters championship in rowing at the 1985 Toronto Masters Games. *Compositions:* has composed seven symphonies, an opera and numerous marches and concerti. *Publications:* Investment Policies of Fire and Casualty Insurance Companies. *Address:* Middendorf Co. Inc., 1730 K Street N.W., 1100, Washington, DC 20006, U.S.A. (Office).

MIDDLEMAS, Robert Keith, D.PHIL., D.LITT., F.R.S.A.; British historian; b. 26 May 1935, Alnwick; s. of Robert James Middlemas and Eleanor Mary Middlemas (née Crane); m. Susan Mary Tremlett 1958; one s. three d.; ed. Stowe School, Pembroke Coll., Cambridge; nat. service 2nd Lieut. Northumberland Fusiliers 1953–55; Clerk House of Commons 1958–67; lecturer in History, Sussex Univ. 1967–76, Reader 1976–86, Prof. 1986–; Visiting Prof. Stanford Univ. and Hoover Inst. 1984, Univ. of Beijing 1989; Dir. ESL and Network S.A. 1998–; mem. U.K. Nat. Cttee. UNESCO 1980–86, co-f. and Ed. Catalyst, A Journal of Public Debate 1985–87; Council mem., Research Cttee. mem. Foundation for Mfg. and Industry 1993–. *Publications:* The Master Builders 1963, The Clydesiders 1965, Baldwin (jtly.) 1969, Diplomacy of Illusion 1972, Thomas Jones: Whitehall Diary (Ed.) 1969–72, Cabora Bassa: Engineering and Politics 1975, Politics in Industrial Society 1979, Power and the Party: Communism in Western Europe 1980, Industry, Unions and Government 1984, Power, Competition and the State (three vols.) 1986–91, Orchestrating Europe: Informal Politics of the Community since 1973 1995. *Leisure interests:* rifle shooting (U.K. nat. team, Canada 1958), sailing, fishing, landscape gardening, building follies. *Address:* West Burton House, West Burton, Pulborough, West Sussex, RH20 1HD, England. *Telephone:* (01798) 831 516.

MIDDLETON, Christopher, M.A., D.PHIL.; British professor of Germanic languages and literature; b. 10 June 1926, Truro; s. of Hubert S. Middleton and Dorothy M. Miller; m. 1953 (divorced); one s. two d.; ed. Felsted School and Merton Coll. Oxford; Lektor in English, Univ. of Zürich 1952–55; Asst. Lecturer in German, King's Coll. Univ. of London 1955–57, lecturer 1957–66; Prof. of Germanic Languages and Literature Univ. of Texas at Austin 1966–; Sir Geoffrey Faber Memorial Prize 1964, Guggenheim Poetry Fellowship 1974–75; Nat. Endowment for Humanities Poetry Fellowship 1980; Tieck-Schlegel Translation Prize 1985, Max Geilinger Stiftung Prize 1987, etc. *Publications:* Torse 3, poems 1948–61 1962, Nonsequences/Selfpoems 1965, Our Flowers and Nice Bones 1969, The Lonely Suppers of W.V. Balloon 1975, Carminalenia 1980, III Poems 1983, Two Horse Wagon Going By 1986, Selected Writings 1989, The Balcony Tree 1992, Andalusian Poems 1993, Intimate Chronicles 1996, That Old Feeling 1997; vols. of prose, essays etc. *Address:* Department of Germanic Languages, University of Texas at Austin, Austin, TX 78712, U.S.A. *Telephone:* (512) 471-4123.

MIDDLETON, Peter, B.A.; British business executive and diplomatist; b. 1940; m. Yvonne Summerson 1968 (divorced 1996); two s. one d.; m. 2nd Anita Mehra 1996; ed. Sorbonne, Hull Univ.; joined a monastery, Paignton, Devon; joined the foreign service, two-year posts in both Indonesia and Tanzania 1969–77; Sr. Embassy Counsellor Paris 1977–82; joined Midland Bank 1985, Midland Int. 1985–87; with Thomas Cook 1987–92; C.E.O. Lloyd's of London (Insurance) 1992–95; Chief Exec. Salomon Bros. Int. 1995–; Hon. LL.D. (Teeside) 1997. *Address:* Salomon Brothers International Ltd, Victoria Plaza, 111 Buckingham Palace Road, London, SW1Y 0SR, England.

MIDDLETON, Sir Peter Edward, G.C.B., M.A.; British fmr. civil servant and business executive; b. 2 April 1934; m. 1st Valerie Ann Lindup 1964 (died 1987); one s. one d.; m. 2nd Connie Owen 1990; ed. Sheffield City Grammar School, Sheffield Univ., Bristol Univ.; Sr. Information Officer, H.M. Treasury 1962, Prin. 1964, Asst. Dir., Centre for Admin. Studies 1967–69, Pvt. Sec. to Chancellor of Exchequer 1969–72, Treasury Press Sec. 1972–75, Head, Monetary Policy Div. 1975, Under-Sec. 1976, Deputy Sec. 1980–83, Perm. Sec. 1983–91; a Deputy Chair. Barclays Group 1991–98, mem. Exec. Bd. 1991–, Chair. BZW Div. 1991–98; mem. Council Sheffield Univ. 1991–, Pro-Chancellor 1997; mem. Bd. United Utilities Group PLC 1993–, Vice-Chair. 1998–; non-exec. mem. Bd. Bass PLC, General Accident PLC; mem. Council Manchester Business School 1985–92; Gov. London Business School 1984–90, Ditchley Foundation 1985–; mem. Nat. Econ. Research Asscn. 1991–; Chair. Inst. of Contemporary History 1992–; mem. Financial Reporting Council 1997–; Visiting Fellow, Nuffield Coll., Oxford 1981–90; Hon. D.Litt. (Sheffield) 1984. *Leisure interests:* music, walking, outdoor sports. *Address:* Barclays Bank PLC, 54 Lombard Street, London, EC3P 3AH, England.

MIDDLETON, Stanley, B.A., M.Ed.; British author and schoolteacher; b. 1 Aug. 1919, Bulwell, Nottingham; s. of Thomas Middleton and Elizabeth Ann Middleton (née Burdett); m. Margaret Shirley Charnley (née Welch) 1951; two d.; ed. Bulwell Highbury School, High Pavement School, Nottingham, Nottingham Univ. Coll., Univ. of Nottingham; fmr. English teacher; fmr. Head of English High Pavement Coll., Nottingham, retd. 1981; Judith Wilson Fellow Emmanuel Coll., Cambridge 1982–83; Booker Prize (for Holiday) 1974; Hon. M.A. (Nottingham), Hon. M.Univ. (Open), Hon. D.Litt. (De Montfort). *Publications:* 38 novels including Harris's Requiem, Wages of Virtue, Holiday, In a Strange Land, Entry into Jerusalem, Valley of Decision, A Place to Stand, Catalysts, Toward the Sea, Brief Hours, Against the Dark, Necessary Ends 1999. *Leisure interests:* music, painting. *Address:* 42 Caledon

Road, Sherwood, Nottingham, NG5 2NG, England. *Telephone:* 0115 962 3085.

MIDLER, Bette; American singer, entertainer and actress; b. 1945, Honolulu; m. Martin von Haselberg 1984; one d.; début as actress in film Hawaii 1965; mem. of cast in Fiddler on the Roof, New York 1966–69, Salvation, New York 1970, Tommy, Seattle Opera Co. 1971; night-club concert performer 1972–; TV appearances include Tonight Show; recordings include The Divine Miss M. 1973, Bette Midler 1973, Broken Blossom 1977, Live at Last 1977, Thighs and Whispers 1979, New Depression 1979, Divine Madness 1980, No Frills 1984, Some People's Lives 1990; film appearances include The Rose 1979, Jinxed 1982, Down and Out in Beverly Hills 1986, Ruthless People 1986, Outrageous Fortune 1987, Big Business 1988, Beaches 1989, Stella 1990, For The Boys 1991, Hocus Pocus 1993, Gypsy (TV), The First Wives Club 1996; After Dark Ruby Award 1973, Grammy Award 1973, Special Tony Award 1973, Emmy Award 1978. *Publications:* A View From A Broad 1980, The Saga of Baby Divine 1983. *Address:* c/o Atlantic Records, 1290 Avenue of the Americas, New York, NY 10104, U.S.A.

MIDORI; Japanese violinist; b. 25 Oct. 1971, Osaka; d. of Setsu Goto; ed. The Professional Children's School and Juilliard School of Music; began violin studies with mother aged four; moved to U.S.A. 1982; début with New York Philharmonic 1982; recording début 1986 aged 14; now makes worldwide concert appearances; Founder and Pres. Midori Foundation 1992; Dorothy B. Chandler Performing Arts Award; New York State Asian-American Heritage Month Award; Crystal Award (Japan), Suntory Award 1994. *Leisure interests:* cooking, reading, listening to music, art. *Address:* c/o ICM Artists Ltd., Oxford House, 76 Oxford Street, London, W1N 0AX, England; Sony Classical, Sony Music Entertainment Inc., 550 Madison Avenue, New York, NY 10022, U.S.A.

MIDWINTER, John Edwin, O.B.E., PH.D., F.R.S., F.ENG., F.I.E.E., F.I.E.E.E., F.INST.P.; British professor of optoelectronics; b. 8 March 1938, Newbury, Berks.; s. of late H. C. Midwinter and of V. J. (née Rawlinson) Midwinter; m. Maureen A. Holt 1961; two s. two d.; ed. King's Coll., London; Sr. Scientific Officer, Royal Radar Establishment 1967–68; Sr. Research Physicist, Perkin-Elmer Corpn., U.S.A. 1968–70; Head, Fibre Optic Devt. British Telecom Research Labs. 1971–77, Head Optical Communications Technology 1977–84; British Telecom Prof. of Optoelectronics, Univ. Coll., London 1984–91, Head, Dept. of Electronic and Electrical Eng. 1988–98, Pender Prof. of Electronic Eng. 1991–, Vice-Provost 1994–; Deputy Pres. IEE 1998– (Vice-Pres. 1994, Chair. Electronics Div. 1991–92); IEE-J.J. Thompson Medal 1987, Faraday Medal 1997. *Publications:* Applied Non-Linear Optics 1972, Optical Fibers for Transmission 1977; over 70 papers on lasers, non-linear optics and optical communications. *Leisure interests:* walking, skiing, writing. *Address:* Department of Electronic and Electrical Engineering, University College, Torrington Place, London, WC1E 7JE, England. *Telephone:* 0171-388 0427.

MIELI, Paolo; Italian journalist; b. 25 Feb. 1949, Milan; two s.; ed. classical lycée and univ.; Asst. to Renzo De Felice, Chair of History of Political Parties, Univ. of Rome; corresp., commentator on home politics, ed. cultural editorial office and then Ed.-in-Chief, Espresso (weekly) 1967–85; worked for Repubblica 1985; joined La Stampa 1986, Ed. 1990; mem. Bd. Govs. Storia Illustrata, Pagina and has collaborated with Tempi Moderni, Questi Istituzioni, Mondo operaio; Ed. Corriere della Sera 1992–; Premio Spoleto 1990, Premio Mediterraneo 1991, Premio Alfio Russo 1995. *Publications:* Litigo a Sinistra, Il Socialismo Diviso, Storia del Partito Socialista Negli Anni della Repubblica. *Leisure interests:* ancient history, skiing. *Address:* c/o Corriere della Sera, RCS Editori, Settore Quotidiani, Via Solferino 28, 20121 Milan, Italy. *Telephone:* (2) 6339. *Fax:* (2) 29009668.

MIELKE, Erich; German politician and shipping clerk; b. 28 Dec. 1907, Berlin; m.; two c.; joined Communist Youth League 1921, CP 1925; fought in Spanish civil war 1936–39; emigrated to U.S.S.R. 1939–45; State Sec., G.D.R. Ministry of State Security 1950–53, 1955–57; Deputy State Sec. for State Security, Ministry of the Interior 1953–55; Minister of State Security 1957–89; mem. Volkskammer (People's Chamber) 1958–89; mem. Cen. Cttee. Socialist Unity Party (SED) 1950–89, cand. mem. Politburo 1971–76, mem. 1976–89; Col.-Gen. 1959, Gen. 1980; Vaterländischer Verdienstorden in Gold (twice), Karl-Marx-Orden and many other decorations; arrested 1990, freed, re-arrested July 1990, accused of numerous crimes April 1991, ruled incapable of standing trial Aug. 1991, found guilty of murder and sentenced to six years in prison Oct. 1993; released Aug. 1995.

MIENO, Yasushi, LL.B.; Japanese central banker; b. 17 March 1924, Tokyo; s. of Masaru Mieno and Fumiko Mieno; m. Kazuko Mori 1951; two s.; ed. Univ. of Tokyo; joined Bank of Japan 1947; Dir. Policy Planning Dept. 1973–75, Market Operations Dept. 1975–78; Exec. Dir. 1978–84; Sr. Deputy Gov. 1984–89; Gov. and Chair. Policy Bd. Bank of Japan 1989–94. *Leisure interests:* reading, walking, art. *Address:* c/o Bank of Japan, 2-1-1, Hongokucho, Nihonbashi, Chuo-ku, Tokyo 100-8630, Japan.

MIERS, Sir David, K.B.E., C.M.G., M.A.; British diplomatist; b. 10 Jan. 1937, Liverpool; s. of the late Col. R. Miers, D.S.O. and Honor Bucknill; m. Imelda Wouters 1966; two s. one d.; ed. Winchester Coll. and Univ. Coll. Oxford; joined diplomatic service 1961; served Tokyo 1963, Vientiane 1966, Paris 1972, Teheran 1977, Beirut 1983; Asst. Under-Sec. FCO 1986; Amb. to Greece 1989–93; to Netherlands 1993–96. *Leisure interest:* open air. *Address:* c/o Foreign & Commonwealth Office, King Charles Street, London, SW1A 2AH, England.

MIERZEJEWSKI, Jerzy; Polish painter and academic; b. 13 July 1917, Kraków; s. of Jacek Mierzejewski and Stanisława Brzezińska; m. Krystyna Szner (died 1994), one s. one d.; ed. Acad. of Fine Arts, Warsaw; lecturer and Prof. State Film School, Łódź; fmr., Dean Film Photography Dept. and Film Directory Dept.; fmr. Pres. Union of Polish Artists and Designers; Minister of Culture and Art Prize (II Class) 1963, Kt.'s Cross Order of Polonia Restituta. *Films include:* Jan Matejko 1954, Jacek Mierzejewski 1968, 25 one-man exhbns.; group exhbns. include Selective Eye, Crown Town Gallery, Los Angeles 1970; works in perm. collections National Museum, Warsaw, Museum of Art Łódź, Stedelijk Museum, Amsterdam and in numerous pvt. collections. *Publications include:* Composition of Film Picture 1955, Some Aspects of Continuity of Film 1963. *Address:* ul. Śmiała 63, 01-526 Warsaw, Poland. *Telephone:* (22) 39-22-43.

MIFFLIN, Fred J.; Canadian politician and fmr. naval officer; b. 1938, Bonavista, Newfoundland; m. Cwenneth Mifflin; three c.; ed. Nat. Defence Coll., Kingston, Ont., U.S. Naval War Coll., Newport, R.I.; joined Navy 1954, assumed first command at sea 1969, commanded destroyers, served in sr. positions relating to UN Confs. on Law of the Sea, fisheries protection, procurement of mil. systems, and int. relations, Head Nat. Defence Secr.; M.P. for Bonavista-Trinity-Conception 1988–; Parl. Sec. to Minister of Nat. Defence and Veterans' Affairs 1993–95; Minister of Fisheries and Oceans 1996–97, of Veterans Affairs and Sec. of State (Atlantic Opportunities Agency) 1997. *Address:* Fisheries and Oceans, Ministry of Veterans Affairs, 66 Slater Street, 16th Floor, Ont., Canada K1A 0P4.

MIFSUD BONNICI, Carmelo, LL.D.; Maltese politician and lawyer; b. 17 July 1933, Cospicua; s. of Lorenzo Mifsud Bonnici and Catherine Buttigieg; ed. Lyceum, Univ. of Malta, Univ. Coll. London; legal consultant, Gen. Workers' Union 1969; Deputy Leader, Maltese Labour Movt. 1980–82, Leader desig. 1982, Leader Labour Party 1984; mem. Parl. 1982–96; Minister of Labour and Social Services 1982–83; Sr. Deputy Prime Minister and Minister of Educ. 1983–84; Prime Minister of Malta and Minister of the Interior and of Educ. 1985–87; Leader of Opposition 1987–92; Lecturer in Industrial and Fiscal Law, Univ. of Malta 1969. *Leisure interest:* reading.

MIFSUD BONNICI, Ugo, B.A., LL.D.; Maltese politician and lawyer; b. 8 Nov. 1932, Cospicua; s. of Carmelo Bonnici; m. Gemma Bianco; three c.; ed. Royal Univ. of Malta; practising lawyer 1955–; mem. Parl. 1966–94; Opposition Spokesman for Educ. 1972–87; Pres. Gen. Council and Admin. Council of Nationalist Party 1977; Minister of Educ. 1987, of Educ. and Interior 1990–92, of Educ. and Human Resources 1992–94, Pres. of Malta April 1994–. *Publications:* newspaper articles. *Address:* The Palace, Valletta (Office); San Anton Palace, Attard, Malta (Residence). *Telephone:* 221221 (Office); 440354 (Residence). *Fax:* 241241 (Office).

MIGAŠ, Jozef, D.PHIL., C.SC.; Slovak politician; b. 7 Jan. 1954, Prušovcia; m.; two c.; ed. Univ. of Kiev; fmrly. with Acad. of Sciences, Košice, Political Univ., Bratislava; f. Party of the Democratic Left, Chair. 1996–; diplomat 1993–96; Chair. Slovak Nat. Council 1998–. *Address:* Slovak National Council, Mudroňova 1, 812 80 Bratislava, Office of the Government of the Slovak Republic, Nám. Slobody 1, 813 70 Bratislava 1, Slovakia. *Telephone:* (7) 534-1111.

MIGRANYAN, Andranik Movsesovich; CAND.HIS.SC.; Russian/Armenian civil servant; b. 10 Feb. 1949, Yerevan; m.; one d.; ed. Moscow State Inst. of Int. Relations, Inst. of Int. Workers' Movt. U.S.S.R. Acad. of Sciences 1972–75; teacher, Prof. Moscow Inst. of Automobile Construction 1976–85; leading researcher Inst. of Econ. and Political Studies Acad. of Sciences 1985–88; Head Cen. for Studies of Social-Political Problems and Interstate Relations of C.I.S. 1992–93; mem. Pres's Council 1993–; chief expert Cttee. on C.I.S. countries of State Duma 1993–96; Prof. Moscow State Inst. of Int. Relations 1994–. *Address:* State Duma, Okhotny Ryad 1, Moscow, Russia.

MÍGUEZ-BONINO, Rev. José, PH.D.; Argentinian professor of theology, clergyman and international church official; b. 5 March 1924, Santa Fé; s. of José Míguez Gándara and Augustina Bonino; m. Noemi Nieuwenhuize 1947; ed. Facultad Evangélica de Teología, Emory Univ., Union Theological Seminary, New York; Methodist minister in Bolivia, later in Argentina 1945–; Prof. of Theology, Facultad Evangélica de Teología, Buenos Aires 1954–70, Rector 1960–70; Prof. of Systematic Theology and Ethics, Protestant Inst. for Higher Theological Studies, Buenos Aires 1970–, Dean of Post-Graduate Studies 1973–; mem. Cen. Cttee. of World Council of Churches (WCC) 1968–75, a Pres. Presidium of WCC 1976–82; Visiting Prof., Facoltà Valdese di Teologia, Rome 1963, Union Theological Seminary, New York 1967–68, Selly Oak Coll., Birmingham, U.K. 1974, Faculté de Théologie Protestante, Strasbourg Univ. 1981; Observer at II Vatican Council 1962–64; Pres. Perm. Ass. for Human Rights (APDH), Argentina; mem. Nat. Constitutional Ass. 1994–, Nuremberg Human Rights Award Jury 1995–(99); Hon. Ph.D. (Candler School of Theol., Free Univ. of Amsterdam 1980), Hon. D.D. (Aberdeen) 1987. *Publications:* Concilio abierto 1968, Integración humana y unidad cristiana 1968, Ama y haz lo que quieras 1972, Theology in a Revolutionary Situation (trans. in Dutch, German, Italian) 1975, Espacio para ser hombres 1975, Christians and Marxists 1976, Toward a Christian Political Ethic 1983, Rostros del Protestantismo en América Latina 1996; articles in Concilium, Expository Times, Evangelische Kommentare. *Address:* Camacuá 252, 1406 Buenos Aires, Argentina. *Telephone:* (1) 654-2184. *Fax:* (1) 656-4239.

MIGULIN, Vladimir Vasiliyevich; Russian physicist; b. 10 July 1911, Furmanov, Ivanov Region; s. of Vasiliy Alekseyevich and Polina Migulin; m. 2nd Marianna Nikolayevna Sokolova; two s. one d.; ed. Faculty of Physics and Mechanics of Polytechnical Inst. of Leningrad; Engineer in Research Inst. of Leningrad 1932–34; Sr. Research Fellow, Chief of Div. Physical Inst. of the Acad. of Sciences of U.S.S.R., Moscow, 1934–51; Asst. lecturer 1935–38, lecturer 1939–46, Prof. 1947–54, 1957–, Deputy Dean of the Faculty of Physics 1954–57, Moscow Univ.; Dir. Inst. of Physical Research at Suchumi 1951–54; Deputy Dir.-Gen. Int. Atomic Energy Agency for the Div. of Training and Tech. Information 1957–59; Ed. Moscow Univ. Bulletin, Physics and Astronomy section 1960–69; Chief, Div. of Inst. of Radio-engineering and Electronics, Acad. of Sciences of U.S.S.R. 1962–69; Dir. Inst. of Terrestrial Magnetism, the Ionosphere and Radio Wave Propagation (IZMIRAN), Acad. of Sciences of U.S.S.R. 1969–89, Adviser 1989–; Vice-Pres. URSI 1972–78, Chair. Soviet (now Russian) Nat. Cttee. URSI 1960–97; mem. Popov Soc. on Radio Tech. and Electrocommunications 1947–80, Hon. mem. 1980–, Chair. History Comm. 1986–; mem. European Physics Soc. 1989–, Int. Acad. of Astronautics 1990–; Corresp. mem. U.S.S.R. (now Russian) Acad. of Sciences 1970–92, mem. 1992–; Chair. Scientific Council on Solar-Terrestrial Physics 1986–; U.S.S.R. State prize for scientific works 1946, 1953; Order of Lenin (twice); several Orders of the Soviet Union and French-Soviet and U.S.-Soviet medals. *Publications:* four books, more than 150 papers and articles in scientific journals on investigations of electrical oscillations in non-linear and parametric systems, investigations of the propagation of radio waves by interference methods, investigations of new methods of receiving of mm and sub-mm e-m waves, ionospheric radio wave propagation, problems of modification of the ionosphere, and solar-terrestrial physics. *Leisure interests:* skiing, tourism, music. *Address:* IZMIRAN, v. Troitsk Moscow Region, 142092, Russia. *Telephone:* (095) 334-09-10 (Office); 242-10-44 (Home). *Fax:* (095) 334-01-24.

MIHAJLOV, Mihajlo; Serbian author, scholar and human rights administrator; b. 26 Sept. 1934, Pančevo; s. of Nicholas Mihajlov and Vera Daniloff; ed. High School, Sarajevo, and Zagreb Univ.; served armed forces 1961–62; freelance writer and translator, magazines, newspapers and radio 1962–63; Asst. Prof. of Modern Russian Literature, Zagreb Univ. 1963–65; freelance writer, western press 1965–66, 1970–74; imprisoned 1966–70, 1974–77; lectures, U.S.A., Europe and Asia 1978–79; Visiting Lecturer, Yale Univ. 1981; Visiting Prof. of Russian Literature and Philosophy, Univ. of Va. 1982–83; Visiting Prof. Ohio State Univ. 1983–84, Univ. of Siegen 1984, Univ. of Glasgow 1985; Commentator on Ideological Matters, Radio Free Europe/Radio Liberty Inc. 1986; Sr. Fellow, Program on Transitions to Democracy, Elliott School of Int. Affairs, George Washington Univ. 1994–; Vice-Pres. Democracy Int.; Chair. Democracy Int. Comm. to Aid Democratic Dissidents in Yugoslavia 1990; mem. Editorial Bd. int. magazine Kontinent 1975–84, Tribuna Magazine, Paris and Forum Magazine, Munich, Contrib. Ed. Religion in Communist Dominated Areas, New York; mem. Int. PEN (French branch 1977, American 1982); Fellow, Nat. Humanities Cen.; mem. Int. Helsinki Group, Cttee. for the Free World; mem. Bd. Int. Gesselschaft für Menschenrechte 1982–, Bd. of Consultants, Centre for Appeals for Freedom 1980, Nat. Cttee. of Social Democrats U.S.A. 1989, Advisory Bd. CAUSA Int. 1986; Trustee, World Constitution and Parl. Asscn. 1982–; Special Analyst for Intellectual and Ideological Events in the Soviet Union and Eastern Europe, Research Div. of Radio Free Europe 1985–86; Int. League for Human Rights Award 1978; Council against Communist Aggression Award 1975, 1978; Ford Foundation Award for the Humanities 1980. *Publications:* Moscow Summer 1965, Russian Themes 1968, Underground Notes 1976, 1982, Unscientific Thoughts 1979, Planetary Consciousness 1982, Djilas versus Marx 1990, Homeland is Freedom 1994, and hundreds of articles in newspapers, magazines and scholarly books (weekly column in Belgrade daily "Borba" (renamed "Nasa Borba" 1995) 1990–). *Leisure interests:* classical music, motoring. *Address:* 1613 Fifth Street, N.W., Washington, DC 20001, U.S.A. (Home). *Telephone:* (202) 232-5161 (Home). *Fax:* (202) 462-4816 (Home).

MIHÁLIK, Vojtech; Slovak poet; b. 30 March 1926, Dolná Streda; m.; three c.; ed. Comenius Univ., Bratislava; Slovak Writers' Publishing House, Bratislava 1949–51; mem. editorial staff Československý voják 1952–54; Sec. Union of Slovak Writers 1954–60; Ed.-in-Chief, Slovak Writers' Publishing House 1960–64; Slovak Centre of Publishing and Book Trade 1964; Deputy to Slovak Nat. Council 1964–, mem. Presidium 1968–69; First Sec. Union of Slovak Writers 1965–67, Chair. 1969–, mem. Presidium 1975–; mem. Cen. Cttee. of CP of Slovakia 1966–68, 1969–71, alt. mem. 1971–76, mem. 1976–81; mem. Presidium Fed. Ass. 1969–71, Deputy Chair. of Fed. Ass. and Chair. of House of Nations 1969–71, Deputy to House of Nations 1971–76; mem. Communità Europea degli Scrittori (COMES) 1962–; Chair. Cttee. for Educ. and Culture, Slovak Nat. Council 1969–70; Chair. Cultural Cttee., House of Nations, Fed. Ass. 1971–76; Dir. Slovensky Spisovatel (Slovak Writer) Publishing House 1977–84; Artist of Merit 1966, Order of Labour 1976, Nat. Artist 1978, Medal of World Peace Council 1980. *Publications:* Sixteen vols. of poetry including: The Plebeian Shirt 1950, The Singing Heart 1952 (State Prize), Archimedes Circles 1960, The Rebel Job 1960 (Prize of Czechoslovak Union of Writers 1961), Appassionata 1965 (Prize of the Slovak Writers' Publishing House), Black Autumn 1970, The Thirteenth Room 1976; Man against Blindness 1974 (critical essays), Sympathy (collection of poems) 1984, We Will Return Alive 1987, The Reverend of Madunice 1990; translations of Greek, Latin, Polish, French, Spanish and American poetry. *Address:* Bratislava, Hollého 15, Slovakia.

MIHOV, Col. Gen. Miho, M.A.; Bulgarian army officer; b. 1 Feb. 1949, Sennik; s. of Dimitar Mihov and Stanka Mihov; m. 1973; one s. one d.; ed. Benkovski Air Force Acad., Dolna Mitropolia, Rakovski Nat. War Coll., Sofia, Gen. Staff Coll., Moscow; Air Squadron Second-in-Command, Commdr., Air Regt. Second-in-Command, Commdr., Corps Second-in-Command, Air Defence Div. Commdr. Air Force C.-in-C., Chief of Gen. Staff Bulgarian Armed Forces 1997–; Gold Medal, Gen. Staff Coll., Medal for Services to Bulgarian Army; Order of Merit and Valour. *Leisure interests:* hunting, skiing. *Address:* General Staff, 3 V. Levski Street, Sofia, Bulgaria. *Telephone:* (02) 52 29 52. *Fax:* (02) 87 32 26.

MIKAZUKI, Akira; Japanese politician, lawyer and academic; lawyer; fmr. Dean, Faculty of Law, Tokyo Univ., Prof. Emer.; Minister of Justice 1993–94. *Address:* House of Representatives, Tokyo, Japan.

MIKHAILOV, Nikolai Vasilyevich, DR. ECON.; Russian politician; b. 14 May 1937, Sevsk, Bryansk Region; ed. Moscow Bauman Higher School of Tech.; with defence industry enterprises 1961–96; Head, Vympel Co. 1986–96; Deputy Sec. Security Council of Russian Fed. 1996–97; State Sec., First Deputy Minister of Defence of Russian Fed. 1997–; Co-Chair., Russian-American Comm. on Econ. and Tech. Co-operation 1998–; U.S.S.R. State Prize, State Prize of Russian Fed. 1997. *Address:* Ministry of Defence, Myasnitskaya str. 37, 103160 Moscow, Russia. *Telephone:* (095) 296 8900 (Office).

MIKHAILOV, Viktor Nikitovich, DR. TECH. SC.; Russian politician; b. 12 Feb. 1934, Moscow; m.; one s.; ed. Moscow Inst. of Physics and Eng.; on staff All-Union Research Inst., Arsamas; worked with group of nuclear bomb constructors; Deputy, First Deputy Minister of Machine Construction of U.S.S.R. (later U.S.S.R. Ministry of Atomic Energy) 1988–1992; Minister of Atomic Energy Russian Fed. 1992; mem. Security Council of Russia; mem. Russian Acad. of Sciences 1997; Lenin's Prize, U.S.S.R. State Prize. *Address:* Ministry of Atomic Energy, B. Ordynka str. 24/26, 101000 Moscow, Russia (Office). *Telephone:* (095) 233 4908, 233 3751 (Office).

MIKHAILOV, Vyacheslav Aleksandrovich, DR. HIST.; Russian politician; b. 13 April. 1938, Dubovka, Volgograd Region; m., two d.; ed. Lvov State Univ.; teacher, secondary school, lecturer, Lvov State Univ.; Head of sector, Inst. of Marxism–Leninism at CPSU Cen. Cttee. 1987–90; Head, Div. of Nat. Policy, CPSU Cen. Cttee. 1990–91; scientific consultant, I and World (magazine), Head, Centre on Int. Problems and Protection of Human Rights 1991–93; Deputy Chair. State Cttee. on Problems of Fed. and Nationality 1993–95; First Deputy Minister on Problems of Nationality and Regional Policy Jan.–July 1995, Minister 1995–98, First Deputy Sec. Security Council June 1998–; Prof. Moscow Inst. of Int. Relations. *Publications:* 3 monographs on nat. problems, numerous articles. *Address:* Security Council, Ipatyevsky per. 4/10, entr. 6, Moscow, Russia. *Telephone:* (095) 206 4326 (Office).

MIKHALCHENKO, Alla Anatolyevna; Russian ballerina; b. 3 July 1957, Moscow; d. of Anatoly Alexandrovich Dmitryev and Irina Antonovna Mikhalchenko; ed. Moscow Choreographic School; dancer with Bolshoi 1976–; First Prize, All-Soviet Competition 1976, First Prize and Distinction, Varna Ballet Competition 1976; First Prize, Moscow Int. Ballet Competition 1977, People's Artist of Russia; roles include Odette-Odile (Swan Lake), Kitri (Don Quixote), Nina (The Seagull), Giselle, Anastasia (Ivan the Terrible), Rita (Golden Age), Shirin (Legend of Love), Serene (Prodigal Son). *Address:* Malaya Gruzinskaya Street, 12/18, Moscow 123242, Russia. *Telephone:* 252 2609 (Home). *Fax:* 292 9032.

MIKHALKOV, Nikita Sergeyevich; Russian film director; b. 21 Oct. 1945, Moscow; s. of Mikhalkov Sergey Vladimirovitch and Konchalovskaya Natalia Petrovna; m. 1st Anastasya Vertinskaya 1966; m. 2nd Tatyana Mikhalkova 1973; two s. two d.; ed. Shchukin Theatre School, State Film Inst. under Mikhail Romm; R.S.F.S.R. People's Artist 1984; mem. Duma 1995–; First Sec. Russian Union of Cinematographers 1997–98, Chair. 1998–; first worked as actor in films: Strolling around Moscow, A Nest of Gentlefolk, The Red Tent; *films directed:* A Quiet Day at the End of the War, At Home Among Strangers, A Stranger at Home 1975, The Slave of Love 1976, An Unfinished Piece for Mechanical Piano 1977, Five Evenings 1978, Several Days in the Life of I. I. Oblomov 1979, Kinsfolk 1982, Without Witnesses 1983, Dark Eyes 1987, The Barber of Siberia; play: An Unfinished Piece for Mechanical Piano, Rome 1987, Urga 1990 (Prize at Venice Biennale 1991), Felix Prize for Best European Film 1993, Nika Prize 1993, Anna from 6 to 18 1994, Burned by the Sun 1994 (Acad. Award for Best Foreign Film and several other awards), Barber of Siberia 1998. *Leisure interests:* sport, hunting. *Address:* Maly Kozikhinsky per. 4, Apt. 16–17, 103001 Moscow, Russia.

MIKHALKOV, Sergey Vladimirovich; Russian playwright, poet, and children's writer; b. 12 March 1913, Moscow; ed. Literary Inst. Moscow; began writing 1928, verses for children 1935; joint author (with El-Registan) Soviet Anthem 1943; mem. CPSU 1950–91; Chief Ed. Fitil 1962–; First Sec. Moscow Branch, R.S.F.S.R. Union of Writers 1965–70, Chair. of Union 1970–91; Deputy to Supreme Soviet of R.S.F.S.R. 1967–70, to U.S.S.R. Supreme Soviet 1970–89; mem. Comm. for Youth Affairs, Soviet of Nationalities; fmr. Corresp. mem. Acad. of Pedagogical Sciences 1970; numerous awards. *Publications:* Dyadya Styopa (Uncle Steve) 1936 and Collected Works (poems, stories, plays) in two vols.; *Film script:* Frontovye podrugi

(Frontline Friends) 1941; *Plays:* Tom Kenti (after Mark Twain) 1938, Krasnyi galstuk (Red Neckerchief), Selected Works 1947, Ilya Golovin, Ya khochu domoi (I Want to Go Home) 1949, Raki (Lobsters) 1952, Zaika-Zaznaika 1955, Sombrero 1958, Pamyatnik Sebe (A Monument to Oneself) 1958, Dikari (Campers) 1959, Collected Works (4 Vols.) 1964, Green Grasshopper 1964, We are Together, My Friend and I 1967, In the Museum of Lenin 1968, Fables 1970, Disobedience Day 1971, The Funny Bone (articles) 1971, Collected Works (3 vols.) 1970–71, Selected Works 1973, Slap in the Face 1974, Bibliographical Index 1975, The Scum 1975, The Lodger 1977, Echo 1980, Almighty Kings 1983, Fables 1987, A Choice for Children (English trans.) 1988. *Address:* Tchaikovskogo str. 28/35, Apt. 67, 121069 Moscow, Russia. *Telephone:* 291-78-15.

MIKHALKOV-KONCHALOVSKY, Andrey Sergeyevich; Russian film director and script-writer; b. 20 Aug. 1937, Moscow; s. of Sergey Mikhalkov and Natalia Konchalovskaya; m. 1st Natalia Arinbasarova 1946; m. 2nd Irina Ivanova 1960; one s. two d.; ed. U.S.S.R. State Inst. of Cinema, Moscow 1961–65; R.S.F.S.R. People's Artist 1980. *Films include:* Roller and Violin (with A. Tarkovsky) 1959, The First Teacher 1965, The Story of Asya Klyachina, who Loved but Did Not Marry 1966, A Nest of Gentlefolk 1969, Uncle Vanya 1971, Romance of Lovers 1974, Siberiada 1979, Maria's Lovers 1984, Runaway Train 1985, Duet for One 1986, Shy People 1987, Homer and Eddie 1988, Tango and Cash 1989, The Inner Circle 1991, Ryaba—My Chicken 1994, Odissea 1997; script-writer (with Tarkovsky) Andrei Rublev 1969; also opera dir. and theatre dir. (productions at La Scala, Bastille). *Address:* Mosfilmovskaya str. 1, Russkaya Ruletka, 119858 Moscow (Studio); Malaya Gruzinskaya 28, Apt. 130, 123557 Russia (Home). *Telephone:* (095) 143-9309 (Studio); 253-5021 (Home). *Fax:* (095) 143-9189.

MIKHEEV, Vladimir Andreyevich, DR. PHYS. SC.; Ukrainian physicist; b. 5 Aug. 1942; m. Tatiana Mikheeva 1969; one s. one d.; ed. Kharkov Polytechnic; researcher 1964–86; discovery of quantum diffusion 1972–77; Head. of Lab. of Ultralow Temperatures, Inst. for Low Temperature Physics and Eng., Ukrainian Acad. of Science 1986–; Visiting Prof. Royal Holloway and Bedford New Coll. 1992; Lenin Prize for Science and Tech. *Address:* 88 Barrington Close, Witney, Oxon., OX8 5FL, England.

MIKI, Akira; Japanese business executive; b. 16 Feb. 1921, Fukushima; s. of Takashi Miki and Teruyo Miki; m. Kiyoko Mizutani 1944; two s. one d.; ed. Kyoto Univ.; joined Japan Iron & Steel Co., Ltd.; Dir. Nippon Steel Corpn. 1973, Man. Dir. 1979, Sr. Man. Dir. 1981, Exec. Vice-Pres. 1983, Vice-Chair. 1987, Chair. 1989; Chair. Soc. of Steel Construction of Japan; Vice-Chair. Fed. of Employers' Asscns.; Blue Ribbon Medal. *Leisure interest:* golf. *Address:* 28-7 Sakura-Shinmachi, 1-chome, Setagatu-ku, Tokyo, Japan.

MIKKELSEN, Richard, M.SC. (ECON.); Danish central banker (retd.); b. 27 April 1920, Copenhagen; m. Ester Overgaard 1944 (died 1993); at Banken for Slagelse og Omegn 1937–45; apptd. Asst. Danmarks Nationalbank 1945, Head of Section 1954, Asst. Head Dept. 1961, Head Dept. 1961, Dir. 1966, Asst. Gov. 1971, Gov. 1982–90; Attaché, Danish-OEEC Del., Paris 1955–57; mem. Bd. European Monetary Agreement 1970–72; Industrial Mortgage Fund 1971–81; mem. Bd. Mortgage Credit Council, Supervisor 1972–81; mem. Bd. Export Finance Corpn. 1975–90; mem. Steering Cttee. and Bd. Employees Capital Pension Fund 1980–91, Industrial Mortgage Credit Fund 1981–91, Monetary Cttee. of EEC 1982–90; Nordic Financial Cttee. 1982–90, Econ. Policy Cttee. of OECD 1982–90; Chair. Financing Fund of 1992 1992–96. *Address:* c/o Danmarks Nationalbank, Havnegade 5, 1093 Copenhagen K, Denmark. *Telephone:* 33-63-63-63.

MIKLOŠKO, Jozef, D.SC.; Slovak politician, mathematician and educationist; b. 31 March 1939, Nitra; s. of Ondrej Mikloško and Marta (née Kutliková) Mikloško; m. Mária Bitterová 1964; two s. two d.; ed. Teacher Training Coll., Komenský Univ., Bratislava; teacher, Nové Zámky 1961–62; scientific worker, Inst. of Tech. Cybernetics, Slovak Acad. of Sciences, Bratislava 1963–90; lecturer, Faculty of Mathematics and Physics, Komenský Univ., Bratislava 1969–89; Head. Int. Base Lab. for Artificial Intelligence 1985–90; Vice-Chair. Christian-Democratic Movt. 1990; Deputy to Slovak Nat. Council 1990–91; Fed. Deputy Premier for Human Rights in Czechoslovak Fed. Repub. 1990–92; Deputy to House of the People, Fed. Ass. June–Dec. 1992; Adviser to Pres. of Slovakia 1993–95; Head DACO publishing house 1995–; Sec. Justice and Peace Comm. 1995–; lecturer and Vice-Pres. Trnava Univ. 1996–; Chair. Solidarity Foundation 1993–, Schiller Foundation for Protection of Life and Human Rights 1995–; mem. World Ecological Acad., Moscow 1994–, Int. Informatization Acad., Moscow 1995–, Slovak Asscn. of Writers 1995–, Slovak Asscn. of Journalists 1997–; Deputy to Town Council, Bratislava V 1994–. *Publications:* 7 books and 100 scientific articles. *Leisure interests:* literature, music, sport. *Address:* Žabotova 2, 81104 Bratislava (Office); Trnava University, Hornopotočná 23, 91843 Trnava, Slovakia. *Telephone:* (7) 397995 (Bratislava); (805) 511438 (Trnava). *Fax:* (7) 397995 (Bratislava); (805) 511129 (Trnava).

MIKÓ, András; Hungarian opera producer; b. 30 June 1922, Budapest; m. Éva Rehák; studied music and designing; started at State Opera Budapest; Chief Producer Budapest Operetta Theatre 1951–52; chief producer Budapest Opera House 1962–87; Prof. of Operatic Stage Acting, Acad. of Music, Budapest 1950–; produced operas on open-air stage Margaret Island, Budapest and Summer Festival plays in Szeged, Covent Garden of London, Bolshoi Theatre of Moscow, Teatro Colón of Buenos Aires, Teatro Liceo of Barcelona, Teatro Zarzuela of Madrid, Festival Savonlinna of Finland, Copenhagen, Turin, Rome, Brussels, Cologne, Helsinki, Berlin and others; Liszt Prize 1961, title of Merited Artist 1967, Eminent Artist 1987, Kossuth Prize 1975. *Address:* Hungarian State Opera, Andrássy ut 22, Budapest VI (Office); Uri utca 44/46, Budapest I, Hungary (Home). *Telephone:* 331-2550 (Office), 156-0382 (Home).

MIKULSKI, Barbara Ann, B.A.; American politician; b. 20 July 1936, Baltimore; d. of William Mikulski and Christina Eleanor Kutz; ed. Mount St. Agnes Coll. and Maryland Univ.; Baltimore Dept. Social Services 1961–63, 1966–70; York Family Agency 1964; VISTA Teaching Center 1965–70; Teacher, Mount St. Agnes Coll. 1969; Teacher, Community Coll., Baltimore 1970–71; Democratic Nominee to U.S. Senate 1974, to House of Reps. 1976; mem. 96th–99th Congresses from 3rd Md. Dist.; Senator from Maryland Jan. 1987–, first woman Democrat elected to U.S. Senate in her own right; Hon. LL.D. (Goucher Coll.) 1973, (Hood Coll.) 1978; mem. Democratic Nat. Strategy Council; mem. Nat. Bd. of Dirs. Urban Coalition; mem. Nat. Asscn. of Social Workers; Democrat. *Address:* U.S. Senate, 709 Hart Office Building, Washington, DC 20510, U.S.A.

MILBURN, Alan, B.A.; British politician; b. 27 Jan. 1958; partner Ruth Briel; one s.; ed. Stokesley Comprehensive School, Lancaster Univ.; co-ordinator Trade Union Studies Information Unit, Newcastle 1984–90; sr. business devt. officer N. Tyneside Municipal Borough Council 1990–92; M.P. for Darlington 1992–; Opposition Front Bench Spokesman on Health 1995–96, on Treasury and Econ. Affairs 1996–97; Minister of State, Dept. of Health 1997–98; Chief Sec. to Treasury 1998–; Chair. Parl. Labour Party Treasury Cttee. 1992–95; mem. Public Accounts Cttee. 1994–95. *Address:* House of Commons, London, SW1A 0AA, England.

MILCHAN, Arnon; American film producer; b. 6 Dec. 1944; has worked in television and theatre as well as film. *Plays produced:* Tomb, It's So Nice to be Civilized, Amadeus (Paris production). *Television:* Masada 1981. *Films:* The Medusa Touch 1978, The King of Comedy 1983, Once Upon a Time in America 1984, Brazil 1985, Stripper 1986, Legend 1986, Man on Fire 1987, The Adventures of Baron Munchausen 1989, Who's Harry Crumb 1989, The War of the Roses 1989, Big Man on Campus 1990, Pretty Woman 1990, Q&A 1990, Guilty by Suspicion 1991, JFK 1991, The Mambo Kings 1992, Memoirs of an Invisible Man 1992, The Power of One 1992, Under Siege 1992, Sommersby 1993, Falling Down 1993, Made in America 1993, Free Willy 1993, The Nutcracker 1993, That Night 1993, Heaven and Earth 1993, The New Age 1993, Striking Distance 1993, Six Degrees of Separation 1993, Second Best 1994, Boys on the Side 1994, The Client 1994, Bogus 1995, A Time to Kill 1996, The Mirror Has Two Faces 1996, Tin Cup 1996. *Address:* Regency Enterprises, 4000 Warner Boulevard, Bldg. 66, Burbank, CA 91522, U.S.A.

MILCZANOWSKI, Andrzej Stanisław; Polish politician and lawyer; b. 26 May 1939, Równe; m. Sławomira Ołtarzewska; one d.; ed. Adam Mickiewicz Univ., Poznań; apprentice, subsequently assesor and subprosecutor in Public Prosecutor's Dist. Office, Szczecin 1962–68; legal adviser to various enterprises, mainly to enterprises of mun. economy, Szczecin 1968–80; mem. Solidarity Independent and Self-governing Trade Union 1980–, mem. Co-ordinating Council of Solidarity Co-ordinate Comm., Solidarity Nat. Exec. Comm., Presidium Nat. Exec. Comm. 1989–; arrested and sentenced to 5 years' imprisonment for organizing strike during martial law, released under amnesty after serving 2 years and 4 months April 1984; casual job 1981–88; legal adviser to Optimum Co. Ltd., Szczecin 1989–90; mem. Interfactory Strike Cttee. of Western Pomerania Regional Br. of Solidarity Trade Union, Szczecin Aug. 1988; participant Round Table debates 1989; Deputy Chief Office for State Protection 1990, subsequently Chief of Office 1990–92; Sec. of State in Ministry of Internal Affairs June–July 1992, Minister of Internal Affairs 1992–95; Freedom Award of Paul Lauritzen Foundation (Denmark) 1988. *Leisure interests:* cross-country races, philosophy, poetry, music, prognosis of socio-political changes.

MILEDI, Ricardo, M.D., F.R.S., F.A.A.A.S., M.R.I.; Mexican professor of biophysics; b. 15 Sept. 1927, Mexico D.F.; m. Ana Mela Garces 1955; one s.; ed. Universidad Nacional Autónoma de Mexico; Research Fellow, Instituto Nacional de Cardiología, Mexico 1954–56; Visiting Fellow, John Curtin School of Medical Research, Canberra, Australia 1956–58; Hon. Research Assoc., Dept. of Biophysics, Univ. Coll. London 1958–59, Lecturer 1959–62, Reader 1962–65, Prof. of Biophysics 1965–75, Foulerton Research Prof. of the Royal Soc. 1975–85, Foulerton Research Prof. and Head of Dept. of Biophysics 1978–85; Distinguished Prof., Dept. of Psychobiology, School of Biological Sciences, Univ. of Calif., Irvine 1984–; Fellow, Third World Acad. of Sciences, American Acad. of Arts and Sciences, A.A.A.S.; Hon. mem. Hungarian Acad. of Sciences; mem. N.A.S. 1989, European Acad. of Arts, Sciences and Humanities 1995, Mexican Acad. of Medicine 1995, Mexican Acad. of Sciences 1995; Dr. h.c. (Univ. del País Vasco, Leioa, Spain) 1992; King Faisal Foundation Int. Prize for Science. *Publications:* numerous published papers. *Address:* Department of Psychobiology, University of California, 2205 Bio Sci II, Irvine, CA 92697-4550, U.S.A. *Telephone:* (714) 824-5693. *Fax:* (714) 824-3522.

MILEIKOWSKY, Curt, DR.TECH.; Swedish business executive; b. 1 May 1923, Stockholm; s. of Gregor Mileikowsky and Margit Wallis; m. Ulla B. Varenius 1947; two s.; ed. Royal Inst. of Tech.; Research engineer, ASEA, Ludvika 1946; Research Asst. to Prof. Lise Meitner 1946–47, Nobel Inst. of Physics 1948–54, ASEA, Västerås 1954; Man. Nuclear Power Dept., ASEA

1958, Exec. Vice-Pres. for Sales 1962; Pres. SAAB, Linköping 1968–78, SAAB-SCANIA, Linköping 1969–78; Chair. Bd. Swedish Export Credit Corpn. *Publications:* Scientific and tech. publs. in Sweden and U.S.A. *Address:* Måsvaegen 8C, S-183 51 Taeby, Sweden (Home).

MILES, John Arthur Reginald, C.B.E., M.A., M.D., F.R.A.C.P., F.R.S.N.Z.; New Zealand microbiologist and epidemiologist; b. 13 May 1913, Sidcup, Kent, England; s. of Albert E. Miles and Mary Watson; m. 1st Ruth H. French 1951 (died 1980); m. 2nd Violet C. Miller 1985; two d.; ed. Monkton Combe School, Bath, Gonville & Caius Coll. Cambridge and St. Thomas's Hosp., London; Capt. Royal Army Medical Corps. 1942–46; Huddersfield Lecturer in Special Pathology, Cambridge 1946–50; Medical Research Fellow, Inst. of Medical and Veterinary Science, Adelaide 1951–55; Prof. of Microbiology Univ. of Otago 1955–79, Prof. Emer. 1979–; Pres. Royal Soc. of N.Z. 1966–70; Hon. Dir. N.Z. MRC Virus Research Unit 1960–79; mem. M.R.C. of N.Z. 1966–72; mem. N.Z. Health Dept. Epidemiology Advisory Cttee. 1961–79; mem. N.Z. Nat. Comm. for UNESCO 1972–76; Pres. Pacific Science Asscn. 1979–83; many other professional appts.; Hon. Life Fellow, Pacific Science Asscn.; N.Z. Asscn. of Scientists Service to Science Award 1972, K. F. Meyer Award, American Soc. of Veterinary Epidemiologists 1983. *Publication:* Infectious Diseases Colonising the Pacific 1996. *Leisure interests:* ornithology, fishing, gardening. *Address:* P.O. Box 17, Capell Avenue, Lake Hawea, Otago 9192, New Zealand. *Telephone:* (03) 443-1695.

MILES, Roy Brian Edward; British art dealer; b. 9 Feb. 1935, Liverpool; s. of Edward Marsh and Elsa McKinley; m. Christine Rhodes 1970; ed. Sorbonne, Paris; Dir. and sole owner, Roy Miles Gallery (largest pvt. gallery in London); major dealer in British and Russian art. *Publications:* articles in magazines, newspapers and journals. *Leisure interest:* classical music.

MILES, Sarah; British actress; b. 31 Dec. 1941; m. Robert Bolt 1967 (divorced 1976), remarried 1988 (died 1995); ed. Royal Acad. of Dramatic Art, London; first film appearance in Term of Trial 1962; with Nat. Theatre Co. 1964–65; Shakespeare stage season 1982–83. *Films include:* Those Magnificent Men in Their Flying Machines 1964, I Was Happy Here 1966, The Blow-Up 1966, Ryan's Daughter 1970, Lady Caroline Lamb 1972, The Hireling 1973, The Man Who Loved Cat Dancing 1973, Great Expectations 1975, Pepita Jiminez 1975, The Sailor Who Fell From Grace With the Sea 1976, The Big Sleep 1978, Venom 1981, Hope and Glory 1987, White Mischief 1988, The Silent Touch; *theatre appearances include:* Vivat! Vivat Regina!, Asylum 1988; *television appearances:* James Michener's Dynasty, Great Expectations, Harem, Queenie, A Ghost in Monte Carlo, Dandelion Dead, Ring Around the Moon, The Rehearsal. *Publications:* Charlemagne (play) 1992, A Right Royal Bastard (memoirs) 1993, Serves me Right (memoirs) 1994, Bolt from the Blue (memoirs) 1996.

MILI, Mohamed Ezzedine; Tunisian international official and telecommunications engineer; b. 4 Dec. 1917, Djemmal; m. Mlle. Zouhir 1950; three s. two d.; ed. Teacher's Training Coll., Tunis, Ecole Normale Supérieure, Paris, Sorbonne and Ecole Nat. Supérieure des Télécommunications, Paris; joined Posts, Telegraphs and Communications (P.T.T.) Admin. 1948; Chief Engineer and Dir.-Gen. of Telecommunications, Ministry of P.T.T. 1957; Tunisian del. to ITU confs. 1956–, mem. ITU Admin. Council 1960–65, Chair. of 19th session 1964; Deputy Sec.-Gen. ITU 1965–67, Sec.-Gen. 1967–82; Sr. mem. I.E.E.E.; Officer, Order of Independence of Tunisia, Commdr. Order of the Tunisian Repub., Commdr. Swedish Order of Vasa, Grand Cross Order of Duarte, Sánchez y Mella with Silver star (Dominican Repub.), Honour Merit Medal (Paraguay), Grand Star of Order of Merit of Telecommunications (Spain), Commdr. of the Order of Leopold (Belgium), Officier, Légion d'honneur, Philip Reis Medal (Fed. Repub. of Germany), Diploma of Honour (Int. Council of Archives) 1978, I.E.E.E. Award for Public Service in the Field of Telecommunications 1984. *Leisure interests:* reading scientific publications, youth movements. *Address:* 5 route de Mon Idée, 1226 Thônex, Geneva, Switzerland (Home). *Telephone:* 022-348-79-19.

MILINGO, Most Rev. Archbishop Emmanuel, DIP.ED.; Zambian ecclesiastic; b. 13 June 1930; s. of Yakobe Milingo and Tomaida Lumbiwe; ed. St. Mary's Presbyteral School, Fort Jameson and Kasina Jr. Seminary and Kachebere Major Seminary, Nyasaland (now Malawi); Curate, Minga Mission 1958–61; studied Pastoral Sociology (Diploma), Rome 1961–62; Univ. Coll. Dublin, Ireland (Dip. Ed.) 1962–63; Parish Priest, St. Ann's Mission, Chipata 1963–66; Sec. for Mass Media, Zambia Episcopal Conf. 1966–69; Archbishop of Lusaka 1969–83, Archbishop Emer. 1983–; Special Del. to Pontifical Comm. for Pastoral Care of Migrants, Refugees and Pilgrims 1983–. *Publications:* Amake Joni, Demarcations, The World in Between, The Flower Garden of Jesus the Redeemer, My Prayers are not heard, Precautions in the Ministry of Deliverance, Against Satan. *Leisure interests:* writing and preaching to make Jesus Christ known and loved. *Address:* Pontificio Consiglio della Pastorale per i Migranti e gli Itineranti, Piazza S. Calisto 16, 00153 Rome, Italy.

MILIUS, John Frederick; American film writer and director; b. 11 April 1944, St. Louis; s. of William Styx Milius and Elizabeth (née Roe) Milius; m. 1st Renée Fabri 1967; two s.; m. 2nd Celia K. Burkholder 1978; ed. Univ. of Southern Calif.; wrote screenplays: The Devil's 8 1969, Evel Knievel 1971, Jeremiah Johnson 1972, The Life and Times of Judge Roy Bean 1973, Magnum Force 1973, Purvis FBI (for TV) 1974, Apocalypse Now 1979 (Acad. Award for Best Screenplay 1980), 1941 (with Francis Ford Coppola, q.v.) 1979, Geronimo: An American Legend (co-writer), Clear and Present Danger (co-writer), wrote and directed: Dillinger 1973, The Wind and the Lion 1975, Big Wednesday 1978, Conan the Barbarian 1981, Red Dawn 1984, Farewell to the King 1989, Navy Seals 1990, Flight of the Intruder 1991, The Texas Rangers 1994. *Address:* c/o International Creative Management, 8942 Wilshire Boulevard, Beverly Hills, CA 90211, U.S.A.

MILLAN, Rt. Hon. Bruce, P.C.; British politician; b. 5 Oct. 1927; s. of David Millan; m. Gwendoline Fairey 1953; one s. one d.; ed. Harris Acad., Dundee; worked as Chartered Accountant 1950–59; M.P. for Craigton Div. of Glasgow 1959–83, for Govan div. of Glasgow 1983–88; EEC (now EU) Commr. for Regional Policy 1989–95; Parl. Under-Sec. of State for Defence (R.A.F.) 1964–66, for Scotland 1966–70; Minister of State, Scottish Office 1974–76, Sec. of State for Scotland 1976–79; Opposition Spokesman for Scotland 1979–83; Hon. F.R.S.E. 1995; Hon. LL.D. (Dundee) 1989, (Abertay Dundee) 1994, (Glasgow) 1995, Hon. Fellow (Paisley) 1991, Hon. D.Litt. (Heriot-Watt) 1991, Dr h.c. (Panteios, Athens) 1995, (Sheffield Hallam) 1996; Labour. *Address:* 1 Torridon Avenue, Glasgow, G41 5LA, Scotland (Home). *Telephone:* 0141-427 6483 (Home).

MILLAR, Fergus Graham Burtholme, M.A., D.PHIL., D.LITT., F.B.A., F.S.A.; British academic; b. 5 July 1935, Edinburgh s. of J. S. L. Millar and J. B. Taylor; m. Susanna Friedmann 1959; two s. one d.; ed. Edinburgh Acad., Loretto School, Trinity Coll., Oxford; Fellow, All Souls Coll., Oxford 1958–64; Fellow and Tutor in Ancient History, The Queen's Coll., Oxford 1964–76; Prof. of Ancient History, Univ. Coll., London 1976–84; Camden Prof. of Ancient History, Univ. of Oxford 1984–; Fellow, Brasenose Coll., Oxford 1984–; Pres. Soc. for the Promotion of Roman Studies 1989–92 (Vice-Pres. 1977–89, 1992–); Pres. Classical Asscn. 1992–93; Publications Sec. British Acad. 1997–; Corresp. mem. German Archaeological Inst. 1977, Bavarian Acad. 1987, Finnish Acad. 1989; Hon. D.Phil. (Helsinki) 1994. *Publications:* several historical studies, The Roman Near East 1993. *Address:* Brasenose College, Oxford, OX1 4AJ (Office); 80 Harpes Road, Oxford, OX2 7QL, England (Home). *Telephone:* (01865) 277874 (Office); (01865) 515782 (Home).

MILLAR, Sir Oliver Nicholas, G.C.V.O., F.B.A.; British art historian and administrator; b. 26 April 1923, Standon, Herts.; s. of Gerald and Ruth Millar; m. Delia Mary Dawnay, C.V.O. 1954; one s. three d.; ed. Rugby School and Courtauld Inst. of Art, Univ. of London; Asst. Surveyor of the King's Pictures 1947–49, Deputy Surveyor of the King's (Queen's from 1952) Pictures 1949–72, Surveyor 1972–88, Surveyor Emer. 1988–; Dir. of the Royal Collection 1987–88; Trustee Nat. Portrait Gallery 1972–95; mem. Reviewing Cttee. on Export of Works of Art 1975–87, Exec. Cttee. Nat. Art Collections Fund 1986–98; Trustee Nat. Heritage Memorial Fund 1988–92. *Publications:* English Art 1625–1714 (with M. D. Whinney) 1957, Abraham van der Doort's Catalogue 1960, Tudor, Stuart and Georgian Pictures in the Collection of H.M. The Queen 1963, 1969, Inventories and Valuations of The King's Goods 1972, The Queen's Pictures 1977, Victorian Pictures in the Collection of H.M. The Queen 1992; numerous catalogues including William Dobson 1951, Age of Charles I 1972, Sir Peter Lely 1976, Van Dyck in England 1982 and for The Queen's Gallery. *Leisure interests:* grandchildren, drawing, gardening, cricket, listening to music. *Address:* The Cottage, Rays Lane, Penn, Bucks., England. *Telephone:* (0149 481) 2124.

MILLER, Andrew, C.B.E., M.A., PH.D., F.R.S.E.; British academic; b. 15 Feb. 1936, Kelty, Fife; s. of William Hamilton Miller and Susan Anderson (née Auld) Miller; m. Rosemary Singleton Hannah Fyvie 1962; one s. one d.; ed. Beath High School, Univ. of Edinburgh; Asst. Lecturer in Chem., Univ. of Edinburgh 1960–62; Post-Doctoral Fellow, CSIRO Div. of Protein Chem., Melbourne 1962–65; Staff Scientist MRC Lab. of Molecular Biology, Cambridge 1965–66; Lecturer in Molecular Biophysics, Oxford Univ. 1966–83; First Dir. European Molecular Biology Lab., Grenoble Antenne, France 1975–80; Prof. of Biochem., Edinburgh Univ. 1984–94, Vice-Dean of Medicine 1991–93, Vice-Provost, Medicine and Veterinary Medicine 1992–93, Vice-Prin. 1993–94; Prin. and Vice-Chancellor, Univ. of Stirling 1994–; mem. Science and Eng. Research Council Biological Sciences Cttee. 1982–85; Council mem., Inst. Laue-Langevin, France 1981–85; mem. Univ. Grants Cttee. Biological Sciences Cttee. 1985–88; Dir. of Research, European Synchrotron Radiation Facility, Grenoble 1986–91; Fellow Wolfson Coll., Oxford 1967–83, Hon. Fellow 1995–; mem. Univ. Funding Council-Biological Science Advisory Panel, Medical Advisory Panel 1989; mem. Council, Grenoble Univ. 1990–91, Royal Soc. of Edin. 1997; mem. Minister of Educ.'s Action Group on Standards in Scottish Schools 1997–. *Publications:* Minerals in Biology (Co-Ed.) 1984; 160 research papers. *Leisure interests:* reading, walking, music. *Address:* Principal's Office, University of Stirling, Stirling, FK9 4LA, Scotland.

MILLER, Arjay, B.S.; American business executive; b. 4 March 1916, Shelby, Neb.; s. of Rawley John Miller and Mary Gertrude Schade; m. Frances M. Fearing 1940; one s. one d.; ed. Univ. of California; Teaching Asst. Univ. of Calif. Berkeley 1937–40; Research Technician, Calif. State Planning Bd. 1941; Economist, Fed. Reserve Bank of San Francisco 1941–43; U.S.A.F. 1943–46; Asst. Treas. Ford Motor Co. 1947–53, Controller 1953–57, Vice-Pres. and Controller 1957–61, Vice-Pres. (Finance) 1961–62, Vice-Pres. (Staff-Group) 1962–63, Dir. 1962–, Pres. 1963–68, Vice-Chair. 1968–69; Dean Graduate School of Business, Stanford Univ. 1969–79, Dean Emer. 1979–; Chair. Public Policy Inst. of Calif. 1997–; Trustee of several insts. and mem. of various cttees.; Hon. D.Jur. (Calif., Nebraska, Washington (St. Louis) Univs., Whitman Coll., Ripon Coll.). *Publication:* An Economic and

Industrial Survey of the Los Angeles and San Diego Areas (with Arthur G. Coons) 1941. *Leisure interests:* archaeology, hunting, forestry. *Address:* 225 Mountain Home Road, Woodside, CA 94062, U.S.A.

MILLER, Arthur, A.B.; American playwright; b. 17 Oct. 1915, New York; s. of Isidore and Augusta (Barnett) Miller; m. 1st Mary Grace Slattery 1940 (divorced 1956); one s. one d.; m. 2nd Marilyn Monroe 1956 (divorced 1961); m. 3rd Ingeborg Morath 1962; one s. one d.; ed. Univ. of Michigan; received Hopwood Award for play-writing, Univ. of Mich. 1936 and 1937, Theatre Guild Nat. Award 1938, New York Drama Critics Circle Award 1947 and 1949, Pulitzer Prize for Drama 1949, Antoinette Perry Award 1953, American Acad. of Arts and Letters Gold Medal for Drama 1959, Anglo-American Award 1966, Creative Arts Award, Brandeis Univ. 1970, Kennedy Centre Award 1984, Nat. Medal of Arts 1993, Olivier Award 1995; Prof. of Contemporary Theatre, Univ. of Oxford 1995–; Hon. D.Litt. (Univ. of E. Anglia) 1984, (Oxford) 1995, (Harvard) 1997; Pres. Int. PEN Clubs Org. 1965–69; Fellow St. Catherine's Coll., Oxford. *Publications:* The Man Who Had All the Luck 1943, Situation Normal 1944, Focus 1945, All My Sons 1947, Death of a Salesman 1949, The Crucible 1953, A View From The Bridge 1955, A Memory of Two Mondays 1955, Collected Plays 1958, The Misfits (screenplay) 1959, After the Fall 1964, Incident at Vichy 1964, I Don't Need You Any More (short stories) 1967, The Price (play) 1968, In Russia (with Inge Morath) 1969, The Creation of the World and Other Business (play) 1972, Up From Paradise 1974, Chinese Encounters 1979, The American Clock 1980, Playing for Time (play) 1981, Elegy for a Lady (play) 1983, Some Kind of Love Story (play) 1983, Salesman in Beijing (journal) 1984, Two Way Mirror 1985, Danger: Memory! (plays) 1986, The Archbishop's Ceiling 1986, Timebends: A Life (autobiog.) 1987, Everybody Wins (screenplay) 1989, The Ride Down Mt. Morgan 1990, The Last Yankee 1990 (play), Broken Glass (play) 1994, Homely Girl (novella) 1995, The Crucible (screenplay) 1995. *Address:* c/o ICM, 40 W. 57th Street, New York, NY 10019 (Office); Tophét Road, Roxbury, CT 06783, U.S.A. (Home).

MILLER, C. Arden, A.O., M.D.; American professor of maternal and child health; b. 19 Sept. 1924, Shelby, Ohio; s. of Harley H. Miller and Mary Thuma; m. Helen Lloyd Meihack 1948; three s. one d.; ed. Oberlin Coll. and Yale Univ. School of Medicine; House Officer, New Haven Hosp., Conn. 1948–51; mem. Faculty, Dept. of Pediatrics, Univ. of Kansas Medical Center 1951–66, Dean of Medical School and Dir. Medical Center 1960–66; Prof. of Pediatrics, Maternal and Child Health, School of Public Health, Univ. of N.C., Chapel Hill 1966–, Vice-Chancellor Health Sciences 1966–71, Chair. Dept. of Maternal and Child Health 1977–87; mem. Inst. of Medicine of N.A.S.; Markle Scholar in Medical Science; Fellow Clare Hall, Cambridge Univ.; Hon. Fellow Royal Soc. of Health; Sedgwick Medal, American Public Health Asscn. 1986, Fulbright Grant to review perinatal care in Western Europe 1986, Robert Felix Award in Community Medicine, Martha Mae Eliot Award in Public Health. *Publications:* Local Health Departments, 15 Case Studies 1981, Monitoring Child Health, Key Indicators 1986. *Leisure interest:* gardening. *Address:* Department of Maternal and Child Health, School of Public Health, The University of North Carolina at Chapel Hill, Chapel Hill, NC 27599; 908 Greenwood Road, Chapel Hill, NC 27514, U.S.A. (Home). *Telephone:* (919) 966-5975 (Office); (919) 942-4320 (Home).

MILLER, G. (George) William, B.S., J.D.; American business executive; b. 9 March 1925, Sapulpa, Okla.; s. of James Dick and Hazel Deane (née Orrick) Miller; m. Ariadna Rogojarsky 1946; ed. U.S. Coast Guard Acad., New London, Univ. of Calif. School of Law, Berkeley; served as line officer in Pacific area, stationed in China for a year; lawyer with Cravath, Swaine and Moore, New York, N.Y. 1952–56; joined Textron Inc. as Asst. Sec. 1956, Vice-Pres. 1957–60, Pres. 1960–74, Chief Exec. Officer 1968–78, Chair. 1974–78; Chair. Fed. Reserve Bd. 1978–79, Sec. of the Treasury 1979–81; Chair. G. William Miller & Co. Inc. 1983–; Chair. Federated Stores Inc. 1990–92; Chair. Bd. Waccamaw Corpn.; Dir. Repligen Corpn., GS Industries Inc., Kleinwort Benson Australia Income Fund Inc., Simon Property Group Inc., Bd. of Trustees Marine Biological Lab.; mem. The Business Council and the Conference Bd. *Address:* 1215 19th Street, N.W., Washington, DC 20036, U.S.A. *Telephone:* (202) 429-1780. *Fax:* (202) 429-0025.

MILLER, George "Kennedy", A.O., M.B., B.S.; Australian film director, producer, writer and doctor; b. 3 March 1945, Brisbane; s. of James Miller and Angela (Balson) Miller; m. Sandy Gore 1985; one d.; ed. Sydney Boys' High School, Univ. of New South Wales Medical School; Resident Medical Officer, St. Vincent's Hosp., Sydney 1971–72; f. Kennedy Miller film co. with the late Byron Kennedy 1977, Chair. 1977–; Writer and Dir. Violence in the Cinema, Part 1 1975, Co-Writer and Dir. Mad Max 1979, Mad Max II (The Road Warrior) 1981, Exec. Producer and Dir. The Dismissal (mini-series) 1982, Dir. The Twilight Zone Movie 1983, Producer Bodyline (mini-series) 1983, The Cowra Breakout (mini-series) 1984, Co-Writer, Producer, Co-Dir. Mad Max Beyond Thunderdome 1985, Producer Vietnam (mini-series) 1986, Dir. Witches of Eastwick 1986, Producer The Riddle of the Stinson, The Clean Machine, Fragments of War 1987, Co-Producer Dead Calm, The Year My Voice Broke 1988, The Bangkok Hilton (mini-series), Flirting 1989, Over the Hill, Dir., Co-Writer, Co-Producer Lorenzos Oil 1990, Co-Producer, Co-Writer Babe 1994 (Golden Globe Award for Best Picture 1996); dir. Contact 1996; Pres. Jury Avoriaz Film Festival 1984; mem. Jury Cannes Film Festival 1988; Chair. Byron Kennedy Memorial Trust 1984–; mem. Bd. of Dirs. Museum of Contemporary Art, Sydney 1987–; Best Dir., Australian Film Inst. 1982, Best Dir. TV Drama, Penguin Awards 1983, Grand Prix Avoriaz 1983, Best Foreign Film, L.A. Film Critics 1983, and numerous other prizes and awards. *Leisure interests:* art, music, sport. *Address:* 30 Orwell Street, King's Cross, N.S.W. 2011, Australia. *Telephone:* (02) 357 2322.

MILLER, Harold T.; American publishing executive; b. 5 Jan. 1923, New Paltz, N.Y.; s. of Harold F. Miller and Grace (Taylor) Miller; m. Marcheta Novak 1947; one s.; ed. Columbia Univ.; high school teacher, Plainfield, N.J. 1948–50; joined Houghton Mifflin Co. 1950, textbook salesman 1950–57, Ed.-in-Chief Test Dept. 1957–62, Asst. Man. Midwestern Regional Office 1962–65, Dir. 1965, Man. 1965–71, Vice-Pres. Educ. Div. 1971–73, Pres. and C.E.O. 1973–79, Pres. 1979–89, C.E.O. and Chair. 1979–90; mem. Bd. of Dirs. Bank of New England Corpn.; mem. Asscn. of American Publrs. (Chair. of Bd. 1977–78), American Antiquarian Soc. *Address:* Houghton Mifflin Co., 1222 Berkeley Street, MA 02116, U.S.A.

MILLER, Jacques Francis, A.O., M.D., PH.D., D.SC., B.A., F.A.A., F.R.S.; Australian medical research scientist; b. 2 April 1931, Nice, France; s. of late Maurice Miller and Fernande Debarnot; m. Margaret D. Houen 1956; ed. Univs. of Sydney and London; Jr. Resident Medical Officer, Royal Prince Alfred Hosp., Sydney 1956; pathological research, Univ. of Sydney 1957; cancer research, Chester Beatty Research Inst., London 1958–65; Head, Experimental Pathology and Thymus Biology Unit, Walter and Eliza Hall Inst., Melbourne 1966–; various other professional appts.; Foreign Assoc., N.A.S.; numerous awards and honours. *Publications:* over 380 papers in scientific journals, mostly on immunology and cancer research. *Leisure interests:* art, photography, music, literature. *Address:* 5 Charteris Drive, East Ivanhoe, Vic. 3079, Australia (Home). *Telephone:* 9345 2555 (Office); 9499 2481 (Home).

MILLER, James Clifford, III, PH.D.; American government official, academic and business executive; b. 25 June 1942, Atlanta, Ga.; s. of James Clifford Miller, Jr. and Annie Moseley; m. Demaris Humphries 1961; one s. two d.; ed. Univs. of Georgia and Virginia; Asst. Prof. Ga. State Univ. Atlanta 1968–69; Economist, U.S. Dept. of Transport 1969–72; Assoc. Prof. of Econs. Texas A & M Univ. 1972–74; Economist, U.S. Council of Econ. Advisers, Washington, D.C. 1974–75; Asst. Dir. U.S. Council of Wage and Price Stability 1975–77; Resident Scholar, American Enterprise Inst. 1977–81; Admin., Office of Information and Regulatory Affairs, Office of Man. and Budget and Exec. Dir. Presidential Task Force on Regulatory Relief 1981; Chair Fed. Trade Comm., Washington 1981–85; Dir. Office of Man. and Budget 1985–89; Distinguished Fellow, Center for Study of Public Choice, George Mason Univ. and Chair. Citizens for a Sound Econ. 1988–; serves on several business bds. and non-profit bds.; Thomas Jefferson Fellow 1965–66; DuPont Fellow 1966–67, Ford Foundation Fellow 1967–68. *Publications:* Why the Draft? The Case for a Volunteer Army 1968, Economic Regulation of Domestic Air Transport; Theory and Policy 1974, Perspectives on Federal Transportation Policy 1975, Benefit—Cost Analyses of Social Regulation 1979, Reforming Regulation 1980, The Economist as Reformer 1989, Fix the U.S. Budget! 1994. *Leisure interests:* politics, economics. *Address:* Citizens for a Sound Economy, 1250 H Street, N.W., Washington, DC 20005, U.S.A.

MILLER, Jonathan Wolfe, C.B.E., M.B., B.CH.; British stage and film director and physician; b. 21 July 1934, London; s. of late Emanuel Miller; m. Helen Rachel Collet 1956; two s. one d.; ed. St. Paul's School, St. John's Coll., Cambridge and Univ. Coll. Hosp. Medical School, London; co-author of and appeared in Beyond the Fringe 1961–64; dir. John Osborne's Under Plain Cover, Royal Court Theatre 1962, Robert Lowell's The Old Glory, New York 1964 and Prometheus Bound, Yale Drama School 1967; dir. at Nottingham Playhouse 1968–69; dir. Oxford and Cambridge Shakespeare Co. production of Twelfth Night on tour in U.S.A. 1969; Research Fellow in the History of Medicine, Univ. Coll., London 1970–73; Assoc. Dir. Nat. Theatre 1973–75; mem. Arts Council 1975–76; Visiting Prof. in Drama, Westfield Coll., Univ. of London 1977–; Exec. Producer Shakespeare TV series 1979–81; Artistic Dir. Old Vic 1988–90; Research Fellow in Neuropsychology, Univ. of Sussex; Dir. of the Year, Soc. of West End Theatre Awards 1976; Fellow, Univ. Coll. London 1981–, Hon. Fellow, St. John's Coll. Cambridge, Royal Coll. of Physicians 1997, Royal Coll. of Physicians (Edin.) 1998; Research Fellow in Neuropsychology, Univ. of Sussex; Dr. h.c. (Open Univ.) 1983; Hon. D.Litt. (Leicester) 1981, (Kent) 1985, (Leeds) 1996, (Cambridge) 1996; Silver Medal (Royal Television Soc.) 1981, Albert Medal (Royal Soc. of Arts) 1992. *Productions:* for Nat. Theatre, London: The Merchant of Venice 1970, Danton's Death 1971, The School for Scandal 1972, The Marriage of Figaro 1974, The Wind in the Willows 1990; other productions The Tempest, London 1970, Prometheus Bound, London 1971, The Taming of the Shrew, Chichester 1972, The Seagull, Chichester 1973, The Malcontent, Nottingham 1973, Arden Must Die (opera) 1973, The Family in Love, Greenwich Season 1974, The Importance of Being Earnest 1975, The Cunning Little Vixen (opera) 1975, All's Well That Ends Well, Measure For Measure, Greenwich Season 1975, Three Sisters 1977, The Marriage of Figaro (English Nat. Opera) 1978, Arabella (opera) 1980, Falstaff (opera) 1980, 1981, Otello (opera) 1982, Rigoletto (opera) 1982, 1984, Fidelio (opera) 1982, 1983, Don Giovanni (opera) 1985, The Mikado (opera) 1986, Tosca (opera) 1986, Long Day's Journey into Night 1986, Taming of the Shrew 1987, The Tempest 1988, Turn of the Screw 1989, King Lear 1989, The Liar 1989, La Fanciulla del West (opera) 1991, Marriage of Figaro (opera), Manon Lescaut (opera), Die Gezeichneten (opera) 1992, Maria Stuarda (opera) Capriccio (opera), Fedora (opera), Bach's St. Matthew Passion 1993, Der Rosenkavalier (opera), Anna Bolena (opera), Falstaff (opera), L'Incoronazione di Poppea (opera), La Boheme (opera) 1994, Così fan Tutte (opera) 1995, Carmen (opera) 1995, Pelléas et Mélisande (opera) 1995, She Stoops to Conquer, London 1995, A Midsummer Night's Dream, London 1996, The Rake's Progress, New York 1997; films: Take a Girl Like You 1969 and several films for television including Whistle and I'll Come to You 1967, Alice in Wonderland 1967, The Body in Question (series) 1978, Henry the Sixth, part one 1983, States of Mind (series) 1983, Subsequent Performances 1986, The Emperor 1987, Jonathan Miller's Opera Works (series) 1997. *Publications:* McLuhan 1971, Freud: the Man, his World, his Influence 1972, The Body in Question 1978, Subsequent Performances 1986, The Don Giovanni Book: myths of seduction and betrayal (Ed.) 1990, On Reflection 1998. *Address:* c/o IMG Artists, Media House, 3 Burlington Lane, London, W4 2TH, England.

MILLER, Karl Fergus Connor; British professor of English literature; b. 2 Aug. 1931; s. of William and Marion Miller; m. Jane E. Collet 1956; two s. one d.; ed. Royal High School, Edin. and Downing Coll., Cambridge; Asst. Prin., H.M. Treasury 1956–57; BBC TV producer 1957–58; Literary Ed. The Spectator 1958–61, New Statesman 1961–67; Ed. The Listener 1967–73; Lord Northcliffe Prof. of Modern English Literature, Univ. Coll., London 1974–92; Ed. London Review of Books 1979–92, Co-Ed. 1989–92. *Publications:* Cockburn's Millennium 1975, Doubles: studies in literary history 1985, Authors 1989, Rebecca's vest (autobiog.) 1993, Boswell and Hyde 1995, Dark Horses (autobiog.) 1998; ed. of several anthologies. *Leisure interest:* football. *Address:* 26 Limerston Street, London, SW10 0HH, England. *Telephone:* 0171-352 1735.

MILLER, Lajos; Hungarian baritone; b. 23 Jan. 1940, Szombathely; s. of Lajos Miller and Teréz Sebestyén; m. Zsuzsa Dobránszky; one s.; studied at Music Acad. of Budapest under Jenö Sipos;. mem. Hungarian State Opera 1968–; won Grand Prix, Fauré singing contest, Paris 1974 and first prize, "Toti dal Monte" singing contest, Treviso, Italy 1975; Liszt Prize 1975, Kossuth Prize 1980; has sung with maj. cos. in France, Germany, Italy, Monaco, Switzerland, Austria, U.K., U.S.A., Belgium, Venezuela, Canada, Chile. *Operatic roles include:* (Verdi) Renato, Rodrigo, Simon Boccanegra, Don Carlos, Rolando (Battaglia di Legnano), Iago, Nabucco, Conte di Luna, Miller, Germont, (Gluck) Orpheus, Orestes, (Mozart) Don Giovanni, Guglielmo, (Giordano) Carlo Gérard, (Leoncavallo) Silvio, (Rossini) Figaro, Guglielmo Tell, (Tchaikovsky) Eugene Onegin, Yeletsky, (Puccini) Scarpia, (Bizet) Escamillo, (Berio) Commandante Ivo, (Donizetti) Enrico, (Rimsky-Korsakov) Grasnoi. *Recorded roles:* Don Carlos (Ernani), Simon Boccanegra, Lycidas, Sharpless (Madame Butterfly), Fanuel, Valentin (Faust), Andrei (War and Peace), Manfredo (Il Giuramento), Chelkalov (Boris Godunov), Belfagor, Zosimo (Maria Egiziaga), Falásar (Semirama). *TV films:* Enrico (Lucia di Lammermoor), Marcello (Tabarro), Silvio (Pagliacci), Loth (Madarasz 'Loth) and two portrait films 1995. *Leisure interests:* tennis, surfing. *Address:* Balogh Ádám utca 28 1026 Budapest; State Opera, Andrássy ut 22, 1061 Budapest, Hungary. *Telephone:* 1.31-2550.

MILLER, Merton Howard, PH.D.; American professor of banking and finance; b. 16 May 1923, Boston, Mass.; s. of Joel L. Miller and Sylvia F. Starr; ed. Harvard and Johns Hopkins Univs.; with Treasury Dept. 1944–47, Fed. Reserve Bd. 1947–49; Asst. lecturer, London School of Econs. 1952; Asst. Prof., Assoc. Prof. Grad. School of Industrial Admin. Carnegie Inst. of Tech. Pittsburgh 1958–61; Prof. of Banking and Finance, Grad. School of Business, Univ. of Chicago 1961–96, Prof. Emer. 1996–; Fellow, Econometric Soc.; mem. American Finance Asscn. (Pres. 1976), American Econ. Asscn., American Statistical Asscn.; Nobel Prize in Econs. (with H. M. Markowitz, q.v.) 1990. *Publications:* Theory of Finance 1972, Macroeconomics 1974, Financial Innovation and Market Volatility 1991. *Address:* University of Chicago Graduate School of Business, 1101 East 58th Street, Chicago, IL 60637, U.S.A.

MILLER, Neal Elgar, M.A., PH.D.; American professor of psychology; b. 3 Aug. 1909, Milwaukee, Wis.; s. of Irving Miller and Lily Miller; m. Marion E. Edwards 1948; one s. one d.; ed. Univ. of Washington, Stanford and Yale Univs.; Asst. in Research, Dept. of Psychology, Yale Univ. 1933–35; Social Science Research Council Fellow, Vienna Psychoanalytic Inst. 1935–36; Research Asst. in Psychology, Inst. of Human Relations, Yale Univ. 1936–41, Research Assoc. 1941–42; Officer in charge of Research, Psychological Research Unit, Army Air Corps, Nashville, Tenn. 1942–44; Dir. of Psychological Research Project (Pilot), H.Q. Flying Training Command, Randolph, Tex. 1944–46; Research Assoc. in Psychology (Assoc. Prof.), Inst. of Human Relations, Yale Univ. 1946–50, Prof. of Psychology 1950–52, James Rowland Angell Prof. of Psychology 1952–66; Prof. The Rockefeller Univ. 1966–80, Prof. Emer. 1981–; Clinical Prof. of Psychology in Medicine, Cornell Univ. Medical Coll. 1970–73, Adjunct Prof. 1973–75; Research Affiliate, Yale Univ. 1985–; Fellow Berkeley Coll. 1955–; Sr. Fellow Inst. of Medicine 1983–; mem. N.A.S., American Acad. of Arts and Sciences, American Philosophical Soc., Inst. of Medicine and numerous professional socs. and orgs.; recipient of Nat. Medal of Science 1965, six hon. degrees and numerous other awards and prizes. *Publications:* 269 publs. *Leisure interests:* gardening, hiking. *Address:* Yale University, Department of Psychology, P.O. Box 208205, New Haven, CT 06520-8205, U.S.A. *Telephone:* (203) 432-4524. *Fax:* (203) 432-7172.

MILLER, Sir Peter North, Kt., M.A., D.SC.; British insurance broker; b. 28 Sept. 1930, London; s. of Cyril T. and Dorothy N. Miller; m. Jane Miller 1991; one s.; two s. one d. by previous marriage; ed. Rugby School and Lincoln Coll. Oxford; joined Thos. R. Miller & Son (Insurance) 1953, Partner 1959, Sr. Partner 1971–, Chair. of Miller Insurance Group 1971–83, 1988–96; mem. Cttee. Lloyds Insurance Brokers' Asscn. 1973–77, Deputy Chair. 1974–75, Chair. 1976–77; mem. Cttee. of Lloyds 1977–80, 1982–89; Chair. of Lloyds 1984–87; mem. Cttee. on Invisible Exports 1975–77; mem. Insurance Brokers' Registration Council 1977–81; Chair. British Cttee. of Bureau Veritas 1980–; one of Her Majesty's Lieuts. for City of London 1987–; Hon. Fellow Lincoln Coll., Oxford 1992–; Commendatore, Ordine al Merito della Repubblica Italiana 1989. *Leisure interests:* all forms of sport (except cricket), particularly running, riding, tennis and sailing, wine, music. *Address:* Dawson House, 5 Jewry Street, London, EC3N 2EX, England. *Telephone:* 0171-488 2345.

MILLER, Petr; Czech politician; b. 27 June 1941, Prague; m. 1st Hana Miller; m. 2nd Eva Miller; one s.; worked as smith, Tatra Smíchov Co., Prague 1955–58; smith, ČKD Praha Co., Prague, Div. Elektrotechnika 1962–89; mem. of Action Team of Co-ordinating Centre, Civic Forum Nov. 1989–; Fed. Minister of Labour and Social Affairs 1989–92; Deputy to House of People, Fed. Ass. 1990–92; mem. Czechoslovak (now Czech) Social Democratic Party 1992–94; Pres. Masaryk Inst. for Employment and Social Policy 1992–; Dir. Personnel Dept., Ecotrans Moravia a.s./PLC 1994–95; Dir. Chemapol Group 1995–; Dir. Project EDUCA 1997–. *Address:* Chemapol Group, Kodaňská 46, Vršovice, 100 00 Prague 10, Czech Republic. *Telephone:* 671 51111.

MILLER, Robert Joseph, B.A., J.D.; American lawyer and politician; b. 30 March 1945, Evanston, Ill.; s. of Ross Wendell Miller and Coletta Jane Doyle; m. Sandra Ann Searles; one s. two d.; ed. Santa Clara and Loyola Univs.; First Legal Advisor Las Vegas Metropolitan Police Dept. 1973–75; J.P. 1975–78; Deputy Dist. Attorney, Clark Co., Las Vegas 1971–73, Dist. Attorney 1979–86; Lieut. Gov. of Nevada 1987–89, 1989–90, Gov. 1991–98; Chair. Nev. Comm. on Econ. Devt., Nev. Comm. on Tourism 1987–91; mem. Nat. Govs. Asscn. (Vice-Chair. Exec. Cttee. 1995–96, Chair. 1996–97, fmr. Chair. Cttee. on Justice and Public Safety, Chair. Legal Affairs Cttee. 1992–94, Lead Gov. on Transport 1992–); Democrat. *Address:* c/o Office of the Governor, Capitol Bldg., Carson City, NV 89710, U.S.A.

MILLER, Robert Stevens, Jr., A.B. M.B.A., J.D.; American business executive; b. 4 Nov. 1941, Portland, Ore.; s. of Robert Stevens Miller and Barbara Weston Miller; m. Margaret Rose Kyger 1966; three s.; ed. Stanford Univ. and Harvard Law School; mem. financial staff, Ford Motor Co., Dearborn, Mich. 1968–71; Investment Man., Ford Motor de Mexico, Mexico City 1971–73; Dir. of Finance, Ford Asia Pacific, Melbourne, Australia 1974–77; Vice-Pres. (Finance), Ford Motor de Venezuela, Caracas 1977–79; Vice-Pres.-Treas., Chrysler Corpn., Detroit, Mich. 1980–81, Exec. Vice-Pres. (Finance) 1981–85, 1985–88, Exec. Vice-Pres. 1988–92; Sr. Partner James D. Wolfensohn Inc. 1992–93; Chair. Morrison Knudson Corpn. 1995–96, Waste Man. Inc. 1997–; Dir. Fed.-Mogul, Pope and Talbot, Coleman, Symantec, Morrison Knudson; mem. Int. Advisory Bd., Creditanstalt Bankverein, Vienna, Austria. *Leisure interest:* model railroading.

MILLER, Stanley Lloyd, PH.D.; American chemist and educator; b. 7 March 1930, Oakland, Calif.; s. of Nathan Harry Miller and Edith (Levy) Miller; ed. Univs. of California (Berkeley) and Chicago; F. B. Jewett Fellow, Calif. Inst. of Tech. 1954–55; Instructor and Asst. Prof., Dept. of Biochem. and Chem., Coll. of Physicians and Surgeons, Columbia Univ. 1955–60; Asst., Assoc. then Full Prof., Dept. of Chem., Univ. of Calif., San Diego 1960–; mem. N.A.S.; Hon. Councillor, Higher Council of Scientific Research of Spain; Oparin Medal, Int. Soc. for the Study of the Origin of Life. *Publication:* The Origins of Life on the Earth (with L. E. Orgel) 1974. *Address:* University of California, San Diego, Department of Chemistry, La Jolla, CA 92093-0317, U.S.A. *Telephone:* (619) 534-3365.

MILLER, Walter Geoffrey Thomas, A.O.; Australian diplomatist; b. 25 Oct. 1934, Tasmania; s. of Walter T. Miller and Gertrude S. Galloway; m. Rachel C. Webb 1960; three s. one d.; ed. Launceston High School and Univs. of Tasmania and Oxford; served in Australian missions in Kuala Lumpur, Djakarta, and at UN, New York; Deputy High Commr., India 1973–75; Amb. to Repub. of Korea 1978–80; Head, Int. Div. Dept. of the Prime Minister and Cabinet, Canberra 1982; Deputy Sec. Dept. of Foreign Affairs 1985–86; Amb. to Japan 1986–89; Dir.-Gen. Office of Nat. Assessments Canberra 1989–95; High Commr. in N.Z. 1996–; Rhodes Scholar 1956. *Leisure interests:* international relations, literature, ballet, tennis, reading, golf. *Address:* Australian High Commission, 75–79 Hobson Street, Thorndon, Wellington, New Zealand.

MILLER, William (see Miller, G. (George) William).

MILLER, Zell Bryan, M.A.; American politician; b. 24 Feb. 1932, Young Harris, Ga.; s. of Stephen G. Miller and Birdie Bryan; m. Shirley Carver 1954; two s.; ed. Young Harris Coll., Univ. of Georgia; Prof. of Political Science and History, Univ. of Ga., Young Harris Coll. 1959–64; mem. Ga. Senate 1960–64; Dir. Ga. Bd. of Probation 1965–67; Deputy Dir. Ga. Dept. of Corrections 1967–68; Exec. Sec. to Gov. of Ga. 1968–71; Exec. Dir. Democratic Cttee. of Ga. 1971–72; mem. State Bd. of Pardons and Paroles, Atlanta 1973–75; Lieut.-Gov. of Ga. 1975–91; Gov. of Georgia 1990–; Pres. Council State Govts. 1991–; Vice-Chair. Southern Gov.'s Asscn. 1991–; Democrat. *Publications:* The Mountains Within Me, Great Georgians, They

Heard Georgia Singing. *Address:* Office of the Governor, State Capitol, Room 203, Atlanta, GA 30334, U.S.A.

MILLERON, Jean-Claude, French economist; b. 8 Jan. 1937, Paris; s. of Pierre A. Milleron and Geneviève Hedouin; m. Marie-France Dannaud 1966; two s. one d.; ed. Ecole Polytechnique, Paris, Ecole Supérieure des Sciences Econ., Paris; with Nat. Inst. of Statistics and Econ. Studies (INSEE), Paris 1963–70, Dir.-Gen. 1987–92; Visiting Research Dept. of Econs., Univ. of Calif. at Berkeley 1970–71; Deputy Dir. Nat. School of Statistics and Econ. Admin. (ENSAE), Paris 1971–78; Head of Dept. of Econs., Planning Commissariat-Gen., Paris 1978–81; Dir. of Forecasting French Ministry of Econ. and Finance 1982–87; Under-Sec.-Gen. Dept. of Econ. and Social Information and Policy Analysis, UN, New York 1992–97; Special Adviser to French Minister of Econ., Finance and Industry 1997–98; Exec. Dir. of IMF and IBRD 1998–; Financial Minister Embassy, Washington 1998–; Fellow Econometric Soc. *Publications:* various books and articles on econ. theory and public econs. *Leisure interests:* jogging, hiking, opera. *Address:* International Monetary Fund, 700 19th Street, N.W., Washington, DC 20431; French Embassy, 4101 Reservoir Road, N.W., Washington, DC 20007, U.S.A. *Telephone:* (202) 623-6505 (IMF); (202) 944-6380 (Embassy). *Fax:* (202) 623-4951 (IMF); (202) 944-6392 (Embassy).

MILLER SMITH, Charles, M.A.; British business executive; b. 7 Nov. 1939, Glasgow; s. of William Smith and Margaret Wardrope; m. Dorothy Adams 1964; one s. two d.; ed. Glasgow Acad. and St. Andrews Univ.; Financial Dir. Vinyl Products, Unilever 1970–73, Head of Planning 1974; Finance Dir. Walls Meat Co. 1976; Vice-Chair. Industan Lever 1979–81; Speciality Chemicals Group 1981; Chief Exec. PPF Int. 1983; Chief Exec. Quest Int. 1986; Financial Dir. Unilever Bd. 1989; Exec. Unilever Foods 1993–94; Exec. Dir. Imperial Chemical Industries PLC 1994–95, Chief Exec. 1995–; Non-Exec. Dir. HSBC Holdings PLC 1996–; Hon. LL.D. (St. Andrews). *Leisure interests:* reading, walking. *Address:* Imperial Chemical Industries PLC, 9 Millbank, London, SW1P 3JF, England. *Telephone:* 0171-834 4444. *Fax:* 0171-834 2042.

MILLIGAN, Spike (Terence Alan); British author and actor; b. 16 April 1918, Ahmednagar, India; s. of L. A. Milligan and Florence Mary Winifred Kettleband; m. 1st June Marlowe; one s. two d.; m. 2nd Patricia Margaret Ridgway (died 1978); one d.; m. 3rd Shelagh Sinclair 1983; ed. Poona, St. Paul's High School, Rangoon, and Brownhill Boys School, Catford; first broadcast as a comedian in Opportunity Knocks 1949; appeared in and wrote scripts for The Crazy People radio series, BBC 1951; appeared in and wrote The Goon Show radio series; TV Writer of the Year Award 1957; Hon. C.B.E. *TV appearances include:* A Show Called Fred, Son of Fred 1956, World of Beachcomber, Q5, Oh in Colour, A Milligan for all Seasons, Marty Feldman's Comedy Machine (also co-wrote: Golden Rose and special comedy award, Montreux 1972), The Melting Pot 1975, Q7 1977, Q8 1978, Q9 1979, There's a lot of it about 1982, Last Laugh Before TV-AM (own show). *Films include:* Postman's Knock 1961, The Bed-Sitting Room 1969, The Magic Christian 1971, The Devils 1971, The Cherry Picker 1972, Digby the Biggest Dog in the World 1972, The Three Musketeers 1973, The Great McGonagall 1975, The Last Remake of Beau Geste 1977, The Hound of the Baskervilles 1978, Monty Python's Life of Brian 1978, History of the World, Part One 1980, Yellowbeard 1982. *Publications:* Dustbin of Milligan 1961, Silly Verse for Kids 1963, Puckoon 1963, The Little Pot Boiler 1965, A Book of Bits 1965, Milliganimals 1968, The Bedside Milligan 1968, The Bed-Sitting Room (co-author) 1969, The Bald Twit Lion 1970, Adolf Hitler, My Part in his Downfall 1971, Milligan's Ark 1971, Small Dreams of a Scorpion 1972, The Goon Show Scripts 1972, More Goon Show Scripts 1973, Rommel: Gunner Who? 1973, Badjelly the Witch 1973, Book of the Goons 1974, The Great McGonagall Scrapbook (with J. Hobbs) 1975, The Milligan Book of Records 1975, Dip the Puppy 1975, Transports of Delight 1975, William McGonagall, the truth at last 1976, Monty, His Part in my Victory 1976, Goblins (with illustrations by Heath Robinson) 1978, Mussolini, His Part in my Downfall 1978, Open Heart University 1978, Spike Milligan's Q Annual 1979, Ubu Roi (play) 1980, Get in the Q Annual 1980, Indefinite Articles and Scunthorpe 1981, Unspun Socks from a Chicken's Laundry 1981, The Goon Cartoon 1982, The 101 Best and Only Limericks of Spike Milligan 1982, Sir Nobonk and the terrible, awful, dreadful, naughty, nasty Dragon 1982, More Goon Cartoons 1983, The Melting Pot 1983, 'There's a Lot of it About' 1983, Vol. 5, War Memoirs, Where Have All the Bullets Gone 1985, Further Transports of Delight 1985, Floored Masterpieces and Worse Verse 1985, Vol. 6, Goodbye Soldier 1986, The Looney, An Irish Fantasy (novel) 1987, The Mirror Running (serious poetry) 1987, Starting Verse for All the Family 1987, The Lost Goon Shows 1987, Milligan's War 1988, William McGonagall meets George Gershwin 1989, It Ends with Magic . . . 1990, Depression and How to Survive It (with Anthony Clare) 1991, Peacework, Vol 7. 1991, Condensed Animals 1991, McGonagall—Freefall 1992, Hidden Words 1993, The Bible According to Spike Milligan 1993, Lady Chatterley's Lover According to Spike Milligan 1994, Wuthering Heights According to Spike Milligan 1994, Fleas, Knees and Hidden Elephants (poetry) 1994, John Thomas and Lady Jane According to Spike Milligan 1995, A Celebration 1996, Black Beauty According to Spike Milligan 1996, Frankenstein According to Spike Milligan 1997, The Goons 1997, Hounds of the Baskervilles According to Spike Milligan 1998. *Leisure interests:* restoration of antiques, oil painting, water colours, gardening, eating, drinking, talking, sleeping, wine, jazz. *Address:* Spike Milligan Productions, 9 Orme Court, London, W2 4RL, England. *Telephone:* 0171-727 1544.

MILLON, Charles, L. ÈS SC.ECON.; French politician; b. 12 Nov. 1945, Belley, Ain; s. of Gabriel Millon and Suzanne Gunet; m. Chantal Delsol 1970; three s. two d.; ed. Ecole Sainte-Marie, Lyon, Faculté de Droit et de Sciences Economiques de Lyon; univ. tutor 1969; legal and taxation adviser 1970–; Mayor of Belley 1977–; Deputy 1981–86, 1988–93, First Vice-Pres. Ass. Nat. 1986–88, Leader Union pour la Démocratie Française in Nat. Ass. 1989; Minister of Defence 1995–97; Local Councillor, Ain 1985–88; Vice-Pres. Regional Council, Rhône-Alpes 1981–88, Pres. 1988–. *Publications:* L'extravagante histoire des nationalisations 1984, L'Alternance-vérité 1986, La Tentation du Conservatisme 1995, La Paix civile 1998. *Leisure interests:* reading, walking, mountaineering. *Address:* Assemblée nationale, 75355 Paris; Conseil Régional Rhône-Alpes, 78 route de Paris, 69260 Charbonnières les Bains, France.

MILLS, Dame Barbara Jean Lyon, D.B.E., Q.C., M.A.; British lawyer; b. 10 Aug. 1940; m.; four c.; ed. St. Helen's School, Northwood and Lady Margaret Hall, Oxford; called to bar, Middle Temple, London 1963, Bencher 1990; Jr. Prosecuting Counsel to Inland Revenue 1977, Sr. Prosecuting Counsel 1979; Jr. Treasury Counsel, Cen. Criminal Court 1981; Recorder, Crown Court 1982–92; Q.C. 1986; Dept. of Trade and Industry Insp. under Section 177 of Financial Services Act 1986 (re Jenkins-British Commonwealth) 1986; mem. Criminal Injuries Compensation Bd. 1988–90; legal assessor to Gen. Medical Council and Gen. Dental Council 1988–90; mem. Parole Bd. 1990; Dir. Serious Fraud Office 1990–92; mem. Gen. Advisory Council of BBC 1991–92; Q.C. (N. Ireland) 1991; Dir. of Public Prosecutions and Head, Crown Prosecution Service 1992–98; Hon. Vice-Pres., Inst. for Study and Treatment of Delinquency 1996; Hon. Fellow, Lady Margaret Hall, Oxford 1991, Soc. for Advanced Legal Studies 1997; Companion of Honour, Inst. of Man. 1993; Hon. LL.D. (Hull, Nottingham Trent) 1993, (London Guildhall) 1994. *Address:* 72 Albert Street, London, NW1 7NR, England. *Telephone:* 0171-388 9206. *Fax:* 0171-388 3454.

MILLS, Hayley Cathrine Rose Vivien; British actress; b. 18 April 1946, London; d. of Sir John Mills (q.v.) and Lady Mills (Mary Hayley Bell); m. Roy Boulting (q.v.) 1971 (divorced 1977); two s.; Elmhurst Ballet School, Inst. Alpine Vidamanette; first film appearance in Tiger Bay 1959; on contract to Walt Disney; films include Pollyanna 1960, The Parent Trap 1961, Whistle Down the Wind 1961, Summer Magic 1962, In Search of the Castaways 1963, The Chalk Garden 1964, The Moonspinners 1965, The Truth about Spring 1965, Sky West and Crooked 1966, The Trouble with Angels 1966, The Family Way 1966, Pretty Polly 1967, Twisted Nerve 1968, Take a Girl Like You 1970, Forbush and the Penguins 1971, Endless Night 1972, Deadly Strangers 1975, The Diamond Hunters 1975, What Changed Charley Farthing? 1975, The Kingfisher Caper 1975, Appointment with Death 1987, After Midnight 1992; first stage appearance as Peter Pan 1969, appeared in The Wild Duck 1970, Trelawny 1972, A Touch of Spring 1975, My Fat Friend 1978, Hush and Hide 1979, The Importance of Being Earnest (Royal Festival Theatre, Chichester), The Summer Party 1980, Talley's Folly 1982, The Secretary Bird 1983, Dial M for Murder 1984, Toys in the Attic 1986, The Kidnap Game 1991, The Card 1994, The King and I 1994, Fallen Angels 1994, Dead Guilty 1995–96, Brief Encounter 1996; TV appearances: The Flame Trees of Thika 1981, Parent Trap II 1986, Good Morning Miss Bliss, Murder She Wrote, Back Home, Tales of the Unexpected, Walk of Life 1990; Silver Bear Award, Berlin Film Festival 1958, British Acad. Award; Special Oscar (U.S.A.). *Publication:* My God (with Marcus Maclaine) 1988. *Leisure interests:* riding, reading, children, cooking, scuba-diving. *Address:* c/o Chatto and Linnit, Prince of Wales Theatre, Coventry Street, London, W1V 7FE, England.

MILLS, Sir John, Kt., C.B.E.; British actor; b. 22 Feb. 1908, North Elmham, Suffolk; s. of Lewis Mills; m. Mary Hayley Bell 1941; one s. two d. (Hayley Mills, q.v.); ed. Norwich High School; debut in chorus of The Five O'Clock Girl 1929; appeared in repertory 1929–30; appeared as The Aunt in Charley's Aunt, London, 1930; has since appeared in numerous West End productions including the following plays by his wife Mary Hayley Bell: Men in Shadow 1942, Duet for Two Hands 1945, Angel 1947, The Uninvited Guest 1952; mem. Council Royal Acad. of Dramatic Art (RADA) 1965–; mem. Bd. Govs. of British Film Inst., Soc. of Film and TV Arts (Vice-Pres.); Chair. Stars Org. for Spastics 1975; Patron, Life mem. Variety Club; numerous theatre and film awards include Best Actor of the Year (for Of Mice and Men) 1939, Best Actor (for Great Expectations) 1947, Venice Film Festival Best Actor Award (for Tunes of Glory) 1960, San Sebastian Film Festival Best Actor Award (for The Family Way) 1968; Acad. Award (Oscar) for role in Ryan's Daughter 1971. Other stage appearances include: Noel Coward's Cavalcade 1931 and Words and Music 1932, Give me a Ring 1933, Jill Darling 1934, Red Night 1936, A Midsummer Night's Dream, She Stoops to Conquer, The Damascus Blade 1950, Figure of Fun 1951, The Uninvited Guest 1952, Ross (Broadway production) 1961, Powers of Persuasion 1963, Veterans 1972, At the End of the Day 1973, Good Companions (musical) 1974, Great Expectations (musical) 1975, Separate Tables 1977, Goodbye, Mr. Chips (musical) 1982, The Housekeeper 1983, Little Lies 1983 and 1984, The Petition 1986, Pygmalion 1987, When the Wind Blows (TV play) 1987. *Film appearances include:* The Midshipmaid, Those Were the Days, Doctor's Orders, Royal Cavalcade, Tudor Rose, O.H.M.S., Goodbye Mr. Chips (1937), Four Dark Hours, Black Sheep of Whitehall, The Young Mr. Pitt, In Which We Serve,

Waterloo Road, This Happy Breed, The Way to the Stars, Scott of the Antarctic, The History of Mr. Polly, The Rocking Horse Winner, Morning Departure, Hobson's Choice, The Colditz Story, Above Us The Waves, Escapade, War and Peace, The Baby and the Battleship, Round the World in 80 Days, Dunkirk, Ice Cold in Alex, Monty's Double, Summer of the Seventeenth Doll, Tiger Bay, Swiss Family Robinson, Tunes of Glory, The Singer Not the Song, Flame in the Streets, Tiara Tahiti, King Rat, The Chalk Garden, Operation Crossbow, The Wrong Box, The Family Way, Chuka, Cowboy in Africa, Adam's Woman, Lady Hamilton, Oh! What a Lovely War, Run Wild, Run Free, A Black Veil for Lisa, Ryan's Daughter, Dulcima, Young Winston, Oklahoma Crude, The Human Factor, Trial by Combat, The Big Sleep, Thirty-Nine Steps, Zulu Dawn, Dr. Strange, Love Boat, Quatermass (TV), Young at Heart (TV) 1980/82, A Woman of Substance (TV), The Masks of Death (TV), Murder with Mirrors (TV), Gandhi 1980, Sahara 1983, A Woman of Substance, Tribute to Her Majesty (film documentary) 1986, A Tale of Two Cities (TV) 1989, Ending Up (TV) 1989, Harnessing Peacocks 1993, The Big Freeze, Martin Chuzzlewit (TV) 1994. *Publications:* Up in the Clouds Gentlemen Please 1980, Book of Famous Firsts 1984. *Leisure interests:* skiing, golf, painting. *Address:* c/o I.C.M. Ltd., 76 Oxford Street, London, W1R 1RB, England.

MILNE, Alasdair David Gordon, B.A.; British broadcasting official; b. 8 Oct. 1930; s. of Charles Gordon Shaw Milne and Edith Reid Clark; m. Sheila Kirsten Graucob 1954 (died 1992); two s. one d.; ed. Winchester Coll., New Coll., Oxford; served with 1st Bn., Gordon Highlanders 1949; joined BBC 1954, Deputy Ed. 1957–61, Ed. of Tonight Programme 1961–62, Head of Tonight Productions 1963–65; Partner Jay, Baverstock, Milne & Co. 1965–67; rejoined BBC 1967, Controller BBC Scotland 1968–72, Dir. of Programmes, BBC TV 1973–77, Man. Dir. TV 1977–82, Deputy Dir.-Gen. BBC 1980–82, Dir.-Gen. 1982–87; Chair., Darrell Waters Ltd. 1988–90; Dir. ABU TV Ltd. 1988–93; Pres. Commonwealth Broadcasting Asscn. 1984–87; BBC Visiting Prof., Univ. of Miami 1989; Dr. h.c. (Stirling) 1983; Hon. Fellow New College, Oxford; Cyril Bennett Award 1987. *Publication:* DG: The Memoirs of a British Broadcaster 1988. *Leisure interests:* piping, salmon fishing, golf. *Address:* 30 Holland Park Avenue, London, W11 3QU, England.

MILNE, Denys Gordon ('Tiny'), C.B.E., M.A.; British petroleum industry executive; b. 12 Jan. 1926, Shetlands; s. of Dr. George Gordon Milne and Margaret Campbell; m. Pamela Mary Senior 1951; two s. one d.; ed. Epsom Coll., Brasenose Coll., Oxford; Colonial Admin. Service, Northern Nigeria 1951–54; joined BP Group 1955, Regional Man., Kano, N. Nigeria 1955, then Sales Man., Ghana, then Gen. Man., Nigeria; returned to London 1965; Regional Co-ordinator, U.K. and Ireland 1966–71, also Dir. Shell-Mex and BP, Chair. Lubricants Producers Ltd.; Dir. Alexander Duckham & Co. Ltd. 1966–71, Chair. 1976–81; Shareholders' Rep. in Southern Africa 1971; First Chair. BP Southern Africa Ltd. 1975; returned to London as Deputy Man. Dir. BP Oil Ltd. 1975; Chief Exec. and Man. Dir. BP Oil Ltd. 1976–81; Pres. Inst. of Petroleum 1977–79; Vice-Pres. U.K. Petroleum Industry Asscn. 1978–79, Pres. 1979–81; Chair. Occupational and Environmental Health Spar Ltd. 1986–, Stag Petroleum Co. Ltd. 1986–; mem. Advisory Cttee. on Energy Conservation 1979–81, Scottish Econ. Council 1978–81; Dir. Silkolene Lubricants Ltd. 1981–91, Fluor (G.B.) Ltd. 1981–90, Aviva Petroleum Inc. 1989– (Chair. 1992–); Chair. Exec. Unit Business in the Community 1981–84; Chair. Horder Centre for Arthritis 1983–96; Dir. Weir Group PLC 1983–92; Chair. Council Epsom Coll. 1990–95. *Leisure interests:* gardening, sailing. *Address:* Westbury, Old Lane, St. John's, Crowborough, East Sussex, TN6 1RX, England. *Telephone:* (01892) 652634.

MILNE, Sir John Drummond, Kt.; British business executive; b. 13 Aug. 1924, Manchester; s. of Frederick John Milne and Minnie E. Milne; m. Joan Akroyd 1948; two s. two d.; ed. Stowe School, Trinity Coll. Cambridge and R.M.C. Sandhurst; served Coldstream Guards; joined Associated Portland Cement Mfrs. 1948, Asst. to Dir. in charge of overseas investment 1953; Pres. Ocean Cement Ltd., Van., B.C. 1957; Dir. Associated Portland Cement Mfrs. Ltd. 1964, Dir. in charge of overseas investments 1968; Man. Dir. and Chief Exec. Associated Portland Cement Mfrs. Ltd. (now known as Blue Circle Industries PLC) 1975; Chair. and Man. Dir. Blue Circle Industries PLC 1983–87, Chair. 1983–89, non-exec. Chair. 1987–89; Chair DRG 1987–89; Chair. Alfred McAlpine PLC 1992–96; Dir. Royal Insurance PLC 1982–95, Witan Investment Co. 1988–96, Avon Rubber PLC 1989–95, Solvay & Cie S.A. 1990–96. *Leisure interests:* golf, shooting, skiing. *Address:* Chilton House, Chilton Candover, Nr. Alresford, Hants., SO24 9TX, England.

MILNE-WATSON, Sir Michael, Bt., Kt., C.B.E.; British company executive; b. 16 Feb. 1910, London; s. of Sir David Milne-Watson, 1st Bart., and the late Lady Olga (Herbert) Milne-Watson; m. Mary Lisette Bagnall 1940 (died 1993); one s.; ed. Eton and Balliol Coll., Oxford; Gas Light and Coke Co. 1933–49, Gov. 1946–49; Chair. North Thames Gas Bd. 1949–64; Chair. Richard Thomas & Baldwins Ltd. 1964–67; mem. Org. Cttee. Nat. Steel Corpn. 1966–67, Deputy Chair. (Admin.) Nat. (now British) Steel Corpn. 1967–69; Chair. William Press Group of Companies 1969–74; Chair. British United Provident Asscn. (BUPA) 1976–81, Vice-Pres. 1981–; Dir. Industrial and Commercial Finance Corpn. Ltd. 1963–80, Commercial Union Assurance Co. Ltd. 1968–81, Finance for Industry Ltd. 1974–80; mem. of Council, Reading Univ. 1972–80 (Pres. 1975–80), Soc. of British Gas Industries Guild 1970–71, Pipeline Industries Guild 1971–72; mem. R.N.V.R. 1943–45, Liveryman, Grocers Company 1947. *Address:* 39 Cadogan Place, London, SW1X 9RX; The Stables, Oakfield, Mortimer, Berks., RG7 3AJ, England. *Telephone:* (01734) 832200 (Berks.).

MILNER, Anthony Francis Dominic, D.MUS., F.R.C.M.; British composer, writer and teacher; b. 13 May 1925, Bristol; s. of Arthur Milner and Mabel Price; ed. Douai School, Woolhampton, Berks. and Royal Coll. of Music, London; Tutor in Music Theory and History at Morley Coll., London 1954–65; part-time Teacher, R.C.M. 1961–80; Extension Lecturer in Music, Univ. of London 1954–65; Lecturer in Music, King's Coll., London Univ. 1965–71, Sr. Lecturer in Music, Goldsmith's Coll. 1971–74, Prin. Lecturer 1974–80; Prin. Lecturer, R.C.M. 1980–89; lectured on variety of musical topics in over 70 univs. and colls. in U.S.A. and Canada 1964–; Dir. and Harpsichordist, London Cantata Ensemble 1954–65; Kt. Order of St. Gregory (Papal Award) 1985. *Compositions:* Symphony No. 1 1972, Symphony No. 2 1978, Symphony No. 3 1987, Concerto for Oboe and Symphony Orchestra 1994, Orchestral Variations 1958, Oratorio: The Water and the Fire 1961, cantatas, chamber music, choral and vocal music, etc. *Leisure interests:* reading, travel. *Address:* 147 Heythorp Street, Southfields, London, SW18 5BT, England.

MILNES, Sherill, M.MUS.ED.; American opera singer; b. 10 Jan. 1935, Hinsdale, Ill.; s. of James Knowlton and Thelma Roe Milnes; m. 2nd Nancy Stokes 1969; one s.; one s. one d. by first marriage; m. 3rd Maria Zouves 1996; ed. Drake Univ., Northwestern Univ.; studied with Boris Goldovsky, Rosa Ponselle, Andrew White, Hermanes Baer; with Goldovsky Opera Co. 1960–65, New York City Opera Co. 1964–67, debut with Metropolitan Opera Co., New York 1965, leading baritone 1965–; has performed with all American city opera cos. and major American orchestras 1962–73; performed in Don Giovanni, Vespri Siciliani and all standard Italian repertory baritone roles, Metropolitan Opera and at San Francisco Opera, Hamburg Opera, Frankfurt Opera, La Scala, Milan, Covent Garden, London, Teatro Colón, Buenos Aires, Vienna State Opera, Paris Opera and Chicago Lyric Opera; recordings for RCA Victor, London Decca, EMI Angel, Phillips, Deutsche Grammophon, 60 albums 1967–; most recorded American opera singer 1978; Chair. of Bd. Affiliate Artists Inc.; three hon. degrees, Order of Merit (Italy) 1984. *Leisure interests:* table tennis, swimming, horse riding. *Address:* c/o Herbert Barrett, 1776 Broadway, Suite 1610, New York, NY 10019, U.S.A.

MILO, Paskal, PH.D.; Albanian politician; b. 22 Feb. 1949, Vlorë; s. of Koço Petromilo and Parashqevi Petromilo; m. Liliana Balla-Milo 1976; one s. two d.; ed. Univ. of Tirana; journalist 1971–74; high school teacher 1975–80; lecturer in History Univ. of Tirana 1981–91, Dean Faculty of History and Philology 1991–92, Prof. 1996; Sec. of State for Educ. 1991; M.P. 1992–96, 1997–, Chair. Parl. Comm. for Educ. and Science 1992–96, Minister of Foreign Affairs 1997–. *Publications:* The End of an Injustice 1984, Albania and Yugoslavia 1918–27 1992, A Good Understanding and Cooperation in the Balkans; From Utopia to Necessity 1997, Albania and the Balkan Entente 1997, Constitutional Rights and Minorities in the Balkans: A Comparative Analysis 1997, The Soviet Union and Albania's Foreign Policy 1944–46 1997, Albania in East-West Relations 1944–45 1998. *Leisure interests:* football, music. *Address:* Ministria e Punëve të Jashtme, Bul. Zhan D'Ark, Tirana, Albania. *Telephone:* (42) 62170. *Fax:* (42) 35899.

MILO, Ronnie; Israeli politician and lawyer; b. 26 Nov. 1949, Tel Aviv; m. Dr. Elisheva Milo 1973; one s. one d.; mem. Knesset 1977–; Chair. Cttee. on Immigration and Absorption 1977–81; mem. Cttee. on Foreign Affairs and Security, Cttee. on Constitution, Law and Justice, Cttee. on Immigration and Absorption 1981–84; mem. Knesset House Cttee. 1984–88; Deputy Minister of Foreign Affairs 1984–86; Minister of the Environment 1988–90, of Police 1990–92; mem. State Comptroller's Cttee.; mem. Likud Party; Chair. World Likud 1991–. *Address:* World Likud, 38 King George Street, Tel-Aviv, Israel.

MILONGO, Andre; Congolese politician; Prime Minister of the Congo 1991–93; Leader Parti congolais du travail (PCT) 1991; now Leader Union pour la démocratie et la République; Presidential Cand. 1992. *Address:* c/o Union pour la démocratie et la République, Brazzaville, Congo.

MILOŠEVIĆ, Slobodan; Serbian politician; b. 20 Aug. 1941, Požarevac, Serbia; m. Mirjana Milošević; one s. one d.; ed. Belgrade Univ.; mem. League of Communists of Yugoslavia (LCY) 1959–; active in student politics; Adviser on Econ. Affairs to Mayor of Belgrade; Deputy Dir. Tehnogas Co. 1960–73, Dir.-Gen. 1973–78; Head, Belgrade Information Service 1966–69; Pres. Beogradska Udružena Banka (Jt. Bank of Belgrade) 1978–83; mem. Presidium, LCY Cen. Cttee. 1983–84; Chair. Belgrade City Cttee. of LCY 1984–86; mem. Presidency of League of Communists of Serbia, Pres. 1986–88; mem. Presidency, Belgrade City Cttee. of League of Communists; mem. Fed. Council's Comm. for Long-Term Stabilization Program; Pres. collective Presidency of Serbia 1989–90; Pres. of Serbia 1990–97; Pres. Socialist Party of Serbia 1990–91; Pres. of Yugoslavia 1997–; Order of Labour with Gold Wreath; Order of Labour with Red Flag. *Publication:* Years of Outcome 1989. *Address:* Office of the President, 11000 Belgrade, Andrićev venac 1, Yugoslavia.

MIŁOSZ, Czesław; Polish/American writer; b. 30 June 1911, Szetejnie, Lithuania; s. of Aleksander and Weronika (Kunat) Miłosz; ed. Univ. of Wilno (now Vilnius, Lithuania); helped form literary group Zagary; first collection of poems published 1933; studied in Paris 1934–35; programmer with Polish Nat. Radio 1935–39; active in Polish resistance, World War II; brought out "underground" an anti-Nazi anthology of poems Pieśń niepodległa (Invincible

Song) and other publications; diplomatic service, Washington Embassy, later Paris 1946–50; went into exile, Paris 1951; with Polish emigrant publishing house Instytut Literacki, Paris 1951–60, still writes for house magazine Kultura; went to U.S.A. 1960, became naturalized American 1970; Prix Littéraire Européen (jointly) for novel Zdobycie władzy (first published in French as La prise du pouvoir) 1953; Visiting Lecturer, Univ. of Calif. at Berkeley 1960, Prof. of Slavic Languages and Literatures 1960–78, Prof. Emer. 1978–; hon. doctorate (Univ. of Michigan, Ann Arbor) 1977, (Brandeis Univ.) 1985, (Harvard Univ.) 1989, (Jagellonian Univ.) 1989, (Rome) 1992; mem. American Acad. of Arts and Letters; Polish PEN Club award for poetry translation 1974; Books Abroad/Neustadt Prize 1978; Nobel Prize for Literature 1980. *Publications include: poetry:* Swiatło dzienne (Daylight) 1953, Traktat poetycki (Poetic Treatise) 1957, Król Popiel i inne wiersze (King Popiel and Other Poems) 1962, Gucio zaczarowany (Bobo's Metamorphosis) 1964, Miasto bez imienia (City Without a Name) 1969, Gdzie słońce wschodzi i kiedy zapada (From Where the Sun Rises to Where it Sets) 1974, Bells in Winter (poems) 1978, Kroniki (Chronicles) 1988, Facing the River 1995, A Book of Luminous Things 1996; *prose:* Zniewolony umysł (The Captive Mind) 1953, Zdobycie władzy (The Usurpers) 1955, Dolina Issy (The Issa Valley) 1955, Native Realm: a Search for Self-Definition 1968, The History of Polish Literature 1969, Emperor of the Earth: Modes of Eccentric Vision (essays) 1977, Year of the Hunter 1994, Striving Towards Being 1997; translations into Polish: The Gospel According to St. Mark, The Book of Psalms, The Book of Job, Five Megloth, Book of Wisdom; into English: Post-war Polish Poetry 1965; Ziemia Ulro (The Land of Ulro) 1977, The Separate Notebooks (poems) 1984, The Unattainable Earth (poems) 1986, Collected Poems 1988, Provinces (poems) 1991, Beginning with my Streets: Baltic Reflections (memoirs) 1992, A Year of the Hunter 1994, Facing the River 1995, A Book of Luminous Things 1996, Striving Towards Being 1996, Road-side Dog 1998; numerous essays, translations. *Address:* c/o Department of Slavic Languages and Literature, University of California, Berkeley, CA 94720, U.S.A.; Polish Writers' Association, ul. Kanonicza 7, 31-002 Cracow, Poland. *Telephone:* (12) 422 47 73 (Cracow). *Fax:* (12) 422 47 73 (Cracow).

MILOV, Leonid Vasilyevich; Russian historian; b. 28 July 1929; m.; one d.; ed. Moscow State Univ.; jr. researcher Inst. of Slavonic Studies U.S.S.R. Acad. of Sciences 1956–60; asst., sr. teacher, docent Moscow State Univ. 1960–66, Prof., Chair. 1976–; head of lab., Inst. of History of U.S.S.R. 1971–76, sr. researcher Inst. of History of U.S.S.R.; Deputy Ed.-in-Chief History of U.S.S.R. (journal) 1966–71; corresp. mem. U.S.S.R. (now Russian) Acad. of Sciences 1990; research in social-econ. history and agrarian history of Russia 17th-18th Centuries, old Russian law. *Publication:* All-Russian Agrarian Market 1974; Tendencies of Agrarian Development in the Russian State of the first half of the 17th Century 1986, From Nestor to Fonvisin (jtly.) 1994. *Leisure interest:* science. *Address:* Moscow State University, Vorobyevy gory, 119899 Moscow, Russia. *Telephone:* (095) 939 2861 (Office); 468-95-66 (Home).

MILOW, Keith; British artist; b. 29 Dec. 1945, London; ed. Camberwell School of Art and Royal Coll. of Art; experimental work at Royal Court Theatre, London 1968; teacher, Ealing School of Art 1968–70; Artist in Residence, Leeds Univ. (Gregory Fellowship) 1970; worked in New York (Harkness Fellowship) 1972–74; teacher, Chelsea School of Art 1975; teacher, School of Visual Arts, New York City 1981–85; lives and works in New York; many one-man exhbns. in England, U.S.A., Belgium, France, Netherlands and Switzerland; over 50 group exhbns. in several countries; works in public collections in 6 countries including Tate Gallery and Victoria and Albert Museum, London, Guggenheim Museum and Museum of Modern Art, New York; Calouste Gulbenkian Foundation Visual Arts Award 1976; equal First Prize Tolly Cobbold/Eastern Arts 2nd Nation Exhbn. 1979; Arts Council of G.B. Major Award. *Address:* 32 West 20th Street, New York, NY 10011, U.S.A. *Telephone:* (212) 929-0124.

MILSOM, Stroud Francis Charles, Q.C., F.B.A.; British academic; b. 2 May 1923, Merton, Surrey; s. of Harry Lincoln Milsom and Isobel Vida Collins; m. Irene Szereszewski 1955; ed. Charterhouse School, Trinity Coll. Cambridge and Univ. of Pennsylvania Law School (as Commonwealth Fund Fellow); Fellow, Trinity Coll. 1948–55; Fellow, Tutor and Dean, New Coll. Oxford 1956–64; Prof. of Legal History, L.S.E. 1964–76; Prof. of Law, Cambridge Univ. 1976–90, Fellow of St. John's Coll. 1976–; called to Bar 1947, Hon. Bencher, Lincoln's Inn 1970, Q.C. 1985; Literary Dir. Selden Soc. 1964–80, Pres. 1985–88; mem. Royal Comm. on Historical Manuscripts 1975–98; Foreign mem. American Philosophical Soc.; Hon. LL.D. (Glasgow) 1981, (Chicago) 1985; Ames Prize, Harvard 1972; Swiney Prize, R.S.A. 1974. *Publications:* Novae Narrationes 1963, Introduction to reissue of History of English Law (Pollock and Maitland) 1968, Historical Foundations of the Common Law 1969, 1981, Legal Framework of English Feudalism 1976, Studies in the History of the Common Law 1985. *Address:* St. John's College, Cambridge, CB2 1TP; 113 Grantchester Meadows, Cambridge, CB3 9JN, England (Home). *Telephone:* (01223) 354100 (Home).

MILSTEIN, César, C.H., PH.D., F.R.S.; British molecular biologist; b. 8 Oct. 1927, Bahía Blanca, Argentina; s. of Lazaro Milstein and Maxima Vapniarsky; m. Celia Prilleltensky 1953; ed. Colegio Nacional, Bahia Blanca, Universidad de Buenos Aires, Instituto de Química Biológica and Univ. of Cambridge; British Council Fellowship, Dept. of Biochemistry, Cambridge Univ. 1958–60; on Scientific Staff, MRC 1960–61; Head of Molecular Biology Div., Instituto Nacional de Microbiología, Buenos Aires, Argentina 1961–63; on Scientific Staff of MRC Lab. of Molecular Biology, Cambridge 1963–95, Head, Div. of Protein and Nucleic Acid Chem. 1983–93, Deputy Dir. 1988–95; Fellow, Darwin Coll., Cambridge 1981–96, Emer. Fellow 1996–; Hon. Fellow Fitzwilliam Coll. Cambridge; Foreign Assoc. N.A.S. 1981; many awards including Nobel Prize in Physiology or Medicine 1984, Ciba Medal and Prize 1978, Wolf Prize in Medicine, Wolf Foundation, Israel 1980, Robert Koch Prize and Medal, Fed. Repub. of Germany 1980, Royal Soc. Wellcome Foundation Prize 1980, Jimenez Diaz Memorial Award, Spain 1981, Gairdner Foundation Annual Award, Canada 1981, Royal Medal, Royal Soc. 1982, Copley Medal 1989, Nat. Biotech. Ventures Award U.S.A. 1990. *Publications:* papers in various scientific journals. *Leisure interests:* theatre, open-air activities, cooking. *Address:* Medical Research Council Laboratory of Molecular Biology, Hills Road, Cambridge, CB2 2QH, England. *Telephone:* (01223) 248011. *Fax:* (01223) 402269, 412178.

MILTON-THOMPSON, Sir Godfrey James, K.B.E., M.A., M.B., F.R.C.P.; British naval surgeon; b. 25 April 1930, Birkenhead, Cheshire; s. of late Rev. James Milton-Thompson and May L. Hoare; m. Noreen H. F. Fitzmaurice 1952; three d.; ed. Eastbourne Coll., Queens' Coll. Cambridge and St. Thomas's Hospital, London; joined R.N. 1955, Sr. Specialist in Medicine, R.N. Hospital, Malta 1962–66; Consultant Physician, R.N. Hospital, Plymouth 1966–69, 1971–75; Hon. Research Fellow, St. Mark's Hospital 1969–70; Prof. of Naval Medicine 1975–80; promoted Surgeon Capt. 1976; Royal Coll. of Defence Studies 1981, Deputy Medical Dir.-Gen. (Naval) 1982–84, Medical Dir.-Gen. (Naval) 1985–90, Deputy Surgeon-Gen. (Research and Training) 1985–87; promoted Surgeon Rear Admiral 1984, Surgeon Rear Adm. (Operational Medical Services) 1984; Surgeon Gen., Defence Medical Services in the rank of Surgeon Vice-Adm. 1988–90; Hon. Physician to H.M. the Queen 1982–90; Chair. Cornwall Community Healthcare Trust 1991–93; Chair. Bd. of Govs., St. Mary's School, Wantage 1996–; Vice-Pres. British Digestive Foundation 1997–; Warden, St. Katharine's House, Wantage 1993–; Hon. Col. 211 (Wessex) Field Hosp., R.A.M.C. (V) 1990–95; Errol-Eldridge Prize 1974; Gilbert Blane Medal 1976; Kt. of St. John, Hospitaller, Order of St. John 1991–95. *Publications:* contributions to medical and scientific literature on gastroenterology. *Leisure interests:* fishing, literature, collecting East Anglian paintings. *Address:* Pool Hall, Menheniot, Cornwall, PL14 3QT, England.

MILUTINOVIĆ, Milan; Serbian politician and diplomatist; b. 12 Dec. 1942, Belgrade; s. of Aleksandar Milutinović and Ljubica Milutinović; m. Olga Milutinović; one c.; ed. Belgrade Univ.; mem. Pres. of Youth League of Yugoslavia; Minister of Science and Educ. of Serbian Repub.; Dir. Serbian Nat. Library; Amb. to Greece; Minister of Foreign Affairs Fed. Repub. of Yugoslavia 1995–97; Pres. of Serbia 1997–. *Publications include:* Still – It Revolves. *Address:* Office of the President, Andrićev venac 1, 11000 Belgrade, Yugoslavia.

MILYUKOV, Yuri Aleksandrovich; Russian banker; b. 29 April 1957; m.; two s.; ed. Moscow Inst. of Physics Eng.; researcher, Lebedev Inst. of Physics U.S.S.R. (now Russian) Acad. of Sciences 1984–87; Chair. Council of Altair 1989–91; f. Moscow Commodity Exchange (MTB) 1990–, Pres. 1993–; mem. Council on Business, Govt. of Russian Fed. 1992–; mem. Bd. Dirs., Russian Industrialists and Entrepreneurs Union 1992–; mem. Presidium, All-Russian Movt. Businessmen for New Russia 1993–94; mem. Co-ordination Council, Round Table of Russian Business 1994–; mem. Beer Lovers Party; mem. Cen. Cttee. 1995–; mem. Political Consultative Council of Russian Presidency 1996; Chair. Rosmed; Chair. Russian Union of Stock Exchanges 1991–. *Leisure interest:* theatre. *Address:* Mira prosp. 69, 129223 Moscow, Russia. *Telephone:* (095) 187 9826 (Office).

MIMS, Cedric Arthur, B.SC., M.D., F.R.C.PATH.; British professor of microbiology; b. 9 Dec. 1924, London; s. of A. H. and Irene Mims; m. Valerie Vickery 1952; two s. two d.; ed. Mill Hill School, Univ. Coll. London, Middx. Hosp. Medical School; Medical Research Officer, E. African Virus Research Inst., Entebbe 1953–56; Research Fellow and Professorial Fellow, John Curtin School of Medical Research, Australian Nat. Univ., Canberra 1957–72; Rockefeller Foundation Fellow, Children's Hosp. Medical Center, Boston 1963–64; Visiting Fellow, Wistar Inst., Philadelphia 1969–70; Prof. of Microbiology Guy's Hosp. Medical School, London 1972–90. *Publications:* The Biology of Animal Viruses (jt. author) 1974, The Pathogenesis of Infectious Disease 1976, Viral Pathogenesis and Immunology (with D. O. White) 1984, Medical Microbiology (jt. author) 1993, When We Die 1998; numerous scientific papers. *Leisure interests:* writing, walking. *Address:* Sheriff House, Hammingden Lane, Ardingly, Sussex, RH17 6SR, England. *Telephone:* (01444) 892243.

MIN HUIFEN; Chinese musician and university professor; b. Nov. 1945, Yixing Co., Jiangsu Prov.; ed. Shanghai Music Inst.; Prof. Shanghai Music Inst. 1993–; mem. 5th Nat. Cttee. CPPCC 1978–82, 6th 1983–87, 7th 1988–92, 8th 1993–; Prize for Excellent Performance, Spring of Shanghai. *Address:* Room 1101 Bldg. 151, Weihai Road, Shanghai 200003, People's Republic of China.

MINAH, Francis Misheck, LL.M.; Sierra Leonean politician and lawyer; b. 19 Aug. 1929, Pujehun; m. Gladys Emuchay; four c.; ed. Methodist Boys' High School, Freetown, King's Coll. (London Univ.), Grays Inn, London; Pres. Sierra Leone Students' Union of Great Britain and Ireland 1960–62; mem. House of Reps. 1967–87; Minister of Trade and Industry 1973–75, of Foreign Affairs 1975–77, of Justice 1977–78; Attorney-Gen. 1978; Minister of Finance 1978–80, of Health 1980–82; Attorney-Gen. and Minister of Justice 1982–84; First Vice-Pres. 1985–87; UNESCO Fellowship to study community devt. in India and Liberia; barrister-at-law.

MINCKWITZ, Bernhard von; German business executive; b. 11 Aug. 1944, Göttingen; m. Cornelia Böhning; mem. Man. Bd. Bertelsmann AG. *Address:* Bertelsmann Fachinformation, Neumarkter Strasse 18, 81644 Munich, Germany. *Telephone:* 089 431 80 329.

MINDADZE, Aleksander Anatol'yevich; Russian scriptwriter; b. 28 April 1949, Moscow; m. Galina Petrovna Orlova; two d.; ed. All-Union State Inst. of Cinematography; screenplays since 1972. *Film scripts include:* Say of the Defence 1977 (Prize of All-Union Film Festival, Prize of Lenin's Komsomol), Spring Mobilisation 1977 (A. Dovzhenko Silver Medal), Turn 1979, Fox Hunt 1980, The Train has Stopped 1982, Parade of Planets 1985, Plumbum or Dangerous Game 1986, Servant 1991, Armavir 1991, Play for a Passenger 1994, Time for a Dancer 1997; Merited Worker of Art of Russia, State Prize of Russia 1984, U.S.S.R. State Prize 1991, Silver Pegas Prize of Cultural Asscn. Ennio Flaiano 1985. *Address:* Usiyevicha str. 8, Apt. 89, 125319 Moscow, Russia. *Telephone:* (095) 155 7534 (Home).

MINFORD, (Anthony) Patrick (Leslie), C.B.E.; British economist; b. 17 May 1943; s. of Leslie Mackay Minford and Patricia Mary Sale; m. Rosemary Irene Allcorn 1970; two s. one d.; ed. Horris Hill, Winchester Coll., Oxford Univ., L.S.E.; Econ. Asst., Ministry of Overseas Devt. 1966; Economist, Ministry of Finance, Malawi 1967–69; Econ. Adviser Courtaulds Ltd. 1970–71; H.M. Treasury 1971–73; H.M. Treasury Del. Washington, D.C. 1973–74; Visiting Hallsworth Fellow Manchester Univ. 1974–75; Edward Gonner Prof. of Applied Econs., Univ. of Liverpool 1976–97; Visiting Prof. Cardiff Business School 1993–97, Prof. of Econs. 1997–; Dir. Merseyside Devt. Corpn. 1988–89; mem. Monopolies and Mergers Comm. 1990–96, Treasury Panel of Independent Econ. Forecasters 1993–96; Ed. Nat. Inst. for Econ. and Social Research Review 1975–76, Liverpool Quarterly Econ. Bulletin 1980–. *Publications:* Substitution Effects, Speculation and Exchange Rate Stability 1978, Unemployment—Cause and Cure 1983, Rational Expectations and the New Macroeconomics 1983, The Housing Morass 1987, The Supply-Side Revolution in Britain 1991, The Cost of Europe (ed.) 1992, Rational Expectations Macroeconomics 1992; articles in journals. *Address:* Cardiff Business School, University of Wales Cardiff, Cardiff, CF1 3EU, Wales.

MINGHELLA, Anthony; British director and playwright; b. Isle of Wight; s. of Eddie Minghella and Gloria Minghella; m. Carolyn Choa; one s.; ed. St. John's Coll., Sandown High School, Univ. of Hull; fmr. drama lecturer, Univ. of Hull; TV includes first series of Inspector Morse (screenplay); Hon. D.Litt. (Hull) 1997; First Hon. Freeman, Isle of Wight 1997. *Films directed include:* Truly, Madly, Deeply, Mr Wonderful, The English Patient. *Publications:* Whale Music 1983, Made in Bangkok 1986, Jim Henson's Storyteller 1988, Interior—Room, Exterior—City 1989. *Plays:* One 1992, Driven to Distraction: A Case for Inspector Morse 1994, Two 1997; The English Patient (screenplay) 1997.

MING-LIANG, Tsai; Taiwanese film director; *Films include:* Rebels of the Neon God 1992, Vive l'Amour 1994, The River 1996, The Hole; Venice Golden Lion Award (for Vive l'Armour) 1994; Berlin Silver Bear Award (for The River) 1996.

MINGOS, David Michael Patrick, D.PHIL., F.R.S.; British university professor; b. 6 Aug. 1944, Basrah, Iraq; s. of Vasso Mingos and Rose Enid Billie Griffiths; m. Stacey Mary Hosken 1967; one s. one d.; ed. Harvey Grammar School, Folkestone, King Edward VII School, Lytham, Univ. of Manchester, Univ. of Sussex; Fulbright Fellow Northwestern Univ. Ill., U.S.A. 1968–70; ICI Fellow Univ. of Sussex 1970–71; lecturer Queen Mary Coll., London Univ. 1971–76; lecturer in Inorganic Chem. Univ. of Oxford 1976–90, Reader 1990–92; Fellow Keble Coll., Oxford 1976–92; Univ. Assessor 1991–92; Sir Edward Frankland BP Prof. of Inorganic Chem., Imperial Coll., Univ. of London 1992–; Dean, Royal Coll. of Science 1996–; visiting professorships in U.S.A., Canada, France, Germany, Switzerland and consultant for various U.K. and U.S. chem. cos.; Gov. Harrow School; mem. numerous editorial bds.; Corday Morgan Medal, Noble Metal Prize, Tilden Medal of Royal Soc. of Chem., Manchott Prize 1995, Michael Collins Award for Innovation in Microwave Chemistry 1996. *Publications:* An Introduction to Cluster Chemistry, Essentials of Inorganic Chemistry 1996, Essential Trends in Inorganic Chemistry 1998, Essentials of Inorganic Chemistry 2 1998. *Leisure interests:* cricket, tennis, walking, gardening, travel. *Address:* Department of Chemistry, Imperial College of Science, Technology and Medicine, South Kensington, London, SW7 2AY, England (Office). *Telephone:* 0171-594 5753 (Office).

MINKIN, Vladimir Isaakovich; Russian chemist; b. 4 March 1935; m.; one d.; ed. Rostov State Univ.; asst., docent, Prof. Rostov State Univ.; corresp. mem. U.S.S.R. (now Russian) Acad. of Sciences 1990, mem. 1994; works on physical and organic chem., quantum chem. of organic compounds, organic photochemistry; U.S.S.R. State Prize; mem. Comm. of Int. Union on Pure and Applied Chem. *Publications include:* Dipole Moments in Organic Chemistry 1968, Quantum Chemistry of Organic Compounds 1986. *Leisure interests:* chess, literature. *Address:* Institute of Physical and Organic Chemistry, Stachki pr. 194/3, 344104 Rostov-Don, Russia. *Telephone:* (8632) 285 488 (Office).

MINKOWSKI, Alexandre, M.D., F.R.A.P., F.R.C.P.; French professor of neonatalogy; b. 5 Dec. 1915, Paris; s. of Eugène Minkowski and Françoise Minkowski; m. Mary Ann Wade 1950; three s. one d.; ed. Paris Univ.; Chef de Clinique 1945–46; Rockefeller Fellow 1946–47; Head, Dept. of Intensive Care 1962; Prof. of Neonatalogy, Paris Univ. 1962–87, Full Prof. 1970–87; Conseiller Régional, Ile de France; mem., the American Pediatric Soc., British Neonatalogy Soc.; Royal Coll. of Child Health and Paediatrics 1998; Commandeur, Légion d'honneur, Croix de Guerre 1939–45, Médaille de la Résistance. *Publications include:* Sauver la santé 1985, l'Art de naître 1987, Mémoires turbulents 1990, Pour les enfants du monde 1991, Ce que je crois 1997, Developmental Neurobiology, Le vieil homme et l'amour; several scientific essays. *Leisure interests:* tennis, skiing, music, ethnography, anthropology. *Address:* Association partage, 27 boulevard Saint-Michel, 75005 Paris, France.

MINKS, Wilfried; German stage director and designer; b. 21 Feb. 1930, Binai, Czechoslovakia; twin s.; ed. Akad. der Künste, Berlin; theatre engagements in Ulm through Intendant Kurt Hübner (worked with Peter Zadek, Peter Palitzsch); Hübner (Intendant), Zadek, Minks, Bremen 1962–73; worked as stage designer with Fassbinder, Gruber, Stein, Zadek, Palitzsch; Prof. of Stage Design, Hochschule für Bildende Kunst, Hamburg 1970–; cr. German Pavilion, Expo 1970, Osaka, Japan; began working as theatre dir. 1971; screenplay and direction for film Die Geburt der Hexe 1979. *Address:* Wellingsbüttler Landstr. 166, 200 Hamburg 63, Germany. *Telephone:* 040/ 503600.

MINNELLI, Liza; American actress and singer; b. 12 March 1946; d. of the late Vincente Minnelli and Judy Garland; m. 1st Peter Allen 1967 (divorced 1972); m. 2nd Jack Haley, Jr. 1974 (divorced 1979); m. 3rd Mark Gero 1979 (divorced 1992). *Films:* Charlie Bubbles 1968, The Sterile Cuckoo 1969, Tell Me that You Love Me, Junie Moon 1971, Cabaret (played Sally Bowles) 1972 (Acad. Award for Best Actress, The Hollywood Foreign Press Golden Globe Award, the British Acad. Award and David di Donatello Award, Italy), Lucky Lady 1976, A Matter of Time 1976, New York, New York 1977, Arthur 1981, Rent-a-Cop 1988, Arthur 2: On the Rocks 1988, Sam Found Out 1988, Stepping Out 1991. *TV Specials:* Liza, Liza with a Z (Emmy Award) 1972, Goldie and Liza Together 1980, Baryshnikov on Broadway 1980 (Golden Globe Award), A Time to Live 1985 (Golden Globe Award). *Theatre:* Best Foot Forward 1963, Flora, the Red Menace 1965 (Tony Award), Chicago 1975, The Act 1977–78 (Tony Award), Liza at the Winter Garden 1973 (Special Tony Award), The Rink 1984, Victor-Victoria 1997. *Recordings:* Liza with a Z, Liza Minnelli: The Singer, Liza Minnelli: Live at the Winter Garden, Tropical Nights, The Act, Liza Minnelli: Live at Carnegie Hall, The Rink, Liza Minnelli at Carnegie Hall, Results 1989. *Address:* Angel Records, 810 7th Avenue, Floor 4, New York, NY 10019; Capital Records Incorporated, 1750 Vine Street, Hollywood, CA 90028, U.S.A.

MINNIGERODE, Gunther von, DR.RER.NAT.; German physicist; b. 6 Oct. 1929, Osterode/Harz; s. of Werner Freiherr von Minnigerode and Margarete von Drachenfels; m. Ulrike Göllerich 1972; two step-s.; ed. Univ. of Göttingen; Asst. Univ. of Göttingen 1959–66, lecturer 1966–67, Prof. of Experimental Physics 1973–; Prof. of Applied Physics Univ. of Cologne 1967–73; mem. Göttingen Acad. *Publications:* articles on low temperature physics and solid state physics in professional journals. *Leisure interest:* farming. *Address:* I. Physikalisches Institute, Bunsenstrasse 9, 37073 Göttingen (Office); Hermann Föge Weg 10, 37073 Göttingen, Germany (Home). *Telephone:* (0551) 397601 (Office); (0551) 58828 (Home).

MINOGUE, Kylie; Australian singer and actress; b. 28 May 1968, Melbourne; started acting aged 11 years in Skyways, The Sullivans, then Neighbours 1986 (all TV series); first female vocalist to have her first (released) five singles obtain silver discs in U.K., 9 Logies (Australian TV Industry awards), Woman of the Decade award 1989. *Records:* singles include: I Should Be So Lucky 1988, Got To Be Certain 1988, The Loco-Motion 1988, Je Ne Sais Pas Pourquoi 1988, Especially For You (with Jason Donovan, q.v.) 1988, Hand On Your Heart 1989, Wouldn't Change a Thing 1989, Never Too Late 1989, Tears On My Pillow 1990, Better the Devil You Know 1990, Step Back in Time 1990, What Do I Have To Do 1991, Shocked 1991, If You Were With Me Now (with Keith Washington) 1991, Give Me Just A Little More Time 1992, Confide In Me 1994; albums: Kylie 1988, Enjoy Yourself 1989, Rhythm of Love 1990, Let's Get To It 1991, Greatest Hits 1992, Kylie Minogue 1994, Some Kind of Bliss 1997, Impossible Princess 1998; several video releases. *Films:* The Delinquents 1989, Streetfighter 1994, Biodome 1996. *Play:* The Tempest 1999. *Address:* c/o Terry Blamey Management, 329 Montague Street, Albert Park, Vic. 3206, Australia; c/o Terry Blamey Management, P.O. Box 13196, London, SW6 2WA, England. *Telephone:* 0171-371 7627. *Fax:* 0171-731 7578.

MINOW, Newton N., J.D.; American lawyer; b. 17 Jan. 1926, Milwaukee, Wis.; s. of Jay A. and Doris (Stein) Minow; m. Josephine Baskin 1949; three d.; ed. Northwestern Univ.; Law Clerk to Supreme Court Chief Justice Vinson 1951; Admin. Asst. to Gov. of Illinois 1952–53; served Stevenson's law firm 1955–57, Partner 1957–61; Chair. Fed. Communications Comm. 1961–63; Exec. Vice-Pres. Gen. Counsel Encyclopaedia Britannica, Chicago 1963–65; mem. Bd. of Trustees, Rand Corpn. 1965–75, 1976–86, 1987, Chair. 1970–72; Partner, Sidley & Austin (fmrly. Leibman, Williams, Bennett, Baird & Minow) 1965–91, of counsel 1991–; Dir. Sara Lee Corpn., Manpower Inc., Aon Corpn.; mem. Bd. of Trustees, Carnegie Corpn. of New York

1987–97, Chair. 1993–97; Annenberg Univ. Prof., Northwestern Univ. 1987–; Dir. The Annenberg Washington Program 1987–96, Big Flower Press 1997–; Trustee Northwestern Univ. 1975–87 (Life Trustee 1987); Life Trustee, Univ. of Notre Dame; Chair. Arthur Andersen & Co. Public Review Bd. 1974–83, Public Broadcasting Service 1978–80; Hon. Chair. and Dir. Chicago Educational TV Assen; Hon. LL.D. (Northwestern Univ.) 1965, (Wisconsin) 1963, (Brandeis) 1963, (Columbia Coll.) 1972; Democrat. *Publications:* Equal Time: The Private Broadcaster and the Public Interest 1964, Presidential Television (co-author) 1973, Electronics and the Future (co-author) 1977, For Great Debates (co-author) 1987, Abandoned in the Wasteland: Children, Television and the First Amendment 1995. *Address:* Sidley & Austin, 1 First National Plaza, Chicago, IL; 179 E. Lake Shore Drive, Chicago, IL, U.S.A. (Home). *Telephone:* (312) 853-7555 (Office).

MINTER, Alan; British boxer (retd.); b. 17 Aug. 1951, Penge, London; s. of Sidney and Anne Minter; m. Lorraine Bidwell 1974; one s. one d.; ed. Sarah Robinson School, Ifield; amateur boxer 1965–72; Amateur Boxing Assen. (A.B.A.) champion 1971; Olympic bronze medallist 1972; 145 amateur fights, 125 wins; professional boxer 1972–82; won British middleweight championship 1975; won Lonsdale Belt outright 1976; won European championship from Germano Valsecchi Feb. 1977, lost it to Gratien Tonna Sept. 1977; forfeited British title Feb. 1977, regained it Nov. 1977; won vacant European title v. Angelo Jacopucci July 1978, retained it v. Tonna Nov. 1978; relinquished British title Nov. 1978; won world middleweight title from Vito Antuofermo, Las Vegas March 1980 (first British boxer to win a world championship in U.S.A. for 63 years); retained title v. Antuofermo June 1980, lost it to Marvin Hagler Sept. 1980; lost European title to Tony Sibson Sept. 1981; retd. from boxing Feb. 1982. *Leisure interest:* golf. *Publication:* Minter: An Autobiography 1980.

MINTOFF, Dominic, B.SC., B.E.&A., M.A.; Maltese politician; b. 6 Aug. 1916, Cospicua; s. of Lawrence Mintoff and Concetta née Farrugia (deceased); m. Moyra de Vere Bentinck 1947; two d.; ed. Univs. of Malta and Oxford; civil engineer in Great Britain 1941–43; practised in Malta as architect 1943–; rejoined and helped reorganize Maltese Labour Party 1944; elected to Council of Govt. and Exec. Council 1945; mem. Legis. Assembly 1947; Deputy Leader of Labour Party, Deputy Prime Minister and Minister for Works and Reconstruction 1947–49; resigned Ministry, Leader of Labour Party 1949–85; Prime Minister and Minister of Finance 1955–58; Leader of the Opposition 1962–71; Prime Minister 1971–84, also Minister of Foreign and Commonwealth Affairs 1971–81 (redesignated Ministry of Foreign Affairs 1978), of the Interior 1976–81, 1983–84; Special Adviser to Prime Minister 1985–87; mem. House of Reps. 1987; Chair. Malta Counter Trade Co. Ltd. *Publications:* several scientific, literary and artistic works. *Leisure interests:* swimming, water skiing, bocci, horse riding. *Address:* "The Olives", Tarxien, Malta.

MINTON, Yvonne Fay, C.B.E.; Australian mezzo-soprano; b. 4 Dec. 1938, Sydney; d. of R. T. Minton; m. William Barclay 1965; one s. one d.; ed. Sydney Conservatorium of Music and studied in London with H. Cummings and Joan Cross; sang with several opera groups in London; début Covent Garden 1965, Prin. Mezzo-soprano 1965–71; U.S. début, Lyric Opera, Chicago (Octavian in Der Rosenkavalier) 1972; Guest Artist, Cologne Opera 1969–, Australian Opera 1972–73, also with Hamburg State Opera, and at Bayreuth, Paris, Salzburg, Metropolitan Opera, New York, Munich and San Francisco; recordings include Der Rosenkavalier, Figaro, La Clemenza di Tito, Mozart's Requiem, Elgar's The Kingdom; many concert appearances; created role of Thea in Tippett's The Knot Garden 1970; Hon. A.R.A.M. *Leisure interests:* reading, gardening. *Address:* c/o Ingpen and Williams, 26 Wadham Road, London, SW15 2LR, England. *Telephone:* 0181-874 3222. *Fax:* 0181-877 3113.

MINTZ, Shlomo; Israeli violinist; b. 30 Oct. 1957, Moscow; s. of Abraham Mintz and Eve (Labko) Mintz; m. Corina Ciacci; two s.; ed. Juilliard School of Music, New York; went to Israel when very young; many concert tours; Premio Accademia Musicale Chigiana, Siena, Italy 1984; Music Dir., conductor, soloist Israel Chamber Orchestra 1989–. *Recordings include:* Violin Concertos by Mendelssohn and Bruch (Grand Prix du Disque, Diapason d'Or) 1981, J. S. Bach Complete Sonatas and Partitas for Solo Violin, The Miraculous Mandarin by Bartok (with Chicago Symphony Orchestra, conducted by Abbado), Compositions and Arrangements by Kreisler (with Clifford Benson, piano), Twenty-four Caprices by Paganini, Two Violin Concertos by Prokofiev (with London Symphony Orchestra, conducted by Abbado), The Four Seasons by Vivaldi (with Stern, Perlman, Mehta). *Address:* ICM Artists Ltd., 40 West 57th Street, New York, NY 10019, U.S.A.

MIOT, Jean Louis Yves Marie; French journalist; b. 30 July 1939, Châteauroux (Indre); s. of René Miot and Madeleine Moreau; two s. three d.; ed. Lycée Jean Giraudoux de Châteauroux and Univ. de Poitiers; Ed. Centre Presse, Poitiers 1964–68; journalist, French Antilles 1968–70; Ed.-in-Chief, later Political Dir. Havre-Presse 1970–74; Man. Dir. France Antilles Martinique Guadeloupe, launched France-Guyane (weekly) 1974–76; Head, Legis. Elections Service, Le Figaro 1977–78; Man. Dir. Berry Républicain, Bourges 1978; Dir. Groupe de Presse Robert Hersant 1978–79; Political corresp. L'Aurore 1979–80; mem. Man. Bd. Société de Gestion and Assoc. Dir. Le Figaro 1980–93; Pres. Advisory Bd. Le Figaro 1993–96; Pres. Syndicat de la Presse Parisienne 1986–96; Pres. Féd. Nat. de la Presse Française 1993–96; Pres. Agence-France-Presse (AFP) 1996–, Syndicat des agences de presse de nouvelles (SANOV) 1996–; mem. Conseil Econ. et Social 1993–96, Comm. de réflexion sur la justice 1997–; Dir. Société Financière de Radio-Diffusion (SOFIRAD) 1995; many other professional appts.; Chevalier, Légion d'Honneur, Officier de l'Etoile Civique, Officer, Order of Lion (Senegal). *Address:* Agence France-Presse, 13 place de Bourse, 75002 Paris, France. *Telephone:* 01.40.41.49.16. *Fax:* 01.40.41.45.92.

MIOU- MIOU (b. Sylvette Hery); French film actress; b. 22 Feb. 1950, Paris; one d. by late Patrick Dewaere; one d. by Julien Clerc; worked as child in Les Halles wholesale market; apprenticed in upholstery workshop; with comedian Coluche helped create Montparnasse café-theatre 1968; stage appearance in Marguerite Duras' La Musica 1985. *Films:* La cavale 1971, Themroc 1972, Quelques missions trop tranquilles 1972, Elle court la banlieue 1972, Les granges brûlées 1972, Les aventures de Rabbi Jacob 1972, Les valseuses 1973, La grande Vadrouille 1974, Lily aime-moi 1974, Pas de Problem 1974, Un génie, deux associés, une cloche 1975, La marche triomphale 1975, F. comme Fairbanks 1976, On aura tout vu 1976, Jonas qui aura vingt ans en l'an 2000 1976, Portrait de province en rouge 1977, Dites-lui que je l'aime 1977, Les routes du Sud 1978, Au revoir à lundi 1978, Le grand embouteillage 1978, La Dérobade 1978, La femme flic 1980, Est-ce bien raisonnable? 1980, La guèle du loup 1981, Josepha 1981, Guy de Maupassant 1982, Coup de foudre 1983, Attention, une femme peut en cacher une autre! 1983, Canicule 1983, Blanche et Marie 1984, Tenue de soirée 1986, Ménage, Les portes tournantes 1988, La lectrice, Milou en mai, Netchaiev is Back, The Jackpot, Le Bal des Casse-Pieds, Germinal.

MIQUEL, Pierre Gabriel Roger; French social historian, broadcaster and administrator; b. 30 June 1930, Montluçon, Allier; s. of Jean Miguel and Suzanne Montagne; m. Maryvonne Jaume 1956; three s.; ed. Lycée de Montluçon, Lycée Henri-IV, Paris, Univ. de Paris; teacher, Lycée d'Avignon 1955–56, de Melun 1956–57, Carnot, Paris 1958–59; Asst. Faculté des lettres, Univ. de Paris 1961-64, Asst. lecturer, Nanterre 1964–70; lecturer Faculté des lettres, Univ. de Lyon 1970–71, Head Dept. Humanities 1971–72, Head Dept. TV Documentaries 1972–74; lecturer Inst. d'etudes politiques, Paris 1970–70; Prof. of Mass Communications, Sorbonne 1975–, fmr. Admin. Bibliothèque Nat.; at Ministry of Works 1957–58, Ministry of Co-operation 1959–61; Head of Documentaries Antenne 2 1975; Pres. Inst. pratique de journalisme 1978–; Commentary for Les oubliés de l'histoire, France-Inter 1987; Chevalier Palmes académiques, Légion d'honneur, Officer, Arts et Lettres, Diplome d'études superieures de philosophie, Agrégé d'histoire, Docteur d'Etat. *Publications:* numerous books on social and media history, including L'affaire Dreyfus 1959, Poincaré 1961, La paix de Versailles et l'opinion politique française 1971, Histoire de la radio et de la télévision 1973, Histoire de la France 1976, La véritable histoire des Français 1977, Les oubliés de l'histoire 1978, Les guerres de religion 1980, La quatrième république 1982, La grande guerre 1983, Histoire de la radio et de la télévision, au temps de la grande guerre 1984, La seconde guerre mondiale 1986, La lionne de Belfort 1987, Les hommes de la Grande guerre 1987, Vive la France 1988, La Grande Révolution 1988, La Troisième République 1989, Les Gendarmes 1990, la Campagne de France de Napoléon ou les Eclairs du Génie 1991, Histoire du monde contemporain 1945–91 1991, le Magasin de chapeaux (novel) 1992, le Second Empire 1993, La guerre d'Algérie 1993, Les Polytechniciens 1994, Le Monde Bascule 1995, Mourir à Verdun 1995, Vincent de Paul 1996, Petite histoire des fleurs de l'histoire 1997, La Main courante, les archives indiscrètes de la police parisienne 1997, les Poilus d'Orient 1998. *Leisure interest:* collecting replicas (in tin) of soldiers of the First Empire. *Address:* 24 rue de la Gare, 77135 Pontcarré, France (Home).

MIRAKHOR, Abbas, PH.D.; Iranian international banking executive and economist; b. 1 July 1941, Teheran; m. Loretta Thomas 1965; two s.; ed. Kansas State Univ., U.S.A.; Asst. and Assoc. Prof. and Chair. Dept. of Econs., Univ. of Alabama 1968–77, Prof. and Chair. Dept. 1977–79, Vice-Chancellor 1979–80; Az-Zahra Univ., Teheran; Prof. and Chair. Grad. Study Dept., Alabama A & M Univ. 1980–83; Prof. of Econs. Fla. Inst. of Tech. 1983–84; Economist, IMF 1984–87, Sr. Economist 1987–90, Exec. Dir. 1990–. *Publications:* numerous articles on econs. *Address:* International Monetary Fund, 700 19th Street, NW, Washington, DC 20431, U.S.A.

MIRANI, Aftab Shahban; Pakistani politician; s. of Ghulam Kadir Shahban Mirani and Begum Sharfunisa Shahban Mirani; m.; one s. three d.; ed. studies in farm man. and agric. in U.S.A.; fmr. Pres. Shikarpur Municipality; mem. Sindh Provincial Ass. (Pakistan People's Party) 1977–90; Chief Minister of Sindh until 1990; mem. Nat. Ass. 1990–; Minister of Defence 1993–96. *Leisure interests:* walking, swimming. *Address:* c/o Ministry of Defence, Pakistan Secretariat, No 11, Rawalpindi 46000, Islamabad, Pakistan.

MIRDHA, Ram Niwas, M.A.; Indian politician; b. 24 Aug. 1924, Kuchera, Rajasthan; s. of late Shri Baldev Ramji Mirdha; m. Indira Mirdha; two s. one d.; ed. Allahabad and Lucknow Univs., Inst. of Int. Studies, Geneva, Switzerland; mem. Rajasthan State Legis. Ass. 1953–67, Minister of Agric., Irrigation and Transport 1954–57, Speaker of Ass. 1957–67; mem. Rajya Sabha 1967–80, Deputy Chair. 1977–80, Minister of State in Ministry of Home Affairs 1970–74, Minister of Defence Production 1974–75, Minister of Supply and Rehabilitation 1975–77, Minister of State for Irrigation 1983–84, Minister of State for External Affairs Aug.-Dec. 1984, Minister of State for Ministry of Communications 1985–86, Minister of Textiles with additional charge for Ministry of Health and Family Welfare 1986–89; mem.

10th Lok Sabha (Parl.) from Barmer in Rajasthan 1991–96; Rep. of India at several int. confs.; Chair. Jt. Parl. Cttee. to enquire into irregularities in securities and banking transactions; Chair. Youth Hostels Asscn. of India; Pres. Indian Heritage Soc., Indian Soc. of Int. Law; mem. Exec. Bd. UNESCO; Hon. Pres. World Fed. of UN Asscns.; fmr. Chair. Nat. Inst. of Sports; Chair. Nat. Acad. of Fine Arts 1976–80. *Leisure interests:* arts, sports, agriculture. *Address:* 7 Lodhi Estate, New Delhi 110003, India. *Telephone:* 4629493 (Home). *Fax:* 91-11-6113469.

MIRICIOIU, Nelly; Romanian opera singer; b. 31 March 1952, Adjud; d. of Voicu Miricioiu and Maria Miricioiu; ed. Conservatoire G. Enesco, Iassy; professional début as Queen of the Night in The Magic Flute in Romania 1970; western European début as Violetta in Scottish Opera production of La Traviata 1981; début at Convent Garden as Nedda in Pagliacci 1982, at La Scala as Lucia in Lucia di Lammermoor 1983; has since appeared at many of the other opera houses of the world including Verona, San Francisco, Vienna, Berlin, Hamburg, Madrid, Florence, and in recitals and concerts; repertoire includes Mimi (La Bohème), Julietta (I Capuleti e I Montecchi), Gilda (Rigoletto), Marguerite and Elena (Mephistofele), Michaela (Carmen), Marguerite (Faust), Violetta (La Traviata), Manon Lescaut; repertoire also includes Anna Bolena and Lucrezia Borgia (by Donizetti), Norma (Bellini), Tancredi (Rossini); made 1st recording, recital Wigmore Hall, London 1986; winner of 10 int. competitions. *Leisure interests:* literature, television, cooking, socializing. *Address:* 53 Midhurst Avenue, Muswell Hill, London, N.10, England. *Telephone:* 0181-883 8596.

MIRONOV, Oleg Orestovich, LL.D.; Russian lawyer; b. 5 June 1939; m.; one s.; ed. Saratov Inst. of Law; asst., teacher, docent, Acting Head of Dept., Prof. Saratov Inst. of Law 1965–82, 1991–93; docent, Prof., Head of Dept. Prorector on scientific work, Volga Social and Political Inst. 1982–91; mem. CP of Russian Fed. 1992–; mem., State Duma 1993–; mem. Cttee. on Law and Legal Reform; mem. Parl. Union of Russia and Belarus; Ombudsman of Russian Fed. elected by State Duma 1998–; mem. Interparl. Ass. of C.I.S. countries on Legal Problems. *Publications:* over 170 articles including monographs on problems of constitutional law, theory of state and law, politology. *Leisure interests:* mountain tourism, Master of Sports. *Address:* Ombudsman's Office, Myasnitskaya str. 47, Moscow, Russia. *Telephone:* (095) 207 3986 (Office).

MIRONOV, Col.-Gen. Valery Ivanovich; Russian army officer; b. 19 Dec. 1943, Moscow; m.; one d.; ed. Moscow High Command School, Frunze Mil. Acad., U.S.S.R. Gen. Staff Acad.; with Soviet troops in Germany 1965–70; Turkestan mil. command 1970–79; Deputy, First Deputy Commdr. army in Afghanistan 1979–82; First Deputy Commdr. of Leningrad Mil. Command 1984–91; Commdr. N.W. group of troops 1991–92; Deputy Minister of Defence of Russia 1992–95; spokesman on problems of deployment and withdrawal of Russian troops from Baltic Repubs; Chief Mil. Expert of Russian Govt. 1995–. *Address:* Ministry of Defence, 103175 Moscow, ul. Myasnitskaya 37, Russia.

MIRONOV, Yevgeniy Vitalyevich; Russian actor; b. 29 Nov. 1966, Saratov; s. of Vitaly Sergeyevich Mironov and Tamara Petrovna Mironova; ed. Saratov School of Theatre Art, Studio School of Moscow Art Theatre; actor Oleg Tabakov Theatre-Studio 1990–; roles in most productions, including David Schwartz (Matrosskaya Tishina, A. Galich), Aleksander Aduyev (Common Story, Goncharov), Bumbarash (Passions over Bumbarash, Kim), Orest (Orestea, Aeschylus), Ivan Karamazov (The Karamazovs and Hell, Dostoyevsky), Maratov (The Last Night of the Last Tsar, Radzinsky); in cinema since 1988–; roles in films by A. Kaidanovsky, A. Mitta, V. Todorovsky, Khotinenko, D. Yevstigneyev, N. Mikhalkov, S. Gazarov including Flutist (Wife of a Keroseneman 1989), Volodya (Lost in Siberia 1989), Sasha (Love 1990 - Prize for best Kinotaurus Festival 1992), Constellation 1992, Young Stars of Europe, Geneva 1992, Cinema Critics Prize - Best Actor of the Year 1992, Volodya Poletayev (Encore, Another Encore 1991 - Prize of Cinema Critics - Best Actor of the Year 1993), Kolya (Moslem 1995 - Cinema Critics Prize - Best Actor of the Year 1995), Misha Vuloch (Limita 1994 - Nika Prize 95), Kolya (Burnt of the Sun 1993 - Prize for supporting actor, Constellation- 95), Khlestakov (Inspector - Prize for Best Actor Role, Ural Festival 1996); Merited Artist of Russia 1996. *Address:* Oleg Tabakov Theatre-Studio, Chaplygina str. 12A, Moscow, Russia. *Telephone:* (095) 916 2121 (Office); 264 1558 (Home).

MIRREN, Helen; British actress; b. 26 July 1945, London; m. Taylor Hackford 1997; first experience with Nat. Youth Theatre culminating in appearance as Cleopatra in Antony and Cleopatra, Old Vic 1965; joined Royal Shakespeare Co. (RSC) 1967 to play Castiza in The Revenger's Tragedy and Diana in All's Well that Ends Well. *Other roles include:* Cressida in Troilus and Cressida, Hero in Much Ado About Nothing, RSC, Stratford 1968; Win-the-Fight Littlewit in Bartholomew Fair, Aldwych 1969, Lady Anne in Richard III, Stratford, Ophelia in Hamlet, Julia in The Two Gentlemen of Verona, Stratford 1970 (the last part also at Aldwych), Tatyana in Enemies, Aldwych 1971; title role in Miss Julie, Elyane in The Balcony, The Place 1971; with Peter Brook's Centre International de Recherches Théâtrales, Africa and U.S.A. 1972–73; Lady Macbeth, RSC, Stratford 1974 and Aldwych 1975; Maggie in Teeth 'n' Smiles, Royal Court 1975; Nina in The Seagull and Ella in The Bed Before Yesterday, Lyric for Lyric Theatre Co. 1975; Margaret in Henry VI (parts 1, 2 and 3), RSC 1977–78; Isabella in Measure for Measure, Riverside 1979; The Duchess of Malfi, Manchester Royal Exchange 1980 and Roundhouse 1981; The Faith Healer, Royal Court 1981; Antony and Cleopatra 1983, 1998, The Roaring Girl, RSC, Barbican 1983, Extremities (Evening Standard Award) 1984, Madame Bovary 1987, Two Way Mirror 1989; Sex Please, We're Italian, Young Vic 1991; The Writing Game, New Haven, Conn. 1993, The Gift of the Gorgon (New York) 1994; A Month in the Country 1994. *Films include:* Age of Consent 1969, Savage Messiah, O Lucky Man! 1973, Caligula 1977, The Long Good Friday, Excalibur 1981, Cal (Best Actress, Cannes) 1984, 2010 1985, White Nights 1986, Heavenly Pursuits 1986, The Mosquito Coast 1987, Pascali's Island 1988, When the Whales Came 1988, Bethune: The Making of a Hero 1989, The Cook, the Thief, his Wife and her Lover 1989, The Comfort of Strangers 1989, Where Angels Fear to Tread 1990, The Hawk, The Prince of Jutland 1991, The Madness of King George 1995, Some Mother's Son 1996, Killing Mrs Tingle 1998. *TV includes:* Miss Julie, The Apple Cart, The Little Minister, As You Like It, Mrs. Reinhardt, Soft Targets 1982, Blue Remembered Hills, Coming Through, Cause Celebre, Red King White Knight, Prime Suspect (B.A.F.T.A. Award) 1991, Prime Suspect II 1992, Prime Suspect III 1993, Prime Suspect: Scent of Darkness 1996 (Emmy Award 1996), Painted Lady 1997, Ayn Rand 1998. *Address:* c/o Ken McReddie Ltd., 91 Regent Street, London, W1R 7TB, England.

MIRRLEES, Sir James Alexander, Kt., M.A., PH.D., F.B.A.; British professor of economics; b. 5 July 1936, Scotland; s. of the late George B. M. Mirrlees; m. Gillian M. Hughes 1961 (died 1993); two d.; ed. Edinburgh Univ. and Trinity Coll., Cambridge; Adviser, M.I.T. Center for Int. Studies, New Delhi 1962–63; Asst. Lecturer in Econs. and Fellow, Trinity Coll., Univ. of Cambridge 1963, Univ. Lecturer 1965; Research Assoc. Pakistan Inst. of Devt. Econs. 1966–67; Fellow, Nuffield Coll. and Edgeworth Prof. of Econs. Univ. of Oxford 1968–95; Prof. of Political Economy, Univ. of Cambridge, Fellow Trinity Coll. 1995–; Adviser to Govt. of Swaziland 1963; Visiting Prof. M.I.T. 1968, 1970, 1976, 1987; Ford Visiting Prof., Univ. of Calif., Berkeley 1986; Visiting Prof., Yale Univ. 1989; mem. Treasury Cttee. on Policy Optimization 1976–78; Pres. Econometric Soc. 1982; Pres. Royal Econ. Soc. 1989–92; Nobel Prize for Econ. 1996; Foreign Hon. mem. American Acad. of Arts and Sciences; Hon. mem. American Econ. Asscn.; Hon. Fellow Royal Soc. of Edin.; Hon. D.Litt. (Warwick) 1982, (Portsmouth) 1997, (Oxford) 1998; Hon. D.Sc.S. (Brunel) 1997; Hon. D.Sc. (Social Sciences) (Edin.) 1997. *Publications:* jt. author of three books and articles in academic journals. *Leisure interests:* music, travel, computing. *Address:* Trinity College, Cambridge, CB2 1TQ, England. *Telephone:* (01223) 339516. *Fax:* (01223) 335475.

MIRSAIDOV, Shukurulla Rakhmatovich, D.ECON.; Uzbekistan politician; b. 14 Feb. 1938, Leninabad; m.; four c.; ed. Tashkent Finance and Econ. Inst.; mem. CPSU 1962–91; on staff State Planning Org. 1964–84; Head Cen. Statistical Dept., Uzbek S.S.R. 1984–85; Chair. Tashkent City Council 1985–86; Head of Dept., CP of Uzbekistan 1988–89; Deputy Premier of Uzbekistan S.S.R. 1989–90; Chair. Council of Ministers 1990–92; Vice-Pres. of Uzbekistan 1991–92; State Sec. for Pres. Karimov 1992; rep. Int. Fund for Privatization and Investments in Uzbekistan 1992–95. *Address:* International Fund for Privatization, Tashkent, Uzbekistan.

MIRVISH, David, C.M.; Canadian theatrical producer; b. 29 Aug. 1944; s. of Edwin Mirvish (q.v.), C.B.E. and Anne Macklin; producer and owner of the Old Vic Theatre, London and The Royal Alexandra and The Princess of Wales Theatres, Toronto; productions and co-productions include: Candide and Too Clever by Half (London), Into the Woods (London), Les Misérables (Canada), The Good Times are Killing Me (New York), Miss Saigon, Crazy for You, Tommy (Toronto); Dir. Williamstown Theatre Festival, U.S.A. –1992, Nat. Gallery of Canada, Nat. Theatre School of Canada 1989–91, Toronto French School; mem. Canadian Cultural Property Export Review Bd. 1983–86; Rayne Award (Royal Nat. Theatre); Toronto Theatre Alliance (Dora) Humanitarian Award, Toronto Arts Award 1994. *Address:* The Old Vic, Waterloo Road, London, SE1 8NB, England; Mirvish Productions, 266 King Street W., Toronto, Ont., Canada. *Telephone:* 0171-928 2651 (London); (416) 593-0351 (Toronto).

MIRVISH, Edwin (Ed), O.C., C.B.E.; Canadian impresario; b. 1914, Colonial Beach, Va., U.S.A.; m. Anne Mirvish; one s.; opened Honest Ed's (Bloor Street Retail Bargain Emporium), Markham St., Toronto in 1940s; bought Royal Alexandra Theatre, Toronto 1962, bought Old Vic Theatre, London, U.K. 1982; Pres. and C.E.O. Honest Ed's Ltd., Royal Alexandra Theatre; Dir. Mirvish Enterprises; opened Ed's Unusual Theatre Museum 1991; bought (with son) Canadian rights to musical Les Misérables 1988; built Princess of Wales Theatre, Toronto 1993; Markham St., Toronto officially renamed Mirvish village 1984; Mirvish Productions have won Dora Awards in Canada and 5 Olivier Awards in U.K., nominated for Tony Awards in U.S.A.; Hon. LL.D. (Trent, Waterloo, York); numerous honours and awards including Order of Ont., Order of Merit, City of Toronto, Distinguished Retailer of the Year Award, Retail Council of Canada, Drama Bench (Toronto) Award for distinguished contrib. to Canadian theatre, Freeman City of London. *Publication:* How to Build an Empire on an Orange Crate (autobiog.) 1993. *Leisure interest:* ballroom dancing. *Address:* Honest Ed's Ltd., 581 Bloor Street W., Toronto, Ont., M6G 1K3, Canada. *Telephone:* (416) 537-2111.

MIRZABEKOV, Andrei Daryevich, D.CHEM.; Russian molecular biologist; b. 19 Oct. 1937, Baku; m. Nataly Romanov 1964; one d.; ed. Inst. of Fine Chemical Technology, Moscow; Lab. Asst. W. Engelhardt Inst. of Molecular Biology of U.S.S.R. Acad. of Sciences 1961, later jr. researcher, Chief of

Dept., Deputy Dir. 1984, Dir. 1985–; fmr. Academician-Sec. Biophysics, Biochem. and Chem. of Physiologically Active Compounds Div. U.S.S.R. Acad. of Sciences; Visiting Scientist, MRC Lab. of Molecular Biology, Cambridge, U.K. 1971, Calif. Inst. of Tech. Pasadena and Harvard Univ. 1975; Vice-Pres. Int. Human Genome Org. (HUGO) 1989–; mem. U.S.S.R. (now Russian) Acad. of Sciences 1987, Academia Europaea 1990; U.S.S.R. State Prize 1969; FEBS Anniversary Prize 1978; Gregor Mendel Medal, Deutsche Akad. der Naturforscher Leopoldina. *Publications:* contribs. to professional journals. *Leisure interests:* philosophy, hiking, skiing. *Address:* W. A. Engelhardt Institute of Molecular Biology, Vavilov Street 32, Moscow 117984, Russia. *Telephone:* (095) 135-23-11 (Office); 331-32-79 (Home).

MIRZOEFF, Edward, C.V.O., C.B.E., M.A.; British television producer; b. 11 April 1936; s. of late Eliachar Mirzoeff and of Penina Asherov; m. Judith Topper 1961; three s.; ed. Hasmonean Grammar School, Queen's Coll. Oxford; market researcher, Social Surveys (Gallup Poll) Ltd. 1958–59, Public Relations Exec., Duncan McLeish & Assocs. 1960–61; Asst. Ed. Shoppers' Guide 1961–63; with BBC TV 1963–, Exec. Producer, Documentaries 1983–; dir. and producer of film documentaries including: (with Sir John Betjeman) Metro-land 1973, A Passion for Churches 1973, The Queen's Realm 1977; Police – Harrow Road 1975, The Regiment 1977, The Front Garden 1979, The Ritz 1981, The Englishwoman and The Horse 1981, Elizabeth R 1992, Torvill and Dean – facing the music 1994, Treasures in Trust 1995; Ed. 40 Minutes 1985–89; Ed. several series including Real Lives 1985, Pandora's Box 1992, The Ark 1993, True Brits 1994, Situation Vacant 1995, The House 1995, Full Circle with Michael Palin 1997, The Fifty Years War: Israel and the Arabs 1998, Richard Dimbleby Lectures 1972–82, A. J. P. Taylor Lectures (three series); Chair. B.A.F.T.A. 1995–97 (Vice-Chair., TV 1991–95); B.A.F.T.A. Awards: Best Documentary 1981, Best Factual Series 1985, 1989, Alan Clarke Award for outstanding creative contribution to TV 1995; Samuelson Award, Birmingham Festival 1988, B.F.I. TV Award 1988, British Video Award 1992, Broadcasting Press Guild Award 1996, Royal Philharmonic Soc. Music Award 1996, Int. Emmy 1996. *Leisure interests:* exploring the London Library, walking in Wiltshire, visiting Venice. *Address:* 9 Westmoreland Road, London, SW13 9RZ, England. *Telephone:* 0181-748 9247.

MIRZOYAN, Edvard Mikhailovich; Armenian composer; b. 12 May 1921, Gori, Georgian S.S.R.; s. of Mikhail Mirzoyan and Luciné Mirzoyan; m. Elena M. Stepanyan 1951; two c.; ed. Yerevan Conservatory; teacher Komitas Conservatory, Yerevan, Armenia 1948–, Prof. 1965–; mem. CPSU 1952–90; Pres. Union of Composers of Armenian S.S.R. 1957–91; Sec. U.S.S.R. Union of Composers 1962–90; mem. Cen. Cttee. of Armenian CP 1964–90; Deputy of Supreme Soviet of Armenian S.S.R.C.P. 1959–90; People's Deputy of U.S.S.R. 1989–91; mem. U.S.S.R. Supreme Soviet 1990–91; Pres. Armenian Peace Fund 1978–; Armenian Meritorious Artist 1958; Armenian People's Artist 1963; U.S.S.R. People's Artist 1981; Order of Cyril and Methodius, Bulgaria 1981. *Compositions include:* Symphonic Dances 1946, Soviet Armenia (cantata), To the Heroes of the War (Symphonic poem), Symphony of Light (ballet), Symphony for strings and timpani 1962, Sonata for cello and piano 1967, Poem for Piano, Lyrical Picture "Shushanik" 1973, In Memory of Aram Khachaturyan 1988, Album for my Granddaughter 1988, Poem for Cello and Piano 1995, Circle "Seasons" based on the words of Chinese poets 1997; string quartet, romances, instrumental pieces, songs, film-music. *Address:* Demirchyan Street 25, Apt. 9, 375002 Yerevan, Armenia. *Telephone:* (2) 52-92-59. *Fax:* (2) 72-36-39.

MIRZOYEV, Gasan Borisovich; Russian lawyer; b. 11 Dec. 1947, Baku, Azerbaijan; ed. Azerbaijan State Univ., Moscow Inst. of Man.; worked at factory, joined militia; State Arbiter of Moscow 1987–; f. and Chair. Presidium, Centre of Law, Moscow, f. and Pres. Bd. of Lawyers Mosyurcenter; Head of Dept. Moscow Int. Inst. of Law, Russian Ministry of Justice; Sec. Dept. of Human Rights; mem. Int. and European Asscn. of Lawyers; Chair. Bd. Dirs. Cen. House of Lawyers; Pres. Guild of Russian Lawyers; Head, Cttee. of Plevako Golden Medal; Merited Lawyer of Russia; main research in law regulation of business. *Publications:* over 100 including monographs on problems of legal protection of business in Russia and protection of human rights. *Leisure interest:* chess. *Address:* Guild of Lawyers, Maly Poluyaroslavsky per. 3/5, 107120 Moscow, Russia. *Telephone:* (095) 917 1196 (Office).

MIRZOYEV, Ramason Zarifovich; Tajikistan diplomatist; b. 15 Feb. 1945, Kulyab Region, Tajikistan; m.; six c.; ed. Tadjik Inst. of Agric.; worked with construction teams Kulyab Region; in Afghanistan 1975–78; since 1983 worked in CP bodies and orgs.; U.S.S.R. People's Deputy 1989–92; Deputy Chair. U.S.S.R. Supreme Soviet 1989–91; Man. Council of Ministers Repub. of Tajikistan 1992–95; Amb. of Tajikistan to Russian Fed. 1995–. *Address:* Tajikistan Embassy, 121069 Moscow Skatertny per. 19, Russia. *Telephone:* (095) 290 6102.

MISCHNICK, Wolfgang; German politician; b. 29 Sept. 1921; s. of Walter Mischnick and Marie Rölig; m. Christine Dietzsch 1949; two s. one d.; ed. High School, Dresden; co-founder, Liberal Democratic Party, Dresden 1945; town official, Dresden 1946–48; mem. Cen. Cttee. of Liberal Democratic Party, Soviet Zone 1946–48; fled to Fed. Germany 1948; mem. Prov. Assembly, Hesse, 1954–57, Parl. Leader of FDP; Fed. Chair. FDP Youth Movement and Ed. Stimmen der jungen Generation 1954–57; mem. Bundestag 1957–94; Deputy Chair. FDP, Hesse 1957–67, Chair. 1967–77; Fed. Minister for Refugees 1961–63; Deputy Chair. FDP 1964–88, FDP Chair. in Bundestag 1968–77; Chair. Supervisory Bd. Gröditzer Stahlwerke GmbH 1991; Hon. Chair. FDP Hessen. *Leisure interests:* sport (especially football), music, history.

MISHCON, Baron (Life Peer), cr. 1978, of Lambeth in Greater London; **Victor Mishcon;** British solicitor and politician; b. 14 Aug. 1915; s. of Rabbi Arnold Mishcon and Queenie Mishcon; m. Joan Estelle Conrad 1976; two s. one d. by previous marriage; ed. City of London School; mem. Lambeth Borough Council 1945–49, Chair. Finance Cttee. 1947–49; mem. for Brixton London Co. Council 1946–65, Chair. Public Control Cttee. 1947–52, Gen. Purposes Cttee. 1952–54, Council 1954–55, Supplies Cttee. 1956–57, Fire Brigade Cttee. 1958–65; mem. for Lambeth, GLC 1964–67, Chair. Gen. Purposes Cttee. 1964–67; mem. Inner London Educ. Authority 1964–67; contested parl. seat (Labour) Leeds N.W. 1950, Bath 1951, Gravesend 1955, 1959; mem. Jt. Cttee. on Consolidation of Bills 1983–85, Law Sub-Cttee., House of Lords European Communities Cttee. 1978–86, House of Lords Select Cttee. on Procedure 1981–83, House of Lords Select Cttee. on Medical Ethics 1993; Opposition Spokesman on Home Affairs, House of Lords 1983–90, on Legal Affairs 1983–92; Vice-Chair. Lords and Commons Solicitors Group 1983–; solicitor, later Sr. Partner Mishcon de Reya (fmrly. Victor Mishcon and Co.) 1988–92, now Consultant; Gov. and Chair. Bd. of Govs. various schools in U.K. 1947–85; mem. Standing Jt. Cttee., Co. of London Sessions 1950–65, Vice-Chair. 1959–61, Nat. Theatre Bd. 1965–67, 1968–90, South Bank Theatre Bd. 1977–82, London Orchestra Bd. 1966–67, Exec. Cttee. London Tourist Bd. 1965–67; mem. Govt. Cttee. of Enquiry into London Transport 1953–54, Departmental Cttee. on Homosexual Offences and Prostitution 1954–57; Vice-Chair. Council of Christians and Jews 1976–77; Vice-Pres. Bd. of Deputies of British Jews 1967–73; Hon. Pres. British Technion Soc.; Vice-Pres. (Past Pres.) Asscn. of Jewish Youth; Pres. British Council of the Shaare Zedek Hosp., Jerusalem; Hon. Q.C. 1992; Hon. Fellow Univ. Coll. London 1993; Hon. LL.D. (Birmingham) 1991; Commdr. Royal Swedish Order of North Star 1954, Star of Ethiopia 1954, Star of Jordan 1995; D.L. Greater London 1954. *Leisure interests:* theatre, music, reading. *Address:* House of Lords, London, SW1A 0PW; 21 Southampton Row, London, W.C.1, England.

MISHIN, Vasiliy Pavlovich; Russian engineer; b. 18 Jan. 1917, Orekhovo-Zuevo, Moscow Region; m.; three c.; ed. Moscow Aviation Inst.; specialist in applied mechanics; mem. CPSU 1943–91; researcher, office of designer V. Bolkhovitinov, worked on first Soviet rocket aircraft –1946; First Deputy Head, Construction Bureau of Sergey Korolev 1946–66; Head, chief constructor of Soviet rockets, space vehicles, orbital space stations 1966–74; discharged by CP Cen. Cttee. 1974; Prof. Moscow Aviation Inst. 1974–90, Councillor 1990–; Deputy of Supreme Soviet R.S.F.S.R. 1966–70; Corresp. mem. U.S.S.R. (now Russian) Acad. of Sciences 1958–66, mem. 1966–; Lenin Prize 1957; Hero of Socialist Labour 1956; Order of Lenin (three), S. P. Korolev Prize and other decorations. *Publications:* numerous articles in the field of applied mechanics. *Address:* Moscow Aviation Institute, Volokolamskoye sh. 4, 125080 Moscow A-80, Russia. *Telephone:* (095) 158-58-59 (Office); (095) 255-45-32 (Home).

MISTRY, Dhruva, R.A., M.A.; Indian sculptor; b. 1 Jan. 1957, Kanjari; s. of Pramodray Mistry and Kantaben Mistry; ed. Univ. of Baroda and R.C.A., London; British Council Scholar 1981–83; artist in residence Churchill Coll., Cambridge 1984–85; Freelance Sculptor-Agent Nigel Greenwood Gallery, London; sculptor in residence, Victoria and Albert Museum, London 1988; Rep. G.B. for the Grand Rodin Prize Exhbn., Japan 1990; one-man exhbns. at Kettle's Yard Gallery, Cambridge 1985, tour to Arnolfini, Bristol 1986, Mostyn Art Gallery, Llandudno 1986, Walker Art Gallery, Liverpool 1986, Nigel Greenwood Gallery, London 1987, 1990, Collins Gallery, Strathclyde 1988; Public collections Tate Gallery, British Council, Arts Council, Victoria and Albert Museum, Walker Art Gallery, Nat. Museum of Wales, Hakone Open Air Museum, Japan. *Publications:* (exhbn. catalogues) Sculptures and Drawings 1985, Cross-sections 1988, Dhruva Mistry, Bronzes 1985–1990. *Leisure interests:* photography, reading, walking. *Address:* c/o Anthony Wilkinson Fine Art, 29 Great Ormond Street, London, WC1N 3HZ, England.

MITA, Katsushige, B.E.E.; Japanese business executive; b. 6 April 1924, Tokyo; s. of Yoshitaro and Fuji Mita; m. Toriko Miyata 1957; two d.; ed. Univ. of Tokyo; joined Hitachi Ltd. 1949; Gen. Man. Omika Works Aug.–Nov. 1971, Kanagawa Works 1971–75, Dir. 1975; Man. Computer Group 1976–78, Exec. Man. Dir. 1977–79, Sr. Exec. Man. Dir. 1979–80, Exec. Vice-Pres. 1980–81; Pres. and Rep. Dir. Hitachi Ltd. 1981–91, Chair. and Rep. Dir. 1991–; Vice-Chair. Keidanren (Japan Fed. of Econ. Orgs.) 1992–; Dr. h.c. (Tufts Univ., U.S.A.) 1991; Blue Ribbon Medal (Japan) 1985; Officier, Légion d'honneur 1993; DSPN Dato (Malaysia) 1993; Will Rogers Award (U.S.A.) 1994. *Leisure interests:* golf, gardening. *Address:* Hitachi Ltd., 6 Kanda-Suragadai 4-chome, Chiyoda-ku, Tokyo 101 (Office); 2423-277, Nara-machi, Aoba-ku, Yokohama-shi, Kanagawa-ken, 227, Japan (Home). *Telephone:* 045 961 7733.

MITCHELL, Arthur; American dancer, choreographer and artistic director; b. 27 March 1934, New York; s. of Arthur and Willie Mae Mitchell; ed. School of American Ballet; with Ballet Theater Workshop 1954; with John Butler Co., 1955; prin. dancer, N.Y. City Ballet 1955–72; dancer, choreographer and actor, Spoleto Festival of Two Worlds 1960; founder and artistic dir. American Negro Dance Co. 1966–; founder, choreographer and artistic dir. Nat. Ballet Co., Brazil 1967; founder, dir. and choreographer Dance Theater of Harlem, N.Y. City 1969–; teacher of dance, Karel Shook Studio, Melissa Hayden School, Cedarhurst, Long Island, Jones-Haywood School of Ballet, Washington; choreographer (with Rod Alexander) Shinbone Alley; has appeared in numerous productions; hon. degrees include: Hon. D.Arts (Columbia Coll., Chicago) 1975, Hon. D.F.A. (N.C. School of the Arts) 1981, (Fordham Univ.) 1983, (Princeton Univ., Williams Coll.) 1986, (Juilliard School) 1990, Hon. D.A. (Harvard) 1987; awards include: Ebony Magazine American Black Achievement Award 1983; Paul Robeson Award, Actors Equity Assen., N.A.A.C.P. Image Awards Hall of Fame 1986; Arnold Gingrich Memorial Award 1987; Banquet of the Golden Plate 1989; Kennedy Center Honor for Lifetime Achievement 1993; Handel Medallion, City of N.Y., American Acad. of Arts and Letters Award for Distinguished Service to the Arts, Barnard Coll. Medal of Distinction, Zenith Award for Fine Arts 1994, Nat. Medal of Arts 1995. *Address:* Dance Theater of Harlem, 466 West 152nd Street, New York, NY 10031, U.S.A. (Office).

MITCHELL, Basil George, M.A., D.D., F.B.A.; British academic; b. 9 April 1917, Bath; s. of George William Mitchell and Mary Mitchell; m. Margaret Collin 1950; one s. three d.; ed. King Edward VI School, Southampton and The Queen's Coll., Oxford; served R.N. 1940–46; Lecturer Christ Church, Oxford 1946–47; Fellow and Tutor Keble Coll., Oxford 1947–67; Nolloth Prof. of the Philosophy of the Christian Religion, Oxford Univ. and Fellow of Oriel Coll. 1968–84, Prof. Emer. 1984–; Stanton Lecturer, Cambridge Univ. 1959–62; Edward Cadbury Lecturer, Birmingham Univ. 1966–67; Gifford Lecturer, Glasgow Univ. 1974–76; Norton Lecturer, Southern Baptist Theological Seminary, Louisville 1989; Sarum Lecturer, Oxford Univ. 1992; Visiting Prof. Princeton Univ., U.S.A. 1963, Colgate Univ., U.S.A. 1976; Nathaniel Taylor Lecturer, Yale Univ., U.S.A. 1986; mem. Church of England Doctrine Comm. 1978–85; Chair. Ian Ramsey Centre, Oxford 1985–89; Hon. D.D. (Glasgow); Hon. D.Lit.Hum. (Union Coll., Schenectady). *Publications:* Faith and Logic (Ed.) 1957, Law, Morality and Religion in a Secular Society 1967, The Philosophy of Religion (Ed.) 1971, The Justification of Religious Belief 1973, Morality: Religious and Secular 1980, How to Play Theological Ping Pong and Other Essays on Faith and Reason 1990, Faith and Criticism 1994. *Leisure interests:* gardening, flower arranging. *Address:* Bartholomew House, 9 Market Street, Woodstock, Oxon., OX20 1SU, England.

MITCHELL, Sir Derek, K.C.B., C.V.O.; British fmr. civil servant and company director; b. 5 March 1922, Wimbledon; s. of the late Sidney Mitchell and Gladys Mitchell; m. Miriam Jackson 1944 (died 1993); one s. two d.; ed. St. Paul's School, London and Christ Church, Oxford; served Royal Armoured Corps and HQ London District 1942–45; served in H.M. Treasury 1947–63, Principal Private Sec. to Chancellor of the Exchequer 1962–63; Principal Private Sec. to Prime Minister 1964–66; Deputy Under-Sec. of State, Dept. of Econ. Affairs 1966–67, Ministry of Agric., Fisheries and Food 1967–69; Econ. Minister, British Embassy, Washington and Exec. Dir. IBRD, IMF, etc. 1969–72; Second Perm. Sec. (Overseas Finance) H.M. Treasury 1973–77; Sr. Adviser, Shearson Lehman Brothers International 1979–88; Dir. Guinness Mahon 1977–78, Bowater Corpn. 1979–84, Bowater Industries PLC 1984–89, Bowater Inc. 1984–93, Standard Chartered PLC 1979–89; mem. Nat. Theatre (now Royal Nat. Theatre) Bd. 1977–96; mem. Bd. French Theatre Season 1997 1996–98; Trustee Nat. Theatre (now Royal Nat. Theatre) Foundation 1982–, Chair. 1989–; mem. Council of Univ. Coll., London 1978–82, Port of London Authority 1979–82; Independent Dir. The Observer Ltd. 1981–93; Dir. the Peter Hall Production Co. Ltd. 1989–90; Trustee Nuffield Trust (fmrly. Nuffield Prov. Hosps. Trust) 1978–. *Leisure interests:* opera, concerts, theatre, travelling. *Address:* 9 Holmbush Road, Putney, London, SW15 3LE, England. *Telephone:* 0181-788 6581. *Fax:* 0181-788 6948.

MITCHELL, Duncan, M.SC., PH.D., F.R.S.S.AF; South African professor of physiology; b. 10 May 1941, Germiston; s. of Thomas and Maud K. (née Abercrombie) Mitchell; m. Lily May Austin 1966; one s. one d.; ed. St. John's Coll., Johannesburg, Univ. of Witwatersrand; mem. scientific staff, Research Org. of Chamber of Mines of South Africa 1964–72, Nat. Inst. for Medical Research, London 1973–75; Prof. of Physiology, Medical School, Univ. of Witwatersrand 1976–. *Publications:* over 140 papers in thermal physiology. *Leisure interests:* nature conservation, ballet. *Address:* Physiology Dept., Medical School, University of the Witwatersrand, Parktown 2193, South Africa. *Telephone:* (11) 647-2359. *Fax:* (11) 643-2765.

MITCHELL, Sir (Edgar) William John, Kt., C.B.E., D.SC., F.R.S., F.INST.P.; British university professor; b. 25 Sept. 1925, Kingsbridge; s. of late Edgar Mitchell and Caroline Mitchell; m. 1st 1948; one s.; m. 2nd Margaret Constance Davies 1985; one step-s. one step-d.; ed. Sheffield and Bristol Univs.; Research Physicist, Metropolitan Vickers 1946–51, Bristol Univ. 1948–50; Research Fellow, Reading Univ. 1951, Lecturer 1952–56, Reader 1956–61, Prof. 1961–78, Deputy Vice-Chancellor 1976–78; Prof. Experimental Philosophy, Head of Clarendon Lab., Oxford Univ. 1978–88; Prof. of Physics, Oxford Univ. 1988–89; Personal Chair., Clarendon Lab. 1988; Chair. U.K. Science and Eng. Research Council 1985–90; Fellow, Wadham Coll., Oxford 1978–92, Emer. Fellow; Vice-Pres. European Science Foundation 1989–92; mem. Scientific Council, Inst. Max von Laue-Paul Langevin, Grenoble, France 1968–75; mem. Council CERN 1985–93 (Vice-Pres. 1990, Pres. 1991–93); MacRobert Award 1990, Glazebrook Medal, Inst. of Physics 1996. *Publications:* numerous scientific papers. *Leisure interests:* opera, mountains, food. *Address:* Wadham College, Oxford, OX1 3PN, England. *Telephone:* (01865) 272267. *Fax:* (01865) 272400.

MITCHELL, George John, B.A., LL.B.; American politician and lawyer; b. 20 Aug. 1933, Waterville, Me.; s. of George J. Mitchell and Mary (née Saad) Mitchell; one d.; called to Bar 1960; Trial Attorney U.S. Dept. of Justice, Washington 1960–62; Exec. Asst. to Senator Edmund Muskie (q.v.) 1962–65; partner Jensen & Baird, Portland 1965–77; U.S. Attorney for Maine 1977–79; U.S. Dist. Judge 1979–80; U.S. Senator from Maine 1980–95; Majority Leader, U.S. Senate 1988–95; Chair. Maine Democratic Cttee. 1966–68; mem. Nat. Cttee. Maine 1968–77; Special Adviser to Pres. Clinton for Econ. Initiatives in Ireland 1995; Chair. Cttee. on Northern Ireland 1995; Democrat; Hon. LL.D. (Queen's, Belfast) 1997; Hon. K.B.E. 1999; Shared Honphouet-Boigny Peace Prize 1999.

MITCHELL, Rt. Hon. Sir James Fitzallen, K.C.M.G.; St. Vincent and the Grenadines politician, agronomist and hotelier; b. 15 May 1931, Bequia, Grenadines; s. of Reginald Mitchell and Lois (née Baynes) Mitchell; m. Patricia Parker 1965 (divorced); four d.; ed. St. Vincent Grammar School, Imperial Coll. of Tropical Agric., Trinidad and Univ. of British Columbia; Agricultural Officer, St. Vincent 1958–60; Ed. Pest Control Articles and News Summaries, Ministry of Overseas Devt., London 1965–66; joined St. Vincent Labour Party (SVLP) 1966; M.P. for the Grenadines 1966–; Minister of Trade, Agric., Labour and Tourism 1967–72 (resgnd.); expelled from SVLP 1972; M.P. (as an ind.) for the Grenadines 1972–79, re-elected in by-election July 1979–; Premier of St. Vincent 1972–74; Prime Minister of St. Vincent and the Grenadines July 1984–, also Minister of Finance and Planning, and fmr. Minister of Foreign Affairs; f., Pres. New Democratic Party 1975; Chair. Caribbean Democrat Union 1991; Vice-Chair. Int. Democrat Union 1992. *Leisure interests:* gardening, sailing. *Address:* Prime Minister's Office, Kingstown, St. Vincent.

MITCHELL, James Richard, P.C., T.D.; Irish politician; b. 19 Oct. 1946, Dublin; s. of Peter Mitchell and Eileen Whelan; m. Patricia Kenny 1973; two s. three d.; ed. Rathmines Coll. of Commerce, Trinity Coll., Dublin; Councillor, Dublin City Council 1974–79, 1991–94; Lord Mayor of Dublin 1976–77, Alderman 1979–81; T.D. (mem. Parl.) 1977–; Shadow Minister for Labour 1977–81, for Public Service Jan.-June 1981; Minister for Justice 1981–82; Shadow Minister for Justice March–Dec. 1982; Minister for Posts and Telegraphs, and for Transport 1982–84, for Communications 1984–87; Shadow Minister for Social Welfare 1987–88, for Labour 1988–91, and for Communications 1989–91, for the Environment 1991–93; mem. EC Council of Ministers (Justice) 1981–82, (Transport) 1982–87, Pres. Council of Ministers (Transport) 1984; Pres. Eurocontrol 1985; Chair. Parl. Select Cttee. on Public Accounts 1993–95, 1997–, on Finance and Gen. Affairs 1995–97; mem. Council of Europe Ass. 1993–, Vice-Pres. 1995–96; Leader Irish Del. to Parl. Ass. of Council of Europe 1995–96; Peace Commr. 1973; Fine Gael. *Publications:* Working Accord, Working Together (papers on industrial democracy and industrial relations); Poverty Traps. *Address:* Leinster House, Kildare Street, Dublin 2 (Office); 4 Rathdown Crescent, Terenure, Dublin 6W, Ireland (Home).

MITCHELL, Joni (Roberta Joan Anderson); Canadian singer and songwriter; b. 7 Nov. 1943, Fort Macleod, Alberta; d. of William A. and Myrtle (née McKee) Anderson; m. 1st Chuck Mitchell 1965 (divorced); m. 2nd Larry Klein 1982; one d. by Brad McGrath; ed. Alberta Coll. *Albums include:* Song to a Seagull, Clouds, Ladies of the Canyon 1970, Blue 1971, For the Roses, Court and Spark 1974, Miles of Aisles, The Hissing of Summer Lawns 1975, Hejira 1976, Don Juan's Reckless Daughter, Mingus 1979, Shadows and Light 1980, Wild Things Run Fast 1982, Dog Eat Dog 1985, Chalk Mark in a Rain Storm 1988, Night Ride Home 1991, Turbulent Indigo 1994 (Grammy Awards for Best Pop Album, Best Art Direction 1996), Hits 1996, Misses 1996. *Songs include:* Both Sides Now, Michael from Mountains, Urge for Going, Circle Game. *TV includes:* Joni Mitchell: Intimate and Interactive (Gemini Award 1996). Jazz Album of Year and Rock-Blues Album of Year for Mingus, Downbeat Magazine 1979, Juno Award 1981, Century Award, Billboard Magazine 1996, Polar Music Prize (Sweden) 1996, Gov. Gen.'s Performing Arts Award 1996, Nat. Acad. of Songwriters Lifetime Achievement Award 1996; inducted into Rock & Roll Hall of Fame 1997, into Nat. Acad. of Popular Music–Songwriters Hall of Fame 1997. *Publication:* Joni Mitchell: The Complete Poems and Lyrics. *Address:* c/o S. L. Feldman & Associates, 1505 W. 2nd Avenue, Suite 200, Vancouver, B.C., V6H 3Y4, Canada.

MITCHELL, Julian; British author; b. 1 May 1935; s. of the late William Moncur Mitchell and Christine Mitchell (née Browne); ed. Winchester and Wadham Coll., Oxford; mem. Literature Panel, Arts Council 1966–69, Welsh Arts Council 1988–92; John Llewellyn Rhys Prize 1965; Somerset Maugham Award 1966. *Publications: novels:* Imaginary Toys 1961, A Disturbing Influence 1962, As Far As You Can Go 1963, The White Father 1964, A Circle of Friends 1966, The Undiscovered Country 1968; *biography:* Jennie: Lady Randolph Churchill (with Peregrine Churchill); *plays:* Half Life 1977, The Enemy Within 1980, Another Country 1981 (SWET Award 1982, filmed 1984), Francis 1983, After Aida (or Verdi's Messiah) 1986, Falling over England 1994, August 1994 (adapted from Uncle Vanya, filmed 1995). *Films:* Arabesque 1965, Vincent and Theo 1990, Wilde 1997; television plays and adaptations; translation of Pirandello's Henry IV. *Leisure interest:* fishing. *Address:* 47 Draycott Place, London, SW3 3DB, England. *Telephone:* 0171-589 1933.

MITCHELL, Katie; British theatre director; Pres. Oxford Univ. Dramatic Soc. 1984; awarded a Winston Churchill Memorial Trust award to research Eastern European theatre in Russia, Lithuania, Georgia, Poland and Germany 1989; awarded a Prince's Trust grant to research dramaturgy in Czechoslovakia and Yugoslavia 1990; f. Classics on a Shoestring Theatre Co. 1990. *Plays directed:* Vinegar Tom (The Old Fire Station), Façade (Edin. Fringe Festival) 1984; The House of Bernarda Alba, The Good Person of Szechwan (Oxford Playhouse), The Maids (Edin. Fringe Festival), The Country Wife (Asst. Dir., Oxford Playhouse) 1985; Gobstopper (King's Head Theatre Club, London) 1986; Hatikva—The Hope (King's Head) 1986; Joking Apart (Asst. Dir., Belgrade Theatre, Coventry), The Way to Go Home (Asst. Dir., Royal Court, London) 1987; Titus Andronicus, The Master Builder, The Man Who Came to Dinner, King Lear, The Plain Dealer, The Man of Mode, Much Ado About Nothing (all as Asst. Dir., R.S.C.) 1989; Arden of Faversham, Vassa Zheleznova and Women of Troy (with Classics on a Shoestring) 1990; A Woman Killed with Kindness 1991, The Dybbuk 1992, Ghosts 1993, Henry VI 1994, The Phoenician Women 1995, The Mysteries 1997, The Beckett Shorts 1997, Uncle Vanya 1998 (R.S.C.); Rutherford and Son (1994), The Machine Wreckers 1995 (Royal Nat. Theatre); The Widowing of Mrs Holroyd 1995 (BBC); Endgame 1996 (Donmar Warehouse); Don Giovanni 1996, Jenůfa 1998 (WNO); Attempts on Her Life 1999 (Piccolo Theatre, Milan); The Maids 1999 (Young Vic, London); Evening Standard Award for Best. Dir. 1996. *Address:* c/o Sebastian Born, The Agency, 24 Pottery Lane, London, W11 4LZ, England.

MITCHELL, Keith Claudius, M.S., PH.D.; Grenadian politician; ed. Presentation Coll., Grenada, Univ. of West Indies, Howard Univ. and American Univ., Washington; cand. for Grenada Nat. Party in 1972 elections; Gen. Sec. New Nat. Party (NNP) 1984–89, Leader Jan. 1989–; Minister of Communication, Works, Public Utilities, Transportation, of Civil Aviation and Energy 1984–87, of Communications, Works, Public Utilities, Co-operatives, Community Devt., Women's Affairs and Civil Aviation March 1988–89; Prime Minister of Grenada and Minister of Finance, External Affairs, Mobilization, Trade and Industry, Information and Nat. Security June 1995–; Capt. Grenada Nat. Cricket Team 1971–74. *Address:* Office of the Prime Minister, The Carenage, St. George's, Grenada. *Telephone:* 440-2255. *Fax:* 440-4116.

MITCHELL, Dame Roma, A.C., D.B.E.; Australian state governor and judge; b. 2 Oct. 1913, Adelaide; d. of Harold Flinders and Maude I. V. (née Wickham) Mitchell; ed. St. Aloysius Coll., Adelaide and Univ. of Adelaide; admitted to Bar, S. Australia 1934, Q.C. 1962; Judge, Supreme Court of S. Australia 1965–83; Chair. Criminal Law and Penal Methods Reform Cttee. of S. Australia 1971–77, Parole Bd. of S. Australia 1974–81, Human Rights Comm. 1981–86, South Australian Council on Child Protection 1988–90; Chancellor, Univ. of Adelaide 1983–90; Gov. S. Australia 1991–96; Dr. h.c. (Adelaide) 1985, (S. Australia) 1994; LL.D. h.c. (Queensland) 1992, (Flinders) 1993; Inst. of Engineers Medal 1994; Commdr. Légion d'honneur 1997. *Leisure interests:* swimming, walking, theatre, opera. *Address:* 256 East Terrace, Adelaide, S.A. 5000, Australia.

MITCHELL, Thomas Noel, PH.D., LITT.D.; Irish academic; b. 7 Dec. 1939; s. of Patrick Mitchell and Margaret Mitchell; m. Lynn S. Hunter 1965; three s. one d.; ed. Nat. Univ. of Ireland and Cornell Univ. N.Y.; Instructor Cornell Univ. 1965–66; Asst. Prof. Swarthmore Coll. 1966–73, Assoc. Prof. 1973–78, Prof. of Classics 1978–79; Prof. of Latin, Trinity Coll. Dublin 1979–91, Fellow 1980–, Sr. Dean 1985–87, Sr. Lecturer 1987–90, Provost 1991–; Cornell Visiting Prof. Swarthmore Coll. 1986; mem. Royal Irish Acad. (Vice-Pres. 1989); mem. American Philosophical Soc. 1996–; Hon. Fellow R.C.P.I. 1992, R.C.S.I. 1993; Hon. LL.D. (Queen's Univ. Belfast) 1992, (Nat. Univ. of Ireland) 1992; D.Hum.Lett. (Swarthmore) 1992; (Lynn Univ., U.S.A.) 1998, (State Univ. of New York) 1998; Hon. Ph.D. (Charles Univ., Prague) 1998. *Publications:* Cicero, The Ascending Years 1979, Cicero, Verrines II.1. 1986, Cicero the Senior Statesman 1990; numerous articles and reviews on Cicero and Roman History. *Leisure interest:* gardening. *Address:* Provost's House, Trinity College, Dublin 2 (Office); Dodona, Blackwood Lane, Malahide, Co. Dublin, Ireland (Home).

MITCHISON, John Murdoch, F.R.S., F.R.S.E.; British cell biologist; b. 11 June 1922, Oxford; s. of late Lord Mitchison and of Naomi M. Haldane (Naomi Mitchison, q.v.); m. Rosalind Mary Wrong 1947; one s. three d.; ed. Winchester Coll., Trinity Coll., Univ. of Cambridge; Army Operational Research 1941–46; Sr. and Research Scholar, Trinity Coll., Univ. of Cambridge 1946–50, Fellow 1950–54; Lecturer in Zoology, Univ. of Edinburgh 1953–59, Reader in Zoology 1959–62, Prof. of Zoology 1963–88, Dean of Faculty of Science 1984–85, Univ. Fellow 1988–92, now Emer. Prof. and Hon. Fellow; J. W. Jenkinson Memorial Lecturer, Univ. of Oxford 1971–72; mem. Edinburgh Univ. Court 1971–74, 1985–88; mem. Council Scottish Marine Biological Asscn. 1961–67; mem. Exec. Cttee. Int. Soc. for Cell Biology 1964–72; mem. Biology Cttee. S.R.C. 1976–79, Science Bd. 1976–79; mem. Royal Comm. on Environmental Pollution 1974–79, Academia Europaea 1989; mem. Working Group of Biological Manpower, Dept. of Educ. and Science 1968–71; Pres. British Soc. for Cell Biology 1974–77; mem. Advisory Cttee. on Safety of Nuclear Installations, Health and Safety Exec. 1981–84; Fellow Inst. Biology 1963. *Publications:* The Biology of the Cell Cycle 1971, numerous papers in scientific journals. *Address:* Institute of Cell, Animal and Population Biology, West Mains Road, Edinburgh, EH9 3JT (Office); Great Yew, Ormiston, East Lothian, EH35 5NJ, Scotland (Home). *Telephone:* (01875) 340530.

MITCHISON, (Nicholas) Avrion, D.PHIL., F.R.S.; British professor of zoology and comparative anatomy; b. 5 May 1928, London; s. of late Baron Mitchison and of Naomi Mitchison (q.v.); m. Lorna Margaret Martin 1957; two s. three d.; ed. Leighton Park School and Univ. of Oxford; Lecturer, later Reader in Zoology, Univ. of Edinburgh 1956–62; Head, Div. of Experimental Biology, Nat. Inst. for Medical Research, Mill Hill 1962–71; Jodrell Prof. of Zoology and Comparative Anatomy, Univ. Coll. London 1970–89; Scientific Dir. Deutsches Rheuma-Forschuengszentrum, Berlin 1990–96; Sr. Fellow, Dept. of Immunology, Univ. Coll. London 1996–; Hon. Dir. Imperial Cancer Research Fund, Tumour Immunology Unit, Univ. Coll. London; Paul Ehrlich Prize; Hon. M.D. (Edin.). *Address:* Department of Immunology, University College London, Windeyer Building, 46 Cleveland Street, London, W1P 6DB (Office); 14 Belitha Villas, London, N1 1PD, England (Home). *Telephone:* 0171-380 9349. *Fax:* 0171-380 9357.

MITRA, Sombhu; Indian actor and stage director; b. 22 Aug. 1915; m. (deceased); one d.; ed. Ballygunge Govt. High School and St. Xavier's Coll., Calcutta; joined Stage, Calcutta 1939; Producer-Dir.-Actor, Indian People's Theatre Asscn. 1943–46; Producer-Dir.-Actor Bohurupee (non-commercial theatre) 1948; fmr. Prof. & Head of Drama Dept., Rabindra Bharati Univ., Calcutta; Fellow Sangeet Natak Akademi, New Delhi; Grand Prix Karlovy Vary Film Festival 1957; Nat. Honour Padma Bhushan 1970, Ramon Magsasay Award 1976. *Productions include:* Four Chapters (Tagore) 1951, An Enemy of the People (Ibsen) 1952, Red Oleanders (Tagore) 1954, The Doll's House (Ibsen) 1958, Sacrifice (Tagore) 1961, The King of the Dark Chamber (Tagore) 1964, Oedipus Rex (Sophocles) 1964, Baki Itihas 1967, Pagla Ghora 1971. *Publications:* Abhinay-Natak-Mancha 1957, Putul Khela 1958, Kanchanranga 1961, Ghurnee 1967, Raja Oidipous 1969, Prasanga Natya 1973.

MITROFANOV, Aleksey Valentinovich; Russian politician; b. 16 March 1962, Moscow; m.; ed. Moscow Inst. of Int. Relations with U.S.S.R. Ministry of Foreign Affairs 1985–88; researcher, Inst. of U.S.A. and Canada 1988–91; producer TV programmes, Leisure Centre Sokol; mem. Higher Council, Liberal Democratic Party of Russia 1991–93; Minister of Foreign Affairs, Shadow Cabinet of Liberal Democratic Party 1992–; mem. State Duma 1993; Deputy Chair. Cttee. on Int. Relations 1993–96, Chair. Cttee. on Geopolitics 1996–. *Address:* State Duma, Okhotny ryad 1, 103265 Moscow, Russia. *Telephone:* (095) 292 5623 (Office). *Fax:* (095) 292 1084 (Office).

MITROPOLSKY, Yuriy Alekseyevich; Ukrainian mathematician; b. 3 Jan. 1917, Shishaki, Poltava Region; s. of Alexy Savvich Mitropolsky and Vera Vasilevna (née Charnish) Mitropolskaya; m. Alexandra (née Lihacheva) Mitropolskaya 1941; one s. one d.; ed. Kiev Univ.; Dir. of Ukrainian Acad. of Sciences Inst. of Maths. 1958–88, Hon. Dir. 1988–; Academician-Sec. Dept. of Maths. and Cybernetics, Ukrainian Acad. of Sciences 1963–93, scientific consultant 1993–; mem. U.S.S.R. (now Russian) Acad. of Sciences 1984; Corresp. mem. Accademia di Bologna 1971–; Lenin Prize 1965; Hero of Socialist Labour 1986. *Publication:* Group-theoretical approach in asymptotic methods of nonlinear mechanics 1988, Nonlinear Mechanics, Groups and Symmetry 1995, Nonlinear Mechanics, One-Frequency Oscillations 1997. *Leisure interests:* travel. *Address:* Ukrainian Academy of Sciences, Vladimirskaya 54, 252601 GSP Kiev 30 (Office); B. Hmelnitchogo Street 42, Apt. 10, 252030 Kiev 30, Ukraine (Home). *Telephone:* (44) 225-23-84, 225-31-93 (Office); 225-20-10 (Home).

MITSOTAKIS, Constantine; Greek politician; b. 18 Oct. 1918, Chania, Crete; m. Marika Yianoukou; one s. three d.; ed. Univ. of Athens; served in army 1940–41; active in Cretan resistance against Nazi occupation, twice arrested and sentenced to death; after War, republished newspaper KIRYX; M.P. for Chania 1946–74, 1977–; Under-Sec. of State for Finance, then Acting Minister for Communications and Public Works 1951; Minister for Finance 1963–64, for Econ. Co-ordination 1965; arrested by mil. junta 1967, released, under house arrest, escaped and lived in exile; returned to Greece 1974; f. Neoliberal Party; joined New Democracy Party 1978, Leader 1984–93; Minister for Econ. Co-ordination 1978-80, for Foreign Affairs 1980–81; Prime Minister of Greece, also with responsibility for the Aegean 1990–93. *Address:* 1 Aravantinou Street, 106 74 Athens, Greece.

MITSUZUKA, Hiroshi; Japanese politician; mem. House of Reps.; fmrly. Minister of Transport, Minister of Int. Trade and Industry, Minister of Foreign Affairs; Minister of Finance 1996–98. *Address:* c/o Ministry of Finance, 3-1-1 Kasumigaseki, Chiyoda-ku, Tokyo 100, Japan.

MITTA, Aleksander Naumovich; Russian film director; b. 29 March 1933, Moscow; ed. Moscow Inst. of Construction Eng., All-Union Inst. of Cinematography; with Mosfilm studio 1961; Prof. Hamburg Univ. 1995–. *Films:* My Friend Kolka 1961, Without Fear and Reproach 1963, One is Ringing, Open the Door 1966 (Grand Prix Int. Festival in Venice), Period, Period, Comma 1973, Twinkle, Twinkle, My Star 1970, The Crew 1980 (Prize of All-Union Film Festival), The Tale of Wandering 1983, Safety Margin 1988, A Step 1988, Lost in Siberia 1991, Alfred Schnittke and His Friends (TV) 1994; Merited Worker of Arts of Russia 1974. *Address:* Malaya Gruzinskaya str. 28, Apt. 105, 123557 Moscow, Russia (Home). *Telephone:* (095) 253 7320 (Home, Moscow); (40) 41234169 (Home, Hamburg). *Fax:* (095) 253 8067.

MITTERRAND, Gen. Jacques; French aerospace executive; b. 21 May 1918, Angoulême, Charentes; s. of Joseph and Yvonne (née Lorrain) Mitterrand; brother of late François Mitterrand; m. Gisèle Baume 1948; two d.; ed. St. Paul Coll., Angoulême, St. Louis Lycée, Paris, St. Cyr Mil. Acad.; served in Air Force 1937–75; participated in devt. and institution of French Nuclear Force; mem. Del. to NATO Perm. Group, Washington, D.C. 1961–64; Gen., Asst. Commdr. French Strategic Air Forces 1965–67, Commdr. 1970–72; Deputy Chief of Staff of Air Force 1968, of Armed Forces 1968–70; Insp. Gen. of Air Force 1972–75; mem. Supreme Air Council 1970–75; Chair. Bd. and Chief Exec., Soc. Nat. Industrielle Aérospatiale (SNIAS) 1975–81; Counsellor to Chair. French Atomic Energy Agency 1975; First Vice-Chair. French Aerospace Industries Asscn. (GIFAS), Chair. 1981–84; Chair. Asscn. Européenne des Constructeurs de Matériel Aérospatial (AECMA) 1978–83; Pres. Office Gén. de l'Air (Oga) 1984–93, Hon. Pres. 1993–; Vice-Chair. Supervisory Bd. of Airbus Industry; Vice-Pres. Turbomeca 1983; mem. Bd. Inst. of Air Transport; Dir. Intertechnique, Turbomeca, Hurel Dubois; Grand Croix, Légion d'honneur, Croix de guerre, Croix de la Valeur militaire, Croix du Combattant; Médaille de l'Aéronautique. *Address:* Oga, 33 Avenue des Champs-Elysées, Paris 75008 (Office); 87 boulevard Murat, 75016 Paris, France (Home).

MITYUKOV, Mikhail Alekseyevich, CAND.IUR.SC.; Russian politician, lawyer and professor; b. 7 Jan. 1942, Ust-Uda, Irkutsk Region; m. Ludmila Aleksandrovna Mityukova; two s. one d.; ed. Irkutsk State Univ.; worked in Khakassia Autonomous Region (now Repub.), Deputy Chair. regional court 1968–87; sr. teacher, Head of Chair of History and Law Abakan State Pedagogical Inst. 1987–90; Russian Fed. People's Deputy and mem. Supreme Soviet, Deputy Chair. then Chair. Cttee. on Law 1990–93; First Deputy Minister of Justice 1993–94; mem. State Duma (Parl.) 1993–95, First Deputy Chair. 1994–95; participated in drafting new Russian Constitution; First Deputy Sec., Security Council of Russia 1996–98; Plenipotentiary Rep. of Pres. Yeltsin in Constitutional Court 1998–. *Address:* Ipat'yevski per. 4-10, 103132 Moscow, Russia (Office).

MIYAI, Jinnosuke, M.A.; Japanese business executive; b. 22 Oct. 1921, Kagawa; m. Takeko Inoue 1948; one d.; ed. The Sixth High School, Univs. of Tokyo and Chicago; Vice-Pres. Shell Sekiyu K.K. 1971–81, Shell Kosan K.K. 1971–81; Dir. Showa Sekiyu K.K. 1974–81; Pres. Shin Nishi Nihon Sikiyu Kaihatsu K.K. 1977–81; Vice-Pres. Showa Yokkaichi Sekiyu K.K. 1982–83, Pres. 1983–85; Pres. Japan Productivity Centre for Socio-economic Devt. 1985–97, Sr. Adviser 1997–; Dr. h.c. Stirling Univ. 1986; Hon. O.B.E. *Address:* 240 Yabe-cho, Totsuka-ku, Yokohama 244-0002, Japan. *Telephone:* (045) 861-4112.

MIYAKE, Issey; Japanese fashion designer; b. (as Kazunaru Miyake) 22 April 1939, Tokyo; ed. Tama Art Univ. Tokyo and La Chambre Syndicale de la Couture Parisienne, Paris; asst. designer to Guy Laroche, Paris 1966–68, to Hubert de Givenchy, Paris 1968–69; designer, Geoffrey Beene (ready-to-wear firm), New York 1969–70; est. Miyake Design Studio, Tokyo 1970; Dir. Issey Miyake Int., Issey Miyake & Assocs., Issey Miyake Europe, Issey Miyake U.S.A. and Issey Miyake On Limits (Tokyo); Exec. adviser and planner, First Japan Culture Conf., Yokohama 1980; work has been exhibited in Paris, Tokyo and at M.I.T. and appears in collections of Metropolitan Museum of Art, New York and Victoria & Albert Museum, London; Japan Fashion Editors' Club Awards, 1974, 1976, Mainichi Design Prize 1977, Pratt Inst. Award (New York) 1979; Dr. h.c. (Royal Coll. of Art) 1993.

MIYAMOTO, Kenji; Japanese politician and writer; b. 17 Oct. 1908, Yamaguchi; s. of Sutekichi and Miyo Miyamoto; m. Sueko Omori 1956; two c.; ed. Tokyo Imperial Univ.; mem. Japanese CP 1931–, (imprisoned 1933–45), mem. Cen. Cttee. 1933–, Gen. Sec. of Cen. Cttee. 1958–70, Chair. Presidium Cen. Cttee. 1970–82, Chair. Cen. Cttee. 1982–97, Chair. Emer. 1997–; mem. House of Councillors 1977–89. *Publications:* Problems of Democratic Revolution 1947, Advance Towards Freedom and Independence 1949, Twelve Years' Letters 1952, World of Yuriko Miyamoto 1954, Perspective of Japanese Revolution 1961, The Path of Our Party's Struggle 1961, Selections from Literary Critiques of Kenji Miyamoto 1966–80, The Road towards a New Japan 1970, Actual Tasks and the Japanese Communist Party 1970, Standpoint of the Japanese Communist Party 1972, Dialogues with Kenji Miyamoto 1972, Kenji Miyamoto with Pressmen 1973, Interviews with Kenji Miyamoto 1975, Kenji Miyamoto on Our Time 1975, Kenji Miyamoto Before the Court under Militarism 1976, Dialogues with Kenji Miyamoto (sequel) 1977, Kenji Miyamoto on Contemporary Politics 1978, Kenji Miyamoto on the 1980s 1981–83, Now Is Turn for JCP 1983, Dialogues on Developments in the World and Japan 1984, Road to Elimination of Nuclear Weapons 1985, People in Retrospect 1985, Selected Works 1985, Kenji Miyamoto on the 1980s (sequel) 1983–86, Fundamental Problems of the Communist Movement 1988, Works in the Early Postwar Period 1987–88, No Future for the Current against History 1991, Immortal Party Based on Scientific Socialism 1991, Twentieth Century and Vitality of Socialism 1992, Japan: Its Present and Future Course 1994, Basic Course of Party Building 1995, Features of Some Party Members 1995, Toward the Progressive Future 1997. *Address:* Central Committee of the Japanese Communist Party, Sendagaya 4-26-7, Shibuya-ku, Tokyo, Japan. *Telephone:* (3) 5474-8421. *Fax:* (3) 3746–0767.

MIYASHITA, Sohei; Japanese politician; mem. LDP; fmr. civil servant in Finance Ministry; mem. for Nagano House of Reps.; Dir.-Gen. Defence Agency 1991–92, Environment Agency 1994–95; Minister of Health and Welfare 1998–. *Address:* Ministry of Health and Welfare, 1-2-2, Kasumigaseki, Chiyoda-ku, Tokyo 100, Japan. *Telephone:* (03) 3503-1711. *Fax:* (03) 3501-4853.

MIYAZAKI, Isamu; Japanese civil servant; Chair. Daiwa Inst. of Research Ltd; fmr. Dir.-Gen. Research Bureau Econ. Planning Agency; Admin. Vice-Minister Econ. Planning Agency, then Minister of State, Dir.-Gen. 1995–96.

MIYAZAWA, Kiichi; Japanese politician; b. 8 Oct. 1919, Tokyo; m. Yoko Miyazawa 1943; two c.; ed. Tokyo Imperial Univ.; Finance Ministry 1942–52, Pvt. Sec. to Minister of Finance 1949; mem. House of Councillors 1953–65; Parl. Vice-Minister of Educ. 1959–60; Minister of State, Dir.-Gen. of Econ. Planning Agency 1962–64, 1966–68, 1977–78; mem. House of Reps. 1967–; Minister of Int. Trade and Industry 1970–71, of Foreign Affairs 1974–76, of Finance 1986–88; Deputy Prime Minister and Minister of Finance 1987–88; Minister of State, Chief Cabinet Sec. 1980–82; Chair. Exec. Council LDP 1984–86; Pres. 1991–93; Prime Minister of Japan 1991–93; Minister of Finance Jan. 1999–. *Publications:* Tokyo-Washington no Mitsudan (Tokyo-Washington secret talks) 1956, Shakaito tono taiwa (Dialogue with the Socialist Party), Utsukushii Nippon heno Chosen (Challenge for Beautiful Japan) 1984. *Leisure interests:* Noh theatre, reading. *Address:* Ministry of Finance, 3-1-1, Kasumigaseki, Chiyoda-ku, Tokyo 100; c/o Liberal Democratic Party, 1-11-23 Nagata-cho, Chiyoda-ku, Tokyo 100, Japan. *Telephone:* (3) 3581-4111- *Fax:* (3) 5251-2105.

MIYET, Bernard; French diplomatist; b. 16 Dec. 1946; m. Dominique Bourguignon 1974; one d.; ed. Inst. of Political Studies, Grenoble, Nat. School of Admin.; Consul Gen. of France, L.A. 1986–89; Deputy Dir.-Gen. Office of Cultural, Scientific and Tech. Relations, Ministry of Foreign Affairs, Paris 1989–91; Perm. Rep. of France to UN, Geneva 1991–93; Amb. responsible for audio-visual services to GATT Uruguay Round, Ministry of Foreign Affairs, Paris 1993–94; Perm. Rep. of France to Org. for Security and Co-operation in Europe, Vienna 1994–97; Under-Sec. for Peacekeeping Operations, UN, New York 1997–; Chevalier Ordre nat du Mérite, Officier des Arts et Lettre. *Address:* United Nations, Department of Peacekeeping Operations, S-3727B, New York, NY 10017, U.S.A. *Telephone:* (212) 963-8079. *Fax:* (212) 963-9222.

MIYOSHI, Shunkichi; Japanese business executive; b. 16 March 1929; ed. Univ. of Tokyo; joined NKK Corpn. 1951, mem. Bd. Dirs. 1982–, Man. Dir. 1985–88, Sr. Man. Dir. 1988–90, Exec. Vice-Pres. 1990–92, Pres. 1992–97, Chair. of Bd. 1997–; Pres. Iron and Steel Inst. of Japan 1992–94; Chair. Japan Inst. of Construction Eng. 1997–, Japan Vocational Ability Devt. Asscn. 1998–, Weights and Measures Admin. Council 1998–; Vice-Chair. Japan Fed. of Employers' Asscns. 1997–; Dir. Japan Iron and Steel Fed. 1992–97, Vice-Chair 1993–94, 1996–97; Exec. mem. Bd. of Dirs. Japan Fed. of Econ. Orgs. 1992–97; mem. Coal Mining Council 1992–97, Electric Power Devt. Co-ordination Council 1996–, Trade Council 1997–, Cen. Environment Council 1997–; Trustee Japan Asscn. of Corp. Executives 1995–. *Leisure interests:* tennis, golf. *Address:* NKK Corporation, 1-1-2 Marunouchi, Chiyoda-ku, Tokyo 100-8202, Japan. *Telephone:* 03-3212-7111. *Fax:* 03-3214-8401.

MIYOSHI, Toru, LL.B.; Japanese judge (retd.); b. 31 Oct. 1927; ed. Univ. of Tokyo; Asst. Judge, Tokyo Dist. Court and Tokyo Family Court 1955; Judge, Hakodate Dist. Court and Hakodate Family Court 1965; Judge, Tokyo Dist. Court (Presiding Judge of Div.) 1975; Pres. Research and Training Inst. for Court Clerks 1982; Pres. Oita Dist. Court and Oita Family Court 1985; Pres. Nagano Dist. Court and Nagano Family Court 1986; Chief Judicial Research Official of Supreme Court 1987; Pres. Sapporo High Court 1990, Tokyo High Court 1991; Justice of Supreme Court 1992; Chief Justice of Supreme Court 1995–97.

MIZRAHI, Isaac; American fashion designer; b. 14 Oct. 1961, Brooklyn, New York; s. of Zeke Mizrahi and Sarah Mizrahi; ed. Yeshiva, Flatbush, High School of Performing Arts, Manhattan, Parsons School of Design; apprenticed to Perry Ellis 1982, full-time post 1982–84; worked with Jeffrey Banks 1984–85, with Calvin Klein 1985–87; started own design firm in partnership with Sarah Hadad Cheney 1987, first formal show 1988, first spring collection Nov. 1988, first menswear line launched April 1990, announced closure of firm Oct. 1998. *Address:* 104 Wooster Street, New York, NY 10012, U.S.A.

MKAPA, Benjamin William, B.A.; Tanzanian politician and journalist; b. 12 Nov. 1938, Masasi; s. of William Matwani and Stephania Nambanga; m. Anna Joseph Maro 1966; two s.; ed. Makerere Univ. Coll.; Admin. Officer, Dist. Officer 1962; Foreign Service Officer 1962; Man. Ed. Tanzania Nationalist and Uhuru 1966, The Daily News and The Sunday News 1972; Press Sec. to Pres. 1974; founding Dir. Tanzania News Agency 1976; High Commr. in Nigeria 1976; Minister for Foreign Affairs 1977–80, for Information and Culture 1980–82; High Commr. in Canada 1982–83; Amb. to U.S.A. 1983–84; Minister for Foreign Affairs 1984–90; M.P. for Nanyumbu 1985–95; Minister for Information and Broadcasting 1990–92, for Science, Tech. and Higher Educ. 1992–95; Pres. of Tanzania Nov. 1995–; Chair. Chama Cha Mapinduzi (CCM) party 1996–. *Leisure interest:* reading. *Address:* Office of the President, P.O. Box 9120, Dar es Salaam, Tanzania.

MKHATSHWA, Smangaliso, PH.D., TH.M.; South African ecclesiastic; b. 26 June 1939, Barberton; s. of Elias Mkhatshwa and Maria Mkhatshwa (née

Nkosi); ordained Catholic priest 1965; Gen. Sec. Southern African Catholic Bishops' Conf. 1980–88; Patron of the United Democratic Front 1983; Gen. Sec. Inst. for Contextual Theology 1988–94; mem. Parl. (ANC) 1994–, mem. Reconstruction And Devt. Standing Cttee. and Educ. Standing Cttee.; Deputy Minister Educ. 1996–; Trustee Kagiso Trust, Matla Trust; Pres. Cen. Transvaal Civics Asscn. (later renamed SANCO Pretoria); Dr. h.c. (Tübingen, Germany, Georgetown, U.S.A.); Steve Biko Award, Indicator Newspaper Award. *Publications:* articles on theology and politics. *Leisure interests:* tennis, music, reading, theatre. *Address:* Private Bag X895 Pretoria 0001; Private Bag X9023, Cape Town, 8000, South Africa.

MKRTUMYAN, Yuri Israelovich, CAND.HIS.SC.; Armenian diplomatist; b. 1 Jan. 1939, Tbilisi; ed. Moscow State Univ.; lab. asst., jr. researcher Inst. of Archaeology and Ethnography, Armenian Acad. of Sciences 1962–71; sr. lecturer Yerevan State Univ. 1971–89; Head Chair of Ethnography, Yerevan State Univ. 1989–94; Sec. CP Cttee. Yerevan State Univ.; mem. Cen. CPSU Cttee., mem. Bureau Cen. Cttee. Armenian CP 1990–91; counsellor to Minister of Foreign Affairs, Repub. of Armenia April–June 1994; Amb. to Russia 1994–96; Prof. Inst. of Ethnography and Archaeology, Acad. of Sciences 1996–. *Publications:* over 40 scientific works on theoretical and regional ethnography in Russian, Armenian and English. *Address:* Institute of Ethnography and Archaeology, Armenian Academy of Sciences, Charentsa Street 15, 375025 Yerevan, Armenia. *Telephone:* (2) 55-68-96 (Office).

MLADENOV, Peter Toshev; Bulgarian politician; b. 22 Aug. 1936, Toshevtsi, Vidin; s. of Tosho Mladenov Gergovski and Stoina Dimitrova Gergovska; m. Galia Spasova Mladenova 1964; one d.; ed. Suvorov School, Sofia, Univ. of Sofia and Moscow State Inst of Int. Relations; Sec., subsequently First Sec., Vidin District Cttee., League of Young Communists 1963–66; Sec. Cen. Cttee. League of Young Communists 1966–69; First Sec. Vidin Dist. Cttee., Bulgarian CP 1969–71; cand. mem. Politburo, Cen. Cttee. Bulgarian CP 1974–77, mem. 1977–90; Deputy to Nat. Assembly; Minister of Foreign Affairs 1971–89; Chair. State Council 1989–90, Pres. of Bulgaria April–July 1990; Gen. Sec. Cen. Cttee. 1989–90; mem. Presidium of Supreme Council –1989, C.-in-C. of Armed Forces 1980–90; Order of Georgi Dimitrov, The Thirteen Centuries of Bulgaria Order. *Leisure interests:* swimming, tennis. *Address:* 10 Veliko Turnovo St., Sofia, Bulgaria. *Telephone:* 446554.

MMARI, Geoffrey Raphael Vehaeli, DIP.ED., PH.D.; Tanzanian university teacher and administrator; b. 24 June 1934, Moshi; s. of late Vehaeli Mmari and of Luisia Mmari; m. Salome Mmari 1959; one s. three d.; ed. Univ. of E. Africa, Univ. of N. Iowa, U.S.A., Univ. of Dar es Salaam; teacher and admin. 1966–69; univ. teacher 1969–; Vice-Chancellor Sokoine Univ. of Agric. 1984–88, Univ. of Dar es Salaam 1988–91; Co-ordinator Open Univ. Planning Office 1991–, Vice-Chancellor Open Univ. 1993–. *Publications:* Understanding of Mathematical Concepts among Secondary School Pupils (Ph.D. dissertation) 1974, Mwalimu: The Influence of Julius Nyerere (ed. with Colin Legum) 1995; ed. secondary math. books series; articles in journals and chapters in books 1960–. *Leisure interests:* reading, travelling, walking. *Address:* The Open University, P.O. Box 23409, Dar es Salaam, Tanzania. *Telephone:* 668445. *Fax:* 668759.

MMUSI, Peter; Botswana politician; fmr. Vice-Pres. of Botswana; Chair. Botswana Democratic Party (BDP) 1993. *Address:* Botswana Democratic Party, Gaborone, Botswana.

MNOUCHKINE, Ariane; French theatre director; has staged productions with the Paris-based Théâtre du Soleil since the 1960s. *Stage productions include:* Les Atrides.

MO, Timothy; British author; b. 30 Dec. 1950, Hong Kong; s. of Peter Mo Wan Lung and Barbara Helena Falkingham; ed. Mill Hill School and St. John's Coll., Univ. of Oxford; fmrly. worked for Times Educational Supplement and New Statesman; fmr. reporter for Boxing News and P.A.Y.E. clerk; Geoffrey Faber Memorial Prize for first novel The Monkey King 1979, E. M. Forster Award for The Redundancy of Courage 1992. *Publications include:* The Monkey King 1979, Sour Sweet 1982, An Insular Possession 1986, The Redundancy of Courage 1991, Brownout on Breadfruit Boulevard 1995. *Address:* c/o 89 Great Russell Street, London, WC1B 3PS, England.

MO WENXIANG; Chinese politician; b. 1923, Xianjin Co., Shandong Prov.; Vice-Minister, Third Ministry of Machine-Building 1978–81, Minister 1981–82, of Aviation Ind. (now Aeronautics Industry) 1982–88; mem. 12th Cen. Cttee. CCP 1982–87; mem. Presidium 6th NPC 1986–88, 7th NPC 1988–93, 8th NPC 1993–; mem. Credentials Cttee., Financial and Econ. Cttee. N.C.P. 1993–, Educ., Science and Public Health Cttee., NPC 1986; Head China-Sudan Friendship Group 1985; Chair. Bd. of Dirs., China Nat. Aero-Tech. Import and Export Corpn. 1986. *Address:* 67 Jiaonan Street, Beijing, People's Republic of China.

MO YAN (b. Guan Moyan); Chinese novelist; b. 1955, Gaomi, Shandong Prov.; ed. PLA Acad. of Arts, Beijing Normal Univ.; joined PLA 1976. *Publications:* Red Sorghum Family, The Song of Heaven's Garlic Shoots, Thirteen Steps, The Herbivora Family, Jiuguo.

MOBBS, Sir (Gerald) Nigel, Kt.; British business executive; b. 22 Sept. 1937, Birmingham; s. of Gerald Aubrey Mobbs and Elizabeth Lanchester; m. Hon. Pamela Jane Berry 1961; one s. two d.; ed. Marlborough Coll. and Christ Church, Oxford; Chair. and C.E.O. Slough Estates PLC 1976–; Chair. Kingfisher PLC 1995–96 (Dir. 1982–96); Chair. Bovis Homes Group PLC 1996–; numerous directorships including Barclays Bank PLC 1979–, The Charterhouse Group PLC 1974–84, Cookson Group PLC 1985–93; Chair. Univ. of Buckingham; mem. Commonwealth War Graves Comm. 1988–97, Cttee. on Corp. Governance 1995–98; Lord Lieut. of Buckinghamshire 1997–; Hon. D.Univ. (Buckingham Univ.) 1993; Hon. D.Sc. (City Univ.). *Leisure interests:* hunting, skiing, golf, riding, travel. *Address:* 234 Bath Road, Slough, Berks., SL1 4EE, England. *Telephone:* (01753) 537171.

MOCK, Alois, LL.D.; Austrian politician; b. 10 June 1934, Euratsfeld; s. of August and Mathilde Mock; m. Edith Partik 1963; ed. Univ. of Vienna, Johns Hopkins Univ., Bologna, and Free Univ., Brussels; mem. Austrian mission to OECD 1962–66; Private Sec. to Fed. Chancellor 1966, Head of Private Office 1968; Minister of Educ. 1969–70; mem. Parl. 1970–; Leader, Austrian People's Party (ÖVP) 1979–89; Leader of Opposition 1979–87; Vice-Chancellor and Minister of Foreign Affairs 1987–89; Chair. European Democratic Union, Vienna 1979–; Chair. Int. Democratic Union, London 1983–87. *Publication:* Standpunkte 1983. *Address:* c/o Österreichische Volkspartei, Lichtenfelsgasse 7, 1010 Vienna, Austria.

MOCUMBI, Pascoal Manuel; Mozambican politician; b. 10 April 1941, Maputo; s. of Manuel Mocumbi Malume and Leta Alson Cuhle; m. Adelina Isabel Bernardino Paindane 1970; two s. two d.; fmr. Minister of Health, fmr. Minister of Foreign Affairs; Prime Minister of Mozambique Dec. 1994–; mem. Frente de Libertação de Moçambique (FRELIMO). *Leisure interests:* jogging, squash, reading. *Address:* Praça da Marinha, Maputo, Mozambique. *Telephone:* 426861/3. *Fax:* 426881.

MOCZULSKI, Leszek Robert, LL.M.; Polish political leader, lawyer, journalist and historian; b. 7 June 1930, Warsaw; s. of Stanisław Moczulski and Janina (née Reimer) Moczulska; m. 1st Małgorzata (née Smogorzewska) Moczulska 1951 (deceased); m. 2nd Maria-Ludwika (née Różycka) Moczulska 1968; two d.; ed. Acad. of Political Science, Warsaw, Warsaw Univ.; reporter on Życie Warszawy (daily) 1950–53, on dailies and weeklies, including Dookoła Świata, Warsaw 1955–57; imprisoned on charges of slandering Poland in foreign press 1957–58, acquitted; associate (pseud. Leszek Karpatowicz) Więź (monthly) 1959–62; head history section Stolica (weekly) 1961–72; ed. of underground journals Opinia 1977–78, Droga 1978–80, Gazeta Polska 1979–80; arrested Aug. 1980 and sentenced to 7 years on charge of attempting to overthrow regime, amnestied Aug. 1984; sentenced to 4 years on charge of heading illegal org. March 1985, amnestied Sept. 1986; victim of reprisals 1946–89, including repeated 48 hr. custody (250 times 1976–80), forbidden to publish, refused passport, prevented from finishing Ph.D.; mem. Polish Journalists' Asscn. 1951–, Theatre Authors and Composers' Union 1960– (mem. Bd. 1972–77), Polish Historical Soc.; active in Movt. for Rights of Man and Citizen (ROPCiO) 1977–80; deputy to Sejm (Parl.) 1991–97; Hon. Chair. Parl. Club of Confed. of Independence of Poland (KPN) 1993–97; Chair. Parl. Cttee. for Polish Connection Abroad 1993–97; mem. Confed. for an Independent Poland (KPN) 1979– (one of f., temporary chair. 1979–80, Chair. 1980–); mem. Polish del. to Parl. Ass., Council of Europe 1992–93, 1995–; Gold Badge of Honour; Officer's Cross of Polonia Restituta Order (London) 1987. *Publications:* numerous contribs. on history, politics and int. affairs, over 20 books including Wojna polska 1939 1972, Rewolucja bez rewolucji 1979, Trzecia Rzeczpospolita—zarys ustroju politycznego 1984, U progu niepodległości 1990, Bez wahania 1992, Trzy drogi 1993, Demokracja bez demokracji 1995, Geopolityka 1999. *Leisure interests:* horse riding, old automobiles, sailing, old maps. *Address:* ul. Jaracza 3 m. 4, 00-378 Warsaw, Poland. *Telephone:* (22) 826-10-43 (Office); (22) 625 26 39 (Home). *Fax:* (22) 826 14 00.

MODI, Vinay Kumar, B.TECH.CHEM.ENG.; Indian industrialist; b. 31 May 1943, Modinagar; s. of the late Rai Bahadur Gujar Mal Modi and Dayawati Modi; m. Chander Bala 1965; one s. one d.; ed. Scindia School, Gwalior, Indian Inst. of Tech., Kanpur; Jt. Man. Dir. Modi Industries Ltd. 1965–; Vice-Chair., Man. Dir. Modi Rubber Ltd. 1976–; Chair. Bombay Tyres Int. Ltd., Gujarat Guardian Ltd., Modi Mirrlees Blackstone Ltd., Shree Acids and Chemicals Ltd., Modistone Ltd. 1989–; various awards from govt. for export performance; prizes from several asscns. *Publications:* various articles on steel, tyres and cement production. *Leisure interests:* golf, tennis, billiards. *Address:* Modi Bhavan, Civil Lines, Modinagar 201204; 55A, Friends Colony (East), New Delhi 110065, India. *Telephone:* 683 5766 (Office); 683 3633 (Home).

MODIANO, Patrick Jean; French novelist; b. 30 July 1945, Boulogne-Billancourt; s. of Albert Modiano and Luisa Colpyn; m. Dominique Zehrfuss 1970; two d.; ed. schools in Biarritz, Chamonix, Deauville, Thônes, Barbizon, coll. in Paris; Prix Roger Nimier 1968, Prix Felix Fénéon 1969, Grand Prix de l'Académie Française 1972, Prix Goncourt 1978; Chevalier des Arts et des Lettres; prix Pierre de Monaco 1984; Grand prix du Roman de la Ville de Paris 1994. *Publications:* La place de l'étoile 1968, La ronde de nuit 1969, Les boulevards de ceinture 1972, Lacombe Lucien (screenplay) 1973, La polka (play) 1974, Villa triste (novel) 1975, Interrogatoire d'Emmanuel Berl 1976, Livret de famille (novel) 1977, Rue des boutiques obscures 1978, Une jeunesse 1981, Memory Lane 1981, De si braves garçons (novel) 1982, Poupée blonde 1983, Quartier perdu 1985, Dimanches d'août 1986, Une aventure de Choura 1986, La fiancée de Choura 1987, Remise de peine (novel) 1988, Catherine Certitude 1988, Vestiaire de l'enfance (novel) 1989, Voyage de noces 1990, Fleurs de ruine (novel) 1991, Un cirque passe (novel) 1992, Chien de Printemps 1993, Du plus loin de l'oubli 1995, Dora Bruder 1997. *Address:* c/o Editions Gallimard, 5 rue Sébastien Bottin, 75007 Paris, France.

MODIGLIANI, Franco, D.JUR., D.SC.; American professor of economics; b. 18 June 1918, Rome, Italy; s. of Enrico Modigliani and Olga Flaschel; m. Serena Calabi 1939; two s.; ed. Liceo Visconti, Univ. of Rome, New School for Soc. Research, New York; Lecturer, New School for Soc. Research, New York, 1943–44, Asst. Prof. of Math. Econ. and Econometrics 1946–48; Assoc. Prof. of Econs., Univ. of Ill. 1949–50, Prof. 1950–52; Prof. of Econs. and Industrial Admin., Carnegie Inst. of Tech. 1952–60; Prof. of Econs., Northwestern Univ. 1960–62; Prof. of Econs. and Finance, M.I.T. 1962–, Inst. Prof. 1970–88, Prof. Emer. 1988–; Academic Consultant, Bd. of Govs., Fed. Reserve System 1966, mem. Cttee. on Monetary Statistics, 1974–76; Sr. Advisor, Brookings Panel on Econ. Activity 1971–; Vice-Pres. Int. Econ. Assen. 1976–83, Hon. Pres. 1983–; Pres. American Finance Assen. 1981; fmr. Pres. Econometric Soc., American Econ. Assen.; mem. N.A.S., American Acad. of Arts and Sciences; LL.D. h.c. (Univ. of Chicago) 1967, Dr. Econs. h.c. (Univ. Catholique de Louvain, Belgium) 1974, Dr. of Econs. and Commerce h.c. (Istituto Universitario di Bergamo) 1979; Hon. D.Hum. Litt. (Bard Coll., New York) 1985, (Brandeis Univ.) 1986, Dr. h.c. (Ill.) 1990; Journal of Business Award 1961, Graham and Dodd Award 1975, 1980, Nobel Prize for Economic Science 1985, Premio Scanno 1997. *Publications:* National Incomes and International Trade 1953, Planning Production, Inventories and Work Force 1960, Role of Anticipations and Plans in Economic Behavior and Their Use in Economic Analysis and Forecasting 1961, New Mortgage Designs for Stable Housing in an Inflationary Environment 1975, The Collected Papers of Franco Modigliani (3 vols.) 1980, (4th and 5th vols.) 1989; co-author of several publs. *Leisure interests:* sailing, swimming, skiing, tennis. *Address:* Massachusetts Institute of Technology, Sloan School of Management, Room E52-443, 50 Memorial Drive, Cambridge, MA 02139 (Office); 25 Clark Street, Belmont, MA 02178, U.S.A. (Home). *Telephone:* (617) 253-7153 (Office); (617) 484-8419 (Home).

MODISE, Joe; South African politician; b. 8 Aug. 1929, Doornfontein; m.; five c.; fmr. lorry driver; active in African Nat. Congress (ANC) Youth League in 1950s; arrested and charged with treason Dec. 1956, charges dropped 1958; joined Umkhonto we Sizwe 1961, left S. Africa 1963; mil. training, Czechoslavakia and U.S.S.R. 1963–64; fmr. Commdr. Umkhonto we Sizwe (mil. wing of ANC); mem. ANC Nat. Exec. Cttee. 1965–; Chair. ANC Mil. Cttee. 1983; returned to S. Africa 1990, Minister of Defence 1994–99. *Address:* c/o Ministry of Defence, Private Bag X427, Pretoria 0001, South Africa.

MÖDL, Martha; German singer; ed. Munich and Nuremberg Conservatoires; numerous appearances at German and foreign opera houses, and at Bayreuth Festivals 1951–; mem. Staatsoper Stuttgart 1953–. *Address:* Perlacherstrasse 19, 8082 Grünwald, Germany.

MODROW, Hans, DR.; German politician; b. 27 Jan. 1928, Jasenitz, Ueckermuende Dist.; s. of Franz Modrow and Agnes (née Krause) Modrow; m. Annemarie Straubing 1950; two d.; apprentice locksmith 1942–45; served in German army in Second World War; prisoner of war 1949; mem. SED 1949; First Sec. of East Berlin City Cttee. 1953–61; mem. East Berlin City Council 1953–71; SED Party School 1954–58; cand. mem. SED Cen. Cttee. 1958–67, mem. Cen. Cttee. 1967–90; Deputy to People's Chamber (Volkskammer) 1958–90; First Sec. SED Dist. Cttee., Berlin-Köpernick 1961–67; Head Dep. for Agitation and Propaganda, SED Cen. Cttee. 1967–71; First Sec., SED Dresden Dist. Cttee. 1973–89; Prime Minister of G.D.R. 1989–90; mem. Bundestag 1990–94, leader Party of Democratic Socialism; on trial for alleged vote-rigging April 1993; found guilty and fined May 1993; to stand trial again for the same offence after appeal court decision that fine was too small; retrial ordered Nov. 1994; given nine-month suspended sentence for electoral fraud 1995; Decorations include Order of Merit of Fatherland 1959, Silver 1969, Gold 1975, Karl Marx Order 1978. *Leisure interests:* politics, culture, sport (active skier). *Address:* Frankfurter Tor 6, 10243 Berlin, Germany. *Telephone:* (030) 2912789.

MOE, George Cecil Rawle, C.H.B., Q.C., M.A., LL.M.; Barbadian fmr. politician and barrister-at-law; b. 12 March 1932, Barbados; s. of Cecil S. and Odessa M. (née Marshall) Moe; m. Olga Louise Atkinson 1957; two s. one d.; ed. Harrison Coll., Oxford Univ. and Columbia Univ., New York; called to the Bar, Middle Temple, London; Magistrate 1960–62; Acting Asst. Legal Draftsman 1962–63; Acting Crown Counsel 1963–66; Sr. Crown Counsel 1967–71; Acting Perm. Rep. to UN 1970–71; Attorney-Gen. and Minister of Legal Affairs 1971–76, also Minister of External Afairs 1972–76; Leader of Senate 1972–76; pvt. practice 1976–79; Puisne Judge (Belize) 1979–81, Chief Justice (Belize) 1982–85; Justice of Appeal, Eastern Caribbean Supreme Court 1985–91, Justice of Appeal, Supreme Court of Barbados 1991–. *Leisure interests:* music, cricket, gardening, swimming. *Address:* P.O. Box 1004, Bridgetown, Barbados. *Telephone:* 432-2357.

MOE, Thorvald, PH.D.; Norwegian economist; b. 4 Oct. 1939, Oslo; s. of Thorvald Moe and Marie Cappelen Moe; m. Nina Kjeldsberg 1968; one s. one d.; ed. Stanford Univ.; held various sr. posts in Ministry of Finance; Dir.-Gen. Econ. Policy Dept. Ministry of Finance 1978–86, Chief Econ. Adviser and Deputy Perm. Sec. 1989–; Amb. to OECD 1986–89; Deputy Sec.-Gen. OECD Dec. 1997–. *Leisure interests:* history, tennis. *Address:* OECD, 19 rue Franqueville, 75116 Paris, France.

MOELLER, Bernd, DR.THEOL.; German professor of Church history; b. 19 May 1931, Berlin; s. of late Max Moeller and Carola Bielitz; m. Irene Müller 1957; three d.; ed. Univs. of Erlangen, Mainz, Basle, Munich and Heidelberg; Research Asst. Univ. of Heidelberg 1956–58, Privatdozent 1958–64; Prof. of Church History, Univ. of Göttingen 1964–, Rector 1971–72; Chair. Verein für Reformationsgeschichte, Heidelberg 1976–; mem. Akademie der Wissenschaften zu Göttingen, Academia Europaea. *Publications:* Reichsstadt und Reformation 1962, Geschichte des Christentums in Grundzügen 1965, Spätmittelalter 1966, Oekumenische Kirchengeschichte (with R. Kottje) I-III 1970–74, Deutschland im Zeitalter der Reformation 1977, Die Reformation und das Mittelalter 1991, Kirchengeschichte. Deutsche Texte (1699–1927) 1994, Städtische Predigt in der Frühzeit der Reformation (with K. Stackmann) 1996. *Address:* Herzberger Landstrasse 26, 37085 Göttingen, Germany. *Telephone:* (0551) 42850.

MOERDANI, Leonardus Benjamin; Indonesian army officer; b. 2 Oct. 1932, Cepu; m. Theresia Hartini Moerdani 1964; one d.; served under Gen. Soeharto in mil. operation to take back Irian Jaya from Netherlands 1962; played key role in restoring diplomatic relations with Malaysia following Pres. Soekarno's armed conflict over Sabah and Sarawak 1963–66; Consul Gen., Kuala Lumpur 1967–71, Seoul 1971–74; Asst. for Intelligence, Dept. of Defence & Security 1974–83; Head Strategic Intelligence Center 1977, Vice-Chief State Intelligence Co-ordinating Agency 1978–83; Commdr. in Chief of the Armed Forces, Commdr. Security & Order Restoration Command, Chief of Strategic Intelligence Agency 1983–88; Minister of Defence & Security 1988–93. *Leisure interest:* golf. *Address:* c/o Ministry of Defence & Security, Jalan Merdeka Barat 13, Jakarta 10110, Indonesia.

MOERSCH, Karl; German politician and journalist; b. 11 March 1926, Calw/Württ.; s. of Karl F. Moersch; m. Waltraut Schweikle 1947; one s.; ed. Univ. of Tübingen; journalist in Ludwigshafen, Bad Godesberg (Deutscher Forschungsdienst) and Frankfurt (Ed. of Die Gegenwart) 1956–58; Head of Press Dept., Freie Demokratische Partei (FDP) 1961–64; free-lance journalist 1964–; fmr. mem. Bundestag; Parl. Sec. of State, Minister of State, Ministry of Foreign Affairs 1970–76; mem. Exec. Bd. of UNESCO 1980–85. *Publications:* Kursrevision—Deutsche Politik nach Adenauer 1978, Europa für Anfänger 1979, Sind wir denn eine Nation? 1982, Bei uns im Staate Beutelsbach 1984, Geschichte der Pfalz 1987, Sueben, Württemberger und Franzosen 1991, Sperrige Landsleute 1996, Es gehet seltsam zu - in Württemberg 1998, and numerous newspaper articles, etc. *Address:* Thouretallee 4, 71638 Ludwigsburg, Germany. *Telephone:* 07141/905745. *Fax:* 01741/905643.

MOERTONO, Maj.-Gen. Amir; Indonesian politician and retd. army officer; ed. Mil. School of Law, Jakarta; Staff Officer with Dept. of Defence during 1950s; attended intelligence course with Lightning Div. of U.S. Army 1959; worked with Sekber Golkar (now Golongan Karya) (Secr. of Functional Groups forming a political front) 1964; Brig.-Gen. 1969; Asst. for Socio-Political Affairs, Hankam (Ministry of Defence and Security) 1969; Maj.-Gen. 1971; Chair. Golongan Karya 1972, Gen. Chair. 1973; retd. from Army 1972. *Address:* Golongan Karya, Jakarta, Indonesia.

MOFFAT, Sir Brian Scott, Kt., O.B.E., F.C.A.; British business executive; b. 6 Jan. 1939; s. of Festus Moffat and Agnes Moffat; m. Jacqueline Cunliffe 1964; one s. (and one s. deceased) one d.; ed. Hulme Grammar School; with Peat Marwick Mitchell & Co. 1961–68; joined British Steel Corpn. (now British Steel PLC) 1968, Man. Dir. Finance 1986–91, Chief Exec. 1991–99, Chair. 1993–; Dir. (non-exec.) Enterprise Oil PLC 1995–, HSBC 1998–. *Leisure interests:* farming, fishing, shooting. *Address:* c/o British Steel PLC, 15 Marylebone Road, London, NW1 3JD, England; Springfield Farm, Earlswood, Chepstow, Gwent, NP6 6AT, Wales (Home). *Telephone:* (01291) 650228.

MOFFATT, Henry Keith, SC.D., F.R.S.; British professor of mathematical physics; b. 12 April 1935, Edinburgh; s. of late Frederick Henry Moffatt and Emmeline Marchant Fleming; m. Katharine (Linty) Stiven 1960; two s. (one deceased) two d.; ed. Edinburgh and Cambridge Univs.; Asst. Lecturer, then Lecturer, Cambridge Univ. 1961–76, Prof. of Mathematical Physics 1980–; Fellow of Trinity Coll., Cambridge 1961–76, 1980–, Tutor 1971–74, Sr. Tutor 1975; Dir. Isaac Newton Inst. for Mathematical Sciences 1996–; Prof. Applied Mathematics, Bristol Univ. 1977–80; part-time Prof. Ecole Polytechnique, Paris 1992–; Ed. Journal of Fluid Mechanics 1966–83; mem. Academia Europaea 1994; Foreign mem. Royal Netherlands Acad. of Arts and Sciences 1991, Acad. des Sciences, Paris 1998; Dr. h.c. (INPG Grenoble) 1987, (State Univ. of New York) 1990; Smiths Prize 1960; Officier des Palmes Académiques. *Publications:* Magnetic Field Generation in Electrically Conducting Fluids 1978, Topological Fluid Mechanics (Ed. with A. Tsinober) 1990, Topological Aspects of the Dynamics of Fluids and Plasmas (Ed. jtly.) 1992. *Leisure interests:* French country cooking, hill walking. *Address:* Trinity College, Cambridge, CB2 1TQ (Office); 6 Banhams Close, Cambridge, CB4 1HX, England. *Telephone:* (01223) 363338.

MOFFO, Anna; opera singer; b. Wayne, Pa., U.S.A.; d. of Nicholas and Regina (Cinti) Moffo; m. Robert Sarnoff 1974; ed. Curtis Inst.; m. Robert Sarnoff 1974; appeared in TV opera Madam Butterfly, Italy; singer opera houses in Paris, London, Salzburg, Vienna, Milan, numerous others abroad; American debut at Lyric Opera Co., Chicago 1957, Metropolitan Opera Co., New York 1959; appeared Voice of Firestone telecast 1957; *operatic roles (soprano) include;* Norma, La Bohème, Mignon, Rigoletto, Falstaff, Madam Butterfly, The Barber of Seville, La Traviata, Thaïs, The Daughter of the Regiment, Stiffelio, Tosca, Hansel and Gretel, Faust, Don Pasquale, Romeo and Juliet, The Magic Flute, Turandot, La Juive, The Marriage of Figaro,

Otello, Il Trovatore, Luisa Miller, La Belle Hélène, The Gypsy Princess; recital tours, U.S.; numerous recordings; Order of Merit (Italy); Young Artists award, Philadelphia Orchestra; Fulbright award for study in Europe; Liebe Augustin Award.

MOGAE, Festus Gontebanye, M.A.; Botswana financial administrator; b. 21 Aug. 1939, Serowe; s. of Dihabano and Dithunya Mogae; m. Barbara Gemma Modise 1968; three d.; ed. Moeng Secondary School, North West London Polytechnic, Univs. of Oxford and Sussex; Planning Officer, Ministry of Devt. Planning 1968–69, Ministry of Finance and Devt. Planning 1970, Sr. Planning Officer 1971, Dir. Econ Affairs 1972–74, Perm. Sec. 1975–76; Alt. Exec. Dir. of IMF 1976–78, Exec. Dir. 1978–80; Alt. Gov. for Botswana, IMF 1971–72, African Devt. Bank 1971–76, IBRD 1973–76; Dir. Botswana Devt. Corpn. 1971–74 (Chair. 1975–76), De Beers Botswana Mining Co. Ltd. 1975–76, Bangwato Concessions Ltd. 1975–76, B.C.L. Sales Ltd. 1975–76, Bank of Botswana 1975–76 (Gov. 1980–81); Gov. IMF 1981–82; Perm. Sec. to Pres. of Botswana 1982–89, Minister of Finance and Devt. Planning 1989–98, Vice-Pres. 1992–98; Pres. of Botswana April 1998–; Pres. Botswana Soc., Botswana Soc. of the Deaf; mem. Jt. Devt. Cttee of World Bank and IMF on the transfer of real resources to developing countries 1992–, Kalahari Conservation Soc., Commonwealth Parl. Assoc., Parliamentarians for Global Action, Global Coalition for Africa; Rep., Commonwealth Fund for Tech. Co-operation 1971–; Officier, Ordre Nat. de la Côte d'Ivoire 1979, du Mali; Presidential Order of Honour of Botswana 1989. *Leisure interests:* reading, tennis, music. *Address:* Ministry of Finance and Development Planning, Private Bag 008, Gaborone, Botswana.

MOGG, John Frederick; British European Community official; b. 5 Oct. 1943, Brighton; m. Anne Smith 1967; one s. one d.; ed. Univ. of Birmingham; fmrly. with Rediffusion group; First Sec. U.K. Perm. Representation at EC, Brussels 1979–82; various appts. in U.K. civil service 1982–89; Deputy Head, European Secr. Cabinet Office 1989–90; Deputy Dir.-Gen. Internal Market and Industrial Affairs, European Comm. 1990–93, Dir.-Gen. Internal Market and Financial Services Directorate-Gen. 1993–. *Address:* European Commission, DG XV 200 rue de la Loi, B-1049 Brussels, Belgium.

MOGGACH, Deborah, B.A.; British writer; b. 28 June 1948, London; d. of Richard Hough and Helen Charlotte Hough; m. Anthony Moggach 1971 (divorced); one s. one d.; ed. Camden School for Girls, Bristol Univ.; TV dramas: To Have and To Hold 1986, Stolen 1990, Goggle-Eyes (adaptation) 1993 (Writers' Guild Award for Best Adapted TV Serial), Seesaw 1998, Close Relations 1998; play for theatre Double Take. *Publications:* (novels) You Must Be Sisters 1978, Close to Home 1979, A Quiet Drink 1980, Hot Water Man 1982, Porky 1983, To Have and To Hold 1986, Driving in the Dark 1988, Stolen 1990, The Stand-in 1991, The Ex-Wives 1993, Seesaw 1996, Close Relations 1997, Tulip Fever 1999; (short stories) Smile 1987, Changing Babies 1995. *Leisure interests:* swimming in rivers, walking round cities. *Address:* c/o Curtis Brown, 28/29 Haymarket, London, SW1Y 4SP, England. *Telephone:* 0171-396 6600. *Fax:* 0171-396 0110.

MOGGIE, Datuk Leo, M.A., M.B.A.; Malaysian politician; b. 1 Oct. 1941, Kanowit, Sarawak; ed. Univs. of Otago and Pennsylvania State Univ.; Dist. Officer, Kapit, Sarawak 1966–68; Dir. Borneo Literature Bureau, Kuching, Sarawak 1968–69; attached to Office of Chief Minister, Kuching 1969–72; Deputy Gen. Man. Borneo Devt. Corpn. Kuching 1973–74; elected to Sarawak State Legis. Ass. and Parl.; Sec.-Gen. Sarawak Nat. Party (SNAP) 1976; Minister of Welfare Services, State Govt. of Sarawak 1976–77, of Local Govt. 1977–78; Minister of Energy, Telecommunications and Posts 1978–89, of Works and Public Utilities 1989–90, of Public Works 1990–95. *Address:* c/o Ministry of Public Works, Jalan Sultan Salahuddin, 50580 Kuala Lumpur, Malaysia.

MOĞULTAY, Mehmet; Turkish politician and lawyer; b. 1945, Tunceli; m.; three c.; ed. Ankara Univ.; ind. lawyer; parl. deputy; fmr. Minister of Labour and Social Security, of Justice 1994–95. *Address:* c/o Ministry of Justice, Adalet Bakanlığı, 06100 Bakanlıklar, Ankara, Turkey.

MOGWE, Archibald Mooketsa, M.B.E., B.A., P.M.S., P.H., M.P.; Botswana politician and teacher; b. 29 Aug. 1921, Kanye; s. of Rev. Morutwana T. Mogwe and Mary (née Leepo) Mogwe; m. Lena Mosele Senakhomo 1953; one s. two d.; ed. schools in Bechuanaland Protectorate, teacher training in S. Africa, Univs. of Reading and Oxford; teacher 1944–57; Educ. Officer 1957–64; transferred to Secr. 1964, Perm. Sec. 1966; worked in Foreign Office 1966–, Sr. Perm. Sec., Sec. to Cabinet and Head of Public Service 1968–74; Minister of Foreign Affairs 1974–84, of Mineral Resources and Water Affairs 1984–89, 1990–94. *Leisure interests:* soccer, classical music, shooting. *Address:* c/o Ministry of Mineral Resources and Water Affairs, Private Bag 0018, Gaborone, Botswana. *Telephone:* 353180 (Home).

MOHAMED, Caabi el Yachroutou; Comoran politician; Minister of Finance 1993–94; Prime Minister of Comoros April–Oct. 1995; Interim Pres. 1995–96; mem. Rally for Democracy and Renewal. *Address:* Office of the Prime Minister, Moroni, Comoros.

MOHAMMED ZAHIR SHAH; fmr. King of Afghanistan; b. 15 Oct. 1914; m. Lady Homira, 4 Nov. 1931; children: Princess Bilqis, Prince Ahmad Shah, Princess Maryam, Prince Mohammed Nadir, Prince Shah Mahmoud, Prince Mohammed Daoud, Prince Mirvis; ed. Habibia High School, Istiqlal Coll. (both in Kabul), Lycée Janson-de-Sailly and Lycée of Montpellier, France; graduated with honours; attended Infantry Officers' School, Kabul 1932; Asst. Minister in Ministry of Nat. Defence 1932–33; acting Minister of Educ. 1933; crowned King 8 Nov. 1933; deposed 17 July 1973, abdicated 24 Aug. 1973, stripped of citizenship 1978 after Communist takeover, citizenship restored 1991.

MOHAN, Ramesh, PH.D.; Indian university vice-chancellor and fmr. professor of English; b. 20 March 1920, Meerut (U.P.); s. of Madan Mohan and Kamal Kumari; m. Vimala Mangalik 1943; three s.; ed. Lucknow Univ., Leeds Univ., U.K.; lecturer in English, Lucknow Univ. 1942–55, Reader 1955–61, Prof. and Head Dept. of English and Modern European Languages 1961–67; Dir. Cen. Inst. of English and Foreign Languages, Hyderabad 1967–85; Vice-Chancellor, Meerut Univ. 1985–88; Visiting Prof. Univ. of Ill., Urbana, U.S.A. 1971, 1975; Consultant, Indira Gandhi Nat. Open Univ., New Delhi 1988–90; Pres. Indian Asscn. of English Studies 1975–80, Asscn. of Indian Univs. 1982–83; mem. Bd. of Dirs., American Studies Research Centre 1969–89, Exec. Council, Univ. of Hyderabad 1974–77, Exec. Bd. Sahitya Akademi, New Delhi 1978–88, Bd. of Dirs., U.S. Educational Foundation of India 1980–81, Governing Council, Indian Inst. of Science, Bangalore 1980–81, Univ. Grants Comm. 1982–85, Council, Asscn. of Commonwealth Univs. 1982–83, Governing Body, Indian Inst. of Advanced Studies, Simla 1984–87; Wilhelm and Jacob Grimm Prize (G.D.R.) 1986. *Publications:* The Political Novels of Anthony Trollope 1961, George Meredith and the Political Novel 1968, Teaching of English at the University Level in India 1968, Syllabus Reform in English 1977, Some Aspects of Style and Language in Indian English Fiction 1978, Indian Writing in English (Ed.) 1978, English by Air 1979, Stylistics and Literary Interpretation 1980, Symphony (collection of poems) 1984, Nehru as a Man of Letters 1989, Radhakrishnan and Higher Education in India 1989, Religion and National Secularism 1993, English in India: Status and Creativity 1993, Crisis in Higher Education 1994, Let Me Say (essays and addresses) 1996, Benjamin Disraeli: Political Novelist 1998; numerous papers on teaching of English and higher educ. in India. *Leisure interests:* music, theatre, reading, writing, jigsaw puzzles. *Address:* Shanti Sadan 36, Nehru Road, Meerut, Uttar Pradesh, India. *Telephone:* 642339.

MOHIEDDIN, Zakaria; Egyptian politician and army officer; b. 7 May 1918; s. of late Abdul Magid Mohieddin and Zeinab Abdul Magid; m. Naila Moustafa 1950; one s. two d.; ed. Mil. Coll. and Staff Officers' Coll., Cairo; fmr. lecturer Mil. Coll. and Staff Officers' Coll. and Dir.-Gen. Intelligence; mem. Revolutionary Council 1952; Minister of the Interior 1953–58; Minister of the Interior U.A.R. 1958–62, Vice-Pres. U.A.R. and Chair. Aswan Dam Cttee. 1961–62; mem. Nat. Defence Cttee. 1962–69, Presidency Council 1962–64; mem. Exec. Cttee. Arab Socialist Union 1964–69; Deputy Prime Minister 1964–65, 1967–68; Prime Minister and Minister of the Interior 1965–66. *Leisure interests:* fishing, shooting, rowing, poultry farming. *Address:* 52 El-Thawra Street, Dokki, Cairo, Egypt. *Telephone:* 349 9421.

MOHN, Reinhard; German publisher; b. 29 June 1921; ed. high school; army service 1939–43; P.O.W. in N. Africa and U.S.A. 1943–46; Pres. and C.E.O. Bertelsmann A.G. 1947–81, Chair. Supervisory Bd. 1981–91; Chair. Bertelsmann Foundation 1991–97. *Address:* c/o Bertelsmann Foundation, Carl-Bertelsmann-Str. 256, Postfach 103, 33311 Gütersloh, Germany. *Telephone:* 05241/817-0. *Fax:* 05241/816677.

MOHORITA, Vasil; Czech politician and businessman; b. 19 Sept. 1952, Prague; s. of Vasil Mohorita and Ludmila Mohoritova; m. Vlasta Mohoritova 1976; one s. one d.; ed. Komsomol Coll., Moscow and CP of Czechoslovakia (CPCZ) Political Coll., Prague; joined CPCZ 1970, mem. Cen. Cttee. 1988–90, First Sec. Cen. Cttee. 1989–90; Chair. Youth Union's Czechoslovak Cen. Cttee. 1987–89; mem. Czechoslovak Nat. Front Presidium 1987; Deputy, Czechoslovak Nat. Council 1985–90; mem. Presidium Fed. Ass. Jan.–Oct. 1990, Deputy to Fed. Ass. House of People 1990; Chair. Communist Deputies Club Jan.–Nov. 1990; Head of Sales, Frut Ovo (pvt. co.); mem. Party of Democratic Left 1993–97; Chair. Party of Democratic Socialism 1997–98. *Publications:* numerous articles. *Leisure interests:* reading historical and political literature, playing the guitar, basketball, tennis.

MOHRT, Michel, L. EN D.; French writer and editor; b. 28 April 1914, Morlaix; s. of Fernand and Amélie (née Gélébart) Mohrt; m. Françoise Jarrier 1955; one s.; ed. Law School, Rennes; lawyer, Marseilles Bar until 1942; Prof. Yale Univ., Smith Coll., Univ. Coll. L.A. 1947–52; Ed. and Head English Translations Section Les Editions Gallimard 1952–; mem. Acad. Française 1985; Officier, Légion d'honneur, Croix de guerre; Grand Prix du roman de l'Académie française for La Prison Maritime 1962; Grand Prix de la Critique Littéraire 1970; Grand Prix de Littérature de l'Académie française 1983. *Publications:* Novels: Le répit, Mon royaume pour un cheval 1949, Les nomades, le serviteur fidèle, La prison maritime 1961, La campagne d'Italie 1965, L'ours des Adirondacks 1969, Deux Américaines à Paris 1974, Les moyens du bord 1975, La guerre civile 1986, Le Télésiège 1989, Un soir à Londres 1991, On liquide et on s'en va 1992; essays: Les intellectuels devant la défaite de 1870, Montherlant, homme libre 1943, Le nouveau roman américain 1956, L'air du large 1969, L'air du large II 1988; Plays: Un jeu d'enfer 1970, La maison du père 1979, Vers l'Ouest 1988, L'Air du temps 1991. *Leisure interests:* sailing, painting. *Address:* c/o Editions Gallimard, 5 rue Sébastien-Bottin, 75007 Paris; 4 bis rue du Cherche-Midi, 75006 Paris, France (Home). *Telephone:* (1) 42-22-42-12 (Home).

MOHTASHAMI, Ali Akbar; Iranian politician; b. 1946, Teheran; s. of Seyed Hossein and Fatemeh Mohtashami; m. Fatemeh Mohtashami 1968;

two s. five d.; studied theology in Iran and Iraq; mil. training in Palestinian camps, Lebanon; went to Paris with Ayatollah Khomeini 1978; returned to Iran and took part in overthrow of monarchy 1979; mem. political advisory office of Ayatollah Khomenei; dir. of Ayatollah's representative delegation in Foundation of the Oppressed 1980; mem. IRIB Supervisory Council 1980–81; Amb. to Syria 1981–85; a founder of Hezbollah in Lebanon; Minister of the Interior 1985; mem. Parl. 1989–91; Chair. Parl. Cttee. on Defence; Sec.-Gen. IPU Group of Iran (Chair. 1989–91); mem. Cttee. to protect the Islamic Revolution of Palestine, Cen. Council of Combatant Clergy. *Leisure interests:* study, sport (especially mountaineering and swimming). *Address:* 80 Sharif Vagafi Street–Ray Street, Teheran, Iran. *Telephone:* 2046569.

MOI, Daniel arap; Kenyan politician; b. 1924, Sacho, Baringo district; ed. African Mission School, Kabartonjo A.I.M. School and Govt. African School, Kapsabet; teacher 1945–57; Head Teacher, Govt. African School, Kabarnet 1946–48, 1955–57, teacher Tambach Teacher Training School, Kabarnet 1948–54; African Rep. mem., Legis. Council 1957–63; Chair. Kenya African Democratic Union (KADU) 1960–61; mem. House of Reps. 1961–; Parl. Sec., Ministry of Educ. April-Dec. 1961; Minister of Educ. 1961–62, Local Govt. 1962–64, Home Affairs 1964–67; Pres. Kenya African Nat. Union (KANU) for Rift Valley Province 1966–67; Vice-Pres. of Kenya 1967–78, concurrently Minister of Home Affairs; Pres. of Kenya and C.-in-C. of the Armed Forces Oct. 1978–; Minister of Defence 1979–; Chair. OAU 1981–82; mem. Rift Valley Educ. Bd., Kalenjin Language Cttee.; Chair. Rift Valley Provincial Court; Kt. of Grace, Order of St. John 1980. *Address:* Office of the President, Harambee House, Harambee Avenue, P.O. Box 30510, Nairobi, Kenya.

MOINOT, Pierre, L. ÈS L.; French civil servant; b. 29 March 1920, Fressines, Deux-Sèvres; m. Madeleine Sarrailh 1947; one s. four d.; ed. Univs. de Paris, Caen and Grenoble; Sr. Civil Servant 1946–; Tech. Adviser, Pvt. Office of André Malraux 1959–61; Dir. Theatres and Cultural Action 1960–62; Admin. Union générale cinématographique 1960–; Pres. Comm. on advances in long films 1964–72, Comm. on Audiovisual Problems 1981–; French Del. to UNESCO 1966; Dir.-Gen. of Arts and Letters 1966–69; Chief Adviser, Audit Office 1967, Pres. 1978, Attorney-Gen. 1983–86; mem. Acad. française 1982–; Prix du Roman de l'Académie française, Prix Sainte-Beuve, Prix des libraires de France, Prix Fémina 1979; Grand Officier, Légion d'honneur, Croix de guerre, Médaille des blessés, Commdr. des Arts et des Lettres, Bronze Star Medal, Chevalier des Palmes académiques, Officier du Mérite agricole and other decorations. *Publications:* Armes et bagages 1951, La chasse royale 1954, La blessure 1956, Le sable vif 1963, Héliogabale 1971, Mazarin 1978, Le guetteur d'ombre 1979, Jeanne d'Arc 1988, La descente du fleuve 1991, Tous comptes faits 1993, T. E. Lawrence en guerre 1994, Attention à la peinture 1997. *Leisure interests:* hunting, carpentry. *Address:* 44 rue du Cherche-Midi, 75006 Paris, France (Home). *Telephone:* (1) 45-44-19-47.

MOISEIWITSCH, Benjamin Lawrence, PH.D.; British professor of applied mathematics; b. 6 Dec. 1927, London; s. of Jacob Moiseiwitsch and Chana Kotlerman; m. Sheelagh M. McKeon 1953; two s. two d.; ed. Royal Liberty School, Romford and Univ. Coll., London; lecturer in Applied Math., Univ. of Belfast 1952–62, Reader in Applied Math. 1962–68, Prof. 1968–93, Prof. Emer. 1993–, Head Dept. of Applied Math. and Theoretical Physics 1977–89, Dean Faculty of Science 1972–75; mem. Royal Irish Acad. *Publications include:* Variational Principles 1966, Integral Equations 1977. *Leisure interest:* music. *Address:* 21 Knocktern Gardens, Belfast, Northern Ireland, BT4 3LZ (Home). *Telephone:* (01232) 273158 (Office).

MOISEYEV, Igor Aleksandrovich; Russian choreographer; b. 21 Jan. 1906, Kiev, Ukraine; m. 1st Tamara Alekseevna Seifert; one d.; m. 2nd Irina Alekseevna Chagadaeva; ed. Bolshoi Theatre School of Choreography; artist and ballet master at the Bolshoi Theatre 1924–39; Dir. of the Choreographic Dept. of the Theatre of People's Art 1936; Founder and Art Dir. of the Folk Dance Ensemble of the U.S.S.R. (now Moiseyev Dance Co.) 1937–; People's Artist of the U.S.S.R. 1953; State Prizewinner 1942, 1947, 1952; Lenin Prize 1967; Hero of Socialist Labour 1976 and other decorations. *Publications:* articles on choreography of national dance. *Address:* Iverskaya str. 31, Moscow; Moiseyev Dance Company, 20 Triumfalnaya Pl., Moscow, Russia. *Telephone:* (095) 299-63-28. *Fax:* (095) 202-20-36.

MOISEYEV, Nikita Nikolayevich, D.PHYS.-MATH.SC.; Russian physicist; b. 23 Aug. 1917, Moscow; m.; two c.; ed. Moscow Univ.; service World War II; worked as teacher Mil. Navigation Acad. 1947–48, Moscow Higher Tech. School 1948–50, Rostov Univ. 1950–56; Prof. Moscow Inst. of Physics and Tech. 1956–61; sr. researcher, Head of Lab., Vice-Dir. Computation Centre, U.S.S.R. Acad. of Sciences 1960–87; concurrently Dean Faculty of Man. and Applied Math., Moscow Inst. of Physics and Tech. 1971–87; adviser Computation Centre, Russian Acad. of Sciences 1987–; Pres. Green Cross Russia; Chair. Council on analysis of critical situations and governmental decisions of the Govt. of Russia 1992–; U.S.S.R. State Prize, Prize of U.S.S.R. Council of Ministers. *Publications:* works on math., mechanics and theory of man., math. modelling of econ. systems, imitation modelling, including Asymptotic Models of Nonlinear Mechanics 1981, Mathematical Problems of System Analysis 1981, People and Cybernetics 1984. *Leisure interest:* mountaineering. *Address:* Computation Centre, Vavilova str. 40, 117967 GSP Moscow (Office); Acad. Zelinsky str. 38, bl. 8, apt. 5, 117334 Moscow, Russia (Home). *Telephone:* (095) 135-24-89 (Office); 135-04-97 (Home). *Fax:* 923-68-33.

MOÏSI, Dominique; French professor of international relations; b. 21 Oct. 1946, Neuilly-sur-Seine; s. of Jules Moïsi and Charlotte Tabakman; m. Diana Pinto-Moïsi 1977; two s.; ed. Lycée Buffon, Paris, Institut d'Etudes Politiques, Paris, Faculté de Droit de Paris, Harvard Univ., U.S.A.; Visiting Lecturer, Hebrew Univ. of Jerusalem 1973–75; Asst. Lecturer, Univ. of Paris X 1975–89; Deputy Dir. Institut français des relations internationales 1979–; lecturer, Ecole Nationale d'Administration 1980–85, Ecole des Hautes Etudes en Sciences Sociales 1988–; Sec.-Gen. Groupe d'Etude et de Recherche des problèmes internationaux 1975–78; Assoc. Prof., Johns' Hopkins Univ. European Centre, Bologna 1983–84; Ed. Politique étrangère 1983–; Prof. Inst. d'etudes politiques, Paris; Bd. Dirs. Salzburg Seminar, Aspen Inst., Berlin; editorial writer for Financial Times and Asahi Shimbun. *Publications:* Crises et Guerres au XXe siècle: analogies et différences 1981, Le nouveau continent: plaidoyer pour une Europe renaissante (with Jacques Rupnik) 1991 etc. *Leisure interests:* music, cinema, tennis, skiing. *Address:* Institut Français des Relations Internationales (IFRI), 27 rue de la Procession, 75015 Paris (Office); 23 avenue Bosquet, 75007 Paris, France (Home). *Telephone:* (33-1) 40.61.60.00 (Office); (33-1) 45.55.94.58 (Home). *Fax:* (33-1) 40.61.60.60.

MOITINHO DE ALMEIDA, José Carlos de Carvalho, L. EN D.; Portuguese judge; b. 17 March 1936, Lisbon; m. Maria de Lourdes Saraiva De Menezes 1959; one s. one d.; Asst. to public prosecutor 1963–68; public prosecutor, Court of Appeal, Lisbon 1962–72; Chef du Cabinet to Minister of Justice 1972–73; Deputy Attorney-Gen. 1974–79; Dir. Office of European Law 1980–86; now Judge, Court of Justice of European Union; Croix de Guerre, Ordre du Mérite. *Publications:* Le contrat d'assurance dans le droit portugais et comparé, La publicité mensongère, Droit communautaire, ordre juridique communautaire, Les libertés fondamentales dans la CEE. *Leisure interests:* swimming, gardening. *Address:* Palais de la Cour de Justice, L-2925 Luxembourg (Office); 32 rue Jean-Pierre Brasseur, 1258 Luxembourg; Vivenda Panorama, Av. do Monaco, 2675 Estoril, Portugal (Homes). *Telephone:* 4303–1 (Office). *Fax:* 43 03 26 00 (Office).

MOJSOV, Lazar, D.IUR.; Macedonian journalist, politician and diplomatist (retd.); b. 19 Dec. 1920, Negotino, Macedonia; s. of Dono and Efka Mojsov; m. Liljana Jankov 1945; two d.; ed. Belgrade Univ.; fmr. mem. Anti-Fascist Assembly for the Nat. Liberation of Macedonia; fmr. Public Prosecutor, Macedonia; Minister of Justice, Macedonia 1948–51; Dir. New Macedonia 1953–58; Pres. Supreme Court of Macedonia 1953; fmr. Head of Press Dept., Fed. Govt of Macedonia; mem. Yugoslav Fed. Parliament and Parliament of Macedonia; mem. Exec. Bd., Socialist League of Working People of Yugoslavia; mem. Exec. Cttee. of Cen. Cttee., Macedonian League of Communists; mem. Cen. Cttee. League of Communists of Yugoslavia –1989 (Pres. of Presidium 1980–81); Amb. to U.S.S.R. 1958–61; Dir. Inst. for Study of Workers' Movements 1961–62; Dir. and Chief Ed. Borba 1962–64; Pres. Int. Cttee. of Fed. Conf. of Socialist Alliance of Working People of Yugoslavia 1965; Amb. to Austria 1967–69; Perm. Rep. to UN 1969–74; Chair. Security Council 1973; Deputy Fed. Sec. for Foreign Affairs 1974–78, Fed. Sec. 1982–84; mem. Collective State Presidency of Yugoslavia 1984–89, Vice-Pres. 1986–87, Pres. 1987–88; Pres. 32nd UN Gen. Assembly 1977; Partisan Memorial medal 1941; Order of Merit for Exceptional Achievements First Class, Order of Merit for Services to the Nation, First and Third Class, Order of Brotherhood and Unity. *Publications:* The Bulgarian Working Party (Communist) and the Macedonian National Question 1948, Vasil Glavinov: First Propagator of Socialism in Macedonia 1949, Concerning the Question of the Macedonian National Minority in Greece 1954, The World Around Us 1977, Historical Themes 1978, Dimensions of nonalignment 1980, Past and Present 1981, Nonalignment Yesterday, Today and Tomorrow 1990. *Leisure interest:* philately.

MOKABA, Peter Ramoshoane; South African politician; b. 1958, Mankeng Township, nr. Pietersburg; ed. Hwiti High School; fmr. journalist and teacher; student leader in revolts in Hwiti High School 1976–77; detained 1977; mil. training in Swaziland, Mozambique and Angola 1980; returned to S. Africa and operated underground 1981; convicted under Terrorism Act 1984 but conviction overturned by Appeal Court; detained again March 1985, July 1985; released on appeal 1986; joined UDF 1985; Nat. Educ. Officer, Nat. Youth League 1986; helped establish Congress of Traditional Leaders of S.A. and formed N. Transvaal People's Congress for migrant workers 1987; Founder and Pres. S.A. Youth Congress 1987–91; detained March 1988, Jan.–Feb. 1990; Nat. Chair. Provincial Youth Comm. of ANC Youth League 1990; Pres. ANC Youth League 1991–93; mem. Nat. Exec. ANC 1991–94; M.P. Nat. Ass. 1994–; Deputy Minister of Environmental Affairs and Tourism 1996–; Chair. ANC Natal Tourism Forum 1993–, Select Cttee. on Environmental Affairs and Tourism 1994–. *Address:* African National Congress, P.O. Box 61884, Marshalltown 2107, South Africa.

MOKRONOSOV, Adolf Trofimovich, D.BIOL.SC.; Russian physiologist; b. 14 June 1928, Lenevskoe, Sverdlovsk Region; m.; two d.; ed. Ural Univ.; mem. CPSU 1963–91; teacher, Prof., Pro-Rector Ural Univ. 1954–83, Deputy Dir. Timiryazev Inst. of Physiology of Plants 1983–88, Dir. 1988–; Head of Chair of Physiology of Plants, Moscow Univ. 1988–93, Prof. 1988–; Corresp. mem. U.S.S.R. (now Russian) Acad. of Sciences 1981, mem. 1987; Ed.-in-Chief Physiology of Plants; Pres. Russian Soc. of Physiology of Plants 1988–93. *Publications:* works on physiology of plants, biochem., ecology and photosynthesis. *Address:* Institute of Physiology of Plants, Botanicheskaya ul. 35, 127276 Moscow, Russia. *Telephone:* (095) 482-32-58, 482-29-04 (Office); 331-32-58 (Home).

MOLCHANOV, Vladimir Kyrillovich; Russian journalist; b. 7 Oct 1950, Moscow; s. of Kyrill Molchanov; m. Consuella Segura; one d.; ed. Moscow State Univ.; with Press Agency Novosti 1973–86; observer U.S.S.R. State Cttee. for TV and Radio 1987–91; artistic dir. studio of independent co. REN-TV 1991–, Observer Reuter-TV 1994–; regular appearances in his own TV programmes Before and After Midnight 1987–93, Before and After 1994–; mem. Acad. of Russian TV, Acad. of Natural Sciences; Prize of Journalists' Union as the best TV journalist 1990 and others. *Publications:* TV films: Remembrance, I, You, He and She, People and Years, Zone, I Still Have More Addresses, Tied with One Chain, August of 1991 (screenplays), Retribution must come (M. Gorky Prize 1982). *Leisure interest:* life in the country. *Address:* REN-TV, Zubovsky blvd. 17, Moscow, Russia. *Telephone:* (095) 425 3558 (Office).

MOLEFE, Popo Simon; South African politician; b. 26 April 1952, Sophiatown; m. 1st Olympia Molefe (divorced); three c.; m. 2nd Boitumelo Plaatje 1991; ed. Naledi High School; microfilm machine operator, photographic printing machine operator 1976–78; mem. SASM 1973–76; mem. Black Peoples's Convention 1974, 1977; First Chair. Azanian People's Org. (AZAPO), Soweto Branch 1979–81; mem. Gen. and Allied Workers Union 1980–83; Sec. Transvaal Region, United Democratic Front (UDF) 1983, Nat. Gen. Sec. 1983–91; mem. Nat. Exec. Cttee. ANC 1991–; charged with treason and murder after detention in 1985, convicted at Delmas Treason Trial, sentenced to 10 years imprisonment after being held in custody for 4 years 1988, released 1989; Chair. ANC Nat. Elections Comm. 1992–94, ANC Alexandra Br. 1990; Vice-Chair. ANC PWV Region 1990–94; Premier N.W. Prov. Parl. 1994–; Sec. Nat. Organizing Comm. of ANC. *Address:* Private Bag X2018, Mmabatho 8681; African National Congress, P.O. Box 61884, Marshalltown 2107, South Africa.

MOLIN, Yuriy Nikolaevich; Russian chemist and physicist; b. 3 Feb. 1934; s. of N. N. Molin and A. F. Kuramova; m. N. G. Molina 1965; two d.; ed. Moscow Inst. of Physics and Tech.; worked in U.S.S.R. Acad. of Sciences Inst. of Chemical Physics 1957–59; various posts in U.S.S.R. Acad. of Sciences Inst. of Chem. Kinetics and Combustion 1959–, Dir. 1974–93, Head of Lab. 1993–; teacher in Univ. of Novosibirsk 1966–, Prof. 1974–; mem. U.S.S.R. (now Russian) Acad. of Sciences 1981; Lenin Prize 1986. *Address:* Institute of Chemical Kinetics and Combustion, Novosibirsk 630090, Russia. *Telephone:* (3832) 331607 (Office); (3832) 355521 (Home). *Fax:* (3832) 342350 (Office).

MOLINA, Alfred; British actor; b. 24 May 1953, London; m. Jill Gascoigne; ed. Guildhall School of Music and Drama; on stage has appeared with RSC and at Nat. Theatre, Royal Court Theatre and Donmar Warehouse; TV appearances include role of Blake in series El C.I.D., Year in Provence, Nervous Energy. *Films include:* Raiders of the Lost Ark 1981, Anyone for Denis 1982, Number One 1984, Eleni 1985, Ladyhawke 1985, A Letter to Brezhnev 1985, Prick Up Your Ears 1987, Manifesto 1988, Not Without My Daughter 1991, American Friends 1991, Enchanted April 1991, Maverick 1994, Hideaway, The Perez Family, The Steal, Species, Before and After, Dead Man, Scorpion Spring, Anna Karenina.

MOLINA, Mario Jose, PH.D.; American professor of atmospheric chemistry; b. 19 March 1943, Mexico City; s. of Roberto Molina-Pasquel and Leonor Henriquez; m. Luisa Y. Tan 1973; one s.; ed. Acad. Hispano Mexicana, Univ. Nacional Autónoma de Mexico (UNAM), Univ. of Freiburg and Univ. of Calif. Berkeley; Asst. Prof. UNAM 1967–68; Research Assoc. Univ. of Calif. Berkeley 1972–73; Research Assoc. Univ. of Calif. Irvine 1973–75, Asst. Prof. 1975–79, Assoc. Prof. 1979–82; Sr. Research Scientist, Jet Propulsion Lab. Calif. 1983–89; Prof. Dept. of Earth, Atmospheric and Planetary Sciences and Dept. of Chem. M.I.T. 1989–97, Inst. Prof. 1997–; mem. N.A.S.; Max Planck Research Award 1994–96; UN Environmental Programme Ozone Award 1995; Nobel Prize for Chemistry 1995; many other awards and distinctions. *Publications:* articles in scientific journals. *Leisure interests:* music, reading, tennis. *Address:* Department of Earth, Atmospheric and Planetary Sciences, Massachusetts Institute of Technology, Room 54-1814, Cambridge, MA 02139 (Office); 8 Clematis Road, Lexington, MA 02173, U.S.A. *Telephone:* (617) 253-5081 (Office). *Fax:* (617) 258-6525 (Office).

MOLINA BARRAZA, Col. Arturo Armando; Salvadorean fmr. Head of State and army officer; b. 6 Aug. 1927, San Salvador; s. of Mariano Molina and Matilde Barraza de Molina; m. María Elena Contreras de Molina; four s. one d.; ed. Escuela Militar, El Salvador, Escuela Superior de Guerra, Mexico, Escuela de Infanteria, Spain; Section and Co. Commdr., Escuela Militar; Artillery Garrison, Asst. Dir. Escuela de Armas, Section and Dept. Chief, Staff HQ; Del. 6th Conf. of American Armed Forces, Peru 1965, 7th Conf. Buenos Aires; Gen. Co-ordinator, 2nd and 3rd Confs. of Defence Council of Cen. American States; Dir. Exec. Comm. for Shipping; Dir. Nat. Cttee. of Caritas, El Salvador; Pres. of El Salvador 1972–77.

MOLINARI, Ricardo E.; Argentinian writer; b. 23 March 1898; s. of Juan Lauriano Molinari and Maria Esther de Molinari; m. Amelia Vegazo; ed. secondary school; has received every poetry prize in Argentina. *Publications include:* El Huésped y la Melancolía 1946, Días donde la Tarde es un Pájaro 1954, Unida Noche 1957, El Cielo de las Alondras y las Gaviotas 1963, Una sombra antigua Canta 1966, La Hoguera Transparente 1970, La Escudilla 1973, Las Sombras del Pájaro Tostado (complete works) 1974. *Address:* Julián Alvarez 2092, Piso 4°, Código Postal 1425, Buenos Aires, Argentina. *Telephone:* 826-1821.

MÖLK, Ulrich, DR.PHIL.; German professor of Romance literature; b. 29 March 1937, Hamburg; s. of Heinrich Mölk and Berta Mölk; m. Renate Mölk 1962; ed. Univs. of Hamburg and Heidelberg; Prof. of Romance Literature, Univ. of Giessen 1967; Prof. of Romance Literature Univ. of Göttingen and Dir. Inst. für Lateinische und Romanische Philologie des Mittelalters 1974–; mem. Acad. of Göttingen, Vice-Pres. 1990–92, Pres. 1992–94. *Publications:* Guiraut Riquier, Las cansos 1962, Trobar clus 1968, Répertoire métrique de la poésie lyrique française 1972, Trotzki, Literaturkritik 1973, Trobadorlyrik 1982, Flaubert, Une Nuit de Don Juan, Edition 1984, Vita und Kult des hl. Metro von Verona 1987, Lohier et Malart 1988, Romanische Franenlieder 1989, Die europaïsche Bedeutungsgeschichte von 'Motiv' 1992, Julien Sorel vor dem Schwurgericht 1994, Impressionistischer Stil 1995, Literatur und Recht 1996. *Address:* Höltystr. 7, 37085 Göttingen, Germany. *Telephone:* (0551) 4 79 78.

MOLL, Kurt; German bass; b. 11 April 1938, Buir; m. Ursula Pade 1968; one s. two d.; ed. Staatliche Hochschule für Musik, Cologne; operatic début Cologne; subsequently sang operatic roles at Aachen, Mainz, Wuppertal, Hamburg; appeared Bayreuth 1968, Salzburg 1970, La Scala, Milan 1972, Covent Garden, London 1975, Metropolitan Opera, New York 1978; Prof. Staatliche Hochschule für Musik, Cologne 1991–. *Address:* Voigtelstr. 22, 50933 Köln, Germany.

MÖLLEMANN, Jürgen W.; German politician; b. 15 July 1945, Augsburg; s. of the late Wilhelm Mölleman and Franziska Reisner; m. Carola M. Appelhoff 1975; three d.; ed. Munster Teachers' Coll.; joined Christian Democratic Union (CDU) 1962, resgnd. 1969; joined Free Democratic Party (FDP) 1970; mem. Deutscher Bundestag 1972–; Educ. Policy Spokesman for FDP Parl. Party in Bundestag 1972–75; mem. FDP Fed. Exec. 1981–; FDP Deputy State Chair. N. Rhine Westphalia 1982–83, Chair. 1983–94, 1998–; Minister of State, Foreign Office 1982–87; Fed. Minister of Educ. and Science 1987–91, of Econs. 1991–93; Health Policy Spokesman for FDP Parl. Party 1994–; Pres. German-Arab Soc. 1993–; Pres. German-Arab Chamber of Trade and Ind. 1996–. *Leisure interest:* modern literature, parachuting. *Address:* Coesfeldweg 59, 48161 Münster, Germany (Home). *Telephone:* 0251 86 82 82.

MÖLLER, Erwin; German business executive; b. 23 Jan. 1939; m.; ed. Tech. Univ. of Darmstadt; Chair. Supervisory Bd. Metaleurop S.A., Foutenay-sous-Bois, VTG Vereinigte Tanklager und Transportmittel GmbH, Hamburg; Chair. Exec. Bd. Preussag A.G.; mem. Supervisory Bd. Hannoversche Lebensversicherung AG, Hannover, Kabelmetal Electro GmbH, Hannover, Salzgitter Stahl GmbH, Düsseldorf; mem. Governing Council DSL Bank, Bonn; Chair. Bd., Dir. Amalgamated Metal Corp. PLC, London; Hon. Consul Grand-Duchy of Luxembourg.

MOLLER, Gordon Desmond, F.N.Z.I.A., F.R.S.A.; New Zealand architect; b. 26 July 1940, Hastings; s. of Oscar Carl Moller and Winifred Daisy Moller; m. Sylvia Anne Liebezeit 1962; one s. two d.; ed. Wellington Coll., Hutt Valley High School, Univ. of Auckland; Dir. Craig Craig Moller architectural practice 1969–; designs include Sky Tower, Sky City, Auckland 1994–97, numerous houses; Chair. Arts Marketing Bd., Aotearoa 1994, 1995; Pres. Wellington Architectural Centre 1972, 1973; Professorial Teaching Fellow Victoria Univ. School of Architecture 1990, 1991; mem. Design Consortium Wellington Civic Centre 1992, 1998; Ed. New Zealand Architect 1976–83; N.Z. Inst. of Architecture Gold Medal for Architecture 1983, 1988; 22 design awards 1970–97. *Leisure interests:* photography, skiing, music, motoring, landscape gardening. *Address:* 150 Hobson Street, Auckland, New Zealand. *Telephone:* (9) 357-0686. *Fax:* (9) 357-0689.

MØLLER, Hans Bjerrum, DR.PHIL.; Danish physicist; b. 11 May 1932, Copenhagen; s. of Oscar B. Møller and Erna Ch. Christensen; m. Inger J. Thorshaug (died 1995); one s. two d.; ed. Tech. Univ. of Denmark and Univ. of Copenhagen; scientist, Risoe Nat. Lab., Denmark 1956–62, Nat. Lab. Brookhaven, U.S.A. 1958–62; Euratom Research Centre, Ispara, Italy 1962–63; Head, State Physics Section, State of Risoe 1964–68, Head, State Physics Dept. 1968–; Dir. of Research, Risoe Nat. Lab. 1982–, Man. Dir., Risoe Nat. Lab. Works 1987–; mem. Royal Danish Acad. of Technical Sciences, Danish Acad. of Sciences and Letters; mem. Bd. of Govs. Jt. Research Centre, Scientific and Tech. Cttee. *Publications:* articles in int. scientific journals. *Address:* Risoe National Laboratory, P.O. Box 49, 4000 Roskilde (Office); Kirsebaerhaven 12, 4000 Roskilde, Denmark (Home).

MØLLER, Maersk Mc-Kinney; Danish shipowner; b. 13 July 1913, Copenhagen; s. of Arnold Peter and Chastine Estelle Mc-Kinney Møller; m. Emma (née Neergaard Rasmussen) Mc-Kinney Møller 1940; three d.; Partner A. P. Møller 1940–, Sr. Partner 1965–; mem. Int. Council Morgan Guaranty Trust Co., New York 1967–84; mem. Bd. IBM Corpn., U.S.A. 1970–84, Advisory Bd. 1984–93; Chair. Steamship Co. of 1912 Ltd., Steamship Co. Svendborg Ltd.; Maersk Line A/S, Odense Steel Shipyard Ltd., Maersk Olie og Gas A/S; Chair. The A. P. Møller and Chastine Mc-Kinney Møller Foundation; hon. mem. Baltic Exchange, London 1991; Peace and Commerce Medal, U.S. Dept. of Commerce 1991; Hon. K.B.E. 1990. *Address:* Esplanaden 50, 1098 Copenhagen K, Denmark.

MOLLISON, Patrick Loudon, C.B.E., M.D., F.R.S.; British professor of haematology and medical author; b. 17 March 1914, London; s. of William M.

Mollison and Beatrice M. Walker; m. 1st Margaret D. Peirce 1940 (dissolved 1964); three s.; m. 2nd Jennifer A. Jones 1973; ed. Univ. of Cambridge and St. Thomas's Hosp. Medical School, London; worked in London Blood Transfusion Service for Medical Research Council 1939–43, then in R.A.M.C.; Dir. MRC Blood Transfusion Research Unit (later Experimental Haematology Unit) at Postgrad. Medical School after demobilization; in charge of Haematology Dept. St. Mary's Hosp., London 1960–79; Prof. of Haematology, Univ. of London 1962–79, Prof. Emer.; Hon. Consultant Immunohaematologist North London Blood Transfusion Centre 1983–; various other professional appointments; several awards and honours. *Publications:* Blood Transfusion in Clinical Medicine 1951; some 200 papers in scientific journals. *Leisure interests:* opera, gardening. *Address:* North London Blood Transfusion Centre, Colindale Avenue, London, NW9 5BG (Office); 60 King Henry's Road, London, NW3 3RR, England (Home). *Telephone:* 0181-200 7777 (Office); 0171-722 1947 (Home).

MOLLOY, Patrick; Irish banker; b. 4 Jan. 1938; m. Ann Lynch; three s. two d.; ed. Trinity Coll. Dublin, Harvard Business School; Asst. Gen. Man. Bank of Ireland 1975–78, Gen. Man. Area East 1978–83, Man. Dir. 1983–91, Group Chief Exec. 1991–. *Leisure interests:* fishing, shooting. *Address:* Bank of Ireland, Lower Baggot Street, Dublin 2, Ireland.

MOLLOY, Robert M., B.COMM.; Irish politician; b. July 1936, Salthill, Galway; s. of Michael Edward and Rita (Stanley) Molloy; m. Phyllis Barry 1972; two s. two d.; ed. St. Ignatius Coll., Univ. Coll., Galway; mem. Dáil Éireann (House of Reps.) 1965–, House Cttee. of Public Accounts 1965–69, House Cttee. on Constitution 1967; Parl. Sec. to Minister for Educ. 1969–70; Minister for Local Govt. 1970–73, for Defence 1977–79, of Energy 1989–93; mem. Galway Co. Council 1967–70, 1974–77, 1985–91, Galway Borough Council 1967–70, 1985–91; Mayor of Galway 1968–69; Chair. Galway Harbour Bd. 1974–77, 1985–91, Lough Corril Navigation Trustees 1985–91; Chair. House Cttee. on Bldg. Land; mem. House Cttee. on State-Sponsored Bodies 1982–87, 1994–, on the Irish Language 1992–, on Enterprise and Econ. Strategy 1994–; mem. Council of Europe 1996–; mem. Governing Body, Univ. Coll., Galway 1977; mem. Exec., Inter-Parl. Asscn.; Dir. Salthill Failte Ltd. 1985–91; Progressive Democrat. *Leisure interests:* swimming, sailing, golf. *Address:* Dáil Éireann, Dublin 2; St. Mary's, Rockbarton, Salthill, Galway, Ireland. *Telephone:* 01-6795417 (Dublin), 091-521765 (Galway). *Fax:* 091-520304 (Galway).

MOLONEY, Thomas Walter, M.A., M.B.A., M.P.H.; American foundation executive; b. 8 Feb. 1946, New York; s. of Thomas Walter Moloney and Anne Heney; ed. Colgate Univ., Columbia Univ.; Program Dir. Nat. Center for the Deaf-Blind, New York 1971–72; Special Asst. to Dir. and Dean, Cornell Univ. Medical Center 1973–74; Asst. Vice-Pres. Robert Wood John Foundation 1975–80; Visiting Lecturer, Princeton Univ. 1975–80; Sr. Vice-Pres., The Commonwealth Fund, New York 1980–92; Dir. of Public Policy and Health Programmes, Inst. for the Future 1992–; mem. Bd. Dirs. New England Medical Center, Boston 1982–89; mem. Bd. Grantmakers in Health, New York 1984–, Chair. 1984–88; Policy Scholar Eisenhower Center, Columbia Univ., New York 1992–, Inst. of Health Policy Studies, Univ. of Calif. at San Francisco 1992–; mem. Nat. Bd. of Medical Examiners 1986–90, Health Advisory Cttee., Gen. Accounting Office, Washington,D.C. 1987–; Bd., Foundation Health Services Research, Washington, D.C. 1989 and other bds.; Fellow of the American Acad. of Arts and Sciences; mem. Inst. of Medicine, N.A.S. *Publications:* Ed. New Approaches to the Medicaid Crisis 1983; numerous articles. *Address:* Institute for the Future, 111 Fifth Avenue, 8th Floor, New York, NY 10003; 72 Norwood Avenue, Upper Montclair, NJ 07043, U.S.A.

MOLSON, Eric H., A.B.; Canadian business executive; b. 16 Sept. 1937, Montreal, P.Q.; s. of Thomas H. P. Molson and Celia F. Cantlie; m. Jane Mitchell 1966; three c.; ed. Selwyn House School, Montreal, Bishop's Coll. School, Lennoxville, Le Rosey, Switzerland, Princeton and McGill Univs. and U.S. Brewers Acad. New York; served as apprentice brewer with Molson Breweries of Canada Ltd., rising through various appts. to Pres.; now Chair. Bd. The Molson Companies Ltd. *Address:* 1225 St. Antoine Street West, Suite 300, Montreal, P.Q. H3C 1B3, Canada.

MOLTKE, Gebhardt von; German diplomatist; b. 28 June 1938, Wernersdorf, Silesia; m. Dorothea von Moltke 1965; one s. one d.; ed. Univs. of Heidelberg, Grenoble, Berlin, Freiburg im Breisgau; practical legal training 1963–67; with Fed. Foreign Office, Bonn 1968–71, Personnel Admin. 1977–82, Head of U.S. Dept. 1986–91; Embassy, Moscow 1971–75; Embassy, Yaoundé 1975–77; Embassy, Washington, D.C. 1982–86; Asst. Sec.-Gen. for Political Affairs NATO 1991–97; Amb. to U.K. Sept. 1997–. *Leisure interest:* tennis. *Address:* Embassy of the Federal Republic of Germany, 23 Belgrave Square/1 Chesham Place, London, SW1X 8PZ, England. *Telephone:* 0171-824 1301. *Fax:* 0171-824 1315.

MOLYNEAUX OF KILLEAD, Baron (Life Peer), cr. 1997 of Killead in the County of Antrim; **James Henry Molyneaux,** K.B.E.; Northern Irish politician; b. 28 Aug. 1920, Crumlin; s. of William Molyneaux and Sarah Gilmore; unmarried; ed. Aldergrove School, Co. Antrim; served R.A.F. 1941–46; mem. Antrim Co. Council 1964–73; Vice-Chair. Eastern Special Care Hosp. Man. Cttee. 1966–73; Chair. Antrim Branch Northern Ireland Asscn. for Mental Health 1967–70; Hon. Sec. S. Antrim Unionist Asscn. 1964–70; M.P. for Antrim South 1970–83, for Lagan Valley 1983–97; Vice-Pres. Ulster Unionist Council 1974; Leader Ulster Unionist Party, House of Commons 1974–97; Leader Ulster Unionist Party 1979–95; mem. Northern Ireland Ass. 1982–86; fmr. J.P. (resgnd. 1987); Deputy Grand Master of Orange Order and Hon. Past Grand Master of Canada; Sovereign Grand Master, Commonwealth Royal Black Inst. 1971. *Leisure interests:* music, gardening. *Address:* House of Lords, London, SW1A 0PW; Aldergrove, Crumlin, County Antrim, Northern Ireland BT29 4AR. *Telephone:* (018494) 22545 (Crumlin).

MOMOH, Maj.-Gen. Joseph Saidu, O.B.E.; Sierra Leonean fmr. Head of State and army officer; b. 26 Jan. 1937, Binkolo, Northern Prov. m. Hannah V. Wilson (died 1996); two d.; ed. West Africa Methodist Collegiate Secondary School, Officers' Training School, Ghana, School of Infantry, Hythe, U.K., Nigeria Defence Acad., Kaduna, Mons Officers' Cadet School, Aldershot, U.K. and Mil. Training Dept., Zaria, Nigeria; commissioned, Royal Sierra Leone Mil. Forces 1963, Deputy Asst. Adjutant and Quartermaster-Gen. 1968, Commdr. First Bn. 1969, Acting Force Commdr. 1971, Brig. 1973, Maj.-Gen. 1983; mem. Parl. 1973–85; Minister of State 1973–85; Pres. of Sierra Leone 1985–92; Minister of Defence and Public Services 1986–92; charged with treason April 1998; sentenced to ten years imprisonment for conspiracy 1998; found not guilty of treason; Order of the Rokel; Order of Nat. Security Merit (Repub. of Korea); Hon. D.C.L. *Leisure interests:* reading, sport.

MOMPER, Walter; German politician; b. 21 Feb. 1945, Sulingen; mem. Berlin Chamber of Deputies 1975–95; Party Whip SPD, Berlin 1985–89, Chair. –1992; Gov. Mayor of Berlin 1989–91. *Address:* Mohrenstrasse 30, 10117 Berlin, Germany. *Telephone:* 2023-2036.

MONBERG, Torben Axel, D.PHIL.; Danish anthropologist; b. 25 July 1929, Copenhagen; s. of Axel S. S. Monberg and Elna Elsa Johansson; m. 1st Bodil B. Melbye (died 1976); m. 2nd Hanne (née Schou) Birthe 1985; one s. two d.; ed. Univ. of Copenhagen; Asst. Prof. of Cultural Sociology, Univ. of Copenhagen 1965–69, Prof. 1969–75; Chief. Curator Nat. Museum of Denmark 1975–80; Prof., Univ. of Hawaii 1972; Hon. Chief Bellona Island, Solomon Islands 1984; Field work on Rennell and Bellona Islands 1958–84, on Tikopia (with Raymond Firth) 1966; mem. Danish Acad. of Sciences. *Publications:* From the Two Canoes, Oral Traditions of Rennell and Bellona Islands (with Samuel H. Elbert) 1965, The Religion of Bellona Island 1966, Mobile in the Trade Wind 1976, Mungiki, Kulturen og dens religion på øen Bellona i Stillehavet 1979, Bellona Island: Beliefs and Ritual Practices 1991; scientific and popular papers. *Address:* Veksebovej 10, 3480 Fredensborg, Denmark. *Telephone:* 42281031. *Fax:* 42284531.

MONDALE, Walter Frederick, LL.B.; American politician and lawyer; b. 5 Jan. 1928, Ceylon, Minn.; s. of Rev. and Mrs. Theodore Sigvaard Mondale; m. Joan Adams 1955; two s. one d.; ed. Minnesota public schools, Macalester Coll., Univ. of Minnesota and Univ. of Minnesota Law School; admitted to Minn. Bar 1956, pvt. practice 1956–60; Attorney-Gen., Minn. 1960–64; U.S. Senator from Minnesota 1964–77; Vice-Pres. of the U.S. 1977–81; mem. Nat. Security Council 1977–81; fmr. Regent Smithsonian Inst.; Counsel with firm Winston and Strawn 1981–87; partner Dorsey and Whitney 1987–93; Amb. to Japan 1993–96; fmr. mem. Bd. Control Data, Columbia Pictures; Democrat-Farm Labor Party; Democratic Cand. for Presidency 1984. *Publication:* The Accountability of Power: Towards a Responsible Presidency 1975. *Leisure interest:* fishing. *Address:* c/o Department of State, 2201 C Street, N.W., Washington, DC 20520, U.S.A.

MONDUZZI, H.E. Cardinal Dino; Italian ecclesiastic; b. 2 April 1922, Brisighella; ordained priest 1945; titular Bishop of Capri 1987; Prefect of the Pontifical Household; cr. Cardinal Feb. 1998. *Address:* Via Monfe della Farina 64, 00186 Rome, Italy. *Telephone:* (6) 69883273. *Fax:* (6) 69885863.

MONEO, José Rafael; Spanish architect and professor of architecture; b. May 1937, Tudela, Navarra; s. of Rafael Moneo and Teresa Vallés; m. 1963; three d.; ed. Madrid Univ. School of Architecture; Fellow, Acad. in Rome 1963–65; Asst. Prof. Madrid School of Architecture 1966–70; Prof. Barcelona School of Architecture 1970–80; Visiting Fellow, Inst. for Architecture and Urban Studies, Cooper Union School of Architecture New York 1976–77; Chair. Dept. of Architecture Harvard Univ. Grad. School of Design 1985–90, Josep Lluís Prof. 1992–; mem. American Acad. of Arts and Sciences, Academia di San Luca di Roma; Hon. Fellow, American Inst. of Architects; Premio di Roma 1962; Gold Medal for Achievement in Fine Arts, Govt. of Spain 1992; Brunner Memorial Prize, American Acad. of Arts and Letters; Schock Prize in the Visual Arts 1993; Dr. h.c. (Leuven) 1993 and other distinctions; work includes: Bankinter Bank, Madrid; Nat. Museum of Roman Art, Mérida; Thyssen Bornemisza Museum; San Pablo Airport, Seville; Manzana Diagonal, Barcelona; Davis Museum, Wellesley Coll. U.S.A. *Address:* Harvard University, Graduate School of Design, Cambridge, MA 02138, U.S.A.; Calle Miño 5, Madrid 28002, Spain. *Telephone:* (34 1) 5642257. *Fax:* (34 1) 5635217.

MONETTE, Richard Jean, O.C., C.M., B.A.; Canadian actor and artistic director; b. 19 June 1944, Montreal, P.Q.; ed. Concordia Univ. Montreal (fmrly. Loyola Coll.); debut as the Prince in Cinderella, St. Michael's Playhouse, Winooski, Vt. 1962; has appeared in numerous productions at Stratford Festival, especially in works of Shakespeare 1965–; dir. of numerous productions, Stratford Festival 1978–, Assoc. Dir. 1988–90, Artistic Dir. 1994–; other appearances at Theatre Toronto, Welsh Nat. Theatre, Open Air Theatre, London, Open Space Theatre, London, St. Lawrence Centre etc.; Artistic Dir. Citadel Theatre Young Co. 1989; regular TV and film appearances 1963–; Tyrone Guthrie Award 1967, Queen's Silver Jubilee Medal 1977; Derek F. Mitchell Artistic Dir.'s Award, Stratford 1984; Dora Mavor Moore Award for Outstanding Direction, St. Joan, Theatre Plus 1991. *Leisure interests:* gardening, cooking. *Address:* Stratford Festival, Box 520, Stratford, Ont., N5A 6V2, Canada. *Telephone:* (519) 271-4040. *Fax:* (519) 271-4904.

MONEY-COUTTS, Sir David Burdett, K.C.V.O., M.A.; British banker; b. 19 July 1931, Oakhill; s. of Hon. Alexander B. Money-Coutts and Mary E. Hobhouse; m. Penelope Utten Todd 1958; one s. two d.; ed. Eton Coll. and New Coll. Oxford; joined Coutts & Co. 1954, Dir. 1958–96, Man. Dir. 1970–86, Chair. 1976–93; Dir. M & G Group 1987–97 (Chair. 1990–97); Dir. Nat. Discount Co. 1964–69, Gerrard & Nat. 1969–99 (Deputy Chair. 1969–89), Nat. Westminster Bank 1976–90 (mem. U.K. Advisory Bd. 1990–92); mem. Council U.C.L. 1987–97; Phoenix Assurance 1978–89, Sun Alliance Assurance 1982–90. *Address:* Magpie House, Peppard Common, Henley-on-Thames, Oxon., RG9 5JG, England.

MONGBE, René Valéry, B.A.; Benin diplomatist; b. 12 Nov. 1939, Agbangnizoun; m.; six c.; ed. Swarthmore Coll., Pa., U.S.A., Univ. of Geneva, Switzerland; began career as civil servant 1966, served in Embassy in France 1969–73, Dir.-Gen., Head of European Desk and Dir. of Research and Planning, Ministry of Foreign Affairs and Co-operation 1973–84, Head Int. Orgs. Desk 1987–90; Amb. to Zaïre 1975–81 (also accred. to Congo 1978–81, to Angola 1980–81); Head Higher Educ. Supervisory Service, Ministry of Secondary and Higher Educ. 1985–87; mem. Supreme Council of the Repub., Chair. Cttee. for Foreign Affairs, Sovereignty, Defence and Security March–Sept. 1990; Perm. Rep. to UN 1990–97. *Address:* c/o Ministry of Foreign Affairs, BP 318, Cotonou, Benin.

MONGE, Luis Alberto: Costa Rican politician; b. 29 Dec. 1925, Palmares; ed. Univs. of Costa Rica and Geneva; mem. Cen. de Trabajadores Rerum Novarum 1947, subsequently Pres.; fmr. Vice-Pres. Inter-American Labor Confed. (CIT); militant mem. Nat. Liberation Army 1948; mem. Nat. Constituent Ass. (Social Democrat) 1949; co-founder Nat. Liberation Party 1951, Sec.-Gen. for 12 years; worked for ILO, Geneva for 3 years; Sec.-Gen. Interamerican Labor Org. (ORIT) for 6 years; served at Ministry of the Presidency, Govt. of José Figueres 1955; mem. Legis. Ass. 1958, 1970, Pres. of Congress 1970–74; Prof. Inter-American School of Democratic Educ. and Dir. Center of Democratic Studies for Latin America (CEDAL); Pres. of Costa Rica 1982–86.

MONGO BETI (pseudonym of Alexandre Biyidi-Awala); Cameroonian writer and teacher; b. 1932, Mbalmayo; s. of Oscar Awala and Régine Alomo; m. Odile Marie Jeanne Lebossé 1963; two s. one d.; ed. Lycée de Yaoundé, Univ. d'Aix-en-Provence and Sorbonne, Paris; exiled from Cameroon, became teacher and writer in Paris; undertook research in sociology, Paris Univ. 1957–59; currently Prof. Lycée Corneille, Rouen; founder of bi-monthly journal, Peuples Noirs-Peuples Africains 1978; Prix Sainte-Beuve for Mission Terminée 1958. *Publications:* Le pauvre Christ de Bomba 1956 (trans. in English), Mission terminée 1957 (trans. in English), Le roi miraculé 1958 (trans in English), Main basse sur le Cameroun, autopsie d'une décolonisation (political essay) 1972 (banned in France), Remember Ruben 1974, Perpétue et l'habitude du malheur 1974, La ruine presque cocasse d'un polichinelle (novel) 1979.

MONGUNO, Alhaji Shettima Ali; Nigerian politician and educationist; b. 1926, Borno; s. of Rahma and Fanna Monguno; m. Ashe Meta 1948 (died 1994); two s. five d.; ed. Borno Middle School, Bauchi Teacher Training Coll., Katsina Higher Coll., and Univ. of Edinburgh; teacher, Borno Middle School 1952–56; M.P. 1956–66; Councillor for Educ., Borno Native Authority 1961–65; Fed. Minister of Air Force 1965, of Int. Affairs 1965–66; Fed. Commr. for Trade and Industry 1967–71, for Mines and Power, Petroleum and Energy 1971–75; Pres. of OPEC 1972–73; Chair. Maiduguri Metropolitan Council 1976–79; Pro-Chancellor Calabar Univ. 1976–80, Univ. of Nigeria 1980–84; mem. Constituent Ass. 1978–79; Deputy Nat. Chair. Nat. Party of Nigeria 1980–84; political detainee 1984–85 (cleared by mil. tribunal); del. to UN Gen. Ass., UNCTAD 1968 and other int. confs.; mem. Bd. of Trustees West African Examinations Council 1976–83; Chair. Bd. of Dirs. FRUCO Co. Nigeria Ltd. 1987–; Chair. Bd. of Trustees Borno Educ. Endowment Fund 1986–87; Co-Pres. Provisional World Constitution and Parl. Asscn. 1992–; mem. Bd. of Trustees, World Environmental Movement for Africa 1986; mem. Commonwealth Countries League Educ. Fund 1996–, Transparency Int. Nigeria 1997–; Hon. D.Litt. (Sokoto) 1984, (Maiduguri) 1996; UNESCO Medal and numerous other int. awards. *Leisure interests:* gardening, reading, cycling. *Address:* P.O. Box 541, Maiduguri, Borno State, Nigeria (Home). *Telephone:* (76) 231170, 342140 (Maiduguri); (1) 5837572, 269534 (Lagos). *Fax:* (76) 231170, 342140 (Maiduguri).

MONICELLI, Mario; Italian film director; b. 16 May 1915; ed. Università degli Studi, Pisa; fmr. Asst. to Pietro Germi; writer of film Riso Amaro; film dir. 1949–; Golden Lion, Venice Film Festival; Silver Medal, Berlin Film Festival; Silver Laurel Medal, San Francisco Film Festival. *Films include:* Guardie e Ladri 1948, The Big Deal of Madonna Street 1955, The Great War 1958, The Organiser 1960, Casanova '70 1963, L'Armata Brancaleone 1965, Vogliamo i Colonnelli, Romanzo popolare, Caro Michele, Amici miei, Un borghese piccolo piccolo, Viaggio con Anita, Temporale Rosy, Camera d'Albergo 1979, Il Marchese del Grillo 1980, 2nd part of Amici Miei 1982, Viva Italia!, Lovers and Liars, Bertoldo, Bertoldino, E Cacasenna, The Two Lives of Mattia Pascal, I Picari, Let's Hope It's a Girl (also wrote screenplay), The Rogues (also co-wrote screenplay), The Obscure Illness (co-wrote screenplay), Looking for Paradise. *Address:* Via del Babuino 135, 06 6780448 Rome, Italy.

MONK, Meredith Jane; American composer, director and choreographer; b. 20 Nov. 1942; d. of Theodore G. Monk and Audrey Lois (Zellman); ed. Sarah Lawrence Coll; Founder and Artistic Dir. House Foundation for the Arts 1968–; formed Meredith Monk & Vocal Ensemble 1978–. *Works include:* Break 1964, 16 Millimeter Earrings 1966, Juice: a theatre cantata 1969, Key 1971, Vessel: an opera epic 1971, Paris 1972, Education of the Girlchild 1973, Quarry 1976, Songs from the Hill 1976, Dolmen Music 1979, Specimen Days: a civil war opera 1981, Ellis Island 1981, Turtle Dreams Cabaret 1983, The Games 1983, Acts from Under and Above 1986, Book of Days 1988, Facing North 1990, Three Heavens and Hells 1992, Atlas: an opera in three parts 1991, New York Requiem 1993, Volcano Songs 1994, American Archaeology 1994, The Politics of Quiet 1996; Golden Eagle Award 1981, Nat. Music Theatre Award 1986, German Critics' Award for Best Recording of the Year 1981, 1986 and many other awards; Dr. h.c. (Bard Coll.) 1988, (Univ. of the Arts) 1989, (Juilliard School of Music) 1998. *Leisure interests:* gardening, horseback riding. *Address:* House Foundation for the Arts, 131 Varick Street, New York, NY 10013, U.S.A.

MONKS, John Stephen, B.A.; British trades union official; b. 5 Oct. 1945, Manchester; s. of Charles Edward Monks and Bessie Evelyn Monks; m. Francine Jacqueline Schenk 1970; two s. one d.; ed. Nottingham Univ.; joined TUC Org. Dept. 1969, Asst. Sec. Employment and Manpower Section 1974, Head Org., Employment Law and Industrial Relations Dept. 1977–87, Deputy Gen.-Sec. 1987–93, Gen.-Sec. Sept. 1993–; mem. Council Advisory, Conciliation and Arbitration Service (ACAS), 1979–95; mem. British Govt. and EU Competitiveness Councils 1997–; mem. Exec. Council, European TUC and Int. Confed. of Free Trade Unions; Trustee Nat. Museum of Labour History 1988–; Gov. Sedgehill Comprehensive School 1987–94, London School of Econs. 1989–, Goldsmiths' Coll. 1994–; Visiting Prof., School of Man., UMIST 1996–; Visiting Fellow, Nuffield Coll., Oxford 1996–; Hon. D.Sc.(UMIST) 1998. *Leisure interests:* gardening, hiking, music, squash. *Address:* Trades Union Congress, Congress House, Great Russell Street, London, WC1B 3LS, England. *Telephone:* 0171-636 4030. *Fax:* 0171-636 0632.

MONNIER, Claude Michel, PH.D.; Swiss journalist; b. 23 March 1938, Rwankéri, Rwanda; s. of Henri Monnier and Olga Pavlov; m. Estela Troncoso Balandrán 1958; two s.; ed. Univs. of Geneva and Mexico, Graduate Inst. of Int. Studies, Geneva; educational tour in Asia and America 1956–58; Research Fellow, Swiss Nat. Fund for Scientific Research, Tokyo 1963–66; Tokyo Corresp. Journal de Genève 1963–66, Foreign Ed. 1966–70, Ed.-in-Chief 1970–80; Ed. Le Temps Stratégique, Geneva 1982–; mem. Bd. French speaking Swiss TV and radio 1989–; mem. Academic Council, Univ. of Lausanne 1998–. *Publications:* Les Américains et sa Majesté l'Empereur: Etude du conflit culturel d'où naquit la constitution japonaise de 1946 1967, Alerte, citoyens! 1989, L'année du Big-Bang 1990, La terre en a marre 1991, La déprime, ça suffit! 1992, Dieu, que la crise est jolie! 1993, Les Rouges nous manquent 1994, La bonté qui tue 1995, Envie de bouffer du lion 1996, Programme d'un agitateur 1997, Le temps des règlements de compte 1998. *Leisure interests:* walking, light aircraft flying. *Address:* Chemin de Saussac 2, 1256 Troinex, Geneva, Switzerland (Home). *Telephone:* (22) 343 95 55 (Home). *Fax:* (22) 343 95 55 (Home).

MONOD, Jérôme; French businessman; b. 7 Sept. 1930, Paris; s. of Olivier and Yvonne (née Bruce) Monod; m. Françoise Gallot 1963; three s.; ed. Wesleyan Univ., U.S.A., Institut d'Etudes Politiques, Ecole Nat. d'Admin.; Auditeur, Cour des Comptes 1957; Rapporteur, Study mission of Sec.-Gen. for Algerian affairs 1958; Chargé de mission, Prime Minister's Office 1959–62; Conseiller Référendaire à la Cour des Comptes 1963; Chief Exec. Dél. à l'Aménagement du Territoire 1967–75; Special Asst. to Prime Minister Jacques Chirac 1975–1976; Sec.-Gen. Rassemblement pour la République (RPR) 1976–78; Chair. Bd., Centre Français du Commerce Extérieur 1980–83; Pres. French Canadian Chamber of Commerce in Paris 1984–86; Vice-Pres. Société Lyonnaise des Eaux 1979–80, Chair. and C.E.O. 1980–97; Vice-Chair. General Waterworks Corpn. (U.S.A.) 1983–93; Vice-Chair., Compagnie de Suez 1995–97, Chair. Supervisory Bd., Suez Lyonnaise des Eaux June 1997–, Chair. Lyonnaise des Eaux de Casablanca June 1997–; Chair. Sino French Holding (China) 1996–; mem. Bd. of Dirs. Total (Cie. Française des Pétroles), Aguas de Barcelona (Spain), Dic-Degrémont (Japan), Lyonnaise American Holding (U.S.A.), Groupe GTM, GTM-Entrepose, Métropole Télévision; mem. Consultative Council Banqe de France, Business Advisory Council, IFC (U.S.A.); mem. Int. Advisory Bd., NatWest Bank; mem. Steering Cttee., fmr. Chair., European Round Table; Commdr., Légion d'honneur, Officier des Arts et des Lettres, Chevalier des Palmes académiques. *Publications:* L'aménagement du territoire 1971, Transformation d'un pays: pour une géographie de la liberté 1975, Propositions pour la France 1977. *Leisure interests:* swimming, climbing. *Address:* Suez Lyonnaise des Eaux, 72 Ave de la Liberté, 92753 Nanterre Cedex; 94 rue du Bac, 75007 Paris, France (Home).

MONOD, Théodore André, D. ÈS SC.; French zoologist; b. 9 April 1902, Rouen; s. of Rev. Prof. Wilfred and Dorina Monod; m. Olga Pickova 1930;

two s. one d.; ed. Ecole Alsacienne and Paris Univ.; Asst. Museum nat. d'histoire naturelle, Paris 1922, Prof. 1942, then Hon. Prof. 1974–; Dir. Inst. Français d'Afrique Noire, Dakar 1938–65; Dean, Faculty of Sciences, Dakar Univ. 1957–58; mem. Inst. de France (Acad. des Sciences) 1963, Acad. des Sciences d'Outremer 1949, Acad. de Marine 1957; Dr. h.c. (Univs. of Cologne and Neuchâtel); Gold Medal, Soc. de Géographie, Royal Geographical Soc. and American Geographical Soc.; Haile Selassie Prize for African Research; Grand Officier, Légion d'honneur, Ordre des Palmes académiques, Order of Golden Ark, Order of Christ, Mérite Saharien, Mérite Nat. Mauritanie, Ordre Nat. Sénégal. *Publications:* Méharées, L'hippopotame et le philosophe, Bathyfolages, Les déserts 1973, L'émeraude des Garamantes: Souvenirs d'un saharien 1984, Sahara désert magique (contrib.) 1986, Déserts (contrib.) 1988, Mémoires d'un Naturaliste Voyageur 1990, Sortie de secours 1991, Le fer de Dieu (contrib.) 1992, Desert libyque 1994, Maxence au désert 1995, Majâbât al-Koubra 1996, Le chercheur d'absolu 1997, Terre et ciel 1997. *Leisure interest:* field natural history. *Address:* 43 rue Cuvier, 75005 Paris (Office); 14 quai d'Orléans, 75004 Paris, France (Home). *Telephone:* (1) 43-26-79-50 (Home).

MONORY, Jacques; French artist; b. 25 June 1934, Paris; s. of Luis José Monory and Angel Foucher; m. 1st Sabine Monirys 1959 (divorced 1968); one s.; m. 2nd Paule Moninot 1993; ed. Ecole de Beaux Arts, Paris; numerous one-man exhbns. in France and throughout Europe since 1955 including Galerie Kléber, Paris 1955, Galerie H. Legendre 1965, Musée de l'Art Moderne, Paris 1971, 1984, Palais des Beaux Arts, Brussels 1971, Stedelijk Museum, Amsterdam 1972, Centre national d'art contemporain, Paris 1974, Louisiana Museum 1975, Galerie Maeght, Zürich 1975, Galerie Maeght, Paris 1976, 1978, 1981, Galerie Maeght, Barcelona 1980, Fuji TV Gallery, Tokyo 1984, Galerie Lelong, Paris 1987, 1989, 1991, 1994, Mayer-Schwartz Gallery, Los Angeles 1990, Galerie Andata Ritorno, Geneva 1992, Champclose 1995, Théâtre, Centre Culturel, Cherbourg 1996, Galerie Grand Café, Saint-Nazaire 1996, Villa Tamaris, La Seyne sur Mer 1996, Galerie Nova Sim, Prague 1997, Municipal Art Museum, Reykjavík 1997, Musée des Beaux Arts, Sables d'Olonne 1998, Musée des Beaux Arts, Chartres 1998, Musée des Beaux Arts, Dole 1999, Galerie Zannettacci, Geneva 1999, Palais des Congrès Paris 1999; work represented in numerous public collections in Europe, U.S.A. and Japan. *Films:* Ex 1968, Brighton Belle 1973, La Voleuse (video) 1986. *Publications:* Document bleu, Diamondback, Les bords de la mort ne sont pas assez vite, Quick, Eldorado. *Leisure interests:* shooting, swimming. *Address:* 9 Villa Carnot, Cachan 94230, France. *Telephone:* 46-65-08-67. *Fax:* 46-65-08-67.

MONORY, René Claude Aristide; French politician and administrator; b. 6 June 1923, Loudun; s. of Aristide and Marguerite (Devergne) Monory; m. Suzanne Cottet 1945; one d.; ed. Ecole primaire supérieure de Thouars; dealer in vehicles and agricultural machinery 1952; Chair. agricultural machinery and oil cos.; Mayor of Loudun 1959–; Pres. Mayors' Asscn. of Vienne; Councillor, Canton of Loudun 1961; municipal judge; Senator for Vienne 1968–77, 1981–86, Rapporteur, Senate Finance Comm. 1976–77; Minister of Industry and Trade 1977–78, of the Economy 1978–81, of Educ. 1986–88; Pres. Conseil général de la Vienne 1979–; Chair. Interim Cttee. of Bd. of Govs., IMF 1981; Pres. Asscn. de l'union républicaine des présidents de conseils généraux 1983–86; mem. Centre des démocrates sociaux (fmr. nat. sec.), First Vice-Pres. 1984–; mem. Union pour la démocratie française; Pres. Conseil régional Poiton-Charentes 1985–86; Senator for Vienne 1988–; Pres. of Senate 1992–98; Founder-Pres. Futuroscope 1987–. *Publications:* Combat pour le bon sens 1983, Des clés pour le futur 1995. *Leisure interests:* big-game fishing, hunting. *Address:* Mairie de Loudun, Hôtel de Ville, BP 65, 86206 Loudun; Palais de Luxembourg, 15 rue de Vaugirard, 75291 Paris Cedex 06, France. *Telephone:* (1) 56-54-31-44, 56-54-31-40. *Fax:* (1) 56-54-31-45.

MONREAL LUQUE, Alberto, DR.ECON.SC.; Spanish politician and economist; b. 18 Nov. 1928, Madrid; s. of Federico Monreal and Irene Luque; m. Maria Elena Alfageme 1961; two s. one d.; ed. Univ. de Madrid; mem. Cuerpo de Economistas del Estado 1957–; Prof. Faculty of Econ. Sciences, Univ. de Madrid 1957–68; Tech. Sec. Ministry of Public Works 1965–68; Sec. of State, Ministry of Educ. and Science 1968–69; Minister of Finance 1969–73; Pres. Tabacalera (Tobacco Monopoly Co.) 1974–82; Pres. Eurotabac 1994–; Econ. Consultant, Superior Council of Commerce, Ministry of the Economy; Deputy Chair. Grupo Anaya (publishers). *Address:* Eurotabac, Monte Esquinza 28, Madrid 28010, Spain. *Fax:* 3104286.

MONTAGNA, Gilberto Luis Humberto; Argentinian civil engineer; b. 1936; m.; four c.; Sec. Chamber of Food Industrialists (CIPA) 1964–84, Vice-Pres. 1984; Sec. Fed. of Food and Derivatives Industries (FIPAA) 1975–84, Pres. 1984–87; Sec. to Coordinator of Food and Derivates Industry (COPAL) 1975–79, now Pres.; Sec. Industrial Transitory Comm. (COTEI) of Union Industrial Argentina (UIA) 1978–79, mem. Advising Exec. Comm. of UIA Comptrolling 1979–81, First Vice-Pres. UIA 1981–89, Pres. 1989; Tech. Adviser, ILO, Geneva 1978; Alt. Del. to ILO 1979, 1980, 1981; founder, currently Vice-Pres. Action for Pvt. Initiative; Vice-Pres. Establecimientos Modelo Terrabusi SAIC; Dir. Terra Garba Sacai y F, Atilena SCA. *Address:* c/o Union Industrial Argentina, Avda Leandro N. Arem 1067, 11°, 1001 Buenos Aires, Argentina.

MONTAGNE SÁNCHEZ, Gen. Ernesto; Peruvian politician and army officer; b. 18 Aug. 1916, Barranco, Lima; s. of Gen. Ernesto Montagne Markholtz and Raquel de Montagne; m. Isabel Landázuri de Montagne; one s. one d.; ed. Military School of Chorrillos; Capt. 1944, Lieut.-Col. 1953, Col. 1958, Brig.-Gen. 1963, Gen. of Div. 1968; taught at various mil. schools; several posts as Div. Chief of Staff; Dir. Chorrillos Mil. School; Dir. Escuela Superior de Guerra; Prefect of Lima; Gen. Commdr. 3rd Mil. Zone; Minister of State for Educ.; Dir. of Personnel; Deputy Chief of Staff of Army; Gen. Commdr. 1st Mil. Zone and Insp. Gen. of Army; Gen. Commdr. of Army, Pres. of Council of Ministers and Minister of War 1968–72; Orden Militar de Ayacucho, Cruz Peruana al Mérito Militar, Orden del Sol, Orden de San Gregorio Magno, and numerous other foreign awards. *Leisure interest:* sailing. *Address:* Lima, Peru.

MONTAGNIER, Luc, L. ÈS SC., D.MED.; French research scientist; b. 18 Aug. 1932, Chabris; s. of Antoine Montagnier and Marianne Rousselet; m. Dorothea Ackermann 1961; one s. two d.; ed. Univs. of Poitiers and Paris; Asst. in Faculty of Science, Paris 1955–60, Attaché 1960, Head 1963, Head of Research 1967; Dir. of Research C.N.R.S. 1974–; Head of Lab. Inst. of Radium 1965–71; Head of Viral Oncology Unit, Pasteur Inst. 1972–, Prof. Pasteur Inst. 1985–; Pres. World Foundation for AIDS Research and Prevention 1993; Vice-Pres. Scientific Council AIDS Research Agency 1989–; mem. Acad. Nat. de Médecine 1989, Acad. des Sciences 1996; Commdr., Légion d'honneur, Commdr. Ordre nat. du Mérite; Lauréat du C.N.R.S. 1964, 1973, Prix Rosen de Cancérologie 1971, Prix Galien 1985, Prix de la Fondation Louis-Jeantet 1986, Prix Lasker 1986, Prix Gairdner 1987, Japan Prize 1988, King Faisal Prize 1993, Warren Alpert Foundation Prize 1998 and many other prizes. *Publications:* Vaincre le SIDA 1986, SIDA: les faits, l'espoir 1987, SIDA et infection par VIH (jtly.) 1989, Des virus et des hommes 1994, Oxidative Stress in Cancer, AIDS and Neurodegenerative Diseases (jt. ed.) 1997, New Concepts in Aids Pathogenesis (jtly.), numerous scientific papers. *Leisure interests:* piano playing, swimming. *Address:* Institut Pasteur, 28 rue du Docteur-Roux, 75015 Paris, France (Office).

MONTAGUE, Diana, A.R.C.M.; British mezzo-soprano opera and concert singer; b. 8 April 1953, Winchester; d. of Mr and Mrs N. H. Montague; m. Philip Doghan 1978; one s.; ed. Testwood School, Totton, Hants., Winchester School of Art and Royal Manchester Coll. of Music; professional début at Glyndebourne 1977; principal mezzo-soprano, Royal Opera House, Covent Garden 1978; freelance artist 1984–; has toured throughout Europe and U.S.A. appearing at Metropolitan Opera and Bayreuth, Aix-en-Provence, Salzburg and Glyndebourne festivals etc. *Leisure interests:* horse riding, country life in general.

MONTANA, Claude; French fashion designer; began career designing jewellery in London, then worked for leather and knitwear firms; first ready-to-wear show 1976; f. Claude Montana Co. 1979; Designer in charge of haute couture, House of Lanvin 1989–.

MONTANA, Joseph C., Jr., B.B.A.; American football player (retd.); b. 11 June 1956, New Eagle, Pa.; s. of Joseph C. Montana, Sr. and Theresa Montana; m. 1st Kim Monses 1975 (divorced); m. 2nd Cass Castillo (divorced 1983); m. 3rd Jennifer Wallace 1984; two d.; ed. Univ. of Notre Dame; quarterback, San Francisco 49ers 1979–93, Kansas City Chiefs 1993–95, commentator NBC TV 1995–; partner Target-Chip Ganassi Racing Team 1995–; mem. Super Bowl Championship Team 1982, 1985, 1989; played in Pro Bowl 1982–85. *Publication:* Cool Under Fire (with Alan Steinberg) 1989. *Address:* c/o IMG, 1 Erieview Plaza, Suite 1300, Cleveland, OH 44114, U.S.A.

MONTANELLI, Indro; Italian journalist and writer; b. 22 April 1909, Fucecchio; s. of Sestilio Montanelli and Maddalena Doddoli; m. Colette Rosselli; ed. Univs. of Florence, Grenoble and Paris (Sorbonne); reporter Paris Soir, United Press Agency; forced into exile because of his reporting on Spanish Civil War, returned to Italy 1939; Special Corresp. Corriere della Sera 1939–73; War Corresp. in Finland, Norway, Spain, Albania and Greece; sentenced to death for an article on Mussolini, escaped after 10 months in prison 1944; Founder, Man. Ed. Il Giornale, Milan 1974–, then Man. Dir., fmr. Ed.-in-Chief –1994; Founder and Ed. La Voce 1994–; has won Bagutta and Marzotto Prizes. *Publications:* some 60 books, including Storia di Roma 1957, Storia dei Greci 1958, Incontri 1961, Garibaldi 1962, Gente qualunque 1963, Dante e il suo secolo 1964, Italia dei secoli bui 1965; *Plays:* I sogni muoino all'alba (also film), Il Generale della Rovere (also film), Kibbutz.

MONTAÑO, Jorge, PH.D.; Mexican diplomatist; b. 16 Aug. 1945, Mexico City; s. of Jorge Montaño and Lucia Montaño; m. Luz Maria Valdes; one s. one d.; ed. Nat. Autonomous Univ. of Mexico, London School of Econs., U.K.; posts with Nat. Inst. of Fine Arts, Ministry of Public Educ., Nat. Autonomous Univ. of Mexico; Dir.-Gen., Office for UN Specialized Agencies, then Dir.-in-Chief for Multilateral Affairs, Ministry of Foreign Affairs 1979–82; fmr. Int. Affairs Adviser to Pres. Salinas de Gortari; fmr. univ. lecturer, Mexico and U.K.; Perm. Rep. to UN 1989–93; Amb. to U.S.A. 1993–95. *Publication:* The United Nations and the World Order 1945–1992 1992. *Address:* Chimalistac No. 6, Colonia San Angel, 01070 México, D.F., Mexico. *Telephone:* (5) 661-9765.

MONTAZERI, Ayatollah Hussein Ali; Iranian religious leader; b. *c.* 1923, Najafabad, Isfahan; ed. Isfahan Theological School; teacher of science and philosophy, Theological School, Qom; arrested after riots over Shah's land reform 1963; visited Ayatollah Khomeini in Iraq 1964; arrested several times and exiled to rural parts of Iran 1964–74; imprisoned 1974–78; Leading Ayatollah of Teheran 1979–80; returned to Qom Feb. 1980; named Grand

Ayatollah 1984; resgnd. as successor to Ayatollah Khomeini March 1989; reported under house arrest. *Address:* Madresseh Faizieh, Qom, Iran.

MONTEFIORE, Rt. Rev. Hugh William, M.A., B.D.; British ecclesiastic; b. 12 May 1920, London; s. of Charles Edward Sebag-Montefiore O.B.E. and Muriel Alice Ruth de Pass; m. Elisabeth Mary Macdonald Paton 1945; three d.; ed. Rugby School, St. John's Coll., Oxford and Westcott House, Cambridge; Chaplain and Tutor, Westcott House 1951–53, Vice-Prin. 1953–54; Fellow and Dean, Gonville and Caius Coll., Cambridge 1954–63; Vicar of Great St. Mary's, Cambridge 1963–70; Bishop of Kingston-upon-Thames 1970–78; Bishop of Birmingham 1978–87; Hon. Asst. Bishop, Diocese of Southwark 1987–; Chair. Transport 2000 1987–92, Friends of the Earth Trust 1992–, Nat. Trust for the Homeless 1992–; Hon. D.D. (Aberdeen) 1976, Birmingham 1985. *Publications include:* Commentary on the Epistle to the Hebrews 1964, The Question Mark 1969, The Probability of God 1985, So Near and Yet So Far 1986, Communicating the Gospel in a Scientific Age 1988, God, Sex and Love 1989, Christianity and Politics 1990, Reclaiming the High Ground (Ed.) 1990, The Gospel and Contemporary Culture 1992, The Womb and the Tomb 1992, Preaching for Our Planet 1992, Credible Christianity 1994, Oh God, What Next? 1995, Reaffirming the Church of England 1995, Time to Change 1997, On Being a Jewish Christian 1998. *Address:* White Lodge, 23 Bellevue Road, Wandsworth Common, London, SW17 7EB, England. *Telephone:* 0181-672 6697. *Fax:* 0181-672 6697.

MONTEGRIFFO, Peter Cecil Patrick, LL.B.; British barrister; b. 28 Feb. 1960, Gibraltar; s. of Dr. Cecil Montegriffo and Lily Zammitt; m. Josephine Perera 1985; two s.; ed. Bayside Comprehensive School, Univ. of Leeds and Lincoln's Inn/Council of Legal Educ.; called to the Bar 1982; practitioner in law firm J. H. Hassan & Partner 1987–88, partner 1988–; Exec.mem. Gibraltar Labour Party/Asscn. for Advancement of Civil Rights (GLP/AACR) 1982–88, Deputy Leader 1988–89, Leader Gibraltar Social Democrats (GSD) 1989–91. *Publications:* numerous articles on Gibraltar as a finance centre. *Leisure interests:* literature (especially political science), economics, music. *Address:* J. A. Hassan & Partners, 57 Line Wall Road, Gibraltar (Office); 10 Gardiner's Road, Gibraltar (Home). *Telephone:* 79000 (Office); 79912 (Home).

MONTGOMERIE, Colin Stuart; British golfer; b. 23 June 1963, Glasgow, Scotland; m. Eimear Wilson 1990; one d.; ed. Baptist Univ., Texas, U.S.A.; won Scottish Stroke Play Championship 1985, Scottish Amateur Championship 1987; turned professional 1987; won Portuguese Open 1989, Scandinavian Masters 1991, Heineken Dutch Open, Volvo Masters 1993, Peugeot Open de España, Murphy's English Open, Volvo German Open 1995, Volvo German Open, Trophée Lancôme 1995; finished 2nd Dubai Desert Classic, Murphy's English Open, Volvo Scandinavian Masters, Volvo Masters 1995; mem. winning European Ryder Cup team 1995. *Leisure interests:* music, cars, DIY, films. *Address:* c/o IMG, Pier House, Strand-on-the-Green, London, W4 3NN; Oxshott, Surrey, England.

MONTGOMERY, David; American photographer; b. 8 Feb. 1937, Brooklyn, New York; m. 2nd Martine King 1983; one s. three d.; ed. Midwood High School; toured U.S.A. as musician; freelance photographer/dir. 1960–; regular contrib. to Sunday Times Colour Magazine, Vogue, Tatler, Rolling Stone, Esquire, Fortune, New York Sunday Times, House and Garden magazines; has photographed H.M. Queen Elizabeth II, H.M. Queen Elizabeth the Queen Mother, T.R.H. Duke and Duchess of York, Rt. Hon. Margaret Thatcher, Rt. Hon. Pierre Trudeau, Mick Jagger, Clint Eastwood, Lord Mountbatten, Lord Hume, H.M. King Hussein, H.R.H. Queen Noor, Rt. Hon. Edward Heath, Rt. Hon. James Callaghan, Baron Thyssen-Bornemisza, Prince and Princess Thurn und Taxis, H.E. Cardinal Basil Hume; numerous awards for photography. *Leisure interests:* flowers and fish keeping, photography, day-dreaming. *Address:* Studio B, 11 Edith Grove, London, S.W.10, England. *Telephone:* 0171-352 6667/8.

MONTGOMERY, David John, B.A.; British newspaper executive; b. 6 Nov. 1948, Bangor, Northern Ireland; s. of William John Montgomery and Margaret Jean Montgomery; m. 1st Susan Frances Buchanan Russell 1971 (divorced 1987); m. 2nd Heidi Kingstone 1989 (divorced 1997); m. 3rd Sophie, Countess of Woolton 1997; ed. Queen's Univ., Belfast; Sub-Ed., Daily Mirror London, Manchester 1973–78, Asst. Chief Sub-Ed. 1978–80; Chief Sub-Ed. The Sun 1980; Asst. Ed. Sunday People 1982; Asst. Ed. News of the World 1984, Ed. 1985–87; Ed. Today 1987–91 (Newspaper of the Year 1988); Man. Dir. News UK 1987–91; Chief Exec. London Live TV 1991–92, Dir. 1991–; Chief Exec. Mirror Group 1992–99; Dir. Satellite Television PLC 1986–91, News Group Newspapers 1986–91, Donohue Inc. 1992–95, Newspaper Publishing 1994–98, Scottish Media Group 1995, Press Asscn. 1996–. *Leisure interests:* swimming, music. *Address:* c/o Mirror Group PLC, One Canada Square, London, E14 5AP; 13 Warrington Crescent, London, W9 1ED, England.

MONTI, Innocenzo; Italian banker; b. 3 Dec. 1909, Salerno; s. of Edoardo Monti and Maria Piera del Bo; m. Lalla Romano 1932; one s.; ed. Turin Univ.; joined Banca Commerciale Italiana, Cuneo Branch 1927; took part in preparations for post-war reconstitution of Bank's admin. 1944; joined Italian Banking Asscn. as mem. Tech. Comm. for Banking Admin. 1951; Adviser to Chair. of Banco de Credito del Perú, Lima 1953; Chief Accountant-Gen. Banca Commerciale Italiana 1966; invited by Bank of Italy to take part in Interbank Convention on Automation Problems (CIPA) 1968; supervised admin. aspects of establishment of branches in New York, London, Singapore, Tokyo, Los Angeles, Chicago, São Paulo 1968–74; Chair. Banca Commerciale Italiana 1976–81, S.I.A. (Interbanking Agency for Automation) 1977–; Chair. Mediobanca, Milan 1978–79, Dir. 1979–; Dir. Banca Commerciale Italiana 1981–; Dir. Associazione Amici di Brera e dei Musei milanesi 1980–, Fondazione G. Feltrinelli, Milan 1982–; Cavaliere di Gran Croce, Ordine al Merito della Repubblica Italiana. *Publications:* L'impiego degli elaborati elettronici nel lavoro bancario 1970, La banca di credito ordinario con filiali operanti in tutto il territorio nazionale 1970, Intervento finale al Convegno IRI "Inflation accounting" 1977. *Leisure interests:* literature, history, music, mountaineering. *Address:* Via Brera 17, 20121 Milan, Italy.

MONTWILL, Alexander, PH.D., D.SC., M.R.I.A., F.INST. P.; Irish professor of physics; b. 28 Oct. 1935, Riga, Latvia; s. of Stanislaw Montwill and Jadwiga Huszcza; m. Ann O'Doherty 1966; one s. four d.; ed. Belvedere Coll., Westland Row Christian Brothers' School, Dublin and Univ. Coll. Dublin; lecturer, Univ. Coll. Dublin 1959–81, Assoc. Prof. 1981–85, Prof. of Experimental Physics 1985, Head Dept. of Physics 1986–95; Visiting Assoc. Prof. City Coll. of New York 1966–68; Visiting Scientist, CERN, Geneva 1965–. *Publications:* 43 publs. on high energy physics. *Leisure interest:* bridge. *Address:* Department of Physics, University College, Belfield, Dublin 4, Republic of Ireland. *Telephone:* (01) 7062210. *Fax:* (01) 2837275.

MONTY, Jean C., M.A., M.B.A.; Canadian business executive; b. 26 June 1947, Montreal; m. Jocelyne Monty; two s.; ed. Coll. Sainte-Marie, Montreal and Univs. of W. Ontario and Chicago; Merrill Lynch, New York, Toronto and Montreal 1970–74; Bell Canada, Montreal 1974; Pres. Télébec Ltée. 1976; Nat. Defence Coll. Kingston, Ont. 1979–80; Bell Canada 1980–92, Pres. 1989, Pres. and C.E.O. 1991–92; Pres. and C.O.O. Northern Telecom Ltd. 1992, Pres. and C.E.O. 1993–98; C.E.O. BCE Inc. 1998–; Dir. Bank of Montreal, Bell-Northern Research Ltd.; mem. Supervisory Bd. Lagardère Group, Paris. *Leisure interest:* golf. *Address:* BCE Incorporated, 1000 Rue de la Gauchetiere, Quebec, H3B 4Y7, Canada. *Telephone:* (514) 397-7244.

MONYAKE, Lengolo Bureng, M.SC., U.E.D.; Lesotho public servant; b. 1 April 1930, Lesotho; s. of Bureng L. Monyake and Leomile Monyake; m. Molulela Mapetla 1957; two s. one d.; ed. Fort Hare Univ. Coll., Univ. of Toronto, Carleton Univ., London School of Economics; headmaster, Jordan High School 1958–61; Dir. of Statistics, Govt. of Lesotho 1968–74, Perm. Sec. 1974–76, Deputy Sr. Perm. Sec. 1976–78; Amb. 1979–83; Man. Dir. Lesotho Nat. Devt. Corpn. 1984–86; Minister for Foreign Affairs 1986–88, for Works 1988; Alt. Exec. Dir. IMF 1988–90, Exec. Dir. 1990–92; Deputy Exec. Sec. Southern African Devt. Community 1993–. *Leisure interests:* tennis, table tennis, music, photography. *Address:* Southern African Development Community, Private Bag 0095, Gaborone, Botswana. *Telephone:* 314016. *Fax:* 372848.

MONZEN, Mitsugi; Japanese business executive; b. 29 May 1918, Kogoshima; three s.; ed. Tokyo Azabu Veterinary Surgeon Speciality Coll.; Dir. Morinaga Milk Industry Co. Ltd. 1968, Man. Dir. 1976, Pres. 1979, Chair. 1985–89; Sr. mem. Bd. 1989–91, Sr. Adviser 1991–; Official Commendation from Japan Milk Products Asscn. 1978. *Leisure interest:* reading. *Address:* 2-13-18 Tsukushino, Machida-si, Tokyo 105, Japan. *Telephone:* (0427) 95-5559.

MOODY, George Franklin; American banker; b. 28 July 1930, Riverside, Calif.; s. of William Clifford and Mildred E. (née Scott) Moody; m. Mary Jane Plank 1950; three s. one d.; ed. Riverside City Coll. and Pacific Coast Banking School; Business Officer, Univ. of Calif., Riverside 1950–52; joined Security Pacific Nat. Bank 1953, Vice-Pres. and Personnel Dir., Los Angeles 1970–71, Sr. Vice-Pres. (Inland Div. Admin.) 1971–73, Exec. Vice-Pres. 1973–78, Vice-Chair. 1978–81, Pres. and C.O.O. 1981–87, Chair. Exec. Cttee. (Security Pacific Corpn.) 1985; Dir. Music Center Operating Co.; Los Angeles Chamber of Commerce (Chair. of Bd. and Dir.).

MOODY-STUART, Mark, M.A., PH.D.; British oil company executive; b. 15 Sept. 1940, Antigua, West Indies; s. of Sir Alexander Moody-Stuart and Judith (née Henzell); m. Judith McLeavy 1964; three s. one d.; ed. Shrewsbury School and St. John's Coll. Cambridge; Shell Internationale Petroleum Mij. 1966–67; Koninklijke Shell E & P Lab. 1967–68; worked with Shell cos. in Spain, Oman, Brunei 1968–72, Chief Geologist, Australia 1972–76, Shell U.K. 1977–78; Brunei Shell Services Man. 1978–79; Man. Western Div. Shell Nigeria 1979–82; Gen. Man. Shell 1978–79; Man. Western Div. Shell Nigeria 1979–82; Gen. Man. Shell Turkey 1982–86; Chair. and C.E.O. Shell Malaysia 1986–89; Exploration and Production Co-ordinator, Royal Dutch/Shell 1990; Dir. Shell Transport & Trading 1990–, Chair. July 1997–; Man. Dir. Royal Dutch/Shell Group 1991–, Chair. Cttee of Man. Dirs. 1998–. *Publications:* papers in scientific journals. *Leisure interest:* sailing. *Address:* Shell International Petroleum Co. Ltd., Shell Centre, London, SE1 7NA, England. *Telephone:* 0171-934 4212.

MOONEY, Harold Alfred, M.A., PH.D.; American professor of biology; b. 1 June 1932, Santa Rosa, Calif.; s. of Harold Walter Stefany and Sylvia A. Hart; m. Sherry L. Gulmon 1974; three d.; ed. Univ. of Calif., Santa Barbara and Duke Univ.; Instructor to Assoc. Prof. Univ. of Calif., L.A. 1960–68; Assoc. Prof. Stanford Univ. 1968–73, Prof. 1975–, Paul S. Achilles Prof. of Environmental Biology 1976–; Guggenheim Fellow 1974; mem. N.A.S., American Acad. of Arts and Sciences, American Philosophical Soc.; Mercer Award (Ecology Soc. of America) 1961, Humboldt Award 1988. *Publications:* 9 books. *Address:* Department of Biological Sciences, 459 Herrin Lab., Stanford University, Stanford, CA 94305 (Office); 2625 Ramona Street, Palo Alto, CA 94306, U.S.A. (Home).

MOONS, Charles M. J. A., D.IUR.; Netherlands jurist; b. 30 May 1917, Gemert; s. of A. J. W. M. Moons and A. M. van der Heyden; m. H. S. de Vriese 1949; three s. two d.; ed. Univ. of Nijmegen; Substitute Public Prosecutor 1940–56, Public Prosecutor 1956–58; Advocate-Gen. Court of Appeal 1958–61; Advocate-Gen. Hoge Raad der Nederlanden (Supreme Court) 1961–66, Judge 1966–76, Vice-Pres. 1976–81, Pres. 1981–87; Judge, Benelux Court 1976–79, Vice-Pres. 1979–83, Pres. 1983; mem. Council of Govs., Leiden Univ. 1968–72; mem. Council of Govs., Royal Mil. Acad. 1970–; Appointing Authority Iran-U.S. Claims Tribunal 1983; Commandeur Orde van de Nederlandsche Leeuw, Orde van Oranje-Nassau; Groot Officier Kroonorde van Belgie; Grand Officier, Ordre Grand-Ducal de la Couronne de Chêne. *Publications:* Conclusions Advocate-General Nederlandse Jurispendentie, 1961–67, De Hoge Raad der Nederlanden, een Portret de Strafkamer 1988. *Leisure interest:* computer science. *Address:* Wassenaarseweg 81, 2596 CM, 's-Gravenhage, Netherlands. *Telephone:* 070-3243571.

MOORBATH, Stephen Erwin, D.PHIL., D.SC., F.R.S.; British earth scientist; b. 9 May 1929, Magdeburg, Germany; s. of Heinz and Else Moosbach; m. Pauline Tessier-Varlêt 1962; one s. one d.; ed. Lincoln Coll., Oxford; Asst. Experimental Officer, Atomic Energy Research Est., Harwell 1948–51; Scientific Officer, A.E.R.E. 1954–56; Research Fellow, Univ. of Oxford 1956–61, Sr. Research Officer, 1962–78, Reader in Geology 1978–92, Prof. of Isotope Geology 1992–96, Emer. Prof. 1996–, Professorial Fellow Linacre Coll. 1990–96, Emer. Fellow 1996; Research Fellow, M.I.T. 1961–62; several awards. *Publications:* numerous contributions to books and scientific journals. *Leisure interests:* music, philately, travel, linguistics. *Address:* Department of Earth Sciences, Oxford University, Parks Road, Oxford, OX1 3PR (Office); 53 Bagley Wood Road, Kennington, Oxford, OX1 5LY, England (Home). *Telephone:* (01865) 274584 (Office); (01865) 739507 (Home).

MOORCOCK, Michael John; British novelist; b. 18 Dec. 1939, London; s. of Arthur Moorcock and June Moorcock; m. 1st Hilary Bailey 1963, 2nd Jill Richies 1978, 3rd Linda M. Steele 1982; one s. two d.; ed. Michael Hall School, Sussex; worked as musician and journalist; Ed. Outlaws Own 1951–53, Tarzan Adventures 1957–59, Sexton Blake Library 1959–61, Current Topics 1961–62; Consulting Ed. New Worlds 1963–; Nebola Award (for Behold the Man) 1967, August Derleith Prize, Guardian Fiction Prize (for Condition of Muzak) 1977, World Fantasy Award (for Gloriana) 1979. *Publications include:* The Eternal Champion sequence 1963–98, Behold the Man 1968, Condition of Muzak 1976, Gloriana 1977, Byzantium Enclaves 1981, The Laughter of Carthage 1984, Mother London 1988, Jerusalem Commands 1992. *Leisure interests:* climbing, travelling, walking, cats, birds. *Address:* c/o Peters, Fraser, Dunlop, 503/4 The Chambers, Chelsea Harbour, London, SW10 0XF, England; P.O. Box 1230, Bastrop, TX 78602, U.S.A. *Telephone:* 0171-344 1000 (London); (512) 321-5000 (U.S.A.). *Fax:* 0171-352 7356 (London); (512) 321-5000 (U.S.A.).

MOORE, Carole Irene, M.S.; Canadian librarian; b. 15 Aug. 1944, Berkeley, Calif., U.S.A.; ed. Stanford and Columbia Univs.; Reference Librarian Columbia Univ. Libraries 1967–68, Univ. of Toronto Library 1968–73; Asst. Head Reference Dept., Univ. of Toronto Library 1973–74, Head 1974–80; Head Bibliographic Processing Dept., Univ. of Toronto Library 1980–86, Assoc. Librarian, Tech. Services 1986–87, Chief Librarian June 1986–; Research Libraries Group Dir. 1994–96; Bd. Dirs. Univ. of Toronto Press 1994–; Columbia Univ. School of Library Service Centenary Distinguished Alumni Award 1987. *Publications:* Labour Relations and the Librarian (ed.) 1974, Canadian Essays and Collections Index 1972–73 1976. *Leisure interest:* gardening. *Address:* Robarts Library, 130 St. George Street, Toronto, Ont. M5S 1A5 (Office); 5 Albemarle Avenue, Toronto, Ont. M4K 1H6, Canada.

MOORE, Charles Hilary, B.A.; British journalist; b. 31 Oct. 1956, Hastings; s. of Richard Moore and Ann Moore; m. Caroline Baxter 1981; twin s. and d.; ed. Eton Coll. and Trinity Coll. Cambridge; editorial staff, Daily Telegraph 1979–81, leader writer 1981–83; Asst. Ed. and political columnist, The Spectator 1983–84, Ed. 1984–90, fortnightly columnist ('Another Voice') 1990–; weekly columnist, The Daily Express 1987–90; Deputy Ed. The Daily Telegraph 1990–92; Ed. The Sunday Telegraph 1992–95, The Daily Telegraph 1995–; Trustee T.E. Utley Memorial Fund. *Publications:* 1936 (ed. with C. Hawtree) 1986, The Church in Crisis (with A. N. Wilson and G. Stamp) 1986, A Tory Seer: the selected journalism of T. E. Utley (ed. with S. Heffer) 1986. *Address:* Daily Telegraph, 1 Canada Square, Canary Wharf, London, E14 5DT, England. *Telephone:* 0171-538 6300.

MOORE, Demi; American actress; b. Roswell, New Mexico; m. Bruce Willis (q.v.); three d.; began acting with small part in TV series; worked as a model, Los Angeles. *Films:* Blame it on Rio, No Small Affair, St. Elmo's Fire, One Crazy Summer, About Last Night . . ., Wisdom, The Seventh Sign, Ghost, Mortal Thoughts (also Co-Producer), The Butcher's Wife, A Few Good Men, Indecent Proposal, Disclosure, The Scarlet Letter, Striptease 1995, The Juror 1996, G.I. Jane 1996, The Hunchback of Notre Dame, Now and Then (also co-producer), Deconstructing Harry 1997. *Television:* General Hospital (series), Bedroom. *Theatre:* The Early Girl (Theatre World award). *Address:* Creative Artists Agency Inc., 9830 Wilshire Boulevard, Beverly Hills, CA 90212, U.S.A.

MOORE, Dudley Stuart John, B.A., B.MUS.; British actor, composer and musician; b. 19 April 1935; s. of the late John Moore and of Ada Francis Huges; m. 1st Suzy Kendall 1958 (dissolved); m. 2nd Tuesday Weld 1975 (dissolved); one s.; m. 3rd Brogan Lane 1988; m. 4th Nicole Rothschild 1994 (divorced 1999); one s.; ed. County High School, Dagenham, Essex, and Magdalen Coll., Oxford. *Stage work:* composed incidental music for Royal Court Theatre productions; with Vic Lewis and John Dankworth jazz bands 1959–60; Beyond the Fringe, London 1960–62, Broadway, New York 1962–64; Play It Again Sam (Globe Theatre) 1970; Behind the Fridge (Cambridge Theatre) 1972–73; Good Evening, Broadway 1973–74; tour of U.S.A. 1975; Royal Command Performance; tours with own jazz piano trio. *TV work:* Not only . . . but also (series with Peter Cook) 1965, 1966, 1970; Goodbye again (ITV); It's Lulu, not to mention Dudley Moore 1972; guest appearances with jazz trio. *Films:* The Wrong Box 1966, Thirty is a Dangerous Age Cynthia 1967, Bedazzled 1968, Monte Carlo or Bust 1969, The Bed-sitting Room 1969, Alice's Adventures in Wonderland 1972, The Hound of the Baskervilles, Foul Play, 10, Wholly Moses, Arthur (Golden Globe Award 1983), Six Weeks, Lovesick, Romantic Comedy, Unfaithfully Yours, Micki and Maude (Golden Globe Award 1985), Best Defense, Santa Claus, Like Father, Like Son, Arthur 2: On the Rocks, Crazy People, Blame it on the Bellboy, The Pickle, A Weekend in the Country; composed music for Bedazzled, Thirty is a Dangerous Age Cynthia, The Staircase, Six Weeks and various TV films. *Albums:* Beyond the Fringe and all that Jazz, The Other Side of Dudley Moore, Today, Dudley Moore Trio-Down Under, Dudley Moore and Cleo Laine—Smilin Through, The Music of Dudley Moore, Songs without Words. *Publications:* Dud and Pete: the Dagenham Dialogues 1971, Dudley Moore—Offbeat 1986, The Complete Beyond the Fringe 1987, Voices of Survival 1988. *Leisure interests:* films, theatre, music. *Address:* c/o Louis Pitt, ICM, 8942 Wilshire Boulevard, Beverly Hills, CA 90211, U.S.A.

MOORE, Francis Daniels, M.D.; American surgeon; b. 17 Aug. 1913, Evanston, Ill.; s. of Philip Wyatt and Caroline (Daniels) Moore; m. 1st Laura Benton Bartlett 1935 (died 1988); two s. three d.; m. 2nd Katharyn Watson Saltonstall 1990; ed. Harvard Coll. and Medical School; Intern and Resident, Mass. Gen. Hosp. 1939–43; Research Fellow, Nat. Research Council 1940–41; Tutor and Asst. Prof. in Surgery, Harvard Medical School 1944–48, Moseley Prof. of Surgery 1948–76, Elliott Carr Cutler Prof. of Surgery 1976–80; Surgeon-in-Chief, Peter Bent Brigham Hosp. 1948–76, Surgeon 1976–80, Surgeon-in-Chief Emer. 1980–; Sr. Consultant in Surgery, Sidney Farber Cancer Center 1976–; Moseley Prof. of Surgery (Emer.), Harvard Medical School 1980–; Pres. Mass. Health Data Consortium Inc. 1981–87; Consultant to Surgeon-Gen. of Army 1981–85; Consultant, NASA 1966–69, 1986–92, mem. Advisory Cttee. (special ref. to radiobiological hazards of prolonged exomagnetospheric voyages); Chair. Ed. Bd. Journal of Clinical Surgery 1981–82; Ed. Staff New England Journal of Medicine 1981–91; mem. N.A.S. 1981; mem. Inst. of Medicine 1993; Hon. M.Ch. (Nat. Univ., Ireland) 1961, Hon. LL.D. (Glasgow) 1965, Hon. S.D. (Suffolk) 1966, Hon. M.D. (Edinburgh) 1975, (Paris) 1976, (Copenhagen) 1979, Hon. D.Sc. (Harvard) 1982; Silver Medal Award of Int. Soc. of Surgery 1959, Harvey Allen Award of American Burns Asscn. 1970, Gold Headed Cane of Univ. of Calif. 1970, Bigelow Medal of Boston Surgical Soc. 1974, Samuel D. Gross Medal of American Surgical Asscn. 1978, Lister Medal of Royal Coll. of Surgeons of England 1978. *Publications:* Metabolic Response to Surgery 1952, Metabolic Care of the Surgical Patient 1959, Give and Take, the Development of Tissue Transplantation 1964, Surgical Manpower in the United States 1975, A Miracle and a Privilege 1995. *Leisure interests:* sailing, music. *Address:* 10 Shattuck Street, Boston, MA 02115, U.S.A. (Office). *Telephone:* (617) 734-0420 (Office). *Fax:* (617) 264-5293.

MOORE, (Georgina) Mary, M.A.; British administrator and writer; b. 8 April 1930, Oxford; d. of late Prof. V. H. Galbraith and Georgina R. Cole-Baker; m. Antony R. Moore 1963; one s.; ed. The Mount School, York and Lady Margaret Hall, Oxford; joined H.M. Foreign (later Diplomatic) Service 1951; served Budapest 1954, U.K. Perm. Del. at UN, New York 1956; First Sec. 1961; resgnd. on marriage 1963; Prin. St. Hilda's Coll., Oxford 1980–90, Hon. Fellow 1990; Trustee, British Museum 1982–92, Rhodes Trust 1984–96, Pilgrim Trust 1991– (Chair. 1993–); mem. Council for Industry and Higher Educ. 1986–90. *Publications:* (all under pseudonym Helena Osborne) novels: The Arcadian Affair 1969, Pay Day 1972, White Poppy 1977, The Joker 1979; plays for radio and TV. *Address:* Touchbridge, Boarstall, Aylesbury, Bucks., HP18 9UJ, England. *Telephone:* (01844) 238247.

MOORE, John A(lexander), PH.D.; American biologist; b. 27 June 1915, Charles Town, W. Va.; s. of George Douglas and Louise Hammond Blume Moore; m. Anna Betty Clark 1938; one d.; ed. Columbia Coll. and Columbia Univ.; Asst. Zoology Dept., Columbia Univ. 1936–39, Chair. 1949–52, Prof. 1954–68; Prof. Biology Dept. Univ. of Calif. (Riverside) 1969–82, Emer. Prof. 1982–; Tutor of Biology, Brooklyn Coll. 1939–41; Instructor at Queens Coll. 1941–48; Asst. Prof. Zoology Barnard Coll. 1943–47, Assoc. Prof. 1947–50, Prof. 1950–68, Chair. Zoology Dept. 1948–52, 1953–54, 1960–66; Walker Ames Prof. Univ. of Washington 1966; Fulbright Research Scholar, Australia 1952–53; mem. Nat. Research Council Comm. on Human Resources 1979–82; Biological Sciences Curriculum Study 1959–76, Comm. on Science Educ. 1967–73 (Chair. 1971–73), A.A.A.S. Project 2061 1985–89, Nat. Research Council: Co-ordinating Council for Educ. 1991–95, Cttee. on Under-graduate Science Educ. 1992–, Nat. Science Resource Center 1994–, Cttee. K-12 Science Educ. 1996–, Marine Biology Lab., A.A.A.S.; Guggenheim Fellowship Award 1959; mem. Genetics Soc. of America, American Soc. of Zoologists (Pres. 1974), American Soc. of Naturalists (Pres. 1972), Soc. for Study Evolution (Pres. 1963), American Acad. Arts and Sciences, N.A.S. *Publications:* Principles of Zoology 1957, Heredity and Development 1963, 1972, A

Guide Book to Washington 1963, Biological Science: An Inquiry into Life 1963, 1968, 1973 (Supervisor), Physiology of the Amphibia (Ed.) 1964, Ideas in Modern Biology (Ed.) 1965, Interaction of Man and the Biosphere (Co-author) 1970, 1975, 1979, Ideas in Evolution and Behavior (Ed.) 1970, Science for Society: A Bibliography 1970, 1971, Readings in Heredity and Development 1972, Dobzhansky's Genetics of Natural Populations (Ed.) 1981, Science as a Way of Knowing—Evolutionary Biology 1984, Science as a Way of Knowing—Human Ecology 1985, Science as a Way of Knowing—Genetics 1986, Science as a Way of Knowing—Developmental Biology 1987, Science as a Way of Knowing—Form and Function 1988, Genes, Cells, and Organisms (12 vols., Ed.) 1988, Science: A Way of Knowing—A Conceptual Framework for Biology (Part I) 1989, (Part II) 1990, (Part III) 1991, Science as a Way of Knowing: The Foundations of Modern Biology 1993. *Leisure interests:* photography, history of American science, history of illumination. *Address:* Department of Biology, University of California, Riverside, CA 92521-0427; 11522 Tulane Avenue, Riverside, CA 92507-6649, U.S.A. (Home). *Telephone:* (909) 787-3142 (Office); (909) 684-0412 (Home). *Fax:* (909) 789-4286.

MOORE, John Colinton, B.COM., A.A.S.A.; Australian politician; b. 16 Nov. 1936; s. of T. R. Moore and D. S. Moore; m. 2nd Jacquelyn Moore; two s.; one d. from previous m.; ed. Armidale School, Queensland, Queensland Univ.; stockbroker 1960; mem. Brisbane Stock Exchange 1962–74; Vice-Pres. and Treas. Queensland Liberal Party 1967–73, Pres. 1973–76, 1984–90; M.P. for Ryan, Queensland 1975–; Minister for Business and Consumer Affairs 1980–82; Opposition Spokesman for Finance 1983–84, for Communications 1984–85, for Northern Devt. and Local Govt. 1985–87, for Transport and Aviation 1987, for Business and Consumer Affairs 1987–89, for Business Privatization and Consumer Affairs 1989–90; Shadow Minister for Privatization and Public Admin. 1994, for Privatization 1994–95, for Industry, Commerce and Public Admin. 1995–96; Minister for Industry, Science and Tourism 1996–97, of Industry, Science and Tech. 1997–98, for Defence 1998–; Vice-Pres. Exec. Council March 1996–; Dir. William Brandt & Sons (Australia), Phillips, First City, Brandt Ltd., Merrill Lynch, Pierce, Fennell and Smith (Australia) Ltd., Citinat, Agricultural Investments Australia Ltd; mem. various int. delegations, Council Order of Australia. *Leisure interests:* tennis, cricket, reading, golf. *Address:* Parliament House, Canberra, A.C.T. 2600, Australia.

MOORE, Capt. John Evelyn, R.N., F.R.G.S.; British editor, author and (retd.) naval officer; b. 1 Nov. 1921, Sant' Ilario, Italy; s. of William John Moore and Evelyn Elizabeth (née Hooper); m. 1st Joan Pardoe 1945; one s. two d.; m. 2nd Barbara Kerry; ed. Sherborne School, Dorset; entered R.N. 1939, specialised in hydrographic surveying, then submarines, commanded H.M. Submarines Totem, Alaric, Tradewind, Tactician, Telemachus; R.N. staff course 1950–51; Commdr. 1957; attached to Turkish Naval Staff 1958–60; subsequently Plans Div., Admiralty, 1st Submarine Squadron, then 7th Submarine Squadron in command; Capt. 1967; served as Chief of Staff, C.-in-C. Naval Home Command; Defence Intelligence Staff; retd. list at own request 1972; Ed. Jane's Fighting Ships 1972–87; Ed. Jane's Naval Review 1982–87; Hon. Prof. of Int. Relations, St. Andrew's Univ. 1990–92. *Publications:* Jane's Major Warships 1973, The Soviet Navy Today 1975, Submarine Development 1976 Soviet War Machine (jtly.) 1976, Encyclopaedia of World's Warships 1978, World War 3 1978, Seapower and Politics 1979, Warships of the Royal Navy 1979, Warships of the Soviet Navy 1981, Submarine Warfare: Today and Tomorrow (jtly.) 1986, Watchers on the Shore 1994; ed. The Impact of Polaris 1998. *Leisure interests:* gardening, swimming, archaeology. *Address:* 1 Ridgelands Close, Eastbourne, East Sussex, BN20 8EP, England. *Telephone:* (01323) 638836.

MOORE, Maj.-Gen. Sir (John) Jeremy, K.C.B., O.B.E., M.C.; British Royal Marines officer; b. 5 July 1928, Lichfield, Staffs.; s. of Lieut.-Col. C. P. Moore, M.C.; m. Veryan Acworth 1966; one s. two d.; ed. Cheltenham Coll.; with Royal Marines 1947–83; Staff Coll., Australia 1963–64; Chiefs of Staff Secr., London 1966–68; C.O. 42 Commando, Royal Marines 1972–73; Purveyor in Mil. Music to Royal Navy 1973–75; Royal Coll. of Defence Studies 1976; Commdr. 3rd Commando Brigade, Royal Marines 1977–79; Maj.-Gen. commanding commando forces, Royal Marines 1979–82; Commdr. of British Land Forces in Falklands conflict 1982, accepted Argentine surrender 14 June 1982, Col. Commdt. 1990–93; Specialist Adviser Commons Select Cttee. on Defence 1984–91; defence consultant; Dir.-Gen. Food Mfrs. Fed. 1984–85, Food and Drink Fed. 1984–85; Chair. Ranleigh Enterprises Ltd., Task (International) Ltd; Pres. Royal Marines Asscn. 1990–93; Hon. Col. Wiltshire Army Cadet Force 1991–93; Hon. Pres. British Biathlon team 1984–88; mem. Parish Council, Bratton, Wilts. 1987–91. *Leisure interests:* governor of two schools, music, sailing, hill walking.

MOORE, Julianne, B.A.; American actress; b. 1961; ed. Boston Univ. School for Arts; with the Guthrie Theatre 1988–89. *Stage appearances include:* Serious Money 1987, Ice Cream with Hot Fudge 1990, Uncle Vanya, The Road to Nirvana, Hamlet, The Father. *Film appearances include:* Tales from the Darkside 1990, The Hand That Rocks the Cradle 1992, The Gun in Betty Lou's Handbag 1992, Body of Evidence 1993, Benny & Joon 1993, The Fugitive 1993, Short Cuts 1993, Vanya on 42nd Street 1994, Roommates 1995, Safe 1995, Nine Months 1995, Assassins 1995, Surviving Picasso 1996, Jurassic Park: The Lost World 1997, The Myth of Fingerprints 1997, Hellcab 1997, Boogie Nights 1997, The Big Lebowski 1998. *Television appearances include:* As the World Turns (series), The Edge of Night (series), Money, Power Murder 1989, Lovecraft 1991, I'll Take Manhattan, The Last to Go, Cast a Deadly Spell. *Address:* c/o Creative Artists Agency, 9830 Wilshire Boulevard, Beverly Hills, CA 90212, U.S.A.

MOORE, Michael, C.B.E., M.B.A., M.A.; British business executive; b. 15 March 1936; m. Jan Moore; one s.; ed. Eton Coll., Magdalen Coll. Oxford and Harvard Business School; called to the Bar 1961; Chair. Tomkins PLC 1984–95, Quicks Group PLC 1993–, Linx Printing Technologies PLC 1993–, London Int. Group PLC 1994–; Jt. Deputy Chair., Clerical Medical & Gen. Life Assurance Soc. 1996–; Chair. Nat. Soc. for Prevention of Cruelty to Children (NSPCC) 1988–95; Chair. Which? 1997–; Trustee Public Concern at Work 1996–. *Leisure interests:* reading, music (especially opera), visiting ruins, tennis. *Address:* 35 New Bridge Street, London, EC4V 6BJ, England.

MOORE, Rt. Hon. Michael Kenneth, P.C., M.P.; New Zealand politician; b. 28 Jan. 1949, Whakatane; s. of late Alan Moore and Audrey Moore; m. Yvonne Dereaney; fmr. social worker, printer etc.; M.P. for Eden 1972–75, Papanui, Christchurch 1978–84, Christchurch North 1984–96, Waimakariri 1996–; Minister of Overseas Trade and Marketing, also Minister of Tourism and Publicity, and of Recreation and Sport 1984–87; Minister of Overseas Trade and Marketing, and of Publicity 1987–88, 1989–90, of External Relations and Int. Trade 1988–90; Minister of Foreign Affairs Jan.-Oct. 1990; Prime Minister Sept.–Oct. 1990; Leader of the Opposition 1990–93; fmr. Assoc. Minister of Finance; Labour. *Publications:* six books including A Pacific Parliament, Hard Labour, Fighting for New Zealand 1993, Children of the Poor 1996. *Address:* Parliament Buildings, Wellington, New Zealand.

MOORE, Patrick Caldwell-, C.B.E.; British astronomer and author; b. 4 March 1923, Pinner, Middx.; s. of late Capt. Caldwell-Moore, M.C. and Gertrude Lilian Moore (née White); ed. privately; Officer, Bomber Command, RAF 1940–45; BBC TV series, The Sky at Night 1957–, radio broadcasts; Ed. Year Book of Astronomy 1962–; Dir. Armagh Planetarium 1965–68; freelance 1968–; composed Perseus and Andromeda (opera) 1975, Theseus 1982; Pres. British Astronomical Asscn. 1982–84, now Vice-Pres.; Hon. D.Sc. (Lancaster) 1974, (Hatfield Polytechnic) 1989, (Birmingham) 1990, (Portsmouth) 1997; Dr. h.c. (Keele) 1994; Goodacre Medal (British Astronomical Asscn.) 1968; Jackson Gwilt Gold Medal (Royal Astronomical Soc.) 1977; Klumpke Medal (Astronomical Soc. of the Pacific) 1979; Minor Planet No. 2602 is named in his honour. *Publications:* numerous, including Guide to the Moon 1976, Atlas of the Universe 1980, History of Astronomy 1983, The Story of the Earth (with Peter Cattermole) 1985, Halley's Comet (with Heather Couper) 1985, Patrick Moore's Armchair Astronomy 1985, Stargazing 1985, Exploring the Night Sky with Binoculars 1986, The A–Z of Astronomy 1986, Astronomy for the Under Tens 1987, Astronomers' Stars 1987, The Planet Uranus (jtly.) 1988, Space Travel for the Under Tens 1988, The Planet Neptune 1989, Mission to the Planets 1990, The Universe for the Under Tens 1990, A Passion for Astronomy 1991, Fireside Astronomy 1992, Guinness Book of Astronomy (revised edn.) 1995, Passion for Astronomy 1995, Stars of the Southern Skies 1995, Teach Yourself Astronomy 1996, Eyes on the Universe 1997. *Leisure interests:* music, cricket, chess, tennis. *Address:* Farthings, 39 West Street, Selsey, Sussex, PO20 9AD, England. *Telephone:* (01243) 603668.

MOORE, Robin James, M.A., PH.D., D.LIT., F.A.H.A.; Australian professor of history; b. 29 April 1934, Melbourne; s. of late F. E. Moore; m. 2nd Rosemary Sweetapple 1976; ed. Univs. of Melbourne and London; Exec. Containers Ltd. 1955–60, Western Mining Corpn. 1960–62; Sir Arthur Sims Travelling Scholar 1962–64; lecturer in Modern Indian History S.O.A.S., London Univ. 1964–71; Prof. of History, Flinders Univ. of South Australia 1971–, mem. of Council 1986–89, Dean Faculty of Social Sciences 1988–97; Smuts Visiting Fellow in Commonwealth Studies, Cambridge Univ. 1974–75; Australian Vice-Chancellor's Cttee. Visiting Fellow, India 1979; Chapman Visiting Fellow Inst. of Commonwealth Studies, Univ. of London 1980–81; Gov. Adelaide Festival of Arts Inc. 1980–94; Pres. Australian Historical Asscn. 1985–86; mem. Bd. Wakefield Press 1985–86; Visiting Prof. Univ. of Tulsa, Okla. 1987. *Publications:* Sir Charles Wood's Indian Policy 1853–1866 1966, Liberalism and Indian Politics 1872–1922 1966, The Crisis of Indian Unity 1917–40 1974, Churchill, Cripps and India 1939–45 1979, Escape from Empire 1983, Making the New Commonwealth 1987, Endgames of Empire 1988, Paul Scott's Raj 1990. *Leisure interests:* music, theatre, reading, walking. *Address:* 2 Palm Street, Medindie, S.A. 5081, Australia.

MOORE, Roger, C.B.E.; British actor; b. 14 Oct. 1927, London; m. 1st Doorn van Steyn (divorced 1953); 2nd Dorothy Squires 1953 (divorced 1969); 3rd Luisa Mattioli; two s. one d.; ed. R.A.D.A.; Special Amb. for UNICEF 1991–. *Films include:* Crossplot 1969, The Man With the Golden Gun 1974, That Lucky Touch 1975, Save Us From Our Friends 1975, Shout At The Devil 1975, Sherlock Holmes in New York 1976, The Spy Who Loved Me 1976, The Wild Geese 1977, Escape To Athena 1978, Moonraker 1978, Esther, Ruth and Jennifer 1979, The Sea Wolves, 1980, Sunday Lovers 1980, For Your Eyes Only 1980, Octopussy 1983, The Naked Face 1983, A View to a Kill 1985, Key to Freedom 1989, Bed and Breakfast 1989, Bullseye! 1989, Fire, Ice and Dynamite 1990, The Quest 1997. *TV appearances include:* The Alaskans, The Saint 1962–69, The Persuaders 1972–73, The Man Who Wouldn't Die 1992, The Quest 1995. *Publication:* James Bond Diary 1973. *Address:* c/o ICM Ltd., 76 Oxford Street, London, W1R 1RB, England.

MOORE OF LOWER MARSH, Baron (Life Peer), cr. 1992, of Lower Marsh in the London Borough of Lambeth, **John Edward Michael Moore;** British politician; b. 26 Nov. 1937; s. of Edward O. Moore; m. Sheila S. Tillotson 1962; two s. one d.; ed. London School of Econs.; with Royal Sussex Regt. Korea 1955–57; Pres. Students' Union L.S.E. 1959–60; banking and stock-broking, Chicago 1962–65; Dir. Dean Witter Int. Ltd. 1968–79, Chair. 1975–79; underwriting mem. Lloyds 1978–92; Exec. Chair. Crédit Suisse Asset Man. 1991–, Energy Saving Trust Ltd. 1992–95 (Pres. 1995–); mem. Parl. for Croydon Cen. 1974–92; Parl. Under-Sec. of State, Dept. of Energy 1979–83; Econ. Sec. to H.M. Treasury June–Oct. 1983, Financial Sec. to H.M. Treasury Oct. 1983–86; Sec. of State for Transport 1986–87, for Dept. of Health and Social Security 1987–88, for Social Security 1988–89; Dir. Monitor Inc. 1990– (Chair. Monitor Europe 1990–), Blue Circle Industries 1993–, Camelot PLC 1994–, Rolls-Royce PLC (Deputy Chair. 1996–), Credit Suisse Investment Man. Australia 1995–, Cen. European Growth Fund PLC 1995–, BEA Assocs. U.S.A. 1996–, TIG Inc. 1997–; mem. Ct. of Govs. L.S.E. 1977–; Conservative. *Address:* House of Lords, Westminster, London, SW1A 0PW, England.

MOORER, Admiral Thomas Hinman, D.S.M., D.F.C.; American naval officer (retd.); b. 9 Feb. 1912, Mount Willing, Ala.; s. of the late Dr. Richard Randolph Moorer and Hulda Hinson; m. Carrie Ellen Foy 1935; three s. one d.; ed. U.S. Naval Acad.; service in U.S. warships 1933–35, aviation squadrons 1936–43; Commdr. of bombing squadron 1943; Gunnery and Tactical Officer, Staff of Commdr., Naval Air Force, Atlantic 1944–45; Strategic Bombing Survey, Japan 1945–56; Naval Aviation Ordnance Test Station 1946–48; Exec. Officer aircraft carrier Midway 1948–49; Operations Officer on Staff of Commdr. Carrier Div. Four, Atlantic Fleet 1949–50; Naval Ordnance Test Station, Inyokern 1950–52; Capt. 1952; Staff of Commdr., Naval Air Force, Atlantic Fleet 1953–55; Aide to Asst. Sec. of Navy for Air 1955–56; Commdr. U.S.S. Salisbury Sound 1956–57; Special Asst., Strategic Plans Div., Office of Chief of Naval Operations, Navy Dept. 1957–58; Rear Adm. 1958; Asst. Chief of Naval Operations (War Gaming Matters) 1958–59; Commdr. Carrier Div. Six 1959–60; Dir. Long Range Plans 1960–62; Vice-Adm. 1962; Commdr. U.S. Seventh Fleet, W. Pacific 1962–64; Adm. 1964; C.-in-C. U.S. Pacific Fleet 1964–65; C.-in-C. U.S. Atlantic Fleet, C.-in-C. Atlantic and Supreme Allied Commdr. Atlantic (NATO Forces) 1965–67; Chief of Naval Operations, U.S. 1967–70; Chair. U.S. Joint Chiefs of Staff 1970–74; Dir. Blount Inc., Montgomery, Ala. 1974–; mem. Asscn. of Naval Aviation (Chair. 1974–); Silver Star Medal 1942, Legion of Merit 1945, Gray Eagle of U.S. Navy Award 1972, Defense Distinguished Service Medal 1973, included in Nat. Aviation Hall of Fame 1987, Nat. Football Foundation and Hall of Fame Gold Medal 1990, and many U.S. and foreign decorations. *Leisure interests:* football, golf, hunting, fishing. *Address:* 9707 Old Georgetown Road, Bethesda, MD 20814, U.S.A. (Home).

MOOREY, (Peter) Roger (Stuart), F.B.A., F.S.A., D.PHIL. (OXON.); British museum curator; b. 30 May 1937, Bush Hill Park, Middx.; s. of the late Stuart Moorey and of Freda (née Harris) Moorey; ed. Mill Hill School, Corpus Christi Coll., Oxford; Asst. Keeper, Ashmolean Museum, Oxford 1961–73, Sr. Asst. Keeper 1973–83, Keeper, Dept. of Antiquities 1983– (Acting Dir. 1997–98); Pres. British School of Archaeology, Jerusalem 1990–; Fellow of Wolfson Coll., Oxford 1976–. *Publications:* Catalogue of the Ancient Persian Bronzes in the Ashmolean Museum 1971, Biblical Lands 1975, Kish Excavations 1923–33 1978, Cemeteries at Deve Hüyük 1980, Excavation in Palestine 1981, Materials and Manufacture in Ancient Mesopotamia 1985, The Bible and Recent Archaeology (with Kenyon) 1987, Ancient Near Eastern Seals in the Ashmolean Museum, vols. 2 and 3 (with Buchanan) 1984, 1988, A Century of Biblical Archaeology 1991, Ancient Mesopotamian Materials and Industries 1994. *Leisure interests:* travelling, walking. *Address:* Ashmolean Museum, Oxford, OX1 2PH, England. *Telephone:* (0865) 278020.

MOORMAN van KAPPEN, Olav, LL.D.; Netherlands legal historian; b. 11 March 1937, The Hague; s. of Karel S. O. van Kappen and Johanna J. Moorman; m. Froukje A. Bosma 1963; one s. one d.; ed. Huygens Lyceum and Utrecht Univ.; Research Asst. Faculty of Law, Utrecht Univ. 1961–64, Jr. Lecturer 1965–68; Sr. Lecturer Faculty of Law, Amsterdam Univ. 1968–71; Asst. Prof. Faculty of Law, Leyden Univ. 1971–72; Prof. of Legal History, Nijmegen Univ. 1971–, Co. Dir. Gerard Noodt Inst. for Legal History 1972–; Visiting Prof. Munster Univ. 1982–83, Poitiers Univ. 1986 Düsseldorf Univ. 1989–90, Univ. René Descarts (Paris V) 1992, 1995; mem. Bd. of Govs. Netherlands School for Archivists 1979–81, Chair. 1981–95; mem. Netherlands Council of Archives 1979–89, Vice-Pres. 1986–89, Pres. 1990–95; mem. Nat. Council of Cultural Heritage 1990–95; mem. editorial Bd., Legal History Review 1983–; mem. Dutch Soc. of Sciences at Haarlem 1982, Royal Netherlands Acad. of Sciences 1986; Corresp. mem. Acad. of Sciences, Göttingen; Dr. h. c. (Univ. René Descartes (Paris V)); Cross of Merit (Fed. Repub. of Germany, 1st Class), Officier, Ordre des Palmes Académiques. *Publications:* several books and numerous articles on various aspects of legal history. *Address:* Institute of Legal Science of Nijmegen University, P.O. Box 9049, 6500 KK Nijmegen, Netherlands. *Telephone:* 024-3612186. *Fax:* 024-3616145.

MOOSA, Mohammed Valli, B.SC.; South African politician; b. 9 Feb. 1957, Johannesburg; m. Elsabé Wessels; ed. Lenasia State Indian High School, Univ. of Durban-Westville; active in S.A. Students' Org., Nat. Indian Congress and other political and trade-union activities; teacher 1979–82; involved in est. of Anti-S.A. Indian Council Cttee. 1982, revival of Transvaal Indian Congress 1983; founder mem. and fmr. mem. Nat. Exec. Cttee. United Democratic Front; fmr. leader Mass Democratic Movt.; detained 1987, escaped 1988; planned Defiance Campaign; detained 1989; involved in Conf. for a Democratic Future 1989; mem. Nat. Reception Cttee. for released ANC leaders 1989–90; with ANC 1990–, mem. Nat. Exec. Cttee. 1991, fmr. mem. Nat. Working Cttee., rep. of negotiating team Convention for a Democratic South Africa 1991–94; Deputy Minister of Provincial Affairs and Constitutional Devt. 1994, Minister 1996–. *Address:* Ministry of Provincial Affairs and of Constitutional Development, 87 Hamilton Street, Arcadia, Pretoria 0083; Private Bag X802, Pretoria 0001, South Africa (Office). *Telephone:* (12) 3340705 (Office). *Fax:* (12) 3213264 (Office).

MORA GRAMUNT, Gabriel; Spanish architect; b. 13 April 1941, Barcelona; s. of Evaristo Mora Gramunt and Josefa Mora Gramunt; m. Carmina Sanvisens Montón 1985; one s.; ed. Tech. Univ. of Architecture, Barcelona (ETSAB); Assoc. Piñón-Viaplana 1967; tutor, ETSAB 1973; in partnership with Jaume Bach Nuñez, Bach/Mora Architects 1976–; Prof. of History of Modern Architecture, EINA School of Design 1978; design tutor, ETSAB 1978–; Visiting Prof. Univ. of Dublin 1993; work includes grass hockey Olympic Stadium, Terrassa 1992, cen. telephone exchange, Olympic Village, Barcelona 1992, apt. bldgs., agric. complex, health clinic etc.; various professional awards. *Publications include:* Junge Architekten in Europa (jtly.) 1983, Young Spanish Architects (jtly.) 1985. *Address:* Passatge Sant Felip, 12 bis, 08006 Barcelona, Spain.

MORAES, Dominic; Indian writer and poet; b. 19 July 1938; s. of late Frank Moraes; m. Leela Naidu 1970; ed. St. Mary's High School, Bombay, and Jesus Coll., Oxford; Consultant UN Fund for Population Activities 1973– (on loan to India); Man. Ed. The Asia Magazine Hong Kong 1972–; Ed. Indian Express; Hawthornden Prize for A Beginning 1957. *Publications include:* A Beginning 1957, Gone Away 1960, My Son's Father (autobiog.) 1968, The Tempest Within 1972–73, The People Time Forgot 1972, A Matter of People 1974, Voices for Life (essays) 1975, Mrs. Gandhi 1980, Bombay 1980, Collected Poems 1957–87 1988, Serendip 1990 (poems). Never At Home 1994 (autobiog.). *Address:* 12 Sargent House, Allana Marg, Bombay 39, India.

MORAHAN, Christopher Thomas; British theatre, television and film director; b. 9 July 1929; s. of late Thomas Morahan and Nancy Barker; m. 1st Joan Murray 1954 (died 1973); m. 2nd Anna Carteret 1974; two s. three d. (one deceased); ed. Highgate School and Old Vic Theatre School; Dir. Greenpoint Films and Head, plays, BBC TV 1972–76. *Stage productions include:* Little Murders, This Story of Yours, The Caretaker, Flint, Melon, Major Barbara, The Handyman, Letter of Resignation, Racing Demon, Equally Divided; for Nat. Theatre (Assoc. 1977–88): State of Revolution, Man and Superman, Wild Honey, The Devil's Disciple; TV productions include: The Jewel in the Crown 1984, In the Secret State 1985, After Pilkington 1987 (Prix Italia 1987), Troubles 1988, The Heat of the Day 1989, Old Flames 1990, Can You Hear Me Thinking? 1990, Ashenden 1991, The Common Pursuit 1992, Unnatural Pursuits 1992, The Bullion Boys 1993, Summer Days Dream 1994, It Might be You 1995, The Peacock Spring 1996, Element of Doubt, A Dance to the Music of Time (two episodes) 1997; films: Clockwise 1986, Paper Mask 1990; BAFTA Award 1985; Emmy Award 1985 and many other awards. *Address:* c/o Whitehall Artists, 125 Gloucester Road, London, SW7 4TE; Highcombe Farmhouse, The Devil's Punchbowl, Thursley, Godalming, Surrey, GU8 6NS, England. *Telephone:* 0171-244 8466; (01428) 607031. *Fax:* (01428) 607989.

MORALES, Armando; Nicaraguan artist; b. 15 Jan. 1927; ed. Inst. Pedagógico de Varones, Managua, Escuela de Bellas Artes, Managua and Pratt Graphic Art Center, New York; first one-man exhbn. Lima 1959, subsequently at Toronto, New York, Washington, D.C., Panama, Bogotá, Detroit, Caracas, Mexico City; Group exhbns. all over N. and S. America and in Europe; numerous awards for painting in the Americas including Carnegie Int. 1964, and award at Arte de América y España Exhbn., Madrid.

MORALES BERMÚDEZ, Gen. Francisco: Peruvian politician and army officer; b. 4 Oct. 1921, Lima; grandson of the late Col. Remiro Morales (President of Peru, 1890-94); m. Rosa Pedraglio de Morales Bermúdez; four s. one d.; ed. Chorillos Mil. School; founder mem. Dept. of Research and Devt., Army Gen. Staff; taught at School of Eng. and at Army Acad. of War; Chief of Staff of First Light Div., Tumbes; Asst. Dir. of Logistics, Dir. of Econ., War Ministry; advanced courses at Superior Acad. of War, Argentina and Centre for Higher Mil. Studies, Peru; appointed to reorganize electoral registration system 1962; Minister of Econ. and Finance 1968–74; Chief of Army Gen. Staff 1974–75: Prime Minister, Minister of War and Commdr.-Gen. of Army Feb.-Aug. 1975; Pres. of Peru 1975–80.

MORAN, 2nd Baron, (cr. 1943), of Manton; **(Richard) John McMoran Wilson,** K.C.M.G.; British diplomatist (retd.); b. 22 Sept. 1924; s. of late Sir Charles McMoran Wilson, 1st Baron Moran; m. Shirley Rowntree Harris 1948; two s. one d.; ed. Eton, King's Coll., Cambridge; served in World War II; H.M.S. Belfast 1943, Sub-Lieut. R.N.V.R. in motor torpedo boats and H.M. Destroyer Oribi 1944–45; Foreign Office 1945; Third Sec., Ankara 1948, Tel-Aviv 1950; Second Sec., Rio de Janeiro 1953; First Sec., Foreign Office 1956; Washington, D.C. 1959; Foreign Office 1961; Counsellor, Pretoria 1965; Head of W. African Dept. of FCO 1968–73, concurrently Amb. to Chad 1970–73; Amb. to Hungary 1973–76, to Portugal 1976–81; High Commr. in Canada 1981–84; sits as independent peer, House of Lords; Chair. All Party Conservation Group of both Houses of Parl. 1992–, Wildlife and Countryside Link 1990–95, Regional Fisheries Advisory Cttee., Welsh

Region, NRA 1989–94 , Salmon and Trout Asscn. 1997–; Pres. Welsh Salmon and Trout Angling Asscn. 1988–95, Radnorshire Wildlife Trust 1994–; Vice-Chair. Atlantic Salmon Trust 1983–95, Vice-Pres. 1995–; mem. Council RSPB 1989–94 (Vice-Pres. 1997–98), Agricultural Sub. Cttee. 1991–95, 1997–; Grand Cross of the Order of the Infante (Portugal) 1978. *Publications:* C.B., a Life of Sir Henry Campbell-Bannerman 1973 (Whitbread Award), Fairfax 1985. *Leisure interests:* fishing, fly-tying, bird watching. *Address:* c/o House of Lords, Westminster, London, SW1A 0PW, England.

MORÁN LÓPEZ, Fernando; Spanish politician; b. 1926, Avilés; m. Maria Luz Calvo-Sotelo; one s. two d.; ed. Institut des Hautes Etudes Internationales, Paris, London School of Econs.; began diplomatic career 1954; Asst. Consul, Spanish Consulate-Gen., Buenos Aires 1956; Sec. Spanish Embassy, Pretoria; transferred to Ministry of Foreign Affairs 1963, specialized in African affairs, Asst. Dir.-Gen. for Africa, Near and Middle East, Political Dir. Dept. of Foreign Policy, later in charge of Africa, Near and Middle East 1971, Dir.-Gen. of African Affairs 1975–77; First Sec. Spanish Embassy, Lisbon; Consul-Gen. Spanish Embassy, London 1974; Partido Socialista Popular cand. for elections to Congress of Deputies 1977; elected Partido Socialista Obrero Español Senator for Asturias, Socialist Spokesman for Foreign Affairs in Senate; Minister of Foreign Affairs 1982–85; Perm. Rep. to the UN 1985–87; Légion d'honneur, Grand Cross of Carlos III, Grand Cross Order of Isabel la Católica 1985. *Publications:* También se muere el Mar 1958, Una política exterior para España. *Address:* Juan XXIII 5, 28040 Madrid, Spain (Home).

MORATH, Ingeborg Hermine, B.A.; American photographer; b. 27 May 1923, Graz, Austria; d. of Prof. Edgar Morath and Mathilde Morath; m. Arthur Miller (q.v.) 1962; one d.; Univ. of Berlin; translator, ed. ISB Feature, Section, Salzburg, Vienna; Ed. Der Optimist (literary monthly) 1945–52; Austria Ed. Heute magazine; freelance writer for magazines and radio; joined Magnum Photos 1952–, mem. 1953–; teacher and lecturer at various univs. including Univ. of Miami, Univ. of Mich. and Harvard Univ.; Great Austrian State Prize for Photography 1992; Hon. D.F.A. (Hartford) 1984. *Publications include:* Fiesta in Pamplona 1956, Venice Observed 1956, From Persia to Iran 1961, Tunisia 1961, Le Masque 1967, In Russia 1969, East West Exercises 1973, Boris Pasternak: My Sister Life 1976, In the Country 1977, Chinese Encounters 1979, Images of Vienna 1982, Salesman in Beijing 1984, Portraits 1987, Russian Journal 1991, Inge-Morath: Photographs from 1952 to 1992 1992, Spain in the Fifties 1994, The Danube 1995, Inge Morath-Pamphona 1997. *Leisure interests:* looking at paintings, travel, hiking. *Address:* Magnum Photos, 151 W. 25th Street, New York, NY 10001-7204 (Office); RRI Box, 232 Tophet Road, Roxbury, CT 06783, U.S.A. (Home). *Telephone:* (212) 929-6000 (Office). *Fax:* (212) 929-9325.

MORAVČÍK, Jozef, LL.D.; Slovak politician; b. 19 March 1945, Očová Zvolen Dist.; m.; two d.; ed. Charles Univ., Komenský Univ.; clerk with Chemapol (trade co.) Bratislava; lecturer Law Faculty, Komenský Univ., Bratislava 1972–85, Head of Dept. of Business Law 1985–90; Dean, Law Faculty 1990–91; Deputy to Slovak Nat. Council 1991–92; mem. Movt. for Democratic Slovakia (MDS) 1991–94; Minister of Foreign Affairs of Č.S.F.R. July–Dec. 1992; Chair. Council of Ministers of C.S.C.E. July–Dec. 1992; Minister of Foreign Affairs, Slovak Repub. 1993–94; Premier, Govt. of Slovakia March–Dec. 1994; Chair. Democratic Union of Slovakia 1994–97; Chair. Policy Planning Council 1997–; Mayor of Bratislava Dec. 1998–. *Address:* Democratic Union of Slovakia, Medená 10, 811 02 Bratislava, Slovakia.

MORAVEC, Ivan; Czech pianist and academic; b. 9 Nov. 1930, Prague; m. 1st (deceased); m. 2nd; one s., one d.; ed. Conservatoire, Prague 1946–51; teacher Acad. of Musical Arts, Prague 1969–; soloist with Czech Philharmonic Orchestra; concert tours Europe, U.S.A., Japan; Player of the Year, Union of U.S. Radio Stations 1997. *Leisure interest:* culture. *Address:* Pod Vyhlídkou 520, 160 00 Prague 6, Czech Republic (Home). *Telephone:* 02-312 3696 (Home).

MORCELI, Noureddine; Algerian athlete; b. 28 Feb. 1970; coached by his brother Abderrahmane Morceli; World Champion, 1500 m. Tokyo 1991, Stuttgart 1993, Gothenburg 1995; fmr. world record-holder at 1500m., 3000m.; world record-holder at mile, 2000m.; participant, Olympic Games, Barcelona 1992, Atlanta 1996 (Gold Medal 1,500 m.). *Address:* c/o Ministry of Youth and Sports, 3 rue Mohamed Belouizdad, Algiers, Algeria.

MORDACQ, Patrick; French government official; b. 20 May 1934, Bordeaux; m. Marie Thérèse de Yturbe 1967; one s. one d.; ed. Ecole Nat. d'Admin.; Commissariat Gen. du Plan d'Equipement et de la Productivité 1963–67; Office of Minister of Equipment and Housing 1968; Head, Office of Foreign Investment, Treasury 1969; Deputy Chair. Comm. of Industry for VIth Plan 1970; Head, Office of Loans, Aid and Guarantees to Business, Treasury 1971; Dir. Soc. Financière pour favoriser l'industrialisation de régions minières 1971–74; Finance Dir. Groupe Jacques Borel Int. 1974–77; Head, Finance Service, Commissariat Gen. du Plan d'Equipement et de la Productivité 1977; Financial Counsellor, French Embassy, Bonn 1979; Head, Regulation of Finance, Treasury 1984–86; Govt. Commr. Centre Nat. des Caisses d'Epargne et de Prévoyance 1984–86; Sec.-Gen. Comm. des Opérations de Bourse 1986–91; Dir. for France EBRD (London) and Financial Counsellor, French Embassies, Poland, Romania and Bulgaria 1991–96; Conseiller-Maître, Cour des Comptes 1996–. *Address:* 13 rue Cambon, 75100 Paris, France (Office). *Telephone:* (1) 42985592. *Fax:* (1) 42989602.

MORDECHAI, Yitzhak, M.A.; Israeli politician and fmr. army officer; b. 1944, Iraq; m. (divorced); two c.; ed. Staff and Command Colls., Tel-Aviv and Haifa Univs.; emigrated to Israel aged five; served in Israeli Defence Forces (IDF) 1962–95, Commdr. of a paratroop unit in the Sinai, 1967 Six Day War, paratroop bn. on Suez Canal front, 1973 Yom Kippur War, Chief Infantry and Paratroopers Officer 1983–86, apptd. Head of IDF HQ Training Dept., rank of Maj.-Gen. 1986, Officer in Command of IDF Southern Command 1986, of Cen. Command 1989, of Northern Command 1991; joined Likud party 1995; mem. Knesset (Parl.) 1996–, Minister of Defence 1996–99; mem. Likud-Tzomet-Gesher group. *Address:* c/o Ministry of Defence, Kaplan Street, Hakirya, Tel-Aviv 67659, Israel.

MORDKOVITCH, Lydia, PH.D., F.R.N.C.M.; Russian violinist; b. 30 April 1944, Saratov, U.S.S.R. (now Russia); d. of Mendel and Golda Shtimerman; m. 1st Leonid Mordkovitch 1962 (divorced); one d.; m. 2nd Malkia Chayoth 1977 (divorced 1983); ed. School for Talented Children, Kishinev, Stoliarski School, Odessa, Nejdanova Conservatoire, Odessa, Tchaikovsky Conservatoire, Moscow and studied with David Oistrakh; went to Israel 1974; has lived in U.K. since 1980; Sr. Lecturer, Kishinev Inst. of Art 1970–73; Sr. Lecturer, Rubin Acad. of Music, Jerusalem 1974–80; Prof. of Violin, Royal Northern Coll. of Music, Manchester, England 1980-, Royal Acad. of Music, London 1995–; soloist in recitals, concerts, on radio and T.V., U.S.S.R., then Europe, U.S.A., S. and Cen. America 1974–; Prizewinner, Young Musicians Competition, Kiev 1967, Long-Thibaud Competition, Paris 1969, Gramophone award (for Shostakovich concertos) 1990, three Diapason d'Or Awards, Woman of the Year Award, American Biog. Inst. 1996 and 1997, recordings include works by Franck, Ravel, Brahms, Bartok, Prokofiev, Honegger, Bloch, Bruch, Achron, Strauss, Fauré, Shostakovich, Moeran, Khachaturian, Kabalevsky, Schubert, Bach, Nielsen, Busoni, Szymanowski, Ysaÿe, Saint-Saens, Walton, Respighi, Alwyn, Ferguson, John Ireland, Dyson, Vaughan Williams, Schnittke, Howells. *Leisure interests:* theatre, literature, art. *Address:* 25B Belsize Avenue, London, NW3 4BL, England. *Telephone:* 0171-873 7373.

MORDYUKOVA, Nonna (Noyabrina) Viktorovna; Russian actress; b. 27 Nov. 1925, Otradnaya, Kuban Territory; ed. All-Union Inst. of Cinematography; debut in 1948 film Young Guard; over 60 films; U.S.S.R. People's Actress 1974; U.S.S.R. State Prize 1949; prize winner int. and all-union festivals. *Roles include:* Somebody Else's Kinsfolk, Ekaterina Voronina, Paternal House, Simple Story, Chairman, Commissar, Small Crane, Russian Field, Quagmire, Relatives. *Publications:* That's Our Life (novel), short stories. *Address:* Rublevskoye Shosse 34, korp. 2, Apt. 549, 121609 Moscow, Russia.

MOREAU, Jeanne; French actress; b. 23 Jan. 1928, Paris; d. of Anatole-Désiré Moreau and Katherine Buckley; m. 1st Jean-Louis Richard 1949 (divorced); one s.; m. 2nd William Friedkin 1977 (divorced); ed. Collège Edgar-Quinet, Conservatoire national d'art dramatique; stage actress with Comédie Française 1948–52; Théâtre Nat. Populaire 1953; Pres. Cannes Film Festival July 1975; Paris Int. Film Festival 1975; Pres. Acad. des Arts et Techniques du Cinéma 1986–88; Pres. Comm. des avances sur recettes 1993–94; Officier, Légion d'honneur, Officier Ordre nat. du Mérite, Commdr. des Arts et Lettres, Moliere Award 1988; European Cinema Prize, Berlin 1997; Fellow B.A.F.T.A., British Acad.; since 1954 has appeared on stage in L'heure éblouissante, La machine infernale, Pygmalion, La chatte sur un toit brûlant, La bonne soupe, La chevauchée sur le lac de Constance, Lulu, L'intoxe, Night of the Iguana, Le Récit de la Servante Zerline 1986, La Célestine 1989, etc. *Films include:* Touchez pas au grisbi, Le salaire du péché, Ascenseur pour l'échafaud, Les amants, Moderato Cantabile, Les liaisons dangereuses, Dialogue des Carmélites, Jules et Jim, Eve, The Victors, La baie des anges, Peau de banane, Le train, Le journal d'une femme de chambre, Mata Hari—H21, The Yellow Rolls-Royce 1964, Viva Maria 1965, Mademoiselle 1965, Chimes at Midnight 1966, L'amour à travers les âges 1967, The Sailor from Gibraltar 1967, The Bride wore Black 1967, The Great Catherine 1968, Le corps de Diane 1970, Une histoire immortelle, Monte Walsh, L'humeur vagabonde, Comptes rebours 1971, Chère Louise 1972, Jeanne, la Française 1972, Nathalie Granger 1972, Je t'aime 1973, Les valseuses 1973, La race des seigneurs 1973, Pleurs 1974, Le jardin qui bascule 1974, Souvenirs d'en France 1974, Lumière (also dir.) 1976, The Last Tycoon 1976, Mr. Klein 1976, Le Petit Théâtre de Jean Renoir 1976, L'adolescente 1978, Madame Rosa 1978, L'intoxe 1980, Plein Sud 1981, Mille milliards de dollars 1982, Au-delà de cette limite votre billet n'est plus valable 1982, Querelles 1982, La truite 1982, Le paltoquet 1986, Sauve-toi Lola 1986, Alberto Express 1989, Nikita 1990, Anna Karamazoff 1989–90, La femme fardée 1990, The Suspended Step of the Stork 1991, Till the End of the World 1991, La Vieille qui Marchait dans la Mer 1991, La Nuit de l'océan 1992, A Demain 1992, The Summer House 1994, Les Cents et Une Nuits 1995, The Proprietor 1996, Un amour de sorcière 1997. *Leisure interest:* reading. *Address:* Spica Productions, 3 rue du bois de Boulogne, 75116 Paris, France.

MOREIRA NEVES, H.E. Cardinal Lucas, O.P.; Brazilian ecclesiastic; b. 16 Sept. 1925, São João del Rei; ordained 1950, elected to the titular Church of Feradi Maggiore 1967, consecrated bishop 1967, Archbishop 1979, transferred to the titular Church of Vescovio 1987, then São Salvador da Bahia 1987; cr. Cardinal 1988, Primate of Brazil. *Address:* Palácio da Sé, Praça da Sé 1, 40020–210, Salvador, Brazil. *Telephone:* (071) 247-4346. *Fax:* (071) 336-4039.

MOREL, Pierre Jean Louis Achille; French diplomatist; b. 27 June 1944, Romans (Drôme); s. of André Morel and Janine Vallernaud; m. Olga Bazanoff 1978; three c.; ed. Lycée du Parc, Lyon, Paris, Ecole nat. d'admin.; Europe Dept., Ministry of Foreign Affairs 1971–73, Analysis and Forecasting Centre 1973–76, First Sec. then Second Counsellor, Embassy, Moscow 1976–79, Ministerial rep., Gen. Secr. interministerial cttee. on European Econ. Co-operation 1979–81, Office of Pres. of Repub., Technical Adviser to Gen. Secr. 1981–85, Dir. Political Affairs, Ministry of Foreign Affairs 1985–86, Amb. and France's rep. Disarmament Conf. Geneva 1989, Head French del. preparatory cttee. Conference on Security and Co-operation in Europe 1990, Diplomatic Adviser, Office of Pres. of Republic 1991–92, Amb. to Georgia 1992–93, to Russia (also accred. to Moldova, Turkmenistan, Mongolia, Tadjikistan and Kyrgyzstan) 1992–96, to China 1996–, Minister Plenipotentiary; Chevalier, Légion d'honneur, Officier Ordre nat. du Mérite. *Publications:* trans. Mantrana 1984, Sauts de Temps 1989, Serpentara 1998 by Ernst Jünger. *Address:* French Embassy, 3 Dong San Jie, San Li Tun, Chao Yangqu, 100020 Beijing, People's Republic of China. *Telephone:* (10) 6532-1331. *Fax:* (10) 6532-4841.

MORELLET, François Charles Alexis Albert; French painter and sculptor; b. 30 April 1926, Cholet, Maine-et-Loire; s. of Charles Morellet and Madeleine Guérineau; m. Danielle Marchand 1946; three s.; ed. Lycée Charlemagne, Institut Nat. des Langues et Civilisations Orientales, Paris; Commercial Dir. then Man. Dir. Morellet-Guérineau 1948–76; artist 1942–; exhbns. Van Abbemuseum, Eindhoven 1971, Centre Nat. d'art contemporain, Paris 1971, Nat. Gallery, West Berlin 1977, Brooklyn Museum, New York 1985, Musée nat. d'art moderne, Paris 1986, Stedelijk Museum, Amsterdam 1986; monumental works include mural at 22 Reade St., Lower Manhattan, New York 1988, neon piece, Grande halle de la Villette, Paris 1988, steel sculpture, La Défense, Paris 1991; Grand prix nat. de sculpture 1987. *Leisure interests:* travel, underwater fishing. *Address:* 83 rue Porte Baron, 49300 Cholet; 8 rue Fallempin, 75015 Paris, France.

MORENILLA, José María, DR. IUR.; Spanish judge; b. 29 Aug. 1926, Granada; s. of Carlos Morenilla and Clotilde Morenilla; m. Joanne Allard 1962; one s. one d.; ed. School of Law, Granada, Columbia Univ., Univ. of Granada; Judge of First Instance 1952; Legal Adviser (in int. law) Ministry of Justice 1978–87; Supreme Court Judge Criminal Section 1987–90, Admin. Section 1990–; Agent/Rep. of Spanish Govt. before European Comm. of Human Rights 1988–90; Judge European Court of Human Rights 1990–; Cross of Honour of San Raimundo de Penãfort. *Leisure interests:* music (opera), reading. *Publications:* Organization of the Courts and Judicial Reform in the United States 1968, Poder Judicial en los Estados Unidos 1979, La Igualdad (Jurídica) de la Mujer en España 1980, Medidas Alternativas de la Prisión 1983, Protección Internacional de los Derechos Humanos 1984, Convenio Europeo de Derechos Humanos—Ambito, Organos, Procedimientos 1985. *Address:* Juan Ramón Jiménez 2, 9°C, 28036 Madrid, Spain. *Telephone:* (91) 457-4591.

MORGAN, Howard James, M.A.; British artist; b. 21 April 1949, N. Wales; s. of Thomas James Morgan and Olive Victoria Morgan (née Oldnall); m. Susan Ann Sandilands 1977 (divorced 1998); two s. one d.; ed. Fairfax High School, Sutton Coldfield, Univ. of Newcastle-upon-Tyne; career artist; numerous Royal and pvt. comms.; perm. display of work at Nat. Portrait Gallery, London; mem. Royal Soc. of Portrait Painters 1986–. *Leisure interests:* riding, 1938 Citröen, books. *Address:* 401½ Wandsworth Road, Battersea, London, SW8 2JP (Studio); 12 Rectory Grove, Clapham Old Town, London, SW4 0EA, England (Home). *Telephone:* 0171-720 1181.

MORGAN, James N. PH.D.; American economist; b. 1 March 1918, Corydon, Ind.; s. of John Jacob Brooke and Rose Ann Davis Morgan; m. Gladys Lucille Hassler 1945; three s. one d.; ed. Northwestern Univ. and Harvard; Asst. Prof. of Econs. Brown Univ. 1947–49; Carnegie Research Fellow Inst. for Social Research, Univ. of Mich. 1949–51, Fellow Center for Advanced Study in the Behavioral Sciences 1955–56, Program Dir. Survey Research Center, Inst. for Social Research 1956–88, Prof. of Econs. 1957–88, Prof. Emer. 1988–; Fellow Wissenschaftskolleg zu Berlin 1983–84; mem. N.A.S.; Fellow American Statistical Asscn., mem. American Acad. of Arts and Sciences, American Gerontological Asscn. *Publications:* Income and Welfare in the United States 1962, Economic Behavior of the Affluent 1965, Economic Survey Methods 1971, Five Thousand American Families (Ed.) 10 Vols. 1972–84, Economics of Personal Choice 1980. *Leisure interests:* travel, photography. *Address:* Institute for Social Research, Thompson Street, Ann Arbor, MI 48104 (Office); 1217 Bydding Road, Ann Arbor, MI 48103, U.S.A. (Home). *Telephone:* (313) 764-8388 (Office); (313) 668-8304 (Home).

MORGAN, Keith John, B.SC., M.A., D.PHIL., F.R.S.C., F.R.A.C.I., F.A.I.M.; British university vice-chancellor; b. 14 Dec. 1929; s. of C. F. J. Morgan and W. Morgan; m. Hilary A. Chapman 1957; one d.; ed. Manchester Grammar School and Brasenose Coll. Oxford; Sr. Research Fellow, Ministry of Supply 1955–57; ICI Research Fellow 1957–58; lecturer, Univ. of Birmingham 1958–64; AEC Research Fellow, Purdue Univ. 1960–61; lecturer, Univ. of Lancaster 1964–65, Sr. lecturer 1965–68, Prof. 1968–86, Pro-Vice-Chancellor 1973–78, Sr. Pro-Vice-Chancellor 1978–86; Vice-Chancellor, Univ. of Newcastle, N.S.W. 1987–93; Visiting Prof. Kobe Univ., Japan 1993; Chair. Hunter Foundation for Cancer Research –1993; Deputy Chair. Hunter Tech. Devt. Centre 1987–93, Hunter Econ. Devt. Council 1989–93, Hunter Fed. Task Force 1991–93; Prof. Univ. of Electro-Communications, Tokyo 1993–95; Visiting Prof., Hiroshima Univ. 1995–97; Hon. D.Sc. (Newcastle) 1993. *Publications:* various scientific, managerial, economic and educational papers. *Leisure interests:* Mozart, mountains, cricket. *Address:* 9B Castle Hill, Lancaster, LA1 1YS, England.

MORGAN, Kenneth Owen, D.PHIL., D.LITT., F.B.A., F.R.HIST.S.; British historian; b. 16 May 1934; s. of David James Morgan and Margaret Morgan (née Owen); m. Jane Keeler 1973 (died 1992); one s. one d.; ed. University Coll. School, London, Oriel Coll., Univ. of Oxford; Lecturer History Dept. Univ. Coll., Swansea 1958–66, Sr. Lecturer 1965–66; Fellow and Praelector Modern History and Politics The Queen's Coll., Univ. of Oxford 1966–89; Prin., Univ. Coll. of Wales, Aberystwyth 1989–95; Pro-Vice-Chancellor, Univ. of Wales 1988–93, Vice-Chancellor 1993–95, Prof. 1989–; Ed. Welsh History Review 1961–; Jt. Ed. 20th Century British History 1994–99; Fellow American Council of Learned Socs. Columbia Univ. 1962–63, Visiting Prof. 1965; Hon. Fellow Univ. Coll., Swansea 1985, Hon. Prof. 1995–; Hon. Fellow The Queen's Coll., Oxford 1992, Univ. of Wales, Cardiff 1997, Trinity Coll., Carmarthen 1998; Supernumerary Fellow, Jesus Coll., Oxford 1991–92; Hon. D. Litt. (Wales), (Glamorgan) 1997. *Publications*: Wales in British Politics 1963, David Lloyd George 1963, Freedom or Sacrilege? 1966, Keir Hardie 1967, The Age of Lloyd George 1971, Lloyd George: Family Letters (ed.) 1973, Lloyd George 1974, Keir Hardie: Radical and Socialist 1975, Consensus and Disunity 1979, Portrait of a Progressive (with Jane Morgan) 1980, Rebirth of a Nation: Wales 1880–1980 1981, David Lloyd George 1981, Labour in Power 1945–51 1984, The Oxford Illustrated History of Britain (ed.) 1984, Labour People 1987, The Red Dragon and The Red Flag 1989, Academic Leadership 1991, The People's Peace: British History 1945–90 1992, Modern Wales: Politics, Places and People 1995, Young Oxford History of Britain and Ireland (Gen. Ed.), 1996, Callaghan: A Life 1997. *Leisure interests*: music, sport, travel. *Address*: The Croft, 63 Millwood End, Long Hanborough, Witney, Oxon., OX8 8BP, England. *Telephone:* (01993) 881341.

MORGAN, Michèle (pseudonym of Simone Roussel); French actress; b. 29 Feb. 1920; d. of Louis Roussel; m. 1st Bill Marshall; one s.; m. 2nd Henri Vidal (deceased); studied with R. Simon (Paris); actress 1936–; Cannes Festival Prize for Best Actress (in Symphonie pastorale) 1946; French "Victoire" for Best Actress 1946, 1948, 1950, 1952, 1955; Médaille de vermeil, Paris 1967; Grand Officier, Légion d'honneur, Officier, Ordre nat. du Mérite, Commdr. des Arts et des Lettres. *Films include:* Quai des brumes, Symphonie pastorale, Fabiola, Les septs péchés capitaux, Les orgueilleux, Obsession, Les grandes manoeuvres, Marguerite de la nuit, Marie Antoinette, Si Paris nous était conté, Le miroir à deux faces, Femmes d'un été, Pourquoi viens-tu si tard? Les scélérats, Fortunat, Le puits aux trois vérités, Les lions sont lâches, Rencontres, Le crime ne paie pas, Landru, Constance aux Enfers, Les yeux cernés, Dis-moi qui tuer, Les centurions, Benjamin, Le chat et la souris 1975, Ils vont tous bien 1989; has also appeared on television and in theatre. *Publications:* Mes yeux ont vu 1965, Avec ces yeux-là 1977, le Fil Bleu 1993. *Address:* Agents Associés, 201 rue du Faubourg Saint-Honoré, 75008 Paris, France.

MORGAN, Peter William Lloyd, M.A.; British business executive; b. 9 May 1936; s. of Matthew Morgan and Margaret Gwynneth (née Lloyd) Morgan; m. Elisabeth Susanne Davis 1964; three d.; ed. Llandovery Coll., Trinity Hall, Cambridge; served Royal Signals 1954–56; joined IBM UK Ltd. 1959, Data Processing Sales Dir. 1971–74, Group Dir. of Data Processing Marketing, IBM Europe, Paris 1975–80, Dir. IBM UK Ltd. 1980–87, IBM UK Holdings Ltd. 1987–89; Dir. Gen. Inst. of Dirs. 1989–94; Dir. South Wales Electricity PLC 1989–95, Chair. 1996; Dir. Nat. Provident Inst. 1990–95, Chair. 1996–; Dir. Firth Holdings PLC 1994–, Zergo Holdings PLC 1994–; Chair. Pace Micro Tech. PLC 1996–; Dir. Asscn. of Lloyd's Mems. 1997–; mem. Econ. and Social Cttee., EC 1994–; Radical of the Year, Radical Soc. 1990; Liveryman Worshipful Co. of Information Technologists 1992. *Leisure interests:* music, history, gardening, skiing, exercising his dogs. *Address:* 40 Catherine Place, London, SW1E 6HL, England. *Telephone:* 0171-828 9989. *Fax:* 0171-630 5735.

MORGAN, Piers Stefan; British journalist; b. 30 March 1965, Guildford; s. of Anthony Pughe-Morgan and Gabrielle Oliver; m. Marion E. Shalloe 1991; two s.; ed. Cumnor House Preparatory School, Chailey School, Sussex, Lewes Priory Sixth Form Coll. and Harlow Journalism Coll.; reporter, Surrey and S. London newspapers 1987–89; Showbusiness Ed. The Sun 1989–94; Ed. The News of the World 1994–95, Daily Mirror 1995–; Atex Award for Nat. Newspaper Ed. of Year 1994. *Publications:* Private Lives of the Stars 1990, Secret Lives of the Stars 1991, Phillip Schofield, To Dream a Dream 1992, Take That, Our Story 1993, Take That: On the Road 1994. *Leisure interests:* cricket, Arsenal Football Club. *Address:* The Daily Mirror, 1 Canada Square, Canary Wharf, London, E14 5AP, England. *Telephone:* 0171-293 3000. *Fax:* 0171-293 3098.

MORGAN, William Newton, M.ARCH., F.A.I.A.; American architect; b. 14 Dec. 1930, Jacksonville, Fla.; s. of Thomas Morgan and Kathleen Fisk Morgan; m. Bernice Leimback 1954; two s.; ed. Duncan U. Fletcher High School, Harvard Coll., Harvard Grad. School of Design and Università degli Studi per Stranieri, Perugia; U.S. Navy 1952–55; Lehman Fellow, Harvard Univ. 1956–57; Fulbright Grantee, Italy 1958–59; Pres. William Morgan Architects, P.A. 1961–; maj. architectural designs: Fla. State Museum Gainsville 1969–70, Jacksonville Police Admin. Bldg. 1971–75, Pyramid Condominium, Ocean City, Md. 1972–74, First Dist. Court of Appeal, Tallahassee

1983–85, Westinghouse H.Q., Orlando 1984–86, U.S. Embassy, Khartoum 1987–91, U.S. Courthouses, Fort Lauderdale 1976–78, Tallahassee 1992–98; Wheelwright Fellow, Harvard Grad. School of Design 1964–65, Visiting Critic 1981–82; Nat. Endowment of the Arts Fellow 1980; Adjunct Prof. of Art History, Jacksonville Univ. 1995–, Univ. of N. Fla. 1997, Univ. of Fla. 1998; Beineke-Reeves Distinguished Prof. of Architecture, Univ. of Fla. 1998–99; numerous awards and distinctions, including A.I.A. Honor for Research and Recording Ancient American Architecture 1998. *Publications:* Prehistoric Architecture in the Eastern United States 1980, Prehistoric Architecture in Micronesia 1988, Ancient Architecture of the Southwest 1994, Pre Columbian Architecture in Eastern North America 1999; numerous articles. *Address:* William Morgan Architects, P.A., 220 East Forsyth Street, Jacksonville, FL 32202 (Office); 1945 Beach Avenue, Atlantic Beach, FL 32233, U.S.A. (Home). *Telephone:* (904) 356-4195 (Office). *Fax:* (904) 356-2808 (Office).

MORGENTHAU, Robert Morris, LL.B.; American lawyer; b. 31 July 1919, New York; s. of Henry Morgenthau, Jr. and Elinor (née Fatman) Morgenthau; m. 1st Martha Pattridge (deceased); one s. four d.; m. 2nd Lucinda Franks 1977; one s. one d.; ed. Deerfield Acad., Amherst Coll., Yale Univ.; barrister, New York 1949; Assoc. of Patterson, Belknap & Webb, New York 1948–53, Partner 1954–61; U.S. Attorney S. Dist. New York 1961–62, 1962–70; Dist. Attorney New York County 1975–; mem. New York Exec. Cttee. State of Israel Bonds; Democratic Candidate for Gov., New York 1962; mem. Bd. of Dirs. P.R. Legal Defense and Educ. Fund; Trustee Baron de Hirsch Fund, Fed. of Jewish Philanthropies; Co. Chair. New York Holocaust Memorial Comm.; Pres. Police Athletic League 1962; mem. Bar Asscn. City of New York; Dr. h.c. (New York Law School) 1968, (Syracuse Law School) 1976, (Union Univ., Albany Law School) 1982, (Colgate Univ.) 1988. *Address:* Office of District Attorney, 1 Hogan Place, New York, NY 10013, U.S.A.

MORI, Hanae; Japanese fashion designer; b. 1926, Shimane; m.; two s.; graduate in Japanese literature; began career as costume designer for films in 1950s and has designed for over 500 films; opened first shop in Shinjuku, Tokyo 1951; now has 67 Hanae Mori shops in Japan, a store in New York, three shops in Paris and one in Monaco; first overseas show New York 1965; couture business and ready-to-wear; mem. Chambre Syndicale de la Haute Couture, Paris (first Asian mem.) 1977–; retrospective exhbn. at The Space, Hanae Mori Bldg. Tokyo 1989; Co-founder Asscn. for 100 Japanese books; launched Hanae Mori perfume brand 1995; Order of Cultural Merit (Japan); Chevalier Légion d'honneur, Ordre des Arts et des Lettres; numerous awards and prizes. *Address:* Hanae Morae Haute Couture, 17-19 avenue Montaigne, 75008 Paris, France.

MORI, Hideo, B.A.; Japanese business executive; b. 1 April 1925, Osaka City; s. of Shigekazu Mori and Ikue Mori; m. Masako (née Okano) Mori; two s.; ed. Kyoto Univ. 1947; joined Sumitomo Chemical Co. Ltd. 1947, Dir. 1977, Man. Dir. 1980, Sr. Man. Dir. 1982, Pres. 1985–93, Chair. 1993–; Chair. Sumitomo Pharmaceuticals Co. Ltd., ICI-Pharma Ltd., Japan Upjohn Ltd., Nippon Wellcome K.K.; Dir. and Counsellor Japan Petrochemical Ind. Asscn.; Exec. Dir. Japan Fed. of Employers' Asscns.; Dir. Japan Tariff Asscn., Nihon Singapore Polyolefin Co. Ltd; Pres. Japan Chemical Industry Asscn. 1990; mem. Bd. of Exec. Dirs., Fed. of Econ. Orgs. (Keidanren); Blue Ribbon Medal 1987. *Leisure interest:* golf. *Address:* Sumitomo Chemical Co. Ltd., 27-1, Shinkawa 2-chome,Chuo-ku, Tokyo, Japan. *Telephone:* (03-3278) 7227.

MORI, Kazuhisa, B.SC.; Japanese nuclear industry executive; b. 17 Jan. 1926, Hiroshima; s. of Tsunezo Mori and Kayo Mori; m. Reiko Iizuka 1953; two s.; ed. Kyoto Univ.; mem. editorial staff, Chuokoron-sha Inc. 1948–55; Chief of Nuclear Energy Devt. Electric Power Devt. Co., Ltd. 1956–65; Man. Programming Div. Tokyo Channel 12 TV, Ltd. 1963–65; Japan Atomic Industrial Forum Inc. (JAIF) 1956–, Exec. Man. Dir. 1978–, Vice-Chair. 1996–; Dir. Nuclear Safety Research Asscn. 1965–; Vice-Pres. Japan Atomic Energy Relations Org. 1976–; Councillor Univ. Alumni Asscn. 1994–; Chevalier, Ordre Nat. du Mérite (France), Order of Civil Merit Seogryu Medal (Korea). *Publications:* Economics of Atomic Power 1956, Atomic Power 1960. *Leisure interests:* fishing, Go (traditional Japanese game). *Address:* Japan Atomic Industrial Forum Inc., 1–13 Shimbashi 1-chome, Minato-ku, Tokyo 105-8605 (Office); 5-20, Sakuragaoka 1-chome, Kugenuma, Fujisawa City, Kanagawa, Japan. *Telephone:* 03-3508-2411 (Office); 0466-26-6228 (Home).

MORI, Taisuke: Japanese steel industry executive; b. 11 Nov. 1920, Tokyo, Japan; s. of the late Yoshitaro Mori and Chie Mori; m. Kikuko Sakashita 1959; two s. one d.; ed. Tokyo Univ. of Commerce and Industry (Hitotsubashi Univ.); Trade Corpn. of Japan (Govt. Agency for Foreign Trade) 1943–46; Ministry of Int. Trade and Industry 1946–50; Kinoshita & Co. Ltd. (Domestic and Int. Tradings) 1951–65; Kobe Steel Ltd. 1965–, Dir. of Bd., Gen. Man., Industrial Machinery Div. 1972–77, Sr. Man. Dir. Machinery Group 1977–79, Exec. Vice-Pres. Machinery Group and Marketing Activities 1979–83, Dir. 1983–, Exec. Vice-Chair. and Sr. Adviser 1983–87; Dir. Heninschfeger Industries Inc. (Exec. Vice-Chair. 1983–87, Sr. Advisor 1987–), Heninschfeger Corpn.; Chair. Steel Castings and Forgings Asscn. of Japan; Vice-Chair. Japan Industrial Machinery Mfrs.' Asscn.; lecturer Int. Univ. of Japan; Medal with Blue Ribbon (related to trade promotion and public services). *Publications:* many articles in magazines and newspapers. *Leisure interests:* golf, fishing, tourism. *Address:* 4-12-17 Shinoharakita-machi, Nadaku, Kobe 657, Japan. *Telephone:* 078-882-0600 (Home).

MORI, Yoshiro; Japanese politician; b. 14 July 1937; m. Chieko Mori; one s.. one d.; ed. Waseda Univ.; with Sankei Newspapers, Tokyo 1960–62; mem. House of Reps, for Ishikawa Pref. Dist. 1 1969–96, Dist. 2 1996–; Deputy Dir.-Gen. Prime Minister's Office 1975–76; Deputy Chief Cabinet Sec. 1977–78; Dir. Educ. Div., Policy Research Council, Liberal Democratic Party (LDP) 1978–81, Deputy Sec. Gen. LDP 1978–79, 1984–85, Chair. Special Cttee. on Educational Reform, Policy Research Council 1984–87, Acting Chair. Policy Research Council 1986, Acting Chair. Gen. Council 1986–87, Chair. Nat. Org. Cttee. 1987–88, Chair. Research Comm. on Educational System, Policy Research Council 1989–91, Chair. Policy Research Council 1991–92, Sec. Gen. LDP 1993–95, Chair. Gen. Council 1996–98, Sec. Gen. LDP 1998–; Chair. Standing Cttee. on Finance, House of Reps. 1981–82, on Rules and Admin. 1991; Minister of Educ. 1983–84, of Int. Trade and Ind. 1992–93, of Construction 1995–96. *Address:* 4-9-16, Seta, Setagaya-ku, Tokyo, Japan.

MORIKAWA, Kosuke, PH.D.; Japanese scientist; b. 28 Sept. 1942, Tokyo; m. Keiko Tanaka 1966; ed. Koyamadai High School, Tokyo Univ.; instructor Tokyo Univ. 1971–75, research assoc. Aarhus Univ., Denmark 1975–77, MRC Lab. of Molecular Biology, Cambridge, U.K. 1978–80; instructor Kyoto Univ. 1980–86, Dir. First Dept. Protein Eng. Research Inst. 1986–, Research Dir. Dept. of Structural Biology 1996–. *Leisure interest:* listening to classical music, particularly by Bach and Mozart. *Address:* 1-22-16 Hiyoshidai, Takatsuki, Osaka 569, Japan. *Telephone:* 0726 89 0519.

MORIKAWA, Toshio, LL.B.; Japanese banker; b. 3 March 1933, Tokyo; m. Sawako Morikawa; two d.; ed. Univ. of Tokyo; joined Sumitomo Bank Ltd, 1955, Dir. 1980, Man. Dir. 1984, Sr. Man. Dir. 1985, Deputy Pres. 1990, Pres. 1993; Chair. Fed. of Bankers' Asscns. 1994–95. *Leisure interests:* golf, driving. *Address:* c/o Sumitomo Bank Ltd., 1-3-2 Marunouchi, Chiyoda-ku, Chuo-ku, Tokyo 541, Japan. *Telephone:* 03-3282-5111.

MORILLON, Gen. Philippe; French army officer; b. 24 Oct. 1935, Casablanca; m. Anne Appert 1958; three d.; ed. Saint Cyr Mil. Acad.; platoon leader, French Foreign Legion during Algerian war of independence; fmr. Divisional Commdr. of French units stationed in Germany; Deputy Under-Sec. for Int. Relations, Ministry of Defence in late 1980s; Commdr. UN Forces in Bosnia-Herzegovina 1992–93; Adviser on Defence to Govt. of France 1993; Commdr. Force d'Action Rapide 1994–96; numerous decorations. *Publications:* Croire et Oser 1993, Paroles de Soldat 1996. *Address:* Ministère de la Défense, 14 rue Saint-Dominique, 75700 Paris, France.

MORIN, Edgar, L. EN. D.; French scientific researcher; b. 8 July 1921, Paris; s. of Vidal Nahoum and Luna Beressi; m. Edwige Lannegrace; two d.; resistance fighter 1942–44; Head Propaganda Dept., French military government, Germany 1945; Ed.-in-Chief Paris newspaper 1947–50; researcher, C.N.R.S. 1950–, Dir. of Research 1970–93, Dir. Emer. 1993; Dir. Review Arguments 1957–62, Communications 1972–; Dir. Centre d'études transdisciplinaires (sociologie, anthropologie, politique) (Cetsap), of Ecole des hautes études en sciences sociales 1977–93; Prix européen de l'Essai Charles Veillon 1987, Prix média de l'Asscn. des journalistes européens 1992, Prix Internacional Catalunya 1994; Officier Légion d'honneur, Commdr., Ordre des Arts et des Lettres. *Publications include:* L'Homme et la Mort 1951, Le Cinéma ou l'Homme imaginaire 1956, Autocritique 1959, Le Vif du sujet 1969, Le Paradigme perdu: la nature humaine 1973, La méthode (4 vols.) 1977–1991, De la nature de l'URSS 1983, Penser l'Europe 1987, Vidal et les siens 1989, Mes démons 1994, Une Année Sisyphe 1995; numerous other publs. *Leisure interests:* music, theatre, movies, literature. *Address:* 7 rue Saint-Claude, 75003 Paris, France. *Telephone:* (01) 42.78.90.99. *Fax:* (01) 48.04.86.35.

MORIN, Jean, L. EN D.; French civil servant; b. 23 June 1916, Melun; s. of Alexis Morin and Berthe France; m. Janine Lamouroux 1942; one s. two d.; ed. Ecole Libre des Sciences Politiques; Sec.-Gen. Inst. Scientifique des Recherches Economiques et Sociales 1939; Auditeur, Cour des Comptes 1941; Dir. of Personnel, Ministry of the Interior 1944; Prefect, Manche 1946; Deputy Dir. du Cabinet to Pres. of Provisional Govt. 1946, to Minister of Foreign Affairs 1947–48; Tech. Adviser, Minister of the Interior 1948–49; Prefect, Maine-et-Loire 1949; Conseiller Référendaire, Cour des Comptes 1949; Prefect, Haute-Garonne and Extraordinary Insp.-Gen. of Admin. (5th Region) 1958–60; Del.-Gen. in Algeria 1960–62; Sec.-Gen. of Merchant Navy 1962–68; Pres. Ass., Inter-Governmental Maritime Consultative Org. 1962–68; Pres. Société auxiliaire minière du Pacifique (Saumipac) 1968–72, Cie. française industrielle et minière du Pacifique 1969–72; Dir. Publicis S.A. 1970, Vice-Pres. 1972, Dir. Publicis Conseil, Pres. 1972–73, mem. Conseil de Surveillance de Publicis S.A. 1987–90; Pres. Communication et Publicité 1972, Intermarco 1974–84, Comité de surveillance Intermarco (Amsterdam); Chair. and Man. Dir. Régie-Presse 1974–83; Vice-Pres. Comité de surveillance Holding Farner (Zürich); Pres. Inst. de la Mer 1974–97, now Hon. Pres., Acad. de Marine 1990–92; Grand Officier, Légion d'honneur, Croix de guerre, Médaille de la Résistance. *Leisure interests:* history, bridge. *Address:* 19 avenue du Maréchal-Franchet-d'Esperey, 75016 Paris, France. *Telephone:* (1) 46-47-59-10.

MORIN, Roland Louis, L.EN D.; French public servant; b. 6 Sept. 1932, Taza, Morocco; s. Fernand and Emilienne (Carisio) Morin; m. Catherine Roussy 1961; one s. one d.; ed. Lycée Gouraud, Rabat, Faculty of Law and Humanities, Bordeaux and Ecole Nat. d'Administration; Auditor, Audit Office 1960; Asst. to Prime Minister and Chargé de Mission, Algeria 1960–61;

Pvt. Recorder Comm. for Verification of Public Accounts, Asst. to Recorder-Gen. 1964; Tech. Counsellor Louis Joxe Cabinet (Minister of State for Admin. Reform) 1966–67, Edmond Michelet Cabinet (Minister of State for Public Office) 1967-68; Referendary Counsellor Audit Office 1967; Asst. to Prime Minister, Departmental Head for Econ. and Financial Programmes and Affairs 1968; Dir. of Financial Affairs, Gen. Del. for Scientific and Tech. Research 1969, Asst. to Del.-Gen. 1970, Asst. Del.-Gen. 1974, Dir. 1978; rejoined Audit Office 1980; Prof. Inst. d'Etudes Politiques de Paris 1965–90; Chargé de Mission with Jean-Pierre Chevènement (Minister of State, Minister for Research and Tech.) 1981–82, Dir. Gen. Research and Technology, Ministry of Research and Industry 1982–86; Conseiller maître, Cour des comptes 1986, Pres. 1993–; mem. Comité national d'évaluation de la recherche (CNER) 1989–94, Commission nationale des comptes de campagne et des financements politiques (CCFP) 1997–; Officier, Légion d'honneur, Ordre Nat. de Mérite, Chevalier, Palmes Académiques, Mérite Agricole. *Publications:* Les sociétés locales d'économie mixte et leur contrôle 1964, Théorie des grands problèmes économiques contemporains. *Leisure interest:* tennis. *Address:* Cour des comptes, 13 rue Cambon, 75001 Paris (Office); 24 Résidence des Gros-Chênes, 91370 Verrières-le-Buisson, France (Home).

MORINIGO, Gen. Higinio; Paraguayan politician and army officer; b. 1897, Paraguarí; ed. Colegio Nacional and Escuela Militar, Asunción; 2nd Lieut. 1919, served Northern Operational Dept. and 2nd and 3rd Infantry Regts. to 1928; Capt. 1927; War Coll., apptd. Staff Maj. Battn. Commdt. Mil. School 1932; Dir. Reserve School; served Chaco War; fmr. Chief of Staff to C.-in-C., Ministry of War and Marine and Ministry of Interior; Gen. 1943; Pres. of Republic 1940–48; exiled in Argentina 1948–51, Brazil 1951–56; returned to Paraguay 1956, now living in Argentina; Cruz del Chaco, Cruz del Defensor and many other decorations; Dr. h.c. (Fordham and Brazil Univs.). *Address:* Calle General Urguiza 625-Acassuso, Buenos Aires, Argentina. *Telephone:* 792-4823.

MORISHIMA, Michio, M.A., F.B.A.; Japanese professor of economics; b. 18 July 1923, Osaka; s. of Kameji and Tatsuo Morishima; m. Yoko Tsuda 1954; two s. one d.; ed. Univ. of Kyoto; Asst. Prof. Univ. of Kyoto 1950–51; Asst. Prof. and Prof. Univ of Osaka 1951–69; Rockefeller Foundation Fellow, Oxford and Yale Univs. 1956–58; Visiting Sr. Fellow, All Souls Coll., Oxford 1963–64; Prof. Univ. of Essex 1968–70; Sir John Hicks Prof. of Econs. L.S.E. 1984–88 (Prof. of Econs. 1970–84), Prof. Emer. 1988–; mem. Econometric Soc., Pres. 1965; Hon. mem. American Econ. Asscn. 1976; Foreign Hon. mem. American Soc. of Arts and Sciences; Bunka Kunsho 1976. *Publications:* Equilibrium, Stability and Growth 1964, Theory of Economic Growth 1969, The Working of Econometric Models 1972, The Theory of Demand: Real and Monetary 1973, Marx's Economics 1973, The Economic Theory of Modern Society 1975, Walras' Economics 1977, Value, Exploitation and Growth 1978, Why has Japan "succeeded"? 1982, The Economics of Industrial Society 1984, Ricardo's Economics 1989, Capital and Credit 1992, Dynamic Economic Theory 1996. *Address:* London School of Economics and Political Science, 10 Portugal Street, London WC2A 2HD (Office); Ker, 31 Greenway, Hutton Mount, Brentwood, Essex, CM13 2NP, England (Home). *Telephone:* 0171-405 7686 (Office).

MORISSETTE, Alanis; Canadian rock singer and songwriter; b. 1 June 1974, Ottawa; acted in TV serial You Can't Do That on Television aged 10; signed contract as songwriter with MCA Publishing aged 14, recorded two albums for MCA's recording division; moved to Toronto, later to L.A., U.S.A. *Albums include:* Jagged Little Pill (co-written with Glen Ballard; 16 million (copies sold worldwide); numerous awards including Brit Award for Best Int. Newcomer, four Grammy Awards including Album of the Year and Best Rock Album, Best Female Award, MTV European Music Awards 1996. *Address:* Maverick Music Co., 8000 Beverly Boulevard, Los Angeles, CA 90048, U.S.A.

MORITA, Akio; Japanese business executive; b. 26 Jan. 1921, Nagoya; s. of S. Kyuzaemon and Shuko (Toda) Morita; m. Yoshiko Kamei 1950; two s. one d.; ed. Osaka Imperial Univ.; Co-Founder Tokyo Tsushin Kogyo K.K. (Tokyo Telecommunications Eng. Corpn.) 1946 (became Sony Corpn. 1958), Exec. Man. Dir. 1958–59, Exec. Vice-Pres. 1959–71, Pres. 1971–76, Chair. and C.E.O. 1976–89, Chair. of Bd. 1989–94, Hon. Chair. 1994–; Pres. Sony Corpn., America 1960–66, Chair. of Bd. 1966–74, Pres. 1968–71, Chair. of Finance Cttee. 1977–81; Chair. Exec. Cttee. Sony Corpn. of America 1974–77, 1981–94; Dir. IBM World Trade Americas/Far East Corpn. 1972–77; Dir. Pan American World Airways Inc. 1980; Vice-Chair. Keidanren (Japan Fed. of Econ. Orgs.) 1986–92, Vice-Chair. Bd. of Councillors 1992–94; Hon. Chair. Council for Better Corp Citizenship 1995– (Chair. 1988–95); Chair. Japan Int. Training Co-operation Org. 1991–95; Vice-Chair. Keizai Koho Center (Inst. for Social and Econ. Affairs), 1992–94; Chair. Japan-U.S. Business Council 1993–94, Foreign Investment in Japan Devt. Inc. 1993–; Japan Chair. Trilateral Comm. 1992–; Hon. mem. I.E.E.E.; Hon. LL.D. (Williams Coll.) 1982, (Univ. of Pa.) 1990; Hon. D.Eng. (Illinois) 1993; Albert Medal, Royal Soc. of Arts 1982, Int. Award, Inst. of Mfg. Engineers 1991, I.E.E.E. Founder's Medal 1994; Légion d'honneur 1984, Commdr.'s Cross, Order of Merit (Fed. Repub. of Germany) 1987, Hon. K.B.E. and numerous other int. distinctions. *Publications:* Gakureki Muyouron 1966, Shin Zitsuryoku Shugi (with Shintano Ishihara, q.v.) 1969, Made in Japan 1986, The Japan that Can Say No (with Shintano Ishihara) 1989. *Leisure interests:* listening to music, playing golf. *Address:* Sony Corporation, 6-7-35, Kitashinagawa 6-chome, Shinagawa-ku, Tokyo 141, Japan. *Telephone:* 03-5448-2111.

MORITS, Yunna Petrovna; Russian poet; b. 2 June 1937, Kiev; m. Yuri Grigor'yevich Vasil'yev; one s.; ed. Gorky Literary Inst.; began publishing poetry 1954; taken part in int. poetry festivals London, Cambridge, Toronto etc.; has made solo singing recordings; mem. Russian PEN, Int. Fed. of Journalists, Russian Acad. of Natural Sciences. *Publications:* nine collections of poetry (trans. in many languages), including The Vine 1970, With Unbleached Thread 1974, By Light of Life 1977, The Third Eye 1980, Selected Poems 1982, The Blue Flame 1985, On This High Shore 1987, In the Den of Voice 1990, A Bunch of Cats 1997 and 6 books for children, including The Great Secret for a Small Company 1987; poems appeared in journal Oktyabr 1993–97; also short stories, essays, scripts for animated cartoons. *Leisure interests:* painting and drawing. *Address:* Astrakhansky per. 5, Apt. 76, 129010 Moscow, Russia. *Telephone:* (095) 280-08-16.

MORIYAMA, Raymond, O.C., M.ARCH, F.R.A.I.C., M.C.I.P., R.C.A., F.R.S.A.; Canadian architect and planner; b. 11 Oct. 1929, Vancouver; s. of John Michi and Nobuko Moriyama; m. Sachiko Miyauchi 1954; three s. two d.; ed. Univ. of Toronto, McGill Univ.; Raymond Moriyama Architects and Planners 1958–70; partner, Moriyama and Teshima Architects 1970–, Prin. 1980–; winner int. competition for Nat. Saudi Arabian Museum, Riyadh 1996; Design Tutor, Univ. of Toronto 1961–63; Chair. Ecological Research Ltd. 1970; Chair. Mid-Canada Conf., Task Force on Environmental and Ecological Factors 1969–70; mem. Bd. and Life mem. Royal Canadian Inst.; Dir. Canadian Guild of Crafts 1973–75; mem. of Council, Ont. Coll. of Arts 1972–73; mem. Advisory Cttee., MBA Programme in Arts Admin., York Univ. 1982; founding mem. Asia Pacific Foundation of Canada 1982; mem. Bd., Multilingual TV; mem. Bd. of Trustees, Royal Ont. Museum; mem. Council's Advisory Cttee., N. York Gen. Hosp.; Fellow Toronto Soc. of Architects 1998; eight hon. doctorates including Univ. of Toronto, McGill Univ., York Univ.; Civic Awards of Merit (Toronto and Scarborough), Governor-General's Medal for Architecture (four times), P.A. Award 1989, Toronto Arts Award 1990, Order of Ont. 1992, Gold Medal, Royal Architectural Inst. of Canada 1997, Best Architect in Toronto Award 1997, 1998, and many other awards. *Leisure interest:* sailing. *Publications:* Great American Goose Egg Co. (Canada) Ltd., The Global Living System and Mid-Canada Task Force Committee on Ecological and Environmental Factors 1970, Can Your Life Become a Work of Art 1975, The Satisfactory City: The Survival of Urbanity 1975, Into God's Temple of Eternity, Drive a Nail of Gold, TANT—Time, Appropriateness, Nature and Transition 1982, Architect as Nature's Collaborator (lecture at McGill Univ.) 1996. *Leisure interests:* fishing, sailing. *Address:* 32 Davenport Road, Toronto, Ont. M5R 1H3, Canada. *Telephone:* (416) 925-4484. *Fax:* (416) 925-4736.

MORIZET, Jacques, L. ÈS L.; French diplomatist; b. 7 March 1921, Saint Mauré; m. Aline Reyss 1948; three s. one d.; ed. Lycée Voltaire, Paris, Sorbonne, Paris, Ecole Nat. d'Admin.; served UN Dept., Ministry of Foreign Affairs 1949–52, German Affairs High Comm. 1952–54, Secr.-Gen. of the Ministry 1954–56; First Sec., Bonn 1956, Second Counsellor 1959; Sec.-Gen.'s Chef du Cabinet 1960–61; Deputy Spokesman of Ministry 1961–62; Dir. of Information Office 1962–63; First Counsellor, Washington 1963–67; Deputy Dir. African Affairs 1967–69; Minister-Counsellor, Rome 1969–72; Embassy Minister, Bonn 1972–75; Amb. to Iraq 1975–80, to Morocco 1980–82, to Fed. Repub. of Germany 1982–86; Ambassadeur de France 1986; Vice-Pres. State Cttee. on Nat. Defence; State Rep. on Bd. of Total/CFP; mem. Haut Conseil franco-allemand de la culture (Sec.-Gen. 1988–), Conseil d'administration d'Euro France Berlin 1988–; Commr. pour la présence française à la foire internationale du livre de Francfort 1989–; Pres. Associaton des Amis de la Bibliothèque de France 1990, Hon. Pres. 1994; Officier Légion d'honneur, Commandeur Ordre du Mérite, Croix de guerre 1939–45, Chevalier du mérite agricole, several foreign decorations. *Publications:* articles and numerous lectures. *Address:* 4 rue Michel Ange, 75016 Paris, France. *Telephone:* 42.88.31.85.

MØRK, Truls; Norwegian cellist; b. 25 April 1961, Bergen; s. of John Mørk and Turid Otterbech; one s.; studied under his father, with Frans Helmerson at Swedish Radio Music School, in Austria with Heinrich Schiff and in Moscow with Natalia Schakowskaya; works closely with Oslo Philharmonic Orchestra under Mariss Jansons; debut, BBC Promenade Concerts 1989; has since appeared with leading European, American and Australian orchestras; regular appearances at int. chamber music festivals; recordings include Dvorak and Shostakovich cello concertos, Haydn concertos with Norwegian Chamber Orchestra, Britten cello suites and recital discs of works by Grieg, Sibelius, Brahms, Rachmaninov and Myaskovksy; prizewinner, Moscow Tchaikovsky Competititon 1982; First Prize, Cassado Cello Competition, Florence 1983, W. Naumburg Competition, New York 1986; UNESCO Prize, European Radio-Union Competition, Bratislava. *Address:* c/o Harrison/Parrott, 12 Penzance Place, London, W11 4PA, England. *Telephone:* 0171-229 9166. *Fax:* 0171-221 5042.

MORLEY, Malcolm, A.R.C.A.; British artist; b. 1931, London; ed. Royal Coll. of Art and Camberwell School of Arts and Crafts, London; one-man exhbns. in New York, Paris, Amsterdam, Cologne, Toronto, Zurich, London, etc.; numerous group exhbns. throughout U.S.A. and Europe; "Malcolm Morley", major retrospective exhbn. organized by Whitechapel Art Gallery, London, travelled to Kunsthalle, Basle, Museum Boymans-van Beuningen, Rotterdam, Whitechapel Art Gallery, London, Corcoran Gallery of Art, Washington D.C., Museum of Contemporary Art, Chicago and Brooklyn Museum,

New York 1983–84; many solo exhbns. in Europe, Canada, U.S.A.; 1st Annual Turner Prize, The Tate Gallery, London 1984, 1991.

MORO, Vincenzo; Italian industrial executive; b. 26 Jan. 1922, Sartirana Lomellina, Pavia; s. of Paolo Moro and Carmelita Gei; m. Gianna Tagliabue 1948; one s. one d.; with Naclon Farmaceutici 1937; joined Filotecnica Salmoiraghi 1939, Sales Dir. 1954–59; Deputy Dir. Alfa Romeo S.p.A. 1959, Special Affairs Dir. 1960, Sales Dir. 1962, Deputy Gen. Man. 1969, Man. Dir. and Gen. Man. 1974–78; Chair. Alfa Romeo Int. S.A. 1978–80, Autodelta 1975–78, Termomeccanica S.p.A. 1978–83, Italgel S.p.A. 1979–80, Frendo Abex S.p.A. 1983–90, Aerimpianti S.p.A. 1980–94, Abex Equipment S.A. 1988–89, Abex Industries S.A. 1988–91, Abex Rail S.A. 1989–90; Vice-Pres. Fiat Diesel do Brasil S.A. 1977–79; mem. Bd. Aerospace Industries Asscn. of Italy 1953–74, Automotive Industries Asscn. of Italy 1968–78, Ducati Meccanica S.p.A. 1980–83, Fonderies B. Piret S.A. 1989–90, IGM S.p.A. (Waste Man. Group) 1990–92, Turisanda S.p.A. 1990–; Vice-Chair. E.E.C. Euroglaces Asscn. 1980; Chair. Fed. European Mfrs. of Friction Materials 1987. *Address:* Via delle Magnolie 2, Appiano Gentile (CO), Italy. *Telephone:* (031) 930830.

MOROCCO, King of (see Hassan II).

MOROSS, Manfred David, B.SC., M.B.A.; business executive; b. 30 Aug. 1931; s. of Dr. H. and A. Moross; m. Edna Fay Jacobson 1956; three s. one d.; ed. Witwatersrand and Harvard Univs.; Dir. Whitehall Financial Group, New York, Whitehall Investment Corpn., New York, Siem Industries Inc., Bermuda. *Leisure interests:* tennis, reading. *Address:* 1 Derry Street, London, W8 5NN (Office); 7 Princes Gate, London, S.W.7, England (Home). *Telephone:* 0171-591 8015 (Office); 0171-589 9020 (Home). *Fax:* 0171-938 1393.

MOROZ, Oleksandr Oleksandrovich; Ukrainian politician; b. 29 Feb. 1944, Buda, Kiev Region; m.; two d.; trained as engineer in Kiev; engineer and mechanic in state farm professional school, dist. and regional enterprises of Selkhoztechnika; sec. regional trade union, First Sec. Dist. CP Cttee.; Head of Agric. Div. Regional CP Cttee.; People's Deputy of Ukrainian S.S.R. (later of Ukraine); one of founders Socialist Party of Ukraine 1991; Chair. Verkhovna Rada (Parl.) 1994–98. *Publications:* author and co-author of a number of legal projects including Code on Land; Where Are We Going?, Choice, Subjects for Meditation and articles. *Address:* Office of the Chairman, Verkhovna Rada, M. Hrushevskoho 5, 252019 Kiev, Ukraine. *Telephone:* (44) 226-28-25, 293-23-15.

MOROZOV, Oleg Viktorovich; Russian politician; b. 5 Nov. 1953, Kazan; m.; one d.; ed. Kazan State Univ.; docent, mem. Int. Acad. of Books and Book Art; Head of Div. Tatar Regional CP Cttee. 1987–89; instructor, asst. to Sec., CPSU Cen. Cttee. 1989–91; consultant, Office of U.S.S.R. Pres. 1991–92; Deputy Dir.-Gen., Biotekhnologiya; Tatarstan mem. State Duma 1993–; mem. Deputies' group New Regional Politics 1994–96; Deputy Chair. Deputies' group Russian Regions 1997–. *Leisure interests:* collecting toy hippopotamuses, serious classical music. *Address:* State Duma, Okhotny ryad 1, 103265 Moscow, Russia. *Telephone:* (095) 292 6788 (Office).

MOROZOV, Vladimir Mikhailovich; Russian opera singer (bass); b. 12 Nov. 1933; ed. Leningrad Conservatory; soloist with Kirov (now Mariinsky) Opera 1959–; mem. CPSU 1965–91; Glinka Prize 1974, U.S.S.R. State Prize 1976; R.S.F.S.R. People's Artist 1976; U.S.S.R. People's Artist 1981. *Roles include:* Varlaam (Boris Godunov), Ivan the Terrible (The Women from Pskov), Grigory (Quiet Flows the Don), Peter the Great (Peter I), Dosifey (Khovanshchina). *Address:* c/o Mariinsky Theatre, Teatralnaya pl. 1, St. Petersburg, Russia.

MORRICE, Norman Alexander; British choreographer; b. 10 Sept. 1931, Agua Dulce, Mexico; s. of Norman Morrice and Helen Vickers; ed. Rambert School of Ballet; joined Ballet Rambert as dancer 1952, Prin. Dancer 1958, Asst. Dir. 1966–70, Dir. 1970–74; freelance choreographer 1974–77; Dir. Royal Ballet Co. 1977–86, Dir. Royal Ballet Choreographic Group 1987–96, Head Choreographic Studies, Royal Ballet School 1987–; first success as choreographer with Two Brothers 1958; second ballet Hazaña (première, Sadler's Wells Theatre, London) 1958; ballet Hazard, Bath Festival 1967; 10 new ballets for Ballet Rambert by 1968; Elizabeth II Coronation Award for services to British ballet; *Ballets include:* 1-2-3, Them and Us, Pastorale Variée, Ladies, Ladies!, Spindrift. *Leisure interests:* literature, music, films. *Address:* c/o Royal Opera House, Covent Garden, London, W.C.2, England. *Telephone:* 0171-240 1200.

MORRICONE, Ennio; Italian film score composer; b. 10 Nov. 1928, Rome; s. of Mario Morricone and Libera Morricone; m. Maria Travia; two s. two d.; ed. Acad. of Santa Cecilia, Rome. *Film scores include:* The Federal, The Basilisks, For a Handful of Dollars (Silver Ribbon Award), For a Few Dollars More, The Good, Bad and the Ugly, Once Upon a Time in the West, Battle of Algiers, Partner, China is Near, Teorema, Decameron, Investigation of a Senior Citizen Above Suspicion, Orca, 1900, The Five Man Army, Fraulein Doktor, The Guns of San Sebastian, A Fine Pair, Pardon, Let's Make Love, Once Upon a Time in the Country, Escalation, Grazie Zia, The Harem, La Cage aux Folles I, II & III, The Mission, The Untouchables, Cinema Paradiso, Casualties of War, Frantic, Hamlet, Bugsy, City of Joy, The Bachelor, In the Line of Fire, A Pure Formality, Frantic, Cinema Paradiso, Wolf, Disclosure, Love Affair, Lolita. *Address:* c/o Piazza SS. Giovanni e Paolo 8, 00184 Rome, Italy.

MORRILL, John Stephen, D.PHIL., F.B.A.; British historian and academic; b. 12 June 1946, Manchester; s. of William Henry Morrill and Marjorie Morrill (née Ashton); m. Frances Mead 1968; four d.; ed. Altrincham Grammar School, Trinity Coll. Oxford; Research Fellow, Trinity Coll. Oxford 1970–74; lecturer in History, Univ. of Stirling 1974–75; Fellow Selwyn Coll. Cambridge 1975–, Sr. Tutor 1989–92, Vice-Master 1994–; Lecturer in History, Cambridge Univ. 1975–92, Reader in Early Modern History 1992–; mem. Council, Royal Historical Soc. 1988–92, Vice-Pres. 1992–96. *Publications:* Cheshire 1630–1660 1974, The Revolt of the Provinces 1976, Reactions to the English Civil War 1981, Oliver Cromwell and the English Revolution 1989, The Impact of the English Civil War 1991, Revolution and Restoration 1992, The Nature of the English Revolution 1992, The British Problem 1534–1707 1996, The Oxford Illustrated History of Tudor and Stuart Britain 1996; 40 articles in learned journals. *Leisure interests:* music, theology, beer. *Address:* Selwyn College, Cambridge, CB3 9DQ (Office); 1 Bradford's Close, Bottisham, Cambridge, CB5 9DW, England (Home). *Telephone:* (01223) 335895 (Office); (01223) 811822 (Home). *Fax:* (01223) 335837.

MORRIS, Christopher, F.C.A.; British chartered accountant; b. 28 April 1942; m. Isabel Ramsden (divorced); two s.; ed. Ampleforth Coll.; articled clerk, Bernard Phillips; qualified 1967; partner Touche Ross & Co. (later Deloitte and Touche) 1970; Nat. Dir. Corp. Special Services 1975, Chair. 1992, now Sr. Partner Corp. Recovery; specialises in insolvency; cases have included liquidation of Laker Airways 1982, British Island Airways, British Air Ferries, Rush & Tompkins, London & County Securities, Polly Peck Int., Bank of Credit and Commerce International (BCCI). *Address:* Hill House, Little New Street, London, EC4A 3TR, England.

MORRIS, Derek James, M.A., D.PHIL.; British economist; b. 23 Dec. 1945, Harrow; s. of Denis William Morris and Olive Margaret Morris; m. Susan Mary Whittles 1975; two s.; ed. Harrow Co. Grammar School, St. Edmund Hall and Nuffield Coll., Oxford; Research Fellow Univ. of Warwick 1969–70; Fellow and tutor of Econs. Oriel Coll., Oxford 1970–98; Econ. Dir. Nat. Econ. Devt. Office 1981–84; Chair. Oxford Econ. Forecasting Ltd. 1984–98; mem. Monopolies and Mergers Comm. 1991–95, Deputy Chair. 1995–98, Chair. 1998–. *Publications include:* The Economic System in the UK. (ed.) 1971, Industrial Economics and Organisation (with D. Hay) 1985, Chinese State-Owned Enterprises and Economic Reform 1994, numerous journal articles on economics. *Leisure interests:* skiing, badminton. *Address:* Monopolies and Mergers Commission, 48 Carey Street, London, WC2A 2JT, England. *Telephone:* 0171-324 1467. *Fax:* 0171-324 1400.

MORRIS, Desmond John, D.PHIL.; British zoologist; b. 24 Jan. 1928, Purton, Wilts.; s. of Capt. Harry Howe and Marjorie (née Hunt) Morris; m. Ramona Joy Baulch 1952; one s.; ed. Dauntsey's School, Wilts., Birmingham Univ. and Oxford Univ.; Head of Granada TV and Film Unit at Zoological Soc. of London 1956–59; Curator of Mammals at Zoological Soc. of London 1959–67; Dir. Inst. of Contemporary Arts, London 1967–68; Research Fellow at Wolfson Coll., Oxford 1973–81; now privately engaged in writing books on animal and human behaviour. *Television:* Zootime (Granada) 1956–67, Life in the Animal World (BBC) 1965–67, The Human Race (Thames TV) 1982, The Animals Roadshow (BBC) 1987–89, The Animal Contract 1989, Animal Country 1991–95, The Human Animal 1994, The Human Sexes 1997. *Publications:* The Ten-spined Stickleback 1958, The Biology of Art 1962, The Mammals: A Guide to the Living Species 1965, Men and Snakes (with Ramona Morris) 1965, Men and Apes (with Ramona Morris) 1966, Men and Pandas (with Ramona Morris) 1966, Primate Ethology (Editor) 1967, The Naked Ape 1967, The Human Zoo 1969, Patterns of Reproductive Behaviour 1970, Intimate Behaviour 1971, Manwatching: A Field-Guide to Human Behaviour 1977, Gestures, Their Origins and Distribution 1979, Animal Days (autobiography) 1979, The Giant Panda 1981, The Soccer Tribe 1981, Inrock (fiction) 1983, The Book of Ages 1983, The Art of Ancient Cyprus 1985, Bodywatching 1985, The Illustrated Naked Ape 1986, Dogwatching 1986, Catwatching 1986, The Secret Surrealist 1987, Catlore 1987, The Animals Roadshow 1988, Horsewatching 1988, The Animal Contract 1990, Animal-Watching 1990, Babywatching 1991, Christmas Watching 1992, The World of Animals 1993, The Naked Ape Trilogy 1994, The Human Animal 1994, Body Talk: A World Guide to Gestures 1994, The Illustrated Catwatching 1994, Illustrated Babywatching 1995, Catworld; A Feline Encyclopedia 1996, Illustrated Dogwatching 1996, The Human Sexes 1997, Illustrated Horse-Watching 1998. *Leisure interests:* painting and archaeology. *Address:* c/o Jonathan Cape, 20 Vauxhall Bridge Road, London, SW1V 2SA, England.

MORRIS, James (Humphry) (see Morris, Jan).

MORRIS, James Peppler; American opera singer; b. 10 Jan. 1947; s. of James Morris and Geraldine Peppler; m. 1st Joanne F. Vitali 1971; one d.; m. 2nd Susan Quittmeyer 1987; one s. one d. (twins); ed. Univ. of Maryland, Peabody Conservatory and Acad. of Vocal Arts; debut at Metropolitan Opera, New York 1970; opera and concert appearances throughout U.S.A., Canada, S. America, Europe and Australia; recordings include Wotan in the New Ring Cycles. *Address:* c/o Colbert Artists Management Inc., 111 West 57th Street, New York, N.Y. 10019, U.S.A.

MORRIS, Jan, M.A. F.R.S.L.; British writer; b. 2 Oct. 1926; editorial staff The Times 1951–56, editorial staff The Guardian 1957–62; Commonwealth Fellowship, U.S.A. 1954; George Polk Memorial Award for Journalism (U.S.A.) 1961; mem. Yr Academi Gymreig; Hon. Fellow, Univ. Coll. Wales;

Hon. F.R.I.B.A.; Dr. h.c. (Univ. of Wales), (Univ. of Glamorgan); Heinemann Award for Literature 1961. *Publications:* (as James Morris) Coast to Coast 1956, Sultan in Oman 1957, The Market of Seleukia 1957, Coronation Everest 1958, South African Winter 1958, The Hashemite Kings 1959, Venice 1960, The Upstairs Donkey (for children) 1962, The Road to Huddersfield 1963, Cities 1963, The Presence of Spain 1964, Oxford 1965, Pax Britannica 1968, The Great Port 1970, Places 1972, Heaven's Command 1973, Farewell the Trumpets 1978; (as Jan Morris) Conundrum 1974, Travels 1976, The Oxford Book of Oxford 1978, Spain 1979, Destinations, The Venetian Empire, My Favourite Stories of Wales, 1980, The Small Oxford Book of Wales, Wales The First Place, A Venetian Bestiary, Spectacle of Empire 1982, Stones of Empire 1983, Journeys 1984, The Matter of Wales 1984, Among the Cities 1985, Last Letters from Hav 1985, Stones of Empire: The Buildings of the Raj 1986, Scotland, The Place of Visions 1986, Manhattan, '45 1987, Hong Kong: Xianggang 1988, Pleasures of a Tangled Life 1989, Ireland Your Only Place 1990, O Canada 1992, Sydney 1992, Locations 1992, Travels with Virginia Woolf (ed.) 1993, A Machynlleth Triad 1994, Fisher's Face 1995, 50 Years of Europe 1997, Wales: Epic Heirs of a Small Country 1999. *Address:* Trefan Morys, Llanystumdwy, Gwynedd, LL52 0LP, Wales. *Telephone:* (01766) 522222. *Fax:* (01766) 522426.

MORRIS, Rt. Hon. John, P.C., Q.C., M.P., LL.D.; British politician and barrister; b. 5 Nov. 1931, Aberystwyth; s. of the late D. W. Morris; m. Margaret M. Lewis J.P. 1959; three d.; ed. Ardwyn, Aberystwyth, Univ. Coll. of Wales, Aberystwyth, Gonville and Caius Coll., Cambridge, and Acad. of Int. Law, The Hague; commissioned Royal Welch Fusiliers and Welch Regt.; Called to Bar, Gray's Inn 1954, Bencher 1985; Labour M.P. for Aberavon Oct. 1959–; Parl. Sec. Ministry of Power 1964–66; Jt. Parl. Sec. Ministry of Transport 1966–68; Minister of Defence for Equipment 1968–70; Sec. of State for Wales 1974–79; a Recorder, Crown Court 1982–; Legal Affairs and Shadow Attorney Gen. 1983–97; Attorney Gen. May 1997–; fmr. Deputy Gen. Sec. and Legal Adviser, Farmers' Union of Wales; mem. U.K. Del., Consultative Assembly, Council of Europe and Western European Union 1963–64; mem. Cttee. of Privileges 1994–97, Select Cttee. on Implementation of the Nolan Report 1995–97; Chair. Nat. Pneumoconiosis Jt. Cttee. 1964–66, Nat. Road Safety Advisory Council 1967–68, Jt. Review of Finances and Man. British Railways 1966–67; mem. N. Atlantic Assembly 1970–74; mem. Courts of Univ. Colls., Aberystwyth, Swansea and Cardiff. *Address:* House of Commons, London, SW1A 0AA, England.

MORRIS, Mark William; American choreographer and dancer; b. 29 Aug. 1956, Seattle, Wash.; s. of William Morris and Maxine Crittenden Morris; Artistic Dir. Mark Morris Dance Group 1980–; Dir. of Dance, Théâtre Royal de la Monnaie, Brussels 1988–91; co-f. White Oak Dance Project (with Mikhail Baryshnikov, q.v.) 1990; performed with various dance cos. including Lar Lubovitch Dance Co., Hannah Kahn Dance Co., Laura Dean Dancers and Musicians, Eliot Feld Ballet and Koleda Balkan Dance Ensemble; created over 70 works for Mark Morris Dance Group including Mythologies 1986, L'Allegro, il Penseroso ed il Moderato 1988, Dido and Aeneas 1989, Nutcracker 1991, Lucky Charms 1994, Rondo 1994, The Office 1994; has created dances for many other ballet cos. including San Francisco Ballet, Paris Opera Ballet, and American Theatre Ballet; Guggenheim Fellowship 1986; Fellow MacArthur Foundation 1991; New York Dance and Performance Award 1984, 1990. *Address:* Mark Morris Dance Group, 225 Lafayette Street, Suite 504, New York, NY 10012, U.S.A. *Telephone:* (212) 219-3660.

MORRIS, Michael Jeremy, M.A.; British performing arts producer; b. 30 March 1958, London; s. of Lawrence Morris and Monica Morris; m. Sarah Culshaw 1991; one s. one d.; ed. Oundle School, Keble Coll. Oxford and City Univ. London; Assoc. Dir. of Theatre, ICA 1981–84, Dir. of Performing Arts 1984–87; mem. Drama and Dance Panel, British Council 1984–90; founding Dir. Cultural Industry Ltd. (presenting and producing contemporary theatre, music and dance) 1987–; Co.-Dir. The Artangel Trust (commissioning outstanding artists to create new work) 1991–; Dir. first production and co-author of libretto of Michael Nyman's opera The Man Who Mistook His Wife for a Hat 1986; Dir. first production and author of libretto of Mike Westbrook's opera Coming Through Slaughter 1994. *Leisure interests:* world music, fine wine, foreign food, popular art. *Address:* 36 St. John's Lane, London, EC1M 4BJ, England. *Telephone:* 0171-336 6781. *Fax:* 0171 336-6782.

MORRIS, Sir Peter John, Kt., M.B., B.S., PH.D., F.R.C.S., F.R.C.A.S., F.A.C.S.; Australian professor of surgery; b. 17 April 1934, Horsham, Vic.; s. of Stanley Henry Morris and Mary Lois (née Hennessy) Morris; m. Jocelyn Mary Gorman 1960; three s. two d.; ed. Univ. of Melbourne; Resident Surgical Officer, St. Vincent's Hosp. 1958–61; Surgical Registrar, Southampton Gen. Hosp., U.K. 1963–64; Clinical Assoc. and Fellow, Mass. Gen. Hosp., Boston, U.S.A. 1964–66; Asst. Prof. of Surgery, Medical Coll., Richmond, Va., U.S.A. 1967; Dir. Tissue Transplantation Labs., Univ. of Melbourne, Australia 1968–74, Reader in Surgery 1971–74; Consultant Surgeon, Lymphona Clinic, Cancer Inst., Melbourne 1969–74; Nuffield Prof. of Surgery, Univ. of Oxford, U.K. 1974–, Dir. Oxford Transplant Centre; Pres. The Transplantation Soc. 1984–86, European Surgical Assсn. 1996–, Vice-Chair. Clinical Medicine Bd., Univ. of Oxford 1982–84; Scientific mem. MRC, London 1983–87; Ed. Transplantation 1979–; Fellow, Balliol Coll., Univ. of Oxford 1974–; mem. UFC 1989–92, Council, Royal Coll. of Surgeons of England; Selwyn Smith Prize (Australia). *Publications:* Kidney Transplantation 1978, Tissue Transplantation 1982, Transient Ischaemic Attacks 1982, Progress in Transplantation 1984, Oxford Textbook of Surgery (with R. Malt) 1993. *Leisure interests:* golf, tennis. *Address:* Nuffield Department of Surgery, John Radcliffe Hospital, Headington, Oxford, OX3 9DU (Office); 19 Lucerne Road, Oxford, OX2 7QB, England (Home). *Telephone:* (01865) 221297 (Office).

MORRIS, Richard Graham Michael, M.A., D.PHIL., F.R.S.E., F.R.S.; British neuroscientist; b. 27 June 1948, Worthing; s. of Robert Morris and Edith Morris; m. Hilary Ann Lewis 1985; two d.; ed. Cambridge and Sussex Univs.; lecturer in Psychology Univ. of St. Andrews 1977–86, MRC Research Fellow 1983–86; Reader, then Prof. of Neuroscience Univ. of Edin. 1986–, Dir. Centre for Neuroscience 1993–97, Chair. Dept. of Neuroscience 1998–; Chair. Brain Research Assсn. 1991–95; Sec. Experimental Psychology Soc. 1983–87; mem. MRC Neuroscience Research Grants Cttee. 1983–87, Neuroscience and Mental Health Bd. 1993–97; Fellow Acad. of Medical Sciences 1998–; Decade of the Brain Lecturer 1998. *Publications:* scientific papers on neural mechanisms of memory. *Leisure interest:* sailing. *Address:* Department of Neuroscience, University of Edinburgh, 1 George Square, Edin., EH8 9JZ, Scotland. *Telephone:* (0131) 650 3520. *Fax:* (0131) 650 6530.

MORRIS, Richard Keith, B.PHIL., M.A., F.S.A.; British archaeologist; b. 8 Oct. 1947; s. of John Richard Morris and Elsie Myra Wearne; m. Jane Whiteley 1972; two s. one d.; ed. Denstone Coll., Staffs., Pembroke Coll., Oxford and Univ. of York; musician 1971–72; Resident Asst. York Minster Archaeological Office 1972–75; Churches Officer Council for British Archaeology 1975–77, Resident Officer, 1978–88, Dir 1991–; Hon. Lecturer School of History, Leeds Univ. 1986–88; Lecturer Dept. of Archaeology, York Univ. 1988–91; Hon. Visiting Prof. York Univ. 1995; Commr. English Heritage 1996–; Frend Medal, Soc. of Antiquaries 1992. *Publications:* Cathedrals and Abbeys of England and Wales 1979, The Church in British Archaeology 1983, Churches in the Landscape 1989, Guy Gibson 1994. *Leisure interests:* music, aviation history, writing. *Address:* Council for British Archaeology, Bowes Morrell House, 111 Walmgate, York, YO1 2UA, England. *Telephone:* (01904) 671417.

MORRIS, William (Bill), F.R.S.A.; British trade union official; b. 19 Oct. 1938, Jamaica; s. of William Morris and Una Morris; m. Minetta Morris 1957 (died 1990); two s.; ed. in Jamaica; Dist. Officer, Transport & Gen. Workers' Union (TGWU), Nottingham 1973, Dist. Sec. Northampton 1977, Nat. Sec. Passenger Services 1979–85, Deputy Gen. Sec. TGWU 1986–92, Gen. Sec. 1992–; mem. TUC Gen. Council 1988–; mem. Comm. for Racial Equality 1977–87, IBA Gen. Advisory Council 1981–86, ITF Exec. Bd. 1986–, Prince of Wales Youth Business Trust 1987–90, BBC Gen. Advisory Council 1987–88, Employment Appeals Tribunal 1988–, Econ. and Social Cttee. EC 1990–, NEDC 1992, Royal Comm. on Lords Reform 1999–; Bd. mem. Project Fullemploy 1985–88; Dir. Unity Trust Bank 1994–; Hon. Fellow City & Guilds 1992; Dr. h.c. (S. Bank Univ.) 1994, (Open Univ.) 1994; Hon. D. Litt. (Westminster) 1998. *Leisure interests:* walking, gardening, watching sports. *Address:* Transport & General Workers' Union, Transport House, 16 Palace Street, London, SW1E 5JD (Office); 156 St. Agnells Lane, Grove Hill, Hemel Hempstead, Herts., HP2 6EG, England. *Telephone:* 0171-828 7788 (Office). *Fax:* 0171-931 7258.

MORRIS, Willie, M.A.; American writer and editor; b. 29 Nov. 1934, Jackson, Miss.; s. of Henry Rae and Marian Weaks Morris; m. 1st Celia Buchan 1958 (divorced 1969); one s.; m. 2nd Jo Anne Shirley Prichard 1991; ed. Yazoo City High School, Miss., Univ. of Texas and New College, Oxford; Ed.-in-Chief The Texas Observer 1960–62; Exec. Ed. Harper's Magazine 1965–67, Ed.-in-Chief 1967–71; Writer-in-Residence Univ. of Miss. 1980–91; Rhodes Scholarship 1956; Fellow, Silliman Coll., Yale Univ.; Houghton-Miflin Literary Fellowship Award 1967; Richard Wright Medal for Literary Excellence; several hon. degrees. *Publications:* The South Today, 100 Years After Appomatox (Ed.) 1966, North Toward Home 1967, Yazoo: Integration in a Deep Southern Town 1971, The Last of the Southern Girls 1973, Good Old Boy 1973, James Jones: A Friendship 1978, The Ghosts of Ole Miss and Other Essays 1981, The Courting of Marcus Dupree, Always Stand in Against the Curve 1983, Homecoming 1989, Good Old Boy and the Witch of Yazoo (children's fiction) 1989, Faulkner's Mississippi 1990, After All, It's Only a Game 1992, New York Days 1993, My Dog Skip 1995, The Ghosts of Medgau Evers 1998; also introductory essay Official Games and Souvenir Program for 1996 Centennial Olympics, Atlanta.

MORRISON, James Douglas, A.O., D.SC., PH.D., F.A.A., F.R.S.E., F.R.A.C.I.; Australian mass spectrometrist; b. 9 Nov. 1924, Glasgow, Scotland; s. of James K. Morrison and Rose Ann Wheeler; m. Christine B. Mayer 1947; three s.; ed. Lenzie Acad., Scotland and Univ. of Glasgow; Instructor Dept. of Chem. Univ. of Glasgow 1946–48; Research Officer, CSIRO 1949, Chief Research Officer 1965–67; Foundation Prof. of Chem. La Trobe Univ. 1967–90, Prof. Emer 1990–; Resident Head, Chisholm Coll. 1972–77; Adjunct Prof. Univ. of Utah 1975–, Univ. of Delaware 1987–; Commonwealth Fund Fellow, Chicago Univ. 1956–57; Visiting Prof. Princeton Univ. 1964, Univ. of Utah 1971; mem. Council, Royal Soc. of Victoria, Pres. 1975–76; mem. Council, Australian Acad. of Science, Vice-Pres. 1986–87; Rennie and Smith Medals, Royal Australian Chemical Inst. *Publications:* articles in scientific journals. *Leisure interests:* fossil hunting, Byzantine studies. *Address:* 40 Central Avenue, Mooroolbark, Vic. 3138, Australia.

MORRISON, (Philip) Blake, PH.D.; British author; b. 8 Oct. 1950, Lancashire; s. of late Arthur Morrison and Agnes O'Shea; m. Katherine Ann Drake 1976; two s. one d.; Ermysted's Grammar School, Skipton, Nottingham

Univ., McMaster Univ., Univ. Coll. London; Poetry and Fiction Ed., Times Literary Supplement 1978–81; Deputy Literary Ed. The Observer 1981–86, Literary Ed. 1987–89; Literary Ed. The Independent on Sunday 1990–94; freelance writer 1995–; Eric Gregory Prize 1980, Somerset Maugham Prize 1984, Dylan Thomas Prize 1985, E.M. Forster Prize 1987, Waterstones/Esquire Prize 1994, J.R. Ackerley Prize 1994. *Publications:* The Movement 1980, Seamus Heaney 1982, Penguin Book of Contemporary British Poetry (Ed.) 1982, Dark Glasses (poetry) 1984, The Yellow House 1987, The Ballad of the Yorkshire Ripper 1987, And When Did You Last See Your Father 1993, The Cracked Pot 1996, As If 1997, Too True 1998, Dr. Ox's Experiment (libretto) 1998. *Leisure interests:* soccer, tennis. *Address:* 54 Blackheath Park, London, SE3 9SJ, England. *Telephone:* 0181-318 9599.

MORRISON, Toni (Chloe Anthony Morrison), M.A.; American novelist; b. 18 Feb. 1931, Lorain, Ohio; d. of George Wofford and Ella Ramah (Willis) Wofford; m. Harold Morrison 1958 (divorced 1964); two c.; ed. Howard Univ., Cornell Univ.; taught English and Humanities, Tex. Southern Univ. 1955–57, Howard Univ. 1957–64; Ed., Random House, New York 1965–; Assoc. Prof. of English, State Univ. of New York 1971–72, Schweitzer Prof. of the Humanities 1984–89; Robert F. Goheen Prof. of the Humanities, Princeton Univ. 1989–; mem. Council, Authors Guild; Nobel Prize for Literature 1993; Commdr. Ordre des Arts et des Lettres. *Publications:* The Bluest Eye 1970, Sula 1974, Song of Solomon 1977, Tar Baby 1983, Beloved 1987 (Pulitzer Prize and Robert F. Kennedy Book Award 1988), Jazz 1992, Playing in the Dark: Whiteness and the Literary Imagination 1992, Nobel Prize Speech 1994, Birth of a Nation'hood: Gaze, Script and Spectacle in the O.J. Simpson Trial 1997. *Address:* Princeton University, 111 Dickinson Hall, Princeton, NJ 08544; c/o Suzanne Gluck, International Creative Management, 40 57th Street West, New York, NY 10019, U.S.A.

MORRISON, Van, O.B.E.; (b. George Ivan Morrison); British singer, songwriter and instrumentalist; 31 Aug. 1945, Belfast; left school aged 15; joined The Monarchs, playing in Germany; formed Them, Belfast, disbanded 1966; moved to New York; first album Blowin' Your Mind 1967; subsequent albums include: Astral Weeks, Moondance 1970, Van Morrison: His Band and Street Choir 1970, Tupelo Honey 1971, Saint Dominic's Preview 1972, Hardnose the Highway 1973, It's Too Late To Stop Now 1970, Veedon Fleece 1974, A Period of Transition 1977, Wavelength 1978, Into the Music 1979, Common One 1980, Beautiful Vision 1982, Inarticulate Speech of the Heart 1983, Live At The Royal Opera House, Belfast 1984, A Sense of Wonder 1985, No Guru, No Method, No Teacher 1986, Poetics Champion Compose 1987, Irish Heartbeat 1988, Avalon Sunset 1989, Enlightenment 1990, Hymns to the Silence 1991, Bang Masters 1991, The Best of Van Morrison 1993, Too Long in Exile 1993, A Night in San Francisco 1994, Days Like This 1995, The Healing Game 1997, Tell Me Something 1997.

MORRITT, Hon. Sir (Robert) Andrew, Kt., C.V.O., Q.C.; **Hon. Mr. Justice Morritt;** British judge; b. 5 Feb. 1938; s. of Robert Augustus Morritt and Margaret Mary Tyldesley Jones; m. Sara Simonetta Merton 1962; two s.; ed. Eton Coll., Magdalene Coll. Cambridge; 2nd Lieut. Scots Guards 1956–58; called to Bar, Lincoln's Inn 1962, Bencher 1984, Q.C. 1977; Jr. Counsel to Sec. of State for Trade in Chancery Matters 1970–77, to Attorney-Gen. in Charity Matters 1972–77; Attorney-Gen. to H.R.H. The Prince of Wales 1978–88; a Judge of High Court of Justice, Chancery Div. 1988–94; a Lord of Appeal in Ordinary 1994–; Pres. Council of the Inns of Court 1997–; mem. Gen. Council of Bar 1969–73, Advisory Cttee. on Legal Educ. 1972–76, Top Salaries Review Body 1982–87. *Leisure interests:* fishing, shooting. *Address:* Royal Courts of Justice, Strand, London, WC2A 2LL, England.

MORROW, Sir Ian Thomas, C.A., F.C.M.A., J.DIP., M.A.; British chartered accountant; b. 8 June 1912, Manchester; s. of the late Thomas George Morrow and Jamesina Hunter; m. 1st Elizabeth Mary Thackray 1940 (dissolved 1967); one s. one d.; m. 2nd Sylvia Jane Taylor 1967; one d.; ed. Dollar Acad., Scotland; Chartered Accountant 1936; Asst. Accountant Brocklehurst-Whiston Amalgamated Ltd. 1937–40; Partner, Robson, Morrow & Co. 1942–51; Financial Dir. The Brush Electrical Eng. Co. Ltd. (now The Brush Group Ltd.) 1951–52, Deputy Man. Dir. 1952–56, Jt. Man. Dir. 1956–57, Man. Dir. 1957–58; Jt. Man. Dir. H. Clarkson & Co. Ltd. 1961–72; Chair. Rowe Bros. & Co. (Holdings) Ltd. 1960–70, Associated Fire Alarms Ltd. 1965–70, Crane Fruehauf Trailers Ltd. 1969–71, Rolls-Royce (1971) Ltd. (Deputy Chair. and Man. Dir. 1971–73), MAI (fmrly. Mills and Allen Int. PLC) 1974–94, Scotia Holdings PLC (fmrly. Efamol Holdings) 1986–95, Beale Dobie & Co. Ltd. 1989–97, Scotia Pharmaceuticals Ltd. 1986–95, Walbrook Insurance Co. Ltd. 1990–92, Fintauro SIM S.p.A. (Milan) 1992–93, Thurne Group Ltd. 1993–; mem. Bd. Scotia Pharmaceuticals Ltd. 1986–95, Insport Consultants 1988–93, etc.; fmr. Dir. The Laird Group PLC (fmr. Chair.) 1973–92, Dir. Hambros Industrial Man. Ltd., Zeus Management Ltd. –1993, Psion PLC 1987–98, C.E. Heath PLC 1988–97, Harlow Ueda Savage (Holdings) Ltd. 1985–88, and numerous other cos.; Council mem. Chartered Inst. of Man. Accountants 1952–70 (Pres. 1956–57; Gold Medallist 1961); Pres. Inst. of Chartered Accountants of Scotland 1981–82; mem. Press Council until 1981; Hon. D.Litt. (Heriot-Watt) 1982, Hon. D.Univ. (Stirling) 1979; Freeman, City of London; Liveryman, Worshipful Co. of Spectacle-makers. *Leisure interests:* reading, music, golf, skiing. *Address:* 2 Albert Terrace Mews, London, NW1 7TA, England (Home). *Telephone:* 0171-722 7110 (Home). *Fax:* 0171-481 1048.

MORSE, Sir (Christopher) Jeremy, K.C.M.G.; British banker; b. 10 Dec. 1928, London; s. of late Francis J. and Kinbarra (née Armfield-Marrow) Morse; m. Belinda M. Mills 1955; three s. one d.; ed. Winchester and New Coll., Oxford; fmrly. with Glyn, Mills & Co., Dir. 1964; Dir. Legal and Gen. Assurance Society Ltd. 1963–64, 1975–87; Exec. Dir. Bank of England 1965–72, Dir. (non-exec.) 1993–97; Alt. Gov. IMF 1966–72; Chair. of Deputies of "Cttee. of Twenty", IMF 1972–74; Deputy Chair. Lloyds Bank Ltd. 1975–77, Chair. 1977–93; Chair. Lloyds Merchant Bank Holdings 1985–88; Dir. (non-exec.) ICI 1981–93, Zeneca 1993–; Chair. Cttee. of London Clearing Bankers 1980–82, City Communications Centre 1985–87; mem. Council, Lloyd's 1987–98; mem. NEDC 1977–81; Pres. Inst. Int. d'Études Bancaires 1982–83, Int. Monetary Conf. 1985–86, Banking Fed. of EC 1988–90, Chartered Inst. of Bankers 1992–93; Vice-Pres. Business in the Community; Chair. City Arts Trust 1977–79, Per Jacobsson Foundation 1987–, Governing Bodies Assсn. 1994–; Chancellor Bristol Univ. 1988–; Pres. Classical Asscn. 1989–90; Fellow, All Souls Coll., Oxford 1953–68, 1983–; Fellow, Winchester Coll. 1966–83, Warden 1987–97; Hon. life mem. British Chess Fed. 1988–; Hon. D.Litt (City) 1977, Hon. D.Sc. (Aston) 1984, Hon. LL.D. (Bristol) 1989. *Leisure interests:* poetry, golf, problems and puzzles, coarse gardening. *Address:* 102A Drayton Gardens, London, SW10 9RJ, England (Home). *Telephone:* 0171-370 2265.

MORSE, Sir Jeremy (see Morse, Sir Christopher Jeremy).

MORTELL, Michael Philip, M.SC., M.S., PH.D.; Irish university administrator; b. 9 Feb. 1941, Cork; m. Patricia Yule 1967; two d.; ed. Charleville Christian Bros. School, Univ. Coll. Cork and Calif. Inst. of Tech.; Asst. Prof. Center for Application of Math. Lehigh Univ. 1967–72; lecturer in Math. Univ. Coll. Cork 1972–89, Registrar 1979–89, Pres. 1989–; Visiting Prof. Univ. of British Col. 1976–77, Univ. of Queensland 1979; Hon. LL.D. (Dublin, Queen's Belfast, Limerick). *Publications:* some 30 papers on nonlinear acoustics. *Leisure interests:* reading, art, gardening, sport. *Address:* President's Office, University College, Cork, Ireland. *Telephone:* 353-21-902201. *Fax:* 353-21-275006.

MORTIER, Gerard; Belgian music director; b. 25 Nov. 1943, Ghent; ed. Univ. of Ghent; engaged in journalism and communications 1966–67; Admin. Asst. Flanders Festival 1968–72; Artistic Planner, Deutsche Oper am Rhein, Düsseldorf 1972–73; Asst. Admin. Frankfurt Opera 1973–77; Dir. of Artistic Production, Hamburg Staatsoper 1977–79; Tech. Programme Consultant, Theatre Nat. de l'Opéra, Paris 1979–81; Dir.-Gen. Belgian Nat. Opera, Brussels 1981–; Dir. Salzburg Music Festival Sept. 1992–. *Address:* c/o Salzburger Festspiele, Hofstallgasse 1, 5020 Salzburg, Austria.

MORTIER, Roland F. J., DR.PHIL.; Belgian university professor; b. 21 Dec. 1920, Ghent; s. of late Arthur Mortier and Berthe Baudson; m. Loyse Triffaux 1948; one s.; ed. Antwerp Atheneum, Univ. Libre de Bruxelles and Univ. of Ghent; Prof., Univ. Libre de Bruxelles 1955–85, Prof. Emer. 1990; Visiting Prof. Toronto, Stanford, Yale, Paris, Cologne, Jerusalem, London, Cleveland, Maryland, Duisburg, Pisa; Vice-Pres. Inst. des Hautes Etudes de Belgique; past Pres. Société Diderot; mem. Acad. Royale de Langue et Littérature Française, Belgium; Foreign mem. Hungarian Acad. of Sciences; corresp. Fellow, British Acad., Academia Europaea; mem. Inst. de France 1993; other professional appts. and affiliations; Dr. h.c. (Montpellier, Göttingen, Jerusalem); Prix Francqui 1965; Prix Montaigne 1983; Prix Counson 1985; Prix de l'Union rationaliste de France 1993. *Publications:* Diderot en Allemagne 1954, Clartés et Ombres du Siècle des Lumières 1969, Le Tableau littéraire de la France au XVIIIe Siècle 1972, La Poétique des Ruines en France 1974, L'Originalité, une nouvelle catégorie esthétique 1982, Le coeur et la raison 1990, Anacharsis Cloots, ou l'Utopie Foudroyée 1995; critical edns. of Voltaire and Diderot. *Leisure interests:* reading, walking, swimming, travel. *Address:* 10 avenue Général de Longueville, B.P. 12, 1150 Brussels, Belgium. *Telephone:* (2) 772 0194. *Fax:* (2) 772 0194.

MORTIMER, James Edward; British trade unionist (retd.); b. 12 Jan. 1921, Bradford, Yorks.; s. of William Ward and Elsie Mortimer; m.; two s. one d.; ed. Jr. Tech. School, Portsmouth, Ruskin Coll., Oxford, L.S.E.; worked in shipbuilding and eng. industries; TUC Scholar, Oxford 1945–46; TUC Econ. Dept. 1946–48; full-time trade union official, Draughtsmen's and Allied Technicians Asscn. 1948–68; Dir. London Co-operative Soc. 1968–71; mem. Nat. Bd. for Prices and Incomes 1968–71; mem. London Transport Exec. 1971–74; Chair. A.C.A.S. (fmrly. Conciliation and Arbitration Service) 1974–81; Gen. Sec. Labour Party 1982–85; mem. Wilberforce Cttee. of Inquiry into the Power Dispute 1970, Armed Forces Pay Review Body 1971–74, Econ. Devt. Cttee. for Chemical Industry 1973–74; Chair. Econ. Devt. Cttee. for Mechanical and Electrical Eng. Construction 1974–82, Editorial Cttee. Socialist Campaign Group News; mem. Cttee. Inst. of Employment Rights; Visiting Fellow, Admin. Staff Coll., Henley 1976–82; Sr. Visiting Fellow, Bradford Univ. 1977–82; Visiting Prof., Imperial Coll. of Science and Tech., London Univ. 1981–83; Hon. D.Litt. (Bradford) 1982. *Publications:* A History of Engineering and Shipbuilding Draughtsmen 1960, British Trade Unions Today (with Clive Jenkins, q.v.) 1965, The Kind of Laws the Unions Ought to Want 1968 (with Clive Jenkins), Industrial Relations 1968, Trade Unions and Technological Change 1971, History of the Boilermakers' Society, Vol. I 1973, Vol. II 1982, Vol. III 1993, A Professional Union: the Evolution of the Institution of Professional Civil Servants (with Valerie Ellis) 1980, A Life on the Left (political autobiog.) 1999. *Leisure interest:* writing. *Address:* 31 Charleston Street, London, SE17 1NG, England. *Telephone:* 0171-708 4415.

MORTIMER, Sir John (Clifford), Kt., C.B.E., Q.C.; British author, barrister and playwright; b. 21 April 1923, Hampstead, London; s. of Clifford and Katherine (née Smith) Mortimer; m. 1st Penelope Fletcher (Penelope Mortimer, q.v.) 1949 (dissolved 1972); one s. one d.; m. 2nd Penelope Gollop; two d.; ed. Harrow, Brasenose Coll., Oxford; called to the Bar 1948, Master of the Bench, Inner Temple 1975; mem. Bd. of Nat. Theatre 1968–; Chair. Council Royal Soc. of Literature 1989; Chair. Council Royal Court Theatre 1990–; Pres. Howard League for Penal Reform 1991–; British Acad. Writers' Award 1979, 1980; Dr. h.c. (Exeter) 1986; Hon. LL.D. (Susquehanna Univ.) 1985; Hon. D.Litt. (St. Andrews) 1987, (Nottingham) 1989, Hon. D. Univ. (Brunel) 1990. *Plays include:* The Wrong Side of the Park 1960, Two Stars for Comfort 1962, The Judge 1967, A Voyage Round My Father 1970 (adapted for TV 1982, Int. Emmy Award), I, Claudius (adaptation from Robert Graves) 1972, Collaborators 1973, Mr. Luby's Fear of Heaven (radio) 1976, Heaven and Hell 1976, The Bells of Hell 1977, The Lady from Maxim's (trans. from Feydeau) 1977, TV adaptations of Rumpole of the Bailey (six series), Brideshead Revisited 1981, Unity Mitford 1981, The Ebony Tower 1984, adaptation of Die Fledermaus 1989, (TV) A Christmas Carol 1994; Under the Hammer (TV Series) 1993. *Publications:* novels: Charade 1947, Rumming Park 1948, Answer Yes or No 1950, Like Men Betrayed 1953, Three Winters 1956, Will Shakespeare 1977, Rumpole of the Bailey 1978, The Trials of Rumpole 1979, Rumpole's Return 1981, Rumpole and the Golden Thread 1983, Paradise Postponed 1985, Rumpole's Last Case 1987, Rumpole and the Age of Miracles 1988, Rumpole à la Carte 1990, Clinging to the Wreckage (autobiog.) 1982, In Character 1983, Character Parts (interviews) 1986, Summer's Lease 1988, The Narrowing Stream, Titmuss Regained 1990, Dunster 1992, Rumpole on Trial 1992, The Best of Rumpole 1993, Murderers and Other Friends (autobiog.) 1993, Rumpole and the Angel of Death 1995, Rumpole and the Younger Generation 1996, Felix in the Underworld 1997, Rumpole's Return 1997, The Third Rumpole Omnibus 1997, The Sound of Trumpets 1998; trans. Die Fledermaus 1988; ed. Great Law and Order Stories 1991, The Oxford Book of Villains 1992, numerous articles in magazines. *Leisure interests:* working, gardening, going to the opera. *Address:* c/o A. D. Peters Ltd., 5th Floor, The Chambers, Chelsea Harbour, Lots Road, London, SW10 0XF; Turville Heath Cottage, Henley on Thames, Oxon., England.

MORTIMER, Penelope Ruth, F.R.S.L.; British author; b. 19 Sept. 1918, Rhyl, N. Wales; d. of Rev. A. F. G. Fletcher and Caroline A. Fletcher (née Maggs); m. 1st Charles Dimont 1937 (dissolved 1949); four d.; m. 2nd John C. Mortimer (q.v.) 1949 (dissolved 1972); one s. one d.; ed. Univ. Coll., London; awarded Whitbread Prize for autobiography About Time 1979. *Publications:* A Villa in Summer 1954, The Bright Prison 1956, With Love & Lizards 1957, Daddy's Gone A-Hunting 1958, Saturday Lunch With The Brownings 1960, The Pumpkin Eater 1962, My Friend Says It's Bulletproof 1967, The Home 1971, Long Distance 1974, About Time (autobiog.) 1979, The Handyman 1983, Queen Elizabeth 1986, Summer Story (screenplay) 1988, Portrait of a Marriage (screenplay) 1990, About Time Too (autobiog.) 1993, Queen Mother 1995. *Leisure interest:* gardening. *Address:* 19 St. Gabriel's Road, London, NW2 4DS, England. *Telephone:* 0181-452 8551. *Fax:* 0181-208 1946.

MORTON, Sir Alastair (see Morton, Sir Robert Alastair).

MORTON, Donald Charles, PH.D., F.A.A.; Canadian astronomer; b. 12 June 1933, Canada; s. of Charles O. Morton and Irene M. Wightman; m. Winifred Austin 1970; one s. one d.; ed. Univ. of Toronto and Princeton Univ.; astronomer, U.S. Naval Research Lab. 1959–61; from Research Assoc. to Sr. Research Astronomer (with rank of Prof.), Princeton Univ. 1961–76; Dir. Anglo-Australian Observatory (Epping and Coonabarabran, N.S.W.) 1976–86; Dir. Herzberg Inst. of Astrophysics, Nat. Research Council of Canada 1986–, now Dir. Gen.; Assoc. Royal Astronomical Soc. 1980; mem. Int. Astronomy Union, Royal Astronomy Soc. (assoc. 1980), Astronomy Soc. of Australia (Pres. 1981–83, Hon. mem. 1986) etc; Fellow Australian Acad. of Sciences. *Publications:* research papers in professional journals. *Leisure interests:* mountaineering, marathon running. *Address:* Herzberg Institute of Astrophysics, National Research Council of Canada, 5071 W. Saanich Road, Victoria, B.C., V8X 4M6, Canada. *Telephone:* (250) 363-0040.

MORTON, Sir (Robert) Alastair, Kt., M.A.; British business executive; b. 11 Jan. 1938, Johannesburg, South Africa; s. of late Harry Newton Morton and Elizabeth Markino; m. Sara Stephens 1964; one s. one d.; ed. St. John's Coll., Johannesburg, Univ. of Witwatersrand, Johannesburg, Univ. of Oxford and M.I.T.; with Anglo-American Corpn. of South Africa, London and Cen. Africa 1959–63; with World Bank Group, Washington, D.C. 1964–67, Industrial Reorganisation Corpn., London 1967–70; Exec. Dir. Investment Trust Group 1970–72; Chair. and CEO, Draymont Securities Ltd. 1972–76; (first) Man. Dir. British Nat. Oil Corpn. (BNOC) 1976–80; Co-int. energy consultancy 1980–81; C.E.O. Guinness Peat Group PLC 1982–87, Chair. 1987; Chair. Guinness Mahon & Co. 1986–87; Dir. British Steel Corpn. (BSC) 1979–82; Chair. Eurotunnel PLC 1987–96, C.E.O., Eurotunnel Group 1990–94, Co-Chair. 1987–90, 1994–96; (first) Chair. Kent Training and Enterprise Council 1989–95; Dir. National Power PLC 1989–, Lucas Industries PLC 1993–96, Lonrho 1998–; Chair. Pvt. Finance Panel advising Chancellor of the Exchequer 1993–95, Strategic Adviser 1997–; Hon. LL.D. (Bath) 1990; D.C.L. (Kent) 1992, D.Univ. (Brunel) 1992; Hon. D.Sc. (Warwick) 1994, (Cranfield); Gold Medal, Inst. of Civil Engineers 1994; Commdr. Légion d'honneur; *Leisure interests:* yachting, walking. *Address:* 6th Floor, Senator House, 85 Queen Victoria Street, London EC4V 4DP; St. Peter's House, 130 Wood Street, London, EC2V 6EQ, England.

MOSBACHER, Robert Adam, B.SC.; American politician and oil and gas executive; b. 11 March 1927, New York; s. of Emil Mosbacher and Gertrude (née Schwartz) Mosbacher; m. Georgette Paulsin 1986; one s. three d.; ed. Washington and Lee Univs.; Ind. oil and gas producer 1948–; Pres. Mosbacher Energy Corp., Houston 1995–; Sec. of Commerce, Washington 1989–92; Chair., C.E.O. Mosbacher Energy Co., Houston; Dir. Texas Bankshares, Houston, New York Life Insurance Co.; Chair. Bd. Dirs., Choate School, Wallingford, Conn.; Dir. Aspen Inst. Centre for Strategic and Int. Studies; Chair. Nat. Finance, George Bush for Pres.; Pres. Ford Finance Cttee.; Gen. Campaign Chair., then Chief Fundraiser 1992 Republican Presidential Campaign; Gen. Chair. Finance, Republican Nat. Cttee., Washington 1992–; Dir. Texas Heart Inst.; mem. Mid-Continent Oil and Gas Asscn. (fmr. Chair.), American Petroleum Inst. (Dir., Exec. Cttee.), Nat. Petroleum Council (fmr. Chair.), All American Wildcatters Asscn. (fmr. Chair.), American Asscn. Petroleum Landmen; Hon. LL.D. (Lee Univ.) 1984. *Address:* Mosbacher Energy Corp., 712 Main Street, Suite 2200, Houston, TX 77002, U.S.A.

MOSBAKK, Kurt; Norwegian politician; b. 21 Nov. 1934, Orkdal; s. of Henrik Mosbakk and Jenny Mosbakk; m. Grete Tidemandsen 1975; two s. one d.; ed. Norwegian Coll. Econs. and Business Admin.; Pvt. Sec. to Minister of Defence 1964–65; Minister of Trade and Shipping 1986–88; County Exec. of Østford 1988–; Deputy Chair. Norwegian Defence Comm. 1990–92; fmr. Deputy Mayor Lørenskog; Chair. Akershus Co. Labour Party 1969–74; Chief Co. Exec. Finnmark Co. 1976; Chair. Bd. Norwegian State Housing Bank 1988–; Chair. Norwegian Tourist Bd. 1990–. *Leisure interest:* literature. *Address:* NORTRA, Drammensvn 40, P.O. Box 2893 Solli, 0230 Oslo, Norway.

MOSCOVICI, Pierre; French politician; b. 16 Sept. 1957; ed. Univ. of Paris X, I, IV, Ecole nat. d'administration; official, Cour des Comptes 1984–88; Adviser, pvt. office of Minister of Nat. Educ., Youth and Sport 1988–89, Special Adviser to Minister 1989–90; Head. Gen. Planning Comm.'s Public Sector Modernization and Finance Dept. 1990; mem. Parti Socialiste (PS) Nat. Council and Nat. Bureau 1990, Nat. Sec. responsible for policy research and devt. 1990–92, 1995–97, Nat. Treas. 1992–94; mem. Doubs Gen. Council, Sochaux-Grand-Charmont canton 1994; Montbéliard municipal councillor 1995; mem. European Parl. 1994–97; Nat. Ass. Deputy for 4th Doubs constituency 1997–; Minister Del. attached to Minister for Foreign Affairs, with responsibility for European Affairs 1997–. *Publications include:* A la recherche de la gauche perdue 1994, L'urgence, plaidoyer pour une autre politique 1997. *Address:* Ministry of Foreign Affairs, 37 quai d'Orsay, 75700 Paris cédex 07, France. *Telephone:* (1) 43.17.53.53. *Fax:* (1) 43.17.52.03.

MOSELEY-BRAUN, Carol, B.A.; American politician and lawyer; b. 16 Aug. 1947; d. of Joseph J. Moseley and Edna A. (Davie); ed. Univ. of Illinois; fmr. Asst. Attorney, Davis, Miner & Barnhill; fmr. Attorney, Jones, Ware & Grenard; fmr. Asst. U.S. Attorney for Northern Dist. of Ill.; mem. Ill. House of Reps. 1978–88; Cook Co. Recorder of Deeds 1988; Senator from Illinois 1993–99; Democrat. *Address:* U.S. Senate, Washington, DC 20510, U.S.A.

MOSER, Sir Claus Adolf, K.C.B., C.B.E., F.B.A.; British statistician; b. 24 Nov. 1922, Berlin; s. of the late Dr. Ernest and Lotte Moser; m. Mary Oxlin 1949; one s. two d.; ed. Frensham Heights School, London School of Econs.; R.A.F. 1943–46; Asst. lecturer in Statistics, L.S.E. 1946–49, lecturer 1949–55, Reader in Social Statistics 1955–61, Prof. of Social Statistics 1961–70; Statistical Adviser Cttee. on Higher Educ. 1961–64; Dir. L.S.E. Higher Educ. Research Unit 1964–; Dir. Royal Opera House Covent Garden 1965–87, Chair. 1974–87; Dir. Cen. Statistical Office, Head of Govt. Statistical Service 1967–78; Visiting Fellow, Nuffield Coll. 1972–80; Vice-Chair. N.M. Rothschild and Sons 1978–84, Dir. 1978–90; Dir. The Economist 1979–93, Chair. Economist Intelligence Unit 1978–84; Warden of Wadham Coll., Oxford 1984–93, Pres. 1989–90; Chair. Harold Holt Ltd. 1990–, British Museum Devt. Trust 1993–, Basic Skills Agency 1997–; Dir. Equity & Law Life Assurance Soc. 1980–87, Int. Medical Statistics Inc. 1982–88, Octopus Publishing Group 1982–87, Property and Reversionary Investments 1986–87; Chancellor, Univ. of Keele 1986–, Open Univ. of Israel 1994–; Pres. British Asscn. 1989–95; Pro-Vice-Chancellor Oxford Univ. 1991–93; Gov. Royal Shakespeare Theatre 1982–93, British American Arts Asscn. 1982–, Pilgrim Trust 1982–, Nat. Comm. on Educ. 1991–95; Hon. Fellow, R.A.M. 1970; mem. Gov. Body, Royal Ballet School 1974–87; Ordre national du Mérite 1976; Hon. Fellow, L.S.E. 1976, Inst. of Educ., Univ. of London 1997; Hon. D.Sc. S. (Southampton) 1975, (Leeds, Surrey, Keele, York, Sussex, City Univs.) 1977, Hon. D.Tech. (Brunel) 1981, Hon. D.Sc. (Wales) 1990, (Liverpool) 1991; Hon. D.Sc.Econ. (London) 1991; Dr. h.c. (Brighton) 1994; Trustee Soros Foundation 1993–; Commdr.'s Cross, Order of Merit (Fed. Repub. of Germany) 1986. *Publications:* Measurement of Levels of Living 1957, Survey Methods in Social Investigation 1958, Social Conditions in England and Wales (co-author) 1958, British Towns (co-author) 1961, and papers in statistical journals. *Leisure interest:* music. *Address:* 3 Regents Park Terrace, London, NW1 7EE, England (Home). *Telephone:* 0171-485 1619 (Home).

MOSER, Jürgen K.; American professor of mathematics; b. 4 July 1928, Königsberg, Germany (now Kaliningrad, Russia); s. of Kurt Moser and Ilse (Strehlke); m. Gertrude Moser 1955; two d.; ed. Univ. of Göttingen; Asst. Prof. New York Univ. 1956, M.I.T. 1957–60; Prof. of Math., New York Univ. 1960, Dir. Courant Inst. of Math. Sciences 1967–70; with Eidgenössische

Tech. Hochschule, Zürich; 1970–95; mem. N.A.S., Foreign mem. Russian Acad. of Sciences, Int. Math. Union (Pres. 1983–86); Sloan Fellow 1961, Guggenheim Fellow 1970–71; G. D. Birkhoff Prize 1968, Craig Watson Medal 1969, L. E. J. Brouder Medal 1984, Georg Cantor Medal 1992, Wolf Prize 1994/95. *Publications:* Lectures on Celestial Mechanics (with C. L. Siegel) 1971, Stable and Random Motions in Dynamical Systems 1973. *Leisure interest:* chamber music. *Address:* ETH-Zürich, Rämistr. 101, 8092 Zurich (Office); Greifenseestr. 49, 8603 Schwerzenbach, Switzerland.

MOSES, Edwin, B.SC.; American athlete; b. 31 Aug. 1955, Dayton, Ohio; m. Myrella Bordt Moses 1982; ed. Fairview High School and Morehouse Coll., Atlanta, Ga.; won gold medal for 400 m. hurdles, Olympic Games, Montreal 1976, (in world record time), Los Angeles 1984; one of only three men to break 48 secs. for 400 m. hurdles; holds record for greatest number of wins consecutively in any event; winner 122 straight races 1977–87, lost to Danny Harris June 1987; retd. 1988, comeback 1991; holder of 10 fastest times ever recorded; mem. Jt. Olympic Cttee. Athletes Comm., Exec. Bd. of U.S.O.C., Bd. of Dirs. Jesse Owens Foundation; U.S. Rep. to Int. Amateur Athletic Fed. 1984–; dynamics engineer, Pomona, Calif.; Chair. U.S.O.C. Substance Abuse Cttee. 1989–. *Leisure interests:* aviation, scientific breakthroughs in athletics. *Address:* Robinson-Humphrey Co., 3333 Peachtree Road N.E., Atlanta, GA 30326,U.S.A.

MOSES, Lincoln Ellsworth, PH.D.; American professor of statistics; b. 21 Dec. 1921, Kansas City; s. of Edward Walter Moses and Virginia (née Holmes) Moses; m. 1st Jean Runnels 1942; m. 2nd Mary Louise Coale 1968; two s. three d.; ed. Stanford Univ.; Asst. Prof. of Educ., Columbia Univ. 1950–52; Asst. Prof. of Statistics, Stanford Univ. and Stanford Medical School 1952–55, Assoc. Prof. 1955–59, Prof. 1959–, Assoc. Dean of Humanities and Sciences 1965–68, 1985–86, Dean of Graduate Studies 1969–75; (First) Admin. Energy Information Admin., U.S. Dept. of Energy 1978–80; Guggenheim Fellow, Fellow at Center for Advanced Study in Behavioral Sciences. *Publications:* (with Herman Chernoff) Elementary Decision Theory 1959, Biostatistics Casebook (Jt. Ed.) 1980, Think and Explain with Statistics 1986. *Leisure interests:* birds, chess. *Address:* Division of Biostatistics, Stanford University Medical Centre, Stanford, CA 94305, U.S.A. *Telephone:* (415) 723-6910.

MOSHANU, Aleksandru, D.HIS.SC.; Moldovan politician; b. 1932, Branishte, Moldova; ed. Moldovan Univ.; sr. researcher, scientific sec. Inst. of History Moldovan Acad. of Sciences 1957–78, sr. teacher, Head of Chair., Dean of History, Chair. Moldovan Univ. 1976–; People's Deputy of Moldova 1990–; mem. of Parl. 1990–, Presidium of Parl., Chair. of Parl. 1990–93; Deputy Chair. Party for Democracy. *Publications:* about 100 scientific articles on recent history of Moldova and European countries. *Address:* House of Parliament, Stefan Celmari prosp. 105, 277073 Chisinău, Moldova.

MOSHER, Gregory Dean, B.F.A.; American theatre producer and director; b. 15 Jan. 1949, New York; s. of Thomas Edward Mosher and Florence Christine Mosher; ed. Oberlin Coll., Ithaca Coll., Juillard School; Dir. Stage 2 Goodman Theatre, Chicago 1974–77, Artistic Dir. 1978–85; Dir. Lincoln Center Theatre 1985–92, Resident Dir. 1992–; producer of new works by Tennessee Williams, Studs Terkel, David Mamet, John Guare, Michael Weller, Wole Soyinka, Elaine May, David Rabe, Mbongeni Ngema, Edward Albee, Spalding Gray, Arthur Miller, Leonard Bernstein, Stephen Sondheim, Richard Nelson, Jerome Robbins; producer: Samuel Beckett's first directing work in U.S., Krapp's Last Tape 1979, Endgame 1980; Dir. Glengarry Glen Ross (David Mamet), Broadway 1984–85, American Buffalo 1975, A Life in the Theatre 1977, Edmond 1982, Speed-the-Plow (David Mamet), Danger: Memory (Miller premiere) 1987, Broadway 1988, London 1989, Our Town (50th Anniversary production, Thornton Wilder), Broadway 1988, Oh Hell, Lincoln Center Theater 1989, Uncle Vanya 1990, Mr Gogol and Mr Preen 1991, A Streetcar Named Desire 1992; two Tony Awards (as producer of revivals: Anything Goes, Our Town). *Address:* Lincoln Center Theater, 150 W 65th Street, New York, NY 10023, U.S.A. *Telephone:* (212) 362 7600.

MOSHINSKY, Elijah, B.A.; British opera director; b. 8 Jan. 1946; s. of Abraham Moshinsky and Eva Moshinsky; m. Ruth Dyttman 1970; two s.; ed. Melbourne Univ. and St. Antony's Coll. Oxford; apptd. to Royal Opera House 1973, Assoc. Producer 1979–; work for Royal Opera includes original productions of Peter Grimes 1975, Lohengrin 1978, The Rake's Progress 1979, Un Ballo in Maschera 1980; Macbeth 1981, Samson et Dalila 1981, Tannhäuser 1984, Otello 1987, Die Entführung aus dem Serail 1987, Attila 1990, Simon Boccanegra 1991, Stiffelio 1993, Aida 1994, Otello 1994, The Makropulos Case 1996, has also produced work for English Nat. Opera, Australian Opera, Metropolitan Opera, New York, Holland Festival, Maggio Musicale, Florence etc.; *theatre productions include:* Troilus and Cressida (Nat. Theatre) 1976, The Force of Habit (Nat. Theatre) 1976, Three Sisters (Albery) 1987, Light Up the Sky (Globe) 1987, Ivanov (Strand) 1989, Much Ado About Nothing (Strand) 1989, Another Time (Wyndham's) 1989, Shadowlands (Queen's) 1989, Cyrano de Bergerac 1992, Genghis Cohn 1993, Danton 1994; Dir. Matador (Queen's) 1991, Becket (Haymarket) 1991, Reflected Glory (Vaudeville) 1992, Richard III 1998; productions for BBC TV of works by Shakespeare, Ibsen and Sheridan. *Leisure interests:* painting, conversation. *Address:* 28 Kidbrooke Grove, London, SE3 0LG, England. *Telephone:* 0181-858 4179.

MOSIER, Frank Eugene; American oil executive; b. 15 July 1930, Kersey, Pa.; s. of Clarence Mosier and Helen Mosier; m. Julia M. Fife 1961; one s. one d.; ed. Univ. of Pittsburgh; joined Standard Oil Co. Cleveland 1953, Vice-Pres. (supply and distribution) 1972–76, (supply and transport) 1976–77, Sr. Vice-Pres. (marketing and refining) 1977–78, (supply and transport) 1978–82, (downstream petroleum dept.) 1982–85, Exec. Vice-Pres. 1985–86, Pres. and C.O.O. 1986–88; with BP America Inc. (following 1987 merger of BP and Standard Oil), Cleveland 1987–, Pres. 1987–88, Vice-Chair. 1988–. *Address:* BP America Inc., 200 Public Square, Cleveland, OH 44114, U.S.A.

MOSIMANN, Anton; Swiss chef and restaurateur; b. 23 Feb. 1947; s. of Otto Mosimann and Olga Mosimann; m. Kathrin Roth 1973; two s.; ed. pvt. school in Switzerland; apprentice, Hotel Baeren, Twann; worked in Canada, France, Italy, Sweden, Japan, Belgium, Switzerland 1962–; cuisinier at Villa Lorraine, Brussels, Les Prés d'Eugénie, Eugénie-les-Bains, Les Frères Troisgros, Roanne, Paul Bocuse, Collonges au Mont d'Or, Moulin de Mougins; joined Dorchester Hotel, London 1975, Maître Chef des Cuisines 1975–88; owner, Mosimann's (fmr. Belfry Club) 1988–, Mosimann's Party Service 1990–, The Mosimann Acad. 1995–, Créative Chefs 1996–; TV programmes include series Cooking with Mosimann 1990, Anton Mosimann Naturally 1991–92, Natürlich, Leichtes Kochen (Swiss TV) 1997, Mosimann's Culinary Switzerland (Swiss TV) 1998; Hon. mem. Chefs' Asscns. of Canada, Japan, Switzerland, S.A.; World Pres. Les Toques Blanches Internationales 1989–93; Dr. of Culinary Arts h.c. (Johnson and Wales Univ., U.S.A.); Hon. D.Sc. (Bournemouth Univ.) 1998; Chevalier du Mérite Agricole; Personalité de l'Année Award 1986, Glenfiddich Award (for TV programme Anton goes to Sheffield) 1986; numerous awards in int. cookery competitions etc. *Publications:* Cuisine à la Carte 1981, A New Style of Cooking: The Art of Anton Mosimann 1983, Cuisine Naturelle 1985, Anton Mosimann's Fish Cuisine 1988, The Art of Mosimann 1989, Cooking with Mosimann 1989, Anton Mosimann—Naturally 1991, The Essential Mosimann 1993, Mosimann's World 1996. *Leisure interests:* jogging, travel, collecting art. *Address:* c/o Mosimann's, 11B West Halkin Street, London, SW1X 8JL, England.

MOSISILI, Bethuel Pakalitha; Lesotho politician; fmrly. Deputy Prime Minister, Minister of Home Affairs, Local Govt. and Rural and Urban Development; fmrly. Deputy Leader Lesotho Congress for Democracy, Leader June 1997–; Prime Minister of Lesotho May 1998–. *Address:* Office of the Prime Minister, P.O. Box 527, Maseru 100, Lesotho. *Telephone:* 311030. *Fax:* 310102.

MOSLER, Hermann, LL.D.; German international lawyer; b. 26 Dec. 1912, Hennef; s. of Karl and Marga (née Loenartz) Mosler; m. Anne Pipberger; five c.; ed. Bonn Univ.; Asst., later Research Fellow, Kaiser Wilhelm Inst. for Foreign Public Law and Public Int. Law 1937; Barrister-at-Law, Bonn 1946; Pvt. Dozent in Public Int. Law, Constitutional Law and Admin. Law, Univ. of Bonn 1946; Ordinary Prof. of Public Law, Univ. of Frankfurt 1949; Visiting Prof. of Int. Law, Georgetown Univ. 1950; Head of Legal Dept., Fed. Ministry of Foreign Affairs 1951–53: Ordinary Prof. Univ. of Heidelberg 1954; Dir. Max-Planck Inst. for Foreign Public Law and Public Int. Law, Heidelberg 1954, now Emer.; mem. Perm. Court of Arbitration 1954–85; Judge of European Court of Human Rights 1959–81; Lectures, Hague Acad. of Int. Law 1957, 1974; ad hoc Judge, Int. Court of Justice 1968–69, Judge 1976–85; mem. Heidelberg Acad. of Sciences 1975, Pres. 1982–86; Hon. Pres. German Soc. of Int. Law 1985; mem. Curatorium, Hague Acad. of Int. Law 1976, Inst. de Droit Int. 1977; Corresp. mem. Austrian Acad. of Sciences 1972, Accad. Naz. Italiana dei Lincei 1991; Dr. Iur. h.c. (Brussels) 1969, (Saarbrücken) 1982, (Univ. de Educación a Distancia, Madrid) 1996. *Publications:* The International Society as a Legal Community 1980, and other publs. on international law, comparative public law, European law. *Address:* 69121 Heidelberg, Mühltalstr. 117a, Germany.

MOSLEY, Max Rufus; British fmr. motor racing driver and lawyer; b. 13 April 1940; s. of the late Sir Oswald Mosley and of the Hon. Lady Diana Mosley (née Freeman-Mitford); m. Jean Marjorie Taylor 1960; two s.; ed. Christ Church Oxford; called to Bar (Gray's Inn) 1964; fmr. Dir. March Cars Ltd., Legal Adviser to Formula One Constructors Asscn., fmr. Formula Two racing driver, Co-Founder March Grand Prix Team; Pres. Fed. Internationale du Sport Automobile (FISA) 1991–93, Fed. Int. de l'Automobile 1993–; Chair. Mfrs. Comm. 1986–91; Hon. Pres. E.P. Automobile Users Group 1994; Chair. European New Car Assessment Prog. 1998–; Order of Merit (Italy) 1994; Sec. Oxford Union Soc. 1960. *Leisure interests:* walking, snowboarding. *Address:* Fédération Internationale de l'Automobile, 2 chemin Blandonnet, 1215 Geneva, Switzerland.

MOSLEY, Nicholas (see Ravensdale, 3rd Baron).

MOSLEY, Walter; American writer; b. 1952, Los Angeles; m. Joy Kellman; ed. Johnson State Coll. *Publications include:* Devil in a Blue Dress 1990, A Red Death 1991, White Butterfly 1992, RL's Dream 1995. *Address:* c/o W. W. Norton, 5th Avenue, New York, N.Y. 10110, U.S.A.

MOSS, David Joseph, C.M.G.; British diplomatist (retd.); b. 6 Nov. 1938, Surrey; s. of late Herbert J. Moss and of Irene Moss; m. Joan L. Tyler 1961; one s. (deceased) one d.; ed. Hampton Grammar School; entered FCO 1957; R.A.F. 1957–59; served Bangkok 1962–65, La Paz 1969–70; First Sec. and Head of Chancery, The Hague 1973–77; Counsellor and Deputy Perm. Rep. U.K. Mission to UN, Geneva 1983–87; Asst. Under-Sec. of State, FCO 1987–90; High Commr. in New Zealand and in Western Samoa 1990–94, in Malaysia 1994–98. *Leisure interests:* walking, reading, listening to music.

MOSS, Kate; British model; b. 16 Jan. 1974, Addiscombe; d. of Peter Edward Moss and Linda Rosina; ed. Croydon High School; has modelled for Face,

Harpers and Queen, Vogue, Dolce & Gabana, Katherine Hamnett, Versace, Yves Saint Laurent; exclusive contract worldwide with Calvin Klein (q.v.) 1992–99; named Female Model of the Year VH-1 Awards 1996. *Film:* Unzipped 1996. *Publication:* Kate 1994. *Address:* Storm Model Management, 1st Floor, 5 Jubilee Place, London, SW3 3TD, England. *Telephone:* 0171-376 7764.

MOSS, Stirling, O.B.E.; British racing driver; b. 17 Sept. 1929, London; s. of Nora Aileen and Alfred Moss; m. 1st Katherine Stuart Moson 1957 (dissolved 1960); m. 2nd Elaine Barbarino 1964 (dissolved 1968); one d.; m. 3rd Susie Paine 1980, one s.; ed. Haileybury and Imperial Service Coll.; bought his first racing car, a Cooper 500, with prize money from show-jumping 1947; British Champion 1951; built his own car, the Cooper-Alta 1953; drove in H.W.M. Formula II Grand Prix team 1950, 1951, Jaguar team 1950, 1951; leader of Maserati Grand Prix team 1954; mem. Mercedes team 1955; leader of Maserati Sports and Grand Prix teams 1956, Aston Martin team 1956; mem. Vanwall, Aston Martin, Maserati teams 1958; winner of Tourist Trophy (TT) race, U.K. 1950, 1951, 1955, 1958, Gold Coupe des Alpes (3 rallies without loss of marks) 1954, Italian Mille Miglia 1955, Sicilian Targa Florio 1955, 8 int. events including New Zealand, Monaco Grand Prix, Nurburgring 1,000 km. (Fed. Repub. of Germany) 1956, Argentine 1,000 km. U.K., Pescara (Italy), Moroccan Grand Prix 1957, 11 events incl. Argentine, Netherlands, Italian Grand Prix and Nurburgring 1,000 km. 1958, 19 events including New Zealand, Portuguese, U.S. Grand Prix 1959, 19 events including Cuban, Monaco, Austrian, S. African Grand Prix 1960, 27 events including Monaco, German, Pacific Grand Prix, Nassau Tourist Trophy 1961; competed in 492 events, finishing in 366, winning 222, during motor racing career 1947–62; retd. from racing after accident at Goodwood, U.K. April 1962, attempted comeback 1980; subsequently took part in many business ventures, consultancy work on vehicle evaluation, property conversion, design; Man. Dir. Stirling Moss Ltd.; Dir. 28 cos.; also journalism and lecturing; Pres. or Patron of 28 car clubs; Hon. F.I.E. 1959; Gold Star, British Racing Drivers' Club 10 times 1950–61, Driver of the Year (Guild of Motoring Writers) 1954; Sir Malcolm Campbell Memorial Award 1957. *Publications include:* Stirling Moss 1953, In the Track of Speed 1957, Le Mans '59 1959, Design and Behaviour of the Racing Car 1963, All But My Life 1963, How to Watch Motor Racing 1975, Motor Racing and All That 1980, My Cars, My Career 1987, Stirling Moss: Great Drives in the Lakes and Dales 1993, Motor Racing Masterpieces 1995. *Leisure interests:* water and snow skiing, theatre and cinema, designing, model making, motor trials, swimming, interior decorating, woodwork, horse jumping and riding. *Address:* c/o Stirling Moss Ltd., 46 Shepherd Street, Mayfair, London, W1Y 8JN (Office); 44 Shepherd Street, London, W1Y 8JN, England (Home). *Telephone:* 0171-499 3272/7967.

MOSSAKOWSKI, Mirosław Jan, M.D.; Polish neurologist and neuropathologist; b. 23 Sept. 1929, Bereza Kartuska; s. of Tadeusz Mossakowski and Janina Mossakowska; m. Bibiana Kamińska; one s.; ed. Medical Acad., Gdańsk; staff Medical Acad., Gdańsk 1950–54, Jr. Asst., Physiological Anatomy Research Centre 1950–53, Asst., Neurological Clinic 1953–54; postgrad. studies 1954–57, Sr. Asst. Research Centre on Histopathology of Nervous System, Polish Acad. of Sciences 1957–58; postgrad. fellow, Neurological Inst., Montreal 1959–60; researcher, Neuropathological Research Centre of Polish Acad. of Sciences 1961–66, Asst. Prof., Head, Research Unit on Nervous Tissue Culture; Visiting Prof., Nat. Inst. of Neurological Diseases and Blindness, N.I.H. Bethesda 1966–67; Staff Centre for Experimental and Clinical Medicine of Polish Acad. of Sciences, Warsaw 1967–, Head, Neuropathology Dept. 1967–86, Deputy Dir. for Research 1967–68, Dir. 1975–; Extraordinary Prof. 1971–79, Ordinary Prof. 1979–; Corresp. mem. Polish Acad. of Sciences (PAN) 1973–86, Ordinary mem. 1986–; Deputy Sec., Medical Sciences Dept., Polish Acad. of Sciences 1968–80, Sec. 1981–95, mem. Presidium of Polish Acad. of Sciences 1975–, Vice-Pres. 1996–; Corresp. mem. Instituto Mexicano de Cultura 1976–; Foreign mem. Russian Acad. of Medical Sciences 1993–; Titular mem. European Acad. of Arts, Sciences and Humanities 1997–; Ed. Neuropatologia Polska (quarterly) 1969–72, 1978–80; mem. numerous int. neurological and pathological socs.; mem. Polish United Workers' Party (PZPR) 1953–90; Dr. h.c. (Medical Acad. Lublin) 1987, (Medical Acad. Gdańsk) 1996; numerous Polish awards and decorations. *Publications:* numerous research works in Polish and foreign journals on pathomorphology and histochemistry of brain tumours, cerebral ischemia and other disorders; Ed. Podstawy neuropatologii (Essentials of Neuropathology) 1981, Experimental and Clinical Neuropathology 1981, Brain Tumours 1997, Histology: nerve tissue and nervous system. *Leisure interests:* mountaineering, 18th century Polish history, colour photography. *Address:* ul. Polna 54 m. 40, 00-644 Warsaw, Poland. *Telephone:* (22) 825 29 86.

MÖSSBAUER, Rudolf, PH.D.; German physicist; b. 31 Jan. 1929, Munich; s. of Ludwig and Erna Mössbauer; m.; one s. two d.; ed. Tech. Hochschule, Munich; Research Asst. Max-Planck Inst., Heidelberg 1955–57; Research Fellow, Tech. Hochschule, Munich 1958–60; Research Fellow, Calif. Inst. of Tech. 1960, Sr. Research Fellow 1961, Prof. of Physics Dec. 1961; Prof. of Experimental Physics, Tech. Univ. of Munich 1964–72, 1977–; Dir. Inst. Max von Laue and of German-French-British High Flux Reactor, Grenoble, France 1972–77; Foreign mem. American Acad. of Arts and Sciences, Accad. Nazionale di Roma; mem. Deutsche Physische Gesellschaft, Deutsche Gesellschaft der Naturforscher, Leopoldina, American Physical Soc., European Physical Soc., Indian Acad. of Sciences, American Acad. of Sciences, N.A.S., Acad. of Sciences of the U.S.S.R., Pontifical Acad. of Sciences, Hungarian Acad. of Sciences; Hon. D.Sc. (Oxford) 1973, (Lille) 1973, (Leicester) 1975, (Birmingham) 1999; Dr. h.c. (Grenoble) 1974; Research Corpn. Award 1960, Röntgen Prize, Univ. of Giessen 1961, Elliot Cresson Medal of Franklin Inst., Philadelphia 1961, Nobel Prize for Physics 1961; Grosses Bundesverdienstkreuz. *Publications:* Papers on Recoilless Nuclear Resonance Absorption and on Neutrino Physics. *Leisure interests:* piano, hiking, photography, languages. *Address:* James-Franck-Str., 85748 Garching bei München (Office); Stümpflingstr. 6A, 82031 Grünwald, Germany (Home).

MOSTAFIZUR RAHMAN, A. S. M.; Bangladeshi politician; b. 8 Jan. 1934; s. of late Khan Bahadur Bazlur Rahman; m. Sufia Ruby; one s. one d.; ed. St. Xavier's Coll. Calcutta, St. Gregory High School, Dhaka Dhaka Govt. Coll. and Pakistan Mil. Acad.; commissioned into Army 1955; artillery officer 1956; served in various units and in Inter-Services Intelligence; Lt.-Col., retd. 1973; in business 1973–77; Deputy Adviser in charge of Home Affairs, Govt. of Pakistan 1977–78; Minister-in-charge, Ministry of Home Affairs 1978–81; mem. Parl. 1979–82, 1991–; mem. Standing Cttee. Bangladesh Nat. Party, Sec.-Gen. 1985–86; Minister of Foreign Affairs 1991–96. *Leisure interests:* shooting, reading, photography. *Address:* Ministry of Foreign Affairs, Topkhana Road, Dhaka, Bangladesh.

MOSTELLER, Frederick, M.A., PH.D.; American professor of mathematical statistics; b. 24 Dec. 1916, Clarksburg, Va.; s. of William R. Mosteller and Helen (Kelley) Mosteller; m. Virginia Gilroy 1941; one s. one d.; ed. Carnegie Inst. of Tech. and Princeton Univ.; Instr. in Math. Princeton Univ. 1942–43, Research Mathematician 1944–45; Lecturer, Dept. of Social Relations Harvard Univ. 1946–48, Assoc. Prof. 1948–51, Prof. of Mathematical Statistics 1951–87, Emer. Prof. 1987–, Chair. Dept. of Statistics 1957–69, 1975–77, Chair. Dept. of Biostatistics, School of Public Health 1977–81, Chair. Dept. of Health Policy & Man. Harvard School of Public Health 1981–87, Roger I. Lee Prof. 1978–87, Prof. Emer. 1987–; Dir. Tech. Assessment Group 1987–; Dir. Center for Evaluation American Acad. of Arts and Sciences 1994–; mem. Faculty, Harvard Medical School 1977–; Miller Research Prof. Univ. of Calif. Berkeley 1974–75; Charles M. and Martha Hitchcock Prof. Univ. of Calif. Berkeley 1984–85; mem. American Acad. of Arts and Sciences, American Philosophical Soc., N.A.S., Royal Statistical Soc.; Myrdal Prize 1978, Lazarsfeld Prize 1979; S. S. Wilks Award 1986, R.A. Fisher Award 1987; five hon. degrees. *Publications:* articles in related field and co-author of numerous books. *Address:* Department of Statistics, Harvard University, 1 Oxford Street, Cambridge, MA 02138, U.S.A. *Telephone:* (617) 495-2583.

MOSTOW, George Daniel, M.A., PH.D.; American professor of mathematics; b. 4 July 1923, Boston, Mass.; s. of Isaac J. Mostow and Ida Rotman; m. Evelyn Davidoff 1947; three s. one d.; ed. Harvard Univ.; Instructor in Math. Princeton Univ. 1947–48; mem. Inst. for Advanced Study 1947–49, 1956–57, 1975, Trustee 1982–92; Asst. Prof. Syracuse Univ. 1949–52; Asst. Prof. Johns Hopkins Univ. 1952–53, Assoc. Prof. 1954–56, Prof. 1957–61; Prof. of Math. Yale Univ. 1961–66, James E. English Prof. of Math. 1966–81, Henry Ford II Prof. of Math. 1981–, Chair. 1971–74; mem. Science Advisory Council, Math. Sciences Research Inst. Berkeley, Calif. 1988–91; mem. Science Advisory Council, Weizman Inst. Rehovoth, Israel 1988–, Bd. of Govs., Weizman Inst. 1988–, Tel Aviv Univ. 1990, Harvard Grad. Council 1989–93; Chair. U.S. Nat. Comm. for Math. 1971–73, 1983–85; Visiting Prof. at numerous univs. etc.; Fulbright scholar; Guggenheim Fellowship 1957–58; mem. N.A.S., American Acad. of Arts and Sciences, American Math. Soc. (Pres. 1987, 1988), Exec. Cttee. Int. Math. Union; many other professional affiliations and distinctions; Steel Prize for Research Paper of Fundamental or Lasting Value (American Math. Soc.) 1993. *Address:* Department of Mathematics, Yale University, New Haven, CT 06520 (Office); 25 Beechwood Road, Woodbridge, CT 06525, U.S.A. (Home).

MOTION, Andrew, M.LITT.; British biographer and poet; b. 26 Oct. 1952; s. of Andrew R. Motion and Catherine G. Motion; m. 1st Joanna J. Powell 1973 (dissolved 1983); m. 2nd Janet Elisabeth Dalley 1985; two s. one d.; ed. Radley Coll. and Univ. Coll., Oxford; Lecturer in English, Univ. of Hull 1977–81; Ed. Poetry Review 1981–83; Poetry Ed. Chatto & Windus 1983–89, Editorial Dir. 1985–87; Prof. of Creative Writing Univ. of E. Anglia, Norwich 1995–; Chair. Literature Advisory Panel Arts Council of England 1996–98; Rhys Memorial Prize for Dangerous Play 1984, Somerset Maugham Award for The Lamberts 1987, Whitbread Biography Award 1993, Hon. D.Litt. (Hull) 1996. *Publications:* poetry: The Pleasure Steamers 1978, Independence 1981, The Penguin Book of Contemporary British Poetry (anthology) 1982, Secret Narratives 1983, Dangerous Play 1984, Natural Causes 1987, Love in a Life 1991, The Price of Everything 1994, Selected Poems 1996–97 1998; criticism: The Poetry of Edward Thomas 1981, Philip Larkin 1982, William Barnes selected poems (ed.) 1994, Salt Water 1997; biography: The Lamberts 1986, Philip Larkin: A Writer's Life 1993, Keats 1997; novels: The Pale Companion 1989, Famous For the Creatures 1991. *Leisure interest:* cooking. *Address:* Dept. of English and American Studies, University of East Anglia, Norwich, NR4 7TJ; c/o Faber & Faber, 3 Queen Square, London, WC1N 3AU, England.

MOTLANA, Nthato Harrison, B.SC., M.B., B.CH.; South African community worker and medical practitioner; b. 1925, Marapyane, Pretoria Dist.; m. Sally Maunye 1953; three s. one d.; ed. Kilnerton High School, and Univs. of Fort Hare and Witwatersrand; Sec. ANC Youth League 1949; participated in ANC Defiance Campaign 1952; arrested, received suspended sentence, banned for five years 1952–57; Resident Houseman, Baragwanath Hosp. 1955–56, subsequently Medical Officer; own medical practice 1957–; founder mem. Black Community Programmes 1972; Vice-Chair. Black Parents Asscn. 1976; detained for six months 1976; Chair. Cttee. of Ten est. to organize civic affairs in Soweto 1977; imprisoned 1977–78; Pres. Soweto Civic Asscn.; active in campaign to ban Black Local Authority Election 1983; frequent guest of overseas govts.; Chair. Population Devt. Council of S. Africa 1993–, Metropolitan Life 1993–, Corporate Africa, Metlife Holdings 1993–, etc.; numerous other professional and public appts.; Citation for Outstanding Community Services (Univ. of Witwatersrand); Dr. h.c. (Dartmouth, U.S.A.). *Address:* c/o Metropolitan Life Ltd., 7 Coen Steytler Avenue, Foreshore, Cape Town, South Africa.

MOTSPAN (MOTPAN), Dumitru; Moldovan politician; b. 3 May 1940; engineer, worked as head agric. enterprises, head local admin.; Chair. Agrarian-Democratic Party; Deputy Chair. of Parl. 1994–97, Chair. March 1997–. *Address:* Parliament House, Stefan Celmari prosp. 105, 277033 Chişinău, Moldova (Office). *Telephone:* (2) 23 25 28 (Office).

MOTSUENYANE, Samuel Mokgethi, B.SC.(AGRIC.); South African business executive; b. 11 Feb. 1927, Potchefstroom; s. of the late Solomon P. and Christina D. Motsuenyane; m. Jocelyn Mashinini 1954; six s.; ed. N. Carolina State Univ., U.S.A., Jan Hofmeyr School of Social Work; Nat. Organizing Sec. African Nat. Soil Conservation Asscn. 1952–59; N.C. State Univ., U.S.A. 1960–62; Pres. NAFCOC 1968–92; Chair. African Business Publications, African Business Holdings, NAFCOC Permanent, Venda Nat. Devt. Corpn., New-Real African Investments; Dir. African Devt. and Construction Holdings, NAFCOC Nat. Trust, Barlow Rand, Blackchain Ltd., numerous other cos.; Chancellor, Univ. of the North (S.A.) 1985–90; Pres. Motsunenyane Comm. to investigate torture and disappearances in ANC detention camps 1992–93; Pres. Boy Scouts of S. Africa 1976–81; Leader of Senate 1994–96; serves on bds. of numerous cos. and orgs.; Harvard Business Award 1977; Dr. h.c. (Univ. of Witwatersrand) 1983; Hon. D.Econ.Sc. (Cape Town) 1986. *Leisure interests:* gardening, reading. *Publications:* numerous articles. *Address:* P.O. Box 911407, Rosslyn 0200, South Africa.

MOTTISTONE, Lord, 4th Baron, cr. 1933, of Mottistone, **David Peter Seely,** C.B.E.; British naval officer (retd.); b. 16 Dec. 1920, London; s. of Maj.-Gen. J. E. B. Seely, 1st Lord Mottistone and Hon. Evelyn Murray; m. Anthea Christine McMullan 1944; two s. three d. (one deceased); ed. Royal Naval Colls., Dartmouth and Greenwich; promoted to Commdr., R.N. 1955, Special Asst. NATO Chief of Allied Staff, Malta 1956–58, in command H.M.S. Cossack 1958–59, rank of Capt. R.N. 1960, Deputy Dir. Signals Div., Admiralty 1961–63, in command H.M.S. Ajax and 24th Escort Squadron 1964–65, Naval Adviser to U.K. High Commr., Ottawa 1965–66, retd. from R.N. in protest at govt.'s defence policy 1967; Dir. of Personnel and Training, Radio Rentals Group of Cos. 1967–69; Dir. Distributive Industries Training Bd. 1969–75, Cake & Biscuit Alliance 1975–82; Lord Lieut. of Isle of Wight 1986–95, Gov., Capt. and Steward 1992–95; Hon. D.Litt. (Bournemouth) 1993; K.St.J. *Leisure interest:* yachting. *Address:* The Old Parsonage, Mottistone, Isle of Wight, PO30 4EE, England.

MOTTRAM, Sir Richard Clive, K.C.B.; British civil servant; b. 23 April 1946; s. of John Mottram and Florence Yates; m. Fiona Margaret Erskine 1971; three s. one d.; ed. King Edward VI Camp Hill School, Birmingham, Univ. of Keele; joined Civil Service 1968, assigned to Ministry of Defence, Asst. Pvt. Sec. to Sec. of State for Defence 1971–72, Prin. Naval Programme and Budget 1973, Cabinet Office 1975–77, Pvt. Sec. to Perm. Under-Sec., Ministry of Defence 1979–81, Asst. Sec. Manpower Control and Audit Procurement Exec. 1981, Pvt. Sec. to Sec. of State for Defence 1982–86, Asst. Under-Sec. of State 1986–89, Deputy Under-Sec. of State (Policy) 1989–92, Second Perm. Sec. Cabinet Office 1992, Perm. Sec. Office of Public Service and Science, Cabinet Office 1992–95, Ministry of Defence 1995–98, Dept. of the Environment, Transport and the Regions 1998–. *Leisure interests:* cinema, tennis. *Address:* Department of the Environment, Transport and the Regions, 6th Floor, Eland House, Bressenden Place, London, SW1E 5DU, England.

MOTULSKY, Arno Gunther, B.S., M.D.; American medical geneticist; b. 5 July 1923, Germany; s. of Herman and Rena (née Sass) Motulsky; m. Gretel Stern 1945; one s. two d.; ed. YMCA Coll., Chicago, Yale Univ., Univ. of Illinois Medical School; Intern, Fellow, Asst. and Sr. Resident (Internal Medicine) Michael Reese Hosp., Chicago 1947–51; Staff mem. in charge of Clinical Investigation, Dept. of Hematology, Army Medical Service Graduate School, Walter Reed Army Medical Center; Research Assoc. in Internal Medicine, George Washington Univ. School of Medicine, Washington 1952–53, Instructor 1953–55, Asst. Prof. 1955–58, Assoc. Prof. 1958–61, Prof. Dept. of Medicine 1961–, Prof. Dept. of Genetics 1961–, Dir. Medical Genetics Training Program 1961–89, Dir. Center for Inherited Diseases 1972–89; Pres. Int. Congress of Human Genetics 1986; Ed. American Journal of Human Genetics 1969–75, Human Genetics 1969–98; mem. American Soc. of Human Genetics, N.A.S. 1976, American Acad. of Arts and Sciences 1978; Hon. D.Sc. (Illinois) 1982, Hon. M.D. (Würzburg) 1991; William Allan Memorial Award 1970, Alexander von Humboldt Award 1984, San Remo Int. Prize for Genetic Research 1988. *Publications:* Human Genetics—Problems and Approaches (with F. Vogel) 1996; about 300 medical and scientific articles. *Leisure interests:* reading, collecting African art, antique maps. *Address:* Division of Medical Genetics, University of Washington, P.O. Box 356423, Seattle, WA 98195 (Office); 4347 53rd N.E., Seattle, WA 98105, U.S.A. (Home). *Telephone:* (206) 543-3593 (Office). *Fax:* (206) 616-4196.

MOTZFELDT, Jonathan; Danish politician; b. 1938; teacher; Lutheran pastor; mem. and Vice-Chair. Greenland Assembly 1971–79; mem. Greenland Parl. (Landsting) 1979–, Chair. 1979–88, 1997; Prime Minister of Greenland 1979–91, Sept. 1997–; Chair. Siumut. *Address:* Greenland Home Rule Government, POB 1015, 3900 Nuuk, Greenland.

MOUBARAK, Samir, PH.D.; Lebanese diplomatist; b. 21 March 1943, Beirut; s. of Moussa Moubarak and Nada Aboussouan; ed. Ecole des Hautes Etudes Commerciales, Paris, Sorbonne, Paris; Political Section, Ministry of Foreign Affairs, Beirut 1967–69; mem. Lebanese Del., Perm. Mission of Lebanon to UN, New York 1969–73; First Sec., Embassy, Paris 1973–77, Chargé d'Affaires a.i., Embassy, Madrid; Special Adviser to Minister of Foreign Affairs, Beirut 1977–82; Amb. to Sweden 1982–88; Amb., Ministry of Foreign Affairs 1988–94; Perm. Rep. of Lebanon to UN, New York 1994–, Vice-Pres. 50th Session UN Gen. Ass. 1995, Vice-Pres. ECOSOC, New York 1996. *Address:* Permanent Mission of Lebanon to the United Nations, 866 United Nations Plaza, Suite 531, New York, NY 10017, U.S.A.

MOUGEOTTE, Etienne Pierre Albert; French journalist; b. 1 March 1940, La Rochefoucauld; s. of Jean Mougeotte and Marcelle Thonon; m. Françoise Duprilot 1972; one s. two d.; ed. Lycée Buffon, Lycée Henri-IV, Paris, Inst. d'études politiques de Paris, Inst. Français de presse; reporter France-Inter 1965-66, Beirut Corresp. 1966–67; Ed. Europe Numéro 1 1968–69; Chief Reporter, Asst. Ed.-in-Chief Information Première (TV) 1969–72; Producer l'Actualité en question 1972; journalist Radio-Télé Luxembourg 1972–73; Ed.-in-Chief Europe 1 1973, News Dir. 1974–81; monthly contrib. Paradoxes 1974–; Editorial Dir. Journal du Dimanche 1981–83, Télé 7 Jours 1983–87; Dir. Gen. Broadcasting TF1 1987–89, Dir. Gen. 1987–, Vice-Pres. Broadcasting 1989–; Vice-Pres. French Fed. of Press Agencies 1975–81; mem. Interprofessional communication group (Gic) 1985–87; Pres. Nat. Videocommunication Syndicate 1982–87, TF1 Films, Tricom; Dir. TF1 1991–; Pres. TF1 Films Productions; Officier, Légion d'honneur, Ordre nat. du Mérite. *Leisure interests:* tennis, golf. *Address:* TF1, 1 quai du Point-du-Jour, 92656 Boulogne-Billancourt cedex, France.

MOULAERT, Jacques, LL.D., M.P.A.; Belgian banker; b. 23 Oct. 1930, Ostend; s. of late Albert Moulaert and of Marie de Neckere; m. Christiane Laloux 1957; four d.; ed. St. Barbara Coll. Ghent, Univ. of Ghent and Harvard Univ.; Gen. Sec. Aleurope S.A. 1961; Asst. Man. Compagnie Lambert 1967; Man. Compagnie Bruxelles Lambert (CBL) 1972; Man. Dir. Groupe Bruxelles Lambert 1979; Chair. Bd. Bank Brussels Lambert (BBL) 1993; Officier, Ordre de la Couronne; Commdr., Ordre de St.-Sylvestre; Commdr., Ordre de Léopold. *Address:* Bank Brussels Lambert, 24 avenue Marnix, 1000 Brussels, Belgium. *Telephone:* (2) 547-21-11. *Fax:* (2) 547-38-44.

MOULAYE, Mohamed, D.SC.; Mauritanian politician and public official; b. 1 Oct. 1936, Ouagadougou, Burkina Faso; s. of El Hassan Moulaye and Maimouna Dem; m. Ginette Marcin 1962; three s. five d.; Founder-mem. Asscn. de la Jeunesse de Mauritanie (AJM) 1956; Sec.-Gen. Section P.R.M. Boutilimit 1960; mem. Nat. Ass. 1965–75; Directeur des finances 1966; Contrôleur financier 1967–75; Minister of Finance 1975–77, 1979; Parl. rapporteur to Comm. des Finances; fmr. mem. IPU; Dir. Office of Pres. of Mauritania 1979–80; Conseiller Econ. et Financier du Chef de l'Etat, Prés. de la Comm. Centrale des Marchés Publics; Pres. Parti du Centre démocratique mauritanien 1992, now Democratic Centre Party (DCP); First Vice-Pres. Action pour le Changement; mem. Conseil général, Banque Centrale de Mauritanie 1980–; Dir. Personnel Air Afrique, Financial Dir. 1985–; Chair. and Man. Dir. Arrachad, Nouakchott 1990; Chevalier, Ordre nat. du mérite (France). *Leisure interests:* reading, cinema. *Address:* B.P. 289, Nouakchott, Mauritania.

MOULE, Rev. Charles Francis Digby, C.B.E., F.B.A.; British university professor and ecclesiastic (retd.); b. 3 Dec. 1908, Hangchow, China; s. of Henry W. Moule and Laura C. Pope; ed. Weymouth Coll., Dorset, Emmanuel Coll., Cambridge and Ridley Hall, Cambridge; ordained deacon 1933, priest 1934; Tutor, Ridley Hall 1933–34; Curate, St. Andrew's, Rugby 1934–36; Vice-Prin., Ridley Hall 1936–44; Fellow, Clare Coll., Cambridge 1944–, Dean 1944–51; Asst. Lecturer in Divinity, Univ. of Cambridge 1944–47, Lecturer 1947–51, Lady Margaret's Prof. 1951–76; Hon. Fellow, Emmanuel Coll., Cambridge; Hon. D.D. (St. Andrews, Cambridge); Collins Biennial Book Prize; Burkitt Medal (British Acad.). *Publications:* Idiom Book of New Testament Greek 1953, Commentary on Colossians and Philemon 1957, The Birth of the New Testament 1962, The Origin of Christology 1977, Essays in New Testament Interpretation 1982, Forgiveness and Reconciliation 1998. *Address:* 1 King's Houses, Pevensey, East Sussex, BN24 5JR, England. *Telephone:* (01323) 762436.

MOULINE, Larbi; Moroccan business executive, diplomatist and consultant; b. 10 Nov. 1934, Rabat; s. of Mohamed Mouline and Habiba Balafrej; m. Naima Mouline 1959; three s. one d.; ed. Ecole Nat. Supérieure des Mines, St. Etienne, France; Man. Dir. O.C.P. (phosphate co.) 1959–74, Pres. Amicale des Hors-Cadres; Gen. Man. Sonasid (steel co.) 1975–83; Amb. to India 1984–86, to Greece 1987–88; Adviser to Minister of Privatization and Econ. Affairs, Minister of Agric. 1989–94; now pvt. consultant; Sec.-Gen. Asscn. des Intervenants Scientifiques (ASSIST), Rabat; (Kt. of the Throne

(Morocco); Order of Phoenix (Greece). *Publications:* A Study on Economic Development Linked to a Steel Complex in Morocco 1977, A Study on Mechanization in Phosphate Mines. *Leisure interests:* reading, music, golf, travel. *Address:* 27 rue Cadi Sanhaji, Souissi, Rabat, Morocco. *Telephone:* (7) 750282. *Fax:* (7) 639501.

MOULTON, Alexander Eric, C.B.E., R.D.I., M.A., F.ENG., F.I.MECH.E., F.P.R.I., F.R.S.A.; British engineer; b. 9 April 1920, Stratford-on-Avon; s. of John Coney and Beryl Latimer Moulton; ed. Marlborough Coll., King's Coll., Cambridge; worked in Engine Research Dept., Bristol Aeroplane Co. 1939–44, Personal Asst. to Sir Roy Fedden 1940–42; established Research Dept. of George Spencer, Moulton & Co. Ltd., originating work on rubber suspensions for vehicles and designing Flexitor, Works Man. then Tech. Dir. 1945–56; f. Moulton Devts. Ltd., Man. Dir. 1956–, devt. work on own designs of rubber suspensions including Hydrolastic and Hydragas 1956, Chair. 1956–67, Man. Dir. 1956–; designed Moulton Coach; f. Moulton Bicycles Ltd. to produce own design Moulton Bicycle 1962, Chair. and Man. Dir. 1962–67, Dir. 1967–; Dir. Alex Moulton Ltd.; Dir. S.W. Regional Bd., Nat. Westminster Bank 1982–87; Hon. Dr. R.C.A.; Hon. D.Sc. (Bath); Design Centre Award 1964, Amb. Award 1964, Bidlake Memorial Plaque 1964, Gold Medal Milan Triennale 1964, Queens Award to Industry for Tech. Innovation (Moulton Devts. Ltd.) 1967, Soc. of Industrial Artists and Designers (S.I.A.D.) Design Medal 1976, Council of the Inst. of Mechanical Engineers James Clayton Prize, Crompton Lanchester Medal (from Automobile Div.), Thomas Hawksley Gold Medal, 1979. *Publications:* various papers on vehicle suspension. *Leisure interests:* steamboating, canoeing, cycling, shooting. *Address:* The Hall, Bradford-on-Avon, Wiltshire, BA15 1AJ, England. *Telephone:* (01225) 862991.

MOULTRIE, James Bertram, B.SC., M.ED.; Bahamian diplomatist; b. 27 Dec. 1944; m.; one s. two d.; ed. Bahamas Teachers' Coll., Univ. of West Indies and Univ. of Miami; Deputy Perm. Rep. of Bahamas to UN 1978–80; del. to numerous int. confs. including those of Caribbean Community, OAS, Commonwealth Heads of Govt. and UN Gen. Ass.; Jr. Minister, Ministry of Foreign Affairs 1987–88; Perm. Rep. to UN 1988–94.

MOUMIN, Amini Ali, M.A.; Comoran diplomatist; b. 30 Aug. 1944, Mutsamudu Anjouan; m.; four c.; ed. King George Coll., Zanzibar, Univ. of Kuwait, Downing Coll., Cambridge, Paris Inst. of Int. Relations and Univ. of Paris-V; Accountant Ministry of Commerce and Industry, Zanzibar 1964–68; Adviser to Pres. of Comoros 1978–79; Chief Africa Dept. Ministry of Foreign Affairs and Co-operation 1979–82, Dir. Political Affairs 1982–86; Perm. Rep. of Comoros to UN 1986–93. *Address:* c/o Ministry of Foreign Affairs, BP 482, Moroni, The Comoros.

MOUNGAR, Fidele; Chadian politician and medical practitioner; b. Logone Region; fmr. head of surgery, Peronne Hosp., Somme, France; Prime Minister of Chad 1993; leader Action pour l'unité et le socialisme (ACTUS), Collectif des Partis pour le Changement (COPAC). *Address:* c/o Action pour l'unité et le socialisme, N'Djamena, Chad.

MOUNT, (William Robert) Ferdinand; British author and journalist; b. 2 July 1939, London; s. of Robin Mount and Julia Mount; m. Julia Lucas 1968; two s. one d.; ed. Eton Coll., Christ Church, Oxford; Political Ed. The Spectator 1977–82, 1985, Literary Ed. 1984–85; Head Prime Minister's Policy Unit 1982–84; Political Columnist, The Times 1984–85, Daily Telegraph 1985–90; Ed. Times Literary Supplement 1991–; Hawthornden Prize (for Of Love and Asthma) 1992. *Publications:* Very Like a Whale 1967, The Theatre of Politics 1972, The Man Who Rode Ampersand 1975, The Clique 1978, The Subversive Family 1982, The Selkirk Strip 1987, Of Love and Asthma 1991, The British Constitution Now 1992, Communism 1992, Umbrella 1994, The Liquidator 1995, Jem (and Sam) 1998. *Address:* 17 Ripplevale Grove, London, N1 1HS, England. *Telephone:* 0171-607 5398.

MOUNTCASTLE, Vernon Benjamin, Jr., M.D.; American neurophysiologist and educator; b. 15 July 1918, Shelbyville, Ky.; s. of Vernon B. Mountcastle and Anna-Francis Marguerite Waugh; m. Nancy Clayton Pierpont 1945; two s. one d.; ed. Roanoke Coll., Salem, Va., and Johns Hopkins Univ. School of Medicine; House Officer, Surgery, The Johns Hopkins Hosp. Baltimore, Md. 1943; with U.S.N. Amphibious Forces 1943–46; through jr. ranks, The Johns Hopkins Univ. School of Medicine 1948–59, Prof. of Physiology 1959, Dir. of Dept. of Physiology 1964–80, Univ. Prof. of Neuroscience 1980–92, Prof. Emer. 1992–; Dir. Bard Labs. of Neurophysiology, Johns Hopkins Univ. 1981–91; Pres. Neurosciences Research Foundation 1981–85; Dir. Neuroscience Research Program 1981–84; Penfield Lecturer, American Univ., Beirut 1971; Sherrington Lecturer, Liverpool Univ. 1974; Sherrington Lecturer, Royal Soc. of Medicine, London, Mellon Lecturer, Univ. of Pittsburgh 1976, Visiting Prof. Collège de France, Paris 1980, and numerous other hon. lectureships; Nat. Pres. Soc. for Neuroscience 1971–72; mem. N.A.S., American Acad. of Arts and Sciences, American Phil. Soc.; Hon. Dr.Sc. (Pa.) 1976, (Roanoke) 1968, (Northwestern) 1985, Hon. M.D. (Zurich) 1983, (Siena) 1984; Lashley Prize, American Phil. Soc. 1974, F. O. Schmitt Prize and Medal, M.I.T. 1975, Gold Medal, Royal Soc. of Medicine 1976, Horwitz Prize, Columbia 1978, Gerard Prize, Soc. for Neuroscience 1980, Int. Prize, Fyssen Foundation Paris 1983, Lasker Award 1983, Nat. Medal of Sciences 1986, McGovern Prize and Medal, A.A.A.S. 1990, Neuroscience Award Fidia Fed. 1990, Australia Prize 1993, Neuroscience Prize, N.A.S. 1998. *Publications:* The Mindful Brain (with G. M. Edelman) 1978, Medical Physiology (two vols.) (Ed. and major contrib.) 14th edn. 1980, Perceptual Neuroscience: The Cerebral Cortex 1998 and more than 50 articles in scientific journals on the physiology of the central nervous system especially on the neuronal mechanisms in sensation and perception. *Leisure interests:* sailing, horsemanship. *Address:* Department of Physiology, The Johns Hopkins University School of Medicine, 725 North Wolfe Street, Baltimore, MD 21205 (Office); 15601 Carroll Road, Monkton, MD 21111, U.S.A. *Telephone:* (301) 955-3635 (Office).

MOUNTER, Julian D'Arcy; British journalist, television director and producer and broadcasting executive; b. 2 Nov. 1944, Cornwall; s. of Francis Mounter and Elizabeth Moore; m. Patricia A. Kelsall-Spurr 1983; two s.; ed. Skinners Grammar School, Tunbridge Wells and Grenville Coll.; reporter various local newspapers 1961–65; journalist The Times 1966–71; Weekend World, London Weekend TV 1971–73; Head of Current Affairs and Documentaries, Westward TV 1973–74; Reporter/Dir. Panorama and Midweek, BBC TV 1974–78; Ed., Inside Business, Thames TV 1978–79, Exec. Producer, Current Affairs 1979–81, Controller, Children's and Young Adults' Dept. 1981–84; Dir. Programmes and Production, Thorn-EMI Satellite and Cable 1984–86; Dir. Cosgrove Hall Ltd. 1981–84, JRA Ltd. 1980–85, Cameralink Ltd. 1980–85, Blackwell Videotec Ltd. 1980–85; Dir.-Gen. and C.E.O. Television New Zealand 1986–91; Chair. South Pacific Pictures Ltd., Broadcast Communications Ltd. 1988–91; Dir. The Listener, Visnews (UK) Ltd. 1987–89, Reuters TV Ltd. 1989–91; Chief Exec. and Pres. Star TV Ltd. Hutchvision Ltd., Media Assets Ltd., Asia News Ltd. 1992–93; Chair. New Media Investments 1994–98, Majestic Films and TV Ltd. 1993–95, Swoffers Ltd. 1995–96, Renown Leisure Group Ltd. 1995–; C.E.O. and Man. Dir. Seven Network Ltd. 1998–; Dir. CTV Ltd.; 1994–99; Trustee Int. Inst. of Communications 1988–95; Dir. Int. Council of Nat. Acad. of Television Arts and Sciences, U.S.A. 1993–; Queen's Medal 1990, for Services to N.Z.; jt. winner, IPC Investigative Journalism award; various television awards. *Leisure interests:* ocean sailing, naval history, music. *Address:* Seven Network Ltd., Mobbs Lane, Epping, NSW 2121, Australia. *Telephone:* (2) 9877-7000. *Fax:* (2) 9877-7111.

MOUREAUX, Philippe; Belgian politician; b. 12 April 1939, Etterbeek; m.; four c.; secondary school teacher 1961–62; Asst., subsequently Prof., Université Libre de Bruxelles 1967–; Adviser, Deputy Prime Minister's Office 1972–73, on staff Prime Minister's Office 1973–74, Chef de cabinet to Deputy Prime Minister 1977–80, Minister of the Interior and Institutional Reforms 1980, of Justice and Institutional Reforms 1980–81, Minister and Chair. Exec. of French Community, responsible for cultural affairs, budget and foreign affairs 1981–85, Feb.–May 1988, Deputy Prime Minister and Minister for the Brussels Region and Institutional Reforms 1988–89, Deputy Prime Minister, Minister for Brussels Region and of Institutional Reforms 1990–92, of Social Affairs 1992–93.

MOUSAWI, Faisal Radhi al-, M.B., B.CH., F.R.C.S.(E.), F.R.C.S.(I.); Bahraini government minister and orthopaedic surgeon; b. 6 April 1944, Bahrain; one s. three d.; ed. Univ. of Cairo, Egypt; fmr. Rotary Intern., Cairo Univ. Hosp., House Officer, Sr. House Officer, Dept. of Surgery, Govt. Hosp., Bahrain, Sr. House Officer, Accident and Orthopaedic Surgery, Cen. Middx. Hosp., London, Orthopaedic Surgery, St. Helier Hosp., Carshalton, Surrey, Gen. Surgery, Nelson Hosp., London, St. Bartholomew's Hosp., London, registrar, Orthopaedic Surgery, Whittington Hosp., London, Gen. and Traumatic Surgery, Wexford Co. Hosp., Ireland; locum consultant, Whittington Hosp. 1983–84; consultant Orthopaedic Surgeon, Salmaniya Medical Centre, Bahrain 1976–, Chair. Dept. of Surgery 1982–84, Chief of Medical Staff June–Aug. 1982, Chair. Dept. of Orthopaedic Surgery; Asst. Prof. Coll. of Medicine and Medical Sciences, Arabian Gulf Univ.; Asst. Under-Sec., Ministry of Health 1982–85, Minister of Health 1995–; mem. Scientific Council, Arab Bd. for Surgery 1979–; Chair. Arab Bd. Cttee. for Sub-specialities in Surgery, Arab Bd. for Orthopaedic Surgery 1990–, Chair. Training Cttee. 1988–; Chair. Nat. Arab Bd. Cttee. and Co-ordinator, Arab Bd. Programme in Surgery, Bahrain; Examiner, Ministry of Health Qualification Examination 1982–, Royal Coll. of Surgeons, Ireland, Part B Fellowship Examination; mem. Editorial Bd. Bahrain Medical Bulletin; Pres. Gulf Orthopaedic Asscn.; mem. European Soc. for Sport Medicine, Knee Surgery and Arthroscopy; Fellow British Orthopaedic Asscn. *Publications:* numerous papers and articles. *Leisure interest:* tennis. *Address:* Ministry of Health, P.O. Box 12, Sheikh Sulman Road, Manama, Bahrain. *Telephone:* 255555. *Fax:* 254459.

MOUSKOURI, Nana (Joanna); Greek singer; b. 13 Oct. 1936, Canea; m. George Petsilas; one s. one d.; ed. Athens Nat. Conservatory; Greek Broadcasting Festival Award 1959, Barcelona Festival Award and numerous awards and prizes; several gold albums since 1959, also over 300 gold and platinum records worldwide; living in Paris 1962–; UNICEF Amb. 1993–94; mem. European Parl. 1994–. *Address:* c/o European Parliament, Centre Européen, Plateau de Kirchberg, 2929 Luxembourg; c/o Polygram, 20 rue des Fossés Saint-Jacques, 75005 Paris, France; Aharnon 289, GR112 53, Athens, Greece. *Telephone:* 1 856 19 02 (Greece). *Fax:* 1 960 05 55.

MOUSSA, Pierre L.; French banker; b. 5 March 1922, Lyon; m. Anne-Marie Trousseau 1957; ed. Ecole Normale Supérieure; Insp. of Finances 1946–50; Tech. Adviser to Sec. of State for Finance 1949–51, Dept. of External Econ. Relations 1951–54, Dir. Econ. Affairs and Planning, Ministry for Overseas Territories 1954–59; Dir. of Civil Aviation, Ministry of Public Works and Transport 1959–62; Dir. Dept. of Operations for Africa, World Bank 1962–64; Pres. French Fed. of Assurance Cos. 1965–69; Pres. Banque de Paris et des Pays-Bas 1969–81, Chair. 1978–81; Chair. Finance and Devt. Inc. 1982–86, Pallas Holdings 1983–92, Dillon, Read Ltd. 1984–87, France Développement (Frandev) 1986–90, Cresvale Partners 1987–94, Pallas Invest 1988–90, Pallas Monaco 1988–96, The Managed Convertible Fund 1990–95, Pallas Ltd. 1992–93, Strand Assocs. Ltd. 1993–, Strand Partners Ltd. 1993–94, The Prometheus Fund 1993–95, West Africa Growth Fund 1997–; Dir. numerous cos.; Officier, Légion d'honneur 1976, Officier, Ordre national du Mérite. *Publications:* L'économie de la zone franc, Les chances économiques de la communauté Franco-Africaine, Les nations prolétaires, Les Etats-Unis et les nations prolétaires, La roue de la fortune, souvenirs d'un financier, Caliban naufragé: les relations Nord/Sud à la fin du XXe siècle. *Address:* 17 Bulstrode Street, London W1M 5FQ; 14 Pelham Place, South Kensington, London, SW7 2NH, England. *Telephone:* 0171-486 1238. *Fax:* 0171-935 0860.

MOUSSAVI, Mir Hussein; Iranian politician; b. 1942, Iran; ed. Nat. Univ., Teheran; joined Islamic Soc. at univ. in Teheran and active in Islamic Socs. since; imprisoned briefly for opposition to the Shah 1973; a founder mem. Islamic Republican Party (IRP) 1979; appointed Chief Ed. IRP newspaper Islamic Republic 1979; Foreign Minister Aug.–Oct. 1981; elected Prime Minister by Majlis (consultative assembly) 1981–89, Adviser to the Pres. 1989. *Address:* Office of the President, Teheran, Iran.

MOUSTIERS, Pierre Jean (Rossi), L. EN D.; French author; b. 13 Aug. 1924, La Seyne (Var); ed. Univs. of Aix-Marseilles and Neuchâtel; Attaché at the Office des Changes, French zone in Germany 1947–49; Chief, Information Services, Nat. Information and Protection Centre for Construction (C.N.I.P.) 1950–60; medical del., pharmaceutical lab. MERCK, Darmstadt 1961, later regional insp.; literary critic Nice-Matin 1970, Radio-Marseille; Hommes et Lectures prize 1962, Grand Prix de littérature sportive, Grand Prix du Roman, Acad. Française for La Paroi 1969, Prix des Maisons de la Presse for L'Hiver d'un Gentilhomme 1972, Grand Prix littéraire de Provence for Une place forte 1975, Prix Louis Philippe Kammans for Une place forte, Prix des libraires for Un crime de notre temps 1977, Grand Prix du Scénario for La ronde de nuit, Prix Acad. Balzac for TV adaptation of Curé de Tours 1980, Sept d'Or for L'Affaire Caillaux, Prix Jean Giono, Italy 1986; Officier des Arts et Lettres; Médaille des Combattants de la Résistance. *Publications:* Le journal d'un geôlier 1957, La mort du Pantin 1961, Le pharisien 1962, La paroi 1969, L'hiver d'un gentilhomme 1971, Une place forte 1974, Un Crime de Notre Temps 1976, Prima Donna 1978, Le Coeur du Voyage 1981, La grenade 1984, Un Aristocrate à La Lanterne 1986, l'Eclat 1990, Un si bel orage 1991, la Flambée 1993, L'Or du torrent 1995, A l'Abri du Monde (Prix Chateaubriant) 1997. *Essay:* Hervé Bazin ou le romancier en mouvement 1973. *Television:* L'hiver d'un gentilhomme 1973, La mort du Pantin 1975, Une place forte 1976, Un crime de notre temps 1977, La ronde de nuit 1978, Antoine et Julie 1981, Bel Ami 1983, L'Affaire Caillaux 1985, Le Coeur du Voyage 1986, L'Eté de la Revolution 1989, L'Interdiction, Pris au piège, Un si bel orage 1995. *Leisure interests:* mountaineering, reading, painting and drawing, taxidermy. *Address:* Campagne Sainte Anne, boulevard des Acacias, 83100 Toulon, France.

MOUT, Marianne Elisabeth Henriette Nicolette, D.LITT.; Netherlands historian; b. 31 May 1945, Wassenaar; d. of Arie Mout and Maria Helena van Tooren; m. 1st Robbert Salomon van Santen (divorced 1979); m. 2nd Peter Felix Ganz 1987; ed. Rijnlands Lyceum, Wassenaar, Univ. of Amsterdam; research student Czechoslovakia 1966, 1967; Asst. Keeper, Jewish Historical Museum, Amsterdam 1969; Ed., Martinus Nijhoff publrs. 1970; lecturer in Modern History, Utrecht Univ. 1975–76; Sr. Lecturer in Dutch History, Leiden Univ. 1976–, Prof. of Cen. European Studies 1990–, Prof. of Modern History 1994–; Man. Ed. Tijdschrift voor Geschiedenis 1981–86; Fellow Netherlands Inst. for Advanced Studies, Wassenaar 1987–88, 1993–94; mem. Bd., Inst. of Netherlands History (Instituut voor Nederlandse Geschiedenis) 1989–; mem. Royal Netherlands Acad. of Arts and Sciences; Corresp. mem. Austrian Acad. of Sciences. *Publications:* Komenský v Amsterodamu (with J. Polišenský) 1970, Bohemen en de Nederlanden in de zestiende eeuw 1975, Plakkaat van Verlatinge 1581 1979, Die Kultur des Humanismus 1998; numerous articles, mainly on 16th–17th-century Dutch and Cen. European history of ideas and cultural history; Ed. and Co-Ed. of several books, including Gerhard Oestreich, Antiker Geist und moderner Staat bei Justus Lipsius 1989. *Address:* P.B. 9515, 2300 RA Leiden (Office); Oranje Nassaulaan 27, 2361 LB Warmond, Netherlands (Home). *Telephone:* 071-5272759, 5272651 (Office). *Fax:* 5272652.

MOWAT, Farley McGill, O.C., B.A.; Canadian author; b. 12 May 1921, Belleville, Ont.; s. of Angus and Helen (née Thomson) Mowat; m. 1st Frances Mowat 1947; two s.; m. 2nd Claire Mowat 1963; ed. Toronto Univ.; served in the Canadian Army 1939–45; Arctic exploration 1947–49; full-time writer 1950–; Hon. D.Litt. (Laurentian Univ.) 1970, (Univ. of Victoria) 1982, (Lakehead Univ.) 1986; Hon. D. Laws (Lethbridge, Toronto, Prince Edward Island, Queen's Univ.); Hon. D.H. (McMaster Univ., Hamilton) 1994; Hon. LL.D. (Queens Univ.) 1995; Gov.-Gen.'s Award, Canadian Centennial Medal, Leacock Medal for Humour, Hans Christian Andersen Award, Anisfield Wolf Award, Mark Twain Award, Gemini Award (best documentary script), Award of Excellence (Atlantic Film Festival) 1990, Canadian Achievers Award, Take Back the Nation Award, Council of Canadians 1991, Author's Award, Author of the Year, Foundation for Advancement of Canadian Letters 1993. *Publications:* People Of The Deer 1952, The Regiment 1955, Lost In The Barrens 1956, The Dog Who Wouldn't Be 1957, Coppermine Journey 1958, The Grey Seas Under 1958, The Desperate People 1959, Ordeal By Ice 1960, Owls in the Family 1961, The Serpent's Coil 1961, The Black Joke 1962, Never Cry Wolf 1963, Westviking 1965, The Curse of the Viking Grave 1966, Canada North 1967, The Polar Passion 1967, This Rock Within The Sea 1968, The Boat Who Wouldn't Float 1969, Sibir 1970, A Whale For The Killing 1972, Tundra 1973, Wake of the Great Sealers (with David Blackwood) 1973, The Snow Walker 1975, Canada North Now 1976, And No Birds Sang 1979, The World of Farley Mowat 1980, Sea of Slaughter 1984, My Discovery of America 1985, Virunga (Woman in the Mist, U.S.A.) 1987, The New Founde Land 1989, Rescue the Earth 1990, My Father's Son 1992, Born Naked 1993, Aftermath 1995; TV documentary: Sea of Slaughter 1990. *Leisure interests:* travel, all facets of nature. *Address:* 18 King Street, Port Hope, Ont., L1A 2R4, Canada.

MOWLAM, Rt. Hon. Marjorie, P.C., PH.D., M.P.; British politician; b. 18 Sept. 1949; d. of Tina Mowlam; m. Peter Norton 1995; ed. Coundon Court Comprehensive School, Coventry, Durham Univ., Iowa Univ., U.S.A.; fmr. lecturer and coll. admin.; elected Labour M.P. for Redcar 1987–; fmr. mem. Opposition Northern Ireland team; mem. Treasury team, with special responsibility for City and Corp. Affairs 1990–92; mem. Shadow Cabinet, Shadow Minister for Citizens' Charter and Women's Affairs 1992–93, for Nat. Heritage 1993–94, Shadow Sec. of State for Northern Ireland 1994–97; Sec. of State for N. Ireland May 1997–. *Leisure interests:* jigsaws, swimming. *Address:* House of Commons, London, SW1A 0AA, England. *Telephone:* (01642) 490404 (Redcar).

MOXLEY, John Howard, III, M.D., F.A.C.P.; American physician and business executive; b. 10 Jan. 1935, Elizabeth, N.J.; s. of John Howard Moxley, Jr. and Cleopatra Mundy Moxley; m. Doris Banchik; three s.; ed. Williams Coll. and Univ. of Colorado School of Medicine; hosp. posts 1961–63; Clinical Assoc. Nat. Cancer Inst., Solid Tumor Branch 1963–65; Sr. Resident Physician, Peter Bent Brigham Hosp. 1965–66; mem. Lymphoma Task Force Nat. Cancer Inst. 1965–77; Instructor in Medicine and Asst. to the Dean, Harvard Medical School 1966–69; Dean, Univ. of Md. School of Medicine and Assoc. Prof. of Medicine 1969–73; Vice-Chancellor for Health Sciences and Dean of School of Medicine, Univ. of Calif., San Diego, and Assoc. Prof. of Medicine 1973–80; Asst. Sec. of Defense for Health Affairs, Dept. of Defense, Washington, D.C. 1979–81; Sr. Vice-Pres., Corp. Planning and Alternative Services, American Medical Int. Inc. 1981–87; Pres. and C.E.O., MetaMedical Inc., Beverly Hills, Calif. 1987–89; Man. Dir. Korn Ferry Int. 1989–; Dir. Nat. Fund for Medical Educ. 1986–, Chair. 1993–; Fellow American Fed. for Clinical Research; mem. Inst. of Medicine (N.A.S.), American Soc. of Clinical Oncology, American Medical Asscn.; Dir. Henry M. Jackson Foundation for the Advancement of Mil. Medicine 1983; Sec. of Defense Medal for Distinguished Public Service and other awards. *Publications:* numerous papers in scientific journals. *Address:* Korn/Ferry International, 1800 Century Park East, Suite 900, Los Angeles, CA 90067 (Office); 8180 Manitoba Street 210, Playa del Rey, CA 90293, U.S.A. (Home). *Telephone:* (310) 843-4123 (Office).

MOXON, (Edward) Richard, M.B., B.CHIR., F.R.C.P.; British medical doctor; b. 16 July 1941, Leeds; s. of late Gerald Richard Moxon and of Margaret Forster Mohun; m. Marianne Graham 1973; two s. one d.; ed. Shrewsbury School, St. John's Coll., Cambridge and St. Thomas' Hosp. Medical School, London; with Hosp. for Sick Children, Great Ormond St., London 1969; Research Fellow in Infectious Diseases, Children's Hosp. Medical Center, Boston, Mass., U.S.A. 1971–74; Asst. Prof. of Pediatrics, Johns Hopkins Hosp., Baltimore, Md., U.S.A. 1974–80, Dir. Eudowood Pediatric Infectious Diseases Unit 1982–84; Action Research Prof. of Paediatrics, Oxford Univ. 1984–; Head, Molecular Infectious Diseases Group, Inst. of Molecular Medicine, John Radcliffe Hosp. 1988–; Visiting Scientist, Dept. of Molecular Biology, Washington Univ., St. Louis, Mo. 1990–91; Fellow, Jesus Coll. Oxford 1974–; Chair. Oxford Vaccine Group 1994–; mem. Steering Group, Encapsulated Bacteria, WHO 1987–93; Chair. MRC sub-cttee. Polysaccharide Vaccines 1986–90; convenor, BPA Immunology and Infectious Diseases Group 1984–89; Teale Lecturer, Royal Coll. of Physicians 1998; Founder Fellow Acad. of Medical Sciences 1998; mem. American Soc. Clinical Investigation; Fellow Infectious Diseases Soc. of America, American Soc. Pediatric Research; Mitchell Lecture, Royal College of Physicians 1992. *Publications:* Neonatal Infections (with D. Isaacs) 1991, A Practical Approach to Pediatric Infectious Diseases (with D. Isaacs) 1996; contribs. to eight other books, many papers on meningitis and molecular basis of bacterial virulence. *Leisure interests:* music, literature, sports. *Address:* Department of Paediatrics, John Radcliffe Hospital, Headington, Oxford, OX3 9DU; 17 Moreton Road, Oxford, OX2 7AX, England (Home). *Telephone:* (01865) 221074 (Office). *Fax:* (01865) 220479.

MOYA PALENCIA, Lic. Mario; Mexican politician and lawyer; b. 14 June 1933, México, D.F.; s. of Mario Moya Iturriaga and Concepción Palencia de Moya; m. Marcela Ibáñez de Moya Palencia 1959; one s. one d.; ed. Univ. Nacional Autónoma de México; Public Relations Dept., Ferrocarriles Nacionales de México 1955–58; in Dept. of Nat. Property 1959–64; Dir. Gen. of Cinematography, Dept. of Interior 1964–68; Pres. of Bd. of Dirs. of Productora e Importadora de Papel, S.A. (PIPSA) 1968–69; Under-Sec., Dept. of Interior 1969; Sec. of Interior 1970–76; fmr. Perm. Rep. to UN; Prof. of Constitutional Law, Univ. Nacional Autónoma de México 1977; Dir.-Gen. Organización Editorial Mexicana (OEM) 1977–79, Fondo Nacional de Fomento al Turismo (FONATUR) 1979–82, Banco Nacional de Turismo 1982; Exec. Pres. Ocean

Garden Products Inc. 1983–; Gen. Man. Exportadores Asscn. S.A. de C.V. 1983–; numerous foreign awards and decorations. *Publications:* La reforma Electoral 1964, Temas Constitucionales 1978, Democracia y Participación 1982. *Leisure interests:* reading, riding. *Address:* Insurgentes Sur Torre B, 4o. piso, C.P. 1000, México 20, D.F., Mexico. *Telephone:* 548-91-84.

MOYANA, Kombo James, M.A., M.PHIL., PH.D.; Zimbabwean banker; b. 4 July 1942, Chipinge; m.; one s. three d.; ed. Columbia Univ. New York; Research Fellow, Inst. de Développement Economique et de Planification, Dakar 1972; Fellow, UNITAR, New York 1973; int. finance economist, Div. of Money, Finance and Devt. UNCTAD, New York and Geneva 1974–80; seconded to Ministry of Econ. Planning and Devt. of Govt. of Zimbabwe 1980; Deputy Gov. Reserve Bank of Zimbabwe 1980, Gov. 1983; Alt. Gov. IMF 1983; Pres. Inst. of Bankers (Zimbabwe) 1985–86; Exec. Sec. Preferential Trading Area (PTA) of Eastern, Cen. and Southern African States until 1991; Chair. Asscn. of African Cen. Banks (AACB) 1991–93. *Leisure interest:* farming. *Address:* P.O. Box 1283, Harare, Zimbabwe. *Telephone:* 790731; 7910721.

MOYERS, Bill D., American journalist; b. 5 June 1934, Hugo, Okla.; s. of Henry Moyers and Ruby Johnson; m. Judith Davidson 1954; two s. one d.; ed. Univ. of Texas, Edinburgh Univ. and Southwestern Baptist Theological Seminary; Exec. Asst. to Senator Lyndon Johnson 1959–60; Assoc. Dir. U.S. Peace Corps 1961–63, Deputy Dir. 1963; Special Asst. to Pres. Johnson 1963–66, Press Sec. to Pres. 1965–66; Publr. of Newsday, Long Island, N.Y. 1966–70; host of This Week, weekly current affairs TV programme 1970; Ed.-in-Chief Bill Moyers Journal, Public Broadcasting Service 1971–76, 1978–81; Contrib. Newsweek 1974–76; Chief Corresp. CBS Reports 1976–78, Sr. News Analyst, CBS News 1981–86; Exec. Ed. Public Affairs TV Inc. 1987–; news analyst NBC News 1995–; mem. American Philosophical Soc., Fellow A.A.A.S.; Emmy awards 1983–90, Gold Baton Award 1991, American Jewish Cttee. Religious Liberty Award 1995, Walter Cronkite Award 1995, Fred Friendly First Amendment Award 1995, Charles Frankel Prize 1997. *Publications:* Listening to America 1971, The Secret Government 1988, Joseph Campbell and the Power of Myth 1988, A World of Ideas 1989, Healing and the Mind 1993, Genesis: A Living Conversion 1996. *Address:* Public Affairs TV Inc., 356 West 58th Street, New York, NY 10019, U.S.A.

MOYNIHAN, Daniel Patrick, PH.D.; American politician, fmr. diplomatist and university professor; b. 16 March 1927, Tulsa, Okla.; s. of John Henry and Margaret A. Phipps Moynihan; m. Elizabeth T. Brennan 1955; two s. one d.; ed. City Coll. of New York, Tufts Univ. and Fletcher School of Law and Diplomacy; Dir. of Public Relations, Int. Rescue Comm. 1954; successively Asst. to Sec., Asst. Sec., Acting Sec. to Gov. of N.Y. State 1955–58; mem. N.Y. Tenure Comm. 1959–60; Dir. N.Y. State Govt. Research Project, Syracuse Univ. 1959–61; Special Asst. to Sec. of Labor 1961–62, Exec. Asst. to Sec. 1962–63, Asst. Sec. of Labor 1963–65; Dir. Jt. Center Urban Studies M.I.T. and Harvard Univ. 1966–69; Prof. of Educ. and Urban Politics, 1966–77, Sr. mem., Kennedy School of Govt., Harvard 1966–77, Asst. to Pres. of U.S.A. for Urban Affairs 1969, Counsellor to Pres. (with Cabinet rank) 1969–70; Amb. to India 1973–74; Perm. Rep. to UN 1975–76; Senator from New York 1977–; Chair. Senate Finance Cttee. 1993–94, Ranking mem. 1995–; Chair. Bd. of Trustees Hirshhorn Museum, Comm. on Reducing and Protecting Govt. Secrecy 1994–97; mem. American Philosophical Soc., American Acad. of Arts and Sciences; Hon. Fellow, L.S.E.; numerous hon. degrees; Democrat. *Publications:* Beyond the Melting Pot (co-author) 1963, Maximum Feasible Misunderstanding, Community Action in the War on Poverty 1969, The Politics of a Guaranteed Income 1973, Coping: Essays in the Practice of Government 1974, A Dangerous Place (with Suzanne Weaver) 1978; Ed.: Defenses of Freedom: The Public Papers of Arthur J. Goldberg 1966, On Understanding Poverty: Perspective from the Social Sciences 1969, Toward A National Urban Policy 1970, Counting Our Blessings: Reflections on the Future of America 1980, Loyalties 1984, Family and Nation 1986, Came the Revolution 1988, On the Law of Nations 1990, Pandaemonium: Ethnicity in international politics 1993, Miles To Go: A Personal History of Social Policy 1996; co-editor of several publs. *Address:* U.S. Senate, 464 Russell Senate Building, Washington, DC 20510, U.S.A. *Telephone:* (202) 224-4451.

MOYOLA, Baron (Life Peer), cr. 1971, of Castledawson in the County of Londonderry; **Rt. Hon. Major James Dawson Chichester-Clark,** P.C.; British politician and farmer; b. 12 Feb. 1923, Castledawson; s. of James Jackson Chichester-Clark and Marion Caroline Chichester; m. Moyra Maud Haughton 1959; one step-s. two d.; ed. Eton Coll.; entered Army 1942, Second Lieut. Irish Guards Dec. 1942; wounded Italy 1944; ADC to Gov.-Gen. of Canada (Field-Marshal Earl Alexander of Tunis) 1947–49; attended Staff Coll., Camberley 1956; retd. from Army as Maj. 1960; M.P. for S. Derry, Parl. of N. Ireland 1960–73, Asst. Whip March 1963, Chief Whip 1963–67; Minister of Agric., N. Ireland 1967–69; Leader of Unionist Party and Prime Minister of N. Ireland 1969–71; Deputy Lieut. N. Ireland 1954. *Leisure interests:* fishing, shooting and skiing. *Address:* Moyola Park, Castledawson, Co. Derry, Northern Ireland (Home).

MPHAHLELE, Es'kia (Ezekiel), M.A., PH.D., D.LITT.; South African author; b. 17 Dec. 1919, Marabastad; s. of Moses Mphahlele and Eva Mphahlele; m. Rebecca Nnana Mphahlele 1945; four s. one d.; ed. teacher training and private study; teacher of English and Afrikaans, Orlando, Johannesburg until 1957; Fiction Ed. Drum magazine 1955; Lecturer in English Literature, Dept. of Extra-Mural Studies, Univ. Coll., Ibadan, Nigeria 1957; fmr. Dir. African Programme for the Congress for Cultural Freedom, Paris; circuit schools inspector Lebowa 1978; Educ. Adviser and Chair. of Bd. Funda Centre, Soweto 1986–; Researcher African Studies Inst., Univ. of Witwatersrand 1979, Prof. of African Literature 1979–88, Head of African Literature 1983–88, Prof. Emer. 1988–; fmr. lecturer Univ. of Nairobi, Univ. of Denver, Univ. of Penn., Dir. Council for Black Educ.; numerous hon. degrees. *Publications include:* Man Must Live, The Living and the Dead (short stories), Down Second Avenue (autobiography), The Wanderers (novel) 1972, In Corner B (short stories), The African Image (essays), Voices in the Whirlwind (essays), Chirundu (novel) 1981, Afrika My Music (autobiog.) 1984, Father Come Home (novel) 1984, Creative Writing Guides: Let's Talk Writing, Prose and Let's Talk Writing, Poetry; The Story of African Literature 1986, Renewal Time 1989; numerous other essays and poems. *Leisure interests:* music, theatre. *Address:* 5444, Zone 5, Pimville, Johannesburg, South Africa. *Telephone:* (011) 933-2273.

MPINGA KASENDA, PH.D.; Democratic Republic of Congo politician and university professor; b. 30 Aug. 1937, Tshilomba; ed. Elisabethville (now Lubumbashi) High School of Social Sciences, Catholic Univ. of Lovanium and Univ. of Bordeaux, France; Teacher, Tshilomba Secondary School 1957–59; studied at Lubumbashi and Lovanium Univ. 1959–65; Asst. lecturer, Lovanium Univ. 1965–66, Prof. 1966–70; Adviser to the Chancellor, Nat. Univ. of Zaire and to the Minister of Public Admin. 1971–72; mem. Political Bureau Mouvement Populaire de la Révolution (MPR) 1972, mem. Perm. Cttee. 1974–80; Deputy People's Commr. 1975, First State Commr. 1977–80; Dir. Makanda Kabobi Inst. (MPR school) 1974–; Commdr., Nat. Order of Zaire and Dem. People's Repub. of Korea, Grand Officier Ordre du Mérite national (Mauritania). *Publications:* Ville de Kinshasa, Organisation politique et administrative 1968, L'administration publique du Zaire 1973, Les reformes administratives au Zaire 1975. *Address:* Institut Makanda Kabobi, avenue de la Gombe, Kinshasa (Office); 384 Quartier Gombele, Kinshasa/Lemba, P.O.B. 850, Democratic Republic of Congo (Home).

MROUDJAE, Ali; Comoran politician; b. 2 Aug. 1939, Moroni; s. of Chohezi Mroudjae and Charif Zahara; m. Nourdine Batouli 1967; three s. five d.; Minister of Foreign Affairs and Co-operation 1979–82; Prime Minister of the Comoros 1982–85; Minister of State for Internal and Social Affairs Jan.–Sept. 1985; and numerous other portfolios; Leader Parti Comorien pour la Démocratie et le Progrès (PCDP). *Leisure interests:* reading, swimming, travelling. *Address:* PCDP, Route Djivani, B.P. 179, Moroni; B.P. 58, Rond Point Gobadjou, Moroni, Comoros. *Telephone:* 73-1733 (PCDP); 73-1266. *Fax:* 73-0650 (PCDP).

MROŻEK, Sławomir; Polish writer; b. 26 June 1930, Borzęcin; m.; fmr. cartoonist, satirist and journalist. *Publications include:* Maleńkie lato 1956, The Elephant 1957, Wesele w Atomicach (Wedding in Atomice) 1959, The Rain 1962 (short stories), The Ugupu Bird (short stories) 1968, Dwa listy 1974, Małe listy 1981; Plays: The Police 1958, What a Lovely Dream, Indyk (Turkey), Karol, Let's Have Fun, The Death of the Lieutenant 1963, Striptease 1964, Tango 1964, On the High Seas, Vatzlav 1970, Druga zmiana (Second Service) 1970, Testarium 1970, Blessed Event 1973, Rzeźnia (Butchery) 1973, Emigrants 1974, Garbus (Humpback) 1975, Utwory sceniczne nowe 1976, Wybór dramatów i opowiadań 1976, Krawiec (Tailor), Opowiadania o lisie (Fox Stories), Drugie danie (Second Dish), Amor 1979, Pieszo 1983, Moniza Clavier 1983; series of satirical drawings: Polska w obrazach (Poland in pictures) 1957, Postępowiec (Progressive man) 1960, Rysunki 1982. *Address:* Zwigzek Literatów Polskich, ul. Królewska 84 m. 18, 30-079 Cracow, Poland. *Telephone:* (12) 636-29-66.

MROZIEWICZ, Robert; Polish politician; b. 20 Sept. 1942, Warsaw; m. Elżbieta Nowik; two s.; ed. Univ. of Warsaw; Asst. Prof. Inst. of History, Polish Acad. of Sciences 1985, asst. Warsaw Univ. 1965–68, Polish Inst. of Int. Affairs 1968–70; Inst. of History, Polish Acad. of Sciences 1971–89; minister-adviser Ministry of Foreign Affairs; Deputy Perm. Rep. to UN, New York, then Perm. Rep. of UN, New York 1990–92; Under-Sec. of State in Ministry of Foreign Affairs; Pres. of UN Social and Economic Council 1992–97, Pres. of Gen. Assembly 1992; Under-Sec. of state for Co-operation with Abroad and Integration with NATO in Ministry of National Defence 1997–; mem. Solidarity Trade Union 1980–; Commdr.'s Cross of Order Polonia Restituta 1995. *Publications:* author and co-author of 6 monographs and various scientific articles. *Address:* Ministry of National Defence, ul. Królewska 1, 00-909 Warsaw 60, Poland. *Telephone:* (22) 827 76 79.

MSIMANG, Mendi, B.A.; South African diplomatist and civil servant; b. 1928, Johannesburg; m. Mantombazana Tshabalala; four c. from previous marriage; ed. Univ. Coll. of Roma, Lesotho; with Rand Steam Laundries, organizer Laundry Workers' Union; asbestos assayer Costa Rican consulate; joined ANC, Personal Sec. to then Sec.-Gen. Walter Sisulu; with Nelson Mandela (q.v.) and Oliver Tambo's law practice–1960; left for U.K.; Rep. ANC Mission to U.K. and Ireland; co-founder South Africa in Fact (ANC newsletter); Ed. Spotlight on South Africa (ANC journal); Admin. Sec. ANC Nat. Exec. Cttee. in Exile, E. Africa br.; collaborated with Oliver Tambo to est. Solomon Mahlangu Freedom Coll., Tanzania; ANC Educ. Officer; Admin. Sec. Treas.-Gen. of ANC's office, Zambia; ANC Chief Rep. to India 1969, to U.K. 1988; returned to S.A. 1990; elected mem. ANC Nat. Exec. Cttee. 1991, Nat. Ass. 1994 (fmr. Chair.); fmr. Chair. ANC Parl. Caucus; High Commr. in U.K. 1995–98; Treasurer ANC 1998–; Chair. Nelson Mandela Children's

Fund; Vice-Pres. Royal Over-Seas League, London; Fellow Rotarian, Rotary Club of London. *Leisure interests:* watching football, golf, jazz/blues, reading, theatre. *Address:* P.O. Box 25929, Monument Park, Pretoria 0105, South Africa.

MSUYA, Cleopa David, B.A.; Tanzanian politician and civil servant; b. 4 Jan. 1931, Chomvu Usangi, Mwanga Dist.; s. of David Kilenga and Maria Ngido; m. Rhoda Christopher 1959; four s. two d.; ed. Makerere Univ. Coll., Uganda; Civil Service, Community Devt. Officer 1956–61, Commr. for Community Devt. 1961–64, Prin. Sec. to Ministry of Community Devt. and Nat. Culture 1964, to Ministries of Land Settlement and Water Devt. 1965–67, to Ministry of Econ. Affairs and Devt. Planning 1967–70 and to Treas. 1970–72; Minister of Finance 1972–75, 1983–85, for Finance, Econ. Affairs and Planning 1985–89, for Industries 1975–80, for Industries and Trade 1990–95; Prime Minister 1980–83, 1994–95; First Vice-Pres. 1994–95; mem. Nat. Ass.; Gov. AFDB, IMF; mem. Bd. of Dirs. of several public corpns. *Address:* c/o Office of the Prime Minister and First Vice-President, P.O. Box 980, Dodoma, Tanzania.

MTHEMBI-MAHANYELE, Sankie, B.A.; South African politician; b. 23 March 1951, Sophiatown; d. of late Mkhomazi Mthembi and Emma Gabaza Mthembi; one d.; ed. Sekano-Ntoane High School, Univ. of the North; fmr. punch card operator Standard Bank; became involved in ANC underground, left S.A. 1977 to work for ANC, with Radio Freedom 1977–81, Ed. women's journal Voice of Women 1979–87, fmr. sub-Ed. Dawn, mem. Nat. Exec. Cttee. of Women 1980–87, 1987–89, Admin. Sec. mission in West Africa 1986–89, Admin. Sec. mission in Sweden 1983–84, Chief Rep. mission for Germany and Austria 1989–93, mem. Nat. Exec. 1993–, Deputy Head Dept. of Int. Affairs 1993–94; Deputy Minister of Welfare 1994–95; Minister of Housing 1995–. *Publications:* Flames of Fury (poetry), One Never Knows (short stories). *Address:* Ministry of Housing, 240 Walker Street, Sunnyside, Pretoria 0002; Private Bag X644, Pretoria 0001, South Africa (Office). *Telephone:* 12-441879 (Office). *Fax:* 12-341-8513 (Office).

MU GUOGUANG; Chinese university professor; b. 22 Jan. 1931, Liaoning; m. Chi Yuanxiang; one s. one d.; Pres. Nankai Univ. 1986–95; mem. Chinese Science Acad. 1991. *Leisure interest:* swimming. *Address:* 94 Weijin Road, Tianjin 300071, People's Republic of China. *Telephone:* 22-3502275.

MUALLA, H. H. Sheikh Rashid bin Ahmad Al; Ruler of Umm Al-Qaiwain; b. 1930; apptd. Deputy Ruler of Umm Al-Qaiwain, succeeded as Ruler on the death of his father Feb. 1981; Chair. Umm Al-Qaiwain Municipality 1967; constituted the Emirate's first municipal council 1975. *Address:* Rulers' Palace, Umm Al-Qaiwain, United Arab Emirates.

MUBARAK, Lt.-Gen. (Muhammad) Hosni; Egyptian politician and air force officer; b. 4 May 1928, Kafr El-Moseilha, Minuffya Governorate; ed. Mil. Acad., Air Acad.; joined Air Force 1950; Dir.-Gen. Air Acad. 1967–69; Air Force Chief of Staff 1969–72; C.-in-C. 1972–75; promoted to Lt.-Gen. 1973; Vice-Pres. of Egypt 1975–81; Vice-Chair. Nat. Democratic Party (NDP) 1976–81; mem. Higher Council for Nuclear Energy 1975–; Sec.-Gen. NDP and Political Bureau 1981–82, Chair. 1982–; Pres. of Egypt Oct. 1981– (Cand. of NDP); Prime Minister 1981–82; Chair. OAU 1989–90; Order of Star of Sinai, Louise Michel Prize 1990. *Address:* Presidential Palace, Abdeen, Cairo, Egypt.

MUDD, Roger Harrison, M.A.; American news broadcaster; b. 9 Feb. 1928, Washington; s. of Kostka and Irma Iris (née Harrison) Mudd; m. Emma Jeanne Spears 1957; three s. one d.; ed. Washington and Lee Univ. and Univ of North Carolina; served with U.S. Army 1945–47; teacher Darlington School, Rome, Ga. 1951–52; Reporter Richmond (Va.) News Leader 1953; News Dir. Station WRNL, Richmond 1953–56; Reporter, radio and TV Station WTOP, Washington 1956–61; Corresp. CBS 1961–80; Chief Washington Corresp. NBC 1980–87, Congressional Corresp. MacNeil/Lehrer News Hour 1987–92, Special Corresp. 1993–; Host The History Channel 1995–; Prof. of Journalism, Princeton Univ. 1992–94, Washington & Lee Univ. 1995–96; Dir. Berlin Comm. 1996–, Va. Foundation for Ind. Colls. 1997–, Nat. Portrait Gallery Comm. 1997–; Bd. Dirs. Media Gen. 1998–. *Address:* c/o 3620 S 27th Street, Arlington, VA 22206, U.S.A. (Office).

MUDENDA, Elijah Haatukali Kaiba; Zambian politician and agriculturist; b. 6 June 1927; ed. Makerere Univ. Coll., Uganda, Fort Hare Univ. Coll., S. Africa, and Univ. of Cambridge; agricultural expert until 1962; mem. Legis. Assembly 1962–64; Parl. Sec. for Agric. 1962–64; mem. Zambian Parl. 1964–; Minister of Agric. 1964–67, of Finance 1967–68, of Foreign Affairs 1968–69, 1970–73, of Devt. and Finance 1969–70; Prime Minister 1975–77, also Minister of Nat. Guidance and Culture 1975–76; mem. Cen. Cttee. United Nat. Independence Party (UNIP), Chair. Political Sub-cttee. 1973–75, Rural Devt. Sub-cttee. 1977–78, Social and Cultural Sub-cttee. 1978–81, Econs. and Finance Sub-cttee. 1981–; Chair. Nat. Comm. for Devt. Planning April-July 1977. *Address:* United National Independence Party, Freedom House, P.O. Box 302, Lusaka, Zambia.

MUDGE, Dirk; Namibian politician; b. 16 Jan. 1928, Otjiwarongo; m. Stienie Jacobs; two s. three d.; Chair. of Turnhalle Constitutional Conf. 1977; Vice-Chair. of Nat. Party and mem. S.W. Africa Exec. Council Sept. 1977; formed Republican Party of S.W. Africa Oct. 1977; Chair. Democratic Turnhalle Alliance (now DTA of Namibia) 1977; mem. Constituent Ass. Nov. 1978–May 1979, Nat. Ass. 1979–83; Pres. Ministers' Council 1980–83, Minister for Finance and Governmental Affairs 1985–89; mem. Nat. Ass. 1991–93. *Address:* DTA of Namibia, P.O. Box 173, Windhoek 9000, Namibia.

MUELLER, Lothar; German financier; b. 27 Jan. 1927, Munich; m. Irmgard Mueller; one s. three d.; with tax authority of Bavaria 1954; Head Bavarian Finance Ministry 1977–79; Pres. Landeszentralbank, Bavaria 1979–94; mem. Cen. Bank Council of the Deutsche Bundesbank; Bayerischer Verdienstorden, Grosses Bundesverdienstkreuz. *Publications:* publs. in public finance, company and tax law, monetary and economic policy. *Address:* Waldparkstrasse 35c, 85521 Riemerling, Germany. *Telephone:* (089) 2889-3200. *Fax:* (089) 2889-3890.

MUFAMADI, Fholisani Sydney; South African politician; b. 28 Feb. 1959, Alexandra; m. Nomsa Mboweni; two d.; pvt. teacher Lamula Secondary School 1980; Gen. Sec. Gen. and Allied Workers' Union 1982; Publicity Sec. United Democratic Front (UDF); Asst. Gen. Sec. Congress of S.A. Trade Unions 1985; mem. Nat. Peace Cttee., helped draft Nat. Peace Accord 1991; mem. ANC Nat. Exec. Cttee., ANC Working Cttee., Cen. Cttee. of S.A. Communist Party, Political Bureau; ANC Rep. at Transitional Exec. Council on Law and Order, Safety and Stability 1993–94; Minister of Safety and Security, Govt. of Nat. Unity 1994–. *Address:* Ministry of Safety and Security, Wachthuis, 7th Floor, 231 Pretorius Street, Pretoria 0002; Private Bag X463, Pretoria 0001, South Africa. *Telephone:* (12) 3392800. *Fax:* (12) 3392819.

MUGABE, Robert Gabriel, B.A., B.ADMIN., B.ED., M.SC.(ECON.), LL.M.; Zimbabwean politician and fmr. teacher; b. 21 Feb. 1924, Kutama; m. 1st Sarah Mugabe (died 1992); one s. (deceased); m. 2nd Grace Marufu 1996; ed. Kutama and Empandeni Mission School, Fort Hare Univ. Coll., S. Africa, Univs. of S. Africa and London; teacher, at Drifontein Roman Catholic School, Umvuma 1952, Salisbury S. Primary School 1953, in Gwelo 1954, Chalimbana Teacher Training Coll. 1955, in Accra, Ghana 1958–60; entered politics 1960; Publicity Sec. of Nat. Dem. Party 1960–61; Publicity Sec. Zimbabwe African People's Union 1961; detained Sept.-Dec. 1962, March-April 1963; escaped to Tanzania April 1963; Co-founder of Zimbabwe African Nat. Union (ZANU) Aug. 1963; Sec.-Gen. Aug. 1963; in detention in Rhodesia 1964–74; Pres. ZANU; mem. Politburo ZANU 1984–; Jt. Leader of Patriotic Front (with Joshua Nkomo) 1976–79; contested Feb. 1980 elections as Leader of ZANU (PF) (name changed to ZANU 1984) Party, Pres. 1988–; Prime Minister of Zimbabwe 1980–87; Pres. of Zimbabwe Jan. 1988–; Minister of Defence 1980–87, also fmrly. of Public Works, Industry and Tech.; Chancellor Univ. of Zimbabwe; attended Geneva Constitutional Conf. on Rhodesia 1976, Malta Conf., 1978, Lancaster House Conf. Sept.–Dec. 1979, Newsmaker of the Year Award (S. African Soc. of Journalists) 1980, Africa Prize 1988; Hon. Dr. (Ahmadu Bello Univ., Nigeria) 1980, (Edin. Univ.) 1984; Int. Human Rights Award (Howard Univ., Washington) 1981, Jawarhal Nehru Award 1992. *Address:* Office of the President, Munhumutapa Building, Samora Machel Avenue, Private Bag 7700, Causeway, Harare, Zimbabwe.

MUGLER, Thierry; French fashion designer; b. 1946, Strasbourg; ed. in Strasbourg; fmr. ballet dancer, Opéra du Rhin, Strasbourg; later window-dresser and clothing designer, Gudule boutique, Paris; designer of fashion collection for André Peters, London; subsequently began career as freelance clothing designer in Amsterdam, later in Paris where he launched Café de Paris collection; designer of menswear and fashion accessories; launched own Thierry Mugler fashion label, Paris 1973; launched Thierry Mugler Diffusion fashion co,; opened own boutique, Place des Victoires, Paris; clothing also sold in dept. stores in U.S.A. and Japan.

MUHAMMAD, Ali Nasser; Yemeni politician; b. 1939, Dathina Rural District; active mem. of Nat. Liberation Front (NLF) 1963–67; Gov. of the Islands 1967, of Second Province 1968; mem. Nat. Front Gen. Command March 1968; Minister of Local Govt. April 1969, of Defence 1969–77, of Educ. 1974–75; mem. Front Exec. Cttee. 1970; mem. Presidential Council of People's Democratic Repub. of Yemen 1971–78, Chair. June–Dec. 1978; Chair. Council of Ministers (Prime Minister) 1971–85; mem. Supreme People's Council (SPC) 1971, Chair. Presidium of SPC (Head of State) 1980–86 (overthrown in coup Jan. 1986); mem. Political Bureau of Nat. Front 1972–75, of United Political Org. Nat. Front 1975–78, of Yemen Socialist Party (YSP) 1978–86, Sec.-Gen. of YSP 1980–86.

MUHAMMADULLAH; Bangladeshi politician and lawyer; b. 21 Nov. 1921, Saicha; m. Serajun Nahar Muhammadullah; three s. two d.; ed. Dacca and Calcutta Univs.; joined Dacca Bar 1950; Lawyer, High Court 1964; mem. Awami League 1950–; Sec. E. Pakistan Awami League 1952–72; mem. E. Pakistan Prov. Assembly 1970; Political Adviser to Acting Pres. Syed Nazrul Islam 1971; Deputy Speaker Bangladesh Constituent Assembly April–Nov. 1972, Speaker 1972–73; Speaker Bangladesh Parl. 1973–74: Acting Pres. of Bangladesh 1973–74, Pres. 1974–75; Minister of Land Admin. and Land Reforms Jan.–Aug. 1975; Vice-Pres. of Bangladesh Aug.–Nov. 1975.

MUHEIM, Franz Emmanuel, L. ÈS L.; Swiss diplomatist (retd.) and academic; b. 27 Sept. 1931, Berne; s. of Hans Muheim and Hélène Ody; m. Radmila Jovanovic 1962; ed. Univs. of Fribourg, Geneva and Paris; joined Fed. Dept. of Foreign Affairs 1960, served successively in Belgrade, Rabat and London 1961–70, Council of Europe, UN and Int. Orgs. Section, Dept. of Foreign Affairs, Berne 1971–77, Deputy Head of Mission, Minister Plenipotentiary, Washington, D.C. 1978–81, Deputy Dir. Political Affairs and Head, Political Div. Europe and N. America, with rank of Amb., Berne 1982–83, Dir. Int. Orgs., Dept. of Foreign Affairs 1984–89, Amb. to U.K. 1989–94;

Pres. Swiss Red Cross; Vice-Pres. Int. Fed. of Red Cross and Red Crescent Socs.; Head of Swiss dels. to int. confs. including UNESCO, Int. Red Cross, Non-Aligned Movement; Fellow Center for Int. Affairs, Harvard Univ., U.S.A. 1981–82; Prof. Bologna Center of Johns Hopkins Univ. 1995–96. *Publications:* (Jt. Ed.) Einblick in die Schweizerische Aussenpolitik: Festschrift für Staatssekretär Raymond Probst 1984; (contrib.) Les organisations internationales entre l'innovation et la stagnation 1984, Multilateralism Today, Geburstag von a. Ständerat Franz Muheim 1993. *Leisure interests:* walking, mountaineering, skiing, photography, music. *Address:* Es Chesaux, 1646 Echarlens, Switzerland. *Telephone:* (026) 915 2474. *Fax:* (026) 915 2450.

MÜHLEMANN, Lukas, M.B.A.; Swiss business executive; ed. Harvard Univ.; fmr. systems eng. IBM; man. consultant McKinsey 1977–94; Chief Exec. Swiss Re 1994; now Chief Exec. Credit Suisse. *Address:* Credit Suisse, Praes, 8070 Zurich, Switzerland.

MUIR, (Isabella) Helen (Mary), C.B.E., M.A., D.PHIL., D.SC., F.R.S.; British biochemist; b. 20 Aug. 1920, Naini Tal, Uttar Pradesh, India; d. of the late Basil Fairlie Muir and Gwladys Helen Muir; ed. Somerville Coll., Univ. of Oxford; Research Fellow Univ. of Oxford 1947–48; Research Scientist Nat. Inst. for Medical Research 1948–54; at St. Mary's Hosp. 1954–66, Empire Rheumatism Council Fellow 1954–58, Pearl Research Fellow 1959–66; Head of Div. Kennedy Inst. of Rheumatology 1966–86, Dir. 1977–90; Bunim Lecturer U.S. Arthritis Asscn. 1978; Visiting Prof. of Biochemistry, Queen Elizabeth Coll. 1981–85, Newcastle Univ. 1995; Hon. Prof. of Biochemistry Charing Cross Hosp. Medical School 1979–90; Gov. Strangeways Research Lab. 1980–90; mem. Arthritis and Rheumatism Council Research Sub-Cttee. 1962–75; mem. Editorial Bd. Biochemical Journal 1964–70, Annals of Rheumatic Diseases 1971–77, Connective Tissue Research 1971–85, Journal of Orthopaedic Research 1983–; Scientific mem. MRC 1973–77; Hon. Fellow Somerville Coll., Oxford 1978; Hon. mem. American Soc. Biological Chemists; Foreign mem. Royal Swedish Acad. of Sciences 1989; mem. Council Royal Soc. 1982–83, Council Chelsea Coll. 1982–85; Wellcome Trustee 1982–90; Hon. D.Sc. (Edin.) 1982, (Strathclyde) 1983, (Brunel) 1990; numerous awards including Heberden Orator and Medallist 1976, Feldberg Prize 1977, Bunim Medal of American Arthritis Asscn. 1978, Co-Winner Basic Science Section Volvo Prize 1980, Neil Hamilton Fairley Medal 1981, CIBA Medal Biochemical Soc. 1981, Steindler Award Orthopaedic Research Soc., U.S.A. 1982, CIBA Int. Award 1993. *Publications:* over 200 articles, mainly on biochemistry of connective tissues in relation to arthritis and inherited diseases; contrib. several specialist books. *Leisure interests:* gardening, music, horses, natural history, ballet. *Address:* c/o School of Biological Sciences, University of Manchester, Stopford Building, Oxford Road, Manchester, M13 9PT; Longlands House, Hornby, Bedale, North Yorkshire, DL8 1NG, England. *Telephone:* (0161) 275 5074.

MUIR, Richard John Sutherland, C.M.G., B.A.; British diplomatist; b. 25 Aug. 1942, London; s. of John Muir and Edna Hodges; m. Caroline Simpson 1965; one s. one d; ed. Stationers' Co. School and Univs. of Reading and Strasbourg; entered H.M. Diplomatic Service 1966; Second Sec. Jeddah 1967–70, Tunis 1970–72; FCO 1972–75; First Sec. Washington, D.C. 1975–79; Prin. Dept. of Energy 1979–81; Counsellor, Jeddah 1981–85; FCO 1985–91; Under-Sec. and Chief Insp. Diplomatic Service 1991–94; Amb. to Oman 1994–98, to Kuwait 1999–. *Leisure interests:* walking, sailing, fishing, opera. *Address:* c/o Foreign and Commonwealth Office, London, SW1A 2AH, England.

MUIR WOOD, Sir Alan (Marshall), Kt., M.A., F.ENG., F.R.S.; British consulting civil engineer; b. 8 Aug. 1921, London; s. of Edward Stephen Wood and Dorothy Wood (née Webb); m. Winifred Leyton Lanagan (Dr. W. L. Wood) 1943; three s.; ed. Abbotsholme School, Derbyshire and Peterhouse, Cambridge; Engineer Officer, R.N. 1942–46; Asst. Engineer, British Rail 1946–50; Research Asst., Docks Exec. 1950–52; Engineer, Sir William Halcrow & Partners 1952–64, Partner, then Sr. Partner 1964–84, Consultant 1984–; Pres. Inst. of Civil Engineers 1977–78; Fellow, Imperial Coll. London; Hon. Fellow, Peterhouse, Portsmouth Polytechnic; Hon. D.Sc. (City Univ.) 1978, (Southampton) 1986, Hon. LL.D. (Dundee) 1985, Hon. D.Eng. (Bristol) 1991; Telford Medal (ICE) 1976, Ewing Medal (ICE and Royal Soc.) 1984, ICE Gold Medal 1998. *Publication:* Coastal Hydraulics 1969, 2nd edn. with C. A. Fleming 1981. *Leisure interests:* music, arts and the countryside. *Address:* Franklands, Bere Court Road, Pangbourne, Berkshire, RG8 8JY, England.

MUJURU, Joyce Teurai-Ropa; Zimbabwean politician; b. 15 April 1955, Mt. Darwin; m. Tapfumanei Ruzambu Solomon Mujuru (Nhongo) 1977; four d.; Minister of Youth, Sport and Recreation 1980–81, of Community Devt. and Women's Affairs 1981–88, of Community and Co-operative Devt. 1989–92; Gov. and Resident Minister of Mashonaland Cen. Prov. 1993–96. *Leisure interests:* church and women's meetings, knitting, sewing, cooking, outdoor life. *Address:* Private Bag 7735, Causeway, Harare, Zimbabwe.

MUKHAMEDOV, Irek Javdatovich; Russian/Tatar ballet dancer; b. 8 Feb. 1960; m. Maria Zubkova; one d.; ed. Moscow Choreographic Inst.; joined Moscow Classical Co.; debut with Bolshoi Ballet in title role of Grigorovich's Spartacus 1981; other roles include Ivan IV in Ivan the Terrible, Jean de Brienne in Raymonda, Basil in Don Quixote, Romeo in Grigorovich's Romeo and Juliet, Boris in Grigorovich's The Golden Age; f. Irek Mukhamedov and Co. 1991–; toured extensively with Bolshoi Ballet and made worldwide guest appearances; joined The Royal Ballet 1990; Covent Garden debut in MacMillan's pas de deux Farewell (with Darcey Bussell) 1990; appeared in musical The King and I, London 1995. *Address:* c/o Royal Ballet, Royal Opera House, Covent Garden, London, WC2E 9DD, England. *Telephone:* 0171-240 1200.

MUKHAMETSHIN, Farid Khairullovich; Russian/Tatar politician; b. 25 May 1947, Almetyevsk, Tatarstan; ed. Almetyevak Higher Professional Tech. School, Ufa Inst. of Oil; metal turner in factories; CP functionary: Sec. Almetyevsk City CP Cttee.; Chair. Exec. Cttee., Almetyevsk City Soviet; Deputy Chair. Council of Ministers, Minister of Trade of Tatar A.S.S.R. 1970–91; Chair. Supreme Soviet of Tatarstan Repub., mem. Council of Feds. 1991–94; Prime Minister of Tatarstan Repub. *Address:* Parliament Buildings, Svobody pl. 1, 420060 Kazan, Tatarstan, Russia. *Telephone:* (8432) 32 05 90 (Office).

MUKHERJEE, Bharati; American (b. Indian) lecturer and author; b. 27 July 1940, Calcutta; s. of Sudhir Lal Mukherjee and Bina Banerjee; m. Clark Blaise 1963; two s.; ed. Univs. of Calcutta, Baroda and Iowa; Prof. of English, McGill Univ.; lecturer Skidmore Coll.; lecturer in literature and creative writing, Queen's Coll., New York; Prof. Univ. of Calif., Berkeley 1990–. *Publications include:* The Tiger's Daughter 1971, The Tiger's Daughter and Wife 1975, Days and Night in Calcutta 1977, Darkness 1985, The Sorrow and the Terror (with Clark Blaise) 1987, The Middleman and Other Stories (Nat. Book Critics Circle Award for Fiction 1988) 1988, Jasmine 1989, The Holder of the World 1993, Leave it to Me 1996. *Address:* c/o Janklow and Nesbit, 598 Madison Avenue, New York, NY 10022; 130 Rivoli Street, San Francisco, CA 94117, U.S.A. *Telephone:* (415) 681 0345. *Fax:* (415) 759 9810.

MUKHERJEE, Pranab Kumar, M.A., LL.B.; Indian politician; b. 11 Dec. 1935, Mirati, Birbhum District, W. Bengal; s. of Mamada Kinkar; m.; two s. one d.; ed. Univ. of Calcutta; started career as lecturer; Ed. Palli-O-Panchayat Sambad (Bengali monthly); founder-Ed. Desher Dak (Bengali weekly) 1967–71; mem. Rajya Sabha 1969–, Leader 1980–88; Deputy Minister of Industrial Devt., Govt. of India 1973; Deputy Minister for Shipping and Transport Jan.–Oct. 1974; Minister of State, Ministry of Finance 1974–75; Minister for Revenue and Banking 1975–77; Minister of Commerce 1980–82, of Finance Jan.–Sept. 1982, of Finance 1982–85, of Commerce 1993–95, of External Affairs 1995–96; Deputy Chair. Planning Comm. with Cabinet rank; f. Rashtriya Samajwadi Congress 1987–; mem. Exec. Cttee. Congress (I) Party 1972–73, All India Congress Cttee. 1986; Treas. Congress (I) Party, mem. Working Cttee., Deputy Leader in Rajya Sabha. *Publications:* Bangla Congress: An Aspect of Constitutional Problems in Bengal 1967, Mid-term Election 1969. *Address:* 2 Jantar Mantar Road, New Delhi 110001, India.

MUKUMBAYEV, Usup Mukambayevich; Kyrgyzstan politician; b. 28 Jan. 1941, Dzholgolot, Kyrgyzia; ed. Kyrgyz State Univ., Higher Courses U.S.S.R. Cttee. of State Security; army service; shepherd Kolkhoz Ak-Suy Region; Sec. CP Cttee. of State Security Cttee. Kyrgyz Repub. 1970–78; Deputy Dir. Dept. of State Security Cttee. Osh Region 1978–80; Dir. Dept. of State Security Cttee. Talass and Osh Regions 1980–86; First Deputy Dir. State Security Cttee. Kyrgyz Repub. 1986–91; Minister of Justice 1991–92; Deputy Parl. (Zhogorku Kenesh) of Kyrgyzstan 1990–, Chair 1996-; Chair. Legislation Asscn. Kyrgyz Parl. *Address:* Zhogorku Kenesh, 720003 Bishkek, Kyrgyzstan (Office). *Telephone:* (3312) 22 55 23 (Office).

MULAMBA NYUNYI WA KADIMA, Gen. (Léonard); Democratic Republic of Congo politician, army officer and diplomatist; b. 1928, Luluabourg (now Kananga); s. of Kadima and Ngalula Mulamba; m. Adolphine N'galula 1956; six s. two d.; ed. Mil. School, Luluabourg; commissioned 1954; Maj. and Deputy Dir. of Cabinet, Ministry of Defence 1961–64; Lieut.-Col. 1962; Col., Chief of Staff and Commr. of Eastern Province (now Haut Zaïre) after re-occupation of Kivu Province 1964–65; Prime Minister 1965–66; Pres. Soc. nationale d'Assurances (SONAS) 1966; Amb. to India 1967–69; Amb. to Japan 1969–76, also accred. to Repub. of Korea 1971–76; Amb. to Brazil 1976–79; Gén. de Division, Gén. de Corps d'Armée 1979; Mil. Medal, Cross of Bravery, Commdr. Ordre de la Couronne (Belgium), Grand Officier Ordre nat. du Léopard (Zaire), Ordre du Mérite (Cen. African Republic), Compagnon de la Révolution. *Leisure interests:* hunting, reading. *Address:* c/o Chancellerie des Ordres Nationaux, B.P. 2014, Kinshasa, Democratic Republic of Congo.

MULCAHY, Sir Geoffrey John, Kt., B.SC., M.B.A.; British business executive; b. 7 Feb. 1942, Sunderland; s. of Maurice Mulcahy and Kathleen (née Blankinsop) Mulcahy; m. Valerie Elizabeth Mulcahy 1965; one s. one d.; ed. King's School, Worcester, Univ. of Manchester, Harvard Univ.; started career in labour relations, marketing and planning with Esso Corpn.; Finance Dir. Norton Abrasives' European Div., then for British Sugar; joined Woolworth Holdings (now Kingfisher PLC) 1983, firstly as Group Financial Dir., then Group Man. Dir. 1984–86, C.E.O. 1986–93, Chair. 1990–95, Group Chief Exec. Kingfisher Group 1995–; Dir. Bass 1989–; Dir. (non-exec.) BNP UK Holdings Ltd. *Leisure interest:* sailing. *Address:* Kingfisher PLC, North West House, 119 Marylebone Road, London, NW1 5PX, England. *Telephone:* 0171-724 7749. *Fax:* 0171-724 1160.

MULDOON, Paul Benedict, B.A.; Irish poet and university lecturer; b. 20 June 1951, Portadown; s. of Patrick Muldoon and Brigid Regan; m. Jean Hanff Korelitz 1987; ed. St. Patrick's Coll., Armagh, Queen's Univ., Belfast;

Radio and TV Producer, BBC Northern Ireland 1973–86; has taught at Cambridge Univ., Univ. of E. Anglia, Columbia Univ., Univ. of Calif. at Berkeley, Univ. of Mass. 1986–; Lecturer, Princeton Univ. 1990–95, Prof. 1995–; Guggenheim Fellowship 1990; T. S. Eliot Prize for The Annals of Chile 1995, American Acad. of Arts and Letters Award for Literature 1996. *Publications:* New Weather 1973, Mules 1977, Why Brownlee Left 1980, Quoof 1983, Meeting the British 1987, Madoc: A Mystery 1990, The Annals of Chile 1995; Selected Poems 1968–83 1986, New Selected Poems 1968–1994 1996, Hay (poems) 1999, Ed. The Faber Book of Beasts 1997. *Address:* Creative Writing Programme, Princeton University, Princeton, NJ 08544, U.S.A.

MULDOWNEY, Dominic John, B.PHIL.; British composer; b. 19 July 1952, Southampton; s. of William Muldowney and Barbara Muldowney (née Lavender); m. Diane Ellen Trevis 1986; one d.; ed. Taunton's Grammar School, Southampton and York Univ.; Composer-in-Residence to Southern Arts Assn. 1974–76; Music Dir., Royal Nat. Theatre 1976–; has composed music for British and int. festivals, for many films and TV and over 50 scores for the theatre. *Publications:* Piano Concerto 1983, Saxophone Concerto 1984, Sinfonietta 1986, Ars Subtilior 1987, Lonely Hearts 1988, Violin Concerto 1989, Three Pieces for Orchestra 1990, Percussion Concerto 1991, Oboe Concerto 1992, Trumpet Concerto 1993, Concerto for 4 Violins 1994 The Brontës (ballet) 1995, Trombone Concerto 1996, Clarinet Concerto 1997, The Fall of Jerusalem (oratorio) 1998. *Leisure interest:* France. *Address:* c/o Music Department, Royal National Theatre, South Bank, London, SE1 1PX, England.

MÜLLER, Claus, DR. RER. NAT.; German university professor and consultant; b. 20 Feb. 1920, Solingen; s. of Michael Müller and Grete (née Porten) Müller; m. Irmgard Döring 1947; two s. one d.; ed. Univs. of Bonn and Munich; Asst. Prof. Göttingen Univ. 1945–46; service in German army and navy 1941–45; lecturer Bonn Univ. 1947–55; Prof. and Dir. Inst. of Math. Sciences, Tech. Univ. of Aachen 1955–85, Prof. Emer. 1985–; Fellow Peterhouse, Cambridge 1948; lecturer, Univ. Coll. Hull 1949; Visiting Prof. and Consultant Corant Inst., New York, Math. Research Center Madison 1955–65. *Publications:* Foundations of the Mathematical Theory of Electromagnetic Waves, Spherical Harmonics, Analysis of Spherical Symmetries 1997; specialist articles in math. *Leisure interest:* music. *Address:* Horbacher Strasse 33, 52072 Aachen, Germany. *Telephone:* (0241) 12661.

MÜLLER, Gerhard, DR.THEOL.; German ecclesiastic; b. 10 May 1929, Marburg/Lahn; s. of Karl Müller and Elisabeth Landau; m. Ursula Herboth 1957; two s.; ed. Marburg, Göttingen and Tübingen; priest in Hanau/Main 1956–57; Deutsche Forschungsgemeinschaft scholarship, Italy 1957–59; Asst., Ecumenical Seminar, Univ. of Marburg 1959–61, Docent, Faculty of Theology 1961–66; guest lecturer, German Historical Inst., Rome 1966–67; Prof. of Historical Theology (Modern Church History), Univ. of Erlangen 1967–82; Evangelical-Lutheran Bishop of Brunswick 1982–94; Hon. Prof. Univ. of Göttingen 1983–; mem. Mainz, Netherlands Acads. and Braunschweiger Wissenschaftliche Gesellschaft; Dr.theol. h.c. (St. Andrews). *Publications:* Franz Lambert von Avignon und die Reformation in Hessen 1958, Nuntiaturberichte aus Deutschland 1530–1532 (2 vols.) 1963, 1969, Die römische Kurie und die Reformation 1523–1534 1969, Die Rechtfertigungslehre 1977, Reformation und Stadt 1981, Zwischen Reformation und Gegenwart 1983, Zwischen Reformation und Gegenwart II 1988, Causa Reformationis 1989; ed. works of Andreas Osiander and a 29-vol. theological encyclopaedia. *Address:* Sperlingstr. 59, 91056 Erlangen, Germany. *Telephone:* 09131/490939.

MÜLLER, K. Alex, PH.D.; Swiss physicist; b. 20 April 1927; ed. Swiss Fed. Inst. of Tech.; lecturer, Univ. of Zurich 1962, Titular Prof. 1970, Prof. 1987–; with IBM Research Lab. Rüschlikon 1963–73, Man. Dept. of Physics 1973–82, Fellow 1982–85, researcher 1985–; Nobel Prize for Physics (with G. Bednorz) for discovery of new superconducting materials 1987, Europhysics prize Hewlett-Packard Co. 1988; Fellow American Physics Soc.; mem. European Physics Soc., Swiss Physics Soc. *Address:* IBM Zürich Research Laboratory, Säumerstrasse 4, CH-8803 Rüschlikon, Switzerland. *Telephone:* 41-1-72 48 111.

MÜLLER, Werner; German politician and business executive; b. 1 June 1946, Essen; m.; two c.; ed. Univs. of Mannheim, Duisberg and Bremen; teacher Ludwigshafen Polytechnic 1970–72; dept. chief Rheinisch-Westfälische electricity co. (RWE) 1973–80; gen. rep. and Chief Exec. VEBA power co. 1980–87; adviser to Minister-Pres. of Lower Saxony 1991–; independent industrial consultant 1997–98; Fed. Minister of Econ. and Tech. 1998–; Independent. *Address:* Ministry of Economics, Villemombler Strasse 76, 53123 Bonn, Germany. *Telephone:* (228) 6150. *Fax:* (228) 615-44-36.

MULLER, Peter, M.ARCH., B.E., F.S.A.S.M.I.; Australian architect; b. 3 July 1927, Adelaide; s. of Clarence Muller and Eva Rankin; m. 1st Rosemary Winn Patrick 1953 (divorced 1964); two s. (one deceased) one d.; m. 2nd Carole Margaret Mason 1964 (divorced 1990); m. 3rd Helen Patricia Hayes 1998; ed. St Peter's Coll., Adelaide, Univ. of Adelaide, S. Australian School of Mines and Industries, Adelaide, Univ. of Penn., U.S.A.; independent architectural practice, Sydney 1953–89, Adelaide 1990–; Visiting tutor Univ. of N.S.W., Sydney 1962, Prin. Regional Design and Research 1978–; Dir. Nat. Capital Devt. Comm., Canberra 1975–77. *Leisure interests:* tennis, music, philosophy. *Address:* 48 Millbank, London, S.W.1, England; P.O. Box 545, Clare, South Australia 5453. *Telephone:* (8) 8842-1772 (Australia). *Fax:* 0171-630 6353 (England); (8) 8842 1771 (Australia).

MULLER, Steven, PH.D.; American university and hospital administrator; b. 22 Nov. 1927, Hamburg, Germany; s. of Werner A. and Marianne (Hartstein) Muller; m. Margie Hellman 1951; two d.; ed. Hollywood High School, Los Angeles, Univ. of Calif., Los Angeles, Oxford Univ., Cornell Univ.; Instructor in Political Science, Wells Coll. 1953; U.S. Army 1954–55; Research Fellow in Social Science, Cornell Univ. 1955–56; Asst. Prof. of Political Science, Haverford Coll. 1956–58; Asst. Prof. of Govt., Cornell Univ. 1958–61, Assoc. Prof. and Dir. Center for Int. Studies 1961–66, Vice-Pres. for Public Affairs 1966–71; Provost, Johns Hopkins Univ. 1971–72, Pres. 1972–90, Pres. Emer. 1990–; Prof. School of Advanced Int. Studies 1993; Pres. Johns Hopkins Hosp. 1972–83; Chair. 21st Century Foundation 1990–96; Chair. of Bd. St. Mary's Coll. of Md.; Co-Chair. American Inst. for Contemporary German Studies; Dir. Van Kampen Closed End Funds, Law/Gibb Corpn., Org. Resources Counselors, Inc., Atlantic Council of the U.S., German Marshall Fund of the U.S.; fmr. mem. Bd. of Dirs., CSX Corpn., Millipore Corpn., Beneficial Corpn., Alex. Brown & Sons Inc.; Commdr.'s Cross of the Order of Merit (Fed. Repub. of Germany). *Publications:* Documents on European Government 1963, From Occupation to Cooperation 1992 (co-ed.), In Search of Germany 1996 (co-ed.), Universities in the Twenty-First Century 1996; articles in learned journals. *Address:* Johns Hopkins University, School of Advanced International Studies, 1619 Massachusetts Avenue, N.W., Suite 711, Washington, DC 20036, U.S.A.

MÜLLER-SEIDEL. Walter, DR. PHIL.; German professor of modern literature; b. 1 July 1918, Schöna; s. of Martin Müller-Seidel and Rosa (née Seidel) Müller; m. Ilse Peters 1950; one s.; ed. Univs. of Leipzig and Heidelberg; lecturer Univ. of Cologne 1958, Privat-dozent 1958–59; Prof. Univ. of Munich 1960–65; Ordinary Prof. 1965, now Emer.; mem. Bayerischen Akademie der Wissenschaften 1974. *Publications:* Versehen und Erkennen: Eine Studie über Heinrich von Kleist 1961, Probleme der literarischen Wertung 1965, Theodor Fontane: Soziale Romankunst in Deutschland 1975, Die Geschichtlichkeit der deutscher Klassik 1983, Die Deportation des Menschen, Kafkas Erzählung 'In der Strafkolonie' im europäischen Kontext 1986, Arztbilder im Wandel. Zum literarischen Werk Arthur Schnitzlers 1997. *Address:* Pienzenauerstrasse 164, 81925 Munich, Germany. *Telephone:* (089) 988250.

MÜLLER-WARMUTH, Werner; German professor of physical chemistry; b. 1 Oct. 1929, Hamburg; s. of Viktor Müller-Warmuth and Luise Müller-Warmuth; m. Inge Schmidtke 1955; two s.; ed. Univs. of Frankfurt and Mainz; with Max Planck Inst. für Chemie, Mainz 1955–65; Euratom Research Center, Ispra, Italy 1965–73; Prof. and Dir. Inst. für Physikalische Chemie, Univ. of Münster 1973–, Rector 1978–82; Pres. Conf. of Univ. Rectors of Nordrhein-Westfalen 1981–83; Hon. Prof., Univ. of Lima. *Publications:* more than 200 scientific publications on physical chem., spectroscopy, materials, etc. *Address:* Institut für Physikalische Chemie, Schlossplatz 4/7, 48149 Münster (Office); Julius-Hart-Strasse 6, 48147 Münster, Germany (Home). *Telephone:* 0251/832421 (Office); 0251/22104 (Home).

MULLIS, Kary Banks, PH.D.; American biochemist; b. 28 Dec. 1944, Lenoir, N.C.; s. of Cecil Banks Mullis and Bernice Alberta Barker Fredericks Mullis; two s. one d. ed. Georgia Inst. of Tech., Univ. of California, Berkeley; lecturer in Biochemistry Univ. of Calif., Berkeley 1972; postdoctoral fellow, Univ. of Kan. Medical School 1973–76, Univ. of Calif., San Francisco 1977–79; researcher Cetus Corp. 1979–86; Dir. Molecular Biology Xytronyx, Inc., San Diego 1986–88; consultant 1988–96; Chair. StarGene, Inc.; Vice-Pres. Histotec, Inc., Vyrex Inc.; Visiting Prof. Univ of S.C.; partner in Questar Int. 1998; Preis Biochemische Analytik Award 1990, Allan Award 1990, Gairdner Foundation Award 1991, Nat. Biotech. Award 1991, R&D Magazine Scientist of the Year 1991, Koch Award 1992, Chiron Corpn. Award 1992, Japan Prize 1992, Calif. Scientist of the Year 1992, shared Nobel Prize for Chem. 1993; devised polymerase chain reaction. *Publications:* numerous articles. *Address:* Vyrex Inc., 2519 Avenida de la Palaya, La Jolla, CA 92037, U.S.A. (Office).

MULLOVA, Viktoria; Russian violinist; b. 27 Nov. 1959, Moscow; d. of Raissa Mullova and Juri Mullov; one s. two d.; studied in Moscow at Cen. Music School and Moscow Conservatory under Leonid Kogan; first prize at Sibelius Competition, Helsinki 1980, Gold Medal, Tchaikovsky Competition, Moscow 1982; left U.S.S.R. 1983; has appeared with most major orchestras and conductors, and at int. festivals. *Recordings include:* Tchaikovsky and Sibelius Violin Concertos with Boston Symphony under Seiji Ozawa (Grand Prix du disque); Bartok, Bach and Paganini solo works; Shostakovich Concerto No. 1; Prokofiev Concerto No. 2; Brahms violin sonatas; J. S. Bach partitas for violin and piano; Mendelssohn concertos; J. S. Bach partitas for solo violin; Brahms violin concerto; Janáček, Prokofiev and Debussy sonatas; J. S. Bach violin concertos, concerto for violin and oboe; Stravinsky concerto; Bartok concerto no. 2. *Leisure interests:* reading, cinema, skiing, tennis, mountain climbing. *Address:* c/o Askonas Holt, Lonsdale Chambers, 27 Chancery Lane, London, WC2A 1PF, England. *Telephone:* 0171-400 1700. *Fax:* 0171-400 1799.

MULRONEY, Rt. Hon. (Martin) Brian, P.C., LL.D.; Canadian politician and former business executive; b. 20 March 1939, Baie Comeau, Que.; s. of Benjamin and Irene (O'Shea) Mulroney; m. Mila Pivnicki 1973; three s. one d.; ed. St. Francis Xavier Univ. and Univ. Laval; called to Bar of Quebec 1965; Partner, Ogilvy, Cope, Porteous, Montgomery, Renault, Clarke & Kirkpatrick, Montreal 1965–76, Sr. Partner, Ogilvy Renault 1993–; Exec.

Vice-Pres. (Corp. Affairs), Iron Ore Co. of Canada 1976–77, Pres. and Dir. 1977–83; Leader, Progressive Party of Canada 1983–93; mem. Parl. 1983–93; Leader of Opposition 1983–84; Prime Minister of Canada 1984–93; Chair. Chase Manhattan Corpn.; Dir. Barrick Gold Corpn. (Chair. Int. Advisory Bd.), Horsham Corpn., Archer Daniels Midland, Petrofina A.A., Proagro Compania Anonima; mem. Int. Advisory Bd., Power Corpn., Chase Manhattan Corpn., China Int. Trust and Investment (CITIC), Bombardier/Aerospace Group, Violi, Byorum & Partners; Trustee Fredom Forum, George Bush Presidential Library; numerous hon. degrees. *Publication:* Where I Stand 1983. *Leisure interests:* tennis, swimming. *Address:* 47 Forden Crescent, Westmount, Que. H3Y 2Y5; Ogilvy Renault, 1981 McGill College Avenue, Suite 1100, Montreal, Quebec H3A 3C1, Canada.

MULUZI, Bakili; Malawi politician and business executive; b. Machinga; ed. Huddersfield Tech. Coll. and coll. in Denmark; clerk, colonial civil service of Nyasaland; fmr. Sec.-Gen. Malawi Congress Party (dismissed 1983); mem. Parl. 1975; held various Cabinet portfolios including Educ. and Minister without Portfolio; business interests in transport and sugar trading; Leader, United Democratic Front 1992–; Pres. of Malawi May 1994–. *Address:* Office of the President, Private Bag 301, Capital City, Lilongwe 3, Malawi. *Telephone:* 782655. *Fax:* 782095.

MUMBENGEGWI, Simbarashe Simbanenduku, B.A., DIP.ED.; Zimbabwean diplomatist, politician and public servant; b. 20 July 1945, Chivi Dist.; s. of Chivandire Davis Mumbengegwi and Dzivaidzo Shuvai Chimbambo; m. Emily Charasika 1983; one s. four d.; ed. Monash Univ., Melbourne, Australia, Univ. of Zimbabwe; active in Zimbabwe African Nat. Union (ZANU) party 1963–, in exile, Australia 1966–72, Deputy Chief Rep. in Australia and Far East 1973–76, Chief Rep. 1976–78, Chief Rep. in Zambia 1978–80, mem. Cen. Cttee. 1984–94; elected M.P. 1980, 1985; Deputy Minister of Foreign Affairs 1981–82, Minister of Water Resources and Devt. 1982, of Housing 1982–84, of Public Construction and Nat. Housing 1984–88, of Transport 1988–90; Perm. Rep. to UN 1990–95; Amb. to Belgium, the Netherlands and Luxembourg, Perm. Rep. to EU 1995–; Perm. Rep. to Org. for the Prohibition of Chemical Weapons (OPCW) 1997–, Chair. Conf. of the State Parties 1997–98, mem. Exec. Council 1997–. *Leisure interests:* reading, photography, jogging, tennis, golf. *Address:* Embassy of Zimbabwe, Square Josephine Charlotte 11, 1200 Brussels, Belgium. *Telephone:* (02) 762 5808. *Fax:* (02) 762 9605.

MUMFORD, David Bryant, PH.D.; American professor of mathematics; b. 11 June 1937, Sussex, England; s. of William Bryant Mumford and Grace Schiott; m. 1st Erika Jentsch 1959 (died 1988); three s. one d.; m. 2nd Jenifer Moore 1989; ed. Harvard Univ.; Prof. of Maths. Harvard Univ. 1967–77, Higgins Prof. 1977–97, Chair. Maths Dept. 1981–84, MacArthur Fellow 1987–92; Prof. of Maths. Brown Univ. 1996–; Pres. Int. Math. Union 1995–; mem. N.A.S., American Acad. of Arts and Sciences; Hon. D.Sc. (Warwick) 1983; Fields Medal 1974. *Publications:* Geometric Invariant Theory 1965, Abelian Varieties 1970, Algebraic Geometry I 1976. *Leisure interest:* sailing. *Address:* Brown University, 182 George Street, Providence, RI 02912 (Office); 65 Milton Street, Milton, MA 02186, U.S.A. (Home). *Telephone:* (617) 547-2639 (Home).

MUNA, Solomon Tandeng; Cameroonian politician (retd.); b. 1912, Ngyn-Mbo, Momo Division; s. of Muna Tayim and Ama Keng Muna; m. Elizabeth Fri Muna 1937; seven s. one d.; ed. Teacher Training Coll., Kumba and Univ. of London Inst. of Educ.; M.P. for Bamenda Dist. 1951; Eastern Nigeria Minister for Public Works 1951; Minister of Works, subsequently Minister of Commerce and Industries, Minister of Finance, Southern Cameroon Region; Fed. Minister of Transport, Mines, Posts and Telecommunications of Cameroon 1961–68; Prime Minister of W. Cameroon 1968–72, also Vice-Pres. Fed. Repub. of Cameroon 1970–72; Minister of State 1972–73; Pres. Nat. Assembly 1973–88; Co-Pres. ACP-EEC States Consultative Assembly 1978–82; fmrly. Chair. Bd. of Dirs. Cameroon Railways, Chair. Higher Cttee. on Cameroon Ports; has represented Cameroon at various int. confs.; mem. Bureau of the Cameroon People's Democratic Movt. (CPDM) 1973–88; Chief Scout of Cameroon 1970–77; Chair. African Scout Cttee. 1973–77, mem. World Bureau of Scouts 1975, Vice-Chair. World Scout Cttee. 1977–81; Commdr., Ordre de la Valeur du Cameroun, Officier, Légion d'honneur and numerous other foreign decorations. *Leisure interests:* horseback riding, stamp collecting, scouting, gardening, inland fish-farming. *Address:* P.O. Box 15, Mbengwi, Momo Division, North West Province, Cameroon. *Telephone:* 36-12-62.

MUNDEBO, (Kurt Allan) Ingemar, FIL.LIC.; Swedish fmr. politician, auditor-general and university teacher; b. 15 Oct. 1930, Långasjö; s. of Magni and Hildegard Gustavsson; m. Lillemor Ericsson 1973; one s. one d.; Asst. in Nat. and Communal Admin. 1950–56; teacher in secondary school 1956–60; Lector in School of Social Studies 1960–64; Head of Dept., Univ. of Stockholm 1964–76; mem. Riksdag (Parl.) 1965–80, Nordic Council 1969–76; Minister of the Budget 1976–80 and Econ. Affairs 1978–79; Gov. Province of Uppsala 1980–86; Dir.-Gen., Swedish Nat. Audit Bureau 1986–93; mem. Folkpartiet (Liberal Party); Kt., Order of North Star, Grand Cross, Icelandic Order of the Falcon, Kt. Commdr. Order of Dannebrog. *Publications:* Ny kris i befolkningsfrågan? 1962, Social Administration 1963, Socialkunskap 1968, Förvaltningskunskap 1970, Våra villkor 1975. *Leisure interest:* Rotarians. *Address:* Gyllenstiernsgatan 15, 115 26 Stockholm, Sweden (Home). *Telephone:* 08-663 1490 (Home).

MUNDELL, Robert Alexander, PH.D.; Canadian professor of economics; b. 24 Oct. 1932, Kingston, Ont.; s. of William Campbell Mundell and Lila Teresa Mundell; m. Barbara Sheff 1957 (divorced 1972); two s. one d.; ed. Univ. of British Columbia, Univ. of Washington, Massachusetts Inst. of Tech., London School of Econs., Univ. of Chicago; Instructor, Univ. of B.C. 1957–58; economist, Royal Comm. on price Spreads of Food Products, Ottawa 1958; Asst. Prof. of Econs., Stanford Univ., U.S.A. 1958–59; Prof. of Econs., Johns Hopkins Univ., School of Advanced Int. Studies, Bologna, Italy 1959–61; Sr. Economist, IMF 1961–63; Visiting Prof. of Econs., McGill Univ. 1963–64, 1989–90; Prof. of Int. Econs., Grad. Inst. of Int. Studies, Geneva, Switzerland 1965–75; Prof. of Econs. Univ. of Chicago 1966–71; Prof. of Econs. and Chair. Dept. of Econs., Univ. of Waterloo, Ont. 1972–74; Prof. of Econs. Columbia Univ., U.S.A. 1974–; Ed. Journal of Political Economy 1966–71; Annenburg Distinguished Scholar in Residence, Univ. of Southern Calif. 1980; Richard Fox Visiting Prof. of Econs., Univ. of Pa. 1990–91; First Rockefeller Visiting Research Prof. of Int. Econs., Brookings Inst. 1964–65; Guggenheim Fellow 1971; Marshall Lectures, Cambridge Univ. 1974; Distinguished Lecturer, Ching-Hua Inst., Taipei, Taiwan 1985; Pres. N. American Econ. and Financial Asscn. 1974–78; Dr. h.c. (Univ. of Paris) 1992, (People's Univ. of China) 1995; Jacques Rueff Prize and Medal 1983. *Publications:* The International Monetary System: Conflict and Reform 1965, Man and Economics 1968, International Economics 1968, Monetary Theory: Interest, Inflation and Growth in the World Economy 1971; numerous papers and articles in journals. *Leisure interests:* painting, tennis, hockey, skiing, art history. *Address:* Department of Economics, Columbia University, Morningside Heights, New York, NY 10027; 35 Clarement Avenue, New York, N.Y. 10027, U.S.A. (Home); Palazzo Mundell, Santa Colomba, Siena, Italy (June-Aug.). *Telephone:* (212) 854-3669 (Office); (212) 749-0630 (Home, U.S.A.); 577-57068 (Italy). *Fax:* (212) 854-8059.

MUNGOSHI, Charles Muzuva; Zimbabwean writer, poet and playwright; b. 2 Dec. 1947, Chivhu; m. Jesesi Jaboon 1976; four s. one d.; ed. secondary school; clerk in book shop, Harare 1969–74; Ed. with the Literature Bureau 1974–81; Dir. and Ed. publisher in Zimbabwe 1981–88; Writer-in-Residence, Univ. of Zimbabwe 1985–87; Visiting Arts Fellow, Univ. of Durham 1990; Noma Award for Publishing in Africa, Book Center/PEN Award, Commonwealth Writers Award (Africa Region). *Publications:* (novels) Makunun'unu Maodzamwoyo (in Shona) 1970, Waiting for the Rain 1975, Ndiko Kupindana Kwamazuva (in Shona) 1975, Kunyarara Hakusi Kutaura? (in Shona) 1983; (short stories) Coming of the Dry Season 1972, Some Kinds of Wounds 1980, Setting Sun and Rolling World 1987, One Day Long Ago: Tales from a Shona Childhood (folk tales) 1991, Walking Still 1997; (poetry) The Milkman Doesn't Only Deliver Milk 1981. *Film:* The Axe (writer and dir.) 1999. *Leisure interests:* travelling reading, acting. *Address:* P.O. Box 1688, Harare (Business); 47/6156 Uta Crescent, Zengeza 1, Chitungwiza, Zimbabwe.

MUNIM, Mohammad Abdul, M. SC. ENG.; Bangladeshi government official; b. 1 Jan. 1935, Bogra; s. of Emdad Ali and Sufia Khatun; m. Dr. Ayesha Akhter 1961; four d.; ed. Imperial Coll. of Science and Tech., London; Commissioned Electrical and Mechanical Engineers Corps, Pakistan Army 1956–71, Bangladesh Army 1974–86, Dir. of Corps, Maj.-Gen.; Gen. Man. GEM Plant 1974–76; Chair. PDB 1979–83; mem. Council of Ministers 1983–90, Minister for Works 1983–85, for Agric. 1985–86, for Commerce 1986–87, of Finance 1987–88, of Health and Family Planning 1988–89, for Agric. 1989–90, of Finance and Planning 1990; mem. consulting firm Agric. and Electrical Power Eng. 1991–. *Leisure interests:* reading, listening to Tagore songs. *Address:* 33 Dhanmondi R.A. Road 7, Dhaka-1205, Bangladesh. *Telephone:* (2) 813334 (Home). *Fax:* (2) 861718.

MUÑIZ, Carlos Manuel, LL.D.; Argentinian diplomatist and university professor; b. 2 Feb. 1922, Buenos Aires; ed. Univ. de Buenos Aires; Under-Sec. of Interior and Justice 1955, of Interior 1955–56; Amb. to Bolivia 1956–59, to Brazil 1959–62, to U.S.A. 1971–73, to Barbados (also to Bahamas) 1984–86; Minister of Foreign Affairs and Worship 1962–63; Prof. of Int. Public Law, Univ. de La Plata 1963–73, also Dir. Int. Law Inst.; Prof. of Constitutional Law, Univ. de Buenos Aires; fmr. Prof. of Int. Law and Int. Relations, Univ. Católica de La Plata; Perm. Rep. to UN 1982–86; Pres. Argentine Council on Foreign Relations (CARI); Founder Instituto del Servicio Exterior de la Nación (ISEN); Pres. Nat. Cttee. for 50th Anniversary of UN; mem. Nat. Acad. of Law and Social Sciences; Silver Laurel Award to Diplomat of the Year, Rotary Club Buenos Aires 1979; decorations from govts. of Bolivia, Brazil, Japan, Peru, Paraguay, Colombia etc. *Publications:* National Basis for an International Policy 1969, Relations between Argentina and Brazil 1979, Diplomacy and Diplomats 1979 and others. *Address:* CARI, Uruguay 1037, 1st Floor, 1016 Buenos Aires, Argentina. *Telephone:* 811-0071/4. *Fax:* 811-0072.

MUNK ANDERSEN, Jens; Danish businessman; b. 21 Dec. 1928, nr. Vorupoer; one s. one d.; ed. Birkeroed, Univ. of Århus; joined Dansk Esso AS 1956, Analyst, Economist 1956–64, Supply Man., Refinery Man., mem. Excom and Bd. of Dirs. 1964–75, Chair. of Bd. and Chief Exec. 1978–86; joined Esso Int., London 1963, Analyst, Supply 1963–64; joined Esso N. Europe AS, Copenhagen, PPD Dir. 1983–85, Pres. 1985–86; Exec. Asst. to Chair. Exxon Corpn., New York 1975–78; Pres. Statoil A/S (fmrly. Dansk Esso A/S) 1986. *Address:* 6A Skjoldhoj Allé, DK-2920 Charlottenlund, Denmark (Home).

MUNK OLSEN, Birger, D.LITT.; Danish professor of medieval culture and philology; b. 26 June 1935, Copenhagen; m. 1st Annalise Bliddal 1964 (divorced 1988); m. 2nd Gudrun Haastrup 1994; two d.; ed. Ecole Normale Supérieure, Sorbonne, Paris and Pontificia Univ. Gregoriana, Rome; Assoc. Prof. of Romance Philology, Univ. of Copenhagen 1961–68; lecturer Univ. Paris-Sorbonne 1968–74; Prof. of Romance Philology, Univ. of Copenhagen 1974–83, Prof. of Medieval Culture and Philology 1983–; Chair. Danish Nat. Research Council for the Humanities 1987–90; Danish Rep. Standing Cttee. for the Humanities, European Science Foundation 1988–92; mem. Royal Danish Acad. 1985– (Vice-Pres., Chair. Humanities Section 1989–95, Pres. 1996–), Danish Council for Research Planning and Policy 1987–89, Acad. Europaea 1988– (Exec. Council 1989–92); Corresp. mem. Acad. des Inscriptions et Belles Lettres (Inst. de France) 1996, mem. 1998–; Vice-Pres. Soc. Int. de Bibliographie Classique 1994–; mem. European Science and Tech. Ass. (ESTA) 1997; Prix Brunet 1984; Kt. Order of Dannebrog, Officier Ordre Nat. du Merite. *Publications:* Les "Dits" de Jehan de Saint-Quentin 1978, L'étude des auteurs classiques latins aux XIe et XIIe siècles, Vols. I–IV 1982–89, I classici nel canone scolastico altomedievale 1991, L'atteggiamento medievale di fronte alla cultura classica 1994, La réception de la littérature classique au Moyen Age 1995. *Address:* Ny Kongensgade 20, 1557 Copenhagen V, Denmark; 51 rue de Tolbiac, 75013 Paris, France; Torshoj 1, Veddinge, 4540 Faarevejle, Denmark. *Telephone:* 33919181 (Copenhagen); (01) 45-84-27-18 (Paris); 20217217 (Faarevejle).

MUÑOZ LEDO, Porfirio; Mexican politician and university professor; b. 1933; ed. Univ. Nacional Autónoma de México; Prof. of Political Science, Univ. Nacional Autónoma de México and El Colegio de México 1958–69; Gen. Sec. Inst. Mexicano del Seguro Social 1966–70; worked for election campaign of Pres. Echeverría (q.v.) 1969; Pvt. Sec. to Pres. Echeverría 1970–72; Sec. for Labour and Social Security 1972–75, for Educ. 1976–77; Perm. Rep. of Mexico to UN 1979–81, 1982–85; Pres. Partido Revolucionario Institutional 1975–77; fmr. Chair Partido de la Revolución Democrática (PRD). *Address:* Partido de la Revolución Demócrata, México D.F., Mexico.

MUNRO, Alice; Canadian writer; b. 10 July 1931, Wingham, Ont.; d. of Robert E. Laidlaw and Anne Chamney; m. 1st James A. Munro 1951 (divorced 1976); three d.; m. 2nd Gerald Fremlin 1976; recipient of Gov.-Gen.'s Award for Literature 1968, Canadian Booksellers' Award 1971, Canada-Australia Literary Prize. *Publications:* Dance of the Happy Shades 1968, Lives of Girls and Women 1971, Something I've Been Meaning to Tell You 1974, Who Do You Think You Are? (appeared as The Beggar Maid in U.S.A. and U.K.) 1978, The Moons of Jupiter 1982, The Progress of Love 1986, Friend of My Youth 1990, Open Secret 1994, Selected Stories 1996, The Love of A Good Woman 1999. *Address:* c/o Alfred A. Knopf Inc., 201 E. 50th Street, New York, NY 10022 (Office); P.O. Box 1133, Clinton, Ont., N0M 1L0, Canada [Home).

MUNRO, J. Richard, B.A.; American publishing executive; b. 1931; m.; ed. Colgate, Columbia and New York Univs.; joined Time Inc. 1957; Pres. Pioneer Press Inc. (Time subsidiary) 1969; Publr. Sports Illustrated 1969–71; Vice-Pres. Time Inc. 1971–75, Group Vice-Pres. for video 1975–79, Exec. Vice-Pres. 1979–80, Pres. 1980–86, C.E.O. 1980–90, Chair. 1986–90, Chair. Exec. Comm. 1990, also Dir.; Chair. Genentech Inc. 1997–; Dir IBM Corpn.; Purple Heart with two Clusters; Hon. Litt. D. (Richmond Univ.) 1983. *Address:* Time Inc., Time & Life Building, 75 Rockefeller Plaza, New York, N.Y. 10019, U.S.A.

MUNS ALBUIXECH, Joaquín, PH.D.; Spanish university professor and international civil servant; b. 25 June 1935, Barcelona; one s.; ed. Univ. of Barcelona and London School of Econs.; Economist, Nat. Studies Div. of OECD 1962–63; Asst. Prof. of Econs. Univ. of Barcelona 1963–65, Prof. of Econs. Univ. of Barcelona 1968–73, Sr. Prof. of Int. Econ. Org. 1973–, Jean Monnet Prof. of European Integration 1991–; Economist, Western Hemisphere Dept. of IMF 1965–68, Exec. Dir. IMF 1978–80; Econ. Adviser to Barcelona City Council 1968–73; Econ. Adviser to Govt. of Spain and to various public and pvt. insts. 1973–78; Exec. Dir. IBRD 1980–82; Adjunct Prof. SIS American Univ. 1982; mem. European Parl. (Liberal Group) 1987–89; mem. Vatican Council of Econ. Advisers 1988–94; mem. Governing Council Bank of Spain 1994–. *Publications:* (in English): Adjustment, Conditionality and International Financing (ed.) 1984; (in Spanish): Industrialization and Growth in the Developing Countries 1972, The European Option for the Spanish Economy 1973, The International Economic Crisis: Thoughts and Proposals 1975, Crisis and Reform of the International Monetary System 1978, History of the Relations between Spain and the IMF 1958–82, Twenty-five Years of the Spanish Economy 1986, The EMU and its Future 1992, Radiography of the Crisis 1993, Spain and the World Bank 1994, Spain and the Euro: Risks and Opportunities (Ed.) 1997; over 30 essays and articles, with special reference to problems of the int. econ. orgs. *Leisure interests:* travel, music. *Address:* C. Muntaner, 268, 08021 Barcelona, Spain. *Telephone:* (3) 2094534. *Fax:* (3) 4140697.

MUNTEAN, Mihai; Moldovan opera singer (tenor); b. 15 Aug. 1943, Kriva, Briceni; s. of Ion Muntean and Elizaveta Muntean; m. Rosentul Galina Andrian 1969; one s. one d.; ed. Kishinev Inst. of Arts, La Scala, Milan; soloist with Moldovan State Acad. Theatre of Opera and Ballet 1971–; Prof., Music Acad. of Moldova 1993–; U.S.S.R. People's Artist, 1986, Moldovan State Prize 1988. *Roles include:* Lensky (Eugene Onegin), Riccardo (Un Ballo in Maschera), Cavaradossi (Tosca), Calaf (Turandot), Hermann (The Queen of Spades), Radames (Aida), José (Carmen), Turriddu (Cavalleria Rusticana), Othello (Othello), Canio (Pagliacci), Manrico (Il Trovatore), Samson (Samson et Dalila), Ismael (Nabucco); performances throughout the world. *Leisure interests:* collecting books, family, children, music. *Address:* 16 N. Iorga Str., Apt. 13, 2012 Chişnău, Moldova. *Telephone:* (2) 237519. *Fax:* (2) 237519.

MÜNTEFERING, Franz; German politician; b. 16 Jan. 1940, Neheim; s. of Franz Müntefering and Anna Schlinkmann; m. Ankepetra Rettich 1995; two d.; apprenticeship in industrial admin. 1954–57; industrial admin. in eng. firm 1957–61; mil. training 1961; mem. Social Democratic Party of Germany (SPD) 1966–, sub-dist. Chair. Hochsauerland 1984–88, mem. dist. exec. W. Westphalia 1984–, dist. Chair. 1992–98, Fed. Business Man. 1995–, Chair. state org. North Rhine Westphalia 1998; mem. Sudern City Council 1969–79; mem. Bundestag 1975–92, Parl. Business Man. SPD Bundestag Parl. group 1991–92; mem. North Rhine Westphalia Landtag 1996–98; Fed. Minister of Transport, Construction and Housing 1998–; mem. IG Metall (eng. TU) 1967–. *Address:* Ministry of Transport, Robert-Schumann-Platz 1, 53175 Bonn, Germany. *Telephone:* (228) 3000. *Fax:* (228) 300-3428.

MURAD, Ferid, B.A., M.D., PH.D.; American professor of pharmacology; s. of John Murad and Henrietta Josephine Bowman; m. Carol A. Leopold 1958; one s. four d.; ed. DePauw Univ., Ind. and Western Reserve Univ., Cleveland, Ohio; Dir. Clinical Research Center, School of Medicine, Univ. of Va. 1971–81, Div. of Clinical Pharmacology 1973–81, Prof. Depts. of Internal Medicine and Pharmacology 1975–81; Prof. Depts. of Internal Medicine and Pharmacology, Stanford Univ. 1981–89, Acting Chair. Dept. of Medicine 1986–88; Chief of Medicine Palo Alto Veterans Admin. Medical Center, Calif. 1981–86; Adjunct Prof. Dept. of Pharmacology, Northwestern Univ., Chicago 1988–96; Chair. Dept. of Integrative Biology and Pharmacology, Univ. of Texas Medical School, Houston 1997– (Prof. and Dir. Depts. of Pharmacology and Physiology), Dir. Inst. of Molecular Medicine 1999–; Vice-Pres. Pharmaceutical Research and Devt., Abbott Labs. 1990–92; C.E.O. and Pres. Molecular Geriatrics Corpn., Lake Bluff, Ill. 1993–95; Albert and Mary Lasker Award for Basic Research 1996; Nobel Prize in Medicine or Physiology 1998. *Publications:* Discovery of Some of the Biological Effects of Nitric Oxide and its Role in Cellular Signaling (Nobel Lecture 1998) 1999. *Leisure interests:* golf, carpentry. *Address:* P.O. Box 20708, MSB, 4.100, Houston, TX 77225, (Office); 3324 Nottingham, West University Place, Houston, TX 77005, U.S.A. (Home). *Telephone:* (713) 500-7509 (Office); (713) 664-3509 (Home). *Fax:* (713) 500-7444 (Office).

MURADOV, Sakhat, D.TECH.SC.; Turkmenistan politician; b. 7 May 1932, Ivanovo, Russia; s. of Nepes Muradov and Nursoltan Muradova; m. Sona Muradova 1954; two s. one d.; ed. Turkmen Agric. Inst.; fmr. mem. CP; Head Dept. of Science and Educ. Central Cttee. Turkmen CP 1965–70; Rector, Turkmen State Univ. 1970–79; Minister for Higher Educ. 1979–85; Rector, Turkmen Polytechnic Inst. 1985–90; fmr. First Deputy Chair. Supreme Soviet of Turkmenistan, Chair. 1990–92; Chair. Turkmenistan Majlis 1992–; Deputy to Supreme Soviet of Turkmenistan, 8th and 12th convocations; Order of Red Banner of Labour (twice), Star of Pres. of Turkmenistan; Certificate of Honour (Presidium of Turkmenistan Supreme Soviet). *Publications:* three books, more than 50 articles. *Leisure interests:* sport, tourism, literature. *Address:* Turkmenistan Mejlis, 17 Gogol Street, 744017 Ashkhabad, Turkmenistan. *Telephone:* (3632) 35-31-25. *Fax:* 25-31-47.

MURAOKA, Takamitsu, PH.D., F.A.H.A.; Japanese academic; b. 9 Feb. 1938, Hiroshima; m. Keiko Kageyama 1965; two s. one d.; ed. Tokyo Kyoiku, The Hebrew Univ., Jerusalem; lecturer in Semitic Languages, Dept. of Near Eastern Studies, Univ. of Manchester, U.K. 1970–80; Prof. of Middle Eastern Studies, Chair. Dept., Melbourne Univ. 1980–91; Prof. of Hebrew, Univ. of Leiden 1991–; Ed. Abr-Nahrain (Leiden) 1980–92; Academic Assoc., The Oxford Centre for Hebrew and Jewish Studies. *Publications:* A Greek-Hebrew/Aramaic Index to I Esdras 1982, Emphatic Words and Structures in Biblical Hebrew 1985, Classical Syriac for Hebraists 1987, A Grammar of Biblical Hebrew (with P. Joüon) 1991, Studies in Qumran Aramaic (ed.) 1992, A Greek-English Lexicon of the Septuagint (Twelve Prophets) 1993, Studies on the Hebrew of the Dead Sea Scrolls and Ben Sira (ed. with J. F. Elwolde) 1997, a Grammar of Egyptian Aramaic (with B. Porten) 1997, Classical Syriac—A Basic Grammar with a Chrestomathy 1997. *Leisure interest:* angling. *Address:* Postbus 9515, Hebreeuws, Rijksuniversiteit, 2300 RA Leiden, Netherlands.

MURATA, Kiyoaki, M.A.; Japanese journalist, educator and author; b. 19 Nov. 1922, Ono, Hyogo; s. of the late Itsuji Murata and of Kazue Murata; m.; two s. one d.; ed. Carleton Coll., Minnesota and Univ. of Chicago; visiting lecturer, Kansei Gakuin Univ. 1949, Meiji Gakuin Univ. 1950, Aoyama Gakuin Univ. 1959–63, Univ. of Tokyo 1960–62; editorial writer, The Japan Times 1957–66, Man. Ed. 1971–76, Exec. Ed. 1976–77, Man. Dir. 1974–83, Ed.-in-Chief 1977–83; Prof. of Int. Communication, Yachiyo Int. Univ. 1988–; Dir. Japan Graphic Inc. 1977–92; special adviser, Japanese del. to UN 1978, 1979; perm. adviser Simul Acad. 1983–; Hon. LL.D. (Carleton College); Vaughn Prize (Japan Newspaper Eds. and Publrs. Asscn.) 1957. *Publications:* Japan's New Buddhism—An Objective Account of Soka Gakkai 1969, Japan—The State of the Nation 1979, An Enemy among Friends 1991. *Leisure interests:* aikido, kendo. *Address:* 19-12 Hiroo 2-chome, Shibuya-ku, Tokyo 150, Japan. *Telephone:* 03-3400-5362.

MURATA, Makoto, B.ENG.; Japanese business executive; b. 26 Dec. 1926, Nagano Pref.; s. of Ichiro Murata and Misue Murata; m. Yukio Kurashina 1953; one s.; ed. Univ. of Tokyo; joined Showa Denko K.K. (SDK) 1948, Dir. 1973, Rep. Dir. and Exec. Vice-Pres. 1983, Rep. Dir., Pres. and C.E.O. 1987–97, Rep. Dir., Chair. 1997–; Chair. Japan Ammonium Sulphate & Urea Industry Asscn. 1988–90, Japan Carbon Asscn. 1991–93, Acetic Acid Mfrs. Asscn. 1991–93, Japan Hygienic Olefine and Styrene Plastics Asscn. 1993–94; Chair. Japan Petrochemical Industry Asscn. 1993–94; Pres. Japan Chemical Industry Asscn. 1996–98; Chair. Asscn. for the Progress of New Chemistry 1998–; Exec. mem. Bd. of Dirs., Japan Fed. of Econ. Orgs. (Keidanren) 1994. *Leisure interests:* golf, hunting. *Address:* Showa Denko K.K., 13-9, Shiba Daimon 1-chome, Minato-ku, Tokyo (Office); 2-12, Miyazaki 6-chome, Miyamae-ku, Kawasaki, Japan (Home). *Telephone:* 44-854-2551 (Home).

MURATA, Ryohei, LL.B.; Japanese diplomatist; b. 2 Nov. 1929, Kyoto; s. of Tahei Murata and Yoshiko Murata; m. Reiko Akama 1958; one d.; ed. Kyoto Univ.; joined Ministry of Foreign Affairs 1953; Deputy Dir.-Gen. Middle Eastern and African Affairs Bureau 1974–76, Treaties Bureau 1976–78; Amb. to United Arab Emirates 1978–80; Dir.-Gen. Middle Eastern and African Affairs Bureau 1980–82, Econ. Affairs Bureau 1982–84; Amb. to Austria 1985–87; Deputy Minister for Foreign Affairs 1987, Vice-Minister 1987–89; Amb. to U.S.A. 1989–91, to Germany 1992–94; Adviser to the Foreign Minister 1994–, to the Sanwa Bank and to Hobel Okura 1995– . *Publication:* Between Friends 1985. *Leisure interest:* contract bridge. *Address:* c/o Ministry of Foreign Affairs, 2-2, Kasumigaseki, Chiyoda ku, Tokyo (Office); 2-37-15, Eifuku, Suginami-ku, Tokyo 168-0064, Japan (Home). *Telephone:* (03) 3327-7633 (Home). *Fax:* (03) 3327-7610.

MURATOVA, Kira Georgievna; Russian/Ukrainian film director; b. 5 Nov. 1934, Soroki, Romania; m. 1st Alexandre Muratov (divorced); m. 2nd Yevgeni Golubenko; ed. All-Union Inst. of Cinematography with Sergey Gerasimov; debut feature film with A. Muratov On Steep Bank; acted in several films; U.S.S.R. State Prize 1989. *Films include:* Our Harvest Bread 1965, Short Meetings 1968, Long Partings 1972 (Fipressi Prize, Locarno 1987), Cognizing the White World 1980, Among Grey Stones 1983, Change of Fate 1988, Asthenic Syndrome 1990 (Nika Prize 1990), The Sentimental Militiaman 1991, Animations 1994, Three Stories 1996. *Address:* Proletarsky blvd. 14B, apt. 15, 270015 Odessa, Ukraine. *Telephone:* 28 65 51 (Home).

MURAYAMA, Tomiichi; Japanese politician; b. 3 March 1924; m. Yoshie Murayama; two d.; ed. School of Political Science and Econs., Meiji Univ.; fmr. sec. of a trade union of Oita Pref. Govt. employees; entered local govt. 1955; mem. Japanese Socialist Party (JSP), now Social Democratic Party of Japan (SDPJ), renamed Democratic League 1995, renamed Shakai Minshuto (Social Democratic Party); Chair. Oita Pref. of JSP, Chair. Diet Affairs Cttee. 1991–93, Chair. SDPJ 1993–96; mem. House of Reps. 1972–; Prime Minister 1994–96; mem. Lower House's Cttee. on Social and Labour Affairs. *Publications:* several books on social and labour affairs. *Leisure interest:* drama appreciation. *Address:* Social Democratic Party, 1-8-1, Nagata-cho, Chiyoda-ku, Tokyo 100 (Office); 3-2-2 Chiyomachi, Oita, Oita 870, Japan (Home). *Telephone:* (03) 3580-1171 (Office); (0975) 32 0033 (Home). *Fax:* (03) 3580-0691.

MURDOCH, (Keith) Rupert, A.C.; American (b. Australian) publisher; b. 11 March 1931, Melbourne, Victoria; s. of the late Sir Keith Murdoch and of Dame Elisabeth Murdoch; m. 1st Patricia Booker (divorced); one d.; m.2nd Anna Maria Torv 1967; two s. one d.; ed. Geelong Grammar School, Victoria, and Worcester Coll., Oxford; inherited Adelaide News 1952; has since built up Cruden Investments, a Murdoch family co. which owns 43 per cent of News Corpn. (Group C.E.O. 1979–, Chair. 1991–); has acquired newspapers, magazines and other interests in Australia, U.K., U.S.A. and Hong Kong, including: Australia—newspapers: The Australian (national), Daily Telegraph, Sunday Telegraph, Daily Mirror (Sydney), Sunday Sun (Brisbane), The News and Sunday Mail (Adelaide), The Sunday Times (Perth); U.S.A.—The Chicago Sun-Times, New York Post, Boston Herald, Mirror Newspapers Ltd., Nationwide News Pty. Ltd., Southdown Press Ltd., Cumberland Newspapers Ltd., (C.E.O. and fmr. Man. Dir. News Ltd. Group and associated cos. as above); magazines: TV Week, New Idea; television: Channel 10 (Sydney), Channel 10 (Melbourne, 50 per cent interest through Ansett Transport); other interests: Bay Books, Santos (energy), fmr. C.E.O. and Jt. Chair. Ansett Transport Industries. U.K.—newspapers: Sun, News of the World (national, acquired 1969), Berrows Org. (regional newspapers), C.E.O., Man. Dir. News Int. PLC (U.K.), Dir. 1969–, Chair. 1969–87, 1994–95, Chair., Pres. News America Publishing Inc.; acquired Times Newspapers Ltd. Feb. 1981, group includes The Times, The Sunday Times, The Times Literary Supplement, The Times Educational Supplement, The Times Higher Education Supplement; Dir. Times Newspapers Holdings 1981–, Chair. 1982–90, 1994–; magazines: City Magazines (Antique Collector's Guide, The Trader, Licensed Bookmaker); television: News Group Productions (U.S.A.), Skyband (U.S.A.), Satellite Television PLC (U.K.), 11.8 per cent stake in London Weekend Television; C.E.O. Sky Television Jan. 1989–, controlling stake in Star TV Asia 1993–; other interests: Townsend Hook (paper), Bemrose (printing), Convoys (transport). U.S.A.—newspapers: New York Post, others in San Antonio and Houston, Chair. News America Publishing Inc., City Post Publishing Corpn.; acquired Triangle Push Inc. 1988, Premiere 1988, William Collins PLC, Glasgow 1989–, acquired 20th Century Fox 1985–, Chair. Fox Productions 1985–, Chair., C.E.O. Fox Inc. USA 1992–, Twentieth Century Fox 1992–; magazines: Star, New York Magazine (including Cue and Village Voice); Today newspaper acquired 1987; Dir. United Technologies (U.S.) 1984; Dir. (non-exec.) Reuters Holdings PLC 1984–90; other interests: New York State Lotto; Commdr. of the White Rose (First Class) 1985; Kt. Order of St. Gregory the Great 1998. *Address:* 1 Virginia Street, London, E1 9XY, England; 2 Holt Street, Surry Hills, Sydney, N.S.W. 2000, Australia; News America Publishing Inc., 1211 Ave. of the Americas, 3rd Floor, New York, NY 10036, U.S.A.

MURDOCH, Lachlan Keith; business executive; b. 8 Sept. 1971; s. of Keith Rupert Murdoch (q.v.) and Anna Maria Torv; m. Sarah O'Hare 1999; ed. Trinity School, Manhattan, Aspen Country Day School, Andover, Princeton Univ.; fmr. Reporter San Antonio Express News, The Times (U.K.); fmr. Sub-Ed., The Sun U.K.; Gen. Man. Queensland Newspapers Pty. Ltd. 1994–95; Exec. Dir. News Ltd. 1995; Dir. Beijing P.D.N. Xinren Information Tech. Co. Ltd. 1995–; Exec. Chair. and C.E.O. News Ltd. 1997–; Deputy Chair. Star Television 1995–; Deputy Chief Exec., News Ltd. 1995–96; Dir. The Herald & Weekly Times Ltd. 1996–, News Corpn. 1996–, Ind. Newspapers Ltd. (N.Z.) 1997–. *Leisure interests:* Greek Philosophy, ancient history, rock climbing. *Address:* News Ltd., 2 Holt Street, Surry Hills, N.S.W. 2010, Australia.

MURENA, H. A.; Argentinian writer; b. 14 Feb. 1923, Buenos Aires; lecturer in Phil., Univ. de Buenos Aires 1968–. *Publications:* Primer testamento (story) 1946, La vida nueva (poetry) 1951, El juez (play) 1953, El pecado original de América (essay) 1954, La fatalidad de los cuerpos (novel) 1955, El centro del infierno (short stories) 1956, El círculo de los paraísos (poetry) 1958, Las leyes de la noche (novel) 1958, El escándalo y el fuego 1959, Homo atomicus 1961, Relámpago de la duración 1962, Ensayos sobre subversión 1962, El demonio de la armonía 1964, Los herederos de la promesa 1965, El nombre secreto (essays) 1969, Epitalámica (novel) 1969, Nímas Nímenos (novel) 1969, La cárcel de la mente (essays) 1970, El coronel de caballería (short stories) 1970, Caina muerte (novel) 1971, F.G. un bárbaro entre la belleza (poetry) 1972. *Address:* San José 910, Buenos Aires, Argentina.

MURKOWSKI, Frank Hughes, B.A.; American politician and banker; b. 28 March 1933, Seattle, Wash.; s. of Frank Michael and Helen (Hughes) Murkowski; m. Nancy R. Gore 1954; two s. four d.; ed. Santa Clara Univ., Seattle Univ.; with Pacific Nat. Bank of Seattle 1957–59, Nat. Bank of Alaska, Anchorage 1959–67, Vice-Pres. in Charge of Business Devt., Anchorage 1965–67; Commr., Dept. of Econ. Devt., Alaska State, Juneau 1967–70; Pres. Alaska Nat. Bank of the North 1971–80, Alaska State Chamber of Commerce 1977; Senator from Alaska 1981–, Chair. Cttee. on Energy and Natural Resources; Vice-Pres. Bd. of Trade, B.C. (Canada) and Alaska; mem. American and Alaskan Bankers' Asscns.; Republican. *Address:* US Senate, 706 Hart Senate Building, Washington, DC 20510, U.S.A.

MUROFUSHI, Minoru; Japanese business executive; ed. Tokyo Univ.; joined C Itoh 1956, Gen. Man. Coal Dept., New York 1963–71, Vice-Pres. C Itoh (America) (now ITOCHU) 1971, mem. Bd. 1985, Chief Exec. 1990–, now also Pres.; mem. Bd. HSBC Holdings 1992–. *Address:* ITOCHU Corporation, 5-1 Kita-Aoyama 2-chome, Minato-ku, Tokyo 107-77, Japan.

MURPHY, Dervla Mary; Irish author and critic; b. 28 Nov. 1931, Cappoquin; d. of Fergus Murphy and Kathleen Rochfort-Dowling; one d.; ed. Ursuline Convent, Waterford; American Irish Foundation Literary Award 1975; Ewart-Biggs Memorial Prize 1978; Irish American Cultural Inst. Literary Award 1985. *Publications:* Full Tilt 1965, Tibetan Foothold 1966, The Waiting Land 1967, In Ethiopia with a Mule 1968, On a Shoestring to Coorg 1976, Where the Indus is Young 1977, A Place Apart 1978, Wheels Within Wheels 1979, Race to the Finish? 1981, Eight Feet in the Andes 1983, Muddling Through in Madagascar 1985, Ireland 1985, Tales from Two Cities 1987, Cameroon with Egbert 1989, Transylvania and Beyond 1992, The Ukimwi Road 1993, South from the Limpopo 1997, Visiting Rwanda 1998, One Foot in Laos 1999. *Leisure interests:* music, reading, swimming, cycling, walking. *Address:* Lismore, Co. Waterford, Ireland.

MURPHY, Eddie (Edward Regan); American film actor; b. 3 April 1951, Brooklyn, New York; s. of Vernon Lynch (stepfather) and Lillian Lynch; m. 2nd Nicole Mitchell; two s. one d.; feature player in Saturday Night Live TV show 1980–84; film debut in 48 Hours 1982; recipient of numerous awards and nominations. *Films include:* 48 Hours 1982, Trading Places 1983, Delirious 1983, Best Defence 1984, Beverly Hills Cop 1984, The Golden Child 1986, Beverly Hills Cop II 1987, Eddie Murphy Raw 1987, Coming to America 1988, Harlem Nights 1989, 48 Hours 2 1990, Boomerang 1992, Distinguished Gentleman 1992, Beverly Hills Cop III 1994, The Nutty Professor 1996, Dr. Dolittle 1998, Holy Man 1998, Life 1998; tours with own comedy show; comedy albums: Eddie Murphy 1982, Eddie Murphy: Comedian 1983, How Could It Be 1984, So Happy 1989; has also released seven record albums of comedy and songs. *Address:* c/o Jim Wiatt, ICM, 8942 Wilshire Boulevard, Beverly Hills, CA 90211, U.S.A.

MURPHY, John A., B.SC., J.D.; American business executive; b. 15 Dec. 1929, New York; s. of John A. Murphy and Mary J. Touhey; m. Carole Ann Paul 1952; four s. two d.; ed. Villanova Univ. and Columbia Univ. Law School; mem. of New York law firm Conboy, Hewitt, O'Brien and Boardman, then joined Philip Morris Inc. as Asst. Gen. Counsel 1962, held various posts in the group, then apptd. Dir. 1971, Pres. 1985–91, Vice-Chair. 1991–92; Pres. and C.E.O. Miller Brewing Co. 1971–78, Chair. and C.E.O. 1978–84,

Pres. 1984–91; mem. Bd. of Dirs. Nat. Westminster Bank, U.S.A.; mem. American and New York Bar Asscns. and Business Cttee., Metropolitan Museum of Art; Roberto Clemente Award, Nat. Asscn. for Puerto Rican Civil Rights, Distinguished Public Service Award, Anti-Defamation League Appeal, Blackbook Humanitarian Award 1982, New York Boys' Club Harriman Award 1982. *Address:* Philip Morris Companies Inc., 100 Park Avenue, New York, NY 10017, U.S.A. *Telephone:* (212) 880-5000.

MURPHY, John Michael; British artist; b. 7 Sept. 1945, St. Albans; s. of James and Maureen (née Tarrant) Murphy; ed. St. Michael's Coll., Hitchin, Luton and Chelsea Schools of Art; one-man exhbns. include Jack Wendler Gallery, London 1973, Museum of Modern Art, Oxford 1975, The New Gallery, ICA, London 1976, Barry Barker Gallery, London 1976, Galerie Arno Kohnen, Düsseldorf 1978, Piwna Warsawa 1980, Arts Council of Northern Ireland Gallery, Belfast 1981, Orchard Gallery, Derry 1982, Vereniging voor het Museum van Hedendaagse Kunt, Ghent 1983, Serpentine and Lisson Galleries, London 1984, Whitechapel Art Gallery, London 1987, Arnolfini, Bristol 1988, Galerie Marca Paz, Madrid 1988, Asher/Faure Gallery, L.A. 1989, Lisson, London 1990, 1992, John Weber Gallery, New York 1991, Christine Burgin Gallery, New York 1991, Galerie Yvon Lambert, Paris 1992, Project Room, John Weber Gallery, New York 1992, Galerie Bruges La Morte, Bruges 1992, Koninklijk Museum voor Schone Kunsten Antwerpen 1993, Saatchi Gallery, London 1996; has participated in several group exhbns. in Britain, Europe and U.S.A.; Arts Council of G.B. Award 1980. *Address:* c/o Lisson Gallery, 67 Lisson Street, London, NW1 5DA, England.

MURPHY, Thomas, D.SC., LL.D., M.D., F.R.C.P.I., F.R.C.S.I., M.R.I.A.; Irish university president and medical practitioner; b. 3 Dec. 1915, Co. Wexford; s. of late John and Mary Murphy; m. Rosaline Byrne 1944; four s.; ed. Clongowes Wood Coll. and Univ. Coll., Dublin; jr. hosp. appts. 1940–43; Medical Officer, Bord na Mona 1943–48; Asst. Medical Officer of Health, Co. Kildare 1948–51; medical staff, Dept. of Health 1951–55; Prof. of Social and Preventive Medicine, Univ. Coll., Dublin 1955–72, Dean, Faculty of Medicine 1962–65, Registrar 1965–72, President 1972–86. *Publications:* 20 articles in scientific journals. *Address:* 11 Crannagh Road, Rathfarnham, Dublin, Ireland. *Telephone:* 4906664.

MURPHY, Tom (Thomas); Irish playwright; b. 23 Feb. 1935, Tuam, Co. Galway; s. of John (Jack) Murphy and Winifred Shaughnessy; m. Mary Lindisfarne Hamilton-Hippisley 1966; two s. one d.; ed. Tuam Vocational School, Vocational Teachers' Training Coll., Dublin; metalwork teacher 1957–62; playwright and theatre dir. 1962–; Hon. D.Litt. (Dublin) 1998; Irish Acad. of Letters Award 1972, Harveys Award 1983, 1985, Independent Newspapers Award 1983, 1989, Drama-Logue Critics' Award 1995, Irish Times ESB Theatre Awards Special Tribute 1997. *Stage plays:* On the Outside 1959, A Whistle in the Dark 1961, A Crucial Week in the Life of a Grocer's Assistant 1966, The Orphans 1968, Famine 1968, The Morning After Optimism 1971, The White House 1972, The Vicar of Wakefield (adaptation) 1974, On the Inside 1974, The Sanctuary Lamp 1975, The J. Arthur Maginnis Story 1976, The Blue Macushla 1980, The Informer (adaptation) 1981, The Gigli Concert 1983, Conversations on a Homecoming 1985, Bailegangaire 1985, A Thief of a Christmas 1986, Too Late for Logic 1989, The Patriot Game 1991, The Seduction of Morality (novel) 1994, Cup of Coffee (In the Apiary) and She Stoops to Folly 1995, The Wake 1997, Plays (four vols.) 1998, Too Late for Logic 1998. *Leisure interests:* music, gardening. *Address:* 4 Garville Road, Dublin 6, Ireland.

MURPHY-O'CONNOR, Rt. Rev. Cormac, S.T.L.; British ecclesiastic; b. 24 Aug. 1932, Reading, Berks.; s. of the late Dr. Patrick George Murphy-O'Connor and Ellen Theresa Cuddigan; ed. Prior Park Coll., Bath, The Venerable English Coll., Rome and Gregorian Univ., Rome; ordained Priest 1956; Parish Priest, Portswood, Southampton 1970–71; Rector Venerable English Coll., Rome 1971–77; Bishop of Arundel and Brighton 1977–; First Chair. Bishops' Cttee. for Europe 1980–83; Co.-Chair. Anglo-R.C. Int. Comm. 1983–; Chair. TVS Religious Advisers Panel 1985–90. *Publication:* The Family of the Church 1984. *Leisure interests:* music, walking and reading. *Address:* St. Joseph's Hall, Greyfriars Lane, Storrington, Pulborough, W. Sussex, RH20 4HE, England. *Telephone:* (01903) 742172. *Fax:* (01903) 746336.

MURRAY, Dame A. Rosemary, D.B.E., D.PHIL., J.P.; British university administrator and chemist; b. 28 July 1913, Havant; d. of late Admiral A. J. L. Murray and Ellen Maxwell Spooner; ed. Downe House School, Newbury, and Lady Margaret Hall, Oxford; Lecturer in Chem., Royal Holloway Coll. 1938–41, Univ. of Sheffield 1941–42; W.R.N.S. 1942–46; Fellow and Tutor, Girton Coll., Cambridge 1946–54; Pres. New Hall, Cambridge 1954–81; Univ. Demonstrator in Chem. 1947–52, Vice-Chancellor Cambridge Univ. 1975–77; J.P., Cambridge 1953–83; Pres. Nat. Inst. of Adult Educ. 1977–80; Dir. Midland Bank 1978–84, The Observer 1981–93; D.L. (Cambridgeshire) 1982; Chair., mem. cttees. and councils in univs., colls. of educ., schools, Wages Councils, Armed Forces Pay Review Body and others; Hon. D.Sc. (Ulster) 1972, (Leeds) 1975, (Pa.) 1975, (Wellesley, S. Calif.) 1976; Hon. D.C.L. (Oxford) 1976; Hon. LL.D. (Sheffield) 1977, (Cambridge) 1988. *Leisure interests:* foreign travel, gardening, book binding, restoring.

MURRAY, Allen Edward, B.S.; American business executive; b. 5 March 1929, New York; s. of Allen Murray and Carla Jones; m. Patricia Ryan 1951; one s. four d.; ed. New York Univ.; trainee, Nat. Bank & Trust Co., New York 1948–49; accountant, Gulf Oil Corpn. 1949–52; various financial positions, Socony-Vacuum Overseas Supply Co. (Mobil) 1952–56; with Mobil Oil Corpn. 1956–94, Vice-Pres. Planning, N. American Div. 1968–69, Vice-Pres. Planning, Supply and Transportation, N. American Div. 1969–74, Exec. Vice-Pres. N. American Div. 1974, Pres. U.S. Marketing and Refining Div., Exec. Vice-Pres. 1975–82; Pres. Worldwide Marketing and Refining 1979–82, Corporate Pres. 1983–84, C.O.O. 1984–86, C.E.O., C.O.O., Chair. Exec. Cttee. 1986–93, Chair., C.E.O. 1993–94; Dir. Metropolitan Life Insurance Co., American Petroleum Inst., Minnesota Mining and Mfg., Martin Marietta Co., Morgan Stanley Group Inc.; mem. Council on Foreign Relations, Business Council, Business Roundtable, Trilateral Cttee., Chase Manhattan Bank Int. Advisory Cttee. *Address:* Mobil Corporation, 375 Park Avenue, #2901, New York, NY 10152 (Office); 3225 Gallows Road, Fairfax, VA 22037, U.S.A.

MURRAY, Anne; British opera singer; b. 27 Aug. 1949, Dublin, Ireland; m. Philip Langridge 1981; one s.; ed. Royal Manchester Coll. of Music; fmrly. performed with English Nat. Opera, Royal Opera; European recital tours 1990, 1993, 1994; has performed in festivals at Aldeburgh, Edin., Munich, Salzburg. *Address:* c/o Lies Askonas, 6 Henrietta Street, London, WC2E 8LA, England.

MURRAY, Bill; American actor and writer; b. 21 Sept. 1950, Evanston, Ill.; m. Margaret Kelly 1980; two s.; ed. Loyola Acad., Regis Coll., Denver, Second City Workshop, Chicago; performer off-Broadway Nat. Lampoon Radio Hour; regular appearances TV series Saturday Night Live; appeared in radio series Marvel Comics' Fantastic Four; film appearances: Meatballs 1977, Mr. Mike's Mondo Video 1979, Where the Buffalo Roam 1980, Caddyshack 1980, Stripes 1981, Tootsie 1982, Ghostbusters 1984, The Razor's Edge 1984, Nothing Lasts Forever 1984, Little Shop of Horrors 1986, Scrooged 1988, Ghostbusters II 1989, What About Bob? 1991, Mad Dog and Glory 1993, Groundhog Day 1993, Ed Wood 1994, Kingpin 1996, Larger Than Life 1996, Space Jam 1996, The Man Who Knew Too Little 1997, With Friends Like These 1998, Veeck as in Wreck 1998, Rushmore 1998, Wild Things 1998; co-producer, dir., actor film Quick Change 1990; Writer, NBC-TV series Saturday Night Live 1977–80; Emmy Award for best writing for comedy series 1977. *Address:* c/o Jessica Tuchinsky, Creative Artists Agency, 9830 Wilshire Boulevard, Beverly Hills, CA 90212, U.S.A.

MURRAY, Denis James, O.B.E.; British journalist; b. 7 May 1951; s. of James Murray and Helen Murray; m. Joyce Linehan 1978; two s. two d.; ed. St Malachy's Coll. Belfast, Trinity Coll. Dublin, Queen's Univ. Belfast; grad. trainee Belfast Telegraph 1975–77, also reporter; Belfast Reporter Radio Telefís Éireann 1977–82; Dublin Corresp. BBC 1982–84, Northern Ireland Political Corresp. 1984–88, Ireland Corresp. 1988–. *Leisure interests:* music, reading, sports, family. *Address:* c/o BBC, Ormeau Avenue, Belfast, BT2 8HQ, Northern Ireland. *Telephone:* (01232) 338000.

MURRAY, John Loyola, B.L., S.C.; Irish judge; b. 27 June 1943, Limerick; s. of John C. Murray and Catherine Casey; m. Gabrielle Walsh 1969; one s. one d.; ed. Crescent Coll., Rockwell Coll., Univ. Coll. Dublin and King's Inns, Dublin; Pres. Union of Students of Ireland 1964–66; barrister-at-law 1967; bencher, Kings Inns 1986; Sr. Counsel, Bar of Ireland 1981; Attorney-Gen. Aug.–Dec. 1982, 1987–91; mem. Council of State 1987–91; Judge, Court of Justice of European Communities 1991–; Hon. LL.D. (Limerick). *Leisure interests:* yachting, travel, art. *Address:* Court of Justice of the European Communities, Plateau de Kirchberg, 2925 Luxembourg. *Telephone:* 43032208. *Fax:* 43032800.

MURRAY, Joseph Edward, M.D., D.SC.; American plastic surgeon; b. 1 April 1919, Milford, Mass.; s. of William A. Murray and Mary DePasquale; m. Virginia Link 1945; three s. three d.; ed. Holy Cross Coll. and Harvard Univ.; Chief Plastic Surgeon, Peter Bent Brigham Hosp. Boston 1964–86, Emer. 1986–; Chief Plastic Surgeon, Children's Hosp. Medical Center, Boston 1972–85, now Emer.; Prof. of Surgery, Harvard Medical School 1970–; Hon. fellow, Royal Australasian Coll. of Surgeons, Royal Coll. of Surgeons of England; mem. American Surgical Asscn., American Soc. of Plastic and Reconstructive Surgery, American Asscn. of Plastic Surgeons etc.; hon. award, American Acad. of Arts and Sciences 1962; Gold Medal, Int. Soc. of Surgeons 1963; Nobel Prize for Medicine 1990; Hon. D.Sc. (Holy Cross Coll.) 1965, (Rockford (Ill.) Coll.) 1966, (Roger Williams Coll.) 1986. *Address:* 108 Abbott Road, Wellesley Hills, MA 02181, U.S.A.

MURRAY, Lowell, M.A.; Canadian politician; b. 26 Sept. 1936, New Waterford, Nova Scotia; s. of late Daniel Murray and Evelyn Yound; m. Colleen Elaine MacDonald 1981; two s.; ed. St. Francis Xavier Univ., Queen's Univ., Ont.; fmr. Chief of Staff to Minister of Justice and Minister of Public Works; Progressive Conservative Nat. Campaign Chair. in Gen. Election 1979, 1981–83; Senator 1979–, Co-Chair. Jt. Senate-House of Commons Cttee. on Official Languages 1980–84, Chair. Standing Senate Cttee. on Nat. Finance 1995–; Chair. Standing Cttee. on Banking, Trade and Commerce 1984–86; Leader of the Senate and Minister of State for Fed.-Provincial Relations 1986–93; mem. Bd. of Trustees, Inst. for Research on Public Policy 1984–86, Trilateral Cttee. 1985–86, Bd. of Dirs. Parl. Int. Forum 1984–86, Dir. Sony of Canada 1995–; Chair. Standing Senate Cttee. on Social Affairs, Science and Tech. 1997–; Progressive Conservative. *Address:* The Senate, Room 502, Victoria Building, Ottawa, Ont., K1A 0A4, Canada.

MURRAY, Noreen Elizabeth, PH.D., F.R.S., F.R.S.E.; British university teacher of molecular biology; b. 26 Feb. 1935, Burnley, Lancs.; d. of John and Lilian G. Parker; m. Kenneth Murray, 1958; ed. Lancaster Girls' Grammar School, King's Coll., Univ. of London, Univ. of Birmingham; Research Assoc. Dept. of Biological Sciences, Stanford Univ., Calif. 1960–64; Research Fellow Botany School, Univ. of Cambridge 1964–67; at Dept. of Molecular Biology, Univ. of Edin., Lecturer, then Sr. Lecturer 1974–80, Reader 1982–88, Prof. of Molecular Genetics 1988–; mem. MRC Molecular Genetics Unit 1968–74; Group Leader, European Molecular Biology Lab., Heidelberg 1980–82; mem. European Molecular Biology Org. 1981–, Biotech. and Biosciences Research Council 1994–; Pres. Genetical Soc. of G.B. 1987–90; Gabor Medal, Royal Soc. 1989. *Publications:* numerous articles in specialist publs. and journals. *Leisure interest:* gardening. *Address:* Institute of Cell and Molecular Biology, University of Edinburgh, King's Buildings, Mayfield Road, Edin. EH9 3JR, Scotland. *Telephone:* (0131) 650-5374.

MURRAY, Patty, B.A.; American politician; b. 11 Oct. 1950, Bothell, Wash.; d. of David L. Johns and Beverly A. (McLaughlin); m. Robert R. Murray 1972; one s. one d.; ed. Washington State Univ.; teacher, Shoreline Community Coll. 1984–87; campaigned against proposed closure of Wash. State parent educ. programme 1980; fmr. mem. Wash. State Senate; instr. Shoreline Community Coll. Seattle 1984–; U.S. Senator from Wash. 1993–; Vice-Chair. Senate Democratic Policy Cttee.; mem. Budget Cttee., Appropriations Cttee. etc.; Democrat. *Address:* U.S. Senate, 111 Russell Senate Office Bldg., Washington, DC 20510; 528 N.W. 203rd Place, Seattle, WA 98177, U.S.A.

MURRAY, Robin MacGregor, M.D., D.SC., F.R.C.P.; British psychiatrist; b. 31 Jan. 1944, Glasgow, Scotland; s. of James. A. C. Murray and Helen MacGregor; m. Shelagh Harris 1970; one s. one d.; ed. Glasgow and London Univs.; jr. posts with Glasgow Univ., Dept. of Medicine 1970–72, with Maudsley Hosp. 1972–75; Sr. Lecturer Inst. of Psychiatry, London 1978–82, Dean 1982–89, Prof. of Psychological Medicine 1989–; Lilly Int. Fellow Nat. Inst. for Mental Health, Bethesda, Md. 1976–77; Prof. King's Coll., School of Medicine and Dentistry 1989–; Pres. Asscn. of European Psychiatrists 1995–; Gaskell Gold Medal and Research Prize (Royal Coll. of Psychiatrists) 1976, Sr. Leverhulme Research Fellow (Royal Soc.) 1993; Kurt Schneider Award 1994, Adolf Meyer Award 1997, Paul Hoch Award 1998, Stanley Dean Award 1999. *Publications:* publs. on schizophrenia, depression, psychiatric genetics and epidemiology, alcoholism and analgesic abuse. *Leisure interests:* Scottish music, reggae, swimming, rollerblading. *Address:* Department of Psychological Medicine, Institute of Psychiatry, de Crespigny Park, London, SE5 8AF, England. *Telephone:* 0171-703 6091. *Fax:* 0171-710 9044.

MURRAY, Dame Rosemary (see Murray, Dame A. Rosemary).

MURRAY, Simon; British banker; b. 25 March 1940, Leicester; s. of Patrick G. Murray and Maxine M. K. Murray; m. Jennifer A. Leila 1966; one s. two d.; ed. Bedford School (sr. exec. programme) and Stanford Business School; Jardine Matheson & Co., Ltd. 1966–73; Dir. Matheson & Co., London 1973–75; Man. Dir. Jardine Eng. Corpn. 1975–80; Man. Dir. Davenham Investments Ltd. 1980–84; Group Man. Dir. Hutchison Whampoa Ltd. 1984–93; Exec. Chair. (Asia/Pacific) Deutsche Bank 1994–. *Publication:* The Legionnaire 1979. *Leisure interests:* squash, jogging, reading. *Address:* 8 Mount Cameron Road, The Peak, Hong Kong. *Telephone:* (852) 2849-6006 (Home).

MURRAY, Stuart, F.R.A.I.A., R.I.B.A.; Australian architect and planner; b. 27 Oct. 1926, Sydney; s. of Cyril Hargreaves Murray and Daphne Williams; m. 1st Elizabeth Grime 1952 (divorced 1965); two s. two d.; m. 2nd Adrienne Solti 1982; ed. Fort Street High School, Sydney, Sydney Tech. Coll. School of Architecture and Univ. of Sydney; Office of Burley Griffin 1944–46; Office of Sydney Ancher 1947–49; Office of Denis Clarke Hall, London 1950–52; partner, Ancher Mortlock & Murray 1953–64; Dir. Ancher Mortlock Murray & Woolley, Architects 1965–75; Stuart Murray & Assocs., Architects & Planners 1976–; Dir. N. Sydney Planning Consultants 1968–72; work includes Great Hall, Univ. of Newcastle (winner, Limited Competition 1968) 1971, Aeronautics School, Univ. of Sydney 1974, North Sydney Devt. Control Plan 1974, Polo Club, Forbes, N.S.W. 1987, school and univ. bldgs., homes and apts. etc. *Publications:* papers on civic design and urban environment. *Leisure interests:* architecture, art, music, literature, philosophy, cooking, travel, walking. *Address:* Stuart Murray & Associates, Suite 1, 144 High Street, North Sydney, N.S.W. 2060, Australia. *Telephone:* (2) 9554779.

MURRAY, Timothy Vincent, F.R.I.B.A., F.R.A.I.C., F.R.I.A.I., M.C.D.; Canadian architect; b. 6 May 1930, Dublin, Ireland; s. of T. J. Murray and M. T. Purcell; m. Juliet J. Taylor 1958; two s. one d.; ed. Rockwell Coll., Cashel, Ireland, Univ. Coll., Dublin and Liverpool Univ.; architect and planner, Lord Holford 1953–55, London Co. Council 1955–57, Fed. Govt. of Canada 1957–58; Prin. and Founding Partner, Murray and Murray Assocs., architects and planners, Ottawa, Toronto, Dublin, Cork, Africa 1959–; Visiting Lecturer/Critic, Carleton Univ., Ottawa, Nova Scotia School of Architecture, Univ. of Dublin, Ireland; Chair. Bd. of Govs., Ashbury Coll. 1985–87; Chair. Design Cttee., Nat. Capital Comm., Fed. Govt. of Canada 1985–87; recipient of several architectural awards; Kt. of St. Gregory, Kt. of St. Lazarus of Jerusalem. *Publications:* articles in professional journals. *Address:* 444 Springfield Road, Ottawa, Ont. K1M 0K4, Canada. *Telephone:* (613) 741-2212.

MURRAY OF EPPING FOREST, Baron (Life Peer), cr. 1985, of Telford in the County of Shropshire; **Rt. Hon. Lionel (Len) Murray,** P.C., O.B.E.; British trade unionist; b. 2 Aug. 1922; m. Heather Woolf 1945; two s. two d.; ed. Wellington Grammar School, Univ. of London, New Coll., Oxford; with Econ. Dept., TUC 1947, Head of Dept. 1954–69; Asst. Gen. Sec. TUC 1969–73, Gen. Sec. 1973–84; mem. Social Science Research Council 1965–70, NEDC 1973–84; Vice-Pres. European Trade Union Confed. 1974–84, Int. Confed. Free Trade Unions 1973–84; mem. Cttee. to Review Functioning of Financial Insts. 1977–80; Bd. of Trustees, Anglo-German Foundation for the Study of Industrial Soc. 1977–86; Vice-Chair. Nat. Children's Home; Vice-Pres. Hearing and Speech Trust, Ironbridge Museum Trust, Wesley's Chapel, Nat. Youth Theatre; Trustee Carnegie U.K. Trust, Crisis at Christmas, Prison Service Trust; Hon. Fellow, New Coll., Oxford 1975, Sheffield City Polytechnic 1979, Queen Mary Coll., London; Hon. D.Sc. (Aston) 1977, (Salford) 1978; Hon LL.D (St. Andrews) 1979, (Leeds) 1985. *Address:* 29 The Crescent, Loughton, Essex 1G10 4PY, England. *Telephone:* 0181-508 4425.

MURTA, Jack Burnett; Canadian politician and farmer; b. 13 May, Carman, Man.; m. Lynda Morris 1977; one s. two d. ed. Univ. of Manitoba; farm owner at Graysville, Man.; M.P. for Lisgar-Man., fmr. Fed. Progressive Conservative Party spokesperson on multi-culturalism, fmr. Caucus spokesperson for Northern Devt., for Transport, fmr. Chair. Transportation Cttee., Agric. Cttee., Parl. Sec. to Pres. of Treasury Bd. 1979, Chair. Fed. Task Force on problems of grain transportation industry 1979, mem. Special subcttee. on Latin America and the Caribbean 1981, Pres. Canadian Agra Int.; Bd. Dirs. Parl. Centre for Foreign Affairs and Foreign Trade 1982; Minister of State for Multiculturalism 1984–85, for Tourism 1985–86; Hon. Canadian Grain Commr.; Progressive Conservative Party. *Address:* 147 Goderich Street, Kincardine, Ont., N2Z 2K9, Canada.

MURTAGH, Peter, M.A.; Irish journalist; b. 9 April 1953, Dublin; s. of Thomas Murtagh and Olive de Lacy; m. Moira Gutteridge 1988; one s. one d.; ed. The High School, Dublin and Trinity Coll. Dublin; reporter, The Irish Times 1981–84; ed. Insight, The Sunday Times, London 1985; reporter, Deputy Foreign Ed. and News Ed. The Guardian, London 1986–94; Ed. The Sunday Tribune, Dublin 1994–97; Journalist of the Year, Ireland 1983; Reporter of the Year, U.K. 1986. *Publications:* The Boss: Charles J. Haughey in Government (with J. Joyce) 1983, Blind Justice: The Sallins Mail Train Robbery (with J. Joyce) 1984, The Rape of Greece 1994. *Leisure interests:* family, newspapers, Ireland. *Address:* Penhanboon, Somerby Road, Greystones, Co. Wicklow, Ireland (Home). *Fax:* 353-1-661 5302 (Office).

MUSA, Said, LL.B.; Belizean politician; b. 19 March 1944, San Ignacio; ed. St. John's Coll., Belize City, Manchester Univ., England; called to the bar London 1966; worked as barrister, Gray's Inn, London 1966–67; circuit magistrate Belize 1967–68, Crown Counsel 1968–70, lawyer pvt. practice 1970–79, 1984–89, 1993–98 (sr. counsel 1983–); Pres. Public Service Union 1969; o-f. People's Action Cttee., Soc. for Promotion of Educ. and Research (SPEAR) 1969; obliged to leave public serivce because of political activities; joined People's United Party (PUP); contested Fort George seat 1974 elections; apptd. Senator to Nat. Ass. by George Price 1974; negotiator in talks to safeguard territorial integrity of Belize on independence 1975–81; mem. House of Reps. for Fort George constituency 1979–98; Attorney-Gen. and Minister for Educ., Sports and Culture 1979–84; Minister of Foreign Affairs, Econ. Devt. and Educ. 1989–93 (negotiated recognition of Belizean sovereignty by Guatemala 1991); Leader of the Opposition 1996–98; Prime Minister, Minister of Finance and Foreign Affairs 1998–; Chair. Fort George Div. PUP 1974–; Chair. PUP 1986–94, Deputy Leader 1994–96, Leader 1996–; co-f. Journal of Belizean Affairs 1972. *Publications:* People's Assemblies, People's Government and articles in nat. press. *Leisure interests:* reading, international affairs, human rights, music, tennis. *Address:* Office of the Prime Minister, New Administrative Building, Belmopan, Belize. *Telephone:* (8) 22346. *Fax:* (8) 20071.

MUSEVENI, Yoweri Kaguta; Ugandan head of state; b. 1944, Ntungamo, Mbarara; s. of Amos Kaguta and Esteri Kokundeka; m. Janet Kataaha; four c.; ed. Mbarara High School, Ntare School, Univ. Coll. of Dar es Salaam; Research Asst. Office of fmr. Pres. Milton Obote (q.v.) 1971; in Tanzania planning overthrow of regime of Idi Amin (q.v.) 1971–79; f. Front for Nat. Salvation (FRONASA) 1972; taught at Moshi Co-operative Coll., Tanzania 1972; participated in Tanzanian invasion of Uganda 1979; Defence Minister in interim Govt. of Uganda Nat. Liberation Front (UNLF) following overthrow of Amin 1979–80; following election of Dr. Obote, amid allegations of ballot-rigging, in 1980, spent five years as leader of National Resistance Army (NRA) waging a guerrilla war 1981–86; President of Uganda (following overthrow of Govt. by NRA forces) and Minister of Defence Feb. 1986–; Chair. Preferential Trade Area (PTA) 1987–88, 1992–93, OAU 1990–91. *Publications:* Selected Essays 1985, Selection of Speeches and Writings, Vol. I: What is Africa's Problem? 1992, Vol. II 1997, Sowing the Mustard Seed—the Struggle for Freedom and Democracy 1997. *Leisure interest:* football. *Address:* Office of the President, P.O. Box 7108, Kampala, Uganda. *Telephone:* 234881. *Fax:* 235459.

MUSGRAVE, Thea, MUS.DOC.; British composer; b. 27 May 1928, Edinburgh; d. of James and Joan (née Hacking) Musgrave; m. Peter Mark 1971; ed. Edinburgh Univ. and Paris Conservatoire (under Nadia Boulanger); Lecturer, Extra-Mural Dept., London Univ. 1958–65; Visiting Prof. Univ. of Calif., Santa Barbara 1970; Distinguished Prof., Queen's Coll., City Univ. of New York 1987; Koussevitzky Award 1972; Guggenheim Fellow 1974–75, 1982–83; Hon. D.Mus. (Council for Nat. Academic Awards, Smith Coll. and

Old Dominion Univ.). *Works include:* Chamber Concerto 1, 2 & 3 1966, Concerto for Orchestra 1967, Clarinet Concerto 1968, Beauty and the Beast (ballet) 1969, Night Music 1969, Horn Concerto 1971, The Voice of Ariadne (chamber opera) 1972–73, Viola Concerto 1973, Space Play 1974, Mary, Queen of Scots (opera) 1976–77, A Christmas Carol (opera) 1978–79, An Occurrence at Owl Creek Bridge (radio opera) 1981, Harriet, A Woman Called Moses 1980–84, Black Tambourine for women's chorus and piano 1985, Pierrot 1985, For the Time Being for chorus 1986, The Golden Echo 1987, Narcissus 1988, The Seasons (orchestral) 1988, Rainbow (orchestral) 1990, Simón Bolivar (opera) 1993, Autumn Sonata 1993, Journey through a Japanese Landscape (marimba concerto) 1993, On the Underground (vocal) 1994, Helios (oboe concerto) 1995, Phoenix Rising (orchestral) 1997; chamber music, songs, choral music, orchestral music. *Leisure interests:* cooking, cinema, reading. *Address:* c/o Novello & Co., 8/9 Frith Street, London, W1V 5TZ, England.

MUSHKETIK, Yuri Mikhailovich; Ukrainian author; b. 21 March 1929, Verkiivka, Chernigiv Region; s. of Mushketik Mikhail Petrovich and Uliana Onufriivna Mushketik; m. Lina Sergiivna Mushketik (née Lushnikova); two d.; ed. Kiev Univ.; mem. CPSU 1951–91; Chair. Bd. Union of Writers of Ukraine 1987–; first works published 1952; T. Shevchenko Ukrainian State Prize 1980, U.S.S.R. State Prize 1987. *Publications include:* Fires in the Middle of the Night 1959, Black Bread 1960, The Heart and the Stone 1961, Drop of Blood 1964, A Bridge Across the Night 1975, White Shadow 1975, Position 1979, Pain 1981, The Boundary 1987, Selected Works (2 vols.) 1989, Hetman's Treasure (novel) 1993, Brother Against Brother (novel) 1995. *Leisure interests:* reading American literature, history of Ukrainian Kozacks. *Address:* Suvorova Str. 3, Apt. 10, 252010 Kiev, Ukraine. *Telephone:* (44) 290-80-04.

MUSOKE, Kintu; Ugandan politician; fmr. Minister of State for Security; Prime Minister of Uganda Nov. 1994–. *Address:* Office of the Prime Minister, P.O. Box 341, Kampala, Uganda. *Telephone:* (41) 259518. *Fax:* (41) 242341.

MUSOKOTWANE, Kebby Sililo Kambulu; Zambian politician and educationist; b. 5 May 1946, Musokotwane; s. of late Chief Musokotwane and Rhoda Chambwa; m. Regina Muzya Sibulowa 1966; four s. three d.; ed. Monze Secondary School, David Livingstone Teachers' Training Coll., Univ. of Zambia; primary school teacher 1965, Demonstration Teacher 1965–71, Deputy Head Teacher 1968–69, Head Teacher 1970, Lecturer 1972–73; M.P. 1973–89; Minister of Water and Natural Resources 1977–78, of Youth and Sport 1979, of Finance and Tech. Co-operation 1979–83, of Gen. Educ. and Culture 1983–85, of Educ., Sport and Culture 1989; Prime Minister 1985–89; High Commr. in Canada 1990; Pres. United Nat. Independence Party (UNIP) 1992. *Leisure interest:* playing tennis. *Address:* Freedom House, P.O. Box 30302, Lusaka, Zambia.

MUSONGE, Peter Mafany; Cameroonian politician; fmr. Gen. Man. Cameroon Devt. Corp. (CDC); mem. Rassemblement démocratique du peuple camerounais (RDPC); Prime Minister of Cameroon Sept. 1996–. *Address:* Office of the Prime Minister, Yaoundé, Cameroon. *Telephone:* 23-57-50. *Fax:* 23-57-63.

MUSSA, Michael; American economist; b. 1944; ed. Univs. of Calif. and Chicago; Asst. Prof. of Econs. Univ. of Rochester; Research Fellow, London School of Econs. and Grad. Inst. of Int. Studies; William H. Abbott Prof. of Int. Business, Univ. of Chicago Grad. School of Business 1980–; Research Assoc. Nat. Bureau of Econ. Research 1981–; fmr. mem. U.S. Council of Econ. Advisers; fmr. Visiting Prof. Asian and Research Depts. of IMF; Econ. Counsellor and Dir. Research Dept. IMF 1991–. *Address:* International Monetary Fund, 700 19th Street, NW, Washington, DC 20431, U.S.A.

MUSTILL, Baron (Life Peer), cr. 1992, of Pateley Bridge in the County of North Yorkshire, **Michael John Mustill,** Kt., P.C., F.B.A.; British judge; b. 10 May 1931; s. of Clement Mustill and late Marion Mustill; m. 1st Beryl R. Davies (divorced); m. 2nd Caroline Phillips; two s. one step d.; ed. Oundle School and St. John's Coll. Cambridge; called to Bar, Gray's Inn 1955, Bencher 1976, Q.C. 1968; Deputy Chair. Hants. Quarter Sessions 1971; Recorder, Crown Court 1972–78; Judge, High Court, Queen's Bench Div. 1978–85; Presiding Judge, North-East Circuit 1981–84; a Lord Justice of Appeal 1985–92; Lord of Appeal in Ordinary 1992–97; Hon. Prof. of Law Univ. of Birmingham 1995–; Pres. British Maritime Law Asscn. 1995–, Chartered Inst. of Arbitrators 1995–98, Asscn. of Average Adjusters 1996–97, Seldon Soc. 1997–; Yorke Distinguished Visiting Fellow Univ. of Cambridge 1996–; mem. Comité Maritime Arbitration 1996–. *Publications:* The Law and Practice of Commercial Arbitration in England (with S. C. Boyd) 1982, Anticipatory Breach of Contract 1990; articles in legal journals. *Address:* House of Lords, London, SW1A 0PW; 42 Laurier Road, London, NW5 1SJ, England.

MUSTONEN, Olli; Finnish pianist and composer; b. 7 June 1967, Helsinki; s. of Seppo Mustonen and Marja-Liisa Mustonen; m. Raija Kerppo 1989; began studies with harpsichord, studied piano with Ralf Gothóni and Eero Heinonen, composition with Einojuhani Rautavaara; has played with many of the world's leading orchestras; appears at maj. festivals including Berlin, Hollywood Bowl, BBC Proms, and Salzburg; Artistic Dir. Turku Music Festival 1990–92; Edison Award 1992, Gramophone Award for Best Instrumental Recording 1992. *Major compositions:* Fantasia (for piano and strings) 1985, Toccata (for piano, string quartet and double bass) 1989, Nonet (for 2 string quartets and double bass) 1995. *Leisure interests:* mathematics, nature, politics, sports. *Address:* c/o Harrison/Parrott Ltd., 12 Penzance Place, London, W11 4PA, England. *Telephone:* 0171-229 9166. *Fax:* 0171-221 5042.

MUTALIBOV, Ayaz Niyazi Ogly; Azerbaijani politician; b. 12 May 1938, Baku; m. Adilia Khanum; two s.; ed. M. Azizbekov Azerbaijani Inst. of Oil and Chemistry; mem. CPSU 1963–91; engineer, later Dir. Baku Refrigerator Manufacturing Plant; Dir. Baku Asscn. for Production of Refrigerators and Household Equipment 1974–77; Second Sec. of Narimanov Dist. Party Cttee. 1977–79; Minister of Local Industry for Azerbaijan S.S.R. 1979–82; Vice-Chair. Council of Ministers Azerbaijan S.S.R. 1982–89, Chair. 1989–91; Pres. Gosplan for Repub. 1982–89; First Sec., Cen. Cttee. Azerbaijan CP 1990–91; U.S.S.R. People's Deputy 1989–91; mem. CPSU Politburo 1990–91; Pres. of Azerbaijan 1990–92; charged with organizing a coup and impeached 1992; lives in Moscow.

MUTALLAB, Alhaji Umaru Abdul; Nigerian government official and accountant; b. 15 Dec. 1939, Katsina, Kaduna State; m.; three d.; ed. Barewa Coll., Zaria, Achimota Coll. of Admin., Ghana, S.W. London Coll., U.K.; mem. of Asscn. of Certified Accountants 1965–; Man. Accountant, Fuller, Jenks, Beecroft Co. Ltd., London 1965–67; Chief Accountant, Defence Industries Corpn. of Nigeria, Kaduna 1967–71; Financial Controller, New Nigeria Devt. Co. 1971–74, Gen. Man. 1974–75; Fed. Commr. for Econ. Devt. 1975–76, for Co-operatives and Supply 1976–78; Exec. Vice-Chair. United Bank for Africa Ltd. 1978–80, C.E.O., Man. Dir. 1980–88; Chair. Africa Merchant Bank April 1989. *Address:* c/o Africa Merchant Bank, Lagos, Nigeria.

MUTALOV, Abdulkhashim Mutalovich; Uzbekistan politician and business executive; b. 1947, Telyau, Tashkent Region; ed. All-Union Inst. of Food Industry; worker Tashkent Factory of Bread Products; army service 1965–79; Dir. Akhangaran Enterprise of Bread Products 1979–86; Deputy Minister of Bread Products Uzbek S.S.R. 1986–87, Minister 1987–91; Deputy Chair. Cabinet of Ministers 1991–92; Prime Minister of Uzbekistan 1992–96; Chair. State grain co. Uzdon Makhsulot 1996–. *Address:* Government House, 700008 Tashkent, Uzbekistan (Office). *Telephone:* (371) 39-82-95. *Fax:* 39-86-01.

MUTEBI II, the Kabaka of Buganda; (Ronald Muwenda Mutebi); b. 1956; s. of late Kabaka Sir Edward Mutesa II (King Freddy); ed. Bradfield Coll., Univ. of Cambridge and North London Polytechnic; lived in exile in England, following overthrow of his father by fmr. Pres. of Uganda Milton Obote (q.v.) 1966–87; worked as double-glazing salesman; returned to Uganda 1987; crowned 36th Kabaka (King) of Buganda, marking restoration of ancient kingdom of Buganda, 31 July 1993. *Leisure interest:* squash. *Address:* Royal Palace, Kampala, Uganda.

MUTI, Riccardo; Italian conductor; b. 28 July 1941; Naples; s. of Domenico Muti and Gilda Sellitto; m. Cristina Mazzavillani 1969; two s. one d.; ed. Naples and Milan Conservatories of Music; Prin. Conductor, Maggio Musicale, Florence 1969–, Philharmonia Orchestra, London 1973–82, Music Dir. 1979–82, Conductor Laureate 1982–; Prin. Guest Conductor Philadelphia Orchestra 1977–80, Prin. Conductor and Music Dir. 1980–92, Conductor Laureate 1992–; Music Dir. La Scala (Milan) 1986–; concert tours in U.S.A. with Boston, Chicago and Phila. Orchestras; concerts at Salzburg, Edinburgh, Lucerne, Flanders and Vienna festivals; also conducted Berlin Philharmonic, Vienna Philharmonic and Concertgebouw Amsterdam; opera: Florence, Munich, Covent Garden, La Scala, Vienna; Accad. di Santa Cecilia, Rome; Accademico Dell'Accademia Cherubini, Florence; Officer Order of Merit (Germany); Diapason d'Oro; Premio Critica Discografia Italiana; Prix Académie nat. du disque 1977; Verdientskreuz (First Class, Germany) 1976, Cavaliere Gran Croce (Italy) 1991, Deutscher Schallplatten Preis; Grand Prix du disque for La Traviata (Verdi), Requiem in C minor (Cherubini) 1982. *Address:* Teatro alla Scala, Via Filodrammtici 2, Milan 20121, Italy.

MUTO, Kabun; Japanese politician; b. 18 Nov 1926; s. of Kaichi Muto; m. Hisako Koketsu 1951; two s.; ed. Kyoto Univ.; worked in family brewing business; mem. House of Reps. 1967–; Parl. Vice-Minister of Home Affairs 1972–73, Minister of Agric., Forestry and Fisheries 1979–80, of Int. Trade and Industry Feb.–Dec. 1990, of Foreign Affairs April–Aug. 1993, Dir.-Gen. Man. and Coordination Agency (State Minister) 1996–97; Chair. Liberal-Democratic Party (LDP) Commerce and Industry Div. 1974–76; Deputy Sec.-Gen. LDP 1978–79; mem. Standing Cttee. on Budget, House of Reps., LDP Finance Cttee.; Vice-Pres. LDP Cttee. on small and medium enterprises, LDP Tax Policy Cttee. etc. *Publications:* Kusa-no-Ne Minshushugi (Grassroots Democracy), Jiminto Saisei no Teigen, Nihon no Sentaku (Japan's Choice) etc. *Address:* c/o Ministry of Foreign Affairs, 2-2 Kasumigaseki, Chiyoda-ku, Tokyo, Japan.

MUTSCHLER, Carlfried, DIPL. ING.; German architect; b. 18 Feb. 1926, Mannheim; s. of Wilhelm Mutschler; m. Isolde Autenrieth 1955; ed. Goethe Real Gymnasium Mannheim, Technische Hochschule Karlsruhe; freelance architect in Frankfurt and Mannheim 1953–; lecturer, Technische Hochschule Stuttgart 1962–63; Hon. Prof., Staedel-Hochschule der Künste, Frankfurt 1976–; mem. Bund Deutscher Architekten 1956–, Chair. Baden-Württemberg 1967–70, 1975–78; mem. Deutscher Werkbund 1956–, Chair. Baden-Württemberg 1963–79; Pres. Künstlerbund Rhein-Neckar 1982–88; Visiting Lecturer, M.I.T., Cambridge, Mass., U.S.A. 1983; mem. Akademie der Künste Berlin, Deutsche Akademie dür Städtebau und Landesplanung; Pres. Freie Akademie der Künste, Mannheim; bldgs. and projects include: Social Bldg. Adox-Foto Frankfurt, Pfingstberg Church, Mannheim 1962, Friedrich-Ebert School, Mannheim 1964, Multi-purpose hall and residential area Mannheim 1975, Max-Planck-Inst. for Astronomy, Heidelberg 1976, Insts. for Univ. of Heidelberg 1969–82; Bab-al-Sheikh, Baghdad, Iraq 1983, Reiss Museum for Archaeology, Mannheim 1988, Stadthaus, Mannheim 1988–90; numerous prizes and awards including Grand Prix int. d'architecture et urbanisme, France 1969, Hugo-Häring-Preis 1977, 1978, 1984, 1988, Grosser BDA-Preis 1978, Le Corbusier-Preis (Germany) 1985. *Publications:* Bauten und Projekte Carlfried Mutschler & Partner 1976, Carlfried Mutschler & Partner 2 1994; numerous articles and papers in architectural magazines etc. *Address:* E 7, 7, 68159 Mannheim, Germany. *Telephone:* (0621) 127550. *Fax:* 1275555.

MUTTER, Anne-Sophie; German violinist; b. 29 June 1963, Rheinfelden/Baden; studied with Prof. Aida Stucki, Winterthur, Switzerland; began musical career playing piano and violin 1969; played in the Int. Music Festival, Lucerne 1976; début with Herbert von Karajan at Pfingstfestspiele, Salzburg 1977; soloist with major orchestras of the world; also plays with string trio and quartet; Guest teacher Royal Acad. of Music, London 1985; est. foundation promoting gifted young string players throughout the world; Hon. Pres. Mozart Soc., Univ. of Oxford 1983; Jugend musiziert Prize (Fed. Repub. of Germany) for violin 1970, for piano 1970, for violin 1974; Künstler des Jahres 'Deutscher Schallplattenpreis', Grand Prix Int. du Disque, Record Acad. Prize, Tokyo 1982, Internationaler Schallplattenpreis 1993; Order of Merit (of Germany, of Bavaria). *Leisure interests:* graphic arts, sport. *Address:* Effnerstrasse 48, 81925 Munich, Germany. *Telephone:* (089) 984418. *Fax:* (089) 9827186.

MUZENDA, Simon Vengai; Zimbabwean politician; b. 28 Oct. 1922; m. Mandy Muzenda 1950; three s. five d. (one deceased); returned to S. Rhodesia (now Zimbabwe) 1950; Sec.-Gen. Voice Asscn. 1953; Chair. Umvuma Branch, Nat. Democratic Party, later Organizing Sec. Victoria Prov. 1960–61; founder mem. Zimbabwe African People's Union (ZAPU) and Admin. Sec. Victoria Prov. 1961–62; imprisoned 1962–64; founder mem. Zimbabwe African Nat. Union (ZANU) 1963, mem. Cen. Cttee. 1964; activity restricted 1964–71; mem. Exec., African Nat. Council, and Sec. of Law and Order 1971; Deputy Admin. Sec. Zambia 1975–76; co-ordinated activities of ZANU from Zambia and formed Zimbabwe People's Army (ZIPA) in conjunction with ZAPU leadership; Deputy Leader of ZANU 1976, Vice-Pres. 1977, mem. Politburo; Deputy Prime Minister 1980–88, Vice-Pres. of Zimbabwe Jan. 1988–; Minister of Foreign Affairs 1980–81, of Energy and Water Resources 1984–85. *Leisure interests:* wrestling, music, traditional music. *Address:* ZANU-PF, 88 Manica Road, Harare, Zimbabwe.

MUZI-FALCONI, Livio; Italian diplomatist; b. 1 Sept. 1936, Oslo, Norway; s. of Baron Filippo Muzi Falconi and Marion Barton; m. Marina Chantre 1961; two s. two d.; ed. Tamalpais School for Boys, San Rafael, CA, Lowell High School, Univ. of San Francisco, Univ. of Genoa; joined Italian diplomatic corps 1960; Lieut, Italian Air Force 1962; Vice Consul Buenos Aires 1963–67; First Sec. Madrid Embassy 1967–70; Dept. of Migratory Affairs Ministry of Foreign Affairs 1970–72; Counsellor London Embassy 1972–77; Consul Gen. Addis Ababa 1977–79; Coordinator European Affairs Ministry of Foreign Affairs 1979–83; Amb. to Nigeria (also accred. to Benin) 1983–87; Minister Embassy, London 1987–92; Deputy Head Italian State Protocol 1992–95; Chief of Protocol Exec. Office of Sec.-Gen. of UN 1995–; elected rep. Italian diplomatic and others Trade Union 1969–73, re-elected 1977–79, 1992–95; Grand Official Order of Repub. 1990; Hon. K.C.M.G. 1991. *Address:* Room S-201A, Protocol and Liaison Service, United Nations, New York, NY 10017 (Office); 455 East 51st Street, Apt. 3C, New York, NY 10022, U.S.A. (Home). *Telephone:* (212) 963-7171. *Fax:* (212) 963-1921.

MUZOREWA, Abel Tendekayi, M.A., D.D., D.H.L.; Zimbabwean ecclesiastic; b. 14 April 1925, Old Umtali; s. of Philemon Haadi Muzorewa and Hilda Takaruda Muzorewa (née Munangatire); m. Margaret Muzorewa (née Chigodora); four s. one d.; ed. Old Umtali Secondary School, Nyadiri United Methodist Mission, Cen. Methodist Coll., Fayette, Mo., Scarritt Coll., Nashville, Tenn., U.S.A.; Pastor, Chiduku N. Circuit 1955–57; studied in U.S.A. 1958–63; Pastor, Old Umtali Mission 1963; Dir. of Youth Work, Rhodesia Annual Conf. 1965; Joint Dir. of Youth Work, Rhodesia Christian Council 1965; Travelling Sec. Student Christian Movt. 1965; Resident Bishop, United Methodist Church 1968–92; Pres. African Nat. Council (ANC) 1971–85, All-Africa Conf. of Churches; Rep. of UANC at Geneva Conf. on Rhodesia 1976; mem. Transitional Exec. Council to prepare transfer to majority rule in Rhodesia 1978–79, Prime Minister of Zimbabwe Rhodesia, Minister of Defence and Combined Operations June–Dec. 1979; attended Lancaster House Conf. 1979; contested March 1980 election as Leader of UANC; detained Nov. 1983–Sept. 1984; fled to U.S.A. 1985, returned to Zimbabwe Nov. 1986; Pres. of United Parties 1994–98; Pres. Coll. of Bishops United Methodist Church of Cen. Africa 1988–92; Bishop of Zimbabwe and Head of United Methodist Church; Hon. D.D. (Cen. Methodist Coll., Mo.) 1960; UN Prize for Outstanding Achievement in Human Rights 1973. *Publications:* Manifesto for African National Council 1972, Rise Up and Walk (autobiog.) 1978. *Leisure interests:* vegetable and flower growing, poultry raising. *Address:* P.O. Box 3408, Harare; P.O. Box 353, Borrowdale, Harare, Zimbabwe. *Telephone:* 4-704127/263-4-860 036/781 505. *Fax:* 745 303.

MUZYKANTSKY, Aleksander Ilyich, CAND. TECH. SC.; Russian politician; b. 4 Feb. 1941; m.; one s. one d.; ed. Moscow Inst. of Railway Transport, Moscow State Univ.; metalworker designing bureau U.S.S.R. Ministry of Transport 1957–58; engineer, sr. researcher, Head of Div. Cen. Research Inst. Projektstalkonstruktsiya 1963–87, Deputy Dir. 1987–90; mem. Movt. for Democratic Russia, took part in Movt. of Democratic Reforms 1988–91–; mem. Moscow Election Comm. 1989; Prefect Moscow Cen. Admin. Dist. 1991–, Deputy Prime Minister Moscow Govt. 1991; mem. Moscow Govt. 1996; *Address:* Central Administrative Okrug, Marksistskaya str. 24, 109147 Moscow, Russia (Office). *Telephone:* (095) 911 1067, 912 5503 (Office).

MWAANGA, Vernon Johnson; Zambian diplomatist and businessman; b. 1939; ed. Hodgson Tech. Coll., Lusaka, Stanford Univ., U.S.A. and Oxford Univ., U.K.; joined Zambian independence movement 1960; mem. United Nat. Independence Party (UNIP) 1961, later Regional Party Sec., Monze and Choma Areas; Deputy High Commr. for Zambia in U.K. 1964–65; Amb. to U.S.S.R. 1965–68; Perm. Rep. to UN 1968–72; Ed.-in-Chief Times of Zambia 1972–73; Minister of Foreign Affairs 1973–75, 1991–92; mem. UNIP Cen. Cttee. 1975; Sr. Business Exec. 1975–; reported detained Sept. 1985; Chair. Curray Ltd., Bank of Credit and Commerce (Zambia) Ltd., Zambia Safaris Ltd.; mem. Int. Public Relations Asscn.; Fellow, London Inst. of Dirs. *Address:* c/o Ministry of Foreign Affairs, P.O. Box RW50069, Lusaka, Zambia.

MWAKAWAGO, Daudi Ngelautwa; Tanzanian politician; b. Sept. 1939; ed. Makerere Univ., Uganda, Victoria Univ. of Manchester, England; Tutor at Kivukoni Coll., Dar es Salaam 1965–72, Vice-Principal 1970, Principal 1971, 1977; Nat. M.P. 1970–75; Minister for Information and Broadcasting 1972–77; Constituent M.P. 1975; mem. Party of Constitution Comm. 1976; mem. Constituent Ass. 1977, Cen. Cttee. Chama cha Mapinduzi 1977–; Minister of Information and Culture 1982–84, of Labour and Manpower Devt. 1984–86, of Industries and Trade 1986–88; now Perm. Rep. of Tanzania to UN, New York; fmr. mem. Historical Asscn. of Tanzania, Nat. Adult Educ. Asscn. of Tanzania, African Adult Educ. Asscn., Income Tax Local Cttee., Bd. of Inst. of Adult Educ., Nat. Advisory Council on Educ.; fmr. dir. Nat. Devt. Corpn., Nat. Museum; Chair. Wildlife Corpn. 1979–; Vice-Chair. Co-operative Coll., Moshi; mem. TIRDO. *Address:* Permanent Mission of United Republic of Tanzania to the United Nations, 205 E. 42nd Street, 13th Floor, New York, NY 10017, U.S.A.

MWANAWASA, Levy Patrick; Zambian lawyer and politician; b. 3 Sept. 1948, Mufulira; m. Maureen Kakubo Mwanawasa 1988; two s. two d.; ed. Univ. of Zambia and Law Practice Inst. Lusaka; admitted to Zambian Bar 1975; Vice-Chair. Law Asscn. of Zambia 1981–83; Solicitor-Gen. for Zambia 1986–87; Legal Chair. Interim Cttee. of Movt. for Multi-Party Democracy 1990, Vice-Pres. March 1991; Vice-Pres. of Zambia 1991–94.

MWINYI, Ali Hassan; Tanzanian politician, teacher and diplomatist; b. 8 May 1925, Kivure, Tanganyika; m. Siti A. Mwinyi 1960; five s. four d.; moved to Zanzibar as a child; schoolteacher, later Prin. Zanzibar teacher-training Coll.; Prin. Perm. Sec. of Educ. Zanzibar 1963–64; Asst. Gen. Man. Zanzibar State Trading Corpn. 1964–70; Minister of State, Office of Pres., Tanzania 1970; later Minister of Health and Home Affairs; Minister of Natural Resources and Tourism 1982–83, of State in Vice-Pres.'s Office 1983–84; interim Pres. of Zanzibar Feb.–April 1984, Pres. April 1984; Vice-Pres. of Tanzania 1984–85, Pres. 1985–95, also fmr. Minister of Defence and Nat. Service; fmr. C.-in.-C. of Armed Forces; mem. Chama Cha Mapinduzi (CCM or Revolutionary Party, Chair. 1990–96). *Address:* c/o State House, Dar es Salaam, Tanzania.

MYASOYEDOV, Boris Fedorovich; Russian chemist; b. 2 Oct. 1930; m.; one s.; ed. Moscow I. Mendeleyev Inst. of Chem. and Tech.; jr., sr. researcher, head of lab, Deputy Dir. V. Vernadsky Inst. of Geochem. and Analytical Chem.; corresp. mem. U.S.S.R. (now Russian) Acad. of Sciences 1990, mem. 1994; research in chem. of radioactive elements, radionucleides, creation and application of chem. sensors and analysers; U.S.S.R. State Prize, V. Khlopin Prize Acad. of Sciences. *Publications:* Chemical Sensors: Possibilities and Perspectives 1990. *Leisure interests:* music, stamp collecting. *Address:* Institute of Geochemistry and Analytical Chemistry, Kosygin str. 19, 117975 Moscow, Russia. *Telephone:* (095) 137 4147 (Office); 420 9081 (Home). *Fax:* (095) 938 2054.

MYERS, Barton, M.ARCH., F.R.A.I.C., F.A.I.A.; American/Canadian architect and planner; b. 6 Nov. 1934, Norfolk, Va.; s. of Barton and Meeta (Burrage) Myers; m. Victoria George 1959; one d.; ed. Norfolk Acad., U.S. Naval Acad. and Univ. of Pennsylvania; Partner, A. J. Diamond & Barton Myers, Toronto 1968–75; Founder and Prin. Barton Myers Assocs., Toronto 1975–87, Barton Myers Assocs., Los Angeles 1981–; Asst. Prof. of Architecture Univ. of Toronto 1968–70; mem. Advisory Cttee. Nat. Capital Comm., Ottawa 1968–74; Founder and Pres. Bd. of Dirs., Trace Magazine 1980–82; Visiting Prof. Harvard Grad. School of Design 1981; Prof. of Architecture Univ. of Calif. (Los Angeles) School of Architecture 1981–; other lectureships and professional appointments; mem. Royal Canadian Acad. of Arts, American Inst. of Architects; recipient of numerous design awards, including RAIC Gold Medal 1994, A.I.A. New Jersey Award 1998. *Major Works by Diamond & Myers Assocs. include:* York Square, Toronto; Ont. Medical Asscn., Toronto; Myers & Wolf Residences, Toronto; Housing Union Bldg., Univ. of Alberta Citadel Theatre, Edmonton; Dundas-Sherbourne Housing, Toronto. *Major works by Barton Myers Assocs. include:* Seagram Museum, Waterloo, Ont.; Library, Unionville; Howard Hughes Center, L.A.; Wang Tower, L.A.; Performing Arts Center, Portland, Ore.; Hasbro Inc. Corp. HQ, R.I.; Phoenix Municipal Center, Ariz. (competition winner); plans for Bunker Hill, L.A.; Pasadena City Centre; Music Center Expansion, L.A.; CBC Network HQ, Toronto; Cerritos Center for the Performing Arts, Calif.; Woodsworth Coll., Univ. of Toronto; N.W. Campus Housing, U.C.L.A.; Art Gallery of Ont. expansion (competition winner); York Univ. Fine Arts Bldg. expansion, Toronto; USC Education Bldg., USC Plaza, L.A.; New Jersey Performing Arts Center, Newark; The Ice House Renovation, Beverly Hills, Calif.; UCSD/Scripps Ocean Atmosphere Research Facility, La Jolla, Calif.; Univ. of New Mexico, Albuquerque (Master Devt. Plan); Federal Courthouse, San Diego, Calif. 1998, Sotheby's Renovation, Beverly Hills, Calif. 1998. *Publications:* Barton Myers Selected and Current Works (in The Master Architect series) 1994, New Stage for a City (monograph) 1998. *Leisure interests:* travel, reading, tennis. *Address:* Barton Myers Associates, 9348 Civic Center Drive, Beverly Hills, CA 90210, U.S.A. *Telephone:* (310) 246-5757. *Fax:* (310) 246-5750.

MYERS, Dale Dehaven, B.S.A.E.; American engineer, business executive and consultant; b. 8 Jan. 1922, Kansas City, Mo.; s. of Wilson A. and Ruth Hall Myers; m. Marjorie Williams 1943; two d.; ed. Univ. of Washington, Seattle; Aerophysics Dept., N. American 1946, Chief Engineer Missile Div. 1954, Vice-Pres. and Program Man. Hound Dog Air Launched Missile Program 1960; Vice-Pres. and Program Man., Apollo Command and Service Modules, N. American 1964; Assoc. Admin. for Manned Space Flight, NASA Headquarters 1970–74, Deputy Admin., NASA 1986–89; U.S. Govt. Rep. to AGARD 1988–89; Pres. N. American Aircraft Operations, Rockwell Int. Corpn. 1974–77, Corporate Vice-Pres. 1974–77; Under-Sec., Dept of Energy, Washington 1977–79; Pres. and C.O.O. Jacobs Eng. Group Inc., Pasadena 1979–84; Pres. Dale Myers and Assocs., Leucadia, 1984–86, 1989–; mem. Bd. of Dirs. Ducommun Inc., 1982–86, Jacob's Eng. Group 1979–86, MacNeal Schwendler Corpn. 1990–98, SYS 1984–86, SAIC's GSC 1993–97, San Diego Aerospace Museum 1992–; mem. NASA Advisory Comm. 1984–86, NASA Aero Comm. 1994–97; Fellow, American Astronautical Soc., American Inst. of Aeronautics and Astronautics; mem. Nat. Acad. of Engineers 1974, Int. Acad. of Astronautics 1991; Hon. Ph.D. (Whitworth Coll.); NASA Public Service Award 1969, NASA Distinguished Service Medal 1971, 1974, D.S.M. (Dept. of Energy) 1979. *Leisure interests:* golf, old cars. *Address:* P.O. Box 232518, Leucadia, CA 92023, U.S.A.

MYERS, Margaret Jane (Dee Dee), B.S.; American political campaign organizer, broadcaster and magazine editor; b. 1 Sept. 1961, Quonset Point, R.I.; d. of Stephen George Myers and Judith Ann Burleigh; ed. Univ. of Santa Clara; Press Asst. Mondale for Pres. Campaign, L.A. 1984, to deputy Senator Art Torres, L.A. 1985; Deputy Press Sec. to Major Tom Bradley, L.A. 1985–87, Tom Bradley for Gov. Campaign 1986; Calif. Press Sec. Dukakis for Pres. Campaign, L.A. 1988; Press Sec. Feinstein for Gov. Campaign, L.A. and San Francisco 1989–90; Campaign Dir. Jordan for Mayor Campaign, San Francisco 1991; Press Sec. Clinton for Pres. Campaign, Little Rock 1991–92, White House, Washington 1993–94; co-host Equal Time, CNBC, Washington 1995–; Ed. Vanity Fair magazine, Washington 1995–; Robert F. Kennedy Award, Emerson Coll., Boston 1993. *Leisure interests:* running, cycling, music, major league baseball. *Address:* CNBC, 1233 20th Street, N.W., Suite 302, Washington, D.C. 20036, U.S.A.

MYERS, Mike; Canadian actor and writer; b. 25 May 1963, Toronto, Ont.; s. of Eric Myers and Bunny (Hind) Myers; m. Robin Ruzan 1993. *Stage appearances:* The Second City, Toronto 1986–88, Chicago 1988–89; *actor and writer:* Mullarkey & Myers 1984–86; *TV show:* Saturday Night Live 1989–94 (Emmy Award for outstanding writing in a comedy or variety series 1989). *Films:* Wayne's World 1992, So I Married an Axe Murderer 1992, Wayne's World II 1993, Austin Powers: International Man of Mystery 1997, Meteor 1998, McClintock's Peach 1998, Just Like Me 1998, It's A Dog's Life 1998, 54 1998, Austin Powers: The Spy Who Shagged Me 1998; *actor:* John and Yoko (TV film) 1985. *Address:* c/o Creative Artists Agency, 9830 Wilshire Boulevard, Beverly Hills, CA 90212, U.S.A.

MYERS, Norman, C.M.G., PH.D., F.R.S.A., F.L.A.; British scientist; b. 24 Aug. 1934, Whitewell, Yorks.; s. of John Myers and Gladys Myers (née Howarth); m. Dorothy Mary Halliman 1965 (separated 1972); two d.; ed. Clitheroe Royal Grammar School, Lancs., Oxford Univ., Univ. of Calif. Berkeley; ind. scientist and consultant in Environment and Devt. with focus on Third World regions of the tropics 1970–; has worked for many int. orgs. and govt. agencies; Man. Dir. Norman Myers Scientific Consultancy Ltd. 1992–; lectures at American univs; Fellow Royal Inst. 1997. *Publications:* The Long African Day 1973, The Sinking Ark 1979 (five scientific/literary awards), A Wealth of Wild Species, The Primary Source, Economics of Ecosystem Management 1985, The Gaia Atlas of Planet Management 1985, Future Worlds: Challenge and Opportunity in an Age of Change 1991, Population, Resources and the Environment: The Critical Challenges (for UN Population Fund) 1991, Tropical Forests and Climate (Ed.) 1992, Ultimate Security: The Environmental Basis of Political Stability 1993, Scarcity or Abundance: A Debate on the Environment (proceedings of a debate with Julian Simon) 1944, Enviromental Exodus: An Emergent Crisis in the Global Arena 1995, Peverse Subsidies: Taxpayer Dollars Undercutting Our Economies and Environments Alike 1998, (jtly.) Biodiversity Hotspots 1999. *Leisure interests:* marathon running, mountaineering, photography. *Address:* Upper Meadow, Old Road, Headington, Oxford, OX3 8SZ, England. *Telephone:* (01865) 750387. *Fax:* (01865) 741538.

MYERSON, Jacob M., M.A.; American economist; b. 11 June 1926, Rock Hill, S.C.; s. of Solomon and Lena (née Clein) Myerson; m. 1st Nicole Neuray 1965 (died 1968); one d.; m. 2nd Helen Hayashi 1974 (died 1995); ed. Washington, D.C., Pennsylvania State Coll., George Washington Univ.; entered U.S. Foreign Service 1950; Economic Analyst for the Office of the U.S. High Commr., Berlin 1950–52, mem. U.S. Regional Mission for the OEEC and Marshall Plan, Paris 1953–56; State Dept. Desk Officer for EC and European Free Trade Area Affairs 1956–60; Chief of Political Section of U.S. Mission to the European Communities, Brussels 1960; Special Asst. to the Under-Sec. of State, Officer in charge of NATO Political Affairs, State Dept., then Deputy Political Adviser and Counsellor to the U.S. Mission to NATO, Brussels 1965–68, Adviser to the U.S. del. at several ministerial sessions of the N. Atlantic Council 1966–70; Econ. Counsellor U.S. Mission to the European Communities, Brussels, then Deputy Chief and Minister Counsellor 1970–75; Amb. to UN Econ. and Social Council, New York 1975–77; Minister Counsellor for Econ. and Commercial Affairs, U.S. Embassy, Paris 1977–80; Deputy Sec.-Gen. of the OECD 1980–88. *Leisure interest:* twentieth century art. *Address:* 2 rue Lucien-Gaulard, 75018 Paris, France.

MYINT MAUNG, U; Myanma diplomatist and administrator; b. 10 March 1921, Magwe; m.; three c.; ed. Univ. of Rangoon; joined Army 1942; has held the following positions: Head of Co-operative Dept.; Chief of Admin. Div. of Burma Socialist Programme Party, also mem. Party Inspection Cttee.; mem. Pyithu Hluttaw (People's Congress) for Magwe Constituency; mem. Bd. of Dirs. of People's Bank of the Union of Burma, Exec. Cttee. of Burma Sports and Physical Fitness Cttee., Cen. Cttee. of Burma Red Cross Soc.; Chair. Resettlement Cttee. of Cen. Security and Admin. Cttee., Independence Award Cttee.; Perm. Rep. to UN 1975–77; Minister of Foreign Affairs 1977–79; Amb. to China –1989; mem. State Council and Attorney-Gen. 1988. *Address:* c/o Ministry of Foreign Affairs, Yangon, Myanmar.

MYNBAEV, Sauat M., CAND.ECON.; Kazakhstan politician; b. 19 Nov. 1962, Taldy-Kurgan; s. of Mukhametbai Mynbaev and Oralbaeva Rakhima; m. Kalieva Zhanar Mynbaev; one d.; ed. Moscow State Univ.; teacher Alma-Ata Inst. of Nat. Economy, later Assoc. Prof. 1989–; Pres. Kazakhstan Exchange 1991–92; First Deputy Chair., Dir. Kazkommerts Bank 1992–95; Deputy Minister of Finance and Dir. of Treasury 1995–98, Minister of Finance Feb. 1998–. *Address:* 60 Republic Avenue, 473000 Astana, Kazakhstan. *Telephone:* (3172) 280065. *Fax:* (3172) 280321.

MYRDAL, Jan; Swedish writer; b. 19 July 1927, Stockholm; s. of the late Gunnar Myrdal and Alva Reimer; m. 1st Nadja Wiking 1948; m. 2nd Maj Liedberg 1953; m. 3rd Gun Kessle 1956; one s. one d.; Sunday Columnist (politics, culture) Stockholms-Tidningen 1963–66, Aftonbladet 1966–72; Chair. and Publr. Folket i Bild/Kulturfront 1971–72, columnist 1972–; Hon. D.Lit. (Upsala Coll., N.J.) 1980; Hon. Ph.D. (Nankai Univ., China) 1993; Chevalier, Ordre des Arts et des Lettres 1990. *Works include:* films: Myglaren 1966, Hjalparen 1968, Balzac or the triumphs of realism 1975, Mexico: Art and Revolution 1991; TV documentaries: Democratic Kampuchea 1978–79, Guerilla Base Area of Democratic Kampuchea 1979, China 1979, 20 films on history of political caricature and posters 1975–87. *Publications:* (in Swedish) novels: Hemkomst 1954, Jubelvår 1955, Att bli och vara 1956, Badrumskranen 1957, Karriär 1975, Barndom 1982, En annan värld 1984; drama: Folkets Hus 1953, Moraliteter 1967, Garderingar 1969, B. Olsen 1972; travel: Resa i Afghanistan 1960, Bortom berg och öknar 1962, Turkmenistan 1966, En världsbild (co-author) 1977, Sidenvägen 1977, Indien väntar 1980; politics: Kina: Revolutionen går vidare 1970, Albansk utmaning 1970, Ett 50-tal 1972, lag utan ordning, Kinesiska frågor, Tyska frågor 1976, Kina efter Mao Tse-tung 1977, Kampuchea och kriget 1978, Kampuchea hösten 1979, Den albanska utmaningen 1968–86, 1987, Mexico, Dröm och längtan 1996; art: Bartom Bergen 1983; essays: Söndagsmorgon 1965, Skriftställning 1968, Skriftställning II 1969, Skriftställning III 1970, Skriftställning IV 1973, V 1975, Klartexter 1978, Skriftställning X 1978, Balzac und der Realismus (in German) 1978, Strindberg och Balzac 1981, Ord och Avsikt 1986, Det nya Stor, Tyskland 1993; autobiography: Rescontra 1962, Samtida bekännelser 1964, Inför nedräkningen 1993, När morgondagarna sjöng 1994, En kärlek 1998, Maj: En kärlek 1998; art: Ansikte av sten, Angkor 1968, Ondskan tar form 1976; Dussinet fullt 1981, Den trettonde 1983, Franska revolutionens bilder 1989, 5 år av frihet 1830–35 1991, När Västerlandet tradde fram 1992, André Gill 1995, Drömmen om det goda samhallet; Kinesiska affischer 1966–1976 1996; (in English) Report from a Chinese Village 1965, Chinese Journey 1965, Confessions of a Disloyal European 1968, Angkor: an essay on art and imperialism 1970, China: the Revolution Continued 1971, Gates to Asia 1971, Albania Defiant 1976, The Silk Road 1979, China Notebook 1975–78 1979, Return to a Chinese Village 1984, India Waits 1984, Childhood 1991, Another World 1993, 12 going on 13 1995. *Leisure interests:* collecting Meccano, computing for fun. *Address:* Kalvängen 70 D, 739 91 Skinnskatteberg, Sweden. *Telephone:* (223) 51012. *Fax:* (223) 51007.

MYSEN, Bjorn O., M.A., PH.D.; American research scientist; b. 20 Dec. 1947, Oslo, Norway; s. of Martin Mysen and Randi Mysen; m. Susanna Laya 1975; two c.; ed. Univ. of Oslo and Pennsylvania State Univ.; Carnegie Foundation Fellow 1974–77; Sr. Scientist, Experimental Geochemist, Carnegie Inst. Washington; mem. Royal Norwegian Acad. of Sciences; Fellow, Mineralogy Soc. of America; F.W. Clarke Medal; Reusch Medal. *Publications:* Structure and Properties of Silicate Melts 1988; more than 160 other scientific publications. *Address:* Geophysical Laboratory, Carnegie Institution of Washington, 5251 Broad Branch Road, N.W., Washington, D.C. 20015, U.S.A. *Telephone:* (202) 686-2410.

MYŚLIWSKI, Wiesław; Polish writer; b. 25 March 1932, Dwikozy n. Sandomierz; ed. Catholic Univ. of Lublin; worked at People's Publishing Cooperative until 1976, Ed. quarterly magazine Regiony 1975–; Ed. fortnightly Sycyna 1994–; numerous awards include Piętak Prize 1968, 1973, Prize of Ministry of Culture and Art 1971, State Prize 1986, Nike Literary Prize 1997; Alfred Jurzykowski Foundation Award, New York 1998. *Novels:* Nagi sad (Naked orchard) 1967, Pałac (Palace) 1970, Kamień na kamieniu (Stone on stone) 1984, Widnokrag (Horizon) 1996. *Plays:* Złodziej (Thief) 1973, Klucznik (Steward) 1978, Drzewo (Tree) 1989. *Address:* ul. Nowoursynowska 119C, 02-797 Warsaw, Poland.

MYTARAS, Dimitris; Greek artist; b. 1934, Chalkis; s. of Basilis Mytaras and Efrosini Mytaras; m. Chariklia Mytaras 1961; one s.; ed. Athens School of Fine Arts and Ecole des Arts Décoratifs, Paris; Prof. Athens School of Fine Arts; has exhibited in many of the world's capitals and has participated in most important Biennales; assoc. with Kreonidis Gallery, Athens, Metropolis Art Galleries, New York, the Inter Art Group, Tokyo and Galérie Flak, Paris; main periods of his painting are: Mirrors 1960–64, Dictatorship 1966–70, Epitaphs 1971–76, Portraits 1977–87, Theatre Scenes 1988–91. *Publications:* D. Mytaras: Peinture 1982, D. Mytaras: Peinture 1990, D. Mytaras: Drawings 1994, D. Mytaras: Parepiptonda. *Address:* Kamariotou 15, 115-24 N. Filothei, Athens, Greece. *Telephone:* 6913658. *Fax:* 6928327.

MYTTON, Graham Lambert, PH.D.; British broadcasting executive; b. 21 Oct. 1942, Sanderstead; s. of Peter Mytton and Sarah Jackson; m. Janet Codd 1966; two d.; ed. Trinity School, Croydon, Purley Grammar School and Univs. of Liverpool, Manchester and Dar es Salaam; Man. BBC Radio studio 1964–66; Research Fellow, Zambia Broadcasting 1970–73; radio producer, BBC African Service 1973–75; current affairs producer, BBC Radio Four 1976; Head, Hausa Language Section, BBC African Service 1976–82; Head, Int. Broadcasting Audience Research, BBC World Service 1982–91, Head, Audience Research and Correspondence 1991–96, Controller, Marketing 1996–; AT&T Guest Lecturer, George Washington Univ. 1995. *Publications:* Mass Communications in Africa 1983, Global Audiences (ed.) 1993, Handbook on Radio and TV Audience Research 1993. *Leisure interests:* stamp collecting, singing. *Address:* BBC World Service, London, WC2B 4PH (Office); Roffeys, The Green, Coldharbour, Dorking, Surrey, RH5 6HE, England (Home). *Telephone:* 0171-257 8139 (Office); (01306) 712122 (Home). *Fax:* 0171-257 8254 (Office).

MZALI, Mohamed, LIC.EN.PHIL.; Tunisian politician; b. 23 Dec. 1925, Monastir; m.; six c.; ed. Sadiky School, Tunis, Univ. of Paris; Teacher at Sadiky School, Lycée Alaoui and Univ. of Zitouna 1950–56; Chef de Cabinet, Ministry of Education 1956–58; mem. Nat. Assembly 1959–; Dir. of Youth and Sports, President's Secr. 1959–64; Dir.-Gen. Radiodiffusion Télévision Tunisienne (RTT) 1964–67; Sec. of State for Nat. Defence 1968–69; Minister of Youth and Sports 1969–70, of Educ. 1969–70, 1971–73, 1976–80, of Health 1973–76; Co-ordinator of Govt. Activities, Dept. of the Pres. March-April 1980; Prime Minister 1980–84, Prime Minister and Minister of the Interior 1984–86; mem. Neo-Destour Party (now Parti Socialiste Destourien) 1947–, mem. Cen. Cttee. 1971–, Sec.-Gen. 1980–86; mem. Int. Olympic Cttee. 1981–; Municipal Councillor, Tunis 1960, 1963; First Vice-Pres. Tunis Town Council 1960–63, Pres. Culture, Youth and Sports Comm. 1960–66; Pres. Ariana Town Council 1959–72; Founder El Fikr (monthly cultural review) 1955; Pres., Tunisian Olympic Cttee. 1962–, Union des Ecrivains Tunisiens 1970–; First Vice-Pres. Int. Olympic Cttee. 1976–80; Pres. Int. Cttee. Jeux Méditerranéens 1979–; mem. Arab Language Acad., Cairo 1976–, Baghdad 1978–, Damascus 1980–, Jordan 1980–; mem. French Sports Acad. 1978–; Grand Cordon, Ordre de l'Indépendance, Ordre de la République, Grand Officier Légion d'honneur and numerous foreign decorations. *Publications:* La Démocratie 1955, Recueil d'Editoriaux d'El Fikr 1969, Prises de positions 1973, Etudes 1975, Points de Vue 1975, Les Chemins de la Pensée 1979, The Word of the Action 1984, The Olympism Today 1984. Living in France in self-imposed exile; fined and sentenced to 15 years forced labour after *in absentia* conviction for corruption 1987.

MZIMELA, Rev. Sipo E., PH.D.; South African ecclesiastic and civil servant; b. 1937, Durban; m.; three d.; in exile 1961, W. Germany 1964–74, U.S.A. 1974; Rector Epiphany Church New Jersey; ordained Episopal Priest New York 1976; worked with S.A. refugees; teacher St. Paul's United Theological Coll., Kenya 1984; founder S.A. Educ. Fund 1987; Assoc. Priest St. Bartholomew's Episcopal Church, Atlanta 1987; Inkatha Freedom Party Rep. to U.S.A. 1990; fmr. Minister of Works, KwaZulu Govt. 1994; Minister of Correctional Services, Govt. of Nat. Unity 1994. *Publications include:* Apartheid. South African Nazism, Whither South Africa Now?, Marching to Slavery—South Africa's Descent to Communism 1983. *Address:* c/o Private Bag X853, Pretoria 0001, South Africa.

N

NÄÄTÄNEN, Risto Kalervo, PH.D.; Finnish professor of psychology; b. 14 June 1939, Helsinki; s. of Prof. Esko K. Näätänen and Rauni (née Raudanjoki) Näätänen; m. Marjatta Kerola 1960; three s.; ed. Univ. of Helsinki; Asst. Dept. of Psychology, Univ. of Helsinki 1965–69, Prof. of Psychology 1975–, Dir. Cognitive Brain Research Unit 1991–; Researcher Acad. of Finland 1969–75, Research Prof. 1983–, Acad. Prof. 1995–; Scientific Organizer (with Prof. G. Rizzolatti) of European Science Foundation Winter School 1990; Fellowships, Dept. of Psychology, UCLA 1965–66, Univ. Dundee, Scotland 1979–80, Univ. Marburg, Germany 1980–81, The Neurosciences Inst., New York 1985–86, Inst. for Advanced Study, Berlin 1988–89; Vice-Pres. Fed. of European Psychophysiology 1994–96, Pres. 1996–; mem. Finnish ViceAcad. of Science and Letters 1980–, Brain Research Soc. of Finland (Pres. 1983–91), Int. Brain Research Org. (Governing Council 1985–91), Nordic Psychophysiology Soc. (Pres. 1992–95), Advisory Council, Int. Asscn. for the Study of Attention and Performance, Governing Council, Fed. of European Psychophysiology Socs.; mem. Finnish Acad. of Science and Letters 1980–, Academia Europaea; Foreign mem. Russian Acad. of Sciences 1994–; Purkinje Medal (Prague) 1988, Finnish Cultural Foundation Prize 1990, First Science Prize (Finland) 1997, State Traffic Safety Medal 1992; Kt., First Class, Order of the White Rose of Finland. *Publications:* Selective Attention and Evoked Potentials 1967, Road-User Behaviour and Traffic Accidents (with H. Summala) 1976, Attention and Brain Function 1992, numerous articles. *Leisure interests:* sports, the Green Movement, traffic safety. *Address:* The Department of Psychology, University of Helsinki, Meritullink 1, 00140 Helsinki (Univ.); Mäkipellontie 12 D, 00320 Helsinki, Finland (Home). *Telephone:* 191 23445 (Office); (3589) 5876121 (Home). *Fax:* 191 22924.

NABARRO, Frank Reginald Nunes, M.B.E., D.SC., F.R.S.; British physicist; b. 7 March 1916, London; s. of Stanley Nunes Nabarro and Leah (née Cohen) Nabarro; m. Margaret Constance Dalziel 1948 (died 1997); ed. Nottingham High School, New Coll. Oxford, Univ. of Bristol; Sr. Experimental Officer Ministry of Supply 1941–45; Royal Soc. Warren Research Fellow, Univ. of Bristol 1944–49; lecturer in Metallurgy, Univ. of Birmingham 1949–53; Prof. of Physics, Univ. of the Witwatersrand, Johannesburg 1953–84, Emer. Prof. 1985–; Consultant South African Council for Scientific and Industrial Research 1985–, Fellow 1994–; Pres. Royal Soc. of S.A. 1989–92; Founder mem. S.A. Acad. of Science 1995; Hon. mem. South African Inst. of Physics, Microscopy Soc. of South Africa; Foreign Assoc. U.S. Nat. Acad. of Eng. 1996–; Hon. F.R.S.S.A.; Beilby Memorial Award, South African Medal (S.A. Asscn. for the Advancement of Science) 1972, De Beers Gold Medal 1980, Claude Harris Leon Foundation Award of Merit 1983, J.F.W. Herschel Medal 1983, R.F. Mehl Award 1995, Platinum Medal, Inst. of Materials 1997. *Publications:* Theory of Crystal Dislocations 1967, Ed. Dislocations in Solids (9 vols.) 1979–92, Vol. 10 (with M.S. Duesbery) 1996, Physics of Creep (with H. Filmer) 1995. *Leisure interests:* gardening, music. *Address:* 32 Cookham Road, Auckland Park, Johannesburg 2092, South Africa. *Telephone:* (011) 716-4420 (Office); (011) 726-7745 (Home). *Fax:* (011) 339 8262.

NACHTIGALL, Dieter, DR. RER. NAT.; German physicist; b. 4 Feb. 1927, Berge; s. of Walter Nachtigall and Emma (née Eisermann) Nachtigall; two s. one d.; ed. Humboldt Univ., Berlin; schoolteacher, G.D.R. 1946–49, lecturer Teacher's Coll. 1949–50; Scientific Asst. and Lecturer, Tech. Univ. of Dresden 1956–59; Research Group Leader Nuclear Research Establishment, Juelich, F.R.G. 1959–65; Research Assoc. CERN, Geneva 1965–66; Group Leader EURATOM BCNM, Geel 1966–71; Prof. of Physics Educ., Paed. Hochschule, Dortmund 1971–81, Univ. of Dortmund 1981–92, Prof. Emer. 1992–, Dean Dept. of Physics 1990–92; Hon. Prof. Xian Highway Inst. 1988; Advisory Prof., East China Normal Univ., Shanghai 1989–; Hon. Prof. Normal Univ. of Chengdu/Sichuan 1993, South West China Normal Univ. at Chongqing 1994; Guangxi Normal Univ. 1995; mem. Int. Comm. on Physics Educ. 1987–93; Medal of Int. Comm. on Physics Education 1998. *Publications:* Physikalische Grundlagen für Dosimetrie und Strahlenschutz Thiemig 1971, Skizzen zur Physik-Didaktik Lang 1986, Neues Physiklernen-Das Teilchen-Konzept Lang 1989, Das Feldkonzept 1990, Das Wellenkonzept 1990, Internalizing Physics—Making Physics Part of One's Life (UNESCO) 1995. *Address:* Auf'm Hilmkamp 15, 58739 Wickede-Wiehagen, Germany. *Telephone:* 02377-3548. *Fax:* 02377-6134.

NADER, Ralph; American lawyer, author and consumer advocate; b. 27 Feb. 1934, Winsted, Conn.; s. of Nadra Nader and Rose Bouziane; ed. Princeton and Harvard Univs.; admitted to Conn. Bar 1958, Mass. Bar 1959, also U.S. Supreme Court; U.S. Army 1959; law practice in Hartford, Conn. 1959–; Lecturer in History and Govt., Univ. of Hartford 1961–63; fmr. Head of Public Citizen Inc. 1980; Lecturer, Princeton Univ. 1967–68; Co-founder Princeton Project 55 1989; mem. American Bar Asscn.; has advanced cause of consumer protection, particularly with regard to car safety in U.S.A.; f. Clean Water Action Project, Disability Rights Center and other organisations; Woodrow Wilson Award (Princeton Univ.) 1972. *Publications:* Unsafe at Any Speed 1965, Who Runs Congress? 1972, Ed. The Consumer and Corporate Accountability 1974, Taming the Giant Corporation (co-author) 1976, The Menace of Atomic Energy (with John Abbotts) 1979, The Lemon Book 1980, Who's Poisoning America? 1981, The Big Boys 1986, Winning the Insurance Game (co-author) 1990, Good Works 1993, No Contest 1996; Contrib. Ed. Ladies Home Journal 1973–, syndicated columnist 1972–. *Address:* Consumer Advocate Center, P.O. Box 19367, Washington, DC 20036; 2000 P Street, N.W., Washington, DC 20036, U.S.A.

NADIR, Asil; Turkish-Cypriot business executive; b. 1 May 1941, Paphos; s. of Irfan Nadir; m. Ayesha Nadir twice (divorced twice); two s.; ed. Univ. of Istanbul; settled in East End of London, England 1963; formed Wearwell cash-and-carry clothing co., Tower Hamlets 1967; est. cardboard-box factory for fruit-packing in Northern Cyprus following partition of island in 1974; Chair. Polly Peck Int. PLC 1980–90; business expanded to include citrus fruit, colour television factory in Turkey, hotels, leisure complexes, Pizza Hut franchise in Turkey, etc.; acquired control of Sansui electronics co.; bought tropical fruit arm of Del Monte Co., making Polly Peck world's third largest fruit trader; cos. became largest employers in Northern Cyprus; owner of several leading Turkish newspapers; set up charitable trust Nadir Health and Educ. Foundation 1989; Polly Peck empire valued at nearly £2 billion when it collapsed and was placed in hands of administrators Oct. 1990; arrested 15 Dec. 1990 following inquiries into his business affairs by Inland Revenue and Serious Fraud Office; indicted on counts of theft and false accounting faced further charges rearrested Sept. 1991; declared bankrupt Nov. 1991; jumped bail and fled to "Turkish Federated State of Northern Cyprus" May 1993. *Address:* c/o Dome Hotel, Kyrenia, "Turkish Federated State of Northern Cyprus".

NAFEH, Ibrahim; Egyptian journalist; b. 1934, Suez, Egypt; m.; two c.; diplomatic corresp., Cairo Radio 1956–60; Econ. Ed., Al-Gumhuriya newspaper 1960–62; econ. Ed. of Al-Ahram (newspaper) 1962–67; Middle East specialist in IBRD, Information Dept. 1971–73; head of al-Ahram econ. dept. 1974–75; Chief Ed. Al-Ahram 1975; now Chair. and Ed. in Chief, Al-Ahram. *Publication:* Translation into Arabic of Lester Pearson's Report: Partners in Devt. 1971. *Address:* Al-Ahram, Sharia al Galaa, Cairo, Egypt. *Telephone:* (2) 745666. *Fax:* (2) 745888.

NAFFAH, Fouad Georges, LIC.EN DROIT; Lebanese politician and lawyer; b. 1 March 1925, Zouk Mikhaël; s. of Georges Naffah and Malvina Takla; m. Zbeide Sfeir; three s. one d.; ed. Coll. des Frères Maristes, Coll. d'Antoura, Univ. St. Joseph, Beirut; elected Deputy for Kesrouan 1960, 1972; Lecturer in Constitutional Law and Lebanese Constitution, Coll. de la Sagesse and Univ. Libanaise; Minister of Agric. March-May 1972, of Finance 1972–73, of Foreign Affairs 1973–74, Centre Bloc. *Address:* P.O.B. 4504, Raouché, Beirut, Lebanon (Home). *Telephone:* 391840, 810385/6.

NAGAKURA, Saburo, DR.SC.; Japanese scientist; b. 3 Oct. 1920, Shizuoka Pref.; m. Midori Murayama 1953; one s.; ed. Shizuoka High School and Tokyo Imperial Univ.; Assoc. Prof., Univ. of Tokyo 1949–59, Prof. 1959–81; Head of Physical Organic Chem. Lab., Inst. of Physical and Chemical Research 1961–81; mem. Science Council of Japan 1972–75; mem. Science Council, Ministry of Educ., Science and Culture 1974–86, 1988–96, Univ. Council 1987–93; Dir.-Gen. Inst. for Molecular Science 1981–87; Pres. Int. Union of Pure and Applied Chem. 1981–83, Chem. Soc. of Japan 1984–85, Okazaki Nat. Research Insts. 1985–88, Grad. Univ. for Advanced Studies 1988–95, Japanese Centre for Int. Studies in Ecology 1993–, Kanagawa Acad. of Science and Tech. 1995–; mem. Japan Acad., Int. Acad. of Quantum Molecular Science, Deutsche Akademie der Naturforscher Leopoldina; Foreign mem. Royal Swedish Acad. of Sciences; Hon. mem. Royal Institution, London, Chem. Soc. of Japan, Korean Acad. of Science and Tech.; Foreign Fellow Indian Nat. Science Acad.; Hon. Fellow Chinese Chem. Soc., Indian Acad. of Sciences; Hon. D.Sc. (Nebraska); Chem. Soc. of Japan Prize 1966, Asahi Prize 1971, Japan Acad. Prize 1978, Jawaharlal Nehru Birth Centenary Medal 1996; Person of Cultural Merit 1985, Order of Cultural Merit 1990. *Publications:* Electronic Theory for Organic Chemistry 1966 and many publs. on electronic structure and dynamic behaviour of excited molecules. *Leisure interest:* appreciation of Japanese paintings. *Address:* 2-7-13 Higashicho, Kichijoji, Musashino, Tokyo 1800002, Japan. *Telephone:* (0422) 22-5777.

NAGANO, Kent; American conductor; studied under Ozawa, Boulez and Bernstein; first achieved int. recognition when he conducted Boston Symphony Orchestra in performance of Mahler's Symphony No. 9 1984; conducted US premiere of Messiaen's The Transfiguration; debut at Paris Opera conducting world premiere of Messiaen's St. François d'Assise; conducted world premiere performances of John Adams' The Death of Klinghoffer in Brussels, Lyon and Vienna; Music Dir. Berkeley Symphony Orchestra, Calif. 1978–; Music Dir. Opera de Lyon 1989; Assoc. Prin. Guest Conductor, London Symphony Orchestra 1990; Music Dir., Prin. Conductor desig. Music Dir., Prin. Conductor 1994–; Hallé Orchestra 1992–94; debut, Metropolitan Opera, New York conducting Poulenc's Dialogues de Carmelites 1994; several awards for operatic recording. *Address:* c/o Van Walsum Management Ltd., 26 Wadham Road, London, SW15 2LR, England. *Telephone:* 0181-874 6344. *Fax:* 0181-877 0077.

NAGARE, Masayuki; Japanese sculptor; b. Nagasaki; m. (divorced); one d.; enrolled in Zen Temple; apprentice to a sword maker; fighter pilot volunteer World War II; works include: Cloud Fortress, New York, Nagare Park, Okushiri, as well as over 2,000 other pieces; several one-man exhbns.

NAGASHIMA, Shigeo, B.A.; Japanese baseball player and manager; b. 20 Feb. 1936, Chiba Pref.; s. of Toshi Nagashima and Chiyo Nagashima; m. Akiko Nishimura 1965; two s. two d.; ed. St. Paul's Univ., Tokyo; professional baseball player, Tokyo Yomiuri Giants 1958–74, Man. 1975–81, 1993–; Rookie of the Year 1958, Most Valuable Player of the Year five times, Best Average Hitter of the Year six times, Most Home-run Hitter of the Year twice, Most Runs batted in Hitter of the Year five times, Man. of Champion Team of the Year three times. *Leisure interest:* golf. *Address:* 3-29-19, Denenchofu, Ohta-ku, Tokyo 145, Japan. *Fax:* 03-3722-3766.

NAGATA, Masao; Japanese business executive; b. 25 March 1931; ed. Keio Univ.; Man. Dir. Kanebo Ltd. 1976, now Chair., C.E.O. *Address:* Kanebo Ltd., 5-90 Tomobuchi-cho 1-chome, Miyakojima-ku, Osaka 534 (Office); 1-25-20 Ookayama, Meguro-ku, Tokyo 152, Japan.

NAGATA, Takao; Japanese business executive; b. 1 Sept. 1911, Kumamoto; ed. Nagasaki College of Commerce; with Hitachi Shipbuilding and Eng. Co. 1934–, Dir. 1951–60, Vice-Pres. 1960–62, Pres. 1962–, Chair. 1979–; Chair. Nippon Admin. Man. Asscn.; Adviser, Japan Fed. of Employers' Asscn.; Pres. Japan Overseas Enterprises Asscn.; Vice-Pres. ILO Asscn. of Japan; Man. Dir. Fed. of Econ. Orgs. (Keidanren); Dir. Hitachi Ltd., Toyo Unpanki Co. Ltd., All Nippon Airways Co. Ltd.; standing mem., Industry and Labour Council of Ministry of Labour.

NAGEL, Günter; German landscape architect; b. 2 Feb. 1936, Dresden; s. of Heinrich Nagel and Erna (née Hempel) Nagel; m. Helga Jähnig 1962; one c.; ed. Dresden, Humboldt Univ., Berlin and Berlin Tech. Univ.; Scientific Asst. Garden and Landscape Design, Berlin Tech. Univ. 1962–70, lectureship in Design, Garden and Lanscape; Freelance landscape architect; lectureships at Fine Arts Univ., Berlin (Prof. 1974) and Tech. Univ. Brunswick 1970–74; Prof. and Dir. Inst. for Park Planning and Garden Architecture, Univ. of Hannover 1977–; mem. German Soc. for Garden Design and Preservation of Natural Resources; Deutscher Werkbund; mem. Bd. of Trustees, Fritz Schumacher Foundation and Karl Foerster Foundation mem. Acad. of Arts, Berlin, German Acad. of Town and Country Planning; exhbn. "Wohnen in den Stadten?" (with H. Luz and F. Spengeli) 1984. *Publications:* Gärten in Cornwall 1975; Freiräume in der Stadtentwicklung 1978; Erholungsraum Stadtlandschaft 1980; Stadtumbau Grunfunktionen im Hamburger Hafen 1983; Gestaltung und Nutzung des Freiraums Strasse 1985, Verbesserung des Wohnumfeldes 1985; Qualität öffentlicher Freiräume 1986. *Address:* Institut Für Grünplanung und Gartenarchitektur, Universität Hannover, Herrenhäuser Strasse 2, 30419 Hannover, Germany. *Telephone:* (0511) 762-2694. *Fax:* (0511) 762-4043.

NAGEL, Ivan; German professor of aesthetics and history of performing arts; b. 28 June 1931, Budapest; ed. Univs. of Heidelberg, Paris, Frankfurt and Durham; Theatre and Music Critic, Deutsche Zeitung 1959–61, Süddeutsche Zeitung 1969–71; Artistic Adviser, Münchner Kammerspiele 1962–69; Gen. Man. Deutsches Schauspielhaus, Hamburg 1972–79; Pres. Int. Theatre Inst. 1972–79; Cultural Corresp. Frankfurter Allgemeine, New York 1980–83; Fellow, Wissenschaftkolleg, Berlin 1983–84, 1988–89; Dir. State Theatre, Stuttgart 1985–88; Prof. for Aesthetics and History of the Performing Arts, Hochschule der Künste, Berlin 1988–96; Dir. Drama Section Salzburg Festival 1997–98; founder and Pres. Theater der Welt (int. theatre festival), Hamburg 1979, 1989, Cologne 1981, Stuttgart 1987; mem. Akad. der Künste, Berlin, Akad. für Sprache und Dichtung, Darmstadt and Akad. der Darstellenden Künste, Frankfurt; mem. PEN Club.; Merck Award, Kortner Award. *Publications:* Autonomie und Gnade: Über Mozarts Opern 1985, Gedankengänge als Lebensläufe: Versuche über das 18. Jahrhundert 1987, Kortner Zadek Stein 1989, Johann Heinrich Dannecker: Ariadne auf dem Panther 1993, Vier Regisseure: Bondy, Castorf, Sellars, Wilson 1996, Der Künstler als Kuppler: Goyas Nackte und Bekleidete Maja 1997. *Leisure interest:* music. *Address:* Keithstr. 10, 10787 Berlin, Germany. *Telephone:* 030/2114710. *Fax:* 030/2114710.

NAGEL, Thomas, PH.D.; American professor of philosophy and law; b. 4 July 1937, Belgrade, Serbia; s. of Walter Nagel and Carolyn Baer Nagel; m. 1st Doris Blum 1968 (divorced 1972); m. 2nd Anne Hollander 1979; ed. Cornell, Oxford and Harvard Univs.; Asst. Prof. of Philosophy, Univ. of Calif. Berkeley 1963–66; Asst. Prof. of Philosophy, Princeton Univ. 1966–69, Assoc. Prof. 1969–72, Prof. 1972–80; Prof. New York Univ. 1980–, Prof. of Philosophy and Law 1986–; Fellow, American Acad. of Arts and Sciences, British Acad. *Publications:* The Possibility of Altruism 1970, Mortal Questions 1979, The View from Nowhere 1986, What Does It All Mean? 1987, Equality and Partiality 1991, Other Minds 1995, The Last Word 1997. *Address:* New York University Law School, 40 Washington Square South, New York, NY 10012, U.S.A. *Telephone:* (212) 998-6225. *Fax:* (212) 995-4526.

NAHNAH, Sheikh Mahfoud; Algerian politician; b. 1939; took part in war of independence against France; f. Harakat el-Mouwahidine (The Unifiers) underground movt. 1970; sentenced to 15 years imprisonment for terrorist activities, released 1981; mem. Islamic Algerian Hamas party; cand. in presidential election Dec. 1995. *Address:* Hamas, Algiers, Algeria.

NAHYAN, Sheikh Sultan bin Zayed an-; Abu Dhabi government official and soldier; b. 1955; ed. in Abu Dhabi, Lebanon, U.K., Sandhurst Univ. Coll.; Commdr. Western Mil. Dist. 1976; Gen. Commdr. U.A.E. Armed Forces 1978; now Deputy Commdr. Abu Dhabi Defence Forces; Deputy Prime Minister 1991. *Address:* P.O.B. 831, Abu Dhabi, United Arab Emirates. *Telephone:* (2) 651881.

NAHYAN, Sheikh Zayed bin Sultan an-; Ruler of Emirate of Abu Dhabi; b. 1926; m.; appointed by his brother Sheikh Shakhbut bin Sultan (Ruler of Abu Dhabi 1928–66) as his personal rep. at inland oasis of Al Ain 1946; paid first official visit to Europe and U.K. with his brother 1953; Ruler of Abu Dhabi 1966–; Pres. Fed. of U.A.E. 1971–; played leading role in establishment of Gulf Cooperation Council. *Leisure interests:* hunting, falconry. *Address:* Presidential Palace, Abu Dhabi, United Arab Emirates.

NAIDOO, Jay; South African trade union official; b. 20 Dec. 1954, Durban; m. L. Page 1992; two s. one d.; ed. Sastri Coll., Durban and Univ. of Durban-Westville; mem. SASO 1977; involved in community orgs., Natal 1976–79; Organizer Fed. of South African Trade Unions (FOSATU) 1980; Gen. Sec. Sweet Food & Allied Workers Union 1982, Congress of South African Trade Unions (COSATU) 1985–93; Minister, Office of the Pres., Govt. of Nat. Unity 1994–1996; Minister of Posts and Telecommunications and Broadcasting 1996–. *Leisure interests:* jazz, skiing cross-country, kids, cycling. *Address:* Iparioli Office Park, Nkululeko House, 339 Duncan Street, Hatfield, Pretoria 0083; Private Bag X860, Pretoria 0001, South Africa. *Telephone:* (12) 4278111. *Fax:* (12) 3626915.

NAIPAUL, Sir Vidiadhar Surajprasad, Kt., C.LIT., B.A.; Trinidadian-born writer; b. 17 Aug. 1932; m. 1st Patricia Ann Hale 1955 (died 1996); m. 2nd Nadira Khannum Alvi 1996; ed. Queen's Royal Coll., Port-of-Spain and Univ. Coll. Oxford; for two years freelance broadcaster with the BBC, producing programmes for the Caribbean area; fiction reviewer on New Statesman 1958–61; grant from Trinidad Govt. to travel in Caribbean and S. America 1961; in India 1962–63, 1975, 1988–89, in Uganda 1965–66, in U.S.A. 1969, 1978–79, 1987–88, in Argentina 1972, 1973–74, 1977, 1991, in Venezuela 1977, 1985, in Iran, Pakistan, Malaysia and Indonesia 1979–80, 1995; Hon. D.Litt. (Univ. of the W. Indies, St. Augustine) 1975, (St. Andrews) 1979, (Columbia) 1981, (Cambridge) 1983, (London) 1988, (Oxford) 1992; John Llewelyn Rhys Memorial Prize 1958, Somerset Maugham Award 1961, Phoenix Trust Award 1962, Hawthornden Prize 1964, W. H. Smith Award 1968, Booker Prize 1971, Jerusalem Prize 1983, Ingersoll Prize 1986, David Cohen British Literature Prize 1993. *Publications:* The Mystic Masseur 1957, The Suffrage of Elvira 1958, Miguel Street 1959, A House for Mr. Biswas 1961, The Middle Passage 1962, Mr. Stone and the Knights Companion 1963, An Area of Darkness 1964, The Mimic Men 1967, A Flag on the Island 1967 (collection of short stories), The Loss of El Dorado 1969, In a Free State 1971, The Overcrowded Barracoon (essays) 1972, Guerrillas 1975, India: A Wounded Civilization 1977, A Bend in the River 1979, The Return of Eva Perón 1980, Among the Believers 1981, Finding the Centre 1984, The Enigma of Arrival 1987, A Turn In The South 1989, India: A Million Mutinies Now 1990, A Way in the World 1994, Beyond Belief 1998, Letters 1999. *Address:* c/o Gillon Aitken Associates Ltd., 29 Fernshaw Road, London, SW10 0TG, England.

NAIR, C. V. Devan (see Devan Nair, C. V.).

NAIR, M. R. R., M.A. (ECON.). LL.B.; Indian business executive; b. 27 Nov. 1937; s. of late Pillai Raman and Janaki Amma; m. Leela Nair; two s.; man. trainee, Bhilai Steel Plant, Hindustan Steel Ltd. 1960; Sr. Man. (Personnel & Admin.) Steel Authority of India Ltd. (SAIL) 1973, Dir. (Personnel), mem. Bd. 1981, Chair. 1992–96; Chief Personnel Man. Hindustan Steel Works Construction Ltd. 1974, Gen. Man. 1977; Man. Dir. Bokaro Steel Plant 1990; founder mem. Acad. of Human Resource Devt.; fmr. Visiting Faculty Int. Centre for Public Enterprises; recipient of numerous awards. *Publications:* articles on man. for nat. and int. magazines and journals. *Leisure interests:* reading, music, driving. *Address:* Steel Authority of India Ltd., Ispat Bhawan, Lodi Road, New Delhi 110 003, India. *Telephone:* 690481.

NAIRNE, Rt. Hon. Sir Patrick Dalmahoy, P.C., G.C.B., M.C., M.A.; British civil servant and university administrator; b. 15 Aug. 1921, London; s. of late C. S. Nairne and E. D. Nairne; m. Penelope Chauncy Bridges 1948; three s. three d.; ed. Radley Coll., Univ. Coll., Oxford; entered civil service 1947; Pvt. Sec. First Lord of Admiralty 1958–60; Defence Sec. 1965–67; Deputy Sec. Ministry of Defence 1970–73; Second Perm. Sec. Cabinet Office 1973–75; Perm. Sec. Dept. of Health and Social Security 1975–81; Master, St. Catherine's Coll., Oxford 1981–88, Chancellor of Essex Univ. 1983–97; Dir. Cen. Independent Television 1982–92; Chair., W. Midlands Bd. 1990–92, Nuffield Council on Bioethics 1991–96; mem. Civil Service Security Appeals Panel 1982, Cttee. of Inquiry into the events leading to the Argentine invasion of the Falklands 1982; U.K. Monitor, Anglo-Chinese Agreement on Hong Kong 1984; Gov. and mem. Council of Man. Ditchley Foundation 1988–; Chair. Comm. on the Conduct of Referendums 1996; Church Commr. 1993–98; Trustee Nat. Maritime Museum 1981–91, Joseph Rowntree Foundation 1982–96, Nat. AIDS Trust 1987–96; Chair. Advisory Bd., Museum of Modern Art, Oxford 1988–98, Pres. 1998; painting exhbns., London 1971–83, 1989, 1992–1997; Hon. LL.D. (Leicester) 1980, (St. Andrews) 1984; Dr. h.c. (Essex) 1983. *Leisure interests:* water-colour painting, calligraphy. *Address:* Yew Tree, Chilson, Chipping Norton, Oxon, OX7 3HU, England. *Telephone:* (01608) 676456.

NAISH, Bronwen, A.R.C.M.; British solo double bass player; b. 19 Nov. 1939; Burley Hants.; d. of E. F. E. Naish and G. J. Grant; m. Roger Best

1959 (divorced 1981); two s. three d.; ed. Holyhead Grammar School and Royal Manchester Coll. of Music; began playing double bass 1966; performance and teaching in northern England and sub-prin. bass, Northern Sinfonia 1967–73; début recital, King's Hall, Newcastle upon Tyne 1971; London début, Purcell Room 1974; returned to N. Wales to concentrate on solo career 1976; Channel Island tours 1980, 1988; Australian tour 1988; est. Slap & Tickle with pianist Maurice Horhut 1988; Edin. Fringe Festival 1989, 1990; commissioning new works for musical saw (recent acquisition) 1990; examiner, Assoc. Bd. of Royal Schools of Music. *Publication:* Another String to my Bow 1982. *Leisure interests:* beekeeping, do-it-yourself. *Address:* Moelfre, Cwm Pennant, Garndolbenmaen, Gwynedd, North Wales, LL5 9AX. *Telephone:* (0176) 675356.

NAJARIAN, John Sarkis, M.D.; American surgeon; b. 22 Dec. 1927, Oakland, Calif.; s. of Garabed L. and Siranoush T. (Demirjian) Najarian; m. Arlys Viola Mignette Anderson 1952; four s.; ed. Univ. of Calif., Berkeley and Univ. of Calif. Medical School, San Francisco; Internship (surgical) Univ. of Calif., San Francisco 1952–53, Residency (surgical) 1955–60; Special Research Fellow (N.I.H.) Univ. of Pittsburgh 1960–61; Sr. Fellow and Assoc. (N.I.H.) Scripps Clinic and Research Foundation, La Jolla, Calif. 1961–63; Asst. Prof. of Surgery, Dir. of Surgical Research Labs. and Chief, Transplantation Service, Univ. of Calif., San Francisco 1963–66, Prof. and Vice-Chair. Dept. of Surgery 1966–67; Prof. and Chair. Dept. of Surgery, Univ. of Minn. Hosps. 1967–93, Regents' Prof. 1985–95; Jay Phillips Chair. 1986–95; many visiting professorships; Pres. American Surgical Asscn. 1988–89, Int. Transplantation Soc. 1994–96, Int. Pediatric Transplant Asscn. 1998–; mem. many editorial boards and professional groups; Hon. Prof. Madrid Univ. 1990; Hon. F.R.C.S. (England); numerous honours. *Publications:* more than 1,200 articles and chapters, co-author several books. *Address:* Surgery Department, University of Minnesota Hospital, Box 195 Mayo, 420 Delaware Street S.E., Minneapolis, MN 55455, U.S.A. *Telephone:* (612) 625-8444.

NAJDER, Zdzisław Marian, PH.D.; Polish civic leader and author; b. 31 Oct. 1930, Warsaw; s. of Franciszek Najder and Józefa Najder (née Kowalska); m. Halina Paschalska 1965; one s.; ed. Warsaw Univ., Oxford Univ.; Asst. Inst. for Literary Research of Polish Acad. of Sciences 1952–57; sr. asst. Aesthetics, Warsaw Univ. 1958–59; staff Twórczość (monthly) 1957–81; taught Polish literature at Columbia and Yale Univs. 1966 and Univ. of California, Berkeley 1966–67; Prof. of Philosophy 1967–68, Regents' Prof. Univ. of Calif. Davis 1968–69; Prof. of English Literature Northern Ill. Univ. 1971–72; visiting scholar Stanford Univ. 1974–75; adviser to Solidarity Trade Union 1980–90; Visiting Fellow St. Antony's College, Oxford 1981, 1988; head Polish section of Radio Free Europe, Munich 1982–87; charged with spying, sentenced to death in absentia by Warsaw Mil. Tribunal in May 1983, stripped of Polish citizenship 1985, sentence revoked Sept. 1989, case dismissed Jan. 1990; mem. editorial staff Kontakt, Paris 1988–91; Chair. Nat. Civic Cttee. 1990–92; Chief Adviser to the Prime Minister 1992; Pres. Civic Inst. 1991–97, Atlantic Club 1991–93; Chair. Joseph Conrad Soc. (Poland) 1994–; Prof. of English Literature, Univ. of Opole 1997–; Prof. School of Foreign Languages and Econs., Częstochowa 1997–; mem. Polish Writers' Union 1956–83, PEN Club 1957–; f. Polish Agreement for Independence 1976; Juliusz Mieroszewski Award 1982, Prize of Modern Language Asscn. 1984, Polish PEN Club Prize 1988; Commdr.'s Cross, Order of Polonia Restituta 1983; Commdr., Ordre nat. du Mérite 1991. *Publications:* academic treatises and literary essays including Conrad's Polish Background 1964, Nad Conradem 1965, Values and Evaluations 1975, Życie Conrada-Korzeniowskiego 1981, Ile jest dróg? 1982, Wymiary polskich spraw 1990, Jaka Polska 1993, Z Polski do Polski poprzez PRL 1995, Conrad in Perspective: Essays on Art and Fidelity 1997, W sercu Europy 1998. *Leisure interests:* travel, walks in forest, 12th century Romanesque art. *Address:* ul. Tyniecka 31 m. 7, 02-621 Warsaw, Poland. *Telephone:* (22) 844 85 36. *Fax:* (22) 844 85 36.

NAJJAR, Mgr. Raouf, PH.D.; Jordanian ecclesiastic; b. 1932, Haifa, Palestine; ed. Latin Seminary, Beit-Jala, nr. Jerusalem, Lateran Univ., Rome; ordained priest, Nazareth 1955; Pres. Church Court (Officialis) 1963–88; Canon of the Holy Sepulchre 1971; Mgr. 1973; acting for Apostolic Del. in Jordan 1988–, for the Apostolic Nunciature 1994–; Pres. Bethlehem Univ. 1988–; Chair. and Gen. Dir. Jordanian Acad. of Music; owner and Ed.-in-Chief Voice of the Holy Land 1968–; Chair. and Gen. Dir. Al Wasifiyyah Vocational Centre 1968–; mem. Bd. Int. Fed. of Catholic Univs., Paris; Distinguished Leadership Award in Church Law, American Biographical Inst.; Prelate ad honorem 1991; Commdr. Italian Repub., Order of Jordan Independence (2nd Degree), Commdr. Ordre Int. de la Paix, Grand Chevalier, Order of St. John of Jerusalem. *Address:* Apostolic Nunciature, P.O. Box 5634, Amman 11183, Jordan. *Telephone:* (6) 694095. *Fax:* (6) 692502.

NAKAE, Toshitada; Japanese journalist; b. 4 Oct. 1929, Chiba City; m. Yohko Nakae 1959; three s.; ed. Tokyo Univ.; local reporter Asahi Shimbun 1953–58, econ. reporter 1958–72, Econ. Ed. 1972–76, Asst. Man. Ed. 1976–78, Man. Ed. 1978–83, Dir. 1982–97, Pres. 1989–96, Special Adviser 1996–. *Publications:* (in English trans.) Cities 1966, The Pulitzer Prize Story 1970, The News Media 1971, The Economy of Cities 1971. *Leisure interests:* driving, listening to music. *Address:* 1-11-1-401 Hamadayama, Suginami-ku, Tokyo, Japan. *Telephone:* (3) 3302-7087.

NAKAE, Yosuke; Japanese diplomatist; b. 30 Dec. 1922, Osaka; s. of Yasuzo Nakae and Itsu Kawase; m. Yasuko Takakura 1959; one s. one d.; ed. Kyoto Univ.; Dir.-Gen. of Asian Affairs Bureau, Ministry of Foreign Affairs 1975; Amb. to Yugoslavia 1978, to Egypt 1982, to People's Repub. of China 1984–87; Commr. Japan Atomic Energy Comm. 1987–91; Pres.'s Adviser, Mitsubishi Heavy Industries Co. Ltd. 1991–. *Publications:* ballet scenarios: Creature 1975, Mobile et Immobile—Mirage à l'Abu-Simbel 1983, Friendship across the Water 1986, Magpies' Bridge 1998; books: Wind Blowing over China 1991, Wonderful Diplomat 1993. *Leisure interest:* writing scenarios for ballet. *Address:* 3-21-5, Eifuku, Suginami, Tokyo 168-0064, Japan. *Telephone:* (3) 3325-7359. *Fax:* (3) 3325-7359.

NAKAGAWA, Shoichi; Japanese politician; b. Hokkaido; s. of Ichiro Nakagawa; fmr. banker; mem. for Hokkaido, House of Reps.; Minister of Agric., Forestry and Fisheries 1998–; Head Policy Research Council of LDP on Agric. and Forestry. *Address:* Ministry of Agriculture, Forestry and Fisheries, 1-2-1, Kasumigaseki, Chiyoda-ku, Tokyo 100, Japan. *Telephone:* (03) 3502-8111. *Fax:* (03) 3592-7697.

NAKAJIMA, Fumio, D.LITT.; Japanese professor; b. 11 Nov. 1904, Tokyo; m. Chizu Takaba 1935; ed. First Prefectural School, First Nat. Coll. and Univ. of Tokyo; Asst. Prof., Univ. of Keijo, Seoul 1928, Assoc. Prof. 1933, Prof. of English Philology 1939; Prof. of English Philology, Univ. of Tokyo 1947–65, Prof. Emer. 1965–; Prof. Tsuda-juku Coll. 1965–73, Pres. 1973–80; Pres. English Literary Soc. of Japan 1952–64, Shakespeare Soc. of Japan 1964–75; mem. Japan Acad. 1974–; Order of the Sacred Treasure (2nd Class) 1975. *Publications:* Imiron 1939, Eigo-no-Joshiki 1944, Bunpo-no-Genri 1949, Eibunpo-no-taikei 1961, Eigo-no-Kozo 1980, Nihongo-no-Kozo 1985. *Address:* 2-24-10, Nishi-koigakubo, Kokubunji, Tokyo 185, Japan. *Telephone:* (0423) 24 5580.

NAKAJIMA, Hiroshi, M.D., PH.D., F.R.C.P.; Japanese international civil servant; b. 16 May 1928, Chiba City; m. Martha DeWitt; two s.; ed. Tokyo Medical Coll. and Univ. of Paris; Scientist, Nat. Inst. of Health and Medical Research, Paris (specializing in neuropsychopharmacology) 1958–67; Dir. of Research and Admin., Nippon Roche Research Centre, Tokyo 1967–73; Scientist, Evaluation and Control of Drugs 1973–76; Chief Drug Policies and Man., WHO HQ, Geneva 1976–79; Dir. WHO Regional Office for the Western Pacific, Manila 1979–88; Dir.-Gen. WHO 1988; Visiting Prof., Univ. of Tokyo 1991; Corresp. mem. Acad. of Pharmacy, Paris; Foreign Assoc. mem. Nat. Acad. of Medicine of France; Kojima Award 1984; Chevalier, Légion d'honneur and numerous other distinctions. *Publications:* more than 60 articles and reviews in the field of medical and pharmaceutical sciences. *Address:* c/o World Health Organization, 20 avenue Appia, CH-1211 Geneva 27, Switzerland. *Telephone:* 791 21 11.

NAKAMURA, Hajime, D.LITT.; Japanese professor of philosophy; b. 28 Nov., 1912, Matsue City; s. of Kiyoji Nakamura and Tomo Nakamura; m. Rakuko Nakamura 1944; two d.; ed. Univ. of Tokyo; Prof. of Indian and Buddhist Philosophy, Univ. of Tokyo 1943–73; f. and Dir. Eastern Inst. Inc. 1973–; mem. Japan Acad. of Sciences 1984–; corresp. mem. Acad. of Sciences, Göttingen, Austrian Acad. of Sciences; Hon. Fellow Royal Asiatic Soc. of Great Britain; Imperial Prize (Japan Acad. of Sciences); Order of Merit. *Publications:* A Comparative History of Ideas 1986, Ways of Thinking of Eastern Peoples, A History of Early Vedànta Philosophy. *Address:* Kugayama 4-37-15, Suginami-ku, Tokyo, Japan.

NAKAMURA, Hisao; Japanese business executive; b. 11 Nov. 1923, Kyoto Pref.; s. of Kinjiro Nakamura and Masao Nakamura; m. Fusako Nagai 1955; one s. one d.; ed. Kyoto Univ.; joined Kuraray Co. Ltd. 1950, Dir. 1972, Man. Dir. 1976, Exec. Vice-Pres. 1981, Pres. 1985–93, Chair. 1993–; Chair. Kurray Trading Co. Ltd. 1984–; Pres. Kyowa Gas Chemical Industries Co. Ltd. 1985–. *Leisure interests:* golf, car-driving, reading. *Address:* 1-12-39 Umeda, Kita-ku, Osaka 530; 52 Nigawa-dai, Takarazuka, Hyogo 665, Japan.

NAKAMURA, Kishiro; Japanese politician; mem. House of Reps. from Ibaraki 1976–; fmr. Dir.-Gen. Science and Tech. Agency; Minister of Construction 1992–93; Chair. House of Reps. Construction Cttee.; mem. Takeshita faction (Obuchi group) of LDP. *Address:* c/o Ministry of Construction, 2-1, Kasumigaseki, Chiyoda-ku, Tokyo, Japan.

NAKAMURA, Shozaburo; Japanese politician; fmr. businessman; mem. LDP; mem. for Minami Kanto bloc. House of Reps.; fmr. Dir.-Gen. Environment Agency, Parl. Vice-Minister of Finance (three times); Minister of Justice 1998–99. *Leisure interests:* skiing, scuba diving. *Address:* c/o Ministry of Justice, 1-1-1, Kasumigaseki, Chiyoda-ku, Tokyo 100, Japan.

NAKAMURA, Tameaki; Japanese business executive; b. 5 Feb. 1930, Fukuoka Pref.; s. of late Tametsugu Nakamura and Kaoru Nakamura; m. Fukuyo Nakamura 1961; two d.; ed. Kumamoto and Kyoto Univs.; joined Sumitomo Metal Industries, Ltd. 1955; Dir. Bd. and Gen. Man. Kokura Steel Works 1984; Man. Dir. 1988; Gen. Man. Kashima Steel Works 1989; Gen. Man. EGL Construction Div. and Sr. Man. Dir. 1990, now Vice-Chair; Pres. and C.E.O. Sumitomo Metal Industries, Ltd. 1992; fmr. mem. Bd. Dirs. Int. Iron and Steel Inst.; Dir. and mem. Policy Bd. Japan Iron and Steel Fed. *Leisure interests:* golf, baseball. *Address:* c/o Sumitomo Metal Industries, Ltd., 5-33 Kitahama 4-chome, Chuo-ku, Osaka 541, Japan.

NAKANISHI, Sekisuke; Japanese politician; fmr. labour union official; Minister of State and Dir.-Gen. Man. and Co-ordination Agency Jan.–Nov. 1996; mem. House of Reps.; mem. Social Democratic Party of Japan (SDPJ). *Address:* c/o Management and Co-ordination Agency, 3-1-1, Kasumigaseki, Chiyoda-ku, Tokyo 100, Japan.

NAKAO, Eiichi; Japanese politician; b. Jan. 1930, Yamanashi Pref.; m.; one s. one d.; ed. Aoyama Gakuin Univ. and Waseda Univ.; mem. House of Reps. 1967–; Chair. Nippon Network Services Co., Ltd. 1970; Parl. Vice-Minister for Agric. and Forestry 1972; Chair. Exec. Council, Liberal-Democratic Party (LDP) 1978; Chair. LDP Nat. Org. Cttee. 1982; Minister of State, Dir.-Gen. Econ. Planning Agency 1987–88; Minister of Int. Trade and Industry 1990–91, of Construction Jan.–Oct. 1996. *Leisure interests:* shigin (recitation of classical Chinese poetry), listening to music. *Address:* 708 Nissho-Iwai Otowa Mansions, 2-4-8 Otsuka, Bunkyo-ku, Tokyo 112, Japan.

NAKASONE, Yasuhiro; Japanese politician; b. 27 May 1917, Takasaki, Gumma Prov.; s. of Matsugoroh and Yuku Nakasone; m. Tsutako Kobayashi 1945; one s. two d.; ed. Tokyo Imperial Univ.; mem. House of Reps.; fmr. Minister of State, Dir.-Gen. of Science & Tech. Agency; Chair. Nat. Org. Liberal-Dem. Party (LDP), Jt. Cttee. on Atomic Energy, Special Cttee. on Scientific Tech., Chair. LDP Exec. Council 1971–72, Sec.-Gen. LDP 1974–76, Chair. 1977–80; Minister of Transport 1967–68; Minister of State and Dir.-Gen. Defence Agency 1970–71; Minister of Int. Trade and Industry 1972–74; Minister of State and Dir.-Gen. of Admin. Man. Agency 1980–82; Prime Minister of Japan 1982–87; Chair. and Pres. Int. Inst. for Global Peace 1988–89, Inst. for Int. Policy Studies 1988–; after involvement in Recruit affair resigned from LDP, rejoined April 1991. *Publications:* Ideal of Youth, Frontier in Japan, The New Conservatism, Human Cities—a proposal for the 21st Century 1980, Tenchiyujou (autobiog.) 1996. *Leisure interests:* golf, swimming, painting. *Address:* 3-22-7, Kamikitazawa, Setagaya-ku, Tokyo, Japan (Home). *Telephone:* (03) 3304-7000 (Home).

NAKAYAMA, Taro, M.D.; Japanese politician; b. 27 Aug. 1924, Osaka; ed. Osaka Medical Coll.; mem. Osaka Pref. Assembly 1955, Parl. Vice-Minister of Labour, Vice-Chair. of Liberal-Democratic Party (LDP) Diet Policy Cttee.; mem. House of Councillors 1968–, Chair. Cabinet Cttee., Steering Cttee.; Minister of State, Dir.-Gen. Prime Minister's Office and Okinawa Devt. Agency 1980–81; Minister of Foreign Affairs 1989–91. *Publications:* five books including Scientific Strategy for the Post-Oil Age 1979. *Address:* 1-7-1 Nagata-Cho, Chiyoda-ku, Tokyo, Japan.

NAKAYAMA, Toshio; Japanese politician; ed. Nihon Univ.; served as pvt. in army; mem. House of Reps. from Ibaraki; fmr. Parl. Vice-Minister of Home Affairs, of Justice; Dir.-Gen. Defence Agency (State Minister) 1992–93; Chair. House of Reps. Security Cttee.; mem. Takeshita Faction (Obuchi group) of LDP.

NAŁĘCZ, Maciej, DR.; Polish scientist; b. 27 April 1922, Warsaw; s. of Aleksander and Stefania Nałęcz; m. Zofia Bozowska 1952; one s.; ed. Warsaw Tech. Univ.; scholarship to Case Inst. of Tech., Cleveland, U.S.A. 1961–62; Assoc. Prof. 1962–72, Prof. 1972–; Corresp. mem. Polish Acad. of Sciences (PAN) 1967–73, Ordinary mem. 1974–, Presidium mem. and Sec. Tech. Sciences Section 1972–80, Deputy Gen. Sec. PAN 1981–83, Deputy to Sejm (Parl.) 1985–89, mem. Presidium 1972–89; Dir. Inst. of Automatic Control 1962–72; Chair. Biomedical Eng. Cttee. of Section IV 1972–; Dir. Inst. of Biocybernetics and Biomedical Eng. 1975–93, Int. Centre of Biocybernetics 1988–; Chair. Nat. Cttee. for Pugwash Confs. 1972–, elected Chair. Pugwash Council 1974, 1977, 1982, 1987, 1992; co-founder and Vice-Chair. European Soc. for Eng. and Medicine (ESEM) 1995–; Visiting Prof. Polytechnic Inst. of Brooklyn 1967–68, Univ. of Hanover, W. Germany 1990; Distinguished Visiting Prof. Ohio State Univ. 1979–80, Campinas Univ., Brazil 1985, Cleveland Clinic Foundation 1985, Waseda Univ., Japan 1988; Scholar in Residence, Int. Fogarty Foundation, N.I.H., U.S.A. 1991–92; mem. Int. Measurement Confed. (IMEKO), Cttee. on Data for Science and Tech. (CODATA) of ICSU, Exec. Cttee. Int. Fed. of Automatic Control 1972–, Int. Soc. of Artificial Organs, Admin. Bd. Int. Fed. for Medical and Biological Eng. 1988–94, Gen. Bd. European Soc. of Engineers and Physicians (co-founder) 1991–, Int. Acad. for Medical and Biological Eng. 1997–; Foreign mem. U.S.S.R. (now Russian) Acad. of Sciences 1976–, Georgian Acad. of Sciences 1996–; Hon. mem. World Org. of Gen. Systems and Cybernetics 1979, Soc. for Theoretical and Applied Electrotechnics 1980, Polish Soc. for Medical Eng. 1995; State Prize, 2nd Class 1972, Nobel Peace Prize (for Pugwash) 1995; Award med tack för värdefull insats (Sweden) 1957, Medal of 30th Anniversary of People's Poland 1974, Kt.'s, Officer's and Commdr.'s with Star Cross of Order Polonia Restituta, Order Banner of Labour, 2nd Class 1972, 1st Class 1978, Copernicus Medal, Polish Acad. of Science, Križik Medal, Czechoslovakian Acad. of Science 1988, Int. Fogarty Center Medal, U.S.A. 1991. *Publications:* The Technology of Hall Generators and Their Use in Measurement and Conversion 1972, Trends in Control Components 1974, Control Aspects of Biomedical Engineering (Ed. and Contrib.) 1987, Computers in Medicine (Ed. and Contrib.) 1987, Problems of Biocybernetics and Biomedical Engineering (Ed. and Contrib.) 1990–91, State of Art and Development of BME in Poland (monograph, Ed. and Co-author) 1994. *Leisure interest:* summer house. *Address:* International Centre of Biocybernetics, Polish Academy of Sciences, ul. Trojdena 4, 02-109 Warsaw, Poland. *Telephone:* (22) 658 28 77. *Fax:* (22) 658 28 72.

NALLET, Henri Pierre; French politician; b. 6 Jan. 1939, Bergerac (Dordogne); s. of Jean Nallet and France Lafon; m. Thérèse Leconte 1963; one s.; ed. Inst. d'Etudes Politiques, Bordeaux; Sec.-Gen. Jeunesse Étudiante Catholique 1963–64; Inst. de Formation des Cadres Paysans 1965–66; Féd. Nat. des Syndicats d'Exploitants Agricoles (FNSEA) 1966–70; Dir. of Research, Dept. of Econ. and Rural Sociology, Inst. Nat. de Recherche Agronomique (INRA) 1970–81; agricultural adviser, Secr. Gen. of Presidency of Republic 1981–85; Minister of Agric. 1985–86; Socialist Deputy to Nat. Ass. 1986–88; Minister of Agric. and Forestry 1988–90, Garde des Sceaux, Minister of Justice 1990–92; Conseiller-Gen. of Yonne 1988–; Mayor of Tonnerre 1989–; Conseiller d'Etat 1992–; Deputy for Yonne 1997–; Pres. del of Nat. Ass. to EU; mem. Parl. Ass. of Council of Europe and of WEU; consultant IBRD 1992–, EU 1992–; Pres. World Council of Nutrition 1985–87. *Publication:* Tempête sur la justice 1992. *Address:* Hôtel de Ville, 89700 Tonnerre; Assemblée Nationale, 233 boulevard St. Germain, 75355 Paris Cedex 07, France.

NAM DUCK-WOO, PH.D.; Korean politician, economist and government official; b. 10 Oct. 1924; s. of Sang Bom Nam and Cha Soon Yoo; m. Hye Sook Choi 1953; two s. one d.; ed. Kook Min. Coll., Seoul, Seoul Nat. Univ. Oklahoma State and Stanford Univs.; with Bank of Korea 1952–54; Asst. Prof., Assoc. Prof., Prof., Dean of Econ. Dept., Kook Min Coll. 1954–64; Prof. Sogang Univ. and Dir. Research Inst. for Econ. and Business 1964–69; Minister of Finance 1969; Gov. for Korea, IMF, IBRD, ADB 1969–72, Chair. Bd. of Govs. Asian Devt. Bank 1970; Deputy Prime Minister and Minister of Econ. Planning Bd. 1974–78; Special Asst. for Econ. Affairs to the Pres. Jan.-Dec. 1979; Prime Minister of Repub. of Korea 1980–82; mem. Advisory Cttee. on Evaluation of Econ. Devt. Plan, Nat. Mobilization Bd. 1964–69; Adviser to Korea Devt. Bank 1964–69; Assoc. mem. Econ. and Scientific Council 1967–69. *Publications:* History of Economic Theory 1958, Price Theory 1965, History of Economic Theory (co-author) 1962, The Determinants of Money Supply and Monetary Policy: in the case of Korea 1954–64 1966, Social Science Research and Population Policy (jt. author) 1980, Changes in the Pattern of Trade and Trade Policy in a Pacific Basin Community 1980. *Leisure interests:* reading, music appreciation.

NAMALIU, Rt. Hon. Sir Rabbie Langanai, K.C.M.G., P.C., M.A.; Papua New Guinea politician; b. 3 April 1947, Raluana, E. New Britain Prov.; s. of Darius Namaliu and Utul Ioan Namaliu; m. Margaret Nakikus 1978 (died 1993); two s. one step. d.; ed. Keravat High School, Univ. of Papua New Guinea; fmrly. scholar and fellow Univ. of Papua New Guinea; tutor and lecturer in History, Univ. of Papua New Guinea; Prin. Pvt. Sec. to Chief Minister 1974; fmr. Prov. Commr., East New Britain, and Chair. Public Services Comm.; held sr. positions in the Office of the Prime Minister and Leader of the Opposition under Mr. Somare; M.P. for Kokopo Open 1982–; Minister for Foreign Affairs and Trade 1982–84, for Primary Industry 1984–85; Deputy Leader Pangu Pati 1985–88, Leader 1988–92; Prime Minister 1988–92; Speaker Nat. Parl. 1994–; Sr. Minister for State 1997–98, for Petroleum and Energy Aug. 1998–; Pres. African Caribbean Pacific Council of Ministers 1984; Co-Pres. ACP/EEC Jt. Council of Ministers 1984; Vacation Scholar A.N.U. 1968; Visiting Fellow Univ. of Calif., Center for Pacific Studies, Santa Cruz, Calif., U.S.A. 1976; Hon. LL.D., M.A. (Victoria, B.C.) 1983; Independence Medal 1975, Queen's Silver Jubilee Medal 1977; Pacific Man of the Year 1988. *Leisure interests:* reading, walking, golf. *Address:* National Parliament, P.O. National Parliament, Waigani, National Capital District; P.O. Box 6655, Boroko, National Capital District, Papua New Guinea. *Telephone:* 3277752/54/55. *Fax:* 3277753.

NAMIR, Ora; Israeli politician; b. 1930; ed. Levinsky and Givat Hashlosha teacher seminaries, Hunter Coll., NY; officer Israel Defence Forces, War of Independence; Sec. Mapai Knesset faction; Sec. Coalition Exec.; Sec.-Gen. Na'amat (Working Women and Volunteers Org.) 1967; Chair. Prime Minister's Cttee. on the Status of Women 1975, Educ. and Culture Cttee. 1977–84, Labour and Social Welfare Cttee. 1984–92; Minister of the Environment 1992–94; fmr. Minister of Labour; mem. Knesset 1973–. *Address:* c/o Knesset, Jerusalem, Israel.

NAMPHY, Lieut.-Gen. Henri; Haitian politician and soldier; fmr. Chief of Haitian Gen. Staff; Head of State and Pres. Nat. Governing Council (formed after overthrow of Jean-Claude Duvalier (q.v.) in coup) 1986–88; Vice-Chair. Legis. 1987–88; now living in exile in Dominica.

NANAYEV, Akmatbek Kasymkulovich; Kyrgyzstan politician; b. 10 Feb. 1941; m. Valentina Petrovna Lyubayeva; one s. one d.; ed. Kyrgyz State Univ., Alma-Ata Higher CP School; metalworker Factory of Physical Equipment 1958–71; Sec. Frunzensky Dist. Comsomol Cttee. 1971–73; second sec. CP Cttee. Device Production Factory 1974–83; Chair. Exec. Bd. Okryabrsky Dist. Cttee. Soviet of people's deputies in Frunze 1983–90; First Sec., Exec. Bd. Frunze City Soviet of People's Deputies 1990–91; Perm. Rep. of Kyrgyz S.S.R. to U.S.S.R. Council of Ministers 1991; Plenipotentiary Rep. of Kyrgyzstan to Russia Nov. 1991–; Amb. to Russia (also accred. to Azerbaijan, Armenia and Georgia) 1992–. *Address:* Kyrgyzstan Embassy, Bolshaya Ordynka str. 64, 109017 Moscow, Russia. *Telephone:* (095) 237-46-01; 237-48-82 (Office).

NANDAN, Satya Nand, C.B.E.; Fijian diplomatist; b. 10 July 1936, Suva; s. of Shiu Nandan and Rajukar Nandan; m. 1st Sreekumari Nandan 1966 (died 1971); m. 2nd Zarine Merchant 1976; one s.; ed. John McGlashan Coll. Dunedin, N.Z., D.A.V. Coll. Suva and Univs. of Wellington and London; called to Bar, Lincoln's Inn, London 1965; barrister and solicitor, Supreme Court of Fiji 1966–; pvt. law practice, Suva 1965–70; Counsellor then Amb. Perm. Mission of Fiji to UN 1970–76; Leader, Fiji del. to Third UN Conf. on Law of Sea 1973–82; Amb. to EEC, (also accred. to Belgium, France, Italy, Luxembourg, Netherlands) 1976–80; Perm. Sec. for Foreign Affairs, Fiji 1981–83; UN Under-Sec.-Gen. for Ocean Affairs and the Law of the Sea and

Special Rep. of UN Sec.-Gen. for Law of the Sea 1983–92; mem. Perm. Mission of Fiji at UN 1993–; Chair. UN Conf. on Straddling Fish Stocks and Highly Migratory Fish Stocks 1993–95; Rep. of Fiji to Int. Seabed Authority 1994–95; Int. Law Adviser to Govt. of Fiji 1994–95; del. to numerous int. confs. etc.; Visiting lecturer, Col. Univ. New York and Univ. of Va., Charlottesville; Sr. Visiting Fellow, US Inst. of Peace 1992; many other professional appts.; Hon.LL.D. (Newfoundland) 1995. *Publications include:* Commentary on 1982 UN Convention on Law of Sea (7 vols.) (ed.); numerous articles on UN and aspects of Law of the Sea. *Leisure interests:* reading, swimming, watching sports in general. *Address:* One United Nations Plaza, 26th Floor, New York, NY 10017 (Office); 301 E 48th Street, New York, NY 10017, U.S.A. (Home).

NANO, Fatos Thanas; Albanian politician; b. 1952, Tirana; fmr. Sec.-Gen. of Council of Ministers, Deputy Chair. Jan.–Feb. 1991, Chair. 1991–92; Leader Socialist Party of Albania 1991; stripped of immunity from prosecution to face charges of embezzlement July 1993; convicted of misappropriation of state funds, of dereliction of duty and of falsifying state documents April 1994; sentenced to 12 years' imprisonment, released and pardoned March 1997; Prime Minister of Albania 1997–98. *Address:* c/o Council of Ministers, Këshilli i Ministrave, Tirana, Albania.

NAPIER, John; British stage designer; b. 1 March 1944; s. of James Edward Thomas Napier and Lorrie Napier (née Godbold); m. 1st Andreanne Neofitou; one s. one d.; m. 2nd Donna King; one s. one d.; ed. Hornsey Coll. of Art, Cen. School of Arts and Crafts; Production designs include: A Penny for a Song, Fortune and Men's Eyes, The Ruling Class, The Fun War, Muzeeka, George Frederick (ballet), La Turista, Cancer, Isabel's a Jezebel, Mister, The Foursome, The Lovers of Viorne, Lear, Jump, Sam Sam, Big Wolf, The Devils (English Nat. Opera), Equus, The Party, Knuckle, Kings and Clowns, Lohengrin (Covent Garden), Macbeth, Richard III, Hedda Gabler, Macbeth, Twelfth Night, The Greeks, Nicholas Nickleby, Cats, Starlight Express, Time, Les Misérables, Miss Saigon, Sunset Boulevard, Burning Blue, Jesus Christ Superstar, Idomeneo (Glyndebourne), Who's Afraid of Virginia Woolf?, An Enemy of the People, Peter Pan, Martin Guerre; designer, co-dir. Siegfried & Roy Show, Las Vegas 1990; film designs include Hook 1991; numerous stage and TV set designs worldwide. *Leisure interest:* photography. *Address:* c/o M.L.R., Douglas House, 16–18 Douglas Street, London, SW1P 4PB, England. *Telephone:* 0171-834 4646. *Fax:* 0171-834 4949.

NAPIER, Rt. Rev. Wilfrid Fox, B.PH., B.TH., M.A.; South African ecclesiastic; b. 8 March 1941, Matatiele; s. of Thomas D. Napier and Mary Davey; ed. Little Flower School, Ixopo, Natal, Univ. of Ireland, Galway and Catholic Univ., Louvain, Belgium; ordained priest 1970; Asst. Pastor, St. Anthony's Parish, Lusikisiki 1971; Parish Priest, St. Francis Parish, Tabankulu 1973; Apostolic Administrator, Diocese of Kokstad 1978; Bishop of Kokstad 1981; Archbishop of Durban 1992–; Vice-Pres. S. African Catholic Bishops' Conf. 1984, Pres. 1987–92, First Vice-Pres. 1994–. *Leisure interests:* gardening, tennis, golf, D.I.Y. mechanics, fishing. *Address:* Archbishop's House, 154 Gordon Road, Durban 4001; P.O. Box 47489, Greyville 4023, South Africa. *Telephone:* (31) 3031417. *Fax:* (31) 231848.

NAPOLI, Jacopo; Italian composer; b. 26 Aug. 1911; ed. S. Pietro a Majella Conservatoire of Music, Naples; obtained diplomas in Composition, Organ and Piano; held Chair of Counterpoint and Fugue at Cagliari Conservatoire, and at Naples Conservatoire; Dir. S. Pietro a Majella Conservatoire of Music, Naples 1955, 1962; Dir. Giuseppe Verdi Conservatoire of Music, Milan –1972, then Dir. St. Cecilia Conservatory, Rome; Dir. Scarlatti Arts Soc. 1955–; works performed in Germany, Spain and on Italian radio. *Works:* (operas) Il Malato Immaginario 1939, Miseria e Nobiltà 1946, Un curioso accidente 1950, Masaniello 1953, I Pescatori 1954, Il Tesoro 1958, (oratorio) The Passion of Christ, Il Rosario 1962, Il Povero Diavolo 1963, Piccola Cantata del Venerdì Santo 1964, (orchestral works) Overture to Love's Labours Lost 1935, Preludio di Caccia 1935, La Festa di Anacapri 1940. *Address:* 55 Via Andrea da Isernia, I-80122, Naples, Italy.

NARANTSATSRALT, Janlav, PH.D.; Mongolian politician; b. 10 June 1957, Ulan Bator; s. of T. Janlav and D. Orgo; m. M. Altantsetseg 1978; two s.; ed. Moscow Land Tenure Systems Univ., Nat. Univ. of Mongolia; Sr. Engineer and Gen. Specialist Land Tenure Inst., Ministry of Agriculture 1981–89; Scientific Researcher and Head of Dept., Land Policy Inst. 1989–91; Head Urban Devt. and Planning Bd., Ulan Bator Municipality 1991–95; Sr. Specialist Office of the Mayor, Ulan Bator 1995–96; Head Land Dept., Ulan Bator 1996; Acting Mayor Ulan Bator 1996–97, Mayor 1997–98; Prime Minister of Mongolia 1998–; Medal of Labour, Anniversary Medals. *Publications:* Land Management Issues in the New Market, Economic Conditions in Mongolia. *Leisure interest:* travelling. *Address:* State House, Ulan Bator 12, Mongolia. *Telephone:* 976 1 372923. *Fax:* 976 1 328329.

NARASIMHA RAO, P. V., B.SC., LL.B.; Indian politician; b. 28 June 1921, Karimnagar, Andhra Pradesh; widower; three s. five d.; ed. Osmania, Bombay and Nagpur Univs.; mem. Andhra Pradesh Legis. Ass. 1957–77, Minister, Govt. of Andhra Pradesh 1962–71, Chief Minister 1971–73; Gen. Sec. All India Congress Cttee. 1975–76; mem. Lok Sabha (Congress (I) Party) 1977–, Prime Minister of India 1991–96, numerous other portfolios; Acting Leader then Pres. Congress (I) 1991–96; Minister of External Affairs, Govt. of India 1980–85, of Defence and Acting Minister of Planning 1985, of Human Resources Devt. and Health and Family Welfare 1985–88, of Human Resources Devt. Feb.–June 1988, of External Affairs 1988–90; Chair. Telugu Acad., Andhra Pradesh 1968–74; Vice.-Pres. Dakshin Bharat Hindi Prachar Sabha 1972. *Publications:* translations into Telugu and Hindi of several famous works; many articles in journals on political matters and allied subjects. *Leisure interests:* Indian Philosophy and culture, writing poems in Telugu and Hindi, music, theatre and cinema. *Address:* Vangara Post, Karimnagar District, Andhra Pradesh, India.

NARASIMHAM, Maidavolu; Indian official; b. 3 June 1927, Bangalore; s. of M. Seshachelapati; m. Shanthy Sundaresan; one s.; ed. Presidency Coll., Madras, and St. John's Coll., Cambridge; joined Reserve Bank of India, Bombay 1950, Sec. 1967, Gov. 1977; Chief of S. Asia Div., IMF 1960–63, Exec. Dir. of IMF for India, Bangladesh and Sri Lanka 1980–82; Exec. Dir. IBRD 1978–80; Additional Sec. Ministry of Finance 1972, Sec. Banking Dept. 1976–78, Sec. Dept. of Econ. Affairs 1982; Finance Sec., Govt. of India 1983; Prin. Admin. Staff Coll. of India, Hyderabad 1983–85, Chair. 1985–; Vice-Pres. Asian Devt. Bank, Manila 1985–88; Norton Prize (Madras Univ.). *Leisure interests:* reading, music. *Address:* "Sukruti", 8-2-681/7, Road No. 12, Banjara Hills, Hyderabad 500 034, India (Home). *Telephone:* (40) 3310994 (Office); 3396511 (Home). *Fax:* (40) 3310994/3312954.

NARAYAN, Rasipuram Krishnaswamy; Indian writer; b. 10 Oct. 1906; ed. Maharaja's Coll., Mysore; Hon. Litt. D. (Leeds) 1967; Hon. mem. American Acad. and Inst. of Arts and Letters 1982. *Publications:* (all in English), novels: Swami and Friends 1935, The Bachelor of Arts, The Dark Room, The English Teacher, Mr. Sampath, The Financial Expert, Waiting for the Mahatma, The Guide 1958, The Man-Eater of Malgudi 1961, Gods, Demons and Others 1964, The Sweet-Vendor 1967, The Painter of Signs 1977, A Tiger for Malgudi 1983, Talkative Man 1986, The World of Nagaraj 1990; short stories: An Astrologer's Day, The Lawley Road, A Horse and Two Goats, Malgudi Days, The Ramayana (prose trans.) 1972, Under the Banyan Tree and Other Stories 1985, The Grandmother's Tale and Other Stories 1993; My Days (autobiog.) 1974. *Address:* c/o Anthony Shiel Associates, 43 Doughty Street, London, WC1N 2LF, England; Yadavagiri, Mysore 2, India.

NARAYANAN, Kocheril Raman, M.A.; Indian diplomatist; b. 4 Feb. 1921, Ozhavoor, Kerala; s. of the late Raman Vaidyan; m. Usha Ma Tint Tint 1951; two d.; ed. Travancore Univ. and London School of Econs., Univ. of London; Lecturer in English Literature, Travancore Univ. 1943; worked in Editorial Dept. of Hindu newspaper, Madras 1944–45; Reporter, Times of India 1945; London Corresp. of Social Welfare (weekly), Bombay 1945–48; entered Foreign Service 1949; Joint Dir. of Orientation Centre for Foreign Technicians, Delhi School of Econs. 1954–55; served Rangoon, Tokyo, London and in Ministry of External Affairs 1949–60; Acting High Commr. in Australia 1961–62; Consul-Gen., Hanoi 1962–63; Dir. of China Div., Ministry of External Affairs 1963–67; Amb. to Thailand 1967–69; Joint Sec. for Policy Planning in Ministry 1969–70; Jawaharlal Nehru Fellow 1970–72; Hon. Prof., Jawaharlal Nehru Univ. 1970–72; Amb. to Turkey 1973–75; Additional Sec. for Policy Planning Div. of Ministry 1975–76; Sec. for the East, Ministry of External Affairs April–May 1976; Amb. to People's Repub. of China 1976–78; mem. Indian del. to UN Gen. Assembly 1979; Amb. to U.S.A. 1980–83; mem. Lok Sabha for Ottapalath, Kerala 1984–; Minister of State for Planning, Govt. of India 1984–85, for External Affairs 1985–86, for Atomic Energy, Space, Electronics and Ocean Devt. 1986–87, for Science and Tech. 1986–89; Vice-Pres. of India 1992–97, concurrently Chair. Rajya Sabha (Council of States); Pres. of India July 1997–; Vice-Pres. Council of Scientific and Industrial Research 1986–; Vice-Chancellor Jawaharlal Nehru University 1979–80; Co-Chair. Indo-U.S. Sub-Comm. on Educ. and Culture 1980; mem. Indian Council for Social Science Research, New Delhi, Exec. Council, Children's Book Trust, Inst. of Defence Studies and Analysis, Indian Asscn. of Social Science Inst.; Hon. Fellow, L.S.E. 1972–; Hon. D.Sc. (Toledo) 1987. *Publications:* India and America—Essays in Understanding, Images and Insights, Non-Alignment in Contemporary International Relations (with Prof. K.P. Mishra), and other works on int. relations, Indian politics, literary subjects. *Leisure interests:* literature, philosophy. *Address:* Office of the President, Rashtrapati Bhavan, New Delhi 110 004, India. *Telephone:* (11) 3015321. *Fax:* (11) 3017290.

NARITA, Yoriaki, D.JUR.; Japanese professor of law; b. Tokyo; s. of Masaji Narita and Masako Narita; m. Akiko Narita 1956; two d.; lecturer, Faculty of Econs., Yokohama Nat. Univ. 1929, Asst. Prof. 1933, Prof. 1943, Dean of Econs. 1982–86, Dir. and Prof., Grad. School of Int. and Business Law 1990–93; Man. Dir. Japan Energy Law Inst. 1993–. *Publications:* Introduction to Modern Administrative Law, Legal Theories and Reform of Local Self-government, Land Policy and Law. *Leisure interest:* collecting stamps. *Address:* 2-20-2, Tomigaya, Shibuya-ku, Tokyo 151, Japan.

NARJES, Karl-Heinz; German politician and public servant; b. 30 Jan. 1924, Soltau; m.; two c.; ed. Hamburg Univ.; submarine commdr. during World War II; with Minstry of Foreign Affairs; Chef de Cabinet to Pres. of European Comm. 1963; Dir.-Gen. Press and Information Directorate of Comm. 1968–69; Minister of the Econ. and of Transport, Schleswig-Holstein Province 1969–73; mem. Bundestag 1972–88, Bundestag Foreign Affairs Comm. 1972–76, 1980–88, Bundestag Econ. Affairs Comm. (Pres. 1972–76, 1980–); Commr. for Internal Market and Industrial Innovation, Customs Union, Environment and Consumer Protection and Nuclear Safety, Comm. of the European Communities 1981–84, for Economic Affairs and Employment 1985–86, for Industrial Affairs, Information Tech., Science and Research, Jt. Research Centre 1986–88, Vice-Pres. Comm. of the European Communities 1985–88.

NARLIKAR, Jayant Vishnu, PH.D., SC.D.; Indian scientist; b. 19 July 1938, Kolhapur; s. of Prof. and Mrs. V. V. Narlikar; m. Mangala S. Rajwade 1966; three d.; ed. Banaras Hindu Univ. and Fitzwilliam Coll., Cambridge; Berry Ramsey Fellow, King's Coll., Cambridge 1963–69; Grad. Staff Mem., Inst. of Theoretical Astronomy, Cambridge 1966–72; Sr. Research Fellow, King's Coll. 1969–72; Jawaharlal Nehru Fellow 1973–75; mem. Science Advisory Council to the Prime Minister 1986–90; Dir. Inter-Univ. Centre for Astronomy and Astrophysics, Pune 1988–; Hon. Prof. Jawaharlal Nehru Centre for Advanced Scientific Research; Homi Bhabha Prof. 1998–; Pres. Cosmology Comm. of IAU 1994–(97); Fellow, Indian Nat. Science Acad. (INSA), Assoc. Royal Astronomical Soc., London; awarded Padma Bhushan by the Indian Govt. 1965, S. S. Bhatnagar Award 1978, Rashtrabhushan Award of FIE Foundation 1981, Rathindra Award 1985, INSA Vainu Bappu Award 1988, INSA Indira Gandhi Award for Science Popularization 1990, UNESCO Kalniga Award 1996. *Publications:* articles on cosmology, general relativity and gravitation, quantum theory, astrophysics etc. in the Proceedings of the Royal Soc., London, The Monthly Notices of the Royal Astronomical Soc., London, The Astrophysical Journal, Nature, Observatory and scientific articles in various magazines; Action at a distance in Physics and Cosmology (with Sir F. Hoyle (q.v.)) 1974, The Structure of the Universe 1977, General Relativity and Cosmology 1978, The Physics Astronomy Frontier (with Sir F. Hoyle) 1980, Violent Phenomena in the Universe 1982, The Lighter Side of Gravity 1982, Introduction to Cosmology 1983, From Black Clouds to Black Holes 1985, Gravity Gauge Theories and Quantum Cosmology (with T. Padmanabhan) 1986, The Primeval Universe 1988. *Address:* IUCAA, Post Bag 4, Ganeshkhind, Pune 411007, India. *Telephone:* (212) 351414. *Fax:* (212) 356417.

NARR, Karl Josef, DR. PHIL.; German professor of prehistory and protohistory; b. 9 June 1921, Düsseldorf; s. of Otto Narr and Gertrud Busch; m. Theresia Pelzer 1952; one s. one d.; ed. Univ. of Bonn; part-time collaborator, State Museum, Bonn and grantee, German Research Council 1950–52; Asst. Seminary of Prehistory and Protohistory, Univ. of Göttingen 1953–59, lecturer, Assoc. Prof. Univ. of Göttingen 1959–65; Prof. of Prehistory and Protohistory, Univ. of Münster 1965–86, Prof. Emer. 1986–; mem. Rheinisch-Westfälische Akad. der Wissenschaften 1976–, Deputy Sec. 1978–79; Fellow, German Archaeological Inst. 1965– (Corresp. mem. 1956–65). *Publications:* six books. *Address:* Nerzweg 48, 48157 Münster/Westfalen, Germany. *Telephone:* (0251) 248148. *Fax:* (0251) 248148.

NARS, Kari, DR.SC.; Finnish banker; m.; two c.; ed. Univ. of Helsinki, Helsinki Swedish School of Econs.; economist, Bank of Finland 1964–66, Sec. of Bank 1967, Head Foreign Exchange Policy Dept. 1972–75, Dir. (Int.) 1977–83; Exec. Man. Dir. Bank of Helsinki 1984–85; Economist, IMF, Washington, D.C. 1967–71; Dir. Council of Econ. Orgs. 1975–76; Dir. of Finance, Ministry of Finance 1986–91, 1994–; Exec. Dir. EBRD, London 1991–94; Chair Admin. Cttee., Social Devt. Fund of Council of Europe 1993–; Alt. Gov. for Finland, IMF 1981–82; mem. Bd. Nordic Investment Bank 1989–91; Co-Chair. Govt. Borrowers' Forum 1988–91. *Publications include:* Corporate Foreign Exchange Strategies 1980, Foreign Financing and Foreign Exchange Strategy (Co-author) 1981, Financial Sector Study on Mozambique – a World Bank study (Co-author) 1992, Cross Currency Swaps (contrib.) 1992; numerous articles and speeches. *Address:* Ministry of Finance, Snellmaninkatu 1A, 00170 Helsinki, Finland. *Telephone:* (90) 160 1.

NARVEKAR, Prabhakar A.; Indian international civil servant; b. 5 Jan. 1932, Mumbai; s. of Ramkrishna Manjunath Narvekar and Indira Narvekar; m. (wife deceased); one s. one d.; ed. Bombay, Columbia and Oxford Univs.; Research Asst. IMF 1953; subsequently held various positions in Asian and European Depts. of IMF; Dir. Asian Dept. IMF 1986–94; Deputy Man. Dir. IMF 1994–97; Special Adviser to Pres. of Indonesia 1997–. *Leisure interest:* reading. *Address:* 600 New Hampshire Avenue, N.W., Suite No. 640, The Watergate, Washington, DC 20037, U.S.A. *Telephone:* (202) 298-6841. *Fax:* (202) 298-6875.

NASCIMENTO, Lopo Fortunato Ferreira do; Angolan politician; b. 10 July 1940, Luanda; s. of Vaz I. do Nascimento and Arminda F. do Nascimento; m. Maria do Carmo Assis 1969; two s. one d.; mem. Presidential Collegiate in transitional Govt. before independence from Portugal Jan.–Nov. 1975; Prime Minister of Angola 1975–78; Minister of Internal Trade 1977–78, of Foreign Trade 1979–82, of Planning 1980–86; Deputy Exec. Sec. UN ECA, Addis Ababa 1979; Head Fifth Mil. Region 1986–90; Gov. Huila Prov. 1986–90; Presidential Adviser for Special Political Affairs 1990–; Head Govt. Del. at negotiations on a peace agreement for Angola 1991; Minister of Territorial Admin. 1991; Sec. Gen Movimento Popular de Libertação de Angola (MPLA) –1993; Deputy Speaker of Parl. *Leisure interests:* music, writing, walking. *Address:* Ambuíla Street 47, P.O. Box 136, Luanda, Angola. *Telephone:* 321.611, 322.522. *Fax:* 321.611, 322.545.

NASH, Charles; Irish boxer; b. 10 May 1951, Londonderry, N. Ireland; s. of Alexander Nash and of late Bridget Nash; m. Elizabeth Nash; one s. one d.; ed. St. Joseph's Secondary School, Londonderry; five times Irish amateur lightweight champion; boxed for Ireland in Olympic Games and European championships; won Irish title in first professional contest Oct. 1975; won vacant British lightweight title v. Johnny Claydon Feb. 1978; won vacant European title v. Andre Holyk June 1979, retained it v. Ken Buchanan Dec. 1979; relinquished British and European titles Jan. 1980 to challenge, unsuccessfully, for world title v. Jim Watt, Glasgow March 1980; regained European title from Francisco Leon Dec. 1980; 25 fights, 23 wins. *Leisure interests:* football, snooker, table tennis, coaching amateur boxers.

NASH, David; British sculptor; b. 14 Nov. 1945, Surrey; s. of Lieut.-Col. W. C. E. Nash and Dora (née Vickery); m. Claire Langdown 1972; two s.; ed. Brighton Coll., Kingston Art School and Chelsea School of Art; has exhibited widely in Britain, Europe, U.S.A. and Japan; first exhbn. Briefly Cooked Apples, York Festival 1973; one-man shows include Loosely Held Grain, Arnolfini Gallery, Bristol 1976, 30 days 2 beech, Kroller Muller Museum, Netherlands 1982, Ki No Inoichi: Ni No Katachi, Japan 1984, Spirit of Three Seasons, Otoineppu, Japan (touring exhbn.) 1993–94, Voyages and Vessels, Joslyn Art Museum, U.S.A. (touring exhbn.) 1994–95; major group exhbns. British Art Now, Guggenheim Museum, New York 1980, Aspects of British Art Today, Japan 1982; works in several public collections including Tate Gallery and Guggenheim Museum. *Publication:* Forms into Time. *Address:* Capel Rhiw, Blaenau Ffestiniog, Gwynedd, Wales, LL41 3NT; c/o Annely Juda Fine Art, 23 Dering Street, London, W1R 9AA, England. *Telephone:* 0171-629 7578 (London). *Fax:* (01766) 831179 (Blaenau Ffestiniog); 0171-491 2139 (London).

NASH, John Forbes, Jr., PH.D.; American mathematician and economist; b. 13 June 1928, Bluefield, W. Va.; s. of John F. Nash and Margaret Virginia Martin Nash; m. Alicia Larde 1957; one s.; ed. Carnegie Mellon Univ., Princeton Univ.; Research Asst., Instructor, Princeton Univ. 1950–51; Moore Instructor, M.I.T. 1951–53, Asst. Prof. 1953–57, Assoc. Prof. 1957–59; Research Assoc. in Mathematics 1966–67; Visiting Research Collaborator, Princeton Univ. 1959–, visiting mem. Inst. of Advanced Study 1956–57, 1961–62, 1963–64; mem. Nat. Acad. of Sciences 1996; Fellow of Econometric Soc., Sloan Fellow, N.S.F. Fellow, Westinghouse Scholar; awarded Von Neumann Medal of Operations Research Soc. of America; shared Nobel Prize for Econs. 1994 for pioneering work on game theory; Business Week Award, Erasmus Univ., Rotterdam 1998; Leroy P. Steele Prize, American Mathematical Soc. 1999. *Publications:* articles on econometric and mathematical theory. *Address:* Department of Mathematics, Princeton University, Fine Hall, Princeton, N.J. 08544, U.S.A.

NASHASHIBI, Nassiriddin; journalist; b. 1924, Palestine; ed. American Univ. of Beirut; Arab Office, Jerusalem 1945–47; Chief Chamberlain, Amman, Jordan 1951; Dir. Gen. Hashemite Broadcasting 1952; Ed. Akhbar al Youm, Cairo; Chief Ed. Al-Gumhuriyah, 1959–65; Rep. of the Arab League 1965–67; Diplomatic Ed. Al-Ahram; freelance journalist in Europe and the Middle East. *Publications:* What Happened in the Middle East 1958, Political Short Stories 1959, Return Ticket to Palestine 1960, Some Sand 1962, An Arab in China 1964, Roving Ambassador 1970, The Ink is Very Black 1976, Order of the Jordanian Star. *Address:* 55 Avenue de Champel, Geneva, Switzerland.

NASIR, Agha, M.A.; Pakistani television executive and playwright; b. 9 Feb. 1937, Meerut, U.P., India; s. of Ali Ahmad Khan and Ghafari Begum; m. Safia Sultana 1957; one s. two d.; Programmes Man. Pakistani TV 1967–68, Additional Gen. Man. 1967, Gen. Man. 1969–72, Dir. Programmes Admin. 1972–86, Deputy Man. Dir. 1986–87, Man. Dir. 1987–88; Man. Dir. Nat. Film Devt. Corpn. 1979; Dir.-Gen. Pakistan Broadcasting Corpn. 1989–92; Chief Exec. Shalimar Recording Co. 1992–; recipient of numerous awards for radio and TV plays; Pride of Performance award from Pres. of Pakistan for services in field of broadcasting 1993. *Publications:* Saat Dramey (plays), Television Dramey (TV plays). *Leisure interest:* reading. *Address:* House No. 23, Street No. 3, F-8/3, Islamabad, Pakistan (Home). *Telephone:* 852619; 263685 (Home).

NASIR, Amir Ibrahim; Maldivian politician; b. 2 Sept. 1926, Malé; s. of Ahmed Didi and Aishath Didi; m. 1st Aishath Zubair 1950; m. 2nd Mariyam Saeed 1953; m. 3rd Naseema Mohamed Kalegefaan 1969; four s. one d.; ed. Ceylon (now Sri Lanka); Under-Sec. of State to Minister of Finance and to Minister of Public Safety, Repub. of Maldives 1954; Minister of Public Safety 1956, of Home Affairs Aug. 1957; Prime Minister (1st term) Dec. 1957, Prime Minister (2nd term) and Minister of Home Affairs, Finance, Educ., Trade, External Affairs and Public Safety Aug. 1959, Prime Minister (3rd term) and Minister of Finance, Educ., External Affairs and Public Safety 1964; Pres. of the Repub. of Maldives 1968–78; in exile in Singapore, tried in absentia 1980 on charges of embezzling public funds and illegally collecting taxes, banished for 25 years, granted pardon by Pres. Gayoom (q.v.) July 1990; Award of Nishan Ghazee ge Izzatheri Veriya, Ranna Bandeiri Kilegefaan; Hon. K.C.M.G. *Leisure interests:* fishing, yachting, gardening.

NASON, John William, A.M.; American educator; b. 9 Feb. 1905, St. Paul, Minn.; s. of Albert J. Nason and Mary E. Eaton; m. 1st Bertha D. White 1935 (died 1955); m. 2nd Elizabeth M. Knapp 1957; two s. one step-s. two step-d.; ed. Chicago Latin School, Phillips Exeter Acad., Carleton Coll., Yale Divinity School, Harvard Graduate School, Oxford Univ.; Instructor in Phil. Swarthmore Coll. 1931–34, Asst. Prof. 1934–40, Pres. 1940–53; Pres. Foreign Policy Asscn. 1953–62, mem. Bd. of Dirs. 1971–80; Pres Carleton Coll. 1962–70; Asst. to American Sec. Rhodes Trust 1934–40; Pres. UN Council Philadelphia 1942–45, Vice-Pres. 1945–47; Pres. World Affairs Council of Philadelphia 1949–51, 1952–53; Fellow and mem. Bd. of Dirs. Soc. for Religion in Higher Educ.; Trustee, Phillips Exeter Acad. 1946–50, 1952–62, Edward W. Hazen Foundation 1945–67, 1968–78, Vassar Coll. 1954–62, Eisenhower Exchange Fellowships 1953–65, Danforth Foundation 1961–68; mem. Educator's Advisory Comm. Esso Educ. Foundation 1964–68; mem.

Visiting Comm. Harvard Graduate School of Educ. 1975–82; Dir. of Studies, Asscn. of Governing Bds. of Univs. and Colls. 1973–75; Dir. of Study of Foundation Trustees for Council on Foundations 1975–77; Dir. of Study of Presidential Selection and Assessment, Asscn. of Governing Bds. 1977–80; Educ. Consultant 1979–; Bd. of Dirs. Adirondack Conservancy Comm. 1977–90, New York State Conservancy 1983–90; Gov. Bruce L. Crary Foundation 1979–93; Hon. LL.D. (Pennsylvania, Carleton, Swarthmore, Hamilton, Brandeis, Johns Hopkins); Litt.D. (Mühlenberg Coll., Hahnemann Medical School and Coll.); L.H.D. (Dropsie Coll., St. Olaf Coll. and Coll. of Wooster, State Univ. of N.Y.). *Publications:* American Higher Education in 1980—Some Basic Issues 1965, Crises of the University 1970, The Future of Trusteeship: The Role and Responsibilities of College and University Boards 1975, Trustees and the Future of Foundations 1977, Presidential Search: A Guide to the Process of Selecting and Appointing College and University Presidents 1979, Presidential Assessment: A Challenge to College and University Leadership 1980, The Nature of Trusteeship 1982, Foundation Trusteeship: Service in the Public Interest 1989. *Leisure interests:* woodworking, reading. *Address:* 12 Crosslands Drive, Kennett Square, PA 19348, U.S.A. *Telephone:* (610) 388-1392.

NASR, Farouk Sayf an-; Egyptian politician; b. Dec. 1922; fmr. Pres. Supreme Constitutional Court; Dir. Tech. Office, Ministry of Justice; worked on the preparation of Laws, on Nationalist Councils; Minister of Justice 1987–. *Address:* Ministry of Justice, Justice Building, (Lazoughli) Cairo, Egypt. *Telephone:* (02) 31176. *Fax:* (02) 3555700.

NASR, Seyyed Hossein, M.S., PH.D.; Iranian/American professor of Islamic studies; b. 7 April 1933, Tehran; s. of Valiallah Nasr and Ashraf Kia; m. Soussan Daneshvari 1958; one s. one d.; ed. Massachusetts Inst. of Tech. and Harvard Univ.; Teaching Asst. Harvard Univ. 1955–58, Visiting Prof. 1962, 1965; Assoc. Prof. of History of Science and Philosophy, Tehran Univ. 1958–63, Prof. 1963–79, Dean, Faculty of Letters 1968–72, Vice-Chancellor 1970–71; Chancellor (Pres.) Aryamehr Univ. 1972–75; First Prof. of Islamic Studies, American Univ. of Beirut 1964–65; Prof. of Islamic Studies, Temple Univ. 1979–84; Univ. Prof. of Islamic Studies, George Washington Univ. 1984–; Visiting Prof. Princeton Univ. 1975, Univ. of Utah 1979; A. D. White Prof.-at-Large, Cornell Univ. 1991–; Founder and first Pres. Iranian Acad. of Philosophy 1974–79; mem. Inst. Int. de Philosophie, Greek Acad. of Philosophy, etc.; Dr. h.c. (Uppsala) 1977, (Lehigh) 1996. *Publications:* numerous books and some 250 articles in Persian, Arabic, English and French in leading int. journals. *Leisure interests:* classical music (both Western and Eastern), tennis, hiking. *Address:* 712 Gelman Library, The George Washington University, Washington, DC 20052, U.S.A. *Telephone:* (202) 994-5704. *Fax:* (202) 994-0458.

NASREEN, Taslima; Bangladeshi author; b. 1962, Mymensingh, E. Pakistan; m. 3rd (divorced); ed. Mymensingh Medical Coll., Dhaka Univ.; practised as a gynaecologist; columnist Ajker Kagoj 1989; left Bangladesh 1994, returned Oct. 1998; winner Sakharov Prize (European Parl.) 1994; *Publication:* Laija (Shame) (novel) 1993.

NĂSTASE, Adrian, LL.M., PH.D.; Romanian academic and politician; b. 22 June 1950, Bucharest; s. of Marin Năstase and Elena Năstase; m. Daniela Miculescu 1985; two s.; ed. Bucharest Univ.; Research Fellow, Inst. of Legal Research, Bucharest 1973–90; Prof. of Public Int. Law, Bucharest Univ. 1990–; Assoc. Prof. of Public Int. Law, Paris-Panthéon Sorborne I 1994–; Minister of Foreign Affairs 1990–92; Speaker Chamber of Deputies 1992–96, Deputy Speaker 1996–; Exec. Pres. Social Democracy Party of Romania 1992–; Vice-Pres. Asscn. of Int. Law and Int. Relations, Bucharest 1977–; Dir. of Studies, Int. Inst. of Human Rights, Strasbourg 1984; Pres. Titulescu European Foundation 1990–92 (Hon. Pres. 1992–); Exec. Pres. Euro-Atlantic Centre, Bucharest 1991–92; Dir. of Research Romanian Inst. of Int. Studies (IRSI) 1994–; mem. Bd. of Dirs. Inst. for East-West Studies, New York 1991–96; mem. Human Rights Information and Documentation System; lecturer at numerous univs. and insts. of int. relations and human rights and speaker at many int. confs.; mem. French Soc. of Int. Law 1984–, American Soc. of Int. Law; Nicolae Titulescu Prize, Romanian Acad. 1994, The Political Man of 1995, Turkish Businessmen's Asscn.; Order of Diplomatic Service Merit 1991, Gwanghwa Medal, Repub. of Korea, Grande Croix de Mérite, Sovereign Order of Malta 1992. *Publications include:* Human Rights: an End-of-the-Century Religion 1992, International Law: Achievements and Prospects (co-author) 1992, Human Rights, Civil Society, Parliamentary Diplomacy 1994, Public International Law (co-author) 1995, Nicolae Titulescu—our contemporary 1995, Parliamentary Humour 1996, International Economic Law II 1996, Romania and the New World Architecture 1996, Documenta universale (with law documents) 1997; *c.* 240 articles and papers. *Leisure interests:* hunting, modern art, collecting antiques, gardening, tennis. *Address:* Parliament Palace, 13 September Street no. 1, s. 5, Bucharest, Romania. *Telephone:* (1) 613.14.50. *Fax:* (1) 312.24.36.

NĂSTASE, Ilie; Romanian lawn tennis player; b. 19 July 1946, Bucharest; m. 1st; one d.; m. 2nd Alexandra King 1984; nat. champion (13–14 age group) 1959, (15–16 age group) 1961, (17–18 age group) 1963, 1964; won the Masters Singles Event, Paris 1971, Barcelona 1972, Boston 1973, Stockholm 1975; winner of singles at Cannes 1967, Travemünde 1967, 1969, Gauhati 1968, Madras 1968, 1969, New Delhi 1968, 1969, Viareggio 1968, Barranquilla 1969, Coruna 1969, Budapest 1969, Denver 1969, Salisbury 1970, Rome 1970, 1973, Omaha 1971, 1972, Richmond 1971, Hampton 1971, Nice 1971, 1972, Monte Carlo 1971, 1972, Baastad 1971, Wembley 1971, Stockholm 1971, Istanbul 1971, Forest Hills 1972, Baltimore 1972, Madrid 1972, Toronto 1972, South Orange 1972, Seattle 1972, Roland Garros 1973, U.S. Open 1973; winner of doubles at Roland Garros (with Ion Ţiriac) 1970, Wimbledon (with Rosemary Casals) 1970, 1972, (with Jimmy Connors) 1975; winner of ILTF Grand Prix 1972, 1973; played 130 matches for the Romanian team in the Davis Cup; "Best Romanian sportsman of the year" 1969, 1970, 1971, 1973. *Publication:* Breakpoint 1986. *Address:* Clubul sportiv Steaua, Calea Plevnei 114, Bucharest, Romania.

NATADZE, Nodar; Georgian politician and academic; b. 27 May 1929, Tbilisi; s. of Revas Natadze and Tina (Tatiana) Natadze; m. Nana Gadyatska 1968; two s.; philologist and Head Dept., Inst. of Philosophy, Georgian Acad. of Sciences; Chair. Popular Front of Georgia 1989–, Nat. Cttee. of United Republican Party of Georgia; mem. Supreme Council (Parl.) of Georgia 1989–90, 1990–91, 1992–95. *Leisure interests:* mountaineering, skiing, literary criticism. *Address:* Panaskerteli str. 16, Apt. 57, Tbilisi, Georgia. *Telephone:* (8832) 381632.

NATHAN, Ove, D.PHIL.; Danish university administrator and professor; b. 12 Jan. 1926, Copenhagen; m. 1956; two d.; ed. Univ. of Copenhagen; Prof. of Physics, Univ. of Copenhagen 1970–96, Rector 1982–93; Jens Rosenkjaer Prize 1974. *Publications:* books on science, articles on nuclear physics, autobiog. *Address:* The Niels Bohr Institute, 17 Blegdamsvej, 2100 Copenhagen Ø (Office); Bernstorffsvej 144, 2900 Hellerup, Denmark. *Telephone:* 35 32 52 44 (Office); 39 62 75 11 (Home).

NATHANS, Daniel, M.D.; American professor of molecular biology and genetics; b. 30 Oct. 1928, Wilmington, Del.; s. of Samuel and Sarah (Levitan) Nathans; m. Joanne Gomberg 1956; three s.; ed. Univ. of Delaware, Washington Univ. School of Medicine; Intern, Columbia-Presbyterian Medical Center, New York, N.Y. 1954–55, Resident 1957–59; Clinical Assoc., Nat. Cancer Inst. 1955–57; Guest Investigator, Rockefeller Univ., New York 1959–62; Asst. Prof. of Microbiology, Johns Hopkins Univ. School of Medicine, Baltimore, Md. 1962–65, Assoc. Prof. 1965–67, Prof. 1967–82, Dir. Dept. of Microbiology 1972–82, Prof. of Molecular Biology and Genetics 1982–; Sr. Investigator, Howard Hughes Medical Inst. 1982–; Non-resident Fellow, Salk Inst., San Diego, Calif. 1983–94; mem. N.A.S., American Philosophical Soc., American Acad. of Arts and Sciences, European Molecular Biology Org.; mem. Pres.'s Council of Advisors for Science and Tech. 1990–93; American Cancer Soc. Scholar in Genetics Dept. of Weizmann Inst. of Science, Rehovoth, Israel 1969; shared Nobel Prize for Physiology or Medicine 1978 with Prof. Werner Arber and Dr. Hamilton Smith (qq.v.) for the application of restriction enzymes to problems of genetics; U.S. Nat. Medal of Science 1993. *Address:* Department of Molecular Biology and Genetics, Johns Hopkins University School of Medicine, 725 North Wolfe Street, Baltimore, MD 21205, U.S.A. *Telephone:* (410) 955-8445. *Fax:* (410) 955-9124.

NATOCHIN, Yury Viktorovich; Russian physiologist; b. 6 Dec. 1932, Charkov, U.S.S.R. (now Ukraine); s. of Victor Natochin and Frida Kohan; m. 1957; one s. one d.; ed. Novosibirsk Inst. of Medicine; jr., sr. researcher Inst. of Evolutionary Physiology and Biochemistry 1959–64, Head of lab. 1964–; Head Physiology Dept., St. Petersburg State Univ. 1996–; Corresp. mem. U.S.S.R. (now Russian) Acad. of Sciences 1987, mem. 1992, Acad.-Sec. Dept. of Physiology 1996–; Ed.-in-Chief Russian Journal of Physiology 1995–; main research in physiology of kidney, functional nephrology, molecular physiology; mem. Int. Acad. of Astronautics, Academia Europaea; Hon. mem. Hungarian Physiology Soc.; L. A. Orbeli Prize, S. Korolev Medal, Jan Parkinje Gold Medal, S. Rach Medal. *Publications include:* Ion-Regulating Function of Kidney 1976, Physiology of Kidney 1982, Problems of Evolutional Physiology of Water-Salt Transport 1984, Kidney 1997, Fluid and Electrolyte Regulation in Spaceflight 1998. *Leisure interests:* photography, poetry, travelling. *Address:* Sechenov Institute of Evolutionary Physiology and Biochemistry, 44 M. Thorez prospekt, 194223 St. Petersburg; Presidium of Russian Academy of Sciences, Leninsky prospekt 32A, 117334 Moscow, Russia. *Telephone:* (812) 552 30 86 (St. Petersburg), (095) 938 51 10 (Moscow). *Fax:* (812) 552 30 86 (St. Petersburg).

NATSUKI, Shizuko; Japanese novelist; b. 21 Dec. 1938, Tokyo; m. Idemitsu Natsuki 1963; one s. one d.; ed. Keio Univ.; screenplay for Only I Know (Japanese TV); Mystery Writers of Japan Prize 1973, Prix du Roman d'Aventures (France) 1989; Literary Award Fukuoka City 1972. *Publications:* 30 novels include The Angel Vanishes 1970, Disappearance 1973, Murder at Mt. Fuji 1984, The Third Lady 1987, Portal of the Wind 1990; 220 novelettes and short stories. *Leisure interests:* go, golf. *Address:* 2-6-1 Oike, Minamiku, Fukuoka Shi 815, Japan. *Telephone:* 092-553 1893. *Fax:* 092-552 0181.

NATTA, Alessandro; Italian politician; b. 1917, Sardinia; m.; fmr. teacher; mem. Partito Comunista Italiano (PCI) 1946–90; M.P. 1948–90; PCI Whip, Chamber of Deputies 1979–83; Gen. Sec. PCI 1985–88; fmr. Ed. Rinascita (PCI newspaper). *Address:* c/o Partito Comunista Italiano, Via delle Botteghe Oscure 4, 00186 Rome, Italy.

NATTRASS, E.M.B. (Sue), F.A.I.M.; Australian arts administrator and director; b. 15 Sept. 1941, Horsham; d. of John Elliott Nattrass and Elizabeth Claven Saul; ed. Univ. of Melbourne and Melbourne Business School; Stage Man., Lighting Designer and Production Dir. 1963–79; Gen. Man. J. C. Williamson Productions Ltd. 1980–83; Dir. Playbox Theatre Co. 1981–84; Theatre Operations Man., Victorian Arts Centre 1983–88, Deputy Gen. Man.

1988–89, Gen. Man. 1989–96; Artistic Dir. Melbourne Int. Festival of the Arts 1997–; numerous public appts. including mem. Drama Advisory Panel, Vic. Ministry for the Arts 1983–85, 1987–88, mem. Bicentennial Arts and Entertainment Cttee. 1987–88; mem. Ministerial Advisory Cttee., Queen Victoria Women's Centre 1993–94, Chair. Appeal Planning Cttee, 1996, patron 1996–; mem. Arts, Entertainment and Communications Sub-Cttee., Victoria Olympic 2000 Cttee. 1995– Amb. for the Arts, City of Melbourne; Premier Award, The AGE Performing Arts Awards, St. Michael's Medal 1996. *Leisure interests:* cooking, walking, staring at trees, the bush. *Address:* P.O. Box 10, Flinders Lane, Melbourne, 8009 Australia (Office); 5 Havelock Street, St. Kilda, Vic. 3182; Australia (Home). *Telephone:* 9534 6269. *Fax:* 952 5 4392.

NAUDÉ, Rev. (Christiaan) Beyers; South African clergyman; b. 1915; s. of Jozua François Naudé and Adriana Johanna Naudé; m. Ilse Weder 1940; three s. one d.; co-f. multi-racial Christian Inst of S.A.; given seven-year Govt. banning order 1977; Gen. Sec. S.A. Council of Churches 1985–87; mem. A.N.C. del. for talks with S.A. Govt 1990; Hon. D. Theol. (Amsterdam) 1972, Hon. D.LL. (Witwatersrand) 1974, (Notre Dame, U.S.A.) 1985, (Limburg) 1989, (Durban–Westville) 1993, Hon. D. Litt. (Cape Town) 1983, (Univ. of the North) 1995; many int. humanitarian awards, including Bruno Kreisky Award, Austria 1979, Robert F. Kennedy Human Rights Award 1985, Herbert Haag Prize, Fed. Repub. of Germany, Hoof-Offisier van die Orde van Oranje-Nassau, Netherlands 1995, Order of Meritorious Service (Gold) 1997. *Address:* 26 Hoylake Road, Greenside 2193, South Africa.

NAUGHTIE, (Alexander) James, M.A.; British journalist; b. 9 Aug. 1951, Aberdeen; s. of Alexander Naughtie and Isabella Naughtie; m. Eleanor Updale 1986; one s. two d.; ed. Univs. of Aberdeen and Syracuse; journalist The Scotsman (newspaper) 1977–84, The Guardian 1984–88, also Chief Political Corresp.; presenter The World at One, BBC Radio 1988–94, The Proms, BBC Radio and TV 1991–, Today, BBC Radio 4 1994–, Book Club BBC Radio 4 1998–; Hon. LL.D. (Aberdeen). *Leisure interests:* books, opera. *Address:* BBC News Centre, London, W12 7RJ, England. *Telephone:* 0181-624 9644.

NAUMAN, Bruce, M.F.A.; American artist; b. 6 Dec. 1941, Fort Wayne, Ind.; ed. Univ. of Wisconsin (Madison) and Univ. of Calif. (Davis); studied with Italo Scango, William Wiley, Robert Arneson, Frank Owen, Stephen Kaltenbach; Instructor San Francisco Art Inst. 1966–68, Univ. of Calif. (Irvine) 1970; numerous one-man shows including L.A. 1972, 1988, 1993, 1994, Düsseldorf 1974, 1989, 1994, Paris 1974, New York 1975, 1976, 1982, 1990, 1991, 1993, 1994, Amsterdam 1978, Basel 1990, Barcelona 1991, Frankfurt-am-Main 1991, Vienna 1991, London 1991, 1992, 1994, Tel Aviv 1992, Munich 1993, Madrid 1993, Washington, D.C. 1995, Copenhagen 1993, Chicago 1995, Athens 1995; has participated in numerous group exhbns. in U.S.A. and Europe; work in many perm. collections including Whitney Museum, Los Angeles County Museum of Art; retrospective Kunsthaus Zurich 1995; Dr. h.c. (San Francisco Art Inst.) 1989; Artist Fellowship Award, Nat. Endowment for the Arts 1968, Max Beckmann Prize (Frankfurt) 1990, Wolf Prize 1993, Aldrich Prize 1995. *Publications:* Pictures of Sculptures in a Room 1966, Clear Sky 1968, Burning Small Fires 1968, Bruce Naumann 1988, Bruce Naumann Prints 1989. *Address:* c/o Leo Castelli Gallery, 420 W. Broadway, New York, NY 10013, U.S.A.

NAUMANN, Gen. Klaus, O.B.E.; German army officer; b. 1939, Munich; m. Barbara Linke; one s. one d.; joined Bundeswehr 1958, Col. staff of German Mil. Rep.-Nato Mil. Cttee. Brussels 1981–84; Brigade Commdr. Armoured Infantry Brigade, Ellwangen 1984–86; Brig. Dept. Head of Force Planning, Gen. Staff, Ministry of Defence 1986–88; Maj.-Gen. Head of Defence Policy & Operations staff 1988–90; Adviser in two-plus-four negotiations on German Unification 1990; Lieut.-Gen., Commdr. first German corps April–Oct. 1991; Insp.-Gen. of the Bundeswehr 1991–; Chair. NATO Mil. Cttee. 1996–99; Great Distinguished Service Cross 1993, Commdr. Legion of Merit 1993, Grand Officer, Légion d'honneur 1994, and numerous other awards and honours. *Address:* c/o NATO HQ, Boulevard Leopold III, 1110 Brussels, Belgium.

NAUMANN, Michael, D.PHIL.; German publisher; b. 8 Dec. 1941, Köthen; s. of Eduard Naumann and Ursula (née Schönfeld) Naumann; m. Christa Wessel 1969; one s. one d.; ed. Univ. of Munich and Queen's Coll., Oxford; Asst. Prof. Univ. of Bochum 1971–76; Florey Scholar Queen's Coll., Oxford 1976–78; Ed., Foreign Corresp. Die Zeit, Hamburg 1978–82; Sr. Foreign Ed. Der Spiegel, Hamburg 1982–84; Publr. Rowohlt Verlag, Reinbek 1984–95; Pres. and C.E.O. Henry Holt and Co., New York 1996–. *Publications:* Der Abbau einer Verkehrten Welt 1969, Amerika liegt in Kalifornien 1983, Strukturwandel des Heroismus 1984, Die Geschichte ist offen 1990. *Leisure interests:* books, motor-cycling. *Address:* Henry Holt and Company, 115 West 18th Street, New York, N.Y. 10011, U.S.A. *Telephone:* (212) 886-1099. *Fax:* (212) 337-0043.

NAUMOV, Vladimir Naumovich; Russian film director and script writer; b. 6 Dec. 1927, Leningrad; m. Natalia Belokhvostikova; one s. one d.; ed. Dept. of Directing, State Inst. of Cinematography (under I. A. Savchenko); Artistic Dir. workshop unit at Mosfilm 1961–89 (with A. Alov until 1983); Chair. Bd. Mosfilm Studios Co. 1989–; Prof. VGIK 1980–; People's Artist of U.S.S.R. 1983; U.S.S.R. State Prize 1984. *Films include:* (in collaboration with Alov to 1983) Uneasy Youth 1955, Pavel Korchagin (based on Ostrovsky's novel How the Steel Was Tempered) 1957, Wind 1959, Peace to Him Who Enters (two prizes at 22nd Venice Film Festival) 1961, A Nasty Story (based on Dostoevsky) 1966 (banned, shown 1989), Flight (based on M. Bulgakov's play) 1971, How the Steel Was Tempered (TV series) 1974, Legend about Til (three prizes at All-Union Festival, First Prize Int. Festival Haugesunde, Norway, Int. Festival Brussels) 1976, Teheran-43 (Golden Prize at 12th Int. Film Festival, Moscow, Golden Prize All-Union Festival) 1981, The Shore (First Prize at 17th Int. Film Festival, Kiev) 1984, The Choice 1987, The Law 1989, Ten Years of Confinement 1990, The White Holiday (two prizes Int. Festival Rimini 1995) 1994. *Address:* Bolshaya Gruzinskaya 39, Apt. 214, 123056 Moscow, Russia. *Telephone:* (095) 147-23-10 (Office); (095) 253-87-32. *Fax:* (095) 938-20-88.

NAVA-CARRILLO, Germán, DR.; Venezuelan diplomatist and politician; b. 21 Aug. 1930, Maracaibo; m.; two c.; ed. Universidad Central de Venezuela; joined Ministry of Foreign Affairs 1955; Minister Plenipotentiary, Chargé d'affaires, London; Asst. Dir.-Gen. of Int. Politics and Chief Div. of Inter-American Affairs, Ministry of Foreign Affairs; Minister-Counsellor, Perm. Mission at UN 1967–69; Amb. and Deputy Perm. Rep. to UN 1969–70; Amb. to Egypt, also accred. to Ethiopia 1970–72; Dir. of Protocol, Ministry of Foreign Affairs 1972–74; Amb. to Costa Rica 1974–75; Dir. of Int. Politics, Ministry of Foreign Affairs 1975–78, Gen. Dir. of Int. Politics and Vice-Minister 1978–79; Perm. Rep. to UN 1979–81; Vice-Minister, Ministry of Foreign Affairs 1984–88, Minister of Foreign Affairs 1988–89; rep. of Venezuela to several UN and other int. confs.; Prof., Int. Studies School, Cen. Univ. of Venezuela 1981. *Address:* c/o Ministry of Foreign Affairs, Casa Amarilla, Biblioteca Central, esq. Principal, Caracas 1010, Venezuela.

NAVARRO NAVARRO, Miguel; Spanish sculptor; b. 29 Sept. 1945, Mislata; s. of Vicente Navarro Navarro and Valentina-Francisca Navarro Navarro; exhbns.: New York 1980, Madrid 1985, 1988, 1989, 1991, Venice 1986, London 1986, Valencia 1988, 1990, 1996, Barcelona 1988, Paris 1994, Derry, Northern Ireland 1996; works in public spaces include: public fountains Valencia 1984, Turis (Valencia) 1986, Minerva Paranoica (sculpture), Castellón 1989, Torre del Sonido (sculpture), Universidad Carlos III, Getafe 1990, Fraternitat (sculpture), Barcelona 1992, Boca de Luna (fountain), Brussels 1994; works in public collections including: Guggenheim Museum, New York, Fundació Caixa de Pensions, Barcelona, Instituto Valenciano de Arte Moderno, Valencia, Museo Nacional Centro de Arte Reina Sofía, Madrid, Fondation Lambert, Brussels, Diputación Prov. de Valencia, Centre Georges Pompidou, Paris, Museu d'Art Contemporani, Barcelona, Colección Argentaria, Madrid, Colección Banco de España, Madrid, Fundación Coca Cola España, Madrid, Fundazion I.C.O., Madrid, Universidad Politécnica de Valencia; Premio Nacional Artes Plast. 1986; Premio Alfons Roig, Valencia 1987. *Leisure interests:* cooking, countryside. *Address:* C/. San Martín 13, 46920 Mislata (Valencia), Spain. *Telephone:* 379 26 24.

NAVASKY, Victor Saul, A.B., LL.B.; American writer and editor; b. 5 July 1932, New York; s. of Macy Navasky and Esther Goldberg; m. Anne Landey Strongin 1966; one s. two d.; ed. Swarthmore Coll., Yale Univ. Law School; Special Asst. to Gov. G. Mennen Williams, Mich. 1959–60; Ed. and Publisher, Monocle Magazine 1961–65; Ed. New York Times magazine 1970–72; Ed.-in-Chief The Nation magazine 1978–94, Editorial Dir. and Publr. 1995–; mem. Bd. PEN, Authors' Guild, Cttee. to Protect Journalists, Man. bd. Swarthmore Coll. 1991–94; American Book Award (for Naming Names) 1981. *Publications:* Kennedy Justice 1971, Naming Names 1980, The Experts Speak (Co-Ed. with C. Cerf) 1984. *Address:* The Nation, 72 Fifth Avenue, New York, NY 10011 (Office); 33 W. 67th Street, New York, NY 10023, U.S.A. (Home).

NAVON, Itzhak; Israeli politician; b. 9 April 1921, Jerusalem; s. of Yosef Navon and Miriam Ben-Atar; m. Ofira Reznikov-Erez; one s. one d.; ed. Hebrew Univ. of Jerusalem; Dir., Hagana Arabic Dept., Jerusalem 1946–49; Second Sec., Israel Legation in Uruguay and Argentina 1949–51; Political Sec. to Foreign Minister 1951–52; Head of Bureau of Prime Minister 1952–63; Head, Dept. of Culture, Ministry of Educ. and Culture 1963–65; mem. Knesset 1965-78; fmr. Deputy Speaker; fmr. Chair. Knesset Defence and Foreign Affairs Cttee.; Chair. World Zionist Council 1973–78; Pres. of Israel 1978–83; Vice-Premier and Minister of Educ. and Culture 1984–90; mem. Mapai Party 1951–65, Rafi 1965–68, Israel Labour Party 1968–; Chair. Wolf Foundation. *Publications:* Romancero Sephardi, Six Days and Seven Gates. *Leisure interests:* theatre, folklore, cantorial music. *Address:* c/o Ministry of Education and Culture, Jerusalem, Israel.

NAVRATILOVA, Martina; American (b. Czechoslovakian) lawn tennis player; b. 18 Oct. 1956, Prague; d. of Miroslav Navratil and Jana Navratilova; professional since 1975, the year she defected to U.S.A.; ranked No. 1 1982–85; Wimbledon singles Champion 1978, 1979, 1982, 1983, 1984, 1985, 1986, 1987, 1990, finalist 1988, 1989; (doubles 1976, 1979, 1982, 1983, 1984, 1985); French Champion 1982, 1984; Australian Champion 1981, 1983, 1985; Avon Champion 1978, 1979, 1981; U.S. Open Champion 1983, 1984, 1986, 1987; 54 Grand Slam Titles (18 singles, 37 women's doubles; holder of 167 singles and 165 doubles titles; world no. 1 for 332 weeks at retirement (Nov. 1994.); 8 Wimbledon titles (1993); set professional women's record for consecutive victories 1984; won 100th tournament of career 1985; only player to win 100 matches at Wimbledon 1991; record of 158 wins (Feb. 1992) in singles beating the record of Chris Evert Lloyd (q.v.); Pres. Women's Tennis Assn. 1979–80; World Champion 1980; Played Federation Cup for Czechoslovakia 1973, 1974, 1975; 1,400 victories (Oct. 1993); 167 singles titles

(Nov. 1994); designer own fashion wear; Dr. h.c. (George Washington) 1996. *Publications:* Being Myself (autobiog.) 1985, The Total Zone (novel with Liz Nickles) 1994, The Breaking Point (with Liz Nickles) 1996. *Leisure interest:* golf. *Address:* IMG, 1 Erieview Plaza, Cleveland, OH 44114, U.S.A.

NAWAR, Ahmed, PH.D.; Egyptian arts administrator; b. 3 June 1945, El sheen Gharbia; s. of Mohamed Ismail Nawar and Fakiha Karam Mostafa Ghali; m. Wafaa Mossallem 1969; three d.; ed. Cairo Univ. and St. Fernando Acad., Madrid; Prof. of Graphics, Faculty of Fine Art, Helwan Univ. 1967–; Dean and f. Faculty of Fine Art, Menia Univ. 1983–88; Head Nat. Centre for Fine Arts, Ministry of Culture 1988–; Head Museums Service, Higher Council for Antiquities 1994–; Gen. Supervisor Nubia Savings Fund 1996–98; State Order of Arts and Sciences, First Class 1979, Nobel Gold Medal 1986, Order of Merit (Spain) 1992, Officier, Ordre des Arts et des Sciences and many others. *Address:* 54 Dimashk, Madenat Al Mohandeseen, Flat 16, Giza, Cairo, Egypt. *Telephone:* (2) 3488279. *Fax:* (2) 3488279.

NAWAZ, S. Shah, M.A.; Pakistani diplomatist; b. 17 March 1917, Dehra Doon, India; s. of Sardar Shah Zaman Khan and Humaira Khanum; m. Maliha Nawaz 1959; ed. St. Stephen's Coll., Delhi; joined foreign service of Pakistan 1950; Deputy High Commr., U.K. 1964–66; Minister, Washington, D.C. 1966–68; Amb. to Iran 1968–72; Dir.-Gen. Ministry of Foreign Affairs 1972–74, Additional Foreign Sec. 1974–77, Foreign Sec. 1977–80, Sec.-Gen. for Foreign Affairs 1980–82; Perm. Rep. to UN 1982–89. *Leisure interests:* hunting, painting. *Address:* c/o Ministry of Foreign Affairs, Constitution Avenue, Islamabad, Pakistan.

NAWAZ SHARIF, Mohammed; Pakistani politician and industrialist; b. 25 Dec. 1949, Lahore; s. of Mian Mohammad Sharif; m. 1971; two s. two d.; ed. Govt. Coll. and Punjab Univ. Law Coll., Lahore; started work in Ittefaq faction industrial group 1969; Finance Minister, Govt. of the Punjab 1981–85, Chief Minister of Punjab 1985–90; Prime Minister of Pakistan 1990–93 (dismissal ruled unconstitutional) resgnd. July 1993, Prime Minister 1997–, also Minister of Defence and Finance; Pres. Pakistan Muslim League, Punjab 1985, Islami Jamhoori Ittehad 1988. *Leisure interests:* social work, photography, hunting, playing cricket. *Address:* Office of the Prime Minister, Islamabad; 180-181-H, Ittefaq Colony, Model Town, Lahore, Pakistan. *Telephone:* 856069/851744/857155 (Home).

NAYAR, Sushila, DR.P.H.; Indian medical practitioner; b. 26 Dec. 1914, Kunjah District, Punjab (now in Pakistan); d. of Brindaban and Tara Devi Nayar; ed. Lahore Coll. for Women, Lady Hardinge Medical Coll., Delhi, Johns Hopkins Univ., U.S.A.; Medical Attendant to Mahatma Gandhi and his Ashram; work for communal harmony in West Punjab, Noakhali; Dir. Mahatma Gandhi Inst. of Medical Sciences 1969–, Prof. of Preventive and Social Medicine 1969, now Hon. Prof.; mem. Delhi Legis. Ass. 1950–56, Speaker 1952–56; mem. Lok Sabha 1957–71, 1977–79; Minister of Health, Local Self-Govt., Country and Town Planning and Family Planning, Govt. of India 1962–67; Pres. S.P.C.A. 1952–62; Chair. Indian Red Cross Soc. 1964–67, Kasturba Gandhi Nat. Memorial Trust 1988–; Pres. Indian Council of Medical Research 1962–67, All-India Inst. of Medical Sciences 1964–67, Kasturba Health Soc. 1964–, Nat. Soc. for Prevention of Blindness 1964–81, Indian Women's League for Peace and Freedom 1955–; mem. Indian Medical Asscn., Public Health Asscn. of India, Indian Council of Child Welfare, Indian Soc. for Rehabilitation of the Handicapped; Pres's Award for Karavas Ki Kahani 1952, Amal Prabha Das Award, Govt. of Assam 1996. *Publications:* Wife of Gandhi, Satyagraha at Work, Gandhiji Awakens India, etc. *Leisure interests:* writing, painting, reading, bridge. *Address:* Kasturba Hospital, Sevagram-442102, Wardha, Maharashtra (Office); N. 1, Tara Apartments, Kalkaji, New Delhi 110019, India. *Telephone:* Wardha 84341 (Office); (Delhi) 6434635 (Home).

NAZARBAYEV, Nursultan Abishevich; Kazakhstan politician; b. 6 July 1940, Chemolgan, Kazakstan; s. of Abish Nazarbayev and Aizhan Nazarbayev; m. Sarah Alplisovna Kounakaeva 1962; three d.; ed. Higher Tech. Course at Karaganda Metallurgical Combine and Higher Party School of Cen. Cttee. CPSU; mem. CPSU 1962–91; worked for Karaganda Metallurgical Plant 1960–64, 1965–69; Sec. Temirtau City Cttee. of Kazak CP 1969–84; Sec. party cttee. of Karaganda Metallurgical Combine 1973–77; Second, then First Sec. Karaganda Dist. Cttee. of Kazak CP 1977–79; Sec. Cen. Cttee. of Kazak CP 1979–84; Chair. Council of Ministers of Kazak S.S.R. 1984–89; U.S.S.R. People's Deputy 1989–91; First Sec. Cen. Cttee. of Kazak CP 1989–91, Socialist Party 1991–; Chair. Kazak Supreme Soviet 1989–90; Pres. Kazak S.S.R. 1990–91, Kazak Repub. 1991–; Chair. World Kazak Union 1992–. *Publications:* 9 books, numerous articles on economics. *Leisure interests:* tennis, water-skiing, horses, reading history books. *Address:* Office of the President, Astana; Respubliki sq. 4, 480091 Alma-Ata, Kazakhstan. *Telephone:* (3272) 62-30-16, 15-11-53.

NAZARENKO, Tatyana Georgievna; Russian painter; b. 24 June 1944, Moscow; m.; ed. Moscow Surikov State Fine Arts Inst.; worked Studio of U.S.S.R. Acad. of Fine Arts 1969–72; mem. U.S.S.R. (now Russian) Union of Painters 1969; solo exhbns. France, U.S.A., Spain, Russia, Germany 1987–; Russian State Prize 1993. *Address:* Moscow Artists' Union, Starosadsky Per. 5, 101000 Moscow, Russia. *Telephone:* (095) 921-51-88.

NAZARIO DE LIMA, Ronaldo Luiz (Ronaldo); Brazilian professional football player; b. 22 Sept. 1976, Rio de Janeiro; s. of Nelio Nazario de Lima and Sonia Nazario de Lima; teams: Social Ramos, Rio (at age 15) (12 games, 8 goals), São Cristóvão, Rio Second Div. (54 games, 36 goals), Cruzeiro, Brazil (60 games, 58 goals), PSV Eindhoven, Holland (56 games, 55 goals), Barcelona, Spain (48 games, 45 goals), Inter(nazionale) Milan 1997–; Brazilian Nat. Team 1994– (29 int. caps, 20 goals); played for winning team World Cup 1994 (at age 17) and Copa America 1997 (Brazil); Spanish Cup and European Cup-Winners Cup (Barcelona) 1996; World Soccer Magazine World Player of the Year 1996, FIFA World Footballer of the Year 1996.

NAZAROV, Talbak; DR. ECON. SC.; Tajikistan politician and academic; b. 15 March 1938, Kulyab; m. Tatyana Grigorievna Teodorovich 1959; one s. one d.; ed. Leningrad Inst. of Finance and Econs.; asst., Deputy Dean Econs. Faculty; Tajik State Univ. 1960–62, Head of Dept., Dean 1965–80; Rector Tajik State Univ. 1982–88; Chair Supreme Soviet Tajik S.S.R. 1986–88; Minister of Public Educ. 1988–90; First Deputy Chair. Council of Ministers, Chair. State Planning Cttee., 1990–91; Minister of Foreign Affairs 1994–; mem. Tajikistan Acad. of Sciences 1980–; Vice-Pres. 1991–94; U.S.S.R. People's Deputy 1989–92; Extraordinary and Plenipotentiary Amb.; Merited Worker of Science and many other awards and medals. *Publications:* books and articles on Tajikistan's economy and external policies. *Address:* Ministry of Foreign Affairs, Rudaki 42, 734051 Dushanbe (Office); Pushkina 6 fl. 10, 734051 Dushanbe, Tajikistan (Home). *Telephone:* (3772) 210259; 232964 (Office).

NAZDRATENKO, Yevgeny Ivanovich; Russian politician; b. 15 Feb. 1949, Severo-Kurilsk, Sakhalin Region; m.; two s.; ed. Far E. Inst. of Tech.; served with Pacific Fleet; Head of sector Bor Co.; mechanic, Vice-Pres., Pres., Primorsk Mining Co., Vostok 1980–93; f., J. Primorsk Corpn. of Mfrs. 1992; Peoples' Deputy of Russian Fed. 1990–93; Head of Admin. Primorsk Territory 1995–; Gov. of Primorsk 1995–; mem. State Duma 1993–95; mem. Council of Feds. of Russia 1996–. *Address:* Office of the Governor, Svetlanskaya str. 22, Vladivostok, Russia. *Telephone:* (423) 22 38 00 (Office). *Fax:* (423) 22 50 10 (Office).

NAZER, Sheikh Hisham Mohi ed-Din; Saudi Arabian politician; b. 1932; ed. Univ. of California; legal adviser 1958; assisted in foundation of OPEC 1960; Deputy Minister of Petroleum 1962–68; with Ministry of Planning 1975–, Acting Minister of Planning 1986–91; Minister of Petroleum and Mineral Resources 1986–95; Pres. Cen. Org. for Planning 1968–; mem. Supreme Council for Petroleum and Minerals 1968–; Chair. SAMAREC, Saudia Arabian Oil Co. *Address:* c/o Ministry of Petroleum and Mineral Resources, P.O. Box 247, Riyadh 11191, Saudi Arabia.

NAZIR-ALI, Rt. Rev. Michael James, M.LITT., M.A., PH.D.; British/Pakistani ecclesiastic; b. 19 Aug. 1949, Karachi; s. of James Nazir-Ali and Patience Nazir-Ali; m. Valerie Cree 1972; two s.; ed. St. Paul's High School, Karachi, St. Patrick's Coll., Karachi, Univ. of Karachi, Fitzwilliam Coll., Cambridge, Ridley Hall, Cambridge, St. Edmund Hall, Oxford and Australian Coll. of Theology in asscn. with Centre for World Religions, Harvard; Tutorial Supervisor in Theology, Univ. of Cambridge 1974–76; Tutor then Sr. Tutor, Karachi Theological Coll. 1976–81; Assoc. Priest Holy Trinity Cathedral, Karachi 1976–79; Priest-in-Charge St. Andrew's Akhtar Colony, Karachi 1979–81; Provost Lahore Cathedral 1981–84; Bishop of Raiwind 1984–86; fmr. Visiting Lecturer, Centre for Study of Islam and Muslim-Christian Relations, Birmingham; Asst. to Archbishop of Canterbury; Co-ordinator of Studies for 1988 Lambeth Conf.; Gen. Sec. Church Missionary Soc. 1989–94; Asst. Bishop, Diocese of Southwark 1990–94; Canon Theologian Leicester Cathedral 1992–94; Bishop of Rochester 1994–; Chair. Mission Theological Advisory Group 1992–, Governing Council, Trinity Coll. Bristol 1996–; Pres. Horticultural Soc., Cambridge 1975; Dir. Oxford Centre for Mission Studies, Christian Aid; mem. Design Group for 1998 Lambeth Conf., Anglican Roman Catholic Int. Comm. 1991–, Bd. of Mission Gen. Synod, Church of England 1992–94, 1996–, Human Fertilization and Embryology Authority 1998–; Fellow St. Edmund Hall, Oxford 1998–; Visiting Prof. of Theological and Religious Studies, Univ. of Greenwich 1996–; Radio Pakistan Prize for English Language and Literature 1964; Burney Award (Cambridge) 1973, 1975; Oxford Soc. Award for Grads. 1973; Langham Scholarship 1974. *Publications:* Islam, a Christian Perspective 1982, Frontiers in Christian–Muslim Encounter 1985, Martyrs and Magistrates: Toleration and Trial in Islam 1989, The Roots of Islamic Tolerance: Origin and Development 1990, From Everywhere to Everywhere 1991, Mission and Dialogue 1995, The Mystery of Faith 1995, Citizens and Exiles 1998; numerous articles on Islam, Christianity, mission, inter-faith dialogue, Anglican and ecumenical affairs. *Leisure interests:* cricket, hockey, table tennis and reading. *Address:* Bishopscourt, Rochester, Kent, ME1 1TS, England. *Telephone:* (01634) 842721. *Fax:* (01634) 831136.

NDAMASE, Tutor Nyangilizwe; South African politician; b. 11 Jan. 1921, Transkei; m. 1st Jessie Tandiwe Ka Solomon Ka Dinizulu 1943 (died 1971); four c.; m. 2nd Ndileka Bikitsha 1975; ed. Healdtown Inst.; became Chief 1947; mem. United Transkeian Territories Gen. Council 1952; M.P. 1963; Paramount Chief of Pondoland (and nominated M.P.) 1974–; Pres. of Transkei 1986–94. *Address:* Umtata, Transkei, South Africa.

N'DIAYE, Babacar; Senegalese banker; b. 11 June 1936, Conakry, Guinea; joined African Devt. Bank 1965, subsequently Group Dir. of Finance, then Vice-Pres. for Finance, Pres. 1985–95; Chair. African Business Round Table; LL.D. (Clark Atlanta Univ., Ga.) 1992, (Lincoln Univ., Pa.) 1993. *Address:* c/o African Development Bank, 01 BP 1387, Abidjan 01, Côte d'Ivoire.

NDIMIRA, Pascal-Firmin; Burundian politician; fmrly. univ. rector, IBRD official; fmrly. Minister of Agric.; Prime Minister of Burundi July 1996–. *Address:* Office of the Prime Minister, Bujumbura, Burundi.

N'DONG, Léon; Gabonese diplomatist; b. 15 Feb. 1935, Libreville; s. of late Jean-Martin Bikègne and of Marthe Kemeboune; m. Chantal Annette Bekale 1971; four s. one d.; ed. School of Law and Econ. Sciences, Rennes, France; Under-Sec. Gen. of Ministry of Foreign Affairs, later Sec.-Gen.; Teacher, Nat. School of Admin. 1969–72; Amb. to Cen. African Repub. and Sudan 1972–73, to Morocco 1973–74, to UN Office at Geneva 1974–76, to UN 1976–80, to U.K. 1980–86, to Fed. Repub. of Germany 1986–90 (also accred. to Norway, Denmark, Finland and Sweden); Amb. du Gabon, Diplomatic Adviser to Prime Minister 1990–; High Commr., Office of Prime Minister 1997–; Commdr. de l'Etoile Equatoriale, Grand Cordon of Order of the Brilliant Star (China), Commdr., Order of Devotion (Malta), Commdr. Nat. Order of Dahomey, Order of Nile (Sudan), Ordre nationale du Mérite (Gabon), Diplomatic Order of Repub. of Korea, Ordre de la Pléïade (France), Grand Officier Etoile Equatoriale, Grand Officier Ordre du Mérite, Officier Courtoisie française. *Leisure interests:* swimming, walking, music, reading, fishing, gardening. *Address:* Office of the Prime Minister, B.P. 546 Libreville, Gábon.

NDUNGANE, Most Rev. Winston Njongonkulu, M.TH., B.D., D.D., A.F.T.S.; South African ecclesiastic; b. 2 April 1941, Kokstad; s. of Foster Ndungane and Tingaza Ndungane; m. 1st Nosipo Ngcelwane 1972 (died 1986), 2nd Nomahlubi Vokwana 1987; one step-s. one step-d.; ed. Lovedale High School, Univ. of Cape Town, Fed. Theological Seminary and King's Coll. London; Rector, St. Nicholas Church, Matroosfontein, Cape Town 1980–81; Provincial Liaison Officer, Johannesburg 1982–84; Prin., St. Bede's Theological Coll. Umtata 1985–86; Exec. Officer, Church of the Prov. of Southern Africa (Anglican) 1987–91; Bishop of Kimberley and Kuruman 1991–96; Archbishop of Cape Town 1996; mem. Bd. SABC, Johannesburg 1992–96. *Publications:* The Commuter Population for Claremont, Cape 1973, Human Rights and the Christian Doctrine of Man 1979. *Leisure interests:* music, walking. *Address:* Bishopscourt, 16 Bishopscourt Drive, Claremont 7700, South Africa. *Telephone:* (021) 761-2531; 451555. *Fax:* (021) 797-1298; 451571.

NDUWAYO, Antoine; Burundian politician; mem. Union pour le progrès national (UPRONA); Prime Minister of Burundi 1995–96. *Address:* c/o Office of the Prime Minister, Bujumbura, Burundi.

NE WIN, U (Maung Shu Maung); Myanma politician and fmr. army officer; b. 24 May 1911; ed. Govt. High School, Prome and Rangoon Univ.; joined Allied Forces 1945; Vice-Chief of Gen. Staff and Major-Gen. 1948; Deputy Prime Minister 1949–50; Gen. 1956; Prime Minister and Minister of Defence 1958–60; Chief of Gen. Staff 1962–72; Prime Minister, Minister of Defence, Finance, and Revenue, Nat. Planning and Justice 1962–63; Prime Minister, Minister of Nat. Planning and Defence 1963; Prime Minister and Minister of Defence, also Chair. of Revolutionary Council 1965–74; Chair. Exec. Cttee. Burma Socialist Programme Party 1973–88; Chair. State Council and Pres. of Burma 1974–81; Legion of Merit (U.S.A.). *Address:* c/o Office of the President, Rangoon, Myanmar.

NEAGU, Paul; British sculptor, painter and fine art lecturer; b. 22 Feb. 1938, Bucharest, Romania; s. of Tudor Neagu and Rozalia Neagu; m. Sibyla Oarcea 1966 (divorced 1972); ed. Inst. Fine Art, Bucharest 1959–65; freelance artist 1965–; emigrated to England 1969; Lecturer in Fine Art, Hornsey School of Art 1972–79; Visiting Lecturer and External Assessor throughout U.K. 1975–; Asst. Prof. Univ. Concordia of Montreal 1982–83; part-time lecturer, Slade School of Art 1985–90; Co-Dir. Generative Art Trust 1995–; Sargant Fellow, British School at Rome 1991–92; Tolly Cobbold Prize 1977; Westminster City Sculpture Prize (Charing Cross Station) 1987. *Publications and exhbns.:* Palpable Art Manifesto! 1969, Generative Art 1972, Gradually Going Tornado 1974, Generative Arts Group 1975, Hyphen 1975, Nine Catalytic Stations 1987, Deep Space and Solid Time 1988, Unnamed 1988, Epagoge 1988–93, Tossing Fish Over Gate 1992, New Hyphen 1993, Ten right angles, ten right angels 1994, Sacramentalia 1995, Reorganisation of nothing 1996, Unnamed—Eschaton 1997, Century's Cross (monument, Bucharest) 1997, Endless edge—Hyphen 1998, Isotope 1998. *Leisure interests:* poetry, philosophy, architecture. *Address:* c/o 31c Jackson Road, London N7 6ES. *Telephone:* 0171-607 7858.

NEAL, Sir Eric James, Kt., A.C., C.V.O., C.ENG., F.I.GAS.E., F.I.E.AUST., F.A.I.M.; Australian state governor and business executive; b. 3 June 1924, London, U.K.; s. of James Neal and May Neal (née Johnson); m. Thelma Joan Bowden 1950; two s.; ed. South Australian School of Mines; Dir. Boral Ltd. 1972–92, Chief Exec. 1973–82, Man. Dir. 1982–87; Dir. Oil Co. of Australia NL 1982–87, Chair. 1984–87; Dir. Westpac Banking Corpn. 1985–92, Chair. 1989–92; Dir. Atlas Copco Australia Ltd. 1986, Chair. 1989–96; Dir. Metal Manufactures Ltd. 1987–96, Chair. 1990–96; Dir. Wormald Int. Ltd. 1978–85, John Fairfax Ltd. 1986–87, Cola-Cola Amatil Ltd. 1987–96, BHP 1988–94; Gov. S. Australia 1996–; mem. Gen. Motors Australia Advisory Council 1987–94; Chief Commr. Council of City of Sydney 1987–88; Int. Trustee, The Duke of Edinburgh's Award Int. Foundation 1988–97; Chair. of Trustees, Sir David Martin Foundation 1991–94; Nat. Pres. Australian Inst. of Co. Dirs. 1990–93; Fellow, Senate, Univ. of Sydney 1989–91; Hon. D.Eng. (Sydney) 1989; Hon. D.Univ. (S. Australia). *Leisure interests:* reading, motor boating, sailing, naval history, opera. *Address:* Government House, Adelaide, South Australia. *Telephone:* (8) 2236166. *Fax:* (8) 2236049.

NEAL, Sir Leonard Francis, Kt., M.A., C.B.E.; British industrial relations official; b. 27 Aug. 1913, London; s. of Arthur Henry Neal and Mary Cahill; m. Mary L. Puttock 1939; one s. one d.; ed. London School of Econs. and Trinity Coll., Cambridge; Deputy Employee Relations Adviser, Esso Petroleum Co. 1962–66; Labour Adviser, Esso Europe Inc. 1966; mem. for Personnel, British Railways Bd. 1967–71; Chair. Comm. on Industrial Relations 1971–74; Chair. MAT Int. Group 1975–84; Chair. Employment Conditions Abroad Ltd. 1977–84; Pres. Asscn. of Supervisory and Exec. Engineers 1974–80; non-exec. Dir. Pilkington Bros. Ltd. 1976–83; Adviser to Bd. of a number of private, commercial and industrial cos.; Chair. Trade Union Reform Cttee. Centre for Policy Studies 1978–85. *Publication:* A Manager's Guide to Industrial Relations (with A. Robertson). *Leisure interests:* gardening, reading.

NEAL, Patricia; American actress; b. 20 Jan. 1926, Packard, Ky., U.S.A.; d. of William Burdette Neal and Eura Mildred Petrey; m. Roald Dahl 1953 (divorced 1983); one s. three d. (and one d. deceased); ed. Northwestern Univ., Ill.; numerous TV appearances; public lectures in America and abroad. *Stage appearances include:* Another Part of the Forest 1946, The Children's Hour 1953, A Roomful of Roses 1954, Suddenly Last Summer 1958, The Miracle Worker 1959; Antoinette Perry Award (Tony) 1946; Academy Award (Oscar) for film Hud 1963. *Films:* John loves Mary 1949, The Hasty Heart 1949, The Fountainhead 1949, The Breaking Point 1950, Three Secrets 1950, Raton Pass 1951, The Day the Earth Stood Still 1951, Diplomatic Courier 1952, Something for the Birds 1953, A Face in the Crowd 1957, Breakfast at Tiffany's 1961, Hud 1963, The Third Secret 1964, In Harms Way 1965, The Subject was Roses 1968, The Road Builder 1970, The Night Digger 1970, The Boy 1972, Happy Mother's Day Love George 1973, Baxter 1973, Widow's Nest 1976, The Passage 1978, All Quiet on the Western Front 1979, Ghost Story 1981, An Unremarkable Life 1989. *Publication:* As I Am (autobiog.) 1988. *Leisure interests:* needlepoint, gardening, cooking. *Address:* 45 East End Avenue, New York, NY 10028, U.S.A. *Telephone:* (212) 772-1268.

NEAME, Ronald; C.B.E.; British film director; b. 23 April 1911, London; s. of Elwin Neame and Ivy Close; m. Beryl Heanly 1933; one s.; messenger and tea boy, British Int. Film Studios 1925; became Dir. of Photography 1932; with Sir David Lean and Anthony Havelock-Allen, formed Cineguild and produced Great Expectations 1946, Oliver Twist 1947 and The Passionate Friends 1948; film dir. 1950–; teacher of film direction, Univ. of Calif., L.A. 1992–. *Films photographed include:* Drake of England 1934, The Gaunt Stranger 1937, Four Just Men, Major Barbara 1940, One of Our Aircraft is Missing 1942, In Which We Serve 1942, This Happy Breed 1943, Blithe Spirit 1945. *Films directed include:* Take My Life 1947, The Golden Salamander 1950, The Card 1950, The Million Pound Note 1953, The Man Who Never Was 1956, Windom's Way 1958, The Horse's Mouth 1959, Tunes of Glory 1960, I Could Go On Singing 1962, The Chalk Garden 1964, Mr. Moses 1965, A Man Could Get Killed 1966, Gambit 1966, The Prime of Miss Jean Brodie 1968, Scrooge 1970, The Poseidon Adventure 1972, The Odessa File 1974, Meteor 1978, Hopscotch 1979, First Monday in October 1980, Foreign Body 1985, The Magic Balloon 1989. *Leisure interests:* painting, photography, stereo and hi-fi equipment. *Address:* 2317 Kimridge Road, Beverly Hills, CA 90210, U.S.A. *Fax:* (310) 271-3044.

NEAOUTIYNE, Paul; New Caledonian politician; b. 1952, St. Michel Village; ed. Univ. of Lyon; teacher of econs. at secondary coll. in Nouméa until 1980; gaoled for participation in pro-independence demonstration 1980; reinstated as teacher 1983; aide to Jean-Marie Tjibaou (Pres. Northern Regional Council) 1985; leader, Party of Kanak Liberation (Palika); Mayor of Poindimie; mem. Northern Provincial Govt.; Pres. Parti de Libération Kanak (PALIKA) (merged with Kanak Socialist Nat. Liberation Front). *Address:* Kanak Socialist National Liberation Front, Nouméa, New Caledonia.

NEARY, Martin Gerard James, L.V.O., M.A., F.R.C.O.; British conductor and organist; b. 28 March 1940; s. of the late Leonard W. Neary and of Jeanne M. Thébault; m. Penelope J. Warren 1967; one s. two d.; ed. City of London School and Gonville & Caius Coll. Cambridge; Asst. Organist, St. Margaret's Westminster 1963–65, Organist and Master of Music 1965–71; Prof. of Organ, Trinity Coll. London 1963–72; Organist and Master of Music, Winchester Cathedral 1972–87; Organist and Master of Choristers, Westminster Abbey 1988–98; has led Westminster Abbey Choir on tours to France, Germany, Switzerland, Hungary, U.S.A., Russia, Ukraine; founder and Conductor Martin Neary Singers 1972–; Chair. Church Services Cttee., Musicians Benevolent Fund 1993–, Herbert Howells Soc. 1993–; Conductor Waynflete Singers 1972–87; Pres. Cathedral Organists Asscn. 1985–88; Pres. Royal Coll. of Organists 1988–90, 1996–98; many organ recitals and broadcasts in U.K., Europe, U.S.A., Canada, the Far East and Australia; many choral premières; guest conductor English Chamber Orchestra, London Symphony Orchestra; numerous recordings; Hon. R.A.M.; Hon. F.T.C.L.; Hon. Fellow Royal School of Church Music; *Publications:* editions of early organ music, contributions to organ journals. *Leisure interest:* watching cricket. *Address:* 2 Little Cloister, Westminster Abbey, London, SW1P 3PL, England. *Telephone:* 0171-222 6923.

NECHAYEV, Andrey Alekseevich; Russian politician and economist; b. 2 Feb. 1953, Moscow; s. of Aleksey Nechayev and Marseliesa Nechayev; m. 1st Elena Belyanova 1975; m. 2nd Margarita Kitova 1986; one s. one d.; m. 3rd Svetlana Serguenko; ed. Moscow State Univ.; mem. CPSU 1984–91;

researcher Cen. Econ.-Math. Inst. U.S.S.R. Acad. of Sciences 1979–86, Inst. of Econ. and Prognosis of Scientific Tech. Progress U.S.S.R. Acad. of Sciences 1986–90; Deputy Dir. Inst. of Econ. Policy Acad. of Nat. Econ. 1990–91; Deputy Minister of Econ. and Finance of Russia 1991–92; Minister of Econ. 1992–93; Pres. Russian Financial Corpn. 1993–, Moscow Finance Club 1994–; mem. Political Consultative Council under Pres. of Russia 1996–, Scientific Council under Security Council of Russia 1997–; Ed.-in-chief Mneniya; Co-Chair. Business Round-table of Russia; Vice-Pres. Moscow Actors Charity Fund. *Publications:* 150 publs., including works on use of math. models in econ. and structural analysis of econ. *Leisure interests:* theatre, art, history, tennis. *Address:* Russian Financial Corporation, Georgievsky per. 1, 103009 Moscow, Russia. *Telephone:* (095) 292-74-82. *Fax:* (092) 292-91-07.

NEDERKOORN, Erik Jan; Netherlands business executive; b. 22 Aug. 1943, Haarlem; m.; two s. one d.; Vice-Pres. Fokker (aircraft mfrs.) 1988–91, Chair. Bd. of Man. and C.E.O. 1991–94; mem. Bd. Deutsche Telekom 1996–. *Address:* c/o Deutsche Telekom, PO Box 2000, 53105 Bonn, Germany.

NEDERLANDER, James Morton; American impresario; b. 31 March 1922, Detroit, Mich.; s. of David T. Nederlander and Sarah L. Applebaum; m. Charlene Saunders 1969; one. s. two d.; ed. Pontiac Sr. High School and Detroit Inst. of Tech.; former usher, box-office asst. and press agent for father's Schubert-Lafayette Theatre; served in U.S.A.F. in W.W. II; Man. Lyceum Theatre, Minneapolis for eight years; returned to Detroit to assist in devt. of Nederlander theatre chain in Detroit and Chicago in 1950s; chain expanded to Broadway with purchase of Palace Theatre 1965; now Chair. Bd. Nederlander Org. 1966–, owners and operators of largest chain of theatres in world including 11 Broadway theatres and Adelphi and Aldwych theatres, London and producers and backers of major Broadway musicals such as Annie, La Cage aux Folles and Will Roger Follies; est. Nederlander TV and Film Production (creating films, mini-series, etc. for TV) in 1980s. *Address:* Nederlander Organization Inc., 810 Seventh Avenue, New York, NY 10019, U.S.A.

NEEDHAM, James J.; American business consultant (retd.); b. 18 Aug. 1926, Woodhaven N.Y.; s. of James Joseph Needham (deceased) and Amelia Pasta Needham; m. 1st Dolores A. Habick 1950 (died 1993); three s. two d.; m. 2nd Patricia H. Campo 1995; ed. Cornell and St John's (Brooklyn) Univs.; with Price Waterhouse & Co., then Partner, Raymond T. Hyer & Co.; joined A. M. Pullen & Co. 1957, subsequently partner, in charge of New York office and mem. Exec. Cttee.; Commr. Securities and Exchange Comm. 1969–72; Chair. New York Stock Exchange 1972–76; Vice-Pres. Int. Fed. of Stock Exchanges 1973–75, Pres. 1976–86; Councilman, Southampton, N.Y. 1990–93; fmrly. Distinguished Prof., Graduate Dir., Coll. of Business Admin., St. John's Univ.; Amb. and Commr. Gen. of U.S. Int. Exposition, Japan 1985; Hon. DLL. (St. John's Univ.) 1972. *Leisure interests:* golf, fishing. *Address:* P.O. Box 1229, Bridgehampton, NY 11932, U.S.A. *Telephone:* (516) 537-3748. *Fax:* (516) 537-2773.

NEEDLEMAN, Jacob, PH.D.; American professor of philosophy; b. 6 Oct. 1934, Philadelphia; s. of Benjamin Needleman and Ida Needleman; m. 1st Carla Satzman 1959 (divorced 1989); one s. one d.; m. 2nd Gail Anderson 1990; ed. Research Assoc., Rockefeller Inst., New York 1960–61, Harvard Coll., Yale Univ.; Assoc. Prof. of Philosophy, San Francisco State Univ. 1962–66, Prof. 1967–; Dir., Center for the Study of New Religions, Graduate Theological Union, Berkeley, Calif. 1977–83; Vice-Pres. Audio Literature Co. 1987–; Rockefeller Humanities Fellow, Fulbright Scholar. *Publications:* The New Religions 1970, A Sense of the Cosmos 1975, Lost Christianity 1980, The Heart of Philosophy 1982, The Way of the Physician 1985, Sorcerers 1986, Money and the Meaning of Life 1991, A Little Book on Love 1996. *Address:* San Francisco State University, Department of Philosophy, 1600 Holloway Ave, San Francisco, CA 94132; 25 San Andreas Way, San Francisco, CA 94132, U.S.A. *Telephone:* (415) 566-1311.

NEEL, James Van Gundia, PH.D., M.D.; American geneticist; b. 22 March 1915, Hamilton, Ohio; s. of Hiram A. Neel and Elizabeth Van Gundia; m. Priscilla Baxter 1943; one d. two s.; ed. Coll. of Wooster, Ohio, and Univ. of Rochester, New York; Inst. of Zoology, Dartmouth 1939–41; Fellow in Zoology, Nat. Research Council 1941–42; Strong Memorial Hosp. 1944–46; Acting Dir. Field Studies, Atomic Bomb Casualty Comm., Nat. Research Council 1947–48; Assoc. Geneticist, Lab. of Vertebrate Biology, Asst. Prof. of Internal Medicine, Univ. of Mich. 1948–51; Geneticist, Inst. of Human Biology 1951–56; Chair. and Lee R. Dice Univ. Prof., Dept. of Human Genetics, Univ. of Mich. Medical School 1956–85, Prof. of Internal Medicine 1957–85, Prof. Emer. 1985–; Pres. 6th Int. Congress of Human Genetics 1981; Dir. Centre Royaumont pour une Science de l'Homme; Consultant Nat. Research Council, WHO, Pan American Health Org., etc.; Cutter Lecturer, Harvard Univ. 1956; Wilhelmina Key Lecturer, American Genetics Assn. 1982; Jacobson Lecture, Univ. of Newcastle-upon-Tyne 1988; Baker Lecture, Pa. State Univ. 1989; Andros Lecture, Univ. of Chicago 1991; mem. N.A.S., American Phil. Soc., Assn. of American Physicians, American Soc. of Human Genetics (Vice-Pres. 1952–53, Pres. 1953–54, Bd. Dir. 1968–70), American Acad. of Arts and Sciences, Inst. of Medicine (N.A.S.), Int. Genetic Epidemiology Soc. (Pres. 1991–92); Hon. Fellow American Coll. of Medical Genetics; Lasker Award 1950, Modern Medicine Award 1960, Allan Award, American Soc. of Human Genetics 1965, Russell Award, Univ. of Mich. 1966, Nat. Medal of Science 1974, Smithsonian Institution Medal 1981, American Coll. of Physicians Laureate Award 1988, Conte Award, Conte Inst. for Environmental Health 1991, James D. Bruce Memorial Award, American Coll. of Physicians 1995. *Publications:* Human Heredity (with W. J. Schull) 1954, A Clinical, Pathological and Genetic Study of Multiple Neurofibromatoses (with F. W. Crowe and W. J. Schull) 1956, Changing Perspectives on the Genetic Effects of Radiation 1963, Effects of Inbreeding on Japanese Children (with W. J. Schull) 1965; Ed. (with Crow) Proc. III Int. Congress Human Genetics. *Address:* University of Michigan, Department of Human Genetics, 4708 Medical Science II, Ann Arbor, MI 48109-0618 (Office); 2235 Belmont, Ann Arbor, MI 48104, U.S.A. (Home). *Telephone:* (313) 9362890.

NÉEL, Louis Eugène Félix; French scientist; b. 22 Nov. 1904, Lyon, Rhône; s. of Louis Néel and Marie-Antoinette Hartsmayer; m. Hélène Hourticq 1931; one s. two d.; ed. Lycée du Parc, Lyon, Lycée Saint-Louis, Paris, and Ecole Normale Supérieure, Paris; Prof., Univ. of Strasbourg 1937–45, Grenoble 1945–76; Scientific Adviser to Navy 1952–82; French Rep. to Scientific Cttee. of NATO 1960–83; Pres. French Physical Soc. 1957; Pres. Int. Union of Pure and Applied Physics 1963–65; Pres. Inst. Nat. Polytechnique, Grenoble 1971–76; Pres. Conseil Supérieur Sûreté Nucléaire 1981–86; mem. Acad. of Sciences (Paris); Foreign mem. Russian Acad. of Sciences, Royal Netherlands Acad., German Leopoldina Acad., Romanian Acad. of Sciences, Royal Soc. (U.K.), American Acad. of Arts and Sciences, Polish Acad. of Sciences; many hon. degrees; Prix Holweck 1952, Gold Medal (C.N.R.S.) 1965, Nobel Prize for Physics 1970; Croix de guerre 1940; Grand Croix, Légion d'honneur. *Publications:* over 200 works on various aspects of magnetism. *Leisure interests:* history, carpentry. *Address:* 15 rue Marcel Allégot, 92190 Meudon, France. *Telephone:* (01) 45-34-36-51.

NEEMAN, Yaakov, J.S.D.; Israeli politician and lawyer; b. 1939, Tel-Aviv; m.; six c.; ed. Hebrew Univ. of Jerusalem, New York Univ. Law School; mem. Israeli Bar Assn. 1966–; Sr. Partner Herzog Fox & Neeman 1972– (with two-year interruption); Visiting Prof. of Law Univ. of Calif. at L.A., U.S.A. 1976, Tel-Aviv Univ. 1977–79, New York Univ. 1989–90, Hebrew Univ. of Jerusalem 1990, 1994; Dir.-Gen. Ministry of Finance 1979–81; Chair. Cttee. of Inquiry into Inter-Relation between Tax Laws and Foreign Currency Restrictions 1977–78, Public Cttee. on Allocation of Distributions by Ministry of Interior 1991–92; mem. Investigation Cttee. on Temple Mount Affair 1991; fmr. mem. several other public cttees.; mem. Bd. of Govs. Bank of Israel 1977–79, 1992–; mem. Cen. Cttee. of World Bank; Minister of Justice 1996, of Finance 1997. *Publications:* seven books and over 30 articles on taxation, corpn. and securities law. *Address:* c/o Ministry of Finance, P.O. Box 13191, 1 Rehov Kaplan, Kiryat Ben-Gurion, Jerusalem 91008, Israel. *Telephone:* (2) 531-7111. *Fax:* (2) 563-7891.

NE'EMAN, Yuval, DIP.ING., D.E.M., D.I.C., PH.D.; Israeli professor of physics; b. 14 May 1925, Tel-Aviv; s. of Gedalia and Zipora Ne'eman; m. Dvora Rubinstein 1951; one d. one s.; ed. Herzliya High School, Tel-Aviv, Israel Inst. of Tech., Haifa, and London Univ.; Hagana volunteer, taking part in activities against British rule in Palestine 1946–47; Hydrodynamical Design Engineer 1946–47; Capt., Israeli Defence Forces (Infantry) 1948, Maj. 1949, Lieut.-Col. 1950; Head of Defence Planning 1952–55; Deputy Dir. Defence Intelligence Div. 1955–57; Defence Attaché, London 1958–60; resigned from Israeli Defence Forces active service May 1960; took part in six day war June 1967; Scientific Dir. Israel Atomic Energy Establishment 1961–63; Research Assoc. Calif. Inst. of Tech., Pasadena 1963–64, Visiting Prof. of Theoretical Physics 1964–65; Prof. of Physics and Head of Dept. Tel-Aviv Univ. 1965–73; Prof. of Physics and Dir. Centre for Particle Theory, Univ. of Texas (Austin) 1968–; Pollak Prof. of Theoretical Physics, Tel-Aviv Univ. 1968–76, Wolfson Prof. Extraordinary in Theoretical Physics 1977–97; Vice-Pres. Tel-Aviv Univ. 1965–66, Pres. 1971–75; Dir. Sackler Inst. of Advanced Studies, Tel-Aviv Univ. 1979–97; Adviser to Head of Mil. Intelligence 1973–74; Special Adviser to Israel Defence Ministry 1975–76; mem. Knesset 1981–90; Minister of Science and Devt. 1982–84, of Science, Devt. and Energy 1990–92; Chair. Steering Cttee. Mediterranean–Dead Sea Conduit 1977–83; Chair. Israel Space Agency 1983–; mem. Israel Atomic Energy Cttee. 1966–84, Israel Nat. Acad. of Sciences 1966–; co-discoverer of Unitary Symmetry Theory; conceived basic field explaining compositeness of nuclear particles; Foreign Hon. mem. American Acad. Arts and Sciences, Hon. Life mem. New York Acad. of Sciences 1973–, Foreign Assoc. Nat. Acad. of Sciences; Hon. D.Sc. (Israel Inst. of Tech.) 1966, (Yeshiva Univ., New York) 1972; Weizmann Prize for Sciences 1966, Rothschild Prize 1968, Israel Prize for Sciences 1969, Albert Einstein Medal and Prize for Physics 1970, Wigner Medal 1982. *Publications:* The Eightfold Way (with M. Gell-Mann) 1964, Algebraic Theory of Particle Physics 1967, One Way to Unitary Symmetry, The Past Decade in Particle Theory (with E. C. G. Sudarshan) 1973, Symétries, Jauges et Variétés de Groupes 1979, Group Theoretical Methods in Physics (with L. P. Horwitz) 1980, To Fulfil a Vision 1981, Twentieth Century Physics (Hebrew) 1981, The Particle Hunters (in Hebrew, with Y. Kirsch) 1983, Policy from a Sober Viewpoint 1984, Dynamical Groups (with A. Barut and A. Bohm) 1989; about 350 articles on physics, astrophysics and philosophy of science. *Leisure interests:* music, history, linguistics. *Address:* Department of Physics and Astronomy, Tel-Aviv University, Ramat Aviv, Tel-Aviv 69978, Israel. *Telephone:* (03) 6408560. *Fax:* (03) 6424264.

NEESON, Liam; British actor; b. Ballymena, Northern Ireland; m. Natasha Richardson 1994; one s.; ed. St. Mary's Teachers' Coll., London; worked as forklift operator, then as architect's asst.; acting debut with Lyric Players' Theatre, Belfast, in The Risen 1976. *Theatre includes:* Of Mice and Men

(Abbey Theatre Co., Dublin), The Informer (Dublin Theatre Festival), Translations (Nat. Theatre, London), The Plough and the Stars (Royal Exchange, Manchester), The Judas Kiss. *Films include:* Excalibur, Krull, The Bounty, The Innocent, Lamb, The Mission, Duet for One, A Prayer for the Dying, Suspect, Satisfaction, High Spirits, The Dead Pool, The Good Mother, Darkman, The Big Man, Under Suspicion, Husbands and Wives, Leap of Faith, Ethan Frome, Ruby Cairo, Schindler's List, Rob Roy, Nell, Before and After, Michael Collins (Best Actor Evening Standard Award 1997), Les Misérables (1998). *Television includes:* Arthur the King, Ellis Island, If Tomorrow Comes, A Woman of Substance, Hold the Dream, Kiss Me Goodnight, Next of Kin, Sweet As You Are.

NEFEDOV, Oleg Matveyevich, D.SC.; Russian chemist; b. 25 Nov. 1931, Dmitrov, Moscow region; s. of Matvey Kondrat'evich Nefedov and Mariya Adolfovna Teodorovich; m. Galina Gimelfarb 1954; one s. one d.; ed. D.I. Mendeleyev Inst. of Chem. and Tech.; worked as jr. then sr. researcher, Head Lab. Zelinsky Inst. of Organic Chem., U.S.S.R. (now Russian) Acad. of Sciences 1957–; corresp. mem. U.S.S.R. (now Russian) Acad. of Sciences 1979–87, mem. 1987–, Academic Sec. Div. of Gen. and Applied Chem. 1988–91, Vice-Pres. 1988–; U.S.S.R. People's Deputy 1989–91; U.S.S.R. State Prize 1983, 1990, N.D. Zelinsky Prize 1987, Prize of U.S.S.R. and Hungarian Acads. 1988, N. Semyonov Prize 1991, A. Karpinsky Prize 1993. *Publications:* The Structure of Cyclopropane Derivatives 1986, Chemistry of Carbenes and Small-sized Cyclic Compounds (ed.) 1989, Carbenes Chemistry 1990; 627 articles and 201 patents. *Leisure interests:* sport, gathering mushrooms. *Address:* Zelinsky Institute of Organic Chemistry, GSP-1, Leninsky prospekt 47, Moscow, Russia. *Telephone:* (095) 237-45-32. *Fax:* (095) 938 1837.

NEFFATI, Chedly; Tunisian politician; b. 15 March 1946, Gabès; m.; three c.; ed. Ecole Nat. d'Admin.; various posts in regional admin. for the Ministry of the Interior and as a del. in Kairouan; Gov. of Kairouan June 1982, of Béja July 1984; Head of Regional Affairs, Ministry of the Interior Aug.–Dec. 1987; Sec. of State for Nat. Security April–Nov. 1988; Minister for the Interior 1988–90, of Justice 1990–91; mem. Rassemblement Constitutionnel Démocratique; Officier de l'Ordre de l'Indépendance (Tunisia). *Address:* c/o Ministry of Justice, avenue Bab Benat, Tunis, Tunisia.

NEGAHBAN, Ezatollah, PH.D.; Iranian archaeologist; b. 1 March 1926; s. of Abdol Amir Negahban and Roghieh Dideban; m. Miriam Lois Miller 1955; five s.; ed. Teheran and Chicago Univs.; Assoc. Prof. Univ. of Teheran 1956–62, Prof. 1962, Founder and Dir. Univ. Inst. of Archaeology 1957, Head, Dept. Archaeology 1968–75, Dean Faculty of Letters and Humanities 1975–78; Prof. Univ. Chicago 1964; Tech. Dir. Iranian Archaeological Service 1960–65; Tech. Adviser to Ministry of Culture 1965–79; Visiting Curator Univ. Museum, Visiting Prof., Univ. of Pa. 1980–; Dir. Museum Iran Bastan 1966–68, Iranian Archaeological Asscn. 1957–65; Sec.-Gen. Int. Congress, Iranian Art and Archaeology, Dir. 5th Congress; excavated at Mehranabad 1961, Marlik 1961–62, Haft Tepe 1966; Dir. Gazvin Plain Expedition (Zaghe, Qabrestan and Sagzabad) 1970; archaeological survey of N.E. Iran 1965, Mazandaran Highlands 1975; mem. German Archaeological Inst., Exec. Cttee. and Perm. Council, Congress of Pre- and Proto-History. *Publications:* The Buff Ware Sequence in Khuzistan 1954, Preliminary Report on the Marlik Excavation 1961–1962 1964, Archaeology of Iran 1973, Metal Vessels from Marlik 1983, Excavations at Haft Tepe 1991, Final Report of Marlik Excavation 1994, Weapons from Marlik 1995, Final Report of Marlik Excavation 1996; and numerous excavation reports and articles in journals. *Leisure interest:* Persian calligraphy. *Address:* 5226 Rexford Road, Philadelphia, PA 19131, U.S.A. *Telephone:* (215) 898-4057 (Office); (215) 877-1821 (Home).

NEGISHI, Takashi, PH.D.; Japanese economist and professor; b. 2 April 1933, Tokyo; s. of Setsuko Negishi and Suteta Negishi; m. Aiko Mori 1964; one d.; ed. Univ. of Tokyo; Research Asst., then Research Assoc., Stanford Univ., Calif. 1958–60; Research Asst., Univ. of Tokyo 1963–65, Assoc. Prof. 1965–76, Prof. 1976–94, Dean Faculty of Econs. 1990–92; Prof., Aoyama Gakuin Univ. 1994–; Fellow Econometric Soc. 1966–, Vice-Pres. 1992–93, Pres. 1994; Pres. Japan Asscn. of Econs. and Econometrics 1985; Pres. The Soc. for the History of Econ. Thought, Japan 1997–99; mem. Exec. Cttee. Int. Econ. Asscn. 1989–92, Science Council of Japan 1985–88, Japan Acad. 1998–; Foreign Hon. mem. American Econ. Asscn. 1989; Japan Acad. Prize 1993. *Publications:* General Equilibrium Theory and International Trade 1972, Microeconomic Foundations of Keynesian Macro Economics 1979, Economic Theories of a Non-Walrasian Tradition 1985, History of Economic Theory 1989, The Collected Essays of Takashi Negishi 1994. *Address:* 2-10-5-301, Motoazabu, Minato-ku, Tokyo 106, Japan. *Telephone:* 3440-0630.

NEGMATULLAEV, Sabit, D.TECH.SC.; Tajikistan physicist; b. 16 Sept. 1937, Ura-Tube; ed. Tajik Polytech. Inst.; mem. CPSU 1966–91; jr. researcher Inst. of Seismology, Tajik Acad. of Sciences, Scientific Sec. 1964–65, Vice-Dir. 1965–69, Dir. 1969–; mem. Tajik Acad. of Sciences 1987, Pres. 1988–95; Chair. Scientific-Publishing Council of Acad. of Sciences; mem. Cen. Cttee. CPSU 1990–91. *Address:* Academy of Sciences of Tajikistan, Rudaki Prospect 33, 734029 Dushanbe, Tajikistan. *Telephone:* (3772) 22-50-83.

NEGRI SEMBILAN, Yang di-Pertuan Besar, Tuanku Jaafar ibni Al-Marhum Tuanku Adbul Rahman: Malaysian Ruler; b. 19 July 1922; m. Tuanku Najihar binti Tuanku Besar Burhanuddin 1943; three s. three d.; ed. Malay School Sri Menanti, Malay Coll. and Nottingham Univ.; entered Malay Admin. Service 1944; Asst. Dist. Officer, Rembau 1946–47, Parti 1953–55; Chargé d'Affaires, Washington, D.C. 1947; First Perm. Sec., Malayan Perm. Mission to the UN 1957–58; First Sec., Trade Counsellor, rising to Deputy High Commr., London 1962–63; Amb. to United Arab Repub. 1962; High Commr. concurrently in Nigeria and Ghana 1965–66; Timbalan Yang di-Pertuan Agong (Deputy Supreme Head of State) 1979–84, 1989–94, Yang di-Pertuan Agong (Supreme Head of State) 1994–. *Leisure interests:* well-planned housing schemes, sports. *Address:* Seremban, Malaysia.

NEGRITOIU, Misu, M.S., PH.D.; Romanian politician and economist; b. 26 May 1950, Dăbuleni, Dolj Co.; s. of Marin and Floarea Negritoiu; m. Paula Urzica 1977; one s. one d.; ed. Bucharest Acad. of Econ. Studies, Law School, Bucharest Univ., HDS Hertfordshire Univ.; foreign trade economist, and then foreign trade co. dir. 1973–90; Minister-Counsellor, Embassy, Washington, Pres. Romanian Devt. Agency 1990–92; Deputy Prime Minister, Chair. Council for Strategy and Econ. Reform Co-ordination 1993; Chief Econ. Adviser to Pres. of Romania 1994–96; mem. Parl. 1996–; Prof. Acad. of Econ. Studies, School of Political Studies and Public Admin., Bucharest; Chair. Bd. of Dirs. Grad. School of Man., M.B.A. Canadian Programme; mem. Romanian Econ. Soc. (SOREC), Romanian Soc. for Club of Rome, Romanian Asscn. for Energy Policy (APER), American Asscn. for Arbitration, Centre for European Policy Studies, Econ. Policy Forum. *Publications:* Jumping Ahead—Economic Development and FDI 1996, International Finance (textbook) 1994); numerous studies and articles on int. and domestic economic issues. *Address:* c/o Chamber of Deputies, Calea 13 Septembrie 1, Bucharest (Office); Str. Mexic 2, ap. 16, sector 1, Bucharest, Romania (Home).

NEGROPONTE, John Dimitri, B.A.; American diplomatist; b. 21 July 1939, U.K.; s. of Dimitri J. Negroponte and Catherine C. Negroponte; m. Diana Mary Villiers 1976; two s. three d.; ed. Yale Univ.; entered Foreign Service 1960, Amb. to Honduras 1981–85; Asst. Sec. of State 1985–87; Deputy Asst. to Pres. for Nat. Security Affairs 1987–89; Amb. to Mexico 1989–93, to the Philippines 1993–95; Special Co-ordinator for post-1999 U.S. Presence in Panama 1996–97; Exec. Vice-Pres. Global Markets McGraw-Hill 1997–. *Leisure interests:* swimming, skiing, reading, history. *Address:* McGraw-Hill Companies, 49th Floor, 1221 Avenue of the Americas, New York, NY 10020 (Office); 4936 Lowell Street, N.W., Washington, DC 20016, U.S.A. (Home).

NEHER, Erwin; German research scientist; b. 20 March 1944, Landsberg; s. of Franz Xaver Neher and Elisabeth Neher; m. Dr. Eva-Maria Neher 1978; three s. two d.; ed. Tech. Univ. Munich, Univ. of Wisconsin, Madison, U.S.A.; Research Assoc., Max-Planck-Institut für Psychiatrie, Munich 1970–72, Max-Planck-Institut für biophysikalische Chemie, Göttingen 1972–75, 1976–83, Research Dir. 1983–; Research Assoc., Yale Univ. New Haven, Conn., U.S.A. 1975–76; Fairchild Scholar, Calif. Inst. of Tech. 1988–89; shared Nobel Prize for Medicine 1991; several nat. and int. scientific awards. *Publications:* Elektronische Messtechnik in der Physiologie 1974, Single Channel Recording (Ed.) 1983. *Address:* Domäne 11, 37120 Bovenden, Germany. *Telephone:* (05594) 93135.

NEHRU, Braj Kumar, B.SC., B.SC.(ECON); Indian civil servant and barrister; b. 4 Sept. 1909, Allahabad; s. of Brijlal Nehru and Rameshwari Nehru; m. Magdalena Friedmann 1935; three s.; ed. Allahabad Univ., London School of Econs., Balliol Coll., Oxford, Inner Temple, London; joined ICS 1934; Asst. Commr. 1934–39; Under-Sec. Dept. of Educ., Health and Lands, Govt. of India 1939; mem. Indian Legis. Ass. 1939; Officer on special duty, Reserve Bank of India, Under-Sec. Finance Dept., Govt. of India 1940, Jt. Sec. 1947; rep. Reparations Conf. 1945, Commonwealth Finance Ministers Conf., UN Gen. Ass. 1949–52, 1960, FAO Confs. 1949–50, Sterling Balances Confs. 1947–49, Bandung Conf. 1955; deputed to enquire into Australian Fed. Finance 1946; mem. UN Advisory Cttee. on Admin. and Budgetary Questions 1951–53; Adviser to Sudan Govt. 1955; Exec. Dir. IBRD (World Bank) 1949–54, 1958–62; Minister, Indian Embassy, Washington 1949–54; Sec. Dept. of Econ. Affairs, Ministry of Finance 1957–58, Commr.-Gen. for Econ. Affairs 1958–61; Amb. to U.S.A. 1961–68; Vice-Pres. Vienna Inst. for Devt. 1962–87; mem. UN Investments Cttee. 1962–, Chair. 1977–91, mem. emer. 1991–; Gov. of Assam and Nagaland 1968–73, of Manipur, Meghalaya and Tripura 1972–73, of Jammu and Kashmir 1981–84, of Gujarat 1984–86; Chair. North-Eastern Council 1972–73; High Commr. in U.K. 1973–77; Chair., Gov. Body Dyal Singh Coll., Indian Advisory Bd. ANZ Grindlays Bank 1988–94, Hindustan Oil Exploration Co. Ltd. 1987–94; Pres. Dyal Singh Coll. Governing Body 1988–, Dyal Singh Library Trust Soc. 1988–, Dyal Singh Coll. Trust Soc. 1988–97; Trustee Tribune Trust 1989– (Chair. 1996–), World Memorial Fund for Disaster Relief 1989–, Indira Gandhi Memorial Trust 1986–; Dir. East India Hotels Ltd. 1988–; Vice-Chair. Vienna Inst. for Devt. 1962–90; mem. Int. Advisory Council of Vienna Inst. for Devt. and Co-operation 1990–; Fellow, L.S.E.; Hon. LL.D. (Mo. Valley Coll.), Hon. Litt.D. (Jacksonville Univ.), Hon. D.Litt. (Punjab Univ.). *Publications:* Australian Federal Finance 1947, Speaking of India 1966, Thoughts on the Present Discontents 1986, Nice Guys Finish Second 1997. *Leisure interests:* reading and writing. *Address:* Fairview, Kasauli 173 204 (H.P.), India. *Telephone:* (01792) 72189.

NEIL, Andrew Ferguson, M.A.; British journalist, writer and broadcaster; b. 21 May 1949, Scotland; s. of James Neil and Mary Ferguson; ed. Paisley Grammar School, Univ. of Glasgow; with Conservative Party Research Dept. 1971–73; with The Economist 1973–83, Ulster Political then Industrial

Corresp. 1973–79, American Corresp. 1979–82, U.K. Ed. 1982–83; Ed. The Sunday Times 1983–94; with Fox TV Network, U.S.A. 1994; Exec. Chair. Sky TV 1988–90; Ed.-in-Chief Sunday Business, The Scotsman, Scotland on Sunday, Edinburgh Evening News, The European 1996–; regular anchorman and TV commentator U.K. and U.S.A.; Contrib. Ed. Vanity Fair, New York 1994–; consultant NBC News 1997–; freelance writer and broadcaster 1994–; Hon. D.Lit. (Napier Univ.) 1998. *Publications:* The Cable Revolution 1982, Britain's Free Press: Does It Have One? 1989, Full Disclosure 1996. *Leisure interests:* dining out in New York, London, Aspen and Côte d'Azur, skiing. *Address:* Glenburn Enterprises, P.O. Box 584, London, SW7 3QY, England. *Telephone:* 0171-240 9968.

NEILAND, Brendan Robert, M.A., R.A.; British artist and professor of painting; b. 23 Oct. 1941, Lichfield; s. of Arthur Neiland and Joan Whiley; m. Hilary Salter 1970; two d.; ed. St. Philip's Grammar School, Birmingham, St. Augustine's Seminary, Ireland, Birmingham School of Art and Royal Coll. of Art; painter and printmaker; gallery artist, Angela Flowers Gallery 1970–78, Fischer Fine Art 1978–92, Redfern Gallery 1992–; one-man shows and group shows throughout Europe, Middle East, America and Australia; lecturer in Fine Art, Brighton Univ. 1983–, Prof. of Painting 1996–; Daler Rowney Award, Royal Acad. Summer Exhbn. 1989. *Publication:* Upon Reflection 1997. *Leisure interests:* cricket, golf, fine wines. *Address:* 7 Roedean Way, Brighton, BN2 5RJ, England; Crepe, La Grévé sur Mignon, 17170 Courcon, France. *Telephone:* (01273) 691833 (Brighton); 05 46 01 62 97 (France). *Fax:* (01273) 691833.

NEILD, Robert Ralph; British economist; b. 10 Sept. 1924, Peterborough; s. of Ralph and Josephine Neild; m. 1st Nora Clemens Sayre (dissolved 1961); 2nd Elizabeth W. Griffiths 1962 (dissolved 1986); one s. four d.; ed. Charterhouse, and Trinity Coll., Cambridge; R.A.F. 1943–44, Operational Research, R.A.F., 1944–45; Secr., UN Econ. Comm. for Europe, Geneva 1947–51; Econ. Section, Cabinet Office (later Treasury) 1951–56; Lecturer in Econs., Fellow and Steward of Trinity Coll., Cambridge 1956–58; Nat. Inst. of Econ. and Social Research 1958–64; Econ. Adviser to Treasury 1964–67; mem. Fulton Cttee. on the Civil Service 1966–68; Dir. Stockholm Int. Peace Research Inst. 1967–71, mem. Governing Bd. 1972–82; Prof. of Econs., Cambridge Univ. 1971–84, Emer. 1984–; mem. Governing Body Queen Elizabeth Coll., Oxford 1978–87; Fellow, Trinity Coll. 1971–, Acorn Investment Trust 1988. *Publications:* Pricing and Employment in the Trade Cycle 1964, The Measurement and Reform of Budgetary Policy (with T. S. Ward) 1978, How to Make up your Mind about the Bomb 1981, An Essay on Strategy 1990, The Foundations of Defensive Defence (ed. with A. Boserup) 1990, The English, the French and the Oyster 1995. *Address:* Trinity College, Cambridge, CB2 1TQ, England. *Telephone:* (01223) 338400.

NEILL, Rt. Hon. Sir Brian (Thomas) Neill, Kt., PC, Q.C., M.A.; British judge; b. 2 Aug. 1923; s. of Sir Thomas Neill and Lady (Annie Strachan) Neill (née Bishop); m. Sally Margaret Backus 1956; three s.; ed. Highgate School, Corpus Christi Coll., Oxford; served Rifle Brigade 1942–46; called to Bar, Inner Temple 1949, Bencher 1976; Q.C. 1968; a Recorder of the Crown Court 1972–78; a Judge of the High Court, Queen's Bench Div. 1978–84; a Lord Justice of Appeal 1985–96; mem. Departmental Cttee. to examine operation of Section 2 of Official Secrets Act 1971; Chair. Advisory Cttee. on Rhodesia Travel Restrictions 1973–78; mem. Court of Assistants 1972–, Master 1980–81. *Publication:* Defamation (with Colin Duncan) 1978. *Address:* c/o Royal Courts of Justice, Strand, London, WC2A 2LL, England.

NEILL, Sam, O.B.E.; New Zealand actor; b. 14 Sept. 1947, N. Ireland; m. Noriko Watanabe; one d.; one s. by Lisa Harrow; ed. Univ. of Canterbury; toured for one year with Players Drama Quintet; appeared with Amamus Theatre in roles including Macbeth and Pentheus in The Bacchae; joined N.Z. Nat. Film Unit playing leading part in three films 1974–78; moved to Australia 1978, to England 1980; TV appearances include: From a Far Country, Ivanhoe, The Country Girls, Reilly: Ace of Spies, Kane and Abel (mini-series). *Films:* Sleeping Dogs 1977, The Journalist, My Brilliant Career, Just Out of Reach, Attack Force Z, The Final Conflict (Omen III), Possession, Enigma, Le Sang des Autres, Robbery Under Arms, Plenty, For Love Alone, The Good Wife, A Cry in the Dark, Dead Calm, The French Revolution, The Hunt for Red October, Until the End of the World, Hostage, Memoirs of an Invisible Man, Death in Brunswick, Jurassic Park, The Piano, Sirens, Country Life, Restoration, Victory, In the Month of Madness, Event Horizon, The Horse Whisperer.

NEILL OF BLADEN, Baron (Life Peer) cr. 1997, of Briantspuddle in the County of Dorset; **Francis Patrick Neill,** Kt., Q.C.; British lawyer; b. 8 Aug. 1926; s. of late Sir Thomas and Annie Strachan (née Bishop) Neill; m. Caroline Susan Debenham 1954; three s. two d. (and one s. deceased); ed. Highgate School and Magdalen Coll., Oxford; served with Rifle Brigade 1944–47; G.S.O. III (Training), British Troops Egypt 1947; called to the Bar, Gray's Inn 1951; Recorder of the Crown Court 1975–78; Judge of the Court of Appeal of Jersey and Guernsey 1977–94; Fellow of All Souls Coll., Oxford 1950–77, Sub-Warden 1972–74, Warden 1977–95; Vice-Chancellor Oxford Univ. 1985–89; Chair., Justice—All Souls Cttee. for Review of Admin. Law 1978–87, Press Council 1978–83, Council for Securities Industry 1978–85; mem. DTI Cttee. of Inquiry into Regulatory Arrangements at Lloyds 1986–87; Bencher, Gray's Inn 1971, Vice Treasurer 1989, Treasurer 1990; mem. Bar Council 1967–71, Vice-Chair. 1973–74, Chair. 1974–75; Chair. Senate of the Inns of Court and the Bar 1974–75; Chair. Cttee. on Standards in Public Life 1997–; Dir. Times Newspapers Holdings Ltd. 1988–97; Hon. Fellow Magdalen Coll., Oxford 1988; Hon. Prof. of Legal Ethics, Birmingham Univ. 1983–84; Hon. D.C.L. (Oxford) 1987; Hon. LL.D. (Hull) 1978, (Buckingham) 1994. *Publication:* Administrative Justice: Some Necessary Reforms 1988. *Leisure interests:* music, forestry. *Address:* 1 Hare Court, Temple, London, EC4Y 7BE, England.

NEIMAN, LeRoy; American artist; b. 8 June 1921, St. Paul, Minn.; s. of Charles Runquist and Lydia Runquist (née Serline); m. Janet Byrne 1957; ed. Art Inst., Chicago, Univ. of Illinois and DePaul Univ.; instructor Art Inst., Chicago 1950–60, Saugatuck (Mich.) Summer School of Painting 1957–58, 1963, School of Arts and Crafts, Winston-Salem, N.C. 1963; instructor in painting Atlanta Youth Council for Poverty Program 1968–69; contrib. to features Playboy magazine 1956–; graphics printmaker 1971–; artist Olympic Games, Munich, ABC TV 1971, official artist Olympic Games, Montreal, ABC TV 1976, U.S. Olympics 1980, 1984; computer artist Superbowl, New Orleans CBS TV 1978; official artist Goodwill Games, Moscow, CNN TV 1986; first official artist Ky. Derby, Louisville 1997; one-man shows in Chicago, London, Paris, New York, Atlanta, Dublin, Caracas, Leningrad, Tokyo, Helsinki, Stockholm, Cadaqués (Spain), Elkhart (Ind.), Oklahoma, Moscow, Youngstown (Ill.) etc.; retrospective exhbns. in Minn., Houston, Tokyo, Ohio, Ky., Paris; two-man show Neiman–Warhol, Los Angeles Inst. of Contemporary Art 1961; group shows in U.S.A., Paris, Milan, London, Munich, Tokyo, St. Petersburg; rep. in perm. collections Minneapolis Inst. of Arts, State Museum, Springfield, Joslyn Museum, Omaha, Wadham Coll., Oxford, Nat. Art Museum Sport, New York, Museo de Bellas Artes, Caracas, Hermitage Museum, St. Petersburg, The Armand Hammer Collection, Los Angeles, Edwin and Ruth Kenney Museum of American Art, Ohio Univ.; work commissioned for Baseball Hall of Fame, Coca Cola, Gen. Mills, Gen. Motors, Ky. Derby, Los Angeles Dodgers 100th Anniversary, Nat. Football League, Newport Jazz Festival, Rocky II, III, IV and V films; executed murals at Merchant Nat. Bank, Hammond, Ind., Continental Hotel, Chicago, Swedish Lloyd ship S.S. Patricia, Stockholm, Sportsmans Park, Chicago; donor and mem. advisory cttee. LeRoy Neiman Center for Print Studies, School of the Arts, Columbia Univ. 1995, LeRoy Neiman Center for Study of American Soc. and Culture, Univ. of Calif. at L.A.; mem. advisory cttee. New York Comm. for Cultural Affairs 1995; numerous hon. doctorates including Franklin Pierce Coll. 1976, St. Francis Coll. 1998, St. Bonaventure Univ. 1999; numerous prizes including Gold Medal, Salon d'Art Moderne, Paris 1961, Award of Merit, Outstanding Sports Artist, AAU 1976, Gold Plate Award, American Acad. of Achievement 1977, Olympic Artist of Century Award 1979, Gold Medal Award, St. John's Univ. 1985. *Publications include:* Art and Lifestyle 1974, Illustrations for new edn. of Moby Dick 1975, Horses 1979, Posters 1980, Carnaval 1981, Winners 1983, Monte Carlo Chase 1988, Big Time Golf 1992, An American in Paris 1994, LeRoy Neiman on Safari 1997. *Address:* Hammer Galleries, 33 West 57th Street, New York, NY 10019; Knoedler Publishing, 19 East 70th Street, New York, NY 10021; LeRoy Neiman Inc., 1 West 67th Street, New York, NY 10023, U.S.A. *Telephone:* (212) 644-4400 (Hammer Galleries); (212) 794-0571 (Knoedler Publishing).

NEISS, Hubert; Austrian international finance official; b. 1935; ed. Hochschule für Welthandel and Univ. of Kansas; economist, European Dept. IMF 1967; Chief, S. Pacific Div. 1973; Resident Rep. of IMF in Indonesia; Deputy Dir. Asian Dept. 1980–91; Dir. Asian Regional Dept. IMF 1991–. *Address:* International Monetary Fund, 700 19th Street, N.W., Washington, DC 20431, U.S.A.

NEÍZVESTNY, Ernst Iosifovich; Russian artist and sculptor; b. 9 April 1925, Sverdlovsk; ed. V. I. Surikov State Inst. of Arts (M. G. Manizer's studio); Soviet Army 1942–45; sculptor at studios of U.S.S.R. Agricultural Exhbn. (later Econ. Achievements of U.S.S.R. Exhbn.) 1953–54; mem. Artists' Union of U.S.S.R. 1955–57; granted permission to emigrate to Geneva 1976; Soviet citizenship restored 1990; mem. Royal Acad. of Fine Arts, Sweden, New York Acad. of Sciences 1986, European Acad. of Arts, Sciences and Humanities, Paris; State Prize 1995; Order of Red Star 1945. *Main works:* Kremlin Builder, First Wings, The Youth, Mother, series: War—is ...; Robots and Semi-robots, Great Mistakes, Nikita Krushchev Memorial, Lotus Blossom, Aswan Dam, Egypt 1968, Monument to the Golden Child, Odessa, Ukraine 1995, Monument to Victims of Stalinism, Magadan, Russia 1990–96, Bust of Boris Yeltsin 1996, Monument to the Kalmykia Deportation 1996. *Publications:* Space, Time and Synthesis in Art 1990, Artist's Fate 1992. *Leisure interests:* building sculpture garden on Shelter Island, New York, U.S.A. *Address:* 81 Grand Street, New York, NY 10013, U.S.A. *Fax:* (212) 226-2603.

NEKROŠIUS, Eimuntas; Lithuanian theatre director and actor; b. 21 Nov. 1952, Pažobris, Lithuania; s. of Petras Nekrošius and Elena Nekrošiené; m. Nadezhda Gultyaeva 1976; two s.; ed. State Inst. of Theatre Art in Moscow; f. Meno Fortas Theatre Studio; Theatre Dir. Kaunas Drama Theatre 1978–79; Theatre Dir. Youth Theatre Lithuanian S.S.R. (now Lithuania), Vilnius 1979–91, Dir. LIFE Int. Theatre Festival 1993–97. *Productions include:* A Taste of Honey 1976, Duokishkis Ballad 1978, Ivanov 1978, Square 1980, Pirosmani 1981, Love and Death in Verona 1982, The Day Lasts More Than Ages 1983, Uncle Vanya 1986, Mozart and Salieri, Don Juan, Plague 1994, Three Sisters 1995; toured with theatre and productions of his own in Russia and other countries. *Film roles include:* Girenas in Flight Through Atlantics 1983, Father in Lessons of Hatred 1984, Minister in Team 1985. U.S.S.R.

State Prize 1987, Award of European Theatre Union 1991, Baltic Ass. Award 1994, Nat. Culture and Art Award, Order of Grand Duke Gediminas. *Address:* Bernardinų 8/8, LT-2000 Vilnius, Lithuania. *Telephone:* (2) 613515, 622727.

NEKVASIL, Lieut.-Gen. Jiří; Czech army officer; b. 24 April 1948, Benešov; m. 1st Jaroslava Papežová; m. 2nd Danuše Kadlečková; two s. two d.; ed. Tech. Inst. Liptovský Mikuláš, Mil. Acad., Kalinin, Acad. of Gen. Staff of Mil. Forces, Moscow; 2nd in Command Czech A.F. and Anti-Air Defence System 1990–92; Commdr. of Gen. Staff 1993–98; Czech Rep. to NATO 1998–; Order of Red Star (U.S.S.R.), Meritorious Legion Order (U.S.A.) 1996. *Leisure interests:* mushrooming, tennis, gardening, photography. *Address:* c/o Ministry of Defence, Tychonova 1, 160 00 Prague 6, Czech Republic. *Telephone:* 330-4-1111.

NELDER, John Ashworth, M.A., D.SC., F.R.S.; British statistician; b. 8 Oct. 1924, Dulverton, Somerset; s. of Reginald Charles Nelder and Edith May Ashworth (née Briggs); m. Mary Hawkes 1955; one s. one d.; ed. Blundell's School, Tiverton, Sidney Sussex Coll., Cambridge Univ.; Head, Statistics Section, Nat. Vegetable Research Station, Wellesbourne 1950–68; Head, Statistics Dept., Rothamsted Experimental Station, Harpenden 1968–84; Sr. Research Fellow, London Business School 1984–87; Originator statistical computer programs Genstat and GLIM; Visiting Prof., Imperial Coll., London 1971–; fmr. Pres., Int. Biometric Soc.; Pres. Royal Statistical Soc. 1985–86; Guy Medal (Silver) of Royal Statistical Soc. *Publications:* Generalized Linear Models (with P. McCullagh), Computers in Biology; more than 120 papers in scientific journals. *Leisure interests:* ornithology, music (especially playing piano). *Address:* Cumberland Cottage, 33 Crown Street, Redbourn, St. Albans, Herts., AL3 7JX, England. *Telephone:* (01582) 792907.

NELISSEN, Roelof J.; Netherlands politician and banker; b. 4 April 1931, Hoofdplaat, Zeeland province; m. A. M. van der Kelen; three s. one d.; ed. grammar school at Dongen and Faculty of Law, Catholic Univ. of Nijmegen; various posts in employers' asscns., Amsterdam and The Hague 1956–69; mem. Second Chamber, States-Gen. (Parl.) 1963–70; Minister of Econ. Affairs 1970–71; First Deputy Prime Minister, Minister of Finance 1971–73; mem. Bd. Man. Dirs. Amsterdam-Rotterdam Bank N.V. 1974–, Vice-Chair. 1979–82, Chair. 1983–92; Chair. Bd. Man. Dirs ABN-AMRO Holding N.V. 1990–92. *Address:* P.O. Box 552, 1250 AN Laren, Netherlands.

NELLIGAN, Kate; Canadian actress; b. 16 March 1951, London, Ont.; d. of Patrick Joseph and Alice (née Dier) Nelligan; ed. St. Martin's Catholic School, London, Ont., York Univ., Toronto, and Cen. School of Speech and Drama, London, England; professional stage début as Corrie in Barefoot in the Park, Little Theatre, Bristol 1972; other parts there and at Theatre Royal for Bristol Old Vic 1972–73 include: Hypatia in Misalliance, Stella Kowalski in A Streetcar Named Desire, Pegeen Mike in The Playboy of the Western World, Grace Harkaway in London Assurance, title role in Lulu, Sybil Chase in Private Lives; London début as Jenny in Knuckle, Comedy Theatre 1974; joined Nat. Theatre Co. at Old Vic to 1975 to play Ellie Dunn in Heartbreak House, also in Plenty and Moon for the Misbegotten 1984; As You Like It for R.S.C., Stratford; Serious Money, Broadway 1988, Spoils of War 1988, Eleni; *films include:* The Count of Monte Cristo, The Romantic Englishwoman, Dracula 1979, Patman, Eye of the Needle 1980, Agent 1980, Without a Trace 1983, Eleni 1986, White Room, The Prince of Tides, Frankie and Johnny, Shadows and Fog, Fatal Instinct, Wolf, How to Make An American Quilt, Up Close and Personal, U.S. Marshals, Stolen Moments (voice). *TV includes:* The Onedin Line, The Lady of the Camellias, Licking Hitler, Measure for Measure, Thérèse Raquin 1980, Forgive our Foolish Ways 1980, Count of Monte Cristo, Victims, Kojak, Love and Hate, Old Times; Evening Standard Best Actress Award 1978. *Leisure interests:* reading, cooking. *Address:* c/o Joe Funicello, International Creative Management, 8942 Wilshire Boulevard, Beverly Hills, CA 90211, U.S.A.

NELSON, E. Benjamin, M.A., J.D.; American politician; b. 17 May 1941, McCook, Neb.; s. of Benjamin E. Nelson and Birdella Nelson; m. Diane Nelson (née Gleason); two s. two d.; ed. Univ. of Nebraska; instructor Dept. of Philosophy, Univ. of Neb. 1963–65; Dir. of Compliance Neb. Dept. of Insurance 1965–72, Dir. 1975–76; admitted to Neb. Bar 1970; Gen. Counsel, Cen. Nat. Insurance Group of Omaha 1972–74, Exec. Vice-Pres. 1977, Pres. 1978–79, Pres. and C.E.O. 1980–81; Attorney of Counsel Kennedy, Holland DeLacy and Svoboda, Omaha 1985–90; Gov. of Nebraska 1990–98; Exec. Vice-Pres. Nat. Asscn. of Insurance Commrs. 1982–85; Chair. Nat. Educ. Goals Panel 1992–94, Govs.' Ethanol Coalition (also f.) 1991, 1994, Midwestern Govs.' Conf. 1994; fmr. Chair. Interstate Oil and Gas Compact Comm., Western Govs.' Asscn. and Co-Lead Gov. on Int. Trade; Pres. Council of State Govts. 1994; Chair. Nat. Resources Cttee. and Co-Lead Gov. on Federalism, Nat. Govs.' Asscn.; Co-Chair. Nat. Summit on Federalism 1995; fmr. Vice-Chair. Democratic Govs.' Asscn.; Hon. LL.D. (Creighton Univ.) 1992, (Peru State Coll.) 1993; Hon. D.Hum.Litt. (Coll. of St. Mary) 1995; numerous awards. *Leisure interests:* spending time with my family, hunting and fishing, reading and collecting clocks. *Address:* c/o Governor's Residence, 1425 H Street, Lincoln, NE 68508, U.S.A. (Home).

NELSON, Gaylord Anton, LL.B.; American politician and lawyer; b. 4 June 1916, Clear Lake, Wis.; s. of Anton Nelson and Mary Bradt; m. Carrie Lee Dotson 1947; two s. one d.; ed. Clear Lake High School (Polk County, Wis.), San José State Coll., Calif., and Wisconsin Univ. Law School; army service 1942–46; admitted to Wis. Bar 1942; Practising Attorney, Madison, Wis. 1946–58; Wisconsin State Senator 1949–58; Gov. of Wisconsin 1958–62; U.S. Senator from Wisconsin 1963–80; Counsellor Wilderness Soc., Washington, D.C. 1981–; Founder of Earth Day 1970; UN Environmental Programme "Environmental Leadership" Award 1982, UN Environment Programme "Only One Earth" Award 1992, Presidential Medal of Freedom 1995; Democrat. *Address:* Wilderness Society, 900 17th Street, N.W., Washington, DC 20006 (Office); 3611 Calvend Lane, Kensington, MD 20895, U.S.A. (Home).

NELSON, Judith, B.A.; American singer; b. 10 Sept. 1939; d. of Virgil D. Nelson and Genevieve W. Manes; m. Alan H. Nelson 1961; one s. one d.; ed. St. Olaf Coll., Northfield, Minn.; Alfred Hertz Memorial Fellowship, Univ. of Calif. Berkeley 1972–73; European debut 1972; specializes in baroque repertoire; has appeared with most of the maj. baroque orchestras in U.S. and Europe including Acad. of Ancient Music, Tafelmusik, Toronto, Philharmonia, San Francisco; has performed with San Francisco, St. Louis, Baltimore and Washington Nat. Symphony Orchestras and Los Angeles Philharmonic; has appeared in opera in Boston, Los Angeles, Brussels, Innsbruck, Venice, Turin and Rome and at Md. Handel Festival; master classes at UCLA, Univ. of Chicago, Bath Summer School, Bruges Festival, Jerusalem Music Center; Hon. D.F.A. (St.Olaf Coll.) 1979. *Leisure interests:* languages, support of local arts orgs., local politics. *Address:* 2600 Buena Vista Way, Berkeley, CA 94708, U.S.A. *Telephone:* (415) 848-1992.

NELSON, Ralph Alfred, M.D., PH.D., F.A.C.P.; American professor of medicine; b. 19 June 1927, Minneapolis; s. of Alfred Walter Nelson and Lydia (née Johnson) Nelson; m. Rosemarie Pokela 1954; three s. two d.; ed. Univ. of Minnesota; Pathology Residency, Univ. of Minnesota 1954–55; Fellowship in Physiology, Mayo Graduate School, Mayo Clinic, Rochester 1957–60, Resident Internal Medicine 1976–78; Asst. Prof. of Nutrition, Cornell Univ. 1961–62; Assoc. Prof. of Physiology, Assoc. Prof. of Nutrition, Mayo Medical School, Rochester 1967–78; Prof. of Nutrition, Dept. of Medicine, Univ. of Ill. 1979–, Prof. of Food Science, Prof. of Physiology, Univ. of Ill. 1979–, Head, Dept. of Internal Medicine, Univ. of Ill. Coll. of Medicine at Urbana-Champaign 1979–, Exec. Head Dept. of Medicine 1989–; Consultant for Nutritional Support Service, Danville Veterans Admin. Hosp.; Dir. of Research, Carle Foundation Hosp., Urbana 1979–; mem. American Physiological Soc., American Inst. of Nutrition, American Soc. of Clinical Nutrition; Mayo Clinic Alumni Award for Outstanding Research 1959. *Publications:* Mayo Clinic Renal Diet Cook Book 1974, numerous learned papers, including over 140 on the metabolism of bears. *Leisure interests:* walking, bicycling, canoeing, mountain hiking. *Address:* Carle Foundation Hospital, Department of Medical Research, 611 West Park Street, Urbana, IL 61801; 2 Illini Circuit, Urbana, IL 61801, U.S.A.

NĚMEC, Jaroslav, DR.SC.; Czech engineer and metallurgist (retd.); b. 15 March 1921, Horaždovice, Klatovy Dist.; s. of Karel Němec and Bohuslava Němcová; m. Zdenka Němcová 1944; ed. Eng. Faculty, Tech. Univ. of Prague (ČVUT); design engineer 1942–45; Dir. of Research and Devt., ČKD Sokolovo 1945–53; Prof., Coll. of Transport (VŠD), Dean 1953–55, Deputy Rector 1955–59; Prof., Head of Materials Dept. and Dept. of Specialization, Faculty of Nuclear and Physical Eng., ČVUT 1969–86, Deputy Dean 1967–74, Deputy Rector 1973–79; Corresp. mem. Czechoslovak (now Czech) Acad. of Sciences (ČSAV) 1972–75, mem. ČSAV 1975–, mem. Presidium 1979–87, Dir. Acad. Inst. of Theoretical and Applied Mech., Prague 1979–87; mem. Czechoslovak Atomic Comm.; Expert Adviser, Skoda Works, ČKD and others; Hon. mem. Int. Conf. on Fracture, Nat. Tech. Museum; mem. various foreign scientific and eng. socs.; Kaplan Medal 1958, All States Prize of Sciences 1965, 1974, Felber Medal 1971, Krížík Medal 1976, Order of Labour 1981, Nat. Prize 1985, Komensky Medal 1986 and many others. *Publications:* over 250 original papers on mechanics, elasticity and strength; 20 books including: Strength of Pressure Vessels under Different Operational Conditions, Toughness and Strength of Steel Parts, Failure of Strength of Plastics (with Acad. Serensen, Moscow), Shape and Strength of Metal Bodies (with Prof. Puchner), New Methods of Calculations of Rigidity and Strength of Machines (with Prof. Valenta), Fracture Dynamics, Dynamics and Reliability of Locomotive Parts, The Problem of Nuclear Equipment, with Special Reference to Reliability and Safety, Endurance of Mechanical Structures (with Dr. Drexler). *Leisure interest:* painting (18 exhbns. held). *Address:* Letohradská 60, 7 Prague 17000, Czech Republic. *Telephone:* 372862.

NEMEIRY, Field Marshal Gaafar Mohammed al- (see Nemery, Field Marshal Gaafar Mohammed al-).

NEMERY, Field Marshal Gaafar Mohammed al-; Sudanese political leader and army officer; b. 1 Jan. 1930, Omdurman; ed. Sudan Military Coll.; fmr. Commdr. Khartoum garrison; campaigns against rebels in Southern Sudan; placed under arrest on suspicion of plotting to overthrow the govt.; led successful mil. coup May 1969; promoted from Col. to Maj.-Gen. May 1969, to Field Marshal May 1979; Chair. Revolutionary Command Council (RCC) 1969–71, C.-in-C. of Armed Forces 1969–73, 1976–85; Minister of Defence May-June 1969, 1972–73, 1974–76, 1978–79; Prime Minister 1969–76, 1977–85; Minister of Foreign Affairs 1970–71, of Planning 1971–72, of Finance 1977–78, of Agric. and Irrigation 1982, of Defence 1983–85; Pres. of Sudan 1971–85 (overthrown in coup); Supreme Commdr. of Armed Forces 1985; stripped of rank of Field Marshal in absentia June 1985; Pres. Political Bureau Sudanese Socialist Union 1971–85, Sec.-Gen. 1971–76, 1979–82; Pres. of OAU 1978–79.

NÉMETH, Miklós; Hungarian politician; b. 24 Jan. 1948, Monok; s. of Andras Nemeth and Margit (née Stajz) Nemeth; m. Erzsebet Szilágy 1971; two s.; ed. Karl Marx Univ. of Budapest; Lecturer in Political Economy Karl Marx Univ. 1971–77; deputy section head Nat. Planning Office 1977–81; worked on staff, later as deputy leader, of HSWP Cen. Cttee. Dept. of Political Economy, Dept. Leader 1987–88; mem. of Cen. Cttee., Secr. 1987–88; mem. Political Cttee. 1987–88; M.P. 1988–90; Prime Minister of Hungary 1988–90; appointed to four-member Presidium of HSWP 1989; mem. Presidium, Hungarian Socialist Party (HSP) Oct.–Dec. 1989 (resgnd.); Vice-Pres. (Personnel and Administration) EBRD 1991–. *Leisure interests:* sailing, tennis. *Address:* c/o European Bank for Reconstruction and Development, One Exchange Square, London, EC2A 2EH, England.

NEMITSAS, Takis Xanthos; Greek-Cypriot fmr. politician and industrialist; b. 2 June 1930, Limassol; s. of Xanthos Nemitsas and Vassiliki Nemitsa; m. 1st Daisy Petrou 1958 (died 1983); three d.; m. 2nd Louki Loucaides 1986; mem. House of Reps. 1976–81; fmr. Pres. Parl. Cttee. on Commerce and Industry; Minister of Commerce and Industry 1988–93; Chair. and Man. Dir. Nemitsas Group 1993–95, Chair. Bd. of Dirs. 1995–; fmr. mem. Bd. Bank of Cyprus, Cyprus Employers' and Industrialists' Fed., Chamber of Commerce and Industry, Cyprus Tourism Org.; fmr. Deputy Chair. Woolworth Cyprus; Grand Cross of Leopold (Belgium), Grand Officer Kt. of the Order of Merit (Italy). *Leisure interest:* swimming. *Address:* Nemitsas Industries Ltd., P.O. Box 124, Limassol, Cyprus. *Telephone:* (5) 369222. *Fax:* (5) 369275.

NEMTSOV, Boris Yefimovich, C.TECH.SC.; Russian politician; b. 9 Oct. 1959, Sochi; m.; one d.; ed. Gorky (now Nizhny Novgorod) State Univ.; researcher then sr. researcher Research Inst. of Radiophysics 1981–91; rep. of Pres. of Russia in Nizhny Novgorod Region 1991; Gov. of Nizhny Novgorod Region 1991–97; People's Deputy of Russia 1990–93; mem. Council of Fed. (Upper House of Parl.) 1993–97; First Deputy Chair. Russian Govt. 1997–98; Minister of Fuel and Power Eng. March–Nov. 1997; f. Young Russia Movt. *Publication:* The Provincial 1997. *Leisure interests:* tennis, windsurfing, fishing.

NEOH, Anthony Francis, LL.B, Q.C., J.P.; Chinese lawyer; b. 9 Nov. 1946, Hong Kong; ed. Univ. of London; teaching 1964–66; Hong Kong Civil Service 1966–79; pvt. practice, Hong Kong Bar 1979–95, Calif. Bar 1984–95; Hong Kong public service in educ., health etc. 1985–; People's Repub. of China public service in teaching, govt. advisory work etc. 1985–; Visiting Scholar, Harvard Univ. 1990–91; now Chair. Securities and Futures Comm. Hong Kong; Chair. IOSCO Tech. Cttee. 1996. *Leisure interests:* reading, music. *Address:* 12th Floor, The Landmark, 15 Queen's Road Central, Hong Kong Special Administrative Region, People's Republic of China. *Telephone:* 2840 9201. *Fax:* 2810 1872.

NERETTE, Justice Joseph; Haitian politician and judge; fmr. mem. Supreme Court of Haiti; named Pres. of Haiti after mil. coup overthrew govt. of Father Jean Aristide (q.v.) 1991–92.

NERLICH, Graham Charles, M.A., B. PHIL., F.A.H.A.; Australian professor of philosophy; b. 23 Nov. 1929, Adelaide; m. Margaret Shirley Rawlinson 1991; three s.; ed. Oxford Univ.; lecturer, Univ. of Leicester 1958–61, Univ. of Sydney 1962–72; Prof. of Philosophy Univ. of Sydney 1972–73; Prof. Emer. Univ. of Adelaide 1974–. *Publications:* The Shape of Space 1976, Values and Valuing 1989, What Spacetime Explains 1994. *Address:* Department of Philosophy, University of Adelaide, Adelaide, South Australia 5005, Australia.

NERLOVE, Marc L., PH.D.; American professor of economics; b. 12 Oct. 1933, Chicago; s. of Samuel Henry Nerlove and Evelyn (née Andelman) Nerlove; two d.; ed. Univ. of Chicago and Johns Hopkins Univ.; Analytical Statistician, U.S. Dept. of Agric., Washington, D.C. 1956–57; Assoc. Prof., Univ. of Minn., Minneapolis 1959–60; Prof., Stanford Univ. 1960–65, Yale Univ. 1965–69; Prof. of Econs., Univ. of Chicago 1969–74; F. W. Taussig Research Prof., Harvard Univ. 1967–68; Visiting Prof., Northwestern Univ., 1973–74, Cook Prof. 1974–82; Prof. of Econs., Univ. of Pa. 1982–86, Univ. Prof. 1986–93; Prof. of Agric. and Resource Econs. Univ. of Md., Coll. Park 1993–; mem. N.A.S.; John Bates Clark Medal 1969; P. C. Mahalinobis Medal 1975. *Publications:* Dynamics of Supply 1958, Distributed Lags and Demand Analysis 1958, Estimation and Identification of Cobb-Douglas Production Functions 1965, Analysis of Economic Time Series: A Synthesis 1979, Household and Economy: Welfare Economics of Endogenous Fertility 1987; numerous articles. *Address:* Department of Agriculture and Research Economics, Maryland University, College Park, MD 20742, U.S.A.

NERO, Franco (b. Francesco Sparanero); Italian actor; b. 1941, Parma; appeared in TV mini-series: The Last Days of Pompeii, Moyles: The Legend of Valentino, 21 Hours at Munich, The Pirate, Young Catherine. *Films:* The Bible 1966, Ojango, Camelot, The Hired Killer, The Wild, Wild Planet, The Brute and the Beast, The Day of the Owl, Sardinia, Mafia, Vendetta, Companeros, Detective Belli, The Mercenary, A Quiet Place in the Country, Tristana, The Virgin and the Gypsy, Battle of the Neretva, Confessions of a Police Captain, The Vacation, Pope Joan, Deaf Smith and Johnny Ears, The Last Days of Mussolini, Force Ten from Navarone, The Roses of the Danzig, Mimi, The Man With Bogart's Face, Enter the Ninja, Mexico in Flames, Querelle, Kamikaze '89, The Salamander, Wagner, Victory March, The Day of the Cobra, Ten Days That Shook the World, Der Falke, The Repenter, The Forester's Sons, Garibaldi: The General, The Girl, Sweet Country, Die Hard 2, Brothers and Sisters, A Breath of Life, Jonathan of the Bears, Conflict of Interest, The Dragon's Ring, Talk of Angels, The Innocent Sleep, The King and Me.

NESTERENKO, Yevgeniy Yevgeniyevich; Russian singer (bass); b. 8 Jan. 1938, Moscow; s. of Yevgeny Nikiforovich Nesterenko and Velta Woldemarovna Baumann; m. Yekaterina Dmitrievna Alexeyeva 1963; one s.; ed. Leningrad Eng. Inst. and Leningrad Conservatoire (V. Lukanin's class); soloist with Leningrad Maly Opera and Ballet Theatre 1963–67; soloist with Kirov Opera 1967–71; teacher of solo singing at Leningrad Conservatoire 1967–71; soloist with Bolshoi 1971–; mem. CPSU 1974–91; mem. staff, Moscow Musical Pedagogical Inst. 1972–74; Chair. of Singing at Moscow Conservatoire 1975–93, Prof. 1981–93; Prof. Vienna Conservatoire 1993–; U.S.S.R. People's Deputy 1989–91. *Roles include:* Boris Godunov, Dosifey (Khovanshchina), Prince Igor, Mephistopheles (Gounod's Faust), Grigori (Dzerzhinsky's Quiet Flows the Don), Kutuzov (War and Peace), Filippo II (Don Carlo), Attila, Zaccaria (Nabucco), Don Pasquale, Sarastro (Magic Flute); Hero of Labour, Lenin Prize 1982, Giovanni Zenatello Prize, Verona 1986, Viotti d'Oro Prize, Chaliapin Prize 1992, Wilhelm Furtwängler Prize 1992, Austrian Kammersänger 1992. *Publication:* Thoughts on My Profession 1985. *Leisure interest:* tea testing. *Address:* Bolshoi Theatre, Teatralnaya pl. 1, 103009 Moscow (Office); Frunzenskaya nab. 24, korp. 1, Apt. 178, 119146 Moscow, Russia (Home). *Telephone:* (095) 242-47-89 (Home).

NESTERIKHIN, Yuri Yefremovich; Russian physicist; b. 10 Oct. 1930, Ivanovo; s. of Yefrem Nesterikhin and Maria Morozova; m. 1954; one s. one d.; ed. Moscow Univ.; mem. CPSU 1960–91; with Inst. of Atomic Energy 1954–61, 1987–, Inst. of Nuclear Physics 1961–67; Prof. 1970; Corresp. mem. of U.S.S.R. (now Russian) Acad. of Sciences 1970, mem. 1981–; Dir. of Inst. of Automation and Electrometrics, Siberian Branch of Acad. of Sciences 1967–87; Head of Synchrotron and Applied Electronics Divs. Kurchatov Inst., Moscow 1987–; Dir. Multimedia Centre, Acad. of Nat. Economy 1992–; mem. Bd. Ranet (jt. stock co.) 1992–95; most important works on plasma physics and thermonuclear synthesis. *Leisure interest:* sauna. *Address:* Kurchatov Institute, Kurchatova ploshchad 46, D-182 Moscow (Office); Leninski Prosp. 13, Apt. 93, 117071 Moscow, Russia. *Telephone:* (095) 196-97-79 (Office); 237-43-47 (Home). *Fax:* (095) 420-22-66.

NESTEROVA, Natalia Igorevna; Russian painter; b. 23 April 1944, Moscow; one s., ed. Moscow Surikov State Fine Arts Inst.; mem. U.S.S.R. (now Russian) Union of Painters; participated in over 170 exhibitions including solo exhbns. Russia, Europe, N. America 1988–; Prof. Russian Acad. of Theatre Art 1992–. *Address:* Moscow Artists Union, Starosadsky per. 5, 101000 Moscow, Russia. *Telephone:* (095) 921-51-88.

NESTEROVA, Natalya Vasilyevna; Russian academic; b. 1952; ed. Moscow State Univ., Moscow Pedagogical Inst.; worked in different higher educ. insts. of Moscow; f. and Pres., Moscow Centre of Educ. 1990–; f., Humanitarian Gymnasium of N. Nesterova 1991–; f. and Rector, New Humanitarian Centre of Educ. (Univ. and Acad. of Dance N. Nesterova) 1992–; f., Acad. of Painting 1994–. *Address:* New Humanitarian Centre of Education, Varshavskoye shosse 38, 115230 Moscow, Russia. *Telephone:* (095) 113 5544 (Office).

NETANYAHU, Benjamin, M.A.; Israeli politician and diplomatist; b. 21 Oct. 1949; m.; two c.; ed. M.I.T.; man. consultant, Boston Consulting Group 1976–78; Exec. Dir. Jonathan Inst. Jerusalem 1978–80; Sr. Man. Rim Industries, Jerusalem 1980–82; Deputy Chief of Mission, Israeli Embassy, Washington, D.C. 1982–84; Perm. Rep. to UN 1984–88, Deputy Minister of Foreign Affairs 1988–91, Deputy Minister, Prime Minister's Office 1991–92, Prime Minister of Israel, Minister of Housing and Construction May 1996–; Leader Likud March 1993–. *Publication:* A Place Among the Nations: Israel and the World 1993, Fighting Terrorism 1996. *Address:* Office of the Prime Minister, P.O. Box 187, 3 Rehov Kaplan, Kiryat Ben-Gurion, Jerusalem 91919, Israel. *Telephone:* 2-6705511. *Fax:* 2-6512631.

NETHERLANDS, H.R.H. Prince of the (Bernhard Leopold Frederik Everhard Julius Coert Karel Godfried Pieter), Prince zur Lippe-Biesterfeld; b. 29 June 1911, Germany; s. of H.S.H. the late Prince Bernhard zur Lippe and Princess Armgard, Baroness von Sierstorpff-Cramm; m. Juliana Louise Emma Marie Wilhelmina, (q.v.), Queen of the Netherlands 1937–80; four d.; ed. Gymnasiums at Zuellichau and Berlin and Univs. of Lausanne, Munich and Berlin; assumed Netherlands nationality 1936; studied at Netherlands Staff Coll.; apptd. mem. State Council; after German invasion of Holland, May 1940, evacuated family to England and returned to Continent with army until fall of France; returned to England and qualified as pilot 1941; appointed Hon. Air Cdre. R.A.F.V.R. 1941; subsequently Chief Netherlands Liaison Officer with British Forces, Col. later Maj.-Gen. and Chief of Netherlands Mission to War Office; visited war fronts in N. Africa and Normandy; maintained liaison throughout the war between Netherlands Underground and the Allied Govts.; appointed Supreme Commdr. (Lieut.-Gen.) Netherlands Armed Forces 1944 and played important part in liberation of Netherlands; decorated for his services in this operation by H.M. Queen Wilhelmina (M.W.O.) and H.M. King George VI (G.B.E.); subsequently resigned from office of Supreme Commdr. 1945; mem. Council for Mil. Affairs of the Realm, and mem. Joint Defence, Army, Admiralty and Air Force Councils; Insp.-Gen. of Armed Forces; Adm., Gen. R. Netherlands A.F., Gen. (Army) 1954–76; Hon. Air Marshal R.A.F. 1964; Hon. Cdre.

R.N.Z.A.F. 1973; mem. Bd. of the Netherlands Trade and Industries Fair; has greatly contributed to post-war expansion of Netherlands trade; founder and regent Prince Bernhard Fund for the Advancement of Arts and Sciences in the Netherlands; Regent Praemium Erasmianum Foundation; Founder-Pres. World Wildlife Fund Int., Pres. W.W.F. Netherlands, Pres. Rhino Rescue Trust; Chair. Achievement Bd. ICBP; Hon. mem. Royal Aeronautical Soc., Royal Inst. Naval Architects, Aeromedical Soc., Royal Spanish Acad.; Hon. degrees (Utrecht) 1946, (Delft) 1951, (Montréal) 1958, (British Columbia) 1958, (Amsterdam) 1965, (Michigan) 1965, (Basel) 1971; many decorations. *Leisure interests:* golf, skiing, filming, photography, hunting. *Address:* Soestdijk Palace, Baarn, Netherlands.

NEUBER, Friedel; German banker; b. 10 July 1935, Rheinhessen; Chair. Man. Bd., Westdeutsche Landesbank Girozentrale (WestLB), Düsseldorf/Münster 1981–; Chair. Supervisory Bd., Preussag AG, Hanover/Berlin, Deutsche Babcock AG, Oberhausen, LTU Lufttransport Unternehmen GmbH & Co. KG, Düsseldorf, LTU Touristik GmbH, Düsseldorf, WestLB (Europa) AG, Düsseldorf; mem. Supervisory Bd. Deutsche Bahn AG, Frankfurt, Douglas Holding AG, Hagen, Friedr. Krupp AG Hoesch-Krupp, Essen, KD Köln-Düsseldorfer Deutsche Rheinschiffahrt AG, Düsseldorf, RWE AG, Essen, STEAG, Essen, VIAG Aktiengesellschaft, Munich, Bank Austria, Vienna, UAP S.A., Paris; Chair. Bd., Verband öffentlicher Banken e.V., Bonn/Bad Godesberg; Pres. Handelshochschule Leipzig 1997–; mem. Bd. of Dirs. Deutsche Girozentrale-Deutsche Kommunalbank, Frankfurt, and of numerous other bds.; Hon. D.Univ. (Duisburg). *Address:* Herzogstr. 15, 40217 Düsseldorf, Germany.

NEUBERGER, Rabbi Julia Babette Sarah, M.A.; British rabbi; b. 27 Feb. 1950, London; d. of late Walter Schwab and of Alice Schwab; m. Anthony John Neuberger 1973; one s. one d.; ed. South Hampstead High School, Newnham Coll. Cambridge and Leo Baeck Coll. London; Rabbi, S. London Liberal Synagogue 1977–89; lecturer and Assoc. Fellow, Leo Baeck Coll. 1979–97; Assoc. Newnham Coll. Cambridge 1983–96; Sec. and Chief Exec. The King's Fund 1997–; Chancellor, Univ. of Ulster 1994–; Chair. Rabbinic Conf. Union of Liberal and Progressive Synagogues 1983–85; Camden and Islington Community Health Services NHS Trust 1993–97; mem. Policy Planning Group, Inst. of Jewish Affairs 1986–90, NHS Complaints Review 1993–94, Gen. Medical Council 1993–, Council, Univ. Coll., London 1993–97, MRC 1995–, Council, Save the Children Fund 1995–96; Visiting Fellow, King's Fund Inst. 1989–91; Trustee, Runnymede Trust 1990–97; Chair. Patients Asscn. 1988–91, Royal Coll. of Nursing Comm. on Health Service; mem. Nat. Cttee. Social Democratic Party 1982–88; mem. Bd. of Visitors, Memorial Church, Harvard Univ. 1994–; other public and charitable appts.; presenter, Choices, BBC TV 1986, 1987; Harkness Fellow, Commonwealth Fund of New York; Visiting Fellow, Harvard Medical School 1991–92; Hon. Fellow, City and Guilds Inst., Mansfield Coll. Oxford; Dr. h.c. (Open Univ.); Dr. h.c. (City Univ. London, Humberside, Ulster, Stirling, Oxford Brookes, Teesside, Nottingham). *Publications:* The Story of Judaism 1986, Days of Decision (ed.) 1987, Caring for Dying Patients of Different Faiths 1987, Whatever's Happening to Women? 1991, A Necessary End (ed. with J. White) 1991, Ethics and Healthcare: the role of Research Ethics Committees in the UK 1992, The Things that Matter 1993, On Being Jewish 1995, Dying Well—A Health Professional's Guide to Enabling a Good Death 1999; contribs. to various books on cultural, religious and ethical factors in nursing; contribs. to Nursing Times; reviews in journals and newspapers. *Leisure interests:* riding, sailing, Irish life, opera, setting up the old girls' network, children. *Address:* The King's Fund, 11–13 Cavendish Square, London, W1M 0AN, England. *Telephone:* 0171-307 2400. *Fax:* 0171-307 2803.

NEUHARTH, Allen H.; American business executive; b. 22 March 1924, Eureka, S. Dakota; m. 1st Loretta F. Helgeland 1946 (divorced 1972); one s. one d.; m. 2nd Lori Wilson 1973 (divorced 1982); m. 3rd Rachel Fornes 1993; ed. Univ. of S. Dakota; reporter, The Associated Press, Sioux Falls, S. Dakota; launched weekly tabloid SoDak Sports 1952; reporter, rising to Asst. Man. Ed., Miami Herald 1954–60; Asst. Exec. Ed. Knight's Detroit (Mich.) Free Press 1960; joined Gannett (newspaper and communications group) 1963, Exec. Vice-Pres. 1966, Pres. and C.O.O. 1970, Pres. and Chief Exec. 1973, Chair., Pres. and C.E.O. 1979, Chair. and C.E.O. 1984–86, Chair. 1986–89, Gannett Foundation, Arlington, Va. 1989–91, Freedom Forum 1991–; f. and Chair. USA Today 1982; Chair. and Pres. American Newspaper Publishers' Asscn. 1979, 1980; numerous awards and seven hon. degrees. *Publication:* Confessions of an S.O.B. 1989. *Address:* Freedom Forum, 1101 Wilson Boulevard, Arlington, VA 22209, U.S.A. (Home).

NEUHAUSER, Duncan von Briesen, PH.D.; American professor of epidemiology and biostatistics; b. 20 June 1939, Philadelphia, Pa.; s. of Edward B. D. Neuhauser and Gernda von Briesen Neuhauser; m. Elinor Toaz Neuhauser 1965; one s. one d.; ed. Harvard Univ. and Univs. of Michigan and Chicago; Research Assoc. (Instructor), Center for Health Admin. Studies, Univ. of Chicago 1965–70; Asst. Prof., then Assoc. Prof., Harvard School of Public Health 1970–79; Assoc. Chair., Program for Health Systems Man., Harvard Business School 1972–79; Consultant in Medicine, Mass. Gen. Hosp. 1975–80; Prof. of Epidemiology and Biostatistics, Case Western Reserve Univ. 1979–, Prof. of Organizational Behaviour 1979–, Prof. of Medicine 1981–, Keck Foundation Sr. Research Scholar 1982–, Prof. of Family Medicine 1990–, Charles Elton Blanchard Prof. of Health Man. 1995–; mem. bioscientific medical staff, Cleveland Metropolitan Gen. Hosp. 1981–; Adjunct mem., Medical Staff, Cleveland Clinic Foundation 1984–; Co-Dir. Health Systems Man. Centre, Case Western Reserve Univ. 1985–; Ed. Medical Care 1983–97, Health Matrix 1982–90; mem. Inst. of Medicine (N.A.S.). *Publications:* (Co-author) Health Services in the U.S., The Efficient Organization 1977, The Physician and Cost Control 1979, Clinical Decision Analysis 1980, Competition, Co-operation or Regulation 1981, The New Epidemiology 1982, Coming of Age 1984, 1995, Clinical CQI 1995, Health Services Management 1997, Health Services Management Case Studies 1997, and scientific papers. *Leisure interests:* sailing, curling. *Address:* Department of Epidemiology and Biostatistics, Medical School, Case Western Reserve University, 10900 Euclid Avenue, Cleveland, OH 44106-4945; 2655 North Park Boulevard, Cleveland Heights, OH 44106-3622 (Home, winter); Parker Point Road, P.O. Box 932, Blue Hill, ME 04614, U.S.A. (Home, summer). *Telephone:* (216) 368-3725 (Office); (216) 321-1327 (Cleveland Heights); (207) 374-5325 (Blue Hill).

NEUKIRCHEN, Karl Josef, DR.RER.POL.; German business executive; b. 17 March 1942, Bonn; Chair. Man. Bd. Klöckner-Humboldt-Deutz AG, Cologne until 1988, Hösch AG, Dortmund 1991–92; Chair. Supervisory Bd. Klöckner-Werke AG Duisburg 1992–95, Dynamit Nobel Ag 1994–; C.E.O. Metallgesellschaft AG Dec. 1993–. *Address:* c/o Metallgesellschaft AG, 60271 Frankfurt am Main, Bockenheimer Landstrasse 73–77, Germany.

NEUMANN, Bernhard Hermann, A.C., DR.PHIL., PH.D., D.SC., F.A.C.E., F.A.A., F.R.S.; British mathematician; b. 15 Oct. 1909, Berlin-Charlottenburg, Germany; s. of late Richard Neumann and Else Aronstein; m. 1st Hanna von Caemmerer 1938 (died 1971); three s. two d.; m. 2nd Dorothea F. A. Zeim 1973; ed. Berlin-Charlottenburg, Univs. of Freiburg, Berlin, Cambridge; Temp. Asst. Lecturer Univ. Coll. Cardiff 1937–40; army service 1940–45; Lecturer Univ. Coll. Hull 1946–48; Lecturer, Sr. Lecturer, Reader, Univ. of Manchester 1948–61; Prof., Head of Dept., Australian Nat. Univ. 1962–74, Emer. Prof., Hon. Fellow 1975–; Sr. Research Fellow, Div. of Math. and Statistics (now Div. of Math. and Information Sciences), CSIRO 1975–77, Hon. Research Fellow 1978–; Visiting Lecturer Australian Univs. 1959, Monash Univ. 1980; Visiting Prof. Tata Inst. Fundamental Research, Bombay 1959, Courant Inst. Math. Sciences, New York Univ. 1961–62, Univ. Wisconsin 1966–67, Vanderbilt Univ. 1969–70, Univ. of Cambridge 1970, Univ. Illinois Urbana-Champaign 1975; Visiting Scientist, Univ. of Manitoba 1979, Univ. of Bielefeld 1987; Visiting Fellow, Fitzwilliam Coll., Cambridge 1970; Matthew Flinders Lecturer of the Australian Acad. of Science 1984; Ed. Proc. of London Math. Soc. 1959–61; Assoc. Ed. Pacific Journal of Math. 1964–92; Foundation Ed. Bulletin of Australian Math. Soc. 1969–79, Hon. Ed. 1979–; mem. Editorial Bd. Zentralblatt Didaktik Math. 1969–84, 1991–, Communications in Algebra 1972–84, Houston Journal of Math. 1974–, Math. Scientist 1975–85; Ed. and Publr. IMU Canberra Circular 1972–99; Editorial Consultant, South-East Asian Math. Bulletin 1987–, Hon. Ed. Algebra Colloquium 1994–; mem. Council London Math. Soc. 1954–61 (Vice-Pres. 1957–59), Council Australian Math. Soc. 1963–79 (Vice-Pres. 1963–64, 1966–68, 1971–73, Pres. 1964–66), Council Australian Acad. Science 1968–71 (Vice-Pres. 1969–71) Foundation Pres. Australian Asscn. Math. Teachers 1966–68, Vice-Pres. 1968–69; Foundation Pres. Canberra Math. Asscn. 1963–65, Vice-Pres. 1965–66; Chair. Aust. Nat. Cttee. Math. 1966–75; Chair. Aust. Sub-Comm., Int. Comm. Math. Instruction 1968–75; mem.-at-large, Int. Comm. on Math. Instruction 1975–82, Exec. Cttee. 1979–82; mem. Exchange Comm., Int. Math. Union (IMU) 1975–79; mem. Acad. Advisory Council, Royal Aust. Naval Coll. 1978–87; Fellow (non-resident) Bruce Hall Australian Nat. Univ. 1963– (mem. Governing Body 1984–97); SERC Visitor, Univ. of Glasgow 1985, Univ. Coll. Cardiff 1991; Fellow Australian Math. Soc. 1994–; Hon. Life mem. Australian Asscn. of Math. Teachers 1975–, Canberra Math. Asscn. 1975–, New Zealand Math. Soc. 1975–; Pres. Amateur Sinfonia of Canberra Inc. 1978–80, Vice-Pres. 1980–81, 1983-84, Hon. Life mem. 1984–; Vice-Pres. Friends of Canberra School of Music 1983–; mem. Governing Bd., Australian Math. Competition 1980–; Chair. Australian Mathematical Olympiad Cttee 1980–86; mem. Comm. for 1988 Int. Mathematical Olympiad 1984–88; Hon. Fellow Inst. Combinatories and its Applications; Hon. D.Sc. (Newcastle, N.S.W.) 1974, (Monash) 1982, (W. Australia) 1995, (Hull, U.K.) 1995; Hon. D.Math. (Waterloo) 1986, Hon. Dr. Rer. Nat. (Humboldt) 1992; Prize of Wiskundig Genootschap te Amsterdam 1949; Adams Prize (Cambridge Univ.) 1951–52. *Publications:* Selected Works of B. H. Neumann and Hanna Neumann, 6 Vols., 1988; over 120 papers in mathematical journals. *Leisure interests:* chamber music, chess, cycling, camping. *Address:* School of Mathematical Sciences, Australian National University, Canberra, A.C.T. 0200; CSIRO-DMIS, G.P.O. Box 664, Canberra, A.C.T. 2601 (Offices); 20 Talbot Street, Forrest, A.C.T. 2603, Australia (Home). *Telephone:* (02) 6216 7257 and (02) 6249 4504 (Offices); (02) 6273 3447 (Home). *Fax:* (02) 6249 5549.

NEUMANN, Robert Gerhard, PH.D.; American diplomatist and educator; b. 2 Jan. 1916, Vienna, Austria; s. of Hugo and Stephanie Taussky; m. Marlen Eldredge 1941 (died 1997); two s.; ed. High School and Consular Acad., Vienna, Univ. of Rennes, Geneva School of Int. Studies, Amherst Coll., Mass., Univ. of Minnesota; Teacher of Political Science and Econs., State Teachers' Coll., Oshkosh, Wis. 1941–42; lecturer in Political Science, Univ. of Wisconsin 1946–47; Asst. Prof., Univ. of Calif., Los Angeles 1947–52, Assoc. Prof. 1952–58, Prof. of Political Science 1958–67, Dir. Inst. of Int. and Foreign Studies 1958–65; Chair. Atlantic and W. European Program 1965–66; Amb. to Afghanistan 1966–73, to Morocco 1973–76; Sr. Assoc. and Project Dir. Centre for Strategic and Int. Studies (CSIS), Georgetown Univ.

1976–79, Coordinator, Middle East Programs 1979–81, Vice-Chair. 1980–81, Dir. Middle East Studies 1982–93, Sr. Adviser CSIS 1982–; Dir. State Dept. Transition Team 1980–81; Amb. to Saudi Arabia April–July 1981; Vice-Chair., Trustee Exec. Cttee. Moroccan-American Foundation 1982–90; Vice-Chair. American-Saudi Business Round Table 1983–84, Chair. 1984–91, Chair. Emer. 1991–; Editorial Writer Los Angeles Times 1952–59; Vice-Pres. American Friends of Afghanistan 1985–93; Advisory Council, Cttee. for a Community of Democracies, U.S.A. 1984–; mem. Exec. Cttee. Islam and the West 1984–88; mem. Int. Inst. for Strategic Studies 1984–, Washington Inst. of Foreign Affairs 1992–; Hon. Medal Univ. of Brussels 1955; Chevalier, Légion d'honneur 1957, Order of the Star, 1st Class (Afghanistan) 1973, Commdr. Order of Merit (Fed. Repub. of Germany) 1974, Grand Officier, Order and Star of Ouissam Alaoui (Morocco) 1976, Kt. Commdr. Cross and Star (Austria) 1991. *Publications:* European and Comparative Government, The Government of Germany 1966, Toward a More Effective Executive-Legislative Relationship in the Conduct of American Foreign Policy 1977 and numerous articles in professional journals. *Leisure interests:* photography, hiking. *Address:* 4986 Sentinel Drive, No. 301, Bethesda, MD 20816, U.S.A.

NEUMEIER, John, B.A.; American choreographer and ballet director; b. 1942, Milwaukee, Wis.; s. of Albert Neumeier and Lucille Neumeier; ed. Marquette Univ., Milwaukee; dance training in Milwaukee, Chicago, Royal Ballet School, London and in Copenhagen with Vera Volkova; soloist, The Stuttgart Ballet 1963; Ballet Dir. Frankfurt 1969; Ballet Dir. and Chief Choreographer, The Hamburg Ballet 1973–; Prof. City of Hamburg 1987; Dir. Hamburg Ballet 1996, Balletintendant 1997–; f. John Neumeier ballet centre, Hamburg 1989; noted for his creation of new works and original interpretations of well-known ballets; founded a ballet training school in Hamburg 1978; appears as soloist, notably in The Chairs with Marcia Haydée, a ballet created for them by M. Béjart. *Works Choreographed Include:* A Midsummer Night's Dream (Mendelssohn/Ligeti), ballets to the Mahler symphonies, Le Sacre (Stravinsky), The Lady of the Camellias (Chopin), Bach's St. Matthew Passion, A Streetcar Named Desire (Prokofiev/Schnittke); Golden Camera Award for TV series of his Ballet Workshops 1978; Dance Magazine Award 1983; Deutscher Tanzpreis 1988; Bundesverdienstkreuz; Hon. D.F.A. (Marquette); Diaghilev Prize 1988, Ordre des Arts et des Lettres, Benois de la Danse 1992, Medal of Honour (City of Tokyo) 1994, Carina-Ari Gold Medal (Sweden) 1994, Nijinsky Medal (Polish Ministry of Culture) 1996. *Address:* Hamburg Ballet, Ballettzentrum Hamburg, Casper-Voght-Str. 54, 20535 Hamburg, Germany.

NEURATH, Hans, PH.D.; American biochemist; b. 29 Oct. 1909, Vienna, Austria; s. of Rudolf and Hedda Samek Neurath; m. 1st Hilde Bial 1935 (divorced 1960); one s.; m. 2nd Susi Spitzer 1960; ed. Elementary and High School, Vienna, and Univ. of Vienna; Research Fellow, Univ. of London 1934–35; Instructor and George Fischer-Baker Fellow, Cornell Univ., N.Y. 1936–38; Asst. Prof., Assoc. Prof., Prof. of Physical Biochem., Duke Univ. 1938–50; Prof. of Biochem., Univ. of Washington, Seattle 1950–80, Prof. Emer. 1980–, Chair. Dept. of Biochem. 1950–75; Scientific Dir. Fred Hutchinson Cancer Research Center (Seattle) 1976–80; Dir. German Cancer Research Centre (Heidelberg) 1980–81; Hon. Prof. Univ. of Heidelberg 1980–; mem. N.A.S.; Foreign mem. Max-Planck Soc.; Hon. mem. Japanese Chemical Soc.; Fellow American Acad. of Arts and Sciences; specializes in biochem. of proteins and enzymes, relation of their structure and function; D.Sc. (Geneva) 1970, (Tokushima) 1977, (Tokyo) 1990. *Publications:* Over 300 original publs. in biochemistry; Ed. Biochemistry 1962–91, Protein Science 1991–. *Leisure interests:* music (piano), mountaineering, skiing. *Address:* University of Washington, Department of Biochemistry, P.O. Box 357350, Seattle, WA 98195 (Office); 5752 60th Avenue N.E., Seattle, WA 98105, U.S.A. (Home). *Telephone:* (206) 543-7893.

NEURRISSE, André, D. EN D., D. ÈS SC.ECON.; French historian and economist; b. 21 April 1916, Pomarez; m. Louise Marie Verdier 1942; two d.; ed. Univs. of Bordeaux and Paris; civil servant, Ministry of Finance 1941–58, Treas.-Paymaster Gen. 1958–82; Consultant to IMF, World Bank and UN 1982–; Man. Dir. Société d'Etudes et des Participations (SEP) 1984–89; Man. Dir. Banque Internationale de Financement et de Négociation (BIFEN) 1985–91; Pres., Dir.-Gen. Union Commerciale de crédit multiservices 1989–91; Officier Légion d'honneur, Commdr. Mérite national, Officier des Palmes académiques etc. *Publications:* Précis de droit budgétaire 1961, La comptabilité économique française 1963, Les règlements internationaux 1972, Histoire du Franc 1974, Les jeux de casino 1977, Histoire de l'impôt 1978, L'économie sociale 1983, Le Trésorier-Payeur Général 1986, Le Franc C.F.A. 1987, Les jeux d'argent et de hasard 1990, Deux mille ans d'impôts 1994, Histoire de la Fiscalité en France 1996, Histoire monétaire de la France. *Address:* 9 rue Docteur Blanche, 75016 Paris, France. *Telephone:* (1) 45 25 89 32. *Fax:* (1) 45 25 89 32.

NEUSTADT, Richard Elliott, PH.D.; American political scientist; b. 26 June 1919, Philadelphia; s. of Richard Neustadt and Elizabeth Neufeld; m. 1st Bertha Cummings 1945 (died 1984); one s. one d.; m. 2nd Shirley Williams (now Baroness Williams of Crosby (q.v.)) 1987; ed. Univ. of Calif. (Berkeley) and Harvard Univ.; Economist, Office of Price Admin. 1942; Staff mem., Bureau of Budget 1946–50, White House 1950–53; Prof. of Public Admin. Cornell Univ. 1953–54, of Govt., Columbia Univ. 1954–65, Harvard Univ. 1965–78; Lucius N. Littauer Prof. of Public Admin. John F. Kennedy School of Govt. 1978–86, Assoc. Dean 1965–75, Dir. Inst. of Politics 1966–71; Douglas Dillon Prof. of Govt., Harvard 1986–89, Prof. Emer. 1989–; mem. Inst. for Strategic Studies 1963; Fellow, American Acad. of Arts and Sciences 1964; Visitor, Nuffield Coll., Oxford 1961–62, Assoc. mem. 1965–67, 1990–93; Visting Prof. of Govt., Univ. of Essex 1994–95; Special Consultant, Sub-Cttee. on Nat. Policy Machinery, U.S. Senate 1959–61; mem. Advisory Bd. on Comm. on Money and Credit 1960–61; Special Consultant to Pres.-Elect Kennedy 1960–61, to Pres. Kennedy 1961–63, to Bureau of Budget 1961–70, to Dept. of State 1962–69; Consultant to Pres. Johnson 1964–66, to Rand Corpn. 1964–78; mem. Council on Foreign Relations 1963, Inst. for Strategic Studies 1968, American Political Science Asscn., Nat. Acad. of Public Admin., American Philosophical Soc.; Fellow American Acad. of Arts and Sciences; Chair. Advisory Cttee. to Comm. on Presidential Debate 1988–96; Trustee, Radcliffe Coll. 1977–80; Democrat. *Publications:* Presidential Power 1960 (revised 1990), Alliance Politics 1970, The Epidemic That Never Was (with Harvey Fineberg) 1983, Thinking in Time (with Ernest May) 1986. *Address:* Kennedy School of Government, Harvard University, Cambridge, MA 02138, U.S.A. *Telephone:* (617) 495-1196. *Fax:* (617) 496-6886.

NEUVO, Yrjö A., PH.D., F.I.E.E.E.; Finnish research professor; b. 21 July 1943, Turku; s. of Olavi Neuvo and Aune (née Vaisala) Neuvo; m. Tuula Halsas 1968; two s. one d.; ed. Cornell Univ. and Helsinki Univ. of Tech.; Acting Prof. Helsinki Univ. of Tech. 1975–76; Prof. of Electronics, Tampere Univ. of Tech. 1976–92; Sr. Vice-Pres., Tech. Nokia Corpn. 1993–; Sr. Research Fellow Acad. of Finland 1979–80, Research Prof. 1984–; Visiting Prof. Univ. of Calif. 1981–82; Hon. M.D. (Tampere Univ. of Tech.) 1992; Commdr. Order of Lion of Finland 1992; I.E.E.E. Bicentennial Award 1986, Asscn. in Finland Hon. Prize 1988; Nokia Prize 1989. *Publications:* over 300 scientific publs. on computer eng. and new technologies. *Address:* Nokia Corporation, P.O. Box 226, 00101 Helsinki, Finland. *Telephone:* (358-0) 18071. *Fax:* (358-0) 176015.

NEUWIRTH, Lucien; French politician; b. 18 May 1924, Saint-Etienne; s. of René Neuwirth and Gabrielle Blanchon; m. Mariette Didier 1952 (deceased); one d.; ed. Lycée Claude Fauriel, Saint-Etienne and Business School; mem. S.A.S.-Free French Forces 1942–46; town councillor, St.-Etienne (Gaullist Party) 1947–65; Man. French Nat. Broadcasting Network in Algeria 1958; Deputy of Loire 1958–81; Gen. Sec. Gaullist Group in Parl. 1959–62; Gen. Councillor of Saint-Etienne 1967; Pres. Council of Loire 1979–94, Hon. Pres. 1994–; Senator, Loire 1983–, Quaestor 1989–; mem. Public Safety Cttee., Algeria 1958; Tech. Councillor Charles de Gaulle cabinet 1958; Officier Legion d'honneur; World War II War Cross, Officer Medal of Resistance, Medal of Freedom, and other French and foreign distinctions. *Publications:* The Fiscal Flail 1977, May Life Be 1979, My War at 16 1986, Mais Après Tout . . . 1994. *Address:* Palais du Luxembourg, 75291 Paris, Cedex 06; 22 Rue du Général de Gaulle, 42000 Saint-Etienne, France. *Telephone:* (1) 423-2216; (77) 33-42-45.

NEVANLINNA, Eero Olavi, DIP. ENG., DR. TECH.; Finnish professor of mathematics; b. 17 April 1948, Helsinki; m. Marja Lähdesmäki 1968; three s. one d.; ed. Helsinki Univ. of Technology; Asst. Math. Helsinki Univ. of Tech. 1971–74; Sr. Researcher Acad. of Finland 1975–77; Assoc. Prof. Applied Math. Oulu Univ. 1978–79; Prof. Math. Helsinki Univ. of Tech. 1980–; Research Prof. Acad. of Finland 1986–92; Visiting Prof. at several U.S. Univs. and at ETH, Zürich; Chair. Rolf Nevanlinna Inst. 1989–90; Chair. Supervisory Bd. Suomi Mutual Life Assurance Co. 1996–98; mem. Bd. Pohjola Insurance Co. Ltd. 1997–; mem. Finnish Acad. of Tech. Sciences 1984, Finnish Acad. of Sciences and Letters 1986, Ed. Bd. BIT, Nat. Cttee. in Math. 1984–. *Publications:* Convergence of Iterations for Linear Equations 1993; about 90 scientific papers, especially in numerical analysis. *Address:* Institute of Mathematics, Helsinki University of Technology, P.O. Box 1100, 02015 Hut, Finland. *Telephone:* (09) 451 3034. *Fax:* (09) 451 3016.

NEVEROV, Valery Ivanovich, C.PHYS.-MATH.SC.; Russian businessman; b. 2 June 1952, Golymanovo, Tumen Region; ed. Urals State Univ., Moscow Inst. of Metallurgy; teacher Udmurtia State Univ., Tumen State Univ. 1982–88; f. co-operative enterprise Effekt 1986; Head Centre of Research Activities of Youth (Spektr) 1988; f. and Dir. Hermes Research Centre 1990–; f. and Pres. Hermes Tumen-Moskva Stock Exchange 1991, Hermes Moscow Jt.-Stock Co.; Pres. Hermes (incorporating more than 50 cos., banks, exchanges), Chair. 1992. *Address:* Hermes, Acad. Korolyov str. 13, 129715 Moscow, Russia. *Telephone:* 216-63-21.

NEVILLE, John, O.B.E.; British actor and theatre director; b. 2 May 1925, Willesden, London; s. of Reginald D. Neville and Mabel L. Fry; m. Caroline Hooper 1949; three s. three d.; ed. Chiswick County Grammar School and Royal Acad. of Dramatic Art, London; with Bristol Old Vic Co., London 1953, played Othello, Iago, Hamlet, Aguecheek and Richard II; mem. Chichester Theatre Co. 1962; created part of Alfie (Alfie by Bill Naughton), London 1963; Dir. Nottingham Playhouse 1963–68, Newcastle Playhouse 1967; Hon. Prof. in Drama, Nottingham Univ. 1967–; Drama Adviser to Howard and Wyndham Ltd.; in musical Mr. & Mrs. 1968; series of TV plays 1968; presented four plays at Fortune Theatre, London with the Park Theatre Co.; appeared in the Apple Cart, Mermaid Theatre, London 1970, The Beggar's Opera, Chichester 1972, Happy Days, Nat. Theatre, London 1977, The School for Scandal, Nat. Theatre 1990, The Dance of Death, Almeida 1995, Beethoven's Tenth, Chichester 1996; went to Canada 1973; staged The Rivals, Nat. Arts Theatre, Ottawa; Dir. opera Don Giovanni, Festival Canada, Ottawa; played Prospero (The Tempest), Judge Brack (Hedda

Gabler), Sir George Croft (Mrs. Warren's Profession), in Sherlock Holmes, New York 1975; Artistic Dir. of Citadel Theatre, Edmonton, Alberta, Canada 1973–78; Artistic Dir. Neptune Theatre, Halifax, Nova Scotia 1978–83; with Stratford Festival Theatre, Ont. 1983–89, Artistic Dir. 1985–89; Dir. Hamlet 1986, Mother Courage, Othello 1987, Three Sisters 1989; film (in title role) Adventures of Baron Munchhausen 1987–88; acted in School for Scandal, Nat. Theatre 1990; Hon. Dr. Dramatic Arts (Lethbridge Univ., Alberta) 1979; Hon. D.F.A. (Nova Scotia Coll. of Art and Design) 1981. *Films acted in include:* Mr. Topaz, Oscar Wilde, Billy Budd, A Study in Terror, Adventures of Baron Munchausen. *Leisure interests:* watching football, listening to music (all kinds), thinking about gardening. *Address:* 139 Winnett Avenue, Toronto. Ont. M6C 3L7, Canada.

NEVIN, John Joseph, B.S., M.B.A.; American business executive; b. 13 Feb. 1927, Jersey City; s. of Edward Vincent Nevin and Anna (née Burns) Nevin; m. Anna Filice 1951; five s. one d.; ed. Univ. of Calif. 1950, Harvard Univ. 1952; served with U.S.N.R. 1945–46; various financial positions; product planning and marketing Ford Motor Co., Dearborn, Mich. 1954–71, Vice-Pres. Marketing 1969–71; Pres. Zenith Radio Corpn., Chicago 1971–76, Chair. 1976–79; Pres. Firestone Tire and Rubber Co., Akron, Ohio 1979–82, 1984–87, C.E.O. 1980–91, Chair. 1981–91; Gen. Chair. Summit County (AKRON) United Way 1983; Dir. American Natural Resources Co., First Chicago Corpn., First Nat. Bank Chicago; mem. Advisory Council J. L. Kellogg Graduate School of Man., Northwestern Univ.; mem. advisory bd. School of Business Admin., Berkeley, Univ. of Calif.; Chair. Bd. Council of Better Business Bureaus 1984–. *Address:* 205 North Michigan Avenue, Suite 3800, Chicago, IL 60601, U.S.A.

NEVO, Ruth, PH.D.; Israeli painter and fmr. professor of humanities; b. 1924, Johannesburg, S.A.; d. of Benjamin Weinbren and Henrietta (née Goldsmith) Weinbren; m. Natan Nevo 1952; three s.; ed. Univ. of the Witwatersrand, Johannesburg and Hebrew Univ., Jerusalem; tutor Dept. of English, Hebrew Univ. 1952, Prof. 1973; Renee Lang Prof. of Humanities 1982–87; full-time painter 1987–; four solo exhbns. 1986, 1991, 1993, 1995, mem. Israel Acad. 1985–, Israel Asscn. of Painters and Sculptors 1989–. *Publications:* The Dial of Virtue 1963, Tragic Form in Shakespeare 1972, Comic Transformations in Shakespeare 1980, Shakespeare's Other Language 1987; trans. Selected Poems by Bialik 1981, Travels by Amichai 1986. *Address:* Hehalutz 22, Jerusalem; Department of English, Hebrew University, Mount Scopus, Jerusalem, Israel. *Telephone:* 02-6523752.

NEWALL, James Edward Malcolm, O.C., B.COMM.; Canadian business executive; b. 20 Aug. 1935, Holden, Alberta; m. Margaret Elizabeth Lick; ed. Prince Albert Coll. Inst., Univ. of Saskatchewan; joined Du Pont Canada Inc. 1957, various posts in marketing and gen. man. in fibres business, leading to Dir. Fibres Group 1972, Vice-Pres., Corp. Devt. 1974, Marketing 1975, Exec. Vice-Pres. 1975, Dir. 1976, Pres. and C.E.O. 1978–89, Chair. 1979, Chair. and C.E.O. du Pont Canada –1994, and responsible for E.I. du Pont's int. businesses outside Canada and U.S.A. 1989–91, Sr. Vice-Pres. E.I. du Pont de Nemours Agricultural Products 1989–91; Vice-Chair., C.E.O. and Dir. Nova Corpn. of Alberta 1991–, Maritime Transport Services 1994–; Chair. Business Council on Nat. Issues; Dir. Alcan Aluminium Ltd., BCE Inc., The Molson Cos. Ltd., Pratt & Whitney Canada Inc., The Royal Bank of Canada; Chair. Business Council on Nat. Issues; fmr. Chair. and Dir. Conf. Bd. of Canada; mem. Advisory Group to Prime Minister on exec. compensation in the public service. *Address:* 801-7th Avenue, S.W., Calgary, Alberta T2P 3P7, Canada.

NEWBERY, David Michael Garrood, PH.D., F.B.A.; British academic economist; b. 1 June 1943, Bucks.; m. Dr. Terri E. Apter 1975; two d.; ed. Portsmouth Grammar School, Trinity Coll., Cambridge; Economist, Treasury of Tanzanian Govt. 1965–66; Univ. Asst. Lecturer, Faculty of Econs. and Politics, Cambridge Univ. 1966–71, Lecturer 1971–86, Reader in Econs. 1986–88, Prof. of Applied Econs. and Dir. Dept. of Applied Econs. 1988–, Fellow Churchill Coll. 1966–; Div. Chief, World Bank 1981–83; Fellow Econometric Soc. 1989; Vice-Pres. European Econ. Asscn. 1994–95, Pres. 1996; mem. Monopolies and Mergers Comm. 1996–; Frisch Medal 1990, Harry Johnson Prize 1993. *Publications:* Project Appraisal in Practice (Co-Author) 1976, The Theory of Commodity Price Stabilization: A Study in the Economics of Risk (with J. E. Stiglitz) 1981, The Theory of Taxation for Developing Countries (with N. H. Stern) 1987, Hungary: An Economy in Transition (with I. Székely) 1993, Tax and Benefit Reform in Central and Eastern Europe 1995; numerous articles. *Address:* Department of Applied Economics, Sidgwick Avenue, Cambridge, CB3 9DE (Office); 9 Huntingdon Road, Cambridge, CB3 0HH, England (Home). *Telephone:* (01223) 335247 (Office); (01223) 360216 (Home). *Fax:* (01223) 335299.

NEWBIGGING, David Kennedy, O.B.E.; British business executive; b. 19 Jan. 1934, Tientsin, China; s. of late D. L. and L. M. Newbigging; m. Carolyn S. Band 1968; one s. two d.; ed. Oundle School; joined Jardine, Matheson & Co., Ltd. 1954, Dir. 1967, Man. Dir. 1970, Chair. and Sr. Man. Dir. 1975–83; Chair. Hongkong & Kowloon Wharf & Godown Co., Ltd. 1970–80; Chair. and Man. Dir. Hongkong Land Co., Ltd. 1975–83; Dir. Hongkong & Shanghai Banking Corpn. 1975–83; Dir. Hongkong Electric Holdings Ltd. 1975–83, Chair. 1982–83; Dir. Hongkong Telephone Co., Ltd. 1975–83; Chair. Jardine, Fleming & Co., Ltd. 1975–83; Dir. Rennies Consolidated Holdings Ltd. 1975–83; Dir. Safmarine and Rennies Holdings Ltd. 1984–85; Dir. Provincial Insurance PLC 1984–86, Deputy Chair. Provincial Group PLC 1985–91; Deputy Chair. Ivory & Sime PLC 1990–95, Chair. 1992–95 (Dir. 1987–95); Dir. NM UK (Chair. 1990–93), Rentokil Group PLC 1986–94 (Chair. 1987–94), PACCAR (U.K.) Ltd. 1986–97, Mason Best Int. Ltd. 1986–90 (Chair. 1987–90), Int. Financial Markets Trading Ltd. 1986–93, United Meridian Corpn. 1987–97, Thai Holdings Ltd. 1989–91, Merrill Lynch Inc., U.S.A. 1997–, Ocean Energy Inc., U.S.A. 1998–; Deputy Chair. Benchmark Group PLC 1996–; Chair. Redfearn PLC March–Dec. 1988; Chair. Faupel Trading Group PLC 1994– (Dir. 1989–), London Capital Holdings PLC March–Dec. 1994; Dir. Wah Kwong Shipping Holdings Ltd. 1992–, Lloyd's Market Bd. 1993–95, Friends' Provident Life Office 1993– (Chair. 1998–); Chair. Equitas Holdings Ltd. 1995–98, Maritime Transport Services Ltd. 1993–95; Trustee, King Mahendra U.K. Trust for Nature Conservation 1988–; Chair. of Trustees, Wilts Community Foundation 1991–97; Chair. of Council, Missions to Seamen 1993–; mem. Legis. Council of Hongkong 1978–82, mem. Exec. Council 1980–84; mem. Int. Council, Morgan Guaranty Trust Co. of New York 1977–85, Supervisory Bd. DAF Trucks NV 1997–; mem. British Coal Corpn. (fmrly. Nat. Coal Bd.) 1984–87, CIN Man. 1985–87. *Leisure interests:* most outdoor sports, Chinese art. *Address:* 15 Old Bailey, London, EC4M 7EF, England. *Telephone:* 0171-506 1000. *Fax:* 0171-248 6332.

NEWBY, (George) Eric, C.B.E., M.C., F.R.S.L., F.R.G.S.; British author; b. 6 Dec. 1919, London; s. of George A. Newby and Hilda Pomroy; m. Wanda Skof 1946; one s. one d.; ed. St. Paul's School; with Dorland Advertising, London 1936–38; apprentice and ordinary seaman, four-masted Finnish barque 1938–39; mil. service 1939–45, Black Watch and Special Boat Section, prisoner-of-war 1942–45; women's fashion business 1946–56; exploration in Nuristan 1956; with Secker and Warburg (publisher) 1956–59; fashion buyer, John Lewis Partnership 1959–63; Travel Ed., The Observer and Gen. Ed. Time Off Books 1964–73; Hon. D.Litt. (Bournemouth) 1994; Hon. Dr. (Open Univ.) 1996. *Publications:* The Last Grain Race 1956, A Short Walk in the Hindu Kush 1958, Something Wholesale 1962, Slowly Down the Ganges 1966, Time Off in Southern Italy 1966, Grain Race: Pictures of Life Before the Mast in a Windjammer 1968, The Wonders of Britain (jtly.) 1968, The Wonders of Ireland (jtly.) 1969, Love and War in the Apennines 1971, The World of Evelyn Waugh (jtly.) 1973, Ganga 1973, World Atlas of Exploration 1975, Great Ascents 1977, The Big Red Train Ride 1978, A Traveller's Life 1982, On the Shores of the Mediterranean 1984, A Book of Traveller's Tales 1985, Round Ireland in Low Gear 1987, What the Traveller Saw 1989, A Small Place in Italy 1994, A Merry Dance Around the World 1995. *Leisure interests:* walking, cycling, gardening. *Address:* Pine View House, 4 Pine View Close, Chilworth, Surrey, GU4 8RS, England. *Telephone:* (01483) 571430.

NEWBY, Howard Joseph, PH.D., F.R.S.A.; British university vice-chancellor; b. 10 Dec. 1947, Derby; s. of Alfred J. Newby and Constance A. Potts; m. Janet Elizabeth Craddock 1970; two s.; lecturer in Sociology, Univ. of Essex 1972–75, Sr. lecturer 1975–79; Prof. of Sociology, Univ. of Wis. 1979–83, Univ. of Essex 1983–88; Chair. Econ. & Social Research Council 1988–94, Chief Exec. 1994; mem. Rural Devt. Comm. 1991–, S. & W. Regional Health Authority 1994–96, European Sciences and Technology Asscn. 1997–; Vice-Chancellor, Univ. of Southampton 1994–; Chair Centre for Exploitation of Science and Tech. 1995–; visiting appts. Univs. of New South Wales 1976, Sydney 1976, Wis. 1977–78, Newcastle upon Tyne 1983–84; six hon. degrees. *Publications include:* Community Studies (jtly.) 1971, The Deferential Worker 1977, Property, Paternalism and Power (jtly.) 1978, Green and Pleasant Land? 1979, The Problem of Sociology (jtly.) 1983, Country Life 1987, The Countryside in Question 1988, Social Class in Modern Britain 1988 (jtly.), The National Trust: The Next 100 Years 1995. *Leisure interests:* family life, gardening, Derby County, railway enthusiasms. *Address:* The Old Mill, Mill Lane, Corston, Malmesbury, Wilts., SN16 0HH, England. *Telephone:* (01703) 592801. *Fax:* (01703) 593159.

NEWCOMBE, John David, A.O., O.B.E.; Australian professional tennis player; b. 23 May 1944, Sydney; s. of George Ernest and Lillian Newcombe; m. Angelika Pfannenberg 1966; one s. two d.; ed. Sydney Church of England Grammar School; winner of Wimbledon Singles Championship 1970, 1971, U.S.A. Singles Championship 1973, Australia Singles Championship 1973, 1975, World Championship Tennis Crown 1974, Wimbledon Doubles Championship 1965–66, 1968–70, 1974; played with Australian Davis Cup Team 1963–67, 1973–76, Capt. (non-playing) 1994–; Pres. Asscn. of Tennis Professionals 1976–78; Pres. Program Tennis Services, Texas Co., Nat. Australia Day Council; Chair. McDonald's Jr. Tennis Australia. *Publications:* The Family Tennis Book 1975, The Young Tennis Player 1981, Bedside Tennis 1983. *Leisure interests:* skiing, waterskiing, golf, fishing. *Address:* c/o Tennis Australia, Batman Avenue, Melbourne, Vic. 3000, Australia.

NEWELL, Frances Mary, F.R.S.A., F.C.S.D.; British design consultant; b. 19 Jan. 1947, Surrey; d. of late Alexander C. Newell and Julie S. Newell; m. John William Sorrell 1974; two s. one d.; Founder and Chair. Newell & Sorrell (identity & design consultants, merged with Interbrand 1997) 1976–97; Group Creative Dir. Interbrand Newell and Sorrell; Chair. City & Guilds Nat. Advisory Cttee. on Art, Craft and Design 1994–96, mem. Colour Group 1996–, City & Guilds Sr. Awards Cttee. 1996–; Bd. Dir. Royal Acad. Enterprises 1996–; mem. Exec. Cttee. Mencap Blue Sky Appeal 1996–98, Advisory Bd. of Nat. Museum of Photography, Film and TV; 11 DBA Design Effectiveness Awards, 5 Silver D&ADs, 5 Clios, 1 Grand Award for British Airways Corp. Identity and 5 Gold Awards in New York Festivals, 2 Art

Directors' Club of Europe Awards. *Leisure interests:* art, travel, gardening. *Address:* Interbrand Newell and Sorrell, 4 Utopia Village, Chalcot Road, London, NW1 8LH, England. *Telephone:* 0171-722 1113. *Fax:* 0171-722 0259.

NEWELL, Mike; British film director; b. 1942, St. Albans, Herts.; s. of Terence William Newell and Mollie Louise Newell; m. Bernice Stegers 1979; one s. one d.; ed. Univ. of Cambridge; trainee dir. Granada TV 1963; TV work includes Big Breadwinner Hog (series) 1968, Budgie (series), Thirty Minute Theatre and other TV plays; dir. European premiere of Tennessee Williams' The Kingdom of the Earth, Bristol Old Vic. *Films:* The Man in the Iron Mask 1976, The Awakening 1979, Bad Blood 1980, Dance with a Stranger 1984, The Good Father 1985, Amazing Grace and Chuck 1986, Soursweet 1987, Common Ground 1990, Enchanted April 1991, Into the West, Four Weddings and a Funeral (B.A.F.T.A. Award for Best Director 1995) 1994, An Awfully Big Adventure 1994, Donnie Brasco 1997. *Address:* Dogstar, 5 Sherwood Street, London, W1V 7RA, England.

NEWELL, Norman Dennis, PH.D.; American palaeontologist and geologist; b. 27 Jan. 1909, Chicago, Ill.; s. of Virgil Bingham Newell and Nellie Clark; m. 1st Valerie Zirkle 1928 (died 1972); m. 2nd Gillian Wendy Wormall 1973; ed. Univ. of Kansas and Yale Univ.; Geologist, Kansas Geological Survey 1929–37; Faculty mem., Univ. of Kansas 1934–37; Assoc. Prof. of Geology Univ. of Wis. 1937–45; Prof. of Geology Columbia Univ. 1945–77, Prof. Emer. 1977–; Curator American Museum of Natural History, New York 1945–77, Curator Emer. 1977–; Consultant on Petroleum Geology, Govt. of Peru 1942–45; mem. N.A.S., American Acad. of Arts and Sciences, American Philosophical Soc., Geological Soc. of America, London Geological Soc., Paleontology Soc. (Pres. 1960–61), Soc. for the Study of Evolution (Pres. 1949), Soc. of Systematic Zoology (Pres. 1972–73); Hon. mem. Canadian Soc. of Petroleum Geologists 1993; awards include N.A.S. Mary Clarke Thompson Medal 1960, Yale Univ. Verrill Medal 1966, American Museum of Natural History Gold Medal for Achievement in Science 1978, Palaeontological Soc. Medal 1979 and A.A.A.S. Scientific Freedom and Responsibility Award 1987, Geological Soc. of America Penrose Medal 1990, American Asscn. of Petroleum Geologists Special Award 1996, Geological Soc. of Peru Medal 1997. *Publications:* Late Paleozoic Pelecypods 1937–42, Geology of the Lake Titicaca Region 1943, Upper Paleozoic of Peru 1953, Permian Reef Complex of the Guadalupe Mountains Region 1953, Geological Reconnaissance of Raroia Atoll 1956, Classification of the Bivalvia 1965, Revolutions in the History of Life 1967, Creation and Evolution: Myth or Reality? 1982, Pectinoid Bivalves of the Permian-Triassic Crisis 1995; scientific and popular articles on evolution, extinction, etc. *Address:* Department of Invertebrates, American Museum of Natural History, Central Park W. and 79th Street, New York, NY 10024 (Office); 135 Knapp Terrace, Leonia, NJ 07605, U.S.A. (Home). *Telephone:* (212) 769-5736 (Office); (201) 944-5596 (Home). *Fax:* (212) 769-5222.

NEWHOUSE, S. I., Jr.; American publishing executive; b. 1928; m. Victoria Newhouse; Chair. Condé Nast Publs. Inc., New York; Chair., C.E.O. Advance Publs. Inc., New York; Henry Johnson Fisher Award, Magazine Publishers' Asscn. 1985. *Address:* c/o Condé Nast Publications, Inc., 350 Madison Avenue, New York, NY 10017; Advance Publishers Inc., 950 Fingerboard Road, Staten Island, NY 10305, U.S.A.

NEWMAN, Edwin Harold; American journalist; b. 25 Jan. 1919, New York; s. of Myron Newman and Rose Parker Newman; m. Rigel Grell 1944; one d.; ed. Univ. of Wisconsin, Louisiana State Univ.; Washington Bureau, Int. News Service 1941, United Press 1941–42, 1945–46; U.S. Navy 1942–45; CBS News, Washington, D.C. 1947–49; freelance, London 1949–52; NBC News, London Bureau 1952–, Rome Bureau 1957–58, Paris Bureau 1958–61; Corresp. and Commentator, NBC News, New York 1961–83; Moderator of presidential cand. debates Ford-Carter 1976, Reagan-Mondale 1984; Columnist, King Features Syndicate 1984–89; freelance journalist and lecturer; appeared as self in numerous TV comedy series and films including The Pelican Brief and Spies like Us; Peabody, Overseas Press Club, Emmy, Univ. of Mo. School of Journalism Award, Chevalier, Legion d'honneur and others. *Publications:* Strictly Speaking 1974, A Civil Tongue 1976, Sunday Punch 1979, I Must Say 1988; articles for Punch, Esquire, Atlantic, Harper's, New York Times, Saturday Review, Chicago Tribune, TV Guide, Sports Illustrated. *Leisure interests:* music, reading. *Address:* c/o Richard Fulton Inc., 66 Richfield Street, Plainview, NY 11803, U.S.A.

NEWMAN, Frank, B.A.; American banker; b. 20 April 1942, Quincy, Mass.; m. Lizabeth Newman; one s.; ed. Harvard Univ.; Man. Peat Marwick Livingston & Co. 1966–69; Vice-Pres. Citicorp 1969–73; Exec. Vice-Pres., Chief Financial Officer Wells Fargo Bank 1973–86; Vice-Chair., Chief Financial Officer Bank America Corp. 1986–93; Under-Sec., Deputy Sec. Treasury Dept. 1993–95; Sr. Vice-Chair. Bankers Trust Co. 1995–, Chair., C.E.O., Pres. 1996–; Alexander Hamilton Award (Treasury Dept.). *Address:* 130 Liberty Street, New York, NY 10006, U.S.A. *Telephone:* 212-250-2500.

NEWMAN, Jocelyn Margaret, LL.B.; Australian politician; b. 8 July 1937; ed. Melbourne Univ.; Senator (Liberal Party) for Tasmania 1986–; Shadow Minister for Defence, Science and Personnel 1988–92, Veterans' Affairs 1990–92; Shadow Minister Assisting Leader on Status of Women 1989–93; Shadow Minister for the Aged and Veterans' Affairs 1992–93; Shadow Minister for Family Health, Shadow Minister Assisting Leader on Family Matters, Chair. Health, Welfare and Veterans' Affairs Group 1993–94; Shadow Minister for Defence 1994–96; Minister for Social Security and Minister Assisting Prime Minister on Status of Women 1996–98, for Family and Community Services 1998–. *Address:* Parliament House, Canberra, A.C.T. 2600, Australia.

NEWMAN, Sir Kenneth (Leslie), Kt., G.B.E.; British police officer; b. 15 Aug. 1926; s. of John William and Florence Newman; m. Eileen Lilian Newman 1949; one s. one d.; ed. Univ. of London; with R.A.F. 1942–46; mem. Palestine Police 1946–48; with Metropolitan Police, London 1948–73, Commdr. New Scotland Yard 1972; with Royal Ulster Constabulary 1973–79, Sr. Deputy Chief Constable 1973, Chief Constable 1976–79; Commandant, Police Staff Coll. 1980–82; Insp. of Constabulary 1980–82; Commr. Metropolitan Police 1982–87; Prof. of Law, Bristol Univ. 1987–88; Registrar Imperial Soc. of Kts. Bachelor 1991–98; Dir. Control Risks 1987–92; Chair. Disciplinary Cttee., Security Systems Inspectorate, British Security Industry Asscn. 1987–95, Asscn. for Prevention of Theft in Shops 1987–91; Pres. Asscn. of Police and Public Security Suppliers 1993–; Vice-Pres. Defence Mfrs. Asscn. 1987–; Trustee Community Action Trust 1987–99, World Humanity Action Trust 1993–; Companion of British Inst. of Man. 1977; Kt. of the Order of St. John of Jerusalem 1984, Queen's Police Medal 1982, numerous foreign decorations. *Address:* c/o New Scotland Yard, Broadway, London, S.W.1, England.

NEWMAN, Nanette; British actress and writer; b. Northampton; d. of Sidney and Ruby Newman; m. Bryan Forbes (q.v.) 1955; two d.; ed. Sternhold Coll., London, Italia Conti Stage School, Royal Acad. of Dramatic Art; *Film appearances include:* The L-Shaped Room 1962, The Wrong Arm of the Law 1962, Seance on a Wet Afternoon 1963, The Wrong Box 1965, The Whisperers 1966, The Madwoman of Chaillot 1968, The Raging Moon (Variety Club Best Actress Award) 1971, The Stepford Wives 1974, International Velvet 1978. *Television appearances include:* The Fun Food Factory, London Scene, Stay with me till Morning, Jessie, Let There Be Love, Late Expectations, The Endless Game 1988. *Publications:* God Bless Love 1972, Lots of Love 1973, All Our Love 1978, Fun Food Factory 1976, The Root Children 1978, Amy Rainbow 1980, That Dog 1980, Reflections 1981, Dog Lovers Coffee Table Book 1982, Cat Lovers Coffee Table Book 1983, My Granny was a Frightful Bore 1983, Christmas Cookbook 1984, Cat and Mouse Love Story 1984, The Best of Love 1985, Pigalev 1985, Archie 1986, The Summer Cookbook 1986, Small Beginnings 1987, Bad Baby 1988, Entertaining with Nanette Newman 1988, Charlie the Noisy Caterpillar 1989, Sharing 1989, ABC 1990, 123 1991, Cooking for Friends 1991, Spider, The Horrible Cat 1992, There's a Bear in the Bath 1993, There's a Bear in the Classroom 1996, Take 3 Cooks 1996. *Leisure interests:* needlepoint, china painting. *Address:* Chatto & Linnit Ltd., 123A King's Road, London, SW3 4PL, England.

NEWMAN, Paul; B.A., L.H.D.; American actor; b. 26 Jan. 1925, Cleveland, Ohio; s. of Arthur Newman and Theresa Fetzer; m. 1st Jacqueline Witte 1949; one s. (died 1978) two d.; m. 2nd Joanne Woodward (q.v.) 1958; three d.; ed. Kenyon Coll. and Yale Univ. School of Drama; Mil. service 1943–46; Best Actor, Acad. of Motion Pictures, Arts and Sciences 1959, 1962, 1964, Hon. Acad. Award 1986, Head cos. Newman's Own, Newman's Own Spaghetti Sauce, Newman's Own Popcorn etc.; Hon. D. Hum. Litt. (Yale) 1988, Franklin D. Roosevelt Four Freedoms Medal 1991, Kennedy Center Honor 1992, Jean Hersholt Humanitarian Award 1994. *Stage appearances include:* Picnic 1953–54, Desperate Hours 1955, Sweet Bird of Youth 1959, Baby Want a Kiss 1964. *Films include:* The Rack 1955, Somebody Up There Likes Me 1956, Cat on a Hot Tin Roof 1958, Rally Round the Flag, Boys 1958, The Young Philadelphians 1958, From the Terrace 1960, Exodus 1960, The Hustler 1962, Hud 1963, The Prize 1963, The Outrage 1964, What a Way to Go 1964, Lady L 1965, Torn Curtain 1966, Hombre 1967, Cool Hand Luke 1967, The Secret War of Harry Frigg 1968, Butch Cassidy and the Sundance Kid 1969, WUSA 1970, Pocket Money 1972, The Life and Times of Judge Roy Bean 1973, The Mackintosh Man 1973, The Sting 1973, The Towering Inferno 1974, The Drowning Pool 1975, Buffalo Bill and the Indians 1976, Silent Movie 1976, Slap Shot 1977, Absence of Malice 1981, The Verdict 1982, Harry and Son (Dir.) 1984, The Color of Money 1986, Fat Man and Little Boy, Blaze 1989, Mr. and Mrs. Bridge 1990, The Hudsucker Proxy 1994, Nobody's Fool 1994, Message in a Bottle 1999. *Directed:* Rachel, Rachel 1968, The Effect of Gamma Rays on Man in the Moon Marigolds 1973, The Shadow Box 1980, When Time Ran Out 1980, Fort Apache: the Bronx 1981, The Glass Menagerie 1987, Super Speedway 1997, Where the Money Is 1998, Twilight 1998. *Address:* Creative Artists Agency, 477 Madison Avenue, New York, NY 10022, U.S.A.

NEWMAN, Peter C., C.C., C.D. Canadian author and journalist; b. 10 May 1929, Vienna, Austria; s. of Oscar and Wanda Newman; m. 1st Christina McCall (divorced); m. 2nd Camilla J. Turner 1978; two d.; m. 3rd Alvina Björklund 1992; ed. Upper Canada Coll., Toronto, Univ. of Toronto and McGill Univ.; Asst. Ed. The Financial Post 1951–55; Ottawa Ed. Maclean's 1955–64; Ottawa Ed. Toronto Daily Star 1964–69, Ed.-in-Chief 1969–71; Ed.-in-Chief, Maclean's 1971–82, Sr. Contributing Ed. 1982–; Dir. Maclean Hunter Ltd. 1972–83, Key Radio Ltd. 1983–; Prof. Creative Writing, Univ. of Victoria 1985–90; several honours and awards including Kt. Commdr. Order of St. Lazarus; Hon. LL.D. (Brock) 1974, (Wilfrid Laurier) 1983, (Royal Mil. Coll.) 1986, (Queens) 1986, Hon. D.Litt. (York) 1975, (British Columbia) 1979. *Publications:* Flame of Power 1959, Renegade in Power 1963, The Distemper of our Times 1968, Home Country 1973, The Canadian Establishment: Vol. I 1975, Bronfman Dynasty 1978, The Acquisitors – The Canadian

Establishment: Vol. II 1981, The Establishment Man 1982, True North – Not Strong and Free 1983, Debrett's Illustrated Guide to the Canadian Establishment 1983, Company of Adventurers 1985, Caesars of the Wilderness 1987, Sometimes A Great Nation 1988, Merchant Princes 1991, The Canadian Revolution 1995, Defining Moments 1996, Titans: How the New Canadian Establishment Seized Power 1998. *Leisure interest:* sailing. *Address:* Box 46, Granthams Landing, B.C. V0N 1X0, Canada. *Telephone:* (604) 886-6814. *Fax:* (604) 886-6815.

NEWMARCH, Michael George, B.SC. (ECON.); British insurance executive; b. 19 May 1938, London; s. of George Langdon Newmarch and Phillis Georgina Newmarch; m. Audrey Ann Clarke 1959; one s. two d.; ed. Tottenham County Grammar School, London Univ.; joined Econ. Intelligence Dept. Prudential Assurance Co. Ltd. 1955; Exec. Dir. Prudential Corpn. 1985, C.E.O. Prudential Financial Services 1987, Chair. Prudential Holborn 1986–89, C.E.O. and Deputy Chair. Prudential Portfolio Mans. Ltd. 1980–90, C.E.O. Prudential Corpn. 1990–95; Dir. (non-exec.) Celltech PLC 1996–; Consultant Price Waterhouse 1997–; Chair. Bourne End Properties PLC 1997–; Vice-Chair. Princess Royal Trust for Carers 1994–; Trustee Berkshire Community Trust 1996–; mem. Advisory Council, Orchestra of the Age of Enlightenment 1994–. *Leisure interests:* salmon fishing, fly-tying, bridge, music, theatre, cinema, travel. *Address:* 27 Paultons Square, London, S.W.3; Craven View, Craven Hill, Hampstead Marshall, nr. Newbury, Berks., England (Homes).

NEWSOM, David Dunlop, A.B., M.S.; American diplomatist; b. 6 Jan. 1918, Richmond, Calif.; s. of Fred Stoddard and Ivy Elizabeth (née Dunlop) Newsom; m. Jean Frances Craig 1942; three s. two d.; ed. Richmond Union High School and California and Columbia Univs.; Reporter, San Francisco Chronicle 1940–41; U.S. Navy 1941–45; Newspaper publr. 1945–47; Information Officer, U.S. Embassy, Karachi 1947–50; Consul, Oslo 1950–51; Public Affairs Officer, U.S. Embassy, Baghdad 1951–55; Dept. of State 1955–59; U.S. Nat. War Coll. 1959–60; First Sec. U.S. Embassy, London 1960–62; Dir. Office of Northern African Affairs, State Dept. 1962–65; Amb. to Libya 1965–69; Asst. Sec. of State for African Affairs 1969–73; Amb. to Indonesia 1974–77, to Philippines 1977–78; Under-Sec. of State for Political Affairs 1978–81; Marshall B. Coyne Research Prof. of Diplomacy, Georgetown Univ.; Prof. (fmrly. lecturer) in Int. Relations Univ. of Va. 1991–95, Cumming Memorial Prof. of Int. Relations 1991–98; interim dean School of Foreign Service Georgetown Univ., Washington 1995–96; Dept. of State Meritorious Service Award 1958, Nat. Civil Service League Career Service Award 1971, Rockefeller Public Service Award 1973, Dept. of State Distinguished Honor Award 1981, John Adams Memorial Fellow in Int. Relations 1986. *Address:* 2409 Angus Road, Charlottesville, VA 22901, U.S.A.

NEWTON, Sir (Charles) Wilfrid, Kt., C.B.E., F.R.S.A., F.C.I.T.; British business executive; b. 11 Dec. 1928, Johannesburg, South Africa; s. of Gore M. and Catherine K. Newton; m. Felicity Mary Lynn 1954; two s. two d.; ed. Highlands North High School, Johannesburg, Univ. of Witwatersrand; Territory Accounting and Finance Man., Mobil Oil Corpn. of South Africa 1955–62; Controller, Mobil Sekiyu K.K., Tokyo 1962–63, Finance Dir. 1965–68; Financial Man. and Deputy Gen. Man., Mobil Oil East Africa Ltd. 1963–65; Chief Financial Officer, Mobil Interests Japan 1965–68; Finance Dir., Turner and Newall Ltd. 1968–74, Man. Dir. Finance and Planning 1974–76, Man. Dir. Plastics, Chemicals and Mining Divs. 1976–79, Group Man. Dir. 1979–82, C.E.O. 1982–; Chair. Mass Transit Railway Corpn. Hong Kong 1983–89, Hong Kong Futures Exchange Ltd. 1987–89, Chair. Jacobs Holdings PLC 1994–, Raglan Properties PLC 1994–99; Chair. and C.E.O. London Regional Transport 1989–94, London Underground Ltd. 1989–93; Chair. G. Maunsell Int. Ltd. 1996–98; Non-exec. Dir. Hong Kong and Shanghai Banking Corpn. 1986–92, Sketchley PLC, HSBC Holdings PLC, Midland Bank PLC, Mountcity Investments Ltd., Maunsell Holdings Ltd.; mem. Inst. of Chartered Accounts of South Africa; Fellow Hong Kong Man. Asscn; Hon. F.Eng., Hon. Fellow Hong Kong Inst. of Engineers. *Leisure interests:* sailing, reading, current affairs, economics. *Address:* Newtons Gate, Ramley Road, Pennington, Lymington, Hants., SO4 8GQ, England. *Telephone:* 0171-629 1339 (Office); (01590) 679750 (Home). *Fax:* 0171-629 0728 (Office); (01590) 677440.

NEWTON, Christopher, C.M., M.A., F.R.C.M.; Canadian actor, director and author; b. 11 June 1936, Deal, Kent; s. of Albert E. Newton and Gwladys M. Emes; ed. Sir Roger Manwood's School, Sandwich, Kent, Univs. of Leeds and Illinois and Purdue Univs.; actor, Stratford Festival, New York; founding Artistic Dir. Theatre Calgary, Calgary, Alberta 1968–71; Artistic Dir. Vancouver Playhouse and founder (with late Powys Thomas), The Playhouse Acting School 1973–79; Artistic Dir. The Shaw Festival, Niagara-on-the-Lake 1979–; Hon. Fellow Ryerson Univ.; Hon. LL.D. (Brock Univ., Guelph); Hon. D.Litt. (Wilfrid Laurier Univ.). *Publications:* plays: You Two Stay Here, the Rest Come with Me, Slow Train to St. Ives, Trip, The Sound of Distant Thunder, The Lost Letter. *Leisure interest:* landscape architecture. *Address:* c/o Shaw Festival, Box 774, Niagara-on-the-Lake, Ont., L0S 1J0 (Office); 22 Prideaux Street, Niagara-on-the-Lake, Ont., L0S 1J0, Canada (Home). *Telephone:* (416) 468-2153 (Office).

NEWTON, David A., M.A., F.B.I.M., F.INST.D.; British company director; b. 6 Oct. 1942; s. of Alexander Newton and Hazel Newton (née Little); m. Kathleen Mary Moore 1965; one. s. one d.; ed. Morecombe Grammar School, Wyvern Business Studies Coll.; Man. Trainee J. Bibby & Sons Ltd. 1964–67; Gen. Man. Anglian Hatcheries Ltd. 1967–73; Agric. Dir. Sovereign Poultry 1973–81; Man. Dir. Ross Poultry Ltd. 1981–83, Buxted Poultry Ltd. 1983–86; Dir. Hillsdown Holdings Ltd. U.K. 1985–96, C.E.O. 1993–96, C.O.O. 1992–93; Chair., Pres., C.E.O. Maple Leaf Mills, Toronto 1987–92, Pres., Deputy Chair. 1992–95; Pres., C.E.O. Canada Packers Inc., Toronto (subsequently Maple Leaf Foods Inc.) 1990–92; Dir. Carr's Milling Industries 1996–, Bodfari Ltd. 1996–, Bernard Matthews PLC 1996–, Prism Rail PLC 1997–, MRCT Ltd. 1997–; Chair. Carr's Milling Industries 1997–; Partner K&D Partnership 1997–; rep. Lancashire County Rugby, Soccer. *Leisure interest:* golf. *Address:* Carr's Milling Industries, Old Croft, Stanwix, Carlisle, CA3 9BA, England. *Telephone:* (01228) 528291.

NEWTON, Helmut; Australian photographer; b. 31 Oct. 1920, Berlin; m. June F. Browne (pseudonym Alice Springs, q.v.) 1948; ed. Heinrich von Treitschke Realgymnasium, Berlin and American School, Berlin; apprentice to fashion and theatre photographer Yva (Else Simon) 1936–38; emigrated to Australia; served Australian Army 1940–45; freelance photographer Melbourne in 1940s; moved to Paris; freelance photographer working for Jardin des Modes, Elle, Queen, Playboy, Nova, Marie-Claire, Stern and French and U.S. edns. of Vogue, etc., 1958–; numerous one-man exhbns. including Paris 1975, 1979, 1981, 1984, 1992, 1993, L.A. 1976, New York 1978, Munich 1982, Shiga, Japan 1990, London 1991, 1995, Milan 1993, Monte Carlo 1995; participant in numerous group shows; work in numerous public collections; Best Photography Award, Art Dirs. Club, Tokyo 1976; American Inst. of Graphic Arts Award 1977, 1980; Gold Medal, Art Dirs. Club, Germany 1978, 1979, Photographers Award for Outstanding Achievements and Contribs. to Photography in 1960s and 1970s, Photographic Soc. of Japan 1989, Grand Prix de la Ville de Paris 1989, Grand Prix Nat. for Photography, France 1990, World Image for Best Portrait Photography, New York 1991; Chevalier des Arts et des Lettres, Grosse Verdienstkreuz des Bunderesrepublik Deutschland, Chevalier des Arts, Lettres et Sciences (Monaco), Commdr. des Arts et des Lettres. *Publications include:* White Women 1976, Sleepless Nights 1978, Special Collection: 24 Photo Lithos 1979, 47 Nudes 1982, World Without Men 1984, Private Property 1984, Pola-Woman 1992, Naked and Dressed in Hollywood 1992, Immorale 1993, Helmut Newton's Illustrated No. 4–Dr. Phantasme 1995.

NEWTON, John Oswald, M.A., PH.D., D.SC., F.A.A.; Australian/British professor of nuclear physics; b. 12 Feb. 1924, Birmingham; s. of O. J. Newton and R. K. Newton; m. 2nd Silva Dusan Sablich 1964; two s. one d.; ed. Bishop Vesey's Grammar School, Sutton Coldfield, St. Catharine's Coll., Cambridge, Cavendish Lab., Cambridge; Jr. Scientific Officer, Telecommunications Research Establishment, Great Malvern 1943–46; Harwell Fellow 1951–54; Prin. Scientific Officer, A.E.R.E. Harwell 1954–59; Sr. Lecturer, Univ. of Manchester 1959–67, Reader 1967–70; Prof. of Nuclear Physics, A.N.U. 1970–89, Head of Dept. of Nuclear Physics, Inst. of Advanced Studies 1970–88, Emer. Prof. and Visiting Fellow in Dept. of Nuclear Physics 1990–; Visiting Physicist, Lawrence Berkeley Lab. (several times since 1956); Visiting Prof. Univ. of Manchester 1985–86. *Publications:* more than 100 publs. in Nuclear Physics and several book chapters. *Leisure interests:* painting, chess, music, walking, tennis. *Address:* Department of Nuclear Physics, IAS, Australian National University, Canberra, A.C.T. 0200 (Office); 21 Ryrie Street, Campbell, A.C.T. 2612, Australia (Home). *Telephone:* (02) 62492074 (Office). *Fax:* (02) 62490748 (Office).

NEWTON, Ronald Gordon, O.B.E., PH.D., D.SC.; British professor of glass technology; b. 19 Nov. 1912, Middx.; s. of Henry J. H. Newton and Thelma C. Hammond; m. 1st Hallé Marsten 1937 (died 1953); m. 2nd Lilian E. Parish 1954 (died 1970); m. 3rd Joyce M. Bagshaw 1971; two. s.; ed. Brighton Grammar School, Brighton Tech. Coll. and Imperial Coll. London; Fellowship, Rubber Growers' Asscn. 1936–37; Research Asscn. of British Rubber Mfrs. 1938–48; British Rubber Producers' Research Asscn. 1948–52 (seconded to Rubber Research Inst. of Malaya 1949–50); Deputy Sec. Int. Rubber Research Bd. 1952–55; Founder-Dir. British Glass Industry Research Asscn. 1955–74; Hon. Visiting Prof. Univ. of York 1974–79; Clayton Memorial Lecture 1972, Twenty-third Mellor Memorial Lecture 1979, Eighth Turner Memorial Lecture 1984; Hon. Prof. of Glass Tech. Univ. of Sheffield 1980–91; Hon. Fellow, Soc. of Glass Tech.; Dr. h.c. (Sheffield) 1990. *Publications:* The Deterioration and Conservation of Painted Glass, A Critical Bibliography 1982, The Conservation of Glass 1989, 1995; many scientific articles on rubber and glass. *Leisure interest:* genealogical research on the name Bagshaw/e. *Address:* Flat 9, Broomgrove Trust, 30, Broomgrove Road, Sheffield, S10 2LR, England. *Telephone:* (0114) 266 1409. *Fax:* (0114) 266 1409.

NEWTON, Sir Wilfrid (see Newton, Sir (Charles) Wilfrid).

NEWTON OF BRAINTREE, Baron (Life Peer) cr. 1997, of Coggeshall in the County of Essex; **Antony Harold (Tony) Newton,** O.B.E., P.C.; British politician; b. Aug. 1937; m. 1st Janet Huxley 1962 (divorced 1986); two d.; m. 2nd Patricia Gilthorpe 1986; one step-s. two step-d.; ed. Friends' School, Saffron Walden, Trinity Coll. Oxford; Pres. Oxford Union 1959; fmr. Sec. and Research Sec. Bow Group; Head Econ. Section, Conservative Research Dept. 1965–70, Asst. Dir. 1970–74; Parl. Cand. for Sheffield, Brightside 1970; M.P. for Braintree 1974–97; Asst. Govt. Whip 1979–81; Lord Commr., Treasury 1981–82; Parl. Under-Sec. for Social Security 1982–84, and Minister for the Disabled 1983–84, Minister of State 1984–86; Minister of State (Health) and Chair. Nat. Health Service Man. Bd. 1986–88; Chancellor Duchy of Lancaster 1988–89; Sec. of State for Social Security 1989–92; Lord

Pres. of the Council and Leader of the House of Commons 1992–97. *Address:* c/o House of Commons, London, SW1A 0AA, England.

NEWTON-JOHN, Olivia, O.B.E.; British singer and actress; b. 26 Sept. 1948, Cambridge; d. of Brin Newton-John and Irene Born; m. Matt Lattanzi 1984; one d.; co-owner Koala Blue 1982–; UNEP Goodwill Amb. 1989–; Humanitarian Award U.S. Red Cross 1999 and numerous other awards. *Recordings* (1971–) *include:* Let Me Be There, If You Love Me, Let Me Know, Clearly Love, Come On Over, Don't Stop Believin', Making a Good Thing Better, Totally Hot, Physical. *Film appearances include:* Grease 1978, Xanadu 1980, Two of a Kind 1983. *TV appearances:* numerous, including It's Cliff Richard (BBC-TV series). *Leisure interests:* horse riding, song writing, cycling, astrology, conservation, animals. *Address:* c/o Bill Sammeth Organization, P.O. Box 960, Beverly Hills, CA 90213, U.S.A.

NEY, Edward Noonan, B.A.; American business executive; b. 26 May 1925, St. Paul, Minn.; s. of John and Marie Noonan Ney; m. 1st Suzanne Hayes 1950 (divorced 1974); one s. two d.; m. 2nd Judith I. Lasky 1974; ed. Amherst Coll.; Account Exec., Young & Rubicam Inc. 1951, Vice-Pres. 1959–63, Sr. Vice-Pres. 1963–67, Exec. Vice-Pres. 1967–68, Pres. Int. Div. 1968–70, Pres. and C.E.O. 1970–72, Pres., C.E.O. and Chair. 1972–83, Chair. and C.E.O. 1983–85, Chair. 1985–86, Chair. PaineWebber/Young Rubicam Ventures 1987–89, Young and Rubicam Ventures 1989–, Vice-Chair. PaineWebber 1987–89; Chair. Bd. of Advisers Burton-Marsteller 1992–; Amb. to Canada 1989–92; Vice-Chair. The Advertising Council 1984–87, Chair. 1987–88; mem. Bd. Int. Broadcasting 1984–, Bd. of Govs. Foreign Policy Asscn. 1980– (Vice-Chair. 1984–87); Dir. Center for Communications 1986–; Chair. Manteller Advertising 1996–; Trustee, Nat. Urban League 1974–, Amherst Coll. 1979–, New York Univ. Medical Center 1979–, Museum of Broadcasting 1982–; mem. Council on Foreign Relations 1974; mem. Bd. Advisory Council, Center for Strategic and Int. Studies 1986–. *Leisure interests:* tennis, paddle tennis, reading. *Address:* Burston-Marsteller, 230 Park Avenue South, New York, NY 10003, U.S.A.

NEYELOVA, Marina Mstislavovna; Russian actress; b. 8 Jan. 1948; m. Kyrill Gevorgyan; one d.; ed. Leningrad Inst. of Theatre, Music and Cinema; actress Moscow Theatre Studio of Film Actors 1968–71, Mossoviet Theatre 1971–74, Sovremennik 1974–; prin. roles in classical and contemporary repertoire including Chekhov's plays; debut in cinema 1968; numerous roles in films including Old, Old Tale 1970, Monologue 1973, Autumn Marathon 1979 (State Prize of Russia), Prison Romance; People's Artist Russian Fed. 1980; U.S.S.R. State Prize 1990, Prize Nika (film I Have Only You) 1994; Order Friendship of Peoples 1996. *Address:* Potapovsky per. 12, 117333 Moscow, Russia (Home).

NEZVAL, Jiří; Czech government official; b. 5 April 1941, Brno; s. of František Nezval and Květa Nezval; m. Silva Moltašová 1963; two d.; ed. Railway Coll. Zilina and Polytechnic Inst. Brno; designer and design office man. in automation of rail transport, Prague; involved in Czechoslovak Scientific and Tech. Soc., Peace Movt.; Fed. Minister of Transport 1990–92; mem. Civic Movt. Party 1991–93, Free Democrats Party 1993– (merged with Liberal Nat. Social Party 1995); Dir. Denzel Praha Co. 1992–; Chair. Union of Motor Car Importers 1995–; Exclusive Mitsubishi dealership in Czech Repub. 1997–. *Leisure interests:* computer art, management systems, reading books, sports (skiing, cycling, volleyball). *Address:* Denzel Praha s.r.o., Revoluční 2, Prague 1, Czech Republic. *Telephone:* 24 81 08 36.

NG, Daniel; Chinese business executive; Chair. McDonald's Restaurants (Hong Kong Special Administrative Region). *Address:* McDonald's Restaurants, Hong Kong Special Administrative Region, People's Republic of China.

NGAPO NGAWANG-JIGME (see Ngapoi Ngawang Jigme).

NGAPOI NGAWANG JIGME, Lieut.-Gen.; Chinese politician; b. 1911, nr. Lhasa, Tibet; captured by Communist troops, Qamdo (Tibetan Mil. Region under his control) 1950; Vice-Chair. Qamdo Liberation Cttee. 1950; First Deputy Commdr. Tibet Mil. Region 1952; Vice-Chair. and Sec. Gen. 1959; Deputy for Xizang, 1st NPC 1954; mem. Nat. Defence Council 1954–Cultural Revolution; Sec.-Gen. Preparatory Cttee. for Establishment of Tibet Autonomous Region (AR) 1956, Vice-Chair. 1959, Acting Chair. 1965; Vice-Chair. Standing Cttee., 3rd CPPCC 1959–64; Head, Cadre School, Lhasa 1961; Vice-Chair. Standing Cttee., 3rd NPC 1965–75, 4th NPC 1975–78, 5th NPC 1978–86, 6th NPC 1983–87, 7th NPC 1988–93; Chair. Tibet AR 1965; Vice-Chair. Tibet AR Revolutionary Cttee. 1968–79; Chair. People's Congress, Tibet AR 1979; Exec. Chair. Presidium 6th NPC 1986; Chair. Tibet Autonomous Regional 5th People's Congress 1988–93; Chair. Nationalities Cttee., NPC, 1979–; Chair. China-Tibet Devt. Foundation April 1992–, Vice-Chair. CPPCC 8th Nat. Cttee. 1993–98, 9th Nat. Cttee. 1998–; Hon. Pres. Asscn. for Well-Known Chinese Figures 1993–. *Publication:* Tibet (with others). *Address:* National Committee of Chinese People's Political Consultative Conference, 23 Taipingqiao Street, Beijing, People's Republic of China.

NGEI, Paul, B.SC.(ECON.); Kenyan politician; b. 1923, Machakos; grandson of Akamba Paramount Chief Masaku; ed. Makerere Coll., Kampala; Army Service, Second World War; founded Wasya wa Mukamba newspaper and Swahili magazine Uhuru wa Mwafrika 1950; Deputy Gen. Sec. Kenya African Union 1951–52; imprisoned and under restriction for connection with Mau-Mau 1953–61; Pres. Kenya African Farmers' and Traders' Union 1961; founded African Peoples' Party 1962; Chair. Maize Marketing Bd. 1963–64; Minister for Co-operatives and Marketing 1964–65, for Housing and Social Services 1965–66, for Housing 1966–74, of Local Govt. 1974–75, unseated by High Court ruling; M.P. for Kagunda Jan. 1976–; Minister of Co-operative Devt. 1976–79, of Works 1979–82, of Livestock Devt. 1982–83, of Lands and Settlement 1983–84, of Environment and Nat. Resources 1984–85, of Water Devt. 1985–87, of Livestock Devt. 1987–88, Minister of Culture and Social Services 1988–89, of Manpower Devt. and Employment 1989–90; Man. Dir. Akamba Carving and Industrial Co. *Address:* c/o Ministry of Manpower Development and Employment, Nairobi, Kenya.

NGO DINH NHU, Madame; Vietnamese politician; widow of Ngo Dinh Nhu, brother and Adviser to the late Pres. Ngo Dinh Diem; arrested by Viet Minh, later escaped 1946; organized first popular demonstration in support of Govt. of Prime Minister Ngo Dinh Diem 1954; Official Hostess for Pres. Ngo Dinh Diem 1955–63; fmr. Deputy, Nat. Assembly, author of "Family Bill"; f. programme of paramilitary service for women Oct. 1961; Founder-Pres. Vietnamese Women's Solidarity Movement.

NGO, Quang Xuan; Vietnamese diplomatist; b. 1 Jan. 1951, Nghe An; s. of Ngo Tri Tai and Dau Thi Nghiem; m. Le Thi Hoa 1975; two d.; ed. Inst. of Int. Relations, Hanoi, Inst. des Hautes Etudes Internationales, Geneva, Diplomatic Acad. of Moscow; Deputy Gen. Dir. Dept. for Multilateral Econ. and Cultural Co-operation, Foreign Ministry 1988–91, Deputy Dir. Int. Orgs. Dept. 1992–93, Dir. of Ministry 1995–; Nat. Rep. to Francophone Community 1990–93; Acting Perm. Rep. to UN 1993–95, Perm. Rep. 1995–; Medal for Diplomatic Service. *Leisure interests:* classical music, tennis. *Address:* Permanent Mission of Viet Nam to the United Nations, 866 United Nations Plaza, Suite 435, New York, NY 10017, U.S.A. *Telephone:* (212) 644-0594. *Fax:* (212) 644-5732.

NGOUPANDE, Jean-Paul; Central African Republic politician and fmr. diplomatist; fmrly. Amb. to France; Prime Minister of Central African Repub. 1996–97. *Address:* c/o Office of the Prime Minister, Bangui, Central African Republic.

NGUBANE, Baldwin Sipho, M.B., CH.B.; South African politician and doctor; b. 22 Oct. 1941, Camperdown; m. Sheila Buthelezi; four c.; ed. St. Francis Coll., Marrianhill, Durban Medical School, Univ. of Witwatesrand, Natal Medical School; fmr. Latin teacher; mem. Inkatha Freedom Party Cen. Cttee. Exec. 1977–; mem. KwaZulu Legis. Ass. 1978–; led KwaZulu Govt. del. to Constitutional negotiations; Minister of Health, KwaZulu Govt. 1991–94; Minister of Arts, Culture, Science and Tech. 1994; mem. S.A. Red Cross Soc. 1977–, Regional Counsellor 1978–; mem. Council Univ. of Zululand; mem. Natal Boxing Bd. of Control. *Leisure interests:* tennis, reading, photography. *Address:* Ministry of Arts, Culture, Science and Technology, Oranje Nassau Bldg., Schoeman Street, Pretoria 0002; Private Bag X727, Pretoria 0001, South Africa (Office). *Telephone:* 12-324-4096. *Fax:* 12-324-2687.

NGUGI, Wa Thiong'o (James); Kenyan novelist; b. 1938, Limuru; ed. Makerere Univ. Coll., Uganda and Leeds Univ., England; Lecturer in Literature, Univ. Nairobi 1967–69; Fellow in Creative Writing, Makerere Univ. 1969–70; Visiting Assoc. Prof. Northwestern Univ., U.S.A. 1970–71; fmr. Sr. Lecturer, then Assoc. Prof. and Chair. Literature Dept., Univ. Nairobi; arrested and detained Dec. 1977, released Dec. 1978; in exile in London 1982–; lecturer in Politics and Literature, Yale Univ. *Publications:* The Black Hermit (play) 1962, Weep Not Child 1964, The River Between 1965, A Grain of Wheat 1967, Homecoming (essays) 1972, Secret Lives (short stories) 1973, Petals of Blood (novel) 1977, The Trial of Dedan Kimathi (with Micere Mugo) 1977, Detained: A Writer's Prison Diary 1981, I'll Marry When I Want (with Ngugi wa Mirii) 1982, Devil on the Cross 1982, Writers in Politics (essays) 1982, Barrel of a Pen (essays) 1983, Decolonising the Mind (essays) 1986, Writing Against Neo-Colonialism 1986, Matigari ma Ngirũũngi (novel in Gĩkũyũ language) 1986, Moving the Centre 1992.

NGUYEN CAO KY, Air Vice-Marshal; Vietnamese politician and air force officer; b. 8 Sept. 1930; ed. High School, Hanoi, and Officers' Training School, Hanoi; Flight Training, Marrakesh until 1954; commanded Transport Squadron 1954, later commdr. Tan Son Nhât Air Force Base, Repub. of Viet Nam; spent six months at U.S. Air Command and Staff Coll., Maxwell Field, Ala., U.S.A.; later Commdr. Air Force, Repub. of Viet Nam; Prime Minister 1965–67; Vice-Pres. Repub. of Viet Nam 1967–71; went to U.S.A. April 1975; owns liquor store. *Publication:* Twenty Years and Twenty Days 1977.

NGUYEN KHANH, Lieut.-Gen.; Vietnamese politician and army officer; b. 1927; ed. Viet Nam Mil. Acad., Dalat, Army Staff Schools, Hanoi and France, and U.S. Command and Gen. Staff Coll., Fort Leavenworth; French Colonial Army 1954, Vietnamese Army 1954; Chief of Staff to Gen. Duong Van Minh 1955; took part in coup against Pres. Diem Nov. 1963; Prime Minister Jan.-Oct. 1964; Chair. Armed Forces Council 1964–65; led coup Jan. 1965; Roving Amb. 1965; mem. Secr. CP of Viet Nam; Vice-Prime Minister and Gen. Sec. Council of Ministers 1987. *Address:* Office of the Vice-Prime Ministers, Hanoi; 1 Hoang Van Thu, Hanoi, Viet Nam.

NGUYEN PHU DUC, LL.D., DR.JUR.; Vietnamese diplomatist; b. 13 Nov. 1924, Son-Tay; m.; two s.; ed. Univ. of Hanoi, Harvard Law School; Perm. Observer to UN 1964–65; Special Asst. for Foreign Affairs to Pres. Thieu 1968; Envoy to Thailand, Khmer Repub., Laos, Indonesia, U.S.A. 1972; Minister of Foreign Affairs 1973; Amb. to Belgium 1974–75; attended confs.

on Viet Nam 1966, 1967, 1968, 1969, 1973, active in negotiations leading to Paris Conf. 1968, and to Paris Agreement 1973.

NGUYEN THI BINH, Madame; Vietnamese politician; b. 1927; ed. Saigon; student political leader in Saigon; organized (with Nguyen Huu Tho) first anti-American demonstration 1950; imprisoned by French authorities 1951–54; Vice-Pres. S. Vietnamese Cttee. for Solidarity with the American People; Vice-Pres. Union of Women for the Liberation of S. Viet Nam; mem. Cen. Cttee. Nat. Liberation Front (NLF); appointed NLF spokesman to four-party peace talks, Paris Nov. 1968; Minister for Foreign Affairs, Provisional Revolutionary Govt. of S. Viet Nam 1969–76 (in Saigon 1975–76); Minister of Educ., Socialist Repub. of Viet Nam 1976–87; Vice-Pres. Vietnamese Women's Union, Hanoi 1976–; Vice-Pres. of Viet Nam 1992–93; Vice-Pres. OSPAA. *Address:* c/o Ministry of Education, 21 Le Thanh Tong, Hanoi, Viet Nam.

NGUYEN VAN LOC, LL.M.; Vietnamese politician, lawyer and writer; b. 24 Aug. 1922, Vinh-Long; s. of Nguyen Van Hanh and Tran Thi Ngo; m. Nguyen Thi Mong Hoa; two s.; ed. Univs. of Montpellier and Paris; Lawyer, Saigon Court of Appeal 1955; Lecturer, Nat. Inst. of Admin. 1965; Chair. People's and Armed Forces Council 1966, People's and Armed Forces Council Political Cttee. 1966; Vice-Chair. Constituent Ass. Electoral Law Preparation Cttee.; mem. Barristers Fraternity 1961–67; Del. in charge of campaigning, Cttee. for Aid to War Victims (Viet Nam Red Cross); Counsellor, Viet Nam Asscn. for Protection of Human and People's Rights; Sec.-Gen., Inter-Schools Asscn. 1965–67; Prime Minister of Repub. of Viet Nam 1967–68; Prof. Univ. of Hóa-Hao 1970; Founder and Rector, Cao-Dai Univ. 1971–75; escaped to Singapore 1983. *Publications:* Uprising (novel) 1946, Rank 1948, New Recruits (novel) 1948, Poems on Liberation (collection) 1949, Recollections of the Green Years 1960, Free Tribune (collection) 1966, Poisonous Water (novel) 1971.

NGUYEN VAN THIEU, Lt.-Gen.; Vietnamese politician and army officer; b. 5 April 1923, Ninh Thlian; m. Nguyen Thi Mai Anh 1951; two s. one d.; ed. Catholic Pellerin School, Hué, and Nat. Mil. Acad., Hué; Viet Nam Nat. Army 1948–54; Repub. of Viet Nam Army 1954–75; Commdr. First Infantry Div. 1960–62, Fifth Infantry Div. 1962–63; Commdr. IV Corps and Armed Forces Chief of Staff 1963–64; Deputy Premier and Minister of Defence 1964–65; Chair. Nat. Leadership Cttee. and Head of State 1965–67; Pres. of Repub. of Viet Nam 1967–75; f. Dan Chu Party 1973; went to Taiwan April 1975 and later to the U.K.; lives in Surrey.

NGUYEN VAN VY, Lieut. Gen.; Vietnamese politician; b. 16 Jan, 1916, Hanoi; ed. Univ., Tong Officers' School and School of Command and Staff, Paris; Chief Mil. Cabinet of Chief of State 1952; Commdr. Coastal Interzone 1954; Acting Chief, Gen. Staff, Vietnamese Army Oct. 1954; Insp.-Gen. Dec. 1954; Asst. Chief of Staff for Training, R.V.N.A.F. Jan. 1964; Asst. to C.-in-C. Nov. 1964; Commdt. Quang Trung Training Centre Feb. 1965; Commdr. Training Command, R.V.N.A.F. June 1966; C.-of-S. Jt. Gen. Staff R.V.N.A.F. 1966–67; Minister of Defence 1968–72; Grand Officer Nat. Order of Viet Nam; Army and Air Force Distinguished Service Orders; Officier, Légion d'honneur.

NGUZA KARL-I-BOND; Democratic Republic of the Congo politician and diplomatist; b. 1938, Musumba; m. N'Landu Kavidi; ed. Catholic schools, Elisabethville (now Lubumbashi), and Univ. of Louvain, Belgium; Announcer, Radio Lubumbashi 1957–60, Radio Kinshasa 1964; mem. of Prime Minister Tshombe's private cabinet 1964; Counsellor, Congolese Embassy, Brussels 1964–66; Govt. Commr. Union Minière 1965–66; Counsellor, Congolese Del. to UN, New York 1966–68; Deputy Perm. Rep. to UN 1968; Minister, later Amb., and Perm. Rep. at UN Office, Geneva 1970–72; State Commr. for Foreign Affairs 1972–74, 1976–77, 1979–80, for Foreign Affairs and Int. Co-operation 1988–90, Minister of State in Office of the Pres. 1992–93; First Deputy Prime Minister in charge of Defence by Pres. Mobutu 1993–94; First State Commr. (Prime Minister) 1980–81, 1991–92; Amb. to U.S.A. 1986–88; mem. Political Bureau of the Mouvement populaire de la révolution 1972–77, 1979–81, Nat. Security Council 1979–81, Dir. 1974–77; Vice-Pres. Exec. Council, presiding over Political, Econ. and Finance Comm. Feb.-Aug. 1977; arrested Aug. 1977; accused of treason and sentenced to death, sentence commuted to life imprisonment Sept. 1977, reinstated March 1979; resgnd. posts while in Brussels April 1981; in exile 1982; returned to Zaire 1985. *Publications:* Mobutu ou l'Incarnation du Mal Zaïrois, Le Zaire de Demain 1984, Un Avenir pour le Zaire 1985. *Address:* c/o Office of the President, Kinshasa-Gombe, Democratic Republic of the Congo.

NHU, Madame (see Ngo Dinh Nhu, Madame).

NI CHIH-FU (see Ni Zhifu).

NI ZHENGYU, D.JUR.; Chinese international jurist; b. 28 July 1906, Wujiang, Jiangsu Province; m. Zhang Fengzhen 1930; one d.; ed. Dongwu Univ., Shanghai, Stanford Univ., Johns Hopkins Univ., U.S.A.; mem. Shanghai Bar Asscn. 1931–; Prosecutor, Int. Mil. Tribunal for the Far East 1946–48; attended many int. confs. as legal consultant to govt. del. of People's Repub. of China; legal adviser to Chinese Foreign Ministry; mem. UN Int. Law Comm. 1981–; Judge, Int. Court of Justice 1985–94; Assoc. mem. l'Institut de Droit 1987–; Pres. Maritime Law Soc. 1995–; LL.D. h.c. *Publications:* The Question of Judicial Jurisdiction in International Law, The Judicial Systems in the United States and the United Kingdom, The Theory and Practice Concerning Jurisdictional Immunities of States. *Address:* c/o The Ministry of Justice, 11 Xiaguangli, Chayang Gu, Beijing, People's Republic of China.

NI ZHIFU; Chinese party official; b. 1933, Chuansha Co., Shanghai; errand boy for a Japanese oil company 1944; ed. elementary school 1945–48; apprentice, a Shanghai printing machine factory 1948; joined trades union 1950; mechanic, Yongding Machine Tool Factory 1953; joined CCP 1958; promoted engineer 1962; active participation in the criticism movt. during the Cultural Revolution; mem. 9th Cen. Cttee. CCP 1969; Chair. Municipal Trade Union Council, Beijing 1973; Second Sec. CCP Cttee., Beijing 1973–76; alt. mem. Politburo, 10th Cen. Cttee. CCP 1973; Vice-Chair. Municipal Revolutionary Cttee., Beijing 1974–78; Second Sec. CCP Cttee., Shanghai 1976–78; First Vice-Chair. Municipal Revolutionary Cttee., Shanghai 1976–78; mem. Politburo, 11th Cen. Cttee. CCP 1977; Pres. All-China Fed. of Trade Unions 1978–93; mem. Politburo 12th CCP Cen. Cttee. 1982–87; mem. 13th CCP Cen. Cttee. 1987–92, 14th CCP Cen. Cttee. 1992–97, 15th CCP Cen. Cttee. 1997–; Sec. Tianjin Municipal Cttee. of CCP 1984–87; Vice-Chair. 7th NPC Standing Cttee. 1988–92; Vice-Chair. Standing Cttee. 8th NPC 1993–98; Hon. Chair. Bd. Dirs. Beijing Science and Eng. Univ. 1995–; Advisor Chinese Asscn. for Promotion of Population Culture 1993–. *Address:* 10 Fuxingmenwai Street, Beijing, People's Republic of China.

NIASSE, Cheikh Moustapha; Senegalese politician; b. 4 Nov. 1939; ed. Lycée Faidherbe, Saint Louis, Univs. of Dakar and Paris, Nat. School of Admin., Dakar; Dir. for Information and Press Affairs, Ministry of Information 1968–69; Dir. de Cabinet at Presidency 1970–78; Minister of Town Planning, Housing and Environment March–Sept. 1978, of Foreign Affairs 1978–84; Minister of Foreign Affairs of the Confed. of Senegambia 1982–84; now Minister of State, Minister of Foreign Affairs and Senegalese Abroad; Political Sec. Union Progressiste Sénégalaise until 1984. *Address:* c/o Ministère des Affaires Etrangères, place de l'Indépendance, Dakar, Senegal.

NIAZI, Maulana Kausar; Pakistani politician and journalist; b. 21 April 1934, Musa Khel, Mianwali Dist., Punjab; three s. one d.; ed. Punjab Univ.; fmr. Ed. Tasneem (daily), Lahore and later Kausar, Lahore; f. Shahab (weekly) 1960; Information Sec. Pakistan People's Party 1970–78, Chair. breakaway Progressive People's Party 1978–; political imprisonment 1970; elected mem. Nat. Assembly while in prison 1970; Adviser to Pres. for Information and Religious Affairs 1971; Minister of Information and Broadcasting, Auqaf and Haj 1972–74, of Religious Affairs 1974–77, of Minority Affairs Overseas 1976–77; detained July 1977; mem. Senate March 1985–; Minister for Information and Broadcasting 1993. *Publications:* several books on religious, historical and literary topics. *Leisure interests:* reading, writing.

NIBBERING, Nicolaas Martinus Maria, PH.D.; Netherlands professor of chemical mass spectrometry; b. 29 May 1938, Zaandam; s. of Dirk Nibbering and Hendrika Clijnk; m. Christina A. de Waart 1964; three s. one d.; ed. Gymnasium B Zaanlands Lyceum Zaandam and Univ. of Amsterdam; mem. Faculty, Univ. of Amsterdam 1967–75, Assoc. Prof. 1975–80, Prof. of Organic Mass Spectrometry 1980–88, Prof. of Chemical Mass Spectrometry 1988–, Scientific Dir. Inst. of Mass Spectrometry 1988–; Visiting faculty mem. Cornell Univ. 1974; Guest Prof. Univ. of Colorado 1980; Chair. 12th Int. Mass Spectrometry Conf., Amsterdam 1991; Chair. European Soc. for Mass Spectrometry 1993–97, Pres. 1997–; Treas. Int. Mass Spectrometry Soc. 1997–; Co-Ed. Scientific Journal of Mass Spectrometry Reviews 1991; Ed. Scientific Journal of Mass Spectrometry 1995–; mem. Royal Netherlands Acad., New York Acad. of Sciences; Unilever Chemistry Prize 1964, Shell Research Chemistry Prize 1968, J. J. Thomson Award 1991, Joannes Marcus Marci Award 1992. *Publications:* articles in books and journals. *Leisure interests:* motorbike races, classical music, opera, musicals, travelling, history. *Address:* Institute of Mass Spectrometry, University of Amsterdam, Nieuwe Achtergracht 129, 1018 WS Amsterdam (Office); Janshof 39, 1391 XK Abcoude, Netherlands (Home). *Telephone:* 20-5255457 (Office); 294-283211 (Home). *Fax:* 20-5256971 (Office).

NICHOL, Lawrence Walter, PH.D., F.A.A.; Australian university vice-chancellor and scientist; b. 7 April 1935, Adelaide; s. of Lawrence G. Nichol and Mavis L. Nichol; m. Rosemary E. White 1963; three s.; ed. Norwood High School and Univ. of Adelaide; Fulbright Scholar, Clark Univ., Mass., U.S.A. 1961–62; Research Fellow, Australian Nat. Univ. (ANU) 1963–65; Sr. Lecturer, Reader, Univ. of Melbourne 1966–70; Prof. ANU 1971–85; Vice-Chancellor, Univ. of New England 1985–88; Vice-Chancellor, ANU 1988–93; David Syme Research Prize 1966; Lemberg Medal 1977. *Publications:* Migration of Interacting Systems 1972, Protein-Protein Interactions 1981. *Address:* Unit 36, 171 Walker Street, North Sydney, N.S.W. 2060, Australia (Home). *Telephone:* (02) 959-3183 (Home).

NICHOLAS, Sir David, Kt., C.B.E.; British television executive and editor; b. 25 Jan. 1930, Tregaron; m. Juliet Davies 1952; one s. one d.; ed. Neath Grammar School, Univ. Coll. of Wales; Nat. Service 1951–53; journalist with Yorkshire Post, Daily Telegraph, Observer; joined ITN 1960, Deputy Ed. Ind. Television News 1963, Ed. 1977–89, C.E.O. 1977–91, Chair. 1989–91; Dir. (non-exec.) Channel 4 TV 1992–97; Chair. Circle Communications Ltd., Sports News TV; Dir. Channel 1, London 1994–; Visiting Ed. 10 U.S. Schools of Journalism 1992–; Hon. LL.D. (Univ. Coll. of Wales, Aberystwyth). *Leisure interests:* walking, sailing. *Address:* Lodge Stables, 2F Kidbrooke Park Road, London, SE3 0LW, England. *Telephone:* 0181-319 2823. *Fax:* 0181-319 2417.

NICHOLAS, (John Keiran) Barry (Moylan), M.A., F.B.A.; British academic lawyer; b. 6 July 1919, London; m. 1st Hildegart Cloos 1948 (died 1995);

one s. one d.; m. 2nd Rosalind Williams 1998; ed. Downside School and Brasenose Coll., Oxford; war service in Royal Signals (Major) 1939–45; Fellow Brasenose Coll., Oxford 1947–78, Tutor 1947–71, Prin. 1978–89; All Souls Reader in Roman Law, Oxford 1949–71, Prof. of Comparative Law 1971–78; Visiting Prof. Tulane Univ. 1960, Rome Univ. 1964, 1993, Fordham Univ. 1968, 1985, Georgetown Univ. 1990; called to the Bar, Inner Temple 1950; Hon. Bencher of Inner Temple; Hon. Dr. (Paris V). *Publications:* Introduction to Roman Law 1962, Jolowicz's Historical Introduction to Roman Law (third edn.) 1972, The French Law of Contract (second edn.) 1992. *Address:* 18A Charlbury Road, Oxford, OX2 6UU, England. *Telephone:* (01865) 558512.

NICHOLAS, Nicholas John, Jr., M.B.A.; American communications executive; b. 3 Sept. 1939, Portsmouth, N.H.; s. of Nicholas John Nicholas; m. Llewellyn Jones 1972; two s. three d.; ed. Princeton and Harvard Univs.; Dir. of Financial Analysis, Time Inc., New York 1964–69, Asst. to Pres. 1970, Asst. Treas. 1971–73, Vice-Pres. 1975–86, Pres. and C.O.O. 1986–; Pres. Manhattan Cable TV 1973–76; Pres. Home Box Office, New York 1976–80, Chair. 1979–81, Chief Financial Officer 1982–. *Address:* Time Inc., Time & Life Building, Rockefeller Center, New York, NY 10020, U.S.A.

NICHOLLS OF BIRKENHEAD, Baron (Life Peer) cr. 1994, of Stoke D'Abernon in the County of Surrey; **Donald James Nicholls,** P.C., M.A., LL.B.; British judge; b. 25 Jan. 1933, Bebington, Cheshire; s. of William Greenhow and the late Eleanor J. Nicholls; m. Jennifer Mary Thomas 1960; two s. one d.; ed. Birkenhead School, Univ. of Liverpool and Trinity Hall, Cambridge; called to Bar, Middle Temple 1958; in practice at Chancery Bar, London 1958–83; Q.C. 1974; Judge, High Court of Justice, Chancery Div. 1983–86; Lord Justice of Appeal 1986–91; Vice-Chancellor, Supreme Court 1991–94; a Lord of Appeal in Ordinary 1994–; Chair. Lord Chancellor's Advisory Cttee. on Legal Educ. and Conduct 1996–97, Jt. Cttee. on Parl. Practice 1997–; a Non-permanent Judge, Hong Kong Court of Final Appeal 1998–; Hon. Fellow, Trinity Hall, Cambridge 1986; Hon. LL.D. (Liverpool) 1987. *Leisure interests:* history, music, walking. *Address:* House of Lords, London, SW1A 0PW, England.

NICHOLS, Mike; American entertainer, stage and film director; b. Michael Igor Peschowsky 6 Nov. 1931, Berlin, Germany; s. of Paul Nikolaievich Peschowsky and Brigitte Landauer; m. 1st Patricia Scot 1957 (divorced); m. 2nd Margot Callas 1974 (divorced); one d.; m. 3rd Annabel Nichols (divorced); m. 4th Diane Sawyer 1988; ed. private schools and Univ. of Chicago; started Playwrights Theatre Club, Chicago which became the Compass Players and later Second City; formed improvised nightclub double-act with Elaine May, touring for two years and recording television programmes and record albums; appeared in An Evening with Mike Nichols and Elaine May New York 1961–62; acted in Shaw's St. Joan and directed The Importance of Being Earnest, Vancouver. *Directed shows:* Barefoot in the Park, New York 1963, The Knack 1964, Luv 1964, The Odd Couple 1965, The Apple Tree 1966, The Little Foxes 1967, Plaza Suite 1968. *Directed films:* Who's Afraid of Virginia Woolf? 1966, The Graduate 1967, Catch-22 1969, Carnal Knowledge 1971, Day of the Dolphin 1973, The Fortune 1975, Gilda Live 1980, Silkwood 1983, Heartburn 1985, Biloxi Blues 1987, Working Girl 1988, Postcards From the Edge 1990, Regarding Henry, Wolf 1994 (co-producer), Mike Nicholas 1995, The Birdcage (co-producer), Primary Colors 1998. *Directed plays:* Streamers 1976, Comedians 1976, The Gin Game 1978, Lunch Hour 1980, The Real Thing 1984, Hurlyburly 1984, Waiting for Godot 1988, Death and the Maiden 1992, Blue Murder 1995; producer Annie (New York) 1977; Antoinette Perry (Tony) awards for direction Barefoot in the Park, Luv, The Odd Couple, Plaza Suite, The Real Thing; Oscar for The Graduate; Emmy award for television programme Julie and Carol at Carnegie Hall; Nat Asscn. Theatre Owners' Achievement Award for direction for Who's Afraid of Virginia Woolf? *Leisure interest:* Arabian horse breeding. *Address:* c/o Mike Ovitz, CAA, 9830 Wilshire Boulevard, Beverly Hills, CA 90212, U.S.A.

NICHOLS, Peter Richard, F.R.S.L.; British playwright; b. 31 July 1927; s. of late Richard G. Nichols and Violet A. Poole; m. Thelma Reed 1960; one s. two d. (and one d. deceased); ed. Bristol Grammar School, Bristol Old Vic School and Trent Park Training Coll.; actor, mostly in repertory 1950–55; schoolteacher 1958–60; mem. Arts Council Drama Panel 1973–75; playwright-in-residence, Guthrie Theatre, Minneapolis; Visiting Writer, Nanyang Coll., Singapore 1994; directed revivals of Joe Egg and Forget-me-not Lane (Greenwich), National Health (Guthrie, Minneapolis), and first productions of Born in the Gardens (Bristol), A Piece of My Mind (Southampton), Blue Murder (Bristol); Tony Award, New York 1985; recipient of several SWET and Evening Standard Drama Awards. *Plays:* A Day in the Death of Joe Egg 1967, The National Health 1969, Forget-me-Not Lane 1971, Chez Nous 1973, The Freeway 1974, Privates on Parade 1977, Born in the Gardens 1979, Passion Play 1980, Poppy (musical) 1982, A Piece of My Mind 1986, Blue Murder 1995. *Films:* Catch Us If You Can 1965, Georgy Girl 1967, Joe Egg 1971, The National Health 1973, Privates on Parade 1983; also work for radio and TV. *Publications:* Feeling You're Behind (memoirs) 1984, Nichols: Plays One and Two 1991. *Leisure interests:* listening to jazz, looking at cities. *Address:* c/o Alan Brodie Representation, 211 Piccadilly, London, W1V 9LD, England.

NICHOLS, Rt. Rev. Vincent Gerard, S.T.L., PH.L., M.A., M.ED.; British ecclesiastic; b. 8 Nov. 1945, Crosby; s. of Henry Joseph Nichols and Mary Russell; ed. St. Mary's Coll., Crosby, Gregorian Univ., Rome, Manchester Univ. and Loyola Univ., Chicago; Chaplain St. John Rigby VI Form Coll., Wigan 1972–77; Priest in inner city of Liverpool 1978–81; Dir. Upholland Northern Inst., Lancs. 1981–84; Gen. Sec. Catholic Bishops' Conf. of England and Wales 1984–91; Auxiliary Bishop of Westminster 1992–; Adviser to Cardinal Hume (q.v.) and Archbishop Worlock at the Int. Synods of Bishops 1980, 1983, 1985, 1987, 1990, 1991; del. of Bishops' Conf. to Synod of Bishops 1994. *Publication:* Promise of Future Glory—Reflections on the Mass 1997. *Address:* Westminster House, Watford Way, Hendon, London, NW4 4TY, England. *Telephone:* 0181-202 2371. *Fax:* 0181-203 8278.

NICHOLSON, Sir Bryan Hubert, Kt., M.A., F.R.S.A., C.B.I.M.; British business executive; b. 6 June 1932; s. of late Reginald H. Nicholson and Clara Nicholson; m. Mary E. Harrison 1956; one s. one d. (and one s. deceased); ed. Palmers School, Grays, and Oriel Coll. Oxford; Man. trainee, Unilever 1955–58; Dist. Man. Van den Berghs 1958–59; Sales Man. Three Hands/Jeyes Group 1960–64; joined Sperry Rand 1964, Sales Dir. U.K. Remington Div. 1964–66, Gen. Man. Australia, Remington Div. 1966–69, Man. Dir. U.K. and France, Remington Div. 1969–72; Dir. Operations, Rank Xerox (U.K.) 1972–76, Dir. Overseas Subsidiaries 1976, Exec. Dir. 1976–84, Chair. Rank Xerox (U.K.) and Rank Xerox G.m.b.H. 1979–84; Chair. Manpower Services Comm. 1984–87, The Post Office 1987–92; Chair. BUPA 1992–, Varity Holdings Ltd. (now Varity Europe Ltd.) 1993–96, Cookson Group PLC 1998–; Dir. (non-exec.) Newsquest PLC 1997–, Action Centre for Europe Ltd. 1997–; Pres. Involvement and Participation Asscn. 1990–94; Chair. CBI Vocational Educ. and Training Task Force 1988–89, C.N.A.A. 1988–91, Nat. Council for Vocational Qualifications 1990–93, CBI Educ. and Training Affairs Cttee. 1990–93, Industrial Soc. 1990–93, Deputy Pres. C.B.I. 1993–94, Pres. 1994–96; Non-exec. Dir. GKN 1990–, Varity Corpn., U.S.A. 1993–96, LucasVarity 1996–, Equitas Holdings Ltd. 1996–; mem. Nat. Econ. Devt. Council 1985–92; Pres. Oriel Soc. 1988–92; Vice-Pres. Nat. Children's Home 1990–; Chancellor Sheffield Hallam Univ. 1992–; Pro-Chancellor and Chair. of Council The Open Univ. 1996–; Chair. United Oxford and Cambridge Univ. Club 1995–97. *Leisure interests:* tennis, bridge, political history. *Address:* Point Piper, Lilley Drive, Kingswood, Surrey, KT20 6JA, England.

NICHOLSON, Ernest Wilson, PH.D., D.D., F.B.A.; British university professor; b. 26 Sept. 1938, Northern Ireland; s. of Ernest Tedford Nicholson and Veronica Muriel Nicholson; m. Hazel Jackson 1962; one s. three d.; ed. Trinity Coll. Dublin, Univ. of Glasgow; Lecturer in Semitic Languages, Trinity Coll. Dublin 1962–67; Lecturer in Divinity, Cambridge Univ. 1967–79, Fellow Univ. Coll. (now Wolfson Coll.) Cambridge 1967–69, Fellow and Chaplain Pembroke Coll. Cambridge 1969–79, Dean 1973–79; Oriel Prof. of The Interpretation of Holy Scripture, Oxford Univ. 1979–90, Provost of Oriel Coll. 1990–; Pro-Vice-Chancellor, Oxford Univ. 1993–; Chair. Jardine Foundation 1993–; Hon. Fellow Trinity Coll. (Dublin), Wolfson Coll. (Cambridge), St. Peter's Coll. (Oxford); Commdr. Order of Merit Italian Repub. *Publications:* Deuteronomy and Tradition 1967, Preaching to the Exiles 1970, Exodus and Sinai in History and Tradition 1973, The Book of Jeremiah 1–25 1973, Kimchi's Commentary on Psalms 120–150 1973, The Book of Jeremiah 26–52 1974, God and His People 1986, The Pentateuch in the Twentieth Century 1998. *Leisure interests:* country walking, music. *Address:* Oriel College, Oxford, OX1 4EW, England. *Telephone:* (01865) 276533.

NICHOLSON, Jack; American actor and film maker; b. 22 April 1937, Neptune, N.J.; s. of John and Ethel May Nicholson; m. Sandra Knight 1961 (divorced 1966); one d.; Cecil B. De Mille Award 1999; Commdr. des Arts et des Lettres. *Films include:* Cry-Baby Killer 1958, Studs Lonigan 1960, The Shooting (produced and acted), Ride the Whirlwind (wrote, produced and acted), Hell's Angels on Wheels 1967, The Trip (wrote screenplay) 1967, Head (co-scripted, co-produced) 1968, Psych-Out 1968, Easy Rider 1969 (Acad. Award for Best Supporting Actor), On a Clear Day You Can See Forever 1970, Five Easy Pieces 1971, Drive, He Said (directed) 1971, Carnal Knowledge 1971, The King of Marvin Gardens 1972, The Last Detail 1973, Chinatown 1974, The Passenger 1974, Tommy 1974, The Fortune 1975, The Missouri Breaks 1975, One Flew over the Cuckoo's Nest 1975 (Acad. Award for Best Actor 1976), The Last Tycoon 1976, Goin' South (actor, dir.) 1978, The Shining 1980, The Postman Always Rings Twice 1981, Reds 1981, The Border 1982, Terms of Endearment 1984 (Acad. Award for Best Supporting Actor), Prizzi's Honor 1984, Heartburn 1985, The Witches of Eastwick 1986, Ironweed 1987, Batman 1989, The Two Jakes (actor, dir.) 1989, Man Trouble, A Few Good Men 1992, Hoffa 1993, Wolf 1994, The Crossing Guard 1995, Mars Attacks!, The Evening Star, Blood and Wine 1996, As Good As It Gets 1997. *Address:* Bresler Kelly Kipperman, 15760 Ventura Boulevard, Suite 1730, Encino, CA 91436, U.S.A.

NICHOLSON, Sir Robin Buchanan, Kt., PH.D., F.ENG., F.R.S.; British metallurgist; b. 12 Aug. 1934, Sutton Coldfield; s. of the late Carroll and Nancy Nicholson; m. 1st Elizabeth Mary Caffyn 1958 (died 1988); one s. two d.; m. 2nd Yvonne Appleby 1991; ed. Oundle School and St. Catharine's Coll., Cambridge; Demonstrator in Metallurgy, Univ of Cambridge 1960–64, lecturer 1964–66, Fellow of Christ's Coll. 1962–66; Prof. of Metallurgy, Univ. of Manchester 1966–72; Dir. of Research Lab., Inco Europe Ltd. 1972–76, Dir. 1975–81, Man. Dir. 1976–81; Co.-Chair. Biogen N.V. 1979–81; Chief Scientist, Cen. Policy Review Staff 1981–83; Chief Scientific Adviser, Cabinet Office 1983–86; Chief. Exec., Chair. Electro-Optical Div., Pilkington PLC 1986–, Dir. Pilkington PLC (fmrly. Pilkington Bros. PLC) 1986–96; Dir. Rolls-Royce 1986–, BP PLC 1987–; Chair. Centre for Exploitation of Science and Tech. 1987–90, Advisory Council on Science and Tech. 1990–93, Pilkington Optronics Ltd. 1991–; Pres. Inst. of Materials 1997–98; mem. Council, Royal Soc. 1983–85, Council for Science and Tech. 1993–, Scottish Advisory Cttee. Imperial Cancer Research Fund 1994–; Hon. D.Sc. (Cranfield, Aston) 1983, (Manchester) 1985, Hon. D.Met. (Sheffield) 1984, Hon. D.Eng. (Birmingham) 1986; Rosenhain Medal, Inst. of Metals 1971; Platinum Medal, Metals Soc. 1981. *Publications:* Precipitation Hardening (with A. Kelly) 1962, Electron Microscopy of Thin Crystals (with Sir P. Hirsch and others) 1965, Strengthening Methods in Crystals (ed. and contributor with A. Kelly) 1971. *Leisure interests:* family life, gardening, music. *Address:* c/o Pilkington Optronics Ltd., Glascoed Road, St. Asaph, Denbighshire, LL17 0LL (Office); Penson Farm, Diptford, Totnes, Devon, TQ9 7NN, England. *Telephone:* (01745) 588003 (Office).

NICKLAUS, Jack William; American golfer; b. 21 Jan. 1940, Columbus, Ohio; s. of L. Charles Nicklaus and Helen (Schoener) Nicklaus; m. Barbara Bash 1960; four s. one d.; ed. Ohio State Univ.; professional golfer 1961–; won U.S. Amateur Championship 1959, 1961; U.S. Open Championship 1962, 1967, 1972, 1980, U.S. Masters 1963, 1965, 1966, 1972, 1975, 1986, U.S. P.G.A. Championship 1963, 1971, 1973, 1975, 1980, British Open Championship 1966, 1970, 1978; by 1973 had won more major championship titles (totals now: 18 as professional, 2 as amateur) than any other player; Australian Open Champion six times, World Series winner five times, record three times individual winner World Cup, six times on winning team; rep. U.S.A. six Ryder Cup matches; 97 tournament victories, 76 official tour victories, 58 times second, 36 times third; won U.S. Sr. Open, U.S.A.; 136 tournament appearances 1996; total earnings over $6m.; has also designed over 100 golf courses in 26 countries; five times U.S. P.G.A. Player of the Year; Golfer of the Century 1988; Athlete of the Decade Award 1970s; Hon. LL.D. (St. Andrews) 1984. *Publications:* My Story 1997, numerous books about golf. *Address:* Golden Bear International Inc., 11780 U.S. Highway 1, North Palm Beach, FL 33408, U.S.A. (Office).

NICKLES, Don; American politician and business executive; b. 6 Dec. 1948, Ponca City, Okla.; s. of Robert and Coeweene Nickles; m. Linda Morrison 1968; one s. three d.; mem. Nat. Guard 1971–76; mem. Okla. State Senate 1978–80, U.S. Senator from Oklahoma, 1981–; Asst. Majority Leader, U.S. Senate; Vice-Pres., Gen. Man. Nickles Machine Co. 1972–80; Republican. *Address:* 133 Hart Senate Office Building, Washington, DC 20510, U.S.A. (Office).

NICKS, Stevie (Stephanie Nicks); American singer and songwriter; b. 26 May 1948, Calif.; songwriter with Lindsey Buckingham; recorded album Buckingham Nicks 1973; joined group Fleetwood Mac 1973; albums with Fleetwood Mac include: Fleetwood Mac 1975, Rumours 1977, Tusk 1979, Fleetwood Mac Live 1980, Mirage 1982, Tango in the Night 1987, Behind the Mask 1990, 25 Years—The Chain 1992; solo albums include: Bella Donna 1981, The Wild Heart 1983, Rock a Little 1985, Time Space 1991, Street Angel 1994; composer of songs Rhiannon, Landslide, Leather and Lace, Dreams, Sara, Edge of Seventeen, If Anyone Falls (with Sandy Stewart), Stand Back (with Prince Rogers Nelson), I Can't Wait (with others), The Other Side of the Mirror, Time Space, Street Angel, Seven Wonders (with Sandy Stewart). *Address:* Modern Records, c/o W.E.A., 1740 Broadway, 20th Floor, New York, NY 10019, U.S.A.

NICKSON, Baron (Life Peer) cr. 1994, of Renagour in the District of Stirling; **David Wigley Nickson,** K.B.E.; British business executive; b. 27 Nov. 1929, Eton; s. of Geoffrey W. Nickson and Janet M. Nickson; m. Helen L. Cockcraft 1952; three d.; ed. Eton and Royal Mil. Acad. Sandhurst; man. trainee, Wm. Collins, Publrs. Glasgow 1954, Dir. 1961, Jt. Man. Dir. 1967, Vice-Chair. 1976, Vice-Chair. and Group Man. Dir. 1979–82, Non-exec. Dir. 1982–85; Non-exec. Dir. Scottish & Newcastle Breweries PLC 1981–95, Deputy Chair. 1982, Chair. 1983–89; Chair. Atlantic Salmon Trust 1989–96 (Vice-Chair. 1985–88), Sec. of State for Scotland's Atlantic Salmon Task Force 1996, Scottish Devt. Agency 1989–90, Scottish Enterprise 1990–92; Deputy Chair. Clydesdale Bank PLC 1989–91, (Chair. 1991–98), Gen. Accident 1993–98; Non-exec. Dir. Gen. Accident Fire & Life Assurance Corpn. PLC, Edinburgh Investment Trust PLC 1983–94; Pres. Confed. of British Industry (CBI) 1986–88; Chair. Top Salaries Review Body 1989–95; Chancellor Glasgow Caledonian Univ. 1993–; Vice-Lord-Lieut. of Stirling and Falkirk 1997–; Hon. D.L., Hon. D.Univ. (Stirling) 1986, Hon. D.BA. (Napier Univ.) 1990, (Paisley Univ.) 1991, Hon. D. Univ. (Glasgow) 1993. *Leisure interests:* fishing, birdwatching, shooting, the countryside. *Address:* Renagour, Aberfoyle, Stirling, FK8 3TF, Scotland (Home). *Telephone:* (01877) 382275 (Home).

NICODIM, Ion; Romanian painter and engraver; b. 26 March 1932, Constanţa; ed. Nicolae Grigorescu Coll. of Fine Arts, Bucharest; mem. of the Romanian Artists' Union; exhbns. Bucharest, Cluj-Napoca, Rome, São Paulo, Cagnes-sur-Mer, Yugoslavia, Vienna, Warsaw, Prague; Prize of the Romanian Artists' Union 1964, 1977; Prize of the Romanian Acad. 1975. *Works:* frescoes, mosaics, tapestries including Praise to Man, at the UN headquarters in New York, painting, graphics, glass, furniture, design, engravings, monumental decorative designs. *Address:* Uniunea Artistilor Plastici, Str. Nicolae Iorga 42, Bucharest, Romania; 60 rue de Domrémy, 75013 Paris, France. *Telephone:* 45.70.87.04.

NICOL, Donald MacGillivray, PH.D., F.B.A., F.R.HIST.S.; British professor of Byzantine history; b. 4 Feb. 1923, Portsmouth; s. of George Manson Nicol and Mary Patterson (née MacGillivray); m. Joan Mary Campbell 1950; three s.; ed. King Edward VII School, Sheffield, St. Paul's School, London, Pembroke Coll. Cambridge and British School of Archaeology at Athens; Lecturer in Classics and Ancient History, Univ. Coll. Dublin 1952–64; Visiting Fellow, Dumbarton Oaks, Washington, D.C. 1964–65; Visiting Prof. of Byzantine History, Indiana Univ., U.S.A. 1965–66; Reader in Byzantine History, Univ. of Edin. 1966–70; Koraës Prof. of Modern Greek and Byzantine History, Language and Literature, King's Coll., Univ. of London 1970–88, now Emer.; Dir. Gennadius Library, Athens 1989–92; Fellow and fmr. Vice-Prin. King's Coll.; Birkbeck Lecturer, Cambridge Univ. 1976–77; Pres. Ecclesiastical History Soc. 1975–76; mem. Royal Irish Acad. *Publications:* The Despotate of Epirus 1957, Meteora: The Rock Monasteries of Thessaly 1963, The Byzantine Family of Kantakouzenos (Cantacuzenus) *c.* 1100–1460 1968, The Last Centuries of Byzantium 1972, Church and Society in the Last Centuries of Byzantium 1979, The Despotate of Epiros: a contribution to the history of Greece in the Middle Ages 1267–1479 1984, Studies in Late Byzantine History and Prosopography 1986, Byzantium and Venice. A Study in Diplomatic and Cultural Relations 1988, A Biographical Dictionary of the Byzantine Empire 1991, The Immortal Emperor, The Life and Legend of Constantine Palaiologos, Last Emperor of the Romans 1992, Ten Byzantine Ladies 1250–1500 1994, The Reluctant Emperor. A Biography of John Cantacuzene, Byzantine Emperor and Monk *c.* 1295-1383 1996, Theodore Spandounes, On the Origin of the Ottoman Emperors (ed. and translator) 1997. *Leisure interest:* bookbinding. *Address:* 4 Westberry Court, Pinehurst, Grange Road, Cambridge, CB3 9BG, England. *Telephone:* (01223) 360955.

NICOLAIDES, Maj.-Gen. Cristino; Argentinian army officer; b. 2 Jan. 1925; ed. Mil. Acad.; Second Lieut., Corps of Engineers, Mil. Acad. 1947; Capt. 1954; Staff Officer army high command; Col. 1970; Dir. School for Combat Services 1974; Brig.-Gen. 1975; led mil. campaign against leftist guerrillas, Córdoba; Commdr. 1st Army Corps 1981–82; C.-in-C of the Army and mem. mil. junta 1982–83.

NICOLET, Claude; French professor of Roman history; b. 15 Sept. 1930, Marseilles; s. of Edmond Nicolet and Suzanne Nicolet; m. 1st Michelle Brousset 1956 (divorced); one s.; m. 2nd Hélène Pierre 1963; three s.; ed. Ecole Normale Supérieure and Ecole Française de Rome; served on Staff of Minister of State Pierre Mendès-France 1956; Editorial Sec. Cahiers de la République 1956–57; mem. Ecole Française de Rome 1957–59; lecturer Univ. of Tunis 1959–61; lecturer and Prof. Univ. of Caen 1961–69; Prof. of Roman History, Univ. of Paris/Sorbonne 1969–; Dir. of Studies, Ecole Pratique des Hautes Etudes (Section IV) 1969–; mem. Inst. for Advanced Studies, Princeton 1966–67, 1972; Prof. Univ. Paris I 1971–; Dir. Era 757, C.N.R.S. 1978–91; Dir. Centre Gustav Glotz 1981–92, Ecole Française de Rome 1992–95; Pres. Soc. for Latin Studies 1983, Conseil scientifique du Centre d'études et des prévisions du ministère de l'Interiéur 1998; mem. Acad. des Inscriptions et Belles Lettres (Inst. de France); Assoc. mem. Academia dei Lincei; Corresp. Fellow British Acad. 1987; Prix Galileo Galilei des Rotary italiens 1994, Grand prix nat. (histoire) 1996, Prix des Culbori di Roma 1997; Chevalier, Légion d'honneur; Officier des Palmes Académiques. *Publications:* fifteen books. *Address:* Institut de France, 23 quai Conti, 75006 Paris; 2 rue de Paradis, 75010 Paris, France. *Telephone:* (1) 47-70-02-91.

NICOLI, Eric Luciano, B.SC.; British business executive; b. 5 Aug. 1950, Pulham Market, Norfolk; s. of Virgilio Nicoli and Ida Nicoli; m. Rosalind West 1977; one. s. one d.; ed. Diss Grammar School, Norfolk, King's Coll., London Univ.; worked briefly in market research, then various positions with Rowntree Marketing Dept. 1972–80; Sr. Marketing Controller, Biscuit Div., United Biscuits 1980–81, Marketing Dir., Biscuits 1981–84, and Confectionery 1982–84; U.K. Business Planning Dir. 1984, Man. Dir. UB Frozen Foods 1985, UB Brands 1986–89, apptd. to Bd. of UB (Holdings) PLC 1989, C.E.O., European Operations 1989–90, Group C.E.O. United Biscuits (Holdings) PLC 1991–; Deputy Chair. BITC 1991–, Per Cent Club 1993–; Dir. (non-exec.) Thorn EMI PLC 1993–. *Leisure interests:* all sports (especially golf), music, food. *Address:* United Biscuits (Holdings) P.L.C., Church Road, West Drayton, Middx., UB7 7PR, England. *Telephone:* (01895) 432100.

NICOLIN, Curt René; Swedish company executive; b. 10 March 1921, Stockholm; s. of Felix and Anna-Lisa Nicolin; m. Ulla Sandén 1946; three s. two d.; ed. Royal Inst. of Tech., Stockholm; with STAL Finspong 1945–61; Interim Pres. Scandinavian Airlines System (SAS) 1961–62; Swedish Chair. SAS 1973–91; Pres. ASEA AB, Västerås 1961–76, Chair. of Bd. 1976–91, Incentive AB 1991–92; Co-Chair. ABB Asea Brown Boveri 1988–91; Hon. Chair. ASEA AB 1991; Hon. Dr. Tech. 1974; Hon. Dr. Laws 1991; Hon. Dr. Econ. 1994; Lucia Trade Award 1996; Commdr., Order of Vasa, First Class 1974, Medal, Order of Seraphim 1991. *Publication:* Private Industry in a Public World 1973, New Strategy for Sweden 1996. *Leisure interests:* tennis, sailing. *Address:* Box 16100, SE-103 22 Stockholm, Sweden. *Telephone:* (8) 613 67 65, 613 67 64. *Fax:* (8) 22 35 67.

NICULESCU, Ştefan; Romanian composer; b. 31 July 1927, Moreni, Dîmboviţa Co.; s. of Lazar Niculescu and Maria Niculescu; m. Colette Demetrescu 1952; ed. Acad. of Music and Theatrical Art, Bucharest Coll. of Engineering, Bucharest, C. Porumbescu Conservatory of Music, Bucharest; studies in electronic music Munich 1966; researcher Inst. for Art History of the Romanian Acad., Bucharest 1960–63; Prof. Ciprian Porumbescu Conservatory, Bucharest 1963–87, 1992–; Sec. for Symphonic, Chamber and Opera Music Romanian Composers' Union 1990–93; Guest, Deutscher Akademischer Austauschdienst, West Berlin 1971–72, Internationaler Frienkurse für Neu

Musik, Darmstadt 1992; mem. Romanian Acad.; Romanian Acad. Prize 1962, French Acad. Prize 1972, Prizes of the Romanian Composers' Union 1972, 1975, 1977, 1979, 1981, 1982, 1984, 1985, 1986, 1988, 1994, Festival Montreux Prize, Int. Record Critics Award 1985, Herder Prize, Vienna 1994. *Works include:* symphonies, cantatas, chamber music; Ison I–II for orchestra; Sincronie I–IV, Aphorismes d'Héraclite, for mixed choir of 20 soloists 1969, Ricercare in uno, for synthesizer, clarinet and violin 1983, Cantos for saxophone and orchestra 1985, Octuplum 1987, Invocatio (choral symphony) 1988, Axion for choir and saxophone 1992, Psalmus for 6 voices 1993, Deisis for orchestra 1995, Litanies for orchestra 1997; stage and film music. *Address:* Intr. Sublocotenent Stăniloiu 4, 73228 Bucharest, Romania (Home); Calea Victoriei 141, 70149 Bucharest (Office). *Telephone:* 6424370 (Home).

NÍ DHOMHNAILL, Nuala, B.A.; Irish poet; b. 16 Feb. 1952, St. Helens, Lancs, England; d. of Séamus Ó Dhomhnaill and Eibhlín Ní Fhiannachta; m. Dogan Leflef 1973; one s. three d.; ed. Laurel Hill Convent, Limerick and Univ. Coll., Cork; travel overseas 1973–80; Writer-in-Residence Univ. Coll., Cork 1992–93; various Oireachtas awards 1982, 1984, 1990, Irish American O'Shaughnessy Award 1988, Ireland Fund Literary Prize 1991. *Publications:* An Dealg Droighinn 1981, Feár Suaithinseach 1984, Feís 1991. *Leisure interests:* swimming, mountain walks, reading. *Address:* 2 Little Meadow, Pottery Road, Cabinteely, Co. Dublin, Ireland. *Telephone:* (1) 2857465. *Fax:* (1) 2834327.

NIE BICHU; Chinese administrator; b. 1928, Taoyuan Co., Hunan Prov.; ed. Eng. Inst. of Beiyang Univ., Tianjin; Deputy Dir. of Tianjin Planning Cttee. 1981–; Vice-Mayor of Tianjin 1983–88; Deputy Sec. of Tianjin CP 1985–; 8th NPC Deputy, Tianjin Municipality; Mayor of Tianjin Municipality 1989–93; Chair. Tianjin Municipal 12th People's Congress Standing Cttee. June 1993–. *Address:* c/o Tianjin People's Government, Dagu Road, Heping District, Tianjin, People's Republic of China.

NIE KUIJU, Vice-Adm.; Chinese naval officer; b. 1929, Yidu Co., Shandong Prov.; joined Red Army 1944, CCP 1945; commdr. of a unit under the South China Sea Fleet 1982; alt. mem. 12th CCP Cen. Cttee. 1982–87, mem. 13th Cen. Cttee. 1987–; Deputy Commdr. PLA Navy 1982; Commdr. E. China Sea Fleet 1985–; Deputy Commdr. Nanjing Mil. Area. Jan. 1988–; promoted Vice-Adm. PLA Navy 1988. *Address:* People's Liberation Army Naval Headquarters, Beijing, People's Republic of China.

NIE LI (LILI), Maj.-Gen.; Chinese administrator; b. 1930; d. of late Marshal Nie Rongzhen; m. Ding Henggao; Vice-Chair. of Scientific and Tech. Cttee. under Comm. of Science, Tech. and Industry for Nat. Defence 1983; promoted Maj.-Gen. PLA 1988; Vice-Chair. of Nat. Examination Cttee. for Science Award; mem. 8th NPC 1994–; Vice-Pres. All-China Women's Fed. 1992–; mem. Internal and Judicial Affairs Cttee. *Address:* National Examination Committee for Science Award, Sanlihe, Beijing, People's Republic of China.

NIEH K'UEI-CHU (see Nie Kuiju).

NIELSEN, Erik H., P.C., D.F.C., Q.C., LL.B.; Canadian politician (retd.); b. 24 Feb. 1924, Regina; s. of late Ingvard Nielsen and Mabel Elizabeth (née Davies) Nielsen; m. 1st Pamela Hall (died 1969); two s. one d.; m. 2nd Shelley Coxford 1983; ed. Dalhousie Univ., Halifax; pilot in R.C.A.F.; called to Bar of Nova Scotia 1951; own legal practice Whitehorse, Yukon 1952; mem. House of Commons for Yukon 1957–87; Chair. Nat. Transportation Agency of Canada 1987–92; Minister of Public Works 1979–80, Deputy Prime Minister 1984–86, Pres. Queen's Privy Council for Canada 1984–85, Minister of Nat. Defence 1985–86; Deputy House Leader, House of Commons, House Leader; Leader, Progressive Conservative Party Feb.–June 1983, later Deputy Leader; Prin. Solar Electric Eng. Distributors, Canada 1992–; Pres., Solar Electric Eng. Hawaii, Inc., U.S.A. 1993–, Electricycle, Inc. (Hawaii), Solar Electric Eng. Distributors, Canada; Fellow Canadian School of Man.; mem. Canadian Bar Asscn., Yukon Law Soc.; Hon. mem. Yukon Chamber of Commerce, Yukon Chamber of Mines, Royal Canadian Mounted Police Veterans' Asscn., House of Commons Protective Staff, Int. Union of Mine, Mill and Smelter Workers; Hon. Vice-Pres. Dawson City Museum and Historical Soc. *Publication:* The House is not a Home: An Autobiography 1989. *Leisure interests:* fishing, flying, hunting, computer science, writing. *Address:* MSPO P.O. Box 31024, Whitehorse, Yukon, Y1A 5P7, Canada. *Telephone:* (403) 633 4571 (Yukon); (604) 244-9450 (Vancouver); (250) 495-6183. *Fax:* (250) 495-7183.

NIEMEYER, Oscar; Brazilian architect; b. 15 Dec. 1907, Rio de Janeiro; s. of Oscar Niemeyer Soares; m. Anita Niemeyer; one d.; ed. Escola Nacional de Belas Artes, Rio de Janeiro; in office of Lúcio Costa 1935; designed Ministry of Educ. and Health Bldg., Rio de Janeiro 1937–43, Brazilian Pavilion, New York World Fair 1939, with others designed UN bldg., New York 1947; Dir. of Architecture for new capital of Brasília and given a free hand in design of public and other bldgs. 1957–; Designer of Bienal Exhbn. Hall, São Paulo, urban area of Grasse (near Nice) 1966, French CP bldg., Paris 1966, Palace of Arches (for Foreign Ministry) Brasília; Lenin Peace Prize 1963, Prix Int. de l'Architecture d'aujourd'hui 1966, shared Pritzker Prize 1988, Prince of the Asturias Prize for the Arts 1989, Royal Gold Medal for Architecture 1998. *Address:* 3940 avenida Atlàntica, Rio de Janeiro, RJ, Brazil.

NIEMI, Irmeli, DR.PHIL.; Finnish fmr. civil servant and university professor; b. 3 Feb. 1931, Helsinki; d. of Taneli Kuusisto and Kyllikki Valtonen; m. Mikko Niemi 1953; one s. two d.; ed. Univ. of Helsinki; freelance translator, literature and theatre critic, ed. 1950–68; Jr. Research Fellow, Acad. of Finland 1968–69; Assoc. Prof. of Comparative Literature and Drama, Univ. of Turku 1970–78, Prof. 1978–81, 1984–90; Dir.-Gen. Dept. of Culture, Ministry of Educ. 1990–96; Sr. Teacher, Theatre Acad. Helsinki 1964–96; Research Prof. Acad. of Finland 1981–84; Chair. Finnish Research Council for the Humanities 1986–88, Bd. of Finnish Nat. Opera 1996–, Finland Festivals 1998–; mem. Science Policy Council of Finland 1986–90. *Publications:* Maria Jotunin näytelmät 1964, Nykydraaman ihmiskuva 1969, Nykyteatterin juuret 1975, The Role of the Spectator 1984, Suomalainen alueteatteri 1978–82 1984. *Leisure interests:* modern music, forest walks, travel. *Address:* Osmalahdentie 437, 21570 Sauvo, Finland. *Telephone:* (02) 4701833. *Fax:* (02) 4701893.

NIEMÖLLER, Klaus Wolfgang, DR.PHIL; German professor of musicology; b. 21 July 1929, Gelsenkirchen; s. of Karl Niemöller and Magarete Helmich; m. Ursel Stoltenberg 1956; four c.; ed. Univ. of Cologne; Research Assoc. Deutsche Forschungsgemeinschaft 1956–58; Asst. Univ. of Cologne 1958–64, Privatdozent 1964, Prof. 1969; Prof. Univ. of Münster 1975–83; Prof. and Dir. Inst. of Musicology, Univ. of Cologne 1983–94, Prof. Emer. 1994–; Chair. Joseph Haydn Inst. Cologne 1977; mem. Bd. Robert Schumann Forschungsstelle, Düsseldorf 1986; Pres. Soc. for Music Research 1989; mem. Düsseldorf Acad. of Sciences; Chair. Institut für deutsche Musikkultur im Östlichen Europa, Bonn 1998; Dent Medal, Royal Musical Asscn. London 1971. *Publications:* Der sprachhafte Charakter der Musik 1980, Report Schostakowitsch-Symposion 1986, Report Symposion Bernd Alois Zimmermann 1989, Report Prokofiev Symposium 1991. *Leisure interests:* chamber music, dressage riding. *Address:* Geranienweg 5, 50769 Cologne, Germany. *Telephone:* (0221) 701160. *Fax:* (0221) 701160.

NIETO GALLO, Gratiniano; Spanish art official; b. 6 March 1917, La Aguilera, Burgos; s. of Francisco and Genoveva Nieto Gallo; m. María de Mergelina Cano-Manuel; one s. one d.; ed. Institución Teresiana, Instituto Ramiro de Maeztu and Univ. de Madrid; Prof., Univ. de Valladolid 1940–52; Dir. Colegio Mayor Santa Cruz de Valladolid 1943–52; Sec. School of Art and Archaeology, Univ. de Valladolid 1940–52; Dir. Colegio Mayor Nebrija, Univ. de Madrid 1952–56; Tech. Sec.-Gen. Directorate of Archives and Libraries 1956–61; attached to Univ. de Murcia 1959–61; Dir.-Gen. of Fine Arts 1961–68; Dir. Cen. Inst. for Conservation and Restoration of Works of Art 1968–; Prof. Univ. Madrid 1968–; Pres. Univ. Autónoma de Madrid 1973; decorations from Spain, Portugal, Malta, Fed. Repub. of Germany, Italy, France and Peru. *Publications:* La Necrópolis Ibérica del Cabecico del Tesoro 1940, 1944, 1947, Las tablas flamencas de la Igl. del Salvador de Valladolid 1941, Criterio de Reconstrucción de Objetos Arqueológicos 1941, El Oppidum de Iruña 1949, Guía Artística de Valladolid 1954, Historia de los Monumentos de Lerma 1959, La cueva artificial del Bronco I de Alguazas 1959, Tendencias Actuales de la Arqueología 1959, Guía de la Exposición Conmemorativa de la Paz de los Pirineos 1963, Las Bellas Artes en España 1963, Conservación del Patrimonio Artístico 1968, Museos de Artes y Costumbres Populares 1968, Conservación de Objetos Arqueológicos 1969, Panorama de los Museos Españoles y cuestiones museológicas 1971, Reflexiones sobre la Universidad 1973. *Leisure interests:* swimming, rowing, mountaineering. *Address:* Universidad Autónoma de Madrid, Km. 15 Carretera de Colmenar Viejo, Canto Blanco, Madrid, Spain.

NIGHTINGALE, (William) Benedict (Herbert), B.A.; British author and theatre critic; b. 14 May 1939, London; s. of R. E. and Hon. Mrs. Nightingale (née Gardner); m. Anne B. Redmon 1964; two s. one d.; ed. Charterhouse School, Magdalene Coll., Cambridge and Univ. of Pennsylvania; general writer, The Guardian 1963–66; Literary Ed. New Society 1966–67; theatre critic, New Statesman 1968–86; Prof. of English, Theatre and Drama Univ. of Mich. 1986–89; Chief Drama Critic The Times 1990–; Sunday theatre critic, New York Times 1983–84. *Publications:* Charities 1972, Fifty British Plays 1982, Fifth Row Center 1986, The Future of the Theatre 1998; numerous articles on cultural and theatrical matters in British and American journals. *Leisure interests:* music, literature, watching soccer. *Address:* 40 Broomhouse Road, London, SW6 3QX, England.

NIGHY, Bill; British actor; b. Croydon, Surrey; partner Diana Quick; one d. *Stage appearances include:* Arcadia, A Map of the World, The Seagull, Skylight. *Film appearances include:* Illuminations. *Television appearances include:* The Men's Room.

NIILUS, Leopoldo Juan (Leopold Johannes); Argentinian lawyer; b. 19 Jan. 1930, Tallinn, Estonia; s. of late Jaan Eduard Niilus and Meta Kiris; m. Malle Reet Veerus 1961; one d.; ed. Faculty of Law, Univ. Buenos Aires, Argentina, Southern Methodist Univ., Dallas, Tex., U.S.A.; left Estonia 1944; fmrly. practising lawyer, Buenos Aires; fmr. Chair. Argentine Student Christian Movt.; fmr. mem. World Student Christian Fed. (WSCF); Dir. Argentine Dept. River Plate Centre of Christian Studies 1966–67; Gen. Sec. ISAL (Comm. for Church and Soc. in Latin America) 1968–69; Dir. Comm. of the Churches on Int. Affairs of WCC, Geneva 1969–81; Dir. Int. Ecumenical Relations, Middle East Council of Churches (MECC) 1982–95; Consultant on int. affairs and human rights, Lutheran World Fed. 1988–95; ind. political consultancy 1996–; participated in mediation for Sudan peace negotiations 1972, peace negotiations, civil war in Guatemala, signed as witness, Oslo accords on Guatemala 1990; Order of Two Niles, 1st grade (Sudan). *Publications:* On Penal Law (essays); numerous articles and essays in ecumenical publs. on peace, disarmament, North-South relations, Middle East, Central

America. *Address:* 7 chemin Champ d'Anier, 1209 Geneva, Switzerland (Home). *Telephone:* (022) 798 32 59 (Office). *Fax:* (022) 788 44 48.

NIINISTÖ SAULI, Väinämö; Finnish politician and lawyer; b. 24 Aug. 1948, Salo; m. (wife deceased); two s.; own law office in Salo 1978–88; Sr. Sec. Turku Court of Appeal 1976; mem. Salo City Council 1977–, Chair. 1989–92, mem. City Bd. 1977–88; mem. Nat. Coalition Party (KOK) Party Council 1979–81, Party Chair. 1994–; mem. Parl. 1987–; Chair. Constitutional Cttee. of Parl. 1993–95; Deputy Prime Minister and Minister of Justice 1995–96; Deputy Prime Minister and Minister of Finance 1996–. *Address:* Ministry of Finance, Snellmanink 1A, 00170 Helsinki, Finland. *Telephone:* (09) 1601. *Fax:* (09) 1603090.

NIITAMO, Olavi Ensio, D.ECON.; Finnish economist; b. 23 Nov. 1926, Kotka; s. of Tenho Armas Niitamo and Alja Elisabet Väliaho; m. Helka Narinen 1953; three s. one d.; ed. Lyceum of Kotka and Univ. of Helsinki; Chief, Econ. Statistics Div., Cen. Statistical Office of Finland 1959–63, Chief, Nat. Income Statistics Div. 1963–71, Chief, Planning Div. 1971–78, Dir. 1979–, Dir.-Gen. 1982–; Docent of Econs., Univ. of Helsinki 1962, Acting Prof. of Econs. 1964–65, Acting Prof. of Econometrics 1970; Acting Prof. of Econs., Univ. of Tampere 1965–66; Visiting Fellow, Univ. of Calif. (Berkeley) and Harvard Univ. 1967–68; mem. Finnish Acad., Cen. Research Bd. 1971–; mem. UN Statistical Comm. 1981–; Hon. Prof. 1981; Hon. Dr. (Turku School of Econs. and Business Man.) 1990; Kt. First Class White Rose of Finland; Commdr. Order of the Lion of Finland 1989. *Publications:* several books and more than 150 articles. *Leisure interests:* family life, car racing, cybernetics of human life. *Address:* Central Statistical Office of Finland, Annankatu 44, 00022 Helsinki (Office); Riihitie 21 A 2, 00330 Helsinki 33, Finland (Home). *Telephone:* 17341 (Office); 487490 (Home). *Fax:* (0) 1734 3562.

NIJENHUIS, Emmie te, PH.D.; Netherlands ethnomusicologist; b. 11 Nov. 1931, Bussum; d. of Dirk te Nijenhuis and W. Margarete Küchenthal; m. 1965–70; one s.; ed. Utrecht Conservatory and Utrecht Univ.; Teacher of Theory and History of Western Music, Zwolle Conservatory 1958–61; Reader Indian Musicology, Utrecht Univ. 1964–88; Visiting Lecturer Oxford and Basel Univs. 1978, 1984; mem. Royal Netherlands Acad. of Sciences 1978. *Publications:* Dattilam: Compendium of Ancient Indian Music 1970, Indian Music, History and Structure 1974, The Ragas of Somanatha, 2 Vols. 1976, Musicological Literature 1977, Sacred Songs of India: Muttusvami Diksitar's Cycle of Hymns to the Goddess Kamala, 2 Vols. 1987, Saṅgītaśiromaṇi, A Medieval Handbook of Indian Music 1992. *Address:* Verlengde Fortlaan 39, 1412 CW Naarden, Netherlands. *Telephone:* 0356949322.

NIJPELS, Eduardus Hermannes Theresia Maria, B.LL.; Netherlands politician; b. 1 April 1950, Den Helder; m. I. M. Pieters; ed. Utrecht Univ.; fmr. Nat. Chair. Young People's Org. of the JOVD; M.P. 1977–; Chair. Standing Cttee. on the Police, Parl. Party of VVD (People's Party for Freedom and Democracy) 1982; mem. Cttee. Liberal Renascence Soc., AVRO Broadcasting Asscn.; Minister of Housing, Physical Planning and the Environment 1986–89; Mayor of Breda 1990; regular columnist for the Algemeen Dagblad newspaper; fmr. mem. Consultative Cttee. on Environmental Activities in the Belgian/Dutch border region (BENEGORA). *Address:* Office of the Mayor, Town Hall, P.O. Box 90156, 4800 RH Breda, Netherlands

NIKOLAYEV, Army Gen. Andrei Ivanovich; Russian army officer; b. 21 April 1949, Moscow; m. Tatyana Yuryevna Nikolayeva; two s.; ed. Moscow Gen. Troops Commdg. School of R.S.F.S.R. Supreme Soviet, M. Frunze Mil. Acad., Gen. Staff Acad.; commdr. of platoon, co., regt.; First Deputy Head Main Admin. of Gen. Headquarters of U.S.S.R. Armed Forces; First Deputy Head of Gen. H.Q. of Russian Army 1992–94; C.-in-C. of Border troops of Russian Fed. 1994–; Head of Fed. Border Troops Service 1995–97; mem. State Duma 1998–; f. Union of People's Power and Labour 1998–. *Leisure interests:* theatre, organ music. *Address:* State Duma, Okhotny Ryad 1, 103265 Moscow, Russia. *Telephone:* (095) 292-80-34.

NIKOLAYEV, Mikhail Yefimovich; Russian politician; b. 13 Nov. 1937, Ordzhonikidze Region, Yakutia; m.; three c.; ed. Omsk Veterinary Inst., Higher CP School; worked as veterinarian, then Sec. Zhigan Regional Comsomol Cttee., First Sec. Yakut Comsomol Cttee., Sec., then First Sec. Verkhneviluysk Regional CP Cttee. 1971–75; Deputy Chair. Council of Ministers Yakut A.S.S.R. 1975–79; Minister of Agric. 1979–85; Sec. Yakut Regional CP Cttee. 1985–89; Chair. Presidium of Supreme Soviet Yakut A.S.S.R. 1989–91; Pres. Repub. of Sakha (Yakutia) 1991–, mem. Council of Fed. of Russia 1996–. *Address:* Office of the President, Kirova str. 11, 677022 Yakutsk, Russia. *Telephone:* (4112) 43 50 50 (Office). *Fax:* 24 06 24 (Office).

NIKOLSKY, Boris Vassilyevich; Russian politician; b. 1 May 1937, Moscow; m.; two c.; ed. Moscow Inst. of Agric. Eng., Higher School Cen. Cttee. CPSU.; master, chief engineer in a factory; Deputy Chair. Moscow Municipal Exec. Cttee. on problems of energy and eng. 1976–82; Sec. Moscow City CP Cttee. 1982–84; Sec., Second Sec. Cen. Cttee. of Georgian CP 1984–; First Deputy Chair. Moscow City Planning Cttee. 1989–; First Deputy Chair. Moscow City Construction Cttee. 1990–; First Deputy Prime Minister Moscow Govt. 1992–. *Address:* Moscow Government, Tverskaya str. 13, 103032 Moscow, Russia (Office). *Telephone:* (095) 229 2424 (Office).

NIKOLSKY, Sergey Ivanovich; Russian physicist; b. 5 June 1923; m.; one s.; ed. Moscow State Univ.; served in Soviet Army 1941–43; mem. of staff of Inst. of Physics, U.S.S.R. (now Russian) Acad. of Sciences 1948–, head of section 1970–73, Deputy Dir. 1973–93, Dir. Dept. of Nuclear Physics 1993–, Corresp. mem. 1984–; numerous publs. on space research, nuclear physics, solid state physics 1947–90; Lenin Prize 1982. *Leisure interest:* history of civilization. *Address:* P. N. Lebedev Institute of Physics, Leninsky Prospekt 53, 117924 Moscow, Russia. *Telephone:* 135-50-11 (Office); 135-00-93 (Home).

NIKONOV, Vyacheslav Alekseyevich, DR. HIS.; Russian politician and academic; b. 5 June 1956, Moscow; s. of Aleksey Dmitrievich Nikonov and Svetlana Vyacheslavovna Molotova; m. 1st Viktoria Makarovna Kostyuk 1976; m. 2nd Olga Mikhailovna Rozhkova 1987; three s.; ed. Moscow State Univ.; researcher Moscow State Univ., on staff Admin. Cen. Cttee. CPSU 1981–90; on staff of Pres. Gorbachev 1990–91; Asst. to Chair. U.S.S.R. State Security Cttee. (KGB) 1991–92; counsellor Dept. of Political Problems Int. Foundation of Econ. and Social Reforms (Foundation Reforma) 1992–93; Pres. Foundation Politika 1993–; mem. State Duma; Chair. Subcttee. on Int. Security and Arms Control 1994–95; Deputy Chair. Cttee. to re-elect the Pres. 1996; Head Analytical Dept. Pres. Yeltsin's Admin. 1996–97. *Publications:* Republicans: From Eisenhower to Nixon 1984, Iran-Contra Affair 1988, Republicans: From Nixon to Reagan 1989, The Age of Change: Russia in the 90s as Viewed by a Conservative 1998. *Leisure interests:* reading, gardening. *Address:* Zlatoustinsky per. 8/7, 101000 Moscow, Russia (Office). *Telephone:* (095) 206 8149 (Office). *Fax:* (095) 206 8661 (Office).

NILES, Thomas Michael Tolliver, M.A.; American diplomatist; b. 22 Sept. 1939, Lexington, Ky.; s. of John Jacob Niles and Rena (née Lipetz) Niles; m. Carroll C. Ehringhaus 1967; one s. one d.; ed. Harvard Univ. and Univ. of Kentucky; Foreign Service Officer, Dept. of State 1962; posts in Moscow, Belgrade and Brussels; Amb. to Canada 1985–89, to Greece 1993–97; Perm. Rep. to the EEC, Brussels 1989; Vice-Pres. Nat. Defense Univ. 1997–; Superior Honor Award, Dept. of State 1982, 1985. *Address:* c/o National Defense Headquarters Library, 101 Colonel By Drive, Ottawa, Ont. K1A 0K2, Canada. *Telephone:* (613) 996-0831. *Fax:* (613) 995-8176.

NILSSON, Birgit (Fru Bertil Niklasson); Swedish opera singer (soprano); b. 17 May 1918, Karup; m. Bertil Niklasson 1948; ed. Stockholm Royal Acad. of Music; with Stockholm Opera 1947–51; sang at Glyndebourne (England) 1951, Bayreuth 1954, 1957–70, Munich 1954–58, Hollywood Bowl, Buenos Aires and Florence 1956, London (Covent Garden) 1957, 1962, 1963, 1973, Milan (La Scala), Naples, Vienna, Chicago and San Francisco 1958, New York (Metropolitan) 1959, Moscow 1964; sang in Turandot, Paris 1968, Elektra, London 1969; particularly well known for her Wagnerian roles (Brünnhilde, Isolde, etc.); Royal Court singer 1954; retd. 1985; Austrian Kammersängerin, Bavarian Kammersängerin and Hon. mem. of the Vienna State Opera 1968; Hon. mem. Royal Acad. of Music (London) 1970; Dr. h.c. Andover Music Univ., Mass., U.S.A., Manhattan School of Music, New York,, Mich. State Univ. of Fine Arts, Sibelius Acad. Helsinki 1997; Medal Litteris et Artibus 1960, Medal for Promotion of Art of Music, Royal Acad. of Music, Stockholm 1968, First Commdr., Order of Vasa 1974, Commdr. Order of St. Olav 1st Class (Norway) 1975, Swedish Gold Medal 1978. *Address:* Box 527, Stockholm C, Sweden.

NIMAH, Hassan Ali Hussain al-, PH.D.; Qatari diplomatist; b. 1940; ed. Cambridge Univ.; joined govt. service 1959; Amb. to India, non-resident Amb. to Sri Lanka, Nepal, Thailand, Singapore 1976–90; Perm. Rep. to UN 1990–97; rep. at numerous meetings of Movement of Non-Aligned Countries and confs. on educ. and literature. *Address:* c/o Ministry of Foreign Affairs, P.O. Box 250, Doha, Qatar.

NIMATALLAH, Yusuf A., PH.D.(ECONS.); Saudi Arabian economist; b. 1936; ed. American Univ., Beirut and Univ. of Mass.; with Banque de l'Indochine 1952–57; Teaching Asst. in Econs., Univ. of Mass. 1963–65; Prof. Monetary and Int. Econs., Univ. of Riyadh (King Saud Univ. 1982–) 1965 (on leave 1973); Adviser to Minister of Finance on Money and Banking, Oil Finance and Planning 1967–73; Adviser to Sultan of Oman on Oil, Finance, Money and Banking; Deputy Chair. and Pres. Cen. Bank of Oman 1975–78; Deputy Chair. UBAF Arab American Bank, New York 1976–78; Exec. Dir. Fund for Saudi Arabia 1979–89. *Address:* c/o Ministry of Finance and National Economy, Airport Road, Riyadh 11177, Saudi Arabia.

NIMERI, Field-Marshal Gaafar Mohammed al- (see Nemery, Field-Marshal Gaafar Mohammed al-).

NIMOY, Leonard; American actor and director; b. 26 March 1931, Boston; s. of Max Nimoy and Dora (née Spinner) Nimoy; m. 1st Sandi Zober 1954 (divorced); one s. one d.; m. 2nd Susan Bay 1988; ed. Boston Coll. and Antioch Univ.; served in U.S. Army 1954–56; trained at the Pasadena Playhouse, Calif. 1960-63. *TV appearances include:* Star Trek 1966–69, Eleventh Hour, The Virginian, Rawhide, Dr. Kildare. *Film appearances include:* Queen for a Day, Rhubarb 1951, Kid Monk Baron, Francis Goes to West Point 1952, Old Overland Trail 1953, Satan's Satellites 1958, The Balcony 1963, Deathwatch 1966, Valley of Mystery (co-producer) 1967, Catlow (co-producer) 1971, Invasion of the Bodysnatchers (co-producer) 1978, Star Trek—the Motion Picture (co-producer) 1979, Star Trek—the Wrath of Khan (co-producer) 1982, Star Trek III—the Search for Spock (also dir.) 1984, Star Trek IV—the Voyage Home (also dir.) 1986, Star Trek V—The Final Frontier 1989, Star Trek VI—The Undiscovered Country 1991, Bonanza: Under Attack 1995, Carpati: 50 Miles, 50 Years 1996, A Life Apart: Hasidism in America (voice) 1997; also directed Three Men and A Baby 1987, The Good Mother 1988, Funny About Love 1990, Holy Matrimony

1994, The Pagemaster (voice), numerous stage appearances. *Publications:* I Am Not Spock (autobiog.) 1975, We Are All Children 1977, Come Be With Me 1979. *Address:* c/o Gersh Agency Inc., 232 North Cannon Drive, Beverly Hills, CA 90210, U.S.A.

NIMR, Nabih An-; Jordanian diplomatist; b. 26 Oct. 1931, Tubas; m. Rabab Al-Nimr 1961; one s. one d.; ed. Alexandria Univ.; Amb. to Syria 1974–78, to Fed. Rep. of Germany (also accred. to Sweden, Denmark, Norway and Luxembourg) 1978–81, to Tunisia and Perm. Rep. to the Arab League 1981–85, to U.K. 1985–87, (also accred. to Ireland 1986–87), to Egypt 1988–; Sec. Gen. Ministry of Foreign Affairs 1987–88. *Address:* Embassy of Jordan, 6 Sharia Juhaini, Cairo, Egypt.

NIN-CULMELL, Joaquín María; Spanish composer, pianist and conductor; b. 5 Sept. 1908, Berlin, Germany; s. of Joaquín Nin and Rosa Culmell; ed. Schola Cantorum and Nat. Conservatoire, Paris; studied privately with Manuel de Falla; Instructor, Middlebury Coll., Vt. 1938, 1939, 1940, Williams Coll. 1940–50; Prof. of Music, Univ. of Calif. 1949–74, Emer. Prof. 1974–, Inst. of Creative Arts 1965–66; has appeared as pianist and conductor with the San Francisco Symphony and other orchestras in the U.S.A. and Europe; Corresp. mem. Royal Acad. of Fine Arts of San Fernando (Madrid 1962). *Compositions:* Piano Concerto, El burlador de Sevilla (ballet), Piano Quintet, Sonata Breve, Tonadas (piano), Twelve Cuban Dances (piano), Three Old Spanish Pieces (orchestra), Diferencias (orchestra), Concerto for cello and orchestra (after Padre Anselmo Viola), Mass in English (for mixed chorus and organ), La Celestina (opera), Cantata for voice and harpsichord or piano and strings (after Padre José Pradas), Le rêve de Cyrano (ballet), incidental music for Shakespeare's Cymbeline, Federico García Lorca's Yerma, Six Sephardic Folksongs (for voice and piano), songs, choral pieces, organ symphony, pieces for guitar, etc. *Publications:* Ed. Spanish Choral Tradition, Prefaces in English and French for the early diaries of Anaïs Nin (Vols. I–IV). *Fax:* (510) 658 0477 (U.S.A.)

NINAGAWA, Yukio; Japanese theatre director; known for his direction of Western classic plays, especially Shakespeare, in a Japanese style; his co. appeared at Edin. Festival with samurai-style Macbeth 1985, Suicide of Love, Nat. Theatre, London 1989, Medea, Suicide for Love and a Noh-inspired version of The Tempest, Barbican Theatre, London 1992; also dir. Tango at the End of Winter.

NINEHAM, Rev. Canon Dennis Eric, M.A., D.D.; British professor of theology and ecclesiastic (retd.); b. 27 Sept. 1921, Southampton; s. of Stanley Martin Nineham and Bessie Edith Gain; m. Ruth Corfield Miller 1946; two s. two d.; ed. King Edward VI School, Southampton, Queen's Coll., Oxford and Lincoln Theological Coll.; Chaplain Queen's Coll., Oxford 1944–54, Fellow 1946–54; Prof. of Biblical and Historical Theology London Univ. 1954–58, Prof. of Divinity 1958–64; Regius Prof. of Divinity Cambridge Univ. 1964–69; Fellow of Emmanuel Coll. 1964–69; Warden Keble Coll., Oxford 1969–79; Prof. of Theology Bristol Univ. 1980–86; Visiting Prof. Rikkyo Univ., Tokyo 1994; Fellow King's Coll., London; Hon. Canon Emer. Bristol Cathedral; Hon. Fellow Keble Coll., Oxford, Queen's Coll., Oxford; Hon. D.D. (Yale) 1965, (Birmingham) 1972. *Publications:* The Gospel of St. Mark 1963, The Use and Abuse of the Bible 1976, Explorations in Theology 1977, Christianity Medieval and Modern: A Study in Religious Change 1993. *Leisure interests:* walking and reading. *Address:* 9 Fitzherbert Close, Iffley, Oxford, OX4 4EN, England (Home). *Telephone:* (01865) 715941.

NINN-HANSEN, Erik, LL.D.; Danish politician; b. 12 April 1922, Skørpinge, Western Zealand; s. of Christian Hansen; in pvt. law practice 1955–; mem. Folketing (Parl.) 1953–94; Minister of Defence 1968–71, of Finance 1971, of Justice 1982–89; Pres. of the Folketing Jan.–Oct. 1989; Nat. Chair. Conservative Youth 1948–50. *Publication:* Syv år for VKR 1974, Fra Christmas til Baunsgaard 1985, Ret Færd mellem jura og politik 1990, Christmas Møller, En stridsmand i dansk politik 1991. *Address:* Bregnegårdsvej 11, 2920 Charlottenlund, Denmark.

NIORDSON, Frithiof Igor Niord, PH.D.; Danish professor of engineering; b. 1 Aug. 1922, Johannesburg, South Africa; s. of Niord Gustafson and Helena de Makeeff; m. 1st Ann-Marie Odqvist 1954; m. 2nd Hanne Oerregaard 1975; two s. three d.; ed. Royal Inst. of Tech., Sweden, Brown Univ., Providence, R.I., U.S.A.; Consulting Eng. 1949–58; Prof. of Mechanical Eng., Tech. Univ. of Denmark 1958–92, Dean 1975–91; mem. NATO Advisory Group for Aerospace Research and Devt. 1963–86; Sec. Danish Cen. of Applied Math. and Mechanics 1968–92; Sec.-Gen. Int. Union of Theoretical and Applied Mechanics 1968–74, Pres. 1974–80, Vice-Pres. 1980–84; Chair. Bd. of Dirs. N. Europe Univ. Computing Cen. 1980; mem. Royal Acad. of Sciences (Sweden), Danish-Soviet Gov. Comm. for Scientific Co-operation 1982–92, Polish Acad. of Sciences; Hon. mem. American Asscn. of Mechanical Engs.; Kt. of the Dannebrog. *Publications:* several books and papers on shell-theory, stability and vibrations. *Leisure interests:* sailing, skiing, riding. *Address:* Geelsvej 19, 2840 Holte, Denmark. *Telephone:* 45 42 50 29. *Fax:* 45 42 59 60.

NIRENBERG, Louis, PH.D.; American professor of mathematics; b. 28 Feb. 1925, Hamilton, Ont., Canada; s. of Zuzie Nirenberg and Bina Katz; m. Susan Blank 1948; one s. one d.; ed. McGill and New York Univs.; Instructor, New York Univ. 1949–51, Asst. Prof. 1951–54, Assoc. Prof. 1954–57, Prof. 1957–; Dir. Courant Inst. of Mathematical Sciences 1970–72; mem. N.A.S., American Acad. of Arts and Sciences, American Philosophical Soc., Accad. dei Lincei, Acad. des Sciences, France, Istituto Lombardo Accad. di Scienze e Lettere, Italy; Hon. Prof. Nankai Univ., Zhejiang Univ.; Hon. D.Sc. (McGill Univ., Univ. of Pisa, Univ. of Paris, Dauphine); Bôcher Prize and Steele Prize of American Mathematical Soc, Crafoord Prize (Royal Swedish Acad. of Sciences) 1982. *Publications:* various papers in mathematical journals. *Leisure interests:* classical music, reading fiction, cinema, walking. *Address:* 221 West 82nd Street, New York, NY 10024, U.S.A. (Home). *Fax:* (212) 995-4121.

NIRENBERG, Marshall Warren, PH.D.; American biochemist; b. 10 April 1927; s. of Harry Edward and Minerva (Bykowsky) Nirenberg; m. Perola Zaltzman 1961; ed. Univ. of Florida and Univ. of Michigan; Postdoctoral Fellow, American Cancer Soc., Nat. Insts. of Health (N.I.H.) 1957–59, U.S. Public Health Service, N.I.H. 1959–60; mem. staff, N.I.H. 1960–, research biochemist 1961–62; research biochemist, Head of Section for Biochemical Genetics, Nat. Heart Inst. 1962–66; Chief, Lab. of Biochemical Genetics, Nat. Heart, Lung and Blood Inst. 1962–; has researched on mechanism of protein synthesis, genetic code, nucleic acids, regulatory mechanism in synthetic macromolecules; mem. New York Acad. of Sciences, A.A.A.S., N.A.S., Pontifical Acad. of Sciences 1974, Deutsche Leopoldina Akad. der Naturforscher; Foreign Assoc. Acad. des Sciences (France) 1989; hon. mem. Harvey Soc.; Molecular Biology Award, Nat. Acad. of Sciences 1962; Medal from Dept. of Health, Educ. and Welfare 1963, Modern Medicine Award 1964, Nat. Medal for Science, Pres. Johnson 1965, Nobel Prize for Medicine (with Holley and Khorana) for interpreting the genetic code and its function in protein synthesis 1968, Louisa Gross Horwitz Prize for Biochemistry 1968. *Address:* Laboratory of Biochemical Genetics, National Heart, Lung and Blood Institute, Building 36, Room IC06, Bethesda, MD 20892, U.S.A.

NISBET, Robin George Murdoch, M.A., F.B.A.; British classical scholar; b. 21 May 1925, Glasgow, Scotland; s. of Robert George Nisbet and Agnes Thomson Husband; m. Anne Wood 1969; ed. Glasgow Acad., Glasgow Univ. and Balliol Coll. Oxford; Fellow and Tutor in Classics, Corpus Christi Coll. Oxford 1952–70, Prof. of Latin 1970–92; Hon. Fellow Balliol Coll. 1989, Corpus Christi Coll. 1992; Kenyon Medal, British Acad. 1997. *Publications:* Commentary on Cicero, In Pisonem 1961, Horace, Odes I, II (with M. Hubbard) 1970, 1978, Collected Papers on Latin Literature 1995. *Address:* 80 Abingdon Road, Cumnor, Oxford, OX2 9QW, England. *Telephone:* (01865) 862482.

NISHANOV, Rafik, CAND.HIST.SC.; Uzbekistan politician (retd.); b. 1926; ed. Tashkent Evening Pedagogical Inst.; mem. CPSU 1949–91; work on kolkhoz 1942–44; work for Tashkent Dist. Komsomol 1944–45; served in Soviet Army 1945–50; instructor, Head of Section, Sec. Oktyabrsky Regional Cttee., Tashkent 1951–56; Head of Section Tashkent City Cttee. 1956–59; Sec. Cen. Cttee. of Uzbek CP 1963–70; Amb. to Sri Lanka 1970–78, to Jordan 1987–85; Minister of Foreign Affairs of Uzbek S.S.R. 1985–91; Chair. of Presidium of Supreme Soviet of Uzbek S.S.R. 1986–91; Deputy Chair. of Presidium of Supreme Soviet of U.S.S.R. 1986–88; First Sec. Uzbek CP 1988–89; U.S.S.R. People's Deputy 1989–91; Chair. U.S.S.R. Council of Nationalities 1989–91; Adviser to Pres. Gorbachev 1991; Vice-Pres. New World-500 Fund; lives in Moscow.

NISHIDA, Mamoru; Japanese politician; b. Ehime Pref.; mem. LDP; mem. for Shikoku, House of Reps.; fmr. Dir.-Gen. Nat. Land Agency; Minister of Home Affairs 1998–. *Address:* Ministry of Home Affairs, 2-1-2, Kasumigaseki, Chiyoda-ku, Tokyo 100, Japan. *Telephone:* (03) 3581-5311. *Fax:* (03) 3593-3758.

NISHIHARA, Haruo, LL.D.; Japanese professor of law; b. 13 March 1928, Tokyo; s. of Keiichi Nishihara and Makoto Tateyama Nishihara; m.; one s.; ed. Waseda Univ.; Asst., School of Law, Waseda Univ. 1953–59, Asst. Prof. 1959–63, Assoc. Prof. 1963–67, Prof. 1967–, Dean School of Law and mem. Bd. of Trustees 1972–76, Exec. Dir. 1978–80, Vice-Pres. 1980–82, Pres. and mem. Bd. of Trustees 1982–95; Hon. LL.D. (Korea Univ.) 1985, (Earlham Coll.) 1988; D. Univ. (Sydney) 1989; Educational Man. Prize (De La Salle Univ.) 1988. *Publications:* On the Theory of "mittelbare Täterschaft" 1962, Traffic Accidents and the Principle of Trust 1962, Particular Aspects of Criminal Law 1974, 1983, General Aspects of Criminal Law 1977, What Governs the Criminal Law? 1979. *Leisure interests:* swimming, skiing. *Address:* 619-18 Nohgaya-cho, Machida-shi, Tokyo, Japan.

NISHIMATSU, Chikara, B.S.M.E.; Japanese business executive; b. 3 Nov. 1931, Osaka; m. Michiko Yamada 1959; two s. one d.; ed. Pratt Inst.; joined Itochu Co., Ltd. 1959, mem. Bd. Dirs. 1984–91, Gen. Man. Itochu Asian Operations 1985, Man. Dir. 1986, Gen. Man. Itochu Europe and Africa Operation 1989–91; Pres. and C.E.O. Matsubo Co. Ltd. (fmrly known as Matsuzaka Co. Ltd.) 1992– (Chair. 1998–). *Address:* 3-21-6, Katsuta-Dao, Yachiyo City, Chiba-ken 276, Japan (Home). *Telephone:* 03-5472-1712 (Office); 047-480-1436 (Home); *Fax:* 0474-854326 (Home).

NISHIMURA, Kiyohiko G., PH.D.; Japanese professor of economics; b. 30 March 1953, Tokyo; s. of Giichi Nishimura and Sumiko Otsuka; m. Yukiko Kurihata 1979; two d.; ed. Univ. of Tokyo, Yale Univ., U.S.A.; Arthur Okun Research Fellow, Brookings Inst., U.S.A. 1981–82; Assoc. Prof. of Econs., Univ. of Tokyo 1983–94, Prof. 1994–; Assoc. Ed. Economic Studies Quarterly 1989–93; Research Assoc. US-Japan Center, New York Univ. 1989–; Dir. Tokyo Centre for Econ. Research 1990–91; Visiting Scholar, M.I.T., U.S.A. 1991–92; Visiting Research Fellow Inst. for Int. Econ. Studies, Sweden 1993; Visiting Prof., Louis Pasteur Univ. 1994, Aarhus Univ. 1996; Special mem.

Econ. Council, Japanese Govt. 1994–; Nikkei Prize 1993, Japan Economist's Prize 1997, Nakahara Prize, Japanese Econ. Asscn. 1998. *Publications:* Stock and Land Prices in Japan (in Japanese) 1990, The Distribution System in Japan (ed., in Japanese) 1991, Imperfect Competition, Differential Information and Microfoundations of Macroeconomics 1992, Macroeconomics of Price Revolution 1996. *Leisure interest:* painting. *Address:* 7-3-1, Hongo, Bunkyo-ku, Tokyo 113 (Office); 1-2-26-403, Higashi-Gotanda, Shinagawa-ku, Tokyo 141, Japan (Home). *Telephone:* (03) 3812-2111. *Fax:* (03) 3818-7082.

NISHIZAWA, Jun-ichi, D.ENG., F.I.E.E.; Japanese electrical engineer and academic; b. 12 Sept. 1926, Sendai; s. of Kyosuke Nishizawa and Akiko (Ishii) Nishizawa; m. Takeko Hayakawa 1956; one s. two d.; ed. Tohoku Univ.; Research Asst., Electrical Communication Research Inst., Tohoku Univ. 1953–54, Asst. Prof. 1954–62, Prof. 1962–90, Dir. 1983–86, 1989–90, Pres. of Univ. 1990–96; Dir. Semiconductor Research Inst., Sendai 1968–; Pres. Iwate Univ.; approx. 520 patents in Japan, 310 patents abroad; mem. Japan Acad.; Foreign mem. Polish Acad. of Sciences, Russian Acad. of Sciences, Korea Acad. of Science and Tech.; Laudise Prize IOCG, Kenneth J. Button Prize. *Publications:* Semiconductor Devices 1961, Semiconductor Materials 1968, Optoelectronics 1977. *Leisure interests:* classical music, reading, pottery, pictures (especially Impressionist school). *Address:* Semiconductor Research Institute, Kawauchi, Aoba-ku, Sendai 980-0862, Japan. *Telephone:* (22) 223 7287. *Fax:* (22) 223 7289.

NISSEL, Siegmund, O.B.E.; British musician; b. 3 Jan. 1922, Munich, Germany; s. of Isidor Nissel and Malvine Nissel; m. Muriel Nissel 1957; one s. one d.; ed. Mittelschule Vienna, London Univ. and violin tuition pvtly. with Prof. Max Weissgärber, Vienna and Prof. Max Rostal, London; Leader, London Int. Orchestra 1947; Founder mem. Second Violin, Amadeus Quartet 1948–87; Prof. of Chamber Music, Musikhochschule, Cologne, Feb. Repub. of Germany 1978–, R.A.M., London 1986– (Dir. for Chamber Music); Hon. mem. R.A.M.; Hon. D.Mus. (York, London); Grosses Verdienstkreuz, Germany; Ehrenkreuz für Wissenschaft und Kunst, Austria. *Leisure interests:* opera and theatre. *Address:* 29 The Park, London, NW11 7ST, England. *Telephone:* 0181-458 2085.

NISSIM, Moshe, LL.D.; Israeli politician; b. 1935, Jerusalem; ed. Hebrew Univ. of Jerusalem; elected to Knesset 1959– (as rep. of Union of Gen. Zionists 1959, subsequently as rep. of Gahal faction of the Liberal Party, then of the Likud Bloc); has served on Defence, Foreign Affairs and Security, Constitution Law and Legislation, Labour and Housing Cttees. in the Knesset; Co-Chair. Likud group 1975–79; Chair. Exec. Cttee., Likud Feb. 1978–; Minister without Portfolio 1978–80, 1988–89; Minister of Justice 1980–86, of Finance 1986–88, of Trade and Industry 1989–92; Deputy Prime Minister 1990–92. *Address:* 6 Shlom Aleichem Street, Jerusalem 92148, Israel.

NITZE, Paul Henry A.B.; American adviser; b. 16 Jan. 1907, Amherst, Mass.; s. of William A. and Anina (Hilken) Nitze; m. 1st Phyllis Pratt 1932 (deceased); two s. two d.; m. 2nd Elisabeth Scott Porter 1993; ed. Harvard Univ.; New York Investment Banker 1929–41; Financial Dir. Office of Co-ordinator of Inter-American Affairs 1941–42; Chief, Metals and Minerals Branch, Bd. of Econ. Welfare, Dir. Foreign Procurement and Devt. 1942–43; Vice-Chair. Strategic Bombing Survey 1944–46; Deputy Dir. Office of Int. Trade Policy 1946–48; Deputy to Asst. Sec. of State for Econ. Affairs 1948–49; Dir. Policy Planning Staff, Dept. of State 1950–53; Pres. Foreign Service Educ. Foundation 1953–61; Asst. Sec. of Defense for Int. Security Affairs 1961–63; Sec. of the Navy 1963–67; Deputy Sec. of Defense 1967–69; mem. U.S. Del. to Strategic Arms Limitation Talks (SALT) 1969–74; Consultant, System Planning Corpn. 1974–81; Head of U.S. Del. to the Intermediate Range Nuclear Forces Negotiations with U.S.S.R. 1981–83; Adviser on Arms Control Matters to the Pres. and the Sec. of State 1984–89; Founder, Diplomat-in-Residence and Distinguished Research Prof. in Strategic Studies and American Foreign Policy, Paul H. Nitze School of Advanced Int. Studies, Johns Hopkins Univ.; mem. and fmr. Pres. Advisory Council, Paul H. Nitze School of Advanced Int. Studies; mem. Bd. of Dirs. Marshall Foundation, Atlantic Council of the U.S., Center for Naval Analyses, Washington Opera, St. Mary's Coll. of Maryland; mem. Council on Foreign Relations; Chair. Washington Inst. of Foreign Affairs; Hon. Vice-Pres. Int. Inst. for Strategic Studies; Hon. LL.D. (Brown Univ., Johns Hopkins Univ., William Coll.); George C. Marshall Medal, Sec. of State's Distinguished Service Award, Sylvanus Thayer Award, Theodore Roosevelt Distinguished Service Medal, Jefferson Award for Public Service, Eric M. Warburg Prize, Sec.-Gen. of NATO Atlantic Award, James Doolittle Award; Medal of Merit, Medal of Freedom, Kt. Commdr.'s Cross (Badge and Star) of Order of Merit, Fed. Repub. of Germany, Grand Officier, Ordre de la Couronne, Belgium, Grosse Goldene Ehrenzeichen des Landes Steiermark, Austria, and awards from the Netherlands and Italy. *Publications:* From Hiroshima to Glasnost: At the Center of Decision—A Memoir 1989, Tension Between Opposites 1993, and numerous articles on U.S. foreign policy, nat. security policy and international affairs. *Leisure interests:* horseback riding, skiing, tennis. *Address:* Paul H. Nitze School of Advanced International Studies, Johns Hopkins University, 1619 Massachusetts Avenue, N.W., Washington, DC 20036 (Office); 2416 Tracy Place, N.W., Washington, DC 20008, U.S.A. (Home).

NIU MAOSHENG; Chinese government official; b. 1939, Beijing; ed. Beijing Agric. Inst.; joined CCP 1961; Vice-Minister of Water Resources 1988–93, Minister 1993–98; Acting Gov. Hebei Prov. 1998–; Deputy Head, Nat. Gen. Headquarters for Flood Prevention and Drought Control; mem. 15th CCP Cen. Cttee. 1997–. *Address:* Hebei Provincial People's Government, Shijiazhuang City, Hebei Province, People's Republic of China.

NIU QUN; Chinese actor; b. Dec. 1949, Tianjin; joined PLA 1971; actor Zhanyou Art Troupe of PLA Beijing Mil. Command 1974–93; actor China Broadcasting Art Troupe 1993–; performs comic dialogues with Feng Gong; numerous prizes. *Publications:* In Various Ingenious Names (5 cassettes of comic dialogues). *Address:* China Broadcasting Art Troupe, Beijing, People's Republic of China.

NIWANO, Nikkyō; Japanese religious leader; b. 15 Nov. 1906, Niigata Pref.; s. of Jūkichi and Mii (Hosaka) Niwano; m. Sai Abè 1930 (died 1994); three s. three d.; ed. Ōike Primary School, Suganuma; Founder Rissho Kosei-kai, a lay Buddhist asscn. with 6.8 million mems. 1938–; Chair. Shinshuren (Fed. of the New Religious Orgs. of Japan) 1965–93, Hon. Chair. 1993–; Pres. Japanese Cttee. for World Conf. on Religion and Peace 1972–96, Hon. Pres. 1996–; Hon. Pres. Int. Asscn. for Religious Freedom 1987–; Pres. Niwano Peace Foundation 1978–92, Hon. Pres. 1992–; Chair. Asian Conf. on Religion and Peace 1977–96, Hon. Pres. 1996–; Hon. Pres. World Conf. on Religion and Peace 1979–; Trustee, Japan Religions League 1967–; Hon. LL.D. (Meadville/Lombard Theol. School) 1975; Imperial Household Agency Medal of Honour with Dark Navy Blue Ribbon 1958, Templeton Foundation Prize for Progress in Religion 1979, Artigiana della Pace, United Nations Plaque 1983, Interfaith Medallion of Int. Council of Christians and Jews 1993; Kt. Commdr. with Silver Star of Order of St. Gregory the Great 1992. *Leisure interests:* calligraphy, ink painting, golf. *Publications:* in English: Buddhism for Today: a Modern Interpretation of the Threefold Lotus Sutra 1976, A Buddhist Approach to Peace 1977, Lifetime Beginner (autobiog.) 1978, The Richer Life 1979, Shakyamuni Buddha 1980, A Guide to the Threefold Lotus Sutra 1981, The Meaningful Life 1982, The Wholesome Family Life 1982, Invisible Eyelashes 1994; in Japanese: Buddhism for Today (5 vols.) 1959–60, A New Interpretation of the Threefold Lotus Sutra (10 vols.) 1964–68, A Guide to the Threefold Lotus Sutra 1975. *Address:* Rissho Kosei-kai, 2-11-1 Wada Suginami-ku, Tokyo 166, Japan. *Telephone:* (03) 3383-1111. *Fax:* (03) 3382-1729.

NIXON, Sir Edwin Ronald, Kt., C.B.E., D.L., M.A.; British business executive; b. 21 June 1925, Leicester; s. of William Archdale Nixon and Ethel Nixon (née Corrigan); m. 1st Joan Lilian Hill 1952 (died 1995); one s. one d.; m. 2nd Bridget Diana Rogers 1997; ed. Alderman Newton's Grammar School, Leicester, and Selwyn Coll., Cambridge; served R.A.F. 1943–47; Man. Accountant, Dexion Ltd. 1950–55; joined IBM as a data processing salesman 1955, various man. posts 1955–65, Man. Dir. 1965–79; Chair. and C.E.O. IBM United Kingdom Holdings Ltd. 1979–86, Chair. 1986–90; Dir. Nat. Westminster Bank PLC 1975–96, Deputy Chair. 1987–96; Dir. Amersham Int. PLC 1987–96, Chair. 1988–96; Dir. U.K.-Japan 2000 Group Ltd. –1996, Partnership Sourcing Ltd. –1996, Lloyd Instruments PLC 1987–91, NatWest Bancorp Inc. 1991–96, Nat. Westminster Bank U.S.A. 1992–96; Chair. London Classical Radio PLC 1989-92, NatWest Pension Trustees Ltd. 1991–96, Leicester BioSciences Ltd. 1996–; mem. Council CBI 1971–96; Council mem. The Open Univ. 1986–92, Univ. of Leicester; Gov. United World Coll. of the Atlantic; Vice-Pres. Opportunities for the Disabled, London Int. String Quartet Competition; Hon. Trustee Inst. of Econ. Affairs; mem. Royal Nat. Theatre Devt. Council 1984–96, Advisory Council The Prince's Youth Business Trust 1987–, The Macmillan Appeal Devt. Bd. 1994–96; Trustee Inst. for Man. Devt. –1996, Jean Sainsbury Royal Opera House Trust, Monteverdi Choir and Orchestra (Chair. 1988–); Friend of Lambeth Palace Library; Patron Asscn. Internationale des Etudiants en Sciences Economiques et Commerciales, G.B. –1996; Hon. Fellow Selwyn Coll. Cambridge, Chartered Inst. of Marketing; Fellow Queen Mary and Westfield Coll. London; Dr. h.c. (Stirling, Manchester, Aston, Brunel, Portsmouth, Leeds Metropolitan). *Leisure interests:* music, golf. *Address:* Starkes Heath, Rogate, Petersfield, Hants., GU31 5EJ, England. *Telephone:* (01730) 821504.

NIXON, John Forster, PH.D., D.SC., F.R.S., F.R.S.A.; British professor of chemistry; b. 27 Jan. 1937, Whitehaven, Cumberland (now Cumbria); s. of Edward Forster Nixon, M.B.E. and Mary Nixon (née Lytton); m. "Kim" Smith 1960; one s. one d.; ed. Univ. of Manchester; Research Assoc. in Chem., Univ. of Southern Calif., Los Angeles 1960–62; ICI Fellow, Cambridge Univ., Inorganic Chem. Dept. 1962–64; Lecturer in Inorganic Chem. Univ. of St. Andrews 1964–66; lecturer in Chem., Univ. of Sussex 1966, Reader 1976, Subject Chair. in Chem. 1981–84, Prof. of Chem. 1986–, Dean School of Chem. and Molecular Sciences 1989–92; Visiting Assoc. Prof. of Chem., Victoria, B.C. 1970–71; Visiting Prof. Simon Fraser Univ., Vancouver B.C. 1975; Chair. Downland Section, Chemical Soc. 1973–74; mem. Int. Cttee. on Phosphorus Chem. 1983; elected titular mem. IUPAC Comm., Inorganic Nomenclature 1985; mem. Inorganic Chem. Panel SERC Cttee. 1986–89; Royal Soc.-Leverhulme Sr. Research Fellow 1993; Corday-Morgan Medal and Prize 1973, Main Group Element Prize 1985, Tilden Lectureship 1991–92 (all Royal Soc. of Chem.). *Publications:* Phosphorus: The Carbon Copy (co-author) 1998, and over 300 publs. in chemical journals, and invited lectures to int. chemical socs. *Leisure interests:* walking, theatre, music, watching cricket, playing tennis, badminton and squash. *Address:* School of Chemistry, Physics and Environmental Science, University of Sussex, Brighton, Sussex, BN1 9QJ (Office); Juggs Barn, The Street, Kingston, Lewes, Sussex, BN7 3PB,

England (Home). *Telephone:* (01273) 678536 (Office); (01273) 483993 (Home). *Fax:* (01273) 677196 (Office).

NIYAZOV, Saparmurad; Turkmenistan politician; b. 19 Feb. 1940, Ashkhabad; m. Muza Alexeevna Niyazova; one s. one d.; ed. Leningrad Polytechnic Inst.; mem. CPSU 1962–91; instructor with Trade Union Org. of mineral prospecting works in Turkmenistan 1959–67; instructor, then deputy head of section of Cen. Cttee. of Turkmen CP 1970–79; head of section and first sec. of Ashkhabad City Cttee. of Turkmen CP 1979–84; party work with Cen. Cttee. of CPSU 1984–85; mem. Cen. Cttee. of CPSU 1986–91; mem. CPSU Politburo 1990–91; Pres. of Council of Ministers of Turkmen S.S.R. 1985; First Sec. of Cen. Cttee. of C.P. of Turkmen S.S.R. 1985–91; Chair. Turkmen Supreme Soviet Jan.–Nov. 1990; Pres. of Turkmenistan 1991–, concurrently Prime Minister 1991–; Chair. Democratic Party of Turkmenistan 1991; Pres. Humanitarian Asscn. of Turkmen People of the World; Mukhtumikuli Prize 1992; title of Turkmenbashi (Father of Turkmen People) conferred by Parl. 1993. *Address:* Office of the President, Karl Marx str. 24, 744017 Ashgabat; Democratic Party of Turkmenistan, Gogolya str. 28, 744014 Ashgabat, Turkmenistan. *Telephone:* (3632) 35-45-34.

NKOMO, Joshua; Zimbabwean politician; b. 19 June 1917; ed. Adam's Coll., Natal, Univ. of S. Africa, Johannesburg; Welfare Officer, Rhodesia Railways, Bulawayo, then Organizing Sec., Rhodesian African Railway Workers' Union 1945–50; Pres. African Congress; employed in insurance and real estate; Pres.-Gen. African Nat. Congress 1957; lived abroad when African Nat. Congress banned 1959; elected Pres. Nat. Dem. Party Aug. 1960; returned to S. Rhodesia; Pres. Zimbabwe African People's Union (ZAPU) 1961–87, amalgamated in African Nat. Council (ANC) 1974–76; imprisoned 1963–64; banished to Nuanetsi area April 1964, to Gonakudzingula Restriction Camp Nov. 1964 and for a further five years Dec. 1968, released Dec. 1974; mem. ANC Exec. 1974–76; involved in constitutional negotiations with Prime Minister Ian Smith 1976; Leader ANC del. at Geneva Conf. on Rhodesia; Joint Leader (with Robert Mugabe, q.v.) of Patriotic Front 1976–80; attended Lancaster House Conf. 1979; contested Feb. 1980 elections as Leader of Patriotic Front; Minister of Home Affairs 1980–81, without Portfolio 1981–82; Sr. Minister in the Pres.'s Office 1988–90; a Vice-Pres. of Zimbabwe Aug. 1990–; Interim Second Vice-Pres. ZANU April 1988; fmr. mem. Cabinet Cttee. on Public Security; Hon. LL.D. (Atlanta) 1979. *Publication:* The Story of My Life 1984. *Address:* Office of the Vice-Presidents, Munhumutapa Building, Samora Machel Avenue, Private Bag 7700, Causeway, Harare, Zimbabwe. *Telephone:* (4) 707091.

NOAH, Harold Julius, M.A., PH.D.; British academic; b. 21 Jan. 1925, London; s. of Abraham Noah and Sophia Cohen; m. 1st Norma Mestel 1945 (divorced 1966); m. 2nd Helen Claire Chisnall 1966; two s. two d.; ed. Stratford Grammar School, L.S.E., King's Coll., London, Teachers Coll. Columbia Univ., New York; Asst. Master then Head of Econs., Henry Thornton School, London 1949–60; Asst., Assoc. and Gardner Cowles Prof. Emer. of Econs. and Educ. Teachers Coll., Columbia Univ., New York 1964–87, Dean 1976–81; Prof. of Educ., State Univ. of New York, Buffalo 1987–91; has received numerous academic honours and awards. *Publications include:* Educational Financing and Policy Goals for Primary Schools: General Report (with Joel Sherman) 1979, The National Case Study: An Empirical Comparative Study of Twenty-one Educational Systems (with Harry Passow and others) 1976, Canada: Review of National Policies for Education 1976, International Study of Business/Industry Involvement in Education 1987, Secondary School Examinations: International Perspectives on Policies and Practice 1993, Doing Comparative Education: Three Decades of Collaboration (with Max Eckstein) 1998. *Address:* Teachers College, Columbia University, Box 169, New York, NY 10027, U.S.A. *Telephone:* (212) 678-3390. *Fax:* (212) 678 4048.

NOAKES, Rt. Rev. George, B.A.; Welsh ecclesiastic (retd.); b. 13 Sept. 1924, Bwlchllan, Dyfed; s. of David John Noakes and Elizabeth Mary Noakes; m. Jane Margretta Davies 1957; ed. Tregaron Co. School, Univ. Coll. of Wales and Wycliffe Hall, Oxford; Curate of Lampeter 1950–56; Vicar of Eglwyswrw with Meline 1956–59, Tregaron 1959–67, Dewi Sant 1967–76; Rector, Aberystwyth 1976–80; Canon, St. David's Cathedral 1977–79; Archdeacon of Cardigan 1979–82; Vicar of Llanychaearn with Llanddeiniol 1980–82; Bishop of St. Davids 1982–91; Archbishop of Wales 1987–91; Hon. D.D. (Univ. of Wales). *Leisure interest:* angling. Address: Hafodlon, Rhydargaeau, Carmarthen, Dyfed, SA32 7DT, Wales. *Telephone:* (01267) 253302.

NOAKES, Michael; British portrait and landscape painter; b. 28 Oct. 1933, Brighton, Sussex; s. of late Basil Noakes and Mary Noakes; m. Vivien Langley 1960; two s. one d.; ed. Downside, Reigate School of Art, The Royal Acad. Schools; mil. service 1954–56; has painted numerous portraits of mems. of royal family including Queen Elizabeth II, Queen Elizabeth The Queen Mother, Prince of Wales, Prince Philip, the Duke and Duchess of York, the Princess Royal, Princess Margaret, The Duchess of Kent, Princess Alice Countess of Athlone, and of other leading figures, including Earl Mountbatten, Earl of Snowdon, Lady Thatcher as Prime Minister, President Clinton, Archbishop Hope when Bishop of London, Duke of Norfolk, Cardinal Hume, Lord Aberconway, Princess Ashraf of Iran, Lord Charteris, Lord Denning, Sir Alec Guinness, Haham Dr. Solomon Gaon, Gen. Sir John Hackett, Robert Hardy, Cliff Michelmore, Robert Morley, Malcolm Muggeridge, Airey Neave, Valerie Hobson Profumo, Sir Ralph Richardson, Lord Runcie when Archbishop of Canterbury, Dame Margaret Rutherford, Dennis Wheatley, Sir Mortimer Wheeler, etc.; exhbns. internationally, including Royal Acad., Royal Inst. of Oil Painters, Royal Soc. of British Artists, of Marine Artists, of Portrait Painters, Nat. Soc. etc.; represented in perm. collections, The Queen, The Prince of Wales, The British Museum, Nat. Portrait Gallery, House of Commons, Frank Sinatra, etc.; mem. Royal Inst. of Oil Painters 1964, Vice-Pres. 1968–72, Pres. 1972–78, Hon. mem. Council 1978–; mem. Royal Soc. of Portrait Painters 1967–, served Council, 1969–71, 1972–74, 1978–80, 1993–95; Gov. Fed. of British Artists 1972–83, a dir. 1981–83; Freeman City of London; Liveryman Co. of Woolmen; Hon. mem. numerous socs. including Nat. Soc., United Soc.; fmr. Chair. Contemporary Portrait Soc.; Platinum Disc Award for record sleeve, Portrait of Sinatra 1977; designed Crown Piece (£5 coin) as a mark of 50th Birthday of Prince of Wales and the work of the Prince's Trust 1998; throughout 1999 will be illustrating The Working Life of Queen Elizabeth II. *Publications:* A Professional Approach to Oil Painting 1968, numerous contribs. to art journals and books on art; has broadcast frequently in U.K. and also in U.S.A. on art subjects. *Leisure interest:* idling. *Address:* 146 Hamilton Terrace, St. John's Wood, London, NW8 9UX, England. *Telephone:* 0171-328 6754. *Fax:* 0171-625 1220.

NOBILO, Mario, M.A., PH.D.; Croatian diplomatist; b. 15 June 1952, Lumbarda, Korcula Island; s. of Donko I. Nobilo and Frana Mušić; m. Ljerkica Šegota 1979; one s. one d.; ed. Univ. of Zagreb; Research Assoc. Dept. of Political and Strategic Studies, Inst. for Int. Relations, Zagreb 1979–89; Guest Prof. in U.S.A., Germany and Spain 1985–90; co-founder and Vice-Pres. Croatian Council of European Movt. 1990–92; Spokesman and Foreign Policy Adviser to Pres. of Croatia 1991–92; Perm. Rep. of Croatia to UN 1992–96, to CSCE 1996–; Decoration of Homeland War 1993. *Publications:* Western Sahara 1984, Namibia 1985, South Africa 1986, Atlas 1989, War Against Croatia 1992. *Leisure interests:* diving, fishing, sailing, do-it-yourself skills.

NOBLE, Adrian Keith, B.A.; British theatre director; b. 19 July 1950; s. of late William John Noble and of Violet Ena (née Wells) Noble; m. Joanne Pearce 1991; one d. one s.; ed. Chichester High School for Boys, Bristol Univ. and Drama Centre, London; Assoc. Dir. Bristol Old Vic 1976–79; Resident Dir. Royal Shakespeare Co. (RSC) 1980–82, Assoc. Dir. 1982–90, Artistic Dir. April 1991–; Guest Dir. Royal Exchange Theatre, Man. 1980–81; Hon. D.Litt. (Birmingham) 1994, (Bristol) 1996. *Stage productions include:* Ubu Rex 1977, A Man's a Man 1977, A View from a Bridge 1978, Titus Adronicus 1978, The Changeling 1978, Love for Love 1979, Timon of Athens 1979, Recruiting Officer 1979, Duchess of Malfi 1980, Dr Faustus 1981, The Forest 1981, A Doll's House 1981, King Lear 1982, Antony and Cleopatra 1982, A New Way to Pay Old Debts 1983, Comedy of Errors 1983, Measure for Measure 1983, Henry V 1984, The Winter's Tale 1984, As You Like It 1985, Mephisto 1986, The Art of Success 1986, Macbeth 1986, Kiss Me Kate 1987, The Plantagenets 1989, The Master Builder 1989, The Fairy Queen, The Three Sisters 1990, Henry IV (parts 1 and 2) 1991, The Thebans 1991, Hamlet, Winter's Tale 1992, Travesties, King Lear, Macbeth 1993, A Midsummer Night's Dream 1994, Romeo and Juliet 1995, The Cherry Orchard 1995, Little Eyolf 1996, Cymbeline 1997, Twelfth Night 1997, The Tempest 1998, Don Giovanni (Kent Opera) 1983; dir. film of A Midsummer Night's Dream 1995. *Address:* Barbican Theatre, London EC2Y 8BQ, England.

NOBLE, Denis, C.B.E., PH.D., F.R.S., F.R.C.P.; British professor of physiology; b. 16 Nov. 1936, London; s. of George Noble and Ethel Rutherford; m. Susan Jennifer Barfield 1965; one s. (adopted) one d.; ed. Emanuel School and Univ. Coll. London; Asst. Lecturer Univ. Coll. London 1961–63; Fellow, Lecturer and Tutor in Physiology Balliol Coll., Oxford 1963–84, Praefectus Balliol Graduate Centre 1971–89, Burdon Sanderson Prof. of Cardiovascular Physiology, Oxford Univ. 1984–, Professorial Fellow 1984–; Visiting Prof., Alberta 1969–70; Ed. Progress in Biophysics 1967–; Founder Dir. Oxsoft Ltd. 1984–, Physiome Sciences Inc. 1994–, Chair. Jt. Dental Cttee. 1984–90; Pres. Medical Section British Asscn. 1992; Gen.-Sec. Int. Union of Physiological Sciences 1993–; Hon. Sec. Physiological Soc. 1974–80, Foreign Sec. 1986–92; Darwin Lecturer British Asscn. 1966; Nahum Lecturer Yale Univ. 1977; Hon. mem. Acad. de Medécine de Belgique; Fellow University Coll., London 1986; Lloyd Roberts Lecturer 1987; Bowden Lecturer, Alderdale Wyld Lecturer 1988; Hon. F.R.C.P., Hon. mem. American Physiological Soc.; Hon. mem. Academia Europaea 1989, Hon. mem. Japanese Physiological Soc. 1998, The Physiological Soc. 1999; Scientific Medal, Zoological Soc. 1970, British Heart Foundation Gold Medal and Prize 1985, Pierre Rijlant Prize (Belgian Royal Acad.) 1991, Baly Medal, Royal Coll. of Physicians (London) 1993. *Publications:* Initiation of the Heartbeat 1975, Electric Current Flow in Excitable Cells 1975, Electrophysiology of Single Cardiac Cells 1987, Goals, No Goals and Own Goals 1989, Sodium-Calcium Exchange 1989, Logic of Life 1993, Ionic Channels and the effect of taurine on the heart 1993, Ethics of Life 1997; scientific papers mostly in Journal of Physiology. *Leisure interests:* Occitan language and music, Indian and French cooking, classical guitar. *Address:* 49 Old Road, Oxford, OX3 7JZ, England. *Telephone:* (01865) 272533 (Office); (01865) 762237 (Home).

NODA, Seiko; Japanese politician; b. 1961; ed. Sophia Univ.; fmr. mem. staff Imperial Hotel; elected mem. Gifu Prefectural Ass. 1987; mem. LDP; mem. for Gifu, House of Reps.; fmr. Parl. Vice-Minister of Posts and Telecommunications, Minister 1998–. *Address:* Ministry of Posts and Telecommunications, 1-3-2, Kasumigaseki, Chiyoda-ku, Tokyo 100, Japan. *Telephone:* (03) 3504-4411. *Fax:* (03) 3504-0265.

NODA, Takeshi; Japanese politician; mem. House of Reps., constituency Kumamoto-1; Chair. Liberal Democratic Party (LDP) Nat. Campaign HQ., Cttee. on Commerce and Industry House of Reps.; fmr. Construction Minister, LDP Deputy Sec. Gen.; Dir. Gen. Econ. Planning Agency (State Minister) 1991–92; Minister for Home Affairs 1999–. *Address:* Ministry of Home Affairs, 2-1-2 Kasumigaseki, Chiyoda-ku, Tokyo 100, Japan.

NODA, Tetsuya, M.A.; Japanese print-making artist and university professor; b. 5 March 1940, Kumamoto Pref.; s. of Tesshin Noda and Sakae Noda; m. Dorit Bartur 1971; one s. one d.; ed. Tokyo Nat. Univ. of Fine Art and Music; Visiting Artist at Alberta Univ., Canada 1984, Betzalel Art Acad., Israel 1985, Canberra Art School, Australia 1990, Columbia Univ., U.S.A. 1998; Prof. Tokyo Nat. Univ. of Fine Arts and Music 1990–; mem. Int. Jury for the British Int. Print Biennale 1976, Korean Int. Print Biennale 1996; one-man shows Fuji TV Gallery 1978, 1983, 1987, 1992; numerous group exhbns. including São Paulo Biennale 1971, Venice Biennale (Graphic Int.) 1972, The Mechanized Image (touring), U.K., Printed Art, A View of Two Decades, Museum of Modern Art, New York 1980, Japanese Prints since 1900, British Museum, London; prizes include Int. Grand Prize (Tokyo Int. Print Biennale) 1968, Grand Prize (Ljubljana Int. Print Biennale) 1977 and Grand Prize of Honour 1987, Grand Prize (Norwegian Int. Print Biennale) 1978, Friends of Bradford Art Galleries and Museum Prize (British Int. Print Biennale) 1986, Gen Yamaguchi Memorial Grand Prize, City of Numazu 1993. *Publications:* several woodcut and silkscreen prints. *Leisure interest:* gardening. *Address:* 2-12-4 Kikkodai, Kashiwa-shi, Chiba-ken, 299-0031, Japan. *Telephone:* (0471) 63-5332. *Fax:* (0471) 63-5332.

NOE PINO, Hugo, PH.D.; Honduran economist; b. 11 Jan. 1955, Tegucigalpa; s. of Roberto Noe and Elidia Pino; m. Vivian Bustamante; two s. one d.; ed. Universidad Nacional Autonoma de Honduras (UNAH), Univ. of Texas at Austin, U.S.A.; fmr. teaching asst., Dept. of Econs., Univ. of Tex.; Pres. Cen. Bank of Honduras 1994–97; Dir. Master's Programme in Econs. for Cen. American and Caribbean Region, UNAH; Pres. Asscn. of Economists of Honduras; mem. Editorial Council of various magazines published in Honduras; Spokesman of Shadow Cabinet 1993. *Publications:* An Assessment of the Campesino Associative Enterprise of Isletas 1987, Honduras: Structural Adjustment and Agrarian Reform 1992. *Leisure interests:* reading, music. *Address:* c/o Banco Central de Honduras, 6a. Y 7a. Ave., la Cll. Apdo. 58-C, Tegucigalpa, Honduras.

NOELLE-NEUMANN, Elisabeth, DR.PHIL.; German professor of communications research; b. 19 Dec. 1916, Berlin; d. of Dr. Ernst Noelle and Eva Schaper; m. 1st Erich P. Neumann 1946 (died 1973); m. 2nd Heinz Maier-Leibnitz 1979; ed. Univ. of Berlin; f. and Dir. Inst. für Demoskopie Allensbach (first German survey research inst.) 1947–; Lecturer in Communications Research, Free Univ. of Berlin 1961–64; Prof. of Communications Research, Univ. of Mainz 1964–, also Dir. Inst. für Publizistik (until 1983); Visiting Prof., Dept. of Political Science, Univ. of Chicago 1978–91, Univ. of Munich 1993–94; Hon. Prof. Moscow External Univ. of the Humanities; Co-Ed. Int. Journal of Public Opinion Research; Dr.oec. h.c. (St. Gallen); Grosses Bundesverdienstkreuz. *Publications include:* Allensbacher Jahrbücher der Demoskopie (10 vols.) (Ed.) 1947–97, Fischer Lexikon Publizistik—Massenkommunikation (Co-Ed.) 1971, 1989, 1994, 1996, Umfragen in der Massengesellschaft: Einführung in die Methoden der Demoskopie 1963, revised edn., Alle, nicht jeder. Einführung in die Methoden der Demoskopie (with T. Petersen) 1996, Öffentlichkeit als Bedrohung 1977, 1979, Die Schweigespirale: Öffentliche Meinung—unsere soziale Haut 1980, Macht Arbeit krank? Macht Arbeit glücklich? 1984 (with B. Strümpel), The Spiral of Silence, Public Opinion—Our Social Skin 1984, 1986, 1993, Die verletzte Nation (with R. Köcher) 1987, Öffentliche Meinung Die Entdeckung der Schweigespirale 1989, 1991, 1996, Demoskopische Geschichtsstunde 1991. *Address:* Institut für Demoskopie Allensbach, Radolfzeller Str. 8, 78476 Allensbach am Bodensee, Germany. *Telephone:* 07533/8050. *Fax:* 07533/3048.

NOELTE, Rudolf; German producer; b. 20 March 1921, Berlin; m. Cordula Trantow; two s.; productions in Berlin, Hamburg, Düsseldorf, Cologne, Frankfurt, Munich, Stuttgart, Vienna, Salzburg, Cardiff and London of works by Sophocles, Shakespeare, Schiller, Goethe, Dürrenmatt, Kafka, Ibsen etc. since 1948; TV producer 1956–; film producer 1968–; opera producer (including works by Mozart, Tchaikovsky, Weber, Smetana and Berg) 1970–; Preis des Verbandes der deutschen Kritiker, Kunstpreis der Stadt Berlin; Bayerischer Maximiliansorden für Wissenschaft und Kunst; Bundesverdienstkreuz. *Address:* Roseweg 4, 86938 Schondorf, Germany. *Telephone:* 08192-8350.

NOGUCHI, Teruhisa, PH.D.; Japanese business executive; b. 22 Oct. 1924, Chiba Pref.; m.; one s. three d.; ed. Schools of Medicine, Kanazawa and Tokyo Univs.; with Nihon Soda Co. 1949–72; with Teijin Ltd. 1972–79, Dir. 1973, Dir. Teijin Inst. for Biomedical Research 1976; with Suntory Ltd. 1979–92, Dir. 1979, Exec. Man. Pharmaceutical Div. 1981, Sr. Man. Dir. 1987–, Chief Exec. 1991; Exec. Vice-Pres. Yamanouchi Pharmaceutical Co. Ltd. 1992–; Adjunct Prof., The Rockefeller Univ. 1984–; Fellow American Acad. of Microbiology; several prizes and awards. *Publications include:* Biochemistry of Interferons 1982, New Trends in Neuro-Science 1984. *Leisure interests:* fine arts, golf. *Address:* 2-18-11, Kugenuma Kaigan, Fujisawa City, Kanagawa Prefecture 251, Japan. *Telephone:* 0466 (36) 4736. *Fax:* 0466 (33) 7708.

NOGUEIRA, Albano Pires Fernandes; Portuguese diplomatist, writer and literary critic; b. 8 Nov. 1911, Arganil; s. of Albano P. D. Nogueira and Albertina F. Nogueira; m. Alda Xavier da Cunha 1937 (died 1998); ed. Coimbra Univ.; entered Diplomatic Service 1941; posts in embassy in Washington, and legation in Pretoria 1944–49; Chargé d'Affaires and Rep. to Allied High Comm. in Japan 1950–52, Rep. of Portuguese Govt. to Japanese Govt. 1952; Counsellor, London 1952; Consul-Gen., Bombay 1955, New York 1955; Deputy Perm. Rep., Mission of Portugal at UN 1955–59; Amb. to EEC 1964; Perm. Rep. to North Atlantic Council 1970–74; Amb. to U.K. 1974–76; Sec.-Gen. Ministry of Foreign Affairs 1977–78; Visiting Prof. Univ. of Minho 1979–80; mem. Int. Asscn. of Literary Critics 1981–. *Publications:* a novel, two books of essays, contribs. to books on NATO, book reviews. *Leisure interests:* writing, reading. *Address:* Avenida Gaspar Corte Real 18, Apt. 4D, 2750 Cascais; Rua Alberto de Oliveira, 5-3, 3000 Coimbra, Portugal. *Telephone:* Cascais 4868264; Coimbra 715035.

NOGUEIRA, Dênio Chagas; Brazilian economist; b. 12 Dec. 1920, Rio de Janeiro; s. of Outubrino Nogueira and Anna Cândida Nogueira: m. Orsina de Fonseca 1956; one s. one d.; ed. Universidade do Brasil and Univ. of Michigan; Head, Finance Dept. Nat. Econ. Council 1951–64; Ed.-in-Chief Conjuntura Econômica 1953; Econ. Consultant to Econ. Comm. for Latin America and OAS on Foreign Investments in Latin American Free Trade Asscn. 1960, to OAS on the Treaty of Montevideo (LAFTA) 1961; Exec. Dir. Superintendency of Money and Credit, Brazil (SUMOC) 1964–65; fmr. Pres. Banco Central do Brasil; Pres. Banco Geral do Brasil. *Publications:* Joint International Business Ventures in Brazil 1959, Foreign Private Investments in LAFTA 1960, Reforma Agraria: Problemas e Soluções 1964. *Leisure interests:* tennis, yachting. *Address:* Banco Geral do Brasil, S.A., Belém, Brazil.

NOGUEIRA, Joaquim Fernando; LL.B.; Portuguese politician; b. Matosinhos, Oporto; m.; four c.; ed. Coimbra Univ.; fmr. Minister for the Presidency and Minister of Justice; fmr. Minister for the Presidency and Minister of Defence; First Vice-Pres. Nat. Political Comm. of Partido Social Democrata (PSD), Political Dir., Leader of PSD 1995–96. *Address:* Partido Social Democrata, Rua de São Caetano 9, 1296 Lisbon Codex, Portugal.

NOGUEIRA-BATISTA, Paulo, M.A.; Brazilian diplomatist; b. 4 Oct. 1929, Recife; m.; four c.; ed. Univ. of Rio de Janeiro and Carleton Univ.; entered Foreign Service 1952; First Sec. Brazilian Embassy, Ottawa 1964–66; Minister-Counsellor, Bonn 1969–70; Head Brazilian Del. to Preparatory Cttee., Tokyo Round of Trade Negotiations, Geneva 1973; Chief Negotiator Tripartite Agreement on Safeguards for the Peaceful Uses of Nuclear Energy between Brazil, the Fed. Repub. of Germany and the IAEA, Vienna 1985; Head. Brazilian Del. ECOSOC, Geneva and UNCTAD 1983–86; Chair. Negotiating Cttee., Gen. System of Trade Preferences among Developing Countries, Geneva March-Oct. 1986; Amb. to UN Office, Geneva 1983–87; Perm. Rep. to UN 1987; Pres. and Chair. Bd. of the Brazilian State Corpn. for Nuclear Activities (NUCLEBRAS) 1975–82. *Address:* c/o Ministry of Foreign Affairs, Palacio do Itamaraty, Esplanada dos Ministérios 70.047 Brasília, DF, Brasil.

NOIRET, Philippe; French actor; b. 1 Oct. 1930, Lille; s. of Pierre Noiret and Lucy Heirman; m. Monique Chaumette 1962; one s.; ed. Lycée Janson-de-Sailly, Paris and Coll. des oratoriens, Juilly; Prix Orange 1972, César for Le vieux fusil 1976, Best Actor at Rio de Janiero Film Festival for Les Ripoux 1984, David Award, Best Foreign Actor for Life and Nothing But 1990. *Stage appearances include:* la Nuit des rois, le Cid, Richard II, Drôle de couple. *Films include:* La Pointe courte 1954, Zazie dans le métro, les Amours célèbres, Tout l'or du monde, Thérèse Desqueyroux, Ballade pour un voyou, Clementine chérie 1963, Cyrano et d'Artagnan, Monsieur 1964, L'une et l'autre 1967, Le vieux fusil 1975, Le taxi mauve, Une semaine de vacances 1980, Les Ripoux 1984, Masques 1987, La femme de mes amours 1989, La vie et rien d'autre (Life and Nothing But) 1989, Cinema Paradiso 1989, Ripoux contre ripoux 1990, Oublier Palerme 1990, Faux et usage de faux 1990, Le Cop 2 1991, J'embarrasse pas 1991, Nous deux 1992, Le Chien leu 1992, Max et Jérémie 1992, Tango 1993, Il Postino 1995, D'Artagnan's Daughter 1995, Le Roi de Paris 1995, les Grands ducs 1996, Fantôme avec chauffeur 1996, Les Palmes de M. Schultz 1997. *Address:* 104 rue des Sablons, 78750 Mareil-Marly, France.

NØJGAARD, Morten, D.PHIL.; Danish professor of romance philology; b. 28 July 1934, Holbaek; s. of Niels Nøjgaard and Annie (née Bay) Nøjgaard; m. Stina Lund 1962; two s. two d.; secondary school teacher Roedovre Statskole 1960–63; research scholar Univ. of Copenhagen 1963–65; Prof. of Romance Philology, Univ. of Odense 1966–; Chief Ed. Orbis Litterarum 1968–; Pres. Asscn. of French Prof. 1962–63, Alliance Française, Odense 1970–; mem. Soc. of Letters (Lund, Sweden) 1978, Royal Danish Acad. of Science 1982, Royal Norwegian Acad. of Science 1991, Royal Swedish Acad. of Antiquities 1997; Fnske Bladfond Research Award 1975, Ordre du Mérite 1980. *Publications:* La Fable Antique, (vols I–II) 1964–67, Elévation et Expansion. Les deux dimensions de Baudelaire 1973, An Introduction to Literary Analysis 1975, Romain-Gary-Emile Ajar, Homo Duplex 1986, Les Adverbes français, Vol. I 1992, Vol. II 1993, Vol. III 1995, Plaisir et vérité, Le paradoxe de l'évaluation littéraire 1993; numerous scientific articles.

Address: Aløkken 48, 5250 Odense SV, Denmark. *Telephone:* 65 96 18 06. *Fax:* 65 93 51 49.

NOLAN, Baron (Life Peer), cr. 1994, of Brasted in the County of Kent; **Michael Patrick Nolan,** Kt., P.C.; British judge; b. 10 Sept. 1928; s. of James T. Nolan and Jane Walsh; m. Margaret Noyes 1953; one s. four d.; ed. Ampleforth and Wadham Coll. Oxford; called to Bar, Middle Temple 1953, Bencher 1975; Q.C. 1968; called to Bar, N. Ireland 1974; Q.C. (N.I.) 1974; a Recorder of Crown Court 1975–82; Judge, High Court of Justice, Queen's Bench Div. 1982–91; Presiding Judge, Western Circuit 1985–88; Lord Justice of Appeal 1991–93; a Lord of Appeal in Ordinary 1994–98; Chair. Comm. of Inquiry into Standards in Public Life 1994–97; Chair. Bd. Inst. of Advanced Legal Studies 1994–; Chancellor Essex Univ. 1997–; Dr. h.c. (Essex) 1996, (Surrey) 1996, LL.D (Warwick) 1998. *Leisure interest:* fishing. *Address:* House of Lords, London, SW1A 0PW, England.

NOLAND, Kenneth Clifton; American artist; b. 10 April 1927, Asheville, N.C.; s. of Harry C. and Bessie (Elkins) Noland; m. 1st Cornelia Langel (divorced); one s. two d.; m. 2nd Stephanie Gordon 1967; m. 3rd Peggy Schiffer (divorced); one s.; m. 4th Paige Rense 1994; ed. Black Mountain Coll., North Carolina and Paris; Teacher Inst. of Contemporary Arts 1950–52, Catholic Univ. 1951–60, Bennington Coll. 1968; one-man shows: Galerie Creuze, Paris 1949, Tibor de Nagy, New York 1957, 1958, French and Co., New York 1959, André Emmerich Gallery, New York 1967, 1973, 1975, 1977–78 1980–83, 1988, 1998, André Emmerich Gallery, Zürich 1973, 1976, 1979, 1982, Nicholas Wilder Gallery, Los Angeles 1967, Salander New York 1989, 1991, O'Reilly Galleries, Gana Art Gallery, Seoul, Korea 1995, also Toronto, Florida, Atlanta, Houston, Beverly Hills, Berlin, Edmonton, Madrid, Milan, Paris, London; work in permanent collections in Museum of Modern Art, Guggenheim Museum, Whitney Museum, Tate Gallery, Stedelijk Museum (Amsterdam), Zürich Kunsthaus and others. *Address:* North Bennington, VT 05257, U.S.A.

NOLL, João Gilberto, B.A.; Brazilian writer; b. 15 April 1946, Porto Alegre; s. of João Noll and Ecila Noll; columnist Folha de São Paulo newspaper; writer-in-residence Univ. of Calif. at Berkeley, also teaching Brazilian Literature 1996, 1997, 1998; Prêmio Jabuti on three occasions. *Publications:* (short stories) O cego e a dançarina; (novels) A fúria do corpo, Bandoleiros, Hotel Atlântico, Harmada, Boulevard. *Leisure interests:* music, travelling. *Address:* Rua Antônio da Silveira 282, C.P. 88062-100, Lagoa da Conceição, Florianópolis, S.C., Brazil. *Telephone:* (48) 2321079.

NOLTE, Nick; American film actor; b. 1942, Omaha; m. Rebecca Linger 1984 (divorced 1995); one s.; ed. Pasadena City Coll., Phoenix City Coll.; stage appearance in The Last Pad 1973; television films 1974–75 and drama series Rich Man, Poor Man 1976; also appeared in repertory groups. *Films:* Return to Macon County 1975, The Deep 1977, Who'll Stop the Rain 1978, North Dallas Forty 1979, Heartbeat 1980, Cannery Row 1982, 48 Hours 1982, Under Fire 1983, The Ultimate Solution of Grace Quigley 1984, Teachers 1984, Down and Out in Beverly Hills 1986, Weeds 1987, Extreme Prejudice 1987, Farewell to the King 1989, New York Stories 1989, Three Fugitives, Everybody Wins, Q & A 1990, Prince of Tides 1990, Cape Fear 1991, Lorenzo's Oil 1992, Blue Chips 1994, I'll Do Anything 1994, Love Trouble 1994, Jefferson in Paris 1994, Mulholland Falls 1996, Mother Night 1996, Afterglow 1997, Affliction 1998, U-Turn, Breakfast of Champions 1998, The Thin Red Line 1998. *Address:* 6153 Bonsall Drive, Malibu, CA 90265, U.S.A.

NOMIYAMA, Akihiko, LL.B.; Japanese business executive; b. 15 June 1934, Fukuoka Pref.; one s. one d.; ed. Tokyo Univ.; joined Nippon Mining Co. 1957, assignments in budget control, corp. financing, Gen. Man. Admin. Dept., Petroleum Operation 1981–92, Man. Dir. Japan Energy Corpn. (formed from merger with Kyodo Oil Co.) 1992–96, Pres., C.E.O. and Dir. 1996–; Vice-Chair. Petroleum Asscn. of Japan. *Leisure interests:* golf, classical music. *Address:* Japan Energy Corporation, 10-1 Toranomon, 2-chome, Minato-ku, Tokyo 105, Japan.

NOMURA, Masayasu, PH.D.; Japanese molecular biologist and academic; b. 27 April 1927, Hyogo-ken; s. of Hiromichi Nomura and Yaeko Nomura; m. Junko Hamashima 1957; one s. one d.; ed. Univ. of Tokyo; Research Assoc., Prof. S. Spiegelman's Lab., Univ. of Ill. and Prof. J. D. Watson's Lab., Harvard Univ. 1957–59, Prof. S. Benzer's Lab., Purdue Univ. 1959–60; Asst. Prof., Inst. for Protein Research, Osaka Univ. 1960–63; Assoc. Prof., Dept. of Genetics, Univ. of Wis. 1963–66, Prof. 1966–70, Elvehjem Prof. of Life Sciences, Inst. for Enzyme Research, with jt. appts. in Depts. of Genetics and Biochem. 1970–84, Grace Bell Prof. of Biological Chem., Univ. of Calif., Irvine 1984–; Fellow A.A.A.S.; mem. American Acad. of Arts and Sciences, N.A.S.; Foreign mem. Royal Danish Acad. of Sciences and Letters, Royal Netherlands Acad. of Arts and Sciences; U.S. Steel Award in Molecular Biology (N.A.S.), Japan Acad. Award 1972, Y. D. Mattia Award (Roche Ints.). *Leisure interests:* hiking, reading. *Address:* University of California, Department of Biological Chemistry, Med. Sci. I, D240, Irvine, CA 92697-1700 (Office); 74 Whitman Court, Irvine, CA 92612, U.S.A. (Home). *Telephone:* (714) 824-4564 (Office); (714) 854-3482 (Home).

NOMURA, Yoshihiro; Japanese professor of law; b. 3 Jan. 1941, Nagoya City; s. of Akio Nomura and Michiko Nomura; m. 1966; three s. one d.; ed. Univ. of Tokyo; Asst. Researcher in Law, Univ. of Tokyo 1963; Lecturer Tokyo Metropolitan Univ. 1966, Assoc. Prof. 1967, Prof. of Civil and Environmental Law 1977–. *Publication:* Automobile Accident Damages 1970, Environmental Law 1981. *Leisure interests:* nature watching, driving. *Address:* Faculty of Law, Tokyo Metropolitan University, Minami-Ohsawa 1-1, Hachiohji-City, Tokyo 192-03, Japan. *Telephone:* (045) 973-2612. *Fax:* (045) 972-0592.

NONAKA, Hiromu; Japanese politician; fmr. Vice-Gov. Kyoto Pref.; Minister of Home Affairs 1994–95; mem. House of Reps. for Kyoto; Dir.-Gen. LDP Election Bureau. *Address:* c/o Ministry of Home Affairs, 2-1, Kasumigaseki, Chiyoda-ku, Tokyo, Japan.

NOOR, Dato Mohamad Yusof, M.A., PH.D.; Malaysian politician and teacher; b. 5 Feb. 1941, Raja, Terangganu; m.; two c.; ed. Islamic Coll., Klang, Selangor, Al Azhar Univ., Ein Shams Univ. and Univ. of Cairo; secondary school teacher 1969–70; Insp. of Secondary Schools, Terengganu State 1970; Prin., Sultan Zainal Abidin Secondary Religious School 1970; lecturer and Head of Coll., Nat. Univ. of Malaysia 1974, Dean, Faculty of Islamic Studies 1975–79, Deputy Vice-Chancellor for Student Affairs 1980–84; mem. Senate 1984; Deputy Minister responsible for Islamic Affairs, Prime Minister's Dept. 1984; mem. House of Reps. 1987–; mem. Supreme Council, United Malays Nat. Org. (UMNO) 1987–; Minister, Prime Minister's Dept. 1987; Chair. Religious Council for Fed. Territory; many other appts. in Islamic and religious field. *Publications:* numerous articles in fields of educ. and Islamic affairs. *Address:* c/o House of Representatives, Parliament Building, Kuala Lumpur, Malaysia.

NOOR AL-HUSSEIN, H.M. Queen of Jordan, B.A.; b. Lisa Najeeb Halaby, 23 Aug. 1951; m. King Hussein I of Jordan (died 1999) 1978; four c.; ed. Princeton Univ.; architectural and urban planning projects in Australia, Iran and Jordan 1974–78; f. in Jordan: Royal Endowment for Culture and Educ. 1979, annual Arab Children's Congress 1980, annual int. Jerash Festival for Culture and Arts 1981, Jubilee School 1984, Noor Al-Hussein Foundation 1985, Nat. Music Conservatory 1986; Chair. Nat. Task Force for Children, Advisory Cttee. for UN Univ. Int. Leadership Acad., Amman; Patron, Gen. Fed. of Jordanian Women, Nat. Fed. of Business and Professional Women's Clubs, Royal Soc. for Conservation of Nature and various cultural, sports and nat. devt. orgs.; Hon. Pres. Jordan Red Crescent; Patron, Int. Union for Conservation of Nature and Natural Resources 1988, Landmine Survivors Network 1998; founding mem. Int. Comm. on Peace and Food 1992; Pres. United World Colls. 1995; Dir. Hunger Project; Hon. Pres. Birdlife Int. 1996–; mem. Int. Eye Foundation Hon. Bd.; mem. Gen. Ass. SOS-Kinderdorf Int.; mem. Int. Council Near East Foundation; Trustee Mentor Foundation; many other affiliations; numerous hon. doctorates, int. awards and decorations for promotion of environmental conservation and awareness, econ. and social devt. of women, children and communities, cross cultural exchange, int. understanding and world peace. *Leisure interests:* skiing, riding, tennis, sailing, reading, photography. *Address:* Royal Palace, Amman, Jordan.

NORA, Simon, L. EN D.; French government official; b. 21 Feb. 1921, Paris; s. of Gaston Nora and Julie Lehman; m. 1st Marie-Pierre de Cosse-Brissac (divorced); one s. one d.; m. 2nd Léone Georges-Picot 1955; one s. two d.; ed. Lycée Janson-de-Sailly, Paris, Facultés de droit et des lettres, Grenoble and Paris, and Ecole nat. d'Admin.; Insp. of Finance 1949, Insp.-Gen. 1971; held various posts in Ministry of Finance 1951–60, 1963–71; Dir–Gen. econ. and energy service, European Coal and Steel Community 1960–63; interministerial del. for colour TV 1967–71; mem. supervisory council, Entreprise minière et chimique 1967–71; in office of PM Jacques Chaban-Delmas 1969–71; Dir.-Gen. Librarie Hachette 1971–74; Dir. Soc. d'études de télévision (Télétudes) 1971–74; Cie. luxembourgeoise de télédiffusion 1972–75; Dir. Ecole nat. d'Admin. 1982–85, France Télécom 1995–, Air France 1995–; Sr. Adviser, Shearson Lehman Brothers Int. 1986, Pres. Advisory Council, Admin. Council Banque Lehman Brothers 1987–95, Sr. Advisor for Europe 1995–; mem. council of ordre nat. de la Légion d'honneur 1989; Commdr., Légion d'honneur (mem. Council 1989–), des Palmes académiques; Croix de guerre; Commdr. Order of Merit (Italy). *Publications:* Rapport sur les entreprises publiques 1967, l'Amélioration de l'habitat ancien (in collab.) 1976, Informatisation de la société (in collab.) 1978. *Address:* 1 Avenue de l'Observatoire, 75006 Paris, France.

NORDAL, Jóhannes, PH.D.; Icelandic economist and banker; b. 11 May 1924, Reykjavík; s. of Prof. Sigurdur Nordal and Olöf Jónsdóttir; m. Dóra Gudjónsdóttir 1953; one s. five d.; ed. Reykjavík Grammar School and L.S.E., London; Chief Economist, Nat. Bank of Iceland 1954–59, Gen. Man. 1959–61; Gov., Central Bank of Iceland (Sedlabanki Islands) 1961–93, (Chair. Bd. of Governors 1964–93); Chair. of Bd. Nat. Power Co. (Landsvirkjun) 1965–96; Gov. IMF for Iceland 1965–93; Ed. Fjármálatíáindi (Financial Review) 1954–94; Co.-Ed. Nýtt Helgafell (literary periodical) 1955–59; Chair. Humanities Div. of Science Fund for Iceland 1958–87, Icelandic Council of Science 1987–, Nat. Library Bd. 1994–; mem. Soc. Scientiarum Islandica 1959–; Grand Kt. Order of Falcon 1966. *Publications:* Iceland 1966, 1974, 1986. *Address:* Sedlabanki Islands, Kalkofnsvegur 1, 150 Reykjavík (Office); Laugarásvegur 11, Reykjavík, Iceland (Home). *Telephone:* 699600 (Office); 33350 (Home).

NORDHAGEN, Per Jonas, D.PHIL.; Norwegian professor of the history of art; b. 30 Oct. 1929, Bergen; s. of Rolf Nordhagen and Elisabeth M. Myhre; m. Inger K. Noss 1978; one s. four d.; ed. Univ. of Oslo; Lecturer, Univ. of Oslo 1962; Assoc. Prof. Univ. of Bergen 1969; Dir. Norwegian Inst. Rome

1973; Sr. Lecturer, Univ. of Oslo 1977; Prof. of History of Art, Univ. of Bergen 1986–; mem. Norwegian Acad. of Sciences. *Publications:* The Frescoes of John VII (705–707 AD) in S. Maria Antiqua, Rome 1968, S. Maria Antiqua, Frescoes of the Seventh Century 1978, The Capri Papers (novel) 1986, Collected Papers in the History of Byzantine and Early Medieval Art 1990, Bergen—Guide and Handbook 1992, The Wooden Architecture of Bergen 1994, The Technique of Early Christian and Byzantine Mosaics 1997, Art and Architecture of Norway, an Outline 1997. *Leisure interests:* skiing, hiking, books, botany. *Address:* Institute of Art History, University of Bergen, Parkv. 22B, 5014 Bergen, Norway. *Telephone:* 55 58 24 76. *Fax:* 55 58 96 57.

NORDHEIM, Arne; Norwegian composer; b. 20 June 1931, Larvik; m. 1st 1956; m. 2nd 1981; two c.; ed. Oslo Conservatory of Music and electronic music studies in Paris, Utrecht, Warsaw and Stockholm; began to compose 1950; first major work Stringquartett 1956; since composed seven works for orchestra and solo instruments, and symphonic music, voice or electronic sound and one ballet score; worked as music critic for several daily newspapers 1959–67; Nordic Council Music Prize 1972, Prix Italia 1980, awarded Norwegian State Residence of Honour 1982, Steffens Prize 1993; Commdr. Order of St. Olav 1997. *Address:* Wergelandsveien 2, 0167 Oslo, Norway. *Telephone:* (47) 22 11 2827. *Fax:* (47) 22 11 3847.

NORDLI, Odvar; Norwegian politician; b. 3 Nov. 1927, Stange, Hedmark; ed. in business admin.; Asst. Baerum Municipal Auditor's Office 1948–49; Chief Clerk, Hedmark County Auditor's Office 1949–57; Dist. Auditor, Vang and Löten 1957–61; mem. Storting (Parl.) 1961; mem. and Deputy Chair. Stange Municipal Council 1952; Chair. Municipal Cttee. of Hedmark Labour Party 1960–; Deputy mem. Cen. Cttee. of Labour Party 1965, Chair. Hedmark Labour Party 1968; Chair. Trade Union and Labour Party Tax Cttee. 1967–68; Vice-Chair. Parl. Municipal Cttee. 1965–69; Chair. Parl. Social Welfare Cttee. 1969–71; Minister of Labour and Municipal Affairs 1971–72; Chair. Comm. of Defence 1974–75; Prime Minister 1976–81; Vice-Pres. Parl. 1981; Leader Parl. Labour Party 1973–76.

NORDLING, Carl, PH.D.; Swedish professor of physics; b. 6 Feb. 1931, Edmonton, Canada; s. of Jarl Nordling and Karin Thorén; m. Gunhild Söderström 1954; two s. one d.; ed. Univ. of Uppsala; Asst. Prof. Univ. of Uppsala 1959–61, lecturer 1962–64, Assoc. Prof. 1965–69, Prof. of Atomic and Molecular Physics 1970–95; Sec.-Gen. Swedish Nat. Science Research Council 1987–93; Chair. Nobel Cttee. for Physics 1992–96. *Publications:* ESCA-Atomic, Molecular and Solid State Structure Studied by Means of Electron Spectroscopy (co-author) 1967, ESCA Applied to Free Molecules (co-author) 1969, Physics Handbook (co-author) 1982; 150 scientific papers on electron, X-ray and laser spectroscopy. *Address:* Department of Physics, University of Uppsala, Box 530, 751 21 Uppsala (Office); Malma Ringv. 45B, 75645 Uppsala, Sweden (Home). *Telephone:* 18 4713545 (Office); 18 302221 (Home). *Fax:* 18 512227.

NORDSTRÖM, Torkel, LL.D.; Swedish fmr. judge; b. 12 March 1910, Halmstad; s. of Thorsten Nordström and Tora Afzelius; m. Vera Starfelt 1937; three d.; ed. Univ. of Lund; Assoc. Judge, Svea Court of Appeal 1946–53, Ordinary Judge 1953–55; Justice of the Supreme Court 1955–77, Chief Justice 1976–77; mem. Drafts Legislation Cttee. 1951–55; Hon. LL.D. (Lund) 1973; Commdr. Grand Cross Order of North Star (Sweden), Icelandic Falcon, Kt. Order of Dannebrog (Denmark), White Rose of Finland, King's Medal. *Publications:* Commentaries on the Citizenship Act 1952 and the Hire Purchase Act 1957, Lagen om företagsinteckning 1966; Ed. Swedish Statute Book (annual) 1974–90. *Leisure interests:* gardening, genealogy. *Address:* Åsbacken 25, S-16766 Bromma, Sweden. *Telephone:* 08/26-06-34.

NORÉN, Lars; Swedish playwright; b. 9 May 1944, Stockholm; s. of Matti Norén and Britt Norén; m. 1st Titti Mörk 1979; m. 2nd Charlott Neuhauser 1993; two d.; started career as a poet; wrote first play 1968; has written 43 plays, performed worldwide; De Nio's Pris 1985, Expressens Reviewers' Prize 1993, Pilot Prize 1994 and many other prizes and awards. *Plays include:* Courage to Kill 1978, Munich-Athens 1981, Night is Day's Mother 1982, Comedians 1985, Hebriana 1987, Autumn and Winter 1987, And Give Us the Shadows 1988, Trick or Treat 1989, Lost and Found 1991, Leaves in Vallombrosa 1992, Blood 1994, Some Kind of Hades 1994, The Clinic 1995, Personkrets 3:1 1997. *Leisure interests:* fishing, hunting. *Address:* c/o Ulla Orre, Draken Teaterförlag, Södermannagatan 27 NB, SE-11640 Stockholm (Agent); Östermalmsgatan 33, S-11426 Stockholm, Sweden, (Home). *Telephone:* (8) 642 7106. (Agent) *Fax:* (8) 643 8108.

NORFOLK, 17th Duke of, cr. 1483; **Miles Francis Stapleton Fitzalan-Howard,** K.G., G.C.V.O., C.B., C.B.E., M.C., D.L.; Earl of Arundel, Baron Beaumont, Baron Maltravers, Earl of Surrey, Baron FitzAlan, Clun, and Oswaldestre, Earl of Norfolk, Baron Howard of Glossop, Earl Marshal and Hereditary Marshal and Chief Butler of England; Premier Duke and Earl; British landowner and fmr. army officer; b. 21 July 1915, London; s. of 3rd Baron Howard of Glossop, M.B.E., and Baroness Beaumont (11th in line), O.B.E.; m. Anne Mary Teresa Constable Maxwell 1949; two s. three d.; ed. Ampleforth Coll., Christ Church, Oxford; 2nd Lieut. Grenadier Guards 1937; served World War II, France, N. Africa, Sicily, Italy, N.W. Europe; Head of British Mil. Mission to Soviet forces, Germany 1957; Commdr. 70 Brigade, King's African Rifles 1961–63; GOC (Maj.-Gen.) 1 Div. 1963–65; Dir. Man. and Support Intelligence, Ministry of Defence 1965-66, Service Intelligence 1966–67; retd. 1967; Chair. Arundel Castle Trustees Ltd. 1976–; D.L. West Sussex 1977–; Dir. Robert Fleming Holdings Ltd. 1969–85; Pres. Building Socs. Asscn. 1982–86; Hon. Master of the Bench of the Inner Temple 1984–; Prime Warden, Fishmongers' Co. 1985–86; Kt. of Sovereign Order of Malta. *Address:* Arundel Castle, West Sussex, BN18 9AB; Carlton Towers, Goole, North Humberside, DN14 9LZ; Bacres House, Hambleden, Henley-on-Thames, Oxon., RG9 6RY, England. *Telephone:* (01903) 882173; (01405) 860243; (01491) 571-350.

NØRGAARD, Carl Aage, DR. JUR.; Danish professor of law; b. 15 Sept. 1924, Denmark; s. of Edvard Nørgaard and Jensine Kristine Kristensen; m. Hedvig Hauberg 1951; one d.; ed. Univs. of Aarhus, Cambridge and Geneva; Asst. Faculty of Law, Univ. of Aarhus 1955–58, Lecturer 1958–64, Prof. 1964–89, Head of Inst. of Public Law 1964–86; Rockefeller Fellowship, Univ. of Geneva 1959–60; mem. European Comm. of Human Rights 1973–95, Second Vice-Pres. 1976–81, Pres. 1981–95, Ind. Legal Adviser for UN concerning the release of political prisoners in Namibia 1989–90; Legal Adviser to S. African Truth and Reconciliation Comm. 1994–; Jur. Dr. h.c. (Lund) 1994; Danish Grand Cross, German Grand Order of Merit with star and sash. *Publications:* The Position of the Individual in International Law 1962, Forvaltningsret-Sagsbehandling 1972, Administration og Borger (with Claus Haagen Jensen) 1972, 1984, 1988; articles in legal periodicals. *Leisure interests:* rowing, gardening. *Address:* Skjoldsbjergvej 2A, Skórring, 8464 Galten, Denmark. *Telephone:* 89-421133 (Office); 86-944047 (Home).

NORIEGA, Gen. Antonio; Panamanian army officer; b. 11 Feb. 1940, Panama City; m. Felicidad Sieiro; three c.; ed. Univ. of Panama, Mil. Acad., Peru; First Lieut. Panama Nat. Guard 1962; Head Panama Intelligence Services 1970; mem. Jt. Chiefs of Staff, Guardia Nacional 1970–81, Chief 1982–83; C.-in-C. Panama Defence Forces 1983–89; overthrown, sought refuge in Vatican Embassy, Panama; extradited on drug charges to Miami, U.S.A. Jan. 1990; residing in high security prison, facing 12 charges of drug trafficking 1990–92; found guilty of 8 of 10 charges (money laundering, cocaine manufacturing and distribution, racketeering and the bldg. of a drug laboratory in Panama) April 1992; sentenced to 40 years' imprisonment; further sentence in absentia of 20 years' imprisonment for murder Oct. 1993; numerous medals; *Publication:* Immortal Ayacucho.

NORMAN, Archie John, M.A., M.B.A.; British business executive; b. 1 May 1954, London; s. of Archibald Percy Norman and Aleida Elizabeth Norman; m. Vanessa Peet 1982; one d.; ed. Univ. of Minnesota, Emmanuel Coll., Cambridge, Harvard Business School; with Citibank N.A. 1975–77; partner, McKinsey & Co. Inc. 1979–86; Group Finance Dir. Kingfisher PLC 1986–91; Chief Exec. Asda Group PLC 1991–96, Chair. 1996–97; M.P. for Tunbridge Wells 1997–; Vice-Chair. Conservative Party 1997–98; Chief Exec. and Deputy Chair. Conservative Party 1998–; Dir. non-exec. Geest 1988–91, British Rail 1992–94, Railtrack 1994–. *Leisure interests:* farming, music, opera, tennis, football. *Address:* House of Commons, Westminster, London, S.W.1, England.

NORMAN, Sir Arthur Gordon, K.B.E., D.F.C.; British business executive; b. 18 Feb. 1917, North Pertherton, Somerset; s. of Christopher William Norman and Mary Christine Milton; m. Margaret Doreen Harrington 1944 (died 1982); three s. two d.; ed. Blundell's School; Thomas De La Rue and Co. 1934–87, Asst. Gen. Man. 1947, Dir. 1951, Man. Dir. 1953; Chair. The De La Rue Co. PLC 1964–77, non-exec. Chair. 1977–87; Dir. Kleinwort, Benson, Lonsdale PLC; R.A.F. 1941–46; Pres. CBI 1968–70; Chair. U.K. Centre for Econ. and Environmental Devt. 1984–96; Vice-Chair. Sun Life Assurance Soc. 1984–87; Dir. SKF (U.K.) Ltd. 1970–87, Kleinwort, Benson, Lonsdale PLC 1985–88; Chair. of Trustees, World Wildlife Fund (U.K.) 1977–84; Treasurer Int. Inst. for Environment and Devt.; mem. Nature Conservancy Council 1980–86. *Leisure interests:* tennis, golf, country life. *Address:* Fir Tree Cottage, Hammoon, Sturminster Newton, Dorset, DT10 2DB, England.

NORMAN, Barry Leslie, C.B.E.; British writer and broadcaster; b. 21 Aug. 1933, London; s. of Leslie Norman and Elizabeth Norman; m. Diana Narracott 1957; two d.; ed. Highgate School, London; Entertainments Ed. Daily Mail, London 1969–71; weekly columnist The Guardian 1971–80; Writer and Presenter of BBC 1 Film 1973–81, 1983–98, The Hollywood Greats 1977–79, 1984, The British Greats 1980, Omnibus 1982, Film Greats 1985, Talking Pictures 1988, Barry Norman's Film Night, BSkyB 1998–; Radio 4 Today 1974–76, Going Places 1977–81, Breakaway 1979–80; Hon. D.Litt. (East Anglia) 1991; Richard Dimbleby Award, BAFTA award 1981, Columnist of the Year award 1990; Hon. D.Litt. (Herts.) 1996. *Publications:* Novels: The Matter of Mandrake 1967, The Hounds of Sparta 1968, End Product 1975, A Series of Defeats 1977, To Nick a Good Body 1978, Have a Nice Day 1981, Sticky Wicket 1984, The Birddog Tape 1992; non-fiction: Tales of the Redundance Kid 1975, The Hollywood Greats 1979, The Movie Greats 1981, Talking Pictures 1987, The Good Night In Guide 1992, 100 Best Films of the Century 1992, The Mickey Mouse Affair 1995, Death on Sunset 1998. *Leisure interest:* cricket. *Address:* c/o Curtis Brown Ltd., Haymarket House, 28–29 Haymarket, London, SW1Y 4SP, England. *Telephone:* 0171-396 6600.

NORMAN, Denis; Zimbabwean politician and farmer; b. 1931, Oxfordshire, U.K.; m.; four c.; emigrated to Rhodesia (now Zimbabwe) 1953; employed as a farm man.; started farming in own right 1959; served on various agricultural cttees. 1961–; Chair. Commercial Grain Producers 1974–76; Minister of Agric. 1980–85, 1995–96, of Transport and Energy 1990–95; Vice-Pres. Commercial Farmers' Union 1976–78, Pres. 1978–80; Pres. Zimbabwe Agricultural Soc. 1993–. *Address:* c/o Ministry of Agriculture, Ngungunyana Building, Private Bag 7701, Causeway, Harare, Zimbabwe.

NORMAN, Gregory John (Greg), A.M.; Australian golfer; b. 10 Feb. 1955, Queensland; m. Laura Andrassy 1981; one s. one d.; turned professional 1976; won Westlakes Classic, Australia 1976, Martini Int., New S. Wales Open, South Seas Classic, Fiji 1978, Martini Int., Hong Kong Open 1979, Australian Open, French Open, Scandinavian Open 1980, Australian Masters, Martini Int., Dunlop Masters 1981, Dunlop Masters, State Express Classic, Benson & Hedges Int. 1982, Australian Masters, Nat. Panasonic New S. Wales Open, Hong Kong Open, Cannes Invitational, Suntory World Match Play Championship 1983, Canadian Open, Victorian Open, Australian Masters, Toshiba Australian PGA Championship 1984, Toshiba Australian PGA Championship, Nat. Panasonic Australian Open 1985, European Open, British Open, Suntory World Matchplay Championship, Panasonic-Las Vegas Invitational, Kemper Open 1986, Australian Masters, Nat. Panasonic Australian Open 1987, Palm Meadows Cup, Australia, PGA Nat. Tournament Players Championship, Australia, Panasonic N.S.W. Open, Lancia Italian Open 1988, Australian Masters, PGA Nat. Tournament Players Championship 1989, Australian Masters, The Memorial Tournament 1990, Canadian Open 1992, British Open, Taiheyo Masters, Japan 1993, Johnnie Walker Asian Classic, The Players Championship 1994, Australian Open, Memorial Tournament, Canon Greater Hartford Open 1995, SA Open 1996, World Championship 1997. *Leisure interests:* fishing, hunting, scuba diving. *Address:* Great White Shark Enterprise Inc., 501 North A1A, Jupiter, FL 33477, U.S.A.

NORMAN, Jessye, M.MUS.; American concert and opera singer; b. 15 Sept. 1945, Augusta, Ga.; d. of Silas and Janie (King) Norman; ed. Howard Univ., Washington, D.C., Peabody Conservatory, Univ. of Michigan; Vocal Winner, Int. Musikwettbewerb, Bayerischer Rundfunk, Munich, Fed. Repub. of Germany 1968; operatic début Deutsche Oper Berlin 1969; début La Scala, Milan 1972, Royal Opera House, Covent Garden 1972; American operatic début, Hollywood Bowl 1972; tours in N. and S. America, Europe, Middle East, Australia; int. festivals incl. Aix-en-Provence, Aldeburgh, Berliner Festwochen, Edinburgh, Flanders, Helsinki, Lucerne, Salzburg, Tanglewood, Spoleto, Hollywood Bowl, Ravinia; with leading orchestras from U.S.A., U.K., Israel, Australia; Hon. Mus.Doc. (Howard) 1982, (Univ. of the South, Sewance) 1984, (Univ. of Mich.) 1987, (Edinburgh) 1989; Hon. D.Mus. (Cambridge) 1989; Grand Prix du Disque (Acad. du Disque Français) 1973, 1976, 1977, 1982; Deutsche Schallplatten Preis für Euryanthe 1975; Cigale d'Or (Aix-en-Provence Festival) 1977; Grammy Award 1980, 1982, 1985, Musician of the Year (Musical America) 1982, IRCAM record award 1982, Alumna Award (Univ. of Michigan) 1982; Commdr., Ordre des Arts et des Lettres 1984. *Leisure interests:* reading, cooking, houseplant growing, fashion designing. *Address:* L'Orchidee, P.O. Box South, Crugers, NY 10521; Philips Records Polygram, 825 8th Avenue, New York, NY 10019, U.S.A.

NORMAN, Marsha; American playwright; b. 21 Sept. 1947, Louisville; d. of Billie Williams and Bertha Conley; m. 1st Michael Norman (divorced 1974); m. 2nd Dann C. Byck Jr. 1978 (divorced); m. 3rd. Timothy Dykman; one s. one d.; ed. Agnes Scott Coll. and Univ. of Louisville; Rockefeller playwright-in-residence grantee 1979–80; American Acad. and Inst. for Arts and Letters grantee; Pulitzer Prize for Drama 1983; Tony Award 1991; many other awards and prizes. *Publications:* plays: Getting Out 1977, Third and Oak 1978, Circus Valentine 1979, The Holdup 1980, 'Night, Mother 1982, Traveler in the Dark 1984, Sarah and Abraham 1987, Four Plays by Marsha Norman (collection) 1988, D. Boone 1992, Loving Daniel Boone 1992, Trudy Blue 1995; The Secret Garden (book of musical lyrics) 1991; TV plays: It's the Willingness 1978, In Trouble at Fifteen 1980, The Laundromat 1985, Third and Oak: The Pool Hall 1989, Face of a Stranger 1991; The Fortune Teller (novel) 1987; books of musicals and lyrics; The Secret Garden 1991, The Red Shoes 1992. *Address:* c/o Jack Tantleff, 375 Greenwich Street, Ste. 700, New York, NY 10013, U.S.A.

NORODOM RANARIDDH, Prince; Cambodian politician; b. 2 Jan. 1944; s. of King Norodom Sihanouk (q.v.); m. 1968; two s. one d.; Pres. United Nat. Front for an Independent, Neutral, Peaceful and Co-operative Cambodia (FUNCINPEC); Co-Chair. Provisional Nat. Govt. of Cambodia, also Minister of Nat. Defence, Interior and Nat. Security June–Sept. 1993; mem. Nat. Ass. May 1993–; Co-Prime Minister and mem. Throne Council Sept.–Oct. 1993; First Prime Minister of Royal Govt. of Cambodia 1993–97; Chair. Nat. Devt. Council 1993–97; found guilty of conspiracy with Khmer Rouges to overthrow the govt., sentenced to 30 years imprisonment; in exile; returned from exile May 1998; Prof. of Public Law. *Leisure interest:* aviation.

NORODOM SIHANOUK, Samdech Preah; King of Cambodia; b. 31 Oct. 1922; s. of late King Norodom Suramarit and Queen Kossamak Neariereath; m. Princess Monique; fourteen c. (six deceased); ed. in Saigon (now Ho Chi Minh City), Viet Nam, and Paris; mil. training in Saumur, France; elected King April 1941, abdicated March 1955; Prime Minister and Minister of Foreign Affairs Oct. 1955, March 1956, Sept. 1956, April 1957; Perm. Rep. to UN Feb.-Sept. 1956; elected Head of State after death of his father 1960, took oath of fidelity to vacant throne 1960, deposed by forces of Lon Nol (q.v.) March 1970; resided in Peking (now Beijing), People's Repub. of China; est. Royal Govt. of Nat. Union of Cambodia (GRUNC) May 1970; restored as Head of State when GRUNC forces overthrew Khmer Repub. April 1975, resigned April 1976; Special Envoy of Khmer Rouge to UN 1979; f. Nat. United Front for an Independent Neutral, Peaceful Co-operative Kampuchea 1981–89; Head of the Popular Socialist Community 1955–70; Head of State in exile of Govt. of Democratic Kampuchea 1982–88, 1989–90; Self-styled Pres. Nat. Govt. of Cambodia (Democratic Kampuchea); Pres. Tripartite Nat. Cambodian Resistance; in exile 13 years, returned to Cambodia Oct. 1991; Chair. Supreme Nat. Council 1991–93; Pres. of Cambodia 1991–93; crowned King of Cambodia Sept. 1993–; C.-in-C. of Armed Forces June 1993–; musician and composer; producer of films including Le Petit Prince. *Publications:* L'Indochine vue de Pékin (with Jean Lacouture) 1972, My War With the C.I.A. (with Wilfred Burchett) 1973, War and Hope: The Case for Cambodia 1980, Souvenirs doux et amers 1981, Prisonnier des Khmers Rouges 1986, Charisme et Leadership 1989. *Leisure interests:* badminton, film making in DPR Korea, French style cooking in Beijing. *Address:* Khemarindra Palace, Phnom Penh, Cambodia.

NORRBACK, Johan Ole; Finnish politician; b. 18 March 1941, Overmark; m. Vivi-Ann Lindqvist 1959; teacher 1966–67; Dist. Sec. Swedish People's Party in Ostrobothnia 1967–71; Exec. Man. Provincial Union of Swedish Ostrobothnia 1971–91; Political Sec. to Minister of Communications 1976–77; mem. Parl. 1979–87, 1991–; mem. Exec. Cttee. Swedish People's Party 1983–, Chair. 1990–; Minister of Defence 1987–90, of Educ. and Science 1990–91, of Transport and Communications 1991–95, for Europe and Foreign Trade 1995–. *Address:* Eduskunta, Helsinki, Finland.

NORRINGTON, Sir Roger Arthur Carver, Kt., O.B.E.; British conductor; b. 16 March 1934; s. of Sir Arthur Norrington and Edith Joyce Carver; m. 1st Susan Elizabeth McLean May 1964 (divorced 1982); one s. one d.; m. 2nd Karalyn Mary Lawrence 1986; one s.; ed. Dragon School, Oxford, Westminster School, Clare Coll., Cambridge, Royal Coll. of Music; freelance singer 1962–72; Prin. Conductor, Kent Opera 1966–84; Guest Conductor many British and European orchestras, appearances BBC Promenade Concerts, and City of London, Bath, Aldeburgh, Edin. and Harrogate festivals; regular broadcasts U.K., Europe, U.S.A.; Prin. Conductor Bournemouth Sinfonietta 1985–89; Assoc. Chief Guest Conductor London Philharmonic Orchestra 1993–; Chief Conductor South German Radio Orchestra 1997–, Camerata Academica Salzburg 1997–; Musical Dir. London Classical Players 1978–97, London Baroque Players 1975–, Schütz Choir of London 1962, Orchestra of St. Lukes, N.Y. 1990–94; Co.-Dir. Early Opera Project 1984–, Historic Arts 1986–; Hon. D.Mus. (Kent) 1994; many gramophone recordings; Cavaliere, Ordine al Merito della Repubblica Italiana. *Leisure interests:* reading, walking, sailing.

NORRIS, David Owen, M.A., F.R.C.O., F.R.A.M.; British pianist and broadcaster; b. 16 June 1953, Northampton; s. of Albert Norris and Amy Norris; two s.; ed. Keble Coll. Oxford and Royal Acad. of Music; Prof. Royal Acad. of Music 1977–89; Dir. Petworth Festival 1986–92; Artistic Dir. Cardiff Festival 1992–95; Gresham Prof. of Music 1993–97; Chair. Steans Inst. for Singers, Chicago 1992–98; First Gilmore Artist Award 1991. *Leisure interests:* naval and detective fiction, wine. *Address:* Aughton Rise, Collingbourne Kingston, Wilts., SN8 3SA, England. *Telephone:* 0181-961 4830.

NORRIS, Steve; British film producer; fmrly. with Rank Org.; fmr. exec. Columbia Pictures, Warner Brothers, Enigma, U.S.A.; fmr. Vice-Pres. Producers' Alliance for Cinema and TV, Chair. Film Cttee.; British Film Commr. Jan. 1998–. *Films include:* Memphis Belle, Being Human, War of the Buttons, The Burning Season, Le Confessionnal, My Life So Far; several awards, including Golden Globe for The Burning Season. *Address:* British Film Commission, 70 Baker Street, London, W1M 1DJ, England. *Telephone:* 0171-224 5000. *Fax:* 0171-224 1013.

NORSHTEIN, Yuri Borisovich; Russian film director, animator and script-writer; b. 15 Sept. 1941, Andreyevka, Penza Region; s. of Basya Girshevna Krichevskaya and Berko Leibovich Norshtein; m. Francesca Alfredovna Yarbusova; one s. one d.; ed. Soyuzmultfilmstudio courses; debut as film dir. The 25th is the First Day 1968 (co-dir. with Arkady Tyurin); cutout film Battle at Kerzhenets 1971 (co-dir. with I. Ivanov-Vano); later with his wife (art dir. Yarbusova): Fox and Hare 1973, Heron and Crane 1974, Hedgehog in Mist 1975, The Tale of Tales 1979, Great Coat (production interrupted 1986, now re-started); Tale of Tales voted in int. survey, L.A. Animation Olympiad, best animated film of all time 1984; Tarkovsky Prize 1989; Grand Prix Zagreb Animation Festival 1980; U.S.S.R. State Prize 1979, Triumph Prize 1995. *Address:* Butlerov str. 4, korp. 2, Apt. 88, 117485 Moscow, Russia (Home). *Telephone:* (095) 335 0821 (Home).

NORTH, Alastair Macarthur, O.B.E., PH.D., D.SC.; British professor of chemistry (retd.); b. 2 April 1932, Aberdeen, Scotland; s. of Norman R. North and Anne North; m. Charlotte Muriel Begg 1957; two s. two d.; ed. Univs. of Aberdeen and Birmingham; Lecturer, Dept. of Inorganic, Physical and Industrial Chem., Univ. of Liverpool; apptd. to Burmah Chair of Physical Chem., Univ. of Strathclyde, Scotland 1967, subsequently Dean of School of Chemical and Materials Science, then Vice-Prin. of the Univ.; Pres. Asian Inst. of Tech. 1983–96; mem. several nat. cttees. on formation of science policy; Sc.D. h.c. (Politechnika Lodzka); Hon. Ph.D. (Ramkhamhaeng Univ.); D.Univ. h.c. (Strathclyde); Dr. h.c. (Inst. Nat. Polytechnique de Toulouse), D. Tech. h.c. (A.I.T.), LL.D. h.c. (Aberdeen); Commdr. des Palmes Académiques; Commdr. Order of King Leopold II (Belgium); Prasidda Prabala Gorkha Dakshin Bahu (Nepal). *Leisure interests:* golf, scuba diving. *Address:* 79/78 Soi 7/1 Mooban Tararom, Ramkhamhaeng Soi 150, Sapansoong, Bangkok 10240, Thailand. *Telephone:* (2) 373 2818. *Fax:* (2) 373 3052.

NORTH, Douglass Cecil, PH.D.; American professor of economics; b. 5 Nov. 1920, Cambridge, Mass.; s. of Henry North and Edith Saitta; m. Elisabeth Willard Case 1972; three s. by previous m.; ed. Univ. of Calif. Berkeley; Asst. Prof. Univ. of Washington 1950–56, Assoc. Prof. 1957–60, Prof. of Econs. 1960–63, Prof. Emer. 1983–, Chair. Dept. of Econs. 1967–79; Dir. Inst. of Econ. Research 1960–66, Nat. Bureau of Econ. Research 1967–87; Luce Prof. of Law and Liberty, Prof. of Econs. Washington Univ. St. Louis 1983–; Pitt Prof. of American History and Inst. Cambridge Univ. 1981–82; mem. Bradley Foundation 1986–; Fellow, Center for Advanced Study on Behavioral Sciences 1987–88; Guggenheim Fellow 1972–73; Fellow, American Acad. of Arts and Sciences; mem. American Econ. Asscn., Econ. History Asscn.; shared Nobel Prize for Econs. 1993; Dr. rer. pol. h.c. (Cologne) 1988, (Zürich) 1993, (Stockholm School of Econs.) 1994, (Prague School of Econs.) 1995. *Publications:* The Economic Growth of the U.S. 1790–1860 1961, Growth and Welfare in the American Past 1971, Institutional Change and American Economic Growth (with L. Davis) 1971, The Economics of Public Issues (with R. Miller) 1971, The Rise of the Western World (with R. Thomas) 1973, Structure and Change in Economic History 1981, Institutions, Institutional Change and Economic Performance 1990. *Address:* Department of Economics, Washington University, Campus Box 1208, Saint Louis, MO 63130, U.S.A.

NORTH, John David, M.A., B.SC., D.PHIL., D.LITT., F.B.A.; British professor of the history of philosophy and the exact sciences; b. 19 May 1934, Cheltenham; s. of J. E. North and G. A. North; m. Marion J. Pizzey; one s. two d.; ed. Merton Coll., Oxford and Univ. of London; Nuffield Foundation Research Fellow Univ. of Oxford 1963–68, Museum of History of Science, Univ. of Oxford 1968–77; Visiting Prof. of History of Science, Aarhus Univ. 1974, Prof. of the History of Philosophy and the Exact Sciences, Univ. of Groningen, 1977–; Visiting Prof. Univs. in Germany, Denmark and U.S.A.; Dean of the Cen. Interfaculty 1981–84, 1991–93; Sec. Perpétuel, Acad. int. d'histoire des sciences, Paris 1983–89, Hon. Sec. Perpétuel 1990–; mem. Royal Netherlands Acad. (mem. Council 1990–93), Deutsche Akad. der Naturforscher Leopoldina; Foreign mem. Royal Danish Acad.; Koyré Medal Acad. Int. d'Histoire des Sciences 1989. *Publications:* The Measure of the Universe 1965, Richard of Wallingford, (3 vols) 1976, The Light of Nature (Ed.) 1985, Horoscopes and History 1986, Chaucer's Universe 1988, Stars, Minds, and Fate 1989, The Universal Frame 1989, The Fontana History of Astronomy 1994, Stonehenge: Neolithic Man and the Cosmos 1996. *Leisure interest:* archaeology. *Address:* Kamperfoelieweg 25, 9765 HJ Paterswolde, Netherlands; 28 Chalfont Road, Oxford, OX2 6TH, England. *Telephone:* 050-3091846 (Netherlands), (01865) 558458 (England).

NORTH, Oliver L.; American marine officer; b. 7 Oct. 1943, San Antonio, Texas; s. of Oliver Clay North and Ann North; m.; c.; ed. U.S. Naval Coll., Annapolis; joined marines, platoon commdr. Viet Nam; marine instructor 1969; leader marine mission, Turkey 1980; mem. Nat. Security Council as Deputy Dir. for Political Mil. Affairs 1981–86; dismissed Nov. 1986 because of involvement with secret operation to sell arms to Iran and the diversion of proceeds from the sales to aid anti-govt. "Contra" guerrillas in Nicaragua; rank of Lieut.-Col. 1983, retd. from Marines 1988; on trial Feb. 1989, found guilty on three counts May 1989, received 3 year suspended sentence and fined $150,000, ordered to do 1,200 hours community work, appeal court reverses one count 1990, three convictions set aside 1990; cleared of all charges 1991; Head V-PAC (political action group); own radio show 1995–; Dr. h.c. (Liberty Univ.) 1988. *Publication:* Under Fire: An American Story 1991.

NORTH, Sir Peter Machin, Kt., C.B.E., Q.C., M.A., D.C.L., F.B.A.; British academic; b. 30 Aug. 1936, Nottingham; s. of Geoffrey Machin North and Freda Brunt (née Smith) North; m. Stephanie Mary Chadwick 1960; two s. one d.; ed. Oakham School, Rutland, Keble Coll., Oxford; Teaching Assoc., Northwestern Univ. Law School, Chicago 1960–61; Lecturer, Univ. Coll. of Wales, Aberystwyth 1961–63, Univ. of Nottingham 1964–65; Fellow and Tutor in Law, Keble Coll., Oxford 1965–76; Chair., Faculty of Law, Univ. of Oxford 1971–75; Prin. Jesus Coll., Oxford 1984–; Pro-Vice-Chancellor, Oxford 1988–93, 1997–, Vice-Chancellor 1993–97; Ed. Oxford Journal of Legal Studies 1987–92; Law Commr. for England and Wales 1976–84; mem. Lord Chancellor's Advisory Cttee. on Legal Educ. 1973–75, Council of Man., British Inst. of Int. and Comparative Law 1976–, Econ. and Social Research Council Cttees. 1982–87, Council, Univ. of Reading 1986–89; Chair. Conciliation Advisory Cttee. 1985–88, Road Traffic Law Review 1985–88, Independent Review of Parades and Marches in Northern Ireland 1996–97; Hon. Fellow, Keble Coll., Oxford, Univ. Coll. of North Wales, Bangor, Trinity Coll., Carmarthen, Univ. of Wales, Aberystwyth; Hon. Bencher, Inner Temple; mem. Inst. de droit int.; Hon. LL.D. (Reading) 1992, (Nottingham) 1996, (Aberdeen) 1997. *Publications:* Occupier's Liability 1971, Modern Law of Animals 1972, Chitty on Contracts (ed.) 1968–89, Private International Law of Matrimonial Causes 1977, Contract Conflicts (ed.) 1982, Cases and Materials on Private International Law (with J.H.C. Morris) 1984, Cheshire and North's Private International Law (ed.) 1970–92, Private International Law Problems in Common Law Jurisdictions 1993, Essays in Private International Law 1993. *Address:* Jesus College, Oxford, OX1 3DW, England. *Telephone:* (01865) 279701. *Fax:* (01865) 279687.

NORTHARD, John Henry, C.B.E., F.ENG., C.B.I.M.; British industrialist; b. 23 Dec. 1926, Pudsey; s. of William Henry Northard and Nellie Northard; m. Marian Josephine Lay 1952; two s. two d.; ed. St. Bede's Grammar School, Bradford, Yorks, Barnsley Mining and Technical Coll.; Colliery Man., Yorkshire 1955–57, Leicestershire 1957–63; Group Man., Leicestershire Colleries 1963–65; Deputy Chief Mining Engineer, Staffordshire Colleries 1965–70; Area Deputy Dir. (Mining), N. Derbyshire 1970–73, Area Dir. 1973–81; Area Dir., Western Area 1981–85; Operations Dir. British Coal Corpn. 1985, Deputy Chair. 1988–92; Chair. British Coal Enterprise Ltd. 1991–93; Pres. Inst. of Mining Engineers 1982; Hon. F.I.M.M.; Serving Brother Order of St. John 1981. *Publications:* numerous papers in various mining eng. insts. and tech. journals. *Address:* Rydal, 196 Ashgate Road, Chesterfield, Derbyshire, S40 4AL, England.

NORTHCOTE, Donald Henry, D.S., F.R.S.; British plant biochemist; b. 27 Dec. 1921, Plymouth; s. of F. Northcote and F. Corbin; m. Eva Marjorie Mayo 1948; two d.; ed. Univs. of London and Cambridge; Demonstrator in Biochem., Univ. of Cambridge 1948, Prof. of Plant Biochem. 1972–, Master of Sidney Sussex Coll. 1976–92; Fellow, St. John's Coll. Cambridge 1960; Hon. Fellow, Downing Coll. Cambridge 1979. *Publications:* 300 papers on plant cell growth and differentiation 1948–. *Leisure interests:* sailing, reading and computing. *Address:* 100 North Street, Burwell, Cambridge, CB5 0BB, England. *Telephone:* (01638) 743924.

NORTON, Hugh Edward, B.A.; British business executive; b. 23 June 1936, London; s. of Lieut.-Gen. Edward F. Norton and I. Joyce Norton; m. 1st Janet M. Johnson 1965 (died 1993); one s.; m. 2nd F. Joy Harcup 1998; ed. Winchester Coll., Trinity Coll. Oxford; joined British Petroleum Co. 1959, Exploration Dept. 1960, in Abu Dhabi, Lebanon and Libya 1962–70, subsequently held appts. in Supply, Cen. Planning, Policy Planning, Regional Directorate Middle East and Int. and Govt. Affairs depts.; Man. Dir. BP's assoc. cos., Singapore, Malaysia, Hong Kong 1978–81, Dir. of Planning 1981–83, Regional Dir. for Near East, Middle East and Indian sub-continent 1981–86, Dir. of Admin. 1983–86, Man. Dir. and C.E.O. BP Exploration Co. 1986–89, Chair. 1989–95, Man. Dir. The British Petroleum Co. PLC 1989–95; Chair. BP Asia Pacific Pvt. Co. Ltd. 1991–95; Dir. Inchcape PLC 1995–, Standard Chartered PLC 1995–, Lasmo PLC 1997–; mem. Council Royal Inst. of Econ. Affairs 1991–. *Leisure interests:* painting, ornithology, tennis, travel. *Address:* c/o BP Asia Pacific Pte Ltd., BP Tower, 25th Storey, 396 Alexandra Road, Singapore 0511.

NORVIK, Harald; Norwegian administrator and executive; b. 21 June 1946, Vadsø; ed. Norwegian School of Econs. and Business Admin., Bergen; Advisor, Nat. Inst. of Tech. 1971–73; Group Sec. for Industrial and Financial Affairs 1973–75; Trainee course Ministry of Foreign Affairs 1975–76; Personal Sec. to Prime Minister 1976–79; Minister of Petroleum and Energy 1979–81; Dir. of Finance Aker mek. Verksted A/S 1981–85, Sr. Exec. Vice-Pres. 1985–86; Pres. Astrup Hoyer A/S 1986–87; now Pres. and Chair. Exec. Bd. Statoil Group; alternating Chair. Bd. Dirs. SAS Norge ASA, Scandinavian Airlines System (S.A.S.); Chair. Supervisory Bd. Den norske Bank; mem. Bd. Orkla Borregaard A.S., Supervisory Council Nycomed A.S.A.; Commr. Order of the Lion of Finland (1st Class), Grosseverdienstkreuz. *Address:* Statoil, 4035 Stavanger, Norway. *Telephone:* 51-80-80-80. *Fax:* 51-80-51-77.

NORWICH, 2nd Viscount, cr. 1952, of Aldwick; **John Julius Cooper,** C.V.O., F.R.S.L., F.R.G.S.; British author and broadcaster; b. 15 Sept. 1929; s. of 1st Viscount Norwich, P.C., G.C.M.G., D.S.O. and the late Lady Diana Cooper; m. 1st Anne Clifford 1952 (divorced 1985); one s. one d.; m. 2nd Mollie Philipps 1989; ed. Upper Canada Coll. Toronto, Eton Coll., Univ. of Strasbourg and New Coll. Oxford; entered Foreign Office 1952; Third Sec. Belgrade 1955–57; Second Sec. Beirut 1957–60; Foreign Office and British del. to Disarmament Conf. Geneva 1960–64; Chair. British Theatre Museum 1966–71, Venice in Peril Fund; mem. Exec. Cttee. Nat. Trust 1969–95; mem. Franco British Council 1972–79; mem. Bd. English Nat. Opera 1977–81; Ed. New Shell Guides to Britain 1987–91; Dir. Robelif Productions Ltd. 1991–94; has made some 30 documentary films for TV, mainly on history and architecture; Commendatore, Ordine al Merito della Repubblica Italiana. *Publications:* (as John Julius Norwich): Mount Athos (with R. Sitwell) 1966, The Normans in the South 1967, Sahara 1968, The Kingdom in the Sun 1970, A History of Venice (Vol. I) 1977, (Vol. II) 1981, Christmas Crackers 1970–79 1980, Britain's Heritage (ed.) 1982, The Italian World (ed.) 1983, Fifty Years of Glyndebourne 1985, A Taste for Travel (anthology) 1985, Great Architecture of the World (general ed.) 1975, The Architecture of Southern England 1985, Byzantium, the Early Centuries 1988, More Christmas Crackers 1980–89 1990, Venice: a Traveller's Companion 1990, Byzantium: The Apogee 1991, Byzantium: Decline and Fall 1995. *Leisure interests:* sight-seeing, walking at night through Venice. *Address:* 24 Blomfield Road, London, W9 1AD, England. *Telephone:* 0171-286 5050. *Fax:* 0171-266 2561.

NORWOOD, Mandi; British magazine editor; b. 9 Oct. 1963; m. Martin Kelly 1995; two d.; ed. Lord Lawson Comprehensive School, Park View Grammar School, Darlington Coll. of Tech. and London Coll. of Fashion; Sub-Ed. then Deputy Chief Sub Look Now magazine 1984–86; freelance journalist 1986–87; Features Ed. Clothes Show magazine Aug.–Oct. 1987; Deputy Ed. More! magazine 1987–89; Ed. Looks magazine 1989–90, Company magazine 1990–95, Cosmopolitan 1995–; mem. Cttee. First Step Centre (charity for victims of violence and abuse); mem. British Soc. of Magazine Eds. 1990; mem. Periodical Publrs. Asscn. Editorial Cttee.; Women's Magazine Ed. of the Year Award, British Soc. of Magazine Eds. 1993. *Address:*

Cosmopolitan, National Magazine House, 72 Broadwick Street, London, W1V 2BP, England. *Telephone:* 0171-439 5442. *Fax:* 0171-439 5016.

NOSIGLIA, Enrique; Argentinian politician; b. 28 May 1949, Posadas; m. Nina Ciarlotti; four c.; ed. Universidad Nacional de Buenos Aires; joined Unión Cívica Radical 1972; mem. Nat. Exec. Movimiento de Renovación y Cambio 1975–80; Sec. Comité de la Capital (Wealth) 1983–87, Pres. 1987; Under-Sec. for Health and Social Affairs, Ministry of Health and Social Affairs 1983–85; Sec. Exec. Comm. Programa Alimentario Nacional (PAN) 1983–85; mem. Consejo para la Consolidación de la Democracia 1986; Minister of the Interior 1987–89.

NOSSAL, Sir Gustav Joseph Victor, A.C., C.B.E., M.B., B.S., PH.D., F.R.C.P., F.R.A.C.P., F.R.C.P.A., F.R.C.PATH., F.R.S.E., F.T.S.E., F.A.A., F.R.S.; Australian medical research scientist; b. 4 June 1931, Bad Ischl, Austria; m. Lyn B. Dunnicliff 1955; two s. two d.; ed. St Aloysius Coll., Sydney, Univs. of Sydney and Melbourne; jr. and sr. resident officer, Royal Prince Alfred Hosp., Sydney 1955–56; Research Fellow, The Walter and Eliza Hall Inst. of Medical Research, Melbourne 1957–59; Asst. Prof., Dept. of Genetics, Stanford Univ. School of Medicine, Calif. 1959–61; Deputy Dir. (Immunology), The Walter and Eliza Hall Inst. of Medical Research 1961–65, Dir. 1965–96; Prof. of Medical Biology, Univ. of Melbourne 1965–96, Prof. Emer., Dept. of Pathology 1996–; Chair. WHO Global Programme for Vaccines and Immunization 1992–; Partner Foursight Assocs. Pty. Ltd. 1996–; Dir., CRA Ltd. 1977–97; Pres. Australian Acad. of Science 1994–98; Foreign Assoc. N.A.S. (U.S.A.); mem. or hon. mem. many other nat. and foreign acads. and learned socs.; Hon. F.R.A.C.O.G.; Robert Koch Gold Medal, Albert Einstein World Award of Science, Emil von Behring Prize, Rabbi Shai Shacknai Prize and many other awards and prizes; Hon. LL.D. (Monash, Melbourne); Hon. M.D. (Mainz, Newcastle, Leeds, U.W.A.); Hon. D.Sc. (Sydney, Queensland, A.N.U., U.N.S.W., La Trobe, McMaster). *Publications:* Antibodies and Immunity 1968, Antigens, Lymphoid Cells and Immune Response 1971, Medical Science and Human Goals 1975, Nature's Defences (1978 Boyer Lectures), Reshaping Life: Key issues in genetic engineering 1984; 500 publications on immunity. *Leisure interests:* golf, literature. *Address:* Department of Pathology, The University of Melbourne, Parkville, Vic. 3052 (Office); 46 Fellows Street, Kew, Vic. 3101, Australia (Home). *Telephone:* (03) 9344-6946 (Office). *Fax:* (03) 9347-5242.

NOSSOL, Bishop Alfons, PH.D.; Polish ecclesiastic and professor of theology; b. 8 Aug. 1932, Brożec, Opole Prov.; ed. Higher Ecclesiastic Seminary in Opole Silesia, Catholic Univ. of Lublin (KUL) asst. prof. 1976, Prof. 1981; ordained priest, Opole 1957; lecturer Higher Ecclesiastic Seminary in Opole Silesia 1962–; lecturer Catholic Univ. of Lublin 1968, head Second Dept. of Dogmatic Theology 1977, Prof. 1981, head Ecumenical Inst. 1983; Prof. Theological Dept. Jan Gutenberg Univ., Mainz 1977; Prof. Pontifical Theology Dept., Wrocław 1978; Prof. Diocesan Theology and Pastoral Inst., Opole 1981; Ordinary Bishop Opole Diocese 1977; High Chancellor Opole Univ. Theological Dept.; mem. Main Council of the Polish Episcopate; leader Academic Council of the Episcopate; leader Episcopate Cttee. for Ecumenism; vice-leader Episcopate Cttee. for Catholic Learning; mem. Christian Unity Support Council, int. cttees. for theological dialogue with the Orthodox Church and the Lutheran Church; mem. European Acad. of Science and Art, Salzburg; Dr h.c. (Munster Univ.) 1991, (Mainz Univ.) 1992, (Christian Acad. of Theology, Warsaw) 1997. *Publications:* Theology for the Service of Faith 1968, Cognito Dei experimentalis 1974, Karol Barth Christology 1979, Truth and Love 1982, Towards a Civilization of Love 1984, Theology Closer to Life 1984, Der Mensch braucht Theologie 1986, Love the Victor of Truth 1987, Gelebte Theologie heute 1991, By Truth to Love 1994, and many academic articles and speeches. *Leisure interests:* classical literature, philosophy, the history of art. *Address:* ul. Książąt Opolskich 19, 45-005 Opole, Poland. *Telephone:* (77) 54 24 18. *Fax:* (77) 53 79 61.

NÖTH, Heinrich; German university professor; b. 20 June 1928, Munich; s. of Hans Nöth and Eugenie Nöth; m. 1951; two d.; ed. Univ. of Munich; Scientific Asst. Univ. of Munich 1952–55, 1957–62, Research Officer 1956, Lecturer 1962–64, Assoc. Prof. 1964–65, Prof. 1965–, Head Inst. of Inorganic Chem. 1969–97, Prof. Emer. 1997–; Pres. German Chemical Soc. 1988–89, 1991–92, Hon. mem.; Pres. Bavarian Acad. of Sciences 1998–(2000); Hon. mem. Austrian Chemical Soc.; Hon. mem. Royal Soc. of Chem.; Foreign mem. Russian Acad. of Sciences; Dr. h.c. (Marburg); D.Sc. h.c. (Leeds); Alfred Stock Medal; Bavarian Order of Maximilian for Science and Art. *Publications:* Nuclear Magnetic Resonance of Boron Compounds; more than 600 original research papers. *Leisure interests:* hiking, gardening, music. *Address:* Eichleite 25A, 82031 Grünwald, Germany. *Telephone:* (089) 641-3461.

NOTT, Rt. Hon. Sir John William Frederic, K.C.B., B.A.; British fmr. politician and business executive; b. 1 Feb. 1932; s. of Richard Nott and Phyllis Nott (née Francis); m. Miloska Sekol 1959; two s. one d.; ed. Bradfield Coll. and Trinity Coll., Cambridge; Lieut. with 2nd Gurkha Rifles, (regular officer) 1952–56; called to the Bar, Inner Temple 1959; M.P. for St. Ives, Cornwall 1966–83; Minister of State at Treasury 1972–74; Sec. of State for Trade 1979–81, for Defence 1981–83; Man. Dir. Lazard Brothers 1983–90, Chair. and C.E.O. 1985–90; Chair. Hillsdown 1993– (Dir. 1991–), Maple Leaf Foods Inc., Toronto 1993–95; Deputy Chair. Royal Insurance PLC 1986–89; Chair. (non-exec.) Etam 1991–95; Dir. Apax Partners & Co. Capital 1996–, Apax Partners & Co. Asset Man. Ltd. 1997–; Pres. Cambridge Union 1959. *Address:* Hillsdown Holdings PLC, 32 Hampstead High Street, London, NW3 1QD, England. *Telephone:* 0171-794 0677. *Fax:* 0171-433 6398.

NOTT, Rt. Rev. Peter John, M.A.; British ecclesiastic; b. 30 Dec. 1933, Belfast, Northern Ireland; s. of Cecil Frederick Wilder Nott and Rosina Mabel Nott; m. Elizabeth May Maingot 1961; one s. three d.; ed. Bristol Grammar School, Dulwich Coll., London, R.M.A. Sandhurst and Fitzwilliam House and Westcott House, Cambridge; served in regular army, commissioned R.A. 1951–55; Curate of Harpenden 1961–64; Chaplain and Fellow of Fitzwilliam Coll. Cambridge 1966–69, Hon. Fellow 1993; Chaplain of New Hall, Cambridge 1966–69; Rector of Beaconsfield 1969–77; Bishop of Taunton 1977–85; Bishop of Norwich 1985–; Archbishop's Adviser to H.M.C. 1980–85; Vice-Chair. Archbishops' Comm. on Rural Areas 1988–90; Pres. S.W. Region of Mencap 1978–84, Somerset Rural Music School 1981–85, Royal Norfolk Agricultural Asscn. 1996. *Address:* Bishop's House, Norwich, NR3 1SB, England. *Telephone:* (01603) 629001.

NOUEL, Philippe, D. EN D.; French lawyer; b. 21 July 1926, Maisons-Laffitte; s. of Jacques Nouel and Jacqueline Vallet; m. Nicole Danet 1955; two s. one d.; ed. Lycée Carnot and Faculté de Droit, Paris; lawyer at English Bar 1952–, Paris Court 1954–; Founding Partner of Gide Loyrette Nouel 1956–; fmr. mem. Council of the Bar, Paris; Fellow A.B.A.; Officier, Légion d'honneur. *Leisure interests:* golf, sailing. *Address:* Gide Loyrette Nouel, 26 cours Albert ler, 75008 Paris (Office); 9 boulevard Raspail, 75007 Paris, France (Home). *Telephone:* (01) 40 75 60 00 (Office).

NOUMAZALAY, Ambroise; Republic of the Congo politician; b. 23 Sept. 1933, Brazzaville; ed. Mathematics Faculty Univ. of Toulouse, France; First Sec. Nat. Revolutionary Movement (MNR); Dir. of Econ. Affairs 1964–66; mem. Nat. Revolutionary Council (CNR) and Sec. Org. Cttee. of the CNR Aug.–Oct. 1968; Prime Minister and Minister of Planning 1966–68; Minister of State in charge of Planning Aug.-Dec. 1968, for Agric., Water Resources and Forests 1968–69; Second Sec. responsible for the Execution of the Plan 1970–71; sentenced to life imprisonment March 1972; amnestied Oct. 1973; Minister of Industry and Manufacturing 1984–85, of Industry and Fisheries 1985–88, of Crafts 1986–88, of Forestry 1988–89; fmr. Sec. Gen. Parti congolais du travail (PCT). *Address:* Parti congolais du travail, Brazzaville, Republic of the Congo.

NOURBAKHSH, Mohsen, PH.D.; Iranian banker; b. 1948, Isfahan; s. of late Hossein Nourbakhsh and of Heshmat Pasra Nourbakhsh; m. Moazzam Karbasizadeh 1976; two s. two d.; ed. Univ. of Teheran, Univ. of Calif., U.S.A.; fmr. Faculty mem. Shahid Beheshti Univ., Teheran; Deputy Minister of Econ. Affairs and Finance 1979–81, Minister 1989–93; Gov. Cen. Bank (Bank Markazi Johhouri Islami Iran) 1981–86, 1994–; M.P. 1988–89; Deputy to the Pres., Econ. Affairs 1993–94. *Leisure interest:* swimming. *Address:* Bank Markazi Johhouri Islami Iran, 23 Ferdowsi Avenue, P.O. Box 11365, Teheran, Iran. *Telephone:* (21) 3110231. *Fax:* (21) 3115674.

NOURISSIER, François; French writer and journalist; b. 18 May 1927, Paris; s. of Paul E. E. Nourissier and Renée Heens; m. 1st Marie-Thérèse Sobesky 1949; two s.; m. 2nd Cécile Muhlstein 1962; one d.; ed. Lycée Saint Louis, Lycée Louis-le-Grand, Paris, Ecole libre des Sciences politiques, Paris, and Faculté de Droit, Paris; on staff of Secours Catholique Int., and work with Int. Refugee Org. 1949–51; Dir. Chalet Int. des Etudiants, Combloux (World Univ. Service) 1951–52; Sec.-Gen. Editions Denoël 1952–56; Editor-in-Chief La Parisienne (review) 1956–58; Literary Adviser to Editions Grasset 1958–95; Literary Dir. Vogue (French) 1964–66, Contributing Ed. Vogue (American) 1964–; Literary Critic Les Nouvelles littéraires 1963–72; Cinema Critic L'Express 1970–72; Literary Critic Le Point 1972–, Le Figaro 1975–, Figaro-Magazine 1978–; mem. l'Acad. Goncourt 1977, Sec.-Gen. 1983–96, Pres. 1996–; Prix Félix Fénéon 1952, Grand Prix de la Guilde du Livre 1965 (Swiss), Grand Prix du Roman de l'Acad. française 1966, Prix Fémina 1970, Prix Prince Pierre de Monaco 1975; Grand Prix de la Ville de Paris 1987; Commdr., Légion d'honneur, Commdr., Ordre nat. du Mérite, Commdr. des Arts et des Lettres. *Publications:* L'eau grise (novel) 1951, Lorca (essay) 1955, Les orphelins d'Auteuil (novel) 1956, Le corps de Diane (novel) 1957, Portrait d'un indifférent 1957, Bleu comme la nuit 1958, Un petit bourgeois 1964, Une histoire française 1966, Les Français (essay) 1967, Le maître de maison 1968, The French (trans. of Les Français) 1970, Cartier-Bresson's France 1971, La crève (novel) 1970, Allemande (novel) 1973, Lettre à mon chien (essay) 1975, Lettre ouverte à Jacques Chirac (essay) 1977, Le musée de l'homme (essay) 1979, L'empire des nuages (novel) 1981, La fête des pères (novel) 1986, En avant, calme et droit (novel) 1987, Bratislava (essay) 1990, Autos Graphie (essay) 1990, Le Gardien des ruines (novel) 1992, Mauvais genre (essay) 1994, le Bar de l'escadrille (novel) 1997, les Plus belles histoires d'amour (anthology) 1997. *Leisure interests:* walking, dogs. *Address:* Editions Grasset, 61 rue des Saints-Pères, 75006 Paris (Office); 23 rue Henri Heine, 75016 Paris; "Sainte Barbe", 84560 Ménerbes, France; En Cerniaz, 1824 Caux (Vaud), Switzerland.

NOUSIAINEN, Jaakko Ilmari, PH.D.; Finnish professor of political science; b. 20 Dec. 1931, Pälkjärvi; s. of Eino J. Nousiainen and Hilja S. Pussinen; m. Eva S. Lukkarinen 1958; one s. one d.; ed. Univ. of Helsinki; Assoc. Prof. of Political Science, Univ. of Jyväskylä 1960–63; Prof. of Political Science, Univ. of Turku 1963–93, Chancellor 1994–97; Research Assoc. W. European Study Centre, Harvard Univ. 1973–74; Research Prof. Finnish Acad. 1987–92. *Publications:* The Finnish Political System 1971, Presidential Leadership in Finland 1985, On the Top of Politics 1992. *Leisure interests:*

reading, sailing. *Address:* Department of Political Science, University of Turku, 20014 Turku (Office); Itäinen Pitkäkatu 24 A 18, 20700 Turku, Finland.

NOUVEL, Jean; French architect; b. 1945, Fumel, Lot-et-Garonne; m. Catherine Richard 1992; one d; two s. by Odil Fillion; ed. Ecole des Beaux Arts, Paris; first maj. bldg., medical centre, Bezons; began Nemausus housing projects, Nîmes 1985; Hon. Prof. Univ. of Buenos Aires; Grand Prix de l'Architecture for Arab cultural centre, Paris 1987; in 1992 completed designs for La Tour Sans Fins, a 1,400 ft. (425m) glass tower to be built in Paris, completed Opéra Lyon, opened 1993, Fondation Cartier, opened 1994, Galeries Lafayette Berlin, opened 1996. *Address:* Architectures Jean Nouvel, 10 Cité d'Angoulême, 75011 Paris, France.

NOVÁK, Jiří, LL.D.; Czech politician and lawyer; b. 11 April 1950, Hranice, Přerov Dist.; m.; one s. one d.; ed. J.E. Purkyně (now Masaryk) Univ., Brno; lawyer 1976–89; mem. Standing Comm. of the Presidium of Czech Nat. Council for Prison System Issues 1989–92; Deputy to Czech Nat. Council Feb.–June 1990; mem. Presidium, Czech Nat. Council 1990–92; Chair. Cttee. on Law and Constitution of Czech Nat. Council 1990–92; Minister of Justice, Czech Repub. 1992–96; Chair. Legis. Council of Govt. of Czech Repub. Feb.–July 1992; mem. Parl. 1996–98; Chair. Parl. Cttee. for Petitions 1996–98; Vice-Chair. Interdepartmental Antidrug Comm. 1996; mem. Civic Democratic Party 1991–98; advocate 1998–. *Address:* Sokolská 60, 120 00 Prague 2 (Office); nám. T. G. Masaryka 15, Lipník/Bečvou, Czech Republic (Home). *Telephone:* 24 94 19 44 (Office).

NOVÁK, Josef, PROF. RNDR.; Czech mathematician; b. 19 April 1905, Třebětín, Letovice; s. of Alois Novák and Františka Loubalová; m. Vladimíra Plocková 1936; one s. one d.; Asst. Univ. of Brno 1935–45, Prof. of Math., Univ. of Brno 1945–48; Czech Technical Univ., Prague 1948–51; Charles Univ. Prague 1952–; Math. Inst. of the Czechoslovak Acad. of Sciences 1952–82; Academician, Czechoslovak (now Czech) Acad. of Sciences 1952–92; Chair. of Math. and Physics Section of the Czechoslovak Acad. of Sciences 1955–61; Chair. Bd. of Math., Czechoslovak Acad. of Sciences 1966–82; Dir. Math. Inst. of the Czechoslovak Acad. of Sciences 1972–76; Chair. Asscn. of Czechoslovak Mathematicians and Physicists 1972–78; mem. Advisory Cttee. for Science and Tech., ECOSOC 1972–76; mem. Scientific Bd. of Int. Math. S. Banach Center 1972–82; Scientific Consultant, Math. Inst. of Czecholsovak (now Czech) Acad. of Sciences 1983–91; Order of Labour 1965, 1982, Gold Medal of Bernard Bolzano 1970, of Palacký Univ., Olomouc 1971, Gold Felber Medal, Czech Tech. Univ. 1975, Gold Medal of Brno Univ. 1976, Gold Medals, Czechoslovak Acad. of Sciences 1980, 1991, Slovak Acad. of Sciences 1991. *Leisure interests:* genetics, music, gardening. *Address:* Jeseniova 39, 13000 Prague 3, Czech Republic. *Telephone:* 42-2-6441187.

NOVAK, Michael, B.T., M.A.; American theologian; b. 9 Sept. 1933, Johnstown, Pa.; s. of Michael J. Novak and Irene Sakmar; m. Karen R. Laub 1963; one s. two d.; ed. Stonehill Coll., North Easton, Mass. and Gregorian Univ., Rome; Teaching Fellow, Harvard Univ. 1961–63; Asst. Prof. of Humanities, Stanford Univ. 1965–68; Assoc. Prof. of Philosophy and Religious Studies, State Univ. of N.Y., Old Westbury 1969–71; Assoc. Dir. Humanities, Rockefeller Foundation 1973–74; Ledden-Watson Distinguished Prof. of Religion, Syracuse Univ. 1976–78; Resident Scholar American Enterprise Inst. 1978–, George Frederick Jewett Prof. of Public Policy Research 1983–, Dir. Social and Political Studies 1987–; Visiting Prof. Univ. of Notre Dame 1987–88; columnist, The Nat. Review 1979–86, Forbes Magazine 1989–; f., publr. Crisis 1982–, Ed.-in-Chief 1993–; mem. Bd. for Int. Broadcasting 1983–; Judge, Nat. Book Awards, DuPont Awards in Broadcast Journalism; Head, U.S. Del. to UN Human Rights Comm., Geneva 1981, 1982; other public appts.; numerous hon. degrees and awards, including Templeton Prize 1994. *Publications include:* Belief and Unbelief 1965, The Spirit of Democratic Capitalism 1982, Freedom with Justice: Catholic Social Thought and Liberal Institutions 1984, Taking Glasnost Seriously 1988, Free Persons and the Common Good 1989, This Hemisphere of Liberty 1990, The Catholic Ethic and the Spirit of Capitalism 1993, Business as a Calling 1996, and numerous articles in journals. *Address:* American Enterprise Institute, 1150 17th Street, Washington, DC 20036, U.S.A. *Telephone:* (202) 862-5839.

NOVARINA, Maurice Paul Joseph; French architect and planner; b. 28 June 1907, Thonon-les-Bains, Haute Savoie; s. of Joseph Novarina and Anaïs Detruche; m. Manon Trolliet 1937; two s.; ed. Ecole Speciale des Travaux Publics and Ecole Nat. Supérieure des Beaux Arts, Paris; Chief Architect of Public Bldgs. and Nat. Palaces; Chief Architect, Reconstruction of the Eure 1947–55; Ancien Prof. Ecole Speciale d'Architecture, Ecole Nat. des Beaux Arts; works include churches, cultural bldgs., schools, hosps., hotels, commercial bldgs. etc.; mem. Acad. des Beaux Arts (Inst. de France), Acad. d'architecture; Commdr., Légion d'honneur, Officier, Ordre Nat. du Mérite, Ordre des Arts et Lettres; several awards and prizes. *Address:* 52 rue Raynouard, 75116 Paris, France.

NOVELLO, Antonia Coello, M.D., M.P.H.; American public health official; b. 23 Aug. 1944, Fajardo, Puerto Rico; m. Joseph Novello 1970; ed. Univ. of Puerto Rico and Johns Hopkins Univ.; intern, Mott Children's Hosp., Univ. of Mich. Ann Arbor 1970–71; Univ. of Mich. Medical Center 1971–73; postgrad. training in nephrology, Dept. of Internal Medicine, Univ. of Michigan Medical Center 1973–74, Dept. of Pediatrics, Georgetown Univ. 1974–75; pvt. practice in pediatrics, Springfield, Va. 1976–78; entered U.S. Public Health Service 1978; various posts at Nat. Insts. of Health, Bethesda, Md. 1978–90, Deputy Dir. Nat. Inst. of Child Health and Human Devt. 1986–90; Clinical Prof. of Pediatrics, Georgetown Univ. Hospital, Washington, D.C. 1986, 1989, Uniformed Services Univ. of the Health Services, Bethesda, Md. 1989; Adjunct Prof. of Pediatrics and Communicable Diseases, Univ. of Mich.; Surgeon-Gen. U.S. Public Health Service 1990–93, UNICEF Special Rep. for Health and Nutrition 1993–; numerous professional appts., memberships and affiliations; recipient of numerous awards, honours and honorary degrees. *Address:* UNICEF, 3 United Nations Plaza, Room 634, New York, NY 10017, U.S.A. *Telephone:* (301) 496-0186. *Fax:* (301) 496-0625.

NOVIKOV, Sergey Petrovich; Russian mathematician; b. 20 March 1938, Gorky; s. Petr Novikov and Ludmila Keldysh; m. Eleonora Tsoi 1962; one s. two d.; ed. Moscow Univ., Steklov Math. Inst.; Corresp. mem. of U.S.S.R. (now Russian) Acad. of Sciences 1966–, mem. 1981–; Prof. Moscow Univ. 1966–; Head Dept., Landau Inst. for Theoretical Physics 1975–, Chair. Dept. of Geometry and Topology, Moscow Univ. 1984–; Head Dept., Steklov Math. Inst. 1983–; Foreign mem. N.A.S., Acad. dei Licei; Hon. mem. London Math. Soc., Serbian Acad. of Art and Science 1988, Academia Europaea 1990, Pontifical Acad. of Sciences 1996; Dr. h.c. (Athens) 1989; Lenin Prize 1967, Field's Medal, Int. Math. Union 1970, Lobachevsky Int. Prize, U.S.S.R. Acad. of Sciences 1981. *Publications:* Algebraic and Differential Topology 1960, General Relativity 1971–75, Soliton Theory 1974 and works on geometry, topology and theory of relativity. *Leisure interest:* history. *Address:* University of Maryland at C.P., College Park, IPST, MD 20742, U.S.A.; Landau Institute for Theoretical Physics, Kosygina 2, 117334 Moscow, Russia. *Telephone:* (301) 405-4836 (Office, U.S.A.); 137-32-44 (Office, Russia); (301) 314 7472 (Home, U.S.A.); 135-12-24 (Home, Russia). *Fax:* (301) 314 9363 (U.S.A.).

NOVODVORSKAYA, Valeria Ilyinichna; Russian politician; b. 17 May 1950; ed. Krupskaya Moscow Region Pedagogical Inst.; in dissident movt. since late 1960s, arrested as student on charge of organizing underground anti-Soviet group 1969; translator Second Moscow Medicine Inst. 1975–90; organized political action against invasion of Czechoslovakia Dec. 1969; arrested, discharged 1972; initiator and participant of anti-Soviet meetings; was arrested 17 times 1985–91; imprisoned for anti-Soviet activities four times 1978, 1985, 1986, 1991; mem. Co-ordination Council of Democratic Union, participated in political seminar Democracy and Humanism 1988; leader Party of Democratic Union 1992; political reviewer Khozyain 1993–95, Stolitsa 1995–. *Publications:* articles in newspapers and magazines. *Leisure interests:* reading, mountain climbing, swimming. *Address:* Democratic Union, Onezhskaya str. 4, Apt. 113, Moscow, Russia. *Telephone:* 453-37-76.

NOVOTNÁ, Jana; Czech tennis player; b. 2 Oct. 1968, Brno (in fmr. Czechoslovakia); d. of Frank Novotny and Libuse Novotna; won U.S. Open Jr. Doubles 1986; turned professional 1987; won her first title Adelaide 1988; Olympic Silver Medal in doubles with Helena Suková 1988; won Australian and U.S. Open mixed doubles with Pugh 1988; won six women's doubles titles 1989; with Suková won Australian Open, French Open and Wimbledon doubles 1990; reached quarter-finals French Open 1991; won 7 doubles titles with Savchenko Neiland 1992; won singles titles Osaka and Brighton 1993; singles titles Leipzig, Brighton and Essen 1994; Olympic Bronze Medal in singles, Silver Medal in doubles with Suková, Atlanta 1996; won Wimbledon singles 1998, Wimbledon women's doubles 1998.

NOVOZHILOV, Genrikh Vasilievich; Russian mechanical engineer; b. 27 Oct. 1925, Moscow; m.; one s.; ed. Moscow Aviation Inst.; mem. CPSU 1951–91; constructor, constructing engineer, leading engineer, Sec. CP Cttee. aviation plant 1948–57; Deputy Constructor-in-Chief, Main Constructor, Constructor-Gen. U.S.S.R. Ministry of Aviation Industry 1958–86; simultaneously First Deputy Constructor-Gen. Moscow Ilyushin Machine Constructing Plant 1964–; Deputy to U.S.S.R. Supreme Soviet 1974–89, U.S.S.R. People's Deputy 1989–91; mem. Cen. CPSU Cttee. 1986–91. *Publications:* works in the field of new samples of aviation tech., including Theory and Practice of Designing Passenger Aircraft 1976, Design, Testing and Production of Wide-Fuselage Passenger Aircraft 1980, essays on History of Constructions and Systems of Aircraft 1983; Hero of Socialist Labour (twice), Lenin Prize and other decorations. *Leisure interests:* tennis, photography. *Address:* S. Ilyushin Machine Construction Plant, Leningradsky prospekt 45G, 125319 Moscow, Russia. *Telephone:* 251-5293, 155-3116.

NOWINA-KONOPKA, Piotr Maria, D.ECON.SC.; Polish politician, economist and publicist; b. 27 May 1949, Chorzów; s. of Mikotaj Nowina-Konopka and Anna Nowina-Konopka; m. Wanda Nowina-Konopka 1975; two d.; ed. Higher School of Econs., Sopot and Gdańsk Univ. 1972; Asst. Gdańsk Tech. Univ. 1972–74; Deputy Head, Centre of Revocatory Maritime Chamber, Gdynia 1977–79; Lecturer, Foreign Trade Econs. Inst. of Gdańsk Univ. 1979–; co-founder and Sec. Catholic Intelligentsia Club in Gdańsk 1980–81; mem. Solidarity Independent Self-governing Trade Union 1980–, Assoc. 1982–, Press Spokesman 1988–89, Chief of Press 1989; mem. Civic Cttee. attached to Lech Wałęsa (q.v.) 1988–91; Lecturer, Gdańsk Theology Inst. 1988–; Minister of State in Chancellery of Pres. of Poland 1989–90; Sec.-Gen. Democratic Union 1990–94; Union for Freedom Sec. for Foreign Affairs 1994–98; Deputy to Sejm (Parl.) 1991–, Vice-Chair. Cttee. for the European Treaty 1992–97; Sec. of State Office of the Cttee. for European Integration 1998; Sec. of State in Chancellery of Prime Minister 1998–; Deputy Chief Negotiator for negotiations with EU 1998–; Deputy Chair. Jt. Parl. Cttee. Poland-European Parl.; mem. Foreign Affairs Comm.; Pres. Polish Robert

Schuman Foundation 1991–; Chevalier Ordre du Mérite. *Leisure interests:* family life, reading, social sciences, yachting, riding. *Address:* Al. Ujazdowskie 37/5, II p., 00 540 Warsaw, Poland (Office). *Telephone:* (22) 6212161. *Fax:* (22) 6297214.

NOWRA, Louis; Australian writer; b. 12 Dec. 1950; Prix Italia 1990, Australia/Canada Award 1993. *Publications:* The Misery of Beauty 1977, Inner Voices 1978, Inside the Islands 1980, The Golden Age 1985, Palu 1988, Byzantine Flowers 1990, Map of the Human Heart 1991, Summer of the Aliens 1991, The Watchtower 1992, Cosi 1992, Radiance 1993, Crow 1994, The Temple 1994, The Incorruptible 1995, Heaven's Burning 1997, Red Nights 1997. *Leisure interests:* cricket, mycology. *Address:* Level 18, Plaza 11, 500 Oxford Street, Bondi Junction, N.S.W. 2011, Australia. *Telephone:* (02) 389 6400.

NOYER, Christian; French banker and civil servant; b. 6 Oct. 1950, Soisy; s. of Alain Noyer and Magdeleine Noyer (née Ogee); m. Martine Broyet; three s. one d.; ed. Univs. of Rennes and Paris, Inst. of Political Science, Ecole Nat. d'Admin.; joined Treasury 1976, Chief of Banking Office, then of Export Credit Office 1982–85, Deputy Dir. in charge of Int. Multilateral Issues 1988–90, then of Debt Man., Monetary and Banking Affairs 1990–92, Dir. of Dept. responsible for public holdings and financing 1991–93, Dir. of Treasury 1993–95; financial attaché French del. to EC, Brussels 1980–82; tech. adviser, then sr. adviser to Minister for Econ. Affairs, Finance and Privatization, Edouard Balladur (q.v.) 1986–88, Chief of Staff to E. Alphandéry 1993, to Jean Arthuis (q.v.) 1995–97; Dir. Ministry for Econ. Affairs, Finance and Industry 1997–98; Vice-Pres. European Cen. Bank June 1998–; Alt. Gov. IMF and World Bank 1993–95; alt. mem. European Monetary Cttee. 1988–90, mem. 1993–95, 1998–; alt. mem. G7 and G10 1993–95; mem. working party no. 3 OECD 1993–95; Chair. Paris Club of Creditor Cos. 1993–97; Chevalier Légion d'honneur, Ordre nat. du Mérite, Commdr. Nat. Order of Lion, Senegal. *Publications:* Banks: The Rules of the Game 1990, various articles. *Leisure interest:* sailing. *Address:* European Central Bank, Kaiserstrasse 29, 60311 Frankfurt am Main, Germany (Office); 53 rue Geoffroy Saint-Hilaire, 75005 Paris, France (Home). *Telephone:* (69) 13-44-0 (Office).

NOYES, Richard Macy, PH.D.; American professor of chemistry; b. 6 April 1919, Champaign, Ill.; s. of William Albert Noyes and Katharine Haworth Macy; m. 1st Winninette Arnold 1946 (died 1972); m. 2nd Patricia Harris 1973; ed. Harvard Coll. and Calif. Inst. of Tech.; Research Assoc. Calif. Inst. of Tech. 1942–46; Instructor Columbia Univ. 1946–49, Asst. Prof. 1949–54, Assoc. Prof. 1954–58; Prof. of Chem. Univ. of Ore. 1958–, Acting Head or Head of Dept. of Chem. 1960–61, 1963–64, 1966–68, 1975–78; Guggenheim Fellow Univ. of Leeds 1955–56; Fulbright Fellow, Vic. Univ. of Wellington 1964; Nat. Science Foundation Sr. Postdoctoral Fellow Max-Planck-Inst. of Physical Chem, Göttingen 1965; Visiting Prof. Oxford 1971–72, Max-Planck-Inst. of Biophysical Chem. 1978–79, 1982–83; mem. N.A.S., American Acad. of Arts and Sciences; Hon. mem. Hungarian Acad. of Sciences; Alexander von Humboldt Sr. American Scientist Award 1978–79. *Publications:* over 200 articles in chemical journals. *Leisure interest:* trying to influence land use decisions regarding forestry and wilderness areas. *Address:* 2014 Elk Avenue, Eugene, OR 97403, U.S.A. (Home). *Telephone:* (503) 344-0639 (Home).

NOZICK, Robert, A.M., PH.D.; American professor of philosophy; b. 16 Nov. 1938, Brooklyn; s. of late Max Nozick and Sophie Cohen; m. 1st Barbara Fierer 1959 (divorced 1981); one s. one d.; m. 2nd Gjertrud Schnackenberg 1987; ed. Columbia Coll. and Princeton Univ.; Instr. Princeton Univ. 1962–63, Asst. Prof. 1963–65; Asst. Prof. Harvard Univ. 1965–67; Assoc. Prof. the Rockefeller Univ. 1967–69; Prof. of Philosophy, Harvard Univ. 1969–, Arthur Kingsley Porter Prof. of Philosophy 1985–98, Pellegrino Univ. Prof. 1998–, Chair. of Dept. 1981–84; Fellow, Center for Advanced Study in Behavioral Sciences 1971–72; Rockefeller Fellowship 1979–80; Nat. Endowment for Humanities Fellowship 1987–88; Guggenheim Fellowship 1996–97; Fellow, American Acad. of Arts and Sciences; Corresp. Fellow, British Acad.; Nat. Book Award 1975; D.Hum.Litt. h.c. (Knox Coll.) 1983; other awards and distinctions. *Publications:* Anarchy, State and Utopia 1974, Philosophical Explanations 1981, The Examined Life 1989, The Nature of Rationality 1993, Socratic Puzzles 1996; articles in professional journals. *Address:* Emerson Hall, Harvard University, Cambridge, MA 02138, U.S.A. *Telephone:* (617) 495-2191.

NOZIERES, Philippe Pierre Gaston François; French physicist; b. 12 April 1932, Paris; s. of Henri Nozieres and Alice Noel; m. Catherine Michel 1982; one d. and one s. one d. by previous m.; ed. Ecole Normale Supérieure and Princeton Univ.; Prof. of Physics, Univ. of Paris 1961–72; Physicist, Laue-Langevin Inst. 1972–76; Prof. of Physics, Grenoble Univ. 1976–83; Prof. of Statistical Physics, Coll. de France 1983–; mem. Acad. des Sciences (Inst. de France); Foreign Assoc. N.A.S. (U.S.A.); Holweck Prize 1976, Prix du CEA (Acad. des Sciences) 1979, Wolf Prize 1985, Gold Medal C.N.R.S. 1988. *Publications:* papers on theoretical physics and statistical physics. *Address:* I.L.L., B.P. 156, 38042 Grenoble Cedex (Office); 15 route de Saint Nizier, 38180 Seyssins, France (Home). *Telephone:* (04) 76.20.72.74 (Office); (04) 76.21.60.28 (Home). *Fax:* (04) 76.88.24.16.

NSEKELA, Amon James, M.A., DIP.ED., F.I.B.A.; Tanzanian fmr. diplomatist, civil servant and banker; b. 4 Jan. 1930, Lupepo, Rungwe; s. of late Ngonile Reuben Nsekela and of Anyambilile Nsekela (née Kalinga); m. Christina Matilda Kyusa 1957; two s.; ed. Rungwe Dist. School, Malangali Secondary School, Tabora Govt. Sr. Secondary School, Makerere Univ. Coll., and Univ. of the Pacific, Calif., U.S.A., teacher 1955–59; Admin. Officer 1960–62; Perm./Prin. Sec. Ministries of External Affairs and Defence, Industries, Mineral Resources and Power, and Treasury 1963–67; Chair. and Man. Dir. Nat. Bank of Commerce 1967–74, 1981–91; Chair. Nat. Insurance Corpn. of Tanzania 1967–69, Tanzania Investment Bank 1981–91, Inst. of Devt. Man., Mzumbe, Morogoro 1982–91; High Commr. in U.K. 1974–81 (also accred. to Ireland) 1980–81; Dir. Tanzania-Zambia Railway Authority 1982–, Computers & Telecoms Systems 1993–; Chair., Council, Univ. of Dar es Salaam 1970–74, Pensioners' Union of Tanzania 1992–; Vice-Pres. Britain–Tanzania Soc.; Hon. D.Lit. (Dar es Salaam) 1990; African Insurance Org. Award 1982; Order of the United Republic of Tanzania. *Publications:* Minara ya Historia ya Tanganyika: Tanganyika hadi Tanzania, Demokrasi Tanzania, Socialism and Social Accountability in a Developing Nation, The Development of Health Services in Mainland Tanzania: Tumetoka Mbali (with Dr. A. L. Nhonoli), Towards National Alternatives 1984, A Time to Act 1984. *Leisure interests:* swimming, darts, reading and writing. *Address:* 9 Lupa Way, P.O. Box 722, Mbeya, Tanzania. *Telephone:* (065) 3487. *Fax:* (065) 2541.

N'SINGA UDJUU ONGWABEKI UNTUBE; Democratic Republic of the Congo politician; b. (as Joseph N'Singa) 29 Oct. 1934, Bandundu; s. of Nshue O. Nsinga and Monkaju Medji; m. Mbu Modiri; four s. five d.; Minister of Justice 1966–69; Minister of State for Home Affairs March–Aug. 1969; Minister of the Interior 1969–70; Minister of State at the Presidency Sept. 1970, dismissed Sept. 1970; mem. Cen. Cttee., Mouvement populaire de la révolution (MPR) 1980–83 (Exec. Sec. 1981–83), First Vice-Chair. 1980–83; First State Commr. 1981–82; State Commr. for Justice 1986–90; Pres. Judiciary Council 1986; mem. Sacred Congregation for the Evangelization of Peoples. *Address:* B.P. 3559, Kinshasa/Gombe, Democratic Republic of the Congo (Home).

NTIBANTUNGANYA, Sylvestre; Burundian politician; b. 8 May 1956, Nyamutobo; m. Eusebie Ntibantunganya (deceased); ed. Nat. Audiovisual Inst. Paris; worked for Burundi State TV and Radio for two years; joined Nat. Secr. Unity for Nat. Progress (UPRONA); in exile in Rwanda 1979–83; founding mem. Sahwanya-Frodebu Party, mem. Exec. Cttee. 1991, Leader 1993–; Chief Ed. Aube de la Démocratie (Frodebu Party newspaper) until 1993; Deputy for Gitega 1993; Minister for External Relations 1993; fmr. Speaker of Parl.; Pres. of Burundi 1994–96; Chair. Nat. Security Council 1996–. *Address:* National Security Council, Bujumbura, Burundi.

NUAIMI, Ali Ibrahim al-, M.S.; Saudi Arabian politician and fmr. oil industry executive; b. 1935, Eastern Prov.; m. 1962; four c.; ed. Int. Coll. Beirut, American Univ. Beirut, and Lehigh Univ., Pennsylvania and Stanford Univ., U.S.A.; Asst. Geologist, Exploration Dept., Aramco 1953, Hydrologist and Geologist 1963–67, worked in Econs. and Public Relations Dept. 1967–69, Vice-Pres. Aramco 1975, Sr. Vice-Pres. 1978, Dir. 1980, Exec. Vice-Pres., Operations 1982, Pres. 1984, C.E.O. 1988; Minister of Petroleum and Mineral Resources 1995–. *Leisure interests:* hunting, hiking. *Address:* P.O. Box 247, Riyadh 11191, Saudi Arabia. *Telephone:* (1) 478 1661. *Fax:* (1) 1980.

NUAIMI, H.H. Sheikh Humaid bin Rashid an-; ruler of Ajman; Ruler of Ajman 1981–; mem. Supreme Council of U.A.E. 1981–; Patron, Sheikh Humaid bin Rashid Prizes for Culture and Science 1983–. *Address:* Ruler's Palace, P.O. Box 1, Ajman, United Arab Emirates.

NUCERA, Louis; French writer; b. 1928, Nice; s. of Ange Nucera and Baptistine Vicini; m. Suzanne Biffi 1970; contrib. Monde des Livres 1980s, Nouvel Observateur, Figaro Magazine, Valeurs Actuelles; Prix Interallié for Le Chemin de la Lanterne 1981, Grand Prix de Littérature (Acad. Française) 1993, Prix Pierre Mac Orlan 1996; Chevalier Légion d'honneur, des Arts et des Lettres. *Publications include:* L'Obstiné 1970, L'Ami 1974, Le Roi René 1976, Avenue des Diables Bleus 1979, Le Chemin de la Lanterne, Le Kiosque à Musique 1984, Mes Rayons de Soleil 1987, Le Chanson de Maria 1989, Le Ruban Rouge 1991, Sa Majesté le chat (essay) 1992, Souvenirs: Mes Ports d'Attache 1994, Ils s'aimaient 1998, several essays. *Leisure interests:* cycling, cats. *Address:* 55 rue Caulaincourt, 75018 Paris; 31 rue Smollett, 06300 Nice, France. *Telephone:* (01) 46 06 28 87 (Paris); (04) 93 26 27 77 (Nice).

NUGIS, Ulo; Estonian politician and business executive; b. 28 April 1944, Tallinn; ed. Minsk Polytech. Inst.; chief engineer Tegur Factory 1970–73; Dir. Ehitusdetail (experimental factory) 1974–80; Dir. Dunamo (Ski Mfg. factory) 1980–86; Dir.-Gen. Production Asscn. Estoplast 1986–1990; mem. Congress of Estonia and Speaker Supreme Soviet of Estonian Repub. 1990–92; mem. Republican Coalition Party (now People's Party of Republicans and Conservatives) 1990–; Chair. Riigikogu (State Ass.) 1992–95, mem. 1995–. *Address:* Riigikogu, Lossi-plats 1A, 0100 Tallinn, Estonia (Office).

NUJOMA, Sam Shafilshuna; Namibian politician; b. 12 May 1929, Etunda Village, Ongandjera Dist.; s. of late Daniel Uutomi Nujoma and Hewi Mpingana Kondombolo; m. Kovambo Theopoldine Katjimune; three s. one d.; ed. Finnish Protestant Mission School, St. Barnabas School, Windhoek; with State Railways until 1957; Municipal Clerk, Windhoek 1957; Clerk in wholesale store 1957–59; elected Leader of Ovamboland People's Org. (OPO) 1959; arrested Dec. 1959; went into exile 1960; Founder, with Herman Toivo ja Toivo (q.v.), and Pres. SWAPO (S.W. Africa People's Org.) April 1960–; appeared before UN Cttee. on S.W. Africa June 1960; set up SWAPO provisional HQ in Dar es Salaam, Tanzania March 1961; arrested on return to Windhoek and formally ordered out of the country March 1966; turned to armed struggle after rejection by Int. Court of Justice of SWAPO complaint against S. Africa Aug. 1966; gave evidence at UN Security Council Oct. 1971; led SWAPO negotiations at numerous int. negotiations culminating in implementation in March 1989 of UN Resolution 435 providing for independence of Namibia; returned to Namibia Sept. 1989; mem. Constituent Ass. Nov. 1989–Feb. 1990; Pres. of Namibia March 1990–, also Minister of Home Affairs 1995–96; Hon. LL.D. (Lincoln Univ., U.S.A., Ahmadu Bello Univ., Nigeria); Hon. Dr. Tech. (Fed. Univ. of Tech., Minna); Grand Master, Order of Merit Grand Cruz (Brazil); Lenin Peace Prize 1973, Frederic Joliot Curie Gold Medal 1980, Ho Chi Minh Peace Award 1988, Indira Gandhi Peace Prize 1990. *Publication:* To Free Namibia 1994. *Address:* Office of the President, State House, Robert Mugabe Avenue, P.M.B. 13339, Windhoek, Namibia. *Telephone:* (61) 220010. *Fax:* (61) 221780.

NUKAGA, Fukushiro; Japanese politician and fmr. journalist; b. 1944; ed. Waseda Univ.; fmr. political and econ. reporter for Sankei Shimbun; fmr. mem. Ibaraki Prefectural Ass.; mem. LDP; mem. for Ibaraki, House of Reps.; fmr. Deputy Chief Cabinet Sec.; Dir.-Gen. Defence Agency 1998–. *Address:* Defence Agency, 9-7-45, Akasaka, Minato-ku, Tokyo 107, Japan. *Telephone:* (03) 3408-5211.

NUMAIRI, Field-Marshal Gaafar al- (see Nemery).

NUMAN, Yasin Said; Yemeni politician; fmr. Deputy Prime Minister and Minister of Fisheries; Prime Minister of Democratic Republic of Yemen 1986–90, Minister of Labour and Civil Service 1986.

NUNES, Manuel Jacinto, PH.D.; Portuguese banker and politician; b. 27 Jan. 1926, Lisbon; of José and Lourença da Conceição Nunes; m. Lutgarda da Silva Rodrigues Nunes 1950; one d.; Prof., Inst. for Advanced Mil. Studies 1953–74; Sec. of State for Finance 1955–59; Vice-Gov. Banco de Portugal 1960–74, Gov. 1974–75, 1980–85; Pres. Caixa Geral de Depósitos 1976–80; Deputy Prime Minister and Minister of Finance and the Plan 1978–79; Econ. Adviser 1985–89; Pres. Lisbon Acad. of Sciences 1980–90; Vice-Pres. Nat. Geographic Soc. 1974–79; Chair. Consultative Comm. for European Econ. Integration; Chair. Portuguese-American Foundation for Devt.; Grand Officer, Order of Christ, Grand Officer, Order of the Southern Cross, Grand Cross of the Viscount of Rio, Distinguished Service Silver Medal, Grand Cross of Prince d. Henrique, Grand Cross of Public Educ., Officier, Légion d'honneur (France), Hon. C.B.E. (U.K.). *Publications:* Structure of the Portuguese Economy 1954, National Income and Budgetary Balance 1957, Economic Growth and Budget Policy 1961, Economic Development and Planning, The Monetary Controversy, From Rome to Maastricht; numerous articles. *Leisure interests:* history, politics, philosophy. *Address:* Fundação Luso-Americana, Rua do Sacramento à Lapa 21, 1200 Lisbon (Office); R. S. Francisco De Sales, 17-A, 1° Esq., 1250 Lisbon, Portugal (Home). *Telephone:* (01) 396 0297 (Office); (01) 386408 (Home).

NUNGESSER, Roland, L. EN D.; French politician; b. 9 Oct. 1925, Nogent-sur-Marne; s. of Léon Nungesser and Aline Sanguinolenti; m. 1st Michèle Jeanne Elizabeth Selignac 1957 (divorced 1981); three d.; m. 2nd Marie-Christine Ventrillon 1981; ed. Ecole Libre des Sciences Politiques, Paris Law Faculty; Commissaire-général du Salon Nautique Int. 1957–62; Vice-Pres. Chambre Syndicale des Industries Nautiques; Pres. Conseil Nat. de la Navigation de Plaisance 1961–67; Regional Chair. 1962; Deputy for Seine 1958–67, Val-de-Marne 1967–95; Sec. Nat. Ass. 1958–60; Sec. of State for Housing 1966–67; Sec. of State at Ministry of Economy and Finance 1967–68; Minister of Youth and Sports May–July 1968; Mayor of Nogent-sur-Marne 1959–95; Pres. Franco-Soviet (Franco-Russian 1992–) Chamber of Commerce 1969–, Liaison Cttee. for Local Councillors 1971, Union of Parisian Region Mayors 1983, Soc. for Protection of Animals (SPA) 1984–88 (Hon. Pres. 1988–); Vice-Pres. Nat. Ass. 1969–74; Pres. Conseil Général du Val de Marne 1970–76; Vice-Pres. Movt. Nat. des élus Iocaus 1976–; Pres. Carrefour du Gaullisme 1979–, Asscn. des Maires de l'Ile-de France 1983–; mem. Rassemblement pour la République; mem. various socs. and asscns; Chevalier Légion d'honneur, Mérite commercial. *Leisure interests:* motor yachting, athletics. *Address:* Assemblée Nationale, 75355 Paris; 18 avenue Duvelleroy, 94130 Nogent-sur-Marne, France. *Telephone:* (01) 48.81.11.22.

NUNN, John Francis, M.D., PH.D., F.R.C.S., F.R.C.A.; British anaesthetist; b. 7 Nov. 1925, Colwyn Bay; s. of Francis Nunn and Lilian Nunn (née Davies); m. Sheila Doubleday 1949; one s. two d.; ed. Wrekin Coll. and Birmingham Univ.; Malayan Medical Service 1949–53; Resident Anaesthetist, Birmingham 1953–56; Leverhulme Research Fellow, Royal Coll. of Surgeons 1957–64; Prof. of Anaesthesia, Univ. of Leeds 1964–68; Head of Div. of Anaesthesia, Clinical Research Centre, and Hon. Consultant Anaesthetist 1968–91; Dean Faculty of Anaesthetics, Royal Coll. of Surgeons 1979–82; Pres. Section of Anaesthetics, Royal Soc. of Medicine 1984–85; Hon. Fellow Royal Soc. of Medicine; Hon. Fellow Australian and New Zealand Coll. of Anaesthetists, Hon. Fellow Faculty of Anaesthetists, Royal Coll. of Surgeons of Ireland; Dr. h.c. (Turin) 1993; Hon. M.D. (Uppsala) 1996. *Publications:* Applied Respiratory Physiology (4th edn.) 1993, General Anaesthesia (Gen. Ed.), Ancient Egyptian Medicine 1996; 220 publs. in scientific journals. *Leisure interests:* Egyptology, model eng., music, skiing, geology. *Address:* 3 Russell Road, Moor Park, Northwood, Middx., HA6 2LJ, England (Home). *Telephone:* (01923) 826363.

NUNN, Sam, LL.B.; American politician and lawyer; b. 8 Sept. 1938, Perry, Ga.; s. of Samuel Augustus Nunn and Elizabeth Cannon; m. Colleen O'Brien 1965; one s. one d.; ed. Georgia Tech. Coll., Emory Univ. and Emory Univ. Law School, Atlanta; pvt. law practice 1964–73; mem. Ga. House of Reps. 1968–72; U.S. Senator from Georgia 1972–96, mem. Armed Services Cttee., Govt. Affairs Ctte., Small Business Cttee.; Partner King & Spalding, Atlanta 1997–; Democrat. *Leisure interest:* golf. *Address:* King & Spalding, 191 Peachtree Street, Atlanta, GA 30303, U.S.A. *Telephone:* (404) 572-4949.

NUNN, Trevor Robert, C.B.E.; British theatre director; b. 14 Jan. 1940, Ipswich; s. of Robert Alexander Nunn and Dorothy May Nunn (née Piper); m. 1st Janet Suzman (q.v.) 1969 (divorced 1986); one s.; m. 2nd Sharon Lee Hill 1986 (divorced 1991); two d.; m. 3rd Imogen Stubbs 1994; one s. one d.; ed. Northgate Grammar School, Ipswich and Downing Coll., Cambridge; Trainee Dir. Belgrade Theatre, Coventry; Assoc. Dir. Royal Shakespeare Co. 1964–86, Artistic Dir. 1968–78, C.E.O. 1968–86, Jt. Artistic Dir. 1978–86, Dir. Emer. 1986–; f. Homevale Ltd. and Awayvale Ltd.; Artistic Dir. Royal Nat. Theatre 1996–; toured U.S.A., Australia with own version of Hedda Gabler 1975; mem. Arts Council of England 1994–; Hon. Litt.D. (Warwick) 1982; Hon. M.A. (Newcastle upon Tyne) 1982, London Theatre Critics' Best Dir. Award for The Revenger's Tragedy and The Winter's Tale 1969, Soc. of Film and TV Arts Award for Antony and Cleopatra 1975, Ivor Novello Award for Best British Musical of 1976 for The Comedy of Errors (Lyrics), Soc. of West End Theatre Awards, Best Musical of the Year, for The Comedy of Errors 1977, Plays and Players Award 1978, 1979 for Best Production (Dir.) and Sydney Edwards Award for Best Director in Evening Standard Drama Awards 1978, 1979, both for Once in a Lifetime, Soc. of West End Theatres Awards, incl. Best Dir., Best New Play, Evening Standard Award, Best Dir., Drama Award for Best Dir., Mr. Abbott Award (Broadway) (all for The Life and Adventures of Nicholas Nickleby); Hon. D.Litt. (Suffolk) 1997. *Productions:* Tango 1965, The Revenger's Tragedy 1965, 1969, The Taming of the Shrew, The Relapse, The Winter's Tale 1969, Hamlet 1970, Henry VIII 1970, Roman Season: Antony and Cleopatra, Coriolanus, Julius Caesar, Titus Andronicus 1970; Macbeth 1974, 1976, Hedda Gabler (own version) 1975, Romeo and Juliet 1976, Comedy of Errors 1976, Winter's Tale (co-dir.) 1976, King Lear (co-dir.) 1976, Macbeth 1976, The Alchemist 1977, As You Like It 1977, Every Good Boy Deserves Favour 1977, Three Sisters 1978, The Merry Wives of Windsor 1979, Once in a Lifetime 1979, Juno and the Paycock 1980, The Life and Adventures of Nicholas Nickleby 1980 (with John Caird) (New York 1981), Cats 1981, All's Well That Ends Well 1981, Henry IV (parts I & II) 1981, 1982, Peter Pan (with John Caird) 1982, Starlight Express 1984, Les Misérables (with John Caird) 1985, Chess 1986, The Fair Maid of the West 1986, Aspects of Love 1989, Othello 1989, The Baker's Wife 1989, Timon of Athens 1991, The Blue Angel 1991, Measure for Measure 1991, Heartbreak House 1992, Arcadia 1993, Sunset Boulevard 1993, Enemy of The People 1997, Mutabilitie 1997. *TV:* Antony and Cleopatra 1975, Comedy of Errors 1976, Every Good Boy Deserves Favour 1978, Macbeth 1978, Shakespeare Workshops Word of Mouth (written and directed by T. Nunn) 1979, The Three Sisters, Othello 1989, Porgy and Bess 1992. *Films:* Hedda (own scripted version), Lady Jane 1985, Twelfth Night 1996. *Operas:* Idomeneo 1982, Porgy and Bess 1986, Così Fan Tutte 1991, Peter Grimes 1992, Katya Kabanova 1994, Not about Nightingales 1998, Oklahoma 1998, Betrayal 1998. *Publication:* British Theatre Design 1989. *Address:* Royal National Theatre, Upper Ground, South Bank, London, SE1 9PX, England. *Telephone:* 0171-452 3333. *Fax:* 0171-452 3350.

NUORVALA, Aarne Johannes; Finnish judge; b. 18 April 1912, Viipuri; s. of Karl Elias Nylenius and Aino Tyyne Ranta; m. Hellin Helena Hintikka 1945; one s. three d.; ed. Helsinki Secondary School and Univ. of Helsinki; Civil Servant, Ministry of Finance 1944; Jr. Cabinet Sec. 1945, Sr. 1946–50; Jr. mem. Comm. for Drafting Legislation 1950–55, Sr. mem. 1955; Extra Justice of Supreme Admin. Court 1955–57, Justice 1957–63; Sec.-Gen. Deputy Prime Minister and mem. Cabinet 1963–64; Chancellor of Justice 1964, Pres. Supreme Admin. Court 1965–82; mem. High Court of Impeachment 1965–82; Chair. Supreme Court of Office 1966–81; Hon. LL.D. *Address:* c/o Korkeavuorenkatu 13A 2, 00130 Helsinki 13, Finland. *Telephone:* 62-66-38.

NURSE, Paul Maxime, M.A., PH.D., F.R.S.; British scientist; b. 25 Jan. 1949, Norfolk; s. of Maxime Nurse and Cissie (née White) Nurse; m. Anne Teresa Talbott 1971; two d.; ed. Harrow County Grammar School, Univ. of Birmingham, Univ. of East Anglia; Research Asst., Microbiology Dept., Twyford Labs., London 1967; Research Fellow, Inst. of Microbiology, Univ. of Bern, Switzerland 1973, Dept. of Zoology, Univ. of Edin. 1974–78, Advanced Research Fellow 1978–80; Sr. Research Fellow, School of Biology, Univ. of Sussex 1980–84; Head Cell Cycle Control Lab., Imperial Cancer Research Fund (ICRF), London 1984–87; Iveagh Prof. of Microbiology, Univ. of Oxford 1987–91, Napier Research Prof. of Royal Soc. 1991–93; Dir. of Research (Labs.) and Head Cell Cycle Labs., ICRF 1993–96, Dir.-Gen. ICRF 1996–; Fleming Lecturer, Soc. of Gen. Microbiology 1984; Florey Lecturer, Royal Soc. 1990; Marjory Stephenson Lecturer, Soc. of Gen. Microbiology 1990; mem. EMBO 1987–; Pres. Genetical Soc. 1990–93; mem. Acad. Europaea 1991; Foreign Assoc. N.A.S. 1995–; Feldberg Prize for Medical Research (U.K./Germany) 1991, CIBA Medal (Biochem. Soc.) 1991, Louis Jeantet Prize for Medicine in Europe, Switzerland 1992, Gairdner Foundation Int. Award, Canada 1992, Royal Soc. Wellcome Medal 1993, Jiménez Díaz Memorial Award and Medal, Spain 1993, Purkyne Medal (Czech Acad.)

1994, Pezcoller Award for Oncology Research (Italy) 1995, Royal Soc. Medal 1995, Dr. Josef Steiner Prize, Switzerland 1996, Dr. H. P. Heineken Prize for Biochem. and Biophysics, The Netherlands 1996, Alfred P. Sloan Jr. Prize and Medal, General Motors Cancer Research Foundation 1997. *Publications:* numerous articles in scientific journals concerned with cell and molecular biology. *Leisure interests:* gliding, astronomy, talking. *Address:* Imperial Cancer Research Fund, P.O. Box 123, Lincoln's Inn Fields, London, WC2A 3PX, England.

NUSSBAUM, Martha Craven, M.A., PH.D.; American professor of philosophy and classics; b. 6 May 1947, New York; d. of George Craven and Betty Craven; m. Alan J. Nussbaum 1969 (divorced 1987); one d.; ed. New York and Harvard Univs.; Jr. Fellow, Soc. of Fellows, Harvard Univ. 1972–75, Asst. Prof. of Philosophy and Classics 1975–80, Assoc. Prof. 1980–83; Assoc. Prof. of Philosophy and Classics, Brown Univ. 1984–85, Prof. of Philosophy, Classics and Comparative Literature 1985–87, David Benedict Prof. 1987–89, Prof. 1989–95; Prof. of Law and Ethics Chicago Univ. 1995–96; Ernst Freund Prof. 1996–; Visiting Prof. of Law, Univ. of Chicago 1994; Fellow, American Acad. of Arts and Science; mem. American Philosophical Asscn. (Chair. Cttee. on Status of Women 1994–97); Brandeis Creative Arts Award 1990; PEN Spielvogel-Diamondstein Award 1991. *Publications:* Aristotle's De Motu Animalium 1978, The Fragility of Goodness 1986, Love's Knowledge 1990, The Therapy of Desire 1994, The Quality of Life (ed. with A. Sen) 1993, Passions and Perceptions (with J. Brunschwig) 1993, Women, Culture and Development (with J. Glover) 1995, Poetic Justice 1996, For Love of Country 1996, Cultivating Humanity 1997, Sex and Social Justice 1998. *Leisure interests:* music, running, hiking. *Address:* University of Chicago, Law School, 111 E. 60th Street, Chicago, Ill 60637, U.S.A..

NÜSSLEIN-VOLHARD, Christiane, PH.D.; German scientist; b. 20 Oct. 1942, Magdeburg; d. of Rolf Volhard and Brigitte Volhard (née Haas); ed. Univ. of Tübingen; Research Assoc., Lab. of Dr. Schaller, Max-Planck-Inst. für Virusforschung, Tübingen 1972–74; Postdoctoral Fellow (EMBO Fellowship), Lab. of Prof. Dr. W. Gehring, Biozentrum Basel, Switzerland 1975–76, Lab. of Prof. Dr. K. Sander, Univ. of Freiburg 1977; Head Group, European Molecular Biology Lab. (EMBL), Heidelberg 1978–80; Group Leader, Friedrich-Miescher-Laboratorium, Max-Planck-Gesellschaft, Tübingen 1981–85, Scientific mem. Max-Planck-Gesellschaft and Dir. Max-Planck-Institut für Entwicklungsbiologie, Tübingen 1985–90, Dir. Dept. of Genetics 1990–; Hon. Sc.D. (Yale); shared Nobel Prize for Medicine 1995; Leibnizpreis der Deutschen Forschungsgemeinschaft, Franz-Vogt-Preis, Univ. of Giessen, Rosenstiel Medal, Brandeis Univ. *Publications:* 55 scientific articles. *Address:* Max-Planck-Institut für Entwicklungsbiologie, Spemannstrasse 35/III, 7400 Tübingen, Germany. *Telephone:* 7071/601 487.

NUTT, Jim, B.F.A.; American artist; b. 28 Nov. 1938, Pittsfield, Mass.; s. of Frank E. Nutt and Ruth Tureman Nutt; m. Gladys Nilsson 1961; ed. School of Art Inst. of Chicago, Washington Univ. and Univ. of Pennsylvania; Prof. of Art, Calif. State Univ. Sacramento 1968–75, School of Art Inst. of Chicago 1990; one-man shows include: Museum of Contemporary Art, Walker Art Center, Minneapolis, Whitney Museum of American Art, New York 1974, San Francisco Art Inst. 1975, Rotterdamse Kunstichting, Rotterdam 1980, Kunsthalle Basel 1992–93, Centro de Arte Reina Sofia, Madrid 1992–93, Setagaya Art Museum 1992–93; Cassandra Foundation Award 1969; Nat. Endowment for the Arts Award 1975, 1990. *Address:* c/o Phyllis Kind Gallery, 136 Greene Street, New York, NY 10012, U.S.A.

NUTTER, Most Rev. Harold Lee, O.C., M.A., M.S.LITT.; Canadian ecclesiastic (retd.); b. 29 Dec. 1923, Welsford, N.B.; s. of William L. Nutter and Lillian A. Joyce; m. Edith M. Carew 1947; one s. one d.; ed. Mount Allison Univ., Dalhousie Univ., Univ. of King's Coll., Halifax; ordained Deacon, Anglican Church of Canada 1946; ordained Priest 1947; Rector, Parish of Simonds and Upham 1947–51; Rector, Parish of Woodstock 1951–57; Rector, Parish of St. Mark, Saint John, N.B. 1957–60; Dean of Fredericton 1960–71, Bishop 1971–89, Archbishop of Fredericton and Metropolitan of the Ecclesiastical Prov. of Canada 1980–89 (retd.); Examining Chaplain to Bishop of Fredericton 1960–71; Co-Chair. New Brunswick Task Force on Social Devt. 1970–71; Pres. Atlantic Council of Churches 1972–74, 1984–86; Vice-Chair. N.B. Police Comm. 1988–98; Vice-Pres. Canadian Bible Soc.; mem. Bd. of Govs. St. Thomas Univ.; Mount Allison Univ., Univ. of Kings Coll.; Hon. D.D. (King's Coll., Halifax, Montreal Diocesan Coll., Wycliffe Coll., Toronto, Trinity Coll., Toronto), Hon. LL.D. (Mount Allison Univ.). *Publication:* New Brunswick Report on Social Development 1971 (Co-author). *Leisure interests:* gardening, skiing. *Address:* 21 Cedar Ridge Drive, Douglas, N.B., E3A 7X2, Canada.

NWACHUKWU, Maj.-Gen. Ike; Nigerian politician; m.; four c.; Commandant Army School of Infantry 1979; Provost Marshal 1979–84; Mil. Gov. of Imo State 1984–85; Adjutant-Gen. 1985–86; Minister of Employment, Labour and Productivity 1986–87, of External Affairs 1988; mem. Commonwealth Cttee. of Foreign Ministers, Lusaka 1988; mem. Governing Council Univ. of Sokoto; Hon. G.C.M.G. *Address:* c/o Ministry of Foreign Affairs, Garki, Area 2, Abuja, Federal Capital Territory, Nigeria.

NYAKYI, Anthony Balthazar, B.A.; Tanzanian diplomatist; b. 8 June 1936, Moshi; m. Margaret Mariki 1969; two s. two d.; ed. Umbwe Secondary School, Moshi, Holy Ghost Secondary School, Pugu, Makerere Univ. Coll., Kampala, Uganda; Dir. Political Div., Ministry of Foreign Affairs 1966–68; Amb. to Netherlands 1968–70, to Fed. Repub. of Germany (also accred. to the Holy See 1970 and Romania 1972) 1970–72; Prin. Sec. Ministry of Foreign Affairs 1972–78, Ministry of Defence and Nat. Service 1978–80; High Commr. in Zimbabwe 1980–81, in U.K. 1981–89; Perm. Rep. to UN 1989–94; UN Special Rep. for Liberia 1994–. *Address:* c/o United Nations Observer Mission in Liberia, P.O. Box 4677, Grand Central Station, New York, NY 10163, U.S.A.

NYAMDOO, Gendengiyin, PH.D.; Mongolian diplomatist; b. 1 April 1934; m.; three c.; ed. Inst. of Int. Relations, Moscow; served in Mongolian Dept. of Legal Affairs and Dept. of Int. Orgs., Ministry of Foreign Affairs 1962–68, Chief of Section of Legal Affairs 1969–72, Dir. of Dept. of Treaties and Legal Affairs 1972–76, 1980–84; Counsellor of Mongolian Mission to the UN 1976–78, Perm. Rep. to UN 1984–88; Amb. to U.S.A. 1989–91, to the U.K. 1995; Foreign Policy Adviser to Prime Minister 1991–92; mem. Constitutional Court 1992–. *Address:* c/o Ministry of External Relations, Government Bldg. 6, Ulan Bator, Mongolia.

NYAMOYA, Albin; Burundian politician; b. 27 July 1924, Ibuye, Ngozi Province; s. of Pierre Nkikanyi and Marie Inamabubwe; m. Mélanie Sinduhije 1946; six s. (one deceased) four d. (one deceased); ed. Ecole Supérieure, Astrida (now Butare, Rwanda); qualified as veterinary surgeon; held various posts at the Ministry of Agric. and Stockbreeding, Ruanda-Urundi 1945–61, Minister of Agric. and Stockbreeding 1961–62; Minister of Interior and Information, Burundi 1962–63; Prime Minister and Minister of State 1964–65; Minister of State 1965–66; Deputy to Nat. Assembly 1963–66; various posts in Ministry of Agric. and Stockbreeding 1966–72, Dir.-Gen. 1970–71, Minister 1971–72; Prime Minister and Minister of the Interior 1972–73; Nat. Exec. Sec., mem. Cen. Cttee., Political Bureau, Unity and Nat. Progress Party until 1973; engaged in pvt. livestock farming and research 1973–76, 1980–; mem. Party Bureau, Chair. Political Comm., mem. Rural Villagization Comm. 1976–78; Adviser to Minister of Agric., Livestock and Rural Devt. 1978–80, to Dept. of Livestock 1980; elected mem. Nat Ass. 1982, mem. various govt. comms. 1982–; Councillor, Mwumba Commune, Ngozi Prov. 1985–91; mem. Party Prov. Cttee., Bujumbura Dec. 1991–; mem. Nat. Comm. studying Nat. Unity 1988–91, Centre de Développement et de Solidarité 1990–91, Comm. de Commercialisation du Café, Office du Café 1991–92; mem. Bd. Société Régionale de Développement du Buyenzi 1983–87, Office Pharmacéutique Vétérinaire 1988–91; Commdr. Ordre du Mérite Civique 1985.

NYANDA, Lieut.-Gen. Siphiwe; South African army officer; b. Soweto; fmrly. sports journalist; trained in fmr. G.D.R. and U.S.S.R. as platoon commander, artilleryman, and in intelligence; mem. African Nat. Congress, fmrly. guerrilla fighter for A.N.C., Commissar of Transvaal Region 1979–86, mem. Nat. Exec. Cttee. 1991–96; Deputy Chief South African Nat. Defence Force 1997–98, Chief 1998–. *Address:* c/o Ministry of Defence, Armscor Building, Block 5, Nossob Street, Erasmusrand 0181; Private Bag X603, Pretoria 0001, South Africa.

NYANJA, Rt. Rev. Peter Nathaniel; Malawi ecclesiastic; b. 10 June 1940, Malawi; m. Irene Matrida Kayamba 1964; seven s. one d.; ed. secondary school; primary school teacher 1963–67; parish priest 1972–77; Diocesan Bishop, Diocese of Lake Malawi 1978–. *Leisure interest:* gardening. *Address:* Diocese of Lake Malawi, P.O. Box 30349, Capital City, Lilongwe 3, Malawi. *Telephone:* 731966 (Office); 722670 (Home).

NYE, John Frederick, M.A., PH.D., F.R.S.; British professor of physics; b. 26 Feb. 1923, Hove; s. of Haydn Percival Nye and Jessie Mary (née Hague) Nye; brother of Peter Nye (q.v.); m. Georgiana Wiebenson 1953; one s. two d.; ed. Stowe School, King's Coll., Cambridge; University Demonstrator, Dept. of Mineralogy and Petrology, Cambridge 1949–51; mem. of Tech. Staff, Bell Telephone Labs., N.J. 1952–53; lecturer in Physics, Bristol Univ. 1953–65, Reader 1965–69, Prof. 1969–88, Prof. Emer. 1988–; Foreign mem. Royal Swedish Acad. of Sciences 1977. *Publications:* Physical Properties of Crystals, Natural Focusing and Fine Structure of Light 1999, numerous papers in scientific journals on glaciers, physics of ice, waves and mathematical catastrophes. *Leisure interest:* gardening. *Address:* H. H. Wills Physics Laboratory, Tyndall Avenue, Bristol, BS8 ITL (Office); 45 Canynge Road, Bristol, BS8 3LH, England (Home). *Telephone:* (0117) 928 8727 (Office); (0117) 973 3769 (Home).

NYE, Joseph S(amuel), Jr., PH.D.; American university dean; b. 19 Jan. 1937; s. of Joseph Nye and Else Ashwell; m. Molly Harding 1961; three s.; ed. Princeton, Oxford and Harvard Univs.; Prof. of Govt. John F. Kennedy School of Govt. Harvard Univ. 1969–, also Dir. Centre for Int. Affairs and Assoc. Dean of Int. Relations; Deputy Under-Sec. Dept. of State, Washington, D.C. 1977–79, consultant 1979; consultant, Dept. of Energy 1979; Chair. Nat. Intelligence Council 1992–; Asst. Sec. of Defense for Int. Security Affairs 1994–95, Dean and Don K. Price Prof. of Public Policy Harvard Univ. Sch. of Govt. 1995–; mem. Trilateral Comm.; Fellow, American Acad. of Arts and Sciences, Aspen Inst.; mem. Council, Int. Inst. of Strategic Studies; mem. Council on Foreign Relations; Dept. of State Distinguished Honor Award 1979. *Publications:* Power and Independence (co-author) 1977, The Making of America's Soviet Policy (ed. and co-author) 1984, Hawks, Doves and Owls (co-author and ed.) 1985, Nuclear Ethics 1986, Fateful Visions (co-ed.) 1988, Bound to Lead: The Changing Nature of American Power (co-ed.) 1990, Understanding International Conflicts: An Introduction to Theory and History 1993. *Leisure interests:* fly fishing, skiing, hiking, squash, gardening. *Address:* c/o Harvard University, Center for International Affairs,

737 Cambridge Street, Cambridge, MA 02141 (Office); 1932 Massachusetts Avenue, Lexington, MA 02173, U.S.A. (Home).

NYE, Peter Hague, B.SC., M.A., F.R.S.; British soil scientist; b. 16 Sept. 1921, Hove, Sussex; s. of Haydn P. Nye and Jessie M. Hague; brother of John Nye (q.v.); m. Phyllis M. Quenault 1953; one s. two d.; ed. Charterhouse, Balliol Coll. Oxford and Christ's Coll. Cambridge; agricultural chemist, Gold Coast 1947–50; lecturer in Soil Science, Univ. Coll. of Ibadan, Nigeria 1950–52; Sr. Lecturer in Soil Science, Univ. of Ghana 1952–60; Research Officer, I.A.E.A. Vienna 1960–61; Reader in Soil Science, Univ. of Oxford 1961–88, Emer. Reader 1988–; Professorial Fellow, St. Cross Coll. Oxford 1966–88 (Sr. Fellow 1982–83), Emer. Fellow 1988–; Pres. British Soc. of Soil Science 1968–69; mem. Council, Int. Soc. of Soil Science 1968–74; Gov. Nat. Vegetable Research Station 1972–88; Visiting Prof. Cornell Univ. 1974, 1981, Univ. of W. Australia 1979, Royal Veterinary and Agricultural Univs. Copenhagen 1990; Hon. Research Prof. Scottish Crop Research Inst. 1995; Fellow Inst. of Professional Soil Scientists; IMPHOS Award 1982; Messenger Lectures, Cornell Univ. 1989. *Publications:* The Soil Under Shifting Cultivation 1961, Solute Movement in the Soil-Root System 1977; articles, mainly in Journal of Soil Science and Plant and Soil. *Leisure interests:* cycling, watching cricket, computing, Scrabble. *Address:* Hewel Barn, Common Road, Beckley, Oxon., OX3 9UR, England. *Telephone:* (01865) 351607.

NYE, Robert, F.R.S.L.; British poet, novelist and critic; b. 15 March 1939, London; s. of Oswald William Nye and Frances Dorothy Weller; m. 1st Judith Pratt 1959 (marriage dissolved 1967); three s.; m. 2nd Aileen Campbell 1968; one d. one step-s. one step-d.; ed. Southend High School; freelance writer 1961–; contributes critical articles and reviews to British periodicals, including The Times and The Scotsman; Poetry Critic, The Times 1971–; Eric Gregory Award 1963, Guardian Fiction Prize 1976, Hawthornden Prize 1977. *Publications include:* (poetry) Juvenilia 1 1961, Juvenilia 2 1963, Darker Ends 1969, Divisions on a Ground 1976, A Collection of Poems 1955–1988 1989, Collected Poems 1995, 1998; (novels) Doubtfire 1967, Falstaff 1976, Merlin 1978, Faust 1980, The Voyage of the Destiny 1982, The Memoirs of Lord Byron 1989, The Life and Death of My Lord Gilles de Rais 1990, Mrs. Shakespeare: The Complete Works 1993, The Late Mr. Shakespeare 1998; several children's books, plays. *Address:* Thornfield, Kingsland, Ballinghassig, Co. Cork, Ireland.

NYEMBO SHABANI, D.SC.(ECON.); Democratic Republic of the Congo politician and professor of economics; b. 5 Aug. 1937, Kayanza; ed. Inst. Saint Boniface, Elisabethville (now Lubumbashi), and Univ. Catholique de Louvain, Belgium; Dir., Bureau of Econ. Co-operation attached to the Prime Minister's Office 1964–65; Research in Econs. Univ. Catholique de Louvain 1967–76; Prof. Faculty of Econ. Science, Nat. Univ. of Zaire Oct. 1976; State Commr. for Nat. Econ. and Industry Feb.–Aug. 1977, for Nat. Econ. 1977–78, for the State Portfolio (Investments) 1978–80, for Agric. and Rural Devt. 1980–81, 1983–84, for Econ., Industry and Foreign Trade 1982–83, for Finance and Budget 1986–88, for Agric. 1988–89; Pres. Gécamines Holdings 1985. *Publications:* L'industrie du cuivre dans le monde, Le progrès économique du Copperbelt Africain, Bruxelles, la Renaissance du Livre 1975. *Address:* B.P. 3. 824, Kinshasa 1, Democratic Republic of the Congo (Home).

NYERERE, Julius Kambarage, M.A.; Tanzanian politician; b. April 1922, Butiama-Musoma, Lake Victoria; s. of Chief Nyerere Burito; m. Maria Magige 1953; five s. two d.; ed. Musoma Native Authority Primary School, Tabora Govt. Sr. Secondary School, Makerere Coll., Uganda and Edinburgh Univ.; teacher, St. Mary's R.C. School, Tabora 1946–49; student at Edinburgh Univ. 1949–52; teacher, St. Francis' R.C. Coll. 1953–55; Founder-Pres. Tanganyika African Nat. Union (TANU) 1954–77; Founder-Chair. Chama Cha Mapinduzi 1977–90; elected mem. Tanganyika Legis. Council 1958, leader Elected Members Org. 1958–60; Chief Minister 1960–61; Prime Minister 1961–62; Pres. of Tanganyika 1962–64, of Tanzania 1964–85; Chair. Defence and Security Cttee. of Tanzania; Minister of External Affairs 1962–63, 1965–72; C.-in-C. of the Armed Forces 1973–85; Chancellor, Univ. of East Africa 1963–70, Univ. of Dar es Salaam 1970–85, Sokoine Univ. of Agric. 1984–; Chair. OAU 1984, South Comm. 1987–90, South Centre 1990–; Third World Award 1981, Distinguished Son of Africa Award 1988, Simón Bolívar Prize 1992. *Publications:* Freedom and Unity—Uhuru na Umoja 1967, Freedom and Socialism—Uhuru na Ujamaa 1968, Ujamaa: Essays on Socialism 1969, Freedom and Development—Uhuru na Maendelo 1973, Crusade for Liberation; Swahili trans. of Julius Caesar and The Merchant of Venice 1969. *Leisure interest:* reading. *Address:* P.O. Box 71000, Dar es Salaam, Tanzania; South Centre, Ch. du Champs d'Anier 17, Case postale 228, 1211 Geneva 19, Switzerland.

NYERS, Rezsö; Hungarian politician and economist; b. 21 March 1923, Budapest; s. of Rezsö Nyers and Julia Nagy; m. Ilona Witz 1946; one s.; printer until 1945; mem. Parl. 1948–53, 1958–98; Vice-Pres. Nat. Asscn. of Co-operatives 1954–56; Minister of Food Industry 1956–57; Pres. Nat. Asscn. of Co-operatives 1957–60; Minister of Finance 1960–62; Sec. Cen. Cttee. HSWP (now HSP) 1962–74; mem. Political Cttee. (now HSP) 1966–75, 1988–89, Chair. 1989–90; Dir. Inst. of Econs., Hungarian Acad. of Sciences 1974–82; Vice-Pres. Hungarian Soc. of Economists 1982–90; Minister of State 1988–89. *Publications:* The Co-operative Movement in Hungary 1963, Gazdaságpolitikánk és a gazdasági mechanizmus reformja (Economic Policy and Reform of Economic Management) 1968, A magyar népgazdaság a szocializmus építésének útján (Hungary's National Economy on the Road towards Socialism) 1973, Útkeresés-reformok 1988. *Leisure interests:* reading, theatre, tennis, philately. *Address:* 1025 Budapest, Özgida utca 22/A, Hungary. *Telephone:* 325-62-84.

NYKVIST, Sven; Swedish cinematographer; b. 1924, Moheda; ed. Stockholm Municipal School for Photographers; asst. photographer, Sandew movie studios 1941–59; photographer, Cinecitta, Rome; filmed nearly 40 feature-length films and several documentaries in Africa including Vördnad för Livet (Albert Schweitzer); Dir. of photography for Ingmar Bergman (q.v.) from 1960; has worked with many other famous directors including John Huston, Caspar Wrede, Richard Fleischer, Roman Polanski, Louis Malle, Alan J. Pakula and Andrei Tarkovsky; numerous Swedish and int. honours and awards inc. Acad. Award for photography in Bergman's Cries and Whispers 1973. *Films include:* with Bergman: The Virgin Spring 1960, Through a Glass Darkly 1960, Winter Light 1963, The Silence 1963, All these Women 1964, Persona 1966, Hour of the Wolf 1968, A Passion 1969, The Touch 1971, Cries and Whispers 1973, Scenes from a Marriage 1973, The Magic Flute 1975, Face to Face 1976, The Serpent's Egg 1977, The Autumn Sonata 1978, The Postman Always Rings Twice 1980, Star 80 1982, The Tragedy of Carmen 1983, Swann in Love 1985, The Sacrifice, Agnes of God 1987, Dream Lover, The Unbearable Lightness of Being 1987, Katinka, Another Woman 1989, The Ox (Dir. only) 1991, New York Stories, Crimes and Misdemeanors, Chaplin, Sleepless in Seattle, With Honors, Kirsten Lavrandatter, Only You, Mixed Nuts, Something to Talk About 1995, Confession. *Publications:* three books. *Address:* c/o Svenska Filminstitutet, Filmhuset Borgvagen 1–5, Box 27126, S-10252 Stockholm 27, Sweden. *Telephone:* (08) 665 1100.

NYRUP RASMUSSEN, Poul; Danish politician; b. 15 June 1943, Esbjerg, Western Jutland; s. of Olof Nyrup Rasmussen and Vera Nyrup Rasmussen; m. 1st (divorced); m. 2nd (divorced); m. 3rd Lone Dybkjar; one c. (deceased); ed. Esbjerg Statsskole and Univ. of Copenhagen; worked for Danish Trade Union Council in Brussels for a year; Chief Economist, Danish Trade Union Council 1981; Man. Dir. Employees' Capital Pension Fund 1986–88; Deputy Chair. Social Democratic Party 1987–92, Chair. 1992–; mem. Parl. 1988–; Prime Minister of Denmark 1993–. *Address:* Office of the Prime Minister, Christiansborg, Prins Jørgens Gaard 11, 1218 Copenhagen K, Denmark. *Telephone:* 33923300. *Fax:* 33111665.

NZAMBIMANA, Lieut.-Col. Edouard; Burundian politician and army officer; Minister of Public Works, Transport and Equipment 1974–76; participated in coup which overthrew Pres. Micombero Nov. 1976; Prime Minister 1976–78 and Minister of Planning 1976–78, of Agric., Livestock and Rural Devt. 1978, of Foreign Affairs and Co-operation 1978–82; Chair. Union Commerciale d'Assurances et de Réassurance (U.C.A.R.). *Address:* Union Commerciale d'Assurances et de Réassurance, B.P. 3012, Bujumbura, Burundi.

NZENGEYA, Bagbeni Adeito; Democratic Republic of the Congo diplomatist; b. Jan. 1941, Kisangari (fmrly. Stanleyville); m.; five c.; ed. Institut des Hautes Etudes d'Outre-mer, Paris, Univ. of Sorbonne, Paris, Int. Law Acad., The Hague, Int. Relations Inst., Geneva; Deputy Chef de Cabinet in charge of Int. Co-operation Dept., Ministry of Foreign Affairs 1969–71; Amb. to Netherlands 1971–72, to Ethiopia and OAU 1972–75; Pres. Perm. Comm. of Public Admin. 1976–80; Perm. Rep. of Zaire to UN Office at Geneva 1980–83; Amb. to India, Indonesia, Sri Lanka and Singapore 1983–85; Perm. Rep. to UN, New York 1985–92, Chair. First Cttee. (Political and Security) 1987–92. *Address:* c/o Department of Foreign Affairs, P.O. Box 7100, Kinshasa-Gombe, Democratic Republic of the Congo.

NZO, Alfred Baphethuxolo; South African politician; ed. World Mission School, Mariazell, Healdtown Mission Inst., Fort Beaufort and Univ. of Fort Hare; Health insp., Alexander Cttee. 1951–58; Sec. Alexander Business Boycott Cttee. 1957; joined African Nat. Congress (ANC) 1950, Chair. Alexandra Br. 1956, full-time organizer Transvaal and Natal Exec. Cttee. 1958; repeatedly banned and arrested as illegal resident 1959–61; served 5-month prison sentence for residence without permit under Urban Areas Act 1961; placed under 24-hour house arrest, Moroka, Soweto 1962–65; detained under 90-day detention Act June 1963, released Feb. 1964; joined external mission of ANC; Deputy Rep., ANC, Cairo 1964–67, Chief Rep., New Delhi 1967–69; Sec.-Gen. ANC 1969–91; mem. ANC del. in talks with S.A. Govt., ANC Nat. Exec. Cttee. 1991–; Minister of Foreign Affairs May 1994–; mem. Nat. Ass; Order of Friendship Among Peoples in Moscow 1985. *Publications:* numerous articles in SECHABA, World Marxist Review and Information Bulletin. *Address:* Ministry of Foreign Affairs, Union Buildings, East Wing, Pretoria, 0002; Private Bag X152, Pretoria 0001, South Africa. *Telephone:* (12) 351005. *Fax:* (12) 3510253.

O

OAKES, John Bertram, A.M., LL.D.; American journalist (retd.); b. 23 April 1913, Elkins Park, Pa.; s. of George W. Ochs Oakes and Bertie Gans Ochs; m. Margery C. Hartman 1945; one s. three d.; ed. Princeton Univ., and The Queen's Coll., Oxford (Rhodes Scholar); Reporter Trenton Times 1936–37; Political Reporter Washington Post 1937–41; served U.S. Army 1941–46; Editor, Review of the Week, Sunday New York Times 1946–49, mem. Editorial Bd. 1949–61, Editorial Page Ed. 1961–76, (originator Op-Ed page 1970), Sr. Ed. 1977–78, Contributing Columnist 1977–90; mem. Pres.'s Comm. on White House Fellows 1964–68; mem. N.Y. State Comm. on the Adirondacks 1988–90, American Philosophical Soc.; Carnegie Foundation Travel Award 1959, Columbia Catherwood Award (for int. journalism) 1961, George Polk Memorial Award 1966 (as editor), Jefferson Award of Unitarians 1968 (service in cause of religious liberty), Dept. of Interior of U.S. Conservation Award 1962, Silurian Soc. Award 1969, Garden Club of America Award 1969, Woodrow Wilson Prize (Princeton Univ.) 1970, John Muir Award, Sierra Club 1974, Audubon Medal, Nat. Audubon Soc. 1976, Environment Award, Natural Resources Defense Council 1977, UN Environment Programme Award 1982; Bronze Star (U.S.); Hon. M.B.E.; Croix de guerre, Médaille de Reconnaissance (France). *Publications:* The Edge of Freedom 1961; contributions to Essays Today 1955, Foundations of Freedom 1958; Tomorrow's American 1977, On the Vineyard 1980, The March to War 1991, Cast a Cold Eye 1991. *Address:* 1120 Fifth Avenue, New York, NY 10128, U.S.A. (Home).

OAKLEY, Ann, PH.D.; British sociologist and writer; b. 17 Jan. 1944; d. of Richard Titmuss; m. Robin Oakley (divorced); three c.; ed. Chiswick Polytechnic and Somerville Coll., Oxford; Prof. of Sociology; Head of Research Unit Inst. of Educ., London Univ. 1991–. *Publications include:* (novels) The Men's Room (adapted for TV 1991), Matilda's Mistake, The Secret Lives of Eleanor Jenkinson 1992, Scenes Orginating in the Garden of Eden 1994, A Proper Holiday 1996; (non-fiction) The Sociology of Housework, From Here to Maternity, The Captured Womb, Taking It Like a Woman (autobiog.) 1992, Social Support and Motherhood 1992, Essays on Women, Medicine and Health 1993. *Address:* c/o Edinburgh University Press, 22 George Street, Edin., EH8 9LF, Scotland.

OAKLEY, Brian Wynne, C.B.E., M.A.; British civil servant; b. 10 Oct. 1927, London; s. of Bernard Oakley and Edna Oakley; m. Marian Elizabeth Wooley 1953; one s. three d.; ed. Sutton Valance and Exeter Coll., Oxford; at T.R.E. (now R.S.R.E.) 1950–53, 1956–69; Scientific Adviser Air Ministry 1953–56; Computer Div., Mintech 1969–73; Requirements Div., Dept. of Industry 1973–78; Sec. Science and Eng. Research Council 1978–83; Deputy Sec. and Dir. Alvey Programme Dept. of Trade and Industry 1983–87; Dir. Logica (Cambridge) Ltd. *Publication:* The Alvey Experiment 1989. *Leisure interests:* theatre, opera, sailing. *Address:* 120 Reigate Road, Ewell, Epsom, Surrey, KT17 3BX, England. *Telephone:* 0181-393 4096.

OATES, Joyce Carol, M.A.; American author; b. 16 June 1938, Lockport, N.Y.; d. of Frederic J. Oates and Caroline Bush; m. Raymond J. Smith 1961; ed. Syracuse Univ. and Univ. of Wisconsin; Prof. of English, Univ. of Detroit 1961–67, Univ. of Windsor, Ont. 1967–87; Writer-in-residence, Princeton Univ. 1978–81, Prof. 1987–; mem. American Acad., Inst. of Arts and Letters; Guggenheim Fellow 1967–68; O. Henry Prize Story Award 1967, 1968, Rea Award for Short Story 1990, Elmer Holmes Bukst Award 1990. *Publications include:* novels: With Shuddering Fall 1965, A Garden of Earthly Delights 1967, Wonderland 1971, Do With Me What You Will 1973, The Assassins 1975, Childwold 1976, The Triumph of the Spider Monkey 1977, Son of the Morning 1978, Unholy Loves 1979, Cybele 1979, Bellefleur 1980, A Sentimental Education 1981, Angel of Light 1981, A Bloodsmoor Romance 1982, Mysteries of Winterthurn 1984, Solstice 1985, Wild Nights 1985, The Lives of the Twins 1987, You Must Remember This 1988, American Appetites 1989, Because It Is Bitter, and Because It Is My Heart 1990, Black Water 1992, Foxfire 1993, What I Lived For 1994, Man Crazy 1997, My Heart Laid Bare 1998, The Collector of Hearts 1999, several volumes of poems including Them 1969 (Nat. Book Award 1970); Nemesis (under pseudonym of Rosamond Smith) 1990, I Lock the Door Upon Myself 1990; George Bellows: American Artist 1995 (biog.); plays, stories, essays; fiction in nat. magazines; Ed. The Oxford Book of American Short Stories 1993. *Address:* c/o John Hawkins, 71 W. 23rd Street, Suite 1600, New York, NY 10010, U.S.A.

OBAME-NGUEMA, Paulin; Gabonese politician; mem. Union nationale pour la démocratie et le développement (UNDD); Prime Minister of Gabon 1994–99. *Address:* c/o Office of the Prime Minister, BP 546, Libreville, Gabon.

OBANDO Y BRAVO, H.E. Cardinal Miguel; Nicaraguan ecclesiastic; b. 2 Feb. 1926, La Libertad (Chontales), Juigalpa; ordained 1958; consecrated Bishop (Titular Church of Puzia di Bizacena) 1968–, Archbishop of Managua 1970–; cr. Cardinal 1985; Chair. Nat. Reconciliation Comm. for Nicaragua 1987. *Address:* Arzobispado, Apartado 3058, Managua, Nicaragua. *Telephone:* (2) 277-1754. *Fax:* (2) 276-0130.

O'BANNON, Frank Lewis, B.A., J.D.; American lawyer and politician; b. June 1930, Louisville, Ky.; s. of Robert Pressley O'Bannon and Rosella Faith Dropsey; m. Judith Asmus 1957; one s. two d.; ed. Indiana Univ.; pvt. practice, Corydon, Ind.; partner Hays, O'Bannon, Funk, Corydon 1966–80, O'Bannon, Funk and Simpson 1990–94, Funk, Simpson, Thompson and Byrd 1995–97; mem. Ind. Senate 1970–89, Asst. Minority Floor Leader 1972–76, Minority Floor Leader 1979–89, Acting Gov. of Indiana 1989–97, Gov. 1997–; Lieut.-Gov. of Ind. 1989–97; Chair. and Dir. O'Bannon Co. Inc.; mem. American Judicature Soc., American Bar Assen.; Democrat. *Address:* Office of the Governor, State House, 200 West Washington Street, Indiana, IN 46204, U.S.A.

OBASANJO, Gen. Olusegun; Nigerian politician and fmr. army officer; b. 5 March 1937, Abeokuta, Ogun State; m. 1st Oluremi Akinbwon; two s. four d.; m. 2nd Stella Abebe; ed. Abeokuta Baptist High School and Mons Officers' Cadet School, U.K.; joined Nigerian Army 1958, commissioned 1959; served in Congo (now Democratic Repub. of the Congo) 1960; promoted Capt. 1963, Major 1965, Lt.-Col. 1967, Col. 1969, Brig. 1972, Gen. 1979; Commdr. Eng. Corps 1963, later Commdr. 2nd Div. (Rear), Ibadan; G.O.C. 3rd Infantry Div. 1969; Commdr. 3rd Marine Commando Div. during Nigerian Civil War, accepted surrender of Biafran forces Jan. 1970; Commdr. Eng. Corps 1970–75; Fed. Commr. for Works and Housing Jan-July 1975; Chief of Staff, Supreme HQ 1975–76; mem. Supreme Mil. Council 1975–79; promoted from Brig. to Lt.-Gen. Jan. 1976; Head of Fed. Mil. Govt. and C.-in-C. of Armed Forces 1976–79; mem. Advisory Council of State 1979; farmer 1979–; Pres. (elect) of Nigeria May 1999–; Fellow, Univ. of Ibadan 1979–81; mem. Ind. Comm. on Disarmament and Security 1980, mem. Exec. Cttee. Inter Action Council of fmr. Heads of Govt.; Chair. Africa Leadership Forum and Foundation; Hon. D. Hum. Litt (Howard); Co-Chair. Eminent Persons Group on S. Africa (EPG) 1985; Hon. LL.D. (Maiduguri) 1980, (Ahmadu Bello Univ., Zaria) 1985, (Ibada) 1988; Grand Commdr. Fed. Repub. of Nigeria 1980; arrested March 1995, interned 1995. *Publications:* My Command 1980, Africa in Perspective 'Myths and Realities' 1987, Nzeogwu 1987, Africa Embattled 1988, Constitution for National Integration and Development 1989, Not My Will 1990, Elements of Development 1992, Elements of Democracy 1993, Africa: Rise to Challenge 1993, Hope for Africa 1993. *Leisure interests:* table tennis, squash, reading, writing. *Address:* P.O. Box 2286, Abeokuta, Ogun State, Nigeria. *Telephone:* 090400208, 039722420. *Fax:* 090402762.

OBASI, Godwin Olu Patrick, PH.D.; Nigerian meteorologist and statistician; b. 24 Dec. 1933, Ogori; s. of A.B.P. Obasi and R.A. Akande; m.; one s. five d.; ed. McGill Univ., Montreal, Canada and Massachusetts Inst. of Tech., U.S.A.; joined Nigerian Meteorological Dept. as Asst. Meteorological Officer 1956, later apptd. Sr. Meteorologist in charge of Research and Training and of Nat. Meteorological Centre for Forecasting Services; Visiting Research Scientist, Fla. State Univ., and Nat. Center for Atmospheric Research, Boulder, Colo., U.S.A. 1973; Sr. Lecturer in Meteorology for WMO/UNDP, Univ. of Nairobi, Kenya 1967–74, Prof., Chair. Dept. of Meteorology, and Dean Faculty of Science 1974–76; Adviser in Meteorological Research and Training, Fed. Govt. of Nigeria, Head Nigerian Inst. for Meteorological Research and Training 1976–78; Dir. Educ. and Training Dept., WMO Secr., Geneva 1978–84, Sec.-Gen. WMO 1984–; mem. British Inst. of Statisticians, Int. Acad. of Sciences of Nature and Society (Armenia br.) 1998; Fellow African Acad. of Sciences 1993, Third World Acad. of Sciences 1996 (Vice-Pres. 1999–), meteorological socs. of Dominican Repub., Ecuador, Colombia, Nigeria, Africa, America, Hon. Fellow Meteorological Socs. of Cuba, Burkina Faso, India; Hon. mem. Acad. of Agricultural and Forestry Sciences, Romania, Kenya Meteorological Soc.; Hon. Dr. Physics (Bucharest) 1991; Hon. LL.D. (Univ. of Philippines) 1992; Hon. D.Sc. (Fed. Univ. of Tech., Nigeria) 1992, (Alpine Geophysical Research Inst., Russian Fed.) 1993, (Univ. of Nairobi) 1998; Gold Plaque Merit Award for Science and Art, Czechoslovakian Acad. of Sciences 1986, Gold Medal for Meteorology and Hydrology, Paraguay 1988, Cross Medal of Air Force, Venezuela 1989, Ogori Merit Award, Kogi State, Nigeria 1991, Washington Climate Award, U.S.A. 1990, Gold Medal Award, African Meteorological Soc. 1993, Recognition of Merit, Nat. Univ. of Asunción, Paraguay 1993, Medal of Merit for Devt. of Hydrology and Meteorology, Slovak Hydrometeorological Inst. 1994, Balkan Physical Union Golden Medal Award, Greece 1997, Medal of Honour and Certificate of Merit, Front for Ebira Solidarity, Okene, Nigeria 1995, Award for Promotion of Hydrometeorology, Viet Nam 1998; Officer Order of Fed. Repub. of Nigeria; Commdr. Nat. Order Côte d'Ivoire, Benin, Burkina Faso; Commdr. Nat. Order of Lion, Senegal, Medal of Freedom of Ho Chi Minh City, Viet Nam, Order of Grand Duke of Gediminas and Medal Order of Gediminas, Lithuania, Presidential Award Medal of Friendship, Viet Nam and other distinctions. *Publications:* many scientific and tech. papers on meteorology and hydrometeorology. *Leisure interests:* tennis, gardening, reading. *Address:* 7 bis avenue de la Paix, 1202 Geneva, Switzerland. *Telephone:* (022) 7308111.

OBEID, Atif Muhammad, M.A., PH.D.; Egyptian politician; m.; two c.; ed. Faculty of Commerce, Cairo Univ. and Univ. of Illinois; mem. Arab League Media Policy Co-ordinating Cttee. 1970; fmr. Prof. of Business Admin. Faculty of Commerce, Cairo Univ. and Pres. Int. Man. Centre; Minister of Cabinet Affairs and Minister of State for Admin. Devt. 1985–93, Minister of the Public Enterprise Sector 1993–. *Address:* Sharia Majlis ash-Sha'ab, Lazoughli Square, Cairo, Egypt. *Telephone:* (2) 3558026. *Fax:* (2) 3555882.

OBEIDAT, Ahmad Abdul-Majeed; Jordanian politician; b. 1938, Hartha, Irbid; m.; five c.; ed. Salahiyah School and Univ. of Baghdad; Teacher, Min. of Educ. 1957; Customs Officer 1961; First Lieut. Gen. Security Service 1962–64; Asst. Dir. Gen. Intelligence Service 1964–74, Dir. 1974–82; Minister of the Interior 1982–84; Prime Minister of Jordan and Minister of Defence 1984–85; partner Law and Arbitration Centre 1985–. *Address:* Law and Arbitration Centre, P.O. Box 926544, Amman, Jordan. *Telephone:* 672222/672333.

OBENG, Letitia Eva, PH.D., F.R.S.A.; Ghanaian environmental consultant; b. 10 Jan. 1925, Anum; d. of Rev. E. V. Asihene and Dora Asihene; m. George A. Obeng 1953; two s. one d.; ed. Univs. of Birmingham and Liverpool, U.K.; lecturer, Coll. of Science and Tech. Kumasi 1952–59; research scientist, Nat. Research Council, Ghana 1960–63; research staff, Ghana Acad. of Sciences 1963–65; Dir. Inst. of Aquatic Biological Council for Scientific and Industrial Research (CSIR), Ghana 1965–74; Sr. Programme Officer and Chair. Soil and Water Task Force, UNEP, Nairobi 1974–80; Dir. and Regional Rep. of UNEP to Africa 1980–85; Distinguished Int. Visitor, Radcliffe Coll., Cambridge, Mass., U.S.A. 1992–93; mem. Exec. Council, Africa Leadership Forum 1991; Trustee, Bd. of Int. Rice Research Inst., Int. Irrigation Man. Inst., Human Ecology Foundation; Dir. Bd. of Stockholm Environment Inst., PANOS etc.; Fellow, Ghana Acad. of Arts and Sciences; Silver Medal, Royal Soc. of Arts. *Publications:* Man-made Lakes (ed.) 1969, Environment and the Responsibility of the Privileged, Environment and Population, The Right to Health in Tropical Agriculture; scientific articles; book chapters. *Leisure interests:* poetry, painting, flowers, Helminth parasites. *Address:* P.O. Box C223, Accra, Ghana.

OBERMEIER, Georg, DR.PHIL.; German business executive; b. 21 July 1941, Munich; m. ; Knorr-Bremse GmbH 1964–72; Bayernwerk AG, Munich, latterly Dir. of Finance and Org. 1973–89; mem. Man. Bd. VIAG AG 1989–, Chair. 1995–98; Chair. Supervisory Bd. Isar-Amperwerke AG, Munich, Rheinhold & Mahla AG, Munich, SKW Trostberg AG, Trostberg; mem. Supervisory Bd. Bayernwerk AG, Munich, Didier-Werke AG, Wiesbaden, Gerresheimer Glas AG, Düsseldorf, Klöckner & Co. AG, Duisburg, Kühne & Nagel Int. AG, Schindellegi, Mobil Oil AG, Hamburg, Schmalbach-Lubeca AG, Brunswick, Thomassen & Drijver Verblifa NV, Deventer, Thyssengas GmbH, Duisburg, VAW Aluminium AG, Berlin/Bonn. *Address:* c/o VIAG AG, Nymphenburger Strasse 37, 80335 Munich, Germany.

OBI, Onyeabo C., LL.B., F.C.I.A.; Nigerian international business lawyer; b. 20 Nov. 1938, Ogidi; s. of Chief Z.C. Obi; m. Evelyn Nnenna Obioha 1967; two s. three d.; ed. London School of Economics, London Univ.; admitted to Bar (Gray's Inn) 1962; in pvt. practice as barrister and solicitor of Supreme Court of Nigeria 1963–; Dir. Nigerian Rubber Bd. 1977–79; Senator of Fed. Repub. of Nigeria 1979–83; mem. of Council (and Vice-Chair. Cttee. on Procedures for Settling Disputes), Section on Business Law, Int. Bar Asscn. 1986–92; mem. Advisory Cttee. on Rules of the Supreme Court of Nigeria (by appt. of Hon. Chief Justice) 1986–. *Leisure interest:* lawn tennis. *Address:* Western House (13th Floor), 8-10 Broad Street, P.O. Box 4040, Lagos, Nigeria. *Telephone:* (01) 263-0843, 263-4604. *Fax:* (01) 263-7609.

OBOLENSKY, Sir Dimitri, Kt., PH.D., D.LITT., F.B.A., F.R.HIST.S.; British professor of history; b. 1 April 1918, Petrograd, Russia; s. of late Prince Dimitri Obolensky and Countess Mary Shuvalov; m. Elizabeth Lopukhin 1947 (divorced 1989); ed. Lycée Pasteur, Paris and Trinity Coll. Cambridge; came to Britain 1937, naturalized 1948; Lecturer, Trinity Coll. Cambridge; Univ. Lecturer in Slavonic Studies 1946; Fellow, Trinity Coll. Cambridge 1942–48; Reader in Russian and Balkan Medieval History, Univ. of Oxford 1949–61, Prof. of Russian and Balkan History 1961–85, Prof. Emer. 1985–; Student of Christ Church, Oxford 1950–85, Student Emer. 1985–; Sr. Assoc. mem. St. Antony's Coll. Oxford 1993–; Visiting Scholar (Fellow), Dumbarton Oaks Center for Byzantine Studies, Harvard Univ. 1952, 1964, 1977, 1981–82; Visiting Prof. at other U.S. univs. etc.; Fellow, Soc. of Antiquaries; corresp. mem. Acad. of Athens; foreign mem. Serbian Acad. of Science and Arts, American Philosophical Soc., Russian Acad. of Sciences 1994; Hon. Fellow Trinity Coll. Cambridge; Dr. h.c. (Sorbonne, Paris, Sofia Univ., Bulgaria); Hon. D.Litt. (Birmingham). *Publications:* The Bogomils: A Study in Balkan Neo-Manichaeism 1948, The Penguin Book of Russian Verse (Ed.) 1962, The Christian Centuries, Vol. II (jtly.) 1969, Byzantium and the Slavs 1971, The Byzantine Commonwealth 1971, Companion to Russian Studies (Ed. jtly.), 3 Vols. 1976–80, The Byzantine Inheritance of Eastern Europe 1982, Six Byzantine Portraits 1988. *Address:* 29 Belsyre Court, Woodstock Road, Oxford, OX2 6HU, England. *Telephone:* (01865) 556496.

OBOTE, (Apollo) Milton; Ugandan politician; b. 1924; s. of the late Stanley Opeto; labourer, clerk, salesman, Kenya 1950–55; founder-mem. Kenya African Union; mem. Uganda Nat. Congress 1952–60; mem. Uganda Legis. Council 1957–71; formed and mem. of Uganda People's Congress 1960–71, then Leader; Leader of the Opposition 1961–62; Prime Minister 1962–66; Minister of Defence and Foreign Affairs 1963–65; assumed full powers of Govt. Feb. 1966; Pres. of Uganda 1966–71 (deposed by mil. coup); in exile in Tanzania 1971–80; returned to Uganda May 1980, re-elected Pres. 1980–85, Minister of Foreign Affairs and Finance 1980–85; deposed by mil. coup 1985; resident in Zambia 1985–. *Address:* c/o Uganda People's Congress, P.O. Box 1951, Kampala, Uganda.

OBOUKHOV, Alexei Aleksandrovich, PH.D.; Russian diplomatist; b. 12 Nov. 1937, Moscow; s. of Alexander Oboukhov and Klaudia Oboukhov; m. Olga Oboukhov 1962; two s; ed. Moscow Inst. of Int. Relations and Univ. of Chicago; joined Ministry of Foreign Affairs 1965; served in Embassy in Thailand; took part in Strategic Arms Limitation Talks (SALT) I and Strategic Arms Reduction Talks (START) II and in the talks on Threshold Test Ban Treaty (TTBT), Moscow 1974; Deputy Dir. U.S. Dept., Ministry of Foreign Affairs 1980–86; mem. Soviet negotiating team in arms control talks, responsible for negotiations on long-range strategic weapons, subsequently for negotiations on medium-range nuclear weapons, Geneva 1985; Deputy Head Soviet Del., Nuclear and Space Talks, Geneva 1987, Head 1988; Head, Dept. of U.S.A. and Canada, Ministry of Foreign Affairs 1989–90; Deputy Minister of Foreign Affairs 1990–91; Amb. to Denmark 1992–96; Amb.-at-large 1996–. *Publications:* numerous texts on diplomatic affairs. *Address:* 117049 Bolshaya Yakimanka str., Moscow, Russia. *Telephone:* 238-00-48.

OBRAZTSOV, Ivan Filippovich; Russian mechanical engineer; b. 28 July 1920, Tver, Tverskaya Prov.; s. of Philipp I. Obraztsov and Pelageia I. Obraztsova; m. Rosa I. Mavrina 1945; two d.; ed. Moscow Aviation Inst.; active service with Soviet Army; mem. CPSU 1944–91; teaching 1944–58; Rector of Moscow Aviation Inst. 1958–72; R.S.F.S.R. Minister of Higher and Intermediate Special Educ. 1972–89; Dir. Inst. of Applied Mechanics, U.S.S.R. (now Russian) Acad. of Sciences 1989–96, Scientific Man. 1996–; Pres. Nat. Cttee. for Theoretical and Applied Mechanics 1981–; Corresp. mem. of U.S.S.R. (now Russian) Acad. of Sciences, mem. 1974; cand. mem. of CPSU Cen. Cttee. 1981–90, U.S.S.R. People's Deputy 1989–91; State Prize 1976, Lenin Prize 1988. *Publications:* works on building, mechanics and theory of cohesion of flying machines. *Leisure interest:* classical music. *Address:* Institute of Applied Mechanics, Leninsky Prosp. 32a, 117334 Moscow, Russia. *Telephone:* 938-18-36 (Office); 202-82-24 (Home).

OBRAZTSOVA, Yelena Vasilyevna; Russian mezzo-soprano; b. 7 July 1939, Leningrad (now St. Petersburg); d. of Vasily Alekseevich Obraztsov and Nataljya Ivanovna Obraztsova (née Bychkova); m. 1st Vyacheslav Makarov (divorced 1983); m. 2nd Algis Žiuraitis 1983 (died 1998); ed. Leningrad Conservatoire (under tuition of Prof. Grigoriyeva); Prof., Moscow Conservatoire 1973–1994; mem. Bolshoi Theatre, Moscow 1964–; has appeared at most leading opera houses of Europe and America, including Vienna State Opera 1975, Metropolitan Opera New York 1976, La Scala Milan 1976, Salzburg 1978, Covent Garden, London 1981 and has toured extensively in Russia and throughout world. *Roles include:* Marina Mniszek in Boris Godunov (debut, Bolshoi 1963), Countess in Queen of Spades, Konchakovna in Prince Igor, Marfa in Khovanshina, Lyubasha in The Tsar's Bride, Helene Bezukhova in War and Peace, Princess de Bouillon in Adriana Lecouvreur, Jocasta in Oedipus Rex, Silvana in La Fiamma, Giovanna Seymour in Anna Bolena, Herodiade, Amneris in Aida, Azucena in Il Trovatore, Eboli in Don Carlos, Santuzza in Cavelleria Rusticana, Ulrica in Un Ballo in Maschera, Adalgiza in Norma, Orfeo in Orfeo ed Euridice, Neris in Medea, Leonora in La Favorita, Aunt Princess in Suor Angelica, Carmen, Charlotte in Werther, Delilah in Samson and Delilah, Judith in Duke Bluebeard's Castle, Granny in The Gambler; recital repertoire includes works by more than 100 composers; several TV appearances; staged Werther at Bolshoi Theatre 1986; Hon. mem. Pushkin Acad. 1995; gold medals at competitions Helsinki 1962, Moscow 1962, 1970, Barcelona 1970, Medal of Granados 1971, Gold Pen of Critics, Wiesbaden 1972, Gold Verdi, Italy 1978, Bartók Memorial Medal, Hungary 1982; State Prize of Russia 1974, Lenin Prize 1976; Gold Star-Hero of Labour, People's Artist of U.S.S.R. and other decorations. *Leisure interests:* dogs, horses, fishing, mushrooms. *Address:* c/o Bolshoi Theatre, Teatralnaya pl. 1, 103009 Moscow, Russia. *Telephone:* 292-31-08. *Fax:* 292-90-32.

OBREGÓN, Alejandro; Colombian painter; b. 4 June 1920; s. of Pedro and Carmen Obregón; three s. one d.; ed. Stonyhurst Coll., England, Middlesex School, Concord, and Museum School of Fine Arts, Boston, U.S.A.; Dir. School of Fine Arts, Bogotá 1949–51, Barranquilla 1956–57; one-man exhbns. Bogotá, Barranquilla, Cali, Paris, Milan, Washington, New York, Lima, Madrid, Barcelona, Munich, São Paulo and Rio de Janeiro; numerous prizes include 1st Nat. Prize Guggenheim Int. 1959; Prize at São Paulo Biennial 1967; represented in numerous galleries including: Museum of Modern Art and Guggenheim Museum, New York, Phillips Gallery, Washington, Museo Nacional, Bogotá, Inst. de Arte Contemporáneo, Lima, Museo de Arte Moderno, Bogotá, Museo Nacional, La Paz, Galerie Creuze, Paris, Galerie Buchholz, Munich, The Vatican Museum, Rome, Galeria Profili, Milan and Inst. Cultura Hispánica, Madrid. *Address:* Apartado Aéreo 37, Barranquilla, Colombia.

O'BRIEN, Conor Cruise, PH.D.; Irish writer and diplomatist; b. 3 Nov. 1917, Dublin; s. of Francis Cruise O'Brien and Katherine Sheehy; m. 1st Christine H. Foster 1939 (dissolved 1962); one s. one d. (and one d. deceased); m. 2nd Maire MacEntee 1962; one s. one d. (both adopted); ed. Sandford Park School, Dublin, Trinity Coll., Dublin; entered Dept. of External Affairs of Ireland 1944, Counsellor, Paris 1955–56, Head UN Section and mem. Irish Del. to UN 1956–60, Asst. Sec.-Gen., Dept. of External Affairs of Ireland 1960; Rep. of Sec.-Gen. of UN in Katanga, Congo (now Shaba, Zaire) May-Dec. 1961; Vice-Chancellor, Univ. of Ghana 1962–65; Regent's Prof. and Holder of Albert Schweitzer Chair in Humanities, New York Univ. 1965–69; mem. Dáil Eireann (House of Reps.) for Dublin (Labour) 1969–77;

Minister for Posts and Telegraphs 1973–77; resgnd. from Labour Party; Senator for Dublin Univ. 1977–79; Ed.-in-Chief The Observer, London 1978–81, Consultant Ed. 1981; Contributing Ed. The Atlantic, Boston; Pro-Chancellor Univ. of Dublin 1973–; Visiting Fellow, Nuffield Coll., Oxford 1973–75; Fellow, St. Catherine's Coll., Oxford 1978; Visiting Prof. Dartmouth Coll., U.S.A. 1984–85; mem. Royal Irish Acad.; Hon. D.Litt. (Bradford) 1971, (Ghana) 1974, (Edinburgh) 1976, (Nice) 1978, (Liverpool) 1987; Hon. LL.D. (Glasgow) 1990; Valiant for Truth Media Award 1979. *Publications:* Maria Cross (under pseudonym Donat O'Donnell) 1952, Parnell and his Party 1957, The Shaping of Modern Ireland (ed.) 1959, To Katanga and Back 1962, Conflicting Concepts of the United Nations 1964, Writers and Politics 1965, The United Nations: Sacred Drama 1967, Murderous Angels (play) 1968, Power and Consciousness (ed.) 1969, Conor Cruise O'Brien Introduces Ireland 1969, Edmund Burke's Reflections on the Revolution in France (ed.) 1969, Camus 1969, A Concise History of Ireland (with Máire Cruise O'Brien) 1972, The Suspecting Glance 1972, States of Ireland 1972, Herod's Reflections on Political Violence 1978, Neighbours: Ewart-Biggs memorial lectures 1978–79 1980, The Siege: the Saga of Israel and Zionism 1986, Passion and Cunning 1988, God Land: reflections on religion and nationalism 1988, The Great Melody: A Thematic Biography of Edmund Burke 1992, Ancestral Voices 1994, On the Eve of the Millennium 1996, The Long Affair: Thomas Jefferson and the French Revolution 1996, Memoir: My Life and Themes 1998. *Leisure interest:* travelling. *Address:* Whitewater, Howth Summit, Dublin, Ireland. *Telephone:* (01) 8322474.

O'BRIEN, Edna; Irish author; b. Tuamgraney, Co. Clare; d. of Michael O'Brien and Lena Cleary; m. Ernest Géblev 1954 (divorced 1964); two s.; ed. convents, Pharmaceutical Coll. of Ireland; engaged in writing from an early age; Yorkshire Post Novel Award 1971, Kingsley Amis Award, Writers' Guild of G.B. Award 1993, European Prize for Literature 1995. *Publications include:* The Country Girls 1960 (film 1983), The Lonely Girl 1962, Girls in Their Married Bliss 1963, August is a Wicked Month 1964, Casualties of Peace 1966, The Love Object 1968, A Pagan Place 1970 (play 1971), Night 1972, A Scandalous Woman (short stories) 1974, Mother Ireland 1976, Johnny I Hardly Knew You (novel) 1977, Arabian Days 1977, Mrs. Reinhardt and other stories 1978, Virginia (play) 1979, Mrs. Reinhardt (adapted for TV) 1981, The Dazzle (children's book), Returning: A Collection of New Tales 1982, A Christmas Treat 1982, A Fanatic Heart (Selected Stories) 1985, Madame Bovary (play) 1987, Vanishing Ireland 1987, Tales for the Telling (children's book) 1987, The High Road (novel) 1988, On the Bone (poetry) 1989, Scandalous Woman and Other Stories 1990, Lantern Slides (stories) 1990, Time and Tide (novel) 1992, House of Splendid Isolation (novel) 1994, Down By the River (novel) 1997, Maud Gonne (screenplay) 1996, Song of Love (play) 1996. *Leisure interests:* reading, walking. *Address:* c/o Wylie Agency, 52 Knightsbridge, London, SW1X 7JP, England. *Telephone:* 0171-235 6394.

O'BRIEN, Gregory Michael St. Lawrence, PH.D.; American university chancellor; b. 7 Oct. 1944, New York; s. of Henry J. O'Brien and Mary A. McGoldrick; m. Mary K. McLaughlin 1968; two d.; ed. Lehigh Univ., Pa. and Boston Univ.; Dean and Prof. School of Social Welfare, Univ. of Wisconsin-Milwaukee 1974–78; Provost and Prof. of Psychology, Univ. of Mich.-Flint 1978–80; Prof. of Psychology, Univ. of S. Fla. 1980–87, also Prof. of Social Work 1980–87, Prof. of Man. 1986–87, Vice-Pres. for Academic Affairs 1980–87, Univ. Provost 1983–87; Chancellor, Univ. of New Orleans 1987–; Chair. Metro Council Govts. Metrovision 1992–; Vice-Chair. State of La. Film and Video Comm. 1993–94 (mem. 1994–); mem. Kellogg Comm. on Future of Land Grant Colls. and State Univs. 1996–. *Address:* Office of the Chancellor, University of New Orleans, Lakefront, New Orleans, LA 70148 (Office); 2468 Lark Street, New Orleans, LA 70122, U.S.A. (Home). *Telephone:* (504) 280-6201 (Office); (504) 288-4878 (Home).

O'BRIEN, Most Rev. Keith Michael Patrick, B.SC., DIP. ED.; British ecclesiastic; b. 17 March 1938, Ballycastle; s. of Mark Joseph O'Brien and Alice Mary Moriarty; ed. St. Patrick's High School, Dumbarton, Holy Cross Acad., Edinburgh, Univ. of Edinburgh, St. Andrew's Coll., Drygrange and Moray House Coll. of Educ.; ordained to priesthood 1965; Chaplain and teacher St. Columba's High School, Dunfermline 1966–71; Asst. Priest St. Patrick's, Kilsyth 1972–75, at St. Mary's, Bathgate 1975–78; Spiritual Dir. St. Andrew's Coll. 1978–80; Rector St. Mary's Coll., Blairs 1980–85; R.C. Archbishop of St. Andrews and Edin. 1985–; Sovereign Mil. Order of Malta, Grand Cross Conventual Chaplain 1985; Equestrian Order of Holy Sepulchre of Jerusalem, Kt. Commdr. with Star 1991. *Address:* 42 Greenhill Gardens, Edinburgh, EH10 4BJ, Scotland. *Telephone:* 0131-447 3337. *Fax:* 0131-447 0816.

O'BRIEN, (Michael) Vincent; Irish racehorse trainer (retd.); b. 9 April 1917, Cork; s. of Daniel P. O'Brien and Kathleen O'Brien (née Toomey); m. Jacqueline Wittenoom 1951; two s. three d.; ed. Mungret Coll., Limerick; started training in Co. Cork 1944, moved to Co. Tipperary 1951; won all principal English and Irish steeplechases, including 3 consecutive Champion Hurdles, 3 consecutive Grand Nationals and 4 Gold Cups; has concentrated on flat racing 1959–; trained winners of 16 English classics, including 6 Derbys; trained Nijinsky, first Triple Crown winner since 1935, also winner of 27 Irish Classics (including 6 Irish Derbys), 1 French Derby, 3 Prix de l'Arc de Triomphe, 2 King George VI and Queen Elizabeth Diamond Stakes, Washington Int., Breeders' Cup Mile, etc.; Hon. LL.D. (Nat. Univ. Ireland) 1983; Dr. h.c. (Ulster) 1995. *Leisure interests:* golf, fishing. *Address:* Ballydoyle House, Cashel, Co. Tipperary, Ireland. *Telephone:* (062) 61222. *Fax:* (062) 61677.

O'BRIEN, Patrick Karl, B.SC.(ECON.), M.A., D.PHIL., F.R.S.A., F.R.HIST.S., F.B.A.; British professor of economic history; b. 12 Aug. 1932, London; s. of William O'Brien and Elizabeth O'Brien; m. Cassy Cobham 1959; one s. two d.; ed. London School of Economics, Nuffield Coll. Oxford; lecturer, S.O.A.S., London Univ. 1963–70; Reader in Econs. and Econ. History, London Univ. 1967–70; Univ. Lecturer in Econ. History and Faculty Fellow, St. Antony's Coll. Oxford 1970–84, Univ. Reader in Econ. History and Professorial Fellow 1984–90; Prof. of Econ. History, London Univ. 1990–95, Sr. Research Fellow and Convener of Programme in Global History, Inst. of Historical Research, London Univ. 1998–. *Publications:* The Revolution in Egypt's Economic System 1966, The New Economic History of Railways 1977, Two Paths to the 20th Century: Economic Growth in Britain and France 1978, The Economic Effects of the Civil War 1988. *Leisure interests:* theatre, Western art, tennis, squash, foreign travel. *Address:* Institute of Historical Research, University of London, Senate House, London, WC1E 7HU (Office); 66 St. Bernard's Road, Oxford, OX2 6EJ, England (Home). *Telephone:* 0171-862 8783 (Office); (01865) 512004 (Home). *Fax:* 0171-862 8763 (Office).

O'BRIEN, Vincent (see O'Brien, Michael Vincent).

O'BRIEN QUINN, James Aiden, B.A., LL.B., Q.C.; Irish lawyer; b. 3 Jan. 1932, Tipperary; s. of the late William Patrick Quinn and Helen Mary Quinn (née Walshe); m. Christel Mary Tyner 1960; two s. one d.; ed. Presentation Coll., Bray, Univ. Coll. Dublin and King's Inns, Dublin; studied banking, Nat. City Bank, Dublin 1949–53; Crown Counsel and Acting Sr. Crown Counsel, Nyasaland (Malawi) 1960–64; Asst. Attorney-Gen. and Acting Attorney-Gen., West Cameroon 1964–66; Procureur-Général près la Cour Suprême Cameroun Occidental 1966–68; Avocat-Général près la Cour Fédérale de Justice, Cameroun 1966–68; Conseiller à la Cour Fédérale de Justice, Yaoundé, Cameroun 1968–72; Président du Tribunal Administratif du Cameroun Occidental 1968–72; Conseiller Technique (Harmonisation des Lois), Yaoundé, Cameroun 1968–72; Attorney-Gen. of Seychelles and British Indian Ocean Territory 1972–76; Chief Justice of Seychelles 1976–77; Acted as Deputy Gov. of Seychelles for a period during 1974; mem. Seychelles dels. on self-govt. and independence constitutions 1975, 1976; Chief Justice of Gilbert Islands (later Kiribati), Pacific Ocean 1977–81; Judge of High Court of Solomon Islands 1977–81; Special Prosecutor, Falkland Is. 1980; Chief Justice of Botswana 1981–87; Chair. of Judicial Service Comm., Botswana 1981; Adjudicator Immigrations Appeals 1990–96; Vice-Pres. Immigration Appeals Tribunal 1996–; B.E.S.O. Adviser, Dominica 1992; Third Place, Inst. of Bankers in Ireland 1950; Chevalier de l'Ordre National de la Valeur, Cameroun 1967; Q.C., Seychelles 1973; Kiribati Independence Medal 1979. *Publications:* Ed. W. Cameroon Law Reports 1961–68 and Gilbert Islands Law Reports, Kiribati Law Reports 1977–79; Magistrates' Courts' Handbook, W. Cameroon 1968, Magistrates' Courts' Handbook, Kiribati 1979. *Leisure interests:* swimming, reading, languages, travel. *Address:* 9 Lorane Court, Langley Road, Watford, Herts., WD1 3LZ, England. *Telephone:* (01923) 232861.

Ó BUACHALLA, Breandán, PH.D.; Irish professor of Irish language and literature; b. 15 Jan. 1936, Cork; s. of Joseph Buckley and Bridget de Courcey; m. Aingeal Ní'n Cháinte 1960; one s. two d.; ed. Sullivan's Quay Boys' School, Cork, Univ. Coll. Cork and Nat. Univ. of Ireland; lecturer, Queen's Univ. Belfast 1959–62, Univ. Coll. Dublin 1962–73; Prof. Dublin Inst. for Advanced Studies 1973–78; Prof. of Modern Irish Language and Literature, Univ. Coll. Dublin 1978; mem. Royal Irish Acad. *Publications:* I mBéal Feirste Cois Cuain, Peadar Ó Doirnín: amhráin, Cathal Buí, Nua-Dhuanaire. *Leisure interests:* walking, fishing. *Address:* Department of Modern Irish, University College, Dublin 4, Ireland. *Telephone:* 01-706 8380.

OBUCHI, Keizo; Japanese politician; 25 June 1937, Gunma Pref.; m. Chizuko Obuchi; one s. two d.; ed. Waseda Univ.; mem. for Gunma Pref. 1963; Parl. Vice-Minister of Posts and Telecommunications 1970, of Construction 1972, Deputy Dir.-Gen. Prime Minister's Office 1973, Dir.-Gen., and Dir.-Gen. Okinawa Devt. Agency 1979, Chief Cabinet Sec. 1987, Minister for Foreign Affairs 1997–98, Prime Minister of Japan 1998–; Chair. House of Reps. Cttee. on Finance 1976, Special Cttee. on Security 1982, Cttee. on Budget 1986; Sec.-Gen. LDP 1991, Vice-Pres. 1994, Pres. 1998–. *Address:* Office of the Prime Minister, 1–6, Nagata-cho, Chiyoda-ku, Tokyo 100, Japan. *Telephone:* (03) 3581-2361.

OCALIK, Paul, LL.B.; Canadian politician; b. Baffin Island; s. of Auyaluk; first Inuit law grad.; called to the bar 1999; mem. Nunavut Ass. 1999–; first Premier of Nunavut April 1999–. *Address:* Government Offices, Iqaluit, Nunavut, Canada.

O'CATHAIN, Baroness, cr. 1991 (Life Peer), of The Barbican in the City of London; **Detta O'Cathain,** O.B.E., B.A., F.A.I.M., F.R.S.A.; British business executive; b. 3 Feb. 1938, Cork, Ireland; d. of Caoimhghin O'Cathain and Margaret Prior; m. William Ernest John Bishop 1968; ed. Loreto School, Rathfarnham, Co. Dublin, Laurel Hill, Limerick, Univ. Coll. Dublin; Asst. Economist, Aer Lingus 1961–66; Group Economist, Tarmac Ltd. 1966–69; Econ. Adviser, Rootes Motors Ltd. 1969–72; Sr. Economist, Carrington Viyella 1972; Market Planning Dir., British Leyland 1973–76; Corp. Planning Exec., Unigate PLC 1976–81; Head of Strategic Planning, Milk Marketing Bd. 1981–83, Dir. and Gen. Man. 1983, Man. Dir. Milk Marketing

1984–88; Man. Dir. Barbican Centre, London 1990–95; Non-exec. Dir. Midland Bank PLC 1984–93, Tesco PLC 1985–, Sears PLC 1987–94, British Airways 1993–, BET PLC 1994–96, BNP (UK) PLC 1995–, Thistle Hotels 1996–, Saur UK PLC, Southeast Water PLC, Mid-Southern Water PLC; Pres. Chartered Inst. of Marketing 1998–. *Leisure interests:* music, reading, swimming, gardening. *Address:* Eglantine, Tower House Gardens, Arundel, West Sussex, BN18 9RU; 121 Shakespeare Tower, Barbican, London, EC2Y 8DR, England. *Telephone:* (01903) 883775 (Arundel); 0171-638 6443 (London). *Fax:* (01903) 883775 (Arundel); 0171-638 6443 (London).

OCCHETTO, Achille; Italian politician; b. 1936, Turin; joined Italian Communist Party (PCI) and Young Communists' Fed. 1953, apptd. Nat. Sec. Young Communists 1962; Sec. PCI Palermo 1969, subsequently Regional Sec. for Sicily; moved to Rome, held succession of party posts 1976; Deputy Leader PCI (name changed to Partito Democratico della Sinistra 1991) 1987–88, Gen.-Sec. 1988–94. *Address:* c/o Partito Democratico della Sinistra, Via delle Botteghe Oscure 4, 00186 Rome, Italy.

OCCHIUTO, Antonino, B.ECON. AND DIPL.; Italian central banker; b. 21 Dec. 1912, Naples; s. of late Stefano Occhiuto and Margherita Ruggiero; m. Valeria Marcucci 1952; one s. two d.; ed. Univ. of Naples; Head of Gen. Secr., Banca d'Italia 1961–64, Head of Personnel Dept 1965–67, Gen. Insp. 1967–69, Deputy Dir.-Gen. 1969–76, Hon. Dir.-Gen. Banca d'Italia 1976–; mem. Bd. of Dirs., BIS 1975–; Chair. Luigi Einaudi Inst. for Monetary, Banking and Financial Studies 1976–; Pres. Istituto Italiano di Credito Fondiario, Istituto di Credito per le Imprese di Pubblica Utilità (ICIPU) 1979–; Grande Ufficiale dell'Ordine al Merito della Repubblica Italiana. *Address:* Istituto di Credito Fondiario, via Piacenza 6, 00184 Rome (Office); Via Nomentana 293, Rome, Italy.

OCHIRBAT, Punsalmaagin, M.SC.; Mongolian politician; b. 23 Jan. 1942, Tudevtei Dist., Zavkhan Prov.; s. of Gonsiin Gendenjav and Tsogtiin Punsalmaa; m. Sharaviin Tsevelmaa 1965; two d.; ed. Mining Inst. of U.S.S.R.; apptd. official at Ministry of Industry 1966, Chief Engineer Sharyn Gol coal mine 1967, Deputy Minister, Ministry of Fuel and Power Industry and Geology 1972–76, Minister 1976; Chair. State Cttee. External Econ. Relations 1985–87, Minister 1987; elected mem. Mongolian People's Revolutionary Party (MPRP) Cen. Cttee. 17th, 18th and 19th Party Congresses and at 1990 Extraordinary Congress; resgnd. from MPRP 1991; elected Deputy to Great People's Hural 9th, 10th and 11th elections, Chair. 1990; Pres. of Mongolia 1990–97, C.-in-C. of the Armed Forces 1993–97. *Address:* Tengeriin Tsag Co. Head Office, Olympic Street 14, Ulan Bator, Mongolia. *Telephone:* (1) 327215. *Fax:* (1) 327233.

OCHMAN, Wiesław; Polish tenor; b. 6 Feb. 1937, Warsaw; s. of Jan Ochman and Bronisława Ochman; m. Krystyna Ochman 1963; one s. one d.; ed. Acad. of Mining and Metallurgy, Cracow 1960, studied with Prof. Gustaw Serafin, Cracow and with Prof. Maria Szłapak, Jerzy Gaczek and Sergiusz Nadgryzowski; début Silesian Opera, Bytom 1960; soloist: Silesian Opera, Bytom 1960–63, Opera in Cracow 1963–64, Great Theatre, Warsaw 1964–75, Deutsche Staatsoper 1967, Hamburgische Staatsoper 1967–, Metropolitan Opera, New York 1975–, La Scala, Milan 1981; Festivals at Glyndebourne, Salzburg, Orange; guest performances in operas in Paris, Munich, Frankfurt am Main, San Francisco, Miami, Chicago, Geneva, Budapest, Staatsoper in Vienna, Grand Theatre in Moscow, Staatsoper and Deutsche Oper in W. Berlin, Teátro Colón in Buenos Aires, Gran Teatre del Liceu in Barcelona, Accademia Santa Cecila in Rome, Carnegie Hall in New York; repertoire includes lead roles in Faust, Don Carlos, Tosca (Cavaradossi), Carmen (Don José), Boris Godunov (Dimitri), Aida (Radames), Halka (Jontek), Jenufa (Laca), Rigoletto (Prince), Don Giovanni (Don Ottavio); participation in TV films including Eugene Onegin, Tcharevitch, Salome, Don Giovanni; numerous recordings; mem. Pres. Council for Culture 1992–95; Minister of Culture and Art Prize 1973, The City of Warsaw Prize 1976, Pres. of Radio and TV Cttee. Prize (1st Class) 1976, Prime Minister Prize (1st Class) 1979, Minister of Foreign Affairs Diploma 1977, 1986, Medal Maecenas of Art 1976, The City of Cracow Gold Award, Medal of Merit for Nat. Culture 1986; Commdr.'s Cross Order of Polonia Restituta. *Leisure interests:* painting, collecting objects of art. *Address:* ul. Miączyńska 46B, 02-637 Warsaw, Poland. *Telephone:* (22) 643 01 58 (Office).

OCKRENT, Christine; French journalist; b. 24 April 1944, Brussels, Belgium; d. of Roger Ockrent and Greta Bastenie; m. Bernard Kouchner (q.v.); one s.; ed. Collège Sévigné, Paris, Cambridge Univ., England and Institut d'études politiques de Paris; journalist, Information Office, EEC 1965–66; Researcher, NBC News, U.S.A. 1967–68; producer and journalist, CBS News, U.S.A. 1968–77; Journalist and Producer, FR3, France 1976–80; Ed. and Anchor, news programme on Antenne 2 1980–85; Chief Ed. RTL 1985–86; Deputy Dir.-Gen. TFI 1986–87; Ed., anchor and producer, news programmes on Antenne 2 1988–92, on France 3 1992–95; Chief Ed. L'Express 1995–96; Deputy Dir. BFM 1996–; Ed.-in-Chief Dimanche Soir programme France 3 1996–; Ed.-in-Chief and Presenter France Europe Express 1997–; Dir. L'Européen 1998–. *Publications:* Dans le Secret des Princes 1986, Duel 1988, Les Uns et Les Autres 1993, Portraits d'ici et d'ailleurs 1994, La Mémoire du coeur 1997, Les Grands patrons 1998. *Address:* France 3, 28 cours Albert ler, 75008 Paris; L'Européen, 94bis rue de Suffren, 75015 Paris, France. *Telephone:* (1) 40 54 31 43.

Ó COFAIGH, Tomás F.; Irish banker; b. 7 Oct. 1921, Dublin; s. of James J. and Sarah (née Leahy) Coffey; m. Joan Kinsella 1953; three s. one d.; ed. O'Connell School, Dublin, Dublin Univ.; entered civil service 1939; Second Perm. Sec., Dept. of Finance 1974–77, Sec.-Gen. 1977–81; Dir. Cen. Bank of Ireland 1977–81, Gov. 1981–87; Alt. Gov. for Ireland, World Bank 1977–81; mem. Cttee. of Govs. of Cen. Banks of mem. States of EEC (Chair. 1984), Bd. of Govs., European Monetary Co-operation Fund (Chair. 1984); Alt. Gov. for Ireland, IMF 1981–87; mem. Nat. Econ. and Social Council (various periods), Council, Exec. Cttee. and Pres. Econ. and Social Research Inst. 1981–, Inst. of Public Admin., Inst. of European Affairs; Hon. LL.D. (Nat. Univ.). *Leisure interests:* music, hill walking, reading. *Address:* c/o Central Bank of Ireland, Dame Street, Dublin 2, Ireland.

O'CONNOR, Charmian Jocelyn, C.B.E., J.P., PH.D., D.SC., F.R.S.N.Z., C.CHEM., F.R.S.C., F.N.Z.I.C.; New Zealand professor of chemistry and university administrator; b. 4 Aug. 1937, Woodville; d. of Cecil J. Bishop and Kathrene M. Bishop; m. Peter S. O'Connor 1963 (divorced 1970); one s. one d.; ed. Univ. of Auckland; Post-doctoral Fellow, Univ. Coll. London 1967, Univ. of Calif. Santa Barbara 1967–68; lecturer, Univ. of Auckland 1958–66, Sr. Lecturer 1967–71, Assoc. Prof. 1972–85, Prof. of Chemistry 1986–, Deputy Vice-Chancellor 1994, Asst. Vice-Chancellor 1988–97; Visiting Prof. Texas A & M Univ. 1972, Nagasaki Univ. 1982, 1986, 1987, Tokushima Univ. 1987, Nagoya Inst. of Tech. 1994, 1996, 1998; numerous awards and prizes. *Publications:* one book, nearly 300 articles in refereed journals and several book chapters. *Leisure interests:* swimming, knitting, watching television. *Address:* Department of Chemistry, The University of Auckland, Private Bag 92019, Auckland, New Zealand. *Telephone:* (09) 3737 599. *Fax:* (09) 3737 422.

O'CONNOR, H.E. Cardinal John, PH.D.; American ecclesiastic and fmr. naval officer; b. 15 Jan. 1920, Philadelphia; s. of Thomas Joseph and Dorothy Magdalene (Gomple) O'Connor; ed. St. Charles Coll., Catholic Univ. of America, Georgetown Univ.; ordained R.C. Priest 1945, Msgr. 1966, consecrated Bishop 1979, Auxiliary Bishop, Vicar-Gen. (Mil. Vicariate) 1979–83; Bishop of Scranton 1983; Archbishop of New York 1984–; cr. Cardinal 1985; served in Chaplain Corps U.S. Navy 1952, rose to rank of Rear Adm., assigned to Atlantic and Pacific fleets, Okinawa and Vietnam. *Publications:* Principles and Problems of Naval Leadership 1958, A Chaplain Looks at Vietnam 1969, In Defense of Life 1981, His Eminence and Hizzoner (with Ed. Koch, q.v.) 1989, A Journey of Faith (with Elie Wiesel) 1990. *Address:* Archdiocese of New York, 452 Madison Avenue, New York, NY 10022; 1011 1st Avenue, New York, NY 10022, U.S.A.

O'CONNOR, Sandra Day; American judge; b. 26 March 1930, El Paso, Tex.; d. of Harry A. and Ada Mae (née Wilkey) Day; m. John Jay O'Connor III 1952; three s.; pvt. practice Phoenix, Ariz. 1959–65; served in Arizona Senate 1969–74, Majority Leader 1973–74; elected Superior Court Judge, Ariz. 1975, Judge of Appeals 1979–81; Judge (Assoc. Justice), U.S. Supreme Court Sept. 1981–; mem. Nat. Bd. Smithsonian Assocs. 1981–. *Address:* Supreme Court Building, 1 First Street, N.E., Washington, DC 20543, U.S.A.

O'CONNOR, Sinead; Irish singer; b. 8 Dec. 1966, Dublin; d. of John O'Connor and the late Marie O'Connor; m. John Reynolds (dissolved); one s. one d.; ed. Dublin Coll. of Music; band mem. Ton Ton Macoute 1985–87; refused to accept Grammy Award for Best Alternative Album 1991. *Singles include:* Heroin 1986, Mandinka 1987, Jump in the River 1988, Nothing Compares 2 U 1990 (MTV Best Video, Best Single Awards 1990, also Best Female Singer), Three Babies 1990, You Do Something To Me (for the Red Hot and Blue compilation) 1990, Silent Night 1991, My Special Child 1991, Visions of You (with Jah Wobble's Invaders of the Heart) 1992, Emperor's New Clothes 1992, Secret Love 1992, Success Has Made a Failure of Our Home 1992. *Albums include:* The Lion and the Cobra 1987, I Do Not Want What I Haven't Got 1990 (Grammy Award for Best Alternative Album 1991, also Rolling Stone Artist of the Year Award 1991, BRIT Award for Best Int. Solo Artist 1991), Am I Not Your Girl? 1992, Universal Mother 1994, Gospeloak 1997. *Video films:* Value of Ignorance 1989, The Year of the Horse 1991. *TV film:* Hush-a-Bye-Baby. *Address:* c/o Principle Management, 30–32 Sir John Rogersons Quay, Dublin 2, Ireland.

ODA, Minoru, D.SC.; Japanese university president; b. 24 Feb. 1923, Sapporo; m. Tomoe Oda 1956; one s. one d.; ed. Osaka Imperial Univ. and Osaka Univ.; Assoc. Prof. Inst. for Nuclear Study, Univ. of Tokyo 1956–66; Prof. Inst. of Space and Aeronautical Science, Univ. of Tokyo 1966–81; Prof. Nat. Inst. of Space and Astronautical Science 1981–84, Dir.-Gen. 1984–88; Pres. Inst. of Physical and Chemical Research 1988–93; Pres. Tokyo Univ. of Information Science 1994–; Dir. Int. Inst. for Advanced Study 1994–, Japan Synchro Radiation Research Inst. 1995–; Visiting Prof. M.I.T. 1963–66; mem. Japan Acad., Pontifical Acad. of Science, Academia Europaea, Indian Acad.; Nishina Memorial Prize 1966; Japan Acad. Award 1975; Von Karman Award (Int. Acad. of Astronomy) 1987; Order of Cultural Merit (Japan) 1993. *Publications:* several academic books; Flowers and Friends (art book) 1993; over 70 scientific papers. *Leisure interests:* mountain trekking, sketching flowers, music. *Address:* 2-25-13 Kyonancho, Musashino, Tokyo 180, Japan. *Telephone:* 81 (0) 422 31 1787. *Fax:* 81 (0) 422 32 2340.

ODA, Shigeru, LL.M., J.S.D., LL.D.; Japanese lawyer; b. 22 Oct. 1924; s. of Toshio and Mioko Oda; m. Noriko Sugimura 1950; one s. one d.; ed. Univ. of Tokyo, Yale Univ.; Research Fellow, Univ. of Tokyo 1947–49; Lecturer Univ. of Tôhoku 1950–53, Assoc. Prof. 1953–59, Prof. 1959–76; Prof. Emer. 1985–; Tech. Adviser, Atomic Energy Comm. 1961–64; Special Asst. to Minister for Foreign Affairs 1973–76; mem. Science Council of Ministry of

Educ. 1969–76, of Council for Ocean Devt. in Prime Minister's Office 1971–76, Advisory Cttee. for Co-operation with UN Univ. 1971–76; Judge, Int. Court of Justice 1976–85, 1985–94, 1994–, Vice-Pres. 1991–94; del. to UN Confs. on Law of the Sea 1958, 1960, 1973–75; Rep. at 6th Gen. Conf. of Inter-Governmental Oceanographic Comm. 1969; consultative positions with bodies concerned with marine questions; Counsel for Fed. Repub. of Germany before Int. Court of Justice 1968; Editor-in-Chief, Japanese Annual of International Law 1973–77; Assoc. Inst. de Droit Int. 1969 (mem. 1979); mem. Curatorium, Hague Acad. of Int. Law 1989–, Bd. of Dirs., Int. Devt. Law Inst., Rome 1994–, Int. Council of Arbitration for Sport 1994–; Hon. mem. American Soc. of Int. Law 1975; mem. Japan Acad. 1994; Hon. D.Jur. (Bhopal Univ.) 1980, (New York Law School) 1981. *Publications:* in Japanese: International Law of the Sea 1956–85 (8 vols.), International Law and Maritime Resources 1971–75; Judicial Decisions relating to International Law before Japanese Courts 1978; in English: International Control of Sea Resources 1962, The International Law of Ocean Development (4 vols.) 1972–79, The Law of the Sea in Our Times (2 vols.) 1977, The Practice of Japan in International Law 1961–70 1982, The International Court of Justice 1987; various articles. *Address:* International Court of Justice, Peace Palace, Carnegieplein 2, 2517 KJ The Hague, The Netherlands (Office).

ODDI, H.E. Cardinal Silvio; Italian ecclesiastic; b. 14 Nov. 1910, Morfasso; ordained 1933; Titular Archbishop of Mesembria 1953; Apostolic Del. in Palestine, Jerusalem and Cyprus 1953–56; Apostolic Internuncio in Egypt and U.A.R. 1956–62; Apostolic Nuncio in Belgium and Luxembourg 1962–69; cr. Cardinal March 1969; fmr. Pres. of the Pontifical Comm. for the Sanctuaries of Loreto and Pompei; fmr. Pontifical Del. for the Basilica of Assisi; fmr. Prefect of the Sacred Congregation for the Clergy; fmr. Camerlengo of Coll. of Cardinals. *Address:* Via delle Grazie 3, 00193 Rome, Italy.

ODDSSON, David; Icelandic politician; b. 17 Jan. 1948, Reykjavík; s. of Oddur Ólafsson and Ingibjörg Kristín Lúdvíksdóttir; m. Ástrídur Thorarensen 1970; one s.; ed. Reykjavík Coll., Univ. of Iceland; mem. Reykjavík City Council 1974–; Mayor of Reykjavík 1982–91; Vice-Chair. Independence Party 1989–91, Chair. 1991–; M.P. 1991–; Prime Minister of Iceland 1991–; Minister of the Statistical Bureau of Iceland. *Publications:* Plays: For My Country's Benefit (Nat. Theatre 1974–75), Icelandic Confabulations (Reykjavík Theatre 1975–76). TV Dramas: Robert Eliasson Returns From Abroad 1977, Stains on the White Collar 1981; Anders Küng-Estonia, a Small Nation under the Yoke of a Foreign Power 1973. *Leisure interests:* bridge and salmon fishing. *Address:* Stjórnarráðshusið v/Laekjartorg, 150 Reykjavík, Iceland. *Telephone:* 5609400. *Fax:* 5624014.

ODELL, Mats; Swedish politician; m.; four c.; ed. Stockholm Univ.; Chair. Union of Christian Democrats 1973–81; mem. Nat. Bd. Christian Democratic Party, mem. Exec. Cttee.; mem. European Unit of Christian Democrats, mem. Political Bureau; Minister of Transport and Communications 1991–94; mem. Vallentuna Municipal Council 1979–, Municipal Exec. Bd.; mem. Vallentuna Parochial Church Council 1970–79. *Leisure interest:* music. *Address:* Vallbostrand, 186 00 Vallentuna, Sweden.

ODGERS, Graeme David William, M.A., M.B.A.; British business executive; b. 10 March 1934, Johannesburg, S.A.; s. of the late William Arthur Odgers and of Elizabeth Minty (née Rennie); m. Diana Patricia Berge 1957; one s. three d. (one deceased); ed. St. John's Coll., Johannesburg, Gonville and Caius Coll., Cambridge, Harvard Business School, U.S.A.; Investment Officer, IFC, Washington D.C. 1959–62; Man. Consultant, Urwick Orr & Partners Ltd. 1962–64; Investment Exec., Hambros Bank Ltd. 1964–65; Dir. Keith Shipton Ltd. 1965–72, C. T. Bowring (Insurance) Holdings Ltd. 1972–74; Chair. Odgers & Co. Ltd. (Man. Consultants) 1970–74; Dir. Industrial Devt. Unit, Dept. of Industry 1974–77; Assoc. Dir. (Finance) Gen. Electric Co. 1977–78; Group Finance Dir., Tarmac PLC, 1979–86, Group Man. Dir. 1983–86, Non-exec. Dir. 1986–87; Non-exec. Dir. Dalgety PLC 1987–93; Part-time Bd. mem. British Telecommunications PLC 1983–86, Govt. Dir. 1984–86, Deputy Chair. and Chief Finance Officer 1986–87, Group Man. Dir. 1987–89; Chief. Exec. Alfred McAlpine 1990–93; Chair. Monopolies and Mergers Comm. 1993–97; Dir. (non-exec.) Southern Electric PLC 1998–. *Leisure interest:* golf. *Address:* Brome House, West Malling, Kent, ME19 6NE, England.

ODJIG, Daphne, C.M.; Canadian artist and muralist; b. 11 Sept. 1919, Wikwemikong (Manitoulin Island), Ont.; d. of Dominic Odjig and Joyce Emily (Peachey) Odjig; m. Chester Beavon 1963; two s. two step-s. one step-d.; mem. Odawa Tribe; numerous solo exhbns. Canada 1967–; numerous group exhbns. in Canada, also London, U.K. 1976, São Paulo, Brazil 1977, Okla., U.S.A. 1978; commissions include: Earthmother, for Canadian Pavilion, Expo 1970, Osaka, Japan; mural depicting Indian legend, Creation of the World, Museum of Man 1972, From Mother Earth Flows the River of Life, Cultural Devt. Div., Ministry of Indian and Northern Affairs 1974; The Indian in Transition, for Nat. Museum of Man. 1978; works in collections of Winnipeg Art Gallery, Ministry of Indian and Northern Affairs, Winnipeg, Nat. Museum of Man, Man. Indian Brotherhood, Canadian Council Art Bank, McMichael Canadian Coll., Kleinberg, Ont., Tom Thompson Gallery, Sir Wilfrid Laurier Univ., Govt. of Israel, Jerusalem, and other; Founding mem. Professional Native Indian Artists' Asscn. Inc. 1973–; mem. Royal Canadian Acad. of Art 1989; LL.D. h.c. (Laurentian Univ.) 1982, (Toronto) 1985, Hon.D.Ed. (Nipissing Univ., Ont.) 1996; Swedish Brucebo Foundation Scholarship 1973, Man. Arts Council Bursary 1973, Canadian Silver Jubilee Medal 1977, Eagle Feather presented by Chief Wakageshig, Wikwemikong Reserve in recognition of artistic accomplishments 1978, Commemorative Medal, 125th Anniversary of Confed. of Canada 1992, Aboriginal Award, Toronto 1998. *Publication:* Nanabush Indian Legends for Children (Author and Illustrator; 10 books) 1971. *Address:* P.O. Box 111, Anglemont, British Columbia, V0E 1A0, Canada. *Telephone:* (250) 955-2974.

ODLING-SMEE, John Charles, M.A.; British official; b. 13 April 1943; s. of late Rev. Charles William Odling-Smee and Katherine Hamilton Odling-Smee (née Aitchison); m. Carmela Veneroso 1996; ed. Durham School, St. John's Coll. Cambridge; Jr. Research Officer Dept. of Applied Econs., Cambridge 1964–65; Asst. Research Officer Inst. of Econs. and Statistics, Oxford 1968–71, 1972–73; Econ. Research Officer Govt. of Ghana 1971–72; Sr. Research Officer Centre for Urban Econs. L.S.E. 1973–75; Econ. Adviser Cen. Policy Review Staff, Cabinet Office 1975–77; Sr. Econ. Adviser HM Treasury 1977–80; Sr. Economist IMF 1981–82; Under-Sec. HM Treasury 1982–89; Deputy Chief Econ. Adviser HM Treasury 1989–90; Sr. Adviser IMF 1990–91, Dir. IMF European II Dept. 1992–. *Publications:* Housing Rent Costs and Subsidies 1978, British Economic Growth 1856–1973 1982; various articles in books and learned journals. *Address:* c/o IMF, 700 19th St, N.W., Washington, DC 20431, U.S.A.

ODONE, Cristina, M.A.; Italian journalist and writer; b. 11 Nov. 1960, Nairobi, Kenya; d. of Augusto Odone and Ulla Sjöström; ed. Oxford Univ.; Vice-Pres. Odone Assocs. consultancy, Washington; Ed. The Catholic Herald, U.K. 1992–96; Diary journalist The Times 1991–; TV reviewer Daily Telegraph 1996–. *Publications:* The Shrine 1996, Renewal 1997, A Perfect Life 1998. *Leisure interests:* travel, walking, entertaining, swimming. *Address:* c/o The Times, 1 Virginia Street, London, E.1., England.

O'DONNELL, Augustine Thomas 'Gus', C.B., B.A., M.PHIL.; British economist; b. 1 Oct. 1952, London; s. of James O'Donnell and Helen O'Donnell (née McLean); m. Melanie Timmis 1979; one d.; ed. Salesian Coll., Battersea, Univ. of Warwick and Nuffield Coll., Oxford; lecturer Dept. of Political Economy, Univ. of Glasgow 1975–79; economist 1979–85; First Sec. (Econ.) Embassy, Washington 1985–88; Sr. Econ. Adviser, H.M. Treasury 1988–89, Press Sec. to Chancellor of the Exchequer 1989–90; Press Sec. to Prime Minister 1990–94; Under-Sec. (monetary group) H.M. Treasury 1994–95, Deputy Dir. Macroeconomic Policy and Prospects Directorate 1995–96, Minister (Econs.) British Embassy, Washington, U.K. Exec. Dir. IMF, World Bank 1997–98, Macroeconomic Policy and Prospects Directorate 1998–; Head of Govt. Econ. Service, HM Treasury 1998–. *Publications:* various articles in econ. journals. *Leisure interests:* football, cricket, tennis. *Address:* HM Treasury, Parliament Street, London, SW1P 3AG, England.

O'DONNELL, Chris; American actor; b. 1970, Winnetka, Ill; m. Caroline Fentress 1997. *Films include:* Men Don't Leave 1990, Fried Green Tomatoes 1991, Scent of a Woman 1992, School Ties 1992, The Three Musketeers 1993, Blue Sky 1994, Circle of Friends 1995, Mad Love 1995, Batman Forever 1995, The Chamber, In Love and War, Batman and Robin, Cookie's Fortune 1998, The Bachelor 1998. *Address:* c/o Kevin Huvane, C.A.A., 9830 Wilshire Boulevard, Beverly Hills, CA 90212, U.S.A.

O'DONOGHUE, John, B.C.L., LL.B.; Irish politician; b. 28 May 1956, Cahirciveen, Co. Kerry; m. Kate Ann Murphy; two s. one d.; ed. Christian Brothers' Secondary School, Cahirciveen, Univ. Coll., Cork, Inc. Law Soc. of Ireland; fmrly. solicitor; mem. Dáil Éireann Feb. 1987–; Minister of State Dept. of Finance 1991–92; fmr. Fianna Fáil Spokesperson on Justice; Minister of Justice, Equality and Law Reform June 1997–; mem. Kerry Co. Council (Chair. 1990–91), mem. various council cttees., Southern Health Bd. Psychiatric Services Cttee., British-Irish Parl. Body. *Leisure interests:* English literature, history, Gaelic games, horse racing. *Address:* Department of Justice, 72–76 St. Stephen's Green, Dublin 2 (Office); Garranearagh, Cahirciveen, Co. Kerry, Ireland (Home). *Telephone:* (1) 6028202 (Office); (66) 72413 (Home). *Fax:* (1) 6615461 (Office); (66) 72667 (Home).

ODUBER, Nelson O.; Aruban politician; Leader Movimentu Electoral di Pueblo (People's Electoral Movt.); Prime Minister of Aruba and Minister of Gen. Affairs 1989–94. *Address:* MEP, Cumana 84, Oranjestad, Aruba.

ODUBER QUIRÓS, Daniel; Costa Rican politician and diplomatist; b. 25 Aug. 1921, San José; s. of Porfirio Oduber and Ana María Quirós; m. Marjorie Elliott Sypher 1950; one s.; ed. Univ. de Costa Rica, McGill Univ., Canada, and Univ. de Paris; Amb. to UN 1949; Head of Public Relations, Partido de Liberación Nacional (PLN) 1951–53, Sec.-Gen. 1956–58, Pres. 1970–77; Minister of Foreign Affairs 1962–64; Head various dels. to UN Gen. Assembly; co-ordinator at the meeting of Presidents of Central America U.S.A. and Panama 1963: PLN Presidential Cand. 1965; Pres. of Congress 1970–74; Pres. of Costa Rica 1974–78; Dr. h.c. (Yale) 1986; Grand Cross Order of Malta, Gran Cruz, Orden de Isabel la Católica (Spain), and numerous other foreign decorations. *Leisure interests:* sports, reading, travel. *Address:* c/o Casa Presidencial, San José, Costa Rica.

ODUM, Eugene P., PH.D.; American ecologist, educator, lecturer and writer; b. 17 Sept. 1913, Newport, N.H.; s. of the late Howard W. Odum and Anna Louise Kranz Odum; m. Martha Ann Huff 1940; one s. (deceased); ed. Univs. of North Carolina and Illinois; Instructor, then Asst. Prof., Assoc. Prof., Prof., Univ. of Georgia 1940–57, Alumni Distinguished Prof. of Zoology 1957, Callaway Prof. of Ecology 1977, Dir. Inst. of Ecology 1960–85, Dir. Emer. and Prof. Emer. 1985–; Instructor-in-charge, Marine Ecology Training Program,

Marine Biological Lab., Woods Hole, Mass. summers 1957–61; pioneer in field of ecosystem ecology as a new "integrative" science; research interests include ecological energetics, estuarine and wetland ecology, ornithology and resource econs.; Fellow A.A.A.S., American Acad. of Arts and Sciences, American Ornithologists' Union; mem. N.A.S., Ecological Soc. of America, American Soc. of Limnology and Oceanography, American Soc. of Mammalogists, American Inst. of Biological Sciences, Wildlife Soc., Soc. for Study of Evolution, American Naturalist Soc.; Institut de la Vie Prize, France 1957; Mercer Award, Ecological Soc. of America 1956, Eminent Ecologist's Award 1974; Conservationist of the Year, Nat. Wildlife Fed. 1976, Tyler Ecology Award 1977; Crafoord Prize, Royal Swedish Acad. 1987.. *Publications:* Fundamentals of Ecology 1953, Ecology 1963, Basic Ecology 1983, Ecology, and Our Endangered Life-support Systems (2nd edn.) 1993 (all translated into several languages); more than 200 papers in scientific journals. *Leisure interests:* natural history, tennis. *Address:* Beech Creek Road, Athens, GA 30606, U.S.A. (Home). *Telephone:* (404) 543-2290 (Home). *Fax:* (706) 542-6040.

ODUMEGWU-OJUKWU, General Chukwuemeka; Nigerian politician and army officer; b. 4 Nov. 1933, Zungeru; s. of Sir Odumegwu Ojukwu, K.B.E. and Grace Ojukwu; m. Bianca Olivia Odinaka Onoh 1994; ed. C.M.S. Grammar School and King's Coll., Lagos, Epsom Coll., U.K., Lincoln Coll., Oxford, Eaton Hall Officer Cadet School, U.K. and Joint Services Staff Coll., U.K.; Admin. Officer, Nigerian Public Service 1956–57; joined Nigerian Army 1957; at Nigerian Army Depot, Zaria 1957; army training in U.K. 1957–58; joined 5th Battalion Nigerian Army 1958; Instructor, Royal West African Frontier Force Training School, Teshie 1958–61; returned to 5th Battalion Nigerian Army 1961; Maj. Army HQ 1961; Deputy Asst. Adjutant and Quartermaster-Gen. Kaduna Brigade HQ 1961; Congo Emergency Force 1962; Lieut.-Col. and Quartermaster-Gen. 1963–64; Commdr. 5th Battalion, Kano 1964–66; Mil. Gov. of E. Nigeria 1966–67; Head of State of Republic of Biafra (E. Region of Nigeria) 1967–70; sought political asylum in Ivory Coast 1970–82; returned to Nigeria 1982; joined Nat. Party of Nigeria 1983–84; imprisoned Jan.-Oct. 1984; then released; disqualified from Presidential candidacy Feb. 1993; left SDP May 1993. *Publications:* Biafra: Random Thoughts 1969, Because I am Involved 1982. *Leisure interests:* sports, music, art, photography, poetry. *Address:* Villaska, 29 Queen's Drive, Ikoyi, Lagos, Nigeria.

O'DWYER, Thomas, M.S., PH.D.; Irish European Union official; b. 13 April 1937, Tipperary; m. Margaret M. Tuohy 1963; three s.; ed. Christian Brothers School, Tipperary, Univ. Coll. Dublin and Cornell Univ.; Marketing Dept. Agricultural Inst. Dublin 1968–73; Head, Dairy Div. European Comm. 1973; Chef de Cabinet to Commr. for Personnel and Admin. 1981; Dir. Org. of Markets in Livestock Products Dec. 1981; Chef de Cabinet to Commr. for Agric. and Rural Devt. 1989; Dir.-Gen. for Co-ordination of Structural Policies and mem. Bd. Dirs. EIB 1990; Dir.-Gen. for Educ., Training and Youth (DG XXII) 1993–98; First Pres. European Foundation for Vocational Training 1994–. *Publications:* contributions to agricultural and econ. journals 1968–73. *Leisure interests:* reading, golf. *Address:* Directorate-General XXII, European Commission, rue de la Loi 200, B-1049 Brussels (Office); Avenue Xavier Henrard 30, 1150 Brussels, Belgium (Home). *Telephone:* (02) 295.85.35; 295.32.51. *Fax:* (02) 295.60.85.

OË, Kenzaburo: Japanese author; b. 1935; m.; two c.; first stories published 1957; Akutagawa prize for novella The Catch 1958; first full-length novel Pluck The Flowers, Gun The Kids 1958; represented young Japanese writers at Peking (now Beijing) 1960; travelled to Russia and Western Europe writing a series of essays on Youth in the West 1961; Shinchosha Literary Prize 1964; Tanizaka Prize 1967; Nobel Prize for Literature 1994. *Publications:* The Catch 1958, Pluck The Flowers, Gun The Kids 1958, Our Age 1959, Screams 1962, The Perverts 1963, Hiroshima Notes 1963, Adventures in Daily Life 1964, A Personal Matter 1964 (English 1969), Football in The First Year of Mannen 1967, The Silent Cry 1989, Nip the Buds Shoot the Kids 1995, Japan, The Ambiguous and Myself (Nobel Prize speech and other lectures) 1995, A Healing Family 1996. *Address:* 585 Seijo-machi, Setagaya-ku, Tokyo, Japan. *Telephone:* 482-7192.

OERTER, Alfred A.; American athlete; b. 19 Sept. 1936, Astoria, N.Y.; s. of Alfred and Mary (Strup) Oerter; m. 1st Corinne Benedetto 1958 (divorced 1975), two d.; m. 2nd Cathy Carroll 1983; competed Olympic Games, winning gold medals at discus, Melbourne 1956, Rome 1960, Tokyo 1964, Mexico 1968; only athlete to win gold medals at four successive Olympic Games; held world records at discus and was first man to throw over 200 feet; current world record holder for Masters track and field; motivational speaker athletic and corporate promotions; mem. track and field Hall of Fame, Olympic Hall of Fame, Olympic Order 1982. *Address:* 19435 Doewood Drive, Monument, CO 80132, U.S.A.

OESTERHELT, Jürgen, LL.D.; German diplomatist; b. 19 Aug. 1935, Munich; s. of Dr. Egon Oesterhelt and Trude Pfohl; m. Katharina Galeiski 1964; one s. one d.; ed. Univ. of Munich and Columbia Univ.; int. lawyer, Paris 1963–64; entered diplomatic service, Bonn 1964; served Moscow 1964–65, New York (UN) 1966–71, Sofia 1971–74, Athens 1977–80; Ministry of Foreign Affairs 1980–92; Amb. to Turkey 1992–95, to U.K. 1995–97, to the Holy See 1997–; Bundesverdienstkreuz; decorations from Greece, Finland, Austria. *Leisure interests:* sports, reading, music. *Address:* German Embassy, Via di Villa Sacchetti 4–6, 00197 Rome, Italy.

OESTREICHER, Rev. Canon Paul, M.A.; British/New Zealand clergyman and journalist; b. 29 Sept. 1931, Meiningen, Germany; s. of Paul Oestreicher, M.D., and Emma Oestreicher (née Schnaus); m. Lore Feind 1958; two s. two d.; ed. Otago and Victoria Univs., N.Z., Bonn Univ., Fed. Repub. of Germany, Lincoln Theological Coll., U.K.; emigrated to New Zealand with parents 1939; Ed. Critic student newspaper, Otago Univ. 1952–53; Humboldt Research Fellow, Bonn Univ. 1955, Berlin 1992; studied industrial mission (Opel, Gen. Motors), Rüsselsheim 1958–59; ordained in Church of England 1959; freelance journalist and broadcaster in Fed. Repub. of Germany and U.K. 1959–; Curate in Dalston, London 1959–61; Programme Producer, Religious Dept., BBC Radio 1961–64; Assoc. Sec., Dept. of Int. Affairs, British Council of Churches, with special responsibility for East-West relations 1964–69, Hon. Sec. East-West Relations Cttee. 1969–81, Asst. Gen. Sec. and Div. Sec. for Int. Affairs 1981–86; Vicar, Church of the Ascension, Blackheath, London 1968–81; Dir. of Lay Training, Diocese of Southwark 1969–72; mem. Gen. Synod of Church of England 1970–86, 1996–97; mem. Exec. Council Amnesty Int. (U.K. Section) 1969–80, Chair. 1974–79; Founder and Trustee, Christian Inst. (of Southern Africa) Fund 1974–94, Chair. Trustees 1983–94; Hon. Chaplain to Bishop of Southwark 1975–80; Hon. Canon of Southwark Cathedral 1978–83, Canon Emer. 1983–86; Public Preacher, diocese of Southwark 1981–86; Dir. Int. Ministry of Coventry Cathedral 1986–97, Canon Residentiary 1986–97, Canon Emer. 1998–; int. consultant 1997–; mem. Council Keston Coll. 1975–83; mem. Nat. Council Campaign for Nuclear Disarmament 1980–82, Vice-Chair. 1983–85, Vice-Pres. 1985–; mem. Soc. of Friends 1982; Hon. D. Litt.; Hon. Citizen Meiningen 1995; Bundesverdienstkreuz (First Class), Germany 1995. *Publications:* Editor: Gollwitzer: The Demands of Freedom (English edn.) 1965, The Christian Marxist Dialogue 1969, (with J. Klugmann) What Kind of Revolution 1969, The Church and the Bomb (jtly.) 1983, The Double Cross 1986; trans. Schulz: Conversion to the World 1967; contributor to British Council of Churches working party reports on Eastern Europe and Southern Africa. *Leisure interests:* horse riding, sauna bathing, Mozart. *Address:* 20 Styvechale Avenue, Coventry, CV5 6DX, England (Home). *Telephone:* (01203) 673704 (Home). *Fax:* (01203) 631448.

OETKER, Rudolf-August; German shipowner and industrialist; b. 20 Sept. 1916, Bielefeld; s. of Rudolf Oetker; m. 3rd Maja von Malaisé 1963; eight c.; Owner Dr. August Oetker, Bielefeld 1944–, Hamburg-Südamerika Dampfschifffahrts-Gesellschaft Eggert und Amsinck, Hamburg 1951–; holder of controlling interest of Bankhaus Hermann Lampe KG, Bielefeld; numerous other business interests. *Leisure interests:* art, tennis. *Address:* Lutterstrasse 14, 33617 Bielefeld, Germany. *Telephone:* 0521/1550.

O'FARRELL, Anthony Gilbert, PH.D., M.R.I.A.; Irish professor of mathematics; b. 28 May 1947, Dublin; s. of Patrick O'Farrell and Sheila O'Farrell, née Curtis; m. Lise Pothin 1972; three s. one d.; ed. Univ. Coll. Dublin, Brown Univ., U.S.A.; Meteorological Officer, Irish Meteorological Service 1967–68; Asst. Prof., Univ. of Calif., Los Angeles 1973–75; Prof. of Math., Maynooth Coll. 1975–, Head of Computer Science 1992–95; Research Assoc., Dublin Inst. for Advanced Studies 1979–; Fellow and Teaching Asst., Brown Univ. 1970–73; mem. Irish Math. Soc. (Pres. 1982–84, Sec. 1984–85, 1987–89), London Math. Soc., Société Mathématique de France, American Math. Soc., Math. Asscn. of America, Irish Meteorological Soc.; Nat. Univ. Travelling Studentship 1969. *Publications:* numerous research papers. *Leisure interests:* literature, walking, music. *Address:* Mathematics Department, NUI Maynooth, Co. Kildare, Ireland. *Telephone:* (01) 708 3914. *Fax:* (01) 708-3913.

O'FARRELL, Patrick James, PH.D.; New Zealand professor of history; b. 17 Sept. 1933, Greymouth; s. of P. V. O'Farrell; m. Deidre G. MacShane 1956; three s. two d.; ed. Marist Bros. High School, Greymouth, Univ. of Canterbury, Christchurch and Australian Nat. Univ. (A.N.U.), Canberra; Research Scholar A.N.U. 1956–59; Lecturer, Sr. Lecturer, Assoc. Prof. Univ. of N.S.W. 1959–72, Prof. of History 1972–; Visiting Prof. Univ. Coll. and Trinity Coll., Dublin 1965–66, 1972–73, Scientia Prof. 1998; N.S.W. Premier's Literary Award 1987. *Publications:* Harry Holland: Militant Socialist 1964, The Catholic Church in Australia 1968, Documents in Australian Catholic History 1969, Ireland's English Question 1971, England and Ireland since 1800 1975, The Catholic Church and Community in Australia 1977, Letters from Irish Australia 1825–1929 1984, The Irish in Australia 1986, Vanished Kingdoms: Irish in Australia and New Zealand 1990, Through Irish Eyes: Australian and New Zealand Images of the Irish, 1788–1948 1994, UNSW: A Portrait 1998. *Leisure interest:* reading thrillers. *Address:* School of History, University of New South Wales, N.S.W. 2052, Australia. *Telephone:* (02) 6972348.

OFFERGELD, Rainer; German politician; b. 26 Dec. 1937, Genoa, Italy; s. of Carlo O. Offergeld and Erna (Buchter) Offergeld; m. Christel Hiller 1967; three d.; ed. Grammar School, Meersburg, and Frankfurt, Freiburg, Lyon and Zürich Univs.; Councillor, Fed. Law and Tax Admins.; Town Councillor and Administrator; Mayor, Lörrach 1984–95; Man. Dir. Thermoselect Südwest GmbH; mem. Bundestag 1969–84; Sec. of State to Minister of Finance 1975–78; Minister for Econ. Co-operation 1978–82; mem. several supervisory bds. *Publications:* numerous publs. on financial policy and devt. aid policy. *Leisure interest:* skiing, music. *Address:* Thermoselect Südwest GmbH, Südendstr. 42, 76135 Karlsruhe, Germany. *Telephone:* 0721 936-3976. *Fax:* 0721 936-2515.

OFFICER, David Adrian, M.A., F.R.S.A.; British artist, art lecturer, television presenter and producer; b. 24 Aug. 1938, Belfast, Northern Ireland; s. of Adrian Charles Officer and Eileen Officer (née Sterritt); ed. Hutcheson's Grammar School, Glasgow, Univ. of Durham and Moray House Coll. of Educ. Edinburgh; Head of Art Dept. Rhyl Grammar School, lecturer in Fine Art, Harrow School 1970–71; lecturer in Art Educ. W. Australian Inst. of Tech. (now Curtin Univ.) Perth 1972–78; ABC TV lecturer, Melbourne and Sydney 1973–78; Festival Artist, Perth 1974; Art Consultant, Whittaker (U.S.A.), Tabuk Mil. Hosp. Saudi Arabia 1979–83; lecturer in Art and Design, United Coll. of Educ. Zimbabwe 1983–85; weekly art and design programmes, ZTV Television, Zimbabwe 1985–87; lecturer in Fine Art, Hillside Teacher's Coll. Bulawayo 1985–87; lecturer in Fine Art and World Art History, Univ. of Anatolia, Turkey 1987–89; Visiting Examiner in Art, Cambridge Univ. 1991–; freelance artist, display artist, art educator, exhbn. organizer; exhbns. in most maj. European cities, and in Sydney, Adelaide, Melbourne and Perth. *Publications:* articles in Liverpool Gazette, festival magazines etc. *Leisure interests:* fine arts, drawing, painting, calligraphy, typography, stained glass, rugby, cricket. *Address:* 86 London Road, Plaistow, London, E.13, England.

OFFORD, Robin Ewart, M.A., PH.D.; British professor of medical biochemistry; b. 28 June 1940, Stondon; s. of Frank Offord and Eileen Offord; m. Valerie Wheatley 1963; one s. two d.; ed. Dame Alice Owen's School, London, Peterhouse Coll., Cambridge; scientific staff (part-time) UKAEA 1959–62; grad. student MRC Lab. for Molecular Biology 1962–65, on scientific staff 1965–66; scientific staff Lab. of Molecular Biophysics, Oxford 1966–72; Fellow Univ. Coll., Oxford Univ. 1968–73, Univ. lecturer in Molecular Biophysics, Oxford 1972–80, tutor in Biochem. and Official Fellow Christ Church Coll., Oxford Univ. 1973–80; Prof., Dir. Dept. of Medical Biochem., Univ. of Geneva 1980–, Pres. Pre-Clinical Medicine 1994–. *Publications:* author, co-author and ed. six scientific books; author and co-author over 150 articles in scientific journals. *Leisure interests:* scuba diving, windsurfing, cross-country skiing, comparative linguistics. *Address:* Department of Medical Biochemistry, University Medical Center, 1 rue Michel Servet, 1211 Geneva 4, Switzerland. *Telephone:* (22) 7025470. *Fax:* (22) 3468758.

OFILI, Chris, M.A.; British artist; b. 1968, Manchester; ed. Chelsea School of Art, Royal Coll. of Art; has exhibited as solo artist in Southampton, and at Serpentine Gallery, London, and at Manchester City Art Gallery; fmr. winner Whitworth Young Contemporaries exhbn.; Turner Prize 1998.

OFNER, Harald, DR.JUR.; Austrian politician; b. 25 Oct. 1932, Vienna; m.; three c.; ed. Univ. of Vienna; private legal practice 1965–; Chair. Lower Austrian FPÖ (Austrian Freedom Party) 1976–89; mem. Nationalrat 1979–83, 1986–; Fed. Minister of Justice 1983–87. *Leisure interests:* history, travel. *Address:* c/o Parliament, Vienna, Austria.

OGATA, Sadako; Japanese United Nations official; b. 1927; Minister, Japan's Mission to UN 1978–79; UN special emissary investigating problems of Cambodian refugees on Thai-Cambodian border; rep. of Japan on UN Comm. for Human Rights 1982–85; fmr. Chair. Exec. Bd. UNICEF; fmr. Dir. Inst. of Int. Relations, Sophia Univ. Tokyo; Dean, Faculty of Foreign Studies, Sophia Univ. until 1990; UN High Commr. for Refugees 1991–; UNESCO Houphouet-Boigny Peace Prize 1996; Ramon Magsaysay Award for Int. Understanding 1997; Dr. h.c. (Harvard) 1994, Hon. D.C.L. (Oxford) 1998. *Address:* Office of the United Nations High Commissioner for Refugees, Casa Postale 2500, 1211 Geneva 2 dépôt, Switzerland. *Telephone:* (22) 7398111. *Fax:* (22) 7319546.

OGATA, Shijuro, M.A.; Japanese banker; b. 16 Nov. 1927, Tokyo; s. of Taketora Ogata and Koto Ogata; m. Sadako Nakamura 1961; one s. one d.; ed. Seikei Higher School, Tokyo, Univ. of Tokyo and Fletcher School of Law and Diplomacy; joined Bank of Japan 1950, Asst. Rep. in London 1962–64, Rep. in New York 1975–78, Adviser to Gov. 1978–79, Dir. Foreign Dept. 1979–81, Exec. Dir. 1981–84, Deputy Gov. for Int. Relations 1984–86; Deputy Gov. The Japan Devt. Bank 1986–91; Dir. Barclays Bank 1991–95, Fuji Xerox 1991–; Adviser Swire Group 1991–, Yamaichi Securities 1991–97; Chair. Barclays Trust & Banking Co. (Japan) Ltd. 1993–97; Head Study Group on UN Finances 1992. *Publications:* International Financial Integration: The Policy Challenges (co-author) 1989, The Yen and the Bank of Japan 1996; several articles on int. monetary issues. *Leisure interests:* reading, writing. *Address:* 3-29-18 Denenchofu, Ota-ku, Tokyo 145-0071, Japan. *Telephone:* 3-3722-4801.

OGI, Adolf; Swiss politician; b. 18 July 1942, Kandersteg; s. of Adolf Ogi and Anna Ogi; m.; two c.; ed. Commercial Coll., La Neuveville, Swiss Mercantile School, London; Man. Soc. for the Devt. and Improvement of Meiringen and the Hasli Valley 1963–64; joined Swiss Ski Asscn. 1964, Tech. Dir. 1969–74, Dir. 1975–81; Maj. in Army, Staff Liaison Officer 1984–87; joined Swiss People's Party 1978, Chair. 1984–87; Nat. Councillor 1979–; mem. Fed. Council and Head Fed. Dept. of Transport, Communications and Energy 1988–; Vice-Pres. Jan.–Dec. 1992, Pres. of Switzerland Jan.–Dec. 1993; Vice-Chair. World and European Cttee., Int. Ski Fed. 1971–83; Dir.-Gen. and mem. of Bd. Intersport Schweiz Holding AG 1981–. *Address:* Federal Department of Transport, Communications and Energy, Bundeshaus-Nord, Kochergasse 10, 3003 Berne, Switzerland. *Telephone:* (031) 614111 (Office).

OGILVIE, Dame Bridget Margaret, D.B.E., SC.D., F.I.BIOL., F.R.C.PATH.; Australian scientist; b. 24 March 1938, Glen Innes; d. of late John Mylne Ogilvie and Margaret Beryl McRae; ed. New England Girls School, Armidale, N.S.W., Univ. of New England, N.S.W., Univ. of Cambridge; Fellow Wellcome Animal Health Trust 1963–66; mem. scientific staff MRC 1966–81; mem. staff of The Wellcome Trust (various capacities) 1979–, Dir. 1991–98; Visiting Prof. Imperial Coll. London; Dir. (non-exec.) Lloyds Bank 1995–, Lloyds TSB Group PLC 1996–, Zeneca Group PLC; mem. U.K. Council for Science and Tech. 1993–, Advisory Council for Chem., Univ. of Oxford 1997–, Nat. Endowment for Science and Tech. 1998–, Australian Health and Medical Research Strategic Review 1998–; Trustee Nat. Museum of Science and Tech. 1992–, Royal Coll. of Veterinary Surgeons Trust Fund 1998–; Chair. Governing Body Inst. for Animal Health 1997–, Cttee. on the Public Understanding of Sciences 1998–; Ian McMaster Fellow; Hon. mem. British and American Socs. of Parasitology, British Veterinary Asscn., Hon. M.R.C.P.; Hon. Asscn. Royal Coll. of Veterinary Surgeons; Hon. Fellow Univ.-Coll. London, Girton Coll. Cambridge; Foundation Hon. Fellow Royal Veterinary Coll.; Hon.D.Sc. (Univs. of Nottingham, Salford, Westminster, Bristol, Glasgow, A.N.U., Buckingham, Dublin, Trent, Oxford Brookes, Greenwich); Hon. LL.D. Trinity Coll.; Univ. Medal (Univ. of New England), Inaugural Distinguished Alumni Award (Univ. of New England). *Publications:* various scientific papers, reviews, book chapters on the immune response to parasitic infections of man and animals 1964–84. *Leisure interests:* the company of friends, looking at landscape, swimming, walking, music, gardening. *Address:* c/o The Wellcome Trust, 183 Euston Road, London, NW1 2BE, England. *Telephone:* 0171-611 8888. *Fax:* 0171-611 8735.

OGILVIE THOMPSON, Julian, M.A.; South African business executive; b. 27 Jan. 1934, Cape Town; s. of the late the Hon. Newton and of Eve Ogilvie Thompson; m. the Hon. Tessa M. Brand 1956; two s. two d.; ed. Diocesan Coll., Rondebosch and Worcester Coll., Oxford; Chair. De Beers Consolidated Mines Ltd. 1985–97, Deputy Chair. 1998–; Chair, Mineral and Resources Corpn. 1982–; Deputy Chair. Anglo-American Corpn. of S.A. Ltd. 1982–90, Chair. 1990–; Dir. Anglo-American Gold Investment Co. Ltd. (Chair. 1976–90), AECI Ltd., Anglo-American Coal Corpn., Nat. Business Initiative, Zambian Copper Investments Ltd.; Hon. LL.D.; Rhodes Scholar 1953; Commdr., Order of Leopold (Belgium), Grand Official, Order of Bernardo O'Higgins (Chile), Presidential Order of Honour (Botswana). *Leisure interests:* golf, fishing, shooting. *Address:* P.O. Box 61587, Marshalltown 2107 (Office); Froome, Froome Street, Athol Ext. 3, Sandton, Tvl., South Africa (Home). *Telephone:* 638.9111 (Office); 884.3925 (Home).

OGILVY, H.R.H. Princess Alexandra, the Hon. Lady, G.C.V.O.; b. 25 Dec. 1936; d. of the late Duke of Kent (fourth s. of King George V) and Princess Marina (d. of late Prince Nicholas of Greece); m. Hon. Angus James Bruce Ogilvy (second s. of late 12th Earl of Airlie, K.T., G.C.V.O., M.C.) 1963; one s. one d.; ed. Heathfield School, Ascot; Chancellor, Univ. of Lancaster; Col.-in-Chief, the King's Own Royal Border Regt., The Queen's Own Rifles of Canada and the Canadian Scottish Regt. (Princess Mary's); Deputy Col.-in-Chief, The Light Infantry; Deputy Hon. Col., The Royal Yeomanry (Territorial Army Voluntary Reserves); Deputy Col.-in-Chief Queen's Royal Lancers 1993–; Patron and Air Chief Commdt., Princess Mary's Royal Air Force Nursing Service; Patron, Queen Alexandra's Royal Naval Nursing Service; Pres. or Patron of many charitable and social welfare orgs.; Hon. Fellow, Royal Coll. of Physicians & Surgeons of Glasgow, Royal Coll. of Anaesthetists, Royal Coll. of Obstetricians & Gynaecologists, Royal Coll. of Physicians; Hon. Liverywoman, Worshipful Co. of Clothworkers, Hon. Freedom, City of Lancaster, City of London; Hon. degrees (Queensland, Hong Kong, Mauritius, Liverpool); decorations from Mexico, Peru, Chile, Brazil, Japan, Finland, Luxembourg, the Netherlands, Canada; rep. H.M. Queen Elizabeth II at independence celebrations of Nigeria 1960 and St. Lucia 1979, 150th anniversary celebrations, Singapore 1969. *Leisure interests:* music, reading, tapestry, outdoor recreations including swimming, skiing, riding. *Address:* Buckingham Palace, London, SW1A 1AA, England. *Telephone:* 0171-930 1860.

OGILVY, David Mackenzie, C.B.E.; British advertising executive; b. 23 June 1911, West Horsley; s. of Francis J. L. and Dorothy (née Fairfield) Ogilvy; m. Herta Lans 1973; one s.; ed. Fettes Coll., Edinburgh, and Oxford Univ.; Assoc. Dir. Audience Research Inst., Princeton 1939–42; with British Security Co-ordination 1942–44; Second Sec. British Embassy, Washington 1944–45; founder 1948, Pres., Ogilvy, Benson and Mather Int., New York 1965–75, Creative Dir. 1973; Chair. Public Participation Cttee., Lincoln Center 1959, United Negro Coll. Fund 1968; Dir. New York Philharmonic 1957–67; Chair. WPP Group 1989–92; Trustee Colby Coll. 1963–69; Trustee and mem. Exec. Council World Wildlife Fund Int. 1975–; mem. American Asscn. of Advertising Agencies, Gov. Eastern Region 1959–61; Hon. Litt.D. (Adelphi) 1977; Parlin Award of American Marketing Asscn. 1972, elected to Advertising Hall of Fame 1977; Officier, Ordre des Arts et des Lettres. *Publications:* Confessions of an Advertising Man 1964, Blood, Brains and Beer (autobiog.) 1978, Ogilvy on Advertising 1983. *Leisure interest:* gardening. *Address:* Château de Touffou, 86300 Bonnes, France (Home).

OGRIS, Werner, DR.IUR.; Austrian professor of law; b. 9 July 1935, Vienna; s. of Alfred Ogris and Maria Erber; m. Eva Scolik 1963; two s.; ed. Univ. of Vienna; Asst. Inst. für Deutsches Recht, Vienna 1958–61; Prof. Freie Univ. Berlin 1962, Univ. of Vienna 1966–; mem. Austrian Acad. of Sciences; corresp. mem. Saxon Acad.; Foreign mem. Royal Netherlands Acad.; Hon. Dr. iur. (Prague, Bratislava); Prize of Theodor-Körner-Stiftung 1961. *Publications:* Der mittelalterliche Leibrentenvertrag 1961, Die Entwicklungsgang der österreichischen Privatrechtswissenschaft im 19. Jahrhundert 1968, Die Rechtsentwicklung in Österreich 1848–1918 1975, Personenstandsrecht 1977, Recht und Macht bei Maria Theresia 1980, Goethe—amtlich und politisch 1982, Jacob Grimm; Ein politisches Gelehrtenleben 1986, Friedrich der Grosse und das Recht 1987, Joseph von Sonnenfels als Rechtsreformer 1988, Zur Entwicklung des Versicherungsaufsichtsrechts und des Versicherungsvertragsrechts in Österreich von 1850 bis 1918 1988, Mozart und das Eherecht seiner Zeit 1991, Deutsche und österreichische Rechtsgeschichte in Japan 1991, Tatort Rechtsgeschichte 1994, Vom Galgenberg zum Ringtheaterbrand 1997. *Leisure interest:* tennis. *Address:* Vienna University, Juridicum, Institut für Österreichische und Deutsche Rechtsgeschichte, Schottenbastei 10–16, A-1010 Vienna (Office); Mariahilferstrasse 71, A-1060 Vienna, Austria (Home). *Telephone:* (4277) 34567 (Office); 586-41-57 (Home). *Fax:* (4277) 34599.

OGURA, Takekazu; Japanese agriculturist; b. 2 Oct. 1910, Fukui Prefecture; s. of Reizô Ogura and Hisako Ogura; m. Chieko Ogura 1937; two s. one d.; ed. Tokyo Imperial Univ.; Posts with Ministry of Agriculture and Forestry 1934–56; lecturer, Faculty of Agriculture, Univ. of Tokyo 1947–61; Dir.-Gen. Food Agency 1956–58; Sec.-Gen. Agriculture, Forestry and Fisheries Research Council 1958–60; Vice-Minister of Agriculture and Forestry 1960–61; Chair. Agriculture, Forestry and Fisheries Research Council 1963–75; Chair. Food and Agric. Policy Research Centre 1967–85, Hon. Chair. 1985–; Commr., Tax Comm., Prime Minister's Office 1963–69, Chair. 1969–90; Pres. Inst. of Developing Economies 1967–72, Chair. 1972–75, Adviser 1975–; mem. Policy Board, The Bank of Japan 1975–83; Chair. Japan FAO Asscn. 1975–80. *Publications include:* (in Japanese): Agricultural Policy of Japan 1965, Japanese Food Industry 1987, Can Japanese Agriculture Survive 1987, For Whom the Food is Produced 1987; (in English): Agricultural Development in Modern Japan 1966, Can Japanese Agriculture Survive? A Historical and Comparative Approach 1982, Toward Structural Reform of Japanese Agriculture 1983, Co-operation in World Agriculture (ed. with Th. Bergmann) 1985, Japanese Agricultural Policy Reconsidered 1993; articles in English and Japanese. *Leisure interest:* reading. *Address:* Food and Agriculture Policy Research Centre, Yushima Tokyu Bldg., 3-37-4 Yushima Bunkyo-ku, Tokyo 113-0034 (Office); 3-1-1006 Otsuka 2-chome, Bunkyo-ku, Tokyo 112-0012, Japan (Home). *Telephone:* (03) 3839-6802 (Office); (03) 3945-1805 (Home). *Fax:* (03) 3839-6803.

O'HALI, Abdulaziz A., PH.D.; Saudi Arabian business executive; b. 1935, Onayza; one s. three d.; ed. Univ. of Puget Sound, Tacoma, Wash. and Claremont Graduate School, Calif.; entered govt. service 1957, held various posts, including Mil. Advisory Dir., Prime Minister's Office, Acting Dir. of Planning and Budgeting, Dir. Cultural and Educ. Directorate, Ministry of Defense and Aviation; retd. with rank of Col. 1979; founding shareholder United Saudi Commercial Bank, Nat. Industrialization Co. 1983; Chair. Saudi Investment Bank; Man. Dir. Gulf Center Man. Consultants; mem. Jt. Econ. and Tech. Comm. of Saudi Arabia and U.S.A., of Saudi Arabia and Germany. *Address:* Saudi Investment Bank, P.O. Box 3533, Riyadh 11481; Gulf Center Management Consultants, P.O. Box 397, Riyadh 11411, Saudi Arabia. *Telephone:* 476-0287. *Fax:* 478-1557.

O'HANLON, Rory; Irish politician and doctor; b. 7 Feb. 1934, Dublin; s. of Michael O'Hanlon and Anna Mary O'Hanlon; m. Teresa Ward 1962; four s. two d.; ed. Blackrock Coll. Dublin and Univ. Coll. Dublin; mem. Dáil 1977–; mem. Monaghan County Council 1979–; Minister of State, Dept. of Health and Social Welfare Oct.–Dec. 1982; Minister of Health 1987–91, for the Environment 1991–92; Deputy Speaker of Dáil 1997–; Fellow Royal Acad. of Medicine; mem. British-Irish Parl. Group 1992–, Jt. Cttee. on Foreign Affairs 1993–; Fianna Fáil. *Leisure interests:* swimming, reading, walking. *Address:* Mullinary, Carrickmacross, Co. Monaghan, Ireland (Home). *Telephone:* (042) 61530 (Home).

O'HARA, Michael John, M.A., PH.D., F.R.S., F.R.S.E.; British scientist; b. 22 Feb. 1933, Sydney, Australia; s. of late Michael Patrick O'Hara and Dorothy Winifred Avis; m. 1st Janet Prudence Tibbits 1962 (divorced 1977); one s. two d.; m. 2nd Susan Howells 1977; two s. one d.; ed. Dulwich Coll. Prep., London, Cranleigh School, Surrey, and Peterhouse, Cambridge; Univ. of Edin., Grant Inst. of Geology 1958–78, Reader 1967, Prof. 1971–; Research Fellow, Carnegie Inst. of Washington Geophysical Lab. 1962–63; Prof., Univ. Coll. Aberystwyth, Dept. of Geology 1978–88, Head of Dept. 1978–87, Prof., Inst. of Earth Sciences 1988–93; Distinguished Research Prof. Earth Sciences Dept., Cardiff Univ. 1994–, Sherman-Fairchild Distinguished Visiting Scholar, Calif. Inst. of Tech. 1984–85; Visiting Prof. Dept. of Earth Sciences, Harvard Univ. 1986; Prof. and Head of Dept., Sultan Qaboos Univ., Oman 1988–90; mem. Natural Environment Research Council 1986–88; mem. Univ. Grants Cttee. 1987–89; Chair. Univ. Grants Cttee. Earth Sciences Review; Hon. mem. Geological Soc. France; Geological Soc. of London Murchison Medal 1983; American Geophysical Union Bowen Award 1984, Geochemistry Fellow, Jt. geochemical socs. of America and Europe 1997. *Publications:* over 100 articles in scientific journals. *Leisure interests:* mountaineering, hill walking. *Address:* University of Wales, College of Cardiff, P.O. Box 914, Cardiff, CF1 3YE, Wales. *Telephone:* (01222) 874830. *Fax:* (01222) 874326.

O'HARE, Joseph Aloysius, M.A., PH.L., S.T.D., PH.D.; American university president and Jesuit priest; b. 12 Feb. 1931, New York; ed. Berchmans Coll., Cebu City, Philippines, Woodstock Coll., Md. and Fordham Univ. New York; Instr. in Humanities, Ateneo de Manila Univ. 1955–58, Assoc. Prof. in Philosophy 1967–72; Assoc. Ed. America Magazine, New York 1972–75, Ed.-in-Chief 1975–84; Pres. Fordham Univ. 1984–; Chair. NY City Campaign Financial Bd.; Chair. NY City Campaign Financial Bd.; numerous hon degrees. *Leisure interests:* contemporary fiction, Irish folk music. *Address:* Office of the President, Fordham University, New York, NY 10458, U.S.A. *Telephone:* (212)-579-2003.

Ó hEOCHA, Colm, PH.D.; Irish university administrator; b. 19 Sept. 1926, Dungarvan, Co. Waterford; s. of Seamas Ó hEocha and Máiréad Drohan; m. Daiden Fahy 1957; two s. four d.; ed. Univ. Coll., Galway and Univ. of Calif. (Los Angeles and La Jolla); teaching asst. UCLA 1950–51; Research Asst. Scripps Inst. of Oceanography, La Jolla 1952–55; Research Assoc. Univ. of Minn. Minneapolis 1961–62; lecturer in Chem. Univ. Coll., Galway 1955–63, Prof. of Biochem. 1963–75, Pres. 1975; Chair. New Ireland Forum 1983–84, European Centre for Higher Educ. Arts Council (Ireland) 1989–; mem. Admin. Bd. Int. Asscn. of Univs. 1986–; Vice-Chair. Liaison Cttee. of Rectors Confs. of Mem. States of the EC 1993–; Hon. Life Mem. Royal Dublin Soc. 1992; Chevalier, Légion d'honneur; Commendatore dell'Ordine al merito della Repubblica Italiana; Commdr. Order of Merit (Poland) 1992; Hon. LL.D. (Queen's Univ., Belfast), (Univ. of Dublin). *Publications:* numerous papers on algal pigments, science and educ. policies. *Leisure interests:* gardening, drinking in good company. *Address:* Chestnut Lane, Bushy Park, Galway, Ireland. *Telephone:* 091.24436.

OHGA, Norio, B.MUS.; Japanese business executive; b. 29 Jan. 1930, Numazu, Shizuoka Pref.; s. of Shoichi Ohga and Toshi Mizuno; m. Midori Matsubara 1957; ed. Tokyo Nat. Univ. of Art, Kunst Universität, Berlin; joined Tokyo Tsushin Kogyo K.K. (Tokyo Telecommunications Eng. Corpn.) as Consultant and Adviser 1953, co. name changed to Sony Corpn. 1958; Gen. Man. Tape Recorder Div. and Product Planning (also in charge of Industrial Design) 1959, Dir. 1964; Sr. Man. Dir. CBS/Sony Inc. 1968, Pres. 1970; Man. Dir. Sony Corpn. 1972, Sr. Man. Dir. 1974, Deputy Pres. 1976, Pres. 1982–95, Chair. 1995–; Chair. CBS/Sony Group Inc. 1980–90; Chair. Sony USA Inc. 1988–, C.E.O. Sony Corpn. 1989–, Pres. 1989–95, Chair. Sony Software Corpn. 1991–; Vice-Chair. Tokyo Chamber of Commerce and Industry 1989–; Chair. Cttee. on New Business, Keidanren 1994–; fmr. Chair. Electronic Industries Asscn. of Japan 1995–; Vice-Chair. Keidanren 1998–; Int. C.E.O. of the Year (George Washington Univ.) 1994; Commdr.'s Cross First Class of the Order of Merit (Austria) 1987; Medal of Honour with Blue Ribbon (Japan) 1988; Commdr.'s Cross Order of Merit (Germany) 1994. *Leisure interests:* yachting and flying. *Address:* Sony Corporation, 6-7-35 Kita Shinagawa 6-chome, Shinagawa-ku, Tokyo 141, Japan. *Telephone:* (03) 448-2111.

OHKUCHI, Shunichi; Japanese business executive; b. 15 Jan. 1918, Tokyo; s. of Tatsuzo and Takae Ohkuchi; m. Kazuko Ohkuchi 1948; two s.; ed. Tokyo Imperial Univ.; Ministry of Agric. and Forestry 1941; mil. service 1942–48; Chief, Import Planning Div., Food Agency, Ministry of Agric. and Forestry; First Sec. Embassy, London 1956–59; Dir. Overseas Fishery Dept., Fishery Agency, Ministry of Agric. and Forestry 1961–64; Deputy Vice-Minister of Agric. and Forestry 1965, Vice-Minister 1968–69; Dir.-Gen. Food Agency, Ministry of Agric. and Forestry 1966–68; retd. from govt. service 1969; Adviser, Nippon Suisan Kaisha Ltd. 1970, Man. Dir., Sr. Man. Dir., then Vice-Pres. 1971–75, Exec. Vice-Pres. 1975–80, Pres. 1980–86, Chair. 1986–. *Leisure interests:* golf, audio (classical music), billiards. *Address:* Nippon Suisan Kaisha Ltd., 2-6-2, Ohtemachi, Chiyoda-ku, Tokyo, Japan.

OHLSSON, Garrick; American pianist; b. 1948, White Plains, New York; winner Chopin Int. Piano Competition, Warsaw 1970; appears regularly with all maj. orchestras and recital series throughout the world. *Address:* c/o Vincent Ryan, Arts Management Group Inc., 150 Fifth Avenue, Suite 845, New York, NY 10011-4311, U.S.A.

OHLSSON, Per Evald Torbjörn; Swedish journalist; b. 3 March 1958, Malmö; s. of Ulla Ohlsson and Torsten Ohlsson; m. Maria Rydqvist-Ohlsson 1989; one s.; ed. Univ. of Lund; Ed. Lundagärd 1980–81; editorial writer Expressen, Stockholm 1981–85; New York Corresp. Sydvenska Dagbladet 1985–88, Ed. in Chief 1990–. *Publications:* 'Över ther' — Banden Över Atlanten 1992, Gudarnas Ö 1993, 100 År Av Tillväxt 1994. *Leisure interests:* music, literature, sports. *Address:* Sydvenska Dagbladet, 205 05 Malmö, Sweden. *Telephone:* 40-28-12-00. *Fax:* 40-93-54-75.

OHNISHI, Minoru; Japanese business executive; b. 28 Oct. 1925, Hyogo Pref.; s. of Sokichi and Mitsu Ohnishi; m. Yaeko Yui 1951; two s.; ed. School of Econs., Tokyo Univ.; joined Fuji Photo Film Co. Ltd. 1948, Man. Tokyo Sales Dept. of Consumer Products Div. 1957–61, Sales Dept. of Industrial Products Div. 1961–62, Fukuoka Branch Office 1962–64, Exec. Vice-Pres. Fuji Photo Film U.S.A. Inc. 1964–68, Man. Export Sales Div. Fuji Photo Film Co. Ltd. 1968–76, Dir. 1972–, Man. Dir. 1976–79, Sr. Man. Dir. 1979–80, Pres. 1980–96, Chair. 1996–; Pres. Photo-Sensitized Materials Mfrs. Asscn. of Japan June 1980–. *Leisure interests:* golf, reading. *Address:* Fuji Photo Film Company Ltd., 26–30 Nishiazabu, 2- chome, Minato-ku, Tokyo 106, Japan.

OHNO, Susumu, PH.D., D.SC.; Japanese/American research scientist; b. 1 Feb. 1928, Seoul, Korea; s. of Kenichi Ohno and Toshiko (Saito) Ohno; m. Midori Aoyama 1951; two s. one d.; ed. Tokyo Univ. of Agric. and Tech. and Hokkaido Univ., Sapporo; Research Staff, Pathology, Tokyo Univ. 1950–53;

Research Assoc., City of Hope, Duarte, Calif., U.S.A. 1953–66, Chair. Biology 1966–81, Ben Horowitz Chair of Distinguished Scientist in Reproductive Genetics, Beckman Research Inst. of The City of Hope 1981–95, Emer. 1996–; Visiting Prof. Tohoku Univ. 1987–, Nat. Inst. of Genetics of Japan 1997; Bd. Dirs. Beckman Research Inst.; Hon. D.Sc. (Pennsylvania); Amory Prize, American Acad. of Arts and Sciences; Kihara Prize, Japanese Soc. of Genetics, Royal Danish Baic Research Prize. *Publications:* Sex Chromosomes and Sex-linked Genes 1967, Evolution by Gene Duplication 1970, Major Sex Determining Genes 1979. *Leisure interests:* horsemanship (dressage), fishing, history, musical transformation of DNA sequences. *Address:* c/o Beckman Research Institute of The City of Hope, 1450 Duarte Road, Duarte, CA 91010; 7329 Oak Drive, Glendora, CA 91740, U.S.A. (Home). *Telephone:* (616) 357-9711 (Office); (616) 963-2214 (Home). *Fax:* (616) 357-1929 (Office); (616) 963-2922 (Home).

OHTA (HARADA), Tomoko, PH.D.; Japanese geneticist; b. 7 Sept. 1933, Aichi-ken; d. of Mamoru Harada and Hatsu Harada; m. Yasuo Ohta 1960 (divorced 1972); one d.; ed. Tokyo Univ., North Carolina State Univ.; researcher Kihara Inst. for Biological Research 1958–62; Post Doctoral Fellow Nat. Inst. of Genetics 1967–69, researcher 1969–76, Assoc. Prof. 1976–84, Prof. 1984–97, Prof. Emer. 1997–, Head Dept. of Population Genetics 1988–97; Vice-Pres. Soc. for the Study of Evolution 1994; Foreign hon. mem. American Acad. of Arts and Sciences 1984; Saruhashi Prize 1981, Japan Acad. Prize 1985, Weldon Memorial Prize (Oxford Univ.) 1986. *Publications:* Evolution and Variation of Multigene Families, Lecture Notes in Biomathematics vol. 37 1980. *Leisure interest:* reading. *Address:* 20-20 Hatsunedai, Mishima-shi, Shizuoka-ken 411, Japan. *Telephone:* (0559) 724638.

OHTANI, Ichiji; Japanese textile executive; b. 31 Aug. 1912, Kobe; s. of Kyosuke Ohtani and Tama Ohtani; m. Atsuko Suzuki 1943; two s. one d.; ed. Kobe Univ.; Dir. Toyobo Co. Ltd. 1964–68, Man. Dir. 1968–72, Senior Man. Dir. 1972–74, Deputy Pres. 1974, Pres. 1974–78, Chair. 1978–83, Counsellor 1983–92, Hon. Sr. Adviser 1992–; Dir. Toyobo Petcord Co. Ltd. 1969–83, Chair. Toyobo Co. Ltd. 1978–83, Counsellor 1983–; Vice-Pres. Industrias Unidas, S.A. 1973–79; Exec. Dir. Fed. of Econ. Orgs. 1976–83; Chair. Japan Spinners' Asscn. 1976–79, Diafibres Co. Ltd. 1977–88; Vice-Pres. Japan Textile Fed. 1976–79; Jr. Vice-Pres. Int. Textile Mfrs. Fed. 1976–78, Sr. Vice-Pres. 1978–80, Pres. 1980–82, Hon. Life mem. 1982–; Blue Ribbon Medal 1979; Order of the Rising Sun (Second Class) 1984. *Leisure interest:* sports. *Address:* Toyobo Co. Ltd., 2-8 Dojima Hama 2-chome, Kita-ku, Osaka 530 (Office); 7-18 Yamate-cho, Ashiya-shi 659, Japan (Home).

OHTANI, Monshu Koshin, M.A.; Japanese ecclesiastic; b. 12 Aug. 1945, Kyoto; s. of Kosho Ohtani and Yoshiko Ohtani; m. Noriko Tanaka 1974; two s. two d.; ed. Tokyo Univ. and Ryukoku Univ.; ordained Priest of Jodo Shinshu Hongwanji-ha Aug. 1960, Monshu (Ecclesiastic Patriarch) Apparent 1970–1977, Monshu April 1977–; Pres. All-Japanese Buddhist Fed. 1978–80, 1988–90. *Leisure interests:* the study of literature, skiing. *Address:* Horikawa-dori, Hanayacho-sagaru, Shimogyo-ku, Kyoto 600, Japan. *Telephone:* (075) 371-5181. *Fax:* (075) 351-1211.

OIDE, Shun; Japanese politician; Chair. Social Democratic Party of Japan; Minister of Posts and Telecommunications 1994–95; mem. House of Reps. for Kanagawa, Dir. Special Cttee. on Security. *Address:* c/o Social Democratic Party of Japan, 1-8-1 Nagata-cho, Chiyoda-ku, Tokyo 100, Japan.

OISTRAKH, Igor Davidovich, F.R.C.M.; Russian violinist; b. 27 April 1931, Odessa; s. of late David Oistrakh; m. Natalia Zertsalova 1960; one s.; ed. State Conservatoire, Moscow; many foreign tours, several concerts with father David Oistrakh; appears with maj. orchestras throughout the world as soloist and conductor; teaches int. master classes; Pres. Russian br. of ESTA, César Franck Foundation; Hon. mem. Beethoven Soc., Bonn, E. Ysaÿe Soc., Brussels; winner of numerous competitions; numerous awards; over 100 recordings; lives in Belgium and Russia.

OIZERMAN, Teodor Ilyich; Russian philosopher; b. 14 May 1914, Petrovervovka; s. of Ilya Davidovich Oizerman and Yelizaveta Abramovna Nemirovskaya; m. Genrietta Kasavina; two s. one d.; ed. Moscow Inst. of History, Philosophy and Literature; Industrial worker 1930–33; Postgraduate 1938–41; Army service 1941–46; Asst. Prof., Moscow Inst. of Econs. 1946–47; Asst. Prof., Prof. Moscow Univ. 1952–54, Head of Chair 1954–68; corresp. mem. U.S.S.R. (now Russian) Acad. of Sciences 1966–81, mem. 1981–; Foreign mem. Acad. of Sciences, GDR 1981–90; mem. Int. Inst. of Philosophy 1982–; Head Dept. of History of Philosophy, Inst. of Philosophy of Acad. of Sciences 1971–87, Adviser to Dir. 1987–; Vice-Pres. U.S.S.R. (now Russian) Philosophical Soc. 1982–95; various decorations. *Publications:* (works have been translated into German, French and English), Development of Marxist theory in Experience of the Revolution of 1848 1955, Philosophie Hegels 1959, The Making of Marxist Philosophy 1962, 1974, 1986, On the History of pre-Marxist Philosophy 1961, Alienation as an Historical Category 1965, Problems of Historical-Philosophical Science 1969, Principal Philosophical Trends 1971, Crisis of Contemporary Idealism 1973, Problems of the History of Philosophy 1973, Philosophy of Kant 1974, Dialectic Materialism and the History of Philosophy 1982, Principles of the Theory of the Historical Process in Philosophy 1986, The Main Trends in Philosophy 1988, Philosophical and Scientific World Outlook of Marxism 1989, Philosophie auf dem Wege zur Wissenschaft 1989, Kant's Theory of Knowledge 1991, and over 500 articles on philosophical problems. *Leisure interest:* walking. *Address:* Institute of Philosophy, Russian Academy of Sciences, Volchonka str. 14, Moscow (Office); Mendeleyev str. 1, Apt. 168, 117234 Moscow, Russia (Home). *Telephone:* 2039198 (Office); 9390137 (Home).

OJEDA PAULLADA, Pedro; Mexican lawyer; b. 19 Jan. 1934, México, D.F.; s. of Manuel Ojeda Lacroix and Adela Paullada de Ojeda; m. Olga Cárdenas de Ojeda 1959; two s. three d.; ed. Univ. Nacional Autónoma de México; Head of Personnel and lawyer, Técnica y Fundación, S.A. de C.V. 1955, Sub-Man. 1955–57; Gen. Man. Industria Química de Plásticos S.A. 1957–58; Deputy Dir.-Gen. Juntas Federales de Mejoras Materiales 1959–65; Dir.-Gen. of Legal Affairs, SCT 1966–70; Sec.-Gen. Presidential Secr. 1970–71; Attorney-Gen. 1971–76; Sec. of Labour and Social Welfare 1976–81; Minister of Fisheries 1982–88; Gen. Coordinator Nat. Food Comm. 1988–91; Pres. Fed. Court of Conciliation and Arbitrage 1995–; Prof. of Law and Economics UNAM (Nat. Autonomous Univ. of Mexico), Prof. of Social Security; represented Mexico on many int. and regional comms. etc., including Pres. Perm. Conf. of Political Parties of Latin America (COPPAL) 1981–82, Chair. World Conf. of Int. Women's Year 1975, 64th Int. Conf. of ILO 1978, World Conf. on Fishing Devt. (FAO) 1984; Fed. Congressman 1991–94; Pres. Energy Comm. of the Mexican Congress 1991–94, Nat. Fed. of Lawyers in the Service of Mexico (FENASEM) 1992–, Tech. Comm. of Foreign Relations of Fundación Mexicana Luis Donaldo Colosio, A.C. 1992–94, Mexican Coll. of Lawyers 1994–, Mexican Acad. of Law and Econs. 1995–; Mexican Soc. of Geography and Statistics, 1994–97; mem. Institutional Revolutionary Party (PRI) 1951–, Pres. Nat. Exec. Cttee 1981–82; mem. Nat. Acad. of History and Geography, American Law and Econs. Asscn. 1991–; Order of Merit (Italy), Gran Cruz al Mérito (Italy), Orden de Isabel la Católica (Spain) and other orders. *Leisure interests:* art, dominoes, reading, tennis. *Address:* Avenida del IMAN 660, 3° piso, Col. Pedregal del Maurel, C.P. 04720, Del. Coyoacán, Mexico, D.F., Mexico. *Telephone:* (5) 568-18 78; (5) 606-88 81. *Fax:* (5) 606-90 70.

OJEDA Y EISELEY, Jaime de, LL.B.; Spanish diplomatist; b. 5 Aug. 1933; ed. Univ. of Madrid, Int. Acad. of The Hague, Naval War Coll. of Madrid and Sr. Center for Nat. Defence Studies (CESEDEN), Madrid; Prof. of Political Law, Complutense Univ. of Madrid 1958; joined diplomatic service 1958; served Washington, D.C. 1962–69; Minister-Counsellor, Beijing 1973–76; Consul-Gen. of Spain in Hong Kong and Macao 1976–79; Assoc. mem. Center for Int. Relations, Harvard Univ. 1979–80; Deputy Perm. Rep. to North Atlantic Council 1982–83, Perm. Rep. to NATO 1983–90; Amb. to U.S.A. 1990–97; Pres. Sr. Council on Foreign Affairs 1997–98; Amb.-in-Residence Shenandoah Univ. 1998–. *Address:* 3770 Leed's Manor Road, Markham, VA 22643, U.S.A. *Telephone:* 540 364 2275. *Fax:* 540 364 9281.

OJUKWU, General Chukwuemeka Odumegwu-, (see Odumegwu Ojukwu, General Chukwuemeka).

OKA, Takeshi, PH.D., F.R.S.C., F.R.S.; Canadian university professor; b. 10 June 1932, Tokyo, Japan; s. of Shumpei Oka and Chiyoko Oka; m. Keiko Nukui 1960; two s. two d.; ed. Univ. of Tokyo; Fellow Japan Soc. for the Promotion of Science 1960–63; Postdoctoral Fellow Nat. Research Council of Canada 1963–65; Research Physicist, Herzberg Inst. of Astrophysics 1965–81; Prof. of Chemistry and Astronomy and Astrophysics, Enrico Fermi Inst., Univ. of Chicago, U.S.A. 1981–; Fellow American Acad. of Arts and Sciences; Robert A. Millikan Distinguished Service Prof. 1989; Steacie Prize 1972, Plyler Prize 1982; Meggers Award 1997, Lippincott Award 1998. *Leisure interest:* history of science. *Address:* 1463 East Park Place, Chicago, IL 60637, U.S.A. *Telephone:* (312) 752-5963.

OKADA, Tokindo, D.SC.; Japanese biologist; b. 2 Feb. 1927, Hyogo-Ken; s. of Rihei Okada and Teruko Okada; m. Ei Waki 1956; one s.; ed. Kohnan High School, Kyoto Univ.; Instructor Kyoto Univ. 1954–59, Assoc. Prof. 1961–66, Prof. 1966–84; Research Fellow Edin. Univ. 1958–59, Fellow Carnegie Inst. of Washington 1964–65; Pres. Int. Soc. of Developmental Biologists 1982–86; Dir.-Gen. Nat. Inst. for Basic Biology 1984–89; Pres. Okazaki Nat. Research Insts. 1989–91; Vice-Pres. Int. Union of Biological Sciences 1991–; Dir. Biohistory Research Hall 1993–; awarded Harrison Prize, Alcon Prize and Naito Memorial prize; Purple Ribbon Medal, Person of Cultural Merit 1995. *Publications:* Differentiation in Development 1984, Ed. Commitment and Instability in Cell Differentiation 1984, Transdifferentiation—Flexibility in Cell Differentiation 1991. *Leisure interest:* music. *Address:* 22 Minamishiba-cho, Shimogamo, Sakyo-ku, Kyoto 606, Japan. *Telephone:* (075) 781 0839. *Fax:* (075) 712 0501.

O'KANE, Dene Philip; New Zealand professional snooker player; b. 24 Feb. 1963, Christchurch; s. of Robert John O'Kane and Lesley Joan Marshall; youngest-ever N.Z. Champion 1980; turned professional 1984; twice World Championship quarter-finalist 1987, 1992; Finalist Hong Kong Open 1989; quarter-finalist many other World Ranking events including British Open, European Open, Asian Open; Overseas (non-British) Player of the Year 1987. *Leisure interests:* golf, skin-diving, Formula One motor-racing, wine, clothes.

O'KANE, Maggie, B.A.; Irish journalist; b. 8 June 1962, Ardglas, Co. Down, N. Ireland; d. of Peter O'Kane and Maura McNeil; m. 1995; one s.; ed. Loreto Convent (Balbriggan, Co. Dublin), Univ. Coll. Dublin, Coll. de Journalistes en Europe, Paris and Coll. of Commerce, Dublin; reporter on Irish TV 1982–84, for Sunday Tribune newspaper 1984–87; reporter, TV Producer and Presenter 1987–89; Foreign Corresp. and Feature Writer, The Guardian 1989–; has reported from world trouble spots: Eastern Europe 1989–91,

Baghdad 1991 (one of only 32 int. journalists to remain in Iraq in Jan. 1991), Kurdistan 1991–92, Yugoslavia 1992–94, Bosnia, Haiti, Cuba 1994–96, etc.; writer and presenter various TV documentaries including documentary Bloody Bosnia (Documentary of the Year, Royal TV Soc. 1994); Journalist of the Year 1992, Foreign Corresp. of the Year 1992, Reporter of the Year (commended) (jt. award) 1994, Amnesty Int. Foreign Corresp. of the Year 1993, James Cameron Award for Journalism 1996. *Publications:* A Woman's World: Beyond the Headlines 1996, Mozambique. *Leisure interests:* swimming, cooking, gym. *Address:* The Guardian, 119 Farringdon Road, London, EC1R 3ER, England. *Telephone:* 0171-278 2332; (01232) 246583.

OKASHA, Sarwat Mahmoud Fahmy, D. ÈS L.; Egyptian author and fmr. diplomatist and politician; b. 18 Feb. 1921, Cairo; s. of Mahmoud Okasha and Saneya Okasha; m. Islah Abdel Fattah Lotfi 1943; two s. one d.; ed. Military Coll. and Cairo Univ.; Cavalry Officer 1939; took part in Palestine war 1948–49, Egyptian Revolt 1952: Mil. Attaché, Berne 1953–54, Paris 1954–56; Counsellor in Presidency of Repub. 1956–57; Egyptian Amb. to Italy 1957–58; U.A.R. Minister of Culture and Nat. Guidance 1958–62; Chair. and Man. Dir. Nat. Bank 1962–66; Deputy Prime Minister and Minister of Culture 1966–67; Minister of Culture 1967–71; Asst. to the Pres. 1971–72; Visiting Prof. Coll. de France 1973; Pres. of Supreme Council for Literature, Art and Social Sciences; Pres. Egypt-France Asscn. 1965–; mem. Exec. Bd. UNESCO 1962–70 (master-minded int. campaign to save temples of Abu Simbel, etc. from the rising waters of the Aswan Dam); Pres. Consultative Cttee., Inst. du Monde Arabe (Paris) 1990–93; Corresp. Fellow British Acad.; Hon.D.Hum.Litt. (American Univ., Cairo) 1995; numerous awards (including UNESCO Gold Medal 1970, State Award for the Arts 1988) and foreign decorations. *Publications:* 50 works (including translations): Ovid's Metamorphoses and Ars Amatoria, Gibran, Khalil's works, Etienne Drioton's Le Théâtre Egyptien, studies of the works of Wagner, The Development of European Music (in Arabic), History of Art (20 vols.), The Muslim Painter and the Divine 1979, Ramsès Recouronné, The Renaissance 1996, The Baroque 1997, The Rococo 1998. *Leisure interests:* horse-riding, golf, music. *Address:* 34 Street 14, Villa 34, Maadi, Cairo, Egypt. *Telephone:* 3505075.

ÖKÇÜN, Gündüz; Turkish politician and university professor; b. 1936; fmr. Dean, Faculty of Political Sciences, Univ. of Ankara; Minister for Foreign Affairs June-July 1977, 1978–79; Republican People's Party. *Address:* c/o Ministry of Foreign Affairs, Ankara, Turkey.

OKE, Timothy R., M.A., PH.D., F.R.S.C.; Canadian/British professor of geography; b. 22 Nov. 1941, Kingsbridge, Devon; s. of late Leslie Oke and of Kathleen Smerdon; m. Margaret Lowe 1967; one s. one d.; ed. Lord Wandsworth Coll., Univ. of Bristol and McMaster Univ.; Asst. Prof. McGill Univ. 1967–70; Asst. Prof. Univ. of British Col. 1970–71, Assoc. Prof. 1971–78, Prof. of Geography 1978–, Head, Dept. of Geography 1991–96; Ed.-in-Chief, Atmosphere-Ocean 1977–80; Hooker Distinguished Visiting Prof. McMaster Univ. 1987; Visiting Fellow, Keble Coll. Oxford 1990–91; Research Scholar (Rockefeller Foundation) Bellagio, Italy 1991; consultant to WMO and other orgs.; Fellow, Royal Canadian Geographical Soc.; Guggenheim Fellow 1990 and other awards and distinctions. *Publications:* Boundary Layer Climates 1978, Vancouver and its Region 1992, The Surface Climates of Canada 1997; more than 100 articles on climate of cities. *Leisure interests:* golf, music, walking, painting. *Address:* Department of Geography, University of British Columbia, 1984 West Mall, Vancouver, B.C., V6T 1Z2 (Office); 3776 West 39th Avenue, Vancouver, B.C., V6N 3A7, Canada (Home). *Telephone:* (604) 822-2900 (Office); (604) 263-7394 (Home). *Fax:* (604) 822-6150.

O'KENNEDY, Michael, M.A.; Irish politician; b. 21 Feb. 1936, Nenagh, Co. Tipperary; s. of Éamonn and Helena (Slattery) O'Kennedy; m. Breda Heavey 1965; one s. two d.; ed. St. Flannan's Coll., Ennis, Univ. Coll. Dublin, King's Inns, Dublin; practised as barrister 1961–70, as Senior Counsel 1973–77, 1982–; mem. Senate 1965–69, 1993–, Front Bench Spokesman on Educ. and Justice, Senate Statutory Instruments Cttee. on the Constitution until 1967; mem. Dáil for North Tipperary 1969–80, 1982–93; Parl. Sec. to Minister of Educ. 1970–72, Minister without Portfolio 1972–73, Minister for Transport and Power 1973; Opposition Spokesman on Foreign Affairs 1973–77; Minister for Foreign Affairs 1977–79, of Finance 1979–80; mem. Comm. of European Communities 1980–82; Commr. for Personnel, Consumer Affairs, Environment 1981–82; Opposition Spokesman for Finance 1982–87, Minister of Agric. 1987–92; mem. All-Parties Cttee. on Irish Relations, Chair. 1973–80; mem. Informal Cttee. on Reform of Dáil Procedure until 1972, Dáil and Senate Joint Cttee. on Secondary Legislation of EEC 1973–80, Anglo-Irish Parl. Body 1993–; mem. Inter-Parl. Union, mem. Exec. of Irish Council of European Movement; Pres. EEC Council of Ministers July–Dec. 1979; Pres. EC Council of Agriculture Ministers Jan.–June 1990; Pres. Re-negotiation EEC/ACP at 2nd Lomé Convention 1979; Nat. Trustee Fianna Fáil. *Leisure interests:* reading, philosophy, history, politics, drama, music, sports. *Address:* Gortlandroe, Nenagh, Co. Tipperary, Ireland. *Telephone:* (067) 31366 (Home).

OKEZIE, Chief Josiah Onyebuchi Johnson, L.S.M., F.M.C.G.P.; Nigerian politician and physician; b. 26 Nov. 1924, Umuahia-Ibeku; s. of Chief Johnson Okezie and Esther Okezie; m. Rose Chioma Onwucheka 1966; three s. one d.; ed. Higher Coll., Yaba, Achimota Coll., Ghana, Yaba Coll. of Medicine, Univ. Coll., Ibadan and Royal Coll. of Surgeons, U.K.; Asst. Medical Officer, Nigerian Civil Service 1950–54; Founder and Medical Supt. Ibeku Central Hosp., Umuahia-Ibeku 1958–69; Sr. Medical Officer in charge of Queen Elizabeth Hosp., Umuahia-Ibeku 1970; Assoc. Editor, The Nigerian Scientist 1961–62; Sec. E. Nigerian Science Asscn. 1961–63; mem. Nigerian Medical Council 1965–66; mem. E. Nigeria House of Assembly 1961–66; Leader, Republican Party 1964–66; Rep. of E. Central State, Fed. Exec. Council 1970; Fed. Commr. for Health 1970–71, for Agric. and Natural Resources 1971–74; mem. Constituent Ass. to draw up 1979 Constitution of Nigeria 1977–78; Chair. Imo State Branch, Nigerian Medical Asscn. 1976, Alvan Ikoku Coll. of Educ., Owerri 1980–82; Chair. Bd. of Dirs. African Continental Bank Ltd. 1982–84; Sec. Nigerian Medical Asscn. (E. Region Branch) 1960–70; Life mem. Nigerian Bible Soc. 1972; Pres. Imo State Scout Council 1976–; Pres.-Gen. Ibeku Egwu ASA Devt. Asscn. 1981–84; Patron Grad. Nurses Asscn. of Nigeria 1987–, Imo State Red Cross Soc., Soc. for Promoting Igbo Language and Culture, Govt. Coll. Umuahia Old Boys' Asscn. 1990–; mem. Gov. Council Imo State Univ., Okigwe 1991–; Kt. of St. Christopher, Anglican Church 1988, Pres. Council of Kts., Umuahia Diocese 1994–97, patron Council of Kts. 1998; installed Chief Ezeomereoha of Bende 1974; invested Ochiagha of Ibeku 1982, traditional title of Eze Udo of Abiriba 1983, title of Onunekwuru Igbo of Umuopara Abia State 1997. *Publications:* The Evolution of Science 1959, Atomic Radiation 1961. *Leisure interests:* English literature, reading poetry, gardening, keeping animals (peacocks, antelopes and rabbits). *Address:* P.O. Box 306, Umuahia-Ibeku, Abia State, Nigeria. *Telephone:* (088) 220673.

OKHOTNIKOV, Nikolai Petrovich; Russian bass; b. 5 July 1937, Glubokoye, Kazakh Repub.; s. of P. Y. Okhotnikov and K. A. Okhotnikov; m. Larkina Tamara 1973; two s.; ed. Leningrad Conservatoire (pupil of I. I. Pleshakov); mem. CPSU 1974–90; soloist with Leningrad Concert Union; with Maly Theatre, Leningrad 1967–71, with Kirov (now Mariinsky) Opera 1971–; teacher of singing at Leningrad (now St. Petersburg) Conservatoire 1976–; Grand Prix, Barcelona 1972, People's Artist of U.S.S.R. 1983, U.S.S.R. State Prize 1985. *Major roles include:* Kochubey in Mazeppa, René in Iolanta, the Miller in Rusalka, Susanin in Glinka's Ivan Susanin, Dosifey in Mussorgsky's Khovanshchina, Kutuzov in Prokofiev's War and Peace, Philip II in Don Carlos, Heinrich in Lohengrin, Gremin in Eugene Onegin, Boris Godunov and Pimen in Boris Godunov, Don Basilio in The Barber of Seville. *Leisure interests:* fishing, photography. *Address:* The Mariinsky Theatre, Teatralnaya pl.1, St. Petersburg; Canal Griboedova 109, Apt. 13, 190068 St. Petersburg, Russia (Home). *Telephone:* 310-57-38.

OKINAGA, Shoichi, M.D., PH.D.; Japanese university president; b. 29 June 1933, Tokyo; s. of Shobei Okinaga and Kin Ino-Okinaga; m. Yoko Ishida 1968; two s.; ed. Univ. of Tokyo; Prin. Teikyo Commercial and Eng. Sr. High School 1961–71; founder and Pres. Teikyo Women's Jr. Coll. 1965–; founder and Pres. Teikyo Univ. 1966–, Prof. of Medicine 1971–; pvt. practice in obstetrics and gynaecology 1971–; Pres. Teikyo Special School of Medical Tech. 1969–; f. Teikyo Univ. of Tech. 1987; Chair. Bd. of Trustees, Teikyo Univ. Foundation 1987–; Chair. Judo Fed. of Tokyo 1987–; f. Teikyo School U.K. 1989, Nishi-Tokyo Univ. 1990; Chair. Salem-Teikyo Univ., U.S.A. 1990–, Teikyo-Loretto Heights Univ., U.S.A. 1990–, Teikyo Westmar Univ., U.S.A. 1990, Teikyo Marycrest Univ., U.S.A. 1991–, Teikyo Post Univ., U.S.A. 1991–; Fellow, Wadham Coll. Oxford 1991, St. Edmund's Coll. Cambridge 1991. *Publication:* Hitasura No Michi (autobiog.) 1984. *Leisure interest:* judo. *Address:* Teikyo University, 2-11-1, Kaga, Itabashi-ku, Tokyo 173, Japan.

OKOGIE, Mgr. Anthony Olubunmi, S.T.L., D.D.; Nigerian ecclesiastic; b. 16 June 1936, Lagos; s. of Prince Michael Okogie and Lucy Adumni Okogie; ed. St. Gregory's Coll., Lagos, St. Theresa Minor Seminary, Ibadan, St. Peter and St. Paul's Seminary, Ibadan, Urban Univ., Rome; ordained priest 1966; Act. Parish Priest, St. Patrick's Church, Idumagbo, Lagos; Asst. Priest, Holy Cross Cathedral, Lagos; Religious Instructor, King's Coll., Lagos; Dir. of Vocations, Archdiocese of Lagos; Man. Holy Cross Group of Schools, Lagos; Master of Ceremonies, Holy Cross Cathedral; Broadcaster of religious programmes, NBC/TV; Auxiliary Bishop of Oyo Diocese 1971–72; Auxiliary Bishop to the Apostolic Admin., Archdiocese of Lagos 1972–73; Archbishop of Lagos April 1973–; Vice-Pres. Catholic Bishops' Conf. of Nigeria 1985–88, Pres. 1988; Nat. Pres. Christian Asscn. of Nigeria 1988–96; mem. Prerogative of Mercy, Religious Advisory Council, Commdr. Order of the Niger 1999. *Leisure interests:* reading, watching films. *Address:* Archdiocese of Lagos, 19 Catholic Mission Street, P.O. Box 8, Lagos, Nigeria. *Telephone:* (1) 2633841. *Fax:* (1) 2633841.

OKOSO, Yoshinori; Japanese business executive; b. 1 Feb. 1915, Kagawa; s. of Atsushi Okoso and Nobu Okoso; m. Hisae Itasaka 1946; one s.; established Tokushima Ham Co., Ltd. 1942; Pres. and Rep. Dir. Nippon Meat Packers, Inc. (name changed following incorporation of Torise Ham Co., Ltd.) 1963; Blue Ribbon Medal 1973; Imperial Medal 1988. *Leisure interest:* golf. *Address:* Nippon Meat Packers Inc., 47 Minami-Honmachi, 4-chome, Higashi-ku, Osaka 541, Japan. *Telephone:* 06-282-3031.

OKPAKO, David Tinakpoevwan, PH.D., C.BIOL., F.I.BIOL., F.N.I.BIOL., F.A.A.S., F.A.S.; Nigerian pharmacologist; b. 22 Nov. 1936, Owahwa, Delta; s. of late Okun Okoro-Okpako Tsere and Obien Rebayi-Tsere; m. Kathleen Gweneth Jones-Williams 1967; one s. one d.; ed. Urhobo Coll. Effurun, Nigerian Coll. of Arts, Science & Tech. Ibadan, Univ. of Bradford and Univ. Coll. London; Visiting Fellow, Corpus Christi Coll. Cambridge 1973–74, 1983–84; Prof. and Head, Dept. of Pharmacology and Therapeutics, Univ.

of Ibadan 1978–81, 1986–87, Dean, Faculty of Pharmacy 1987–91; Pres. W. African Soc. for Pharmacology 1987–90; Foundation Pres. Nigeria Inst. of Biology 1990–92; Chair. Council, Nigerian Field Soc. 1991–; Visiting Scientist, Research Inst. Hosp. for Sick Children, Univ. of Toronto; now working as consultant pharmacist and pharmacologist. *Publications:* Principles of Pharmacology—A Tropical Approach 1991, Pharmacological Methods in Phytotherapy Research, Vol. 1. Selection, Preparation and Pharmacological Evaluation of Plant Material (with E. M. Williamson and F. J. Evans) 1996; articles in professional journals; book chapters. *Leisure interests:* golf, tennis, reading. *Address:* P.O. Box 20334, University of Ibadan Post Office, Oyo Road, Ibadan; 22 Sankore Avenue, University of Ibadan, Ibadan, Nigeria. *Telephone:* (023) 400550.

OKRI, Ben, F.R.S.L.; Nigerian author; b. 15 March 1959, Minna; s. of Silver Okri and Grace Okri; ed. John Donne's School, Peckham, London, Children's Home School, Sapele, Nigeria, Christ High School, Ibadan, Urhobo Coll. Warri and Univ. of Essex, U.K.; staff writer and librarian, Afriscope magazine 1978; poetry ed. West Africa magazine 1983–86; broadcaster with B.B.C. 1983–85; Fellow Commoner in Creative Arts, Trinity Coll. Cambridge 1991–93; mem. Int. PEN, a Vice-Pres. English Centre of Int. PEN 1997–; mem. Soc. of Authors; Hon. D.Litt. (Westminster) 1997; Commonwealth Prize for Africa 1987, Paris Review Aga Khan Prize for Fiction 1987, Booker Prize (for The Famished Road) 1991, Premio Letterario Internazionale, Chianti Ruffino-Antico Fattore 1992, Premio Grinzane Cavour 1994, The Crystal Award (World Econ. Forum, Switzerland) 1995. *Publications:* Flowers and Shadows 1980, The Landscapes Within 1982, Incidents at the Shrine 1986, Stars of the New Curfew 1988, The Famished Road 1991, An African Elegy (vol. of poems) 1992, Songs of Enchantment 1993, Astonishing the Gods 1995, Birds of Heaven (essays) 1996, Dangerous Love (novel) 1996, A Way of Being Free (non-fiction) 1997, Infinite Riches (novel) 1998, Mental Fight (epic poem) 1999, poems, essays, short stories. *Leisure interests:* chess, music, travel, theatre, dancing, cinema, art, games, riddles, silence. *Address:* c/o Orion Books, Orion House, 5 Upper St. Martin's Lane, London, WC2H 9EA, England.

OKUDA, Hiroshi; Japanese business executive; b. 29 Dec. 1932; ed. Hitotsubashi Univ.; fmr. Exec. Dir. Toyota Motor Corpn, Pres. Aug. 1995–; Deputy Chair. Keidanren. *Leisure interests:* music appreciation, reading. *Address:* 1-12-5 Umezonocho, Okazaki, Aichi 444, Japan. *Telephone:* (0564) 21-7348.

OKULOV, Valery Mikhailovich; Russian business executive and pilot; b. 22 April 1952, Kirov; m. Yelena Yeltsin (d. of Pres. Boris Yeltsin q.v.); two c.; ed. Acad. of Civil Aviation; navigator, instructor, Sverdlovsk aviation team 1976–85; leading navigator, First Deputy Dir.-Gen. Aviation Co. Aeroflot 1996–97, Dir.-Gen. 1997–. *Address:* Aeroflot, Leningradsky prosp. 37, korp. 9, 125836 Moscow, Russia. *Telephone:* (095) 155 5045 (Office).

OKUN, Daniel A., SC.D.; American professor of environmental engineering and consulting engineer; b. 19 June 1917, New York; m. Beth Griffin 1946; one s. one d.; ed. Cooper Union, New York, California Inst. of Tech., Pasadena and Harvard Univ.; Sanitary Engineer, U.S. Public Health Service 1940–42; served U.S. Army 1942–46; Assoc., Malcolm Pirnie Inc., Consulting Engineers 1948–52; Assoc. Prof., then Kenan Prof., Univ. of N.C. 1952–87, Kenan Prof. Emer. 1987–; Head, Dept. of Environmental Sciences and Eng. 1955–73, Dir. Inst. of Environmental Health Studies 1965–73, Dir. Int. Programmes, Dept. of Environmental Sciences and Eng. 1954–84, Chair. of Faculty, Univ. of N.C. 1970–73; Consultant to local, State and Nat. Govts., int. agencies and industry 1952–; mem. Environmental Advisory Council Rohm and Haas Inc. 1985–92; Chair. Water Science and Tech. Bd., Nat. Research Council 1991–94; Pres. Chapel Hill Chapter N.C. Civil Liberties Union 1991–93; Kappe Lecturer, American Acad. of Environmental Engineers; mem. Nat. Acad. of Eng., Inst. of Medicine (N.A.S.), Comm. on Human Rights N.A.S. 1991–94; Hon. mem. American Soc. of Civil Engineers; Eddy and Fair Medals, Water Environment Fed.; Fair Award, American Acad. of Environmental Engineers; Billard Award, New York Acad. of Sciences; Freese Award, American Soc. of Civil Engineers; Friendship Medal, British Inst. of Water and Environmental Man., Best Paper Award, Educ. Div., and Abel Wolman Award of Excellence, American Waterworks Asscn., Boyd Award, Asscn. of Metropolitan Water Agencies, Founders' Award, Asscn. of Environmental Eng. Professionals, Thomas Jefferson Award, Univ. of N.C. *Publications:* Water and Wastewater Engineering (with Fair and Geyer), Elements of Water Supply and Wastewater Disposal (with Fair and Geyer), Regionalization of Water Management, Community Wastewater Collection and Disposal (with George Ponghis), for WHO, Surface Water Treatment for Communities in Developing Countries (with Schulz). *Leisure interests:* squash, tennis, reading. *Address:* Department of Environmental Sciences and Engineering, CB 7400, University of North Carolina, Chapel Hill, NC 27599 (Office); 204 Carol Woods, 750 Weaver Dairy Road, Chapel Hill, NC 27514, U.S.A. (Home). *Telephone:* (919) 966-4898 (Office); (919) 918-3500 (Home). *Fax:* (919) 966 7115.

OKUN, Lev Borisovich; Russian theoretical physicist; b. 7 July 1929, Sukhinichi, Kaluga Dist.; s. of B. G. Okun and B. R. Ginzburg; m. Erica Gulyaeva 1954; one s. two d.; ed. Moscow Physics and Eng. Inst.; mem. of staff of Inst. of Experimental and Theoretical Physics, now Head of Lab. 1954–; main work has been on the theory of elementary particles; Corresp. mem. of U.S.S.R. (now Russian) Acad. of Sciences 1966–90, mem. 1990–, mem. Bureau Nuclear Physics Div.; mem. Science Policy Cttee. CERN 1981–86, Super Conducting Super Collider Lab., Dallas 1989–93; mem. Extended Scientific Council of DESY 1992–98, Bd. Int. Science Foundation 1993–97, Council of Scientists of Int. Asscn. for the Promotion of Co-operation with Scientists from the Independent States of the fmr. Soviet Union (INTAS), Brussels 1993–97; mem. Acad. Europaea 1991; Hon. Life mem. New York Acad. of Sciences 1993; Loeb Lecturer, Harvard Univ. 1989; Regents Prof. Univ. Calif. Berkeley 1990; Buhl Lecturer, Carnegie Mellon Univ. 1991, Visiting Prof., CERN 1992; Fermi Lecturer, Scuola Normale Superiore, Pisa 1993, Schrödinger Professorship (Univ. of Vienna) 1994, AUI Distinguished Lecturer, Brookhaven Nat. Lab. (U.S.A.) 1995; invited lecturer numerous maj. int. confs. on high energy physics; Matteucci Prize (Italy) 1988, Lee Page Prize (Yale Univ.) 1989, Karpinsky Prize (F.V.S. Foundation, F.R.G.) 1990, Humboldt Research Award 1993, Bruno Pontecorvo Prize (Jt. Inst. for Nuclear Research, Dubna) 1996, Open Soc. Inst. Prize 1997. *Publications include:* The Weak Interaction of Elementary Particles 1963, Leptons and Quarks 1981, Particle Physics: The Quest for the Substance of Substance 1984, A Primer in Particle Physics 1987, The Relations of Particles 1991; more than 200 research and review articles in leading physics journals. *Address:* Institute of Theoretical and Experimental Physics, 117218 B. Cheremushkinskaya 25, Moscow, Russia. *Telephone:* 123-31-94. *Fax:* 883-96-01 (Office); 124-19-41 (Home).

OLAFSSON, Thröstur; Icelandic government official and business consultant; b. 4 Oct. 1939, Husavík; m. 1st Monika Büttner 1966 (divorced), 2nd Thorunn Klemenzdóttir 1975; three s. one d. (and one s. deceased); ed. Akureyri Gymnasium, Free Univ. of Berlin, Ruhr Univ., Bochum, Germany; economist, Nat. Bank of Iceland 1968–69, Civil Servants' Org. 1969–71; specialist adviser to Minister of Industry 1971–73; Man. Dir. Mál og Menning (publishing co.) 1979–80; Asst. to Minister of Finance 1980–83; Man. Dir. Gen. Workers and Transport Union 1983–88; Exec. Dir. Mikligardur Ltd. 1989–90; Political Asst. to Minister of Foreign Affairs 1991–95; Chair. Bd. of Dirs. Gen. Bank of Iceland 1994–98; Sec.-Gen. Social Democratic Party's Parl. Group 1995–97; consultant 1997–98; Chair. Bd. Icemarkt Ltd. 1989–, Icelandic Int. Devt. Agency 1991–95; Gen. Man. Iceland Symphony Orchestra 1998–; mem. Admin. Council of Europe Social Devt. Fund. *Publications:* numerous articles on Icelandic econs. and politics. *Leisure interests:* music, literature, skiing, forestry. *Address:* Brædraborgarstígur 21 B, 101 Reyjavík, Iceland. *Telephone:* 551 9698. *Fax:* 563 0580.

OLAH, George Andrew, PH.D.; American professor of chemistry; b. 22 May 1927, Budapest, Hungary; s. of Julius Olah and Magda Krasznai; m. Judith Lengyel 1949; two s.; ed. Tech. Univ. Budapest; mem. Faculty, Tech. Univ. Budapest 1949–54; Assoc. Dir. Centre for Chemical Research, Hungarian Acad. of Sciences 1954–56; research scientist, Dow Chemical Canada Ltd. 1957–64, Dow Chemical Co. Framingham, Mass. 1964–65; Prof. of Chem. Case Western Reserve Univ. 1965–69, C. F. Mabery Research Prof. 1969–77; Donald P. and Katherine B. Loker Distinguished Prof. of Chemistry and Dir. Hydrocarbon Research Inst. Univ. of S. Calif. Los Angeles 1977–; consultant to industry; numerous visiting professorships; Fellow, A.A.A.S., Chemical Inst. of Canada; Foreign Fellow Royal Soc. (U.K.), Canadian Royal Soc.; mem. N.A.S., Italian Acad. of Sciences, Hungarian Acad. of Sciences, European Acad. of Arts, Sciences and Humanities, German, British and Swiss Chem. Socs. etc.; Dr. h.c. (Durham) 1988, (Budapest) 1989, (Munich) 1990, (Crete) 1994, (Southern Calif., Case Western, Szeged, Veszprem) 1995, (Montpellier) 1996, (N.Y. State Univ.) 1998; Alexander von Humboldt Sr. U.S. Scientist Award 1979; Pioneer of Chem. Award, American Inst. of Chemists 1993; Nobel Prize for Chem. 1994; other awards and distinctions. *Publications:* Friedel-Crafts Reactions (Vols. I–IV) 1963–64, Carbonium Ions (Vols. I–V) 1969–76 (with P. Schleyer), Friedel-Crafts Chemistry 1973, Carbocations and Electrophilic Reactions 1973, Halonium Ions 1975, Superacids (with G. K. S. Prakash and J. Somer) 1984, Hypercarbon Chemistry (with others) 1987, Nitration (with R. Malhotra and S. C. Narang) 1989, Cage Hydrocarbons 1990, Electron Deficient Boron and Carbon Clusters (with K. Wade and R. E. Williams) 1991, Synthetic Fluorine Chemistry (with Chambers and Prakash) 1992, Hydrocarbon Chemistry 1995; book chapters; numerous scientific papers. *Leisure interests:* reading, swimming. *Address:* Loker Hydrocarbon Research Inst., University of Southern California, Los Angeles, CA 90089 (Office); 2252 Gloaming Way, Beverly Hills, CA 90210, U.S.A. (Home). *Telephone:* (213) 740 5976. *Fax:* (213) 740 5087.

OLANG', Most Rev. Festo Habakkuk; Kenyan ecclesiastic; b. 11 Nov. 1914, Maseno; m. Eseri Olang' 1937; four s. eight d.; ed. Alliance High School, St. Paul's Theological Coll., Wyclif Hall, Oxford; Teacher Maseno Secondary School 1936–39; on staff Butere Girls' School 1940–45; ordained Deacon 1945; consecrated Bishop 1955; Bishop of Maseno 1961–70; Archbishop of Kenya (Anglican Church) 1970–79. *Address:* c/o P.O. Box 1, Maseno, Kenya. *Telephone:* Maseno 1.

OLARREAGA, Manuel; Uruguayan international civil servant and academic; b. 1 June 1937, Salto; s. of Manuel Olarreaga and Hilda Leguisamo; m. Marina Rico 1966; three s.; ed. Univ. of Paris; Minister-Counsellor, Uruguay's Perm. Del. to GATT 1982–87; First Exec. Sec. Latin American and Caribbean Program of Commercial Information to Support Foreign Trade 1988–91; Co-ordinator, Admin. Secr. of MERCOSUR 1991–96, Head, Regulations Div. 1997–, Ed. Official Bulletin of MERCOSUR 1997–; Prof. of Int. Marketing, Catholic Univ. of Uruguay 1993–; Chair. Cttee. of Countries Participating in Protocol Relating to Trade between Developing Countries, GATT; Deputy Chair. 18th, 19th and 20th Consultative Groups,

UNCTAD–GATT Int. Trade Centre. *Publications:* several publs. on int. trade. *Leisure interests:* reading, collecting antique keys. *Address:* Luis Piera 1992, Piso 1°, CP 11200, Montevideo (Office); Tomás Diago 769, Ap. 601, CP 11300, Montevideo, Uruguay. *Telephone:* (05982) 402 9024 (Office); (05982) 710 2433 (Home). *Fax:* (05982) 400 0958 (Office).

ÓLASON, Vésteinn, PH.D.; Icelandic academic and university administrator; b. 14 Feb. 1939, Hofn.; s. of Óli K. Gudbrandsson and Adalbjörg Gudmundsdóttir; m. Unnur Alexandra Jónsdóttir 1960; one s. one d.; ed. Menntaskólinn Laugarvatni, Univ. of Iceland; lecturer in Icelandic Language and Literature Univ. of Copenhagen 1968–72, in Comparative Literature Univ. of Iceland 1972–80, docent Icelandic Literature 1980–85; Prof. of Icelandic Univ. of Oslo 1985–91; Prof. of Icelandic Literature Univ. of Iceland 1991–, Dean Faculty of Arts 1993–95, Prorektor 1993–94; mem. Icelandic Research Council 1994–, Standing Cttee. for the Humanities of European Science Foundation 1996–; Iceland Literary Prize for Non-Fiction 1993. *Publications:* Sagnadansar: Edition and Study 1979, The Traditional Ballads of Iceland 1982, Islensk Bókmenntasaga I–II (History of Icelandic Literature 870–1720) 1992–93, Dialogues with the Viking Age: Narration and Representation in the Sagas of the Icelanders 1998, over 100 articles in professional publs. *Address:* Faculty of Arts, University of Iceland, IS-101 Reykjavík (Office); Nylendugata 43, IS–101 Reykjavík, Iceland (Home). *Telephone:* 525-4424 (Office); 552-1792 (Home). Fax: 525-4410.

OLAZABAL, José María; Spanish golfer; b. 5 Feb. 1966, Fuenterrabía, Spain; won Italian Open, Spanish Open and British Boys' Amateur Championships 1983, Belgian Int. Youth Championship 1984, Spanish Open Amateur Championship 1984, British Youths' Amateur Championship 1985; turned professional 1995; winner World Series of Golf 1990, 1994, The Int. (USA) 1991, U.S. Masters 1994, 1999; mem. European Ryder Cup Team 1987, 1989, 1991, 1993, 1997.

OLBRYCHSKI, Daniel; Polish actor; b. 27 Feb. 1945, Łowicz; m.; one s. one d.; ed. State Higher School of Drama, Warsaw; Actor Nat. Theatre 1969–77; mem. Polish Film Union; State Prize (2nd Class) 1974; numerous awards at Polish and foreign film festivals; Officier ordre des arts et des lettres. *Roles include:* Koral in Wounded in the Forest 1964, Rafał Olbromski in Ashes 1965, boxer in Boxer 1966, Marek in Jowita 1967, Daniel in All for Sale 1968, Azja in Mr. Wołodyjowski 1969, Angel of Death in Agnus Dei 1970, Tadeusz in Landscape After Battle 1970, Bolesław in The Birch Wood 1971, Wit in Family Life 1971, Pan Młody in The Wedding 1972, Mateusz in Pilatus und Andere 1972, Kmicic in The Flood 1974, Karol Borowiecki in The Promised Land 1975, Przybyszewski in Dagny 1976, Wiktor in The Maids of Wilko 1978, Jan in Little Tin Drum 1978, Saint-Genis in The Trout 1982, Pisarz in Flash-Back 1983, Love in Germany 1983, I'm Against 1985, Leon in Rosa Luxemburg 1986, Ga-ga 1986, Siekierezada 1986, Pitt in Tiger's Fight 1987, Pestka 1995, Old Tuchajbej in With Fire and Sword 1998, Gerwazy in Mr. Tadeusz 1998. *Stage appearances:* Hamlet 1970, Rhett in Gone With the Wind, Cyd 1985, Cześnik in Revenge 1998; TV: Raskolnikow in Crime and the Punishment 1980, Chello 1985. *Leisure interests:* tennis, horses, family life. *Address:* Teatr Polski, ul. Karasia 2, 00-327 Warsaw, Poland. *Telephone:* (22) 826-48-80. *Fax:* (22) 826 92 78.

OLDENBOURG, Zoé; French writer; b. 31 March 1916, Petrograd (now St. Petersburg), Russia; d. of Sergius Oldenbourg and Ada Starynkevitch; m. Henri Idalie 1948; one s. one d.; ed. Lycée Molière and Sorbonne, Paris; in France 1925–, studied history and literature at the Sorbonne; studied theology, Great Britain 1938; mem. Jury of Prix Fémina 1961–; Prix Fémina for La pierre angulaire (The Cornerstone) 1953, Chevalier, Légion d'honneur 1981, Officier de l'Ordre du Mérite des Arts et Lettres. *Publications:* Argile et cendres 1946, La pierre angulaire 1953, Bûcher de Montségur 1959, Les brûlés 1961, Les cités charnelles 1961, Les Croisades 1963, Catherine de Russie 1965, Saint Bernard 1969, La joie des pauvres 1970, L'épopée des cathédrales 1973, Que vous a donc fait Israël? 1974, Visages d'un autoportrait 1977, La joie-souffrance 1980, Le procès du rêve 1982, L'évêque et la vieille dame 1983, Que nous est Hécube? 1984, Les amours égarées 1987, Déguisements 1989, Aliénor 1992. *Address:* 4 rue de Montmorency, 92100 Boulogne-Billancourt, France.

OLDENBURG, Claes; American artist; b. 28 Jan. 1929, Stockholm, Sweden; s. of Gösta Oldenburg and Sigrid E. Lindfors; brother of Richard Oldenburg (q.v.); m. 1st Pat Muschinski 1960 (divorced 1970); m. 2nd Coosje van Bruggen 1977; ed. Yale Coll. and Art Inst. of Chicago; Apprentice reporter, City News Bureau, Chicago 1950–52; various odd jobs 1952–53; first group exhbn., Club St. Elmo, Chicago 1953; participated in other local shows, Chicago and Evanston 1953–56; moved to New York 1956; part-time job at Cooper Union Museum Library 1956–61; exhibited in group show, Red Grooms's City Gallery 1958–59; first public one-man show, Judson Gallery, New York 1959; two-man show with Jim Dine (q.v.), Judson Gallery Nov.–Dec. 1959; has since participated in numerous exhbns. of contemporary art throughout U.S.A. and Europe; several one-man shows at Sidney Janis Gallery, New York; works included in XXXII Biennale, Venice 1964; IX Bienal do Museu de Arte Moderno, São Paulo 1967; installed Giant Soft Fan in Buckminster Fuller's (q.v.) dome for U.S. Pavilion, Expo 67, Montreal 1967; travelling one-man exhbn. sponsored by Museum of Modern Art, New York shown at Tate Gallery, London and other European galleries 1970; mem. American Acad., Inst. of Arts and Letters; Wilhelm Lehmbruck Sculpture Award 1981, Wolf Prize for the Arts 1989, Dr. h.c. (R.C.A.) 1996. *Publications:* Claes Oldenburg, Proposals for Monuments and Buildings 1965–69 1969, Claes Oldenburg, Drawings and Prints 1969, Notes in Hand 1971, Raw Notes 1973, Claes Oldenburg: Multiples in Retrospect 1991. *Address:* c/o Pace Gallery, 32 East 57th Street, New York, NY 10022, U.S.A.

OLDENBURG, Richard Erik, A.B.; American museum director; b. 21 Sept. 1933, Stockholm, Sweden; s. of Gösta Oldenburg and Sigrid E. Lindfors; brother of Claes Oldenburg (q.v.); m. Harriet L. Turnure 1960 (died 1998); ed. Harvard Coll.; Man. Ed., The Macmillan Co. 1964–69; Dir. of Publications, Museum of Modern Art, New York 1969–71; Acting Dir. Museum of Modern Art Jan.–June 1972, Dir. 1972–94, Dir. Emer., Hon. Trustee 1995–; Chair. Sotheby's N. and S. America 1995–. *Leisure interest:* reading. *Address:* Sotheby's Inc., 1134 York Avenue, New York, NY 10021 (Office); 447 East 57th Street, New York, NY 10021, U.S.A. (Home).

OLDFIELD, Bruce, O.B.E.; British fashion designer; b. 14 July 1950; brought up in Dr. Barnardo's charity home; ed. Ripon Grammar School, Sheffield City Polytechnic, Ravensbourne Coll. of Art and St. Martin's Coll. of Art; grew up at Dr. Barnardo's, Ripon; established own fashion house, producing designer collections 1975; began making couture clothes for individual clients 1981; opened retail shop selling couture and ready-to-wear 1984; apptd. to Man. Bd., British Knitting and Clothing Export Council 1989; designed for films Jackpot 1974, The Sentinel 1976; Vice-Pres. Barnardo's 1998; Hon. Fellow Sheffield Polytechnic 1987, Royal Coll. of Art 1990, Durham Univ. 1991. *Publication:* Seasons 1987. *Leisure interests:* music, reading, driving, working, cooking. *Address:* 27 Beauchamp Place, London, S.W.3, England. *Telephone:* 0171-584 1363. *Fax:* 0171-584 6972.

OLDMAN, Gary; British actor; b. 21 March 1958, New Cross, South London; m. 1st Lesley Mannille; one s.; m. 2nd Uma Thurman; m. 3rd Dorya Fiorentino; one s.; ed. Rose Bruford Drama Coll.; studied with Greenwich Young People's Theatre; acted with Theatre Royal, York and then with touring co.; appeared at Glasgow Citizens Theatre in Massacre at Paris, Chinchilla, Desperado Corner, A Waste of Time; London stage appearances: Minnesota Moon, Summit Conference, Real Dreams, The Desert Air (RSC), War Play I, II, III (RSC), Serious Money (Royal Court), Women Beware Women (Royal Court), The Pope's Wedding; appeared in The Country Wife, Royal Exchange Theatre, Manchester; TV appearances include: Remembrance, Meantime (Channel 4); Honest, Decent and True (BBC); Rat in the Skull (Central), The Firm, Heading Home, Fallen Angels. *Films:* Sid and Nancy, Prick Up Your Ears, Track 29, Criminal Law, We Think The World of You, Chattahoochee, State of Grace, Exile, Before and After Death, Rosencrantz and Guildenstern are Dead, JFK, Dracula, True Romance, Romeo is Bleeding, Immortal Beloved, Murder in the First, Dead Presidents, The Scarlet Letter, Basquiat, Nil by Mouth 1997, The Fifth Element 1997, Air Force One 1997.

O'LEARY, Hazel, B.A.; American politician and lawyer; b. 17 May 1937, Newport News, Va.; d. of Russell Reid and Hazel Palleman; m. John F. O'Leary 1980; one s.; fmr. prosecutor, then an Asst. Attorney-Gen., N.J.; fmr. Vice-Pres. and Gen. Counsel, O'Leary Assocs. (consultants on energy econs. and planning); fmr. mem. staff Dept. of Energy and Fed. Energy Admin., joined Northern States Power Co., Minn. 1989, subsequently Exec. Vice-Pres.; Sec. of Energy 1993–97; Democrat. *Address:* c/o Department of Energy, James Forrestal Building, 1000 Independence Avenue, S.W., Washington, DC 20585, U.S.A.

O'LEARY, Michael; Irish politician and barrister; b. 8 May 1936, Cork; s. of John O'Leary and Margaret McCarthy; ed. Univ. Coll., Cork, Kings Inns Dublin; Deputy Pres. Nat. Students' Union 1960–61; Educ. Officer, Irish TUC 1962–65; T.D. for Dublin North Cen. 1965–82, for Dublin S.W. 1982–87; spokesman on Industry and Commerce, Labour, Foreign Affairs and Educ. 1965–73; Minister for Labour 1973–77; Deputy Prime Minister and Minister of Energy 1981–82; fmr. Leader, Labour Party (resgnd.); Pres. 2nd European Regional Conf., ILO 1974, Annual Conf. 1976, EEC Council of Ministers for Social Affairs Jan.–June 1975; mem. European Parl. 1979–81; resgnd. from Labour Party 1982 and joined Fine Gael Party; mem. Hon. Soc. of the Middle Temple.

O'LEARY, Terence Daniel, C.M.G., M.A.; British diplomatist (retd.); b. 18 Aug. 1928, London; s. of the late Daniel O'Leary and Mary O'Leary; m. Janet Douglas Berney 1960 (died 1997); twin s. one d.; ed. Dulwich Coll., St. John's Coll., Cambridge; commissioned officer Queen's Royal Regt. 1946–48; worked in industry 1951–53; Asst. Prin. Commonwealth Relations Office (later FCO) 1953, subsequently served New Zealand, India, Tanganyika, Australia, South Africa, and in Cabinet Office and as Sr. Directing Staff, Nat. Defence Coll. 1978–81; High Commr. in Sierra Leone 1981–84, in New Zealand, and concurrently W. Samoa, and Gov. of Pitcairn 1984–87; Sr. British Officer EC Monitoring Mission, Yugoslavia 1991–92; Chair. Petworth Preservation 1989–; Councillor, Petworth 1993–97. *Leisure interests:* gardening, croquet, walking. *Address:* Glebe Cottage, Bartons Lane, Petworth, West Sussex, GU28 0DA, England. *Telephone:* (01798) 344137.

OLECHOWSKI, Andrzej, M.A., PH.D.; Polish politician and economist; b. 9 Sept. 1947, Cracow; m. Irena Olechowska 1971; two s.; ed. Cen. School of Planning and Statistics, Warsaw; Assoc. Econ. Affairs Officer, UNCTAD Multilateral Trade Negotiations Project, Geneva 1974–78; Head, Dept. of Analysis and Projections, Foreign Trade Research Inst. Warsaw 1978–82; Econ. Affairs Officer, UNCTAD, Geneva 1982–84; Economist, IBRD, Washington, D.C. 1985–87; Adviser to Gov. Nat. Bank of Poland 1987; Dir. World Bank Cooperation Bureau, Nat. Bank of Poland 1988; Dept. Dir. Ministry of Foreign Econ. Relations 1988–89; Deputy Gov. Nat. Bank of Poland 1989–91; Sec. of State, Ministry of Foreign Econ. Relations 1991–92; Minister of Finance Feb.–May 1992; Sr. Adviser, EBRD 1992–93; Econ. Adviser to Pres. of Repub. 1992–93; Minister of Foreign Affairs 1993; Chair. Bd. Dirs. Bank Handlowy w Warszawie S.A.; Commr. U.S.-Poland Action Comm.; Pres. Polish League for European Econ. Cooperation. *Address:* Bank Handlowy w Warszawie SA, ul. Traugutta 7/9, 00-067 Warsaw, Poland.

OLECHOWSKI, Tadeusz, M.A.; Polish diplomatist and politician; b. 10 Jan. 1926, Vilnius; m.; one c.; ed. Faculty of Law, Jagiellonian Univ., Cracow and Acad. of Trade, Cracow; Chief of Polish Trade Mission, Rangoon 1955; Commercial attaché, Polish Embassy, Burma 1956; Deputy Dir. Metalexport 1957–58; with Ministry of Foreign Trade 1958–61; Commercial Attaché, Rome 1961–64; Vice-Minister of Foreign Trade 1965–69; Amb. to France 1969–72, 1976–80; Minister of Foreign Trade 1972–74; Amb. to Egypt, Yemen and Sudan 1974–76; Under-Sec. of State, Ministry of Foreign Affairs 1980–83; Amb. to Federal Repub. of Germany 1983–86; Under-Sec. of State, Ministry of Foreign Affairs 1986–88; Minister of Foreign Affairs 1988–89; Adviser for Foreign Affairs to Chair. of Council of Ministers 1989–90; Amb. to Belgium (also accred. to Luxembourg and NATO) 1990–92; fmr. mem. Polish United Workers' Party (PZPR); Commdr.'s and Knight's Cross of Polonia Restituta Order, Order of Banner of Labour, 2nd Class; other decorations. *Leisure interest:* gardening.

OLEKSY, Józef, D.ECON.; Polish politician and economist; b. 22 June 1946, Nowy Sącz; s. of Józef Oleksy and Michalina Oleksy; m. Maria Oleksy 1983; one s. one d.; ed. Main School of Commerce, Warsaw, Int. Faculty of Comparative Law, Strasbourg; scientific worker Main School of Commerce, Warsaw 1969–98; worker Cen. Cttee. Polish United Workers' Party (PZPR) 1978–81; Minister, mem. of Council of Ministers 1989; mem. Polish Group of IPU; deputy to Sejm (Parl.) 1989–; Speaker of Sejm 1993–95; Prime Minister 1995–96; Chair. Social Democracy of Polish Repub. 1996–97; Pres. Polish Council of Young Scientists 1969–76; participant Historical Compromise in Poland Round Table 1989. *Publications:* numerous articles on econ. and int. affairs. *Leisure interests:* walking, history, futurology, parapsychology. *Address:* ul. Wiktorii Wiedeńskiej 5 m. 4, 02-954 Warsaw, Poland. *Telephone:* 6423636. *Fax:* 6211153.

OLESEN, Aase, Danish politician; b. 24 Sept. 1934, Horsens; teacher 1956–58; housewife 1958–70; Co-owner Tormod Olesen's architectural practice 1970–; mem. Folketing (Parl.) 1974–77, 1979–; mem. Exec. Cttee and General Council, Radical Liberal Party 1986, Sec. to Parl. Group 1980–; Chair. Parl. Social Cttee. 1987–88; Minister of Social Affairs 1988–90. *Address:* c/o Folketing, Christianborg, 1218 Copenhagen K, Denmark.

OLESEN, Poul; Danish physicist; b. 28 April 1939, Aalborg; s. of Viktor Olesen and Herdis Olesen; m. Birgitte Sode-Mogensen 1984; ed. Univ. of Copenhagen; Research Assoc. Univ. of Rochester, New York 1967–69; Research Assoc. CERN, Geneva 1969–71, Visiting Fellow 1985; Assoc. Prof. of Theoretical Physics, The Niels Bohr Inst. Copenhagen 1971–97, Prof. 1997–, Chair. Research Cttee. 1993–95, mem. Governing Body 1996–; mem. Faculty of Science, Univ. of Copenhagen 1989–, Exec. Cttee. 1990–93, Research Cttee. 1998–; mem. Royal Danish Acad.; Hermer Prize. *Publications:* articles in int. journals on particle physics. *Address:* The Niels Bohr Institute, Blegdamsvej 17, 2100 Copenhagen Ø (Office); Malmmosevej 1, 2840 Holte, Denmark (Home). *Telephone:* 31 42 16 16 (Office).

ØLGAARD, Anders, DR.POLIT.; Danish professor of economics; b. 5 Sept. 1926, Aabenraa; s. of Axel Ølgaard and Anna Lebeck; m. Alice Christiansen 1951; three c.; ed. Univ. of Copenhagen; Civil servant, Econ. Secr. 1953–60; Prof. of Econs., Univ. of Copenhagen 1962–96; Adviser in Malaysia, Harvard Univ. Devt. Advisory Service 1968–69; mem., Econ. Council 1966–68; Chair. 1970–76; Pres. Danish Econ. Assen. 1983–88. *Publications:* Growth, Productivity and Relative Prices 1966, The Danish Economy, EEC Economic and Financial Series 1980. *Address:* Institute of Economics, University of Copenhagen, 6 Studiestraede, 1455 Copenhagen (Office); 12 Lerbaekvei, 2830 Virum, Denmark (Home). *Telephone:* 35-323018 (Office); 45-851239.

OLHAYE, Roble, M.B.I.M.; Djibouti diplomatist; b. 24 April 1944; m.; five c.; ed. Commercial School of Addis Ababa; worked in area of financial and admin. man. in various orgs. in Ethiopia engaged in communication, printing, export trade, insurance and mfg. 1964–73; regional accountant, TAW Int. Leasing Corpn. Nairobi 1973, Financial Dir. 1975; independent consultant 1980–82; Hon. Consul of Djibouti to Kenya 1980–85; founded (as jt. venture with Middle East Bank of Dubai) Banque de Djibouti et du Moyen Orient, S.A. 1982; Perm. Rep. to UNEP and UN Centre for Human Settlements (Habitat), Nairobi 1986–88; Perm. Rep. to UN 1988–. *Address:* Permanent Mission of Djibouti to the United Nations, 866 United Nations Plaza, Suite 4011, New York, NY 10017, U.S.A.

OLINS, Wally (Wallace), M.A., F.C.S.D.; British business executive; b. 19 Dec. 1930; s. of Alfred Olins and Rachel Olins (née Muscovitch); m. 1st Renate Steinart 1957 (divorced 1989), two s. one d.; m. 2nd Dornie Watts 1990, one d.; ed. Highgate School, St. Peter's Coll., Oxford; nat. service with army in Germany 1950–51; with S.H. Benson Ltd., London 1954–57; with Benson, India 1957–62; with Caps Design Group, London 1962–65; joined Wolff Olins 1965, now Chair.; Vice-Pres. SIAD 1982–85; visiting lecturer Design Man. London Business School 1984–89; Visiting Prof. Man. School Imperial Coll., London 1987–89, Lancaster Univ. 1992–, Copenhagen Business School 1993–, Duxx, Centro de Excelencia Empresarial, Mexico 1992; Chair. Design Dimension Educ. Trust 1987–93; Trustee Design Museum 1988–93; mem. Council R.S.A. 1989–95; mem. Devt. Trust Royal Philharmonic Orchestra 1994–; Dir. Glasgow 1999 1996–; Dir. Health Educ. Authority 1996–; mem. Master's Council St. Peter's Coll., Oxford 1995–. *Leisure interests:* looking at buildings, shopping for books, theatre, old cars. *Publications:* The Corporate Personality 1978, The Wolff Olins Guide to Corporate Identity 1983, The Wolff Olins Guide to Design Management 1985, Corporate Identity 1989, International Identity 1995, New Guide to Identity 1996, numerous articles in design and man. publs. *Address:* Wolff Olins, 10 Regents Wharf, All Saints Street, London, N1 9RL, England. *Telephone:* 0171-713 7733.

OLIPHANT, Sir Mark Laurence Elwin, A.C., K.B.E., F.R.S., F.A.A., F.T.S., M.A., PH.D.; British physicist and administrator; b. 8 Oct. 1901, Adelaide, Australia; s. of Harold George Oliphant and Beatrice Fanny Tucker; m. Rosa Louise Wildbraham 1925 (died 1987); one s. one d.; ed. Adelaide Univ., and Trinity Coll., Cambridge; Messel Research Fellow, Royal Soc. 1931; Lecturer and Fellow, St. John's Coll. 1934; Asst. Dir. Research, Cavendish Lab., Cambridge 1935; Prof. and Dir. of Dept. of Physics Birmingham Univ. 1937–50, Vice-Principal Sept. 1948–49; Dir. of post-graduate Research School of Physical Sciences, Australian Nat. Univ. 1950–63, Prof. of Physics of Ionised Gases, Inst. of Advanced Studies (Australian Nat. Univ.) 1964–67, Prof. Emer.; Prof. of Particle Physics 1950–64; Pres. Australian Acad. of Sciences 1954–57; Gov. of S. Australia 1971–76; Hon. Fellow, St. John's Coll., Cambridge 1952, Australian Nat. Univ. 1968–71; Hon. LL.D. (St. Andrews), Hon. D.Sc. (Toronto, Flinders, Belfast, Melbourne, Birmingham, New South Wales, Australian Nat. Univ. and Adelaide); K.St.J. *Publications:* Rutherford: Recollections of the Cambridge Days 1972, and various technical and scientific papers. *Leisure interests:* music, gardening, carpentry. *Address:* 28 Carstensz Street, Griffith, A.C.T. 2603, Australia. *Telephone:* (062) 2950417.

OLIPHANT, Patrick, D.HUM.LITT.; American political cartoonist, artist and sculptor; b. 24 July 1935, Adelaide, Australia; s. of Donald K. Oliphant and Grace L. Price; m. 1st Hendrika deVries 1958 (divorced 1978); one s. two d.; m. 2nd Mary A. Kuhn 1983 (divorced 1994); copyboy, press artist, Adelaide Advertiser 1953–55, cartoonist 1955–64; cartoonist, Denver Post 1964–75, Washington Star 1975–81; independent cartoonist syndicated through Universal Press Syndicate 1980–; Hon. L.H.D. (Dartmouth Coll.) 1981; awards include Pulitzer Prize 1967, Nat. Cartoonist of Year Award 1968, 1972, Washington Journalism Review 'Best in the Business' Award 1985. *Publications:* The Oliphant Book 1969, Four More Years 1973, An Informal Gathering 1978, Oliphant, A Cartoon Collection 1980, The Jellybean Society 1981, Ban This Book 1982, But Seriously Folks 1983, The Year of Living Perilously 1984, Make My Day! 1985, Between Rock and a Hard Place 1986, Up to Here in Alligators 1987, Nothing Basically Wrong 1988, What Those People Need is a Puppy 1989, Fashions for the New World Order 1991, Just Say No 1992, Waiting for the Other Shoe to Drop 1994, Off to the Revolution 1995, Maintain the Status Quo 1996. *Leisure interests:* skeet and trap shooting, tennis, swimming, bicycling, reading. *Address:* Universal Press Syndicate, 4520 Main Street, Suite 700, Kansas City, MO 64112; c/o Susan Conway Gallery, 1214 Thirtieth Street Northwest, Washington DC 20007, U.S.A.

OLITSKI, Jules, M.A.; American painter and sculptor; b. 27 March 1922, Snovsk, Russia; s. of late Jevel Demikovsky and of Anna Zarnitsky; m. 1st Gladys Katz 1944 (divorced 1951), one d.; m. 2nd Andrea Hill Pearce 1956 (divorced 1974), one d.; m. 3rd Kristina Gorby 1980; ed. Beaux Arts Inst., N.Y., New York Univ.; Assoc. Prof. of Art, State Univ. Coll., New Paltz 1954–55; Curator New York Univ. Art Educ. Gallery 1955–56; Art Instructor, Co-ordinator Fine Arts Dept., C. W. Post Coll., Long Island Univ. 1956–63; Art Teacher Bennington Coll., Vt. 1963–67; one-man exhbns. of paintings, drawings and sculpture in U.S.A. at Corcoran Gallery, Washington, D.C. 1967, 1974, 1975, Metropolitan Museum of Art, New York 1969, retrospective exhbn. at Museum of Fine Arts, Boston 1973, Galleria dell'Ariete, Milan 1974, Knoedler Contemporary Arts, New York 1974–77, Waddington Gallery, London 1975, Boston Museum of Fine Art 1977, Galeria Wentzel, Fed. Repub. of Germany 1975, 1977, Hirshhorn Museum, Washington 1977, Edmonton Art Gallery, Canada 1978; one-person exhbns. at Galerie Huit, Paris 1950, Kasmin Gallery, London 1964–75, 1989, David Mirvish Gallery, Toronto 1964–78, André Emmerich Gallery, New York 1966–89, 1995, Zürich 1973–74, Gallery One, Toronto 1981–89, Yares Gallery, Ariz. 1983–89, Gallery Camino Real, Fla. 1988–97, Salander-O'Reilly Galleries, New York 1989–94, Long Fine Art, New York 1994–97 and many others in U.S.A. and abroad; numerous group exhbns. in U.S.A., Canada, France, Fed. Repub. of Germany, Switzerland, Spain; represented in many perm. collections in U.S.A.; Fellow American Acad. of Arts and Sciences 1993; Assoc. Nat. Academician, Nat. Acad. of Design 1993; chosen for Carnegie Int. 1961, 1967, for Venice Biennale 1966; Second Prize Carnegie Int. 1961, First Prize Corcoran Biennal 1967, Award for Distinction in the Arts Univ. Union (S. Carolina) 1975. *Publications:* The Courage of Conviction (essay) 1985, How I Got My First New York Show (essay) 1989, A Letter to Kristina: The Courage to Grow Old (essay) 1989. *Address:* c/o Salanders O'Reilly Galleries Inc., 20 E. 79th Street, New York, NY 10021, U.S.A.

OLIVA, L. Jay, PH.D.; American university president; b. 23 Sept. 1933, Walden, N.Y.; s. of Lawrence Oliva and Catherine Mooney; m. Mary E. Nolan 1961; two s.; ed. Manhattan Coll. and Univs. of Freiburg and Paris; Univ. Fellow, Syracuse Univ. 1955–57, Research Assoc. 1957–58, Univ. Research Inst. 1959–60; Instr., Assoc. Prof. of History, New York Univ. 1960–69, Prof. of History 1969–, Deputy Vice-Chancellor 1970–75, Vice-Pres. for Academic Planning and Service 1975–77, Vice-Pres. for Academic Affairs 1977–80, Provost and Exec. Vice-Pres. for Academic Affairs 1980–83, Chancellor and Exec. Vice-Pres. for Academic Affairs 1983–91, Pres. 1991–; mem. Council on Foreign Relations 1992–; other academic and professional appts.; Hon. D. Hum. Lit. (Manhattan Coll.) 1987, (Hebrew Union Coll.) 1992; Hon. LL.D. (St. Thomas Aquinas Coll.); Hon. D. Lit. (Univ. Coll. Dublin) 1993; Medal of the Sorbonne 1992. *Publications include:* Misalliance: A Study of French Policy in Russia During the Seven Years War 1964, Russia and the West from Peter to Kruschev (ed.) 1965, Russia in the Era of Peter the Great 1969, Peter the Great (ed.) 1970, Catherine the Great (ed.) 1971. *Leisure interests:* athletics, music, reading. *Address:* New York University, 70 Washington Square South, New York, NY 10012, U.S.A. *Telephone:* (212) 998-2345. *Fax:* (212) 995-3679.

OLIVE, David Ian, M.A., PH.D., F.R.S.; British professor of theoretical physics; b. 16 April 1937, Staines; m. Jenifer Tutton 1963; two d.; ed. Royal High School, Edinburgh and Univs. of Edinburgh and Cambridge; Fellow, Churchill Coll., Cambridge 1963–70; Asst. Lecturer, Lecturer, Univ. of Cambridge 1965–71; staff mem. CERN Theory Div. 1971–77; Lecturer, Reader, Blackett Lab. Imperial Coll., London 1977–84, Prof. of Theoretical Physics 1984–92; Research Prof. in Physics, Univ. of Wales, Swansea 1992–. *Publications:* The Analytic S-Matrix (with others) 1965; many scientific papers and articles on the theory of elementary particles and their symmetries. *Leisure interests:* golf, listening to music. *Address:* Department of Physics, University of Wales Swansea, Singleton Park, Swansea, SA2 8PP (Office); 4 Havergal Close, Caswell, Swansea, SA3 4RL, Wales (Home). *Telephone:* (01792) 295842 (Office).

OLIVEIRA, Gen. Araken de; Brazilian army officer; ed. Escola Militar, Realengo, Command and Gen. Staff School and Catholic Univ.; Instructor, Escola Militar Realengo and Command and Gen. Staff School; Gunnery Officer, then Operations Officer, First Howitzer Battalion, Brazilian Expeditionary Force; with Command and Gen. Staff, Officer in War Minister's Office; promoted to rank of Gen.; Chief, President's Office, Nat. Oil Council, later Pres.; Pres. Petrobrás 1974–78; Commdr., Order of Merit and several other mil. honours. *Address:* c/o Petrobrás, Avenida República do Chile 65, C.P. 809, Rio de Janeiro, RJ, Brazil.

OLIVEIRA, Manoel de; Portuguese film director; b. 1908, Oporto. *Films include:* Douro, Faina Fluvial 1931, Aniki-Bóbó 1942, O Pinto e a Cidade 1956, O Pão 1959, O Acto da Primavera 1963, A Caça 1964, O Passado e Presente 1972, Benilde ou A Virgem Mãe 1975, Amor de Perdição 1979, Francisca 1981.

OLIVER, Roland, PH.D., F.B.A.; British Africanist; b. 30 March 1923, Srinagar, Kashmir; s. of Douglas Gifford Oliver and Lorimer Janet Donaldson; m. 1st Caroline Linehan 1947 (died 1983), one d.; m. 2nd Suzanne Miers 1990; ed. Cambridge Univ.; Lecturer, SOAS., Univ. of London 1948–49, 1950–57, Reader 1958–63, Prof. of African History 1963–86, Hon. Fellow 1992; organized first confs. on history and archaeology of Africa, London Univ. 1953, 1957, 1961; founded and edited Journal of African History 1960–73; Pres. British Inst. in E. Africa 1981–93; Chair. Minority Rights Group, Distinguished Africanist Award, American African Studies Assen. 1989. *Publications:* The Missionary Factor in East Africa 1952, Sir Harry Johnston and the Scramble for East Africa 1957, The Dawn of African History 1961, Short History of Africa (with J. D. Fage) 1962, History of East Africa (with G. Mathew) 1963, Africa since 1800 (with A. Atmore) 1967, Africa in the Iron Age (with B. M. Fagan) 1975, The African Middle Ages 1400–1800 (with A. Atmore) 1980, The African Experience 1991, The Realms of Gold 1997; Gen. Ed. Cambridge History of Africa 8 vols. 1975–86. *Address:* Frilsham Woodhouse, near Thatcham, Berkshire, RG18 9XB, England. *Telephone:* (01635) 201407. *Fax:* (01635) 202716.

OLIVER of AYLMERTON, Baron (Life Peer), cr. 1986, of Aylmerton in the County of Norfolk; **Peter Raymond Oliver,** Kt., P.C.; British lawyer; b. 7 March 1921; s. of David Thomas Oliver and Alice Maud Oliver; m. 1st Mary Chichester Rideal 1945 (died 1985), one s. one d.; m. 2nd Wendy Anne Oliver 1987; ed. The Leys, Cambridge, Trinity Hall, Cambridge; Mil. Service 1941–45; called to Bar, Lincoln's Inn 1948, Bencher 1973; Q.C. 1965; Judge of the High Court of Justice, Chancery Div. 1974–80; mem. Restrictive Practices Court 1976–80; Chair. Review Body on Chancery Div. of High Court 1979–81; Lord Justice of Appeal 1980–85; Lord of Appeal in Ordinary 1986–92; Hon. Fellow, Trinity Hall, Cambridge 1980. *Leisure interests:* gardening, music. *Address:* House of Lords, London, SW1A 0PW (Office); 24 Westbourne Park Road, London, W.2, England (Home). *Telephone:* 0171-229 1058 (Home).

OLLILA, Esko Juhani, LL.M.; Finnish bank executive; b. 14 July 1940, Rovaniemi; s. of Heikki Armas Ollila and Lempi Maria (née Häggman) Ollila; m. Riitta Leena, née Huhtala 1963; two s.; Man. Dir. Rovaniemi Savings Bank 1971–75; Man. Dir. and Chair. Bd. Regional Devt. Fund of Finland 1975–79; mem. Bd. Skopbank 1979–83; Minister of Trade and Industry 1982–83; Minister of Finance 1986–87; mem. Bd. Bank of Finland 1983–; Chair. Finnish Nat. Fund for Research and Devt. (SITRA) 1991–95, mem. 1995–; mem. Supervisory Bd. Finnish Guarantee Bd. 1995–; Chair. Advisory Bd. Baltic Investment Fund 1995–. *Address:* c/o Bank of Finland, P.O. Box 160, 00101 Helsinki, Finland. *Telephone:* (9) 1831. *Fax:* (9) 661676.

OLLILA, Jorma, M.SC.; Finnish business executive; b. 15 Aug. 1950, Seinäjoki; m. Liisa Annikki Metsola; two s. one d.; ed. Univ. of Helsinki, London School of Econs. and Helsinki Univ. of Tech.; mem. Man. Bd. Citibank Oy 1983–85; Vice-Pres. Int. Operations, Nokia 1985–86, Deputy mem. Bd. of Dirs. 1989–90, Sr. Vice-Pres. Finance 1986–89, mem. Group Exec. Bd. 1986–, Pres. Nokia Mobile Phones 1990–92, Pres. Nokia 1992–, C.E.O. 1992–, Chair. Group Exec. Bd. 1992–95; Chair. Bd. MTV Oy; mem. Bd. Oy Dipoli Ab, ICI PLC; mem. Supervisory Bd. NKF Holding N.V., Tietotehdas Oy, Industrial Mutual Insurance Co., Pohjola Insurance Co. Ltd., Sampo Insurance Co. Ltd., Pension-Varma Mutual Insurance Co., Oy Rastor AB; mem. Bd. and Exec. Cttee. Confed. of Finnish Industries and Employers; Chair. Council, Finnish Foreign Trade Assen.; Vice-Chair. Bd., Finnish Section, Int. Chamber of Commerce; Knight, Order of White Rose of Finland. *Address:* Office of the President, Nokia Group, Keilalahdentie 4, P.O. Box 226, 00045 Helsinki, Finland.

OLMERT, Ehud; Israeli politician and lawyer; b. 1945, Binyamina; m.; four c.; ed. Hebrew Univ.; columnist for Yediot Achronot (daily evening paper); mem. Likud Party; mem. Knesset 1973–; Minister of Minorities 1988–90, of Health 1990–92; Mayor of Jerusalem 1993–. *Address:* c/o Knesset, Jerusalem (Office); 29 November Street, Jerusalem, Israel (Home).

OLMI, Ermanno; Italian film director; b. 24 July 1931, Bergamo; fmr. clerk, Edison-Volta electric plant; later dir. and produced sponsored documentary films; made first feature film 1959, founded production co. 22 December S.P.A. 1961 and helped found Hypothesis Cinema. *Films include:* Il Tempo si è Fermato 1959, Il Posto 1961, I Fidanzati 1963, E Venne un Uomo 1965, Un Certo Giorno 1969, I Recuperanti 1970, Durante l'Estate 1971, La Circostanza 1974, L'Albero degli Zoccoli (Palme d'Or, Cannes) 1978, Legend of a Holy Drinker 1988, Il Segreto Del Bosco Vecchio.

OLOVSSON, Ivar (Olov Göte), DR.SC.; Swedish professor of inorganic chemistry; b. 15 Oct. 1928, Rödön; s. of Erik Olovsson and Anna Andersson; m. Kristina Jonsson 1950; three s. one d.; ed. Univ. of Uppsala; Teaching Asst. Univ. of Uppsala 1953–57, Asst. Prof. 1961–64, Assoc. Prof. 1965–69, Prof. of Inorganic Chem. 1969–93; Research Assoc. Univ. of Calif. Berkeley 1957–59, 1964–65; Guest Prof. Lab. de Cristallographie, Grenoble 1977–78, Univ. of Konstanz 1982–83; mem. Royal Soc. of Sciences 1970 (Pres. 1996–97), Royal Acad. of Sciences of Sweden 1974; Gold Medal, Royal Acad. of Sciences of Sweden 1961; Gold Medal, Swedish Chem. Soc. 1965; Kt. of Northern Star 1975; Chevalier des Palmes Académiques 1981. *Publications:* about 90 scientific papers, mainly in field of structural chem. *Leisure interests:* outdoor life, mountaineering, skiing, music. *Address:* Ångström Laboratory of Inorganic Chemistry, P.O. Box 538, 751 21 Uppsala (Office); Murklevägen 27, 756 46 Uppsala, Sweden (Home). *Telephone:* 018-4713721 (Office); 018-302276 (Home). *Fax:* 018-513548.

OLSEN, Olaf, PH.D.; Danish archaeologist, historian and fmr. museum director; b. 7 June 1928, Copenhagen; s. of the late Prof. Albert Olsen and of Agnete Bing; m. 1st Jean Catherine Dennistoun Sword, one s; m. 2nd Rikke Agnete Clausen 1971; ed. Copenhagen Univ.; Asst., Medieval Dept., Nat. Museum 1950–58, Asst. Keeper 1958–71, State Antiquary and Dir. Nat. Museum 1981–95; Prof. of Medieval Archaeology, Aarhus Univ. 1971–81; Dir. Hielmstierne-Rosencrone Foundation 1979–; Vice-Pres. Det kgl. nordiske Oldskriftselskab 1981–95, Royal Danish Acad. of Sciences and Letters 1983–89; founding mem. Academia Europaea 1988; Dir. numerous archaeological excavations, mainly of Viking ships and fortresses and medieval churches and monasteries; Hon. Fellow, Soc. of Antiquaries; Dr. h.c. (St. Petersburg Univ.) 1994; GEC Gad Foundation Prize 1966, 1992, Hartmann Prize 1995. *Publications:* numerous books and papers on history and medieval archaeology. *Address:* Strevelshovedvej 2, Alrø, 8300 Odder, Denmark. *Telephone:* 86552128. *Fax:* 86552128.

OLSON, Mancur, PH.D.; American professor of economics; b. 22 Jan. 1932, Grand Forks, N.D.; s. of Mancur L. Olson, Sr. and Clara Olson (née Fuglesten); m. Alison Gilbert 1959; two s. one d.; ed. North Dakota State Univ., Oxford and Harvard Univs.; First Lieut. U.S. Air Force 1960–61; lecturer in Econs., Princeton Univ. 1960–61, Asst. Prof. of Econs. 1963–67; Deputy Asst. Sec. (Social Indicators), U.S. Dept. of Health, Educ. and Welfare 1967–69; Prof. of Econs. Univ. of Md. 1970–79, Distinguished Univ. Prof. of Econs. 1979–; founder and Prin. Investigator, Center for Institutional Reform and the Informal Sector (I.R.I.S.) 1990–; Hon. Fellow, Univ. Coll., Oxford. *Publications:* The Logic of Collective Action 1965 (Best Book Award), Towards a Social Report (jtly.) 1969, The No Growth Society 1975, A New Approach to the Economics of Health Care 1981, The Rise and Decline of Nations 1982, How Bright are Northern Lights 1992. *Leisure interests:* reading, running. *Address:* Department of Economics, University of Maryland, College Park, MD 20742 (Office); 4316 Claggett-Pineway, Hyattsville, MD 20782, U.S.A. (Home). *Telephone:* (301) 405-3497 (Office). *Fax:* (301) 314-6334 (Office).

OLSSON, Curt G., B.SC.ECON.; Swedish banker; b. 20 Aug. 1927, Mjällby; s. of N. E. Olsson and Anna (née Nilsson) Olsson; m. Asta Olsson 1954; two d.; Man. Dir. Swedish Bank Giro Centre 1959; Deputy Man. and Head of

Marketing, Skandinaviska Banken, Stockholm 1964, Man. and Head of Central Management Group 1966, Man. Dir. (Stockholm Group) 1970; Man. Dir. Skandinaviska Enskilda Banken, Stockholm Group 1972; Man. Dir. and Chief Exec. Head Office, Stockholm 1976–82, 1st Deputy Chair. of Bd. 1982–84, Chair. 1984–96; Dir. Fastighets AB Hufvudstaden; mem. Royal Swedish Acad. of Eng. Sciences; Consul Gen. h.c. for Finland; Hon. D.Econ.; Kt., Order of Vasa, H.M. King Carl XVI Gustaf's Gold Medal, Commdr. Royal Norwegian Order of Merit, Commdr. Order of the Lion of Finland. *Address:* Skandinaviska Enskilda Banken, 106 40 Stockholm, Sweden. *Telephone:* 22 19 00.

OLSSON, Karl Erik; Swedish politician; b. 1938, Häglinge, Kristianstad; m. Sonja Olsson; three c.; ed. Colleges of Agric.; farmer Nygård Farm 1963–; Chair. Nat. Centre Party Youth League 1971–74; mem. Centre Party Nat. Bd. 1981–92, Asst. Vice-Chair. 1986–87, Vice-Chair. 1987–92; M.P. 1976–79, 1985–; mem. Bd. Nuclear Power Inspectorate 1977–91, Foundation for the Promotion of Literature 1980–91, Swedish Univ. of Agric. Sciences 1986–91; Chair. Standing Cttee. on Agric. 1985–91; Minister of Agric. 1991–94. *Publications:* Bonde i lokalsamhället, Tankar. *Address:* c/o Ministry of Agriculture, Drottninggt. 21, 103 33 Stockholm, Sweden.

OLSZEWSKI, Jan Ferdynand; Polish politician and lawyer; b. 20 Aug. 1930, Warsaw; m.; ed. Warsaw Univ.; mem. underground Boy Scouts WWII; Research Asst. Legal Sciences Dept. Polish Acad. of Sciences 1951–56; journalist Po Prostu 1956–57; banned from working as a journalist 1957; mem. Crooked Circle Club 1956–62; Trial Lawyer 1962–68; suspended from the Bar by Justice Minister for defending students involved in anti-Communist demonstrations 1968; returned to work as Attorney 1970; Defence Counsel for anti-Communist Ruch Organization 1972; founder leader Polish Independence Alliance 1975–81; co-founder Workers' Defence Cttee. (KOR) 1976–77; drafted (jtly.) Statute of the Free Trade Union of Coast Workers 1980; Adviser Solidarity Nat. Comm. 1980–; Legal Adviser Secretariat of Polish Episcopate; Plenipotentiary to family of Father Jerzy Popiełuszko during trial of his killers; Rep. Solidarity-opposition in sub-commn. on legal and judicial reform 1989; mem. Pres. Lech Wałęsa's Advisory Cttee. Jan.–Nov. 1991; Deputy to Sejm (Parl.) 1991–93, 1997–; Prime Minister of Poland 1991–92; Co-founder and Pres. Movt. for the Repub. 1992–94; co-founder and Leader Movt. for the Reconstruction of Poland (ROP) 1995–; Leader 'Homeland' Patriotic Movt. 1997–; Founder-mem. Civic Inst. and Atlantic Club. *Address:* Sejm RP, ul. Wiejska 4/6/8, 00-902 Warsaw, Poland. *Telephone:* (22) 694-25-00.

O'MALLEY, Desmond Joseph, B.C.L.; Irish politician and solicitor; b. 2 Feb. 1939, Limerick; s. of Desmond J. O'Malley and Una O'Malley; m. Patricia McAleer 1965; two s. four d.; ed. Crescent Coll., Limerick, Nat. Univ. of Ireland; practised as solicitor 1962; mem. Dáil (House of Reps.) for Limerick East 1968–; mem. Limerick Corpn. 1974–77; Parl. Sec. to Taoiseach (Prime Minister) and to Minister for Defence 1969–70; Minister for Justice 1970–73; Opposition Spokesman on Health 1973–75, on Industry and Commerce 1975–77; Minister for Industry and Commerce 1977–81, 1989–92, for Energy 1977–79; Opposition Spokesman on Industry and Commerce 1981–82; Minister for Trade, Commerce and Tourism 1982; Opposition Spokesman on Energy 1983–84; fmrly. Fianna Fáil (expelled 1984); co-f. and Leader of Progressive Democrats Party 1985–93, now Spokesman on Foreign Affairs and Northern Ireland and Party Whip; Chair. Foreign Affairs Cttee. *Leisure interest:* golf. *Address:* Leinster House, Kildare Street, Dublin 2, Ireland. *Telephone:* (01) 6183750.

OMAN, Julia Trevelyan, C.B.E., R.D.I., F.C.S.D., DES.R.C.A.; British designer; b. 11 July 1930, London; d. of Charles Chichele Oman and Joan Trevelyan; m. Dr. (now Sir) Roy Strong (q.v.) 1971; ed. Royal Coll. of Art; Designer BBC Television 1955–67 (including TV film Alice in Wonderland 1966); designer for theatre: Brief Lives (London and New York) 1967, 1974, Country Dance 1967, Forty Years On 1968, The Merchant of Venice 1970, Othello 1971, Getting On 1971, The Importance of Being Earnest (Burgtheater, Wien) 1976; ballet: Enigma Variations (Royal Ballet, London) 1968; opera: Eugene Onegin (Covent Garden) 1971, Un Ballo in Maschera (Hamburg) 1973, La Bohème (Covent Garden) 1974, A Month in the Country (Royal Ballet, London) 1976, Die Fledermaus (Covent Garden) 1977, Le Papillon (Ashton, Pas-de-Deux) 1977; films: The Charge of the Light Brigade (art dir.) 1967, Laughter in the Dark (art dir.) 1968, Julius Caesar (production designer) 1969, Straw Dogs (design consultant) 1971; exhbns.: Samuel Pepys (Nat. Portrait Gallery) 1970, Hay Fever (Danish TV) 1979; Designer Mme Tussaud's Hall of Historical Tableaux 1979, Hay Fever (Lyric, Hammersmith) 1980, The Wild Duck (Lyric, Hammersmith) 1980, Sospiri (Ashton, Pas-de-Deux) 1980, The Bear's Quest for the Ragged Staff—A Spectacle, Warwick Castle 1981, Swan Lake, Boston Ballet 1981, The Shoemaker's Holiday, Nat. Theatre 1981, Die Csárdasfürstin, Kassel, Fed. Repub. of Germany 1982, Separate Tables 1982, Otello, Stockholm 1983, Arabella, Glyndbourne Opera 1984, Nutcracker, Royal Ballet Covent Garden 1984, The Consul, Edin. and U.S.A. 1985, Mr. & Mrs. Nobody 1986, A Man for All Seasons (Chichester Festival and Savoy, London) 1987, The Best of Friends 1988, Enigma Variations (Birmingham Royal Ballet) 1994, Beatrix (Chichester) 1996; Dept. Educ. and Science Visiting Cttee., Royal Coll. of Art 1980; Dir. Oman Productions Ltd.; Hon. D. Litt. (Bristol) 1987; Silver Medal, Royal Coll. of Art; Royal Scholar, Royal Coll. of Art; elected, Royal Designer for Industry (R.D.I.), Designer, Royal Coll. of Art; Designer of the Year Award 1967, ACE Award for Best Art Dir., NCTA, U.S.A. 1983. *Publications:* Street Children (with B. S. Johnson) 1964, Elizabeth R. (with Roy Strong) 1971, Mary Queen of Scots (with Roy Strong) 1972, The English Year (with Roy Strong) 1982, A Celebration of Gardens (with Roy Strong) 1991, A Country Life (with Roy Strong) 1994, On Happiness (with Roy Strong) 1997. *Address:* c/o Oman Productions, The Laskett, Much Birch, Hereford, HR2 8HZ, England.

OMAND, David Bruce; British civil servant; b. 15 April 1947; s. of the late J. Bruce Omand and Esther Omand; m. Elizabeth Wales 1971; one s. one d.; ed. Glasgow Acad., Corpus Christi Coll., Cambridge; Asst. Prin. Ministry of Defence 1970, Pvt. Sec. to Chief Exec. (Procurement Exec.) 1973, Asst. Pvt. Sec. to Sec. of State 1973–75, 1979–80, Prin. 1975, Asst. Sec. 1981, Pvt. Sec. to Sec. of State 1981–82; Asst. Under Sec. of State (Man. Strategy) 1988–91, Deputy Under Sec. of State (Policy) Ministry of Defence 1992–96, Dir. Govt. Communications HQ 1996–; Defence Counsellor FCO U.K. Del. to NATO, Brussels 1985–88. *Leisure interests:* opera, hill-walking. *Address:* Government Communications Headquarters, Priors Road, Cheltenham, Glos., GL52 5AJ, England.

OMAR, Chamassi Said; Comoran politician; fmr. naval officer; Prime Minister of Comoros 1998–. *Address:* Office of the Prime Minister, B.P. 421, Moroni, Comoros. *Telephone:* (73) 2413.

OMAR, Dato Abu Hassan Bin Haj; Malaysian politician; b. 15 Sept. 1940, Bukit Belimbing, Kuala Selangor; m. Datin Wan Noor bint Haj Daud; five c.; ed. Univ. of Hull; fmr. Deputy State Sec. State of Selangor and Deputy Sec.-Gen. Ministry of Land and Fed. Devt.; mem. Parl. 1978–; Parl. Sec. Ministry of Commerce and Industry 1978–80; Deputy Minister of Defence 1980–81, of Transport 1981–84; Minister of Welfare Services 1984–86, of Fed. Territory 1986–87, of Foreign Affairs 1987–91, of Domestic Trade and Consumer Affairs 1991; mem. UMNO Supreme Council 1978–; recipient of several awards. *Leisure interests:* gardening, photography. *Address:* c/o Ministry of Domestic Trade and Consumer Affairs, Tingat 19, 22--24 and 40, Menara Maybank, 100 Jalan Tun Perak, 50050 Kuala Lumpur, Malaysia.

OMAR, Dullah, B.A., LL.B.; South African politician and legal representative; b. 26 May 1934, Cape Town; m. Farida Ally; three c.; ed. Trafalgar High School, Cape Town, Univ. of Cape Town; defence lawyer for political prisoners serving sentences on Robben Island; legal rep. to trade unions, civic and religious orgs.; Nat. Vice-Pres. Nat. Asscn. of Democratic Lawyers, Pres. Cape Town br.; Attorney and Advocate Supreme Court 1982; Chair. United Democratic Front W. Cape Region 1987–88, Vice-Pres. 1988–91; Dir. Community Law Centre, Univ. of W. Cape –1994; Minister of Justice (also with responsibility for the intelligence services 1995–) Govt. of Nat. Unity 1994–; Commr. Human Rights Comm. of S.A.; mem. ANC Nat. Exec. Comm., ANC Constitutional Comm.; Trustee S.A. Legal Defence Fund. *Address:* Presidia Building, 8th Floor, Corner Pretorius and Paul Kruger Streets, Pretoria 0002; Private Bag X276, Pretoria 0001, South Africa. *Telephone:* (12) 3238581. *Fax:* (12) 3111708.

OMAR, Ibrahim Amin, B.A.; Egyptian civil servant; b. 1 Dec. 1936, Kafr El Moselha; s. of Amin Ebraim Omar; m. Afaf Ghazy 1971; three d.; ed. Cairo Univ.; mem. Nat. Guards 1953; Bd. mem. Menufia Governorate 1967; Head, Safag Port 1982, Areesh City 1990; Sec.-Gen. Al Aswan Governorate 1995–; Sec., Head Cttee. of Interior Front 1969; mem. Nat. Democratic Party, 1981; State Prize, Science Day 1957. *Publication:* Planning and Developing Education Policy in Egypt. *Leisure interests:* reading, swimming, shooting. *Address:* 28 Abdel Aziz Fahmay Street, Kafr El Mosselha, Menufia, Egypt. *Telephone:* 221543.

OMAR, Dato Napsiah binti, M.SC.; Malaysian politician; b. 21 April 1943; m. (husband deceased); ed. Australian Nat. Univ. Canberra and Cornell Univ. New York; Admin. Officer, Fed. Land Devt. Authority, Kuala Lumpur 1967–69; started Women's and Family Devt. Programme 1967; lecturer, Agricultural Coll. Malaya Serdang 1972; Co-ordinator, Food Tech., Home and Food Tech. Div. Agricultural Univ. 1972–73, Deputy Head, Dept. of Home Tech. 1973–76, Head, Dept. of Human Devt. Studies 1978–80, Warden, Fourth Residential Coll. 1974–82; Assoc. Prof. Dept. of Human Devt. Studies 1981; Deputy Minister of Housing and Local Govt. 1981–87; Minister of Public Enterprises 1988–90; mem. Exec. Cttee. UMNO Women Malaysia and Chair. of Unity Bureau, UMNO Malaysia 1987–90; Chair. Econ. Bureau, UMNO 1986–88. *Address:* c/o Ministry of Public Enterprises, WISMA PKNS, 3rd Floor, Jalan Raja Lant, 50652 Kuala Lumpur, Malaysia.

O'MEARA, Mark; American golfer; b. 13 Jan. 1957, Goldsboro, N.C.; ed. Long Beach State Univ.; professional golfer 1980–; mem. Ryder Cup team 1985, 1989, 1991, 1997; won U.S. Amateur Championship 1979, Greater Milwaukee Open 1984, Bing Crosby Pro-Am 1985, Hawaiian Open 1985, Fuji Sankei Classic 1985, Australian Masters 1986, Lawrence Batley Int. 1987, AT&T Pebble Beach Nat. Pro-Am 1989, 1990, 1992, 1997, H-E-B Tex. Open 1990, Walt Disney World/Oldsmobile Classic 1991, Tokia Classic 1992, Argentine Open 1994, Honda Classic 1995, Bell Canada Open 1995, Mercedes Championships 1996, Greater Greensboro Open 1996, Brick Invitational 1997, U.S. Masters 1998, British Open 1998; tied (with Corey Pavin) Bob Hope Chrysler Classic 1990; All-American Rookie of Year, Long Beach State Univ. 1981. *Address:* c/o PGA, Box 109601, Avenue of Champions, Palm Beach Gardens, FL 33410, U.S.A.

OMINAMI PASCUAL, Carlos, D.SC.ECON.; Chilean politician; b. 1951; m.; fmr. Research Assoc. at various insts. in France including Centro

Latinoamericano de Economía y Política Internacional (CLEPI), Chile; Assessor of Industrial Policy, Ministries of Cooperation and Industry, Govt. of France 1981–83; Regional Assessor, Int. Relations Programme for Latin American of CEPAL; Assessor, ILPES; Head, Econ. Comm. Chilean Socialist Party 1986–89; deputy co-ordinator of the econ.-social platform of the Parties for Democracy 1988–89; Vice-Pres. Partido por la Democracia (PPD) 1989–90; Minister of the Economy 1990. *Address:* c/o Ministry of the Economy, Teatinos 40, Santiago, Chile. *Telephone:* 717436.

OMIRBEK, Baigeldi; Kazakhstan politician; b. 15 Apr. 1939, Yernazar, Zhambyl Region; m.; three c.; ed. Almaty Inst. of Veterinary Sciences, Acad. of Social Sciences Cen. CPSU Cttee.; various posts in Dist. Dept. of Agric. Man. 1962–74; First Deputy Chair. Regional Dept. on Agric. Man. 1974–75; First Sec. Kurdai Regional Cttee., Chair. Zhambyl Regional Exec. Cttee., First Sec. Zhambyl Regional Cttee. CP of Kazakhstan, Chair. Zhambyl Soviet of People's Deputies 1975–92; Head Zhambyl Regional Admin. 1992–95; Counsellor to Pres. of Kazakhstan 1995–96; Chair. Senate (Parl.) Jan. 1996–. *Address:* House of Parliament, Astara, Kazakhstan. *Telephone:* (3172) 327892 (Office).

Ó MÓRÁIN, Dónall; Irish public official; b. 6 Sept. 1923, Co. Kerry; s. of Mícheál Ó Móráin and Eibhlín Ní Loingsigh; m. Maire Beaumont 1949; three s. two d.; ed. Coláiste Muire, Dublin, Univ. Coll., Dublin, and King's Inns, Dublin; called to the Bar 1946; Man. Ed. of Retail Food Trade Journal 1946–50; Gen. Man., printing and publishing firm 1951–63; Founder, Gael-Linn (voluntary nat. cultural and social asscn.) 1953, Chair. 1953–63, Dir.-Gen. 1963–88, Chair. and Life mem. of Bd. 1988–; Chair. Convocation of Nat. Univ. of Ireland 1955–84; Chair. Inisfree Handknits Group 1965–; mem. Radio Telefis Éireann Authority 1965–70, Chair. 1970–72, 1973–76; mem. Language Consultative Council, Dept. of Finance 1965–75; Dir. Glens of Antrim Tweed Co. Ltd. 1967–79; mem. Irish Comm. for UNESCO 1966–, Irish Film Industry Comm. 1967–69; Chair. Consultative Council to Radio na Gaeltachta (first local radio service in Ireland) 1971–76; Hon. LL.D. (Nat. Univ. of Ireland) 1979; founder and Man. Dir. Anois, Sunday newspaper 1984–96; Man. Dir. Gael-Linn Educational Publications 1996–. *Leisure interests:* fowling, salmon fishing. *Address:* 32 Sydney Avenue, Blackrock, Dublin, Ireland. *Telephone:* (01) 2880541. *Fax:* (01) 6767030.

OMOROGBE, Oluyinka Osayame, LL.M.; Nigerian university lecturer and legal practitioner; b. 21 Sept. 1957, Ibadan; d. of Samuel O. Ighodaro and Irene E. B. Ighodaro; m. Allan Omorogbe 1984; one s. one d.; ed. Univ. of Ife and L.S.E.; Nat. Youth Service 1979–80; Pvt. Legal Practitioner 1980–81; Lecturer Dept. of Jurisprudence and Int. Law, Univ. of Benin 1983–90, Head of Dept. 1988–89; Sr. Lecturer Univ. of Lagos 1990–; Dir. Centre for Petroleum, Environment and Devt. Studies, Lagos 1996–; mem. Exec. Cttee. Petroleum Energy and Mining Law Asscn. of Nigeria 1986–; mem. Int. Bar Asscn., African Soc. of Int. and Comparative Law; Treas. Nigerian Soc. of Int. Law 1994–97, Sec. 1997–. *Publications:* numerous articles on petroleum and energy law, and int. econ. law in int. journals. *Leisure interests:* cooking, baking, handcrafts. *Address:* P.O. Box 9261, Ikeja, Lagos, Nigeria.

ONDAATJE, Michael; Canadian author; b. 12 Sept. 1943, Colombo, Sri Lanka; s. of Philip Mervyn Ondaatje and Enid Doris Gratiaen; two s.; ed. Dulwich Coll. London, Queen's Univ. and Univ. of Toronto, Canada. *Publications include:* poetry: The Dainty Monsters 1967, The Man with Seven Toes 1968, There's a Trick with a Knife I'm Learning to Do 1979, Secular Love 1984; fiction: The Collected Works of Billy the Kid, Coming Through Slaughter, Running in the Family, In the Skin of a Lion, The English Patient (shared the Booker Prize for Fiction 1992). *Address:* 2275 Bayview Road, Toronto, Ont., N4N 3MG, Canada.

ONDARTS, Raúl Agustín; Argentinian business executive and politician; b. 28 Aug. 1915, Buenos Aires; s. of Juan Ondarts and Juana Ansolabehere; m. Norah Elsa Unia 1942; three s. two d.; ed. Univ. de Buenos Aires; private engineering practice 1938–75; Under-Sec. for Industry 1957; Del. Econ. Conf. OAS 1957; Pres., with rank of Amb., Argentine purchasing Comm. in European communist countries 1958; Sec. of State for Communications 1962; Under-Sec. for Economy and Labour 1967; Vice-Pres. and Pres. of Exec. Cttee. Hidronor 1968–70; Pres. Metallurgical Industries of San Martín (TAMET SA) 1970–75; Pres. Iron and Steel Industry's Centre 1971–77; Pres. Yacimientos Petrolíferos Fiscales Sociedad del Estado 1977–80; Pres. Centre of Engineers and Union of Engineers 1958–60; mem. Acad. de Ingeniería de Argentina. *Leisure interests:* sport, reading. *Publications:* La Ingeniería y los Ingenieros (essay), articles in technical periodicals published in Brazil, Italy, U.K. and Japan. *Address:* c/o Avda. Pres. Roque Sáenz Peña 777, Buenos Aires, Argentina. *Telephone:* 46-7271.

O'NEAL, Ryan; American actor; b. 20 April 1941, Los Angeles; s. of Charles and Patricia (Callaghan) O'Neal; m. 1st Joanna Moore 1963 (divorced 1967), one s. one d. (Tatum O'Neal, q.v.); m. 2nd Leigh Taylor-Young 1967, one s.; one s. by Farrah Fawcett. *TV appearances include:* Dobie Gillis, Two Faces West, Perry Mason, The Virginian, This is the Life, The Untouchables, My Three Sons, Bachelor Father, Empire, Peyton Place. *Films include:* The Big Bounce 1969, Love Story 1970, The Wild Rovers 1971, What's Up, Doc? 1972, The Thief Who Came to Dinner 1973, Paper Moon 1973, Oliver's Story 1978, The Main Event 1979, So Fine 1981, Partners 1982, Irreconcilable Differences 1983, Fever Pitch 1985, Tough Guys Don't Dance 1986, Chances Are 1989, Faithful 1996, Hakcs 1997, Burn Hollywood Burn 1997, Zero Effect 1998.

O'NEAL, Shaquille Rashaun; American professional basketball player; b. 6 March 1972, Newark; s. of Philip A. Harrison and Lucille O'Neal; ed. Louisiana State Univ.; Centre Orlando Magic 1992–96; Los Angeles Lakers 1996–; mem. Nat. Basketball Asscn. (NBA) All-Star team 1993, Dream Team 11 1994. *Films:* Blue Chips 1994, Kazaam 1996. *Address:* c/o Los Angeles Lakers, 3900 West Manchester Boulevard, Inglewood, CA 90306, U.S.A.

O'NEAL, Tatum; American actress; b. 1963, Los Angeles; d. of Ryan O'Neal (q.v.) and Joanna Moore; m. John McEnroe (q.v.) 1986; two s. one d.; *Film appearances include:* Paper Moon 1973, The Bad News Bears 1976, Nickelodeon 1976, International Velvet 1978, Little Darlings 1980, Circle of Two 1980, Certain Fury 1985, Little Noises 1992, Basquiat 1996. *Address:* c/o Innovative Artists, 1999 Avenue of the Stars, Suite 2850, Century City, CA 90067, U.S.A.

O'NEIL, William Andrew, O.C., B.SC., F.R.S.A.; Canadian international public servant and engineer; b. 6 June 1927, Ottawa; s. of Thomas Wilson and Margaret (Swan) O'Neil; m. Dorothy Muir 1950; one s. two d.; ed. Univ. of Toronto; engineer, Fed. Dept. of Transport, Ottawa 1949–53, Resident Engineer, Special Projects Br. 1954; Div. Engineer, St. Lawrence Seaway Authority 1955–59, Regional Dir. 1960–63, Dir. of Construction 1964–70; Deputy Admin., Marine Services, Canadian Marine Transportation Admin. 1975–79; Commr., Canadian Coast Guard and Deputy Admin., Marine Admin. 1979–89; Pres. St. Lawrence Seaway Authority 1980–89; Chair. Council Int. Maritime Org. 1980–89, Sec.-Gen. 1990–; mem. Bd. of Govs. World Maritime Univ. 1983–89, subsequently mem. Exec. Council of Bd. of Govs. and Bd. of Trustees of Capital Fund; Chair. Governing Bd., Int. Maritime Law Inst., Malta 1991–; Canadian del. to Perm. Int. Asscn. of Navigation Congresses 1984–90; Chair. Canadian Cttee. Lloyd's Register of Shipping 1987–88; mem. Int. Maritime Bureau 1991–; Chancellor World Maritime Univ. 1991–; Dir. Canarctic Shipping Co.; Pres. Seaway Int. Bridge Corpn.; mem. Bd. of the Thousand Islands Bridge Authority 1980–90; mem. Asscn. of Professional Engineers of Ont., American Soc. of Civil Engineers; Foreign mem. Royal Acad. of Eng. (U.K.); Fellow Chartered Inst. of Transport (U.K.); Hon. Commodore, Canadian Coast Guard; Hon. mem. Canadian Maritime Law Asscn., Honourable Co. of Master Mariners, U.K., Int. Maritime Pilots Asscn., Int. Fed. of Shipmasters' Asscns., NUMAST (Nat. Union of Marine Aviation and Shipping Transport Officers) (U.K.), Soc. of Naval Architects and Marine Engineers (U.S.A.), Soc. of Naval Architects and Marine Engineers, Singapore, Int. Asscn. of Lighthouse Authorities, Co. of Master Mariners, India 1998; Hon. Fellow The Nautical Inst., U.K., Royal Inst. of Naval Architects 1998; Hon. Dip. Canadian Coast Guard Coll.; Hon. LL.D. (Malta), (Memorial Univ. of Newfoundland) 1996; Hon. D.Sc. (Nottingham Trent) 1994; Eng. Medal, Asscn. of Professional Engineers of Ont., Distinguished Public Service Award, U.S. Govt., Admirals' Medal 1994, Seatrade Personality of the Year Award 1995, NUMAST Award (U.K.) 1995, Professional Engineers Ont. Gold Medal, mem. Eng. Alumni Hall of Distinction, Univ. of Toronto 1996, Silver Bell Award, Seamen's Church Inst. New York 1997; Commdr., Ordre Nat. des Cèdres (Lebanon) 1995, Grand Cross, Orden Vasco Nuñez de Balboa (Panama) 1998, Cdre. Award, Conn. Maritime Asscn. 1998, Dioscun Prize, Lega Navale Italiana (Italy) 1998. *Leisure interests:* reading, swimming, golf. *Address:* International Maritime Organization, 4 Albert Embankment, London, SE1 7SR (Office); 15 Ropers Orchard, London, SW3 5AX, England (Home). *Telephone:* 0171-587 3100.

O'NEILL, Michael, B.A., M.B.A.; American banker; b. 31 Oct. 1946; m.; two s.; ed. Princeton Univ. and Univ. of Virginia; U.S. Marine Corps 1969–71; joined Continental Bank 1974, worked in Belgium, Hong Kong and London (Country Man.); ind. consultant 1985–88; returned to Continental Bank as Chief Financial Officer heading merger negotiations with BankAmerica; responsible for pvt. equity business BankAmerica Corpn. following 1994 merger, Vice-Chair., Chief Financial Officer 1995, then Pres. Prin. Investing and Wealth Man. and mem. Policy Cttee. Transition (fmr. Chair.); Group Chief Exec. and Dir. Barclays PLC and Barclays Bank PLC March 1999. *Address:* c/o Barclays PLC, 54 Lombard Street, London, EC3P 3AH, England.

O'NEILL, Paul H., M.P.A.; American business executive; b. 4 Dec. 1935, St. Louis, Mo.; s. of John Paul O'Neill and Gayland Elsie Irvin; m. Nancy Jo Wolfe 1955; one s. three d.; ed. Fresno State Coll., Indiana Univ., Claremont Grad. School and George Washington Univ.; computer systems analyst, U.S. Veterans Admin.; later engineer, Morris-Knudsen, Anchorage, Alaska; mem. staff, Office of Man. and Budget 1967–77, Deputy Dir. 1974–77; Vice-Pres. Planning, Int. Paper Co. 1977, Sr. Vice-Pres. Planning and Finance 1981, Sr. Vice-Pres. paperboard and packaging Div. 1983, Pres. 1985–87; Chair., C.E.O. Aluminum Co. of America (Alcoa) 1987–; Dir. Manpower Demonstration Research Group, Aluminum Co. of America, Lucent Technologies, Eastman Kodak Co.; Chair. Rand; many other business and community affiliations; Dr. h.c. (Clarkson Univ.) 1993. *Address:* Alcoa, 425 Sixth Avenue, Suite 31, Pittsburgh, PA 15219, U.S.A. (Office).

O'NEILL, Robert John, A.O., M.A., B.E., D.PHIL., F.A.S.S.A.; Australian historian and army officer; b. 5 Nov. 1936, Melbourne; s. of Joseph Henry O'Neill and Janet Gibbon O'Neill; m. Sally Margaret Burnard 1965; two d.; ed. Scotch Coll. Melbourne, Royal Mil. Coll. of Australia, Melbourne Univ., Brasenose Coll. Oxford; served in Australian army 1955–68, Fifth Bn. Royal

Australian Regt., Vietnam (despatches) 1966–67, Maj. 1967–68 (resgnd.); Rhodes scholar, Vic. 1961; Official Australian Historian for the Korean War 1969–82; Head Strategic and Defence Studies Centre, Australian Nat. Univ. 1971–82; Dir. Int. Inst. of Strategic Studies, London 1982–87; Chichele Prof. of the History of War Oxford Univ. 1987–; Dir. Grad. Studies Modern History Faculty, Oxford 1990–92; Fellow All Souls Coll. Oxford 1987, Hon. Fellow Brasenose Coll. Oxford, Sr. Fellow in Int. Relations Australian Nat. Univ. 1969–77, Professorial Fellow 1977–82; Trustee Imperial War Museum 1990–, Deputy Chair. 1996–98, Chair. 1998–; Gov. Ditchley Foundation 1989–, Int. Peace Acad. 1990–; Chair. Bd. Centre for Defence Studies and Bd. Centre for Australian Studies, Univ. of London 1990–95; Chair. Council, Int. Inst. of Strategic Studies 1996–; Dir. The Shell Transport and Trading Co. 1992–, and two mutual funds of Capital Group, Los Angeles 1992; mem. Advisory Bd. Investment Co. of America 1988–; mem. Commonwealth War Graves Comm. 1990, The Rhodes Trust 1995–; Hon. Col. 5th (V) Battalion, The Royal Greenjackets 1993–. *Publications:* The German Army and the Nazi Party 1933–39 1966, Vietnam Task 1966, General Giap: politician and strategist 1969, (ed.) The Strategic Nuclear Balance 1975, (ed.) The Defence of Australia: fundamental new aspects 1977, (ed.) Insecurity: the spread of weapons in the Indian and Pacific Oceans 1978, (co-ed.) Australian Dictionary of Biography Vols 7–12, 1891–1939, 1979–91, (co-ed.) New Directions in Strategic Thinking 1981, Australia in the Korean War 1950–53: Vol. I Strategy and Diplomacy 1981, Vol. II Combat Operations 1985, (co-ed.) Australian Defence Policy for the 1980s 1982, (ed.) Security in East Asia 1984, (ed.) The Conduct of East-West Relations in the 1980s 1985, (ed.) New Technology and Western Security Policy 1985, (ed.) Doctrine, the Alliance and Arms Control 1986, (ed.) East Asia, the West and International Security 1987, (ed.) Security in the Mediterranean 1989 (co-ed.) The West and the Third World 1990, (co-ed.) Securing Peace in Europe 1945–62 1992, (co-ed.) War, Strategy and International Politics 1992; articles in numerous journals. *Leisure interests:* local history, walking. *Address:* All Souls College, Oxford, OX1 4AL, England.

O'NEILL, Terence Patrick; British photographer; b. 30 July 1938, London; s. of Leonard Victor O'Neill and Josephine Mary O'Neill; m. 1st Vera Day; one s. one d.; m. 2nd Faye Dunaway (q.v.) 1981; one s.; ed. Gunnersbury Grammar School; fmr. modern jazz drummer in leading London jazz clubs; army service as physical training instructor; subsequently took up photography, took first photographs of Beatles and Rolling Stones early 1960s; went to Hollywood 1962; has photographed leading actors and actresses, rock and classical musicians, political and sports personalities, mems. of British and other royal families; work published in The Sunday Times, Time, Life, Newsweek, Tatler, Elle, Paris Match, Stern etc. and other newspapers and magazines, in 52 countries, and used on about 500 front covers worldwide a year. *Leisure interests:* music, food, wine, art in all forms, literature.

O'NEILL, William Atchison; American politician; b. 11 Aug. 1930, Hartford, Conn.; s. of the late Joseph O'Neill and of Frances O'Neill; m. Natalie Scott Damon 1962; ed. schools, East Hampton, Conn., New Britain Teacher's Coll., Conn., and Univ. of Hartford, Conn.; served with U.S.A.F. 1950–53; mem. East Hampton Democratic Town Cttee. 1954–78; mem. House of Reps., Conn., from 52nd Assembly Dist. 1966–78, Asst. Majority Leader 1971–72, Asst. Minority Leader 1973–74, Majority Leader 1975–78; mem. Conn. Gov.'s Finance Advisory Cttee. 1968–74; Chair. House Cttee. on Exec. Nominations; State Chair. Ella Grasso for Gov. Cttee. 1974; Chair. Democratic State Cen. Cttee. 1975–78; Lieut.-Gov. of Conn. 1979–80, Gov. of Connecticut 1980–90; mem. Nat. Gov.'s Asscn.; mem. American Legion; Hon. Alumnus Award, Univ. of Hartford 1981.

O'NEILL OF BENGARVE, Baroness (Life Peer) cr. 1999, of The Braid in the County of Antrim; Onora Sylvia O'Neill, C.B.E., PH.D., F.B.A.; British philosopher and college principal; b. 23 Aug. 1941, Aughafatten, N. Ireland; d. of late Sir Con O'Neill and of Lady Garvey (née Rosemary Pritchard); m. Edward Nell 1963 (divorced 1976); two s.; ed. St. Paul's Girls' School, London, Somerville Coll. Oxford and Harvard Univ., U.S.A.; Asst. Prof. Barnard Coll. Columbia Univ. 1970–76, Assoc. Prof. 1976–77; Lecturer, Univ. of Essex 1977–78, Sr. Lecturer 1978–82, Reader 1982–87, Prof. 1987–92; Prin. Newnham Coll. Cambridge 1992–; Chair. Nuffield Foundation 1998–, Human Genetics Advisory Cttee. 1997–; Dr. h.c. (E. Anglia) 1995, (Essex) 1996. *Publications:* Faces of Hunger: An Essay on Poverty, Development and Justice 1986, Constructions of Reason: Explorations of Kant's Practical Philosophy 1989, Towards Justice and Virtue: A Constructive Account of Practical Reasoning 1996. *Leisure interests:* walking, talking. *Address:* Newnham College, Cambridge, CB3 9DF, England. *Telephone:* (01223) 330469. *Fax:* (01223) 359155.

ONG, John Doyle, M.A., L.L.B.; American business executive; b. 29 Sept. 1933, Uhrichsville, Ohio; s. of Louis Brosee and Mary Ellen (née Liggett) Ong; m. Mary Lee Schupp 1957; two s. one d.; ed. Ohio State Univ., Harvard Univ.; admitted to Ohio Bar 1958; Asst. Counsel B. F. Goodrich Co., Akron 1961–66, Group Vice-Pres. 1972–73, Exec. Vice-Pres. 1973–74, Vice-Chair. 1974–75, Pres. 1975–84, Dir. 1975–77, C.O.O. 1978–79, Chair. Pres. and C.E.O. 1979–84, Chair. 1984–97, C.E.O. 1984–96, Chair. Emer. 1997–; Asst. to Pres. Int. B. F. Goodrich Co., Akron 1966–69, Vice-Pres. 1969–70, Pres. 1970–72; Dir. Cooper Industries, The Kroger Co., Ameritech Corpn.; Chair. Ohio Business Roundtable 1994–97; mem. Bd. Dirs. Nat. Alliance for Business; Pres. Bd. of Trustees, Western Reserve Acad., Hudson 1977–95; Trustee John S. and James L. Knight Foundation 1995–, Univ. of Chicago 1991–. *Leisure interests:* fishing, hunting. *Address:* 230 Aurora Street, Hudson, OH 44236, U.S.A. (Home).

ONG, Tan Sri Haji Omar Yoke-Lin; Malaysian politician and diplomatist; b. 23 July 1917, Kuala Lumpur; m. Toh Puan Datin (Dr.) Hajjah Aishah 1974; three s. one d.; mem. Kuala Lumpur Municipal Council 1952–55; co-founder Alliance Party; mem. Fed. Legis. Council 1954; Malayan Minister of Posts and Telecommunications 1955–56, of Transport 1956–57, of Labour and Social Welfare 1957–59, of Health and Social Welfare 1959–72; M.P. 1959–72; Vice-Pres. Commonwealth Parl. Asscn. 1961; Amb. to UN 1962–64, to U.S.A. 1962–72, also accred. to Canada 1966–72 and Brazil 1967–72; Minister without Portfolio 1964–73; Pres. of the Senate 1973–80; Chair. Asian Int. Merchant Bankers Bhd., Malaysian Oxygen Bhd., Omariff Holdings Sdn. Bhd., Syarikat Ong Yoke Lin Sdn. Bhd., OYL Industries Sdn. Bhd., Raza Sdn. Bhd.; Dir. Esso Malaysia Berhad, Hume Industries (Malaysia) Berhad, Malayan Flour Mills Bhd., United Chemical Industries Bhd.; Pro-Chancellor Nat. Univ. of Malaysia 1987; Council mem. Inst. of Strategic Studies, Malaysia; Vice-Pres. UN Malaysia Asscn.; Hon. LL.D. (Hanyang Univ.) Seoul 1978, Hon. Ph.D. (Malaysia); S.S.M. 1979; Panglima Mangku Neyara (Malaysia) 1959; Order of First Homayon (Iran) 1969, Grand Cross (1st Class) Fed. Rep. of Germany; Order of Civil Merit (1st Class) Rep. of Korea, Commdr. Ordre nat. du Mérite. *Leisure interests:* golf, photography, swimming. *Address:* Asian International Merchant Bankers Ltd., UMBC Annexe 9-11 Floors, Jalem Salaiman, Kuala Lumpur (Office); Malaysian Oxygen Bhd., 13 Jalan 222, 46100 Petaling Jaya, Selangor Darul Ehsan; 44 Pesiaran Duta, Kuala Lumpur, Malaysia (Home). *Telephone:* 03-274 9011 (Office); 03-254 6637/255 9731 (Home).

ONG, Romualdo Añover, B.SC.; Philippine diplomatist; b. 25 April 1939, Manila; s. of late Juan Salido Ong and of Adelaida Añover; m. 1st Cecilia Hidalgo 1964 (deceased); m. 2nd Farita Aguilucho 1994; two s. two d.; ed. Ateneo de Manila and Univ. of the Philippines; joined Ministry of Foreign Affairs 1968; served Bonn 1972–75, Geneva 1975–79, Minister Counsellor, Beijing 1979–82; Special Asst. to Deputy Minister for Foreign Affairs 1983; Asst. Minister for ASEAN Affairs 1984–85; Sr. Econ. Consultant, Tech. Secr. for Int. Econ. Relations/Bd. of Overseas Econ. Promotion 1985; Amb. to Australia (also accred. to Vanuatu) 1986–89; Asst. Sec. for Asian and Pacific Affairs, Dept. of Foreign Affairs, Manila 1990–93; Amb. to Russia 1993–94, to People's Repub. of China 1994–. *Leisure interests:* reading, car driving, basketball, hiking, movies, listening to music. *Address:* Philippines Embassy, 23 Xiu Shui Bei Jie, Jian Guo Men Wai, Beijing, People's Republic of China. *Telephone:* (10) 6532-1872. *Fax:* (10) 6532-3761.

ONG TENG CHEONG, M.A.; Singaporean politician and architect; b. 22 Jan. 1936, Singapore; m. Ling Siew May 1963; two s.; ed. Chinese High School and Univs. of Adelaide and Liverpool; joined Planning Dept., Ministry of Nat. Devt. 1967, later seconded to UNDP (Special Fund) assistance in Urban Renewal and Devt. Project; est. own architectural practice with wife 1971; mem. Parl. 1972–93; Sr. Minister of State for Communications 1975–78, also Acting Minister for Culture 1977; Minister for Communications, concurrently Minister for Culture 1978; Minister for Communications and Labour 1981–83; Sec.-Gen. Nat. Trades Union Congress 1983–93; Minister without Portfolio 1983–85; Second Deputy Prime Minister 1985–90, Deputy Prime Minister 1990–93; Pres. of Singapore 1993–. *Address:* Office of the President, Istana, Singapore 2388, Singapore.

ÖNHON, Candemir; Turkish diplomatist; b. 30 Oct. 1933, Istanbul; s. of Saim Önhon and Münire Önhon; m. Birsen Kap 1959; one s. one d.; ed. Univ. of Ankara; cand. officer, Political Dept. 1956; mil. service 1956–57; NATO Dept. 1958–60; Second Sec., then First Sec. Turkish Perm. Del. to NATO 1960–64; Consul, Consulate-Gen. Comotini, Greece 1964–65; Dir. of Section, NATO Dept. 1965–66, Dept. of Cyprus/Greece 1966–67; Counsellor, Nicosia 1967–69, Athens 1969–72; Deputy Head, Middle East Political Dept. 1972; Chief of Cabinet of Presidency of Repub. 1973–76; Rep. of Turkey (with rank of Amb.), Nicosia 1976–79; Amb. to Finland 1979–82; Under-Sec. of Information, Office of Prime Minister 1982–84; Sr. Adviser and Insp. Ministry of Foreign Affairs 1984–86; Amb. to Egypt 1986–91, to U.K. 1991–95. *Leisure interests*: horse-riding, hunting, photography, cinematography. *Address:* c/o Ministry of Foreign Affairs, Dişişlerı Bakanlığı, Yeni Hizment Binasi, 06520 Ankara, Turkey.

O'NIONS, Robert Keith, M.A., PH.D., F.R.S.; British geochemist; b. 26 Sept. 1944, Birmingham; s. of William Henry O'Nions and Eva Stagg; m. Rita Bill 1967; three d.; ed. Univ. of Nottingham, Univ. of Alberta; Postdoctoral Fellow, Univ. of Alberta 1969–70; Unger Vetlesen Postdoctoral Fellow, Univ. of Oslo 1970–71; Demonstrator in Petrology, Univ. of Oxford 1971–72, Lecturer in Geochemistry 1972–75; Assoc. Prof. and Prof. of Geology, Columbia Univ. 1975–79; Royal Soc. Research Prof., Univ. of Cambridge 1979–95; Fellow Clare Hall Cambridge 1980–95; Prof. of Physics and Chemistry of Minerals, Univ. of Oxford 1995–; Fellow St. Hughes Coll. Oxford 1995–; Fellow, American Geophysical Union 1979–; mem. Norwegian Acad. of Sciences; J. B. Macelwane Award 1979; Bigsby Medal 1983, Holmes Medal 1995, Lyell Medal 1995. *Publications:* numerous publications in scientific journals on the subject of geochemistry. *Address:* Department of Earth Sciences, University of Oxford, Parks Road, Oxford, OX1 3PR, England. *Telephone:* (01865) 272969. *Fax:* (01865) 272072.

ÖNNERFORS, Alf, PH.D.; Swedish university professor; b. 30 Nov. 1925, Hovmantorp; s. of Carl-Oscar Önnerfors and Karin Widerström; m. 1st Ingrid Åhlén 1949; m. 2nd Ute Michaelis 1964; three s.; ed. Univ. of Uppsala; Lecturer, then Assoc. Prof., Univ. of Uppsala 1957–62, Univ. of Lund 1962–63; Prof., Freie Universität Berlin, West Berlin 1963–70, Univ. of Cologne, Fed. Repub. of Germany 1970–91; research into Latin language and literature; mem. Rheinisch-Westfälische Akademie der Wissenschaften, Ed. Lateinische Sprache u. Literatur des Mittelalters 1974–93. *Publications:* Pliniana (dissertation) 1956, In Medicinam Plinii studia philologica 1963, Die Hauptfassungen des Sigfrid-Offiziums 1968, Vaterporträts in der römischen Poesie 1974, Willem Jordaens, Conflictus virtutum et viciorum 1986, Antike Zaubersprüche 1991, Das medizinische Latein von Celsus bis Cassius Felix 1993, Magische Formeln im Dienste römischer Medizin 1993, Zu Person und Werk des Publius Flavius Vegetius Renatus 1993, Classica et Mediaevalia. Abhandlungen und Aufsätze 1997; critical edns. of Cicero, Ad Atticum 13-16 1960, Medicina Plinii (Corpus Med. Lat.) 1964, C. de Bridia, Hystoria Tartarorum 1967, Physica Plinii Bambergensis (ed. princeps) 1975, Tacitus, Germania (Teubner) 1983, Vegetius, Epitoma rei militaris 1995; about 75 papers and essays in int. reviews and journals of Classical and Medieval Philology. *Leisure interests:* riding (military), chemistry, pharmacology. *Address:* Rudeboksvägen 199, 22655 Lud; 36051 Hovmantorp, Sweden. *Telephone:* (046) 158887; (0478) 19039.

ONSLOW OF WOKING, Baron (Life Peer), cr. 1997, of Woking in the County of Surrey; **Cranley Gordon Douglas Onslow,** K.C.M.G., P.C., M.P.; British politician; b. 8 June 1926, Bexhill; s. of the late F.R.D. Onslow and M. Onslow; m. Lady June Hay 1955; one s. three d.; ed. Harrow School, Oriel Coll. Univ. of Oxford, Geneva Univ.; served R.A.C., Lieut. 7th Queen's Own Hussars 1944–48, Capt. 3rd/4th Co. of London Yeomanry 1948–52; joined Foreign Service 1951, Third Sec. Embassy, Rangoon 1953–55, Consul, Maymyo, N. Burma 1955–56, resgnd. 1960; served Dartford Rural Dist. Council 1960–62, Kent County Council 1961–64; M.P. for Woking 1964–97; Parl. Under-Sec. of State for Aerospace and Shipping, Dept. of Trade and Industry 1972–74, Opposition Spokesman on Health and Social Security 1974–75, on Defence 1975–76; Minister of State, Foreign and Commonwealth Office 1982–83; mem. Exec. 1922 Cttee. 1968–72, 1981–82, 1983–92, Chair. 1984–92; U.K. del. to Council of Europe and WEU 1977–81; Chair. Conservative Aviation Cttee. 1970–72, 1979–82, Select Cttee. on Defence 1981–82; mem. Select Cttee. on Trade and Industry 1992–97; Chair. Nautical Museums Trust 1983–97; Dir. Argyll Group PLC 1983–93; mem. Council Nat. Rifle Asscn., Salmon and Trout Asscn., Anglers' Conservation Asscn.; Conservative. *Publication:* Asian Economic Development (Ed.) 1965. *Leisure interests:* fishing, shooting, watching cricket. *Address:* c/oHouse of Lords, London, S.W.1, England.

ONWUMECHILI, Cyril Agodi, PH.D.; Nigerian professor of physics and administrator; b. 20 Jan. 1932, Inyi; s. of Nwaime and Akuviro (née Orji) Onwumechili; m. Cecilia Bedeaka (née Anyadibe) 1958; two s. one d.; ed. King's Coll., Lagos, Univ. Coll., Ibadan and Univ. of London; Professor 1962–; Dir. of chain of observatories 1960–66; Dean, Faculty of Science, Univ. of Ibadan 1965–66; Prof. and Head of Dept. Univ. of Nigeria 1966–73, 1976–78, Dean, Faculty of Science 1970–71, Dean, Faculty of Physical Sciences 1973–76, 1978; Visiting Prof. of Geophysics, Univ. of Alaska 1971–72; Consultant, Inst. for Space Research, Nat. Research Council of Brazil 1972; Vice-Chancellor, Univ. of Ife, Ile-Ife 1979–82; Deputy Pres. Anambra State Univ. of Tech., Enugu 1983–84, Pres. 1984–85, Vice-Chancellor 1985–86; Consultant U.N. Econ. Comm. for Africa 1987, Commonwealth Science Council 1988; mem. Int. Scientific Programmes Cttee., Int. Symposia on Equatorial Aeronomy 1972–, UN Advisory Cttee. on Science and Tech. for Devt. 1981–83; Vice-Pres. Asscn. of African Univs. 1984–89, Consultant 1990–; mem. American Geophysical Union, Soc. for Terrestrial Magnetism and Electricity of Japan; Fellow U.K. and Nigerian Inst. of Physics 1969; Foundation Fellow and Former Pres. Nigerian Acad. of Science; U.K. Chartered Physicist 1986; Fellow African Acad. of Sciences 1987, Third World Acad. of Sciences 1989; Foundation Fellow, Science Asscn. of Nigeria 1974; chair. or mem. of many nat. and int. bds. and councils; Hon. D.Sc. (Ife) 1977, (Enugu State Univ.) 1992. *Publications:* The Equatorial Electrojet 1997; numerous scientific articles. *Leisure interests:* swimming, table tennis, lawn tennis. *Address:* 69 Lansdowne Drive, Hackney, London, E8 3EP, England; P.O. Box 9059, Uwani, Enugu, Nigeria. *Telephone:* 0171-249 3260 (London); (042) 254 987 (Enugu).

ONYEAMA, Charles Dadi, LL.B.; Nigerian judge; b. 5 Aug. 1917, Eke, Enugu; s. of Chief Onyeama; m. 1st Susannah Ogwudu 1950, 2nd Florence Wilcox 1966; five s. two d.; ed. King's Coll., Lagos, Achimota Coll., Gold Coast, Univ. Coll., London and Brasenose Coll., Oxford; Cadet Admin. Officer, Nigeria 1944; mem. Legis. Council of Nigeria and Eastern House of Ass. 1946–51; mem. Nigerianization Comm. and mem. Gen. Conf. and Constitutional Drafting Cttee. 1948–50; Chief Magistrate, Nigeria 1952–56; Acting High Court Judge, W. Nigeria 1956–57; High Court Judge, Lagos 1957–64; Acting Chief Justice, Lagos High Court 1961 and 1963; Justice of Supreme Court of Nigeria 1964–66; Judge Int. Court of Justice, The Hague 1967–76; Chair. Cttee. on the Prerogative of Mercy, Nigeria 1976–79, Ife Univ. Teaching Hospitals Complex Bd. 1976–79, Orthopaedic Hospitals Man. Bd. 1979–; Judge, World Bank Admin. Tribunal 1982–; Hon. LL.D.; Commdr. of the Fed. Repub. of Nigeria. *Leisure interest:* reading. *Address:* 1 Church Road, P.O. Box 602, Enugu, Nigeria.

ONYSZKIEWICZ, Janusz, D.MATH.; Polish government official and mathematician; b. 18 Dec. 1937, Lvov; s. of Stanislaw and Franciszka Onyszkiewicz; m. 1st Witoslawa Boretti (died 1967); m. 2nd Alison Chadwick (died 1978); m. 3rd Joanna Jaraczewska 1983; two s. three d.; ed. Warsaw Univ.; Asst., Math. Engines Inst., Polish Acad. of Sciences, Warsaw 1958–61; Asst. later, Sr. Asst. Faculty of Math., Informatics and Mechanics, Math. Inst., Warsaw Univ. 1963–67, lecturer 1967–75, now Sr. lecturer; lecturer, Univ. of Leeds 1976–79; lectured at many univs. abroad; mem. Polish Teachers' Union (ZNP) 1969-80, Ind. Self-governing Trade Union of Science, Tech. and Educ. Workers 1980, Deputy Chair. Br. at Warsaw Univ. Sept.–Oct. 1980; adviser to Interfactory Founding Cttee. of Solidarity Ind. Self-governing Trade Union–Mazovia Region, subsequently mem. Presidium of Nat. Comm. of Solidarity Trade Union, Bd. and Press Spokesman of Mazovia Region of Solidarity Trade Union; Press Spokesman Nat. Understanding Comm. and First Nat. Congress of Solidarity Trade Union 1980–81; interned 1981–82; arrested April 1983, released under amnesty July 1983; sentenced to six weeks' confinement May 1988; Press Spokesman Nat. Exec. Comm., Solidarity Trade Union; mem. Civic Cttee. attached to Lech Wałęsa (q.v.) 1988–91; participant Round Table debates, mem. team for mass media and opposition press spokesman Feb.–April 1989; Deputy to Sejm (Parl.) 1989–; Vice-Minister of Nat. Defence 1990–92, Minister 1992–93, 1997–; Chair. Defence Cttee., Council of Ministers 1997–; mem. Democratic Union Parl. Club 1991–94, Freedom Union Parl. Club 1994–; mem. Nat. Council Freedom Union 1996; mem. Euro-Atlantic Asscn. 1994– (Pres. 1994–98); mountaineer and speleologist, participant mountaineering expeditions in Himalayas, Hindu Kush, Karakoram, Pamir; Hon. D.Sc. (Leeds) 1991; Gold Medal 'For outstanding sporting achievements'. *Publications:* 15 works on foundations of math., including Complete Abstract Logics 1979; co-author Zdobycie Gasherbrumów 1977. *Leisure interests:* climbing, caving, tourism. *Address:* Ministerstwo Obrong Narodowej, ul. Klonowa 1, 00-909 Warsaw, Poland. *Telephone:* (22) 621-02-61. *Fax:* (22) 845-53-78.

OOKA, Makoto; Japanese writer and professor; b. 16 Feb. 1931, Mishima City; s. of Hiroshi Ooka and Ayako Ooka; m. Kaneko Aizawa 1957; one s. one d.; ed. Tokyo Nat. Univ.; journalist with Yomiuri (newspaper), foreign news section 1953–63; Asst. Prof. Meiji Univ., Tokyo 1965–70, Prof. 1970–87; Pres. Japan Poets' Asscn. 1979–81; Prof. Nat. Univ. for Fine Arts and Music 1988–93; Pres. Japan PEN Club 1989–93; mem. Int. Advisory Bd. of Poetry Int., Rotterdam; mem. Japan Art Acad. 1995–; Yomiuri Prize for Literature, Kikuchi Kan Prize, Hanatsubaki Prize for Poetry, Golden Wreath Prize, Struga Poetry Evenings Macedonia 1996, Asahi Prize 1996, Person of Cultural Merit 1997; Officier Ordre des Arts et des Lettres. *Publications:* Poetry: Memories and the Present 1956, For a Girl in Springtime 1978, City of Water 1981, Odes to the Waters of my Hometown 1989, A String Around Autumn 1982, Elegy and Benediction 1991, The Afternoon in the Earthly Paradise 1992, What the Kite Thinks, a linked poem with three American poets 1994, Beneath the Sleepless Tossing of the Planets 1995, The Last Will of Fire 1995, Dans l'Océan du Silence 1998; Criticism: The Banquet and the Solitary Mind, Aesthetics of Japanese Poetry 1978, Japanese Poetry; Past and Present, A Poet's Anthology 1979–, an anthological series for the newspaper Asahi, The Range of Japanese Poetry 1994; English translations: The Colours of Poetry—Essays on Classic Japanese Verse 1991; The Poetry and Poetics of Ancient Japan 1997; French translations: Poèmes de tous les jours 1993, Propos sur le vent et autres poèmes 1995, Poésie et Poétique du Japon Ancien 1995. *Address:* 5-11-5, Jindaiji Minami-cho, Chofu-shi, Tokyo 182, Japan. *Telephone:* (0424) 835202. *Fax:* (0424) 811135.

OPEL, John Roberts, B.A., M.B.A.; American data processing company executive; b. 5 Jan. 1925, Kansas City, Mo.; s. of Norman J. Opel and Esther (Roberts) Opel; m. Julia Carole Stout 1953; two s. three d.; ed. Westminster Coll., Fulton, Mo. and Univ. of Chicago; joined Int. Business Machines Corpn. (IBM) 1949, Sales Rep. 1949, Vice-Pres. 1966, Sr. Vice-Pres. 1969, Dir. 1972–94, Pres. 1974–83, and C.E.O. 1980–85, Chair. 1983–86, Chair. Exec. Cttee. 1986–93; Vice-Chair. The Business Council 1983; Dir. Fed. Res. Bank of New York Co. Inc. (Chair. 1987–89), Pfizer Inc., Prudential Insurance Co. of America, Time Inc.; Trustee, Westminster Coll., Univ. of Chicago, Inst. for Advanced Study; mem. Bd. of Govs. of Wilson Council, United Way of America, Task Force on Market Mechanisms 1987; Vice-Chair. Business Council; mem. Council on Foreign Relations, Policy and Planning Cttees. of Business Round Table. *Address:* c/o IBM Corporation, 590 Madison Avenue, New York, NY 10022, U.S.A.

OPIE, Julian Gilbert, B.A.; British artist; b. 12 Dec. 1958, London; s. of Roger G. Opie and Norma Opie; m. Lisa K. Milroy 1984; ed. Magdalen Coll. School, Oxford, Chelsea School of Art, London and Goldsmiths' School of Art, London; exhibited Young Blood, Riverside Studios, London 1983, Sculpture 1983, Rotterdam 1983, The Sculpture Show, Hayward Gallery, London 1983, Making Sculpture, Tate Gallery, London 1983, Perspective, Basle Art Fair, Basle 1984, Home and Abroad, Serpentine Gallery, London 1984, Myth and Symbol, Tokyo Museum of Modern Art 1984, The British Show touring Australia 1984, Paris Biennale, Paris 1985, Anniotanta, Ravenna 1985, British Sculpture Louisiana Museum, Denmark 1986, De Sculptura, Vienna 1986, Correspondence Europe, Stedelijk Museum, Amsterdam 1986, Prospect 86, Frankfurt 1986; one-person exhbns. at Lisson Gallery, London 1983, Kunstverein Köln, Cologne 1984 and Groningen Museum, Netherlands 1985, ICA, London 1985, Lisson Gallery 1985, 1986, Franco Toselli Gallery, Milan 1985; works in the collections of The British Council,

The Contemporary Arts Soc., Tate Gallery, Cincinnati Museum of Modern Art, Documenta 8, Kassel 1987, Stedelijk Museum, Amsterdam. *Publications:* Julian Opie, Kunstverein Köln: Catalogue of Works 1984, Julian Opie Drawings, ICA, London, Julian Opie New Works, Lisson Gallery. *Leisure interests:* art, music, films, books, architecture, travel, a 1981 Chevrolet Caprice Classic, supermarkets, fast food restaurants, hotel lobbies, petrol stations. *Address:* Lisson Gallery, 66–68 Bell Street, London, NW1 6SP, England. *Telephone:* 0171-262 1539.

OPIE, Lionel Henry, M.D., PH.D., M.R.C.P., F.A.C.C., F.R.S.S.A.; South African professor of medicine; b. 6 May 1933, Hanover, S.A.; s. of Prof. William Henry Opie and Marie Opie (née Le Roux); m. Carol June Sancroft Baker 1969; two d.; ed. Diocesan Coll., Rondebosch, Cape Town, Univ. of Cape Town, Oxford Univ., England; Intern, Groote Schuur Hosp. 1956; Sr. House Officer, Dept. of Neurology, Radcliffe Infirmary, Oxford, England 1957–59; House Physician (Endocrinology), Hammersmith Hosp., London 1959; Asst. in Medicine, Peter Bent Brigham Hosp., Boston, Mass., U.S.A., Samuel A. Levine Fellow in Cardiology, Harvard Medical School 1960–61; Asst. Resident in Medicine, Toronto Gen. Hosp., Canada 1961–62; Consultant Physician, Karl Bremer Hosp. and Univ. of Stellenbosch, S.A.; Out-Patient Asst. Physician, Radcliffe Infirmary, Wellcome Research Fellow, Dept. of Biochemistry, Oxford Univ. 1964–66; Part-Time Registrar, Hammersmith Hosp., London 1966–67; Research Fellow, Dept. of Biochemistry, Imperial Coll., London 1966–68; Sr. Registrar in Medicine (Cardiology), Hammersmith Hosp. 1967–69, Consultant in Medicine 1969; Sr. Specialist Physician, Groote Schuur Hosp. 1971; Assoc. Prof. of Medicine, Univ. of Cape Town 1975, Dir. MRC Research Unit for Ischaemic Heart Disease 1976, Personal Chair in Medicine, Prof. of Medicine 1980–; Dir. Hypertension Clinic 1979–; Visiting Prof. Div. of Cardiovascular Medicine, Stanford Univ. School of Medicine, Calif., U.S.A. 1991–94; British Heart Foundation Sr. Fellow and Visiting Prof. St. Thomas' Hosp., London 1992; Pres. Southern Africa Cardiac Soc. 1980–82; Chair. Council on Cardiac Metabolism, Int. Soc. and Fed. of Cardiology 1980; Pres. Southern Africa Hypertension Soc. 1986; Chair. Cttee. Cardiovascular Drugs, Int. Soc. and Fed. Cardiology 1990; mem. British Cardiac Soc., Physiological Soc. (U.K.), S.A. Socs. of Cardiology, Pharmacology, Biochemistry and Hypertension, Int. Hypertension Soc. *Publications:* over 300. *Address:* Heart Research Unit, Department of Medicine, University of Cape Town Medical School Observatory 7925; 66A Dean Street, Newlands 7700, South Africa (Home). *Telephone:* 47-1250 (ext. 358) (Univ.); 685-3855 (Home).

OPLE, Blas F.; Philippine politician; b. 3 Feb. 1927, Hagonoy, Bulacan; s. of Felix Ople and Segundina Fajardo; m. Susana Vasquez 1949; five s. two d.; ed. Philippine public and pvt. schools, Far Eastern Univ. and Manuel L. Quezon Univ., Manila; copy Ed. and columnist The Daily Mirror, Manila 1950–53; Asst. to Pres. Ramon Magsaysay on labour and agrarian affairs 1954–57; writer and labour leader 1958–64; Head, Propaganda Div., Ferdinand E. Marcos' presidential campaign 1965; Special Asst. to Pres. Marcos and Commr. Social Security System 1966; Sec. of Labour 1967–78, Minister of Labour and Employment 1978–86; founder and Leader Partido Nacionalista ng Pilipinas (PNP) 1986–; Chair. Nat. Manpower and Youth Council 1967–71; mem. Bd. of Trustees, Land Bank 1968; Chair. Govt. Group, Int. Labour Conf. 1969, Pres. Int. Labour Conf. 1975–76; Chair. Asian Labour Ministers' Conf. 1967; various govt. and civic awards. *Address:* 61 Visayas Avenue, Project 6, Quezon City, Philippines. *Telephone:* 98-20-56.

OPPENHEIM, Dennis A., M.F.A.; American artist; b. 6 Sept. 1938, Washington; s. of David Oppenheim and Katherine Belknap; m. Karen Cackett (divorced); one s. two d.; ed. Coll. of Arts and Crafts, Oakland, Calif., Stanford Univ.; Prof. of Art, Yale Univ. 1969, State Univ. of New York at Stony Brook 1969; Guggenheim Foundation Sculpture Grant 1972; Nat. Endowment for the Arts Sculpture Grant 1974; numerous individual and group exhbns. at galleries in U.S.A. and Europe since 1968; works in many public collections including Museum of Modern Art, New York, Tate Gallery, London, Stedelijk Museum, Amsterdam and Musée d'Art Moderne, Paris. *Publications:* Catalyst 1967–70, Indentations 1974; articles in journals. *Leisure interest:* computer programming. *Address:* 54 Franklin Street, New York, NY 10013, U.S.A.

OPPENHEIM, Sir Duncan Morris, Kt.; British tobacco manufacturer and solicitor; b. 6 Aug. 1904, St. Helen's; s. of Watkin Oppenheim and Helen Oppenheim (née McKechnie); m. 1st Joyce Mitcheson 1932 (deceased), 2nd Susan Macnaghten 1936 (deceased); one s. one d.; ed. Repton School; Asst. Solicitor Messrs. Linklaters & Paines, London 1929; Solicitor to and Dir. of China Assoc. Co. of British-American Tobacco Co. Ltd. 1934; Asst. Solicitor, British-American Tobacco Co. London 1935, Solicitor 1936–49, Dir. 1943–72, Deputy Chair. 1947–49, Vice-Chair. 1949–53, Chair. 1953–66, Pres. 1966–72; Chair. Tobacco Securities Trust Ltd. 1969–74; Deputy Chair. Commonwealth Devt. Finance Co. Ltd. 1968–74; Chair. Royal College of Art Council 1956–72, Pro-Provost 1967–72; Chair. Council of Industrial Design 1960–72; Dir. Lloyds Bank Ltd. 1956–75, Equity, Law Life Assurance Soc. Ltd. 1966–80; Chair. British Nat. Cttee. of Int. Chamber of Commerce 1963–74, Overseas Investment Cttee., CBI 1970–74, Court of Govs., Admin. Staff Coll., Henley 1963–71; Chair. Royal Inst. of Int. Affairs 1966–71; Gov. Repton School 1959–79; mem. Advisory Cttee. Victoria and Albert Museum, London 1966–79, Crafts Council 1971–83; Deputy Chair. 1977–83; Trustee and mem. Council, St. John's Smith Square 1972–94, Chair. Council 1990–94; Hon. Dr. and Sr. Fellow, Royal Coll. of Art; Hon. Fellow Chartered Soc. of Designers; Bicentenary Medal, Royal Soc. of Arts 1969. *Leisure interests:* painting, sailing. *Address:* 43 Edwardes Square, London, W.8, England. *Telephone:* 0171-603 7431.

OPPENHEIM-BARNES, Baroness (Life Peer), cr. 1989, of Gloucester in the County of Gloucestershire; **Sally Oppenheim-Barnes,** P.C.; British fmr. politician; b. 26 July 1930; d. of Mark Viner and Jeanette Viner; m. 1st Henry M. Oppenheim 1949 (died 1980), one s. two d.; m. 2nd John Barnes 1984; ed. Sheffield High School, Lowther Coll., N. Wales; fmr. Exec. Dir. Industrial & Investment Services Ltd.; fmr. Social Worker, School Care Dept. ILEA; M.P. for Gloucester 1970–87; Vice-Chair. Conservative Party Parl. Prices and Consumer Protection Cttee. 1971–73, Chair. 1973–74; Opposition Spokesman on Prices and Consumer Protection 1974–79; mem. Shadow Cabinet 1975–79; Minister of State (Consumer Affairs), Dept. of Trade 1979–82; Chair. Nat. Consumer Council 1987–89; Dir. (non-exec.) Main Bd. Boots Co. PLC 1982–93, Fleming High Income Trust 1989–97, HFC Bank PLC 1989–98; Conservative; fmr. Nat. Vice-Pres. Nat. Union of Townswomen's Guilds; Pres. Glos. Dist. Br. BRCS; fmr. Trustee Clergy Rest House Trust. *Leisure interests:* tennis, bridge. *Address:* Quietways, The Highlands, Painswick, Glos., GL6 6SL England.

OPPENHEIMER, Harry Frederick, M.A.; South African industrialist (retd.); b. 28 Oct. 1908, Kimberley; s. of late Sir Ernest Oppenheimer and May Pollak; m. Bridget Denison McCall 1943; one s. one d.; ed. Charterhouse and Christ Church, Oxford (Hon. student); Chair. Anglo-American Corpn. of S. Africa Ltd. –1983, Chair. De Beers Consolidated Mines Ltd. 1957–84 (Dir. 1934–94), Chair. E. Oppenheimer and Son; M.P. 1947–58; Chancellor Cape Town Univ. 1967–96; Hon. D.Econ. (Natal); Hon. LL.D. (Leeds, Witwatersrand and Rhodes); Hon. D.Litt. (Cape Town). *Leisure interests:* horse breeding, racing. *Address:* P.O. Box 61631, Marshalltown 2107; Brenthurst, Federation Road, Parktown, Johannesburg, South Africa (Home).

OPPENHEIMER, Nicholas Frank, M.A.; South African business executive; b. 8 June 1945, Johannesburg; s. of Harry F. Oppenheimer (q.v.); m. Orcillia M. L. Lasch 1968; one s.; ed. Harrow School and Christ Church, Oxford; Chair. De Beers Consolidated Mines Ltd., Anglo-American Gold Investment Co. 1990–; Deputy Chair. Anglo-American Corpn. of S.A. Ltd.; Dir. Elandsrand Gold Mining Co. Ltd., De Beers Holdings Ltd., De Beers Industrial Corpn. Ltd., E. Oppenheimer & Son. (Pty.) Ltd., Vaal Reefs Exploration and Mining Co. Ltd.; Dir. (non-exec.) Minorco. *Leisure interests:* squash, golf. *Address:* Little Brenthurst, Third Avenue, P.O. Box 61631, Marshalltown 2107, South Africa.

OPPENLÄNDER, Karl Heinrich, D.ECON.; German economist; b. 17 Jan. 1932, Dörzbach; m. Cäcilie Oppenländer 1958; one s. one d.; ed. Univ. of Munich; entered IFO Inst. for Econ. Research 1958, Head of Dept. 1966, mem. Exec. Cttee. 1972, Pres. (Prof.) 1976–; Lecturer, Univ. of Tübingen 1975, Univ. of Munich 1976–, Univ. of Augsburg 1980–83. *Publications:* Die moderne Wachstumstheorie 1963, Der investitionsinduzierte technische Fortschritt 1976. *Address:* IFO Institut für Wirtschaftsforschung, Poschingerstrasse 5, 81679 Munich, Germany. *Telephone:* 089-92-24-279.

ORAZMUKHAMEDOV, Nury Orazovich; Turkmenistan politician; b. 1949, Mary; ed. Turkmen Polytech. Inst.; master, engineer, chief engineer Turkmencentrstroi 1971–; head Ashkhabad construction units; Deputy Chair. State Construction Cttee. 1990–91; Minister of Construction of Turkmenistan 1991–94; Minister of Construction and Architecture 1994–95; Head of Admin. Khikim Ashkhabad Feb. 1995; Amb. of Turkmenistan to Russian Fed. Dec. 1996–. *Address:* Embassy of Turkmenistan, Filippovsky per. 22, 121019 Moscow, Russia (Office). *Telephone:* (095) 291-66-36. *Fax:* (095) 291-09-35.

ORBÁN, Viktor, LL.D., PH.D.; Hungarian politician and lawyer; b. 31 May 1963, Székesfehérvár; s. of Győző Orbán; m.; one s. two d.; ed. Loránd Eötvös Univ. of Budapest and Pembroke Coll., Oxford; trainee sociologist Mans. School of Ministry of Agric. and Food Industry; researcher Middle'Europe Research Group 1989–91; co-f. Hungarian opposition group Fed. of Young Democrats (FIDESZ) 1988, Spokesman 1989; represented FIDESZ political sub-cttee. of Opposition Round Table Discussion 1989; M.P., leader of FIDESZ Parl. Group 1990–94, Prime Minister (FIDESZ) July 1998–; Chair. Parl. Cttee. on European Integration Affairs 1994–98; Pres. FIDESZ 1993–, New Atlantic Initiative Hungarian Cttee. 1996–98; Vice-Pres. Liberal Int. 1992–, mem. Bureau 1993–; rep. of Hungary Trilateral Comm. *Leisure interest:* playing soccer. *Address:* H-1055 Budapest, Kossuth Lajos tér 1–3; 1357 Budapest, Pf. 2, Hungary. *Telephone:* 268-3000, 269-5353. *Fax:* 268-4740.

ORBELIAN, Konstantin Agaparonovich; Armenian composer; b. 29 July 1928, Armavir; s. of A. Orbelian and S. (née Atarbecova) Orbelian; m. Nellie Orbelian 1986; ed. Yerevan Conservatoire (Mirzoyan composition class); mem. CPSU 1961–89; work with Armenian State Orchestra of Light Music 1946–, Artistic Dir. and Chief Conductor 1956–; lives in U.S.A.; People's Artist of Armenia 1974, People's Artist of U.S.S.R. 1979. *Compositions include:* Immortality (ballet) 1969, two symphonies 1961, 1967, string quartet 1956, film music, popular songs. *Leisure interest:* sport. *Address:* Demirchyan Str. 27, Apt. 12, 3750002 Yerevan, Armenia. *Telephone:* (02) 52-35-26.

ORDJHONIKIDZE, Yosif Nikolayevich; Georgian/Russian politician; b. 9 Feb. 1948, Borzhomi, Georgia; m.; two c.; ed. Tbilisi Polytech. Inst.;

different posts Tbilisi Aviation factory; about 20 years' Komsomol service; First Sec. Regional Komsomol Cttee., First Sec. Cen. Komsomol Cttee. of Ga. Sec. U.S.S.R. Cen. Komsomol Cttee.; Pres. Union of Innovation Enterprises 1989; Deputy Chair., First Deputy Chair. Exec. Cttee. Moscow City Council 1990–; Deputy Prime Minister Moscow Govt., Head Dept. of Int. Relations 1992–. *Address:* Moscow Government, Tverskaya str. 13, 103032 Moscow, Russia (Office). *Telephone:* (095) 229 6360, 229 0812 (Office).

OREFFICE, Paul F(austo); B.S.; American company executive; b. 29 Nov. 1927, Venice, Italy; s. of Max and Elena (Friedenberg) Oreffice; m. Franca Giuseppina Ruffini 1956; one s. one d.; ed. Purdue Univ.; joined Dow Chemical Int., Midland, Mich. 1953, Mediterranean Area Sales Man., Milan, Italy 1955–56, Man. Dow Quimica do Brazil, São Paulo 1956–63, Gen. Man. Dow. Int., Spain 1963–65, Gen. Man. Dow Chemical Latin America 1965–67, Pres. Dow Chemical Inter-American Ltd. 1967–69, Financial Vice-Pres. The Dow Chemical Co. 1969–75, Dir. Dow Chemical Co. 1971–, Pres. Dow Chemical U.S.A. 1975–78, Chair. Exec. Cttee. Dow Chemical Co. 1978–87, Pres. and C.E.O. 1978–86, Chair., Pres. and C.E.O. 1986–87, Chair. Bd. 1987–92; Dir. Cigna Corpn., Northern Telecom Ltd. 1983, The Coca-Cola Company 1985, Morgan Stanley Group Inc. 1987; Chair. American Enterprise Inst., Bd. of Overseers Inst. for Civil Justice; Bd. of Govs. Nat. Parkinson Foundation; mem. The Business Council; Encomienda del Mérito Civil (Spain) 1966; Hon. D.Eng. (Purdue) 1976, Hon. Dr. Industrial Management (Lawrence Inst. of Tech.), Science (Saginaw Valley State Coll.), Business Admin. (Tri-State Univ.). *Leisure interests:* tennis, bridge, golf, various other sports. *Address:* c/o 2030 Willard H. Dow Center, Midland, MI 48674, U.S.A. (Office).

O'REGAN, (Andrew) Brendan; Irish business executive; b. 15 May 1917, Co. Clare; s. of James and Norah O'Regan; m. (Rita) Margaret Barrow 1950; two s. three d.; ed. Blackrock Coll., Dublin; Comptroller, Sales and Catering, Shannon Airport 1943–73; Chair. Bord Fáilte Eireann 1957–73, Shannon Free Airport Devt. Co. 1959–78, State Agencies Devt. Co-operation Org. (DEVCO) 1974–79, 1988–89; Chair. Co-operation N. 1979–82, Pres. 1982–; Pres. Co-operation Ireland Inc. (N.Y.) 1982–90; Chair. Irish Peace Inst. 1984–90, Pres. 1990–; Chair. Shannon Centre for Int. Co-operation 1987–90, Pres. 1990–; Fellow, Inst. of Engineers of Ireland 1977, Irish Hotel and Catering Inst. 1977; Hon. LL.D. (Nat. Univ. of Ireland) 1978; United Dominions Trust Endeavour Award for Tourism 1973, American Soc. of Travel Agents—Hall of Fame 1977, British Airways Tourism Endeavour Award 1980, Clare Person of the Year 1983, Rotary's Paul Harris Award. *Publications:* numerous speeches and articles on peace through managed co-operation. *Leisure interests:* reading, walking. *Address:* The Bungalow, Main Street, Newmarket-on-Fergus, Co. Clare; 51/52 Marina Village, Malahide, Co. Dublin, Ireland. *Telephone:* 01-8454523.

O'REILLY, Anthony J. F., B.C.L.; company executive; b. 7 May 1936, Dublin, Ireland; s. of John Patrick and Aileen (O'Connor) O'Reilly; m. 1st Susan Cameron 1962 (divorced); three s. three d.; m. 2nd Chryss Goulandris 1991; ed. Univ. Coll., Dublin; qualified as solicitor 1958; Demonstrator and Lecturer, Univ. Coll., Cork 1960–62; Personal Asst. to Chair., Suttons Ltd., Cork 1960–62; Dir. Robert McCowen & Sons Ltd., Tralee 1961–62; Gen. Man. Bord Bainne (Irish Dairy Bd.) 1962–66; Man. Dir. and C.E.O., Comhlucht Siuicre Eireann Teo. (Irish Sugar Co.) 1966–69; Jt. Man. Dir. Heinz-Erin Ltd. 1967–70, Man. Dir. H. J. Heinz Co. Ltd., U.K. 1969–71, Sr. Vice-Pres. N. America and Pacific H. J. Heinz Co. 1971–72, Exec. Vice-Pres. and C.O.O. 1972–73, Pres. and C.O.O. 1973–79, Chair. 1978–, Pres. 1979–90, C.E.O. 1979–98; Chair; European Advisory Bd. Bankers Trust 1992–, Independent Newspapers Group, Newspapers Holdings (fmrly. Argus Newspapers, S.A.), Fitzwilton PLC, Atlantic Resources, Dublin; numerous other commercial appointments; Fellow B.I.M., R.S.A.; Dr. h.c. (Bradford) 1991, Hon. LL.D. (Leicester) 1992. *Publications:* Prospect 1962, Developing Creative Management 1970, The Conservative Consumer 1971, Food for Thought 1972. *Address:* H. J. Heinz Company, P.O. Box 57, 600 Grant Street, Pittsburgh, PA 15219; Mobil Corporation, 150 East Forty Second Street, New York, NY 10017 (Office); 835 Fox Chapel Road, Pittsburgh, PA 15238, U.S.A.

O'REILLY, Francis Joseph, B.A., B.A.I., LL.D., M.R.I.A.; Irish university chancellor and fmr. banker; b. 15 Nov. 1922, Dublin; s. of Lieut.-Col. C. J. O'Reilly; m. Teresa Williams 1950; three s. seven d.; ed. Ampleforth Coll. and Trinity Coll. Dublin; Chair. Irish Distillers Group 1966–83; Dir. Ulster Bank 1961–90, Chair. 1982–89; Dir. Nat. Westminster Bank 1982–89; Chair. Coll. des Irlandais, Paris 1988–; Chancellor, Univ. of Dublin 1985–; Hon. LL.D. (Dublin) 1978, (Nat. Univ. of Ireland) 1986. *Leisure interests:* racing, gardening, reading. *Address:* Trinity College, Dublin 2 (Office); Rathmore, Naas, Co. Kildare, Ireland (Home). *Telephone:* (01) 772941 (Office); (045) 862136 (Home).

OREJA AGUIRRE, Marcelino; Spanish diplomatist and government official; b. 13 Feb. 1935; entered diplomatic service 1958; Dir. Tech. Office of Minister of Foreign Affairs 1962; fmr. Asst. Dir., Prof. of Foreign Affairs at Escuela Diplomática; mem. Dels. to UN, IMF, IDB, OECD; mem. interministerial cttee. drafting bill for religious freedom; Dir. of Int. Relations, Banco de España 1971–74; Under-Sec. for Information and Tourism 1974, for Foreign Affairs Dec. 1975; Minister of Foreign Affairs 1976–80; elected Deputy for Guipúzcoa and Alava in 1979 and 1982; Govt. Rep. in Basque Country 1980–82; Sec. Gen. Council of Europe 1984–89; EC Commr. for Energy, Eurotom Supply Agency and Transport 1994–95, for Relations with European Parl., with mem. States, Culture and Public Affairs Jan. 1995–; Senator by royal appointment June 1977. *Address:* European Union, 200 rue de la Loi, 1049 Brussels, Belgium; 81 Núñez de Balboa, E-28006 Madrid, Spain.

OREK, Osman Nuri; Cypriot politician and lawyer; b. 26 Dec. 1925, Nicosia; s. of the late Ahmet Mustafa Orek and of Muride Ahmet; m. Neriman Orek 1958; one s. one d.; ed. Turkish Lycée, Nicosia, Univ. of Istanbul and Middle Temple, London; Founder-mem. Cyprus-Turkish Asscn., London, Chair. 1951–52; Sec. Nicosia Branch, Cyprus Turkish Nat. Union Party 1953–55, Sec.-Gen. 1955–60; Deputy Chair. High Council of Evcaf 1956–60; rep. Turkish Cypriot Community at London Conf. 1959 and subsequent Joint Cttee.; Minister of Defence 1959–67; mem. Exec. Council of Turkish Cypriot Provisional Admin. for Defence 1967–74, concurrently for Internal Affairs 1967–70, and External Affairs 1967–72; mem. Exec. Council of Autonomous Turkish Cypriot Admin. for Vice-Presidency and Defence 1974–75; Vice-Pres. "Turkish Federated State of Cyprus" ("TFSC") 1975–76, Minister of Defence 1975–76; Pres. "TFSC" Legis. Ass. 1976–78; Prime Minister April–Dec. 1978; Leader of Nat. Unity Party 1978; M.P. "TFSC" 1979–81; mem. Constituent Ass. T.R.N.C. 1983–85; Chair. Bar Council of TRNC 1988–91; Adjunct Lecturer in Law, Faculty of Econs. and Business Admin., E. Mediterranean Univ., Famagusta, TRNC, 1989–; Dr. h.c. (E. Mediterranean Univ.) 1997; Grand Cross of Merit, Fed. Repub. of Germany. *Publications:* International Political Institutions 1990, Orek's Student Companion for Business Law 1991, An Introduction to Political Organisation 1994. *Leisure interests:* swimming, water-skiing, hunting. *Address:* Orek and Associates Law Office, Mufti Raci Street, Nicosia, Mersin 10 (Office); 10 Ismail Beyoglu Street, P.O. Box 506, Lefkoşa, Mersin 10, Turkey (Home). *Telephone:* 392-22-72859 (Office); 392-22-86283 (Home). *Fax:* 392-22-86399.

OREKHOV, Ruslan Gennadyevich; Russian politician; b. 14 Oct. 1963, Kalinin (now Tver); m.; two c.; ed. Kazakh State Univ.; engineer-researcher Kazakh State Univ. 1985–87; Head of div. Alma-Ata Dist. Exec. Cttee. 1987–88; instructor Moscow Dist. Exec. Cttee. 1989–90; expert U.S.S.R. Union of Lawyers 1990; leading expert Cttee. on Law Supreme Soviet of Russian Fed. 1990–91; Head Div. of Service of State Counsellors Russian Fed. 1991–93; Head State Dept. of Law; Russian Presidency 1993–94; Co-Chair. Expert Council on Law, Russian Presidency 1994–96; Deputy Head of Admin. Russian Presidency, Head Dept. of State Law 1996–. *Address:* Ilyinka str. 8/4, entrance 20, Moscow, Russia (Office). *Telephone:* (095) 206 4578 (Office).

ORELLANA, José Roberto, M.S.; Salvadorean banker; b. 20 Jan. 1944, San Salvador; s. of Roberto Orellana and Aida Milla; m. Julia Raquel Aguilar 1977; four c.; ed. Trinity Coll., Conn., U.S.A., Stanford Univ.; Vice-Pres., Gen. Man. Banco Cuscatlán 1971–81; Dir. Fundación Salvadoreña para el Desarrollo Económico y Social (FUSADES) 1984–89; now Pres. Banco Cen. de Reserva de El Salvador; Alt. Gov. Interamerican Devt. Bank 1989–95, IMF 1989–, World Bank 1989–, Banco Centroamericano de Integración Económica 1989–. *Address:* Banco Central de Reserva de El Salvador, Alameda Juan Pablo II y 17 Avenida Norte, San Salvador, El Salvador. *Telephone:* 281-8402. *Fax:* 281-8401.

ORGAD, Ben Zion; Israeli composer; b. 21 Aug. 1926, Germany; two s.; ed. Acad. of Music in Jerusalem and Brandeis Univ., U.S.A.; studied violin with Kinory and Bergman and composition with Paul Ben-Haim and Josef Tal; studied in U.S.A. under Aaron Copland (q.v.) and Irving Fine; Supervisor of Musical Educ., Israel Ministry of Educ. and Culture 1950–88; Chair. Israel Composers' League; recipient of several awards for compositions. *Compositions include:* cantatas: The Story of the Spies (UNESCO Koussevitsky Prize 1952), Isaiah's Vision; orchestral: Building a King's Stage, Choreographic Sketches, Movements on 'A', Kaleidoscope, Music for Horn and Orchestra, Ballad for Orchestra, Dialogues on the First Scroll; Hatsvi Israel (baritone and orchestra), Suffering for Redemption (mezzo-soprano, choir and orchestra), Out of the Dust (for solo and instruments); Ballada (for violin), Taksim (for harp), Monologue (for viola); works for soloists and orchestra, songs, piano pieces, etc. *Address:* 14 Bloch Street, Tel-Aviv 64161, Israel (Home). *Telephone:* 5242833.

ORGAN, (Harold) Bryan; British artist; b. 31 Aug. 1935, Leicester; s. of Harold Victor and Helen Dorothy Organ; m. 2nd Sandra Mary Mills 1982; ed. Loughborough Coll. of Art; Royal Acad. Schools, London; Lecturer in Drawing and Painting, Loughborough 1959–65; One-man Exhbns.: Leicester Museum and Art Gallery 1959, Redfern Gallery, London 1967, 1969, 1971, 1973, 1975, 1978, 1980, Leicester 1973, 1976, New York 1976, Baukunst, Cologne 1977, Turin 1981; Represented: Kunsthalle, Darmstadt 1968, Mostra Mercatao d'Arte Contemporanea, Florence 1969, 3rd Int. Exhbns. of Drawing Germany 1970, São Paulo Museum of Art, Brazil; Works in private and public collections in England, France, Germany, Italy, Switzerland, U.S.A., Canada, Brazil, Hon. M.A. (Loughborough) 1974, Hon. D.Litt. (Leicester) 1985. *Portraits include:* Sir Michael Tippett 1966, David Hicks 1968; Mary Quant 1969, Princess Margaret 1970, Elton John 1973, Viscount Stockton 1980, The Prince of Wales 1980, The Princess of Wales 1981, Lord Denning 1982, Sir James Callaghan 1982, H.R.H. The Duke of Edinburgh 1983. *Leisure interest:* cricket. *Address:* c/o Redfern Gallery, 20 Cork Street, London, W1X 2HL; The Stables, Marston Trussell, Nr. Market Harborough, Leics, LE16 9TX, England. *Telephone:* 0171-734 1732 (London).

O'RIORDAN, Timothy, M.A., PH.D., F.R.S.A.; British professor of environmental sciences; b. 21 Feb. 1942, Edinburgh; s. of Kevin O'Riordan and Norah O'Riordan; m. Ann Philip 1968 (died 1992); two d.; ed. Univs. of Edinburgh and Cambridge and Cornell Univ.; Asst. Prof. Dept. of Geography, Simon Fraser Univ. Vancouver, B.C. 1967–74; Visiting lecturer, Univ. of Canterbury, New Zealand 1970; Visiting Assoc. Prof. Clark Univ., Worcester, Mass. 1972; Reader Univ. of East Anglia 1974, Prof. of Environmental Sciences 1980–; Chair. Environment Cttee. Broads Authority 1989–, Environment Science & Soc. Programme, European Science Foundation 1989–; Adviser Environmental Research Directorate 1996–97; mem. Environmental Advisory Council, Dow Chemicals 1992–, Eastern Group PLC 1995–; D. L. Norfolk 1998; Gill Memorial Prize, Royal Geographical Soc. *Publications:* Environmentalism 1976, Countryside Conflicts 1986, Sizewell B: An Anatomy of the Inquiry 1987, The Greening of the Machinery of Government 1990; ed. Interpreting the Precautionary Principle 1994, The Politics of Climate Change in Europe 1996, Ecotaxation 1996. *Leisure interests:* classical double bass playing, jogging, cycling, swimming. *Address:* School of Environmental Sciences, University of East Anglia, Norwich, NR4 7TJ; Wheatlands, Hethersett Lane, Colney, Norwich, NR4 7TT, England. *Telephone:* (01603) 810534. *Fax:* (01603) 250588.

ORLOV, Viktor Petrovich, CAND. GEOL. SC., D.SC. ECON.; Russian politician; b. 23 March 1940, Chernogorsk, Krasnoyarsk Region; s. of Petr Orlov and Eva Orlova; m.; three d.; ed. Tomsk State Univ., Acad. of Nat. Econ. at U.S.S.R. Council of Ministers; geologist, chief geologist, team leader W. Siberian Geological Survey 1968–75; Chief Engineer Geological Exploration, Iran 1975–78; chief geologist, Deputy Head Geological Div. Amalgamation Tsentrgeologiya 1979–81, Dir. Gen. 1986–90; Deputy Head Geology and Production Depts., Ministry of Geology Russian Fed. 1981–84, 1986–; Deputy Minister of Geology U.S.S.R. 1990–; First Deputy Chair. State Cttee. on Geology Russian Fed. 1990–92; Chair. Cttee. on Geology and Use of Mineral Resources Russian Fed. 1992–96; Minister of Natural Resources Russian Fed. 1996–. *Leisure interests:* fishing, hunting. *Address:* Ministry of Natural Resources, B. Gruzinskaya str. 4/6, 123812 Moscow, Russia (Office). *Telephone:* (095) 254 7633. *Fax:* (095) 943 0013.

ORLOV, Yuri Fedorovich; Russian physicist and human rights activist; b. 13 Aug 1924, Moscow; worked in a factory; served in army in World War II; ed. Moscow Univ.; mem. staff of Inst. of Theoretical and Experimental Physics until dismissed for political reasons 1956; subsequently worked in Yerevan; obtained doctorate 1963, became an expert on particle acceleration; mem. staff Inst. of Physics 1956–62, Inst. of Earth Magnetism 1962–73; Corresp. mem. Armenian Acad. of Sciences; returned to Moscow 1972; dismissed from post after pleading on behalf of Andrei Sakharov 1973; co-founder and Chair. Helsinki Monitoring Group following signing of Helsinki Agreement 1975; arrested 1977, on trial 1978 and sentenced to seven years in strict-regime labour camp followed by five years' exile; wrote account of prison conditions, smuggled out and printed in Belgian newspaper 1979; released from labour camp and exiled to Kobyai, nr. Yakutsk, Siberia 1984; left U.S.S.R. Oct. 1986, living in U.S.A.; U.S.S.R. Citizenship restored 1990.

ORME, Baron (Life Peer), cr. 1997, of Salford in the County of Greater Manchester; **Rt. Hon. Stanley Orme,** P.C.; British politician; b. 5 April 1923, Sale, Cheshire; s. of Sherwood Orme; m. Irene Mary Harris 1951; ed. elementary and tech. schools, Nat. Council of Labour Colls. and Workers' Educ. Asscn. classes; Shop Steward, Amalgamated Union of Engineering Workers (AUEW) 1949–64; Councillor, Sale Borough Council 1957–65; M.P. for Salford W. 1964–83, for Salford E. 1983–97; Minister of State, Northern Ireland Office 1974–76, Dept. of Health and Social Security April-Sept. 1976; Minister for Social Security 1976–79; Opposition Spokesman for Health and Social Security 1979–80, for Industry 1980–83, for Energy 1983–87; Chair. Parl. Labour Party 1987–92; Chair. AUEW Parl. Group of Labour M.P.s 1977; Hon. Dr. Sc. (Salford) 1985. *Address:* 8 Northwood Grove, Sale, Cheshire, M33 3DZ, England (Home).

ORMESSON, Comte Jean d'; French author, journalist and international official; b. 16 June 1925; s. of Marquis d'Ormesson; nephew of late Comte Wladimir d'Ormesson; m. Françoise Béghin 1962; one d.; ed. Ecole Normale Supérieure; Deputy Sec.-Gen. Int. Council for Philosophy and Humanistic studies (UNESCO) 1950–71, Sec.-Gen. 1971; staff of various govt. ministers 1958–66; Deputy Ed. Diogène (int. journal) 1952–72, mem. Man. Cttee. 1971–; mem. Council ORTF 1960–62, Programme Cttee. 1973; mem. Control Comm. of Cinema 1962–69; mem. Editorial Cttee. Editions Gallimard 1972–74; Ed.-in-Chief, Columnist, Le Figaro 1974–77, Dir.-Gen. 1976–, leader writer, columnist 1977–; mem. Acad. Française 1973; Pres., Soc. des amis de Jules Romains 1974–; Grand Prix du Roman (Acad. Française) for novel La gloire de l'empire 1971; Officier, Légion d'honneur, Commdr. des Arts et des Lettres, Officier, Ordre nat. du Mérite, Chevalier des Palmes académiques. *Publications:* L'amour est un plaisir 1956, Du côté de chez Jean 1959, Un amour pour rien 1960, Au revoir et merci 1966, Les illusions de la mer 1968, La gloire de l'empire 1971, Au plaisir de Dieu 1974, Le vagabond qui passe sous une ombrelle trouée 1978, Dieu, sa vie, son oeuvre 1981, Mon dernier rève sera pour vous 1982, Jean qui grogne et Jean qui rit 1984, Le vent du soir 1985, Tous les hommes en sont fous 1985, Bonheur à San Miniato 1987, Garçon de quoi écrire (jtly). 1989 (prix de Mémorial 1990), Histoire du juif errant 1991, Tant que vous penserez à moi, entretien avec Emmanuel Berl 1992, La Douane de mer 1994, Presque rien sur presque tout 1996, Casimir mène la grande vie 1997, Une autre histoire de la littérature française 1997; numerous articles in Le Figaro, Le Monde, France-Soir, Paris Match, etc. *Address:* c/o Le Figaro, 37 rue du Louvre, Paris 75001; 1 rue Miollis, 75015 Paris (Offices); 10 avenue du Parc-Saint-James, 92200 Neuilly-sur-Seine, France (Home).

ORMOND, Julia; British actress; b. 1965; m. Rory Edwards (divorced); ed. Guildford High School, Cranleigh School, Farnham Art School and Webber Douglas Acad.; worked in repertory, Crucible Theatre, Sheffield, Everyman Theatre, Cheltenham and on tour with Royal Exchange Theatre, Manchester; appeared in Faith, Hope and Charity (Lyric, Hammersmith), Treats (Hampstead Theatre); West End debut in Anouilh's The Rehearsal (Almeida); TV appearances: Traffik (Channel 4 series), Ruth Rendell Mysteries, Young Catherine 1990. *Films:* The Baby of Macon, Legends of the Fall, First Knight, Sabrina, Smilla's Sense of Snow 1997, The Barber of Siberia 1998. *Address:* c/o CAA, 9830 Wilshire Boulevard, Beverly Hills, CA 90212, U.S.A.

ORMOND, Richard Louis, M.A.; British museum director; b. 16 Jan. 1939, Bath; s. of Conrad E. Ormond and Dorothea Gibbons; m. Leonée Ormond 1963; two s.; ed. Marlborough Coll., Brown Univ. U.S.A. and Christ Church, Oxford; Asst. Keeper, Nat. Portrait Gallery 1965–75, Deputy Dir. 1975–83; Head of Picture Dept. Nat. Maritime Museum 1983–86; Dir. Nat. Maritime Museum 1986–. *Publications:* J.S. Sargent 1970, Catalogue of Early Victorian Portraits in the National Portrait Gallery 1973, Lord Leighton 1975, Sir Edwin Landseer 1982, The Great Age of Sail 1986, F.X. Winterhalter and the Courts of Europe 1987, Frederic, Lord Leighton (co-author) 1996, Sargent Abroad (co-author) 1997, John Singer Sargent: The Early Portraits (co-author) 1998, John Singer Sargent (co-author) 1998. *Leisure interests:* opera, theatre. *Address:* 8 Holly Terrace, London, N6 6LX, England. *Telephone:* 0181-340 4684.

ORMOS, Mária, PH.D.; Hungarian historian; b. 1 Oct. 1930, Debrecen; d. of János Ormos and Elza Förster; one s. one d.; ed. Kossuth Lajos Univ., Debrecen; Asst. lecturer, Historic Science Inst. 1963; mem. Hungarian Acad. of Sciences 1993, mem. of Presidium; Univ. Prof. 1982; Rector Janus Pannonius Univ. of Pécs 1984–92; mem. Nat. Cttee of Historians; Pres. Italian-Hungarian Mixed Cttee of Historians; Vice-Pres. Asscn. d'histoire des relations internationales; mem. European Acad. of Arts, Sciences and Humanities. *Publications:* Franciaország és a keleti biztonság 1931–36 (France and the Eastern security) 1969, Merénylet Marseilleben (Assassination in Marseille) 1984, Mussolini: a political portrait 1987, Nazism and Fascism, 1987, Never as long as I shall live 1989, Civitas fidelissima 1921 1990, From Padova to Trianon 1991, Hitler 1993, Magyarország a világháborúk korában 1914–45 (Hungary in the Age of the World Wars 1914–45) 1997. *Leisure interests:* music, books, theatre. *Address:* c/o Janus Pannonius University, 7621 Pécs, Rókus u. 2, Hungary. *Telephone:* (36-72) 315-942.

ORNSTEIN, Donald Samuel, PH.D.; American mathematician; b. 30 July 1934; s. of Harry Ornstein and Rose (Wisner) Ornstein; m. Shari Richman 1964; two s. one d.; ed. Swarthmore Coll. and Univ. of Chicago; mem. Inst. for Advanced Study, Princeton 1956–58; Instructor, Univ. of Wisconsin 1958–60; Asst. Prof. Stanford Univ. 1960–63, Sloan Fellow and Assoc. Prof. 1963–65, Assoc. Prof. 1965–66, Prof. of Math. 1966–; Visiting Prof. Cornell Univ. and New York Univ. (Courant Inst.) 1967–68, Hebrew Univ. Jerusalem 1975–76, Mathematical Sciences Research Inst. Berkeley 1983–84; mem. N.A.S., American Acad. of Arts and Sciences; Bocher Prize, American Math. Soc. 1974. *Publications:* mathematical papers in many journals since 1959. *Address:* Department of Mathematics, Stanford University, Stanford, CA 94305-2125 (Office); 857 Tolman Drive, Stanford, CA 94305, U.S.A. (Home). *Fax:* (415) 725-4066 (Office).

O'ROURKE, Mary; Irish politician; b. 31 May 1937, Athlone; d. of P. J. Lenihan; m. Enda O'Rourke; two s.; ed. St. Peter's Convent, Univ. Coll. Dublin and St. Patrick's Coll. Maynooth, Co. Kildare; fmr. secondary school teacher; mem. Westmeath County Council 1979–; mem. Dáil 1982; Minister for Educ. 1987–91, of Health 1991–92, for Trade and Marketing 1992–93; Fianna Fáil. *Address:* Aisling, Arcadia, Athlone, Co. Westmeath, Ireland. *Telephone:* (0902) 75065. *Fax:* (0902) 78218.

ORR, Christopher John, R.A.; British artist; b. 8 April 1943, London; m. Catherine Terris 1985; one s. one d.; ed. Royal Coll. of Art; worked as artist and teacher, latterly as a tutor and visiting lecturer, Royal Coll. of Art 1976–, Prof. and Course Dir. of Printmaking 1998–; one man touring exhbns. The Complete Chris Orr 1976, Many Mansions 1990; numerous exhbns. worldwide; Fellow Royal Soc. of Painters and Printmakers. *Address:* 7 Bristle Hill, Buckingham, MK18 1EZ, England. *Telephone:* (01280) 815255. *Fax:* (01280) 815255.

ORR, Sir David Alexander, Kt., M.C., LL.D., F.R.S.A.; British business executive; b. 10 May 1922, Dublin, Ireland; s. of Canon A. W. F. Orr and Grace Robinson; m. Phoebe R. Davis; three d.; ed. High School and Trinity Coll., Dublin; with Unilever 1948–82; Marketing Dir., Hindustan Lever, Bombay 1955; mem. Overseas Cttee., Unilever 1960; Vice-Pres. Lever Brothers Co., New York 1963, Pres. 1965; Dir. Unilever PLC 1967–82, Vice-Chair. 1970–74, Chair. 1974–82; Chair. British Council 1985–92; Dir. Rio Tinto-Zinc Corpn. 1981–92, Shell Transport and Trading Co. 1982–92, Inchcape PLC 1982–92 (Chair. 1983–86, 1991–92, Deputy Chair. 1986–91), Bank of Ireland 1982–90; Chair. Sea Perfect PLC 1994–96; Pres. Liverpool School of Tropical Medicine 1981–89, Vice-Pres. 1989–; Pres. Coll. of Speech and Language Therapists 1992–96; Children's Medical Charity 1990–96; Trustee Leverhulme Trust 1979–81, Chair. 1982–91; Chair. Charles Wallace (India) Trust 1991–98; Chancellor The Queen's Univ. Belfast 1992–; Council mem. L.S.E.; Hon. LL.D. (Trinity Coll. Dublin) 1978, (Liverpool Univ.) 1989, (Queen's Univ., Belfast) 1992, (Nat. Univ. of Ireland) 1993; Hon. D.Univ. (Surrey) 1982; Commdr. of Order of Oranje Nassau (Netherlands) 1979. *Leisure interests:* books, travel and sport. *Address:* 81 Lyall Mews West, London, SW1X 8DJ; Home Farm House, Shackleford, Godalming, Surrey, GU8 6AH, England. *Telephone:* (01483) 810350 (Home).

ORREGO VICUÑA, Francisco, PH.D.; Chilean lawyer and diplomatist; b. 12 April 1942, Santiago; m. Soledad Bauza; three c.; ed. schools in Chile, Argentina, Spain and Egypt, Univ. of Chile and L.S.E.; fmr. Dir. Inst. of Int. Studies Univ. of Chile; fmr. Visiting Prof. Stanford Univ., Univ. of Paris II Law School, Univ. of Miami Law School; participated in projects for Acad. of Int. Law, The Hague, UNITAR and various studies and projects undertaken by univs. in Europe, U.S.A., Asia and Latin America; fmr. legal adviser to OAS; fmr. Del. Law of Sea Conf.; fmr. int. ed., El Mercurio (daily newspaper); Amb. to U.K. 1983–85; Prof. of Int. Law, Inst. of Int. Studies, Law School, Univ. of Chile 1985–; Pres. Chilean Council on Foreign Relations; mem. Chilean-U.S. Comm. for Settlement of Disputes; Conciliator and Arbitrator of ICSID 1995–; Judge and Vice-Pres. Admin. Tribunal of IBRD; Commr. UN Compensation Comm. 1998; mem. Inst. of Int. Law. *Publications:* Antarctic Resources Policy 1983, Antarctic Mineral Exploitation 1988, The Exclusive Economic Zone 1989, The Changing International Law of High Seas Fisheries 1999, and other books and articles. *Address:* Institute of International Studies, University of Chile, P.O. Box 14187 Suc. 21, Santiago 9, Chile. *Telephone:* 2745377. *Fax:* 2740155.

ORRELL-JONES, Keith, M.A.; British business executive; b. 15 July 1937; s. of Francis George Orrell-Jones and Elsie Orrell-Jones; m. Hilary Kathleen Orrell-Jones (née Pegram) 1961; four s.; ed. The High School, Newcastle-under-Lyme, St. John's Coll., Cambridge; Chief Exec. ARC Ltd. 1986–89; Dir. Consolidated Gold Fields PLC 1989; Dir. Blue Circle Industries PLC 1990, Chief Exec. 1992–; N.E. Dir. Smiths Industries PLC 1990, Chair. 1998–. *Leisure interests:* music, particularly opera, field sports. *Address:* 765 Finchley Road, London, NW11 8DS, England.

ORSETTI, Christian Ernest, L. EN D.; French diplomatist; b. 1 April 1923, Montpellier; s. of Antoine Orsetti and Marie-Louise Couffinhal; m. Marie-Antoinette Vincent 1946; three d.; ed. Univ. of Montpellier, Ecole Libre des Sciences Politiques; holder of numerous government posts since 1945, including: Sec.-Gen. for Haute-Marne 1952, Tarn-et-Garonne 1955, Fougères 1960; Cabinet Dir. for Minister of Agric. 1962–64, then Minister for Material Resources 1966–67; Auditor to Inst. des Hautes Etudes de Défense Nat. 1972–73; Prefect for Martinique 1973–75; with Ministry of Foreign Affairs 1977; Hon. Prefect 1989; Amb. of Monaco to France 1977–; Vice-Pres. then Pres. Jury du prix des Ambassadeurs; mem. and Chair. Bd. Dirs. Institut de paléontologie humaine, Fondation Prince Albert de Monaco; Officier Légion d'honneur, Commdr. Ordre nat. du Mérite, Ordre du Mérite Agricole, Officier des Palmes Académiques, etc. *Address:* 12 avenue Georges-Mandel, 75116 Paris (Office); Ambassade de la Principauté de Monaco, 22 boulevard Suchet, 75116 Paris (Office); 6 rue Foucault, 75116 Paris, France (Home).

ORTEGA SAAVEDRA, Daniel; Nicaraguan politician and fmr. resistance leader; b. 11 Nov. 1945, La Libertad, Chontales; s. of Daniel Ortega and Lidia Saavedra; m. Rosario Murillo; seven c.; ed. Univ. Centroamericano, Managua; joined Frente Sandinista 1963; active in various underground resistance movts. against regime of Anastasio Somoza from 1959 and was several times imprisoned and tortured for revolutionary activities; ed. El Estudiante, official publ. of Frente Estudiantil Revolucionaria and directed org. of Comités Cívicos Populares in Managua 1965; mem. Nat. Directorate of FSLN (Sandinista Liberation Front) 1966–67; imprisoned 1967–74; resumed position with FSLN and with José Benito Escobar became involved in further revolutionary activities; fought on front in two-year mil. offensive which overthrew Somoza regime 1979; mem. Junta of Nat. Reconstruction Govt. 1979, Co-ordinator of Junta 1981–85, Pres. of Nicaragua 1985–90; Gen. Sec. FSLN. *Address:* c/o Frente Sandinista de Liberación Nacional, Costado Oeste Parque El Carmen, Managua, Nicaragua. *Telephone:* (2) 66-0845. *Fax:* (2) 66-1560.

ORTIZ, Cristina; Brazilian concert pianist; b. 17 April 1950, Bahia, Brazil; d. of Silverio M. Ortiz and Moema F. Ortiz; m. Jasper W. Parrott 1974; two d.; ed. Conservatório Brasileiro de Música, Rio de Janeiro, Acad. Int. de Piano (with Magda Tagliaferro), Paris and Curtis Inst. of Music, Philadelphia (with Rudolph Serkin); First Prize Van Cliburn Int. Competition, Texas 1969; has since appeared in concerts with the Vienna Philharmonic, Berlin Philharmonic, the Concertgebouw, Chicago Symphony, N.Y. Philharmonic, Israeli Philharmonic, L.A. Philharmonic, all the leading British orchestras etc. and has undertaken many tours of North and South America, the Far East, N.Z. and Japan; has recorded extensively for EMI, Decca, Pantheon, Collins Classics and Pickwick Records. *Leisure interests:* tennis, swimming, gardening, reading, hiking, holidaying. *Address:* c/o Harrison-Parrott Ltd., 12 Penzance Place, London, W11 4PA, England. *Telephone:* 0171-229 9166.

ORTIZ, Francis Vincent, M.S.; American diplomatist (retd.); b. 14 March 1926, Santa Fé; s. of Frank V. Ortiz and Margaret Delgado Ortiz; m. Mary Dolores Duke 1953; three s. one d.; ed. Georgetown, George Washington, New Mexico, Madrid Univs. and American Univ. of Beirut, Lebanon; diplomatic posts in Ethiopia and Mexico 1953–57; Special Asst. to Under-Sec. of State 1957–60, to Amb. to Mexico 1961–63; Country Dir. for Spain and Portugal 1963–67, for Argentina, Uruguay and Paraguay 1973–75; Head, Political Section and Chargé d'Affaires, Peru and Uruguay 1967–73; Deputy Exec. Sec. of State 1975–77; Amb. to Barbados, Grenada, St. Lucia and Dominica 1977–79, to Guatemala 1979–80, to Peru 1981–83, to Argentina 1983–86; Diplomat in Residence, Latin American Inst., New Mexico Univ. 1986–88; Special Asst. to Under-Sec. of State for Man. 1988–90; Political Adviser, C.-in-C., Southern Command 1980–81; mem. American Foreign Service Assn.; Hon. Dr. Iur. (New Mexico); Superior Service Award, Order of Civil Merit of Spain, Order of the Kts. of Malta; Meritorious Honor Award, Presidential Chamizal Medal (Mexico), Grand Cross Order of Mayo (Argentina), and others. *Leisure interests:* history, tennis. *Address:* 663 Garcia Street, Santa Fe, NM 87501, U.S.A. *Telephone:* (505) 984-2586. *Fax:* (505) 984-2741.

ORTIZ DE ROZAS, Carlos; Argentinian diplomatist and lawyer; b. 26 April 1926, Buenos Aires; s. of late Alfredo Ortiz de Rozas and Susana del Valle; m. Carmen Sarobe 1952; ed. Univ. de Buenos Aires; entered foreign service 1948; Chargé d'Affaires, Bulgaria 1952–54; Sec. Greece 1954–56; mem. Cabinet, Argentine Ministry of Foreign Affairs 1958–59; Counsellor, Argentine Mission at UN 1959–61; subsequently Dir.-Gen. Policy Dept., Ministry of Foreign Affairs and later Minister at embassies in U.A.R. and U.K.; Amb. to Austria 1967–70; Chief Rep. to Conf. of Cttee. on Disarmament, Geneva 1969 (Chair. of Cttee. 1979); Perm. Rep. to UN 1970–77; Amb. to U.K. 1980–82, to France 1984–89, to U.S.A. 1991–93; Under-Sec. of State for Foreign Relations 1990; Head of Argentine Special Mission to Holy See 1982–83; Pres. UN Security Council 1971, 1972; mem Advisory Bd. to Sec.-Gen. on Disarmament 1978–92; Prof. of Int. Relations, Univ. of Belgrano, Buenos Aires 1995–; Dir. Del. of Conf. on Law of the Sea 1973, First (Political and Security) Cttee. of the 29th General Assembly 1974; has held several teaching posts including Prof. of Public Law and Int. Relations, Univ. del Salvador, Buenos Aires (now mem. Bd. of Dirs.); Pres. Bunge and Born Foundation 1994–; decorations from Italy, Chile, Brazil, Greece, Japan, Peru, Thailand, Egypt, Austria, Nicaragua, the Republic of Korea, Spain, Holy See and France. *Address:* Avenida Gelly y Obes 2263, 1425 Buenos Aires, Argentina.

ORTLEB, Rainer, DR.RER.NAT., DR.SC.TECH.; German politician and computer scientist; b. 5 June 1944, Gera; m.; one s. one d.; ed. Dresden Tech. Univ. and Rostock Univ.; Asst. lecturer, Dresden Tech. Univ. 1971–82; Sr. Asst. lecturer, Computer Centre, Rostock Univ. 1982–84, lecturer, Computer Science Dept. 1984–, lecturer, Ship Eng. Dept. 1986–, Assoc. Prof. 1989–; Chair. Rostock Liberal Party Org. 1987–90; fmr. Chair. Liberal LDPD Party and mem. fmr. GDR Parl. 1990; mem. Bundestag 1990–; Deputy Fed. Chair. Free Democratic Party (FDP) 1990–; Fed. Minister for Special Tasks 1990–91; Fed. Minister for Educ. and Science 1991–94. *Leisure interests:* art, music. *Address:* c/o Bundesministerium für Bildung und Wissenschaft, Heinemannstrasse 2, 53175 Bonn, Germany.

ORTOLI, François-Xavier; French economist; b. 16 Feb. 1925, Ajaccio, Corsica; s. of Antoine Ortoli and Angèle Tessarech; m. Yvonne Calbairac 1946; one s. three d.; ed. Hanoi Faculty of Law, and Ecole Nat. d'Administration, Paris; Insp. of Finances 1948–51; Tech. Adviser to the Office of the Minister of Econ. Affairs and Information 1951–53; Technical Adviser, Office of the Minister of Finances 1954; Asst. Dir. to the Sec. of State for Econ. Affairs and Sec.-Gen. Franco-Italian Cttee. of EEC 1955; Head, Commercial Politics Service of Sec. of State for Econ. Affairs 1957; Dir.-Gen. of the Internal Market Div. of EEC 1958; Sec.-Gen. Inter-Ministerial Cttee. for Questions of European Econ. Co-operation, Paris 1961; Chef de Cabinet to Prime Minister 1962–66; Commr.-Gen. of the Plan 1966–67; Minister of Works 1967–68, of Educ. 1968, of Finance 1968–69, of Industrial and Scientific Devt. 1969–72; Pres. Comm. of European Communities 1973–76; Vice-Pres. for Econ. and Monetary Affairs 1977–84; Pres., Dir. Gen. TOTAL 1984–90, Hon. Chair. 1990–; Dr. h.c. (Oxford and Athens Univs.); Commdr. Légion d'honneur, Médaille militaire, Croix de guerre 1945, Médaille de la Résistance, etc. *Address:* Tour Total, 24 cours Michelet, 92069 Paris la Défense (Office); 18 rue de Bourgogne, 75007 Paris, France (Home). *Telephone:* (1) 41.35.31.84 (Office). *Fax:* (1) 41.35.33.46.

OSBALDESTON, Gordon Francis, P.C., C.C., B.COMM., M.B.A., LL.D.; Canadian company director; b. 29 April 1930, Hamilton, Ont.; s. of John E. and Margaret (Hanley) Osbaldeston; m. Geraldine M. Keller 1953; three s. one d.; ed. St. Jerome's Coll., Kitchener, Ont. and Univs. of Toronto and Western Ontario; Sec. Treasury Bd. 1973–76; Deputy Minister, Dept. of Industry, Trade and Commerce 1976–78; Sec. Ministry of State for Econ. Devt. 1978–82; Under-Sec. of State for External Affairs 1982; Clerk of Privy Council and Sec. to Cabinet 1982–86; Sr. Fellow, School of Business Admin., Univ. of Western Ontario 1986–95, Prof. Emer., Western Business School, Univ. of W. Ont. 1995–; Dir. Du Pont Canada, Great West Lifeco Inc., London Life Insurance Co., Bell Canada; Vanier Medal, Inst. of Public Admin. of Canada 1990. *Publications:* Keeping Deputy Ministers Accountable 1989, Organizing to Govern 1992. *Leisure interests:* golf, stamp collecting. *Address:* 1353 Corley Drive, London, Ont. N6G 4L4, Canada.

OSBORN, Eric Francis, PH.D., D.D., F.A.H.A.; Australian professor of New Testament and early church history; b. 9 Dec. 1922, Melbourne; s. of William F. Osborn and Hilda P. Osborn; m. Lorna G. Grierson 1946; two s.; ed.

Wesley Coll. Melbourne, Queen's Coll., Univ. of Melbourne and Queens' Coll., Cambridge; army service 1942–44; Methodist Minister in country parishes 1948–51, 1954–57; research student, Cambridge 1952–54; Prof. of New Testament and Early Church History, Queen's Coll. Univ. of Melbourne 1958–87, Pres. United Faculty of Theology 1987; Guest Prof. Univ. of Strasbourg 1981–82; Visiting Prof. La Trobe Univ. 1990–97; Guest Prof. Augustinanum Lateran Univ., Rome 1997. *Publications:* The Philosophy of Clement of Alexandria 1957, Justin Martyr 1973, Ethical Problems in Early Christian Thought 1976, The Beginning of Christian Philosophy 1981, La Morale dans la Pensée Chrétienne Primitive 1984, Anfänge Christlichen Denkens 1986, The Emergence of Christian Theology 1993, Tertullian, First Theologian of the West 1997. *Leisure interests:* swimming, running. *Address:* 2 Ocean Road, Point Lonsdale, Vic. 3225, Australia. *Telephone:* (03) 52582827 (Home); 03-93472249.

OSBORN, Frederic (Derek) Adrian, C.B., B.A., B.PHIL.; British government official; b. 14 Jan. 1941, Dorset; s. of Rev. George Osborn and Betty Osborn; m. Caroline Niebuhr Tod 1971; one s. one d.; ed. Leys School, Cambridge and Balliol Coll. Oxford; Ministry of Housing and Local Govt. 1965–70; with Dept. of Transport 1975–77, Dept. of Environment 1977–95, Dir.-Gen. (Deputy Sec.) 1990–95; Chair. European Environment Agency 1995–; Chair. UNED, UK 1996–, Earth Centre 1996–, Joseph Rowntree Foundation Steering Group on Reconciling Environmental and Social Objectives 1998–, mem. Bd. Earth Centre 1996–; England and Wales Environment Agency 1996–98, Severn Trent PLC 1998–; Special Adviser House of Commons Environmental Audit Cttee. 1998–; mem. Royal Soc. for Protection of Birds 1996–; Visiting Fellow Green Coll., Oxford 1996–97; Visiting Prof., School of Public Policy, Univ. Coll., London 1998–. *Publications:* Earth Summit II 1998, contribs. to Journal of Environmental Law etc. *Leisure interests:* music, reading. *Address:* European Environment Agency, c/o Department of Environment, 2 Marsham Street, London, SW1P 3EB, England. *Telephone:* 0171-276 3570. *Fax:* 0171-276 0590.

OSBORNE, Richard de Jongh, A.B.; American business executive; b. 19 March 1934, Bronxville, New York; s. of Stanley De Jongh and Elizabeth Ide Osborne; m. Cheryl A. Archibald 1957; two s. two d.; ed. Milton (Massachusetts) Acad., and Princeton Univ.; Cuno Eng. Corpn. 1956–60; Planning and Marketing Exec., Finance, IBM 1960–69; Investment Adviser, Sherman M. Fairchild 1969–70; Exec. Vice-Pres. Fairchild Camera & Instrument Corpn. 1970–74; Vice-Pres. Finance, ASARCO Inc. 1975–77, Exec. Vice-Pres. 1977–81, Pres. 1981–85, Chair., Pres. and C.E.O. 1985–; Dir. and Chair. (non-exec.) Grupo Mexico S.A. de C.V.; Dir. Southern Peru Copper Corpn., Schering-Plough Corpn., B.F. Goodrich Co., The Tinker Foundation; Chair. Int. Copper Research Asscn.; Dir., Council of the Americas. *Address:* ASARCO Inc., 180 Maiden Lane, New York, NY 10038 (Office); 40 East 94th Street, Apartment 32B, New York, NY 10128, U.S.A. (Home).

OSCARSSON, Per Oscar Heinrich; Swedish actor; b. 28 Jan. 1927, Stockholm; s. of Ing. Einar Oscarsson and Theresia Küppers; m. Bärbel Krämer 1960; one s. two d.; ed. Royal Dramatic School; Royal Dramatic Theatre 1947–52, Gothenburg Town Theatre 1953–59, TV-Theatre 1966–67; now works mainly as free-lance film-actor; Best Actor Award, Cannes 1966; New York Critics Award for Best Actor 1968; Silver Hugo Best Actor Award, Chicago Int. Film Festival 1969; appeared on stage in Hamlet 1953, Candida 1961, Waiting for Godot 1963; films: The Doll 1962, My Sister My Love 1965, Hunger 1965, Ole Dole Doff 1967, It's Up to You 1968, Close to the Wind 1970, A Last Valley, Salem Comes to Supper 1971. *Leisure interests:* reading and riding.

OSHEROFF, Douglas Dean, PH.D.; American physicist and researcher; b. 1 Aug. 1945, Aberdeen, Wash.; s. of William Osheroff and Bessie Anne (Ondov) Osheroff; m. Phyllis S. K. Liu 1970; ed. California Inst. of Tech., Cornell Univ.; mem. tech. staff Bell Labs., Murray Hill, N.Y. 1972–82, Head Solid State and Low Temperature Physics Research Dept. 1982–87; Prof. Stanford Univ., Calif. 1987–, J. G. Jackson and C. J. Wood Prof. of Physics 1992–, Chair. Physics 1993–96; co-discoverer superfluidity in liquid 3He 1971, nuclear antiferromagnetic resonance in solid 3He 1980; Fellow American Physical Soc., American Acad. of Arts and Sciences, N.A.A.; co-recipient Simon Memorial Prize, British Inst. of Physics 1976, Oliver E. Buckley Solid State Physics Prize 1981, John D. and Catherine T. MacArthur Prize Fellow 1981, shared Nobel Prize for Physics 1996. *Address:* Department of Physics, Stanford University, Stanford, CA 94305-4060, U.S.A.

OSHIMA, Nagisa; Japanese film director; b. 31 March 1932, Kyoto; m. Akiko Koyama 1960; two s.; ed. Kyoto Univ.; with Shochiku Co. 1954–59; formed own film company 1959; Pres. Dirs'. Guild of Japan 1980–; has also directed television films. *Films:* Ai To Kibo No Machi (A Town of Love and Hope) 1959, Seishun Zankoku Monogatari (Cruel Story of Youth) 1960, Taiyo No Hakaba (The Sun's Burial) 1960, Nihon No Yoru To Kiri (Night and Fog in Japan) 1960, Shiiku (The Catch) 1961, Amakusa Shiro Tokisada (The Rebel) 1962, Etsuraku (The Pleasures of the Flesh) 1965, Yunbogi No Nikki (Yunbogi's Diary) 1965, Hakuchu No Torima (Violence at Noon) 1966, Ninja Bugeicho (Band of Ninja) 1967, Nihon Shunka-ko (A Treatise on Japanese Bawdy Song) 1967, Muri Shinju Nihon No Natsu (Japanese Summer: Double Suicide) 1967, Koshikei (Death By Hanging) 1968, Kaettekita Yopparai (Three Resurrected Drunkards) 1968, Shinjuku Dorobo Nikki (Diary of a Shinjuku Thief) 1968, Shonen (Boy) 1969, Tokyo Senso Sengo Hiwa (He Died After the War, or The Man Who Left His Will on Film) 1970, Gishiki (The Ceremony) 1971, Natsu No Imooto (Dear Summer Sister) 1972, Ai no Corrida (In the Realm of the Senses) 1976, Ai no Borei (Empire of Passion) 1978, Merry Christmas, Mr. Lawrence 1982, Max, mon amour 1985, Kyoto, My Mother's Place 1991. *Address:* Oshima Productions, 2-15-7 Akasaka, Minato-ku, Tokyo, Japan.

OSIPOV, Victor Ivanovich; Russian geologist; b. 15 April 1937; ed. Moscow State Univ.; Dir. scientific station 1959–61; lecturer, Prof. Moscow State Univ. 1964–90; Deputy Dir. Inst. of Lithosphere 1990; Dir. Centre of Eng. Geology and Geoecology (now Inst. of Geoecology) Russian Acad. of Sciences; corresp. mem., U.S.S.R. (now Russian) Acad. of Sciences 1991–; main research in eng. geology, environmental protection; State Prize 1988. *Leisure interests:* travelling, sports, gardening. *Address:* Institute of Geoecology, Ulansky per. 13, 101000 Moscow, Russia. *Telephone:* (095) 135 8325 (Office).

OSIPOV, Yuri Sergeyevich; Russian mathematician and technician; b. 7 July 1936, Tobolsk; m.; one d.; ed. Urals State Univ.; corresp. mem. U.S.S.R. (now Russian) Acad. of Sciences 1984, mem. 1987, Pres. 1991–; staff mem., Inst. of Mechanics and Math., Urals Scientific Cen. Acad. of Sciences 1959, Dir. 1990–93; Prof., Urals Univ. 1961–70; fmr. Head of Chair of Moscow State Univ.; Dir. Steklov Math. Inst. 1993–; Lenin Prize 1976. *Publications:* works on the theory of man., differential equations and their application. *Address:* Russian Academy of Sciences, Leninsky prospekt 14, 117901 GSP-1, Moscow; Steklov Mathematical Institute, 42 Vavilov Street, 117966 Moscow, Russia. *Telephone:* 954-35-06 (Acad.); 135-2291 (Inst.).

OSIPYAN, Yuri Andreyevich; Russian physicist; b. 15 Feb. 1931; m.; three c.; ed. Moscow Steel Inst.; mem. CPSU 1959–91; on staff of Cen. Inst. of Metallo-Physics (sr. researcher) 1955–62; Deputy Dir. of U.S.S.R. (now Russian) Acad. of Sciences Inst. of Crystallography 1962–63; on staff of U.S.S.R. (now Russian) Acad. of Sciences Inst. of Solid State Physics 1963–, Prof. 1970–, Deputy Dir. then Dir. 1973–; Corresp. mem. of U.S.S.R. (now Russian) Acad. of Sciences 1972, mem. 1981–, Vice-Pres. 1988–97, mem. Presidium 1997–; Dean, Prof. and head of Faculty of Moscow Inst. of Physics and Tech. 1963–73; mem. Pres. Council 1990–91; Pres. Int. Union for Theoretical and Applied Physics 1990–; Hero of Socialist Labour 1986; U.S.S.R. People's Deputy 1989–91; P.N. Lebedev Gold Medal 1984, A. P. Karpinsky Prize, City of Hamburg 1991. *Publications:* works on solid state physics. *Address:* Institute of Solid State Physics, Chernogolovka, Noginsky region, Moscow District, 142432, Russia. *Telephone:* 913-23-24.

OSKANYAN, Vartan; Armenian politician; b. 1955, Syria; m.; two s.; ed. Yerevan Polytechnic Inst., Tufts Univ. Massachusetts, Harvard Univ., Fletcher School of Law and Diplomacy; f. and Ed. Armenian Int. Magazine; on staff Armenian Ministry of Foreign Affairs 1992–; Head, del. to Karabakh Negotiations 1994–, Deputy Head, Middle E. Dept., Head, Dept. of N. America 1992–94; Deputy Foreign Minister 1994–97, First Deputy Foreign Minister 1997–98, Minister April 1998–. *Address:* Ministry of Foreign Affairs, Marshal Bagramyan prosp. 10, 375019 Yerevan, Armenia. *Telephone:* (3742) 52 35 31 (Office).

OSKARSON, Peter; Swedish theatre director; b. 13 June 1951, Stockholm; s. of Per-Otto Oskarson and Margareta Du Rietz; m. Gunilla Kindstrand 1983; one s. four d.; ed. Actors' School, Stockholm; Artistic Dir. Skånska Teatern Landskrona 1973–82, Folkteatern Gävleborg 1982–90; Head, Helsingegården, inst. for theatre and popular arts, N. Scandinavia 1990–; Artistic Dir. Oskarsons Lager Orion Theatre 1993–; Gen. Man. Folkteatern Gävleborg 1997–; Artistic Adviser Peking Opera, Anhui, Hefei, China 1996–; plays produced also at Royal Opera House and at Royal Dramatic Theatre, Stockholm, Drottningholm Theatre, Staatsoper, Stuttgart, Intiman, Seattle, U.S.A., Oper der Stadt, Bonn, Swedish TV etc.; mem. Swedish Theatre Acad. 1993–, Swedish World Culture Forum 1998–; Alf Sjöberg Prize, Swedish Acad. Theatre Prize, Svenska Dagbladet Thalia Prize, Expressen Theatre Prize, Gävle and Gävleborg Culture Prize, Malmö Thalia Prize. *Address:* Helsingegården, S-820 40 Järvsö, Sweden. *Telephone:* (46) 701-409500. *Fax:* (46) 651 41595.

OSMAN, Ahmed, LL.B., LL.M.; Moroccan politician and diplomatist; b. 3 Jan. 1930, Oujda; m. H.R.H. Princess Lalla Nezha (sister of King Hassan II, q.v.) 1965; one s.; ed. Royal High School, Rabat, Univ. of Rabat and Univ. of Bordeaux, France; Head of the Legal Section, Royal Cabinet 1956; joined Ministry of Foreign Affairs 1957; Sec.-Gen. Ministry of Nat. Defence 1959–61; Amb. to Fed. Repub. of Germany 1961–62; Under Sec.-of-State for Industry and Mines 1963–64; Pres. and Gen. Man. Moroccan Navigation Co. 1964–67; Amb. to U.S.A., Canada and Mexico 1967–70; Minister of Admin. Affairs 1970–71; Dir. of Royal Cabinet 1971–72; Prime Minister 1972–79; Parl. Rep. for Oujda 1977–; Pres. Rassemblement Nat. des Indépendants 1978; mem. Nat. Defence Council 1979–; Minister of State 1983; Pres. Chamber of Reps. 1984; participated in UN sessions 1957, 1958, 1960, 1961, 1968, Conf. on Maritime law 1958, Conf. of the League of Arab States 1961. *Leisure interests:* bridge, sports, reading. *Address:* R.N.I., 6 rue Laos, Rabat, Morocco.

OSMAN, Amal Abd ar-Rahim, PH.D.; Egyptian politician; m.; ed. Univs. of Cairo and Rome; perm. mem. of most political and social confs.; Minister of Social Insurance and Social Affairs 1978–97. *Publications:* several works on criminal law. *Address:* c/o Ministry of Social Insurance, 3 Sharia El Alfi, Cairo, Egypt.

OSMAN, Osman Ahmed, B.SC.; Egyptian civil engineer (retd.); b. 1917, Ismailia; s. of Ahmed Mohamed Osman; m. Samia Ismail Wahbi 1947; four

s. one d.; ed. Cairo Univ.; Chair. The Arab Contractors (Osman Ahmed Osman & Co) 1949–73, and of its assoc. companies, Saudi Enterprises, Kuwaiti Eng. Co., The Arab Contractors (Libya), The Libyan Co. for Contracting and Devt., The Osman Ahmed Osman & Co. (Abu Dhabi, Arabian Gulf); Minister of Reconstruction 1973–76, and of Housing 1975–76; Deputy Premier, responsible for Popular Devt. Jan.–May 1981; mem. People's Ass. 1976–, Pres. Chamber of Reps. (Speaker) 1984–92; mem. Consultative Council 1957; Chair. Syndicate of Engineers March 1979; mem. Inter Action Council (union of fmr. heads of states and govts.) 1983; Hon. LL.D. (Ricker Coll. of North East) 1976; Repub. Medal (1st Class), Soviet Hero of Labour Medal, Nile Medal (1st Class) 1980; Chief works undertaken include: (in Egypt) Aswan High Dam, Suez Canal deepening and widening, Port Said Shipyard, Cairo Int. Airport, Salhia reclamation project, High Dam Electric Power Transmission Lines, Giza Bridge and Ramsis Bridge over the Nile; (in Saudi Arabia) Dhahran Airport, Riyadh Mil. Coll., Dammam Mil. Barracks; (in Kuwait) Municipality Centre, Kuwait sewer system, secondary schools, Sabahia roads and drainage system; (in Libya) Benghazi drainage system, Stadium, and Highway; (in Iraq) Kirkuk Feeder Canal No. 2 and 3; (in Jordan) Khaled Ibn El-Walid Dam and Tunnels; (in Abu Dhabi) Zayed City, Ruler's Palace Kharj Mil. Base and City, Taif Mil. Base, numerous airports, hospitals and land reclamation. *Publications:* The High Dam (lecture) 1966, My Experience 1981. *Leisure interests:* fishing, football. *Address:* c/o Osman Ahmed Osman & Co., 34 Adly Street, Cairo, Egypt. *Telephone:* 3935011. *Fax:* 3937674.

OSMOND, Charles Barry, F.R.S., F.A.A., PH.D.; Australian professor of biology; b. 20 Sept. 1939, Australia; s. of Edward Charles Osmond and Joyce Daphne (née Krauss) Osmond; m. 1st Suzanne Ward 1962 (divorced 1983), one s. one d.; m. 2nd Cornelia Gauhl 1983; ed. Wyong High School and Univs. of New England and Adelaide; Postdoctoral fellow, Univ. of Calif. at Los Angeles 1965–66, Univ. of Cambridge 1966–67; Research Fellow, Dept. of Environmental Biology, Research School of Biol. Sciences, A.N.U. 1967, subsequently Fellow, Sr. Research Fellow, Prof. of Biol. 1978–87, 1991–; Exec. Dir. Biol. Science Center, Desert Research Inst., Univ. of Nevada 1982–86; Arts and Sciences Prof., Dept. of Botany, Duke Univ. 1987–91; Dir. Research School of Biol. Sciences, A.N.U. 1991–98, also Visiting Fellow; Sr. Fulbright Fellowship, Univ. of Calif. (Santa Cruz) 1973–74; Guest Prof., Technical Univ., Munich 1974; Overseas Fellow, Churchill Coll., Cambridge 1980; Forschungspreis, Alexander von Humboldt Foundation, Univs. of Darmstadt and Göttingen 1997–98; mem. Australian Nat. Comm. for UNESCO 1980–82; mem. Council, Australian Acad. of Sciences 1982–85. *Publications:* numerous publications in plant physiology. *Address:* 7 Needham Place, Stirling, A.C.T. 2611, Australia.

OSMUNDSEN, Terje, PH.D.; Norwegian administrator and business executive; b. 1 Feb. 1957, Stavanger; s. of Siri Osmundsen and Tor Osmundsen; m. Manuela Ramin 1987; two d.; ed. Univ. of Oslo, St. Olaf's Coll., Minn., U.S.A., American Univ., Washington, D.C., U.S.A.; Research Assoc. Norwegian Mfrs. Asscn. 1980; Counsellor, Ministry of Planning 1981; First Political Sec. to Prime Minister 1981–85; Research Counsellor, Norwegian Embassy, Paris 1985–86; Project Dir. "Scenarios for Norway towards Year 2000", Norwegian School of Man. 1986–87; Vice-Pres. Saga Petroleum 1988; Man. Business Planning/Asst. Dir., Strategic Planning Dept., Alcatel N.V., Paris 1989–91; Deputy Dir.-Gen., Confed. of Norwegian Business and Industry 1991–93; Sr. Vice-Pres. Kvaerner a.s. 1994–. *Publications include:* The New Industrial Age 1991. *Leisure interests:* reading, family, sports. *Address:* Kvaerner a.s., Hoffsreien 1, P.O. Box 100, Skøyen, 0212 Oslo, Norway. *Telephone:* 22 96 70 00. *Fax:* 22 52 01 22.

OSOGO, James Charles Nakhwanga, M.P.; Kenyan politician and teacher; b. 10 Oct. 1932, Bukani; m. Maria Nakhubal Obara 1959; seven s. one d.; ed. Port Victoria Primary School, St. Mary's High School, Yala, Railway Training School, Nairobi and Kagumo Teachers' Training Coll.; Teacher, Sigalame School 1955, Withur School 1956, Barding School 1957, Ndenga School 1958, Port Victoria School 1959; Headmaster Kibassanga School 1960, Nangina School 1961–62; Vice-Chair. Kenya Nat. Union of Teachers, Central Nyanza 1958–62; mem. Kenya House of Reps. 1963–81, 1992–; Asst. Minister, Ministry of Agric. 1963–66; Minister for Information and Broadcasting 1966–69; Minister of Commerce and Industry 1969–73, also acting Minister of Agric. 1970; Minister for Local Govt. 1973–74, of Health 1974–79, of Agric. 1979–80, of Livestock Development 1980–82; Asst. Minister for Commerce and Industry 1992; Chair. Kenya Youth Hostels Asscn. 1964–70, Patron 1970–; Elder, Order of the Golden Heart (Kenya), Order of the Star of Africa (Liberia), Grand Cordon of the Star of Ethiopia, Grand Cross of the Yugoslav Flag. *Leisure interests:* volley ball, reading. *Address:* P.O. Box 1, Port Victoria, Kenya.

OSPANOV, Marat Turdybekovich; Kazakhstan politician and economist; b. 17 Sept. 1949, Aktyubinsk; s. of Turdybek Ospanov and Rauza Zeinulovna; m. Bahyt Akhmetkalievna 1975; one s. one d.; ed. G. Plekhanov Moscow State Inst. of Nat. Economy, S. Kirov Kazakh State Univ.; lecturer Aktyubinsk State Inst. of Medicine 1973–90; Deputy Chair. Cttee. Supreme Soviet of Kazakhstan 1990–91; Deputy Head, Head Chief Taxation Inspection, First Deputy Minister of Finance, Repub. of Kazakhstan 1991–94; Deputy Chair. Supreme Soviet of Kazakhstan 1994–95; Chair. Cttee. on Foreign Investments Cabinet of Ministers 1995–96; Chair. Majilis (Lower Chamber of Parl.), Repub. of Kazakhstan 1996–; mem. Int. Econ. Acad. "Eurasia" 1997–. *Publications:* 5 monographs and more than 50 publs. on econ. and agrarian problems, and on taxation, budget and investment policies. *Leisure interest:* music. *Address:* House of Parliament, Astana, Kazakhstan. *Telephone:* (3172) 32 79 90.

OSPEL, Marcel; Swiss banker; b. 8 Feb. 1950; ed. Higher School of Econs. and Man., Basel; joined Dept. of Planning and Marketing Swiss Bank Corpn. (SBC) 1977, with SBC Capital Markets, London, New York 1980, Dir. 1987, mem. Enlargement Group 1990, C.E.O. Capital Markets and Treasury 1992, SBC Warburg 1995, Group Pres. 1996–; C.E.O. Union Bank of Switzerland 1998–. *Address:* Union Bank of Switzerland, Bahnhofstr. 45, 8021 Zürich; Swiss Bank Corporation, Aeschenplatz 6, 4002 Basel, Switzerland. *Telephone:* (61) 2882020; (61) 2341111. *Fax:* (61) 2884576; (61) 2365111.

OST, Friedhelm; German politician; b. 15 June 1942, Castrop-Rauxel; s. of Franz Ost and Barbara Ost; m. Erika Herrmann 1968; three s. two d.; ed. Univs. of Freiburg and Cologne; bank employee 1966–69; Adviser, Bundesverband Deutscher Banken 1969–72; Econ. Ed., moderator and commentator, Zweites Deutsches Fernsehen (ZDF) 1973–85; State Sec. and Head, Govt. Press and Information Dept. 1985–89; Econ. and Political Adviser to German Fed. Chancellor and freelance journalist and public relations consultant 1989–90; Gen. Man. Wirtschaftsvereinigung Bergbau until end of 1990; mem. CDU 1980–; mem. Bundestag 1990–, Chair. Econ. Cttee; Adviser Frankfurter Rothschild GmbH 1997–; mem. Russian Acad. of Sciences. *Address:* Heiersmauer 69, 33098 Paderborn, Germany.

OSTEN, Suzanne (Carlota); Swedish playwright and theatre and film director; b. 20 June 1944, Stockholm; d. of Carl Otto Osten and Gud Osten; one d.; ed. Lund Univ.; started directing while a student 1963; ran fringe theatre group performing in schools, prisons, public areas, etc.; joined City Theatre, Stockholm 1971; f. Unga Klara Stadsteatern ind. repertory co. 1975; has written and directed over 30 plays, numerous radio and TV productions; began directing films 1980; Prof. Dramatic Inst. 1995–; Nat. Theatre Critics Prize 1982; Guldbagge Award for Direction (for The Mozart Brothers) 1986; Paris-Creteil Prize 1993; several other awards and prizes. *Films include:* Mamma—Our Life is Now 1982, The Mozart Brothers 1986, Lethal Film 1988, Guardian Angel 1990, Speak Up It's So Dark 1992, Only You and Me 1994, Carmen's Revenge 1996.

OSTERBROCK, Donald E., PH.D.; American astronomer; b. 13 July 1924, Cincinnati, Ohio; s. of William C. Osterbrock and Elsie W. Osterbrock; m. Irene Hansen 1952; one s. two d.; ed. Univ of Chicago; Instructor Princeton Univ. 1952–53; Instructor, then Asst. Prof. Calif. Inst. of Technology 1953–58; Asst. Prof., then Assoc. Prof., Univ. of Wis. 1958–61, Prof. of Astronomy 1961–73, Chair. Dept. of Astronomy 1967–68, 1969–72; Visiting Prof., Univ. of Chicago 1963–64; Letters Ed., Astrophysical Journal 1971–73; Prof. of Astronomy, Univ. of Calif., Santa Cruz 1972–92, Prof. Emer. 1993–; Dir. Lick Observatory 1972–81; Hill Family Prof., Univ. of Minn. 1977–78; Visiting Prof., Ohio State Univ. 1980, 1986; Guggenheim Fellow 1960–61, 1982–83, Nat. Science Sr. Foundation Fellow 1968–69; Assoc., Royal Astronomical Soc. 1976; mem. Nat. Acad. of Sciences, American Acad. of Arts and Sciences, American Philosophical Soc., Wisconsin Acad. of Sciences, Arts and Letters, American Astronomical Soc. (Vice-Pres. 1975–77, Pres. 1988–90); Corresp. mem. Mexican Acad. of Sciences 1998; Hon. D.Sc. (Ohio State Univ.) 1986, (Univ. of Chicago) 1992, (Univ. of Wis.-Madison) 1997; Univ. of Chicago Alumni Asscn. Professional Achievement Award 1982, Henry Norris Russell Lectureship, American Astronomical Soc. 1991, Catherine W. Bruce Medal, Astronomical Soc. of the Pacific 1991, Antoinette de Vaucouleurs Memorial Lectureship and Medal (Univ. of Texas) 1994, Gold Medal, Royal Astronomical Soc. 1997. *Publications:* Astrophysics of Gaseous Nebulae 1974, James E. Keeler, Pioneer American Astrophysicist and the Early Development of American Astrophysics 1984, Astrophysics of Gaseous Nebulae and Active Galactic Nuclei 1989, (with J. R. Gustafson and W. J. S. Unruh) Eye on the Sky: Lick Observatory's First Century 1988, Pauper and Prince: Ritchey, Hale and Big American Telescopes 1993; numerous scientific papers in Astrophysical Journal and Publications of the Astronomical Society of the Pacific, etc. *Leisure interests:* drama, hiking, conservation. *Address:* Lick Observatory, University of California, Santa Cruz, CA 95064; 120 Woodside Avenue, Santa Cruz, CA 95060, U.S.A. (Home). *Telephone:* (831) 459-2605 (Office). *Fax:* (831) 426-3115.

ÖSTMAN, Arnold; Swedish conductor; b. 1939, Malmo, Sweden; ed. Univs. of Paris and Stockholm; fmr. lecturer State Acad. of Music and Drama, Stockholm; Artistic Dir. Vadstena Acad. 1969, f. Norrlands Operan 1974, Gen. Admin. and Artistic Dir. Drottningholm Court Theatre 1979–92; has conducted at opera houses including: Covent Garden, Parma, Paris Bastille, Trieste, Cologne, Bonn, Toulouse, Nice, Vienna, Wexford, Madrid, Washington, Lausanne; symphonic conductor with orchestras including: the German radio orchestras of Hamburg, Cologne, Stuttgart and Baden-Baden, the Stuttgart Philharmonic, Orchestre nat. de France, de Lille, orchestra of La Fenice, Venice, Adelaide Symphony Orchestra, Orchestra Sinfonia Siciliana, Scottish Chamber Orchestra, Acad. of Ancient Music, London, Royal Concertgebouw Orchestra, Amsterdam etc.; works regularly with Netherlands Radio Chamber Orchestra (symphonic and operatic); recordings include: Così fan tutte, Le Nozze di Figaro, Don Giovanni, Die Zauberflöte (Diapason d'Or and Deutsche Schallplattenpreis); co-producer two TV films: Christina the Winter Queen, Gustav III (both winners of Prix d'Italia). *Address:* Haydn Rawstron (UK) Ltd., 36 Station Road, London, SE20 7BQ, England. *Telephone:* 0181-659 2659. *Fax:* 0181-676 9119.

OSTRIKER, Jeremiah (Paul), PH.D.; American professor of theoretical astrophysics; b. 13 April 1937, New York; s. of Martin Ostriker and Jeanne Sumpf; m. Alicia S. Suskin 1958; one s. two d.; ed. Harvard Univ. and Univ. of Chicago; Postdoctoral Fellow, Cambridge Univ., England 1964–65; Research Assoc. and Lecturer, Princeton Univ. 1965–66, Asst. Prof. 1966–68, Assoc. Prof. 1968–71, Prof. 1971–, Chair. Dept. of Astrophysical Sciences and Dir. Observatory 1979–95, Charles A. Young Prof. of Astronomy 1982–; Provost, Princeton Univ. 1995–; mem. Editorial Bd. and Trustee, Princeton Univ. Press 1982–84, 1986; Visiting Prof. Harvard Univ. and Regents Fellow Smithsonian Inst. 1984–85, 1987; mem. N.A.S. 1974–, mem. Council 1992–95, mem. Bd. of Govs. 1993–95; mem. American Acad. of Arts and Sciences, American Astronomical Soc., Int. Astronomical Union, American Philosophical Soc. 1994; Assoc. mem. Royal Astronomical Soc. 1994; Fellow A.A.A.S. 1992; Hon. F.R.A.S. 1994; Nat. Science Foundation Fellowship 1960–65; Alfred P. Sloan Fellowship 1970–72; Sherman Fairchild Fellowship of CalTech 1977; Hon. D.Sc. (Univ. of Chicago) 1992; Helen B. Warner Prize (American Astronomical Soc.) 1972, Henry Norris Russell Prize 1980; Vainu Bappu Memorial Award (Indian Nat. Science Acad.) 1993. *Leisure interest:* squash. *Address:* Office of the Provost, 3 Nassau Hall, Princeton University, Princeton, NJ 08544 (Office); 33 Philip Drive, Princeton, NJ 08540, U.S.A. (Home). *Telephone:* (609) 258-3026 (Office); (609) 924-5737 (Home).

OSTROVSKY, Mikhail Arkadievich, D.BIOL.SC.; Russian physiologist and biophysicist; b. 22 Feb. 1935, Leningrad; m. Raisa Brook; two s.; ed. Moscow State Univ.; jr., sr. researcher Inst. of Higher Nervous Activity and Neurophysiology 1959–70, Head of Sensory Reception Lab., Inst. of Chemical Physics U.S.S.R. (now Russian) Acad. of Sciences 1970–; Prof. Moscow State Univ. 1977–; Visiting Prof., Univ. of Md. at Coll. Park 1994–; Corresp. mem. U.S.S.R. (now Russian) Acad. of Sciences 1990, mem. 1994; Ed. Russian Sensory Systems 1987–; Chair. Expert Comm. on Physiology and Medicine of Russian Foundation for Basic Research 1992–; mem. Int. Brain Research Organization 1980, Russian Pavlov Physiological Soc. 1976, Int. Eye Research Asscn. 1989; mem. Bd. and Chair. Cttee. for Relations with E. European Neuroscience Asscns. *Publications:* more than 100 articles and papers on photoreception, visual pigments, phototransduction, eye screening pigments, light damage to eye structures; patents for devices and methods in biochem., medicine and optics; invented UV blue light-absorbing intraocular lenses. *Address:* ul. Kosygina 4, 117334 Moscow, Russia. *Telephone:* (095) 135-70-73; (095) 939-73-57 (Office); (095) 434-15-35 (Home). *Fax:* (095) 938-21-56; (095) 137-41-01.

OSTROWER, Fayga; Brazilian painter, engraver and author; b. 14 Sept. 1920, Łódź, Poland; m. Heinz Ostrower 1941; one s. one d.; ed. Fundação Getúlio Vargas, Rio de Janeiro; Fulbright Scholar, U.S.A.; Lecturer in Theory of Composition and Analysis, Museum of Modern Art, Rio de Janeiro 1954–70, Univ. Federal de Minas Gerais 1966–70; Post-graduate Prof., Univ. Rio de Janeiro 1982–; Vice-Pres. Brazilian Cttee., Int. Soc. of Educ. through Art, UNESCO 1983; John Hay Whitney Lecturer, Spelman Coll., Atlanta 1964; mem. Jury Bienal of São Paulo and Nat. Show of Fine Arts, Rio de Janeiro; mem. Int. Jury Bienal Grabado Inter-Americano, Puerto Rico 1995; Vice-Pres. Brazilian Cttee., Int. Asscn. of Plastic Arts, Int. Council of ICIS (Int. Centre for Integrative Studies, New York); Pres. INSEA (Int. Soc. for Educ. through Art, Brazil); mem. Bd. Cultural Council, Museum of Modern Art, Rio de Janeiro, Escola de Artes Visuais Parque Lage, Rio de Janeiro; Counsellor, Instituto Cultural Brasil-Alemanha, Goethe Institut, Rio de Janeiro; elected mem. State Council for Culture, Rio de Janeiro; numerous one-person exhbns. and works in collections in the Americas and Europe; Special Show Mexico Bienal 1981, Puerto Rico Bienal 1995; Hon. mem. Accad. delle Arti del Disegno, Florence; numerous prizes including awards at São Paulo Bienal in 1955, 1957, 1961, 1963, Venice Biennale 1958, 1962, Venezuela Bienal 1967, Rio de Janeiro City Award 1969, II Biennale Internazionale della Grafica, Florence 1970, Grand Int. Prize Venice, Grand Nat. Award for the Arts 1994, Grand Nat. Prize of Art 1995, Grand Prize of Fine Arts, Brazilian Ministry of Culture 1998; Chevalier Order of Rio Branco, Hon. Citizenship of Rio de Janeiro, Ordem do Mérito Cultural. *Publications:* Criatividade e Processos de Criação 1977, Universos de Arte 1983, Acasos e Criação Artística 1990, Goya, Life and Work 1990, Os Caprichos de Goya 1995, Goya, Artista Revolucionário e Humanista 1997, A Sensibilidade do Intelecto 1998. *Leisure interest:* art. *Address:* Avenida Rui Barbosa 532, apdo. 1001, Rio de Janeiro, RJ 22250-020, Brazil. *Telephone:* 551.3015. *Fax:* 551.8916.

OSTRY, Sylvia, C.C., PH.D., F.R.S.C.; Canadian economist; b. Winnipeg; d. of Morris J. Knelman and B. (Stoller) Knelman; m. Bernard Ostry; two s.; ed. McGill and Cambridge Univs.; Chief Statistician, Statistics Canada 1972–75; Deputy Minister of Consumer and Corpn. Affairs and Deputy Registrar Gen. 1975–78; Chair. Econ. Council of Canada 1978–79; Head, Econ. and Statistics Dept., OECD 1979–83; Deputy Minister (Int. Trade) and Co-ordinator for Int. Econ. Relations, Dept. of External Affairs 1984–85; Amb., Multilateral Trade Negotiations and Personal Rep. of the Prime Minister, Econ. Summit, Dept. of External Affairs 1985–88; Per Jacobsson Foundation Lecture, Washington 1987; Sr. Research Fellow, Univ. of Toronto 1989–90; Volvo Distinguished Visiting Fellow, Council on Foreign Relations, New York 1989; Chair. Centre for Int. Studies, Univ. of Toronto 1990–; Chancellor, Univ. of Waterloo 1991–97; Western Co-Chair. Blue Ribbon Comm. for Hungary's Econ. Devt. 1990–94; Chair. Council Canadian Inst. for Int. Affairs 1990–94; Dir. Power Financial Corpn.; Chair. Int. Advisory Council, Bank of Montreal; mem. several learned socs. and professional orgs.; Fellow American Statistical Asscn.; Sylvia Ostry Foundation annual lecture series launched 1992; seventeen hon. degrees; Outstanding Achievement Award, Govt. of Canada 1987. *Publications include:* International Economic Policy Co-ordination (with Michael Artis) 1986, Governments and Corporations in a Shrinking World: The Search for Stability 1990, The Threat of Managed Trade to Transforming Economies 1993, Technonationalism and Technoglobalism: Conflict and Cooperation (with Richard Nelson) 1995, Rethinking Federalism: Citizens, Markets and Governments in a Changing World (jtly.) 1995, The Halifax G7 Summit: Issues on the Table (ed. with Gilbert Winham) 1995, Who's On First? The Post Coldwar Trading System 1997; articles on labour econs., demography, productivity, competition policy. *Leisure interests:* films, theatre, contemporary reading.

O'SULLEVAN, Sir Peter John, Kt., C.B.E.; racing correspondent and commentator; b. 3 March 1918; s. of the late Col. John Joseph O'Sullevan and Vera O'Sullevan; m. Patricia Duckworth 1951; ed. Hawtreys, Charterhouse and Collège Alpin, Switzerland; attached to Chelsea Rescue Services 1939–45; then editorial work and MSS. reading with Bodley Head publr.; Racing Corresp., Press Asscn. 1945–50, Daily Express 1950–86, Today 1986–87; race-broadcaster 1946–98 (from Australia, South Africa, Italy, France, U.S.A. etc.); first regular TV (BBC) horse-racing commentator to work without a race-reader; commentator on first televised Grand National 1960, world's first televised electronic horse race from Atlas computer at London Univ. (transmitted by BBC) 1967, first horse race transmitted live via satellite from New York 1980; Dir. Int. Racing Bureau 1979–93, Racing Post Ltd. 1985–95; mem. Jockey Club 1986–; numerous awards for services to horse-racing include Derby Award for Racing Journalist of the Year (with the late Clive Graham) 1971, Racehorse Owner of the Year award, Horserace Writers' Asscn. 1974, Sport on TV award, Daily Telegraph 1994, Services to Racing Award, Daily Star 1995, Lester's Award, Jockeys' Asscn. 1996. *Publication:* Calling the Horses: A Racing Autobiography 1989. *Leisure interests:* travel, reading, art, food and wine. *Address:* 37 Cranmer Court, London, SW3 3HW, England. *Telephone:* 0171-584 2781.

O'SULLIVAN, John B.A.; British editor and journalist; b. 25 April 1942, Liverpool; s. of Alfred M. O'Sullivan and Margaret (née Corner) O'Sullivan; ed. London Univ.; Jr Tutor Swinton Conservative Coll. 1965–67, Sr. Tutor 1967–69; Ed. Swinton Journal 1967–69; London Corresp. Irish Radio and TV 1970–72; Editorial Writer and parl. sketchwriter Daily Telegraph 1972–79; Ed. Policy Review 1979–83; Asst. Ed. Daily Telegraph 1983–84; Columnist The Times 1984–86, Assoc. Ed. 1986–87; Editorial Page Ed. New York Post 1984–86; Ed. Nat. Review 1988–97, Ed.-at-Large 1998–; Columnist Sunday Telegraph 1988–; Dir. of Studies Heritage Foundation 1979–83; Special Adviser to the Prime Minister 1987–88; Founder, Co-Chair. The New Atlantic Initiative 1996–; Conservative cand. for Parl. 1970; mem. Exec. Advisory Bd. Margaret Thatcher Foundation, Advisory Council Social Affairs Unit, Hon. Bd. Civic Inst., Prague; Fellow Inst. of Politics, Harvard Univ. 1983. *Leisure interests:* reading, cinema, theatre, dining out. *Address:* National Review, 215 Lexington Avenue, New York, NY 10016, U.S.A. *Telephone:* (212) 679-7330.

O'SULLIVAN, Sonia; Irish athlete; b. 28 Nov. 1969, Cóbh, Co. Cork; d. of John O'Sullivan and Mary O'Sullivan; ed. accountancy studies in Villanova, U.S.A.; Gold Medal 1500m., Silver Medal 3000m., World Student Games 1991; holds seven nat. (Irish) records; set new World record (her first) in 2000m. TSB Challenge, Edin. 1994, new European record in 3000m. TSB Games London 1994, Gold Medal in 3000m. European Athletic Championships, Helsinki 1994; winner Grand Prix 3000m., second overall 1993; Silver Medal, 1500m., World Championships, Stuttgart 1993; Gold Medal, 5000m., World Championships, Gothenburg 1995; Gold Medal World Cross Country Championships 4km, 8km 1998; Gold Medal European Championships 5000m., 10,000m. 1998; Female Athlete of the Year 1995. *Leisure interests:* mountain biking, reading, films. *Address:* c/o Kim McDonald, 201 High Street, Hampton Hill, Middx., TW12 1NL, England. *Telephone:* 0181-941 9732. *Fax:* 0181-941 9734.

OSWALD, Adm. of the Fleet, Sir (John) Julian (Robertson), G.C.B.; British naval officer; b. 11 Aug. 1933, Selkirk, Scotland; s. of George Oswald and Margaret (née Robertson) Oswald; m. Veronica Thompson 1958; two s. three d.; ed. Beaudesert Park, Minchinhampton; Britannia Royal Naval Coll., Royal Coll. of Defence Studies; joined R.N. 1947; served in H.M. ships Devonshire, Vanguard, Verulam, Newfoundland, Jewel, Victorious, Naiad; specialised in Gunnery 1960; commanded H.M.S. Yarnton 1962–63, H.M.S. Bacchante 1971–72, H.M.S. Newcastle 1977–79; Ministry of Defence 1972–75; R.N. Presentation Team 1979–80; Capt. Britannia, R.N. Coll. 1980–82; Asst. Chief of Defence Staff (Progs.) 1982–84, (Policy and Nuclear) 1985; Flag Officer, Third Flotilla, Commdr. Anti-Submarine Warfare, Striking Fleet 1985–87; C.-in-C., Fleet, Allied C.-in-C., Channel and C.-in-C., E. Atlantic Area 1987–89; First Sea Lord and Chief of Naval Staff 1989–93; First and Prin. Aide-de-Camp to H.M. the Queen 1989–93; Chair. Aerosystems Int. 1995–; Dir. Sema Group PLC 1993–, BAe Sema 1995–, James Fisher & Sons 1993–, Marine and Gen. Mutual Life Assurance 1994–; Chair. Maritime Trust 1994–, Nat. Historic Ships Cttee. 1995–, Ends of the Earth 1996–; Pres. Sea Cadet Asscn. 1994–; Gov. Portsmouth Univ. 1994–. *Leisure interests:* gliding, travel, stamp collecting, music, tennis. *Publications:* defence and strategy articles in specialised journals, book reviews.

Address: c/o Naval Secretary, Victory Building, HM Naval Base, Portsmouth, PO1 3LS, England.

OSYKA, Sergey Grigoryevich; Ukrainian politician; b. 1955; ed. Kiev State Univ.; worked as researcher and teacher Kiev State Univ., then chief consultant Comm. of Foreign Affairs Verkhovna Rada (Parl.) of Ukraine 1991–92; adviser to Prime Minister Kuchma 1992–93; Deputy, First Deputy Minister of External Econ. Relations 1993–94, Minister of Foreign Econ. Relations and Trade 1994–. *Address:* c/o Ministry of External Economic Relations, Lvivska pl. 8, 252053 Kiev, Ukraine. *Telephone:* 44-226-27-33.

OTA, Seiichi; Japanese politician; b. 1946, Fukuoka Pref.; ed. Keio Univ.; fmr. Asst. Prof. of Econs., Fukuoka Univ.; mem. LDP; mem. Shinshinto 1994–95; mem. for Fukuoka, House of Reps.; fmr. Parl. Vice-Minister of Finance, Chair. House of Reps. Finance Cttee.; Dir.-Gen. Man. and Co-ordination Agency 1998–. *Address:* Management and Co-ordination Agency, 3-1-1, Kasumigaseki, Chiyoda-ku, Tokyo 100, Japan. *Telephone:* (03) 3581-6361.

OTAKA, Tadaaki; Japanese conductor; b. 8 Nov. 1947, Kamakura; s. of Hisatada Otaka and Misaoko Otaka; m. Yukiko Otaka 1978; ed. Toho Music School, Toho Music Acad., Vienna Acad.; began studying violin 1951; 2nd Prize Minon Conductors' Competition 1969; apptd. Chief Conductor Tokyo Philharmonic Orchestra 1971–, Conductor Laureate 1991–; Chief Conductor Sapporo Symphony 1981–86; Prin. Conductor BBC Welsh Symphony Orchestra (now BBC Nat. Orchestra of Wales) 1987–95, Conductor Laureate 1996–; Chief Conductor Yomiuri Nippon Symphony Orchestra 1992–; Music Dir. and Prin. Conductor Kioi Sinfonietta (Tokyo) 1995–; Hon. Fellowship (Welsh Coll. of Music and Drama) 1993; Dr. h.c. (Univ. of Wales) 1993; Suntory Music Award 1992; Hon. C.B.E. 1997. *Leisure interests:* fishing, tennis, cooking. *Address:* c/o Harold Holt Ltd., 31 Sinclair Road, London, W14 0NS, England. *Telephone:* 0171-603 4600.

OTČENÁŠEK, Karel, D.THEOL.; Czech ecclesiastic; b. 13 April 1920, České Meziříčí nr. Opočno; s. of František Otčenášek and Žofie Otčenášková; ed. Papal Lateran Univ., Rome; ordained priest 1945; secretly made bishop of Hradec Králové Diocese without approval from communist authorities 1950; sentenced to 13 years' imprisonment by communist regime 1954; pardoned 1962; labourer 1962–65; ecclesiastical admin. 1965–89; Bishop of Hradec Králové Diocese 1990–98, Archbishop 1998–; Dr. h.c. (Pedagogical Univ. Hradec Králové) 1996; Golden Medal of Honour, Charles Univ. Prague 1995; Scout Orders of Lily of Honour and of Silver Wolf; Order of T. G. Masaryk 1996; František Ulrich Prize, Hradec Králové 1998. *Leisure interests:* scouting, travelling, social service. *Address:* Biskupství Královéhradecké, Velké náměsti 35, 500 01 Hradec Králové, Czech Republic. *Telephone:* (49) 551 23 11. *Fax:* (49) 551 28 50.

OTCHAKOVSKY-LAURENS, Paul, L. EN D.; French publisher; b. 10 Oct. 1944, Valreas, Vaucluse; s. of Zelman Otchakovsky and Odette Labaume; adopted s. of Berthe Laurens; m. Monique Pierret 1970; one s. one d.; ed. Coll. and Lycée de Sablé sur Sarthe, Coll. Montalembert de Courbevoie, Coll. St. Croix de Neuilly and Faculté de Droit, Paris; Reader, Editions Christian Bourgois 1969–70; Dir. of Collection, Editions Flammarion 1970–77; Dir. of Collections, then Dir. of Dept. Editions Hachette 1977–82; Pres. Dir.-Gen. Editions P.O.L. 1983–; Commdr. des Arts et Lettres. *Address:* Editions P.O.L., 33 rue Saint-André-des-Arts, 75006 Paris, France.

OTHMAN BIN WOK; Singaporean company director and fmr. journalist and politician; b. 8 Oct. 1924, Singapore; m. Asnah Bte Suhaimi (now called Lina Binte Abdullah) 1975; one s. two d.; ed. Telok Saga Malay School, Raffles Inst. and London School of Journalism; worked on Utusan Melayu as reporter, News Ed. then Deputy Ed. 1946–63; mem. People's Action Party 1954–; M.P. for Pasir Panjang Constituency 1963–81; Minister for Social Affairs 1963–77; Amb. to Indonesia (also accred. to Papua New Guinea) 1977–80; Dir. Overseas Investment Pte. Ltd. 1981–, Overseas Trustees Ltd. 1982–, Overseas Investment Nominees Pte. Ltd. 1982–, Biohealth Int. (S) Pte. Ltd. 1983–, Autologous Blood Bank (S) Pte. Ltd. 1987–, Sembawang Eng. Pte. Ltd. 1989–97, Utusan Melayu (S) Pte. Ltd. 1988–, Gainall Pte. Ltd. 1992–, Property Services Int. 1993–, Hale Medical Clinic (Concourse) Pte. Ltd. 1995–, Mindsets (Pte.) Ltd. 1996–, Bright Steel Pte. Ltd. 1996–; Chair. Lion Asiapac Ltd. 1996; Perm. mem. Presidential Council for Minority Rights 1981–; mem. Singapore Tourist Promotion Bd. 1981–94, Sentosa Devt. Corpn. 1981–97; Hon. Consul Principality of Monaco 1996–; Order of Nila Utama for Distinguished Service, Jasa Utama Star for Outstanding Services (Indonesia). *Address:* Overseas Investment Private Ltd., 300 Beach Road, # 02-01, The Concourse, Singapore 199555. *Telephone:* 3929881.

OTMAN ASSED, Mohamed; Libyan politician; b. Oct. 1922, Fezzan; s. of Ahmed al-Badawi Assed and Fatima Nuweir; m. Lola Seif 1959; nine s.; ed. Libyan religious and Arabic schools; Teacher 1942–43; in Liberation Movement; Head of Fezzan Del. in Legis. Ass. 1950–51; Rep. for Fezzan, UN Council for Libya 1951; Deputy 1952–64; Minister of Health, Fed. Govt. 1951–58, of Econ. Affairs Feb.-Oct. 1960; Prime Minister 1960–63; pvt. business 1964–; emigrated to Morocco 1969; Order of Independence 1954, Order of Independence (Tunisia) 1957, Order of the Throne (Morocco) 1962, Mohamed Ali al-Sanoussi Medal 1964. *Address:* Villa Rissani, Route Oued Akrach, Souissi, Rabat, Morocco. *Telephone:* 75-16-25; 75-11-83.

O'TOOLE, Peter Seamus; Irish actor; b. 2 Aug. 1932, Connemara, Co. Galway; s. of Patrick Joseph O'Toole; m. 1st Siân Phillips (q.v.) 1960 (divorced 1979); two d.; m. 2nd Karen Brown 1983 (divorced); one s.; ed. Royal Acad. of Dramatic Art; office boy, later reporter for Yorkshire Evening News; Nat. Service as signalman, Royal Navy; joined Bristol Old Vic Theatre Co., playing 73 parts 1955–58; West End debut in musical play Oh, my Papa 1957; toured England in play The Holiday; appeared in The Long, the Short and the Tall 1959; Stratford season 1960, playing Shylock, Petruchio, and Thersites; stage appearances in Pictures in the Hallway 1962, Baal 1963, Ride a Cock Horse, Waiting for Godot 1971, Dead Eyed Dicks 1976, Present Laughter 1978; Bristol Old Vic Theatre Season 1973; inaugurated Britain's Nat. Theatre Co.; appeared with Abbey Theatre Co. in Waiting for Godot, Man and Superman 1976; fmr. Assoc. Dir. Old Vic Theatre Co.; Artistic Dir., North American Tour of Royal Alexandra Theatre Co. playing Present Laughter and Uncle Vanya 1978; Macbeth, Old Vic 1980; Man and Superman 1982–83, Pygmalion 1984, 1987, The Apple Cart 1986, Jeffrey Bernard is Unwell 1989, Our Song 1992. *Films include:* Kidnapped 1959, The Day they Robbed the Bank of England 1959, Lawrence of Arabia 1960, Becket 1963, Lord Jim 1964, The Bible 1966, What's New Pussycat? 1965, How to Steal a Million 1966, Night of the Generals 1967, Great Catherine 1967, The Lion in Winter 1968, Goodbye Mr. Chips 1969, Brotherly Love 1970, Country Dance 1970, Murphy's War 1971, Under Milk Wood 1972, The Ruling Class 1972, Man of La Mancha 1972, Rosebud 1974, Man Friday 1975, Foxtrot 1975, Rogue Male (TV) 1976, Caligula 1977, Power Play 1978, Stuntman 1978, Zulu Dawn 1978, Masada (TV) 1981, The Antagonists 1981, My Favourite Year 1981, Svengali (TV) 1982, Supergirl 1984, Banshee (TV) 1986, Club Paradise 1986, The Last Emperor 1986, High Spirits 1988, On a Moonlit Night 1989, The Dark Angel (TV) 1989, Creator 1990, King Ralph 1990, Wings of Fame 1991, Rebecca's Daughters 1992, Our Song 1992, Civies (TV) 1992; Commdr. des Arts et des Lettres 1988. *Publications:* Loitering with Intent 1992, Loitering with Intent 2: The Apprentice 1996. *Address:* c/o William Morris Agency, 31–32 Soho Square, London, W1V 5DG; Guyon House, Hampstead High Street, London, N.W.3, England.

OTSASON, Rein, DR.ECON.SC.; Estonian economist; b. 24 May 1931, Tartu; s. of August Otsason and Marta Otsason; m. Valentina Otsason 1979; one s.; Dir. Inst. of Econ., Acad. of Sciences of Estonia; Deputy Chair. Council of Ministers of Estonian S.S.R. (now Estonia) 1988–89, State Planning Cttee. 1988–89; Pres. Bank of Estonia 1989–91, Credit Bank of Estonia 1992–. *Publications:* works on monetary policy and currency reforms. *Address:* Eesti Krediidipank, Narva Mnt. 4, EE 0100 Tallinn, Estonia. *Telephone:* (3726) 313530. *Fax:* (3726) 313533.

OTTEWILL, Ronald Harry, O.B.E., M.A., PH.D., F.R.S.; British professor of physical chemistry; b. 8 Feb. 1927, Southall, Middx.; s. of Harry A. and Violet D. (née Bucklee) Ottewill; m. Ingrid G. Roe 1952; one s. one d.; ed. Southall County School, Queen Mary Coll., London and Fitzwilliam Coll., Cambridge; Asst. Lecturer, Queen Elizabeth Coll., London 1951–52; Nuffield Fellowship, Dept. of Colloid Science, Univ. of Cambridge 1952–55, Sr. Asst. in Research 1955–58, Asst. Dir. of Research 1958–63; Lecturer in Physical Chem., Univ. of Bristol 1964–66, Reader in Colloid Science 1966–71, Prof. of Colloid Science 1971–82, Leverhulme Prof. of Physical Chem. 1982–92, Emer. Prof. of Physical Chem. 1992–, Dean, Faculty of Science 1988–90, Head of School of Chem. 1990–92; Sr. Research Fellow Univ. of Bristol 1996–; mem. NATO Research Grants Cttee. 1980–84, Chair. 1984; mem. Science Bd. SERC 1982–85, Chair. Neutron Beam Cttee. 1982–85; mem. Scientific Council Inst. Laue Langevin 1981–86; mem. Council Faraday Soc. (now Faraday Div. of Royal Soc. of Chem.) 1981–, Hon. Treas. 1985–89, Vice-Pres. 1986–89, 1991–, Pres. 1989–91; Monsanto Lecturer 1979, Alexander Lecturer, Royal Australian Chem. Inst. 1982; Liversidge Lecturer, Royal Soc. of Chem. 1985–86; Founders Lecturer SCI 1985; Xerox Lecturer, Canada 1987; Rideal Lecture, Royal Soc. of Chem. 1990, Dunning Lecture, Univ. of Bristol 1992; Langmuir Lecturer, A.C.S. 1988; Orica Lecture, Melbourne Univ. 1998; Chem. Soc. Medal 1974, Wolfgang Ostwald Prize, Kolloid Gesellschaft 1979, Bude Medal, Collège de France 1981, Faraday Soc. C.I.S.G. Medal 1993. *Publications:* 298 papers in scientific journals, ed. 10 books. *Leisure interests:* gardening, walking, music. *Address:* School of Chemistry, Cantock's Close, University of Bristol, Bristol, BS8 1TS (Office); The Glen House, Holt Close, Wickham, Hants., PO17 5EY, England (Home). *Telephone:* (0117) 928 7647 (Office); (01329) 834745 (Home). *Fax:* (0117) 925 1295.

OTUNBAYEVA, Rosa Isakovna, C.PHIL.SC.; Kyrgyzstan politician and diplomatist; b. 23 Aug. 1950; m.; one s. one d.; ed. Moscow Univ.; sr. teacher, Head of Chair Kyrgyz Univ. 1975–81; Second Sec. Regional CP Cttee. in Frunze, Sec. City CP Cttee. 1979–86; Vice-Chair. Council of Ministers, Minister of Foreign Affairs of Kyrgyz S.S.R. 1986–89; Exec. Sec. U.S.S.R. Comm. on UNESCO Problems 1989–90, Chair. 1990–91; Amb. of U.S.S.R. to Malaysia 1991–92; Vice-Prime Minister and Minister of Foreign Affairs of Repub. of Kyrgyzstan Feb.–May 1992; Amb. of Kyrgyzstan to U.S.A. 1992–94 (also accred. to Canada); Minister of Foreign Affairs 1994–97. *Address:* c/o Ministry of Foreign Affairs, 205 Abdumomunov Str., Bishkek, Kyrgyzstan 720003. *Telephone:* (996-2) 220545. *Fax:* (996-2) 225735.

OTUNGA, H.E. Cardinal Maurice Michael: Kenyan ecclesiastic; b. Jan. 1923, Chebukwa; ordained priest 1950; consecrated titular Bishop of Tacape 1957; Bishop of Kisii 1961; titular Archbishop of Bomarzo 1969; Archbishop of Nairobi 1971; created Cardinal by Pope Paul VI 1973; Primate of Kenya 1983–; Dir. Castrense for Kenya. *Address:* Archbishop's House, P.O. Box 14231, Nairobi, Kenya. *Telephone:* (2) 441919. *Fax:* (2) 471320.

OU GEPING; Chinese administrator; b. 1930, Feicheng Co., Shandong Prov.; ed. Shandong Univ.; joined CCP 1962; Chair. Environmental Protecting Comm. of State Council 1987; Chair. Environmental Protecting Cttee. 8th NPC 1994–. *Address:* Standing Committee, National People's Congress, Tiananmen Square, Beijing 100010, People's Republic of China.

OUAIDOU GUELENDOUKSIA, Nassour; Chadian politician; fmrly. Sec.-Gen. in Office of the Pres.; Prime Minister of Chad May 1997–. *Address:* Office of the Prime Minister, N'Djamena, Chad.

OUATTARA, Alassane D., D.SC.; Côte d'Ivoirian financial official; b. 1 Jan. 1942, Dimbokro; ed. Drexel Inst. of Tech., Phila. and Univ. of Pennsylvania, U.S.A.; Economist, IMF 1968–73; Sr. Staff mem. in charge of missions Banque Centrale des Etats de l'Afrique de l'Ouest (BCEAO) 1973–75, Special Adviser to the Gov. and Dir. of Research 1975–82, Vice-Gov. 1983–84, Gov. 1988–90; Dir. African Dept., IMF 1984–88, Counsellor to Man. Dir. 1987–88; Prime Minister of Côte d'Ivoire and Minister of Economy and Finance 1990–93; Deputy Man. Dir. IMF 1994–; Pres. CNUCED 1979–80; mem. Bd. Dirs., Global Econ. Action Inst.; Expert Adviser Comm. sur les Corpns. Transnat.; Hon. Gov. BCEAO; Commdr. Ordre du Lion du Sénégal, Ordre du Mono du Togo, Ordre Nat. du Niger, Grand Officier Ordre Nat. de Côte d'Ivoire. *Address:* 700 19th Street, N.W., Suite 12-300H, Washington, DC 20431, U.S.A. *Telephone:* (202) 623-4553. *Fax:* (202) 623-4305.

OUCHI, Tsutomu, D. ECON.; Japanese professor of economics and politician; b. 19 June 1918, Tokyo; s. of Hyoe Ouchi; m. Setsuko Otsuka 1944; one s. one d.; ed. The Daiichi Kotogakko and Tokyo Imperial Univ.; researcher Japan Inst. of Agric. 1942–46; Assoc. Prof. Univ. of Tokyo 1947–60, Prof. 1960–79, Prof. Emer. 1979–; Prof. Shinshu Univ. 1979–84, Prof. Emer. 1984–; Prof. Daito Bunka Univ. 1987–91; Dean Faculty of Econs., Univ. of Tokyo 1968–69; Vice-Pres. Univ. of Tokyo 1972–73; Dir. Nat. Fed. of Univ. Co-operative Asscns. 1988–; Chair. Central Cttee. for Security of Employment 1976–88, Employment Cttee., Ministry of Labour 1988–96; mem. Japan Acad. 1981–; Mainichi Press Prize, Nasu Prize, Nihon Keizai Press Prize. *Publications:* Agricultural Crisis 1954, American Agriculture 1965, State Monopolistic Capitalism 1970, American Agriculture in the 1960's 1975, Japanese Agriculture 1978, Methodology of Economics 1980, Principles of Economics (2 vols) 1981–82, Imperialism, (2 vols.) 1984–85, World Economy 1991. *Leisure interests:* skiing, trekking. *Address:* 26–19 Hyakunin-cho II, Shinjuku-ku, Tokyo 169 0073, Japan. *Telephone:* (03) 3371-3760.

OUEDDEI, Goukouni; Chadian politician; b. 1944, Zouar; formed the Second Army of the Front de Libération Nationale du Tchad (FROLINAT) 1972; head of Northern Armed Forces Command Council 1977–; Chair. Revolutionary Cttee., Popular Armed Forces of FROLINAT 1978–84; Chair. Provisional State Council of Chad after Kano peace agreement March–April 1979, in charge of Information; Minister of State for the Interior in Shawa Govt. April–Sept. 1979; Pres. of Chad and Head of State (Governement d'union nationale de transition-GUNT) 1979–82 (deposed); Pres. GUNT forces in N. Chad 1982–86, Pres. Conseil suprême de la Révolution 1985–86; leader Front de Libération nationale du Tchad (FROLINAT). *Address:* c/o Conseil Suprême de la Révolution, Badai, Chad.

OUÉDRAOGO, Gérard Kango; Burkinabè politician; b. 19 Sept. 1925, Ouahigouya; s. of Jean Ouédraogo and Christine Ouédraogo; m. 1947; Rep. to French West African Fed. 1952; Deputy to French Nat. Assembly 1956–59; co-founder Mouvement Démocratique Voltaïque; mem. Parl. 1957–65; Minister of Finance 1958–59; Amb. to U.K. 1961–66; Adviser, Ministry of Foreign Affairs; Pres. Union Démocratique Voltaïque 1970–74, now Commr.; Prime Minister 1971–74; Pres. Nat. Ass. 1978–80; Jr. Pres. ACP/EEC Lomé Convention 1970–80; Leader Rassemblement Démocratique Africain (RDA); Deputy and Pres. Parl. Group RDA, Assemblée des Députés du Peuple; Grand Officier Ordre Nat. Burkina Faso; Grand Officier du Mérite Français; Grand Officier Légion d'honneur; several other decorations. *Address:* 01-BP 347, Ouagadougou, Burkina Faso. *Telephone:* (226) 2 30 68 53; (226) 55 02 00 (Ouahigouya).

OUEDRAOGO, Idrissa; Burkinabè film director; ed. film school in Burkina Faso; Grand Jury Prize, Cannes Film Festival 1990; Etalon de Yenenga (Grand Prix) for Tilaï, Pan-African Film Festival (Fesparo), Ouagadougou 1991. *Films include:* Yaaba, Tilaï, Samba Traore 1993, Lumiè et Compagnie 1995, Kini and Adams 1997. *Address:* FEPACI, 01 B.P. 2524, Ouagadougou, Burkina Faso.

OUEDRAOGO, Kadré Désiré; Burkinabè politician; fmr. Gov. of Cen. Bank of West African States; Prime Minister of Burkina Faso Feb. 1996–; independent. *Address:* Office of the Prime Minister, Ouagadougou, Burkina Faso.

OUELLET, Hon. André, P.C., B.A., LL.L.; Canadian fmr. politician and lawyer; b. 6 April 1939, St.-Pascal, Quebec; s. of Dr. Albert Ouellet and Rita Turgeon; m. Edith Pagé 1965; two s. two d.; ed. Pensionnat St.-Louis de Gonzague, Quebec Seminary, Ottawa and Sherbrooke Univs.; M.P. for Papineau 1967–93; Parl. Sec. to Minister for External Affairs 1970, to Minister for Nat. Health and Welfare 1971; Postmaster Gen. 1972–74; Minister for Consumer and Corp. Affairs 1974–76, 1980–84, for Urban Affairs 1976–79, for Public Works 1978–79, for Canada Post Corpn. 1980–83, for Labour 1983, for Regional Econ. Devt. 1983–84; Pres. Privy Council 1984; Govt. Leader of Commons 1984; Opposition Transport Critic 1984; Opposition External Affairs Critic 1987; Opposition Critic for Fed. Provincial Relations 1990; Minister for Foreign Affairs 1993–96; Chair. Canada Post Corpn. 1996–; Liberal. *Leisure interests:* tennis, swimming, squash, skiing, reading and collecting works of art. *Address:* Canada Post Corporation, 2701 Riverside Drive, Suite N1250, Ottawa, Ont. K1A 0B1, Canada.

OUMAROU, Ide; Niger public servant; b. 1937, Niamey; s. of Ounténi Oumarou and Salay Hamsatou; m. 1st Fatimata Diallo 1962, 2nd Adiara Garba 1968, 3rd Mariana Alhéri 1985; six s. four d.; ed. William Ponty School, Dakar, Senegal and Institut des Hautes Etudes d'Outre-mer, Paris; started as journalist in Ministry of Information, Niger 1960; Ed. Le Niger 1961–63; Dir. of Information 1963–70, Comm.-Gen. for Information 1970–72; Dir.-Gen. Office of Posts and Telecommunications 1972–74; Head of Cabinet of Pres. of Supreme Mil. Council 1974–79; Perm. Rep. UN New York 1979–83, non-perm. mem. Security Council 1980–81, Pres. Security Council May 1980–Aug. 1981, Vice-Pres. 35th Session UN Gen. Ass., Chair. Group of French-speaking Perm. Reps. to UN; Minister of Foreign Affairs 1983–85; Sec.-Gen. OAU 1985–89; Counsellor-Minister of State, President's Office 1989–91; mem. Cttee. of Eminent Persons reviewing Treaty of Community of W. African States; mem. Cttee. created by UN Sec.-Gen. for Prevention of Natural Disasters 1990–; mem. Cttee., The Hunger Project, New York and its jury for Leadership Prize for the Elimination of Hunger in Africa; Chevalier, Ordre des Arts et des Lettres (France) 1984; several other decorations, France, Germany, Tunisia, Saudi Arabia and Togo. *Publications include:* Gros Plan (Grand Prix littéraire d'Afrique noire, Paris 1978), Le Représentant 1984; several plays. *Address:* c/o Ministry of Foreign Affairs, Niamey, Niger. *Telephone:* 73 21 00 (Home).

OUMAROU, Mamane; Niger politician; m.; Prime Minister of Niger 1988–90; mem. Mouvement Nat. de la société de développement (MNSD). *Address:* c/o Office of the Prime Minister, Niamey, Niger.

OURISSON, Guy, DR.SC., PH.D.; French chemist; b. 26 March 1926, Boulogne-sur-Seine; s. of Jacques Ourisson and Colette Ourisson (née de Bosredon); m. 1st Paula Baylis 1950 (deceased 1958), 2nd Nicole Heiligenstein 1959 (divorced); one s. two d. from previous marriage; ed. Ecole Normale Supérieure, Paris, Harvard Univ.; Maître de Conférences, Univ. Louis Pasteur, Strasbourg 1955–58, Prof. of Chem. 1958–, Pres. of Univ. Louis Pasteur 1971–75; Dir. of Univ. Studies, Ministry of Educ. Nat. 1981–82; Dir. Inst. of Chem. of Natural Products, C.N.R.S., Gif/Yvette 1984–89; Chair. Scientific Council, Rhône-Poulenc 1988–92, Compagnie Générale des Eaux 1993–; Pres. of many scientific cttees. in France; Chair. Publications Cttee., IUPAC 1973–77, Sec.-Gen. 1975–83; Regional Ed. Tetrahedron Letters 1965–; Pres. Fondation Alsace; Vice-Pres. Acad. of Sciences 1997–; Sec.-Gen. Fondation Alfred Kastler de l'Académie des Sciences; mem. jury Prix Körber; mem. Acad. Leopoldina (Halle), Acad. Europaea, American Acad. of Arts and Sciences, Danish, Swedish, Indian, Rheinland-Westphalia, Serbian and French Acads. of Sciences; Hon. mem. Chemical Socs. of Belgium, U.K., Switzerland; awards from Chemical Socs. of France, Fed. Repub. of Germany, Belgium, U.K., U.S.A.; Officier, Légion d'honneur; Commdr., Ordre national du Mérite; Commdr. des Palmes académiques; Order of Sacred Treasure (Japan). *Publications:* over 400 on chem. and on ethics of science. *Address:* Centre de Neurochimie, 5 rue Blaise Pascal, 67084 Strasbourg (Office); 10 rue Geiler, 67000 Strasbourg, France (Home). *Telephone:* (03) 88-60-05-13; (03) 88-11-04-21 (Home). *Fax:* (03) 88-60-76-20.

OUSELEY, Sir Herman (George), Kt.; British civil servant and race relations adviser; various public service posts 1963–86; Race Relations Adviser Lambeth Borough Council 1979–81, GLC 1981–84; Dir. of Educ. ILEA 1986–88, Chief Exec. 1988–90; Chief Exec. London Borough of Lambeth 1990–93; Chair. Comm. for Racial Equality 1993–; mem. Council Policy Studies Inst. 1988–, Inst. of Race Relations 1990–, Inst. of Educ., Univ. of London 1995–; mem. Advisory Council Prince's Youth Business Trust 1993–; Chair. Uniting Britain Charitable Trust 1997–, Presentation Educ. and Employment Charitable Trust 1997–; Patron Presentation Housing Asscn. 1990–. *Publications:* The System 1981, pamphlets and articles on local govt., public services, employment, training and race equality issues. *Address:* Elliot House, 10–12 Allington Street, London, SW1E 5EH, England (Office).

OUSMANE, Sembene; Senegalese writer and film-maker; b. 1 Jan. 1923, Ziguinchor, Casamance region; plumber, bricklayer, apprentice mechanic; served in Europe in World War II; docker in Marseille; studied film production in U.S.S.R. under Marc Donski; Founder Ed. first Wolof language monthly, Kaddu; first prize for novelists at World Festival of Negro Arts, Dakar 1966; numerous int. awards. *Films:* Borom Sarret 1963, niaye 1964, La noire de ... 1966, Mandabi 1968, Taaw 1971, Emitai 1971, Xala 1974, Ceddo 1977, Camp de Thiaroye 1988 (Jury Prize, Venice), Guelwaar 1992. *Publications:* novels: Le docker noir 1956, O pays mon beau peuple 1957, Les bouts de bois de Dieu 1960, Voltaïque 1962, L'harmattan 1964, Vehi-Ciosane suivi du mandat 1966, Xala 1974, Fat Ndiay Diop 1976, Dernier de l'empire 1979, Niiwam 1987, God's Bits of Wood 1995, Guelwaar 1996. *Address:* P.O. Box 8087 Yoff, Dakar, Senegal. *Telephone:* 823 51 66. *Fax:* 823 51 66.

OUSSET, Cécile; French pianist; b. 23 Jan. 1936, Tarbes; ed. Paris Conservatoire; French début with Orchestre de Paris; British début, Edin. Festival 1980; U.S. début with L.A. Philharmonic 1984; prizewinner, Van Cliburn, Queen Elisabeth of Belgium, Busoni and Marguerite Long-Jacques Thibaud competitions; Grand Prix du Disque for recording of Brahms 2nd Piano Concerto; other recordings include concertos by Rachmaninov, Liszt, Saint-

Saëns, Ravel, Grieg and Mendelssohn and recitals of Chopin, Debussy and Liszt.

OUTRAM, Dorinda, M.A., PH.D.; British historian; b. 11 Dec. 1949, Leicester; d. of Ernest Albert Outram and Rosemary Elenor Collins; m. 1976 (divorced 1980); one s.; ed. Univ. of Cambridge; Research Fellowship British Acad. 1974, Univ. of Reading 1975; Lectureship and Research Fellowships, Univ. of London 1977–81; Asst. Prof. Univ. of Montreal 1981–82; Research Fellowship, Girton Coll., Cambridge 1982–84; Lecturer in Modern History, Univ. Coll., Cork 1984–98; Clark Prof. of History, Univ. of Rochester, N.Y. 1998–; Visiting Prof. Griffith Univ., Australia 1990; Landon Clay Visiting Assoc. Prof. Harvard Univ. 1991–92; Editorial Dir., Comité int. pour l'édition de la correspondance de Georges Cuvier 1983–; mem. Editorial panel, Dictionary of Irish Biography 1984–; Ed. Bulletin of the Irish Asscn. for Research in Women's History 1987–88; Trustee, British Soc. for History of Science; Hon. Sec. Irish Nat. Cttee. for Research in Women's History 1988–; Vellacott Historical Essay Prize, Cambridge 1971; Royal Soc. of London Research Award 1982; C.N.R.S. Research Award, Paris 1982. *Publications:* Science, Vocation and Authority in Post-Revolutionary France; Georges Cuvier 1984, Uneasy Careers and Intimate Lives: Women in Science 1987, The Body and the French Revolution 1989, The Enlightenment 1994, numerous articles. *Leisure interest:* walking. *Address:* Department of History, University of Rochester, Rochester, NY 14627, U.S.A.

OUVRIEU, Jean-Bernard; French diplomatist; b. 13 March 1939; m. Arabella Cruse 1968; one s. two d.; ed. Ecole Nat. d'Administration; Head of Mission, Office of Prime Minister 1968–69; served Perm. Mission to European Communities, Brussels 1971–74, Baghdad 1975–77, Washington 1977–79; Deputy Dir., Office of Minister of Foreign Affairs 1979–80; Rep. to Governing Council of IAEA 1981–85; Amb. to Repub. of Korea 1985–87, to Brazil 1989–93, to Japan 1993–98; Dir. of Econ. and Financial Affairs, Ministry of Foreign Affairs 1987–89; Officier, Légion d'honneur, Officier, Ordre nat. du Mérite. *Address:* c/o Ministry of Foreign Affairs, 37 quai d'Orsay, 75007 Paris; 23 Square des Peupliers, 75013 Paris, France.

OUYAHIA, Ahmed; Algerian politician and diplomatist; fmr. Sec. of State for Co-operation and Maghreb Affairs; Prime Minister of Algeria 1996–98. *Address:* c/o Office of the Prime Minister, rue Docteur Saâdane, Algiers, Algeria.

OUYANG SHAN; Chinese author, party and cultural official; b. 1908, Ouyang Yangyi, Guangdong Prov.; active in Guangdong dialectical literary movt., studied under Lu Xun in Shanghai 1930s; active in Fed. of Literary and Art Circles, Yun'an 1940–; Deputy Dir. Cultural and Educ. Dept., Guangdong Prov. People's Congress, Chair S. China Fed. of Literary and Art Circles 1951–; Pres. S. China Inst. of People's Literature and Art 1952–; published self-criticism in Yangtze Literature and Art Feb. 1952; Chair Canton branch of Union of Chinese Writers 1953–66; Council mem. China-Pakistan Friendship Asscn. 1956–66; Standing Cttee. mem. Guangdong Prov. CPPCC Cttee. 1959–66; mem. 3rd NPC Sept. 1964; criticized 1964; purged 1966; rehabilitated 1978; Vice-Chair. Guangdong Prov. People's Congress 1979–81; mem. Cen. Advisory Cttee. of CCP Cen. Cttee. 1982–; Hon. Vice-Chair. Chinese Writers' Asscn. 1996–. *Publications:* Stranger in the Village, The Proud Lady, Three-Family Lane, Bitter Struggle. *Address:* Central Advisory Committee of the Central Committee of the Chinese Communist party, Zhongnanhai, Beijing, People's Republic of China.

OUYANG ZIYUAN; Chinese scientist; b. Oct. 1935; Chair. Chinese Soc. of Mineralogy, Petrology and Geochem.; Vice-Chair. Chinese Soc. of Space Research; mem. Chinese Sciences Acad. 1992; a Vice-Chair. Guizhou Prov. 9th People's Congress 1998–. *Address:* Institute of Geochemistry, Guiyang City, Guizhou Province, People's Republic of China.

OVCHINIKOV, Vladimir Pavlovich; Russian pianist; b. 1 Jan. 1958, Beleby, Urals; ed. pvtly. under Anna Artobolevskaya and Moscow Conservatoire (under Alexey Nasedkin); Silver Medal (jtly. with Peter Donohoe), Moscow Tchaikovsky Competition 1982; First Prize, Leeds Int. Piano Competition 1987; London debut, Barbican Hall 1987; has since given recitals in UK, Europe, U.S.A., Canada and Japan and appeared with BBC Symphony, Royal Liverpool Philharmonic, Netherlands Philharmonic, Moscow Philharmonic and other maj. orchestras; lecturer, Keyboard Studies, Royal Northern Coll. of Music 1994–. *Address:* c/o Manygate Management, 13 Cotswold Mews, 30 Battersea Square, London, SW11 3RA, England. *Telephone:* 0171-223 7265. *Fax:* 0171-585 2830.

OVCHINNIKOV, Lev Nikolayevich; Russian geologist; b. 9 Oct. 1913, Perm; s. of Nicolai Alexandrovich Ovchinnikov and Marija Michailovna Ovchinnikova; m. Ludmila Ovchinnikova 1952; three s. one d.; ed. Uralsk Univ.; mem. CPSU 1944–91; Head of Lab. for Mineralogy and Geochemistry, Inst. of Mining and Geology, Uralsk Br. U.S.S.R. (now Russian) Acad. of Sciences 1946–62; Dir. Inst. of Geology 1962–66; Dir. Inst. of Mineralogy, Geochemistry and Crystallochemistry 1966–86, Head Div. of Metallogeny 1986–; Corresp. mem. U.S.S.R. (now Russian) Acad. of Sciences 1964–. *Publications:* Genesis of Ore Deposits 1988, Applied Geochemistry 1990, Prognosis of Ore Deposits 1992, and numerous other publs., mainly on geology of the Urals, ore deposits and geochemical methods in geological prospecting. *Leisure interests:* fishing, mycology. *Address:* Institute of Mineralogy, Geochemistry and Crystallochemistry of Rare Elements, Veresayeva str. 15, 121357 Moscow, Russia. *Telephone:* 2351-24-28 (Office); 124-99-75 (Home).

OVENDEN, Graham Stuart, M.A., A.R.C.A., A.R.C.M.; British art historian, artist and poet; b. 11 Feb. 1943, Alresford, Hants.; s. of the late Henry Ovenden and Gwendoline D. Hill; m. Ann. D. Gilmore 1969; one s. one d.; ed. Alresford Dames School, Itchen Grammar School, Southampton, Southampton Coll. of Art, Royal Coll. of Music and Royal Coll. of Art; corresp. and critic, Architecture Design Magazine. *Publications:* Illustrators of Alice 1971, Victorian Children 1972, Clementina, Lady Harwarden 1973, Pre-Raphaelite Photography 1972, Victorian Erotic Photography 1973, Aspects of Lolita 1975, A Victorian Album (with Lord David Cecil) 1976, Satirical Poems and Others 1983, The Marble Mirror (poems) 1984, Lewis Carroll Photographer 1984; Graham Ovenden . . . A Monograph with essays by Laurie Lee, etc. 1987, Sold With All Faults (poems) 1991; photographs: Alphonse Mucha 1973, Hill & Adamson 1973; contributions on art to numerous journals. *Leisure interests:* music (very seriously indeed), architecture, social science. *Address:* Barley Splatt, Panters Bridge, Mount, nr. Bodmin, Cornwall, England.

OVERBEEK, Jan Theodoor Gerard, DRS.CHEM., PH.D.; Dutch professor of physical chemistry; b. 5 Jan. 1911, Groningen; s. of Dr. A. A. Overbeek and J. C. (van Ryssel) Overbeek; m. Johanna Clasina Edie 1936; four d.; ed. Univ. of Utrecht; Asst. at Univ. of Ghent, Belgium 1935–36, Univ. of Utrecht 1936–41; Scientific Officer, N. V. Philips, Eindhoven 1941–46; Prof. of Physical Chem., Univ. of Utrecht 1946–81, Vice-Pres. of Univ. 1971–76; Visiting Prof., M.I.T., Cambridge, Mass., U.S.A. 1952–53, 1966–67, 1969–81, 1984–88, Columbia Univ., New York 1956, Univ. of Southern Calif., Los Angeles 1959–60; Ed. Advances in Colloid Interface Science –1967, Ed. Emer. 1990–; mem. Bd. Verenigde Bedrijven Bredero, Utrecht 1963–83; mem. Royal Netherlands Acad. of Arts and Sciences 1953–; Foreign mem. Royal Flemish Acad. of Sciences (Belgium) 1957–; Foreign Hon. mem. American Acad. of Arts and Sciences 1969–; Hon. Fellow Royal Soc. of Chem. (London) 1983; Hon. mem. Royal Netherlands Chem. Soc. 1993–, Kolloid-Gesellschaft 1993–; Hon. D.Sc. (Clarkson Coll. of Tech., Potsdam, N.Y.) 1967, (Univ. of Bristol) 1984; Wolfgang-Ostwald-Preis (Kolloid-Gesellschaft) 1989; Kt., Order of Netherlands Lion. *Publications:* Theory of Stability of Lyophobic colloids (with E. J. W. Verwey) 1948, Colloid Science (with H. R. Kruyt) Vol. I 1952, Vol. II 1949, The Electrical Double Layer (with A. L. Loeb, P. H. Wiersema) 1960; An Introduction to Physical Chemistry (with H. R. Kruyt) 1954, Colloid and Surface Chemistry Vols. I–IV 1971–74, Electrochemistry Vols. I, II & III 1981; numerous articles and study guides on colloid and surface science. *Leisure interests:* outdoor activities, hiking, photography. *Address:* Zweerslaan 35, 3723HN Bilthoven, Netherlands (Home). *Telephone:* 030-2532391 (Office); 030-2282882 (Home).

OVERHAUSER, Albert Warner, PH.D.; American physicist; b. 17 Aug. 1925, San Diego; s. of Clarence Albert Overhauser and Gertrude Irene (Pehrson) Overhauser; m. Margaret Mary Casey 1951; four s. four d.; ed. Univ. of California at Berkeley; service with USNR 1944–46; Research Assoc., Univ. of Ill. 1951–53; Asst. Prof. of Physics, Cornell Univ. 1953–56, Assoc. Prof. 1956–58; Supervisor, Solid State Physics, Ford Motor Co., Dearborn, Mich. 1958–62, Man. Theoretical Sciences 1962–69, Asst. Dir. of Physical Sciences 1969–72, Dir. 1972–73; Prof. of Physics Purdue Univ., W. Lafayette, Ind. 1973–74, Stuart Dist. Prof. of Physics 1974–; Fellow American Physics Soc., American Acad. of Arts and Sciences; mem. N.A.S.; Hon. D.Sc. (Chicago) 1979, Hon. D. Laws (Simon Fraser Univ., Canada) 1998; Oliver E. Buckley Solid State Physics Prize (American Physics Soc.) 1975, Alexander von Humboldt Sr. U.S. Scientist Award 1979, Nat. Medal of Science 1994. *Address:* Department of Physics, Purdue University, West Lafayette, Ind. 47907; 236 Pawnee Drive West, Lafayette, IN 47906, U.S.A. (Home). *Fax:* (317) 494-0706.

OVERY, Richard James, PH.D., F.R.Hist.S.; British professor of history; b. 23 Dec. 1947, London; s. of James Herbert Overy and Margaret Grace Overy (née Sutherland); m. 1st Tessa Coles 1969 (dissolved 1976); m. 2nd Jane Giddens 1979 (dissolved 1992); m. 3rd Kim Turner 1992; one s. four d.; ed. Sexey's Blackford Grammar School, Somerset, Gonville and Caius Coll., Cambridge; Research Fellow Churchill Coll., Cambridge 1972–73; Fellow and Coll. lecturer Queen's Coll., Cambridge 1973–79; Univ. Asst. Lecturer Cambridge Univ. 1976–79; lecturer in History King's College, Univ. of London 1980–88, Reader in History 1988–92, Prof. of Modern History 1992–; T. S. Ashton Prize 1983, Cass Prize for Business History 1987. *Publications:* The Air War 1939–45 1980, Goering: The 'Iron Man' 1984, The Road to War 1989, War and Economy in the Third Reich 1994, Why the Allies Won 1995, Times Atlas of the Twentieth Century 1996, Russia's War 1997. *Address:* Department of History, King's College, Strand, London, WC2R 2LS, England. *Telephone:* 0171-836 5454. *Fax:* 0171-873 2502.

OVETT, Stephen Michael, M.B.E.; British athlete; b. 9 Oct. 1955, Brighton, Sussex; m. Rachel Waller 1981; ed. Brighton College of Art; competed Olympic Games, Montreal 1976, finished 5th in 800 m., reached semi-final of 1500 m.; Moscow 1980, won gold medal at 800 m. and bronze medal at 1500 m.; European Junior Champion at 800 m. 1973; European Champion at 1500 m. 1978 and silver medallist at 800 m. 1974 and 1978; world record holder at 1500 m., fmr. world record holder at mile; holder of record for greatest number of mile/1500 m. victories (45 to 1980); also winner of major titles at 5,000m. *Leisure interest:* art.

OVITZ, Michael; American film industry executive; b. Dec. 1946, Chicago; m. Judy Reich 1969; three c.; ed. Birmingham High School and Univ. of

Calif. Los Angeles; tour guide at Universal Studios while at coll.; joined William Morris Agency, Beverly Hills 1968; with three others formed Creative Artists Agency (CAA) 1975, Pres. 1975–95; Pres. Walt Disney Co. 1995–97; Head Livent Inc. Toronto 1998–; f. Artists Man. Group 1999; agency represents many of top Hollywood actors, writers, dirs., producers. *Address:* c/o Dreyer Edmonds & Assocs., 355 S. Grand Avenue, Suite 4150, Los Angeles, CA 90071, U.S.A.

OWADA, Hisashi; Japanese diplomatist and international lawyer; b. 18 Sept. 1932, Niigata; s. of Takeo Owada and Shizuka Tamura; m. Yumiko Egashira 1962; three d.; (one d. Masako, m. Crown Prince Michiko); ed. Univs. of Tokyo and Cambridge; Pvt. Sec. to Prime Minister 1976–78; Minister-Plenipotentiary, U.S.S.R. 1981–84; Dir.-Gen. Treaties Bureau and Office for Law of the Sea 1984–87; Deputy Vice-Minister, Ministry of Foreign Affairs 1987–88; Amb. to OECD 1988–89; Deputy Minister, Ministry of Foreign Affairs 1989–91, Vice-Minister for Foreign Affairs 1991–93; Adviser to Minister for Foreign Affairs 1993–94, 1999–; Adjunct Prof. Tokyo Univ. 1963–88, Col. Law School 1994–; Visiting Prof. Harvard Univ. 1979–81, 1987, 1989, N.Y. Univ. Law School; Amb. and Perm. Rep. to UN 1994–98; Pres. Japan Inst. of Int. Affairs 1999–; Associé de l'Institut de Droit Int. *Publications:* U.S.–Japan Economic Interaction in an Independent World 1981, Japanese Perspectives on Asian Security 1982, Practice of Japan in International Law 1984, From Involvement to Engagement: A New Course for Japanese Foreign Policy 1994, Diplomacy 1997. *Leisure interests:* music, skiing. *Address:* Japan Institute of International Affairs, Kasimigaseki Bldg. 11/F, 3-2-5 Kasumigaseki, Chiyoda-ku, Tokyo, 100-6011 Japan. *Telephone:* (03) 3503-6625. *Fax:* (03) 3503-7292.

OWEN, Baron (Life Peer) cr. 1992, of the City of Plymouth; **David Anthony Llewellyn Owen,** C.H., P.C., M.A., M.B., B.CHIR.; British politician; b. 2 July 1938, Plymouth; s. of Dr. John William Morris Owen and Mary Llewellyn; m. Deborah Schabert 1968; two s. one d.; ed. Bradfield Coll., Sidney Sussex Coll., Cambridge, St. Thomas' Hosp.; house appointments, St. Thomas' Hosp. 1962–64, Neurological and Psychiatric Registrar 1964–66, Research Fellow, Medical Unit 1966–68; M.P. for Sutton Div. of Plymouth 1966–74, for Devonport Div. of Plymouth 1974–92; Parl. Private Sec. to Minister of Defence, Admin. 1967; Parl. Under-Sec. of State for Defence, Royal Navy 1968–70; Opposition Defence Spokesman 1970–72, resigned over party policy on EEC 1972; Parl. Under-Sec. of State, Dept. of Health and Social Security (DHSS) March-July 1974; Minister of State, DHSS 1974–76, FCO 1976–77; Sec. of State for Foreign and Commonwealth Affairs 1977–79; Opposition Spokesman for Energy 1979–80; co-f. Social Democratic Party (SDP) 1981; Chair. Parl. Cttee. 1981–82; Deputy Leader SDP 1982–83, Leader 1983–87, 1988–92; now Independent Social Democrat; Chair. Decision Tech. Int. 1970–72, Palme Comm. on Disarmament and Security Issues 1980–89, Ind. Comm. on Int. Humanitarian Issues 1983–88; EC Co-Chair. Int. Conference on Fmr. Yugoslavia 1992–95, Carnegie Comm. on Preventing Deadly Conflict 1994–; Exec. Chair. Middx. Holdings 1995–; Dir. (non-exec.) Coats Viyella 1994–; Dir. Abbott Laboratories 1996–; f. New Europe 1999; Chair. Humanitas; Chancellor Liverpool Univ. 1996–. *Publications:* Ed.: A Unified Health Service 1968; Contributor: Social Services for All 1968; Author: The Politics of Defence 1972, In Sickness and in Health—The Politics of Medicine 1976, Human Rights 1978, Face the Future 1981, A Future that Will Work 1984, A United Kingdom 1986, Personally Speaking to Kenneth Harris 1987, Our NHS 1988, Time to Declare (autobiog.) 1991, Seven Ages (Poetry) 1992, Balkan Odyssey 1995; articles in Lancet, Neurology and Clinical Science. *Leisure interest:* sailing. *Address:* House of Lords, London, SW1A 0PW; 78 Narrow Street, Limehouse, London, E14 8BP, England (Home). *Telephone:* 0171-787 2751; 0171-987 5441 (Home). *Fax:* (01442) 876108.

OWEN, Clive; British actor; b. 1965; ed. Royal Acad. of Dramatic Arts; m. Sarah-Jane Fenton. *Television appearances include:* Precious Bane, Vroom, Chancer (series), Sharman (series). *Film appearances include:* Close My Eyes 1991, Century, Bent 1998. *Stage appearances include:* Design for Living 1994, Closer 1997.

OWEN, Sir Geoffrey (David) Kt., M.A.; British newspaper editor; b. 16 April 1934; s. of L. G. Owen; m. 1st Dorothy J. Owen 1961 (died 1991); two s. one d.; m. 2nd Miriam Marianna Gross 1993; ed. Rugby School and Balliol Coll. Oxford; joined Financial Times as feature writer and industrial corresp. 1958, U.S. corresp. 1961, industrial ed. 1967; Exec. Industrial Reorganization Corpn. 1967–69; Dir. of Admin. Overseas Div. British Leyland Int. 1969, Dir of Personnel and Admin. 1972; Deputy Ed. Financial Times 1974–80, Ed. 1981–90; Dir. Business Policy Programme, Centre for Economic Performance, L.S.E. 1991–; mem. Council Foundation for Mfg. and Industries 1993–. *Publication:* Industry in the U.S.A. 1966. *Address:* London School of Economics and Political Science, Houghton Street, London, WC2A 2AE, England.

OWEN, Kenneth Frederick; South African journalist; b. 18 Feb. 1935, Johannesburg; m. Catherine F. Hamilton 1985; one s.; ed. Lydenberg High School, Transvaal; Asst. Ed. Sunday Times 1977; Man. Ed. Rand Daily Mail 1981; Ed. Sunday Express 1982; Ed. Business Day 1986; Ed. Sunday Times 1990–96. *Leisure interests:* sailing, reading, politics, writing. *Address:* P.O. Box 1090, Johannesburg, 2000 (Office); 49 Maple Drive, Athol, 2196, South Africa (Home).

OWEN, Ray David, PH.D., SC.D.; American biologist; b. 30 Oct. 1915, Genesee, Wis.; s. of Dave Owen and Ida Hoeft Owen; m. June Johanna Weissenberg 1939; one s.; ed. Carroll Coll., Wis., Univ. of Wisconsin; Research Fellow, Wisconsin 1941–43, Asst. Prof. of Genetics and Zoology 1943–47; Gosney Fellow, Calif. Inst. of Tech. 1946–47, Assoc. Prof. 1947–53, Prof. 1953–83, Chair. Div. of Biology 1961–68, Vice-Pres. for Student Affairs and Dean of Students 1975–80, Prof. Emer. 1983; Research Participant, Oak Ridge Nat. Lab. 1957–58; mem. Genetics Soc. of America (Treas. 1957–60, Vice-Pres. 1961, Pres. 1962), Nat. Acad. of Sciences, American Acad. of Arts and Sciences, American Philosophical Soc., Soc. for the Study of Evolution, American Asscn. of Immunologists; served on numerous scientific cttees. *Publications:* General Genetics (with Srb and Edgar) 1952, 1965; numerous research papers. *Address:* Division of Biology, 156-29, California Institute of Technology, Pasadena, CA 91125, U.S.A. (Office). *Telephone:* (626) 395-4960 (Office). *Fax:* (626) 449-0756.

OWEN, Robert John Richard, M.A.; British financial official; b. 11 Feb. 1940, London; s. of Thomas R. Owen and Margaret Fletcher; m. Beatrice M. Voelker 1962 (divorced); two s. one d.; ed. Repton School and Oriel Coll. Oxford; Foreign Office 1961–68, served British Embassy, Washington 1964–68; H.M. Treasury 1968–70; Morgan Grenfell & Co., Ltd. 1970–79, Dir. 1973; Dir. Merchant Banking Div. Lloyds Bank Int., Ltd. 1979–82, Dir. Far East Div. 1982–84; Dir. of Investment Banking, Lloyds Bank PLC and Chair. Lloyds Merchant Bank, Ltd. 1984–88; Adviser to Hong Kong Govt. on implementation of Securities Review Cttee. Report 1988–89; Chair. Securities and Futures Comm. of Hong Kong 1989–92; Dir. European Capital Co. Ltd. 1992–, Regulatory Bd. and Council of Lloyd's of London 1993–; Deputy Chair. Nomura Int. Ltd., Hong Kong 1993–; Dir. Yaohan Int. Holdings 1993–, Int. Securities Consultancy Ltd. 1995–, Regent Pacific Group Ltd. 1998–. *Leisure interests:* mountain walking, collecting oriental paintings and carvings. *Address:* c/o European Capital Co. Ltd., 3 Lombard Street, London, EC3V 9AA, England.

OWEN-JONES, Lindsay, B.A.; British business executive; b. 17 March 1946, Wallasey; s. of Hugh A. Owen-Jones and Esmee (Lindsay) Owen-Jones; m. 1st Violaine de Dalmas 1984; one d.; m. 2nd Cristina Furno 1994; ed. Univ. of Oxford and European Inst. of Business Admin. (INSEAD); Product Man. L'Oréal 1969, Head, Public Products Div., Belgium 1971–74, Man. SCAD (L'Oréal subsidiary), Paris 1974–76, Marketing Man. Public Products Div., Paris 1976–78, Gen. Man. SAIPO (L'Oréal subsidiary, Italy) 1978–81, Chair. 1991–, Pres. COSMAIR Inc. (exclusive L'Oréal agent) U.S.A. 1981–83, Vice-Pres. L'Oréal Man. Cttee. 1984, mem. Bd. of Dirs. 1984, Pres. and C.O.O. 1984–88, Chair. and C.E.O. Sept. 1988–; Dir. Banque Nat. de Paris 1989–, Lafarge (fmrly. Lafarge Coppé) 1993–, Air Liquide 1994–; Officier, Légion d'honneur. *Leisure interest:* private helicopter pilot. *Address:* L'Oréal, 41 rue Martre, 92117 Clichy Cedex, France (Home). *Telephone:* (1) 47-56-70-00 (Office).

OWENS, Bill; American politician; m. Frances Owens; two s. one d.; fmrly. with Touche Ross & Co., Gates Corpn.; State Treas., Colorado 1994–99; Gov. of Colorado 1999–; fmrly. guest host Mike Rosen, Ken Hamblin and Chuck Baker talk shows; Republican. *Publications:* contrib. to professional journals. *Address:* Office of the Governor, State Capitol Building, Room 136, Denver, CO 80203, U.S.A.

OWUSU, Victor; Ghanaian politician; b. 26 Dec. 1923, Agona-Ashanti; ed. Univs. of Nottingham and London; called to the Bar, Lincoln's Inn 1952; practising barrister 1952–67; M.P. for Agona-Kwabre 1956–61; Attorney-Gen. 1966–69; concurrently Minister of Justice 1967–69; Minister of External Affairs April 1969, 1969–71; Attorney-Gen. and Minister of Justice 1971–72; Leader fmr. Popular Front Party 1979 (political activity suspended by Flt.-Lieut. Jerry Rawlings Jan. 1982); Presidential Cand. 1979; has served on several govt. comms. and corpns.; fmr. mem. Council of Univ. of Ghana, Legon, Council of Univ. of Science and Technology, Kumasi and Cen. Legal Council of Ghana. *Address:* Popular Front Party, Accra, Ghana.

OXBURGH, Sir Ernest Ronald, K.B.E., PH.D., F.R.S.; British geologist; b. 2 Nov. 1934, Liverpool; s. of Ernest Oxburgh and Violet Bugden; m. Ursula Mary Brown 1934; one s. two d.; ed. Liverpool Inst., Univ. of Oxford and Univ. of Princeton, U.S.A.; Departmental Demonstrator, Univ. of Oxford 1960–61, Lecturer in Geology 1962–78, Fellow, St. Edmund Hall 1964–78, Emer. Fellow 1978, Hon. Fellow 1986; Prof. of Mineralogy and Petrology, Univ. of Cambridge 1978–91, Head of Dept. of Earth Sciences 1980–88; Professorial Fellow, Queens' College, Cambridge 1989–91; Chief Scientific Adviser, Ministry of Defence 1988–93; Rector Imperial Coll. of Science, Tech. and Medicine Sept. 1993–; Fellow, Trinity Hall Cambridge 1978–82, Hon. Fellow 1983; Pres. Queens' Coll. Cambridge 1982–89; Dir. Shell Transport and Trading 1996–, Nirex 1996–97; Sherman Fairchild Distinguished Scholar, Calif. Inst. of Tech. 1985–86; Pres. European Union of Geosciences 1985–87; mem. Nat. Cttee. of Inquiry into Higher Educ. (Dearing Cttee.) 1996–97; Trustee Natural History Museum 1993–, Chair. of Trustees 1999–; Foreign mem. Venezuelan Acad. of Sciences 1992, Deutsche Acad. der Naturforscher Leopoldina 1994; Hon. Fellow Univ. Coll., Oxford 1983; Hon. mem. Geologists' Asscn.; D.Sc. h.c. (Paris) 1986, (Leicester) 1990, (Loughborough) 1991, (Edin.) 1994, (Birmingham, Liverpool) 1996; Bigsby Medal, Geological Soc. of London 1979. *Publications:* The Geology of the Eastern Alps (Ed. and Contrib.) 1968, Structural, Metamorphic and Geochronological Studies in the Eastern Alps 1971 and contribs. to Nature, Journal of Geophysical Research, Tectonophysics, Journal of the Geological Soc. of London and other learned journals. *Leisure interests:* reading, walking and various sports. *Address:* Imperial College of Science, Technology and Medicine, SW7 2AZ, England.

ØYANGEN, Gunhild; Norwegian politician; b. 31 Oct. 1947, Levanger; m.; Chair. Agdenes Labour Party, mem. Co. Council 1982–, mem. Nat. Bd. of Labour Party, Agricultural Cttee. 1985–; Minister of Agric. 1986–89; M.P. and Deputy Leader Agric. Cttee. 1989–90; Minister of Agric. 1990; Leader Social Cttee. in Parl. 1996–. *Address:* c/o Ministry of Agriculture, Akersgt. 42, P.O. Box 8001, Dep., 0030 Oslo, Norway.

ØYE, Harald Arnljot, DR.TECH.; Norwegian professor of inorganic chemistry; b. 1 Feb. 1935, Oslo; s. of Leiv C. Øye and Ingrid H. Øye; m. Tove Stiegler 1963; two s. one d.; ed. Norwegian Inst. of Tech.; Postdoctoral Fellow, Argonne Nat. Lab. Ill. U.S.A. 1963–64; Assoc. Prof. Inst. of Inorganic Chem. Norwegian Inst. of Tech. 1965–72, Prof. and Head of Inst. Norwegian Univ. of Science and Tech. (fmrly. Norwegian Inst. of Tech.) 1973–90, 1992–; Pres. Norwegian Acad. of Tech. Sciences 1985–92, Hon. Fellow 1993–; guest scientist at various insts. in Germany, Italy, U.S.A.; Brotherton Distinguished Prof. Univ. of Leeds 1985; awards from NATO Science Foundation, Alcoa Science Foundation, U.S. Nat. Research Council, Norwegian Nat. Science Prize for Outstanding Research 1997. *Publications:* Cathodes in Aluminium Electrolysis (with M. Sørlie) 1989; more than 300 publs. on electrowinning of aluminium and magnesium, characterization of silicon, carbon technology, transport properties, molten salt chemistry, spectroscopy and thermodynamics of high temperature systems. *Leisure interests:* reading, outdoor activities. *Address:* Institute of Inorganic Chemistry, Norwegian University of Science and Technology, 7034 Trondheim (Office); Steinhaugen 5, 7049 Trondheim, Norway (Home). *Telephone:* 73 594016 (Office); 73 937558 (Home).

OYÉ-MBA, Casimir, D. EN D.; Gabonese banker; b. 20 April 1942, Nzamaligue Village, Libreville; s. of Ange Mba and Marie-Jeanne Nse; m. Marie-Françoise Razafimbelo 1963; one s. two d.; ed. Univs. of Rennes and Paris; trainee Banque Centrale, Libreville 1967–69, Asst. Dir. 1969–70, Dir. 1970–73; Nat. Dir. Banque pour le Gabon 1973–76; Asst. Dir.-Gen. Banque Centrale 1977–78; Gov. Banque des Etats de l'Afrique Centrale 1978–; Prime Minister of Gabon 1990–94; Minister of Foreign Affairs and Co-operation 1994–; Acting Gov. IMF for Gabon 1969–76; Pres. Asscn. des Banques Centrales Africaines 1987–; Rep. of Komo-Mondah Dist. 1990–; mem. political bureau, Gabonese Democratic Party 1991; Campaign Man. for Pres. Omar Bongo 1993; Légion d'honneur; Gabon, Cameroon, Congo and Equatorial Guinea decorations. *Leisure interests:* football, tennis, cinema, reading. *Address:* Ministry of Foreign Affairs and Co-operation, P.O. Box 2245, Libreville, Gabon. *Telephone:* 72-95-21. *Fax:* 76-12-72.

ÖYMEN, Onur Basaran, PH.D.; Turkish diplomatist; b. 1940, Istanbul; s. of Münir Raşit Öymen and Nebahat Öymen; m. Nedret Gürsel 1971; one s. one d.; ed. Galatasay Lisesi, Istanbul, Univ. of Ankara; joined Ministry of Foreign Affairs 1964; mil. service 1964–66; Second Sec. NATO Dept., Ministry of Foreign Affairs 1966–68, First Sec. Perm. Del. to Council of Europe, Strasbourg 1968–72, Chief of Section, Policy Planning Dept., Ministry of Foreign Affairs 1972–74, Counsellor Turkish Embassy, Nicosia 1974–78; Special Adviser to Minister of Foreign Affairs 1978–80; Counsellor Turkish Embassy, Prague 1980–82, Turkish Embassy, Madrid 1982–84, Head Policy Planning Dept., Ministry of Foreign Affairs 1984–88, Amb. to Denmark 1988–90, to Germany 1990–95; Under-Sec. Ministry of Foreign Affairs 1995–97; Perm. Rep. of Turkey to NATO 1997–; Bureaucrat of the Year, Nokta Review 1995, Diplomat of the Year, Asscn. of Turkish Industrialists and Business 1995, 1996, 1997; Abdi Ipekçi Special Peace Award, Milliyet newspaper 1997. *Publications:* Türkiye 'nin Gücü (Turkish Strength) 1998, trans. into Turkish of Science and Common Sense by Oppenheimer. *Address:* Turkish Delegation to NATO, Boulevard Léopold III, 1110 Brussels, Belgium. *Telephone:* (32 2) 707 68 01. *Fax:* (32 2) 707 68 33.

OZ, Amos, B.A.; Israeli author; b. 4 May 1939, Jerusalem; m. Nily Zuckermann 1960; three c.; ed. Hebrew Univ. Jerusalem; Kibbutz Hulda 1957–86; teacher of literature and philosophy, Hulda High School and Givat Brenner Regional High School 1963–86; Visiting Fellow, St. Cross Coll. Oxford; Writer-in-residence Hebrew Univ. Jerusalem 1975; Visiting Prof. Univ. of Calif. at Los Angeles (Berkeley); Writer-in-residence, and Prof. of Literature Colorado Coll., Colorado Springs 1984–85; Prof. of Hebrew Literature, Ben Gurion Univ. 1987–, Agnon Chair in Modern Hebrew 1990–; Visiting Prof. of Literature, Writer in Residence, Boston Univ. 1987; Writer in Residence, Hebrew Univ. 1990–, and Prof of Literature, Princeton Univ. 1997; Holon Prize 1965, Brenner Prize 1976; Zeev Award for Children's Books 1978; Bernstein Prize 1983, Bialik Prize 1986; Prix Femina, Paris 1989 (for novel Black Box), German Publrs.' Int. Peace Prize 1992, Luchs Prize for Children's Books (Germany) 1993, Hamore Prize 1993, Israeli Prize for Literature 1998; Officier des Arts et des Lettres (France). *Publications:* novels: Elsewhere, Perhaps 1966, My Michael 1968, Touch the Water, Touch the Wind 1973, A Perfect Peace 1982, Black Box 1987, To Know a Woman 1989, Fima 1991, Don't Pronounce It Night 1994; novellas and short stories: Where the Jackals Howl 1965, Unto Death 1971, The Hill of Evil Counsel 1976; essays: Under this Blazing Light 1979, In the Land of Israel 1983, The Slopes of Lebanon 1987, Israel, Palestine and Peace 1994; Different People (selected anthology) 1974; Soumchi (children's story) 1978, Panther in the Basement (novel) 1995, A Story Begins 1996. *Address:* Ben Gurion University of the Negev, P.O.Box 653, Beersheva 84105, Israel.

OZAWA, Ichiro; Japanese politician; b. 24 May 1942, Mizusawa; m. Kazuko Fukuda 1973; three s.; mem. House of Reps.; Minister of Home Affairs 1985–87; fmr. Deputy Chief Cabinet Sec.; fmr. Dir.-Gen. Liberal-Democratic Party (L.D.P.) Election Bureau; Sec.-Gen. L.D.P. 1989–91; Chair. Cttee. on Rules and Admin.; left LDP 1993; co-founder Shinseito (Japan Renewal Party) 1993; Sec.-Gen. Shinshinto (New Frontier Party) 1994–95, Pres. 1995–97. *Publication:* Blueprint for A New Japan 1993. *Address:* Room 605, Daiichi Giia Kaikan, Nagata-cho, Chiyoda-ku, Tokyo 100, Japan.

OZAWA, Seiji; Japanese conductor; b. 1 Sept. 1935, Shenyang, China; m. 1st Kyoko Edo, 2nd Vera Ilyan; one s. one d.; ed. Toho School of Music, Tokyo (under Prof. Hideo Saito), Tanglewood, U.S.A., and in West Berlin under Herbert von Karajan; Asst. Conductor (under Leonard Bernstein), New York Philharmonic 1961–62 (including tour of Japan 1961); guest conductor, San Francisco Symphony, Detroit Symphony, Montreal, Minneapolis, Toronto and London Symphony Orchestras 1961–65; Music Dir. Ravinia Festival, Chicago 1964–68; Music Dir. Toronto Symphony Orchestra 1965–69, Boston Symphony Orchestra 1973–; toured Europe conducting many of the major orchestras 1966–67; Salzburg Festival 1969; Music Dir. San Francisco Symphony Orchestra 1970–76; Music Dir. Boston Symphony 1973–; toured U.S.A., France, Fed. Repub. of Germany, China 1979, Austria, U.K. 1981, Japan 1981, 1986, toured England, Netherlands, France, Germany, Austria and Belgium 1988; now makes frequent guest appearances with most of the leading orchestras of America, Europe and Japan; has conducted opera at Salzburg, Covent Garden, La Scala, Vienna Staatsoper and Paris Opera; conducted world premiere, Messiaen's St. Francis of Assisi, Paris 1983; First Prize, Int. Competition of Orchestra Conductors, France 1959, Koussevitsky Prize for outstanding student conductor 1960, Laureate, Fondation du Japon 1988; many recordings; Hon. D.Mus. (Univ. of Mass., New England Conservatory, Wheaton Coll., Norton, Mass.). *Leisure interests:* golf, tennis, skiing. *Address:* c/o Ronald A. Wilford Columbia Artists Management Inc., Conductors Division, 165 West 57th Street, New York, NY, U.S.A.; c/o Harold Holt Ltd., 31 Sinclair Road, London, W14 0NS, England.

OZBEK, (Ibrahim Mehmet) Rifat, B.A.; Turkish/British couturier; b. 8 Nov. 1953, Istanbul; s. of Melike Osbek and Abdulazim Mehmet Ismet; ed. St. Martin's School of Art, London; worked with Walter Albini for Trell; designer Monsoon Co.; launched O for Ozbek (now Future Ozbek) 1987; presented first collection 1984; British Fashion Council Designer of the Year 1988, 1992. *Address:* c/o OZBEK (London) Ltd., 18 Haunch of Venison Yard, London, W1Y 1AF, England. *Telephone:* 0171-408 0625. *Fax:* 0171-629 1586.

OZICK, Cynthia, M.A.; American author; b. 17 April 1928, New York; d. of William Ozick and Celia Regelson; m. Bernard Hallote 1952; one d.; ed. New York Univ. and Ohio State Univ.; mem. PEN, Authors League, American Acad. of Arts and Sciences, American Acad. and Inst. of Arts and Letters; Guggenheim Fellow 1982; Mildred and Harold Strauss Living Award, American Acad. of Arts and Letters 1983; Rea Award for short story 1986, PEN/Spiegel-Diamonstein Award for the Art of the Essay 1997, Harold Washington Literary Award, City of Chicago 1997; Hon. L.H.D. (Yeshiva) 1984, (Hebrew Union Coll.) 1984, (Williams Coll.) 1986, (Hunter Coll.) 1987, (Jewish Theological Seminary) 1988, (Adelphi) 1988, (State Univ. of N.Y.) 1989, (Brandeis) 1990, (Bard Coll.) 1991, (Spertus Coll.) 1991. *Publications:* Trust 1966, The Pagan Rabbi and Other Stories 1971, Bloodshed and Three Novellas 1976, Levitation: Five Fictions 1982, Art & Ardor: Essays 1983, The Cannibal Galaxy 1983, The Messiah of Stockholm 1987, Metaphor & Memory: Essays 1989, The Shawl 1989, What Henry James Knew: And Other Essays on Writers 1993, Blue Light (play) 1994, Portrait of the Artist as a Bad Character and Other Essays on Writing 1995, The Shawl (play) 1996, Fame & Folly: Essays 1996, The Puttermesser Papers (novel) 1997, The Best American Essays 1998 (guest Ed.); also poetry, criticism, reviews, translations, essays and fiction in numerous periodicals and anthologies. *Address:* c/o Alfred A. Knopf Co., 201 E. 50th Street, New York, NY 10022, U.S.A.

OZIM, Igor; Slovenian violinist; b. 9 May 1931, Ljubljana; s. of Rudolf Ozim and Marija Kodric; m. Dr. Breda Volovsek 1963; one s. one d.; ed. Akad. za glasbo Ljubljana, Royal Coll. of Music; studied with Prof. Max Rostal; Prof. of Violin, Akad. za glasbo Ljubljana 1960–63, Staatliche Hochschule für Musik, Cologne 1963–96, Berne Conservatoire 1985–, Hochschule für Musik, Vienna 1996–; concerts throughout Europe; First Prize, Int. Carl-Flesch Competition, London 1951, Munich 1953. *Address:* Breibergstrasse 6, 50939 Cologne, Germany. *Telephone:* (221) 414707.

P

PAAR, Vladimir, D.SC.; Croatian physicist; b. 11 May 1942, Zagreb; s. of Vladimir Paar and Elvira Paar; m. Nada Paar-Pandur 1968; three s. one d.; ed. Zagreb Univ.; Research Assoc. Zagreb Univ. 1973–76, Prof. 1981; Visiting Prof. in Copenhagen, Zurich, Paris, Moscow, Munich, Amsterdam, Livermore (Calif.) and Rio de Janeiro; participation in numerous int. confs.; mem. Croatian Acad. of Arts and Sciences; mem. Croatian Physical Soc., European Physical Soc. *Publications:* author and ed. of several books and over 300 papers on atomic nucleus structure, symmetry, supersymmetry and deterministic chaos, energetics and scientific econ. devt. *Leisure interests:* soccer, tennis, presenting science in the media. *Address:* Gajeva 26, Samobor, Croatia (Office). *Telephone:* (01) 4680 321 (Office). *Fax:* (01) 4680 336.

PAASIO, Pertti Kullervo, M.SC.; Finnish politician; b. 2 April 1939, Helsinki; s. of Rafael Paasio and Mary Wahlman; m. Kirsti Johansson 1967; two s. two d.; ed. Turku Univ.; regional organizer, Nuoret Kotkat (Young Falcons) 1963–66; mem. Turku City Council 1965–91; Sec. for Tourism, City of Turku 1967–73; Political Sec. Ministry of Finance 1972; Head of Turku Labour Exchange 1973–87; Vice-Pres. Int. Falcon Movt. 1975–81; Chair. Young Falcons Fed. 1978–81; Political Sec. to Prime Minister 1975; mem. Parl. 1975–79, 1982–96; mem. Exec. Cttee. Social Democratic Party of Finland 1978–91; mem. Presidential Electoral Coll. 1978, 1982, 1988; Leader, Social Democratic Parl. Group 1984–87; Chair. Social Democratic Party 1987–91; Deputy Prime Minister, Minister for Foreign Affairs 1989–91; Chair. Parl. Cttee. for Foreign Affairs 1991–96; mem. European Parl. 1996–, Quaestor 1997–. *Leisure interests:* photography, caravanning. *Address:* European Parliament, Rue Wiertz, 1000 Brussels, Belgium; Eerikinkatu 30, 20100 Turku, Finland. *Telephone:* (02) 414 5002 (Finland). *Fax:* (02) 414 5003 (Finland).

PACEA, Ion; Romanian painter; b. 7 Sept. 1924, Salonica; s. of Dumitru Pacea and Ecaterina Pacea (née Girtu); m. Lucrezia Hagi; one s. one d.; ed. The Fine Arts Acad. Bucharest; Sec., Vice-Pres. Romanian Fine Arts Union; Hon. mem. Romanian Acad. 1994–; has held exhbns. in Romania and Sofia, Prague, Berlin, Dresden, Venice, Le Havre, Tokyo, Aachen, Munich, Rome, Turin, Edinburgh, Washington, Salzburg; Romanian Acad. Award 1963, The Great Prize of the Romanian Fine Arts Union "Trionfo 81" Rome, Omaggio a Picasso, Rome, First Prize of Moldovan Repub. 1995. *Address:* 1 Pictor Rosenthal, 29 Pangratti, Bucharest, sector 1, Romania.

PAČES, Václav, DR.SC.NAT, D.SC.; Czech biochemist; b. 2 Feb. 1943, Prague; m. Magdalena Tomková Pačes 1966; two s.; ed. Charles Univ., Prague, Univ. of Chicago, McMaster Univ., Canada; scientific worker, Inst. of Organic Chemistry, Czech Acad. of Sciences, Prague 1970–77; independent scientific worker Inst. of Molecular Genetics Czech Acad. of Sciences 1977–86; Yale Univ., New Haven, Conn., 1990–91; Vice-Pres. Czech Acad. of Sciences 1993–97; State Prize for Science 1989; Prize for Popularization of Science 1992. *Publications:* Molecular Biology of the Gene, Prague 1982; Molecular Genetics 1983; Antibiotics, Mechanism of Action and Resistance (jtly.) 1987; Highlights of Modern Biochemistry 1989. *Leisure interests:* skiing, golf, music, hiking. *Address:* Institute of Molecular Genetics, Czech Acad. of Sciences, Flemingovo nám. 2, Prague 6 – 160 00, Czech Republic. *Telephone:* 242 405 21 (Office).

PACH, Zsigmond Pál; Hungarian historian; b. 4 Oct. 1919; s. of Lipót Pach and Rózsa Weisz; m. Klára Edit Sós 1945; one s. one d.; ed. Budapest Univ. of Arts and Sciences; High School Teacher 1943–48; Reader, Budapest Univ. of Econs. 1948–52, Prof. for Econ. History 1952–63, Rector 1963–67, Prof. Emer. 1995–; Deputy Dir. Hungarian Acad. of Sciences Inst. of History 1949–56, Dir. 1967–89; mem. Editorial Bd. Jahrbuch für Wirtschaftsgeschichte, Berlin 1960–91, The Economic History Review 1966–75; Ed.-in-Chief Acta Historica, Hungarian Acad. of Science 1973–92; mem. Hungarian Acad. of Science (Vice-Pres. 1976–85), Istituto Int. di Storia Economica, Exec. Cttee. Int. Econ. History Asscn. (Pres. 1978–82, Hon. Pres. 1982–); Foreign mem. U.S.S.R. (now Russian) Acad. of Sciences 1982, Bulgarian Acad. of Sciences 1985; Hon. Dr. Tartu Univ. 1982, Budapest Univ. of Econs. 1989; Kossuth Prize 1949, State Prize 1978, Laureate of Hungarian Repub. 1989. *Publications:* Gazdaságtörténet— a feudalizmus hanyatlásáig (Economic History up to the decline of Feudalism) 1947, Az eredeti tőkefelhalmozás Magyarországon (Previous accumulation of capital in Hungary) 1952, A földesuri gazdaság "porosz-utas" fejlődése Oroszországban a 19. sz. második felében (Development of the "Prussian type" manorial economy in Russia in the second part of the 19th century) 1958, Nyugateurópai és magyarországi agrárfejlődés a 15–17. sz.-ban (West-European and Hungarian development of agrarian relations in the 15th to 17th centuries) 1963, Die ungarische Agrarentwicklung im 16–17. Jahrhundert 1964, Problemi razvitiya vengerskoy marxistskoy istoricheskoy nauki 1966, A nemzetközi kereskedelmi utvonalak 15–17. sz.-i áthelyeződésének kérdéséhez (On the shifting of international trade routes in the 15th to 17th centuries) 1968, The Role of East Central Europe in International Trade: 16th and 17th Centuries 1970, Le commerce du Levant et la Hongrie au Moyen Age 1976, Történetszemlélet és történettudomány (History and its View) 1978, The Transylvanian Route of Levant Trade at the Turn of the 15th and 16th Centuries 1980, East Central Europe and World Trade at the Dawn of Modern Times 1982, Business Mentality and Hungarian National Character 1985, Történelem és nemzettudat (History and National Consciousness) 1987, Le Développement de l'Historiographie Hongroise après 1945, 1987, Von der Schlacht bei Mohács bis zur Rückeroberung Budas 1988, A harmincadvám eredete (The Origins of the Frontier Customs Duty in Hungary) 1990, The East-Central European Aspect of Overseas Discoveries and Colonization 1990, Colony or Periphery? The Position of East Central Europe in the 16th and 17th Centuries 1992, A Levante-történetírás fordulata 1879 és 1918 között (The Turnabout in the Historiography of the Levant between 1879 and 1918) 1993, Hungary and the European Economy in Early Modern Times 1994, The Oldest Guild Privilege of Clothmakers in Hungary (Debrecen) 1995, Hogyan lett a harmincadvámból huszad? 1996, A hazai posztóipar 16. századi történetéből (History of Nat. Clothing Industry in the Sixteenth Century) 1998. *Leisure interest:* history. *Address:* Németvölgyi ut 72/C, H-1124 Budapest, Hungary. *Telephone:* 3-558 133.

PACHAURI, Rajendra K., PH.D.; Indian research director; b. 20 Aug. 1940, Nainital; s. of A.R. Pachauri; m. Saroj Pachauri; three d.; ed. N.C. State Univ., U.S.A.; Asst. Prof. N.C. State Univ. 1974–75; mem. Sr. Faculty, Admin. Staff Coll. of India 1975–79, Dir. Consulting and Applied Research Div. 1979–81; Dir. Tata Energy Research Inst. New Delhi 1981–; Visiting Prof. W. Va. Univ. 1981–82; Visiting Fellow, Energy Dept. IBRD 1990; Pres. Int. Asscn. for Energy Econs. 1988, Chair. 1988–90; Pres. Asian Energy Inst. 1992–; mem. World Energy Council 1990–93; Adviser on Energy and Sustainable Man. of Natural Resources to the Admin., UNDP 1994–. *Publications:* The Dynamics of Electrical Energy Supply and Demand 1975, Energy and Economic Development in India 1977, International Energy Studies 1980, Energy Policy for India: An Interdisciplinary Analysis 1980, The Political Economy of Global Energy 1985, Global Energy Interactions 1986, Contemporary India 1992; scientific papers; newspaper articles. *Leisure interests:* cricket, flying, golf. *Address:* Tata Energy Research Institute, Darbari Seth Block, Habitat Place, New Delhi 110003, India. *Telephone:* 11-4622246, 4601550. *Fax:* 11-4621770, 4632609.

PACHE, Bernard; French business executive and engineer; b. 13 Oct. 1934, Sallanches; s. of Joseph Pache and Sabine Pache (née Minjoz); m. Yvette Vitaly 1959; three s. (one deceased); ed. Ecole Polytechnique de Paris and Ecole des Mines de Paris; mining engineer 1957–; Asst. to Dir. of Mines 1963–65; Tech. Adviser to Minister of Industry 1965–67; Chief Mining Engineer 1967; joined Compagnie Pechiney 1967, Asst. to Dir., Uranium and Nuclear Activity Dept., then Dir. of Mines Div., Nuclear Branch of Pechiney Ugine Kuhlmann 1969–73; Gen.-Man. Société des Electrodes et Refractaires Savoie (SERS) 1972–73; Chair. Compagnie Générale d'Electrolyse du Palais 1972–76; Gen.-Man. Société Cefilac 1973–74; Dir. and Gen. Man. Société Française d'Electrométallurgie 1974–79; Dir. of Industrial Policy, Pechiney Ugine Kuhlmann Group 1979–83, Deputy Dir. of Pechiney 1983–84, Chair. and C.E.O. 1985–86, Hon. Pres. 1986–; Dir.-Gen. Charbonnages de France 1986, Chair. and C.E.O. 1987–92, Hon. Pres. 1992–; Pres., Dir.-Gen. Cie. des Machines Bull 1992–93, Hon. Pres. 1993–; Pres. Directoire de l'Entreprise minière et chimique 1994–, la Fondation Georges 1994–, Energy Comm. Nat. Council of French Employers (CNPF) 1996–; Officier Légion d'honneur; Officier Ordre Nat. du Mérite. *Address:* Entreprise minièrve et chimique, 62 rue Jeanne d'Arc, 75641 Paris; Résidence de l'Observatoire, 8 rue Bel Air, 92190 Meudon, France (Home). *Telephone:* 46-26-32-90 (Home).

PACHECO, Máximo; Chilean economist; b. 12 Feb. 1953, Santiago; s. of Máximo Pachecho and Adriana Matte; m. Soledad Flanagan 1976; four d.; Man. Banco Osorno; Man. Planning, Banco Talca; Gen. Man. Leasing Andino 1983–90; Exec. Dir. Cabildo S.A. 1982–90, Jucosa 1987–90; Pres. Chilean Leasing Asscn. 1984–90; Faculty mem. Univ. de Chile; C.O.O. Codelco-Chile; Exec. Vice-Pres. for Chile and Latin America, Carter Holt Harvey 1994–. *Address:* Miraflores 222, 13th Floor, Santiago, Chile. *Telephone:* (56-2) 638-3585. *Fax:* (56-2) 632-9311.

PACINO, Al (Alfredo James); American actor; b. 25 April 1940, New York; s. of Salvatore and Rosa Pacino; ed. High School for the Performing Arts, New York, The Actors Studio; worked as messenger and cinema usher; Co-artistic Dir. The Actors Studio, Inc., New York 1982–83; mem. Artistic Directorate Globe Theatre 1997–; Broadway début in Does a Tiger Wear a Necktie? 1969; appeared with Lincoln Center Repertory Co. as Kilroy in Camino Real 1970; other New York appearances include The Connection, Hello Out There, Tiger at the Gates and The Basic Training of Pavlo Hummel 1977, American Buffalo 1981 (U.K. 1984), Julius Caesar 1988, Salome 1992; appearances at Charles Playhouse, Boston, include: Richard III 1973 (repeated on Broadway 1979), Arturo Ui 1975, Rats (director) 1970; films include: Me, Natalie 1969, Panic in Needle Park 1971, The Godfather 1972, Scarecrow 1973, Serpico 1974, The Godfather Part II 1974, Dog Day Afternoon 1975, Bobby Deerfield 1977, And Justice For All 1979, Cruising 1980, Author! Author! 1982, Scarface 1983, Revolution 1985, Sea of Love 1990, Dick Tracy 1991, The Godfather Part III 1990, Frankie and Johnny 1991, Glengarry Glen Ross 1992, Scent of a Woman (Acad. Award for Best Actor 1993) 1992, Carlito's Way 1994, City Hall 1995, Heat 1995, Donny

Brasco 1996, Looking for Richard 1996 (also producer, dir.), Tony Award 1996, Devil's Advocate 1997; Nat. Soc. of Film Critics Award, The Godfather; British Film Award, The Godfather Part II. *Address:* c/o Rick Nicita, C.A.A., 9830 Wilshire Boulevard, Beverly Hills, CA 90212, U.S.A.

PACKER, James Douglas; Australian media company executive; s. of Kerry Francis Packer (q.v.) and Roslyn Packer; ed. Cranbrook School, Sydney; worked as a 'jackeroo' on a family-owned cattle station, Newcastle Walters; joined family business as magazine sales rep.; Dir. Publishing & Broadcasting Ltd. (PBL) 1991–, Man. Dir. 1996–, Exec. Chair. 1998–; Dir. Australian Consolidated Press Group Ltd. 1991–, Gen. Man. 1993–; Dir. Nine Network Australia Ltd. 1992–, Huntsman Corpn. (Utah) 1994–, Optus Vision Pty. Ltd. 1995–, Valassas Inserts, U.S.A. *Address:* Consolidated Press Ltd., Level 3, 54–58 Park Street, Sydney, N.S.W. 2000, Australia.

PACKER, Kerry Francis Bullmore, A.C.; Australian business executive; b. 17 Dec. 1937, Sydney; s. of late Sir Frank and Lady Packer; m. Roslyn Weedon 1963; one s. one d.; ed. Cranbrook School, Geelong Church of England Grammar School; Chair. Consolidated Press Holdings Ltd. 1974–; Dir. Publishing and Broadcasting Ltd. 1994–; business interests include pastoral property, ski resort, investment portfolio, magazine publishing and TV broadcasting. *Leisure interests:* polo, golf, cricket, tennis. *Address:* Consolidated Press Holdings Ltd., 54 Park Street, Sydney, N.S.W. 2000, Australia. *Telephone:* (02) 9282 8000. *Fax:* (02) 9264 6969.

PACKER, Richard John, M.SC.; British government official; b. 18 Aug. 1944; s. of late George Packer and Dorothy Packer; m. 1st Alison Sellwood; two s. one d.; m. 2nd Lucy Neville-Rolfe; four s.; ed. City of London School and Univ. of Manchester; joined Ministry of Agric., Fisheries and Food (MAFF) 1967; on secondment, First Sec., Office of Perm. Representation to EEC 1973–76; Prin. Pvt. Sec. to Minister, Ministry of Agric., Fisheries and Food 1977–78, Asst. Sec. 1979–85, Under-Sec. 1985–89, Deputy Sec. 1989–93, Perm. Sec. 1993–. *Leisure interests:* philosophy, history, arts, sport. *Address:* Ministry of Agriculture, Fisheries and Food, 17 Smith Square, London, SW1P 3JR, England.

PACKER, William John; British artist, art critic and teacher; b. 19 Aug. 1940, Birmingham; s. of Rex Packer and Molly Wornham; m. Clare Winn 1965; three d.; ed. Windsor Grammar School, Wimbledon School of Art; teacher 1964–77; art critic, Financial Times 1974–; first exhibited Royal Acad. 1963; most recent one-man exhbn. Piers Feltham Gallery, London 1996; mem. Fine Art Bd. of Council for Nat. Academic Awards and Specialist Adviser 1976–83, Specialist Adviser 1983–87; mem. Advisory Cttee. to Govt. Art Collection 1977–84, Crafts Council 1980–87; sole selector first British Art Show (Arts Council) 1979–80, external examiner various art schools 1980–; Inaugural Henry Moore Memorial Lecture, Florence 1986; Hon. F.R.C.A.; Hon. R.B.A.; Hon. R.B.S.; Nat. Diploma in Design. *Publications:* Fashion Drawing in Vogue 1983, Henry Moore 1985. *Leisure interests:* hockey, riding, Venice. *Address:* 39 Elms Road, Clapham, London, SW4 9EP, England. *Telephone:* 0171-622 1108. *Fax:* 0171-622 1108.

PACKWOOD, Bob, LL.B.; American politician and lawyer; b. 11 Sept. 1932, Portland, Ore.; m. Georgie Oberteuffer 1964 (divorced); one s. one d.; ed. Williamette Univ., N.Y. Univ.; practised law in Portland 1958–68; mem. Oregon House of Reps. 1962–68; U.S. Senator from Oregon 1969–95 (resgnd.); Chair. Senate Commerce, Science and Transportation Cttee. 1981–85; fmr. mem. Senate Finance Cttee. (Chair. 1985–86), Senate Small Business Cttee., Bd. Dirs. New York Univ.; Hon. LL.D. (Yeshiva Univ.) 1982, (Gallaudet Coll.) 1983; several awards. *Address:* Sunrise Research, 2201 Wisconsin Avenue, N.W., Suite 120, Washington, DC 20007, U.S.A.

PADGAONKAR, Dileep, PH.D.; Indian journalist; b. 1 May 1944, Poona; s. of Vasant Padgaonkar and Shakuntala (née Kattakar) Padgaonkar; m. Latika Tawadey 1968; two s.; ed. Fergusson Coll., Poona, Institut des Hautes Etudes Cinématographiques, Paris, Sorbonne, Paris; Paris Corresp. of The Times of India 1968–73, Asst. Ed., Bombay and Delhi 1973–78, Assoc. Ed. 1986–88, Ed. 1988–; Information Chief for Asia and Pacific, UNESCO 1978–81; Deputy Dir. Office of Public Information, Paris 1981–85, Acting Dir. 1985–86, Acting Dir. Communication Sector 1986. *Publication:* When Bombay Burned (Ed.) 1993. *Leisure interests:* reading, classical music, contemporary art, cooking. *Address:* The Times of India, Times House, 7 Bahadur Shah Zafar Marg, New Delhi 110 002 (Office); C-313, Defence Colony, New Delhi-110024, India (Home). *Telephone:* (11) 331-2277 (Office); 469 7949 (Home).

PADILLA ARANCIBIA, Gen. David; Bolivian politician and army officer; Career officer with regional commands; Pres. of Bolivia and C.-in-C. of the Armed Forces 1978–79. *Address:* c/o Oficina del Presidente, La Paz, Bolivia.

PADIYARA, H.E. Cardinal Anthony; Indian ecclesiastic; b. 11 Feb. 1921, Manimala, Changanacherry; s. of Kuruvila and Annamma Padiyara; ordained 1945, elected to Ootacamund 1955, consecrated bishop 1955, prefect to Chaganacherry of the Syro-Malabarese 1970; Archbishop of Ernakulam 1985; cr. Cardinal 1988; made first Maj. Archbishop of Syro-Malabar Church 1992. *Address:* c/o Major Archbishop's House, Post Box No. 2580, Cochin 682031, Kerala, India.

PADMANABAN, A., M.A.; Indian civil servant and writer; b. 14 Dec. 1928, Pinji, Ranipet, Tamil Nadu; m. Seetha Padmanaban 1961; two s. one d.; fmrly. with Indian Admin. Service; Chief Sec. Govt. of Tamil Nadu 1986–87, adviser to Gov. 1988–89; mem. Union Public Service Comm. 1989–93; Gov. of Mizoram 1998–; Indian Ed. Poet Int.; Pres. Authors' Guild of India; Vice-Pres. World Acad. of Arts and Culture, U.S.A.; Gov. Indian Council for Cultural Affairs; Eminent Poet Award, Int. Acad., India, Nat. Integration Award 1994, Michael Madhusudan Award. *Poetry includes:* Rain Drops 1986, Light a Candle 1987, Buddha 1987, Untouchable's Journey 1991, My Dream 1992, Cosmic Accident 1995. *Other publications:* biographical sketches, Dalits at the Cross-Roads: Their Struggle Past and Present 1996. *Leisure interests:* freelance writing, social work. *Address:* Office of the Governor, Raj Bhavan, Aizawl 791 001, Mizoram, India. *Telephone:* (389) 323200. *Fax:* (389) 323344.

PADOA-SCHIOPPA, Tommaso, M.SC.ECON.; Italian banker and economist; b. 23 July 1940, Belluno; s. of Fabio Padoa and Stella Schwarz; m. Fiorella Kostoris 1966; one s. two d.; ed. Università Commerciale Luigi Bocconi, Milan, Massachusetts Inst. of Tech., U.S.A.; with insurance co., Bremen, Fed. Repub. of Germany 1959–60, C. & A. Brenninkmeyer 1966–68; Economist, Research Dept., Banca d'Italia, Rome 1970–79, Head, Money Market Dept. 1975–79, Direttore Centrale for Econ. Research 1983–84, Deputy Dir.-Gen. 1984–; Economic Adviser, the Treasury 1978–79; Dir.-Gen. Econ. and Financial Affairs, Comm. of EC 1979–83; mem. Group of Thirty; Chair. Banking Advisory Cttee., Comm. of EC 1988–91, Cen. Bank's Working Group on EC Payment Systems 1991–, Group of Ten Basle Cttee. on Banking Supervision at BIS 1993–; mem. Bd. European Cen. Bank 1998–. *Publications include:* The Management of an Open Economy with One Hundred Per Cent Plus Wage Indexation (with F. Modigliani, in Essays in International Finance) 1978, Money, Economic Policy and Europe 1985, The Road to Monetary Union in Europe 1994. *Address:* Banca d'Italia, Via Nazionale 91, 00187 Rome, Italy. *Telephone:* (00396) 47922512.

PADVA, Genrikh Pavlovich; Russian barrister; b. 20 Feb. 1931, Moscow; s. of Pavel Padva and Eva Rappoport; one d.; ed. Moscow Inst. of Law; Kalinin Pedagogical Inst.; mem. Kalinin Bar 1953, Presidium 1965–71, of Moscow Bar 1970–, of the Presidium 1986; one of founders of the U.S.S.R. (now Russian) Union of Barristers, Deputy-Chair. of the Exec. Board 1990; Vice-Pres. of the Int. Asscn. of Lawyers 1990, acted as a barrister on maj. political and economic trials in 1970s, was a lawyer for many dissidents, rendered legal advice to the families of Andrei Sakharov, singer Vladimir Vysotsky, Anatoliy Lukyanov, (q.v.); investigated some maj. econ. and criminal cases in late 1980s–1990s, a founder and Dir.-Gen. of Russian-American Law Firm 1990–. *Publications:* articles in specialized journals and newspapers on legal problems. *Address:* B. Sukharevskiy per. 15 Apt. 15, 103051 Moscow, Russia (Home). *Telephone:* 234-46-00 (Home). *Fax:* 974 2425.

PAEMEN, Hugo; Belgian diplomatist and international civil servant; with Dept. of Foreign Affairs 1963–77; fmr. Econ. Minister, Embassy, Washington; later Deputy Dir. Gen. External Relations EU; EU Amb. to U.S.A. 1995. *Address:* 3rd Floor, 2300 M Street, N.W., Washington DC 20037, U.S.A.

PAENIU, Bikenibeu, M.SC.; Tuvaluan politician and economist; b. 10 May 1956, Bikenibeu, Tarawa; m. Foketi Paeniu; two s. two d.; ed. King George V School, Tarawa, Univ. of S. Pacific, Suva and Univ. of Hawaii; worked in Agric. Div. Tuvalu; later Asst. Economist, South Pacific Comm. Nouméa; returned to Tuvalu 1988; Prime Minister of Tuvalu 1989–93. *Address:* c/o Office of the Prime Minister, Fongafale, Tuvalu.

PAFFRATH, Hans-Georg; German art dealer; b. 12 April 1922, Düsseldorf; s. of Hans Paffrath and Eleonore (née Theegarten) Paffrath; m. Helena née Baroness Åkerhielm 1958; two s. three d.; ed. Gymnasium; war service 1941–45; art dealer 1945–; fmr. Royal Swedish Consul-Gen. for North Rhine Westphalia. *Leisure interest:* riding. *Address:* Königsallee 46, Düsseldorf 40212, Germany. *Telephone:* (0211) 326405.

PAGANO, Gino; Italian industrialist; b. 2 Sept. 1921, Naples; ed. Naples Univ.; joined ANIC (Associazione Nazionale dell'Industria Chimica) 1951, Man. Dir. 1967–, Vice-Pres. 1970–72, Pres. 1972–76, 1980; co-ordinator, chemical and nuclear sector, ENI –1975; Pres. SIR Finanziaria S.p.A. 1980–; Consultant Bastogi S.p.A. 1978–80; Pres. SAPIR Porto Intermodale Ravenna S.p.A. 1974–76, 1980–; Vice-Pres. Associazione Italiana di Ingegneria Chimica 1973–; mem. Bd. Dirs. Hydrocarbons Int., Consultative Bd. Liquifar Agropecuaria do Brasil 1981–. *Address:* c/o ANIC, San Donato Milanese, Milan, Italy. *Telephone:* 02-53531.

PAGBALHA GELEG NAMGYAI; Chinese administrator; b. 1940, Litang Co., Sichuan Prov.; was confirmed by the Qangdin Lamasery as 11th incarnation of a living Buddha 1942; Vice-Chair. CPPCC 1959; mem. Presidium 4th NPC 1975–78; mem. Presidium 5th NPC 1978–82; Vice-Chair. People's Govt. of Tibet Autonomous Region 1979–83; Vice-Pres. Buddhist Asscn. of China 1980–; Exec. Chair. 6th CPPCC 1983–88; Acting Chair., Tibet Autonomous Region People's Congress 1983–86; Vice-Chair. Tibetan Autonomous Region Cttee. of CPPCC and Vice Chair. Standing Cttee. of Tibetan Autonomous Regional People's Congress 1983–88; Vice-Chair, CPPCC 7th Nat. Cttee. 1988–92; Vice-Chair. Standing Cttee. 8th NPC 1993–98, 9th NPC 1998–; Chair. People's Political Consultative Conference of Tibetan Autonomous Region 1993–; Pres. China Tibet Devt. Foundation. *Address:* Standing Committee of National People's Congress, Beijing, People's Republic of China.

PAGE, Ashley; British classical dancer and choreographer; b. 9 Aug. 1956, Rochester, Kent; s. of John H. Laverty and Sheila R. Medhurst; ed. St. Andrews, Rochester, Royal Ballet, Lower and Upper Schools; joined Royal

Ballet Co. 1975, soloist 1980, Prin. 1984, House Choreographer; leading roles in classical and modern repertoire; created numerous roles for MacMillan, Ashton and other leading choreographers; Choreographer Royal Opera House 1984; with numerous cos. in London, Europe; Frederick Ashton Choreographer Award 1982, Frederick Ashton Memorial Comm. Award 1990, Time Out Dance Award 1994. *Leisure interests:* art, driving, films, music, reading, theatre, travel. *Address:* c/o The Royal Ballet, Royal Opera House, Covent Garden, London, WC2E 7QA, England.

PAGE, Bruce; British journalist and publisher; b. 1 Dec. 1936, London; s. of Roger and Amy B. Page; m. 1st Anne Gillison 1964 (divorced 1969); m. 2nd Anne L. Darnborough 1969; one s. one d.; ed. Melbourne High School and Melbourne Univ.; trained as journalist, Melbourne Herald 1956–60; Evening Standard, London 1960–62; Daily Herald, London 1962–64; various exec. posts, Sunday Times, London 1964–76; Assoc. Ed. Daily Express 1977; Ed. New Statesman 1978–82; Dir. Direct Image Systems and Communications 1992–95; Dir. Report and Accounts Ltd. 1996–; various awards for journalism. *Publications:* co-author: Philby, the Spy who Betrayed a Generation, An American Melodrama, Do You Sincerely Want to be Rich?, Destination Disaster, Ulster (contrib.), The Yom Kippur War, The British Press. *Leisure interests:* reading, sailing, computers. *Address:* 32 Lauderdale Tower, Barbican, London, EC2Y 8BY; Beach House, Shingle Streeet, Shottisham, Suffolk, IP12 3BE, England. *Telephone:* 0171-628 3847; (01394) 411427.

PAGE, Ewan Stafford, PH.D., C.B.I.M.; British university vice-chancellor; b. 17 Aug. 1928, Leicester; s. of Joseph W. Page and Lucy Stafford; m. Sheila M. Smith 1955; three s. one d.; ed. Univs. of Cambridge and London; lecturer in Statistics, Durham Colls. 1954–57; Dir. Durham Univ. Computing Lab. 1957–64; Prof. of Computing & Data Processing, Univ. of Newcastle-upon-Tyne 1965–79, Dean, Faculty of Science 1969–72, Pro-Vice-Chancellor 1972–78; Vice-Chancellor, Univ. of Reading 1979–93; mem. Gen. Optical Council 1984–, Vice-Chair. 1989–; Hon. Fellow, American Statistical Asscn., British Computer Soc., Newcastle Polytechnic; Hon. D.Sc. (Reading); Chevalier, Ordre des Palmes Académiques 1991. *Publications:* Information Representation and Manipulation in a Computer, Introduction to Computational Combinatorics, Information Representation and Manipulation using Pascal (with L. B. Wilson). *Leisure interests:* golf, music, reading, vegetable gardening. *Address:* High View, Charlcombe Lane, Bath, BA1 5TT, England. *Telephone:* (01225) 422073.

PAGE, Geneviève (pseudonym of Geneviève Bonjean); French actress; b. 13 Dec. 1927, Paris; d. of Jacques Bonjean and Germaine Lipmann; m. Jean-Claude Bujard 1959; one s. one d.; ed. Lycée Racine, Paris, Sorbonne, Paris, Conservatoire nat. d'art dramatique; prin. actress in the Comédie Française, the Jean-Louis Barrault company and TNP Jean Vilar; has appeared in many famous classical and tragic stage roles, including Les larmes amères de Petra von Kant (Critics' Prize for Best Actress 1980), La nuit des rois, L'aigle à deux têtes, Angelo, tyran de Padoue 1984, Perséphone 1988, Mère Courage 1988, Le Balcon 1991, Paroles de poètes 1992, La peste 1992, La Femme sur le lit 1994 (Colombe Prix, Plaisir du Théâtre Best Actress), Les Orandes Forêts 1997, Delicate Balance 1998. *Films include:* Ce siècle a cinquante ans, Pas de pitié pour les femmes, Fanfan la tulipe, Lettre ouverte, Plaisirs de Paris, Nuits andalouses, L'étrange désir de M. Bard, Cherchez la femme, L'homme sans passé, Foreign Intrigue, The Silken Affair, Michael Strogoff, Un amour de poche, Song Without End, Le bal des adieux, El Cid, Les égarements, Le jour et l'heure, L'honorable correspondence, Youngblood Hawke, Le majordome, Les corsaires, Trois chambres à Manhattan, Grand Prix, Belle de jour, Mayerling, A Talent for Loving, The Private Life of Sherlock Holmes, Les Gémeaux, Décembre, Buffet Froid, Beyond Therapy 1987, les Bois noirs 1991; *TV:* La Nuit des rois 1962 (Best Actress TV 1962), La Chambre 1964, La Chasse aux hommes 1976, Athalie 1980, Les gens ne sont pas forcément ignobles 1990; Chevalier du Mérite sportif. *Address:* 52 rue de Vaugirard, 75006 Paris, France.

PAGE, Jennifer Anne, C.B.E., B.A.; British civil servant and business executive; b. 12 Nov. 1944; d. of Edward Page and Olive Page; ed. Barr's Hill Grammar School, Coventry and Univ. of London; entered civil service 1968, Prin. Dept. of Employment 1974, Asst. Sec. Dept. of Transport 1980; seconded BNOC 1981, London Dockland's Devt. Corpn. 1983; Sr. Vice-Pres. Pallas Invest SA 1984–89; Chief Exec. English Heritage (Historic Bldgs. and Monuments Comm.) 1989–95; Chief Exec. Millennium Comm. 1995–97, New Millennium Experience Co. Ltd. 1997–; mem. Bd. Railtrack Group 1994–, Equitable Life Assurance Soc. 1994–. *Address:* New Millennium Experience Company Ltd., 110 Buckingham Palace Road, London, SW1W 9SB, England. *Telephone:* 0171-808 8200.

PAGLIA, Camille, PH.D.; American professor of humanities; b. 2 April 1947, Endicott, N.Y.; d. of Pasquale Paglia and Lydia Paglia; ed. State Univ of New York at Binghamton, Yale Univ.; Faculty mem. Bennington Coll. 1972–80; Visiting Lecturer, Wesleyan Univ. 1980, Yale Univ. 1980–84; Asst. Prof., Phil. Coll. of Performing Arts (now Univ. of the Arts) 1984–87, Assoc. Prof. 1987–91, Prof. of Humanities 1991–. *Publications:* Sexual Personae: Art and Decadence from Nefertiti to Emily Dickinson 1990, Sex, Art, and American Culture: Essays 1992, Vamps and Tramps: New Essays 1994, Alfred Hitchcock's The Birds 1998. *Address:* Department of Liberal Arts, University of the Arts, 320 South Broad Street, Philadelphia, PA 19102, U.S.A. *Telephone:* (215) 875-2235. *Fax:* (212) 980-3671 (Agent).

PĄGOWSKA, Teresa; Polish painter; b. 12 June 1929, Warsaw; m. Henryk Tomaszewski (q.v.); one s.; ed. High School of Plastic Arts, Poznań; Prof. Acad. of Fine Arts, Warsaw 1988; Hon. mem. Asscn. Réalités Nouvelles 1963, Nouvelle Ecole de Paris 1964; numerous one-man and group exhbns. in Poland and abroad; works in numerous collections; City of Warsaw Prize 1989, Alfred Jurzykowski Foundation Award, New York 1990, Kt.'s Cross Order of Polonia Restituta, Golden Cross of Merit. *Address:* ul. Jazgarzewska 13, 00-730 Warsaw, Poland. *Telephone:* (22) 40 11 51.

PAHANG, H.R.H. Sultan of, Sultan Haji Ahmad Shah Al-Mustain Billah ibni Al-Marhum Sultan Abu Bakar Ri'Ayatuddin Al-Muadzam Shah, D.K.P.; Malaysian Ruler; b. 24 Oct. 1930, Istana Mangga Tunggal, Pekan; m. Tengku Hajjah Afzan binti Tengku Muhammad 1954; ed. Malay Coll. Kuala Kangsar, Worcester Coll., Oxford, Univ. Coll., Exeter; Tengku Mahkota (Crown Prince) 1944; Capt. 4th Battalion, Royal Malay Regt. 1954; Commdr. of 12th Infantry Battalion of Territorial Army 1963–65, Lieut.-Col.; mem. State Council 1955; Regent 1956, 1959, 1965; succeeded as Sultan 1974; Timbalan Yang di Pertuan Agong (Deputy Supreme Head of State of Malaysia) 1975–79, Yang di Pertuan Agong (Supreme Head of State) 1979–84, 1985; Constitutional Head of Int. Islamic Univ. 1988; Hon. D.Litt. (Malaya) 1988; Hon. LL.D. (Northrop, U.S.A.) 1993. *Address:* Istana Abu Bakar, Pekan, Pahang, Malaysia.

PAHLAVI, Farah Diba; fmr. Empress of Iran; b. 14 Oct. 1938; d. of Sohrab and Farida Diba; m. H.I.M. Shah Mohammed Reza Pahlavi 1959 (died 1980); two s. two d.; ed. Jeanne d'Arc School and Razi School, Teheran, and Ecole Spéciale d'Architecture, Paris; Foreign Assoc. mem. Fine Arts Acad., France 1974; fmr. Patron Farah Pahlavi Asscn. (admin. of Social Educ. Asscn.), Iran Cultural Foundation, and 34 other educational, health and cultural orgs.; left Iran Jan. 1979; living in Egypt June 1980.

PAHR, Willibald P., DR.IUR.; Austrian administrator and politician; b. 5 June 1930, Vienna; m. Ingeborg Varga 1960; one s. one d.; ed. Univ. of Vienna and Coll. of Europe, Bruges, Belgium; Asst. in Inst. of Int. Law and Int. Relations, Univ. of Vienna 1952–55; served Fed. Chancellery 1955–76, Head of Section 1968, Head of Dept. 1973, Dir.-Gen. 1975–76; Fed. Minister for Foreign Affairs 1976–83; Amb. to Fed. Repub. of Germany 1983–85; Sec.-Gen. World Tourism Org. 1986–88; Special Commr. for Refugees and Migration 1990–95. *Publications:* Der österreichische Status der dauernden Neutralität 1967, several articles in Revue des Droits de l'Homme, numerous articles on current int. problems in various periodicals; co-editor Grundrechte, die Rechtsprechung in Europa (journal). *Address:* ICMPD, Möllwaldplatz 4, 1040 Vienna, Austria.

PAIGE, Elaine, O.B.E.; British singer and actress; b. 5 March 1948, Barnet; d. of Eric Bickerstaff and Irene Bickerstaff; ed. Aida Foster Stage school; West End theatre appearances in Hair 1968, Jesus Christ Superstar 1973, Grease (played Sandy) 1973, Billy (played Rita) 1974, created roles of Eva Perón in Evita 1978 and Grizabella in Cats 1981, Abbacadabra (played Carabosse) (London) 1983, Chess (played Florence) 1986, Anything Goes (played Reno Sweeney) 1989, Piaf 1993–94, Sunset Boulevard (played Norma Desmond) 1995–96, The Misanthrope (played Célimène) 1998; 14 solo albums; 4 multi-platinum albums, 8 consecutive gold albums; Soc. of West End Theatre Award (Best Actress in a Musical for the role of Eva Perón in Evita) 1978, Variety Club Award for Showbusiness Personality of the Year, and Recording Artist of the Year 1986, British Asscn. of Songwriters, Composers and Authors (BASCA) Award 1993. *Leisure interests:* antiques, gardening, skiing, tennis. *Address:* c/o EP Records, M, M and M, Pinewood Studios, Pinewood Road, Iver, Bucks., SL10 0NH, England. *Telephone:* (01753) 650808. *Fax:* (01753) 650705.

PAIGE, Victor Grellier, C.B.E., C.I.P.D., F.C.I.T., C.I.M.; British administrative official; b. 5 June 1925; s. of Victor Paige and Alice (née Grellier) Paige; m. Kathleen W. Harris 1948; one s. one d.; ed. East Ham Grammar School and Univ. of Nottingham; Roosevelt Scholar 1954; Deputy Personnel Man. Boots Pure Drug Co., Ltd. 1957–67; Controller of Personnel Services, CWS Ltd. 1967–70, Dir. Manpower Org. 1970–74; Exec. Vice-Chair. (Admin.) Nat. Freight Corpn. (later Nat. Freight Co.) 1974–77, Deputy Chair. 1977–82; Dir. and Deputy Chair. Nat. Freight Consortium 1982–85, non-exec. Dir. 1985–87; Chair. Port of London Authority 1980–85; Chair. Nat. Health Service Man. Bd. and 2nd Perm. Sec., Dept. of Health and Social Security 1985–86; Pres. Inst. of Admin. Man. 1984–90; Chair. Viking Press Ltd. 1994–; other professional appointments; Commdr. Order of Oranje Nassau. *Publications:* contribs. on management to technical press. *Leisure interests:* reading, wood-carving, sport (especially athletics). *Address:* Queen's Wood, Frithsden, Berkhamsted, Herts., England. *Telephone:* (01442) 865030.

PAIK, Kun Woo; South Korean pianist; b. 10 March 1946; ed. Juilliard School, New York and in London and Italy; interpreter of piano works of Ravel, Liszt, Scriabin and Prokofiev; has played with orchestras throughout N. America and Europe, notably Indianapolis Symphony, Rotterdam Philharmonic, Royal Philharmonic, London Symphony, BBC Symphony (soloist, Last Night of the Proms 1987), Orchestre Nat. de France, Polish Radio Nat. Symphony; recitals at all maj. European music festivals; three Diapason d'Or awards; lives in Paris. *Address:* c/o Worldwide Artists (London) Ltd., 12 Rosebery Avenue, Thornton Heath, Surrey, CR7 8PT, England. *Telephone:* 0181-771 3444.

PAIK, Nam June; Korean/American kinetic artist; b. 1932, Korea; ed. Univ. of Tokyo, Japan; left S. Korea 1949, moved permanently to N.Y. 1964;

mem. Fluxus (anarchic, neo-dadaist movement) 1961; *major works include:* Urmusik 1961, Opera Sextronique, performed N.Y. 1967, The K-456 Robot; *major exhibitions include:* Galerie Parnassus, Wuppertal, Germany 1963, Video Works 1963–68, Hayward Gallery, London 1988.

PAIN, Emil Abramovich, PH.D.; Russian sociologist; b. 6 Dec. 1948, Voronezh; m.; one s.; ed. Voronezh State Univ.; researcher on problems of regional sociology and ethnology, problems of nat. conflicts, Voronezh State Univ. and Inst. of Ethnography U.S.S.R. Acad. of Sciences 1974–91; during perestroika was expert of Deputies' Comm. on Deported Peoples and Problems of Crimea Tartars 1989–91; Head Cen. Ethnopolitical Studies Int. Asscn. of Foreign Policy 1991–92; mem. Pres.'s Council 1993–97; mem. Expert-Analytical Dept. of Pres. of Russia 1994–98.

PAINTAL, Autar Singh, M.D., PH.D., F.R.C.P., F.R.S., F.R.S.E.; Indian professor of physiology; b. 24 Sept. 1925; s. of Dr. Man Singh and Rajwans Kaur; one s. two d.; ed. Forman Christian Coll., Lahore, Lucknow and Edinburgh Univs.; lecturer, King George's Medical Coll. Lucknow Univ. 1949; Rockefeller Fellow 1950; lecturer, Univ. of Edinburgh 1951; Control Officer, Tech. Devt. Establishment Labs., Ministry of Defence, Kampur 1952–54; Prof. of Physiology, All India Inst. of Med. Sciences, Delhi 1958–64; Prof. of Physiology and Dir. Vallabhbhai Patel Chest Inst., Delhi Univ. 1964–; now Dir.-Gen. Indian Council of Medical Research; Dean Faculty of Med. Sciences, Delhi Univ. 1966–77; Fellow, Indian Acad. of Medical Sciences, Indian Nat. Science Acad. and other learned socs.; Pres. Nat. Coll. of Chest Physicians 1981–86, Indian Science Congress 1984–85; numerous awards and distinctions including R.D. Birla Award 1982, Nehru Science Award 1983, Acharya J. C. Bose Medal 1985; Hon. D.Sc. (Benares Hindu Univ.) 1982, (Delhi) 1984, (Aligarh Muslim Univ.) 1986, other hon. degrees. *Publications:* articles in professional journals. *Leisure interests:* swimming, rowing, bird watching. *Address:* DST Centre for Visceral Mechanisms, Vallabhbhai Patel Chest Institute, Delhi University, P.O. Box 2101, Delhi 110007, India.

PAIS, Abraham, B.SC., M.SC., PH.D.; American physicist; b. 19 May 1918, Amsterdam, Netherlands; s. of Isayah Pais and Kaatje van Kleef; m. 1st Lila Atwill 1956 (divorced 1962), one s.; m. 2nd Agnes Ida Benedicte Nicolaisen 1990; ed. Univs. of Amsterdam and Utrecht; Rask Oersted Fellow, Inst. of Theoretical Physics, Copenhagen 1946; Fellow, Inst. of Advanced Study, Princeton 1946–50, Prof. 1950–63; Prof. Rockefeller Univ. 1963–81, Detlev Bronk Prof. Rockefeller Univ. 1981, Prof. Emer. 1988; Staff mem. Lawrence Radiation Lab., Berkeley, Calif. 1958–; Consultant Brookhaven Nat. Laboratory, Upton, N.Y.; Guggenheim Fellow 1960; Fellow American Physical Soc.; mem. N.A.S., American Acad. Arts and Sciences, Royal Danish Acad. of Sciences and Letters, Royal Swedish Acad. of Sciences, American Philosophical Soc., Council for Foreign Relations; Corresp. mem. Royal Acad. of Sciences, Netherlands; Oppenheimer Prize 1979, American Book Award and American Inst. of Physics Award for Subtle is the Lord 1983, Physica Prize (Netherlands) 1992, Nat. Science Medal, Royal Acad. of Sciences of Netherlands 1993, Gemant Award, American Inst. of Physics 1993, Lewis Thomas Prize 1995. *Publications:* Subtle is the Lord (biography of Albert Einstein) 1983, Inward Bound 1987, Niels Bohr's Times 1991, Einstein Lived Here 1994, A Tale of Two Continents 1997, contributions to Physical Review, Physical Review Letters, Physics Letters, Annals of Physics and other physics journals. *Leisure interests:* squash, swimming, mountaineering. *Address:* Department of Physics, Rockefeller University, New York, NY 10021 (Office); 1161 York Avenue, New York, NY 10021, U.S.A. (Home). *Telephone:* (212) 327-8833 (Office); (212) PL3-3083 (Home).

PAISLEY, Rev. Ian Richard Kyle, D.D., M.P., F.R.G.S.; British politician and minister of religion; b. 6 April 1926; s. of Rev. J. Kyle Paisley and Isabella Paisley; m. Eileen E. Cassells 1956; two s. (twins) three d.; ed. Ballymena Model School, Ballymena Tech. High School and S. Wales Bible Coll. and Reformed Presbyterian Theological Coll., Belfast; ordained 1946; Minister, Martyrs Memorial Free Presbyterian Church 1946–; Moderator, Free Presbyterian Church of Ulster 1951; founded The Protestant Telegraph 1966; M.P. (Democratic Unionist) 1974– (Protestant Unionist 1970–74) resgnd. seat Dec. 1985 in protest against the Anglo-Irish Agreement; re-elected Jan. 1986; M.P. (Protestant Unionist) for Bannside, Co. Antrim, Parl. of N. Ireland (Stormont) 1970–72, Leader of the Opposition 1972, Chair. Public Accounts Cttee. 1972; mem. N. Ireland Ass. 1973–74, elected to Second N. Ireland Ass. 1982; mem. European Parl. 1979–; M.P. for Antrim N. N.I. Ass. 1998–; mem. Constitutional Convention 1975–76; Leader (co-founder) of Democratic Unionist Party 1972; Chair. Agric. Cttee. and Cttee. of Privileges 1983; Pres. Whitefield Coll. of the Bible, Laurencetown, Co. Down 1979–; Co-Chair. World Congress of Fundamentalists 1978; mem. Political Cttee. European Parl., N.I. Ass. 1998–; mem. Int. Cultural Soc. of Korea 1977. *Publications:* History of the 1859 Revival 1959, Christian Foundations 1960, Ravenhill Pulpit Vol. I 1966, Vol. II 1967, Exposition of the Epistle to the Romans 1968, Billy Graham and the Church of Rome 1970, The Massacre of Saint Bartholomew 1972, Paisley, the Man and his Message 1976, America's Debt to Ulster 1976, Ulster—the facts 1981 (jtly.), No Pope Here 1982, Dr. Kidd 1982, Those Flaming Tennents 1983, Crown Rights of Jesus Christ 1985, Be Sure: 7 Rules for Public Speaking 1986, Paisley's Pocket Preacher 1986, Jonathan Edwards, The Theologian of Revival 1987, Union with Rome 1989, The Soul of the Question 1990, The Revised English Bible: An Exposure 1990, What a Friend We Have in Jesus 1994, Understanding Events in Northern Ireland: An Introduction for Americans 1995, My Plea for the Old Sword 1997, The Rent Veils at Calvary 1997, A Text a Day Keeps the Devil Away 1997. *Address:* The Parsonage, 17 Cyprus Avenue, Belfast, BT5 5NT, N. Ireland.

PAK SONG CHOL; Korean politician; Amb. to Bulgaria 1954; Minister of Foreign Affairs 1959; mem. Cen. Cttee. Workers' Party of Korea (WPK) 1961, mem. Political Bureau 1980–; Vice-Premier and Minister of Foreign Affairs 1966; Second Vice-Premier 1970; Political Commissar of WPK 1970; Premier 1976; mem. Cen. People's Cttee. 1977; Vice-Pres. Democratic People's Repub. of Korea 1977–; mem. Presidium, Democratic Front for Reunification of Fatherland 1991. *Address:* Office of the Vice-President, Pyongyang, Democratic People's Republic of Korea.

PÁL, László; Hungarian politician and electrical engineer; b. 5 September, 1942, Budapest; m.; two c.; ed. Inst. of Energetics, Moscow, Political Acad., Budapest; Research Inst. for Electrical Eng. 1966–69; mem. Nat. Cttee. for Technological Devt. 1969–89; State Sec. Ministry of Industry 1989–90; mem. of Parl. 1990–97; Minister of Industry 1994–95; Chair. Bd. Hungarian Oil and Gas Co.; Lóránd Eötvös Award 1986, János Neumann Award 1988. *Address:* 1117 Budapest, Okt. 23. str. 18, Hungary. *Telephone:* (36-1) 209-0101. *Fax:* (36-1) 209-0051.

PÁL, Lénárd; Hungarian physicist; b. 7 Nov. 1925, Gyoma; s. of Imre Pál and Erzsébet Varga; m. Angela Danóci 1963; one d.; ed. Budapest and Moscow Univs.; Dept. Head, Cen. Research Inst. for Physics, Budapest 1953–56, Deputy Dir. 1956–69, Dir. 1970–74, Dir.-Gen 1974–78; Prof. of Nuclear Physics, Eötvös Lóránd Univ. Budapest 1961–77, 1989–98; Pres. State Office for Tech. Devt. 1978–80, 1984–85, Nat. Atomic Energy Comm. 1978–80, 1984–85; mem. Science Policy Cttee., Council of Ministers 1978–85; Sec. Cen. Cttee. Hungarian Socialist Workers' Party 1985–88; Corresp. mem. Hungarian Acad. of Sciences 1961–73, mem. 1973, Gen. Sec. 1980–84, Pres. Intercosmos Council 1980–84; Foreign mem. Acad. of Sciences of the U.S.S.R. 1976, of G.D.R. 1982, of Czechoslovakia 1983, Russian Acad. of Sciences 1996; mem. Leibniz Soc. e.V. 1994; Gold Medal, Order of Labour 1956, 1968; Kossuth Prize 1962; Memorial Medal 25th Anniversary of the Liberation 1970; Kurtchatov Memory Medal (U.S.S.R.) 1970; Gold Medal of the Hungarian Acad. of Sciences 1975, Eötvös Lóránd Physical Soc. Medal 1976, Red Banner Order of Labour (U.S.S.R.) 1975, Red Banner of Work 1985. *Publications:* Science and Technical Development 1987, Science and Technology Policies in Finland and Hungary 1985; approximately 275 articles in Hungarian and foreign scientific journals. *Leisure interests:* hunting, angling. *Address:* Széher út 21/A, 1021 Budapest II, Hungary. *Telephone:* 275-07-25. *Fax:* 275-07-25.

PALADE, George Emil; American scientist; b. 19 Nov. 1912, Iaşi, Romania; s. of Emil Palade and Constanţa Cantemir; m. 1st Irina Malaxa 1941 (died 1969), one s. one d.; m. 2nd Marilyn Farquhar 1970; ed. Hasdeu Lyceum, Buzău, Univ. of Bucharest; went to the U.S.A. 1946; naturalized U.S. citizen 1952; Instructor, Asst. Prof. of Anatomy, School of Medicine, Univ. of Bucharest 1935–45; Visiting Investigator, Asst., Assoc., Prof. of Cell Biology, Rockefeller Univ. 1946–73; Prof. of Cell Biology, Yale Univ. 1973–83, Sr. Research Scientist 1983–90; Dean Scientific Affairs, Univ. of Calif. San Diego, School of Medicine 1990–; Fellow American Acad. of Arts and Sciences; mem. N.A.S., Pontifical Acad. of Sciences; Foreign mem. Royal Soc.; Albert Lasker Basic Research Award 1966, Gairdner Special Award (Canada) 1968, Hurwitz Prize 1970, Nobel Prize for Medicine 1974, Nat. Medal of Science 1986. *Leisure interest:* history. *Address:* University of California at San Diego, Division of Cellular and Molecular Medicine, M-002, La Jolla, CA 92093, U.S.A.

PALAU, Luis; American evangelist and writer; b. 27 Nov. 1934, Buenos Aires, Argentina; s. of Luis Palau Sr.; m. Patricia Marilyn Scofield 1961; four s.; ed. St. Alban's Coll., Buenos Aires, Multnomah School of the Bible, Portland, Ore., U.S.A.; mem. staff Bank of London, Buenos Aires and Cordoba 1952–59; moved to U.S.A. 1960; worked as interpreter for Billy Graham 1962; began Spanish radio broadcasts as missionary in Colombia 1967; began evangelistic ministry as part of Overseas Crusades 1968; made crusade broadcasts to all Latin America 1975; named Pres. Overseas Crusades 1976; f. Luis Palau Evangelistic Asscn. 1978; first major crusade in U.S.A., San Diego 1981; crusades on four continents 1982; Dr. h.c. (Talbot Theological Seminary) 1977, (Wheaton Coll.) 1985. *Publications:* Heart After God 1978, My Response 1985, Time To Stop Pretending 1985, So You Want To Grow 1986; 26 books and booklets in Spanish; works have been transl. into 30 languages. *Leisure interest:* family. *Address:* P.O. Box 1173, Portland, OR 97207, U.S.A. *Telephone:* (503) 643-0777.

PALAZZINI, H.E. Cardinal Pietro, S.T.D., J.U.D.; Vatican ecclesiastic; b. 19 May 1912, Piobbico, Pesaro; s. of Giovanni Palazzini and Luigia Conti; ed. Lateran Univ.; ordained 6 Dec. 1934; advocate of the Sacred Roman Rota; fmr. Asst. Dir. Pontificio Seminario Maggiore; Prof. of Moral Theology, Lateran Univ. 1945–56; Under-Sec. Sacred Congregation for the Religious 1956–58; Sec. Sacred Congregation for the Clergy 1962; cr. Cardinal by Pope Paul VI 1973; fmr. Prefect Sacred Congregation for the Causes of Beatification and Canonization of Saints; Hon. mem. Pontifical Acad.; *Publications:* Il Monoteismo dei Padri Apostolici 1946, Indissolubilità del Matrimonio 1952, Il Diritto Strumento di Riforma in S. Pier Damiani 1956, Theologia Moralis (with A. Lanza) 4 vols. 1953–63, Morale Cattolica e Morale Protestante 1961, La Coscienza 1963, Morale dell'Attualità 1963, S. Pier Damiani il Superfluo 1972, Vita Sacramentale (3 vols.) 1972–86, Dizionario dei concili 6 vols. 1963–67, Dictionarium morale et canonicum 4 vols. 1962–68

(Dir.); Vita e virtù cristiane 1975, Avviamento allo studio della morale Cristiana 1976, Pio IX nel primo centenario della morte 1978, Francesco Faà di Bruno, scienziato e prete 1980, La Santissima Vergine 1984. *Address:* Via Proba Petronia 83, 00136 Rome, Italy. *Telephone:* 06 3452 555.

PALECKIS, Justas Vincas; Lithuanian diplomatist; b. 1 Jan. 1942, Samara, Russia; m. Laima Paleckiene; two s. one d.; ed. Vilnius State Univ., Higher Diplomatic School, U.S.S.R. Ministry of Foreign Affairs; contrib. Komjamunimo Tiesa (daily) 1963–66; Third Sec. U.S.S.R. Embassy to Switzerland; Second, First Sec., Counsellor, U.S.S.R. Embassy to G.D.R.1969–82; Deputy Dir., Dir. of sector Lithuanian CP Cen. Cttee. 1983–89; Sec., Ind. Lithuanian CP Cen. Cttee. 1989–90; Deputy Dir. Dept. of Foreign Affairs, Lithuanian Repub. Supreme Soviet 1990–92; lecturer Inst. of Journalism, Vilnius State Univ. 1990–93; lecturer Inst. of Int. Relations and Political Science, Vilnius State Univ. 1993–95; adviser on Foreign Affairs to Lithuanian Pres. 1993–96; Amb. to U.K. 1996– (also accred. to Ireland and Portugal 1997–). *Publications:* Swiss Pyramids 1974, At the Foot of Swiss Pyramids 1985. *Leisure interests:* reading, theatre, gardening, tennis, swimming (mem. Lithuanian water polo team). *Address:* Embassy of Lithuania, 84 Gloucester Place, London, W1H 3HN, England (Office); K. Donelaicio 20-5, LT-2000 Vilnius, Lithuania (Home). *Telephone:* (0171) 48666401 (Office); (3702) 635445 (Home).

PALEOKRASSAS, Yannis, M.SC.; Greek politician; b. 27 March 1934, Athens; m. Natalia Gritzala; three c.; ed. London School of Econs.; Planning Div. Ministry of Coordination 1959–63; Doxiades Assocs. (devt. consultants), Ghana, Athens and Detroit 1963–68; Gen. Man. London, Windward Shipping Ltd. 1968–70; Financial Consultant, J.C. Caras Group of cos. 1970; Man. Dir. Planning & Devt. Co. S.A. Athens 1972–74; joined American Express Int. Banking Corpn. 1974–77; with others est. ERGOBANK 1975, Gen. Man. 1975–77; Under-Sec. of State, Ministry of Coordination 1977–80, Alt. Minister 1980–81, Minister of Coordination 1981; Deputy to Greek Parl. (New Democracy Party) 1980–90; Minister of Finance 1990–92, of Industry, Energy and Tech. Aug.–Dec. 1992; mem. European Comm. for the Environment, Nuclear Security, Civil Protection and Fisheries 1993–95. *Publications:* numerous books, studies and reports on econs. of transport and shipping, human resource devt., urban and regional planning, growth and devt., banking and financial man. *Leisure interests:* painting, scuba diving, church choir singing, carpentry.

PALEY, Grace; American writer and teacher; b. 11 Dec. 1922, The Bronx, New York, N.Y.; d. of Isaac Goodside and Manya Ridnik Goodside; m. 1st Jess Paley 1942; one s. one d.; m. 2nd Robert Nichols 1972; ed. Hunter Coll. and New York Univ.; teaching staff Sarah Lawrence Coll. 1966, Columbia Univ., New York 1984; mem. Inst. of American Writers, American Acad., Inst. of Arts and Letters; Guggenheim Fellow; Edith Wharton Award, New York State. *Publications:* The Little Disturbances of Man 1959, Enormous Changes at the Last Minute 1974, Later the Same Day 1984, Leaning Forward (poems) 1985, Long Walks and Intimate Talks 1991, New and Collected Poems 1992, The Collected Stories 1994. *Address:* P.O. Box 620, Thetford, VT 05074, U.S.A.

PALIN, Michael Edward, B.A.; British actor and writer; b. 5 May 1943; s. of the late Edward Palin and Mary Palin; m. Helen M. Gibbins 1966; two s. one d.; ed. Birkdale School, Sheffield, Shrewsbury School, Brasenose Coll. Oxford; Pres. Transport 2000; actor and writer: Monty Python's Flying Circus, BBC TV 1969–74, Ripping Yarns, BBC TV 1976–80; actor: Three Men in a Boat, BBC 1975: writer: East of Ipswich, BBC TV 1987, Number 27, BBC TV, The Weekend (play for stage) 1994; actor and co-author, films: And Now for Something Completely Different 1970, Monty Python and the Holy Grail 1974, Monty Python's Life of Brian 1979, Time Bandits 1980, Monty Python's "The Meaning of Life" 1982; actor, writer and co-producer The Missionary 1982; actor, co-scriptwriter American Friends 1991; actor in: Jabberwocky 1976, A Private Function 1984, Brazil 1985, A Fish Called Wanda 1988 (Best Supporting Film Actor, BAFTA Award 1988), GBH (Channel 4 TV) 1991, Fierce Creatures 1997; TV series: contrib. to Great Railway Journeys of the World, BBC TV 1980, 1993, Around the World in 80 Days 1989, Pole to Pole 1992, Palin's Column 1994, Pole to Pole: The Photographs 1994, Full Circle 1997, Full Circle: The Photographs 1997. *Publications include:* Monty Python's Big Red Book 1970, Monty Python's Brand New Book 1973, Montypithonscrapbook 1979, Dr. Fegg's Encyclopaedia of All World Knowledge 1984, Limericks 1985, Around the World in 80 Days 1989, Pole to Pole 1992, Hemingway's Chair 1995, Palin's Pacific, Full Circle 1997; for children: Small Harry and the Toothache Pills 1981, The Mirrorstone 1986, The Cyril Stories 1986; Dr. h.c. (Sheffield) 1992. *Leisure interests:* reading, running, railways. *Address:* Mayday Management, 34 Tavistock Street, London, WC2E 7PB, England. *Telephone:* 0171-497 1100. *Fax:* 0171-497 1133.

PALITZSCH, Peter; German theatre director; b. 11 Sept. 1918, Deutmannsdorf; s. of Alwin Palitzsch and Johanna Strauss; m. Tanja von Oertzen; Dramatic Adviser and Stage Dir. Berliner Ensemble; Dir. of Production, Schauspiel Stuttgart; mem. Bd. of Dirs. Schauspiel Frankfurt-am-Main; freelance dir. throughout Germany and other European countries. *Address:* Waldpromenade 28, 82131 Gauting; Bundesratufer 5, 10555 Berlin, Germany. *Telephone:* 089 8503634 (Gauting); 030 391 27 57 (Berlin).

PALKHIVALA, Nani Ardeshir; Indian businessman and lawyer; b. 16 Jan. 1920, Bombay; s. of Ardeshir Nanabhoy and Sheherbanoo A. Palkhivala; m. Nargesh H. Matbar 1945; ed. St. Xavier's Coll. and Govt. Law Coll., Bombay; Sr. advocate, Supreme Court of India; Amb. to U.S.A. 1977–79; Chair. Assoc. Cement Cos. Ltd., Tata Exports Ltd., Tata Unisys Ltd., Tata Zambia Ltd.; Vice-Chair. SKF Bearings India Ltd.; Dir. Tata Sons Ltd., Tata Industries Ltd., Indian Hotels Co. Ltd., Tata Iron and Steel Co. Ltd., Nat. Organic Chemical Industries Ltd., Tata Exports South East Asia Ltd., Tata Namibia (P.) Ltd., etc.; Prof. Law, Calcutta Univ.; Pres. Forum of Free Enterprise; Chair. Income-tax Appellate Tribunal Bar Asscn.; Chair. Assoc. Cement; Hon. mem. Acad. of Political Science, New York 1975; Hon. LL.D. (Princeton) 1978, (Lawrence) 1979, (Annamalai) 1986. *Publications:* The Law and Practice of Income-tax (co-author) 8th edn. 1990, Taxation in India 1960, Our Constitution Defaced and Defiled 1975, India's Priceless Heritage 1980, We, The People 1984. *Leisure interests:* motoring, history, literature. *Address:* Cement House, 121 Maharshi Karve Road, Bombay 400 020; "Commonwealth", 181 Backbay Reclamation, Bombay 400 020, India.

PALLANT, John, B.A.; British advertising executive; b. 10 Aug. 1955; s. of Dennis Pallant and Doreen (née Hirst) Pallant; ed. St. John's Coll., Southsea, Univ. of Reading; copywriter Griffin & George Ltd. 1977, Acroyd Westwood Assocs. 1977, Collett Dickenson Pearce 1980, Gold Greenless Trott 1982, Boase Massimi Politt 1978, copywriter and creative group head 1983; copywriter Saatchi & Saatchi 1988, Group Head 1991, Deputy Creative Dir. and Exec. Bd. Dir. 1995, Creative Dir. 1996–97, Jt. Exec. Creative Dir. 1997–; numerous awards. *Address:* Saatchi & Saatchi, 80 Charlotte Street, London, W1A 1AQ, England. *Telephone:* 0171-636 5060. *Fax:* 0171-637 8489.

PALLISER, Rt. Hon. Sir (Arthur) Michael, G.C.M.G., P.C., M.A., F.R.S.A.; British diplomatist; b. 9 April 1922, Reigate, Surrey; s. of late Admiral Sir Arthur Palliser, K.C.B., D.S.C., and of Lady Palliser (née Margaret E. King-Salter); m. Marie M. Spaak (d. of late Paul-Henri Spaak) 1948; three s.; ed. Wellington Coll. and Merton Coll., Oxford; war service in Coldstream Guards (mentioned in despatches) 1942–46; entered diplomatic service 1947; Foreign Office 1947–49, 1951–56; posted to Athens 1949–51, Paris 1956–60; Head of Chancery, Dakar 1960–62; Counsellor and seconded to Imperial Defence Coll. 1963; Head of Planning Staff, Foreign Office 1964; a Pvt. Sec. to Prime Minister 1966–69; Minister, Paris 1969–71; Amb. and Head, U.K. Del. to EEC 1971–72; Amb. and U.K. Perm. Rep. to European Communities 1973–75; Perm. Under-Sec., Head of Diplomatic Service 1975–82; Chair. Council, Int. Inst. for Strategic Studies 1983–90; Deputy Chair. Midland Bank PLC 1987–91; Deputy Chair. Midland Montagu (Holdings) 1987–93; Vice-Chair. Samuel Montagu and Co. Ltd. 1983–84, 1993–96 (Chair. 1984–85, 1986–93); Dir., Arbor Acres Farm Inc., Booker PLC, BAT Industries PLC, Eagle Star (Holdings), Shell Transport and Trading Co. PLC 1983–92, United Biscuits PLC 1983–89; Pres. China-Britain Trade Group 1992–96; Deputy Chair. British Invisible Exports Council 1987–95; Dir. XCL Ltd. 1994–; Chair. Major Projects Asscn. 1994–98; Vice-Chair. Salzburg Seminar 1996–; Pres. Int. Social Service (U.K.) 1982–96; Chair. City and E. London Confed. of Medicine and Dentistry 1989–95; Gov. Wellington Coll. 1982–92; mem. Security Comm. 1983–92; mem. Bd. Royal Nat. Theatre 1988–96; Assoc. Fellow Centre for Int. Affairs, Harvard Univ. 1982; Hon. Fellow Merton Coll., Oxford 1986, Queen Mary and Westfield Coll., London Univ. 1990; Chevalier, Order of Orange-Nassau, Commdr., Légion d'honneur. *Address:* 12B Wedderburn Road, London, NW3 5QG, England.

PALMAR, Sir Derek, Kt., F.C.A.; British business executive; b. 25 July 1919, Romford; s. of the late Lieut.-Col. F. J. Palmar and Hylda (née Smith) Palmar; m. 1st Edith Brewster 1946 (died 1990), one s. one d.; m. 2nd Shuna Pyman 1992; ed. Dover Coll.; R.A. 1941–46; Staff Coll.; Lieut.-Col. 1945; with Peat, Marwick Mitchell & Co. 1937–57; Dir. Hill Samuel Group 1957–70, Industrial Adviser Dept. of Econ. Affairs 1965–67; Pres. Bass PLC 1987–89 (Dir. 1970–76, C.E.O. 1976–84, Chair. 1976–87); Chair. Yorkshire TV 1982–93, Boythorpe 1986–93; Dir. Grindlays Bank Ltd. 1973–85, Grindlays Holdings PLC 1979–85, United Newspapers 1986–93, Centre for Policy Studies Ltd. 1983–88, CM Group Holdings Ltd. 1986–93, Consolidated Venture Trust PLC 1984–93, Drayton Consolidated Trust PLC 1982–93; mem. Dover Harbour Bd. 1964–75, British Railways Bd. 1969–72, Prince's Trust 1984–; Chair British Rail Southern Regional Advisory Bd. 1972–79; Chair. Leeds University Foundation Trust 1986–89, Zoological Soc. of London Devt. Trust 1986–88; Accounting Standards Comm. 1982–84; World Wildlife Fund (U.K.) 1982–85; Trustee, Civic Trust 1979–89, Police Dependants' Trust 1979–, Queen Elizabeth's Foundation for Disabled People Devt. Trust 1993–96; Vice-Pres. Brewers' Soc. 1982– (Chair. 1982–84); mem. Alcohol Educ. and Research Council 1982–87, Ct. Brewers' Co. 1982–88; Freeman, City of London. *Leisure interests:* shooting, gardening. *Address:* Church Farm, Naunton, Cheltenham, Glos., England.

PALMER, Arnold Daniel; American professional golfer and business executive; b. 10 Sept. 1929, Latrobe, Pa; s. of Milfred J. Palmer and Doris Palmer; m. Winifred Walzer 1954; two d.; ed. Wake Forest Univ., N.C.; U.S. Coast Guard 1950–53; U.S. Amateur Golf Champion 1954; professional golfer 1954–; winner of 92 professional titles, incl. British Open 1961, 1962, U.S. Open 1960, U.S. Masters 1958, 1960, 1962, 1964, Canadian P.G.A. 1980, U.S. Srs. Championship 1981, and more than $4 million in prize money; mem. U.S. Ryder Cup team 1961, 1963, 1965, 1967, 1971, 1973, Captain 1963, 1975; Pres. Arnold Palmer Enterprises, three automobile agencies, one aviation service co., Latrobe Country Club, Bay Hill Club; mem. Bd. of dirs. Latrobe Area Hospital; Hon. Nat. Chair. Nat. Foundation March of Dimes 1971–90; designer numerous golf courses; Hon. LL.D. (Wake

Forest, Nat. Coll. of Educ.), Hon. D.H. (Thiel Coll.), Hon. D.H.L. (Fla. Southern Coll.); Athlete of Decade, Associated Press 1970; Sportsman of the Year, Sports Illustrated 1960; Hickok Belt, Athlete of Year 1960. *Publications:* My Game and Yours 1965, Situation Golf 1970, Go for Broke 1973, Arnold Palmer's Best 54 Golf Holes 1977, Arnold Palmer's Complete Book of Putting 1986, Play Great Golf 1987, Arnold Palmer: A Personal Journey (with Thomas Hauser) 1994, A Golfer's Life (with James Dodson) 1999. *Leisure interests:* bridge, occasional hunting. *Address:* P.O. Box 52, Youngstown, PA 15696, U.S.A. (Home and Office). *Telephone:* (412) 537-7751 (Home).

PALMER, Frank Robert, D.LITT., F.B.A.; British professor of linguistics; b. 9 April 1922, Westerleigh, Glos.; s. of George Samuel Palmer and Gertrude Lilian (née Newman) Palmer; m. Jean Elisabeth Moore 1948; three s. two d.; ed. Bristol Grammar School, New College, Oxford, Merton College, Oxford; Lecturer in Linguistics, School of Oriental and African Studies (SOAS), Univ. of London 1950–60; Prof. of Linguistics, Univ. Coll. of North Wales, Bangor 1960–65; Prof. of Linguistic Science, Univ. of Reading 1965–87, Dean, Faculty of Letters and Social Sciences 1969–72; Vice-Pres., Philological Soc.; Chair. Linguistics Assen. (G.B.) 1965–68, Ed. Journal of Linguistics 1969–79, Linguistic Soc. of America Prof., Buffalo, U.S.A. 1971; Distinguished Visiting Prof. Univ. of Del., Newark, U.S.A. 1982. *Publications:* The Morphology of the Tigre Noun 1962, A Linguistic Study of the English Verb 1965, Ed. Selected Papers of J. R. Firth (1951–58) 1968, Ed. Prosodic Analysis 1970, Grammar 1971, 1984, The English Verb 1974, 1987, Semantics 1976, 1981, Modality and the English Modals 1979, 1990, Mood and Modality 1986, Jt. Ed. Studies in the History of Western Linguistics in Honour of R. H. Robins 1986, Grammatical Roles and Relations 1994, Ed. Grammar and Meaning: Essays in Honour of Sir John Lyons 1995. *Leisure interests:* gardening, crosswords. *Address:* 'Whitethorns', Roundabout Lane, Winnersh, Wokingham, Berks., RG41 5AD, England. *Telephone:* (0118) 978 6214.

PALMER, Rt. Hon. Sir Geoffrey Winston Russell, K.C.M.G., P.C., A.C., B.A., LL.B., J.D.; New Zealand fmr. politician and professor; b. 21 April 1942, Nelson; s. of Leonard R. and Jessie P. Palmer; m. Margaret E. Hinchcliff 1963; one s. one d.; ed. Nelson Coll., Victoria Univ. of Wellington and Univ. of Chicago; solicitor, Wellington 1964–66; Lecturer in Political Science, Vic. Univ. 1968–69; Prof. of Law, Univ. of Iowa and Univ. of Va., U.S.A. 1969–73; Principal Asst. to Australian Nat. Comm. of Inquiry on Rehabilitation and Compensation 1973; Prof. of English and New Zealand Law, Victoria Univ. 1974–79; Visiting Fellow, Wolfson Coll., Oxford 1978; mem. Parl. for Christchurch Cen. 1979–90; Deputy Leader N.Z. Labour Party 1983–89; Deputy Prime Minister, Minister of Justice and Attorney-Gen. 1984–89, for the Environment 1987–90; Prime Minister of New Zealand 1989–90; Minister in Charge of N.Z. Security Intelligence; Prof. of Law Victoria Univ. 1991–95, Univ. of Iowa 1991–95; Partner Chen & Palmer, Wellington 1995–; Ida Beam Distinguished Visiting Prof. of Law, Univ. of Iowa 1991; UN Environment Programme Global 500 Laureate 1991. *Publications:* Unbridled Power?—An Interpretation of New Zealand's Constitution and Government 1979, Compensation for Incapacity—A Study of Law and Social Change in Australia and New Zealand 1979, Environmental Politics—A Greenprint for New Zealand 1990, New Zealand's Constitution in Crisis 1992, Public Law in New Zealand (with Mai Chen) 1993, Environment—the international challenge 1995, Bridled Power 1997. *Leisure interests:* cricket, golf, playing the trumpet, fishing. *Address:* 63 Roxburgh Street, Mount Victoria, Wellington, New Zealand. *Telephone:* (4) 8015185.

PALMER, Robert B., M.S.; American business executive; b. 1940; ed. Texas Tech. Univ.; Vice-Pres. Semiconductor Operations, Digital Equipment Corpn., of Mfg., now Pres., C.E.O. 1992–, Chair. 1995–98. *Address:* Digital Equipment Corporation, 111 Powdermill Road, Maynard, MA 01754, U.S.A.

PALMER, Thomas Joseph, C.B.E., M.A.; British business executive; b. 11 Sept. 1931, Cheddar; m. Hilary Westrup 1955; two s. two d.; ed. King's School, Bruton and Trinity Coll. Cambridge; Gen. Man. (Admin.), Legal & General Group PLC 1972–78, Gen. Man. (Int.) 1978–84, Group Chief Exec. 1984–91, Dir. 1972–91; Chair. Asscn. of British Insurers 1989–91, Laser Richmount Ltd. 1991–93, Personal Investment Authority 1993–, Springman Tipper Campbell Partnership 1993–; Dir. Nat. Power PLC 1991–96, S.I.B., Halifax Bldg. Soc. 1991–93, Sedgwick Group PLC, Investors Compensation Scheme 1992–93; Hon. Fellow, London Business School. *Leisure interests:* mountain walking, langlauf, gardening, reading. *Address:* 1 Canada Square, Canary Wharf, London, E14 5AZ, England. *Telephone:* 0171-538 8860.

PALMSTIERNA, Jacob, C.B.E.; Swedish banker; b. 28 April 1934, Lund; s. of Carl Palmstierna and Anne-Marie Palmstierna; m. Hanne Wedell-Wedellsborg 1994; two s. one d.; ed. Wharton School of Finance, Stockholm School of Econ.; with Stockholms Enskilda Bank 1960–69; Exec. Vice-Pres. Skandinaviska Enskilda Banken 1969–76, Pres. 1976–89, Man. Exec., C.E.O., Chair. 1989–91; Vice-Chair. Nord Banken 1991–92, Chair. 1992–98; Chair. Siemans-Elema AB 1996–, Bilia AB 1997–; Vice-Chair. Merita Nord Banken 1998–99, Chair. 1999–; Hon. D. Econ.; King Carl X Gustaf's Medal (Sweden); Grosse Verdienstkreutz (Germany). *Leisure interests:* golf, hunting. *Address:* Merita Nord Banken, SE-105 71, Stockholm, Sweden. *Telephone:* 8-614 7800. *Fax:* 8-105069.

PALOUŠ, Radim, PH.D.; Czech university rector (retd.); b. 6 Nov. 1924, Prague; m. Anna Štausová 1949; two s.; ed. Charles Univ. of Prague, Pedagogical Univ.; lecturer in Analytical Chem., Faculty of Natural Sciences 1957–59, Inst. of Univ. Studies, Tech. Univ. of Prague 1960; Chair. Educ. Techniques Dept., Faculty of Pedagogics, Prague 1968–69; Rector Charles Univ. 1990–94; Vice-Chair. Czechoslovak Asscn. of the Roman Club 1991–; mem. numerous acads. and orgs.; Dr. h.c. (Pittsburgh) 1990, (Omaha) 1990, (Int. Acad. for Philosophy) 1991, (Cracow) 1991, (Moravian Coll., U.S.A.) 1991; Czechoslovak Acad. Prize for 1989, TGM Prize, Prague 1997. *Publications include:* Die Schule den Alten 1979, The Godchildren 1977, Expedice 1984, The Time of Education 1983, The Czech Experience 1984. *Leisure interests:* carpentry, tennis. *Address:* Charles University, Ovocný trh 3-5, 116 36 Prague 1 (Office); Újezd 17, 101 00 Prague 1, Czech Republic (Home). *Telephone:* 22 08 15 (Office).

PAL SINGH, Krishna; Indian politician; b. 2 Aug. 1922, V. Birhuli, Shahdol Dist., Madhya Pradesh; politically active at school and in higher educ.; Pres. Students' Union, Rewa, organized students' congress and congress volunteer corps; worked with Sindhi refugees during communal riots of 1947–48; became follower of Bhai Paramanandji 1942, joined Quit India movt., arrested and served prison sentence; after independence became trades union leader, continuing to campaign for causes of students, kisans, colliery workers and other labourers; Vice-Pres. M.P. Unit of All India Trades Union Congress; joined Socialist Party 1946 and became Pres. of party in fmr. Vindya Pradesh and Pres. Samyukta Socialist Party, M.P.; joined Congress Party 1965; mem. A.I.C.C. and M.P.C.C., later Gen. Sec. and Vice-Pres. M.P.C.C. and special invitee A.I.C. Working Cttee.; M.P. Vidhan Sabha 1962–90; served five times as Minister with many different portfolios, finance, law, etc., becoming Deputy Leader; Gov. of Gujarat; party and political observer gen. and party elections in Indian states; Pres. Friends of Soviet Union, India-China Soc., M.P. Unit of Nepal Friendship Soc., India-Africa Friendship Asscn. and Gen. Sec. All India Indo-Arab Friendship Soc. *Address:* Raj Bhavan, Gandhinagar, Gujarat, India.

PÁLSSON, Thorsteinn; Icelandic politician; b. 29 Oct. 1947; m. Ingibjórg Rafnar; three c.; ed. Commercial Coll., Reykjavík and Univ. of Iceland; Chair. Vaka (student's union) 1969–70; Ed. Vísir 1975; Dir. Confed. of Icelandic Employers 1979–; M.P. 1983–; Chair. Independence Party 1983–91; Minister of Finance 1985–87, Prime Minister of Iceland 1987–88, Minister of Fisheries 1991–, of Justice 1991–, also of Ecclesiastical Affairs. *Address:* Althing, 150 Reykjavík, Iceland.

PALTRIDGE, Garth William, PH.D., F.A.A.; Australian research scientist; b. 24 April 1940, Brisbane; s. of T.B. Paltridge and A.T. Savage; m. Kay L. Petty 1965; one s. one d.; ed. Brisbane Boys' Coll., and Queensland and Melbourne Univs.; Postdoctoral Fellow, New Mexico Tech. 1965; Sr. Scientific Officer R.S.R.S., U.K. 1966; research scientist, CSIRO Div. of Meteorological Physics 1967; Exec. Dir. P.I.E.C.E. of Australian Inst. of Petroleum 1980; Chief Research Scientist, CSIRO Div. of Atmospheric Research 1981–89; Dir. Co-operative Research Centre for Antarctic and Southern Ocean Environment, Univ. of Tasmania 1991–; WMO Research Prize. *Publications:* Radiative Processes in Meteorology and Climatology; 100 research papers on environmental topics. *Leisure interests:* golf, history, furniture and cabinet making. *Address:* Antarctic Co-operative Research Centre, University of Tasmania, GPO 252C, Hobart, Tasmania 7001 (Office); 97 Hampden Road, Battery Point, Hobart, Tasmania 7004, Australia (Home).

PALTROW, Gwyneth; American actress; b. 1973, Los Angeles; d. of Bruce Paltrow and Blythe Danner; ed. Spence School, New York and Univ. of Calif. at Santa Barbara; appeared with her mother at Williamstown Theater Festival 1990. *Films include:* Flesh and Bone 1993, Hook, Moonlight and Valentino, The Pallbearer, Seven, Emma 1996, Sydney, Kilronan, Great Expectations 1998, Sliding Doors 1998, A Perfect Murder 1998, Shakespeare in Love (Acad. Award for Best Actress) 1998, The Talented Mr. Ripley 1999. *Address:* c/o Rick Kurtzman, CAA, 9830 Wilshire Boulevard, Beverly Hills, CA 90212; Screen Actors Guild, 5757 Wilshire Boulevard, Los Angeles, CA 90036, U.S.A.

PALUMBO, Baron (Life Peer) cr. 1991, of Walbrook in the City of London; **Peter Garth Palumbo,** M.A.; British property developer; b. 20 July 1935, London; s. of Rudolph Palumbo and Elsie Palumbo; m. 1st Denia Wigram 1959 (died 1986), one s. two d.; m. 2nd Hayat Morowa 1986, one s. two d.; ed. Eton Coll. and Worcester Coll., Oxford; Gov. L.S.E. 1976–94; Hon. mem. Emmanuel Coll., Cambridge 1994–; Trustee, Mies van der Rohe Archive 1977–, The Tate Gallery 1978–85, Whitechapel Art Gallery Foundation 1981–87; Trustee and Hon. Treas. Writers and Scholars Educational Trust 1984–; Chair. The Tate Gallery Foundation 1986–87, Painshill Park Trust Appeal 1986–96; Chair. The Arts Council of G.B. 1989–94; Chancellor Univ. of Portsmouth 1992–; Trustee Natural History Museum 1994–, Design Museum 1995–; mem. Council, Royal Albert Hall 1995–; Gov. RSC 1995–; Hon. F.R.I.B.A.; Hon. Fellow Inst. of Structural Eng.; mem. Livery, Salters' Co.; Dr. h.c. (Portsmouth) 1993; Nat. Order of Southern Cross, Brazil. *Leisure interests:* music, travel, gardening, reading. *Address:* Bagnor Manor, Bagnor, Newbury, Berks., RG16 8AG, England. *Telephone:* (01635) 40930.

PAMFILOVA, Ella Aleksandrovna; Russian politician; b. 12 Sept. 1953, Tashkent Region, Uzbekistan; d. of Alexandre Lekomtsev and Polina Lekomtseva; m. Nikita Leonidovich Pamfilov 1976 (divorced 1993); one d.; ed. Moscow Inst. of Power Eng.; foreman Cen. factory Mosenergo, Chair. trade union at factory 1981–89; U.S.S.R. People's Deputy 1989–91; Sec. Comm. of Supreme Soviet on Privileges Jan.–Nov. 1991; Russian Fed. Minister for

Social Security 1991–94; mem. State Duma (Parl.) 1993–, mem. Cttee. on Security 1995–; Chair. Council on Social Policy under Presidential Admin. 1994; f. Healthy Russia Movt. 1996. *Leisure interest:* gardening. *Address:* State Duma, Okhotny Ryad 1, 103009 Moscow, Russia. *Telephone:* 292-88-43. *Fax:* 292-70-14.

PAN CHENGDONG; Chinese mathematician; b. 1930; mem. Chinese Acad. of Sciences 1992–; Pres. Shandong Univ.; Science and Tech. Progress Award. *Address:* Shandong University, 25 Shanda Road S., Jinan 250100, Shandong Province, People's Republic of China.

PAN HONG; Chinese film actress; b. 4 Nov. 1954, Shanghai; m. Mi Jingshan (divorced 1990); ed. Shanghai Drama Acad. 1973–76; actress, Shanghai Film Studio, Shanghai 1977–80, Omei Film Studio, Chengdu 1980–; mem. 5th Nat. Cttee., Fed. of Literary and Art Circles 1988–; 3rd Golden Rooster Best Actress Award for A Middle-aged Women 1983; 8th Golden Rooster Best Actress for Well 1988. *Films include:* The Last Aristocrat, A Slave's Daughter, Camel Bell in the Desert, A Bitter Smile. *Address:* Omei Film Studio, Tonghui Menwai, Chengdu City, Sichuan Province, People's Republic of China. *Telephone:* 22991 (Chengdu).

PAN RIYUAN, Lieut.-General; Chinese army officer; b. Feb. 1933, Laiyang City, Shandong Prov.; ed. Jinzhou Artillery School and PLA Mil. Acad.; joined PLA 1948; Base Commdr. and Chief of Staff, PLA Second Artillery 1990; Deputy Commdr. PLA Second Artillery 1994–; mem. CCP 1956–; Deputy to 7th NPC 1988. *Address:* c/o Ministry of National Defence, Jingshanqian Jie, Beijing, People's Republic of China.

PAN RONGWEN, M.D.; Chinese physician; b. 1 July 1931, Jiangsu Prov.; d. of Pan Yu Qi and Pan Cao Shi; m. Lu Shi Cai 1960; one s. one d.; alt. mem. 12th CCP Cen. Cttee. 1982; Physician-in-Charge, Changzheng Hosp. 1982, Vice-Pres. 1983–, Prof. 1986–. *Address:* Changzheng Hospital, 428 Feng Yang Road, Shanghai 200003, People's Republic of China. *Telephone:* 21-3275997 Ext. 201.

PANAYIDES CHRISTOU, Tasos, M.A., M.P.A.; Cypriot diplomatist; b. 9 April 1934, Ktima-Paphos; s. of Christos Panayi and Efrosini Savva; m. Pandora Constantinides 1969; two s. one d.; ed. Paphos Gymnasium, Cyprus Teacher's Training Coll., Univ. of London, and Univ. of Indiana; Teacher, Cyprus 1954–59; First Sec. to Pres. (Archbishop Makarios), then Dir. President's Office 1960–69; Amb. to Fed. Repub. of Germany (also to Austria and Switzerland) 1969–79; Sec. and Dean, Commonwealth Group, Bonn 1976–79; High Commr. in U.K. (also Amb. to Denmark, Iceland, Norway and Sweden) 1979–90; Perm. Sec. of Ministry of Foreign Affairs and Amb. to Iceland 1990–94; Amb. to Sweden 1994–96 (also to Denmark, Finland, Iceland, Norway, Latvia, Lithuania and Estonia); Chair. AVRA Shipmanagement S.A. 1997–; Chair. Commonwealth Foundation Grants Cttee. 1985–88, Commonwealth Fund for Tech. Co-operation (C.F.T.C.) 1986–89, Finance Cttee. of Commonwealth Secr. 1988–90, SCOSO (Commonwealth Steering Cttee. of Senior Officials) 1994–95; Rep. to IAEA 1976–79; Fellow, Ealing Coll.; Grand Cross (with Star and Sash) of Fed. Repub. of Germany, Grand Cross (with Star and Sash) of Austria, Thyateira Archbishopric Grand Cross (in Gold), Grand Cross (in Gold) of the Patriarchate of Antioch 1984, Freeman of City of London 1984; Hon. G.C.V.O. 1990, Hon. LL.D. (Birmingham) 1991. *Leisure interests:* history, swimming, reading. *Address:* 116 Kolokotroni Street, 185-35 Piraeus, Greece. *Telephone:* (1) 418-1601. *Fax:* (1) 418-1608.

PANCHENKO, Aleksandr Mikhailovich, D.HIST.SC.; Russian historian; b. 25 Feb. 1937, Leningrad (now St. Petersburg); m.; one s.; ed. Karlov Univ., Prague; researcher, Head of Div., Prof. Inst. of Russian Literature (Pushkin House), U.S.S.R. (now Russian) Acad. of Sciences 1962–; mem. Russian Acad. of Sciences 1991–; State Prize 1995. *Publications:* Russian Poetic Culture of the XVII Century 1973, Laughter in Ancient Russia 1984, Russian Culture on the Eve of Reforms of Peter the Great and works on the history of Russian poetry, culture of old and new periods, cultural relationship of Slavic literatures, numerous articles on Russian History and Culture. *Address:* Pushkinsky Dom, Institute of Russian Literature, Naberezhnaya Makarova 4, 199034 St. Petersburg, Russia. *Telephone:* 812/218-0902.

PANCIROLI, Most Rev. Romeo; Vatican ecclesiastic; b. 21 Nov. 1923, Italy; s. of Anthony Panciroli and Celestine Cavazzoni; ordained Priest 1949; teacher of natural ethics and sociology 1951–59; Vatican Secr. of State 1960; Attaché to Apostolic Nunciature, Nigeria 1961–64; Sec. to Pontifical Comm. for Social Communications 1965–76; Consultant to Pontifical Cttee. for revision of Canon Law 1975–83; Dir. Vatican Press Office and Spokesman of Holy See 1976–84; Information Officer and mem. Papal Suite with Pope John Paul II in His journeys to 54 countries 1978–84; Titular Archbishop of Noba 1984–; Apostolic Pro-Nuncio to Liberia, Guinea, The Gambia 1984–92; Apostolic Del. to Sierra Leone 1984–92; Apostolic Nuncio to Iran 1992–99. *Publications:* Words on the Faith, Papal Messages in Asia and Australia, Audience Pontifical Suite. *Leisure interests:* reading, fine arts, clasical music, travelling. *Address:* Borgo S. Spirito, 10-00193 Rome, Italy.

PANDAY, Basdeo; Trinidad and Tobago politician; Minister of Foreign Affairs 1986–91; mem. Nat. Alliance for Reconciliation (NAR), expelled 1988; f. and Leader United Nat. Congress (UNC); Prime Minister of Trinidad and Tobago Nov. 1995–. *Address:* Office of the Prime Minister, Level 19, Central Bank Tower, Eric Williams Plaza, Independence Square, Port of Spain, Trinidad and Tobago. *Telephone:* 623-3655. *Fax:* 627-3444.

PANDIT, Jasraj, D.MUS.; Indian musician; b. 28 Jan. 1930, Hissar, Hariyana; s. of Motiram Pandit and Krishnabai Pandit; m. Madhura Pandit 1962; one s. one d.; studied under elder brother Maniram Pandit; belongs to Mewati Gharana (school of music); has conducted extensive research in Haveli Sangeet and successfully presented the original Pure Haveli Sangeet with its devotional content intact; has established an Ashram Motiram Sangeet Natale Acad. with main object of propagating Indian classical music by teaching bright students free of charge; mem. advisory bd. of radio and TV; numerous awards and honours, including Rajeev Gandhi Award for professional excellence, Padma Bhushan and Sangeet Martand. *Works include:* compositions for opera, ballet and short films etc. including Kan Khani Sunyo Kare, Geet Govindam, Sur, Laya Aur Chhanda. *Publication:* Sangeet Saurabh. *Leisure interests:* teaching, travel, sport. *Address:* Rajkamal Building, 138 Shivaji Park, Bombay 400016, India. *Telephone:* 4456281. *Fax:* 4147654.

PANDOLFI, Filippo Maria, PH.D.; Italian politician; b. 1 Nov. 1927, Bergamo; fmr. company dir.; mem. Chamber of Deputies for Brescia-Bergamo 1968; mem. Comm. on Finance and the Treasury; fmr. Under-Sec. of State in Ministry of the Budget; Minister of Finance 1976–78, of the Treasury 1978–80, of Industry 1980–81, 1982–83, of Agric. 1983–88; EEC Commr. for Science, Research, Telecommunications and Information Tech. 1989–92; Christian Democrat.

PANETTA, Leon, LL.B.; American politician and lawyer; b. 28 June 1938, Monterey, Calif.; s. of Carmelo Panetta and Carmelina Panetta; m. Sylvia Varni 1962; three s.; ed. Univ. of Santa Clara; served U.S. Army 1964–66; Legis. Asst. to Senator Thomas Kuchel, Washington 1966–69; Dir. U.S. Office of Civil Rights 1969–70; Exec. Asst. to Mayor of New York 1970–71; partner Panetta, Thompson and Panetta, Monterey 1971–76; mem. U.S. House of Reps. 1977–93, mem. House Budget Cttee. 1979–85, Chair. 1989–92; Head of Office of Man. and Budget 1993–94; Chief of Staff to Pres. Clinton 1994–97; Democrat. *Address:* c/o 252 Old Executive Office, Washington, DC 20503, U.S.A.

PANFILOV, Gleb Anatolyevich; Russian film director; b. 21 May 1934, Magnitogorsk; m. Inna Mikhailovna Churikova; one s.; grad. Sverdlovsk Polytechnic Inst. as chemical engineer and Mosfilm Studios (course in directing); work as dir. in Sverdlovsk, Leningrad (now St. Petersburg), Moscow 1976–; R.S.F.S.R. People's Artist 1984, R.S.F.S.R. State Prize 1985; *films include:* No Ford in the Fire (scenario: Yevgeniy Gabrilovich) 1968 (Grand Prix Locarno 1969), Début 1970, both starring Inna Churikova, I Wish to Speak 1975, Valentina 1981, Vassa Zheleznova 1983, The Theme 1986, The Mother 1991; stage productions at Lenkom Theatre incl. Hamlet 1986, Sorry (A. Galin) 1992. *Address:* Universitetski Prosp. 6, Korp. 4, Apt. 68, 117333 Moscow, Russia. *Telephone:* 137-89-67.

PANGALOS, Theodoros, PH.D.; Greek politician; b. Aug. 1938, Elefsis; m.; one s. one d.; ed. Athens and Sorbonne Univs.; a founder of the Grigoris Lambrakis Youth Movt.; stood as EDA candidate in 1964 election; active in dissident movement during mil. dictatorship; deprived of Greek citizenship by junta 1968; Lecturer and Researcher specializing in Econ. Devt., Programming and Town and Country Planning, Sorbonne, Paris, and Head of Econ. Devt. Inst. 1969–78; practises as lawyer in Athens; Legal Adviser to trade unions in Megarida; active in movt. to protect environment, a founder mem. of Citizens Against Pollution, Socialist M.P. for Attila; Alt. Minister of Foreign Affairs 1986–87, 1993–94, 1996–99; Minister of State for EEC Affairs 1987–88; Minister of Transport and Communication 1994–96, of Foreign Affairs 1996–99; an Ed. of newspaper The Thriasio and the Megara, and periodical ANTI. *Publications:* several works on economics, sociology and philosophy. *Address:* 16–18 Pireos Street, 104 31 Athens, Greece.

PANGGABEAN, Gen. Maraden Saur Halomoan; Indonesian politician and army officer; b. 29 June 1922, Tarutung, N. Sumatra; s. of M. Patuan Natoras and Katharina Panjaitan; m. Meida Seimima Matiur Tambunan; one s. three d.; studied mil. affairs in various mil. acads. including the Advanced Infantry Officer Course, U.S.A.; mil. posts include C.-in-C. of the Army 1968, Vice-Commdr. Armed Forces 1969–73, C.-in-C. 1973–78; Deputy Commdr. for Restoration of Security and Order 1968, Commdr. 1969–73, Exec. Officer Command 1973–78; Minister of State for Defense and Security 1969–73, Minister 1973–78; Acting Minister of Home Affairs 1973; Minister Co-ordinator for Political and Security Affairs 1978–83; Acting Foreign Minister 1978–83; Chair. Bd. of Guidance, GOLKAR 1973–78, Vice-Chair. 1978–83; Chair. Exec. Presidium, Bd. of Guidance, GOLKAR 1978–83; mem. People's Consultative Ass. 1973–78, 1978–83, 1983–; War of Independence Medal, Service Award Medal, Best Son of the Nation Medal, Rep. of Indonesia Medal and numerous other medals and awards. *Leisure interests:* golf, jogging, gymnastics, hunting, reading. *Address:* Jalan Teuku Umar 21, Jakarta, Indonesia. *Telephone:* 378012.

PANHOFER, Walter; Austrian concert pianist; b. 3 Jan. 1910, Vienna; s. of Josef and Maria Panhofer; m. Gertraut Schmied 1956; two s.; ed. Akademie für Musik und darstellende Kunst, Hochschule für Musik und darstellende Kunst, Vienna; concerts in Austria, Germany, England, Switzerland, Italy and Yugoslavia; performed with Vienna Philharmonic and Vienna Symphony Orchestras and Royal Philharmonic and London Chamber Orchestras, England; has toured with, and made records with Vienna Octet; master classes in Brussels, Vienna and in Italy; has adjudicated many times at Int. Beethoven piano competition, Vienna; Ehrenkreuz für Wissenschaft und

Kunst. *Leisure interests:* mountains, skiing, books. *Address:* Erdbergstrasse 35/9, A-1030 Vienna, Austria. *Telephone:* 757902.

PANIČ, Milan; Serbian politician and businessman; b. 20 Dec. 1929, Belgrade; m. Seli Vin; one s. (deceased) two d.; ed. Belgrade, South Carolina and Heidelberg Univs.; emigrated to U.S.A. 1956; f. and Chair. ICN Pharmaceutical Co. 1960; returned to Yugoslavia 1991; Prime Minister of Yugoslavia July–Dec. 1992; cand. for Presidency of Serbia 1992; Dir. Galenica Co., Belgrade and Moscow; mem. Bd. Fund for Interdisciplinary Scientific Research (ISRF); Corresp. mem. Californian Inst. of Tech.; mem. American Nuclear Soc., Swiss Chemical Soc., Int. Soc. of Haemotherapy. *Leisure interests:* tennis, cycling (fmr. Yugoslav Champion). *Address:* 1050 Arden Road, Pasadena, CA 91106, U.S.A.

PANICHAS, George Andrew, F.R.S.A., M.A., PH.D., LITT.D.; American writer and university professor; b. 21 May 1930, Springfield, Mass.; s. of Andrew Panichas and Fannie Dracouli Panichas; ed. Springfield Classical High School, American Int. Coll., Trinity Coll. and Nottingham Univ., England; Instructor in English, Univ. of Maryland 1962, Asst. Prof. 1963, Assoc. Prof. 1966, Prof. 1968–92; Co-Dir. of Conf. "Irving Babbitt: Fifty Years Later" 1983; mem. Richard M. Weaver Fellowship Awards Cttee. 1983–88; Academic Bd. Nat. Humanities Inst. 1985–, Advisory Bd. Humanitas 1993–; Editorial Adviser, Modern Age: A Quarterly Review 1972–77, Assoc. Ed. 1978–83, Ed. 1984–; mem. advisory Bd. Continuity: A Journal of History 1984; Ingersoll Prizes Jury Panel 1986; Earhart Foundation Award 1982. *Publications:* Adventure in Consciousness: The Meaning of D. H. Lawrence's Religious Quest 1964, Renaissance and Modern Essays: Presented to Vivian de Sola Pinto in Celebration of his Seventieth Birthday (Ed. with G. R. Hibbard and A. Rodway) 1966, Epicurus 1967, Mansions of the Spirit: Essays in Literature and Religion (Ed.) 1967, Promise of Greatness: The War of 1914–1918 (Ed.) 1968, The Politics of Twentieth-Century Novelists (Ed.) 1971, The Reverent Discipline: Essays in Literary Criticism and Culture 1974, The Burden of Vision: Dostoevsky's Spiritual Art 1977, The Simone Weil Reader (Ed.) 1977, Irving Babbitt: Representative Writings (Ed.) 1981, The Courage of Judgment: Essays in Criticism, Culture and Society 1982, Irving Babbitt in Our Time (Ed. with C. G. Ryn) 1986, Modern Age: The First Twenty-Five Years. A Selection (Ed.) 1988, The Critic as Conservator: Essays in Literature, Society and Culture 1992, In Continuity: The Last Essays of Austin Warren (Ed.) 1996, The Critical Legacy of Irving Babbitt: An Appreciation 1999, Growing Wings to Overcome Gravity: Criticism as the Pursuit of Virtue 1999; also numerous articles, translations and reviews for books and journals published in U.S. and Europe. *Leisure interests:* hiking, playing racquetball, keeping physically fit, listening to music. *Address:* P.O. Box AB, College Park, MD 20741 (Office); 4313 Knox Road, Apartment 402, College Park, MD 20740, U.S.A. (Home). *Telephone:* (301) 779-1436 (Home).

PANIGRAHI, Sanjukta; Indian dancer and choreographer; b. 24 Aug. 1934, Berhampur; d. of late Abhiram Mishra and of Shakuntala Mishra; m. Raghunath Panigrahi 1960; two s.; first performance aged four; has toured extensively in Europe giving lecture demonstrations and performances in Odyssi style; has appeared at int. festivals of music. dance and drama in India, U.S.S.R., Australia, Japan, Indonesia, U.K. etc.; conducts regular workshops at cultural and educ. insts. abroad; Life Pres. Kalinga Kala Kshetra and the Natyotkala; mem. Gen. Council Orissa Sangeet Natak Acad.; mem. Gov. Bd. Utkal Sangeet Mahavidyalaya, Bhubaneswar; mem. various social and cultural orgs.; several awards including Cen. Sangeet Natak Akad. Award. 1976, State Akad. Award 1977, Padmashree (Govt. of India) 1978, Tirupati Nat. Award 1987, All-India Critics Asscn. Award 1989. *Publications:* articles in journals in India and abroad. *Address:* Plot No. 4114/A, Ashok Nagar East, Unit II, Bhubaneswar 751009, Orissa, India. *Telephone:* 50638.

PANINA, Yelena Vladimirovna, CAND.POL.SC.; Russian civil servant; b. 29 April 1948; m. Aleksander Andreyevich Panin; one d.; ed. Moscow Inst. of Finance; on staff Control-Audit Dept. Ministry of Finance, Russian Fed. 1970–75; Head of Dept., Deputy Dir.-Gen. Production Union 1975–86; Sec. Dist. CP Cttee. Moscow Region 1986–88; Head of Dept. Moscow CP City Cttee. 1988–91; Dir.-Gen. U.S.S.R. Trade Chamber 1991–92; mem. Exec. Bd. Russian Union of Businessmen 1992–; Chair. Russian Zemsvto Movt. 1993–; Deputy Head World Russian People's Sobor 1995–; Co-Chair., Coordinator Moscow Confed. of Businessmen 1992–; Dir.-Gen. Centre of Business Projects (Interbuzinesproekt) 1992–97; mem. State Duma 1997–. *Address:* State Duma, Okhotny Ryad 1, Moscow Interbisnesproekt, Novy Arbat 21, Moscow, Russia (Office). *Telephone:* (095) 292 9326; 291 9874 (Office).

PANKIN, Boris Dmitriyevich; Russian diplomatist and essayist; b. 20 Feb. 1931, Frunze (now Bishkek); m.; two s. one d.; ed. Moscow State Univ.; journalist and literary critic 1957–; Ed. Komsomolskaya Pravda 1965–73; Chair. Bd. U.S.S.R. Copyright Agency 1973–82; U.S.S.R. Amb. to Sweden 1982–90, to Czechoslovakia 1990–91; Foreign Minister Aug.–Dec. 1991; Russian Amb. to U.K. 1991–94; now living in Sweden; U.S.S.R. State Prize 1982. *Publications:* Severe Literature, Time and Word, Boundaries and Books, The Last 100 Days of the Soviet Union.

PANNENBERG, Wolfhart Ulrich, DR. THEOL.; German professor of systematic theology; b. 2 Oct. 1928, Stettin; s. of Kurt B. S. Pannenberg and Irmgard Pannenberg; m. Hilke S. Schütte 1953; ordained as Lutheran Minister 1955; Privatdozent, Heidelberg 1955; Prof. of Systematic Theology, Wuppertal 1958, Univ. of Mainz 1961, Univ. of Munich 1967–; Head, Inst. of Ecumenical Theology, Munich; mem. Bavarian Acad. of Sciences, British Acad. of Sciences; Hon. D.D. (Glasgow, Manchester, Trinity Coll. Dublin, Cambridge). *Publications:* What is Man? 1962, Jesus: God and Man 1968, Revelation as History 1969, Theology and the Kingdom of God 1969, Basic Questions in Theology (Vol. I) 1970, (Vol. II) 1971, The Apostle's Creed 1972, Theology and the Philosophy of Science 1976, Human Nature, Election and History 1977, Anthropology in Theological Perspective 1985, Christianity in a Secularized World 1989, Metaphysics and the Idea of God 1990, Systematic Theology (Vol. 1) 1991, Grundlagen der Ethik 1996, Theologie und Philosophie 1996, Problemgeschichte der neueren evangelischen Theologie in Deutschland 1997. *Leisure interests:* history, music, philosophy. *Address:* Sudetenstrasse 8, 82166 Gräfelfing, Germany. *Telephone:* (089) 85 59 15.

PANNI, Marcello; Italian conductor and composer; b. 24 Jan. 1940, Rome; s. of Arnaldo Panni and Adriana Cortini; m. Jeanne Colombier 1970; one d.; ed. Accademia di Santa Cecilia, Rome under Goffredo Petrassi and Conservatoire Nat. Supérieur, Paris; conducting début, Festival of Contemporary Music, Venice 1969; has since achieved renown in field of avant-garde music conducting first performances of works by Berio, Bussotti, Cage, Feldman, Donatoni, Clementi, Sciarrino, Pennisi, Vandor, Ferrero and others at all major European festivals and for Italian Radio; regular guest conductor for Accademia di Santa Cecilia, the Italian radio orchestras and other European orchestras performing full range of baroque, classical and modern works; Musical Dir. Bonn Opera House 1994–97, Nice Opera House 1997–; opera début with The Barber of Seville, Hamburg 1977 and has since conducted opera in all the principal opera houses in Europe; American debut with Elisir d'amore, Metropolitan Opera, New York 1988; conducted world premiere of Bussotti's Cristallo di Rocca (opera) at La Scala 1983; Milhaud Prof. of Composition and Conducting, Mills Coll., Oakland, Calif. 1980–84. *Works include* symphonic and chamber music and music for experimental theatrical works; operas: Hanjo (one act) 1994, Il Giudizio di Paride (one act) 1996, The Banquet 1998. *Leisure interests:* arts, sport. *Address:* 3 Piazza Borghese, 00186 Rome, Italy. *Telephone:* 06/6873617.

PANNICK, David Philip, Q.C., B.C.L., M.A.; British barrister; b. 7 March 1956, London; s. of Maurice A. Pannick and Rita L. Pannick; m. Denise Sloam 1978; two s. one d.; ed. Bancroft's School, Essex and Hertford Coll. Oxford; called to the Bar 1979, Q.C. 1992; Fellow, All Souls Coll. Oxford 1979–; Jr. Counsel to the Crown (Common Law) 1988–92; columnist on law, The Times 1991–. *Publications:* Sex Discrimination Law 1985, Judges 1987, Advocates 1992. *Leisure interests:* reading, watching television, jogging. *Address:* Blackstone Chambers, Temple, London, EC4Y 7BH, England. *Telephone:* 0171-583 1770. *Fax:* 0171-822 7222.

PANNONE, Rodger John, F.R.S.A.; British solicitor; b. 20 April 1943, Minehead, Somerset; s. of Cyril Pannone and Violet Weeks; m. Patricia Todd 1966; two s. one d.; ed. St. Brendan's Coll. Bristol and Coll. of Law, London and Manchester Polytechnic; articled clerk, Casson & Co. Salford; joined W.H. Thompson 1969, later partner; joined Conn Goldberg (now Pannone & Partners) 1973, Sr. Partner 1991–; lecturer and broadcaster on legal affairs; mem. Lord Chancellor's Advisory Cttee. on Civil Justice; fmr. mem. Supreme Court Rule Cttee.; Gov. Coll. of Law; Fellow, Manchester Metropolitan Univ.; mem. Council, Law Society of England and Wales, Pres. 1993–94; Hon. mem. Canadian Bar Asscn.; Hon. Fellow Soc. of Chiropodists, Birmingham Univ. 1998; D.Litt. h.c. (Salford), Hon. LL.D. (Nottingham Trent). *Publications:* legal articles. *Leisure interests:* walking slowly, food and drink. *Address:* Pannone & Partners, 123 Deansgate, Manchester, M3 2BU, England. *Telephone:* 0161-832 3000. *Fax:* 0161-834 2067.

PANOFSKY, Wolfgang Kurt Hermann, A.B., PH.D.; American scientist; b. 24 April 1919, Berlin, Germany; s. of Erwin Panofsky and Dorothea Mosse Panofsky; m. Adele Dumond 1942; three s. two d.; ed. Princeton Univ. and California Inst. of Tech.; in U.S.A. 1934–; mem. of staff Radiation Laboratory, Calif. Univ. 1945–51; Asst. Prof. 1947–48, Assoc. Prof. 1948–51; Prof. Stanford Univ. 1951–89, Prof. Emer. 1989–, Dir. High Energy Physics Laboratory 1953–61, Dir. Linear Accelerator Center 1962–84, Dir. Emer. 1984–; Consultant Office of Science and Tech., Exec. Office of Pres. 1965–73; Consultant, Arms Control and Disarmament Agency 1968–81; mem. President's Science Advisory Cttee. 1960–64; mem. Panel Office of Science and Tech. Policy 1977–; mem. N.A.S., American Physical Soc. (Vice-Pres. 1974, Pres. 1975), American Acad. of Arts and Sciences, Accad. Naz. dei Lincei 1994; Hon. D.Sc. (Case Inst. of Tech., Saskatchewan, Columbia, Hamburg, Yale, Rome); Dr. h.c. (Princeton, Beijing, Uppsala); Lawrence Prize, U.S. Atomic Energy Comm. 1961; Calif. Scientist of Year Award 1967, Nat. Medal of Science 1969, Franklin Medal 1970, Enrico Fermi Award, Dept. of Energy 1979, Shoong Foundation Award for Science 1983; Officier, Légion d'honneur. *Leisure interest:* music. *Address:* Stanford Linear Accelerator Center, Stanford University, P.O. Box 4349, Palo Alto, CA 94309 (Office); 25671 Chapin Road, Los Altos, CA 94022, U.S.A. (Home). *Telephone:* (415) 926-3988.

PANOV, Alexander Nikolayevich, C.HIS.SC.; Russian diplomatist; b. 6 July 1944, Moscow; m. 1967; one d.; ed. Moscow Inst. of Int. Relations; diplomatic service 1968–; asst. man., translator Embassy, Japan 1968–71; teacher Moscow Inst. of Int. Relations 1971–77; Third, Second Sec. Perm. U.S.S.R. Mission to UN, New York 1977–82; First Sec. Second Far East Dept. U.S.S.R. Ministry of Foreign Affairs 1982–83; First Sec., Counsellor Embassy, Japan 1983–86; Deputy Chief, Chief of Div., Deputy Chief Dept.

of Countries of Pacific Ocean and South-East Asia, U.S.S.R. Ministry of Foreign Affairs 1988–90, Chief 1990–92; Russian Amb. to Korean Repub. 1992–94; Deputy Minister of Foreign Affairs 1994–96; Amb. to Japan 1996–. *Publications:* Postwar Reforms in Japan 1945–52, Japanese Diplomatic Service (articles in periodicals), Beyond Distrust to Trust. *Address:* Russian Embassy, Minato-ku, Azabu-dai 2-1-1, Tokyo, Japan. *Telephone:* 83583-4224.

PANSA CEDRONIO, Paolo, LL.D., LIC.POL.SC.; Italian diplomatist; b. 15 Nov. 1915, Naples; s. of Ciro Pansa Cedronio and Elina Stammelluti; ed. Univs. of Naples and Florence; entered Italian diplomatic service 1940; Sec., Italian Embassy, Washington 1945–49; Sec., Italian Del. to NATO, London and Paris 1951–55; Head of Service, Ministry of Foreign Affairs, Rome 1955–61; Minister, Italian Embassy, London 1961–66; Amb. to Chile 1966–70, to Canada 1970–71; Deputy Sec.-Gen. NATO 1971–78; Amb. to U.S.A. 1978–81; mem. Cttee. of Patrons, Atlantic Treaty Asscn., Paris; alt. Pres. NATO Appeals Bd., Brussels; fmr. mem. Consiglio del Contenzioso Diplomatico, Ministry of Foreign Affairs, Rome; mem. Istituto Studi Ricerca Difesa, Centro Conciliazione Internazionale, Circolo Studi Diplomatici, Rome; Croce di Guerra, Cavaliere di Gran Croce al Merito della Repubblica Italiana, Gran-Cruz Orden al Mérito de Chile, Officier, Légion d'honneur, etc. *Address:* Palazzo Borghese, Largo Fontanella Borghese 19, 00186 Rome, Italy. *Telephone:* 06-687 6128.

PANT, Krishna Chandra; M.SC.; Indian politician; b. 10 Aug. 1931, Bhowali, Nainital Dist.; s. of late Pandit Govind Ballabh Pant; m. Ila Pant 1957; two s.; ed. St. Joseph's Coll., Nainital, Univ. of Lucknow; Mem. Lok Sabha for Nainital 1962–77, re-elected 1978–; Minister of Finance 1967–69, of Steel and Heavy Eng. 1969–70, of Home Affairs and Head, Depts. of Science, Electronics and Atomic Energy 1970–73; Minister of Irrigation and Power 1973–74, of Energy 1974–77, 1979–80, of Educ. Jan.–Sept. 1985, of Steel and Mines 1985–87, of Defence 1987–89; Chair. Advisory Bd. on Energy 1983–84; First Vice-Pres. Human Rights Comm. 1966; Leader del. to Int. Conf. on Human Rights, Teheran 1968; del. to various other int. confs.; mem. Nat. Integration Council; Hon. Fellow Inst. of Engineers; Hon. D.Sc. (Udaipur). *Leisure interests:* welfare work, reading, travelling, sports.

PANT, Sumitranandan; Indian poet; b. 1900, Kausani; s. of G. Pant; Fellow of Sahitya Acad.; Padma Bhushan 1961; Jnan Pith Award 1969. *Publications:* Vina Granthi 1919, Jyotsna (drama) 1922, Pallav 1926, Vina-Gramthi 1930, Gunjan 1931, Birth of Poetry, Jyotsna (drama) 1934, Panch Kahaniyan (short stories) 1936, Uygvani-Gramya 1938, Swarana Kiran 1946, Uttara 1948, Gradya Path (essays) 1953, Atima 1955, Vani 1957, Chidambara (poetry) 1958, Kala Aur Boodhachand (Acad. Award Winner) 1959, Lokayatan (epic, Soviet Nehru Award Winner) etc. *Address:* 18/B.7, K. G. Marg, Allahabad, Uttar Pradesh, India. *Telephone:* Allahabad 3540.

PANYARACHUN, Anand; Thai diplomatist and politician; b. 9 Aug. 1932; s. of Phya and Khunying Prichanusat; m. M. R. Sodsee Panyarachun Chakrabandh 1956; two d.; ed. Bangkok Christian Coll., Dulwich Coll., London, and Univ. of Cambridge; joined Ministry of Foreign Affairs 1955; Sec. to Foreign Minister 1959; First Sec. Perm. Mission to UN 1964, Counsellor 1966, Acting Perm. Rep. 1967–72, concurrently Amb. to Canada; Amb. to U.S.A. concurrently Perm. Rep. to UN 1972–75, Amb. to Fed. Repub. of Germany 1977; Perm. Under-Sec. of State for Foreign Affairs 1975–76; del. to several sessions of UN Gen. Ass. and SEATO Council; Chair. Group of 77 on Law of Sea 1973; Rep. to UN Econ. and Social Council 1974–75; Chair. Thai Del. to 7th Special Session of UN Gen. Ass., Vice-Chair. Ad Hoc Cttee. 7th Special Session, Sept. 1975; Chair. Textport Int. Corpn. Ltd.; Pres. ASEAN-CCI Council 1980; Vice-Chair. Saha-Union Corpn. Ltd. 1979; Vice-Pres. Asscn. Thai Industries; Vice-Chair. ASEAN-U.S. Business Council 1980; Dir. Sime Darby 1982; Acting Prime Minister 1991–92; Prime Minister of Thailand 1992; UNICEF Amb. for Thailand 1996; Ramon Magsaysay Award 1997. *Leisure interests:* tennis, squash, reading. *Address:* Government House, Thanon Nakhon Pathom, Bangkok 10300, Thailand.

PANZA di BIUMO, Giuseppe, D.JUR.; Italian art collector; b. 23 March 1923, Milan; s. of Ernesto Panza di Biumo and Maria Mantegazza; m. Rosa G. Magnifico 1955; four s. one d.; ed. self-taught in art history; 80 works of art acquired by Museum of Contemporary Art, Los Angeles 1984; 220 works of art acquired by Guggenheim Museum 1990; 150 works of art in gift to Guggenheim Museum, 200 works of art in gift to Museo Cantonale d'Arte, Lugano, 70 to Museum of Contemporary Art, Los Angeles, 133 works of art and the 18th-century villa in Biumo. *Publications:* Art of the Sixties and Seventies 1988, Panza di Biumo: The Eighties and Nineties from the Collection 1992. *Address:* P.O. Box 3183, 6901 Lugano; Sentiero Vinorum 2, 6900 Massagno, Switzerland. *Telephone:* 91-9676021; 91-9682353. *Fax:* 91-9676125.

PAO, Eugene; Chinese jazz guitarist; ed. Univ. of Washington; played in local groups while at univ.; joined father's trading co. upon return to Hong Kong; began playing at Rick's Cafe; subsequently joined Hong Kong's Jazz Club where he leads a four-man band 1988–; CDs include By the Company You Keep.

PAOLOZZI, Sir Eduardo Luigi, Kt., C.B.E., R.A.; British sculptor; b. 7 March 1924, Leith, Scotland; s. of Alfonso Rudolfo Paolozzi and Carmella (Rossi) Paolozzi; m. (divorced); three d.; ed. Edinburgh Coll. of Art and Slade School of Fine Art, Oxford and London; first exhibitions, Mayor Gallery, London 1947, 1948, 1949; teacher of textile design, Cen. School of Art and Design 1949–55; Lecturer in sculpture, St. Martin's School of Art 1955–58; Visiting Prof. Hochschule für Bildende Künste, Hamburg 1960–62; Visiting Lecturer, Univ. of Calif., Berkeley 1968; tutor in Ceramics, Royal Coll. of Art 1968–89; Prof. in Ceramics, Fachhochschule, Cologne 1976–81, Prof. of Sculpture at Akad. der Bildenen Künste, Munich 1981–90; Visiting Prof. R.C.A. 1989–; Prof. Master Class, Int. Summer Acad., Salzburg 1982; H.M. Sculptor in Ordinary, Scotland 1986–; one-man exhbns. have included Hanover Gallery, London 1958, 1967, Betty Parsons Gallery, N.Y. 1960, 1962, Robert Fraser Gallery, London 1964, 1966, Museum of Modern Art, N.Y. 1964, Pace Gallery, N.Y. 1966, 1967, Stedelijk Museum, Amsterdam 1968, Tate Gallery, London 1971, Victoria and Albert Museum 1977, Nationalgalerie, Berlin retrospective 1975, Kölnischer Kunstverein, Cologne 1979, Museum für Kunst und Gewerbe, Hamburg 1982, Royal Scottish Acad. 1984, Lenbachhaus, Munich 1984, Museum Ludwig, Cologne 1985, Museum of Mankind, London 1986, Royal Acad., London 1986, Serpentine Gallery 1987, Nat. Portrait Gallery 1988, Talbot Rice Art Gallery, Edin. 1989, Stadtmuseum, Munich 1990, Goethe Inst., London 1991, and other galleries in U.K., U.S.A., Canada, Netherlands, Germany; has participated in numerous group exhbns. including Venice Biennale 1952, 1960, São Paulo Biennale 1957, 1963, New Images of Man, Museum of Modern Art, N.Y. 1959, 2nd 3rd and 4th Int. Biennial Exhbns. of Prints, Museum of Modern Art, Tokyo 1960, 1962, 1964, British Art Today (travelling exhbn., tour of U.S.A.) 1962, 7th Int. Art Exhbn., Tokyo 1963, Neue Realisten und Pop Art, Akad. der Künste, Berlin 1964, Premier Bienniale Exhbn., Cracow 1966, Sculpture from Twenty Nations, Guggenheim Museum, N.Y. 1967, Pop Art Redefined, Hayward Gallery, London 1969, Expo 70, Osaka 1970, Hayward Annual Arts Council Exhbn. 1977, Nat. Gallery of Scotland 1980, 20th Century British Sculpture, London 1981, West-Kunst, Cologne 1981, English Painters 1900–82, Museo Municipal of Madrid 1983, British Museum 1990, Pompidou Centre 1990, Royal Acad. 1991; designed mosaics for Tottenham Court Road underground station, London; Fellow, Univ. Coll. London 1986; apptd. Her Majesty's Sculptor-in-Ordinary for Scotland 1986; Trustee Nat. Portrait Gallery 1988–, Dean Gallery, Paolozzi Collection, Edin.; corresp. mem. Bayerische Akad. der Schönen Künste 1990; Dr. h.c. R.C.A., London; Hon. D.Litt. (Univ. of Glasgow) 1980, (Heriot-Watt Univ., Edin.) 1987, (London) 1987, (St. Andrews) 1994, (Birmingham) 1996; British Critics' Prize 1953, Copley Foundation Award 1956, Bright Foundation Award 1960, Blair Prize, 64th Annual American Exhbn., Chicago 1961, 1st Prize for Sculpture, Carnegie Int. Exhbn., Pittsburgh 1967, Saltire Soc. Award 1981, Grand Prix d'honneur, 15th Int. Print Biennale, Ljubljana 1983; Invited Artist, Cleveland Sixth Int. Drawing Biennale 1983, Goethe Medal 1991; Cavaliere Ufficiale, Ordine al Merito (Italy) 1991; Hon. Fellow Royal Glasgow Inst. of Fine Arts 1993. *Address:* 107 Dovehouse Street, London, SW3 6JZ, England.

PAPACOSTEA, Serban, D.HIST.; Romanian historian; b. 25 June 1928, Bucharest; s. of Petre G. Papacostea and Josefina Papacostea; ed. Univ. of Bucharest; scientific researcher and Dir., "Nicolae Iorga" Inst. of History, Bucharest; mem. editorial bd. Revue Roumaine d'Histoire, Studii si materiale de istorie medie (Studies and Materials of Medieval History), Il Mar Nero (Rome); Corresp. mem. Romanian Acad., Accademia Ligure di Scienze e Lettere; Prize of the Roman Acad. 1971. *Publications:* Istoria României (The History of Romania) (in collaboration) 1964, 1998, Istoria poporului român (History of the Romanian People) 1970 (in collaboration), Nochmals Wittenberg und Byzanz: die Moldau im Zeitalter der Reformation 1970, Oltenia sub stăpînirea austriacă, 1718–1739 (Oltenia under Austrian Rule, 1718–1739) 1971, Venise et les Pays Roumains au Moyen Age, in Venezia e il Levante fino al secolo XV, 1973; Stephan der Grosse, Fürst der Moldau 1975; Kilia et la politique orientale de Sigismond de Luxembourg 1976, Die politischen Voraussetzungen für die wirtschaftliche Vorherrschaft des Osmanischen Reiches im Schwarzmeergebiet 1453–1484 1978; La fondation de la Valachie et de la Moldavie et les Roumains de Transylvanie 1978, "Quod non iretur ad Tanam": Un aspect fondamental de la politique génoise dans la Mer Noire au XIVe siècle 1979, Inceputurile politicii comerciale a Tării Româneşti şi Moldovei (The Beginnings of Trade Policy in Wallachia and Moldavia) 1983, La fin de la domination génoise à Licostomo 1985, La Valachie et la crise de structure de l'Empire Ottoman (1402–1413) 1986, La Mer Noire: du monopole byzantin à la domination des Latins aux Détroits 1988, La première crise des rapports byzantino-génois après Nymphaion: le complot de Guglielmo Guercio (1264) 1988, Geneza statului in Evul mediu Românesc (The Formation of the Medieval Romanian State) 1988, Gênes, Venise et la Mer noire à la fin du XIIIe siècle 1990, Byzance et la Croisade au Bas-Danube à la fin du XIVe siècle 1991, Jews in the Romanian Principalities during the Middle Ages 1993, Romanii in Secolul XIII intre Cruciata şi Imperial Mongol 1993, Une révolte antigénoise en mer Noire et la riposte de Gênes (1432–1434) 1994, Captive Clio: Romanian Historiography under Communist Rule 1996, Un tournant de la politique génoise en mer Noire au XIVe siècle 1997, Gênes, Venise et la Croisade de Varna 1997. *Address:* Institutul de Istorie "Nicolae Iorga", Bd. Aviatorilor 1, Bucharest (Office); Caragea Vodă 19, 71149 Bucharest, Romania (Home). *Telephone:* 6509045 (Office); 2114455 (Home).

PAPADIMITRIOU, George, D.JUR.; Greek professor of law; b. 1944, Thessaloniki; s. of Alexandros Papadimitriou and Argiri Papadimitriou; m. Anna Papadimitriou Tsatsou 1976; one s.; ed. Univs. of Thessaloniki, Heidelberg and Paris I; Research Fellow, Inst. für Int. Recht, Kiel 1971–72, Max Planck Inst. of Foreign, Public and Int. Law, Heidelberg 1972–74; lecturer,

Thessaloniki Univ. Law School 1975–79; Prof. of Constitutional Law, Thrace Univ. 1979–84, Univ. of Athens 1984–; Dean, Dept. of Political Science and Public Admin. Univ. of Athens 1993; Legal Advisor to Prime Minister 1996–; mem. several nat. and foreign learned socs. *Publications include:* Die Stellung der allgemeinen Regeln des Voelkerrechts im innerstaatlichen Recht 1972, The Dispute of the Aegean Shelf and the Cyprus Problem 1975, Constitutional Law. The Electorate 1981, The European Parliament: Problems, Realities and Perspectives 1984, Constitutional Problems 1989–91, Democracy and European Integration 1993, Constitutional Problems 1992–93 1995. *Address:* 30 Sina Street, Athens 10672 (Office); 15 Lombardou Street, Athens 11473, Greece (Home). *Telephone:* 3635137, 3617443 (Office); 6437414 (Home). *Fax:* 3629353.

PAPADONGONAS, Alexandros; Greek politician and naval officer; b. 11 July 1931, Tripolis; s. of Dionisios and Vasiliki Papadongonas; m. Niki Maidonis 1976; one s. one d.; ed. Greek Naval Acad., Naval War Coll., U.S. Naval Schools, NATO Defence Coll.; has served on Greek fleet vessels and submarines and has held staff positions; organized with other Navy officers movt. of Navy against the dictatorship; arrested May 1973 and removed from service; returned to Navy July-Nov. 1974; M.P. 1974–93; Minister of Merchant Shipping 1974–77, of Communications 1977–80; Deputy Minister of Defence 1990–91, Minister of Merchant Shipping 1992–93; mem. Council of Europe 1982–89, 1991; Pres. Greek Del. to Parl. Ass. of OSCE 1993–; mem. North Atlantic Ass.; Medal of Mil. Valour, Commdr. Order of the Phoenix, Officer Order of George I; New Democracy Party. *Leisure interests:* sailing, scuba diving, underwater archaeology. *Address:* 11 Nikis Street, Athens 105 57, Greece. *Telephone:* 3255150.

PAPADOPOULOS, Georgios; Greek politician and army officer (retd.); b. 5 May 1919, Eleochorion, Achaia; m. 1st Nekee Vassiliadis 1941 (divorced), two c.; m. 2nd Despina Gaspari 1970, one d.; ed. War Acad., Artillery School, and Officers' Training School in Middle East; Second Lieut. 1940, Lieut. 1943, Capt. 1946, Maj. 1949, Lieut.-Col. 1956, Col. 1960, Brig. and retd. Dec. 1967; served on Albanian front in Greek-Italian war 1940; joined nat. resistance units during German occupation; Staff Officer 1944–45, Intelligence Officer 1945–46; Commdr. Artillery Battery 1946; Training Officer, Artillery School 1946–48; Commdr. 131st Mountain Artillery Unit 1948, 144th Mountain Artillery Unit 1948–49; then Artillery Instructor and Unit Commdr. 1949–54; Intelligence Bureau, Army Gen. Staff 1954; Chief of Staff, Artillery Div. 1955–57; Cen. Intelligence Service 1959–64; Commdr. 117th Field Artillery Unit 1964–65, First Army Force 1965–66; at Third Staff Bureau, Army Gen. Staff 1966–67; led mil. coup to overthrow govt. April 1967, Minister to Prime Minister's Office April-Dec. 1967; Prime Minister, Minister of Defence and Minister to Prime Minister's Office 1967–73, also Minister of Educ. 1969–70, of Foreign Affairs 1970–73, Regent 1972–73; Pres. of Repub. of Greece June-Nov. 1973, arrested Oct. 1974, sentenced to death for high treason and insurrection Aug. 1975 (sentence commuted to life imprisonment); Leader Nat. Political Society (EPEN) 1984–88; Commdr. Royal Order of Phoenix; Medal of Mil. Merit, and numerous other medals. *Publication:* To Pistero Mas (Credo) 1968. *Leisure interests:* ancient Greek authors, book collecting, hunting, the countryside. *Address:* Korydallos Prison, 181 00 Korydallos, Greece.

PAPAIOANNOU, Miltiades; Greek politician and lawyer; b. 1946, Kalavryta, Achaia; ed. Panteio Univ., Law Faculty of Athens; Panhellenic Socialist Movt. (PASOK) M.P.; Deputy Minister, Ministry of Internal Affairs 1982–85, Minister of Justice 1985, Deputy Minister, Prime Minister's Dept. and Govt. Spokesman 1985–86, Gen. Sec. Ministry of Nat. Economy 1993–96; Minister of Labour and Social Security 1998–; mem. Exec. Bureau and Cen. Cttee. PASOK. *Publications:* numerous articles on politics, econs., public admin., local govt. and regional devt. *Address:* Ministry of Labour and Social Security, Odos Pireos 40, 104 37 Athens, Greece. *Telephone:* (01) 5291111. *Fax:* (01) 5249805.

PAPANDREOU, George A., M.SC.; Greek politician; b. 16 June 1952, St. Paul, Minn., U.S.A.; ed. Amherst Coll., Md., U.S.A., Stockholm Univ., Sweden, London School of Econs.; Panhellenic Socialist Movt. (PASOK) M.P. for Achaia (Patras) 1981–93; Under-Sec. for Cultural Affairs 1985–87, Minister of Educ. and Religious Affairs 1988–89, Deputy Minister of Foreign Affairs 1993–98, Alt. Foreign Minister 1998–; mem. Cen. Cttee. PASOK 1984–, Exec. Cttee. 1987–88, Sec. for Greek Diaspora 1990–; mem. Bd. Foundation of Mediterranean Studies, for Research and Self-Educ.; Fellow Center for Int. Affairs, Harvard Univ. 1992–93, Botsis Foundation for Promotion of Journalism 1988. *Address:* Ministry of Foreign Affairs, Odos Zalokosta 2, 106 71 Athens, Greece. *Telephone:* (01) 3610581. *Fax:* (01) 3624195.

PAPANDREOU, Vasso, PH.D.; Greek politician; b. 1953, Valimitika Aeghiou; ed. Athens, London and Reading Univs.; lecturer, Athens Univ.; Research Asst. Exeter and Oxford Univs.; Dir. Hellenic Org. of Small and Medium-sized Businesses, Athens 1981–85; mem. Admin. Council, Greek Commercial Bank; fmr. Minister for Industry, Energy and Tech., fmr. Minister for Commerce; founder mem. Greek Socialist Party 1974, mem. Cen. Cttee. Exec. Bureau 1984–88; Commr. for Social Affairs, Employment, Educ., Comm. of European Communities 1989–92; Vice-Pres. Council of Europe Parl. Ass. 1995–96; Minister for Devt. 1996–; Minister of the Interior Feb. 1999–; Hon. Litt.D. (Sheffield) 1992; Dr. h.c. (C.N.A.A., London) 1992, (P. Sabatier, Toulouse) 1993; Chevalier Légion d'honneur, Grand-Croix, Belgium. *Publications:* Multinational Companies and Less Developed Countries: The Case of Greece 1981, numerous papers on politics and econs. *Address:* Ministry of the Interior, Odos Stadiou 27, 101 83 Athens; 15 Omirou Street, 10672 Athens, Greece. *Telephone:* 3223521 (Office); 3646480. *Fax:* 3240631 (Office); 3634995.

PAPANTONIOU, Yiannos, PH.D.; Greek politician; b. 1949; ed. Univs. of Athens, Wisconsin, U.S.A., Paris, Cambridge; lecturer Dept. of Econs., Univ. of Athens, Researcher Centre of Planning and Econ. Research 1977–78; staff mem. Econs. Dept. OECD, Paris 1978–81; Panhellenic Socialist Movt. (PASOK) M.E.P. 1981–84; Special Adviser to Prime Minister on EC Affairs; Deputy Minister for Nat. Economy 1985–89, Minister of Trade 1989; M.P. for first dist. of Athens 1989–; Alt. Minister for Nat. Economy 1993–94, Minister of Nat. Economy 1994–. *Address:* Ministry of National Economy, Plateia Syntagmatos, 105 63 Athens, Greece. *Telephone:* (01) 3230931. *Fax:* (01) 3232218.

PAPATHANASSIOU, Aspassia; Greek actress; b. 1918, Amphissa; m. Costas Mavromatis 1944; ed. Dramatic Art School of National Theatre of Greece; played a variety of leading roles with various Greek theatrical groups; founder-mem. Piraikon Theatre; has toured extensively in Europe and N. and S. America; appeared at Int. Festivals in Berlin, Paris, Florence and Vienna; has given over 450 performances of ancient tragedy; appeared on T.V. in England, U.S.S.R., U.S.A. and several other countries; Paris Théâtre des Nations 1st Prize; Gold Medal of City of Athens 1962; Silver Palladium Medal for best European actress 1963. *Address:* 38 Xenokratous Street, 106 76 Athens, Greece.

PAPAZYAN, Vahan, C.HIS.SC.; Armenian politician, diplomatist and historian; b. 26 Jan. 1957, Yerevan; m.; one s.; ed. Yerevan Univ.; researcher Inst. of History, Armenian Acad. of Sciences 1980–91; Counsellor to Pres. of Armenia 1991–92; Chargé d'Affaires of Armenia to France 1992–93; Minister of Foreign Affairs 1993–96; staff Acad. of Sciences 1996–. *Publications:* works on history of Armenian-Iranian relations and trade routes in Middle Ages. *Address:* c/o Ministry of Foreign Affairs, 10 Bagramian Avenue, 375019 Yerevan, Armenia. *Telephone:* (3742) 523531. *Fax:* 527022.

PAPIERNIK-BERKHAUER, Emile, D. EN MED., F.R.C.O.G.; French obstetrician and gynaecologist; b. 14 Feb. 1936, Paris; m. Martine Czermichow 1961; two s. one d.; ed. Univ. of Paris; Asst. Prof. Faculté de Médecine René Descartes, Paris and Maternité de Port-Royal, Paris 1966–72; Prof. of Obstetrics and Gynaecology, Univ. of Paris-Orsay and Chair. Dept. of Obstetrics and Gynaecology, Hôpital Béclère, Clamart 1972–90; Dir. Research Unit 187, Inst. de la santé et de la recherche médicale (INSERM) (Physiology and Psychology of Human Reproduction) 1979–; Bd. Dirs. Collège nat. des gynécologues-accoucheurs; Fellow, American Acad. of Pediatrics, Royal Coll. of Obstetricians and Gynaecologists; Chevalier, Légion d'honneur. *Publication:* Le prix de la vie 1988, Le Guide Papiernik de la Grossesse (jtly.) 1991. *Leisure interest:* collector of contemporary painting. *Address:* Hôpital Antoine Béclère, 157 rue de la Porte de Trivaux, 92140 Clamart (Office); 35 rue Imbergeres, 92330 Sceaux, France (Home).

PAPON, Maurice Arthur Jean, L. EN D.; French politician; b. 3 Sept. 1910, Gretz-Armainvilliers (Seine-et-Marne); s. of Arthur Papon and Marie Dussiau; m. Paulette Asso 1932; one s. two d.; ed. Lycée Louis-le-Grand, and Facultés de Droit et de Lettres, Paris; Ed., Ministry of Interior 1935–36; Attachée, Cabinet of the Under-Sec. of State 1936, Foreign Affairs 1937–39; Sec.-Gen. Gironde 1942–44; Prefect and Dir. of Cabinet of the Comm. of the Repub. of France 1944–45; Deputy Dir. for Algeria at Ministry of Interior 1946–47; Prefect of Corsica 1947–49, Constantine, Algeria 1949–51; Sec.-Gen., Prefecture of Police 1951–54, Protectorate of Morocco 1954–55; Tech. Adviser, Cabinet of Sec. of State for Interior 1956; Insp.-Gen. for Admin., E. Algeria 1956–58; Prefect of Police, Paris 1958–66; Pres., Dir.-Gen. Sud-Aviation 1967–68; elected Deputy for Cher, Nat. Ass. 1968, 1973, 1978; Pres. Ass. Finance Comm. 1972–73, Rapporteur 1973–78; Minister of the Budget 1978–81; Mayor of Saint-Amand-Montrond 1971–82; Chair. and Man. Dir. Verreries champenoises, Rheims; Hon. Prefect of Police 1972; sentenced to ten years imprisonment for crimes against humanity April 1998; Commdr., Légion d'honneur, Commdr., Ordre du Mérite Civil and mil. awards. *Publications:* L'ère des responsables 1954, Vers un nouveau discours de la méthode 1965, Le Gaullisme ou la loi de l'effort 1973, Les Chevaux du Pouvoir 1988.

PAPOULIAS, George Dimitrios; Greek diplomatist; b. 19 May 1927; s. of Dimitrios G. Papoulias and Caterina Kontopoulou; m. Emily Pilavachi 1974; one d.; ed. Univ. of Athens; entered diplomatic service 1955; served Athens, New Delhi, Bonn; Deputy Perm. Del. to UN and int. orgs. Geneva 1964–69; Dir. Political Affairs, Ministry of Northern Greece 1969–70; Minister, Paris and Perm. Rep. to UNESCO 1971–74; mem. Bd. of Dirs. Resettlement Fund, Council of Europe 1971–74; Perm. Rep. to UN, New York 1975–79; Amb. to Turkey 1979–83, to U.S.A. 1983–89; Alt. Minister and Minister for Foreign Affairs 1989, 1990; Amb. to U.K. (also accred. to Iceland) 1990–93; Commdr. Order of the Phoenix, Order of George I; other foreign orders and decorations. *Leisure interests:* archaeology, history. *Address:* Rigillis 16, Athens 10674, Greece.

PAPOULIAS, Karolos, PH.D.; Greek politician and lawyer; b. 1929; s. of late Maj.-Gen. Gregorios Papoulias; ed. Univs. of Athens, Madrid, Bonn and Cologne; fmr. practising lawyer in Athens; lived in Germany 1962–74; worked for Greek radio programme of Deutsche Welle; mem. Greek democratic del. at Gen. Ass. of Council of Europe during period of mil. dictatorship in Greece; mem. Parl. 1977–; mem. Cen. Cttee. Panhellenic Socialist Movt. (PASOK); Sec.-Gen. Centre for Mediterranean Studies, Athens; Deputy Minister for Foreign Affairs 1981–84, Alt. Minister 1984–85, Minister of Foreign Affairs 1985, 1993–96; Alt. Minister for Defence 1989–90. *Address:* c/o Parliament Buildings, Syntagma Square, Athens, Greece.

PAPOUTSIS, Christos; Greek politician and economist; b. 11 April 1953, Larissa; Pres. Greek Nat. Union of Students 1978–80; Special Adviser on Public Admin. Ministry of Presidency of Govt. 1981–84; mem. Exec. Bureau Pan-Hellenic Socialist Movt. (PASOK); mem. European Parl. 1984–, Vice-Pres. Socialist Group 1987–; leader, PASOK del. to European Parl.; mem. Presidium, Party of European Socialists 1988–; Commr. for Energy and Euratom Supply Agency, Small and Medium Enterprises (SME) and Tourism, European Comm. 1995–. *Address:* Commission of the European Communities, 200 rue de la Loi, 1049 Brussels, Belgium.

PAPP, László; Hungarian boxer (retd.); b. 25 March 1926; s. of Imre Papp and Erzsébet Burgus; m. Erzsébet Kovács 1950; one s.; original profession mechanic; three times Olympic Champion and twice European champion; professional boxer 1956–64 and professional European Champion 1962–64; official coach with the Hungarian amateur boxing fed. 1968–93; Labour Order of Merit, Sport Order of Merit, Olympic Silver Order of Merit, World Boxing Council Order 1989, Int. Fair Play Prize 1993. *Leisure interest:* angling. *Address:* Ora-utca 6, 1125 Budapest, Hungary.

PAPPALARDO, H.E. Cardinal Salvatore, D.S.T.; Italian ecclesiastic; b. 23 Sept. 1918, Villafranca; s. of the late Alfio Pappalardo and Gaetana Coco; ed. Pontifical Univ. Lateranensis; ordained Priest 1941; Counsellor, Vatican Secr. of State 1947–65; Apostolic Pronuncio, Indonesia 1965–69; Pres. Pontifical Ecclesiastical Acad., Rome 1969–70; Archbishop of Palermo 1970; Vicar-Gen. of Catania; cr. Cardinal by Pope Paul VI 1973; mem. Congregations for the Clergy, for the Eastern Churches. *Address:* Arcivescovado, Via Matteo Bonello 2, 90134 Palermo, Italy.

PAPPANO, Antonio; conductor; b. London; studied piano, composition and conducting in U.S.A. with Norma Verrilli, Arnold Franchetti and Gustav Meier; worked as pianist and asst. conductor with New York City Opera, Gran Teatro del Liceo, Barcelona, Frankfurt Opera, Lyric Opera of Chicago and the Bayreuth Festival (asst. to Daniel Barenboim for Tristan und Isolde, Parsifal and the Ring cycle); opera conducting debut with Norwegian opera, later Music Dir.; has also conducted opera at Vienna Staatsoper (debut conducting new production of Wagner's Siegfried 1993), San Francisco Opera, Théâtre du Châtelet, Berlin Staatsoper, E.N.O., Covent Garden (debut conducting La Bohème 1990) and the Teatro Comunale, Florence; has conducted many world-class orchestras including Chicago Symphony Orchestra, Cleveland Orchestra, Los Angeles Philharmonic, L.S.O., Berlin Philharmonic, Orchestre de Paris, Oslo Philharmonic, Berlin Radio Symphony Orchestra; Prin. Guest Conductor Israel Philharmonic Orchestra 1997–; Music Dir. Théâtre Royal de la Monnaie, Brussels 1992–99; opera repertory includes Britten, Wagner, Strauss, Verdi and Shostakovich (Lady Macbeth of Mtsensk); concert repertoire includes Shostakovich, Berlioz, Berg, Beethoven, Mozart, Bartok, Messiaen and Debussy; piano accompanist for La Monnaie int. recital series; Music Dir. Royal Opera House, Covent Garden March 1999–. *Recordings include:* Puccini's La Rondine (Gramophone Award for Best Opera Recording and Record of the Year 1997), Il Trittico 1999, Britten's The Turn of the Screw (Théâtre Royal de la Monnaie production) (Choc du Monde de la Musique, Prix de l'Acad. du Disque Lyrique Grand Prix Int., Orphée d'Or) 1999, Werther 1999. *Address:* Royal Opera House, Covent Garden, Floral Street, London, England.

PAPPAS, Spyros; Greek civil servant and European Union official; b. 1 Jan. 1953, Athens; m. Frady Karkanis; one s. one d.; ed. Univ. of Athens, Panteios School of Econ. and Political Studies, Univ. of Paris, Directorate for European Affairs, INSEAD; fmr. naval Petty Officer; barrister, Athens 1976; Auditor Council of State 1978, Counsel 1983; Special Adviser in Prime Minister's Legal Office 1981; mem. Cen. Comm. for Drafting of Laws 1982; est. Nat. Centre of Public Admin., Sec.-Gen. 1985; est. Inst. of Permanent Training 1985; Assoc. Prof. European Inst. of Public Admin., Maastricht 1988, Dir. of Faculty 1989, Dir.-Gen. 1990, Prof. of European Law 1992; Dir.-Gen. for Consumer Policy EC 1995, for Information, Communication, Culture and Audiovisual Media 1997–; Chair. Bd. of Govs. Int. East-West Acad. (IOWA); mem. Supreme Council Church of Greece 1984, Comm. of Information on National Affairs, Inst. for Admin. Studies, Asscn. of the Judges of the Council of State, Inst. of Public Admin.; Cttee. for Drafting of the Encyclopedia of Admin., Centre for European Policy Studies Int. Advisory Council, Scientific Council of Academia Istropolitana Bratislava Inst. of Advanced Studies, Foundation for Hellenic Culture; assoc. mem. Asscn. of European Magistrates for Democracy and Liberty (MEDEL); substitute bd. mem. Open Univ., Athens; cr. European Centre of Judges and Lawyers 1992; hon. State Scholar 1970–73; First Prize Michel Stassinopoulos Foundation for Admin. Law 1976; Scholar of Council of Europe 1977; Officer Order of Merit, Luxembourg 1994. *Publications:* La Constitution de la Grèce de 1975 1976, Le régime de Planification en Grèce 1977, Le Tribunal de Première Instance 1990, Tendances actuelles et évolution de la jurisprudence de la cour de justice des Communautés européennes: suivi annuel Vol. I 1993, Vol. II 1995 (Ed.), Procédures Administratives Nationales: Préparation et mise en oeuvre des décisions communautaires: Etudes comparatives (Ed.) 1994, EC Competition Law: Financial Aspects (Co-Ed.) 1994, The Changing Role of Parliaments in the European Union (Co-Ed.) 1995, The European Union's Common Foreign and Security Policy: The Challenges of the Future 1996, Politiques publiques dans l'Union européenne 1996. *Address:* Directorate-General X, European Commission, 200 rue de la Loi, 1049 Brussels, Belgium.

PAQUET-SEVIGNY, Thérèse, PH.D.; Canadian United Nations official; b. 3 Feb. 1934, Sherbrooke, Quebec; d. of René Paquet and Marie-Reine Cloutier; m. Robert Sévigny 1956; one s. one d.; ed. Sorbonne-Paris Univ. and Univ. of Montreal; journalism and communications research for La Tribune and L'Actualité, Montreal and for Montreal and Laval Univs. 1952–61; Man. Dir. for Consumer Research, Steinberg Limitée 1961–66; various appts. at Communications Depts. Montreal Univ., McGill Univ. and Ecole des Hautes Etudes Commerciales, Montreal 1969–76; Vice-Pres. for Research and Planning, BCP Publicité Limitée 1969–71, Vice-Pres. and Man. Dir. 1974–81, Pres. and Chief of Operations 1981–83; Vice-Pres. RSGL Publicité Limitée 1971–74; Vice-Pres. for Communications, Canadian Broadcasting Corpn. (CBC) 1983–87; Under-Sec.-Gen. for Public Information, United Nations 1987; Prof. of Communications Quebec Univ., Montreal (UQAM) 1993–; Dir., UNESCO Chair. in Communication and Int. Devt. 1993–; Int. Consultant 1993–; Sec.-Gen. Orbicom (Int. Network of UNESCO Chairs in Communications); Dr. h.c. (Sherbrooke) 1991, (Bishop's Univ.) 1991. *Publications:* articles in books and journals. *Leisure interests:* reading, films, walking, friends. *Address:* 1509 Sherbrooke Street, West, Apartment 29, Montreal, Que. H3G 1M1, Canada.

PARAYRE, Jean-Paul-Christophe; French building and civil engineering executive; b. 5 July 1937, Lorient; s. of Louis and Jeanne (Malarde) Parayre; m. Marie-Françoise Chaufour 1962; two s. two d.; ed. Lycées in Casablanca (Morocco) and Versailles, Ecole Polytechnique, Paris, Ecole Nat. des Ponts et Chaussées; Engineer, Dept. of Highways 1963–67; Tech. Adviser, Ministry of Social Affairs 1967, Ministry of Econ. and Finance 1968; Dir. of Mech. Industries at Ministry of Industry and Research 1970–74; Chief Adviser to Pres. and Gen. Man. Banque Vernes et Commerciale 1974; Man. of Planning, Automobile Div. of Peugeot 1975; Man. Automobile Div. of Peugeot-Citroën 1976, Chair. Bd. of Dirs. Peugeot S.A. 1977–84, mem. Supervisory Bd. 1984; mem. Supervisory Bd. Soc. Dumez 1977–84 (Dir.-Gen. 1984, Chair. 1988–90, Pres. 1991–92); Pres., Dir.-Gen. Fided Financière (affil. to Dumez) 1985; Vice-Pres., Dir.-Gen. Lyonnaise des Eaux-Dumez 1990–92, Vice-Pres. 1990–93; Pres. Supervisory Bd. Razel 1991; Pres. Bolloré Technologies Jan–Sept. 1994, Scac-Delmas-Vieljeux 1994, Pres. Saga 1996–; Vice-Pres., Dir.-Gen. Bolloré Group 1994–; Dir. Crédit National 1978–, Albatros investissement 1994, Bolloré 1994, Coflexip 1995, Stena Int. B.V. 1995, Tarmac PLC 1995, Delmas 1996, Financière de l'Odet; Dir. (non-exec.) Tarmac 1994–; Chevalier, Légion d'honneur, Officier Ordre nat. du Mérite. *Leisure interests:* golf, tennis. *Address:* Groupe Bolloré, 31–32 quai de Dion Bouton, 92811 Puteaux cedex; 38 quai du Point du jour, 92100 Boulogne-Billancourt, France.

PARBO, Sir Arvi Hillar, Kt., A.C., B.ENG.; Australian mining engineer; b. 10 Feb. 1926, Tallinn, Estonia; s. of Aado Parbo and Hilda Rass; m. Saima Soots 1953; two s. one d., ed. Estonia, Germany and Univ. of Adelaide; joined Western Mining Corpn. Ltd. 1956, Mining Eng. 1956, Underground Man. Nevoria Mine 1958, Tech. Asst. to Man. Dir. Western Mining Corpn. 1960, Deputy Gen. Supt. W. Australia 1964, Gen. Man. Western Mining Corpn. Ltd. 1968, Deputy Man. Dir. 1970, Man. Dir. 1971–86, Vice-Chair. 1973, Chair. 1974–86, Exec. Chair. 1986–90, Chair. (non-exec.) 1990–; Chair. Alcoa of Australia Ltd. 1978–96, Broken Hill Pty. Co. Ltd. 1989–92, Munich Reinsurance Co. of Australia Ltd. 1984–98, Zurich Australian Insurance Group 1985–98; Dir. Aluminium Co. of America 1980–98, Hoechst Australian Investments Pty. Ltd. 1981–97, Sara Lee Corpn. 1991–98; Pres. Australia-Japan Business Co-operation Cttee. 1985–91; mem. Chase Manhattan Int. Advisory Cttee. 1983–, Degussa AG Supervisory Bd. 1988–93; Pres. Australian Inst. Mining and Metallurgy 1990; Chair. of the Year Australian Inst. of Co. Dirs. 1995. *Publication:* Down Under: Mineral Heritage in Australia 1992. Leisure interests: reading, carpentry. *Address:* Longwood, Highbury Road, Vermont South, Vic. 3133, Australia (Home).

PARDEE, Arthur Beck, PH.D.; American biochemist; b. 13 July 1921, Chicago, Ill.; s. of Charles A. Beck and Elizabeth Beck; m. Ruth Sager; three s. from previous m.; ed. Univ. of California (Berkeley), California Inst. of Tech.; Postdoctoral Fellow, Univ. of Wisconsin 1947–49; Instructor, Asst. and Assoc. Prof. Univ. of Calif. (Berkeley) 1949–61; Sr. Postdoctoral Fellow, Pasteur Inst. 1957–58; Prof. and Chair. Biochemical Sciences, Princeton Univ. 1961–67, Prof. of Biochemistry 1967–75; Donner Prof. of Science, Princeton 1966; Prof. Dana Farber Cancer Inst. and Biochemical Pharmacology Dept., Harvard Medical School 1975–; mem. N.A.S., American Chemical Soc., American Soc. of Biological Chemists (Treasurer 1964–70, Pres. 1980–81); American Asscn. for Cancer Research (Pres. 1985–86), American Acad. of Arts and Sciences, American Soc. of Microbiologists, Japanese Biochemical Soc.; mem. Council American Cancer Soc. 1967–71; Paul Lewis Award (American Chemical Soc.) 1960, Krebs Medal (Fed. of European Biochemical Socs.) 1973, Rosensteil Award (Brandeis Univ.) 1975. *Publications:* articles on bacterial physiology and enzymology in synchronous cultures, cell division cycle events, growth regulation in cancer and normal cells, enzymology of DNA synthesis, repair of damaged DNA; Experiments in Biochemical Research Techniques (co-author) 1957. *Leisure interests:*

music, tennis, travel, art. *Address:* Dana Farber Cancer Institute, 44 Binney Street, Boston, MA 02115 (Office); 30 Codman Road, Brookline MA 02445, U.S.A. (Home). *Telephone:* (617) 732-3372 (Office). *Fax:* (617) 632-3372.

PARDO, Luis María de Pablo; Argentinian professor of law and politician; b. 15 Aug. 1914, Buenos Aires; s. of Augusto de Pablo Pardo and Luisa Gosset; m. Aida Quinteros Sánchez de Bustamente; one s. two d.; ed. Law Faculty, Univ. de Buenos Aires, postgraduate Univ. of Georgetown (Washington, D.C.); Dir. of Courses, Law and Social Sciences Faculty, Univ. de Buenos Aires, Prof. adjunct of Int. Public Law, Faculty of Econ. Sciences 1947–51; Prof. titular of Int. Public Law, Univ. Católica, Argentina, then Prof. titular of Int. Relations 1961–; also Prof. of Int. Public Law and Int. Policy, Naval War School, and lecturer at Aeronautical Staff's Officers School 1966–; imprisoned 1951, 1952, and 1953 for anti-Peronist activities, exiled to Brazil until 1955; Minister of the Interior designate 1955; Legal Adviser to Ministry for Foreign Relations and Worship 1958–61; Rep. UN 2nd Sea Law Conf. 1960; Tech. Adviser at 5th, 6th and 7th "Reunión de Consulta" of American Foreign Ministers; Amb. to Chile 1961; Legal Adviser of Chancellery at the "Rio Encuentro" Affair; Legal Adviser of the "Tech. Argentine-Uruguayan Mixed Comm. for the Salto Grande"; Minister for Foreign Relations and Worship 1970–72; Judge adjunct of Supreme Court; Grand Cross of Orders Cruzeiro del Sur, Rio Branco (Brazil), Bernardo O'Higgins (Chile), Del Sol (Peru), Al Mérito (Ecuador), and many other decorations, incl. from German and Japanese Govts. *Publications:* manual of International Public Law for use of Navy Officers, The Geographic Position of Argentina as a Factor of its Foreign Policy 1947, The Tendency towards Federation within Interamerican Relations 1947, Dominant Economics within the International Order, Foreign Policy 1952, The Contemporary International System and Argentine International Policy 1973. *Address:* Paraná 976, Buenos Aires (Office); Avenida Quintane 325, 1014 Buenos Aires, Argentina (Home). *Telephone:* 44-43-50/42-29-80 (Office); 44-27-34 (Home).

PARET, Peter, PH.D., D.LIT., LITT.D.; American historian; b. 13 April 1924, Berlin, Germany; s. of Dr. Hans Paret and Suzanne Aimée Cassirer; m. Isabel Harris 1961; one s. one d.; ed. Univ. of Calif. and Univ. of London; Research Assoc. Center of Int. Studies, Princeton Univ. 1960–62; Visiting Asst. Prof. Univ. of California, Davis 1962–63, Assoc. Prof. 1963–66, Prof. of History 1966–69; Prof. of History, Stanford Univ. 1969–77, Raymond A. Spruance Prof. in Int. History 1977–86; Andrew W. Mellon Prof. in the Humanities, Inst. for Advanced Study, Princeton 1986–97, Andrew W. Mellon Prof. Emer. 1997–; mem. American Philosophical Soc., Historische Kommission zu Berlin; Fellow, American Acad. of Arts and Sciences, Royal Historical Soc., Leo Baeck Inst.; Hon. Fellow L.S.E., Thomas Jefferson Medal, Samuel Eliot Morison Medal; several hon. degrees. *Publications:* Guerrillas in the 1960s (with John Shy) 1961, French Revolutionary Warfare 1964, Yorck and the Era of Prussian Reform 1966, The Berlin Secession 1980, Makers of Modern Strategy (ed.) 1986, Art as History 1988, Carl von Clausewitz: On War (ed. and trans. with Michael Howard) 1976, 1984, Clausewitz and the State 1985, Carl von Clausewitz, Historical and Political Writings (ed. and trans.) 1991, Understanding War 1992, Persuasive Images (with Beth Lewis and Paul Paret) 1992, Sammler, Stifter und Museen (ed. with Ekkehard Mai) 1993, Imagined Battles 1997. *Address:* School of Historical Studies, Institute for Advanced Study, Princeton, NJ 08540, U.S.A. *Telephone:* (609) 734 8344. *Fax:* (609) 924 8399.

PARFIT, Derek, M.A., F.B.A.; British academic; b. 11 Dec. 1942, Chengtu, China; s. of Norman Parfit and Jessie Browne; ed. Oxford Univ.; Fellow All Souls Coll., Oxford 1967–, Sr. Research Fellow 1984–; Visiting Prof. Dept. of Philosophy, Harvard, Princeton and New York Univs.; Fellow American Acad. of Arts and Sciences. *Publication:* Reasons and Persons 1984. *Leisure interest:* architectural photography. *Address:* All Souls College, Oxford, OX1 4AL, England. *Telephone:* (01865) 279379. *Fax:* (01865) 279299.

PARIZEAU, Jacques, PH.D.; Canadian politician; b. 9 Aug. 1930, Montreal; s. of Gérard Parizeau and Germaine (Biron) Parizeau; m. 1st Alicja Poznanska 1956, one s. one d.; m. 2nd Lisette Lapointe 1992; ed. Ecole des Hautes Etudes Commerciales, Montreal, Institut d'Etudes Politiques, Paris, London School of Econs.; Adviser to Govt. of Quebec 1961–65; elected Deputy for Assomption, Montreal 1976–84, 1989–; fmr. Minister of Finance, Prov. of Quebec (resgnd. 1985); mem. Exec. Cttee. Parti Québecois 1969, Pres. 1988; Premier of Quebec 1994–95 (resgnd.) *Publications:* The Terms of Trade of Canada 1966, numerous articles. *Leisure interests:* reading, music. *Address:* 88 S. Grand Alle est, Québec, P.Q. G1A 1A2, Canada.

PARK, Charles Rawlinson, A.B., M.D.; American professor of physiology; b. 2 March 1916, Baltimore, Md.; s. of Edwards A. Park and Agnes Bevan Park; m. Jane Harting 1953; one s.; ed. Harvard Coll. and Johns Hopkins School of Medicine; Intern in Medicine, Johns Hopkins 1942; Asst. Resident then Chief Resident, Harvard 1943–44; U.S. army 1944–47; Welch Fellow in Biochemistry, Wash. Univ. 1947–52; Prof. of Physiology and Chair. of Dept., Vanderbilt School of Medicine 1952–84, Prof. of Molecular Physiology and Biophysics, Emer. 1984–; Adjunct Prof. Biochemistry, Mehoorry Medical Coll. 1993–; mem. Bd., Life Insurance Fund, Howard Hughes Medical Inst. 1964–84, Juvenile Diabetes Foundation, Int. Inst of Cellular and Molecular Pathology, Nat. Inst. of Heart, Lung and Blood (Nat. Insts. of Health); mem. Editorial Bd., Journal of Biological Chem.; mem. American Physiological Soc., American Soc. of Biological Chemists, American Soc. of Clinical Investigation (Vice-Pres. 1961), Asscn. of American Physicians, N.A.S.; Banting Medal for Research, American Diabetes Asscn. *Publications:* approx. 120 scientific papers in journals of biochemistry and physiology 1942–; major topics concern action of hormones, diabetes, metabolic regulation, sugar and fat transport into mammalian cells. *Leisure interests:* music, reading, outdoor sports. *Address:* Department of Molecular Physiology and Biophysics, Vanderbilt School of Medicine, Nashville, TN 37232; 5325 Stanford Drive, Nashville, TN 37215, U.S.A. (Home). *Telephone:* (615) 936-0721 (Office); (615) 665-1228 (Home). *Fax:* (615) 322-7236.

PARK, Dame Merle Florence, D.B.E.; British ballerina; b. 8 Oct. 1937, Salisbury, Rhodesia (now Harare, Zimbabwe); m. 1st James Monahan, C.B.E. 1965 (divorced 1970; died 1985), one s.; m. 2nd Sidney Bloch 1971, one s.; ed. Elmhurst Ballet School and Royal Ballet School; joined Royal Ballet 1954; first solo role 1955; opened own ballet school 1977; Dir. Royal Ballet School 1983–98; Prin. Royal Ballet; repertoire includes Façade, Coppelia, Sleeping Beauty, La Fille Mal Gardée, Giselle, Les Sylphides, The Dream, Romeo and Juliet, Triad, The Nutcracker, La Bayadère, Cinderella, Shadow Play, Anastasia, Pineapple Poll, Swan Lake, The Firebird, Walk to the Paradise Garden, Dances at a Gathering, Shadow, Don Quixote, Deux Pigeons, Serenade, Scène de Ballet, Wedding Bouquet, Les Rendezvous, Mirror Walkers, Symphonic Variations, Daphnis and Chloë, Serenade, In the Night, Laurentia, Mamzelle Angot, Manon, Apollo, Flower Festival, Le Corsaire, The Moor's Pavane, Aureole, Elite Syncopations, Lulu, The Taming of the Shrew, Mayerling, Birthday Offering, La Fin du Jour, Adieu, Isadora, Raymonda, etc.; Adelaine Genée Medal, Queen Elizabeth Award, Royal Acad. of Dancing 1982 and many other certificates and medals. *Leisure interests:* travel, lying in the sun, listening to music. *Address:* c/o Royal Ballet School, 144 Talgarth Road, London, W14 9DE, England.

PARK, Nicholas W., C.B.E., B.A.; British film animator; b. 1958, Preston, Lancs.; ed. Sheffield Art School and Nat. Film and TV School, Beaconsfield; joined Aardman Animations 1985; BAFTA Award for Best Short Animated Film for A Grand Day Out 1990; Acad. Awards for Creature Comforts 1991, A Grand Day Out 1994, A Close Shave 1996. *Films include:* A Grand Day Out 1989, Creature Comforts 1990, The Wrong Trousers 1993, A Close Shave 1995. *Address:* Aardman Animations Ltd., Gas Ferry Road, Bristol, BS1 6UN, England. *Telephone:* 0117-984 8485. *Fax:* 0117-984 8486.

PARK, Robert, O.B.E., PH.D., F.R.S.N.Z., F.I.P.E.N.Z., F.I.C.E., F.ENG.; New Zealand professor of civil engineering; b. 13 Aug. 1933, Suva, Fiji; s. of James Park and Loloma Park; m. Kathleen Costello 1956; three s. two d.; ed. Grammar School, Suva, Canterbury Univ., N.Z. and Univ. of Bristol; Asst. Eng. Christchurch Drainage Bd. 1955–56; lecturer in Civil Eng. Canterbury Univ. 1956–59, Univ. of Bristol 1959–65; Sr. Lecturer and Reader, Canterbury Univ. 1965–68, Prof. of Civil Eng. 1968–, Head of Dept. 1978–92, Deputy Vice-Chancellor 1993–; Vice-Pres. Int. Asscn. for Earthquake Eng. 1996–; Pres. N.Z. Nat. Soc. for Earthquake Eng. 1983–85; Pres. N.Z. Prestressed Concrete Inst. 1975–77; mem. Council N.Z. Concrete Soc.; recipient of several professional awards in N.Z., U.S.A. and U.K. *Publications:* Reinforced Concrete Structures (with T. Paulay) 1975, Reinforced Concrete Slabs (with W. L. Gamble) 1980; book chapters and about 260 tech. papers. *Leisure interests:* gardening, reading, watching sport. *Address:* 27 Gothic Place, Ilam, Christchurch 4, New Zealand. *Telephone:* 03-358-5837.

PARK CHOONG-HOON, Maj.-Gen.; Korean politician and retd. air force officer; b. 19 Jan. 1919, Cheju-Do Prov.; s. of Park Chong-Sil; m. Chung Kyungsook 1943; two s. four d.; ed. Doshisha Commercial Coll., Japan; Trade Affairs Dir. of Minister of Commerce and Industry, Repub. of Korea 1948; retired as Air Force Maj. Gen. 1961; Vice-Minister of Commerce and Industry 1961, Minister of Commerce and Industry 1963; Deputy Premier and Minister of Econ. Planning 1967–69; Prime Minister May–Sept. 1980, Acting Pres. Aug.–Sept. 1980; Standing mem. Econ. and Scientific Council 1970–71; Chair. AIRC 1971–73, Korean Traders' Asscn., Naeoe Business Journal (daily), Korea Industrial Devt. Research Inst. 1980–; Pres. Trade Press 1973–; Chair. Korea-Saudi Arabia Econ. Co-operation Cttee. 1974–, Korea–U.S. Econ. Council 1974–80; mem. Advisory Council of State Affairs Jan. 1981–. *Leisure interest:* golf. *Address:* 1-36, Seongbuk-dong, Seongbuk-ku, Seoul, Republic of Korea. *Telephone:* 762-2750.

PARK SUNG SANG, PH.D.; Korean economist; b. 10 Dec. 1923, Kyungsang-bukdo; s. of late Soon Young Park and Nan Kyo Chung; m. Chang Sook Kim 1947; one s. two d.; ed. Kukmin Univ. and American Univ. Grad. School; Asst. Gov. Bank of Korea 1972–76; Deputy Pres. Small and Medium Industry Bank 1976–80, Pres. 1980–81; Pres. Korea Int. Econ. Inst. Oct.-Nov. 1981, Korea Scientific and Technological Information Center 1981–82, Korea Inst. for Industrial Econs. and Tech. 1982–83; Chair. and Pres. Export-Import Bank of Korea 1983–85; Gov. Bank of Korea 1986–88; Pres. Korea Inst. for Industrial Econs. and Tech. 1988. *Publication:* Growth and Development 1977. *Leisure interest:* golf. *Address:* c/o Korea Institute for Industrial Economics and Technology, 206-9, Cheonryangri-dong, Dongdaemun-ku, Seoul (Office); No. 1-303 Hanshinbang-bae Villa, 610-46 Banpodong, Socho-ku, Seoul, Republic of Korea (Home). *Telephone:* 966-6501 (Office); 533-1477 (Home).

PARK OF MONMOUTH, Baroness (Life Peer) cr. 1990, of Broadway in the County of Hereford and Worcester; **Daphne Margaret Sybil Désirée Park,** C.M.G., O.B.E.; British fmr. diplomatist and college principal; b. 1 Sept. 1921; ed. Rosa Bassett School and Somerville Coll. Oxford; W.T.S. (Field Aid Nursing Yeomanry) 1943–47; entered Foreign Office 1948; served UK

Del. to NATO 1952, Moscow 1954, Leopoldville 1959, Lusaka 1964, Consul-Gen. Hanoi 1969–70, Chargé d'Affaires a.i. Ulan Bator 1972, F.C.O. 1973–79, retd.; Hon. Research Fellow, Univ. of Kent 1971–72; Prin. Somerville Coll. Oxford 1980–89, Pro-Vice-Chancellor, Univ. of Oxford 1985–89; Chair. Royal Comm. on Historical Monuments of England 1989–94; mem. Thatcher Foundation 1992–; other public appts.; Hon. LL.D. (Bristol) 1988. *Leisure interests:* good talk, politics, difficult places. *Address:* House of Lords, London, SW1A 0PW, England.

PARKER, Alan William, C.B.E.; British film director and writer; b. 14 Feb. 1944, London; s. of William Parker and Elsie Parker; m. Annie Inglis 1966 (divorced 1992); three s. one d.; ed. Owen's School, Islington, London; Advertising Copywriter 1965–67; TV Commercials Dir. 1968–78; wrote screenplay Melody 1969; Chair. Dir's. Guild of G.B. 1982–, British Film Inst. 1998–; mem. British Screen Advisory Council 1985–; *wrote and directed:* No Hard Feelings 1972, Our Cissy 1973, Footsteps 1973, Bugsy Malone 1975, Angel Heart 1987, A Turnip Head's Guide to the British Cinema, Come See the Paradise 1989, The Road to Wellville 1994; *directed:* The Evacuees 1974, Midnight Express 1977, Fame 1979, Shoot the Moon 1981, The Wall 1982, Birdy 1984, Mississippi Burning 1988, The Commitments (BAFTA Award for Best Dir.) 1991, Evita 1996, Angela's Ashes 1998; Vice-Chair. Dirs.' Guild of G.B. 1982–; mem. British Screen Advisory Council 1985–; British Acad. of Film and TV Arts Michael Balcon Award for Outstanding Contrib. to British Film, Nat. Review Bd. Best Dir. Award for Mississippi Burning 1988. *Publications:* (novels) Bugsy Malone 1976, Puddles in the Lane 1977; (cartoon) Hares in the Gate 1983; Making Movies 1998; Lifetime Achievement Award Dirs. Guild of Great Britain. *Leisure interest:* cartooning. *Address:* c/o Creative Artists' Agency, 9830 Wilshire Boulevard, Beverly Hills, CA 90212, U.S.A.

PARKER, Sir Eric Wilson, Kt., F.C.A.; British business executive; b. 8 June 1933; s. of Wilson Parker and Gladys Edith Wellings; m. Marlene Teresa Neale 1955; two s. two d.; ed. The Priory Grammar School for Boys, Shrewsbury; articled clerk with Wheeler, Whittingham & Kent, Shrewsbury 1950–55; nat. service, Pay Corps 1956–58; Taylor Woodrow Group 1958–64; joined Trafalgar House Group 1965, Finance/Admin. Dir. 1969, Deputy Man. Dir. 1973, Group Man. Dir. 1977, Group Chief Exec. 1983–92, Deputy Chair. 1988–93; Chair. Caradon PLC 1998; Pres. Racehorse Owners Asscn. 1998; Dir. (non-exec.) Criterion Properties 1997–, Ministry of Defence Quartermaster Gen. Bd. 1997–, British Borneo PLC 1998–, European Real Estates, Sweden 1998–; Cttee. mem. Teenage Cancer Trust; owns Crimbourne Stud. *Leisure interests:* golf, horse racing, wines. *Address:* Crimbourne Stud, Crimbourne Lane, Wisborough Green, Nr. Billingshurst, West Sussex, RH14 0HR, England (Home). *Telephone:* (01403) 700400. *Fax:* (01403) 700776.

PARKER, Eugene N., PH.D.; American physicist (retd.); b. 10 June 1927, Houghton, Mich.; s. of Glenn H. Parker and Helen M. Parker; m. Niesje Meuter 1954; one s. one d.; ed. Mich. State Univ. and Calif. Inst. of Tech.; Instructor, Dept. of Mathematics and Astronomy, Univ. of Utah 1951–53, Asst. Prof., Dept. of Physics 1953–55; at Univ. of Chicago 1955–, Prof. Dept. of Physics 1962–95, Prof. Dept. of Astronomy 1967–95; mem. N.A.S. 1967–, Norwegian Acad. of Sciences 1988–; Hon. D.Sc. (Michigan State Univ.) 1975; Dr. h.c. (Utrecht) 1986; Space Science Award, A.I.A.A. 1964, John Adam Fleming Award, American Geophysical Union 1968, Henryk Arctowski Medal, N.A.S. 1969, Henry Norris Russell Lecture, American Astronomical Soc. 1969, George Ellery Hale Award, Solar Physics Div. American Astronomical Soc. 1978, Sydney Chapman Medal, Royal Astronomical Soc. 1979, Distinguished Alumnus Award, Calif. Inst. of Tech. 1980, James Arthur Prize Lecture, Harvard Smithsonian Center for Astrophysics 1986, U.S. Nat. Medal of Science 1989, William Bowie Medal, American Geophysics Union 1990, Karl Schwarzschild Medal (F.R.G.) 1990, Gold Medal (Royal Astronomical Soc.) 1992, Bruce Medal (Astronomical Soc. of the Pacific) 1997, Adion Medal (Observatoire de Nice) 1997. *Publications:* Interplanetary Dynamical Processes 1963, Cosmical Magnetic Fields 1979, Spontaneous Current Sheets in Magnetic Fields 1994. *Leisure interests:* hiking, history, wood-carving. *Address:* 1323 Evergreen Road, Homewood, IL 60430, U.S.A. (Home). *Telephone:* (708) 798 3497 (Home).

PARKER, Franklin, B.A., M.S., ED.D.; American writer and educationalist; b. 2 June 1921, New York; m. Betty June Parker 1950; ed. Berea Coll., Ky., Univ. of Illinois, Peabody Coll. Vanderbilt Univ., Nashville, Tenn.; Librarian and Speech Teacher, Ferrum Coll., Va. 1950–52, Belmont Coll., Nashville, Tenn. 1952–54, Peabody Coll. Vanderbilt Univ. 1955–56; Assoc. Prof. of Educ., State Univ. Coll., New Paltz, N.Y. 1956–57, Univ. of Tex. 1957–64; Prof., Univ. of Okla. 1964–68; Claude Worthington Benedum Prof. of Educ., West Va. Univ., Morgantown 1968–86; Distinguished Prof. Emer., Center for Excellence in Educ. 1986–89; Visiting Distinguished Prof. Western Carolina Univ. 1989–94; Consultant Macmillan Merrill (Publrs.), Teachers Coll. Press, William C. Brown 1988–; several visiting professorships; Sr. Fulbright Research Scholar, Zambia 1961–62; Distinguished Alumnus Award, Peabody Coll., Vanderbilt Univ. 1970, Berea Coll., Kentucky 1989. *Publications include:* African Development and Education in Southern Rhodesia 1960, Government Policy and International Education 1965, Church and State in Education 1966, Strategies for Curriculum Change: Cases from 13 Nations 1968, International Education: Understandings and Misunderstandings 1969, George Peabody, A Biography 1971, American Dissertations on Foreign Education: Abstracts of Doctoral Dissertations (20 vols.) 1971–91, What We Can Learn From China's Schools 1977, Education in Puerto Rico and of Puerto Ricans in the U.S.A. Vol. 1 1978, Vol. 2 1984, British Schools and Ours 1979, Women's Education (2 vols.) 1979–81, U.S. Higher Education: Guide to Information Sources 1980, Education in the People's Republic of China, Past and Present: Annotated Bibliography 1986, Education in England and Wales: Annotated Bibliography 1991, Academic Profiles in Higher Education 1993, Tennessee Encyclopaedia of History and Culture (mem. editorial bd.) 1998, many articles, contributions to encyclopaedias.

PARKER, Sir Peter, K.B.E., Kt., L.V.O., M.A.; British business executive; b. 30 Aug. 1924, Malo-les-Bains, France; s. of late Tom Parker and of Dorothy Mackinlay Parker; m. Gillian Rowe-Dutton 1951; three s. one d.; ed. in France and China, Bedford School, London Univ., Lincoln Coll., Oxford, Cornell and Harvard Univs.; worked for Philips Electrical 1951–53; Head, Overseas Dept., Industrial Soc. 1953–54; Sec., Duke of Edinburgh Study Conf. 1954–56; Chair. Eng. Group, Booker McConnell 1957–70; mem. Org. Cttee., later of Main Board, British Steel Corpn. 1966–67; mem. Mech. Eng. EDC 1966–70; Chair. British Pump Mfrs. Asscn. 1966–69) Dillons Univ. Bookshop 1967–75, London Univ. Computing Services 1969–76, Dawnay Day Group Ltd. 1971–76, British Railways Bd. 1976–83, mem., later Deputy Chair. Court of London Univ. 1964–; Chair. Mitsubishi Electric UK Ltd. 1983–96, Parkdale Holdings PLC 1988–89, Art Advisers Ltd. 1989–91, CLM Advisers PLC 1993, Mitsubishi Electric Europe 1996–, Apricot Computers Ltd. 1990–, Scruttons PLC 1993–, Whitehead Mann Group PLC 1984–, Arcadian Int. PLC 1990–98, Fidelity Japan OTC, Regional Markets Fund Ltd. 1990–, The Young Vic 1993–, Accuread 1996–, Court of Govs. of L.S.E. 1988–; Deputy Chair. CLM Insurance Fund PLC 1994–, Group 4 Securitas; Dir. UK.-Japan 2000 Group Rebound IPD Ltd. 1992–; mem. British Tourist Authority 1969–75; Chair. Rockware Group Ltd. 1971–76, 1983–92; Chair. Westfield Coll., London Univ. 1970–76, Econ. Devt. Cttee. for the Clothing Industry 1971–78, Landel Insurance Holdings Ltd. 1971–75, Target Group PLC 1984–87, B.I.M. 1984–86; Vice-Chair. H. Clarkson (Holdings) Ltd. 1984–93; mem. Bd. British Airways 1971–81; Dir. Int. Research and Devt. Co. Ltd. 1970–75, Renold Ltd. 1971–76, Shipping Industrial Holdings Ltd. 1971 (Chair. 1972–75), Fullemploy Ltd. 1973–76; Chair. (non-Exec.) Bardon Group PLC 1989–94; Pres. British Asscn. of Industrial Editors 1971–74, British Mechanical Eng. Confed. 1972–74, British Graduates Asscn. Advisory Council 1972, Design and Industry Asscn.; Chair. Nat. Theatre Devt. Council 1985–91, The Japan Festival 1991 1987–92; Dimbleby Lecture (BBC TV) 1983; mem. Inst. for Social Work Training 1970–76, York and Humberside Devt. Asscn. Ltd. -1976, Foundation for Man. Educ., Nat. Theatre Bd. 1986–91; Trustee, British Architectural Library Trust 1984; Council mem. Museum of Modern Art, Oxford 1984–; Dir. Metropolitan Radio 1983–91; Vice-Chair. Friends of the Earth Trust Ltd. 1988, Trustees of H.R.H. The Duke of Edinburgh's Commonwealth Study Conf. (U.K. Fund); Companion and mem. Council, Inst. of Man.; Visiting Fellow, Nuffield Coll., Oxford 1980 (Hon. Fellow); Hon. Fellow, Westfield Coll., Lincoln Coll., Oxford, Soc. of Industrial Artists and Designers, Open Univ., S.O.A.S., London Business School, Manchester Metropolitan Univ., R.I.B.A.; Hon. LL.D. (London Univ., Bath, Birmingham, Westminster); Bicentenary Medal, R.S.A. 1990; Grand Cordon, Order of Sacred Treasure (Japan) 1991. *Publication:* For Starters: The Business of Life (autobiog.) 1989. *Leisure interests:* rugby, swimming, theatre, browsing. *Address:* Fountain House, 130 Fenchurch Street, London, EC3M 5EE, England. *Telephone:* 0171-621 1472. *Fax:* 0171-283 7470.

PARKER, Robert Brown, PH.D.; American writer; b. 17 Sept. 1932, Springfield, Mass.; s. of Carroll Snow Parker and Mary Pauline (née Murphy) Parker; m. Joan Hall 1956; two s.; ed. Colby Coll., Boston Univ.; served with U.S. Army 1954–56; Co-Chair. Parker-Farman Co. 1960-62; lecturer Boston Univ. 1962–64; mem. faculty Lowell State Coll., Mass. 1964–66; lecturer Suffolk Univ. 1965–66; mem. faculty Bridgewater State Coll. 1966–68; Asst. Prof. of English Northeastern Univ., Boston 1968–73, Assoc. Prof. 1973–76, Prof. 1976–79; screenwriter with Joan Parker 1985–; mem. Writer's Guild of America; Hon. D.Litt. (Northeastern Univ.) 1987. *Publications include:* Promised Land 1976 (Edgar Allen Poe Award for Best Novel, Mystery Writers of America 1976), Three Weeks in Spring (with Joan Parker) 1978, A Savage Place 1981, Surrogate: A Spenser Short Story 1982, Love and Glory 1983, Parker on Writing 1985, Pale Kings and Princes 1987, Poodle Springs (with Raymond Chandler) 1989, Stardust 1990, A Year at the Races 1990, Paper Doll 1993, All Our Yesterdays 1994, Spenser's Boston 1994, Thin Air 1995, Chance 1996, Small Vices 1997, Night Passage 1997. *Screenwriting includes:* Spenser: For Hire 1985–88 (series), Blues for Buder 1988, High Rise 1988, A Man Called Hawk (series) 1989–90, Spenser: Ceremony 1993, Spenser: Pale Kings and Princes 1993.

PARKER, Sarah Jessica; American actress; b. 25 March 1965, Nelsonville, Ohio; m. Matthew Broderick (q.v.) 1997. *Stage appearances include:* The Innocents 1976, The Sound of Music 1977; Annie 1978, The War Brides 1981, The Death of a Miner 1982, To Gillian on Her 37th Birthday 1983–84, Terry Neal's Future 1986, The Heidi Chronicles 1989. *Film appearances include:* Rich Kids 1979, Somewhere Tomorrow 1983, Firstborn 1984, Footloose 1984, Girls Just Want to Have Fun 1985, Flight of the Navigator 1986, L.A. Story 1991, Honeymoon in Vegas 1992, Hocus Pocus 1993, Striking Distance 1993, Ed Wood 1994, Miami Rhapsody 1995, If Lucy Fell 1996, Mars Attacks! 1996, The First Wives Club 1996, Extreme Measures 1996, 'Til There was You 1997, A Life Apart: Hasidism in America 1997; numerous

TV appearances. *Address:* c/o Kevin Huvane, Creative Artists Agency, 9830 Wilshire Boulevard, Beverly Hills, CA 90212, U.S.A.

PARKER, (Thomas) John, D.SC.(ENG.), SC.D., F.ENG.; British business executive; b. 8 April 1942, Downpatrick, Northern Ireland; s. of Robert Parker and Margaret Elizabeth Parker (née Bell); m. Emma Elizabeth Blair 1967; one s. one d.; ed. Belfast Coll. of Tech.; Ship Design Staff, Harland and Wolff PLC 1963–69, Ship Production Man. 1969–71, Production Drawing Office Man. 1971–72, Sales and Projects Dept. Gen. Man. 1972–74; Man. Dir. Austin & Pickersgill 1974–78; Bd. mem. for Shipbuilding (Marketing and Operations), British Shipbuilders 1978–80, Corpn. Deputy Chief Exec. 1980–83; Chair. and C.E.O. Harland and Wolff Holdings PLC 1983–93, Dir. (non-exec.) 1993–; Chair. Harland-MAN Engines 1983–93; Bd. mem. Industrial Devt. Bd. for Northern Ireland 1983–87; mem. Gen. Cttee. Lloyds Register of Shipping 1983– (Chair. Technician Cttee. 1996); Bd. mem. QUBIS 1984–93; British Coal Bd. mem. 1986–93; Deputy Chair. 1993–94, Chief Exec. Babcock Int. Group PLC 1993, Chair. 1994–; Dir. (non-exec.) GKN PLC 1993–, BG PLC 1997–; Vice-Pres. Royal Inst. of Naval Architects 1985–93, Pres. 1996–(99); Chair. Council of European Shipbuilders Asscn. 1993. *Publications:* A Profile of British Shipbuilders 1979, British Shipbuilders—A Period of Constructive Change (Marintec Conf., Shanghai) 1981, The Challenge of Change in Shipbuilding Today (ICCAS '85 Conf., Trieste) 1985. *Leisure interests:* reading, music, ships, sailing. *Address:* Babcock International Group, The Lodge, Church Street, Amersham, Bucks., HP7 0DD, England. *Telephone:* (01494) 727296.

PARKINSON, Baron (Life Peer), cr. 1992, of Carnforth in the County of Lancashire; **Cecil Edward Parkinson,** P.C., M.A.; British politician and chartered accountant; b. 1 Sept. 1931; s. of Sidney Parkinson; m. Ann Mary Jarvis 1957; three d.; one d. by Sarah Keays; ed. Royal Lancaster Grammar School and Emmanuel Coll., Cambridge; joined Metal Box Co. as man. trainee; joined West, Wake, Price & Co. (chartered accountants) as articled clerk 1956, Partner 1961–71; f. Parkinson Hart Securities Ltd. 1967, Chair. 1967–79, Dir. 1967–79, 1984–; Dir. several other cos. 1967–79; Branch Treas. Hemel Hempstead Conservative Asscn. 1961–64, Constituency Chair. 1965–66, Chair. and ex officio mem. all cttees. 1966–69; Chair. Herts. 100 Club 1968–69; Pres. Hemel Hempstead Young Conservatives 1968–71, Northampton Young Conservatives 1969–71; contested Northampton, Gen. Election 1970; M.P. for Enfield West 1970–74, for Hertfordshire South 1974–83, for Hertsmere 1983–92; Sec. Conservative Backbench Finance Cttee. 1971–72; Parl. Pvt. Sec. to Minister for Aerospace and Shipping 1972–74; Asst. Govt. Whip 1974, Opposition Whip 1974–76; Opposition Spokesman on Trade 1976–79; Minister of State for Trade 1979–81; Paymaster-Gen. 1981–83; Chair. Conservative Party 1981–83, 1997–98; Sec. of State for Trade and Industry June–Oct. 1983, for Energy 1987–89, for Transport 1989–90; Chair. Conservative Way Forward Group 1991–; Chancellor of the Duchy of Lancaster 1982–83; Leader, Inst. of Dirs. Parl. Panel 1972–79; Sec. Anglo-Swiss Parl. Group 1972–79, Chair. 1979–82; Chair. Anglo-Polish Conservative Soc. 1986–, Chemical Dependency Centre Ltd. 1986–, Jarvis (Harpenden) Holdings, Usborne 1991–, Midland Expressway Ltd. 1993–, Dartford River Crossing Ltd. 1993–; Dir. Babcock Int. 1984–87, Sports Aid Foundation, Save and Prosper 1984–87, Tarmac 1984–87, Sears PLC 1984–87. *Publication:* An Autobiography: Right at the Centre 1992. *Leisure interests:* skiing, reading, golf. *Address:* c/o House of Lords, London, SW1A 0PW, England.

PARKINSON, Michael; British television and radio presenter and writer; b. 28 March 1935, Barnsley; m. Mary Heneghan 1959; three s.; ed. Barnsley Grammar School; began career as journalist with local paper, then worked on The Guardian, Daily Express, Sunday Times, Punch, The Listener etc.; joined Granada TV as interviewer/reporter 1965; joined 24 Hours (BBC) as reporter; Exec. Producer and Presenter, London Weekend TV 1968; Presenter Cinema 1969–70, Tea Break, Where in the World 1971, hosted own chat show "Parkinson" 1971–82, The Boys of '66 1981, Presenter TV-AM 1983–84, Give Us a Clue 1984–92, All Star Secrets 1984–86, The Skag Kids 1985, Desert Island Discs (BBC Radio 4) 1986–88, The Help Squad 1991–92, Ghost Watch 1992, Parkinson on Sport (BBC Radio 5) 1994–97, Going for a Song 1995–, A League Apart, 100 Years of Rugby League (BBC 2) 1995, Parkinson: The Interviews 1995–97, Parkinson's Sunday Supplement (BBC Radio 2) 1996–, Auntie's All Time Greats 1997, Parkinson 1998–; columnist for Daily Mirror 1986–90, for Daily Telegraph 1991–; Parkinson One-to-One 1987–88; Ed., Catalyst 1988–; has worked extensively on Australian TV; f. and Dir. Pavilion Books 1980–97; Sports Feature Writer of the Year (British Sports Journalism Awards) 1995, Fellow BFI for contrib. to TV 1997. *Publications:* Football Daft 1968, Cricket Mad 1969, Sporting Fever 1974, George Best: An Intimate Biography 1975, A-Z of Soccer (jt. author) 1975, Bats in the Pavilion 1977, The Woofits 1980, Parkinson's Lore 1981, The Best of Parkinson 1982, Sporting Lives 1992, Sporting Profiles 1995. *Address:* c/o Parkinson Partnership, 48 Gray's Inn Road, WC1X 8LT, England.

PARLY, Jeanne-Marie; French civil servant; b. 1 April 1935, Toulouse; sr. lecturer Univ. de Clermont-Ferrand 1967–68; fmrly. sr. lecturer, Prof. Univ. of Paris IX, Prof. 1985–89; with Ministry of Nat. Educ. 1984, 1993–, adviser 1997–98, Dir. 1998–; Rector Acad. of Caen 1989–. *Address:* c/o Ministry of National Education, 110 rue de Grenelle, 75700 Paris, France. *Telephone:* (1) 49-55-10-10. *Fax:* (1) 45-51-53-63.

PARMINTER, Kate; British charity administrator; fmrly. grad. trainee Nestlé; fmrly. mem. Horsham Dist. Council; fmrly. Head Press and Public Affairs R.S.P.C.A.; Dir. Council for the Protection of Rural England 1998–. *Address:* Council for the Protection of Rural England, Warwick House, 25 Buckingham Palace Road, London, SW1W 0PP, England. *Telephone:* 0171-976-6433. *Fax:* 0171-976 6373.

PARODI, Anton Gaetano; Italian journalist and playwright; b. 19 May 1923, Castanzaro Lido (Calabria); s. of Luigi Parodi and Grazia Scicchitano; m. Piera Somino 1952; two c.; ed. Università degli Studi, Turin and Genoa; journalist 1945–; professional journalist 1947–; Corresp. of Unità, Budapest 1964–; Premio nazionale di teatro Riccione 1959, 1965, Premio nazionale di teatro dei giovani 1947 and numerous other prizes. *Plays include:* Il gatto, Il nostro scandalo quotidiano, L'ex-maggiore Hermann Grotz, Adolfo o della nagia, Filippo l'Impostore, Una corda per il figlio di Abele, Quel pomeriggio di domenica, Dialoghi intorno ad un'uovo, Una storia della notte, Pioggia d'estate, Cielo di pietra. I giorni dell'Arca, Quello che dicono.

PARR, Robert Ghormley, PH.D., A.B.; American physical chemist and educator; b. 22 Sept. 1921, Chicago, Ill.; s. of Leland Wilbur Parr and Grace Ghormley; m. Jane Bolstad 1944; one s. two d.; ed. Western High School, Washington, D.C., Brown Univ., Univ. of Minnesota; Asst. Prof. of Chem., Univ. of Minn. 1947–48; Asst. Prof. to Prof. of Chem., Carnegie Inst. of Tech. 1948–62, Chair. of Gen. Faculty 1960–61; Prof. of Chem. Johns Hopkins Univ. 1962–74, Chair. of Dept. of Chem. 1969–72; William R. Kenan, Jr. Prof. of Theoretical Chem. Univ. of N.C. 1974–90, Wassily Hoeffding Prof. of Chemical Physics 1990–; Guggenheim Fellow and Fulbright Scholar Univ. of Cambridge 1953–54; Sloan Fellow 1956–60; Visiting Prof. at Univ. of Ill. 1962, State Univ. of New York at Buffalo and Pa. State Univ. 1967, Japan Soc. for Promotion of Sciences 1968, 1979; Firth Prof. Univ. of Sheffield 1976; Visiting Prof. Univ. of Berlin 1977, Duke Univ. 1996–97; Fellow Univ. of Chicago 1949, Research Assoc. 1957; Nat. Science Foundation Sr. Postdoctoral Fellow, Univ. of Oxford and CSIRO, Melbourne 1967–68; mem. of numerous academic and scientific socs., including A.A.A.S., American Physical Soc., American Chemical Soc., N.A.S., American Acad. of Arts and Sciences; mem. Int. Acad. of Quantum Molecular Science, Vice-Pres. 1973–79, Pres. 1991–97; Trustee Inst. for Fundamental Chemistry Kyoto 1988–; Dr. h.c. (Louvain) 1986, (Jagiellonian) 1996; N.C. Inst. of Chemists Distinguished Chemists Award 1982, Langmuir Award in Chemical Physics, American Chemical Soc. 1994. *Publications:* The Quantum Theory of Molecular Electronic Structure 1963; Density—Functional Theory of Atoms and Molecules 1989; more than 200 scientific articles in specialist publs., fmr. mem. Editorial Bd. numerous specialist magazines and reviews. *Address:* Department of Chemistry, University of North Carolina, Chapel Hill, NC 27599 (Office); 701 Kenmore Road, Chapel Hill, NC 27154, U.S.A. (Home). *Telephone:* (919) 929-2609 (Home).

PARRA, Nicanor; Chilean poet; b. 5 Sept. 1914, San Fabián; s. of Nicanor P. Parra and Clara S. Navarrete; m. 1st Ana Troncoso 1948; m. 2nd Inga Palmen; seven c.; ed. Univ. de Chile, Brown Univ., U.S.A., and Oxford; Prof. of Theoretical Mechanics, Univ. de Chile 1964–; has given poetry readings in Los Angeles, Moscow, Leningrad, Havana, Lima, Ayacucho, Cuzco; Premio Municipal de Poesía, Santiago 1937, 1954; Premio Nacional de Literatura 1969. *Publications:* Poetry: Cancionero sin nombre 1937, Poemas y antipoemas 1954, La cueca larga 1958, Antipoems 1958, Versos de salón 1962, Discursos (with Pablo Neruda) 1962, Deux Poèmes (bi-lingual) 1964, Antología (also in Russian) 1965, Antología de la Poesía Soviética Rusa (bilingual) 1965, Canciones Rusas 1967, Defensa de Violeta Parra 1967; Scientific Works: La Evolución del Concepto de Masa 1958, Fundamentos de la Física (trans. of Foundation of Physics by Profs. Lindsay and Margenau) 1967, Obra Gruesa 1969. *Address:* Julia Bernstein, Parcela 272, Lareina, Santiago, Chile.

PARRA-ARANGUREN, Gonzalo; Venezuelan judge and university professor; b. 5 Dec. 1928, Caracas; ed. Cen. Univ. of Venezuela, Inter-American Law Inst., Univ. of New York, Ludwig-Maximilians Univ., Munich; Prof., Cen. Univ. of Venezuela, Caracas 1956–, Andrés Bello Catholic Univ., Caracas 1957–; Judge, Second Court of First Instance (commercial matters), Fed. Dist. and State of Miranda, Caracas 1958–71; First Assoc. Judge, Chamber of Cassation (civil, commercial and labour matters) of Supreme Court of Justice 1988–92, elected Alt. Judge 1992; mem. nat. group for Venezuela, Perm. Court of Arbitration, The Hague 1985; Judge Int. Court of Justice 1991–; has acted as arbitrator in Venezuela and abroad on pvt. commercial matters; mem. Legal Advisory Cttee. of Ministry of Foreign Affairs 1984–, of Nat. Congress 1990–; mem. Acad. of Political and Social Sciences of Caracas 1966– (Pres. 1993–95), Inst. of Int. Law 1979–; rep. Venezuela at several sessions of The Hague Conf. on Pvt. Int. Law. *Publications:* several books and numerous articles in Venezuelan and foreign journals on law of nationality, pvt. int. law and int. civil procedural law. *Address:* International Court of Justice, Peace Palace, Carnegieplein 2, 2517 KJ The Hague, Netherlands. *Telephone:* (70) 392-44-41. *Fax:* (70) 364-99-28.

PARRATT, James Roy, D.SC., D.SC. (MED.), PH.D., F.E.S.C., F.R.C.PATH., F.R.S.E.; British professor of cardiovascular pharmacology; b. 19 Aug. 1933, London; s. of James J. Parratt and Eunice E. King; m. Pamela J. Lyndon 1957; two s. one d.; ed. St. Clement Danes Holborn Estate Grammar School, London and Univ. of London; Nigerian School of Pharmacy 1958–61; Dept. of Physiology, Univ. Coll. Ibadan, Nigeria 1961–67; Univ. of Strathclyde, Glasgow 1967–, Reader 1970, Personal Prof. 1975, Prof. of Cardiovascular Pharmacology 1983–, Head, Dept. of Physiology and Pharmacology 1986–90,

Chair. School of Pharmacy and Pharmacology 1988; Vice-Pres. European Shock Soc.; Fellow Royal Pharm. Soc., Inst. of Biology; mem. Council, Int. Soc. for Heart Research (European Section); Hon. mem. Hungarian Pharmacological Soc., Slovak Medical and Cardiological Socs., Czech Cardiological Soc.; M.D. h.c. (Albert Szent Gyorgyi Univ. Medical School); Gold Medal, Univ. of Szeged, Hungary, Gold J.E. Purkyne Medal, Acad. of Sciences of the Czech Repub. *Leisure interests:* active within Baptist denomination in Scotland and in Christian mission. *Address:* Department of Physiology and Pharmacology, University of Strathclyde, Strathclyde Institute for Biomedical Sciences, 27 Taylor Street, Glasgow, G4 0NR; 16 Russell Drive, Bearsden, Glasgow, G61 3BD, Scotland. *Telephone:* (0141) 942-7164. *Fax:* (0141) 552-2562.

PARRAVICINI, Giannino; Italian economist and financial official; b. 3 July 1910, Castellanza (Varese); s. of Renzo Parravicini and Edvige Parravicini; m. Carla Benini; two c.; ed. Univs. of Pavia, Vienna, Berlin, Paris and London; with Banca d'Italia 1935–60, latterly Chief Exec.; Chair. Bd. of Dirs. Istituto Centrale per il Credito a Medio Termine 1962–78; mem. Bd. of Dirs. EFIM and Finsider until 1975; Chair. Banco di Sicilia 1979–92; Prof. of financial science, Univs. of Pavia, Florence and Milan 1954–72; Prof. of Monetary and Credit Economics, Rome Univ. 1972–85, Prof. Emer. 1985–; Hon. Chair. Ente Luigi Einaudi; has participated in numerous official cttees. and was charged with formation of monetary and currency system in Somalia; fmr. Head, UN Financial Office, Léopoldville (now Kinshasa, Democratic Republic of the Congo); Hon. Pres. A.B.I. (Italian Bankers Asscn.); Nat. mem. Accademia dei Lincei; Knight Grand Cross and Cavaliere del Lavoro. *Leisure interests:* historical and political works. *Address:* 10 Piazza Cavour, 10-00193 Rome, Italy.

PARRIS, Matthew; British writer and broadcaster; b. 7 Aug. 1949, Johannesburg, S. Africa; s. of Leslie F. Parris and Theresa E. (née Littler) Parris; ed. Waterford School, Swaziland, Clare Coll., Cambridge and Yale Univ.; FCO 1974–76; with Conservative Research Dept. 1976–79; mem. Parl. (Conservative) for W. Derbyshire 1979–86; Presenter Weekend World 1986–88; Parl. Sketch Writer for The Times 1988–; mem. Broadcasting Standards Council 1992–97; Edgar Wallace Trophy (London Press Club) 1990, Columnist of the Year 1992, British Press Award 1996; Hon. D.Univ. (Sheffield Hallam) 1997. *Publications:* Inca-Kola, A Traveller's Tale of Peru 1990, So Far So Good . . . (selected pieces) 1991, Look Behind You! (Sketches and Follies from the Commons) 1993, Scorn 1994, Great Parliamentary Scandals 1995, Read My Lips (with Phil Mason) 1996, Scorn with Added Vitriol 1996, I Couldn't Possibly Comment 1997, The Great Unfrocked: 2000 Years of Church Scandals 1997. *Address:* c/o The Times, Pennington Street, London, E1 9XN; The Spout, Gratton, Bakewell, Derbyshire, DE45 1LN, England.

PARROTT, Andrew Haden, B.A.; British conductor and scholar; b. 10 March 1947, Walsall; s. of R. C. Parrott and E. D. Parrott; m. 1st Emma Kirkby 1971; m. 2nd Emily Van Evera 1986; one d.; ed. Queen Mary's Grammar School, Walsall, Merton Coll., Oxford; Dir. of Music Merton Coll., Oxford 1969–71; Founder, Conductor and Dir., Taverner Choir, Taverner Consort and Taverner Players 1973–; BBC Promenade Concerts début 1977; fmr. musical Asst. to Sir Michael Tippett; freelance orchestral and operatic conductor; occasional writer, broadcaster, lecturer, continuo-player and singer; Open Post-Mastership, Merton Coll. 1966–69; Leverhulme Fellowship 1984–85. *Publications include:* Transposition in Monteverdi's Vespers of 1610 (Early Music, Nov. 1984), New Oxford Book of Carols 1992, Performing Purcell: The Purcell Companion 1995. *Recordings include:* medieval, renaissance and 20th-Century music, Monteverdi, Purcell, Vivaldi, Bach, Handel, Mozart. *Address:* Allied Artists, 42 Montpelier Square, London, SW7 1JZ, England. *Telephone:* 0171-589 6243.

PARRY, Martin, O.B.E., PH.D.; British environmentalist; b. 12 Dec. 1945; s. of John Fyson Parry and Frances Joan Stewart; m. Cynthia Jane Mueller 1968; two d.; ed. Durham and West Indies Univs.; Prof. of Environmental Man. and Dir. Oxford Univ. Environmental Change Unit 1991–94; Prof. of Environmental Man., Dept. of Geography, Univ. Coll. London 1994–; Dir. Jackson Environment Inst. 1996–; fmrly. with Birmingham Univ.; Chair. U.K. Climate Change Review Group. *Publications:* Climatic Change, Agric. and Settlement 1976, Climate Change and World Agriculture 1990, Economic Implications of Climate Change in Britain 1995. *Address:* Department of Geography, University College London, Gower Street, London, WC1E 6BT, England.

PARSONS, Charles Dacre, PH.D.; American professor of philosophy; b. 13 April 1933, Cambridge, Mass.; s. of Talcott Parsons and Helen Walker Parsons; m. Marjorie Louise Wood 1968; one s. one d.; ed. Harvard Coll., King's Coll., Cambridge, Harvard Univ.; Jr. Fellow, Soc. of Fellows, Harvard Univ. 1958–61; Asst. Prof. of Philosophy, Cornell Univ. 1961–62, Harvard Univ. 1962–65; Assoc. Prof. of Philosophy, Columbia Univ. 1965–69, Prof. 1969–89, Chair. Dept. of Philosophy 1976–79, 1985–89; Prof. of Philosophy, Harvard Univ. 1989–, Edgar Pierce Prof. of Philosophy 1991–; Ed. The Journal of Philosophy 1966–90, consulting ed. 1990–; Sec. Asscn. for Symbolic Logic 1971–76, Vice-Pres. 1986–89, Pres. 1989–92; Santayana Fellow, Harvard 1964–65, NEH Fellow 1979–80, Guggenheim Fellow 1986–87; Fellow Center for Advanced Study in The Behavioural Sciences 1994–95; Fellow American Acad. of Arts and Sciences 1982–. *Publications:* Mathematics in Philosophy 1983, Kurt Gödel, Collected Works, vol. III (Ed. with Solomon Feferman et al.) 1995; articles on logic and philosophy. *Address:* Department of Philosophy, Emerson Hall, Harvard University, Cambridge, MA 02138 (Office); 16 Ellery Square, Cambridge, MA 02138, U.S.A. (Home). *Telephone:* (617) 495-2191 (Office).

PARSONS, Peter John, M.A., F.B.A.; British academic; b. 24 Sept. 1936, Surbiton, Surrey; s. of Robert John Parsons and Ethel Ada Parsons (née Frary); ed. Raynes Park County Grammar School and Christ Church, Oxford; Lecturer in Documentary Papyrology, Oxford Univ. 1960–65, Lecturer in Papyrology 1965–89, Regius Prof. of Greek 1989–; Student (Fellow) Christ Church Oxford 1964–; J. H. Gray Lecturer, Cambridge Univ. 1982; Hon. Ph.D. (Berne) 1985; Hon. D.Litt. (Milan) 1994, Hon. Ph.D. (Athens) 1995. *Publications:* The Oxyrhynchus Papyri (jtly.) vols. XXXI 1966, XXXIII and XXXIV 1968, LIV 1987, LIX 1992, LX 1994, (solely) vol. XLII 1973, Supplementum Hellenisticum (with H. Lloyd-Jones) 1983; articles in learned journals. *Leisure interests:* music, cinema, cooking, eating. *Address:* Christ Church, Oxford, OX1 1DP, England. *Telephone:* (01865) 276223.

PARSONS, Roger, D.SC., PH.D., F.R.S.; British professor of chemistry; b. 31 Oct. 1926, London; s. of Robert H. A. Parsons and Ethel Fenton; m. Ruby M. Turner 1953; three s. one d.; ed. King Alfred School, London, Strathcona High School, Edmonton, Alberta and Imperial Coll., London; Asst. Lecturer, Imperial Coll. 1948–51; Deedes Fellow, Univ. Coll., Dundee 1951–54; Lecturer, Univ. of Bristol 1954–63, Reader 1963–79; Dir. Lab. d'Electrochimie Interfaciale du CNRS, Meudon, France 1977–84; Prof. of Chem. Univ. of Southampton 1985–92, Prof. Emer.; Pres. Faraday Div., Royal Soc. of Chemistry 1991–93; D. Univ. (Buenos Aires) 1997; Prix Pascal, Palladium Medal, Breyer Medal, Galvani Medal. *Publications:* Electrochemical Data 1956, Electrical Properties of Interfaces (with J. Lyklema); Co-Ed. Standard Potentials in Aqueous Solution 1985, Electrochemistry in Research and Development 1985; over 200 scientific papers. *Leisure interests:* listening to music, going to the opera. *Address:* c/o Department of Chemistry, Southampton University, Southampton, SO17 1BJ, England. *Telephone:* (01703) 593371.

PARSURAMAN, Armoogum (Dassen), B.A.; Mauritian politician; b. 30 June 1951; m.; ed. Univ. of Mauritius; mem. Legis. Ass. June 1982–; Minister of Educ., Arts and Culture 1983–92, of Educ. and Science 1992–95; Chair. Parti Socialiste Mauricien (PSM); Vice-Pres. MSM 1986–; mem. MSM/PMSD/Labour Party Govt. –1990, MSM/MMM Govt. 1990–; Chair. Public Accounts Cttee. 1982–83, Mauritius Ex-Servicemen Welfare Fund; mem. Local Govt. Comm., Select Cttee. on Industrial Relations Act. *Address:* c/o Ministry of Education, Science and Technology, Government Centre, Port Louis, Mauritius.

PÄRT, Arvo; Estonian composer; b. 11 Sept. 1935, Paide; ed. Tallinn Conservatory (student of Heino Eller); worked as sound producer for Estonian radio 1957–67; teacher at Tallinn Conservatory 1967–78; emigrated to Berlin 1980. *Works include:* Meie Aed (Our Garden) 1959, Stride of the World, Perpetuum mobile 1963, Symphony no. 2 1966, Pro et contra 1966, Song for the Beloved 1973, Tabula rasa 1977, Arbos 1977, Sumna 1980, Cantus in Memory of Benjamin Britten 1980, An den Wassern zu Babylon 1984, St. John Passion 1982, Stabat Mater 1985, Festina Lente 1989, Miserere 1989. *Address:* c/o Deutsche Akademie der Musik und Darstellende Künste, Berlin, Germany.

PARTON, Dolly Rebecca; American singer, composer; b. 19 Jan. 1946, Sevier County, Tenn.; d. of Robert Lee and Avie Lee (née Owens) Parton; m. Carl Dean 1966; radio appearances include Grand Ole Opry, WSM Radio, Cass Walker Program; appeared in films Nine to Five 1980, The Best Little Whorehouse in Texas 1982, Rhinestone 1984, Steel Magnolias 1989, Straight Talk 1991; *albums include:* Here You Come Again (Grammy award 1978), Real Love 1985, Just the Way I Am 1986, Heartbreaker, Great Balls of Fire, Rainbow 1988, White Limozeen 1989, Home for Christmas 1990, Eagle When She Flies 1991, Slow Dancing with the Moon 1993, Honky Tonk Angels 1994, The Essential Dolly Parton 1995, Just the Way I Am 1996, Super Hits 1996, I Will Always Love You and Other Greatest Hits 1996 (with others); *composed numerous songs including:* Nine to Five (Grammy Award 1981); Vocal Group of the Year award (with Porter Wagoner) 1968, Vocal Duo of the Year, All Country Music Asscn. 1970, 1971; Nashville Metronome Award 1979; Female Vocalist of the Year 1975, 1976; Country Star of the Year 1978; People's Choice 1980; Female Vocalist of the Year, Academy of Country Music 1980; East Tenn. Hall of Fame 1988. *Publication:* Dolly: My Life and Other Unfinished Business 1994. *Address:* RCA, 6 W. 57th Street, New York, NY 10019, U.S.A.

PARTRIDGE, Derek William, C.M.G.; British diplomatist; b. 15 May 1931, London; s. of late Ernest Partridge and Ethel E. Buckingham; ed. Preston Manor Co. Grammar School, Wembley, Middx.; entered Foreign Office 1949; R.A.F. 1949–51; served Oslo 1954–56, Jeddah 1956, Khartoum 1957–60, Sofia 1960–62, Manila 1962–65, Djakarta 1965–67, Brisbane 1972–74, Colombo 1974–77; FCO 1977–86; High Commr. in Sierra Leone 1986–91; mem. Southwark Borough Council (Lib. Dem.) 1994–. *Address:* 16 Wolfe Crescent, London, SE16 1SF, England. *Telephone:* 0171-231 2759. *Fax:* 0171-231 2759.

PARTRIDGE, Frank David Peregrine; British art dealer; b. 14 Sept. 1955, London; s. of John A. Partridge and Caroline M. Cust; m. Susan A. Hince 1982; three d.; ed. Elstree and Harrow Schools; Dir. Partridge Fine Arts 1981–. *Leisure interests:* shooting, tennis, skiing, golf, sailing, bridge. *Address:* 7 Thurloe Square, London, SW7 2TA, England.

PARTRIDGE, John Albert, C.B.E., R.A., F.R.I.B.A.; British architect; b. 26 Aug. 1924, London; s. of George Partridge and Gladys Partridge; m. Doris Foreman 1953; one s. one d.; ed. Shooter's Hill Grammar School, Woolwich, and Polytechnic School of Architecture, London; London County Council Housing Architects' Dept. 1951–59; Sr. and Founding Partner, Howell, Killick, Partridge & Amis (HKPA) 1959–95; Vice-Pres. R.I.B.A. 1977–79, Concrete Soc. 1979–81; R.I.B.A. Hon. Librarian 1977–81; Chair. R.I.B.A. Architectural Research Steering Cttee. 1978–84, Clients Advisory Steering Cttee. 1990–94; Gov. Building Centre, London 1981–96; Chair. Asscn. of Consultant Architects 1983–85; mem. NEDO Construction Research Strategy Cttee. 1983–86; Architect mem. FCO Advisory Bd. on the Diplomatic Estate 1985–94; External Examiner in Architecture, Univ. of Bath 1975–78, 1992, Thames Polytechnic 1978–86, Univ. of Cambridge 1979–81, Univ. of Manchester 1982–, South Bank Polytechnic (London) 1981–86, Brighton Polytechnic 1987–91, Royal Coll. of Art 1991–94. *Major works include:* Wolfson Rayne and Gatehouse Bldg., St. Anne's Coll., Oxford, New Hall and Common Room, St. Antony's Coll., Oxford, Wells Hall, Univ. of Reading, Middlesex Polytechnic Coll. of Art, Cat Hill, Medway Magistrates Court, The Albany, Deptford, Hall of Justice, Trinidad & Tobago, in asscn. with ACLP, Trinidad; Warrington Crown Courthouse, Basildon Courthouse, Haywards Heath Magistrates Courthouse, Japanese Univ. Coll., Chaucer Coll., Univ. of Kent; exhbns. of HKPA work at Heinz Gallery, London 1983, Puck Bldg., New York 1983; 35 Nat. Design Awards for HKPA 1965–. *Publications:* articles in the tech. press and architectural papers to conferences. *Leisure interests:* looking at buildings, travel, sketching, taking photographs, listening to music. *Address:* Cudham Court, Cudham, Nr. Sevenoaks, Kent, England. *Telephone:* (01959) 571294. *Fax:* (01959) 570478.

PARTRIDGE, Linda, B.A., D.PHIL., F.R.S., F.R.S.E.; British biometrist; b. 18 March 1950, Bath; d. of George Albert Partridge and Ida Partridge (née Tucker); m. 1st Vernon French (divorced 1989); m. 2nd Michael John Morgan 1996; ed. Convent of Sacred Heart, Tunbridge Wells, Univ. of Oxford; demonstrator, then lecturer, Reader, Prof. of Evolutionary Biology Univ. of Edin. 1976–1993; Weldon Prof. of Biometry Univ. Coll. London 1994–; NERC Research Prof. 1997–. *Leisure interests:* sailing, gardening. *Address:* Department of Biology, University College London, Wolfson House, 4 Stephenson Way, London, NW1 2HE (Office); 68 Gladsmuir Road, London, N19 3JU, England (Home). *Telephone:* 0171-380 7418 (Office). *Fax:* 0171-383 2048 (Office).

PARTRIDGE, Sir Michael John Anthony, K.C.B., M.A.; British civil servant; b. 29 Sept. 1935, Stourbridge, Worcs.; s. of Dr. John Henry Partridge and Ethel Green; m. Joan Elizabeth Hughes 1968; two s. one d.; ed. Merchant Taylors' School, St. John's Coll., Oxford Univ.; joined Home Civil Service (Ministry of Pensions and National Insurance–MPNI) 1960, Pvt. Sec. to Perm. Sec. 1962–64, Prin. MPNI 1964–71, Asst. Sec. 1971–76, Under Sec. 1976–81, Deputy Sec. 1981–83; Deputy Under-Sec. of State, Home Office 1983–87; Second Perm. Sec. Dept. of Health and Social Security 1987–88; Perm. Sec. Dept. of Social Security 1988–95; Sr. Treas. Methodist Church Finance Div. 1980–96; Hon. Fellow St. John's Coll. Oxford 1991–; Dir. (non-exec.) Norwich Union 1996–, Stationery Office 1997–; Chair. Bd. of Govs. Middx. Univ. 1997–; Gov. Merchant Taylors' School 1992—; Liveryman Merchant Taylors' Co. 1987. *Leisure interests:* do-it-yourself, Greece, reading, skiing. *Address:* 27 High View, Pinner, Middx., HA5 3NZ, England. *Telephone:* 0181-868 0657. *Fax:* 0181-429 4532.

PASANELLA, Giovanni, F.A.I.A.; American architect; b. 13 Jan. 1931, New York; two s.; ed. Cooper Union, New York, Yale Univ.; designer, Edward L. Barnes, New York 1959–64; Prin. Giovanni Pasanella, New York 1964–76; co-owner Pasanella & Klein, New York 1976–; Architecture Critic, Univ. of Ky., Lexington 1963, Yale Univ. 1964; Adjunct Prof. of Architecture, Columbia Univ. 1965–87, Project Dir. Inst. of Urban Environment 1965–68; Visiting Fellow Urban Studies, Inst. of Architecture 1975; Consultant Architect to Chair. New York City Planning Comm. 1967; mem. Bd. of Trustees Il Piccolo Teatro dell'Opera, Brooklyn, New York 1986; Yale Univ. Travelling Fellow 1958–59; Fellow A.I.A.; mem. Soc. of Architectural Historians; Architecture Award, Architectural Record 1974, 1975. *Address:* Pasanella & Klein, 330 W. 42nd Street, New York, NY 10036, U.S.A.; Villa Cannizzaro, via Fondi Camaiore, Lucca, Italy. *Telephone:* 0584 989297.

PASCAL, Jean-Baptiste Lucien, L. EN D., DIPL.; French banker; b. 26 Nov. 1930, Bordeaux; s. of Ernest Pascal and Paule de Battisti; m. Christiane Gardelle 1962; three s. (one deceased); ed. Univ. of Paris; attached to Banque Nat. pour le Commerce et l'Industrie 1954; Head of Supplies Mission for the Devt. of Algeria and Jt. Govt. Commr. for Crédit Populaire de France in Algeria 1959; Head of Bureau for Financial Co-operation to Sec. of State for Algerian Affairs 1963; mem. Crédit Commercial de France (CCF) 1965, Deputy Dir. Cen. Admin. CCF 1967, Dir.-Gen. d'Interbail 1971, Dir. Cen. Admin. 1973–, Admin. Dir.-Gen. 1974, Vice-Pres. Dir.-Gen. d'Interbail 1976–; Dir. Crédit Commercial de France 1977; Pres. Dir.-Gen. Banque Hervet 1986–89; Pres. Admin. Council SOFEC 1991–; Pres. GOBTP 1993–97, Pres. Conseil de Surveillance du GOBTP 1997–, Interbail 1996– (Chair. Bd. Dirs. 1996–97); Dir. French Asscn. of Financial Cos., Vice-Pres. 1995–97. *Publication:* La Décolonisation de l'Europe—Querelle des Continents 1964. *Leisure interests:* alpinism, hunting. *Address:* GOBTP, 251 Boulevard Pereire, 75017 Paris (Office); 14 rue Jules Claretie, 75116 Paris, France (Home).

PASCAL-TROUILLOT, Ertha; Haitian politician and attorney; b. 13 Aug. 1943, Pétionville; m. Ernst Trouillot 1971 (died 1987); one d.; ed. at law school; Judge, Lower Court 1980, Supreme Court 1986; Acting Pres. of Haiti 1990–91. *Address:* c/o Office du Président, Palais National, Port-au-Prince, Haiti.

PASCHKE, Fritz, DR.TECH.SC.; Austrian electrical engineer; b. 2 March 1929, Graz/Goesting; s. of late Eduard Paschke and Stefanie Mittellehner; m. Gertrud P. Kutschera 1955; two d.; ed. Tech. Univs. of Graz and Vienna; Asst. Tech. Univ. Vienna 1953–55; consultant, New York 1955–56; mem. tech. staff, RCA David Sarnoff Research Center 1956–61; Components Div. Siemens AG, Munich 1961–66; Prof. of Gen. Electronics, Tech. Univ. Vienna 1965–, Dean, School of Electrical Eng. 1970–71, Rector/Pro-Rector 1971–76, Head, Inst. für Allgemeine Elektrotechnik und Elektronik 1980–; Vice-Pres. Austrian Nat. Science Foundation 1974–82; Ludwig Boltzmann Award 1977, Cardinal Innitzer Award 1984, Erwin Schrödinger Award (Austrian Acad.) 1988, Award of City of Vienna for Science and Tech. 1988 etc.; Dr. h.c. (Budapest) 1974. *Publications:* articles in professional journals. *Leisure interests:* art, hiking, swimming. *Address:* Technical University of Vienna, Karlsplatz 13, 1040 Vienna, Austria. *Telephone:* 0222-58801-3836.

PASCHKE, Karl Theodor; German diplomatist; b. 12 Nov. 1935, Berlin; s. of Adolf Paschke and Adele Cornill; m. Pia-Irene Schwerber 1963; one s. one d.; ed. Univs. of Munich and Bonn; Consul, New Orleans, La., U.S.A. 1964–68; Deputy Chief of Mission, Kinshasa 1968–71; Dean, Foreign Office Training School, Bonn 1972–77; Press Counsellor, Washington, D.C. 1977–80; Spokesman, German Foreign Office, Bonn 1980–84; Amb. to UN Orgs. Vienna 1984–86; Minister, Washington, D.C. 1987–90; Dir.-Gen. for Personnel & Man. German Foreign Office, Bonn 1990–94; Under-Sec.-Gen. for Internal Oversight Services, UN, New York 1994–. *Publication:* Reform der Attache-Ausbildung 1975. *Leisure interest:* music, especially jazz. *Address:* Under-Secretary-General for Internal Oversight Services, United Nations, Room S-3327-A, New York, NY 10017, U.S.A. *Telephone:* (212) 963-6196. *Fax:* (212) 963-7010.

PASCO, Richard Edward, C.B.E.; British actor; b. 18 July 1926, Barnes; s. of Cecil George Pasco and Phyllis (née Widdison) Pasco; m. 1st Greta Watson 1956 (dissolved 1964); one s.; m. 2nd Barbara Leigh-Hunt 1967; ed. Colet Court and King's Coll. School, Wimbledon, Cen. School of Speech and Drama; first appearance on stage, Q Theatre 1943; served in H.M. forces 1944–48; Old Vic Co. 1950–52; Birmingham Repertory Co. 1952–55; Hon. Assoc. Artist, Royal Shakespeare Co.; played Fortinbras in Hamlet (Moscow and London) 1955; English Stage Co. 1957, played in The Member of the Wedding, Look Back in Anger, The Entertainer, Man from Bellac and The Chairs. *Roles include:* The Entertainer (New York) 1958, Moscow Youth Festival in Look Back in Anger 1959, Teresa of Avila (Dublin Theatre Festival and Vaudeville) 1961, Henry V, Love's Labour's Lost (Bristol Old Vic, Old Vic and tour to Europe) 1964; Hamlet, Bristol Old Vic, 1965, Measure for Measure, Peer Gynt, Man and Superman, Hamlet 1966; toured U.S.A. and Europe 1967; joined R.S.C. 1969; *roles include:* Polixenes in The Winter's Tale, Proteus in The Two Gentlemen of Verona, Buckingham in Henry VIII 1969, Major Barbara, Richard II, Duchess of Malfi 1971, Becket in Murder in the Catherdral, Medraut in the Island of the Mighty 1972, Richard and Bolingbroke in Richard II 1973–74; The Marrying of Ann Leete 1975, Jack Tanner in Man and Superman 1977, Trigorin in The Seagull 1978, Timon in Timon of Athens 1980, Clarence in Richard III 1980, in The Forest 1981, La Ronde 1982, joined Nat. Theatre 1987: *roles:* Father in Six Characters in Search of an Author 1987, Pavel in Fathers and Sons 1987, Charlie Southwark in Racing Demon, Sir Peter Edgcombe in Murmuring Judges, Mr. Birling in An Inspector Calls, Malcolm Pryce in Absence of War, Boss Findley in Sweet Bird of Youth 1994; tours with R.S.C. to Japan, Australia 1970, Japan 1972; Hon. Assoc. Artist of R.S.C. 1972; has made broadcasts and recordings of plays and verse, including complete sonnets of Shakespeare. *TV appearances include:* Henry Irving, The Three Musketeers, Savages, As You Like It, Julius Caesar, British in Love, Trouble with Gregory, Philby, The House Boy, Number 10—Disraeli, The Plot to Murder Lloyd George, Let's Run Away to Africa, Sorrell and Son, Drummonds, etc. *Films include:* Room at the Top, Yesterday's Enemy, The Gorgon, Rasputin, Watcher in the Woods, Wagner, Arch of Triumph, Inspector Morse, etc. *Publications:* Time and Concord: Aldeburgh Festival Recollections (contrib.) 1997, Acting in Stratford (contrib.) 1997. *Leisure interests:* music, gardening, preservation of rural England. *Address:* c/o Michael Whitehall Ltd., 125 Gloucester Road, London, SW7 4TE, England.

PASCUAL, Ramon, D.SC.; Spanish professor of physics; b. 4 Feb. 1942, Barcelona; s. of Josep Montserrat; m. Maria Lluisa Roca 1966; two s. one d.; Junta de Energía Nuclear, Madrid 1963–64; Teaching Asst. Univ. of Valencia 1964–67; Asst. Prof. of Quantum Mechanics, Univ. Complutense de Madrid 1967–70; Prof. of Mathematical Physics, Univ. of Zaragoza Jan.–Sept. 1970; Prof. Univ. Autónoma de Madrid 1970–71; Prof. of Theoretical Physics, Univ. Autónoma de Barcelona 1971–, Dean, Faculty of Science 1976–79, Vice-Rector for Academic Affairs 1979–80, Rector 1986–90; Visiting Scientist, CERN, Geneva, 1969, 1970, 1977, 1978, 1981, 1983, 1986, Faculty of Science, Paris (Orsay) 1972, 1975, Rutherford Appleton Lab. Oxford 1975; other professional appts.; mem. Real Sociedad Española de Física y Química, European Physical Soc., Real Acad. Ciencias y Artes de Barcelona. *Publications:* over 40 articles in scientific journals etc. *Address:* Universidad Autónoma de Barcelona, Edificio C, 08193 Bellaterra, Barcelona, Spain. *Telephone:* (3) 518-1307.

PASHIN, Valentin Mikhailovich; Russian engineer; b. 25 July 1937, m.; two c.; ed. Leningrad Inst. of Vessel Construction; on staff St. Petersburg Krylov Research Inst. 1960–, Dir. 1990–; corresp. mem. Russian Acad. of Sciences 1991, mem. 1997–; main research in theoretical fundamentals of modern methods of optimization of vessels by computation; Hero of Russian Fed. 1994, U.S.S.R. State Prize 1985. *Address:* Central A.N. Krylov Research Institute, Moskovskoye shosse 44, 199034 St. Petersburg, Russia. *Telephone:* (812) 291 9623 (Office); (812) 268 7590 (Home).

PASINETTI, Luigi Lodovico, M.A., PH.D.; Italian professor of economics; b. 12 Sept. 1930, Bergamo; s. of Giovanni Pasinetti and Romilda Arzuffi; m. Carmela Colombo 1966; one s.; ed. Univ. Cattolica del Sacro Cuore, Milan, Univ. of Cambridge, Harvard Univ.; Research Fellow, Nuffield Coll., Oxford 1960–61; Fellow and Lecturer in Econs., King's Coll., Cambridge 1961–73; Lecturer, then Reader in Econs., Univ. of Cambridge 1961–76; Prof. Faculty of Econs., Univ. Cattolica del Sacro Cuore 1976–, Chair. 1980–83; Wesley Clair Mitchell Visiting Research Prof. of Econs., Columbia Univ., New York 1971, 1975; Visiting Research Prof., Indian Statistical Inst., Calcutta and New Delhi 1979; Visiting Prof. of Econs., Univ. of Ottawa, Carleton Univ. 1981, Kyoto Univ. 1984, Univ. of Southern Calif. 1985; Visiting Fellow, Gonville and Caius Coll., Cambridge 1989; McDonnell Distinguished Scholars Fellow, WIDER, the UN Univ., Helsinki 1992; Visiting Prof. Univ. of Sydney 1993; Visiting Fellow Trinity Coll. Cambridge 1997; mem. Council and Exec. Cttee. Int. Econ. Asscn. 1980–; Pres. Italian Econ. Asscn. 1986–89, mem. of Council 1989–; Pres. Confed. European Econ. Asscns. 1992–93; Pres. European Soc. for the History of Econ. Thought 1995–97; Fellow Econometric Soc. 1978–; mem. Accademia Lincei, Rome 1986–; Dr. h.c. (Fribourg) 1986; St. Vincent Prize for Econs. 1979, Invernizzi Prize for Econs. 1997; Gold Medal (First Class) for Educ., Culture and Arts 1982. *Publications:* Growth and Income Distribution 1974, Lectures on the Theory of Production 1977, Structural Change and Economic Growth 1981, Structural Change and Adjustment in the World Economy (with P. Lloyd) 1987, Structural Economic Dynamics 1993, Economic Growth and the Structure of Long-Term Development (with R. M. Solow) 1994; numerous articles on income distribution, capital theory and economic growth. *Leisure interests:* tennis, climbing, music. *Address:* c/o Faculty of Economics, Università Cattolica del Sacro Cuore, Largo A. Gemelli 1, 20123 Milan, Italy. *Telephone:* (02) 72342470. *Fax:* (02) 72342406.

PASKAI, H.E. Cardinal László; Hungarian ecclesiastic; b. 8 May 1927, Szeged; ed. high-school, Szeged; joined Franciscan Order, professed his vows 1949; assumed diocesan service 1950; ordained priest 1951; Episcopal liturgist 1952–55, Szeged; Prof. of Philosophy, Theological Acad., Szeged 1955–65, simultaneously Apostolic Prefect 1955–62, Spiritual 1962–65; Spiritual Prefect, Central Seminary of Budapest 1965–69; commissioned lecturer 1965–67, leading Prof. of Philosophy, Theological Academy, Budapest 1967–78; Rector of Seminary 1973–78; appointed titular Bishop of Bavagaliana and Apostolic Gov. of Veszprém 1978; Diocesan Bishop of Veszprém 1979, coadjutor with right of succession to Archbishop of Kalocsa 1982; Archbishop of Esztergom (now Esztergom-Budapest) and Primate of Hungary 1987–; created Cardinal 1988; Chair. Hungarian Catholic Bench of Bishops 1986–90. *Address:* Úri u. 62, 1014 Budapest, Hungary. *Telephone:* (1) 202-5611. *Fax:* (1) 202-5458.

PASQUA, Charles Victor; French politician; b. 18 April 1927, Grasse; s. of André Pasqua and Françoise Rinaldi; m. Jeanne Joly 1947; one s.; ed. College de Grasse, Inst. d'Etudes Juridiques, Nice and Faculté de Droit, Aix-en-Provence; Rep. Société Ricard 1952, Insp. 1955, Regional Dir. 1960, Dir. French Sales 1962, Dir.-Gen. French Sales and Export 1963; Pres.-Dir.-Gen. Société Euralim 1967–71; Commercial Consultant 1972–; Deputy to Nat. Ass. (UDR) 1968–73; Sec.-Gen. UDR 1974–76; Senator, Hauts de Seine 1977–86, 1988–93, 1995–; Pres. RPR Group in Senate 1981–86, 1988–93; Minister of the Interior and Administration 1986–88, 1993–95; Political adviser Exec. Comm. of RPR 1998–; Chevalier, Légion d'honneur; Médaille de la France libre. *Publications:* La libre entreprise — un état d'esprit 1964, L'ardeur nouvelle 1985, Que demande le peuple 1992, Demain, la France (Vol. I): La Priorité Sociale (jtly.) 1992. *Address:* Sénat, 75291 Paris; Conseil Général, Hôtel du Département, 2-16 Blvd Soufflot, 92015 Nanterre Cedex, France.

PASQUAL, Lluís; Spanish theatre and opera director; b. 5 June 1951; founder and Dir. Lliure Theatre, Barcelona 1976; worked in Poland; became asst. to Giorgio Strehler, Italy 1978; apptd. Dir. Centro Dramatico Nacional, Teatro Maria Guerrero, Madrid 1983; Dir. Odéon, Théâtre de l'Europe, Paris 1990–; Teacher Inst. Teatral de Barcelona; numerous prizes; Officier des Arts et des Lettres, France. *Plays directed include:* Luces de Bohemia (Valle Inclan) 1984, Sans Titre (Lorca) 1990, Le Balcon (Genet) 1991, Tirano Banderas (Valle Inclan) 1992; Le Chevalier d'Olmédo (Lope de Vega) 1992, El Publico (Lorca) 1986. *Operas directed include:* (Teatro de la Zarzuela, Madrid); Samson et Dalila (Saint-Saëns) 1982, Falstaff (Verdi) 1983, Don Carlo (Verdi) 1985, Il Trittico (Puccini) 1987, Il Turco in Italia (Rossini) 1990; La Vera Storia (Berio), Paris 1985, Maggio Musicale, Florence 1986, Falstaff, Bologna 1987. *Address:* c/o Théâtre National de l'Odéon, 1 place Paul Claudel, 75006 Paris, France. *Telephone:* 43.25.80.92. *Fax:* 40.46.95.31.

PASQUINI, Pierre Emile Joseph, L. EN. D., L. ÈS L.; French politician and lawyer; b. 16 Feb. 1921, Sétif, Algeria; s. of Aimé Pasquini and Clotilde Tabet; one s. one d.; ed. Lycée Louis-le-Grand, Paris, Facultés de Droit et des Lettres, Algiers; Admin. Overseas Territories 1945; lawyer, Bar of Nice 1946–; Deputy Mayor of Nice 1947–65; Deputy (UNR) to Nat. Ass. 1958–67; RPR Deputy to Nat. Ass. 1978–81, 1986, 1988–95; Vice-Pres. Nat. Ass. 1962–65, 1978–79; Minister of War Veterans and Victims of War May–Nov. 1995; Deputy Minister (with responsibility for Veterans and War Victims) 1995–97; Commdr. Légion d'honneur, Commdr. Ordre Nat. du Mérite, Croix de Guerre. *Publications:* Virginie, Le Guérisseur (comedies); Elle a parlé (book); Vol nuptial (ballet); L'Ane de Zigliara (screenplay). *Address:* 40 rue Pastorelli, 06000 Nice; Mairie, 20220 L'Ile-Rousse, France. *Telephone:* 93-85-98-60. *Fax:* 93-62-56-64.

PASSACANTANDO, Franco, D.ECON.; Italian economist; b. 7 Aug. 1947, Rome; m. Miriam Veronesi 1987; three s. one d.; ed. Rome and Stanford Univs.; Head Money Market Div., Research Dept., Bank of Italy 1981–85, Task Force on the Reform of the Italian Payment System 1986–89, Dir. Monetary and Financial Sector, Research Dept. 1990–95; mem. Group of Experts in Banking, Financial Markets Cttee. OECD 1979–86, Group of Monetary Experts 1991; mem. Group of Experts on Payment Systems BIS 1980–90, Working Party on Multilateral Netting Obligations, Cttee. on Interbank Netting Schemes 1990, Eurocurrency Standing Cttee. 1991–92; Exec. Dir. World Bank 1995–, Chair. Budget Cttee.; Fulbright, Einaudi and Stringher fellowships. *Leisure interests:* making movies, art. *Publications:* White Paper on the Payment System in Italy 1988, Le Banche e il Finanziamento delle Imprese 1997 and articles on monetary policy in professional journals. *Address:* The World Bank, 1818 H Street, N.W., Washington, D.C. 20433 (Office); 3503 Shepherd Street, Chevy Chase, MD 20815, U.S.A. (Home). *Telephone:* (202) 458-1169 (Office); (301) 718-8144 (Home).

PASSMORE, John Arthur, A.C., M.A., F.A.H.A., F.A.S.S.A.; Australian professor of philosophy; b. 9 Sept. 1914, Manly; s. of F. M. Passmore and Ruby Moule; m. Annie D. Sumner 1936; two d.; ed. Sydney Boys' High School and Sydney Univ.; Tutor, Lecturer and Sr. Lecturer in Philosophy, Sydney Univ. 1935–49; Prof. of Philosophy, Otago Univ., Dunedin, N.Z. 1950–54; Reader in Philosophy, Inst. of Advanced Studies, A.N.U. 1955–58, Prof. 1959–79, now Prof. Emer.; Univ. Fellow, History of Ideas, A.N.U. 1981–82, Visiting Fellow in History of Ideas 1983–93, Visiting Fellow in Historical Studies 1995–; Visiting Distinguished Prof. in Russell Studies and Gen. Ed. Russell Project, McMaster Univ., Canada 1984–90, Gen. Ed. 1991; Visiting Prof. Brandeis Univ. 1960; Visiting Fellow, All Souls, Oxford 1970, 1978, Clare Hall, Cambridge 1973; Pres. Australian Acad. of Humanities 1974–77; Corresp. Fellow, British Acad.; Foreign Fellow, American Acad. of Arts and Sciences, Royal Danish Acad. of Arts and Letters; Hon. D.Litt. (Sydney, McMaster, Wollongong). *Publications:* Ralph Cudworth 1951, Hume's Intentions 1952, A Hundred Years of Philosophy 1957, Philosophical Reasoning 1961, The Perfectibility of Man 1970, Man's Responsibility for Nature 1974, Science and its Critics 1978, The Philosophy of Teaching 1980, The Limits of Government 1981, Recent Philosophers 1985, Serious Art 1991, Memoirs of a Semi-detached Australian 1997. *Leisure interests:* theatre, film, travel, walking. *Address:* c/o Historical Studies, RSSS, Australian National University, 0200 Canberra, A.C.T.; 6 Jansz Crescent, Manuka, A.C.T. 2603, Australia. *Telephone:* (02) 62957745. *Fax:* (02) 62493969.

PASTINEN, Ilkka Olavi, M.POL.SC.; Finnish diplomatist; b. 17 March 1928, Turku; s. of Martti Mikael and Ilmi Saga Karlström Pastinen; m. Eeva Marja Viitanen 1950; two d.; ed. Åbo (Turku) Akad., Inst. d'Etudes Politiques, Paris, Inst. Int. des Sciences et Recherches Diplomatiques; entered Foreign Service 1952; served Stockholm 1955–57, Mission to UN 1957–59; Deputy Chief of Mission, Beijing 1962–64; Deputy Chief of Mission, London 1966–69; Amb., Deputy Perm. Rep. to UN and Deputy Rep. to Security Council 1969–70; Asst. Sec.-Gen. UN and Special Rep. of Sec.-Gen. of UN to Cttee. for Disarmament 1971–75; Amb., Perm. Rep. to UN 1977–82; Amb. to U.K. 1983–91. *Publication:* Excellency from Upstairs (memoirs) 1994, A Diva and a Diplomat (memoirs) 1996. *Leisure interests:* golf, music, bridge. *Address:* Maneesikatu 1-3B, Helsinki, Finland.

PASTOR DE LA TORRE, Celso, LL.B.; Peruvian diplomatist; b. 20 Dec. 1914; m. (wife deceased); four c.; ed. Bogotá, Berlin, Catholic Univ. of Peru; Amb. to U.S.A. and Rep. to IBRD and IMF 1963–68; Perm. Rep. to UN 1983–84; Consultant to various int. cos., Chair. Int. Insurance Co. –1983; f. and fmr. Sec.-Gen. of Acción Popular Party 1956; promoter of numerous exhbns. of Peruvian Culture in U.S.A. *Publications:* Escuela Pictórica del Cuzco. *Address:* c/o Ministerio des Asuntos Exteriores, Lima, Peru.

PASTRANA-ARANGO, Andrés, LL.D.; Colombian politician; b. 17 Aug. 1954, Bogotá; s. of Misael Pastrana-Borrero (fmr. Pres. of Colombia) and María Cristina Arango de Pastrana; m. Nohra Puyana Bickenbach; one s. two d.; ed. Colegio San Carlos de Bogotá, Colegio Mayor de Nuestra Señora del Rosario Law School, Harvard Univ.; Man. Dir. Revista Guión (publ.) 1978–79; Man. Dir. Datos y Mensajes S.A. News Broadcasting Co. 1979–80; Dir. TV Hoy News 1980–87; Councillor Bogotá City Council 1982–86, Chair. Jan.–April 1983, 1984–85; Mayor of Bogotá 1988–90; Senator 1991–93; founder and Presidential Cand. of Nueva Fuerza Democrática 1994; Pres. of Colombia Aug. 1998–; mem. Int. Union of Local Authorities (IULA), Exec. Cttee. 1989, Pres. Latin American Chapter 1988–89; Vice-Pres. Latin American Union of Capital Cities; Co-Dir. World Mayors' Conf. on Drug Addiction, New York 1989, Madrid 1990; Sec. Gen. Union of Latin American Parties 1992–; Adviser to UN Univ., Tokyo 1994; Dir. and f. UN Leadership Acad., Jordan; fmr. Chair. Bogotá Telephone Co., Bogotá Aqueduct and

Sewerage Co., Electricity and Public Utilities Co. of Bogotá, Inst. for Urban Devt., Dist. Planning; Colombian Jr. Chamber Exec. of the Year 1981, King of Spain Int. Journalism Award 1985, Simón Bolivar Nat. Journalism Award 1987, King of Spain Nat. Journalism Award 1987, Bogotá Circle of Journalists Nat. Award 1987, Nat. Police Distinguished Service Order, UNESCO Order, Grand Cross, Civilian Order of Merit 1988, Order of Merit, Colombian Publishing Industry 1988, Civilian Defence Order 1989, Order of Santa Barbara, Colombian Navy 1990, José María Córdova Order of Mil. Merit 1990. *Publication:* Hacia la formulación de un derecho ecológico (Towards the formulation of an ecological law). *Address:* Oficina del Presidente, Carrera 8 No 7-26, Bogotá, Colombia.

PASTUKHOV, Boris Nikolayevich; Russian politician; b. 10 Oct. 1933, Moscow; m. Janna Pastukhova; two d.; ed. Bauman Higher Tech. Coll., Moscow; mem. CPSU 1959–91; First Sec. Bauman Regional Komsomol Cttee., Moscow 1959–61; Second Sec. Moscow City Komsomol Cttee. 1961–62, First Sec. 1962–64; Second Sec. All-Union Komsomol Cttee. 1964–77, First Sec. 1977–82; Chair. U.S.S.R. State Cttee. for Publishing, Printing and Bookselling, U.S.S.R. Goskomizdat 1982–86; mem. Presidium, Supreme Soviet of the U.S.S.R. 1978–83; U.S.S.R. Amb. to Denmark 1986–89, to Afghanistan 1989–92; Deputy Foreign Minister of Russia 1989–96; First Deputy Foreign Minister 1996–98; mediator in negotiations between Georgia and Abkhazia; Minister for C.I.S. Affairs 1998–. *Address:* Ministry of C.I.S. Affairs, Nikolski per., Moscow, Russia. *Telephone:* (095) 206-72-71.

PASUGSWAD, Suwan, M.A.; Thai international civil servant; b. 19 March 1937, Songkhla; s. of Dam Pasugswad and Kate Pasugswad; m. 1973; two d.; ed. Univ. of Bangkok and Queen's Univ. Ont., Canada; Asst. to Exec. Dir. IBRD and affiliates 1975–78; Alt. Exec. Dir. Asian Devt. Bank, Manila 1985–87, Exec. Dir. 1987–89; Deputy Dir.-Gen. Fiscal Policy Office, Ministry of Finance 1992–94; Exec. Dir. IBRD and affiliates 1994–97. *Leisure interests:* swimming, gardening. *Address:* 123/4 Soi Bangkrabue, Samsen Road, Dusit, Bangkok, Thailand. *Telephone:* (662) 243-8751. *Fax:* (662) 273-9167/9168.

PATAKI, George, B.A.; American politician and lawyer; b. 24 June 1945, Peekskill, N.Y.; m. Elizabeth Rowland; two s. two d.; ed. Yale Univ.; Assoc. Dewey Ballantine PC (law firm), New York 1970–74; partner, Plunkett & Jaffee PC (law firm), White Plains and New York; co-owner, Pataki's Farm, Peekskill, N.Y.; Mayor of Peekskill 1982–84; fmr. mem. New York State Ass.; mem. New York State Senate 1993–95; Gov. of New York 1996–; Republican. *Address:* State Capitol, Office of the Governor, Albany, New York, NY 12224, U.S.A.

PATASSE, Ange-Félix; Central African Republic politician; b. 25 Jan. 1937; ed. French Equatorial Coll.; Agricultural inspector 1959–65; Dir. of Agric. 1965; Minister of Devt. 1965; Minister of State for Transport and Power 1969–70, concurrently Minister of State for Devt. and Tourism 1969–70; Minister of State for Agric., Stock-breeding, Waters and Forests, Hunting, Tourism, Transport and Power Feb.-June 1970; Minister of State for Devt. June-Aug. 1970; Minister of State for Transport and Commerce 1970–72, for Rural Devt. 1972–73, of Health and Social Affairs 1973–74; Minister of State for Tourism, Waters, Fishing and Hunting 1974–76, Prime Minister 1976–78, also Keeper of the Seals Sept.-Dec. 1976; Vice-Pres. Council of the Cen. African Revolution Sept.-Dec. 1976; Leader Mouvement pour la libération du peuple centrafricain; under house arrest Oct. 1979, escaped, recaptured and detained Nov. 1979; Cand. in Pres. Election March 1981; took refuge in French Embassy March 1982, fled to Togo April 1982; lived in France, returned to C.A.R.; elected Pres. of Cen. African Repub. Oct. 1993–. *Address:* Office of the President, Palais de la Renaissance, Bangui, Central African Republic.

PATE, John Stewart, PH.D., F.A.A., F.R.S.; British professor of botany; b. 15 Jan. 1932; s. of H. S. Pate and M. M. Pate; m. Elizabeth L. Sloan 1959; three s.; ed. Campbell Coll. Belfast and Queen's Univ. Belfast; lecturer in Botany, Univ. of Sydney 1957–60; lecturer in Botany, Queen's Univ. Belfast 1960–65, then Reader, Personal Chair. in Plant Physiology 1970–83; Prof. of Botany, Univ. of W. Australia 1974–. *Publications:* Restionoceae of Allied Families of Australia 1998 (co.Ed.), books, research articles, reviews, chapters for textbooks and conf. proceedings. *Leisure interests:* music, reading, nature study, committed Christian. *Address:* 83 Circe Circle, Dalkeith, W.A. 6009, Australia. *Telephone:* (9) 3866070.

PATEL, A. K., M.B.; Indian politician and medical practitioner; b. 1 July 1931, Vadu, Mehsana Dist., Gujarat; s. of Kalidas Patel; m.; two s. one d.; ed. B.J. Medical Coll., Ahmedabad; mem. Gujarat Legis. Ass. - 1984; mem. for Mehsana, Lok Sabha 1984–, Minister of State for Chemicals and Fertilizers; Pres. Bharatiya Janata Party, Gujarat 1982–85; Man. Trustee S.R.S.T. Gen. Hosp., Vijapur, Asha Educ. Trust, Girls' Coll., Vijapur; Trustee St. Joseph Public School, Vijapur. *Leisure interests:* reading, swimming, riding, sports. *Address:* Ministry of Chemicals and Fertilizers, Shastri Bhavan, New Delhi 110 001, India. *Telephone:* (011) 3383695. *Fax:* (011) 3386222.

PATEL, Indraprasad Gordhanbhai, PH.D.; Indian economist; b. 11 Nov. 1924, Baroda; s. of Gordhanbhai Patel and Kashiben Patel; m. Alaknanda Dasgupta 1958; one d.; ed. Baroda Coll., Bombay Univ., King's Coll., Cambridge and Harvard Univ.; Prof. of Econs. and Principal Baroda Coll., Maharaja Sayajirao Univ., Baroda 1949–50; Economist and Asst. Chief, Financial Problems and Policies Div., IMF 1950–54; Deputy Econ. Adviser, Indian Ministry of Finance 1954–58; Alt. Exec. Dir. for India, IMF 1958–61; Chief Econ. Adviser, Ministry of Finance, India 1961–63, 1965–67, Econ. Adviser Planning Comm. 1961–63; Special Sec. Ministry of Finance 1968–69, Sec. 1970–72; Deputy Admin., UN Devt. Programme 1972–77; Gov. Reserve Bank of India 1977–82; Dir. Indian Inst. of Man., Ahmedabad, India 1982–84; Dir. L.S.E. 1984–90; mem. Comm. on Global Governance; Chair. Aga Khan Rural Support Programme, Indian Inst. of Man. 1996–, Ahmedabad and Indian Council for Research on Int. Econ. Relations, Delhi 1997–; Trustee Int. Food Policy Research Inst., Washington, D.C.; Visiting Prof., Delhi School of Econs., Delhi Univ. 1964; Hon. Fellow King's Coll., Cambridge 1986, L.S.E. 1990; Hon. D.Litt. (Sardar Patel Univ.) 1980, (M.S. Univ. of Baroda) 1993; Hon. Dr. Civil Laws (Univ. of Mauritius) 1990; Hon. K.B.E. 1990; Padmavibhushan 1990. *Publications:* On the Economics of Development 1986, Essays in Economic Policy and Economic Growth 1986, Economic Reform and Global Change 1998 and articles on inflation and econ. devt., monetary and credit policy, etc. *Leisure interests:* reading, music. *Address:* 12 Amee Co-operative Housing Society, Diwali Pura, Old Padra Road, Vadodara 390015, India. *Telephone:* (0265) 339026. *Fax:* (0265) 333658.

PATEL, Jayadevappa Halappa, B.A., LL.B.; Indian politician; b. 1 Oct. 1930, Kariganur; s. of Halappa Patel and Mahadevamma Patel; m.; three s.; ed. Mysore and Belgaum Univs.; elected to Lok Sabha from Shimmoga Constituency 1967, to Karnataka Legis. Ass. from Channagiri Constituency 1978, 1983; served as cabinet minister 1983, resgd. 1984, re-elected 1985; co-founder Janata Dal Party 1989, later Pres.; Deputy Chief Minister of Karnataka, Minister of Power and of Tourism 1994–96, Chief Minister of Karnataka 1996–. *Address:* No. 1, Cauvery, High Grounds, Bangalore, 560 001 Karnataka, India. *Telephone:* (0) 2258928; 2251449. *Fax:* (0) 2253414; 2254424.

PATEL, Jeram, F.R.S.A.; Indian painter and graphic designer; b. 20 June 1930; ed. Sir J. J. School of Art, Bombay, Central School of Arts and Crafts, London; Reader in Applied Arts, M.S. Univ., Baroda (now Vadodara) 1960–61, 1966–76, Prof. 1976; Reader in Visual Design, School of Architecture, Ahmedabad 1961–62; Deputy Dir. All India Handloom Bd. 1963–66; mem. Group 1890 (avant-garde group of Indian artists), Lalit Kala Akademi; one-man exhbns. in London 1959, New Delhi 1960, 1962–65, in Calcutta 1966; in Tokyo Biennale 1957–63, São Paulo Biennale 1963; represented in Nat. Gallery of Modern Art, New Delhi, Art Soc. of India, Bombay, Sir J. J. Inst. of Applied Art, Bombay, and in private collections in U.S.A., London, Paris and Tokyo; Lalit Kala Akademi Nat. Awards 1957, 1964; Bombay State Award 1957; Silver Medal, Bombay Art Soc. 1961; Gold Medal Rajkot Exhbn. *Address:* Faculty of Fine Arts, M.S. University, Vadodara 2, India.

PATEL, Sir Praful Raojibhai Chaturbhai, Kt.; British race relations adviser and company director; b. 7 March 1939, Jinja, Uganda; s. of Raojibhai Chaturbhai Patel and Maniben Jivabhai Lalaji Patel; ed. Govt. Secondary School and London Inst. of World Affairs (Extra-Mural Dept., Univ. Coll., London); Sec. Uganda Students' Union 1956–58; del. to Int. Youth Assembly, New Delhi 1958; studied and lectured on politics and econs. in Africa and Middle East before arrival in Britain as student 1958, where developed commercial activities 1962; spokesman for Asians in U.K. following Commonwealth Immigrants Act 1968; Hon. Sec. All Party Parl. Cttee. on U.K. Citizenship 1968–; mem. Council, U.K. Immigrants Advisory Service 1970–; mem. Uganda Resettlement Bd. 1972–74, Hon. Sec. Uganda Evacuees Resettlement Advisory Trust 1974–; Pres. Nava Kala India Socio-Cultural Centre, London 1962–75; Chair. Bd. of Trustees, Swaminarayan Hindu Mission, U.K. 1970–76; Jt. Convenor, Asian Action Cttee. 1976; Convener Manava Trust 1979–; frequent appearances on radio and television programmes concerned with immigration and race relations. *Publications:* many articles in newspapers and journals on race relations and immigration. *Leisure interests:* cricket, campaigning and lobbying, current affairs, interfaith co-operation. *Address:* 60 Bedford Court Mansions, Bedford Avenue, London, WC1B 3AD, England; Taj Mahal Hotel, Apollo Bunder, Bombay, 400001 India. *Telephone:* 0171-580 0897 (London). *Fax:* 22 2872711 (India).

PATEMAN, John Arthur, F.R.S., F.R.S.E., F.R.S.A.; Australian geneticist; b. 18 May 1926, London, England; s. of John Pateman and Isobel May (née Kirk) Pateman; m. Mary D. F. Phelps 1952; one s. two d.; ed. Clacton County High School, Univ. Coll., Leicester; Lecturer in Genetics, Univ. of Sheffield 1954–57; Sr. Lecturer in Botany, Univ. of Melbourne 1957–60; Lecturer in Genetics, Cambridge Univ., Fellow, Churchill Coll. 1960-67; Prof. of Biology, Flinders Univ., S. Australia 1967–70; Prof. of Genetics, Univ. of Glasgow 1970–79; Prof. and Head, Dept. of Genetics, A.N.U. 1979–88, Prof. Emer.; Exec. Dir., Centre for Recombinant DNA Research 1982–88. *Publications:* numerous articles in scientific journals. *Leisure interests:* reading, music, walking.

PATERSON, Sir Dennis Craig, Kt., B.S., M.D., F.R.C.S., F.R.A.C.S.; Australian orthopaedic surgeon; b. 14 Oct. 1930, Adelaide; s. of Gilbert Charles Paterson and Thelma Drysdale Paterson; m. Mary Mansell Hardy 1955; one s. three d.; ed. Collegiate School of St. Peter, Adelaide, Univ. of Adelaide; Resident Medical Officer, Royal Adelaide Hosp. 1954, Adelaide Children's Hosp. 1956; Registrar, Robert Jones and Agnes Hunt Orthopaedic Hosp., Oswestry, Shropshire, England 1958–60; Sr. Registrar, Royal Adelaide Hosp. 1960–62; Consultant Orthopaedic Surgeon, Repatriation Gen. Hosp., Adelaide 1962–70; Asst. Hon. Orthopaedic Surgeon, Adelaide Children's Hosp. 1964–66, Sr. Hon. Orthopaedic Surgeon 1966–70, Dir. and Chief Orthopaedic Surgeon 1970–95, mem. Bd. of Man., Chair. Medical Advisory Cttee., Medical

Staff Cttee. 1976–84; Sr. Hon. Orthopaedic Surgeon, Queen Victoria and Modbury Hosps., Adelaide 1970; Sr. Visiting Consultant Orthopaedic Surgeon, Royal Adelaide Hosp.; Clinical Assoc. Prof. Orthopaedic Surgery Univ. of Adelaide 1990–; mem. Bd. of Orthopaedic Surgery, R.A.C.S. 1974–82, 1984–87, Chair. 1977–82, mem. Court of Examiners 1974–84; Censor-in-Chief, Australian Orthopaedic Asscn. 1976–80, Dir. Continuing Educ. 1982–86; Pres. Crippled Children's Asscn. of S. Australia 1970–84; Pres. Int. Soc. of Orthopaedic Surgery and Traumatology (SICOT) 1987–90; Chair. S. Australia Road Safety Consultative Council 1994–, Trauma Systems Cttee. of S. Australia 1994–; mem. Bd. Man. McLaren Vale and Fleurian Visitor Centre 1995–; Queen's Jubilee Medal 1977; L.O. Betts Medal in Orthopaedic Surgery 1980. *Publications:* Electrical Stimulation and Osteogenesis (Thesis) 1982; over 60 articles in scientific journals. *Leisure interests:* golf, tennis, gardening. *Address:* 31 Myall Avenue, Kensington Gardens, South Australia 5068, Australia (Home). *Telephone:* (08) 267 7223 (Office); (08) 332 3364 (Home).

PATERSON, Rt. Rev. John Campbell, B.A., L.TH.; New Zealand ecclesiastic; b. 4 Jan. 1945, Auckland; s. of Thomas Paterson and Mary Paterson; m. Marion Reid Anderson 1968; two d.; ed. King's Coll., Univ. of Auckland, St. John's Coll.; asst. curate Whangarei 1969–71; vicar Waimate N. Maori pastorate 1971–76; priest-in-charge Hokianga 1973–74, Bay of Islands 1974–75; chaplain Queen Victoria School 1976–82; asst. priest Maori Mission 1976–82; Sec. Bishopric of Aotearoa 1978–87; provincial sec. 1986–92; mem. Anglican Consultative Council 1990–96; Gen. Sec. of Anglican Church, Aotearoa, Polynesia and N.Z. 1992–95, Presiding Bishop and Primate 1998–; Bishop of Auckland 1995–. *Address:* Bishopscourt, P.O. Box 37242, Parnell, New Zealand. *Telephone:* (9) 302-7202. *Fax:* (9) 303-3321

PATERSON, Mervyn Silas, F.A.A., SC.D.; Australian geophysicist; b. 7 March 1925, South Australia; s. of Charles Paterson and Edith M. Michael; m. Katalin Sarosy 1952; one s. one d.; ed. Adelaide Technical High School, Univs. of Adelaide and Cambridge; research, Aeronautical Research Labs. Melbourne 1945–53; A.N.U., Canberra 1953–, Prof. Research School of Earth Sciences 1987–90, Visiting Fellow and Emer. Prof. 1990–; Dir. Paterson Instruments Pty. Ltd.; Fellow, American Mineralogical Soc., American Geophysical Union; Hon. Fellow, Geological Soc. of America. *Publications:* Experimental Rock Deformation: The Brittle Field 1978; about 100 research papers in rock deformation and materials science. *Leisure interests:* walking, reading. *Address:* Research School of Earth Sciences, Australian National University, Canberra 0200, Australia. *Telephone:* (02) 6249 2497 (Office). *Fax:* (02) 6249 0738.

PATHAK, Rahunandan Swarup, LL.B., M.A.; Indian judge; b. 25 Nov. 1924, Bareilly, Uttar Pradesh; s. of Gopal Swarup Pathak (fmr. Vice-Pres. of India) and Prakashwati Pathak; m. Asha Pathak; three s.; ed. Allahabad Univ.; enrolled as advocate, Allahabad High Court 1948, Supreme Court of India 1957; Additional Judge, Allahabad High Court 1962–63, Judge 1963–72; Chief Justice, Himachal Pradesh High Court 1972–78; Judge, Supreme Court of India 1978–86; Chief Justice of India 1986–89; Judge, Int. Court of Justice, The Hague 1989–91; Pro-Chancellor Univ. of Delhi 1986–89; Hon. Pres. World Peace Through Law Center, Washington, D.C.; Pres. Indian Law Inst. 1986–89, Indian Soc. of Int. Law, Int. Law Asscn. (Regional Branch) India 1986–89; Pres. Indian Council of Legal Aid and Advice, Indian Soc. of Int. Law 1989–; Pres. Commonwealth Games, Kuala Lumpur 1998; Vice-Pres. Olympic Games, Nagano 1998; mem. Indian Council of Arbitration 1991–, Int. Council for Arbitration of Sport 1994–; del. to numerous int. confs., cttees. etc.; Hon. Bencher, Gray's Inn, London; Hon. LL.D. (Agra and Punjab Univs.), Hon. D. Litt. (Kashi Vidhyapeeth, Varanasi). *Publications:* numerous lectures and research papers. *Address:* 6 Akbar Road, New Delhi, 110011, India. *Telephone:* 301-9224.

PATNAIK, Janaki Ballav, M.A.; Indian politician; b. 3 Jan. 1927, Rameswar, Puri District, Orissa; s. of Gokulanand and Rambha Devi; m. Jayanti Patnaik; one s. two d.; ed. Banaras Univ.; Sub-Ed. Eastern Times 1949, Jt. Ed. 1950, Ed. (also for Prajatantra) 1952–67; Ed. Paurusha; led tenants' agitation in Madhupur, Cuttack District 1953; mem. Sahitya Akademi, Orissa 1956–57, Lok Sabha 1971–77, 1980–; Minister of State for Defence, Govt. of India 1973–77; Minister of Tourism, Civil Aviation and Labour Jan.–Dec. 1980; Chief Minister of Orissa State 1980–89, 1995–98. *Address:* c/o Chief Minister's Secretariat, Bhubaneswar, India.

PATON, Boris Yevgeniyevich; Ukrainian metallurgist; b. 27 Nov. 1918, Kiev; s. of Evgeny Oskarovich Paton and Natalya Viktorovna Paton; m. Olga Borisovna Milovanova 1948; one d.; ed. Kiev Polytechnic Inst.; Dir. E. O. Paton Electric Welding Institute of Ukrainian S.S.R. (now Ukrainian) Acad. of Sciences 1953–; corresp. mem. Ukrainian S.S.R. (now Ukrainian) Acad. of Sciences 1951–58, mem. 1958–, Pres. 1962–; mem. U.S.S.R. (now Russian) Acad. of Sciences 1962, mem. Presidium 1963–; Pres. Engineering Acad. 1991–; Chair. of Co-ordination Council on Welding in U.S.S.R. (now Russian) 1958–; Chair. of Scientific Council of U.S.S.R. (now Russian) Acad. of Sciences "New processes of production and treatment of metallic materials" 1964–; Chair. of Co-ordination Bd. of CMEA on joint works in the field of welding 1972–; Chair. of U.S.S.R. (now Russian) Nat. Cttee. on Welding 1976–; mem. of editorial bd. and ed.-in-chief of a number of scientific and tech. journals; author of numerous books, articles and inventions; Honoured Scientist of Ukrainian S.S.R. 1968; Honoured Inventor of U.S.S.R. 1983; Foreign mem. of Acad. of Sciences of Bulgaria 1969, Czechoslovakia 1973, Bosnia and Herzegovina 1975, G.D.R. 1980, Royal Swedish Acad. of Engineering 1986; mem. CPSU 1952–91, cand. mem. Cen. Cttee. of CPSU 1961–1966, mem. 1966–91; mem. Central Cttee. of CP of Ukraine 1960–91; Deputy to U.S.S.R. Supreme Soviet 1962–89; Vice-Chair. Soviet of the Union U.S.S.R. Supreme Soviet 1966–89; Deputy to Ukrainian S.S.R. Supreme Soviet 1959–90, mem. of Pres. 1963–80; People's Deputy of the U.S.S.R. 1989–91; State Prize 1950, Lenin Prize 1957, numerous other awards. *Leisure interest:* tennis. *Address:* E. O. Paton Electric Welding Institute, 11 Bozhenko Street, Kiev-5, Ukraine. *Telephone:* (381 44) 227 31 83.

PATSATSIA, Otar; Georgian politician; b. 15 May 1929, Zugdidi; s. of Ambako Patsatsia and Luba Patsatsia; m. Nunu Gulua 1957; one s. one d.; ed. Leningrad Inst. of Tech.; engineer, Deputy Dir., Dir. Zugdidi Paper Factory 1955–65; elected First Sec. Zugdidi Regional CP Cttee. but removed for his refusal to follow orders of Cen. CPSU Admin.; Dir.-Gen. Gruzbumprom, Zugdidi 1966–92, on initiative of E. Shevarnadze appointed Head of Zugdidi Region Adm., controlled by adversaries of fmr. Pres. Gamsakhurdia 1992–93; Prime Minister of Georgia 1993–95; U.S.S.R. People's Deputy 1989–90; mem. Georgian Parl. 1995–; Hero of Socialist Labour. *Leisure interest:* hunting. *Address:* Parliament Building, Tbilisi, Georgia.

PATTAKOS, Stylianos; Greek politician; b. 8 Nov. 1912, Crete; s. of George and Maria Pattakos; m. Dimitra Nickolaidou 1940; two d.; ed. high school, cadet school, War Coll. and Nat. Defence Acad.; commissioned 1937, promoted Maj.-Gen. Dec. 1967, retd.; Minister of the Interior 1967–73, Deputy Premier Dec. 1967; First Deputy Premier 1971–73; arrested Oct. 1974, sentenced to death for high treason and insurrection Aug. 1975 (sentence commuted to life imprisonment).

PATTEN, Christopher, C.H., P.C.; British politician; b. 12 May 1944; m. Mary Lavender Thornton 1971; three d.; ed. St. Benedict's School, Ealing, Balliol Coll., Oxford; worked in Conservative Party Research Dept. 1966–70, Dir. 1974–79; seconded to Cabinet Office 1970; at Home Office, then personal asst. to Lord Carrington, Party Chair. 1972–74; M.P. for Bath 1979–92; Parl. Pvt. Sec. (PPS) to Leader of the House 1979–81, to Social Services Sec. 1981–83; Parl. Under-Sec. for Northern Ireland 1983–85; Minister of State for Educ. 1985–86; Overseas Devt. Minister 1986–89; Sec. of State for the Environment 1989–90; Chancellor of the Duchy of Lancaster and Chair. of the Conservative Party 1990–92; Gov. of Hong Kong 1992–97; Chair. Comm. charged with reform of Royal Ulster Constabulary 1998–; Dir. Independent Newspapers 1998–; Hon. F.R.C.P. (Edin.) 1994. *Publication:* East and West 1998. *Address:* c/o Coutts & Co., Campbells Office, 440 Strand, London, WC2R 0QS, England.

PATTERSON, Harry (pseudonym Jack Higgins), B.SC.(SOC.), F.R.S.A.; British/Irish novelist; b. 27 July 1929; s. of Henry Patterson and Rita Higgins Bell; m. 1st Amy Margaret Hewitt 1958 (divorced 1984), one s. three d.; m. 2nd Denise Leslie Ann Palmer 1985; ed. Roundhay School, Leeds, Beckett Park Coll. for Teachers, London School of Econs.; N.C.O., The Blues 1947–50, tried numerous jobs including clerk and circus tent hand 1950–58; schoolmaster, lecturer in liberal studies, Leeds Polytechnic, Sr. Lecturer in Educ., James Graham Coll. and Tutor in School Practice, Leeds Univ. 1958–72; full-time writer since age of 41; Hon. D.Univ. (Leeds Metropolitan Univ.) 1995. *Publications include:* (as Jack Higgins) Prayer for the Dying 1973 (filmed 1985), The Eagle has Landed 1975, Storm Warning 1976, Day of Judgement 1978, Solo 1980, Luciano's Luck 1981, Touch the Devil 1982, Exocet 1983, Confessional 1985 (filmed 1985), Night of the Fox 1986, A Season in Hell 1989, Memoirs of a Dancehall Romeo 1989, The Dark Side of the Island 1989, The Cold Harbour 1989, The Eagle Has Flown 1990, Thunder Point 1993, Angel of Death 1995, Year of the Tiger 1996, The President's Daughter 1996, Drink with the Devil 1998; (as Harry Patterson) The Valhalla Exchange 1978, To Catch a King 1979 (filmed 1983), Dillinger 1983, Walking Wounded (play) 1987; others under pseudonyms Martin Fallon, Hugh Marlowe, Henry Patterson. *Leisure interests:* tennis, old movies. *Address:* c/o Ed Victor Ltd., 6 Bayley Street, London, WC1B 3HB, England.

PATTERSON, Rt. Hon. Percival James; Jamaican politician and lawyer; b. 10 April 1935, Cross Road, St. Andrew; s. of Henry Patterson and Ina James; m. (divorced); one s. one d.; ed. Univ. of West Indies, London School of Econs.; called to Bar, Middle Temple 1963, Jamaican Bar 1963; mem. People's Nat. Party (PNP) 1958–, Party Organizer 1958–60, mem. Nat. Exec. Council, mem. Party Exec. 1964–69; nominated to Senate 1967, Leader of Opposition Business in Senate 1969–70; mem. for S.E. Westmoreland, House of Reps. 1970–80, 1989–; Minister for Industry, Foreign Trade and Tourism 1972; Deputy Prime Minister and Minister for Foreign Trade 1978; Campaign Dir. for PNP, elections 1972, 1976, 1989; Deputy Prime Minister and Minister for Devt., Planning and Production 1989, for Finance and Planning 1990–91, of Defence 1993–; Prime Minister 1992–; Queen's Counsel, Inner Bar 1984; Adviser to Govt. of Belize 1982; Pursell Trust Scholarship, Leverhulme Scholarship; Sir Hugh Parry Prize for Excellence, L.S.E. *Leisure interests:* jazz, Jamaican music, spectator sports including cricket, boxing, track and field events and tennis. *Address:* Office of the Prime Minister, Jamaica House, Hope Road, Kingston 6, Jamaica. *Telephone:* (809) 927-9639; 929-4364. *Fax:* (809) 929-0005.

PATTERSON, Walter Cram, M.SC.; Canadian analyst and writer; b. 4 Nov. 1936, Winnipeg; s. of Walter Thomas Patterson and Thirza Helen Cram; m. Cleone Susan Davis 1966; two d.; ed. Kelvin High School, Winnipeg,

Univ. of Manitoba; Ed. Your Environment 1970–73, (European) Ed. Bulletin of the Atomic Scientists 1979–81; First 'Energy Campaigner' Friends of the Earth 1972–78; ind. analyst, writer 1978–93; with Gorleben Int. Review 1978–79; Course tutor Open Univ. 1981–91; Series Adviser BBC TV Drama Edge of Darkness 1984–85; Specialist Adviser House of Commons Select Cttee. on Environment 1985–86, on Energy 1991–92; Assoc. Fellow Energy and Environmental Programme Royal Inst. of Int. Affairs 1991–93, Sr. Research Fellow 1993–; Companion, Inst. of Energy 1991. *Leisure interests:* baseball, beer, computers, languages, music, orchids, playing with the family, travel. *Publications:* Nuclear Power 1976–86, The Fissile Society 1977, Coming to a Boil 1978, The Plutonium Business 1984, Going Critical 1985, Advanced Coal-Use Technology 1987, The Energy Alternative 1990, Coal-Use Technology in a Changing Environment 1990, Coal-Use Technology: New Challenges, New Responses 1993, Power from Plants 1994, Rebuilding Romania: Energy, Efficiency and the Economic Transition 1994, Electric Futures 1997, Transforming Electricity 1999. *Address:* Royal Institute of International Affairs, Chatham House, St. James's Square, London, SW1Y 4LE (Office); Garden Court, Hervines Road, Amersham, Bucks., HP6 5HS, England (Home). *Telephone:* 0171-957 5736 (Office); (01494) 726267 (Home). *Fax:* 0171-957 5710 (Office); (01494) 726748 (Home).

PATTINSON, Rev. Sir (William) Derek, Kt., M.A.; British administrator; b. 31 March 1930, Barrow-in-Furness; s. of late Thomas William Pattinson and Elizabeth Pattinson; ed. Whitehaven Grammar School, The Queen's Coll., Oxford; Home Civil Service 1952–70; Asst. Prin., Inland Revenue Dept. 1952, Pvt. Sec. to Chair. of Bd. 1955–58, Prin. 1957; Prin., H.M. Treasury 1962–65; Asst. Sec., Inland Revenue 1965–68; Asst. Sec., H.M. Treasury 1968–70; Assoc. Sec.-Gen., Gen. Synod of Church of England 1970–72, Sec.-Gen. 1972–90; ordained deacon 1991, priest 1992; Asst. Curate, St Gabriel's, Pimlico 1991–; Prin. Soc. of Faith 1992–; Chair. Liddon Trustees 1972–; Master, Worshipful Co. of Parish Clerks 1986, Vice-Pres. SPCK; Stanhope Historical Essay Prize, Oxford 1957. *Address:* 9 Strutton Court, Great Peter Street, London, SW1P 2HH, England. *Telephone:* 0171-222 6307.

PATTULLO, Sir (David) Bruce, Kt., C.B.E., B.A., F.C.I.B.S., F.R.S.E.; British banker; b. 2 Jan. 1938; s. of late Colin Pattullo and Elizabeth Bruce; m. Fiona Nicholson 1962; three s. one d.; ed. Rugby School and Hertford Coll. Oxford; Gen. Man. Bank of Scotland Finance Co. Ltd. 1973–77; Dir. British Linen Bank Ltd. 1977–98, Chief Exec. 1977–78; Deputy Treas. Bank of Scotland 1978, Treas. and Gen. Man (Chief Exec.) 1979–88, Dir. 1980–98, Group Chief Exec. 1988–96, Deputy Gov. 1988–91, Gov. 1991–98; three hon. degrees. *Leisure interests:* tennis, hill walking. *Address:* 6 Cammo Road, Edinburgh, EH4 8EB, Scotland.

PATZAICHIN, Ivan; Romanian canoeist; b. 26 Nov. 1949, Mila, Tulcea Co.; m.; one d.; ed. Coll. for Physical Educ. and Sport, Bucharest; World champion: simple canoe 1,000m. (Tampere 1973, Sofia 1977) and 10,000m. (Belgrade 1978, 1982); double canoe 500m. (Duisburg 1979) and 1,000m. (Copenhagen 1970, Nottingham 1981, Tampere 1983); Olympic champion simple canoe 500m. (Munich 1972) and double canoe 1,000m. (Mexico City 1968, Moscow 1980, Los Angeles 1984); numerous silver and bronze medals at World and Olympic Championships; 25 times nat. champion of Romania. *Address:* Clubul Sportiv Unirea Tricolor, Soseaua Stefan cel Mare nr. 9, Bucharest, Romania.

PATZIG, Guenther, DR.PHIL.; German professor of philosophy; b. 28 Sept. 1926, Kiel; s. of Admiral Conrad Patzig and Gertrud Patzig (née Thomson); m. Christiane Köhn 1948; one s. one d.; ed. Gymnasiums in Kiel and Berlin-Steglitz, Univs. of Göttingen and Hamburg; Asst. Philosophisches Seminar, Göttingen 1953–60, Privatdozent 1958–60, Prof. of Philosophy 1963–91; Prof. of Philosophy, Univ. of Hamburg 1960–63; UNESCO Fellowship in Philosophy 1951–52; Howison Memorial Lecturer, Berkeley 1971; Keeling Lecturer, London 1992; mem. Göttingen Acad. of Sciences (Pres. 1986–90), Wissenschaftskolleg, Berlin 1984–85, Oslo Acad. of Sciences 1997–; Lower Saxony Prize for Science 1983. *Publications:* Die aristotelische Syllogistik 1959, Sprache und Logik 1970, Ethik ohne Metaphysik 1971, Tatsachen, Normen, Sätze 1980, Aristoteles Metaphysik Z: Text, Übersetzung, Kommentar (with M. Frede) 1988, Gesammelte Schriften Vols. I–IV 1993–96, Die Rationalität der Moral 1996. *Address:* Philosophisches Seminar, Universität Göttingen, Humboldtallee 19, 37073 Göttingen; Ottfried-Müller-Weg 7, 37075 Göttingen, Germany. *Telephone:* (0551) 42929. *Fax:* (0551) 39-9607.

PAU, Louis-François, PH.D., D.SC., M.B.A.; French computer and aerospace technology expert; b. 29 May 1948, Copenhagen, Denmark; s. of Louis Pau and Marie-Louise Van Jessen; m. 1st Miki Miyamoto 1983 (divorced 1990); one d.; m. 2nd Maria Jonkovskaia; ed. Ecole Nat. Supérieure de l'Aéronautique et de l'Espace, Paris Univ., Inst. d'Etudes Politiques, Paris; served in Air Force 1970–72; Asst. Prof., Tech. Univ., Denmark 1972–74; Prof. and Dept. Head, Ecole Nat. Supérieure Télécommunications, Paris 1974–82; Assoc. Prof., M.I.T., U.S.A. 1977–78; Science and Tech. Counsellor, French Embassy, Washington, D.C. 1979–82; Professorial Lecturer, Univ. of Md., College Park, Md. 1980–82; Sr. Scientist, Battelle Memorial Inst. 1982–86; Research Prof., Tech. Univ., Denmark 1986–90; CSK Prof., Univ. of Tokyo 1988–90; Tech. Dir., Digital Equipment Corpn. (Europe) 1990–95; Gen. Man. Ericsson Utvecklings (Engineering) AB, Sweden 1995–; consultant to several int. corpns.; adviser to several govts. and govt. agencies, U.S.A., Asia and Europe; mem. Review Bds., Singapore, EEC, U.S.A.; Vice-Pres. (Tech.) Int. Fed. of Automatic Control 1982–86; F.I.E.E.E.; Fellow Japan Soc. of Promotion Sciences; Fellow British Computer Soc.; many awards and prizes. *Publications:* eight books (Author), 12 books (Ed.), more than 250 papers on computers and software, aerospace tech. and financial/econ. models. *Leisure interests:* ballet, flying, travel. *Address:* Ericsson, P.O. Box 1505, 12525 Älvsjö, Sweden (Office); 33 chemin d'Aubagne, 13600 Ceyreste, France. *Telephone:* (8) 727 3000 (Office); 42.83.06.92 (France). *Fax:* (8) 647 8276.

PAUK, György; British violinist; b. 26 Oct. 1936, Budapest, Hungary; m. Susan Mautner 1959; one s. one d.; ed. Franz Liszt Acad. of Music, Budapest under Zathureczky, Leo Weiner and Zoltán Kodály; concerts all over East Europe 1952–58, and over the rest of the world; settled in Western Europe 1958, The Netherlands 1958–61, England 1961–; Prof. of Violin, Royal Acad. of Music 1987–; Artistic Dir. Mozart Bicentenary Festival, London 1991; has recorded numerous concertos, the complete violin/piano music of Mozart and Schubert, all Handel's sonatas, all Brahms's sonatas, Mozart string quintets, all Bartok's music for solo, duo and sonatas; first performances of Penderecki's violin concerto, U.K., Japan, Sir Michael Tippett's Triple Concerto, London 1980, Lutoslawski's Chain 2, U.K., Netherlands, Hungary, with composer conducting, Sir Peter Maxwell's violin concerto, Switzerland, Germany; Hon. mem. and Prof. Guildhall School of Music and Drama, London, Royal Acad. of Music 1987; Hon. R.A.M. 1990; Paganini Prize 1956, Sonata Competition Prize, Munich 1957, Jacques Thibaud Prize 1959, Grand Prix for Bartók Records (Ovation Magazine, U.S.A.) 1982, Best Record of 1983 (Gramophone Magazine), Grammy nomination for most recent Bartók records 1995; Highest civilian award, Hungarian Govt. 1998. *Leisure interests:* football, tennis, theatre, reading, swimming, my family. *Address:* 27 Armitage Road, London, N.W.11, England. *Telephone:* 0181-455 5042.

PAUL, Baron (Life Peer), cr. 1996, of Marylebone in the City of Westminster; **Swraj Paul,** M.SC., F.R.S.A.; British industry executive; b. 18 Feb. 1931, India; s. of Payare Paul and Mongwati Paul; m. Aruna Vij 1956; three s. one d. (and one d. deceased); ed. Punjab Univ., Massachusetts Inst. of Tech., U.S.A.; joined family-owned Apeejay Surrendra Group as Partner 1953; moved to U.K. and est. Natural Gas Tubes Ltd. 1966; Founder-Chair. Caparo Group Ltd. 1978–, Caparo Industries PLC 1981–; Chair. Caparo Inc., U.S.A. 1988–, Armstrong Equipment Ltd. 1989–, CREMSA, Spain 1989–, ENSA, Spain 1989–; Founder-Chair. Indo-British Assen. 1975–; Pres. Family Service Unit 1997–; Pro-Chancellor, Thames Valley Univ. 1998–; Trustee Police Foundation 1997–; Hon. Ph.D. (American Coll. of Switzerland, Leysin) 1986; Hon. D.Sc. (Econ.) (Hull) 1992; Hon. D.Litt. (Westminster) 1996; D. Univ. (Bradford) 1997. Corp. Leadership Award, M.I.T. 1987; Padma Bhushan 1983. *Publications:* Indira Gandhi 1984, Beyond Boundaries 1998. *Address:* Caparo House, 103 Baker Street, London, W1M 1FD, England. *Telephone:* 0171-486 1417.

PAUL, Robert Cameron, C.B.E., M.ENG., F.ENG., F.I.CHEM.E.; British chemical engineer; b. 7 July 1935, Uxbridge; m. Diana Kathleen Bruce 1965; two d.; ed. Rugby School and Corpus Christi Coll., Cambridge; Nat. Service (2nd Lieut. in Royal Engineers) 1953–55; Imperial Chemical Industries (ICI) 1959–86; Deputy Chair. ICI Mond Div. 1979–86; Deputy Chair. and Man. Dir. Albright and Wilson 1986–95, Chief Exec. 1995–97; Dir. (non-exec.) Courtaulds PLC 1994–; Pres. Chemical Industries Asscn. 1995–97; Hon. D.Eng. *Leisure interests:* music (piano) and golf. *Address:* 2 Devonshire Place, Kensington, London, W8 5UD, England.

PAULA, Alejandro Felippe "Jandi"; Netherlands Antilles prime minister and librarian; Govt. Librarian 1973–93; Prime Minister of Netherlands Antilles 1993–94. *Address:* c/o Office of the Prime Minister, Curaçao, Netherlands Antilles.

PAULAUSKAS, Arturas; Lithuanian politician; b. 23 Aug. 1963; m. Jolanta Paulauskiene; two s. one d.; ed. Vilnius State Univ.; Deputy Prosecutor Kaisiadoris 1979–82; Prosecutor Varena 1982–87; instructor Cen. Cttee. CP 1987; Deputy Prosecutor-Gen., Prosecutor-Gen. of Lithuania 1987–95; Deputy Prosecutor-Gen. of Lithuania 1995; Cand. in Pres. Elections 1997.

PAULS, Raymond; Latvian composer and jazz pianist; b. 12 Jan. 1936, Riga; ed. Latvian Conservatory; Artistic Dir. and Chief Conductor of Latvian State Radio and TV 1985–88; Chair. Latvian State Cttee. for Culture, later Minister of Culture 1988–93 (first non-communist Minister in U.S.S.R. since 1920s); Counsellor to Pres. 1993–97; elected to Parl. (Sacima) 1998; Latvian State Prize 1979; U.S.S.R. People's Artist 1985. *Compositions include:* musicals Sister Kerry, Sherlock Holmes, many popular songs, jazz pieces. *Address:* Veidenbaum Str. 41/43, Apt. 26, 6001 Riga, Latvia. *Telephone:* (3712) 27-55-88.

PAUNIO, Jouko Juhani Kyösti, D.SC.S.; Finnish economist and international official; b. 18 May 1928, Helsinki; s. of Tauno Erhard Paunio and Saara Elina Paunio; m. 1st Terttu Jääskeläinen 1949 (divorced 1978), three s.; m. 2nd Riitta-Leena Heiskanen 1979, one d.; ed. Univ. of Helsinki; Head Research Dept., Bank of Finland 1959–66; Prof. of Econs., Univ. of Helsinki 1966; Research Prof., Acad. of Finland 1972–75; Assoc. Dean, Faculty of Social Sciences, Univ. of Helsinki 1969, 1976–77, 1978, 1980; Dir. of Gen Econ. Analysis Div., UN Econ. Comm. for Europe 1981–86; Research Assoc., Univ. of Calif. at Berkeley 1962–63; Scientific Adviser to Bank of Finland 1966–76; Ford Foundation Research Fellow, Harvard Univ. 1969–70; Chair. Dept. of Econs., Univ. of Helsinki 1970–76, 1989; mem. Exec. Cttee. Int. Econ. Asscn. 1974–80; Chair. Nordic Econ. Research Council 1986–89; mem. Finnish Acad. of Science and Letters 1971 (Pres. 1992, Chair. Soc. Science

Section 1990–); mem. Finnish Soc. of Sciences and Letters 1973; Dr. h.c. (Åbo Acad.) 1988, (Turku School of Econs.) 1989; Commdr. Order of the Finnish Lion 1983, Commdr. Order of the Finnish White Rose 1992; Special Prize, Finnish Cultural Foundation 1976. *Publications:* A Study in Theory of Open Inflation 1959, A Theoretical Analysis of Growth and Cycles 1969 and numerous articles on macroeconomic theory and application. *Leisure interests:* long distance running, literature. *Address:* University of Helsinki, Aleksanterink 7, 00100 Helsinki, Finland. *Telephone:* 1912524.

PAVAROTTI, Luciano, D.MUS.; Italian opera singer; b. 12 Oct. 1935, Modena; s. of Fernando Pavarotti and Adele (Venturi) Pavarotti; m. Adua Veroni 1961; three d.; ed. Istituto Magistrale; tenor range; début as Rodolfo in La Bohème at Reggio nell'Emilia 1961, Staatsoper Vienna, Royal Opera House, London 1963, La Scala 1965, Metropolitan Opera House, New York 1968, Paris Opera and Lyric Opera of Chicago 1973; début as Edgardo in Lucia di Lammermoor in U.S.A. (Miami) 1965; La Scala tour of Europe 1963–64; recitals and concerts abroad including the U.S.A. and Europe 1973–, tour of U.S.S.R. 1990; Pavarotti in the Park (London) 1991; about 30 albums 1964–79; appeared in MGM film Yes, Giorgio 1981; hon. degree (Pa.) 1979; Noce d'Oro Nat. Prize, Luigi Illica int. prize, first prize Gold Orfeo (Acad. du Disque Lyrique de France), Grammy Award for best classical vocal soloist 1981 and many other prizes; Grand Officer, Italian Repub., Légion d'honneur. *Publications:* Pavarotti: My Own Story (with William Wright), Grandissimo Pavarotti 1986, Pavarotti: My World (with William Wright) 1995. *Leisure interests:* tennis, painting, equitation. *Address:* c/o Herbert Breslin, 119 West 57th Street, New York, N.Y. 10019, U.S.A. (Office); Via Giardini 941, 41040 Saliceta, Modena, Italy (Home).

PAVIĆ, Milorad, D.PHIL.; Serbian poet and historian; b. 15 Oct. 1929, Belgrade; m. Branka Pavić; one s. one d.; ed. Belgrade Univ.; journalist, Radio Belgrade 1958–63, Prosveta Publrs. 1963–74; Prof., Dean, Faculty of Philosophy, Novy Sad Univ. 1974–82; Prof., Belgrade Univ. 1982–94; lecturer, Univ. of Paris (Sorbonne); mem. Serbian Acad. of Sciences and Arts; numerous prizes and awards. *Publications:* 4 novels, 5 collections of short stories, 2 collections of poetry, 1 play, more than 10 historical and literary monographs, including: (novels): Dictionary of Kharzars 1984, Landscape Painted with Tea 1988, The Inner Side of the Wind 1991, The Last Love in Tsarigrad 1994, The Fishkin Hat 1995; (poetry): The Iron Curtain 1973, St. Mark's Horses 1978, Borzoi 1979, The Inverted Glove 1989; numerous articles and essays. *Address:* Vojvode Breme str. 9, Belgrade, Yugoslavia.

PAVLE, Patriarch (Pavle Gojko Stojcevic); Serbian ecclesiastic; b. 1 Sept. 1914, Kućanci, Slavonia; ed. High School, Belgrade, Orthodox Theological Faculty, Belgrade and Theological Faculty, Athens; worked as catechist of refugee children at St. Trinity Monastery, Serbia during World War II; became a monk in 1948, hieromonk 1954, Archimandrite 1957; teacher, Theological Seminary, Prizren, Kosovo 1950–51; Bishop, Raska-Prizren Diocese/Kosovo-Metohija 1957–91; 44th Patriarch of Serbia Dec. 1990–, Archbishop of Péc, Metropolitan of Belgrade-Karlovci; Dr. h.c. (Theological Faculty, Belgrade) 1992, (St. Vladimir Theological Seminary, New York) 1992. *Publications:* ed. of liturgical books in Serbian and in Old Church Slavonic; articles in liturgics in monthly journal Glasnik. *Address:* Kralja Petra 5, P.O. Box 182, 11001 Belgrade, Yugoslavia. *Telephone:* 00 381 11/638-161, 635-699. *Fax:* 00 381 11/638-161.

PAVLETIĆ, Vlatko; Croatian literary researcher and politician; b. 2 Sept. 1930, Zagreb; s. of Mate Pavletić and Mira Pavletić; m. Neda Majnarić; one s.; ed. Zagreb Univ.; started as drama man. at Zagreb People's Theatre (HNK); Prof. Zagreb Drama Arts Acad.; Ed.-in-Chief numerous edns.; Artistic Dir. Adria Filmstudio; mem., Vice-Pres. Croatian Acad. of Sciences and Arts –1992; Minister of Educ., Culture and Sports of Croatian Repub. 1990–92; mem. of Parl. (Sabor) 1992–95; Pres. of Parl. 1995–; mem. Croatian Writers' Asscn; mem. Croatian PEN. *Publications:* A Door-knocker in your Hand 1952, The Destiny of an Automaton 1953, How Writers Wrote 1956, Croatian Literary Critics 1958, A Moment of the Present 1959, An analysis one cannot do without 1961, Plays by Ivo Vojnovic 1962, Goran with Himself 1963, Croatian Poets between Two Wars, The Golden Book of Croatian Poetry 1970, Against Barbarism 1971, Work in Reality 1971, Ujevic in the Paradise of his Hell 1978, The Restrained Wrath 1978, Essays and Reviews 1982, The Witness of the Apocalypse 1983, Men's Life 1987, Key to Modern Poetry 1986, A Trap for Generations 1987, A Puzzle without a Solution 1987, How to Read Poetry 1987, Common Life's Poesy 1991, Baudelaire's Flowers of Evil 1993, Critical Miniatures (a panorama of Croatian writers and works) 1997. *Address:* Croatian PEN-Centre, HDZ, Rubetićeva str. 7, 10000 Zagreb, Croatia. *Telephone:* (01) 461 6000 (Home).

PAVLÍČEK, František, PH.D.; Czech playwright; b. 20 Nov. 1923, Lukov, Zlín Dist.; s. of František Pavlíček and Růžena Šmídová; m. 1st Alena Břízová 1971, one s. one d.; m. 2nd Eva Košlerová 1991; ed. Charles Univ., Prague; Script Ed.-in-Chief, Czechoslovak Film Co. 1956–65; Dir. Theatre Na Vino-hradech 1965–70, signed Charter 77, served long-term imprisonment sentence; Dir.-Gen. Czechoslovak Radio, Prague 1990–91; Czechoslovak State Prize. *Works:* 15 plays for stage and TV, including the Little Mermaid 1992, In Praise of Debauchery 1994, Muž v pozadí (Mastermind) 1995, 20 screenplays, 80 radio plays and The End of Patriarchate (novel) 1992, Zrcadlení (The Reflection) 1997. *Leisure interests:* writing plays, history. *Address:* M. Pujmanové 25, 140 00 Prague 4, Czech Republic (Home).

PAVLOV, Valentin Sergeyevich, D.ECON.; Russian politician and banker; b. 26 Sept. 1937, Moscow; ed. Moscow Inst. of Finance; economist; worked in Finance Ministries of R.S.F.S.R. 1959–66, U.S.S.R. 1966–79; State Planning Cttee. 1979–86; Chair. State Price Cttee. 1986–89; Minister of Finance 1989–91; Prime Minister Jan.–Aug. 1991; arrested 22 Aug. 1991 as an accomplice in the failed coup d'état of Aug. 1991; charged with conspiracy Jan. 1992, on trial 1993–94, released on amnesty 1994; consultant for various cos. including Doveriye Trust; Chair. of Bd. ChaspromBank 1995–96; Adviser to Promstroybank 1996–. *Publications:* On Taxation of the Population: Has the chance been missed?; numerous articles. *Address:* Promstroybank, Tversikoy blvd. 13, 103867 Moscow, Russia. *Telephone:* 200-79-00.

PAVLYCHKO, Dmytro Vasylovych; Ukrainian poet and politician; b. 1929, Ivano-Frankovsk; ed. Lvov Univ.; started publishing in early 1950s; mem. CPSU 1954–88; keen advocate of de-Stalinisation from 1962; f. Taras Shevchenko Ukrainian Language Soc. 1988, for protection of language; Chair. inaugural Congress of the Popular Movt. of the Ukraine for Perestroika (Rukh); Deputy to Ukrainian Supreme Soviet 1990; Chair. Parl. Cttee. for Int. Affairs 1991; Amb. to Slovakia 1995. *Publications include:* My Hand 1955, The Day 1960, Bread and Banner 1968, Sonnets 1978, Turned to the Future 1986. *Address:* Radvanská 35, 811 01 Bratislava, Slovakia. *Telephone:* (07) 5331-672. *Fax:* (07) 5312-651.

PAWAR, Sharadchandra Govindrao, B.COM.; Indian politician; b. 12 Dec. 1940, Katychiwadi, Poona; s. of Govindrao Jijaba Pawar; m.; one d.; Head State Level Youth Congress; Gen. Sec. Maharashtra Pradesh Congress Cttee.; elected to State Legis. 1967, held Portfolios of Home and Publicity, and Rehabilitation; Minister of State and Educ. and Youth Welfare, Home, Agric. and Industries and Labour; Chief Minister of Maharashtra 1978–80, 1988–91, Minister of Defence 1991–92; Pres. Nat. Congress (opposition) 1981–86; rejoined Congress (I) 1986; fmr. Pres. Congress Forum for Socialistic Action; Sec. Defence Cttee; mem. Lok Sabha 1996–; Leader of Opposition March 1998–; Pres. Maharashtra Kabbadi Asscn., Maharashtra Olympic Asscn., Agricultural Devt. Foundation. *Address:* 6 Gurudwara Rakabgany Road, New Delhi-110001; Ramalayan, 44-A Peddev Road, Mumbai-40026, India. *Telephone:* 3737670.

PAWLAK, Waldemar, M.SC.; Polish politician; b. 5 Sept. 1959, Pacyna, Płock Prov.; m.; two s. one d.; ed. Warsaw Univ. of Tech.; farm man. 1984–; mem. United Peasant Party (ZSL) 1984–90; Deputy to Sejm (Parl.) 1989–; mem. Polish Peasant Party (PSL) 1992–; Chair. Council of Ministers (Prime Minister) of Poland June–July 1992, 1993–95. *Leisure interests:* philosophy, information science, computers. *Address:* Sejm RP, ul. Wiejska 4/6/8, 00-902 Warsaw, Poland. *Telephone:* (22) 694 25 00.

PAWSON, Anthony James, PH.D., F.R.S., F.R.S.C.; British molecular biologist; b. 18 Oct. 1952, Maidstone; s. of Henry Anthony Pawson and Hilarie Anne Pawson (née Bassett); m. Margaret Ann Luman 1975; two s. one d.; ed. London Univ.; Asst. Prof. Dept. of Microbiology, Univ. of British Columbia 1981–85; Sr. Scientist Samuel Lunenfeld Research Inst., Mount Sinai Hosp., Toronto 1985–, Head of Programme in Molecular Biology and Cancer 1994–; Assoc. Prof. Dept. of Medical Genetics, Univ. of Toronto 1985-88, Prof. 1989–; Gairdner Foundation Int. Award 1994; Dr. H. P. Heineken Prize for Biochemistry and Biophysics, Royal Netherlands Acad. of Arts and Sciences 1998; American Asscn. for Cancer Research-Pezcoller Foundation Award for Cancer Research 1998. *Publications:* over 200 papers in various scientific journals. *Leisure interests:* reading, theatre, fly-fishing. *Address:* Samuel Lunenfeld Research Institute, Mount Sinai Hospital, 600 University Avenue, Room 1084, Toronto, Ont. M5G 1X5, Canada. *Telephone:* (416) 586-8262. *Fax:* (416) 586-8869.

PAWSON, John; British architect; lived three years in Japan before studying architecture; bldgs. designed include Lesley Woodington Gallery, Hawk St., London, Neuendorf House, Majorca, Calvin Klein Store, Madison Ave., New York, Jigsaw clothes shop, Bond St., London.

PAXMAN, Jeremy Dickson, M.A.; British journalist and author; b. 11 May 1950, Leeds; s. of Arthur Keith Paxman and Joan McKay Dickson; ed. Malvern Coll., St. Catharine's Coll., Cambridge; journalist, Northern Ireland 1973–77; reporter, BBC TV Tonight and Panorama programmes 1977–85, Presenter BBC TV Breakfast Time 1986–89, Newsnight 1989–, Univ. Challenge 1994–, Start the Week, Radio 4, 1998–; Royal TV Soc. Award for Int. Reporting, Richard Dimbleby Award, B.A.F.T.A. 1996, Interview of the Year, Royal TV Soc. 1997, 1998, Voice of the Viewer and Listener Presenter of the Year 1994, 1997. *Publications:* A Higher Form of Killing (co-author) 1982, Through the Volcanoes 1985, Friends in High Places 1990, Fish, Fishing and the Meaning of Life 1994, The Compleat Angler 1996, The English 1998; numerous articles in newspapers and magazines. *Leisure interests:* flyfishing, skiing, daydreaming. *Address:* c/o BBC TV, London, W12 7RJ, England.

PAYE, Jean-Claude; French diplomatist; b. 26 Aug. 1934, Longué; s. of Lucien Paye and Suzanne (née Guignard) Paye; m. Laurence Jeanneney 1963; two s. two d.; ed. Inst. d'Etudes Politiques and Ecole Nat. d'Admin.; Head, private office of Mayor of Constantine 1961–62; Sec. of Embassy, Algiers 1962–63; Ministry of Foreign Affairs 1963–65; special adviser, Office of Sec. of State for Scientific Research 1965, Office of Minister for Social Affairs 1966; Head of private office of M Barre (Vice-Pres. of Comm. of European Communities) 1967–73; Counsellor, Bonn 1973–74; Deputy Head,

Office of Minister for Foreign Affairs 1974–76; Counsellor to Prime Minister Raymond Barre 1976–79; Sec.-Gen. Interministerial Cttee. for European Econ. Co-operation questions 1977–79; Dir. Econ. and Financial Affairs, Ministry for External Relations 1979–84; Sec.-Gen. OECD 1984–; Conseiller d'Etat 1996; ministre plénipotentiaire hors classe 1986; Chevalier, Légion d'honneur, Officier, Ordre National du Mérite. *Address:* Conseil d'Etat, 75100 Paris RP (Office); 1 place Alphonse Deville, 75006 Paris (Home). *Telephone:* 45492030. *Fax:* 45492006.

PAYNE, Anthony Edward, B.A.; British composer; b. 2 Aug. 1936, London; s. of Edward Alexander Payne and late (Muriel) Margaret Payne; m. Jane Manning (q.v.); ed. Dulwich Coll., London and Durham Univ.; freelance musical journalist, musicologist, lecturer, etc. with various publs. and BBC Radio, active in promoting "new music", serving on cttee. of Macnaghten Concerts (Chair. 1967) and Soc. for the Promotion of New Music (Chair. 1969–71), composed part-time 1962–73; full-time composer 1973–; tutor in Composition, London Coll. of Music 1983–85, Sydney Conservatorium 1986, Univ. of W. Australia 1996; Milhaud Prof., Mills Coll., Oakland, Calif. 1983; Artistic Dir. Spitalfields Festival; Composition Tutor Univ. of Western Australia 1996; Contrib. Daily Telegraph 1964–, The Times 1964–, The Independent 1986–, Country Life 1995–; mem. Cttee. Asscn. of Professional Composers. *Compositions:* Phoenix Mass 1972, Concerto for Orchestra 1976, The World's Winter 1976, String Quartet 1978, The Stones and Lonely Places Sing 1979, Song of the Clouds 1980, A Day in the Life of a Mayfly 1981, Evening Land 1981, Spring's Shining Wake 1981, The Spirit's Harvest 1985, The Song Streams in the Firmament 1986, Fanfares and Processional 1986, Half Heard in the Stillness 1987, Consort Music 1988, Sea-Change 1988, Time's Arrow 1990, The Enchantress Plays 1991, Symphonies of Wind and Rain 1991, A Hidden Music 1992, The Seeds Long Hidden 1993, Empty Landscape-Heart's Ease 1995, completion of Elgar's Third Symphony 1997, Piano Trio 1998; Radcliffe Award 1975, Int. Jury Choice for Int. Soc. for Contemporary Music Festival 1976 (Concerto for Orchestra), Gramophone Critics' Choice 1977 (The Music of Anthony Payne). *Publications:* Schoenberg 1968, The Music of Frank Bridge 1984, Elgar's Third Symphony: The Story of the Reconstruction 1998. *Leisure interests:* English countryside, cinema. *Address:* 2 Wilton Square, London, N1 3DL; c/o J. & W. Chester, 8–9 Frith Street, London W1V 5TZ, England. *Telephone:* 0171-359 1593. *Fax:* 0171-226 4369.

PAYNE, Nicholas; British opera company director; b. 4 Jan. 1945, Bromley; m. Linda Jane Adamson 1986; two s.; ed. Eton Coll. and Trinity Coll. Cambridge; joined finance dept. of Royal Opera House; Subsidy Officer, Arts Council of G.B. 1970–76; Financial Controller, Welsh Nat. Opera 1976–82; Gen. Admin. Opera North 1982–93; Dir. The Royal Opera 1993–98; Gen. Dir. ENO Aug. 1998–. *Address:* English National Opera, St. Martin's Lane, London, W.C.2, England.

PAZ ESTENSSORO, Víctor; Bolivian politician; b. 2 Oct. 1907; s. of Domingo Paz Rojas and Carlos Estenssoro de Paz; m. 1st Carmela Cerruto Calderón 1936, one s. one d.; m. 2nd Teresa Cortez Velasco, three d.; ed. Univ. Mayor de San Andrés; Finance official 1932–33; Deputy Tarija 1938–39 and 1940–41; Pres. Banco Minero 1939; Prof. Econ. History, Univ. of La Paz 1939–41; Minister of Finance 1941–44; Pres. of Bolivia 1952–56, 1960–64, 1985–90; Amb. to the U.K. 1956–59; Prof. Econ. Devt. Theory, Planning Inst. Nat. Eng. Univ. de Lima 1966; fmr. Leader of Movimento Nacional Revolucionario; presidential candidate in inconclusive elections 1979, 1980. *Publications:* Esquema de la Organización Política y Administrativa de Bolivia, Aspecto de la Economía Boliviana, Revolución y Contrarrevolución, Proceso y Sentencia de la Oligarquía Boliviana, La Revolución Boliviana, Discursos Parlamentarios, Discursos y Mensajes, Contra la Restauración por la Revolución Nacional, La Obra, Maestra de los Restauradores, El Imperativo Nacional, Presencia de la Revolución Nacional. *Leisure interest:* photography. *Address:* c/o Palacio de Gobierno, Plaza Murillo, La Paz, Bolivia.

PAZ ZAMORA, Jaime, LIC.; Bolivian politician; b. 15 April 1939, Cochabamba; ed. Colegio Jesuita, Sucre, Seminario Mayor de Villa Allende en Córdoba, Argentina, and Catholic Univ. of Louvain, Belgium; Pres. de la Fed. de Estudiantes Latino-americanos (Belgium); Prof. of Sociology, Univ. Mayor de San Andrés; Prof. of Int. Relations, Dir. Univ. Extension; f. Movimiento de la Izquierda Revolucionaria; cand. Vice-Pres. 1978 and 1980; first Vice-Pres. of the Andean Parl.; Vice-Pres. Repub. of Bolivia and Pres. Nat. Congress 1982–84; Pres. Repub. of Bolivia 1989–93; mem. Exec. Cttee. of the Asoc. Latino-Americana de Derechos Humanos; mem. Movimiento de la Izquierda Revolucionaria (MIR).

PAZNYAK, Zenon; Belarus politician; fmr. anti-Communist dissident; founder mem. Byelorussian Popular Front (BPF) Oct. 1988, Leader 1989; elected in Minsk to Supreme Soviet as mem. Byelorussian Democratic Bloc 1990–; cand. in Pres. elections 1994; lives abroad. *Address:* c/o Byelorussian Popular Front, P.O. Box 208, 220040 Minsk, Belarus. *Telephone:* (02) 31-48-93.

PEACOCK, Sir Alan, Kt., D.S.C., M.A., F.B.A., F.R.S.E.; British economist; b. 26 June 1922, Ryton-on-Tyne; s. of Alexander D. Peacock and Clara M. Peacock; m. Margaret Martha Astell-Burt 1944; two s. one d.; ed. Grove Acad., Dundee High School, Univ. of St. Andrews; Lecturer in Econs., Univ. of St. Andrews 1947–48; Lecturer in Econs., L.S.E. 1948–51, Reader in Public Finance 1951–56; Prof. of Econ. Science, Univ. of Edin. 1956–62; Prof. of Econs., Univ. of York 1962–78; Prof. of Econs. and Prin. Univ. Coll. at Buckingham 1980–83, Vice-Chancellor 1983–84, Prof. Emer. 1985–; Research Prof. in Public Finance, Heriot-Watt Univ. 1987–; Chief Econ. Adviser, Dept. of Trade and Industry 1973–76; Pres. Int. Inst. of Public Finance 1966–69, Hon. Pres. 1975–; mem. Royal Comm. on Constitution 1970–73, Social Science Research Council 1971–72; Trustee, Inst. of Econ. Affairs, Council, London Philharmonic Orchestra 1975–79; Chair. Arts Council Enquiry into Orchestral Resources 1969–70, Scottish Arts Council 1986–92; mem. Bd. of Dirs. English Music Theatre Ltd. 1975–77; Chair. Hebrides Ensemble 1994–; mem. Council of Man., Nat. Inst. of Econ. and Social Research 1977–86; non-exec. Dir. Economist Intelligence Unit 1977–84; Exec. Dir. David Hume Inst. 1985–90; non-exec. Dir. Caledonian Bank PLC 1989–96; Chair. Cttee. on Financing the BBC 1985–86; Hon. Pres. Atlantic Econ. Soc. 1981–82; Hon. Fellow L.S.E. 1980–; Foreign mem. Accademia Naz. dei Lincei, Rome 1996–; Keynes Lecturer, British Acad. 1994; Dr. h.c. (Stirling) 1974, (Catania) 1991, (Brunel) 1989, (York) 1997; Hon. Dr.Econ. (Zürich) 1984; Hon. D.Sc. (Buckingham) 1986; Hon. D.Soc. Sci. (Edin.) 1990; Hon. LL.D. (St. Andrews, Dundee) 1990. *Publications:* Economics of National Insurance 1952, Growth of Public Expenditure in United Kingdom (with J. Wiseman) 1961, Economic Theory of Fiscal Policy (with G. K. Shaw) 1971, The Composer in the Market Place (with R. Weir) 1975, Welfare Economics: A Liberal Reinterpretation (with Charles Rowley), The Credibility of Liberal Economics 1977, The Economic Analysis of Government 1979, The Political Economy of Taxation (ed. with Francesco Forte) 1980, The Regulation Game (Ed.) 1984, Public Expenditure and Government Growth (Ed. with F. Forte) 1985, Corporate Takeovers and the Public Interest (with G. Bannock) 1991, Public Choice Analysis in Historical Perspective 1991, Paying the Piper: Culture, Music and Money 1993, Cultural Economics and Cultural Policies (Ed. with Ilde Rizzo), The Political Economy of Economic Freedom 1997, The Political Economy of Heritage (Ed.) 1998, and numerous articles in professional journals on economics, public finance, social policy. *Leisure interest:* writing music. *Address:* David Hume Institute, 21 George Square, Edinburgh, EH8 9LD; 146/4 Whitehouse Loan, Edinburgh, EH9 2AN, Scotland. *Telephone:* (0131) 650 4633/(0131) 447 5917. *Fax:* (0131) 667-9111.

PEACOCK, Hon. Andrew Sharp, LL.B., M.P.; Australian diplomatist and fmr. politician; b. 13 Feb. 1939, Melbourne; s. of the late A. S. Peacock and Iris Peacock; m. 1st Susan Peacock (divorced), three d.; m. 2nd Margaret Peacock 1983 (divorced); ed. Scotch Coll., Univ. of Melbourne; Pres., Victorian Liberal Party 1965–66; mem. House of Reps. for Kooyong, Vic. 1966–94; fmr. partner Rigby and Fielding, solicitors; fmr. Chair. Peacock & Smith Pty. Ltd., engineers; Minister for the Army and Minister Assisting the Prime Minister 1969–71, Assisting the Treas. 1971–72; Minister for External Territories 1972; mem. Opposition Exec. 1973–75, Spokesman on Foreign Affairs 1973–75; Minister for Foreign Affairs 1975–80, for the Environment Nov.–Dec. 1975, for Industrial Relations 1980–81, for Industry and Commerce 1982–83; Leader Parl. Liberal Party 1983–85; Opposition Spokesman on Foreign Affairs 1985–87; Deputy Leader of the Opposition and Shadow Treas. 1987–89; Leader of the Opposition 1989–90; Shadow Attorney-Gen. and Shadow Minister for Justice 1990–92; Shadow Minister for Trade 1992–93, for Foreign Affairs 1993–94; Chair. Parl. Political Strategy Cttee. 1994; Amb. to U.S.A. 1997–; Chair. Int. Democrat Union 1989–92, Australian Horse Council 1996. *Leisure interests:* horse racing, Australian Rules Football, surfing, reading. *Address:* Australian Embassy, 1601 Massachusetts Avenue, Washington, DC 20036, U.S.A. *Telephone:* (202) 797 3133. *Fax:* (202) 797 3209.

PEACOCK, William James, A.C., PH.D., F.R.S., F.A.A., F.A.I.A.S., F.T.S.E.; Australian research scientist; b. 14 Dec. 1937, Leura, N.S.W.; s. of William Edward Peacock and Evelyn Alison Peacock; m. Margaret Constance Woodward 1961; one s. two d.; ed. Univ. of Sydney; Visiting Research Scientist, Genetics, CSIRO, Canberra 1963; Fellow, Dept. of Biology, Univ. of Oregon 1963–64, Visiting Assoc. Prof. 1964–65; Research Consultant, Biology Div., Oak Ridge Nat. Lab., U.S.A. 1965; Sr. Research Scientist, Div. of Plant Industry, CSIRO, Canberra 1965–69, Prin. Research Scientist 1969–73, Sr. Prin. Research Scientist 1973–77, Chief Research Scientist 1977–78, Chief 1978–; Adjunct Prof. of Biology, Univ. of Calif., San Diego 1969–70; Visiting Prof. of Biochem., Stanford Univ. 1970–71; Visiting Distinguished Prof. of Molecular Biology, Univ. of Calif., Los Angeles 1977; Scientific Adviser, Australian Genetic Eng. Ltd.; Foreign Fellow, Indian Nat. Science Acad. 1990; Foreign Assoc., N.A.S. 1990; Hon. D.Sc. 1996; Edgeworth David Medal, Royal Soc. of N.S.W. 1967, Lemberg Medal, Australian Biochemical Soc. 1978, N.I. Vavilov Medal 1987, BHP Bicentennial Prize 1988, Burnet Medal, Australian Acad. of Science 1989, CSIRO Medal 1989. *Publications:* about 250 research papers on molecular biology, cytogenetics and evolution; ed. of six books. *Leisure interests:* squash, bush-walking, skiing. *Address:* CSIRO Plant Industry, G.P.O. Box 1600, Canberra, A.C.T. 2601 (Office); 16 Brassey Street, Deakin, A.C.T. 2601, Australia (Home). *Telephone:* (02) 6246 5250 (Office); (02) 6281 4485 (Home). *Fax:* (02) 6246 5530.

PEACOCKE, Christopher Arthur Bruce, D.PHIL., F.B.A.; British professor of philosophy; b. 22 May 1950, Birmingham; s. of Arthur Peacocke and Rosemary Peacocke; m. Teresa Rosen 1980; one s. one d.; ed. Magdalen Coll. School, Exeter Coll. Oxford and Harvard Univ. (Kennedy Scholar); Sr. Scholar, Merton Coll. Oxford 1972–73; Jr. Research Fellow, Queen's Coll. Oxford 1973–76; Visiting Lecturer, Univ. of Calif. Berkeley 1975–76; Prize

Fellow, All Souls Coll. Oxford 1975–79; Visiting Prof. Univ. of Mich. 1978; Fellow, New College, Oxford and Common Univ. Fund Lecturer in Philosophy, Oxford Univ. 1979–85; Visiting Prof. Univ. of Calif. Los Angeles 1981; Visiting Fellow, Australian Nat. Univ. Canberra 1981, 1998; Fellow, Center for Advanced Study in Behavioural Sciences, Stanford 1983–84; Susan Stebbing Prof. of Philosophy, King's Coll. London 1985–88; Pres. Mind Assn. 1986; Waynflete Prof. of Metaphysical Philosophy, Oxford Univ. and Fellow of Magdalen Coll. Oxford 1989–; Leverhulme Personal Research Professorship 1996–; Visiting Prof. New York Univ. 1996–(99); Wilde Prize 1971, Webb-Medley Prize 1971, John Locke Prize 1972. *Publications:* Holistic Explanation: Action, Space, Interpretation 1979, Sense and Content 1983, Thoughts: An Essay on Content 1986, A Study of Concepts 1992, Being Known 1999; papers in Philosophical Review, Journal of Philosophy etc. *Leisure interests:* music, visual arts. *Address:* Magdalen College, Oxford, OX1 4AU, England. *Telephone:* (01865) 276000. *Fax:* (01865) 276932.

PEARCE, Sir Austin William, Kt., C.B.E., F.ENG., D.SC., PH.D.; British business executive; b. 1 Sept. 1921, Plymouth; s. of late William T. Pearce and of Florence Pearce; m. 1st Maglona Winifred Twinn 1947 (died 1975), 2nd Florence Patricia Grice 1979 (died 1993); three d. and two step-d.; ed. Devonport High School for Boys, Birmingham Univ. and Harvard Business School; joined Esso Petroleum Co. 1945, Dir. 1963–80, Man. Dir. 1968–71, Chair. 1972–80, Dir. Esso Europe Inc. 1972–80; Chair. Irish Refining Co. Ltd. 1965–71, U.K. Petroleum Industry Advisory Cttee. 1977–80; Pres. Inst. of Petroleum 1968–70; Pres. Pipeline Industries Guild 1973–75; Pres. Oil Industries Club 1975–76; Pres. U.K. Petroleum Industry Assn. 1979–80; Vice-Pres. Soc. of British Aerospace Cos. 1981–82, Pres. 1982–83; Vice-Pres. Eng. Employers' Group 1983–87; Dir. Williams and Glyn's Bank Ltd. 1974–85, Deputy Chair. 1980–83, Chair. 1983–85; Dir. Royal Bank of Scotland Group 1978–92, a Vice-Chair. 1985–92; Dir. British Aerospace 1977–87, Chair. 1980–87; Chair. Oxford Instruments 1987–91; Dir. Pearl Assurance PLC 1985–91, Jaguar PLC 1986–93, Smiths Industries 1987–92, Home Group Ltd. 1998–; Chair. CBI Industrial Policy Cttee. 1982–85; Chair. Warden Housing Assn. 1994–, Martlets Hospice 1994–98; mem. Advisory Council on Energy Conservation 1974–80, Energy Comm. 1977–79; mem. of Bd., English-Speaking Union 1974–80; mem. Comm. on Energy and the Environment 1978–81; Chair of Trustees Science Museum, London 1986–94; Pro-Chancellor Univ. of Surrey 1985–94, Pro-Chancellor Emer. 1994–; mem. Takeover Panel 1987–92; Patron Nat. Training Awards 1988; Treasurer Royal Soc. of Arts 1988–93; Hon. D.Sc. (Exeter, Southampton) 1985, (Salford, Cranfield) 1987; Hon. D. Eng. (Birmingham) 1986; Hon. D. Univ. (Surrey) 1993. *Leisure interests:* golf, general handicrafts. *Address:* Treeps House, 2 High Street, Hurstpierpoint, West Sussex, BN6 9TY, England. *Telephone:* (01273) 832927.

PEARCE, Sir (Daniel Norton) Idris, C.B.E., T.D., D.L., F.R.I.C.S.; British chartered surveyor; b. 28 Nov. 1933, Neath; s. of Lemeul George Douglas Pearce and Evelyn Mary Pearce; m. Ursula Helene Langley 1963 (divorced 1997); two d.; ed. West Buckland School, Coll. of Estate Man.; joined Richard Ellis 1959, Partner 1961–92, Man. Partner 1981–87, Consultant 1992–; Chair. English Estates 1989–94; Chair. Higher Educ. Funding Council for Wales 1992–96; mem. Advisory Panel for Institutional Finance in New Towns 1974–80; mem. Property Services Agency Advisory Bd. 1981–86; Property Adviser to Nat. Health Service Man. Bd. 1985–90; mem. FCO Advisory Panel on Diplomatic Estate 1985–, Financial Reporting Review Panel 1991–92, UFC 1991–93; Vice-Chair. Greater London TA & VRA 1991–94; mem. Gen. Council The Royal Inst. of Chartered Surveyors 1989–95, mem. Exec. Cttee. 1984–91, Pres. 1990–91, Chair. Int. Assets Valuation Standards Cttee. 1981–86; Chair. Higher Educ. Funding Council for Wales 1992–96; Deputy Chair. Urban Regeneration Agency 1993–; Dir. (non-exec.) Swan Hill 1993–, Nat. Mortgage Bank 1992–97, Innisfree Man. Ltd. 1996–, Redburgh Ltd. 1996–98, Millennium and Copthorne Hotels PLC 1996–; Gov. Peabody Trust 1992–; Hon. D.Sc. City Univ., London, Salford Univ., Oxford Polytechnic; Hon. D.Sc. Tech. (Univ. of E. London); Hon. D.Eng. Bristol, Univ. of W. of England; Thames Polytechnic, Centenary Fellowship 1991; Hon. Fellow, Coll. of Estate Man., Univ. of Wales, Cardiff 1997; Hon. Col., 135 Independent Topological Squadron Royal Engineers (V). *Publications:* articles on valuation and property matters. *Leisure interests:* reading, opera, ballet, travel. *Address:* Richard Ellis, Berkeley Square House, London, W1X 6AN (Office). *Telephone:* 0171-629 6290 (Office).

PEARCE, David William, M.A.; British professor of economics; b. 11 Oct. 1941, Harrow; s. of William Pearce and Gladys Pearce; m. Susan M. Reynolds 1966; two s.; ed. Harrow Weald County Grammar School and Lincoln Coll. Oxford; Sr. lecturer in Econs. Southampton Univ. 1967–74; Dir. Public Sector Econs. Research Centre, Leicester Univ. 1974–77; Prof. of Econs. Aberdeen Univ. 1977–83 (Dir. 1991–96, Assoc. Dir. 1996–), Univ. Coll. London 1983–; Adviser to Sec. of State for Environment 1989–92; Dir. Centre for Social and Econ. Research on the Global Environment (CSERGE), Univ. Coll. London 1990–; UN 'Global 500' Award for Services to World Environment; Giuseppe Mazzotti Prize for Literature. *Publications:* Blueprint for a Green Economy 1989, Economics of Natural Resources and the Environment 1990, Sustainable Development 1990, Economic Valuation and the Natural World 1993, World Without End (jtly.) 1993, Economics of Biodiversity 1994, The Causes of Tropical Deforestation (jtly.) 1994, Blueprint 4: Sustaining the Earth: Capturing Global Value 1995, Blueprint 5: The Social Costs of Road Transport (jtly.) 1996, Acid Rain: Counting the Cost (co-Ed.) 1997. *Leisure interests:* collecting antique porcelain/china, birdwatching. *Address:* CSERGE, University College London, Gower Street, London, WC1E 6BT; 90 Kimbolton Road, Bedford, MK40 2PE, England. *Telephone:* 0171-380 7874. *Fax:* 0171-916 2772.

PEARCE, Reynold, M.A.; British fashion designer, ed. Nottingham Trent Univ., Cen. St. Martin's Coll. of Art and Design; worked for John Galliano (q.v.); design asst. for Roland Klein; launched Pearce Fionda collection with Andrew Fionda (q.v.) 1994; with Andrew Fionda received British Apparel Export Award for best New Designer 1994, New Generation Award Lloyds Bank British Fashion Award 1995, Int. Apparel Fed. World Young Designers Award 1996, Glamour Category Award (British Fashion Awards) 1997. *Address:* Pearce Fionda, Studio S, 25 Horsell Road, London, N5 1XL, England. *Telephone:* 0171-609 6470. *Fax:* 0171-609 6470.

PEARL, Valerie Louise, D.PHIL., F.R.H.S., F.S.A.; British professor of history and college president; b. 31 Dec. 1926, Newport, Mon.; d. of the late C. R. Bence, M.P. and F. Bowler; m. Morris L. Pearl 1949; one d.; ed. King Edward VI High School, Birmingham and St. Anne's Coll. Oxford; Sr. Research Studentship, Westfield Coll. London 1962; Leverhulme Research Award 1962; Graham Research Fellow, lecturer in History, Somerville Coll. Oxford 1965–68; Reader in History of London, Univ. Coll. London 1968–76, Prof. 1976–81; Pres. New Hall, Cambridge 1981–(Sept. 1995); McBride Visiting Prof. Bryn Mawr Coll. Pennsylvania 1974; Founder and Ed.-in-Chief, The London Journal 1973–77; Woodward Lecturer, Yale Univ. 1974; Literary Dir. Royal Historical Soc. 1975–77; Gov. Museum of London 1978–92; Stow Commemorative Lecturer 1979; Ford Special Lecturer, Oxford 1980; Syndic, Cambridge Univ. Library, Cambridge Univ. Press 1982–92; Commr. Royal Comm. on Historical Manuscripts 1983–92; Hon. Fellow St. Anne's Coll. Oxford. *Publications:* London and the Outbreak of the Puritan Revolution 1625–43 1961, Contrib. to The Interregnum; Puritans and Revolutionaries, Co-Ed. and Contrib. History and Imagination (vol. in honour of Hugh Trevor-Roper) 1981, Ed Stow's Survey of London 1985, Change and Continuity in 17th-Century London 1981, (Japanese edn. 1992); articles and contribs. to books, encyclopedias and learned journals. *Leisure interests:* walking, gardening, swimming. *Address:* c/o New Hall, Cambridge, CB3 0DF, England. *Telephone:* (01223) 351721.

PEARLSTEIN, Philip, M.A.; American artist; b. 24 May 1924, Pittsburgh; s. of David Pearlstein and Libbie Kalser; m. Dorothy Cantor 1950; one s. two d.; ed. Carnegie Inst. of Tech. and New York Univ.; Instructor Pratt Inst. 1959–63; visiting critic, Yale 1962–63; Asst. Prof. to Prof., Art Dept. Brooklyn Coll. 1963–82, now Distinguished Prof. Emer.; numerous one-man shows at Allan Frumkin Gallery, New York 1962–83, Frumkin Gallery Chicago 1960–81, and other galleries in U.S.A., U.K. and Europe; participant in numerous group exhbns. at Whitney Museum of American Art and elsewhere; work in perm. collections including Whitney Museum and Museum of Modern Art, New York; mem. American Acad. of Arts and Letters; Fulbright Fellow 1958–59; Guggenheim Fellow 1971–72.

PEARLSTINE, Norman, LL.B.; American journalist; b. 4 Oct. 1942, Philadelphia; s. of Raymond Pearlstine and Gladys (Cohen) Pearlstine; m. Nancy Colbert Friday 1988; ed. Haverford Coll., Univ. of Pennsylvania; staff reporter Wall Street Journal, Dallas, Detroit, L.A. 1968–73, Tokyo Bureau Chief 1973–76, Man. Ed. Asian Wall Street Journal, Hong Kong 1976–78; Exec. Ed. Forbes Magazine, L.A. 1978–80; Nat. News Ed. Wall Street Journal, New York 1980–82, Ed. and Publr. Wall Street Journal Europe, Brussels 1982–83, Man. Ed. and Vice-Pres. Wall Street Journal, New York 1983–91, Exec. Ed. 1991–92; Pres. and C.E.O. Friday Holdings L.P., New York 1993–94; Ed.-in-Chief Time Inc. 1994–; Ed. of Year Award, Nat. Press Foundation 1989; mem. New York Historical Soc., Council on Foreign Relations. *Address:* Time Inc., 1271 Avenue of the Americas, New York, NY 10020, U.S.A.

PEARS, David Francis, M.A., F.B.A.; British university professor; b. 8 Aug. 1921, London; s. of Robert Pears and Gladys Meyers; m. Anne Drew 1963; one s. one d.; ed. Westminster School and Balliol Coll., Oxford; Research Lecturer, Christ Church, Oxford 1948–50, Student 1959–88; Fellow and Tutor, Corpus Christi Coll., Oxford 1950–59; Prof. of Philosophy, Oxford Univ. 1985–88; mem. Inst. Int. de Philosophie, Pres. 1988–90; Foreign Hon. Fellow American Acad. of Arts and Sciences 1996. *Publications:* Bertrand Russell and the British Tradition in Philosophy 1967, Ludwig Wittgenstein 1971, Some Questions in the Philosophy of Mind 1975, Motivated Irrationality 1983, The False Prison: A Study of the Development of Wittgenstein's Philosophy, (Vol. 1) 1987, (Vol. 2) 1988, Hume's System: An Examination of the First Book of His Treatise 1990. *Leisure interests:* entomology, visual art. *Address:* 7 Sandford Road, Littlemore, Oxford, OX4 4PU, England.

PEARSE, Anthony Guy Everson, M.D., F.R.C.P.; British professor of histochemistry; b. 9 Aug. 1916, Birchington, Thanet; s. of Capt. R.G. Pearse and Constance Evelyn Steels; m. Elizabeth Himmelhoch 1947; one s. three d.; ed. Trinity Coll., Cambridge; House Physician, St. Bartholomew's Hosp., London 1940; Surgeon-Lieut., R.N.V.R. 1941–46; Lecturer in Pathology, Royal Postgraduate Medical School, London 1947–57; Consultant Pathologist, Hammersmith Hosp., London 1951–81; Reader and Prof. of Histochemistry, London Univ. 1965–81, Prof. Emer. 1981–; Fulbright Fellow and Visiting Prof. of Pathology, Alabama Univ. 1953–54; Pres., Royal Microscopical Soc. 1972–74; Hon. mem. Mark Twain Soc. 1977; mem. Deutsche Akad. der Naturforscher Leopoldina; Hon. mem. Pathological Soc. 1990; Hon. M.D.

(Basel) 1960, (Krakow) 1978; Horton Smith Prize, Cambridge Univ. 1950; John Hunter Prize, Royal Coll. of Surgeons 1978; Ernst Jung Prize for Medicine 1979, Fred W. Stewart Prize in Oncology 1979, Jan Swammerdam Medal, Dutch Soc. for Advancement of Natural Sciences 1988, Schleiden Medal, Deutsche Akademie der Naturforscher Leopoldina 1989. *Publication:* Histochemistry, Theoretical and Applied, several edns. 1953–91. *Leisure interests:* horticulture, farming, sailing, ship modelling. *Address:* Church Cottage, Church Lane, Cheriton Bishop, Exeter, EX6 6HY, England. *Telephone:* (01647) 24231.

PEARSE, Barbara Mary Frances, B.SC., PH.D., F.R.S.; British/Swiss scientist; b. 24 March 1948, England; d. of Reginald W. B. Pearse, D.SC., F.R.A.S. and Enid Alice (née Mitchell) Pearse; m. Mark Steven Bretscher 1978; one s. one d.; ed. Lady Eleanor Holles School and Univ. Coll., London; Postdoctoral Fellow MRC Lab. of Molecular Biology 1972–81, staff scientist 1981–; Visiting Prof. Stanford Medical Center, U.S.A. 1984–85; mem. European Molecular Biology Org.; Fellow Univ. Coll. London 1996; Jack Drummond Prize 1968, K.M. Stott Prize 1979, European Molecular Biology Org. Gold Medal 1987. *Publication:* European Molecular Biology Org. Review 1987. *Leisure interests:* garden and woodland. *Address:* Medical Research Council, Laboratory of Molecular Biology, Hills Road, Cambridge, CB2 2QH (Office); Ram Cottage, 63 Commercial End, Swaffham Bulbeck, Cambridge, CB5 0ND, England (Home). *Telephone:* (01223) 248011 (Office); (01223) 811276 (Home).

PEARSE, Sir Brian, Kt., F.C.I.B.; British banker; b. 23 Aug. 1933; s. of Francis and Eileen Pearse; m. Patricia M. Callaghan 1959; one s. two d.; ed. St. Edward's Coll., Liverpool; joined Martin's Bank Ltd. 1950; joined Barclays Bank 1969, Local Dir., Birmingham 1972, Gen. Man. 1977, C.E.O., N. America 1983, Finance Dir. Barclays Bank PLC 1987–91; Chief Executive Midland Bank 1991–94; Pres. Chartered Inst. of Bankers 1993–94; Chair. Housing Corpn. 1994–97, British Invisibles 1994–97, Lucas Industries PLC 1994–96, LucasVarity PLC 1996–98; Dir. British American Chamber of Commerce 1987–98; Dir. (non-exec.) Smith & Nephew 1993–; Dir. British Overseas Trade Board 1994–97; Gov. Univ. of Plymouth 1997–; Deputy Chair. Britannic Assurance PLC 1997–. *Leisure interests:* rugby football, opera. *Address:* c/o LucasVarity PLC, 44–46 Park Street, London, W1Y 4DJ, England. *Telephone:* 0171-493 6793. *Fax:* 0171-491 0096.

PEARSON, Ralph Gottfried, PH.D.; American professor of chemistry; b. 12 Jan. 1919, Chicago, Ill.; s. of Gottfried Pearson and Kerstin Pearson (née Larson); m. Lenore Johnson 1941 (died 1982); two s. one d.; ed. Lewis Inst., Northwestern Univ.; First Lieut. U.S.A.F. 1944–46; Asst. Prof. Chem. Dept., Northwestern Univ. 1946–52, Assoc. Prof. 1952–57, Prof. 1957–76; Prof. of Chem. Univ. of Calif., Santa Barbara 1976–89, Prof. Emer. 1989–; mem. N.A.S.; fmr. Guggenheim Fellow; Inorganic Award, American Chemical Soc. *Publications:* Kinetics and Mechanism 1953, Mechanisms of Inorganic Reactions 1958, Hard and Soft Acids and Bases 1974, Symmetry Rules for Chemical Reactions 1976. *Leisure interests:* classical music, hiking. *Address:* c/o Chemistry Department, University of California, Santa Barbara, CA 93106 (Office); 715 Grove Lane, Santa Barbara, CA 93105, U.S.A. (Home). *Telephone:* (805) 893-3745 (Office); (805) 687-7890 (Home).

PEART, Sir (William) Stanley, Kt., M.B., B.S., M.D., F.R.C.P., F.R.S.; British professor of medicine; b. 31 March 1922, South Shields; s. of J. G. Peart and M. Peart; m. Peggy Parkes 1947; one s. one d.; ed. King's Coll. School, Wimbledon, and St. Mary's Hospital Medical School, London; Lecturer in Medicine, St. Mary's Hospital, London 1950–56, Prof. of Medicine 1956–87, Prof. Emer. 1987–; Master, Hunterian Inst. Royal Coll. of Surgeons 1988–92; Chair. Medical Research Soc. 1968, Beit Trust Advisory Bd. 1980, Northwick Park Inst. for Medical Research 1994–; mem. Medical Research Council 1969; mem. Advisory Bd. for the Research Councils 1973; Trustee, Wellcome Trust 1975–94 (Deputy Chair. 1991–94, Consultant 1994–); Councillor, Royal Coll. of Physicians 1977; Stouffer Prize 1968. *Publications:* Clinical Atlas of Hypertension 1991; articles in The Biochemical Journal, Journal of Physiology, The Lancet; chapters in textbooks on renal disease and high blood pressure. *Leisure interests:* reading and tennis. *Address:* 17 Highgate Close, London, N6 4SD, England. *Telephone:* 0181-341 3111. *Fax:* 0181-341 3111.

PEASE, Rendel Sebastian, M.A., SC.D., F.R.S.; British physicist; b. 2 Nov. 1922, Cambridge; s. of Michael Stewart Pease and Helen Bowen Pease (née Wedgwood); m. 1st Susan Spickernell 1952 (died 1996); two s. three d.; m. 2nd Jean Frances White 1998; ed. Bedales School and Trinity Coll., Cambridge; Scientific Officer, Ministry of Aircraft Production at Operational Research Unit, HQ, R.A.F. Bomber Command 1942–46; Research at A.E.R.E., Harwell 1947–61; Div. Head, Culham Lab. for Plasma Physics and Nuclear Fusion, U.K. Atomic Energy Authority (U.K.A.E.A.) 1961–67, Dir. of Culham Lab. 1968–81, Programme Dir. of Fusion 1981–87; Gordon-Godfrey Visiting Prof. of Theoretical Physics, Univ. of N.S.W. 1984, 1988, 1991; Chair. British Pugwash Group 1988–, Council mem. Pugwash Confs. on Science and World Affairs 1992–; Consultant Pease Partners 1988–96; Royal Soc. Assessor, Nuclear Physics Board, S.E.R.C. 1987–93; Visitor, Blackett Lab., Imperial Coll. 1991–; Visiting Scientist, Princeton Univ. 1964–65; Asst. Dir. U.K.A.E.A. Research Group 1967; Vice-Pres. Inst. Physics 1973–77, Royal Soc. 1986–87; Chair. Int. Fusion Research Council 1976–84, Plasma Physics Comm., I.U.P.A.P. 1976–78, W. Ilsley Physics Comm. 1996–; Pres. Inst. of Physics 1978–80; Hon. D.Univ. (Surrey) 1973; Hon. D.Sc. (Aston) 1981, (City) 1987; Hon. Fellow European Nuclear Soc. 1990. *Leisure interest:* music. *Address:* The Poplars, West Ilsley, Newbury, Berks. RG20 7AW, England. *Telephone:* (01635281) 237. *Fax:* (01635281) 688.

PÉBEREAU, Georges Alexandre; French engineer and business executive; b. 20 July 1931, Digne, Basses-Alpes; s. of Alexandre Pébereau and Yvonne Raybaud; m. Bernadette Potier 1954; three d.; ed. Lycées Buffon, Saint-Louis, Paris, Ecole Polytechnique; engineer roads and bridges in various wards 1955–64; Pres. Asscn. des ingénieurs des ponts et chaussées 1964; teacher of Urban Man. École nat. des ponts et chaussées 1964; Chief-Eng., Dept. Seine-St.-Denis 1965, Tech. Counsellor to Ministry of Equipment 1966, Dir. Office Ministry of Equipment and Housing 1967–68; Dir. Land and Urban Man. 1966–68; Vice-Pres. Cttee. action concertée Urbanisation 1967–68; at Cie. industrielle des télécommunications (Cit) 1968–70, Jt. Dir.-Gen. 1968–69, Dir.-Gen. 1969–70; Admin.-Dir.-Gen. Cie. industrielle des télécommunications (Cit-Alcatel) 1970–83, Pres., Dir.-Gen. 1982–86, Hon. Pres. 1986–; at Cie. Gén d'électricité 1970–86, Dir. then Jt. Dir.-Gen. 1970–72, Admin. 1971, Dir.-Gen. 1972, then Chair., Pres. and C.E.O. Admin., Dir. –1986; Hon. Pres. 1986; Co-owner Cie. Privée de Banque 1987; Chair. Marceau Investissements 1987–, Indra Finance 1987–; Pres. Délia Finance 1997–; Dir. numerous eng. cos.; mem. Cttee. de direction et de conseil d'admin. 1970–; mem. conseil d'admin. de la Société des sucreries de Bourbon 1995–, of Musée du Louvre 1996; Commdr. Légion d'honneur, Commdr., Ordre nat. du Mérite. *Address:* 10-12 Avenue de Mesine, 75008 Paris (Office); 19 avenue Charles Floquet, 75007 Paris, France (Home).

PÉBEREAU, Michel Jean Denis; French banker; b. 23 Jan. 1942, Paris; s. of Alexandre Pébereau and Yvonne Raybaud; m. Agnès Faure 1962; two s. two d.; ed. Lycées Buffon and Louis-le-Grand, Paris, Ecole Polytechnique and Ecole Nat. d'Admin.; various appts. in Ministry of Economy and Finance 1970–81; Man. Dir. Crédit Commercial de France 1982–87; Chair. and C.E.O. 1987–93; Chair. and C.E.O. Banque Nationale de Paris (BNP) 1993–; Dir. BNP, Cie. Européenne de Publication, S.A. des Galeries Lafayette, Lafarge Coppée, Saint-Gobain, Lagardère Groupe, Rhône Poulenc, Elf, U.A.P., Renault, Financière BNP, Cie. d'Investissements de Paris, Banque Pour l'Expansion Industrielle, BNP UK Holdings Ltd.; Chair. Banking Operations Comm. of Asscn. Française des Banques; Deputy Chair. Comm. for Control of Cinema Films 1981–85, Comm. for Selective Aid for Film Distribution 1987–88; Lecturer Inst. d'Etudes Politiques Paris 1967–78, Prof. 1980–, mem. Man. Cttee. 1984–; Lecturer Ecole Nat. de Statistiques et d'Admin. Economique 1968–79; Inspecteur Général des Finances; mem. Supervisory Bd. Axa-UAP 1997–, Dresdner Bank 1997–; Pres. Comm. d'exploitation bancaire de l'Association française des banques; Chevalier, Légion d'honneur; Chevalier, Ordre Nat. du Mérite. *Publications:* La politique économique de la France (3 vols.); science fiction book reviews for scientific magazine La Recherche 1983–. *Leisure interest:* piano. *Address:* Banque Nationale de Paris, 16 boulevard des Italiens, 75450 Paris; 14 bis rue Mouton-Duvernet, 75014 Paris, France.

PECK, Gregory, B.A.; American actor; b. 5 April 1916, La Jolla, Calif.; m. 1st Greta Konen Rice 1942 (divorced 1954), two s. (one s. deceased); m. 2nd Veronique Passani 1955, one s. one d.; ed. California Univ.; mem. Nat. Council on Arts 1965–67, 1968–; Pres. Acad. of Motion Picture Arts and Sciences 1967–70; Medal of Freedom Award 1969; Acad. Award (Oscar) best actor 1962; Screen Actors' Guild Annual Award for Outstanding Achievement 1970; Acad. of Motion Picture Arts and Sciences Jean Hersholt Humanitarian Award 1968, Life Achievement Award 1988, Career Award, Cannes Film Festival 1989; Commdr., Ordre des Arts et des Lettres (France), Kennedy Center Honor 1991, Officier, Légion d'honneur. *Appeared in plays including:* The Doctor's Dilemma, The Male Animal, Once in a Lifetime, The Play's the Thing, You Can't Take it With You, The Morning Star, The Willow and I, Sons and Soldiers. *Films include:* Days of Glory 1943, Keys of the Kingdom 1944, Spellbound 1945, The Valley of Decision 1945, Duel in the Sun 1946, The Macomber Affair 1947, Gentleman's Agreement 1947, The Paradine Case 1948, Yellow Sky 1949, Twelve O'Clock High 1949, The Great Sinner 1949, Captain Horatio Hornblower 1951, David and Bathsheba 1951, The Snows of Kilimanjaro 1952, Roman Holiday 1953, The Purple Plain 1954, The Man in the Grey Flannel Suit 1956, Moby Dick 1956, Designing Woman 1957, The Big Country, The Bravados 1958, Pork Chop Hill 1959, On the Beach 1959, Beloved Infidel 1959, Guns of Navarone 1961, Cape Fear 1962, To Kill a Mocking Bird 1962, How the West Was Won 1963, Captain Newman, M.D. 1963, Behold a Pale Horse 1964, Mirage 1964, Arabesque 1965, The Stalking Moon 1968, Mackenna's Gold 1969, The Chairman 1969, Marooned 1969, I Walk the Line 1970, Shoot Out 1971, Billy Two-Hats 1972, The Omen 1976, MacArthur 1977, The Boys from Brazil 1978, The Sea Wolves 1980, The Blue and the Gray 1981 (TV), The Scarlet and the Black 1983 (TV), Amazing Grace and Chuck 1987, The Old Gringo 1989, Other People's Money, Cape Fear 1991, Sinatra: 80 Years My Way 1995, A Salute to Martin Scorsese 1997, Moby Dick 1998; producer The Dove 1974, The Portrait 1993. *Address:* c/o Academy of Motion Picture Arts and Sciences, 8949 Wilshire Boulevard, Beverly Hills, CA 90211, U.S.A.

PECKER, David J., C.P.A.; American publishing executive; b. 24 Sept. 1951; ed. Pace and New York Univs.; m. Karen Balan 1987; fmrly. Sr. Auditor Price Waterhouse & Co.; fmrly. Man. Financial Reporting Diamandis Communications Inc., also Dir. Financial Reporting, Dir. Accounting, Asst. Controller; Exec. Vice-Pres. Hachette Magazines Inc. 1990–91, Pres. 1991–92, Pres., C.E.O. 1992–; mem. Fashion Group's Int. Advisory Bd., N.Y. City Partnership Cttee., American Man. Asscn.; mem. Bd. Dirs. Pace Univ.,

Drug Enforcement Agents Foundation 1995–. *Address:* Hachette Magazines Incorporated, 1633 Broadway, Floor 45, New York, NY 10019, U.S.A.

PECKER, Jean-Claude; French astronomer; b. 10 May 1923, Reims; s. of Victor-Noel Pecker and Nelly Catherine Herrmann; m. 2nd Annie A. Vormser 1974; one s. two d. (by previous m.); ed. Lycée de Bordeaux, Univs. of Grenoble and Paris (Sorbonne) and Ecole Normale Supérieure; Research Asst. C.N.R.S. 1946–52; Assoc. Prof. Univ. of Clermont-Ferrand 1952–55; Assoc. Astronomer, Paris Observatory 1955–62, Astronomer 1962–65; Dir. Nice Observatory 1962–69; Prof. Coll. de France 1963–89, Hon. Prof. 1989–; Asst. Gen. Sec. Int. Astronomical Union 1961–63, Gen. Sec. 1964–67; Pres. Comité Nat. Français d'Astronomie 1970–73; Dir. Inst. Astrophysique, Paris 1971–78; Pres. Soc. Astronomique de France 1973–76; Pres. French Asscn. for Advancement of Science 1978; Chair. Orientation Cttee., Sciences-Industries Museum, La Villette 1983–85; Chair. Nat. Cttee. Scientific and Tech. Culture 1985–87; Vice-Chair. French Comm. for UNESCO 1991–96; Perm. Rep. to UNESCO of Int. Humanist and Ethical Union; Vice-Chair. Scientific Cttee. Musées de France 1988–; Assoc. Royal Soc. of Science, Liège 1967; Corresp. Bureau des Longitudes 1968; Assoc. Royal Astronomical Soc. 1968; Corresp mem. Acad. des Sciences, France 1969, mem. 1977; mem. Acad. Nat. Bordeaux 1977, Acad. Royale Belgique 1979, Acad. European of Science, Arts and Letters 1982, Int. Acad. of Humanism 1983 (Sec.), Acad. Europaea 1988 (Council mem., Vice-Pres. 1989–92); Prix Forthuny, Inst. de France, Prix Stroobant Acad. des Sciences de Belgique 1965, Prix Manley-Bendall de l'Acad. de Bordeaux 1966, Prix des Trois Physiciens 1969; Janssen Medal Astronomical Soc., France 1967, Prix Jean Perrin, Soc. Française de Physique 1973, Medal Univ. de Nice 1972, Adion Medal 1981, Prix Union Rationaliste 1983, Personnalité de l'année 1984, Janssen Medal (Photographic Soc. of France) 1989, Lodén Prize, Royal Astronomical Soc. of Sweden 1996; Commdr., Palmes académiques, Commdr. Légion d'honneur, Commdr., Ordre nat. du Mérite. *Publications include:* L'astronomie au jour le jour (with P. Couderc and E. Schatzman) 1954, Astrophysique générale (with E. Schatzman) 1959, Le ciel 1959, L'astronomie expérimentale 1969, Les laboratoires spatiaux 1969, Papa, dis-moi: L'astronomie, qu'est-ce que c'est? 1971; Ed. L'astronomie nouvelle 1971, Clefs pour l'Astronomie 1981, Sous l'étoile soleil 1984, Astronomie (Ed.) 1985, Pour comprendre l'univers (with Delsemme and Reeves) 1988, L'avenir du soleil 1990, Le promeneur du ciel 1992, Le soleil est une étoile 1992, Débat sur les phénomènes paranormaux 1997, Understanding the Universe 1998. *Leisure interests:* painting, poetry. *Address:* Annexe du Collège de France, 3 rue d'Ulm, 75005 Paris (Office); Pusat-Tasek, Les Corbeaux, 85350 L'Ile d'Yeu, France (Home). *Telephone:* (01) 44 27 16 95 (Collège de France). *Fax:* (01) 44 27 11 85 (Collège de France); (02) 51 59 43 59 (L'Ile d'Yeu).

PECKHAM, Sir Michael John, Kt., M.A., M.D., F.R.C.P., F.R.C.PATH., F.R.C.R., F.R.C.S.; British medical practitioner and university professor; b. 2 Aug. 1935, Panteg, Wales; s. of Gladys Mary Peckham (née Harris) and William Stuart Peckham; m. Catherine Stevenson King 1958; three s.; ed. St. Catharine's Coll. Cambridge, Univ. Coll. Hosp. Medical School; Sr. Lecturer, Inst. of Cancer Research 1972–74, Prof. and Hon. Consultant, Inst. of Cancer Research and Royal Marsden Hosp. 1974–86, Dean Inst. of Cancer Research 1984–86; Dir. British Postgrad. Medical Fed. 1986–90; Ed.-in-Chief European Journal of Cancer 1990–95; Dir. of Research and Devt., Dept. of Health 1991–95; Dir. School of Public Policy, Univ. Coll. London 1996–; Vice-Chair. Imperial Cancer Research Fund 1987–90; Founding Pres. British Oncological Asscn. 1986–88; Pres. Fed. of European Cancer Socs. 1989–91, European Soc. for Therapeutic Radiology and Oncology 1983–85; Foreign Assoc. mem. N.A.S. Inst. of Medicine 1994–; Hon. Fellow St. Catherine's Coll., Cambridge 1998; Hon. Dr. (Besançon); Hon. D.Sc. (Loughborough), (Exeter) 1996; Dr. h.c. (Catholic Univ. of Louvain) 1993. *Publications:* books and articles on cancer research and cancer treatment. *Leisure interest:* painting. *Address:* School of Public Policy, University College London, 29 Tavistock Square, London, WC1H 9EZ, England. *Telephone:* 0171-504 4966. *Fax:* 0171-504 4969.

PECKOVÁ, Dagmar; Czech opera singer (mezzo soprano); b. 4 April 1961, Chrudim; m. 2nd Aleš Kaspřík 1997; one s.; ed. Prague Conservatory; with Music Theatre, Prague 1982–85; soloist with numerous cos. including Czech Philarmony 1985–, with State Opera Berlin 1985–91, with Semper Opera, Dresden 1987–88; concert tours Austria, Switzerland, Germany, U.K., France, U.S.A. 1997–99; First Prize Antonin Dvořák Competition 1982; European Foundation for Music prize 1993. *Recordings include:* Martinů — Nipponari 1991, Mozart — Che Bella 1994, Janáček — Moravian Folk Poetry in Song 1994, Mahler — Adagietto, Kindertotenlieder 1996, Live in Prague 1996, Songs of Mahler and Berio 1997, Janáček—Kátă Kabanová 1997. *Leisure interests:* reading, no time, car driving. *Address:* Krocinova 1, 110 00 Prague 1, Czech Republic. *Telephone:* 242 292 93 (Office); 24229293 (Home). *Fax:* 24229293.

PÉCSI, Márton; Hungarian geographer; b. 29 Dec. 1923, Budapest; s. of Dani de Pécsi and Róza Simon; m. Dr. Éva Donáth 1954; one d.; ed. Pázmány Péter Univ. Budapest; Lecturer, Faculty of Natural Sciences, Eötvös Loránd Univ., Budapest 1949, Prof. 1966–; Ed.-in-Chief, Studies in Geography in Hungary; mem. ed. bd. six int. geographical periodicals; Pres. Hungarian Geographical Soc. 1981–89, Hon. Pres. 1989–; Visiting Prof. at several foreign univs.; mem. Hungarian Acad. of Sciences Research Inst. of Geography 1952–; corresp. mem. Hungarian Acad. of Sciences 1965, Full mem. 1976–; mem. Österreichische Akad. der Wissenschaften 1981–, Deutsche Akad. der Naturforscher Leopoldina, Halle 1985, Acad. of Sciences of Slovenia, Acad. Scientiarium Gottingensis 1989–, Acad. of Sciences of Poland 1993–, New York Acad. of Sciences 1998–; Hon. mem. several nat. geographic socs.; Hon. mem. Int. Union for Quaternary Research INQUA; Pres. INQUA Comm. on Loess 1977–91, on Paleographic Atlas of the Quaternary 1991–96; State Prize 1975, Széchenyi Prize 1990, World Lifetime Achievement Award 1993. *Publications:* A magyarországi Dunavölgy kialakulása (Development and Geomorphology of the Danube Valley in Hungary) 1960, Geomorphology 1975; co-author and ed. Landscapes of Hungary (six vols.), National Atlas of Hungary 1989, Atlas of Paleoclimates and Paleoenvironments of the Northern Hemisphere 1992, Quaternary and Loess Research 1993, Löss: Herkunft, Gliederung, Landschatten 1996, Geomorphological Regions of Hungary 1996, and more than 500 articles. *Leisure interest:* photography. *Address:* Geographical Research Institute of the Hungarian Academy of Sciences, P.O. Box 64, Andrássy ut 62, 1388 Budapest (Office); Dozsa u. 7, 2747 Törtel, Hungary (Home). *Telephone:* (1) 3317-325; 3116-838 (Office); (53) 376.243 (Home). *Fax:* (1) 3317-991 (Office); (53) 376.243 (Home).

PEDERSEN, Carl Th., DR.PHIL.; Danish academic; b. 28 June 1935, Nykøbing Mors; s. of Søren Pedersen and Signe Pedersen; m. Anna M. G. Pedersen 1960; two d.; ed. Univ. of Copenhagen; Assoc. Prof. Univ. of Copenhagen 1960, Univ. of Caen 1968–69; Prof. of Chem. Odense Univ. 1972, Dean, Faculty of Science 1976–83, Rector 1983–93; Chair. Bd. Int. Science Park, Odense 1990–93; Guest Prof. Univ. of Queensland, Australia, Univ. of Tokyo 1993; mem. Danish Acad. of Tech. Sciences; Fyns Stiftidendes Forskerpris 1975. *Publications:* publs. on the chemistry of organic sulphur compounds in scientific journals. *Address:* Campusvej 55, 5230 Odense M (Office); Benediktes Alle 2, 5250 Odense SV, Denmark (Home). *Telephone:* 66158600 (Office); 66130459 (Home).

PEDERSEN, Gert K., M.SC., DR.PHIL.; Danish mathematician; b. 13 April 1940, Copenhagen; m. Dorte Olesen 1971; two s. one d.; ed. Univ. of Copenhagen; Lecturer, Univ. of Copenhagen 1968–75, Prof. of Math. 1975–; Co-ordinator European Network in Operator Algebra 1994–; Chair. Danish Math. Soc. 1974–78; mem. Royal Danish Acad., Vice-Pres. 1987–93; mem. Royal Norwegian Acad.; awarded Knud Sand Domicile 1988; Kt. of Dannebrog 1990. *Publications:* C*-algebras and their automorphism groups 1979, Analysis Now 1988; numerous articles on operator algebra in scientific journals. *Leisure interest:* music. *Address:* Mathematical Institute, Universitetsparken 5, 2100 Copenhagen Ø (Office); Kildeskovsvej 81, 2820 Gentofte, Denmark (Home). *Telephone:* 35320723 (Office); 39681744 (Home). *Fax:* 35320704 (Office); 39681788 (Home).

PEDERSEN, K. George, O.C., PH.D.; Canadian professor and university president (retd.); b. 13 June 1931, Peace River, Alberta; s. of Hjalmar Pedersen and Anna Jensen; m. 1st Joan Vanderwarher 1953 (died 1988), 2nd Penny Jones 1988; one s. one d.; ed. Chilliwack Sr. High School and Univs. of B.C., Washington and Chicago; school teacher, N. Vancouver school system 1952–56; Vice-Prin., North Star Elementary School 1956–59; Prin. Carisbrooke Elementary School 1959–61; Vice-Prin., Handsworth Secondary School 1961–63; Prin., Balmoral Secondary School 1963–65; Research Assoc. Univ. of Chicago 1965–68; Asst. Prof. Ont. Inst. for Studies in Educ. and Univ. of Toronto 1968–70; Assoc. Dir. Midwest Admin. Center, Univ. of Chicago 1970–72; Dean, Faculty of Educ. Univ. of Vic. 1972–75, Vice-Pres. (Academic) 1975–78; Pres. and Vice-Chancellor Simon Fraser Univ. 1979–83, Univ. of B.C. 1983–85, Univ. of Western Ont. 1985–94, Univ. of Northern B.C. 1998–, Royal Roads Univ. 1995–96; Fellow, Canadian Coll. of Teachers, Royal Soc. for Encouragement of Arts; Univ. of Chicago Scholarships 1965–68, Canada Council Scholarships 1966–68; Ford Foundation Fellowship 1967–68; Hon. LL.D. (McMaster) 1996; Commemorative Medal 1992; Order of Ont. 1994. *Publications:* The Itinerant Schoolmaster 1973; book chapters and numerous articles. *Leisure interests:* fishing, golf. *Address:* 2232 Spruce Street, Vancouver, B.C., V6H 2P3, Canada. *Telephone:* (604) 733-2400. *Fax:* (604) 733-2400.

PEDERSEN, Richard Foote, PH.D.; American university administrator and fmr. diplomatist; b. 21 Feb. 1925, Miami, Ariz.; s. of Ralph M. Pedersen and Gertrude M. Pedersen; m. Nelda Newell Napier 1953; one s. two d.; ed. Univ. of the Pacific, Stanford and Harvard Univs.; Foreign Affairs Officer, UN Econ. and Social Affairs, Dept. of State 1950–53; Econ. and Social Affairs Adviser, Perm. Mission to UN 1953, held successive posts of Adviser on Political and Security Affairs, Sr. Adviser and Chief of Political Section, Counsellor, Sr. Adviser to Perm. Rep. to UN, with rank of Amb.; Deputy U.S. Rep. in UN Security Council 1967–69; Counsellor, Dept. of State 1969–73; Amb. to Hungary 1973–75; Sr. Vice-Pres. United States Trust Co. 1975–78; Pres. American Univ. in Cairo 1978–90; Dir. int. programs, Calif. State Polytechnic Univ., Pomona 1990–95; mem. Council on Foreign Relations, New York, Royal Inst. of Int. Affairs, London, UNA of U.S.A., Middle East Inst., American Soc. of Int. Law, L.A. World Affairs Council, Advisory Bd. Fulbright Cultural Enrichment Program, S. Calif., American Foreign Service Asscn., Pacific Council on Int. Policy, Asia Soc.; Bd. mem. Center for Civic Educ. 1995–; Chair. Advisory Bd. School of Int. Studies, Univ. of the Pacific 1997–; Advisory Bd. mem. Nat. Council on US/Arab Relations 1985–; Advisory Council mem. Center for Near Eastern Studies, UCLA 1996–; Hon. LL.D. (George Williams Coll.) 1964, (Univ. of the Pacific) 1965, (American Univ. in Cairo) 1997; Order of Sacred Treasure, Japan, Order of Arts and Sciences, Egypt. *Leisure interests:* swimming, YMCA, Egyptology.

Address: 2503 North Mountain Avenue, Claremont, CA 91711 (Home). *Telephone:* (909) 399 5246 (Home).

PEDERSEN, Thor; Danish politician; b. 14 June 1945, Søllerød; s. of Laurits Pedersen; ed. Copenhagen Univ.; fmr. mem. staff, Assessments Div.; fmr. Man. Dir. of a construction co., North Zealand; fmr. Mayor of Helsinge; mem. Folketing (Parl.) 1985–; Minister of Housing 1986–87, of the Interior 1987–93, of Nordic Affairs 1988, of Economic Affairs 1992–93. *Address:* Folketing, Copenhagen, Denmark.

PEDERSON, Donald Oscar, PH.D.; American professor of electrical engineering and computer science; b. 30 Sept. 1925, Hallock, Minn.; s. of Oscar Jorgan Pederson and Beda Emelia (Dahlof) Pederson; m.; one s. three d.; ed. Iowa State and Stanford Univs.; Research Assoc., Stanford Univ. 1951–53; mem. Tech. Staff, Bell Telephone Labs., Murray Hill, N.J. 1953–55; mem. Faculty, Univ. of Calif., Berkeley 1955, Dir. Electronics Research Lab. 1960–64, fmr. Prof. of Electrical Eng. and Computer Science, Chair. Dept. 1983–85, presently Buttner Prof. of Electrical Eng.; Guggenheim Fellow; mem. N.A.S., Nat. Acad. of Eng. *Publications:* Principles of Circuit Synthesis 1959, Elementary Circuit Properties of Transistors 1964, Multistage Transistor Circuits 1965, Electronic Circuits 1965, Introduction to Electronic Devices, Circuits and Systems 1966; contribs. to numerous engineering publs. *Address:* c/o Department of Electrical Engineering and Computer Science, 516 Cory Hall, University of California, Berkeley, CA 94720; 1436 Via Loma, Walnut Creek, CA 94598, U.S.A. (Home).

PEDNYCYA, Kazys; Lithuanian lawyer; b. 16 Nov. 1949, Plaskunai, Kaisiadoriai Region, Lithuania; m. Viktorija Pednyciene; two s.; ed. Vilnius State Univ.; interrogator Kedainai Regional Public Prosecutor's Office 1972–76; Asst. Public Prosecutor Panevezys City 1976–84; Supervision Prosecutor, Lithuanian Repub. Reformatories 1984–91; Judge, Lithuanian Repub. Supreme Court 1991–92; Sr. Customs Official, Lithuanian Repub. 1992–93; Asst. Dir.-Gen. Lithuanian Nat. Security Dept. 1993–97; Gen. Public Prosecutor 1997–. *Address:* LR Generaline Prokuratura, A. Smetonos 4, LT-2702, Vilnius (Office); Justiniskiu 36-20, LT-2000 Vilnius, Lithuania (Home). *Telephone:* (370) 61 16 20 (Office); (370) 22 83 38 (Home). *Fax:* (370) 61 18 26 (Office).

PEERS, Most Rev. Michael Geoffrey, B.A. (HONS.), L.TH.; Canadian ecclesiastic; b. 31 July 1934; s. of Geoffrey H. Peers and Dorothy E. Mantle; m. Dorothy E. Bradley 1963; two s. one d.; ed. Univs. of British Columbia and Heidelberg and Trinity Coll. Toronto; ordained priest 1960; Curate, Ottawa 1959–65; Univ. Chaplain, Diocese of Ottawa 1961–66; Rector, St. Bede's, Winnipeg 1966–72, St. Martin's, Winnipeg with St. Paul's Middlechurch 1972–74; Archdeacon of Winnipeg 1969–74; Rector, St. Paul's Cathedral, Regina 1974–77; Dean of Qu'Appelle 1974–77; Bishop of Qu'Appelle 1977–82; Archbishop of Qu'Appelle and Metropolitan of Rupert's Land 1982–86; Primate, Anglican Church of Canada 1986–; mem. Cen. Cttee. World Council of Churches 1991–; Hon. D.D. (Trinity Coll. Toronto) 1978, (St. John's Coll. Winnipeg) 1981, (Kent Univ.) 1988, (Montreal Diocesan Coll.) 1989, (Coll. of Emmanuel and St. Chad, Saskatoon) 1990; Hon. D.C.L. (Bishop's Univ., Lennoxville) 1993. *Address:* 600 Jarvis Street, Toronto, Ont., M4Y 2J6; 195 Westminster Avenue, Toronto, Ont., M6R 1N9, Canada. *Telephone:* (416) 924-9192.

PEERTHUM, Satteeanund; Mauritian diplomatist; b. 15 March 1941; m.; three c.; ed. People's Friendship Univ., Moscow; Sr. Research Fellow Inst. of Oriental Studies, Moscow 1973–74; Head History Dept., Bhojoharry Coll., Mauritius several times between 1975 and 1987; Sr. Research Fellow School of Mauritian Asian and African Studies, Mahatma Gandhi Inst. 1985–87; founding mem. Mouvement Socialiste Militant; mem. Mauritian Parl. and Minister of Labour and Industrial Relations 1982–83; Chair. Sugar Industry Devt. Fund Boards of Mauritius 1984–87; Perm. Rep. to UN 1987–96; Chair. Nat. Steering Cttee. for the Teaching of Mauritian History; mem. Advisory Cttee. African Cultural Centre of Mauritius 1986–87; fmr. mem. Court Nat. Univ. of Mauritius. *Address:* Permanent Mission of Mauritius to the United Nations, 211 East 43rd Street, Suite 2000, New York, NY 10017, U.S.A. *Telephone:* (212) 949-0190.

PEI IEOH MING, M.ARCH., F.A.I.A., R.I.B.A.; American architect; b. 26 April 1917, Canton, China; s. of Tsu Yee Pei and Lien Kwun Chwong; m. Eileen Loo 1942; three s. one d.; ed. Shanghai, Massachusetts Inst. of Tech. and Harvard Univ.; in U.S.A. 1935–; naturalized citizen 1954; architectural practice 1939–, Webb and Knapp Inc. 1948–55, Pei, Cobb, Freed & Partners (fmrly. I. M. Pei & Partners) 1955–96, independent architect 1996–; Asst. Prof. Harvard Graduate School of Design 1945–48; Wheelwright Traveling Fellowship, Harvard Univ. 1951; M.I.T. Traveling Fellowship 1940; Fellow A.I.A.; mem. Nat. Council on the Humanities 1966–70, American Acad. of Arts and Sciences, Nat. Acad. of Design, American Acad. of Arts and Letters (Chancellor 1978–80), Nat. Council on the Arts 1981–84, R.I.B.A., Urban Design Council (New York), Corpn. of M.I.T. 1972–77, 1978–83, American Philosophical Soc., Institut de France (Foreign Assoc.); Hon. D.F.A. (Pennsylvania) 1970, (Rensselaer Polytechnic Inst.) 1978, (Northeastern Univ.) 1979, (Univs. of Mass., Rochester, Brown) 1982, (New York Univ.) 1983; Hon. LL.D. (Chinese Univ. of Hong Kong) 1970, Hon. D.H.L. (Columbia Univ., Univs. of Colorado, Rochester, Hong Kong, American Univ. of Paris); Hon. Prof. Tonji Univ., Shanghai 1985; Brunner Award, Nat. Inst. of Arts and Letters 1961; Medal of Honor N.Y. Chapter A.I.A. 1963, The Thomas Jefferson Memorial Medal for Architecture 1976, Gold Medal (American Acad. of Arts and Letters) 1979, Gold Medal (American Inst. of Architects) 1979, La Grande Medaille d'Or (Académie d'Architecture) 1981, Pritzker Architecture Prize 1983, Asia Soc. Award 1984, Medal of Liberty 1986, Nat. Medal of Arts 1988, Praemium Imperiale (Japan Art Asscn.) 1989, Univ. of Calif. Gold Medal 1990, Calbert Award for Excellence 1991, Presidential Medal of Freedom 1992, Edward MacDowell Medal 1998, Commdr., Ordre des Arts et des Lettres; Officier, Légion d'honneur 1988. *Projects include:* Mile High Center (Denver); M.I.T. Earth Science Bldg. (Cambridge, Mass.); U.S. Embassy Bldg. (Montevideo); East-West Center, Univ. of Hawaii; redevt. projects in New York, Philadelphia, Washington, Chicago, Pittsburgh and Singapore; Nat. Center for Atmospheric Research (Boulder, Colorado); Grave of Robert F. Kennedy; Nat. Airlines Terminal (Kennedy Int. Airport); Washington Sq. East (Philadelphia); Everson Museum of Art (Syracuse N.Y.); Nat. Gallery of Art East Bldg. (Washington, D.C.); Wilmington Tower (Wilmington, Del.); John Fitzgerald Kennedy Library Complex (Boston, Mass.); Canadian Imperial Bd. of Commerce Complex (Toronto); Des Moines Art Center Addition (Des Moines, Iowa); Cleo Rogers Memorial County Library (Columbus, Ind.); planning projects in Boston, Oklahoma City and New York; Master Plan Columbia Univ. (N.Y.) 1970; Dallas Municipal Bldg. (Dallas); Raffles City (Singapore); Overseas-Chinese Banking Corpn. Centre (Singapore); Herbert F. Johnson Museum of Art (Ithaca, N.Y.); New West Wing, Museum of Fine Arts (Boston, Mass.); Mellon Art Center, The Choate School (Wallingford, Conn.), Sunning Plaza (Hong Kong), Fragrant Hills Hotel (Beijing), Javits Convention Center, Texas Commerce Tower (Houston), Meyerson Symphony Center, IBM (Purchase, N.Y.), Le Grand Louvre (Paris), Bank of China (Hong Kong), Luce Chapel (Taiwan), Rock-and-Roll Hall of Fame in Cleveland 1995, Museum of Modern Art, Athens, Bilbao Estuary Project, Four Seasons Hotel, New York, Musee Miko, Kyoto 1998. *Address:* Pei Cobb Freed & Partners, 600 Madison Avenue, New York, NY 10022 (Office); 11 Sutton Place, New York, NY 10022, U.S.A. (Home). *Telephone:* (212) 751-3122 (Office).

PEI SHENGJI; Chinese ethnobiologist; b. 15 July 1938, Zitong, Sichuan; s. of Pei Hua-di and Bai-Yi-hua; m. Shen Peiqiong 1965; one s. two d.; ed. Chengdu Agric. School, Sichuan Prov.; advanced training at Univ. of Hawaii 1983–84; fmr. Dir. Yunnan Inst. of Tropical Botany; Deputy Dir. Kunming Inst. of Botany, Chinese Acad. of Sciences 1987–90; Div. Head, Mountain Environment Man., Int. Centre for Integrated Devt., Kathmandu 1990–95; research in biodiversity and indigenous knowledge. *Publications:* Botanical Gardens in China 1984, Iconographic Chinese Material Medica (Vol. 8) 1990, Flora of China, Vol. 13-2, Palmae 1991, Ethnobotany in China, Edible Flowers of China 1991, Biodiversity in Agroecosystems of Southeast Asia: Concepts, Approaches and Methodologies (ed. with Percy Sajasi) 1995, Ethnobotany of Indigenous Non-wood Forest Products in Xishuangbanna of Yunnan in Southwest China 1995, and forty-five articles. *Leisure interests:* photography, stamp collecting, excursions, visiting temples. *Address:* International Centre for Integrated Development, P.O. Box 3226, Kathmandu, Nepal. *Telephone:* (1) 525313. *Fax:* (1) 524509.

PEI YANLING; Chinese actress; b. Aug. 1947, Shuning Co., Hebei Prov. *Performances include:* The Man and the Ghost, Lotus Lantern and others. Vice-Chair. Hebei Fed. of Literary and Art Circles 1993–; mem. 7th CPPCC 1987–92, 8th 1993–. *Address:* Hebei Federation of Literary and Art Circles, Shijiazhuang City, People's Republic of China.

PEICHL, Gustav; Austrian architect; b. 18 March 1928, Vienna; Prof. Acad. of Fine Arts, Vienna; important bldgs. include: Austrian Broadcasting Stations in Salzburg, Linz, Innsbrück, Dornbirn 1970–72, Graz 1979–80, Eisenstadt 1981–83; EFA Radio Satellite Station, Aflenz 1976–79; PEA-Phosphate Elimination Plant, Berlin-Tegel; design for Papal visit to Vienna 1984; art and exhbn. centre, Bonn 1986–92; extension to Städel Museum, Frankfurt-am-Main; ÖMV-Center, Vienna 1991–; rehearsal stage of Burgtheater, Vienna 1991–93; Award of City of Vienna for Architecture, Austrian State Award, Reynolds Memorial Award, Styria Award for Architecture, Mies van der Rohe Award, Berlin Architectural Award; Verleihung der Grossen Verdienst-Kreuzes des Verdienstordens 1996. *Address:* Opernring 4, A-1010 Vienna, Austria. *Telephone:* 512-32-07; 512-32-48. *Fax:* 512-32-48/71.

PEIMBERT, Manuel, PH.D.; Mexican astronomer; b. 9 June 1941, Mexico City; s. of Gonzalo Peimbert and Catalina Sierra; m. Silvia Torres-Peimbert 1962; one s. one d.; ed. Universidad Nacional Autónoma de México (UNAM) and Univ. of Calif. Berkeley; Research Asst. Instituto de Astronomía, UNAM 1960–63; Research Asst. Univ. of Calif. Berkeley 1963–64, Postdoctoral Fellow 1967–68; Prof. Faculty of Sciences, UNAM 1968–, Instituto de Astronomía 1970–; on sabbatical leave at Univ. Coll. London 1976, Tokyo Astronomical Observatory 1986; Vice-Pres. Int. Astronomical Union 1982–88; Foreign Assoc. N.A.S.; Fellow, Third World Acad. of Sciences; Assoc. Royal Astronomical Soc.; Science Prize, Acad. de la Investigación Científica 1971; Guillaume Budé Medal, Coll. de France 1974; Investigador ad Honorem, F. J. Duarte Center for Astronomy, Venezuela 1981; Mexican Nat. Prize in Science and Arts 1981; UNAM Science Prize 1988. *Publications:* more than 100 research papers in int. journals of astronomy and astrophysics. *Address:* Instituto de Astronomía, Universidad Nacional Autónoma de México, Apartado Postal 70-264, Mexico D.F., México 04510. *Telephone:* 525-6223906. *Fax:* 525 6160653.

PEINEMANN, Edith; German concert violinist; b. 3 March 1939, Mainz; d. of Robert Peinemann and Hildegard (née Rohde) Peinemann; studied under her father and later with Heinz Stauske and Max Rostal at the Guildhall School of Music, London; First Prize, ARD competition, Munich 1956; since then has performed with leading orchestras and conductors worldwide; Prof. of Music, Frankfurt. *Leisure interests:* art, hiking, cooking, cross-county skiing.

PEIRIS, Gamini Lakshman, D.PHIL., PH.D.; Sri Lankan academic; b. 13 Aug. 1946, Colombo; s. of Glanville S. Peiris and Lakshmi C. Salgado; m. Savitri N. Amarasuriya 1971; one d.; ed. St. Thomas' Coll. Mount Lavinia, Univ. of Ceylon and New Coll. Oxford; Prof. of Law, Univ. of Colombo 1979, Dean, Faculty of Law 1982–88; Vice-Chancellor, Univ. of Colombo –1994; Dir. Nat. Film Corpn. of Sri Lanka 1973–88; Commr. Law Comm. of Sri Lanka 1986–; mem. Inc. Soc. of Legal Educ. 1986–; Visiting Fellow, All Souls Coll. Oxford 1980–81; Butterworths Visiting Fellow, Inst. of Advanced Legal Studies, Univ. of London 1984; Distinguished Visiting Fellow, Christ's Coll. Cambridge 1985–86; Smuts Visiting Fellow in Commonwealth Studies, Univ. of Cambridge 1985–86; Chair. Cttee. of Vice-Chancellors of the Univs. of Sri Lanka; Vice-Chair. Janasaviya Trust Fund; mem. Securities Council of Sri Lanka 1987–; mem. Pres. Comm. on Youth Unrest 1989; mem. Nat. Educ. Comm., Exec. Cttee. of Asscn. of Teachers and Researchers in Intellectual Property Law, Bd. of Govs. of Inst. of Fundamental Studies; assoc. mem. Int. Acad. of Comparative Law; Presidential Award 1987. *Publications:* Law of Unjust Enrichment in South Africa and Ceylon 1971, General Principles of Criminal Liability in Ceylon 1972, Offences under the Penal Code of Sri Lanka 1973, The Law of Evidence in Sri Lanka 1974, Criminal Procedure in Sri Lanka 1975, The Law of Property in Sri Lanka 1976, Landlord and Tenant in Sri Lanka 1977; numerous articles on comparative and admin. law, and law of evidence. *Leisure interest:* walking. *Address:* 37 Kirula Place, Colombo 5, Sri Lanka. *Telephone:* 582488.

PEIROTES, Yves Jean-Marie, M.SC.; French business executive; b. 7 Nov. 1940, Epinal, Vosges; s. of Marcel Georges Peirotes and Germaine Eugénie Schaeffer; m. 1st Victoria Longacre 1968 (divorced 1981); two s.; m. 2nd Viviane France Bastiani 1987; ed. Lycée de Belfort, Lycée Kleber, Strasbourg, Ecole Polytechnique, Paris, Ecole Nat. Supérieure du Génie Maritime, Paris, Univ. of Calif. at Berkeley; prin. engineer Maritime Eng., Del. Ministérielle pour l'Armement 1966–70; Head of Logistics, Strafor, Strasbourg 1971–72, Tech. and Industrial Devt. Dir. 1972–77; Gen. Man. Industrial Equipment Div., Forges de Strasbourg 1997–81; Man. Dir. Air Industrie 1981–84; Chair., Man. Dir. Sofiltra Poelman 1981–84; Deputy Man. Dir. Cie. Industrielle et Financière de Pompey 1984–85; Gen. Man. White Goods Div. Electrolux France 1985–90, White Goods & Floor Care Appliances Div. 1990–94, Man. Dir. Electrolux S.A. 1995–97, Chair. and Man. Dir. 1997–; Chair. Usines et Fonderies Arthur Martin 1985–; Pres. Bureau Départemental d'Industrialisation des Ardennes 1987–91; mem. Advisory Bd. Senlis branch, Banque de France 1995–; Chevalier, Ordre nat. du Mérite. *Leisure interests:* skiing, jogging, swimming. *Address:* Electrolux, 43 ave. Félix Louat, 60300 Senlis (Office); 6 place Winston Churchill, 92200 Neuilly sur Seine, France (Home). *Telephone:* (03) 44.62.28.00 (Office). *Fax:* (03) 44.62.21.89.

PEISACH, Max, PH.D., D.SC., F.R.S.S.A., F.R.P.S.L.; South African nuclear analytical chemist; b. 3 Aug. 1926, Birzai, Lithuania; s. of Hyman Peisach and Sonia Kantor; m. Eunice Sheila Glick 1950; one s. three d.; ed. Boys' High School, Worcester, S.A., Univ. of Cape Town; demonstrator, Univ. of Cape Town 1948–49, Jr. lecturer 1949–50, lecturer 1950–53; Research Officer, Nat. Chemical Research Lab., S. African Council for Scientific and Industrial Research 1953–57, Sr. Research Officer 1957–60; Head, Isotope Production, Israel Atomic Energy Comm. 1960–63; Head Chem. Div., Southern Univs. Nuclear Inst. 1963–83; Head Nuclear Analytical Chem. Div., Nat. Accelerator Centre 1983–91, Chief Specialist Researcher 1986–91; mem. Int. Cttee. on Modern Trends in Activation Analysis 1969–91, Hon. Life mem. 1994–; Nat. Rep., IUPAC Comm. on Radiochemistry 1985–96; Research Consultant, Witwatersrand Chem. Ion-Beam Analysis Group 1992–98; Research Fellow, Solid State and Materials, Nat. Accelerator Centre 1994; Research Adviser, Dept. of Materials and Interfaces, Weizmann Inst., Rehovot, Israel 1995–; Assoc. Royal Soc. of Chem. (London) 1951–61, Fellow 1962–86; Fellow Royal Soc. of S.A. 1984–, Royal Philatelic Soc. London 1966–; mem. S. African Chemical Inst. 1952–96, Sr. mem. 1996–98, Life mem. 1998–; AE & CI Gold Medal 1965, Roll of Distinguished Philatelists (S.A.) 1966, Int. Hevesy Medal 1981, S.A. Chemical Inst. Gold Medal 1986; Hon. Citizen, State of Tenn., U.S.A. 1965, Order of the Postal Stone (S.A.) 1988. *Publications:* Elemental Analysis by Particle Accelerators; many scientific papers; research papers on nuclear analytical chem.; book chapters on specialized analytical topics. *Leisure interests:* philately, numismatics. *Address:* Sderot Ye'elim 30/4, Shchunat Heh, Beersheba, 84739 Israel. *Telephone:* (07) 644-2232.

PEKKANEN, Raimo Oskari, LL.D.; Finnish judge; b. 29 July 1927, Kivennapa; m. Eeva Niittyla 1953; two s.; ed. Univ. of Helsinki; State Admin. 1950–60; researcher and teacher, Helsinki School of Econ. and Univ. of Tampere 1961–67; Acting Prof. in Labour Law, Univ. of Helsinki 1967–68; Justice, Supreme Admin. Court of Finland 1969–90; Sec.-Gen. Ministry of Justice (on leave of absence from Supreme Admin. Court) 1982–90; Judge, European Court of Human Rights 1990–; Commdr. Order of Finnish Lion, Order of Finnish White Rose. *Publications:* Mixed Type Contract of Employment 1966, On Commencement and Termination of Employment Relationship 1968, On Participation in Water System Regulation 1968; articles in legal publs. *Leisure interests:* fly fishing, skiing. *Address:* Nyyrikimtie 8, 02100 Espoo, Finland. *Telephone:* (9) 455 4557.

PELÉ (Edson Arantes do Nascimento); Brazilian football player and author; b. 23 Oct. 1940, Três Corações, Minas Gerais State; s. of João Ramos do Nascimento and Celeste Arantes; m. Rosemeri Cholbi 1966 (divorced 1978); one s. two d.; m. Assiria Lemos 1994; ed. Santos Univ.; first played football at Baurú, São Paulo; Baurú Atlético Clube; joined Santos F.C. 1955; first int. game v. Argentina; played in World Cup 1958, 1962, 1966, 1970; finished career with New York Cosmos; Chair. Pelé Soccer Camps 1978–; Dir. Santos F.C. 1993–; Special Minister for Sports, Govt. of Brazil 1994–98; Dir. Soccer Clinics; three World Cup winners' medals; two World Club Championship medals; 110 int. caps, 97 goals for Brazil; 1,114 appearances for Santos, 1,088 goals; career total 1,282 goals in 1,364 games, 9 league championship medals, 4 Brazil cup medals; most goals in season 53 (1958); has appeared in several films, including Escape to Victory 1981, A Minor Miracle 1983, Hot Shot 1986; has composed numerous songs in Samba style; Goodwill Amb. for 1992, UN Conf. on Environment and Devt., Rio de Janeiro; Int. Peace Award 1978, WHO Medal 1989; Hon. K.B.E. 1997. *Publications:* Eu Sou Pelé 1962, Jogando com Pelé 1974, My Life and the Beautiful Game 1977, Pelé Soccer Training Program 1982, The World Cup Murders (novel) 1988. *Address:* 75 Rockefeller Plaza, New York, NY 10019, U.S.A.

PELHAM, Hugh Reginald Brentnall, M.A., PH.D., F.R.S.; British research scientist; b. 26 Aug. 1954, Shawford; s. of late Reginald Arthur Pelham and of Pauline Mary Pelham; ed. Marlborough Coll. and Christ's Coll., Cambridge; Research Fellow, Christ's Coll., Cambridge 1978–84; Postdoctoral Fellow, Carnegie Inst. of Washington, Baltimore, Md. 1979–81; mem. Scientific Staff, MRC Lab. of Molecular Biology, Cambridge 1981–; mem. European Molecular Biology Org. 1985, Acad. Europaea 1990, Acad. of Medical Sciences 1998; Colworth Medal 1988, European Molecular Biology Org. Medal 1989, Louis Jeantet Prize for Medicine 1991, King Faisal Int. Prize for Science 1996. *Publications:* articles on molecular and cell biology in scientific journals. *Address:* MRC Laboratory of Molecular Biology, Hills Road, Cambridge, CB2 2QH, England. *Telephone:* (01223) 248011. *Fax:* (01223) 412142.

PELIKAN, Jaroslav, PH.D.; American professor of history; b. 17 Dec. 1923, Akron, O.; s. of Rev. Jaroslav Pelikan and Anna Buzek; m. Sylvia Burica 1946; two s. one d.; ed. Concordia Jr. Coll. Fort Wayne, Ind., Concordia Theological Seminary, St. Louis and Univ. of Chicago; mem. Faculty, Valparaiso Univ. 1946–49, Concordia Theological Seminary 1949–53, Univ. of Chicago 1953–62; Titus Street Prof. Yale Univ. 1962–72, Sterling Prof. 1972–96, Dean, Grad. School 1973–78, William C. DeVane Lecturer 1984–86; Vice-Pres. American Acad. of Arts and Sciences 1976–79, Pres. 1994–(97); mem. Council, American Philosophical Soc. 1984–87, Smithsonian Inst. 1984–90; Dir. Univ. Support Services Inc. 1992–94; mem. Council of Scholars, Library of Congress; mem. Bd. Nat. Humanities Center; many other professional appts; recipient of numerous awards, medals and hon. degrees. *Publications include:* From Luther to Kierkegaard 1950, Fools for Christ 1955, The Riddle of Roman Catholicism 1959, Luther the Expositor 1959, The Shape of Death 1961, The Light of the World 1962, Obedient Rebels 1964, The Finality of Jesus Christ in an Age of Universal History 1965, Spirit versus Structure 1968, Development of Doctrine 1969, Historical Theology 1971, The Christian Tradition (5 vols.) 1971–89, Scholarship and its Survival 1983, The Vindication of Tradition 1984, Jesus through the Centuries 1985, The Mystery of Continuity 1986, Bach among the Theologians 1986, The Excellent Empire 1987, The Melody of Theology 1988, Confessor Between East and West 1990, Imago Dei 1990, Eternal Feminines 1990, The Idea of the University: A Reexamination 1992, Christianity and Classical Culture (Gifford Lectures) 1993, Faust the Theologian 1995, The Reformation of the Bible/The Bible of the Reformation 1996, Mary Through the Centuries 1996; ed. of many other vols. *Address:* c/o Department of History, Yale University, 1504A, Yale Station, New Haven, CT 06520-7425 (Office); 156 Chestnut Lane, Hamden, CT 06518, U.S.A. (Home). *Telephone:* (203)-432-1375 (Office); (203)-288-3030 (Home). *Fax:* (203) 248-7402.

PELIKÁN, Jiří; Czech politician and journalist; b. 7 Feb. 1923, Olomouc; s. of Julius Pelikán and Božena Pelikán (née Šternová); m. 1st Libuše Hynková; one d.; m. 2nd Jitka Frantová; ed. Univ. of Political and Social Sciences, Prague; mem. of illegal CP 1939, sentenced as part of resistance movement 1940, released after six months; Pres. Int. Union of Students 1953–63; Dir.-Gen. Czech TV 1963–68; Chair. Parl. Cttee. for Foreign Affairs 1968; expelled from CP and from political functions 1969; emigrated to Italy 1970; Publr. Listy 1970–; mem. European Parl. for Socialist Party of Italy 1979–89; returned to Czechoslovakia 1989; Medal for Merit (Czech Repub.) 1998. *Publications:* five books on the Prague Spring and revolution in Cen. and E. Europe, various articles published in Italy and Czech Repub. *Leisure interests:* reading, politics. *Address:* Listy, Václavské nám. 17, 110 00 Prague 1, Czech Republic. *Telephone:* (24) 22-62-87.

PELISSIER, Jacques Daniel Paul; French civil servant and railway administrator; b. 4 Feb. 1917, Versailles; s. of Jean Pelissier and Camille Bertrand; m. Jeanine Picard 1946; one s.; ed. Lycée Pasteur, Lycée Hoche, Lycée Chaptal, Inst. Nat. Agronomique; engineer, external service of Ministry of Agric. 1938–44; Sec.-Gen. Landes 1944, Ardennes 1945; Sous-préfet hors cadre, Chef du Cabinet to Minister of Agric. 1946; Asst. Chef du Cabinet, Minister of Industry and Commerce 1948; Sec.-Gen. Indre-et-Loire

1950; Sous-préfet, Saumur 1954; Dir. for Gen. Govt. of Algeria, in Ministry for Algeria and in Gen. Del. of Govt. in Algeria 1956–60; Préfet hors cadre 1957; Préfet, Aude 1960, Hérault and Region of Languedoc-Roussillon 1964, Ille-et-Vilaine and Region of Brittany 1967, Rhône and Region of Rhône-Alpes 1972; Préfet hors cadre, Dir.-Gen. of Admin., Ministry of the Interior April 1974; Dir. du Cabinet for Prime Minister May 1974; Chair. Bd. of Dirs. Soc. Nat. des Chemins de Fer Français 1975–81; Pres. Office de Tourisme de Paris 1983; Adviser to Prime Minister 1986–88; Prés. délégué Supervisory Bd. of Palais Omnisports Paris-Bercy 1983–; Hon. Préfet, Admin. de la Cie. Int. des Wagons-Lits et du Tourisme; Grand Officier, Légion d'honneur, Grand Officier, Ordre nat. du Mérite, Croix de guerre, Médaille de la Résistance. *Address:* 14 rue des Barres, 75004 Paris, France.

PELIZA, Major Sir Robert John, K.B.E., O.B.E., E.D., M.H.A.; Gibraltarian politician; b. 16 Nov. 1920, Gibraltar; s. of Robert Peliza and Emily Victory; m. Irma Risso 1950; three s. four d.; ed. Christian Brothers' Coll., Gibraltar; served in Gibraltar Reg. 1939–61, Hon. Col. 1993–; co. dir. 1962–; City Councillor 1945–48; Leader, Integration with Britain Party 1967; elected mem. House of Ass. 1969–84; Chief Minister of Gibraltar 1969–1972; Leader of the Opposition 1972; Speaker, House of Assembly 1989–96; Founder Gibraltar branch of European Movt. 1976– (Patron 1995–); Pres. Gibraltar branch, Commonwealth Parl. Asscn. 1989–96. *Leisure interests:* painting, writing, swimming, walking and sports in general. *Address:* 203 Water Gardens, Gibraltar. *Telephone:* 78387. *Fax:* 78387.

PELL, Claiborne de Borda, A.M.; American politician; b. 22 Nov. 1918, New York City; s. of Herbert Claiborne and Matilda (née Bigelow) Pell; m. Nuala O'Donnell 1944; two s. two d.; ed. Princeton and Columbia Univs.; Limited Partner, Auchinloss, Parker and Redpath; U.S. Coastguard 1941–45; Capt. U.S.C.G.R. (retd.); U.S. Foreign Service Officer; instructor and Lecturer, Naval and Mil. Govt. Schools 1944–45; served State Dept., Czechoslovakia, Italy, Washington 1945–52; Co.-dir. and trustee 1952–60; Consultant, Dem. Nat. Cttee. 1953–60; U.S. Del. to Inter-Govtl. Maritime Consultative Org. (IMCO) London 1959; Senator from Rhode Island 1961–97; Chair. Foreign Relations Cttee. 1987–95; 46 hon. degrees; Légion d'honneur, Crown of Italy, six Grand Crosses, etc.; Democrat. *Publications:* Rochambeau and Rhode Island 1954, Megalopolis Unbound 1966, Challenge of the Seven Seas (with Harold L. Goodwin) 1966, Power and Policy 1972. *Address:* Ledge Road, Newport, RI 02840, U.S.A.

PELLEGRINO, Edmund Daniel, M.D.; American professor of medicine; b. 22 June 1920, Newark, N.J.; m. Clementine Coakley; two s. four d.; ed. Xavier High School, New York, St. John's Univ., Jamaica and New York; Prof. and Chair. Dept. of Medicine, Univ. of Medical Center 1959–66; Vice-Pres. for Health Sciences, Dean of School of Medicine, Dir. of Health Services Center and Prof. of Medicine, State Univ. of New York 1966–73; Chancellor and Vice-Pres. for Health Affairs, Univ. of Tenn. and Prof. of Medicine and Medical Humanities, Univ. of Tenn. Center for Health Sciences 1973–75; Pres. and Chair. Bd. of Dirs. Yale-New Haven Medical Center and Prof. of Medicine, Yale Univ. 1975–78; Pres. and Prof. of Philosophy and Biology, Catholic Univ. of America, Washington, D.C., concurrently Prof. of Clinical Medicine and Community Medicine, Georgetown Univ. Medical School 1978–82; John Carroll Prof. of Medicine and Medical Humanities, Georgetown Univ. Medical Center 1982–, Dir. Kennedy Inst. of Ethics 1983–88, Dir. Centre for Advanced Study Ethics 1988–94, Dir. for Clinical Bioethics 1991–, Chief (a.i.) Div. of Gen. Internal Medicine 1993–94; Ed. Journal of Medicine and Philosophy 1983–; Fellow or mem. of 20 scientific, professional and honorary socs. including Inst. of Medicine of N.A.S.; mem. numerous nat. cttees. and bds.; recipient of numerous awards and 39 hon. degrees; Kt. of Malta; Kt. Order St. Gregory the Great. *Publications:* ten books and some 400 research papers in learned journals. *Leisure interests:* music, cooking, reading. *Address:* Center for Clinical Bioethics, Georgetown University, Washington, DC 20007, U.S.A. (Office).

PELLI, César, M.ARCH.; American architect; b. 12 Oct. 1926, Tucumán; s. of Victor Vicente Pelli and Teresa S. Pelli (née Suppa); m. Diana Balmori 1950; two s.; ed. Univs. of Tucumán, Illinois at Urbana Champaign; Project Designer Eero Saarinen Offices, Mich., Conn. 1954–64; Dir. of Design Daniel, Mann, Johnson and Medenhall (DMJM) 1964–68; Partner in Charge of Design Gruen Assocs 1968–77; Prof. of Architecture 1977–, Dean Yale School of Architecture 1977–84; Prin. César Pelli and Assocs. 1977–; mem. American Acad. of Arts and Letters; Fellow A.I.A.; numerous awards and prizes including UN City Competition First Prize, Vienna 1969, Arnold W. Brunner Prize Nat. Inst. Arts and Letters 1978, A.I.A. Honor Award for Fed. Office Bldg., Lawndale, San Bernardino City Hall, Calif., Arnold M. Brunner Memorial Prize Nat. Acad. of Design 1991, A.I.A. Honor Award 1994; A..I.A. Firm Award 1989, Gold Medal 1995. *Buildings* include: Pacific Design Centre, Los Angeles, Calif. 1973, U.S. Embassy, Tokyo, Japan 1975, Museum of Modern Art, New York 1984, Herring Hall, Rice Univ. 1984, World Financial Centre, New York 1985–87, Canary Wharf Tower, London 1990, Carnegie Hall Tower, New York 1991, Cincinnati Arts Theatre 1995. *Publications:* César Pelli (monograph) 1991, César Pelli, in The Master Architect series 1993; various articles in specialist journals. *Address:* c/o César Pelli and Associates, c/o Janet Kagan, 1056 Chapel Street, New Haven, CT 06510, U.S.A.

PELLY, Derek ("Derk") Roland, M.A., A.I.B.; British banker; b. 12 June 1929, Welwyn Garden City; s. of the late Arthur Roland Pelly and Phyllis Elsie Henderson; m. Susan Roberts 1953; one s. two d.; ed. Marlborough Coll. and Trinity Coll., Cambridge; joined Barclays Bank Ltd. (various positions) 1952, Local Dir., Chelmsford 1959, Sr Local Dir., Luton 1969; Vice-Chair. Barclays Bank Int. Ltd. 1977, full-time Vice-Chair. 1979; Group Vice-Chair. Barclays Bank PLC 1985, Group Deputy Chair. and Chair. Barclays Int. Ltd. 1986–88; Gov. London House for Overseas Graduates 1985–91; Dir. The Pvt. Bank and Trust Co. 1989–94. *Leisure interest:* painting. *Address:* Kenbank, St. John's Town of Dalry, Kircudbrightshire, DG7 3TX, Scotland. *Telephone:* (01644) 430424.

PELTASON, Jack W., PH.D.; American university president (retd.); b. 29 Aug. 1923, St. Louis, Mo.; s. of Walter Peltason and Emma Hartman; m. Suzanne Toll 1945; one s. two d.; ed. Univ. of Missouri and Princeton Univ.; Asst. Prof. Smith Coll. 1947–51; Asst. Prof. of Political Science, Univ. of Ill., Urbana-Champaign 1951–52, Assoc. Prof. 1953–59, Dean Coll. of Liberal Arts and Sciences 1960–64, Chancellor 1967–77; Vice-Chancellor Univ. of Calif. Irvine 1964–67, Chancellor 1984–92, Pres. Univ. of Calif. 1992–95, Pres. Emer. 1995–; Pres. American Council on Educ. 1977–84, Bren Foundation 1997–; mem. numerous bds., cttees. etc.; Fellow, American Acad. of Arts and Sciences; 22 hon. degrees and other awards. *Publications include:* Federal Courts in the Political Process 1955, Fifty-Eight Lonely Men: Southern Federal Judges and School Desegregation 1961, Understanding the Constitution 1997, Government by the People; co-author of several other books; articles in journals and encyclopedias and book chapters etc. *Leisure interests:* reading, writing, family. *Address:* Department of Politics and Society, University of California at Irvine, Irvine, CA 92717-5100 (Office); 18 Whistler Court, Irvine, CA 92612, U.S.A. (Home). *Telephone:* (714) 856-3315. *Fax:* (714) 856-2102.

PEÑA, Federico, LL.B.; American politician, civil servant and lawyer; b. 15 March 1947, Laredo, Tex.; m. Ellen Hart 1988; two d.; ed. Univ. of Texas; fmr. partner, law firm Pena & Pena; mem. Colo. Legis. 1979–83; served two terms as Mayor of Denver 1983–91; f. Pena Investment Advisors Inc. 1991; apptd. part-time legal consultant to law firm Brownstein Hyatt Farber & Strickland, Denver 1992; Sec. of Transportation 1993–97, of Energy 1997–98. *Address:* c/o Department of Energy, Forrestal Bldg., 1000 Independence Avenue, S.W., Washington, DC 20585, U.S.A.

PEÑA, Paco; Spanish flamenco guitarist; b. 1 June 1942, Córdoba; s. of Antonio Peña and Rosario Pérez; m. Karin Vaessen 1982; two d.; int. concert artist since 1968; f. Paco Peña Flamenco Co. 1970; f. Centro Flamenco Paco Peña, Córdoba 1981, Misa Flamenca 1991; Prof. of Flamenco, Rotterdam Conservatory, Netherlands 1985; composed Misa Flamenca 1991; Ramón Montoya Prize 1983. *Address:* c/o Wim Visser, Staalstraat 10–12, 1011 JL Amsterdam, Netherlands; c/o Karin Vaessen, 4 Boscastle Road, London, NW5 1EG, England. *Telephone:* (20) 6233700 (Amsterdam). *Fax:* (20) 6208212 (Amsterdam), 0171-485 2320 (London).

PEÑA ABIZANDA, Eduardo; Spanish government official; Dir.-Gen. of Transport, Spain until 1991; Insp.-Gen. of European Comm. 1991–95.

PEÑALOSA, Enrique; Colombian economist; b. 31 Aug. 1930, Soacha; s. of Vicente Peñalosa and Abby Camargo; m. 1st Cecilia Londoño 1953 (divorced 1980), 2nd Pamela Gibson 1980; four s. one d.; Econ. Ed. Semana weekly review 1952; Asst. in Nat. Planning Office 1952–53; IBRD Training Course 1954, missions in Colombia 1955; private econ. consultant 1956–61; mem. Comisión Paritaria Económica 1957, City Council, Bogotá 1958–62, Nat. Council for Petroleum Affairs 1958, Advisory Cttee. of Partido Liberal 1959; First Exec. Dir. Corpn. Autónoma Regional de la Sabana de Bogotá 1961; First Gen. Man. Colombian Inst. for Agrarian Reform 1961–68; Minister of Agric. 1968–69; Alt. Exec. Dir. Inter-American Devt. Bank 1970–71, Admin. Man. 1971–74; Sec.-Gen. UN Conf. on Human Settlements (Habitat) 1974–76; Amb. to UN 1987–90; Chair. Colombian Preparatory Comm. for UN Conf. on Environment and Devt. 1991–92, Head Colombian del. to Conf. June 1992; Dir. Research Centre and Special Projects of Univ. Externado de Colombia, Bogotá 1994–; Pres. Bogotá Free Trade Zone 1994–; Fellow, Adlai Stevenson Inst. of Int. Affairs 1972–74; Order of Orange-Nassau (Netherlands); Legion of Agricultural Merit (Peru), Grand Cross, Order of San Carlos (Colombia), Grand Cross, Nat. Merit Order (Ecuador). *Address:* Calle 70 7–60, Santa Fe de Bogotá, Colombia (Office). *Telephone:* 3450600. *Fax:* 2123463.

PENCHAS, Shmuel, M.D., D.I.C., M.SC.; Israeli professor of health administration; b. 12 Feb. 1939, Romania; s. of Nathan Penchas and Liuba Penchas; four s.; ed. Hebrew Univ. Hadassah Medical School, Haifa Technion Grad. School, Imperial Coll., Univ. Coll. London, Harvard Univ.; physician, Hadassah Univ. Hosp., Jerusalem 1967–76, Dir. of Computing 1977–78; Deputy Dir.-Gen. Hadassah Medical Org. 1978, Dir.-Gen. 1981–88; Chair. Israel Asscn. of Hosp. Dirs. 1984–91, Foreign Assoc. Inst. of Medicine of N.A.S. (U.S.A.); Consultant to Hadassah (Women's Zionist Org. of America); mem. Romanian Nat. Acad. of Science; Dr. h.c. *Publications:* articles in professional journals. *Address:* Hadassah Mt. Scopus Hospital, P.O.B. 24035, Jerusalem 91240, Israel. *Telephone:* 5844300. *Fax:* 5844750.

PENDERECKI, Krzysztof; Polish composer and conductor; b. 23 Nov. 1933, Dębica, Cracow Prov.; s. of Tadeusz Penderecki and Zofia Penderecka; m. Elżbieta Solecka 1965; one s. one d.; ed. Jagiellonian Univ., Cracow and State Higher Music School, Cracow; studied composition first with Skołyszewski, later with Malawski and Wiechowicz, Cracow; graduated from

State Higher Music School, Cracow 1958; Lecturer in Composition, State Higher Music School (now Music Acad.), Cracow 1958–66, Prof. Extraordinary 1972–75, Prof. 1975–; Rector Cracow Conservatory 1972–87; Prof. of Composition, Folkwang Hochschule für Musik, Essen 1966–68; Musical Adviser, Vienna Radio 1970–71; Prof. of Composition, Yale Univ., U.S.A. 1973–78; mem. Presidential Council of Culture 1992–; Hon. mem. R.A.M., London 1974; Corresp. mem. Arts Acad. of G.D.R., Berlin 1975; Extraordinary mem. Arts Acad. of W. Berlin 1975; mem. Royal Acad. of Music, Stockholm 1976, Acad. Nat de Sciences, Belles-Lettres et Arts, Bordeaux etc.; Hon. mem. Accad. Nazionale di Santa Cecilia, Rome 1976, Acad. Int. de Philosophie et de l'Art, Berne 1987; Corresp. mem. Academia Nacional de Bellas Artes, Buenos Aires 1982; Fellow Royal Irish Acad. of Music; Hon. Prof. Moscow Conservatory 1997, Cen. Beijing Conservatory 1998; Dr. h.c. (Univ. of Rochester, N.Y.) 1972, (St. Olaf Coll., Northfield, Minn.) 1977, (Katholieke Univ., Leuven) 1979, (Univ. of Bordeaux) 1979, (Georgetown Univ., Washington, D.C.) 1984, (Univ. of Belgrade) 1985, (Univ. Autónoma, Madrid) 1987; Hon. D.Mus. (Glasgow) 1995 and many others; Fitelberg Prize for Threnody for the Victims of Hiroshima 1960, also UNESCO award 1959, Polish Minister of Culture and Art Prize 1961, (First Class) 1981, Cracow Composition Prize for Canon 1962, North Rhine-Westphalia Grand Prize for St. Luke's Passion 1966, also Pax Prize (Poland) 1966, Alfred Jurzykowski Foundation Award, Polish Inst. of Arts and Sciences in America 1966, Prix Italia 1967/68, State Prize (1st Class) 1968, Gustav Charpentier Prize 1971, Gottfried von Herder Prize 1977, Prix Arthur Honegger for Magnificat 1978, Grand Medal of Paris 1981, Sibelius Prize (Wihouri Foundation, Finland) 1983, Order of Banner of Labour (1st Class) 1983, Premio Lorenzo il Magnifico (Italy) 1985, Wolf Foundation Award 1987, Grammy Award Nat. Acad. of Recording Arts and Sciences for the best contemporary composition 1988, Officier, Ordre de Saint-Georges de Bourgogne (Belgium) 1990, Grawemeyer Award for Music Composition 1992, Grand Cross Order of Merit (Fed. Repub. of Germany) 1990, City of Strasbourg Medal 1995, Crystal Award, World Econ. Forum, Davos 1997, Business Center Club Special Award, Warsaw 1998. *Works include:* Psalms of David (for choir and percussion) 1958, Emanations (for 2 string orchestras) 1958, Strophes (for soprano, speaker and ten instruments) 1959, Anaklasis (for strings and percussion) 1960, Dimensions of time and silence (for 40-part mixed choir and chamber ensemble) 1960, String Quartet no. 1 1960, no. 2 1968, Threnody for the Victims of Hiroshima (for 52 strings) 1960, Polymorphia (for strings) 1961, Psalms (for tape) 1961, Fluorescences (for large orchestra) 1961, Sonata for cello and orchestra 1964, St. Luke's Passion 1965–66, Capriccio per oboe e 11 archi 1965, De natura sonoris (for large orchestra) 1966, Dies irae (for soprano, tenor, bass, chorus and large orchestra) 1967, The Devils of Loudun (opera) 1968, Cosmogony 1970, De natura sonoris II (for wind instruments, percussion and strings) 1970, Russian Mass Utrenja 1971, Partita (for harpsichord, guitars, harp, double bass and chamber orchestra) 1972, Symphony no. 1 1973, Canticum Canticorum Salomonis (for 16 voices and chamber orchestra) 1973, Magnificat (for bass solo, voice ensemble, double choir, boys' voices and orchestra) 1974, When Jacob Awoke (for orchestra) 1974, Violin Concerto 1977, Paradise Lost (opera) 1978, (Christmas) Symphony No. 2 1980, Te Deum 1979–80, Lacrimosa 1980, Cello Concerto no. 2 1982, Viola Concerto 1983, Polish Requiem 1980–84, Black Mask (opera) 1986, Der unterbrochene Gedanke (for string quartet) 1988, Adagio (for orchestra) 1989, Ubu Rex (opera) 1991, Benedicamus Domine 1992, Benedictus 1992, Flute Concerto 1992–93, Quartet for Clarinet and String Trio 1993, Violin Concerto no. 2 1995, Seven Gates of Jerusalem (oratorio) 1996. *Leisure interest:* dendrology. *Address:* ul. Cisowa 22, 30-229 Cracow, Poland. *Telephone:* (12) 22 57 60. *Fax:* (12) 25 16 60.

PENG CHONG: Chinese politician; b. 1909, Zhangzhou, Fujian; joined CCP 1933; Political Commissar, regt. of New 4th Army 1938; Deputy Sec.-Gen. prov. People's Govt., Fujian 1950; Mayor of Nanjing 1955–59; First Sec. Municipal CCP Cttee., Nanjing 1955-60; Deputy for Jiangsu, 2nd NPC 1958; alt. Second Sec. CCP Cttee., Jiangsu 1960; Political Commissar Nanjing militia 1960; First Sec. Municipal CCP Cttee., Nanjing 1962–68; Second Sec. CCP Cttee., Jiangsu 1965–68; Vice-Chair. Prov. Revolutionary Cttee., Jiangsu 1968–74; alt. mem. 9th Cen. Cttee. CCP 1969; Sec. CCP Cttee., Jiangsu 1970–74; alt. mem. 10th Cen. Cttee. CCP 1973; Chair. Prov. Revolutionary Cttee., Jiangsu 1974–76; Second Political Commissar, PLA Nanjing Mil. Region 1975–80; Third Sec. CCP Cttee., Shanghai 1976–79; Second Vice-Chair. Municipal Revolutionary Cttee., Shanghai 1976–79; Chair. Municipal CPPCC Cttee., Shanghai 1977–79; mem. 11th Cen. Cttee. CCP 1977; Head, Group in Charge of Snail Fever Prevention, Cen. Cttee. CCP 1978–; Deputy for Shanghai, 5th NPC 1978; Vice-Chair. Nat. Cttee, 5th CPPCC 1978–80; First Sec. CCP Cttee., Shanghai 1979–80; Chair. Municipal Revolutionary Cttee., Shanghai 1979–80; Mayor of Shanghai 1980; Sec. 11th Cen. Cttee. CCP 1980–82; Vice-Chair. Standing Cttee., 5th NPC 1980–83; mem. 12th Cen. Cttee. CCP 1982–87; Vice-Chair. Standing Cttee., 6th NPC 1983–88; mem. Presidium 6th NPC 1986–; Chair. Law Cttee., NPC 1983–87; Vice-Chair. 7th NPC 1988–93; mem. Presidium of 14th CCP Nat. Congress Oct. 1992; Pres. China Int. Cultural Exchange Centre 1984–; Exec. mem. China Welfare Inst. 1978–; Hon. Pres. Gymnastics Asscn. 1983–, Soc. for Industry and Commerce Admin. 1991–, China Foundation for Heroism Awards. *Address:* Standing Committee, National People's Congress, Tian An Men Square, Beijing, People's Republic of China.

PENG DIXIAN; Chinese politician and economist; b. 1908, Meishan Co., Sichuan Prov.; ed. in Japan; joined China Democratic League 1947, Vice-Chair. 1988–; joined CCP 1984; Perm. mem. 8th Nat. Cttee. CPPCC 1993–.

PENG HUANWU, PH.D.; Chinese physicist; b. 1915, Changchun; ed. Tsinghua Univ., Univ. of Edin.; Deputy Dir. Inst. of Modern Physics under Acad. Sinica 1953–; Deputy, 1st NPC 1956–59, 2nd NPC 1959–64, 3rd NPC 1964–66; Deputy Dir. Inst. of Atomic Energy under Acad. Sinica 1958–; Dir. Inst. of Theoretical Physics under Acad. Sinica 1978–82; mem. Acad. Sinica 1955. *Address:* The Institute of Theoretical Physics, Academia Sinica, Zhong Guan Cun, Beijing 100080, People's Republic of China.

PENG MING-MIN; Taiwanese politician; b. 1923; ed. in Japan and Nat. Taiwan Univ.; lost left arm during U.S. bombing raid on Nagasaki; fmr. Chair. Political Science Dept., Nat. Taiwan Univ.; arrested for activities supporting self-determination for Taiwan 1964 and sentenced to eight years' imprisonment; sentence commuted to house arrest; escaped into exile in U.S.A.; returned home 1992; joined Democratic Progressive Party (DDP) 1995; DDP Cand. Presidential Elections March 1996. *Address:* Democratic Progressive Party, 14th Floor, 128 Ming Sheng East Road, Sec. 3, Taipei, Taiwan.

PENG PEIYUN; Chinese administrator; b. 1929, Liuyang Co., Hunan Prov.; ed. Qinghua Univ.; joined CCP 1946; Minister of State Family Planning Comm. 1988–98; mem. 14th CCP Cen. Cttee. 1992, 15th CCP Cen. Cttee. 1997–; State Councillor 1993–98; Chair. Coordination Cttee. for the Handicapped (State Council) 1993–; Chair. Nat. Cttee. for Patriotic Public Health Campaign 1994–, Cttee. for Women and Children's Work; Pres. Chinese Asscn. for Promotion of the Population Culture, Soc. of Population; Vice-Chair. Standing Cttee. of 9th NPC 1998–. *Address:* Standing Committee of National People's Congress, Beijing, People's Republic of China.

PENG SHILU, M.ENG.SC.; Chinese state official and physicist; b. 1925, Haifeng Co., Guangdong Prov.; s. of late Peng Pai and Cai Suping; m. Ma Shuying 1958; two c.; ed. St. Joseph's English Inst., Hong Kong, Yan'an Inst. of Natural Science, Harbin Polytechnical Univ., Dalian Coll. of Eng., Kazan Inst. of Chem. Eng., Moscow Inst. of Chem. Eng., Moscow Inst. of Power Eng.; joined E. River Column of Red Army 1939; joined CCP 1945; Deputy Dir. Nuclear Power Lab., Inst. of Atomic Energy 1958–64; Assoc. Prof. of Physics, Chinese Univ. of Science and Tech. 1962–65; Chief Engineer and Deputy Dir. of Inst. of Nuclear Power 1964–73; Vice-Pres. Acad. of Marine Architecture 1974–79; 1st Chief Designer of Chinese Nuclear Submarine; Vice-Minister and Chief Engineer, 6th Ministry of Machine Building 1979–83; Vice-Minister of Water Resources and Electric Power, Dir. and Gen. Man. Daya Bay Nuclear Power Plant 1983–86; Chair. and Chief Engineer, Science and Tech. Cttee., Ministry of Nuclear Industry 1986–; Hon. Pres. Chinese Nuclear Soc.; Pres. Chinese Nuclear Power Soc. 1984–; mem. Chinese Acad. of Eng. 1994–; Science and Tech. Consultant to CNNC 1990–; alt. mem. 12th CCP Cen. Cttee. 1982–87; mem. Standing Cttee. of CCP, Guangdong Prov. 1983–84; mem. Standing Cttee. 8th NPC 1993–98; Prizewinner, Conf. of State Science 1978, Top Grade Award of Nat. Prize of Science and Tech. Progress 1985, Nat. Defence Distinguished Service Medal 1988, Ho Leung Ho Lee Foundation Science and Tech. Progress Award 1996. *Publications:* Present Status and Prospects of Nuclear Power Development in China — Proceedings of the Sixth PBNC 1987, Calculation and Analysis of Electricity Price in Connection-grid of 2X600 Mwe PWR Nuclear Power Plant, in Nuclear Power Engineering, Vol. 14, No. 2 1993. *Address:* P.O. Box 2102, Beijing, People's Republic of China. *Telephone:* 68512211.

PENGO, H.E. Cardinal Polycarp; Tanzanian ecclesiastic; b. 5 Aug. 1944, Mwazye; ordained priest 1971; Bishop 1984; Coadjutor 1990, Archbishop of Dar es Salaam 1992; cr. Cardinal Feb. 1998. *Address:* Archbishop's House, P.O. Box 167, Dar es Salaam, Tanzania. *Telephone:* (051) 113223. *Fax:* (051) 850941.

PENINGTON, David Geoffrey, A.C., M.A., D.M., F.R.C.P., F.R.A.C.P., F.R.C.P.A.; Australian university vice-chancellor and medical practitioner; b. 4 Feb. 1930, Melbourne; s. of Geoffrey A. Penington and Marjorie D. Fricke; m. 1st Audrey M. Grummitt 1956 (divorced), 2nd Sonay Hussein 1984; two s. two d.; ed. Scotch Coll. Melbourne, Univ. of Melbourne and Magdalen Coll. Oxford; lecturer, Medical Coll. London Hosp. 1957–60, physician, London Hosp. 1963–67; First Asst. Medicine, Univ. of Melbourne 1968–70; Prof. and Chair. of Dept. Univ. of Melbourne 1970–87, Chair. Bd. of Social Studies 1970–75, Dean, Faculty of Medicine 1978–87, Vice-Chancellor 1988–95; partner Foursight 1996–; physician, St. Vincent's Hosp. Melbourne 1970–87; Research Fellow, Wolfson Coll. Oxford 1975–76; Foundation Chair. N. Richmond Family Care Centre 1973–75; mem. Man. Bd. Walter & Eliza Hall Inst. 1978–84, Cancer Inst. 1978–87; mem. Australian Red Cross Nat. Council 1976–83; Pres. Haematology Soc. of Australia 1975–77; Vice-Pres. Int. Soc. of Haematology 1978–82; Chair. Working Party on AIDS (later AIDS Task Force) 1983–87, Australian Higher Educ. Industrial Asscn. 1989–91, Drug Advisory Council, Vic. 1995–96, other professional appts.; Dir. non-exec. Pacific Dunlop Ltd. 1991–; Dir. Murdoch Inst. for Research into Birth Defects 1996– and numerous cos.; partner Foursight 1996–; mem. Victoria Advisory Bd. Ernst and Young 1996–. *Publications:* De Gruchy's Clinical Hematology in Medicine (ed.) 1978, 1989; publs. in experimental clinical haematology. *Address:* 131/461 St. Kilda Road, Melbourne, Vic. 3004, Australia.

PENN, Arthur; American theatre and film director; b. 27 Sept. 1922, Philadelphia; m. Peggy Maurer 1955; one s. one d.; joined Army theatre company during World War II; worked in television 1951–53; taught at Actors' Studio mid-1970s; produced plays for Broadway theatre including The Miracle Worker, All the Way Home, Toys in the Attic, Two for the Seesaw, In the Council House, Wait Until Dark, Sly Fox, Monday after the Miracle. *Films:* The Left-Handed Gun 1957, The Miracle Worker 1962, Mickey One 1964, The Chase 1965, Bonnie and Clyde 1967, Alice's Restaurant 1969, Little Big Man 1971, Night Moves 1975, The Missouri Breaks 1976, Four Friends 1981, Target 1985, Dead of Winter 1987, Penn and Teller Get Killed; Co-Dir. Visions of Eight 1973. *Address:* c/o Bell and Co., 535 Fifth Avenue, 21st Floor, New York, NY 10017, U.S.A.

PENN, Irving; American photographer; b. 16 June 1917, Plainfield, N.J.; s. of Harry Penn and Sonia Penn; m. Lisa Fonssagrives 1950; one s.; painter 1941; first photographs published in Vogue 1943; retrospective exhbn. Museum of Modern Art, New York 1984. *Publications:* Moments Preserved (collection of 300 photographs) 1960, Worlds in a Small Room 1974, Inventive Paris Clothes 1909–1939 1977, Flowers 1980, Passage 1991. *Address:* Irving Penn Studio, 89 Fifth Avenue, New York, NY 10003, U.S.A.

PENN, Sean; American actor; b. 17 Aug. 1960, Burbank, Calif.; s. of Leo Penn and Eileen (née Ryan) Penn; m. 1st Madonna (q.v.) 1985 (divorced); m. 2nd Robin Wright 1996; two c. *Theatre appearances include:* Heartland (Broadway debut), Slab Boys, Hurlyburly 1988. *Film appearances:* Taps 1981, Fast Times at Ridgemont High 1982, Bad Boys 1983, Crackers 1984, Racing with the Moon 1984, The Falcon and the Snowman 1985, At Close Range 1986, Shanghai Surprise 1986, Colors 1988, Judgement in Berlin 1988, Casualties of War 1989, We're No Angels 1989, State of Grace 1990, Carlito's Way 1993, Dead Man Walking 1996 (Best Actor Award Berlin Film Festival 1996), U Turn 1997, She's So Lovely 1997, Hurlyburly 1998, As I Lay Dying 1998, Up at the Villa 1998, The Thin Red Line 1998; dir., writer The Indian Runner 1991, The Crossing Guard 1995. *Address:* William Morris Agency, 151 S. El Camino Drive, Beverly Hills, CA 90212, U.S.A.

PENNANEACH, Biova-Soumi, M.SC.; Togolese diplomatist; b. 5 Oct. 1941, Lomé; m. 1972; two s. four d.; ed. State Univ. of Moscow and Laval Univ. Quebec; active trade unionist since 1966; Head, Soils Analysis Labs. 1966–74, 1976–80; Dir. Agricultural and Land Legislation Service 1980–82; Prefect of Tchaoudjo and the Lakes and Tech. Adviser, Nat. Science Inst. 1982–87; Dir. Office of Minister of Rural Devt. 1987–90; Under-Sec.-Gen. Nat. Confed. of Workers of Togo 1988–90; Perm. Rep. to UN 1990–96; Vice-Pres. 46th session of UN Gen. Ass. 1991. *Publications:* numerous, on conservation and environment protection. *Address:* c/o Ministry of Foreign Affairs and Cooperation, Place du Monument aux Morts, Lomé, Togo.

PENNANT-REA, Rupert Lascelles, M.A.; British business executive and journalist; b. 23 Jan. 1948, Harare, Zimbabwe; s. of Peter A. Pennant-Rea and Pauline E. Pennant-Rea; m. 1st Elizabeth L. Greer 1970 (divorced 1975); m. 2nd Jane Hamilton 1979 (divorced 1986), one s. one d.; m. 3rd Helen Jay 1986, one s. two step-d.; ed. Peterhouse, Zimbabwe, Trinity Coll. Dublin and Univ. of Manchester; with Confed. of Irish Industry 1970–71, Gen. and Municipal Workers' Union 1972–73, Bank of England 1973–77; with The Economist 1977–93, Ed. 1986–93; Deputy Gov. of Bank of England 1993–95; Chair. The Stationery Office 1996–, Plantation and Gen. 1997–; Consultant World Bank 1995–, numerous other appointments. *Publications:* Gold Foil 1979, Who Runs the Economy? (jtly.) 1980, The Pocket Economist (jtly.) 1983, The Economist Economics (jtly.) 1986. *Leisure interests:* music, tennis, fishing, family. *Address:* The Stationery Office, 51 Nine Elms Lane, London, SW8 5DR, England. *Telephone:* 0171-873 8781.

PENNIE, Michael William, A.R.C.A.; British sculptor; b. 23 Oct. 1936, Wallasey, Cheshire; s. of George A. Pennie and Isabel Duff; m. 1st Norah Kimmit 1959 (divorced 1977); m. 2nd Marlene Stride 1985; two s. one d.; ed. Bede Collegiate for Boys, Sunderland, Sunderland Coll. of Art and Royal Coll. of Art; Visiting Lecturer, Bath Acad. of Art, Winchester and Wimbledon Schools of Art, Norwich Coll. of Art and Brighton Polytechnic 1962–82; Sr. Lecturer, Bath Coll. 1985–, now Prof.; Co-Organizer, Sculpture in the City, Bath 1986; Consultant, Goodwill Art Service 1992–; one-man shows include ICA Gallery, London 1965, Welsh Arts Council Gallery, Cardiff 1971, Angela Flowers Gallery, London 1971, 1973, 1976, 1981, Ensembles Artiste, Bath 1989, Drawings of African Sculpture, S.O.A.S., Univ. of London 1991, Michael Pennie: Carving and Drawing 1976–1995, Art Gallery and Museum 1995, Nat. Museum and Art Gallery, Accra, Ghana 1995; Curator touring exhbns. 'African' 1988, 'LOBI' 1994–96, 'West African Albums' 1999–2001; numerous group shows 1961–; participant, Forma Viva, Yugoslavia 1980, Making Sculpture Tate Gallery, London 1983; works in various public collections including Victoria and Albert Museum and Arts Council of G.B., Southern Arts Coll.; several research trips to W. Africa 1994–; Consultant Horniman Museum and Gardens. *Publications:* Where Shall We Put This One? 1987, Smoke of the Savannah 1989, African Assortment: African Art in Museums in England and Scotland 1991, Friday's Rain Takes a Long Time to Stop 1994, Some Sculptors and African Art 1995, Marriage Poles of the Lobi 1996, Adventures with Lobi—An abc 1998. *Leisure interest:* African music. *Address:* 117 Bradford Road, Atworth, Melksham, Wilts., SN12 8HY, England. *Telephone:* (01225) 705409. *Fax:* (01225) 705409.

PENROSE, Oliver, PH.D., F.R.S., F.R.S.E.; British professor of mathematics; b. 6 June 1929, London; s. of Lionel S. Penrose and Margaret Leathes; m. Joan L. Dilley 1953; three s. (one deceased) one d.; ed. Central Collegiate Inst. London, Canada, Univ. Coll. London and King's Coll. Cambridge; Mathematical Physicist, English Electric Co. Luton 1952–55; Research Asst. Yale Univ. 1955–56; lecturer, Reader, Imperial Coll. London 1956–69; Prof. of Math. Open Univ. 1969–86, Heriot-Watt Univ. 1986–94, Prof. Emer. 1994–. *Publications:* Foundations of Statistical Mechanics 1969; about 70 papers in scientific journals. *Leisure interests:* music, chess. *Address:* 29 Frederick Street, Edinburgh, EH2 2ND, Scotland. *Telephone:* (0131) 225 5879.

PENROSE, Sir Roger, Kt., PH.D., F.R.S.; British professor of mathematics; b. 8 Aug. 1931, Colchester; s. of Lionel Penrose; m. 1st Joan Wedge 1959 (divorced 1981), three s.; m. 2nd Vanessa Thomas 1988; ed. Univ. Coll. School, Univ. Coll. London and St. John's Coll. Cambridge; Asst. Lecturer, Bedford Coll. London 1956–57; Research Fellow, St. John's Coll. Cambridge 1957–60; NATO Research Fellow, Princeton and Syracuse Univs. 1959–61; Research Assoc. King's Coll. London 1961–63; Visiting Assoc. Prof. Univ. of Tex. Austin 1963–64; Reader, Birkbeck Coll. London 1964–66, Prof. of Applied Math. 1966–73; Rouse Ball Prof. of Math. Univ. of Oxford 1973–98, Prof. Emer. 1998–; Fellow, Univ. Coll. London 1975; Hon. Fellow, St. John's Coll. Cambridge 1987; Visiting Prof. Yeshiva, Princeton and Cornell Univs. 1966–67, 1969; Lovett Prof. Rice Univ. Houston 1983–87; Distinguished Prof. of Physics and Math. Syracuse Univ. 1987–93, Francis and Helen Pentz Distinguished Prof. of Physics and Math., Pa. State Univ. 1993–; mem. London Math. Soc., Cambridge Philosophical Soc., Inst. for Math. and its Applications, Int. Soc. for Gen. Relativity and Gravitation; Dr. h.c., (New Brunswick) 1992, (Surrey) 1993, (Bath) 1994, (London) 1995, (Glasgow) 1996, (Essex) 1996, (St. Andrews) 1997, (Santiniketon) 1998, Hon. D.Univ. (Open Univ.) 1998; Adams Prize (Cambridge Univ.) 1966–67; Dannie Heinemann Prize (American Physics Soc. and American Inst. of Physics) 1971, Eddington Medal (with S. W. Hawking) (Royal Astronomical Soc.) 1975; Royal Medal (Royal Soc.) 1985; Wolf Foundation Prize for Physics (with S. W. Hawking) 1988, Dirac Medal and Prize, Inst. of Physics 1989, Einstein Medal 1990, Naylor Prize, London Math. Soc. 1991. *Publications:* Techniques of Differential Topology in Relativity 1973, Spinors and Space-time (with W. Rindler), (Vol. I) 1984, (Vol. II) 1986, The Emperor's New Mind 1989, The Nature of Space and Time (with S. Hawking) 1996, The Large, the Small and the Human Mind 1997; articles in scientific journals. *Leisure interests:* three-dimensional puzzles, doodling at the piano. *Address:* Mathematical Institute, 24–29 St. Giles, Oxford, OX1 3LB, England. *Telephone:* (01865) 273538.

PENZIAS, Arno Allan, PH.D.; American astrophysicist; b. 26 April 1933, Munich, Germany; s. of Karl Penzias and Justine Penzias; m. 1st Anne Barras Penzias 1954; one s. two d.; m. 2nd Sherry Chamovelevit 1996; ed. City Coll. of New York, Columbia Univ.; mem. tech. staff Bell Laboratories, Holmdel, N.J. 1961–72, Head Radiophysics Research Dept. 1972–76, Dir. Radio Research Lab. 1976–79, Exec. Dir. Research, Communications Sciences Div. 1979–81, Exec. Dir. Research, Bell Labs., Murray Hill, N.J. 1979–81, Vice-Pres. Research 1981–95, Vice-Pres., Chief Scientist 1995–; Lecturer, Princeton Univ. 1967–72, Visiting Prof. Astrophysical Sciences Dept. 1972–85; Harvard Coll. Observatory Research Assoc. 1968–80; Adjunct Prof., S.U.N.Y. at Stony Brook 1974–84; discovered cosmic microwave background radiation 1965; Assoc. Ed., Astrophysical Journal 1978–82; mem. Editorial Bd. Annual Review of Astronomy and Astrophysics 1974–78, AT & TBL Tech. Journal 1978–84 (Chair. 1981–84); mem. Bd. of Trustees of Trenton State Coll. 1977–79, Visiting Cttee. of Calif. Inst. of Tech. 1977–79; mem. Astronomy Advisory Panel of N.S.F. 1978–79, Industrial Panel on Science and Tech. 1982–, Bd. of Overseers, School of Eng. and Applied Science Univ. of Pa. 1983–86; mem. Union of Councils for Soviet Jews Advisory Bd. 1983–; mem. Bd. of Dirs. IMNET 1986–91; mem. Fachbeirat 1978–85 (Chair. 1981–83); mem. Council on Competitiveness 1989–; Dir. Grad. Faculties Alumni, Columbia Univ. 1987–; Vice-Chair. Cttee. Concerned Scientists; mem. Nat. Acad. Eng., American Astronomical Soc., World Acad. Art and Science; Fellow A.A.A.S., American Physical Soc.; Nobel Prize for Physics 1978; Henry Draper Medal, N.A.S. 1977; Herschel Medal, Royal Astronomical Soc. 1977, Pender Award 1992 and numerous other prizes, awards, lectureships; numerous hon. degrees. *Publications:* Ideas and Information 1989, Harmony 1995, over 80 scientific papers in various journals. *Leisure interests:* swimming, jogging, skiing. *Address:* AT & T Bell Laboratories, 600 Mountain Avenue, Murray Hill, NJ 07974, U.S.A. *Telephone:* (908) 582-3361.

PEPPER, John Ennis Jr.; American business executive; b. 2 Aug. 1938, Pottsville, Pa.; s. of John Ennis Pepper, Sr. and Irma O'Connor; m. Frances Graham Garber 1967; three s. one d.; ed. Yale Univ.; with Procter & Gamble Co. 1963–, Gen. Man. Italian subsidiary 1974–77, Vice-Pres. and Gen. Man. packaged soap div. 1977–80, Group Vice-Pres. 1980–84, Exec. Vice-Pres. 1984–86, Pres. 1986–95, Chair., C.E.O. Jan. 1995–; Co-Chair. Gov.'s Educ. Council of State of Ohio; Dir. Xerox, Motorola; mem. adv. council Yale School of Man., other appointments. *Address:* Procter & Gamble Co., 1 Procter & Gamble Plaza, Cincinnati, OH 45202, U.S.A.

PEPPER, Michael, SC.D., F.R.S., F.INST.P.; British physicist; b. 10 Aug. 1942, London; s. of Morris Pepper and Ruby Pepper; m. Dr. Jeannette D. Josse 1973; two d.; St. Marylebone Grammar School, London and Reading Univ.; Physicist, Mullard Research Lab. 1967–69; physicist engaged in solid state device research, Allen Clark Research Centre, Plessey Co. 1969–73; research at Cavendish Lab., Cambridge 1973–, Prof. of Physics, Univ. of Cambridge 1987–; Man. Dir. Toshiba Cambridge Research Centre Ltd. 1991–; Warren Research Fellow of Royal Soc. 1978–86; Sr. Research Fellow, Trinity Coll., Cambridge 1982–87, Professorial Fellow 1987–; Sr. Research Fellow, GEC Hirst Research Centre 1982–87; Visiting Prof. Bar-Ilan Univ., Israel 1984; Fellow American Physical Soc.; Hon. D.Sc. (Bar-Ilan) 1993, (Linkoping) 1997; Guthrie Prize and Medal, Inst. of Physics 1985; Hewlett-Packard Prize, European Physical Soc. 1985, Hughes Medal of the Royal Soc. 1987. *Publications:* numerous papers on solid state physics and semiconductors in scientific journals. *Leisure interests:* travel, music, whisky tasting. *Address:* Cavendish Laboratory, Madingley Road, Cambridge, CB3 0HE; Toshiba Cambridge Research Centre Ltd., 260 Cambridge Science Park, Milton Road, Cambridge, CB4 4WE, England. *Telephone:* (01223) 337330; (01223) 424666.

PERAHIA, Murray; American pianist and conductor; b. 19 April 1947, New York; s. of David Perahia and Flora Perahia; m. Naomi (Ninette) Shohet 1980; two s.; ed. High School of Performing Arts, Mannes Coll. of Music; studied with Jeanette Haien, Arthur Balsam, Mieczyslaw Horszowski; début, Carnegie Hall 1968; won Leeds Int. Pianoforte Competition 1972, Avery Fisher Award 1975, Gramophone Record Award 1997; Kosciusko Chopin Prize 1965; has appeared with many of world's leading orchestras and with Amadeus, Budapest, Guarneri and Galimir string quartets; regular recital tours N. America, Europe, Japan; Co-Artistic Dir. Aldeburgh Festival 1983–89; numerous recordings including complete Mozart Piano Concertos. *Address:* c/o Edna Landau, IMG, 22 E. 71st Street, New York, NY 10021, U.S.A.

PERAK, H.H. Sultan of, Sultan Azlan Muhibbuddin Shah ibni Al-Marhum Sultan Yussuf Ghafarullahu—Lahu Shah; Malaysian ruler; b. 19 April 1928, Batu Gajah; m. Tuanku Bainun Mohamed Ali 1954; two s. three d.; ed. Govt. English School (now Sultan Yussuf School), Malay Coll. and Univ. of Nottingham; called to Bar, Lincoln's Inn; Magistrate, Kuala Lumpur; Asst. State Sec., Perak; Deputy Public Prosecutor; Pres. Sessions Court, Seremban and Taiping; State Legal Adviser, Pahang and Johore; Fed. Court Judge 1973; Chief Justice of Malaysia 1979; Lord Pres. 1982–83; Raja Kechil Bongsu (sixth-in-line) 1962, Raja Muda (second-in-line to the throne) 1983; Sultan of Perak Jan. 1984–; Yang di-Pertuan Agong (Supreme Head of State) 1989–94; Pro-Chancellor Univ. Saina Malaysia 1971, Chancellor Univ. of Malaya 1986; Hon. Col.-in-Chief Malaysian Armed Forces' Engineers Corps.; Man. Malaysian Hockey Team 1972; Pres. Malaysian Hockey Fed., Asian Hockey Fed.; Vice-Pres. Int. Hockey Fed., Olympic Council of Malaysia.

PERBEN, Dominique; French politician and civil servant; b. 11 Aug. 1945, Lyon; s. of Jacques Perben and Agnès Berthier; m. 1st Annick Demoustier 1968; m. 2nd Corinne Garnier 1996; one s. two d. from previous marriage; ed. Paris Univ., Inst. of Political Studies, Paris; Pvt. Sec. to Maine-et-Loire Prefect 1972–75, to Norbert Ségard (Sec. of State for Postal Services and Telecommunications) 1977; Sec.-Gen. Territoire de Belfort 1975–76; Head of Mission Del. of Devt. of Belfort Region 1977, Pres.'s Office Regional Council at Rhône-Alpes 1983–86; Admin. Télédiffusion de France 1980; with Ministry of the Interior 1981; Mayor of Chalon-sur-Saône 1983–; Vice-Pres. Regional Council Saône-et-Loire 1985–88, R.P.R. Deputy 1986–93, 1997–; R.P.R. Nat. Sec. of Local Elections 1984–86, of General Elections 1986–88, of Communication 1988–89, Asst. Sec.-Gen. 1990–93; Minister of Overseas Territories 1993–95, for the Civil Service, Admin. Reform and Decentralization 1995–97. *Address:* Assemblée nationale, 126 rue de l'Université, 75355 Paris; Mairie, BP 92, Place de l'Hôtel de Ville, 71321 Chalon-sur-Saône cedex, France. *Telephone:* (1) 47 83 01 23 (Chalon).

PERCEVAL, John de Burgh, A.O.; Australian artist and ceramic potter; b. 1 Feb. 1923, Bruce Rock, W. Australia; m. 1944 (dissolved); one s. three d.; ed. Trinity Grammar School; began painting at age 13 (self-taught); mem. and former Sec. Contemporary Artists' Soc.; major retrospective exhbn. Nat. Gallery of Vic. and Art Gallery of N.S.W. 1992; represented in all major Australian art galleries, including Victoria, N.S.W., Queensland, S. Australia, W. Australia, Melbourne, Monash and Canberra, Nat. Gallery of Australia; Zwemmer Galleries, Hayward, Tate, London; Mertz Art Fund, Washington, U.S.A.; Toronto Art Gallery; pvt. collections internationally; the subject of several monographs; illustrated On My Island by Geoffery Dutton; Mona McCaughey Prize 1957, shared Wynne Prize 1961; Fellow in Creative Arts, Australian Nat. Univ., Canberra 1965; Emeritus Medal for Services to Govt., Australian Council 1995; *Address:* Unit 2/13 Terry Street, Balwyn, Vic. 3101, Australia.

PERCOVICH ROCA, Luis; Peruvian politician; b. 14 July 1931, Yungay, Ancash; s. of Alfredo Pércovich Jaramillo and Rosa Roca de Pércovich; m. Haydée Bambarén de Pércovich 1961; two s. one d.; Nat. Deputy 1963–68; Vice-Dean Chemical Pharmaceutical School of Peru 1967–68; Pres. Chamber of Deputies 1981–82; Minister of Fisheries Jan.–April 1983, Minister of the Interior 1983–84; Prime Minister of Peru and Minister of Foreign Affairs 1984–85; mem. Acción Popular (AP); Nat. Org. Sec. and Vice-Nat. Sec. Gen. Acción Popular, 1983–85; Acción Popular Del. Frente Democrático du Perú gen. election 1990. *Leisure interests:* nat. and int. econ. devt., sport. *Address:* Los Eucaliptos 355-13A, San Isidro, Lima 27, Peru. *Telephone:* 440-1705/441-5221. *Fax:* 440-4624/440-0445.

PERCY, Charles Harting; American politician and business executive; b. 27 Sept. 1919, Pensacola, Fla.; s. of Edward H. and Elisabeth (née Harting) Percy; m. Jeanne Valerie Dickerson 1943 (deceased), one s. two d. (one deceased); m. 2nd Loraine Diane Guyer 1950, one s. one d.; m. 3rd Diane Guyer 1990; ed. Univ. of Chicago; Lieut. Sr. Grade U.S. Naval Air Corpn. 1943–45; sales trainee, apprentice, Bell & Howell 1938, Man., War Co-ordinating Dept. 1941–43, Asst. Sec. 1943–46, Corpn. Sec. 1948–49, Pres., C.E.O. 1949–63, Chair. Bd. 1961–66; Senator from Illinois 1967–85; Pres. Charles Percy and Assocs. Inc. 1985–; Chair. Foreign Relations Cttee. 1981–85; Chair. Inst. of Int. Educ. 1985–89; Chair. and Pres. Hariri Foundation 1985–; Officer U.S.N. 1943–45; Chair. U.S. Int. Cultural and Trade Center Pres. Comm. 1988–; Republican. *Publications:* Growing Old In the Country of the Young 1974, I Want To Know about the United States Senate 1976. *Leisure interests:* reading, travel, swimming, tennis, skiing. *Address:* Charles Percy and Associates Inc., 900 19th Street N.W., Suite 700, Washington, DC 20006; 1691 34th Street, N.W., Washington, DC 20007, U.S.A.

PÉREC, Marie-José Juliana; French athlete; b. 9 May 1968, Basse-Terre, Guadeloupe; d. of José Pérec and Joëlle Pérec; ed. Inst. Nat. du Sport et de l'Educ. Physique; Indoor European Champion 1989, Bronze Medallist, European Championships 1990, Gold Medallist 400-metres, World Championships, Tokyo 1991, Olympic Games, Barcelona 1992, European Championships, Helsinki 1994, World Athletics Championships, Gothenburg 1995, Olympic Games, Atlanta 1996; Gold Medallist 200-metres, Olympic Games, Atlanta 1996; also fashion model. *Leisure interest:* fashion. Address: c/o Ars Athletica, 20 rue de Madrid, 75008 Paris, France.

PEREIRA, Aristides Maria; Cape Verde politician; b. 17 Nov. 1923, Boa Vista; s. of Porfírio Pereira Tavares and Maria das Neves Crus Silva; m. Carlina Fortes 1959; one s. two d.; ed. Lycée du Cap-Vert; began career as radio-telegraphist; Head, Telecommunications Services, Bissau, Portuguese Guinea (now Guinea-Bissau); founded Partido Africano da Independência da Guiné e Cabo Verde (PAIGC) with the late Amílcar Cabral 1956; mem. Political Bureau, Cen. Cttee., PAIGC 1956–70; fled to Repub. of Guinea 1960; Asst. Sec.-Gen. PAIGC 1964–73, Sec.-Gen. 1973–81; Sec.-Gen. Partido Africano da Independência de Cabo Verde (PAICV) 1981; mem. Perm. Comm. of Exec. Cttee. for Struggle in charge of Security, Control and Foreign Affairs 1970; Pres. Repub. of Cape Verde 1975–91; Dr. h.c. (Univs. of Rhode Island, Sacred Heart of Bridport, U.S.A., Coimbra, Portugal, Usmane Danfodyo Univ., Sokoto, Nigeria); mem. Orders of Santiago of the Sword and Infante Dom Henrique (Portugal), Médaille, Ordre du Lyon (Senegal), Médaille Amílcar Cabral (Guinea-Bissau), Médaille de Fidélité au Peuple (Repub. of Guinea), Grand Cordon of Nat. Order of Southern Cross (Brazil), Agostinho Neto Medal, First Class (Angola), Amílcar Cabral Medal, First Class (Cape Verde). *Leisure interests:* swimming, tennis, music. *Address:* c/o Prainha, P.O. Box 172, Praia, Cape Verde.

PEREIRA, Sir (Herbert) Charles, Kt., PH.D., D.SC., F.R.S.; British agricultural scientist; b. 12 May 1913, London; s. of Mr. and Mrs. H. J. Pereira; m. Irene Beatrice Sloan 1941; three s. one d.; ed. Prince Albert Coll., Sask., Canada, St. Alban's School, Herts., England, London Univ. and Rothamsted Experimental Station, Herts.; war service with Royal Engineers in Western Desert, Italy and Germany (mentioned in dispatches); Soil Scientist Coffee Research Team Kenya 1946–52; Head of Physics Div., E. African Agricultural and Forestry Research Org. 1952–55, Deputy Dir. 1955–61; Dir. Agricultural Research Council of Cen. Africa 1961–67; Consultant in Land Use Hydrology (I.H.D. Programme) FAO 1968–69; Dir. E. Malling Research Station, Kent, England 1969–72; Chief Scientist, Deputy Sec. Ministry of Agric., Fisheries and Food 1972–77; Consultant in tropical agricultural research 1978–; mem. World Bank Tech. Advisory Cttee. to C.G.I.A.R. 1971–76; mem. Bd. of Trustees, Royal Botanical Gardens, Kew 1983–86; Pres. Tropical Agric. Assen. 1990–; Trustee Marie Stopes Int. 1991–; Hon. Fellow, Royal Agricultural Soc. of England 1976; Life Fellow Inst. of Biology 1992; Hon. D.Sc. (Cranfield) 1977; Haile Sellassie Prize for Research in Africa 1966; Chevalier, Ordre du mérite agricole, Paris 1991. *Publications:* Land Use and Water Resources 1973, Policy and Practice in Watershed Management 1989, scientific papers on tillage and weed competition, soil fertility and water relations, catchment area research, tropical soil structure. *Address:* Peartrees, Nestor Court, Teston, Maidstone, Kent, ME18 5AD, England. *Telephone:* (01622) 813333.

PEREK, Luboš, RN.DR., DR.SC.; Czech astronomer (retd.); b. 26 July 1919, Prague; s. of Zdeněk Perek and Vilemina (née Trapp) Perek; m. Vlasta Straková 1945; ed. Masaryk Univ., Brno, and Charles Univ., Prague; Asst. Astronomical Inst., Masaryk Univ., Brno 1946, Head 1953; Head, Stellar Dept., Astronomical Inst. of Czechoslovak Acad. of Sciences, Prague 1956, Dir. Astronomical Inst. 1968–75; Vice-Pres. Comm. of the Galactic Structure and Dynamics, Int. Astronomical Union 1961–64, Asst. Gen. Sec., Int. Astronomical Union 1964–67, Gen. Sec. 1967–70; Chief, Outer Space Affairs Division, UN Secr. 1975–80; Visiting Prof., Dearborn Observatory, Evanston, Ill. 1964; mem. Czechoslovak Astronomical Soc., Exec. Cttee. Int. Council of Scientific Unions 1967–70, Vice-Pres. 1968–70; Chair. Int. Astronautical Fed. 1980–82; mem. Leopoldina Acad., Int. Acad. of Astronautics, Int. Inst. of Space Law, Nat. Acad. of the Air and Space, Toulouse; Assoc. mem. Royal Astronomical Soc.; silver plaque for services to science 1969, gold plaque 1989, Janssen Medal, Paris 1992. *Publications include:* Catalogue of Galactic Planetary Nebulae (with L. Kohoutek) 1967, about 40 articles on geostationary orbits, definition of space, space debris and environment of space. *Leisure interest:* collecting seashells. *Address:* Kouřimská 28, 130 00 Prague 3, Czech Republic. *Telephone:* (2) 738680. *Fax:* (2) 769023.

PERELLA, Joseph Robert, M.B.A., C.P.A.; American investment banker; b. 20 Sept. 1941, Newark; s. of Dominic Perella and Agnes Perella; m. Amy Gralnick 1974; ed. Lehigh and Harvard Univs.; public accountant, Haskins & Sells, New York 1964–70; consultant IBRD, Washington, D.C. 1971; Assoc. The First Boston Corpn. New York 1972–74, Asst. Vice-Pres. 1974–75, Vice-Pres. 1975-78, Man. Dir. 1978–88; Chair. Wasserstein, Perella & Co. New York 1988–93; mem. operating cttee. Morgan Stanley 1993–. *Address:* Morgan Stanley & Co. Inc., 1251 Avenue of the Americas, New York, NY 10020, U.S.A.

PERELMAN, Ronald Owen, M.B.A.; American business executive; b. 1943, Greensboro, N.C.; s. of Raymond Perelman and Claudia (née Cohen) Perelman; m. Faith Golding (divorced); four c.; ed. Univ. of Pa. and Wharton School of Finance; with Belmont Industries Inc. 1966–78; Dir., Chair. and C.E.O. MacAndrews & Forbes Group, Inc., New York City 1978–; Dir., Chair. and C.E.O. Revlon Group, Inc., New York City 1985–; Andrews Group Inc., New York 1985–; Chair. Nat. Health Labs., La Jolla, Calif. 1985–; Chair. Technicolor Inc., Hollywood, Calif.; Dir. Four Star Int. Inc., Compact Video Inc. *Address:* Revlon Group Inc., 625 Madison Avenue, New York, NY 10022; MacAndrews & Forbes Group Inc., 35 E. 62nd Street, New York, NY 10021, U.S.A. (Offices).

PERÉNYI, Miklós; Hungarian cellist and composer; b. 5 Jan. 1948, Budapest; s. of László Perényi and Erzsébet Seeger; m. Tünde Angermayer; one s.; started playing cello at age 6, first public recital at age 9, Budapest; ed. Music Acad. of Budapest; Prof. of Violoncello Liszt Ferenc Acad. of Music, Budapest 1974–; numerous int. appearances; holder of Liszt Prize 1970, Kossuth Prize 1980, Eminent Artist title. *Leisure interests:* swimming, cycling.

PERERA, Liyanagé Henry Horace, B.A.; Sri Lankan international official; b. 9 May 1915, Yatiyantota, Ceylon; s. of L. H. Perera and Maud Mildred Sirimane; m. Sita Trixie Senarat 1942; one s. three d.; ed. St. Benedict's Coll., Colombo, Univ. Coll., London, Univ. of Ceylon; Sr. Master in Govt. and History, Ceylon 1936–59; Asst. Registrar, Aquinas Univ. Coll., Colombo 1960–61; Educ. Dir. World Fed. of UN Asscns. 1961–63, Deputy Sec.-Gen. and Educ. Dir. 1963–66, Sec.-Gen. 1966–76; Consultant, Pontifical Comm. for Peace and Justice 1969–76; Special Asst. for Asia and the S. Pacific, World Confed. of Orgs. of the Teaching Profession 1976–84; Consultant to World Fed. UN Asscns. 1985–; Sec. Masaryk Study Centre for UN Studies, Geneva; mem. Int. Cttee. Adult Educ. (UNESCO) 1963; Pres. Non-Governmental Orgs. in Consultative status with UN Econ. and Social Council 1969–72, Co-ordinator for Int. Year of the Child; Sec. Strategic Planning Cttee. WFUNA (World Fed. of UN Asscns.), Hon. Pres. 1967–, Hon. Treas. and mem. WFUNA Business Council 1993–, Acting Sec.-Gen. WFUNA 1996–; lectures regularly in Asia and the S. Pacific on human rights; has organized and conducted nine seminars on educ. about the UN and 15 summer courses on the UN and its agencies, and numerous other confs., seminars and courses, and given keynote addresses at int. confs. on educ. and soc., educ. and work, educ. for a technological age, the elimination of all forms of discrimination against women; has lectured in Europe and Asia on Human Rights, Environment and Devt.; Hon. Pres. World Fed. of UN Asscns.; Vice-Pres. NGO Comm. against Racism; William Russel Award 1974, Int. Asscn. of Educators for World Peace Award, Gold Medal (Czechoslovak Soc. for Int. Relations). *Publications:* Ceylon and Indian History, Groundwork of Ceylon and World History, Ceylon Under Western Rule, Guides to the Study of the Status and Working Conditions of the Teacher, ILO Conventions and Trade Unionism, The Convention on the Rights of the Child, The Convention on the Elimination of all Forms of Discrimination against Women, Ed. Human Rights in Hinduism, Buddhism, Christianity and Islam 1988; numerous published papers on the UN, human rights, environmental protection, global security, national sovereignty etc. *Leisure interests:* swimming, tennis, photography, stamp collecting and reading. *Address:* 22 avenue Luserna, 1203 Geneva, Switzerland. *Telephone:* 344-07-37. *Fax:* 733-48-38.

PERERA, Wahalatantrige D.R.; Sri Lankan diplomatist and attorney; b. 4 Aug. 1928, Colombo; s. of Dr. Richard P. Perera and Violet L. Perera; m. Irangani L. Perera (née Agalawatte) 1957; one s. one d.; ed. Royal Coll. of Sri Lanka and Sri Lanka Law Coll.; advocate Supreme Court of Sri Lanka 1954; apptd. Crown Counsel, Criminal Br. Attorney-Gen.'s Dept. 1956–64, 1966–70; Head Legal Branch, Sri Lanka Army HQ, Colombo 1964–66; entered Pvt. Practice 1970; Del. Law Asia Conf., Seoul, apptd. Vice-Chair. Standing Cttee. on Law and Drugs 1981; Rep. Asian Lawyers Legal Inquiry, Bangkok, Vice-Pres. All Asia Bar Asscn. 1981; apptd. Pres.'s Counsel 1981; Perm. Rep. to UN 1988–91; Vice-Pres. Medico Legal Soc. of Sri Lanka 1983–86, Pres. 1987–; Adjunct Prof. John Jay Coll. of Criminal Justice, City Univ. of New York 1989–. *Leisure interests:* music, swimming. *Address:* c/o Ministry of Foreign Affairs, Republic Building, Colombo 1, Sri Lanka.

PERES, Shimon; Israeli politician; b. 1923, Poland; s. of Isaac and Sara Persky; m. Sonia Gelman; two s. one d.; ed. New York Univ., Harvard Univ.; immigrated to Palestine 1934; fmr. Sec. Hano'ar Ha'oved Movt.; mem. Haganah Movt. 1947; Head of Israel Naval Service, Ministry of Defence 1948; Head of Defence Mission in U.S.A.; Deputy Dir.-Gen. of Ministry of Defence 1952–53, Dir.-Gen. 1953–59, Deputy Minister of Defence 1959–65; mem. Knesset 1959–; mem. Mapai Party 1959–65, founder mem. and Sec.-Gen. Rafi Party 1965, mem. Labour Party after merger 1968, Chair. 1977–92, 1995–97; Minister for Econ. Devt. in the Administered Areas and for Immigrant Absorption 1969–70, of Transport and Communications 1970–74, of Information March–June 1974, of Defence 1974–77, of Foreign Affairs 1992–95; Acting Prime Minister April–May 1977; Leader of the Opposition 1977–84, 1996–97; Prime Minister of Israel 1984–86; Minister of the Interior and of Religious Affairs 1984–85, of Defence 1995–96; Prime Minister 1995–96; Vice-Premier and Minister of Foreign Affairs 1986–88, Vice-Premier and Finance Minister 1988–90; shared Nobel Prize for Peace 1994; Int. Council of Christians and Jews Interfaith Gold Medallion 1997. *Publications:* The Next Step 1965, David's Sling 1970, Tomorrow is Now 1978, From These Men 1979, Witness (autobiog.) 1993, The New Middle East 1993, Battling for Peace 1995, and numerous political articles in Israeli and foreign publications. *Address:* The Knesset, Jerusalem, Israel.

PERESYPKIN, Oleg Gerasimovich, D.HIST., M.SC.ECON.; Russian diplomatist and orientalist; b. 12 Aug. 1935, Baku; s. of Gerasim Peresypkin and Anna Kochergina; m. Natalia Ushakova 1957; one d.; ed. Moscow Inst. of Int. Relations; Counsellor, Embassy, Yemen Arab Repub. 1971–76; Adviser, Near Eastern Countries Dept., U.S.S.R. Ministry of Foreign Affairs 1976–80; Amb. to Yemen Arab Repub. 1980–84, to Libya 1984–86; mem. Collegium of Foreign Ministry 1985–; Rector Diplomatic Acad. 1986–93; Chief Adviser on Near Eastern and N. African Countries, Ministry of Foreign Affairs 1993–96; Amb. to Lebanon 1996–; Pres. Imperial Orthodox Palestine Soc. 1989–. *Publications:* Iraqi Oil 1969, Yemen Revolution 1979, On the New East Crossroads 1979, Fifth Season 1991, Oriental Patterns 1993, Informal Notes 1997. *Leisure interests:* travelling, reading. *Address:* Russian Embassy, Mar Elias str., El-Tina, Beirut, Lebanon; P.O. Box 5220, Lebanon. *Telephone:* (1) 867560. *Fax:* (1) 303837.

PERETTI, Jean-Jacques Marie Paul de; French politician; b. 21 Sept. 1946, Clermont-Ferrand; Nat. Sec. RPR 1988; Mayor of Sarlat 1989; Conseiller Général, Dordogne 1992; Regional Councillor, Aquitaine 1992; Deputy to Nat. Ass. 1993–95; Minister of Overseas Depts. May–Nov. 1995, Deputy Minister 1995–97. *Address:* Mairie, 24200 Sarlat-la-Canéda, France.

PERETZ, David Lindsay Corbett, C.B., M.A.; British international finance official; b. 29 May 1943; s. of Michael Peretz and April Peretz; m. Jane Wildman 1966; one s. one d.; ed. The Leys School Cambridge and Exeter Coll. Oxford; Asst. Prin. Ministry of Tech. 1965–69; Head of Public Policy and Institutional Studies, Int. Bank Research Org. 1969–76; Prin. H.M. Treasury 1976–80, Asst. Sec. External Finance 1980–84, Prin. Pvt. Sec. to Chancellor of Exchequer 1984–85, Under-Sec. (Home Finance) 1985–86, (Monetary Group, Public Finance) 1986–90; U.K. Exec. Dir. IMF and IBRD and Econ. Minister, Washington, D.C. 1990–94; Deputy Dir. Int. Finance, H.M. Treasury 1994–; U.K. G7 Financial Sherpa 1994–. *Leisure interests:* walking, sailing, listening to music. *Address:* H.M. Treasury, Parliament Street, London, SW1P 3AG, England.

PERETZ, Yitzhak Haim; Israeli politician; b. 1939, Morocco; m.; four c.; ordained rabbi; fmr. Chief Rabbi of Raanana; mem. Shas Party; mem. Knesset 1984–; Minister without Portfolio 1984, of the Interior 1984–87, without Portfolio 1987–88, of Immigrant Absorption 1988–92. *Address:* The Knesset, Jerusalem, Israel.

PEREZ, Vincent; Swiss actor; ed. Conservatoire, Paris. *Film appearances include:* Cyrano de Bergerac, La Reine Margot, Indochine, The Crow: City of Angels, Amy Foster.

PEREZ BALLADARES, Ernesto, M.B.A.; Panamanian politician; b. 29 June 1946, Panama City; s. of Ernesto Pérez Balladares Sr. and María Enriqueta González Revilla; m. Dora Boyd; two s. three d.; ed. Univs. of Notre Dame and Pennsylvania; Dir., Corp. Credit Official for Cen. America and Panama, Citibank 1971–75; Minister of Finance and the Treasury 1976–81, of Planning and Econ. Policy 1981–82; founding mem. Partido Revolucionario Democrático (PRD) 1979, Sec.-Gen. 1982, 1992; Dir.-Gen. Instituto de Recursos Hidráulicos y Electrificación (IRHE) 1983; Pres. of Panama 1994–; Pres. Golden Fruit, S.A., Inversionista el Torreón, S.A.; mem. Legislation Comm., PRD Political Comm.; Order of Sacred Treasure (1st class) (Japan) 1980, Orden Aguila Azteca en Grado de Bando (Mexico) 1981. *Address:* Office of the President, Palacio Presidencial, Valija 50, Panamá 1, Panama. *Telephone:* 27-4062. *Fax:* 27-0076.

PÉREZ DE CUÉLLAR, Javier; Peruvian diplomatist; b. 19 Jan. 1920, Lima; m. Marcela Temple; two c.; ed. Catholic Univ., Lima; joined Foreign Ministry 1940, diplomatic service 1944; served as Sec. in embassies in France, U.K., Bolivia, Brazil (later Counsellor); Dir. Legal and Personnel Dept., Dir. of Admin., of Protocol and of Political Affairs, Ministry of External Relations 1961–63; Amb. to Switzerland 1964–66; Perm. Under Sec. and Sec.-Gen. Foreign Office 1966–69, Amb. to U.S.S.R. (concurrently to Poland) 1969–71, to Venezuela 1978; Perm. Rep. to UN 1971–75; mem. UN Security Council 1973–74, Pres. 1974; Special Rep. of UN Sec.-Gen. in Cyprus 1975–77; UN Under-Sec.-Gen. for Special Political Affairs 1979–81; UN Sec.-Gen. 1982–91; Pres. World Comm. on Culture and Devt. UN/UNESCO 1992–, Int. Disability Foundation 1992–, Fondation de l'Arche de la Fraternité 1993–; Dir. Repub. Nat. Bank of New York 1992–; Pres. Cand. in 1995 Elections; fmr. Prof. of Diplomatic Law, Acad. Diplomática del Perú and Prof. of Int. Relations, Acad. de Guerra Aérea del Perú; del. to First UN Gen. Assembly 1946–47 and other int. confs.; Montague Burton Visiting Prof. of Int. Relations, Univ. of Edinburgh 1985; mem. Acad. Mexicana de

Derecho Int. 1988–; Olaf Palme Prize for Public Service 1989; Hon. Dr. (Univ. of Nice) 1983, (Jagiellonian, Charles and Sofia Univs., Univ. of San Marcos and Vrije Univ., Brussels) 1984, (Carleton Univ., Ottawa, Sorbonne Univ., Paris) 1985, (Osnabruck) 1986, (Univs. of Mich., Coimbra, Mongolian State, Humbolt, Moscow State) 1987, (Univ. of Leiden) 1988, (Cambridge) 1989, (Univ. of Kuwait) 1993, (Oxford) 1993; Prince of Asturias Prize for Ibero-American Co-operation; Alexander Onassis Foundation Prize 1990, Four Freedoms Award (Franklin Delano Roosevelt Inst.) 1992. *Publication:* Manual de Derecho Diplomático 1964. *Address:* 18 avenue de la Bourdonnais, 75007 Paris, France; Avenida A. Miro Quesada, 1071 Lima, Peru.

PÉREZ ESQUIVEL, Adolfo; Argentinian human rights leader, architect and sculptor; ; b. 26 Nov. 1931, Buenos Aires; m. Amanda Pérez 1956; three s.; ed. Nat. School of Fine Arts, Buenos Aires; trained as architect and sculptor; Prof. of Art, Manuel Belgrano Nat. School of Fine Arts, Buenos Aires 1956–71; Prof. Faculty of Architecture and Urban Studies; Univ. Nacional de la Plata; gave up teaching to concentrate on non-violent human rights movement; f. Servicio Paz y Justicia en America Latina, Buenos Aires 1973, Sec.-Gen. 1974–86, Sec. Gen. 1974–86; co-founder Ecumenical Movement for Human Rights, Argentina; Pres. Perm. Ass. for Human Rights; arrested 1977, released May 1978; visited Europe 1980; Pres. Int. League for the Rights and Liberation of Peoples 1987; fmr. Rector UN Univ. for Peace; Nobel Prize for Peace 1980; Hon. Citizen of Assisi 1982. *Address:* University for Peace, Apdo. Postal 199, 1250 Escalzu, Costa Rica; Servicio Paz y Justicia, Piedras 730, CP 1070, Buenos Aires, Argentina.

PÉREZ FERNÁNDEZ, Pedro, LIC.ECON.; Spanish international finance official; b. 1949; ed. Univ. of Madrid; Adviser to Minister, Ministry of Planning 1975–76, Div. Dir. 1976–77; Deputy Dir.-Gen. of Econ. Research, Ministry of Economy and Chair. Bd. of Prices, Ministry of Economy and Finance 1982–84; concurrently lectured in econs. at Univ. of Madrid; fmr. Chair. Tabacalera S.A.; fmr. mem. bd. of dirs. of several govt. agencies; Exec. Dir. IMF 1984–86. *Publications:* co-author of book on Spanish econ. policy; several articles on budgetary policy, prices and econ. issues. *Address:* c/o PSOE, Ferraz 68 y 70, 28008 Madrid, Spain.

PÉREZ GODOY, Gen. Ricardo Pío; Peruvian politician and army officer; b. 9 June 1905; ed. Colegio Santo Tomás de Aquino and Escuela de Oficiales del Ejército; Dir.-Gen. of Training, Peruvian Army 1956–57; Controller-Gen. of Army 1958–59; Chief of Staff of Jt. Command of Armed Forces 1960–62; Prefect of Dept. of Arequipa 1952–53, 1955–56; Pres. of Mil. Junta of Govt. of Peru 1962–63; mem. Centro de Altos Estudios Históricos del Perú; now Gen. of a Division; numerous decorations. *Publications:* include Teoría de la Guerra y Doctrina de Guerra, La Maniobra y la Batalla. *Address:* Blasco Núñez de Balboa 225, Miraflores, Lima, Peru.

PÉREZ JIMÉNEZ, Col. Marcos; Venezuelan politician and army officer; b. 1914; ed. Caracas Mil. School and Lima War Coll.; Army Chief of Staff in Acción Democrática Govt.; mem. of subsequent three-man Junta and Minister of Defence; Pres. of Venezuela 1952–58; extradited from U.S.A. to Venezuela Aug. 1963; imprisoned in Venezuela 1963–68; went to Madrid; faced corruption charges, imprisoned May 1994.

PÉREZ-LLORCA, José Pedro; Spanish politician and lawyer; b. 30 Nov. 1940, Cadiz; s. of José and Carmen Pérez-Llorca; m. Carmen Zamora Bonilla 1965; one s. one d.; ed. Madrid Central (Complutense) Univ., Univs. of Freiburg and Munich; entered diplomatic service 1964; adviser Spanish del. to 21st and 22nd Gen. Ass. of UN and 5th extraordinary emergency session; Legal Adviser to Parl. 1968; Higher Council for Foreign Affairs 1970; practised law, Madrid 1970–; mem. Cortes 1977–82; fmr. parl. leader Unión de Centro Democrático (UCD); mem. Comm. for drawing up Constitution 1978; Minister of the Presidency 1979–80, Minister for Relations with Parl. Jan.–May 1980, Minister for Territorial Admin. May–Oct. 1980, Minister for Foreign Affairs 1980–82; pvt. law practice 1983–; Chair. AEG-Ibérica SA, Urquiso Leasing SA; Dir. Robert Bosch Española SA; Prof. of Constitutional Law, School of Diplomacy. *Address:* Plaza de la Marina Española 8, 28071 Madrid, Spain.

PÉREZ RODRÍGUEZ, Carlos Andrés; Venezuelan politician; b. 27 Oct. 1922, Rubio; m. Blanca Rodríguez de Pérez; one s. five d.; ed. Univ. Central de Venezuela; Pvt. Sec. to Pres. Rómulo Betancourt 1945; mem. Chamber of Deputies 1947–48, 1958–74; in exile 1949–58; Chief Ed. La República, San José 1953–58; Minister of the Interior 1963–64; Sec.-Gen. Acción Democrática 1968; Pres. of Venezuela 1974–79, 1989–93; suspended, to stand trial on embezzlement charges; barred from returning to office Sept. 1993; found guilty of misappropriation of public funds May 1996 and sentenced to two years and four months' imprisonment, served as house arrest owing to age.

PERHAM, Richard Nelson, M.A., PH.D., SC.D., F.R.S., F.R.S.A.; British professor of biochemistry; b. 27 April 1937, London; s. of Cyril Perham and Helen Thornton; m. Nancy Lane 1969; one s. one d.; ed. Latymer Upper School, London and St. John's Coll., Cambridge; MRC Scholar, MRC Lab. of Molecular Biology, Cambridge 1961–64; Helen Hay Whitney Fellow, Dept. of Molecular Biophysics, Yale Univ. 1966–67; Univ. Lecturer in Biochemistry, Univ. of Cambridge 1969–77, Reader in Biochemistry of Molecular Structures 1977–89, Prof. of Structural Biochemistry 1989–; Fellow, St. John's Coll., Cambridge 1964–, Pres. 1983–87; Fogarty Int. Scholar, N.I.H., U.S.A. 1990–93; mem. European Molecular Biology Org., Academia Europaea; Max Planck Prize 1993, Novartis Medal and Prize 1998. *Publications:* Instrumentation in Amino Acid Sequence Analysis; over 200 papers and articles in learned journals. *Leisure interests:* gardening, theatre, opera, rowing, antiques (18th century). *Address:* Department of Biochemistry, University of Cambridge, 80 Tennis Court Road, Cambridge, CB2 1GA (Office); St. John's College, Cambridge, CB2 1TP (Office); 107 Barton Road, Cambridge, CB3 9LL, England (Home). *Telephone:* (01223) 333663 (Office); (01223) 338764 (Coll.); (01223) 363752 (Home). *Fax:* (01223) 333667 (Office); (01223) 363752 (Home).

PERI FAGERSTROM, Gen. René Alberto; Chilean politician, police officer and writer; b. 21 Dec. 1926; m. Graciela Mundaca; two s. one d.; ed. Carabineros Escuela de Instituto Superior de Carabineros, Academia de Seguridad Nacional; civil servant; journalist; Head First Carabineros Inspection Zone, Antofagasta 1976–77; Head Higher Carabineros Council of Assessors 1978–79; Minister of Land and Settlement (now Nat. Property) 1979; several literary prizes. *Publications:* (short stories): Mundo Aparte 1958, Ronda Rondando 1962, Caranchos 1968, Dioses Difuntos 1969, Orilla Adentro 1970, Caer en Desgracia 1972, Los Genocidas 1975, Los Barbados 1976, Cuentos de Niños y Pajaros. novels: Las Hermanas González 1967, Dos Mujeres 1974. poems: Turnos 1963, Sol Mayor 1976, Uranidas Go Home (science fiction) 1966. essays: Bajo Dos Carabinas 1977, Paja Brava 1978, Los Batallones Bulnes y Valparaíso 1980.

PÉRIER, François (pseudonym of François Pillu); French actor; b. 10 Nov. 1919, Paris; m. 1st Jacqueline Porel 1941; two s. (one deceased) one d.; m. 2nd Marie Daems 1949; m. 3rd Colette Boutouland 1961; ed. Conservatoire Nat. d'Art Dramatique, Paris; Co-Dir. Théâtre de la Michodière, Paris 1951–65; has appeared in numerous plays including Les jours heureux, Les J 3, Les mains sales, Bobosse, Le ciel de lit, Gog et Magog, La preuve par quatre, Le Diable et le Bon Dieu, Ne réveillez pas Madame, Le tube, Equus, Coup de chapeau, Amadeus, Tartuffe. *Films include:* Premier bal 1941, Lettres d'amour 1942, Un revenant, Le silence est d'or 1946, Orphée 1949, Les évadés 1954, Gervaise 1955, Le Notti di Cabiria 1956, Bobosse 1958, Le testament d'Orphée 1960, L'amant de cinq jours 1961, La visita 1963, Les enfants du palais (TV) 1967, Z 1968, Le cercle rouge 1970, Max et les ferrailleurs 1971, Juste avant la nuit 1971, L'attentat 1972, Antoine et Sébastien 1973, Stavisky, Sarah (TV) 1974, Dr. Françoise Gailland 1975, Police Python 357 1976, Mazarin (TV) 1978, La raison d'etat 1978, La guerre des polices 1979, Le bar du téléphone 1980, Le battant 1983, Le Tartuffe 1984, Soigne ta droite 1987, Lacenaire 1990, le Pagaille 1991, Voyage à Rome 1992; has also appeared on TV; British Film Acad. Award 1956, Victoria du Cinéma Français 1957, Médaille George Méliès 1976, Grand Prix nat. du Théâtre 1977, Molière d'honneur 1988; Commdr., Ordre des Arts et des Lettres. *Publications:* Profession menteur 1989, Mes Jours Heureux 1994. *Address:* c/o Artmedia, 10 avenue Georges V, Paris 75008, France.

PERIGOT, François; French business executive; b. 12 May 1926, Lyons; s. of Jean-Paul Perigot and Marguerite de la Tour; m. 2nd Isabelle Paque 1986; one s. one d. from fmr. marriage; ed. Lycée de Bastia, Faculté de Droit, Paris and Inst. d'Etudes Politiques, Paris; joined Unilever group (France) 1955, Head of Personnel 1966; Pres.-Dir.-Gen. Thibaud Gibbs et Cie. 1968–70; Dir. Unilever (Spain) 1971–75; Pres.-Dir.-Gen. Unilever (France) 1976–86; mem. Exec. Council, Conseil Nat. du Patronat Français (CNPF) 1981–86, Pres. 1986–94; Pres., Dir.-Gen. Compagnie du Plâtre 1987; Vice-Pres. Union des confédérations de l'industrie et des employeurs d'Europe (UNICE) 1988–92, Pres. 1994; mem. Social and Econ. Council (CES) 1989–, Admin. Bd. French Centre for Foreign Trade 1995; Officier, Légion d'honneur; numerous foreign decorations. *Leisure interests:* yachting, riding. *Address:* 4 rue Quentin Bauchart, 75008 Paris; Conseil économique et social, 1 avenue Iéna, 75016 Paris, France.

PERIN, François; Belgian politician, professor of law and writer; b. 31 Jan. 1921, Liège; ed. Univ. of Liège; mem. of Socialist Party 1943–64; Asst. Chef de Cabinet to Minister of Interior 1954–57; Asst. to Prof. of Public Law 1954–58; Dir. of Studies, Faculty of Law, Univ. of Liège 1958, Prof. of Constitutional Law 1967; Deputy to Nat. Ass. 1965–; Pres. Rassemblement Wallon 1968–74; Minister of Institutional Reforms 1974–76; mem. co-founders Parti Réformateur Libéral (PRL) 1976–; author of Les invités du Dr. Klaust, staged Théâtre Arlequin, Liège 1998–99. *Publications:* La démocratie enrayée—essai sur le régime parlementaire belge de 1918 à 1958 1960, La Belgique au défi: Flamands Wallons à la recherche d'un état 1962, La décision politique en Belgique (co-author) 1965, Le régionalisme dans l'intégration européenne 1969, Germes et bois morts dans la société politique contemporaine 1981, Histoire d'une nation introuvable 1988, Franc parler: témoignage sur la double crise du Christianisme et du Rationalisme 1996. *Leisure interests:* music, concerts, history of religions, philosophy and science. *Address:* 10 rue Chevaufosse, 4000 Liège, Belgium. *Telephone:* 04-2236782.

PERINETTI, André Louis; French administrator and theatre director; b. 7 Aug. 1933, Asnières; m. Fatiha Bel-el-Abbas 1974; two s. one d.; ed. Collège Turgot, Law Faculty of Paris, Univ. of Theatre of Nations; theatre dir. 1965-83; Gen. Man. Théâtre Cité Universitaire 1968–72, Nat. Theatre of Strasbourg 1972–75, Nat. Theatre of Chaillot, Paris 1974–81; Consultant, UNESCO 1974, Ministry of Culture 1982–83; Sec.-Gen. Int. Theatre Inst. (UNESCO) 1984–; Chevalier, Légion d'honneur; Chevalier des Arts et Lettres. *Leisure interests:* theatre, music, tennis. *Address:* 109 ave. Charles de Gaulle, 92200 Neuilly, France. *Fax:* 45.66.50.40.

PERIŠIC, Zoran; Serbian film director, writer, producer and visual effects supervisor; b. 16 March 1940, Zemun, Yugoslavia; Dir. Sky Bandits/Gunbus (film) 1986; Producer-Dir. The Phoenix and the Magic Carpet 1994; Dir.-Writer Captain Cook's Travels (TV, animated series), Magic Fountain (TV, animated series), In Search of the Real Dracula (documentary), etc.; cr. visual effects for 2001 – A Space Odyssey, Superman 1, 2 and 3, Return to Oz, Cliffhanger and other films; several patents, including ZOPTIC front-projection system and 3D cinematography; Acad. Award (Oscar) for Outstanding Achievement in Visual Effects (for Superman – the Movie), B.A.F.T.A. Award for Outstanding Contrib. to the Cinema, American Acad. Tech. Achievement Award for the invention and devt. of the ZOPTIC dual-zoom front-projection system. *Publications:* Special Optical Effects, The Animation Stand, Photoguide to Shooting Animation. *Leisure interest:* flying (pvt. pilot's licence). *Address:* c/o L'Epine Smith & Carney Associates, Suite 60/61, Kent House, 87 Regent Street, London, W1R 7HF, England.; c/o The Chasin Agency, 8899 Beverly Bldg., Suite 716, Los Angeles, CA 90048, U.S.A.

PERIŠIN, Ivo, D.ECON.; Croatian economist and banker; b. 4 July 1925, Split; s. of Duje and Filomena Tadin Perišin; m. Magda Martinič 1949; one s. one d.; ed. Zagreb Univ.; Prof. of Econ., Zagreb Univ.; Chief of post-univ. studies in banking and financial markets; fmr. Under-Sec., Fed. Secr. for Finance; Gov. Nat. Bank of Yugoslavia (Narodna Banka Jugoslavije) 1969–72; Pres. Exec. Council, Socialist Repub. of Croatia 1972–74; Pres. Parl. 1974–78; Pres. Fed. Council for Devt. and Econ. Policy 1978–88; mem. Croatian Acad. of Science; Partisan Memorial Award, Order of People's Merit, Order of the Repub., Medal for Valour. *Publications:* Money and Credit Policy 1964, Money and Economic Development 1961, Economics of Yugoslavia, Inflation 1965, Financial Dictionary 1967, Money, Credit and Banking 1975, Transformation of Monetary System 1975, Money, Monetary System and Associated Work 1978, Essays on the Reform of the Monetary System 1979, Interest Rates and Savings 1980, Inflation 1985, World Financial Whirlpool (a contrib. to Studies of Modern Banking and Financial Markets) 1988, series on financial transformation 1991–94. *Address:* Ksaverska cesta 13, Zagreb, Croatia. *Telephone:* 4677212.

PERISSICH, Riccardo; Italian international civil servant; b. 24 Jan. 1942, Milan; m. Anne Treca 1989; writer on foreign policy for Il Punto (Rome weekly) 1962; Italconsult S.p.a. (consulting engineers) 1962–64; Head of EC Studies, Istituto Affari Internazionali, Rome 1966–70; joined Comm. of EC, Brussels 1970; Chef de Cabinet of Altiero Spinelli 1970–76, to Cesidio Guazzaroni 1976; Dir. Directorate A (energy savings and energy forecasts) 1977–81; Chef de Cabinet of Antonio Giolitti (regional policy) 1981–84, of Carlo Ripa di Meana (institutional affairs) 1985–86; Dir., later Deputy Dir.-Gen. Directorate-Gen. for Industry 1986, Dir.-Gen. 1990–94; Dir. Public and Econ. Affairs Pirelli S.p.A. 1994–; Vice-Pres. Assolombarda 1995–. *Publications:* Gli eurocrati fra realtà e mitologia 1969, Europa America: materiali per un dibattito (with S. Silvestri) 1970. *Address:* Pirelli S.p.A., Viale Sarca 222, 20126 Milan, Italy.

PERISSOL, Pierre-André Daniel; French politician and engineer; b. 30 April 1947, Nice; s. of Louis Perissol and Aline Cardiec; ed. Lycée Massena, Nice, Ecole Polytechnique, Ecole Nat. des Ponts et Chaussées; Dir. of Planning, Saint-Quentin-en-Yvelines new town 1972–74; Adviser to Sec. of State for Housing 1974–76; Chief Eng. Ecole Nat. des Ponts et Chaussées 1986; Dir.-Gen. Soc. Centrale de Crédit Immobilier 1977–91, Pres., Dir.-Gen. 1991–92, Pres. 1993–95; Founder and Dir.-Gen. Groupe Arcade 1980–91, Pres. 1991–95; Pres. Coopérer pour Habiter 1982, Aiguillon Construction 1987, Fed. Nat. (now Chambre Syndicale) des Sociétés de Crédit Immobilier 1988, Caisse Centrale de Crédit Immobilier 1990–93; Regional Councillor, Ile-de-France 1983–86; Councillor, Paris 1983–95; Deputy Mayor of Paris responsible for Educ. 1989–93; RPR Deputy to Nat. Ass. 1993–95; Minister of Housing May–Nov. 1995, Deputy Minister 1995–97; Mayor of Moulins 1995–; Vice-Pres. Regional Council of Auvergne 1998–; Chevalier, Légion d'honneur, Ordre Nat. du Mérite. *Publication:* Le Défi social 1985. *Leisure interests:* travel, tennis. *Address:* Mairie, 03000 Moulins, France (Office).

PERKIN, James Russell Conway, D.PHIL.; British/Canadian university president; b. 19 Aug. 1928, Northants.; s. of William Perkin and Lily Drage; m. Dorothy Bentley 1953; two s. one d.; ed. Daventry Grammar School, Northants. and Univ. of Oxford; Minister, Altrincham Baptist Church, Cheshire 1955–62; lecturer in New Testament Greek, New Coll. Edinburgh 1963–65; Assoc. Prof. of New Testament Interpretation, McMaster Divinity Coll. Hamilton, Ont. 1965–69; Prof. of Religious Studies and Head of Dept. Acadia Univ. N.S. 1969–77, Dean of Arts 1977–80, Vice-Pres. (Academic) 1980–81, Acting Pres. 1981–82, Pres. 1982–93; mem. Soc. for New Testament Studies, Canadian Soc. for Study of Religion; Hon. D.D. (McMaster) 1986; Hon. D.Litt (Acadia) 1995. *Publications:* Such is Our Story (with E. A. Payne) 1955, Study Notes on Romans 1957, Resurrection in Theology and Life 1966, Handbook for Biblical Studies 1973, Scripture Then and Now 1975, In Season 1978, With Mind and Heart 1979, Crucial Questions 1980, Seedtime and Harvest 1982, Arrows in the Mind 1984, Morning in his Heart: Life and Writings of Watson Kirkconnell (with J. Snelson) 1986, Morning in his Heart: a Biographical Sketch of Watson Kirkconnell 1987, Commonplace Book 1986, Reflections and Insights 1993, Ordinary Magic 1995, Devotional Diary 1998; book chapters, essays, articles and reviews. *Leisure interests:* tennis, reading, gardening, sailing, classical music. *Address:* Box 355, Wolfville, N.S. B0P 1X0, Canada.

PERKINS, David D(exter), PH.D.; American biologist and geneticist; b. 2 May 1919, Watertown, New York; s. of Dexter M. and Loretta F. (Gardiner) Perkins; m. Dorothy L. Newmeyer 1952; one d.; ed. Univ. of Rochester and Columbia Univ.; mem. Faculty, Stanford Univ. 1949, Prof. of Biology 1961–; Research Fellow, Univ. of Glasgow, Scotland 1954–55, Columbia Univ. 1962–63, A.N.U., Canberra 1968–69; mem. India-U.S. Exchange Scientists' Program 1974; Ed. Genetics 1963–67; mem. Int. Genetics Fed. Exec. Bd. 1978–83, Genetics Soc. of America (Pres. 1977), N.A.S.; Nat. Insts. of Health Research Career Award 1964–89, Merit Award 1987–(96), Guggenheim Fellow 1983–85; Genetics Soc. of America Morgan Medal 1994. *Publications:* The cytogenetics of Neurospora (with E. G. Barry) 1977, Chromosomal loci of Neurospora crassa (with others) 1982. *Address:* Department of Biological Sciences, Stanford University, Stanford, CA 94305; 345 Vine Street, Menlo Park, CA 94025, U.S.A. (Home). *Fax:* (415) 723-6132.

PERKINS, Donald H., C.B.E., M.A., PH.D., F.R.S.; British professor of physics; b. 15 Oct. 1925, Hull; s. of G. W. Perkins and G. Perkins; m. Dorothy M. Maloney 1955; two d.; ed. Imperial Coll. London; Sr. 1851 Scholar, Univ. of Bristol 1949–52, G. A. Wills Research Assoc. 1952–55; Visiting Scientist, Univ. of Calif. 1955–56; Lecturer, then Reader in Physics, Univ. of Bristol 1956–65; Prof. of Elementary Particle Physics, Univ. of Oxford 1965–93, Fellow St Catherine's Coll. 1965–; mem. SERC 1985–89; Hon. D.Sc. (Sheffield) 1982, (Bristol) 1995; Guthrie Medal, Inst. of Physics 1979, Holweck Medal (Société française de physique) 1992, Royal Medal, Royal Soc. of London 1997. *Publications:* Study of Elementary Particles by the Photographic Method (with C. F. Powell and P. H. Fowler) 1959, Introduction to High Energy Physics 1972. *Leisure interests:* squash, skiing, lepidoptera. *Address:* 2A Blenheim Drive, Oxford, OX2 8DG, England (Home). *Telephone:* (01865) 311717 (Home).

PERKINS, Edward J., D.P.A.; American diplomatist; b. 8 June 1928, Sterlington, La.; m. Lucy Liu; two d.; ed. Univ. of Calif., Lewis, Clark Coll., Univ. of Maryland and Univ. of S. Calif.; Chief of Personnel, Army and Air Force Exchange Service, Taiwan 1958–62; Deputy Chief, Okinawa, Japan 1962–64, Chief of Personnel and Admin. 1964–66; Asst. Gen. Services Officer, Far East Bureau, AID 1967–69, Man. Analyst 1969–70; Asst. Dir. Foreign Man. U.S. Operations, Mission to Thailand 1970–72; Staff Asst. Office of Dir.-Gen. of Foreign Service 1972; Personnel Officer 1972–74; Admin. Officer, Bureau of Near Eastern and South Asian Affairs 1974–75; Man. Analysis Officer, Office of Man. Operations, Dept. of State 1975–78; Counsellor for Political Affairs, Accra 1981–83; Deputy Chief of Mission, Monrovia 1983–85; Dir. Office of West African Affairs, Dept. of State 1985; Amb. to Liberia 1985–86, to South Africa 1986–89; Dir.-Gen. Foreign Service, Washington 1989–92; Perm. Rep. to UN 1992–93; Amb. to Australia 1993–96; William J. Crowe Prof., interim Exec. Dir. Int. Programs Center, Univ. of Okla. 1996–; Trustee Lewis and Clark Coll. 1994–, Asia Soc. 1997–, Inst. of Int. Educ. 1997–; Gov. Jt. Center for Political and Econ. Studies, Georgetown Univ. 1996–; mem. Advisory Council Univ. Office of Int. Programs Pa. State Univ. 1997–; mem. Advisory Bd. Inst. of Int. Public Policy 1997–. *Address:* International Programs Center, University of Oklahoma, 339 W. Boyd Street, Rm. 400, Norman, OK 73069, U.S.A.

PERKINS, Fred; business executive; fmr. Vice-Pres. Europe, McGraw-Hill; Chief Exec. The Stationery Office (formerly Her Majesty's Stationery Office) 1996–. *Address:* The Stationery Office, 51 Nine Elms Lane, London, SW15 5DR, England. *Telephone:* 0171-873 0011.

PERKINS, Kieren John, O.A.; Australian swimmer; b. 14 Aug. 1973, Brisbane; s. of Kevin Perkins and Gloria Perkins; m. Symantha Liu 1997; one d.; ed. Brisbane Boys' Coll., Univ. of Queensland; winner Gold Medal Olympic Games, Barcelona 1992 for 1,500 m. Freestyle event (world record), also Silver Medal, winner Gold Medal Olympic Games, Atlanta 1996, again for 1,500 m. (making him first swimmer to hold Olympic, World, Commonwealth and Pan Pacific titles simultaneously), winner two Gold Medals, World Championships, Rome 1994 (world and Commonwealth records for 400 m. Freestyle), four Gold Medals, Commonwealth Games, Canada 1994 (world and Commonwealth records for 800 m. and 1,500 m. Freestyle); holder of 10 Australian, 11 Queensland and 10 Brisbane records and two Commonwealth and one Australian "standard time" records; holder of All-Time Australian records Men's Open 400 m., 800 m., 1,500 m. Freestyle and 800 m. and 1,500 m. Freestyle Short Course events; numerous Australian swimming and sports personality awards, World Oceania Award, L.A. Amateur Athletic Foundation Award 1992, Australian Sports and Tourism Amb., Australia Tourist Comm. 1993, Advance Australia Award 1993, World Male Swimmer of the Year 1994, FINA Award 1994. *Leisure interests:* music, horse riding, reading, surfing, boating, fishing, jet skiing. *Address:* Kieren Perkins Management, G.P.O. Box 232, Brisbane, Queensland 4001, Australia. *Telephone:* (7) 3211 1500. *Fax:* (7) 3211 1501.

PERKINS, Lawrence Bradford, Jr., B.A., B.ARCH., M.B.A.; American architect; b. 13 Jan. 1943, Chicago, Ill.; s. of Lawrence B. Perkins and Margery Perkins; m. Phyllis Friedman 1966; three d.; ed. Cornell and Stanford Univs. and City Coll. of New York; President, Omnidata Services 1971–73; Man. Partner, Llewellyn-Davies Assocs. 1973–77; Sr. Vice-Pres., Partner, Perkins and Will 1977–81; Partner Attia & Perkins 1981–83; Pres. Perkins Eastman Architects 1983–; Dir. Settlement Housing Fund 1991–, Helen Keller Int. 1993–; Dir. New York City A.I.A., N.Y. Foundation for Architecture; Fellow, American Inst. of Architects, Epsilon Asscn. (Pres. 1993–96); various design awards. *Publications:* articles in professional journals and chapters for professional textbooks. *Address:* Perkins Eastman & Partners, 115 Fifth Avenue, New York, NY 10003 (Office); 4 Rectory Lane, Scarsdale, NY 10583, U.S.A. (Home). *Telephone:* (212) 353-7200 (Office); (914) 723-8875 (Home). *Fax:* (212) 353-7676 (Office).

PERKOFF, Gerald Thomas, M.D.; American physician; b. 22 Sept. 1926, St. Louis; s. of Nat Perkoff and Ann Schwartz; m. Marion Helen Maizner 1947; one s. two d.; ed. Washington Univ.; Intern, Salt Lake City Gen. Hosp. 1948–49, Resident 1950–52; Instructor, then Assoc. Prof. of Medicine, Utah Univ. 1954–63; Chief, Medical Service of Salt Lake Va. Hosp. 1961–63; Assoc. Prof. then Prof. of Medicine, Wash. Univ. School of Medicine, St. Louis 1963–79; Founder, Dir., Medical Care Group of Wash. Univ. 1968–78; Chief of Medical Service, St. Louis City Hosp. 1963–68; Prof. of Medicine, Univ. of Mo. 1979–91, Prof. Emer. 1991–; Deputy Dir. Robert Wood Johnson Foundation Generalist Physician Initiative 1991–; Curators Prof. of Family and Community Medicine and of Internal Medicine, Curators Prof. Emer.; Carrer Research Prof. of Neuromuscular Diseases, Nat. Foundation of Neuromuscular Diseases 1961; Henry J. Kaiser Sr. Fellow of the Center for Advanced Study in the Behavioral Sciences, Stanford, Calif. 1976–77, 1985–86. *Publications:* one book and over 125 scientific papers. *Leisure interests:* music, photography, books. *Address:* School of Medicine, University of Missouri, Department of Family and Community Medicine, M228 Medical Sciences, Columbia, MO 65212 (Office); 1300 Torrey Pines Drive, Columbia, MO 65203, U.S.A. (Home).

PERL, Martin Lewis, PH.D.; American research physicist and educator; b. 24 June 1927, New York; three s. one d.; ed. Polytechnic Inst. of New York and Columbia Univ.; Chemical Engineer, General Electric Co. 1948–50; Asst., then Assoc. Prof. of Physics, Univ. of Mich. 1955–63; Prof. of Physics, Stanford Linear Accelerator Center, Stanford Univ. 1963–; research in experimental elementary particle physics 1955–; discovered the elementary particle tau lepton 1975–78; Chief Financial Officer, The Invention Co.; mem. N.A.S.; Hon. D.Sc. (Chicago) 1990; Wolf Prize in Physics 1982, shared Nobel Prize in Physics 1995. *Publications:* High Energy Hadron Physics 1974, Reflections on Experimental Science 1996, articles on science and soc. issues and on physics educ. *Leisure interests:* mechanical antiques. *Address:* Stanford Linear Accelerator Center, Stanford University, Stanford, CA 94305; 3737 El Centro Avenue, Palo Alto, CA 94306, U.S.A. *Telephone:* (926) 926-2652. *Fax:* (926) 926-4001.

PERLEMUTER, Vlado; French pianist; b. 26 May 1904, Kaunas, Lithuania; s. of Léon Perlemuter and Gucia Wachs; m. Jacqueline Deleveau 1935; ed. Conservatoire nat. supérieur de musique, Paris; studied with Moszkowski and Cortot; specialist in Ravel and Chopin; Prof. of Pianoforte, Paris Conservatoire 1951–; has appeared in concerts and recitals in Europe, N. Africa, N. America and Far East; Hon. F.R.A.M., London, Fellow Royal Northern Coll. of Music 1991; Prix Diémer; Grand Officier Légion d'honneur, Commdr. des Arts et des Lettres. *Publication:* Ravel d'après Ravel (with H. Jourdan-Morhange). *Leisure interests:* art galleries, French and English literature, rugby and tennis on television, world affairs. *Address:* 21 rue Ampère, 75017 Paris, France.

PERLIS, H.R.H. The Raja of; Tuanku Syed Putra ibni al-Marhum Syed Hassan Jamalullail, D.K., S.P.M.P., D.K.(M)., D.M.N., S.M.N., D.K. (SELANGOR), D.K.(KELANTAN), D.K.(KEDAH), D.K.(PAHANG), D.K.(BRUNEI), S.P.D.K.(SABAH), D.P.(SARAWAK), D.K.(JOHOR), D.K.(NEGERI SEMBILAN), D.K.(PERAK), D.K.(TERENGGANU), D.K.M.B.(BRUNEI), K.C.M.G.; Malaysian ruler; b. 25 Nov. 1920, Arau, Perlis; s. of Syed Hassan Ibni Almarhum Syed Mahmud Jamalullail and Puan Wan Teh Binti Edut; m. H.R.H. Tengku Budriah Binti al-Marhum Tengku Ismail, D.K., D.M.N., S.M.N., S.P.M.K. 1941; eight s. six d.; appointed Bakal Raja (Heir-Presumptive) of Perlis April 1938; attached to Courts in Kangar 1940; worked for a year in the Land Office, Kuala Lumpur, and for a year in the Magistrates' Court, Kuala Lumpur; in private business during Japanese occupation; ascended throne 4 Dec. 1945; Timbalan Yang di-Pertuan Agung (Deputy Paramount Ruler) of Malaya April-Sept 1960, Yang di-Pertuan Agung (H.M. the Paramount Ruler) 1960–65, of Malaysia 1963–65; Chancellor Univ. of Science Malaysia 1971–; numerous decorations. *Leisure interests:* golf, tennis, fishing and shooting. *Address:* Istana Arau, Perlis; and Istana Kenangan Indah, Perlis, Malaysia. *Telephone:* 04-9767212. *Fax:* 04-9761373.

PERLMAN, Itzhak; Israeli violinist; b. 31 Aug. 1945, Tel-Aviv; s. of Chaim Perlman and Shoshana Perlman; m. Toby Lynn Friedlander 1967; two s. three d.; ed. Tel-Aviv Acad. of Music, Juilliard School, U.S.A.; gave recitals on radio at the age of 10; went to U.S.A. 1958; studied with Ivan Galamian and Dorothy De Lay; first recital at Carnegie Hall 1963; has played with major American orchestras 1964–; has toured Europe regularly and played with major European orchestras 1966–; debut in U.K. with London Symphony Orchestra 1968; toured Poland, Hungary, Far East; played with Israel Philharmonic Orchestra in fmr. Soviet Union; appearances at Israel Festival and most European Festivals; numerous recordings; Hon. degrees from Univ. of S. Caroline, Yale, Harvard and Yeshivah Univs.; several Grammy awards; Medal of Liberty 1986. *Address:* c/o IMG Artists, 22 East 71st Street, New York, NY 10021, U.S.A.; c/o Harold Holt Ltd., 31 Sinclair Road, London W14 0NS, England.

PERLOT, Enzo; Italian diplomatist; b. 17 Nov. 1933, Mezzolombardo; s. of the late Augusto and Ida (Paoli) Perlot; m. Ulla Segerstrale 1970; two c.; ed. Univ. of Rome; entered Foreign Ministry 1959; served at Presidency of the Repub. 1965–68; Consul in Munich and Counsellor in Embassy in Vienna 1968–70; served in Office of Prime Minister 1970–72; Spokesman and Dir.-Gen. of Information of EEC Comm. 1978–80; Amb. to Portugal 1983–87; Dir.-Gen. for Political Affairs 1987–91; Perm. Rep. of Italy to N. Atlantic Council, Brussels 1991–93, then to EU 1993–95; Amb. to Germany 1996–. *Address:* Italian Embassy, Karl-Finkelnburg-Str. 51, 53173 Bonn, Germany. *Telephone:* (228) 822-0. *Fax:* (228) 822-169.

PERÓN, María Estela (Isabelita) (see Martínez de Perón).

PEROT, (Henry) Ross; American industrialist; b. 27 June 1930, Texarkana, Tex.; s. of Mr. and Mrs. Gabriel Ross Perot; m. Margot Birmingham 1956; four c.; ed. U.S. Naval Acad.; U.S. Navy 1953–57; with IBM Corpn. 1957–62; formed Electronic Data Systems Corpn. 1962, Chair. of Bd. and C.E.O. 1982–86; Dir. Perot Group, Dallas 1986–; f. Perot Systems Corpn., Washington 1988–, Chair. 1988–92, 1992–, mem. Bd. 1988–; Chair. Bd. of Visitors U.S. Naval Acad. 1970–; Cand. for Presidency of U.S.A. 1992, 1996; f. Reform Party 1995. *Publications:* Not For Sale at Any Price 1993, Intensive Care 1995. *Leisure interest:* horses. *Address:* The Perot Group, 12377 Merit Drive, Suite 1700, Dallas, TX 75251, U.S.A.

PERPIÑA-ROBERT, Fernando; Spanish diplomatist; b. 17 April 1937, San Sebastian; s. of Benito Perpiña and Cármen Peyra; m. Alba Navarro Feussier 1964; two s. two d.; ed. Univ. of Barcelona; joined Diplomatic Service 1965, Consul Gen. Boston, U.S.A. 1978, Minister Counsellor, Bonn 1982, Under-Sec. of State, Ministry of Foreign Affairs, Madrid 1985, Sec. Gen. Foreign Affairs, Madrid 1988, Amb. to Germany 1991–96; numerous Spanish and foreign decorations. *Leisure interest:* bridge. *Address:* c/o Ministerio des Asuntos Exteriores, Plaza de la Provincia 1, 28071, Madrid, Spain.

PERRAULT, Dominique; French architect; b. 9 April 1953, Clermont-Ferrand; s. of Jean Perrault and Thérèse Souchon; m. Aude Lauriot-dit-Prévost 1986; three c.; ed. Univ. of Paris and Ecole Nat. des Ponts et Chaussées; in practice as architect in Marais dist. of Paris; works include Electronic Engineers Acad. at Marne-la-Vallée; winner in 1989 of competition to design and plan new Bibliothèque de France (received Prix Mies Van Der Röhe 1997), Olympic swimming pool, Berlin 1991, re-devt. of town centre, Tremblay-en-France 1995; consultant to city of Nantes 1990–, Bordeaux 1992; Dir. l'Institut français d'architecture; mem. Salzburg Urban Cttee. 1994–; Grand prix nat. d'architecture 1993; Chevalier, Légion d'honneur. *Publication:* An Atmosphere of Falling Meteors. *Address:* Perrault Architecte, 26 rue Bruneseau, 75629 Paris cedex 13, France.

PERREIN, Michèle Marie-Claude; French writer; b. 30 Oct. 1929, La Réole; d. of Roger Barbe and Anne-Blanche Perrein; m. Jacques Laurent (divorced); ed. Univ. of Bordeaux, Centre de Formation des Journalistes; literary ed. and contrib. to periodicals Arts-Spectacles, la Parisienne, Marie-Claire, La Vie Judiciaire, Votre Beauté, Le Point, F. Magazine, Les Nouvelles Littéraires. *Publications:* La Sensitive 1956, Le Soleil dans l'oeil 1957, Barbastre 1960, La Flemme 1961, Le Cercle 1962, Le Petit Jules 1965, M'oiselle S, la Chineuse 1970, La Partie de plaisir 1971, Le Buveur de Garonne 1973, Le Mâle aimant 1975, Gemma Lapidaire 1976, Entre Chienne et louve 1978, Comme une fourmi cavalière 1980, Ave Caesar 1982, Les Cotonniers de Bassalane 1984, La Margagne 1989; *plays:* l'Hôtel Racine 1966, a+b+c = la Clinique d'anticipation, 1971, l'Alter-Auto 1971; film collaborator La Vérité 1959. *Leisure interests:* tapestry, swimming, skating. *Address:* Le Cloître, 33580 Saint-Ferme, France (Home).

PERRY, Baron (Life Peer), cr. 1979, of Walton in the County of Buckinghamshire; **Walter Laing Macdonald Perry,** Kt., O.B.E., M.D., D.SC., F.R.C.P., F.R.S.; British university professor; b. 16 June 1921, Dundee; s. of Fletcher Smith Perry and Flora Macdonald Macdonald; m. 1st Anne Grant 1946; three s.; m. 2nd Catherine Crawley 1971; two s. one d.; ed. Dundee High School and St. Andrews Univ.; Medical Officer in Colonial Service, Nigeria 1944–46, in the R.A.F. 1946–47; Medical Research Council 1947–52; Dir. Dept. of Biological Standards, Nat. Inst. for Medical Research 1952–58; Prof. of Pharmacology, Edin. Univ. 1958–68, Vice-Prin. 1967–68; Vice-Chancellor, Open Univ. 1969–81, Fellow 1981–; Chair. Videotel Int. 1981, Pres. 1996; Consultant to UN Univ. 1981–88; Chair. Bd. of Govs. Int. Technological Univ. 1987–89; Hon. Dir. Int. Centre for Distance Learning 1983; Chair. Continuing Educ. Standing Cttee. 1985–88, Research Defence Soc. 1994; several hon. degrees. *Publications:* Open University 1976; several chapters in other books. *Leisure interests:* golf, music. *Address:* Glenholm, 2 Cramond Road South, Davidson's Mains, Edinburgh, EH4 6AD. Scotland (Home). *Telephone:* (0131) 336 3666 (Home).

PERRY, John Richard, PH.D.; American professor of philosophy; b. 16 Jan. 1943, Lincoln, Neb.; s. of Ralph R. Perry and Ann Roscow Perry; m. Louise E. French 1962; two s. one d.; ed. Doane Coll., Crete, Neb. and Cornell Univ.; Asst. Prof. of Philosophy, Univ. of Calif. at Los Angeles 1968–72, Assoc. Prof. 1972–74; Assoc. Prof. of Philosophy, Stanford Univ. 1974–77, Prof. of Philosophy 1977–85, Henry Waldgrave Stuart Prof. of Philosophy 1985–, Chair. Dept. of Philosophy 1976–82, 1990–91, Dir. Center for Language and Information 1982–83, 1985–86, 1993–; Woodrow Wilson Fellow 1964; Danforth Fellow 1964–68; Guggenheim Fellow 1975–76; Hon. D.Litt. (Doane Coll.) 1982. *Publications:* A Dialogue on Personal Identity and Immortality 1978, Situations and Attitudes (with J. Barwise) 1983, The Problem of the Essential Indexical and Other Essays 1993. *Leisure interests:*

reading, windsurfing, grandchildren. *Address:* Centre for the Study of Language and Information, Stanford University, Stanford, CA 94305, U.S.A. *Telephone:* (415) 723-1224. *Fax:* (415) 723-0758.

PERRY, Sir Michael Sydney, C.B.E., M.A.; British business executive; b. 26 Feb. 1934, Eastbourne; s. of Sydney Albert Perry and Jessie Kate (née Brooker) Perry; m. Joan Mary Stallard 1958; one s. two d.; ed. King William's Coll., Isle of Man, St. John's Coll., Oxford Univ.; Chair. Lever Brothers (Thailand) Ltd. 1973–77, Centrica 1997–, Nippon Lever (Japan) 1981–83, UAC Int. Ltd. 1985–87, Unilever PLC 1992–96, Dunlop Slazenger Group 1996–; Pres. Lever y Asociados (Argentina) 1977–81; Dir. Unilever PLC NV 1985– (Vice-Chair. 1992–96), Bass PLC 1991– (Deputy Chair. 1996–); Dir. (non-exec.) British Gas 1994–97, Marks & Spencer 1996–; Chair. Shakespeare Globe Trust 1993–; Pres. Liverpool School of Tropical Medicine 1997–; Pres. Advertising Asscn. 1993–96; Trustee Leverhulme Trust; Commdr. Order of Oranje Nassau. *Leisure interest:* music. *Address:* Bridges Stone Mill, Alfrick, Worcester, WR6 5HR, England.

PERRY, Robert Palese, PH.D.; American molecular biologist; b. 10 Jan. 1931, Chicago; s. of Robert P. Perry, Sr. and Gertrude Hyman; m. Zoila Figueroa 1957; one s. two d.; ed. Univ. of Chicago and Northwestern Univ.; Postdoctoral Fellow Oak Ridge Nat. Lab. 1956–57, Univ. of Pa. 1957–59, Univ. of Brussels 1959–60; Staff mem. Inst. for Cancer Research, Fox Chase Cancer Center 1960–, Sr. mem. 1969–, Stanley Reimann Chair in Research 1994–; Prof. of Biophysics, Univ. of Pa. 1973–95; UNESCO Tech. Asst. Expert Univ. of Belgrade 1965; Guggenheim Fellow Univ. of Paris 1974–75; Chair. Exec. Cttee. Int. Cell Research Org. (UNESCO) 1982–85; mem. N.A.S.; Dr. h.c. (Univ. of Paris VII). *Publications:* more than 100 articles in int. scientific journals. *Address:* Institute for Cancer Research, Fox Chase Cancer Center, 7701 Burholme Avenue, Philadelphia, Pa. 19111 (Office); 1808 Bustleton Pike, Churchville, PA 18966, U.S.A. (Home).

PERRY, Ruth; Liberian politician; b. Tewor Dist., Grand Cape Mount Co.; m. McDonald M. Perry (deceased); seven c.; fmrly. with Chase Manhattan Bank of Liberia; Senator from Cape Mount Co. 1986–90; Chair. Council of State (of Liberian Nat. Transitional Govt.) 1996–97; mem. Women's Initiatives in Liberia. *Address:* c/o Office of the President, Monrovia, Liberia.

PERRY, Seymour Monroe, B.A., M.D., M.A.C.P.; American physician; b. 26 May 1921, New York; m. Judith Carol Kaplan 1951; two s. one d.; ed. Univs. of California and Southern California, Los Angeles; numerous positions in hosps. and public health orgs. 1951–83, including Assoc. Scientific Dir. for Clinical Trials, Chemotherapy, Nat. Cancer Inst., 1966–71, Assoc. Dir. for Program Planning, Div. of Cancer Treatment 1971–74, Deputy Dir. 1973–74, Assoc. Dir. for Medical Applications of Research, N.I.H. 1978–80; Dir. Nat. Center for Health Care Tech., U.S. Dept. of Health and Human Services 1980–82; Asst. Surgeon Gen., U.S. Public Health Service 1980–82; Sr. Fellow and Deputy Dir. Inst. for Health Policy Analysis 1983–89; Prof. of Medicine and Prof. of Community and Family Medicine, Georgetown Univ. Medical Center 1983–94, Adjunct Prof. 1994–, Interim Chair. Dept. 1989–90, Chair. Dept. 1990–93; Sr. Scholar, Medical Tech. Inst. 1993–; Dir. WHO Collaborating Center for Health Tech. Assessment 1995–; Pres. Int. Soc. of Tech. Assessment in Health Care 1985–87; mem. Inst. of Medicine, N.A.S., and many other professional asscns.; numerous awards. *Publications:* numerous articles on studies of tumour cell growth and bio-chemistry and on medical tech. assessment and health public policy. *Leisure interests:* gardening, photography, squash. *Address:* 4733 Bethesda Avenue, Suite 510, Bethesda, Md., U.S.A. *Telephone:* (301) 652-4005. *Fax:* (301) 652-8355.

PERRY, Simon Frank, C.B.E., B.A.; British film producer; b. 5 Aug. 1943, Farnham; s. of Frank Horace Perry and Brenda Mary Dorothea Perry; ed. Eton Coll., King's Coll.; worked in theatre production (RSC, Bristol Old Vic, London West End) 1965–69, TV production (Anglia TV, Yorkshire TV) 1969–74; independent filmmaker 1974–77; entertainment trade journalist (Variety Magazine etc.) 1978–80; administrator Nat. Film Devt. Fund 1980–82; feature film producer 1982–; Chief Exec. British Screen Finance 1991–; Chevalier Ordre des Arts et des Lettres. *Films include:* Knots, Eclipse, Another Time, Another Place, Nineteen Eighty-Four, White Mischief, The Playboys. *Leisure interests:* cinema-going, cycling, European travel. *Address:* Studio C, Chelsea Studios, 416 Fulham Road, London, SW6 1EB, England. *Telephone:* 0171-386 5119. *Fax:* 0171-386 5119.

PERRY, William, PH.D.; American politician and civil servant; b. 11 Oct. 1927, Vandergift, Pa.; m. Leonilla Mary Green 1947; three s. two d.; ed. Stanford Univ., Pennsylvania State Univ.; Prof. School of Eng., Stanford Univ., Co-Dir. Center for Int. Security and Arms Control (affil. to Stanford Univ.); Under-Sec.-of-Defense for Research and Eng. 1976–81; Mil. Tech. Adviser to Pres. Clinton 1993; Deputy Sec. of Defense 1993–94, Sec. of Defense 1994–97; Prof. Stanford Univ. 1997–, Sr. Fellow 1997–; Chair. Tech. Strategies and Alliances; Dir. United Technologies Corpn., FMC Corpn., Sylvania/Gen. Telephone's Electronic Defense Labs.; served on U.S. Govt.'s Foreign Intelligence Advisory Bd.; mem. Nat. Acad. of Eng., N.A.S. Cttee. on Int. Security and Arms Control; Fellow American Acad. of Arts and Sciences; Trustee Carnegie Endowment for Int. Peace; several nat. and int. decorations. *Address:* School of Engineering, Stanford University, Stanford, CA 94305, U.S.A.

PERRY OF SOUTHWARK, Baroness (Life Peeress), cr. 1991, of Charlbury in the County of Oxfordshire; **Pauline Perry,** M.A., F.R.S.A.; British university administrator; b. 15 Oct. 1931, Wolverhampton; d. of John Welch and Elizabeth Cowan; m. George W. Perry 1952; three s. one d.; ed. Girton Coll. Cambridge; Univ. lecturer in Philosophy, Univs. of Man., Mass., Exeter and Oxford 1956–59, 1961–63, 1966–70; Insp. 1970, Staff Insp. 1975, H.M. Chief Insp. of Schools 1981–86; Vice-Chancellor, South Bank Univ. (fmrly. South Bank Polytechnic) 1987–93; Pres. Lucy Cavendish Coll. Univ. of Cambridge 1994–; Chair. Dept. of Trade and Industry Expert Group for Educ. and Training Sector 1993–98; mem. Prime Minister's Advisory Group on the Citizen's Charter 1993–97; mem. House of Lords Select Cttee. on Science and Tech. 1992–95, on Scrutiny of Delegated Powers 1995–, on Cen. and Local Govt. Relations 1995–96; mem. Bd. of Patrons, Royal Soc. Appeal 1995–; Vice-Pres. City & Guilds of London Inst. 1994–; Chair. Judges Panel on Citizen's Charter 1997–; mem. Cambridge Univ. Foundation 1997–; Hon. Fellow, Coll. of Preceptors; Fellow, Swedish Acad. of Sciences (Pedagogy); Hon. LL.D. (Aberdeen, Bath); Hon. D.Litt. (Sussex, South Bank); Hon. D.Univ. (Surrey); Hon. D.Ed. (Wolverhampton); Liveryman Worshipful Co. of Bakers; Freeman City of London. *Publications:* three books, several chapters and numerous articles. *Leisure interests:* music, walking. *Address:* Lucy Cavendish College, Cambridge, CB3 0BU; House of Lords, London, SW1A 0PW, England. *Telephone:* (01223) 332192 (Cambridge). *Fax:* (01223) 332178 (Cambridge).

PERSSON, Göran; Swedish politician; b. 20 Jan. 1949, Vingaker; m. Gunnel Persson; two c.; ed. Orebro Univ.; Org. Sec. Swedish Social Democratic Youth League 1971; Adult Educ. Officer, Södermanland 1971; Studies Sec. Workers' Educ. Asscn. Sörmland 1972–73, 1974–76; Chair. Katrineholm Educ. Authority 1977–79; mem. Parl. 1979–84; Municipal Commr. Katrineholm 1985–89; Minister with special responsibility for schools and educ., Ministry of Educ. and Cultural Affairs 1989–91, of Finance 1994–96; Prime Minister of Sweden March 1996–; Leader Social Democratic Labour Party 1996–; Vice-Chair. Bd. Oppunda Savings Bank 1976–89, Nordic Museum 1983–89; Chair. Södermanland Co-operative Soc. 1976–89; Chair. Södermanland Co. Bd. of Educ. 1982–89; Accountant, Swedish Co-operative Wholesale Soc. 1988–89. *Address:* Office of the Prime Minister, Sagerska Palace, Stroengarten 18, Stockholm, Sweden.

PERSSON, Jörgen; Swedish director of photography; b. 10 Sept. 1936, Helsingborg; s. of Erik W. Persson and Thyra Liljeroth; m. Anne von Sydow 1969; two s.; ed. High School and Swedish Film School; Dir. of Photography (Features) 1965–; Felix Award, Paris 1989 and Swedish awards. *Films include:* Elvira Madigan 1967, Ådalen-31 1969, My Life as a Dog 1986, Pelle the Conqueror 1988, Best Intentions 1991, Sofi 1991, Young Indy, The House of the Spirits 1993, Jerusalem 1995, Smilla's Sense of Snow 1996, Digging to China 1996, Les Misérables 1997. *Leisure interests:* MC-off road sport, classic cars. *Address:* Rydbolundsvagen 7, 18531 Vaxholm, Sweden.

PERUTZ, Max Ferdinand, O.M., C.H., PH.D., F.R.S.; British biochemist and crystallographer; b. 19 May 1914, Vienna, Austria; s. of Hugo and Adele Perutz; m. Gisela Peiser 1942; one s. one d.; ed. Theresianum, Vienna, and Univs. of Vienna and Cambridge; Dir. Medical Research Council Unit for Molecular Biology, Cavendish Laboratory, Univ. of Cambridge 1947–62; Chair. Medical Research Council Laboratory of Molecular Biology, Univ. Postgraduate Medical School, Cambridge 1962–79, mem. scientific staff 1979–; Reader Davy Faraday Research Laboratory, Royal Inst. 1954–68; Chair. European Molecular Biology Org. 1963–69; Fullerian Prof. Physiology at Royal Inst. 1973–79; Hon. Dr. Phil (Vienna, Edinburgh, Aarhus, Norwich, Saltzburg); Hon. Sc.D. (Cambridge) 1981; Hon. D.Sc. (Wales) 1995, numerous other hon. degrees; Foreign Assoc. N.A.S. 1970; Foreign mem. Acad. des Sciences 1976, Accad. dei Lincei, Rome 1984; shared Nobel Prize for Chem. with Dr. (later Sir) John Kendrew (q.v.) for researches into blood chem. 1962; Royal Medal, Royal Soc. 1971, Copley Medal, Royal Soc. 1979. *Publications:* Proteins and Nucleic Acids: Structure and Function 1962, Atlas of Haemoglobin and Myoglobin (with G. Fermi) 1981, Ging's ohne Forschung besser 1983, Is Science Necessary: Essays on Science and Scientists 1989, Mechanisms of Cooperativity and Allosteric Control in Proteins 1990, Protein Structures: new approaches to disease and therapy 1992, Science Is No Quiet Life 1997, I Wish I'd Made You Angry Earlier 1998, various papers on the structure of proteins. *Leisure interests:* skiing, mountaineering. *Address:* 42 Sedley Taylor Road, Cambridge, CB2 2PN, England. *Telephone:* (01223) 248011 (Office).

PERVYSHIN, Erlen Kirikovich; Russian industrial manager; b. 25 June 1932; ed. Moscow Electrotechnical Inst. of Communications; mem. Int. Engineer Acad.; engineer 1955–, then Head of Ass. Section, Deputy Chief Engineer, Head of Admin., Manager of Design and Ass. Trust, Dir. Gen. All-Union Scientific production asscn.; Deputy U.S.S.R. Minister of Radio Industry 1970–74, Minister of Communications Equipment Mfg. 1974–89, of Communications 1989–91; Chair. Telecom 1991–; Pres. ORB & TEL Co., Andrew Int. Corpn. 1997–. *Address:* Goubkina str. 8, Moscow 17966, Russia. *Telephone:* (095) 135-00-98/135-44-30. *Fax:* (095) 938-37-96.

PESCATORE, Pierre, D.IUR.; Luxembourg diplomatist and professor of law; b. 20 Nov. 1919, Luxembourg; s. of Ferdinand Pescatore and Cunégonde Heuertz; m. Rosalie Margue 1948; three s. one d.; Ministry of Foreign Affairs 1946–67, Sec., later mem., Del. to UN Gen. Ass. 1946–52; Legal Adviser, Min. of Foreign Affairs 1950–58; Dir. for Political Affairs, Min. of Foreign Affairs 1958–64; Minister Plenipotentiary 1959; Sec.-Gen. Ministry of Foreign Affairs 1964–67; Judge, Court of Justice of the European Communities

1967–86, Perm. Court of Arbitration 1969, Pres. Luxembourg Nat. Group; Admin. Tribunal ILO 1986–; served on several GATT Panels 1989–; Prof. Law Faculty and Inst. for European Legal Studies, Univ. of Liège; Lectured Hague Acad. of Int. Law 1961; mem. Inst. de Droit International 1965–; Dr. h.c. (Nancy, Geneva, Tübingen, Leiden, Neuchâtel Univs.). *Publications:* complete bibliography to 1987 appears in Liber Amicorum Pierre Pescatore 1987; Handbook of GATT Dispute Settlement (loose-leaf) 1991–. *Address:* 16 rue de la Fontaine, 1532 Luxembourg. *Telephone:* 46-07-97 (Office); 22-40-44 (Home). *Fax:* 46-61-42.

PESCI, Joe; American film actor; b. 9 Feb. 1943. *Films include:* Death Collector 1976, Raging Bull 1980, I'm Dancing as Far as I Can 1982, Easy Money 1983, Dear Mr Wonderful 1983, Eureka 1983, Once Upon a Time in America 1984, Tutti Dentro 1984, Man On Fire 1987, Moonwalker 1988, Backtrack 1988, Lethal Weapon II 1989, Betsy's Wedding 1990, Goodfellas (Acad. Award for Best Supporting Actor) 1991, Home Alone 1990, The Super 1991, JFK 1991, Lethal Weapon III 1992, Home Alone II 1992, The Public Eye 1992, My Cousin Vinny 1992, A Bronx Tale 1993, With Honours 1994, Jimmy Hollywood 1994, Casino 1995, 8 Heads in a Duffel Bag 1997, Gone Fishing 1997, Lethal Weapon 4 1998.

PESCUCCI, Gabriella; Italian costume designer; b. Castiglioncello, Tuscany; ed. Accademia di Belle Arti, Florence; worked as asst. to Piero Tosi on set of Luchino Visconti's films Death in Venice and Ludwig; solo debut designing costumes for Charlotte Rampling in Italian film adaptation of 'Tis Pity She's a Whore 1971; designed costumes for Maria Callas in Medea, for Sean Connery in The Name of the Rose, Montserrat Caballé in Norma at La Scala, Milan, and for City of Women, Once Upon a Time in America, The Adventures of Baron Munchausen, The Scarlet Letter, and for The Age of Innocence (Acad. Award 1996); other prizes and awards include two Donatello Davids from Italian Acad. of Cinema and two B.A.F.T.A. Awards.

PEŠEK, Libor; Czech conductor; b. 22 June 1933, Prague; ed. Prague Acad. of Musical Arts; studied conducting with Karel Ancerl, Vaclav Neumann and Václav Smetáček; f. Prague Chamber Harmony 1958; Chief Conductor Slovak Philharmonic 1980–81; Conductor-in-Residence Czech Philharmonic Orchestra 1982–, Germany tour 1998; Prin. Conductor and Artistic Adviser Royal Liverpool Philharmonic Orchestra 1982–97, Hon. Conductor 1997–; Visiting Conductor Prague Symphony Orchestra 1989–; Pres. Prague Spring Festival Sept. 1994–; conducted Nat. Theatre Orchestra, Prague, Prokoviev's Romeo and Juliet 1998; has conducted Philharmonia, London Symphony, Royal Philharmonic, BBC Philharmonic, Oslo Philharmonic, Danish Radio, Los Angeles Philharmonic and Cincinnati, Dallas, Minnesota, Pittsburgh, Cleveland, Montreal, Indianapolis and Philadelphia orchestras, Orchestra of La Scala, Milan and Orchestre de Paris; many recordings including works by Dvořák, Suk, Janáček, Martinů and Britten; Hon. K.B.E. Hon. mem. Preston Univ. 1997; Classic Prize for Extraordinary Merit in Musical Culture (Czech Repub.) 1997. *Leisure interests:* physics, Eastern philosophy, literature. *Address:* c/o IMG Artists (Europe), Media House, 3 Burlington Lane, London, W4 2TH, England.

PESENTI, Antonio; Italian politician and economist; b. 15 Oct. 1910, Verona; s. of Romeo Pesenti and Amalia Bisoffi; m. Adriana Ghiadistri 1947; ed. Univs. of Pavia, Vienna, Berne, Paris, London School of Econs.; lecturer Sassari Univ. 1935; active in underground anti-Fascist movement 1930–35; took part in Italian anti-Fascist Congress in Brussels 1935; arrested and sentenced to 24 years' imprisonment by special tribunal; released Sept. 1943; Under-Sec., later Minister of Finance 1944–45; lecturer on Finance, Univ. of Rome 1945; Prof. Univ. of Parma 1948, of Pisa 1960–71, of Rome 1971; Ed. Critica Economica; fmr. mem. Italian Constituent Ass.; Pres. Econ. Centre for Reconstruction; M.P. 1948, mem. Senate 1953–; mem. fmr. CP. *Publications:* Politica finanziaria e monetaria dell'Inghilterra 1934, La politica monetaria delle Devisenverordnungen 1933, I soggetti passivi dell'obbligazione doganale 1934, Ricostruire dalle rovine 1945, Scienza delle Finanze e diritto finanziario 1961, Manuale d'Economia Politica, 2 vols. 1970. *Leisure interests:* chess, mountaineering, rowing. *Address:* Via Nomentana 372, Rome; and 41 Via Nomentana, Istituto di Economia, Rome, Italy. *Telephone:* Rome 897530.

PEŠIĆ, Vesna; Serbian politician, philosopher and lawyer; b. 6 May 1940, Groska; ed. Belgrade Univ.; on staff Inst. of Social Sciences 1964–72, Inst. of Social Politics 1972–78; sr. researcher Inst. of Philosophy and Social Theory, teacher Higher School for Social Workers 1978–91; one of founders Union for Yugoslavian Democratic Initiative (IZDI) 1991–, Helsinki Cttee. in Belgrade, Cen. of Antimil. Actions Daily Time; mem. Cttee. for Freedom of Speech and Self-Expression; Chair. Civil Union of Serbia; active participant opposition block Union of Reform Forces of Serbia; mem. Skuptsina (Parl.) of Serbia; participant mass demonstrations of protest against S. Milošević 1996–97; author of books, articles in scientific journals and periodicals; Award for Democracy Nat. Foundation of Democracy, Washington, 1993. *Publications include:* Social Traditions and Style of Life 1977, Ethnomethodology and Sociology 1985, Social Deviations: Criticism of Social Pathology (with I. Jancović) 1981, Brief Course of Equality 1988, Theory of Changes and Parsons Concept of Contemporary Soc. 1990, Yugoslavian Military Crisis and World Movement 1992, Nationalism, War and Disintegration of Communist Federation 1993.

PESMAZOGLU, John Stevens, PH.D.; Greek politician, economist, university professor and central banker; b. 1 March 1918, Chios; s. of Stephanos G. Pesmazoglu and Angela Lorenzou; m. Miranda Economou 1945; two s.; ed. Varvakion High School, Athens, Univ. of Athens, and St. John's Coll., Cambridge; served in Greek Albanian campaign 1940–41 and in liberation of Greece 1944–45; research student, Cambridge 1945–49; Lecturer in Political Economy, Univ. of Athens 1950–67, Prof. 1967–70; Dir.-Gen. Greek Ministry of Co-ordination in charge of econ. devt. and external financial relations 1951–55; Econ. Adviser Bank of Greece 1955–60; Alt. Gov. for Greece, IMF 1955–67; Deputy Gov. Bank of Greece 1960–67; Leader of Greek mission to negotiations for European Free Trade Area and asscn. of Greece with Common Market 1957–61; Chair. Interdepartmental Cttee. for European Co-operation 1962–65; Trustee Royal Hellenic Research Foundation 1959–68; Pres. Soc. for the Study of Greek Problems 1971–72; exiled by mil. govt. May-Dec. 1972; in prison April–Aug. 1973; Minister of Finance July–Oct. 1974; M.P. 1974–81, 1985–89; mem. European Parl. 1981–84, 1989–94, Hon. mem. 1994; Co-Pres. Jt. Parl. Comm. Greece-European Communities 1975–79; Pres. Party of Democratic Socialism 1979–84; Hon. Fellow St. John's Coll., Cambridge; Pres. Acad. of Athens 1996; Azchon Megas Rhetor, Oecumenical Patriarchate, Grand Cross, Greek Order of Phoenix, Grand Commdr. Royal Order of George I, Commdr. Légion d'honneur, Grand Commdr. of the Yugoslav Standard with Gold Crown, Grand Commdr. German Order of Merit. *Publications:* Studies and articles on the int. trade cycle, economic devt. and monetary policies and on European integration with special reference to Greece's membership of the European Community. *Leisure interest:* painting. *Address:* 6 Neophytou Vamva Street, 10674 Athens, Greece. *Telephone:* (301) 7212458. *Fax:* (301) 7236326.

PETERLE, Lozje; Slovenian politician; b. 5 July 1948, Čužnja Vas, Trebnje; ed. Ljubljana Univ.; worked as consultant in town planning, environmental protection and landscape man.; Pres. Slovenian Christian Democrats (SKD) 1989–; Prime Minister of Slovenia 1990–92; Minister of Foreign Affairs 1993–94; Chair. Parl. Cttee. on European Affairs 1997–; Vice-Pres. European Union of Christian Democrats 1993–. *Address:* Slovenian Christian Democrats (SKD), Beethovnova 4, 1000 Ljubljana, Slovenia. *Telephone:* (61) 1262 179.

PETERS, Janis; Latvian diplomatist, writer and poet; b. 30 June 1939, Liepāja Region, Latvia; s. of Janis Peters and Zelma Peters; m. Baiba Kalniņa 1969; one s.; started as journalist in Latvian newspapers, later freelance; Chair. Bd. of Latvian Writers' Union 1985–89; participant democratic movt. for independence; Chair. Org. Cttee. People's Front of Latvia 1988; U.S.S.R. People's Deputy 1989–90; Perm. Rep. of Council of Ministers of Latvia to Russia 1990–91, then Amb. to Russian Fed. 1991–97; mem. Govt. del. to negotiations with Russia 1992–; Hon. mem. Latvian Acad. of Sciences 1990–, Latvian Univ. 1991–; Cavaliere di San Marco 1993. *Publications:* more than 30 books of poetry, prose and essays in Latvian, Russian and English. *Leisure interests:* gardening, car-driving. *Address:* Vesetas str. 8, apt. 12, 1013 Riga, Latvia. *Telephone:* (02) 370-774.

PETERS, Jonathan C., B.SC., M.B.A.; Saint Vincent and the Grenadines diplomatist; b. 18 Jan. 1946, Georgetown; m. (divorced); four c.; ed. Hunter Coll., New York, Fairleigh Dickinson Univ., Rutherford, N.J. and Pupil Teachers' Training Centre, St. Vincent; Asst. Teacher Ministry of Educ. 1962–67; Sr. Instructor Ministry of Agric. 1967–72; Asst. Man. Schaefer Brewing Co., New York 1972–75; with Merrill Lynch Futures, New York 1975–86; Perm. Rep. to UN 1986–89. *Address:* c/o Ministry of Foreign Affairs, Kingstown, Saint Vincent and the Grenadines.

PETERS, Lenrie Leopold Wilfred, M.A., F.R.C.S.; Gambian surgeon; b. 1 Sept. 1932, Banjul; s. of Lenrie Peters and Keria Peters; m. (divorced); ed. Boys' High School, Banjul, Prince of Wales Secondary School, Freetown, Sierra Leone, Trinity Coll., Cambridge; surgeon specialist, Westfield Clinic, Banjul 1972–; farmer, Chair. and Chief Exec. Farato Farms Export Ltd. 1981–99; Chair. Colloquium Cttee., Lagos 1977, Bd. of Govs. Gambia Coll. 1979–87, W. African Examinations Council 1988–91, Nat. Consultative Cttee. The Gambia 1995–; Fellow Int. Coll. of Surgeons 1992; Distinguished Friend of W. African Examinations Council; Officer of Repub. of The Gambia. *Publications:* The Second Round (novel) 1965; poems: Satellites 1967, Katchikali, Selected Poems; anthologies. *Leisure interests:* tennis, music, reading. *Address:* Westfield Clinic, Kanifing (Office); P.O. Box 142, Banjul, The Gambia (Home). *Telephone:* 392219 (Office); 495419 (Home). *Fax:* 495419.

PETERS, Wallace, M.D., D.SC., F.R.C.P.; British professor of parasitology; b. 1 April 1924, London; s. of Henry Peters and Fanny Peters; m. Ruth Scheidegger-Frehner 1954; ed. Haberdashers Aske's Hampstead School, St. Bartholomew's Hosp. Medical Coll., Univ. of London; Physician West and East Africa, including R.A.M.C. 1947–53; Scientist-Entomologist and Malariologist, WHO, in Liberia and Nepal 1953–55; Malariologist, Territory of Papua and New Guinea 1956–61; Research Assoc., CIBA Pharmaceutical Co., Basle 1961–66; Prof. of Parasitology, Liverpool School of Tropical Medicine 1966–79, Dean 1975–78; Prof. of Medical Protozoology, London School of Hygiene and Tropical Medicine 1979–89; Hon. Consultant in Parasitology, Camden Area Health Authority 1978–89, on malariology, to Army 1986–89; Jt. Dir. Public Health Lab. Service Malaria Reference Centre 1979–89; Hon. Research Fellow Inst. of Parasitology (IIP) 1992–; Pres. Royal Soc. of Tropical Medicine and Hygiene 1987–88 (Vice-Pres. 1982–83, 1985–87); mem. Expert Advisory Panel on Malaria of WHO 1967–; Hon. Fellow Royal Soc. of Tropical Medicine and Hygiene; Hon. mem. American Soc. of Tropical Medicine and Parasitology; Dr. h.c. (Univ. René Descartes, Paris) 1992; King Faisal Int.

Prize, Medicine 1983, Rudolf Leuckart Medallist, German Soc. of Parasitology 1980, Le Prince Medallist, American Soc. of Tropical Medicine and Hygiene 1994. *Publications:* Checklist of Ethiopian Butterflies 1952, Chemotherapy and Drug Resistance in Malaria 1970, 1987, Rodent Malaria (co-ed.) 1978, Atlas of Tropical Medicine and Parasitology (with H. M. Gilles) 1977, 1995, Pharmacology of Antimalarials (2 vols.) (co-ed.) 1984, Leishmaniases in Biology and Medicine (co-ed.) 1987, Atlas of Arthropods in Clinical Medicine 1992. *Leisure interests:* photography, entomology, writing. *Address:* CABI Bioscience, 395a Hatfield Road, St. Albans, Herts., AL4 0XU, England. *Telephone:* (01727) 833151. *Fax:* (01727) 868721.

PETERS, Winston R.; New Zealand politician and lawyer; fmr. M.P. for Tauranga; Minister of Maori Affairs, Minister in charge of the Iwi Transition Agency, Chair. Cabinet Cttee. on Treaty of Waitangi Issues 1990–91; independent M.P. 1993–, now New Zealand First Party; leader New Zealand First Party 1993–; Deputy Prime Minister, Treas. 1996–98; fmr. mem. Nat. Party. *Address:* c/o Parliament Buildings, Wellington, New Zealand.

PETERSDORF, Robert George, M.D.; American physician and medical educator; b. 14 Feb. 1926, Berlin, Germany; s. of Hans H. Petersdorf and Sonja Petersdorf; m. Patricia Horton Qua 1951; two s.; ed. Brown and Yale Univs.; Instructor in Medicine, Yale Univ. 1957–58; Asst. Prof. of Medicine, Johns Hopkins Univ. 1958–59; Assoc. Prof. of Medicine, Univ. of Washington School of Medicine 1960–62, Prof. 1962–79, Chair. Dept. of Medicine 1964–79; Prof. of Medicine, Harvard Medical School 1979–81; Pres. Brigham and Women's Hosp., Boston 1979–81; Vice-Chancellor for Health Sciences and Dean, School of Medicine, Univ. of Calif., San Diego 1981–86; Pres. Asscn. of American Medical Colls. 1986–94, Pres. Emer. 1994–; Distinguished Prof. Univ. of Wash. 1994–; Distinguished Physician VA Medical Center 1994–; Ed. Harrison's Principles of Internal Medicine 1968–90; mem. editorial bds. of several scientific journals; Master American Coll. of Physicians, Royal Soc. of Medicine, Royal Coll. of Physicians, London, American Acad. of Arts and Sciences, A.A.A.S.; mem. Inst. of Medicine of N.A.S. and numerous professional orgs.; numerous hon. degrees and prizes. *Publications:* over 400 papers in professional and scientific journals. *Address:* 1219 Parkside Drive, East Seattle, WA 98112, U.S.A.

PETERSEN, George Bouet, D.SC., M.A., D.PHIL., F.N.Z.I.C., F.R.S.N.Z.; British/New Zealand professor of biochemistry; b. 5 Sept. 1933, Palmerston North, N.Z.; s. of George C. Petersen and Elizabeth S. Petersen; m. Patricia J.E. Caughey 1960; four d.; ed. Univs. of Otago and Oxford; scientist, DSIR Plant Chemistry Div. Palmerston North 1959–60, 1963–67; Departmental Demonstrator in Biochemistry, Univ. of Oxford 1961–63; Head, Dept. of Biochemistry, Univ. of Otago 1968–91; Prof. of Biochemistry 1968–99, Prof. Emer. 1995–; Deputy Dean, Otago Medical School 1991–95; Pres. Acad. Council Royal Soc. of N.Z. 1997–; Visiting Research Fellow, Harvard Univ. 1964; Royal Soc. Commonwealth Bursar, MRC Lab. of Molecular Biology, Cambridge 1973–74, 1981; Carnegie Corpn. of New York Travel Grantee 1964; Marsden Medal, N.Z. Asscn. of Scientists 1995; Officer, N.Z. Order of Merit. *Publications:* numerous papers on aspects of nucleic acid chemistry and biochemistry in various scientific journals. *Leisure interests:* music, literature, book collecting. *Address:* 47 Maori Road, Dunedin, New Zealand. *Telephone:* (03) 4770784.

PETERSEN, Jan; Norwegian politician; b. 11 June 1946, Oslo; m.; two c.; with Norwegian Consumers' Asscn., Norwegian Agency for Devt. Co-operation (NORAD); Chair Young Conservatives 1971–73; Mayor of Oppegård 1976–81; Chair. Standing Cttee. on Foreign Affairs 1985–86, now Deputy Chair.; Leader Akershus Conservative Party 1992–94, Conservative Party (Høyre) April 1994–; mem. Storting (Parl.); mem. Storting Standing Cttee. on Local Govt. 1981–85; Chair. Political Cttee. of N. Atlantic Ass. 1996–. *Address:* Høyre, Stortingst. 20, P.O. Box 1536 Vika, 0117 Oslo, Norway.

PETERSEN, Niels Helveg, LL.D.; Danish politician; b. 17 Jan. 1939, Odense; ed. Copenhagen Univ. and Stanford Univ., Calif., U.S.A.; mem. Folketing (Parl.) 1966–74, 1977–; Chef de Cabinet to Danish Commr. for the European Communities 1974–77; mem. Parl. Foreign Affairs Cttee. 1968–74, Market Cttee. 1972–74, 1977–78, 1982–88, 1990–93, Parl. Politico-Econ. Cttee. 1982–84; Social Liberal Party Spokesman on Political Affairs 1968–74, 1977–78, Chair. Parl. Group 1978–88; Minister for Econ. Affairs 1988–90, for Foreign Affairs Jan. 1993–. *Address:* Ministry for Foreign Affairs, Asiatisk Plads 2, Copenhagen K, Denmark. *Telephone:* 33 92 00 00. *Fax:* 31 54 05 33.

PETERSEN, Wolfgang; German film director and producer; b. 14 March 1941, Emden; ed. German Film and TV Acad.; Asst. Stage Dir. Ernst Deutsch Theatre, Hamburg. *Films include:* Smog (Prix Futura Award 1975), For Your Love Only, Scene of the Crime, The Consequence 1977, Black and White Like Day and Night 1978, Das Boot 1981, The Neverending Story 1984, Enemy Mine 1985, Shattered 1991, In the Line of Fire 1993, Outbreak 1995. *director/producer:* Air Force One 1997, The Red Corner 1997. *Address:* c/o CAA, 9830 Wilshire Boulevard, Beverly Hills, CA 90212, U.S.A.

PETERSON, David, P.C., LL.D., Q.C.; Canadian politician; b. 28 Dec. 1943, Toronto; s. of Clarence Peterson; m. Shelley Matthews 1974; two s. one d.; ed. Univ. of Western Ont., Univ. of Toronto; called to the Bar 1969; Chair. and Pres. C. M. Peterson Co. Ltd. and Cambridge Acceptance Corpn. 1969–75; M.P. for London Centre 1975, re-elected 1977, 1981; elected Leader Ont. Liberal Party 1982, won election for Liberal Party 1985; Premier of Ont. 1985–90; Sr. Partner Cassels Brock & Blackwell; Chair. Cassels, Pouliot, Douglas, Mackimmie, Noriega; numerous directorships; Chair. Toronto Raptors Basketball Club, Chapters Inc.; Dir. Young Pres.' Org., Council for Canadian Unity, etc; Adjunct Prof., York Univ.; several hon. degrees; Chevalier, Légion d'honneur 1994, Ordre de la Pléiade, Int. Ass. of French-speaking Parliamentarians 1995; Liberal. *Address:* Suite 2100, 40 King Street, W., Toronto, Ont. M5H 3C2, Canada.

PETERSON, Oscar Emmanuel, O.C.C.; Canadian jazz pianist; b. 15 Aug. 1925; s. of Daniel Peterson and Olivia John; m. 1st Lillian Alice Ann Peterson 1947; two s. three d.; m. 2nd Sandra Cythia King 1966; m. 3rd Charlotte Peterson; one s.; m. 4th Kelly Ann Green 1990; one d.; ed. Montreal High School; studied with Paul deMarky; f. Advanced School of Contemporary music, Toronto; Chancellor York Univ. (Canada) 1991–94, Chancellor Emer. 1994–; Carnegie Hall début with Jazz at the Philharmonic 1949; leader trio with Ray Brown and Herb Ellis; more than 300 compositions, including Hymn to Freedom, Canadiana Suite; 12 hon. degrees; Genie and Gemeni film awards for music scores, 7 Grammys, American Jazz Hall of Fame 1989, Gov.-Gen.'s Award for Lifetime Achievement 1992, Glenn Gould Prize 1993, NARAS Grammy Award for Lifetime Achievement 1997, Loyola Medal 1997; Chevalier, Order of Quebec, Order of Ont. *Publications:* Oscar Peterson New Piano Solos 1965, Jazz Exercises and Pieces 1965, Jazz Playbook (Vol. 1A) 1991 (Vol. 1B) 1993. *Leisure interests:* audio, photography, astronomy, boating. *Address:* Regal Recordings Ltd., 2421 Hammond Road, Mississauga, Ont. L5K 1T3, Canada. *Telephone:* (905) 855-2370.

PETERSON, Paul E., PH.D.; American political scientist; b. 16 Sept. 1940, Montevideo, Minn.; s. of Alvin C. Peterson and Josephine M. Telkamp; m. Carol D. Schnell 1963; two s. one d.; ed. Concordia Coll., Moorhead, Minn. and Univ. of Chicago; Asst. Prof., then Assoc. Prof. and Prof., Depts. of Political Science and Educ., Univ. of Chicago 1967–83, Chair. Cttee. on Public Policy Studies 1981–83; Dir. Governmental Studies, The Brookings Inst., Washington, D.C. 1983–87; Benjamin H. Griswold III Prof. of Public Policy, Dept. of Political Science, Johns Hopkins Univ. 1987–88; Prof. Dept. of Govt., Harvard Univ. 1988–89, Henry Lee Shattuck Prof. of Govt. 1989, Dir. Centre for American Politics Studies 1989; Research Assoc. Nat. Opinion Research Center 1978–83; Acad. Visitor, Dept. of Govt., L.S.E., England 1977–78; John Simon Guggenheim Fellowship, German Marshall Fund of the U.S. Fellowship 1977–78; mem. Nat. Acad. of Educ., American Acad. of Arts and Sciences; Gladys Kammerer Award for best book publ. 1976 on U.S. nat. policy (for School Politics Chicago Style), Woodrow Wilson Foundation Award for best book publ. 1981 (for City Limits), both from American Political Science Asscn. *Publications:* Urban Politics and Public Policy (with S. David) 1973, Race and Authority in Urban Politics (with J. D. Greenstone) 1973, School Politics Chicago Style 1976, City Limits 1981, The Politics of School Reform, 1870–1940 1985, The New Urban Reality (Ed.) 1985, The New Direction in American Politics (Ed. with J. Chubb) 1985, When Federalism Works (with B. Rabe and K. Wong) 1987, Political Institutions and Effective Government, Can the Government Govern? 1989, Welfare Magnets (with Mark Rom) 1991, The Urban Underclass (with C. Jencks) 1991, The President, the Congress and the Making of Foreign Policy 1994, The Price of Federalism 1995 (Aaron Wildovsky Award 1996), Classifying by Race 1995, The New American Democracy (with M. Fiorina). *Leisure interests:* tennis, piano. *Address:* 5 Midland Road, Wellesley, MA 02181, U.S.A. *Fax:* (617) 496-5149.

PETERSON, Peter G., M.B.A.; American business executive and government official; b. 5 June 1926, Kearney, Neb.; s. of George and Venetia (née Paul) Peterson; m. 1st Sally Hornbogen 1953 (divorced 1979); four s. one d.; m. 2nd Joan Ganz Cooney 1980; ed. M.I.T., Northwestern Univ. and Univ. of Chicago; Market Analyst, Market Facts Inc., Chicago 1947–49, Assoc. Dir. 1949–51, Exec. Vice-Pres. 1951–53; Dir. of Marketing Services, McCann-Erickson (advertising firm) 1953, Vice-Pres. 1954–58, Gen. Man. Chicago Office 1955–57, Dir., Asst. to Pres. co-ordinating services regional offices 1957–58; Exec. Vice-Pres. and Dir. Bell & Howell 1958–61, Pres. 1961–63, C.E.O. 1963–71, Chair. of Bd. 1968–71; Asst. to Pres. of U.S.A. for Int. Econ. Affairs 1971–72, also Exec. Dir. Council on Int. Econ. Policy; Sec. of Commerce 1972–73; Chair. Bd. Lehman Bros. Kuhn Loeb Inc. (fmrly. Lehman Bros. Inc.), New York 1973–83; Chair. The Blackstone Group 1985–; mem. Ind. Comm. on Int. Devt. Issues, Trilateral Comm.; Pres. Clinton's Bipartisan Comm. on Entitlement Reform 1994; nominated as Amb. to Vietnam May 1996; Dir. Minnesota Mining and Mfg. Co., Rockefeller Center Properties Inc.; fmr. Dir. Federated Dept. Stores, Black and Decker Mfg. Co., Gen. Foods Corpn., RCA, Continental Group, Cities Service; mem. Inst. of Int. Econs. (Chair Bd.); Trustee, Museum of Modern Art, New York; Per Jacobsson Lecture 1984; Man of Vision Award 1994. *Publications:* Facing Up: How to Rescue the Economy from Crushing Debt and Restore the American Dream, On Borrowed Time (co-author), Readings in Market Organization and Price Policies (Ed.). *Address:* The Blackstone Group, 345 Park Avenue, New York, NY 10154 (Office); 435 E. 52nd Street, Apartment 11G, New York, NY 10022, U.S.A. (Home).

PETERSON, Rudolph A.; American banker; b. 6 Dec. 1904, Svenljunga, Sweden; s. of Aaron Peterson and Anna (Johannsson) Peterson; m. 1st Patricia Price 1927 (deceased), 2nd Barbara Welser Lindsay 1962; one s. one d. one step-s. three step-d.; ed. Univ. of Calif. (Berkeley) Coll. of Commerce; Asst. Man. San Francisco, successively Vice-Pres. and Gen. Man. Mexico City, Div. Operations Man., Chicago, Commercial Credit Co. 1926–36;

Dist. Man. Fresno, later Vice-Pres. San Francisco, Bank of America Nat. Trust and Savings Asscn. 1936–46, Vice-Chair. of Bd. of Dirs. 1961–63, Pres. 1963–70, Chair. Exec. Cttee. 1970–75, Hon. Dir. 1975–; Pres. Allied Building Credits 1946–52; Vice-Pres. Transamerica Corpn. 1952–55; Pres. Man. Exec. Officer, Bank of Hawaii, Honolulu 1956–61; Pres. and C.E.O. BankAmerica Corpn. 1963–70, Chair. Exec. Cttee. 1970–76, Dir. –1981, Hon. Dir. 1981–; Dir. Nat. Parks Foundation 1968–70, Chair. 1980–87; Chair. The Asia Foundation 1980–90, Calif. Acad. of Sciences 1980–85, Euro-Canadian Bank 1982–94; Di Giorgio Corpn. 1969–89; Dir. Alza Corpn., 1969–96, etc.; Admin. UN Devt. Programme (UNDP) 1972–76; Hon. D.Hum.Litt. (Univ. of Redlands) 1967, Hon. LL.D. (Univ. of Calif.) 1968, Commdr. Royal Order of Vasa (Sweden) 1964, Grand Cross of Civil Merit of Spain 1965, Order of Merit of Italian Repub. 1967. *Leisure interests:* gardening, reading. *Address:* 86 Sea View, Piedmont, CA 94611, U.S.A. *Telephone:* (510)-547-5461.

PETERSON, Russell Wilbur, PH.D.; American politician and conservationist; b. 3 Oct. 1916, Portage, Wis.; s. of John Anton Peterson and Emma Marie Anthony; m. 1st Eva Lillian Turner 1937; two s. two d.; m. 2nd June Bigelow-Jenkins 1995; ed. Portage High School and Univ. of Wisconsin; with Du Pont Company for 26 years, various research, sales and man. assignments to Dir. Research and Devt. Div. of Devt. Dept. 1968; Vice-Pres. Nat. Municipal League 1968–78; Gov. of Del. 1969–73; Chair. Cttee. on Law Enforcement, Justice and Public Safety, Nat. Govs. Conf. 1971, Mid-Atlantic Govs. Conf. 1971; Vice-Chair. Council of State Govts. 1971; Chair. President's Nat. Advisory Comm. on Criminal Justice Standards and Goals 1971–72; Chair. of Bd., Textile Inst.; Chair. Exec. Cttee., Comm. on Critical Choices for Americans 1973; Chair. Council on Environmental Quality 1973–76; Pres. and C.E.O. of New Directions, citizens' action org. focused on global problems 1976–77; Special Adviser to Aspen Inst. for Humanistic Studies 1976–77; Dir. A.A.A.S. 1977–82, U.S. Asscn. of Club of Rome 1975–80, Population Crisis Cttee. (now called Population Action Int.) 1973–, World Wildlife Fund 1976–82, Office of Tech. Assessment, U.S. Congress 1978–79, Global Tomorrow Coalition 1981–91; Pres. Nat. Audubon Soc. 1979–85 (Pres. Emer. 1985–), Better World Soc. 1985–87; Chair. Advisory Bd. Solar Energy Research Inst. 1979–81; mem. President's Three Mile Island Comm. 1979; Regional Councillor, Int. Union for the Conservation of Nature (IUCN) 1981–88, Vice-Pres. 1984–88; mem. World Environment Prize Cttee., U.N. Environment Programme 1989–; Pres. Int. Council for Bird Preservation 1982–90, Pres. Emer. 1990–; Chair. Earth Lobby 1992–97; Visiting Prof. Dartmouth Coll. 1985, Carleton Coll. 1986, Univ. of Wisconsin-Madison 1987; mem. Linnaean Soc., American Ornithologists' Union; Hon. D.Sc. (Williams Coll., Butler Univ., Alma Coll., Fairleigh Dickinson) 1976, (State Univ. of N.Y.) 1981, Hon. Dr. Humanics (Springfield Coll.), Hon. D.Eng. (Stevens Inst. of Tech.), Hon. LL.D. (Gettysburg Coll.), (Univ. of Wis.) 1984, (Monmouth Coll.) 1982, (Salisbury State Univ.) 1988, Hon. L.H.D. (Ohio State Univ., Northland Coll.), Hon. D.Hum. Litt. (Meadville/Lombard Theological School 1992); Vrooman Award 1964, Nat. Conf. of Christians and Jews 1966 Citizenship and Brotherhood Award, Josiah Marvel Cup for Humanitarian and Civic Work, Commercial Devt. Asscn. Honor Award 1971, Gold Medal Award World Wildlife Fund 1971, Golden Plate Award American Acad. of Achievement 1971, Conservationist of the Year, Nat. Wildlife Fed. 1971, Parsons Award, American Chemical Soc. 1974, Nat. Audubon Soc. Medal 1977, Swedish American of the Year 1982, Robert Marshal Award of The Wilderness Soc. 1984, Order of the Golden Ark (Netherlands) 1985, Environmental Law Inst. Award 1990, Lifetime Achievement Award, Global Tomorrow Coalition 1994, Lifetime Achievement Award, League of Conservation Voters 1996, Liberty Bell Award, Del. Bar Asscn. 1998; Democrat 1996– (fmrly. Republican). *Publications:* Rebel with a Conscience (memoirs) 1999, various articles on autoxidation, new product developments, crime reduction, environmental quality, conservation and population. *Leisure interest:* nature study. *Address:* 11 E. Mozart Drive, Wilmington, DE 19807, U.S.A. *Telephone:* (302) 995-0736. *Fax:* (302) 995-9137.

PETERSON, Thage G.; Swedish politician; b. 1933, Berg, Kronoberg; ed. Inst. of Social Studies, Lund 1955–57; Municipal Treas. Community Centre Asscn. 1957–59, head 1967–71; Sec. and Vice-Chair. Social Democratic Youth Union 1964–67; elected to Parl. 1970; Under-Sec. of State to Cabinet 1971–75; Chair. Stockholm County br. of Socialdemokratiska Arbetareparitet (Social Democratic Labour Party—SDLP) 1974–89; mem. SDLP Exec. Cttee. 1975–90; Minister without Portfolio 1975–76; SDLP spokesman for Industrial Policy 1976–82; mem. SDLP Parl. Group Exec. and head of Research Div.; Minister of Industry 1982–88, of Justice 1988, of Defence 1994–97, Minister in the Prime Minister's Office 1997–; Speaker of Parl. 1988–91; Chair. Standing Cttee. on the Constitution 1991–94. *Address:* Office of the Prime Minister, 103 33 Stockholm, Sweden.

PETERSON, Walter; American politician, educationist and real estate executive; b. 19 Sept. 1922, Nashua, New Hampshire; s. of Walter and Helen Reed Peterson; m. Dorothy Donovan 1949; one s. one d.; ed. New Hampton School, Coll. of William and Mary, Univ. of New Hampshire, Dartmouth; formed real estate firm 'The Petersons' with father and brother 1948, now Realtor and Treas.; elected to New Hampshire House of Reps. 1961, Majority Leader 1963, Speaker of the House 1965–68; Gov. of New Hampshire 1969–73; Partner Petersons Inc. 1973–75; Pres. Franklin Pierce Coll., New Hampshire 1975–; mem. N.H. Post Secondary Educ. Comm.; Dir. N.H. Coll. and Univ. Council, Nat. Asscn. of Ind. Colls. and Univs., Cheshire Financial Corpn.; Chair. New England Bd. of Higher Educ.; Republican. *Address:* Franklin Pierce College, Rindge, New Hampshire 03461 (Office); East Mountain Road, Peterborough, NH 03458, U.S.A. (Home). *Telephone:* 603-924-3259.

PETHRICK, Richard Arthur, PH.D., F.R.S.C., F.R.S.E., C. CHEM., F.R.S.A.; British professor of chemistry; b. 26 Oct. 1942, Yate; s. of Arthur T. A. Pethrick and Lavinia M. Pethrick; m. Joan Knowles Hume 1975; one s.; ed. Univs. of London and Salford; Lecturer, Dept. of Pure and Applied Chem. Univ. of Strathclyde 1970, Sr. Lecturer 1978, Reader 1981, Prof. of Chem. 1983–, Head Dept. 1992–95; mem. Editorial Bd. British Polymer Journal 1979–93, Int. Journal of Polymeric Materials 1990–, Polymer News 1991–, Trends in Polymer Science 1992–, Polymer Int. 1993–; Ed. Polymer Yearbook 1983–; Visiting Prof. Univ. of Punjab 1979; British Council Visiting Lecturer, Australia 1985, 1989; Royal Soc. Visiting Lecturer, U.K.-China Del., Beijing 1992; mem. Int. Swedish Tech. Review Cttee. for Polymer Science 1988; mem. Polymers and Composites Cttee., SERC 1993–, Large Area Displays Cttee. EPSRC 1994–; IRC Review Cttee. 1995–; Chair. Science Sector Scottish Vocational Awards Council 1995–; elected to Hon. Craft of Weavers of Glasgow 1991; Elder Merrylea Church, Church of Scotland 1995. *Publications:* Molecular Motion in High Polymers 1979; over 300 scientific papers and numerous book chapters and review articles. *Leisure interests:* Scottish country dancing, walking. *Address:* 40 Langside Drive, Newlands, Glasgow, G43 2QQ, Scotland. *Telephone:* 0141-548 2260/2795 (Office); 0141-637 5134 (Home).

PETIT, Pierre, L. ÈS L.; French composer; b. 21 April 1922, Poitiers; s. of Roger and Yvonne (née Bouchet) Petit; m. 3rd Liliane Fiaux 1974; four s. one d. from previous marriages; ed. Lycée Louis-le-Grand, Université de Paris à la Sorbonne and Conservatoire de Paris; Head of Course, Conservatoire de Paris 1951–; Dir. of Light Music, Office de Radiodiffusion et Télévision Française (ORTF) 1960–64, Dir. of Musical Productions, ORTF 1964–70, Chamber Music 1970–; Producer, Radio-Télévision luxembourgeoise (R.T.L.) 1980; Dir.-Gen. Ecole Normale de Musique de Paris 1963–; Pres. Jury Concours Int. Marguerite Long 1981–; Music Critic, Figaro; mem. Gov. Council Conservatoire de Paris; Vice-Pres. soc. des auteurs et compositeurs dramatiques 1985–; Premier Grand Prix de Rome 1946; Chevalier, Légion d'honneur, Officier des Arts et Lettres, Ordre nationale du Mérite, Officier de l'Ordre du Cèdre du Liban. *Compositions include:* Suite for four 'cellos 1945, Zadig (ballet) 1948, Ciné-Bijou (ballet) 1952, Feu rouge, feu vert 1954, Concerto for piano and orchestra 1956, Concerto for organ and orchestra 1960, Furia Italiana 1960, Concerto for two guitars and orchestra 1965. *Publications:* Verdi 1957, Ravel 1970, Mozart 1991. *Address:* 114 bis boulevard Malesherbes, 75017 Paris (Office); 28 rue Cardinet, 75017 Paris, France (Home). *Telephone:* (01) 47.63.85.72.

PETIT, Roland; French dancer and choreographer; b. 13 Jan. 1924, Villemomble; s. of Edmond and Victoria (née Repetto) Petit; m. Zizi Jeanmaire (q.v.) 1954; one s.; ed. Paris Opera Ballet School; Premier Danseur Paris Opera 1940–44; founded Les Vendredis de la Danse 1944, Les Ballets de Champs-Elysées 1945, Les Ballets de Paris 1948; Dir. Paris Opera Ballet 1970; founded Les Ballets de Marseilles; Officier, Légion d'honneur, Officier des Arts et des Lettres, Ordre. nat. du Mérite. *Works include:* Le rossignol et la rose, Le jeune homme et la mort, Les demoiselles de la nuit, Deuil en vingt-quatre heures, Le loup, Cyrano de Bergerac, Carmen, Les forains, La belle au bois dormant, Hans Christian Andersen, Folies Bergères, L'éloge de la folie, Paradise Lost, Pelléas et Mélisande, Les intermittences du coeur 1975, La symphonie fantastique 1975, Die Fledermaus 1980, Soirée Debussy, Le mariage du ciel et de l'enfer 1985, Fantôme de l'opéra, Charlot danse avec vous, Pink Floyd Ballet, Marcel et la belle excentrique 1992, la Chauve-Souris 1993, Camera Obscura 1994, Passcaille 1994; numerous films and plays. *Address:* 20 boulevard Gabes, 13008 Marseilles, France.

PETKOV, Petko Danev; Bulgarian politician; b. 2 March 1942, Dobrotich; ed. Higher Naval School, Varna; joined Dimitrov Young Communist League 1956, Bulgarian Communist Party (BCP) 1973; worked for 1st Coast Artillery Regt., Varna, radio mechanic for Navigation Maritime Bulgare Shipping Co., designer at Resprom Plant, Varna, Deputy Man., then Man. of Radio Navigation Equipment Works, Varna, Man. Dir. of Cherno More Research and Industry Combined Works; First Sec., BCP Municipal Cttee., Varna Sept. 1987–; alt. mem., BCP Cen. Cttee.; alt. mem., Political Bureau Dec. 1989–. *Address:* Bulgarian Communist Party, Sofia, Bulgaria.

PETKOVSKI, Tito; Macedonian politician; b. 23 Jan. 1945, Psacha, Kriva Palanka; m. Tanja Petkovska; two d.; ed. Kriva Palanka High School, Skopje Univ.; worked in Municipal court Kriva Palanka, Repub. Bureau on Urban Planning and Communal Issues; political career started as deputy in Karposh Communal Ass., deputy City Ass. Skopje; later Vice-Pres. Exec. Council City Ass. Skopje; Sec. Cen. Cttee. League of Communists of Macedonia—Party for Democratic Prosperity; mem. Cttee. on Constitutional Problems, Ass. Repub. of Macedonia; Vice-Pres. first multi-party Ass. of Macedonia 1994–96; co-ordinator Parl. Group Social-Democratic Union of Macedonia; mem. Council of Inter-Parl. Union; Pres. Ass. (Sobranje) Repub. of Macedonia 1996–. *Publications include:* legal articles on housing policy, town planning and land devt. *Address:* 11 Oktombri blvd., 91000 Skopje, Macedonia. *Telephone:* (91) 112255. *Fax:* (91) 237947 (Office).

PETO, Richard, M.SC., M.A., F.R.S.; British professor of medicine; b. 14 May 1943; s. of Leonard Huntley Peto and Carrie Clarinda Peto; m. 1st Sallie Messum 1970 (divorced); two s.; partner Gale Mead; two s.; ed. Trinity Coll.,

Cambridge, Imperial Coll., London; Research Officer MRC 1967–69; with Univ. of Oxford 1969–72, lecturer Dept. of Regius Prof. of Medicine 1972–75, Reader in Cancer Studies 1975–92, Imperial Cancer Research Fund Prof. of Medical Statistics and Epidemiology 1992–. *Publications include:* Natural History of Chronic Bronchitis and Emphysema 1976, Quantification of Occupational Cancer 1981, The Causes of Cancer 1983, Diet, Lifestyle and Mortality in China 1990, Mortality from Smoking in Developed Countries 1950–2000 (jtly.) 1994. *Leisure interests:* science, children. *Address:* Radcliffe Infirmary, Oxford, OX2 6HE, England. *Telephone:* (01865) 552830; (01865) 558379.

PETRAKOV, Nikolai Yakovlevich, DR.ECON.SC.; Russian economist; b. 1 March 1937; m. Tat'yana Aleksandrovna; one s. one d.; ed. Moscow Univ.; mem. CPSU 1964–90; mem. staff Inst. of Tech.-Econ. Research 1959–61, Econ. Inst. 1961–65, then Head of Lab.; Deputy Dir., Cen. Mathematics-Econ. Inst., U.S.S.R. Acad. of Sciences 1965–91; corresp. mem. U.S.S.R. (now Russian) Acad. of Sciences 1984–90, mem. 1990–; U.S.S.R. People's Deputy 1989–91; Dir. Inst. for Market Problems 1991–; Adviser to Pres. Yeltsin Jan. 1994; mem. Political Consultative Council 1991; mem. State Duma (Parl.) 1993–95; Chair. Bd. Savings Investment Bank 1996–. *Publications:* papers and articles on the problems of pricing policies and on socialist economics. *Address:* Institute for Market Problems, Krasikova Str. 32, 117418 Moscow (Office); Acad. Zelinski Str. 38, korp. 8, Apt. 40, 117334 Moscow, Russia (Home). *Telephone:* 129-10-00 (Office); 135-14-46 (Home).

PETRASSI, Goffredo; Italian composer; b. 16 July 1904, Zagarolo; s. of Eliseo Petrassi and Erminia Calzoletti; m. Rosetta Acerbi 1962; one d.; ed. Conservatorio S. Cecilia, Rome; Supt. Teatro Fenice, Venice 1937–40; Pres. Int. Soc. for Contemporary Music 1954–56; now Prof. of Composition, Accad. S. Cecilia. *Works include:* orchestral: Partita 1932, First Concerto 1933, Second Concerto 1951, Récréation Concertante (Third Concerto) 1953, Fourth Concerto 1954, Fifth Concerto 1955, Invenzione Concertata 1957, Quartet 1957; operas and ballets: Follia di Orlando 1943, Ritratto di don Chisciotte 1945, Il Cordovano 1948, Morte dell'Aria 1950; choral works: Salmo IX 1936, Magnificat 1940, Coro di Morti 1941, Noche Oscura 1951, Mottetti 1965; voice and orchestra Quattro Inni Sacri 1942; chamber music: Serenata 1958, Trio 1959, Suoni Notturni 1959, Propos d'Alain 1960, Concerto Flauto 1960, Seconda Serenata-Trio 1962, Settimo Concerto 1964, Estri 1966–67, Beatitudines 1968, Ottetto di Ottori 1968, Souffle 1969, Ottavo Concerto 1970–72, Elogio 1971, Nunc 1971, Ala 1972, Orationes Christi 1975, Alias 1977, Grand Septuor 1978, Violasola 1978, Flou 1980, Romanzetta 1980, Poema 1977–80, Sestina d'Autunno 1981–82, Laudes Creaturarum 1982. *Address:* Via Ferdinando di Savoia 3, 00196 Rome, Italy. *Telephone:* 3201056.

PETRE, Zoe, PH.D.; Romanian historian; b. 23 Aug. 1940, Bucharest; m. (husband deceased); two s.; ed. Bucharest Univ.; Prof. and Dean, History Faculty, Univ. Bucharest 1990–; specialist in ancient world history; Assoc. Prof. École des Hautes Études en Sciences Sociales, Centre de Recherches Comparées sur les Sociétés anciennes, Paris 1982; Sr. Advisor to Pres. of Romania 1996–; mem. Romanian socs. of Classical Studies, Historical Sciences, and Anthropology, Asscn. pour l'encouragement des études grecques, France; Vice-Pres. of the Nat. Cttee. of South-East European Studies. *Publications:* Commentaire aux "Sept cratre Thèbes" d'Eschyle (with Liam Lupas) 1981, Civilizalia greacs di originule democratiei 1993– and articles in scientific journals specializing in ancient history, culture, philology. *Address:* Universitatea Bucureşti, B-dul M. Kogălniceanu 64, 70609 Bucharest; Str. Stupinei 39, 73106 Bucharest, Romania.

PETRENKO, Aleksey Vasilyevich; Russian actor; b. 26 March 1938; ed. Kharkov Theatre Inst.; acted with various prov. cos. in the U.S.S.R., including Lensovet Theatre 1967–81, Moscow Art Theatre 1978–83, Moscow Taganka Theatre, Russia 1985–; R.S.F.S.R. People's Artist 1988. *Films include:* King Lear 1971, Marriage 1978, Agony (role of Grigoriy Rasputin) 1981, A Cruel Romance 1984, 20 Days Out of War 1987, The Servant 1989, Balthazar's Feasts or The Night with Stalin 1990, The Small Bees 1995, and many others. *Address:* Nikitsky Blvd. 9, Apt. 39, 121019 Moscow, Russia. *Telephone:* 291-48-51.

PETRI, Michala; Danish musician; b. 7 July 1958, Copenhagen; d. of Kanny Sambleben and Hanne Petri; m. Lars Hannibal; two d.; ed. Staatliche Hochschule für Musik und Theater, Hanover; recorder player; first concert as soloist in Tivoli 1969; since 1969 has toured extensively all over the world; has played with Pinchas Zukerman, James Galway and Keith Jarrett; several prizes. *Publications:* ed. of several works for Wilhelm Hansen and Moeck. *Address:* Nordskraenten 3, 2980 Kokkedal, Denmark. *Telephone:* 45 86 25 77.

PETRIDES, Paul; Greek historian and university professor; b. 19 Aug. 1947, Thessaloniki; m. Lina Voreopoulou; ed. Thessaloniki and Vienna Univs.; prof. Thessaloniki Univ. 1982–; Visiting Prof. at Panteion Univ.; Chair. Hellenic Lyric Stage 1989–93; Vice-Chair. G. Papandreou Cultural Foundation, Kapodistrias Foundation; Chair. Cultural Cttee. of Law Faculty, Thessaloniki Univ.; Chair. Macedonian News Agency; recipient of several awards and prizes. *Publications include:* The Diplomatic Action of John Kapodistrias for Greeks 1974, Die Jonische Frage auf den Wiener Kongress, Griechenland und Grossmaechte, Political and Social History of Greece, Contemporary Political History of Greece. *Leisure interests:* painting, music. *Address:* 5 P. Mela Street, 552 36 Panorama, Thessaloniki, Greece. *Telephone:* (031) 341.682.

PETRIE, James Colquhoun, C.B.E., F.R.C.P. (U.K.), F.R.C.P. (E.), F.F.P.M., F.R.C.P.I.; British professor of medicine; b. 18 Sept. 1941; s. of the late Dr. James B. Petrie and of Dr. Cairine R. Petrie; m. Dr. Xanthe Forbes 1984; two s. two d.; ed. Robert Gordon's Coll., Aberdeen, Univ. of Aberdeen; Sr. lecturer Univ. of Aberdeen 1971–81, Reader 1981–85, Prof. of Clinical Pharmacology 1985–, Head Dept. of Medicine and Therapeutics 1994–; Hon. Consultant Physician Aberdeen Royal Hosps. 1971–; Assessor R.C.P.E. 1992–; jt. ed. and writer of numerous publs. *Leisure interests:* skiing, golf. *Address:* 126 Desswood Place, Aberdeen, AB15 4DQ, Scotland.

PETRIE, Sir Peter (Charles), Bt., C.M.G.; British diplomatist; b. 7 March 1932, London; s. of Sir Charles Petrie, Bt., C.B.E. and Lady Petrie; m. Countess Lydwine von Oberndorff 1958; two s. one d.; ed. Westminster School and Christ Church, Oxford; Second Sec. U.K. del to NATO 1958–62; First Sec. New Delhi 1961–63; Chargé d'affaires, Kathmandu 1963–64; Cabinet Office, London 1965–67; FCO 1967–69; First Sec. later Counsellor, U.K. Perm. Mission at UN, New York 1969–73; Counsellor, Bonn 1973–76; FCO 1976–79; Minister, Paris 1979–85; Amb. to Belgium 1985–89; European Adviser to Gov. of Bank of England 1989–; mem. Franco-British Council 1995, Chair. British Section 1997–; Acad. de Compatabilité (Paris) 1997–; mem. Council, City Univ. 1997–. *Leisure interests:* gardening, golf. *Address:* 40 rue Lauriston, 75116 Paris, France; 16a Cambridge Street, London, SW1V 4QH, England.

PETRILLI, Giuseppe; Italian administrator; b. 24 March 1913, Naples; s. of Michele Petrilli and Anna Pellegrino; m. Angela Roberti 1939; one s. two d.; ed. Univ. of Rome; Pres. Inst. Nat. d'Assurances contre les maladies 1950–58; mem. Council of Economy and Work; mem. EEC Comm., Pres. Social Affairs Section 1958–60; Pres. Inst. for Industrial Reconstruction (IRI) 1960–79; Sec.-Gen. of the European Christian Democratic Union (UEDC) 1978–82; Pres. Int. Council of European Movt. 1981–85; Senator of the Republic 1979–87; Cavaliere del Lavoro 1965. *Address:* Via T. Salvini 55, 00197 Rome, Italy.

PETROV, Aleksander Aleksandrovich; Russian scientist; b. 3 Feb. 1934; ed. Moscow Inst. of Physics and Eng.; Head of Div., Computation Centre Russian Acad. of Sciences; corresp. mem. Russian Acad. of Sciences 1991, mem. 1997–; main research in problems of optimal perspective analysis and methods of estimating potential possibilities of econs., math. modelling of complex systems; U.S.S.R. State Prize 1980. *Address:* Computation Centre, Vavilova str. 40, 117967, GSP-1, Moscow, Russia. *Telephone:* (095) 135 3023 (Office).

PETROV, Andrei Pavlovich; Russian composer; b. 2 Sept. 1930, Leningrad; s. of Pavel Platonovich Petrov and Olga Petrovna Vaulina; m. Natalia Fishkova 1954; one d.; ed. Leningrad Conservatory; Chair. Leningrad (now St. Petersburg) Composers' Union 1964–; mem. CPSU 1957–90; State Prize 1967, 1976, U.S.S.R. People's Artist 1980; *Compositions include:* Radda and Loiko (Symphonic poem), Violin Concerto, Piano Concerto, Symphonies No. 1, 2, 3, 4, The Creation of the World (ballet), Peter the Great (opera), Mayakovsky Begins (opera), Pushkin (choral dance work), Master and Margarita (ballet music), God-children of Katherine the Great (musical) 1995–96; also operettas, songs, music for numerous films including The Promised Heaven 1992 (Nika Prize). *Leisure interest:* travelling. *Address:* Petrovskaya nab. 4, Apt. 75, 197046 St. Petersburg, Russia. *Telephone:* (812) 232-29-63. *Fax:* (812) 315-13-02.

PETROV, Nikolai Arnoldovich; Russian pianist; b. 14 April 1943, Moscow; m. Larisa Petrova; one d.; ed. Moscow Conservatory (pupil of Yakov Zak); debut in Moscow 1962; soloist of Moscow Philharmonic 1966–; toured many countries of Europe and America as soloist and with maj. conductors and orchestras; took part in music festivals; first performer of music by contemporary Russian composers, including Rodion Shchedrin, first performances in Russia of works by Bach, Beethoven, Mozart, Debussy, Ravel, Liszt; Prof. Moscow Conservatoire 1994–; Founder and Pres. Acad. of Russian Art 1995; Vice-Pres. Int. Asscn. The World of Culture 1993; State Prize of Russia 1993; People's Artist of Russia, Musician of the Year (Musikalnaya Zhizn journal) 1994. *Address:* Kutuzovsky prospekt 26, apt. 23, 121 165 Moscow, Russia. *Telephone:* 561-6747.

PETROV, Rem Viktorovich; DR.MED.SC.; Russian immunologist; b. 22 March 1930, Serafimovitch; s. of Victor Ivanovich Petrov and Kutniak Evdokia Emelianovna; m. 1st Tatiana Kuk 1960 (died 1970), 2nd Natalia Emetz 1978; one s. one d.; ed. Voronezh Medical Inst.; mem. CPSU 1956–91; research work at various grades in U.S.S.R. (now Russian) Ministry of Health Inst. of Bio-Physics 1959–83, Head of Lab. 1983–; Pres. U.S.S.R. (now Russian) Immunology Soc. 1983–; Dir. of U.S.S.R. (now Russian) Ministry of Health Inst. of Immunology 1983–88; mem. of Acad. of Medical Sciences 1978–; concurrently Head of Dept. of Immunology of Second Moscow Inst. of Medicine 1974–; mem. Int. Scientific Advisory Bd. of UNESCO 1996–; mem. U.S.S.R. (now Russian) Acad. of Sciences 1984–, Vice-Pres. 1988–; mem. Acad. of Agric. 1991–; Ed. Sciences in Russia 1989; mem. World Acad. of Art and Sciences 1989–, New York Acad. of Sciences 1992–, Washington Acad. of Sciences 1993–; Dr. h.c. (Bar-Ilan Univ.) 1990, (Madrid Polytechnic Univ.) 1994; L. Mechnikov Gold Medal, Acad. of Medical Sciences 1987; Hero of Labour 1990, Order of Lenin 1990. *Publications:* Essays on the New Immunology 1976, Immunology and Immunogenetics 1981, Immunology 1982, Me or Not Me 1983, Suppressor B-lymphocytes 1988, The Thymus and Bone Marrow Derived Immunoregulatory Peptides 1992. *Leisure interests:* fishing, hunting, wooden handwork. *Address:* Russian Academy of Sciences, Leninsky pr. 14, 117901 Moscow, Russia. *Telephone:* (095) 954-3276. *Fax:* (095) 237-8101.

PETROV, Yuriy Vladimirovich; Russian politician; b. 18 Jan. 1939, Nizhni Tagil; ed. Uralsk Polytech. Inst. and Higher Party School of CPSU Cen. Cttee.; mem. CPSU 1962–91; Dept. Head, Second Sec., First Sec., of Nizhnetagil City Cttee. 1969–77; Sec. Sverdlovsk Dist. Cttee. 1977–85, First Sec. 1985–88; mem. CPSU Cen. Cttee. 1986–91; Deputy of U.S.S.R. Supreme Soviet 1986–91; mem. State Comm. for Industry 1986–87; Chair. Comm. for Transport and Communications 1987–88; Amb. to Cuba 1988–90; Adviser, Head of Staff of Russian Pres. 1990–93; Pres. State Investments Corpn. 1993–; Chair. Realists Union 1994–. *Address:* State Investments Corporation, Myasnitskaya 35, Moscow, Russia. *Telephone:* 208-99-44.

PETROVICS, Emil; Hungarian composer; b. 9 Feb. 1930, Nagybecskerek (now Zrenjanin, Yugoslavia); s. of Jovan Petrovics and Erzsébet Weninger; divorced; one d.; studied at Conservatory, graduated from Music Acad. of Budapest; Musical dir. Petőfi Theatre 1960–64; Lecturer Coll. of Dramatic and Cinematographic Arts 1964–; Prof. of Composition Music Acad., Budapest; Dir. Hungarian State Opera 1986–90; mem. Hungarian Parl. 1967–85; mem. Széchenyi Acad. of Arts, Budapest 1991–, Serbian Acad. of Sciences and Arts, Belgrade 1993–; Erkel Prize 1960, 1963, Kossuth Prize 1966, holder of titles Merited Artist 1975, Eminent Artist 1982. *Compositions for musical stage:* C'est la guerre (single act) 1961, Crime and Punishment 1969; Book of Jonah (oratorio) 1965; Lysistrate (comic opera for concert performance) 1962 (all performed in Czechoslovakia, Finland, France, Fed. Repub. of Germany, Hungary and Yugoslavia); Salome (ballet) 1984; 2nd to 5th Cantatas: There Let Me Die 1972, Fanny's Posthumous Papers 1978, We All Must Go 1980, Letters from Turkey 1981, 6th Cantata: We Take a Rest. *Instrumental music:* Concerto for Flute 1957, String Quartet 1958, Symphony for Strings 1964, Quintet for Winds 1966, Rhapsody No. 1 and No. 2 for Violin and Viola solo 1982, 1983, Concertino for trumpet and orchestra 1990, 2nd string quartet 1991, Rhapsody No 2 for Violoncello Solo 1991, Vörösmarty—Overture for orchestra 1993, Cantata No. 7: Pygmalion, for mixed chorus, narrator and orchestra 1994–95, Lament and Consolation (three poems for tenor voice and piano) 1996, Piangendo e Meditando, for string orchestra 1997, Cantata No. 9: By the Danube 1998; other works for chorus, incidental film and stage music. *Publication:* Ravel 1959. *Address:* Attila utca 39, 1013 Budapest, Hungary. *Telephone:* (01) 375-60-32.

PETROVSKY, Artur Vladimirovich, PH.D.; Russian psychologist; b. 14 May 1924, Sevastopol; m. Ivetta Sinelnikova; one s., one d.; ed. Moscow Pedagogical Inst.; teacher, sr. teacher Vologda Pedagogical Inst. 1947–58; asst. prof. Moscow State Pedagogical Inst., Prof. 1952–66; Chair. Psychology Dept. 1966–92; corresp. mem. U.S.S.R. Acad. of Pedagogical Sciences 1968, mem. 1971; Academician-Sec. Dept. of Psychology and Age Physiology 1968–76, 1997–, Vice-Pres. 1976–79, Pres. 1992–97; mem. Russian Acad. of Educ. 1991. *Publications:* History of Soviet Psychology 1967, General Psychology 1970, 1976–86, Problems of history and theory of Psychology: selected works 1984. Essays on Psychology 1985, Psychology in U.S.S.R. 1990, Psychology of each of us 1992, History of psychology (co-author Yaroshevsky) 1994. *Leisure interests:* collecting fiction books. *Address:* Russian Academy of Pedagogical Sciences, 119900 Moscow, Russia. *Telephone:* (095) 246-86-26.

PETROVSKY, Boris Vasiliyevich; Russian surgeon; b. 27 June 1908, Essentuki; s. of Vasiliy Petrovsky and Lydia Petrovsky; m. Ekaterina Timofeeva; one d.; ed. First Moscow Univ.; physician at various hospitals 1930–50; mem. CPSU 1942–91; Head of Chair of Surgery, Second Moscow Inst. of Medicine 1951–56; Head of Chair of Hospital Surgery, First Moscow Medical Inst., and Dir. Inst. of Clinical and Experimental Surgery (now Scientific Centre of Surgery), Acad. of Medical Sciences 1956–; Minister of Health of U.S.S.R. 1965–80; Deputy to U.S.S.R. Supreme Soviet 1962–84; Cand. mem. Cen. Cttee. of CPSU 1966–81; mem. U.S.S.R. (now Russian) Acad. of Medical Sciences 1957–, U.S.S.R. (now Russian) Acad. of Sciences 1966–, Russian Medico-technical Acad. 1994–; Honoured Scientific Worker of R.S.F.S.R., Lenin Prize 1960, Hero of Socialist Labour 1968, Order of Lenin (four times) and other awards. Main works: has studied problems of blood transfusion, oncology, surgery of vessels and organs of thoracic cavity, surgical treatment of congenital and acquired heart diseases, kidney transplant. *Publications:* Drip Transfusion of Blood and Blood-Substitute Compounds 1948, Surgical Treatment of Vascular Wounds 1949, Surgical Treatment of Carcinoma of the Oesophagus and Cardia 1950, Blood Transfusion in Surgery 1954, Surgery of Mediastinum 1960, Surgery of patent arterial duct 1963, Cardiac aneurysms 1965, Resection & plastic repair of bronchi 1966, Prosthetic replacement of heart valves 1966, Surgery of diaphragm 1966, Oesophageal diverticuli 1968, Surgery for renovascular hypertension 1968, Selected lectures in clinical surgery 1968, Kidney transplantation 1969, Surgery of aortic arch branches 1970, Surgery of peripheral vessels 1970, Atlas of thoracic surgery 1973–74, Surgical hepatology 1972, Microsurgery 1976, Basics of Hyperbaric Medicine 1976, Tracheo-Bronchial Surgery 1978, Surgical Treatment of Chronic Ischemic Heart Diseases 1978, Surgical Diseases 1980, Reconstructive Surgery for Extrabiliary Duct Disorders 1980, Emergency Cardiovascular Surgery 1980, Surgeon and Life 1989, Two Persons—One Life (memoirs) 1991, Surgery for portal hypertension: Atlas 1994; Big Medical Encyclopaedia 30 vols. (Ed.-in-Chief). *Leisure interests:* book collection and gardening. *Address:* c/o National Research Centre for Surgery, Abrikosovskyi 2, Moscow 119874, Russia. *Telephone:* (095) 248-92-65 (Office); 246-43-85 (Home). *Fax:* (095) 230 24 80.

PETROVSKY, Vladimir Fyodorovich, D.HIST.; Russian diplomatist and lecturer; b. 29 April 1933, Volgograd; s. of Fyodor Petrovsky and Anna Khritinina; m. Myra Mukhina; one d.; ed. Moscow Inst. of Int. Relations; with U.S.S.R. (now Russian) Ministry of Foreign Affairs 1957–; staff mem. U.S.S.R. Mission to UN 1957–61, mem. Office of the Foreign Minister, U.S.S.R. Ministry of Foreign Affairs 1961–64; mem. UN Secr. 1964–71; with Dept. of planning of int. policy, U.S.S.R. Ministry of Foreign Affairs 1971–78, Head of Dept. 1978–79, Head Dept. of Int. Orgs. 1979–86, Deputy Minister 1986–91, First Deputy Minister Aug.–Dec. 1991; Exec. Sec. CSCE Conf. on Human Dimension 1991; UN Under-Sec.-Gen. for Political Affairs 1992; Dir.-Gen. UN Office, Geneva, 1993–; Sec.-Gen. Conf. on Disarmament 1994–; mem. Acad. of Natural Sciences of Russian Fed. *Publications:* The Foreign Service of Great Britain 1958, The Diplomacy of 10 Downing Street 1964, US Foreign Policy Thinking: Theories and Concepts 1976, The Doctrine of National Security in US Global Strategy 1980, Disarmament: Concept, Problems, Mechanisms 1983, Security in the Era of Nuclear and Outer Space Technology 1985. *Leisure interests:* art, memoirs. *Address:* Office of the Director-General, Palais des Nations, 1211 Geneva 10, Switzerland. *Telephone:* (022) 917 2100. *Fax:* (022) 917 0002.

PETRUSHEVSKAYA, Liudmila Stefanovna; Russian author and playwright; b. 26 May 1938, Moscow; d. of Stefan Antonovitsh Petrushevskij and Valentina Nikolaevna Jakovleva; m. 1st Evgenij Kharatian 1939; one s.; m. 2nd Boris Pavlov 1940; one s. one d; ed. Moscow Univ.; newspaper and radio journalist 1957–73; started writing short stories 1968, plays and folk tales 1971; stage productions and publ. of works were forbidden for many years; first underground performance 1975, first official performance, Tallin 1979; mem. Bayerische Akad. der Schönen Kunste 1997; Int. A. Pushkin Prize (Germany) 1991, prizes for the best short story of the year from "Ogoniok" 1988, 1989 and "Oktiabr" 1993, 1996, Grand Prize for play The Time: Night, Annual All-Russian Theatre Festival of Solo Theatre, Perm 1995, Moscow-Penne Prize (Russia/Italy) 1996. *Plays include:* Two Windows 1971, Music Lessons 1973, Cinzano 1973, Love 1974, The Landing 1974, Andante 1975, The Execution, A Glass of Water, Smirnova's Birthday 1977–78, Three Girls in Blue 1980, Colombina's Flat 1981, Moscow Choir 1984, The Golden Goddess 1986, The Wedding Night 1990, The Men's Quarters 1992; co-author of screenplay Tale of Tales (prize for best animated film of all time, Los Angeles 1980). *Publications:* Immortal Love 1988, Songs of the 20th Century 1988, On the Way to the God Eros 1993, The Mystery of the House 1993, Girl's House 1998; (children's books) Vasilli's Treatment 1991, Once Upon a Time There Was a Trrrr! 1994, Real Fairy Tales 1997, The Alphabet's Tale 1997; Complete Works (5 vols.) 1996. *Leisure interests:* watercolour painting. *Address:* Staroslobodsky per. 2a, Apt. 20, 107113 Moscow, Russia. *Telephone:* 269-74-48. *Fax:* 269-74-48.

PETRY, Heinz, DIPL. ING; German industrial executive; b. 12 Jan. 1919, Rheinhausen; s. of Heinrich Petry and Elise Petry (née Maas); m. Liselotte Petry (née Gebauer) 1945; two s. one d.; ed. Berlin Tech. Coll., Stuttgart Univ.; construction engineer in dredger mfg., Krupp Industrie- und Stahlbau, Rheinhausen 1946, Deputy Head of Dept. 1950, given proxy of firm 1961, Head of Dept. 1962, Deputy mem. of Man. Bd. 1965, mem. 1966, Spokesman 1973; mem. Man. Bd., Friedrich Krupp GmbH, Essen 1974–, Deputy Chair. 1975–76, Chair. 1976–80; mem. Supervisory Bd. AG Weser, Bremen, Krupp-Koppers GmbH, Essen. *Leisure interests:* hunting, golf, films. *Address:* Kaiserstrasse 238, 47800 Krefeld, Germany.

PETTENGILL, Gordon Hemenway, PH.D.; American professor of planetary physics; b. 10 Feb. 1926, Providence, R.I.; s. of Rodney G. Pettengill and Frances (Hemenway) Pettengill; m. Pamela Wolfenden 1967; one s. one d.; ed. M.I.T. and Univ. of California at Berkeley; staff mem., M.I.T. Lincoln Lab. 1954–68, Assoc. Leader, Haystack Observatory 1965–68; Dir. Arecibo Observatory, Puerto Rico (operated by Cornell Univ.) 1968–70; Prof. of Planetary Physics, Dept. of Earth and Planetary Sciences, M.I.T. 1971–; Dir. M.I.T. Center for Space Research 1984–90; involved in the study of the solar system using radar and radio techniques; discovered 3/2 spin-orbit resonance of Mercury 1965; pioneered delay-doppler radar mapping of planets; prin. investigator of Pioneer Venus Radar Mapper 1978–81, Magellan Venus Radar Mapper 1990–; mem. N.A.S., American Acad. of Arts and Sciences, A.A.A.S., American Physical Soc., American Astronomical Soc., Int. Radio Science Union; Guggenheim Fellow 1980/81; Magellan Premium of the American Philosophical Soc. 1994. *Leisure interests:* ornithology, sailing. *Address:* Room 37–641, Massachusetts Institute of Technology, 77 Massachusetts Avenue, Cambridge, MA 02139, U.S.A. *Telephone:* (617) 253-4281.

PETTIGREW, Pierre S., B.A., M.PHIL.; Canadian politician; b. 1951; ed. Univ. de Québec à Trois-Rivières, Univ. of Oxford; Dir. Political Cttee. NATO Ass., Brussels 1976–78; Exec. Asst. to Leader of Quebec Liberal Party 1978–81; Foreign Policy Adviser to Prime Minister, Privy Council Office 1981–84; Vice-Pres. Samson Belair Deloitte and Touche Int. (Montreal) 1985–95; Minister for Int. Co-operation, Minister with special responsibility for la Francophonie 1996–97, for Papineau-St. Denis, of Human Resources

Devt. 1997–; Co-Chair. First Nat. Forum on Canada's Int. Relations 1994. *Address:* House of Commons, Human Resources Development Canada, 140 promenade du Portage, Hull, PQ, K1A 0J9, Canada.

PETTIT, Philip Noel, PH.D.; Irish/Australian professor of social and political theory; b. 20 Dec. 1945, Ballinasloe, Ireland; s. of Michael A. Pettit and Bridget C. Molony; m. Eileen McNally 1978; two s.; ed. Maynooth Coll., Nat. Univ. of Ireland, Queen's Univ. Belfast, Northern Ireland; lecturer, Univ. Coll. Dublin 1968–72, 1975–77; Research Fellow, Trinity Hall Cambridge, U.K. 1972–75; Prof. of Philosophy, Univ. of Bradford, U.K. 1977–83; Professorial Fellow, Research School of Social Sciences, A.N.U., Canberra 1983–89, Prof. of Social and Political Theory 1989–; Visiting Prof. of Philosophy, Columbia Univ., New York 1997–; Fellow Acad. of Social Sciences, Australia, Australian Acad. of Humanities; Hon. mem. Italian Soc. for Analytical Philosophy; Univ. Medal, Univ. of Helsinki 1992. *Publications:* Concept of Structuralism 1975, Judging Justice 1980, Semantics and Social Science (with G. Macdonald) 1981, Not Just Deserts: A Republican Theory of Criminal Justice (with J. Braithwaite) 1990, The Common Mind: An Essay on Psychology, Society and Politics 1992, Republicanism: A Theory of Freedom and Government 1997. *Leisure interests:* walking, tennis. *Address:* Research School of Social Sciences, Australian National University, Canberra, A.C.T. 0200 (Office); 34 Euree Street, Reid, A.C.T. 2614, Australia (Home). *Telephone:* (02) 6249 2632 (Office); (02) 6249 1012 (Home). *Fax:* (02) 6247 8522.

PETTITI, Louis Edmond; French barrister; b. 14 Jan. 1916, Asnières; s. of Louis Pettiti and Clothile Mussino; m. Zina Cyrin 1952; two s.; ed. Park Univ.; joined the Bar, Paris 1935, Pres. 1978–79; Judge European Court of Human Rights 1980–; Vice-Pres. Soc. de législation comparée 1977; Pres. Soc. des Prisons 1985–88; mem. Nat. Cttee. of Human Rights 1985–89, French Branch, UNESCO 1985–89 (Pres. 1997), Bicentenary Mission 1987–89; UNESCO Prize 1978; Commdr., Ordre nat. du Mérite, Officer, Légion d'honneur, several foreign decorations. *Publications:* le procès Charansky 1979, Mission en Iran 1982, Audio Visuel (with others), Le Rôle actuel du Conseil d'Europe 1983, La cour européenne des droits de l'homme 1983, Liberté d'expression 1985, Aspects juridiques des droits de l'homme, Transexuels et droit 1992, Droits Fondamentaux. *Address:* 4 square La Bruyère, 75009 Paris, France.

PEUGEOT, Pierre; French business executive; b. 11 June 1932, Valentigney; s. of Rodolphe Peugeot and Clémence Seyrig; m. Liliane Seydoux Fornier de Clausonne 1955; two s. two d.; ed. Lycée Janson-de-Sailly, Paris and Centre de perfectionnement dans l'admin. des affaires, Paris; joined gen. man. Peugeot S.A., mem. Bd. and Dir.-Gen. 1972–; Gen. Man. and Vice-Pres. Admin. Bd. Aciers et Outillage Peugeot; Gen. Man. Ets. Peugeot Frères, Cie. Industrielle de Delle, Imprimerie Berger-Lavault; Vice-Pres. Equipements et Composants pour l'Automobile (ECIA) 1987–; Pres. Société foncière, financière et de participations 1991–, Bd. Dirs. of Gefco 1993–98 (Hon. Pres. 1998–); Pres. Advisory Bd. PSA Group Peugeot Citroën 1998–; Adviser on foreign trade 1969–; Chevalier, Légion d'honneur, Croix de la Valeur militaire. *Address:* Peugeot, 75 avenue de la Grande-Armée, 75116 Paris; Gefco, 77–81 rue du Mans, BP 313, 92402 Courbevoie Cedex, France.

PEUGEOT, Roland; French motor-car executive; b. 20 March 1926, Valentigney; s. of Jean-Pierre and Colette (née Boillat-Japy) Peugeot; m. Colette Mayesky 1949; two s.; ed. Lycées Janson-de-Sailly and Saint-Louis, Paris, and Harvard Business School, Mass., U.S.A.; Pres. Etablissements Peugeot Frères 1959–; Pres. du Conseil de Surveillance de Peugeot S.A. 1972–; mem. Bd. Automobiles Peugeot 1982–; Pres. Peugeot Talbot Belgique 1985; Dir. of subsidiaries and other cos. including L'Union et Le Phénix Espagnol 1974–, Champagne Laurent Perrier 1992–; Officier, Légion d'honneur, Officier des Arts et des Lettres. *Address:* 75 avenue de la Grande Armée, 75116 Paris (Office); 170 avenue Victor-Hugo, 75116 Paris, France (Home).

PEYNAUD, Pierre Jean Emile, PH.D.; French oenologist and engineer; b. 29 June 1912, Bordeaux; s. of Antoine Peynaud and Alexine (née Ferrier) Peynaud; m. Yvonne Jameau 1938; two s.; ed. Bordeaux Faculty of Science; Oenologist for Calvet, Bordeaux 1928–49; Head of Research, Bordeaux Centre of Oenology and Head of Educ., Bordeaux Inst. of Oenology 1949–77; Tech. Adviser on Oenology, France and abroad; mem. French Soc. and Soc. of Expert Chemists; Chevalier, Légion d'honneur; Officier des Palmes Académiques et du Mérite Agricole. *Publications:* Traité d'Oenologie 1947, Knowing and Making Wine 1986, The Taste of Wine 1987, Le Vin et les Jours 1988; 300 articles and scientific papers. *Address:* 26 avenue de Maréchal-de-Lattre-de-Tassigny, 33400 Talence, France.

PEYREFITTE, Alain; French politician, diplomatist and writer; b. 26 Aug. 1925, Najac, Aveyron; s. of Jean Peyrefitte and Augustine (Roux) Peyrefitte; m. Monique Luton 1948; one s. four d.; ed. Lycée de Montpellier, Univ. of Montpellier, Paris (Sorbonne), Ecole Normale Supérieure, Ecole Nationale d'Administration; Sec. Bonn 1949–52; Chargé, quai d'Orsay and Lecturer, Ecole Nat. d'Admin. 1952–54; Consul-Gen., Cracow 1954–56; Deputy Dir. of European Orgs. 1956–58; Counsellor of Foreign Affairs 1958; elected Deputy for Seine-et-Marne, Nat. Ass. 1958, 1962, 1967, 1968, 1973, 1978, defeated 1981 but won by-election 1982, elected 1986, 1988, 1993; Senator 1995–; Mayor of Provins 1965–; Rep. European Parl. and UN Gen. Ass. 1959–62; Sec. of State to Prime Minister (Information) April 1962, Minister for Repatriates Sept. 1962; Minister for Information 1962–66; Minister for Scientific Research and Atomic Questions 1966–67; Minister of Educ. 1967–68; Chair. Comm. of Cultural Educ. and Social Affairs, Nat. Ass. 1968–72; Rep. at UN Gen. Ass. 1969–71, 1993–95; Sec.-Gen. UDR (Gaullist Party) 1972–73; Minister of Admin. Reform and Planning 1973–74, of Culture and the Environment March–May 1974, of Justice 1977–81; mem. Acad. Française 1977–, Acad. of Moral and Political Sciences 1987–; Chair. Editorial Bd. Le Figaro 1983–; Chevalier Légion d'honneur, Commdr. des Palmes académiques, des Arts et Lettres. *Publications:* Rue d'Ulm, Le sentiment de confiance, Les roseaux froissés, Le mythe de Pénélope, Faut-il partager l'Algérie?, Quand la Chine s'éveillera, Le mal français, Réponses à la violence, Les chevaux du lac Ladoga (La Justice entre les extrêmes), Quand la rose se fanera, Chine immuable et changeante, Encore un effort M. le Président, L'aventure du XXe siècle, L'Empire immobile, Images de l'Empire immobile, La Tragédie chinoise, La Vision des Chinois (Un choc de cultures, I), La France en Désarroi, C'était de Gaulle, Du "miracle" en économie (leçons au Collège de France), la Société de confiance, La Chine s'est éveillée, Le Regard des Anglais (Un choc de cultures, II). *Leisure interests:* skiing, water skiing, riding. *Address:* 111 rue du Ranelagh, Paris 16e., France. *Telephone:* (1) 42.36.22.56. *Fax:* (1) 42.21.62.80.

PEYREFITTE, (Pierre) Roger, B.A.; French author; b. 17 Aug. 1907, Castres (Tarn); s. of Jean Peyrefitte and Eugénie Jamme; ed. Coll. d'Ardouane (Hérault), du Caousou (Toulouse), Lycée (Foix), Toulouse Univ., Ecole des Sciences Politiques, Paris; joined Diplomatic Service 1931; Attaché, Ministry of Foreign Affairs 1931–33, 1938–40; Sec. Athens 1933–38; resigned 1940; re-instated 1943, mem. Del. of French Govt. in occupied France 1943–44; dismissed 1945; re-instated by judgement of Council of State 1962; judgement annulled 1978. *Publications:* Les amitiés particulières (Prix Théophraste Renaudot) 1944–45, Mademoiselle de Murville 1946, Le prince des neiges 1947, L'oracle 1948, Les amours singulières 1949, La mort d'une mère 1950, Les ambassades 1951, Du Vésuve à l'Etna 1952, La fin des ambassades 1953, Les clés de St. Pierre 1955, Jeunes proies 1956, Chevaliers de Malte 1957, L'exilé de Capri 1959, Le spectateur nocturne 1960, Les fils de la lumière 1961, La nature du prince 1963, Les Juifs 1965, Notre amour 1967, Les Américains 1968, Des Français 1970, La Coloquinte 1971, Manouche 1972, La muse garçonnière 1973, Tableaux de chasse ou la vie extraordinaire de Fernand Legros 1976, Propos secrets 1977, La jeunesse d'Alexandre 1977, L'enfant de coeur 1978, Roy 1979, Les conquêtes d'Alexandre 1979, Propos Secrets II 1980, Alexandre le Grand 1981, L'Illustre écrivain 1982, La soutane rouge 1983, Voltaire, sa Jeunesse et son Temps 1985, L'innominato, nouveaux propos secrets 1989, Réflexion sur De Gaulle 1992, Voltaire et Frédéric II 1992, Retours en Sicile 1996, C'était de Gaulle 1998 (Vol. 2). *Leisure interests:* walking, collecting antiques. *Address:* 9 avenue du Maréchal Maunoury, 75016 Paris, France.

PEYRELEVADE, Jean; French business executive; b. 24 Oct. 1939, Marseille; s. of Paul Peyrelevade and Nadia Benveniste; m. Anne Chavy 1962; three s. one d.; ed. Faculté de droit de Paris, Ecole Nat. de l'aviation civile; fmr. armaments and aviation engineer; Dir. Dept. of Foreign Business, Crédit Lyonnais 1973–82; Asst. Dir. Cabinet of M Pierre Mauroy 1982; Pres. Cie. Financière de Suez 1983–86; Pres. Banque Stern 1986–88; Chair. Union des Assurances de Paris 1988–93; Chair. Crédit Lyonnais Nov. 1993–; Govt. Rep. on Bd. of Renault 1996–; mem. Econ. and Social Council 1994–. *Publications:* la Mort du Dollar 1974, l'Economie de Spéculation 1978, Economie de l'Entreprise 1989, Pour un Capitalisme Intelligent 1993. *Address:* Crédit Lyonnais SA, 19 blvd. des Italiens, 75002 Paris (Office); 61 avenue Charles de Gaulle, 92200 Neuilly-sur-Seine, France (Home).

PEYTON OF YEOVIL, Baron (Life Peer), cr. 1983, of Yeovil in the County of Somerset; **John Wynne William Peyton,** P.C.; British politician; b. 13 Feb. 1919, London; m. 2nd Mary Constance Wyndham 1966; two s. (one deceased) one d. from first marriage; ed. Eton Coll. and Trinity Coll. Oxford; called to the Bar 1945; Conservative M.P. for Yeovil 1951–83; Parl. Sec., Ministry of Power 1962–64; Minister for Transport Industries 1970–74; Shadow Leader of Commons 1974–76; Opposition Spokesman for Agric. 1976–79; Chair. Texas Instruments Ltd. 1974–90; Chair. British Alcan Aluminium PLC 1987–91; Chair. Zoo Operations Ltd. 1988–91. *Publication:* Without Benefit of Laundry (autobiog.) 1997. *Address:* The Old Malt House, Hinton St. George, Somerset, TA17 8SE, England (Home).

PFAFF, Judy; American artist; b. 22 Sept. 1946, London, England; ed. Wayne State Univ., Detroit, S. Illinois Univ., Univ. of Washington and Yale Univ.; numerous solo exhbns. including Webb & Parsons Gallery, New York 1974 and Daniel Weinberg Gallery, Los Angeles 1984; numerous group exhbns. including Razor Gallery, New York 1973 and Holly Solomon Gallery, New York 1984, Whitney Museum of American Art, Contemporary Art Museum, Houston, Tex., Wacoal Art Center, Tokyo, Japan, Brooklyn Museum, Venice Biennale, Museum of Modern Art, New York; Guggenheim Fellowship for Sculpture.

PFEFFER, Philip Maurice, M.A.; American company executive; b. 20 Jan. 1945, St. Louis; s. of Philip McRae and Jeanne (Kaufman) Pfeffer; m. Pamela Jean Korte 1965; three s.; ed. South Illinois Univ., Vanderbilt Univ.; joined Genesco Inc., Nashville 1968, Pres. Genesco Export co. 1970–75; Dir. Financial Planning, Ingram Distribution Group Inc., Nashville 1976–77, Vice-Pres. Finance and Admin. 1977–78, Exec. Vice-Pres. 1978, Pres. and C.E.O. 1978–81, Dir. 1978–95, Chair. of Bd. and C.E.O. 1981–95, Exec. Vice-Pres. Ingram Industries Inc. 1981–95, Dir. 1981–95; Pres. and C.O.O. Random House 1996–; Instructor in Finance and Econs., Univ. of Tenn., Nashville 1968–77; lecturer in Corp. Finance, Vanderbilt Univ. 1972–77. *Leisure* *interests:* scouting, sailing, water sports, landscaping. *Address:* Random House Inc., 201 East 50th Street, New York, NY 10022 (Office); 836 Treemont Court, Nashville, TN 37220, U.S.A. (Home).

PFEIFFER, Didier-Bernard, LIC. EN DROIT; French business executive; b. 3 Nov. 1938, Paris; s. of Jacques Pfeiffer and Denise Pontzen; m. Maryse Bloch 1961; three d.; ed. Lycée Pasteur, Neuilly, Univ. de Paris, Inst. d'études politiques de Paris, Ecole Nat. d'Admin.; civil servant Treasury Dept., Ministry of Economy and Finance 1966–68, Head of Dept. Office of Minister of Econ. and Finance 1968–71; Financial Attaché French Embassy, Washington 1971; a Deputy Dir. World Bank 1972; Dir. Financial Operations l'Union des Assurances de Paris (UAP) 1973, Dir. of Investments 1976–84, Man. Dir. 1984–91, Dir. 1991–94, Vice-Pres. and Man. Dir. 1994–96; Pres. Supervisory Bd. UAP-Vie, UAP-IARD 1994–96; Pres. Vinci-BV 1994, Groupe des assurances nationales (GAN) 1996–; Pres. Société d'Actions sélectionnées (Sicav) 1976, La Réunion-Vie 1989, Groupement des assurances de personnes (GAP) de la Féd. Française des assurances 1989–; fmr. Vice-Pres. Scor SA, UAP Int.; Dir. Parfinance, Fibelpar SA, Electrafina 1996–; Asst. Prin. la Sofres; Chevalier, Légion d'honneur, Officier, Ordre nat. du Mérite. *Address:* GAN, 2 rue Pillet-Will, 75448 Paris, Cédex 9 (Office); 38 rue de Courcelles, 75008 Paris, France (Home). *Telephone:* (1) 42476082 (Office); (1) 42251282 (Home).

PFEIFFER, Eckhard, M.B.A.; American computer executive; Exec. Vice-Pres., Chief Operations Officer, Head of Int. Operations, Compaq Computer Corpn. 1983–91, Pres., C.E.O. 1991–99. *Address:* Compaq Computer Corporation, P.O. Box 692000, 20555 State Highway, Houston, TX 77269, U.S.A.

PFEIFFER, Michelle; American actress; b. 29 April 1957, Orange Co., Calif.; m. 1st Peter Horton (divorced 1987); one adopted d.; m. 2nd David Kelly 1993; one s.; ed. Fountain Valley High School. *Films include:* Grease 2, Into the Night, The Witches of Eastwick, Sweet Liberty, Married to the Mob, Tequila Sunrise 1989, Dangerous Liaisons 1989, The Fabulous Baker Boys 1989, The Russia House 1989, Love Field, Frankie and Johnny 1991, Batman Returns 1992, The Age of Innocence 1993, Wolf 1994, My Posse Don't Do Homework 1994, Dangerous Minds, Up Close and Personal, To Gillian On Her 37th Birthday, One Fine Day 1997, A Thousand Acres 1997, Privacy 1997, The Story of US 1999. *Address:* ICM, 8492 Wilshire Blvd., Beverly Hills, CA 90211, U.S.A.

PFLIMLIN, Pierre, DR. EN D.; French politician; b. 5 Feb. 1907, Roubaix; s. of Jules Pflimlin and Léonie (née Schwartz) Pflimlin; m. Marie-Odile Heinrich 1939 (deceased); one s. two d.; ed. Lycée de Mulhouse, Institut Catholique, Paris, and Strasbourg Univ.; mem. of Bar, Strasbourg 1933–64; served French Army 1939–40; elected Deputy for Bas-Rhin, Nat. Ass. 1946, 1951, 1956, 1958, 1962; Under-Sec. for Nat. Economy 1946; Minister of Agric. 1947–49, 1950–51, for Foreign Econ. Relations 1951–52, for Overseas Territories 1952–53, of Finance 1955–56 and 1957–58; Prime Minister May 1958; Minister of State, de Gaulle Cabinet, 1958–59; Pres. Mouvement Républicain Populaire 1956–59; Co-Pres. "Centre Démocratique" Group, Nat. Ass. 1962–63; Mayor of Strasbourg 1959–83; Minister of Co-operation, April-May 1962; Pres. of Ass. of Council of Europe 1963–66; mem. European Parl. 1979–89, Pres. 1984–87; Pres. Consortium of Rhine Navigation 1971–81; Croix de guerre. *Publications:* Perspectives sur notre économie, L'industrie de Mulhouse (with H. Laufenburger), La structure économique du IIIe Reich (with H. Laufenburger), L'Alsace—Destin et volonté (with René Uhrich), L'Europe communautaire (with Raymond Legrand-Lane), Mémoires d'un Européen de la IVe à la Ve République 1991. *Address:* 24 avenue de la Paix, 67000 Strasbourg, France. *Telephone:* 88 37 32 35.

PHAM THE DUYET; Vietnamese fmr. politician and trades union leader; economist; fmr. mine man.; fmr. Pres. Viet Nam Gen. Confed. of Labour; leader CP of Hanoi, Viet Nam 1987. *Address:* Communist Party of Viet Nam, 1 Hoang Van Thu, Hanoi, Viet Nam.

PHAM VAN DONG; Vietnamese politician; b. 1 March 1906, Quang Nam Province (S. Viet Nam); close collaborator of Ho Chi Minh; underground communist worker from 1925; imprisoned by French authorities for seven years; upon release in 1936, resumed revolutionary activities; a founder of the Revolutionary League for the Independence of Viet Nam (the Viet-Minh) 1941; mem. Lao Dong (Viet Nam Workers') Party (now CP of Viet Nam) 1951–; Minister for Foreign Affairs, Democratic Repub. of Viet Nam 1954–61, Prime Minister 1955–76; Prime Minister, Socialist Repub. of Viet Nam 1981–86 (called Chair. Council of Ministers 1981–86), Adviser Dec. 1986–; Vice-Chair. Nat. Defence Council July 1976. *Address:* c/o Office of the Chairman, Council of Ministers, Hanoi, Viet Nam.

PHAM VAN KY; Vietnamese writer; b. 1916; ed. Secondary School, Hanoi, and Univ. of Paris; went to France 1939; prepared thesis on religion for the Institut des Hautes Etudes Chinoises; Grand Prix du Roman, Académie Française 1961. *Publications:* Fleurs de jade (poems), L'homme de nulle part (short stories) 1946, Frères de sang (novel) 1947, Celui qui régnera (novel) 1954, Les yeux courroucés (novel) 1958, Les contemporains (novel) 1959, Perdre la demeure (novel) 1961, Poème sur soie (poems) 1961, Des femmes assises çà et là (novel) 1964, Mémoires d'un eunuque (novel) 1966, Le rideau de pluie (play) 1974.

PHAN VAN KHAI; Vietnamese politician; b. 25 Dec. 1933, Saigon (now Ho Chi Minh City); involved in revolutionary activities from 1947, in N. Viet Nam 1954–60; joined CP 1959; student, Moscow Nat. Univ. of Econs. 1960–65; fmrly. with Gen. Dept. of State Planning Cttee., fmr. econ. researcher; in communist-controlled areas of S. Viet Nam 1973; Deputy Dir. Aid Planning Dept. of Nat. Reunification Cttee. 1974–75; Deputy Dir. Planning Dept., Ho Chi Minh City 1976–78, Dir. 1979–80; Deputy Mayor, Ho Chi Minh City 1979–80, Perm. Deputy Mayor 1981–84, Mayor 1985–89; Chair. People's Cttee. of Ho Chi Minh City 1985–89; perm. mem. Ho Chi Minh City CP Cttee. 1979–80, Deputy Sec. 1981–84; alt. mem. CP Cen. Cttee. 1982–84, mem. 1984–, mem. Political Bureau 1991–; Chair. State Planning Cttee. 1989–91; Deputy Chair. Council of Ministers 1991–92; Perm. Deputy Prime Minister of Viet Nam 1992–97; Prime Minister of Viet Nam Sept. 1997–. *Address:* Office of the Prime Minister, Hanoi, Viet Nam.

PHANTOG; Chinese mountaineer; b. Aug. 1939, Xigazê, Tibet; d. of Cirhen Phantog and Cijiu Phantog; m. Jia-shang Deng 1963; one s. two d.; ed. Cen. Coll. of Nationalities; first Chinese woman to climb Everest 1975; Deputy Dir. Wuxi Sports and Physical Culture Comm. 1981–. *Leisure interests:* table tennis, badminton. *Address:* Wuxi Sports and Physical Culture Commission, Jiangsu, People's Republic of China. *Telephone:* 225810.

PHARAND, Donat, O.C., Q.C., LL.M., LL.D., S.J.D., F.R.S.C.; Canadian professor of international law; b. 7 Dec. 1922, Hanmer, Ont.; s. of Alphonse Pharand and Georgina Henri; three s. one d.; ed. Dalhousie Univ., Université de Paris, Hague Acad. of Int. Law and Univ. of Michigan; law practice 1956–59; Prof. of Law, Common Law Section, Univ. of Ottawa 1959–65, Chair. Dept. of Political Science 1965–67, Prof. of Int. Law, Civil Law Section 1968–88, Prof. Emer. 1988, on leave as Academic in Residence, Dept. of External Affairs 1977–78, Dir. Grad. Studies, Faculty of Law 1979–82; Visiting Prof. and Lecturer, McGill Univ. 1970, Univ. of N.S.W. 1976, Louvain 1976, Thessalonica 1977, Toulouse 1980, Nantes 1980, Dalhousie 1983, Los Andes, Bogota 1985; Pres. Canadian Council on Int. Law 1976–78. *Publications:* The Law of the Sea of the Arctic, with special reference to Canada 1973, The Northwest Passage: Arctic Straits 1984, Canada's Arctic Waters in International Law 1988, The Continental Shelf and the Exclusive Economic Zone (with U. Leanza) 1993. *Leisure interests:* travelling, reading, cottaging. *Address:* The Rockcliffe Arms, 124 Springfield Road, Apt. 100, Ottawa, Ont., K1M 2C8, Canada.

PHARAON, Ghaith Rashad, PH.D., M.B.A.; Saudi Arabian business executive; b. 7 Sept. 1940, Riyadh; ed. Stanford Univ., Harvard Univ.; Founder Saudi Arabia Research and Devt. Corpn. (Redec) 1965, now Chair. of Bd. and Dir.-Gen.; Chair. Bd. Saudi Arabian Parsons Ltd., Saudi Automotive Industries Ltd., Redec Daelim Ltd., Interstal, Saudi Chemical Processors Ltd., Arabian Maritime Co., Saudi Inland Transport, etc.; Vice-Chair. Jezirah Bank Ltd., Saudi Light Industries Ltd., Arabian Chemical Industries Ltd.; mem. Bd. Okaz Publications, Tihama; Commendatore (Italy); King Abdul Aziz Award. *Address:* P.O. Box 1935, Jeddah (Office); Ghaith Pharaon Residence, Ruwais, Jeddah, Saudi Arabia (Home).

PHELAN, John Joseph, Jr., B.B.A.; American fmr. stock exchange executive and company director; b. 7 May 1931, New York; ed. Adelphi Univ., New York; with Nash and Co. stockbrokers, New York 1955–62, partner 1957–62; Man. partner Phelan and Co., New York 1962–72; Sr. partner Phelan, Silver, Vesce, Barry and Co., New York 1977–80; Pres. New York Stock Exchange 1980–84, Chair. and C.E.O. 1984; Chair. New York Futures Exchange 1979–85, Presidential Bd. of Advisors on Pvt. Sector Initiatives 1986–; Trustee Emer. Adelphi Univ.; mem. Bd. Dirs. Avon Products, Eastman Kodak, Met Life, Merrill Lynch, Sonat Inc.; mem. Securities Industries Assen. (mem. Governing Bd. 1978–79, Exec. Cttee. 1979–80); Hon. LL.D. (Adelphi) 1987, (Hamilton Coll.) 1980, (Niagara) 1985; Dr. h.c. (Notre Dame Univ.) 1986; Kt. Sovereign Mil. Order of Malta; Kt. Holy Sepulchre, Jerusalem, other awards and decorations. *Address:* 108 Forest Avenue, Locust Valley, New York, NY 11560, U.S.A.

PHELPS, Edmund Strother, PH.D.; American economist; b. 26 July 1933, Evanston, Ill.; s. of Edmund S. Phelps and Florence Stone Phelps; m. Viviana Montdor 1974; ed. Amherst Coll. and Yale Univ.; Research Economist, RAND Corpn. 1959–60; taught Yale Univ. 1960–66; Prof., Univ. of Pa. 1966–71, Columbia Univ. 1971–78, New York Univ. 1977–78, Columbia Univ. 1979–82, McVickar Prof. of Political Econ., Columbia Univ. 1982–; Sr. Adviser Brookings Inst. 1976–; Econ. Adviser EBRD 1991–94; mem. N.A.S.; Hon. D. H. (Amherst Coll.). *Publications:* Golden Rules of Economic Growth 1966, Microeconomic Foundations of Employment and Inflation Theory (Ed.) 1970, Studies in Macroeconomic Theory: vol. 1, 2 1979, 1980, Political Economy: an Introductory Text 1985, The Slump in Europe 1988, Seven Schools of Macroeconomic Thought 1990, Structural Slumps 1994, Rewarding Work 1997. *Leisure interest:* music. *Address:* Department of Economics, Columbia University, New York, NY 10027 (Office); 45 East 89th Street, New York, NY 10128, U.S.A. *Telephone:* (212) 722-6688; (212) 854-2060.

PHIEU, General Le Kha; Vietnamese politician and army officer; political commissar; has held political posts throughout mil. career; Chief Political Dept., Vietnamese Army; Sec.-Gen. Vietnamese Communist Party 1997–. *Address:* Communist Party of Viet Nam, 1 Hoang Van Thu, Hanoi, Viet Nam.

PHILARET (Kyrill Varfolomeyevich Vakhromeyev); Russian ecclesiastic; b. 21 March 1935, Moscow; s. of Varfolomey and Aleksandra V.

Vakhromeyev; ed. Moscow Theological Seminary and Moscow Theological Acad.; became monk 1959, ordained as a priest 1961; lecturer, Asst. Prof., Moscow Theological Acad. 1961–65, Rector 1966–73; Bishop of Tikhvin 1965, of Dmitrov 1966; Vice-Chair. Dept. of External Church Relations, Moscow Patriarchate 1968–71, Chair. 1981–; Archbishop 1971; Archbishop of Berlin and Middle Europe 1973–78; Metropolitan 1975, of Minsk and Byelorussia 1978, of Minsk and Grodno, Patriarchal Exarch of All Byelorussia 1989, of Minsk and Slutsk, of All Belarus; Perm. mem. Holy Synod of Russian Orthodox Church 1981–, Chair. Foreign Relations Dept. 1987–89, Theological Comm. 1993–; Medal of Frantsysk Skorina; Order of St. Vladimir, Order of St. Sergey of Radonezh, Order of Friendship of the Peoples, Order of Daniil of Moscow. *Publications:* Russian Orthodox Church Relations to Western Non-Orthodox Churches, St. Cyril and Methodius' Works in the Territory of The Russian State in Russian Historical Literature, Patriotic Character of Patriarch Aleksiy, etc. *Address:* 220004 Minsk, 10 Osvobozdeniya Street, Belarus. *Telephone:* 23 44 95; 23 25 70. *Fax:* 22 11 19.

PHILIP, John Robert, A.O., B.C.E., D.SC., F.A.A., F.R.S.; Australian physicist and mathematician; b. 18 Jan. 1927, Ballarat, Victoria; s. of the late Percival N. Philip and Ruth (née Osborne) Philip; m. Frances J. Long 1949; two s. one d.; ed. Scotch Coll., Melbourne and Queen's Coll., Melbourne Univ.; Research Asst. Melbourne Univ. 1947–48; Engineer Queensland Irrigation Comm. 1948–51; joined research staff at CSIRO 1951, Sr. Principal Research Scientist 1961–63, Chief Research Scientist and Asst. Chief, Div. of Plant Industry 1963–71, Chief, Centre for Environmental Mechanics 1971–80, 1983–91, Assoc. mem. CSIRO Exec. 1978; First Dir. Inst. of Physical Sciences 1980–83; CSIRO Fellow 1991–92, Fellow Emer. 1992–; Visiting Fellow Commonership, Trinity Coll. Cambridge 1994; numerous visiting appointments at univs. in U.K. and U.S.A.; Foreign mem. All-Union (now Russian) Acad. of Agricultural Sciences 1991; Foreign Assoc. U.S. Nat. Acad. of Eng. 1995; numerous honours and awards, including Int. Hydrology Prize (UNESCO, WMO and Int. Asscn. of Hydrological Sciences) 1995. *Publications:* some 300 papers in scientific journals on soil and porous medium physics, fluid mechanics, hydrology, micrometeorology, physical chem., mathematical and physical aspects of physiology and ecology. *Leisure interests:* reading, writing, architecture. *Address:* CSIRO Land and Water, G.P.O. Box 1666, Canberra, A.C.T. 2601 (Office); 42 Vasey Crescent, Campbell, A.C.T. 2612, Australia (Home). *Telephone:* (02) 6246-5645 (Office); (02) 6247-8958 (Home). *Fax:* (02) 6246-5560.

PHILIPPOU, Andreas N., PH.D.; Cypriot politician and university professor; b. 15 July 1944, Katokopia; s. of Nicholas Philippou and Maria G. Protopapa; m. Athina Roustani 1984; three d.; ed. Pancyprian Gymnasium, Athens Univ., Greece, Univ. of Wisconsin, U.S.A.; Teaching and Research Asst., Univ. of Wis., Asst. Prof. of Math., Univ. of Tex., El Paso, Asst. then Assoc. Prof. of Math., American Univ. of Beirut, Lebanon, Prof. of Business Admin., Beirut Univ. Coll., Prof. of Math., subsequently Pres. of Math. Dept., and Vice-Rector, Univ. of Patras, Greece; Minister of Educ. 1988–90; Pres. Preparatory Cttee. for establishment of Univ. of Cyprus, then first Pres. Interim Governing Bd. of Univ. 1988–90; mem. House of Reps. 1991–, mem. House Cttees. on Educ. and the Budget, Council of IPU, Rapporteur for Kosovo 1998, for the Middle East 1999; fmr. Vice-Pres. Hellenic Aerospace Industry; Hon. Pres. Math. Asscn. of Cyprus; Grande Ufficiale Repub. of Italy. *Leisure interests:* swimming, sailing. *Publications:* 56 research papers, ed. 7 books. *Address:* 26 Atlantis Street, 2107 Nicosia, Cyprus. *Telephone:* 2-336360. *Fax:* 2-336366.

PHILIPS, Sir Cyril Henry, Kt., M.A., PH.D., D.LITT., LL.D.; British professor of oriental history; b. 27 Dec. 1912, Worcester; s. of William H. Philips and Mary E. Philips; m. 1st Dorcas Rose 1939 (deceased); one s. (deceased) one d.; m. 2nd Joan Rosemary Marshall 1975; ed. Rock Ferry High School and Univs. of Liverpool and London; Asst. Lecturer in Indian History, S.O.A.S., London Univ. 1936, Lecturer 1939, Sr. Lecturer 1945; war service 1940–46; Prof. of Oriental History and Head Dept. of History, S.O.A.S. 1946–80, Dir. S.O.A.S. 1957–76; Vice-Chancellor, Univ. of London 1972–76; Chair. Royal Comm. on Criminal Procedure 1978–80, India Cttee. of Inter-Univ. Council and British Council 1972, Police Complaints Bd. 1980–85; Adviser to Sec. of State for Home Affairs 1985–87; Pres. Royal Asiatic Soc. 1979–88; mem. Council, Chinese Univ. of Hong Kong 1965–78, Inter-University Council for Higher Educ. Overseas 1967–78; Chair. Council on Tribunals 1986–90; Hon. D.Litt. (Warwick) 1967, LL.D. (Hong Kong Univ.) 1971; Hon. D.Litt. (Bristol) 1983, (Sri Lanka); Bishop Chavasse Prize, Gladstone Memorial Fellow, Frewen Lord Prize (Royal Empire Soc.), Alexander Prize (Royal Historical Soc.), Sir Percy Sykes Memorial Medal, James Smart Police Medal 1979, Bengal Asiatic Soc. Gold Medal 1984. *Publications:* The East India Company 1940, 1961, Handbook of Oriental History 1951, 1960, Correspondence of David Scott 1951, Historians of India, Pakistan and Ceylon 1961, The Evolution of India and Pakistan 1962, Politics and Society in India 1963, Fort William India House Correspondence 1964, History of the School of Oriental and African Studies 1917–1967 1967, The Partition of India 1970, The Correspondence of Lord William Bentinck; Governor General of India 1828–35 1977, The Police in Politics 1982, Reform of the Police Complaints System 1984, Beyond the Ivory Tower 1995. *Address:* c/o School of Oriental and African Studies, Malet Street, London, WC1E 7HP, England. *Telephone:* 0171-637 2388.

PHILIPSON, Lennart Carl, M.D., DR.MED.SCI.; Swedish professor of microbiology; b. 16 July 1929, Stockholm; s. of late Carl Philipson and Greta Svanstrom; m. Malin Jondal 1954; three s.; ed. Univ. of Uppsala; Asst. Prof. Inst. of Virology, Univ. of Uppsala 1958–59; Asst. Prof., Assoc. Prof. Swedish Medical Research Council, Univ. of Uppsala 1961–68; Founder and Dir. Wallenberg Lab. Univ. of Uppsala 1967–76; Prof. and Chair. Dept. of Microbiology, Univ. of Uppsala 1968–82; Dir.-Gen. European Molecular Biology Lab., Heidelberg 1982–93; Dir. Skirball Inst. of Biomolecular Medicine, New York Univ. Medical Center 1993–97; Prof. Dept. of Cell Biology, New York Univ. School of Medicine 1993–; Hon. Prof. Heidelberg Univ. 1985; Dr. h.c. (Turku) 1987, (Umeå) 1994. *Publications:* over 250 scientific publs. in fields of virology, microbiology, immunology, molecular biology and biochemistry. *Leisure interests:* sailing, golf. *Address:* New York University Medical Center, Skirball Institute, 3rd Floor, 550 First Avenue, New York, NY 10016, U.S.A. *Telephone:* (212) 263-8950. *Fax:* (212) 263-8951.

PHILLIPS, Alfredo; Mexican international finance official; b. 2 Sept. 1935, Mexico; s. of Howard S. Phillips and Dolores Olmedo; m. Maureen Greene 1960; two s. one d.; ed. Univs. of Mexico and London and American Univ.; Deputy Chief of Dept. of Banks and Chief, Dept. of Econ. and Fiscal Planning, Secr. of Finance and Public Credit, Mexico 1960–65; Sr. Loan Officer, Inter-American Devt. Bank, 1965–66; Alt. Exec. Dir., IMF 1966–68, Exec. Dir. 1968–70; Prof. of Trade Cycles, School of Business Admin., Univ. Iberoamericana Mexico 1961–63; Sec., Group of Latin American Govs. to the IMF and IBRD 1968–70; Man. Banco de México 1971–75, Deputy Dir. 1975–82; Treas. Bd. of Dirs. of Latin-American Bank for Foreign Trade 1978–, Vice-Chair. Deputies of Group of 24 1978–79, Chair. Deputies Intergovernmental Group of 24 on Int. Monetary Affairs 1979–; Dir.-Gen. Foreign Trade Nat. Bank Mexico 1982–88; Amb. to Canada 1989. *Leisure interests:* golf, swimming. *Address:* c/o Secretariat of State for Foreign Affairs, Ricardo Flores Magón 1, Tlatelolco, 06995 México, DF, Mexico.

PHILLIPS, David, PH.D., F.R.S.C.; British professor of physical chemistry; b. 3 Dec 1939, Kendal, Westmorland (now Cumbria); s. of Stanley Phillips and Daphne Ivy Phillips (née Harris); m. Caroline L. Scoble 1970; one d.; ed. South Shields Grammar Tech. School and Univ. of Birmingham; Postdoctoral Fellow and Fulbright Scholar, Univ. of Tex., U.S.A. 1964–66; Visiting Scientist, Acad. of Sciences of U.S.S.R. 1966–67; Lecturer, Dept. of Chem., Univ. of Southampton 1967–73, Sr. Lecturer 1973–76, Reader 1976–80; Wolfson Prof. of Natural Philosophy, Royal Institution of G.B. 1980–89, Acting Dir. 1986, Deputy Dir. 1986–89; Prof. of Physical Chem., Imperial Coll. of Science, Tech. and Medicine 1989–, Head Dept. of Chem. 1992–; Spinks Lecturer, Univ. of Sask. 1979; Wilsmore Fellow, Univ. of Melbourne 1983–90; Vice-Pres. and Gen. Sec. B.A.A.S. 1987–89, Nyholm Lecturer, Royal Soc. of Chem. 1994; Faraday Award for Public Understanding of Science, Royal Soc. 1997. *Publications:* Time-correlated single-photon counting 1984, Polymer Photophysics 1985, Time-Resolved Laser Raman Spectroscopy 1987, Jet Spectroscopy and Dynamics 1994. *Leisure interests:* music, theatre, popularization of science. *Address:* Department of Chemistry, ICSTM, Exhibition Road, London, SW7 2AZ (Office); 195 Barnett Wood Lane, Ashtead, Surrey, KT21 2LP, England. (Home). *Telephone:* 0171-594 5716 (Office); (013722) 74385 (Home).

PHILLIPS, Sir Horace, K.C.M.G.; British diplomatist (retd.); b. 31 May 1917, Glasgow, Scotland; s. of Samuel Phillips and Polly Yaffie; m. Idina Morgan 1944; one s. one d.; ed. Hillhead High School, Glasgow; Inland Revenue Dept., London 1935–39; Indian Army 1940–47; Consul, Persia and Afghanistan 1947–50; Foreign Office 1951–53; Chargé d'affaires, Saudi Arabia 1953–56; Aden Protectorate Sec. 1956–60; Counsellor, Teheran 1960–64; Deputy Political Resident, Persian Gulf 1964–66; Amb. to Indonesia 1966–68; High Commr. in Tanzania 1968–72; Amb. to Turkey 1973–77; Resident Rep. of Taylor Woodrow Int. in Iran 1978–79, in Hong Kong 1979–83, in Bahrain 1984–85, Beijing 1985–87; Lecturer in Diplomacy, Bilkent Univ., Ankara, Turkey 1988–92, 1997, Erciyes Univ., Kayseri, Turkey 1993–94; Hon. LL.D. (Glasgow); Order of the Taj (Iran). *Publications:* Envoy Extraordinary: A Most Unlikely Ambassador 1995, Ihsan Doğramaci: A Remarkable Turk 1997. *Leisure interests:* languages, long-distance driving. *Address:* 34A Sheridan Road, Merton Park, London, SW19 3HP, England. *Telephone:* 0181-542 3836.

PHILLIPS, John Harber, A.C., LL.B.; Australian judge and author; b. 18 Oct. 1933, Melbourne; s. of Anthony Phillips and I. Muriel Phillips; m. Helen Rogers 1962; two s. one d.; ed. Presentation Convent, De La Salle Coll. and Univ. of Melbourne; mem. Bar of Victoria 1959–84; Q.C. 1975; Judge, Supreme Court of Victoria 1984–90; Judge, Fed. Court of Australia 1990–91; Chief Justice of Victoria 1991–; Chair. Nat. Inst. of Forensic Science, Victoria Inst. of Forensic Medicine, Council of Australia and N.Z. Law Reform, Vic. Law Foundation, Vic. Council of Legal Educ., Attorney-Gen.'s Council of Law Reform. *Publications:* Forensic Science and the Expert Witness (jtly.), Advocacy with Honour, The Trial of Ned Kelly; plays: By a Simple Majority—The Trial of Socrates, Conference with Counsel, The Cab-Rank Rule, The Eureka Advocates. *Address:* Chief Justice's Chambers, 210 William Street, Melbourne 3000, Australia. *Telephone:* (03) 6036139. *Fax:* (03) 9603 6200.

PHILLIPS, Leon Francis, PH.D.; New Zealand professor of chemistry and novelist; b. 14 July 1935; m. Pamela A. Johnstone 1959; two s.; ed. Westport Tech. Coll., Christchurch Boys' High School, Univs. of Canterbury (N.Z.) and Cambridge; Upper Atmosphere Chem. Group, McGill Univ. 1961; lecturer, Univ. of Canterbury 1962, Prof. of Chem. 1966–; Visiting Prof. Univ. of Washington 1968, Monash Univ. 1969; Visiting Fellow, Balliol Coll. Oxford

1975, Japan Soc. for Promotion of Science 1984; Visiting Scholar, Rice Univ., Houston 1987; SERC Research Fellow Univ. Birmingham 1989; Harkness Fellow 1968; Fulbright Award 1980; Corday-Morgan Medal (Royal Soc. of Chem.), Hector Medal, (Royal Soc. of N.Z.), Easterfield and ICI prizes (N.Z. Inst. of Chem.). *Publications:* Basic Quantum Chemistry, Electronics for Experimenters, Chemistry of the Atmosphere (with M. J. McEwan), First Year Chemistry (with J. M. Coxon and J. E. Fergusson); over 150 scientific papers; novels: Fire in his Hand 1978, The Phoenix Reaction 1979, Ritual Fire Dance 1980. *Leisure interests:* sailing, skiing, reading, writing. *Address:* University of Canterbury, Private Bag 4800, Christchurch 1; 12 Maidstone Road, Christchurch 4, New Zealand.

PHILLIPS, Owen Martin, PH.D., F.R.S.; American professor of science and engineering; b. 30 Dec. 1930, Parramatta, N.S.W., Australia; s. of Richard Keith Phillips and Madeline Constance (Lofts); m. Merle Winifred Simons 1953; two s. two d.; ed. Univ. of Sydney, Australia and Univ. of Cambridge; ICI Fellow, Univ. of Cambridge 1955–57, Fellow, St. John's Coll. 1957–60; Assoc. Prof., Johns Hopkins Univ., Baltimore, Md., U.S.A. 1960–63; Asst. Dir. of Research, Cambridge Univ. 1961–64; Prof. of Geophysical Mechanics and Geophysics, Johns Hopkins Univ. 1963–75, Chair. Dept. of Earth and Planetary Sciences 1968–78, Decker Prof. of Science and Eng. 1978–; Assoc. Ed., Journal of Fluid Mechanics 1964–95; mem. U.S. Nat. Acad. of Eng.; Adams Prize, Cambridge Univ. 1965, Sverdrup Gold Medal, American Meteorological Soc. 1974. *Publications:* The Dynamics of the Upper Ocean 1966 (Russian edns. 1969, 1979), The Heart of the Earth 1968, The Last Chance Energy Book 1979, Wave Dynamics and Radio Probing of the Ocean Surface (Ed.) 1985, Flow and Reactions in Permeable Rocks 1991; many research publs. in the tech. literature. *Leisure interest:* sailing. *Address:* The Johns Hopkins University, Baltimore, MD 21218; 23 Merrymount Road, Baltimore, MD 21210, U.S.A. *Telephone:* (410) 516-7036. *Fax:* (410) 516-7933.

PHILLIPS, Roger Julian Noel, PH.D., F.INST.P.; British research physicist (retd.); b. 25 Dec. 1930, Jinan, China; s. of E.L. Phillips and E.B. Phillips (née Gibbon); m. Audrey Helen Symons 1954; two s. two d.; ed. Lunghwa Acad., Shanghai, Mill Hill School, London, Trinity Coll. Cambridge; Research Fellow, A.E.R.E., Harwell 1955–58, Staff mem. 1958–67; Head of High Energy Physics Theory Group, Rutherford Lab., Chilton, Oxon. 1968–91, Head of Theory and Data Handling Div., Rutherford Appleton Lab., Chilton 1987–91; Visiting Prof., Univ. of Calif. at Riverside 1971, Univ. of Wis. 1977; Visiting Fellow Japan Soc. for the Promotion of Science 1979; Mayhew Prize, Cambridge 1952, Rutherford Medal and Prize, Inst. of Physics 1990. *Publications:* Collider Physics (with V. Barger) 1987; over 250 papers in scientific journals. *Leisure interests:* hiking, sketching, sailing, travel, languages, music. *Address:* 14 Holland Road, Abingdon, Oxon., OX14 1PH, England. *Telephone:* (01235) 521926.

PHILLIPS, Siân, B.A.; British actress; b. Bettws, Wales; d. of D. Phillips and Sally Phillips; m. 1st Peter O'Toole (q.v.) 1960 (divorced 1979); two d.; m. 2nd Robin Sachs 1979 (divorced 1992); ed. Pontardawe Grammar School, Univ. of Wales (Cardiff Coll.), RADA; child actress BBC Radio Wales and BBC TV Wales; newsreader and announcer and mem. BBC repertory co. 1953–55; toured for Welsh Arts Council with Nat. Theatre Co. 1953–55; Arts Council Bursary to study drama outside Wales 1955; 1978 Chichester Festival Season; Royal TV Soc. annual televised lecture 1992; Fellow, Cardiff Coll. (Univ. of Wales) 1982; Hon. Fellow Polytechnic Wales 1988, Gov. Welsh Coll. of Music and Drama; mem. Gorsedd of Bards (for services to drama in Wales) 1960; Hon. D.Litt. (Wales) 1984. *Stage appearances include:* Hedda Gabler 1959, Ondine and The Duchess of Malfi 1960–61 (first RSC season at Aldwych), The Lizard on the Rock 1961, Gentle Jack, Maxibules and the Night of the Iguana 1964, Ride a Cock Horse 1965, Man and Superman and Man of Destiny 1966, The Burglar 1967, Epitaph for George Dillon 1972, A Nightingale in Bloomsbury Square 1973, The Gay Lord Quex 1975, Spinechiller 1978, You Never Can Tell, Lyric, Hammersmith 1979, Pal Joey, Half Moon and Albery Theatres 1980 and 1981, Dear Liar 1982, Major Barbara, Nat. Theatre 1982, Peg (musical) 1984, Love Affair 1984, Gigi 1986, Thursday's Ladies 1987, Brel (musical) 1987–88, Paris Match 1989, Vanilla 1990, The Manchurian Candidate 1991, Painting Churches 1992, Ghosts (Cardiff and touring, Wales) (Artist of the Year nomination) 1993, The Lion in Winter 1994, Marlene, An Inspector Calls, Broadway 1995, A Little Night Music, Royal Nat. Theatre 1995–96, Marlene 1996–97, int. tour 1998. *Films include:* Becket 1963, Goodbye Mr. Chips (Critics' Circle Award, New York Critics' Award and Famous Seven Critics' Award 1969), Laughter in the Dark 1968, Murphy's War 1970, Under Milk Wood 1971, The Clash of the Titans 1979, Dune 1983, Ewok II, The Two Mrs Grenvilles, ("Siân" Cineclaire), Valmont 1988, Dark River 1990, Age of Innocence 1992, House of America 1996. *TV appearances include:* Shoulder to Shoulder 1974, How Green was my Valley (BAFTA Award) 1975, I, Claudius (Royal Television Soc. Award and BAFTA Award 1978) 1976, Boudicca, Off to Philadelphia in the Morning 1977, The Oresteia of Aeschylus 1978, Crime and Punishment 1979, Tinker, Tailor, Soldier, Spy 1979, Sean O'Casey (RTE) 1980, Churchill: The Wilderness Years 1981, How Many Miles to Babylon 1982, Smiley's People 1982, George Borrow 1983, A Painful Case (RTE), Beyond All Reason, Murder on the Exchange, The Shadow of the Noose (BBC series) 1988, Snow Spider (HTV serial) 1988, Freddie & Max, Emlyn's Moon, Perfect Scoundrels 1990, Heidi 1992, The Borrowers (series) 1992, 1993, The Chestnut Soldier (B.A.F.T.A. nomination) 1992, Huw Weldon TV Lecture 1993, Summer Silence (HTV musical), The Vacillations of Poppy Carew (BBC), Mind to Kill (TV film series), Scolds Bridle 1997, The Aristocrats (series) 1998, Alice Through the Looking Glass (feature film) 1998. *Recordings include:* Bewitched, Bothered and Bewildered, Pal Joey, Peg, I Remember Mama, Gigi, A Little Night Music 1990, A Little Night Music (2) 1995, Marlene 1996. *Publication:* Siân Phillips' Needlepoint 1987. *Leisure interests:* canvas embroidery, gardening, painting. *Address:* c/o Saraband Ltd., 265 Liverpool Road, London, N1 1HS, England.

PHILLIPS, Tom, M.A., N.D.D., R.A., R.E.; British artist, writer and composer; b. 24 May 1937, London; s. of David John Phillips and Margaret Agnes Arnold; m. 1st Jill Purdy 1961 (divorced 1988), one s. one d.; m. 2nd Fiona Maddocks 1995, two step-d.; ed. St. Catherine's Coll., Oxford and Camberwell School of Art; one-man exhbns. AIA Galleries, Angela Flowers Gallery, Marlborough Fine Art and Waddingtons, London, Galerie Ba Ma, Paris, S. London Gallery, Dulwich Picture Gallery; several int. group exhbns.; touring retrospective exhbn. London, The Hague, Basel, Paris etc. 1975; 50 years of Tom Phillips, Angela Flowers Gallery 1987, retrospective exhbns. Nat. Portrait Gallery, London 1989, N.C. Museum of Art, U.S.A. 1990, Royal Acad. 1992, South London Art Gallery 1998, Dulwich Picture Gallery 1998; publ. music scores 1965–; first performance opera IRMA, York Univ. 1973, revival ICA, London 1983 (CD 1986); collaborations with Jean-Yves Bosseur and John Tilbury on music works/performances 1970–84, Retrospective Concert ICA 1992; Music Works CD 1996, Six of Hearts CD 1997; worked with Peter Greenaway on TV version of Dante's Inferno, as published, translated and illustrated by the artist, broadcast 1990 (1st Prize Montreal TV Festival 1990, Italia Prize 1991); Curator exhbn. "Africa: The Art of a Continent", Royal Acad. London, Gropius Bau, Berlin, Guggenheim Museum, New York 1995–96; Vice-Chair. Copyright Council 1985–89; Chair. Royal Acad. Library, Frua Foundation 1997–; Chair. Exhbns. Royal Acad; mem. Royal Soc. of Painter-Etchers and Engravers; Hon. Fellow St. Catherine's Coll., Oxford, Leeds Univ. (Bretton Hall); John Moores Prize 1969; Frances Williams Memorial Prize V&A 1983. *Publications:* Trailer 1971, A Humument 1973, Works and Texts to 1974 1975, Dante's Inferno 1983, Heart of a Humument 1985, Where are They Now? The Class of '47 1990, Works and Texts II 1992, Merely Connect (with Salman Rushdie) 1994, Africa: The Art of a Continent 1995, Aspects of Art 1997, Music in Art 1997. *Leisure interests:* collecting African art, travel. *Address:* 57 Talfourd Road, London, S.E.15, England. *Telephone:* 0171-701 3978. *Fax:* 0171-703 2800.

PHILLIPS, Warren Henry, B.A.; American publisher and newspaper executive; b. 28 June 1926, New York City; s. of Abraham and Juliette Phillips; m. Barbara Anne Thomas 1951; three d.; ed. Queens Coll.; Copyreader Wall Street Journal 1947–48, Foreign Corresp., Germany 1949–50, Chief, London Bureau 1950–51, Foreign Ed. 1951–53, News Ed. 1953–54, Man. Ed. Midwest Edition 1954–57, Man. Ed. Wall Street Journal 1957–65, Publr. 1975–88; Exec. Ed. Dow Jones & Co. 1965–70; Vice-Pres. and Gen. Man. Dow Jones & Co. Inc. 1970–71, Editorial Dir. 1971–88, Exec. Vice-Pres. 1972, Pres. 1972–79, C.E.O. 1975–90, Chair. 1978–91, mem. Bd. of Dirs. 1972–97, Dir. Emer. 1997–; Pres. American Council on Educ. for Journalism 1971–73; Co-Publr. Bridge Works Publishing Co. 1992–; mem. Bd. of Dirs. Public Broadcasting Service 1991–97; Pres. American Soc. of Newspaper Eds. 1975–76; mem. Pulitzer Prizes Bd. 1977–87; Trustee, Columbia Univ. 1980–93, Trustee Emer. 1993–; mem. Visitors' Cttee. Kennedy School of Govt., Harvard Univ. 1984–90, 1992–97; mem. Corp. Advisory Bd. Queens Coll. 1986–90, Foundation Bd. of Trustees 1990–97; Hon. L.H.D. (Pace) 1982, (Queens Coll.) 1987, (Long Island) 1987; Hon. J.D. (Portland) 1973. *Publication:* China: Behind the Mask (with Robert Keatley) 1973. *Address:* Bridge Works Publishing, P.O. Box 1798, Bridgehampton, NY 11932, U.S.A. *Telephone:* (516) 537-3418. *Fax:* (516) 537-5092.

PHILLIPS, William, M.A.; American educationalist and author; b. New York; s. of Edward Phillips and Marie (née Berman) Phillips; ed. New York Univ., Columbia Univ.; Ed. Partisan Review 1934–; fmr. ed. Dial Press, Criterion Books, Random House, Chilmark Press; Assoc. Prof. New York Univ. 1960–63; Prof. English Rutgers Univ. 1963–78, Boston Univ. 1978–; Grantee Rockefeller Foundation 1977–78; mem. Co-ordinating Council Literary Magazines of America, Chair. 1967–75, Hon. Pres. and Chair. 1975; mem. Authors League. *Publications:* A Sense of the Present 1967, A Partisan View: Five Decades of the Literary Life 1983, Short Stories of Dostoyevsky (Ed.), Great American Short Novels (Ed.), Our Country, Our Culture 1994, Sixty Years of Great Fiction from Partisan Review (Ed.) 1997. *Address:* Partisan Review, 236 Bay State Road, Boston, MA 02215 (Office); 1 Lincoln Place, No. 16D, New York, NY 10023, U.S.A. (Home).

PHILLIPS, William D.; American physicist; b. 5 Nov. 1948, Wilkes-Barre, Pa.; s. of William Cornelius Phillips and Mary Catherine (Savine); m. Jane Van Wynen 1970; two d.; with Nat. Inst. of Standards and Tech.; Adjunct Prof. Univ. of Md. 1991–; mem. N.A.S.; Fellow American Physical Soc., American Acad. of Arts and Sciences; shared Nobel Prize for Physics 1997 for developing methods of cooling matter to very low temperatures using lasers, Schawlow Prize in Laser Sciences 1998. *Address:* National Institute of Standards and Technology, Gaithersburg, MD 20899, U.S.A.

PHILLIS, Robert Weston, B.A., F.R.S.A., F.R.T.S.; British broadcasting executive; b. 3 Dec. 1945, Croydon; s. of Francis W. Phillis and Gertrude G. Phillis; m. Jean Derham 1966; three s.; ed. John Ruskin Grammar School and Univ. of Nottingham; apprentice, printing industry 1961–65; Thomson Regional Newspapers Ltd. 1968–69; British Printing Corpn. Ltd. 1969–71;

lecturer in industrial relations, Univ. of Edin. and Scottish Business School 1971–75; Visiting Fellow, Univ. of Nairobi 1974; Personnel Dir., later Man. Dir. Sun Printers, Ltd. 1976–79; Man. Dir. Independent TV Publs. Ltd. 1979–82; Man. Dir. Cen. Independent TV PLC 1981–87, Dir. Non-Exec. 1987–91; Group Man. Dir. Carlton Communications PLC 1987–91; Chief Exec. Independent TV News 1991–93; Man. Dir. BBC World Service 1993–94, Deputy Dir.-Gen. BBC 1993–97, Chair. BBC Worldwide 1994–97; C.E.O. Guardian Media Group 1997–; Chair. ITV Network Programming Cttee. 1984–86, ITV Film Purchase Group 1985–87, Zenith Productions 1984–91; Dir. (Non-Exec.) ITN Ltd. 1982–87; Dir. and Trustee TV Trust for the Environment; Vice-Chair. (Int.), Int. Council, Nat. Acad. of TV Arts and Sciences 1994–97 (Life Fellow), (Dir. 1985–93); Vice-Pres. European Broadcasting Union 1996–; Hon. Prof. Univ. of Stirling 1997; Fellow, Royal TV Soc. (Chair. 1989–92, Vice-Pres. 1994). *Leisure interests:* family, sport, news, travel. *Address:* Guardian Media Group, 164 Deansgate, Manchester, M60 2RR, England.

PHOOFOLO, Monyane Paanya, B.A.; Lesotho diplomatist; b. 7 Dec. 1946, Ha Phoofolo, Berea; m.; two c.; ed. Univ. of Botswana, Lesotho and Swaziland; fmr. Perm. Sec. Ministry of Transport and Communications; later Man. Dir. Lesotho Telecommunications Corpn.; Prin. Sec. Ministry of Works 1986; Amb. to China 1986–88 (also accred. to Japan); High Commr. in India and Malaysia March–Sept. 1988; del. to various int. confs.; Perm. Rep. to UN 1988–94. *Address:* c/o Ministry of Foreign Affairs, Maseru, Lesotho.

PHOSA, Nakedi Mathews, LL.B.; South African politician; b. 1 Sept. 1952, Nelspruit; s. of Paul M. Phosa and Reshoketjoe (née Mabitsela) Phosa; m. Yvonne Nkwenkwezi 1984; one s. two d.; ed. Univ. of the North; legal adviser ANC, Johannesburg, Chair. ANC Mpumalanga br. 1990–; Premier Mpumalanga Prov. Legislature 1994; mem. ANC Nat. Exec. Cttee., ANC Nat. Negotiations Comm., Police Bd. under Nat. Peace Accord; Hon. LL.D (Boston) 1995. *Publications:* poetry: Ophir, New Classics, Staff Rider, Standpunte. *Address:* Private Bag 1862, Nelspruit 1200, South Africa.

PHOUNSAVANH, Nouhak; Laotian politician; ed. primary school; owner of bus and truck business; visited Peking (now Beijing) in a Viet-Minh del. for Conf. of Asian and Pacific Region 1952; rep. of Pathet Lao at Geneva Conf. on Indochina with Viet-Minh del. 1954; became Minister of Foreign Affairs in Free Lao Front (Neo Lao Issara) resistance Govt.; Deputy for Sam Neua to Nat. Assembly 1957; arrested 1959, escaped 1960; led Lao Patriotic Front (Neo Lao Hak Sat) del. to Ban Namone peace talks 1961; mem. People's Party of Laos 1955; mem. Lao Patriotic Front, mem. Standing Cttee. 1964, of Cen. Cttee.; now mem. Political Bureau; Vice-Chair. Council of Ministers and Minister of Finance 1975–82, Vice-Chair. Council of Ministers 1975–90, then First Vice-Chair; Pres. of Laos 1992–98; Deputy Gen. Sec. Lao People's Revolutionary Party. *Address:* c/o Office of the President, Vientiane, Laos.

PIANO, Renzo; Italian architect; b. 14 Sept. 1937, Genoa; s. of Carlo Piano and Rosa Odone; m. 1st Magda Ardnino 1962; two s. one d.; m. 2nd Emilia Rossato 1992; ed. Milan Polytechnic School of Architecture; worked with Louis I. Kahn, Phila., U.S.A., Z.S. Makowsky, London 1965–70, with Richard Rogers (as Piano & Rogers) 1977–, with Peter Rice (as Atelier Piano & Rice) 1977–; currently has offices in Genoa, Paris, Berlin (Renzo Piano Bldg. Workshop). *Completed projects include:* office bldg. for B&B, Como 1973, Georges Pompidou Centre, Paris 1977, IRCAM Inst. for Acoustic Research, Paris 1977, housing, Rigo Dist., Perugia 1982, office bldg. for Olivetti, Naples 1984, office bldg. for Lowara, Vicenza 1985, museum for Menil Collection, Houston, U.S.A. 1988, HQ for Light Metals Experimental Inst., Novara 1988, S. Nicola Football Stadium, Bari 1989, Underground stations for Ansaldo, Genoa 1990, Bercy commercial centre, Paris 1990, cruise ships for P&O 1991, housing, Paris 1991, Thomson factories, Guyancourt, France 1991, HQ for Credito Industriale Sardo, Cagliari 1992, Lingotto congress and concert hall, Turin 1994, Kansai Int. Airport, Osaka, Japan 1994, Meridien Hotel, Lingotto and Business Centre, Turin 1995, Harbour Authorities HQ, Genoa 1995, cinema, offices, contemporary art gallery, conf. centre, landscaping, Cité Int., Lyon 1996, Ushibuka Bridge, Kumamoto, Japan 1996, Museum of Science and Tech., Amsterdam 1997, Museum of Beyeler Foundation, Basle 1997, Debis Bldg. HQ, Daimler Benz, Berlin 1997, Cultural Centre J.-M. Tjibao, Nouméa, New Caledonia 1998, Mercedes-Benz Design Centre, Stuttgart 1998, Daimler-Benz Potsdamer Platz project including Imax theatre, offices, housing, shops, Berlin 1998, Lodi Bank HQ, Milan 1998. *Projects in progress include:* Auditorium Roma, contemporary art gallery, Varnamö, Sweden, office block, Sydney, Australia, PTT Telecom office tower, Rotterdam, Harvard Univ. Art Gallery master plan, renovation and extension, HQ newspaper Il Sole/24 Ore, Milan; work shown at exhbns. Europe, U.S.A., Australia, Japan 1967–; numerous lectures worldwide; Hon. Fellow Union Int. des Architectes 1978, A.I.A, 1981, R.I.B.A., 1985, American Acad. of Arts and Letters 1994; Dr. h.c. (Stuttgart) 1990, (Delft) 1992; Compasso d'Oro Award, Milan 1981, R.I.B.A. Gold Medal 1989, Kyoto Prize, Japan 1990, Neutra Prize, Pomona, Calif. 1991, Goodwill Amb. of UNESCO for Architecture 1994, Premio Michelangelo 1994, Art Prize of Akademie der Künste, Berlin 1995, Praemium Imperiale, Tokyo 1995, Erasmus Prize, Amsterdam 1995, The Pritzker Architecture Prize, Washington, D.C. 1998 and other prizes and awards; Commdr. des Arts et des Lettres, Légion d'honneur, Cavaliere di Gran Croce, Officer, Ordre Nat. du Mérite. *Publications:* author or co-author of 12 books on architecture. *Leisure interest:* sailing. *Address:* Renzo Piano Building Workshop, Via P.P. Rubens 29, 16158 Genoa, Italy. *Telephone:* (010) 61711. *Fax:* (010) 6171.350.

PIAVKO, Vladislav Ivanovich; Russian tenor; b. 4 Feb. 1941, Krasnoyarsk; s. of Nina Piavko and step-s. of Nikolai Bakhin; m. Irina Arkhipova; two s. two d.; ed. State Inst. of Theatrical Art, Moscow; studied under S. Rebrikov, Moscow, R. Pastorino, La Scala, Milan; mem. CPSU 1978–89; soloist with Bolshoi Opera 1965–89, Berliner Staatsopera 1989–92; teacher of singing and dramatic art, State Inst. of Theatrical Art 1980–89, Dean of School 1983–89; producer at Mosfilm 1980–83; has also sung at Teatro Colón, Buenos Aires, Teatro Comunale, Florence, Opéra La Bastille, Paris, Nat. and Smetana Operas, Prague, Metropolitan, New York, Kirov, St. Petersburg, and in many other houses; also at many int. festivals: numerous recordings for leading int. labels including EMI, HMV, Philips, Chant du Monde, Columbia; Academician, Acad. of Art of Russia 1992; Gold Medal in tenor section, Vervier Int. Competition 1969, Silver Medal, Tchaikovsky Int. Competition 1970, Gold Medal and Pietro Mascagni Silver Medal, Livorno 1984, Gold Plank of Cisternino, Italy 1993; People's Artist of U.S.S.R. 1983, of Kyrgyzstan 1993 and other awards. *Major roles include:* Hermann in Queen of Spades, Andrei in Mazeppa, Dmitry and Shuisky in Boris Godunov, Andrei and Golitsin in Khovanshchina, Radames, Otello, Manrico in Trovatore, Cavaradossi in Tosca, Pinkerton in Madam Butterfly, Don José in Carmen, Turiddu in Cavalleria Rusticana, Guglielmo Ratcliff. *Leisure interests:* poetry, photography, cars. *Address:* Bryusov per. 2/14, Apt. 27, 103009 Moscow, Russia. *Telephone:* 229-43-07.

PIBULSONGGRAM, Nitya, M.A.; Thai diplomatist; b. 1941; m.; ed. Dartmouth Coll. and Brown Univ.; entered Foreign Service as Third Sec. Foreign News Div. Information Dept. June 1968; served in former SEATO Div., Thailand's Int. Org. Dept. 1969–72; Office of Sec. to Minister of Foreign Affairs 1973, Office of Under-Sec. of State, Policy Planning Div. 1974; Head Southeast Asia Div., Political Dept. 1975; First Sec. Perm. Mission to UN 1976–79, Deputy Perm. Rep. 1979–80, Perm. Rep. 1988–96; Deputy Dir-Gen. Information Dept., Foreign Ministry 1980, Political Dept. 1981; Amb.-at-Large 1982; Dir.-Gen. Dept. of Int. Org. 1983–88; Amb. to U.S.A. 1996–. *Address:* Royal Thai Embassy, 1024 Wisconsin Avenue, N.W., Washington, DC 20007, U.S.A. *Telephone:* (202) 944-3600. *Fax:* (202) 944-3611.

PICADO, Sonia, LIC. EN D.; Costa Rican diplomatist, international civil servant and lawyer; b. 20 Dec. 1936; d. of Antonio de Picado and Odile Sotela; m. (divorced); one s. one d.; ed. Univ. of Costa Rica; Dean, Law Faculty of Costa Rica 1980–84, Cathedratical Chair. 1984; Co-Chair. Int. Comm. for Central American Recovery and Devt. 1987–89; mem. Cttee. of Jurists, World Conf. on Refugees, UNHCR, Geneva 1988–89; Exec. Dir. Inter-American Inst. of Human Rights 1988–94; Vice-Pres. Inter-American Court of Human Rights 1991–; Amb. to U.S.A. 1994–; Max Planck/Humboldt Award (Germany) 1991; Leonidas Proaño Award (Ecuador) 1991. *Publications:* Women and Human Rights 1986, Philosophic Fundamentals of Human Rights in Latin America 1987, Religion, Tolerance and Liberty: A Human Rights Perspective 1989, Peace, Development and Human Rights 1989. *Address:* Costa Rican Embassy, 2114 S. Street, N.W., Washington, DC 20008, U.S.A. *Telephone:* (202) 234-2945. *Fax:* (202) 265-4795.

PICARD, Dennis J.; American business executive; b. 1932; ed. Northeastern Univ.; Sr. Vice-Pres., Gen. Man. Missile Systems Div. Raytheon Co., Lexington, Mass., 1985–89, Pres. 1989–90, Chair., C.E.O. 1990– (also Bd. Dirs.); mem. Defence Policy Advisory Cttee. on Trade, President's Export Council. *Address:* Raytheon Co., 141 Spring Street, Lexington, MA 02173, U.S.A.

PICASSO, Paloma; French designer; b. 19 April 1949, Paris; d. of Pablo Picasso and Françoise Gilot; m. Rafael Lopez-Cambil (Lopez-Sanchez) 1978 (divorced 1998); ed. Univ. of Paris, Sorbonne; studied jewellery design and fabrication; fashion jewellery for Yves St. Laurent 1969; jewellery for Zolotas 1971, costumes and sets for Parisian theatre productions, L'Interprétation 1975, Succès 1978; created Paloma Picasso brand; creations designed by her for the Paloma Picasso brand include: jewellery for Tiffany & Co. 1980, fragrance (Paloma Picasso 1984, Minotaure 1992, Tentations 1996) and cosmetics for L'Oréal, women's accessories for Lopez-Cambil Ltd. 1987, eyewear for Metzler Optik Partner AG, bone china, crystal, silverware and tiles for Villeroy & Boch, home linens for KBC, fabrics and wall coverings for Motif; Paloma Picasso boutiques in Japan, Hong Kong, Taipei, Kaoshiung, Singapore, Honolulu, Guam; pieces in perm. collections of Smithsonian Inst. (Washington, D.C.), Musée des Arts Décoratifs (Paris) and Die Neue Zamlang (Munich); Council of Fashion Design of America (CFDA) Accessory Award 1989. *Address:* Quintana Roo Ltd., 291A Brompton Road, London, SW3 2DY, England. *Telephone:* 0171-589 9030. *Fax:* 0171-589 7712.

PICCARD, Jacques Ernest Jean; Swiss scientist; b. 28 July 1922, Brussels, Belgium; s. of Auguste Piccard and Marianne (Denis) Piccard; m. Marie-Claude Maillard 1953; two s. one d.; ed. Univ. of Geneva and Inst. Universitaire de Hautes Etudes Internationales, Geneva; Asst. Prof. of Econs., Geneva 1946–48; consultant scientist to several American orgs. for deep sea research; collaborated with father, Prof. Auguste Piccard, in construction of bathyscaph Trieste; built first mesoscaph Auguste Piccard; has made more than 100 dives in Mediterranean and Pacific, one to 35,800 feet (deepest ever dive at that time, Jan. 1960) and approx. 700 dives in European lakes with submersible F.A.-FOREL; Chief Scientist, research submarine Ben Franklin for the Grumman-Piccard Gulf Stream Drift Mission, Summer 1969; Founder and Pres. Foundation for the Study and Preservation of Seas and Lakes; built research submersible F.A.-FOREL 1978; Visiting Prof. of Oceanic Eng. at Stevens Inst. of Tech., Hoboken, New Jersey; Hon. D.Sc. (American Int. Coll. and Hofstra Univ.); Croix de guerre (France), U.S. Distinguished Public Service award 1960, Officier, Ordre de Léopold (Belgium). *Publications:* The Sun beneath the Sea 1971, several technical papers. *Leisure interests:* reading, walking, swimming, diving.

PICCOLI, Michel; French actor; b. 27 Dec. 1925, Paris; s. of Henri Piccoli; m. 1st Juliette Greco 1966; m. 3rd Ludivine Clerc 1978; one s. from fmr. marriage; ed. Collège d'Annel, Collège Ste. Barbe, Paris; Man. of the Théâtre de Babylone for two years before joining the Madeleine Renaud and Jean-Louis Barrault Theatre Co.; appeared in Phèdre at the Théâtre Nationale Populaire; Best Actor, Cannes 1980 (for Salto nel Vuoto); Chevalier Légion d'honneur, Ordre nationale du Mérite. *Films include:* Le point du jour 1946, Parfum de la dame en noire 1949, French Cancan 1955, The Witches of Salem 1956, Le mépris 1963, Diary of a Chambermaid 1964, De l'amour 1965, Lady L 1965, La curée 1965, Les demoiselles de Rochefort 1967, Un homme de trop 1967, Belle de jour 1967, Dillinger is Dead 1968, The Milky Way 1969, Topaz 1969, The Discreet Charm of the Bourgeoisie 1972, Themroc 1972, Blowout 1973, The Infernal Trio 1974, Le fantôme de la liberté 1974, La faille 1975, Léonar 1975, Sept morts sur ordonnance 1976, La dernière femme 1976, Savage State 1978, Le divorcement 1979, Le saut dans le vide 1979, Le mors aux dents 1979, La città delle donne 1980, Salto nel Vuoto 1980, La passante du sans-souci 1982, Adieu Bonaparte 1985, The Night is Young 1986, L'homme voilé, Maladie d'amour, la Rumba 1987, Y a bon les blancs, Blanc de Chine 1988, Milou en mai 1990, Martha et moi 1991, La Belle Noiseuse 1991, Les Equilibristes, le Voleur d'enfants 1991, le Bal des cassepieds 1992, Archipel 1993, Rupture(s) 1993, Les Cent et une Nuits 1995, Réalisateur de Alors voilá 1997. *Publication:* Dialogues égoistes 1976. *Address:* 11 rue des Lions Saint-Paul, 75004 Paris, France.

PICHLER, Joseph A., PH.D.; American business executive; b. 3 Oct. 1939, St. Louis, Mo.; s. of late Anton Pichler and Anita Pichler; m. Susan Eyerly 1962; two s. two d.; ed. Notre Dame Univ. of Chicago; Dean Univ. of Kan. 1974–80; Exec. Vice-Pres. Dillon Companies Inc. 1980–82, Pres. 1982–84, Pres. and C.E.O. 1984–86, C.E.O. 1986–88; Exec. Vice-Pres. The Kroger Co. 1985–86, Pres. and C.O.O. 1986–90, Pres. and C.E.O. June–Sept. 1990, Chair. of Bd. and C.E.O. Sept. 1990–; Woodrow Wilson Fellow 1961, Ford Foundation Doctoral Fellow 1962–64, Standard Oil Industrial Relations Fellow 1964; Performance Award, U.S. Dept. of Labor Manpower Admin. 1969. *Publications:* Inequality: The Poor and the Rich in America (with Joseph W. McGuire) 1969, Ethics, Free Enterprise, and Public Policy (with Richard T. DeGeorge) 1978. *Leisure interests:* fly fishing, music, reading. *Address:* The Kroger Co., 1014 Vine Street, Cincinnati, OH 45202, U.S.A.

PICHOIS, Claude, D. ÈS L.; French professor; b. 21 July 1925, Paris; s. of Léon Pichois and Renée Bardou; m. Vincenette Rey 1961; ed. Lycée Carnot, Paris, H.E.C., Faculté des lettres, Sorbonne, Paris; Postgrad. Trainee, then Research Asst., C.N.R.S. 1953–56; lecturer, Faculté des lettres, Aix-en-Provence 1956–61; Prof., Univ. of Basle, Switzerland 1961–70; Distinguished Professor of French, Vanderbilt Univ., Nashville, Tenn., U.S.A. 1970–98, Prof. Emer. 1998–; Visiting Prof., Inst. for Research in the Humanities, Madison, U.S.A. 1968; Prof., Facultés de Namur, Belgium 1978–79, Sorbonne Nouvelle, Paris 1979–90; Dr. h.c. (Neuchâtel) 1983, (Trinity Coll. Dublin) 1984. *Publications:* Le vrai visage du général Aupick, beau-père de Baudelaire 1955, L'Image de la Belgique dans les lettres françaises 1957, L'Image de Jean-Paul Richter dans les lettres françaises 1963, Philarète Chasles et la vie littéraire au temps du romantisme (2 vols.) 1965, Baudelaire à Paris 1967, Baudelaire, études et temoignages 1967, 1976, Correspondance et Oeuvres complètes de Baudelaire, (4 vols.) 1973, 1975–76, Album Baudelaire 1973, Vitesse et Vision du monde 1973, Album Colette 1984; (co-author) Baudelaire et Asselineau 1953, Baudelaire devant ses contemporains 1957, 1967, Iconographie de Charles Baudelaire 1960, La Littérature comparée 1967, 1983, Oeuvres complètes de Gérard de Nerval, vol. I, vol. II 1984, Vol. III 1993, Oeuvres de Colette, vol. I 1984, vol. II 1986, Vol. III 1991, Baudelaire (biography) 1987, Le musée retrouvé de Charles Baudelaire (co-author) 1992, Baudelaire/Paris (co-author) 1993, Gérard de Nerval (biography, co-author) 1995, Poulet-Malassis, l'éditeur de Baudelaire 1996 (biography); edns. of poetry by Laforgue, five collections of letters by Colette; numerous articles. *Address:* 3 rue Pierre-Demours, 75017 Paris, France; Box 6312 Sta. B., Vanderbilt University, Nashville, TN 37235, U.S.A. *Telephone:* (1) 45.72.05.82 (France); (615) 322-6900 (U.S.A.).

PICKARD, Sir (John) Michael, Kt., F.C.A., C.B.I.M.; British business executive; b. 29 July 1932, Banstead, Surrey; s. of late John Stanley and of Winifred Joan Pickard; m. Penelope Jane Catterall 1959; one d. three s.; ed. Oundle School; Finance Dir. British Printing Corpn. 1965–68, Man. Dir. Trusthouses Ltd. 1968–70, Trusthouse Forte Ltd. 1970–71; Chair. Happy Eater Ltd. 1972–86, Grattan PLC 1978–84, Courage Ltd and Imperial Brewing & Leisure Ltd. 1981–86; C.E.O. Sears PLC 1986–92; Chair. Bullough PLC 1996– (Dir. 1995–), London Docklands Devt. Corpn. 1992–98, Servus Holdings PLC 1997–, Nat. House-Building Council 1998–, London First Centre 1998–; Dir. (non-exec) Brown Shipley Holdings PLC 1986–93, Electra Investment Trust PLC 1989–, Nationwide Bldg. Soc. 1991–94, Pinnacle Clubs Ltd. 1992–, Bentalls PLC 1993–, United Racecourses (Holdings) Ltd. 1995–; mem. Bd. London First 1992– (Chair. 1998–); mem. Cttee. The Automobile Asscn. 1994–; Hon. LL.D. (E. London) 1997. *Leisure interests:* sport, education. *Address:* 16 Grosvenor Hill Court, Bourdon Street, London, W1X 9HT, England.

PICKENS, Jo Ann; American soprano singer; b. 4 Aug. 1950, Robstown, Tex.; d. of Anne Belle Sanders; started singing career in Chicago Lyric Opera; has perfomed in recital and concert around the world and appeared with conductors including Solti, Dorati, Rattle, Norrington, Pesek and Sanderling; also appears in opera notably Berlioz's The Trojans 1987 and Armide 1988; Award, Int. Competition for Singers, Paris 1980; Metropolitan Opera Regional Auditions 1981; Benson & Hedges Gold Award 1981. *Address:* c/o Norman McCann International Artists, Ltd., The Coach House, 56 Lawrie Park Gardens, London, SE26 6XJ, England.

PICKENS, Thomas Boone, Jr., B.S.; American oil company executive; b. 22 May 1928, Holdenville, Okla.; s. of Thomas Boone Pickens and Grace Molonson Pickens; m. Beatrice L. Carr 1972; ed. Okla. State Univ.; geologist, Phillips Petroleum Co. 1951–55; Founder, Pres., Chair. Bd. Mesa Petroleum Co., Amarillo, Tex.; Gen. Partner, Mesa Inc. 1985–; mem. Nat. Petroleum Council 1970–; Founder, Chair. United Shareholders Asscn. Washington. *Publication:* Boone 1987. *Address:* 6909 Vassar Avenue, Dallas, TX 75205, U.S.A.

PICKERING, Sir Edward Davies, Kt.; British journalist; b. 4 May 1912; s. of George Pickering and Louie Pickering; m. 1st Margaret Soutter 1936 (divorced 1947); one d.; m. 2nd Rosemary Whitton 1955; two s. one d.; ed. Middlesbrough High School; Chief Sub-Ed. Daily Mail 1939; R.A. 1940–44; Staff of Supreme HQ Allied Expeditionary Force 1944–45; Man. Ed. Daily Mail 1947–49, Daily Express 1951–57, Ed. Daily Express 1957–62; Dir. Beaverbrook Newspapers 1956–63; Man. Dir. Beaverbrook Publications 1962–63; Editorial Dir. and Dir. The Daily Mirror Newspapers Ltd. 1964–68; Editorial Dir. Int. Publishing Corpn., Chair. I.P.C. Newspaper Div. and Chair. Daily Mirror Newspapers Ltd. 1968–70; Chair. I.P.C. Magazines Ltd. 1970–74; Chair. Mirror Group Newspapers Ltd. 1974–77; mem. Press Council 1964–69, 1970–82, Vice-Chair. 1977–82; Chair. Commonwealth Press Union 1977–86; Exec. Vice-Chair. Times Newspapers Ltd. 1982–, Chair. The Times Supplements Ltd. 1989–; Dir. Reed Publishing Holdings 1977–81, Times Newspapers Holdings 1981–; Treas. Int. Fed. of the Periodical Press 1971–75; Vice-Pres. Periodical Publrs. Asscn. 1971–94; mem. Press Complaints Comm. 1991–96; Hon. D.Litt. (City Univ., London) 1986. *Address:* 23 Rutland Gate, London, SW7 1PD, England.

PICKERING, Thomas Reeve, M.A.; American diplomatist; b. 5 Nov. 1931, Orange, N.J.; s. of Hamilton Reeve Pickering and Sarah P. Chasteney; m. Alice Jean Stover 1955; one s. one d.; ed. Bowdoin Coll., Brunswick, Me., Fletcher School of Law and Diplomacy, Medford, Mass., Univ. of Melbourne, Australia; Lieut. Commdr. U.S.N. 1956–59; joined Dept of State 1959, Intelligence Research Specialist 1960, Foreign Affairs Officer 1961, Arms Control and Disarmament Agency 1961–62; mem. U.S. Del. to Disarmament Conf., Geneva 1962–64; Prin. Officer, Zanzibar 1965–67; Deputy Chief of Mission, Dar es Salaam 1967–69; Deputy Dir. Bureau of Politico-Mil. Affairs 1969–73; Exec. Sec. Dept. of State, Special Asst. to Sec. of State 1973–74; Amb. to Jordan 1974–78; Asst. Sec. of State, Bureau of Oceans, Environment and Science 1978–81; Amb. to Nigeria 1981–83; Amb. to El Salvador 1983–85, to Israel 1985–88; Perm. Rep. to UN 1989–92, Amb. to India 1992–93, to Russia 1993–96; Under-Sec. of State for Political Affairs 1997–; Pres. Eurasia Foundation 1996–97. *Leisure interests:* archaeology, scuba, photography, carpentry. *Address:* Department of State, 2201 C Street, NW, Washington, DC 20520, U.S.A. *Telephone:* (202) 647-6575. *Fax:* (202) 647-6047.

PICKERING, William Hayward, M.S., PH.D.; American scientist; b. 24 Dec. 1910, Wellington, N.Z.; s. of Albert William and Elizabeth Hayward Pickering; m. 1st Muriel Bowler 1932 (died 1992); one s. one d.; m. 2nd Inez Chapman 1994; ed. Calif. Inst. of Tech.; Calif. Inst. of Tech. 1936–, Prof. of Electrical Eng. 1946–, Dir. Jet Propulsion Laboratory 1954–76, Prof. Emer. 1980–; mem. Scientific Advisory Bd. U.S.A.F. 1945–48; Chair. Panel on Test Range Instrumentation Research and Devt. Bd. 1948–49; directed devt. of Army Corporal and Sergeant missiles 1950–55, and many spacecraft, including Explorer I, Ranger, the first U.S. spacecraft to photograph the moon, Mariner II, first spacecraft to return scientific data from the vicinity of a planet (Venus), Mariner IV, first spacecraft to photograph Mars, Surveyor, first U.S. spacecraft to soft-land on the moon and return scientific data; Dir. Research Inst., Univ. of Petroleum and Minerals, Saudi Arabia 1976–78; Pres. Pickering Research Corpn., Pasadena, Calif. 1980–, Lignetics Inc. 1983–; mem. Advisory Cttee. Dept. of Aeronautics and Astronautics, Univ. of Wash., U.S. Tech. Panel on Earth Satellite Programs IGY 1956–58, Army Scientific Advisory Panel 1963–65; Pres. A.I.A.A. 1963; Fellow I.E.E.E.; Hon. Fellow A.I.A.A.; mem. N.A.S., American Asscn. Univ. Profs., American Geophysical Union, Nat. Acad. of Eng., A.A.A.S., Royal Soc. of New Zealand, Int. Acad. of Astronautics; mem. Int. Astronautics Fed., Pres. 1965–66; Hon. mem. New Zealand Inst. of Eng., and Aerospace Medical Asscn.; Fellow, American Acad. of Arts and Sciences; Hon. D.Sc. (Occidental Coll., Clark Univ., Univ. of Bologna) 1974; Meritorious Civilian Service Award U.S. Army 1945, Distinguished Civilian Service Award U.S. Army 1959, Columbus Gold Medal 1964, Prix Galabert Award 1965, Robert H. Goddard Memorial Trophy 1965, Crozier Gold Medal 1965, Spirit of Saint Louis Medal 1965, Distinguished Service Medal NASA 1965, Louis W. Hill Award 1968, Edison Medal (I.E.E.E.) 1972, Nat. Medal of Science 1975, Herman Oberth Engineering Award (Fed. Repub. of Germany) 1978, François-Xavier Bagnoud

Aerospace Prize 1993, Japan Prize for Aerospace Technology 1994, and many other awards; Hon. K.B.E.; Italian Order of Merit. *Leisure interests:* swimming, fishing, hiking, gardening. *Address:* 294 St. Katherine Drive, Flintridge, CA 91011, U.S.A. (Home). *Telephone:* (626) 797-7510 (Office). *Fax:* (626) 797-1209.

PICKETT, John Anthony, PH.D., C.CHEM., F.R.S., F.R.S.C., F.R.E.S.; British research chemist; b. 21 April 1945, Leicester; s. of Samuel Victor Pickett and Lilian Frances Hoar; m. Ulla Birgitta Skalen 1970; one s. one d.; ed. King Edward VII Grammar School, Coalville, Univ. of Surrey; Postdoctoral Fellowship, UMIST (organic chem.) 1970–72; Sr. Scientist, Chem. Dept., Brewing Research Foundation, Surrey 1972–76; Prin. Scientific Officer, Dept. of Insecticides and Fungicides, Rothamsted Experimental Station 1976–83, Individual Merit (Grade 5), and Head Dept. Insecticides and Fungicides, (now Biological and Ecological Chem. Dept.), Inst. of Arable Crops Research, Rothamsted 1984–; Special Prof., Univ. of Nottingham 1991–; Pres. Int. Soc. of Chemical Ecology (ISCE) 1995; Hon. mem. Academic Staff Univ. of Reading 1995; Rank Prize for Nutrition and Crop Husbandry 1995. *Research:* chemical ecology, and insect pheromones in particular. *Publications:* over 200 papers, including patents. *Leisure interest:* jazz trumpet playing. *Address:* Biological and Ecological Chemistry Department, IACR-Rothamsted, Harpenden, Herts., AL5 2JQ (Office); 53 Parkfield Crescent, Kimpton, Nr. Hitchin, Herts., SG4 8EQ, England (Home). *Telephone:* (01582) 763133, Ext. 2321 (Office); (01438) 832832 (Home). *Fax:* (01582) 762595.

PIËCH, Ferdinand; German business executive; b. 17 April 1937, Vienna; ed. Eidgenössische Technische Hochschule (ETH), Zürich; joined Porsche KG in engine testing 1963, Tech. Man. 1971; joined Audi NSU Auto Union AG 1972, Divisional Man. Gen. Testing 1973, Tech. Devt. Man., Ingolstadt 1974, mem. Bd. of Man. 1975, Vice-Chair. Bd. of Man. 1983, Chair. Bd. of Man. of Audi AG 1988; mem. Supervisory Bd. Volkswagen AG 1992, Dir., Head of Research and Devt. 1995–, responsible for Production Optimisation and Purchasing 1996–; Dr. tech. h.c. (Tech. Univ. Vienna) 1984, Dr. h.c. (Ben Gurion Univ.) 1997; Distinguished Service Medal (1st Class) 1984. *Address:* Volkswagen AG, 38436 Wolfsburg, Germany. *Telephone:* 05361 9-0. *Fax:* 05361 9-28282.

PIEL, Gerard, A.B.; American editor and publisher; b. 1 March 1915, New York; s. of William Piel and Loretto (Scott) Piel; m. 1st Mary Tapp Bird 1938 (divorced 1955); two s. (one deceased); m. 2nd Eleanor Virden Jackson 1955; one d.; ed. Phillips Acad., Andover, Mass. and Harvard Coll.; Editorial Assoc., Science Ed., Life 1938–45; Asst. to Pres., Henry J. Kaiser Co. and associated enterprises 1945–46; Organizer, Pres. Scientific American Inc., Publr. Scientific American 1947–84, Chair of Bd. 1984–87, Chair. Emer. 1987; Chair. Comm. Delivery Personal Health Services, New York 1966–68, Trustees, Foundation for Child Devt.; mem. Bd. Overseers Harvard Univ. 1966–68, 1973–79; Trustee American Museum of Natural History, Radcliffe Coll. 1962–80, Phillips Acad., New York Botanical Garden, Henry J. Kaiser Family Foundation, Mayo Foundation, American Bd. of Medical Specialities, René Dubos Center for Human Environment; mem. Council on Foreign Relations, American Philosophical Soc., Inst. of Medicine; Fellow American Acad. of Arts and Sciences, A.A.A.S. (Pres. 1985, Chair. 1986); George Polk Award 1961, Kalinga Prize 1962, Bradford Washburn Award 1966, Arches of Science Award 1969, Rosenberger Medal, Univ. of Chicago 1973, A. I. Djavakhishvili Medal (Univ. of Tbilisi), Publr. of the Year, Magazine Publrs. Assen. 1980. *Publications:* Science in the Cause of Man 1962, The Acceleration of History 1972, Only One World 1992. *Address:* 1115 Fifth Avenue, New York, NY 10128; Lakeville, CT 06039, U.S.A. (Homes).

PIENAAR, Jacobus Francois, LL.B.; South African rugby player; b. 21 Jan. 1967, Vereeniging; s. of Johan Pienaar and Valerie Du Toit; m. Nerene Pienaar 1996; ed. Patriot High School and Rand Afrikaans Univ.; capped for S. African Schools 1985, S. African Under 20 1987, S. African Barbarians 1990; Capt. S. African Rugby Team 1993–; Capt. Transvaal 1993–; captained S. Africa to World Cup victory 1995; Int. Rugby Player of Year 1994; British Rugby Writers' Lifetime Achievement Award 1995; holds record for most tests as Capt. of S.A. (24, Jan. 1996). *Leisure interests:* golf, spending time at home. *Address:* c/o South African Rugby Football Union, P.O. Box 99, Newlands 7725, South Africa. *Telephone:* 27 (21) 685 3038. *Fax:* 27 (21) 685 6771.

PIENE, Otto; German artist and educator; b. 18 April 1928, Laasphe, Westphalia; s. of Otto and Anne (Niemeyer) Piene; m. Elizabeth Olson 1988; one s. three d.; ed. Acad. of Fine Arts, Munich and Düsseldorf and Univ. of Cologne; organized Night Exhbns., f. Group Zero, Düsseldorf, with Heinz Mack 1957–66; Visiting Prof., Graduate School of Art, Univ. of Pa. 1964; Prof. of Environmental Art, School of Arch., M.I.T. 1972–, Dir. Center for Advanced Visual Studies, M.I.T. 1974–93, Acting Dir. 1993–94, Dir. Emer. 1994–; Prof. Emer. M.I.T. 1993–; one-man exhbns. include: Galerie Heseler, Munich 1971, 1972, 1975, 1977–79, 1981, 1983, Galerie Heimeshoff, Essen 1974, 1977, 1983, 1988, Galerie Schoeller, Düsseldorf 1976, 1977, 1980, 1984, 1987, 1991, 1995, Galerie Löhrl, Mönchengladbach 1986, 1988, 1991, 1996, Gallery 360°, Tokyo 1991, 1992; retrospective exhbn. Museum am Ostwall, Dortmund 1967, Hayden Gallery, M.I.T. 1975, Karlsruhe 1988, Städt. Kunstmuseum, Düsseldorf 1996; group exhbns. include Tate Gallery 1964, Düsseldorf 1973, Antwerp 1979, Paris 1983, London, Berlin 1987, New York 1988–89, Copenhagen 1992; performed works include Olympic Rainbow 1972, Sky Events, SAC 1981, 1982, 1983, 1986, Sky Dance, Guggenheim 1984, Dialogue de Têtes, Reims 1990; Les fleurs du Mal, Quebec 1996; works in museums in many countries; D.F.A. h.c. (Univ. of Md.) 1995; recipient of several awards and prizes. *Publications:* (with Heinz Mack) Zero 1, Zero 2 1958, Zero 3 1961; More Sky 1973; author and ed. Zero 1973, Art Transition 1975–76, Centerbeam 1980, Sky Art Conference Catalog 1981, 1982, 1983, 1986, Lightsorot 1988, Feuerbilder und Texte 1988, Überblick 1991. *Address:* Center for Advanced Visual Studies, Massachusetts Institute of Technology, N51, 265 Massachusetts Avenue, Cambridge, MA 02139 (Office); 383 Old Ayer Road, Groton, MA 01450, U.S.A. (Home and Studio); Hüttenstr. 104, Atelier 40215 Düsseldorf, Germany (Studio). *Telephone:* (617) 253-4415 (Office); (978) 448-5240 (Home and Studio). *Fax:* (617) 253-1660 (Office); (978) 448-6716 (Home and Studio).

PIENIĄŻEK, Szczepan Aleksander, M.PH., M.S., PH.D.; Polish pomologist; b. 27 Dec. 1913, Słup, near Garwolin; s. of Józef and Zofia Pieniążek; m. Janina Praska 1939; one s. one d.; ed. Warsaw Univ., Cornell Univ., Ithaca, N.Y., U.S.A.; Instructor Rhode Island Univ. 1942–45, Asst. Res. Prof. 1945–46; Assoc. Prof., Warsaw Agric. Univ. 1946–54, Prof. 1954–68, Chair. Dept. Pomology 1946–68; Corresp. mem. Polish Acad. of Sciences 1952–64, mem. 1964–; mem. Presidium 1964–89, Vice-Pres. 1975–80; Dir. Res., Inst. of Pomology, Skierniewice 1951–83; mem. Polish Botanical Soc. 1936–, Hon. mem. 1980–; mem. American Soc. for Horticultural Science 1938–, Fellow 1974–; mem. Int. Soc. for Horticultural Science 1958–, Vice-Pres. 1966–70, Pres. 1970–74, Hon. Life mem. 1976–, Chair. Fruit-Growing Section 1962–66; Co-Chair. Council of the Foundation for Devt. of Polish Agric. 1988–; Foreign mem. Bulgarian Acad. of Agric. Science 1968, G.D.R. (now German) Acad. of Agric. Science 1968, V.I. Lenin All-Union (now Russian) Acad. of Agric. Science 1970; Corresp. mem. Agric. Acad. of France 1976–79, mem. 1979–; Dr. h.c. (Cracow Agric. Acad.) 1973, (Bonn Univ.) 1983, (Warsaw Agric. Acad.) 1983, (Szczecin Agric. Acad.) 1984, (Agric. Acad., Poznań) 1985; Officer's Cross, Order of Polonia Restituta 1954, Commdr.'s Cross 1973; Order of Banner of Labour, 2nd Class 1959; State Prize (1st Class) 1978, Order of the Builders of People's Poland 1977, Grand Officier, Ordre de l'Encouragement Public (France) 1981, Meritorious Agronomist of People's Poland 1985, Chevalier, Ordre nat. du Mérite (France) 1990, and other decorations. *Publications:* Dookoła Sadowniczego Świata (Round the Fruit-Growing World) 1965, Gdy Zakwitną Jabłonie (When the Apple Trees Bloom) 1971, Sadownictwo (Textbook of Pomology) 1976, Sady w kwiecie (Orchards in Bloom) 1990, Rozkwitły Sady (Orchards in Bloom) 1991. *Leisure interest:* growing tropical fruit plants in pots indoors. *Address:* Niemodlinsk 65, 04-635 Warsaw, Poland. *Telephone:* (22) 815-36-49.

PIERCE, John Robinson, B.S., M.S., PH.D.; American electrical engineer; b. 27 March 1910, Des Moines, Ia.; s. of the late John S. and Harriett A. Robinson Pierce; m. 1st Martha Peacock 1938 (divorced 1964); one s. one d.; m. 2nd Ellen Richter 1964 (died 1986); m. 3rd Brenda Woodard 1987; ed. Calif. Inst. of Tech.; Bell Telephone Laboratories 1936–71, Dir. of Electronics Research 1952–55, Dir. of Research, Electrical Communications 1955–58, Communications Principles 1958–61; Exec. Dir. Research-Communications Principles and Systems Div. 1961–65, Research-Communications Sciences Div. 1965–71; Prof. of Eng., Calif. Inst. of Tech. 1971–80, Emer. 1980–, Chief Technologist, Jet Propulsion Lab. 1979–82; Visiting Prof. of Music, Stanford Univ., Visiting Prof. Emer. 1983–; mem. N.A.S., Nat. Acad. of Eng. (Founders Award 1977), American Philosophical Soc., Royal Acad. of Sciences (Sweden); Fellow, Acoustical Soc. of America, American Physical Soc., Inst. of Electrical and Electronics Engineers, American Acad. of Arts and Sciences; Valdemar Poulsen Medal 1963, President's Nat. Medal of Science 1963, Marconi Int. Fellowship 1979, Japan Prize 1985, Nat. Acad. of Eng. Charles Stark Draper Award 1995, and many other medals and trophies. *Publications:* Theory and Design of Electron Beams 1954, Traveling Wave Tubes 1950, Electrons, Waves and Messages 1956, Man's World of Sound 1958, Symbols, Signals and Noise 1961, The Research State: A History of Science in New Jersey 1964, Electrons and Waves 1964, Quantum Electronics 1966, Waves and Messages 1967, Science, Art and Communication 1968, Almost All About Waves 1973, Introduction to Communication Sciences and Systems 1980, Signals, the Telephone and Beyond 1981, The Science of Musical Sound 1983, (revised edn.) 1992, Information Technology and Civilization (with Hiroshi Inose) 1984, Current Directions in Computer Music Research 1989 (ed.), Signals, The Science of Telecommunications 1990. *Leisure interests:* writing, science fiction, music. *Address:* 4008 El Cerrito Road, Palo Alto, CA 94306, U.S.A. *Telephone:* (650) 493-5197 (Home).

PIERCE, Mary; Canadian tennis player; b. 15 Jan. 1975, Montreal, Canada; s. of Jim Pierce and Yannick Pierce; turned professional 1989; moved to France 1990; rep. France in Fed. Cup 1991; first career title, Palermo 1991; runner-up French Open 1994; winner Australian Open 1995, Tokyo Nichirei 1995; semi-finalist Italian Open, Canadian Open 1996; finalist Australian Open 1997. *Address:* c/o WTA, 133 First Street N.E., St. Petersburg, FL 33701, U.S.A.

PIERCE, Samuel Riley, Jr., A.B, J.D., LL.M., LL.D., L.H.D., D.C.L., D.LITT.; American public official and lawyer; b. 8 Sept. 1922, Glen Cove, Long Island, N.Y.; s. of Samuel R. and Hettie E. (Armstrong) Pierce; m. Barbara Penn Wright 1948; one d.; ed. Cornell, New York, Yale Univs.; admitted to New York bar 1949, Supreme Court bar 1956; Asst. Dist. Attorney, County of New York 1949–53; Asst. U.S. Attorney, Southern Dist., N.Y. 1953–55; Asst. to Under-Sec., Dept. of Labor, Washington, D.C. 1955–56; Assoc. Counsel,

Counsel Judiciary Sub-Cttee. on Antitrust, House of Reps. 1956–57; pvt. law practice 1957–59, 1961–70, 1973–81, 1989–; on faculty New York Univ. School of Law 1958–70; Judge, N.Y. Court Gen. Sessions 1959–61; Gen. Counsel, Head of Legal Div., U.S. Treasury Dept., Washington 1970–73; Gov. American Stock Exchange 1977–80; U.S. Sec. of Housing and Urban Devt. 1981–89; mem. Nat. Wiretapping Comm. 1973–76; Advisory Group Commr. Internal Revenue Service 1974–76; mem. Nat. Advisory Cttee., Comptroller of Currency 1975–80; dir. numerous cos; mem. A.B.A.; Fellow American Coll. of Trial Lawyers; numerous medals and awards; Republican. *Publications:* articles in professional journals. *Address:* 16 West 77th Street, New York, NY 10024, U.S.A.

PIERCY, Marge, M.A.; American novelist, poet and essayist; b. 31 March 1936, Detroit; d. of Robert Douglas Piercy and Bert Bernice Piercy (née Bunnin); m. Ira Wood 1982; ed. Michigan and Northwestern Univs.; instructor Gary Extension, Ind. Univ. 1960–62; Poet-in-Residence Kan. Univ. 1971; Distinguished Visiting Lecturer Thomas Jefferson Coll., Grand Valley State Colls. 1975, 1976, 1978, 1980, Elliston Poetry Fellow Cincinnati Univ. 1986; DeRoy Distinguished Visiting Prof. Mich. Univ. 1992; mem. Writer Bd. 1985–86; mem. Bd. dirs. Transition House, Mass. Foundation for the Humanities and Public Policy 1978–85; Gov.'s Appointee to Mass. Cultural Council 1990–91, Mass. Council on Arts and Humanities 1986–89; mem. Artistic Advisory Bd. ALEPH Alliance for Jewish Renewal, American Poetry Centre 1988–, Literary Advisory Panel (Poetry), N.E.A. 1989; Ed. Leapfrog Press 1997–; Literary award, Gov. of Mass.'s Comm. on Status of Women 1974, Nat. Endowment of Arts Award 1978, Golden Rose Poetry Prize 1990, Notable Book Award 1997 and many others; mem. PEN, NOW, American Poetry Soc. etc. *Publications:* Breaking Camp 1968, Hard Loving 1969, Going Down Fast 1969, Dance the Eagle to Sleep 1970, Small Changes 1973, To Be of Use 1973, Living in the Open 1976, Woman on the Edge of Time 1976, The High Cost of Living 1978, Vida 1980, The Moon is Always Female 1980, Braided Lives 1982, Circles on the Water 1982, Stone, Paper, Knife 1983, My Mother's Body 1985, Gone to Soldiers 1988, Available Light 1988 (May Sarton Award 1991), Summer People 1989, He, She and It 1991, Body of Glass 1991 (Arthur C. Clarke Award 1993), Mars and Her Children 1992, The Longings of Women 1994, Eight Chambers of the Heart 1995, City of Darkness, City of Light 1996, What Are Big Girls Made Of? 1997, Storm Tide 1998. *Address:* P.O. Box 1473, Wellfleet, MA 02667, U.S.A.

PIERER, Heinrich von; German business executive; b. 26 Jan. 1941, Erlangen; ed. studies in law and econs.; joined Siemens' Legal Dept. 1969; in charge of KWU power station unit (Siemens' power plant div.) 1977; Commercial Dir. KWU 1988; mem. Admin. Bd. Siemens AG 1989, Deputy Chief Exec. 1991, Chief Exec. 1992–, also Pres. *Leisure interest:* tennis. *Address:* Siemens AG, Wittelsbacherplatz 2, 80333 Munich, Germany.

PIERONEK, Bishop Tadeusz; Polish ecclesiastic and professor of theology and canon law; b. 24 Oct. 1934, Radziechowy n. Żywiec; ed. Jagiellonian Univ., Kraków, Higher Ecclesiastic Seminary, Kraków, Catholic Univ. of Lublin, Lateral Univ., Rome; ordained Priest, Kraków 1957; notary Metropolitan Curia, Kraków; prefect Higher Ecclesiastic Seminary, Kraków; lecturer Catholic Theology Acad., Warsaw 1967–76, asst. prof. 1975; lecturer and head Dept. of Canon Law, Pontifical Acad. of Theology, Kraków 1965–, Prof. 1985; Visiting Prof. Santa Croce Univ., Rome 1985–; Cufrut Titular Bishop 1992; Deputy Gen. Sec. Polish Episcopate 1992–93; Gen. Sec. Polish Episcopate Conf. 1993–98; Gen. Sec. Second Plenary Synod, Poland 1987; Rector Pontifical Acad. of Theology, Kraków 1998–. *Publications:* The Church Is Not Afraid of Freedom 1998 and over 100 articles. *Leisure interests:* Polish poetry, landscape tourism, cooking, classical music, painting, folklore. *Address:* Papieska Akademia Teologiczna, ul. Kanonicza 25, 31-002 Kraków, Poland. *Telephone:* (12) 421 84 16.

PIEROTH, Elmar; German politician and viticulturist; b. 9 Nov. 1934, Bad Kreuznach; s. of Philip Pieroth; m. Hannelore Ribow 1957; six c.; ed. Stefan Georg Gymnasium, Bingen and Univs. of Mainz and Munich; has run Weingut Ferdinand Pieroth GmbH since 1955; creator of Pieroth-Modell; devt. work in Togo 1960; initiator Bad Kreuznach talks; mem. Bundestag 1969–81; mem. Berlin Chamber of Deputies 1981–; Senator for Economy and Labour, Berlin 1981–89, 1995–, for Finance, Berlin 1991–95; mem. CDU. *Publications:* Die Union in der Opposition (with G. Golter) 1970, Chancen der Betriebe durch Umweltschutz (with L. Wicke) 1988. *Address:* 105 Martin-Luther-Strasse, 10825 Berlin, Germany.

PIERRE, Abbé (see Groués, Henri).

PIERRE, Eric; Haitian politician; fmr. economist; Prime Minister of Haiti 1997–98. *Address:* c/o Office of the Prime Minister, Port-au-Prince, Haiti.

PIERRE-BROSSOLETTE, Claude, L. EN D.; French civil servant; b. 5 March 1928, Paris; s. of Pierre Brossolette and Gilberte (née Bruel); m. Sabine Goldet 1953; two d.; ed. Lycée Henri-IV, Faculty of Law of Paris Univ., Ecole nat. d'admin.; Inspecteur adjoint des Finances 1952, Insp. 1955; served under two successive Ministers in Office of Minister of Econ. and Financial Affairs 1956; Asst. to Financial Adviser, Embassy in U.S.A. 1957; served Direction des Finances Extérieures 1958; Tech. Adviser, Office of Minister of Finance 1960–62, Asst. Dir. of Office 1962, Deputy Dir. 1963; Asst. Dir. of External Financial Affairs in Direction du Trésor 1964, later Chef de Service 1966; Sec.-Gen. Conseil nat. du Crédit 1967–71; served in office of Valéry Giscard d'Estaing, Minister of Econ. and Financial Affairs 1969–71; Dir. du Trésor, Ministry of Econ. and Financial Affairs 1971; Censeur, Banque de France, Crédit nat. 1971; Vice-Chair. Caisse nat. des Télécommunications 1971–74; Dir. SNCF (Nat. Railways Bd.) 1971–74, Air France 1971–74; Sec.-Gen. of Presidency of the Repub. 1974–76; Chair. Crédit Lyonnais 1976–82, Omnium financier pour l'Industrie nat. (OFINA) 1976, Europartners Securities Corpn., Banque Stern 1982–86 (Vice-Chair. 1986); Assoc. Man. Worms et Cie 1986–92; Admin. Crédit Nat. 1976–81; Pres. Démachy et Assocs. 1987; mem. Conseil nat. du Crédit 1976–81, Conseil de Surveillance de la Cie. Bancaire 1976, Dir. Société Air-liquide, Crédit Foncier de France 1978–82, Générale Occidentale 1979–82, Péchiney Ugine Kuhlmann 1980–82, Lyonnaise des Eaux 1980, B.S.N. 1981, Norsolor 1988; Pres. Supervisory Council Câbles Pirelli 1992–95, Pres. 1995–; Vice-Pres. Eurofin 1992–95, Pres. 1995–96; Pres. Caisse de refinancement hypothécaire 1995; Adviser to Pres. of Merrill Lynch Int. 1993–97, Chair. Supervisory Bd. Merrill Lynch France 1997–; Dir. GTM-Enterpose 1993–; Officier, Légion d'honneur, Commdr. de l'Ordre nat. du Mérite, Chevalier de l'Ordre des Palmes académiques, Médaille de la Résistance. *Address:* Banque Eurofin, 41 rue de la Bienfaisance, 75008 Paris; 37 avenue d'Iéna, 75116 Paris, France (Home). *Telephone:* 54201644 (France).

PIERRET, Alain Marie, B.A.; French diplomatist (retd.); b. 16 July 1930, Mourmelon; s. of Henri Pierret and Yvonne Delhumeau; m. Jacqueline Nanta 1958; three d. (one deceased); ed. Faculties of Arts (Sorbonne) and Law, Paris and Ecole Nat. de la France d'Outre-Mer; reserve officer (navy) 1953–55; District Commr. Togo 1955–59, Sahara (S. Algeria) 1959–61; Sec. of Embassy, Sierra Leone 1961–63, South Africa 1963–66; Africa Div. Ministry of Foreign Affairs 1966–69; Counsellor, Moscow 1969–72; Head, Soviet Affairs Bureau, Ministry of Foreign Affairs 1972; mem. French Del. to Conf. on Security and Co-operation in Europe Helsinki 1972–75; Counsellor, Belgrade 1975–80; Amb. to Niger 1980–82; Asst. Sec. of State for UN Affairs and Int. Orgs. 1983–86; Amb. to Israel 1986–91, to Belgium 1991–93, to the Holy See 1993–95; Pres. Interministerial Cttee. for Agric. and Food (CIAA) 1996–; mem. study mission into the spoliation of Jews in France during Second World War 1997; Del. to Conf. on Nazi Gold, London 1997, to Conf. on Holocaust-era Assets, Washington, D.C. 1998; Officier Légion d'honneur, Croix de Guerre (Vietnam), Grand Cross Order Pius IX (Holy See). *Address:* i 117, 26 rue du Cdt. Mouchotte, 75014 Paris, France.

PIERRET, Christian; French politician and economist; b. 12 March 1946, Bar-le-Duc; m. Marie-Odile Schibler 1978; one d. (and three d. from previous marriages); ed. Faculty of Law and Econs., Paris, Ecole Nat. d'Administration; civil servant, Ministry for the Economy and Finance, then Cour des Comptes 1972–78; fmr. Lorraine regional councillor and mem. Vosges Gen. Council; Nat. Ass. Deputy for Vosges 1978–93, 1997–; Minister of State attached to Minister for the Economy, Finance and Industry, with responsibility for Industry 1997–; Mayor of Saint-Dié-des-Vosges 1989–97, Deputy May 1997–; Chair. Caisse Nat. d'Epargne 1986–93; Vice-Chair. Accor Hotels group 1993–96; Chair. Parl. Study Group on Textile and Clothing industry 1988–, France-Israel Parl. Friendship Group 1988–; Vice-Chair. France-Great Britain Parl. Friendship Group 1988–; Regional councillor of Lorraine 1998–; mem. Comité pour l'union monétaire de l'Europe (CUME). *Publications:* Plan et autogestion, Socialisme et multinationales; many articles in various publs. *Address:* Ministry for the Economy, Finance and Industry, 139 rue de Bercy, 75572 Paris cedex 12; Hôtel de ville, 88100 Saint-Dié; Assemblée nationale, 75355 Paris, France. *Telephone:* (1) 40.04.04.04. *Fax:* (1) 43.43.75.97.

PIETREWICZ, Mirosław Piotr, PH.D.; Polish politician and economist; b. 2 Jan. 1941, Nowa Wieś, Suwałki Prov.; m.; four c.; ed. Main School of Planning and Statistics (SGPiS); worked in Inst. of Finance; Sr. Asst. Chair. of Finance, SGPiS 1968–71; mem. Ed. Bd. Wieś Współczesna 1971, Man. Econ. Section 1973, Asst. Chief Ed. 1981; Head, Agrarian Policy Div. Inst. for Devt. of Countryside and Agric. Polish Acad. of Sciences, Asst. Prof. 1979; returned to Chair. of Finance, SGPiS (Main School of Commerce from 1990) 1985, Prof. 1987, Asst. Dean, Dept. of Finance and Statistics, Asst. Dean, Coll. of Man. and Finance 1993; mem. Scientific Council of Pres. of Nat. Bank of Poland 1990; mem. Social Council for Planning 1992; mem. United Peasants' Party (ZSL) 1961–89; mem. Solidarity Trade Union 1980–84; mem. Exec. Cttee. Polish Peasants' Party (PSL) 1992–93; Minister-Head of Cen. Planning Office 1993–95; Deputy Prime Minister 1995–97; Minister of Treasury 1996–97; Deputy to Sejm (Parl.) 1997–; mem. Parl. Comm. for Public Finance. *Address:* Sejm RP, ul. Wiejska 4/6/8, 00-902 Warsaw, Poland. *Telephone:* (22) 621 26 27; 694 23 21.

PIETRUSKI, John Michael, B.S.; American business executive; b. 12 March 1933, Sayreville, N.J.; s. of the late John M. Pietruski, Sr. and Lillian Christensen Pietruski; m. Roberta Jeanne Talbot 1954; two s. one d.; ed. Sayreville High School and Rutgers Univ.; First Lieut. U.S. Army 1955–57; Mfg. Man., Industrial Eng. Man., Procter & Gamble Co. 1954–63; Pres. Medical Products and Hosp. Divs., C.R. Bard, Inc. 1963–77; Pres. Pharmaceutical Group, Sterling Drug Inc. 1977–81, Corp. Exec. Vice-Pres. 1981–83, Pres. and C.O.O. 1983–85, Chair. and C.E.O. 1985–88, mem. Bd. of Dirs. 1977–88; Pres. Dansara Co. 1988–; Chair. Bd. Texas Biotech. Corp. 1990–; mem. Bd. of Dirs. Irving Bank Corpn. 1985–89, Associated Dry Goods Corpn. 1985–88, Hershey Foods Corpn. 1987–, Cytogen Corpn. 1989–94, Gen. Public Utilities Corpn. 1989–, Lincoln Nat. Corpn. 1989–, McKesson Corpn 1990–, Professional Detailing Inc. 1998–; mem. Pharmaceutical Mfrs. Asscn. 1985–88; Trustee Rutgers Univ. Foundation 1985–94; Regent, Concordia

Coll. 1993–; Hon. LL.D. *Leisure interests:* boating, fishing, travelling, athletics. *Address:* Suite 3408, One Penn Plaza, York, NY 10119; 27 Paddock Lane, Colts Neck, NJ 07722, U.S.A. (Home). *Telephone:* (212) 268-5510 (Office).

PIGEAT, Henri Michel; French administrator; b. 13 Nov. 1939, Montluçon; s. of Eugène Pigeat and Odette Micard; m. Passerose Cyprienne Rueff 1976; one d.; ed. Inst. des Sciences Politiques, Paris, and Ecole Nat. d'Admin.; Civil Servant Office of Gen. Admin. and Public Service 1965–69; Head Office of Sec. of State for Public Service 1969–71, Tech. Adviser 1971–72; Head of Information Services, Office of Sec. of State for Public Service and Information 1973; Sec.-Gen. Interministerial Cttee. for Information 1973–74; Asst. Gen. Dir. Information, Gen. Office of Information 1974, Dir. 1975–76; Dir. Information and Broadcasting Service 1976–; Deputy Man. Dir. Agence France-Presse 1976–79, Chair. and Man. Dir. 1979–86; Chair. and Man. Dir. IBIS S.A.: Prof. Univ. of Paris II; Prof. Inst. d'Etudes Politiques de Paris 1986–92; Dir. Soc. nat. des entreprises de presse 1974–76; Dir. Soc. financière de radiodiffusion (Sofirad) 1972–76; fmr. Dir. E1, R.M.C., Sud Radio, S.N.E.P., T.D.F., Europe 1, Radio Monte Carlo; Maître de confs. Inst. d'études politiques, Paris 1966–73, Ecole nat. d'admin. 1967–69, Inst. int. d'admin. publique 1966–73; Pres. Dir.-Gen. Burson Marsteller 1987–89; Pres. Quicom SA; mem. Exec. Cttee. Int. Inst. of Communications, London, Pres. of French section; mem. Int. Press Inst.; Chevalier, Ordre nat. du Mérite; Commdr. Nat. Order of Fed. Repub. of Germany. *Publications:* La France contemporaine, L'Europe contemporaine (both jointly) 1966–70, Saint Ecran ou la Télévision par câbles 1974, Du Téléphone à la Télématique, La télévision par cable commence demain 1983, Le nouveau désordre mondial de l'information 1987, les Agences de presse 1997, Médias et déontologie 1997. *Address:* 3 rue de la Bourse, 75002 Paris; 23 quai Anatole France, 75007 Paris, France (Home). *Telephone:* 45.51.70.01 (Home).

PIGGOTT, Lester Keith; British jockey and trainer; b. 5 Nov. 1935; s. of Keith Piggott and Iris Rickaby; m. Susan Armstrong 1960; two d.; rode over 100 winners per year in U.K. alone in several seasons since 1955; rode 3,000th winner in U.K. 27 July 1974; Champion Jockey 11 times (1960, 1964–71); frequently rode in France; equalled record of 21 classic victories 1975; won 29 English classic victories by Oct. 1985; 4,349 winners by Oct. 1985; retd. Oct. 1985; races won include: the Derby (9 times): 1954 (on Never Say Die), 1957 (on Crepello), 1960 (on St. Paddy), 1968 (on Sir Ivor), 1970 (on Nijinsky), 1972 (on Roberto), 1976 (on Empery), 1977 (on The Minstrel), 1983 (on Teenoso); St. Leger (8 times); Prix de l'Arc de Triomphe (3 times): 1973 (on Rheingold), 1977 and 1978 (on Alleged); Washington, D.C. Int. 1968 (on Sir Ivor, first time since 1922 an English Derby winner raced in U.S.A.), 1969 (on Karabas), 1980 (on Argument); trainer 1985–87; sentenced to 3 years' imprisonment for tax fraud Oct. 1987; stripped of O.B.E. June 1988; released after 12 months for good behaviour, returned to racing Oct. 1990; retd. as jockey 1995; achieved a record of 30 classic wins 1992. *Publication:* Lester: The Autobiography of Lester Piggott 1995. *Leisure interests:* swimming, water skiing, golf. *Address:* Beech Tree House, The Green, Tostock, Bury St. Edmonds, Suffolk, 1P30 9NY; 6 Pier House, Cheyne Walk, London, SW3 5HG, England. *Telephone:* 0171-352 1520.

PIGOTT-SMITH, Tim; British actor and director; b. 13 May 1946, Rugby; s. of Harry Pigott-Smith and Margaret Pigott-Smith; m. Pamela Miles 1972; one s.; ed. Bristol Univ., Bristol Old Vic Theatre School; began stage career at Bristol Old Vic; mem. R.S.C. 1972–75; dir. Company by Samuel Beckett, Edin. Fringe Festival 1988; Artistic Dir. Compass Theatre 1989; Dir. The Royal Hunt of the Sun 1989, Playing the Wife 1992, Hamlet, Regent's Park 1994. *Stage appearances include:* As You Like it, Major Barbara, Benefactors, Bengal Lancer 1985, Antony and Cleopatra, Coming into Land 1987, Entertaining Strangers, Cymbeline, The Winter's Tale, The Tempest 1988, Julius Caesar 1990, Amadeus 1991, Old Times 1993, Jane Eyre 1993, The Picture of Dorian Gray 1994, Retreat, The Letter 1995, Mary Stuart 1996, The Alchemist, Heritage 1997, The Iceman Cometh 1998. *TV appearances include:* Hamlet, Antony and Cleopatra, Glittering Prizes, North and South, Wings, Eustace and Hilda, Lost Boys, Measure for Measure, Fame is the Spur, The Hunchback of Notre Dame, The Jewel in the Crown, Dead Man's Folly, Life Story 1990, The Chief 1990, 1991, 1992, The Adventures of Christopher Columbus, Bullion Boys 1993, The Shadowy Third, Calcutta Chronicles 1995. *Film appearances include:* Aces High 1975, Joseph Andrews 1977, Sweet William, Richard's Things 1978, The Day Christ Died 1979, Clash of the Titans 1981, Escape to Victory, State of Emergency, Life Story 1986, The Remains of the Day 1993. *Publication:* Out of India 1986. *Leisure interests:* music, reading. *Address:* c/o Peters Fraser & Dunlop, 503 The Chambers, Chelsea Harbour, Lots Road, London, SW10 0XF, England.

PIKAIZEN, Viktor Aleksandrovich; Russian violinist; b. 15 Feb. 1933, Kiev; s. of Alexander Pikaizen and Regina Bayerskaya; m. Irina Piitskaya 1958; one d.; ed. Moscow Conservatory (pupil of David Oistrakh); taught at Moscow Conservatory 1966–86; Prof. of Violin, Ankara State Conservatoire 1993–; Second Prize, Int. Kubelik Violinists' Competition, Prague 1949; G. Thibault Competition, Paris 1957, Tchaikovsky Competition, Moscow 1958, First Prize, Paganini Competition, Genoa 1965, Grand Prix Chant du Monde 1969, R.S.F.S.R. People's Artist 1989; numerous recordings. *Leisure interest:* chess. *Address:* I. Bahriye Ügok Gad. 15/4 B., Evlen, Ankara, Turkey; Chekhova Str. 31/22, Apt. 37, Moscow, Russia. *Telephone:* (312) 2124421 (Ankara); 299-09-85 (Moscow). *Fax:* (312) 2124421 (Ankara).

PIKE, Edward Roy, PH.D., F.R.S., C.PHYS., C.MATH., F.INST.P., F.I.M.A.; British physicist; b. 4 Dec. 1929, Perth, W. Australia; s. of Anthony Pike and Rosalind Irene Davies; m. Pamela Sawtell 1955; one s. two d.; ed. Southfield Grammar School, Oxford, Univ. Coll., Cardiff, M.I.T., U.S.A.; Sr. Scientific Officer Royal Signals and Radar Establishment Physics Group 1960, Prin. Scientific Officer 1967, Deputy Chief Scientific Officer 1973, Chief Scientific Officer 1984–91; Clerk Maxwell Prof. of Theoretical Physics, Univ. of London at King's Coll. 1986–, Head School of Physical Sciences and Eng. 1991–94; fmr. Fulbright Scholar; Royal Soc. Charles Parsons Medal and Lecture 1975, MacRobert Award (jtly.) and lecture 1977, Worshipful Co. of Scientific Instrument Makers Annual Achievement Award (jtly.) 1978, Guthrie Medal and Prize, Inst. of Physics 1996. *Publications:* The Quantum Theory of Radiation (jtly.) 1995, Light Scattering and Photon Correlation Spectroscopy (jtly.) 1997; Ed.: Photon Correlation and Light-Beating Spectroscopy 1974, High Power Gas Lasers 1975, Photon Correlation Spectroscopy and Velocimetry 1977, Frontiers in Quantum Optics 1986, Fractals, Noise and Chaos 1987, Quantum Measurement and Chaos 1987, Squeezed and Non-classical Light 1988, Photons and Quantum Fluctuations 1988, Inverse Problems in Scattering and Imaging 1992; numerous papers in scientific journals. *Leisure interests:* music, languages, woodwork. *Address:* 3A Golborne Mews, North Kensington, London, W.10, England.

PIKE, Sir Philip, Kt., Q.C.; British judge; b. 6 March 1914, Jamaica; s. of Ernest B. and Dora C. (née Lillie) Pike; m. 1st Phyllis Kelvin Calder 1943; one s. one d.; m. 2nd Millicent Locke Staples 1959 (died 1996); ed. De Carteret School and Munro Coll., Jamaica, and Middle Temple, London; Crown Counsel Jamaica 1947–49; Legal Draftsman Kenya 1949–52; Solicitor-Gen., Uganda 1952–58; Attorney-Gen., Sarawak 1958–65; Chief Justice High Court, Borneo 1965–68; Judge and Acting Chief Justice, Malawi 1969–70; Chief Justice, Swaziland 1970–72; Coronation Medal; decorations from Malaysia and Sarawak. *Leisure interests:* golf, gardening. *Address:* 3 Earlewood Court, Penhaligon Way, Robina, Queensland 4226, Australia.

PIKHOYA, Rudolf Germanovich, D.HIST.SC.; Russian historian; b. 27 Jan. 1947, Polevskoe, Sverdlovsk Region; m.; one s.; ed. Ural Univ.; with Ural Univ. 1971–, sr. researcher Ural Scientific Centre, U.S.S.R. Acad. of Sciences 1981–86; Pro-rector Ural Univ. 1986–90; Chair. Cttee. on problems of archives, Council of Ministers of Russian Fed. 1990–, Chief, Archive Service of Russia 1992–96; participated in movt. for making secret documents of the Communist period public; Vice-Pres. Int. Fund for Democracy, Dir. of Research Programmes 1996–. *Leisure interest:* music. *Address:* International Fund for Democracy, Malaya Gruzinskaya str. 15, Bldg. 3, Moscow, Russia. *Telephone:* 252-57-26.

PILARCZYK, Most Rev. Daniel Edward, M.A., PH.D., S.T.D., American ecclesiastic; b. 12 Aug. 1934, Dayton, Ohio; s. of Daniel J. Pilarczyk and Frieda S. Hilgefort; ed. St. Gregory Seminary, Ohio, Pontifical Urban Univ. Rome, Xavier Univ. Cincinnati and Univ. of Cincinnati; ordained Roman Catholic priest 1959; Asst. Chancellor, Archdiocese of Cincinnati 1961–63; Faculty, Athenaeum of Ohio (St. Gregory Seminary) 1963–74, Vice-Pres. 1968–74, Trustee 1974–; Rector, St. Gregory Seminary 1968–74; Synodal Judge, Archdiocesan Tribunal 1971–82; Dir. of Archdiocesan Educ. Services 1974–82; Auxiliary Bishop of Cincinnati 1974–82, Archbishop 1982–; Vice-Pres. Nat. Conf. of Catholic Bishops 1986–89; Pres. Nat. Conf. of Catholic Bishops 1989–92; Chair. Episcopal Bd. Int. Comm. on English in Liturgy 1987–97; numerous professional appts.; Hon. LL.D. (Xavier Univ.) 1975, (Calumet Coll.) 1982, (Univ. of Dayton) 1990, (Marquette Univ.) 1990, (Thomas More Coll.) 1991, (Coll. of Mount St. Joseph) 1994, (Hebrew Union Coll./Jewish Inst. of Religion) 1997. *Publications:* Twelve Tough Issues 1988, We Believe 1989, Living in the Lord 1990, The Parish: Where God's People Live 1991, Forgiveness 1992, What Must I Do? 1993, Our Priests: Who They Are and What They Do 1994, Lenten Lunches 1995, Bringing Forth Justice 1996, Thinking Catholic 1997, Practicing Catholic 1998; numerous articles in newspapers and journals. *Address:* 100 East Eighth Street, Cincinnati, OH 45202, U.S.A. (Home). *Telephone:* 421-3131.

PILGER, John Richard; Australian journalist, film-maker and author; b. 9 Oct. 1939, Sydney; s. of Claude Pilger and Elsie Pilger (née Marheine); m. (divorced); one s. one d.; ed. Sydney High School, Journalism Cadet Training, Australian Consolidated Press; journalist Sydney Daily/Sunday Telegraph 1958–62; Reuters, London 1962; Foreign Corresp. (latterly Chief Foreign Corresp.) Daily Mirror, London 1963–86; columnist New Statesman London 1991–; freelance contrib. The Guardian, London, The Independent, London, New York Times, Melbourne Age, The Nation, New York; Documentary film-maker, Granada TV U.K. 1969–71, Associated Television 1972–80, Cen. Television U.K. 1980–; credited with alerting much of int. community to horrors of Pol Pot régime in Cambodia, also occupation of East Timor; Hon. D. Litt. (Staffordshire Univ.) 1994, Hon. Ph.D. (Dublin City Univ.) 1995, Hon. D.Arts (Oxford Brookes Univ.) 1997; Descriptive Writer of the Year, U.K. 1966, Journalist of the Year, U.K. 1967 and 1979, Int. Reporter of the Year, U.K. 1970, Reporter of the Year, U.K. 1974, Richard Dimbleby Award, British Acad. of Film and TV Arts 1991, U.S. Acad. Award (Emmy) 1991, Reporteurs sans frontières, France 1993, George Foster Peabody Award (U.S.A.) 1992. *Publications:* The Last Day 1975, Aftermath: The Struggle of Cambodia and Vietnam 1981, The Outsiders 1983, Heroes 1986, A Secret Country 1989, Distant Voices 1992, Hidden Agendas 1998. *Feature film:* The Last Day 1983. *Documentary films include:* Cambodia: Year Zero 1979 (and four other films on Cambodia), The Quiet Mutiny 1970, Japan Behind the Mask 1986, The Last Dream 1988, Death of a Nation 1994, Flying the Flag: Arming the World 1994, Inside Burma 1996, Breaking The Mirror:

The Murdoch Effect 1997, Apartheid Did Not Die 1998, Hidden Agendas 1998. *Leisure interests:* swimming, sunning, mulling. *Address:* 57 Hambalt Road, London, SW4 9EQ, England. *Telephone:* 0181-673 2848. *Fax:* 0181-772 0235.

PILLSBURY, Edmund Pennington, PH.D.; American museum director; b. 28 April 1943, San Francisco, Calif.; s. of Edmund P. Pillsbury and Priscilla K. (Giesen) Pillsbury; m. Mireille Marie-Christine Bernard 1969; one s. one d.; ed. Yale Univ. and Univ. of London; David E. Finley Fellow, Nat. Gallery of Art, Washington, D.C. 1967–70; Ford Foundation Fellow, Cleveland Museum of Art 1970–71; Curator, European Art, Yale Univ. Gallery and Lecturer, History of Art, Yale Univ. 1972–76; Dir. Yale Center, British Art and Adjunct Prof. of History of Art Yale Univ. 1976–80; C.E.O. Paul Mellon Centre, Studies in British Art, London 1976–80; Dir. Kimbell Art Museum and Vice-Pres. Kimbell Art Foundation 1980–; mem. Presidential Task Force on Arts and Humanities 1981, The Century Asscn. 1991; Adjunct Prof. Tex. Christian Univ. 1985; Chevalier, Ordre des Arts et des Lettres. *Publications:* Florence and the Arts 1971, David Hockney: Travels with Pen, Pencil and Ink 1977, The Graphic Art of Federico Barocci 1978. *Leisure interests:* skiing, running, reading. *Address:* Kimbell Art Museum, 3333 Camp Bowie Boulevard, Fort Worth, TX 76107 (Office); 1110 Broad Avenue, Fort Worth, TX 76107, U.S.A. (Home). *Telephone:* (817) 332-8451.

PILON, Jean-Guy, O.C., B.A., LL.L.; Canadian poet; b. 12 Nov. 1930, St. Polycarpe; s. of Arthur Pilon and Alida Besner; m. 2nd Denise Viens 1988; two s. by 1st marriage; ed. Univ. de Montréal; founded Liberté (review) 1959, Ed. 1959–79; Head of Cultural Programmes and Producer Radio-Canada 1970–88; Les Ecrits (literary review); mem. Académie des lettres du Québec 1982, Royal Soc. of Canada 1967–; Prix de Poésie du Québec 1956, Louise Labé 1969, France-Canada 1969, van Lerberghe (Paris) 1969, du Gouverneur gén. du Canada 1970, Athanase David 1984; Ordre Nat. du Québec 1988, Ordre des Arts et des Lettres (France) 1992. *Publications (poems):* La Fiancée du matin 1953, Les Cloîtres de l'été 1955, L'Homme et le jour 1957, La Mouette et le large 1960, Recours au pays 1961, Pour saluer une ville 1963, Comme eau retenue 1969 (enlarged edn. 1986), Saisons pour la continuelle 1969, Silences pour une souveraine 1972. *Address:* 5724 Côte St-Antoine, Montréal, P.Q., H4A 1R9, Canada.

PILSWORTH, Michael John, M.A.; British television executive; b. 1 April 1951, Leeds; s. of Alwyne Pilsworth and Catherine Pilsworth (née Silverwood); m. Stella Frances Pilsworth (née Hore) 1972; one s. one d.; ed. King Edward VI Grammar School, Retford, Univ. of Manchester; Research Asst. Inst. of Advanced Studies, Manchester Polytechnic 1972–73; Research Associate Univ. of Manchester 1973–75, lecturer 1973–77; Research Fellow, Centre for TV Research 1977–79, Univ. of Leeds 1979–81; researcher, London Weekend 1982–83; Head of Programme Devt. TV South 1984–86, Controller Corp. Devt. 1987–88; Chief Exec. M.G.M.M. Communications Ltd. 1988–89; Man. Dir Alomo Productions Ltd. 1990–92, Selec TV P.L.C. 1992–93; Chief Exec. Chrysalis Visual Entertainment Ltd. 1993–. *Publications:* co-author Broadcasting in the Third World 1977. *Leisure interests:* reading, cinema, gardening. *Address:* 1 Church Lane, Eaton Bray, Beds., LU6 2DJ, England.

PIMENTA, H.E. Cardinal Simon Ignatius; Indian ecclesiastic; b. 1 March 1920, Bombay; s. of late Joseph Pimenta and Rosie Pimenta; ordained 1949, elected to the titular Church of Bocconia 1971, consecrated bishop 1971, coadjutor bishop 1977, Archbishop of Bombay 1978–97 (retd.); cr. Cardinal 1988. *Address:* Archbishop's House, 21 Nathalal Parekh Marg, Bombay-400 001, India. *Telephone:* (022) 202.10.93; 204.96.96. *Fax:* (022) 285.38.72.

PIMLOTT, Benjamin (Ben) John, F.B.A., PH.D., F.R.HIST.S.; British professor of politics and contemporary history; b. 4 July 1945; s. of the late John Alfred Ralph Pimlott, C.B., and Ellen Dench Howes Pimlott; m. Jean Ann Seaton 1977; three s.; ed. Rokeby School, Wimbledon, Marlborough Coll. and Oxford and Newcastle Univs.; lecturer Newcastle Univ. 1970–79; Resident Assoc. L.S.E. 1979–81; lecturer Birkbeck Coll., Univ. of London 1981–86, Reader 1986–87, Professor of Politics and Contemporary History 1987–98; British Acad. Thank Offering to Britain Fellow 1972–73, Nuffield Foundation Resident Fellow 1977–78; Chair. E.S.R.C. Whitehall Programme Commissioning Panel 1993–94, Steering Cttee. 1994–; contested parl. seat at Arundel 1974, Cleveland and Whitby 1974, 1979; political columnist Today 1986–87, The Times 1987–88, New Statesman (political ed.) 1987–88, Sunday Times 1988–89; Ed. Samizdat 1988–90; Warden Goldsmiths Coll. 1998–; mem. Exec. Fabian Soc. 1987–, Chair. 1993–94. *Publications:* Labour and the Left in the 1930s 1977, Hugh Dalton 1985 (Whitbread Biography Prize), Harold Wilson 1992, Frustrate Their Knavish Tricks 1994, The Queen 1996, Editor: Trade Unions in British Politics (with Chris Cook) 1982, Fabian Essays in Socialist Thought 1984, The Second World War Diary of Hugh Dalton 1940–45 1986, The Political Diary of Hugh Dalton 1918–40, 1945–60 1987, The Media in British Politics (with Jean Seaton) 1987, The Alternative (with A. Wright and T. Flower) 1990, Tackling the Inner Cities (with S. MacGregor) 1990; articles in learned journals and articles and reviews in national newspapers and other publs. *Address:* 9 Milner Place, London, N1 1TN, England. *Telephone:* 0171-609 1793.

PIMLOTT, Steven; British theatre and opera director; b. 18 April 1953, Manchester; m. Daniela Bechly 1991; two s. one d.; ed. Univ. of Cambridge; began career in regional theatre and opera; work directed includes: The Park 1984, Twelfth Night (Crucible Theatre, Sheffield) 1986, Samson et Delila (Bregenz) 1988, Carmen (Earl's Court, London) 1990, Sunday in the Park with George (Nat. Theatre) 1990, Molière's The Miser (Nat. Theatre) 1991, Joseph and the Amazing Technicolour Dreamcoat (Palladium, London) 1991, (Broadway) 1993, Julius Caesar (RSC, Stratford) 1991, Murder in the Cathedral (R.S.C., Stratford) 1993, La Bohème (E.N.O.) 1993, Unfinished Business (R.S.C., Barbican) 1994, Butterfly Kiss (Almeida) 1994, Measure for Measure (R.S.C., Stratford) 1994, The Strip (Royal Court) 1995, Macbeth (Hamburg-Staatsoper) 1997, Camino Real (R.S.C.), Never Land (Royal Court), Bad Weather (R.S.C.), musical staging of Doctor Doolittle (Triumph Apollo) 1998; Dir. 1996/97 R.S.C. Season, including productions of As You Like It and The Learned Ladies, 1998/99 R.S.C. The Other Place, including Antony and Cleopatra; Assoc. Dir. R.S.C. *Address:* c/o Harriet Cruickshank, 97 Old South Lambeth Road, London, SW8 1XU; Old House, Old House Road, Great Horkesley, Colchester, Essex, CO6 4EQ, England.

PINA-CABRAL, João De, D.PHIL.; Portuguese social anthropologist; b. 9 May 1954; s. of Daniel de Pina Cabral and Ana A. de Pina Cabral; ed. Univ. of Witwatersrand, Johannesburg and Univ. of Oxford; Auxiliary Prof. Dept. of Social Anthropology, ISCTE, Lisbon 1982–84, Assoc. Prof. 1988–; Gulbenkian Fellow in Portuguese Studies, Univ of Southampton 1984–86; Research Fellow, Inst. of Social Sciences, Univ. of Lisbon 1986–92, Sr. Research Fellow 1992–. *Publications:* Death in Portugal (co-ed.) 1983, Sons of Adam, Daughters of Eve 1986, Os Contextos da Antropologia 1991, Europe Observed (co-ed.) 1992, Aromas de Urze e de Lama 1993, Em Terra de Tufões 1993. *Address:* Instituto de Ciências Sociais, Universidade de Lisboa, Avenida Forças Armadas, P-1600 Lisbon, Portugal. *Telephone:* 7932272. *Fax:* 7964953.

PINARD, Rt. Hon. Yvon, B.A., LL.L.; Canadian politician and lawyer; b. 10 Oct. 1940, Drummondville, Quebec; s. of Jean-Jacques Pinard and Cécile Chassé; m. Renée Chaput 1964; two d.; ed. Immaculate Conception School, Drummondville, Nicolet Seminary, Sherbrooke Univ.; Pres. Sherbrooke Univ. Law Faculty 1963; admitted to Quebec Bar 1964; Pres. and founder Drummond Caisse d'Entraide Economique; Pres. Drummond Co. Liberal Asscn. 1968–70; mem. Admin. Council Centre Communautaire d'Aide Juridique Mauricie-Bois-Francs region; mem. Commonwealth Parl. Asscn. and Canadian Del. Interparl. Union; mem. House of Commons 1974–84; Parl. Sec. to Pres. of Privy Council Oct. 1977; Pres. of H.M. the Queen's Privy Council for Canada 1980–84; Judge Federal Court of Canada, Trial Div. Judge 1984–; mem. ex-officio Fed. Court of Appeal 1984–; Liberal. *Address:* Federal Court of Canada, Ottawa, Ont., K1A 0H9, Canada.

PINAULT, François; French business executive; b. 21 Aug. 1936, Champs Géraux, Côtes-du-Nord; s. of François Pinault and Eugénie Gabillard; m. Mary Campbell 1970; two s. two d.; ed. Coll. Saint-Martin, Rennes; worked in father's timber co. at age 16; f. Société Pinault, Rennes 1963, Prés.-Dir.-Gén. 1970; Pres. Co. française de l'Afrique occidentale (CFAO) 1990–91; Vice-Pres. Supervisory Bd. Groupe Pinault-Printemps 1992; Prés.-Dir.-Gén. Artémis S.A.; Head Christie's U.K. 1998–; owns vineyard Chateau Latour, Vail ski resort in Colo., luggage mfr. Samsonite and majority shareholding in French real estate investment co. Sefimeg; Officier, Légion d'honneur, Croix de la Valeur Militaire. *Leisure interests:* cinema, theatre, art collecting, cycling, walking. *Address:* Artémis SA, 5 blvd. de Latour Maubourg, 75007 Paris, France; Christies International PLC, 8 King Street, London, S.W.1, England.

PINCOTT, Leslie Rundell, C.B.E., F.C.A., F.INST.M.S.M., C.B.I.M.; British company executive; b. 27 March 1923, London; s. of Hubert George and Gertrude Elizabeth (Rundell) Pincott; m. Mary Mae Tuffin 1944 (died 1996); two s. one d.; ed. Mercers School, Holborn, London, Harvard Business School, U.S.A.; Lieut. in R.N.V.R. 1942–46; qualified as chartered accountant; joined Esso Petroleum Co. Ltd. 1950, Comptroller 1958–60, seconded to Exxon Corpn. 1968–70, Man. Dir. Esso Petroleum Co. 1970–78; Chair. Oxford Univ. Business Summer School 1975–78; Vice-Chair. Remploy Ltd. 1979–87 (Dir. 1975–79); Dir. British Railways Southern Bd. 1977–86, Chair. 1986–89; Pres. Dist. Heating Asscn. 1977–79; Chair. Canada Perm. Trust (UK) Ltd. 1978–80, Dir. in Toronto; Dir. George Wimpey PLC 1978–85, Brown & Root-Wimpey Highlands Fabricators Ltd. 1984–91; Deputy Chair., Chair. Price Comm. 1978–80; Chair. Stone-Platt Industries Ltd. 1980–82, Edman Communications Group PLC 1982–87, Printing Industries Econ. Devt. Cttee. 1982–88; mem. Investment Cttee., London Devt. Capital Devt. Fund 1984–; Chair. The Hurlingham Club 1989–92; mem. Bd. Wandle Housing Asscn. 1996, Chair. 1998–. *Leisure interests:* tennis, walking, travel, swimming. *Address:* 6 Lambourne Avenue, Wimbledon, London, SW19 7DW, England (Home). *Telephone:* 0181-947 1305 (Home).

PINDLING, Rt. Hon. Sir Lynden Oscar, K.C.M.G., P.C.; Bahamian politician; b. 22 March 1930; s. of Arnold Franklin and Viola Pindling; m. Marguerite McKenzie 1956; two s. two d.; ed. Govt. High School, Bahamas, and London Univ.; Lawyer 1952–67; mem. House of Ass.; Leader of Progressive Liberal Party 1992; Premier of Bahamas 1967–69, Prime Minister 1969–92; Minister of Econ. Affairs 1969–82, 1984–90, of Defence 1983–84, of Tourism 1990–92. *Leisure interests:* swimming, boating, travel. *Address:* P.O. Box N-8174, Nassau, Bahamas.

PINEAU-VALENCIENNE, Didier; French company director; b. 21 March 1931, Paris; s. of Maurice and Madeleine (née Dubigeon) Pineau-Valencienne; m. Guillemette Rident 1964; one s. three d.; ed. Lycée Janson-de-Sailly, Paris, Dartmouth Univ. (U.S.A.) and Harvard Business School; Man. Asst. Banque Parisienne pour l'Industrie 1958, Prin. Man. Asst. 1962, Dir.

1964–67, Dir.-Gen. 1969 and Admin. 1971; Pres. and Dir.-Gen. Carbonisation et Charbons Actifs (CECA) 1972–74, Société Resogil 1975–76; Dir.-Gen. Société Celogil 1975–76; Admin. Isorel 1976; Dir. of Admin. and Strategy and Planning Rhone-Poulenc S.A. 1976–77, Dir.-Gen. (Polymer Div.) 1978; Admin. Quartz et Silice; Admin., Vice-Pres., Dir.-Gen. Schneider S.A. 1980–81, Pres. Dir.-Gen. 1981–; Pres., Dir.-Gen. Jeumont-Schneider 1987–89, Pres. Schneider Industries Services Int. 1991–92, Schneider Electric SA 1993–; Asst. Admin. Société Electrorail S.A. 1980–; Dir. Merlin-Gérin 1981–, Pres. Dir.-Gen. 1989–; Chair. Empain-Schneider Group 1981–, Société Parisienne d'Etudes et de Participations 1982–; Chair. and Man. Dir. Creusot-Loire 1982–84; Dir. Paribas 1989–98, Whirlpool Corpn. 1992–; Pres. Admin. Council, Tech. Univ. of Compiègne 1992–96; Pres. Inst. de L'Entreprise 1993–96, Hon. Pres. 1996–; Vice-Pres. and Pres. Comm. Sociale du Couseil nat. du patronat français (CNPF) 1997–; Chair. Advisory Bd. Sisie 1997–98; fmr. teacher Ecole des Hautes Etudes Commerciales; Officier, Légion d'honneur, Officier Ordre nat. du Mérite. *Leisure interests:* tennis, skiing, collecting books. *Address:* Schneider, 64/70 avenue Jean Baptiste Clément, 92646 Boulogne-Billancourt, France.

PINHEIRO FARINHA, João de Deus; Portuguese judge; b. 8 March 1919, Redondo; s. of Simão Martins Pereira and Isabel Gapete (Pinheiro) Farinha; m. Maria das Dores Pombinho 1947; ed. Liceu Nacional André da Gouveia and Univ. of Lisbon; Deputy Public Prosecutor 1943–50; Insp. of Prison Services 1944–49; Judge, Leiria Industrial Court 1950–51; Judge in lower courts 1951–66; Asst. Public Prosecutor 1957–58; Pres. Corregitor (3rd Civil Chamber) 1966–70; Judge, Coimbra and Lisbon Appeal Courts 1970–74; Attorney-Gen. 1974; Minister of Justice 1975–76, of Foreign Affairs 1991–92; Commr. of the European Communities (now European Comm.) for Openness, Communication and Culture 1993–95, for Relations with African, Caribbean and Pacific Countries, South Africa, the Lomé Convention Jan. 1995–; mem. Perm. Court of Arbitration 1975; Pres. Court of Accounts 1977–91; Judge, European Court of Human Rights 1977–, Supreme Court of Justice 1978–; Vice-Pres. Int. Comm. on Civil Status 1977–79, Pres. 1980; Hon. D.Eng. (Birmingham) 1992; Gold Medal of Penitentiary Social Merit (Spain), Medal of Council of Europe. *Publications:* many legal publications. *Leisure interests:* travel, philosophy, religion. *Address:* European Commission, 200 rue de la Loi, 1049 Brussels, Belgium; Avenida Dr. Baraona 14, 7170 Lisbon, Portugal (Home). *Telephone:* 99197 (Home).

PINKAYAN, Subin, PH.D.; Thai politician and engineer; b. 16 June 1934, Chiang Mai; m. Boonsri Pinkayan; one s.; ed. Chulalongkorn Univ., Asian Inst. of Tech. and Univ. of Colo.; researcher Univ. of Colo.; eng. consultant, Mekong Cttee.; Irrigation Dept. 1967–74; Project Dir. Asian Inst. of Tech. 1974; lecturer Chulalongkorn Univ.; assoc. prof. Asian Inst. of Tech.; Social Action Party M.P. for Chiang Mai 1983–; fmr. Univ. Affairs Minister; Deputy Leader Social Action Party; Minister of Foreign Affairs Sept.–Dec. 1990. *Address:* c/o Ministry of Foreign Affairs, Saranrom Palace, Bangkok 10200, Thailand.

PINKER, Sir George Douglas, K.C.V.O., F.R.C.S.ED., F.R.C.O.G.; British gynaecologist and obstetrician; b. 6 Dec. 1924; s. of Ronald D. Pinker and Queenie E. Dix; m. Dorothy E. Russell; three s. one d.; ed. Reading School and St. Mary's Hosp., London; fmrly. consultant gynaecological surgeon, Bolingbroke Hosp. and resident officer, Nuffield Dept. of Obstetrics, Radcliffe Infirmary, Oxford; fmrly. consultant gynaecological surgeon, Queen Charlotte's Hosp., London; consulting gynaecological surgeon and obstetrician, St. Mary's Hosp. Paddington and Samaritan Hosp. 1958–; consulting gynaecological surgeon, Middx. and Soho Hosps. 1969–; consultant gynaecologist, King Edward VII Hosp. for Officers, London 1974–; Surgeon-Gynaecologist to H.M. Queen Elizabeth II 1973–90; mem. Royal Coll. of Obstetricians and Gynaecologists, Pres. 1987–90. *Publications:* co-author of three books on obstetrics and gynaecology. *Leisure interests:* music, gardening, sailing, skiing, fell walking. *Address:* 96 Harley Street, London, W1N 1AF; Sycamore House, Willersey, Broadway, Worcs., WR12 7PJ, England. *Telephone:* 0171-935 7254 (London).

PINKER, Robert Arthur, M.SC.; British professor of administration; b. 27 May 1931; s. of Dora Elizabeth Pinker and Joseph Pinker; m. Jennifer Farrington Boulton 1955 (died 1994); two d.; ed. Holloway Co. School, London School of Econs.; Head Sociology Dept., Goldsmiths' Coll., London Univ. 1964–72, Lewisham Prof. of Social Admin., Goldsmiths' Coll. and Bedford Coll. 1972–74; Prof. of Social Studies, Chelsea Coll. 1974–78; Prof. of Social Work Studies, L.S.E. 1978–93, Prof. of Admin. 1993–96, Emer.-Prof. of Social Admin. 1996–, Pro-Dir. L.S.E. 1985–88; Pro-Vice-Chancellor for Social Sciences, London Univ. 1989–90; Chair. Editorial Bd. Journal of Social Policy 1981–86; Chair. British Library Project on Family and Social Research 1983–86; mem. Council, Advertising Standards Authority 1988–95, Press Complaints Comm. 1991– (Privacy Commr. 1994–), Council, Direct Mail Accreditation and Recognition Centre 1995–, Bd. of Man. London School of Hygiene and Tropical Medicine 1990–; Chair. Govs. Centre for Policy on Ageing 1988–94, Central Westminster Police/Community Consultative Group 1997–. *Publications:* English Hospital Statistics 1861–1938 1964, Social Theory and Social Policy 1971, The Idea of Welfare 1979, Social Work in an Enterprise Society 1990. *Leisure interests:* reading, writing, travel, unskilled gardening. *Address:* 76 Coleraine Road, Blackheath, London, SE3 7PE, England. *Telephone:* 0181-858 5320.

PINNOCK, Trevor, C.B.E., A.R.C.M., F.R.A.M.; British harpsichordist and conductor; b. 16 Dec. 1946, Canterbury; s. of Kenneth and Joyce Pinnock; ed. Canterbury Cathedral School, Royal Coll. of Music, London; Jt. F. Galliard Harpsichord Trio, début, London 1966, solo début, London 1968, Dir. The English Concert 1973–; Artistic Dir., Prin. Conductor Nat. Arts Centre Orchestra, Ottawa 1991–96; has toured Western Europe, U.S.A., Canada, Australia, Japan with The English Concert, as solo harpsichordist and as orchestral/opera conductor; début Metropolitan Opera, New York 1988. *Recordings* include Handel, J. S. Bach, C. P. E. Bach, Rameau, Vivaldi, Scarlatti, 16th-, 17th- and 18th-century harpsichord music, and most of the standard baroque orchestral/concerto/choral repertoire. *Address:* c/o Askonas Holt Ltd., 27 Chancery Lane, London, WC2A 1PF, England.

PINOCHET UGARTE, Gen. Augusto; Chilean army officer; b. 25 Nov. 1915; m. María Lucía Hiriat Rodríguez; two s. three d.; ed. Mil. Acad., School of Infantry, Acad. of War, Acad. of Nat. Defence; Army career 1933–98, Col. 1966, Brig.-Gen. 1969, Div. Gen. 1970, Gen. 1973; Instructor Acad. of War 1954, Deputy Dir. 1964; Asst. to Under-Sec. of War 1954; mem. Chilean mil. mission to U.S.A. 1956; Instructor Acad. of War, Ecuador 1956–59; C.-in-C. VI Army Div., Chief of Army Staff 1969; C.-in-C. of Armed Forces 1973–98; Senator for Life 1998–; led coup to depose President Salvador Allende Sept. 1973; Pres. Gov. Council of Chile 1973–74; Pres. of Chile 1974–90; arrested in London Oct. 1998 and charged on 32 counts of torture and murder; Law Lords rule that he does not enjoy immunity from sovereign prosecution 1998; Home Sec. allows proposed extradition to Spain Dec. 1998; Lords ruling overturned 1998, ruling on immunity sustained after further hearings March 1999; Home Sec. authorizes start of further extradition proceedings April 1999; Case on appeal; Pres. Junta Militar; Mil. Star, Grand Mil. Merit Cross, High Command Hon. Officer (Ecuador), Abdón Calderón Parra Medal (Ecuador), Order of Mil. Merit (Colombia), Grand Cross of Military Merit (Spain). *Publications:* Geopolítica—Diferentes Etapas para el Estudio Geopolítico de los Estados 1968, Geografía de Chile 1968, Geografía de Argentina, Perú y Bolivia 1972, Guerra del Pacífico 1879—Primeras Operaciones Terrestres 1972.

PINÓS, Carmen; Spanish architect; b. 23 June 1954, Barcelona; ed. Escuela Superior de Arquitectura de Barcelona, Int. Lab. of Architecture with Urban Design (ILAUD), Urbino, Columbia Univ.; partnership with Enric Miralles, Barcelona 1983–91, projects included Cemetery of Igualada, Barcelona (Barcelona City Prize), Barcelona Olympics Archery Grand (Biannual Prize for European Architecture); est. own architectural practice 1991, projects include Footbridge, Petrer (Alicante), Hogar School of Morella (Nat. Prize for Architecture 1995); fmr. visiting Prof. Acad. Van Boukunst, Amsterdam; Ecole Speciale d'Architecture, Paris; Plym Prof. Univ. of Ill. at Urbana–Champaign 1994–95; currently Prof. Kunstakademie, Dusseldorf; MOPU competition (1st Prize) 1982; Mies Van de Rohe Prize; numerous other awards. *Major works:* El Croquis 1986, Arte Cemento 1987, Baumeister 1989. *Address:* Av. Diagonal 490, 3º2º, 08006 Barcelona, Spain. *Telephone:* 416-0372. *Fax:* 415-3719.

PINSENT, Matthew, M.B.E.; British oarsman; b. 10 Oct. 1970, Henley-on-Thames; ed. Eton Coll. and Univ. of Oxford; rep. U.K. at Jr. World Championships 1987, 1988, gold medal in coxless pairs (with Tim Foster) 1988; bronze medal, coxed four, World Championships 1989, coxless pair 1990; mem. two winning University Boat Race crews; teamed up with Steve Redgrave (q.v.) in coxless pairs 1990; gold medal, coxless pairs (with Redgrave), World Championships 1991, 1993, 1994, 1995, Olympic Games, Barcelona 1992, Atlanta 1996; gold medal, coxless fours 1997, 1998. *Leisure interest:* golf. *Address:* c/o British International Rowing Office, 6 Lower Mall, London, W6 9DJ, England. *Telephone:* 0181-741 7580. *Fax:* 0181-563 2265.

PINSKY, Robert Neal, PH.D.; American poet; b. 20 Oct. 1940, Long Branch, N.J.; s. of Milford Simon Pinsky and Sylvia Pinsky (née Eisenberg); m. Ellen Jane Bailey 1961; three d.; ed. Rutgers Univ., Stanford Univ.; taught English Univ. of Chicago 1967–68, Wellesley Coll. 1968–80; Prof. of English Univ. of Calif., Berkeley 1980–89; Prof. Boston Univ. 1980–89, Prof. of Creative Writing 1989–; Poet Laureate of U.S.A. Sept. 1997–; Visiting Lecturer, Harvard Univ.; Hurst Prof. Washington Univ., St. Louis; Poetry Ed. New Repub. magazine 1978; Artists Award American Acad. of Arts and Letters 1979, Saxifrage Prize 1980, William Carlos Williams Prize 1984, Shelley Memorial Award 1996; Guggenheim Fellow 1980; mem. A.A.A.S. *Publications:* Landor's Poetry 1968, Sadness and Happiness 1975, The Situation of Poetry 1977, An Explanation of America 1980, History of my Heart 1980, Poetry and the World 1988, The Want Bone 1990, The Inferno of Dante 1994, The Figured Wheel: New and Collected Poems 1966–96 1996. *Address:* Department of English, Boston University, 236 Bay State Road, Boston, MA 02215, U.S.A.

PINTASILGO, Maria de Lourdes; Portuguese politician, engineer and diplomatist; b. 18 Jan. 1930, Abrantes; d. of Jaime de Matos Pintasilgo and Amélia Ruivo da Silva Pintasilgo; ed. Inst. Superior Técnico, Lisbon; mem. Research and Devt. Dept. Companhia União Fabril (CUF) 1954–60; Pres. Pax Romana 1956–58; Int. Vice-Pres. The Grail 1965–69; mem. women's ecumenical liaison group 1966–70; mem. Corporative Chamber Comm. on Politics and Gen. Admin. 1969–74; Founder and Chair. Nat. Comm. on Status of Women 1970–74; mem. Portuguese del. to UN Gen. Ass. 1971–72; Sec. of State for Social Security, First Provisional Govt. 1975; Minister of Social Affairs 1974–75; Amb. to UNESCO 1976–79, mem. Exec. Bd. UNESCO 1976–80; Prime Minister 1979–80; Adviser to Pres. of Repub. 1981–85; independent cand. for Presidency of Portugal 1986; M.E.P. 1987–89; mem.

Advisory bd. World Policy Inst., New School for Social Research 1982–, UNU Council 1983–89, Club of Rome 1984–, UN Advisory Cttee. on Science and Tech. for Devt. 1989–91, Nat. Council of Ethics for Life Sciences 1990–; mem. InterAction Council of Fmr. Heads of State and Govt. 1983–94; mem. World Policy Inst. 1989–; mem., then Chair. Bd. of UNU/WIDER (World Inst. for Devt. Econs. Research), Helsinki 1990–; Pres. Independent Comm. on Population and Quality of Life 1992–96; Chair. working group on Equality and Democracy, Council of Europe, Strasbourg 1993–94. *Publications:* several books and articles on political issues, socio-cultural action and the women's movt. *Leisure interest:* poetry. *Address:* Alameda Santo António dos Capuchos 4–5°, 1150 Lisbon, Portugal. *Telephone:* (1) 354 31 68. *Fax:* (1) 314 25 14.

PINTER, Frances Mercedes Judith, PH.D.; American publisher; b. 13 June 1949, Venezuela; d. of George Pinter and Vera Hirschenhauser Pinter; m. David Percy 1985; Research Officer, Centre for Criminological Research, Oxford Univ., U.K. 1976–79; Man. Dir. Pinter Publrs. 1979–94; Chair., Independent Publrs. Guild 1979–82, Publrs. Asscn. E. European Task Force 1990–; Man. Dir. Cen. European Univ. Press 1994–96; Deputy Chair. Book Devt. Council 1985–89; mem. Bd. UK Publrs. Asscn. 1987–92, IBIS Information Services 1988–90, Libra Books 1991–; Exec. Dir. Centre for Publishing Devt. 1994–, Open Soc. Inst. 1994–. *Leisure interests:* reading, travelling, hiking. *Address:* 25 Belsize Park, London, NW3 4DU, England (Home).

PINTER, Harold, C.B.E., C.LIT.; British playwright; b. 10 Oct. 1930, London; m. 1st Vivien Merchant 1956 (divorced 1980, died 1982); one s.; m. 2nd Lady Antonia Fraser (q.v.) 1980; ed. Hackney Downs Grammar School, London; actor mainly in English and Irish prov. repertory 1949–58; playwright 1957–; Assoc. Dir. Nat. Theatre 1973–83; Dir. United British Artists 1983–85; Jt. Ed. Publr. Greville Press 1988–; Bd. mem. Cricket World 1989–; Hon. D.Litt. (Reading) 1970, (Birmingham) 1971, (Glasgow) 1974, (East Anglia) 1974, (Stirling) 1979, (Brown) 1982, (Hull) 1986, (Sussex) 1990, (Bristol) 1998; Shakespeare Prize, Hamburg 1973, Austrian Prize for European Literature 1973; Pirandello Prize 1980, Commonwealth Award for Dramatic Arts, Washington, D.C. 1981, Donatello Prize 1982; Hon. Fellow (Queen Mary Coll.) 1987; Chilean Order of Merit 1992; David Cohen British Literature Prize 1995; Special Olivier Award 1995. *Plays:* The Room 1957, The Dumb Waiter 1957, The Birthday Party 1957, A Slight Ache 1958, The Hothouse 1958, The Caretaker 1959, A Night Out 1959, Night School 1960, The Dwarfs 1960, The Collection 1961, The Lover 1962, Tea Party (TV play) 1965, The Homecoming 1964, The Basement (TV play) 1966, Landscape 1967, Silence 1968, Night (one act play) 1969, Old Times 1970, Monologue (one act play) 1972, No Man's Land 1974, Betrayal 1978, Family Voices 1980, Other Places 1982, A Kind of Alaska 1982, Victoria Station 1982, One for the Road 1984, Mountain Language 1988, The New World Order 1991, Party Time 1991, Moonlight 1993, Ashes to Ashes 1996. *Screenplays:* The Caretaker 1962, The Servant 1962, The Pumpkin Eater 1963, The Quiller Memorandum 1965, Accident 1966, The Birthday Party 1967, The Go-Between 1969, Langrishe Go Down 1970, A la Recherche du Temps Perdu 1972, The Last Tycoon 1974, The French Lieutenant's Woman 1980, Betrayal 1981, Victory 1982, Turtle Diary 1984, The Handmaid's Tale 1987, Reunion 1988, The Heat of the Day 1988, The Comfort of Strangers 1989, The Trial 1989. *Plays directed:* The Man in the Glass Booth London 1967, N.Y. 1968, Exiles 1970, 1971, Butley 1971, (film) 1973, Next of Kin 1974, Otherwise Engaged 1975, The Rear Column 1978, Close of Play 1979, Quartermaine's Terms 1981, Incident at Tulse Hill 1982, The Trojan War Will Not Take Place 1983, The Common Pursuit 1984, Sweet Bird of Youth 1985, Circe and Bravo 1986, Vanilla 1990, The New World Order 1991, Party Time 1991, Party Time (TV) 1992, Oleanna 1993, Ashes to Ashes 1995, Twelve Angry Men 1996, The Late Middle Classes 1999. *Publications:* Poems and prose 1949–77 1978, The Proust Screenplay (with Joseph Losey and Barbara Bray) 1978, Collected Poems and Prose 1986, 100 Poems by 100 Poets (co-ed.) 1986, The Dwarfs (novel) 1990. *Leisure interest:* cricket. *Address:* c/o Judy Daish Associates, 2 St. Charles Place, London, W10 6EG, England

PINTILIE, Lucian; Romanian stage and film director; b. 9 Nov. 1933, Tarutino (Bessarabia); s. of Victor Pintilie and Amelia Pintilie; ed. Bucharest Theatrical and Cinematographic Art Inst.; career at Lucia Sturdza Bulandra Theatre, directing The Cherry Orchard by Chekhov, D'ale carnavalului by I. L. Caragiale, The Inspector General by Gogol; staged several plays by Chekhov, Gorki, Ibsen, Eugène Ionesco, Pirandello and Strindberg abroad; also operas such as Rigoletto, Carmen, The Magic Flute etc. *Films:* Duminică la ora 6 (At Six o'clock on Sunday), Reconstituirea (The Reconstruction 1969), Salonul nr. 6 (Ward no 6) 1973 (Yugoslavia), De ce trag clopotele Mitică? (What Do The Bells Toll For Mitică?) 1980 and Balanța (The Oak) 1992, O Vară de Neuitat (An Unforgettable Summer) 1994, Prea tirziu (Too Late) 1996, Terminus Paradis (Last Stop Paradise) 1998. *Address:* 44 Mihail Kogălniceanu Blvd., Bucharest, Romania. *Telephone:* 315.47.15.

PINTO BALSEMÃO, Dr. Francisco José Pereira; Portuguese politician, lawyer and journalist; b. 1 Sept. 1937, Lisbon; s. of Henrique Pinto Balsemão and Maria Adelaide C. P. Pinto Balsemão; m. Mercedes Presas Pinto Balsemão 1975; three s. two d.; Ed.-in-Chief review Mais Alto 1961–63; Sec. to Man. Bd. Diário Popular, later Man. –1971; f. weekly Expresso 1973; mem. Nat. Assembly during Govt. of Dr. Marcello Caetano; f. Popular Democratic Party (PPD), later renamed Social Democratic Party (PSD), with late Dr. Sá Carneiro and Joaquim Magalhães Mota (q.v.) May 1974; Vice-Pres. Constituent Assembly 1975; Opposition Spokesman on Foreign Affairs 1977; mem. Assembly of the Repub. Dec. 1979–; Minister Without Portfolio and Deputy Prime Minister 1980; Prime Minister of Portugal 1981–83; Pres. Instituto Progresso Social e Democracia, Francisco dá Carneiro 1983–; Chair. Int. Relations Cttee. and mem. Political Cttee. PSD, party leader 1980–83; Head Sociedad Independente de Comunicação (SIC); Pres. European Inst. for the Media 1990; Head Sociedade Independente de Comunicação; Chair. Sojornal and Controjornal (Media) Groups. *Address:* Rua Duque de Palmela, 37-2° Dt°, 1296, Lisbon Codex, Portugal. *Telephone:* 526141.

PINTO BARBOSA, António Manuel; Portuguese economist and diplomatist; b. 31 July 1917, Murtoza; s. of Manuel Maria Barbosa Junior and Mariana Vieira Pinto Barbosa; m. Maria das Dôres Soares; two s.; ed. Universidade Técnica de Lisboa; teacher 1941–50; Prof. Inst. of Higher Econ. and Financial Sciences 1951–; Pres. Comm. for Reorganization of Industrial Resources 1951–54; Under-Sec. of State at Treasury 1951–54; Minister of Finance and Gov. IBRD 1955–65; mem. Council of State; Gov. Bank of Portugal and Gov. IMF 1966–74; Chair. Higher Studies Inst., Acad. of Sciences; Grand Cross, Order of Christ, Order of Prince Henry and of Isabel la Católica (Spain). *Publications:* L'industrie des conserves au Portugal 1941, L'économie, aspects positifs et aspects théologiques 1943, L'économie du Café 1945, La crise des exportations métropolitaines pour l'étranger 1950, La tâche du Ministre des Finances 1955, Banco de Fomento Nacional 1959, L'activité du Ministre des Finances 1960, La défense de la stabilité financière 1962, Communication du Ministre des Finances sur le crédit extérieur 1962, La phase actuelle des finances portugaises 1964, La dévaluation de 1949 et le commerce extérieur portugais 1966, Portuguese Economic Development in the Presence of the Post-war Foreign Policies of the U.S. 1969, La reforme du systeme monétaire international et ses vicissitudes 1973, Keynes e o accordo de Bretton-Woods 1977, Problemas monetarios internacionais de actualidade 1983, A reabilitação do quantitativo na Economia 1984, Olado menos visivel do Plano Marshall: sua actualidade. *Address:* Rua António Saldanha 3, Barrio do Restelo, Lisbon, 1400, Portugal.

PIONTEK, Heinz; German writer; b. 15 Nov. 1925, Kreuzburg, Silesia; m. Gisela Dallmann 1951; ed. Theologisch-Philosophische Hochschule, Dillingen; Berlin Prize for Literature 1957, Andreas Gryphius Prize, Esslingen 1957; mem. Bavarian Acad. of Fine Arts 1960–, Central PEN of Fed. Repub. of Germany; Rom-Preis, Villa Massimo 1960, Münchner Literatur Preis 1967, Eichendorff-Preis 1971, Tukan-Preis 1971, Literatur Preis des Kulturkreises im BDI 1974, Georg-Büchner-Preis 1976, Werner-Egk-Preis 1981, Oberschlesischer Kulturpreis 1984; Bundesverdienstkreuz (1st Class) 1985, Kultur-Preis Schlesien des Landes Niedersachsen 1991, Bayerischer Verdienstorden 1992. *Publications:* Die Furt (poems) 1952, Die Rauchfahne (poems) 1953, Vor Augen (stories) 1955, Wassermarken (poems) 1957, Buchstab-Zauberstab (essays) 1959, Aus meines Herzens Grunde (anthology) 1959, John Keats: Poems 1960, Weisser Panther (radio play) 1962, Mit einer Kranichfeder (poetry) 1962, Kastanien aus dem Feuer (stories) 1963, Windrichtungen (journey reports) 1963, Neue deutsche Erzählgedichte (anthology) 1964, Klartext (poetry) 1966, Die mittleren Jahre (novel) 1967, Liebeserklärungen (essays) 1969, Männer, die Gedichte machen (essays) 1970, Die Erzählungen 1971, Tot oder lebendig (poems) 1971, Deutsche Gedichte seit 1960 (ed.) 1972, Helle Tage anderswo (travel reports) 1973, Gesammelte Gedichte 1974, Dichterleben (novel) 1976, Wintertage-Sommernächte (short stories) 1977, Juttas Neffe (novel) 1979, Was mich nicht loslässt (poetry) 1981, Lieb', Leid und Zeit und Ewigkeit (anthology) 1981, Zeit meines Lebens (autobiog. vol. 1) 1984, Werke in sechs Bänden (collected works) 1985, Helldunkel (poetry) 1987, Jeder Satz ein Menschengesicht (anthology) 1987, Stunde der Überlebenden (autobiog. vol. 2) 1989, Werkauswahl in 2 Bänden (poems and stories) 1990, Nach Markus (Story) 1991, Morgenwache (poems) 1991, Goethe unterwegs in Schlesien (novel) 1993. *Address:* Dülfer Strasse 97, 80995 Munich, Germany.

PIORE, Emanuel Ruben, B.A., PH.D.; American physicist; b. 19 July 1908, Wilno, Poland (now Vilnius, Lithuania); s. of Ruben and Olga Piore; m. Nora Kahn 1931; one s. two d.; ed. Univ. of Wisconsin; Chief Scientist U.S.N. Office of Naval Research 1951–55; Vice-Pres. for Research, Avco Corpn 1955–56; Dir. of Research, Int. Business Machines Corpn., York 1956–60, Vice-Pres. for Research and Eng. 1960–63, Vice-Pres. and Group Exec. 1963–65, Vice-Pres. and Chief Scientist 1965–75, mem. Bd. of Dirs.; mem. Nat. Science Bd. 1961–; Adjunct Prof., Rockefeller Univ. 1974–80; Fellow, American Physical Soc., Inst. of Electrical and Electronics Engineers, American Acad. of Arts and Sciences, A.A.A.S., Royal Soc. of Arts (U.K.); mem. Nat. Acad. of Sciences, Nat. Acad. of Eng., American Philosophical Soc.; consultant to President's Science Advisory Cttee.; mem. Bd. American Inst. of Physics, Stark Draper Lab., Nat. Information Bureau, SIAM, N.Y. State Foundation for Science, New York Bd. for Higher Educ. 1976–; visiting cttees. at M.I.T., Harvard, Johns Hopkins, Tulane, Mich. State Univ.; mem. several cttees. of Nat. Research Council; Treas. of Nat. Cttee. of Research 1968–80; mem. Bd. Science Research Assocs., Health Advancement Inc., Paul Revere Investors, Guardian Mutual Fund; Hon. D.Sc. (Union and Wisconsin); Kaplun Int. Prize; Industrial Research Inst. Medal 1967. *Address:* 2 Fifth Avenue, New York, NY 10011, U.S.A. *Telephone:* (212) 260-9594.

PIOT, Peter, M.D., PH.D.; Belgian public health official and professor; b. 17 Feb. 1949, Leuven; m. Greet Kimzeke 1975; two c.; ed. Univs. of Ghent, Antwerp and Washington; Asst. in Microbiology, Inst. of Tropical Medicine, Antwerp 1974–78, Prof., Head Dept. of Microbiology 1981–92; Sr. Fellow,

Microbiology and Infectious Diseases, Washington Univ. 1978–79; Asst. Prof. of Public Health, Free Univ. Brussels 1989–94; Assoc. Dir. Global Program AIDS, WHO 1995, Exec. Dir. Jt. UN Program on HIV/AIDS, Geneva 1995–; Dir. WHO Collaborating Centre on AIDS, Antwerp; Bd. Dirs. Project SIDA, Zaire, STD/AIDS Project, Kenya; Chair. WHO Steering Cttee. on the Epidemiology of AIDS 1989–92; NATO Fellow 1978–79; mem. Royal Acad. of Medicine, Int. AIDS Soc. (Pres. 1992–), numerous socs. in Europe, U.S.A., Africa; De Kerkheer Prize for Medicine 1989, Health Research Award (Belgium) 1989, Public Health Award, Flemish Community 1990; AMICOM Award for Medicine 1991, H. Breurs Prize 1992, A. Jaunioux Prize 1992, van Thiel Award 1993, Glaxo award for infectious diseases 1995; cr. baron by King Albert II, Officier, Ordre Nat. du Léopard (Zaire), Ordre du Lion (Senegal). *Publications:* AIDS and HIV Infection in the Tropics (with J. M. Mann) 1988, Handbook on AIDS Prevention in Africa (with P. Lamptey) 1990; AIDS in Africa 1991, Hepatitis B and STD in Heterosexuals (with F. André) 1991, AIDS in Africa: A Handbook for Physicians (co-author) 1992, Reproductive Tract Infections in Women (co-author 1992); articles on AIDS and other sexually transmitted diseases. *Leisure interests:* cooking, hiking, music, literature. *Address:* UNAIDS, 20 Avenue Appia, 1211 Geneva 27, Switzerland (Office). *Telephone:* 791-4510 (Office). *Fax:* 7914179 (Office).

PIOTROVSKY, Mikhail Borisovich, D.HIST.; Russian art researcher; b. 9 Dec. 1944, Yerevan, Armenia; s. of Boris Piotrovsky; m. Irina Leonidovna Piotrovskaya; one s. one d.; ed. Leningrad State Univ., Cairo Univ.; researcher Leningrad Inst. of Oriental Studies U.S.S.R. Acad. of Sciences 1967–91; First Deputy Dir. State Hermitage, St. Petersburg 1991–92, Dir 1992–; Corresp. mem. Russian Acad. of Sciences 1997–; mem. Acad. of Humanitarian Sciences; mem. Presidium, Cttee. on State Prizes of Russian Presidency, Presidium, Russian Cttee. of UNESCO; mem. Int. Council of Museums; consultant to European Parl.; main research in ancient and medieval history of Near E., Muslim art in archaeology. *Publications:* over 150 scientific works. *Address:* State Hermitage, Dvortsovaya nab. 34, 191065 St. Petersburg, Russia (Office). *Telephone:* (812) 311 9645.

PIOVANELLI, H.E. Cardinal Silvano; Italian ecclesiastic; b. 21 Feb. 1924; ordained 1947; consecrated Bishop (Titular Church of Tubune, Mauritania) 1982; Archbishop of Florence 1983–; cr. Cardinal 1985. *Address:* Arcivescovado, Piazza S. Giovanni 3, 50129 Florence, Italy. *Telephone:* (055) 239.88.13.

PIPER, Klaus; German publisher; b. 27 March 1911, Munich; s. of late Rheinhard Piper and Gertrud Engling; ed. Maximilians-Gymnasium, Munich; with R. Piper & Co., Munich (book publishers) 1932–, Partner 1941–53, sole Man. Dir. 1953; mem. Finance Cttee. of German Booksellers Asscn., Cen. PEN of Fed. Repub. of Germany 1955–, Rotary Club, Asscn. of Literary Publishers, Max-Planck-Gesellschaft zur Förderung der Wissenschaften; Hon. D.Lit. (Washington, St. Louis) 1986, Hon. Dr. (Ludwig Maximilians Univ., Munich) 1987; Golden Cultural Medal, Italian Ministry of Foreign Affairs 1963, Distinguished Service Cross (First Class), Fed. Repub. of Germany. *Publications:* Offener Horizont 1953, Nach 50 Jahren 1904–1954 1954, Stationen—Piper-Almanach 1904–1964 1964, Piper-Almanach 1964–74 1974; Ed.: Reinhard Piper Mein Leben als Verleger 1964, Erinnerungen an Karl Jaspers (co-editor). *Leisure interests:* music, art, philosophy, literature, horse-riding. *Address:* R. Piper & Co. Verlag, Georgenstrasse 4, 80799 Munich (Office); Pienzenauerstrasse 63, 8000 Munich, Germany (Home). *Telephone:* (089) 38-18-01-0 (Office); (089) 98-84-73 (Home).

PIPPARD, Sir (Alfred) Brian, Kt., M.A., PH.D., SC.D., F.R.S.; British professor of physics; b. 7 Sept. 1920, London; s. of Prof. A. J. S. Pippard, F.R.S. and F. L. O. (Tucker) Pippard; m. Charlotte Frances Dyer 1955; three d.; ed. Clifton Coll., and Clare Coll., Cambridge; Scientific Officer Radar Research and Devt. Establishment 1941–45; Demonstrator in Physics, Cambridge Univ. 1946, Lecturer 1950, Reader 1959–60, J. H. Plummer Prof. of Physics 1960–71; Cavendish Prof. of Physics 1971–82, now Emer.; Pres. of Clare Hall, Cambridge 1966–73; Pres. Inst. of Physics 1974–76; Hughes Medal (Royal Soc.) 1959, Holweck Medal 1961, Dannie-Heineman Prize (Göttingen) 1969, Guthrie Medal (Inst. of Physics) 1970. *Publications:* Elements of Classical Thermodynamics 1957, Dynamics of Conduction Electrons 1962, Forces and Particles 1972, Physics of Vibration 1978, 1982, Response and Stability 1985, Magnetoresistance in Metals 1989; many papers in Proc. of the Royal Society, etc. *Leisure interest:* music. *Address:* 30 Porson Road, Cambridge, CB2 2EU, England. *Telephone:* (01223) 358713.

PIQUET, Nelson; Brazilian racing driver; b. 17 Aug. 1952, Rio de Janeiro; first Grand Prix, Germany 1978; mem. Ensign Grand Prix team 1978, BS McLaren team 1978, Brabham team 1978–85, Williams team 1986–87, Lotus team 1988–89, Benetton team 1990; winner of 22 Grand Prix; Formula One World Champion 1981, 1983, 1987; lives in Monaco.

PIRELLI, Leopoldo; Italian business executive; b. 27 Aug. 1925, Varese; s. of Alberto Pirelli and Ludovica Zambeletti; one s. one d.; ed. Politecnico, Milan; Chair. Pirelli and Co., Milan—1996, also Partner; Deputy Chair. Soc. Int. Pirelli, Basel; Dir. Riunione Adriatica di Sicurtà (RAS), Milan, Generale Industrie Metallurgiche, Florence; Cavaliere del Lavoro della Repubblica. *Address:* Via Gaetano Negri 10, 20123 Milan, Italy. *Telephone:* (02) 85.351.

PIRES, Gen. Pedro Verona Rodrigues; Cape Verde politician; b. 29 April 1934, Sant' Ana, Fogo; s. of Luís Rodrigues Pires and Maria Fidalga Lopes Pires; m. Adélcia Maria da Luz Lima Barreto Pires 1975; two d.; ed. Licee Gil Eanes de São Vicente, Faculty of Science, Lisbon Univ., Portugal; left Portugal to join Partido Africano da Independência da Guiné e Cabo Verde (PAIGC) 1961; mem. PAIGC dels. 1961–63; involved in preparation for liberation of Cape Verde 1963–65; mem. Cen. Cttee. of PAIGC 1965, of Council of War, PAIGC 1967; re-elected mem. of Commissão Permanente do Comité Executivo da Luta (CEL) and of Council of War 1970; involved in admin. of liberated areas of southern Guinea-Bissau 1971–73; Pres. Nat. Comm. of PAIGC for Cape Verde 1973 (reaffirmed as mem. of Council of War and CEL), appointed an Asst. State Commr. in first govt. of Repub. of Guinea-Bissau 1973–74; negotiated independence agreements of Cape Verde and Guinea-Bissau 1974; Dir. PAIGC policies during transitional govt. before independence of Cape Verde 1975; elected Deputy in Nat. Popular Ass. of Cape Verde June 1975–, re-elected 1980; Prime Minister of Cape Verde 1975–91, with responsibility for Finance, Planning and Co-operation; elected Deputy Gen. Sec. Partido Africano da Independência de Cabo Verde (PAICV) 1981, Sec. Gen. 1990–93, Chair. Gen. 1993–; mem. Perm. Comm. of CEL 1977; Amílcar Cabral Medal 1976. *Leisure interests:* philosophy, sociology, politics. *Address:* c/o PAICV, CP 22, Praia, Santiago, Republic of Cape Verde.

PIRES DE MIRANDA, Pedro, M.ENG.; Portuguese diplomatist and business executive; b. 30 Nov. 1928, Leiria; s. of A. and A. Pires de Miranda; m. Maria Helena Pires de Miranda 1957; one s. two d.; ed. Lisbon Univ.; with William Halcrow & Partners, London; Sales Man. Companhia Portuguesa de Petróleos BP 1955–67, int. petroleum operations with BP, London 1967–70; Commercial Man. Petrosul 1972–73; Dir. Sonap 1973–75; Asst. Bd. of Dirs. for Marketing Affairs, Companhia Brasileira de Petróleos Ipiranga 1975–76; Minister of Commerce and Tourism 1978; Pres. Comm. for Integration in EEC 1979; Amb. at large 1980–; Minister for Foreign Affairs 1985–87; Chair. ALCANTARA (Tate & Lyle Portugal); mem. Bd. of Trustees Fundação Oriente, Fundação Luso Americana; Dir. (non-exec.) Petrogal (Petróleos de Portugal, S.A.); Grand Officier Légion d'honneur, Grand Officier de l'Ordre de Mérite Civil Français, Grand Officier de l'Ordre du Faucon Islandais, Grand Croix Ordem Nacional do Cruzeiro do Sul, Ordem do Rio Branco do Sul, Ordem da Aguia Azteca, Ordre Royal Suédois de l'Etoile Polaire, Gran Cordón de la Orden del Libertador, Grand Croix Order of Honour (Greece). *Leisure interest:* sport. *Address:* Avenida da India 10, 1300 Lisbon, Portugal. *Telephone:* 310 2500. *Fax:* 310 2958.

PIRIE, Madsen Duncan, M.A., PH.D.; British political philosopher; b. 24 Aug. 1940; s. of Douglas G. Pirie and Eva Madsen; ed. Univs. of Edinburgh and St. Andrews; Republican Study Cttee. 1974; Distinguished Visiting Prof. of Philosophy, Hillsdale Coll. Mich. 1975–78; Pres. Adam Smith Inst. 1978–; mem. Citizens' Charter Advisory Panel 1991–95; R.C. Hoiles Fellow 1975. *Publications:* Freeports 1983, Test Your IQ 1983, Book of the Fallacy 1985, Privatization 1988, Micropolitics 1988, Boost Your IQ 1990, The Sherlock Holmes I.Q. Book 1995. *Leisure interest:* calligraphy. *Address:* P.O. Box 316, London, SW1P 3BJ, England.

PIRINSKI, Georgi Georgiev; Bulgarian politician; b. 10 Sept. 1948, New York, U.S.A.; m.; two c.; ed. Higher Econ. Inst., Sofia; fmr. Deputy Minister of Foreign Econ. Relations and Deputy Prime Minister; mem. Parl.; Minister of Foreign Affairs 1995–97; Bulgarian Socialist Party. *Address:* c/o Council of Ministers, Blvd. Dondukov 1, 1000 Sofia, Bulgaria.

PIRIZ-BALLON, Ramiro; Uruguayan diplomatist; b. 20 April 1938, Montevideo; m.; two c.; ed. Wellington Coll. (U.K.) and Univ. of Geneva; joined legal dept. of ILO, Geneva 1958; Third Sec. Ministry of Foreign Affairs 1964; Chef de Cabinet to Minister of Foreign Affairs 1965; served Uruguay Embassy, Moscow 1966–72; Minister-Counsellor, London, concurrently Perm. Rep. to IMCO (now IMO) 1975–80; interregional adviser on maritime legislation of IMO and other posts 1980–85; Amb. to Egypt 1985–90 (also accred. to Jordan); Perm. Rep. to UN 1990–95. *Address:* c/o Ministry of Foreign Affairs, 18 de Julio 1205, Montevideo, Uruguay.

PIRUBHAKARAN, Vellupillai; Sri Lankan guerrilla leader; b. 26 Nov. 1954, Velvettithurai, Jaffna peninsula; m.; one s. one d.; joined Tamil movement 1970; f. Tamil New Tigers guerrilla movt. (Liberation Tigers of Tamil Eelam since 1976) 1972.

PIRZADA, Syed Sharifuddin, S.PK.; Pakistani politician and lawyer; b. 12 June 1923, Burhanpur; s. of S. Vilayat Ali Pirzada and Butul Begum; m. 1st Rafia Sultana (died 1960); m. 2nd Safiya Pirzada; two s. three d.; ed. Univ. of Bombay; Sec. Muslim Students Fed. 1943–45; Hon. Sec. to Quaid-i-Azam, Jinnah 1941–44; Sec. Bombay City Muslim League 1945–47; Prof., Sind Muslim Law Coll. 1947–54; Adviser to Constitution Comm. of Pakistan 1960–61; Chair. Co. Law Comm. 1962; Pres. Karachi High Court Bar Asscn., Pakistan Br. 1964–67; Attorney-Gen. of Pakistan 1965–66, 1968–72, 1977–89; Minister of Foreign Affairs 1966–68, April–Oct. 1993; Minister of Justice 1979–84; mem. or Pres. several asscns. and socs.; led Pakistan Del. to Session of UN Gen. Ass. 1966–67; mem. Panel of Perm. Court of Arbitration; mem. Int. Law Comm. 1981–86; Sec.-Gen. Org. of Islamic Conf. 1984–88; Chair. Heritage Council and Amb.-at-large with rank of Fed. Minister 1989–93. *Publications include:* Evolution of Pakistan 1962, Fundamental Rights and Constitutional Remedies in Pakistan 1966, Some Aspects of Quaid-i-Azam's Life 1978, Collected Works of Quaid-i-Azam Mohammad Ali Jinnah (vol. I) 1985, (vol. II) 1986. *Leisure interest:* bridge. *Address:* c/o Ministry of Foreign Affairs, Constitution Avenue, Islamabad, Pakistan.

PISANI, Edgard, L.ÈS L.; French politician; b. 9 Oct. 1918, Tunis, Tunisia; s. of François and Zoë (née Nani) Pisani; m. Isola Chazereau (deceased); m.

4th Carmen Berndt 1984; one s.; two s. two d. from previous marriages; ed. in Tunis and Paris; Resistance during World War II; Sous-Préfet, Dir. de Cabinet of Chief Commr. of Police 1944–45; Dir. de Cabinet of Minister of the Interior 1946; Préfet, Haute-Loire 1946–47, Haute-Marne 1947–54; Senator, Haute-Marne 1954–61, 1974–81; Minister of Agric. 1961–66, of Equipment 1966–67; County councillor and Mayor of Montreuil-Bellay 1963–75; Deputy for Maine-et-Loire, Nat. Assembly 1967–68; mem. Ind. Comm. on Int. Devt. Issues; mem. Comm. for Foreign Affairs and Defence; mem. European Parl. 1979–; mem. Socialist Group; Commr. for Devt. Aid, Comm. of European Communities 1981–84; French High Commr. in New Caledonia 1984–85; Minister for New Caledonian Affairs May–Nov. 1985; Chargé de Mission, Cabinet du Président 1986–92; Pres. Institut du Monde Arabe 1988–95; Pres. du Centre Int. des Hautes Etudes Agronomiques Méditerranéenes; Publr. quarterly review L'Evènement Européen 1987–; Prix 30 Jours d'Europe. *Publications:* La région: pour quoi faire?, Le général indivis, Utopie foncière, Socialiste de raison, Défi du monde—campagne d'Europe, La France dans le conflit économique mondial, La main et l'outil 1984, Pour l'Afrique 1988, Persiste et Signe 1992, Pour une agriculture marchande et ménagère 1994. *Address:* 31 rue Lhomond, 75005 Paris, France.

PISCHETSRIEDER, Bernd; German business executive; b. 15 Feb. 1948, Munich; ed. Technical Univ. Munich; joined BMW AG, Munich as production planning eng. 1973; Production Dir. BMW South Africa (Pty.) Ltd. 1982–85; Dir. for Quality Control, BMW AG 1985–87, for Tech. Planning 1987–90; Deputy mem. Admin. Bd. in charge of Production 1990, mem. Admin. Bd. 1991, Chair. Admin. Bd. 1993–99; fmr. Chair. Rover; mem. Advisory Bd. Allianz-Versicherung, Munich; Dr. h.c. (Birmingham) 1996. *Address:* c/o BMW AG, 8000 Munich, Germany.

PISCHINGER, Franz Felix, DR. TECHN. E.H.; Austrian academic; b. 18 July 1930, Waidhofen; s. of Franz Pischinger and Karoline Pischinger; m. Elfriede Pischinger 1957; four s. one d.; ed. Technical Univ. Graz; technical asst. Technical Univ. Graz 1953–58; Head of Research Dept. Inst. of Internal Combustion Engines, Prof. List (AVL) 1958–62; leading positions in research and devt. Kloeckner-Humboldt-Deutz AG, Cologne, Fed. Germany 1962–70; Dir. Inst. for Applied Thermodynamics, Aachen Tech. Univ. 1970–97; Pres. FEV Motorentechnik, Aachen 1978–; Vice-Pres. DFG (German Research Soc.) 1984–90; Fellow SAE 1996; Dr. h.c. (Tech. Univ. Graz) 1994; Herbert Akroyd Stuart Award 1962, Carl-Engler-Medaille DGMK, Deutsche Wissenschaftliche Gesellschaft für Erdöl, Erdgas und Kohle, Hamburg 1990, Medal of Honour, Verein Deutscher Ingenieure 1993; Osterreichischer Ehrenring, Bundesverdienstkreuz, Cross of Honour for Science and Art, First Class. *Publications:* articles in professional journals. *Address:* FEV Motorentechnik, Neuenhofstrasse 181, 52078 Aachen (Office); Im Erkfeld 4, 52072 Aachen, Germany (Home). *Telephone:* 241 5689-100 (Office).

PISKOTIN, Mikhail Ivanovich; Russian lawyer, political scientist and journalist; b. 1924, Udmurt Region, Urals; ed. Kazan Law Inst.; active service Second World War 1942–45 on various fronts, wounded; worked at Ministry of Justice, Bashkir A.S.S.R. 1949–50; post-graduate study at Inst. of State and Law, U.S.S.R. Acad. of Sciences 1950–52; Ed.-in-Chief of journal Soviet State and Law 1978–87; head of Centre of Political Science Research, Inst. of State and Law 1987–89; Ed. of journal on new legislation The People's Deputy (now Russian Fed.) 1990–96, Political Observer 1996–; Adviser to Chair. of Constitutional Court of Russia 1997–. *Publications include:* Socialism and State Administration 1984. *Address:* Constitutional Court, Il'ynka str. 21, 103132 Moscow, Russia. *Telephone:* (095) 206-92-25.

PITAKAKA, Sir Moses Puibangara, G.C.M.G.; Solomon Islands politician; b. 24 Jan. 1945, Zaru Village, Solomon Islands; m. 1967; three s. four d.; Gov.-Gen. of the Solomon Islands 1994–. *Leisure interests:* walking, reading. *Address:* Government House, P.O. Box 252, Honiara, Solomon Islands. *Telephone:* 22222. *Fax:* 23335.

PITCHER, Sir Desmond Henry; British company executive; b. 23 March 1935, Liverpool; s. of George Charles Pitcher and Alice Marion (née Osborne) Pitcher; m. 1st Patricia Ainsworth 1961 (divorced 1973); two d.; m. 2nd Carol Ann Rose 1978 (divorced); two s.; m. 3rd Norma Barbara Niven 1991; ed. Liverpool Coll. of Tech., Commerce; Man. Dir. then Vice-Pres. Int. Div. The Sperry Corpn. 1961–76; Man. Dir. British Leyland Truck and Bus Div. 1976–78, Plessey Telecommunications and Office Systems Ltd. 1978–83; Group Chief Exec. The Littlewoods Org. PLC 1983–93, Vice-Chair. 1993–95; Chair. The Mersey Barrage Co. Ltd. 1986–96, The Merseyside Devt. Corpn. 1991–98, The North West Water Group PLC (now United Utilities) 1993–98 (Dir. 1990–98); Dir. Everton Football Club Co. Ltd. 1987–90, Deputy Chair. 1990–; Dir. Northern Advisory Bd. of Nat. Westminster Bank PLC 1989–92, Dir. (non-exec.) Nat. Westminster Bank 1994–98; Dir. Liverpool School of Tropical Medicine 1996–. *Leisure interests:* football, golf, 19th century history, opera, sailing. *Address:* Ouston Hall, Cheshire, CW8 2RG, England. *Telephone:* (01606) 854649.

PITHART, Petr; Czech politician and academic; b. 2 Jan. 1941, Kladno; s. of Vilém Pithart and Blažena (née Krystýnková); m. Drahomíra Hromádková 1964; one s. one d.; ed. Charles Univ., Prague (Faculty of Law); Dept. of Theory of State and Law, Charles Univ. 1964–70; scholarship Oxford Univ. 1969–70; labourer 1970–72; co. lawyer 1972–77; signed Charter 77; labourer 1977–79; clerk with Central Warehouses, Prague 1979–89; Spokesman Co-ordination Centre, Civic Forum 1989–90; Prime Minister of Czech Repub. 1990–92; Deputy to Czech Nat. Council 1990–92; mem. and Chair. Senate 1996–98, Vice-Chair. 1998–; Sr. Research Fellow Cen. European Univ., Prague 1992–94; teacher, Faculty of Law, Charles Univ., Prague 1994–; Chief Ed. periodical The New Presence. *Publications:* numerous articles and essays; Defence of Politics 1974, "1968" 1978, History and Politics 1992, Czechs in the History of Modern Times (co-author) 1992. *Leisure interests:* politics, history, hiking, fishing. *Address:* Senate of the Czech Republic, Valdštejnské nám. 4, 118 11 Prague 1 (Office); Dražického nam. 10/65, 11800 Prague 1, Czech Republic (Home). *Telephone:* (02) 279351 (Office); (02) 539764 (Home).

PITIRIM, (Konstantin Vladimirovich Netchaev); Metropolitan of Volokolamsk and Yuriev, D.THEOL.; Russian ecclesiastic; b. 8 Jan. 1926, Michurinsk; ed. Moscow Theological Acad.; deacon Moscow Patriarch Cathedral 1945–54, Archimandrite 1956; insp. Moscow Theological Acad. 1956–; Ed. Magazine of Moscow Patriarchy 1962–; consecrated as bishop 1963; Bishop of Volokolamsk, Vicar of Moscow Eparchy 1963–71; man. Smolensk Eparchy 1964–65; Archbishop of Volokolamsk 1971–86; Chair. Publishing Bd. of Moscow Patriarchy 1986–; U.S.S.R. People's Deputy 1989–91; Vice-Pres. Int. Foundation for Survival and Development of Humanity; one of f. Acad. of World Civilizations; Pres. Slavic Foundation of Russia. *Publications:* numerous books and articles on theological and philosophical themes. *Leisure interests:* philosophy, music. *Address:* Moscow Patriarchy, Publishing Department, Pogodinskaya 20, 119435 Moscow, Russia. *Telephone:* 246-98-48.

PITMAN, Sir Brian Ivor, Kt., F.I.B.; British banker; b. 13 Dec. 1931, Cheltenham; s. of Ronald Ivor Pitman and Doris Ivy Pitman (née Short); m. Barbara Mildred Ann Darby 1954; two s. one d.; ed. Cheltenham Grammar School; Asst. Gen. Man. Lloyds Bank PLC 1973–75, Jt. Gen. Man. 1975–76; Exec. Dir. (U.K. and Asia-Pacific Div.), Lloyds Bank Int. Ltd. 1976–78; Deputy Chief Exec. Lloyds Bank Int. Ltd. 1978–82; Deputy Group Chief Exec., Lloyds Bank PLC 1982–83, Group Chief Exec. and Dir. 1983–97, Chair. 1997–; Deputy Chief Exec. and Dir. TSB Bank PLC 1995–97, Deputy Chair. 1997–; Group Chief Exec. and Dir. Lloyds TSB Group PLC 1995–97, Chair 1997–; Pres. Chartered Inst. of Bankers 1997–98; fmr. Pres. British Bankers Assn.; Dir. Carlton Communications PLC 1998–; Chair. Next PLC 1998–; Hon. D.Sc. (City Univ.) 1996. *Leisure interests:* golf, cricket, music. *Address:* Lloyds TSB Group PLC, 71 Lombard Street, London, EC3P 3BS, England.

PITMAN, Jennifer Susan, O.B.E.; British racehorse trainer; b. 11 June 1946; d. of George and Mary Harvey; m. 1st Richard Pitman 1965 (divorced); two s.; m. 2nd David Stait 1997; ed. Sarson Secondary Girls' School; Nat. Hunt trainer 1975–99; Dir. Jenny Pitman Racing Ltd. 1975–; winners include: Corbiere (Welsh Nat. 1982, Grand Nat. 1983), Burrough Hill Lad (Welsh Nat. 1984, Cheltenham Gold Cup 1984, King George VI Gold Cup 1984, Hennessey Gold Cup 1984), Smith's Man (Whitbread Trophy 1985), Gainsay (Ritz Club Nat. Hunt Handicap 1987, Sporting Life Weekend Chase 1987), Garrison Savannah (Cheltenham Gold Cup 1991), Wonderman (Welsh Champion Hurdle 1991), Don Valentino (Welsh Champion Hurdle 1992), Royal Athlete (Grand Nat. 1995), Willsford (Scottish Nat. 1995); first woman to train Grand Nat. winner 1983; numerous awards including Racing Personality of the Year, Golden Spurs 1983, Commonwealth Sports Award 1983, 1984, Piper Heidsieck Trainer of the Year 1983–84, 1989–90, Variety Club of G.B. Sportswoman of the Year 1984. *Publication:* Glorious Uncertainty (autobiog.) 1984, Jenny Pitman: The Autobiography 1999. *Address:* Jenny Pitman Racing Ltd., Weathercock House, Upper Lambourn, Hungerford, Berks., RG17 8QT, England. *Telephone:* (01488) 71714.

PITSUWAN, Surin, PH.D.; Thai politician; b. 28 Oct. 1949, Nakhon Si Thammarat; s. of Ismael Pitsuwan and Sapiya Pitsuwan; m. Alisa Ariya 1983; three s.; ed. Claremont McKenna Coll., Harvard Univ.; columnist The Nation Review and Bangkok Post newspapers 1980–92; Congressional Fellow, Office of U.S. Rep. Geraldine Ferraro (q.v.) 1983–84; Academic Asst. to Dean of Faculty of Political Science and to Vice-Rector for Academic Affairs, Thammasat Univ. 1985–86; M.P. from Nakhon Si Thammarat Prov. 1986–; Sec. to Speaker of House of Reps. 1986; Asst. Sec. to Minister of Interior 1988; Deputy Minister of Foreign Affairs 1992–94, Minister of Foreign Affairs 1997–; Democrat. *Leisure interest:* reading. *Address:* Ministry of Foreign Affairs, Saranrom Palace, Bangkok 10200, Thailand. *Telephone:* (2) 224-0617. *Fax:* (2) 226-1374.

PITT, Brad; American film actor; b. 18 Dec. 1963, Shawnee, Okla.; s. of Bill Pitt and Jane Pitt; ed. Univ. of Missouri; TV appearances include Dallas (series), Glory Days (series), Too Young to Die? (film), The Image (film). *Films include:* Cutting Glass, Happy Together 1989, Across the Tracks 1990, Contact, Thelma and Louise 1991, The Favor 1992, Johnny Suede 1992, Cool World 1992, A River Runs Through It 1992, Kalifornia 1993, Legend of the Fall 1994, Interview With The Vampire 1994, 12 Monkeys 1995, Seven 1996, Sleepers, Mad Monkeys, Tomorrow Never Dies 1996, Seven Years in Tibet 1997, The Devil's Own 1997, Meet Joe Black 1998. *Address:* Creative Artists Agency, 9830 Wilshire Boulevard, Beverly Hills, CA 90212, U.S.A.

PITT, Sir Harry Raymond, Kt., PH.D., F.R.S.; British mathematician and university administrator; b. 3 June 1914, West Bromwich; s. of Harry and Florence Pitt; m. Clemency C. Jacoby 1940; four s.; ed. King Edward's School, Stourbridge and Peterhouse, Cambridge; Bye-Fellow, Peterhouse,

Cambridge 1936–39; Choate Memorial Fellow, Harvard Univ. 1937–38; Univ. of Aberdeen 1939–42; Air Ministry and Ministry of Aircraft Production 1942–45; Prof. of Math., Queen's Univ., Belfast 1945–50; Deputy Vice-Chancellor, Univ. of Nottingham 1950–64; Visiting Prof., Yale Univ. 1962–63; Vice-Chancellor, Univ. of Reading 1964–79; Chair. Univs' Cen. Comm. on Admissions, and Standing Conf. on Univ. Entrance Oct. 1975–79; Vice-Pres. Inst. of Mathematics 1980–84, Pres. 1984–85; Hon. LL.D. (Nottingham, Aberdeen); Hon. D.Sc. (Reading, Belfast). *Leisure interests:* reading, travel. *Publications:* Tauberian Theorems 1957, Measure, Integration and Probability 1963, Measure and Integration for Use 1985, papers in scientific journals. *Address:* 105 Manor Green Road, Epsom, Surrey, KT19 8LW, England.

PITTMAN, James A., Jr., M.D.; American professor of medicine; b. 12 April 1927, Orlando, Fla.; s. of James A. Pittman and Jean C. Garretson; m. Constance Ming Chung Shen 1955; two s.; ed. Davidson Coll. N.C., and Harvard Medical School; Clinical Assoc. Nat. Insts. of Health, Bethesda, Md. 1954–56; Instructor in Medicine, Univ. of Alabama 1956–59, Asst. Prof. 1959–62, Assoc. Prof. 1962–64, Prof. of Medicine 1964–, Prof. of Physiology and Biophysics 1967–92, Dean, School of Medicine 1973–92, Distinguished Prof. 1992–; Consultant, Children's Hosp. Birmingham, Ala. 1962–71; Prof. of Medicine, Georgetown Univ. School of Medicine, Washington, D.C. 1971–73; Sr. Adviser Int. Council on Control of Iodine Deficiency Diseases 1994–96; Fellow, American Coll. of Physicians, Asscn. American Physicians, American Chemical Soc. etc.; Hon. D.Sc. (Davidson Coll.) 1980, (Albama) 1984. *Publications:* Diagnosis and Treatment of Thyroid Disease 1963; articles in professional journals. *Leisure interests:* flying, scuba diving, hunting, sailing. *Address:* University of Alabama School of Medicine, Seventh Avenue South, Birmingham, AL 35294 (Office); 5 Ridge Drive, Birmingham, AL 35213, U.S.A. (Home). *Telephone:* (205) 934-3414 (Office).

PITTMAN, Robert Warren; American media executive; b. 28 Dec. 1953, Jackson, Miss.; s. of Warren E. Pittman and Lanita (née Hurdle) Pittman; m. Sandra Hill 1979; one s.; ed. Millsaps Coll., Oakland, Pittsburg and Harvard Univs.; disc jockey WJDX-FM (Miss.) 1970–72; disc jockey WRIT (Milwaukee) 1972; Research Dir. WDRQ (Detroit) 1972–73; programme dir. WPEZ (Pittsburg) 1973–74; with WMAQ-WKQZ (N.Y.) and NBC Radio 1974–77; with WNBC (N.Y.) 1977–79; exec. producer Album Tracks NBC TV 1977–78; Dir., Vice-Pres., Sr. Vice-Pres. Warner Amex Satellite Entertainment Co. (now MTV Networks Inc.) 1979–82, Pres., C.E.O. 1985–86; Exec. Vice-Pres., C.O.O. MTV Networks Inc. 1983–85; Pres., C.E.O. Quantum Media Inc. 1987–89; Exec. Adviser Warner Communications Inc. 1989–90; Pres., C.E.O. Time Warner Enterprises 1990–95; C.E.O. Six Flags Entertainment 1991–95; Man. Partner, C.E.O. Century 21 Real Estate 1995–96; Pres., C.E.O. America On-Line Networks 1996–; Chair. N.Y. Shakespeare Festival 1987–94; Dir. numerous cos.; numerous awards. *Address:* America On-Line, 2200 AOL Way, Sterling, VA 20166, U.S.A.

PIVETTI, Irene; Italian politician; d. of Grazia Gabrielli; m. Paolo Taranta 1988 (separated 1992); ed. Catholic Univ. of the Sacred Heart, Milan; journalist; mem. Parl. 1992–, Speaker 1995–96; fmr. mem. Northern League. *Address:* Camera dei Deputati, Rome, Italy.

PIVOT, Bernard; French journalist; b. 5 May 1935, Lyons; s. of Charles Pivot and Marie-Louise Pivot (née Dumas); m. Monique Dupuis 1959; two d.; ed. Centre de formation des Journalistes; on staff of Figaro littéraire, then Literary Ed.; Figaro 1958–74; Chronique pour sourire, on Europe 1 1970–73; Columnist, Le Point 1974–77; producer and presenter of Ouvrez les guillemets 1973–74, Apostrophes, Channel 2 1975–90, Bouillon de culture 1991–; Ed. Lire 1975–93; Dir. Sofica Créations 1986–; mem. Conseil supérieur de la langue française 1989–; Grand Prix de la Critique l'Académie française 1983, Prix Louise Weiss, Bibliothèque Nat. 1989; Chevalier du Mérite agricole. *Publications:* L'Amour en vogue (novel) 1959, La vie oh là là! 1966, Les critiques littéraires 1968, Beaujolaises 1978, Le Football en vert 1980, Le Métier de lire. Réponses à Pierre Nora 1990, Remontrances à la ménagère de moins de cinquante ans (essay) 1998. *Leisure interests:* tennis, football, gastronomy. *Address:* France 2, 22 Avenue Montaigne, 75008 Paris; 7 avenue Niel, 75017 Paris, France (Home).

PIWOWSKI, Marek; Polish film director, writer, actor, journalist; b. 24 Oct. 1935, Warsaw; s. of Władisław and PiwowskihJadwiga Piwowski; ed. State Acad. of Film, Łodź, Univ. of Warsaw; visiting Prof. City Univ. of New York; actor in 11 films; dir. of 12 films which have won 17 int. film festival awards. *Films include:* Kirk Douglas 1967, Flybeater 1967, A Cruise 1970, Psychodrama 1970, Corkscrew 1971, Blue Hair 1972, How to recognize the Vampire 1974, Foul play 1977, Trouble is my Business 1988, Catch 22 1990, Kidnapping Agata 1993, The Parade Step 1997, The Barracuda's Kiss 1998, The Knife in the Head of Dino Baggio 1998. *Leisure interests:* sailing, skiing, gliders, windsurfing. *Address:* ul. Promenada 21, 00-778 Warsaw, Poland. *Telephone:* (22) 41-80-80. *Fax:* (22) 41-80-80.

PIYASHEVA, Larisa Ivanovna, D.ECON.SC.; Russian economist; b. 10 July 1947, Moscow; m. Boris Pinsker (divorced); two d.; ed. Plekhanov Inst. of Nat. Econ.; researcher Inst. of Int. Workers' Movt. U.S.S.R. Acad. of Sciences 1969–91; Head, Chair. of Econs., Prof., Moscow State Open Univ. 1991–93; Head Finance-Economy Dept. of Council of Fed. Staff 1994–; Dir. F. von Hayek Pvt. Inst. of Econs. and Law 1995–; Dir.-Gen. Dept. of Moscow Maj. Office Feb.–Sept. 1992. *Publications:* monographs and scientific articles on problems of Soviet economy. *Address:* Serpukhovskoy Val 17/23, Apt. 9, 113191 Moscow, Russia. *Telephone:* 292-12-83.

PIZA, Arthur Luiz de; Brazilian painter and printmaker; b. 1928; painter and exhibitor 1943–; moved to Paris 1952; regular exhibitor at Bienal of São Paulo 1951–63, and Biennale of Ljubljana 1957–81, at Triennali of Grenchen since 1958; one-man exhbns. in Brazil, Germany, Yugoslavia, U.S.A., France, Switzerland, Sweden, Spain, Belgium and Italy; works in many important museums and private collections; Purchase Prize 1953, and Nat. Prize for Prints São Paulo Biennale 1959, Prizes at biennales at Ljubljana 1961, Santiago 1966, Venice 1966, Grenchen Triennale 1961, biennales of Norway and Mexico 1980, Puerto Rico 1991, Nat. Asscn. of Critics Grand Prize, Brazil 1994. *Address:* 16 rue Dauphine, 75006 Paris, France.

PLANCHON, Roger; French theatrical director and playwright; b. 12 Sept. 1931, Saint-Chamond; s. of Emile and Augusta (née Nogier) Planchon; m. Colette Dompietrini 1958; two s.; bank clerk 1947–49; Founder Théâtre de la Comédie, Lyon 1951; Dir. Théâtre de la Cité, Villeurbanne 1957–72; Co-Dir. Théâtre Nat. Populaire 1972–; Pres. Fondation Molière 1987–; aims to popularize the theatre by extending its units and recreating the classics within a modern social context; Prix Ibsen (for Le cochon noir) 1974; *acted in films:* Le grand frère 1982, Danton 1983, Un amour interdit, La septième Cible 1984, Camile Claudel 1988, Radio Corbeau 1989, Jean Galmot, aventurier 1990, l'Année de l'éveil 1991, Louis, enfant roi 1992; *plays:* has directed and acted in over 60 plays by Shakespeare, Molière, Racine, Marivaux, Brecht, Adamov, Vinaver, Dubillard and himself, most recently: Ionesco 1983, L'avare 1986, George Dandin 1987, Andromaque (dir.) 1989, Le Vieil Hiver 1990, Fragile Forêt 1990, Les libertins 1994, No Man's Land 1994, Occupe-Toi d'Amélie! 1995, Le Radeau de la Méduse 1995, La Tour de Nesle 1996, Le Triomphe de l'Amour 1996; *films:* (wrote and directed): Dandin 1987, Louis, enfant roi 1992, Lautrec 1998; Pres. Rhône-Alpes Cinéma; Prix Georges Lherminier du Syndicat de la critique dramatique 1986, 1998; Chevalier des Arts et des Lettres, Croix de guerre, Chevalier Légion d'honneur. *Publications:* Plays: La remise 1961, Patte blanche 1965, Bleus, blancs, rouges ou les Libertins 1967, Dans le vent 1968, L'infâme 1969, La langue au chat 1972, Le cochon noir 1973, Gilles de Rais 1976. *Address:* Théâtre National Populaire, 8 place Lazare Goujon, 69627 Villeurbanne Cedex, France. *Telephone:* (4) 78.03.30.30. *Fax:* (4) 78.84.03.20.

PLANT OF HIGHFIELD, Baron (Life Peer) cr. 1991, of Weelsby in the County of Humberside, **Raymond Plant,** PH.D., D.LITT.; British academic and university administrator; b. 19 March 1945, Grimsby; s. of Stanley Plant and Marjorie Plant; m. Katherine Dixon 1967; three s.; ed. Havelock School, Grimsby, King's Coll. London and Univ. of Hull; Lecturer, Sr. Lecturer in Philosophy, Univ. of Manchester 1967–79; Prof. of Politics, Univ. of Southampton 1979–94; Master, St. Catherine's Coll. Oxford 1994–; Pro-Chancellor Southampton Univ. 1996–; Hon. D.Litt. (Hull, London Guildhall). *Publications:* Hegel 1973, Community and Ideology 1974, Political Philosophy and Social Welfare 1981, Philosophy, Politics and Citizenship 1984, Conservative Capitalism 1989, Modern Political Thought 1991, Democracy, Representation and Elections 1992. *Leisure interests:* music, opera, politics. *Address:* Master's Lodgings, St. Catherine's College, Oxford, OX1 3UJ, England. *Telephone:* (01865) 271762.

PLANTEY, Alain Gilles; French government official; b. 19 July 1924, Mulhouse; m. Christiane Wioland 1955; four d.; ed. Univs. of Bordeaux and Paris à la Sorbonne; Staff of Council of State 1949; French Del. to UN 1951–52; Master of Requests Council of State 1956–; Legal Adviser OEEC 1956–57; Prof. Ecole Royale d'Administration, Cambodia, Faculté de Droit and Ecole Nationale d'Administration, Paris 1957–62; Gen. Sec. Agence France-Presse 1958; Asst. Sec.-Gen. for the Community and African and Malagasy Affairs at the Presidency 1961–66; Amb. in Madagascar 1966–72; Asst. Sec.-Gen. WEU 1972–82; Chair. Standing Armaments Cttee. 1972–82; Conseiller d'Etat 1974–; Chair. Int. Court of Arbitration, ICC 1989–96; mem. Conseil Int. de l'Arbitrage en matière de Sport (CIAS); mem. Acad. of Moral and Political Sciences (Inst. of France), American Acad. of Social and Political Science; Chair. Int. Inst. of Law; Vice-Pres. Inst. Charles de Gaulle; numerous decorations. *Publications:* La réforme de la justice marocaine 1949, La justice répressive et le droit pénal chérifien 1950, Au coeur du problème berbère 1952, Traité pratique de la fonction publique 1956, La formation et le perfectionnement des fonctionnaires 1957, La communauté 1962, Indépendance et coopération 1964–77, Prospective de l'État 1975, Droit et pratique de la fonction publique internationale 1977, Réformes dans la fonction publique 1978, La négociation internationale 1980, 1994, International Civil Service: Law and Management 1981, Derecho y Práctica de la Función Pública Internacional y Europea 1982, De la politique entre les Etats: principes de diplomatie 1987, La Fonction publique, traité général 1992, Tratado de Derecho Diplomático 1992. *Address:* 6 avenue Sully-Prudhomme, Paris 75007, France (Home). *Telephone:* (01) 45.55.26.49 (Home).

PLANTIN, Marcus; British broadcasting executive; b. 23 Oct. 1945; s. of Charles P. Plantin and Vera H. Plantin; m. Kate Benfield 1980; two s.; ed. Surbiton Co. Grammar School, Guildford School of Acting; Producer BBC TV 1978–84; joined London Weekend TV, Head Light Entertainment 1985–87, Controller of Entertainment 1987–90, Dir. of Programmes 1990–92, 1997; Dir. London Weekend Productions and LWT Holdings 1990–92; Network

Dir. ITV 1992–97, Man. ITV Network Centre 1995–97. *Leisure interests:* reading, gardening, swimming. *Address:* LWT, London Television Centre, Upper Ground, London, SE1 9LT, England.

PLANTU (pseudonym of Plantureux, Jean Henri); French artist; b. 23 March 1951, Paris; s. of Henri Plantureux and Renée Seignardie; m. Chantal Meyer 1971; three s. one d.; ed. Lycée Henri IV, Paris; political cartoonist, Le Monde 1972–, L'Express 1991–; caricaturist, Droit de réponse (TV show) 1981–87; Grand Prix de l'humour noir Granville; Prix du Reportage (film on Yasser Arafat) 1991. *Publications:* Pauvres chéris 1978, La Démocratie? Parlons-en 1979, Les Cours de caoutchouc sont trop élastiques 1982, C'est le goulag 1983, Pas nette, la planète! 1984, Politic-look 1984, Bonne année pour tous 1985, Ça manque de femmes 1986, A la Soupe 1987, Wolfgang, tu feras informatique 1988, Ouverture en bémol 1988, Des fourmis dans les jambes 1989, C'est la lutte finale 1990, Un Vagne Souvenir 1990, Reproche-Orient 1991, Le Président Hip-Hop! 1991, le Douanier se fait la malle 1992, Ici Maastricht, les Européens parlent aux Européens 1992, Cohabitation à l'Eau de Rose 1993, Le Pire est derrière nous! 1994, Le Petit Mitterrand Illustré 1995, Le Petit Chirac et le Petit Balladur Illustrés 1995, Le Petit Raciste Illustré 1995, Le Petit Communiste Illustré 1995, Le Petit Socialiste Illustré 95, Magic Chirac 1995, les Années vaches folles 1996, Pas de photos 1997, La France dopée 1998. *Address:* Le Monde, 21 bis rue Claude Bernard, 75005 Paris, France.

PLASKETT, Thomas George, M.B.A.; American business executive; b. 24 Dec. 1943, Kansas City, Mo.; s. of Warren Plaskett and Frances Winegar Plaskett; m. Linda Maxey 1968; one s. one d.; ed. Gen. Motors Inst. and Harvard Univ.; with General Motors 1968–74; Asst. Controller, American Airlines 1974–75, Vice-Pres. (Marketing Admin.) 1975–76, Sr. Vice-Pres. (Finance) 1976–80, Sr. Vice-Pres. (Marketing) 1980–87; Pres. Continental Airlines 1987–88; Chair., Pres. and C.E.O. Pan American Corpn. 1988–91; Man. Dir. Fox Run Capital Assocs. 1991–; Acting C.E.O. and Pres. Greyhound Lines Inc. 1994–95, Chair., Dir. 1995–; mem. Bd. Dirs. Tandy Corpn. *Leisure interests:* squash, skiing, golf. *Address:* 5215 N O'Connor Boulevard, Suite 1070, Irving, TX 75039, U.S.A.

PLASTOW, Sir David Arnold Stuart, Kt., F.B.I.M., F.R.S.A.; British business executive; b. 9 May 1932, Grimsby, Lincs.; s. of James Stuart Plastow and Marie Plastow; m. Barbara Ann May 1954; one s. one d.; ed. Culford School, Bury St. Edmunds; apprenticed Vauxhall Motors Ltd. 1950; joined Rolls-Royce Ltd., Motor Car Div. Crewe 1958, Marketing Dir. Motor Car Div. 1967–71, Man. Dir. 1971–72; Man. Dir. Rolls-Royce Motors Ltd. 1972–74, Group Man. Dir. 1974–80; Regional Dir. Lloyds Bank 1974–76; Dir. Vickers Ltd. 1975–92, Man. Dir. 1980–86, Chief. Exec. 1980–92, Chair. 1987–92; Chair. Inchape PLC 1992–95; Dir. GKN Ltd. 1978–84; Dir. Legal & General 1985–87, Guinness PLC 1986–94, Deputy Chair. 1987–89, Jt. Deputy Chair. 1989–94; Deputy Chair. (non-exec.) TSB Group PLC 1991–95; Dir. (non-exec.) Lloyds TSB 1996–; non-exec. Dir. Cable and Wireless PLC 1991–93; Trustee Royal Opera House Trust 1992–93 (Chair. 1992–93); mem. Bd. Tenneco Inc. (Houston) 1985–92; non-exec. Gov. BUPA 1990–95 (Deputy Chair. 1992–95); Pres. Soc. of Motor Mfrs. and Traders Ltd. 1976–78, Deputy Pres. 1978–80; Pres. Motor Industry Research Asscn. 1978–81; Vice-Pres. Inst. of Motor Industry 1974–82; Chair. Grand Council, Motor and Cycle Trades Benevolent Fund 1976–78; mem. Eng. Council 1981–83, Council CBI, Council, Manchester Business School, Court of Manchester Univ., Council, Regular Forces Employment Asscn., Council, Industrial Soc., Chair. 1983–87, British Overseas Trade Bd. 1980–83, British North American Cttee.; Dir. Tenneco Inc. 1985–92, 1996–; Chair. Medical Research Council 1990–98; Chancellor, Luton Univ. 1993–; Companion British Inst. of Man.; Patron, Coll. of Aeronautical and Automobile Eng. 1972–79; Chair. of Govs. Culford School, Bury St. Edmunds; Hon. D.Sc. (Cranfield Inst. of Tech.) 1978; Young Businessman of the Year Award (The Guardian) 1976; Liveryman, Worshipful Co. of Coachmakers and Coach Harness Makers. *Leisure interests:* golf, music. *Address:* Lloyds TSB Group PLC, 71 Lombard Street, London, EC3P 3BS, England.

PLATÉ, Nikolai Alfredovich; Russian chemist; b. 4 Nov. 1934, Moscow; m.; one s. one d.; ed. Moscow State Univ.; jr., sr. researcher, Head of lab. Moscow State Univ. 1956; Dir. A. Topchiyev Inst. of Petrochemical Synthesis; Corresp. mem. U.S.S.R. (now Russian) Acad. of Sciences 1974, mem. 1987; Deputy Acad.-Sec. Dept. of Gen. and Tech. Chem, Sec.-Gen. for Science; mem. European Acad. of Sciences, American Chem. Soc.; research in polymers of medical application, chem. modifications of polymers, liquid crystal polymers, synthetic polymeric membranes; U.S.S.R. State Prize 1985, V. Kargin Prize, S. Lebedev Prize, Herald Russian Acad. of Sciences. *Publications:* Ed.-in-Chief Vysokomolekulyarnye Soyedinenya; books and articles in scientific periodicals. *Leisure interests:* tennis, driving. *Address:* Presidium of Russian Academy of Sciences, Leninsky prospekt 14, 117901 Moscow; Institute of Petrochemical Synthesis, Leninsky prospekt 29, 117912 Moscow, Russia. *Telephone:* (095) 954 4485 (Academy), 952 5927 (Institute). *Fax:* (095) 230 2224.

PLATER, Alan Frederick, F.R.S.L., F.R.S.A.; British writer; b. 15 April 1935, Jarrow-on-Tyne; s. of Herbert Richard Plater and Isabella Scott Plater; m. 1st Shirley Johnson 1958 (divorced 1985); two s. one d.; m. 2nd Shirley Rubinstein 1986; three step-s.; ed. Kingston High School and King's Coll. Newcastle-upon-Tyne; trained as architect; full-time writer 1960–; has written extensively for radio, TV, films and theatre, also for The Guardian, Listener, New Statesman, etc.; Co.-Chair. Writers' Guild of G.B. 1986–87, Pres. 1991–95; Hon. Fellow, Humberside Coll. of Educ. 1983; Hon. D.Litt. (Hull) 1985; Hon. D.C.L. (Northumbria) 1997; Royal TV Soc. Writers' Award 1988, BAFTA Writers' Award 1988, and many other awards. *Plays include:* A Smashing Day, Close the Coalhouse Door, And a Little Love Besides, Swallows on the Water, Trinity Tales, The Fosdyke Saga, Fosdyke Two, On Your Way, Riley!, Skyhooks, A Foot on the Earth, Prez, Rent Party (musical), Sweet Sorrow, Going Home, I Thought I Heard a Rustling, Shooting the Legend, All Credit to the Lads. *Films include:* The Virgin and the Gypsy, It Shouldn't Happen to a Vet, Priest of Love, Keep the Aspidistra Flying. *TV includes:* series Z Cars, Softly Softly; adaptations: Barchester Chronicles, The Fortunes of War, A Very British Coup, Campion, A Day in Summer, A Few Selected Exits; plays, biographies etc. *Publications:* The Beiderbecke Affair 1985, The Beiderbecke Tapes 1986, Misterioso 1987, The Beiderbecke Connection 1992, Oliver's Travels 1994; plays and shorter pieces in various anthologies. *Leisure interests:* reading, theatre, snooker, jazz, grandchildren, talking and listening. *Address:* c/o Alexandra Cann Representation, 12 Abingdon Road, London, W8 6AF, England. *Telephone:* 0171-938 4002.

PLATINI, Michel; French professional footballer and sportsman; b. 21 June 1955, Joeuf; s. of Aldo Platini and Anna Pillenelli; m. Christele Bigoni 1977; one s. one d.; professional footballer A.S. Nancy-Lorraine 1973–79 (winners Coupe de France 1978), A.S. St.-Etienne 1979–82 (French nat. champions 1981), Juventus, Turin 1982–85 (Italian nat. champions, winners European Cup Winners' Cup 1984, European Championship Cup 1985); player with French nat. team 1982, 1984 (winners European Cup), 1985 (winners Artemio Franqui Intercontinental Cup), 1986; co-presenter, ed. and consultant French TV 1985–88, consultant 1993–; f. and Pres. Michel Platini Foundation 1987–; Jt. Pres. French 1998 World Cup Organising Cttee.; Chevalier, Légion d'honneur, Officier, Ordre nat. du Mérite; Ballon d'or du meilleur footballeur européen 1983, 1984, 1985, Soulier d'or européen, Meilleur buteur du championnat d'Italie 1983, 1984, 1985. *Publication:* Ma vie comme un match 1987. *Address:* French 1998 World Cup Organising Committee, 17–21 ave. du Général Mangin, 75204 Paris Cédex 16, France.

PLATONOV, Vladimir Mikhailovich; Russian politician; b. 24 Dec. 1954, Moscow; m.; one s. one d.; ed. Lumumba Univ. of Peoples' Friendship; worked in machine-construction factory 1972–75; investigator Prosecutor's Office, Deputy Prosecutor Moskvoretsky dist. of Moscow 1983–91; pvt. law practice, Exec. Dir. Avtum Co. 1991–94; mem. Moscow City Duma 1993, Chair. (Speaker) 1994–; mem. Party Block Choice of Russia; mem. Russian Council of Fed. 1996–; Chair. Cttee. on Constitutional Law Feb. 1996–. *Address:* Moscow City Duma, Petrovka str. 22, 103051 Moscow, Russia (Office). *Telephone:* (095) 923 5080 (Office).

PLATONOV, Vladimir Petrovich, D.SC.; Belarus mathematician; b. 1 Dec. 1939, Staiki, Byelorussian S.S.R.; s. of Petr Platonov and Anna Platonova; m. Valentina Platonova 1974; two d.; ed. Byelorussian State University; Asst. Prof. Byelorussian State Univ. 1963, Prof. 1968, Head of Algebra Dept. 1967–71; corresp. mem. Acad. of Sciences of Byelorussian S.S.R. (now Belarus) 1969, mem. 1972 (Pres. 1987–92); Head Algebra Dept., Inst. of Math. 1971–93, Dir. 1977–92, lecturer; mem. Inst. for Advanced Studies, Princeton, N.J. 1991–92; Prof., Univ. of Mich., U.S.A. 1993, of Univ. of Bielefeld 1994, of Univ. of Waterloo, Canada 1995–; mem. U.S.S.R. (now Russian) Acad. of Sciences 1987, Belarus Acad. for Educ. 1995, New York Acad. of Sciences 1995; Hon. mem. Chinese-Henan Acad. of Sciences; Foreign mem. Indian Nat. Science Acad.; People's Deputy of the U.S.S.R. 1989–91; Lenin Prize 1978, Humboldt Prize 1993. *Publications include:* Algebraic groups and number theory 1991, Finite-dimensional division algebras 1992. *Leisure interest:* literature. *Address:* Department of Pure Mathematics, University of Waterloo, Waterloo, Ont., N2L 3G1, Canada *Telephone:* (519) 885-1211, Ext. 3484. *Fax:* (519) 725-0160.

PLATT, Nicholas, M.A.; American diplomatist and educational administrator; b. 10 March 1936, New York; m. Sheila Maynard; three s.; ed. Harvard Coll. and Johns Hopkins Univ. School of Advanced Int. Studies; Chinese language student, Taiwan 1963; Political Officer, Hong Kong 1964–68, Beijing 1973–74, Tokyo 1974–77; staff mem. President Nixon's del. to China 1972, later mem. U.S. Liaison Office, Beijing; Dir. for Japanese Affairs, Dept. of State 1977–78; Nat. Security Council staff mem. specializing in Asian Affairs 1978–79; Deputy Asst. Sec. for Defense 1980–81; Acting Asst. Sec. of State for UN Affairs 1981–82; Amb. to Zambia 1982–84, to the Philippines 1987–91, to Pakistan 1991–92; Pres. Asia Soc. 1992–; Special Asst. to Sec. of State and Exec. Sec. Dept. of State 1985–87; mem. Bd. dirs. Fiduciary Trust Int; mem. Int. Advisory Bd. Financial Times 1998–. *Address:* The Asia Society, 725 Park Avenue, New York, NY 10021 (Office); 131 East 69th Street, New York, NY 10021, U.S.A. (Home).

PLATT, Stephen (Steve), B.SC.ECON.; British journalist; b. 29 Sept. 1954, Stoke-on-Trent; s. of Kenneth Platt and Joyce Pritchard; one d. by Diane Louise Paice; partner Anna Elizabeth Sutton; ed. Longton High School, Stoke-on-Trent, Wade Deacon School, Widnes and London School of Econs.; teacher, Moss Brook Special School, Widnes 1972–73; Dir. Self Help Housing Resource Library, Polytechnic of N. London 1977–80; coordinator, Islington Community Housing 1980–83; freelance writer and journalist 1983–; News Ed., subsequently Acting Ed. New Society 1986–88; Ed. Midweek 1988–89, Enjoying the Countryside 1988–; Ed. New Statesman and Society 1991–96. *Leisure interests:* football, walking, countryside, gardening, breeding frogs,

Paddington Bear. *Address:* 46 Tufnell Park Road, London, N7 0DT, England. *Telephone:* 0171-263 4185.

PLATT, Trevor, PH.D., F.R.S., F.R.S.C.; British/Canadian oceanographer; b. 12 Aug. 1942, Salford, England; s. of John Platt and Lily Platt; m. Shubha Sathyendranath 1988; ed. Nottingham, Toronto and Dalhousie Univs.; research scientist Bedford Inst. of Oceanography, Canada 1965–72, Head of Biological Oceanography 1972–; Huntsman Medal, Hutchinson Medal, Rosenstiel Medal. *Publications:* numerous papers in learned journals. *Leisure interests:* cycling, fly-fishing, languages. *Address:* Bedford Institute of Oceanography, Dartmouth, N.S., B2Y 4A2, Canada. *Telephone:* (902) 426-3793. *Fax:* (902) 426-9388.

PLAVINSKY, Dmitri Petrovich; Russian artist; b. 27 April 1937, Moscow; m. Maria Plavinskaya; three d.; ed. Moscow Regional Art Coll.; painter and lithographer; solo exhbns. include Dubna 1970, Alex Lamond Gallery, New York 1993, Mimi Ferzt Gallery, New York 1995; numerous group exhbns. including Grosvenor Gallery, London 1964, ICA London 1977, Phillips Auctioneers, London 1989, Museum of Modern Art, New York 1967, Metropolitan Museum, New York 1977, San Francisco 1965, 1977, Florence 1969, Frankfurt 1969, Lugano 1970, Cologne 1970, Copenhagen 1971, Venice 1977, Tokyo 1978, Berne 1988, Warsaw 1994, Kassel 1995. *Address:* Arbat str. 51, korp. 2, Apt. 97, 121002 Moscow, Russia. *Telephone:* 241-32-29.

PLAYER, Gary (Jim); South African professional golfer; b. 1 Nov. 1935, Johannesburg; s. of Francis Harry Audley Player and late Muriel Marie Ferguson; m. Vivienne Verwey 1957; two s. four d.; first overseas player for 45 years to win U.S. Open Championship 1965; Winner, British Open Championship 1959, 1968, 1974; Piccadilly World Match Play Champion 1965, 1966, 1968, 1971, 1973; U.S. Open Champion 1965; U.S. Masters Champion 1961, 1974, 1978; U.S. Professional Golf Asscn. Champion 1962, 1972; Winner, South African Open 13 times; South African P.G.A. Champion 1959, 1960, 1969, 1979, 1982; Winner, Australian Open 7 times; Quadel Senior Classic Champion 1985; third player ever to win all four major World professional titles; holds world record for lowest 18-hole score in any Open Championship (59 in the Brazilian Open 1974); Sr. Tour victories include: Sr. British Open 1988, 1990, 1997, Sr. P.G.A. Champion 1986, 1988, 1990, Long Island Sr. Classic; runs own business and breeds thoroughbred racehorses; Hon. LL.D. (St. Andrews) 1995, (Ulster) 1997. *Publication:* Gary Player: The Autobiography 1991. *Address:* P.O. Box 785629, Sandton 2146, South Africa.

PŁAŻYŃSKI, Maciej; Polish politician; b. 10 Feb. 1958, Młynary, Elbląg Prov.; m.; two s. one d.; ed. Gdańsk Univ.; co-founder Independent Students Union (NZS) 1980, leader NZS Univ. Board, Gdańsk 1980; participant Young Poland Movt.; organizer of strikes and activist for underground Solidarity during martial law; founder and chair. Gdańsk Height Services Work Cooperative 1983 (employing many unemployed Solidarity activists); Chair. 'Lech Będkowski' Political Thought Club, Gdańsk 1988; co.-f. Liberal Congress in Gdańsk; mem. Republican Coalition 1990 (later Conservative Party); Gdańsk Voivoda 1990–96; Vice-Chair. Gdansk Region Solidarity Election Action (AWS) 1996; Deputy to Sejm (Parl.) 1997–; Sejm Marshal 1997–; mem. Solidarity Election Action Parl. Club. *Address:* Kancelaria Sejmu RP, ul. Wiejska 4/6/8, 00-902 Warsaw, Poland. *Telephone:* (22) 628 09 09.

PLESSNER, Yakir, PH.D.; Israeli economist; b. 18 Jan. 1935, Haifa; s. of Martin Plessner and Eva Plessner; m. Ora Ester Frenkel 1959; one s. one d.; ed. Iowa State Univ. and Hebrew Univ. of Jerusalem; Visiting Lecturer, Pa. Univ. 1971–73; Research Consultant, The World Bank 1977–78; Econ. Advisor to Israel's Minister of Finance 1981–83; Deputy Gov. Bank of Israel 1982–85; mem. Israel's Securities Authority 1982–85; Joseph and Esther Foster Visiting Prof., Brandeis Univ. 1985–86; Visiting Prof. Dartmouth Coll. 1987–88; Sr. Lecturer, The Hebrew Univ. of Jerusalem 1973–; Fellow, Jerusalem Center for Public Affairs 1991; The Oded Levine Prize of the Operations Research Soc. of Israel. *Publications:* The Marketing of Israel's Citrus Fruit in Major European Markets 1976; regular columnist for Globes and Hadashot (daily newspapers); several articles in learned society journals. *Leisure interests:* music, photography, tennis.

PLEŞU, Andrei Gabriel, PH.D.; Romanian philosopher; b. 23 Aug. 1948, Bucharest; s. of Radu Pleşu and Zoe Pleşu; m. Catrinel Maria Lăcrămioara, 1972; two s.; Prof. Acad. of Fine Arts 1991–92; Prof. Dept. of Philosophy Univ. of Bucharest 1992–, Dir. of Dilemma (weekly); Rector of New Europe Coll., Bucharest; Minister of Foreign Affairs Dec. 1997—; New Europe Prize 1993, Prize of Brandenburg Acad. of Sciences, Berlin 1996; Commdr. des Arts et des Lettres 1990. *Publications:* Travel to the World of Forms, Picturesque and Melancholy, Francesco Guardi, The Eye and the Things, Minima Moralia, The Language of Birds (books); numerous papers and articles. *Address:* Alee Modrogan No 14, 73222 Bucharest 1 (Office) Str. Paris 14, Bucharest 1, Romania (Home). *Telephone:* 210 230 7570 (Office); 230 1488 (Home). *Fax:* 210 230.75.70 (Office); 230 1488 (Home).

PLETNEV, Mikhail Vasilievich; Russian pianist, conductor and composer; b. 14 April 1957, Arkhangelsk; ed. Moscow State Conservatory with Yakov Flier and Lev Vlasenko (piano), Albert Leman (composition); First Prize Int. Tchaikovsky competition in Moscow 1978; gave recitals and played with orchestras in maj. cities of Europe and America; gained reputation as Russian music interpreter; f. and Chief Conductor Russian Nat. Orchestra 1990–; tours with orchestra in various countries; teacher in Moscow Conservatory 1981–; People's Artist of Russia 1990, State Prize of Russia 1982, 1993. *Address:* Starokonyushenny per. 33, Apr. 16, Moscow, Russia. *Telephone:* 241 43 39 (Home).

PLIATZKY, Sir Leo, K.C.B., M.A.; British civil servant; b. 22 Aug. 1919, Salford; m. Marian Jean Elias 1948 (died 1979); one s. one d.; ed. Manchester Grammar School, City of London School, Corpus Christi Coll., Oxford; Army service 1940–45 (mentioned in despatches); Research Sec., Fabian Soc. 1946–47; Ministry of Food 1947–50, Treasury 1950–77, Second Perm. Sec. in charge of Public Expenditure 1976–77; Perm. Sec., Dept. of Trade 1977–79; retained on special duties for the Prime Minister Sept. 1979–Jan. 1980; Visiting Prof. City Univ. 1980–84; Non-exec. Dir. Assoc. Communications Corpn. 1980–82, Cen. Independent Television PLC 1981–89; Part-time mem. B.A. Bd. 1980–84, non-exec. Dir. British Airways PLC 1984–85; Trustee, History of Parl. Trust (Treas. 1982–94); Dir. Ultramar Co. PLC 1980–90; Assoc. Fellow, L.S.E. 1982–84, Visiting Fellow 1985–86; Hon. Fellow, Corpus Christi Coll., Oxford; Hon. D.Litt. (Salford) 1986. *Publications:* Getting and Spending: Public Expenditure, Employment and Inflation 1982, Paying and Choosing: The Intelligent Person's Guide to the Mixed Economy 1985, The Treasury under Mrs. Thatcher 1989. *Address:* 27 River Court, Upper Ground, London, SE1 9PE, England. *Telephone:* 0171-928 3667.

PLIMPTON, George Ames, M.A.; American author and editor; b. 18 March 1927, New York; s. of Francis Plimpton and Pauline Ames; m. 1st Freddy M. Espy 1968 (divorced 1988); one s. one d.; m. 2nd Sarah Dudley 1991; two d.; ed. Phillips Exeter Acad. and Harvard and Cambridge Univs.; Ed.-in-Chief, Paris Review 1953–, Paris Review Edns. (subsequently Doubleday & Co.) 1965–72, Paris Review Edns. (subsequently British American Publs.) 1987–; Instr. Barnard Coll. 1956–58; Assoc. Ed. Horizon 1959–61; Dir. American Literature Anthology Program 1967–71; Assoc. Ed. Harper's 1972–81; contributing ed. Food & Wine 1978; TV host, Dupont Plimpton Special 1967–69, Greatest Sports Legends 1979–81, The Ultimate High 1980, Survival Anglia 1980–, Writers' Workshop 1982, Masterpiece Theater 1983–, Challenge 1987; special contrib. Sports Illustrated 1968–; mem. Bd. Dirs. Film Investors 1979–82, Leisure Dynamics 1983–85; Commr. of Fireworks, New York 1973–; Trustee, WNET 1973–81, African Wildlife Leadership Foundation 1980–, N.Y. Zoological Soc. 1985–, etc.; mem. Bd. of Dirs. Dynamite Museum, Nat. Tennis Foundation, Squaw Valley Center for Written & Dramatic Arts, Authors Trust of America, Friends of the Masai Mara, etc.; mem. Linnean Soc., PEN, American Pyrotechnics Asscn., Pyrotechnics Guild Int. etc.; numerous awards and hon. degrees. *Publications:* Rabbit's Umbrella 1956, Out of My League 1961, Paper Lion 1966, The Bogey Man 1968, Mad Ducks and Bears 1973, One for the Record 1974, Shadow-Box 1976, One More July 1976, Sports! (with N. Leifer) 1978, A Sports Bestiary (with A. Roth) 1982, Fireworks 1984, Open Net 1985, The Curious Case of Sidd Finch 1987, The X-Factor 1990, The Best of Plimpton 1990; ed. American Journey: The Times of Robert Kennedy (with J. Stein) 1970, Pierre's Book 1971, The Fancy 1973, Edie, An American Biography (with J. Stein) 1982, D.V. (with C. Hemphill) 1984, and seven vols. of Writers at Work 1957–87; numerous articles. *Address:* Paris Review Inc., 541 East 72nd Street, New York, NY 10021, U.S.A.

PLISETSKAYA, Maiya Mikhailovna; Russian ballerina; b. 20 Nov. 1925, Moscow; m. Rodion Shchedrin; ed. Moscow Bolshoi Theatre Ballet School; soloist Bolshoi Ballet 1943–90; Artistic Dir. Ballet Roma Opera 1984–85, Nat. Ballet of Spain 1987–89; f. Maiya Plisetskaya Int. Ballet Competition, St. Petersburg 1994; Pres. Imperial Russian Ballet 1996–; Hon. mem. Portuguese Dance Centre; Hon. Prof. Moscow Univ. 1993; First Prize, Budapest Int. Competition 1949; People's Artist of the R.S.F.S.R. 1951; People's Artist of the U.S.S.R. 1959, Anna Pavlova Prize 1962, Lenin Prize 1964, Hero of Socialist Labour 1985, Légion d'honneur 1986, and other decorations. *Main ballet roles:* Odette-Odile (Swan Lake, Tchaikovsky), Raimonda (Raimonda, Glazunov), Zaryema (The Fountain of Bakhchisarai, Asafiev), Kitri (Don Quixote, Minkus), Juliet (Romeo and Juliet, Prokofiev), Girl-Bird, Syunmbike (Shuralye, Yarullin), Laurencia (Laurencia, Krein), Aegina (Spartak, Khachaturian); ballets by R. Shchedrin: Carmen (Carmen Suite), Anna (Anna Karenina) 1972, Nina (The Seagull) 1980, Lady with a Lap Dog 1983, La folle de Chaillot 1992, Kurazuka (ballet by Béjart) 1995. *Publication:* I am Maiya Plisetskaya. *Address:* Theresien Str. 23, 80333 Munich, Germany; Tverskaya 25/9, Apt. 31, 103050 Moscow, Russia (Homes). *Telephone:* (089) 28 58 34 (Munich); (095) 2997239 (Moscow).

PLOIX, Hélène Marie Joseph, M.A., M.B.A.; French business executive; b. 25 Sept. 1944, Anould; d. of René Ploix and Antoinette Jobert; m. Alexandre Lumbroso 1988; ed. Calif. and Paris Univs.; Man. Consultant McKinsey and Co., Paris 1968–78; Special Asst. to Cabinet of Sec. of State for Consumer Affairs 1977–78; Dir. Cie. Européenne de Publication 1978–82; Chair. Banque Industrielle et Mobilière Privée 1982–84; mem. of Bd. Comm. des Opérations de Bourse 1983–84; Adviser to Prime Minister for Econ. and Financial Affairs 1984–86; Exec. Dir. IMF and World Bank, representing France 1986–89; Deputy C.E.O. Caisse des dépôts et consignations 1989–95; Chair. Caisse autonome de refinancement 1990–95, CDC Participations 1992–95; Chair. and C.E.O. Pechel Industries 1997; Chevalier de l'Ordre National du Mérite. *Leisure interest:* golf. *Address:* 9 avenue Percier, 75008 Paris, France.

PLORITIS, Marios; Greek author, journalist and director; b. 19 Jan. 1919, Piraeus; m.; ed. Athens Univ.; f. mem. Art Theatre 1942; film and theatre reviewer 1945–67; Dir. Niki Newspaper 1962–63; Dir. Theatro Review 1965–67; prof. at Art Theatre Dramatic School 1957–67; Dir. Courrier de la Resistance Grecque, Paris 1968–69; prof. Univ. Paris VIII 1970–72; Prof. Athens Univ. 1991–; fmr. Chair. Union of Greek Film Reviewers, Greek Center of Theatre, Soc. of Authors; has translated in Greek more than 120 plays and has directed more than 30 plays. *Publications include:* Masks 1967, Dynasties and Tyrants 1974, Politics 1980, Brecht and Hitler 1984, Art, Language and Power 1989. *Address:* 51 Marasli Street, 106 76 Athens, Greece.

PLOWDEN, Baron (Life Peer), cr. 1959; **Edwin Noel Plowden,** G.B.E., K.C.B.; British administrator; b. 6 Jan. 1907, Strachur, Argyll, Scotland; s. of the late Roger H. Plowden; m. Bridget Horatia Richmond, D.B.E. (Lady Plowden, q.v.), 1933; two s. two d. (one deceased); ed. Switzerland and Pembroke Coll., Cambridge; temp. Civil Servant Ministry of Econ. Warfare 1939–40; Ministry of Aircraft Production 1940–46; mem. Aircraft Supply Council, Chief Exec. 1945–46; Chief Planning Officer and Chair. Econ. Planning Bd. in Cabinet Office and Treasury 1947–53; Vice-Chair. Temporary Council Cttee. of NATO 1951–52; Chair. Desig. U.K.A.E.A. 1953–54, Chair 1954–59; Chair. Cttee. of Enquiry into Control of Public Expenditure 1959–61, Cttee. of Enquiry into Org. of Representational Service Overseas 1963–64, Cttee. of Enquiry into Aircraft Industry 1964–65, Standing Advisory Cttee. on Pay of Higher Civil Service 1968–70, Cttee. of Enquiry into Structure of Electricity Supply Industry 1974–75, Enquiry into CBI's Aims and Organisation 1974–75; Deputy Chair. Cttee. of Enquiry into Police Pay and Related Matters 1977–79; mem. Top Salaries Review Body 1977–81, Chair. 1981–89; Pres. AMDEA 1976–87; mem. Advisory Council, Civil Service Coll. 1970–76, Eng. Industries Council 1976, Ford European Advisory Council 1976–83, mem. Int. Advisory Bd. Southeast Bank N.A. 1983–86; Chair. Tube Investments Ltd. 1963–76, Pres. 1976–90; Dir. Nat. Westminster Bank Ltd. 1960–77, Commercial Union Assurance Co. Ltd 1946–78; Pres. London Graduate School of Business Studies 1976–90; Chair. Governing Body 1964–76; Chair. CBI Cos. Cttee. 1976–80, Vice-Chair. Pres.'s Cttee. 1977–80; Chair. Equity Capital for Industry Ltd. 1976–82, Police Complaints Bd. 1976–81, Police Negotiating Bd. 1979–82; Visiting Fellow, Nuffield Coll., Oxford 1956–64; Hon. Fellow, Pembroke Coll., Cambridge 1958; Hon. D.Sc. (Pennsylvania State) 1958, (Aston) 1972, Hon. D.Litt. (Loughborough) 1976. *Publication:* An Industrialist in the Treasury 1989. *Address:* Martels Manor, Dunmow, Essex, CM6 1NB, England. *Telephone:* (01371) 872141.

PLOWDEN, Lady (Bridget Horatia), D.B.E.; British administrator; b. 5 May 1910; d. of late Admiral Sir H. W. Richmond and Lady Richmond; m. Edwin Noel Plowden (Lord Plowden, q.v.) 1933; two s. two d. (one deceased); ed. Downe House; Dir. Trust House Forte Ltd. 1961–72; J.P., Inner London Area Juvenile Panel 1962–71; Chair. Cen. Advisory Council for Educ. (England) 1963–66, Professional Classes Aid Council 1978–86, Advisory Cttee. for Educ. of Romany and other Travellers 1970–83 (Pres. 1983–), Metropolitan Architectural Consortium for Educ., Bd. of Govs. Philippa Fawcett Coll. of Educ. 1967–76, Robert Montefiore Comprehensive School 1968–79; co-opted mem. Educ. Cttee. Inner London Educ. Authority 1967–73, Vice-Chair. ILEA School Sub-Cttee. 1967–70; Vice-Chair. Gov. BBC 1970–75; Chair. IBA 1975–80, Manpower Services Comm. N. London Area Man. Bd. 1983–88; Pres. Pre-Schools Playgroups Asscn. 1972–82 (Vice-Pres. 1982–), Harding Housing Asscn.; Chair. Mary Fielding Guild (fmrly. Working Ladies Guild) 1945–88, Pres. 1992–. mem. Nat. Theatre Bd. 1976–88; Pres. Nat. Inst. of Adult Continuing Educ. 1980–88; Pres. RELATE (fmrly. Nat. Marriage Guidance Council) 1982–93; Liveryman, Goldsmiths Co. 1979–; Fellow, Royal Television Soc. 1980; Hon. Fellow, Coll. of Preceptors 1973, Vice-Pres. Inst. of Preceptors 1984, Pres. 1987; Hon. LL.D. (Leicester) 1968, (Reading) 1970, (Open Univ.) 1974, (London) 1976; Hon. D.Litt. (Loughborough) 1976; *Address:* Martels Manor, Dunmow, Essex, CM6 1NB, England. *Telephone:* (01371) 872141.

PLOWDEN, David, B.A.; American writer, photographer and teacher; b. 10 Sept. 1932, Boston; s. of Roger Stanley Plowden and Mary Plowden (née Butler); m. 1st Pleasance Coggeshall (divorced 1976); m. 2nd Sandra Schoellkopf 1977; three s. one d.; ed. Yale Univ.; Asst. to Trainmaster, Great Northern Railway 1955–56; self-employed photographer/writer 1962–; Assoc. Prof. Ill. Inst. of Tech. Inst. of Design 1978–85; lecturer Univ. of Iowa School of Journalism 1985–88; Visiting Prof. Grand Valley State Univ. 1988–; John Simon Guggenheim Memorial Fellowship 1968, Smithsonian Inst. Award 1970–71, 1975–76; Iowa Humanities Award and Nat. Endowment for the Humanities Award 1987–88. *Publications:* Lincoln and His America 1970, The Hand of Man on America 1971, Floor of the Sky, The Great Plains 1972, Commonplace 1974, Bridges, The Spans of North America 1974, Tugboat 1976, Steel 1981, An American Chronology 1982, Industrial Landscape 1985, A Time of Trains 1987, A Sense of Place 1988, End of an Era 1992, Small Town America 1994, Imprints 1997. *Address:* 609 Cherry Street, Winnetka, IL 60093, U.S.A. *Telephone:* (847) 446-2793. *Fax:* (847) 446-2795.

PLOWRIGHT, David Ernest, C.B.E.; British television executive; b. 11 Dec. 1930, Scunthorpe; s. of William E. Plowright and Daisy M. Plowright; m. Brenda M. Key 1953; one s. two d.; ed. Scunthorpe Grammar School; reporter, Scunthorpe Star 1950; freelance correspondent and sports writer 1952; reporter, feature writer and briefly equestrian corresp., Yorkshire Post 1954; News Ed. Granada TV 1957, Producer, Current Affairs 1960, Exec. Producer, Scene at 6.30 1964, Exec. Producer, World in Action 1966, Head of Current Affairs 1968, Dir. 1968, Controller of Programmes 1969, Jt. Man. Dir. 1975–81, Man. Dir. 1981–87; Chair. Granada TV Ltd. 1987–92; Dir. Granada Int. 1975–92, Granada Group 1981–92, Independent TV News 1981–88, Superchannel 1986–89, British Satellite Broadcasting 1987–90; Deputy Chair. Channel 4, U.K. 1992–97; Visiting Prof. of Media Studies, Univ. of Salford May 1992–; TV broadcast and production consultant 1992–; Dir. Tate Gallery, Liverpool 1988–91; B.A.F.T.A. Fellowship 1992; Hon. D.Litt. (Salford) 1989; Hon. Dr. Arts (Liverpool) 1991. *Leisure interests:* television, theatre, yachting. *Address:* Westways, Wilmslow Road, Mottram, St. Andrew, Cheshire, SK10 4QT, England.

PLOWRIGHT, Joan Anne, C.B.E.; British actress; b. 28 Oct. 1929, Brigg, Lancashire; d. of William Plowright and Daisy (née Burton); m. 1st Roger Gage 1953 (divorced), 2nd Sir Laurence (later Lord) Olivier 1961 (died 1989); one s. two d.; ed. Scunthorpe Grammar School and Old Vic Theatre School; mem. Old Vic Company, toured South Africa 1952–53; first leading rôle in The Country Wife, London 1956; mem. English Stage Company 1956; at Nat. Theatre 1963–74; Vice-Pres. Nat. Youth Theatre; mem. Council English Stage Co.; Best Actress (Tony) Award for A Taste of Honey, New York 1960; Best Actress (Evening Standard) Award for St. Joan 1964; Variety Club Award 1976 for The Bed Before Yesterday, Best Actress Soc. of West End Theatre (Filumena) 1978, Variety Club Film Actress of the Year Award for Drowning by Numbers 1987, Golden Globe Award for Stalin 1993, Golden Globe Award for Enchanted April 1993, 18th Crystal Award for Women in Film, U.S.A. 1994. *Plays and films acted in include:* The Chairs 1957, The Entertainer 1958, Major Barbara and Roots 1959, A Taste of Honey 1960, Uncle Vanya 1962, 1963, 1964, St. Joan 1963, Hobson's Choice 1964, The Master Builder 1965, Much Ado About Nothing 1967, Tartuffe 1967, Three Sisters 1967, 1969 (film 1969), The Advertisement 1968, 1969, Love's Labour's Lost 1968, 1969, The Merchant of Venice, 1970, 1971–72, Rules of the Game, Woman Killed with Kindness 1971–72, Taming of the Shrew, Doctor's Dilemma 1972, Merchant of Venice (TV film) 1973, Rosmersholm 1973, Saturday Sunday Monday 1973, Eden's End 1974, The Sea Gull 1975, The Bed Before Yesterday 1975, Equus (film) 1976, Daphne Laureola (TV film) 1977, Saturday Sunday Monday (TV film) 1977, Filumena 1977, Enjoy 1980, Who's Afraid of Virginia Woolf? 1981, Richard Wagner (film) 1982, Cavell 1982, Britannia Hospital (film) 1981, Brimstone and Treacle (film) 1982, The Cherry Orchard 1983, The Way of the World 1984, Mrs Warren's Profession 1985, Revolution 1985, The House of Bernardo Alba 1986, Drowning by Numbers (film) 1987, Uncle Vanya 1988, The Dressmaker (film) 1988, The Importance of Being Earnest (TV) 1988, Conquest of the South Pole 1989, And a Nightingale Sang 1989, I Love You to Death 1989, Avalon (film) 1990, Time and the Conways 1991, Enchanted April (film) 1991, Stalin 1991, Denis the Menace, A Place for Annie 1992, A Pin for the Butterfly, Last Action Hero 1993, Widow's Peak (film) 1994, On Promised Land 1994, Return of the Natives 1994, Hotel Sorrento 1994, A Pyromaniac's Love Story 1994, The Scarlet Letter 1994, Jane Eyre 1994, If We Are Women (play) 1995, Surviving Picasso (film) 1995, Mr. Wrong (film) 1995, 101 Dalmatians (film) 1996, The Assistant (film) 1996, Shut Up and Dance (film) 1997, Tom's Midnight Garden (film) 1997, It May Be the Last Time (TV film) 1997, America Betrayed 1998, Tea with Mussolini 1998. *Address:* c/o The Malthouse, Horsham Road, Ashurst, Steyning, West Sussex, BN44 3AR, England.

PLOWRIGHT, Rosalind Anne, L.R.A.M.; British soprano; b. 21 May 1949; d. of Robert Arthur Plowright and Celia Adelaide Plowright; m. James Anthony Kaye 1984; one s. one d.; ed. Notre Dame High School, Wigan, Royal Northern Coll. of Music, Manchester; career began London Opera Centre 1973–75; Glyndebourne Chorus and Touring Co. 1974–77; debut with English Nat. Opera as Page in Salome 1975, Miss Jessel in Turn of the Screw 1979 (SWET award), at Covent Garden as Ortlinde in Die Walküre 1980; has sung also in Switzerland, Germany, France, Spain, Portugal, Italy, the Netherlands, Denmark, Austria, Greece, U.S.A., Argentina, Chile, Israel. *Principal roles include:* Ariadne, Alceste, Médée, Norma, Tosca; title role and Elizabeth I in Mary Stuart, Maddalena in Andrea Chénier, Antonia in The Tales of Hoffman, Donna Anna in Don Giovanni, Vitellia in La Clemenza di Tito, Madame Butterfly, Manon Lescaut, Suor Angelica, Giorgetta in Il Tabarro, Aida, Abigaille in Nabucco, Desdemona in Otello, Elena in I Vespri Siciliani, Leonora in Il Trovatore, Amelia in Un Ballo in Maschera, Leonora in La Forza del Destino, Violetta in La Traviata, Kundry in Parsifal; recitals and concerts in U.K., Europe and U.S.A.; several opera recordings; First Prize 7th Int. Competition for Opera Singers, Sofia 1979, Prix Fondation Fanny Heldy, Acad. Nat. du Disque Lyrique 1985. *Leisure interest:* fell walking. *Address:* 83 St. Mark's Avenue, Salisbury, Wilts., SP1 3DW, England.

PLUMB, Baron (Life Peer), cr. 1987, of Coleshill in the County of Warwickshire; **(Charles) Henry Plumb,** Kt., F.R.S.A.; British politician; b. 27 March 1925; s. of Charles Plumb and Louise Plumb; m. Marjorie Dorothy Dunn 1947; one s. two d.; ed. King Edward VI School, Nuneaton; mem. Council Nat. Farmers Union 1959, Vice-Pres. 1964, 1965, Deputy-Pres. 1966–69, Pres. 1970–79; mem. Duke of Northumberland's Cttee. of Inquiry on Foot and Mouth Disease 1967–68; Chair. British Agricultural Council 1975–79; Pres. Nat. Fed. of Young Farmers' Clubs 1976–; Pres. Royal Agricultural Soc. of England 1977, Deputy Pres. 1978; Pres. Int. Fed. of Agricultural Producers 1979–82; mem. (Conservative) European Parl. 1979–, Chair. Agricultural Cttee. 1979–82, Leader, European Democratic Group (Conservative) 1982–87, 1994–, Pres. European Parl. 1987–89, Leader British Conservatives in European Parl. 1994–, Chair. EU/ACP Jt. Ass. for Africa/Caribbean/Pacific Countries 1994, Vice-Pres. EPP Group in European Parl. 1994–; Chancellor Coventry Univ. 1995–; Chair. Agricultural Mortgage Corpn. 1994–95; Fellow Royal Agric. Soc.; Hon. D.Sc. (Cranfield) 1983; D. L. (Warwick); Order of Merit, Fed. Repub. of Germany; R.A.S.E. Gold Medal 1978. *Leisure interests:* fishing, shooting. *Address:* The Dairy Farm, Maxstoke, Coleshill, Warwicks., B46 2QJ; 2 Queen Anne's Gate, London, SW1H 9AA, England. *Telephone:* (01675) 463133 (Coleshill), 0171-222 0411 (London).

PLUMB, Sir John Harold, Kt., PH.D., LITT.D., F.B.A.; British historian; b. 20 Aug. 1911, Leicester; s. of late James Plumb and Sara Ann Plumb; ed. Univ. Coll., Leicester, Christ's Coll., Cambridge; Ehrman Research Fellow King's Coll. Cambridge 1939–46; Foreign Office 1940–45; Fellow, Christ's Coll. 1946–, Steward 1948–50, Tutor 1950–59, Vice-Master 1964–68, Master 1978–82; Lecturer in History, Univ. of Cambridge 1946–62, Reader in Modern English History 1962–65, Prof. of Modern English History 1966–73, now Prof. Emer.; Visiting Prof. Columbia Univ. 1960, Distinguished Visiting Prof. New York City Univ. 1971–72, 1976, Washington Univ. 1977; Ed. History of Human Society 1959–; European Advisory Ed. to Horizon 1959–; Historical Adviser, Penguin Books 1960–92; Ed. Pelican Social History of Britain 1982–; mem. Council of British Acad. 1977–80; Trustee, Nat. Portrait Gallery 1961–82, Fitzwilliam Museum 1985–92; Hon. foreign mem. American Acad. of Arts and Sciences 1970; Hon. D.Litt. (Leicester) 1968, (East Anglia) 1973, (Bowdoin Coll., U.S.A.) 1974, (Univ. of Southern Calif.) 1978, (Westminster Coll., U.S.A.) 1983. *Publications:* England in the Eighteenth Century 1950, West African Explorers (with C. Howard) 1951, Chatham 1953, Sir Robert Walpole Vol. I 1956, Vol. II 1960, The First Four Georges 1956, The Renaissance 1961, Men and Places 1963, Crisis in the Humanities 1964, The Growth of Political Stability in England 1675-1725 1967, The Death of the Past 1969, In the Light of History 1972, The Commercialisation of Leisure 1974, Royal Heritage (with Sir Huw Wheldon) 1977; also televised version of Royal Heritage 1977, New Light on the Tyrant George III 1978, Georgian Delights 1980, Royal Heritage: The Reign of Elizabeth II 1980, The Birth of a Consumer Society (with Neil McKendrick and John Brewer) 1982, The Making of an Historian: Collected Essays of J. H. Plumb 1988, The American Experience (vol. 2) 1989. *Address:* Christ's College, Cambridge, CB2 3BU, England. (Home). *Telephone:* (01223) 362852. *Fax:* (01223) 334919.

PLUMBRIDGE, Robin Allan, M.A.; South African business executive; b. 6 April 1935, Cape Town; s. of late C. O. Plumbridge and late M. A. Plumbridge; m. Celia Anne Millar 1959; two s. two d.; ed. St. Andrews Coll., Grahamstown, Univs. of Cape Town and Oxford; joined Gold Fields of South Africa Ltd. 1957, Asst. Man. 1962–65, Man. 1965–69, Exec. Dir. 1969–80, C.E.O. 1980–95, Chair. 1980–; Chair. World Gold Council 1993–95; Dir., Standard Bank Investment Corpn. 1980–, Newmont Mining Corpn. 1983–; Hon. LL.D. *Address:* P.O. Box 61525, Marshalltown 2107 (Offices); 17 Woolston Road, Westcliff, Johannesburg 2193, South Africa (Home). *Telephone:* (11) 639 2406 (Office). *Fax:* (11) 639 2552.

PLUMMER, (Arthur) Christopher (Orme), C.C.; Canadian actor; b. 13 Dec. 1929, Toronto; m. 1st Tammy Lee Grimes 1956; one d.; m. 2nd Patricia Audrey Lewis 1962 (divorced 1966); m. 3rd Elaine Regina Taylor 1970; public and pvt. schools in Montreal, P.Q.; professional debut as Faulkland in The Rivals, Ottawa Repertory Theatre; Broadway debut in Starcross Story 1951–52; Maple Leaf Award 1982; numerous appearances in theatres in U.S.A. have included: Mark Antony in Julius Caesar, Ferdinand in The Tempest, Earl of Warwick in Anouilh's The Lark, The Narrator in Stravinsky's L'Histoire du Soldat, The Devil in J.B., 1951–61, The Resistible Rise of Arturo Ui and The Royal Hunt of the Sun 1965–66, The Good Doctor 1973, Iago in Othello 1981, Macbeth 1988, No Man's Land 1994, Barrymore 1996 (Tony Award for Best Leading Actor in a Play 1997); played many leading Shakespearian roles in productions by the Stratford Canadian Festival Co.; British debut in title role of Richard III, Stratford on Avon 1961 and then in London as Henry II in Anouilh's Becket; a leading actor in the Nat. Theatre Co. of Great Britain 1971–72; has appeared in Nat. Theatre productions of Amphytrion 38, Danton's Death 1971; many TV roles including Hamlet in BBC/Danish TV production, Hamlet in Elsinore, Jesus of Nazareth 1977. *Films include:* The Fall of the Roman Empire, The Sound of Music, Inside Daisy Clover, Triple Cross, Oedipus the King, Nobody Runs Forever, Lock Up Your Daughters, The Royal Hunt of the Sun, Battle of Britain, Waterloo, The Pyx, The Spiral Staircase, Conduct Unbecoming, The Return of the Pink Panther, The Man Who Would be King, Aces High 1976, The Disappearance 1977, International Velvet 1978, The Silent Partner 1978, Hanover Street 1979, Murder by Decree 1980, The Shadow Box 1980, The Disappearance 1981, The Janitor 1981, The Amateur 1982, Dreamscape 1984, Playing for Keeps 1985, Lily in Love 1985, Dragnet 1987, Souvenir 1988, Shadow Dancing, Mindfield 1989, Where the Heart Is 1989, Star Trek VI: The Undiscovered Country 1991, Malcolm X 1992, Wolf 1994, Dolores Claiborne 1994, Twelve Monkeys 1995, Skeletons 1996, The Arrow 1997. *Leisure interests:* piano, skiing, tennis, old cars. *Address:* c/o Lou Pitt, ICM, 8942 Wilshire Boulevard, Beverly Hills, CA 90211, U.S.A.

PLYUSHCH, Ivan Stepanovich; Ukrainian politician; b. 11 Sept. 1941, Borzna, Chernigov Dist.; ed. Ukrainian Agricultural Acad.; mem. CPSU 1962–91; worked as agronomist, dir. of collective farms, Dir. Sovkhoz 1959–74, party work in Kiev Dist. Cttee. 1975–84; Deputy Chair. Kiev Dist. Soviet 1984–90, Chair. 1990; Deputy to Ukrainian Supreme Soviet 1990–; First Deputy Chair. Supreme Council 1991–92, Chair. 1992–94. *Address:* Verkhovna Rada, M. Hrushevskoho 5, 252019 Kiev, Ukraine.

POATY-SOUCHALATY, Alphonse Mouissou; Republic of the Congo politician; fmr. Minister of Trade and Small and Medium-sized Enterprises; Prime Minister of the Congo 1989–90; mem. Parti congolais du travail (PCT). *Address:* c/o Office of the Prime Minister, Brazzaville, Republic of the Congo.

POCHINOK, Aleksander Petrovich, CAND. ECON.; Russian politician; b. 12 Jan. 1958, Chelyabinsk; m.; one d.; ed. Chelyabinsk Polytech. Inst., Inst. of Econs. Urals br. U.S.S.R. Acad. of Sciences; with Chelyabinsk Inst. of Econs. 1985–89; People's Deputy Russian Fed.; mem. Supreme Soviet, Chair. Comm. on Budget, Planning, Taxation and Prices 1990–93; mem. State Duma, Deputy Chair., Chair. Subcttee. on Budget, Taxation, Banks and Finance 1993–97; mem. Political Council Democratic Union of Russia 1994; Head State Taxation Service Russian Fed. 1997–98; Head Financial Dept. of Govt. Admin. 1998–. *Leisure interests:* chess, tourism. *Address:* Krasnopresnenskaya Embankment 2, Moscow, Russia (Office). *Telephone:* (095) 205-68-75.

PODESTÁ SILVA, Carlos Marcial; Paraguayan politician; b. 5 June 1942, Asunción; s. of Julio Podestá Bóveda and Amalia Silva Ojeda; m.; ed. Colegio "Sagrado Corazón de Jesús", Nat. Univ. of Asunción, Univ. of Guadalajara; Dir. of Communications, of Planning and Public Admin., then Man. Dir. Instituto de Bienestar Rural 1972–83; business consultant 1983–92; councillor Entidad Binacional Itaipú 1992–93; Pres. Nat. Emergency Cttee. May 1993–; Minister of the Interior 1993–95; titular mem. Governing Bd. Asociación Nacional Republicana (Partido Colorado).

PODHORETZ, John, A.B.; American writer and editor; b. 18 April 1961, N.Y.; s. of Norman Podhoretz and Midge (née Rosenthal) Podhoretz; m. Elisabeth Hickey 1996; ed. Univ. of Chicago; Exec. News Ed. Insight Magazine 1985–87; contrib. ed. U.S. News and World Report 1987–88; speechwriter to Pres. of U.S.A. 1988–89; Asst. Man. Ed. Washington Times 1989–91; Sr. Fellow Hudson Inst. 1991–94; TV critic N.Y. Post 1994–95; Deputy Ed. The Weekly Standard 1995–97; J.C. Penney/Mo. Award for Excellence in Feature Sections 1990. *Publication:* Hell of a Ride: Backstage at the White House Follies 1989–93 1993. *Address:* 1211 Avenue of the Americas, 10th Floor, New York, NY 10036, U.S.A.

PODHORETZ, Norman, M.A., B.H.L.; American author and editor; b. 16 Jan. 1930, Brooklyn; s. of Julius Podhoretz and Helen (née Woliner) Podhoretz; m. Midge R. Decter 1956; one s. three d.; ed. Columbia Univ., Jewish Theological Seminary and Univ. of Cambridge; Assoc. Ed. Commentary 1956–58, Ed.-in-Chief 1960–95, Ed.-at-Large 1995–; Ed.-in-Chief, Looking Glass Library 1959–60; Chair. New Directions Advisory Comm. U.S. Information Agency 1981–87; mem. Council on Foreign Relations, Comm. on the Present Danger, Comm. for the Free World; Sr. Fellow Hudson Inst. 1995–; Fulbright Fellow 1950–51; Hon. LL.D. (Jewish Theological Seminary); Hon. L.H.D. (Hamilton Coll.), (Boston) 1995, (Adelphi) 1996; Hon. D. Hum. Litt. (Yeshiva) 1991, (Boston) 1995, (Adelphi) 1996. *Publications:* Doings and Undoings, The Fifties and After in American Writing 1964, Making It 1968, Breaking Ranks 1979, The Present Danger 1980, Why We Were in Vietnam 1982, The Bloody Crossroads 1986, Ex-Friends 1999. *Address:* 165 East 56th Street, New York, NY 10022, U.S.A.

PODRAZHANETS, Iosif Nikolayevich; Russian diplomatist; b. 16 Aug. 1938, Ivansevichi, Belarus; m.; two c.; ed. Moscow Inst. of Int. Relations, Diplomatic Acad. of U.S.S.R. Ministry of Foreign Affairs; with U.S.S.R. Ministry of Foreign Affairs 1968; translator, Embassy, Iceland 1968–71; attaché, Scandinavian Dept. Russian Ministry of Foreign Affairs 1971–74, Counsellor Dept. of U.S.A. and Canada 1986–92, Dir. Dept. of N. America 1992–97; Third, Second Sec. Embassy, Iceland 1974–76; Second Sec. U.S.A. Dept. 1978–81; First Sec. Embassy, Washington 1981–86; Amb. to Brazil 1997–. *Address:* Russian Embassy, SES, Av. das Nações, Lote A. CEP 70476, Brasilia, DF, Brasil. *Telephone:* (5561) 223 3094, (5561) 223 4094 (Office). *Fax:* (5561) 226 7319 (Office).

PÖGGELER, Otto, D.PHIL.; German professor of philosophy; b. 12 Dec. 1928, Attendorn; m. 1959, two c.; ed. Bonn Univ.; Prof. of Philosophy, Bochum Univ. 1968–94, Prof. Emer. 1994–; Dir. Hegel Archives; mem. Rheinland-Westphalia Acad. of Sciences 1977–; Festschriften for O. Pöggeler, Philosophie und Poesie (Ed. A. Gethmann-Siefert) published 1988, and Idealismus mit Folgen (Ed. H.-J. Gawoll and Ch. Jamme) published 1994. *Publications:* Etudes hégéliennes 1985, Martin Heidegger's Path of Thinking 1987, Schritte zu einer Hermeneutischen Philosophie 1994, Über die moderne Kunst. Heidegger und Klees Jenaer Rede von 1924 1995. *Address:* Hegel-Archiv der Ruhr-Universität, 44780 Bochum (Office); Paracelsusweg 22, 44801 Bochum, Germany (Home). *Telephone:* (0234) 700 2208 (Office); (0234) 701160 (Home).

POGORELICH, Ivo; Croatian concert pianist; b. 20 Oct. 1958, Belgrade; s. of I. and D. Pogorelich; m. Aliza Kezeradze 1980 (died 1996); ed. Tchaikovsky Conservatoire of Moscow, then studied with Aliza Kezeradze; f. Bad Wörishofen Festival (Germany) 1988; inaugurated Ivo Pogorelich Int. Solo Piano Competition, Pasadena, CA 1993; UNESCO Goodwill Amb. 1988; f. Sarajevo Charitable Foundation (to raise funds for people of Bosnia in fields of medicine and health) 1994; Fellow-Commoner, Balliol Coll. Oxford 1993;

First Prize Casagrande Competition, Terni, Italy 1978; First Prize Montreal Int. Music Competition, Canada 1980; Special Prize, Int. Chopin Competition, Warsaw 1980; numerous recordings for Deutsche Grammophon, starting with a Chopin recital in 1981 and including works by Beethoven, Schumann, Ravel, Prokofiev and the Tchaikovsky Piano Concerto No. 1; has appeared in major concert halls throughout the world. *Address:* c/o Kantor Concert Management, 67 Teignmouth Road, London, NW2 4EA, England. *Telephone:* 0181-208 2480. *Fax:* 0181-208 2490.

POGORELOV, Aleksey Vasiliyevich; Ukrainian mathematician; b. 3 March 1919, Korocha (Belgorod Dist.); ed. Zhukovsky Air Force Acad., Kharkov Univ.; m.; one s.; Chair. Geometry Dept., Univ. of Kharkov 1947–59; Head of Dept. of Geometry, Research Inst. of Math., Ukrainian Acad. of Sciences, Kiev 1959–60, Corresp. mem. 1960, mem. 1961–; Head of Dept. of Geometry at Physical-Tech. Inst. of Low Temperatures at Ukrainian Acad. of Sciences, Kharkov, concurrently Prof., Univ. of Kharkov 1960–; Corresp. mem. U.S.S.R. (now Russian) Acad. of Sciences 1960–76, mem. 1976–; primarily concerned with problems of solid geometry, theory of shells; U.S.S.R. State Prize 1950, Lobachevsky Prize 1959; Lenin Prize 1962. *Publications:* more than 200 scientific papers. *Address:* Physical-Technical Institute of Low Temperatures at Ukrainian Academy of Sciences, Leninprospekt 47, 310164, Kharkov 164, Ukraine. *Telephone:* 30-85-84 (Office); 43-75-22 (Home).

POGUE, Lloyd Welch, A.B., LL.B. (J.D.), S.J.D., F.R.S.A., F.R.AE.S.; American retd. lawyer, government official and author; b. 21 Oct. 1899, nr. Grant, Montgomery Co., Ia.; s. of Leander Welch Pogue and Myrtle Viola Casey; m. Mary Ellen Edgerton 1926; three s.; ed. Grinnell Coll., Ia., Univ. of Nebraska, Univ. of Michigan and Harvard Law Schools; Assoc. Ropes & Gray (law firm), Boston 1927–33, Partner in New York affiliated firm, Searle, James & Crawford 1933–38; Gen. Counsel, Fed. Civil Aeronautics Authority (later Civil Aeronautics Bd.) 1939–41; mem. and Chair. Civil Aeronautics Bd. 1942–46; U.S. del. to int. aviation confs.; resgnd. to resume pvt. practice of law alone 1946; f. Pogue & Neal 1946; with 14 lawyers, merged with Jones, Day, Cockley & Reavis (Cleveland law firm) to form Jones, Day, Reavis & Pogue 1967; Washington Man. Partner 1967–79; author, lecturer, recorder for the blind 1981–84; Docent at Nat. Air and Space Museum 1982–95; Benjamin Franklin Fellow, Royal Soc. of Arts; mem. Nat. Aeronautic Asscn. (fmr. Pres.), Canadian Aeronautics and Space Inst.; Hon. mem. A.I.A.A.; mem. numerous socs.; Achievement Awards, Golden Eagle Award (Soc. of Aerospace Execs.), Elder Statesman of Aviation Award (Nat. Aeronautic Asscn.), First recipient L. Welch Pogue Award for Lifetime Aviation Achievement, est. by McGraw-Hill Org. 1994. *Publications:* International Civil Air Transport—Transition Following World War II 1979, Pogue/Pollock/Polk Genealogy as Mirrored in History, From Scotland to Northern Ireland/Ulster, Ohio, and Westward 1990 (winner 7 awards), Airline Deregulation, Before and After: What Next? (Lindbergh Memorial Lecture) 1991, The International Civil Aviation Conference (1944), and its sequel, The Anglo-American Bermuda Air Transport Agreement (1946) 1994, Major Milestones in Airline Development 1999; numerous legal articles. *Leisure interests:* writing, genealogy, history. *Address:* 5204 Kenwood Avenue, Chevy Chase, MD 20815-6604, U.S.A. *Telephone:* (301) 654-7233.

PÖHL, Karl Otto; German economist; b. 1 Dec. 1929, Hanover; m. Dr. Ulrike Pesch; two s. two d.; ed. Univ. of Göttingen; Head of Dept. Ifo-Research Inst., Munich 1955–60; econ. journalist 1961–67; mem. Man. Bd. of the Federal Asscn. of German Banks, Cologne 1968–69; Head of Dept. Fed. Ministry of Econ. Affairs 1970–71; Head of Econ. and Fiscal Policy Dept., Fed Chancellor's Office 1971–72; State Sec. Fed. Ministry of Finance 1972–77; Vice-Chair. Deutsche Bundesbank 1977–79, Pres. 1980–91; Dir. Zürich Insurance, Trizec Hahn Corpn., Gabelli Funds, Bogner; partner Bankhaus Sal Oppenheimer Jr. et Cie 1992–98; Dr. h.c. (Georgetown, Ruhr Univ.) 1983, (Tel Aviv Univ.) 1986, (Maryland) 1987, (Buckingham, London) 1992. *Address:* Sal Oppenheim Jr. & Cie KgaA, Bockenheimer Landstrasse 20, 60323 Frankfurt am Main, Germany.

POIROT-DELPECH, Bertrand M.A.H.; French writer and journalist; b. 10 Feb. 1929, Paris; s. of Jean Poirot-Delpech and Jeanne Hauvette; one s. two d.; ed. Univ. of Paris; journalist 1951–; theatre critic for Le Monde 1959– and La Nouvelle Revue Française; literary critic Le Monde 1972–; Pres. Syndicat Professionel de la Critique Dramatique et Musicale 1967–71, Hon. Pres. 1986; mem. Acad. Française 1986; Commdr. Ordre nat. du Mérite, Officier Légion d'honneur; Prix Interallié 1958, Grand Prix du roman de l'Académie Française 1970. *Publications:* Le Grand dadais 1958, La Grasse Matinée 1960, l'Envers de l'eau 1963, Finie la comédie, Au Soir le Soir 1969, La Folle de Lituanie 1970, Les Grands de ce monde 1976, Saïd et moi 1980, Marie Duplessis la Dame aux Camélias 1981, La Légende du siècle 1981, Feuilleton (1972–1982) 1983, Le Couloir du dancing 1983, l'Eté 36 1984, Bonjour Sagan 1985, Monsieur Barbie n'a rien à dire 1987, Le Golfe de Gascogne 1989, Traversées 1989, Discours de réception du commandant Cousteau sous la Coupole 1989, Discours de Réception de Michel Serres 1990, Rue des Italiens (jtly.) 1990, L'Amour de L'Humanité 1994, Diagonales 1996, Théâtre d'ombres 1998. *Address:* Académie Française, 23 rue de Conti, 75006 Paris; Le Monde, 21 bis rue Claude Bernard, 75242 Paris (Office); 14 rue Saint-Guillaume, 75007 Paris, France (Home).

POITIER, Sidney; American actor; b. 20 Feb. 1927, Miami; s. of Reginald and Evelyn Poitier; m. 1st Juanita Hardy; four d.; m. 2nd Joanna Shimkus 1975; two d.; ed. Western Senior High School, Nassau, Governors High School, Nassau; army service 1941–45; acted with American Negro Theatre 1946; appeared in Anna Lucasta 1948, A Raisin in the Sun 1959; mem. Bd. of Dirs. Walt Disney Co. 1994–, Pres. 1994–; Amb. to Japan from the Commonwealth of the Bahamas; Silver Bear Award, Berlin Film Festival 1958; New York Film Critics Award 1958; Academy Award (Oscar) Best Actor of 1963 (for Lilies of the Field); Cecil B. De Mille Award 1982, Life Achievement Award American Film Inst. 1992, Kennedy Center Honors 1995; Hon. K.B.E. 1974. *Appeared in the following films:* Cry the Beloved Country 1952, Red Ball Express 1952, Go, Man, Go 1954, Blackboard Jungle 1955, Goodbye My Lady 1956, Edge of the City 1957, Something of Value 1957, The Mark of the Hawk 1958, The Defiant Ones 1958, Porgy and Bess 1959, A Raisin in the Sun 1960, Paris Blues 1960, Lilies of the Field 1963, The Long Ships 1964, The Bedford Incident 1965, The Slender Thread 1966, A Patch of Blue 1966, Duel at Diablo 1966, To Sir with Love 1967, In the Heat of the Night 1967, Guess Who's Coming to Dinner 1968, For Love of Ivy 1968, The Lost Man 1970, They Call Me Mister Tibbs 1970, The Organization 1971, The Wilby Conspiracy 1975, Shoot to Kill 1988, Deadly Pursuit 1988, Separate But Equal (TV) 1992, Sneakers, Children of the Dust (TV) 1995, To Sir with Love, II (TV) 1996; has appeared in and directed Buck and the Preacher 1972, Warm December 1973, Uptown Saturday Night 1974, Let's Do It Again 1975, A Piece of the Action 1977, One Man, One Vote 1996; directed Stir Crazy 1980, Hanky Panky 1982, Go for It 1984, Little Nikita 1987, Ghost Dad 1990, Sneakers. *Publication:* This Life 1980. *Leisure interests:* football, tennis, gardening. *Address:* c/o CAA, 9830 Wilshire Boulevard, Beverly Hills, CA 90210, U.S.A.

POIVRE D'ARVOR, Patrick, L. EN D.; French journalist; b. 20 Sept. 1947, Reims (Marne); s. of Jacques Poivre and Madeleine France Jeuge; m. Véronique Courcoux 1971; five c. (two deceased); ed. Lycée Georges-Clemenceau, Reims, Insts. d'études politiques, Strasbourg and Paris, Faculties of Law, Strasbourg, Paris and Reims, Ecole des langues orientales vivantes; Special Corresp., France-Inter 1971, journalist 1971–74, Head Political Dept. 1975–76, Deputy Chief Ed., Antenne 2 1976–83, Presenter, evening news programme 1976–83, 1987–, Deputy Dir. News 1989–; Producer and Compère, A nous deux, Antenne 2 1983–86, A la folie, TF1 1986–88; Compère, Tous en Scène, Canal Plus 1984–85; Compère and Producer Ex libris 1988–; Presenter and Producer magazine programme Le Droit de savoir, TF1 1990–94; Leader-writer Paris-Match, Journal du Dimanche 1984–85. *Publications:* Mai 68-Mai 78 1978, Les Enfants de l'aube 1982, Deux amants 1984, Le Roman di Virginie 1985, Les Derniers trains de rêve 1986, La Traversée du miroir 1986, Rencontres 1987, Les Femmes de ma vie 1988, L'Homme d'images 1992, Lettres à l'absente 1993, Les Loups et la bergerie 1994, Elle n'était pas d'ici 1995, Anthologie des plus beaux poèmes d'amour 1995, Un héros de passage 1996, Lettre ouverte aux violeurs de vie privée 1997, Une trahison amoureuse 1997, La fin du monde (collection) 1998. *Address:* TF1, 1 quai du Point du Jour, 92100 Boulogne-Billancourt, France.

POKORNI, Zoltán, A.B.; Hungarian politician and academic; b. 10 Jan. 1962, Budapest; s. of János Pokorni and Klara Vincz; m. Andrea Beck; two s.; ed. Loránd Eötvös Univ., Budapest; lecturer Toldy Ferenc High School, Budapest 1987–94; f. mem., spokesman, writer Democratic Trades Union of Teachers 1993–; joined Fed. of Young Democrats (FIDESz) 1993, Vice-Pres. 1994–; M.P. 1994–98; Deputy Head Parl. Group 1994, Head 1997–98; personal rep. of Budapest XIIth Dist. 1998–; fmrly. Head FIDESz Dept. for Educ. Politics; Minister of Educ. 1998–; mem. Educ. for Democracy 1991–, Pro Scolis Urbis 1992–. *Address:* Oktatási Minisztérium, 1055 Budapest, Szalay u. 10-14, Hungary. *Telephone:* (1) 302-0600.

POKROVSKY, Boris Aleksandrovich; Russian opera stage director; b. 23 Jan. 1912, Moscow; s. of Aleksandr Pokrovsky and Elisaveta Stulova; m. 1st Anna Nekrasova 1936; m. 2nd Irina Maslennikova 1961; one s. one d; ed. Lunacharsky Inst. of Theatre; stage dir., artistic dir. Gorky Opera Theatre 1937–43; stage dir. Moscow Bolshoi Theatre 1937–82, Dir.-Gen. 1952–63, 1967–82; f. and artistic dir. Moscow Chamber Music Theatre 1972–; first opera productions in Bolshoi Theatre of many operas by Russian composers, incl. Francesca da Rimini by Rachmaninov, Semen Kotko and The Gambler by Prokofiev, Dead Souls by Shchedrin; worked with Rostropovich on new productions of Eugene Onegin 1969, Khovanshchina 1995, Bolshoi Theatre; many productions in Moscow Chamber Music Theatre, including The Rake's Progress by Stravinsky, Don Giovanni by Mozart; many productions in European countries, including Life with the Idiot by A. Schnittke, Amsterdam 1993; Prof. Lunacharsky Inst. of Theatre 1954–; Hon. Pres. Int. Inst. of Theatre 1986; U.S.S.R. People's Artist 1961, Lenin Prize 1980, State Prizes of U.S.S.R. and Russia; Golden Mask Theatre Prize 1996. *Publications:* 10 books and many articles. *Leisure interests:* music, reading. *Address:* Moscow Chamber Music Theatre, Nikolskaya str. 17, 103012 Moscow, Russia. *Telephone:* 929-13-24. *Fax:* 921-06-72.

POKROVSKY, Valentin Ivanovich, DR.MED.; Russian physician; b. 1 April 1929; m. Nina Yakovlevna Pokrovskaya; one s.; ed. First Moscow Medical Inst.; mem. CPSU 1959–91; mem. U.S.S.R. (now Russian) Acad. of Medical Sciences 1982–, Pres. 1987–; Dir. Central Scientific Research Inst. of Epidemiology 1971–; mem. of Presidium of U.S.S.R. (now Russian) Fed. of Space Flight; has studied problems of AIDS treatment, meningitis and intestinal diseases; Chair. Scientific Soc. of Microbiologists, Epidemiologists and Parasitologists; mem. Physicians for the Prevention of Nuclear War; mem. WHO Expert Cttee.; mem. WHO Global Cttee. on AIDS and Diarrhoeal

Diseases; mem. Bd. Int. Fed. of Infectionists; Hon. mem. Soc. of Microbiologists of Czech Repub.; U.S.S.R. People's Deputy 1989–91; V. Timakov Prize; D. Ivanovsky Prize. *Publications:* Symptoms, Treatment and Diagnostics of Salmonellesis in Adults 1981, Immuno-ferment Analysis 1985, Symptoms, Pathogenesis and Treatment of Cholera 1988, Small Medical Encylopaedia (Ed.) 1991, Encyclopaedia of Health 1992. *Address:* Russian Academy of Medical Sciences, ul. Solyanka 14, 109801 Moscow, Russia. *Telephone:* 298-21-52. *Fax:* 298-21-64.

POLAK, Jacques Jacobus, PH.D.; Netherlands international official and economist; b. 25 April 1914, Rotterdam; s. of James and Elisabeth F. Polak; m. Josephine Weening 1937; two s.; ed. Gymnasium Erasmianum, Rotterdam, and Univ. of Amsterdam; economist, League of Nations, Geneva, and Princeton, N.J. 1937–43; economist, Netherlands Embassy, Washington, D.C. 1943–44; Asst. Financial Adviser, Econ. Adviser, UN Relief and Rehabilitation Admin., Washington, D.C. 1944–46; IMF, Washington, D.C. 1947–86, Chief, Statistics Div. 1947–48, Asst. Dir. Research Dept. 1948–52, Deputy Dir. Research Dept. 1952–58, Dir. 1958–79; Econ. Counsellor 1966–79, Adviser to Man. Dir. 1980, Exec. Dir. for Cyprus, Israel, Netherlands, Romania and Yugoslavia 1981–86; Sr. Adviser, OECD Devt. Centre 1986–89; Pres. Per Jacobsson Foundation 1987–; Professorial Lecturer, Johns Hopkins Univ. 1949–50, 1987; George Washington Univ. 1950–55; Fellow, Econometric Soc. *Publications include:* The Dynamics of Business Cycles (with Jan Tinbergen) 1950, An International Economic System 1952, Financial Policies and Development 1989, Economic Theory and Financial Policy: The Selected Essays of Jacques J. Polak 1994. *Address:* c/o International Monetary Fund, Washington, DC 20431 (Office); 3420 Porter Street, N.W., Washington, DC 20016, U.S.A. *Telephone:* (202) 623-8834 (Office); (202) 966-6126 (Home).

POLAK, Julia Margaret, M.D., D.SC., F.R.C.PATH., M.R.C.P.; British professor and consultant in histopathology; b. 29 June 1939, Buenos Aires, Argentina; m. Daniel Catovsky; two s. one d.; ed. Univ. of Buenos Aires; various hosp. posts, Buenos Aires 1961–67; Asst. lecturer, Dept. of Histochemistry, Royal Postgrad. Medical School, London 1968–69, lecturer 1970–73, Sr. lecturer 1973–79, Reader 1982–84, Prof. 1984–, Chair. Dept. 1992–; Hon. Consultant in Histopathology, Hammersmith Hosp. 1979–, Deputy Dir. Dept. of Histopathology 1988–; Chair. British Endocrine Pathologists Group 1988–. *Publications:* 19 books, numerous articles, book chapters and case reports etc. *Address:* Department of Histochemistry, Royal Postgraduate Medical School, Hammersmith Hospital, Du Cane Road, London, W12 0NN; 8 Denbigh Road, Ealing, London, W13 8PX, England (Home). *Telephone:* 0181-743 2030 (Ext. 3231); 0181-740 3231 (direct line); 0181-997 0600 (Home). *Fax:* 0181-743 5362.

POLAŃSKI, Roman; French film director, writer and actor; b. 18 Aug. 1933, Paris; s. of Ryszard Polański and Bule Katz-Przedborska; m. 1st Barbara Kwiatkowska-Lass (divorced), m. 2nd Sharon Tate 1968 (died 1969); m. 3rd Emmanuelle Seigner; ed. Polish Film School, Łódź; Dir. Two Men and a Wardrobe 1958, When Angels Fall, Le Gros et Le Maigre, Knife in the Water (prize at Venice Film Festival 1962), The Mammals (prize at Tours Film Festival 1963), Repulsion (prize at Berlin Film Festival 1965), Cul de Sac (prize at Berlin Film Festival 1966), The Vampire Killers 1967, Rosemary's Baby 1968, Macbeth 1971, What? 1972, Lulu (opera), Spoleto Festival 1974, Chinatown (Best Dir. Award. Soc. of Film and TV Arts 1974, Le Prix Raoul-Levy 1975) 1974, The Tenant 1976, Rigoletto (opera) 1976, Tess (Golden Globe Award) 1980, Vampires Ball 1980, Amadeus (play) 1981, Pirates 1986, Frantic 1988, Tales of Hoffmann (opera) 1992, Bitter Moon (dir., produced, written) 1992, Death and the Maiden 1994, Dance of the Vampire (play) 1997; has acted in: A Generation, The End of the Night, See You Tomorrow, The Innocent Sorcerers, Two Men and a Wardrobe, The Vampire Killers, What?, Chinatown, The Tenant, Pirates, Metamorphosis (play) 1988, Icons, A Pure Formality. *Publication:* Roman (autobiography) 1984. *Address:* c/o Agents Associés Georges Beaume, 3 quai Malaquais, 75006 Paris, France.

POLANYI, John Charles, C.C., PH.D., F.R.S., F.R.S.C., F.R.S.E.; Canadian professor of chemistry and physics; b. 23 Jan. 1929, Berlin, Germany; s. of Michael Polanyi and Magda Polanyi (née Kemeny); m. Anne Ferrar Davidson 1958; one s. one d.; ed. Manchester Grammar School and Manchester Univ., England; Postdoctoral Fellow, Nat. Research Council of Canada 1952–54; Research Assoc., Princeton Univ., U.S.A. 1954–56; Lecturer, Univ. of Toronto, Canada 1956–57, Asst. Prof. 1957–60, Assoc. Prof. 1960–62, Prof. of Chem. 1962, Univ. Prof. of Chem. 1974–; many Visiting Lectureships; mem. numerous prof. asscns.; Hon. Foreign mem. A.A.A.S.; Foreign Assoc., N.A.S., U.S.A.; Hon. degrees from over 30 univs.; shared Nobel Prize for Chemistry 1986; Marlow Medal, Faraday Soc. 1962; British Chemical Soc. Award 1971; Chemical Inst. of Canada Medal 1976; Henry Marshall Tory Medal, Royal Soc. of Canada 1977; Wolf Prize in Chem. (shared with G. Pimentel) 1982; Izaak Walton Killam Memorial Prize 1988; Royal Medal, Royal Soc. 1989. *Publications:* Co-Ed.: The Dangers of Nuclear War 1979; author of over 200 scientific papers. *Address:* Department of Chemistry, University of Toronto, 80 St. George Street, Toronto, Ont., M5S 1A1; 142 Collier Street, Toronto, Ont., M4W 1M3, Canada (Home). *Telephone:* (416) 978-3580 (Univ.); (416) 961-6545 or 961-6548 (Home).

POLE, Jack Richon, PH.D., F.B.A., F.R.HIST.S.; British historian; b. 14 March 1922, London; s. of Joseph Pole and Phoebe Rickards; m. Marilyn Mitchell 1952 (divorced 1988); one s. two d.; ed. King Alfred School, London, King's Coll. London, Queen's Coll. Oxford and Princeton Univ., U.S.A.; served in army, rank of Capt. 1941–46; Instructor in History, Princeton Univ. 1952–53; Asst. Lecturer, then Lecturer in American History, Univ. Coll. London 1953–63; Reader in American History and Govt., Cambridge Univ. and Fellow of Churchill Coll. 1963–79, Vice-Master of Churchill Coll. 1975–78; Rhodes Prof. of American History and Insts., Oxford Univ. and Fellow of St. Catherine's Coll. 1979–89, Emer. Fellow 1989–; Visiting Prof. Univs. of Berkeley, Calif. 1960–61, Ghana 1966, Chicago 1969, Beijing 1984, William and Mary Law School 1991; Goleib Fellow New York Univ. Law School 1990; Hon. Vice-Pres. Int. Comm. for the History of Representative and Parl. Insts. 1991–. *Publications:* Political Representation in England and the Origins of the American Republic 1966, Foundations of American Independence 1972, The Pursuit of Equality in American History 1978, (revised and enlarged edn.) 1993, Paths to the American Past 1979, The Gift of Government: Political Responsibility from the English Restoration to American Independence 1983, Colonial British America (co.-ed.) 1984, The American Constitution: For and Against 1987, The Blackwell Encyclopedia of the American Revolution (co-ed.) 1991, Freedom of Speech: Right or Privilege? 1998, Blackwell Companion to the American Revolution 1999; series Co-Ed. Early America: History, Context, Culture. *Leisure interests:* cricket, painting, writing. *Address:* St. Catherine's College, Oxford (Office); 20 Divinity Road, Oxford, OX4 1LJ, England (Home). *Telephone:* (01865) 271757 (Office); (01865) 246950 (Home). *Fax:* (01865) 271768.

POLESE, Kim, B.S.; American computer executive; ed. Univs. of California, Berkeley and Washington; Product Man. Sun Microsystems 1988–95; co-f. Marimba Inc. 1996–, also Pres., C.E.O. *Address:* Marimba Incorporated, 440 Clyde Avenue, Maintain View, CA 94043 U.S.A.

POLETTI, Alan Ronald, D.PHIL., F.R.S.N.Z.; New Zealand professor of physics; b. 19 Oct. 1937, New Plymouth; s. of John Poletti and Pearl Poletti; m. 1st Dorothy M. Martin 1961 (died 1994); three s. one d.; m. 2nd Marcia M. Stenson 1996; ed. Univ. of Oxford; Prof. of Physics, Univ. of Auckland 1969–98, Head of Dept. of Physics 1986–92. *Publications:* over 100 scientific papers. *Leisure interest:* sailing. *Address:* Department of Physics, University of Auckland, Private Bag 92019, Auckland, New Zealand. *Telephone:* 9-3737-599 (Ext. 8853).

POLEZHAYEV, Leonid Konstantinovich; Russian politician; b. 30 Jan. 1940, Omsk; m.; two s.; ed. Omsk Inst. of Agric.; different posts in agric. orgs. Pavlodar Region Kazakhstan; 1965–76; Head of construction Irtysh-Karaganda Canal 1976–82; First Deputy Chair. Karaganda Regional Exec. Cttee. 1982–87; Head. Omsk Regional Dept. of Melioration and Water Resources 1987–89; Deputy Chair., Chair. Omsk Regional Exec. Cttee. 1989–90; Head Admin. of Omsk Region 1991; Gov. Omsk Region Dec. 1995–; mem. Russian Council of Fed. 1993–; corresp. mem. Russian and Int. Acads. of Eng.; Hon. Prof. Omsk State Univ.; Chair. Council of Interregional Asscn. Sibirskoe Soglasheniye; Co-Chair. Consulting Council of admin. Heads of Boundary Territories of Russia and Kazakhstan. *Address:* Office of the Governor, Krasny put str. 1, 644002 Omsk, Russia (Office). *Telephone:* (3812) 24 40 11, 24 14 15 (Office). *Fax:* 24 23 72 (Office).

POLGÁR, László; Hungarian bass opera and concert singer; b. 1 Jan. 1947, Somogyszentpál; s. of Lajos Polgár and Anna Kántor; m. Ágnes Gergely; three d.; ed. Liszt Ferenc Music Acad., Budapest 1967–72; scholarship holder 1972–73; soloist State Opera House, Budapest 1973–; postgraduate study under Hans Hotter, Hochschule für Musik und Darstellende Kunst, Vienna 1979–81. *Song competition winner:* Dvořák, Karlovy Vary 1971, Schumann, Zwickau 1974, Erkel, Budapest 1975, Hungarian Radio 1977, Ostende 1977, Hugo Wolf, Vienna 1980, Pavarotti competition, Philadelphia 1981; Lieder recitalist; also sings oratorio (Verdi: Requiem, etc.); début in Seneca (Monteverdi: L'Incoronazione di Poppea); appearances in Staatsoper, Vienna; Royal Opera House, Covent Garden; Salzburg Festival, Zürich, Munich, Hamburg, Hanover, Paris, Madrid, Venice, Bologna, Florence, Rome, Moscow, Prague, Dresden, Berlin, Stockholm, Buenos Aires, Metropolitan Opera, New York, Philadelphia, Los Angeles, Pittsburgh, Pa.; Liszt Prize 1985, Merited Artist Title 1986. *Operatic roles include:* Osmin, Sarastro, Leporello, Figaro, Publius (La Clemenza di Tito), Bellini: Oroveso (Norma), Rodolfo (La Sonnambula), Basilio (Il Barbiere di Sevilla), Don Geronio (Il Turco in Italia), Philippo II (Don Carlo), Il Guardiano (La Forza del Destino), Conte Walter (Luisa Miller), Fiesco (Simone Boccanegra), Ramphis (Aida), Gurnemanz (Parsifal), Marke (Tristan), Collin (La Bohème), Timur (Turandot), Bluebeard (Duke Bluebeard's Castle), Rocco (Fidelio), Gremin (Eugene Onegin), Boris Godunov. *Address:* 1113 Budapest Ábel Jenő utca 12, Hungary. *Telephone:* 36/1/668-285.

POLIAKOFF, Stephen; British playwright and film director; s. of Alexander Poliakoff and Ina Montagu; m. Sandy Welch 1983; one d. one s.; ed. Westminster School and Univ. of Cambridge; TV plays include: Caught on a Train (BAFTA Award), She's Been Away (Venice Film Festival Prize); plays: Clever Soldiers 1974, The Carnation Gang 1974, Hitting Town 1975, City Sugar 1976, Strawberry Fields (Nat. Theatre) 1978, Shout Across the River (RSC) 1978, The Summer Party 1980, Favourite Nights 1981, Breaking the Silence (RSC) 1984, Coming in to Land (Nat. Theatre) 1987, Playing with Trains (RSC) 1989, Sienna Red 1992, Sweet Panic (Hampstead) 1996, Blinded by the Sun (Nat. Theatre) 1996, Talk of the City 1998; films: Hidden City, Close My Eyes 1992, Century 1995, The Tribe 1998, Food of Love 1998. *Publications:* Plays One 1989, Plays Two 1994, Plays Three; all plays. *Leisure* *interests:* watching cricket, going to the cinema. *Address:* 33 Devonia Road, London, N1 8JQ, England. *Telephone:* 0171-354 2695.

POLI BORTONE, Adriana; Italian politician; b. 25 Aug. 1943, Lecce; m.; two c.; graduated in classics; Assoc. Prof. of Latin Literature, Univ. of Lecce; Movimento Sociale Italian (MSI) party Deputy 1983–94, Alleanza Nazionale Deputy March 1994–; Minister of Agric. 1994–95. *Address:* c/o Ministero delle Politiche Agricole Alimentari e Forestali, Via XX Settembre, 00187 Rome, Italy.

POLING, Harold Arthur, M.B.A.; American business executive; b. 14 Oct. 1925, Troy, Mich.; s.of Plesant Arthur Poling and Laura Elizabeth (née Thompson) Poling; m. Marian Sarita Lee 1957; one s. two d.; ed. Monmouth Coll. and Ind. Univ.; with Ford Motor Co., Dearborn, Mich. 1951–59, 1960–, Asst. Controller Transmissions and Chassis Div. 1964–66, Controller 1966–67, Engine and Foundry Div. 1967–69, Product Devt. Group 1969–72, Vice-Pres. of Finance Ford of Europe, 1972–75, Pres. Ford of Europe, Inc., Brentwood, U.K. 1975–77, Chair. 1977–79, Exec. Vice-Pres. Ford Motor Co., Dearborn, Mich. 1979, Pres. and C.O.O. 1985–87, Vice-Chair. and C.O.O. 1987–90, Chair. and C.E.O. 1990–93, Chair. 1993–94; Sec. Motor Vehicle Mfg. Asscn.; mem. Pres.'s Export Council, Pres.'s Comm. on Environment; mem. Bd. of Dirs. Shell Oil Co.; Co-Chair. Steering Cttee. Barbara Bush Foundation for Family Literacy; mem. Nat. 4-H Council and numerous other orgs.; Hon. degrees (Monmouth Coll.) 1981, (Hofstra Univ.) 1986, (Indiana) 1990, (Detroit) 1990, (Mich. State) 1992; Leadership Award, Eng. Soc., Detroit 1987, Man of the Year (Automotive Industries magazine) 1988, Horatio Alger Award 1991. *Address:* c/o Ford Motor Co., P.O. Box 1899, Room 118, Dearborn, MI 48121-1899, U.S.A.

POLISHCHUK, Lubov Grigoryevna; Russian actress; b. 21 May 1949, Omsk; m.; one s. one d.; ed. Creative Workshop of Variety Arts at Russian Concert Agency, Moscow Lunacharsky Inst. of Theatre Art; in variety shows 1965–76; actress Theatre Hermitage 1980–87; leading actress Theatre School of Contemporary Play 1989–; in cinema 1976–. *Films include:* Zatsepin Family 1976, Twelve Chairs 1976, Love with Privileges, Play of Imagination; Merited Artist of Russian Fed. *Address:* Tsandera str. 7, Apt. 386, 129075 Moscow, Russia (Office). *Telephone:* (095) 215 66 18 (Home).

POLKINGHORNE, Rev. Canon John Charlton, K.B.E., M.A., PH.D., SC.D., F.R.S.; British ecclesiastic and physicist; b. 16 Oct. 1930, Weston-super-Mare; s. of George B. Polkinghorne and Dorothy E. Charlton; m. Ruth I. Martin 1955; two s. one d.; ed. Perse School, Cambridge, Trinity Coll., Cambridge and Westcott House, Cambridge; Lecturer, Univ. of Edin. 1956–58; Lecturer, Univ. of Cambridge 1958–65, Reader 1965–68, Prof. of Math. Physics 1968–79; Fellow, Trinity Coll., Cambridge 1954–86; curate, St. Michael & All Angels, Bedminster 1982–84; Vicar of St. Cosmus and St. Damian in the Blean 1984–86; Hon. Prof. of Theoretical Physics, Univ. of Kent 1984–89; Fellow and Dean, Trinity Hall, Cambridge 1986–89, Hon. Fellow 1989–; Pres. Queens' Coll., Cambridge 1989–96, Fellow 1989–, Hon. Fellow 1996–; Six Preacher, Canterbury Cathedral 1996–; mem. Human Genetics Advisory Comm. 1996–; Hon. D.D. (Kent) 1994; Hon. D.Sc. (Exeter) 1994, (Leicester) 1995. *Publications:* The Analytic S-Matrix (jointly) 1966, The Particle Play 1979, Models of High Energy Processes 1980, The Way the World Is 1983, The Quantum World 1984, One World 1986, Science and Creation 1988, Science and Providence 1989, Rochester Roundabout 1989, Reason and Reality 1991, Science and Christian Belief 1994, Quarks, Chaos and Christianity 1994, Serious Talk 1995, Scientists as Theologians 1996, Beyond Science 1996, Searching for Truth 1996, Belief in God in an Age of Science 1998, Science and Theology 1998. *Leisure interest:* gardening. *Address:* Queen's College, Cambridge, CB3 9ET, England.

POLLACK, Ilana, B.A.; Israeli librarian; b. 13 Aug. 1946, Tel Aviv; d. of Mala First and Leon Pinsky; m. Joseph Pollack 1977 (died 1994); two s.; ed. Re'alit High School, Rishon Le Zion, Tel Aviv Univ. and Hebrew Univ. Jerusalem; served in Israeli Army 1964–66; joined Weizmann Inst. of Science, Rehovot as Librarian 1966, Librarian in charge of Physics Faculty Library 1975, Chief Librarian, Weizmann Inst. 1983–. *Address:* Wix Library, Weizmann Institute of Science, Rehovot 76100 (Office); 22 Shenkin Street, Rishon Le-Zion 75282, Israel (Home). *Telephone:* (08) 9343583 (Office); (03) 9692186 (Home). *Fax:* (08) 9344176.

POLLACK, Sydney; American film director; b. 1 July 1934, Lafayette, Ind.; s. of David Pollack and Rebecca Miller; m. Claire Griswold 1958; one s. two d.; ed. Neighborhood Playhouse Theatre School, New York; Asst. to Sanford Meisner 1954, Acting Instructor 1954–57, 1959–60; Army service 1957–59; Exec. Dir. The Actors Studio (West Coast br.); appeared on Broadway in The Dark is Light Enough 1954, A Stone for Danny Fisher 1955; TV appearances include Aloa Presents; Dir. The Chrysler Theatre, Ben Casey 1962–63 (for TV); Acad. Award for Best Dir. and Best Picture 1986. *Films directed:* The Slender Thread 1965, This Property is Condemned 1966, The Scalphunters 1967, Castle Keep 1968, They Shoot Horses, Don't They? 1969–70, Jeremiah Johnson 1971–72, The Way We Were 1972–73, The Yakuza 1974, Three Days of the Condor 1974–75, Bobby Deerfield 1976, The Electric Horseman 1978–79, Absence of Malice 1981, Tootsie 1982 (produced), Song Writer 1984, Out of Africa 1985 (produced), Havana 1989, The Firm 1993, Sabrina 1996; producer The Fabulous Baker Boys 1989, The Last Ship 1990, King Ralph (co-exec. producer), Dead Again (exec. producer), Presumed Innocent 1990, Sense and Sensibility 1995 (exec. producer); co-producer Bright Lights, Big City 1988; acted in The Player, Death Becomes Her, Husbands and Wives. *Address:* Mirage Enterprises, De Mille Bldg. 110, 5555 Melrose Avenue, Los Angeles, CA 90212; CAA, 9830 Wilshire Boulevard, Beverly Hills, CA 92012, U.S.A.

POLLEN, Arabella Rosalind Hungerford; British couturier and business executive; b. 22 June 1961, Oxford; d. of Peregrine Pollen and Patricia Pollen; m. Giacomo Dante Algranti 1985; two s.; ed. l'Ecole Française, New York, Nightingale Bamford, Hatherop Castle School, Glos., St. Swithins, Winchester and Queen's Coll., London; f. Arabella Pollen Ltd. in jt. venture with Namara Ltd. 1981; bought out Namara Ltd. and entered jt. partnership with Peregrine Marcus Pollen 1983–; Designer for other labels 1983–. *Leisure interests:* music/piano, literature.

POLLINI, Maurizio; Italian pianist; b. 5 Jan. 1942, Milan; has played with Berlin and Vienna Philharmonic Orchestras, Bayerischer Rundfunk Orchestra, London Symphony Orchestra, Boston, New York, Philadelphia, Los Angeles and San Francisco Orchestras; has played at Salzburg, Vienna, Berlin, Prague Festivals; recordings for Polydor Int.; First Prize Int. Chopin Competition, Warsaw 1960.

POLLITT, John, M.D., F.R.C.P., F.R.C.PSYCH., D.P.M.; British consultant physician in psychological medicine; b. 24 Aug. 1926, London; s. of Charles E. Pollitt and Sarah J. Pollitt; m. Erica E. Pollitt 1953; two d.; ed. City of London School, St. Thomas's Hosp. Medical School (Univ. of London) and Mass. Mental Health Center (Harvard Medical School; various posts, Dept. of Psychological Medicine, St. Thomas's Hosp.; Sr. Registrar, St. Andrew's Hosp. Northampton; Rockefeller Research Travelling Fellow, Mass. Mental Health Center 1959–60; Physician in Psychological Medicine, St. Thomas's Hosp. 1961–85, Physician in charge of Dept. of Psychological Medicine 1972–79, now. Hon. Consulting Physician in Psychological Medicine; Regional Postgraduate Dean, S.E. Thames Region (Univ. of London) 1979–83; Medical Dir. Hayes Grove Priory Hosp. 1983–86; Planck Prize, Gaskell Gold Medal and Prize, Bronze Medal and Prize, Royal Medico-Psychological Asscn. *Publications:* Depression and its Treatment 1965, Psychological Medicine for Students 1973, Psychiatric Emergencies in Family Practice 1987; several chapters in textbooks and articles in professional journals. *Leisure interests:* painting, printing, graphic arts, horology. *Address:* 152 Harley Street, London, W1N 1HH, England. *Telephone:* 0171-935 8868; 0181-318 2453.

POLLOCK, Admiral of the Fleet Sir Michael (Patrick), G.C.B., L.V.O., D.S.C.; British naval officer; b. 19 Oct. 1916; m. 1st Margaret Steacy 1940 (died 1951); two s. one d.; m. 2nd Marjory Rees (née Bisset) 1954; one step-d.; ed. Royal Naval Coll., Dartmouth; entered Navy 1930, specialized in gunnery 1941; served in Warspite, Vanessa, Arethusa and Norfolk, Second World War; Capt. Plans Div. of Admiralty and Dir. of Surface Weapons; commanded H.M.S. Vigo and Portsmouth Squadron 1958–59, H.M.S. Ark Royal 1963–64; Asst. Chief of Naval Staff 1964–66; Flag Officer, Second-in-Command, Home Fleet 1966–67; Flag Officer, Submarines, and NATO Commdr., Submarines, E. Atlantic 1967–69; Controller of the Navy 1970–71; Chief of Naval Staff and First Sea Lord 1971–74; First and Prin. Naval Aide-de-Camp to the Queen 1972–74; Chair. Naval Insurance Trust 1975–85, Liddle-Hart Trustee 1976–81; Bath King of Arms 1976–85. *Leisure interests:* shooting, reading, travel. *Address:* The Ivy House, Church Stoke, Montgomery, Powys, SY15 6DU, Wales.

POLOZKOVA, Lidia Pavlovna; Russian speed-skater; b. 8 March 1939, Zlatoust; d. of Pavel I. Skoblikov and Klavdia N. Skoblikova; m. Alexander G. Polozkov; one s.; title of Honoured Master of Sports 1960; six gold medals in Winter Olympic Games 1960 and 1964; all-round world champion 1963–64; won 40 gold medals for breaking records, 25 at world championships and 15 in U.S.S.R.; mem. CPSU 1964–91; Head Dept. of Physical Educ., Moscow Higher School of the All-Union Trade Union Movt. 1974–88; Sr. Vice-Pres. of All-Union Trade Unions Soc. for Physical Culture and Sports 1988–92; Vice-Pres. Russian Speed-Skating Fed. 1992–95, Hon. mem. 1995–; Head, Fund for Support of Sports Veterans 1997–; two orders and various medals. *Publications:* numerous publs. on sport and physical culture. *Leisure interests:* reading, theatre, forest walking, sports, knitting. *Address:* c/o Russian Speed-Skating Federation, Luzhnetskaya nab. 8, Moscow, Russia. *Telephone:* 201-10-40.

POLTORANIN, Mikhail Nikiforovich; Russian politician and journalist; b. 22 Nov. 1939, Leninogorsk, East Kazakhstan Region; m.; two s.; ed. Kazakh State Univ., Higher CP School; corresp., ed.-in-chief local newspapers in Altai 1966–68, Exec. Sec. Kazakhstanskaya Pravda 1970–75, corresp. Pravda in Kazakhstan 1975–86, Ed.-in-Chief Moskovskaya Pravda 1986–88, Political corresp. Press Agency Novosti 1988–90; U.S.S.R. People's Deputy 1989–91; Minister of Press and Mass Media of Russia 1990–92, Deputy-Chair. of Govt. (Deputy Prime Minister) of Russia Feb.–Nov. 1992, Dir. Fed. Information Agency 1992–93; mem. State Duma (Parl.) 1993–95; Chair. Cttee. on Information Policy and Communications 1994–95; Chair. Bd. Moment of Truth Corpn. 1994–96; mem. Bd. of Dirs. TV-3 Russia. *Address:* TV-3, Leningradsky prosp. 22/2, 125040 Moscow, Russia. *Telephone:* 213-30-52.

POLVINEN, Tuomo Ilmari, PH.D.; Finnish professor of history; b. 2 Dec. 1931, Helsinki; s. of Eino Ilmari Polvinen and Ilona Vihersalo; m. Eeva-Liisa Rommi 1965; two d.; ed. Univ. of Helsinki; Docent, Univ. of Helsinki 1965; Prof. of Modern History, Tampere Univ. 1968–70; Dir.-Gen. Nat.

Archives of Finland 1970–74; Prof. of Modern History Univ. of Helsinki 1974–93; Research Prof. Acad. of Finland 1979–95; Urho Kekkonen Prize 1981. *Publications:* Venäjän vallankumous ja Suomi 1917–1920, I-II 1967, 1971, Suomi kansainvälisessä politiikassa 1941–47, I-III 1979, 1980, 1981, Between East and West: Finland in International Politics 1944–47 1986, J. K. Paasikivi, Valtiomiehen elämäntyö Vol. 1, 1870–1918 1989, Vol. 2, 1918–1939 1992, Vol. 3, 1939–1944 1995, Imperial Borderland. Bobrikov and the Attempted Russification of Finland, 1898–1904 1995. *Address:* Ruusulankatu 8 A 9, 00260 Helsinki, Finland. *Telephone:* 408 554.

POLWARTH, 10th Baron; **Henry Alexander Hepburne Scott,** T.D., D.L., M.A., LL.D., F.R.S.E., F.R.S.A.; Scottish administrator, banker and chartered accountant; b. 17 Nov. 1916, Edinburgh; s. of Hon. Walter Thomas Hepburne Scott and Elspeth Glencairn Campbell; m. 1st Caroline Margaret Hay 1943 (divorced 1969); one s. three d.; m. 2nd Jean Jauncey (née Cunninghame Graham) 1969; two step-s. one step-d.; ed. Eton Coll. and King's Coll., Cambridge; Deputy-Gov. Bank of Scotland 1960–66, Gov. 1966–72, Dir. 1974–87; mem. Western Hemisphere Exports Council 1958–64; Partner Chiene and Tait, Edin. 1950–68; Chair. Gen. Accident, Fire and Life Assurance Co. 1968–72; Minister of State, Scottish Office 1972–74, given special responsibility for oil devt. in Scotland 1973–74; Chair. Oil Devt. Council for Scotland 1973–74; Dir. ICI 1969–72, 1974–81, Halliburton Co. 1974–87, Canadian Pacific Ltd. 1975–86, Sun Life Assurance Co. of Canada 1975–84, Brown and Root (U.K.) 1977; mem. Historic Bldgs. Council for Scotland 1953–66; Chancellor Univ. of Aberdeen 1966–86; Chair. Scottish Nat. Orchestra 1975–79; mem. British Section, Franco-British Council 1981–90; mem. House of Lords Select Cttee. on Overseas Trade 1984–85; Vice-Lord Lieut. Borders Region 1975–90; Hon. LL.D. (Univs. of St. Andrews, Aberdeen), Hon. D.Litt. (Heriot Watt), Hon. Dr. (Stirling). *Leisure interests:* country pursuits, travel, the arts. *Address:* Wellfield Parva, Hawkchurch, Axminster, Devon, EX8 5UT, England. *Telephone:* (01297) 678735.

POLYAKOV, Vladimir Porfiriyevich, PH.D.; Russian diplomatist; b. 5 March 1931, Smolensk; s. of Porfiriy and Yevdokia Polyakov; m. Nelly Polyakov 1953; one s.; ed. Inst. of Oriental Studies, Moscow; Diplomatic Service 1956–; Counsellor, Syria 1961–66; various posts in Ministry of Foreign Affairs 1966–68; Counsellor-Minister, Egypt 1968–71; Amb. to Sudan 1971–72, to People's Democratic Repub. of Yemen 1972–74, to Egypt 1974–81 (expelled Sept. 1981); Foreign Ministry section chief for Near East and North Africa 1982–90; U.S.S.R. then Russian Amb. to Egypt 1990–95; Deputy Insp.-Gen., Ministry of Foreign Affairs, Amb.-at-large 1996–. *Leisure interest:* politics. *Address:* Ministry of Foreign Affairs, Smolenskaya-Sennaya 32/34, Moscow, Russia.

POLZE, Werner, DR.RER.POL.; German banker; b. 26 March 1931, Altenburg; m. Margitta Polze 1956; one d.; ed. School of Economics, Berlin, Akademie für Staats- und Rechtswissenschaften, Babelsberg (Inst. of Int. Relations); worked for Deutsche Notenbank, Berlin, G.D.R. 1956–66; joined Deutsche Aussenhandelsbank AG 1966, Exec. Vice-Pres. 1969–78, Pres. 1978–91, Spokesman for the Bd. 1991–; Deputy Chair. Supervisory Bd., DIHB Deutsche Industrie- und Handelsbank AG, Berlin 1990–. *Address:* Deutsche Aussenhandelsbank Aktiengesellschaft, Unter den Linden 26/30, 10117 Berlin, Germany.

POMMIER, Jean-Bernard; French pianist and conductor; b. 17 Aug. 1944, Beziers; two d. by Irena Podleska; ed. Conservatoire de Paris; as pianist has appeared with conductors including: Herbert von Karajan, Bernard Haitink, Pierre Boulez, Riccardo Muti, Gennadi Rozhdestvensky, Leonard Slatkin, Zubin Mehta and Daniel Barenboim; has conducted numerous orchestras including Chamber Orchestra of Europe, Orchestre de Paris; debut with Royal Liverpool Philharmonic Orchestra 1991; Artistic Dir. Northern Sinfonia, Newcastle upon Tyne 1996–; performances worldwide; masterclasses in Chicago, London, Lausanne and Melbourne; Officier, Ordre nat. du mérite; awards include: Int. Competition of Young Musicians, Berlin, Prix de la Guilde des artistes solistes Français, Diapason d'Or, Tchaikovsky Prize, Moscow. *Recordings include:* Mozart Piano Concerti (with Sinfonia Varsovia), Poulenc Piano Concerti (with City of London Sinfonia), Brahms Cello Sonatas and Violin Sonatas, Complete Beethoven Piano Sonatas. *Address:* Opéra & Concert, 1 rue Volney, 75002 Paris, France.

POMODORO, Arnaldo; Italian sculptor and theatrical designer; b. 23 June 1926, Morciano di Romagna; s. of Antonio Pomodoro and Beatrice Luzzi; has worked as jeweller and goldsmith 1950–; artist-in-residence, Stanford Univ. 1966–67, Univ. of Calif. (Berkeley) 1968; lecture course, Mills Coll., Oakland, Calif. 1979–82; Hon. D.Litt. (Dublin) 1992; Int. Sculpture Prize, São Paulo Biennale, Brazil 1963, Premio Nazionale di scultura, Venice Biennale 1964, Int. Sculpture Prize (Carnegie Inst., Pittsburgh) 1967, Henry Moore Grand Prize (Hakone Open-Air Museum, Japan) 1981, Praemium Imperiale for Sculpture (Japan Art Assen.) 1990; Cavaliere di Gran Croce dell' Ordine al merito. *Exhibitions include:* Milan 1955, Bolles Galleries, San Francisco and N.Y. 1960–61, Montreal World Fair 1967, Milan 1974, Marlborough Gallery, N.Y. 1976, Musée d'art moderne de la Ville de Paris 1976, Copenhagen 1983–, Fort Belvedere, Florence 1984–, Tokyo, Osaka and San Francisco 1985, Trinity Coll. Dublin, Mills Coll., Oakland 1986, Marisa Del Re Gallery, New York 1987, 43rd Venice Biennale and Brisbane World Expo 1988, Vatican Museums 1990, Palace of Youth, Moscow 1991, Post and Telecoms HQ, Darmstadt 1992, Kanagawa, Tomaya, Kurashiki, Nishinomiya 1994, UN Plaza, New York 1996, Marlborough Gallery, New York 1996, Fortezza and Palazzo Mediceo, San Leo 1997. *Theatrical designs include:* Semiramide, Rome 1982, Orestea, Gibellina, Sicily 1983–85, Alceste, Genoa 1987, Oedipus Rex, Siena 1988, Cleopatra, Gibellina, Sicily 1989, I Paraventi at Bologna 1990, Nella solitudine dei campi di cotone by Koltès, Rome 1991, More stately mansions by O'Neill, Rome 1992, Oreste by Alfieri, Rome 1993, Stabat Mater by Tarantino, Rome 1994–95, Moonlight by Pinter, Brescia, Rome 1995, Antigone by Anouilh, Taormina 1996. *Publications:* L'arte lunga 1992, Arnaldo Pomodoro 1995. *Leisure interests:* photography, theatre, literature. *Address:* Via Vigevano 5, 20144 Milan, Italy. *Telephone:* 02 58104131.

PONCE ENRILE, Juan, LL.M.; Philippine public official and lawyer; b. 14 Feb. 1924, Gonzaga, Cagayan; s. of Alfonso Ponce Enrile and Petra Furagganan; m. Cristina Castañer 1957; one s. one d.; ed. Ateneo de Manila, Univ. of the Philippines and Harvard Law School; practising corpn. lawyer and Prof. of Taxation 1955–66; Under-Sec. of Finance 1966–68; Acting Sec. of Finance; Acting Insurance Commr.; Acting Commr. of Customs; Sec. of Justice 1968–70; Sec. of Nat. Defence 1970–71 (resgnd.), 1972–78, Minister 1978–86 (reappointed under Aquino Govt. 1985); Chair. Cttee. on Nat. Security, Defense, Peace and Order; mem. Senate and Opposition Leader (Nacionalista Party) 1987; arrested Feb. 1990, released March 1990; mem. Finance, Appropriations and Steering Cttees.; Chair., Bds. of Dirs. Philippine Nat. Bank until 1978, Nat. Investment and Devt. Co., United Coconut Planters Bank, Nat. Disaster Control Center; Dir. Philippine Communications Satellite Corpn.; Trustee and Sec., Bd. of Trustees, Cultural Centre of the Philippines; Chair. Exec. Cttee., Nat. Security Council; mem. Bd., Nat. Econ. and Devt. Authority, Energy Devt., Philippine Nat. Oil Co., Nat. Environmental Protection Council, Philippine Overseas Telecommunications Corpn., Philippine Crop Insurance Corpn.; mem. numerous law and commercial asscns.; two hon. degrees; Mahaputra Adipranada Medal; Philippine Legion of Honor. *Publications:* A Proposal on Capital Gains Tax 1960, Income Tax Treatment of Corporate Merger and Consolidation Revisited 1962, Tax Treatment of Real Estate Transactions 1964; also various articles on law, the military and government. *Leisure interests:* reading, golf, tennis, swimming, water-skiing, fishing. *Address:* 2305 Morado Street, Dasmariñas Village, Makati, Metro Manila, Philippines (Home). *Telephone:* 78-97-26 and 79-03-90.

PONCELET, Christian; French politician; b. 24 March 1928, Blaise; s. of Raoul and Raymonde (née Chamillard) Poncelet; m. Yvette Miclot 1949; two d.; ed. Coll. Saint-Sulpice, Paris and Ecole Professionelle des Postes, Télégraphes et Télécommunications; Deputy to Nat. Assembly for the Vosges 1962–78; Deputy Sec.-Gen. U.D.R. 1971–76, responsible for social affairs; Sec. of State, Ministry of Social Affairs 1972–73, Ministry of Employment, Labour and Population 1973–74; Sec. of State for the Civil Service attached to Prime Minister March–May 1974; Sec. of State for the Budget, Ministry of Econ. Affairs and Finance 1974–77, for Relations with Parl. 1977; Conseiller général, Remiremont 1963–73; Pres. Conseil Général des Vosges 1976; Sénateur des Vosges 1977–, Pres. of Senate 1998–; mem. European Parl. 1979–80; mem. R.P.R. (fmr. U.D.R.), Bureau Politique RPR 1979; Mayor of Remiremont 1983–; Nat. Sec., R.P.R. in Charge of Problems in Society 1984; Pres. Comm. for Finance, Budgetary Control and Econ. Accounts of the Nation to the Senate 1986–98. *Address:* Palais du Luxembourg, 75291 Paris cedex 06; 17 rue des Etats-Unis, 88200 Remiremont, France.

PONGPANIT, Montri; Thai politician and engineer; b. 9 Nov. 1943; m. Thida Pongpanit; two c.; ed. Germany; Highways Dept.; sr. position B. Grimm & Co.; joined Social Action Party 1979; in Office of the Prime Minister; Deputy Communications Minister; Deputy Interior Minister, Deputy Party Sec.-Gen. 1983; fmr. Commerce Minister; Minister of Transport and Communications 1988–90; fmr. leader Social Action Party. *Address:* c/o Social Action Party, Bangkok 10300, Thailand. *Telephone:* (2) 243-0100. *Fax:* (2) 243-3224.

PONIATOWSKI, Prince Michel Casimir, L. EN D.; French politician and civil servant; b. 16 May 1922, Paris; s. of Prince Charles-Casimir Poniatowski and the late Princess Poniatowski (née Anne de Caraman-Chimay); m. Gilberte de Chavagnac 1946; three s. one d.; ed. Ecoles des Roches, Verneuil-sur-Avre, and Univ. de Paris; with Ministry of Finance 1948–56; Financial Attaché in Washington 1956–57; Asst. Dir. du cabinet to Minister of Finance 1957–58; Econ. and Financial Counsellor in Morocco 1958; Asst. Dir. du cabinet to Prés. du Conseil 1958; Dir. du cabinet to Sec. of State for Finance, later to Minister of Finance 1959–62; Dir. du Cabinet, Ministry of Finance 1962; Del. for Foreign Investment, Overseas Finance Admin. 1962; Head of Mission Ministry of Finance 1962–65, Dir. of Insurance 1963–67; Ind. Republican Deputy 1967–73; Sec.-Gen. Féd. des Républicains indépendants 1967–70, Pres. 1975; Mayor of Isle-Adam 1971–; Minister of Health and Social Security 1973–74; Minister of State and of the Interior 1974–77; Roving Amb. (Personal Envoy of Pres.) 1977–81; mem. European Parl. 1979–89; Pres. Comm. for Devt. and Cooperation, European Parl. 1979–84, Inst. de Prospective Politique 1979, Comm. for Energy, Research and Tech. to the European Parl. 1986; Senator from Val-d'Oise 1989–95; Chevalier, Légion d'honneur, Médaille militaire, Chevalier, Ordre national du Mérite, Croix de guerre 1939–45, Commdr. Isabela la Católica, Officier du Ouissam alaouite. *Publications:* L'avenir des pays sous-développés 1954, Histoire de la Russie d'Amérique et de l'Alaska 1959, Talleyrand aux Etats-Unis 1967,

Les choix de l'espoir 1970, Cartes sur table 1972, Les Jagellons 1973, Conduire le changement 1975, Cadoudal, Moreau et Pichegru 1977, L'avenir n'est écrit nulle part 1978, Louis-Philippe et Louis XVIII 1980, L'histoire est libre 1982, Talleyrand et le Directoire 1982, Garnerin, premier parachutiste du monde 1983, Lettre ouverte au Président de la République 1983, L'Europe ou la Mort 1984, Le Socialisme à la Française 1985, Les Technologies Nouvelles, la chance de l'homme 1986, Talleyrand et le Consultat 1986, Talleyrand et l'ancienne France 1988, Talleyrand 1789–1799 1989, Qui survive la France 1991, la Catastrophe socialiste 1991, Mémoires (vol. 1) 1997. *Address:* Mairie, 45 Grande Rue, 95290 l'Isle-Adam; 22 boulevard Jean Mermoz, 92200 Neuilly-sur-Seine, France. *Telephone:* 47.45.45.30.

PONIMAN, Gen. S.; Indonesian politician and army officer; b. 18 July 1926, Solo, Cen. Java; ed. Dutch Elementary School, Dutch Jr. High School and Army Staff and Command Coll.; held various army staff and command posts 1945–70; Commdr. Army Strategic Command (KOSTRAD) 1973; Commdr. of Territorial Defence, Command 1/Medan, N. Sumatra 1974; Deputy Commdr. of Army 1977; Commdr. of Army 1980; Minister of Defence and Security 1983–88. *Address:* c/o Ministry of Defence and Security, Jln. Merdeka Barat 13, Jakarta, Indonesia.

PONOMAREV, Aleksander Sergeyevich; Russian journalist and manager; b. 13 Oct. 1956; m. Nadezhda Ponomareva; one s. one d.; ed. Saratov State Univ.; Komsomol work 1979–87; Deputy Ed.-in Chief Cen. Youth Programme Section, U.S.S.R. Cen. TV 1987–88, Ed.-in-Chief 1988–91; Dir. Creative Union of Experimental TV, Ostankino 1992–93, First Deputy Dir.-Gen. Oskankino 1992–93; Co-founder and Vice-Pres. Moscow Ind. Broadcasting Corpn. (MNVK), Dir.-Gen. 1993–97. *Address:* MNVK Moscow Independent Broadcasting Corporation, Ilyinka str. 15, Bldg. 1, 103070 Moscow, Russia. *Telephone:* (095) 206 0302, 206 0285 (Office).

PONOMAREVA, Ksenya Yuryevna; Russian journalist; b. 19 Sept. 1961; m.; one s. one d.; ed. Moscow State Univ.; on staff Kommersant Publrs. 1993–95; First Deputy Dir. Information and Political Broadcasting Russian Public TV 1995–96; concurrently gen. producer information programmes 1996–97; Dir.-Gen. Russian Public TV 1997–98. *Address:* Akademika Koroleva str. 12, 127000 Moscow, Russia (Office). *Telephone:* (095) 217 9838, 215 1895 (Office).

PONS, Bernard Claude, D. EN MED.; French politician and doctor; b. 18 July 1926, Béziers, Hérault; s. of Claude Pons and Véronique Vogel; m. Josette Cros 1952; one s. three d.; ed. Lyceés, Marseilles and Toulouse and Faculté de Médecine, Montpellier; gen. practitioner, Cahors 1954; Deputy to Nat. Ass. 1967–69, 1973–86, 1988–95, 1997–, Pres. RPR Group 1988–95; Conseiller-Gen. Cajarc canton 1967–78; Sec. of State, Ministry of Agric. 1969–73; mem. Conseil-Gen. Ile-de-France 1978; Sec.-Gen. RPR 1979–84; Paris City Councillor 1983–; Pres. Admin. Council, Paris Câble 1984–; Rep. to Ass. of EC 1984–85; Minister for Overseas Departments and Territories 1986–88; Minister of Town and Country Planning, Equipment and Transport May–Nov. 1995, for Capital Works, Housing, Transport and Tourism 1995–97. *Address:* Paris TV câble, 4 villa Thoréton, 75015 Paris; Assemblée nationale, 75355 Paris, France.

PONSOLLE, Patrick; French business executive; b. 20 July 1944 Toulouse; s. of Jean Ponsolle and Marie-Rose Courthaliac; m. Nathalie Elie Lefebvre 1983; two s. also two s. two d. from previous m.; ed. Lycées Janson-de-Sailly and Henry IV, Paris, Ecole normale supérieure de la rue d'Ulm, Ecole nationale d'administration; civil servant Ministry of Econs. and Finance 1973–77; Financial Attaché Embassy, Washington 1977–79; head of mission for Dir. of Forecasting, Ministry of Econs. and Finance 1980; Sec. Gen. Nat. Accounts and Budgets Comm. 1980–81; Deputy Chief of Staff to Budget Minister 1981–83; Deputy Dir., Asst. Man. Dir. Compagnie de Suez 1983–87, Man. Dir. 1988, Chief Exec. 1991–93; Vice-Chair., Man. Dir. then Chair., Man. Dir. Suez Int. 1985; Chair. Soc. financière pour la France et les pays d'outre mer (Soffo) 1990–96; Co-Chair. Eurotunnel Group, Chair. Eurotunnel S.A. 1994–, Exec. Co-Chair. 1996–; Dir. Unichem PLC 1998–; Dir. numerous cos. including France Télécom, Banque Indosuez; chair. numerous bodies. *Address:* Eurotunnel S.A., 140 boulevard Malesherbes, 75017 Paris (Office); 3 rue Danton, 75006 Paris, France (Home).

PONTECORVO, Gillo (brother of the late Bruno and of Guido Pontecorvo, q.v.); Italian film director; b. 1919, Pisa; Golden Lion Award, Venice for La Battaglia di Algeri. *Films include:* Die Windrose ep Giovanna 1956, La Grande Strada Azzurra 1958, Kapò 1960, La Battaglia di Algeri (Battle of Algiers) 1966, Queimada! 1969, Ogro 1979.

PONTECORVO, Guido, DR.AGR., PH.D., F.R.S. (brother of the late Bruno and of Gillo Pontecorvo, q.v.); British geneticist and university professor; b. 29 Nov. 1907, Pisa; s. of Massimo Pontecorvo and Maria Pontecorvo (née Maroni); m. Leonore Freyenmuth 1939 (died 1986); one d.; ed. Università degli Studi, Pisa, and Univ. of Edinburgh; Asst. and later Regent of Section, Ispettorato Compartimentale Agrario, Florence 1930–38; Research Student, Inst. of Animal Genetics, Edin. 1938–40, Dept. of Zoology, Univ. of Glasgow 1941–43; Lecturer, Inst. of Animal Genetics, Univ. of Edin. 1943–45; Lecturer, Sr. Lecturer, Reader, Dept. of Genetics, Univ. of Glasgow 1945–56, Prof. 1956–68; Hon. Dir. Medical Research Council Unit for Cell Genetics 1964–68; mem. staff, Imperial Cancer Research Fund 1968–75, Hon. Consultant Geneticist 1975–80; Jesup Lecturer, Columbia Univ. 1956, Messenger Lecturer, Cornell Univ. 1957, Leeuwenhoek Lecturer, Royal Soc. 1962; Gandhi Memorial Lecturer, Raman Inst. 1983; J. Weigle Memorial Lecturer, Calif. Inst. of Tech. 1984; Visiting Prof. Albert Einstein Coll. of Medicine, New York 1964, 1965, Washington State Univ. 1967; Royal Soc. Leverhulme Visiting Prof. Dept. of Biophysics, Rio de Janeiro 1969, Dept. of Biology, Pahlavi Univ., Iran 1974; Visiting Prof. Univ. Coll., London 1968–75, King's Coll., London 1969–70, Middlebury Coll., Vermont 1971, Univ. of Teheran 1975; Prof. Ospite Linceo, Scuola Normale Superiore, Pisa 1976–80; Raman Prof., Indian Acad. of Science 1982; Pres. Genetical Soc. 1964–65, Hon. mem. 1982; Vice-Pres. Inst. of Biology 1969–71; mem. Council, Soc. for Gen. Microbiology 1959–60; Fellow Royal Soc. of Edin. 1946 (mem. Council 1958–61), of London 1955 (mem. Council 1958–59); Fellow Linnean Soc. London 1971; Foreign mem., Danish Royal Acad. 1966, Indian Nat. Science Acad. 1984; Hon. mem. Indian Acad. of Sciences 1983, Peruvian Soc. Medical Genetics 1969, Accademia Nazionale delle Science detta dei XL 1993; Foreign Assoc. N.A.S. (U.S.A.) 1984; Hon. Foreign mem. American Acad. of Arts and Sciences 1958; Emer. mem. Acad. Europaea 1990; Hon. D.Sc. (Leicester) 1968, (East Anglia) 1974, (Camerino) 1974; Hon. LL.D. (Glasgow) 1978; Hansen Prize (Carlsberg Foundation) 1961, Darwin Medal (Royal Soc.) 1978, Campano d'Oro (Pisa) 1979. *Publication:* Trends in Genetic Analysis, numerous articles on genetics and a few on high altitude botany. *Leisure interests:* alpine plant photography. *Address:* 60 Thornhill Square, London, N1 1BE, England. *Telephone:* 0171-700 5320.

PONTI, Carlo, LL.D.; French film producer; b. 11 Dec. 1913, Magenta, Milan, Italy; s. of the late Leone Ponti and Maria Ponti (née Zardone); m. 1st Giulania Fiastri 1946; one s. one d.; m. 2nd Sophia Loren (q.v.) 1966; two s.; ed. Università degli Studi, Milan; legal practice in office of Milan barrister 1935–38; film producer 1938–; French citizen 1965–; Major films produced: Roma Città Aperta 1945 (New York Critics Prize 1947), To Live in Peace 1945, Attila 1953, Ulysses 1953, La Strada 1954 (Oscar), War and Peace 1955, Two Women 1960, (Oscar Award for best foreign actress) Boccaccio '70 1961, Yesterday, Today, Tomorrow 1963 (Oscar), Marriage, Italian Style 1964, Casanova '70 1964, Lady L 1965, Dr. Zhivago 1965 (six Oscars), The 25th Hour 1966, Blow Up 1966 (Cannes Film Festival Award), The Girl and the General 1966, More than a Miracle 1966, Ghosts, Italian Style 1967, Smashing Time 1967, Diamonds for Breakfast 1967, Best House in London 1968, A Place for Lovers 1968, Zabriskie Point 1969, Sunflower 1969, Priest's Wife 1970, Love Stress 1971, Mortadella 1971, Red, White and ... 1972, Massacre in Rome 1973, Run Run Joe 1973, Verdict 1974, The Passenger 1974, Blood Money 1975, The Cassandra Crossing 1977, The Naked Sun 1979, A Special Day, Saturday, Sunday, Monday; Officier des Arts et des Lettres. *Address:* Chalet Daniel, Bürgenstock, Nidwalden, Switzerland; 32 Avenue George V, Paris 75008, France; Palazzo Colonna, 1 Piazza d'Ara Coeli 1, Rome, Italy.

PONTI, Michael; American concert pianist; b. 29 Oct. 1937, Freiburg, Germany; s. of Joseph Ponti and Zita Wüchner; m. 1st Carmen Wiechmann 1962 (divorced 1971); one s. two d.; m. 2nd Beatrice van Stappen 1984; one s.; studied under Prof. Gilmour McDonald and Prof. Erich Flinsch; début in Vienna 1964, in New York 1972; has toured extensively all over the world; over 80 recordings; Busoni Award, Italy 1964. *Address:* Heubergstrasse 32, 8116 Eschenlohe, Germany. *Telephone:* (08824) 594.

PONTOIS, Noëlla-Chantal; French ballet dancer; b. 24 Dec. 1943, Vendôme, Loir et Cher; d. of Jean Pontois and Josette Usal; one d.; entered ballet school of Opéra de Paris 1953, joined corps de ballet 1960, prima ballerina 1966, danced Sleeping Beauty with John Gilpin, London Festival Ballet 1967, named Danseuse Etoile, Opéra de Paris, danced Giselle with Rudolf Nureyev 1968, guest Danseuse Etoile 1984–93, farewell performance in The Nutcracker 1993, ballet teacher at Opéra de Paris 1988–; Prix René Blum, Prix Anna Pavlova, Gran Prix Nat. de la danse; Chevalier, Ordre du Mérite; Chevalier, Légion d'honneur, des arts et lettres; Officier, ordre nat. du Mérite. *Address:* c/o Théâtre national de l'Opéra, 8 rue Scribe, 75009 Paris (Office); 25 rue de Maubeuge, 75009 Paris, France (Home).

POOLE, David James, P.P.R.P., A.R.C.A.; British artist; b. 5 June 1931, London; s. of Thomas Herbert Poole and Catherine Lord; m. Iris Mary Toomer 1958; three s.; ed. Stoneleigh Secondary Modern School, Wimbledon School of Art, Royal Coll. of Art; Sr. Lecturer in Painting and Drawing, Wimbledon School of Art 1961–77; Pres. Royal Soc. of Portrait Painters 1983–91; work in H.M. The Queen's collection, London and in pvt. collections in Bermuda, Canada, France, Germany, Italy, S. Africa, Saudi Arabia, Switzerland and U.S.A. *Portraits include:* H.M. Queen Elizabeth II, H.R.H. Prince Philip, H.M. Queen Elizabeth the Queen Mother, H.R.H. Prince Charles, H.R.H. Prince Andrew, H.R.H. Prince Edward, H.R.H. The Princess Royal, Lord Mountbatten, mems. of Govt., armed forces, industry, commmerce, medicine and acad. and legal professions. *Leisure interests:* travel and food, particularly in France. *Address:* Trinity Flint Barn, Weston Lane, Weston, Petersfield, Hants., GU32 3NN; Studio 6, Burlington Lodge, Rigault Road, Fulham, London, SW6 4JJ, England. *Telephone:* (01730) 265075 (Petersfield); 0171-736 9288 (London).

POOS, Jacques F., D. ÈS SC. COMM. ET ECON.; Luxembourg politician; b. 3 June 1935, Luxembourg; m.; three c.; ed. Athénée Grand-Ducal, Luxembourg; ed. Univ. of Lausanne and Luxembourg Int. Univ.; Ministry of Nat. Economy 1959–62; Service d'Etudes et de Statistiques Economiques (STATEC) 1962–64; Dir. Imprimerie Coopérative 1964–76; Pres. SYTRAGAZ

1970–76; Deputy 1974–76; Minister of Finance, Gov. IBRD, IMF, EIB 1976–79; Dir. Banque Continentale du Luxembourg S.A. 1980–82, Banque Paribas (Luxembourg) S.A. 1982–84; Vice-Pres. Parti Socialiste 1982; Deputy Prime Minister and Minister of Foreign Affairs, Foreign Trade and Co-operation 1984–, also of Foreign Trade and Co-operation; Pres. EC 1991. *Publications:* Le Luxembourg dans le Marché Commun 1961, Le modèle Luxembourgeois 1981, La Crise Economique et Financière; est-elle encore maitrisable? 1984. *Address:* Ministry of Foreign Affairs, Foreign Trade and Co-operation, 5 rue Notre Dame, 2240 Luxembourg. *Telephone:* 478-1. *Fax:* 22-31-44.

POPESCU, Dan Mircea, D.JUR.; Romanian politician; b. 6 Oct. 1950, Bucharest; m.; one c.; ed. Faculty of Law, Bucharest Univ.; legal adviser, then researcher at Inst. of Political Science, Bucharest, and lecturer in Int. Relations, Acad. of Socio-Political Studies, Bucharest 1975–; mem. Council Nat. Salvation Front, then mem. of Provisional Council of Nat. Union; presidential adviser for matters of domestic policy Dec. 1990; Minister of State for Living Standards and Social Security 1991; Minister of Labour and Social Protection 1991–92, Minister of State, Minister of Labour and Social Protection 1992–96; Deputy Prime Minister 1992–96; Vice-Pres. Party of Social Democracy in Romania; Senator 1992–. *Publications:* books and studies in the field of political science. *Address:* The Senate, Bucharest, Romania.

POPESCU, Dumitru Radu; Romanian author; b. 19 Aug. 1935, Păpusa Village, Bihor County; ed. Colls. of Medicine and Philology, Cluj; reporter literary magazine Steaua 1956–69; Ed.-in-Chief literary magazine Tribuna 1969–82, Contemporanul 1982; alt. mem. Cen. Cttee. Romanian CP 1968–79; mem. Cen. Cttee. Romanian CP 1979–90; Chair. Romanian Writers' Union 1980–90; Prize of the Writers' Union 1964, 1969, 1974, 1977, 1980; in custody Jan. 1990; Prize of the Romanian Acad. 1970. *Major works:* collections of short stories: Fuga (Flight) 1958, Fata de la miazăzi (A Girl from the South) 1964, Somnul pământului (The Earth's Sleep) 1965, Dor (Longing) 1966, Umbrela de soare (The Parasol) 1967, Prea mic pentru un război aşa de mare (Too Little for Such a Big War) 1969, Duios Anastasia trecea (Tenderly Anastasia Passed) 1967, Leul albastru (The Blue Lion) 1981; *novels:* Zilele săptămînii (Weekdays) 1959, Vara oltenilor (The Oltenians' Summer) 1964, F 1964, Vînătoarea regală (Royal Hunt) 1973, O bere pentru calul meu (A Beer for My Horse) 1974, Ploile de dincolo de vreme (Rains beyond Time) 1976, Impăratul norilor (Emperor of the Clouds) 1976; *plays:* Vara imposibilei iubiri (The Summer of Impossible Love) 1966, Vis (Dream) 1968, Aceşti îngeri trişti (Those Sad Angels) 1969, Pisica în noaptea Anului nou (Cat on the New Year's Eve) 1970, Pasărea Shakespeare (The Shakespeare Bird) 1973, Rezervaţia de pelicani (The Pelican Reservation) 1983, Iepurele şchiop (The Lame Rabbit) 1980, Orasul îngerilor (The Angel's City) 1985; *poems:* Cîinele de fosfor (The Phosphorus Dog) 1981; *essays:* Virgule (Commas) 1978.

POPESCU, Ioan-Iovitz, PH.D.; Romanian professor of optics and plasma physics; b. 1 Oct. 1932, Burila-Mare; s. of Dumitru and Elvira Popescu; m. Georgeta-Denisa Chiru 1963; ed. Univ. of Bucharest; Asst. Prof. of Optics and Gaseous Electronics, Univ. of Bucharest 1955–60, Prof. Faculty of Physics 1972–, Dean 1972–77, Rector of Univ. 1981–89; Head of Plasma Physics Lab., Inst. of Physics, Bucharest 1960–67, Scientific Deputy Dir. 1970–72; Dir. Inst. of Physics and Radiation Tech. 1977–81, Romanian Centre for Induced Gamma Emission 1995–; Alexander von Humboldt Dozenteristipendium, Kiel Univ. 1967–69; Corresp. mem. Romanian Acad. 1974, mem. 1990 (Pres. Physics Section 1990–92); Labour Order of Romania 1964, Prize for Physics (Romanian Acad.) 1965, Scientific Merit Order 1981, Hon. Citizen Mehedintzi Co. 1997. *Publications:* Ionized Gases 1965, General Physics 1971–75, Plasma Physics and Applications 1981, Plasma Spectroscopy 1987, Optics 1988, The Nobel Prizes for Physics 1901–1998 1998; 165 scientific papers cited in about 1,000 foreign works; numerous articles on gas discharges and pioneering works in optogalvanic and multiphoton spectroscopy. *Address:* Str. Fizicienilor 6, Bloc M4, Apt. 6, 76900 Bucharest Măgurele, Romania. *Telephone:* 7.80.66.80.

POPLE, John Anthony, M.A., PH.D., F.R.S.; British professor of theoretical chemistry; b. 31 Oct. 1925, Burnham, Somerset; s. of Keith Pople and Mary Jones; m. Joy Cynthia Bowers 1952; three s. one d.; ed. Univ. of Cambridge; Research Fellow Trinity Coll., Cambridge 1951–54, Lecturer in Math. 1954–58; Research Assoc., Nat. Research Council, Ottawa during summer 1956, 1957; Supt. Basic Physics Div., Nat. Physical Laboratory, Teddington (U.K.) 1958–64; Ford Visiting Prof. of Chem., Carnegie Inst. of Tech., Pittsburgh, Pa. 1961–62; Carnegie Prof. of Chemical Physics, Carnegie-Mellon Univ., Pittsburgh 1964–74, Acting Head, Dept. of Chem. 1967, John Christian Warner Univ. Prof. of Natural Sciences 1974–93; Trustees' Prof. of Chemistry, Northwestern Univ., Evanston 1993–; mem. A.C.S. 1965–, Int. Acad. of Quantum Molecular Science 1967–; Foreign Assoc., Nat. Acad. of Sciences 1977; Fellow, American Physical Soc. 1970–, American Acad. of Arts and Sciences 1971–; Smith's Prizeman (Cambridge) 1950, Marlow Medal of Faraday Soc. 1958, A.C.S. Awards: Irving Langmuir 1970, Harrison Howe 1971, Gilbert Newton Lewis 1973, Pittsburgh 1975, Morley Medal, American Chemical Soc. 1976, Pauling Award 1977, Oesper Award, Univ. of Cincinnati Dept. of Chemistry 1984, Davy Medal, Royal Soc. 1988, Wolf Prize for Chem. 1992, Nobel Prize for Chem. 1998. *Publications:* co-author: High Resolution Magnetic Resonance 1959, Approximate Molecular Orbital Theory 1970, Ab initio Molecular Orbital Theory 1986; also over 450 publs. in scientific journals. *Leisure interest:* music. *Address:* Department of Chemistry, Northwestern University, 2145 Sheridan Road, Evanston, IL 60208; 1500 Sheridan Road, Apt. 7K, Wilmette, IL 60091, U.S.A. (Home). *Telephone:* (847) 491-3403 (Office); (847) 251-3389 (Home). *Fax:* (847) 491-7713 (Office); (847) 251-3396 (Home).

POPOFF, Frank Peter, M.B.A.; American business executive; b. 27 Oct. 1935, Sofia, Bulgaria; s. of Eftim Popoff and Stoyanka Kossoroff; m. Jean Urse; three s.; ed. Indiana Univ.; with Dow Chemical Co. 1959–, Exec. Vice-Pres. 1985–87, Pres. 1987–92, C.E.O. 1987–96, Chair. 1992–; Exec. Vice-Pres., then Pres. Dow Chemical European subsidiary, Switzerland 1976–85; Dir. Dow Corning Corpn., Chemical Bank & Trust Co., Midland, The Salk Inst., American Express; mem. Société de Chimie Industrielle (American Section), Chemical Mfrs. Assen. (Bd. Dirs.). *Address:* Dow Chemical Co., 2030 Dow Center, Midland, MI 48674, U.S.A.

POPOV, Dmitar; Bulgarian politician and judge; fmr. judge and Chair. Sofia Municipal Court; Prime Minister of Bulgaria 1990–91. *Address:* c/o Office of the Prime Minister, Sofia, Bulgaria.

POPOV, Gavriil Kharitonovich, D.ECON.; Russian politician and economist; b. 31 Oct. 1936, Moscow; s. of Khariton Popov and Theodora Popov; m. Irina Popov 1968; two s.; ed. Moscow State Univ.; mem. CPSU 1959–90; teacher at Moscow Univ. 1960–89, Dean of Econ. Faculty 1977–80; introduced man. and business studies to Moscow Univ., Prof. 1971–; Ed.-in-Chief of journal Voprosy ekonomiki (Questions of Economics) 1988–90; People's Deputy of U.S.S.R. 1989–91; Co-Chair. Inter-regional Group of Deputies, pressing for radical change; Chair. Moscow City Soviet 1990–91; Mayor of Moscow 1991–92 (resgnd.); mem. Consultative Council 1991– (Chair, Foreign Policy Cttee 1996–); Pres. Int. Univ. 1991–, Int. Union of Economists 1991–; Chair. Russian Democratic Reform Movt. (RDDR) 1992–, Leader Social Democracy Bloc 1995–; M. Lomonosov Prize. *Publications include:* more than a dozen books on theory of man., and current political and econ. problems. *Leisure interest:* bees. *Address:* # 4, Nikitsky Pereulok, RDDR, 103009 Moscow, Russia. *Telephone:* 956-69-90. *Fax:* 956-80-77.

POPOV, Mihai; D.HIS.SC.; Moldovan diplomatist and philologist; b. 1949, Chebruchi, Sloboza Region, Moldova; ed. Chişinău (Kishinev) State Univ., Diplomatic Acad. in Moscow; worked as Komsomol and CSPU functionary in Kishinev 1973–83; diplomatic service since 1983; First Counsellor, U.S.S.R. Embassy, Romania 1986–92; Minister-Counsellor, Moldovian Embassy Russia 1992–93; Amb. to Belgium 1993–94; Minister of Foreign Affairs 1994–96; Amb. to France 1996–. *Address:* Ministry of Foreign Affairs, Piaţa Marii Adunări Naţionale 1, 277033 Chişinău, Moldova. *Telephone:* (3742) 23-39-40. *Fax:* (3742) 23-23-02.

POPOV, Oleg Konstantinovich; Russian circus actor; b. 31 July 1930, Vyrubovo, Moscow Region; m. H. Lehman; ed. Moscow State Circus School; clown on slack wire at Tbilisi Circus 1950; clown at Saratov Circus 1951; appeared in France, Britain, Poland, etc.; clown at Moscow Circus 1955–; film role in Unauthorized Persons Not Admitted 1986; People's Artist of the U.S.S.R. 1969; Winner of Warsaw Int. Festival of Circus Art 1956, Oscar Prize, Brussels 1958; Order of Red Banner and other decorations. *Publication:* My Hero in the anthology Fires of the Manezh 1961; lives in Germany.

POPOV, Viktor Ivanovich, D.S.; Russian diplomatist (retd.); b. 19 May 1918, Moscow; m. Natalia Aleksandrovna Popova; two s.; ed. Moscow Inst. of History and Philosophy, Higher Diplomatic School of U.S.S.R. Ministry of Foreign Affairs; joined Ministry of Foreign Affairs 1954, Counsellor, Democratic Repub. of Viet Nam 1960–61, Embassy in Australia 1967–68, Minister-Counsellor, Embassy in U.K. 1968; Rector of Acad. of Diplomacy of U.S.S.R. and Amb. on special assignments, including Iran and Afghanistan, UN Gen. Assembly and UNESCO 1968; Amb. to U.K. 1980–86; Counsellor, Foreign Ministry 1986–91; Prof. Moscow State Univ., Diplomatic Acad. 1991–; mem. Cen. Auditing Comm. of CPSU 1981–87; U.S.S.R. State Prize in History, Merited Scientific Worker of the R.S.F.S.R., many other Soviet and foreign awards. *Publications:* Anglo-Soviet Relations 1927–29, Anglo-Soviet Relations 1929–37, History of Diplomacy series (co-author), The Country of Traditions Changes 1991, Margaret Thatcher 1991, Life in Buckingham Palace 1993, Queen's Counsellor–Superagent of the Kremlin 1995, Queen Elizabeth II and the Royal Family 1996, and other publications on international relations and U.S.S.R. foreign policy. *Leisure interests:* tennis, angling. *Address:* Leontyevski per. 14, Apt. 2, 103009 Moscow, Russia. *Telephone:* 229-89-36.

POPOV, Maj.-Gen. Yevgeniy Pavlovich; Russian automation specialist; b. 14 Feb. 1914, Moscow; m.; two s.; ed. Bauman Higher Tech. Coll., Moscow; engineer-mechanic with an Air Force squadron 1939–43; mem. CPSU 1942–91; teacher at A. F. Mozhaisky Acad. of Mil. Aviation and Eng., Leningrad 1943–64; Prof. 1948; Chair. Dept. of Automation and Remote Control, Mozhaisky Inst. 1949–; Chair. Section of Applied Problems, Presidium of U.S.S.R. Acad. of Sciences 1964–71; Head of Chair. at Bauman Higher Coll., Moscow 1971–; Head of Scientific Educational Centre "Robototechnika" 1981–; Corresp. mem. U.S.S.R. (now Russian) Acad. of Sciences 1960–, mem. 1992; U.S.S.R. State Prize 1949, 1972, 1984, many other awards. *Publications:* The Dynamics of Automatic Control Systems 1954, Apply Theory of Control Process for Nonlinear Systems 1973, Robotics and Flexible Manufacturing Systems 1987, Theory of Linear Automatic Control Systems 1989, Fundamentals of Robotics 1990 and many other important works concerned with the theory of automatic controls. *Address:* Centre Robototechnica, Moscow Bauman State Technical University, Izmaylowskaya pl. 7, Moscow 105037, Russia. *Telephone:* 165-17-01 (Office); 915-32-41 (Home). *Fax:* 367-86-90.

POPOV, Yevgeny Anatolyevich; Russian writer; b. 5 Jan. 1946, Krasnoyarsk; m. Svetlana Anatoliyevna Vasilyeva; one s.; ed. Moscow Inst. of Geological Survey; worked as geologist in various regions 1968–73; mem. U.S.S.R. Union of Writers 1978, expelled 1979, readmitted 1988; Assoc. mem. Swedish PEN 1980–; a founder and mem. Bd. Russian PEN 1989–. *Publications:* The Merriment of Old Russia (short stories) 1981, Awaiting Untreacherous Love (short stories) 1989, Wonderfulness of Life (novel) 1990, A Plane to Cologne (short stories) 1991, On the Eve, On the Eve (novel) 1993, The Soul of a Patriot (novel) 1994, Green Musicians (novel) 1998, Thirteen (essays) 1999; (play) Badly Tempered Piano. *Address:* Leningradsky prospect 26, korp. 2, Apt. 52, 125040 Moscow, Russia. *Telephone:* 212-33-97. *Fax:* 212-33-97.

POPOVIČ, Štěpán, C.SC.; Czech engineer; b. 28 Dec. 1945, Ústí nad Labem; m. Iva Popovič; one s. one d.; ed. Mechanical Eng. and Textile Coll., Liberec, Econs. Univ., Prague; with Sklo Union Teplice 1968–89, Dir.-Gen. 1989; Dir.-Gen. Glav Union 1991–; Pres. Union of Industry and Transport 1992–; Man. of the Year 1993, 1998. *Leisure interests:* sport, music, playing the piano. *Address:* Svaz průmyslu a dopravy České republiky, Prague 1, 110 00 Mikulandská 7, Glav Union Teplice 415, Czech Republic. *Telephone:* 24 91 56 79; 041 72 77 81.

POPPER, Frank Geoffrey, D. ÈS L.; British/French art historian; b. 17 April 1918, Prague, Czech Republic; s. of Otto Popper and Paula Goldman; m. 1st Hella Guth 1946; m. 2nd Aline Dallier 1973; ed. Univ. of Paris IV (Paris-Sorbonne); voluntary service in R.A.F. 1941–46; Dir. of shipping and travel agencies 1947–53; mem. research group Inst. of Aesthetics, Paris 1961–68; Asst. Prof. of Aesthetics and the Science of Art, Univ. of Paris VIII (Vincennes à St.-Denis) 1969–71, Dir. of Art Dept. 1970–83, Temp. Reader 1971–73, Reader 1973–75, Prof. 1975–, Full Prof. 1976–; Emer. Prof. 1985–; also organises art exhbns.; Chevalier, Ordre Nat. du Mérite, Officier, Ordre des Arts et des Lettres. *Publications include:* Kunst-Licht-Kunst (exhbn. catalogue) 1966, Lumière et Mouvement (exhbn. catalogue) 1967, Naissance de l'Art Cinétique 1967, Origins and Development of Kinetic Art 1968, Art, Action and Participation 1975, Agam 1976, Electra, Electricity and Electronics in the Art of the Twentieth Century (exhbn. catalogue) 1983, Art of the Electronics Age 1993, Réflexions sur l'Exil, l'Art et l'Europe 1998. *Leisure interests:* chess, music, literature. *Address:* 6 rue du Marché Saint-Honoré, 75001 Paris, France. *Telephone:* (1) 42.61.21.38. *Fax:* (1) 42.61.21.38.

POPTSOV, Oleg Maksimovich; Russian writer and journalist; b. 27 May 1934, Leningrad; m. 2nd Inna Vladimirovna Danilevich; four d.; ed. Leningrad Acad. of Wood and Tech.; worked in Komsomol; First Sec. Leningrad Regional Komsomol Cttee., Cen. Komsomol Cttee; Ed.-in-Chief Selskaya Molodezh 1968–90; Chair. All-Russia State TV and Radio Broadcasting Co. 1990–96; Sec. Moscow Org. of U.S.S.R. Union of Writers 1980–86; People's Deputy of Russia 1990–93. *Publications include:* Do Not Expect Letters 1974, Is Not Subjected to Appeal 1972, The Nominative 1976, The Wedding March of Mendelssohn 1978, Orpheus Does not Bring Luck 1980, It is Not Yet Late 1982, In Search of His Own Alibi 1987, A Banal Subject 1988, And Power, And Captivity 1989, Selected Works 1989, Chronicle of the Times of Tsar Boris 1994. *Address:* Klimashkina str. 12, Apt. 139, 123557 Moscow, Russia. *Telephone:* 252-10-77.

POROKHOVSHCHIKOV, Aleksander Shalvovich; Russian actor, film director and scriptwriter; b. 31 Jan. 1939, Moscow; s. of Mikhail Nikolaevich Dudin and of late Galina Aleksandrovna Porokhovshchikova; m. Irina Valeryevna Zhukova 1995; ed. Chelyabinsk Inst. of Medicine, Shchukin High School of Theatre Art; worked in Satire Theatre 1966–71, Taganka Theatre 1971–81, A. Pushkin Theatre 1981–; f. first Russian pvt. film studio Rodina 1987–, Dir. Studio; Pres. Cultural Centre "House of A. A. Porokhovshchikov 1871"; People's Artist of Russia. *Roles in drama productions include:* Profitable Position, Inspector, Lighting but not Warming, Optimistic Tragedy. *Roles in films include:* Ring 1973, The Star of Captivating Happiness 1975, Diamonds for the Proletariat Dictatorship 1976, Seek the Wind 1979, Family Circle 1980, Living Target 1989, Heir 1992. *Films directed:* The Ninth of May 1988. Dir., scriptwriter and actor: Uncensored Memory 1991 (Main Prize Scochi Film Market, Russia 1993, Spectators Prize, Tver Film Festival, Golden Sail Prize, St.-Raphaël Russian Film Festival, France 1994). *Leisure interests:* music, piano playing, jazz band, nature, diving. *Address:* Prospekt Mira 180, Apt. 169, 129366 Moscow, Russia. *Telephone:* (095) 245-26-47. *Fax:* (095) 245-26-47.

PORPHYRIOS, Demetri; Greek architect; ed. Princeton Univ.; teacher Architectural Assen., London; Architect, designed an extension to Magdalen Coll., Oxford Univ.; fmr. mem. Council Inst. of Architecture. *Publications include:* Classical Architecture.

PORRITT, Sir Jonathon (Espie), 2nd Bt., cr. 1963., B.A.; British environmentalist; b. 6 July 1950; s. of late Lord Porritt; m. Sarah Staniforth 1986; two d.; ed. Eton Coll. and Magdalen Coll. Oxford; school teacher, London 1975–84; Head of English, Burlington Danes School, London 1980–84; Chair. Ecology Party 1979–80, 1982–84; parl. cand. at gen. elections in 1979, 1983; Dir. Friends of the Earth 1984–90, Forum for the Future 1996–; Consultant J. Sainsbury 1991–; Hon. LL.D. (Nottingham) 1991, Hon. D.Litt. (Westminster) 1997. *Publications:* Seeing Green: The Politics of Ecology 1984, Friends of the Earth Handbook 1987, The Coming of the Greens 1988, Save the Earth (ed.) 1990, Where on Earth are we going? 1991, Captain Eco (for children) 1991. *Leisure interest:* walking. *Address:* 9 Lypiatt Terrace, Cheltenham, Glos., GL50 2SX, England.

PORTER, Andrew, M.A.; British music critic; b. 26 Aug. 1928, Cape Town, S.A.; s. of Andrew Ferdinand and Vera Sybil (Bloxham) Porter; ed. Diocesan Coll., Rondebosch, Cape Town, University Coll., Oxford; Music critic The Financial Times 1950–74; Ed. The Musical Times 1960–67; music critic The New Yorker 1972–92, The Observer 1992–97, Times Literary Supplement 1997–; Visiting Fellow All Souls Coll., Oxford 1973–74; Bloch Prof., Univ. of Calif., Berkeley 1981; ASCAP—Deems Taylor Award 1975, 1978, 1982, Nat. Music Theater Award 1988; mem. American Acad. of Arts and Sciences 1984. *Publications:* A Musical Season 1974, Wagner's Ring 1976, Music of Three Seasons 1978, Music of Three More Seasons 1981, Verdi's "Macbeth": A Sourcebook (ed. with David Rosen) 1984, Musical Events: A Chronicle 1980–83 1987, 1983–86 1989, The Song of Majnun 1991. *Leisure interest:* architecture. *Address:* 9 Pembroke Walk, London, W8 6PQ, England.

PORTER, Sir Leslie, Kt., F.I.C.D., C.B.I.M.; British company executive; b. 10 July 1920, London; s. of Henry Alfred and Jane (Goldstein) Porter; m. Shirley Cohen 1949; one s. one d.; ed. Holloway Coll.; served British Army 1939–46; joined Tesco PLC, superstores, supermarkets, chain stores 1959, Man. Dir. and Deputy Chair. 1972–73, Chair. and Chief Exec. 1973–85, Pres. 1985–90; Chair. Sports Aid Foundation 1985–88, Hon. Vice-Pres. 1988–; fmr. Pres. Inst. Grocery Distribution (IGD); mem. President's Council, Baptist Coll. of Hong Kong; Chair. Int. Bd. Govs. Tel Aviv Univ. 1986–89, Hon. Chair. 1989–, Chancellor 1993–; Vice-Pres. Nat. Playing Fields Assen.; Chair. Euro-Consultants & Lampol Devts. 1990–; mem. Lloyds 1994–; Hon. Ph.D. (Tel Aviv) 1973. *Leisure interests:* golf, yachting, tennis, bridge.

PORTER, Neil Anthony, PH.D., D.SC., F.INST.P., M.R.I.A.; British professor of electron physics; b. 4 Sept. 1930, Manchester; s. of Francis Porter and Nora Porter; m. Sheila B. Dunn 1959; one d.; ed. St. Bede's Coll. Manchester, Univ. of Manchester and Dublin Inst. for Advanced Studies; Asst. Univ. Coll. Dublin 1953–54; Jr. and Sr. Research Fellowship, A.E.R.E. Harwell 1954–58; Coll. Lecturer, Univ. Coll. Dublin 1958–64, Prof. of Electron Physics 1964–88, Prof. Emer. 1989–; Visiting Prof. Univ. of Tokyo 1981, Weizmann Inst., Israel 1986–87; Hon. Consultant A.E.R.E., Harwell 1963–73, Harvard-Smithsonian Center for Astrophysics 1972–90. *Publications:* approximately 100 publs. on high energy astrophysics and 10 publs. on the history of science; one book. *Leisure interests:* music, history of science, theology. *Address:* Department of Physics, University College, Belfield, Dublin 4 (Office); 5 Westerton Rise, Dublin 16, Ireland (Home). *Telephone:* 01-2693244 (Office); 01-2987870 (Home).

PORTER, Nyree Dawn, O.B.E., A.R.A.D.; New Zealand actress; b. 22 Jan. Napier; d. of K. N. Porter and E. M. Millard; m. 1st Bryon O'Leary 1958 (died 1970); m., 2nd Robin Halstead 1975 (divorced 1989); one d.; trained as ballet dancer; arrived in U.K. 1958; appeared in Look Who's Here! (revue), Fortune Theatre, London, Ducks and Lovers, Arts Theatre, Come Blow Your Horn, Song at Twilight (by Noel Coward) 1998–99, and numerous other West End shows; leading roles in Sunday in the Park with George, Nat. Theatre 1990, The Winslow Boy 1994, Great Expectations 1994; TV and film appearances since 1960, including Lady Bertram in Mansfield Park 1996, Hilary and Jackie 1998; recipient of various drama awards and nominations. *Leisure interests:* Alexander Technique, philosophical books, helping develop a better understanding of eating disorders. *Address:* c/o Jean Diamond, London Management, 2–7 Noel Square, London, W1V 3RB, England. *Telephone:* 0171-287 9000.

PORTER, Peter Neville Frederick, F.R.S.L.; Australian poet; b. 16 Feb. 1929, Brisbane, Australia; s. of William R. Porter and Marion Main; m. 1st Jannice Henry 1961 (died 1974); two d.; m. 2nd Christine Berg 1991; ed. Church of England Grammar School and Toowoomba Grammar School; fmr. journalist in Brisbane; came to U.K. 1951; worked as clerk, bookseller and advertising writer; full-time writer and broadcaster 1968–; Hon. D. Litt (Melbourne) 1985, (Loughborough) 1987. *Publications:* Once Bitten, Twice Bitten 1961, Penguin Modern Poets, No. 2 1962, Poems, Ancient and Modern 1964, A Porter Folio 1969, The Last of England 1970, Preaching to the Converted 1972, After Martial (translation) 1972, Jonah (with A. Boyd) 1973, The Lady and the Unicorn (with A. Boyd) 1975, Living in a Calm Country 1975, New Poetry I (jt. ed.) 1975, The Cost of Seriousness 1978, English Subtitles 1981, Collected Poems 1983 (Duff Cooper Prize), Fast Forward 1984, Narcissus (with A. Boyd) 1985, The Automatic Oracle 1987 (Whitbread Poetry Award), Mars (with A. Boyd) 1988, A Porter Selected 1989, Possible Worlds 1989, The Chair of Babel 1992, Millennial Fables 1995, New Writing (Co-ed. with A. S. Byatt) 1997, The Oxford Book of Modern Verse (ed.) 1997, The Shared Heritage: Australian and English Literature 1997, ed. The Oxford Book of Modern Australian Verse 1997, Dragons in Their Pleasant Places 1997, Collected Poems 1961–1999 1999. *Leisure interests:* buying records and listening to music, travelling in Italy. *Address:* 42 Cleveland Square, London, W2 6DA, England. *Telephone:* 0171-262 4289.

PORTER, Robert, M.A., D.M., D.SC., F.R.A.C.P., F.A.A.; Australian professor of medical research; b. 10 Sept. 1932, Port Augusta, S. Australia; s. of William

J. and late Amy (née Tottman) Porter; m. Anne D. Steell 1961; two s. two d.; ed. Univs. of Adelaide and Oxford; House Physician and House Surgeon, Radcliffe Infirmary, Oxford 1959–60; Univ. Lecturer in Physiology, Oxford 1961–67; Medical Tutor and Fellow, St. Catherine's Coll., Oxford 1963–67; Prof. of Physiology, Monash Univ. 1967–80, Dean 1989–98, Deputy Vice-Chancellor 1992–93; Dir. John Curtin School of Medical Research and Howard Florey Prof. of Medical Research, A.N.U. 1980–89; Planning Dean (Medicine) James Cook Univ. of N. Queensland, Townsville 1998–; Rhodes Scholar 1954; Radcliffe Travelling Fellow in Medical Science 1963–64; Sr. Fulbright Fellow, Washington Univ. School of Medicine, St. Louis 1973; Fogarty Scholar-in-Residence, Nat. Inst. of Health, Bethesda 1986–87. *Publications:* Corticospinal Neurones: Their Role in Movement (with C. G. Phillips) 1977, Corticospinal Function and Voluntary Movement (with R. N. Lemon) 1993; articles on neurophysiology. *Leisure interest:* sport. *Address:* Room 119, Humanities II, James Cook University, Townsville, Queensland 4811 (Office); 90 Bayview Road, Balnarring Beach, Vic. 3926, Australia. *Telephone:* (7) 4781 5330 (Office); (3) 5983 1518 (Home).

PORTER OF LUDDENHAM, Baron (Life Peer), cr. 1990, of Luddenham in the county of Kent; **George Porter,** O.M., M.A., PH.D., SC.D., F.R.S.; British professor of chemistry; b. 6 Dec. 1920, Stainforth; s. of late John Smith Porter and of Alice Ann Porter; m. Stella Brooke 1949; two s.; ed. Thorne Grammar School, Leeds Univ. and Emmanuel Coll., Cambridge; war service in R.N.V.R.; Demonstrator Physical Chemistry, Univ. of Cambridge 1949–52, Asst. Dir. of Research 1952–54; Prof. of Physical Chemistry, Univ. of Sheffield 1955–63, Firth Prof. and Head of Dept. of Chemistry 1963–66; Prof. of Chemistry, The Royal Institution, London 1963–66, Dir. 1966–85, Fullerian Prof. of Chemistry 1966–88, Emer. Prof. 1988–; Pres. The Royal Soc. 1985–90; Chancellor Leicester Univ. 1986–95; Gresham Prof. of Astronomy, Gresham Coll. 1990–94; Prof. 1987–, Chair. Centre for Photomolecular Sciences, Imperial Coll. of Science, Tech. and Medicine 1990–; Pres. Comité Int. de Photobiologie 1968–72; Pres. Chemical Soc. 1970–72, Faraday Div. 1973–74, Nat. Asscn. for Gifted Children 1975–80; mem. Aeronautical Research Council 1964–66, of Council Open Univ. 1969–75, Science Museum Advisory Council 1970–73; Trustee, British Museum 1972–74; mem. Science Research Council 1976–80, Science Bd. 1976–80; Pres. Research and Devt. Soc. 1977–82; mem. R.S.A. Council 1978–80; Dir. of Applied Photophysics Ltd. 1971–; Pres. The Asscn. for Science Educ. 1985; Pres. British Asscn. for the Advancement of Science 1985–86; Foreign mem. Acad. of Sciences, Lisbon 1983, Inst. of Fundamental Studies, Sri Lanka 1985; Foreign Corresp. mem. La Real Acad. de Ciencias, Madrid 1978; Hon. mem. New York Acad. of Sciences 1968, Leopoldina Acad. 1970, Pontifical Acad. of Sciences 1974, Société de Chimie Physique (now Société Française de Chimie) 1979, Chemical Soc. of Japan 1982, American Philosophical Soc. 1986, Acad. dei Lincei 1988, Hungarian Acad. of Sciences 1988; Foreign Hon. mem. American Acad. of Arts and Sciences 1979; mem. Académie Int. de Lutèce 1979, U.S.S.R. Acad. of Sciences 1988, Acad. Europaea 1988; Foreign Assoc. U.S. Nat. Acad. of Sciences, Washington; Corresp. mem. Göttingen Acad. of Sciences; Hon. Fellow Inst. of Patentees & Investors 1970; Hon. Fellow, Emmanuel Coll., Cambridge; Hon. Prof. of Physical Chem., Univ. of Kent; Visiting Prof., Univ. Coll., London, Dept. of Chem. 1967–, Imperial Coll., London 1978–; Hitchcock Prof. Univ. of Calif. at Berkeley 1978; Robertson Memorial Lecturer 1978; Romanes Lecturer Oxford 1978; Hon. Prof. Chinese Acad. of Sciences, Dalian 1980; Counsellor, Inst. for Molecular Sciences, Okazaki, Japan 1980–83; numerous hon. degrees; Hon. Freeman of the Salters' Co. 1981; Corday-Morgan Medal Chemical Soc. 1955; Liversidge Lecturer, Chem. Soc. 1969; shared with Prof. R. G. W. Norrish half of Nobel Prize for Chem. for work on photo-chem. 1967; Davy Medal, Royal Soc. 1971; Fairchild Distinguished Scholar, Calif. Inst. Tech. 1974; 1976 Kalinga Prize for the Popularisation of Science 1977; Robertson Prize of the Nat. Acad. of Sciences 1978; Rumford Medal (Royal Society) 1978; Communications Award of the European Physical Society 1978, Faraday Medal of Chemical Soc. 1980, Longstaff Medal of RSC 1981, Humphry Davy Lecturer at Royal Soc. 1985, Richard Dimbleby Lecture (BBC) 1988, Michael Faraday Award (Royal Soc.) 1991. *Publications:* Chemistry for the Modern World 1962, Progress in Reaction Kinetics (Ed.), and numerous scientific papers; B.B.C. Television series: Laws of Disorder 1965, Time Machines 1969–70, Natural History of a Sunbeam 1976, Chemistry in Microtime 1996. *Leisure interest:* sailing. *Address:* Departments of Chemistry and Biochemistry, Imperial College, London, SW7 2AY, England.

PORTES, Richard David, D.PHIL.; American/British professor of economics; b. 10 Dec. 1941, Chicago, Ill.; s. of Herbert Portes and Abra Halperin Portes; m. Barbara Diana Frank 1963; one s. one d.; ed. Yale Univ., Balliol and Nuffield Colls. Oxford; Official Fellow and Tutor in Econs., Balliol Coll. Oxford 1965–69; Asst. Prof. of Econs. and Int. Affairs, Princeton Univ. 1969–72; Prof. of Econs., Birkbeck Coll., London Univ. 1972–94, Head Dept. 1975–77, 1980–83, 1994; Prof. of Econs., London Business School 1995–; Pres. Centre for Econ. Policy Research, London 1983–; Directeur d'Etudes, Ecole des Hautes Etudes en Sciences Sociales, Paris 1978–; fmr. Rhodes Scholar, Woodrow Wilson Fellow, Danforth Fellow; Guggenheim Fellow 1977–78; British Acad. Overseas Visiting Fellow 1977–78; Research Assoc., Nat. Bureau of Econ. Research, Cambridge, Mass. 1980–; Visiting Prof., Harvard Univ. 1977–78; Vice-Chair. Econs. Cttee. Social Science Research Council 1981–84; Sec.-Gen. Royal Econ. Soc. 1992–; mem. Bd. of Dirs. Soc. for Econ. Analysis 1967–69, 1972–80 (Sec. 1974–77); mem. Royal Inst. of Int. Affairs 1973– (Research Cttee. 1982–94), Council on Foreign Relations 1978–, Hon. Degrees Cttee., Univ. of London 1984–89; Fellow Econometric Soc. 1983–; mem. Council, Royal Econ. Soc. 1986– (mem. Exec. Cttee. 1987–); mem. Council, European Econ. Asscn. 1992–96; Co-Chair. Bd. of Govs. and Sr. Ed., Economic Policy 1985–; mem. and fmr. mem. several editorial bds.; mem. Franco-British Council 1996–. *Publications:* The Polish Crisis 1981, Deficits and Detente 1983; (Jt. Ed.) Threats to International Financial Stability 1987, ed.: Global Macroeconomics: policy conflict and cooperation 1987, Blueprints for Exchange Rate Management 1989, Macroeconomic Policies in an Interdependent World 1989, The EMS in Transition: a CEPR Report 1989, External Constraints on Macroeconomic Policy: The European Experience 1991, The Path of Reform in Central and Eastern Europe 1991, Economic Transformation of Central Europe 1993, European Union Trade with Eastern Europe 1995, Crisis? What Crisis? Orderly Workouts for Sovereign Debtors 1995; numerous papers and contribs. to learned journals. *Address:* Centre for Economic Policy Research, 90–98 Goswell Road, London, EC1V 7RR, England. *Telephone:* 0171-878 2915. *Fax:* 0171-878 2999.

PORTILLO, Rt. Hon. Michael Denzil Xavier, M.P., M.A.; British politician; b. 26 May 1953; s. of Luis G. Portillo and Cora W. Blyth; m. Carolyn C. Eadie 1982; ed. Harrow Co. Boys' School and Peterhouse, Cambridge; Ocean Transport & Trading Co. 1975–76; Conservative Research Dept. 1976–79; Special Adviser to Sec. of State for Energy 1979–81; Kerr McGee Oil (U.K.) Ltd. 1981–83; Special Adviser to Sec. of State for Trade and Industry 1983, to Chancellor of Exchequer 1983–84; M.P. for Enfield, Southgate 1984–97; Asst. Govt. Whip 1986–87; Parl. Under Sec. of State, Dept. of Health and Social Security 1987–88; Minister of State, Dept. of Transport 1988–90; Minister of State for Local Govt. and Inner Cities 1990–92; Chief Sec. to the Treasury 1992–94; Sec. of State for Employment 1994–95, for Defence 1995–97; freelance writer and broadcaster 1997–; adviser to Kerr McGee Corpn.; mem. Int. Comm. for Missing Persons in fmr. Yugoslavia; Conservative. *Publications:* Clear Blue Water 1994, Democratic Values and the Currency 1998. *Address:* c/o Conservative Party, 32 Smith Square, London, SW1P 3HH, England.

PORTISCH, Lajos; Hungarian chess player and singer; b. 4 April 1937; s. of Lajos Portisch Sr. and Anna Simon; mem. MTK-Sport Club; top ranking player of Hungary's selected team 1962–; nine times Hungarian champion; holder of Int. Grand Master title 1961–; European team Bronze Medallist 1961, 1965, 1973, team Silver Medallist 1970, 1977, 1980; Olympic Team Bronze Medallist 1956, 1966, Silver 1970, 1972, 1980, Gold 1978; qualified eight times as cand. for the individual chess world title; holder of Master Coach qualification; bass-baritone singer, gives regular concerts; Labour Order of Merit (golden degree). *Publication:* Six Hundred Endings (co-author with B. Sárközi) 1973. *Leisure interest:* music. *Address:* Hungarian Chess Federation, 1055 Budapest, Néphadsereg utca 10, Hungary. *Telephone:* 111-6616.

PORTZAMPARC, Christian de; French architect; b. 9 May 1944, Casablanca, Morocco; m. Elizabeth Jardim Neves 1982; two s.; ed. Ecole Supérieure des Beaux Arts; work includes Hautes Formes housing complex, south-east Paris; City of Music, Parc de la Villette, Paris; office bldg. for Crédit Lyonnais, Lille; two small housing projects in Japan and Germany, Zac Massena-Seine-Rive-gauche; retrospective exhbn., Pompidou Centre 1996. *Publications:* la Cité de la musique 1986, Scènes d'atelier, Généalogie des formes 1996, Christian de Portzamparc, Le Dantec 1995, Christian de Portzamparc 1996; Pritzker Prize for Architecture 1994, Equerre d'argent Award 1995; Commdr. des Arts et des Lettres. *Address:* 1 rue de l'Aude, 75014 Paris, France.

POSCH, Fritz (Friedrich), DR.PHIL.; Austrian historian; b. 30 March 1911, Wenireith bei Hartberg, Steiermark; s. of Franz Posch and Johanna Posch; m. Edeltraud Elsässer; ed. Univ. of Graz, Inst. für österreichische Geschichtsforschung, Vienna 1936–38; mil. service and prisoner-of-war 1940–48; with Land Govt. of Steiermark 1948–76, Dir. of Archives 1956–76; Hon. Prof. Univ. of Graz 1962; Pres. Styrian Historical Asscn. 1975–90, Hon. Pres. 1990; Chair. Comm. for the Historical Atlas of the Austrian Alpine Regions, Acad. of Sciences; mem. Austrian Acad.; hon. mem. numerous socs.; Grosses Ehrenzeichen der Republik Österreich, Österreichisches Ehrenkreuz für Wissenschaft und Kunst 1 Klasse, Bürger der Landeshauptstadt Graz 1990, Grosses Goldenes Ehrenzeichen des Landes Steiermark mit dem Stern 1991; many other awards and prizes. *Publications:* around 370 publs. including: Siedlungsgeschichte der Oststeiermark 1941, Die Besiedlung des Weizer Bodens 1956, Flammende Grenze 1968, Atlas zur Geschichte des steirischen Bauerntums 1976, Grosse geschichtliche Landeskunde der Steiermark (3 vols.) 1978–90, Die Zinsregister des Chorherrenstiftes Vorau aus dem 15. Jahrhundert 1986, Siedlung und Bevölkerung in Österreich im Hochmittelalter 1991. *Leisure interest:* mountain walking. *Address:* 8046 Rannach 44, Austria. *Telephone:* 0316/69-14-053 (Rannach).

POSNER, Michael Vivian, C.B.E.; British economist; b. 25 Aug. 1931; s. of Jack Posner; m. Rebecca Posner 1953; one s. one d.; ed. Whitgift School and Balliol Coll. Oxford; Research Officer, Oxford Inst. of Statistics 1953–57; Asst. lecturer, lecturer, then Reader in Econs. Univ. of Cambridge 1958–79, Fellow, Pembroke Coll. 1960–83, Chair. Faculty Bd. of Econs. 1974–75; Visiting Prof. Brookings Inst. Washington, D.C. 1971–72; Dir. of Econs. Ministry of Power 1966–67; econ. adviser to H.M. Treasury 1967–69, econ. consultant 1969–71; consultant to IMF 1971–72; energy adviser, Nat. Econ. Devt. Office (NEDO) 1973–74; econ. adviser, Dept. of Energy 1974–75; deputy chief econ. adviser, H.M. Treasury 1975–76; Chair. Social Science

Research Council 1979–83; Econ. Dir. NEDO 1984–86; mem. British Railways Bd. 1976–84, Post Office Bd. 1978–79; mem. Advisory Council for Energy Conservation 1974–82, Standing Cttee. on Energy and Environment 1978–81; mem. Council, Policy Studies Inst. 1978–83, Sr. Research Fellow 1983–84; Sec.-Gen. European Science Foundation 1986–93; Dir. Railways (British Rail) Pension Trustee Co. 1986–; Prof. Grad. School of Int. Business, Univ. of Bristol 1996–; Hon. D.Ed. (C.N.A.A.) 1989; Hon. LL.D. (Bristol) 1992. *Publications:* Italian Public Enterprise (co-author) 1966, Fuel Policy: a study in applied economics 1973, Energy Economics (co-author) 1981; ed. and author of other books and articles on econs. *Leisure interest:* country life. *Address:* Rushwood, Jack Straw's Lane, Oxford, OX3 0DN, England. *Telephone:* (01865) 63578.

POSNETT, Sir Richard Neil, K.B.E., C.M.G., M.A.; British colonial administrator and diplomatist (retd.); b. 19 July 1919, Kotagiri, India; s. of Rev. Charles Walker Posnett and Phyllis Posnett (née Barker); m. Shirley Margaret Hudson 1959; two s. one d. (two s. one d. by previous marriage); ed. Kingswood School, St. John's Coll., Cambridge; R.A.F. 1940; Colonial Admin. Service, Uganda 1941–62; Chair. Uganda Olympic Cttee. 1954–58; Judicial Adviser 1960; Perm. Sec. for Social Devt., External Affairs, Trade and Industry 1961–63; Foreign Office 1964–66; U.K. Mission to UN 1966–70; briefly H.M. Commr., Anguilla 1969; Head of West Indian Dept., FCO 1970–72; Gov. and C.-in-C., Belize 1972–76; mission to Ocean Island (Banaba) 1977; FCO Adviser on Dependent Territories 1977–79; High Commr. in Uganda April–Nov. 1979; Gov. and C.-in-C. Bermuda 1981–83; U.K. Commr., Bd. of British Phosphate Commrs. 1978–81; Lord Chancellor's Panel of Ind. Inspectors 1983–89; Gov. Kingswood School 1983–93; Pres. Godalming-Joigny Friendship Asscn.; mem. Royal Inst. of Int. Affairs, Royal African Soc., Royal Forestry Soc.; Fellow, Royal Commonwealth Soc.; first ascent South Portal Peak, Ruwenzori 1942; K. St. J. 1972. *Publications:* articles in World Today and Uganda Journal. *Leisure interests:* skiing, golf, growing trees. *Address:* Bahati, Old Kiln Close, Churt, Surrey, England. *Telephone:* (01428) 714147.

POSNETTE, Adrian Frank, C.B.E., SC.D., F.R.S.; British research scientist; b. 11 Jan. 1914, Birmingham; s. of F. W. Posnette and E. Posnette (née Webber); m. Isabelle La Roche 1937; one s. two d.; ed. Cheltenham Grammar School, Christ's Coll. Cambridge and Imperial Coll. of Tropical Agriculture, Trinidad; Econ. Botanist, Gold Coast Govt. (Colonial Service) 1937–44; Head of Botany and Plant Pathology, W. African Cacao Research Inst. 1944–49; Virologist, E. Malling Research Station, England 1949–57, Head, Plant Pathology Dept. 1957–69, Deputy Dir. E. Malling Research Station 1969–72, Dir. 1972–79; Scientific Adviser, Chocolate Confectionery Alliance, London 1979–85; Hon. Prof. in Plant Sciences, Wye Coll., Univ. of London 1971–78; Jones-Bateman Cup, Royal Horticultural Soc. 1958, Victoria Medal of Honour 1982; Ridley Medal, Fruiterers' Co. 1978. *Publications:* Virus Diseases of Cacao in West Africa (in Annals of Applied Biology), Virus Diseases of Apples and Pears (Ed.) 1963, over 100 research papers on virus diseases of fruit crops in scientific journals. *Leisure interests:* gardening, ornithology. *Address:* Gwyn, Sutton Valence, Maidstone, Kent, ME17 3AD, England. *Telephone:* (01622) 843234.

POSOKHIN, Mikhail Mikhailovich; Russian architect; b. 10 July 1940, Moscow; s. of Mikhail Vasilyevich Posokhin and Galina Arkadyevna Posokhina; m. 1st (divorced); one s.; m. 2nd; one d.; ed. Moscow Inst. of Architecture; chief architect Dept. of civil and residential construction Mosproyekt-1 1976–80; head of workshop on designing residential area Chertanovo 1980–82; head of workshop Dept. of Public Construction Mosproyekt-2 1982–; Deputy Chair. Cttee. on architecture and construction of Moscow 1994; author of designs of numerous residential complexes and public edifices including Victory Memorial, restoration of Cathedral of Christ the Saviour, business centre on Vosstanya Square, trade complex on Manege Square, reconstruction of The Kremlin and others. *Address:* Mosproyekt-2, 2 Brestskaya str. 5, 123056 Moscow, Russia. *Telephone:* (095) 200-56-47 (Office).

POST, Herschel, M.A., LL.B.; American investment banker; b. 9 Oct. 1939; s. of late Herschel E. Post and of Marie C. Post; m. Peggy Mayne 1963; one s. three d.; ed. Yale and Harvard Univs. and New Coll. Oxford; Assoc. Davis, Polk & Wordwell (attorneys) 1966–69; Exec. Dir. Parks Council of New York City 1969–72; Deputy Admin., Parks, Recreation and Cultural Affairs Admin. New York 1973; Vice-Pres. and Man. Euro-clear Operations, J.P. Morgan & Co. Brussels 1974–78; Vice-Pres. and Deputy Head, Int. Investment Dept. J.P. Morgan, London 1978–83; Pres. Posthorn Global Asset Man. London 1984–90, Shearson Lehman Global Asset Man., London 1984–90; Deputy Chair. London Stock Exchange 1988–, Chair. Trading Markets Managing Bd. 1990–; Trustee, Earthwatch Europe 1988– (Chair. 1997–), Monteverdi 1997–; C.O.O. Lehman Brothers Int. Ltd. 1990–94, Coutts & Co. 1994–95 (C.E.O., Deputy Chair. 1995–). *Address:* Coutts & Co., 440 Strand, London, WC2R 0QS, England. *Telephone:* 0171-753 1000.

POSTE, George, B.V.SC., PH.D., F.R.S., F.R.C.V.S., F.R.C.Path.; British research scientist; b. 30 April 1944; s. of the late John H. Poste and of Kathleen B. Poste; m. Linda Suhler 1992; one s. two d.; ed. Bristol Univ.; lecturer Royal Postgrad. Medical School, Univ. of London 1969–72; Prof. of Experimental Pathology S.U.N.Y. 1973–80; Vice-Pres. Research and Devt. SmithKline Beecham 1980–88, Research and Devt. Technologies 1989–92, Chair., Pres. Research and Devt. 1992–97, Chief Science and Tech. Officer 1997–; Research Prof. Univ. of Pa. 1981–, Univ. of Tex. Medical Center 1986–; Fleming Fellow Lincoln Coll., Oxford 1995–, Pitt Fellow Pembroke Coll., Cambridge 1996–; mem. Human Genetics Advisory Cttee. 1996–; mem. Bd. Govs. Center for Molecular Medicine and Genetics, Stanford Univ. 1992–; mem. Alliance for Ageing 1992–; Jt. Ed. Cell Surface Reviews 1976–83, New Horizons in Therapeutics 1984–; Hon. F.R.C.P. 1993; Hon. D.Sc. 1987, Hon. LL.D. (Bristol) 1995. *Publications:* numerous reviews and papers in learned journals. *Leisure interests:* automobile racing, mil. history, photography, desert exploration. *Address:* SmithKline Beecham Pharmaceuticals, New Frontiers Science Park, Harlow, Essex, CM19 5AW, England. *Telephone:* (01279) 644333. *Fax:* (01279) 644400.

POSTGATE, John Raymond, D.PHIL., D.SC., F.R.S.; British professor of microbiology; b. 24 June 1922, London; s. of Raymond William and Daisy (née Lansbury) Postgate; m. Mary Stewart 1948; three d.; ed. Woodstock School, Kingsbury County School, Balliol Coll., Oxford; Sr. Research Investigator, Nat. Chemical Lab. 1949–50, Sr. Prin. 1950–59; Prin., Sr. Prin. Scientific Officer Microbiology Research Establishment 1959–63; Asst. Dir. AFRC Unit of Nitrogen Fixation, Royal Veterinary Coll. 1963–65; Asst. Dir. AFRC Unit of Nitrogen Fixation, Univ. of Sussex 1965–80, Dir. 1980–87 and Prof. of Microbiology Univ. of Sussex 1965–87, Prof Emer. 1987–; Visiting Prof. Univ. of Ill. 1962–63, Ore. State Univ. 1977–78; Pres. Inst. of Biology 1982–84, Soc. for Gen. Microbiology 1984–87; Hon. D.Sc. (Bath); Hon. LL.D. (Dundee). *Publications:* Microbes and Man 1969, 1986, 1992, Biological Nitrogen Fixation 1972, Nitrogen Fixation 1978, 1987, 1998, The Sulphate-Reducing Bacteria 1979, 1984, The Fundamentals of Nitrogen Fixation 1982, A Plain Man's Guide to Jazz 1973, The Outer Reaches of Life 1994, A Stomach for Dissent: The Life of Raymond Postgate (with Mary Postgate) 1994. *Leisure interest:* listening to jazz and attempting to play it. *Address:* 1 Houndean Rise, Lewes, Sussex, BN7 1EG, England. *Telephone:* (01273) 472675.

POSTLETHWAITE, Pete; British actor; b. 16 Feb 1946, Lancashire; *Theatre includes:* Macbeth, Bristol. *Films include:* The Last of the Mohicans, In the Name of the Father, Romeo and Juliet, Alien 3, Dragonheart, Distant Voices, Still Lives, Brassed Off, The Lost World: Jurassic Park, Amistad, The Serpent's Kiss.

POSUVALYUK, Viktor Viktorovich, C.HIS.SC.; Russian diplomatist; b. 7 May 1940, Moscow; m.; one d.; ed. Inst. of Oriental Languages, Moscow State Univ.; translator U.S.S.R. Ministry of Foreign Affairs 1964–65; Attache U.S.S.R. Embassy, Yemen 1965-67; Attache, Third Sec. Div. of Near E. Countries, Ministry of Foreign Affairs 1967–69; Second, then First Sec., counsellor Embassy, Iraq 1974–76; counsellor then Head Sector of Near E. Countries, Ministry of Foreign Affairs 1976–80; counsellor Embassy, Syria 1980–85; Deputy Chief Div. of Near E., Ministry of Foreign Affairs 1985–86; Deputy Chief Dept. Near E. Countries and N. America, Ministry of Foreign Affairs 1986–88; Amb. to Oman 1988–90; U.S.S.R. (later Russian) Amb. to Iraq 1990–92; Dir. Dept. of Africa and Near E. Countries, mem. Exec. Bd. Russian Ministry of Foreign Affairs 1992–94; Deputy Minister of Foreign Affairs 1994–. *Publications:* Problems of Political Devt. of Modern Iraq, articles on contemporary Arab world. *Address:* Ministry of Foreign Affairs, Smolenskaya-Sennaya str. 32/34, Moscow, Russia. *Telephone:* 244-12-90.

POTANIN, Vladimir Olegovich; Russian politician and banker; b. 3 Jan. 1961, Moscow; m.; one s., one d.; ed. Moscow Inst. of Int. Relations; staff-mem. U.S.S.R. Ministry of Foreign Trade 1983–90; Head Econ. Co. Interros 1991–92; Vice-Pres., Pres. Joint-Stock Commercial Bank Int. Financial Co. 1992–93; Pres. UNEXIM Bank 1993–, Interross Co.; First Deputy Chair. Govt. of Russian Fed. 1996–97; concurrently Head Interdept. Comm. on Co-operation with Int. Financial-Econ. Orgs. and Group of Seven; mem. bds. of dirs. of maj. industrial cos. *Address:* UNEXIM Bank, Mashi Poryvaevoy str. 11, 107078 Moscow; Interross, Grokholski per. 12, 129010 Moscow, Russia. *Telephone:* (095) 232-37-27; (095) 207-24-57. *Fax:* 975-22-02.

POTAPOV, Leonid Vassilyevich; Russian politician; b. 23 Feb. 1960, Ivanovo-Frankovsk Region, Ukraine; m.; one s. one d.; ed. Kolomya Pedagogical School, Higher Komsomol school at Cen. Komsomol Cttee., Acad. of Nat. Econs. at Russian Govt.; Sec. Kholmsk Dist. Komsomol Cttee. Novgorod Region 1986–88; Dir. Sovkhoz Trudovik Novgorod Region 1991; U.S.S.R. People's Deputy 1989–91; Head of Admin. Novgorod Region 1995–; mem. Russian Council of Fed. 1993–. *Address:* Government House, Sukhe-Bator str. 9, 670001 Ulan Ude, Buryatia, Russia (Office). *Telephone:* (3012) 21 51 86, 21 22 32 (Office). *Fax:* (3012) 21 02 51 (Office).

POTAPOV, Lieut.-Gen. Vladimir Yakovlevich; Russian army officer; b. 1947; ed. Kazan Higher Mil. Tank School, Frunze Mil. Acad., Gen. Staff Mil. Acad.; deputy commdr., commdr. of motorized regt., deputy commdr., commdr. of div.; Head of Gen. Staff, First Deputy Army Commdr., then Army Commdr.; Head of Gen. Staff, First Deputy Commdr., N. Caucasus Mil. Command 1995; Deputy Head, Dept. of Man., State Mil. Inspectorate of Russian Presidency 1997–98; Deputy Sec., Security Council of Russian Fed. 1998–. *Address:* Security Council of Russian Federation, Ipatyevsky per. 4/10, entr. 6, Moscow, Russia. *Telephone:* (095) 206 3596 (Office).

POTILA, Antti, M.SC.; Finnish business executive; b. 1 Nov. 1938, Kokemäki; s. of Erkki Potila and Helvi Potila (née Ekroos); m. Marjatta Rintala 1962; one d.; ed. Technical Univ. of Helsinki and Helsinki School of Econs. and Business Admin.; Sales Engineer, ASEA, Melbourne, Australia 1964; various positions with Oy Strömberg Ab 1964–78, Pres. and C.E.O. 1979–83;

Pres. and C.E.O. Rauma-Repola Corpn. 1984–86; Pres. and C.E.O. Finnair Oy 1987–, Chair. subsidiaries of Finnair Oy 1987–; mem. Bd. of several Finnish cos. and industrial orgs.; Commdr. Order of the Lion of Finland 1982. *Address:* Finnair Oy, P.O. Box 15, 01053 Finnair (Office); Ullankatu 1 A 3, 00140 Helsinki, Finland (Home). *Telephone:* 0-81881 (Office).

POTRČ, Miran; Slovenian politician and lawyer; b. 27 March 1938, Maribor, Slovenia; s. of Ivan Potrč and Olga Potrč; m. Zdenka Potrč 1992; one d.; ed. Univ. of Ljubljana; with Secr. of Justice and Public Admin. Maribor 1962–63; Head, Legal Dept. Mariborska Livarna (Maribor Foundry) 1963–68; Sec. communal cttee. of League of Communists of Maribor 1968–73; mem. Presidency of Cen. Cttee. League of Communists of Slovenia and Pres. Comm. for Socio-Economic Matters and Social Policy 1973; mem. Exec. Cttee. Presidency of Cen. Cttee. of League of Communists of Slovenia 1974–78; Vice-Pres. Repub. Council of Trade Unions of Slovenia 1978–80; mem. Presidency, Trade Unions of Yugoslavia 1980–82, Pres. 1980–81; Head, Del. of Skupshtina (Parl.) of S.R. of Slovenia in Fed. Chamber of Repubs. and Provs. 1982–86; Pres. Skupshtina of S.R. of Slovenia 1986–90; mem. Parl. of Repub. of Slovenia, Head Parl. Group and mem. Presidium, Party of Democratic Reforms of Slovenia 1990–; fmr. Pres. Council, Univ. of Maribor. *Address:* Assembly of the Republic of Slovenia, Tomšičeva 5, 61000 Ljubljana, Slovenia. *Telephone:* 061/215-895.

POTTAKIS, Yannis A.; Greek politician; b. 1939, Corinth; m. Constantina (Alexopoulou) Pottaki; two s. one d.; ed. Univs. of Athens and Munich; founding mem. of Pasok; mem. Parl. 1977–; Alt. Minister of Nat. Economy 1982–83, Minister of Finance 1983–84, of Agric. 1985–89, of Justice 1995–96; Alt. Minister of Foreign Affairs; Chair. Council of Budget Ministers of EEC 1983. *Address:* 15 Chimaras Street, 14671 Nea Erythrea, Greece. *Telephone:* 8001 631.

POUJADE, Pierre; French newspaper executive; b. 1 Dec. 1920, St. Céré; m. Yvette Seva 1944; three s. two d.; served in R.A.F., Second World War; after 1945 became publisher and bookseller, also active in politics; mem. St. Céré Municipal Council 1951; Founder Pres. Union de Défense de Commerçants et Artisans; Founder, Union et Fraternité Française; Founder Dir. Union et Défense (daily), Fraternité Française (weekly); Pres. Confédération Nat. des Travailleurs Indépendants 1970; Pres. Caisse Nat. d'Assurance Maladie Obligatoire 1971–; Pres. Nat. Asscn. l'Utilisation des Resources Energetiques Français (ANUREF) 1979, Pres.-Founder l'Asscn. Occitanie-Caraïbes; mem. Comm. Nat. de Carburants de Substitution 1983; mem. Conseil Economique et Social; led econ. and social mission to Romania 1990; creator of "La Vallée Heureuse" (gastronomic and tourist centre), La Bastide-l'Evêque; Founder and Pres. Centre de Formation Avicole, and Ferme Pieste, Château de Gouzou; Dir. Caisse Régionale, Midi-Pyrénées 1972–; f. Union pour la Défense des Libertés 1978; Founder and Pres. Asscn. Fraternité Occitanie-Roumanie 1991; Croix du combattant volontaire, Medaille des Evadés, Hon. Pres. Conféderation européene des indépendants (Cedi) 1993. *Publications:* J'ai choisi le combat, A l'heure de la colère 1977, etc. *Leisure interest:* sport, particularly football and rugby. *Address:* "Vallée Heureuse", La Bastide-l'Evêque, 12200 Villefranche-de-Rouergue, France. *Telephone:* (65) 299188.

POULIDES, Fotis George; Greek diplomatist and shipping entrepreneur; b. 21 Nov. 1914, Athens; s. of late George F. Poulides and Theano Antonopoulou; one s.; ed. Athens Coll. and Univ. of London; began career in shipping, Piraeus and London 1932; Dir. of Maritime Services of Int. Red Cross (supervising ships carrying food between Canada and Greece) 1942–46; founder and Pres. Medov S.p.A. (shipping enterprises), Genoa 1947–; initiated regular passenger service between Italy and Australia 1949; founder, Medov Lines 1960; Chair. of several shipping cos., shipping insts. and confs.; joined Cyprus diplomatic service 1961; Amb. and Perm. Rep. to UN Agencies for Food and Agric. Rome 1979–; assoc. with Baltic and Int. Maritime Council (BIMCO), Copenhagen 1946–, Vice-Pres. 1981–85, mem. Exec. Cttee. 1989–92, Vice-Pres. 1993–95; nominated Counsellor 1995, honoured for 50 years' asscn. with BIMCO 1995; Cavaliere Grande Croce Ordine al Merito della Repubblica Italiana, Commdr., Order of Phoenix (Greece), Commdr., Ordre du Mérite Maritime (France). *Leisure interests:* reading, philately. *Address:* Via XX Settembre 29, 16121 Genoa (Office); Piazza Farnese 44, 00186 Rome (Embassy); Via Mylius 6, 16128 Genoa, Italy (Home). *Telephone:* (10) 593674 (Office, Genoa); (6) 6865758 (Embassy, Rome); (10) 562033 (Home).

POULSEN, Ole Lønsmann, LL.M.; Danish diplomatist; b. 14 May 1945, Lyngby; s. of Aage Lønsmann Poulsen and Tove Alice Poulsen; m. Zareen Mehta 1973; two s.; ed. Univs. of Poona, India, and Copenhagen; with Danchurchaid 1969–73; Head of Section, Ministry of Foreign Affairs 1973–76, Asian Devt. Bank, Manila 1976–77, First Sec., New Delhi 1977–80; Alt. Exec. Dir. World Bank, Washington, D.C. 1980–83, Deputy Head of Dept., Ministry of Foreign Affairs 1983–85, Head of Dept. 1985–88, Under-Sec. and Amb. 1988–92, Amb. in Vienna, Ljubljana and Sarajevo, Amb. to UN orgs. in Vienna 1992–93, State Sec., Amb. 1993–96, Amb. to U.K. 1996–; Kt. First Order of Dannebrog. *Leisure interests:* art, music, literature, sports. *Address:* Royal Danish Embassy, 55 Sloane Street, London, SW1X 9SR, England. *Telephone:* 0171-333 0200. *Fax:* 0171-333 0270.

POUND, Robert Vivian, M.A.; American physicist; b. 16 May 1919, Ridgeway, Ont., Canada; s. of V. E. Pound and Gertrude C. Prout; m. Betty Yde Andersen 1941; one s.; ed. Univ. of Buffalo and Harvard Univ.; Research Physicist, Submarine Signal Co., Boston, Mass. 1941–42; Staff mem. Radiation Laboratory, M.I.T. 1942–46; Jr. Fellow, Soc. of Fellows, Harvard Univ. 1945–48, Asst. Prof. 1948–50, Assoc. Prof. 1950–56, Prof. 1956–68, Mallinckrodt Prof. of Physics 1968–89, Prof. Emer. 1989–; Chair. Dept. of Physics 1968–72, Dir. Physics Labs. 1975–83; Zernike Prof. Groningen Univ. 1982; Visiting Prof. Coll. de France 1973, Univ. of Florida 1987; Visiting Fellow, Joint Inst. for Lab. Astrophysics, Univ. of Colorado 1979–80; Visiting Scientist Brookhaven Nat. Lab. 1986–87; Research Fellow, Merton Coll., Oxford 1980; mem. N.A.S.; Foreign Assoc. Académie des Sciences; Fellow, American Acad. of Arts and Sciences, American Physical Soc., A.A.A.S.; Fulbright Research Scholar, Oxford Univ. 1951; Fulbright Lecturer, Ecole Normale, Paris 1958; Guggenheim Fellow 1957–58, 1972–73; B. J. Thompson Memorial Award, Inst. of Radio Engineers 1948, Eddington Medal, Royal Astronomical Soc. 1965, Nat. Medal of Science (Pres. of U.S.A.) 1990. *Publications:* Microwave Mixers 1948; papers on nuclear magnetism, electric quadrupole interactions, directional correlations of gamma rays, effect of gravity on gamma rays. *Address:* Lyman Laboratory of Physics, Harvard University, Cambridge, MA 02138 (Office); 87 Pinehurst Road, Belmont, MA 02178, U.S.A (Home). *Telephone:* (617) 495 2873 (Office); (617) 484 0254 (Home).

POUNDS, Kenneth Alwyne, C.B.E., PH.D., F.R.S.; British professor of space physics; b. 17 Nov. 1934, Leeds; s. of Harry Pounds and Dorothy Pounds (née Hunt); m. 1st Margaret Connell 1961; two s. one d.; m. 2nd Joan Mary Millit 1982; one s. one d.; ed. Salt High School, Shipley, Yorks. and Univ. Coll. London; Dir. X-ray Astronomy Group, Univ. of Leicester 1973–94, Prof. of Space Physics 1973–, Head of Dept. of Physics and Astronomy 1986– (on leave of absence 1994–98); Chief Exec. Particle Physics and Astronomy Research Council 1994–98; Pres. Royal Astronomical Soc. 1990–92; mem. Academia Europaea, Int. Acad. of Astronautics; Fellow Univ. Coll. London 1993; Gold Medal of Royal Astronomical Soc. 1990. *Publications:* over 170 scientific publs. *Leisure interests:* sport, music. *Address:* Department of Physics and Astronomy, University, Leicester, LE1 7RH (Office); 12 Swale Close, Oadby, Leics., LE2 4GF, England (Home). *Telephone:* (0116) 252 3509 (Office); (0116) 271 9370 (Home). *Fax:* (0116) 252 3311.

POUNGUI, Ange Edouard; Republic of the Congo politician, economist and banker; began career in school, student unions; apptd. mem. Nat. Council for Revolution 1968, then mem. Political Bureau, Minister for Finance 1971–73, Vice-Pres. Council of State and Minister for Planning 1973–76; Prime Minister of The Congo 1984–89; fmr. Pres. Union pour le Renouveau Democratique (URD); worked for IMF and African Devt. Bank, then Dir.-Gen. Cen. African Bank 1976–79, then C.E.O. Congolese Commercial Bank; Dir. Cen. Bank of the Congo 1994–. *Address:* Bank of the Central African States, P.O. Box 126, Brazzaville, Republic of the Congo.

POUNTAIN, Sir Eric John, Kt., C.B.I.M., F.F.B., F.I.H.E.; British business executive; b. 5 Aug. 1933, Cannock Wood, Staffs.; s. of Horace and Elsie Pountain; m. Joan Sutton 1960; one s. one d.; ed. Queen Mary's Grammar School, Walsall; joined F. Maitland Selwyn & Co., auctioneers and estate agents 1956, Jt. Principal 1959; f. Midland and General Devts. Ltd. (housebuilders) 1964; Chief Exec. John McLean & Sons Ltd. (following their takeover of Midland and General) 1969; Chief Exec. Tarmac Housing Div. (following takeover of John McLean by Tarmac Ltd.) 1974, Dir. Tarmac Ltd. 1977, Group Chief Exec. 1979–92, Deputy Chair. and Chief Exec. 1982, Chair. Tarmac PLC 1983–94 (non-exec. 1992–94); non-exec. Dir. James Beattie PLC 1984–, Deputy Chair. 1985–87, Chair. 1987–; non-exec. Dir. IMI PLC 1988– (Chair. 1989–), United Newspapers (now United News & Media) 1992–, Lloyds Chemists 1993–97, J.W. Maunders Group PLC 1994–; Trustee Lichfield Cathedral Trust 1995–, Crimestoppers Trust 1995–. *Leisure interests:* farming, horse-breeding. *Address:* James Beattie PLC, 71/78 Victoria Street, Wolverhampton, WV1 3PQ, England.

POUNTNEY, David Willoughby, C.B.E., M.A.; British opera director; b. 10 Sept. 1947, Oxford; s. of E. W. Pountney and D. L. Byrt; m. Jane R. Henderson 1980; one s. one d.; ed. St. John's Coll. Choir School, Cambridge, Radley Coll. and St. John's Coll. Cambridge; Dir. of Productions, Scottish Opera 1976–80, English Nat. Opera (ENO) 1982–94; numerous productions for all maj. British cos. including a Janáček cycle for Welsh Nat. Opera/Scottish Opera; has worked in U.S.A. (Chicago, Houston, San Francisco, Metropolitan Opera, New York), Paris, Berlin, Rome, Amsterdam, Vienna, Zürich and Munich; Janáček Medal, SWET Award; Chevalier, Ordre des Arts et Lettres (France). *Publications:* Powerhouse; several translations from German, Italian, Russian and Czech. *Leisure interests:* gardening, cooking, croquet. *Address:* Suite 130, 78 Marylebone High Street, London, W1M 4AP, England. *Telephone:* (017060) 328437. *Fax:* (017060) 328437.

POUPARD, H.E. Paul; French ecclesiastic; b. 30 Aug. 1930; ordained 1954; Titular Bishop of Usula 1979, Archbishop 1980; cr. Cardinal 1985; Priest of S. Prassede; Pres. Pontifical Council for Culture 1982–. *Publications include:* Les Religions 1987, L'Eglise au Défi des Cultures 1989, Dieu et la Liberté 1992, Nouvelle Europe 1993, Après Galilée, Science et Foi, Nouveau Dialogue 1994, What Will Give Us Happiness 1992. *Address:* Piazza San Calisto, 00120 Vatican City, Italy. *Telephone:* (06) 6988 7393. *Fax:* (06) 6988 7368; (06) 6988 7165.

POWATHIL, Most Rev. Joseph, M.A., D.D.; Indian ecclesiastic; b. 14 Aug. 1930, Kurumpanadam; s. of Ulahannan Joseph Powathil; ordained R.C. Priest 1962; lecturer in Econs., St. Berchmans's Coll., Changanacherry 1963–72; Auxiliary Bishop of Changanacherry, Titular Bishop of Caesarea

Philipi, 1972, consecrated Bishop 1972; 1st Bishop of Kanjirappally Diocese, Kerala 1977–86; Archbishop of Changanacherry 1985–; Chair. Kerala Catholic Bishops' Conf. and Chair. Educational Comm. 1993; Pres. Catholic Bishops' Conf. of India 1994; Perm. mem. Syro Malabar Bishops' Synod 1993; Chair. CBCI Comm. for Educ. and Clergy, KCBC Comm. for Devt., Justice and Peace, SMBC Comm. for Ecumenism; mem. Pontifical Comm. for Dialogue with the Orthodox Syrian Church; Chair. Religious Fellowship Foundation 1994; Hon. mem. Pro-Oriente, Vienna 1994. *Address:* Archbishop's House, P.O. Box 20, Changanacherry 686 101, Kerala, India. *Telephone:* (4814) 20040. *Fax:* (4814) 22540.

POWELL, Anthony Dymoke, C.H., C.B.E.; British writer; b. 21 Dec. 1905, London; s. of Lieut.-Col. P. L. W. Powell, C.B.E., D.S.O., and Maud Mary Wells-Dymoke; m. Lady Violet Pakenham 1934; two s.; ed. Eton Coll. and Balliol Coll., Oxford; served Second World War in Welch Regiment and Intelligence Corps; mem. U.S. Acad. of Arts and Sciences; Hon. mem. Modern Languages Asscn. of America; fmr. Trustee of Nat. Portrait Gallery; Hon. D.Litt. (Sussex, Leicester, Kent, Oxford, Bristol, Wales); Hon. Fellow, Balliol Coll., Oxford 1974; James Tait Black Prize (for At Lady Molly's), W. H. Smith Award 1974, The Hudson Review Bennett Award 1984, Ingersoll Foundation T. S. Eliot Prize for Creative Writing 1984; Orders of White Lion (Czechoslovakia), Léopold II (Belgium), Oaken Crown and Croix de Guerre (Luxembourg). *Publications:* Afternoon Men 1931 (performed as a play 1963), Venusberg 1932, From a View to a Death 1933, Agents and Patients 1936, What's Become of Waring 1939, John Aubrey and His Friends 1948, Selections from John Aubrey 1949, the Music of Time series: A Question of Upbringing 1951, A Buyer's Market 1952, The Acceptance World 1955, At Lady Molly's 1957, Casanova's Chinese Restaurant 1960, The Kindly Ones 1962, The Valley of Bones 1964, The Soldier's Art 1966, The Military Philosophers 1968, Books Do Furnish a Room 1971, Temporary Kings 1973, Hearing Secret Harmonies 1975, To Keep the Ball Rolling (memoir, incl. Infants of the Spring Vol. I 1976, Messengers of Day Vol. II 1978, Faces in my Time Vol. III 1980, The Strangers All are Gone Vol. IV 1982), A Dance to the Music of Time (novel-cycle, omnibus edn.) 1977, O, How the Wheel Becomes It 1983, the Fisher king 1986, the Album of Music of Time (ed. Violet Powell) 1987, Journals 1982–86 1995, Journals 1990–1992; plays: The Garden God, The Rest I'll Whistle 1971; criticism: Miscellaneous Verdicts 1990, Under Review 1992, Journals 1982–1986 1995, Journals 1987–1989 1996, Journals 1990–1992 1997. *Address:* The Chantry, Nr. Frome, Somerset, England. *Telephone:* (01373) 836314.

POWELL, Sir (Arnold Joseph) Philip, Kt., C.H., O.B.E., R.A., R.I.B.A., A.A.DIPL.(HONS.); British architect; b. 15 March 1921, Bedford; s. of late Canon A. C. Powell and late Mary Winnifred (née Walker); m. Philippa Eccles 1953; one s. one d.; ed. Epsom Coll. and Architectural Asscn. School of Architecture; partner Powell and Moya Architects 1946–; partner Powell, Moya and Partners 1976–91; Treas. R.A. 1985–95; won Westminster City Council's Pimlico Housing Competition (Churchill Gardens) 1946, Festival of Britain Vertical Feature (Skylon) Competition 1950; R.I.B.A. Bronze Medals, R.I.B.A. Awards, Housing Medals, Civic Trust Awards, Concrete Soc. Award, Carpenter's Award, R.I.B.A. Royal Gold Medal for Architecture 1974; mem. Royal Fine Art Comm. 1969–94. *Works include:* Churchill Gardens Flats, Westminster 1948–62; houses and flats at Gospel Oak, London 1954, houses at Chichester 1950, Toy's Hill 1954, Oxshott 1954, Leamington 1956, Baughurst (Hants.) 1954; "Skylon", Festival of Britain 1951; Mayfield School, Putney 1955, Plumstead Manor School, Woolwich 1970; extensions to Brasenose Coll. Oxford 1961 and Corpus Christi Coll. Oxford 1969, picture gallery and undergraduates' rooms, Christ Church, Oxford 1967, new bldgs. at St. John's Coll. Cambridge 1967, Queens' Coll., Cambridge 1978; Chichester Festival Theatre 1962; Public Swimming Baths, Putney 1967; mental hosp. extensions, Fairmile 1957, Borocourt 1965, hospitals at Swindon, Slough, High Wycombe, Wythenshawe, Woolwich, Maidstone, Ashington and Great Ormond St. (London) 1961–93; British Pavilion at Expo 70, Osaka, Japan; Museum of London 1977; Dining rooms at Bath Acad. of Art 1970 and Eton Coll. 1975; Wolfson Coll., Oxford 1974; Headquarters, London & Manchester Assurance, nr. Exeter 1978, Nat. Westminster Bank, Shaftesbury Ave., London 1982, new bldgs. for Royal Holloway and Bedford New Coll., Egham 1986, Queen Elizabeth II Conf. Centre, Westminster 1986. *Address:* 16 The Little Boltons, London, SW10 9LP, England.

POWELL, Sir Charles David, K.C.M.G., B.A.; British fmr. diplomatist and business executive; b. 6 July 1941; s. of Air Vice-Marshal John Frederick Powell; m. Carla Bonardi 1964; two s.; ed. King's School, Canterbury, New Coll. Oxford; joined Diplomatic Service 1963, Third Sec., Foreign Office 1963–65, Second Sec., Helsinki 1965–67, at FCO 1968–71, First Sec. and Pvt. Sec. to Amb., Washington, D.C. 1971–74, First Sec. Bonn 1974–77, FCO 1977–80 (Counsellor 1979, Special Counsellor for Rhodesia negotiations 1979–80), Counsellor, Perm. Representation to European Communities 1980–84; Pvt. Sec. to Prime Minister 1984–91; Sr. Dir. Jardine Matheson and assoc. cos. 1991–; Dir. Nat Westminster Bank (Chair. Int. Advisory Bd.) 1991–, LVMH, Arjo Wiggins Appleton 1993–, J. Rothschild Name Co., Louis-Vuitton-Moet-Hennessy 1995–; mem. Int. Advisory Council, Textron Corpn.; Chair. Singapore-British Business Council 1994–; Vice-Pres. China-Britain Trade Group 1993–; Trustee Aspen Inst. *Address:* c/o Matheson & Co., 3 Lombard Street, London, EC3V 9AQ, England.

POWELL, Gen. Colin Luther, M.B.A.; American army officer; b. 5 April 1937, New York; s. of Luther Powell and Maud A. McKoy; m. Alma V. Johnson 1962; one s. two d.; ed. City Univ. of New York and George Washington Univ.; commissioned U.S. Army 1958, Lieut. Gen. 1986; Commdr. 2nd Brigade, 101st Airborne Div. 1976–77; Exec. Asst. to Sec. Dept. of Energy 1979; Sr. Mil. Asst. to Sec. Dept. of Defense 1979–81; Asst. Div. Commdr. 4th Infantry Div. Fort Carson, Colo. 1981–83; Mil. Asst. to Sec. of Defense 1983–86; assigned to U.S. V Corps, Europe 1986–87; Nat. Security Adviser, White House, Washington 1987–88; C.-in-C. US Forces, Fort McPherson, Ga. April–Sept. 1989; Chair. Jt. Chiefs of Staff 1989–93; Hon. LL.D. (Univ. of West Indies) 1994; Legion of Merit, Bronze Star, Air Medal, Purple Heart, Pres. Medal of Freedom, Pres. Citizen's Medal, Hon. K.C.B. 1993, Order of Jamaica. *Publication:* A Soldiers' Way (autobiog. with Joseph E. Persico) 1995. *Address:* Suite 767, 909 N. Washington Street, Alexandria, VA 22314, U.S.A.

POWELL, Earl Alexander, III, A.M., PH.D.; American art museum director; b. 24 Oct. 1943, Spartanburg, S.C.; s. of Earl Alexander Powell and Elizabeth Duckworth; m. Nancy Landry 1971; three d.; ed. Williams Coll. and Harvard Univ.; Teaching Fellow, Harvard Univ. 1970–74; Curator, Michener Collection, Univ. of Texas, Austin 1974–76, also Asst. Prof. of Art History; Museum Curator, Sr. Staff Asst. to Asst. Dir. and Chief Curator, Nat. Gallery of Art, Washington, D.C. 1976–78, Exec. Curator 1979–80; Dir. L.A. Co. Museum of Art 1980–92, Nat. Gallery of Art, Washington, D.C. 1992–; other professional appts.; Trustee American Fed. of Arts, Nat. Trust for Historic Preservation, White House Historical Asscn.; mem. Asscn. of Art Museum Dirs., Cttee. for the Preservation of the White House, O'Keefe Museum Nat. Advisory Bd., Pres.'s Cttee. on the Arts and Humanities; King Olav Medal 1978, Williams Bicentennial Medal 1995, Mexican Cultural Inst. Award 1996, Grand Official Order of the Infante D. Henrique, Chevalier des Arts et des Lettres. *Publications:* American Art at Harvard 1973, Selections from the James Michener Collection 1975, Abstract Expressionists and Imagists: A Retrospective View 1976, Milton Avery 1976, The James A. Michener Collection (catalogue) 1978, Thomas Cole monograph 1990. *Address:* Office of Director, National Gallery of Art, 6th Street & Constitution Avenue, N.W., Washington, DC 20565, U.S.A.

POWELL, Jonathan Leslie; British television producer; b. 25 April 1947, Faversham, Kent; s. of James Dawson Powell and Phyllis N. Sylvester (née Doubleday); m. Sally Brampton 1990; one d.; ed. Sherborne School and Univ. of East Anglia; script ed. and producer of drama, Granada TV 1970–77; producer, drama serials, BBC TV 1977–83, Head of Drama Series and Serials 1983–87; Controller BBC 1 1987–92; Dir. Drama and Co-productions, Carlton TV 1993–; Royal TV Soc. Silver Award 1979–80. *Television serials include:* Testament of Youth 1979 (BAFTA award), Tinker, Tailor, Soldier, Spy 1979, Pride and Prejudice 1980, The Bell 1982, Smiley's People 1982 (Peabody Medal, U.S.A.), The Old Men at the Zoo 1983, Bleak House 1985, Tender is the Night 1985, A Perfect Spy 1987. *Leisure interest:* fly fishing. *Address:* c/o Carlton U.K. Television, 35–38 Portman Square, London, W1H 9FU; 139 Randolph Avenue, Maida Vale, London, N.W.9, England (Home). *Telephone:* 0171-486 6688 (Office).

POWELL, Jonathan Nicholas, M.A.; British political adviser; b. 14 Aug. 1956, Fulbeck; s. of Air Vice-Marshal John Frederick Powell and Geraldine Ysolda Powell; partner Sarah Helm; two s. one d.; ed. Univ. Coll., Oxford, Univ. of Pennsylvania; with BBC 1978, Granada TV 1978–79; joined FCO 1979, served in Lisbon 1980–83, FCO, London 1983–85, CSCE, Vienna 1985–89, FCO, London 1989–91, Washington 1991–95; Chief of Staff to Leader of the Opposition 1995–97, to Prime Minister May 1997–. *Leisure interests:* walking, skiing. *Address:* c/o 10 Downing Street, London, SW1A 2AA, England. *Telephone:* 0171-270 3000.

POWELL, Michael James David, SC.D., F.R.S.; British mathematician; b. 29 July 1936; s. of William James David Powell and Beatrice Margaret Powell (née Page); m. Caroline Mary Henderson 1959; one s. (deceased) two d.; ed. Eastbourne Coll. and Peterhouse, Cambridge; mathematician at A.E.R.E., Harwell 1959–76; John Humphrey Plummer Prof. of Applied Numerical Analysis, Cambridge Univ. 1976–, Professorial Fellow, Pembroke Coll. 1978–; George B. Dantzig Prize in Math. Programming 1982, Naylor Prize, London Math. Soc. 1983, Gold Medal Inst. of Math. Applications 1996. *Publications:* Approximation Theory and Methods 1981; papers on numerical mathematics, especially approximation and optimization calculations. *Leisure interests:* canals, golf, walking. *Address:* Department of Applied Mathematics and Theoretical Physics, University of Cambridge, Silver Street, Cambridge, CB3 9EW (Office); 134 Milton Road, Cambridge, CB4 1LE, England (Home).

POWELL, Sir Philip (see Powell, Sir (Arnold Joseph) Philip).

POWELL, Robert; British actor; b. 1 June 1944, Salford, Lancs.; s. of John W. and Kathleen C. Powell; m. Barbara Lord 1975; one s. one d.; ed. Manchester Grammar School; first job, Victoria Theatre, Stoke-on-Trent 1964; Hon. M.A. (Salford) 1990; *television roles include:* Doomwatch 1970, Jude the Obscure 1971, Jesus of Nazareth 1977, Pygmalion 1981, Frankenstein 1984, Hannay (series) 1988, The Sign of Command 1989, The First Circle 1990, The Golden Years 1992, The Detectives 1992; *theatre roles include:* Hamlet 1971, Travesties (RSC) 1975, Terra Nova 1982, Private Dick 1982, Tovarich 1991, Sherlock Holmes 1992; *films include:* Mahler 1974, Beyond Good and Evil 1976, Thirty Nine Steps 1978, Imperative 1981,

Jigsaw Man 1982, Shaka Zulu 1985, D'Annunzio 1987, The Mystery of Edwin Drood 1993; Best Actor, Paris Film Festival 1980, Venice Film Festival 1982. *Leisure interests:* golf, tennis, cricket, computers. *Address:* c/o Jonathan Altaras Associates Ltd., 13 Shorts Gardens, London, WC2H 9AT, England. *Telephone:* 0171-836 8722. *Fax:* 0171-836 6066.

POWELL, Sandy; British costume and set designer; b. 7 April 1960; ed. St. Martin's Coll. of Art and Design, Cen. School of Art, London; costume designer for Mick Jagger on Rolling Stones European Urban Jungle tour 1990, all shows by The Cholmondoleys and The Featherstonehaughs; stage sets include: Edward II (R.S.C.), Rigoletto (Netherlands Opera); costumes for films include: Cobachan, The Last of England, Stormy Monday, The Pope Must Die, Edward II (Evening Standard Award), Caravaggio, Venus Peter, The Miracle, The Crying Game, Orlando (Best Tech. Achievement Award, Evening Standard Awards 1994, Being Human, Interview with a Vampire, Rob Roy, Michael Collins, The Butcher Boy, The Wings of the Dove. *Address:* c/o London Management, 2–4 Noel Street, London, W1V 3RB, England. *Telephone:* 0171-287 9000. *Fax:* 0171-287 3036.

POWIS, Alfred, O.C., B.COM.; Canadian business executive; b. 16 Sept. 1930, Montreal, P.Q.; s. of Alfred Powis Sr. and Sarah Champe McCulloch; m. Louise Margaret Finlayson 1977; two s. one d.; ed. Westmount High School and McGill Univ.; employee, Investment Dept., Sun Life Assurance Co. 1951–55; Internal Auditor, Noranda Inc. 1955, Asst. Treas. 1958, Asst. to Pres. 1962, Exec. Asst. 1963, Dir. 1964, Vice-Pres. 1966, Exec. Vice-Pres. 1967, Pres. and C.E.O. 1968–77, Chair. and Pres. 1977–82, Chair. and C.E.O. 1982–93, Chair. 1990–95; Hon. Pres. Copper Devt. Asscn. 1983–; Dir., Noranda Aluminium Inc. 1995–; Vice-Pres. and Dir., Northwood Pulp Ltd., Brunswick Mining and Smelting Corpn. Ltd.; Dir. Wire Rope Industries Ltd., Noranda Forest Inc., Noranda Sales Corpn. Ltd., Noranda Exploration Co. Ltd., Noranda Australia Ltd., Norcen Energy Resources Ltd., Quebec Smelters Ltd., Waite Amulet Mines Ltd., Kerr Addison Mines Ltd., Canadian Imperial Bank of Commerce, Dal. File Group, Inc., Ford Motor Co. of Canada Ltd., Gulf Canada Ltd., Sun Life Assurance Co., Sears Canada Ltd., Brascan Ltd. 1982–; Vice-Chair. Bd. of Trustees, Toronto Hosp. *Address:* P.O. Box 755, BCE Place, Suite 4100, Toronto, Ont. M5J 2T3 (Office); 73 Summerhill Avenue, Toronto, Ont. M4T 1A9, Canada (Home).

POYNTER, John Riddoch, A.O., PH.D., F.A.H.A., F.A.S.S.A.; Australian historian and university administrator; b. 13 Nov. 1929, Coleraine, Victoria; s. of Robert Poynter and Valetta Riddoch; m. 1st Rosslyn M. Rowell 1954 (divorced 1983); two d.; m. 2nd Marion Davidson 1984; ed. Trinity Grammar School, Kew, Victoria, Trinity Coll. Univ. of Melbourne and Magdalen Coll. Oxford; Dean, Trinity Coll. Univ. of Melbourne 1953–64, Ernest Scott Prof. of History 1966–75, Dean, Faculty of Arts 1971–73, Pro Vice-Chancellor 1972–75, Deputy Vice-Chancellor (Research) 1975–82, Deputy Vice-Chancellor 1982–89, Deputy Vice-Chancellor (Academic) 1989–90, Dean, Faculty of Music, Visual and Performing Arts 1991–93, Asst. Vice-Chancellor (Cultural Affairs) 1991–94, now Professional Assoc., Australian Centre; Nuffield Dominion Travelling Fellow, London and Oxford 1959; Visiting Fellow, A.N.U. 1968, Carnegie Fellow, Fulbright Grant, U.S.A. 1968; Section Ed. Australian Dictionary of Biography 1972–90; Australian Sec. Rhodes Trust 1974–97; Chair. Melbourne Univ. Press 1976–88; mem. Bd. Australian-American Educ. Foundation 1977–84; Rhodes Scholar 1951; Chevalier, Ordre des Palmes Académiques. *Publications:* Russell Grimwade 1967, Society and Pauperism 1969, A Place Apart 1996, Doubts and Certainties 1997. *Leisure interest:* music. *Address:* The University of Melbourne, Parkville, Vic. 3052 (Office); 38 Brougham Street, North Melbourne, Vic. 3051, Australia (Home). *Telephone:* (03) 9344 7202 (Office); (03) 9329 8163 (Home).

POYNTZ, Rt. Rev. Samuel Greenfield, M.A., B.D., PH.D.; Irish ecclesiastic; b. 4 March 1926, Manitoba, Canada; s. of Rev. James Poyntz and Catherine Greenfield; m. Noreen H. Armstrong 1952; one s. two d.; ed. Portora Royal School, Enniskillen and Trinity Coll., Dublin; curate, St. George's, Dublin 1950–52, Bray 1952–55, St. Michan and St. Paul, Dublin 1955–59; Incumbent, St. Stephen, Dublin 1959–67, St. Ann, Dublin 1967–70, St. Ann with St. Stephen, Dublin 1970–78; Archdeacon of Dublin 1974–78; Examining Chaplain, Archbishop of Dublin 1974–78; Bishop of Cork, Cloyne and Ross 1978–87; Bishop of Connor 1987–95; Chair. Irish Council of Churches 1986–88; Vice-Pres. British Council of Churches 1987–90; D.Litt. h.c. (Univ. of Ulster) 1995. *Publications:* The Exaltation of the Blessed Virgin Mary 1953, Journey Towards Union 1975, Our Church—Praying with our Church Family 1983. *Leisure interests:* stamp collecting, rugby football, travel. *Address:* 10 Harmony Hill, Lisburn, Co. Antrim, BT27 4EP, Northern Ireland. *Telephone:* (01846) 679013.

POŽELA, Juras; D.PHYS.; Lithuanian physicist; b. 5 Dec. 1925, Moscow; s. of Karolis Požela and Eugenija Tautkaitė; m. Rima Poželienė 1953; one s. one d.; ed. Vilnius State Univ. and Moscow M. Lomonosov Univ.; Researcher, Sr. Researcher, Sector Man., Dir. Inst. of Physics and Math., Lithuanian Acad. of Sciences 1952–67; Dir. Semiconductor Physics Inst. 1967–85, Sr. Researcher 1996–; mem. Seimas (Parl.) 1992–96; Academician Lithuanian Acad. of Sciences 1968, Pres. 1984–92; mem. U.S.S.R. (now Russian) Acad. of Sciences 1984, European Acad. of Sciences and Arts 1991, Academia Europaea 1993; Lenin Prize 1978, Hero of Socialist Labour 1985, U.S.S.R. State Prize. *Publications include:* Plasma and Current Instabilities in Semiconductors 1981, High Speed Transistors 1989; over 200 articles, 9 monographs; about 100 inventions. *Leisure interests:* hunting, chess. *Address:* Lithuanian Academy of Sciences, Gedimino Prospect 3, Vilnius 2600; Semiconductor Physics Institute, A. Goštauto 11, Vilnius 2600 (Office); M. Paco 7/2, apt. 7, 2055 Vilnius, Lithuania (Home). *Telephone:* (3702) 62 71 22 (Office); 72-70-22 (Home).

POZNER, Vladimir Gerald Dmitri Vladimirovich; Russian broadcaster; b. 1 April 1934, Paris; m. 1st (divorced); one d.; m. 2nd Yekaterina Orlova; ed. Moscow Univ.; worked as trans. of medical biological literature, literary sec. of poet Samuel Marshak 1959–61; Sr. Ed., Exec. Sec. Soviet Life 1961–67, Sputnik 1967–70; commentator U.S.A. and Britain Broadcasting Service of U.S.S.R. TV and Radio Cttee. 1970–86; political observer Cen. TV 1986–91; regular appearances in Pozner-Donahue show, Multimedia Entertainment Inc. (U.S.A.) 1991–95; Meetings with Vladimir Pozner (Moscow Channel, Russia) 1991–94, If 1995, We 1995–, Man in a Mask 1996–; author of film scripts; Pres. Acad. of Russian TV 1996; Communicator of Year Prize of Soviet Journalists' Union 1986; Communicator of Year Medal of the Better World Soc. (with Phil Donahue q.v.). *Publications:* Parting with Illusions 1990, Remembering War (with E. Keyssar 1990), Eyewitness 1991, numerous articles in Russian and American newspapers and magazines. *Telephone:* (095) 202-7161 (Moscow), (212) 3553454 (New York). *Fax:* 095/230-2941 (Moscow), (212) 644-1193 (New York).

PRABHJOT KAUR; Indian poet and politician; b. 6 July 1924, Langaryal; d. of Nidhan Singh; m. Brig. Narenderpal Singh 1948; two d.; ed. Khalsa Coll. for Women, Lahore, and Punjab Univ.; first collected poems published 1943 (aged sixteen); represented India at numerous int. literary confs.; mem. Legis. Council, Punjab 1966; Ed. Vikendrit; mem. Sahitya Akademi (Nat. Acad. of Letters), Exec. Bd. 1978; mem. Cen. Comm. for UNESCO, Nat. Writers Cttee. of India; received honours of Sahitya Shiromani 1964 and Padma Shri 1967; title of Rajya Kavi (Poet Laureate) by Punjab Govt. 1964, the Sahitya Akademi Award 1964, Golden Laurel Leaves, United Poets Int., Philippines 1967, Grand Prix de la Rose de la France 1968, Most Distinguished Order of Poetry, World Poetry Soc. Intercontinental, U.S.A. 1974; Woman of the Year, U.P.L.I., Philippines 1975, Sewa Sifti Award 1980, NIF Cultural Award 1982, Josh Kenya Award 1982, Delhi State Award 1983, Fellow Emer., Govt. of India. *Publications:* 50 books, including: Poems: Supne Sadhran 1949, Do Rang 1951, Pankheru 1956, Lala (in Persian) 1958, Bankapasi 1958, Pabbi 1962, Khari 1967, Plateau (French) 1968, Wad-darshi Sheesha 1972, Madhiantar 1974, Chandra Yug 1978, Dreams Die Young 1979, Shadows and Light (Bulgarian) 1980, Him Hans 1982, Samrup 1982, Ishq Shara Ki Nata 1983, Shadows (English and Danish) 1985; Short Stories: Kinke 1952, Aman de Na 1956, Zindgi de Kujh Pal 1982, Main Amanat Naheen (Hindi), Kuntith, Casket (English); autobiog.: Jeena vi 9k Ada Hai. *Leisure interests:* reading, travel. *Address:* D-203, Defence Colony, New Delhi 110024, India. *Telephone:* 49622756; 4626045.

PRADA, Michel André Jean Edmond; French civil servant; b. 2 April 1940, Bordeaux; s. of Robert and Suzanne (Bouffard) Prada; m. Annick Saudubray 1963; two s. three d.; ed. Lycée Montesquieu Bordeaux, Faculté de Droit et Inst. d'Etudes Politiques de Bordeaux, Ecole Nat. d'Admin.; Inspecteur des Finances with Ministry of Econ. and Finance 1966–; Chargé de Mission, Inspection Générale des Finances 1969; Chargé de Mission, Direction de la Comptabilité Publique 1970, Asst. Director 1974, Head of Service 1977, Dir. de la Comptabilité Publique 1978–85; Dir. of Budget, Ministry of the Economy, Finance and the Budget 1986–88; Chair. Bd. Dirs. Credit d'équipement des petites et moyennes entreprises (PME) 1988–; Chair. Comm. des Opérations de Bourse 1995–; Chair. Admin. Council Banque de l'entreprise 1989, Orchestre de Paris 1989–, Exec. Cttee. Int. Org. of Securities Comms. (IOSCO) 1996–98, Tech. Cttee. of IOSCO 1998–; fmr. mem. Nat. Cttee. on Foreign Trade and Tourism, Econ. and Social Council, Nat. Credit Council; Officier, Légion d'honneur, Ordre nat. du Mérite. *Address:* Commission des Opérations de Bourse, 17 place de la Bourse, 75002 Paris (Office); 2 rue Cart, 94160 Saint-Mandé, France (Home). *Telephone:* 01.53.45.63.04 (Office).

PRADHAN, Trilochan, PH.D.; Indian scientist; b. 3 Jan. 1929, Ghanashalia, Orissa; s. of Ramachandra and Ahalya Dakshinaray; m. Sanjukta Pradhan 1959; one s. one d.; ed. Utkal Univ., Benares Hindu Univ. and Univ. of Chicago; lecturer in Physics, Ravenshaw Coll. Cuttack 1951–62; Assoc. Prof. Saha Inst. of Nuclear Physics, Calcutta 1962–67, Prof. and Head, Div. of Theoretical Nuclear Physics 1967–74; Dir. Inst. of Physics, Bhubaneshwar 1974–89, Prof. Emer. 1989–; Vice-Chancellor, Utkal Univ. 1989–91; Meghnad Saha Award 1980, Padma Bhusan Award 1990. *Publications:* about 60 papers on theoretical physics in the areas of elementary particles, atomic physics, plasma physics. *Leisure interests:* gardening, indoor games. *Address:* Institute of Physics, Bhubaneswar 751005, India. *Telephone:* (0674) 581770 *Fax:* (0674) 581142.

PRADIER, Henri Joseph Marie; French engineer; b. 5 Nov. 1931, Sainte-Colombe-lès-Vienne, Rhône; s. of Camille Pradier and Anne-Marie Côte; m. 1st Marie-France Michot (deceased); two s.; m. 2nd Brigitte Dapvril 1973; one s. one d.; ed. Institution Robin, Vienne, Lycée du Parc, Lyons and Ecole Polytechnique; Consulting Engineer 1955–58; Shell Française 1958–67 and 1970–; Man. Dir. Shell du Maroc 1967–79, Vice-Pres. Distribution 1975–84; Man. Dir. Shell Française 1984–92, now Hon. Pres.; Dir. Société pour l'Utilisation Rationnelle des Gaz (Butagaz) 1975, Shell Chimie 1984, hosp. works, Françaises de L'Ordre de Malte (OHFOM) 1992–95, St. Joseph and St. Luke Hospital, Lyon 1994–97, Bioconversion SA 1998–, Publicis communication 1998–; Chevalier Légion d'honneur, Officier Ordre d'Orange Nassau. *Leisure interests:* gardening, sailing, swimming. *Address:* 52 rue du Ranelagh, 75016 Paris, France.

PRADO ARANGUIZ, Jorge José; Chilean politician and agriculturalist; b. 25 March 1937, Santiago; m. Magdalena Lira Lecaros; two s.; ed. Colegio Padres Franceses, Universidad Católica de Chile; scholarships to study agricultural admin., org. of co-operatives and irrigation tech. in France, Norway and Israel; mem. Man. staff fruit-growing enterprise Casas de Pencahue, San Vicente de Tagua Tagua; partner of livestock enterprise Mapullay, Bucalemu, Santo Domingo; fmr. Man. and Dir. A.F.P. Planvital; active in farmers' unions; Vice-Chair. Confederacion de Productores Agrícolas 1973–75; mem. Bd. Sociedad Nacional de Agricultura 1967, Deputy Chair. 1981–82; Minister of Agric. 1982–88; Chair. 1989–91; Dir. Banco O'Higgins 1989–91, Grupo Empresas G.C.T. 1989–91; mem. Exec. Bd. Universidad Mayor 1989–91. *Address:* Tenderini 187, Santiago, Chile. *Telephone:* 337773.

PRAKKE, Lucas, LL.D.; Netherlands professor of law; b. 20 Feb. 1938, Groningen; m. Margaretha M. O. de Bruijn Kops 1965; two s.; ed. Gemeentelijk Lyceum, Doetinchem, Univ. of Amsterdam and Columbia Univ. Law School, New York; Asst. Prof. of Law, Univ. of Amsterdam 1963–72, Prof. of Dutch and Comparative Constitutional Law 1972–, Dean, Faculty of Law 1981–83; Judge, Civil Service Appeal Tribunal 1977–89; mem. Royal Comm. on Constitution 1982–85; mem. Royal Netherlands Acad. *Publications:* Principles of Constitutional Interpretation in the Netherlands 1970, Toetsing in het publiekrecht 1972, Pluralisme en staatsrecht 1974, Het bestuursrecht van de landen der Europese Gemeenschappen 1986, Bedenkingen tegen het toetsingsrecht (Report of Netherlands Lawyers' Asscn.) 1992, Swamping the Lords, Packing the Court, Sacking the King. Address on 'dies natalis' of Univ. of Amsterdam 1994, Handboek van het Nederlandse staatsrecht 1995, Het staatsrecht van de landen van de Europese Unie (5th edn.) 1998. *Leisure interests:* history, music, walking. *Address:* Faculteit der Rechtsgeleerdheid, University of Amsterdam, Postbus 1030, 1000 BA Amsterdam (Office); Koedijklaan 15, 1406 KW Bussum, Netherlands (Home). *Telephone:* 020-5253966 (Office); 035-6989520 (Home).

PRAMOEDYA ANANTA TOER; Indonesian novelist; b. 20 Feb. 1925, Blora, East Java; worked with Domei Japanese news agency to 1945; studied as stenographer; wrote first book Sepulah Kepala Nika (Ten Chiefs of Nika), Jakarta 1945; manuscript lost before printing; 2nd Lieut., Indonesian revolution, Bekasi, east of Jakarta; with Voice of Free Indonesia producing Indonesian language magazine; arrested by Dutch July 1947; wrote first major works, Bukit Duri gaol; ed. Indonesian Library of Congress after release to 1951; arrested on order of Gen. A. H. Nasution (q.v.) in connection with book on overseas Chinese 1960; released 1961; aligned with communist-sponsored cultural groups; leading figure in Lekkra, Indonesian Communist Party cultural asscn.; arrested Nov. 1966; with first political prisoners on Buni island; released Jan. 1980; 7 novels (one published so far), one drama and 2 minor works composed in prison, Buni 1966–80; novels banned May 1981; Ramon Magsaysay Award for Journalism 1995. *Novels include:* Keluarga Guerilya, Bumi Manusia (The World of Man) 1973, Anak Seluruh Bangsa (A Child of All Nations), Jajak Langkah (Strides Forward), Bumah Kaca (The Greenhouse), The Buru Tetralogy, House of Glass.

PRANCE, Sir Ghillean Tolmie, Kt., D.PHIL., F.R.S.; British botanist; b. 13 July 1937, Brandeston, Suffolk; s. of Basil Camden Prance and Margaret Hope Prance (née Tolmie); m. Anne Elizabeth Hay 1961; two d.; ed. Malvern Coll., Keble Coll. Oxford; Research Asst., The New York Botanical Garden 1963–66, Assoc. Curator 1966–68, Krukoff Curator of Amazonian Botany 1968–75, Dir. of Botanical Research 1975–81, Vice-Pres. 1977–81, Sr. Vice-Pres. 1981–88, Dir. Inst. of Economic Botany 1981–88; Dir. Royal Botanic Gardens, Kew 1988–99; Dir. of Research, The Eden Project 1999–; Adjunct Prof., City Univ. of New York 1968–; Dir. of Graduate Studies, Instituto Nacional de Pesquisas da Amazonia, Brazil 1973–75; Exec. Dir. Org. for Flora Neotropica 1975–88; Visiting Prof. in Tropical Studies, Yale Univ. 1983–88; Visiting Prof., Reading Univ. 1988–; Chair. Bentham-Moxon Trust 1988–99; Pres. Linnean Soc. of London 1997–; Trustee Au Sable Inst. of Environmental Studies 1984–, Margaret Mee Amazon Trust 1988–96, Worldwide Fund for Nature Int. 1989–93, Horniman Museum 1990–; Pres. Asscn. of Tropical Biology 1979–80, American Asscn. of Plant Taxonomists 1984–85, Systematics Asscn. 1988–91; mem. Bd. of Govs. Lovaine Trust Co. Ltd. 1989–; Council mem. Royal Horticultural Soc. 1990–; Corresp. mem. Botanical Soc. of America 1994; Hon. mem. British Ecological Soc. 1996–; Fil. Dr. h.c. (Göteborg) 1983; D.Sc. h.c. (Univ. of Kent at Canterbury) 1994, (Portsmouth) 1994, (Kingston) 1994, (St. Andrews) 1995, (City Univ., New York) 1998, Dr. h.c. (Bergen) 1996, (Sheffield) 1997, (Liverpool) 1998; Henry Shaw Medal, Missouri Botanical Garden 1988, Linnean Medal 1990, Int. Cosmos Prize 1993, Patron's Medal (Royal Geographical Soc.) 1994, Asa Gray Award (American Soc. of Plant Taxonomists) 1998, Int. Award of Excellence (Botanical Research Inst. of Tex.) 1998. *Publications:* Arvores de Manaus 1975, Extinction is Forever 1977, Biological Diversification in the Tropics 1981, Amazonia—Key Environments 1985, Tropical Forests and World Climate 1986, Leaves 1986, White Gold 1989, Wildflowers for All Seasons 1989, Out of the Amazon 1992, Bark 1993, Rainforests of the World 1998; Ed. 13 books; numerous scientific and gen. articles. *Leisure interests:* squash, bird watching. *Address:* The Old Vicarage, Silver Street, Lyme Regis, Dorset, DT7 3HS, England.

PRANDINI, Giovanni; Italian politician; b. 1943, Brescia; studied econs. and commerce; fmr. Christian Democrat (DC) Deputy; Senator for Chiari 1987–; fmr. hosp. admin., Under-Sec. for Foreign Trade, mem. Chamber of Deputies Finance and Treasury Comm., Defence Comm.; fmr. Minister for the Merchant Navy; Minister of Public Works 1989–92. *Address:* c/o Ministry of Public Works, Piazza Porta Pia, 00198 Rome, Italy. *Telephone:* (06) 84821.

PRAPAS CHARUSATHIRA, General (see Charusathira, General Prapas).

PRASAD, Ashoka, M.D.; Indian psychiatrist and university professor; b. 10 May 1955, Patna; s. of late Judge Jahnavi Prasad and Usha Prasad; ed. Colvin Taluqdar's Coll., Lucknow, G.S.V.M. Medical Coll. Kanpur; Resident in Paediatrics and Psychiatry, Castlebar Gen. Hosp., Eire, Resident in Psychiatry, Royal Edin. Hosp., Edin. 1980–83; Research Fellow, Depts. of Biochem. and Psychiatry, Univ. of Leeds 1983–85; Kate Stillman Lecturer in Psychiatry, Univ. Coll. Hosp. and Queen Charlotte's Hosp., London 1984–86; Consultant Psychiatrist, Whipps Cross Hosp., Claybury Hosp. and Thorpe Coombe Hosp., London 1986–87; in charge of Psychopharmacology and Hon. Sr. Lecturer, Mental Health Research Inst. and Monash Univ., Melbourne, Australia, Assoc. Dept. of Psychiatry, Univ. of Melbourne 1987; Visiting Specialist, Kingseat Hosp., N.Z. 1988; Consultant Psychiatrist, Claybury Hosp., London and St. Margaret's Hosp., Essex 1988–89; at Dept. of Psychiatry, Dalhousie Univ., Canada, Dept. of Psychology, St. Mary's Univ., Canada 1989; J. Ernest Runions Fellow, Dept. of Psychiatry, Univ. of B.C., Vancouver 1989–90; Prof. of Psychiatry, Hahnemann Univ., Phila. 1990–91; Adjunct Prof. of Medical Anthropology, Columbia Univ. 1990–91, of Anthropology, Univ. of Pa. 1991; Medical Dir. Phila. Consultation Center 1990–92; currently hon. consultant to several bodies, including Jain TV, India, for medical programmes, Hon. Adviser 1993–; several visiting professorships including Harvard Univ. 1986, 1991; Murphy Award 1987, Blueler Award 1987. *Publications:* five books including Biological Basis and Therapy of Neuroses; over 125 publs. in various journals. *Address:* 1 Avas Vikas, Betia Hata, Gorakhpur 273001, India. *Telephone:* (0551) 334020. *Fax:* (0551) 332845.

PRATCHETT, Terry, O.B.E.; British writer; b. 28 April 1948, Beaconsfield, Bucks.; m. Lyn Marian Purves 1968; one d. *Publications:* The Carpet People 1971, The Dark Side of the Sun 1976, Strata 1981, The Colour of Magic 1983, The Light Fantastic 1986, Equal Rites 1987, Mort 1987, Sourcery 1988, Wyrd Sisters 1988, Pyramids 1989, Truckers 1989, Guards! Guards! 1989, The Unadulterated Cat 1989, Eric 1990, Good Omens (with Neil Gaiman) 1990, Moving Pictures, 1990, Diggers 1990, Wings 1990, Reaper Man 1991, Witches Abroad 1991, Small Gods 1992, Only You Can Save Mankind 1992, Lords and Ladies 1992, Johnny and the Dead 1993, Men At Arms 1993, Soul Music 1993, The Streets of Ankh-Morpork (with Stephen Briggs) 1993, The Discworld Companion (with Stephen Briggs) 1994, Interesting Times 1994, A Company Discworld 1995, Maskerade 1995, The Discworld Map (with Stephen Briggs) 1995, Johnny and the Bomb 1996, Feet of Clay 1996, Hogfather 1996, The Pratchett Portfolio (with Paul Kidby) 1996, Jingo 1997, The Last Continent 1998, A Tourist's Guide to Lancre (with Stephen Briggs) 1998, Carpe Jugulum 1998, Discworld Diary 1998, The Death Trilogy 1998. *Address:* c/o Colin Smythe, P.O. Box 6, Gerrards Cross, Bucks., SL9 8XA, England.

PRATT, (John) Christopher, O.C., C.C., R.C.A., B.F.A.; Canadian painter and printmaker; b. 9 Dec. 1935, St. John's, Newfoundland; s. of John Kerr Pratt and Christine Emily (Dawe) Pratt; m. Mary Frances West 1957; two s. two d.; ed. Prince of Wales Coll., St. John's Newfoundland, Memorial Univ. of Newfoundland, Mount Allison Univ., Sackville, N.B. and the Glasgow School of Art, Scotland; taught as specialist in art, Memorial Univ. 1961–63; freelance artist 1963–; has exhibited widely in Europe and N. America including a major retrospective organized by Vancouver Art Gallery 1985–86; mem. Mount Carmel Town Council 1969–73, Postage Stamp Design Cttee., Ottawa 1970–73, The Canada Council 1976–82, Memorial Univ. Bd. of Regents 1972–75; Hon. D. Litt. (Memorial) 1972, Hon. LL.D. (Mount Allison) 1973, (Dalhousie) 1986. *Leisure interest:* offshore sailing. *Address:* P.O. Box 87, Mount Carmel, St. Mary's Bay, Newfoundland, AOB 2M0, Canada.

PRAWER, Siegbert Salomon, M.A., D.LITT., PH.D., LITT.D., F.B.A.; British university teacher and author; b. 15 Feb. 1925; s. of Marcus and Eleonora Prawer; brother of Ruth Prawer Jhabvala (q.v.); m. Helga Alice Schaefer 1949; one s. two d. (and one s. deceased); ed. King Henry VIII School, Coventry, Jesus Coll., Christ's Coll., Cambridge; Adelaide Stoll Research Student, Christ's Coll., Cambridge 1947–48; Asst. Lecturer, then Lecturer, then Sr. Lecturer, Univ. of Birmingham 1948–63; Prof. of German, Westfield Coll., London Univ. 1964–69; Taylor Prof. of German Language and Literature, Oxford 1969–86, Prof. Emer. 1986–; Co-editor, Oxford Germanic Studies 1971–75, Anglica Germanica 1973–79; Visiting Prof. City Coll., New York 1956–57, Univ. of Chicago 1963–64, Harvard Univ. 1968, Hamburg Univ. 1969, Univ. of Calif., Irvine 1975, Otago Univ., N.Z. 1976, Univ. of Pittsburgh 1977, Australian Nat. Univ., Canberra 1980, Brandeis Univ. 1981–82; Resident Fellow, Knox Coll., Dunedin, N.Z. 1976; Fellow Queen's Coll., Oxford 1969–86, Supernumerary Fellow 1986–90, Hon. Fellow 1990, Dean of Degrees 1976–93; Hon. Dir. London Univ. Inst. of Germanic Studies 1967–69, Hon. Fellow 1986; Pres. British Comparative Literature Asscn. 1984–87, Hon. Fellow 1989; Hon. mem. Modern Languages Asscn. of America 1986; mem. German Acad. of Literature 1989; Pres. English Goethe Soc.

1992–95, Vice-Pres. 1995–; Hon. Fellow Jesus Coll. Cambridge 1996–; Hon. D.Phil. (Cologne) 1985; Hon. D.Litt. (Birmingham) 1988; Goethe Medal 1973, Gold Medal, German Goethe Soc. 1995; Isaac Deutscher Memorial Prize 1977, Gundolf-Prize of the German Acad. 1986. *Publications:* German Lyric Poetry 1952, Mörike und seine Leser 1960, Heine's Buch der Lieder: A Critical Study 1960, Heine: The Tragic Satirist 1962, The Penguin Book of Lieder 1964, The Uncanny in Literature (inaugural lecture) 1965, Heine's Shakespeare, a Study in Contexts (inaugural lecture) 1970, Comparative Literary Studies: An Introduction 1973, Karl Marx and World Literature 1976, Caligari's Children: The Film as Tale of Terror 1980, Heine's Jewish Comedy: A Study of His Portraits of Jews and Judaism 1983, Coalsmoke and Englishmen 1984, A. N. Stencl—Poet of Whitechapel 1984, Frankenstein's Island–England and the English in the Writings of Heinrich Heine 1986, Israel at Vanity Fair: Jews and Judaism in the Writings of W. M. Thackeray 1992, Breeches and Metaphysics, Thackeray's German Discourse 1997; edited: Essays in German Language, Culture and Society (with R. H. Thomas and L. W. Forster) 1969, The Romantic Period in Germany 1970, Seventeen Modern German Poets 1971; screenplay: Das Kabinett des Dr. Caligari 1996, Breeches and Metaphysics: Thackeray's German Discourse 1997; numerous articles on German, English and comparative literature. *Leisure interest:* portrait drawing. *Address:* 9 Hawkswell Gardens, Oxford, OX2 7EX, England.

PRAWIRO, Radius, M.A.; Indonesian politician, economist and banker; b. 29 June 1928, Yogjakarta; ed. Senior High School, Yogjakarta, Nederlandsche Economische Hoogeschool, Rotterdam, Econ. Univ. of Indonesia; Sec. Defence Cttee., Yogjakarta during revolution 1945; with Army High Command, Yogjakarta 1946–47; Angauta Tentara Pelajar (Army) 1948–51; Officer in Govt. Audit Office, Ministry of Finance 1953–65; Vice-Minister, Deputy Supreme Auditor, mem. Supreme Audit Office 1965–66; Gov. Bank Indonesia 1966–73; Chair. Indonesian Asscn. of Accountants 1965–; Gov. IMF for Indonesia 1967–72, Alt. Gov. Asian Devt. Bank 1967–72; Minister of Trade 1973–78, of Trade and Co-operatives 1978–83, of Finance 1983–88, Co-ordinating Minister of Econs., Finance, Industry and Devt. Supervision 1988–93; Chair. Bd. of Govs. IBRD, IDA, IFC 1971–72; mem. Econ. Council of the Pres. 1968, Nat. Econ. Stabilization Council 1968, Gov. Bd. Christian Univ. of Indonesia, Supervisory Bd. Trisakti Univ.; Order of Sacred Treasure. *Address:* Jalan Imam Bonjol 4, Jakarta, Indonesia (Home).

PREBBLE, Mark, PH.D.; New Zealand civil servant; b. 12 May 1951, Auckland; s. of Archdeacon K. R. Prebble and Mary Prebble; m. 1st Fenella Druce 1974 (died 1977); m. 2nd Lesley Bagnall 1978; two s. two d.; ed. Auckland Grammar School, Auckland Univ. and Victoria Univ. of Wellington; with Treasury, Govt. of N.Z. 1977–82, Dept. of Labour 1982–85; Seconded to Prime Minister and Cabinet as Man. Change Team on Targeting Social Assistance 1991–92; Minister (Econ.) N.Z. High Comm., London 1992–93; Deputy Sec. of Treasury 1993–98; Chief Exec. Dept. of Prime Minister and Cabinet 1998–. *Publications:* Smart Cards: Is it Smart to Use a Smart Card? 1990, Information, Privacy and the Welfare State 1990, Incentives and Labour Supply: Modelling Taxes and Benefits (ed., with P. Rebstock) 1992, New Zealand: The Turnaround Economy 1993 and articles in econ., public policy and educational journals. *Leisure interests:* walking and family. *Address:* Department of the Prime Minister and Cabinet, Parliament Buildings, Wellington, New Zealand. *Telephone:* (4) 471 9700. *Fax:* (4) 499 2109.

PREBBLE, Richard William, O.B.E., B.A., LL.B.; New Zealand politician and lawyer; b. 7 Feb. 1948, U.K.; s. of Archdeacon K.R. Prebble; m. Nancy Prebble 1970; ed. Auckland Boys' Grammar School, Auckland Technical Inst. and Auckland Univ.; admitted as barrister and solicitor, N.Z. Supreme Court 1971; admitted to Bar, Fiji Supreme Court 1973; M.P. for Auckland Cen. 1975–; Jr. Opposition Whip 1978–79; Minister of Transport, of Railways, Minister of Civil Aviation and Meteorological Services, Minister of Railways, Minister of Pacific Island Affairs, Assoc. Minister of Finance 1984–87; Minister of State-Owned Enterprises, Postmaster-Gen., Minister of Works and Devt. and Minister of Pacific Island Affairs 1987–88, of Railways, Police, State Owned Enterprises and Pacific Island Affairs Jan.–Oct. 1990; N.Z. Labour Party. *Leisure interests:* Polynesian and Melanesian culture, opera, drama. *Address:* Parliament Buildings, Wellington, New Zealand. *Telephone:* 719-957.

PREM CHAND, Lieut.-Gen. D.; Indian army officer (retd.) and United Nations official; b. 1916, Muzaffargarh, now West Pakistan; s. of the late Dewan and Mrs. Khem Chand; ed. Govt. Coll., Lahore and Staff Coll., Quetta; commissioned Indian Army 1937; served in Gen. Staff, Army HQ, New Delhi 1947, later apptd. Mil. Asst. to Chief of Army Staff; commanded Regimental Centre of First Gurkha Rifles; Instructor, Defence Services Staff Coll., Wellington; subsequently apptd. Deputy Dir. of Mil. Training, Dir. of Personnel Services, Dir. of Mil. Intelligence, New Delhi; Chief of Staff, HQ Western Command, Simla 1961, Commanded Brigade and Div. in Western Command; Gen.-Officer, Katanga Area, UN Operation in the Congo 1962–63; Commanded Div. in Eastern Command, Chief of Staff, HQ Eastern Command, Calcutta; Dir. Gen. Nat. Cadet Corps; retd. 1967 then held admin. post in industrial concern; Commdr. UN Force in Cyprus (UNFICYP) 1969–76; UN Sec. Gen.'s. Rep. for Rhodesia 1977; UNTAG Force Commdr., Namibia 1989; Head of UN Transition Assistance Group, Namibia 1989; rank of Lieut.-Gen. 1974; Param Vishisht Seva Medal. *Leisure interests:* music and trekking. *Address:* c/o UN Information Centre, 55 Lodi Estate, New Delhi, India.

PREM TINSULANONDA, Gen.; Thai politician and army officer; b. 26 Aug. 1920; ed. Suan Kularb School and Chulachomklao Royal Mil. Acad., Bangkok; started mil. career as Sub-Lieut. 1941; Commdr. Cavalry HQ 1968; Commdr.-Gen. 2nd Army Area 1974; Asst. C.-in-C. Royal Thai Army 1977; Deputy Minister of Interior, Govt. of Gen. Kriangsak Chomanan 1977; Minister of Defence 1979–87, later C.-in-C.; Prime Minister of Thailand 1980–88; Chair. Petroleum Authority of Thailand (PTT) 1981; Ramathipbodi Order, King of Thailand, Seri Maharajah Mangku Negara (Malaysia) 1984. *Address:* c/o H.M. Privy Council, Grand Palace, Thanon Na Phra Lan, Bangkok 10200 (Office); 279 Sri Ayutthaya Road, Sisao Theves, Bangkok 10300, Thailand.

PRENDERGAST, Peter Thomas, D.F.A., M.F.A.; Welsh painter and draughtsman; b. 27 Oct. 1946, Abertridwr; s. of Martin and Mary Prendergast; m. Lesley A. Riding 1967; two s. two d.; ed. Cwmaber Sec. School, Cardiff Coll. of Art, Slade School of Fine Art and Reading Univ.; part-time lecturer, Liverpool Coll. of Art 1970–74; teacher, Ysgol Dyffryn Ogwen, Bethesda 1975–80; now part-time lecturer in Painting and Drawing at tech. coll.; one-man exhbns. Liverpool 1973, Bangor Univ. 1974, 1979, 1986, Welsh Arts Council Gallery 1975, Llandudno 1982, Durham 1982, Campden Arts Centre 1982, Swansea 1983, Bath 1987, Agnews, London 1993, Nat. Museum of Wales 1993, From Land and Sea, Scarborough, Swansea 1993, Boundary Gallery, London 1996; group exhbns. at Tate Gallery 1984, Rocks and Flesh at Norwich Art School Gallery 1985, Ways of Telling 1989, Natural Element 1989, Mixe 1990, Scarborough City Art Gallery 1991, Welsh art exhbn. San Francisco 1993, Barcelona 1995 and elsewhere; represented in Group Wales exhbn., Czechoslovakia 1986–87, Artists in the Parks, Victoria and Albert Museum, London, Experience of Landscape, Arts Council of G.B. Touring exhbn.; comms. for Rural Devt. Body for Wales, Nat. Trust Gardens 1991, Nat. Museum of Wales; painting of Bethesda reproduced in book Green Bridge: Short Stories from Wales; included in book The New Wales; featured in TV film Conflicts 1991; commissioned to paint the gardens of Wales 1991–; included in exhbn. 175 years of Agnews 1992; Govt. scholarship to U.S.A. 1993; Hon. D.Litt. (Glamorgan) 1995. *Publications:* Road to Bethesda 1982, Hard Won Image 1984, Self Portrait 1988, Inspiration of Landscape 1989, From Land and Sea (with Len Tabover), The Gaze of Love 1993. *Leisure interests:* sport, music, reading. *Address:* c/o Agi Katz Fine Art, Boundary Gallery, 98 Boundary Road, London, NW8 0RH, England; Tan-y-Graig, Deiniolen, Caernarfon, LL55 3EE, N. Wales, United Kingdom. *Telephone:* (01248) 354683 (Caernarfon).

PRENDERGAST, Sir (Walter) Kieran, K.C.V.O., C.M.G.; British diplomatist; b. 2 July 1942, Campbeltown, Scotland; s. of late Lieut.-Commdr. J. H. Prendergast and Mai Hennessy; m. Joan Reynolds 1967; two s. two d.; ed. Salesian Coll. Chertsey and St. Edmund Hall, Oxford; Asst. Pvt. Sec. to successive Secs. of State, FCO 1976–78; has served at Istanbul, Ankara, Nicosia, The Hague, U.K. Mission to UN, New York and Tel Aviv; seconded to staff of last Gov. of Rhodesia (Lord Soames) during transition to independence in Zimbabwe; High Commr. in Zimbabwe 1989–92, in Kenya 1992–95; Amb. to Turkey 1995–97; UN Under Sec.-Gen. for Political Affairs 1997–. *Leisure interests:* family, reading, wine. *Address:* United Nations, United Nations Plaza, New York, NY 10017, U.S.A. *Telephone:* (212) 963-5055. *Fax:* (212) 963-5065.

PRENTICE, Baron (Life Peer), cr. 1992, of Daventry in the County of Northamptonshire; **Reginald Ernest Prentice,** Kt., J.P.; British politician, public affairs consultant and company director; b. 16 July 1923, Thornton Heath, Surrey; s. of Ernest George Edward Prentice and Elizabeth Prentice; m. Joan Godwin 1948; one d.; ed. Whitgift School and London School of Econs.; temp. civil servant 1940–42; Royal Artillery 1942–46; student at London School of Econs. 1946–49; mem. staff Transport and Gen. Workers Union, Asst. to Legal Sec., in charge of Union's Advice and Service Bureau 1950–57; M.P. for East Ham (North) 1957–74, for Newham North-East 1974–79; Minister of State, Dept. of Educ. and Science Oct. 1964–66; Minister of Public Building and Works 1966–67, of Overseas Devt. 1967–69; Sec. of State for Educ. and Science 1974–75; Minister for Overseas Devt., with Cabinet rank June 1975–Dec. 1976 (resigned); resigned as Transport and Gen. Workers' Union-sponsored M.P. 1976; resigned from Labour Party and joined Conservative Party Oct. 1977; Conservative M.P. for Daventry 1979–87; Minister for Social Security and Minister for the Disabled 1979–81. *Publication:* (jt. author) Right Turn 1978. *Leisure interests:* walking, swimming and golf. *Address:* Wansdyke, Church Lane, Mildenhall, Marlborough, Wilts., SN8 2LU, England. *Telephone:* 01672-515397.

PRESCOTT, John Barry, A.C., B.COMM.; Australian business executive; b. 22 Oct. 1940; m. Jennifer Mary Louise Cahill; one s. three d.; ed. North Sydney Boys' High School, Univ. of New South Wales; Gen. Man. Transport, Broken Hill Proprietary Co. Ltd. (BHP) 1982–87, Exec. Gen. Man. and C.E.O. BHP Steel 1987–91, Dir. BHP 1988–98, Man. Dir. and C.E.O. BHP 1991–98; Dir. Tubemakers 1988–92; mem. Advisory Bd. Booz. Allen 1991–; mem. Defence Industry Cttee. 1988–93, Bd., Business Council of Australia 1995–97; Chair. Mfg. Council 1990–95; Patron Australian Quality Council 1990–; mem. Int. Council of J.P. Morgan 1994–, Asia Pacific Advisory Cttee. of New York Stock Exchange 1995– (Vice-Chair. 1997–), Council of World Econ. Forum, Bd. of The Walter and Eliza Hall Inst. of Medical Research

1994–, Bd. of Trustees, The Conf. Bd. 1995–. *Leisure interests:* tennis, golf. *Address:* The Broken Hill Proprietary Co. Ltd., Level 48, BHP Tower, 600 Bourke Street, Melbourne 3000 (Office); Cathkin, 43 Middle Crescent, Brighton 3186, Australia (Home). *Telephone:* (03) 9609 3242 (Office).

PRESCOTT, John Leslie, P.C., M.P., DIP. ECON POL.; British politician and trade unionist; b. 31 May 1938, Prestatyn, Wales; s. of John Herbert Prescott and Phyllis Prescott; m. Pauline Tilston 1961; two s.; ed. WEA correspondence courses, Ruskin Coll., Oxford, Hull Univ.; trainee chef 1953–55; steward in Merchant Navy 1955–63; Recruitment Officer, Gen. & Municipal Workers Union 1965; contested Southport for Labour 1966; Full-time official Nat. Union of Seamen 1968–70; M.P. Kingston upon Hull (East) 1970–83, Hull (East) 1983–97, Kingston upon Hull East 1997–; mem. Select Cttee. Nationalized Industries 1973–79, Council of Europe 1972–75, European Parl. 1975–79; P.P.S. to Sec. of State for trade 1974–76; Opposition Spokesman on Transport 1979–81, Regional Affairs and Devolution 1981–83, on Transport 1983–84, on Employment 1984–87, on Energy 1987–89, on Transport 1988–93, on Employment 1993–94; Deputy Prime Minister and Sec. of State for the Environment, Transport and the Regions May 1997–; Deputy Leader of Labour Party 1994–; mem. Shadow Cabinet 1983–97; mem. Nat. Exec. Council 1989–; Labour. *Publication:* Not Wanted on Voyage: A report of the 1966 seamen's strike 1966, Alternative Regional Strategy: A framework for discussion 1982, Planning for Full Employment 1985, Real Needs—Local Jobs 1987, Moving Britain into the 1990s 1989, Moving Britain into Europe 1991, Full Steam Ahead 1993, Financing Infrastructure Investment 1994, Jobs and Social Justice 1994. *Address:* House of Commons, London, SW1A 0AA, England.

PRESS, Frank, PH.D.; American geophysicist; b. 4 Dec. 1924, Brooklyn, New York; s. of Solomon and Dora (Steinholz) Press; m. Billie Kallick 1946; one s. one d.; ed. Coll. of City of New York and Columbia Univ.; Research Associate, Columbia Univ. 1946–49, Instructor, Geology 1949–51, Asst. Prof. of Geology 1951–52, Assoc. Prof. 1952–55; Prof. Geophysics, Calif. Inst. of Tech. 1955–65, Dir. Seismological Lab. 1957–65; Co-editor Physics and Chemistry of the Earth 1957–; Chair. Dept. of Earth and Planetary Sciences, M.I.T. 1965–77; Dir. Office of Science and Tech. Policy, Exec. Office of Pres., and Science and Tech. Adviser to Pres. 1977–80; Consultant to U.S. Navy 1956–57, U.S. Dept. of Defense 1958–62, NASA 1960–62, and 1965–; mem. U.S. del. Nuclear Test Ban Conf. Geneva 1959–61, Moscow 1963; Pres. Science Advisory Comm. 1961–64; Chair. Bd. of Advisors Nat. Center for Earthquake Research of the U.S. Geophysical Survey 1966–76; Planetology Subcomm. NASA 1966–70; Chair. Earthquake Prediction Panel Office of Science and Tech. 1965–66; Fellow American Acad. of Arts and Sciences 1966; Fellow Royal Astronomical Soc., mem. N.A.S. 1958, Pres. 1981–93; Cecil & Ida Green Sr. Fellow Carnegie Inst. of Washington, Washington, DC 1993–97; partner Washington Advisory Group 1996–; mem. Nat. Science Bd. 1970–77; fmr. Pres. American Geophysical Union; Chair. Cttee. on Scholarly Communication with People's Repub. of China 1975–77; mem. U.S.-U.S.S.R. Working Group in Earthquake Prediction 1973; fmr. mem. Exec. Council Nat. Acad. of Sciences; Hon. LL.D. (City Univ. of N.Y.) 1972, Hon. D.Sc. (Notre Dame Univ.) 1973, (Univ. of Rhode Island, of Arizona, Rutgers Univ., City Univ. of New York) 1979; Townsend Harris Medal Coll. of the City of New York, Royal Astronomical Soc. Gold Medal (U.K.) 1971, Day Medal Geological Soc. of America, Interior 1972, NASA Award 1973, Killian Faculty Achievement Award, M.I.T. 1975, Japan Prize 1993, Nat. Medal of Science 1994, Philip Hauge Abelson Prize, A.A.A.S. 1995. *Publications:* Earth (with R. Siever) 1986, Understanding Earth 1997. *Leisure interests:* skiing, sailing. *Address:* Suite 616 S., 2500 Virginia Avenue, Washington DC 20037, U.S.A.

PRESS, Tamara Natanovna; Russian athlete; b. 10 May 1937, Kharkov; mem. CPSU 1962–91; ed. Leningrad Construction Engineering Inst. and Higher Party School of Cen. Cttee. of CPSU; women's champion in shot-put at Olympic Games 1960, 1964, at discus 1964, women's champion of Europe in discus throwing three times, between 1958–62, and sixteen times women's champion of U.S.S.R. between 1958–66; worked for All-Union Cen. Council of Trade Unions 1967–91; Deputy Chair. Russian Olympic Cttee.; Vice-Pres. Sports Soc. Rossiya 1992–; Order of Lenin, Order of Badge of Honour, Honoured Master of Sports of U.S.S.R. 1960. *Address:* Sports Society Rossiya, Tolmachevski per. 4, Moscow, Russia. *Telephone:* 238-63-87.

PRESSLER, Larry, M.A., J.D.; American politician; b. 29 March 1942, Humboldt, S.D.; s. of Antone Pressler and Loretta Claussen; m. Harriet Dent 1982; one d.; ed. Univ. of South Dakota, Univ. of Oxford, England, Harvard Kennedy School of Govt. and Harvard Law School; Lieut. in U.S. Army, Viet Nam 1966–68; mem. House of Reps. 1975–79; Senator from South Dakota 1979–97; mem. several Senate Cttees.; Congressional Del. to 47th UN Gen. Ass. 1992; mem. U.S. Comm. on Improving the Effectiveness of the UN 1993; Sec. U.S. Del. to Inter-Parl. Union 1981; Dir. U.S.A.F. Bd. of Visitory 1987–; Chair. Commerce, Science and Transport Cttees., U.S. Senate 1995–96; founder Pressler and Assocs., Washington 1997–; Republican. *Publications:* U.S. Senators from the Prairie 1982, Star Wars: The SDI Debates in Congress 1986. *Leisure interests:* running, tennis. *Address:* 1919 Pennsylvania Avenue Northwest, # 800, Washington, DC 20006 (Office); 114 Fourth Street Southeast, Washington, DC 20003, U.S.A. (Home).

PRESTON, Paul, M.A., D.PHIL., F.R.HIST.S.; British professor of history; b. 21 July 1946, Liverpool; s. of Charles R. Preston and Alice Hoskisson; m. Gabrielle P. Ashford-Hodges 1983; two s.; ed. St. Edward's Coll. Liverpool, Oriel Coll. Oxford and Univ. of Reading; Research Fellow, Centre for Mediterranean Studies, Rome 1973–74; lecturer in History, Univ. of Reading 1974–75; lecturer in Modern History, Queen Mary Coll. London 1975–79, Reader 1979–85, Prof. of History 1985–91; Prof. of Int. History, L.S.E. 1991–; regular contrib. to Times Literary Supplement; columnist in Diario 16 and El Sol, Madrid; Comendador, Orden del Mérito Civil (Spain). *Publications:* The Coming of the Spanish Civil War 1978, The Triumph of Democracy in Spain 1986, The Spanish Civil War 1986, The Politics of Revenge 1990, Franco: A Biography 1993, Las tres Españas del 36 1998. *Leisure interests:* classical music, especially opera, modern fiction. *Address:* Department of International History, London School of Economics, Houghton Street, London, WC2A 2AE (Office); 10 Woodland Gardens, Muswell Hill, London, N10 3UA, England (Home). *Telephone:* 0171-955 7107 (Office); 0181-883 4058 (Home). *Fax:* 0171-955 7107 (Office); 0181-482 9865 (Home).

PRESTON, Peter John, M.A.; British journalist; b. 23 May 1938, Barrow-upon-Soar, Leicestershire; s. of John Whittle Preston and Kathlyn Preston (née Chell); m. Jean Mary Burrell 1962; two s. two d.; ed. Loughborough Grammar School and St. John's Coll., Oxford; editorial trainee, Liverpool Daily Post 1960–63; Political Reporter, The Guardian 1963–64, Educ. Corresp. 1965–66, Diary Ed. 1966–68, Features Ed. 1968–72, Production Ed. 1972–75, Ed. The Guardian 1975–95; Ed.in-Chief The Guardian 1995, Observer 1995–96; Editorial Dir. Guardian Media Group 1996–98; Co-Dir. Guardian Foundation 1997–98; mem. Scott Trust 1979–; Chair. Int. Press Inst. 1995–97, Asscn. of British Eds. 1996–; Hon. D.Litt. (Loughborough) 1982, (E. Anglia, City Univ.) 1997. *Leisure interests:* football, films, four children. *Address:* The Guardian, 119 Farringdon Road, London, EC1R 3ER, England. *Telephone:* 0171-278 2332.

PRESTON, Reginald Dawson, F.R.S., D.SC.; British professor of biophysics; b. 21 July 1908, Leeds; s. of Walter Cluderay and Eliza Preston (née Dawson); m. 1st Sarah Jane Pollard 1935 (deceased); m. 2nd Eva Frei 1963; one s. (deceased), two d.; ed. West Leeds High School, Univ. of Leeds and Cornell Univ., U.S.A.; Research Asst., Botany Dept., Univ. of Leeds 1931–32, 1851 Exhbn. Fellow 1932–35; Rockefeller Foundation Fellow, Cornell Univ. 1935–36; Asst. Lecturer, Lecturer, Sr. Lecturer, Botany Dept., Univ. of Leeds 1936–49, Reader in Plant Biophysics 1949–53, Prof. 1953–62, Prof. and Founder Head, Astbury Dept. of Biophysics 1962–73, Emer. Prof. 1973–, Dean of Science 1955–58, Chair. Bd. of Science and Tech. 1958–61, Library Cttee. 1964–73, School of Biological Sciences 1970–73; Visiting Prof., Botany Dept., Imperial Coll., Univ. of London 1976–79; Scientific Consultant to Hicksons Timber Impregnation Co. 1957–61; Fellow Inst. of Physics, Linnean Soc., Int. Acad. of Wood Science; Hon. Fellow Royal Microscopical Soc.; Hon. mem. Soc. for Experimental Biology, British Biophysical Soc., Int. Asscn. of Wood Anatomists; Anselme Payen Medal and Award, American Chemical Soc.; Distinguished Service Medal, Leeds Philosophy and Literature Soc. *Publications:* Molecular Architecture of Plant Cell Walls 1952, Physical Biology of Plant Cell Walls 1974; some 200 articles in scientific journals. *Leisure interests:* music, walking, gardening. *Address:* 117 St. Anne's Road, Leeds, LS6 3NZ, West Yorkshire, England. *Telephone:* (0113) 2785248.

PRESTON, Simon John, M.A., MUS.B., F.R.A.M., F.R.C.M., F.R.C.O., F.R.C.C.O., F.R.S.A.; British organist and choirmaster; b. 4 Aug. 1938, Bournemouth; ed. Canford School, King's Coll., Cambridge; Sub Organist Westminster Abbey 1962–67; Acting Organist St Albans Abbey 1967–68; Organist and Lecturer in Music, Christ Church, Oxford 1970–81; Organist and Master of the Choristers Westminster Abbey 1981–87; Conductor Oxford Bach Choir 1971–74; Artistic Dir., Calgary Int. Organ Festival; Patron, Univ. of Buckingham; mem. Royal Soc. of Musicians, Council of Friends of St. John's Smith Square; over 30 recordings; Edison Award 1971; Grand Prix du Disque 1979, Performer of the Year Award, American Guild of Organists 1987. *Leisure interests:* croquet, theatre, opera. *Address:* Little Hardwick, Langton Green, Tunbridge Wells, Kent, TN3 0EY, England. *Telephone:* (01892) 862042.

PRETI, Luigi; Italian politician; b. 23 Oct. 1914; fmr. lawyer and professor of philosophy and pedagogy; mem. Constituent Assembly 1946–47, Chamber of Deputies 1947–, Vice-Pres. 1980–83; Pres. Internal Affairs Comm. Chamber of Deputies; Under-Sec. of State to Treas. (War Pensions Dept.) 1954; Minister for Finance 1958–59, 1966–68, of Foreign Trade 1962–63, without Portfolio Dec. 1963–66, for the Budget 1968–69, of Finance 1970–72, of Transport and Civil Aviation 1973–74, of the Merchant Navy March–Aug. 1979, of Transport 1979–80; Chair. Nat. Council, Partito Socialista Democratico Italiano. *Publications:* Il concetto di status 1942, Il Governo nella Costituzione della Repubblica 1954, Le lotte agrarie nella Valle Padana 1955, Diritto elettorale politico 1957, Giovinezza, giovinezza 1964, I miti della razza e dell'Impero 1968, Dialoghi della Nuova Frontiera 1970, Interpretazione di Dubcek 1971, Italia malata 1972, Un ebreo nel fascismo 1974, Il compromesso storico 1975, La sfida tra democrazia e autoritarismo 1980, Mussolini giovane 1982, Giolitti, i riformisti e gli altri 1985, Anno duemila, la pace nel mondo 1986, Il pianeta terra in pericolo 1989, Giovani di Mussolini 1990, Extracomunitari in Italia e in Europa, Romanzo del 18 aprile, L'Italia nella tempesta 1993. *Address:* Partito Socialista Democratico Italiano, Piazza di Spagna 35, Rome; Via P. Costa 34, 40125 Bologna, Italy.

PRÊTRE, Georges; French conductor; b. 14 Aug. 1924, Waziers; s. of Emile and Jeanne (Dérin) Prêtre; m. Gina Marny 1950; one s. one d.; ed. Lycée and Conservatoire de Douai, Conservatoire national supérieur de musique de Paris and Ecole des chefs d'orchestre; Dir. of Music, Opera Houses of Marseilles, Lille and Toulouse 1946–55, Dir. of music Opéra-comique, Paris, 1955–59, at l'Opéra 1959; Dir.-Gen. of Music at l'Opéra 1970–71; conductor of the symphonic asscns. of Paris and of principal festivals throughout the world; also conducted at La Scala, Milan and major American orchestras; Conductor Metropolitan Opera House, New York 1964–65, La Scala, Milan 1965–66, Salzburg 1966; First Visiting Conductor, Vienna Symphony Orchestra 1985–, Opéra Bastille (Turandot) 1997, Opéra-Comique (Pelleas et Melisande) 1998; Officier, Légion d'honneur 1971, Haute Distinction République Italienne 1975, Commdr. République Italienne 1980; Europa Prize 1982; Victoire de la musique Award for Best Conductor 1997. *Leisure interests:* riding, swimming, aviation. *Address:* Salle Gaveau, 45 rue de la Boétie, 75008 Paris (Office); Château de Vaudricourt, à Naves, par Castres, 81100 France. *Telephone:* (63) 59 06 91.

PRETTY, Katharine Bridget (Kate), PH.D.; British archaeologist and college principal; b. 18 Oct. 1945, Cheshire; d. of Maurice Walter Hughes and Bridget Elizabeth Whibley Hughes (née Marples); m. 1st Graeme Lloyd Pretty (divorced 1975); m. 2nd Tjeerd Hendrik van Andel 1988; ed. King Edward VI High School for Girls, Birmingham and New Hall, Cambridge; Fellow and lecturer New Hall, Cambridge Univ. 1972–91, Emer. Fellow 1995–, Chair, Faculty of Archaeology and Anthropology 1991–, Council of the School of Humanities and Social Sciences 1997–; Principal Homerton Coll., Cambridge Univ. 1991–; Chair. RESCUE, British Archaeological Trust 1978–83. *Leisure interests:* archaeology, botany and gardening. *Publications:* The Excavations of Wroxeter Baths-Basilica 1997. *Address:* Homerton College, Hills Road, Cambridge, CB2 2PH, England. *Telephone:* (01223) 507131. *Fax:* (01223) 507130.

PRÉVAL, René; Haitian politician; b. 17 Jan. 1943, Port-au-Prince; m.; two c.; spent ten years in exile in U.S.A.; founding mem. Group for Defence of Constitution; Chair. Cttee. 'Pa Blié' investigating disappearance of persons under Duvalier regime 1987–91; Prime Minister Feb.-Sept. 1991; Pres. of Haiti Feb. 1996–. *Address:* Office of the President, Palais National, Port-au-Prince, Haiti. *Telephone:* 22-4020.

PREVIN, André George; American conductor, pianist and composer; b. (as Andreas Ludwig Priwin) 6 April 1929, Berlin, Germany; s. of Jack and Charlotte (née Epstein) Previn; m. 1st Betty Bennett (divorced); two d.; m. 2nd Dory Langan 1959 (divorced 1970); m. 3rd Mia Farrow (q.v.) 1970 (divorced 1979); three s. three d.; m. 4th Heather Hales 1982; one s.; ed. Berlin and Paris Conservatories; Music Dir. Houston Symphony, U.S. 1967–69; Music Dir. and Principal Conductor, London Symphony Orchestra 1968–79, Conductor Emer. 1979–; composed and conducted approx. 50 film scores 1950–65; Guest conductor of most major world orchestras, also Royal Opera House, Covent Garden, Salzburg, Edinburgh, Osaka, Flanders Festivals; Music Dir. London South Bank Summer Music Festival 1972–74, Pittsburgh Symphony Orchestra 1976–84, Los Angeles Philharmonic Orchestra 1984–89; Music Dir. Royal Philharmonic Orchestra 1985–86, Prin. Conductor 1987–92; Conductor Laureate, London Symphony Orchestra 1992–; series of television specials for BBC and for American Public Broadcasting Service; Television Critics Award 1972; Acad. Award for Best Film Score 1959, 1960, 1964, 1965; Hon. K.B.E. 1995. *Major works:* Symphony for Strings 1965, Overture to a Comedy 1966, Suite for Piano 1967, Cello Concerto 1968, Four Songs (for soprano and orchestra) 1968, Two Serenades for Violin 1969, Guitar Concerto 1970, Piano Preludes 1972, Good Companions (musical) 1974, Song Cycle on Poems by Philip Larkin 1977, Every Good Boy Deserves Favour (music, drama, text by Tom Stoppard, q.v.) 1977, Pages from the Calendar (for solo piano) 1977, Peaches (for flute and strings) 1978, Principals 1980, Outings (for brass quintet) 1980, Reflections 1981, Piano Concerto 1984, Triolet for Brass 1987, Variations for Solo Piano 1991, Six Songs for Soprano and Orchestra on texts by Toni Morrison 1991, Sonata for Cello and Piano 1992, The Magic Number (for soprano and orchestra) 1995, Trio for Bassoon, Oboe and Piano 1995, Sonata for Violin 1996, Sonata for Bassoon and Piano 1997, Streetcar Named Desire (opera) 1998. *Publications:* Music Face to Face 1971, Orchestra (ed.) 1977, Guide to Music 1983, No Minor Chords: My Days in Hollywood 1992. *Leisure interests:* collecting contemporary art, fencing, American folk art. *Address:* c/o Columbia Artists, 165 W. 57th Street, New York, NY 10019, U.S.A.; Barbican Centre, Silk Street, London, EC2Y 8DS, England.

PRICE, Antony, M.A.; British fashion designer; b. 5 March 1945, Yorks.; s. of Peter Price and Joan Price; ed. Bradford Coll. of Art and Royal Coll. of Art; designer for Sterling Cooper 1968–72, for Plaza 1972–79; Chair. of own fashion co. 1979–; British Glamour Award 1989. *Leisure interests:* tropical plants, tropical ornithology, modern and classical music. *Address:* 468 Kings Road, London, S.W.10, England.

PRICE, Charles H., II; American business executive and fmr. diplomatist; b. 1 April 1931, Kansas City, Mo.; s. of Charles Harry Price and Virginia (née Ogden) Price; m. Carol Ann Swanson 1969; two s. three d.; ed. Univ. of Mo.; Pres. and Dir. Linwood Securities Co., Kansas City 1960–81; Chair. and Dir., Price Candy Co., Kansas City 1969–81, American Bancorpn., Kansas City 1960–81; Chair. and C.E.O. American Bank and Trust Co., Kansas City 1973–81; Amb. to Belgium 1981–83, to U.K. 1983–89; Chair. Ameribanc Inc. 1989–92, Pres., C.O.O. 1990–92; Chair. Bd. of Dirs. Mercantile Bank Kansas City, Mo. 1992–96, mem. Bd. of Dirs. 1996–; mem. Bd. of Dirs. Hanson PLC, New York Times Co., Texaco Inc., Mercantile Bancorp. Inc., 360° Communications Inc., Midwest Research Inst. (Chair. 1990–93), St. Luke's Hosp. Kansas City 1970–81 (Hon. Dir. 1989–); Hon. Fellow Regent's Coll., London 1986; several hon. degrees; William Booth Award, Salvation Army 1985, World Citizen of Year Award, Mayor of Kansas City 1985, Trustee Citation Award Midwest Research Inst. 1987, Distinguished Service Award Int. Relations Council 1989, Mankind Award, Cystic Fibrosis Foundation 1990, Chancellor's Medal, Univ. of Mo. 1992, William F. Yates Medallion, William Jewell Coll. 1996. *Leisure interests:* shooting, golf, tennis. *Address:* One West Armour Boulevard, Suite 300, Kansas City, MO 64111–2089, U.S.A. *Telephone:* (816) 360-6175.

PRICE, Frank; American television and cinema producer and executive; b. 17 May 1930, Decatur, Ill.; s. of William and Winifred (née Moran) Price; m. Katherine Huggins 1965; four s.; ed. Michigan State Univ., served with U.S.N. 1948–49; writer and story Ed., CBS-TV, New York 1951–53; with Columbia Pictures, Hollywood 1953–57, NBC-TV 1957–58; producer, writer, Universal Television, Calif. 1959–64, Vice-Pres. 1964–71, Sr. Vice-Pres. 1971–73, Exec. Vice-Pres. 1973–74, Pres. 1974–78; Pres. Columbia Pictures 1978–79, Chair. and C.E.O. 1979–83; Chair. and C.E.O. MCA Motion Picture Group 1983–86, Price Entertainment 1991–; Chair. Columbia Pictures 1990–91; Dir. Sony Pictures Entertainment, Savoy Pictures; Exec. Producer The Virginian 1961–64, Ironside 1965, Kojak, Six Million Dollar Man, Bionic Woman, Rockford Files, Quincy, Rich Man, Poor Man, The Tuskegee Airmen 1996; mem. Writers Guild America; Peabody Award 1996. *Address:* Price Entertainment Inc., 23660 Malibu Colony Road, Malibu, CA 90265, U.S.A.

PRICE, Rt. Hon. George Cadle, P.C.; Belizean politician; b. 15 Jan. 1919; s. of William Cadle Price and Irene Price; ed. St. John's Coll., Belize City, and St. Augustin Seminary, Mississippi; City Councillor 1947–62; founder-mem. People's United Party (PUP) 1950, Sec. PUP 1950–56, Leader PUP 1956–; Pres. Gen. Workers' Union 1947–52; mem. Legislative Council, British Honduras (now Belize) 1954–65; mem. Exec. Council 1954–57, 1961–65; Mayor, Belize City 1956–62; mem. House of Reps. 1965–84, Cabinet 1965–84; fmr. mem. for Nat. Resources; First Minister 1961–63, leader of del. to London for self-Govt. constitutional talks; Premier 1964–81, Prime Minister of Belize 1981–84, 1989–93, Minister of Finance and Econ. Planning 1965–84, of Foreign Affairs 1981–84, 1989–90; mem. Privy Council 1982–; Chair. Reconstruction and Devt. Corpn.; Outstanding Alumnus Award (St. John's Coll.) 1971. *Address:* c/o House of Representatives, Belmopan, Belize.

PRICE, James Gordon, B.A., M.D.; American university professor; b. 20 June 1926, Brush, Colo., U.S.A.; s. of John Hoover Price and Laurette (Dodds) Price; m. Janet Alice McSween 1949; two s. two d.; ed. Univ. of Colorado; intern, Denver Gen. Hosp.; pvt. practice, family medicine, Brush, Colo. 1952–78; Prof. Dept. of Family Practice, Univ. of Kan. 1978–93 (Chair. 1978–90), Dean, School of Medicine 1990–93; nationally syndicated newspaper column, Your Family Physician 1973–86; Medical Ed., Curriculum Innovations 1973–93; mem. Inst. of Medicine, N.A.S.; Charter Fellow American Acad. of Family Physicians. *Leisure interest:* computer programming. *Address:* 12205 Mohawk Road, Leawood, KS 66209, U.S.A. *Telephone:* (913) 491-3072.

PRICE, Leontyne; American soprano; b. 10 Feb. 1927, Laurel, Miss.; d. of James A. and Kate (Baker) Price; m. William Warfield 1952 (divorced 1973); ed. Central State Coll., Wilberforce, Ohio and Juilliard School of Music; appeared as Bess (Porgy and Bess), Vienna, Berlin, Paris, London, New York 1952–54; recitalist, soloist 1954–; soloist Hollywood Bowl 1955–59, 1966; opera singer NBC-TV 1955–58, San Francisco Opera Co. 1957–59, 1960–61, Vienna Staatsoper 1958, 1959–60, 1961; recording artist RCA-Victor 1958–; appeared Covent Garden 1958–59, 1970, Chicago 1959, 1960, 1965, Milan 1960–61, 1963, 1967, Metropolitan Opera, New York 1961–62, 1963–70, 1972, Paris Opéra as Aida 1968, Metropolitan Opera as Aida 1985 (retd.); numerous recordings; Hon. Vice-Chair. U.S. Cttee. UNESCO; Fellow, American Acad. of Arts and Sciences; Trustee Int. House; Hon. D.Mus. (Howard Univ., Cen. State Coll., Ohio); Hon. D.H.L. (Dartmouth); Hon. Dr. of Humanities (Rust Coll., Miss.); Hon. D.Hum.Litt. (Fordham); Presidential Medal of Freedom, Order of Merit (Italy), Nat. Medal of Arts 1985. *Address:* c/o Columbia Artists Management Inc., 165 West 57th Street, New York, NY 10019; 1133 Broadway, New York, NY 10010, U.S.A.

PRICE, Dame Margaret Berenice, D.B.E.; British opera singer; b. 13 April 1941, Tredegar, Wales; d. of late Thomas Glyn Price and of Lilian Myfanwy Richards; ed. Pontllanfraith Grammar School and Trinity Coll. of Music, London; operatic debut with Welsh Nat. Opera in Marriage of Figaro; renowned for Mozart operatic roles; has sung in world's leading opera houses and festivals; has made many recordings of opera, oratorio, concert works and recitals, and many radio broadcasts and television appearances; Hon. Fellow, Trinity Coll. of Music; Fellow Coll. of Wales 1991; Hon. D.Mus. (Wales) 1983; Elisabeth Schumann Prize for Lieder, Ricordi Prize for Opera, Silver Medal of the Worshipful Co. of Musicians. *Major roles include:* Countess in Marriage of Figaro, Pamina in The Magic Flute, Fiordiligi in Cosí fan Tutte, Donna Anna in Don Giovanni, Konstanze in Die Entführung, Amelia in Simone Boccanegra, Agathe in Freischütz, Desdemona in Otello, Elisabetta in Don Carlo, Aida and Norma, Amelia in Ballo in Maschera. *Leisure interests:* cookery, reading, walking, swimming, driving. *Address:* c/o Bayerische Staatsoper München, Max Josef Platz 2, 80539 Munich, Germany.

PRICE, Michael F.; American financial executive; b. 1952; m. (divorced); three s.; ed. Univ. of Oklahoma; with Heine Securities 1975–97, Research Asst., Man., C.E.O.; Pres., C.E.O. Franklin Mutual Advisers Inc. (fmrly. Heine Securities) 1997–; Pres., Chair. Bd. Dirs. Franklin Mutual Series Fund Inc. *Address:* Franklin Mutual Advisers Incorporated, 51 John F. Kennedy Parkway, Short Hills, NJ 07078, U.S.A.

PRICE, Nicholas Raymond Leige (Nick); golfer; b. 28 Jan. 1957, Durban, South Africa; m.; one s. one d.; turned professional 1977; won Asseng Invitational 1979, Canon European Masters 1980, Italian Open, S. African Masters 1981, Vaals Reef Open 1982, World Series of Golf 1983, Trophée Lancôme, ICI Int. 1985, West End S. Australian Open 1989, GTE Byron Nelson Classic, Canadian Open 1991, Air N.Z./Shell Open, PGA Championships, H-E-B Texas Open 1992, The Players Championship, Canon Greater Hartford Open, Sprint Western Open, Federal Express St. Jude Classic, ICL Int., Sun City Million Dollar Challenge 1993, British Open, ICL Int. Honda Classic, Southwestern Bell Colonial, Motorola Western Open, PGA Championship, Bell Canadian Open 1994, Alfred Dunhill Challenge, Hassan II Golf Trophy, Morocco, Zimbabwe Open 1995. *Leisure interests:* water skiing, tennis, fishing, flying. *Address:* c/o P.G.A. Tour, 100 Avenue of the Champions, Palm Beach Gardens, FL 33410, U.S.A.

PRICE, Paul Buford, PH.D.; American physicist; b. 8 Nov. 1932, Memphis, Tenn.; s. of the late Paul Buford and Eva (Dupuy) Price; m. Jo Ann Baum 1958; one s. three d.; ed. Davidson Coll., Univ. of Virginia, Univ. of Bristol, Univ. of Cambridge; Physicist Gen. Electric Research Lab., New York 1960–69; Visiting Prof. Tata Inst. of Fundamental Research, Bombay, India 1965–66; Adjunct Prof. of Physics Rensselaer Polytechnic Inst. 1967–68; Prof. of Physics Univ. of Calif. at Berkeley 1969–, Chair. Dept. of Physics 1987–91, William H. McAdams Prof. of Physics 1990–92, Dean, Physical Sciences 1992–; Dir. Space Science Lab. 1979–85; NASA Consultant on Lunar Sample Analysis Planning Team; mem. Bd. Dirs. Terradex Corpn. 1978–86; mem. Visiting Cttee., Bartol Research Inst. 1991–94, Advisory Cttee., Indian Inst. of Astrophysics 1993–; Fellow and Chair. Cosmic Physics Div. American Physical Soc.; Fellow American Geophysical Union, American Astronomical Soc.; mem. Space Science Bd., N.A.S., Sec. Physical and Math. Sciences Class of N.A.S. 1985–88, Chair. 1988–91, mem. Steering Group on Future of Space Science (N.A.S.) 1994–; Regional Dir. Calif. Alliance for Minority Participation 1994–; Hon. Sc.D. (Davidson Coll.) 1973; Distinguished Service Award, (American Nuclear Soc.) 1964, Ernest O. Lawrence Memorial Award of Atomic Energy Comm. 1971, NASA Medal for Exceptional Scientific Achievement 1973. *Publications:* (jointly) Nuclear Tracks in Solids, numerous research papers in specialized journals. *Leisure interests:* skiing, travel. *Address:* Physics Department, University of California, Berkeley, 366 LeConte Hall, Berkeley, CA 94720; 1056 Overlook Road, Berkeley, California, U.S.A. *Telephone:* (510) 642-4982 (Office); (510) 548-5206 (Home). *Fax:* (510) 643-8497.

PRIDEAUX, Sir Humphrey Povah Treverbian, Kt., O.B.E., M.A.; British business executive; b. 13 Dec. 1915, London; s. of Walter Treverbian Prideaux and Marion Fenn Prideaux (née Arbuthnot); m. Cynthia V. Birch Reynardson 1939; four s.; ed. St. Aubyns, Eton Coll. and Trinity Coll. Oxford; Regular army officer 1936–53; Dir. Navy, Army & Air Force Insts. 1956–63, Chair. 1963–73; Chair. Lord Wandsworth Foundation 1966–92, Trustee 1963–92; Deputy Chair. Liebig's Extract of Meat Co. Ltd. 1968–69, Dir. 1966–69; Chair. Oxo Ltd. 1968–72; Dir. W. H. Smith & Son (Holdings) Ltd. 1969, Vice-Chair. 1977–81; Dir. Brooke Bond Oxo Ltd. 1969–70; Chair. Brooke Bond Liebig 1972–81; Pres. London Life Asscn Ltd. 1973–83, Dir. 1964–88; Vice-Chair. Morland & Co. 1981–82, Chair. 1983–93; Dir. Grindlays (Holdings) PLC 1982–85; Dir. Grindlays Bank PLC 1984–85. *Leisure interests:* country pursuits. *Address:* Kings Cottage, Buryfields, Odiham, Hook, Hants., RG29 1NE, England. *Telephone:* (01256) 703658.

PRIESTMAN, Jane, O.B.E., F.C.S.D.; British design management consultant; b. 7 April 1930; d. of late Reuben Stanley Herbert and Mary Elizabeth Herbert (née Ramply); m. Arthur Martin Priestman 1954 (divorced 1986); two s.; ed. Northwood Coll., Liverpool Coll. of Art; design practice 1954–75; Design Man., Gen. Man. Architecture and Design British Airports Authority 1975–86; Dir. Architecture and Design British Railways Bd. 1986–91; Visiting Prof. De Montfort Univ. 1997–; mem. London Regional Transport Design Panel 1985–88, Jaguar Styling Panel 1988–91, Percentage for Art Steering Group, Arts Council 1989–91; Council mem., Design Council 1996–; Gov. Commonwealth Inst. 1987–98, Kingston Univ. 1988–96; Hon. F.R.I.B.A., F.R.S.A.; Hon. D.Des. (De Montfort) 1994; Dr h.c. (Sheffield Hallam) 1998. *Leisure interests:* textiles, city architecture, opera, travel. *Address:* 30 Duncan Terrace, London N1 8BS. *Telephone:* 0171-837 4525. *Fax:* 0171-837 4525.

PRIGENT, Michel; French editor; b. 29 Sept. 1950, Paris; s. of Jean Prigent and Germaine Morvan; m. Elisabeth Depierre 1974; two s.; ed. Lycées Henri IV and Louis-le-Grand, Ecole Normale Supérieure and Sorbonne, Paris; joined Presses Universitaires de France 1974, Sec. to Bd. of Dirs. 1978, Editorial Dir. 1985; Prés. du Directoire 1994; Pres. Editeurs de Sciences Humaines et Sociales 1984–90; Officier, Ordre nat. du Mérite. *Publications:* La liberté à refaire 1984, Le héros et l'Etat dans la tragédie de Pierre Corneille 1986. *Leisure interest:* walking. *Address:* Presses Universitaires de France, 108 boulevard Saint-Germain, 75006 Paris (Office); 17 rue de Tournon, 75006 Paris, France (Home). *Telephone:* (01) 46.34.12.01 (Office).

PRIGOGINE, Ilya, Viscount, PH.D.; Belgian university professor; b. 25 Jan. 1917, Moscow, U.S.S.R.; s. of Roman Prigogine and Julia Wichman; m. Marina Prokopowicz 1961; two s.; ed. Univ. Libre de Bruxelles; Prof. at Univ. Libre de Bruxelles 1951–87, Prof. Emer. 1987–; Dir. Instituts Internationaux de Physique et de Chimie 1959–; Extraordinary Chair. Enrico Fermi Inst. for Nuclear Studies and Inst. for the Study of Metals, Univ. of Chicago, U.S.A. 1961–66; Dir. Ilya Prigogine Center for Statistical Mechanics, Thermodynamics and Complex Systems, Univ. of Texas 1967–; Assoc. Dir. of Studies, Ecole des Hautes Etudes en Sciences Sociales, France 1987–; mem. Exec. Council Fondation Erasme, Brussels 1983, Haut Conseil de la Francophonie, Paris 1984–88; Distinguished Visitor, Inst. for Advanced Study, Princeton Univ. 1993; Special Adviser to EC 1993; Hon. Prof. Banarashindu Univ. 1988; Hon. Pres. Univ. Philosophique Européenne, Paris 1985; mem. Académie Royale de Belgique 1958, Pres. Classe des Sciences 1968–70; Foreign Hon. mem. American Acad. of Sciences and Arts 1960; Fellow Acad. of Sciences of New York 1962; mem. Romanian Acad. of Science 1965; mem. Royal Soc. of Sciences, Uppsala, Sweden 1967; Foreign Assoc. N.A.S (U.S.A.) 1967; mem. corresp. de la Soc. Royale des Sciences, Liège 1967; corresp. mem. Class of Physics and Mathematics, Acad. of Sciences, Göttingen 1970, Österreichische Akad. der Wissenschaften, Vienna 1971; mem. Deutsche Akad. der Naturforscher Leopoldina 1970, Acad. Int. de Philosophie des Sciences, Acad. Européenne des Sciences, des Arts et des Lettres, Paris 1980; foreign mem. Akad. der Wissenschaften der D.D.R., Berlin 1980; Hon. mem. Chemical Soc. of Poland 1971, Royal Chem. Soc. (Belgium) 1987, Biophysical Soc. (China); American Chem. Soc. Centennial Foreign Fellow 1976; mem. corresp. of Rheinische Westfälische Akad. der Wissenschaften, Düsseldorf, Foreign Fellow of the Indian National Science Acad. 1979; mem. Bd. Lawrence Hall of Sciences, Univ. of Calif. 1982; mem. Accad. Mediterranea delle Scienze, Catania, Italy 1982; Foreign mem. U.S.S.R. Acad. of Sciences 1982; Extraordinary Scientific mem. Max-Planck Foundation (Fed. Repub. of Germany) 1984; mem. Emer. Academia Europaea G.B. 1989; Dr. h.c. (Univs. of Newcastle-upon-Tyne 1966, Poitiers 1966, Chicago 1969, Bordeaux 1972, Uppsala 1977, Liège 1978, Aix-en-Provence 1978, Georgetown 1980, Rio de Janeiro 1981, Cracow 1981, Stevens Inst. of Tech., Hoboken 1981, Heriot-Watt, Edinburgh 1985, François Rabelais, Tours, 1986, Univs. of Nanjing 1986, Beijing 1986, Buenos Aires 1989, Cagliari, Italy 1990, Minn., U.S.A. 1990, Siena 1990); Prix. Francqui 1955, Prix Solvay 1965; Svante Arrhenius Gold Medal, Acad. Royale des Sciences, Sweden 1969; Bourke Medal, Chemical Soc. 1972, Cothenius Gold Medal, Deutsche Akad. der Naturforscher Leopoldina (Halle) 1975, Rumford Medal 1976, Nobel Prize for Chem. 1977, Médaille Descartes 1979, Honda Prize 1983, Gold Medal, Padua Univ. 1988, Gravity Research Foundation Award for 1988, U.S.A. (with others), Artificial Intelligence Scientific Achievement Award, Tokyo 1990, and numerous other prizes and awards; Commandeur, Ordre des Arts et des Lettres (France), Ordre Nat. du Mérite (France), Légion d'honneur (France), Order of Rising Sun, with Gold and Silver Medal, Japan. *Publications:* Traité de Thermodynamique, conformément aux méthodes de Gibbs et de De Donder (with R. Defay) 1944, 1950, Etude Thermodynamique des Phénomènes Irréversibles 1947, Introduction to Thermodynamics of Irreversible Processes 1962, The Molecular Theory of Solutions (with A. Bellemans and V. Mathot) 1957, Non-Equilibrium Statistical Mechanics 1962, Non-Equilibrium Thermodynamics, Variational Techniques and Stability (with R. J. Donnelly and R. Herman) 1966, Kinetic Theory of Vehicular Traffic (with R. Herman) 1971, Thermodynamic Theory of Structure Stability and Fluctuations (with P. Glansdorff) 1971, Self-Organization in Non Equilibrium systems, from Dissipative Structures to order through fluctuations (with G. Nicolis) 1977, From Being to Becoming, Time and Complexity in the Physical Sciences 1980, La nouvelle alliance, les métamorphoses de la science (with I. Stengers) 1981, Order out of Chaos—Man's new Dialogue with Nature 1984, Exploring Complexity (with G. Nicolis) 1987, Entre le Temps et l'Éternité (with I. Stengers) 1988. *Leisure interests:* music, arts. *Address:* Avenue Fond'Roy 67, 1180 Brussels, Belgium. *Telephone:* (2) 374 2952.

PRIGOV, Dmitry Aleksandrovich; Russian poet and artist; b. 5 Nov. 1940, Moscow; m. Nadezhda Georgiyevna Burova; one s.; ed. Moscow Higher School of Arts; worker Likhachev Automobile Factory 1957–59, 1964; architect Main Dept. of Architecture of Moscow 1967–72; freelance 1972–; has taken part in art exhbns. in Moscow, Leningrad, Jerusalem, Prague, Germany, Italy, U.S.A.; mem. Russian Painters' Union, Russian Writers' Union; Pushkin Prize (Germany). *Publications include:* Tears of Heraldic Soul 1990, Poet Ohne Personlichkeit, Der Militioner und die Andere, Sixty Drops of Blood 1993, The Place of God (play) 1995, The Fifties' ABC (play) 1995, The Appearance of the Verse after its Death (poetry) 1996; publs. in magazines in Russia and other countries. *Address:* Volgina str. 25, korp. 2, Apt 207, 117437 Moscow, Russia (Home). *Telephone:* 330 4950 (Home). *Fax:* 330 4950 (Home).

PRIMAKOV, Yevgeniy Maksimovich, D.ECON.; Russian politician and economist; b. 29 Oct. 1929, Kiev; m.; one d.; ed. Moscow Inst. of Oriental Studies; worked for State Comm. on Broadcasting and Television 1953–62; mem. CPSU 1959–91; Columnist and Deputy Ed. (Asia and Africa Desk), Pravda 1962–70; Deputy Dir. Inst. of World Econ. and Int. Relations, U.S.S.R. (now Russian) Acad. of Sciences 1970–77, Dir. 1985–, Dir. Inst. of Oriental Studies 1977–85; elected to Congress of People's Deputies of the U.S.S.R. 1989; mem. CPSU Cen. Cttee. 1989–91; cand. mem. Politburo 1989–90; Chair. Soviet of the Union June 1989–March 1990; mem. Presidential Council 1989–90; Pres. Gorbachev's Special Envoy to Gulf 1990–91; Dir. Central Intelligence Service of U.S.S.R. 1991, Foreign Intelligence Service of Russian Fed. 1991–96; Minister of Foreign Affairs 1996–98; Chair of Govt. (Prime Minister) 1998–99; Chair. Exec. Council of Russia and Belarus Union 1998–99; mem. Security Council 1996–; corresp. mem. U.S.S.R. (now Russian) Acad. of Sciences 1974, mem. 1979, Acad.-Sec., mem. of Presidium 1988–91; specialist on Egypt and other Arab countries; Chief Ed. of and contributor to a number of collective works, including: International Conflicts 1972, The Energy Crisis in the Capitalist World 1975, Nasser Prize 1975, U.S.S.R. State Prize 1980. *Publications include:* Egypt under Nasser (with I. P. Belyayev) 1975, The War Which Could Be Avoided 1991. *Address:* c/o Government of Russia, Krasnopresnenskaya Embankment 2, 103274 Moscow, Russia.

PRIMAROLO, Dawn; British politician; b. 2 May 1954; m. 1st 1972 (divorced); one s.; m. 2nd Thomas Ian Ducat 1990; ed. Thomas Bennett Comprehensive School, Crawley, Bristol Polytechnic, Bristol Univ.; mem. Avon Co. Council 1985–87; M.P. for Bristol S. 1987–; Opposition Front Bench Spokesman on Health 1992–94, on Treasury Affairs 1994–97; Financial Sec. H.M. Treasury 1997–98, Paymaster Gen. 1998–; Labour. *Address:* House of Commons, London, SW1A 0AA; P.O. Box 1002, Bristol, BS99 1WH, England. *Telephone:* (0117) 909-0063 (Bristol).

PRIMATESTA, H.E. Cardinal Raúl Francisco; Argentinian ecclesiastic; b. 14 April 1919, Capilla del Señor; ordained 1942; consecrated titular Bishop of Tanais 1957; Bishop of San Rafael 1961–65; Archbishop of Córdoba 1965–; created Cardinal by Pope Paul VI 1973; mem. Congregation for the Clergy. *Address:* Arzobispado, Avenida H. Irigoyen 98, 5000 Córdoba, Argentina. *Telephone:* (51) 422-1015. *Fax:* (51) 425-5082.

PRINCE (Prince Rogers Nelson); American musician and actor; b. 7 June 1958, Minneapolis; s. of John L. Nelson and Mattie (née Shaw) Nelson; m. Mayte Garcia 1996; one s. (deceased); singer, songwriter and actor; recipient three Grammy awards 1985; mem. Prince and the Revolution. *Albums include:* For You 1978, Dirty Mind 1979, Controversy 1981, 1999 1983, Purple Rain 1984, Around the World in a Day 1985 (Best Soul/Rhythm and Blues Album of the Year, Down Beat Readers' Poll 1985), Parade 1986, Sign of the Times 1987, Lovesexy 1988, Batman (film soundtrack) 1989, Diamonds and Pearls 1991, (symbol as title) 1992, Come 1994. *Films include:* Purple Rain 1984 (Acad. Award for Best Original Score), Under the Cherry Moon 1986, Grafitti Bridge 1990. *Address:* Warner Bros. Records, 75 Rockefeller Plaza, New York, NY 10019, U.S.A.

PRINCE, Harold (Hal), LITT.D.; American theatrical director; b. 30 Jan. 1928, New York; s. of Milton A. and Blanche (Stern) Prince; m. Judith Chaplin 1962; one s. one d.; ed. Emerson Coll.; co-produced Pajama Game 1954–56 (Antoinette Perry Award), Damn Yankees 1955–57 (Antoinette Perry Award), New Girl in Town 1957–58, West Side Story 1957–59, Fiorello! 1959–61 (Antoinette Perry Award, Pulitzer Prize), Tenderloin 1960–61, A Call on Kuprin 1961, They Might Be Giants 1961, Side by Side by Sondheim 1976; produced Take Her, She's Mine 1961–62, A Funny thing Happened on the Way to the Forum 1962–64 (Antoinette Perry Award), Fiddler on the Roof 1964–72 (Antoinette Perry Award), Poor Bitos 1964, Flora the Red Menace 1965; dir., producer She Loves Me! 1963–64, London 1964, Superman 1966, Cabaret 1966–69 (Antoinette Perry Award), London 1968, Zorba 1968–69, Company 1970–72 (Antoinette Perry Award), London 1972, A Little Night Music 1973–74 (Antoinette Perry Award) (London 1975), Pacific Overtures 1976; co-dir., producer Follies 1971–72; co-producer, dir. Candide 1974–75, Merrily We Roll Along 1981; dir. A Family Affair 1962, Baker Street 1965, Great God Brown 1972–73, The Visit 1973–74, Love for Love 1974–75, On the Twentieth Century 1978, Evita, London 1978, Broadway 1979, Los Angeles 1980, Chicago 1980, Australia 1980, Vienna 1981, Mexico City 1981, Sweeney Todd, the Demon Barber of Fleet Street 1979–80, London 1980, A Doll's Life 1982, Diamonds 1984, Grind 1985, The Phantom of the Opera (Tony Award for Best Dir. 1988) 1986, Play Memory, End of the World, Rosa 1987, Grandchild of Kings (The O'Casey Project) (author and dir.) 1992, Kiss of the Spider Woman (Toronto, London) 1992, (New York, Vienna) 1993, Show Boat (Toronto) 1993, (New York) 1994, (nat. tour) 1996, Candide 1997, Parade 1998. *Operas:* Ashmedai 1976, Silverlake 1980, Don Giovanni 1989 (New York City Opera); Madame Butterfly 1982; Candide 1982; Willie Stark 1982 (Houston Opera Co.); Turandot 1983 (Vienna Staatsoper); Faust 1990, 1991 (Metropolitan Opera), La Fanciulla del West 1991 (Chicago Lyric Opera, San Francisco Opera); co-producer films The Pajama Game 1957, Damn Yankees 1958; dir. films Something for Everyone 1970, A Little Night Music 1978; mem. Council, Nat. Endowment Arts, League of New York Theatres; Critic Circle awards, Best Music Award, Evening Standard; Commonwealth Award 1982; John F. Kennedy Center Awards 1994. *Address:* Suite 1009, 10 Rockefeller Plaza, New York, NY 10020, U.S.A.

PRINGLE, James Robert Henry, M.A.; British economist and journalist; b. 27 Aug. 1939, Surrey; s. of John and Jacqueline (née Berry) Pringle; m. Rita Schuchard 1966; ed. King's School, Canterbury, King's Coll., Cambridge, and London School of Econs.; asst. to Ed., then Asst. Ed. The Banker, London 1963–67; mem. editorial staff The Economist, London 1968; Asst. Dir., later Deputy Dir. Cttee. on Invisible Exports 1969–72; Ed. The Banker 1972–79; Exec. Dir. Group of Thirty, Consultative Group on Int. Econ. and Monetary Affairs, New York 1979–86; Sr. Fellow, World Inst. for Devt. Econs. Research of the UN Univ. 1986–89; Sr. Research Fellow, the David Hume Inst. Edin. 1989–91; Dir. Graham Bannock and Partners 1989–97; Ed.-in-Chief, Central Banking 1990–; Head, Public Policy Centre, The World Gold Council 1997–. *Publications:* Banking in Britain 1973, The Growth Merchants 1977, The Central Banks (Co-author) 1994, International Financial Institutions 1998. *Leisure interests:* classical music, the theatre. *Address:* 27 Peel Street, London, W8 7PA, England. *Telephone:* 0171-727 5801.

PRIOR, Baron (Life Peer), cr. 1987, of Brampton in the County of Suffolk; **James Michael Leathes Prior,** P.C.; British politician and farmer; b. 11 Oct. 1927, Norwich; s. of the late C. B. L. Prior and A. S. M. Prior; m. Jane P. G. Lywood 1954; three s. one d.; ed. Charterhouse and Pembroke Coll., Cambridge; M.P. for Lowestoft 1959–83, for Waveney 1983–87; Parl. Private Sec. to Pres. of Bd. of Trade 1963, to Minister of Power 1963–64, to Rt. Hon. Edward Heath 1965–70; Vice-Chair. Conservative Party 1965, 1972–74; Minister of Agric., Fisheries and Food 1970–72, Lord Pres. of Council 1972–74; Shadow Spokesman on Home Affairs March–June 1974, on Employment June 1974–79; Sec. of State for Employment 1979–81, for Northern Ireland 1981–84; Chair. GEC 1984–98; Dir. Barclays PLC 1984–89, J. Sainsbury PLC 1984–92, United Biscuits 1974–79, 1984–94; mem. Tenneco European Advisory Council 1986–97, AIG Advisory Council; Dir. Arab-British Chamber of Commerce; Chair. Royal Veterinary Coll.; Chancellor Anglia Polytechnic Univ. *Publication:* A Balance of Power 1986. *Leisure interests:* cricket, tennis, golf, gardening. *Address:* House of Lords, London, SW1A 0PW, England.

PRISTAVKIN, Anatoliy Ignatevich; Russian author and government official; b. 17 Oct. 1931, Lyubertsy, Moscow; m. 1st V. Golubkova 1960 (divorced 1975); one s. one d.; m. 2nd Mary Berejnaya 1986; one d.; ed. Gorky Inst. of Literature; first works published 1956; Prof., Gorky Inst. of Literature 1981–; Leader of April Independent Asscn. of Writers 1989–; Chair. Comm. for Grace, under Pres. of Russian Fed. 1992; U.S.S.R. State Prize 1987, Deutsche Jugendliteratur Prize 1991. *Publications:* Little Stories 1959, A Lyrical Book 1969, A Golden Cloud (Nochevala tuchka zolotaya) 1987, The Small Cuckoos 1989, Ryazanka 1990, The Small Cuckoos 1995. *Address:* Leningradskij prosp. 26-2, apt. 53, Moscow, Russia. *Telephone:* 206-43-60 (Office); 212-82-36 (Home). *Fax:* 206-43-38.

PRITCHARD, David E., PH.D.; American professor of physics; b. 15 Oct. 1941, New York; s. of Edward M. Pritchard and Blanche M. Allen Pritchard; m. Andrea Hasler; two s.; ed. California Inst. of Tech. and Harvard Univ.; Postdoctoral Fellow, MIT, Cambridge, Mass. 1968, instructor 1968–70, Asst. Prof. 1970–75, Assoc. Prof. 1975–80, Prof. of Physics 1980–; Div. Assoc. Ed. Physics Review Letters 1983–88; Distinguished Traveling Lecturer LSTG/ American Physical Soc. (A.P.S.) 1991–93; Fellow A.A.A.S., A.P.S., American Acad. of Arts and Sciences; Broida Prize, A.P.S. 1991. *Publications:* numerous scientific papers, articles and contribs. to books. *Leisure interests:* piano playing, sailing. *Address:* Department of Physics, Massachusetts Institute of Technology, 77 Massachusetts Avenue, Room 26–237, Cambridge, MA 02139, U.S.A. *Telephone:* (617) 253-6812. *Fax:* (617) 253-4876.

PRLIĆ, Jadranko; Croat politician and university professor; b. 10 June 1959, Djakovo; m. Ankica Prlić; two d.; ed. Univs. of Mostar and Sarajevo; worked as a journalist; joined teaching staff Univ. of Mostar 1987; Chair. governing Council of Mostar 1987–88; fmr. Gen. Man. Apro-Mostar agricultural enterprise; Vice-Pres. Govt. of Bosnia and Herzegovina 1992–94; following signing of Washington (1994) and Dayton (1995) Agreements: Deputy Prime Minister and Minister of Defence; mem. Parl. of Bosnia and Herzegovina and Minister of Foreign Affairs Feb. 1996–. *Publications:* Policy of Fluctuating Foreign Exchange Rates 1990; numerous articles in field of int. economy, particularly finance, and political issues. *Leisure interests:* tennis, soccer, econ. and political literature, etc. *Address:* Ministry of Foreign Affairs, Musala Street 2, 71000 Sarajevo, Bosnia and Herzegovina. *Telephone:* (071) 667 979. *Fax:* (071) 444 766.

PROBST, Raymond R., DR.IUR.; Swiss diplomatist (retd.); b. 6 March 1919, Geneva; s. of Friedrich Probst and Suzanna Guigovsky; m. Annemarie Rey 1945; one s. one d.; ed. Univ. of Berne; Attaché, Dept. of Foreign Affairs 1942–47; Second Sec., Athens 1947–52; First Sec. Washington, D.C. 1952–56; Head, Political Div. West, Dept. of Foreign Affairs 1956–66; Amb. and del. of Swiss Govt. for Trade Rels. 1966–76; Amb. to U.S.A. 1976–80; Sec. of State for Foreign Affairs 1980–84; Hon. Pres. Swiss Foreign Relations Asscn.; fmr. Vice-Chair. Hoffman La Roche, Basle; fmr. mem. Bd. Financière Crédit Suisse-First Boston; Hon. mem. Int. Cttee. of Red Cross, Geneva; mem. Bd. Swiss Archaeological School in Greece; Adviser to Ministry of Foreign Affairs, Latvia, Oct.–Nov. 1991. *Publications:* "Good Offices" in the Light of Swiss International Practice and Experience 1989, and several other publs. on defence matters, foreign affairs, int. law etc.; Co-Ed. Schweiz. Handbuch für Aussenpolitik. *Leisure interests:* reading, art, skiing, swimming. *Address:* Brunnadernstrasse 76, 3006 Berne, Switzerland. *Telephone:* (31) 352.45.91.

PROCHNOW, Herbert Victor, B.A., M.A., PH.D.; American banker and writer; b. 18 May 1897, Wilton, Wisconsin; m. Laura Virginia Stinson 1928 (died 1977); one s.; ed. Univ. of Wisconsin and Northwestern Univ.; with First Nat. Bank of Chicago 1929–73, rising from asst. cashier to Dir. 1960–68, Pres. 1962–68, Hon. Dir. 1968–73; Sec. Fed. Advisory Council of Fed. Reserve System 1945–94; Consultant to Sec. of State 1955, 1957; Deputy Under-Sec. of State for Econ. Affairs 1955–56; Alt. Gov. for U.S. of World Bank and IMF 1955–56; Dir. Annual Summer Graduate School of Banking, Univ. of Wisconsin 1945–82; Chair. U.S. Del. Gen. Agreement on Tariffs and Trade,

Geneva 1956; fmr. Asst. Prof. Business Admin., Indiana Univ., lectured Loyola and Northwestern Univs.; financial columnist, Chicago Tribune 1968–70; Pres. Chicago Asscn. of Commerce and Industry 1964, 1965; Commdr. of the Order of Vasa of Royal Govt. of Sweden 1965, Commdr., Cross of the Order of Merit of Germany 1968; several awards and hon. degrees. *Publications:* The Public Speaker's Treasure Chest (with Herbert V. Prochnow, Jr.) 1942, 1964, 1977, 1986, Great Stories from Great Lives 1944, Meditations on the Ten Commandments 1946, The Toastmaster's Handbook 1949, Term Loans and Theories of Bank Liquidity 1949, The Successful Speaker's Handbook 1951, 1001 Ways to Improve your Conversation and Speeches 1952, Meditations on the Beatitudes 1952, The Speaker's Treasury of Stories for all Occasions 1953, Speaker's Handbook of Epigrams and Witticisms 1955, Speaker's Treasury for Sunday School Teachers 1955, The Toastmaster's and Speaker's Handbook 1955, A Treasury of Stories, Illustrations, Epigrams and Quotations for Ministers and Teachers 1957, Meditations on the Lord's Prayer 1957 (as Inspirational Thoughts on the Lord's Prayer 1970), The New Guide for Toastmasters and Speakers 1956, A Family Treasury of Inspiration and Faith 1958, 1991, The New Speaker's Treasury of Wit and Wisdom 1958, The Complete Toastmaster 1960, Effective Public Speaking 1960, Speaker's Book of Illustrations 1960, A Dictionary of Wit, Wisdom and Satire (with Herbert V. Prochnow, Jr.) 1962, 1000 Tips and Quips for Speakers and Toastmasters 1962, 1992, Practical Bank Credit (co-author) 1963, 1400 Ideas for Speakers and Toastmasters 1964, The Successful Toastmaster (with Herbert V. Prochnow, Jr.) 1966, A Treasury of Humorous Quotations (with Herbert V. Prochnow, Jr.), A Speaker's Treasury for Educators, Convocation Speakers, etc., A Tree of Life, Speakers' Source Book, 1001 Quips, Stories and Illustrations for All Occasions 1973, The Speaker's and Toastmaster's Handbook 1973, 1993, The Changing World of Banking (with Herbert V. Prochnow, Jr.) 1974; co-author: The Next Century is America's 1938; editor American Financial Institutions 1951, Determining the Business Outlook 1954, The Federal Reserve System 1960, World Economic Problems and Policies 1965, The Five-Year Outlook for Interest Rates 1968, The One-Bank Holding Company 1969, The Eurodollar 1970, The Five-Year Outlook for Interest Rates in the U.S. and Abroad 1972, Dilemmas Facing the Nation 1979, The Toastmaster's Treasure Chest (with Herbert V. Prochnow Jr.) 1979, 1988, Bank Credit 1981, A Treasure Chest of Quotations for All Occasions 1983, Toastmaster's Quips and Stories 1983. *Address:* 1 First National Plaza, Chicago, IL 60603 (Office); 2950 Harrison Street, Evanston, IL 60201, U.S.A. (Home).

PROCKTOR, Patrick, R.A., R.W.S.; British artist; b. 12 March 1936, Dublin; s. of Eric C. Procktor and Barbara W. Hopkins; m. Kirsten Andersen 1973 (died 1984); one s.; ed. Highgate School and Slade School; one-man exhbns. Redfern Gallery 1963–; designer of windows for AIDS recreation centre, St. Stephen's Hosp. Fulham 1988; retrospective tour, England and Wales 1990; poster for Antony and Cleopatra and exhbn. at Royal Nat. Theatre. *Publications:* One Window in Venice 1974, Coleridge's Rime of the Ancient Mariner (new illustrated edn.) 1976, A Chinese Journey (aquatint landscapes) 1980, Sailing through China by Paul Theroux (illustrations), Patrick Procktor Prints 1959–85 (catalogue raisonné) 1985, A Shropshire Lad by A. E. Housman (new illustrated edn.) 1986, Self-Portrait (memoir) 1991, P.P. by John McEwen (illustrations) 1997. *Leisure interest:* Russian ballet. *Address:* 26 Manchester Street, London, W1M 5PG, England. *Telephone:* 0171-486 1763.

PROCTER, Jane Hilary Elizabeth; British journalist; b. London; d. of Gordon H. Procter and Florence Bibby Procter; m. Thomas C. Goldstaub 1985; one s. one d.; ed. Queen's Coll. Harley St. London; ed. Tatler 1990–. *Publication:* Dress Sense. *Leisure interests;* skiing, sailing. *Address:* Tatler, Vogue House, 1 Hanover Square, London, W1R 0AD, England. *Telephone:* 0171-499 9080.

PRODI, Romano; Italian politician; b. 1939; m. Flavia Prodi Franzoni; two s.; ed. Catholic Univ. of Milan; Prof. of Econs. and Industrial Policy, Univ. of Bologna 1971–; Minister of Industry 1978–79; Chair. Scientific Cttee. Econ. Research Inst. Nomisma, Bologna 1981–95; Chair. Istituto per le Ricostruzione Industriale (IRI) 1982–89, 1993–94; Prof. of Industrial Org. and Policy, Univ. of Bologna 1990–93; f. l'Olivo (coalition of centre-left parties) 1995; Pres. Council of Ministers (Prime Minister) 1996–98; Pres. (desig.) European Comm. 1999–; mem. Asscn. di cultura e politica, Il Mulino, Bologna, Asscn. Italiana degli Economisti, Rome; Hon. mem. Real Academia de Ciencias Morales y Políticas, Madrid; Hon. Fellow L.S.E.; numerous hon. degrees. *Publications:* author of numerous scientific publs. with particular reference to questions of European industrial policies, public enterprises in Italy and comparative analysis of econ. systems. *Address:* Commission of the European Communities, 200 rue de la Loi, 1049 Brussels, Belgium. *Telephone:* (2) 299-11-11. *Fax:* (2) 295-01-38.

PROFUMO, John Dennis, C.B.E.; British fmr. politician; b. 30 Jan. 1915; s. of the late Baron Albert Profumo, K.C.; m. Valerie Hobson 1954; one s.; ed. Harrow, Brasenose Coll., Oxford; with 1st Northamptonshire Yeomanry 1939; Brig. Chief of Staff, U.K. Mission in Japan 1945; M.P. (Kettering Div.) 1940–45, (Stratford-on-Avon) 1950–63; Parl. Sec., Ministry of Transport and Civil Aviation 1952–57, Parl. Under-Sec. of State for the Colonies 1957–58, for Foreign Affairs 1958–59; Minister of State for Foreign Affairs 1959–60; Sec. of State for War 1960–63; Dir. Provident Life Asscn. of London 1975–, Deputy Chair. 1978–82; mem. Bd. of Visitors, H.M. Prison, Grendon 1968–75; Chair. Toynbee Hall 1982–85, Pres. 1985–. *Leisure interests:* fishing, gardening, do-it-yourself.

PROKEŠ, Jozef, D.SC.; Slovak politician; b. 12 June 1950, Nitra; s. of Jozef Prokeš and Elena Manicová; m. 1979; one s. one d.; ed. Komenský Univ., Bratislava –1973; research student with Inst. of Physics, Slovak Acad. of Sciences, Bratislava 1973–82; worked for Heavy Current Electrotechnical Works, Čab 1982–85; research worker Inst. of Measurements, Slovak Acad. of Sciences, Bratislava 1985–89; co-f. Forum of Coordinating Cttees. of Workers in Slovakia 1989; Chair. Independent Trade Unions 1990; Chair. Trade Union of Research Workers of Slovak Acad. of Sciences 1990; Deputy to Slovak Nat. Council 1990–92; Chair. Slovak Nat. Party (SNP) 1991–92, Hon. Chair. 1992–; Vice-Pres., Slovak Nat. Council 1992–93; Deputy Premier of Slovak Govt. 1993–94; Deputy to Nat. Council 1994–; Vice-Chair. Foreign Cttee. of Nat. Council 1994–98; Head Slovak del. to CSCE 1993–94; mem. Slovak del. to WEU 1995. *Address:* National Council of the Slovak Republic, Mudroňova 1, 812 80 Bratislava, Slovakia.

PROKHOROV, Aleksandr Mikhailovich; Russian physicist; b. 11 July 1916, Atherton, Australia; s. of Mikhail Ivanovich Prokhorov and Mariya Ivanovna Prokhorova; m. Galina Alekseyevna Shelepina; one s.; ed. Leningrad State Univ.; Physicist, P. N. Lebedev Inst. of Physics, U.S.S.R. Acad. of Sciences 1946–83, Vice-Dir. 1972; Academician-Sec., Section Physics and Astronomy, U.S.S.R. (now Russian) Acad. of Sciences 1973–; Corresp. mem. U.S.S.R. (now Russian) Acad. of Sciences (Dept. of Pure and Applied Physics) 1960–66, mem. 1966, mem. Presidium (Academician-Sec.) 1973–; Dir. Gen. Physics Inst. 1983–; mem. American Acad. of Arts and Sciences 1971; mem. CPSU 1950–91; a pioneer in field of quantum electronics; Lenin Prize 1959; Chair. Soviet Nat. Cttee. U.R.S.I.; Ed.-in-Chief of Soviet (now Russian) Encyclopaedia 1969–; Nobel Prize for Physics for work in field of quantum electronics 1964; Lomonosov Gold Medal 1988; Hero of Socialist Labour 1969, 1986, Order of Lenin (twice), and other decorations. *Publications:* works on paramagnetic lasers, open resonators, gas-dynamic and solid-state lasers, powerful infrared and visible spectrum lasers, nonlinear optics, interactions of powerful laser irradiation with matter. *Address:* General Physics Institute, 38 Vavilov Str., 117942 Moscow, Russia. *Telephone:* 135-13-31; 231-23-31 (Office); 146-96-02 (Home).

PROSSER, Sir Ian Maurice Gray, Kt., B. COMM., F.C.A., C.B.I.M.; British business executive; b. 5 July 1943, Bath; s. of Maurice and Freda Prosser; m. Elizabeth Herman 1964; two d.; ed. King Edward's School, Bath, Watford Grammar School and Univ. of Birmingham; Cooper Bros. (chartered accts.) 1964–69; Bass Charrington Ltd. 1969–82, Financial Dir. 1978; Vice-Chair. and Financial Dir. Bass PLC 1982–84, Vice-Chair. and Group Man. Dir. 1984–87, Chair. and C.E.O. 1987–; Chair. The Brewers' Soc.; Dir. Lloyds TSB Group PLC 1988–, BP 1997–. *Leisure interests:* bridge, gardening. *Address:* Bass PLC, 20 North Audley Street, London, W1Y 1WE, England. *Telephone:* 0171-409 1919.

PROST, Alain Marie Pascal; French motor racing team owner and fmr. racing driver; b. 24 Feb. 1955, Lorette; s. of André Prost and Marie-Rose Karatchian; two s.; ed. Coll. Sainte-Marie, Saint-Chamond; French and European Champion, Go-Kart Racing 1973, French Champion 1974–75; French and European Champion, Formula Three Racing 1979; joined Marlboro MacLaren Group 1980; winner French, Netherlands and Italian Grand Prix 1981; World Champion 1985, 1986, 1989, 1993; winner Brazilian, French, Mexican, Spanish and British Grand Prix 1990, South African, San Marino, Spanish, European, Canadian, French, British, German Grand Prix 1993; Silverstone Grand Prix 1993; Estoril Grand Prix; 51 Grand Prix wins; technical consultant to McLaren Mercedes 1995; f. Prost Grand Prix team 1997; Officier, Légion d'honneur; Hon. O.B.E. 1994. *Address:* Prost-Grand Prix, 7 avenue Eugène Freyssinet, 78286 Guyancourt Cedex, France.

PROTHEROE, Alan Hackford, C.B.E., T.D., D.L., F.INST.M.; British journalist and broadcasting executive; b. 10 Jan. 1934, St. David's, Wales; s. of Rev. B. P. Protheroe and R. C. M. Protheroe; m. Anne Miller 1956; two s.; ed. Maesteg Grammar School, Glamorgan; Reporter, Glamorgan Gazette 1951–53; 2nd Lieut., The Welch Regt. 1954–56; Reporter, BBC Wales 1957–59, Industrial Corresp. 1959–64, Ed. News and Current Affairs 1964–70; Asst. Ed., BBC TV News 1970–72, Deputy Ed. 1972–77, Ed. 1977–80; Asst. Dir. BBC News and Current Affairs 1980–82; Asst. Dir.-Gen. BBC 1982–87; Man. Dir. The Services Sound and Vision Corpn. 1987–94; Founder-mem. Asscn. of British Eds., Chair. 1987; Chair. Europac Group Ltd.; Dir. Visnews Ltd. 1982–87; Dir. Defence Public Affairs Consultants Ltd. 1987–; Chair. Europac Group Ltd 1990–, Challenger Marketing Communications 1996–; rank of Hon. Col. T.A. 1991–96; Chair. E. Wessex Reserve Forces Asscn.; mem. Inst. of Public Relations; mem. Man. Bd. Royal British Legion; Deputy Lieut. for Bucks. *Publications:* contribs. to journals on media and defence affairs. *Leisure interests:* travel, photography. *Address:* Amberleigh House, Chapman Lane, Flackwell Heath, Bucks., HP10 9BD, England. *Telephone:* (01628) 528492. *Fax:* (01628) 533209.

PROTOPAPAS, Nakos; Cypriot politician and fmr. civil engineer; b. 27 Aug. 1927, Phrenaros Village, Famagusta Dist.; s. of Gabriel Protopapas and Paulina Protopapa; m. Theodora Konstandopoulou 1953; three s.; ed. Paphos Gymnasium, Civil Eng. Inst. of Moscow, and Lomonosov Univ., U.S.S.R., Int. Inst. of Seismic Eng., Milan Polytechnic, Italy; studies also in Hungary and U.K.; pvt. practice 1962–64; joined Public Works Dept., Ministry of Communications and Works 1964, Nicosia Dist. Engineer 1984–87, retd. as Sr. Exec. Engineer 1987; Minister of Communications and Works 1988–90; pvt. practice 1990–; consultant to various cos. in Cyprus and abroad; Pres. Cyprus Civil Engineers' and Architects' Asscn. 1974–88; Vice-Pres. Civil Servants' Trade Union 1985–. *Leisure interests:* reading, theatre, music, sports, jogging, swimming. *Address:* Nicodemou Mylona 30, Flat No. 6, Nicosia, Cyprus. *Telephone:* (2) 477474. *Fax:* (2) 366425.

PROULX, Edna Ann (E. Annie), M.A.; American writer; b. 22 Aug. 1935, Norwich, Conn.; d. of George Napoleon Proulx and Lois Nellie Gill; m. 3rd James H. Lang 1969 (divorced 1990); three s. one d.; ed. Sir George Williams (now Concordia) Univ., Montreal and Univ. of Vermont; freelance journalist, Vt. 1975–87; f. Vershire Behind the Times newspaper, Vershire, Vt.; short stories appeared in Blair & Ketchums Country Journal, Esquire, etc.; Vt. Council Arts Fellowship 1989, Ucross Foundation Residency, Wyo. 1990, 1992; mem. PEN; Guggenheim Fellow 1993; active anti-illiteracy campaigner; Hon. Dr. Hum. Litt. (Maine) 1994; stories listed in Best American Short Stories 1983, 1987; Alumni Achievement Award, Univ. of Vt. 1994, New York Public Library Literary Lion 1994, Dos Passos Prize for Literature 1996, American Acad. of Achievement Award 1998. *Publications:* Heart Songs and Other Stories 1988, Postcards 1992 (PEN/Faulkner Award for Fiction 1993), The Shipping News 1993 (Chicago Tribune's Heartland Prize for Fiction, Irish Times Int. Fiction Prize, Nat. Book Award for Fiction (all 1993), Pulitzer Prize for Fiction 1994), Accordion Crimes 1996, Best American Short Stories of 1997 (Ed.); numerous articles. *Leisure interests:* fly fishing, canoeing, playing the fiddle. *Address:* P.O. Box 230, Centennial, WY 82055, U.S.A. *Fax:* (307) 742-6159.

PROXMIRE, William, M.A.; American politician (retd.); b. 11 Nov. 1915, Lake Forest, Ill.; s. of Theodore Stanley and Adele (Flanigan) Proxmire; m. Ellen Hodges; ed. Yale and Harvard Univs.; U.S. Army Intelligence Service 1941–46; State Assemblyman (Dem.) for Wisconsin 1951–52; Senator from Wisconsin 1957–89; Chair. Senate Banking Cttee. 1975–81; Pres. Artcraft Press, Waterloo, Wisconsin 1954–57; Commentator NBC 1989–; Democrat. *Publications:* Can Small Business Survive?, Uncle Sam, Last of the Big Time Spenders, You Can Do It!, The Fleecing of America, Your Joy Ride to Health 1993.

PRUNSKIENĖ, Kazimiera, D.ECON.SCI.; Lithuanian politician; b. 26 Feb. 1943, Shvenchioniu Region; d. of Ona Stankevičienė and Pranas Stankevičius; m. 1st Povilas Prunskus 1961; m. 2nd Algimantas Tarvydas 1990 (divorced); one s. two d.; ed. Vilnius State Univ.; teacher, then Dean of Faculty, Vilnius State Univ. 1965–85; Deputy Dir. Inst. of Econ. Agric. 1986–88; People's Deputy of the U.S.S.R. 1989–90, mem. U.S.S.R. Supreme Soviet 1989–90; Deputy Chair. Council of Ministers of Lithuania 1989–90, Chair. 1990–91; mem. Lithuanian Parl. 1990–92, 1996–; Pres. Lithuanian-European Inst. 1991–; Pres. pvt. consulting firm K. Prunskienė-Consulting 1993–; Founder and Pres. Lithuanian Women's Asscn. (now Party) 1992–, Chair. 1995–; mem. CEPS Int. Advisory Council 1992–, Int. Cttee. for Econ. Reform and Co-operation 1994–; Pres. Baltic Women's Basketball League 1994–; mem. Council of Women World Leaders 1997–. *Publications:* Amber Lady's Confession 1991, Leben für Litauen 1992, Behind the Scenes 1992, Challenge to Dragon 1992, Price of Liberation 1993, Markt Balticum 1994, Transformation, Co-operation and Conversion 1996, Science and Technology Policy of the Baltic States and International Co-operation 1997, Intellectual Property Rights in Central and Eastern Europe: the Creation of Favourable Legal and Market Preconditions 1998. *Leisure interests:* sports, music, literature, knitting, cooking, walking in the forest. *Address:* Lithuanian-European Institute, Vilniaus st. 45-13, 2001 Vilnius (Office); Kriviu 53a-13, 2007 Vilnius, Lithuania (Home). *Telephone:* (02) 222 114, 222 834 (Office). *Fax:* (02) 221 955.

PRYCE, George Terry, C.B.E.; British business executive; b. 24 March 1934, Montgomery; s. of Edwin Pryce and Hilda Florence Pryce (née Price); m. Thurza Elizabeth Tatham 1957; two s. one d.; ed. Welshpool Boys' Grammar School, Nat. Coll. of Food Technology; various man. positions in food industry; Tech. Dir. a large nat. frozen food co. early 1960s; Man. Dir. numerous cos. in food processing and mfg. industry 1965–; Asst. Man. Dir. Dalgety (U.K.) Ltd. 1970–71, Man. Dir. 1971, mem. Bd. 1972, Chair. 1978–89; Dir. Dalgety Ltd. 1972–89, Man. Dir. 1978–81, Chief Exec. 1981–89; Chair. Dalgety Spillers Ltd. 1980–89; Chief Exec. Dalgety PLC 1981–89; Chair. Solway Foods Ltd. 1990–94, Horticulture Research Int. Ltd. 1990–97, York House Group Ltd. 1995–, G. T. Pryce (Farms) Ltd.; Dir. H. P. Bulmer Holdings PLC 1984–94, Jas Bowman & Sons Ltd. 1991–; Fellow Inst. of Food, Science and Tech.; Gov. Nat. Coll. of Food Tech. 1981–. *Leisure interest:* golf. *Address:* 89 Brookmans Avenue, Brookmans Park, Hatfield, Herts., AL9 7QG, England.

PRYCE, Jonathan; British actor; b. 1 June 1947, North Wales; s. of Isaac Price and Margaret Ellen Price (née Williams); partner Kate Fahy; two s. one d.; ed. Royal Acad. of Dramatic Art; Patron Friends United Network. *Stage appearances include:* The Comedians, Nottingham Old Vic 1975, New York 1976 (Tony Award), Hamlet, Royal Court Theatre, London (Olivier Award) 1980, The Caretaker, Nat. Theatre 1981, Accidental Death of an Anarchist, Broadway 1984, The Seagull, Queen's Theatre 1985, Macbeth, RSC 1986, Uncle Vanya 1988, Miss Saigon, Drury Lane 1989 (Olivier and Variety Club Awards) 1991, New York (Tony and Drama Desk Awards), Oliver!, London Palladium 1994. *Television appearances in:* Roger Doesn't Live Here Anymore (series) 1981, Timon of Athens 1981, Martin Luther 1983, Praying Mantis 1983, Whose Line Is It Anyway? 1988, The Man from the Pru 1990, Selling Hitler 1991, Mr Wroe's Virgins 1993, Thicker than Water 1993. *Films include:* Something Wicked This Way Comes 1982, The Ploughman's Lunch 1983, Brazil 1985, The Doctor and the Devils 1986, Haunted Honeymoon 1986, Jumpin' Jack Flash 1987, Consuming Passions 1988, The Adventures of Baron Munchausen 1988, The Rachel Papers 1989, Glen Garry Glen Ross 1992, Barbarians at the Gate 1992, Great Moments in Aviation 1993, The Age of Innocence 1993, A Business Affair 1993, Deadly Advice 1994, Carrington 1995 (Best Actor, Cannes Film Festival 1995, Best Actor, Evening Standard Film Awards 1996), Evita 1996, Tomorrow Never Dies 1997, Regeneration 1997, Ronin 1998. *Recordings:* Miss Saigon 1989, Nine—The Concert 1992, Under Milkwood 1992, Cabaret 1994, Oliver! 1995. *Leisure interests:* painting, drawing. *Address:* c/o Julian Belfrage Assocs., 46 Albemarle Street, London, W1X 4PP, England; c/o Paradigm, 200 W. 57th Street, Suite 900, New York, NY 10019, U.S.A.

PRYCE-JONES, Alan Payan, T.D.; British writer and editor; b. 18 Nov. 1908; s. of late Col. Henry Morris Pryce-Jones; m. 1st Thérèse Fould-Springer 1934 (died 1953); one s.; m. 2nd Mary Jean Kempner Thorne 1968 (died 1969); ed. Eton Coll. and Magdalen Coll., Oxford; Asst. Ed. The London Mercury 1928–32; Ed. The Times Literary Supplement 1948–59; served in France, Austria, Italy, Second World War 1939–45, Lieut.-Col. 1945; Trustee Nat. Portrait Gallery 1950–61; Dir. The Old Vic Trust 1950–61; mem. Council of Royal Coll. of Music 1956–61; Program Assoc. (Humanities and Arts) Ford Foundation 1961–63; Book Critic New York Herald-Tribune 1963–67; Theatre Critic, Theatre Arts 1963–. *Publications:* The Spring Journey 1931, People in the South 1932, Beethoven 1933, 27 Poems 1935, Private Opinion 1936, Prose Literature 1945–50, The Bonus of Laughter (autobiog.) 1987; libretto for Berkeley's opera Nelson 1954; The American Imagination (Ed.) 1960, Vanity Fair (libretto) 1962. *Leisure interests:* music, travelling. *Address:* 46 John Street, Newport, RI 02840, U.S.A.

PRYOR, David Hampton, LL.B.; American politician; b. 29 Aug. 1934, Camden, Ark.; s. of Edgar and Susan (née Newton) Pryor; m. Barbara Lunsford 1957; three s.; ed. Univ. of Arkansas; admitted to Arkansas Bar 1964; mem. Ark. House of Reps. 1961–66; served in Congress, House of Reps. 1966–72; Gov. of Arkansas 1974–79; Senator from Arkansas 1979–96; mem. American Bar Asscn., Arkansas Bar Asscn.; Democrat.

PRYOR, Richard; American actor and writer; b. 1 Dec. 1940, Peoria, Ill.; s. of Leroy and Gertrude (née Thomas) Pryor; two s. two d.; served with U.S. Army 1958–60; owner Richard Pryor Enterprises Inc., Los Angeles 1975–; has written film scripts for: Blazing Saddles 1973, Lily 1974, Adios Amigos 1976, The Bingo Long Travelling All-Stars and Motor Kings 1976, Car Wash 1976, Silver Streak 1976, Greased Lightning 1977, Which Way is Up? 1977, Blue Collar 1978, Stir Crazy 1980; *film appearances include:* Lady Sings the Blues 1972, Hit 1973, Wattstax 1973, Uptown Saturday Night 1974, Blue Collar 1978, California Suite 1978, The Wiz 1978, Richard Pryor Live in Concert 1979, Wholly Moses, In God We Trust, Bustin' Loose 1981, Some Kind of Hero 1982, Superman III 1983, The Toy 1984, Brewster's Millions 1985, Jo Jo Dancer Your Life is Calling (also wrote, produced and dir.) 1986, Moving 1988, See No Evil, Hear No Evil 1989, Harlem Nights, Another You 1991, Lost Highway 1996, Mad Dog Time 1996; Kennedy Center Mark Twain Prize 1998. *Address:* c/o Edward Astern, Indigo Promotions, 16633 Ventura Boulevard, Suite 1450, Encino, CA 91436, U.S.A.

PTASHNE, Mark Stephen, PH.D.; American professor of biochemistry; b. 5 June 1940, Chicago, Ill.; s. of Fred Ptashne and Mildred Ptashne; ed. Reed Coll. and Harvard Univ.; Jr. Fellow, Harvard Soc. of Fellows 1965–68; Lecturer, Dept. of Biochemistry and Molecular Biology, Harvard Univ. 1968–71, Prof. 1971–, Chair. Dept. of Biochemistry and Molecular Biology 1980–83; Herchel Smith Prof. of Molecular Biology 1993–; Guggenheim Fellow 1973–74; Fellow American Acad. of Arts and Sciences; mem. N.A.S.; Prix Charles-Léopold Mayer, Acad. des Sciences, Inst. de France (with W. Gilbert and E. Witkin) 1977; Eli Lilly Award 1975; shared Louisa Gross Horwitz Prize 1985; Gairdner Foundation Int. Award (with Charles Yanofsky) 1985; Feodor Lynen Lecturer 1988, Cancer Research Foundation Award 1990. *Publications:* A Genetic Switch 1986, A Genetic Switch II 1992; 122 papers in scientific journals 1950–89. *Leisure interests:* classical music, opera. *Address:* Department of Biochemistry and Molecular Biology, Harvard University, 7 Divinity Avenue, Cambridge, MA 02138, U.S.A. *Telephone:* (617) 495-2336.

PU HAIQING; Chinese politician; b. 1940, Sichuan Prov.; ed. Chongqing Univ.; joined CCP 1973; Man. Chongqing Iron and Steel Co.; Vice-Gov. Sichuan Prov.; Mayor of Chongqing Municipality, Vice-Sec. CCP Chongqing Mun. Cttee. 1997–; mem. 15th CCP Cen. Cttee. 1997–. *Address:* Chongqing Municipal Government, Chongqing, People's Republic of China.

PU NAI-FU; Taiwanese author; b. Nanjing; m.; ed. Beijing Russian-Language Jr. Coll.; imprisoned for various periods in labour-reform camps during anti-intellectual campaigns in China; moved to Hong Kong, subsequently to Taiwan 1983. *Publications include:* Romance in the Arctic, The Woman in the Pagoda, Books Without Names (6 vols.), The Scourge of the Sea, Red in Tooth and Claw.

PU SHAN, PH.D.; Chinese academic; b. 27 Nov. 1923, Beijing; m. Chen Xiuying 1951; ed. in U.S.A.; Vice-Pres. Chinese Soc. of World Economy 1980–85, Pres. 1985–97, Hon. Pres. 1997–; Dir. Inst. of World Econs. and

Politics 1982–88; mem. Nat. Cttee., CPPCC 1988–98, Standing Cttee. mem. 1993–98; Pres. Grad. School, Chinese Acad. of Social Sciences 1991–94. *Address:* Chinese Academy of Social Sciences, Beijing 100732, People's Republic of China.

PU TA-HAI; Taiwanese government official; b. 3 April 1922, Meihsien, Kwangtung; m.; one s. two d.; ed. Chinese Mil. Acad., Chinese Army Command and Gen. Staff Coll. and Chinese Armed Forces Staff Coll.; Section Chief (Col.), Taiwan Peace Preservation H.Q. 1956–57; Dept. Head (Col.), Gen. H.Q., Chinese Army 1957–60; Dept. Head (Maj.-Gen.), Personnel Div., Ministry of Nat. Defence 1963–68; Dept. Head (Maj.-Gen.), Taiwan Garrison Gen. H.Q. 1968–72; Dept. Head, Cen. Personnel Admin., Exec. Yuan 1972–78; Dir. Dept. of Personnel, Taipei City Govt. 1978–81, Taiwan Provincial Govt. 1981–84; Deputy Dir.-Gen. Central Personnel Admin., Exec. Yuan 1984, Dir.-Gen. 1984–93; Nat. Policy Adviser to the Pres. 1993–. *Leisure interests:* tennis, badminton. *Address:* Office of the Director-General, Central Personnel Administration, Executive Yuan, 109 Huai Ning Street, Taipei, Taiwan. *Telephone:* (02) 361-7072.

PUAPUA, Rt. Hon. Sir. Tomasi, KT., P.C.; Tuvaluan politician; b. 10 Sept. 1938; m. 1971; two s. two d.; ed. Fiji School of Medicine and Univ. of Otago, N.Z.; medical practitioner; Prime Minister of Tuvalu 1981–90, also Minister for Civil Service Admin., Local Govt. and Minister for Foreign Affairs; Speaker of Parl. 1993–. *Leisure interests:* athletics, rugby, tennis, volleyball, cricket, soccer, fishing, pig and poultry farming, gardening. *Address:* c/o Office of the Prime Minister, Vaiaku, Funafuti, Tuvalu.

PUCK, Theodore Thomas B.S., PH.D.; American professor of medicine and biochemistry, biophysics and genetics; b. 24 Sept. 1916, Chicago, Ill.; s. of Joseph and Bessie Puckowitz; m. Mary R. Hill 1946; three d.; ed. Univ. of Chicago; Univ. Fellow, Dept. of Chem., Univ. of Chicago 1938–40, Research Assoc., Dept. of Medicine 1941–45, Asst. Prof. Depts. of Medicine and Biochem. 1945–47; mem. Comm. on Airborne Infections, Army Epidemiological Bd., Office of Surgeon-Gen. 1944–46; Sr. Fellow, Calif. Inst. of Tech., Pasadena 1947–48; Prof. and Chair. Dept. of Biophysics, Univ. of Colo. Medical Center 1948–67; Research Prof. of Biochem., Biophysics and Genetics, Univ. of Colo. Medical Center 1967–86, Distinguished Prof. 1986–; Research Prof. of American Cancer Soc. 1966–; Prof. Dept. of Medicine, Univ. of Colo. Health Sciences Center 1981–, Distinguished Prof., Dept. of Medicine, Univ. of Colo. 1986–; Dir. Eleanor Roosevelt Inst. for Cancer Research 1962–95, Sr. Fellow 1995–; Fogarty Int. Scholar, N.I.H. 1997–98; mem. N.A.S. 1960–, Editorial Bd., Encyclopaedia Britannica 1980–87, Paideia Group; Fellow, American Acad. for Arts and Sciences 1967–; Lasker Award 1958, Borden Award 1959, Stearns Award, Univ. of Colo. 1959, General Rose Memorial Hosp. Award 1960, Distinguished Service Award of Univ. of Chicago Med. Alumni Asscn. 1969, Gross Horwitz Prize of Columbia Univ. in Cell Biology and Biochemistry 1973, Inst. of Med. 1974, Gordon Wilson Medal (American Clinical and Climatological Asscn.) 1977, Annual Award, Environmental Mutagen Soc. 1981, A.A.A.S. Award and Lectureship 1983, Heritage Foundation Scholar 1983, E. B. Wilson Medal of American Soc. for Cell Biology 1984, Bonfils—Stanton Award in Science 1984, A.R.C.S. Man of Science Award 1987, Hon. Award of Tissue Culture Asscn. 1987, Who's Who Worldwide Award for Outstanding Achievement 1990, Porter Hosp. Medal 1992. *Publications:* The Mammalian Cell as a Micro organism: Genetic and Biochemical Studies in Vitro 1972; many papers (some jointly) in the field of somatic cell genetics, also airborne infection, virus interaction with host cells, mammalian cell biochemical genetics, human cytogenetics, mammalian radiation biology and cancer. *Leisure interests:* skiing, hiking, travel, music. *Address:* Eleanor Roosevelt Institute for Cancer Research, 1899 Gaylord Street, Denver, CO 80206, U.S.A. (Home). *Telephone:* 303-333-4515 (Office).

PUDDEPHATT, Andrew Charles, B.A.; British administrator; b. 2 April 1950, Luton; s. of Andrew Ross Puddephatt and Margaret Deboo; two c.; ed. Kingsbury School, Dunstable and Sidney Sussex Coll., Cambridge; Deputy Leader Hackney Council 1984–85, Leader 1986–89; Dir. Nat. Council for Civil Liberties 1989–95; Dir. Charter 88 1995–99; Exec. Dir. Article 19 in Int. Centre Against Censorship 1999–. *Leisure interests:* music, cinema, walking. *Address:* c/o Article 19, International Centre Against Censorship, Lancaster House, 33 Islington High Street, London, N1 9LH, England. *Telephone:* 0171-278 9292. *Fax:* 0171-713 1356.

PUDDEPHATT, Richard John, PH.D., F.R.S., F.R.S.C.; British/Canadian professor of chemistry; b. 10 Oct. 1943; s. of Harry Puddephatt and Ena Puddephatt; m. Alice Poulton 1969; one s. one d.; ed. Univ. Coll. London; teaching postdoctoral Fellow Univ. of W. Ontario 1968–70, Prof. of Chemistry 1978–; lecturer Univ. of Liverpool 1970–77, sr. lecturer 1977–78. *Publications include:* The Chemistry of Gold 1978, The Periodic Table of the Elements 1986. *Leisure interest:* gardening. *Address:* Department of Chemistry, University of Western Ontario, London, Ont., N6A 5B7, Canada. *Telephone:* (519) 679-2111. *Fax:* (519) 661-3022.

PUENZO, Luis; Argentinian film director; b. 24 Feb. 1949, Buenos Aires; worked as story-board designer in advertising, becoming advertising Dir. f. Cinemania 1974. *Films include:* Luces de mis zapatos (Lights of my Shoes) 1973, Cinco años de vida (Five Years of Life) 1975, The Official Story 1985 (Palme d'Or, Cannes, Oscar for Best Foreign Film 1986, and 47 other int. awards), Gringo viejo (Old Gringo) 1989. *Address:* c/o Instituto Nacional de Cinematografía, Lima 319, 1073 Buenos Aires, Argentina.

PUGACHEVA, Alla Borisovna; Russian singer; b. 5 April 1949, Moscow; m. 2nd Filipp Kirkorov; one d.; ed. M. Ippolitov-Ivanov Music High School, A. Lunacharsky State Inst. of Theatre Art; debut as soloist of Lipetsk vocal-instrumental group 1970; O. Lundstrem Jazz orchestra 1971; soloist Veselye Rebyata Ensemble 1973–78; f. Song Theatre 1988; numerous prizes and awards including 3rd prize All-Union Contest Moscow, 1974; Grand Prix Int. Competition Golden Orpheus Bulgaria 1975, Int. Festival Sopot 1978; repertoire includes numerous songs by popular Soviet composers such as R. Pauls, A. Muromtsev, A. Zatsepin and others, also songs of her own; acted in films; several concert programmes; tours in U.S.A., Germany, Switzerland, India, France, Italy and other countries; f. Theatre of Songs 1988, Alla Co. 1993, Alla Magazine 1993; U.S.S.R. People's Artist, Ovation Prize 1994, State Prize of Russia 1995. *Address:* State Variety Theatre, Bersenevskaya nab. 20/2, 109072 Moscow (Office); Tverskaya-Yamskaya str. 5–7, Moscow, Russia (Home). *Telephone:* 250-95-78 (Home).

PUGIN, Nikolai Andreyevich; Russian industrialist; b. 30 June 1940; ed. Gorky Polytechnic Inst.; worker, foreman at car factory 1958–75; chief engineer at gear-box factory 1975–81; Tech. Dir. 1981–83, Gen. Dir. of Gorky Automobile Works 1983–86; Minister of Automobile Industry 1986–88, of Automobile and Agricultural Machines Industry 1988–91; mem. Russian Eng. Acad. 1991–; mem. Russian Acad. of Natural Science 1992–; Pres. ASM Holding, Inc. (mfrs. of motor vehicles and farm machinery in CIS) 1992–; Chair. Bd. GAZ Co. (Nizhni Novgorod); now Ind. Financial Group Nizhegorodskiye Automobili) 1994–. *Address:* ASM Holding, 21/5 Kuznetsky Most, 103895 Moscow; GAZ, Lenina prosp. 9, 603046, Nizhni Novgorod, Russia. *Telephone:* (095) 921-68-21; 924-53-85 (both Moscow). *Telephone:* (8312) 561070 (Nizhni Novgorod). *Fax:* (095) 924-39-00.

PUIG, Lluis de Maria; Spanish politician and historian; b. 20 July 1945, Bascara, Gerona; m.; two c.; ed. Autonomous Univ. of Barcelona, Ecole des Hautes Etudes de la Sorbonne, Paris; worked in anti-Franco opposition as active mem. of underground Catalan and socialist orgs.; Prof. of Contemporary History, Autonomous Univ. of Barcelona; Socialist mem. Cortes for Gerona 1979–; mem. Catalonian Socialist Party Bureau 1986–; Pres. Gerona Fed. of Socialist Party 1993–; mem. Council of Europe Ass. 1983–, Chair. Sub-Cttee. on European Social Charter 1984–89, Vice-Pres. Ass. 1993–96; mem. Spanish del. to WEU Ass. 1990–, Vice-Chair. Socialist Group 1992–96, Defence Cttee. 1992–94, Chair. Political Cttee. 1994–96, mem. Presidential Cttee. 1994–, Pres. WEU Ass. 1997–; Sec. Alexander Cirici Inst. for European Co-operation 1986–96, Pres. 1996–; Dr. h.c. (Ovidius Univ. of Constanta, Romania) 1998. *Publications:* several books on history of 19th and 20th century Catalonia, books and essays on Europe, articles on domestic and int. politics. *Address:* Assembly of Western European Union, 43 avenue du Président Wilson, 75775 Paris Cedex 16, France. *Telephone:* (01) 53.67.22.00. *Fax:* (01) 53.67.22.01.

PUISSOCHET, Jean-Pierre, LL.D.; French international judge and lawyer; b. 3 May 1936, Clermont-Ferrand; s. of René Puissochet and Hélène Puissochet (née Brengues); m. Eliane Millet 1973; one d.; ed. Lycée du Parc, Lyon, Inst. for Political Studies, Lyon, Ecole Nat. d'Admin., Paris; Auditeur, Conseil d'Etat 1962, Maître des Requêtes 1968, Conseiller 1985; Dir. Legal Service, Council of EC 1968–70, Dir.-Gen. 1970–73; Dir.-Gen. Agence Nat. pour l'Emploi 1973–75; Dir. of Legal Affairs, OECD 1979–85; Legal Adviser, Dir. of Legal Affairs, Ministry of Foreign Affairs 1987–94; Judge, Court of Justice of the European Communities 1994–; mem. Perm. Court of Arbitration, The Hague 1990–; Officier, Légion d'honneur, Officier Ordre du Mérite. *Publications:* The Enlargement of the EC 1974; numerous articles on Community and int. law. *Address:* Court of Justice of the European Communities, Plateau du Kirchberg, L-2925 (Office); 15 rue Jean-Pierre Brasseur, L-1258, Luxembourg (Home). *Telephone:* 4303.2246 (Office). *Fax:* 4303.2000.

PUJA, Frigyes; Hungarian politician; b. 1921, Battonya, County Békés; s. of János Puja and Danica Vrányés; m. Emma Répás; one d.; ed. Party Acad.; joined Communist Party 1944; Sec. of Party, District Battonya 1945–46; mem. Party Cttee., Deputy Head of Appointments Cttee., County Csanád 1946–49; Sub-Dept. Leader Cen. Bd. of Hungarian Working People's Party 1949–53; Amb. to Sweden 1953–55, to Austria 1955–59; Deputy Foreign Minister 1959–63; Head Foreign Dept., Cen. Cttee. of Hungarian Socialist Workers' Party 1963–68; mem. Cen. Cttee. HSWP 1966–88; First Deputy Foreign Minister 1968–73; Sec. of State for Foreign Affairs 1973; Minister of Foreign Affairs 1973–83; Amb. to Finland 1983–86; Labour Order of Merit, golden degree 1970, Order of the Banner of Hungarian People's Repub. (medal) 1986. *Publications:* The Problems of Coexistence 1967, Unity and Debate in the International Communist Movement 1969, Why is the Warsaw Treaty Organization Necessary? 1970, The Road to Security 1971, Principles and Doctrines 1972, Socialist Foreign Policy 1973, The Liberated Battonya 1979, Characteristics and Perspectives of the Détente Process 1980, Hungarian Foreign Policy 1981, Flaming Years 1986, From the Typesetter's Stand to the Ministerial Chair 1988, and various articles on int. affairs.

PUJOL I SOLEY, Jordi, M.D.; Spanish politician, pharmacologist and businessman; b. 9 June 1930, Barcelona; s. of Florenci and Maria Pujol i Soley; m. Marta Ferrusola 1956; seven s.; ed. Faculty of Medicine, Univ. of Barcelona; worked in pharmaceutical industry 1953–60; f. Banca Catalana group 1959, Man. Dir. 1959–76; f. Convergencia Democratica de Catalunya 1974; Councillor, provisional Generalitat 1977–80; mem. Congress, Madrid 1977, 1979; Head Convergència i Unió Parl. Group in Congress 1977–80;

mem. Catalan Parl. 1980–; Pres. Generalitat de Catalunya 1980–; Vice-Pres. Ass. of European Regions 1988–92, Pres. 1992–96. *Publications include:* Una política per Catalunya 1976, Construir Catalunya 1980, Als joves de Catalunya 1988, La Força serena i constructiva de Catalunya 1991, Pensar Europa 1993. *Leisure interests:* reading, walking, cycling. *Address:* Palau de la Generalitat, Plaça Sant Jaume s/n, Barcelona 2, Spain. *Telephone:* 402.46.00. *Fax:* 318.34.88.

PULJIĆ, H.E. Cardinal Vinko; Bosnia and Herzegovina ecclesiastic; b. 8 Sept. 1945, Priječani, Banja Luka, Bosnia and Herzegovina; s. of Ivan Puljić and Kaja Puljić (née Pletikosa); ed. seminary of Šalata, Zagreb and at Đakovo; ordained priest Đakovo 1970; parish vicar Banja Luka, parish priest Sasina, then Ravska; ecclesiastic, Zmajević seminary, Zadar 1978–87; parish priest Bosanska Gradiška 1987–90; Vice-Rector Catholic Theological Seminary of Vrhbosnia, Sarajevo 1990; Archbishop of Vrhbosnia 1990; cr. Cardinal 1994; travelled to many countries in Europe and N. America to publicise the suffering caused by the war in Bosnia and Herzegovina and discuss possible solutions; Hon. Dr. Humanitarian Science (Grand Valley State Univ., Mich., U.S.A.) 1995; Humanist of the Decade and Golden Diploma of Humanism, Int. League of Humanists, Sarajevo 1995. *Address:* Nadbiskupski Ordinarijat, Kaptol 7, BH 71000 Sarajevo, Bosnia and Herzegovina.

PULLMAN, Bill; American actor; b. 1955, Hornell, N.Y.; ed. Univ. of Massachusetts; m. Tamara Pullman; three c.; fmr. drama teacher, bldg. contractor, dir. of a theatre group; started acting in fringe theatres, New York; moved to L.A. *Films include:* Ruthless People, A League of Their Own, Sommersby, Sleepless in Seattle, While You Were Sleeping, Caspar, Independence Day, Lost Highway 1997, The End of Violence 1997, The Thin Red Line 1998, Brokedown Palace 1998, Zero Effect 1998. *Address:* c/o J. J. Harris, 9560 Wilshire Boulevard, Suite 50, Beverly Hills, CA 90212, U.S.A.

PUNGOR, Ernö, PH.D.; Hungarian chemist; b. 30 Oct 1923, Vasszécsény; s. of József Pungor and Franciska Faller; m. 1st Erzsébet Lang 1950, 2nd Dr. Tünde Horváth 1984; two s. one d.; ed. Pázmány Univ., Budapest; Corresp. mem. Hung. Acad. of Sciences 1967, mem. 1976–; Asst. Prof. Eötvös Univ., Budapest 1948–53, Assoc. Prof. 1953–62; Prof. Chemical Univ., Veszprém 1962–70; Dir. Inst. for Gen. and Analytical Chemistry, Tech. Univ., Budapest 1970–90, now Prof. Emer.; Head Research Group for Tech. Analytical Chem. of Hungarian Acad. of Sciences 1970–93, Pres. Nat. Comm. for Tech. Devt. 1990–94; Minister for Tech. Devt. 1990–94; Gen. Dir. Bay Zoltán Foundation for Applied Research 1994–; Pres. Asscn. of Eds. of European Chemical Journals 1977; mem. Int. Fed. of Scientific Eds. Asscn. 1981–87; Chair. Working Party of Analytical Chemists of Fed. of European Chemical Socs. 1981–87; Chair. Analysis Div. of Hungarian Chemical. Soc.; Head Analysis Group, Hungarian Acad. of Sciences; mem. IUPAC 1973, Pres. Hungarian Nat. Adhering Org. of IUPAC 1985–; Vice-Pres. Electroanalytical Cttee. 1985–87; mem. Scientific Advisory Bd. of Org. for the Prohibition of Chemical Weapons; Hon. mem. Czechoslovak Acad. Science Chemical Section 1966, Egyptian Pharmaceutical Soc. 1973, Austrian Analytical and Micro-analytical Soc. 1977, Chemical Soc. of Finland 1979, Analytical Chemical Soc. of Japan 1981, Finnish Tech. Soc. 1990, Royal Soc. 1992, Indian Acad. of Sciences 1993, Royal Soc. of Chemistry 1993; Hon. Prof., Agricultural Univ. of Lima 1973; Redwood Lecturer for English Soc. for Analytical Chemistry 1979; Dr. h.c. (Tech. Univ. of Vienna), (Bucharest) 1993, (Tech. Univ. of Budapest) 1993; Robert Boyle Gold Medal (Royal Soc.) 1986, Talanta Gold Medal 1987, Excellent Inventor Gold Medal 1987, Gold Medal of Hungarian Acad. of Science 1988, Gold Medal, Inst. of Analytical Chemists of Tech. Univ. of Vienna 1988; Hon. Prof. Árpád Acad., U.S.A. 1990, elected mem. Cen. European Hall of Fame for Eng. Sciences and Tech. (ITI, U.S.A.) 1991; Eur. Ing. 1992; Fraunhofer Medal (Germany) 1993, Boyle Gold Medal, Royal Soc. of Analytical Chem., U.K. 1996, Hon. Medal, Fed. of European Chemical Socs. 1997; Österreich-Ungarisch Corvinus Kreis Ehrenmitgliedschaft 1994, Grosse Deutsche Verdienstkreuz 1995, Officier, Ordre nat. du Mérite 1996; developed new theory of adsorption indicators; pioneering work in the field of ion-selective electrodes and in flow-through analytical techniques. *Leisure interest:* history. *Address:* Institute for General and Analytical Chemistry, Technical University of Budapest, St. Gellért tér 4, 1111 Budapest; Bay Zoltán Foundation, Kondorfa u. 1, 1116 Budapest, Hungary. *Telephone:* (1) 463-4054 (Univ. Inst.); (1) 463-0502 (Bay Foundation). *Fax:* (1) 463-3408 (Univ. Inst.); (1) 463-0505 (Bay Foundation).

PUOLANNE, Ulla Kaija, B.SC.(ECON.); Finnish politician; b. 28 June 1931, Lahti; d. of Eero Raivo and Maili Raivo; divorced; financial officer, Puolanne eng. firm 1960–82; mem. Parl. 1975–91; Chair. Conservative Party Parl. Group 1984–87; Second Minister of Finance 1987–91. *Leisure interest:* swimming.

PURCELL, James Nelson, M.P.A.; American international official; b. 16 July 1938, Nashville, Tenn.; s. of James N. Purcell Sr.; m. Walda Primm 1961; two d.; ed. Furman Univ., Syracuse Univ. New York; Budget Analyst, U.S. Atomic Energy Comm. 1962–66; Man. Analyst, Agency for Int. Devt. 1966–68; Deputy Dir. Budget Preparation Staff, Office of Man. and Budget (OMB) 1968–72; Sr. Examiner Int. Affairs Div. OMB 1972–74; Chief Justice, Treasury Br. OMB 1974–76; Chief Resources Programming and Man. Div., Bureau for Educ. and Cultural Affairs, Dept. of State 1976–77; Deputy Budget Dir., Dept. of State 1977–78; Exec. Dir. Bureau of Admin. Dept. of State 1978–79; Deputy Asst. Sec., Programmes and Budget, Bureau for Refugee Programs, Dept. of State 1979–82, Dir., Asst. Sec. Bureau for Refugee Programmes 1982–87; Dir.-Gen. Int. Org. for Migration (IOM) 1988–; mem. American Soc. of Public Admin.; Distinguished Honor Award, State Dept. *Address:* IOM, C.P. 71, 17 Route des Morillons, 1211 Geneva 19 (Office); 6 Château-Banquet, 1202 Geneva, Switzerland (Home).

PURDUM, Robert L., B.S.; American business executive; b. 1935, Wilmington, Ohio; m. Arlene Peterson; three s.; ed. Purdue Univ.; served U.S.N. and Indiana Toll Road Comm. 1956–62; joined Armco Inc. 1962, Dist. Eng., Metal Products Div. 1962–66, sales staff 1966–72, Dist. Man. 1972–76, Gen. Man. 1976–78; Pres. Midwestern Steel Div. 1978–80, Area Vice-Pres. 1980–82, Group Vice-Pres., C.E.O. Mfg. Services Group 1982–86, Exec. Vice-Pres. and C.O.O. 1986, Pres. and C.O.O. 1986–90, Pres., C.E.O. 1990–. *Leisure interests:* tennis, hunting, fishing, travel. *Address:* Armco Inc., 301 Grant Street, Floor 15, Pittsburgh, PA 15219 (Office); 26 Horizon Drive, Mendham, NJ 07945, U.S.A. (Home).

PURDY, Alfred, O.C.; Canadian author; b. 30 Dec. 1918, Wooler, Ont.; s. of Alfred Purdy and Eleanor Purdy; m. Eurithe Parkhurst 1941; one s.; ed. Dufferin Public School, Trenton, Ont., Albert Coll. Belleville, Ont. and Trenton Coll. Inst.; served Royal Canadian Air Force in World War II; Writer-in-Residence Loyola Univ. 1973–74, Univ. of Manitoba 1975–76, Univ. of W. Ont. 1977–78; recipient of numerous awards including Gov.-Gen.'s Literary Award for Poetry 1966, Jubilee Medal 1978, Governor-Gen.'s Award 1987. *Publications include:* The Enchanted Echo 1944, Pressed on Sand 1955, Emu, Remember 1957, The Crafte So Longe To Lerne 1956, Poems for All the Annettes 1962, the Blur In Between 1963, The Cariboo Horses 1965, North of Summer 1967, Wild Grape Wine 1968, Love in a Burning Building 1970, Storm Warning 1971, On the Bearpaw Sea 1973, Sex and Death 1973, In Search of Owen Roblin 1974, Sundance at Dusk 1976, At Marsport Drugstore 1977, No Other Country 1977, A Handful of Earth 1977, No Second Spring 1978, Moths in the Iron Curtain 1978, The Stone Bird 1981, Bursting into Song 1982, Morning and It's Summer 1982, Birdwatching at the Equator 1983, The Bukowski/Purdy Letters 1964–1974 1983, Piling Blood 1984, Selected Poems 1986, The Woman on the Shore 1990, A Splinter in the Heart (novel) 1990, Cougar Hunter 1993, Margaret Lawrence-Al Purdy: A Friendship in Letters 1993, Reaching for the Beaufort Sea 1993, Starting from Ameliasburgh: the Collected Prose of Al Purdy 1995; vols. of poetry, short stories, radio and TV plays, articles etc. *Leisure interest:* travelling. *Address:* c/o Harbour Publishing, P.O. Box 219, Madeira Park, B.C., V0N 2H0, Canada.

PURDY, James; American writer; b. 1923; ed. Chicago and Spain; interpreter, editor and other posts in Cuba, Mexico, Washington, D.C.; American Acad. of Arts and Letters Morton Dauwen Zabel Award for Fiction 1993, Oscar Williams and Gene Durwood Award for Poetry 1995. *Publications:* novels: Don't Call Me by My Right Name 1956, 63: Dream Palace 1956, Color of Darkness 1957, Malcolm 1959, The Nephew 1960, Cabot Wright Begins 1963, Eustace Chisholm and the Works 1967, Sleepers in Moon-Crowned Valleys (Part I Jeremy's Version 1970, Part II The House of the Solitary Maggot 1971), I Am Elijah Thrush 1972, In a Shallow Grave 1976, Narrow Rooms 1978, On Glory's Course 1983, Garments The Living Wear 1989, Out With the Stars 1992, Kitty Blue: A Fairytale 1993, Gertrude of Stony Island Avenue 1997; plays: Children is All 1962, A Day After the Fair 1977, How I Became a Shadow (eight plays) 1979, Proud Flesh 1980, Scrap of Paper 1981, The Berry-Picker 1981, Foment 1997; An Oyster is a Wealthy Beast (story and poems) 1967, Mr. Evening 1968 (story and poems), On the Rebound 1970 (story and poems), The Running Sun (poems) 1971, Sunshine is an Only Child (poems) 1973, Lessons and Complaints (poems) 1978, Mourners Below 1981, Dawn 1985, Don't Let the Snow Fall (poem) 1985, In the Hollow of His Hand 1986, The Candles of your Eyes (collected stories) 1987, Are You in the Winter Tree? 1987, The Brooklyn Branding Parlors (poems) 1987, Garments the Living Wear 1989, Collected Poems 1990; L.P. Recordings: 63: Dream Palace 1968, Eventide and Other Stories 1969. *Leisure interest:* walking in forests. *Address:* 236 Henry Street, Brooklyn, NY 11201, U.S.A. *Telephone:* (718) 858-0015.

PURKISS, Clive John, PH.D.; British policy research director; b. 6 Sept. 1939, Beckenham, Kent; s. of Charles Purkiss and Dorothy Barnard; m. Gillian Henley 1963; three d.; ed. Eltham Coll., St. Peter's Coll. Oxford, London School of Econs., Lancaster Univ.; Civil Engineer, Sir Halcrow & Partners 1961–63; Operational Research Scientist, British Iron & Steel Research Asscn. 1963–68; Sr. Consultant, Int. Systems Research Ltd. 1968–70; Tech. Dir. Inst. of Manpower Studies 1970–75, Dir. 1975–85; Dir. European Foundation for the Improvement of Living and Working Conditions 1985–; Chair. E. Glendalough School 1994–; mem. Council, Tavistock Inst. 1990–; Vice-Pres. Manpower Soc. 1992–. *Publications:* articles on employment policy in professional journals. *Leisure interests:* travel, garden design, scuba, theatre. *Address:* European Foundation for the Improvement of Living and Working Conditions, Wyattville Road, Loughlinstown, Co. Dublin, Ireland. *Telephone:* 01-282 6888.

PURPURA, Dominick Paul, M.D.; American professor of neuroscience; b. 2 April, 1927, New York; s. of John R. Purpura and Rose Ruffino; m. Florence Williams 1948; three s. one d.; ed. Columbia Univ. and Harvard Medical School; Chair. and Prof., Dept. of Anatomy, Albert Einstein Coll. of Medicine 1967–74, Dept. of Neuroscience 1974–82, Prof. and Chair. of Neuroscience 1974–82, Dean, Albert Einstein Coll. of Medicine 1984–; Dir. Rose F. Kennedy Center for Research in Mental Retardation and Human Devt. 1972–82; Dean, Stanford Univ. School of Medicine 1982–84; Pres. Soc. for Neuroscience 1982–83, Int. Brain Research Org. 1987–, Vice-Pres. for Medical Affairs UNESCO 1961–; Fellow N.Y. Acad. of Sciences; mem. Inst. of Medicine (N.A.S.), N.A.S. *Publications:* numerous scientific papers. *Address:* Albert Einstein College of Medicine, Belfer Building, Room 312, 1300 Morris Park Avenue, Bronx, NY 10461, U.S.A. *Telephone:* (718) 430-2801. *Fax:* (718) 430-8822.

PURSOO, Eugene, B.A.; Grenadian administrator and public servant; b. 26 March 1946, Soubise, St. Andrew; m.; four c.; ed. Fordham Univ., New York, U.S.A.; Accounting Man., Muscular Dystrophy Assen., New York 1972–90; Perm. Rep. to UN, New York 1990–95. *Address:* c/o Ministry of Foreign Affairs, St George's, Grenada.

PURVES, Sir William, Kt., C.B.E., D.S.O.; British retd. banker; b. 27 Dec. 1931, Kelso, Scotland; s. of Andrew Purves and Ida Purves; m. 1st Diana T. Richardson 1958 (divorced 1988); two s. two d.; m. 2nd Rebecca Jane Lewellen 1989; ed. Kelso High School; Nat. Bank of Scotland, Kelso 1948–54; joined the Hongkong and Shanghai Banking Corpn. 1954, Chief Accountant 1970–74, Man., Tokyo 1974–76, Sr. Man. Overseas Operations 1976–78, Asst. Gen. Man. Overseas Operations 1978–79, Gen. Man. Int. 1979–82, Exec. Dir. 1982–84, Deputy Chair. 1984–86, Chair. and C.E.O. 1986–92, Exec. Chair. HSBC Holdings PLC 1992–98; Pres. Int. Monetary Conf. 1992, mem. Exec. Council Hong Kong 1987–93; Chair. British Bank of the Middle East 1986–88, Midland Bank PLC 1994–98 (Dir. 1987–); Dir. HSCB Americas Inc. 1984–88; Deputy Chair. (non-exec.) Alstom S.A.; Dir. (non-exec.) Shell Transport and Trading Co. PLC, East Asiatic Co. A.S.; Chair. Royal Hong Kong Jockey Club 1992–93; Fellow Chartered Inst. of Bankers (CIOB), Fellow CIOB Scotland; mem. Gen. Cttee. Scottish Rugby Union 1997–; Trustee Imperial War Museum, Nat. Museums of Scotland; Hon. D. Univ. (Stirling) 1987; Hon. D.Laws (Sheffield) 1993; Hon. LL.D. (Nottingham) 1997; Hon. D. Business Admin. (Hong Kong Polytechnic) 1993, (Strathclyde) 1996; Dr. h.c. (Hong Kong), (Nottingham) 1997, (Napier) 1998, (Hong Kong Open) 1998. *Leisure interests:* golf, rugby. *Address:* 87 Chester Square, London, SW1W 9HT, England. *Telephone:* 0171-823 6775. *Fax:* 0171-824 8351.

PURY, David de; Swiss business executive and fmr. diplomatist and government official; b. 4 Dec. 1943; ed. Geneva Univ.; fmr. mem. of bar, Geneva; in govt. service, from 1970–86, held various diplomatic posts with Foreign Ministry, Berne, The Hague, Brussels, Washington, Amb., Del. for trade agreements, Chief Negotiator in Uruguay Round of GATT 1986–91; Gov. for Switzerland, IDB 1986–88; Chair. OECD Trade Cttee. 1989–91; co-founder and Chair. de Pury Pictet Turrettini & Co. Ltd. (asset man. and int. investment) 1996–; Chair. and Publ. Le Temps (daily newspaper) 1998–; Chair. Bd. EIC Electricity Investment Co.; mem. Bd. Dirs. Nestlé Group, Zürich Financial Services Group, Groupe Schneider (Paris), Electrowatt Eng. and other cos.; mem. European Advisory Bd. Bankers Trust; Chair. BBC Brown Boveri Ltd., Co-Chair. ABB Asea Brown Boveri Group 1992–96; mem. Exec. Cttee. Geneva Grad. Inst. for Int. Studies, Bd. of Trustees Int. Crisis Group, Council of World Econ. Forum. *Address:* de Pury Pictet Turrettini & Co. Ltd., Binzmühlestrasse 14, 8050 Zürich, Switzerland. *Telephone:* (01) 318 34 01. *Fax:* (01) 318 34 11.

PURYEAR, Martin, M.F.A.; American artist; b. 23 May 1941, Washington, D.C.; s. of Reginald T. Puryear and Martina A. Morse; ed. Catholic Univ., Swedish Royal Acad. Stockholm and Yale Univ.; Asst. Prof. Fisk Univ. Nashville 1971–73, Univ. of Md., Coll. Park 1974–77; Assoc. Prof. of Art, Univ. of Ill. 1978–86, Prof. 1986–88; Louis Comfort Tiffany Foundation Grant 1981; Guggenheim Fellow 1982; Best Artist Prize, São Paulo Biennial 1989.

PUSTOVOITENKO, Valery Pavlovich; Ukrainian politician; b. 1947, Nikolayev Region, Ukraine; m.; two c.; ed. Dnipropetrovsk Inst. of Construction Eng.; People's Deputy of Ukraine; engineer, Chair. Dnipropetrovsk City Soviet; Head election campaign of Pres. Kuchma 1994; mem. Ukrainian Cabinet of Ministers 1994–97; Head Ukrainian Football Fed. 1996–; mem. People's Democratic Party of Ukraine; Prime Minister of Ukraine 1997–. *Address:* Government Offices, Hrushevskoga 12/2, 252008 Kiev, Ukraine. *Telephone:* (381) 226 2472; (381) 226 32 63 (Office).

PUTILIN, Nikolai Georgiyevich; Russian baritone; b. 1954; ed. Krasnoyarsk Inst. of Arts; lessons with Nikola Nikolov in Bulgaria; started as singer of Variety Theatre; soloist of Syktyvkar Musical Theatre, Komi Repub. 1983–85; Kazan Opera Theatre 1985–92; Kirov (Mariinsky) Theatre in St. Petersburg 1992–; Prize-winner Int. Chaliapin Competition 1989; *repertoire includes:* over 40 leading roles toured Metropolitan-Opera, La Scala, Teatro Comunale di Firenza, Covent Garden, Bolshoi Theatre and others. *Address:* Mariinsky Theatre, Teatralnaya pl. 1, St. Petersburg, Russia (Office). *Telephone:* (812) 114 4441 (Office).

PUTIN, Col. Vladimir Vladimirovich; Russian politician; b. 7 Oct. 1952, Leningrad (now St. Petersburg); m.; two c.; ed. Leningrad State Univ.; on staff KGB U.S.S.R., with First Chief Dept. of KGB and in Germany 1975–90; adviser to Pro-rector Leningrad State Univ. 1990; adviser to Chair. of Leningrad City Exec. Cttee. 1990–91; Chair. Cttee. on Foreign Relations, St. Petersburg Mayor's Office 1991; First Deputy Chair. St. Petersburg Govt., Chair. Cttee. on Foreign Relations 1994–96; Deputy Head, First Deputy Head, Admin. of Russian Presidency, Head, Main Control Dept. 1997–98; Dir. Fed. Security Service of Russian Fed. 1998–. *Address:* Federal Security Service, Lubyanka str. 1/3, 101000 Moscow, Russia. *Telephone:* (095) 224 6224 (Office).

PUTNAM, Hilary, PH.D.; American university professor; b. 31 July 1926, Chicago, Ill.; s. of Samuel Putnam and Riva Sampson; m. 1st Erna Diesendruck 1948 (divorced 1962); one d.; m. 2nd Ruth A. Hall 1962; two s. one d.; ed. Cen. High School of Philadelphia, Univ. of Pa., Harvard Univ. and Univ. of Calif. at Los Angeles; Asst. Prof. of Philosophy, Princeton Univ. 1953–60, Assoc. Prof. 1960–61; Prof. of Philosophy of Science, M.I.T. 1961–65; Prof. of Philosophy, Harvard Univ. 1965, Walter Beverly Pearson Prof. of Mathematical Logic and Modern Math. 1976–; Guggenheim Fellow 1960–61; Corresp. mem. British Acad.; many other fellowships; two hon. degrees. *Publications:* Meaning and the Moral Sciences 1978, Reason, Truth and History 1981, Philosophical Papers (3 vols.) 1975–83, The Many Faces of Realism 1987, Representation and Reality 1989, Realism with a Human Face 1990, Renewing Philosophy 1992. *Leisure interests:* hiking, cooking, languages. *Address:* Faculty of Arts and Sciences, Harvard University, Cambridge, MA 02138 (Office); 116 Winchester Road, Arlington, MA 02174, U.S.A. (Home).

PUTTNAM, Baron (Life Peer), cr. 1997, of Queensgate in the Royal Borough of Kensington and Chelsea; **David Terence Puttnam,** Kt., C.B.E., F.R.G.S.; British film producer; b. 25 Feb. 1941, London; s. of Leonard Arthur and Marie Beatrix Puttnam; m. Patricia Mary Jones 1961; one s. one d.; ed. Minchenden Grammar School, London; advertising 1958–66, photography 1966–68, film production 1968–; Chair. Enigma Productions Ltd. 1978–, Spectrum Strategy Ltd.; Dir. Nat. Film Finance Corpn. 1980–85, Anglia TV Group 1982–, Village Roadshow Corpn. 1989–, Survival Anglia 1989–, Chrysalis Group 1993–96; Chair., C.E.O. Columbia Pictures, U.S.A. 1986–88; Pres. Council for Protection of Rural England 1985–92; Hon. Special Lecturer in Drama, Bristol Univ. 1984–86, Visiting Industrial Prof. 1986–96; Gov. Nat. Film and TV School 1974–, (Chair. 1988–96), L.S.E. 1997–; mem. Visiting Cttee., R.C.A. 1985–, Governing Council Royal Photographic Soc., Bd. Landscape Foundation; Trustee, Tate Gallery 1985–92, Science Museum; Chancellor Univ. of Sunderland; Chair. Nat. Endowment for Science, Tech. and the Arts, Nat. Museum of Photography, Film and Television, British Council Films and TV Advisory Cttee.; Vice-Pres. B.A.F.T.A.: mem. Educ. Standards Task Force, Arts Council Lottery Panel 1993–97; Hon. F.C.S.D.; Hon. degrees (Bristol, Leicester, Manchester, Leeds, Bradford, Westminster, Humberside, Sunderland, Cheltenham and Glos., Kent, London Guildhall Univs., Royal Scottish Acad., Imperial Coll. London); Special Jury Prize for The Duellists, Cannes 1977, two Acad. Awards and four BAFTA Awards for Midnight Express 1978, four Acad. Awards (including Best Film), three BAFTA Awards (including Best Film) for Chariots of Fire 1981, three Acad. Awards and nine BAFTA Awards for The Killing Fields 1985; Michael Balcon Award for outstanding contribution to the British Film Industry, BAFTA 1982; Palme d'Or (Cannes), one Acad. Award and three BAFTA Awards for The Mission 1987; Officier, Ordre des Arts et des Lettres 1986. *Productions include:* That'll Be The Day, Mahler, Bugsy Malone, The Duellists, Midnight Express, Chariots of Fire, Local Hero, The Killing Fields, Cal, Defence of the Realm, Forever Young 1984, The Mission 1985, Mr Love 1986, Memphis Belle 1989, Meeting Venus 1990, Being Human 1993, War of the Buttons 1993, Le Confessional 1995, My Life So Far 1998. *Publications:* Rural England: Our Countryside at the Crossroads 1988, Undeclared War: The Struggle to Control the World's Film Industry 1997. *Address:* Enigma Productions, 29A Tufton Street, London, SW1P 3QL, England. *Telephone:* 0171-222 5757. *Fax:* 0171-222 5858.

PUYANA, Rafael; Colombian harpsichordist; b. 14 Oct. 1931, Bogotá; s. of Ernesto Puyana and Alicia de Puyana; studied under Wanda Landowska; lives in Spain and Paris; Colombia's Amb. to UNESCO, Paris; teacher of harpsichord Cursos Manuel de Falla, Granada, and Summer Acad. Musica en Compostela, Santiago de Compostela 1976–; gives performances throughout the world; works written for and dedicated to him by several composers including Federico Mompou, Xavier Montsalvatge, Julian Orbón, Alain Louvier and Stephen Dodgson; appeared in film about life of Domenico Scarlatti (BBC-TV and Televisión Española); Grand Prix du Disque (twice), Deutsche Schalplatten Preis for recording of works by François Couperin; Orden de Isabel la Católica (for his contrib. to study and performances of Spanish baroque and contemporary harpsichord music) 1996. *Leisure interest:* collecting 17th and 18th century keyboard instruments, and Spanish and S. American colonial art. *Address:* 88 rue de Grenelle, 75007 Paris, France; Monasterio de los Descalzos Viejos, Aptdo. 254, 29400 Ronda, Málaga, Spain.

PUYOL ANTOLIN, Rafael; Spanish university rector; b. 26 Feb. 1945, Telde, Las Palmas; m. Dolores Martínez-Ferrando; four c.; ed. Universidad Complutense; Asst. Prof. of Human Geography; Faculty of Geography and History, Universidad Complutense 1975–78, Assoc. Prof. 1978–82, Prof. 1982–, Rector of Univ. 1995–97; mem. editorial bds. various journals; Pres. Population Group, Asociación de Geógrafos Españoles 1986–; Vice-Pres. Exec. Cttee. Real Sociedad Geográfica. *Publications:* Emigración y desigualdades regionales en España 1979, Población y Espacio 1982, Población y recursos 1984, Población española 1988, Los grandes problemas demográficos 1993, La Unión Europea 1995. *Leisure interests:* music, reading. *Address:* C/Marbella, 50, 28034 Madrid, Spain (Home). *Telephone:* (91) 372.04.80 (Home). *Fax:* (91) 394.34.72.

PUZO, Mario; American author; b. 15 Oct. 1920, New York; s. of Antonio Puzo and Maria (Le Conti) Puzo; m. Erika Lina Broske 1946; five c.; ed. New School for Social Research, Columbia Univ.; literary reviewer various magazines; fmr. civil servant; fmr. Ed. Male Magazine. *Publications:* The Dark Arena 1955, The Fortunate Pilgrim 1964, The Runaway Summer of Davie Shaw 1966, The Godfather 1969, The Godfather Papers and Other Confessions 1972, Inside Las Vegas 1977, Fools Die 1978, The Sicilian 1984, The Fourth K 1991, The Last Don 1996. *Screenplays:* The Godfather (with Francis Ford Coppola (q.v.); Acad. Award Best Adapted Screenplay 1972, Screen Award Writers Guild of American W. 1972, Golden Globe Award Best Screenplay 1973) 1972, The Godfather Part II (with Coppola; Acad. Award Best Adapted Screenplay 1974, Screen Award Writers Guild of American W. 1974) 1974, Earthquake (with George Fox) 1974, Superman (with Robert Benton, David Newman and Leslie Newman) 1978, Superman II (with D. Newman and L. Newman) 1981, The Cotton Club (with Coppola and William Kennedy) 1984, The Godfather Part III (with Coppola; Golden Globe Award Best Screenplay 1990) 1990, Christopher Columbus: The Discovery (with John Briley and Cary Bates) 1992. *Address:* c/o Candida Donadio and Associates, 121 West 27th Street, New York, NY 10001, U.S.A.

PYAVKO, Vladislav Ivanovich; Russian tenor; b. 4 Feb. 1941, Krasnoyarsk; s. of Nina Piavko and step-s. of Nikolai Bakhin; m. Irina Arkhipova; two s. two d.; ed. State Inst. of Theatrical Art, Moscow; studied under S. Rebrikov, Moscow, R. Pastorino, La Scala, Milan; mem. CPSU 1978–89; soloist with Bolshoi Opera 1965–89, Berliner Staatsopera 1989–92; teacher of singing and dramatic art, State Inst. of Theatrical Art 1980–89, Dean of School 1983–89; producer at Mosfilm 1980–83; has also sung at Teatro Colón, Buenos Aires, Teatro Comunale, Florence, Opéra la Bastille, Paris, Nat. and Smetana Operas, Prague, Metropolitan, New York, Kirov, St. Petersburg, and in many other houses; also at many int. festivals: numerous recordings for leading int. labels including EMI, HMV, Philips, Chant du Monde, Columbia; Academician, Acad. of Art of Russia 1992; Gold Medal in tenor section, Vervier Int. Competition 1969, Silver Medal, Tchaikovsky Int. Competition 1970, Golde Medal and Pietro Mascagni Silver Medal, Livorno 1984, Gold Plank of Cisternino, Italy 1993; People's Artist of U.S.S.R. 1983, of Kyrgyzstan 1993 and other awards. *Major roles include:* Hermann in Queen of Spades, Andrei in Mazeppa, Dmitry and Shuisky in Boris Godunov, Andrei and Golitsin in Khovanshchina, Radames, Otello, Manrico in Trovatore, Cavaradossi in Tosca, Pinkerton in Madam Butterfly, Don José in Carmen, Turiddu in Cavalleria Rusticana, Guglielmo Ratcliff. *Leisure interests:* poetry, photography, cars. *Address:* Bryusov, per. 2/14, Apt. 27, 103009 Moscow, Russia. *Telephone:* 229-43-07.

PYE, William Burns, A.R.C.A., F.R.B.S.; British sculptor; b. 16 July 1938, London; s. of Sir David Pye and Virginia Pye; m. Susan Marsh 1963; one s. two d.; ed. Charterhouse School, Wimbledon School of Art, Royal Coll. of Art; Visiting Prof., Calif. State Univ. 1975–76; Kinetic sculpture Revolving Tower 1970; made film Reflections 1971; sculpture 'Zemran' 1971; introduction of tensioned cables with less emphasis on volume 1972; combined working on commissions with smaller work and installations 1972–75; first visit to Far East for one-man show (retrospective) 1987; Slipstream and jetstream (water sculptures) commissioned by British Airports Authority, Gatwick Airport 1988; Balla Frois (100 ft. long water sculpture) commission for Glasgow Garden Festival 1988; Alpheus water feature for Gatwick Sterling Hotel 1989; Arethusa water feature for Unicorn House, Euston Rd., London 1989; Chalice water sculpture for 123 Buckingham Palace Rd., London 1990; created Water Wall and Portico for British Pavilion, Expo '92, Seville, Spain; Epidavros at Dolby Labs.; Aventino at Mercury House; Cristos at St. Christopher's Place; Water Sculpture at Trinity Hospice, London; Tetra Trellis at Tetra Pak UK 1993; Downpour at British Embassy, Oman; Cascade at Market Square, Derby 1994; Confluence in Salisbury Square, Hertford 1994; Water Cone at Antony House, Cornwall for Nat. Trust 1996; bronze of Lord Hurd for Nat. Portrait Gallery 1996; Archimedes, floating sculpture at W. India Quay, London 1997, Cader Idris at Cen. Square, Cardiff 1998; Prism for Cathay Pacific at Hong Kong Airport 1999; Hon. F.R.I.B.A. 1993; Prix de Sculpture (Budapest) 1981, Vauxhall Mural Prize 1983, Peace Sculpture Prize 1984, A.B.S.A. award for best commission of new art in any medium 1988, Art at Work award for best site specific commission 1988, Royal Ueno Museum Award, Japan 1989. *Leisure interest:* playing the flute. *Address:* 43 Hambalt Road, London, SW4 9EQ; The Studio, 31 Bellevue Road, London, SW17 7EF, England. *Telephone:* 0181-682 2727 (Studio). *Fax:* 0181-682 3218.

PYM, Baron (Life Peer), cr. 1987, of Sandy in the County of Bedfordshire; **Francis Leslie Pym,** P.C., M.C., D.L.; British politician; b. 13 Feb. 1922, Abergavenny, Wales; s. of Leslie Ruthven Pym and Iris Rosalind Orde; m. Valerie Fortune Daglish 1949; two s. two d.; ed. Eton Coll. and Magdalene Coll., Cambridge; served with 9th Queen's Royal Lancers (N. African and Italian campaigns) 1942–46; mem. Liverpool Univ. Council 1949–53, Herefordshire Co. Council 1958–61; Hon. Fellow, Magdalene Coll.; M.P. for Cambridgeshire 1961–83; for Cambridgeshire S.E. 1983–87; Opposition Deputy Chief Whip 1967–70, Govt. Chief Whip and Parl. Sec. to Treasury 1970–73; Sec. of State for Northern Ireland 1973–74; Opposition Spokesman for Agric. 1974–76, for House of Commons Affairs and Devolution 1976–78, for Foreign and Commonwealth Affairs 1978–79; Sec. of State for Defence 1979–81; Chancellor of Duchy of Lancaster, Paymaster-Gen. and Leader of the House of Commons Jan.–Sept. 1981; Lord Pres. of the Council and Leader of the House of Commons 1981–82; Sec. of State for Foreign and Commonwealth Affairs 1982–83; Chair. Diamond Cable Communications PLC 1995–, Philip N. Christie 1990–93; Dir. Christie Brockbank Shipton Ltd. 1994–; Pres. Cambridge Univ. Conservative Asscn. 1982–87, Atlantic Treaty Asscn. 1985–88; Chair. English-Speaking Union of the Commonwealth 1987–92. *Publications:* The Politics of Consent 1984, Sentimental Journey 1998. *Leisure interest:* gardens. *Address:* Everton Park, Sandy, Beds., SG19 2DE, England.

PYNCHON, Thomas, B.A.; American novelist; b. 8 May 1937, Glen Cove, N.Y.; s. of Thomas R. Pynchon; ed. Cornell Univ.; fmr. editorial writer, Boeing Aircraft Co. *Publications include:* V (Faulkner prize for Best First Novel of 1963) 1963, The Crying of Lot 49 (Rosenthal Foundation Award 1967) 1966, Gravity's Rainbow (Nat. Book Award) 1973, Mortality and Mercy in Vienna 1976, Low-Lands 1978, Slow Learner (short stories) 1984, Vineland 1989, Deadly Sins 1994, Mason & Dixon 1996; contrib. short stories to various publs., including Saturday Evening Post. *Address:* c/o Little Brown and Co., 34 Beacon Street, Boston, MA 02108, U.S.A.

PYNE, Natasha; British actress; b. 9 July 1946, Crawley, Sussex; d. of John Pyne and Iris Pyne; m. Paul Copley 1972; ed. Hurlingham Comprehensive School, London; entered film industry 1961; mem. Young Vic Theatre Co. and Exchange Co., Manchester 1980–81; mem. BBC Radio Drama Co. 1985–87; *stage plays include:* A Party for Bonzo (Soho Poly) 1985–87, Twelfth Night (Middle East and Africa Tour) 1989–90, Rafts and Dreams 1990, Alfie (U.K. Tour) 1992–93; *films include:* The Idol, Taming of the Shrew, Breaking of Bumbo, One of Our Dinosaurs is Missing, Madhouse; *TV plays include:* Father Dear Father (series), Hamlet, Silas Marner; BBC Play for Today: A Brush with Mr Porter on the Road to Eldorado 1981, Van der Valk (Thames TV) 1990–91, The Bill (Thames TV series) 1991, 1993, Virtual Murder (BBC TV) 1992, McLibel! (Channel 4 drama-documentary) 1997, Cadfael III (TV film series) 1997; *radio work includes:* On May-Day (BBC Radio 4 and BBC World Service) 1986, The Snow Queen 1994, Galileo 1995, Ben Hur (serial) 1995, Westway (BBC World Service serial) 1997–98, Yours PC (BBC Radio 4 series) 1997; mem. BBC Radio Drama Co. 1994–95. *Leisure interests:* cycling, reading, cooking, travel, photography. *Address:* c/o Kate Feast Management, 10 Primrose Hill Studios, Fitzroy Road, London, NW1 8TR, England. *Telephone:* 0171-586 5502. *Fax:* 0171-586 9817.

Q

QABOOS BIN SAID; Omani ruler; b. 18 Nov. 1940, Salalah; s. of late H.H. Said bin Taimur; 14th descendant of the ruling dynasty of Albusaid Family; m. 1976; ed. privately in U.K., R.M.A., Sandhurst; Sultan of Oman (following deposition of his father) July 1970–, also Prime Minister, Minister of Foreign Affairs, Defence and Finance; Hon. K.C.M.G. *Leisure interests:* reading, horse-riding, music. *Address:* Diwan of the Royal Court, P.O. Box 632, Muscat 113, Sultanate of Oman. *Telephone:* 738711.

QADDAFI, Col. Mu'ammar al- (see Gaddafi, Col. Mu'ammar al-).

QADHAFI, Col. Mu'ammar al- (see Gaddafi, Col. Mu'ammar al-).

QASIMI, H.H. Sheikh Sultan bin Mohammed al–, PH.D.; Ruler of Sharjah; b. 1 July 1939; ed. Exeter Univ.; Minister of Educ. 1972; Ruler of Sharjah 1972–; Fellow Doram Univ.; Dr. h.c. (Khartoum Univ., Faisalabad Univ., Pakistan); Distinguished Personality Prize (Exeter Univ.) 1993. *Address:* Ruler's Palace, Sharjah, United Arab Emirates.

QASSIMI, H. H. Sheikh Saqr bin Muhammad Al; Ruler of Ras Al-Khaimah; b. 1920; Ruler of Emirate of Ras Al-Khaimah 1948–; Chair. Rulers' Council of Trucial States –1971; mem. Supreme Council of United Arab Emirates 1972–. *Address:* The Ruler's Palace, Ras Al-Khaimah, United Arab Emirates.

QATAR, Emir of (see Thani, Sheikh Khalifa bin Hamad al-).

QI HUAIYUAN; Chinese diplomatist and state official; b. 1930, Echeng Co., Hubei Prov.; ed. North China People's Univ., Harbin Foreign Languages Coll.; Vice-Minister of Foreign Affairs 1986, Dir. Foreign Affairs Office of State Council 1991–98; mem. 14th CCP Cen. Cttee. 1992–97; Pres. Chinese People's Asscn. for Friendship with Foreign Countries (CPAFFC) 1994–, Vice-Chair. Foreign Affairs Cttee., 9th Nat. Cttee. of CPPCC 1998–. *Address:* Chinese People's Association for Friendship with Foreign Countries, 1 Taijichang Dajie, Beijing 100740, People's Republic of China. *Telephone:* (010) 65125505.

QIAN GUANLIN; Chinese politician; b. Oct. 1946, Funing, Jiangsu Prov.; ed. Shanghai Foreign Trade Inst.; joined CCP 1973; Dir. Customs Head Office 1993; mem. CCP 14th Cen. Cttee. for Discipline Inspection 1992–97; alt. mem. CCP 15th Cen. Cttee. 1997–. *Address:* Customs Head Office, Beijing, People's Republic of China.

QIAN GUOLIANG, Lieut.-Gen.; Chinese army officer; b. Wujiang, Jiangsu Prov.; PLA civilian work; rank of Commdr. 1985, of Lieut-Gen. 1994; alt. mem. Cen. Cttee. 13th CCP Nat. Congress 1987–92, Cen. Cttee. 14th CCP Nat. Congress 1992-; Chief of Staff, Jinan Mil. Region 1994–96; Deputy Mil. Region Commdr. 1996, Commdr. 1996–; mem. 15th CCP Cen. Cttee. 1997–. *Address:* c/o People's Liberation Army, Ministry of National Defence, Jingshanqian Jie, Beijing, People's Republic of China.

QIAN LINGXI; Chinese university professor and civil engineer; b. 16 July 1916, Wuxi, Jiangsu; Pres. Dalian Univ. of Tech. 1981; Pres. Chinese Soc. of Theoretical and Applied Mechanics 1982–; mem. Chinese Acad. of Sciences 1955–, Congress Cttee. and Gen. Ass. of Int. Union of Theoretical and Applied Mechanics 1984–, Founding Council of Int. Asscn. for Computational Mechanics 1985–; Dept. of Tech. Science, Acad. Sinica 1985–; Dr. h.c. (Univ. of Liege) 1987. *Address:* c/o Dalian University of Technology, Research Institute of Engineering Mechanics, Dalian, 116024 Liaoning, People's Republic of China.

QIAN LINZHAO (Tsien Ling-Chao), PH.D.; Chinese scientist; b. 9 July 1906, Wuxi Co., Jiangsu Prov.; s. of Qian Bo-Gui and Hua Kai-Sen; one s. two d.; ed. London Univ., and in France; went on a study tour to U.S.A. 1947–48; Deputy, 3rd NPC 1964; Vice-Pres., Univ. of Science and Tech. 1979; mem. Dept. of Math. and Physics, Academia Sinica 1955–; Carey Foster Prize. *Address:* c/o University of Science and Technology of China, Hefei, Anhui, People's Republic of China. *Telephone:* (0551) 3602203.

QIAN LIREN; Chinese party official; b. 20 Aug. 1924, Jiaxing Co., Zhejiang Prov.; s. of Qian Xunyi and Hu Suxian; m. Zheng Yun 1952; one s. one d.; joined CCP 1940; Deputy Sec.-Gen. All-China Fed. of Democratic Youth 1953; Sec.-Gen. All-China Students' Fed. 1956; Dir. Int. Liaison Dept. Communist Youth League 1959-Cultural Revolution; Vice-Chair. All-China Fed. of Youth 1962; mem. Standing Council Chinese People's Asscn. for Friendship with Foreign Countries 1974–78; Perm. Rep. UNESCO 1978–81; Deputy Dir. Int. Liaison Dept., Cen. Cttee. CCP 1982–83, Dir. 1983–85; mem. CCP Cen. Cttee. 1985–92, Chair. Foreign Affairs Cttee. 1995–98; mem. 8th Nat. Cttee. 1993–98; mem. Propaganda and Ideological Work Leading Group 1988; Vice-Pres. Chinese Asscn. for Int. Understanding 1995–; Hon. Pres. Newspaper Operation and Man. Asscn. 1988; Dir. Renmin Ribao (People's Daily) 1985–89. *Leisure interests:* reading, swimming. *Address:* c/o Chinese Association for International Understanding, 15 Wanshou Road, Beijing 100036, People's Republic of China. *Telephone:* 68276033. *Fax:* 68212861.

QIAN QICHEN; Chinese diplomatist and state official; b. Jan. 1928, Tiading Co., Shanghai; m. Zhou Hanqiong; one s. one d.; ed. Shanghai Datung Middle School and in U.S.S.R.; joined CCP 1942; Second Sec. Embassy, U.S.S.R. 1955–62, Counsellor 1972–74; Amb. to Guinea and Guinea Bissau 1974–76; Dir. Information Dept., Ministry of Foreign Affairs 1977–82; Vice-Minister, Foreign Affairs 1982–88, Minister 1988–98; alt. mem. 12th CCP Cen. Cttee. 1982, mem. 1985, mem. 13th Cen. Cttee. 1987–92, 14th Cen. Cttee. 1992–97, Deputy Head Cen. Foreign Affairs Leading Group; mem. Politburo CCP 1992–; mem. 15th CCP Cen. Cttee. 1997–; Leader Special Admin. Region Preparatory Cttee. (to establish post-1997 Govt. in Hong Kong) 1993–97; Chinese Special Envoy, 2–11th Round Sino-Soviet Consultations 1983–87; Head of Chinese Del., First Round Sino-Soviet Border Talks 1987; Deputy Dir. Comm. for Commemorating 40th Anniversary of UN 1985; Vice-Chair. Organizing Cttee. for Int. Year of Peace 1985; State Councillor 1991–93; Vice-Premier of State Council 1993–. *Address:* State Council, Beijing, People's Republic of China.

QIAN RENYUAN, F.A.I.C.; Chinese chemist; b. 19 Sept. 1917, Changshu, Jiangsu; s. of Qian Nantie and Miao Lingfen; m. 1st Hu Miaozhen 1951 (divorced 1956); m. 2nd Ying Qicong 1961 (divorced 1994); one d.; m. 3rd Yu Yansheng 1996; ed. Zhejiang Univ., Univ. of Wisconsin, U.S.A.; Assoc. Prof. Xiamen Univ. 1948–49, Zhejiang Univ. 1949–51; Prof. Inst. of Physical Chem. Acad. Sinica 1951–53, Inst. of Chem. 1956–; Deputy Dir., Inst. of Chem., Acad. Sinica 1977–81, Dir. 1981–85; Pres. Chinese Chemical Soc. 1982–86, Exec. Pres. 1984–85; Chair. Polymer Div., Chinese Chemical Soc. 1986–94; mem. Chem. Div., Acad. Sinica 1980; Assoc. mem. IUPAC Comm. on Polymer Characterization & Properties 1985–(97); Science Premium, (3rd class), Acad. Sinica 1956, Advanced Individual Award, Acad. Sinica 1977, Science Award Nat. Science Congress 1978, State Invention Award, (3rd class), State Comm. of Science and Tech. 1980, SINOPEC Science and Tech. Progress Award, (1st class) 1987, Acad. Sinica Natural Science Award (1st class) 1989, 1993, (2nd class) 1992, State Natural Science Award (2nd class) 1988, 1992, State Science & Tech. Progress Award (1st class) 1989, Qiushi Prize for Distinguished Scientists 1994, Int. Award, The Soc. of Polymer Science, Japan 1995. *Publications:* over 250 papers in Chinese and int. journals, over 50 reviews and book chapters, 2 books and 2 patents. *Address:* Institute of Chemistry, Academia Sinica, P.O. Box 2709, Beijing 100080, People's Republic of China. *Telephone:* 6255-5505. *Fax:* 6256-9564.

QIAN SHUGEN, Lieut.-Gen.; Chinese army officer; b. Feb. 1939, Wuxi City, Jiangsu Prov. ed. Chongqing Artillery School, PLA Mil. Acad. and Univ. of Nat. Defence; mem. CCP 1956–; entered army 1954; Deputy Div. Commdr. 47th Army 1981; Div. Commdr. 139th Div. 1983; Deputy Army Commdr. 47th Army 1984; Army Commdr. 47th Group Army 1985; Chief of Staff, Lanzhou Mil. Region 1992; Deputy Political Commissar, Lanzhou Mil. Region 1993; Asst. to Chief of Gen. Staff 1994; Deputy Chief, PLA Gen. Staff 1995–; rank of Lieut.-Gen. 1993; alt. mem. 14th CCP Cen. Cttee. 1992–97; mem. 15th CCP Cen. Cttee. 1997–. *Address:* c/o Ministry of National Defence, Jingshanqian Jie, Beijing, People's Republic of China. *Telephone:* (1) 6370000.

QIAN WEICHANG (Wei-zang Chien), M.A., PH.D.; Chinese physicist and applied mathematician; b. 9 Oct. 1912, Wuxi, Jiangsu; s. of Prof. Chien Shen-Yi and Chien Wang Shui Ying; m. Kong Xiang-Ying 1939; one s. two d.; ed. Nat. Tsing-Hua Univ. and Univ. of Toronto; Research Engineer Jet Propulsion Lab., Calif. Inst. of Tech. 1942–46; returned to China 1946; Prof. of Physics and Applied Maths, Qinghua Univ. Beijing 1946–83, Dean of Studies 1949–58, Vice-Pres. 1956–58; mem. Standing Cttee. All China Fed. of Scientific Socs. 1950–58; mem. Standing Cttee., All China Democratic Youth League 1949–58; Head Mechanics Section, Inst. of Math., Acad. Sinica 1951–55; Vice-Dir. Inst. of Mechanics; Dir. Inst. of Automation 1955–58; mem. Acad. Sinica 1954–58, 1980–; mem. Polish Acad. of Sciences 1956–; mem. State Council Comm. for Scientific Planning 1956–58; Jiangsu Prov. Deputy to NCP 1954–58, 1975–78; labelled as rightist 1958; Pres. Shanghai Univ. of Tech. 1982, Shanghai Univ. 1994–; Dir. Shanghai Inst. of Applied Math. and Mechanics 1984–; Vice-Chair. CPPCC 7th Nat. Cttee. 1987–93, 8th Nat. Cttee. 1993–98, 9th Nat. Cttee. 1998–; Chair. Science, Educ., Culture, Public Health and Sports Cttee.; Vice-Chair. Chinese Democratic League, Cen. Cttee. 1983–97, Hon. Chair. 1997–; mem. Draft Cttee. Hong Kong Basic Law 1986–91; Vice-Chair. Draft Cttee. Macao Basic Law 1988–93; Pres. (Exec.) Asscn. for Peaceful Reunification Promotion 1988–; Pres. Soc. of Chinese Language Information Processing 1980–, Chinese Overseas Exchanges Asscn. 1990–; Ed.-in-Chief, Applied Maths. and Mechanics (Chinese and English Ed.) 1980–; mem. Editorial Bd., Int. Journal of Eng. Science (U.S.A.) 1982–, Advances in Applied Maths. (U.S.A.) 1984–, Journal of Thin-Walled Structure (U.S.A.) 1986–, Finite Elements in Analysis and Design (U.S.A.), Chinese Encyclopedia 1983–; mem. Jt. Chinese-U.S. Editorial Bd., Chinese Ed., Concise Encyclopedia Britannica 1983–; Nat. Science Award 1955, 1982; Beijing Municipal Award for Discoveries 1974, Shanghai Municipal Award for Technological Discoveries 1985. *Publications:* Scientific Discoveries in Chinese History 1953, Theory of Elasticity 1956, Theory of Torsion for Elastic Columns 1956, Large Deflection of Circular Plates 1957, Variational Principles and Finite Elements Methods 1980, Generalized Variational Principles 1984, Mechanics of Penetration

1985 (Nat. Prize for Best Publ. 1988), Green's Function and Variational Principles in the Problems of Electro-magnetic Fields and Waves 1989, Selected Works of Qian Wei-chang 1989, Applied Mathematics 1991, Foundation of Strength Computation in Electrical Machinery 1993; numerous articles for scientific papers on physics, applied maths. and mechanics. *Address:* 149 Yanchang Road, Shanghai University, Shanghai 200072; Chinese People's Political Consultative Conference, National Committee, Beijing 100811, People's Republic of China. *Telephone:* (021) 5663 9822 (Shanghai), (010) 6619 1111 (Beijing).

QIAN XINBO; Chinese journalist; b. 14 Jan. 1923, Jiading Co., Jiangsu Prov.; m. Chen Meixia 1953; one s. one d.; ed. Yanjing Univ.; council mem. of New China News Agency 1982–; Vice-Pres. and Sec.-Gen. of Feb. Journalism Soc. 1984–90; Deputy Dir. of Journalism Inst. Acad. of Social Sciences 1982–90. *Publications:* On News' Role of Guidance; Five Historical Periods of Development of Chinese Journalism. *Address:* 6-1-502 Tuanjiehu Beili, Beijing 100026, People's Republic of China. *Telephone:* 5029648.

QIAN XUESEN, PH.D.; Chinese scientist; b. 11 Dec. 1910, Shanghai; m. Jiang Ying 1947; one s. one d.; ed. Jiaotong Univ. Shanghai, Calif. Inst. of Tech.; with M.I.T. 1935; Dir. Rocket Section, US Nat. Defence Science Advisory Bd. 1945–49; Prof., M.I.T. 1946–49, Calif. Inst. of Tech. 1949–55; Dir. China Inst. of Mechanics 1956; Pres. Dynamics Soc. 1956–63; Vice-Chair. Science and Tech. Comm. for Nat. Defence 1978–; mem. Dept. for Math. Physics and Chem., Acad. of Sciences 1957–; mem. 9th CCP Cen. Cttee. 1969–73, 10th 1973–77, 11th 1977–82, 12th 1982–85; Vice-Minister Comm. for Science, Tech. and Industry for Nat. Defence 1982–87, Sr. Adviser 1987–; Pres. Dynamics Soc. 1957–82; Chair. China Asscn. for Science and Tech. 1986–91, Hon. Chair. 1991–; Hon. Pres. Astronautics Soc. 1980–, Soc. of Systems Eng. 1980–; Vice-Chair. Nat. Cttee. 6th CPPCC 1986–88, 7th 1988–93, 8th 1993–98; Sr. Fellow Chinese Acad. of Sciences and Chinese Acad. of Eng. 1998–. *Address:* Chinese Academy of Sciences, Beijing, People's Republic of China.

QIAN YONGCHANG; Chinese politician; b. 1933, Shanghai City; joined CCP 1953; alt. mem. 12th Cen. Cttee. CCP 1982–87, mem. 13th Cen. Cttee. 1987–; Vice-Minister of Communications 1982–84, Minister 1984–91; Chair. Bd. of Dirs., Hong Kong China Merchants Group 1985–. *Address:* c/o Ministry of Communications, Beijing, People's Republic of China.

QIAN YUNLU; Chinese politician; b. Nov. 1944, Dawu, Hubei Prov.; ed. Hubei Univ.; joined CCP 1965; Vice-Sec. CCP Hubei Prov. Cttee. 1983-98; Sec. CCP Wuhan City Cttee. 1991–98; Chair. Hubei Prov. People's Political Consultative Conf. 1998; Deputy Gov. of Guizhou Prov. 1998–; alt. mem. CCP 14th and 15th Cen. Cttee. 1992–. *Address:* Guizhou Provincial People's Government, Guiyang, People's Republic of China.

QIAN ZHENGYING; Chinese government official; b. 1923, Jiaxing Co., Zhejiang Prov.; m. Huang Xinbai; ed. Dadong Univ., Shanghai; joined CCP 1941; Vice-Minister of Water Conservancy 1952–67; Minister of Water Conservancy and Electrical Power 1970–74, Minister 1974–88; Adviser to State Council 1981–82, mem. 1982–; Vice-Chair. CCP Nat. Comm., Chair. Women, Youth and Legal Affairs Cttee.; Adviser to State Flood Control HQ 1988–; mem. 11th Cen. Cttee. of CCP 1977–82, 12th Cen. Cttee. 1982–87, 13th Cen. Cttee. 1987–92; mem. 14th Cen. Cttee. 1992–97; Vice-Chair. CPPCC 7th Nat. Cttee. 1988–92, 8th 1993–98, 9th Nat. Cttee. 1998–; Pres. Red Cross Soc. of China 1994–, China–India Friendship Asscn., China Award Foundation for Teachers of Middle and Primary Schools and Kindergartens; Gold Medal (Somalia). *Address:* National Committee of Chinese People's Political Consultative Conference, 23 Taipingqiao Street, Beijing, People's Republic of China.

QIANG XIAOCHU; Chinese party official; b. Shaanxi; Second Sec. CCP Cttee., Sungkiang 1951; mem. Prov. People's Govt., Sungkiang 1951; Chair. Sungkiang (when merged with Heilongjiang) 1952; Deputy Sec. CCP Cttee., Heilongjiang 1954, Sec. Secr., CCP Cttee. 1956; First Sec. Secr., CCP Sungari River Dist. Cttee. 1958; Alt. Sec. Secr., N.E. Bureau 1961; leading mem. 7th Ministry of Machine-Building 1976; First Sec. CCP Cttee., Jilin 1981; mem. 12th Cen. Cttee., CCP 1982–87; First Political Commissar, PLA Jilin Mil. Dist. 1982–; Sec. Cen. Cttee. for Discipline Inspection 1985–87; Deputy Head Leading Group for Rectification of Party Style within Cen. Depts. 1986–, mem. Cen. Advisory Comm. 1987–. *Address:* Communist Party Committee, Jilin Province, People's Republic of China.

QIAO SHI; Chinese party official; b. Dec. 1924, Dinghai Co., Zhejiang Prov.; m. Yu Wen; joined CCP 1940; Sec. CP branch, Shanghai Middle School 1942; Deputy Sec. Shanghai Dist. CP; Sec. Youth Cttee., Hangzhou CP 1950–; Dir. Designing Inst. of Jiuquan Iron and Steel Co. 1960–63; Sec. Afro-Asian Solidarity Cttee. 1965–Cultural Revolution; Deputy Dir. Int. Liaison Dept., CCP Cen. Cttee. 1978–82, Dir. 1982–83; mem. 12th Cen. Cttee., CCP 1982, 13th Cen. Cttee. 1985, 1987–92, 14th Cen. Cttee. 1992–97; mem. Politburo 1985, and Standing Cttee. of Politburo 1987–; Vice-Premier, State Council 1986–88; Alt. mem. Secr., Cen. Cttee. 1982–85, mem. 1985; Dir. Org. Dept., CCP Cen. Cttee. 1984–85; Sec. Cen. Cttee. of Political Science and Law 1985–87; Head Leading Group for Rectification of Party Style within Cen. Depts. 1986–; Sec. Cen. Comm. for Discipline Inspection 1987–93; mem. Politburo, Standing Cttee. of Politburo, Secr. CPC Cen. Cttee. 1989–92; Perm. mem. Politburo 14th Cen. Cttee. 1992–97; Chair. Standing Cttee. 8th NPC 1993–98. *Address:* c/o International Liaison Department, Central Committee, Communist Party, Beijing, People's Republic of China.

QIAO SHIGUANG; Chinese artist; b. 5 Feb. 1937, Guantao Co., Hebei Prov.; s. of Qiao Lu De and Wang Hao Ling; m. Luo Zhen Ru 1961; two d.; Prof. Cen. Acad. of Arts and Design; Founder-Chair. Chinese Soc. of Lacquer Painting 1990 (group exhbn. Beijing 1990); Dir. Chinese Artists Asscn.; Dir. Int. Culture of Lacquer 1992–; Founder Korea-China Lacquer Art Exchange Exhbn., Seoul 1994; solo exhbns. of lacquer paintings Tokyo 1989, 1990, 1994, Kyoto 1989, Japan 1990, Paris 1992, Anano 1993, China Art Gallery 1996, Seoul 1996. *Publications:* Selected Lacquer Paintings of Qiao Shiguang 1993, The Skill and Artistic Expression of Lacquer Painting 1995, Collection of Qiao Shiguang's Lacquer Paintings 1996. *Leisure interests:* calligraphy, writing poetry. *Address:* The Central Academy of Arts and Design, 34 Dong Huan Bei Lu, Beijing 100020 (Office); 3 602 Building, 6 Hong Miao Bei Li, Chao Yang District, Beijing 100025, People's Republic of China (Home). *Telephone:* 5082233-2246 (Office); 65948311 (Home).

QIN HUASUN; Chinese diplomatist; b. Sept. 1935, Jiangsu Prov.; Counsellor and Deputy Perm. Rep. to Office of UN and other int. orgs. Geneva 1984–87, Perm. Rep. Vienna 1987–90; Dir.-Gen. Dept. of Int. Orgs. and Confs. Ministry of Foreign Affairs 1990–93; Asst. Minister of Foreign Affairs 1993–95; Perm. Rep. to UN 1995–97. *Address:* Ministry of Foreign Affairs, 225 Chaoyangmennei Dajie Dongsi, Beijing 100701, People's Republic of China.

QIN WENCAI; Chinese industrialist; b. Feb. 1925, Shanxi; s. of Qin Wanrong and Qin Wangshi; m. Zhang Huang 1950; one s. three d.; Vice-Minister, Minister of Petroleum Industry, Vice-Pres. Petroleum Corpn. of People's Repub. of China 1979–82, China Enterprises Man. Asscn. 1991–, China Entrepreneurs Asscn. 1991–; Pres. China Nat. Offshore Oil Corpn. 1982–87; Chair. China Offshore Oil Service Co., Hong Kong 1985–; Chair. Consultative Cttee. 1987–; Pres. Capital Enterprises Club 1990–. *Leisure interests:* reading, sport. *Address:* Jia 2, Dong San Huan Road, Chaoyang District, P.O. Box 4705, Beijing, People's Republic of China. *Telephone:* 64662114.

QIN YI; Chinese film actress; b. 2 Feb. 1922, Shanghai; Outstanding Film Artist Prize 1992. *Films include:* Remote Love, Song of Youth, Fog is no Fog 1993, and others; mem. 6th CPPCC 1983–87, 7th 1987–92, 8th 1993–. *Address:* Shanghai Film Studio, 595 Caoxi North Road, Shanghai 200030, People's Republic of China.

QING XIAO; Chinese business executive; b. 1947; joined China Int. Trust and Investment Corpn. (CITIC) 1986; served as Deputy Gen. Man., then Gen. Man. Business Dept., Pres. CITIC Devt. Co. Ltd., Chair. CITIC Australia; Vice-Pres. CITIC 1994–95, Pres. 1995–. *Address:* China International Trust and Investment Corporation (CITIC), 6 Xianyuannan Lu, Chaoyang Qu, Beijing 100004, People's Republic of China. *Telephone:* 4660088. *Fax:* 4661186.

QIU CHUNPU; Chinese business executive; b. 1930; joined CCP 1958; Chair. of Bd. of Dirs., China Nat. Nonferrous Metals Industry Corpn. 1993–. *Address:* China National Nonferrous Metals Industry Corporation, 9 Xizhang Hutong, Xicheng District, Beijing 100814, People's Republic of China.

QUADFLIEG, Will; German actor and director; b. 15 Sept. 1914, Oberhausen; m. 1st Benita Vegesack 1940; five c.; m. 2nd Margaret Jacobs 1963; ed. private drama studies; first stage appearances in Giessen, Gera, Düsseldorf; with Volksbühne, Berlin 1937–40, Schiller-Theater, Berlin 1940–45, Schauspielhaus, Hamburg 1946–50; guest appearances at Zürich, Salzburg Festival, Ruhr Festival and Burgtheater, Vienna; tours in Germany, Austria and Switzerland; noted for recitation of works of classical and contemporary poets; major stage roles in works of Goethe, Schiller, Shakespeare, Ibsen, Strindberg, etc. *Film appearances include:* Der Maulkorb, Der grosse Schatten, Lola Montez, Faust; mem. Freie Akad. der Künste, Hamburg, Deutsche Akad. der Darstellenden Künste, Frankfurt; Grosser Hersfeld Preis 1980; Medaille für Kunst und Wissenschaft 1984; Grosses Bundesverdienstkrenz. *Publication:* Wir Spielen Immer 1976. *Leisure interest:* music. *Address:* 27711 Osterholz-Scharmbeck, Germany.

QUADRIO CURZIO, Alberto; Italian professor of economics; b. 25 Dec. 1937, Tirano-Valtellina; s. of Saverio F. Quadrio Curzio and Anna (Isella) Quadrio Curzio; m. Maria Luisa Bottasso 1964; one s. one d.; ed. Faculty of Political Sciences, Catholic Univ., Milan, St. John's Coll., Cambridge; Assoc. Prof. of Econs, Univ. of Cagliari 1965–68; Assoc. Prof. of Econs., Univ. of Bologna 1968–72, Prof. 1972–75, Chair., Faculty of Political Sciences 1974–75; Prof. of Econs, Catholic Univ., Milan 1976–, Dir. Centre of Econ. Analysis 1977–, Chair. Faculty of Political Sciences 1989–; Dir., Economia Politica (quarterly review) 1984–; mem., Italian Nat. Research Council 1977–88; Pres. Italian Econs. Asscn. 1995–98; mem. Comm. Pontificia Justitia et Pax, Consult Stato Città Vaticano, Accademia Naz. dei Lincei, Istituto Lombardo, Accademia di Scienze e Lettere; St. Vincent Award 1984, W. Tobagi Award 1996, Cortima Ulisse Int. Award 1997. *Publications:* about 200, including (since 1980) Rent, Income Distribution, Order of Efficiency and Rentability 1980, The Gold Problem: Economic Perspectives 1982, Planning Manpower Education and Economic Growth 1983, Sui Momenti costitutivi della Economia Politica (co-author) 1983–84, Technological Scarcity: an Essay on Production and Structural Change 1986, The Exchange-Production Duality and the Dynamics of Economic Knowledge (with R. Scazzieri) 1986, Industrial Raw Materials: a Multi-Country, Multi-Commodity Analysis (co-author) 1986, The agro-technological system towards 2000: a European perspective (co-ed. and co-author) 1988, Produzione ed efficienza con tecnologie globali (co-author) 1987, Le scarsita relative 1988, Rent, Distribution and Economic Structure (essays) 1990, Structural Rigidities and Dynamic Choice of Technologies (co-author) 1991, Issues on International Development and Solidarity 1992, On Economic Science: Its Tools and Economic Reality 1993, The Management of Municipal Solid Waste in Europe. Economic, Technological and Environmental Perspectives (co-ed.) 1994, Innovation, Resources and Economic Growth (co-ed. and co-author) 1994, Risorse, Tecnologie, Rendita (co-author) 1996, Noi, l'Economia e l'Europa 1996. *Leisure interest:* skiing. *Address:* Facoltà di Scienze Politiche, Università Cattolica del Sacro Cuore, Largo Gemelli, 1-20123 Milan (Office); Via A. Saffi 31, 20123 Milan, Italy (Home). *Telephone:* 02/72.34.24.74 (Office). *Fax:* 02/72.34.24.75.

QUAID, Dennis; American actor; b. 9 April 1954, Houston, Tex.; s. of William Rudy Quaid and Juanita B. Quaid; m. 2nd Meg Ryan (q.v.) 1991; one s.; ed. Univ. of Houston; appeared on stage in Houston before moving to Hollywood; appeared on stage in New York with brother, Randy Quaid, in True West; performs with rock band The Electrics; wrote songs for films The Night the Lights Went Out in Georgia, Tough Enough, The Big Easy; television appearances: Bill: On His Own, Johnny Belinda, Amateur Night at the Dixie Bar and Grill, Everything That Rises. *Films:* September 30 1955, 1978, Crazy Mama, Our Winning Season, Seniors, Breaking Away, I Never Promised You a Rose Garden, Gorp, The Long Riders, All Night Long, Caveman, The Night the Lights Went Out in Georgia, Tough Enough, Jaws 3-D, The Right Stuff, Dreamscape, Enemy Mine, The Big Easy, Innerspace, Suspect, D.O.A., Everyone's All-American, Great Balls of Fire, Lie Down With Lions, Postcards From the Edge, Come and See the Paradise, A 22 Cent Romance, Wilder Napalu, Flesh and Bone, Wyatt Earp, Something To Talk About 1995, Dragonheart 1996, Criminal Element 1997, Going West 1997, Gang Related 1997, Savior 1997, Switchback 1997, The Parent Trap 1998, On Any Given Sunday 1999.

QUAN SHUREN; Chinese party and government official; b. 1930, Xinmin Co., Liaoning Prov.; joined CCP 1949; Mayor of Fushun 1980–81; Sec. CCP Cttee., Fushun City 1981–82; Gov. of Liaoning 1983–86; Sec. 7th CCP Prov. Cttee., Liaoning 1983–85, Deputy Sec. 1985–86, Sec. 1986–93; Chair. Liaoning Prov. 8th People's Congress Standing Cttee. 1993–; Alt. mem. 12th CCP Cen. Cttee. 1985–87, mem. 13th Cen. Cttee. 1987–92, mem. 14th Cen. Cttee. 1992–; Deputy to 6th NPC, to 8th NPC, Liaoning Prov. *Address:* Liaoning Provincial Committee, Shenyang, Liaoning Province, People's Republic of China.

QUAN ZHENGHUAN; Chinese mural artist, painter and university professor; b. 16 June 1932, Beijing; d. of Quan Liang-Su and Qin Xiao-Qing; m. Li Hua-Ji 1959; two d.; Prof. and mem. Academic Cttee., Cen. Acad. of Applied Arts; mem. Standing Cttee. of Artists' Asscn. of China. *Murals include:* The Story of the White Snake (Beijing Int. Airport), Jin Wei filled the Ocean (Beijing Yian Jing Hotel). *Leisure interests:* Beijing Opera, old movies of 1930–1940s, football. *Address:* 6/F Hongmiao Beili, 10025, Beijing, People's Republic of China. *Telephone:* 501 5522-13.

QUANT, Mary, O.B.E., F.S.I.A.; Welsh fashion, cosmetic and textile designer; b. 11 Feb. 1934, London; d. of Jack Quant and Mildred (née Jones) Quant; m. Alexander Plunket Greene 1957 (died 1990); one s.; ed. Goldsmiths Coll. of Art, London; started career in Chelsea, London 1954; Dir. Mary Quant Group of cos. 1955–, Jt. Chair. Mary Quant Ltd.; Dir. (non-exec.) House of Fraser 1997–; mem. Design Council 1971–74, U.K.-U.S.A. Bicentennial Liaison Cttee. 1973, Advisory Council Victoria and Albert Museum 1976–78; restrospective exhbn. of 1960s fashion, London Museum 1974; Sr. Fellow, Royal Coll. of Art 1991; Hon. Fellow Goldsmiths Coll., Univ. of London 1993; Hon. F.R.S.A. 1995; Sunday Times Int. Fashion Award, Rex Award (U.S.A.), Annual Design Medal, Soc. of Industrial Artists and Designers, Piavolo d'Oro (Italy), Royal Designer for Industry, Hall of Fame Award, British Fashion Council (for outstanding contrib. to British fashion) 1990. *Publications:* Quant by Quant 1966. Colour by Quant 1984, Quant on Make-up 1986, Mary Quant Classic Make-up and Beauty Book 1996. *Address:* Mary Quant Ltd., 3 Ives Street, London, SW3 2NE, England. *Telephone:* 0171-584 8781. *Fax:* 0171-589 9443.

QUARRACINO, H. E. Cardinal Antonio; Argentinian ecclesiastic; b. 8 Aug. 1923, Salerno, Italy; ed. San José Seminary, La Plata; ordained priest 1945; fmr. Prof. Mercedes Diocese Seminary; fmr. Sec. Mercedes Diocesan Curia; fmr. ecclesiastical adviser to Diocesan Council of Catholic Youth Action; fmr. Prof. of Theology Santa María de los Buenos Aires Pontifical Catholic Univ. of Argentina; Bishop of Nueve de Julio 1962–68, of Avellaneda 1968–85; Archbishop of La Plata 1985–90; Archbishop of Buenos Aires and Primate of Argentina 1990–98; cr. Cardinal June 1991; Sec.-Gen. Latin American Council of Bishops 1978, Pres. 1982–87; Pres. Argentinian Bishops' Conf. 1990–96; mem. Pontifical Council for the Promotion of Christian Unity, Pontifical Council for the Pastoral Care of Health Workers, Cardinals' Council for the Study of the Economy and Org. of the Holy See, Pontifical Comm. for Latin America; hon. mem. Argentinian Acad. of Music 1995; Grand Cross of Belgrano Award 1995; Dr. h.c. Catholic Univ. of Puerto Rico. *Address:* c/o Arzobispado Rivadavia 415, 1002 Buenos Aires, Argentina.

QUARRIE, Donald; Jamaican athlete; b. 25 Feb. 1951, Kingston; competed Olympic Games, Munich 1972, reaching semi-final of 200 m.; Montreal 1976, won gold medal at 200 m. and silver medal at 100 m.; Moscow 1980, won bronze medal at 200 m.; competed Commonwealth Games, Edinburgh 1970, won gold medals at 100 m., 200 m. and 4×100 m. relay; Christchurch 1974 won gold medals at 100 m. and 200 m.; Edmonton 1978 won gold medal at 100 m.; one of only four men to break 20 secs. for 200 m.; World record holder for hand-timed 100 m., 200 m. and 220 yards. *Address:* c/o P.O. Box 272, Kingston 5, Jamaica, West Indies.

QUAYLE, James Danforth (Dan), B.S., J.D.; American politician; b. 4 Feb. 1947, Indianapolis; s. of James C. Quayle and Corinne (Pulliam) Quayle; m. Marilyn Tucker 1972; two s. one d.; ed. DePauw Univ., Greencastle, Ind., Indiana Univ.; served in Ind. Nat. Guard; court reporter Huntington Herald Press, Indiana 1965–69, Assoc. Publr. and Gen. Man. 1974–76; mem. Consumer Protection Div., Office of Attorney-Gen., Ind. 1970–71; Admin. Asst. to Gov. of Ind. 1971–73; Dir. Indiana Inheritance Tax Div. 1973–74; admitted to Indiana bar 1974; teacher of business law Huntington Coll. 1975; mem. U.S. House of Reps. 1977–79; Senator from Indiana 1981–88; Vice-Pres. of U.S.A. 1989–93; Chair. Nat. Space Council 1989; with Circle Investors 1993–; Distinguished Visiting Prof. American Grad. School of Int. Man. 1997; mem. Huntington bar asscn.; mem. Hoosier State Press Asscn.; Chair. Council on Competitiveness; Republican. *Publications:* Standing Firm 1994, The American Family 1995. *Address:* 6263 North Scottsdale Road, Suite 292, Scottsdale, AZ 85250, U.S.A.

QUEFFÉLEC, Anne; French concert pianist; b. 17 Jan. 1948, Paris; d. of Henri Queffélec and Yvonne Pénau; m. Luc Dehaene 1983; two s.; ed. Conservatoire National, Paris (First Prize for Piano 1965, for Chamber Music 1966); since 1968 has played all over Europe, Japan (seven tours), Israel, Africa, Canada and U.S.A.; has played with BBC Symphony, London Symphony, Royal Philharmonic, Bournemouth Symphony, Hallé, Scottish Chamber, City of Birmingham Symphony, Miami Symphony, NHK Tokyo, Tokyo Symphony orchestras, Nouvel orchestre philharmonique de Radio-France, Orchestre nat. de Radio-France, Orchestre de Strasbourg, Ensemble Intercontemporain, etc., under conductors including Zinman, Groves, Leppard, Marriner, Boulez, Semkow, Skrowaczewski, Eschenbach, Gardiner, Pritchard, Atherton, etc.; has played at numerous festivals including Strasbourg, Dijon, Besançon, La Roque-d'Anthéron, la Grange de Meslay, Bordeaux, Paris, King's Lynn, Bath, Cheltenham, London Proms; judge in several int. piano competitions; First Prize, Munich Int. Piano Competition 1968, Prizewinner, Leeds Int. Piano Competition 1969, Best Interpreter of the Year, Victoires de la Musique 1990; has made about 20 records for Erato-RCA and Virgin Classics of music by Scarlatti, Chopin, Schubert, Fauré, Ravel (all his piano works), Debussy, Liszt, Hummel, Beethoven, Mendelssohn, Bach, Satie, and complete piano works of Henri Dutilleux 1996; Chevalier Légion d'honneur. *Leisure interests:* literature, cycling, theatre, friends, humour, art exhibitions, children. *Address:* 15 avenue Corneille, 78600 Maisons-Laffitte, France. *Telephone:* 39-62-25-64. *Fax:* 39.62.25.64.

QUELER, Eve; American conductor; b. New York; ed. Mannes Coll. of Music, New York, City Coll. of New York, piano with Isabella Vengerov, conducting with Carl Bamberger, Joseph Rosstock, Walter Susskind and Igor Markevich; began as pianist, asst. conductor New York City Opera 1958 and 1965–70; later became a conductor; guest-conducted Philadelphia, Cleveland, Montréal Symphony, New Philharmonia, Australian Opera, Opéra de Nice, Opera de Barcelona, San Diego Opera, Edmonton Symphony, Nat. Opera of Czechoslovakia, Hungarian State, Hungarian Operahaz, Hamburg Opera, Pretoria, Hamilton, Ont. and various other orchestras; Music Dir. Opera Orchestra of New York 1968; Musician of the Month, Musical American Magazine; Dr. h.c. (Russell Sage Coll., Colby Coll.); Martha Baird Rockefeller Fund for Music Award. *Recordings:* Puccini's Edgar, Verdi's Aroldo, Massenet's Le Cid, Boito's Nerone, Strauss' Guntram. *Publications:* articles in Musical America Magazine. *Leisure interest:* organic gardening. *Address:* c/o Alix Barthelmes, Manager Opera Orchestra, 239 W. 72nd Street, New York, NY 10023, U.S.A.

QUENÉ, Theo; Netherlands civil servant; b. 29 July 1930, Oostzaan; s. of G. J. Quené and Th. A. M. Quené-Francois; m. 1st A. J. Boterenbrood 1956, 2nd Dr A. C. Ritter 1986; two s. three d.; ed. Agricultural Univ., Wageningen; Govt. Official Ministry of Housing and Physical Planning 1956–67, Dir. Nat. Physical Planning Agency 1967–72, Dir.-Gen. for physical planning 1972–76, Sec.-Gen. 1976–78; Chair. Scientific Council for Govt. Policy 1978–85; Chair. Socio-Economic Council 1985–; mem. Royal Netherlands Acad. of Arts and Sciences 1971, numerous acads. in Netherlands and abroad; Dr. h.c. (Agric. Univ. Wageningen); Kt. Order of the Dutch Lion. *Leisure interests:* nature protection, literature. *Address:* Leidsegracht 56, 1016 CN Amsterdam, Netherlands (Home). *Telephone:* (020) 6253663.

QUESTIAUX, Nicole Françoise; French politician; b. 19 Dec. 1930, Nantes; d. of Pierre Valayer and Elisabeth Mills; m. Paul Questiaux 1951; one s. one d.; ed. Lycée de Casablanca, Morocco, Ecole Nat. d'Admin.; Auditor, Conseil d'Etat 1955, mem. 2nd sub-section, Disputes section, Maître des Requêtes 1962, Govt. Commr. assemblée du contentieux 1963–74; Conseiller d'Etat 1980–81; Minister of State May–June 1981, Minister of Nat. Solidarity 1981–82; Pres. 4th Sub-section Conseil d'Etat 1983–; Pres. Conseil du Centre d'étude des revenus et des coûts 1984–92, of public works div. of Conseil d'Etat 1988–95. *Publications:* Le contrôle de l'administration et la protection des citoyens (with Guy Braibant and Céline Wiener) 1973, Traité du social; Situations, luttes politiques, institutions (with Jacques Fournier) 1976. *Address:* 13 avenue de Bretteville, 92200 Neuilly-sur-Seine, France (Home).

QUEYRANNE, Jean-Jack; French politician; b. Nov. 1945; s. of Maurice Queyranne and Jeanne Bonavent; First Deputy Mayor of Villeurbanne (Rhône) 1977–88; Parti Socialiste (PS) mem. Rhône Gen. Council 1979–90; Nat. Ass. Deputy (alt.) for Rhone 1981–93; mem. PS Steering Cttee., Deputy Nat. Sec. responsible for cultural policy 1983, for press and culture 1985, Party Spokesman 1985, Nat. Del. and Spokesman 1987, Nat. Sec. responsible for audiovisual policy 1988, mem. Nat. Council 1993–94; Mayor of Bron (Rhône) 1989–; Nat. Ass. Deputy for Rhône 1997–; Minister of State attached to Minister of the Interior, with responsibility for Overseas Depts. and Territories 1997–. *Address:* Ministry of Overseas Departments and Territories, 27 rue Oudinot, 75358 Paris 07 SP; Mairie, Square Weingarten, 69500 Bron, France. *Telephone:* (1) 53.69.20.00. *Fax:* (1) 43.06.60.30.

QUIGLEY, Sir (William) George (Henry), Kt., C.B., PH.D., C.B.I.M.; British banker; b. 26 Nov. 1929; s. of William G. C. Quigley and Sarah H. Martin; m. Moyra A. Munn 1971; ed. Ballymena Acad. and Queen's Univ. Belfast; Asst. Prin., N. Ireland Civil Service 1955; Perm. Sec. Dept. of Manpower Services, N. Ireland 1974–76, Dept. of Commerce 1976–79, Dept. of Finance 1979–82, Dept. of Finance and Personnel 1982–88; Deputy Chair. Ulster Bank, Ltd. 1988–89, Chair. 1989–; Dir. Irish-American Partnership 1989–, Short Brothers 1989–, Nat. Westminster Bank 1990–99, Scottish Fee Support Review 1998–; mem. Council, N. Ireland Chamber of Commerce and Industry, mem. Qualifications and Curriculum Authority 1997–; Professorial Fellow, Queen's Univ. Belfast 1988; Hon. LL.D. (Queen's), D.Univ. (Ulster) 1998. *Leisure interests:* historical research, reading, music, gardening. *Address:* Ulster Bank Ltd., 47 Donegall Place, Belfast, BT1 5AU, Northern Ireland.

QUILES, Paul; French politician; b. 27 Jan. 1942, Saint Denis du Sig, Algeria; s. of René Quilès and Odette Tyrode; m. Josephe-Marie Bureau 1964; three d.; ed. Ecole Polytechnique, Paris; engineer, Shell Française 1964–78; Socialist Deputy to Nat. Ass. 1978–83, 1986–88, 1993–; Mayor of Cordes-sur-Ciel (Tarn); Minister of Town Planning and Housing 1983–85, and Transport 1984–85, of Defence 1985–86, of Posts, Telecommunications and Space 1988–91, of Public Works, Housing, Transportation and Space Research 1991–92, of the Interior and Public Security 1992–93; Socialist Deputy to Nat. Ass. 1993–; Mayor of Cordes-sur-Ciel 1995–; mem. Econ. and Social Council 1974–75. *Publications:* La Politique n'est pas ce que vous croyez 1985, Nous vivons une époque intéressante 1992. *Address:* Assemblée nationale, 75355 Paris, France.

QUILLEY, Denis; British actor; b. 26 Dec. 1927, London; s. of Clifford Charles Quilley and Ada Stanley; m. Stella Chapman 1949; one s. two d.; ed. Bancrofts School, Essex; worked as asst. stage man., Birmingham repertory theatre; understudied Richard Burton in The Lady's Not for Burning; joined Nottingham Playhouse 1952; subsequently joined Nat. Theatre Co. *Musicals include:* Grab me a Gondola, Candide, Irma La Douce (New York and U.S. tour), Robert and Elizabeth, The Boys from Syracuse, Sweeney Tod (SWET Award for Best Musical Actor), La Cage aux Folles. *Stage appearances include:* Twelfth Night, Lady Windermere's Fan, Major Barbara, The Dolls' House, As You Like It (Orlando), Much Ado About Nothing (Benedick), The Entertainer (Archie Rice), Macbeth, School for Scandal, The Cherry Orchard, Candida, Hamlet (Claudius), Tamburlaine (Bajazeth), Antony and Cleopatra (Antony), Deathtrap, The White Devil, Privates on Parade (SWET Award for Best Comedy Performance), Venus Observed 1992, Sweeney Todd 1993, The Merry Wives of Windsor (Falstaff) 1995, A Patriot for Me 1995, The Tempest 1996, Troilus and Cresoida 1999; (with Peter Hall Co., Old Vic) Gloucester in King Lear, Pozzo in Waiting for Godot 1997. *Films include:* Murder on the Orient Express, Evil under the Sun, Privates on Parade, Life at the Top, Where the Spies Are, Anne of the Thousand Days, King David, Mr Johnson, A Dangerous Man 1991, Sparrow 1994. *Television appearances include:* The Desperate People (serial), The Little White God, Murder in the Cathedral, No. 10, Rhinestone Cowboy, Rich Tea and Sympathy 1991, The Marriage of Figaro 1994. *Address:* c/o Bernard Hunter Associates, 13 Spencer Gardens, London, SW14 7AH, England. *Telephone:* 0181-878 6308.

QUINE, Willard Van Orman, M.A., PH.D., LL.D., L.H.D., D.LITT.; American professor of philosophy; b. 25 June 1908, Akron, Ohio; s. of Cloyd R. Quine and Hattie van Orman Quine; m. 1st Naomi Ann Clayton; two d.; m. 2nd Marjorie Boynton 1948; one s. one d.; ed. Oberlin Coll. and Harvard Univ.; Sheldon Travelling Fellow (Harvard) to Vienna, Prague and Warsaw 1932–33; Jr. Fellow, Soc. of Fellows, Harvard 1933–36, Faculty Instructor in Philosophy 1936–41, Assoc. Prof. 1941–48, Prof. of Philosophy 1948–56, Edgar Pierce Prof. of Philosophy, Harvard Univ. 1956–78, Emer. Prof. 1978–; U.S.N.R. 1942–46; Visiting Prof. Univ. of São Paulo, Brazil 1942, George Eastman Visiting Prof., Oxford Univ. 1953–54; Shearman Lecturer, Univ. of London 1954; Pres. Asscn. for Symbolic Logic 1953–55; mem. Inst. for Advanced Study, Princeton Univ. 1956–57; Fellow, Center for Advanced Study in Behavioral Sciences, Stanford Univ. 1958–59; Gavin David Young Lecturer, Adelaide Univ., Australia 1959; Visiting Prof. Tokyo Univ. 1959; Fellow, Wesleyan Univ. Center for Advanced Study 1965; Visiting Prof. Rockefeller Univ. 1968, Coll. de France 1969; Paul Carus Lecturer, New York 1971, Saville Fellow, Oxford 1973–74; Pres. American Philosophical Asscn. 1958; mem. Inst. Int. de Philosophie, Acad. Int. de Philosophie des Sciences, Inst. Brasileiro de Filosofia, N.A.S.; Corresp. mem. Inst. de France; Fellow, American Acad. of Arts and Sciences, N.A.S., American Philosophical Soc.; Corresp. Fellow British Acad., Norwegian Acad.; Hon. D.Litt. (Oxford Univ.) 1970, (Cambridge Univ.) 1978 and 15 other hon. degrees; Butler Medal (Columbia Univ.), František Palacký Gold Medal (Czechoslovak Acad. of Sciences 1991, Charles Univ. Silver Medal 1993, Rolf Schock Prize in Philosophy and Logic (Royal Swedish Acad. of Science) 1993, Kyoto Prize in Creative Arts and Moral Sciences 1996. *Publications:* A System of Logistic 1934, Mathematical Logic 1940, Elementary Logic 1941, O Sentido da Nova Lógica 1944, Methods of Logic 1950, From a Logical Point of View 1953, Word and Object 1960, Set Theory and its Logic 1963, The Ways of Paradox 1966, Selected Logic Papers 1966, Ontological Relativity 1969, Philosophy of Logic 1970, Web of Belief (with J. S. Ullian) 1970, The Roots of Reference 1973, Theories and Things 1981, The Time of My Life 1985, The Philosophy of W. V. Quine (co-author) 1986, Quiddities 1987, La Scienza e i Dati di Senso 1987, Pursuit of Truth 1989, Perspectives on Quine (co-author) 1989, The Logic of Sequences 1990, From Stimulus to Science 1995. *Leisure interests:* languages, geography. *Address:* Department of Philosophy, Harvard University, Emerson Hall, Cambridge, MA 02138; 38 Chestnut Street, Boston, MA 02108, U.S.A. *Telephone:* (617) 723-6754.

QUINLAN, Sir Michael Edward, G.C.B., M.A.; British foundation executive; b. 11 Aug. 1930, Hampton; s. of late Gerald Quinlan and Roseanne Quinlan; m. Mary Finlay 1965; two s. two d.; ed. Wimbledon Coll. and Merton Coll. Oxford; civil servant 1954–92; Air Ministry 1954–64; Ministry of Defence 1964–70; Defence Counsellor, U.K. Del. to NATO 1970–73; Under-Sec. Cabt. Office 1974–77; Deputy Under-Sec. of State (Policy and Programmes), Ministry of Defence 1977–81; Deputy Sec. (Industry), Treasury 1981–82; Perm. Sec. Dept. of Employment 1983–88; Perm. Under-Sec. of State, Ministry of Defence 1988–92; Dir. Ditchley Foundation 1992–99; Dir. Lloyds TSB Group 1996–98, Pilkington PLC 1992–98; Visiting Prof. King's Coll. London 1992–; Trustee, Science Museum. *Publications:* Thinking About Nuclear Weapons 1997; numerous articles on defence issues and public service issues. *Leisure interests:* cricket, music, golf. *Address:* c/o Ditchley Foundation, Ditchley Park, Enstone, Chipping Norton, Oxon., OX7 4ER, England. *Telephone:* (01608) 677346. *Fax:* (01608) 677399.

QUINLAN, Mike, B.S., M.B.A.; American business executive; b. 4 Dec. 1944, Chicago; s. of Robert Joseph Quinlan and Kathryn (Koerner); m. Marilyn DeLashmutt 1966; two s.; ed. Loyola Univ.; part-time mailroom worker McDonald's 1963, Asst. Buyer 1966, Pres. (U.S.A.) 1980–82, C.E.O. 1987–98, Chair. 1989–. *Address:* McDonald's Corporation, McDonald's Plaza, 1 Kroc Drive, Oakbrook, IL 60521, U.S.A.

QUINN, Aidan; American actor; b. 8 Mar. 1959, Chicago; worked with various theatre groups in Chicago before moving to New York; off-Broadway appearances in Sam Shepard's plays Fool for Love and A Lie of the Mind; appeared in Hamlet, Wisdom Bridge Theater, Chicago, numerous other plays; TV film: An Early Frost. *Films:* Reckless 1984, The Mission, All My Sons, Stakeout, Desperately Seeking Susan, Crusoe, The Handmaid's Tale, At Play in the Fields of the Lord, Avalon, Legends of the Fall, Mary Shelley's Frankenstein 1994, The Stars Fell on Henrietta 1994, Haunted 1994, Michael Collins 1996, Looking For Richard 1996, Commandments 1996, The Assignment 1997, Wings Against The Wind 1998, This is My Father 1998, Practical Magic 1998, Blue Vision 1998, The Imposters 1998. *Address:* CAA, 9830 Wilshire Boulevard, Beverly Hills, CA 90212, U.S.A.

QUINN, Anthony Rudolph Oaxaca; American actor-director; b. 21 April 1915, Chihuahua, Mexico; s. of Frank and Nellie (Oaxaca) Quinn; m. 1st Katherine de Mille 1937 (divorced); one s. three d.; m. 2nd Iolanda Addolori 1966 (divorced 1997); three s.; m. 3rd Kathy Benvin 1997; one s.; ed. Los Angeles; first appeared on stage 1936. *Films include:* Viva Zapata, Lust for Life, La Strada, Man from Del Rio, The Black Orchid, Warlock, Last Train from Gun Hill, Heller in Pink Tights, Savage Innocents, Guns of Navarone, Barabbas, Lawrence of Arabia, The Visit, Zorba the Greek, The Twenty-Fifth Hour, Guns for San Sebastian, The Secret of Santa Vittoria, The Shoes of the Fisherman, The Magus, A Dream of Kings, The Last Warrior, Flap, Across 110th Street, The Don is Dead 1973, The Marseille Contract 1974, Mohammed, Messenger of God (retitled The Message in the United Kingdom) 1976, The Children of Sanchez 1977, The Greek Tycoon 1977, The Passage 1978, Caravans 1979, Lion of the Desert 1981, High Risk 1982, Ghosts Can't Do It 1989, Revenge 1988, The Old Man and the Sea (TV) 1989, The Actor 1989, Jungle Fever 1990, Only the Lonely 1991, Mobsters 1991, A Walk in the Clouds 1995, Project Mankind 1996, Il Sindaco 1996, Seven Servants 1996; acted in musical version of Zorba the Greek, U.S.A. 1982–86; Dir. The Buccaneer 1958; Venice Film Festival Award for La Strada 1954, American Motion Picture Acad. Awards for Best Supporting Actor in Viva Zapata 1952, and Lust for Life 1956. *Publications:* The Original Sin (autobiog.), One Man Tango (with Daniel Paisner) memoirs 1995. *Address:* P.O. Box 479, Bristol, RI 02809, U.S.A.

QUINN, Brian, C.B.E., M.A., PH.D., F.R.S.A.; British banker; b. 18 Nov. 1936; s. of Thomas Quinn and Margaret Cairns; m. Mary Bradley 1961; two s. one d.; ed. Glasgow, Manchester and Cornell Univs.; economist, African Dept. IMF 1964–70; Rep. IMF, Sierra Leone 1966–68; joined Bank of England 1970, Econ. Div. 1970–74, Chief Cashier's Dept. 1974–77, Head Information Div. 1977–82, Asst. Dir. 1982–88, Head of Banking Supervision 1986–88, Exec. Dir. 1988–96; Chair. Nomura Bank Int. 1996–; Vice-Chair. Celtic PLC 1996–; Dir. (non-exec.) Bankgesellschaft Berlin U.K. PLC, Britannia Asset Man., Nomura Holdings Europe. *Publications:* contribs. to books and journals. *Leisure interests:* fishing, golf, cycling. *Address:* Nomura Bank International, 1 St. Martins-le-Grand, London, E.C.1, England. *Telephone:* 0171-236 8811.

QUINN, Ruairi, B.ARCH., M.R.I.A.I., R.I.B.A.; Irish politician and architect; b. 2 April 1946, Dublin; s. of Malachi and Julia Quinn; m. 1st Nicola Underwood 1969 (divorced), one s. one d.; m. 2nd Liz Allman 1990, one s.; ed. Blackrock Coll. and Univ. Coll., Dublin; School of Ekistics, Athens 1970–71; Architects' Dept. Dublin Corpn. 1971–73; Partner, Burke-Kennedy Doyle and Partner 1973–82; mem. Dublin Corpn. 1974–77, 1981–82; mem. Seanad Éireann 1976–77, 1981–82; mem. Dáil Éireann 1977–81, 1982–; Minister of State, Dept. of the Environment 1982–83; Minister for Labour and Minister for the Public Service 1983–87; Deputy Leader Labour Party 1989; Dir. of Elections for Pres. Mary Robinson (q.v.); Labour Spokesperson on Finance and Econ. Affairs 1990; Minister for Enterprise and Employment 1993–94, for Finance 1994–97; Leader Irish Labour Party 1997–. *Leisure interests:* athletics, reading. *Address:* Dáil Eireann, Kildare Street, Dublin 2; 23 Strand Road, Sandymount, Dublin 4, Ireland.

QUIÑONES AMEZQUITA, Mario Rafael; Guatemalan lawyer and diplomatist; b. 4 June 1933; s. of the late Hector Quiñones and of Elisa de Quiñones; m. Yolanda de Quiñones 1963; two s. two d.; ed. Univ. of San Carlos and Univ. of Rio Grande do Sul, Brazil; lawyer and notary with law firm of Viteri, Falla, Quiñones, Umaña, Orellana y Cáceres 1959–; Prof. of Law, Rafael Landívar Univ. 1962–, Dean Dept. of Legal and Social Sciences 1974–82; Vice-Pres. of Landívar Univ. 1978–82, Pres. March–Oct. 1982; Perm. Rep. to UN 1982–84; Minister of Foreign Affairs 1986–87; Vice-Pres. N. and Cen. American Region, Union of Latin Notaries 1978; Pres. Asscn. of Lawyers and Notaries of Guatemala 1977; mem. Guatemalan Del. UN Comm. on Int. Trade Law 1974. *Address:* 6A Calle 5-47, Zona 9, Guatemala City, Guatemala. *Fax:* (502) 2-345145.

QUINTERO, José; Panamanian theatre director; b. 15 Oct. 1924, Panama City; s. of Carlos Rivira Quintero and Consuelo (née Palmerola) Quintero; ed. Goodman Theatre, Chicago, Univ. of Southern California, Los Angeles City Coll.; producer and Dir. Circle in the Square Theatre 1951–63; currently lecturer in Directing and Acting Univ. of Houston, Fla. State Univ.; Caballero de la Orden de Vasco Nunez de Balboa; numerous awards including South East Theatre Conf. Award for Life Achievement; named to Theatre Hall of Fame; mem. Dirs. Guild of America, Soc. of Stage Dirs. and Choreographers, American Fellows of Theatre. *Plays directed include:* Desire Under the Elms, Cradle Song, La Ronde, The Iceman Cometh, The Girl on the Via Flaminia, Summer and Smoke, The King and the Duke, Burning Bright, Yerma, Dark of the Moon, The Balcony, Our Town, Plays for Bleecker Street, A Moon for the Misbegotten, The Innkeepers, Portrait of a Lady, Gabrielle, In the Summer House, The Skin of Our Teeth, Long Days Journey into Night, A Touch of the Poet, Look We've Come Through, Great Day in the Morning, Strange Interlude, Diamond Orchid, Anna Christie, Faith Healer, Clothes for a Summer Hotel, Welded, Cat on a Hot Tin Roof, Private Lives, Our Town. *Films directed include:* The Roman Spring of Mrs Stone, Hughie (TV film), Medea (TV film); also Dir. Eugene O'Neill Play for Nat. Public Radio 1988, 1993. *Address:* The Lantz Office, 888 7th Avenue, Suite 2500, New York, NY 10106, U.S.A.

QUINTON, Baron (Life Peer) cr. 1982, of Holywell in the City of Oxford and County of Oxfordshire; **Anthony Meredith Quinton,** F.B.A.; British academic; b. 25 March 1925, Gillingham, Kent; s. of the late Richard Frith Quinton and Gwenllyan Letitia Quinton; m. Marcelle Wegier 1952; one s. one d.; ed. Stowe School, Christ Church, Oxford; served in R.A.F., Flying Officer and Navigator 1943–46; Fellow, All Souls Coll., Oxford 1949–55, New Coll., Oxford 1955–78; Pres. Trinity Coll., Oxford 1978–87; Visiting Prof., Swarthmore Coll., Pa. 1960, Stanford Univ., Calif. 1964, New School for Social Research, New York 1976–77; Dawes Hicks Lecturer, British Acad. 1971; Gregynog Lecturer, Univ. of Wales Aberystwyth 1973; T. S. Eliot Lecturer, Univ. of Kent, Canterbury 1976; Robbins Lecturer, Univ. of Stirling 1988; R.M. Jones Lecturer, Queen's Univ., Belfast 1988; Tanner Lecturer, Univ. of Warsaw 1988; Pres., Aristotelian Soc. 1975–76, Soc. for Applied Philosophy 1988–91, Royal Inst. of Philosophy 1990–98, Asscn. of Ind. Libraries 1991–98, Friends of Wellcome Inst. 1992–; Gov., Stowe School 1963–84, Chair. of Govs. 1969–75; Fellow, Winchester Coll. 1970–85; Fellow, New Coll., Oxford 1998; Del., Oxford Univ. Press 1970–76; mem. Arts Council 1979–81; mem. Bd. of Eds. Encyclopaedia Britannica 1985–; mem. Peacock Cttee.; Chair. British Library 1985–90, Kennedy Memorial Trust 1990–97. *Publications:* Political Philosophy (Ed.) 1967, The Nature of Things 1973, Utilitarian Ethics 1973, trans. of K. Ajdukiewicz's Problems and Theories of Philosophy (with H. Skolimowski) 1973, The Politics of Imperfection 1978, Francis Bacon 1980, Thoughts and Thinkers 1982, Hume 1998. *Leisure interests:* sedentary pursuits. *Address:* A-11 Albany, Piccadilly, London, W1V 9RD; Mill House, Turville, Henley-on-Thames, Oxon. RG9 6QL, England. *Telephone:* 0171-287 8686 (London); (01491) 638777 (Oxon.).

QUINTON, Sir John Grand, Kt., M.A., F.C.I.B.; British banker; b. 21 Dec. 1929; s. of William Grand and Norah May (née Nunn) Quinton; m. Jean Margaret Chastney 1954; one s. one d.; ed. Norwich School, St. John's Coll., Cambridge; Asst. Gen. Man. Barclays Bank Ltd. 1968, Local Dir. Nottingham Dist. Barclays Bank Ltd. 1969–71, Regional Gen. Man. 1971–75, Gen. Man. Barclays Bank Ltd. and Dir. Barclays Bank UK Ltd. 1975–84, Dir. Barclays Bank PLC and Sr. Gen. Man. 1982–84, Deputy Chair. Barclays Bank PLC 1985–87, Chair. 1987–92; Chair. (non-exec.) Wimpey 1993–95; Chair. Motability Finance Ltd. 1978–84, Gov. 1985– (Hon. Treas. 1998–); Chair. Cttee. of C.E.O.s., Cttee. of London Clearing Bankers 1982–83; Chair. Office of the Banking Ombudsman 1987–92, Cttee. of London and Scottish Bankers 1989–91; Dir. (non-exec.) Norwich and Peterborough Bldg. Soc. 1993– (Deputy Chair. 1996–); Treas. Inst. of Bankers 1980–86; mem. City Capital Markets Cttee. 1981–86; mem. N.E. Thames Regional Health Authority 1974–87; mem. Accounting Standards Cttee. 1982–85; Gov. Royal Shakespeare Theatre 1986–; Pres. Chartered Inst. of Bankers 1989–90; Chair. Botanic Gardens Conservation Int. 1988–; Chair. Football Asscn. Premier League 1992–, Metropolitan Police Cttee. 1995–; Trustee Royal Acad. 1987–93, Thrombosis Research Inst. 1993–. *Leisure interests:* gardening, music, golf. *Address:* Chenies Place, Chenies, Bucks., WD3 6EU, England.

QUIRK, Baron (Life Peer), cr. 1994, of Bloomsbury in the London Borough of Camden; **(Charles) Randolph Quirk,** Kt., C.B.E., PH.D., D.LITT., FIL.DR., D.U., F.B.A.; British university professor and official; b. 12 July 1920, Isle of Man; s. of late Thomas and Amy Randolph Quirk; m. 1st Jean Williams 1946; two s.; m. 2nd Gabriele Stein 1984; ed. Cronk y Voddy School, Douglas High School, Isle of Man, Univ. Coll., London; served in R.A.F. 1940–45; Lecturer in English, Univ. Coll., London 1947–54; Commonwealth Fund Fellow, Yale Univ. and Univ. of Mich., U.S.A. 1951–52; Reader in English Language and Literature, Univ. of Durham 1954–58, Prof. of English Language 1958–60; Quain Prof. of English, Univ. Coll., London 1960–81; Special Univ. Lectures, London 1960; Dir. Univ. of London Summer School of English 1962–67; Survey of English Usage 1959–83; mem. Senate, Univ. of London 1970–85 (Chair. Academic Council 1972–75), Court 1972–85; Vice-Chancellor, Univ. of London 1981–85; Pres. Inst. of Linguists 1983–86, British Acad. 1985–89, Coll. of Speech Therapists 1987–91; Gov. British Inst. of Recorded Sound, English-Speaking Union; Chair. Cttee. of Enquiry into Speech Therapy Services, British Council English Cttee. 1976–80, Hornby Educational Trust 1979–93; mem. BBC Archives Cttee. 1975–79, British Council 1983–91; Trustee Wolfson Foundation 1987–; Lee Kwan Yew Fellow, Singapore 1985–86; Vice-Pres. Foundation of Science and Tech. 1986–90; Hon. degrees (Lund, Uppsala, Poznan, Nijmegen, Paris, Liège, Helsinki, Prague, Reading, Leicester, Salford, London, Newcastle, Bath, Durham, Essex, Open Univ., Glasgow, Bar Ilan, Brunel, Sheffield, Richmond Coll., Aston); Fellow of Queen Mary Coll., Univ. Coll., London, Academia Europaea, King's Coll., London; Foreign Fellow, Royal Belgian Acad. Sciences 1975, Royal Swedish Acad. 1986, Finnish Acad. of Sciences 1992, American Acad. of Arts and Sciences 1995; Hon. Fellow, Coll. of Speech Therapists, Inst. of Linguists; Hon. Master Grays Inn Bench 1983; Jubilee Medal (Inst. of Linguists) 1973. *Publications:* The Concessive Relation in Old English Poetry 1954, Studies in Communication (with A. J. Ayer and others) 1955, An Old English Grammar (with C. L. Wrenn) 1955, Charles Dickens and Appropriate Language 1959, The Teaching of English (with A. H. Smith) 1959, The Study of the Mother-Tongue 1961, The Use of English (with supplements by A. C. Gimson and J. Warburg) 1962, Prosodic and Paralinguistic Features in English (with D. Crystal) 1964, A Common Language (with A. H. Marckwardt) 1964, Investigating Linguistic Acceptability (with J. Svartvik) 1966, Essays on the English Language—Medieval and Modern 1968, Elicitation Experiments in English (with S. Greenbaum) 1970, A Grammar of Contemporary English 1972 (with S. Greenbaum, G. Leech, J. Svartvik) 1972, The English Language and Images of Matter 1972, A University Grammar of English (with S. Greenbaum) 1973, The Linguist and the English Language 1974, Old English Literature: A Practical Introduction (with V. Adams, D. Davy) 1975, A Corpus of English Conversation 1980; contrib. to many others incl. Charles Dickens (ed. S. Wall) 1970, A New Companion to Shakespeare Studies 1971, The State of the Language 1980, Style and Communication in the English Language 1982, A Comprehensive Grammar of the English Language (with S. Greenbaum, G. Leech and J. Svartvik) 1985, Words at Work: Lectures on Textual Structure 1986, English in Use (with Gabriele Stein) 1990, A Student's Grammar of the English Language (with S. Greenbaum) 1990, Grammatical and Lexical Variance in English 1995; papers in linguistic and literary journals. *Address:* University College, Gower Street, London, WC1E 6BT, England.

QUIRK, James Patrick, A.O., PH.D., F.A.A.; Australian agricultural scientist; b. 17 Dec. 1924, Sydney; s. of J. P. Quirk; m. Helen M. Sykes 1950; one s. one d.; ed. Christian Brothers High School, Lewisham, St. John's Coll., Univ. of Sydney and Univ. of London; Research Scientist, CSIRO Div. of Soils, Soil Physics Section 1947; CSIRO Sr. Postgraduate Studentship, Physics Dept., Rothamsted Experimental Station, England 1950; Research Scientist, Sr. Research Scientist, CSIRO 1952–56; Reader in Soil Science, Dept. of Agricultural Chem., Waite Agricultural Research Inst., Univ. of Adelaide 1956–62; Carnegie Travelling Fellow, U.S.A. 1960; Foundation Prof. and Head, Dept. of Soil Science and Plant Nutrition, Univ. of W.A. 1963–74, (Emer. Prof. 1974–), Dir. Inst. of Agric. 1971–74, Dir., Waite Agricultural Research Inst. and Prof. 1974–89; Emer. Prof. and Hon. Research Fellow, Univ. of W.A. 1990–; Prof. Fellow, Dept. Applied Math., A.N.U. 1990–; Commonwealth Visiting Prof., Oxford Univ. 1967; Fellow Australian Acad. of Science (Sec. Biological Sciences 1990–94), Australian Inst. of Agricultural Science, Australian Acad. of Technological Sciences (mem. Council 1996–), American Soc. of Agronomy, Australian and N.Z. Asscn. for the Advancement of Science; Hon. mem. Int. Soc. of Soil Science 1998; Brindley Lecturer (U.S.A.) 1992; Hon. D.Sc. Agric. (Louvain, Belgium) 1978, (Melbourne) 1990, (Western Australia) 1991, (Sydney) 1997; Prescott Medal for Soil Science 1975, Medal of the Australian Inst. of Agricultural Science 1980, Farrer

Memorial Medal 1982, Mueller Medal 1988, Distinguished Service Award (Soil Science Soc. of America) 1996. *Publications:* 200 scientific publs. *Leisure interests:* reading, tennis. *Address:* Faculty of Agriculture, University of Western Australia, Nedlands 6009, Western Australia (Office); 70 Archdeacon Street, Nedlands 6009, Western Australia. *Telephone:* (08) 9386 5948 (Office). *Fax:* (08) 9380 2504.

QURAISHI, Abdul Aziz Bin Said Al, M.B.A., F.I.B.A. ; Saudi Arabian government official; b. 1930, Hail; s. of Zaid al-Quraishi and Sheikhah Abdul Aziz; m. Amal Abdul Aziz al-Turki 1965; one s. two d.; ed. Univ. of Southern California, U.S.A.; Gen. Man. State Railways 1961–68; Pres. Gen. Personnel Bureau 1968–74; Minister of State 1971–74; Gov. Saudi Arabian Monetary Agency 1974–83; fmr. Gov. for Saudi Arabia, IMF, Arab Monetary Fund; fmr. Alt. Gov. for Saudi Arabia, Islamic Devt. Bank; fmr. mem. Bd. of Dirs. Supreme Council for Petroleum and Mineral Affairs, Gen. Petroleum and Mineral Org., Public Investment Fund, Pension Fund, Man. Dir. Ali Zaid Al-Quraishi & Bros., Riyadh 1983–; fmr. Chair. Nat. Saudi Shipping Co., Riyadh 1983; Vice-Chair. Saudi Int. Bank, London 1983–; mem. Int. Advisory Bd., Security Pacific Nat. Bank of Los Angeles 1983–; King Abdul Aziz Medal (Second Class), Order of Brilliant Star with Grand Cordon (Taiwan), Order of Diplomatic Merit, Gwan Ghwa Medal (Repub. of Korea), King Leopold Medal (Commdr. Class), Belgium, Emperor of Japan Award, Order of Sacred Treasure (First Class) 1980. *Address:* Malaz, Riyadh, Saudi Arabia (Office); P.O. Box 1848, Riyadh 11441, Saudi Arabia (Home).

QURESHI, Moeen Ahmad, M.A., PH.D.; Pakistani economist and international official; b. 26 June 1930, Lahore; s. of Mohyeddin Ahmad Qureshi and Khursheed Jabin; m. Lilo Elizabeth Richter 1958; two s. two d.; ed. Islamia Coll. and Govt. Coll., Univ. of Punjab and Indiana Univ., U.S.A.; Social Science Consultant, Ford Foundation, Pakistan 1953; Hon. Lecturer, Univ. of Karachi 1953–54; Asst. Chief, Planning Comm., Govt. of Pakistan 1954–56, Deputy Chief 1956–58; Economist, IMF 1958–61, Div. Chief 1961–65, Adviser Africa Dept. 1965–66, Resident Rep. Ghana 1966–68, Sr. Adviser 1968–70; Econ. Adviser IFC 1970–74, Vice-Pres. 1974–77, Exec. Vice-Pres. 1977–81; Vice-Pres. Finance, World Bank 1979–80, Sr. Vice-Pres. Finance 1980–87, Sr. Vice-Pres. Operations 1987–91; Acting Prime Minister of Pakistan July–Oct. 1993. *Publications:* various articles in economic journals. *Leisure interests:* tennis, collecting antiques. *Address:* c/o Office of the Prime Minister, Islamabad, Pakistan.

R

RÄÄTS, Jaan; Estonian composer; b. 15 Oct. 1932, Tartu; s. of Peeter Rääts and Linda Rääts; m. 1st Marianne Rääts 1958; m. 2nd Ebba Rääts 1983; three c.; ed. Tallinn Conservatory (pupil of Heino Eller); mem. CPSU 1964–90; Music Dir. Estonian TV 1966–74; Prof. Tallinn Conservatory 1978–; Chair. Estonian Composers' Union 1974–93; People's Artist of the Estonian S.S.R. 1977. *Compositions include:* 10 symphonies, 18 concertos, 9 piano sonatas, 9 piano cycles. *Leisure interests:* technology, science. *Address:* c/o Estonian Composers' Union, A. Lauteri Street 7, 10145 Tallinn, Estonia. *Telephone:* 6466536 (Office); 421-645 (Home).

RABAEUS, Bengt, M.A.; Swedish diplomatist; b. 4 May 1917, Vara; m. Birgitta M. Svensson 1946; three s.; ed. Kungliga Universitet i Uppsala; entered Foreign Service 1946, served Prague, Paris, Swedish Del. to UN (New York); Counsellor, Swedish Del. to OEEC, Paris 1957–59; Head of UN Political Div., Foreign Office, Stockholm 1959–61; First Counsellor, Paris 1961–62; Amb. to Algeria 1963–66; Deputy Sec.-Gen. European Free Trade Asscn. (EFTA) 1966–72, Sec.-Gen. 1972–76; Deputy Perm. Under-Sec. of State, Ministry of Foreign Affairs 1976–78; Amb. and Perm. Rep. to European Communities 1978–83; Chair. Swedish Pulp and Paper Asscn. 1983–89. *Address:* Stureparken 3, S-114 26, Stockholm, Sweden.

RABAN, Jonathan, F.R.S.L.; British author and critic; b. 14 June 1942; s. of Rev. Peter J. C. P. Raban and Monica Sandison; m. 1st Caroline Cuthbert 1985 (divorced 1992); m. 2nd Jean Cara Lenihan 1992; one d.; ed. Univ. of Hull; Lecturer in English and American Literature, Univ. Coll. of Wales, Aberystwyth 1965–67, Univ. of E. Anglia 1967–69; Heinemann Award, Royal Soc. of Literature and Thomas Cook Award for Old Glory 1982, Thomas Cook Award for Hunting Mister Heartbreak 1991, Nat. Book Critics Circle Award and PEN/West Creative Nonfiction Award for Bad Land 1997. *Publications:* The Technique of Modern Fiction 1969, Mark Twain: Huckleberry Finn 1969, The Society of the Poem 1971, Soft City 1973, Arabia Through the Looking Glass 1979, Old Glory 1981, Foreign Land 1985, Coasting 1986, For Love and Money 1987, God, Man & Mrs Thatcher 1989, Hunting Mister Heartbreak 1990, The Oxford Book of the Sea (Ed.) 1992, Bad Land: An American Romance 1996. *Leisure interest:* sailing. *Address:* c/o Aitken & Stone Ltd., 29 Fernshaw Road, London, SW10 0TG, England.

RABASSA, Gregory, PH.D.; American professor of Romance languages; b. 9 March 1922, Yonkers, N.Y.; s. of Miguel Rabassa and Clara Macfarland; m. 1st Roney Edelstein 1957 (divorced 1966); one d.; m. 2nd Clementine Christos 1966; one d.; ed. Dartmouth Coll. and Columbia Univ.; mil. service 1942–45; Instructor in Spanish, Columbia Univ. 1947–52, Assoc. Instructor 1952–58, Asst. Prof. 1958–63, Assoc. Prof. of Spanish and Portuguese 1963–68; Prof. of Romance Languages, Queens Coll., Flushing, N.Y. 1968–86, Distinguished Prof. 1986–; Assoc. Ed. Odyssey Review 1961–64; mem. Renaissance Soc. of America, PEN Club and other professional asscns.; Fulbright-Hays Fellow, Brazil 1965–66; Guggenheim Fellow 1988–; Dr. h.c. (Dartmouth Coll.) 1982; Nat. Book Award for translation 1967, New York Gov.'s Arts Award 1985, Wheatland Translation Prize 1988, Literature Award, American Acad. and Inst. of Arts and Letters 1989, Sandrof Award (Nat. Book Critics Circle) 1993, New York Public Library Literary Lion Award 1993; Croce al Merito di Guerra (Italy), Order of San Carlos (Colombia), Gabriela Mistral Medal (Chile) 1996. *Address:* 140 East 72nd Street, New York, NY 10021, U.S.A. *Telephone:* (212) 439-6636.

RABBANI, Burhanuddin: Afghanistan politician and academic; professor; Chair. Jamiat-i Islami (Islamic Union of Afghan Mujahidin) IUAM; named Pres. of Afghanistan during civil war by Leadership Council 1992, elected by Council Dec. 1992; fled from Kabul with govt. Sept. 1996; now based in Mazar-i-Sharif.

RABEE, Hayder K. Gafar, B.A.; Iraqi teacher of calligraphy; b. 22 Feb. 1962, Najaf; m. Ahalam A. Al-Zahawi 1986; two s. one d.; ed. Inst. of Fine Arts; calligrapher, Baghdad TV 1982–88; worked as designer, newspapers and magazines 1989–91; teacher, Inst. of Fine Arts, Baghdad 1992–, Head. Calligraphy Dept. (evening classes) 1995–; Gold Medal, 2nd World Festival 1992, Third World Festival 1993, Gold Medal for Creativity, Dar As-Salaam 1st Nat. Festival 1993. *Publication:* Proposed Alphabetic Study for Arabic Calligraphy in Printing. *Leisure interest:* chess. *Address:* Department of Calligraphy, Institute of Fine Arts, Al-Mansur, Baghdad, Iraq.

RABEMANANJARA, Jacques; Malagasy writer and politician; b. *c.* 1913; mem. French Nat. Ass. as rep. for Madagascar 1946; initiated the Democratic Movt. for the restoration of Malagasy independence in harmony with France; arrested during the Malagasy insurrection of 1947 and exiled in France; helped to inaugurate the review and publishing house Présence africaine; winner of Le grand Prix de la Francophonie awarded by the Acad. Française 1988. *Publications: poems:* Dieux malgaches, Rites millénaires, Antsa, Lamba, Ode à Ranavalo, Antidote, Ordalies; *political works:* Témoignage malgache et colonialisme, Nationalisme et problèmes malgaches, Premiers jalons pour une politique de la culture.

RABETAFIKA, Joseph Albert Blaise, L. ÈS L., M.A., M.ED.; Malagasy diplomatist; b. 3 Feb. 1932, Tananarive (now Antananarivo); m. Jeanne Razafintsalama 1956; one s. two d.; teacher in U.K., France and Madagascar 1953–59; joined Ministry of Defence, France 1960; mem. Madagascar del. to independence negotiations with France 1960; Counsellor in charge of cultural affairs and information, Madagascar diplomatic mission, France 1960–63; Perm. Del. to UNESCO, Paris 1961–63; Head, del. to IBE Confs., Geneva 1961–63; mem. del. to UN Gen. Ass. 1962–69; Dir. of Cabinet Foreign Ministry 1964–67; Consul-Gen., New York 1968; Perm. Rep. to UN 1969–93; Amb. to Canada 1970, to Cuba 1974; Vice-Pres. ECOSOC 1973; Chair. Group of 77 1973; Pres. UN Security Council 1985, 1986. *Leisure interests:* classical music, jazz, reading, violin playing. *Address:* 801 2nd Avenue, Suite 404, New York, NY 10017, U.S.A.

RABIN, Oskar; Russian painter; b. 1928, Moscow; m. Valentina Kropovnitsky; one s.; student of artist and teacher Yevgeny Kropovnitsky; worked in Riga 1946–48; thereafter student of Surikov Art Inst., Moscow; later expelled for unorthodox views; worked until 1958 as loader on railways and on construction sites, painting clandestinely; employed in arts & design centre 1958–67; f. Leonozovo group in Moscow; exhibited in "Festival of Youth" Exhbn., Moscow 1957; one-man show Grosvenor Gallery, London 1965; two open-air exhbns. in Cheremushki, outside Moscow and organized by s. (both officially bulldozed) 1974; "Twenty Russian Artists", Moscow (Bee-keeping Pavilion, VDNKh) 1975; forced to emigrate 1977; now lives in Paris; "Unofficial Art in the Soviet Union", London 1977; other exhbns. in Fed. Repub. of Germany, Switzerland, Austria, France, Poland, USA (Chicago), Tbilisi, Denmark, Moscow. *Publication:* Memoirs: Three Lives 1986.

RABINOVITCH, B(enton) Seymour, PH.D., F.R.S.; Canadian professor of chemistry; b. 19 Feb. 1919, Montreal, P.Q.; s. of Samuel Rabinovitch and Rachel Shachter; m. 1st Marilyn Werby 1949 (deceased), 2nd Flora Reitman 1980; two s. two d. from 1st marriage; ed. McGill Univ.; Royal Soc. of Canada Research Fellow 1946–47; Milton Research Fellow, Harvard Univ. 1947–48; Asst. Prof. Univ. of Washington, Seattle 1948–53, Assoc. Prof. 1953–57, Prof. Dept. of Chem. 1957–85, Prof. Emer. 1985–; Fellow, American Acad. of Arts and Sciences, American Physics Soc.; mem. Silver Soc.; Hon. D.Sc., (Technion Univ., Haifa) 1991; Guggenheim Fellowship 1961; Peter Debye Award, Michael Polyani Medal. *Publications:* Textbook of Physical Chemistry 1964, Antique Silver Servers 1991; Ed. Annual Reviews of Physical Chemistry 1975–85; 220 research papers. *Leisure interest:* silversmithing. *Address:* Department of Chemistry, Box 351700, University of Washington, Seattle, WA 98195 (Office); 12530 42nd Avenue, N.E., Seattle, WA 98125, U.S.A. (Home).

RABINOWITZ, Harry, M.B.E.; British composer and conductor; b. 26 March 1916, Johannesburg, S. Africa; s. of Israel Rabinowitz and Eva (née Kirkel) Rabinowitz; m. Lorna T. Anderson 1944; one s. two d.; ed. Athlone High School, Johannesburg and Guildhall School of Music, London; Conductor, BBC Radio 1953–60; Musical Dir. BBC Television Light Entertainment 1960–68; Head, of Music, London Weekend Television 1968–77; freelance composer and conductor 1977–; Music Dir. (TV) Julia and Friends 1986, Paul Nicholas and Friends 1987, series New Faces 1987; has appeared with London Symphony and Royal Philharmonic Orchestras in U.K. and with the Los Angeles Philharmonic and Boston Pops Orchestras and Orchestra of St. Luke's in U.S.A.; Musical Dir. for world premières of Cats and Song & Dance; Musical Dir. (films) Chariots of Fire, Lord of the Flies, Camille Claudet, Shirley Valentine, La Baule-les Pins, La Fille des Collines, Eve of Destruction, Jesuit Joe, Jeanne, Putain du Roi, Ballad of the Sad Café, Howards End, The Remains of the Day, La Fille de d'Artagnan, Death and the Maiden, Jefferson in Paris, Secret Agent, Alien Empire (BBC TV), The Stupids, The English Patient, Tonka, Surviving Picasso, Wings of the Dove, World of Moss, My Story So Far, City of Angels, Soldiers' Daughters Don't Cry; has composed and conducted several TV scores and conducted numerous film scores; awarded B.A.S.C.A. Gold Badge for Services to British Music 1985, Radio and TV Industries Award for Best TV Theme 1984, All-Music Gold Award 1991; Freeman City of London 1995. *Leisure interests:* listening to others making music, edible fungi hunting, wine-tasting. *Address:* 11 Mead Road, Cranleigh, Surrey, GU6 7BG, England. *Telephone:* (01483) 278676.

RABKIN, Mitchell T., M.D.; American physician and hospital administrator; b. 27 Nov. 1930, Boston, Mass.; s. of Morris A. Rabkin and Esther Quint Rabkin; m. Adrienne M. Najarian 1956; one s. one d.; ed. Harvard Coll. and Harvard Medical School; trained in medicine, Mass. Gen. Hosp., Boston; U.S. Public Health Service, Nat. Inst. of Health, Bethesda, Md. 1957–59; Chief Resident in Medicine, Mass. Gen. Hosp. 1962, medical staff 1963–66; Gen. Dir. Beth Israel Hosp., Boston 1966–80, Pres. 1980–96; Prof. of Medicine, Harvard Medical School 1983–; C.E.O. CareGroup, Boston 1996–98; Distinguished Inst. Scholar, Inst. for Educ. and Research, Beth Israel Deaconess Medical Centre, Boston 1998–; mem. N.A.S. Inst. of Medicine; mem. Trustee Advisory Cttee. Duke Univ. Health System 1998–; Fellow A.A.A.S., A.C.P.; Hon. D.Sc. (Brandeis), (Curry Coll., Milton, Mass.). *Address:* Beth Israel Deaconess Medical Centre, Institute for Education and Research, 330 Brookline Avenue, Boston, MA 02215, U.S.A.

RABUKA, Maj.-Gen. Sitiveni Ligamamada, O.B.E., M.SC.; Fijian politician and army officer; b. 13 Sept. 1948, Nakobo; s. of Kolinio E.V. Rabuka and Salote Lomaloma; m. Suluweti Camamaivuna Tuiloma 1975; one s. two d.; ed. Provincial School Northern, Queen Victoria School, N.Z. Army schools, Indian Defence Services Staff Coll. and Australian Jt. Services Staff Coll.; Sr. Operational Plans Officer UNIFIL, Lebanon 1980–81; Chief of Staff, Fiji July–Dec. 1981; SO 1 Operations and Training, Fiji Army 1982–83, 1985–87; Commdr. Fiji Bn., Sinai 1983–85; staged coup 14 May 1987; Adviser on Home Affairs and Head of Security May–Sept. 1987; staged second coup 25 Sept. 1987; declared Fiji a Repub. 7 Oct. 1987; Commdr. and Head of Interim Mil. Govt. of Fiji Sept.–Dec. 1987; Commdr. Fiji Security Forces 1987–91; Minister for Home Affairs, Nat. Youth Service and Auxiliary Army Services 1987–90; Deputy Prime Minister 1991, Minister for Home Affairs 1991; Prime Minister of Fiji June 1992–, fmrly. Minister for Home Affairs, Immigration, Fijian Affairs and Rural Devt., and Foreign Affairs, now with special responsibility for the Constitutional Review and the Agricultural, Landlords and Tenants Act; Pres. Fijian Political Party (FPP); Commdr., Légion d'honneur, O. St. J. *Publication:* No Other Way 1988. *Leisure interests:* golf, rugby. *Address:* Office of the Prime Minister, Government Buildings, P.O. Box 2353, Suva, Fiji. *Telephone:* 211201. *Fax:* 306034.

RACAN, Jvica; Croatian politician and lawyer; b. 24 Feb. 1944, Ebersbach, Germany; ed. Zagreb Univ.; research asst. Inst. for Social Man., Zagreb; mem. Bd. Cen. Cttee. of SKY (Union of Communists of Yugoslavia) 1986–89; Chair. Cen. Cttee. Croatian Union of Communists 1989–90; Pres. Social Democratic Party 1990–; elected to Croatian Parl. 1990–. *Address:* Trg Grage Iblera 9, 41000 Zagreb, Croatia (Office). *Telephone:* (41) 452 055 (Office).

RACHMANIN, Vladimir Olegovich; Russian diplomatist; b. 1958, Moscow; ed. Moscow Inst. of Int. Relations; on staff U.S.S.R. (later Russian) Ministry of Foreign Affairs 1980–; Deputy Dir. First Asian Dept. 1996–98; Dir. Dept. of Information and Press 1998–. *Address:* Smolenskaya-Sennaya 32/34, Moscow, Russia. *Telephone:* (095) 244 4119 (Office). *Fax:* (095) 244 4112 (Office).

RACICOT, Marc F., B.A.; American politician and lawyer; b. 24 July 1948, Thompson Falls, Mont.; s. of William E. Racicot and Patricia E. (Bentley) Racicot; m. Theresa J. Barber 1970; two s. three d.; ed. Carroll Coll., Helena, Mont., Univ. of Montana; called to Bar, Mont. 1973; served U.S. Army 1973–76, Chief Trial Counsel U.S. Army, Kaiserslautern, Fed. Repub. of Germany 1975–76, resgnd. 1976; Deputy Co. Attorney, Missoula (Mont.) Co. 1976–77; Asst. Attorney-Gen. State of Mont. 1977–89, Attorney-Gen. 1989–93; Gov. of Montana 1993–; Republican. *Address:* State Capitol, Room 204, Helena, MT 59620, U.S.A.

RADCLIFFE, Most Rev. Timothy Peter Joseph, O.P., M.A.; British ecclesiastic; b. 22 Aug. 1945, London; s. of Hugh Radcliffe and Marie-Therese Pereira; ed. Downside School, Le Saulchoir, Paris and St. John's Coll. Oxford; entered Dominican Order 1965; Chaplain to Imperial Coll.; Prior of Blackfriars, Oxford 1982–88; Chair. new Blackfriars 1983–88; Provincial of Prov. of England 1988–92; Pres. Conf. of Maj. Religious Superiors of England and Wales 1991–; Grand Chancellor, Pontifical Univ. of St. Thomas (The Angelicum) 1992–, Univ. of Santo Tomas, Manila 1992–, Ecole Biblique, Jerusalem 1992–, Faculty of Theology, Fribourg, 1992–; Master, Order of Preachers 1992–; Hon. Fellow, St. John's Coll. Oxford; Hon. S.T.D. (Providence Coll. R.I.); Hon. LL.D (Barry Univ., Fla.) 1996; Hon. D.Hum. Litt. (Ohio Dominican Coll.) 1996. *Publication:* El Manantial de la Esperanza 1998. *Leisure interests:* walking, reading long novels. *Address:* Convento di S. Sabina, Piazza Pietro d'Illiria 1, Aventino, 00153 Rome, Italy. *Telephone:* (06) 5794555. *Fax:* (06) 5750675.

RADDA, George Karoly, C.B.E., M.A., D.PHIL., F.R.S.; British medical research director and professor of molecular cardiology; b. 9 June 1936, Gyor, Hungary; s. of Gyula Radda and Anna Bernolak; m. 1st Mary O'Brien 1961 (divorced 1995), two s. one d.; m. 2nd Sue Bailey 1995; ed. Pannonhalma and Eötvös Univ., Budapest and Merton Coll. Oxford; Research Assoc., Univ. of Calif., U.S.A. 1962–63; Lecturer in Organic Chem., St. John's Coll., Oxford Univ. 1963–64, Fellow and Tutor in Organic Chem., Merton Coll. 1964–84, Lecturer in Biochem, Oxford Univ. 1966–84, British Heart Foundation Prof. of Molecular Cardiology 1984–; Professorial Fellow, Merton Coll. 1984–, Head Dept. of Biochem. 1991–96; Chair. MRC Cell. Bd. 1988–92; mem. MRC Council 1988–92, Chief Exec. MRC (on leave from Oxford Univ.) 1996–; mem. Council, Royal Soc. 1990–92, ICRF 1991–96; Hon. Dir. MRC Biochemical and Clinical Magnetic Resonance Unit 1988–96; Ed. Biochemical and Biophysical Research Communications 1977–84; Man. Ed. Biochimica et Biophysica Acta 1977–, Chair. 1989–95; Founder mem. Oxford Enzyme Group 1970–87; Pres. Soc. for Magnetic Resonance in Medicine 1985–86; Fellow Int. Soc. of Magnetic Resonance in Medicine 1995; mem. European Molecular Biology Org. 1997–; Hon. F.R.C.R. 1985; Hon. M.R.C.P. 1987; Hon. Fellow American Heart Asscn. and Citation for Int. Achievement 1987; Hon. F.R.C.P. 1997; Hon. Dr. Med. (Berne) 1985, (London) 1991; Hon. D.Sc. (Stirling) 1998; Colworth Medal, Biochemical Soc. 1969, CIBA Medal and Prize 1983, Feldberg Prize 1982, British Heart Foundation Prize and Gold Medal for cardiovascular research 1982, Gold Medal, Soc. for Magnetic Resonance in Medicine 1984, Buchanan Medal, Royal Soc. 1987, Rank Prize in Nutrition 1990. *Publications:* articles in books and scientific journals. *Leisure interests:* opera, jazz, swimming. *Address:* Medical Research Council, 20 Park Crescent, London, W1N 4AL, England. *Telephone:* 0171-636 5422 *Fax:* 0171-436 6179.

RADEBE, Jeffrey Thamsanqa (Jeff), LL.B.; South African politician; b. 18 Feb. 1953, Cato Manor; ed. Isibonelo High School; joined Black Consciousness Movt. 1970; co-founder Kwamashu Youth Org. 1972; articled clerk with A. J. Gumede & Phyllis Naidoo, E. S. Mchunu & Co. 1976–77; with Radio Freedom 1977–78; Deputy Chief ANC Rep., Tanzania 1981; headed clandestine political movement of ANC and South African Communist Party (SACP) 1986, Head Political Dept. and Co-ordinator of 12-day hunger strike on Robben Island; arrested and sentenced to 10 years on Robben Island 1986, sentence reduced to 6 years, released 1990; Sec. interim leadership group of SACP 1990–91; Deputy Chair. ANC Southern Natal Region 1990–91, Chair. 1991–; Minister of Public Works, Govt. of Nat. Unity 1994–; Hon. LL.M. (Leipzig Univ., Germany). *Address:* Central Government Building, corner Bosman and Vermeuleu Streets, Pretoria 0002; Private Bag X890, 0001 Pretoria, South Africa. *Telephone:* (12) 3241510. *Fax:* (12) 3256380.

RADER, Gen. Paul A., B.A., B.D., M.TH., D.MISS.; American religious leader; b. 14 March 1934, New York; m. Kay Fuller 1956; one s. two d.; ed. Asbury Theological Seminary, Southern Baptist Theological Seminary, Salvation Army's School for Officers' Training, New York, Fuller Theological Seminary; mem. staff Salvation Army Training School, Seoul, Korea 1962–67, Vice-Prin. 1967–71, Training Prin., then Educ. Officer, then Asst. Chief Sec. Salvation Army in Korea 1973–77, Chief Sec. with rank of Lieut.-Col. 1977–84; Prin. School for Officers' Training, Suffern, New York 1984–87, Div. Leader 1987–89; Chief Sec. U.S.A. Eastern Territory 1989; rank of Commr. 1989; Commdr. U.S.A. Western Territory 1989–; Pres. The Salvation Army Calif. Corps 1989–; rank of Gen. of The Salvation Army July 1994. *Address:* The Salvation Army, 639 Sabrina Way, Vista, CA 92084, U.S.A.

RADI, Essam Radi Abd al-Hamid; Egyptian politician and engineer; m.; two c.; ed. Faculty of Eng.; headed engineers of northern region of armed forces; held posts in Ministry of Irrigation in Egypt and Sudan; Gov. of Damietta 1980; Minister of Irrigation 1985–87, of Public Works and Water Resources 1987–97. *Address:* c/o Ministry of Public Works and Water Resources, Sharia Corniche en-Nil, Imbaba, Giza, Egypt.

RADNER, Roy, PH.D.; American economist; b. 29 June 1927, Chicago; s. of Ella and Samuel Radner; m. 1st Virginia Honoski (died 1976), one s. three d. (one d. deceased); m. 2nd Charlotte V. Kuh 1978; ed. Hyde Park High School, Chicago and Univ. of Chicago; served U.S. army 1945–48; Research Assoc., Cowles Comm., Univ. of Chicago 1951–54, Asst. Prof. 1954–55; Asst. Prof. of Econs. Yale Univ. 1955–57; Assoc. Prof. of Econs. and Statistics, Univ. of Calif., Berkeley 1957–61, Prof. 1961–79, Chair. Dept. of Econs. 1965–69; Distinguished mem. tech. staff, AT&T Bell Labs. 1979–95; Research Prof. of Econs. New York Univ. 1983–95, Prof. of Econs. and Information Systems 1995–96, L.N. Stern School Prof. of Business 1996–; Guggenheim Fellow 1961–62 and 1965–66; Overseas Fellow, Churchill Coll. Cambridge, U.K. 1969–70, 1989; Assoc. Ed. Journal of Econ. Theory 1968–, Games and Economic Behavior 1989, Economic Theory 1990, Review of Economic Design 1994, Review of Accounting Studies 1994; mem. N.A.S., Inst. of Math. Statistics; Fellow American Acad. of Arts and Sciences, Econometric Soc. (Pres. 1973); Distinguished Fellow American Econ. Asscn., A.A.A.S. *Publications:* Optimal Replacement Policy (with others) 1967, Decision and Organization (co-ed.) 1972, Economic Theory of Teams (with J. Marschak) 1972, Demand and Supply in U.S. Higher Education (with L. S. Miller) 1975, Education as an Industry (co-ed.) 1976, Mathematicians in Academia (with C. V. Kuh) 1980, Information, Incentives, and Economic Mechanisms (co-ed.) 1987, Perspectives on Deterrence 1989, Bargaining with Incomplete Information 1992, and many articles. *Leisure interests:* music, backpacking, cross-country skiing. *Address:* Stern School of Business, New York University, MEC 9-68, 44 W. Fourth Street, Suite 9–68, New York, NY 10012 (Office); 3203 Davenport Street, N.W., Washington, DC 20008, U.S.A. (Home). *Telephone:* (212) 998-0813. *Fax:* (212) 995-4228.

RADULOVIĆ, Miloš, DR.ECON.; Yugoslav (Montenegrin) politician; b. 22 Feb. 1929, Spuž, Montenegro; s. of Nikolai Radulović and Andja Radulović, m. Slavka Radulović; two c.; ed. School of Econ., Podgorica; Prof. Univ., Dean School of Econ., Podgorica; Pres. Univ. of Montenegro, Podgorica; mem., then Speaker Chamber of Repub.; Chair. IPU Yugoslav Group, Savezna Skupština of Yugoslavia; mem. Presidency of Montenegro; Amb. to U.K. (also accred. to Ireland) 1996–. *Address:* Yugoslav Embassy, 5 Lexham Gardens, London, W8 5JJ, England. *Telephone:* 0171-370 5210. *Fax:* 0171-370 3838.

RADZHABOV, Safarali; Tajikistan politician; b. 2 Sept. 1955, Fayzabad Dist.; m. 1976; two s. six d.; ed. Dushanbe State Pedagogical Inst.; Dir. Special Training Centre, Fayzabad Dist. 1980–86; Tech. Coll. N2U, Fayzabad Dist. 1986–90; Deputy of Tajikistan Supreme Soviet 1990–95; Sec., Deputy Chair., Chair. Cttee. on Legislation and Human Rights 1990–95; Chair. Majlisi Oli (Parl.) of Tajikistan 1995–; Dr. h.c. (Tajik State Agrarian Univ.) 1998. *Publications:* Independence is Sacred 1997, Majlisi Oli 1998. *Address:* Majlisi Oli, Rudaki Str. 42, 734051 Dushanbe, Tajikistan. *Telephone:* (3772) 21-22-53. *Fax:* (3772) 22-92-81.

RADZINOWICZ, Sir Leon, N.Z.C.M., LL.D., F.B.A.; British criminologist and law historian; b. 15 Aug. 1906, Łódź, Poland; m. 1st Irene Szereszewski 1933 (divorced 1955), one s. one d.; m. 2nd Mary Ann Nevins 1958 (divorced 1979); m. 3rd Isolde Klarmann 1979; ed. Cracow, Geneva, Paris, Rome and Cambridge Univs.; Lecturer, Geneva Univ. 1928–31; reported on Belgian penal system 1930; Lecturer, Warsaw Free Univ. 1932–36, Asst. Prof. 1936–39; visited England to report on English penal system for Polish Ministry of Justice 1938; Asst. Dir. of Research, Cambridge Univ. 1946–49, Fellow of Trinity Coll. 1948–, Dir. Dept. of Criminal Science 1949–59, First Wolfson Prof. of Criminology 1959–73, Dir. Inst. of Criminology 1960–72; Vice-Pres. Int. Soc. for Social Defence; Vice-Pres. Assoc. Int. de Droit Pénal, Paris 1947–; Head UN Social Defence Section 1947–48; mem. Royal Comm. on Capital Punishment 1949–53, Home Office Advisory Council on Treatment of Offenders 1950–63, on the Penal System 1966–74, Royal Comm. on English Penal System 1964–66; Hon. Foreign mem. American Acad. of Arts and Sciences; First Pres. British Acad. of Forensic Sciences 1960–61, Hon. Vice-Pres. 1961–; First Chair. Scientific Council, European Problems of Crime, Council of Europe 1963–69; Assoc. Fellow, Silliman Coll., Yale Univ. 1966–; Adjunct Prof. of Law and Criminology, Columbia Law School 1966–75; Walter E. Meyer Visiting Prof., Yale Law School 1962–63; Visiting Prof. Univs. of Va. 1968–75, of Philadelphia and Camden 1968, Univ. of Penn. 1970–73, Rutgers Univ. 1968–72, 1979–81, Minnesota Law School 1979, John Jay Coll. of Criminal Justice 1978–79, Benjamin Cardozo Law School 1978–81; Consultant to Ford Foundation on UN Criminology Inst. Rome 1962, to Ford Foundation and Bar Asscn., New York, on teaching and research in crime 1964–65, to Presidential Nat. Cttee. on Violence 1968, to Minister of Justice, N.S.W. and Nat. Justice and Crime, Canberra 1973, to Univ. of Cape Town Inst. of Crime 1972; Chief Rapporteur IX UN Crime Congress, Kayto 1970; Dir. Securicor 1974; Hon. mem. American Law Inst. 1981; Visitor Princeton Inst. of Advanced Studies 1975; Hon. LL.D. (Leicester) 1965, (Edin.) 1988; Chevalier de l'Ordre de Léopold 1930; J. B. Ames Prize and Medal, Harvard Law School 1950; Coronation Medal 1953; Bruce Smith Sr. Award for outstanding contribution to Criminal Justice Sciences of the U.S. 1976, Sellin-Glueck Award of the American Soc. of Criminology 1976, Joseph Andrews Award of American Law Library Asscn. (with Roger Hood); Chevalier, Ordre de Léopold 1930. *Publications:* numerous books and articles in Polish, French, Italian and English on criminology and penology; History of English Criminal Law and Its Administration from 1750 Vol. I 1948, Vols. II and III 1956, Vol. IV 1968, Vol. V (with Roger Hood) 1986; In Search of Criminology 1961, The Need for Criminology 1965, Ideology and Crime 1966, Ed. Cambridge Studies in Criminology (52 vols.); ed. (with Marvin E. Wolfgang) Crime and Justice (3 vols.) 1971, (with Roger Hood) Criminology and the Administration of Criminal Justice: A Bibliography 1976, (with Joan King) The Growth of Crime 1977, The Cambridge Instutute of Criminology 1988, The Roots of the International Association of Criminal Law 1991, Adventures in Criminology 1998. *Leisure interests:* travelling, dinner parties. *Address:* The Quadrangle, Apt. 2311, 3300 Darby Road, Haverford, PA 19041-1095, U.S.A.; Trinity College, Cambridge, CB2 1TQ, England. *Telephone:* (610) 649-6803 (Haverford).

RADZINSKY, Edvard Stanislavovich; Russian dramatist; b. 23 Sept. 1936, Moscow; s. of Stanislav Radzinsky and Sofia Radzinsky; m. Yelena Timofeyevna Denisova; ed. Inst. of History and Archival Science, Moscow; author and narrator of TV series Mysteries of History 1997–. *Plays include:* My Dream is India 1960, You're all of Twenty-Two, you Old Men! 1962, One Hundred and Four Pages on Love 1964, Kolobashkin the Seducer 1967, Socrates 1977, Lunin 1980, I Stand at the Restaurant 1982, Theatre of the Time of Nero and Seneca 1984, Elderly Actress in the Role of Dostoevsky's Wife 1986, Sporting Scenes 1987, Our Decameron 1989. *Publications:* (novels): The Last of the Romanovs 1989, Our Decameron 1990; (non-fiction): The Last Tsar: The Life and Death of Nicholas II 1992, God Save and Restrain Russia 1993, Stalin 1996, Mysteries of History 1997, Mysteries of Love 1998, Fall of Gallant Century 1998, Rasputin 1999, The Theatrical Novel (memoirs) 1999; Collected Works (7 vols.) 1998–99. *Address:* c/o Lynn C. Franklin Associates, 386 Park Avenue South, New York, N.Y. 10016, U.S.A.; Usievicha Street 8, Apt. 98, 125319 Moscow, Russia *Telephone:* 155-75-31.

RAE, Alexander Lindsay, N.Z.C.M., O.B.E., PH.D., M.AGR.SC., F.R.S.N.Z.; New Zealand professor of animal science; b. 3 Aug. 1923, Eltham; s. of Thomas Rae and Annie Rae; m. Fiona D. Thomas 1957; ed. Massey Agricultural Coll. and Iowa State Univ.; Jr. Lecturer in Sheep Husbandry, Massey Agricultural Coll. 1944-50; Prof. of Sheep Husbandry, Massey Univ. 1951–80, Prof. in Animal Science 1980–89, Emer. 1989–; Fellow, N.Z. Inst. of Agricultural Science, Australian Asscn. of Animal Breeding and Genetics; Trustee N.Z. Animal Breeding Trust 1991–; N.Z. Soc. of Animal Production McMeekan Memorial Award 1977, Sir Ernest Marsden Medal for Outstanding Service to Science 1982, Massey Univ. Award for Distinguished Service 1990. *Publications:* research papers on animal genetics and breeding in scientific journals. *Leisure interest:* fishing. *Address:* 16 Wallace Place, Palmerston North, New Zealand (Home). *Telephone:* 0-6-357 8611 (Home).

RAE, Barbara, R.A., R.S.A., R.S.W.; British artist and lecturer; b. 1943, Scotland; one s.; ed. Edinburgh Coll. of Art; lecturer Glasgow School of Art 1975–96; Trustee British School, Rome 1997–, Hospitalfield House, Arbroath 1997–; mem. Bd. Royal Fine Art Comm. 1995–; Invited Artist, Royal Acad., London 1994, 1995, 1996, Royal Hibernian Acad., Dublin 1995, 1996; numerous group exhbns. U.K., U.S.A., Germany, Netherlands, Spain; works in public and pvt. collections including Scottish Nat. Gallery of Modern Art, Scottish Arts Council, Univs. of Edin., Glasgow and York, Royal Bank of Scotland, Bank of England, TSB Group PLC, H.R.H. the Duke of Edinburgh, Lord Avonside; several awards including Guthrie Award, R.S.A. 1977, Sir William Gillies Travel Award 1983, Calouste Gulbenkian Printmaking Award 1983. *Leisure interests:* interior decoration, gardening, antique collecting. *Address:* c/o Art First, 9 Cork Street, London, W1X 1PD, England.

RAE, Robert (Bob) Keith, P.C., B.PHIL.; Canadian politician and lawyer; b. 2 Aug. 1948, Ottawa; s. of Saul Rae and Lois George; m. Arlene Perly 1980; three d.; ed. public school in Washington, D.C., Int. School of Geneva, Univ. of Toronto and Balliol Coll. Oxford; fmr. volunteer, legal aid clinics in Toronto and asst. counsel for United Steelworkers of America and Union of Injured Workers; mem. Canadian Fed. Parl. 1978–82; Provincial Leader, New Democratic Party (NDP), Ont. 1982–96; mem. Ont. Provincial Legis. 1982–95; Premier of Ontario 1990–95; partner Goodman Phillips & Vineberg 1996–; mem. Security Intelligence Review Cttee. *Publications:* From Protest to Power 1996, The Three Questions: Prosperity and the Public Good 1998. *Address:* Goodman Phillips & Vineberg, 250 Yonge Street, Suite 2400, Toronto, Ont., M5B 2M6, Canada. *Telephone:* (416) 979-221, ext. 655.

RAFELSON, Bob; American film director; b. 1933, New York. *Films directed include:* Head 1968, Five Easy Pieces 1970 (New York Film Critics Award), The King of Marvin Gardens 1972, Stay Hungry 1976, The Postman Always Rings Twice 1981, Black Widow 1987, Mountains of the Moon 1990, Man Trouble 1992, Wet 1993, Armed Response 1994, Blood and Wine 1997, Poodle Springs 1998.

RAFFARIN, Jean-Pierre; French politician; b. 3 Aug. 1948, Poitiers; s. of Jean Raffarin and Renée Michaud; m. Anne-Marie Perrier 1980; one d.; ed. Lycée Henri IV, Poitiers, Faculté de Droit, Paris-Assas and Ecole Supérieure de Commerce, Paris; Marketing Dept. Cafés Jacques Vabre 1973–76; Adviser, Office of Minister of Labour 1976–81; Pres. Crédit Immobilier Rural de la Vienne 1978–95; lecturer, Inst. d'Etudes Politiques, Paris 1979–88; Dir.-Gen. Bernard Krief Communication 1981–88; Gen. Del. Inst. Euro-92 1988–89; Nat. Del., Deputy Sec.-Gen. and mem. Political Bureau, Parti Républicain 1977–; City Counciller, Poitiers 1977–95; Conseiller Régional 1986–88; Pres. Conseil Régional, Poitou-Charentes 1988–; mem. European Parl. 1989–95; Deputy Sec.-Gen. and Spokesman for Union pour la Démocratie Française 1993; Pres. Comm. Arc Atlantique 1994; Minister of Small and Medium-Sized Businesses, of Commerce and Craft Industry 1995–97; Sec.-Gen. U.D.F. 1995–; mem. Senate 1995–; Deputy Mayor of Chasseneuil-du-Poitou 1995–; Vice-Pres. Démocratie libérale 1997–. *Publications:* La vie en jaune 1977, La publicité nerf de la communication 1983, L'avenir a ses racines 1986, Nous sommes tous les régionaux 1988, Pour une morale de l'action 1992, le Livre de l'Atlantique 1994. *Leisure interests:* contemporary painting, regional literature. *Address:* Hôtel de la Région, 15 rue de l'Ancienne Comédie, BP 575, 86021 Poitiers; Sénat, Palais du Luxembourg, 75291 Paris; 7 route de Saint-Georges, 86360 Chasseneuil-du-Poitou, France (Home).

RAFI, Brig. Gen. Mohammed; Afghanistan politician; b. 1944, Kabul; ed. Kabul Mil. Univ. and Mil. Acad. of the U.S.S.R.; mem. People's Democratic Party of Afghanistan 1973, mem. Cen. Cttee. 1978, Politburo 1981; fmr. Minister of Public Works, Defence and Deputy Pres. of Revolutionary Council of Afghanistan; Deputy Chair. Council of Ministers and Minister of Defence 1986–88; Vice-Pres. of Afghanistan 1988–92; Order of the Red Banner.

RAFSANJANI, Hojatoleslam Ali Akhbar Hashemi; Iranian politician; b. 1934, Rafsanjan; ed. Qom; Speaker, Islamic Consultative Ass. 1980–89; Deputy Chair. Council of Experts (f. to appoint eventual successor to Ayatollah Khomeini); mem. Islamic Repub. Party; Acting C.-in-C. of the Armed Forces 1988–89; Vice-Chair. Cttee. to revise the Constitution 1989; Pres. of Iran 1989–97; Chair. Council to Determine the Expediency of the Islamic Order; fmr. First Deputy Speaker Majlis-E-Khobregan. *Address:* c/o Islamic Republican Party, Dr. Ali Shariati Avenue, Teheran, Iran.

RAGNEMALM, Hans, LL.D.; Swedish judge; b. 30 March 1940, Laholm; m. Vivi Ragnemalm 1961; Assoc. Prof. of Public Law, Univ. of Lund 1970–75; Prof. of Public Law, Univ. of Stockholm 1975–87, Dean, Faculty of Law 1984–87; Parl. Ombudsman 1987–92; Judge, Supreme Admin. Court 1992–94; Judge, Court of Justice of European Communities 1995–. *Publications:* Appealability of Administrative Decisions 1970, Extraordinary Remedies in Administrative Procedure Law 1973, Elements of Administrative Procedure Law 1977, The Constitution of Sweden 1980, Administrative Justice in Sweden 1991; numerous other books and articles. *Address:* Court of Justice of the European Communities, 2925 Luxembourg. *Telephone:* 352-4303-2890. *Fax:* 352-4303-2037.

RAGON, Michel; French writer and lecturer; b. 24 June 1924, Marseille; s. of Aristide Ragon and Camille Sourisseau; m. Françoise Antoine 1968; worked in manual jobs since the age of 14; lived in Paris 1945–, bookseller on the Seine embankments 1954–64; art critic, architectural historian, novelist; Lecturer at l'Ecole Nat. Supérieure des Arts Decoratifs à Paris 1972–85; Prix de l'Académie Française et de l'Académie d'Architecture. *Publications:* Histoire mondiale de l'architecture et de l'urbanisme modernes 1971–78, L'homme et les villes 1975, L'espace de la mort 1981, L'art abstrait 1973–74, L'art pour quoi faire? 1971, 25 ans d'art vivant 1969, Histoire de la littérature prolétarienne en France 1974, L'accent de ma mère 1980, Ma soeur aux yeux d'Asie 1982, Les mouchoirs rouges de Cholet 1984, La louve de Mervent 1985, Le marin des sables 1988, La mémoire des vaincus 1990, Le Cocher du Boiroux 1992, Journal de l'Art Abstrait 1992, Le roman de

Rabelais 1994, les Coquelicots sont revenus 1996. *Address:* 4 rue du Faubourg Poissonnière, 75010 Paris, France.

RAHMAN, Shah (Mohammad) Azizur; Bangladeshi politician and lawyer; b. 23 Nov. 1925, Kushtia; Gen. Sec. All-India Muslim Students' Fed., All-Bengal Muslim Students' League 1945–47; Chair. E. Pakistan Combined Opposition Party 1964; Leader Awami League Parl. Party and Deputy Leader of Opposition, Nat. Assembly of Pakistan 1965–69; Sr. Advocate, Supreme Court of Bangladesh; mem. Bangladesh Parl. for Daulatpore, Kushtia Constituency; Leader of the House; Minister of Labour and Industrial Welfare 1978–79; Prime Minister 1979–82, also Minister of Educ. 1979–82, of Law and Parl. Affairs, Local Govt., Rural Devt. and Co-operatives, and Religious Affairs Feb.–March 1982; mem. Bangladesh Bar Council. *Publication:* The Strategy of Development in Bangladesh (with Mahabub Hossain) 1990. *Address:* c/o Office of the Prime Minister, Dhaka, Bangladesh.

RAHMANI, Chérif; Algerian politician; b. 16 Jan. 1945, Ain Oussera; m.; four c.; ed. Ecole Nat. d'Admin.; Inspecteur Gen.; Sec. Gen. to the Ministry of the Interior; Minister of Youth and Sport 1988–89, of Equipment 1989–90. *Address:* c/o Ministry of Equipment, Le Grand Séminaire, Koulsa, Algeria.

RAHMANI, Mawlawi Mohammed Arsala; Afghanistan politician; fmr. Deputy Prime Minister; Minister of Religious Guidance, Endowment and the Haj; Prime Minister of Afghanistan 1994–95. *Address:* c/o Office of the Prime Minister, Shar Rahi Sedarat, Kabul, Afghanistan.

RAIDI; Chinese politician; b. 1938, Biru, northern Tibet; ed. Cen. Nationalities Inst., Beijing; Sec. CCP Cttee., Nagu Region 1972; Sec. CCP Cttee., Tibet Autonomous Region 1975–77, Deputy Sec. (Exec.) 1977–; Chair. Peasants' Fed. of Tibet 1975; alt. mem. 11th CCP Cen. Cttee. 1977–82; Vice-Chair. Revolutionary Cttee., Tibet Autonomous Region 1977–79; Vice-Chair. People's Congress of Tibet 1979–83, Chair. 1986; Chair. Tibet Autonomous Regional 6th People's Congress 1993–; Deputy Sec. CCP Tibet Autonomous Regional Cttee. 1985–; 8th NPC Deputy, Tibet Autonomous Region; mem. 12th CCP Cen. Cttee. 1982, 14th 1992–97, 15th 1997–. *Address:* Tibet Autonomous Region Chinese Communist Party, Lhasa, Tibet, People's Republic of China.

RAIKIN, Konstantin Arkadyevich; Russian actor and theatre director; b. 8 July 1950; s. of Arkady Raikin; m.; one d.; ed. M. Shchukin Theatre High School, Moscow; with theatre Sovremennik 1970–81, debut in Valentin and Valentina; 38 roles including 15 leading, acted in plays of Shakespeare and Russian classics; actor State Theatre of Miniatures (Satirikon) under Arkady Raikin 1981–87, Artistic Dir. 1988–; acts in most productions of the theatre (Hamlet 1998), leading roles in TV productions and films; Prize for Best Acting, Belgrade Festival 1990, People's Artist of Russia 1992, State Prize 1995. *Address:* Theatre Satirikon, Sheremetyevskaya str. 8, Moscow, Russia. *Telephone:* (095) 289 2698 (Office).

RAIMOND, Jean-Bernard; French diplomatist and politician; b. 6 Feb. 1926, Paris; s. of Henri Raimond and Alice Auberty; m. Monique Chabanel 1975; two d.; ed. Ecole Normale Supérieure and Ecole Nationale d'Administration; C.N.R.S. 1951–53; Dept. of Political Affairs and Cen. Admin. of Ministry of Foreign Affairs 1956–66; Deputy Dir. Europe 1967; Asst. Dir. Office of Minister of Foreign Affairs 1967; Tech. Counsellor, Office of Prime Minister 1968–69; Sec.-Gen. Presidency of the Repub. 1969–73; Amb. to Morocco 1973–77; Dir. for N. Africa and the Levant 1977–78; Dir. Office of Minister of Foreign Affairs 1978; Dir.-Gen. for Cultural Relations, Ministry of Foreign Affairs 1979–81; Amb. to Poland 1982–84, to U.S.S.R. 1984–86; Minister of Foreign Affairs 1986–88; Amb. to Holy See, Rome 1988–91; Deputy to Nat. Ass. from Bouches-du-Rhône (R.P.R.) 1993–; Amb. de France 1991; Advisor to the Pres. of the Servier Laboratory 1992–; Pres. French-Russian Friendship Soc. (Sofarus), France–Italy Asscn.; Officier, Légion d'honneur; Commdr., Ordre Nat. du Mérite; Chevalier des Palmes Académiques; Order of Ouissan Alaouite (Morocco), Grand Cross, Order of Pius IX (Holy See). *Publications:* Le Quai d'Orsay à l'épreuve de la cohabitation 1989, Le choix de Gorbatchev 1992. *Address:* Servier SA, 22 rue Garnier, 92200 Neuilly-sur-Seine (Office); Assemblée Nationale, 75355 Paris Cedex 07 (Office); 12 rue des Poissonniers, 92200 Neuilly-sur-Seine (Home).

RAIMONDI, Ruggero; Italian opera singer; b. 3 Oct. 1941, Bologna; m. Isabel Maier 1987; operatic début in La Bohème, Spoleto Festival 1964; début at Metropolitan Opera, New York in Ernani 1970; other engagements include Don Giovanni, Le Nozze di Figaro, Faust, Attila, Don Carlos, Boris Godunov, Don Quichotte, Don Pasquale, Otello, Contes d'Hoffmann. *Films:* Don Giovanni 1978, Six Characters in Search of an Author 1981, La Vie est un Roman 1982, Carmen 1983; operas produced include: Don Giovanni, Nancy 1986; Citizen of Honour, Athens; Officier des Arts et Lettres, Chevalier de l'Ordre de Malte, Commendatore della Repubblica Italiana. *Address:* c/o M. Gromof, 140 bis rue Lecourbe, 75015 Paris, France.

RAINE, Craig Anthony, B.A., B.PHIL.; British writer; b. 3 Dec. 1944, Shildon, Co. Durham; s. of Norman Edward and Olive Marie Raine; m. Ann Pasternak Slater 1972; three s. one d.; ed. Exeter Coll., Oxford; Lecturer, Exeter Coll., Oxford Univ. 1971–72, 1975–76, Lincoln Coll. 1974–75, Christ Church 1976–79; Books Ed. New Review 1977–78; Ed. Quarto 1979–80; Poetry Ed. New Statesman 1981; Poetry Ed. Faber and Faber Ltd. 1981–91; Fellow in English, New Coll., Oxford 1991–; Kelus Prize 1979, Southern Arts Literature Award 1979, Cholmondeley Poetry Award 1983. *Publications:* The Onion, Memory 1978, A Martian Sends a Postcard Home 1979, A Free Translation 1981, Rich 1984, The Electrification of the Soviet Union (opera) 1986, A Choice of Kipling's Prose (ed.) 1987, The Prophetic Book 1988; '1953' (play) 1990, Haydn and the Valve Trumpet: Literary Essays 1990, Rudyard Kipling: Selected Poetry (ed.) 1992, History: The Home Movie 1994, Clay. Whereabouts Unknown 1996, New Writing 7 1998.

RAINE, Kathleen Jessie, M.A., F.R.S.L.; British poet; b. 1908; d. of late George Raine and Jessie Raine; m. Charles Madge (divorced, died 1996); one s. one d.; ed. Girton Coll., Cambridge; Fellow, Girton Coll., Cambridge 1956; co-Ed. Temenos (review) 1982–93; W. H. Smith Literary Award and other English and American poetry prizes and awards; Blake scholar; Hon. D.Litt. (Leicester) 1974, (Durham) 1979; Queens Medal for Poetry 1992; Officier, Ordre des Arts et des Lettres. *Publications:* Stone and Flower 1943, Living in Time 1946, The Pythoness 1949, The Year One 1952, Collected Poems 1956, The Hollow Hill (poems) 1965, Blake and Tradition (Andrew Mellon Lectures) 1969, Selected Writings of Thomas Taylor the Platonist (with George Mills Harper) 1969, William Blake, Selected Poems 1970, The Lost Country (poems) 1971, On a Deserted Shore (poems) 1972, Faces of Day and Night 1973, Farewell Happy Fields (autobiog.) 1973, The Land Unknown (autobiog.) 1975, The Oval Portrait (verse) 1977, The Lions Mouth (autobiog.) 1977, The Oracle in the Heart (poems) 1979, Collected Poems 1981, The Human Face of God 1982, The Presence (poems) 1988, Selected Poems 1988, Visages du Jour et de la Nuit 1989, India Seen Afar 1990, Golgonooza, City of the Imagination 1991, Living with Mystery (poems) 1992; criticism: Defending Ancient Springs 1967, Yeats, the Tarot and the Golden Dawn 1973, Death in Life and Life in Death 1973, David Jones and the Actually Loved and Known 1978, From Blake to a Vision 1978, Blake and the New Age 1979, The Inner Journey of the Poet and other papers 1982, L'imagination créatrice de William Blake 1986, Yeats the Initiate 1986. *Address:* 47 Paultons Square, London, SW3 5DT, England.

RAINES, Franklin Delano, J.D.; American public servant and fmr. investment banker; b. 14 Jan. 1949, Seattle; s. of Delano Thomas and Ida Mae (Fortson) Raines; m. Wendy Farrow 1982; three d.; ed. Harvard Univ., Oxford Univ.; Assoc. Dir. Seattle Model Cities Program 1972–73; Assoc. Preston, Thorgrimson, Ellis, Holman & Fletcher, Seattle 1976–77; Asst. Dir. White House Domestic Policy Staff, Washington, D.C. 1977–78, Assoc. Dir. U.S. Office of Man. and Budget 1978–79, Dir. 1996–98; Vice-Pres. Lazard Frères & Co., New York 1979–82, Sr. Vice-Pres. 1983–84, Gen. Partner 1985–90, Ltd. Partner 1990–91; Vice-Chair. Fed. Nat. Mortgage Asscn. 1991–96; Chair., C.E.O. Design Fannie Mae, Washington 1998–; mem. New York Stock Exchange (allied); mem. Bd. Overseers Harvard Univ.; Trustee Univ. Puget Sound, German Marshall Fund of U.S., French-American Foundation, American Museum of Natural History and other bodies; Rhodes Scholar 1971. *Leisure interests:* running, tennis.

RAINIER III, His Serene Highness Prince, Louis Henri Maxence Bertrand; Prince of Monaco; b. 31 May 1923; s. of the late Comte Pierre de Polignac and the late Princess Charlotte, Duchess of Valentinois; m. Grace Patricia Kelly 1956 (died 1982); one s. two d.; ed. Summerfields School, Hastings (England), Montpellier Univ., and Ecole Libre des Sciences Politiques, Paris; Hereditary Prince of Monaco 1944; succeeded his grandfather Prince Louis II 1949; founded Monaco Red Cross 1948, American Friends of Monaco 1952, Prix Rainier 1955, Grand Master, Ordre de St. Charles de Monaco, Grand Croix, Légion d'honneur, Belgian, Swedish, Greek, Lebanese, Italian, Netherlands and San Marino orders; served in French army as Lieut. and Col. 1944–45. *Address:* Palais princier, B.P. 518, MC 98015, Monaco cedex.

RÄISÄNEN, Heikki Martti, M.A., D.THEOL.; Finnish professor of New Testament exegesis; b. 10 Dec. 1941, Helsinki; s. of Martti Olavi Räisänen and Saara Ilona Itkonen; m. Leena Marjatta Wright 1974; three s. one d.; ed. Univ. of Helsinki; lecturer in New Testament Exegesis, Univ. of Helsinki 1969–74, Acting Assoc. Prof. in Biblical Languages 1971–74, Prof. of New Testament Exegesis 1975–; Research Prof. Acad. of Finland 1984–94; Dir. Exegetical Inst., Univ. of Helsinki 1975–84, 1995–96, Vice-Dean of the Theological Faculty 1978–80, Dir. Centre of Excellence 1994–; Chief Ed. Vartija 1989–; mem. Cttee. Finnish Exegetical Soc. 1969–85, Chair. 1980–85; mem. Finnish Acad. of Sciences 1978–, Cttee. Soc. for New Testament Studies 1986–89; Fulbright Visiting Scholar, Harvard 1970–71, Visiting Scholar, Cambridge Univ. 1978, Humboldt Visiting Scholar, Tübingen 1980–82; Edward Cadbury Lectures, Univ. of Birmingham 1996; Hon. D.D. (Edin.) 1990. *Publications:* Die Mutter Jesu im Neuen Testament 1969, Das Koranische Jesusbild 1971, The Idea of Divine Hardening 1972, Das "Messiasgeheimnis" im Markusevangelium 1976, Paul and the Law 1983, The Torah and Christ 1986, The "Messianic Secret" in Mark's Gospel 1990, Beyond New Testament Theology 1990, Jesus, Paul and Torah 1992, Marcion, Muhammad and the Mahatma 1997; numerous books in Finnish; numerous articles on early Christianity. *Leisure interest:* soccer. *Address:* Vantaanjänne 1 B 11, 01730 Vantaa, Finland. *Telephone:* (9) 898422.

RAISMAN, John Michael, C.B.E., C.B.I.M., M.A.; British business executive; b. 12 Feb. 1929, Lahore, India; s. of Sir Jeremy and Renee Mary (née Kelly) Raisman; m. Evelyn Anne Muirhead 1953; one s. three d.; ed. Rugby School, Queen's Coll., Oxford; joined Shell Int. Petroleum Co. Ltd. 1953, served in Brazil 1953–60; Gen. Man., Shell Panama 1960–62; Asst. to Exploration and Production Co-ordinator, Shell Int. Petroleum, Maatschappij 1963–65; Gen. Man., Shell Co. of Turkey Ltd. 1965–69; Pres. Shell Sekiyu KK 1970–73;

Head of European Supply and Marketing, Shell Int. Petroleum 1974–77; Man. Dir., Shell U.K. Oil 1977–78; Deputy Chair. and C.E.O, Shell U.K. Ltd. 1978–79, Chair. and C.E.O. 1979–85; Chair. Shell Chemicals U.K. Ltd. 1979–85; Dir. Vickers 1981–90, Glaxo Holdings PLC 1982–90, Lloyds Bank 1985–95, Lloyds TSB 1996–98, Lloyds Merchant Bank Holdings 1985–87, Candover 1990–, Tandem Computers 1991–97, British Biotech. 1993–98 (Chair. 1995–98); Deputy Chair. British Telecom 1987–91; mem. Pres.'s Cttee. of Confed. of British Industry (CBI), Chair. Europe Cttee. of CBI 1980–88; Chair. Council of Industry for Man. Educ. (CIME) 1981–85, Chair. Oil Industry Emergency Cttee. (OIEC) 1981–85, Advisory Council, London Enterprise Agency 1979–85, Investment Bd. Electra Candover Partners 1985–95, Electronics Industry EDC 1986–88, Business Forum of European Movement, Council for Industry and Higher Educ. 1991–98; Deputy Chair. Nat. Comm. on Educ. 1991–95; Gov. Nat. Inst. of Econ. and Social Research 1981–; mem. Governing Council of Business in the Community 1982–85; mem. Council, Inst. for Fiscal Studies 1982–92; mem. Royal Comm. on Environmental Pollution 1986–87; Chair. Bd. Trustees R.A. 1986–96; Pro-Chancellor Aston Univ. 1987–93; Hon. D.Univ. (Stirling) 1983, Hon. LL.D. (Aberdeen) 1985, (Manchester) 1986, (UWE) 1994; Hon. D.Sc. (Aston) 1992. *Leisure interests:* golf, travel, skiing, opera. *Address:* Netheravon House, Netheravon Road South, London, W4 2PY, England. *Telephone:* 0181-742 1000. *Fax:* 0181-742 1000.

RAITT, Bonnie Lynn; American blues singer and guitarist; b. 8 Nov. 1949, Burbank, Calif.; d. of John Raitt; ed. Radcliffe Coll.; performer blues clubs, E. Coast; concert tours U.K. 1976, 1977; *albums include:* Nick of Time 1989 (1990 Grammy Awards for rock—best vocal performance, female pop—best vocal performance, female album of the year), I'm in the Mood (with John Lee Hooker; 1990 Grammy Award for blues—best traditional record), Luck of the Draw 1991 (1992 Grammy Award for rock—best vocal performance, female, for best duet), Longing in their Hearts 1994 (Grammy Award for best pop album), Road Tested 1996; *songs include:* Something to Talk About (1992 Grammy Award for best pop vocal performance, female), Good Man, Good Woman (with Delbert McClinton; 1992 Grammy Award for best vocal by a duo or group, rock); numerous Grammy nominations. *Address:* P.O. Box 626, Los Angeles, CA 90078, U.S.A.

RAJAN, Mannaraswamighala Sreeranga, M.A., D.LITT; Indian university professor; b. 4 Aug. 1920, Badikayalapalli, Andhra Pradesh; s. of late M. V. Bhatrachar and Rangamma; m. Padma Rajan 1946; one s. two d.; ed. Univ. of Mysore and Columbia Univ. New York; govt. service 1944–47; Asst. Sec. Asian Relations Org. New Delhi 1947–48; Admin. Sec. and Research Sec. Indian Council of World Affairs 1949–59; joined Indian School of Int. Studies 1959; Research, Inst. of Commonwealth Studies, Univ. of London 1960–61; Prof. of Commonwealth Studies 1962–71, concurrently Dir. Indian School of Int. Studies 1965–71; Prof. of Int. Org. Jawaharlal Nehru Univ. 1971–84, Prof. Emer. 1986–; Ed. International Studies (journal) 1963–74, India Quarterly 1975–81, Foreign Affairs Reports 1975–81, The Nonaligned World 1983–84; Presidential Adviser, Repub. of Nauru, Chief. Sec. and Sec. for External Affairs 1984–86; Asian Fellow, A.N.U., Canberra 1971–72; Fellow, UN Inst. for Training and Research, New York 1974–76; Fellow Inst. for Advanced Studies, Univ. of Edin. 1989–90. *Publications:* United Nations and Domestic Jurisdiction 1958, Post-War Transformation of the Commonwealth 1963, India in World Affairs 1954–56 1964, Nonalignment, India and the Future 1970, Sovereignty over Natural Resources 1978, The Expanding Jurisdiction of the United Nations 1982, India's Foreign Policy and Relations (with A. Appadorai) 1985, Studies on Nonalignment and the Nonaligned Movement 1986, India and the Commonwealth 1990, The Future of Nonalignment and the Nonaligned Movement 1990, Nonalignment and the Nonaligned Movement: Retrospect and Prospect 1990, Studies on India's Foreign Policy 1992, Nonalignment and the Nonaligned Movement in the Present World Order 1994, The United Nations and World Politics 1995, World Order and the United Nations 1995, Recent Essays on India's Foreign Policy 1997, International and Area Studies in India (Ed.) 1997, India and International Affairs 1998; articles in books and learned journals, ed. of six books. *Leisure interest:* cooking. *Address:* School of International Studies, Jawaharlal Nehru University, New Delhi, 110 067, India.

RAJARATNAM, Sinnathamby; Singapore politician; b. 25 Feb. 1915, Ceylon (now Sri Lanka); ed. Raffles Inst., Singapore, King's Coll., London; brought to Malaya at age of six months; Assoc. Ed. Singapore Standard 1950–54; Editorial Staff Straits Times 1954–59; mem. Malayanization Cttee. 1955; mem. Minimum Standards of Livelihood Cttee. 1956; Convenor and Founder-mem. of People's Action Party; Assemblyman (now M.P.) for Kampong Glam constituency 1959–; Minister for Culture 1959–65, for Foreign Affairs 1965–80, also for Labour 1968–71, Second Deputy Prime Minister (with responsibility for Foreign Affairs) 1980–85; Sr. Minister, Prime Minister's Office 1985–88; Distinguished Sr. Fellow Inst. of Southeast Asian Studies 1988; Order of Temasek (First Class) 1990. *Address:* c/o Heng Mui Keng Terrace, Pasir Panjang, Singapore 0511.

RAJNA, Thomas, D.MUS.; British composer and pianist; b. 21 Dec. 1928, Budapest; s. of late Dr. Nandor Rajna and Hella Eisen; m. Anthea Valentine Campion 1967; one s. two d.; ed. Nat. Musical School, Budapest, Franz Liszt Acad. of Music, Budapest and Royal Coll. of Music, London; freelance composer, pianist and teacher, London 1951–63; Prof. of Piano, Guildhall School of Music 1963–70; Lecturer, Univ. of Surrey 1967–70; Sr. Lecturer in Piano, Faculty of Music, Univ. of Cape Town 1970–, Assoc. Prof. 1989; *compositions include* film and ballet music, orchestral and chamber music, two piano concertos, Amarantha (opera in 7 scenes), Video Games (for orchestra), Rhapsody for clarinet and orchestra 1995, Fantasy for violin and orchestra 1996, Suite for violin and harp 1997; *recordings:* works by Stravinsky, Messiaen, Scriabin, Granados, Liszt, Schumann, Dohnanyi and own compositions; Fellow, Univ. of Cape Town 1981; Hon. D.Mus. (Cape Town) 1985, Liszt Prize, Budapest 1947, Artes Award (SABC) 1981, Cape Tercentenary Foundation Merit Award 1997. *Publications:* Preludes for Piano, Music for Violin and Piano 1989–90, Dialogues for clarinet and piano, Concerto for harp and orchestra. *Leisure interests:* chess, swimming. *Address:* 10 Wyndover Road, Claremont, Cape 7700, South Africa. *Telephone:* (021) 613937. *Fax:* (021) 613937.

RAKHIMOV, Murtaza Gubaidullovich; Bashkir politician; b. 7 Feb. 1934, Tavakanovo, Bashkiria; s. of Gubaidulla Zufarovich Rakhimov and Galima Abdullovna Rakhimova; m. Luiza Galimovna Rakhimova; one s.; ed. Ufa Oil Inst.; operator, then chief of oil rig, chief chemist, Chief Engineer, Dir. Ufa Oil Processing Plant 1956–90; U.S.S.R. People's Deputy 1990–92; Chair. Supreme Soviet Repub. of Bashkortostan 1993–, Pres. 1994–; mem. Russian Council of Fed. (Parl.) 1993–. *Leisure interests:* sports, music, literature. *Address:* The Republic House, 46 Tukayev Street, 450101, Ufa, Bashkortostan, Russia. *Telephone:* (3472) 50 24 06. *Fax:* (3472) 50 01 75.

RAKHMONOV, Emomali; Tajikistan politician; b. 5 Oct. 1952, Dangara; ed. Tajik Univ.; worked as electrician, salesman, sec. trade union and CP cttees.; dir. sovkhoz in Dangar Region 1988–92; Chair. Kulyab Regional Exec. Soviet 1992; Chair. Supreme Soviet (Majlisi Oli) Repub. of Tajikistan 1992–94; Pres. of Tajikistan 1994–. *Address:* Office of the President, Dushanbe, Tajikistan.

RAKOTOARIJAONA, Lieut.-Col. Désiré; Malagasy politician and army officer; b. 1934; Minister of Finance Feb.–June 1975; mem. Supreme Revolutionary Council 1975–88; Prime Minister 1977–88; mem. Front National pour la Défense de la Révolution Socialiste Malgache. *Address:* c/o Office du Premier Ministre, Antananarivo, Madagascar.

RAKOTOMAVO, Pascal; Malagasy politician; Prime Minister of Madagascar 1997–98. *Address:* c/o Office of the Prime Minister, B.P. 248, Mahazoarivo, 101 Antananarivo, Madagascar.

RAKOTONIAINA, Justin; Malagasy politician, teacher and diplomatist; b. 1933, Betsileo; fmr. professor of Law, Univ. of Madagascar; Amb. to Algeria, also accred. to Tunisia and Guinea 1973–75; Minister of Nat. Educ. 1975–76; Prime Minister of Madagascar 1976–77; mem. Supreme Revolutionary Council.

RAKOTOVAHINY, Emmanuel; Malagasy politician; fmr. Chair. Union nationale pour la démocratie et le développement (UNDD); fmr. Minister of State for Rural Devt. and Land Reform; Prime Minister of Madagascar 1995–96. *Address:* c/o Office of the Prime Minister, Antananarivo, Madagascar.

RAKOWSKI, Mieczysław Franciszek, DR.HIST.; Polish politician and journalist; b. 1 Dec. 1926, Kowalewko, Szubin district; m. 1st Wanda Wiłkomirska (q.v.) 1952 (separated); two s.; m. 2nd Elżbieta Kępińska; ed. Higher School of Social Sciences, Cracow and Inst. of Social Sciences, Warsaw; worked at Cen. Cttee. of Polish United Workers' Party (PZPR) 1949–52, 1955–57; Sub-editor, Polityka 1957, Editor-in-Chief 1958–82; Chair. Gen. Board, Polish Journalists' Asscn. 1958–61; Deputy mem. Cen. Cttee., PZPR 1964–75, mem. 1975–90; Deputy to Sejm 1972–89, Deputy Chair. PZPR Sejm Deputies' Club 1980; Deputy Chair. Council of Ministers 1981–85; Chair. Cttee. for Trade Unions of Council of Ministers 1981–85; Vice-Marshal (Deputy Speaker) of Sejm 1985–88; Chair. Socio-Econ. Council attached to Sejm 1985–88; mem. Political Bureau PZPR Cen. Cttee. 1987–90; Sec. PZPR Cen. Cttee. 1988–89; First Sec. PZPR Cen. Cttee. 1989–90; Chair. Council of Ministers (Prime Minister) 1988–89; Ed.-in-Chief monthly Dziś, Przegląd społeczny 1990–; Presenter, TV programme Świat i Polityka (World and Politics); fmr. Chair. Polish Yachting Union; Order of Banner of Labour 1st and 2nd Class, Gold Cross of Merit, State Prize 2nd Class 1976, Commdr.'s Cross with Star of Order of Polonia Restituta, and other decorations. *Publications:* NRF z bliska (Fed. Rep. of Germany from a Short Distance) 1958, New World 1959, Socjal-demokratyczna Partia Niemiec w okresie powojennym 1949–54 (Social-Democratic Party of Germany in Post-war Period) 1960, Świat na zakręcie (The World in Turning) 1960, Zachód szuka ideologii (The West Looks for Ideology) 1961, Ameryka wielopiętrowa (Many-storied America), Klimaty w RFN (Climates of the Fed. Rep. of Germany), Polityka Zagraniczna PRL (The Foreign Policy of the Polish People's Republic) 1974, Dymisja Kanclerza (Chancellor's Dismissal) 1975, Spełnione i niespełnione 1978, Przesilenie grudniowe (December Crisis) 1981, Partnerstwo (Partnership) 1982, Czas nadziei i rozczarowań (Time of Hopes and Disappointments), Vol. 1 1985, Vol. 2 1987, Ein schwieriger Dialog 1986, Jak to się stało 1993; co-author: The Polish Upswing 1971–75 1975. *Leisure interests:* joinery, angling, yachting. *Address:* Miesięcznik "Dziś", ul. Poznańska 3, 00-680 Warsaw, Poland. *Telephone:* (22) 621 01 21.

RALL, J. Edward, M.D., PH.D.; American research scientist, physician and research administrator; b. 3 Feb. 1920, Naperville, Ill.; s. of Edward Everett Rall and Nell Platt Rall; brother of David Platt Rall; m. Caroline Domm 1944 (deceased); one s. one d.; ed. North Central Coll., Ill., Northwestern Univ., Chicago and Univ. of Minnesota; served U.S. army, Medical Corps

1946–48; Attending Physician, Memorial Hosp., New York City 1950–55; Assoc., Sloan-Kettering Inst., New York and Asst. Prof. of Medicine, Cornell Univ. 1951–55; Chief, Clinical Endocrinology Branch, Nat. Inst. of Arthritis, Metabolism and Digestive Diseases (later named Nat. Inst. of Arthritis, Diabetes and Digestive and Kidney Diseases—NIADDK), N.I.H. 1955–62, assigned to Collège de France, Paris and Nat. Inst. for Medical Research, London 1961–62; Dir. Div. of Intramural Research, NIADDK 1962–83; Acting Deputy Dir. for Science, N.I.H. 1981–82, Deputy Dir. for Intramural Research 1983–91, Sr. Scientist 1991–; mem. N.A.S., American Acad. of Arts and Sciences. *Publications:* over 150 biomedical research articles on thyroid gland and radiation. *Leisure interests:* pre-Columbian art, linguistics, music, theatre, gardening. *Address:* National Institute of Health, Building 10, Room 8N307, Bethesda, MD 20892 (Office); 3947 Baltimore Street, Kensington, MD 20895, U.S.A. (Home). *Telephone:* (301) 402-2486 (Office). *Fax:* (301) 402-0387.

RALLIS, George J., LL.D.; Greek politician and lawyer; b. 26 Dec. 1918; m. Helene Voultsos 1950; two d.; ed. Athens Univ.; served Reconnaissance Groups 1940–41 and Tank Corps 1945–48; elected Deputy for Athens 1950–58, 1961–67, 1974–93; mem. Greek del. to European Council, Strasbourg 1953–58; Minister to Prime Minister's Office 1954–56, of Public Works and Communications 1956–58, of the Interior 1961–63, of Public Order April 1967; under house arrest April–May 1967, in prison and exile May–Sept. 1968; Minister to Prime Minister's Office and of Educ. 1974–77, for Co-ordination and Planning 1977–78, for Foreign Affairs 1978–80, Prime Minister of Greece 1980–81; mem. Popular Party 1950, Nat. Rally 1951, Nat. Radical Union 1956, New Democratic Party 1974–87, 1989–; Medal of Valour, War Cross with two bars, D.S.M., and several foreign awards. *Publications:* John Rallis 1946, The Possibility of Increasing the Yield of Greek Agriculture 1952, Democracy and Communism 1959, The Truth about the Greek Politicians (in Greek) 1971, The Technique of Violence 1972, Ores Efthynis 1984, Koitazontas Piso 1993. *Leisure interest:* golf. *Address:* 4 Kanari Street, 106 71 Athens, Greece. *Telephone:* 01-3617 340.

RALPH, Richard Peter, C.M.G., C.V.O., M.SC.; British diplomatist; b. 27 April 1946, London; s. of Peter Ralph and late Evelyn Marion Ralph; m. Margaret Elisabeth Coulthurst 1970; one s. one d.; ed. The King's School, Canterbury, Edinburgh Univ.; Embassy, Vientiane, Laos 1970–73, Lisbon, Portugal 1974–77; FCO 1977–81; High Comm., Harare, Zimbabwe 1981–84; FCO 1984–89; Embassy, Washington, D.C. 1989–93; Amb. to Latvia 1993–95; Gov. Falkland Islands 1996–, concurrently Commr. S. Georgia and S. Sandwich Islands. *Leisure interests:* reading, music, art, motorcycling. *Address:* Government House, Stanley, Falkland Islands. *Telephone:* 27433. *Fax:* 27434.

RAMA, Carlos M., PH.D.; Uruguayan writer, lawyer, professor and editor; b. 26 Oct. 1921, Montevideo; s. of Manuel Rama and Carolina Facal; m. Judith Dellepiane 1943; one s. one d.; ed. Univ. de la República and Univ. de Paris; Journalist 1940–48, 1972–; Exec. Sec. of Uruguayan Bar Asscn. 1940–49; Prof. of Universal History in secondary schools 1944–48; Ed. Nuestro Tiempo 1954–56, Gacetilla Austral 1961–73; Prof. of Sociology and Social Research, Prof. of Contemporary History, Prof. of Theory and Methodology of History, Univ. de la República 1950–72; Prof. of Latin American History, Univ. Autónoma de Barcelona 1973–; Pres. PEN Club Latinoamericano en España; Sec. Gen. Grupo de Estudios Latinoamericanos de Barcelona; Commdr., Order of Liberation (Spain); Officier des Palmes académiques (France). *Publications:* La Historia y la Novela 1947, 1963, 1970, 1974, Las ideas socialistas en el siglo XIX 1947, 1949, 1963, 1967, 1976, Ensayo de Sociología Uruguaya 1956, Teoría de la Historia 1959, 1968, 1974, 1980, Las clases sociales en el Uruguay 1960, La Crisis española del siglo XX 1960, 1962, 1976, Itinerario español 1961, 1977, Revolución social y fascismo en el siglo XX 1962, Sociología del Uruguay 1965, 1973, Historia del movimiento obrero y social latinoamericano contemporáneo 1967, 1969, 1976, Los afrouruguayos 1967, 1968, 1969, 1970, Garibaldi y el Uruguay 1968, Uruguay en Crisis 1969, Sociología de América Latina 1970, 1977, Chile, mil días entre la revolución y el fascismo 1974, España, crónica entrañable 1973–77, 1978, Historia de América Latina 1978, Fascismo y anarquismo en la España contemporánea 1979. *Leisure interest:* gardening. *Address:* c/o Monte de Orsá 7, Vallvidrera, Barcelona 17, Spain.

RAMA RAU, Santha; Indian writer; b. 24 Jan. 1923, Madras, Tamil Nadu; d. of late Sir Benegal Rama Rau and Dhanvanthi Handoo; m. 1st Faubion Bowers 1951 (divorced 1966); one s.; m. 2nd Gurdon W. Wattles 1970 (died 1995); two step-s. two step-d.; ed. St. Paul's Girls' School, London, and Wellesley Coll., U.S.A.; numerous journeys in Europe, India, America, S. E. Asia, Japan and Russia; fmr. teacher Hani Freedom School, Tokyo; English teacher at Sarah Lawrence Coll., Bronxville, N.Y. 1971–73; Hon. doctorates from Bates, Brandeis, Roosevelt and Russell Sage Colls.; Achievement Awards from Wellesley Coll., Asia Soc., New York, The Secondary Educ. Bd., N.J., The Asscn. of Indians in America. *Publications:* Home to India 1945, East of Home 1950, This is India 1953, Remember the House 1955, View to the South-East 1957, My Russian Journey 1959, A Passage to India (dramatization of E. M. Forster novel) 1962, Gifts of Passage (autobiog.) 1962, The Cooking of India 1969, The Adventuress 1971, A Princess Remembers 1976, An Inheritance 1979; numerous articles and short stories. *Leisure interests:* opera, reading, travel. *Address:* R.R.I., Box 22, Leedville Road, Amenia, NY 12501; 16 Sutton Place, New York, NY 10022, U.S.A. *Telephone:* (914) 373-9124 (Amenia); (212) 755-3684 (New York).

RAMACHANDRAN, Cherubala Pathayapurayil, F.I.BIOL., DR.MED.SCI.; Malaysian professor and medical scientist; b. 3 June 1936, Kuala Lumpur; s. of K.K. Madhavan Nair and Kamalam M. Nair; m. Githa Priya Darshini 1966; one s. one d.; ed. St. John's Inst., Kuala Lumpur, Christian Coll., Madras, India, Univ. of London, U.K., Univ. of Liverpool, U.K., Tulane Univ., U.S.A., Univ. of Tokyo, Japan; Wellcome Trust Research Scholar and Demonstrator in Medical Parasitology, Liverpool School of Tropical Medicine 1959–62, Research Fellow in Tropical Medicine Inst. for Medical Research, Kuala Lumpur 1962–63, Head Filariasis Research Div. 1967–70; Asst. Prof. in Medical Parasitology Faculty of Medicine, Univ. of Malaysia, Kuala Lumpur 1963–67, Assoc. Prof. in Medical Parasitology and Head School of Biological Sciences University Sains Malaysia, Penang 1970–72, Prof. and Dean 1972–79; Sr. Scientist Human Resource Devt. Tropical Disease Research WHO, Geneva, Switzerland 1979–87, Man. Research and Devt. Filariasis Research Programme, Tropical Disease Research, WHO, Switzerland 1987–92; Chief Filariasis Research and Control, WHO, Geneva 1992–96; Prof. of Clinical Parasitology, Universiti Putra, Malaysia 1996–; Fellow Liverpool School of Tropical Medicine, U.K., Malaysian Scientific Asscn.; fmr. Pres. Malaysian Soc. of Parasitology and Tropical Medicine, mem. Council World Fed. of Parasitologists; Sandosham Medal (Malaysia) 1974; Mary Kingsley Medal for Tropical Medicine (U.K.) 1998. *Publications:* numerous scientific papers in learned journals. *Leisure interests:* squash, photography, music. *Address:* Apt-8A-4-4, Belvedere Bukit Tunku, 50480 Kuala Lumpur, Malaysia. *Telephone:* 9486101, ext. 2531 (Office); 2987275 (Home). *Fax:* 2986152.

RAMADHANI, Most Rev. John Acland, B.A.; Tanzanian ecclesiastic; b. 1 Aug. 1932, Zanzibar; s. of Augustine Ramadhani and Mary Majaliwa; ed. Univ. of E. Africa, Queen's Coll. Birmingham and Univ. of Birmingham; Prin. St. Andrew's Teacher Training Coll., Korogwe 1967–69; Warden, St. Mark's Theological Coll., Dar es Salaam 1977–79; Bishop of Zanzibar and Tanga 1980–; Archbishop of the Prov. of Tanzania 1984–97. *Leisure interest:* reading. *Address:* Diocese of Zanzibar and Tanga, P.O. Box 35, Korogwe, Tanzania. *Telephone:* Korogwe 22 (Office); Korogwe 68 (Home).

RAMAHATRA, Gen. Victor; Malagasy politician and army officer; b. 6 Sept. 1945, Antananarivo; s. of Pierre Longin Ramahatra and Marie Lucile Ratsimandresy; m. Nivonirina Rajoelson 1971; two s. one d.; officer in Corps of Engineers; mil. engineer; Prime Minister of Malagasy Repub. 1987–91; consultant, civilian sector; mem. Asscn. des Ingénieurs Diplômés de l'Ecole Supérieure du Génie Militaire d'Angers, Asscn. des Anciens Elèves de Saint-Cyr. *Leisure interests:* jogging, basketball, reading, march/walking, swimming. *Address:* P.O. Box 6004, Antananarivo 101, Madagascar. *Telephone:* 240-80 (Office); 231-72 (Home). *Fax:* 231-72.

RAMALINGASWAMI, Vulimiri, M.D., D.PHIL., D.SC. (OXON.), F.R.C.P., F.R.C.PATH., F.R.S.; Indian medical scientist; b. 8 Aug. 1921, Srikakulam, Andhra Pradesh; s. of Vulimiri Gumpaswami and Vulimiri Sundaramma Gumpaswami; m. Kuppa Surya Prabha 1947; one s. one d.; ed. Andhra Univ. and Univ. of Oxford, England; Pathologist for Indian Council of Medical Research at the Nutrition Research Labs., Coonor, South India 1947–54; Asst. Sec. and Deputy Dir. Indian Council of Medical Research 1954–57; Prof. of Pathology and Head of Dept., All-India Inst. of Medical Sciences, Ansari Nagar, New Delhi 1957–69, Dir. and Prof. of Pathology 1969–79, now Prof. Emer.; Dir.-Gen. Indian Council of Medical Research 1979–86; Pres. Indian Nat. Science Acad. 1979–80; Nat. Research Prof. 1995–; Jacobson Lecturer, Newcastle-upon-Tyne Univ. 1971, Jaques Parisot Lecturer, WHO 1975, Jawaharlal Nehru Memorial Lecturer 1975; Scholar-in-Residence, Fogarty Int. Centre, Nat. Insts. of Health, Bethesda, Md. 1976; Pres. Indian Asscn. for Advancement of Medical Educ. 1974–; Chair. Global Advisory Cttee. on Medical Research, WHO 1982–86, Task Force on Health Research for Devt., Geneva 1991–92; Fellow, Indian Acad. of Medical Science 1961, Royal Coll. Pathologists; Hon. Fellow, American Coll. of Physicians 1970–; Foreign Assoc., Nat. Acad. of Sciences, U.S.A. 1973–; D.Sc. h.c. (Andhra Univ.) 1967; Hon. Dr.Med. (Karolinska Inst.) 1974; Silver Jubilee Research Award, Medical Council of India 1974, Leon Bernard Foundation Award, WHO, Geneva 1976, J. C. Bose Medal, Indian Nat. Science Acad. 1977, Birla Award for Medical Research 1980; Padma Bhushan 1971. *Publications:* author and co-author of many papers, articles, lectures, monographs and books. *Leisure interests:* literature, music, sports. *Address:* X-29 Hauz Khas, New Delhi 110016, India. *Telephone:* (11) 685-6719. *Fax:* (11) 462-2707.

RAMANANTSOA, Maj.-Gen. Gabriel; Malagasy politician and army officer; b. 13 April 1906, Tananarive; ed. Lycée de Tananarive, de Marseille, Ecole Spéciale Militaire, Saint-Cyr, Inst. des Hautes Etudes de Défense Nationale; Asst. to Chief Officer Ecole Mil. Préparatoire des Enfants de Troupe 1932; assigned to Colonial Infantry Regt. of Morocco, French Army 1931, 1935–36; rank of Capt. 1940; returned to Madagascar, organized Ecole Supérieure d'Educ. Physique, Fianarantsoa 1941, 1943–46; Dept. of Colonial Troops, Ministry of Defence, Paris 1946, 1953–59; in charge of War Veterans, Mil. Office of French High Comm., Madagascar 1948–53; served with French Army in Viet Nam 1953; Lieut.-Col., Col. 1959, Brig.-Gen. 1961, Maj.-Gen. 1967; participated in Franco-Malagasy negotiations for independence 1960; Chief of Gen. Staff of the Malagasy Armed Forces 1960–72; Head of Govt.,

Prime Minister, Minister of Defence, Minister of Planning 1972–75. *Address:* c/o Présidence de la République, Antananarivo, Madagascar.

RAMANUJAM, Gopala; Indian trade unionist; b. 2 Feb. 1916; Founder-Sec. Indian Nat. Trade Union Congress; Pres. Indian Nat. Textile Workers Fed. 1956, Indian Nat. Plantation Workers Fed. 1960; Pres. Indian Nat. Trade Union Congress 1958–59, 1985, Gen. Sec. 1965–86; Man. Ed. Indian Worker 1965–86; Dir. Industrial Finance Corpn. 1968–72; Chair. Cotton Corpn. of India 1974–76, Workers' Educ. Review Cttee. and Cen. Bd. for Workers' Educ. 1981–90, 1992–; mem. Nat. Cttee. on Labour 1967–69; Nat. Award of Padma Bhushan 1985. *Publications:* From the Babul Tree, Industrial Relations—A Point of View, The Payment of Bonus Act, The Payment of Gratuity Act, The Third Party, The Honey Bee, Management—Ring Side View, Indian Labour Movement. *Address:* c/o 4 Bhai Veer Singh Marg, New Delhi 110011, India (Office). *Telephone:* 8264644.

RAMAPHOSA, Matamela Cyril; South African trade union leader; b. 17 Nov. 1952, Johannesburg; s. of Samuel Ramaphosa and Erdmuth Ramaphosa; m. Tshepo Motsepe; two s. two d.; ed. Sekano-Ntoane High School, Soweto, Univ. of Turfloop; Chair. Univ. br. S. African Students' Org. 1974; imprisoned under Section Six of Terrorism Act for 11 months, then for 6 months in 1976; returned to law studies and qualified 1981; apptd. legal adviser, Council of Unions of S. Africa; Gen. Sec. Nat. Union of Mineworkers 1982–91; Sec.-Gen. African National Congress (ANC) 1991–96; Visiting Prof. of Law, Stanford Univ. 1991; M.P. 1994–96; Chair. of Constitutional Ass. 1994–96; Deputy Exec. Chair. New Africa Investments Ltd. 1996–; with Nat. Empowerment Consortium 1996–. *Address:* New Africa Investments, Ltd., P.O. Box 782922, Sandton 2146, South Africa. *Telephone:* (011) 463-1744. *Fax:* (011) 463-3269.

RAMATHLODI, Ngoako, LL.M.; South African politician; fmr. Chair. African Nat. Congress (ANC), Northern Transvaal; Deputy Registrar (student affairs), Exec. Asst. to Prin. Univ. of the N.; in exile 1979, Commdr. Unkhonto weSizwe; Head Political and Mil. ANC Council, Zimbabwe 1986; Political Sec., Asst. to Oliver Tambo and Nelson Mandela (q.v.) 1988–92; Premier of Northern Prov. 1994–98; ANC. *Address:* c/o African National Congress, 51 Plein Street, Johannesburg 2001, South Africa.

RAMBAUD, Patrick; French writer; b. 21 April 1946, Paris; s. of François Rambaud and Madeleine de Magondeau; m. Phamthi Tieu Hong 1988; mil. service with French A.F. 1968–69; co-f. Actual magazine 1970–84; Prix Camartine 1981. *Publications:* (as sole author) La Saignée 1970, Comme des rats 1980, Fric-Frac 1984, La Mort d'un ministre 1985, Comment se tuer sans en avoir l'air 1987, Virginie Q. 1988 (Prix de l'Insolent 1988), Bernard Pivot reçoit . . . 1989, Le Dernier voyage de San Marco 1990, Ubu Président ou L'Imposteur 1990, Les Mirobolantes aventures de Fregoli 1991, Mururoa mon amour 1996, Le Gros secret 1996, La Bataille 1997 (Prix du roman de l'Acad. Française 1997, Prix Goncourt 1997), Les Aventures de Mai 1998; (with Michel-Antoiner Burnier) Les Aventures communautaires de Wao-le-Laid 1973, Les Complots de la liberté: 1832 1976 (Prix Alexandre Dumas 1976), Parodies 1977, 1848 1977, Le Roland Barthes sans peine 1978, La Farce des choses et autres parodies 1982, Le Journalisme sans peine 1997; (with Jean-Marie Stoerkel) Frontière suisse 1986; (with Bernard Haller) Le Visage parle 1988; (with Francis Szpiner) Les Carnets secrets d'Elena Ceaucescu 1990; (with André Balland) Oraisons funèbres des dignitaires politiques qui ont fait leur temps et feignent de l'ignorer 1996. *Leisure interests:* writing, cooking, walking. *Address:* c/o Editions Grasset, 61 rue des Saints-Pères, 75006 Paris, France. *Telephone:* (1) 44.39.22.00.

RAMBERT, Charles Jean Julien, F.R.S.A.; French architect; b. 23 March 1924, Arrigny, Marne; s. of Jean Rambert; m. Françoise Coleda 1949; three s.; ed. Lycée Pierre-Corneille, Rouen, Inst. Saint-Aspais, Melun, and Ecole Nat. Supérieure des Beaux-Arts; Architect 1952–, Govt. registered architect 1953; Prof. of Construction and History of Art, Ecole de secrétariat technique du bâtiment 1957–82; Arbitrator-expert, Tribunal de Commerce 1960, and de Grande Instance, Versailles 1963, Cour d'Appel de Paris 1971–, Tribunal Administratif de Paris 1979–; Sec. Soc. of Registered Architects 1954–57, Sec.-Gen. 1957, 1st Vice-Pres. 1968; Ed.-in-Chief L'Architecture française 1964–75; Counsellor, Ordre des Architectes de Paris 1964, Treas. 1969, Pres. 1976–78; Pres. Cie. des Experts-Architectes, Paris 1978; Asst. Dir. of Studies, Ecole Nat. Supérieure des Beaux Arts 1965, Prof. of History of Architecture 1969–89; mem. Union Franco-Britannique des Architectes 1969; Fellow, Royal Soc. of Arts 1971; mem. Acad. d'Architecture 1978, Vice-Pres. 1981; Chevalier, Légion d'honneur, Officier des Arts et Lettres 1967 and other awards. *Publications:* Constructions scolaires et universitaires 1955, L'habitat collectif, Problème urbain 1957, Maisons familiales de plaisance 1959, Magasins 1961, Histoire de l'architecture civile en France 1963, French adapatation of World Architecture 1964, Architecture des origines à nos jours 1968, (English translation 1969), L'architecture française 1969, L'architecture occidentale 1974 (Audio-visual series), Architecture hispano-mauresque 1980, L'architecture américaine des XIXe et XXe siècles: Chicago, New York. *Leisure interests:* history of art, literature, painting.

RAMEL, Baron Stig, M.A.; Swedish administrator; b. 24 Feb. 1927, Lund; s. of Malte Ramel and Elsa née Nyström; m. Ann Marie Wachtmeister 1953; two s. two d.; ed. studies in political science; attaché, Ministry of Foreign Affairs 1953; Swedish Embassy, Paris 1954–56; del. to OECD, Paris 1956–58; Swedish Embassy, Washington, D.C. 1958–60; Ministry of Foreign Affairs 1960–66; Vice-Pres. and Pres. Gen. Swedish Export Asscn. 1966–72; Exec. Dir. Nobel Foundation, Stockholm 1972–92, Chair. 1992–94; mem. Royal Swedish Acad. of Sciences, King Charles XVI Gustaf Medal; Commdr. Order of Vasa Isabella Catholica and St. Olav, hon. doctorates from Gustavus Adolphus Coll. and Loretto Heights Coll. *Leisure interests:* literature, painting, skiing, orienteering. *Address:* Nobel Foundation, Sturegatan 14, Box 5232, S-102 45 Stockholm, Sweden. *Telephone:* 8-663 09 20.

RAMFORS, Bo C. E.; Swedish business executive; b. 2 June 1936, Stockholm; s. of Arthur Ramfors and Anna (née Gärdmark) Ramfors; m. Gudrun Lindquist 1962; ed. Univ. of Lund; officer, Reserve of the Royal Marine; official, Swedish Chamber of Commerce, Paris, France 1964–65; joined Hambros Bank Ltd., London, England 1966, Dir. 1972–76; Finance Dir. Statsföretag, Stockholm 1976–78, Vice-Pres. 1978–80; Deputy Man. Dir. Skandinaviska Enskilda Banken (Malmö) 1980–83 (Gothenburg) 1983–84, Man. Dir. 1985–89, Man. Dir. and Group C.E.O. 1989–92; Chair. W. Sweden Chamber of Commerce, NOLATO-Koncernen, GMI-Gothenburg Man. Inst.; mem. Bd. Förvaltnings AB Bure, Swedish Exhib. and Congress Centre, Gothenburg, Fastighets AB Regnbågen, Rail Forum Sweden, Scandinavian Link, Univ. of Gothenburg, Ruben Rausing Foundation. *Leisure interests:* shooting, fishing, music. *Address:* c/o Skandinaviska Enskilda Banken, Östra Hamngatan 24, 405 04 Gothenburg, Sweden (Office).

RAMGOOLAM, Navinchandra, L.R.C.P.; Mauritian politician, medical practitioner and barrister; b. 14 July 1947, Mauritius; s. of Sir Seewoosagur Ramgoolam (first Prime Minister of Mauritius) and Lady Sushill Ramgoolam; m. Veena Ramgoolam 1979; ed. Royal Coll. of Surgeons, Dublin, London School of Econs. and Inns of Court School of Law, London; called to the Bar, Inner Temple 1993; Leader, Mauritius Labour Party 1991–, Pres. 1991–92; Leader of Opposition and mem. Nat. Ass. 1991–95; Prime Minister of Mauritius Dec. 1995–, also Minister of Defence and Internal Security, External Communications, etc.; Licentiate, Royal College of Surgeons in Ireland. *Leisure interests:* reading, music, water skiing, chess. *Address:* Government Centre, Port Louis; 85 Sir Seewoosagur Ramgoolam Street, Port Louis, Mauritius. *Telephone:* 2011001. *Fax:* 2088619.

RAMÍREZ MERCADO, Sergio; Nicaraguan politician and author; b. 5 Aug. 1942, Masatepe, Masaya; s. of late Pedro Ramírez Gutiérrez and Luisa Mercado Gutiérrez; m. Gertrudis Guerrero Mayorga 1964; one s. two d.; ed. Univ. Autónoma de Nicaragua; was active in revolutionary student movt. and founding mem. of Frente Estudiantil Revolucionario 1962; mem. Cen. American Univ. Supreme Council (CSUCA), Costa Rica 1964, Pres. 1968; mem. Int. Comm. of FSLN (Sandinista Liberation Front) 1975; undertook tasks on diplomatic front, propaganda and int. work on behalf of FSLN leading to overthrow of regime 1979; mem. Junta of Nat. Reconstruction Govt. 1979–; Vice-Pres. of Nicaragua 1984–90; minority leader, Speaker, Nat. Ass. 1990–94; Leader Movimiento de Renovación Sandinista (MRS) 1994–; MRS pre-cand. for presidency 1996; Dr. h.c. (Cen. Univ. of Ecuador); Bruno Kreisky Prize 1988; Chevalier Ordre des Arts et des Lettres 1993. *Publications include:* Cuentos 1963, El cuento centroamericano 1974, Charles Atlas también muere 1976, El cuento nicaragüense 1976, Castigo divino 1988, Confesión de amor 1991, Clave de sol 1992, Cuentos 1994, Oficios compartidos 1994, Un baile de máscaras 1995. *Leisure interests:* classical music, reading. *Address:* MRS, Tienda Katty lc. Abajo, Apdo. 24, Managua, Nicaragua. *Telephone:* (2) 78-0279. *Fax:* (2) 78-0268.

RAMÍREZ VÁZQUEZ, Pedro; Mexican architect; b. 16 April 1919, Mexico; s. of Dolores Vázquez and Max Ramírez; m. Olga Campuzano 1947; two s. two d.; ed. Univ. Nacional Autónoma de México; Prof. of Design and City Planning, Nat. School of Architecture, Univ. Nacional Autónoma de México; Sec. of Human Settlements and Public Works of Mexican Govt. 1976–82; Chair. Organizing Cttee., Games of XIX Olympiad; lecturer Autonomous Univ. of Mexico 1984; Dir. Inst. of Urban Devt. and Ecology 1988; Dir. of display design Nubia Museum, Egypt 1985; Pres. Soc. of Mexican Architects and Nat. Coll. of Architects of Mexico 1953–58; founding mem. Int. Acad. of Architecture, Sofia 1985; Hon. mem. Council of Socs. of Architects of Spain; Dr. h.c. (Pratt Inst. New York) 1982; Gold Medal of the French Acad. of Architecture 1978, Grand Prix of Twelfth Milan Triennial for prefabricated rural school project, Gold Medal, Eighth São Paulo Biennial for Nat. Museum of Anthropology, Mexico City, Nat. Prize of the Arts 1972. *Major works include:* co-author of design for Nat. School of Medicine, Univ. City; plans for several cities in Mexico; numerous prefabricated schools in Mexico (also used in S. America, Europe and Asia); buildings in Mexico City; Secr. of Foreign Affairs, Aztec Stadium, Cía. Mexicana de Aviación, Omega Co., and Congress bldg., Nat. Museum of Anthropology, Japanese Embassy; Guadeloupe Shrine for 10,000 persons; Cathedral of Villahermosa, Tabasco; Cultural Centre, Tijuana; Monument to Fray Antón de Montesinos, Dominican Repub.; Mexican pavilions at Brussels, Seattle and New York World Fairs; museums of Ciudad Juárez and Mexico City; Nat. Gallery of History and Nat. Gallery of Modern Art, Mexico City; Offices of Int. Olympic Cttee., Lausanne, Switzerland 1981; Olympic Museum Switzerland 1985; Cen. Library and Museum of Anthropology, Toluca, Mexico 1985; Museum of the Major Temple, Mexico City 1985; Dir. of Design for World Trade Center, Mexico City 1988; Museum of Prehispanic Art, Puebla 1988; Chapel of the Virgin of Guadalupe, Vatican 1991. *Leisure interests:* industrial design and design of lead glass objects. *Address:* Avenida de las Fuentes 170, México 01900, D.F., Mexico. *Telephone:* 595-4388.

RAMJUTTUN, Dinesh, M.B., B.S.; Mauritian politician and medical practitioner; b. 13 Oct. 1946; m.; two c.; mem. Legis. Ass. 1982–; Sec.-Gen.

Mauritian Socialist Party 1982, Mauritian Socialist Movt. 1986; Minister of Works 1986–87; Minister of Social Security, Nat. Solidarity and Reform Inst. 1987–90. *Address:* c/o Ministry of Social Security, National Solidarity and Reform Institutions, 13 Lislet Geoffrey Street, Port Louis, Mauritius.

RAMO, Simon, B.S., PH.D.; American engineering executive; b. 7 May 1913, Salt Lake City, Utah; s. of Benjamin and Clara (née Trestman) Ramo; m. Virginia May Smith 1937; two s.; ed. Univ. of Utah and Calif. Inst. of Tech.; with Gen. Electric Co., Schenectady 1936–46; Lecturer, Union Coll. 1941–46; Dir. Research Electronics Dept., Guided Missiles Research and Devt., Vice-Pres. and Dir. of Operations, Hughes Aircraft Co., Culver City 1946–53; Exec. Vice-Pres., Dir., Ramo-Wooldridge Corpn., L.A. 1953–58; Pres. Space Tech. Labs. Div. Ramo-Wooldridge Corpn. 1957–58; Scientific Dir. U.S.A.F. Ballistic Missiles Programme 1954–58; Dir. TRW Inc. 1954–85, Exec. Vice-Pres. 1958–61, Vice-Chair. 1961–78, Chair. Exec. Cttee. 1969–78, Chair. Scientific and Tech. Cttee. 1978, Chair. TRW-Fujitsu Co. 1980–83; Research Assoc. Calif. Inst. of Tech. 1946, Visiting Prof. 1978–; Chair. Cen. for Study of American Experience, Univ. of Southern Calif. 1978–80; Faculty Fellow John F. Kennedy School of Govt., Harvard Univ. 1980–84; mem. White House Energy Research and Devt. Advisory Council 1973–75; mem. U.S. State Dept. Cttee. on Science and Foreign Affairs 1973–75; Chair. President's Cttee. on Science and Tech. 1976–77; mem. Advisory Council to Sec. of Commerce 1976–77; Chair. Aetna, Jacobs & Ramo Venture Capital 1987–90, Allenwood Ventures 1987–; Dir. Union Bancorp Inc., Union Bank, Atlantic Richfield Co., U.S. Chamber of Commerce; Trustee, Calif. Inst. of Tech., American Museum of Electricity; mem. advisory council Gen. Atomics Corp. 1988–; Aurora Capital Partners 1991–, Chartwell Investments 1992–; Consultant, President's Science Advisory Cttee.; Advisor Axiom Venture Partners 1997–; Fellow, American Physical Soc., Inst. of Aeronautics and Astronautics, American Acad. of Arts and Sciences, A.A.A.S., American Astronautical Soc., Inst. for the Advancement of Eng., Inst. of Electrical and Electronic Engineers; Founder mem. Nat. Acad. of Eng.; mem. N.A.S. 1973–, Int. Acad. of Astronautics, American Philosophical Soc., Sr. Execs. Advisory Council, Nat. Industrial Conf. Board, Advisory Council on Japan/U.S. Econ. Relations, U.S. Chamber of Commerce Council on Trends and Perspective; Hon. D.Sc., D.Eng., LL.D.; Presidential Medal of Freedom 1983, Pioneer Award, Int. Council on System Eng. 1997, and numerous other awards. *Publications:* Fields and Waves in Modern Radio (with J. R. Whinnery) 1944, 1953, Introduction to Microwaves 1945, Fields and Waves in Communication Electronics (with J. R. Whinnery and Theodore Van Duzer) 1965, Cure for Chaos 1969, Century of Mismatch 1970, Extraordinary Tennis for the Ordinary Player 1970, The Islands of E, Cono & My 1973, The Business of Science 1988. *Leisure interests:* tennis, the violin. *Address:* 9200 W. Sunset Boulevard, Suite 801, Los Angeles, CA 90069, U.S.A.

RAMON, Haim; Israeli politician and lawyer; b. 1950, Jaffa; Chair. Public Council for Youth Exchanges; Nat. Sec. Labour Party's Young Guard 1978–84; co-ordinator Finance Cttee.-Labour Party 1984–88, Chair. Labour Party 1988–92; Minister of Health 1992–94, of the Interior 1995–96; mem. Knesset 1983–; served on numerous cttees. 1983–92 (Labour). *Address:* c/o Knesset, Jerusalem, Israel.

RAMOS, Gen. Fidel; Philippine politician and army officer; b. 1928; s. of Narciso Ramos; m.; five d.; ed. Nat. Univ. Manila, U.S. Mil. Acad. West Point and Univ. of Illinois; active service in Korea and Viet Nam; Deputy Chief of Staff 1981; Chief of Staff, Philippines Armed Forces 1986–98; Leader People's Power Party; Sec. of Nat. Defence Jan. 1988–98, Cand. for Pres. May 1992; Pres. of the Philippines June 1992–98; Légion d'honneur 1987. *Address:* c/o Office of the President, Presidential Guest House, Malacañang Palace Compound, J. P. Laurel Street, San Miguel, Metro Manila, Philippines.

RAMOS-HORTA, José, M.A.; Indonesian political activist; b. 26 Dec. 1949, Dili, E. Timor; s. of late Francisco Horta and of Natalina Ramos Filipe Horta; m. Ana Pessoa 1978 (divorced); one s.; ed. Hague Acad. of Int. Law, Int. Inst. of Human Rights, Strasbourg, Columbia Univ., Antioch Univ.; journalist and broadcaster 1969–74; Minister for External Affairs and Information, E. Timor 1975; Perm. Rep. of FRETILIN to UN, N.Y. 1976–89; Public Affairs and Media Dir. Mozambican Embassy, Washington 1987–88; f., Dir., lecturer Diplomacy Training Programme, Univ. of N.S.W. 1990–, Visiting Prof. 1996–; Special Rep. Nat. Council of Maubere Resistance 1991–; mem. Bd. E. Timor Human Rights Centre, Melbourne; Sr. Assoc. mem. St. Antony's Coll., Oxford 1987–; received Unrepresented Nations and People's Org. Award 1996; shared Nobel Peace Prize 1996 (with Mgr. Carlos Ximenes Belo q.v.); Order of Freedom (Portugal) 1996. *Publications:* Funu: the Unfinished Saga of E. Timor 1987, articles in numerous publs. worldwide. *Leisure interest:* tennis. *Address:* Rua São Lazaro 16, 1°, 1150 Lisbon, Portugal. *Telephone:* (1) 886-3727. *Fax:* (1) 886-3791.

RAMOS ROSA, António; Portuguese poet and literary critic; b. 17 Oct. 1924, Faro; m. Agripina Costa Marques 1963; one d.; Dir. literary reviews Árvore 1951–53, Cassiopeia 1955, Cadernos do Meio-Dia 1958–60; Prize of Portuguese Centre of Int. Asscn. of Literary Critics 1980, PEN Club's Poetry Prize 1980, Portuguese Asscn. of Writers' Grand Prize 1989, Pessoa Prize 1988, Prize of Liège Poetry Biennial 1991, European Poet of the Decade (Collège de l'Europe) 1991, Jean Malrieux Prize (Marseille) 1992; Grand Oficial, Order of Santiago da Espada; Great Cross, Order of Infante Dom Henrique. *Publications:* numerous vols. of poetry including Delta seguido de Pela Primeira Vez 1996, Nomes de Ninguém 1997, À Mesa do Vento seguido de As Espirais de Dioniso 1997, A Imobilidade Fulminante 1998; (essays): Poesia, Liberdade Livre 1962, A Poesia Moderna e a Interrogação do Real 1979, Incisões Oblíquas 1987, A Parede Azul 1991. *Address:* Av. Barbosa du Bocage, 3–5° E, 1000 Lisbon, Portugal. *Telephone:* (01) 796 41 83.

RAMPAL, Jean-Pierre Louis; French flautist; b. 7 Jan. 1922, Marseille; s. of Joseph and Andrée (née Roggero) Rampal; m. Françoise-Anne Bacqueyrisse 1947; one s. one d.; ed. Univ. de Marseille; world-wide tours 1945–; participant in major festivals in Rio de Janeiro, Aix, Menton, Salzburg, Edinburgh, Prague, Athens, Zagreb, Granada, Tokyo, etc.; Ed. for Ancient and Classical Music, Int. Music Co., New York City 1958–; mem. French Musicological Soc.; Pres. Asscn. Musique et Musiciens 1974–; Commdr., Légion d'honneur; Commdr., ordre des Arts et Lettres, Ordre nat. du mérite; Grand Prix du Disque 1954, 1956, 1959, 1960, 1961, 1963, 1964, 1978; Oscar du Premier Virtuose Français 1956, Prix Edison 1969, Léonie Sonning Danish Music Prize 1978, Prix d'honneur du Prix Mondial du Disque de Montreux 1980. *Publications:* La Flûte 1978, Musique, ma vie 1991. *Leisure interests:* tennis, deep-sea diving, movie-making. *Address:* 15 avenue Mozart, 75016 Paris, France. *Telephone:* 42.88.28.96.

RAMPHAL, Sir Shridath Surendranath, G.C.M.G., O.E., O.M., O.N.Z., A.C., Q.C., S.C., LL.M., F.R.S.A.; Guyanese international official, barrister and politician; b. 3 Oct. 1928, New Amsterdam; s. of James I. Ramphal and Grace Ramphal (née Abdool); m. Lois Winifred King 1951; two s. two d.; ed. Queen's Coll., Georgetown, King's Coll., London, Harvard Law School; Crown Counsel, British Guiana 1953–54; Asst. to Attorney-Gen. 1954–56; Legal Draftsman 1956–58; Solicitor-Gen. 1959–61; Legal Draftsman, West Indies 1958–59; Asst. Attorney-Gen., West Indies 1961–62; Attorney-Gen., Guyana 1965–73; mem. Nat. Assembly 1965–75; Minister of State for External Affairs 1967–72, Minister of Foreign Affairs 1972–75, of Justice 1973–75; Commonwealth Sec.-Gen. 1975–90; Chancellor Univ. of Guyana 1988–92, Univ. of Warwick 1989–, Univ. of West Indies Oct. 1989–; Queen's Counsel 1965 and Sr. Counsel, Guyana 1966; mem. Int. Comm. of Jurists, Ind. Comm. on Int. Devt. Issues, Ind. Comm. on Disarmament and Security Issues, Ind. Comm. on Int. Humanitarian Issues, World Comm. on Environment and Devt., South Comm., Carnegie Comm. on Deadly Conflict, Bd. of Govs. Int. Devt. Research Center, Canada, Exec. Cttee. of Int. Inst. for Environment and Devt., Council of Int. Negotiation Network Carter Center, Georgia, U.S.A. 1991–; Patron One World Broadcasting Trust; Chair. UN Cttee. for Devt. Planning 1984–87, West Indian Comm. 1990–92, Bd. Int. Inst. for Democracy and Electoral Assistance (IDEA) 1995–, Advisory Cttee. Future Generations Alliance Foundation 1995–97; Pres. World Conservation Union—IUCN 1990–93; Int. Steering Cttee. Leadership for Environment and Devt. Program Rockefeller Foundation 1991–98; Co-Chair. Comm. on Global Governance 1992–; Adviser to Sec.-Gen. of UNCED 1992; Chief Negotiator on Int. Econ. Issues for the Caribbean Region 1997–; Hon. LL.D. (Panjab Univ.) 1975, (Southampton) 1976, (Univ. of the West Indies) 1978, (St. Francis Xavier Univ., Halifax, Canada) 1978, (Aberdeen) 1979, (Cape Coast, Ghana) 1980, (London) 1981, (Benin, Nigeria) 1982, (Hull) 1983, (Yale) 1985, (Cambridge) 1985, (Warwick) 1988, (York Univ., Ont., Canada) 1988, (Malta) 1989, (Otago, N.Z.) 1990; Hon. D.H.L. (Simmons Coll., Boston) 1982, Hon. D.C.L. (Oxon.) 1982, (East Anglia) 1983, (Durham) 1985, Hon. Dr. (Surrey) 1979, (Essex) 1980, Hon. D.Hum.Litt. (Duke Univ., U.S.A.) 1985, Hon. D.Litt. (Bradford) 1985, (Indira Gandhi Nat. Open Univ.) 1989, Hon. D. Sc. (Cranfield Inst. of Tech.) 1987; Arden and Atkin Prize, Gray's Inn 1952, Int. Educ. Award (Richmond Coll., London) 1988, R.S.A. Albert Medal 1988; John Simon Guggenheim Fellowship 1962; Hon. Bencher of Gray's Inn 1981; Fellow, King's Coll., London 1975, L.S.E. 1979, R.S.A. 1981, Magdalen Coll., Oxford 1982; Order of the Repub. (Egypt) 1973; Grand Cross, Order of the Sun (Peru) 1974; Grand Cross, Order of Merit (Ecuador) 1974, Order of Nishaan Izzuddeen (Maldives) 1989, Grand Commdr., Order of the Niger 1990, Grand Commdr., Order of the Companion of Freedom (Zambia) 1990, Nishan-e-Quaid-i-Azam (Pakistan) 1990, Order of the Caribbean Community 1991, Commdr. Order of the Golden Ark 1994. *Publications:* One World to Share: Selected Speeches of the Commonwealth Secretary-General 1975–79, Nkrumah and the Eighties (1980 Kwame Nkrumah Memorial Lectures), Sovereignty or Solidarity (1981 Callander Memorial Lectures), Some in Light and Some in Darkness: The Long Shadow of Slavery (Wilberforce Lecture) 1983, The Message not the Messenger (STC Communication Lecture) 1985, The Trampling of the Grass (Econ. Comm. for Africa Silver Jubilee Lecture) 1985, For the South, a Time to Think 1986, Making Human Society a Civilised State (Corbishley Memorial Lecture) 1987, Inseparable Humanity: An Anthology of Reflections of Shridath Ramphal 1988, An End to Otherness (six speeches) 1990, Our Country, The Planet 1992 and contributions in journals of legal, political and international affairs, including International and Comparative Law Quarterly, Caribbean Quarterly, Public Law, Guyana Journal, The Round Table, Royal Society of Arts Journal, Foreign Policy, Third World Quarterly, International Affairs. *Leisure interests:* photography, cooking. *Address:* 1 The Sutherlands, 188 Sutherland Avenue, London, W9 1HR, England.

RAMPHELE, Mamphela Aletta, M.B., CH.B., B.COM., D.P.H.; South African university administrator and community health researcher; b. 28 Dec. 1947, Pietersburg; d. of Pitsi Eliphaz Ramphele and Rangoato Rahab Ramphele (née Mahlaela); two s.; ed. Setotolwane High School, Pietersburg, Univ. of Natal; community health worker Black Community Programmes, Ktown

1975–77, Ithuseng Community Health Programme, Tzaneen 1978–84; Sr. Researcher Dept. Social Anthropology, Univ. of Cape Town 1986–, Deputy Vice-Chancellor 1991–95, Vice-Chancellor 1996–; Researcher and Consultant to Western Cape Hostel Dwellers' Asscn. 1986–92; Dir. (non-exec.) Anglo-American 1992–95, Old Mutual 1993–; Founder mem. Black Consciousness Movt. 1969; mem. NAMDA 1985–; Hon. D.Hum.Litt. (Hunter Coll., New York) 1984; Hon. M.D. (Natal) 1989; Hon. D.Sc. (Univ. Coll., London) 1997. *Publications:* Children on Frontline (UNICEF report) 1987, Uprooting Poverty—The South African Challenge (with David Philip) 1989, A Bed Called Home: Life in Migrant Labour Hostels of Cape Town (with David Philip) 1993, Mamphela Ramphele: A Life (with David Philip) 1995. *Leisure interests:* reading, walking. *Address:* University of Cape Town, Private Bag, Rondebosch 7700, Cape, South Africa. *Telephone:* (21) 650 2105/6. *Fax:* (21) 689 2440.

RAMPHUL, Sir Indurduth, Kt.; Mauritian banker; b. 10 Oct. 1931, Montagne Blanche; m. Taramatee Seedoyal 1962; one s. one d.; ed. Univ. of Exeter, U.K.; Asst. Sec., Ministry of Finance 1966–67; Man., Bank of Mauritius 1967–70, Chief. Man. 1970–73, Man. Dir. 1973–82, Gov. 1982–96. *Address:* c/o Bank of Mauritius, P.O. Box 29, Port Louis; 9 Buswell Avenue, Quatre Bornes, Mauritius (Home).

RAMPLING, Charlotte; British actress; b. 5 Feb. 1946, London; m. 2nd Jean-Michel Jarre (q.v.) 1978; two s. (one s. from previous marriage); one step-d.; film debut 1963. *Films include:* The Knack 1963, Rotten to the Core, Georgy Girl, The Long Duel, Kidnapping, Three, The Damned 1969, Skibum, Corky 1970, 'Tis Pity She's a Whore, Henry VIII and His Six Wives 1971, Asylum 1972, The Night Porter, Giordano Bruno, Zardoz, Caravan to Vaccares 1973, The Flesh of the Orchid, Yuppi Du 1974–75, Farewell My Lovely, Foxtrot 1975, Sherlock Holmes in New York, Orca—The Killer Whale, The Purple Taxi 1976, Stardust Memories 1980, The Verdict 1983, Viva la vie 1983, Beauty and Sadness 1984, He Died with his Eyes Open 1985, Max mon Amour, Max my Love 1985, Angel Heart 1987, Paris by Night 1988, Dead on Arrival 1989, Helmut Newton, Frames from the Edge, Hammers Over the Anvil 1991, Time is Money 1992, La marche de Radetzky (TV film) 1994, Asphalt Tango 1995; numerous TV plays. *Address:* c/o Artmédia, 10 avenue George V, 75008 Paris, France. *Telephone:* (1) 44-31-22-00.

RAMQVIST, Lars Henry, PH.D.; Swedish business executive; b. 2 Nov. 1938, Grängesberg; s. of Henry Ramqvist and Alice Ramqvist; m. Barbro Pettersson 1962; one s. one d.; ed. Univ. of Uppsala; Section Head, Stora Kopparberg AB 1962–65; with Axel Johnson Inst. 1965–80, Pres. 1975–80; joined L.M. Ericsson Telephone Co. as Vice-Pres. and head of Information Systems Div. 1980, Pres. and C.E.O. 1990–98, Chair. 1998–, Pres. subsidiary RIFA AB 1984–86, Ericsson Radio AB 1988–90; mem. Bd. Swedish Eng. Employers' Asscn., Asscn. of Swedish Eng. Industries and Fed. of Swedish Industries; mem. Prime Minister's Special Industry Advisory Cttee. 1994–; mem. Royal Swedish Acad. of Science, Royal Swedish Acad. of Eng. Sciences. *Address:* Telefonaktiebolaget L.M. Ericsson, S-12625 Stockholm, Sweden. *Telephone:* (8) 719 4602. *Fax:* (8) 744 3574.

RAMSBOTHAM, Hon. Sir Peter (Edward), G.C.M.G., G.C.V.O.; British diplomatist and administrator; b. 8 Oct. 1919, London; s. of 1st Viscount Soulbury; m. 1st Frances Blomfield 1941 (died 1982); two s. one d.; m. 2nd Zaida Hall 1985; ed. Eton Coll. and Magdalen Coll., Oxford; entered diplomatic service 1948; served in Political Div., Allied Control Comm., Berlin 1948–50; First Sec., Foreign Office 1950–53; Head of Chancery, U.K. del. to UN, New York 1953–57; Foreign Office 1957–62; Head of Chancery, British Embassy, Paris 1962–67; Foreign Office 1967–69; High Commr. to Cyprus 1969–71; Amb. to Iran 1971–74, to U.S.A. 1974–77; Gov. and C.-in-C. of Bermuda 1977–80; Dir. Commercial Union Assurance Co. 1980–90, Lloyds Bank Ltd. 1980–90, Chair. Lloyds Bank Southern Region 1984–90; Chair. Ryder-Cheshire Foundation for the Relief of Suffering 1982–; World Memorial Fund for Disaster Relief 1992–96; Hon. Fellow Magdalen Coll., Oxford 1991; Hon. LL.D. (Akron Univ.) 1975, (William and Mary Coll.) 1975, (Maryland Univ.) 1976, (Yale Univ.) 1977; Croix de guerre 1945, K.St.J. 1976; D.L. Hants. 1992. *Leisure interests:* gardening, fishing. *Address:* East Lane, Ovington, Alresford, Hants, SO24 0RA, England (Home). *Telephone:* (0196273) 2515.

RAMSEY, Norman Foster, M.A., PH.D., D.SC.; American scientist; b. 27 Aug. 1915, Washington, D.C.; s. of Brigadier-Gen. and Mrs. Norman F. Ramsey; m. 1st Elinor Stedman Jameson 1940 (died 1983); four d.; m. 2nd Ellie Welch 1985; ed. Columbia, Harvard and Cambridge Univs.; Assoc. Univ. of Illinois 1940–42; Asst. Prof. Columbia Univ. 1942–46; Research Assoc. M.I.T. Radiation Lab. 1940–43; Expert Consultant to Sec. of War 1942–45; Group Leader and Asscn. Division Head, Los Alamos Lab. of Atomic Energy Project 1943–45; Chief Scientist of Atomic Energy Lab., Tinian 1945; Assoc. Prof. Columbia Univ. 1945–47; Head Physics Dept., Brookhaven Nat. Lab. 1946–47; Assoc. Prof. Harvard Univ. 1947–50; Dir. Harvard Nuclear Lab. 1948–50 and 1952–53; Air Force Scientific Advisory Cttee. 1947–55; Dept. Defence Panel on Atomic Energy 1953–58; Prof. of Physics, Harvard Univ. 1950–66, Sr. Fellow, Harvard Soc. Fellows 1970–; Higgins Prof. of Physics, Harvard Univ. 1966–86; Prof. Emer. 1986–; Scientific Adviser NATO 1958–59; Gen. Advisory Cttee., Atomic Energy Comm. 1960–72; Dir. Varian Associates 1963–66; Pres. Univs. Research Asscn. 1966–81; Eastman Prof., Oxford Univ. 1973–74; Luce Prof. of Cosmology, Mount Holyoke Coll. 1982–83, Prof. of Physics, Univ. of Va. 1983–84; Research Fellow, Jt. Inst. Lab. Astrophysics, Univ. of Colo. 1986–87; Distinguished Prof., Univ. of Chicago 1987–88; Prof., Williams Coll. 1989; Visiting Prof., Univ. of Mich. 1989–92; Vice-Pres. American Physical Soc. 1977 (Pres. 1978); Chair. Physics Div. American Asscn. for Advancement of Science 1977; mem. N.A.S., American Acad. of Arts and Sciences, American Philosophical Soc., French Acad. of Sciences; Visiting Cttee. Nat. Bureau of Standards 1982–; Trustee, Carnegie Endowment for Int. Peace 1962–85 and the Rockefeller Univ. 1976–90; Chair. Bd. of Govs., American Inst. of Physics 1980–86; Hon. D.Sc. (Case Western Reserve Univ.) 1968, (Middlebury Coll.) 1969, (Oxford) 1973, (Rockefeller) 1986, (Sussex) 1989, (Chicago, Houston) 1990, (Mich. 1993), (Philadelphia Coll. of Pharmacy and Science) 1995; Hon. D.C.L. (Oxford) 1990; other hon. degrees; Presidential Order of Merit, Lawrence Award 1960, Davisson-Germer prize 1974, Award for Excellence in Science (Colombia Univ.) 1980, Medal of Honor of I.E.E. 1984, Monie Ferst Prize 1985, Rabi Prize 1985, Karl Compton Award 1986, Rumford Premium 1985, Oersted Medal 1988, Nat. Medal of Science 1988, Nobel Prize in Physics (jt.) 1989, Pupin Medal 1992, Erice Science for Peace Prize 1992, Einstein Medal 1993, Bush Award 1995. *Publications:* Nuclear Moments 1953, Nuclear Two-Body Problems 1953, Molecular Beans 1955, 1985, Quick Calculus 1965, 1985; and numerous articles in the Physical Review. *Leisure interests:* skiing, walking, sailing, swimming, tennis, reading, conversation, music. *Address:* Lyman Physics Laboratory, Harvard University, Cambridge, MA 02138; 24 Monmouth Court, Brookline, MA 02146, U.S.A. *Telephone:* (617) 495-2864. *Fax:* (617) 496-5144.

RANARIDDH, Prince (see Norodom Ranariddh, Prince).

RANCHOD, Bhadra, B.A., LL.B., LL.M., LL.D.; South African diplomatist and lawyer; b. 11 May 1944, Port Elizabeth; s. of Ghalloo Ranchod and Parvaty Ranchod; m. Vibha M. Desai 1980; two d.; ed. Univs. of Cape Town, Oslo and Leiden; Sr. Lecturer, Dept. of Private Law, Univ. of Durban-Westville 1972, Prof. of Private Law 1974, Dean, Faculty of Law 1976–79; Advocate of Supreme Court 1973–; mem. Bd. of Govs. S. African Broadcasting Corpn.; mem. S. African Law Comm.; mem. Human Sciences Research Council, numerous cttees. and public bodies etc.; Visiting Scholar, Columbia Univ., New York 1980–81; Amb. and Head of S. African Mission to European Communities 1986–92; Minister of Tourism 1993–94; Chair. Minister's Council in House of Dels. 1993–94; M.P. 1994–96; Deputy Speaker, Nat. Ass. 1994–96; High Commr. in Australia (also accred. to New Zealand and Fiji Islands) 1996–. *Publications:* Foundations of the South African Law of Defamation (thesis) 1972, Law and Justice in South Africa 1986; about 100 papers on human rights issues. *Leisure interests:* jogging, reading, travel. *Address:* South African High Commission, Rhodes Place State Circle, Yarralumla, Canberra, A.C.T. 2600, Australia. *Telephone:* (02) 6273 2424. *Fax:* (02) 6273 3543.

RANDALL, Michael Bennett; British freelance journalist; b. 12 Aug. 1919; ed. St. Peter's School, Seaford, and Canford School; Asst. Ed., Sunday Chronicle 1952–53; Ed. Sunday Graphic 1953; Asst. Ed. Daily Mirror 1953–56; Asst. Ed. News Chronicle 1956–57; Asst. Ed. Daily Mail 1957–61, Deputy Ed. 1961–63, Ed. 1963–66; Man. Ed. (News) Sunday Times 1967–72, Senior Man. Ed. 1972–78; Hannen Swaffer Award as Journalist of 1965–66. *Publication:* The Funny Side of the Street 1988. *Address:* Flat One, 39 St. Anne's Crescent, Lewes, East Sussex, BN7 1SB, England.

RANDLE, Sir Philip John, Kt., M.A., PH.D., M.D., F.R.C.P., F.R.S.; British biochemist and medical practitioner; b. 16 July 1926, Nuneaton; s. of Alfred J. and Nora A. Randle; m. Elizabeth A. Harrison 1952; one s. (deceased) three d.; ed. Sidney Sussex Coll., Cambridge and Univ. Coll. Hosp. Medical School, London; house physician and house surgeon, Univ. Coll. Hosp. 1951; MRC Research worker, Dept. of Biochem., Univ. of Cambridge 1952–55; Research Fellow, Sidney Sussex Coll. 1954–57; Lecturer in Biochem. Univ. of Cambridge 1955–64; Fellow and Dir. of Medical Studies, Trinity Hall, Cambridge 1957–64; Prof. and Head of Dept. of Biochem., Univ. of Bristol 1964–75; Prof. of Clinical Biochem. Univ. of Oxford and Fellow, Hertford Coll., Oxford 1975–93, Emer. Prof. and Emer. Fellow 1993–; Pres. Biochemical Soc. 1995–; Hon. Fellow Trinity Hall 1988; Fellow Univ. Coll. London 1990; Hon. D.Sc. (Oxford Brookes) 1997; Minkowski Prize 1966, Ciba Medal 1984. *Publications:* numerous articles in scientific and medical journals. *Leisure interests:* travel, wherever and whenever possible. *Address:* 11 Fitzherbert Close, Iffley, Oxford, OX4 4EN; Department of Clinical Biochemistry, Radcliffe Infirmary, Oxford, OX2 6HE, England. *Telephone:* (01865) 773115. *Fax:* (01865) 224000.

RANDOLPH, Denys, B.SC., C.ENG., C.B.I.M., F.R.S.A., M.R.AE.S., F.I.PROD.E., F.I.E.E., F.INST.D.; British company executive; b. 6 Feb. 1926, Ealing, London; s. of late Harry Beckham Randolph and Margaret Randolph; m. Marjorie Hales 1951; two d.; ed. Saint Paul's School, Hammersmith, Queen's Univ., Belfast; mil. service, Royal Engineers 1944–48; postgraduate apprenticeship 1952–54; Exec. Dir. Graviner Ltd. 1964–65, Wilkinson Sword (Int.) Ltd. 1965–66; Man. Dir. Hand Tools Div., Wilkinson Sword Ltd. 1966–69, Group Man. Dir. 1970–71, Chair. and Man. Dir. 1971–72, Chair. Wilkinson Sword Ltd. 1972–80, Pres. and Special Consultant 1980–85; Chair. Graviner Ltd. 1969–79; Exec. Deputy Chair. British Match Corpn. (now Wilkinson Match Ltd.) 1973–75, Chair. Wilkinson Match Ltd. 1976–79; Dir. Duport Ltd. 1975–81; Chair. Inst. of Dirs. 1976–79, Vice-Pres. 1979–96; Chair. Poitires Eyots Ltd. 1972–93, Pains Fireworks Ltd. 1980–84, Woodrush Investments Ltd. 1980–93, Haddon Rockers Ltd. 1980–87, P.L.C. Peters Ltd. 1981–84,

Peters Jackson Ltd. 1981–84; Propr. Clapcot Vineyards 1986–98; Dir. Henley Distance Learning Ltd. 1985–95, Partnership Wines Ltd. 1995–; Gov. Admin. Staff Coll., Henley 1976–91; Past Master, Worshipful Co. of Scientific Instrument Makers; Past Master, Worshipful Co. of Cutlers; mem. Royal Aeronautical Soc.; Fellow, Inst. of Production Eng., Royal Horticultural Soc. *Publication:* From Rapiers to Razor Blades: the Development of the Light Metals Industry. *Leisure interests:* yachting, golf, viticulture. *Address:* Ickleton Fields, Wantage Road, Streatley, Reading, Berks, RG8 9PY, England.

RANGOONWALA, Mohamed Aly; Pakistani business executive; b. 20 May 1924, Rangoon, Burma; s. of V. M. Gany; m. Banu 1952; five s. one d.; joined father's business aged 12; began own business, Bombay 1940; moved to Pakistan 1948; became founder Chair. and Dir. several commercial, financial and business orgs.; served on Govt. bodies; extended business operations abroad (Asia, Europe, N. America) 1970; fmr. Chair. Nat. Bank of Pakistan, Fed. of Pakistan Chambers of Commerce and Industry; Pres. Pakistan Nat. Cttee., ICC 1976–; Pres. ICC 1981, mem. Presidency 1981–; Chair. World Memon Foundation, Z. V. M. Rangoonwala Trust; Star of Service (Pakistan); Grosse Verdienstkreuz (Fed. Repub. of Germany). *Address:* V. M. House, West Wharf, Karachi, Pakistan; c/o 123 George Street, London, W1H 5TB, England. *Telephone:* 201165 or 201660 (Karachi); 0171-493 3266 or 0171-493 3013 (London).

RANIS, Gustav, PH.D.; American professor of economics; b. 24 Oct. 1929, Darmstadt, Germany; s. of Max Ranis and Bettina Goldschmidt; m. Ray Lee Finkelstein; two s. one d.; ed. Brandeis Univ., Yale Univ.; Social Science Research Council Fellow (Japan) 1955–56; Jt. Dir., Pakistan Inst. of Devt. Econs., Karachi, Pakistan 1959–61; Assoc. Dir. Econ. Growth Center, Yale Univ. 1961–65, Dir. 1967–75; Assoc. Prof. of Econs., Yale Univ. 1961–64, Prof. of Econs. 1964–82, Frank Altschul Prof. of Int. Econs. 1982–; Dir. Yale Center for Int. and Area Studies 1996–; Dir. Yale-Pakistan Project 1970–71; Asst. Admin. for Program and Policy, Agency for Int. Devt., Dept. of State 1965–67, Consultant 1962–65, 1967–71, 1984–; Ford Foundation Faculty Fellow Colegio de Mexico, Mexico City 1971–72, Visiting Prof. Univ. de los Andes, Colombia 1976–77; Consultant UN FAO 1979–; Chief of Mission, ILO Comprehensive Employment Strategy Mission to the Philippines 1973, World Bank/CARICOM Project on Production and Investment Incentives in the Caribbean 1980–82; mem. Oversight Cttee. Int. Conf. on Intellectual Property Rights, Nat. Research Council 1991–; mem. Editorial Advisory Bd. Journal of Int. Devt. 1995–, Oxford Devt. Studies 1996–; mem. Bd. of Trustees and Brandeis Chair. Acad. Affairs Cttee. Brandeis Univ.; Fellow Inst. for Advanced Study, Berlin 1993–94; Dr. h.c. Brandeis Univ. 1982. *Publications:* Development of Labor Surplus Economy: Theory and Policy (jtly.) 1964, Growth with Equity: The Taiwan Case (jtly.) 1979, Comparative Technology Choice in Development (jtly.) 1988, Linkages in Developing Economics: A Philippine Study (jtly.) 1990, The State of Development Economics, Science and Technology: Lessons for Development Policy (jtly.) 1990, Taiwan: From Developing to Mature Economy (ed.) 1992, The Political Economy of Development Policy Change (jtly.) 1992, Japan and the U.S. in the Developing World (ed.) 1997, Growth and Development from an Evolutionary Perspective (with John C. H. Fei) 1997. *Leisure interests:* tennis, squash, hiking. *Address:* Yale Center for International and Area Studies, 34 Hillhouse Avenue, P.O. Box 208206, New Haven, CT 06520-8206 (Office); 7 Mulberry Road, Woodbridge, CT 06525, U.S.A. (Home). *Telephone:* (203) 432-3410 (Office); (203) 397-2560 (Home). *Fax:* (203) 432-9383.

RANK, Sir Benjamin Keith, Kt., C.M.G., M.B., M.S., L.R.C.P., F.R.C.S., F.R.A.C.S., F.A.C.S.; Australian surgeon; b. 14 Jan. 1911, Heidelberg, Victoria; s. of Wreghitt Rank and Bessie Rank (née Smith); m. Barbara Lyle Facy 1938; one s. three d.; ed. Melbourne Univ.; war service 1939–46 (Lieut.-Col.); Hon. Plastic Surgeon, Royal Melbourne Hosp. 1946–66, Consulting Surgeon 1966–85, Chair. Bd. of Postgraduate Educ. 1968–75, mem. Bd. of Man. 1976–82, Medical Adviser to Bd. of Man. 1971–75; Consulting Plastic Surgeon to Dept. of Repatriation, also to Queen Victoria Hosp. and Royal Victorian Eye and Ear Hosp.; Chief Reparative Surgeon, Peter MacCallum Clinic 1964–79; Chair. Cttee. of Man., Victorian Plastic Surgery Unit, Preston and Northcote Community Hosp. 1966–86; Visiting Prof. Harvard Univ. 1976; Pres. British Asscn. of Plastic Surgeons 1965; Pres. Royal Australasian Coll. of Surgeons 1966–68, Syme Orator 1976, Stawell Orator 1977; Pres. St. John's Ambulance Council, Victoria 1983–88, Chair. 1978–83, mem. Motor Accident Bd., Victoria 1972–82; Foundation Chair. Australian Coll. of Speech Therapy, Hon. Fellow 1965; Hon. Fellow, Royal Coll. of Surgeons of Canada 1969, of Edinburgh 1973; Hon. D.Sc. (Punjabi Univ.) 1970; K.St.J. 1989. *Publications:* Surgery of Repair as Applied to Hand Injuries (co-author) 1963, Jerry Moore and Some of His Contemporaries 1975, Heads and Hands: an Era of Plastic Surgery 1987; more than 60 papers in British, American and Australian journals. *Leisure interests:* golf, gardening, painting. *Address:* 12 Jerula Avenue, Mount Eliza, Vic. 3930, Australia (Home).

RANK, Joseph McArthur; British business executive; b. 24 April 1918, Kingswood, Surrey; s. of the late Rowland Rank and of Margaret (née McArthur); m. The Hon. Moira, d. 3rd Baron Southborough 1946; one s. one d.; ed. Loretto School; joined Mark Mayhew Ltd., Flour Millers 1936; R.A.F. 1940–46; Jt. Man. Dir. Joseph Rank Ltd. 1955–65; Deputy Chair. and C.E.O. Rank Hovis McDougall Ltd. 1965–69, Chair. 1969–81, Pres. 1981–88, Hon. Pres. April 1988–; Chair. British Nutrition Foundation Ltd. 1968–69, Millers Mutual Asscn. 1969–81, Hon. Pres. 1991–; Dir. Royal Alexandra and Albert School 1952–, Chair. Governing Body 1975–84; Pres. Nat. Asscn. of British and Irish Millers 1957–58, 1978; First High Sheriff of East Sussex 1974–75; Hon. F.R.C.P. 1978. *Address:* 22 Coulson Street, London, SW3 3NA, England. *Telephone:* 0171-589 7973.

RÁNKI, Dezsö; Hungarian pianist; b. 8 Sept. 1951, Budapest; s. of József Ránki and Edith Jecsmen; m. Edit Klukon 1979; two c.; ed. Ferenc Liszt Music Acad., Budapest (under Pál Kadosa); has given recitals and appeared with several leading orchestras throughout Europe, including Berlin Philharmonic, Concertgebouw and London Philharmonic; regular concert tours N. America and Japan; four-hands piano recitals with Edit Klukon in many European cities 1982–; has taught piano at Budapest Music Acad. since 1973; First Prize, Int. Schumann Competition, Zwickau, G.D.R. 1969, Grand Prix Int. du Disque (Paris) 1972, Liszt Prize 2nd Degree 1973, Kossuth Prize 1978. *Leisure interests:* gramophone records, sound tapes, books, gardening. *Address:* Caecilia, 29 rue de la Coulouvrenière 1204 Geneva, Switzerland (Agent); H-1112 Budapest, Ördögorom Lejtó 11/B, Hungary (Home). *Telephone:* 8091520.

RANKIN, Sir Alick Michael, Kt., C.B.E., D.L., F.R.S.A.; British company director; b. 23 Jan. 1935, London; s. of Col. Niall Rankin and Lady Jean Rankin, D.C.V.O.; m. 2nd Suzetta Nelson 1976; one s. three d.; ed. Eton Coll. and Oxford Univ.; Scots Guards 1953–55; worked in investment banking, Wood Gundy & Co. Ltd., Toronto, Canada 1956–59; with Scottish & Newcastle Breweries PLC (now Scottish and Newcastle PLC) 1960–97, C.E.O. 1983–91, Deputy Chair. 1988–89, Chair. 1989–97; Dir. (non-exec.) Christian Salvesen 1986–97 (Chair. 1992–97), Sears PLC 1991–, Securities Trust of Scotland PLC 1991–, Scottish Financial Enterprise 1991– (Chair. 1991–94), James Finlay PLC 1994–, B.A.T. Industries PLC 1993–95; Dir. Bank of Scotland 1987; Dir. Gen. Accident PLC 1995–, Deputy Chair. 1995–97, Chair. 1997–98; mem. Brewers' Co. 1985–; Chair. Brewers' Soc. 1990–91, Vice-Pres. 1991–; Chair. Holyrood Brewery Foundation 1991–97; Deputy Chair. CGU PLC 1998–; Dir. Edin. Festival Society 1996–; D.L. (Edin.) 1996. *Leisure interests:* shooting, fishing, golf, tennis. *Address:* Tullymoy House, Glenalmond, Perthshire, PH1 3SL, Scotland. *Telephone:* (01738) 800469.

RANNEY, Helen M., M.D.; American physician; b. 12 April 1920, Summer Hill, New York; d. of Arthur C. Ranney and Alesia (Toolan) Ranney; ed. Barnard Coll. and Coll. of Physicians and Surgeons, Columbia Univ.; Asst. Prof. of Clinical Medicine, Columbia Univ. 1958–60; Assoc. Prof. of Medicine, Albert Einstein Coll. of Medicine 1960–65, Prof. 1965–70; Prof. of Medicine, State Univ. of New York, Buffalo 1970–73; Prof. of Medicine, Dept. of Medicine, Univ. of Calif., San Diego 1973–90, Prof. Emer. 1990–, Chair. 1973–86; Distinguished Physician, Department of Veterans' Affairs Medical Center, San Diego, Calif. 1986–91; mem. staff Alliance Pharmaceutical Corpn., San Diego 1991–; mem. N.A.S., Asscn. of American Physicians, American Acad. of Arts and Sciences, American Soc. for Clinical Investigation, Inst. of Medicine. *Publications:* papers in medical journals concerned with haemoglobin. *Address:* c/o Alliance Pharmaceutical Corporation, 3040 Science Park Road, San Diego, CA 92121 (Office); 6229 La Jolla Mesa Drive, La Jolla, CA 92037, U.S.A. (Home). *Telephone:* (619) 558-4316 (Office). *Fax:* (619) 678-4178.

RANQUE, Denis; French business executive; b. 1952; fmrly. with Industry Ministry; joined Thomson group as Head of Planning 1983, fmrly. Dir.-Gen. Thomson Tubes Electroniques, fmrly. Pres., Man. Dir. Thomson Sintra ASM, Pres. Thomson Marconi Sonar 1997–, Head Thomson-CSF 1998–. *Address:* Thomson-CSF, 173 blvd. Haussmann, 75415, Paris, France.

RANTANEN, Paavo Ilmari, M.SC.POL.; Finnish diplomatist and business executive; b. 28 Feb. 1934, Jyvaškylä; s. of Vilho Rantanen and Jenny Auer; m. Ritva Lehtinen 1956; two s. one d.; ed. Univ. of Helsinki and Acad. for Int. Law, The Hague; entered Ministry of Foreign Affairs 1958; served Vienna, Belgrade and Paris 1958–71; Counsellor, Finnish Embassy, Brussels and Mission of Finland to EC, Brussels 1971–73; Counsellor, Deputy Chief of Special Mission of Finland to CSCE, Geneva 1973–74; Amb.-at-Large 1974–76; Ministry of Foreign Affairs 1976–81; Perm. Rep. of Finland, UN Orgs. Geneva 1981–86; Amb. to U.S.A. 1986–88; mem. Exec. Bd. Int. Relations and Trade Policy, Nokia Group 1988–95, April–Dec. 1995; Minister of Foreign Affairs Feb.–April 1995; Chair Finnish Inst. for Int. Trade 1996–; mem. numerous bds. *Address:* Confederation of Finnish Industry and Employers, Eteläranta 10, 00130 Helsinki (Office); Laivurinkatu 39 A 4, 00150 Helsinki, Finland (Home). *Telephone:* 358-0-68681 (Office); 358-0-622 1285 (Home). *Fax:* 358-0-68682316 (Office).

RANTZEN, Esther, O.B.E., M.A.; British television presenter; b. 22 June 1940; d. of Harry Rantzen and Katherine Rantzen; m. Desmond Wilcox 1977; one s. two d.; ed. North London Collegiate School and Somerville Coll. Oxford; studio man. making dramatic sound effects, BBC Radio 1963; presenter, That's Life, BBC TV 1973–94, scriptwriter 1976–94; producer, The Big Time (documentary series) 1976; presenter, Esther Interviews . . . 1988, Hearts of Gold 1988, 1996, Drugwatch, Childwatch, The Lost Babies (also producer), Esther (talk show) 1994–, The Rantzen Report 1996–, etc.; mem. Nat. Consumer Council 1981–90, Health Educ. Authority 1989–95; Chair. ChildLine; numerous charitable activities; BBC TV Personality of 1975, Variety Club of G.B.; Richard Dimbleby Award, BAFTA 1988, Snowdon Award for Services to Disabled People 1996, Royal TV Soc. Hall of Fame

Award 1998, etc. *Publications:* Kill the Chocolate Biscuit (with D. Wilcox) 1981, Baby Love 1985, The Story of Ben Hardwick (with S. Woodward) 1985, Once Upon a Christmas 1996. *Leisure interests:* work and fantasy. *Address:* BBC TV, White City, 201 Wood Lane, London, W12 7RJ; Noel Gay Artists, 22 Dean Street, London, W1V 5AL, England. *Telephone:* 0181-752 5252/ 0171-836 3941.

RAO, Calyampudi Radhakrishna, M.A., SC.D., F.N.A., F.R.S.; Indian statistician; b. 10 Sept. 1920, Hadagali, Mysore State; s. of C. D. Naidu and A. Laxmikanthamma; m. Bhargavi Rao 1948; one s. one d.; ed. Andhra and Calcutta Univs.; Research at Indian Statistical Inst. 1943–46, Cambridge Univ. 1946–48; Prof. and Head of Div. of Theoretical Research and Training 1949–64; Dir. Research and Training School, Indian Statistical Inst. 1964–71, Sec. and Dir. 1972–76, Jawaharlal Nehru Prof. 1976–84; Univ. Prof., Univ. of Pittsburgh 1979–88; Nat. Prof., India 1987–92; Eberly Prof. of Statistics, Penn State Univ. 1988–; Ed. Sankhya (Indian Journal of Statistics); Fellow, Inst. of Mathematical Statistics, U.S.A., Pres. 1976–77; Treas. Int. Statistical Inst. 1961–65, Pres. 1977–79; Pres. Int. Biometric Soc. 1973–75; Pres. Forum for Interdisciplinary Math.; mem. N.A.S.; Hon. Fellow, Royal Statistical Soc.; Fellow, American Statistical Asscn., Econometric Soc., Third World Acad. of Sciences; Hon. Prof. Univ. of San Marcos, Lima; Hon. mem. Int. Statistical Inst., Inst. of Combinatorics and Applications; Foreign mem. Lithuanian Acad. of Sciences; Hon. Foreign mem. American Acad. Arts and Sciences; Hon. Fellow, King's Coll., Cambridge Univ.; Hon. Life mem. Biometric Soc.; Hon. D.Sc. (20 univs.); Hon. D.Litt. (Delhi); Bhatnagar Memorial Award for Scientific Research; Padma Bhushan; Guy Silver Medal Royal Statistical Soc., Meghnad Saha Medal, Nat. Science Acad., J. C. Bose Gold Medal, Wilks Memorial Medal, Calcutta Univ. Gold Medal, Mahalanobis Birth Centenary Gold Medal. *Publications include:* Advanced Statistical Methods in Biometric Research, Linear Statistical Inference and its Application, Generalized Inverse of Matrices and its Applications, Characterization Problems of Mathematical Statistics 1973, Estimation of Variance Components and its Applications (with J. Kleffe) 1988, Statistics and Truth 1989, Choquet Deny Type Functional Equations with Applications to Stochastic Models (with D. N. Shanbhaq) 1994, Linear Models: Least Squares and Alternatives (with H. Toutenburg) 1995, Matrix Algebra and Its Applications to Statistics and Econometrics (with M. B. Rao) 1998; over 250 research papers in mathematical statistics. *Leisure interest:* writing humorous essays. *Address:* Department of Statistics, Penn State University, 326 Thomas Bldg., University Park, PA 16802, U.S.A. *Telephone:* (814) 865-3194 (Office); (814) 234-6209 (Home). *Fax:* (814) 863-7114 (Office); (814) 234-0372 (Home).

RAO, Chintamani Nagesa Ramachandra, D.SC., PH.D., F.N.A., F.R.S.; Indian professor of chemistry; b. 30 June 1934, Bangalore; s. of H. Nagesa Rao; m. Indumati Rao 1960; one s. one d.; ed. Mysore, Banaras and Purdue Univs.; Lecturer, Indian Inst. of Science, Bangalore 1959–63; Prof. later Sr. Prof., Indian Inst. of Tech., Kanpur 1963–77, Dean of Research and Devt. 1969–72; Chair. Solid State and Structural Chem. Unit and Materials Research Lab., Indian Inst. of Science 1977–84, Dir. of Inst. 1984–94; Albert Einstein Research Prof. and Pres. Jawaharlal Nehru Centre for Advanced Scientific Research 1994–; Visiting Prof. Purdue Univ., U.S.A. 1967–68, Oxford Univ. 1974–75; Prof. ILSC, Bangalore; Fellow King's Coll. Cambridge Univ. 1983–84; Past Pres. IUPAC; fmr. Chair. Science Advisory Council to Prime Minister of India, Editorial Boards of 15 int. journals; Foreign mem. Serbian and Slovenian Acads. of Science, Yugoslavia, N.A.S., Russian, Czechoslovak and Polish Acads. of Sciences, Pontifical Acad. of Sciences, American Acad. of Arts and Sciences, American Philosophical Soc., Materials Socs. of Japan and Korea, Int. Acad. of Ceramics; Founding mem. Third World Acad. of Sciences; Hon. Foreign mem. Korean Acad. of Science and Tech.; Hon. mem. Japan Acad.; Corresp. mem. Brazilian Acad. of Sciences; Titular mem. European Acad. of Arts, Sciences and Humanities; Foreign mem. Academia Europaea; fmr. Pres. Indian Acad. of Sciences; Past Pres. Indian Nat. Science Acad., St. Catherine's Coll., Oxford 1974–75; American Chem. Soc. Centennial Foreign Fellow 1976; Jawaharlal Nehru Fellow, Indian Inst. of Tech.; Hon. Fellow Royal Soc. of Chemistry 1989, Univ. of Wales, Cardiff 1997; Nehru Visiting Prof., Cambridge Univ.; Linnett Visiting Prof., Cambridge Univ. 1998; Hon. D.Sc. (Purdue Univ., U.S.A.), (Bordeaux) 1982, 1983, (Sri Venkateswara) 1984, (Roorkee) 1985, (Banares) 1986, (Osmania, Mangalore) 1986, (Manipur) 1987, (Anna, Mysore, Burdwan) 1988, (Wrocław) 1989, (Wales) 1994, (Notre Dame) 1996, (I.I.T., Bombay) 1997; Royal Soc. of Chem. Medal (London) 1981, Marlow Medal, Faraday Soc. 1967, Bhatnagar Award 1968, Padma Shri 1974, Fed. of Indian Chamber of Commerce and Industry Award for Physical Sciences 1977, Sir C. V. Raman Award 1978, S. N. Bose Medal of Indian Nat. Science Acad. 1980, Jawaharlal Nehru Award 1988, Hevrovsky Gold Medal, Czechoslovakia 1989, Blackett Lecturer, Royal Soc. 1991, CSIR Golden Jubilee Prize 1991, N.A.S. Int. Science Lecture, U.S.A. 1993, Sahabdeen Int. Award of Science, Sri Lanka 1994, Third World Acad. of Sciences Medal 1995, Albert Einstein Gold Medal, UNESCO 1996, Asutosh Mookerjee Medal 1996, Shatabdi Puraskar, Indian Scientific Congress 1999; Padma Vibhushan 1984. *Publications:* Ultraviolet Visible Spectroscopy 1960, Chemical Applications of Infrared Spectroscopy 1963, Spectroscopy in Inorganic Chemistry 1970, Modern Aspects of Solid State Chemistry 1970, Solid State Chemistry 1974, Educational Technology in Teaching of Chemistry 1975, Phase Transitions in Solids 1978, Preparation and Characterization of Materials 1981, The Metallic and Non-Metallic States of Matter 1985, New Directions in Solid State Chemistry 1986, Chemistry of Oxide Superconductors 1988, Chemical and Structural Aspects of High Temperature Oxide Superconductors 1988, Bismuth and Thallium Superconductors 1989, Chemistry of Advanced Materials 1992, Chemical Approaches to the Synthesis of Inorganic Materials 1994, Transition Metal Oxides 1995; more than 900 original research papers. *Leisure interests:* gourmet cooking, general reading. *Address:* Jawaharlal Nehru Centre for Advanced Scientific Research, Indian Institute of Science Campus, Bangalore 560012 (Office); JNC President's House, Indian Institute of Science Campus, Bangalore 560012, India (Home). *Telephone:* 3345491/8462762 (Office); 3369410 (Home). *Fax:* 3442468/8462766.

RAO, Raja; Indian writer; b. 21 July 1909; ed. Nizam Coll., Hyderabad, Univs. of Montpellier and Paris; Prof. of Philosophy, Univ. of Texas –1980, Prof. Emer. 1980–; Neustadt Int. Prize for Literature 1988. *Publications:* Kanthapura, Cow of the Barricades, The Serpent and The Rope, The Policeman and the Rose (short stories in French and English), The Cat and Shakespeare, Comrade Kirillov, The Chessmaster and his Moves 1988 (novels), On the Ganga Ghat (stories) 1989. *Address:* c/o Department of Philosophy, College of Humanities at Austin, University of Texas, Austin, TX 78712, U.S.A.

RAO BIN; Chinese business executive; b. 1928, Jilin Prov. ed. Shanghai Univ.; joined CCP 1949; Vice-Minister of Machine Bldg. 1960–82; Gen. Man., China Nat. Automotive Industry Corpn. 1993–. *Address:* China National Automotive Industry Corporation, 12 Fuxing Menwai Street, Beijing 100860, People's Republic of China.

RAOUL, Major Alfred; Republic of the Congo politician, army officer and diplomatist; b. 1938; ed. Mil. Acad., Saint-Cyr, France; Adjutant to C.-in-C. of Congolese Armed Forces 1963–65; Dir. of Corps of Engineers 1965; Sec. in charge of Defence, Directorate of Nat. Revolutionary Council Aug. 1968; Prime Minister of Congo (Brazzaville) 1968–69, concurrently Minister of Defence 1968–69, concurrently Minister of State Planning and Admin. Sept.-Dec. 1969; Head of State 1968–69; Vice-Chair. Council of State 1969–71; sentenced to 10 years' imprisonment March 1972, released Aug. 1972; Amb. to Egypt 1978–80, to Belgium 1980–84, to EEC 1980–84; fmr. mem. Political Bureau of Congolese Workers' Party (P.C.T.); 2nd Sec. Cen. Cttee. of P.C.T. *Address:* c/o Ministry of Foreign Affairs, Brazzaville, Republic of the Congo.

RAOULT, Eric, L. ÈS SC.ECON.; French politician; b. 19 June 1955, Paris; m. Béatrice Abollivier 1990; ed. Inst. d'Etudes Politiques, Paris and Inst. Français de Presse; Parl. Asst. to Claude Labbé; Town Councillor, Raincy 1977; Deputy Mayor of Raincy 1983–95, Mayor 1995–; mem. Cen. Cttee. of RPR 1982–; Deputy to Nat. Ass. 1986–1995, Vice-Pres. 1993–95; Regional Councillor, Ile de France 1992; Minister of Integration and the Fight against Exclusion May–Nov. 1995, Deputy Minister with responsibility for Urban Affairs and Integration 1995–97. *Address:* Mairie, 93340 Le Raincy, France.

RÂPEANU, Valeriu; Romanian literary critic, historian and editor; b. 28 Sept. 1931, Ploiestiori, Prahova Co.; s. of Gheorghe and Anastasia Râpeanu; m. Sanda Marinescu 1956; one s.; ed. Univ. of Bucharest; journalist 1954–69; Vice-Chair. of the Romanian Cttee. of Radio and TV 1970–72; Dir. Mihai Eminescu Publishing House, Bucharest 1972–90; Prof. Spinu Haret Univ., Bucharest; mem. Romanian Writers' Union; fmr. mem. Cen. Cttee. Romanian CP; mem. Int. Assoc. of Literary Critics. *Publications:* the monographs George Mihail-Zamfirescu 1958, Al. Vlahuţă 1964, Noi şi cei dinaintea noastră (Ourselves and Our Predecessors) 1966, Interferenţe spirituale (Spiritual Correspondences) 1970; Călător pe două continente (Traveller on Two Continents) 1970, Pe drumurile tradiţiei (Following Traditions) 1973, Interpretări si înţelesuri (Interpretations and Significances) 1975, Cultură si istorie (Culture and History), two vols., 1979, 1981; Tărâmul unde nu ajungi niciodată (The Land You Could Never Reach) 1982, Scriitori dintre cele două războaie (Writers between the two World Wars) 1986, La vie de l'histoire et l'histoire d'une vie 1989, N. Iorga, Mincea Eliade, Nae Ionescu 1993, N. Iorga 1994; ed. vols. by Nicolae Iorga, Gh. Brătianu, Al. Kiriţescu, Cella Delavrancea, Marcel Mihalovici, I. G. Duca, Gh.I. Brătianu, George Enescu, C. Rădulescu-Motru, C. Brâncuşi; anthology of Romanian drama; essays on François Mauriac, Jean d'Ormesson, Marcel Proust, Aaron Copland, André Malraux, Jean Cocteau. *Leisure interests:* music, art. *Address:* Str. Mecet 21, Bucharest, Romania.

RAPHAEL (pseudonym of Rafael Martos); Spanish singer; b. Jaén; m. Natalia Figueroa 1972; two s. one d.; first prize winner at Salzburg Festival children's singing competition aged 9; subsequently won numerous other competitions; began professional career in Madrid nightclub 1960; first best-selling record Los Hombres Lloran También 1964; rep. of Spain, Eurovision Song Contest 1966, 1967; U.S. debut 1967; toured U.S.S.R. 1968, Japan 1970, Australia 1971; Broadway debut 1974; celebrated 25th anniversary as professional singer with open-air concert at Bernabé Stadium, Madrid 1985; appearances in 16 feature films including Cuando Tú Bo Estás 1966, The Hobo 1968; has sold 220 million records; 250 Gold Discs, 21 Platinum Discs etc. *Address:* c/o Arie Kaduri Agency, Inc., 16125 N.E. 18th Avenue, North Miami Beach, FL 33162, U.S.A.

RAPHAEL, Farid; Lebanese politician and banker; b. 28 Oct. 1933, Dlebta, Kesrouan; s. of Elie Raphael and Evelyne Khalife; m. Ilham Abdel Ahad 1970; one s. three d.; ed. Univ. of St. Joseph, Beirut, Univ. of Lyons, France; with Cie. Algérienne de Crédit et de Banque, Beirut 1956–67; Founder and Gen. Man. Banque Libano-Française S.A.L. 1967–79, Chair. and Gen. Man.

1979–; Founder and Vice-Pres. Banque Libano-Française (France) S.A. (now Banque Française de l'Orient S.A.), Paris 1976–85, Chair. and Gen. Man. 1985–89, Adviser to BFO-France 1989–; Minister of Justice, Finance, Posts, Telephones and Telecommunications 1976–79. *Address:* Banque Libano-Française, B.P. 11-808, Immeuble Liberty Plaza, Hamra, Beirut, Lebanon (Office); Banque Française de l'Orient, 33 rue de Monceau, 75008 Paris, France (Office); Rue St. Charles, Imm. Colette Eddé, Brazilia, Hazmieh, Beirut, Lebanon (Home). *Telephone:* (1) 340350. *Fax:* (1) 340355 (Office).

RAPHAEL, Frederic Michael, M.A., F.R.S.L.; American writer; b. 14 Aug. 1931, Chicago, Ill.; s. of Cedric Michael Raphael and Irene Rose Mauser; m. Sylvia Betty Glatt 1955; two s. one d.; ed. Charterhouse, St. John's Coll., Cambridge; Lippincott Prize 1961, U.S. Acad. Award 1966, Royal TV Soc. Award 1976. *Publications:* novels: Obbligato 1956, The Earlsdon Way 1956, The Limits of Love 1960, Lindmann 1963, Orchestra and Beginners 1967, Like Men Betrayed 1970, April, June and November 1972, California Time 1975, The Glittering Prizes 1976, Heaven and Earth 1985, After the War 1988, A Double Life 1993; short stories: Sleeps Six 1979, Oxbridge Blues 1980, Think of England 1986, The Hidden I (illustrated by Sarah Raphael) 1990, The Latin Lover and Other Stories 1994, Old Scores 1995, Coast to Coast 1998; biography: Somerset Maugham and his World 1977, Byron 1982; essays: Cracks in the Ice 1979, Of Gods and Men (illustrated by Sarah Raphael) 1992, France, the Four Seasons 1994, The Necessity of Anti-Semitism 1997, Historicism and its Poverty 1998, Karl Popper 1998; translations: Catullus (with K. McLeish) 1978, The Oresteia of Aeschylus 1979, Aeschylus (complete plays, with K. McLeish) 1991, Euripides' Medea (with K. McLeish) 1994, Euripides: Hippolytus-Bacchar (with K. McLeish) 1997, Sophokles Aias (with K. McLeish) 1998; screenplays: Nothing But the Best 1965, Darling 1966, Far from the Madding Crowd 1968, Two for the Road 1968, Richard's Things 1980, Oxbridge Blues 1984, After the War 1989, The Man in the Brooks Brothers Shirt (ACE award 1991), Armed Response 1995, Eyes Wide Shut 1998; plays: From the Greek 1979, The Daedalus Dimension (radio) 1982, The Thought of Lydia (radio) 1988, The Empty Jew (radio) 1993. *Leisure interests:* tennis, travel. *Address:* Lagardelle, St. Laurent-la-Vallée, 24170 Belves, France; c/o Deborah Rogers, Rogers, Coleridge-White, 20 Powis Mews, London, W11 1JN, England.

RAPOSO, Mario; Portuguese politician; b. Jan. 1929, Coimbra; ed. Univ. of Coimbra; Sub-Insp. for Social Assistance and Sec. to Minister of Finance, resigned to practise Law 1955; mem. Gen. Council, Ordem dos Advogados (Law Soc.) 1972–74, Chair. 1975–77; mem. Exec. Cttee. First Nat. Congress of Lawyers 1972, Cttee. for Judicial Reform, High Court of Justice 1974; Minister of Justice, Third Constitutional Govt.; mem. Ass. of the Repub. 1978–79, for Social Democratic Party (PSD) Dec. 1979–; Minister of Justice 1980–81, 1985–87; mem. Council of State 1991–. *Address:* c/o PSD, Rua de São Caetano 9, 1296 Lisbon, Codex, Portugal.

RAPPENEAU, Jean-Paul; French film director and screenplay writer; b. 8 April 1932, Auxerre, Yonne; s. of Jean Rappeneau and Anne-Marie (Bornhauser) Rappeneau; m. Claude-Lise Cornély 1971; two s.; ed. Lycée Jacques-Amyot, Auxerre, Faculté de droit, Paris; Asst. Dir. 1953–57; 10 César Awards 1990 (including Best Director, Best Picture), Golden Globe Award for best foreign film 1990, U.S. Nat. Review Bd. Best Foreign Film 1990; wrote screenplays for Signé Arsène Lupin 1959, Le Mariage (in La Française et l'Amour) 1959, Zazie dans le métro 1960, Vie privée 1961, Le Combat dans l'île 1961, L'Homme de Rio 1962; Grand Prix Nat. du Cinéma 1994; Chevalier Légion d'honneur, Officier Ordre Nat. du Mérite, Officier des Arts et Lettres. *Films directed include:* short films: La Maison sur la place, Chronique provinciale 1958; wrote and dir. La Vie de château 1966 (Prix Louis-Delluc), Les Mariés de l'An Deux 1970, Le Sauvage 1975, Tout feu, tout flamme 1982; Dir. and jt. adaptor Cyrano de Bergerac 1990, Le hussard sur le toit 1994. *Address:* 24 rue Henri Barbusse, 75005 Paris, France.

RAPSON, Ralph, M.ARCH.; American architect; b. 13 Sept. 1914, Alma, Mich.; s. of Frank and Mable (née Nickols) Rapson; m. Mary Dolan; two s.; ed. Alma (Mich.) Coll., Univ. of Mich. Coll. of Architecture, and Cranbrook Acad. of Art; practising architect 1941–; f., now proprietor Ralph Rapson and Assocs.; Head Dept. of Architecture Chicago Inst. of Design 1942–46; Assoc. Prof. of Architecture M.I.T. School of Architecture 1946–54 (leave of absence to execute designs in Europe for State Dept. 1951–53); Prof. and Head of School of Architecture, Univ. of Minnesota 1954–84; Visiting Prof. Univ. of Va.; mem. American Inst. of Architects, Int. Congress of Modern Architecture; Dir. Walker Art Gallery; fmr. Chair. Editorial Bd. Northwest Architect; numerous awards include Parker Medal 1951, American Inst. of Architects Honor Award for U.S. Embassy, Stockholm 1954, two Merit Awards 1955, Honour Award 1958. *Designs include:* projects for U.S. Government, several churches and schools, commercial, industrial and residential buildings, particularly U.S. Embassy, Stockholm, U.S. Embassy, Copenhagen, U.S. Consulate, Le Havre, St. Peter's Lutheran Church (Edina, Minn.), Fargo (N.D.) Civic Center, St. Paul (Minn.) Arts and Science Center, American Embassy, Beirut, Dr. William G. Shepherd House, St. Paul, Tyrone Guthrie Repertory Theatre, Minn. (Designs also executed for Embassies at Athens, The Hague and Oslo.) *Address:* Ralph Rapson & Assocs., 409 Cedar Avenue, Minneapolis, MN 55454 (Office); 1 Seymour Avenue, Minneapolis, MN 55404, U.S.A. (Home).

RASHEED, Natheer al-; Jordanian business executive and civil servant; b. 19 June 1929, Salt; s. of Ahmad al-Rasheed and Sahah al-Hiary; m. Rabia al-Rasheed 1961; four s. one d.; ed. mil. courses with British Army and Staff Coll.; Dir. Gen. Intelligence in Jordan 1969–73; Chief, Bd. of Dirs. Jordan Mines Phosphate Co. 1976; Senator 1989–; recipient of three medals. *Leisure interests*: horse-riding (polo), shooting. *Address*: P.O. Box 6583, Amman, Jordan. *Telephone*: (06) 893102/3 (Office); (06) 5523366 (Home). *Fax*: (06) 893117.

RASHID, Hussain; Malaysian stockbroker and banker; fmrly. with London Stock Exchange; est. own brokerage house 1983; est. Rashid Hussain group of financial services companies 1996; Chair. Exec. Cttee. Khazanah govt. holding co. *Address:* c/o D.C.B. Bank Bhd., Menara T.R., 18th Floor, 161B Jalan Ampang, P.O. Box 10145, 50907 Kuala Lumpur, Malaysia. *Telephone:* 3-261-2444. *Fax:* 3-261-9541.

RASHID, Mohammed bin Ahmad al, PH.D.; Saudi Arabian politician and academic; b. 1944, Al-Majma'a; m.; five s. two d.; ed. Imam Mohammed Bin Saud Islamic Univ., Riyadh, Univ. of Indiana, Univ. of Oklahoma; teacher Inst. of Religious Studies, Riyadh 1964–65; Grad. Asst. Coll. of Shari'a and Islamic Studies, Makkah 1965–66; sent on mission to U.S.A. by King Abdulaziz Univ. 1966–72; Asst. Prof. King Saud Univ. 1972–79, Assoc. Prof. 1979–89, Vice Dean Coll. of Educ. 1974–76, Dean 1976–79; Dir. Gen Arab Bureau of Educ. for Gulf States 1979–88; Founder of Arab Gulf States Univ. and Vice-Pres. of Founding Cttee. 1979–88; Prof. of Educ. King Saud Univ. 1989–94; mem. Saudi Nat. Council 1994–95; Minister of Educ. 1995–; Distinguished Fulbright Fellow 1988–89, Distinguished Fellow World Council for Teacher Training 1989, Gold Medal of Merit (Arab League Educ. Cultural and Scientific Org.). *Publications:* numerous articles and research papers in professional journals. *Leisure interests:* walking, swimming, reading. *Address:* Ministry of Education, P.O. Box 3734, Airport Road, Riyadh 11481, Saudi Arabia. *Telephone:* (1) 411-5777. *Fax:* (1) 411-2051.

RASI-ZADE, Artur Tair ogly; Azerbaijani politician and engineer; b. 26 Feb. 1935, Gyanja; m.; one d.; ed. Azerbaijan Inst. of Industry; engineer, Deputy Dir. Azerbaijan Inst. of Oil Machine Construction 1957–73, Dir. 1977–78; chief engineer Trust Soyuzneftemash 1973–77; Deputy Head Azerbaijan State Planning Cttee. 1978–81; Head of section Cen. Cttee. of Azerbaijan CP 1981–86; First Deputy Prime Minister 1986–92; adviser Foundation of Econ. Reforms 1992–96; Asst. to Pres. Aliyev Feb.-May 1996; First Deputy Prime Minister May-Nov. 1996; Prime Minister Nov. 1996–. *Address:* Council of Ministers, Lermontov str. 68, 370066 Baku, Azerbaijan. *Telephone:* (8922) 980008.

RASMUSSEN, Poul Nørregaard, DR. POL.; Danish professor of economics; b. 9 May 1922, Hylke; s. of Anders Rasmussen and Christine (née Nørregaard) Rasmussen; m. Karen Aase Bruun 1948 (died 1984); two d.; ed. Univs. of Aarhus and Copenhagen; Research Assoc. Univ. of Oslo 1947–48; Econ. Affairs Officer UN ECE, Geneva 1948–51; Reader in Econs., Univ. of Copenhagen 1951–56, Prof. 1956–88, Prof. Emer. 1988–. *Publications:* Studies in Inter-Sectoral Relations 1956, Forelaesninger om biblioteksbenyttelse og opgaveskrivning 1958, Matematik for økonomer (with Lange Stething) (vols. 1 & 2) 1958–59, Om økonomiens metode 1963, Forelaesninger for økonomer om biblioteksbenyttelse og opgaveskrivning 1966, Noter og kommentarer til Don Patinkin: Money, Interest and Prices (with Niels Thygesen) 1967, The Economics of Technological Change 1976. *Address:* Bagsvaerdvej 248, Bagsvaerd 2880, Denmark. *Telephone:* (45) 44-44-57-80.

RASPUTIN, Valentin Grigoriyevich; Russian author; b. 15 March 1937, Ust-Uda (Irkutsk); ed. Irkutsk Univ.; first works published 1961; elected People's Deputy 1989; mem. Presidential Council 1990–91; U.S.S.R. State Prize 1977, 1987; Hero of Socialist Labour 1987. *Publications:* I Forgot to Ask Lyosha 1961, A Man of This World 1965, Bearskin for Sale 1966, Vasilii and Vasilisa 1967, Deadline 1970, Live and Remember, Stories, 1974, Parting with Matera 1976, Live and Love 1982, Fire 1985, Collected Works (2 vols.) 1990, Siberia, Siberia 1991. *Address:* 5th Army Street 67, Apt. 68, 664000 Irkutsk, Russia. *Telephone:* (3952) 4-71-00.

RASSADIN, Stanislav Borisovich; Russian literary critic; b. 4 March 1935, Moscow; s. of Boris Matvejevich Rassadin and Varvara Georgievna; m. Alina Yegorovna Petukhova-Yakunina 1962; ed. Moscow Univ. *Publications include:* Poetry of Recent Years 1961, Nikolai Nosov: A Bio-Critical Account 1961, Talk with the Reader: Essay on Literature 1962, The Role of the Reader 1965, Linden Alley 1966, Pushkin the Dramatist 1977, Fonvizin 1980, The Test with a Show: Poetry and Television 1984, Suppositions about Poetry 1988, The Genius and the Villainy or the Case of Sukhovo-Kobylin 1989, After the Flood 1990, I am Choosing Freedom 1990, Very Simple Mandelstam 1994, Russians (Russkiye, ili Iz dvorjan v intelligenty) 1995. *Leisure interest:* work. *Address:* Kosygina Street 5, Apt. 335, 117334 Moscow, Russia. *Telephone:* (095) 137-81-84.

RATEB M. SOAD, Aisha, PH.D.; Egyptian diplomatist and professor of law; b. 22 Feb. 1928, Cairo; d. of Mohamed Soad Rateb; m. 1953 (separated); two s.; ed. in Cairo and Paris; now Prof. of Int. Law, Univ. of Cairo; Minister of Social Affairs and Social Insurance 1971–77; Amb. to Denmark 1979, to Fed. Repub. of Germany 1981; Amb. Ministry of Foreign Affairs; numerous awards and distinctions. *Publications:* Principles of International Law, International Organizations, Neutrality, International Arab Relations, Some Legal Aspects of the Arab-Israeli Conflict, Legal Studies, etc. *Address:* Faculty of Law, University of Cairo, P.O. Box 12611, Orman, Giza, Cairo; 6 Ibn Malek Street, Giza, Cairo, Egypt.

RATHBONE, Julian, B.A.; British writer; b. 10 Feb. 1935, London; s. of Christopher Fairrie Rathbone and Decima Doreen Prost; ed. Clayesmore School, Magdalene Coll., Cambridge; teacher of English, Ankara, London, W. Sussex 1959–73; full-time writer 1973–; contrib. The Times, The New Statesman, Literary Review, The Guardian, The Independent; received Swanage Int. Poetry Prize, Crime Writers Short Story Silver Dagger, Deutsche Krimi Preis. *Publications:* thirty novels, poetry, radio plays and screenplays, including: King Fisher Lives 1976, Joseph 1979, A Last Resort 1980, A Spy of the Old School 1982, Wellington's War 1984 (non-fiction), Nasty, Very 1984, Lying in State 1985, Intimacy 1995, Blame Hitler 1997, The Last English King 1997. *Leisure interests:* music, painting, film, books. *Address:* Sea View, School Road, Thorney Hill, near Christchurch, Dorset, BH23 8DS, England. *Telephone:* (01425) 673313. *Fax:* (01425) 673313.

RATHER, Dan, B.A.; American broadcaster and journalist; b. Oct. 1931, Wharton, Tex.; m. Jean Goebel; one s. one d.; ed. Sam Houston State Coll., Univ. of Houston, Tex., S. Tex. School of Law; writer and sports commentator with KSAM-TV; taught journalism for one year at Houston Chronicle; with CBS; with radio station KTRH, Houston for about four years; News and Current Affairs Dir. CBS Houston TV affiliate KHOU-TV late 1950s; joined CBS News 1962; Chief London Bureau 1965–66; worked in Viet Nam; White House 1966; anchorman CBS Reports 1974–75; co-anchorman 60 Minutes CBS-TV 1975–81; anchorman Dan Rather Reporting CBS Radio Network 1977–; co-ed. show Who's Who CBS-TV 1977; anchorman Midwest desk CBS Nat. election night 1972–80; CBS Nat. Political Consultant 1964–; anchorman Man. Ed. CBS Evening News with Dan Rather 1981–, Co-anchorman 1993–; anchored numerous CBS News Special Programmes, including coverage of presidential campaigns in 1982 and 1984; as White House correspondent accompanied Pres. on numerous travels including visits to Middle East,. U.S.S.R., People's Repub. of China; ten Emmy awards; numerous acad. honours; Distinguished Achievement for Broadcasting Award, Univ. of S. Calif. Journalism Alumni Asscn, Bob Considine Award 1983. *Publications:* The Palace Guard 1974 (with Gary Gates), The Camera Never Blinks Twice (with Mickey Herskowitz) 1977, I Remember (with Peter Wyden) 1991, The Camera Never Blinks Twice: The Further Adventurers of a Television Journalist 1994. *Address:* CBS News, 524 West 57th Street, New York, NY 10019, U.S.A. (Office).

RATHKE, Heinrich Karl Martin Hans, DR.THEOL.; German ecclesiastic; b. 12 Dec. 1928, Mölln, Kreis Malchin; s. of Paul and Hedwig (née Steding) Rathke; m. Marianne Rusam 1955; six s. one d.; ed. Univs. of Kiel, Erlangen, Tübingen and Rostock; parish priest, Althof bei Bad Doberan 1954–55, Warnkenhagen, Mecklenburg 1955–62, Rostock Südstadt 1962–70; Priest in charge of community service and people's mission, Mecklenburg 1970–71; Bishop of the Evangelical-Lutheran Church of Mecklenburg 1971–84; Presiding Bishop of the United Evangelical Lutheran Church of the G.D.R. 1977–81; Pastor in Crivitz/Mecklenburg 1984–91; Bishop and Pastor Emer. 1991–; Asst. Bishop, Evangelical-Lutheran Church of Kazakhstan 1991–93; Hon. D.Theol. (Rostock) 1999. *Publication:* Ignatius von Antiochien und die Paulusbriefe 1967, Gemeinde heute und morgen 1979, Einstehen für Gemeinschaft in Christus 1980. *Address:* Schleifmühlenweg 11, 19061 Schwerin, Germany. *Telephone:* 0385-562887.

RATLIFF, Floyd, PH.D.; American university professor; b. 1 May 1919, La Junta, Colo.; s. of Charles Frederick Ratliff and Alice Hubbard; m. Orma Vernon Priddy 1942; one d.; ed. Pueblo Junior Coll., Colorado Coll. and Brown Univ.; U.S. Army 1941–45; Nat. Research Council Postdoctoral Fellow, Johns Hopkins Univ. 1950–51; Instructor, Harvard Univ. 1951–52, Asst. Prof., 1952–54; Assoc., Rockefeller Inst. 1954–58, Assoc. Prof., Rockefeller Univ. 1958–66, Prof. 1966–89, Emer. 1989–; Pres. Harry Frank Guggenheim Foundation 1983–89, Esperanza 1992–93; mem. Nat. Acad. of Sciences, American Acad. of Arts and Sciences, American Philosophical Soc.; mem. Editorial Bd. Journal of General Physiology 1969–86; mem. Bd. of Scientific Counsellors of Nat. Eye Inst. 1970–73, Educ. Cttee. of the China Inst. in America 1977; Hon. D.Sc. (Colo. Coll.) 1975; Howard Crosby Warren Medal (Soc. of Experimental Psychologists) 1966, Edgar D. Tillyer Award (Optical Soc. of America) 1976, Medal for Distinguished Service, Brown Univ. 1980, Pisart Vision Award, Distinguished Scientific Contribution Award of American Psychological Asscn. 1984, William James Fellow (American Psychological Soc.) 1989. *Publications:* Mach Bands: Quantitative Studies on Neural Networks in the Retina 1965, Studies on Excitation and Inhibition in the Retina (editor) 1974, Paul Signac and Color in Neo-Impressionism 1992. *Leisure interests:* Oriental art (Chinese ceramics of the Sung dynasty). *Address:* 2215 Calle Cacique, Santa Fe, NM 87505, U.S.A. (Home).

RATNER, Gerald Irving; British business executive; b. 1 Nov. 1949; s. of Leslie Ratner and Rachelle Ratner; m. 1st (divorced 1989); two d.; m. 2nd Maria Ratner; one s. one d.; ed. Town and Country School, London; Man. Dir. Ratners Group 1984, Chair. 1986–91, C.E.O. 1986–92, Dir. –1992; Dir. (non-exec.) Norweb 1991; consultant Tobacco Dock 1993–; Dir. Workshop Health Fitness Club 1997–. *Leisure interests:* keeping fit, chess, art. *Address:* Hampton Lodge, Church Road, Bray, Berks., SL6 1UP, England.

RATSIRAHONANA, Norbert; Malagasy politician; Pres. Constitutional High Court – 1996; Prime Minister of Madagascar 1996–97. *Address:* c/o Office of the Prime Minister, Antananarivo, Madagascar.

RATSIRAKA, Adm. Didier; Malagasy politician and naval officer; b. 4 Nov. 1936, Vatomandry; ed. Coll. Saint Michel, Tananarive (now Antananarivo), Lycée Henri IV, Paris, Ecole Navale, Lanveoc-Poulmic (France), Ecole des Officiers "Transmissions", Les Bormettes, and Ecole Supérieure de Guerre Navale, Paris; had several naval postings 1963–70; Mil. Attaché, Paris 1970–72; Minister of Foreign Affairs 1972–75; Pres. Supreme Council of Revolution June 1975–; Prime Minister and Minister of Defence June-Dec. 1975; Pres. Democratic Repub. of Madagascar 1976–93 (relinquished exec. powers Aug. 1991), Feb. 1997–; Sec.-Gen. Avant-garde de la révolution malgache 1976–, Front nat. pour la défense de la révolution socialiste malgache 1977–; Hon. Citizen, New Orleans, U.S.A. 1981. *Publications:* Stratégies pour l'an 2000. *Address:* c/o Présidence de la République, Antananarivo, Madagascar.

RATTANAKOSES, Gen. Mana; Thai politician; b. 16 Sept. 1925, Nakhon Phanom Muang Dist.; s. of Luang Apibal Bancha; m. Pol Col Chalerm; four c.; ed. Chulachomklao Royal Mil. Acad.; mil. career until 1986; MP for Nakhon Prov. 1986–; fmr. Deputy Educ. Minister; Minister of Educ. 1988–90; Deputy Prime Minister Sept.–Dec. 1990; Co-Founder, Sec.-Gen. Rassadorn Party. *Address:* c/o Office of the Deputy Prime Minister, Rassadorn Party, Bangkok, Thailand.

RATTLE, Sir Simon, K.B.E.; British conductor; b. 19 Jan. 1955, Liverpool; m. 1st Elise Ross 1980 (divorced 1995); two s.; m. 2nd Candace Allen 1996; ed. Royal Acad. of Music; won John Player Int. Conducting Competition 1973; has conducted Bournemouth Symphony, Northern Sinfonia, London Philharmonic, London Sinfonietta, Berlin Philharmonic, Los Angeles Philharmonic, Stockholm Philharmonic, Vienna Philharmonic, Philadelphia Orchestra, Boston Symphony orchestras, etc.; début at Queen Elizabeth Hall, London 1974, Royal Festival Hall, London 1976, Royal Albert Hall, London 1976; Asst. Conductor, BBC Symphony Orchestra 1977; Assoc. Conductor, Royal Liverpool Philharmonic Soc. 1977–80; Glyndebourne début 1977, Royal Opera, Covent Garden début 1990; Artistic Dir., London Choral Soc. 1979–84; Prin. Conductor and Artistic Adviser, City of Birmingham Symphony Orchestra (CBSO) 1980–90, Music Dir. 1990–98; Artistic Dir. South Bank summer music 1981–83; Jt. Artistic Dir. Aldeburgh Festival 1982–93; Prin. Guest Conductor, Los Angeles Philharmonic 1981–94, Rotterdam Philharmonic 1981–84; Prin. Guest Conductor Orchestra of the Age of Enlightenment 1992–; more than 30 recordings with CBSO; Hon. D.Mus. (Liverpool) 1991, (Leeds) 1993; Hon. Fellow St. Anne's Coll. Oxford 1991; Edison Award (for recording of Shostakovich's Symphony no. 10) 1987, Grand Prix du Disque (Turangalîla Symphony) 1988, Grand Prix Caecilia (Turangalîla Symphony, Jazz Album) 1988, Gramophone Record of the Year Award (Mahler's Symphony no. 2) 1988, Gramophone Opera Award (Porgy and Bess) 1989, Int. Record Critics' Award (Porgy and Bess) 1990, Grand Prix de l'Acad. Charles Cros 1990, Gramophone Artist of the Year 1993, Montblanc de la Culture Award 1993, Toepfer Foundation Shakespeare Prize (Hamburg) 1996, Gramophone Award for Best Concerto recording (Szymanowski Violin Concertos Nos. 1 and 2), Albert Medal (R.S.A.) 1997, Choc de l'Année Award (for recording of Brahms Piano Concerto op. 15) 1998; Officier des Arts et des Lettres 1995. *Address:* c/o Askonas Holt Ltd., Lonsdale Chambers, 27 Chancery Lane, London, WC2A 1PF, England. *Telephone:* 0171-400 1700.

RATTNER, Steven Lawrence, A.B.; American financial executive; b. 5 July 1952, New York; s. of George Seymour Rattner and Selma Ann Silberman; m. P. Maureen White 1986; three s. one d.; ed. Brown Univ.; Asst. to James Reston, New York Times Corresp., Washington, New York and London 1974–82; Assoc. Vice-Pres. Lehman Brothers Kuhn Loeb, New York 1982–84; Assoc. Vice-Pres., Prin., Man. Dir. then Head communications group Morgan Stanley and Co., New York 1984–89; Man. Dir. then Head communications group Lazard Frères and Co. 1989–97, Deputy C.E.O. 1997–; Dir. Falcon Cable Holding Group 1993–; Trustee Brown Univ. 1987–93, 1994–, Educational Broadcasting Corpn. 1990– (Vice-Chair. 1994–), Metropolitan Museum of Art 1996–; Dir. New York Outward Bound Center 1990–; Harvey Baker Fellow, Brown Univ. 1974, Poynter Fellow Yale Univ. 1979; mem. Council on Foreign Relations, assoc. mem. Royal Inst. for Int. Affairs. *Publications:* contribs. to various news publs. including New York Times, Wall Street Journal, Los Angeles Times, Newsweek. *Address:* 998 Fifth Avenue, New York, NY 10028, U.S.A. (Home).

RATUSHINSKAYA, Irina Borisovna; Russian poet; b. 4 March 1954; m. Igor Gerashchenko 1979; ed. Odessa Pedagogical Inst.; teacher Odessa Pedagogical Inst. 1976–83; arrested with husband, Moscow 1981; lost job, arrested again, 17 Sept. 1982, convicted of 'subverting the Soviet régime' and sentenced 5 March 1983 to seven years' hard labour; strict régime concentration camp Aug. 1983, released Sept. 1986; settled in U.K. 1986–; f. Democracy and Independence Group April 1989–; poetry appeared in samizdat publs., West European Russian language journals, translations in American and British press and in U.S.S.R. 1989–. *Publications include:* Poems (trilingual text) 1984, No, I'm Not Afraid 1986, Off Limits (in Russian) 1986, I Shall Live to See It (in Russian) 1986, Grey Is the Colour of Hope 1989, In the Beginning 1990, The Odessans 1992. *Address:* c/o Vargius Publishing Houses, Kuzakova str. 18, 107005 Moscow, Russia. *Telephone:* (095) 785-09-62.

RATZINGER, H.E. Cardinal Joseph Alois; German ecclesiastic; b. 16 April 1927, Marktl; s. of Joseph Ratzinger and Maria Peintner; ed. Univ. of Munich; Chaplain 1951; Prof. of Theology, Freising 1958, Bonn 1959, Münster 1963, Tübingen 1966, Regensburg 1969; Archbishop 1977; Cardinal

1977; Archbishop of München-Freising; Titular Bishop of Velletri–Segni; Chair. Bavarian Bishops' Conf.; Prefect, Sacred Congregation for the Doctrine of the Faith Nov. 1981–; Pres. Int. Theological Comm., Pontifical Biblical Comm.; mem. Secr. Synod of Catholic Bishops 1983–; mem. Congregation for Public Worship 1985–. *Publications:* books and articles on theological matters. *Address:* Palazzo del S. Uffizio II, 00193 Rome, Italy. *Telephone:* (6) 6988-3357. *Fax:* (6) 6988-3409.

RAU, Johannes; German politician; b. 16 Jan. 1931, Wuppertal; s. of Ewald and Helene (Hartmann) Rau; m. Christina Delius 1982; one s. two d.; mem. North Rhine-Westphalian Diet 1958–, Minister-Pres. North Rhine-Westphalian Land 1978–98; Chair. North Rhine-Westphalian Parl. Group Social Democratic Party (SPD) 1967–70, mem. Exec. Bd. 1968–, Chair. Dist. Bd. 1977–, mem. Presidency 1978–, Deputy Chair. 1982–; Pres. Bundesrat 1982–83, 1994–95; Lord Mayor, City of Wuppertal 1969–70; Minister of Science and Research, North Rhine-Westphalia 1970–78; Dr. h.c. (Düsseldorf) 1985, (Open Univ.) 1986, (Haifa) 1986, (Theological Acad. Budapest of the Reformed Church, Hungary) 1987; D.Theol. (Bochum) 1997; Grand Cross Order of Merit of Fed. Repub. of Germany and decorations from other countries. *Publications:* Oberstufenreform und Gesamthochschule 1970 (co-author), Die neue Fernuniversität 1974. *Leisure interests:* stamp-collecting, especially Israeli stamps, literature, art. *Address:* Haroldstrasse 2, 40213 Düsseldorf, Germany. *Telephone:* (0211) 83701.

RAU, Santha Rama (see Rama Rau, Santha).

RAUSCH, Jean-Marie Victor Alphonse; French politician; b. 24 Sept. 1929, Sarreguemines, Moselle; s. of Victor Rausch and Claire Hessemann; m. 2nd Nadine Haven 1980; two s. by first m.; ed. Lycée de Sarreguemines and Ecole française de meunerie, Paris; Dir. Moulin Rausch, Woippy 1953–76; Admin. Soc. Anonyme des Moulins Rausch, Woippy 1976–77; Pres. departmental milling syndicate 1967–81; Pres. Millers' Union of Moselle 1974–80; Conseiller-Gen. Metz III 1971, 1976, 1982–88, Pres. of Council 1979–82; Mayor of Metz 1971–; Pres. Lorraine Regional Council 1982–92; mem. Nat. Statistical Council 1979, Conseil Nat. du Crédit 1984; numerous other civic, public and professional appts.; Minister of Foreign Trade 1988–91, of Foreign Trade and Tourism 1990–91, of Posts and Telecommunications 1991–92; Deputy Minister attached to Minister of Econ. and Finance in charge of Commerce and Labour April–Oct. 1992; Senator (Moselle) 1974–83, 1983–88, 1992–; Pres. Médiaville 1995–, Metz-interactive 1995–; Grand Prix de la littérature micro-informatique 1987. *Publication:* Le laminoir et la puce: la troisième génération industrielle 1987. *Leisure interests:* photography, skiing. *Address:* Sénat, Palais du Luxembourg, 75291 Paris cedex 06; Mairie de Metz, B.P. 21025, 57036 Metz Cedex (Office); 4 rue Chanoine Collin, 57000 Metz, France (Home). *Telephone:* 03.87.55.51.50. *Fax:* 03.87.74.73.80.

RAUSCHENBACH, Boris Viktorovich, D.TECH.SC.; Russian mechanical scientist; b. 18 Jan. 1915, St. Petersburg; s. of Victor Rauschenbach and Leontine Rauschenbach; m. Vera Ivanchenko 1941; two d.; ed. Leningrad Inst. of Civil Aviation Engs.; engineer Research Inst., Ministry of Armaments, sr. engineer aviation factory 1937–47; Chief of Div. Inst. No 1, Ministry of Aviation Industry 1948–60; Deputy Head Cen. Bureau of Experimental Machine Construction, Ministry of Gen. Tool Construction (Deputy of Sergey Korolev) 1960–74; Scientific Chief of Div. Research-Production enterprise Energia 1974–78; Head of Chair of Theoretical Mechanics, Prof. Moscow Inst. of Physics and Tech.; Corresp. mem. U.S.S.R. (now Russian) Acad. of Sciences 1966, mem. 1984; mem. Russian Acad. of Natural Sciences; Chair. Scientific Council History of World Culture, U.S.S.R Acad. of Sciences; Chair. Supervisory Bd., Russian Br. of The Open Soc. Inst. (New York); mem. Int. Acad. of Astronautics; one of leaders of movt. for restoring the rights of ethnic Germans living in Russia; Lenin Prize; Hero of Socialist Labour; B. Petrov Gold Medal. *Publications:* over a hundred scientific works on theory of automatic man., applied mechanics, eng. psychology, theory of instability, including Vibrational Burning, Management of Control of Space Vehicles, Space Vehicles, Spatial Constructions in Old Russian Painting, Theory and Perspectives. *Leisure interests:* history of art, theology. *Address:* Moscow Institute of Physics and Technology, Institutsky per. 9, 141700 Dolgoprudny, Moscow oblast, Russia. *Telephone:* (095) 408-78-66.

RAUSCHENBERG, Robert; American artist; b. 22 Oct. 1925, Port Arthur, Tex.; s. of Ernest and Dora Rauschenberg; m. Susan Weil 1950 (divorced 1952); one s.; ed. Kansas City Art Inst., Acad. Julien, Paris, Black Mountain Coll., North Carolina and Art Students League, New York; travel in Italy and North Africa 1952–53; Designer of stage-sets and costumes for Merce Cunningham Dance Co. 1955–65, lighting for Cunningham Co. 1961–65; costumes and sets for Paul Taylor Dance Co. 1957–59; Choreography in America 1962–; affiliated with Leo Castelli Gallery, New York City 1957–, Sonnabend Gallery, New York and Paris; works in Tate Gallery, London, Albright-Knox Gallery, Buffalo, Whitney Museum of American Art, New York City, Andrew Dickson White Museum, Cornell Univ., Museum of Modern Art, N.Y., Goucher Coll. Collection, Towson, Maryland, Cleveland Museum of Art, Cleveland, Ohio, Kunstsammlung, Noedheim, Westfalen, Germany, etc.; numerous one-man shows in U.S.A. and Europe; exhbn. at Stedelijk Museum, Amsterdam 1968; travelling retrospective exhbn. organized by Smithsonian Inst. Nat. Collection of Fine Art 1976–78, retrospective exhbn. Staatliches Kunstmuseum, Berlin 1980; mem. American Acad. and Inst. of Arts and Letters; First Prize Int. Exhbn. of Prints, Gallery of Modern Art, Ljubljana 1963, Venice Biennale 1964, Corcoran Biennial Contemporary American Painters 1965, Grammy Award 1984. *Address:* c/o Avanti Editions, 22 E 72nd Street, New York, N.Y. 10021, U.S.A.

RAVANELLI, Fabrizio; Italian footballer; b. 11 Dec. 1968, Perugia; forward; played for Perugia 1986–89, Avellino 1989, Casertana 1989–90, Reggiana 1990–92, Juventus 1992–96, Middlesbrough, U.K. 1996–97, for Italy 1995–, for Marseilles 1997–.

RAVEN, Peter Hamilton, PH.D.; American botanist, administrator and educator; b. 13 June 1936, Shanghai, China; s. of Walter Raven and Isabelle (née Breen) Raven; m. Tamra Engelhorn 1968; one s. three d.; ed. Univ. of California, Berkeley and Univ. of California, Los Angeles; Nat. Science Foundation Postdoctoral Fellow, British Museum, London 1960–61; Taxonomist, Rancho Santa Ana Botanical Garden, Claremont, Calif. 1961–62; Asst. Prof., then Assoc. Prof. of Biological Sciences, Stanford Univ. 1962–71; Dir. Mo. Botanical Garden 1971–, Engelmann Prof. of Botany, Washington Univ., St. Louis, Mo. 1976–; Adjunct Prof. of Biology, Univ. of Mo., St. Louis 1973–; Chair. Nat. Museum Services Bd. 1984–88; mem. Nat. Geographic Soc. Comm. on Research and Exploration 1982, Governing Bd. Nat. Research Council 1983–86, 1987–88, Bd. World Wildlife Fund (U.S.A.) 1983–88, N.A.S. Comm. on Human Rights 1984–87, Smithsonian Council 1985–90; Home Sec. N.A.S. 1987–95; Pres. Org. for Tropical Studies 1985–88; Fellow, American Acad. of Arts and Sciences, Calif. Acad. of Sciences, A.A.A.S., Linnean Soc. of London and John D. Raven and Catherine T. MacArthur Foundation Fellow, Univ. of Missouri 1985–90; Foreign mem. Royal Danish Acad. of Sciences and Letters, Royal Swedish Acad. of Sciences; several hon. degrees; Distinguished Service Award, American Inst. of Biological Sciences 1981; Int. Environmental Leadership Medal of UNEP 1982, Int. Prize in Biology, Japanese Govt.; other awards and prizes. *Publications:* Papers on Evolution (with Ehrlich and Holm) 1969, Biology of Plants 1970, Principles of Tzeltal Plant Classification 1974, Biology 1985, Modern Aspects of Species (with K. Iwatsuki and W. J. Bock) 1986, Understanding Biology (with G. Johnson) 1988; more than 400 professional papers; Ed.: Coevolution of Animals and Plants 1975, Topics in Plant Population Biology 1979, Advances in Legume Systematics 1981, Biology (with G. B. Johnson) 1986, Understanding Biology 1988; contribs. to many other publs. *Leisure interests:* reading, collecting plants. *Address:* Missouri Botanical Garden, P.O. Box 299, St. Louis, MO 63166-0299, U.S.A. *Telephone:* (314) 577-5111. *Fax:* (314) 577-9595.

RAVEN, Simon Arthur Noel, M.A.; British author; b. 28 Dec. 1927, London; s. of A. G. Raven and E. K. Raven (née Christmas); m. Susan Mandeville Kilner 1951 (marriage dissolved 1957); one s.; ed. Charterhouse, King's Coll., Cambridge; Nat. Service 1946–48, served with Parachute Regt. and Officer Training School, Bangalore; research at Cambridge Univ. 1948–52; Lieut. in King's Shropshire Light Infantry 1953, served in Fed. Repub. of Germany and Kenya (rank of Capt. 1956), resgnd. 1957; since 1957 has worked as novelist, critic and playwright. *Publications include:* novels: The Feathers of Death 1959, Alms for Oblivion (10 vol. sequence) 1964–76, Shadows on the Grass (autobiography) 1982, September Castle (novel) 1983, The First-Born of Egypt (7 vol. sequence) 1986–92, The Old School (memoirs) 1986, The Old Gang 1988, Bird of Ill Omen (Memoirs) 1989, "Is There Anybody There?" Said the Traveller (memoirs) 1991, The Islands of Sorrow 1994, Remember Your Grammar, and Other Haunted Stories; TV dramatizations: The Pallisers 1974, Edward and Mrs. Simpson 1978, The Blackheath Poisonings 1992, Remember Your Grammar, and Other Haunted Stories 1998. *Leisure interests:* travel, reading, cricket, horse racing. *Address:* c/o Curtis Brown, 28/29 Haymarket, London, SW1Y 4SF, England.

RAVENSDALE, 3rd Baron, cr. 1911; **Nicholas Mosley,** M.C.; British writer; s. of the late Sir Oswald Mosley and of Lady Cynthia Curzon; b. 25 June 1923; m. 1st Rosemary Salmond 1947 (divorced 1974, died 1991); three s. one d.; m. 2nd Verity Bailey (née Raymond) 1974; one s.; ed. Eton, Balliol Coll., Oxford. *Novels include:* Accident 1964, Impossible Object 1968, Natalie, Natalia 1971, Catastrophe Practice 1979 (three plays and a short novel), Hopeful Monsters (Whitbread Book of the Year 1990), Children of Darkness and Light 1996. *Biographies include:* Rules of the Game: Sir Oswald and Lady Cynthia Mosley 1896–1933 1982, Beyond the Pale 1933–1980 1983, Efforts at Truth (autobiog.) 1994. *Address:* 2 Gloucester Crescent, London, NW1 7DS, England.

RAVERA, Denis, LL.M.; Monegasque civil servant and sports official; b. 8 June 1948, Monaco; m.; one c.; joined Monaco Civil Service 1971, Sec. to Dept. of Public Works and Social Affairs 1971–79, Chief Sec. 1979–84, Dir.-Gen. 1984–91; Chef de Cabinet Minister of State 1991–; Sec.-Gen. Féd. Monégasque de la Natation, Conféd. Mondiale des Sports de Boules; Vice-Pres. Bobsleigh Section, Monaco Sports Asscn.; mem. Monaco Olympic Cttee.; Officier, Ordre de Saint-Charles, Légion d'honneur, Médaille en vermeil de l'Educ. Physique et des Sports. *Address:* Ministère de l'Etat, Monte Carlo, Monaco.

RAVITCH, Diane, PH.D.; American historian; b. 1 July 1938, Houston, Tex.; d. of Walter Cracker and Ann Celia (née Katz) Silvers; m. Richard Ravitch 1960 (divorced 1986); three s. (one deceased); ed. Wellesley Coll., and Columbia Univ.; Adjunct Asst. Prof. of History and Educ. Teachers' Coll., Columbia Univ. 1975–78, Assoc. Prof. 1978–83, Adjunct Prof. 1983–91; Dir. Woodrow Wilson Nat. Fellowship Foundation 1987–91; Chair. Educational Excellence Network 1988–91; Asst. Sec. Office of Research and Improvement Dept. of Educ., Washington 1991–93, Counsellor to Sec. of Educ.

1991–93; Visiting Fellow Brookings Inst. 1993–94; Sr. Research Scholar N.Y. Univ. 1994–98, Research Prof. 1998–; Adjunct Fellow Manhattan Inst. 1996–; Trustee New York Historical Soc. 1995–98; New York Council on the Humanities 1996–; mem numerous public policy bodies; Hon. D.Hum.Litt. (Williams Coll.) 1984, (Reed Coll.) 1985, (Amherst Coll.) 1986, (State Univ. of New York) 1988, (Ramopo Coll.) 1990, (St. Joseph's Coll., N.Y.) 1991; Hon. L.H.D. (Middlebury Coll.) 1997, (Union Coll.) 1998. *Publications:* The Great School Wars: New York City 1805–1973 1974, The Revisionists Revised 1978, The Troubled Crusade: American Education 1945–1980 1983, The Schools We Deserve 1985, What Do Our 17-Year-Olds Know? (with Chester E. Finn, Jr.) 1987, The American Reader (ed.) 1990, The Democracy Reader (ed. with Abigail Thernstrom) 1992, National Standards in American Education 1995, Debating the Future of American Education (ed.) 1995, Learning from the Past (ed. with Maris Vinovskis) 1995, New Schools for a New Century 1997 (ed. with Joseph Viteretti) 1997; 300 articles and reviews. *Address:* New York University, 26 Washington Place, New York, NY 10003, U.S.A. *Telephone:* (212) 998-5146.

RAVIV, Moshe; Israeli diplomatist; b. 1935, Bukovina, Romania; m.; two s. one d.; ed. Univ. of London; went to Israel 1948; entered diplomatic service 1961; Second Sec. London 1961, Minister, London 1983–88; has also served in Washington, DC and as Amb. to the Philippines; Deputy Dir.-Gen. responsible for information, Israeli Ministry of Foreign Affairs until 1993; Amb. to U.K. 1993–98. *Address:* c/o Ministry of Foreign Affairs, Hakirya, Romema, Jerusalem 91950, Israel.

RAVONY, Francisque; Malagasy politician; fmr. First Deputy Prime Minister, Transitional Govt.; Prime Minister of Madagascar 1993–95, also fmr. Minister of Finance and Budget; Leader Cttee. for the Support of Democracy and Devt. in Madagascar; Chair. Union des Forces Vivas Democratiques 1998–. *Address:* Union des Forces Vivas Democratiques, Antananarivo, Madagascar.

RAWIRI, Georges; Gabonese diplomatist and government official; b. 10 March 1932, Lambaréné, Gabon; m.; two c.; ed. Protestant school, Ngomo, and Lycée Jean-Baptiste Dumas, Ales.; Head Tech. Centre Garoua Radio Station 1957, Libreville Radio Station 1959; a founder of Radio Gabon 1959; Dir. Radiodiffusion Gabonaise 1960, Radio-Télévision Gabonaise 1963; Counsellor for Foreign Affairs 1963; Minister of Information, Tourism, Posts and Telecommunications 1963–64; Minister of State and Amb. to France 1964–71, also accred. to Israel, Italy, Spain, U.K., Malta 1965–71, and Switzerland 1967–71; Minister of State for Foreign Affairs and Co-operation 1971–74, of the Govt. Office 1974–75, of Transport 1975–79, Civil Aviation 1975–78 and the Merchant Navy 1975–79, Asst. to the Deputy Prime Minister 1978–79; Deputy Prime Minister, and Minister of Transport 1980–83, First Deputy Prime Minister 1986, Minister for Transport and Public Relations 1983–86, First Deputy Prime Minister, Minister of Rail, Road and Inland Water Transport, Water and Forest Resources and Social Communications 1986–89, Fisheries, Food Resources and Nat. Parks 1989–90; now Pres. Compagnie de Manutention et de Chalandage d'Owendo (COMACO); Grand Officer Ordre de l'Etoile Equatoriale and decorations from Mauritania, France, Malta and Côte d'Ivoire; Médaille d'Or des Arts, Sciences et Lettres; Grand Officier Ordre Int. du Bien Public. *Address:* COMACO, B.P. 2131, Libreville, Gabon.

RAWLINGS, Flight-Lieut. Jerry; Ghanaian Head of State and air force officer; b. 22 June 1947, Accra; s. of John Rawlings and Madam Victoria Agbotui; m. Nana Konadu Agyeman; one s. three d.; ed. Achimota School and Ghana Military Acad., Teshie; commissioned as Pilot Officer 1969, Flight-Lieut. 1978; arrested for leading mutiny of jr. officers May 1979; leader mil. coup which overthrew Govt. of Supreme Mil. Council June 1979; Chair. Armed Forces Revolutionary Council (Head of State) June-Sept. 1979; retd. from armed forces Nov. 1979, from air force Sept. 1992; leader mil. coup which overthrew Govt. of Dr. Hilla Limann (q.v.) Dec. 1981; Head of State Jan. 1982–; Chief of the Defence Staff Nov. 1982–; Chair. Provisional Nat. Defence Council 1981–Jan. 1993; elected Pres. of Ghana Nov. 1992, inaugurated Pres. Jan. 1993. *Leisure interests:* boxing, diving (deep sea), swimming, horse riding, carpentry. *Address:* P.O. Box 1627, Osu, Accra, Ghana. *Telephone:* 665415.

RAWLINS, Surgeon-Vice-Adm. Sir John Stuart Pepys, K.B.E., F.R.C.P., F.F.C.M., F.R.AE.S.; British consultant; b. 12 May 1922, Amesbury, Wilts.; s. of Col. Comdt. Stuart W. H. Rawlins and Dorothy P. Rawlins; m. Diana M. Freshney Colbeck 1944; one s. three d.; ed. Wellington Coll., Univ. Coll., Oxford and St. Bartholomew's Hosp., London; Surgeon-Lieut. R.N.V.R. 1947; Surgeon-Lieut. R.N., R.A.F. Inst. of Aviation Medicine 1951; R.N. Physiological Lab. 1957; Surgeon-Commdr. R.A.F. Inst. of Aviation Medicine 1961; H.M.S. Ark Royal 1964; US Naval Medical Research Inst. 1967–70; Surgeon-Capt. 1969; Surgeon-Cdre., Dir. of Health and Research (Naval) 1973; Surgeon-Rear-Adm. 1975; Dean of Naval Medicine and Medical Officer in charge of Inst. of Naval Medicine 1975–77; Acting Surgeon Vice-Adm. 1977; Medical Dir.-Gen. (Navy) 1977–80; Hon. Physician to H.M. The Queen 1975–80; Dir. Diving Unlimited Int. Ltd.; Pres. Soc. for Underwater Tech. 1980–84; Chair. Deep Ocean Tech. Inc., Deep Ocean Eng. Inc. 1982–90, Trident Underwater Systems Inc. 1986–, Gen. Offshore Corpn. (U.K.) Ltd. 1988–90, Europa Hosps. Ltd.; fmr. consultant to Chemical Defence Establishment, Porton Down and British Airways PLC; designed first anti-G suit accepted in R.N. and R.A.F., first protective helmet for R.N. and R.A.F. aircrew, designed and developed an aircraft underwater escape system; Hon. Research Fellow, Univ. of Lancaster, Univ. Coll., Oxford; Hon. D.Tech., Robert Gordon Univ.; numerous awards and medals including Royal Navy's Man of the Year 1964, Gilbert Blane Medal (Royal Coll. of Surgeons) 1971, Chadwick Naval Prize 1975, Nobel Award of Inst. of Explosive Engineers 1987. *Publications:* numerous papers in fields of aviation and diving medicine and underwater tech. *Leisure interests:* fishing, stalking, riding, judo. *Address:* Little Cross, Holne, Newton Abbot, South Devon, TQ13 7RS, England. *Telephone:* (01364) 631-249. *Fax:* (01364) 631-400.

RAWLINS, Peter Jonathan, M.A., F.C.A., F.R.S.A.; British business executive and accountant; b. 30 April 1951, London; s. of Kenneth Raymond Ivan Rawlins and Constance Amande Malzy; m. Louise Langton 1973; one s. one d.; ed. St. Edward's School and Keble Coll. Oxford; with Arthur Andersen & Co., Chartered Accountants, London 1972–85, partner 1983–85; seconded as Personal Asst. to C.E.O. and Deputy Chair. Lloyd's of London 1983–84; Dir. Sturge Holdings PLC 1985–89, Man. Dir. R. W. Sturge & Co. 1985–89, Dir. Sturge Lloyd's Agencies Ltd. 1986–89; Dir. Wise Speke Holdings Ltd. 1987–89; C.E.O. The London Stock Exchange 1989–93; business strategy consultant 1994–; Man. Dir. (Europe, Middle East and Africa) Siegel & Gale Ltd. 1996–; Dir. Scala Business Solutions NV 1998–. *Leisure interests:* the performing arts, tennis, squash, shooting, travelling. *Address:* 70A Redcliffe Gardens, London, SW10 9HE, England. *Telephone:* 0171-370 0666. *Fax:* 0171-341 9691.

RAWLINSON OF EWELL, Baron (Life Peer), cr. 1978, of Ewell in the County of Surrey; **Peter Anthony Grayson Rawlinson,** Kt., P.C., Q.C.; British politician and lawyer; b. 26 June 1919, Birkenhead, Cheshire (now Merseyside); s. of Lieut.-Col. A. R. Rawlinson and Ailsa Grayson Rawlinson; m. 1st Haidee Kavanagh 1940; three d.; m. 2nd Elaine Angela Dominguez 1954; two s. one d.; ed. Downside and Christ's Coll., Cambridge; served in Irish Guards 1939–46; mentioned in despatches 1943; called to the Bar, Inner Temple 1946, Treas. 1984; mem. of Parl. 1955–78; Recorder of Salisbury 1961–62; Solicitor-Gen. 1962–64; mem. Bar Council 1966–68; Attorney-Gen. 1970–74; Attorney-Gen., Northern Ireland 1972–74; Leader Western Circuit 1975–82; mem. Senate, Inns of Court 1968; Chair. of the Bar 1975–76; Chair. of Senate, Inns of Court and Bar 1975–76, Pres. 1986–87; Recorder of Kingston-upon-Thames 1975–; Dir. Daily Telegraph PLC 1985; Hon. mem. American Bar Asscn.; Hon. Fellow, Christ's Coll., Cambridge, American Coll. of Trial Lawyers; Conservative. *Publications:* War Poems and Poetry today 1943, Public Duty and Personal Faith—the example of Thomas More 1978, A Price Too High (autobiog.) 1989, The Jesuit Factor: A Personal Investigation 1990, The Colombia Syndicate (novel) 1991, Hatred and Contempt (novel) 1992, His Brother's Keeper (novel) 1993, Indictment for Murder (novel) 1994, The Caverel Claim (novel) 1998. *Leisure interest:* painting. *Address:* Wardour Castle, Tisbury, Wilts., SP3 6RH, England. *Telephone:* (01747) 871900.

RAWNSLEY, Andrew Nicholas James, M.A.; British journalist; b. 5 Jan. 1962; s. of Eric Rawnsley and Barbara Rawnsley (née Butler); m. Jane Leslie Hall 1990; three d.; ed. Rugby School, Sidney Sussex Coll. Cambridge; with BBC 1983–85, The Guardian 1985–93 (political columnist 1987–93); Assoc. Ed. and political columnist The Observer 1993–; Presenter Channel 4 TV series A Week in Politics 1989–97, ITV series The Agenda 1996–, Bye Bye Blues 1997, Blair's Year 1998, The Westminster Hour (radio) 1998–; Student Journalist of the Year 1983, Young Journalist of the Year 1987. *Leisure interest:* House of Commons. *Address:* The Observer, 119 Farringdon Road, Farringdon, London, EC1R 3ER, England. *Telephone:* 0171-278 2332.

RAWSON, Jessica Mary, C.B.E., F.B.A.; British archaeologist and college warden; b. 20 Jan. 1943; d. of Roger Quirk and Paula Quirk; m. John Rawson 1968; one d.; ed. New Hall, Cambridge and Univ. of London; Asst. Prin. Ministry of Health 1965–67; Asst. Keeper II, Dept. of Oriental Antiquities, British Museum 1967–71, Asst. Keeper I 1971–76, Deputy Keeper 1976–87, Keeper 1987–94; Warden, Merton Coll. Oxford 1994–; Visiting Prof. Kunsthistorisches Inst. Heidelberg 1989, Univ. of Chicago 1994; Chair. Oriental Ceramic Soc. 1993–96; Hon. D.Sc. (St. Andrews) 1997; Hon. D.Litt. (Sussex) 1998, (Royal Holloway, London) 1998. *Publications:* Chinese Jade Throughout the Ages (with J. Ayers) 1975, Animals in Art 1977, Ancient China, Art and Archaeology 1980, Chinese Ornament: the lotus and the dragon 1984, Chinese Bronzes: art and ritual 1987, The Bella and P.P. Chiu Collection of Ancient Chinese Bronzes 1988, Western Zhou Ritual Bronzes from the Arthur M. Sackler Collections 1990, Ancient Chinese and Ordos Bronzes (with E. Bunker) 1990, The British Museum Book of Chinese Art (ed.) 1992, Chinese Jade from the Neolithic to the Qing 1995, the Mysteries of Ancient China (ed.) 1996. *Address:* Merton College, Oxford, OX1 4JD, England. *Telephone:* (01865) 276352. *Fax:* (01865) 276282.

RAY, Ajit Nath, M.A.; Indian judge; b. 29 Jan. 1912, Calcutta; s. of Sati Nath Ray and Kali Kumari Debi; m. Himani Mukherjee 1944; one s.; ed. Presidency Coll., Calcutta, Oriel Coll., Oxford and Gray's Inn, London; fmrly. practised as a barrister, Calcutta High Court; Judge, Calcutta High Court 1957–69; Judge, Supreme Court of India 1969–73, Chief Justice of India 1973–77; Hon. Fellow, Oriel Coll., Oxford; Pres. Int. Law Asscn. 1974–76, Vice-Pres. 1977–, Vice-Pres. Ramakrishna Inst. of Culture 1981–; mem. Int. Permanent Court of Arbitration 1976–; Pres. Governing Body Presidency Coll., Calcutta 1957–69; Founder-Pres. Soc. for the Welfare of the Blind 1958–80; Treas. Asiatic Soc. 1961–63, Vice-Pres. 1963–65; mem. Karma

Samiti Visva Bharati Santiniketan 1963–65, 1967–69, Life mem. 1969–. *Address:* 15 Panditia Place, Calcutta 700 029, India. *Telephone:* 475-5213.

RAY, Robert Francis; Australian politician; b. 8 April 1947, Melbourne; m. Jane Ray; ed. Rushden State Coll.; fmr. tech. school teacher; Senator from Victoria 1980–; mem. Australian Labor Party (ALP) Nat. Exec. 1983–98; Minister for Home Affairs and Deputy Man. of Govt. Business in the Senate 1987–88, for Transport and Communications Jan.-Sept. 1988, for Immigration, Local Govt. and Ethnic Affairs and Minister assisting Prime Minister for Multicultural Affairs 1988–90, for Defence 1990–96; Deputy Leader of Govt. in Senate 1993–96. *Leisure interests:* films, billiards, tennis, watching Australian Rules football, golf and cricket. *Address:* Suite 3, Level 2, Illoura Plaza, 424 St. Kilda Road, Melbourne, Vic. 3004, Australia.

RAY, Siddhartha Shankar; Indian politician and lawyer; b. 20 Oct. 1920, Calcutta; s. of the late Sudhir Chandra Ray and Shrimati Aparna Devi (Das); m. Maya Bhattacharya 1947; ed. Presidency Coll., Univ. Law Coll., Calcutta; called to the Bar, Inner Temple, London; Sr. Advocate, Supreme Court 1969; corporate, commercial and constitutional lawyer; appeared in all Courts in India including the Supreme Court, the East Pakistan High Court, the Pakistan Supreme Court (Dacca Circuit Bench) and Tribunal of Arbitration, Int. Chamber of Commerce, Paris; mem. West Bengal Legis. Ass. 1957–71, 1972–77, 1991–92; mem. Lok Sabha 1971–72, Jr. Cen. Govt. Counsel 1954–57; Minister of Law and Tribal Welfare, Govt. of West Bengal 1957–58; Leader of the Opposition, West Bengal Ass. 1969–71, 1991–92; Cabinet Minister for Educ., Culture, Social Welfare and West Bengal Affairs, Govt. of India 1971–72; Chief Minister of West Bengal 1972–77; Gov. of Punjab and Admin. of Chandigarh 1986–89; Amb. to U.S.A. 1992–; High Commr. in the Commonwealth of the Bahamas 1994–; Gen. Sec. Calcutta Univ. Law Coll. Union 1941–43; Under-Sec. Calcutta Univ. Inst. 1941–44; Univ. Blue in cricket, football and tennis; Individual Champion Athletics, Calcutta Univ. Law Coll. 1941, 1942; mem. Working Cttee. Indian Nat. Congress, All India Congress Cttee., Congress Parl. Bd.; Pres. Cricket Asscn. of Bengal 1982–84; mem. Indian Nat. Trust for Art and Cultural Heritage; Trustee Jawaharlal Nehru Memorial Fund (mem. Exec. Cttee.); Trustee Nehru Scholarship Trust for Cambridge Univ.; Hon. LL.D. (Drury Coll., Missouri) 1993. *Leisure interests:* reading, music and sports. *Address:* Indian Embassy, 2107 Massachusetts Avenue, N.W., Washington, DC 20008, U.S.A; 2 Beltala Road, Calcutta 700026, India (Home). *Telephone:* (202) 939-7010 (U.S.A.); 4753465 (Calcutta).

RAYES, Ghazi al; Kuwaiti diplomatist; b. 23 Aug. 1935; ed. Univ. of Cairo, Egypt; Third Sec. Ministry of Foreign Affairs 1962; Kuwaiti Embassy, Washington and Beirut 1965–67; Chair. Int. Affairs Section, Ministry of Foreign Affairs 1967–70; Counsellor, Kuwaiti Embassy, Beirut 1970–73; Amb. to Bahrain 1974–80, to United Kingdom 1980–93, to People's Repub. of China 1993–97; Head, Follow-up and Co-ordination Office and Head, Protocol Dept., Ministry of Foreign Affairs 1997–. *Address:* c/o Ministry of Foreign Affairs, P.O. Box 3, 13001 Safat Gulf Street, Kuwait City, Kuwait.

RAYMOND, Lee R., PH.D.; American oil company executive; b. 13 Aug. 1938, Watertown, South Dakota; m. Charlene Raymond 1960; ed. Univ. of Wisconsin, Univ. of Minnesota; various eng. positions Exxon Corpn., Tulsa, Houston, New York and Caracas, Venezuela 1963–72, Man. Planning, Int. Co. Div., New York 1972–75, Pres. Exxon Nuclear Co. Div. 1979–81, Exec. Vice-Pres. Exxon Enterprises Inc. Div. 1981–83, Sr. Vice-Pres. and Dir. Exxon Corp. 1984–86, Pres. and Dir. 1987–93, Chair. and C.E.O. 1993–; Vice-Pres. Lago Oil, Netherlands Antilles 1975–76, Pres. and Dir. 1976–79; Pres. and Dir. Esso Inter-American Inc., Coral Gables, Fla. 1983–84, Sr. Vice-Pres. and Dir. 1984–; mem. Bd. Dirs. J. P. Morgan & Co. Inc., New York, Morgan Guaranty Trust Co. of New York, American Petroleum Inst.; mem. Bd. Dirs. Nat. Action Council for Minorities in Eng. Inc., New York 1985–, New American Schools Devt. Corpn. 1991–, Project Shelter PRO-AM 1991–; mem. American Petroleum Inst. (mem. Bd. Dirs. 1987–), The Business Roundtable, American Council on Germany 1986–, British-N. American Cttee. 1985–, Visitors' Cttee. Univ. of Wis. Dept. of Chem. Eng. 1987–, Dallas Cttee. on Foreign Relations 1988–, The Conf. Bd. 1991–, Bd. of Govs., Dallas Symphony Asscn. *Address:* Exxon Corporation, 225 East John W. Carpenter Freeway, Irving, TX 75062, U.S.A.

RAYMOND, Paul; British publisher, impresario and property owner; b. 15 Nov. 1925; one s. one d. (deceased); ed. St. Francis Xaviers Coll. Liverpool, Glossop Grammar School, Derbyshire; with R.A.F. 1944–47; musician, impresario, night club proprietor; owner Raymond's Review Bar, numerous cen. London properties; publr. Mayfair, Men Only, Club Int., Men's World, Razzle, Escort, Model Directory; mem. Grand Order of Water Rats. *Address:* Paul Raymond Organisation Ltd., 2 Archer Street, London, W1V 7HF, England. *Telephone:* 0171-292 8022. *Fax:* 0171-734 5030.

RAYNAUD, Jean-Pierre; French sculptor; b. 20 April 1939, Courbevoie; s. of André Raynaud and Madeleine Dumay; ed. Ecole d'Horticulture du Chesnay; first one-man exhbn. Galerie Larcade, Paris 1965; numerous other one-man shows in France, Europe, U.S.A., Japan, Israel; retrospective exhbns. The Menil Collection, Houston, Museum of Contemporary Art, Chicago and Int. Centre of Contemporary Art, Montréal 1991, CAPC, Bordeaux 1993; work includes windows at Cistercian Abbey at Noirlac, Cher 1976–77; large sculpture in gardens of Fondation Cartier pour l'Art Contemporain, Jouy-en-Josas 1985; Autoportrait for City of Québec 1987; Container Zero, Pompidou Centre, Paris 1988; Carte du Ciel, Grande Arche, Paris La Défense 1989; Grand Prix National de Sculpture 1983; Prix Robert Giron, Palais des Beaux Arts, Brussels 1985; Grand Prix de Sculpture de la Ville de Paris 1986, Prix d'honneur de la Biennale de Venise 1993; Officier des Arts et des Lettres, Chevalier du Mérite, Légion d'honneur. *Address:* 50 rue Yvan Tourgueniev, 78380 Bougival, France.

RAYNAUD, Pierre; French health inspector; b. 20 Oct. 1917, Paris; s. of Clément Raynaud and Lucienne Massinon; m. Denise Mouton 1940; one s. one d.; Dir. of hosps. 1945–63; Adviser to Ministry of Health 1956–58; expert in int. tech. co-operation 1962–68; Deputy Insp.-Gen. of Health 1963–71, Insp.-Gen. 1971–80; Pres. Fed. Hospitalière de France 1980–88, Hon. Pres. 1988–; founder, Hosp. Cttee. of the EC; Commdr., Légion d'honneur, Commdr. Ordre Nat. du Mérite, Officier de la santé publique. *Publications:* Histoire des hôpitaux en France 1982. *Leisure interest:* collecting books. *Address:* 6 square Angiviller, 78120 Rambouillet, France. *Telephone:* (1) 34-83-11-23.

RAYNE, Baron (Life Peer), cr. 1976, of Prince's Meadow in Greater London; **Max Rayne,** Kt.; British company director; b. 8 Feb. 1918, London; s. of Phillip Rayne and Deborah Rayne; m. 1st Margaret Marco 1941 (marriage dissolved 1960); one s. two d.; m. 2nd Lady Jane Antonia Frances Vane-Tempest-Stewart 1965; two s. two d.; ed. Cen. Foundation School and Univ. Coll., London; Royal Air Force 1940–45; Chair. London Merchant Securities PLC 1960–; Deputy Chair. British Lion Films 1967–72; Deputy Chair. First Leisure Corpn. PLC 1984–92, Chair. 1992–95; Dir. Housing Corpn. (1974) Ltd. 1974–78, dir. of other cos.; Gov. St. Thomas's Hospital 1962–74, Special Trustee 1974–92; Gov. Royal Ballet School 1966–79, Malvern Coll. 1966–, Centre for Environmental Studies 1967–73; mem. Gen. Council King Edward VII's Hospital Fund for London 1966–95; mem. Council St. Thomas's Hospital Medical School 1965–82, Council of Govs., United Medical Schools of Guy's and St. Thomas's Hospitals 1982–89; mem. RADA Council 1973–, South Bank Bd. 1986–92; Chair. London Festival Ballet Trust 1967–75, Nat. Theatre Bd. (now Royal Nat. Theatre Bd.) 1971–88; f. Patron Rayne Foundation 1962–; f. mem. Motability 1979–96, Life Vice-Pres. 1996; Trustee Henry Moore Foundation 1988–; Hon. Vice-Pres. Jewish Care (fmrly. Jewish Welfare Bd.) 1966–; Vice-Pres. Yehudi Menuhin School 1987– (Gov. 1966–87); Hon. Fellow, Univ. Coll., London 1966, London School of Econs. 1974, Darwin Coll., Cambridge 1966, Royal Coll. of Psychiatrists 1977, King's Coll. Hosp. Medical School 1980, Univ. Coll. Oxford 1982, King's Coll., London 1983, Westminster School 1989, Royal Coll. of Physicians 1992, UMDS, Guy's and St. Thomas's 1992; Hon. LL.D., (London) 1968; Officier, Légion d'honneur 1987. *Address:* 33 Robert Adam Street, London, W1M 5AH, England. *Telephone:* 0171-935 3555.

RAYNES, Edward Peter, M.A., PH.D., F.R.S.; British physicist; b. 4 July 1945, York; s. of Edward Gordon Raynes and Ethel Mary Raynes; m. Madeline Ord 1970; two s.; ed. St. Peter's School, York, Gonville and Caius Coll. and the Cavendish Lab., Cambridge; with Royal Signals and Radar Establishment, Malvern 1971–92, Deputy Chief Scientific Officer 1988–92; Chief Scientist Sharp Laboratories of Europe Ltd. 1992–, Dir. of Research 1995–; Visiting Prof., Dept. of Eng. Science, Univ. of Oxford 1996–98, Prof. of Optoelectronic Eng. 1998–; Rank Opto-Electronic Prize 1980, Paterson Medal, Inst. of Physics 1986, Special Recognition Award, Soc. of Information Display 1987. *Publications:* numerous scientific publs. and patents; The Physics, Chemistry and Applications of Liquid Crystals (Jt. Ed.). *Leisure interests:* choral and solo singing. *Address:* Department of Engineering Science, University of Oxford, Parks Road, Oxford, OX1 3PJ, England. *Telephone:* (01865) 273024. *Fax:* (01865) 273905.

RAZ, Joseph, D.PHIL., F.B.A.; professor of the philosophy of law; b. 21 March 1939; ed. Hebrew Univ. Jerusalem and Univ. of Oxford; lecturer, Faculty of Law and Dept. of Philosophy, Hebrew Univ. 1967–71, Sr. lecturer 1971–72; Fellow and Tutor in Law, Balliol Coll. Oxford 1972–85, also mem. sub-faculty of philosophy 1977–; Ed. (with Prof. A. M. Honoré), The Clarendon Law Series 1984–92; Prof. of Philosophy of Law, Univ. of Oxford and Fellow, Balliol Coll. 1985–; Visiting Prof., School of Law, Columbia Univ., New York 1995–; Foreign hon. mem. American Acad. of Arts and Sciences; Dr. h.c. (Katholieke Univ. Brussels) 1994. *Publications:* The Concept of a Legal System 1970, Practical Reason and Norms 1975, The Authority of Law 1979, The Morality of Freedom 1986, Ethics in the Public Domain 1994. *Address:* Balliol College, Oxford, OX1 3BJ, England. *Telephone:* (01865) 277721. *Fax:* (01865) 277803.

RAZAFINDRATANDRA, H.E. Cardinal Armand Gaétan; Malagasy ecclesiastic; b. 7 Aug. 1925; ed. Inst. Catholique de Paris; ordained priest 1954; parochial and teaching assignments; consecrated Bishop of Majunga 1978; Archbishop of Antananarivo 1994–; Pres. Bishops' Conf. of Madagascar; mem. Sec.-Gen.'s Special Council for Africa; Congregation for Evangelization of Peoples, Pontifical Council for the Laity; cr. Cardinal 1994; Cardinal-Priest, Basilica of Saint Sylvester and Saint Martin of the Hills, Rome 1994. *Address:* Archevêché, Andohalo, 101 Antananarivo, Madagascar. *Telephone:* (2) 20726.

RAZAK, Dato Sri Mohamad Najib bin tun Haj Abdul, B.A.; Malaysian politician; b. 23 July 1954, Kuala Lipis, Pahang; m. Tengku Puteri Zainah bint Tengku Iskandar; three c.; ed. Univ. of Nottingham; Exec. Patronas 1974–78; Pengerusi Majuternak 1977–78; M.P. 1976–; Deputy Minister of Energy, Telecommunications and Posts 1978–80, of Educ. 1980–81, of Finance 1981–82; mem. State Ass. for Pakan constituency 1982; apptd. Menteri

Besar Pahang 1982; Minister of Youth and Sports 1986–90; mem. UMNO Supreme Council 1981–; Vice-Pres. UMNO Youth 1982–; Chair. Pahang Foundation 1982–86. *Address:* c/o Ministry of Culture, Youth and Sports, 15th Floor, Wisma Keramat, Jalan Gurney, 50570 Kuala Lumpur, Malaysia.

RAZALEIGH HAMZAH, Tengku Tan Sri Datuk, P.S.M., S.P.M.K.; Malaysian politician and fmr. company executive; b. c. 1936; s. of late Tengku Mohamed Hamzah bin Zainal Abidin (fmr. Chief Minister of Kelantan); ed. Queen's Univ., Belfast, and Lincoln's Inn, London; Chair. of Kelantan Div. of United Malays' Nat. Org. (UMNO) in early 1960s; mem. Kelantan State Assembly for some years; Exec. Dir. Bank Bumiputra 1963, Chair., Man. Dir. 1970; Exec. Dir. PERNAS 1971–74; Chair. Malaysian Nat. Insurance; led trade mission to Beijing 1971; a Vice-Pres. UMNO 1975; Pres. Assoc. Malay Chambers of Commerce until Oct. 1976; Chair. PETRONAS (Nat. Oil Co.) 1974–76; Minister of Finance 1976–84, of Trade and Industry 1984–87; Chair. IMF Meetings 1978, Asram Devt. Bank 1977–, Islamic Devt. Bank 1977.

REA, Stephen; actor; b. 1949, Belfast, Northern Ireland; m. Dolours Price 1983; two s.; ed. Queen's Univ., Belfast; formed (with Brian Friel, q.v.) Field Day Theatre Co. 1980. *Stage appearances include:* The Shadow of a Gunman, The Cherry Orchard, Miss Julie, High Society, Endgame, The Freedom of the City, Translations, Communication Card, St. Oscar, Boesman and Lena, Hightime and Riot Act, Double Cross, Pentecost, Making History, Someone Who'll Watch Over Me 1992 (Broadway, New York), Uncle Vanya 1995 (Broadway); *directed:* Three Sisters, The Cure at Troy. *Films include:* Angel 1982, Danny Boy 1984, Company of Wolves 1985, The Doctor and the Devils 1985, Loose Connections 1988, Life is Sweet 1991, The Crying Game 1992, Bad Behavior 1993, Princess Caraboo 1993, Angie 1994, Interview with the Vampire 1994, Prêt-à-Porter 1994, All Men are Mortal 1994, Citizen X 1994, The Devil and the Deep Blue Sea 1994, The Butcher Boy 1998; *TV appearances include:* Four Days in July, Lost Belongings, Scout, St. Oscar, Not with a Bang, Hedda Gabler, Crime of the Century. *Address:* c/o Peters, Fraser & Dunlop Ltd., 503 The Chambers, Lots Road, Chelsea Harbour, London, SW10 0XF, England.

READ, Sir John Emms, Kt., F.C.A., F.I.B.; British business executive (retd.); b. 29 March 1918, Brighton; s. of William E. Read and Daysie E. (née Cooper) Read; m. Dorothy M. Berry 1942; two s.; ed. Brighton, Hove and Sussex Grammar School and Admin. Staff Coll., Henley-on-Thames; Commdr. Royal Navy 1939–46; Adm.'s Sec. to Asst. Chief of Naval Staff, Admiralty 1942–45, Naval Sec., British Admiralty Tech. Mission, Ottawa 1945–46; Ford Motor Co. 1946–64, Dir. of Sales 1961–64; Exec. Dir. EMI Ltd. 1965, Man. Dir. 1966–69, C.E.O. 1969–79, Deputy Chair. 1973–74, Chair. 1974–79; Deputy Chair. Thorn EMI Ltd. 1979–80, Dir. 1981–87; Chair. Trustee Savings Bank Cen. Bd. 1980–88, Trustee Savings Banks (Holdings) Ltd. 1980–86, TSB England and Wales 1983–86, TSB Group PLC 1986–88, (Dir. TSB England and Wales PLC 1986–88), United Dominions Trust Ltd. 1981–85; Dir. Dunlop Holdings Ltd. 1971–84, Thames Television Ltd. 1973–88 (Deputy Chair. 1981–88), Capitol Industries-EMI Inc., U.S.A. 1970–83, Wonderworld PLC 1986–97, FI Group PLC 1989–94, Nat. Youth Film Foundation 1987–90, Cadmus Investment Man. Ltd. 1993–98, Cafman Ltd. (now Cafcash) 1994–, Cafinvest Ltd. 1994–96; mem. P.O. Bd. 1975–77, Royal Naval Film Corpn. 1975–83, British Overseas Trade Bd. 1976–79; Chair. Electronics Econ. Devt. Comm. 1976–80, Armed Forces Pay Review Body 1976–83, Nat. Electronics Council 1977–80, Gov. Admin. Staff Coll., Henley 1974–92; mem. Council of CBI 1977–89, President's Cttee. 1977–84, Chair. Finance Cttee. 1978–84; Trustee, Westminster Abbey Trust 1978–87, Charity Aid Foundation 1985– (Pres. 1994–98), Crimestoppers Trust 1987–; Chair. Cttee. of Man. Inst. of Neurology 1980–97, Brain Research Trust 1982–; Pres. Sussex Asscn. of Boys' Clubs 1982–97, Cheshire Homes, Seven Rivers, Essex 1979–85; Vice-Pres. Inst. of Bankers 1982–89; mem. Cttee. of London and Scottish Bankers 1986–88; mem. Governing Body, British Postgraduate Medical Fed. 1982–96; Fellow, R.S.A. 1975–90; Companion, Inst. of Radio Engineers, B.I.M.; Hon. Fellow Henley Man. Coll.; Hon. D. Univ. (Surrey) 1987. *Leisure interests:* music, the arts, sport. *Address:* 41 Portman Square, London, W1H 9FH, England (Office). *Telephone:* 0171-935 7888 (Office).

READ, Piers Paul, M.A., F.R.S.L.; British writer; b. 7 March 1941, Beaconsfield; s. of Herbert Edward Read and Margaret Ludwig; m. Emily Albertine Boothby 1967; two s. two d.; ed. Ampleforth Coll., York and St. John's Coll., Cambridge; Artist-in-Residence, Ford Foundation, W. Berlin 1964; Sub-Ed. Times Literary Supplement, London 1965; Harkness Fellow Commonwealth Fund, New York 1967–68; Council mem. Inst. of Contemporary Arts (ICA), London 1971–75; Cttee. of Man. Soc. of Authors, London 1973–76; mem. Literature Panel Arts Council, London 1975–77; Adjunct Prof. of Writing, Columbia Univ., New York 1980; Chair. Catholic Writers' Guild 1992–97; Bd. mem. Aid to the Church in Need 1991–; Trustee Catholic Library 1997–; Sir Geoffrey Faber Memorial Prize, Somerset Maugham Award, Hawthornden Prize, Thomas More Award (U.S.A.), James Tait Black Memorial Prize. *Publications:* Game in Heaven with Tussy Marx 1966, The Junkers 1968, Monk Dawson 1969, The Professor's Daughter 1971, The Upstart 1973, Alive: The Story of the Andes Survivors 1974, Polonaise 1976, The Train Robbers 1978, A Married Man 1979, The Villa Golitsyn 1981, The Free Frenchman 1986, A Season in the West 1988, On the Third Day 1990, Ablaze: The Story of Chernobyl 1993, A Patriot in Berlin 1995, Knights of The Cross 1997. *Leisure interest:* family life. *Address:* 50 Portland Road, London, W11 4LG, England. *Telephone:* 0171-727 5719. *Fax:* 0171-460 2499.

REAGAN, Nancy Davis (Anne Francis Robbins), B.A.; American fmr. First Lady; b. 6 July 1921, New York; d. of Kenneth Robbins and Edith (née Luckett) Robbins, step-d. of Loyal Davis; m. Ronald Reagan (q.v.) 1952; one s. one d., one step-s. one step-d.; ed. Smith Coll., Mass.; contract actress Metro-Goldwyn-Mayer 1949–56; fmr. author syndicated column on prisoners-of-war and soldiers missing in action; civic worker active on behalf of Viet Nam war veterans, sr. citizens, disabled children and drug victims; mem. Bd. of Dirs. Revlon Group Inc. 1989–; Hon. Nat. Chair. Aid to Adoption of Special Kids 1977; one of Ten Most Admired American Women, Good Housekeeping Magazine 1977, Woman of Year, L.A. Times 1977, perm. mem. Hall of Fame of Ten Best Dressed Women in U.S., Lifetime Achievement Award, Council of Fashion Designers of U.S.A. 1988. *Films include:* The Next Voice You Hear 1950, Donovan's Brain 1953, Hellcats of the Navy 1957. *Publications:* Nancy 1980, To Love A Child (with Jane Wilkie), My Turn (memoirs) 1989. *Address:* 2121 Avenue of the Stars, 34th Floor, Los Angeles, CA 90067, U.S.A.

REAGAN, Ronald Wilson; American politician and former actor; b. 6 Feb. 1911, Tampico, Ill.; s. of John Edward and Nelle (Wilson) Reagan; m. 1st Jane Wyman 1940 (divorced 1948); one s. one d.; m. 2nd Nancy (née Davis) Reagan (q.v.) 1952; one s. one d.; ed. Northside High School, Dixon, Ill., and Eureka Coll., Eureka, Ill.; U.S.A.F. 1942–46; Gov. of Calif. 1967–74; Pres. of U.S.A. 1981–89; Dir. Nat. Review Bd. 1989; Chair. Republican Govs. Asscn. 1969; fmr. film actor and producer, radio sports announcer (at Des Moines, Iowa) and Ed., Cen. Broadcasting Co.; operated horse-breeding and cattle ranch; Player and Production Supervisor, Gen. Electric Theater TV for eight years; fmr. Pres. Screen Actors Guild, Motion Picture Industry Council; mem. Bd. of Dirs. Cttee. on Fundamental Educ., St. John's Hosp.; Dr. h.c. (Notre Dame, Ind.) 1981, (Nat. Univ. of Ireland) 1984; Hon. Citizen of Berlin 1992; Foreign Assoc. mem. Acad. des Sciences morales et politiques 1989; Hon. G.C.B.; Grand Cordon, Supreme Order of the Chrysanthemum (Japan) 1989; numerous other awards including Presidential Medal of Freedom 1993, Matsunaga Medal of Peace 1993; Republican. *Films acted in include:* Love is on the Air 1937, Accidents Will Happen 1938, Dark Victory 1939, Hell's Kitchen 1939, Brother Rat and a Baby 1940, Santa Fé Trail 1940, International Squadron 1941, Nine Lives are Not Enough 1941, King's Row 1941, Juke Girl 1942, Desperate Journey 1942, This is the Army 1943, Stallion Road 1947, That Hagen Girl 1947, The Voice of the Turtle 1947, Night unto Night 1948, John Loves Mary 1949, The Hasty Heart (Great Britain) 1949, Louisa 1950, Storm Warning 1951, Bedtime for Bonzo 1951, Hong Kong 1952, Prisoner of War 1954, Law and Order 1954, Tennessee's Partner 1955, Hellcats of the Navy 1957, The Killers 1964. *Publications:* Where's the Rest of Me? (autobiography), reprinted as My Early Life 1981, Abortion and the Conscience of the Nation 1984, Speaking my Mind: Selected Speeches 1990, An American Life (autobiog.) 1990. *Address:* 2121 Avenue of the Stars, 34th Floor, Los Angeles, CA 90067, U.S.A.

REARDON, Raymond (Ray), M.B.E.; British snooker player; b. 8 Oct. 1932, Tredegar, Wales; s. of Benjamin Reardon and Cynthia Jenkins; m. 1st Susan Carter (divorced); one s. one d.; m. 2nd Carol Lovington 1987; ed. Georgeton Secondary Modern School, Tredegar; six times World Snooker Champion 1970–78; Benson & Hedges Masters Champion 1976; twice Welsh Champion. *Publications:* Classic Snooker 1974, Ray Reardon (autobiography) 1982. *Leisure interest:* golf.

REBE, Bernd Werner, DR.IUR.; German university president; b. 5 Sept. 1939, Braunlage; s. of Werner Rebe and Liselotte Rebe; m. Bärbel Bonewitz 1964 (died 1993); two s.; ed. Univ. of Kiel, Freie Univ. Berlin and Univ. of Bielefeld; Prof. of Civil Law, Commercial Law, Competition Law and Corpn. Law, Univ. of Hannover 1975, Vice-Pres. Univ. of Hannover 1979–81; Pres. Tech. Univ. of Brunswick 1983–; mem. Senate W. German Rectors' Conf. 1988; Pres. Rectors' Conf. of Lower Saxony 1989. *Publications:* Die Träger der Pressefreiheit nach dem Grundgesetz 1970, Privatrecht und Wirtschaftsordnung 1978, Arbeitslosigkeit—unser Sicherheit? 1983, Neue Technologien und die Entwicklung von Wirtschaft und Gesellschaft 1984, Verfassung und Verwaltung des Landes Niedersachsen 1986, Nutzen und Wahrheit: Triebkräfte der Wissenschaftsentwicklung 1991, Die Universität heute—Leitinstitution ohne Leitbild? 1991, Umweltverträgliches Wirtschaften—Wettbewerbsvorteile, Marktchancen, Wohlstandssicherung 1993, Denkerkundungen. Reden wider die Vordergründigkeit 1995, Die unvollendete Einheit. Bestandsaufnahme und Perspektiven für die Wirtschaft 1996. *Leisure interests:* swimming, skiing, tennis, history, politics. *Address:* Technical University of Brunswick, Pockelsstrasse 14, 38106 Brunswick (Office); Am Mühlenstieg 10, 38126 Brunswick, Germany (Home). *Telephone:* 531 3914111 (Office); (0531) 691917 (Home).

REBEK, Julius, Jr., PH.D.; American professor of chemistry; b. 11 April 1949, Beregszasz, Hungary; s. of Julius Rebek Sr. and Eva Racz; m. (divorced); two d.; ed. Univ. of Kansas and Mass. Inst. of Tech. (M.I.T.); Asst. Prof. Univ. of Calif. Los Angeles 1970–76; Assoc. Prof., then Prof. Univ. of Pittsburgh 1976–79; Prof. Dept. of Chem. M.I.T. 1989–96, Camille Dreyfus Prof. of Chem. 1991–; Dir. Skaggs Inst. for Chemical Biology, Scripps Research Inst. 1996–; consultant to several cos.; Sloan Fellow; Guggenheim Fellow; von Humboldt Fellow; Cope Scholar Award 1991, James Flack Norris Award in Physical Chem. 1997. *Publications:* 120 publs. in scientific journals.

Leisure interest: tennis. *Address:* Scripps Research Institute, 10550 Torrey Pines Road, La Jolla, CA 92037 (Office); 100 Memorial Drive, Cambridge, MA 02192, U.S.A. (Home). *Telephone:* (617) 492-6427.

REBELO DE SOUSA, Baltasar; Portuguese politician; b. 16 April 1922, Lisbon; s. of Antonio J. and Joaquina L. Rebello de Souza; m. Maria Das Neves F. Duarte 1947; three s.; ed. Faculty of Medicine, Univ. of Lisbon; Under-Sec. of State for Educ. 1955–61; Vice-Pres. Overseas Council 1963–68; Gov.-Gen. of Mozambique 1968–70; Deputy to Nat. Assembly; Minister of Health and Corpns. 1970–73, in charge of Emigration Problems 1971–73, of Overseas Provs. 1973–74; Minister of Parl. Affairs 1982–83; Pres. Lusiada Acad. for Sciences, Literature and Arts S.P. Brazil 1984–87; mem. Portuguese dels. to int. orgs.; Dir. of enterprises-S.P. Brazil; Univ. Prof. Legal Medicine (Brazil); mem. Bd. of Dirs. Asscn. of Social Service and Portuguese League against Cancer; fmr. Prof. Inst. of Social Service; numerous orders and decorations. *Publications:* Integral Preparation of Youth 1951, Unitary Concept of Medical Assistance and Social Assurance, Religion and Life 1952, Forms and Perspectives of Popular Culture 1956, A Big Land and a Great People, One Year of Gov. 1968, Social State—Reflections and Basic Concepts 1969, Pax Lusitana 1970, Social Political Perspectives (3 vols.) 1971, 1972, 1973; Legal Medicine Basics 1976. *Leisure interests:* African and sociology studies, travel, reading and writing. *Address:* Rua S. Bernardo 102, 1200 Lisbon, Portugal. *Telephone:* 608150 (Lisbon).

REBEYROLLE, Paul; French artist; b. 3 Nov. 1926; ed. Lycée Gay-Lussac, Limoges; exhbns. at Salon des Indépendants, Salon d'Automne, Salon de Mai, Salon de la Jeune Peinture (France); Dir. Salon de Mai; works in collections in England, Sweden, Belgium, U.S.A., Poland, Italy, Japan, etc.; rep. at Dunn Int. Exhbn., London 1963; First Prize, La Jeune Peinture 1950, Fénéon Prize 1951, First Prize at French Section, Paris Biennale 1959.

REBUCK, Gail, B.A., F.R.S.A.; British publishing executive; b. 10 Feb. 1952, London; d. of Gordon Rebuck and Mavis Rebuck; m. Philip Gould 1985; two d.; ed. Lycée Français de Londres, Univ. of Sussex; Production Asst., Grisewood & Dempsey (Children's Book Packager) 1975–76; Ed., later Publr. Robert Nicholson Publs. London Guidebooks 1976–79; Publr. Hamlyn Paperbacks 1979–82; Founder Partner Century Publishing Co. Ltd., Publishing Dir. Non-Fiction 1982–85, Publr. Century Hutchinson 1985–89, Chair. Random House Div., Random Century 1989–91, Chair. and Chief Exec. Random House UK Ltd., 1991–; mem. COPUS 1995–97, Creative Industries Task Force 1997–; Trustee IPPR 1993–; Gov. Hallfield Schools, London 1994–. *Leisure interests:* reading, travel. *Address:* Random House UK Ltd., 20 Vauxhall Bridge Road, London, SW1V 2SA, England. *Telephone:* 0171-840 8886. *Fax:* 0171-233 6120.

RECHENDORFF, Torben; Danish politician; b. 1 April 1937; teacher and prin. at various schools, Frederiksberg and Hørsholm 1960–81; Sec.-Gen. Conservative People's Party 1981; Minister of Ecclesiastical Affairs 1988, and of Communications 1989–93; mem. Folketing (parl.) 1990–; leader Conservative People's Party 1993–95. *Address:* Conservative People's Party, Nyharu 4, P.O. Box 1515, 1020, Copenhagen K, Denmark.

RECHTER, Yacov; Israeli architect; b. 14 June 1924, Tel Aviv; s. of Ze'ev Rechter; m. Hanna Marron; five c.; ed. Technion, Hebrew Tech. Inst., Haifa; Architect, Ze'ev Rechter's practice 1946–47, served in Israeli Army 1947–49; partner, Rechter-Zarhi-Rechter Architects, Tel Aviv 1950–60, Rechter-Zarhi Architects, Peri Engineer, Tel Aviv 1960–73, in pvt. practice as Yacov Rechter Architect, Tel Aviv 1973–95, as Yacov Rechter—Amnon Rechter Architects 1995–; Assoc. Prof. of Architecture, Technion; Haifa 1987; Chair. Advisory Bd., America–Israel Cultural Foundation –1980; Chair. Bd. for Plastic Arts, Tel Aviv Fund for Literature and Arts 1984–87, Ministry of Culture 1989–95; mem. Council of Higher Educ. 1983–88; mem. Bd. of Dirs., Tel Aviv Museum of Art 1984–87, of Wolf Prize (Judge, Wolf Prize for Architecture) 1987–; mem. Asscn. of Engineers and Architects in Israel. *Projects include:* (hotels): Tel Aviv Hilton 1965, Jerusalem Hilton (now Holiday Inn) 1974, Dan Panorama, Tel Aviv 1976, Carlton, Tel Aviv 1980, Noga-Hilton, Geneva 1980, Sheraton King Solomon, Jerusalem 1981, Jerusalem Laromme Hotel 1983, Holiday Inn, Ashkelon 1996, Holiday Inn, Lod 1996; (hosps. and clinics): Lynn Out-patient Clinic, Haifa 1965, Out-patient Clinic, Ramat Gan 1972, Kaplan Hosp., Rehovot 1974, Carmel Hosp., Haifa 1978, Hadassah Hosp., Mt. Scopus, Jerusalem 1979, Poria Hosp., Tiberias 1992; (public bldgs.): Tel Aviv Law Courts 1965, Conservatoire, Beer Sheva 1974, Yad Lebanim Museum and Memorial, Herzlia 1975, Migdal Insurance Co. HQ, Tel Aviv 1977, Discount Bank Computer and Admin. Centre, Tel Aviv 1982, Bank Leumi Le'Israel Computer Centre, Lod 1987, Lev Ashdod Shopping Centre, Ashdod 1992, Elementary School, Kfar Saba 1993, Tel Aviv Opera House 1994, Law Courts, Acre 1995, Cen. Bldg. for Israel Broadcasting Authority, Jerusalem 1996; (univs.) Master Plan for Weizmann Inst., Rehovot 1975, Hebrew Univ. Cen. Library, Jerusalem 1981, Grad. School of Business Admin., Technion, Haifa 1988, Life Sciences Library, Weizmann Inst. 1990, Campus for Coll. of Business Admin. and Faculty of Law, Rishon Le'Zion 1995, Master Plan for Haifa Univ. Campus 1995; (housing & urban planning) Gan Yacov Public Garden, Tel Aviv 1966, Namir Square, Tel Aviv 1975, Merom Naveh project, Ramat Gan 1975–, N.W. zone of Gilo', Jerusalem 1977–80, Ma'aloth-Elram dwellings, Jerusalem 1982, Tel Aviv Waterfront Devt. 1983, Tadiran Ind. and Scientific Research Centre, Holon 1987, Master Plan for Big Block devt., Tel Aviv 1988, Master Plan for Tet Vav quarter, Ashdod 1988, Makom Ba'Zamereth dwellings, Jerusalem 1988, Plan of Golda Centre, Tel Aviv 1988, Cultural Centre, Herzlia 1988, Train Compound Devt. Jerusalem 1996; Rokach Prize (for Gan Yacov), Tel Aviv 1968, Israel Prize for Architecture 1973; Arie Elhanany Prize 1983. *Address:* 150 Arlozorov Street, Tel Aviv 62098 (Office); 56 Hanassi Street, Herzlia-Pitvah 46666, Israel (Home). *Telephone:* (3) 5249115 (Office). *Fax:* (3) 5224123 (Office).

REDDAWAY, William Brian, C.B.E., M.A., F.B.A.; British economist; b. 8 Jan. 1913, Cambridge; s. of William Fiddian Reddaway and Kate Waterland (née Sills) Reddaway; m. Barbara A. Bennett 1938; three s. one d.; ed. Oundle School, and King's Coll., Cambridge; Asst. Bank of England 1934–35; Research Fellow in Econs. Univ. of Melbourne 1936–37; Fellow of Clare Coll., Cambridge 1938–; Bd. of Trade 1940–47; Lecturer, Cambridge Univ. 1947–55, Dir. Dept. of Applied Econs. 1955–70, Reader in Applied Econs. 1957–69, Prof. of Political Economy 1969–80, now Prof. Emer.; Econ. Adviser, Org. for European Econ. Co-operation (OEEC) 1951–52, Confed. of British Industries 1972–83; Research Assoc. Centre for Int. Studies, New Delhi 1959–60; Visiting Lecturer, Econ. Devt. Inst., Washington, DC 1966–67; Econ. Consultant, World Bank 1966–; Visiting Prof. Inst. of Devt. Studies, Dacca 1974–75; Head Inst. of Fiscal Studies Study on Sr. Man.'s Taxation 1977–79; mem. Royal Comm. on the Press 1961–62; mem. Nat. Bd. of Prices and Incomes 1967–71; Editor, London and Cambridge Economic Bulletin 1951–74, Economic Journal 1971–76; Regional Adviser, Econ. Comm., W. Asia 1979–80; Adam Smith Prize, Cambridge 1934. *Publications:* The Russian Financial System 1935, The Economics of a Declining Population 1939, The Measurement of Production Movements 1948, The Development of the Indian Economy 1962, The Effects of U.K. Direct Investment Overseas (interim report) 1967, (final report) 1968, The Effects of the Selective Employment Tax (first report) 1970, (final report) 1973, An Alternative Economic Strategy 1981, Some Key Issues for the Development of the Economy of Papua New Guinea 1986, and numerous articles in learned journals, also contrib. chapters to numerous books. *Leisure interests:* walking, skating, chess, current affairs. *Address:* 12 Manor Court, Grange Road, Cambridge, CB3 9BE, England. *Telephone:* (01223) 350041.

REDFORD, Robert; American actor; b. 18 Aug. 1937, Santa Monica, Calif.; m. Lola Van Wegenen (divorced); three c.; ed. Van Nuys High School, Univ. of Colorado; *Films include:* War Hunt 1961, Situation Hopeless But Not Serious 1965, Inside Daisy Clover 1965, The Chase 1965, This Property is Condemned 1966, Barefoot in the Park 1967, Tell Them Willie Boy is Here 1969, Butch Cassidy and the Sundance Kid 1969, Downhill Racer 1969, Little Fauss and Big Halsy 1970, Jeremiah Johnson 1972, The Candidate 1972, How to Steal a Diamond in Four Uneasy Lessons 1972, The Way We Were 1973, The Sting 1973, The Great Gatsby 1974, The Great Waldo Pepper 1974, Three Days of the Condor 1975, All the President's Men 1976, A Bridge Too Far 1977, The Electric Horseman 1980, Brubaker 1980, The Natural 1984, Out of Africa 1985, Legal Eagles 1986, Havana 1991; Dir. Ordinary People 1980 (Acad. Award and Golden Globe Award for Best Dir. 1981), Milagro Beanfield War 1988 (also produced), Promised Land (exec. producer) 1988, Sneakers 1992, A River Runs Through It (also dir.) 1992, Quiz Show (dir.) 1994, The River Wild 1995, Up Close and Personal 1996, The Horse Whisperer 1997; Audubon Medal 1989, Dartmouth Film Soc. Award 1990. *Address:* c/o 1223 Wilshire Boulevard, 412 Santa Monica, CA 90403; Creative Artists Agency, 9830 Wilshire Boulevard, Beverly Hills, CA 90212, U.S.A.

REDGRAVE, Lynn; British actress; b. 8 March 1943, London; d. of late Sir Michael Redgrave and Rachel Kempson; sister of Vanessa Redgrave (q.v.); m. John Clark; one s. two d.; Broadway debut in Black Comedy; other stage appearances include: My Fat Friend 1974, Mrs Warren's Profession, Knock Knock, Misalliance, St. Joan, Twelfth Night (American Shakespeare Festival), Sister Mary Ignatius Explains It All for You, Aren't We All?, Sweet Sue, Les Liaisons Dangereuses; one-woman show Shakespeare for My Father (US and Canada tours, also in Melbourne and London 1996) 1993, Moon over Buffalo 1996; numerous television appearances. *Films:* Tom Jones, Girl With Green Eyes, Georgy Girl, The Deadly Affair, Smashing Time, The Virgin Soldiers, The Last of the Mobile Hot-Shots, Viva La Muerta Tua, Every Little Crook and Nanny, Everything You Always Wanted to Know About Sex, Don't Turn the Other Cheek, The National Health, The Happy Hooker, The Big Bus, Sunday Lovers, Morgan Stewart's Coming Home, Midnight, Getting It Right, Shine, Gods and Monsters. *Address:* c/o John Clark, P.O. Box 1207, Topanga, CA 90290, U.S.A. *Telephone:* (310) 455-1334. *Fax:* (310) 455-1032.

REDGRAVE, Steve, C.B.E.; British oarsman; b. 23 March 1962, Marlow; m. Ann Redgrave; one s. two d.; ed. Marlow Comprehensive School; rep. U.K. at Jr. World Championships 1979; Hon. D.C.L. (Durham Univ.) 1997; stroke, British coxed four, gold medal winners, Los Angeles Olympic Games 1984; gold medals, single scull, coxless pair (with Andy Holmes) and coxed four, Commonwealth Games 1986, coxed pair (with Holmes), World Championships 1986; coxless pair gold medal and coxed pair silver medal (with Holmes), World Championships 1987; gold medal (with Holmes), coxless pair and bronze medal, coxed pair, Olympic Games, Seoul 1988; silver medal (with Simon Berrisford), coxless pairs, World Championships 1989; bronze medal, coxless pair (with Matthew Pinsent, q.v.), World Championships, Tasmania 1990; gold medal, coxless pair (with Pinsent), World Championships, Vienna 1991; gold medal, Olympic Games, Barcelona 1992; gold medal, World Championships, Czech Repub. 1993; gold medal, Indianapolis,

1994; gold medal, Finland 1995; gold medal, Olympic Games, Atlanta 1996; gold medal, coxless four (with Pinsent, Foster, Cracknell), Aiguebelette 1997, Gold Medal, coxless four, Cologne 1998. *Address:* c/o British International Rowing Office, 6 Lower Mall, London, W6 9DJ, England. *Telephone:* 0181-741 7580. *Fax:* 0181-563 2265.

REDGRAVE, Vanessa, C.B.E.; British actress; b. 30 Jan. 1937; d. of the late Sir Michael Redgrave and Rachel Kempson; sister of Lynn Redgrave (q.v.); m. the late Tony Richardson 1962 (divorced 1967, died 1991); two d.; ed. Queensgate School, London, and Cen. School of Speech and Drama; Evening Standard Award, Best Actress 1961 and Variety Club Award 1961; Award for Best Actress, Cannes Film Festival 1966 for Morgan—A Suitable Case for Treatment; Award for Leading Actress, U.S. Nat. Soc. of Film Critics and Best Actress Award, Film Critics' Guild (U.K.) for Isadora Duncan 1969; Acad. Award (Best Supporting Actress) for Julia 1978; Award (TV for Best Actress) for Playing for Time 1981; Laurence Olivier Award 1984; Dr. h.c. (Mass.) 1990; co-f. Moving Theatre 1974; mem. Workers' Revolutionary Party (Cand. for Moss Side 1979); Fellow B.F.I. 1988. *Stage appearances in:* A Midsummer Night's Dream 1959, The Tiger and the Horse 1960, The Taming of the Shrew 1961, As You Like It 1961, Cymbeline 1962, The Seagull 1964, 1985, The Prime of Miss Jean Brodie 1966, Daniel Deronda 1969, Cato Street 1971, Threepenny Opera 1972, Twelfth Night 1972, Anthony and Cleopatra 1973, 1986, Design for Living 1973, Macbeth 1975, Lady from the Sea 1976 and 1979 (Manchester), The Aspern Papers 1984, Ghosts 1986, A Touch of the Poet 1988, Orpheus Descending 1988, A Madhouse in Goa 1989, The Three Sisters 1990, Lettice and Lovage 1991, When She Danced 1991, Isadora 1991, Heartbreak House 1992, The Master Builder 1992, Maybe 1993, The Liberation of Skopje 1995, John Gabriel Borkman 1996; Dir. and acted in Antony and Cleopatra, Houston, Tex. 1996, John Gabriel Borkman 1996; *films include:* Morgan—A Suitable Case for Treatment 1965, Sailor from Gibraltar 1965, Camelot 1967, Blow Up 1967, Charge of the Light Brigade 1968, Isadora Duncan 1968, The Seagull 1968, A Quiet Place in the Country 1968, Dropout, The Trojan Women 1970, The Devils 1970, The Holiday 1971, Mary Queen of Scots 1971, Katherine Mansfield (BBC TV) 1973, Murder on the Orient Express 1974, Winter Rates 1974, 7% Solution 1975, Julia 1977, Agatha 1978, Yanks 1978, Bear Island 1979, Playing for Time (CBS TV) 1979, Playing for Time 1980, My Body My Child (ABC TV) 1981, Wagner 1982, The Bostonians 1983, Wetherby 1984, Prick Up Your Ears 1987, Comrades 1987, Consuming Passions 1988, King of the Wind 1989, Diceria dell'intore 1989, The Ballad of the Sad Cafe 1990, Howards End 1992, Breath of Life, The Wall, Sparrow, They, The House of the Spirits, Crime and Punishment, Mother's Boys, Little Odessa, A Month by the Lake 1996, Mission Impossible 1996, Looking for Richard 1997, Wilde 1997, Mrs Dalloway 1997, Bella Mafia (TV) 1997, Deep Impact 1998; produced and narrated documentary film The Palestinians 1977. *Publications:* Pussies and Tigers 1963, An Autobiography 1991. *Leisure interest:* changing the status quo. *Address:* c/o James Sharkey Assocs., 21 Golden Square, London, W1R 3PA, England.

REDGROVE, Peter William, F.R.S.L.; British author, poet and analytical psychologist; b. 2 Jan. 1932; s. of late Gordon G. Redgrove and Nancy Lena Cestrilli-Bell; m. Penelope Shuttle; one d. (and two s. one d. by previous m.); ed. Taunton School and Queens' Coll., Cambridge; scientific journalist and editor 1954–61; Visiting Poet, Buffalo Univ., New York 1961–62; Gregory Fellow in Poetry, Leeds Univ. 1962–65; Resident Author and Sr. Lecturer in Complementary Studies, Falmouth School of Art 1966–83; O'Connor Prof. of Literature, Colgate Univ., New York; recipient of several awards including Queen's Gold Medal for Poetry 1996. *Publications:* novels: In the Country of the Skin 1973, The Terrors of Dr Treviles 1974, The Glass Cottage 1976, The God of Glass 1979, The Sleep of the Great Hypnotist 1979, The Beekeepers 1980, The Facilitators, or, Madame Hole-in-the-Day 1982; stories: The One Who Set Out to Study Fear 1989; short fiction: The Cyclopean Mistress 1993; psychology and sociology: The Wise Wound 1978, The Black Goddess and the Sixth Sense 1987, Alchemy for Women (with Penelope Shuttle) 1995; numerous vols. of poems, including The Collector and Other Poems 1960, The Force and Other Poems 1966, Dr. Faust's Sea-Spiral Spirit and Other Poems 1972, The Weddings at Nether Powers, and Other New Poems 1979, The Working of Water 1984, The Mudlark Poems and Grand Buveur 1986, In the Hall of the Saurians 1987, Poems 1954–87 1987, The First Earthquake 1989, Dressed as for a Tarot Pack 1990, Under the Reservoir 1992, The Laborators 1993, My Father's Trapdoors 1994, Abyssophone 1995, Assembling a Ghost 1996, Orchard End 1997, What the Black Mirror Saw 1997; anthologies and radio and television plays, etc; articles in magazines and journals. *Leisure interests:* work, photography, judo, yoga. *Address:* c/o David Higham Associates, 5–8 Lower John Street, Golden Square, London, W1R 4HA, England.

REDHEAD, Michael Logan Gonne, PH.D., F.B.A.; British academic; b. 30 Dec. 1929, London; s. of Robert Arthur Redhead and Christabel Lucy Gonne Browning; m. Jennifer Anne Hill 1964; three s.; ed. Westminster School, Univ. Coll. London; Prof. of Philosophy of Physics, Chelsea Coll., London 1984–85, King's Coll. London 1985–87; Prof. of History and Philosophy of Science, Cambridge Univ. 1987–97; Fellow Wolfson Coll. Cambridge 1988–, Vice-Pres. 1992–96; Co-Dir. Centre for Philosophy of Natural and Social Science, L.S.E. 1998–; Tarner Lecturer, Trinity Coll. Cambridge 1991–94; Visiting Fellow All Souls Coll. Oxford 1995; Pres. British Soc. for Philosophy of Science 1989–91; Lakatos Award for Philosophy of Science 1988. *Publications:* Incompleteness, Nonlocality and Realism 1987, From Physics to Metaphysics 1995. *Leisure interests:* poetry, music, tennis. *Address:* 34 Coniger Road, London, SW6 3TA, England. *Telephone:* 0171-736 6767. *Fax:* 0171-731 7627.

REDSTONE, Sumner Murray, LL.B.; American business executive and lawyer; b. 27 May 1923, Boston; s. of Michael Redstone and Belle (Ostrovsky) Redstone; m. Phyllis Gloria Raphael 1947; two c.; ed. Harvard Univ.; called to Bar of Mass. 1947; Special Asst. to U.S. Attorney-Gen., Washington, D.C. 1948–51; partner, law firm of Ford, Bergson, Adams, Borkland & Redstone, Washington, D.C. 1951–54; Pres. and C.E.O. Nat. Amusements Inc., Dedham, Mass. 1967–, Chair. Bd. 1986–87; Chair. Bd., Viacom Int. Inc., New York 1987–; Prof., Boston Univ. Law School 1982, 1985–86; Chair. Corp. Comm. on Education Tech. 1996–; mem. Corpn., New England Medical Center 1967–; Trustee Children's Cancer Research Foundation; Sponsor, Boston Museum of Science; mem. Bd. of Dirs. Boston Arts Festival, John F. Kennedy Library Foundation; mem. Nat. Asscn. of Theatre Owners, Theatre Owners of America, Motion Picture Pioneers (mem. Bd. of Dirs.), Boston Bar Asscn., Mass. Bar Asscn.; Army Commendation Medal, Legends in Leadership Award, Emory Univ. 1995, Lifetime Achievement Award American Cancer Society 1995, Trustees Award Nat. Acad. of TV Arts and Sciences 1997, numerous other awards. *Address:* National Amusements Inc., P.O. Box 9126, Dedham, MA 02027 (Office); 98 Baldpate Hill Road, Newton, MA 02159, U.S.A. (Home).

REDWOOD, Rt. Hon. John (Alan), D.PHIL., M.P.; British politician; b. 15 June 1951, Dover, Kent; s. of William Charles Redwood and Amy Emma Champion; m. Gail Felicity Chippington 1974; one s. one d.; ed. Kent Coll. Canterbury and Magdalen and St. Antony's Colls. Oxford; Fellow, All Souls Coll. Oxford 1972–85; Investment Adviser, Robert Fleming & Co. 1973–77; Dir. (fmrly Man.) N.M. Rothschild & Sons 1977–87; Dir. Norcros PLC 1985–89, Jt. Deputy Chair. 1986–87, Chair. (non-exec.) 1987–89; Head, Prime Minister's Policy Unit 1983–85; M.P. for Wokingham 1987–; Parl. Under-Sec. of State, Dept. of Trade & Industry 1989–90, Minister of State 1990–92, Minister of State, Dept. of Environment 1992–93; Sec. of State for Wales 1993–95; unsuccessful cand. for leadership of Conservative Party 1995; Opposition Front Bench Spokesman on Trade and Industry July 1997–; Parliamentarian of the Year Awards 1987, 1995, 1997. *Publications:* Reason, Ridicule and Religion 1976, Public Enterprise in Crisis 1980, Value for Money Audits (with J. Hatch) 1981, Controlling Public Industries (with J. Hatch) 1982, Going for Broke 1984, Equity for Everyman 1986, Popular Capitalism 1989, The Global Marketplace 1994, The Single European Currency (with others) 1996, Our Currency, Our Country 1997. *Leisure interests:* water sports, village cricket. *Address:* House of Commons, London, SW1A 0AA, England. *Telephone:* 0171-219 4205 (Office); 0171-976 6603 (Home).

REECE, Sir (James) Gordon, Kt.; British public relations executive; b. 28 Sept. 1929; m. (divorced); six c.; ed. Ratcliffe Coll. and Downing Coll. Cambridge; fmr. reporter, Liverpool Daily Post & Echo and Sunday Express; producer, ITV 1960–70; Jt. Man. Dir. RM EMI Ltd. 1970–74; Adviser to Rt. Hon. Margaret Thatcher (now Baroness Thatcher q.v.), Leader of Conservative Party 1975–79; Dir. of Publicity, Conservative Cen. Office 1978–80; Vice- Pres. Occidental Petroleum Corpn. 1980–85, public affairs consultant 1985–. *Address:* c/o Wells Fargo Bank, 10850 Wilshire Boulevard, Los Angeles, CA 90025, U.S.A.

REED, Bruce; American official; fmr. aide to Pres. Clinton; Asst. to Pres., Head Domestic Policy Council 1997–. *Address:* The White House, 1600 Pennsylvania Ave., NW, Washington, D.C. 20500, U.S.A. *Telephone:* (202) 456-2216. *Fax:* (202) 456-2878.

REED, Charles Bass, B.S., M.A., ED.D.; American university chancellor; b. 29 Sept. 1941, Harrisburg, Pa.; s. of late Samuel Ross Reed and Elizabeth Johnson Reed; m. Catherine A. Sayers 1964; one s. one d.; ed. George Washington Univ.; Asst. Prof., then Assoc. Prof., George Washington Univ. 1963–70; Asst. Dir., Nat. Performance-based Teacher Educ. Project 1970–71; Co-ordinator, Research and Devt. in Teacher Educ., Fla. Dept. of Educ. 1971–72, Assoc. for Planning and Co-ordination 1972–74, Dir. Office of Educational Planning, Budgeting and Evaluation 1974–79; Educ. Policy Co-ordinator, Exec. Office of Gov. Bob Graham 1979–80, Dir. of Legis. Affairs 1980–81, Deputy Chief of Staff 1981–84, Chief of Staff 1984–85; Chancellor, State Univ. System of Fla. 1985–98, Calif. State Univ. System 1998–, Bd. Dirs. Fla. Progress Corpn., Capital Health Plan; Chair. Bd. Dirs. Regional Tech. Strategies Inc.; Fullbright 50th Anniversary Distinguished Fellow, Peru 1996; mem. Council on Foreign Relations; Dr. h.c. (George Washington, Stetson and St. Thomas Univs., Waynesburg Coll., Pa.). *Address:* State University System of Florida, 325 West Gaines Street, Tallahassee, FL 32399, U.S.A. *Telephone:* (904) 488-4234 (Office). *Fax:* (904) 922-6565.

REED, Ishmael Scott; American author; b. 22 Feb. 1938, Chattanooga; s. of Bennie S. Reed and Thelma Coleman; m. 1st Priscilla Rose 1960 (divorced 1970); two s.; m. 2nd Carla Blank; one d.; Dir. Reed & Cannon Co.; Assoc. Fellow, Calhoun House, Yale Univ. 1982–; co-publr., Quilt magazine; Sr. Lecturer, Univ. of Calif. Berkeley; mem. usage panel, American Heritage Dictionary; Assoc. Ed. American Book Review; Exec. Producer Personal Problems (video soap opera); collaborator in multi media Bicentennial mystery, The Lost State of Franklin (winner Poetry in Public Places contest 1975); Chair. Berkeley Arts Comm.; Advisory Chair. Co-ordinating Council of Literary Magazines; Pres. Before Columbus Foundation; Nat. Endowment for Arts Writing Fellow 1974; Nat. Inst. of Arts and Letters Award 1975; Guggenheim Fellow 1975; Michaux Award 1978, ACLU Award 1978; mem. authors Guild of America, PEN. *Publications:* novels: The Free-Lance Pallbearers 1967, Yellow Back Radio Broke Down 1969, Mumbo Jumbo 1972, The Last Days of Louisiana Red 1974, Flight to Canada 1976, The Terrible Twos 1982, Cab Calloway Stands in For the Moon 1986, Japanese By Spring 1993; several vols. of poetry and essays. *Address:* c/o Penguin U.S.A., 375 Hudson Street, New York, NY 10014, U.S.A.

REED, John Francis (Jack), B.S., J.D.; American politician; b. 12 Nov. 1949, Providence, R.I.; s. of Joseph Reed and Mary Monahan; ed. U.S. Mil. Acad. and Harvard Univ.; commissioned, 2nd Lieut. U.S. Army 1971, served with 82nd Airborne Div. 1973–77; Asst. Prof. U.S. Mil. Acad. West Point, N.Y. 1977–79; resgnd. from Army 1979; called to Bar, D.C. 1982, Rhode Island 1983; Assoc. Sutherland, Asbill & Brennan, Washington 1982–83, Edwards & Angelli, Providence 1983–89; mem. Rhode Island Senate 1984–90; mem. 102-104th Congresses 1990–96; Senator from Rhode Island 1996–; Vice-Chair. N.E.-Midwest Congressional Coalition; Democrat. *Leisure interests:* reading, hiking. *Address:* United States Senate, 339 Russell Senate Office Building, Washington, D.C. 20510, U.S.A.

REED, John Shepard, M.S.; American banker; b. 7 Feb. 1939, Chicago; m. 1st (divorced), four c.; m. 2nd Cindy McCarthy 1994; ed. Washington and Jefferson Coll., M.I.T., Alfred P. Sloan School of Man., M.I.T.; served with U.S. Army Eng. Corps, Korea; fmr. Trainee Goodyear Tire & Rubber; joined Citicorp/Citibank 1965, fmrly. responsible for operating group, consumer business, fmr. Sr. Vice-Pres., Chair. and Chief Exec. 1984–; named Jt. Chair. and Chief Exec. (desig.) of Citigroup (proposed merger between Citicorp and Travelers Group) May 1998; Chair. Coalition of Service Industries, Services Policy Advisory Cttee. to the U.S. Trade Rep.; Dir. Philip Morris Inc., Monsanto Co.; mem. Business Council, Business Roundtable Policy Cttee.; mem. Bd. M.I.T., Bd. Memorial Sloan-Kettering Cancer Center, Rand Corp., Spencer Foundation, American Museum of Natural History. *Address:* Citicorp, 399 Park Avenue, New York, NY 10043, U.S.A.

REED, Lou, B.A.; American musician; b. 2 March 1942, Brooklyn, New York; s. of Sidney Joseph Reed and Toby (Futterman) Reed; m. Sylvia Morales 1980; ed. Syracuse Univ.; songwriter and recording artist 1965–; founder mem. Velvet Underground band 1966–70; toured with Andy Warhol's The Exploding Plastic Inevitable; poet; film actor; solo albums include: Lou Reed 1972, Rock 'N' Roll Animal 1972, Berlin 1973, Sally Can't Dance 1974, Metal Machine Music 1975, Lou Reed Live 1975, Coney Island Baby 1976, Walk on the Wild Side 1977, Street Hassle 1978, Live, Take No Prisoners 1978, Vicious 1979, The Bells 1979, Growing Up in Public 1980, Rock 'n' Roll Diary 1967–80, Blue Mask, Legendary Hearts 1983, New York 1989, Songs for Drella (with John Cale) 1990, Magic and Loss 1992, Set the Twilight Reeling 1996; several albums with Velvet Underground; Rock and Roll Hall of Fame 1996. *Publication:* Between Thought and Expression (selected lyrics) 1991. *Address:* c/o William Morris Agency, 151 El Camino Drive, Beverly Hills, CA 90212, U.S.A.

REEDER, Franklin S.; American consultant and fmr. government official; b. 25 Oct. 1940, Philadelphia, Pa.; s. of late Simon Reeder and Hertha Strauss; m. Anna Marie Seroski 1962; one s. two d.; ed. Univ. of Pennsylvania and George Washington Univ.; Treasury Dept. 1961–64; Defense Dept. 1964–70; Office of Man. and Budget, Exec. Office of Pres. of U.S.A. 1970–71, 1980–97, Dir. 1995–97; Deputy Dir. House Information System, U.S. House of Reps. 1971–80; consultant in information and governance. *Leisure interests:* running, swimming, bicycling, watching baseball. *Address:* The Reeder Group, 3200 N. Nottingham Street, Arlington, VA 22207, U.S.A. *Telephone:* (703) 536-6635.

REEDY, George Edward; American government official and educationist; b. 5 Aug. 1917, East Chicago, Ind.; s. of George E. Reedy and Mary Mulvaney Reedy; m. 1st Lillian Greenwald 1948 (died 1984); two s.; m. 2nd Ruth Brial Wissman 1988; ed. Univ. of Chicago; Congressional Corresp. United Press, Washington, D.C. 1938–41, 1946–51; U.S. Army Air Corps 1942–45; Staff Dir. U.S. Senate Minority Policy Cttee. 1953–54, Majority Policy Cttee. 1955–60; Special Asst. to Vice-Pres. Lyndon B. Johnson 1961–63, Press Sec. to the Pres. 1964–65, Aide to the Pres. 1965–66, Special Consultant to the Pres. 1968–69; Pegram Lecturer, Brookhaven Nat. Radiation Lab. 1971; Adjunct Prof. of Political Science, State Univ. of New York 1971–72; Dean College of Journalism 1972–76; Lucius W. Nieman Prof. of Journalism, Marquette Univ. 1972–90, Emer. Prof. 1991–; American Specialist lecturing in South America 1976, Asia 1977, under U.S. State Dept. Cultural Exchange Program in India and Indonesia 1984, under U.S. Information Agency; mem. and chair. numerous govt. comms. and bds. of enquiry 1966–68; Vice-Pres. for Planning, Struthers Wells Corpn. 1966–68; mem. Pres.'s Comm. on White House Fellowships 1993–; lecturer, LaFarge Inst. for Lifelong Learning, Milwaukee, Wis. 1997–; Fellow, Woodrow Wilson Int. Center for Scholars 1970; Duke Univ. Fellow in Communications 1973–74; Poynter Fellow, Univ. of Indiana 1974; Hon. D.Cn.L., Episcopal Seminary Nashota 1981, Legum Dr. h.c. (Marquette) 1998; Marquette Teaching Excellence Award 1985. *Publications:* Who Will Do Our Fighting for Us? 1969, The Twilight of the Presidency 1970, The Presidency in Flux 1973, Lyndon B. Johnson, A Memoir 1982, The U.S. Senate: Paralysis or Search for Consensus 1986, The Twilight of the Presidency: Johnson to Reagan (an update) 1987, From the Ward to the White House: The Irish in American Politics 1991, Mass Media and the Public Dialogue 1992. *Leisure interests:* music, fishing. *Address:* St. John's Tower, 1840 N. Prospect # 304, Milwaukee, WI 53202, U.S.A. (Home). *Telephone:* (414) 272-8281 (Home).

REES, Charles Wayne, C.B.E., D.SC., F.R.S.C., F.R.S.; British professor of organic chemistry; b. 15 Oct. 1927, Cairo, Egypt; s. of Percival C. Rees and Daisy A. Beck; m. Patricia M. Francis 1953; three s.; ed. Farnham Grammar School and Univ. Coll., Southampton; Lecturer in Organic Chem. Birkbeck Coll., London 1955–57, King's Coll., London 1957–63, Reader 1963–65; Prof. of Organic Chem. Univ. of Leicester 1965–69, Univ. of Liverpool 1969–78; Hofmann Prof. of Organic Chem., Imperial Coll., London 1978–93, Emer. Prof. 1993–; Visiting Prof., Univ. of Sunderland 1997–; Tilden Lecturer, Royal Soc. of Chem. 1973–74, Pedler Lecturer 1984–85; August Wilhelm von Hofmann Lecturer, German Chem. Soc. 1985; Pres. Royal Soc. of Chem. 1992–94; Hon. D.Sc. (Univ. of Leicester) 1994; Int. Award in Heterocyclic Chemistry 1995. *Publications:* some 390 research papers in scientific journals and 20 books. *Leisure interests:* music, wine, London. *Address:* Department of Chemistry, Imperial College, London, SW7 2AY, England. *Telephone:* 0171-594 5768. *Fax:* 0171-594 5800.

REES, Sir Dai (David Allan), Kt., PH.D., D.SC., F.I.BIOL., F.R.S.C., F.R.S.; British scientist; b. 28 April 1936, Silloth; s. of James A. Rees and Elsie Bolam; m. Myfanwy Owen 1959; two s. one d.; ed. Hawarden Grammar School, Clwyd and Univ. Coll. of N. Wales, Bangor; Univ. of Edinburgh 1960, Asst. Lecturer in Chem. 1961, Lecturer 1962–70, Section Man. 1970–72; Prin. Scientist Unilever Research, Colworth Lab. 1972–82; Assoc. Dir. (part-time) MRC Unit for Cell Biophysics Kings Coll., London 1980–82; Dir. Nat. Inst. for Medical Research 1982–87; Sec., then Chief Exec. MRC 1987–96, MRC scientist 1996–; Chair. European Medical Research Councils 1989–; Pres. European Science Foundation 1994–; Visiting Professorial Fellow, Univ. Coll., Cardiff 1972–77; Hon. F.R.C.P. 1986, F.R.C.P.(E.) 1998; Philips Lecture Royal Soc. 1984; mem. Royal Soc. Council 1985–87; Hon. Fellow, King's Coll., London 1989, Univ. Coll. of N. Wales 1988; Hon. D.Sc. (Edinburgh) 1989, (Wales) 1991, (Stirling) 1995, (Leicester) 1997; Colworth Medal, Biochem. Soc. 1970; Carbohydrate Award, Chem. Soc. 1970. *Publications:* articles on carbohydrate biochem. and cell biology. *Leisure interests:* river cruising, reading, listening to music. *Address:* National Institute for Medical Research, The Ridgeway, Mill Hill, London, NW7 1AA, England. *Telephone:* 0181-959 3666. *Fax:* 0181-906 4477.

REES, Hubert, D.F.C., D.SC., F.R.S.; British professor of agricultural botany; b. 2 Oct. 1923, Llangennech, Wales; s. of Owen Rees and Tugela Rees; m. Mavis Rosalind Hill 1946; one s. two d.; ed. Llandovery and Llanelli Grammar Schools and Univ. Coll. of Wales, Aberystwyth; served R.A.F. 1942–46; lecturer, Genetics Dept., Univ. of Birmingham 1950–59; Sr. lecturer, Univ. Coll. of Wales, Aberystwyth 1960–66, Reader 1966–67, Prof. of Agricultural Botany 1967–90. *Publications:* Chromosome Genetics 1977, B Chromosomes 1982. *Leisure interest:* fishing. *Address:* Irfon, Llanbadarn Road, Aberystwyth, Wales. *Telephone:* (01970) 623668.

REES, Sir Martin John, Kt., M.A., PH.D., F.R.S.; British professor; b. 23 June 1942; s. of Reginald J. Rees and Joan Rees; m. Caroline Humphrey 1986; ed. Shrewsbury School and Trinity Coll., Cambridge; Fellow, Jesus Coll., Cambridge 1967–69; Research Assoc. Calif. Inst. of Tech. 1967–68, 1971; mem. Inst. for Advanced Study, Princeton 1969–70, Prof. 1982–96; Visiting Prof. Harvard Univ. 1972, 1986–87; Prof. Univ. of Sussex 1972–73; Plumian Prof. of Astronomy and Experimental Philosophy, Univ. of Cambridge 1973–91, Royal Soc. Research Prof. 1992–; Astronomer Royal 1995–; Fellow, King's Coll., Cambridge 1969–72, 1973–; Dir. Inst. of Astronomy 1977–82, 1987–91; Regents Fellow, Smithsonian Inst. 1984–88; mem. Council Royal Soc. 1983–85, 1993–95; Pres. Royal Astronomical Soc. 1992–94, British Assscn. for the Advancement of Science 1994–95; Trustee British Museum 1996–, Inst. for Advanced Study, Princeton, U.S.A. 1998, Nat. Endowment for Sciences, Tech. and Arts 1998; Hon. Fellow Trinity Coll. and Jesus Coll., Cambridge, Indian Acad. of Sciences, Univ. of Wales, Cardiff 1998; Foreign hon. mem. American Acad. of Arts and Sciences; Foreign Assoc. N.A.S.; mem. Academia Europaea 1989, Pontifical Acad. of Sciences 1990; Foreign mem. American Philosophical Soc., Royal Swedish Acad. of Science, Russian Acad. of Sciences, Norwegian Acad. of Arts and Science, Accad. Lincei (Rome), Royal Netherlands Acad.; Hon. D.Sc. (Sussex) 1990, (Leicester) 1993, (Copenhagen, Keele, Uppsala, Newcastle) 1995, (Toronto) 1997, (Durham) 1999; Heinemann Prize, American Inst. of Physics 1984, Gold Medal (Royal Astronomical Soc.) 1987, Guthrie Medal, Inst. of Physics 1989, Balzan Prize 1989, Robinson Prize for Cosmology 1990, Bruce Medal, Astronomical Soc. of Pacific 1993, Science Writing Award, American Inst. of Physics 1996, Bower Award (Franklin Inst.) 1998; Officier, Ordre des Arts et des Lettres. *Publications:* Perspectives in Astrophysical Cosmology 1995, Gravity's Fatal Attraction (with M. Begelman) 1995, Before the Beginning 1997; edited books; articles and reviews in scientific journals. *Address:* King's College, Cambridge, CB2 1ST, England. *Telephone:* (01223) 337548 (Office).

REES, Rt. Hon. Merlyn (see Merlyn-Rees, Baron).

REES, Roger; British actor; b. 5 May 1944, Aberystwyth, Wales; ed. Camberwell and Slade Schools of Art; with R.S.C. 1967–; Assoc. Dir. Bristol Old Vic Theatre Co. 1986–. *Stage appearances include:* Hindle Wakes 1964, The Taming of the Shrew, Othello, Major Barbara, Macbeth, Twelfth Night, The Suicide, The Adventures of Nicholas Nickleby, Hapgood, Hamlet, Love's

Labours Lost, The Real Thing, Double Double (also writer), Indiscretions, The End of the Day. *Film appearances include:* Star 80 1983, Keine Storung Bitte, Mountains of the Moon, If Looks Could Kill, Stop! Or My Mom Will Shoot, Robin Hood: Men in Tights, Sudden Manhattan. *Television appearances include:* A Christmas Carol, Place of Peace, Under Western Eyes, Bouquet of Barbed Wire, Saigon: The Year of the Cat, Imaginary Friends, The Adventures of Nicholas Nickleby, The Comedy of Errors, Macbeth, The Voysey Inheritance, The Ebony Tower, The Finding, The Return of Sam McCloud, Charles & Diana: Unhappily Ever After, The Tower, The Possession of Michael D. *Television appearances include:* Cheers, Singles, M.A.N.T.I.S.

REES-MOGG, Baron (Life Peer) cr. 1988, of Hinton Blewett in the County of Avon; **William Rees-Mogg,** Kt.; British journalist; b. 14 July 1928, Bristol; s. of late Edmund Fletcher and Beatrice (née Warren) Rees-Mogg; m. Gillian Shakespeare Morris 1962; two s. three d.; ed. Charterhouse and Balliol Coll., Oxford; Pres. Oxford Union 1951; Financial Times 1952–60, Chief Leader Writer 1955–60, Asst. Ed. 1957–60; City Ed. Sunday Times 1960–61, Political and Econ. Ed. 1961–63, Deputy Ed. 1964–67; Ed. of The Times 1967–81, Dir. The Times Ltd. 1968–81; Vice-Chair. BBC 1981–86; Chair. Arts Council 1982–88; Chair. Broadcasting Standards Council 1988–93; mem. Exec. Bd. Times Newspapers Ltd. 1968–81, Dir. 1978–81; Dir. Gen. Electric Co. 1981–97; Chair. and Propr. Pickering and Chatto Ltd. (Publrs.) 1983–; Chair. Sidgwick and Jackson 1985–89, Int. Business Communications PLC 1994–; Dir. M & G Group 1987, Pvt. Bank and Trust Co. 1993–, Value Realisation Trust PLC 1996–; columnist The Times 1992–; mem. Int. Cttee. Pontifical Council for Culture 1983–87; Hon. LL.D. (Bath) 1977, (Leeds) 1992. *Publications:* The Reigning Error: the Crisis of World Inflation 1974, An Humbler Heaven 1977, How to Buy Rare Books 1985, Blood in the Streets (with James Dale Davidson) 1988, The Great Reckoning (with James Dale Davidson) 1992, Picnics on Vesuvius 1992, The Sovereign Individual 1997. *Leisure interest:* collecting. *Address:* 17 Pall Mall, London, SW1Y 5NB, England. *Telephone:* 0171-930 3088. *Fax:* 0171-839 4509.

REESE, Colin Bernard, M.A., PH.D., SC.D., F.R.S.; British professor of chemistry; b. 29 July 1930, Plymouth; s. of late Joseph Reese and Emily Reese; m. Susanne L. Bird 1968; one s. one d.; ed. Dartington Hall School and Clare Coll., Cambridge; Research Fellow, Clare Coll. 1956–59, Harvard Univ. 1957–58; Official Fellow and Dir. of Studies in Chem., Clare Coll. 1959–73; Demonstrator in Chem., Univ. of Cambridge 1959–63, Asst. Dir. of Research 1963–64, Univ. Lecturer in Chem. 1964–73; Daniell Prof. of Chem., King's Coll. London 1973–98, Fellow 1989, Prof. of Organic Chem. 1999–. *Publications:* scientific papers mainly in chemistry journals. *Address:* Department of Chemistry, King's College London, Strand, London, WC2R 2LS, England. *Telephone:* 0171-873 2260. *Fax:* 0171-873 2899.

REEVE, Sir Anthony, K.C.M.G., K.C.V.O., M.A.; British diplomatist (retd.); b. 20 Oct. 1938, Wakefield; s. of Sidney Reeve and Dorothy (née Mitchell) Reeve; m. 1st Pamela Margaret Angus 1964 (divorced 1988); one s. two d.; m. 2nd Susan Doull (née Collins) 1997; ed. Queen Elizabeth Grammar School, Wakefield, Marling School, Stroud and Merton Coll., Oxford; joined Lever Bros. and Assocs. 1962–65; entered Diplomatic Service 1965; Middle East Centre for Arab Studies 1966–68; Asst. Political Agent, Abu Dhabi 1968–70; First Sec. FCO 1970–73; First Sec., later Counsellor Washington 1973–78; Head of Arms Control and Disarmament Dept. FCO 1979–81; Counsellor, Cairo 1981–84; Head Southern Africa Dept., FCO 1984–86; Asst. Under Sec. of State 1986–88; Amb. to Jordan 1988–91; Amb. to, later High Commr. in, S.A. 1991–96; Chair. Foundation, S.A. 1998–; Dir. (non-exec.) Barclays Pvt. Bank 1997–, Union Castle Travel Ltd. *Leisure interests:* music, golf. *Address:* Box Cottage, Horsley, Stroud, Glos., GL6 0QB, England. *Telephone:* (01453) 832891. *Fax:* (01453) 832608.

REEVE, Christopher; American actor; b. 25 Sept. 1952, New York; one s. one d.; m. Dana Morosini; one s.; ed. Cornell Univ.; TV appearances since 1973 include Anna Karenina 1985; appeared on stage in New York in Street Smart 1986, The Winter's Tale 1989; appeared in more than 110 stage productions in U.S.A. and England; *TV appearances include:* Anna Karenina 1985, The Great Escape 1988. *Films include:* Somewhere in Time, Superman, Superman 2, Deathtrap, Monsignor, Superman 3, The Bostonians, The Aviator, Superman 4, Street Smart 1988, Switching Channels 1988, Noises Off 1992, The Remains of the Day 1993, Morning Glory 1993, Speechless 1994, The Rhinehart Theory 1994, Village of the Damned 1995, A Step Toward Tomorrow 1996. *Address:* c/o Scott Henderson, William Morris Agency, 151 El Camino Drive, Beverly Hills, CA 90212, U.S.A.

REEVE, Michael David, M.A., F.B.A.; British academic; b. 11 Jan. 1943; s. of Arthur Reeve and Edith Mary Barrett; m. Elizabeth Klingaman 1970; two s. one d.; ed. King Edward's School, Birmingham, Balliol Coll., Oxford; Harmsworth Sr. Scholar, Merton Coll., Oxford 1964–65; Woodhouse Research Fellow, St. John's Coll., Oxford 1965–66; Tutorial Fellow, Exeter Coll., Oxford 1966–84, Emer. Fellow 1984–; Kennedy Prof. of Latin and Fellow Pembroke Coll., Univ. of Cambridge 1984–; Visiting Prof. Univ. of Hamburg 1976, McMaster Univ. 1979, Univ. of Toronto 1982–83; Ed., Classical Quarterly 1981–86; Corresp. mem. Akad. der Wissenschaften, Göttingen 1990–; Foreign mem. Istituto Lombardo, Milan 1993–. *Publications:* Longus, Daphnis and Chloe 1982, contributions to Texts and Transmission 1983, Cicero, Pro Quinctio 1992; articles in European and American journals. *Leisure interests:* chess, music, gardening, mountain walking. *Address:* Pembroke College, Cambridge, CB2 1RF, England.

REEVES, Christopher Reginald, C.B.I.M.; British merchant banker; b. 14 Jan. 1936, Cardiff; s. of Reginald Reeves and Dora Tucker; m. Stella Jane Whinney 1965; three s.; ed. Malvern Coll.; served in Rifle Brigade, Kenya and Malaya 1955–58; Bank of England 1958–63; Hill Samuel & Co. Ltd. 1963–67; joined Morgan Grenfell & Co. Ltd. 1968, Dir. 1970, Head of Banking Div. 1972, Deputy Chair. 1975–84, Chief Exec. 1980–84, Chair. and Group Chief Exec. 1984–87; Sr. Adviser, Pres. Merrill Lynch Int. Ltd. 1988, Vice-Chair. 1989–93, Chair. 1993–98, Deputy Chair. 1998–; Chair. Merrill Lynch Europe 1993–98; Chair. Merrill Lynch and Co. Inc. 1998–; Dir. Cornhill Insurance (fmrly. Allianz Int. Insurance Co. Ltd.) 1983–, BICC PLC 1982–, Int. Freehold Properties SARL 1988–96, Andrew Weir and Co. Ltd. 1982–92, Oman Int. Bank 1984–, India Fund 1989–, India Growth Fund 1989–, Austro-Hungary Fund 1990–95, Merrill Lynch Africa Ltd. (fmrly. Smith Borkum Hare (Pty.) Ltd.) 1996–, DSP Merrill Lynch 1997–; mem. City Univ. Business School Council 1986–93, CBI Council 1998–; Gov. Dulwich Coll. Preparatory School 1977–; Treas. City Univ. 1992–. *Leisure interests:* sailing, shooting, skiing. *Address:* 64 Flood Street, London, SW3 5TE, England.

REEVES, Keanu; American actor; b. 2 Sept. 1964, Beirut, Lebanon; ed. Toronto High School for Performing Arts; training at Second City Workshop; Toronto stage debut in Wolf Boy; other stage appearances in For Adults Only, Romeo and Juliet; with rock band Dogstar 1996–; TV films: Letting Go 1985, Act of Vengeance 1986, Babes in Toyland 1986, Under the Influence 1986, Brotherhood of Justice 1986, Save the Planet (TV special) 1990. *Films:* Prodigal, Flying 1986, Youngblood 1986, River's Edge 1987, Permanent Record 1988, The Night Before 1988, The Prince of Pennsylvania 1988, Dangerous Liaisons 1988, 18 Again 1988, Bill and Ted's Excellent Adventure 1988, Parenthood 1989, I Love You to Death 1990, Tune In Tomorrow 1990, Bill and Ted's Bogus Journey 1991, Point Break 1991, My Own Private Idaho 1991, Bram Stoker's Dracula 1992, Much Ado About Nothing 1993, Even Cowgirls Get the Blues, Little Buddha 1993, Speed 1994, Johnny Mnemonic 1995, A Walk in the Clouds 1995, Chain Reaction, Feeling Minnesota, The Devil's Advocate 1996, The Last Time I Committed Suicide 1997, The Matrix 1998. *Address:* c/o Erwin Stoff, 9830 Wilshire Boulevard, Beverly Hills, CA 90212, U.S.A.

REEVES, Marjorie Ethel, C.B.E., PH.D., D.LITT., F.R.HIST.S., F.B.A.; British university teacher (retd.); b. 17 July 1905, Bratton, Wilts.; d. of Robert John Reeves and Edith Sarah (née Whitaker) Reeves; ed. Trowbridge Girls' High School, Wilts., St. Hugh's Coll. Oxford and Westfield Coll. London; History Mistress, Roan School for Girls, Greenwich, London 1927–29; History Lecturer, St. Gabriel's Coll., London 1931–38; Tutor, later Fellow, St. Anne's Coll. Oxford and Univ. Lecturer 1938–72, Vice-Prin. St. Anne's Coll. 1948–68; Hon. Citizen of San Giovanni, Italy 1994; Hon. D.Litt. (Bath) 1992, Medlicott Medal 1993. *Publications:* The Influence of Prophecy in the Later Middle Ages 1969, The Figurae of Joachim of Fiore 1972, Joachim of Fiore and the Prophetic Future 1976, Sheepbell and Ploughshare 1978, Joachim of Fiore and the Myth of the Eternal Evangel in the Nineteenth Century (with Warwick Gould) 1987, Competence, Delight and the Common Good: reflections on the crisis in higher education 1988, The Diaries of Jeffrey Whitaker 1739–1741 (with J. Morrison) 1989, Prophetic Rome in the High Renaissance Period (ed.) 1992, Pursuing the Muses: A Study of Culture and Education from Two Collections of Family Papers 1700–1900 1996, Christian Thinking and Social Order, 1930 to the Present Day (ed. and contrib.) 1999; numerous books in the Then and There Series. *Leisure interests:* gardening, music. *Address:* 38 Norham Road, Oxford, OX2 6SQ, England. *Telephone:* (01865) 557039.

REEVES, Most Rev. Sir Paul Alfred, G.C.M.G., G.C.V.O., M.A., L.TH.; New Zealand ecclesiastic and administrator; b. 6 Dec. 1932, Wellington; s. of D'Arcy Lionel Reeves and Hilda Mary Reeves; m. Beverley Watkins 1959; three d.; ed. Wellington Coll., Vic. Univ. of Wellington, St. John's Theological Coll., Auckland and St. Peter's Coll., Oxford; Deacon 1958; Priest 1960; Curate, Tokoroa, N.Z. 1958–59, St. Mary the Virgin, Oxford 1959–61, Kirkley St. Peter, Lowestoft 1961–63; Vicar, St. Paul, Okato, N.Z. 1964–66; Lecturer in Church History St. John's Coll., Auckland 1966–69; Dir. of Christian Educ. Diocese of Auckland 1969–71; Bishop of Waiapu 1971–79, of Auckland 1979; Primate and Archbishop of New Zealand 1980–85; Visiting Prof., Univ. of Auckland 1997; Gov.-Gen. of New Zealand 1985–90; Rep. of Anglican Church to UN 1991–93; Chair. Environmental Council 1974–76; Dean Te Rau Kahikatea Theological Coll., Auckland 1994–95; Deputy Leader Comm. of Observers S. African elections 1994; Leader Comm. of Observers Ghanaian elections 1996; Chair. Fijian Constitutional Review Comm., 1995–96; Hon. Fellow St. Peter's Coll., Oxford 1980, Hon. D.C.L. (Oxon.) 1985; Hon. LL.D. (Vic., N.Z.); Hon. DD. (General, New York); Dr. h.c. (Edin.) 1994; K.St.J. 1986. *Leisure interests:* swimming, sailing, jogging. *Address:* 16E Cathedral Place, Parnell, Auckland, New Zealand. *Telephone:* (9) 3022913. *Fax:* (9) 3099912.

REEVES, Saskia; British actress; b. London; d. of Peter Reeves; ed. Guildhall School of Music and Drama, London; toured S. America, India and Europe with Cheek By Jowl theatre co. appearing in A Midsummer Night's Dream and The Man of Mode; subsequent stage appearances include: Metamorphosis (Mermaid), Who's Afraid of Virginia Woolf? (Young Vic), Measure for Measure (Young Vic), Separation (Hampstead Theatre), Smelling A Rat (Hampstead Theatre), Ice Cream (Royal Court); appeared in BBC TV In My Defence Series; other TV credits. *Films:* December Bride, Close My Eyes, The Butterfly Kiss, Much Ado About Nothing 1998.

REFALO, Michael, B.A.(HONS), LL.D., M.P.; Maltese politician and lawyer; b. 25 Feb. 1936; s. of Edward Refalo; m. Blanche Smith; one s. three d.; ed. St. Aloysius Coll., Univ. of Malta; lawyer 1961; fmr. Pres. of Students' Council; mem. Parl. 1971–; Parl. Sec. for Tourism 1987–94; Minister for Youth and the Arts 1994–95; Minister for Justice and the Arts 1995–96; Shadow Minister and Opposition Spokesman on Tourism 1996–98; Minister for Tourism 1998–; ed. for nine years of Sunday Nationalist Party newspaper; Nationalist Party. *Publications:* editorials and articles in other newspapers. *Address:* Ministry of Tourism, Pallazzo Spinola, St. Julian's, Malta. *Telephone:* (356) 383847/8. *Fax:* (356) 383834.

REFFELL, Adm. Sir Derek Roy, K.C.B.; British naval officer; b. 6 Oct. 1928, Wanstead; s. of Edward (Roy) Reffell and Murielle Reffell; m. Janne Gronow Davis 1956; one s. one d.; ed. Culford School, Suffolk, Royal Naval Coll., Dartmouth; C.O., H.M.S. Sirius 1966–67; Exec. Officer, Royal Naval Coll., Dartmouth 1968–69; Capt., H.M.S. Hermes 1974–76; Dir. Naval Warfare 1976–78; Commodore, Amphibious Warfare 1978–79; Asst. Chief of Naval Staff (Policy) 1979–82; Flag Officer 3rd Flotilla and NATO Commdr. Anti-submarine Warfare Group 2 1982–83; Flag Officer, Naval Air Command 1983–84; Controller of the Navy 1984–89; Adm. 1988; Gov. and C.-in-C. Gibraltar 1989–93; Master, Hon. Co. of Coachmakers of London 1998–99; King's Medal, Royal Naval Coll. Dartmouth 1945, Shadwell Testimonial 1958; K. St. J. *Leisure interests:* winemaking, golf, painting. *Address:* c/o Lloyds Private Banking, 50 Grosvenor Street, London, W1X 9FA, England.

REFSHAUGE, Major-Gen. Sir William Dudley, A.C., Kt., C.B.E., E.D., M.B., B.S., F.R.C.O.G., F.R.A.C.S., F.R.A.C.P., F.R.A.C.M.A., F.R.A.C.O.G.; Australian health official; b. 3 April 1913, Melbourne; s. of Francis C. Refshauge and Margaret I. Brown; m. Helen E. Allwright 1942; four s. one d.; ed. Hampton High School and Scotch Coll., Melbourne and Melbourne Univ.; Resident Medical Officer, Alfred Hosp., Melbourne 1939, Women's Hosp. Melbourne 1946; served in Australian Army Medical Corps 1939–46; mentioned in despatches four times; Registrar, Women's Hosp. 1946–47, Medical Supt. 1948–51; Deputy Dir.-Gen. Army Medical Services 1951–55, Dir.-Gen. 1955–60; Commonwealth of Australia Dir.-Gen. of Health 1960–73; Chair. Nat. Health and Medical Research Council 1960–73, Commonwealth Council for Nat. Fitness 1960–73, Commonwealth Health Insurance Council 1960–73, etc.; mem. Exec. Bd., WHO 1967–70, Chair. 1969–70; Pres. World Health Assembly 1971; Sec.-Gen. World Medical Asscn. 1973–76; Patron Australian Sports Medicine Asscn., Totally and Permanently Incapacitated Asscn. (T.P.I.) 1983–, 15 Field Ambulance Asscns., Medical Asscn. for Prevention of War, Life Educ. Centre, A.C.T., Hospice Soc., A.C.T., 2/2 Field Regt. Asscn.; Nat. Trustee Returned Services League of Australia 1963–73, 1976–; Chair. Bd. of Man. Canberra Girls Grammar School 1977; mem. Bd. of Dirs. Walter and Eliza Hall Inst. of Medical Research 1977–85, Chair. Medical Research Ethics Cttee. 1980–85; mem. Bd. of Dirs. Nat. Cttee. Sir Robert Menzies Foundation 1979–90; Hon. Consultant Australian Foundation on Alcoholism and Drugs of Dependence 1979–89; Chair. Blood Transfusion Cttee., Red Cross Soc. (A.C.T.) 1980; Pres. 1st Pan-Pacific Conf. on Drugs and Alcohol 1980; mem. Bd. of Dirs. Int. Council on Alcohol and Additions (I.C.A.A.) 1982–89, Deputy Pres. 1985–89; Chair. Interim Bd. of Man., Menzies School of Health Research, Darwin 1983–85, Chair. Bd. of Man. 1985–86; Deputy Chair. Research Grants Advisory Cttee. Menzies Foundation 1980–85; Chair. Planning Cttee., Centre for Population Health Research, Univ. of Tasmania 1986–87; Chair. Research into Drug Abuse Advisory Cttee. (Australian Drug Offensive) 1986–88; Hon. Fellow Royal Soc. of Health; Hon. M.D. (Sydney); Anzac Peace Prize 1990, Meritorious Service Medal, R.S.L. 1992. *Publications:* articles in Medical Journal of Australia and New Zealand Medical Journal. *Leisure interests:* bowls, rug-making, gardening. *Address:* 26 Birdwood Street, Hughes, A.C.T. 2605, Australia. *Telephone:* 2810943.

REGAN, Donald Thomas; American financial executive; b. 21 Dec. 1918, Cambridge, Mass.; s. of William F. Regan and Kathleen (née Ahern) Regan; m. Ann Gordon Buchanan 1942; two s. two d.; ed. Harvard Coll.; U.S. Marine Corps 1940–46, attaining rank of Lt.-Col.; joined Merrill Lynch 1946, partner 1953; Vice-Pres. Merrill Lynch, Pierce, Fenner & Smith Inc. 1959, Exec. Vice-Pres. 1964, Chair. of Bd. and Chief Exec. Officer 1971–81; Chair. of Bd. and Chief Exec. Officer Merrill Lynch and Co. Inc. 1973–81; Pres. Regdon Assocs. 1987–; Sec. of the U.S. Treasury 1981–85, White House Chief of Staff 1985–87; Vice-Chair. Bd. of Dirs. of NYSE 1972–75; mem. Policy Cttee. of Business Roundtable 1978–80; Trustee, Cttee. for Econ. Devt. 1978–80, Charles E. Merrill Trust and Univ. of Pennsylvania; Hon. LL.D. (Hahnemann Medical Coll. and Hospital, Univ. of Penn., Tri-State Coll.); Commdr. Légion d'honneur. *Publications:* A View from the Street 1972, For the Record: From Wall Street to Washington 1988. *Address:* Marketplace Center, 240 McLaws Circle, Suite 142, Williamsburg, VA 23185, U.S.A. *Telephone:* (757) 220-5177. *Fax:* (757) 220-6270.

REGÀS, Rosa: Spanish writer; b. 1934, Barcelona; m.; five c.; ed. Barcelona Univ.; with Seix Barral 1964-70, with Edhasa (both publrs.); translator UN; f. and ed. La Gaya Ciencia; Premio Nadal for Azul 1994. *Publications include:* Memoria de Almator (novel) 1991, Azul (novel) 1993.

REGESTER, Michael; British public relations executive; b. 8 April 1947, Godalming; s. of Hugh Regester and Monique Levrey; m. 1st Christine Regester 1969 (divorced 1993); two d.; m. 2nd Leanne Moscardi 1994; one s. one d.; ed. St. Peter's School, Guildford; Man. Public Affairs, Gulf Oil Corpn., Europe, W. Africa and Middle East 1975–80; co-founder and jt. Man. Dir. Traverse-Healy and Regester Ltd. 1980–87; Man. Dir. Charles Barker Traverse-Healy Ltd. 1987–89; Man. Dir. Regester PLC 1990–94; partner Regester Larkin 1994–. *Publications:* Crisis Management 1987, Investor Relations (with N. Ryder) 1990, Issues and Crisis Management (with J. Larkin) 1997. *Leisure interests:* sailing, golf, tennis, opera, cooking. *Address:* Regester Larkin Ltd., 16 Doughty Street, London, WC1N 2PL, England (Office). *Telephone:* 0171-831 3839. *Fax:* 0171-831 3632.

REGGIANI, Serge; Italian-born French actor and singer; b. 2 May 1922, Reggio nell'Emilia; s. of Ferruccio Reggiani and Letizia Spagni; m. 1st Janine Darcey; one s. (deceased) one d.; m. 2nd Annie Noël; two s. one d.; ed. Conservatoire Nat. d'Art Dramatique; theatrical roles in Britannicus, Les parents terribles, Un homme comme les autres, Les trois mousquetaires, Les séquestrés d'Altona, etc.; Chevalier, Légion d'honneur, Ordre nat. du Mérite, Officier des Arts et des Lettres. *Films include:* Le carrefour des enfants perdus, Les portes de la nuit, Manon, Les amants de Vérone, La ronde, Casque d'or, Napoléon, Les salauds vont en enfer, Les misérables, Marie Octobre, La grande pagaille, La guerre continue, Tutti a casa, Le Doulos, Le guépard, Marie-Chantal contre le Docteur Kah, Les aventuriers, La 25e heure, La mafia fait la loi, L'armée des ombres, Comptes à rebours, Touche pas à la femme blanche 1974, Vincent, François, Paul . . . et les autres 1974, Le chat et la souris 1975, Une fille cousue de fil blanc 1977, L'empreinte des géants, Fantastica, La terrasse 1980, Mauvais sang 1986, L'Apiculture 1986, Ne réveillez pas un flic qui dort 1988, Coupe Franche 1989, Il y a des jours . . . et des lunes 1990, J'ai engagé un tueur 1991, De force avec d'autres 1993, le Petit garçon 1993; albums include Nos quatre vérités 1997; Exhbn. of paintings Vekava Gallery, Paris 1997. *Publications:* La question se pose 1990, Dernier courrier avant la nuit 1995. *Address:* c/o Charley Marouani, 37 rue Marbeuf, 75008 Paris; c/o Artmédia, 10 avenue Georges V, 75008 Paris, France.

REGIS, John; British athlete; b. 13 Oct. 1966, Lewisham; s. of Antony Regis and Agnes Regis; winner, UK 200m 1985 (tie), 100m 1988, Amateur Athletics Asscn. 200m 1986–87; UK record for 200m, World Championships 1987; World Championships Bronze Medallist 200m, Silver Medal, Olympic Games Seoul 1988, 300m indoor record holder Commonwealth Games 1990; Silver Medal 200m 1991, Gold Medal 4 x 100m relay 1991; Gold Medal 200m, 4 x 100m relay, 4 x 400m relay 1993; Gold Medal World Cup 1994, mem. British team Olympic Games, Atlanta 1996. *Address:* c/o Belgrave Harriers Athletic Club, Batley Croft, 58 Harvest Road, Englefield Green, Surrey, England.

REGNIER, Charles; German actor and theatrical director; b. 22 July 1914, Freiburg; m. 1st Pamela Wedekind 1941 (died 1986); one s. two d.; m. 2nd Sonja Ziemann 1989; ed. school of dramatic art; acted in Vienna, Zürich, Hamburg, Cologne, Munich, Düsseldorf, Bochum and Wuppertal; appeared in many films including Band in Gold, Sacha Guitry, Scribe, Jamiaque 1989; trans. works of Giraudoux, Cocteau, Maugham, Feydeau, Labiche, Mauriac, Colette, Barillet-Gredy, Dorin; German Critics' Prize 1955. *Address:* Neherstr. 7, 81675 Munich, Germany.

REGO, Paula; British artist; b. 26 Jan. 1935, Lisbon, Portugal; d. of José Figueiroa Rego and Maria de San José Paiva Figueiroa Rego; m. Victor Willing (died 1988); one s. two d.; ed. St. Julian's School, Carcavelos, Portugal, Slade School of Fine Art, University Coll. London; numerous one-person exhbns. since 1979 in London, Lisbon, Amsterdam, Plymouth, Manchester and Bristol; retrospective exhbns. at Gulbenkian Foundation, Lisbon 1989, Serpentine Gallery, London 1989, 1992, Tate Gallery, Liverpool 1997; included in many mixed exhbns. in Paris, Rome, São Paulo, Tokyo, Madrid, Baden-Baden, New York, U.K.; Assoc. Artist to Nat. Gallery 1990; Sr. Fellow Royal Coll. of Art 1989. *Publication:* Peter Pan (etchings) 1992. *Address:* c/o Marlborough Fine Art, 6 Albemarle Street, London, W1X 4BY, England. *Telephone:* 0171-629 5161.

REGY, Claude; French theatre director; b. 1 May 1923, Nîmes; dir. plays by Marguerite Duras, Harold Pinter, James Saunders, Tom Stoppard, Edward Bond, David Storey 1960–70, by Nathalie Sarraute, Peter Handke, Botho Strauss 1970–80, by Maeterlinck, Wallace Stevens, Leslie Kaplan, Victor Slavkine 1980–90, by Gregory Motton, Henri Meschonnic 1990–96; dir. Ivanov (Chekhov) 1985, Huis-Clos (J. P. Sartre) 1990 (both at Comédie Française); dir. operas Die Meistersinger (Wagner), Théâtre du Chatelet 1990, Jeanne d'Arc au Bûcher (Honegger), Opéra Bastille 1992; Artistic Dir. Les Ateliers Contemporains 1980–; Grand Prix Nat. du Théâtre 1992, Grand Prix des Arts de la Scène de la Ville de Paris 1994; Officier des Arts et des Lettres. *Publication:* Espaces Perdus 1991. *Leisure interest:* country house. *Address:* 68 rue J. J. Rousseau, 75001 Paris, France. *Telephone:* 01.48.87.95.10 (Office); 01.42.33.34.11 (Home). *Fax:* 01.48.87.45.01.

REHN, Elisabeth, D.SC.; Finnish international official and politician; b. 6 April 1935; m. Ove Rehn 1955; one s. three d.; fmr. leader Swedish People's Party in Parl.; fmr. Minister of Defence, fmr. Minister for Women's Equality; cand. in Finnish Presidential election 1994; M.E.P. 1995–96; UN Special Rapporteur for Human Rights in fmr. Yugoslavia 1995–98; Special Rep. of Sec.-Gen. of the UN in Bosnia and Herzegovina Jan. 1998–. *Leisure interests:* fine arts, sports, nature. *Address:* UNMIBH, O/SRSG, Geodetski Zavod, Mese Selimovica 69, 71210 Ilidza, Sarajevo, Bosnia and Herzegovina.

REHNQUIST, William H., LL.B., M.A.; American judge; b. 1 Oct. 1924, Milwaukee, Wis.; s. of William Benjamin Rehnquist and Margery Peck

Rehnquist; m. Natalie Cornell 1953; one s. two d.; ed. Stanford and Harvard Univs.; law clerk to U.S. Supreme Court Justice R. H. Jackson 1952–53; private practice, Evans, Kitchel and Jenckes, Phoenix, Ariz. 1953–57, Cunningham, Messenger, Carson & Elliott 1957–60, Powers & Rehnquist 1960–69; Asst. Attorney-Gen., Office of Legal Counsel, Dept. of Justice 1969–71; Assoc. Justice, Supreme Court of U.S.A. 1971–86, Chief Justice Sept. 1986–; Hon. Master of the Bench, Middle Temple, London 1986–; mem. American Bar Assen., American Judicature Soc., etc. *Publications:* Grand Inquests 1992, All the Laws But One: Civil Liberties in Wartime 1998. *Address:* Supreme Court of the United States, 1 First Street, N.E., Washington, DC 20543, U.S.A.

REICH, Robert Bernard, M.A., J.D.; American politician and political economist; b. 24 June 1946, Scranton, Pa.; s. of Edwin Saul and Mildred Dorf (Freshman) Reich; m. Clare Dalton 1973; two s.; ed. Dartmouth Coll., Oxford Univ. (U.K.), Yale Univ.; Asst. Solicitor-Gen., U.S. Dept. of Justice, Washington 1974–76; Dir. of Policy Planning FTC, Washington 1976–81; mem. Faculty John F. Kennedy School of Govt., Harvard Univ. 1981–; fmr. Econ. Adviser to Bill Clinton; Sec. of Labor 1993–97; Prof. Brandeis Univ. Grad. School for Advanced Studies in Social Welfare 1997–; Chair. Biotechnology Section U.S. Office Tech. Assessment, Washington 1990–91; Chair. Editorial Bd. The American Prospect 1990–; mem. Bd. of Dirs., Econ. Policy Inst., Washington; Contributing Ed. The New Republic, Washington 1982–93; Rhodes Scholar 1968. *Publications:* The Next American Frontier 1983, Tales of a New America 1987, The Power of Public Ideas (Co-author) 1987, The Work of Nations 1991, Putting People First 1997, Locked in the Cabinet 1997. *Address:* Brandeis University, 415 South Street, Waltham, MA 02254; c/o Department of Labor, 200 Constitution Ave., N.W., Washington, DC 20210-0001, U.S.A.

REICH, Steve, M.A.; American composer; b. 3 Oct. 1936, New York; s. of Leonard Reich and June Carroll; m. Beryl Korot 1976; two s.; ed. Cornell Univ., Juilliard School of Music, Mills Coll.; studied composition with Berio and Milhaud; also studied at the American Soc. for Eastern Arts and in Accra and Jerusalem; f. own ensemble 1966; Steve Reich and Musicians have completed numerous tours world-wide 1971–; his music performed by major orchestras and ensembles in United States and Europe; recipient of three Rockefeller Foundation Grants 1975–81, a Guggenheim Fellowship and an award from the Koussevitzky Foundation 1981; Grammy Award for best contemporary composition, for Different Trains 1990; mem. American Acad. of Arts and Letters 1994–. *Major works include:* Drumming 1971, The Desert Music 1984, Tehillim 1982, Eight Lines for Chamber Orchestra 1985, Music for 18 Musicians, Vermont Counterpoint, The Four Sections 1987, Different Trains 1988, The Cave (with Beryl Korot) 1993, City Life 1995, Proverb 1996. *Recordings include:* Come Out, Violin Phase, It's Gonna Rain, Four Organs, Drumming, Six Pianos, Music for Mallet Instruments, Voices and Organ, Music for a Large Ensemble, Octet, and Variations for Winds, Strings and Keyboards, Music for 18 Musicians, The Desert Music, Electric Counterpoint, Different Trains, The Four Sections, Nagoya Marimbas, City Life, Proverb, Hindenburg (in collaboration with Beryl Korot). *Address:* c/o IMG Artists, 22 E. 71st Street, New York, NY 10021, U.S.A.

REICH-RANICKI, Marcel; German literary critic; b. 2 June 1920, Wloclawek; s. of David Reich and Helene Auerbach; m. Teofila Langnas 1942; one s.; in Berlin 1929–38; deported to Poland 1938; publrs., reader and literary critic, Warsaw until 1958; returned to Germany 1958; regular literary critic Die Zeit 1960–73; guest lecturer in U.S. univs. 1968–69; regular guest Prof. of Modern German literature in Univs. of Stockholm and Uppsala 1971–75; Man. Ed. Frankfurter Allgemeine Zeitung 1973–88; Hon. Prof. Univ. of Tübingen 1974–; Heine-Plakette 1976, Ricarda Huch Prize 1981, Goethe-Plakette 1984, Thomas-Mann-Preis 1987, Ludwig-Börne-Preis 1995; Dr. Phil. h.c. *Publications:* Deutsche Literatur in West und Ost 1963, Literarisches Leben in Deutschland 1965, Literatur der kleinen Schritte 1967, Lauter Verrisse 1970, Uber Ruhestörer-Juden in der deutschen Literatur 1973, Zur Literatur der DDR 1974, Nachprüfung, Aufsätze über deutsche Schriftsteller von gestern 1977, Entgegnung, Zur deutschen Literatur der siebziger Jahre 1979, Betrifft Goethe 1982, Lauter Lobreden 1985, Nichts als Literatur, Aufsätze und Anmerkungen 1985, Mehr als ein Dichter, Über Heinrich Böll 1986, Thomas Mann und die Seinen 1987, Herz, Ärzt und Literatur 1987, Thomas Bernhard, Aufsätze und Reden 1990, Max Frisch, Aufsätze 1991, Reden auf Hilde Spiel 1991, Ohne Rabatt—Über Literatur aus der DDR, Der doppette Boden 1992, Günter Grass, Aufsätze 1992, Die Anwälte der Literatur 1994, Martin Walser 1994, Vladimir Nabokov 1995, Ungeheuer oben. Über Bertolt Brecht 1996, Der Fall Heine 1997. *Leisure interests:* literature, theatre, music. *Address:* Gustav-Freytag-Strasse 36, 60320 Frankfurt am Main, Germany.

REICHARDT, Robert Heinrich, D. PHIL; Austrian/Swiss professor of sociology, social philosophy and methodology of the social sciences; b. 2 May 1927, Basel; s. of Heinrich Reichardt and Magdalena (née Bachlehner) Reichardt; m. Dr. Isolde Dünhofen; ed. Univ. of Basel; Research Assoc. Princeton Univ. 1960–61; Asst. Inst. for Social Sciences, Univ. of Basel 1962–64; Dir. Dept. for Sociology, Inst. for Higher Studies, Vienna 1964–66; Prof. Univ. of Vienna 1966; Exec. Dir. Inst. for Research on Socio-Econ. Devt., Austrian Acad. of Sciences 1977–84, Head Comm. for Sociology of Arts and Music 1990–; mem. Austrian Acad. of Sciences 1978–; Fellow Collegium Ramazzini Carpi, Italy 1990, Academia Artium et Scientiarum Europaea 1991; Co-operative Prize, Univ. of Basel 1960, Gold Medal of Honour, City of Vienna 1993. *Publications:* Die Schallplatte als kulturelles und ökon. Phänomen, Bedürfnisforschung im Dienste der Stadtplanung, Überleben wir den technischen Fortschritt (with others), Einführung in die Soziologie für Juristen. *Leisure interests:* composition, playing the piano.

REICHMANN, Paul; Canadian business executive; b. 1930, Vienna, Austria; s. of Renée Reichmann; moved to Toronto 1954; with brothers Ralph and Albert Reichmann formed Olympia & York Construction Co. (business engaged mainly in property but with investments in Gulf Canada, The Consumers Gas Co., Abitibi-Price, real estate, transportation and food retailing); completed First Canadian Place, Toronto (five million sq. ft of offices) 1975; purchased eight office bldgs. in Manhattan, New York 1976; completed bldg. of World Financial Center in New York 1986; took control of Canary Wharf project in London's Docklands 1987. *Address:* c/o Olympia & York, 1 Canada Square, Canary Wharf, London, E14 5AB, England. *Telephone:* 0171-418 2000.

REID, Allen (Alan) Forrest, A.M., PH.D., F.A.A., F.T.S.; Australian scientist; b. 26 March 1931, New Zealand; s. of V. C. Reid and L. E. Reid; m. Hetty Mackay Blythe 1986; two s. one d. two step-d.; ed. Univ. of N.Z., Christchurch, A.N.U., Canberra, Cornell Univ., New York; joined CSIRO 1959, research scientist 1972–82, Chief research scientist 1972–82, Chief Div. of Mineral Engineering 1982–84, Dir. Inst. of Energy and Earth Resources 1984–87, Inst. of Minerals, Energy and Construction 1988–97; Dir. (non-exec.) Queensland Metals Corpn. Ltd. 1989–, Minproc Tech. Pty. Ltd.; Chair. Australia Environmental Resources NL 1996–97, Dir. 1997–; Chair. Man. Bd. Australian Petroleum Co-operative Research Centre; CSIRO Rivett Medal 1970. *Leisure interests:* travel, art, gardening. *Address:* c/o Queensland Metals Corporation Ltd., Level 6 Toowong Tower, 9 Sherwood Road, Toowong, Queensland 4066, Australia.

REID, Harry, J.D.; American politician; b. 2 Dec. 1939, Searchlight, Nevada; s. of Harry Reid and Inez Reid; m. Landra Joy Gould; four s. one d.; ed. George Washington Univ.; City Attorney, Henderson, Nev. 1964–66; Trustee, Southern Nev. Memorial Hosp. Bd. 1967–69, Chair. Bd. of Trustees 1968–69; mem. Nev. Ass. 1969–70; Lieut.-Gov. of Nev. 1970–74; Chair. Nev. Gaming Comm. 1977–81; Congressman, U.S. House of Reps., Washington 1983–87; Senator from Nevada Jan. 1987–; mem. numerous senate cttees.; mem. Bd. of Dirs. of American Cancer Soc., of Legal Aid Soc., of YMCA; Nat. Jewish Hosp., Humanitarian Award 1984; Hon. LL.D. (Southern Utah State Coll.) 1984; Democrat. *Address:* U.S. Senate, Washington, DC 20510, U.S.A.

REID, Sir Martin, K.B.E., C.M.G., M.A.; British diplomatist (retd.); b. 27 Aug. 1928, London; s. of the late Marcus Reid and Winifred Mary Stephens; m. Jane Elizabeth Harwood 1956; one s. three d.; ed. Merchant Taylors' School, and Brasenose Coll., Oxford; entered British Foreign Service 1953, and served in Paris, Rangoon, London, Georgetown and Bucharest 1954–70; Deputy High Commr., Malawi 1970–73; Prin. Pvt. Sec. to successive Secs. of State for Northern Ireland 1973–74; Head of Cen. and Southern African Dept., FCO 1974–78; Minister of British Embassy, S. Africa 1979–82; attached to Civil Service Selection Bd. 1983; British High Commr. in Jamaica and Amb. (non-resident) to Haiti 1984–87; Research Adviser, FCO 1987–88; Hon. Sec. Friends of Student Christian Movt. 1988–91; one-man exhbns. of painting, London 1983, Kingston, Jamaica 1987, Dulwich, London 1989, 1991, 1994. *Publication:* Camille Pissarro 1993. *Leisure interests:* painting, chess. *Address:* 43 Carson Road, London, SE21 8HT, England. *Telephone:* 0181-670 6151.

REID, Sir Norman Robert, Kt., D.LITT., D.A., F.M.A., F.I.I.C.; British art gallery director; b. 27 Dec. 1915, London; s. of Edward Reid and Blanche Drouet; m. Jean Lindsay Bertram 1941; one s. one d.; ed. Wilson's Grammar School, London, Edinburgh Coll. of Art, and Edinburgh Univ.; Maj. Argyll and Sutherland Highlanders 1939–46; Tate Gallery 1946–79, Dir. 1964–79; Fellow, Int. Inst. for Conservation of Historic and Artistic Works, Sec.-Gen. 1963–65, Vice-Chair. 1966–79; Chair. British Council Fine Art Cttee. 1968–76; paintings in Tate Gallery, London, Scottish Nat. Gallery of Modern Art and many pvt. collections; Officer, Order of Aztec Eagle (Mexico). *Leisure interests:* painting, gardening. *Address:* 50 Brabourne Rise, Park Langley, Beckenham, Kent, England (Home).

REID, Ogden Rogers, A.B.; American journalist and diplomatist; b. 24 June 1925, New York, N.Y.; s. of Ogden Reid and Helen Miles Rogers; m. 1949; six c.; ed. Yale Univ.; Reporter New York Herald Tribune 1950–51, various depts. 1952–53; Pres. and Ed. New York Herald Tribune S.A., Paris 1953–59, Dir. 1953–; Vice-Pres. New York Herald Tribune Inc. 1954–55, Pres. and Ed. 1955–58, Dir. 1950; Amb. to Israel 1959–61; Chair. New York State Comm. Against Discrimination 1961–62; Vice-Chair. and Dir. Duratek Corpn.; Vice-Chair. Council of American Ambs.; Dir. Panama Canal Co. 1956–59, Mass. Mutual Life Insurance Co. 1957–60, Nat. Patent Devt. Corpn., Gen. Physics Corpn., Interferon Sciences, Inc.; Congressman for Westchester County, N.Y. 1962–74; Nacional do Cruzeiro do Sul, Brazil 1956; Chair. Bard Coll. Center; Trustee, Caribbean Cen. American Action; Chevalier, Légion d'honneur 1957; Hon. LL.D., Adelphi Coll. (N.Y.); Hon. Fellow, Bar-Ilan Univ., Israel 1959; Democrat. *Publication:* How Strong is America? The Score on National Defense (with Robert S. Bird) 1950. *Leisure interests:* sailing, skiing, hunting, fishing.

REID, Sir Robert Paul (Bob), Kt., M.A.; British businessman; b. 1 May 1934; m. Joan Mary Reid 1958; three s.; ed. St. Andrews Univ.; joined Shell

1956, Sarawak Oilfields 1956–59, Head of Personnel Nigeria 1959–67; Africa and S. Asia Regional Org. 1967–68, Personal Asst. and Planning Adviser to Chair. Shell & BP Services, Kenya 1968–70, Man. Dir. Nigeria 1970–74, Man. Dir. Thailand 1974–78; Vice-Pres. Int. Aviation and Products Training 1978–80, Exec. Dir. Downstream Oil, Shell Co. of Australia Int. Petroleum Co. 1984–90, Chair. and Chief Exec. Shell U.K. 1985–90; Chair. Foundation for Man. Educ. 1986–; Chair. British Railways Bd. 1990–95, London Electricity PLC 1994–97, Sears PLC 1995–, Rosyth 2000 1995–; a Deputy Governor Bank of England 1997; Dir. AVIS 1997–, Sun Life Assurance Co. of Canada 1997–; Chancellor Robert Gordon Univ. 1993–; Hon. LL.D. (St. Andrews) 1987, (Aberdeen) 1988. *Leisure interests:* golf, sailing. *Address:* Sears PLC, 40 Duke Street, London, W1A 2HP, England. *Telephone:* 0171-200 5999.

REID, Timothy Escott, M.A., M.LITT.; Canadian economist, management consultant, educator and public servant; b. 21 Feb. 1936, Toronto, Ont.; s. of Escott Meredith Reid and Ruth (Herriot) Reid; m. Julyan Fancott 1962; one s. one d.; ed. Univ. of Toronto, Yale Univ., Oxford Univ. (Rhodes Scholar), Harvard Business School; Exec. Sec. Canadian Inst. of Public Affairs 1962–63; Asst. to Pres., Asst. Prof. of Econs., Sec. Faculty of Graduate Studies, Research Assoc. for Public Policy, York Univ. 1963–72; mem. Legis. Ass., Ontario 1967–71; Prin. Admin., Economist, Manpower and Social Affairs, OECD, Paris 1972–74; joined Public Service of Canada 1974, subsequently Deputy Sec. Treasury Bd., Office of Comptroller-Gen. of Canada, Asst. Deputy Minister, Planning and Co-ordination, Dept. of Regional Econ. Expansion, Exec. Dir. Regional and Industrial Program Affairs, Dept. of Regional Industrial Expansion, Asst. Deputy Minister responsible for Tourism Canada 1984–85; Dir. and mem. exec. cttee. Canada Mortgage and Housing Corpn. 1980–82, Canadian Labour Market and Productivity Centre 1989 (Co-Chair. Bd. of Dirs. 1993–); headed 18-nation study visit to Japan 1984; Dean Faculty of Business and Prof. of Business Man., Ryerson Polytechnical Inst. 1985–89; Commr. Ont. Securities Comm. 1987–89; Pres. Canadian Chamber of Commerce 1989–; mem. Bd. of Dirs. Canadian Exec. Service Org. 1991–; Consultant, U.S. Nat. Science Foundation 1979–82; mem. Int. Trade Advisory Cttee. (ITAC), Govt. of Canada 1991–; mem. Canadian dels. to 6th and 7th annual APEC Leaders Meetings 1995, 1996. *Leisure interests:* skiing, tennis, skating, swimming, jogging. *Address:* Canadian Chamber of Commerce, 350 Sparks Street, Suite 501, Ottawa, ON K1R 7S8, Canada. *Telephone:* (613) 238-4000. *Fax:* (613) 238-7643.

REID CABRAL, Dr. Donald J.; Dominican politician, lawyer and businessman; b. 9 June 1923, Santiago de los Caballeros; s. of William C. Reid and Auristela Cabral de Reid; m. Clara A. Tejera 1949; two d.; ed. Univ. de Santo Domingo; Pres. Reid & Pellerano C.A. 1949–; Pres. Automobile Dealers' Asscn. 1949–62; Vice-Pres. Council of State 1962–63; Minister of Foreign Affairs Sept.-Dec. 1963; Amb. to UN 1963; Amb. to Israel 1963; Pres. Triumvirate which ruled Dominican Repub. 1963–65; Minister of Foreign Affairs 1964; Minister of Armed Forces 1964–65; Sec. of State without Portfolio 1988. *Leisure interests:* gardening, sailing, scuba-diving. *Address:* Cervantes 8, Santo Domingo, D.N., Dominican Republic. *Telephone:* 565-4481/4; 5-5677/8; 689-3389.

REIDY, Carolyn Kroll, PH.D.; American publishing executive; b. 2 May 1949, Washington, D.C.; d. of Henry and Mildred Kroll; m. Stephen Kroll Reidy 1974; ed. Middlebury Coll. Vt. and Indiana Univ.; various positions, Random House, New York 1975–83; Dir. of Subsidiary Rights, William Morrow & Co., New York 1983–85; Vice-Pres. Assoc. Publr., Vintage Books, Random House, New York 1985–87; Assoc. Publr., Random House (concurrent with Assoc. Publr. and Publr. of Vintage Books) 1987–88; Publr., Vintage Books 1987–88, Anchor Books, Doubleday, New York 1988; Pres. and Publr., Avon Books, New York 1988–92; Pres. and Publr., Simon and Schuster 1992–; Dir. NAMES Project 1994–98. *Address:* c/o Simon and Schuster, 1230 Avenue of the Americas, New York, NY 10020, U.S.A. *Telephone:* (212) 698-7323.

REIJNDERS, Lucas, PH.D.; Netherlands university professor; b. 4 Feb. 1946, Amsterdam; s. of C. Reijnders and C. M. Reijnders-Spillekom; one c.; ed. Univ. of Amsterdam; Dir. Environmental Inst. Univ. of Groningen 1974–80, mem. staff Nat. Environmental Office 1980–, Prof. of Environmental Science Univ. of Amsterdam 1988–; Prof. of Environmental Science Open Univ. 1999–; winner Gouden Ganzeveer 1990, Erewimpel ONRI 1992. *Publications:* Food in the Netherlands 1974, A Consumer Guide to Dutch Medicines 1980, Plea for a Sustainable Relation with the Environment 1984, Help the Environment 1991, Environmentally Improved Production and Products 1995, Agriculture in the Low Countries 1997. *Leisure interests:* 19th century literature. *Address:* Anna van den Vondelstraat 10, 1054 GZ Amsterdam, Netherlands. *Telephone:* 020-5256269. *Fax:* 020-5256272.

REILLY, Sir (D'Arcy) Patrick, G.C.M.G., O.B.E., M.A.; British diplomatist; b. 17 March 1909, Ootacamund, India; s. of Sir D'Arcy Reilly and Florence (née Wilkinson) Reilly; m. 1st Rachel Mary Sykes 1938 (died 1984); two d.; m. 2nd Ruth Norrington 1987; ed. Winchester Coll., and New Coll., Oxford; Fellow All Souls Coll., Oxford 1932–39, 1969–, Hon. Fellow, New Coll., Oxford 1972–; entered Diplomatic Service 1933; served Teheran 1935–38, Foreign Office 1938, Algiers 1943, Paris 1944, Athens 1945; Counsellor, Athens 1947; Imperial Defence Coll. 1949; Asst. Under-Sec. of State, Foreign Office 1950–53; Minister in Paris 1953–56; Deputy Under-Sec., Foreign Office 1956; Amb. to U.S.S.R. 1957–60; Deputy Under-Sec. Foreign Office 1960–64; Official Head U.K. Del. to UN Conf. on Trade and Devt.; Amb. to France 1965–68; Pres. London Chamber of Commerce and Industry 1972–75, Vice-Pres. 1975–; Chair. Banque Nat. de Paris Ltd. 1969–80, United Bank for Africa 1969–74, Univ. of London Management Cttee., British Inst. in Paris 1970–79, Council, Bedford Coll., Univ. of London 1970–75; Hon. D.Litt. (Bath); Commdr., Légion d'honneur 1979. *Leisure interests:* travel, architecture, gardening. *Address:* Flat 2, 75 Warrington Crescent, London, W9 1EH, England. *Telephone:* 0171-289 5384.

REILLY, (David) Nicholas (Nick), M.A., F.I.M.I.; British business executive; b. 17 Dec. 1949; s. of the late John Reilly and of Mona (née Glynne Jones) Reilly; m. Susan Haig 1976; one s. two d.; ed. Harrow School, St Catharine's Coll. Cambridge; investment analyst 1971–74; joined Gen. Motors 1974, Finance Dir. Moto Diesel Mexicana 1980–83, Supply Dir. Vauxhall Motors 1984–87, Vice-Pres. IBC 1987–90, Mfg. Dir. Vauxhall Ellesmere Port 1990–94, Vice.-Pres. Quality Gen. Motors Europe 1994–96, Chair., Man. Dir. Vauxhall Motors 1996–, Chair. IBC Vehicles 1996–; mem. Bd. Saab G.B. 1996–; Chair. Chester, Ellesmere, Wirral Training and Enterprise Council 1990–94. *Leisure interests:* tennis, swimming, sailing, golf, watching sports, music, opera, theatre. *Address:* Vauxhall Motors, Griffin House, Osborne Road, P.O. Box 3, Luton, Beds., LU1 3YT, England. *Telephone:* (01582) 427578.

REINA IDIAQUEZ, Carlos Roberto; Honduran politician; b. 13 March 1926; m. Bessie Watson; one s. (deceased), three d.; ed. Nat. Autonomous Univ. of Honduras, Univs. of London, Cambridge and Paris (Sorbonne) and London Inst. of Int. Affairs; Court Judge, Tegucigalpa 1953; served Embassy of Honduras, Paris 1960–65; Deputy to Nat. Constituent Ass. 1965; Dir. El Pueblo (official Liberal daily) 1966; Francisco Morazán Deputy for Nat. Congress 1971–77; Judge, Inter-American Court of Human Rights 1979; lecturer in Law, Nat. Autonomous Univ. of Honduras; regular lecturer at foreign univs.; Pres. of Honduras 1993–98. *Publications:* El Reto Democrático en Centro America, Honduras: Realidad Nacional y Crisis. *Address:* c/o Office of the President, Casa Presidencial, 6a Avda 1a Calle, Tegucigalpa, Honduras.

REINER, Rob; American actor, writer and director; b. 6 March 1947, New York; s. of Carl Reiner and Estelle (née Lebost) Reiner; m. 1st Penny Marshall 1971 (divorced); m. 2nd Michele Singer 1989; ed. Univ. of Calif. at Los Angeles; has appeared with comic improvisation groups The Session and The Committee; scriptwriter for Enter Laughing 1967, Halls of Anger 1970, Where's Poppa 1970, Summertree 1971, Fire Sale 1977, How Come Nobody's on Our Side 1977; TV appearances: All In The Family 1971–78, Free Country 1978, Thursday's Game 1974, More Than Friends 1978, Million Dollar Infield 1972; directed: This is Spinal Tap 1984, The Sure Thing 1985, Stand By Me 1986, The Princess Bride 1987, Misery 1990; Co-producer and dir. When Harry Met Sally 1989, A Few Good Men 1992, North, The American President 1995, Ghosts of Mississippi 1996. *Address:* c/o Castle Rock Entertainment, 335 North Maple Drive, Suite 135, Beverly Hills, CA 90210, U.S.A.

REINHARD, Keith Leon; American advertising executive; b. 20 Jan. 1935, Berne, Ind.; s. of Herman Reinhard and Agnes Reinhard; m. Rose-Lee Simons 1976; two d.; four s. one d. by previous marriage; ed. public schools in Berne; commercial artist, Kling Studios, Chicago 1954–56; man. tech. communications dept. Magnavox Co., Fort Wayne, Ind. 1957–60; creative/account exec. Biddle Co., Bloomington, Ill. 1961–63; Exec. Vice-Pres., Dir. Creative Services and Pres. Needham, Harper & Steers Inc., Chicago 1964; then Chair. and C.E.O. Needham, Harper & Steers/U.S.A., Chicago; also Dir. Needham, Harper & Steers Inc.; Chair. and C.E.O. DDB Needham Worldwide Inc. New York 1986–, Chair. Exec. Cttee. 1989–. *Address:* DDB Needham Worldwide Inc., 437 Madison Avenue, New York, NY 10022, U.S.A.

REINHARDT, John Edward, M.S., PH.D.; American professor of political science and fmr. diplomatist; b. 8 March 1920, Glade Spring, Va.; s. of Edward Vinton Reinhardt and Alice Miller; m. Carolyn L. Daves 1947; three d.; ed. Knoxville Coll., Univs. of Chicago and Wisconsin; Instructor in English, Knoxville Coll. 1940–41, Fayetteville State Coll. 1941–42; U.S. Army 1942–46; grad. student 1946–50; Prof. of English, Virginia State Coll. 1950–56; Visiting Prof. of English, Atlanta Univ. 1953; Asst. Cultural Officer, American Embassy, Philippines 1956–58; Dir. American Cultural Center, Kyoto, Japan 1958–62; Dir. of Field Programs, American Embassy, Tokyo 1962–63; Cultural Attaché, Teheran 1963–66; Deputy Asst. Dir. of U.S. Information Agency for Far East 1966–68, for Africa 1968–70, for Far East 1970–71; Amb. to Nigeria 1971–75; Asst. Sec. of State for Public Affairs 1975–77; Dir. U.S. Information Agency 1977–78, Int. Communication Agency 1978–80, Acting Dir. Nat. Museum of African Art, Smithsonian Inst. 1981–83, Acting Asst. Sec. for History and Art 1983, Asst. Sec. 1983–84; Dir. Div. of Int. Activities 1984–87; Prof. of Political Science, Univ. Vermont, Burlington 1987–90, Prof. Emer. 1990–. *Leisure interests:* gardening, photography. *Address:* 6801 Laverock Court, Bethesda, MD 20817, U.S.A.

REINHARDT, Max, F.R.S.A.; British publisher; b. 30 Nov. 1915, Istanbul, Turkey; s. of Ernest Reinhardt and Frieda (née Darr) Reinhardt; m. 1st Margaret Leighton 1947 (divorced 1955); m. 2nd Joan MacDonald 1957; two d.; ed. English High School for Boys, Istanbul, Ecole des Hautes Etudes Commerciales, Paris, London School of Economics; Chair. Reinhardt Books Ltd. 1948–, Nonesuch Press Ltd. 1985–; Chair. The Bodley Head Group of Publishers 1957–87; Jt. Chair. Chatto, Virago, Bodley Head and Jonathan

Cape Ltd. 1973–86; mem. Council, Publishers' Asscn. 1963–69, Royal Acad. of Dramatic Art 1965–96, The Pilgrims 1966–. *Leisure interests:* swimming, bridge. *Address:* Flat 2, 43 Onslow Square, London, SW7 3LR, England. *Telephone:* 0171-589 5527.

REINO, Fernando, LIC. EN DER.; Portuguese diplomatist; b. Aug. 1929, Felgar, Moncorvo; s. of Abel Reino and Julia Janeiro Reino; m. Maria Gabriela Vaz Reino 1962; two d.; ed. Univ. of Coimbra, Univ. of Strasbourg, NATO Defence Coll.; entered the Foreign Service 1958, Political and NATO Depts., Lisbon 1958–60, Portuguese del. to NATO, Paris 1960–61, Portuguese Embassy, Tokyo 1961–62, Chargé d'affaires titular, Antananarivo 1962–63, Consul-Gen. Cape Town 1963–66, Chargé d'affaires, Tunis 1966–71, Deputy Head of Mission to the E.E.C. 1971–73; Dir. Int. Econ. Org. Dept., Lisbon 1973–74; Head of Co-operation and Tech. Assistance Dept. and Co-ordinator Nat. Decolonization Comm. 1974–75; Amb. to Norway and Iceland 1977–80, Head of Civilian Staff of the Pres. 1980–81; Perm. Rep. to the UN and other Int. Orgs., Geneva 1981–85; Amb. to Spain 1985–88; Perm. Rep. to UN 1989–92; Emer. Prof. Univ. of Coimbra; Chancellor, Nat. Orders. *Leisure interests:* writing, reading, music, golf, gardening. *Address:* Quinta do Rio Touro, Azoia, 2710 Sintra, Portugal. *Telephone:* 929.2862. *Fax:* 929.2360.

REINSHAGEN, Gerlind; German author; b. 4 May 1926, Königsberg; d. of Ekkehard Technau and Frieda Technau; m. 1949; ed. studies in pharmacy; freelance author of novels, theatre and radio plays, screenplays, poetry, essays and criticism; mem. German PEN; mem. Deutsche Akad. der darstellenden Künste; recipient of various awards. *Publications:* plays: Doppelkopf 1968, Leben und Tod der Marilyn Monroe 1971, Himmel und Erde 1974, Sonntagskinder 1976, Frühlingsfest 1980, Eisenherz 1982, Die Clownin 1985, Die Feuerblume 1987, Tanz, Marie 1989, Die fremde Tochter 1992, Drei Wünsche frei 1992; novels: Rovinato 1981, Die flüchtige Braut 1984, Zwölf Nächte 1989, Jäger am Rand der Nacht 1993, Am grossen Stern 1996; Gesammelte Stücke (collected pieces) 1986; contribs. to theatrical journals and yearbooks etc. *Address:* Rheingaustrasse 2, 12161 Berlin, Germany. *Telephone:* 030/821 71 71.

REINSHAGEN, Maria; Swiss business executive; b. 23 Jan. 1936; one s. one d.; fmr. primary school teacher, Zürich; fmr. Dir. Prints Dept. Felix Landau Gallery, Los Angeles; joined Christie's 1978, mem. European Bd. 1985, London Bd. Mem. 1990, head of Zürich office, Deputy Chair. Switzerland, Vice-Chair. Europe 1996; mem. Bd. Union Bank of Switzerland 1994–. *Address:* c/o Christie's (Int.) AG, Steinwlesplatz, 8032 Zürich, Switzerland. *Telephone:* 01-268 10 10. *Fax:* 01-268 10 11.

REISCH, Georg, D.IUR.; Austrian diplomatist; b. 23 May 1930, Vienna; s. of Walter Reisch and Maria Pokorny; m. Monika Krisch 1957; two s. one d.; ed. Univ. of Agric., Vienna, Univ. of Vienna and Iowa State Coll.; Ministry of Agric. Vienna 1956–57; OEEC, Paris 1957–60; Ministry of Foreign Affairs 1960–63; Chef de Cabinet, Ministry of Foreign Affairs 1968–70; Amb. to Kenya 1970–76; Ministry of Foreign Affairs 1976–83; Perm. Rep. of Austria to UN, EFTA, GATT and other int. orgs. Geneva 1983–88; Sec.-Gen. EFTA 1988–94; Grand Decoration of Honour (Austria) and decorations from U.K., Spain, Germany, France, Portugal and Liechtenstein.

REISS, Howard, PH.D.; American professor of chemistry; b. 5 April 1922, New York; s. of Isidor Reiss and Jean Goldstein; m. Phyllis F. Kohn 1945; one s. one d.; ed. New York and Columbia Univs.; Manhattan project, U.S. Army 1944–46; Instr., Asst. Prof. Boston Univ. 1949–51; mem. tech. staff, Cen. Research Lab. Celanese Corpn. of America 1951–52, Bell Telephone Labs. 1952–60; Asst. Dir. Edgar C. Bain Lab. for Fundamental Research, U.S. Steel Corpn. 1957; Assoc. Dir., Dir. Research Dept. Atomics Int. Div. North American Aviation Inc. 1960–62; Vice-Pres. Research, Pres., Dir. North American Aviation Science Center 1962–67; Vice-Pres. Research, Aerospace and Systems Group, North American Rockwell Corpn. 1967–68; Prof. of Chem., Univ. of Calif., L.A. 1968–91, Prof. Emer. 1991–; Van Arkel Hon. Chair in Chem., Univ. of Leiden, Netherlands 1994; Visiting Fellow Princeton Materials Inst. 1996; mem. N.A.S.; Fellow A.A.A.S.; several awards and distinctions. *Publications:* The Methods of Thermodynamics 1965; articles in professional journals. *Leisure interests:* reading, carpentering, sports. *Address:* c/o Department of Chemistry and Biochemistry, University of California, Los Angeles, CA 90024 (Office); 16656 Oldham Street, Encino, CA 91436, U.S.A. (Home). *Telephone:* (818) 784-4089 (Home).

REISS, Timothy James, M.A., PH.D., F.R.S.C.; British/Canadian professor of literature; b. 14 May 1942, Stanmore, Middx.; s. of James Martin Reiss and Joan Margaret Ping; m. 2nd Patricia J. Hilden 1988; two s. one d. from previous m.; ed. Hardye's School, Dorchester, Manchester Univ., Sorbonne, Paris and Univ. of Illinois; Instructor to Asst. Prof. Yale Univ. 1968–73; Assoc. Prof. Univ. de Montréal 1973–79, Prof. and Chair. of Comparative Literature 1979–84; Prof. of Comparative Literature, Modern Languages and Philosophy, Emory Univ. 1983–86, Samuel C. Dobbs Prof. of Comparative Literature and French 1986–87; Prof. and Chair. of Comparative Literature New York Univ. 1987–94, Prof. 1994–; Morse Fellow 1971–72; Canada Council Sr. Fellow 1977–78; SSHRC of Canada Sr. Fellow 1983–84; ACLS Fellow 1986–87; Guggenheim Fellow 1990–91; Fellow Acad. of Literary Studies; several other awards and visiting professorships. *Publications:* Toward Dramatic Illusion 1971, Science, Language and the Perspective Mind (ed.) 1973, Tragedy and Truth 1980, De l'ouverture des disciplines (ed.) 1981, The Discourse of Modernism 1982, Tragique et tragédie dans la tradition occidentale (ed.) 1983, The Uncertainty of Analysis 1988, The Meaning of Literature 1992 (Forkosch Prize 1992), Sisyphus and Eldorado (ed.) 1997, Knowledge, Discovery and Imagination in Early Modern Europe 1997; more than 100 essays and book chapters. *Address:* Department of Comparative Literature, New York University, 19 University Place, 4th Floor, New York, NY 10003 (Office); 1721 8th Street, Berkeley, CA 94710, U.S.A. (Home). *Telephone:* (212) 998-8795 (Office).

REISZ, Karel; British film director; b. 21 July 1926, Ostrava, Czechoslovakia; s. of Dr. Josef and Frederika Reisz; m. 1st Julia Coppard (dissolved); m. 2nd Betsy Blair 1963; three s.; ed. Leighton Park School, Reading, and Emmanuel Coll., Cambridge; came to England 1939; served with Czechoslovak section of R.A.F. 1944–46; free-lanced as journalist, lecturer and teacher; Films Officer, Ford Motor Co.; now film dir. and producer. *Films:* Momma Don't Allow (Co-dir. with Tony Richardson) 1954, Every Day Except Christmas (producer) 1958, We Are the Lambeth Boys 1958 (Both for Fords), Saturday Night and Sunday Morning 1959, This Sporting Life (producer) 1962, Night Must Fall 1963, Morgan—A Suitable Case for Treatment 1965, Isadora 1969, The Gambler 1974, Dog Soldiers 1977, The French Lieutenant's Woman 1981, Sweet Dreams 1985, Everybody Wins 1989, The Gigli Concert 1991. *Stage productions:* Gardenia 1991, The Gigli Concert, The Deep Blue Sea 1991, A Doll's House 1993, Moonlight 1994–95, Happy Days 1996, A Kind of Alaska 1997, Long Days Journey into Night 1998. *Publication:* The Technique of Film Editing 1953. *Leisure interest:* gardening.

REITER, Janusz; Polish diplomatist and journalist; b. 6 Aug. 1952, Kościerzyna; s. of Stanisław Reiter and Hilda Reiter; m. Hanna Reiter 1975; two d.; ed. Warsaw Univ.; Foreign affairs commentator Życie Warszawy (daily) 1977–81 (dismissed during martial law); jt. founder of Foundation for Int. Ventures and Industrial Centre for Int. Studies in Warsaw; mem. Dziekania Club of Political Thought; staff writer Przegląd Katolicki (weekly) 1984–89, daily Gazeta Wyborcza and Polish TV 1989–90; Amb. to Fed. Repub. of Germany 1990–95; Chair. of Bd. and Dir. Centre for Int. Relations, Warsaw 1998–; co-founder Council for Foreign Policy; mem. Bd. Wissenschaftskolleg (Inst. for Advanced Study), Berlin; mem. Advisory Bd. of Prime Minister. *Leisure interests:* reading, travelling, pet dog. *Address:* Al. Ujazdowskie 47 m. 14, 00-536 Warsaw, Poland. *Telephone:* (22) 622 10 69. *Fax:* (22) 622 10 71.

REITH, Peter; Australian politician; b. 15 July 1950, Melbourne; s. of A. C. Reith and E. V. Reith (née Sambell); m. Julie Treganowan 1971; four s.; ed. Monash Univ.; Supreme Court 1975; worked as solicitor 1976–82; mem. Westernport Waterworks Trust and Cowes Sewerage Authority 1977–82; Councillor Shire of Phillip Island 1976–81, Pres. 1980–81; mem. various cttees. and authorities; M.P. for Flinders 1982–83, 1984–; Deputy Leader of the Opposition 1990–93; Shadow Treasurer 1990–93; Shadow Special Minister of State 1993, responsible for Mabo 1994; Shadow Minister for Defence and Shadow Minister with responsibility for Mabo Jan.–May 1994; Shadow Minister for Defence May–Sept. 1994; Shadow Minister for Foreign Affairs 1994–95, for Industrial Relations and Man. of Opposition Business in the House 1995–96; Minister for Industrial Relations and Leader of the House of Reps. and Minister Assisting the Prime Minister for the Public Service 1996–97; Minister for Workplace Relations and Small Business and Leader of the House of Reps. 1997–98, Minister for Employment, Workplace Relations and Small Business and Leader of the House of Reps. 1998–; mem. Asscn. of Christian Community Colls.; co-ordinator Free Legal Aid Services; founding sec., mem. Newhaven Coll. *Publication:* The Reith Papers. *Leisure interests:* tennis, reading. *Address:* Shop 4, 184 Salmon Street, P.O. Box 274, Hastings, Vic. 3915; Parliament Buildings, Canberra, A.C.T. 2600, Australia. *Telephone:* (03) 5979 3188 (Hastings); (06) 6277 7111 (Canberra).

REITMAN, Ivan, MUS.B.; Canadian film director and producer; b. 27 Oct. 1946, Komarmo, Czechoslovakia; s. of Leslie Reitman and Clara R. Reitman; m. Genevieve Robert 1976; one s. two d.; ed. McMaster Univ.; moved to Canada 1951. *Stage shows produced:* The Magic Show 1974, The National Lampoon Show 1975, Merlin 1983 (also dir.). *Films:* (dir. and exec. producer) Cannibal Girls 1973; (producer) They Came From Within 1975, Death Weekend 1977, Blackout 1978, National Lampoon's Animal House 1978, Heavy Metal 1981, Stop! Or My Mom Will Shoot 1992, Space Jam 1996, Private Parts 1996; (producer and dir.) Foxy Lady 1971, Meatballs 1979, Stripes 1981, Ghostbusters 1984, Legal Eagles 1986, Twins 1988, Ghostbusters II 1989, Kindergarten Cop 1990, Dave 1993, Junior 1994; (exec. producer) Rabid 1976, Spacehunter: Adventures in the Forbidden Zone 1983, Big Shots 1987, Casual Sex? 1988, Feds 1988, Beethoven 1992, Beethoven's 2nd 1993, Commandments 1996. *TV series:* (producer and dir.) Delta House 1978. *TV films:* (exec. producer) The Late Shift 1996, Fathers' Day 1997; mem. Dirs. Guild of America. *Address:* c/o CAA, 9830 Wilshire Boulevard, Beverly Hills, CA 90212, U.S.A.

REITZ, Edgar; German film director; b. 1932. *Films include:* Mahlzeiten (appeared in U.K. as Lust for Love) 1966–67, Die Reise nach Wien 1973, Picnic 1975, Stunde Null 1976, Deutschland im Herbst (with others) 1977–78, Der Schneider von Ulm 1978, Heimat 1980–84, Die zweite Heimat 1991.

RELIGA, Zbigniew, M.D.; Polish surgeon, cardiologist and politician; b. 16 Dec. 1938, Miedniewice; s. of Eugeniusz Religa and Zofia Religa; m. Anna Wajszczuk 1962; one s. one d.; ed. Medical Acad., Warsaw; worked in Surgical Ward of Wolski Hosp., Warsaw 1966–80; Cardiac Inst., Warsaw 1980–84; Head of Cardiac Surgery Dept. and Clinic, Silesian Med. Acad., Katowice

1984–, Prof. 1995–, Rector 1996–; inventor Polish mechanical heart assist devices, total artificial heart, bioliogical heart valve; Chair. Non-Party Bloc in Support of Reforms (BBWR) 1993–95; Chair. Polish Republican Party 1995–98; Senator 1993–97; mem. Conservative Peasant Party (SKL) 1998–; Dr. h.c. (Lvov Medical Univ., Ukraine), (Medical Acad., Białystok); numerous Polish and foreign awards including Kt.'s Cross of Order of Polonia Restituta 1986, (with Star) 1995. *Publications:* over 100, including books on cardiac surgery, transplantation and total artificial heart. *Leisure interest:* fishing. *Address:* Al. 3 Maja 2 m. 175, 00-391 Warsaw, Poland.

RELPH, Michael; British film producer, writer, designer and director; s. of late George Relph and Deborah (née Nansen) Relph; m. 1st Doris Gosden 1938; one s.; m. 2nd Maria Barry 1949; one d.; fmr. Assoc. Producer and Producer, Ealing; Founder/Dir. Allied Film Makers; Chair. Film Production Asscn. of GB 1971–76, BFI Production Bd. 1971–76; Producer mem. Cinematograph Films Council 1971–76; Exec. in charge of Production, Kendon Films 1979–80; Art Dir., Ealing on films Champagne Charley, Nicholas Nickleby, Dead of Night, Saraband for Dead Lovers; Hon. D.Litt. (De Montfort Univ.) 1998. *Films produced include:* The Captive Heart, Frieda, The Blue Lamp, Kind Hearts and Coronets, The Square Ring, I Believe in You (co-author, screenplay), The Ship That Died of Shame, The Rainbow Jacket, The Smallest Show on Earth, Sapphire, League of Gentlemen, Victim, Man in the Moon (co-author, screenplay), Life For Ruth, The Mind Benders, A Place to Go, (author, screenplay), Woman of Straw (co-author, screenplay), Masquerade (co-author, screenplay), The Assassination Bureau (author, screenplay), The Man Who Haunted Himself (co-author), Scum, An Unsuitable Job for a Woman (co-producer), Heavenly Pursuits 1986, Seven Against the West (author, screenplay), Mrs Warren's Profession (co-author, screenplay), Seven Against the West (screenplay with Fay Weldon), My Mother's Profession (screenplay), William Tell: the untold story; production consultant The Torrents of Spring 1989. *Films directed:* Davy, Rockets Galore. *Address:* 71 The Maltings, Westgate, Chichester, West Sussex, PO19 3DN, England. *Telephone:* (01243) 839811.

REMEDIOS, Alberto Telisforo, C.B.E.; British opera singer; b. 27 Feb. 1935, Liverpool; s. of Albert and Ida Remedios; m. 1st Shirley Swindells 1958; one s.; m. 2nd Judith Hosken 1965; one s. one d.; studied with Edwin Francis, Liverpool; joined Sadler's Wells Opera Co. 1955; now sings regularly with English Nat. Opera and Royal Opera House, Covent Garden; has made numerous appearances in U.S.A., Canada, Argentina, Germany, France and Spain, and appeared in concert with major British orchestras; records include Wagner's Der Ring des Nibelungen and Tippett's A Midsummer Marriage; Queen's Prize, Royal Coll. of Music; First Prize, Int. Singing Competition, Sofia, Bulgaria; Sir Reginald Goodall Award Wagner Soc. 1995. *Leisure interests:* football, motoring, record collecting. *Address:* c/o Stuart Trotter, 21 Lanhill Road, London, W9 2BS, England. *Telephone:* 0171-289 6315.

REMENGESAU, Tommy E., Jr., B.S.; Palau politician; b. 28 Feb. 1956, Koror; s. of Thomas O. Remengesau, Sr. and Ferista Esang Remengesau; m. Debbie Mineich; two s. two d.; ed. Grand Valley State Univ., Mich., Michigan State Univ.; Admin./Planner, Palau Bureau of Health Services 1980–81; Public Information Officer, Palau Legislature 1981–84; Senator, Nat. Congress 1984–92; Vice-Pres. and Minister of Admin. 1993–; rep. to IMF 1997–; twice Grand Champion All-Micronesia Fishing Derby. *Leisure interest:* fishing. *Address:* Office of the Vice-President, P.O. Box 6011, Koror, 96940, Palau. *Telephone:* 488-2702. *Fax:* 488-1310.

REMINGTON, Deborah Williams, B.F.A.; American artist; b. 25 June 1935, Haddonfield, N.J.; d. of Malcolm van Dyke Remington and Hazel Irwin Stewart; one-woman shows include Dilexi Gallery, San Francisco 1962, 1963, 1965, San Francisco Museum of Art 1964, Bykert Gallery, New York 1967, 1969, 1972, 1974, Galerie Darthea Speyer, Paris 1968, 1971, 1973, 1992, Pyramid Gallery, Washington, D.C. 1976, Zolla-Lieberman Gallery, Chicago 1976, Hamilton Gallery, New York 1977, Portland Center for Visual Arts, Portland, Ore. 1977, Ramon Osuna Gallery, Washington, D.C. 1983, Newport Harbor Art Museum, Calif. 1983, Oakland (Calif.) Museum of Art 1984, Adams Middleton Gallery, Dallas, Tex. 1984, Ianuzzi Gallery, Phoenix, Ariz. 1985, Jack Shainman Gallery, New York 1987, Shoshana Wayne Gallery, Los Angeles 1988; participant in numerous group shows in U.S.A., France, Switzerland, Portugal etc.; work in many public collections including Whitney Museum, New York, Pompidou Centre, Paris and Bibliothèque Nationale, Paris; Nat. Endowment Fellowship 1979–80; Guggenheim Fellowship 1984–85. *Leisure interests:* gardening/horticulture. *Address:* 309 West Broadway, New York, NY 10013, U.S.A. *Telephone:* (212) 925-3037.

REMNICK, David J., A.B.; American journalist; b. 29 Oct. 1958, Hackensack, N.J.; s. of Edward C. Remnick and Barbara (née Seigel) Remnick; m. Esther B. Fein; two s.; ed. Princeton Univ.; reporter The Washington Post 1982–91; staff writer The New Yorker 1992–, now Ed.; Pulitzer Prize 1994; Livingston Award 1991; George Polk Award 1994; Helen Bernstein Award 1994. *Publications include:* Lenin's Tomb: The Last Days of the Soviet Empire 1993. *Address:* The New Yorker, 20 West 43rd Street, New York, NY 10036 (Office); 322 West 72nd Street, New York, NY 10023, U.S.A. (Home).

REMY, Pierre-Jean (see Angremy, Jean-Pierre).

REN JIANXIN; Chinese fmr. chief justice; b. Aug. 1925, Fencheng (now Xiangfen) Co., Shanxi Prov.; ed. Eng. Coll., Beijing Univ.; joined CCP 1948; Sec., Secr. N. China People's Govt. 1948–49; Sec. Gen. Office, Cen. Comm. for Political Science and Law, Sec. Cen. Comm. for Legis. Affairs 1949–54; Sec. Legis. Affairs Bureau, State Council 1954–59; Section Leader, Division Chief, China Council for the Promotion of Int. Trade (CCPIT) 1959–71, Dir. Legal Dept., CCPIT, lawyer 1971–81, Vice-Chair. CCPIT 1981–83; Vice-Pres. Supreme People's Court 1983–88, Pres. 1988–98; Sec.-Gen. Leading Group of Cen. Cttee. for Political Science and Law 1989, Deputy Sec. and Sec.-Gen. Cen. Cttee. 1990; Chair. Soc. of Chinese Judges 1994–; Hon. Chair China Law Soc. (fmr. Vice-Pres.), China Foreign Econ. Trade and Arbitration Cttee., China Maritime Arbitration Cttee. (fmr. Chair.); Hon. Pres. China Int. Law Soc. (fmr. Vice-Pres.); Dir. China Training Centre for Sr. Judges; Prof. (part-time) Beijing Univ.; mem. 13th CCP Cen. Cttee. 1987–92, 14th CCP Cen. Cttee. 1992–97, Sec. Secr. 14th CCP Cen. Cttee. 1992; Sec. CCP Cen. Comm. for Political Science and Law 1992–98; Vice-Chair. 9th Nat. Cttee. CPPCC 1998–. *Address:* National Committee of Chinese People's Political Consultative Conference, 23 Taipingqiao Street, Beijing, People's Republic of China.

REN MEIE, PH.D.; Chinese scientist and university professor; mem. Dept. of Earth Sciences, Academica Sinica 1985–; Prof. at Geography Dept. of Nanjing Univ. 1986–; Chair. of Asscn. for Devt. and Man. of Coastal Zones 1986–; Victoria Medal (Royal Soc. of Geography) 1986. *Address:* Geography Department, Nanjing University, Nanjing City, Jiangsu Province, People's Republic of China.

REN WUZHI; Chinese state official; b. 12 Sept. 1929, Xingxian Co., Shanxi Prov.; s. of Ren Jin Huo and Ren Zhuo Huan; m. Zhang Miao Wen 1952; one s. two d.; joined CCP 1949; Dir. State Bureau of Religious Affairs 1984–93. *Leisure interests:* reading newspapers and books. *Address:* State Bureau of Religious Affairs, No. 22 Xi An Men Street, Beijing, People's Republic of China.

RENDELL OF BABERGH, Baroness (Life Peer), cr. 1997, of Aldeburgh in the County of Suffolk, **Ruth Barbara Rendell,** C.B.E., F.R.S.L.; British crime novelist; b. 17 Feb. 1930; d. of Arthur Grasemann and Ebba Kruse; m. Donald Rendell 1950, marriage dissolved 1975, remarried 1977; one s.; ed. Loughton County High School; Arts Council Nat. Book Award for Genre Fiction 1981, Sunday Times Award for Literary Excellence 1990 and other awards; Dr. h.c. (Essex) 1990. *Publications include:* From Doon with Death 1964, A Judgment in Stone 1976, The Lake of Darkness 1980, An Unkindness of Ravens 1985, Live Flesh 1986, Heartstones 1987, Talking to Strange Men 1987, Wolf to the Slaughter 1987, The Veiled One 1988, A Warning to the Curious—The Ghost Stories of M. R. James 1988, The Bridesmaid 1989, Suffolk 1989, The Third Wexford Omnibus 1989, Mysterious 1990, Going Wrong 1990, The Strawberry Tree 1990, Walking on Water 1991, The Copper Peacock 1991, Kissing the Gunner's Daughter 1992, The Ruth Rendell Omnibus 1992, The Crocodile Bird 1993, The Third Ruth Rendell Omnibus 1994, No Night is too Long 1994, Simisola 1994, Blood Lines, Long and Short Stories 1995; (ed.) The Reason Why: An Anthology of the Murderous Mind 1995, The Brimstone Wedding 1996; (under pseudonym Barbara Vine) A Dark-Adapted Eye 1986, A Fatal Inversion 1987, The House of Stairs 1988, Gallowglass 1990, King Solomon's Carpet 1991, Asta's Book 1993, The Children of Men 1994, No Night Is Too Long 1994, The Keys to the Street 1996, The Brimstone Wedding 1996, The Chimney Sweeper's Boy 1998, A Sight For Sore Eyes 1998; several vols. of short stories. *Leisure interests:* reading, walking, opera. *Address:* Nussteads, Polstead, Suffolk, CO6 5DN; 26 Cornwall Terrace Mews, London, NW1 5LL; House of Lords, London, SW1A 0PW, England.

RENDLE, Michael Russel, M.A.; British business executive; b. 20 Feb. 1931, Kuala Lumpur, Malaya; s. of late H. C. R. Rendle; m. Heather Rinkel 1957; two s. two d.; ed. Marlborough Coll. and New Coll., Oxford; joined Anglo-Iranian Oil Co. (now British Petroleum) 1954; served in U.K., Trinidad, Aden; Man. Dir. BP Trinidad 1967–70, BP Australia 1974–78; Dir. BP Trading (London) 1978–81; a Man. Dir. BP Co. 1981–86; Chair. TBI PLC (fmrly. Markheath PLC) 1991–94; Deputy Chair. Imperial Continental Gas Asscn. 1986–87, British-Borneo Petroleum Syndicate 1986–, Tace PLC 1991; Dir. Willis Faber PLC (now renamed Willis Corroon PLC) 1985–98, Petrofina SA 1986–87, FIM Ltd. 1989– (Chair. 1992–), Campbell and Armstong PLC 1992–98 (Chair. 1996–98), OIS Int. Inspection PLC 1993–96 (Chair. 1995–96), M.D.U. Ltd. 1998–; mem. London Bd. Westpac Banking Corp. 1978–89; mem. British Overseas Trade Bd. 1982–86, INSEAD Int. Council and U.K. Advisory Bd. 1984–86; Chair. UNICE Social Affairs Cttee. 1984–87; mem. Marlborough Coll. Council 1987–95. *Leisure interests:* golf, music, various outdoor sports. *Address:* c/o Willis Corroon PLC, 10 Trinity Square, London, EC3P 3AX, England. *Telephone:* 0171-481 7152. *Fax:* 0171-481 7171.

RENÉ, (France) Albert; Seychelles politician and barrister; b. 16 Nov. 1935, Seychelles; s. of Price René and Louisa Morgan; m. 1st Karen Handley 1956; one d.; m. 2nd Geva Adam 1975; one s.; m. 3rd Sarah Zarquani 1993; one d.; ed. St. Louis Coll., Victoria, Seychelles Coll., St. Maurice, Switzerland, St. Mary's Coll., Southampton, U.K., King's Coll., London; called to Bar 1957; founder and Leader, Seychelles People's United Party (later Seychelles People's Progressive Party) 1964–; M.P. 1965–; Minister of Works and Land Devt. 1975–77; Prime Minister 1976–77; Pres. of Seychelles 1977–, also C.-in-C., Minister of Econ. Devt. and Housing 1977–78, of Internal Affairs and Finance 1977–79, of Finance 1977–78, of Youth and Community Devt. 1978–80, of Finance and Industries 1981–89, of Planning and External Relations 1984–89, of Industry 1986–93, of Community Devt. 1993, of

Defence 1986–93, of Tourism 1988–89; Order of the Golden Ark 1982. *Leisure interests:* gardening, fishing. *Address:* The State House, Victoria, Mahé, Seychelles. *Telephone:* 224391; 224155. *Fax:* 224200.

RENFREW OF KAIMSTHORN, Baron (Life Peer), cr. 1991, of Hurlet in the District of Renfrew, **Andrew Colin Renfrew,** PH.D., SC.D., F.B.A., F.S.A.; British professor of archaeology; b. 25 July 1937, Stockton-on-Tees; s. of the late Archibald Renfrew and Helena D. Renfrew; m. Jane M. Ewbank 1965; two s. one d.; ed. St. Albans School, St. John's Coll., Cambridge, and British School of Archaeology, Athens; Lecturer in Prehistory and Archaeology, Univ. of Sheffield 1965–70, Sr. Lecturer 1970–72, Reader in Prehistory and Archaeology 1972; Prof. of Archaeology and Head of Dept., Univ. of Southampton 1972–81; Disney Prof. of Archaeology Univ. of Cambridge 1981–, Dir. McDonald Inst. for Archaeological Research 1990–; Fellow St. John's Coll., Cambridge 1981–86, Master Jesus Coll., Cambridge 1986–97; Visiting Lecturer, Univ. of Calif. at Los Angeles 1967; Rivers Memorial Medal, Huxley Memorial Medal, Royal Anthropological Inst. *Publications:* The Emergence of Civilization 1972, Before Civilization 1973, The Explanation of Culture Change (ed.) 1973, British Prehistory (ed.) 1974, Transformations: Mathematical Approaches to Culture Change 1979, Problems in European Prehistory 1979, An Island Polity 1982, Theory and Explanation in Archaeology (ed.) 1982, Approaches to Social Archaeology 1984, The Archaeology of Cult 1985, Peer, Polity Interaction and Socio-Political Change (ed.) 1986, Archaeology and Language: The Puzzle of Indo-European Origins 1987, The Idea of Prehistory 1988, The Cycladic Spirit 1991, The Archaeology of Mind (co-ed. with E. Zubrow) 1994. *Leisure interests:* contemporary arts, coins. *Address:* McDonald Institute for Archaeological Research, Downing Street, Cambridge, CB2 3ER, England. *Telephone:* (01223) 333521. *Fax:* (01223) 333536.

RENGER, Annemarie; German politician; b. 7 Oct. 1919, Leipzig; d. of Fritz Wildung and Martha (née Scholz) Wildung; m. 1st Emil Renger 1938 (killed in 2nd World War); one s.; m. 2nd Aleksandar Renger-Lončarević 1965 (died 1973); private sec. to Dr. Kurt Schumacher 1945–52; managed SPD offices Berlin May-Dec. 1946; mem. Bundestag 1953–; SPD Parliamentary Group Man. 1969–72; Pres. Bundestag 1972–76, Jt. Vice-Pres. 1976–90; mem. SPD 1945–; mem. Presidium 1961–73; mem. for ten years of advisory assembly of European Council and Assembly of West European Union; Vice-Pres. Int. Council of Social Democratic Women of the Socialist International 1972–76; Hon. Fellow Hebrew Univ., Jerusalem; Hon. D.Univ. (Ben Gurion, Beersheva, Israel); Grosses Bundesverdienstkreuz. *Address:* Bundeshaus, 53113 Bonn, Germany. *Telephone:* 161.

RENNERT, Wolfgang; German conductor, music and opera director; b. 1 April 1922, Cologne; s. of Dr. Alfred Rennert and Adelheid (née Nettesheim) Rennert; m. 1st Anny Schlemm 1957; m. 2nd Ulla Berkéwicz 1971 (divorced 1975); one s.; ed. Mozarteum Salzburg; Chief Conductor and Deputy Dir. of Music, Frankfurt 1953–67; Head of Opera, Staatstheater am Gärtnerplatz 1967–71; Dir. of Music and Dir. of Opera, Nat. Theatre, Mannheim 1980–85; Perm. Guest Conductor, State Opera, Berlin 1972–; Guest Conductor, Royal Opera, Copenhagen 1975–79; Prin. Guest Conductor, Semperoper, Dresden 1991–; Prin. Guest Conductor, Portuguese Symphony Orchestra, Lisbon 1998–; guest appearances with Vienna State Opera, Munich and Hamburg Operas, Royal Opera House Covent Garden, San Francisco Opera, Dallas Opera, Salzburg Festival, Munich Festival, and Venice, Rome and Palermo opera houses. *Address:* 12203 Berlin, Holbeinstrasse 58, Germany. *Telephone:* 030-833 3094.

RENNIE, Heughan Bassett (Hugh), C.B.E., B.A., LL.B.; New Zealand lawyer, government official and fmr. broadcasting executive; b. 7 April 1945, Wanganui; s. of the late W. S. N. Rennie, O.B.E. and of Reta Rennie, Q.S.M.; m. 1st Caroline Jane Harding 1967 (died 1992); three s.; m. 2nd Penelope Jane Ryder-Lewis 1998; ed. Wanganui Collegiate School, Victoria Univ., Wellington; part-time law clerk, Wanganui 1960–67, legal officer N.Z. Electricity, Wellington 1967–70; barrister and solicitor Macalister Mazengarb Parkin and Rose (later Macalister Mazengarb Perry Castle), Wellington 1970–91, partner 1972–, sr. litigation partner 1982–, Chair. 1989–91; sole barrister, Wellington 1991–95; Q.C. 1995; specialist practice in medical, media and aviation law; Chair. Broadcasting Corpn. of N.Z. (BCNZ) 1984–88; Chair. Govt. Cttee. on Restructuring BCNZ 1988, Ministerial Inquiry into Auckland Power Supply Failure 1998; Chair. Chatham Is. Enterprise Trust 1990–, Policy Cttee., Dictionary of N.Z. Biography 1991–; Dir. Fourth Estate Group 1970–88, United Broadcasters Ltd. 1981–84, Roydhouse Publishing Ltd. 1981–88, Fletcher Challenge Ltd. 1992–, BNZ Finance Ltd. 1993–97, Forestry Trust Man. Ltd. 1995–, Bank of N.Z. 1997–; Ed. Wellington Dist. Law Soc. newspaper 1973–84; mem. N.Z. Law Soc. cttees. on professional advertising and public affairs 1981–84, N.Z. Council for Law Reporting 1983–87, Govt. Advisory Cttee. to statutory mans. of Equiticorp 1989–; mem. Sir David Beattie Chair of Communications Trust Bd. (VUW) 1986–90, Scientific Cttee., Nat. Heart Foundation 1988–94; N.Z. Gen. Counsel Medical Protection Soc. (U.K.) 1983–; Trustee Broadcasting History Project Trust Bd. 1988–, Cartoon Archive Trust Bd. 1991–95; mem. American Soc. for Medicine and the Law 1988–, Int. Bar Asscn. 1991–; N.Z. Medal 1990. *Leisure interests:* history, travel, writing, cycling, reading. *Address:* Harbour Chambers, 10th Floor, Equinox House, 111 The Terrace, Wellington (Office); 45 Grant Road, Thorndon, Wellington 1 (Home); P.O. Box 10-242, Wellington, New Zealand (Postal). *Telephone:* (04) 499-2684 (Office); (04) 472-9503 (Home). *Fax:* (04) 499-2705 (Office); (04) 472-9257 (Home).

RENO, Janet, B.A., LL.B.; American lawyer; b. 21 July 1938, Miami, Fla.; d. of Henry Reno and Jane Wood; ed. Cornell and Harvard Univs.; admitted Fla. Bar 1963; Assoc. Brigham & Brigham 1963–67; partner, Lewis & Reno 1967–71; Staff Dir. Judiciary Comm. Fla. House of Reps. Tallahassee 1971–72; Admin. Asst. State Attorney, 11th Judicial Circuit Fla., Miami 1973–76, State Attorney 1978–93; partner, Steel, Hector & Davis, Miami 1976–78; U.S. Attorney-Gen. March 1993–; mem. American Bar Asscn., American Law Inst., American Judicature Soc.; Democrat. *Address:* Department of Justice, 10th Street and Constitution Avenue, N.W., Washington, DC 20530, U.S.A. *Telephone:* (202) 633-2000. *Fax:* (202) 633-1678.

RENO, Jean; French actor; b. Casablanca, Morocco. *Films:* Claire de Femme, Le Dernier Combat, Subway, Signes Extérieurs de Richesse, Notre Histoire, I Love You, The Big Blue, La Femme Nikita, L'homme au Masque d'Or, L'Opération Corned Beef, Loulou Graffiti, The Professional (Leon), French Kiss, The Visitors (also wrote screenplay), Beyond the Clouds, For Roseanna. *Address:* Chez Les Films du Dauphin, 25 rue Yves-Toudic, 75010 Paris, France.

RENSCHLER, Andreas; German business executive; joined Daimler-Benz 1988, fmrly. Asst. to Chair., led projects in Latin America and developing 4-wheel drive vehicles, now Pres. Mercedes-Benz U.S. International, Inc. *Address:* Mercedes-U.S. International Inc., P.O. Box 100, Tuscaloosa, AL 35403-0100, U.S.A.

RENTCHNICK, Pierre, M.D.; Swiss physician and editor of medical publications; b. 17 July 1923, Geneva; s. of Jacques Rentchnick and Blanche (Spiegel) Rentchnick; m. Paule Adam 1948; one s.; ed. Univs. of Geneva and Paris; Ed.-in-Chief, Médecine et Hygiène, Geneva 1956–93, Recent Results in Cancer Research, Heidelberg and New York 1962–83, Bulletin de l'Union internationale contre le cancer, Geneva 1962–80; f. Kiwanis-Club, Geneva 1966, Pres. 1976–77; f. Int. Soc. for Chemotherapy 1959; mem. New York Acad. of Sciences, Medical Soc. of Prague, French Soc. of Pathology. *Publications:* Esculape chez les Soviets 1954, Klinik und Therapie der Nebenwirkungen 1963, Esculape chez Mao 1973, Ces malades qui nous gouvernent 1976, Les orphelins mènent-ils le monde? 1978, Ces malades qui font l'Histoire 1983, Ces nouveaux malades qui nous gouvernent 1988–96; numerous publs. on antibiotics in infectious diseases, on ethical problems, euthanasia etc. *Leisure interests:* skiing, golf, swimming, art (Netzuke). *Address:* La Taupinière, Chemin Bouchattet 8, 1291 Commugny, Vaud, Switzerland. *Telephone:* 776 22 64.

RENTON OF MOUNT HARRY, Baron (Life Peer), cr. 1997, of Offham in the County of East Sussex; **(Ronald) Tim(othy) Renton,** P.C.; British politician; b. 28 May 1932; s. of R. K. D. Renton and Mrs Renton; m. Alice Fergusson 1960; two s. three d.; ed. Eton Coll., Magdalen Coll., Oxford; joined C. Tennant Sons & Co. Ltd 1954, with Tennants subsidiaries in Canada 1957–62, Dir. 1964–73, Man. Dir. Tennant Trading Ltd. 1964–73; Dir. Silvermines Ltd. 1967–84, Australia and New Zealand Banking Group 1967–76, J. H. Vavasseur & Co. Ltd. 1971–74; mem. BBC Gen. Advisory Council 1982–84; contested (Conservative) Sheffield Park 1970; M.P. for Mid-Sussex 1974–97; Parl. Pvt. Sec. to Rt. Hon. John Biffen, M.P. 1979–81, to Rt. Hon. Geoffrey Howe, M.P. 1983–84; Parl. Under Sec. of State FCO 1984–85, Minister of State FCO 1985–87; Parl. Sec. to H.M. Treasury and Govt. Chief Whip 1989–90, Minister for the Arts and for the Civil Service 1990–92; mem. Select Cttee. on Nationalised Industries 1974–79, Vice-Chair. Conservative Parl. Trade Cttee. 1974–79, Chair. Conservative Foreign and Commonwealth Council 1982–84; mem. Select Cttee. on Nat. Heritage 1995–97; mem. House of Lords European Communities Cttee. 1997–; Vice-Pres. Conservative Trade Unionists 1978–80, Pres. 1980–84; Chair. Outsider Art Archive 1995–, Sussex Downs Conservation Bd. 1997–; Vice-Chair. British Council 1992–98; Dir. (non-exec.) Fleming Continental European Investment Trust PLC, Chair. 1999–; Parl. Consultant Robert Fleming Holdings 1992–97; Fellow Industry and Parl. Trust 1977–79; mem. Advisory Bd., Know-How Fund for Cen. and Eastern Europe; mem. APEX, Council Roedean School 1982– (Pres. 1998–), Devt. Council, Parnham Trust, Criterion Theatre Trust; Trustee Mental Health Foundation 1985–89; Founding Pres. (with Mick Jagger) of Nat. Music Day. *Publications:* The Dangerous Edge 1994, Hostage to Fortune 1997. *Leisure interests:* writing, gardening, mucking about in boats, listening to opera. *Address:* House of Lords, London, SW1A 0PW, England.

RENTZEPIS, Peter, PH.D.; American scientist; b. 11 Dec. 1934, Kalamata, Greece; s. of Michael and Leucai Rentzepis; m. Alma Elizabeth Keenan; two s.; ed. Denison, Syracuse and Cambridge Univs.; mem. Tech. Staff Research Labs. Gen. Electric Co., New York, then mem. Tech. Staff, Bell Labs., N.J., Head, Physical and Inorganic Chem. Research Dept.; Presidential Chair. Univ. of Calif. 1985–; Prof. of Chemistry, 1986–; Adjunct Prof. of Chem., Univ. of Pa., of Chem. and Biophysics, Yale Univ. 1980–; Visiting Prof., Rockefeller Univ., 1971, M.I.T. –1975, of Chemistry Univ. of Tel-Aviv; mem. numerous academic cttees., editorial and advisory bds. including U.S. Army Cttee. on Energetic Materials Research and Tech. 1982–83; Dir. NATO Advanced Study Inst. 1984–; mem. Bd. of Dirs. KRIKOS—Science and Tech. for Greece, Bd. of Dirs. The Quanex Corpn. 1984; Fellow N.A.S. 1978, American Physical Soc., A.A.A.S., etc.; mem. Nat. Acad. of Greece 1980; American Chem. Soc. Peter Debye Prize in Physical Chemistry, American Physical Soc. Irving Lungmuize Prize in Chemical Physics, Scientist of the Year 1978, and other awards; Hon. Sc.D. (Denison) 1981, (Carnegie-Mellon)

1983; Hon. D.Phil. (Syracuse) 1980. *Publications:* over 300 on lasers, photochemistry, picosecond spectroscopy. *Address:* Department of Chemistry, University of California, Irvine, CA 92717, U.S.A. *Telephone:* (714) 856 5934.

RENWICK OF CLIFTON, Baron (Life Peer), cr. 1997 of Chelsea in the Royal Borough of Kensington and Chelsea, **Robin William Renwick,** K.C.M.G., M.A.; British diplomatist and business executive; b. 13 Dec. 1937; s. of Richard and Clarice Renwick; m. Annie Colette Giudicelli 1965; one s. one d.; ed. St. Paul's School, Jesus Coll., Cambridge and Univ. of Paris (Sorbonne); army 1956–58; entered Foreign Service 1963; Dakar 1963–64; Foreign Office 1964–66; New Delhi 1966–69; Pvt. Sec. to Minister of State, Foreign and Commonwealth Office (FCO) 1970–72; First Sec., Paris 1972–76; Counsellor Cabinet Office 1976–78; Head Rhodesia Dept., FCO 1978–80; Political Adviser to Gov. of Rhodesia 1980; Visiting Fellow Center for Int. Affairs, Harvard 1980–81; Head of Chancery, Washington 1981–84; Asst. Under-Sec. of State, FCO 1984–87; Amb. to S. Africa 1987–91, to U.S.A. 1991–95; Chair. Save and Prosper 1996–98, Fluor Daniel (U.K.); Dir. Robert Fleming (Chair. Robert Fleming U.S. 1998–), Richemont, British Airways 1996–, Liberty Int., Canal Plus, Billiton, Fluor Corpn. 1997–; Trustee The Economist; Hon. LL.D. (Witwatersrand) 1991, (American Univ. in London) 1993, Hon. D.Litt. (Coll. of William and Mary) 1993. *Publication:* Economic Sanctions 1981, Fighting with Allies 1996, Unconventional Diplomacy in Southern Africa 1997. *Leisure interests:* tennis, fishing, islands. *Address:* House of Lords, Westminster, London, SW1A 0PW, England.

REPIN, Vadim Valentinovich; Russian violinist; b. 31 Aug. 1971, Novosibirsk; s. of Viktor Antonovich Repin and Galina Georgievna Repina; m. Nato Gabunia; ed. Novosibirsk Music School with Zakhar Bron; prize winner int. competitions: Veniawsky in Poznan 1982, Tibor Varga in Mion 1985, Queen Elizabeth in Brussels 1990; toured Europe since 1985; debut in London (Barbican) 1988, in U.S.A. 1990.

REPŠE, Einars, B.S.; Latvian banker; b. 9 Dec. 1961, Jelgava; s. of Aivars-Rihards Repše and Aldona Repše (née Krasauska); m. Diana Vagale 1988; two s. one d.; ed. Univ. of Latvia; engineer Latvian Acad. of Sciences 1986–90; mem. Parl. 1990–91; Gov. Bank of Latvia 1991–; Commdr. Order of the Three Stars 1997. *Leisure interest:* aviation. *Address:* Bank of Latvia, 2A K. Valdemara Str., 1050 Riga, Latvia. *Telephone:* 7022-260. *Fax:* 7022-268.

RESCHER, Nicholas, PH.D.; American philosopher and author; b. 15 July 1928, Hagen, Germany; s. of Erwin Hans Rescher and Meta Anna Rescher; m. 1st Frances Short 1951 (divorced 1965); one d.; m. 2nd Dorothy Henle 1968; two s. one d.; ed. Queens Coll., New York, Princeton Univ.; Assoc. Prof. of Philosophy, Lehigh Univ. 1957–61; Prof., Univ. of Pittsburgh 1961–, Dir. Center for Philosophy of Science 1982–89; Consultant RAND Corpn. 1954–66, Encyclopaedia Britannica 1963–64, North American Philosophical Publs. 1980–; Ed. American Philosophical Quarterly 1964–94; Sec.-Gen. Int. Union of History and Philosophy of Science 1969–75; Pres. American Philosophical Asscn. (Eastern Div.) 1989–90; mem. Academia Europea, Institut Int. de Philosophie, Académie Internationale de Philosophie des Sciences; Guggenheim Fellow 1970–71; Hon. mem. Corpus Christi Coll. Oxford; visiting lectureships at Univs. of Oxford, Munich, Konstanz, W. Ontario, and others; several hon. degrees; Alexander von Humboldt Prize 1983. *Publications:* more than 70 books including The Coherence Theory of Truth 1973, Methodological Pragmatism 1977, Scientific Progress 1978, The Limits of Science 1984, Ethical Idealism 1987, Rationality 1988, A System of Pragmatic Idealism (3 vols.) 1992–94, Pluralism 1993, Predicting the Future 1997; numerous articles in many areas of philosophy. *Leisure interests:* reading history and biography. *Address:* 5818 Aylesboro Avenue, Pittsburgh, PA 15217, U.S.A. *Telephone:* (412) 624-5950 (Office); (412) 521-6768 (Home). *Fax:* (412) 383-7506.

RESHETNIKOV, Fedor Grigorevich; Russian physical chemist; b. 25 Nov. 1919, Sumy, Ukraine; s. of Grigory Pavlovich Reshetnikov and Elisaveta Ivanovna Reshetnikova; m. Tatyana Frolovna Reshetnikova 1948; one d.; ed. Moscow Inst. of Non-Ferrous Metals, Dzerzhinsky Artillery Acad.; engineer, metallurgy works, Kazakhstan 1942, Perm 1944–45; mem. CPSU 1947–91; scientific research work 1946–; Head Lab., First Deputy Dir., V. A. Bochvar All Union Scientific and Research Inst. of Inorganic Materials 1966–92, adviser 1992–; Corresp. mem. U.S.S.R. (now Russian) Acad. of Sciences 1974–92, mem. 1992–; U.S.S.R. State Prize 1951, 1975, 1985. *Publication:* Development, Production and Operation of Nuclear Power Reactor Fuels, and numerous articles. *Leisure interests:* touring, fishing. *Address:* Scientific Research Institute of Inorganic Materials, Rogov Street 5, Moscow; Peschany Ln. 4, Apt. 310, 123060 Moscow, Russia (Home). *Telephone:* (095) 196-66-61 (Office); 198-26-80 (Home). *Fax:* (095) 925-28-96.

RESHETNIKOV, Felix Mikhailovich, LL.D.; Russian lawyer; b. 29 Dec. 1930, Moscow; ed. Moscow State Univ.; on staff Marx-Engels-Lenin Inst. 1953–62; docent, Prof. Lumumba Univ. of Friendship of Peoples 1962–70; Dir. Inst. of Legislation and Comparative Jurisdiction of Russian Govt.; main research in criminal law and criminology in foreign cos., comparative studies of law and history of political theories, took part in devt. of Criminal Law Code 1991, Draft Law on state protection of victims, witnesses and others; Merited Lawyer of Russian Fed. *Publications:* over 130 scientific works and 10 monographs including Modern American Criminal Law 1991, Legal Systems of Countries of the World 1993. *Leisure interests:* studying foreign languages, handling of dogs. *Address:* c/o Ministry of Justice, 101 434 Moscow, ul. Yermolovoi 10A, Russia. *Telephone:* (095) 209-60-55. *Fax:* (095) 209-60-98.

RESNAIS, Alain; French film director; b. 3 June 1922, Vannes; s. of Pierre and Jeanne (née Gachet) Resnais; m. Florence Malraux 1969; ed. Institut des Hautes Etudes Cinématographiques, Paris; Special Prize (Cannes) for Mon Oncle d'Amerique 1980; Grand Prix du Cinéma 1986; Légion d'honneur. *Short films directed (1948–59) include:* Van Gogh 1948, Guernica (with Robert Hessens) 1950, Les statues meurent aussi (with Chris Marker) 1952, Nuit et brouillard 1955. *Feature films include:* Hiroshima mon amour 1959, L'année dernière à Marienbad 1961, Muriel 1963, La guerre est finie 1966, Je t'aime, je t'aime 1968, Stavisky 1974, Providence 1977, Mon oncle d'Amérique 1980, La vie est un roman 1983, L'amour à mort 1984, Mélo 1986, I want to go home 1989, Smoking/No Smoking 1993 (César awards for best dir., best film), On Connait La Chanson 1998 (César Award for Best French Film). *Address:* 70 rue des Plantes, 75014 Paris, France (Home).

RESNIK, Regina; American opera singer (mezzo-soprano); b. 30 Aug. 1924; d. of Samuel Resnik and Ruth Resnik; m. 1st Harry W. Davis 1947; one s.; m. 2nd Arbit Blatas 1975; ed. Hunter Col., New York; opera début as Lady Macbeth, New Opera Co. 1942; Mexico City 1943; New York City Opera 1943–44; Metropolitan Opera 1944–1983; sang 80 roles, soprano and mezzo-soprano, became regular mem. Royal Opera, London, Vienna State Opera, Bayreuth, Salzburg, San Francisco, Chicago, La Scala, Milan, Paris, Buenos Aires, Berlin, Brussels, etc.; Stage Dir. for maj. productions Hamburg, Venice, Sydney, Vancouver, Strasbourg, Warsaw, Lisbon, Madrid, Wiesbaden; appeared on Broadway in Cabaret 1987, in A Little Night Music, New York City Opera, 50th anniversary celebrations Danny Kaye Playhouse; Trustee Hunter Foundation, Metropolitan Opera Guild Bd.; Dr. h.c. (Hunter) 1991; Lincoln Center and Vienna State Opera awards; President's Medal, Commdr. Ordre des Arts et des Lettres, France. *Address:* American Guild of Musical Artists, 1727 Broadway, New York, NY 10019, U.S.A.

RESSIN, Vladimir Iosifovich, PH.D.; Russian politician and civil engineer, b. 21 Feb. 1936, Minsk (now in Belarus); s. of Josif Ressin and Rosa Ressina; m. 1959; one d.; ed. Moscow Ore Inst.; worked in orgs. of U.S.S.R. Ministry of Coal Industry and Ministry of Ass. and Special Construction; Deputy, First Deputy, then Head, Moscow Dept. of Eng. and Construction 1974–; Head, Moscow Industrial Construction Dept. 1985–; Chair. Moscow Construction Cttee. 1989–91; Deputy Chair. Exec. Cttee., Moscow City Council 1989–91; Deputy Premier, Moscow City Govt. 1991–92, First Deputy Premier 1992–; Head, Dept. of Moscow Perspective Devt. 1992–; Prof. Russian G. V. Plekhanov Econ. Acad.; mem. Russian Acad. of Architecture and Construction Sciences, Russian Eng. Acad.; author of 30 inventions; awarded 16 State Prizes; other awards and distinctions include Distinguished Constructor of Russian Fed., Honoured Constructor of Moscow, Order of Russian Orthodox Church (two). *Publications:* five books, 90 other publs. *Leisure interest:* work. *Address:* Moscow City Government, Department of Moscow Perspective Development, Nikitsky per. 5, 103009 Moscow, Russia. *Telephone:* (095) 925-46-26, 291-09-47.

RESTAD, Gudmund; Norwegian politician; b. 19 Dec. 1937, Smøla; s. of Ola Restad and Olga Marie Dalen; m. Britt Jorun Wollum 1959; three c.; ed. officers' training school (anti-aircraft artillery), business school, police training school; sergeant at Ørland airport 1959–61, country police Ørland and Orkdal 1961–67; detective constable/inspector Crime Police Centre 1967–73; training in police investigation in Denmark and Germany 1967; lecturer Nat. Police Training School 1973–75; sergeant in Smøla 1975–85; mem. Parl. 1985–; Chair. Local Council, Smøla 1980–85, mem., Chair., Deputy Chair. Nordmøre Interkommunale Kraftlag (Nordmøre Electricity Bd.) 1982–91; mem. Bd. Central Police Org. 1969–73, Møre og Romsdal Centre Party 1982–83, The Centre Party 1983–89; mem. Judiciary Cttee. Storting (Parl.) 1985–89; mem./Deputy Chair. Finance Cttee. 1989–97; Minister of Finance and Customs 1997–. *Address:* Akersgt. 42, POB 8001 Dep., 0030 Oslo, Norway. *Telephone:* 22-24-90-90. *Fax:* 22-24-95-05.

RÉTORÉ, Guy; French theatre director; b. 7 April 1924; s. of Hervé Rétoré and Aline Henry; ed. Univ. of Paris; Public Relations Dept., S.N.C.F. until 1955; Actor and Producer, Théâtre de Boulevard until 1955; formed "La Guilde" (theatrical company), Menilmontant, East Paris 1954; opened Théâtre de Menilmontant 1958; Dir. Maison de la Culture, Menilmontant 1962; Dir. Théâtre de l'Est Parisien 1963– (also gives concerts, ballets, films and conferences). *Plays produced include:* La fille du roi (Cosmos) 1955, Life and Death of King John 1956, Grenadiers de la reine (Farquhar, adapted by Cosmos) 1957, L'avare (Molière), Les caprices de Marianne (Musset), La fleur à la bouche (Pirandello), Le médecin malgré lui (Molière), Le manteau (Gogol, adapted by Cosmos) 1963, La Locandiera (Goldoni), Arden of Faversham 1964, Monsieur Alexandre (Cosmos) 1964, Macbeth (Shakespeare) 1964, Turcaret (Lesage) 1965, Measure for Measure (Shakespeare) 1965, Le voyage de Monsieur Perrichon (Labiche) 1965, Live Like Pigs (Arden), The Silver Tassie (O'Casey) 1966–67, Les 13 soleils de la rue St. Blaise (A. Gatti), La machine (Jean Cosmos) 1968–69, Lorenzaccio (Musset), L'opéra de quat'sous (Brecht), Major Barbara (Shaw) 1969–70, Les ennemis (Gorki), L'âne de l'hospice (Arden) 1970–71, Sainte Jeanne des abattoirs (Brecht) 1971–72, Macbeth (Shakespeare) 1972–73, Androclès et le lion 1974–75, Coquin de coq (O'Casey) 1975–76, L'ôtage (Claudel) 1976–77, Le camp du drap d'or 1980, Fin de partie, tueur sans gage 1981, Le Chantier 1982, Clair d'usine 1983, 325000 francs 1984, Entre passions et prairie (Denise Bonal)

1987, Arturo Ui 1988, Clair de Terre 1989, Chacun pleure son Garabed 1991; Chevalier Légion d'honneur, Officier Ordre nat. du Mérite, Officier des Arts et des Lettres. *Address:* TEP, 159 avenue Gambetta, 75020 Paris, France. *Telephone:* 43.63.20.96.

REUBER, Grant Louis, O.C., PH.D., LL.D., F.R.S.C.; Canadian economist; b. 23 Nov. 1927, Mildmay, Ont.; s. of Jacob Daniel Reuber and Gertrude Catherine Reuber; m. Margaret Louise Julia Summerhayes 1951; three d.; ed. Walkerton High School, Univ. of W. Ontario, Harvard Univ., Sidney Sussex Coll., Cambridge; with Econ. Research Dept. Bank of Canada 1950–52; Econ. and Int. Relations Div. Dept. of Finance 1955–57, Deputy Minister of Finance Govt. of Canada 1979–80; at Univ. of W. Ontario 1957–78, Asst. Prof. 1957–59, Assoc. Prof. 1959–62, Prof. Econ. Dept. 1962–78, Dean of Social Science 1969–74, Acad. Vice-Pres. and Provost, mem. Bd. of Govs. 1974–78; Chair. Ont. Econ. Council 1973–78; Sr. Vice-Pres. and Chief Economist Bank of Montreal 1978–79, Exec. Vice-Pres. 1980–81, Dir., Deputy Chair. and Deputy Chief Exec. 1981–83, Pres. 1983–87, Deputy Chair. 1987–90; Chancellor Univ. of Western Ont. 1988–93; Lecturer, Grad. School of Business, Univ. of Chicago 1992–93; Chair. Canada Deposit Insurance Corpn. 1993–, Canada Merit Scholarship Foundation 1994–. *Publications:* The Cost of Capital in Canada (with R. J. Wonnacott) 1961, (with R. E. Caves): Canadian Economic Policy and the Impact of International Capital Flows 1970, Private Foreign Investment in Development 1973, Canada's Political Economy 1980. *Leisure interests:* tennis, reading. *Address:* P.O. Box 156, Toronto-Dominion Centre, Toronto, Ont. M5K 1H1 (Office); 90 Glen Edyth Drive, Toronto, Ont., M4V 2V9, Canada (Home). *Telephone:* (416) 973-3082 (Office); (416) 924-4971. *Fax:* (416) 954-3819 (Office); (416) 954-6238 (Home).

REUTER, Edzard; German business executive; b. 16 Feb. 1928, Berlin; s. of Ernst Reuter and Hanna Kleinert; ed. Univs. of Göttingen and Berlin; Asst. Prof., Free Univ. of Berlin 1954–56; various exec. posts in Bertelsmann Publishing Group 1957–64; with Daimler-Benz AG 1964–, various financial assignments, then Sec. 1964–71, Head of Corp. Planning and Org. 1971–73, deputy mem. Bd. of Man. 1973–76, full mem. 1976–96, Chief Financial Officer 1980–87, Chair. 1987–95; Chair. Supervisory Bd. AR AEG AG (merger with AEF 1989); Chair. Superviory Bd. Airbus Industries 1994–. *Publication:* Schein und Wirklichkeit 1998. *Address:* Daimler-Benz AG, Postfach 800230, 70546 Stuttgart, Germany.

REUTERSWÄRD, Carl Fredrik; Swedish artist, writer and sculptor; b. 4 June 1934, Stockholm; s. of Wilhelm Reuterswärd and Therese Ingestrom; m. 1st Anna Tesch 1958 (divorced 1968); two s. two d.; m. 2nd Mona Moller-Nielsen 1974; one s.; ed. Ecole de Fernand Leger, Paris and Royal Coll. of Art, Stockholm; first artist to use lasers 1965; Prof. Royal Coll. of Art, Stockholm 1965–70; since 1952 active in drawing, painting, sculpture, holography, scenography, graphics, design and architectural comms.; principal themes: Nonsens 1952–58; Cigars and Games 1958–63; Exercise 1958–64; Lazy Lasers and Holy Holos 1965–74; a trilogy: Kilroy (anybody) 1962–72, CAVIART (a somebody) 1972–82; works in public collections in Sweden, U.S.A., Fed. Repub. of Germany, France, England, Netherlands, Norway and Denmark, including National museum, Stockholm, Museum of Modern Art, New York, Städtische Kunsthalle, Düsseldorf, Musée National d'Art Moderne, Paris, Tate Gallery, London and Stedelijk Museum, Amsterdam; Non-Violence, bronze sculpture on perm. display in front of UN bldg., New York, since 1988. *Publications:* Kafka, Wahlstrom and Widstrand 1981, Caviart 1982, Making Faces 1984, Mes Autres Moi 1989. *Address:* 6 rue Montolieu, 1030 Bussigny/Lausanne, Switzerland. *Telephone:* 021-7010514.

REUTOV, Oleg Aleksandrovich; Russian organic chemist; b. 5 Sept. 1920, Makeyevka, Donetsk Region; s. of Alexander Reutov and Anastasiya Reutov; m. Nina Reutov 1946; one d.; ed. Moscow Univ.; Soviet Army 1941–45; mem. CPSU 1942–91; Instructor, Moscow Univ. 1945–54, Prof. 1954–; Head of Dept. of Organic Chem. Moscow Univ. 1978–94, Adviser to Rector 1994–; research into physical organic chemistry and organometallic chemistry; Soviet expert on chemical and biological warfare, UN 1969–; Deputy Chair. Soviet Peace Cttee. 1974–91; Corresp. mem. U.S.S.R. (now Russian) Acad. of Sciences 1958–64, mem. 1964–; Ed. Metallo-organic Chemistry Journal; Lenin Prize 1984. *Publications:* Theoretical Problems of Organic Chemistry 1956, Fundamentals of Theoretical Organic Chemistry 1967, Reaction Mechanisms of Organometallic Compounds (co-author) 1968, CH-Acids (co-author) 1978, Ambident Anions (co-author) 1983, Reactions of Organometallic compounds as a redox process (co-author) 1981, Advances in Organometallic Chemistry (co-author) 1984, Organic Chemistry (textbook, co-author) 1997. *Leisure interest:* fishing. *Address:* Department of Chemistry, University of Moscow, 119899 Moscow B-234, Russia. *Telephone:* (095) 939-12-34.

REVEL, Jean-François; French writer; b. 19 Jan. 1924, Marseilles; s. of Joseph Ricard and France Mathez; m. 2nd Claude Sarraute 1966; one s; one s. one d. by first m.; two step-s.; ed. Ecole Normale Supérieure and Sorbonne, Paris; teacher of Philosophy and French Literature, Institut Français, Mexico, later Florence 1952–56; teacher of Philosophy, Lille and Paris 1956–63; Literary Adviser Editions Julliard and Pauvert 1961–66, Editions Laffont 1966–77; Columnist L'Express 1966–81, Dir. 1978–81; Ed. and Columnist Le Point magazine 1982; Columnist Europe 1 1989–92, Radio télévision Luxembourg (RTL) 1995–; Konrad Adenauer Prize 1986, Chateaubriand Prize 1988, J. J. Rousseau Prize 1989, Prix du livre politique 1997. *Publications:* novel: Histoire de Flore 1957; essays: Pourquoi des philosophes? 1957, Pour l'Italie 1958, Le style du général 1959, Sur Proust 1960, La cabale des dévots 1962, En France 1965, Contrecensures 1966, Histoire de la philosophie occidentale Vol. I 1968, Vol. II 1970, Ni Marx ni Jésus 1970, Les idées de notre temps 1972, La tentation totalitaire 1976, Descartes inutile et incertain 1976, La nouvelle censure 1977, Un festin en paroles 1978, La grâce de l'état 1981, Comment les démocraties finissent 1983; Le rejet de l'état 1984, Une anthologie de la poésie française 1984, Le terrorisme contre la démocratie 1987, La connaissance inutile 1988, le regain démocratique 1992, L'absolutisme inefficace 1992, Histoire de la Philosophie Occidentale, de Thalès à Kant 1994, Un festin en paroles 1995, Le voleur dans la maison vide, mémoires 1997, Le moine et le philosophe 1997, l'Œil et la connaissance, Ecrits sur l'art 1998. *Leisure interests:* riding, swimming. *Address:* 55 quai de Bourbon, 75004 Paris, France. *Telephone:* (1) 43-54-65-87. *Fax:* (1) 47.00.76.93

REVERDIN, Olivier, D. ÈS L.; Swiss professor, politician and editor; b. 15 July 1913, Geneva; s. of Henri Reverdin and Gabrielle Bouthillier de Beaumont; m. Renée Chaponnière 1936; two s. one d.; ed. Univs. of Geneva and Paris, and Ecole Française d'Athènes; school teaching, Geneva and France 1938–41; Attaché Swiss Legation, Rome 1941–44; Lecturer and Asst. Prof. Ancient Greek Literature, Univ. of Geneva 1945–58, Ordinary Prof. 1958–83, Hon. Prof. 1983–; Parl. Ed. Journal de Genève, Berne 1945–54, and Man. Ed. 1955–59, Man. 1959–67, Chair. 1972–79; Deputy (Liberal) of Geneva at the Conseil Nat. 1955–71, at Conseil des Etats 1971–79; Chair. Fondation Hardt pour l'Etude de l'Antiquité Classique 1959–95; Chair. Soc. Suisse des Sciences Humaines 1960–68; mem. Nat. Council for Scientific Research 1963–80, Chair. 1968–80; rep. Consultative Ass., Council of Europe 1964–74, Chair. of the Cultural and Scientific Cttee. 1966, of the Cttee. for Science and Tech. 1967–69, Pres. of the Ass. 1969–72; Chair. Fondation pour le Lexicon Iconographicum Mythologiae Classicae 1973–81; Vice-Pres. European Science Foundation 1974–77; Chair. Montres Rolex, S.A. 1973–92, Hon. Chair. 1992–; Chair. Sodeco Saia, S.A. 1975–90, Fondation Baur Collections 1984–, Fondation Baur 1984–; Hon. mem. Soc. for the Promotion of Hellenic Studies (London); Hon. Fellow Acad. of Athens, Österreichische Akad. der Wissenschaften and Royal Belgian Acad. of Sciences, Arts and Humanities; Hon. Dr. h.c. (Heidelberg, Strasbourg, Ecole Polytechnique Lausanne, Bucharest, Neuchâtel, Paris-Sorbonne); Robert Schuman Medal. *Publications:* La religion de la cité platonicienne 1945, La guerre du Sonderbund vue par le Général Dufour 1948, 1987, Quatorze calvinistes chez les Topinambous 1957, La Crète, berceau de la civilisation occidentale 1960, Connaissance de la Suisse 1964, Entretiens sur l'Antiquité Classique, Vols. I–XLI (Ed.) 1954–96, La vision de Dorothéos 1984, Les premiers cours de grec au Collège de France 1984, Henri Estienne à Genève 1988, Impressions grecques en Suisse aux XVIe et XVIIe siècles 1991. *Leisure interests:* horticulture, ornithology. *Address:* 8 rue des Granges, 1204 Geneva, Switzerland. *Telephone:* 022-311 51 91.

RÉVÉSZ, Tamas Mihaly; Hungarian broadcasting executive and fmr. professor of law; b. 1945, Budapest; m.; two c.; Prof. of Law, Univ. Eötvös Loránd, Budapest 1983–96; Pres. Nat. Radio and TV Comm. 1996–. *Publications:* Freedom of the Press and National Papers in the Second Half of the 19th Century in Hungary 1986, The Past of Hungarian Legal History and its Tasks for the Future 1987, The Present and the Future of Legal History 1987. *Address:* National Radio and Television Commission, Reviczky u. 5, 1088 Budapest VIII, Hungary.

REXRODT, Günter, DR. RER. POL.; German politician; b. 12 Sept. 1941, Berlin; m. Ingrid Hoyermann 1983; one c.; ed. Freie Univ. Berlin; Berliner Bank, Berlin 1961–62; Standard Elektrik Lorenz AG, Berlin 1963–64; Adviser on Industrial Man., Industrie- und Handelskammer, Berlin 1968–72, Dir. Dept. of Political Tech. 1972–74, mem. Man. Bd. and Dir. Industry Dept. 1974–79; Dir. Industry Dept. Senator for Econs. and Transport, Berlin Senate 1979–82; Sec. of State to Senator for Econs. and Transport 1982–85; Senator for Finance, Berlin 1985–89; joined Citibank, New York April–Dec. 1989; Chair. Man. Bd. Citibank AG, Frankfurt 1990–91; mem. Man. Bd. Treuhandanstalt (agency responsible for privatization of state enterprises of fmr. E. Germany), Berlin 1991–93; mem. FDP 1980–; Deputy Chair. Landesverband Berlin 1983–87, 1989–; mem. Bundesvorstand 1990–95; Minister for the Economy 1993–98. *Leisure interests:* astrophysics, sailing. *Address:* c/o Bundesministerium für Wirtschaft, 5300 Bonn; Villemombler Str. 76, 53123 Bonn, Germany.

REYNALDO, Jacinto; Dominican Republic politician; Vice-Pres. Dominican Republic; Partido Reformista Social Cristiano (PRSC) Cand. for Presidency May 1996. *Address:* Office of the Vice-President, Santo Domingo, Dominican Republic.

REYNOLDS, Albert; Irish politician; b. 3 Nov. 1935, Rooskey, Co. Roscommon; m. Kathleen Coén; two s. five d.; ed. Summerhill Coll., Sligo; fmr. Chair. C & D Petfoods; mem. Longford County Council 1974–79; mem. Dáil 1977–; Minister for Posts and Telegraphs and Transport 1979–81; Minister for Industry and Energy March–Dec. 1982; Minister for Industry and Commerce 1987–88, for Finance and the Public Service 1988–89, of Finance 1989–91, Taioseach 1992–94; Vice-Pres. Fianna Fáil 1983–92, Pres. 1992–94; Chair. Longford Recreational Devt. Centre; mem. Bd. of Govs. European Investment Bank; Gov. for Ireland, Bd. of Govs. World Bank, Int. Monetary Fund; Dir. Jefferson Smurfit 1996–; Hon. LL.D. (Univ. Coll., Dublin) 1995. *Address:* Government Buildings, Upper Merrion Street, Dublin 2; Mount Carmel House, Dublin Road, Longford, Ireland. *Telephone:* (1) 6685333.

REYNOLDS, Anna, F.R.A.M.; British opera and concert singer; b. 5 June 1936, Canterbury; d. of Paul Grey Reynolds and Vera Cicely Turner; ed. Benenden School, Royal Acad. of Music; studied with Professoressa Debora Fambri, Rome; has appeared at many int. festivals including Spoleto, Edinburgh, Aix-en-Provence, Salzburg Easter Festival, Vienna, Bayreuth, Tanglewood; has sung with leading orchestras all over the world including Chicago Symphony, New York Philharmonic, Berlin Philharmonic, London Symphony, etc.; has appeared in opera performances in New York Metropolitan, La Scala, Milan, Covent Garden, Bayreuth, Rome, Chicago Lyric Opera, Teatro Colón, Buenos Aires, Teatro Fenice, Venice and many others; has recorded for Decca, EMI, Polydor, Philips. *Leisure interests:* reading, piano, travel, world-wide correspondence. *Address:* Peesten 9, 8658 Kasendorf, Germany. *Telephone:* 09228 1661.

REYNOLDS, Burt; American actor; b. 11 Feb. 1936, Waycross, Ga.; s. of Burt Reynolds Sr.; m. 1st Judy Carne (divorced 1965); m. 2nd Loni Anderson 1988; one adopted s.; ed. Florida State Univ.; mem. Dirs. Guild of America; Golden Globe for Best Supporting Actor for Boogie Nights 1997. *Stage appearances include:* Mister Roberts, Look, We've Come Through, The Rainmaker; *films include:* Angel Baby 1961, Operation CIA 1965, Navajo Joe 1967, Impasse 1969, Skullduggery 1970, Deliverance 1972, Everything You've Always Wanted to Know about Sex But Were Afraid to Ask 1972, The Man Who Loved Cat Dancing 1973, Hustle 1975, Silent Movie 1976, Gator (also dir.) 1976, Nickelodeon 1976, Smokey and the Bandit 1977, Starting Over 1979, Cannonball Run 1981, Sharky's Machine (also dir.) 1981, City Heat 1984, Stick (also dir.) 1984, Rent A Cop 1987, Breaking In 1988, Switching Channels 1988, Physical Evidence 1989, Breaking In 1989, B. L. Stryker 1989, Modern Love 1990, Alby's House of Bondage 1990, Cop and a Half 1993, Striptease 1996, Mad Dog Time 1996, Boogie Nights 1997, Raven 1997, Waterproof 1998, Mystery Alaska 1998, The Hunter's Moon 1998. *Television appearances include:* Riverboat, Pony Express, Gunsmoke, Hawk, Dan August, B. L. Stryker, Evening Shade 1990–94, The Cherokee Kid 1996; mem. Dirs. Guild of America. *Publication:* My Life (autobiog.) 1994. *Address:* Sutton & Associates, 145 South Fairfax Avenue, Suite 310, Los Angeles, CA 90036, U.S.A.

REYNOLDS, Francis Martin Baillie, Q.C., D.C.L., F.B.A.; British professor of law; b. 11 Nov. 1932, St. Albans; s. of Eustace Baillie Reynolds and Emma Holmes; m. Susan Shillito 1965; two s. one d.; ed. Winchester Coll. and Worcester Coll. Oxford; Bigelow Teaching Fellow, Univ. of Chicago 1957–58; lecturer, Worcester Coll. Oxford 1958–60, Fellow 1960–; barrister, Inner Temple 1960, Hon. Bencher 1979; Reader in Law, Univ. of Oxford 1977, Prof. of Law 1992–; Ed. The Law Quarterly Review 1987–; Visiting lecturer, Univ. of Auckland 1971, 1977; Visiting Prof. Nat. Univ. of Singapore 1984, 1986, 1988, 1990–92, 1994, 1996, 1997, Univ. Coll. London 1987–89, Univ. of Otago 1993, Univ. of Sydney 1993, Univ. of Auckland 1995; Hon. Q.C. *Publications:* Bowstead and Reynolds on Agency, 13th–16th edns. 1965–96, Benjamin's Sale of Goods, 1st–5th edns. (jtly.) 1974–97. *Leisure interests:* music, walking. *Address:* Worcester College, Oxford, OX1 2HB, England. *Telephone:* (01865) 278300. *Fax:* (01865) 511894.

REYNOLDS, John Hamilton, PH.D.; American professor of physics; b. 3 April 1923, Cambridge, Mass.; s. of Horace Mason Reynolds and Catharine Whitford Coffeen; m. Anne Burchard Arnold 1975; two s. three d. (by previous marriages); ed. Harvard Coll. and Univ. of Chicago; Assoc. physicist, Argonne Nat. Laboratory 1950; Asst. Prof. to Prof. of Physics, Univ. of Calif. at Berkeley 1950–61, Prof. 1961–88, Emer. 1989–; Chair. Dept. of Physics, Univ. of Calif. 1984–86; Research Prof. Miller Inst. for Basic Research in Science 1959–61, 1967–68, Faculty Research Lecturer 1974; Guggenheim Fellow, Univ. of Bristol, England 1956–57, Nat. Science Foundation Sr. Postdoctoral Fellow and Visiting Prof. Univ. of São Paulo, Brazil 1963–64; Guggenheim Fellow, Los Alamos, N.M. 1987; Fulbright-Hays Research Award (Portugal) 1971–72; mem. N.A.S.; Dr. h.c. (Univ. of Coimbra, Portugal) 1987; U.S.-Australia Co-operative Science Program award (Perth) 1978–79; Berkeley Citation 1988; John Price Wetherill Medal of Franklin Inst., J. Lawrence Smith Medal of N.A.S., Leonard Medal, Meteoritical Soc., NASA Exceptional Scientific Achievement Medal. *Publications:* Research papers and reviews in fields of mass spectroscopy, isotope studies in meteorites, geochronology, solar system chronology, extinct radioactivity, and lunar samples. *Leisure interests:* swimming, sailing, brewing, microcomputers. *Address:* Department of Physics, University of California, Berkeley, CA 94720, U.S.A. *Telephone:* (510) 642-4863. *Fax:* (510) 643-8497.

REYNOLDS, Sir Peter William John, Kt., C.B.E.; British business executive; b. 10 Sept. 1929, Singapore; s. of Harry and Gladys Reynolds; m. Barbara Anne Johnson 1955; two s.; ed. Haileybury Coll.; with Unilever Ltd. 1950–70, Trainee, Man. Dir., then Chair., Walls Ltd.; Asst. Group Man. Dir. Ranks Hovis McDougall 1971, Group Man. Dir. 1972–81, Chair. 1981–89, Deputy Chair. 1989–93; mem. Consultative Bd. for Resources Devt. in Agric. 1982–84; Deputy Chair. AvisEurope PLC 1988–; Dir. of Industrial Devt. Bd. for Northern Ireland 1982–89, Guardian Royal Exchange Assurance PLC 1986–; Chair. of Resources Cttee. of Food and Drink Fed. 1983–86; Dir. Boots Co. PLC 1986–, Guardian Royal Exchange PLC 1986–, Avis Europe Ltd. 1988–, Cilva Holdings PLC 1989–, Nationwide Anglia Bldg. Soc. 1990–92, Pioneer Concrete (Holdings) 1990–; mem. Peacock Cttee. 1985–86; High Sheriff of Buckingham 1990–91. *Leisure interests:* beagling, riding (occasionally), watching rugby football, reading, gardening. *Address:* Rignall Farm, Rignall Road, Great Missenden, Bucks., HP16 9PE, England. *Telephone:* (0124 06) 4714.

REZA, (Evelyne Agnès) Yasmina; French dramatist, actress and comedian; b. 1 May 1955, Paris; d. of the late Jean Reza and of Nora (née Heltaï) Reza; one s. one d.; ed. Lycée de Saint-Cloud, Paris Univ. X, Nanterre, Ecole Jacques Lecoq.; Chevalier des Arts et des Lettres; Prix du jeune théâtre Beatrix Dussane-André Roussin de l'Acad. française 1991. *Stage appearances include:* La Malade imaginaire 1977, Antigone 1977, Un sang fort 1977, La Mort de Gaspard Hauser 1978, L'An Mil 1980, Le Piège de Méduse 1983, Le Veilleur de nuit 1986, Enorme changement de dernière minute 1989, La Fausse suivante 1990. *Plays directed include:* Birds in the Night 1979, Marie la louve 1981. *Plays written include:* Conversations après un enterrement 1987 (Molière Award for Best Author, Prix des Talents nouveaux de la Soc. des auteurs et compositeurs dramatiques, Johnson Foundation prize), La Traversée de l'hiver 1989, La Métamorphose (adapted) 1988, Art 1994, L'Homme du Hasard. *Screenplays written include:* Jusqu'à la nuit (also dir.) 1984, Le Goûter chez Niels 1986, A demain 1992. *Address:* c/o Marta Andras (Marton Play), 14 rue des Sablons, 75116 Paris, France.

REZEK, Francisco, LL.B.; Brazilian judge and politician; b. 18 Jan. 1944, Cristina, Minas Gerais; ed. Fed. Univ. of Minas Gerais, Sorbonne, Oxford Univ., Harvard Univ., The Hague Acad. of Int. Law; Attorney of the Repub., Supreme Court 1972–79; Prof. of Int. and Constitutional Law Univ. of Brasilia 1971–, Chair. Law Dept. 1974–76, Dean Faculty of Social Studies 1978–79; Prof. of Int. Law Rio Branco Inst. 1976–; Justice of Supreme Court 1983–90, April 1992–; Foreign Minister 1990–92; mem. Perm. Court of Arbitration 1987–; Judge Int. Court of Justice, The Hague Feb. 1997–. *Publications:* Droit des traités: particularités des actes constitutifs d'organisations internationales 1968, La conduite des relations internationales dans le droit constitutional latino-américain 1970, Direito dos Tratados 1984, Public International Law 1989. *Address:* International Court of Justice, Peace Palace, Carnegieplein 2, 2517 KJ The Hague, Netherlands.

REZNIK, Genry Markovich, CAND.JUR.; Russian barrister; b. 11 May 1938, Leningrad; m. Larissa Yulianovna Reznik; one s.; ed. Kazakhstan Univ., Moscow Inst. of Law; professional volleyball mem. U.S.S.R. youth team; investigator Investigation Dept., Ministry of Internal Affairs Kazakh Repub.; barrister since 1985; Dir. Inst. of Defence Int. Union of Advocates; mem. Moscow Helsinki Group 1989–; participated in 22 civil trials; f. Reznik, Gagarin and Partners. *Publications:* over 100 articles on criminal law. *Address:* Schmidtovskiy pr. 3, 123100 Moscow, Russia. *Telephone:* (095) 205 2709 (Office).

RHALLYS, George J. (see Rallis, George J.).

RHEIMS, Maurice; French art critic; b. 4 Jan 1910, Versailles; s. of Gen. Léon and Jeanne (née Lévy) Rheims; m. Lili Krahmer 1951 (divorced); one s. (deceased) two d.; ed. Ecole du Louvre, Sorbonne, Paris; Auctioneer, Paris 1935–72; mem. Acad. Française 1976–; Pres. Cultural Devt. Fund, Foundation of France; Vice-Pres. Admin. Council Nat. Library 1983–; Pres. prix Vasari 1986–; Animator with Antenne 2 of Haute Curiosité 1988–; mem. Nat. Org. Cttee. European Architectural Heritage Year; Grand Officier, Légion d'honneur, Croix de guerre, Médaille de la Résistance, Officier des Arts et des Lettres, Commdr. Order of Merit (Italy). *Publications:* La vie étrange des objets 1960, La main, la vie de Gauguin, Vie de Toulouse-Lautrec (co-author), Le cheval d'argent, Un carpaccio en Dordogne, L'objet 1900, L'art 1900 ou le style Jules Verne, Dictionnaire des mots sauvages, La vie d'artiste, La sculpture au XIXème siècle 1971, Le luthier de Mantoue 1972, Les chefs d'oeuvre des musées de Province 1974, Haute curiosité 1975, Les collectionneurs 1981, Le Saint-Office 1983; film scripts Martin Soldat 1966, L'homme pressé 1977, L'enfer de la curiosité 1979, Amour de l'art 1984, Attila, laisse donc ta petite soeur tranquille 1985, Haarlem . . . noir 1986, Les greniers de Sienne 1988, Les fortunes d'Appollon 1990, Apollon à Wall Street 1992, En tous mes Etâts. Entretiens avec François Duret-Robert 1993, Les Forêts d'Argent 1995, Une Mémoire vagabonde 1997. *Address:* 25 rue du Faubourg-Saint-Honoré, 75008 Paris, France. *Telephone:* 4265 5399.

RHINES, Peter Broomell, PH.D.; American oceanographer and atmospheric scientist; b. 23 July 1942, Hartford, Conn.; s. of Thomas B. Rhines and Olive S. Rhines; m. 1st Marie Lenos 1968 (divorced 1983); m. 2nd Linda Mattson Semtner 1984; one s.; ed. Loomis School, M.I.T., Trinity Coll., Cambridge, England; Sloan Scholar, M.I.T. 1960–63, N.S.F. Fellow 1963–64; Marshall Scholar, Cambridge 1964–67; Asst. Prof. of Oceanography M.I.T. 1967–71; Research Scientist, Cambridge Univ. 1971–72; mem. Scientific Staff, Woods Hole Oceanographic Inst. 1972–84, Dir. Center for Analysis of Marine Systems 1979–82, oceanographic research cruises 1972–95; Prof. of Oceanography and Atmospheric Sciences, Univ. of Washington, Seattle 1984–; Guggenheim Fellow, Christ's Coll. Cambridge, England 1979–80; Natural Environment Research Council Visiting Fellow, U.K. 1983; Fellow American Geophysical Union, American Meteorological Soc., Queen's Fellow in Marine Sciences, Australia; mem. N.A.S.; de Florez Award, M.I.T. 1963, Stommel Research Award, American Meteorological Soc. 1998. *Publications:* research papers on general circulation of the oceans, waves and climate; contribs. to films on oceanography for BBC and Public Broadcasting System, U.S.A. *Leisure interests:* classical guitar, conversation and the out-of-doors. *Address:* School of Oceanography, University of Washington, Box 357940, Seattle, WA 98195 (Office); 5753 61st Avenue N.E., Seattle, WA 98105, U.S.A. (Home). *Telephone:* (206) 522-5753 (Home).

RHOADS, James Berton, PH.D.; American archivist; b. 17 Sept. 1928, Sioux City, Iowa; s. of James H. Rhoads and Mary K. Rhoads; m. S. Angela Handy 1947; one s. two d.; ed. Univ. of California (Berkeley) and the American Univ., Washington, D.C.; held various positions in the Nat. Archives 1952–65; Asst. Archivist, Civil Archives 1965–66; Deputy Archivist of U.S.A. 1966–68; Archivist of U.S.A. 1968–79; Pres. Rhoads Assocs. Int. 1980–84; Dir. Graduate Program in Archives and Records Man., Western Washington Univ. 1984–94, Prof. of History 1987–94, Prof. Emer. 1994–, Dir. Center for Pacific Northwest Studies 1994–97; mem. Cttee. on Soviet-American Archival Co-operation 1986–91, Bd. of Trustees Washington State Historical Soc. 1986–95, Washington State Historical Records Advisory Bd. 1990–, Acad. of Certified Archivists 1989– (Pres. 1992–94); Fellow, Soc. of American Archivists, Pres. 1974–75; Pres. Int. Council on Archives 1976–79; Vice-Pres. Intergovernmental Council on Gen. Information Program, UNESCO 1977–79, and mem. numerous other related orgs. *Publications:* numerous articles in professional journals. *Leisure interests:* reading, philately. *Address:* 3613 Illinois Lane, Bellingham, WA 98226, U.S.A. *Telephone:* (360) 676-1235.

RHODES, Frank Harold Trevor, PH.D.; American geologist and university president; b. 29 Oct. 1926, Warwickshire, England; s. of Harold C. Rhodes and Gladys (Ford) Rhodes; m. Rosa Carlson 1952; four d.; ed. Univ. of Birmingham; Post-doctoral Fellow, Fulbright Scholar, Univ. of Ill. 1950–51, Visiting Lecturer in Geology summers of 1951–52, Asst. Prof., Univ. of Ill. 1954–55, Assoc. Prof. 1955–56, Dir. Univ. of Ill. Field Station, Wyoming 1956; Lecturer in Geology, Univ. of Durham 1951–54; Prof. of Geology and Head Dept. of Geology, Univ. of Wales, Swansea 1956–68, Dean Faculty of Science 1967–68; Prof. of Geology and Mineralogy, Coll. of Literature, Science and Arts, Univ. of Michigan 1968–77, Dean 1971–74, Vice-Pres. for Academic Affairs 1974–77; Pres. Cornell Univ. 1977–94, Prof. of Geology 1977–95; Chair. Nat. Science Foundation 1995–; Dir. John Heinz III Centre for Science, Econs. and the Environment 1996–; Vice-Pres. Dyson Charitable Trust 1996–; Prin. Washington Advisory Group 1997–; mem. Nat. Science Bd. 1987– (Chair. 1994–96); Trustee Andrew W. Mellon 1984–; numerous hon. degrees. *Publications:* The Evolution of Life 1962, Fossils 1963, Geology 1972, Evolution 1974, Language of the Earth 1981; over 70 major scientific articles and monographs, and some 60 articles on educ. *Address:* Cornell University, 3104 Snee Hall, Ithaca, N.Y. 14853, U.S.A.

RHODES, Richard L., B.A.; American writer; b. 4 July 1937, Kansas City; s. of Arthur Rhodes and Georgia Collier Rhodes; m. Ginger Untrif 1993; two c.; ed. East High School, Kansas City, Mo., Yale Univ.; Trustee Andrew Drumm Inst., Independence, Mo. 1990–, Menninger Foundation, Topeka, Kan. 1993–; Fellowships: John Simon Guggenheim Memorial Foundation 1974–75, Nat. Endowment for the Arts 1978, Ford Foundation 1981–83, Alfred P. Sloan Foundation 1985, 1993, 1995, MacArthur Foundation Program on Peace and Int. Co-operation 1990–91; Hon. D.Hum.Litt. (Westminster Coll., Fulton, Mo.) 1988; Nat. Book Critics Circle Award for general non-fiction 1987, Nat. Book Award for non-fiction 1987, Pulitzer Prize for general non-fiction 1988 (all for The Making of the Atomic Bomb). *Publications:* (non-fiction) The Inland Ground: An Evocation of the American Middle West 1970, The Ozarks 1974, Looking for America: A Writer's Odyssey 1979, The Making of the Atomic Bomb 1987, Farm: A Year in the Life of an American Farmer 1989, A Hole in the World: An American Boyhood 1990, Making Love: An Erotic Odyssey 1992, Nuclear Renewal: Common Sense about Energy 1993, Dark Sun: The Making of the Hydrogen Bomb 1995, How To Write 1995, Trying To Get Some Dignity: Stories of Triumph Over Childhood Abuse (with Ginger Rhodes) 1996, Deadly Feasts: Tracking the Secrets of a Terrifying New Plague 1997, Visions of Technology 1999; (fiction) The Ungodly 1973, Holy Secrets 1978, The Last Safari 1980, Sons of Earth 1981. *Address:* c/o Janklow & Nesbit Assocs., 598 Madison Avenue, New York, NY 10021, U.S.A. *Telephone:* (212) 421-1700.

RHODES, Zandra Lindsey, C.B.E., F.C.S.D., F.S.I.A.D.; British textile and fashion designer; b. 19 Sept. 1940, Chatham, Kent; d. of Albert James Rhodes and Beatrice Ellen (née Twigg); ed. Medway Coll. of Art and Royal Coll. of Art; set up print factory and studio 1965; began producing dresses using own prints 1966; founder-partner and designer, Fulham Clothes Shop, London 1967–68; freelance designer, producing own collections for British and U.S. markets 1968–75; founder and Man. Dir. (with Anne Knight and Ronnie Stirling) Zandra Rhodes (U.K.) Ltd. and Zandra Rhodes (Shops) Ltd. 1975–86; opened first shop in London 1975; Man. Dir. all Zandra Rhodes Cos. 1975–; other shops in Bloomingdale's, New York, Marshall Field's, Chicago, Seibu, Tokyo, and Harrods, London; licences include: Wamsutta sheets and pillowcases (U.S.A.) 1976, Eve Stillman Lingerie (U.S.A.) 1977, CVP Designs, interior fabrics and settings (U.K.) 1977, Philip Hockley decorative furs (U.K.) 1986, Zandra Rhodes saris (India) 1987, Littlewoods catalogues (U.K.) for printed T-shirts and intasia sweaters 1988, Hilmet silk scarves and men's ties (U.K.) 1989, Bonnay perfume (U.K.) 1993, Coats Patons needlepoint (U.K.) 1993, Pologeorgis Furs (U.S.A.) 1995, Zandra Rhodes II handpainted ready-to-wear collection (Hong Kong) 1995, Grattons Catalogue sheets and duvets (U.K.) 1996; work has featured in numerous exhbns. and is represented in many perm. collections including Victoria & Albert Museum, London, Metropolitan Museum of Art, New York, Smithsonian Inst. Washington and Museum of Applied Arts and Sciences, Sydney; retrospectives in El Paso, Texas 1984, Columbus, Ohio 1987, Tokyo 1987, 1991, Athenaeum Library, La Jolla 1996; water-colour exhbns. in New York, Los Angeles, New Orleans 1989, f. Zandra Rhodes Museum of Fashion and Textiles, U.K. 1996; Hon. Fellow, Kent Inst. of Art and Design 1992; Hon. D.F.A. (Int. Fine Arts Coll., Miami) 1986; Dr. h.c. (R.C.A.) 1986; Hon. D.D. (C.N.A.A.) 1987; Designer of the Year, English Fashion Trade 1972, Royal Designer for Industry 1974, Emmy Award for Best Costume Designs in Romeo and Juliet on Ice, CBS TV 1984, Alpha Award, New Orleans 1985, 1991, Woman of Distinction Award, Northwood Inst., Dallas 1986, Observer Award as top U.K. Textile Designer 1990, Hall of Fame Award, British Fashion Council 1995. *Publications:* The Art of Zandra Rhodes 1984, The Zandra Rhodes Collection by Brother 1988. *Leisure interests:* travelling, drawing, gardening, cooking. *Address:* 87 Richford Street, Hammersmith, London, W6 7HJ (factory); 79–85 Bermondsey Street, London, SE1 3XF, England. *Telephone:* 0171-403 5333 (Office).

RHYS-JAMES, Shani, B.A.(HONS.); British artist and painter; b. 2 May 1953, Australia; d. of Harold Marcus Rhys-James and Jeannie James-Money; m. Stephen West 1977; two s.; ed. Parliament Hill Girls School, Loughborough Coll. of Art and Cen. St. Martin's Coll. of Art and Design; regular exhbns. with Martin Tinney, Cardiff 1991–99, Stephen Lacey, London; work in art collections of Nat. Museum of Wales, Newport Museum and Art Gallery, Usher Gallery, Arts Council of England, Gallery of Modern Art, Glasgow; many TV appearances including documentary Blood Ties; mem. Royal Cambrian Acad. 1994; BBC Wales Visual Artist Award 1994, BP Nat. Portrait Award, Gold Medal for Fine Art Royal Nat. Eisteddfod, First Prize Hunting/Observer Prize, and others. *Leisure interests:* piano, films, plays, books, writing poetry. *Address:* Dolpebyll, Llangadfan, Welshpool, Powys, SY21 0PU, Wales. *Telephone:* (01938) 820469. *Fax:* (01938) 820469.

RI JONG OK; Korean politician; Minister of Light Industry 1951; mem. Cen. Cttee. Workers' Party of Korea (WPK) 1956; Vice-Premier 1960; Political Commissar of WPK 1960–70, Alt. Political Commissar 1973; mem. Cen. People's Cttee. 1972; Vice-Premier 1976; Premier 1977; Del. to Supreme People's Ass. 1986, 1990; Supreme Commdr. of Korean People's Army 1991; title of Marshal conferred 1992; Chair. Nat. Defence Cttee. 1993–; mem. Political Bureau of Cen. Cttee. of WPK; Vice-Pres. of Democratic People's Repub. of Korea. *Address:* Office of the Vice-President, Pyongyang, Democratic People's Republic of Korea.

RIBAS REIG, Oscar, LL.B.; Andorran politician, industrialist and banker; b. 26 Oct. 1936, Sant Julia de Loria; m.; five c.; ed. Univ. of Barcelona, Univ. of Fribourg, Switzerland; M.P. 1972–75, 1976–79, Head of Govt. 1982–84, 1990–94. *Address:* c/o Office of the Head of Government, Andorra la Vella, Andorra.

RIBEIRO, Ignacio; Brazilian fashion designer; m. Suzanne Clements (q.v.) 1992; ed. Cen. St. Martin's Coll. of Art and Design, London; fmrly. designer, Brazil; design consultant in Brazil with wife 1991–93; f. Clements Ribeiro with wife, London 1993; first collection launched Oct. 1993, numerous collections since; first solo show London Fashion Week March 1995; fashion shows since in London, Paris, Brazil, Japan; consultant to cos. in U.K. and Italy; winners Designer of the Year New Generation Category 1996. *Address:* Clements Ribeiro Ltd., 48 S. Molton Street, London, W1X 1HE, England. *Telephone:* 0171-409 7719. *Fax:* 0171-409 1741.

RIBEIRO, João Ubaldo Osório Pimentel, LL.B., M.S.; Brazilian writer and journalist; b. 23 Jan. 1941, Itaparica, Bahia; s. of Manoel Ribeiro and Maria Felipa Osório Pimentel Ribeiro; m. 1st Maria Beatriz Moreira Caldas 1962; m. 2nd Mônica Maria Roters 1971; m. 3rd Berenice de Carvalho Batella Ribeiro 1982; one s. three d.; ed. Fed. Univ. of Bahia Law School, and School of Admin., and Univ. of Southern California, U.S.A.; Reporter, Jornal da Bahia, Salvador 1958–59, City Ed. and Columnist 1960–63; Chief Ed. Tribuna da Bahia 1968–73; Columnist O Globo, Rio de Janeiro, O Estado de São Paulo, São Paulo; Editorial-writer Folha de S. Paulo 1969–73; Prof. of Political Science, Fed. Univ. of Bahia 1965–71, Catholic Univ of Bahia 1967–71; mem. Brazilian Acad. of Letters; Jabuti Prize (Brazilian Book Chamber) 1971, 1984; Golfinho de Ouro (Govt. of Rio) and many others. *Publications:* (novels) Setembro Não Tem Sentido 1968, Sargento Getúlio 1971, Vila Real 1980, Viva o Povo Brasileiro 1984, O Sorriso do Lagarto 1989; (short stories) Vencecavalo e o Outro Povo 1973, Livro de Histórias 1983; Ein Brasilianer in Berlin (autobiog.) 1994. *Leisure interests:* microscopy (protozoa), music (Bach), sports (soccer, fishing). *Address:* c/o Editora Nova Fronteira S.A., Rua Bambina 25, 22251-050 Rio de Janeiro, R.J.; Rua General Urquiza, 147/401, 22431-040 Rio de Janeiro, R.J., Brazil (Home). *Telephone:* (021) 537-8770 (Office); (021) 239-8528 (Home). *Fax:* (021) 286-6755.

RIBERA, José António Moya; Portuguese diplomatist; b. 19 July 1946, Oporto; s. of António Ribera y Romero and Maria Margarida da Silva Pereira Moya; m. Maria Filomena Leite Pereira de Magalhães 1976; one s. one d.; ed. Liceu Alexandre Herculano, Oporto and Univ. of Oporto; joined Ministry of Foreign Affairs 1972; Sec. The Hague 1976–78; Consul, Vigo, Spain 1978–81; Counsellor, Kinshasa 1981–85; Counsellor, Perm. Mission of Portugal at EC, Brussels 1985–89; Deputy Dir.-Gen. for EC, Ministry of Foreign Affairs 1989–92; Rep. of Portugal at EC Intergovernmental Conf. for Political Union (Maastricht Treaty) 1990–92; Perm. Rep. of Portugal to UNESCO 1992–; Kt. Commdr. of Infante D. Henrique Order, Officer of Mil. Order of Cristo, Grand Cross, Order of Merit, decorations from Netherlands, Zaïre, Brazil. *Leisure interests:* history, genealogy. *Address:* Permanent Representative of Portugal to UNESCO, Miollis 1, 75015 Paris (Office); ave Foch 41, 75016 Paris, France (Home). *Telephone:* (1) 45.68.30.55/7 (Office); 44.05.01.06 (Home). *Fax:* (1) 45.67.82.93.

RIBERHOLDT, Gunnar; Danish diplomatist; b. 7 Nov. 1933, Naestved; s. of Poul G. Riberholdt and Erna M. Andersen; one s. one d.; ed. U.S. univs. and Univ. of Copenhagen; Ministry of Foreign Affairs 1958–62; Sec. of Embassy, Danish Perm. Mission to European Communities 1962–64, Deputy Head of Mission 1964–65; Head of Section, Ministry of Foreign Affairs 1965–69; Econ. Counsellor, Paris 1969–72; Dir. Ministry of Foreign Affairs 1973–75; Dir.-Gen. European Econ. Affairs 1975–77; Amb., Perm. Rep. of Denmark to European Communities (now EU) 1977–84, 1992–94; Amb. to France 1984–91; Amb., Personal Rep. of Minister for Foreign Affairs to Intergovernmental Confs. on Political Union and on Econ. and Monetary Union 1991–92; Amb., Head Danish Del. to OECD 1991–92; Perm. Rep. to NATO 1995–. *Address:* NATO , 1110 Brussels, Belgium.

RIBOUD, Antoine Amédée Paul; French business executive; b. 24 Dec. 1918, Lyons; s. of Camille Riboud and Hélène Frachon; m. Lucette Hugonnard-Roche 1943; three s. one d.; ed. Ecole Supérieure de Commerce, Paris; joined Verreries Souchon-Neuvesel 1943, mem. Bd. of Dirs. and Sec.-Gen. 1952–62, Vice-Pres. 1962–65, Dir.-Gen. 1962–66, Pres. 1965–66; Pres. and Dir.-Gen. Soc. Boussois-Souchon-Neuvesel 1966–73; Pres. Boussois-Souchon-Neuvesel-Gervais-Danone 1973–96, Hon. Pres. 1996–; Vice-Pres. Cie. Gervais-Danone 1973–76, Pres. 1976–; Dir., later Dir.-Gen. Verreries de Gironcourt 1963–68; Dir., later Pres. and Dir.-Gen. Soc. des Eaux minérales d'Evian-les-Bains 1966–70; Vice-Pres. Glaverbel-Mecaniver, Brussels 1969–76, Pres. 1976–; Dir. Fiat 1989–; mem. supervisory council Générale Biscuit 1986–; Pres., Dir.-Gen. Union centrale des arts décoratifs (Ucad) 1989–94; Pres. and Dir.-Gen. Soc. européenne de brasseries 1970–76, Dir. 1976–; Pres. Soc. moderne de boissons 1972; Dir. Cie. financière de Paris et des Pays-Bas, Pricel, Cie. française Philips, Soc. des eaux minérales d'Evian, Dahlbusch, Vereenig de Glasfabrieken (Netherlands), Soc. pour l'exploitation et la vente des produits Fruité et Eva; Pres. Centre Nat. d'information pour la productivité des entreprises 1969–70, Asscn. Progrès et Environnement 1971; mem. Loan Cttee. Crédit Nat., Cercle de l'Union; Officier des Arts et des Lettres. *Address:* Groupe Danone, 7 rue de Téhéran, 75381 Paris Cedex 08 (Office); 13 rue Laurencin, 69002 Lyons, France (Home).

RICCI, Christina; American film actress; b. Santa Monica, Calif.; began acting career in commercials. *Films:* Mermaids 1990, The Hard Way 1991, The Addams Family 1991, The Cemetery Club 1993, Addams Family Values 1993, Casper 1995, Now and Then 1995, Gold Diggers: The Secret of Bear Mountain 1995, That Darn Cat 1996, Last of the High Kings 1996, Bastard Out of Carolina 1996, Ice Storm 1997, Little Red Riding Hood 1997. *Address:* c/o ICM, 8942 Wilshire Boulevard, Beverly Hills, CA 90211, U.S.A.

RICCI, Nino, M.A.; Canadian writer; b. 23 Aug. 1959, Leamington; s. of Virginio Ricci and Amelia Ricci (née Ingratta); m. Erika de Vasconcelos 1997; ed. York and Concordia Univs., Toronto; Pres. Canadian Centre, Int. PEN 1995–96; Gov.-Gen.'s Award 1990, Betty Trask Award 1991, Winifred Holtby Award 1991. *Publications:* (novels) Lives of the Saints 1990, In a Glass House 1993, Where She Has Gone 1997. *Address:* c/o Irene Skolnick, Curtis Brown, 70 Astor Place, New York, NY 10003, U.S.A.

RICCI, Ruggiero; American violinist; b. 24 July 1918, San Francisco; s. of Pietro Ricci and Emma Bacigalupi; m. 1st Ruth Rink 1942; m. 2nd Valma Rodriguez 1957; m. 3rd Julia Whitehurst Clemenceau 1978; two s. three d.; ed. under Louis Persinger, Mischel Piastro, Paul Stassévitch and Georg Kulenkampff; début with Manhattan Symphony Orchestra, New York 1929; first tour of Europe 1932; served U.S.A.F. 1942–45; Prof. of Violin, Univ. of Mich. 1982–87, Mozarteum, Salzburg, Austria 1989–; now makes annual tours of U.S.A. and Europe; has made 13 tours of S. America, five tours of Australia, two tours of Japan and three tours of U.S.S.R.; played the first performances of the violin concertos of Ginastera, Von Einem and Veerhoff; made first complete recording of Paganini caprices; specializes in violin solo literature; Cavaliere Order of Merit (Italy). *Address:* Johann-Wolf-str. 16A, Salzburg, Austria; Intermusica, Stephen Lumsden, 16 Duncan Terrace, London, N1 8BZ, England. *Telephone:* 0171-278 5455 (London). *Fax:* 0171-278 8434 (London).

RICE, Dorothy P., B.A.; American academic; b. 11 June 1922, Brooklyn, New York; d. of Gershon Pechman and Lena Schiff; m. John D. Rice 1943; three s.; ed. Brooklyn Coll., New York, Univ. of Wisconsin, and George Washington Univ., Washington, D.C.; Dept. of Labor 1941–42; War Production Bd. 1942–44; Nat. War Labor Bd. 1944–45; Nat. Wage Stabilization Bd. 1945–47; Health Economist, Public Health Service 1947–49, Public Health Analyst 1960–62, 1964–65; Social Science Analyst, Social Security Admin. 1962–64, Chief, Health Insurance Research Branch 1965–72, Deputy Asst. Commr. Office of Research and Statistics 1972–76; Dir. Nat. Center for Health Stats. Hyattsville, Md. 1976–82; Prof.-in-Residence, Dept. of Social and Behavioural Sciences, Inst. for Health and Aging, Univ. of Calif., San Francisco 1982–, Inst. for Health Policy Studies, Univ. of Calif., San Francisco 1982–94, Prof. Emer. 1994–; numerous honours and awards. *Publications:* more than 200 articles in professional journals. *Address:* Institute for Health and Aging, Department of Social and Behavioral Sciences—N631, School of Nursing, University of California, San Francisco, CA 94143-0646 (Office); 13895 Campus Drive, Oakland, CA 94605, U.S.A. (Home). *Telephone:* (415) 476-2771. *Fax:* (415) 502-5208.

RICE, Stuart Alan, B.S., A.M., PH.D.; American professor of chemistry; b. 6 Jan. 1932, New York City; s. of Laurence Harlan Rice and Helen Rayfield; m. 1st Marian Coopersmith 1952 (died 1994); two d.; m. 2nd Ruth O'Brien 1997; ed. Brooklyn Coll. and Harvard Univ.; Asst. Prof. Dept. of Chem. and Inst. for the Study of Metals, Univ. of Chicago 1957–59, Assoc. Prof. Inst. for the Study of Metals (later James Franck Inst.) 1959–60, 1960–69, Louis Block Prof. of Chem. 1969, Louis Block Prof. of Physical Sciences 1969–, Chair. Dept. of Chemistry 1971–77, Frank P. Hixon Distinguished Service Prof. 1977–, Dean, Div. of Physical Sciences, Univ. of Chicago 1981–95; mem. N.A.S., Nat. Science Bd. 1980–; Foreign mem. Royal Danish Acad. of Science and Letters 1976; Alfred P. Sloan Fellow 1958–62, Guggenheim Fellow 1960–61, Nat. Science Foundation Sr. Postdoctoral Fellow and Visiting Prof. Univ. Libre de Bruxelles 1965–66; Nat. Insts. of Health Special Research Fellow and Visiting Prof. H. C. Orsted Inst., Univ. of Copenhagen 1970–71; Fairchild Distinguished Scholar, Calif. Inst. of Tech. 1979; Fellow, American Acad. of Arts and Sciences; Newton-Abraham Prof., Oxford Univ. 1999–(2000); Bourke Lecturer, Faraday Soc. 1964; Baker Lecturer, Cornell Univ. 1985–86; Centenary Lecturer, Royal Soc. of Chemistry 1986–87; John Howard Appleton Lecturer, Brown Univ. 1995; lecturer, numerous univs. in U.S.A. and abroad; Hon. D.Sc. (Brooklyn Coll., Notre Dame Coll.) 1982; A. Cressy Morrison Prize in Natural Sciences, New York Acad. of Sciences 1955, A.C.S. Award in Pure Chem. 1962, Marlow Medal, Faraday Soc. 1963, Llewellyn John and Harriet Manchester Quantrell Award 1970, Leo Hendrik Baekeland Award 1971, Peter Debye A.C.S. Prize 1985, Joel Henry Hildebrand Award, A.C.S., etc. *Publications:* Poly-electrolyte Solutions (with Mitsuru Nagasawa) 1961, Centennial Medal, Harvard Univ. 1997, Statistical Mechanics of Simple Liquids (with Peter Gray) 1965, Physical Chemistry (with R. S. Berry and John Ross) 1980; and 550 papers on chemical physics in scientific journals. *Leisure interests:* reading, carpentry. *Address:* The James Franck Institute, The University of Chicago, 5640 Ellis Avenue, Chicago, IL 60637 (Office); 5517 S. Kimbark Avenue, Chicago, IL 60637, U.S.A. (Home). *Telephone:* (773) 702-7199 (Office); 667-2679 (Home).

RICE, Thomas Maurice, PH.D.; American theoretical physicist; b. 26 Jan. 1939, Dundalk, Ireland; s. of James Rice and Maureen Rice; m. Helen D. Spreiter 1966; one s. two d.; ed. Univ. Coll. Dublin and Univ. of Cambridge; Asst. lecturer, Dept. of Mathematical Physics, Univ. of Birmingham 1963–64; Research Assoc. Dept. of Physics, Univ. of Calif. at San Diego, La Jolla 1964–66; Bell Laboratories, Murray Hill, N.J. 1966–81; Prof. of Theoretical Physics, Eidgenössische Technische Hochschule (ETH), Zürich 1981–; mem. N.A.S.; Hon. mem. Royal Irish Acad; Hewlett-Packard Europhysics Prize 1998. *Address:* Theoretische Physik, ETH-Hönggerberg, 8093 Zürich, Switzerland. *Telephone:* (01) 633-2581. *Fax:* (01) 633-1115.

RICE, Sir Tim(othy) Miles Bindon, Kt.; British songwriter and broadcaster; b. 10 Nov. 1944, Amersham; s. of Hugh Gordon Rice and Joan Odette Rice; m. Jane Artereta McIntosh 1974 (died 1990); one s. one d.; ed. Lancing Coll.; with EMI Records 1966–68, Norrie Paramor Org. 1968–69; Founder and Dir. GRRR Books Ltd. 1978–, Pavilion Books Ltd. 1981–97; Chair. Foundation for Sport and the Arts 1991–; mem. Main Cttee. MCC 1992–94, 1995–. *Lyrics for musicals* (music by Andrew Lloyd Webber, q.v.): Joseph and the Amazing Technicolor Dreamcoat 1968, Jesus Christ Superstar 1970, Evita 1976, Blondel (music by Stephen Oliver) 1983, Chess (music by Benny Andersson and Bjorn Ulvaeus) 1984, Cricket (with A. L. Webber) 1986, Starmania 1989–90, Tycoon (with music by Michael Berger) 1992, Aladdin (film musical, music by Alan Menken) 1992, The Lion King (with music by Elton John) 1993, Beauty and the Beast 1994; some lyrics for stage version of Beauty and the Beast (music by Alan Menken) 1994, Heathcliff (music by John Farrar) 1995, King David (music by Alan Menken) 1997, Aida (music by Elton John) 1998, El Dorado (music by Elton John) 1999; numerous awards including Golden Globe and Acad. Award for Can You Feel the Love Tonight (from The Lion King) 1995, for You Must Love Me (from film Evita) 1997. *Publications:* Evita (with Andrew Lloyd Webber) 1978, Joseph and the Amazing Technicolor Dreamcoat 1982; ed. Heartaches Cricketers' Almanack 1975–; over 20 books in the series Guinness Book of British Hit Singles, Albums etc. (with Jonathan Rice, Paul Gambaccini and Mike Read), Treasures of Lords 1989, Oh, What a Circus (autobiog.) 1995, The Complete Eurovision Song Contest Companion (jtly.) 1998. *Leisure interests:* cricket, history of popular music, chickens. *Address:* c/o Lewis & Golden, 40 Queen Anne Street, London, W1M 0EL, England.

RICE, Victor Albert; Canadian company executive; b. 7 March 1941, Hitchin, Herts., England; s. of Albert Edward and Rosina Emmeline (Pallant) Rice; financial posts in U.K. with Ford 1957–64, Cummins Engines 1964–67 and Chrysler 1968–70; Comptroller N. European Operations, Massey-Ferguson's Perkins Engines Group 1970, then Dir. Finance and Dir. Sales and Market Devt., Deputy Man. Dir. Operations 1974; Comptroller Massey-Ferguson Ltd., Toronto, Canada 1975, Vice-Pres. Staff Operations 1977; mem. Bd. of Dirs., Pres. and C.O.O. Massey-Ferguson (now Varity Corpn.) 1978, Chair. and C.E.O. 1980–; Chief Exec. Varity PLC (fmrly. Lucas Industries) 1996–. *Leisure interests:* golf, music. *Address:* Lucas Varity Inc., 672 Delaware Avenue, Buffalo, NY 14209, U.S.A.

RICH, Adrienne, A.B.; American writer; b. 16 May 1929, Baltimore; d. of Arnold Rich and Helen Elizabeth Jones; m. Alfred Conrad (died 1970); three s.; ed. Radcliffe Coll.; Teacher, New York poetry centre 1966–67; Visiting Lecturer, Swarthmore Coll. 1967–69; Adjunct Prof., Columbia Univ. 1967–69; Lecturer, City Coll. of New York 1968–70, Instructor 1970–71,

Asst. Prof. of English 1971–72, 1974–75; Visiting Prof. of Creative Literature, Brandeis Univ. 1972–73; Prof. of English, Rutgers Univ. 1976–79; Prof.-at-Large, Cornell Univ. 1981–87; Lecturer and Visiting Prof, Scripps Coll. 1983, 1984; Prof. of English and Feminist Studies, Stanford Univ. 1986–93; Marjorie Kovler Visiting Lecturer, Univ. of Chicago 1989; mem. American Acad. of Arts and Letters, American Acad. of Arts and Sciences, PEN; Hon. Litt.D. (Wheaton Coll.) 1967, (Smith Coll.) 1979, (Brandeis Univ.) 1987, (Wooster Coll.) 1989, (Harvard) 1990, (City Coll. of New York) 1990; Guggenheim Fellow 1952, 1961; Acad. of American Poets Fellowship 1993; MacArthur Fellowship 1994–(99); Yale Series of Younger Poets Award 1951, Ridgely Torrence Memorial Award, Poetry Soc. of America 1955, Shelley Memorial Award 1971, Nat. Book Award 1974, Ruth Lilly Prize 1987, Brandeis Medal in Poetry 1987, Nat. Poetry Assen. Award 1989, L.A. Times Book Award 1992, Frost Silver Medal (Poetry Soc. of America) 1992, The Poets' Prize 1993, American Acad. of Poets Dorothea Tanning Award 1996. *Publications:* A Change of World 1951, The Diamond Cutters and Other Poems 1955, Snapshots of a Daughter-in-Law 1963, Necessities of Life 1962–65, 1965–68 1969, Leaflets, Poems 1965–68, The Will to Change 1971, Diving into the Wreck 1973, Of Woman Born: Motherhood as Experience and Institution 1976, On Lies, Secrets and Silence: Selected Prose 1966–78 1979, A Wild Patience Has Taken Me This Far: Poems 1978–81 1981, The Fact of a Doorframe: Poems 1950–84 1984, Blood, Bread and Poetry: Selected Prose 1979–85 1986, Your Native Land, Your Life 1986, Time's Power: Poems 1985–88 1989, An Atlas of the Difficult World: Poems 1988–91 1991, Collected Early Poems, 1950–1970 1993, What Is Found There: Notebooks on Poetry and Politics 1993, Dark Fields of the Republic: Poems 1991–95 1995. *Address:* c/o W. W. Norton Co., 500 Fifth Avenue, New York, NY 10110, U.S.A.

RICH, Alexander, M.D.; American molecular biologist; b. 15 Nov. 1924, Hartford, Conn.; s. of Max Rich and Bella Shub; m. Jane Erving King 1952; two s. two d.; ed. Harvard Coll. and Harvard Medical School; served U.S. Navy 1943–46; Research Fellow, Gates and Crellin Labs., Calif. Inst. of Tech. 1949–54; Chief of Section on Physical Chem., Nat. Inst. of Mental Health 1954–58; visiting Scientist, Cavendish Lab., Cambridge, U.K. 1955–56; Assoc. Prof. of Biophysics, M.I.T. 1958–61, Prof. 1961–, William Thompson Sedgwick Prof. of Biophysics 1974–; Fairchild Distinguished Scholar, Calif. Inst. of Tech., Pasadena 1976; Visiting Prof., Coll. de France, Paris 1987; Sr. Consultant, Office of Science and Tech. Policy, Exec. Office of the Pres. 1977–81; Chair. Perm. Science Cttee., American Acad. of Arts and Sciences 1967–71, Basic Research Cttee. of Nat. Science Bd. 1978–82, Biotech. Programme of N.A.S. Cttee. on Scholarly Communication with the People's Republic of China 1986–; Co-Chair. Scientific and Academic Advisory Cttee. of Weizmann Inst. of Science, Israel 1987–; mem. or fmr. mem. numerous cttees. etc., including Corpn., Marine Biological Lab., Woods Hole, Mass., 1965–77, 1987–, Advisory Bd. N.A.S. Acad. Forum 1975–82, Scientific Advisory Bd. Stanford Synchrotron Radiation Project 1976–80, U.S.–U.S.S.R. Jt. Comm. on Science and Tech. 1977–82, Council Pugwash Conferences on Science and World Affairs 1977–82, Bd. of Dirs. Medical Foundation, Boston, Mass. 1981–90, Governing Bd. Nat. Research Council 1985–88, Cttee. on U.S.S.R. and E. Europe of Nat. Research Council 1986–, Exec. Cttee., Council of N.A.S. 1985–88, External Advisory Cttee. of Center for Human Genome Studies, Los Alamos, N.M. 1989–, Nat. Critical Technologies Panel of Office of Science and Tech. Policy, Washington, D.C. 1990–91; on editorial bd. of numerous publs., including Journal of Molecular Evolution 1983–, Proteins, Structure, Function and Genetics 1986–91, Genomics 1987–, Journal of Biotechnology 1987, EMBO Journal 1988–90; mem. American Chem. Soc. and other socs., N.A.S. 1970– (mem. Exec. Cttee. 1985–88), Pontifical Acad. of Sciences, The Vatican 1978, American Philosophical Soc. 1980; Sr. mem. Inst. of Medicine, Washington, DC 1990; Fellow, Nat. Research Council 1949–51, American Acad. of Arts and Sciences 1959, Guggenheim Foundation 1963, A.A.A.S. 1965; Foreign mem. French Acad. of Sciences 1984; Hon. mem. Japanese Biochemical Soc. 1986; Assoc. mem. European Molecular Biology Org. 1984; Hon. Dr. (Rio de Janeiro) 1981, Hon. Ph.D. (Weizmann Inst.) 1992; Skylab Achievement Award, NASA 1974; Theodore von Karmen Award 1976, Presidential Award, New York Acad. of Science 1977, James R. Killian Faculty Achievement Award, (M.I.T.) 1980, Jabotinsky Medal, New York 1980, Merck Award, American Soc. of Biochemistry and Molecular Biology, Washington 1998, and numerous other awards. *Publications:* Structural Chemistry and Molecular Biology (co-ed.) 1968; Primary and Tertiary Structure of Nucleic Acids and Cancer Research (co-ed.) 1982; 450 publications in the field of molecular structure of nucleic acid components, nucleic acids and polynucleotides, physical chem. of nucleotides and polynucleotides, molecular structure of proteins, mechanism of protein synthesis, molecular biology of the nucleic acids, X-ray crystallography, origin of life. *Leisure interests:* ocean sailing in small boats, growing tomato plants, collecting fossils. *Address:* Department of Biology, Room 68-223, Massachusetts Institute of Technology, Cambridge, MA 02139 (Office); 2 Walnut Avenue, Cambridge, MA 02140, U.S.A. (Home). *Telephone:* (617) 253-4715 (Office); (617) 547-1637 (Home). *Fax:* (617) 253-8699 (Office).

RICH, Frank Hart, Jr., A.B.; American journalist; b. 2 June 1949, Washington, D.C.; s. of Frank Hart Rich and Helene Aaronson; m. 1st Gail Winston 1976; two s.; m. 2nd Alexandra Rachelle Witchel 1991; ed. Harvard Coll.; Film Critic and Sr. Ed. New Times Magazine 1973–75; Film Critic, New York Post 1975–77; Film and TV Critic, Time Magazine 1977–80; Chief Drama Critic, New York Times 1980–93, Op-Ed. Columnist 1994–. *Address:* The New York Times, 229 West 43rd Street, New York, NY 10036, U.S.A. *Telephone:* (212) 556 7414.

RICH, Patrick Jean Jacques; French business executive; b. 28 March 1931, Strasbourg; s. of late Henri Rich; m. Louise Dionne 1961; two s. one d.; ed. Univ. of Strasbourg and Harvard Univ.; worked for Alcan Aluminium Ltd. in Guinea, France, U.K., Argentina, Spain and Italy 1959–70, Area Gen. Man. for Latin America 1971–75, Exec. Vice-Pres. Europe, Latin America and Africa 1976–77, mem. Bd. 1978–86; Exec. Vice-Pres. Alcan Aluminium Ltd. and C.E.O Aluminium Co. of Canada 1978–81; Exec. Vice-Pres. Europe, Africa, Middle East and Chair. Alcan Aluminium S.A. 1978–86; C.E.O Société Générale de Surveillance Holding SA, Geneva 1987–89; Deputy Chair. BOC Group PLC 1990–91, Chief Exec. 1991–92, Chair. 1992–94 (non-exec. 1994) and Chief Exec. 1992–94; Chair. Royal Packaging Industries Van Leer, Netherlands 1988–95, IMEC Research Project 1995–; Trustee Bernard van Leer Foundation 1982–; Gov. Van Leer Group Foundation 1982–, Van Leer Jerusalem Inst. 1995–; Croix de la Valeur Militaire. *Leisure interests:* opera, walking, skiing, piano playing, reading, sailing. *Address:* Mandarin D, 3962 Crans Montana, Switzerland. *Telephone:* (27) 481 45 89. *Fax:* (27) 480 11 29.

RICHARD, Baron (Life Peer), cr. 1990, of Ammanford in the County of Dyfed; **Ivor Seward Richard,** M.A., Q.C.; British politician, lawyer and diplomatist; b. 30 May 1932, Cardiff; s. of Seward Thomas and Isabella Irene Richard; m. 1st Geraldine Moore 1956 (dissolved 1961); one s.; m. 2nd Alison Mary Imrie 1962 (dissolved 1984); one s. one d.; m. 3rd Janet Armstrong Jones 1989; one s.; ed. Cheltenham Coll., Pembroke Coll., Oxford; called to the Bar 1955; M.P. for Barons Court 1964–74; Parl. Pvt. Sec. to Sec. of State for Defence 1966–69; Under-Sec. of State for Defence for Army 1969–70; Queen's Counsel 1971; Perm. Rep. to UN 1974–79; Commr. of European Communities for Social Affairs, Employment, Education and Vocational Training Policy 1981–84; Leader of Opposition in the House of Lords 1992–97; Lord Privy Seal and Leader of the House of Lords, 1997–98; Chair. World Trade Centre Wales Ltd. (Cardiff) 1985–97; Chair. Rhodesia Conf., Geneva 1976; Counsel to Chadbourne, Parke, Whiteside and Wolff, New York 1979–81; Hon. Fellow, Pembroke Coll. 1981–; Labour. *Publications:* Europe or the Open Sea 1971, We, the British 1983, Unfinished Business: Reforming the House of Lords 1998, and articles in various political journals. *Leisure interests:* playing piano, watching football, talking. *Address:* House of Lords, Westminster, London, S.W.1, England.

RICHARD, Alain; French politician; b. 29 Aug. 1945; m. Elisabeth Couffignal 1988; one s. one d. and one s. by previous m.; ed. Lycée Henri IV, Paris, Univ. of Paris, Institut d'Etudes Politiques, Ecole Nat. d'Admin.; Auditor, Conseil d'Etat 1971, Maître des requêtes 1978, Conseiller d'Etat 1993; teacher Univs. of Reims, Paris I and Institut d'Etudes Politiques; Mayor, Saint-Ouen l'Aumône 1977–97, Deputy 1978–93, Senator for Val d'Oise 1995–97; Vice-Pres. Commission des lois 1981–86, Nat. Ass. 1987–88; Minister of Defence 1997–; founder and Vice-Pres. Forum for Man. of Towns 1985–97; mem. Nat. Office, Parti Socialiste Unifié 1972–74; mem. Cttee. Parti Socialiste 1979, Exec. Bd. 1988. *Address:* Ministry of Defence, 14 rue Saint-Dominique, 00450 Armées (Office); 28 rue René Clair, 95310 Saint-Ouen l'Aumône, France.

RICHARD, Sir Cliff, Kt., O.B.E.; British singer and actor; b. (as Harry Rodger Webb) 14 Oct. 1940, India; s. of Rodger and Dorothy Webb; ed. Riversmead School, Cheshunt; first successful record Move It 1958; plays guitar; own television series on BBC and ITV; various repertory and variety seasons; Top Box Office Star of Great Britain 1962–63, 1963–64; awarded Gold Discs (for sales over a million each) for Living Doll, The Young Ones, Bachelor Boy, Lucky Lips, Congratulations, Power to All Our Friends, Devil Woman, We Don't Talk Anymore, Daddy's Home, Mistletoe and Wine; also 32 Silver Discs (for sales over 250,000); Ivor Novello Award for Outstanding Achievement 1989. *Films:* Serious Charge 1959, Expresso Bongo 1960, The Young Ones 1961, Summer Holiday 1962, Wonderful Life 1964, Finders Keepers 1966, Two a Penny 1968, His Land, Take Me High 1973; appeared in musicals Time, Dominion Theatre, London 1986–87, Heathcliff, Hammersmith Apollo, London 1996–97. *Publications:* Questions 1970, The Way I See It 1972, The Way I See It Now 1975, Which One's Cliff? 1977, Happy Christmas from Cliff 1980, You, Me and Jesus 1983, Mine to Share 1984, Jesus, Me and You 1985, Single-Minded 1988, Mine Forever 1989, My Story: A Celebration of 40 Years in Showbusiness 1998. *Leisure interest:* tennis. *Address:* c/o P.O. Box 46C, Esher, Surrey, KT10 0RB, England. *Telephone:* (01372) 467752.

RICHARD, Jean Barthélemy, D. ÈS L.; French historian; b. 7 Feb. 1921, Kremlin-Bicêtre; s. of Pierre Richard and Amélie Grandchamp; m. Monique Rivoire 1944; three s. two d.; ed. Ecole des Chartes, Ecole Française de Rome and Sorbonne, Paris; Asst. archivist, Dijon 1943–55; Prof. Univ. of Dijon 1955–88, Dean, Faculté des Lettres 1968–71; mem. Acad. des Inscriptions, Inst. de France and other learned socs.; Chevalier, Légion d'honneur, Commdr. Ordre du Mérite, Commdr. Palmes académiques. *Publications:* Latin Kingdom of Jerusalem 1953, Les ducs de Bourgogne 1954, L'Esprit de la Croisade 1969, La papauté et les missions d'Orient 1977, Histoire de la Bourgogne 1978, Saint Louis 1983, Le livre des remembrances de la secrète du royaume de Chypre 1983, Histoire des Croisades 1996; four vols. in Variorum Reprints on Crusades and Oriental History 1976–92. *Leisure interests:* garden and forest activities. *Address:* 12 rue Pelletier de Chambure,

21000 Dijon; Les Billaudots, 71540 Igornay, France. *Telephone:* 03-80-66-10-28; 03-85-82-82-98.

RICHARDS, Ann Willis, B.A.; American state governor; b. 1 Sept. 1933, Waco, Tex.; d. of Cecil Willis and Ona Willis; m. David Richards; two s. two d.; ed. Baylor Univ. and Univ. of Tex.; fmr. schoolteacher; County Commr. Travis County, Austin 1977–82; mem. Pres.'s Advisory Comm. on Women 1979; State Treas. State of Texas, Austin 1983–91; mem. State Banking Bd. of Tex. 1982; Chair. Texas Depository Bd. 1983; Sr. Advisor Verner, Liipfert, Bernhard, McPherson & Hand, Austin 1995–; mem. various bds. and cttees. etc.; Gov. of Texas 1991–95; Democrat. *Address:* Verner, Liipfert, Bernhard, McPherson & Hand, P.O. Box 684746, Austin, TX 78768, U.S.A.

RICHARDS, Frederic Middlebrook, PH.D.; American biochemist; b. 19 Aug. 1925, New York; s. of George and Marianna Richards; m. 1st Heidi Clark 1948 (divorced 1955); two d.; m. 2nd Sarah Wheatland 1959; one s.; ed. Mass Inst. of Tech. and Harvard Univ.; Research Fellow, Physical Chem., Harvard Univ. 1952–53; Nat. Research Council Fellow, Carlsberg Lab., Denmark 1954; Nat. Science Foundation Fellow, Cambridge Univ., U.K. 1955; Asst. Prof. of Biochemistry, Yale Univ. 1955–59, Assoc. Prof. 1959–62, Prof. 1963–89, Chair. Dept. of Molecular Biology and Biophysics 1963–67, Dept. of Molecular Biophysics and Biochemistry 1969–73, Henry Ford II Prof. of Molecular Biophysics 1967–89, Sterling Prof. of Molecular Biophysics 1989–91, Sterling Prof. Emer. 1991–; mem. Council Int. Union of Pure and Applied Biophysics 1975–81; Dir. Jane Coffin Childs Memorial Fund for Medical Research 1976–91, Bd. Dirs. 1997–; Corpn. mem. Woods Hole Oceanographic Inst. 1977–83, 1985–91; mem. Scientific Bd. Whitney Lab. for Experimental Marine Biology and Medicine 1979–84, Nat. Advisory Research Resources Council N.I.H. 1983–87, Board of Trustees, Cold Spring Harbor Lab. 1986–91, Medical Advisory Bd., Howard Hughes Medical Inst. 1989–92, Donaghue Foundation for Medical Research 1991–92, N.A.S., American Acad. of Arts and Sciences, American Chem. Soc., American Soc. of Biological Chemistry (Pres. 1978–80), Biophysical Soc. (Pres. 1972–73), American Crystallographic Asscn., Conn. Acad. of Science and Eng. Guggenheim Fellow 1967–68; Hon. D.Sc. (New Haven) 1982; Pfizer-Paul Lewis Award 1965; Kaj Linderstrøm-Lang Prize 1978, Merck Award of American Soc. for Biochemistry and Molecular Biology 1988, Stein and Moore Award of Protein Soc. 1988. *Publications:* various original research articles in scientific journals in the general field of protein and enzyme chemistry. *Leisure interests:* sailing. *Address:* Department of Molecular Biophysics and Biochemistry, Yale University, P.O. Box 208114, 260 Whitney Avenue, New Haven, CT 06520 (Office); 69 Andrews Road, Guilford, CT 06437, U.S.A.

RICHARDS, Isaac Vivian Alexander ("Viv"), O.B.E.; Antiguan cricketer; b. 7 March 1952, St. John's, Antigua; s. of Malcolm Richards; m. Miriam Lewis; one s. one d.; ed. Antigua Grammar School; right-hand batsman, off-break bowler; played for Leeward Islands 1971–91 (Capt. 1981–91), Somerset 1974–86, Queensland 1976–77, Glamorgan 1990–93; 121 Tests for W. Indies 1974–91, 50 as Capt., scoring 8,540 runs (average 50.2) including 24 hundreds, and holding 122 catches; scored record 1,710 runs in a calendar year (11 Tests in 1976); scored 36,212 first-class runs (114 hundreds, only W. Indian to score 100 hundreds); toured England 1976, 1979 (World Cup), 1980, 1983 (World Cup), 1984, 1988 (as Capt.), 1991 (as Capt.); 187 limited-overs ints. scoring 6,721 runs (11 hundreds including then record 189 not out v. England at Old Trafford 1984); Dr. h.c. (Exeter) 1986. *Publications:* (with David Foot) Viv Richards (autobiog.), Hitting Across The Line (autobiog.) 1991. *Leisure interests:* music, football. *Address:* West Indies Cricket Board, P.O. Box 616, St. John's, Antigua.

RICHARDS, Sir John (Charles Chisholm), K.C.B., K.C.V.O.; British military officer (retd.); b. 21 Feb. 1927, Wallasey; s. of Charles Richards and Alice Milner; m. Audrey Hidson 1953; two s. one d.; ed. Worksop Coll. Notts.; joined Royal Marines 1945; served in commando units and HM Ships worldwide; Canadian Army Staff Coll. 1959–61; Naval Staff in Ministry of Defence 1963–64; Instructor Army Staff Coll. Camberley 1965–67; C.O. 42nd and 45th RM Commandos; Chief of Staff, British Defence Staff, Washington, D.C. and del. to UN 1972–74; Brig. commdg. 3rd Commando Brigade 1975–77; Maj.-Gen. 1977; Commdt.-Gen. Royal Marines (with rank of Lieut.-Gen.) 1977–81; Rep. Col. Commdt. Royal Marines 1989–90; H.M. Marshal of the Diplomatic Corps 1982–92; Dir. (non-exec.) DSC Communications (Europe) Ltd. 1986–93, Andrew Ltd. 1987–94; Extra Equerry to H.M. The Queen 1992; Freeman, City of London 1982; numerous foreign awards including decorations from Fed. Repub. of Germany, France, Netherlands, Spain, Mexico, Italy, Norway, Senegal, U.A.E., Malawi, Bahrain, Qatar and Oman. *Leisure interests:* golf, gardening, swimming, military history. *Address:* 49 Albany Mews, Kingston-upon-Thames, KT2 5SL, England. *Telephone:* 0181-287 8940.

RICHARDS, Keith (Keith Richard); British musician and songwriter; b. 18 Dec. 1943, Dartford; s. of Bert Richards and Doris Richards; m. 1st Anita Pallenberg; two s. (one deceased) one d.; m. 2nd Patti Hansen 1983; two d.; ed. Sidcup Art School; lead guitarist, vocalist with the Rolling Stones 1962–; composer (with Mick Jagger q.v.), numerous songs and albums 1964–, including: The Rolling Stones Now! 1964, Aftermath 1966, Flowers 1967, Beggars' Banquet 1968, Let it Bleed 1969, Sticky Fingers 1971, Hot Rocks 1972, Exile on Main Street 1972, Goat's Head Soup 1973, It's Only Rock and Roll 1974, Metamorphosis 1975, Black and Blue 1976, Some Girls, Emotional Rescue 1980, Tattoo You 1981, Still Life 1982, Under Cover 1983, Dirty Work 1986, Hail Hail Rock 'n' Roll 1987 (with Chuck Berry), Talk is Cheap (solo) 1988, Steel Wheels 1989, Flashpoint 1991, Voodoo Lounge 1994, Stripped 1995; *Films:* Sympathy for the Devil 1970, Gimme Shelter 1970, Ladies and Gentlemen, the Rolling Stones 1974, Let's Spend the Night Together 1983, Hail Hail Rock 'n' Roll 1987 (with Chuck Berry, Eric Clapton and Friends), Flashpoint 1991. *Address:* c/o Solo-ITG Agency, 55 Fulham Road, London, SW6 3JJ, England.

RICHARDS, Peter, M.D., PH.D., F.R.C.P.; British professor of medicine; b. 25 May 1936, London; s. of Dr William Richards and Barbara Taylor; m. 1st Anne Marie Larsen 1959 (dissolved); m. 2nd Carol Anne Seymour; one s. three d.; ed. Monkton Combe School, Emmanuel Coll. Cambridge, St. George's Hosp. Medical School and Royal Postgrad. Medical School; MRC Clinical Research Fellow and tutor in Medicine, Royal Postgrad. Medical School 1964–67; lecturer, St. Mary's Hosp. Medical School 1967–70; Consultant Physician, N.W. Surrey Hosps. 1970–73; Sr. lecturer and Consultant Physician, St. George's Hosp. and Medical School 1973–79; Dean, St. Mary's Hosp. Medical School 1979–95; Prof. and Hon. Consultant Physician, St. Mary's Hosp. 1979–95; Pro-Rector (Medicine), Imperial Coll. of Science, Tech. and Medicine, London 1988–95; Medical Dir. and Consultant Physician, Northwick Park and St. Mark's NHS Trust 1995–99; Pres. Hughes Hall, Cambridge; Fulbright Award, Univ. of Calif. San Francisco 1990; various professional appts. *Publications:* The Medieval Leper 1977, Understanding Water, Electrolytes and Acid/Base Metabolism 1983, Learning Medicine 1983, Living Medicine 1990, Student's Guide to Entry to Medicine 1996, New Learning Medicine 1997; scientific papers on renal disease, metabolism, student selection and educ. *Leisure interests:* social history, music, cycling, mountain walking, Finland. *Address:* Hughes Hall, Cambridge, CB1 2EW, England. *Telephone:* (01223) 334890. *Fax:* (01223) 311179.

RICHARDS, Sir Rex Edward, Kt., D.SC., F.R.S.C., F.R.S.; British professor of chemistry and university administrator (retd.); b. 28 Oct. 1922, Colyton, Devon; s. of H. W. and E. N. Richards; m. Eva Edith Vago 1948; two d.; ed. Colyton Grammar School, Devon, St. John's Coll., Oxford; Fellow of Lincoln Coll., Oxford 1947–64; Dr. Lee's Prof. of Chem., Oxford 1964–70; Fellow of Exeter Coll., Oxford 1964–69; Warden Merton Coll., Oxford 1969–84; Vice-Chancellor Univ. of Oxford 1977–81; Chancellor Exeter Univ. 1982–98; Tilden Lecturer 1962; Research Fellow, Harvard Univ. 1955; Hon. Fellow of St. John's Coll. and Lincoln Coll., Oxford 1968, Merton Coll., Oxford 1984; Assoc. Fellow, Morse Coll., Yale 1974–79; Chair. Oxford Enzyme Group 1969–83; Dir. Oxford Instruments Group 1982–91; Dir. Leverhulme Trust 1985–93; Pres. Royal Soc. of Chem. 1990–92; mem. Chem. Soc. Council 1957, 1988, Faraday Soc. Council 1963, Royal Soc. Council 1973–75, Advisory Bd. for Research Councils 1980–82, Advisory Council for Applied Research and Devt. 1984–87; Dir. IBM United Kingdom Holdings, IBM (U.K.) 1978–82; Chair. British Postgraduate Medical Fed. 1986–93; Trustee of CIBA Foundation 1978–97, Nat. Heritage Memorial Fund 1979–84, Tate Gallery 1982–88, 1991–93, Nat. Gallery 1982–93, Henry Moore Foundation 1989– (Vice-Chair. 1993–94, Chair. 1994–); Foreign Assoc. Acad. des Sciences, Inst. de France 1995–; Hon. F.R.C.P. 1987; Hon. F.B.A. 1990; Hon. F.R.A.M. 1991; Hon. Fellow Thames Polytechnic 1991; Hon.D.Sc. (East Anglia) 1971, (Exeter) 1975, (Leicester) 1978, (Salford) 1979, (Edinburgh) 1981, (Leeds) 1984, (London) 1994, (Oxford Brookes) 1998, (Warwick) 1999; Hon. D.Litt. (Dundee) 1977, (Kent) 1987; Hon. Sc.D. (Cambridge) 1987; Corday-Morgan Medal of Chemical Soc. 1954, Davy Medal, Royal Soc. 1976, Award in Theoretical Chem. and Spectroscopy, Chemical Soc. 1977, Epic Award 1982, Medal of Honour, Bonn Univ. 1983, Royal Medal, Royal Soc. 1986. *Publications:* numerous contributions to scientific journals. *Leisure interest:* painting and sculpture. *Address:* 13 Woodstock Close, Oxford, OX2 8DB, England (Home). *Telephone:* (01865) 513621. *Fax:* (01865) 513621.

RICHARDSON, Baron (Life Peer), cr. 1979, of Lee in the County of Devon, **John Samuel Richardson,** Bt., Kt., L.V.O., M.A., M.D., F.R.C.P.; British consultant physician; b. 16 June 1910, Sheffield; s. of Major John Watson Richardson and Elizabeth Blakeney Roberts; m. Sybil Trist 1933; two d.; ed. Charterhouse, Trinity Coll., Cambridge and St. Thomas's Hospital Medical School; various appointments at St. Thomas's Hosp. and Royal Postgraduate Medical School; with R.A.M.C. during Second World War; Consulting Physician at St. Thomas's Hosp.; Consultant Physician to Metropolitan Police 1957–80, London Transport Bd. 1964–80; Consultant Emer. to Army; Pres. Gen. Medical Council 1973–80; Chair. Council for Postgraduate Medical Educ. in England and Wales 1972–80, Armed Forces Medical Advisory Bd. 1975; mem. Council Royal Coll. of Physicians; fmr. Pres. Royal Soc. of Medicine, Int. Soc. for Internal Medicine, British Medical Asscn.; Past-Master, Worshipful Soc. of Apothecaries of London; Hon. Fellow, Trinity Coll., Cambridge, Hon. F.R.C.P. (Edin., Ireland), Hon. Fellow, Royal Coll. of Physicians and Surgeons (Glasgow), Royal Coll. of Psychiatrists, Royal Coll. of Surgeons of England, Royal Coll. of Gen. Practitioners, Faculty of Community Medicine; Hon. D.Sc. (Nat. Univ. of Ireland, Univ. of Hull), Hon. D.C.L. (Newcastle), Hon. LL.D. (Nottingham, Liverpool); Hadden Prize and Bristowe Medal, St. Thomas's Hosp. 1936, Perkins Fellowship 1939–40; Hon. Bencher, Gray's Inn 1974, 1st De Lancy Law Prize (Royal Soc. of Medicine) 1978, Gold Medal B.M.A. 1980, Guthrie Medal, R.A.M.C. 1980; C. St. J. *Publications:* The Practice of Medicine 1960, Connective Tissue Disorders 1963, Anticoagulant Prophylaxis and Treatment (jointly) 1965. *Leisure interest:* gardening. *Address:* Windcutter, Lee, North Devon, EX34 8LW, England. *Telephone:* (01271) 863198.

RICHARDSON, Elliot Lee, A.B., LL.B.; American government official and lawyer; b. 20 July 1920, Boston, Mass.; s. of Dr. Edward P. Richardson and Clara Shattuck Richardson; m. Anne Francis Hazard 1952; two s. one d.; ed. Harvard Coll. and Harvard Law School; Law Clerk, Court of Appeals Judge L. Hand 1947–48, Supreme Court Justice Felix Frankfurter 1948–49; Asst. Sec. (Legislation), U.S. Dept. of Health, Educ. and Welfare 1957–59, Acting Sec. April-July 1958; U.S. Attorney for Mass. 1959–61; Special Asst. to U.S. Attorney-Gen. 1961; Lieut.-Gov. of Mass. 1965–67; Attorney-Gen. of Mass. 1967–69; U.S. Under-Sec. of State 1969–70; Sec. of Health, Educ. and Welfare 1970–72, of Defense 1972–73; Attorney-Gen. of U.S.A. May-Oct. 1973, resgnd.; Dir. Study of Operations of State and Local Govt., Woodrow Wilson Int. Center 1974; Amb. to U.K. 1975–76; Sec. of Commerce 1976–77; Amb.-at-large and Special Rep. of U.S. Pres. to Law of the Sea Conf. 1977–80; Sr. partner Milbank, Tweed, Hadley and McCloy, Washington 1980–92; Personal Rep. of UN Sec.-Gen. for Nicaraguan Elections 1989–90; Special Rep. of Pres. of U.S.A. for multilateral assistance initiative for Philippines 1989–94; Chair. Council on Ocean Law, Hitachi Foundation; Co-Chair. Nat. Council of UNA-U.S.A.; Bd. Dirs. American Acad. of Diplomacy, Oak Industries; Fellow A.A.A.S., American Bar Foundation; mem. A.B.A; Hon. degrees from Harvard, Ulster, Edin. and many other univs. and colls.; Hon. Bencher, Middle Temple 1975; Presidential Medal of Freedom 1998. *Publications:* The Creative Balance 1976, Reflections of a Radical Moderate 1996; numerous articles. *Address:* Milbank, Tweed, Hadley and McCloy, 1825 I Street, N.W., Suite 1100, Washington, DC 20006 (Office); 10450 Lottsford Road, 1005 Mitchelville, MD 20721, U.S.A. (Home).

RICHARDSON, George Barclay, C.B.E., M.A.; British university administrator (retd.); b. 19 Sept. 1924, London; s. of George Richardson and Christina Richardson; m. Isabel A. Chalk 1957 (dissolved 1999); two s.; ed. Aberdeen Cen. Secondary School and other schools in Scotland, Aberdeen Univ. and Corpus Christi Coll. Oxford; Admiralty Scientific Research Dept. 1944; Lieut. R.N.V.R. 1945; Intelligence Officer, H.Q. Intelligence Div. British Army of the Rhine 1946–47; Third Sec. H.M. Foreign Service 1949; student, Nuffield Coll. Oxford 1950; Fellow, St. John's Coll. Oxford 1951–88; Univ. Reader in Econs., Univ. of Oxford 1969–73; Warden, Keble Coll. Oxford 1989–94; Pro-Vice-Chancellor, Univ. of Oxford 1988–94; Del. Oxford Univ. Pres. 1971–74, Sec. to Dels. and Chief Exec. 1974–88; mem. Econ. Devt. Cttee. for Electrical Eng. Industry 1964–73, Monopolies Comm. 1969–74, Royal Comm. on Environmental Pollution 1973–74; Econ. Adviser, UKAEA 1968–74; mem. Council, Publishers' Asscn. 1981–87; Hon. D.C.L. (Oxford); Hon. LL.D. (Aberdeen). *Publications:* Information and Investment 1960, 1991, Economic Theory 1964, The Economics of Imperfect Knowledge 1998, articles in academic journals. *Leisure interests:* reading, music, swimming. *Address:* 33 Belsyre Court, Observatory Street, Oxford, OX2 6HU, England. *Telephone:* (01865) 510113. *Fax:* (01865) 510113.

RICHARDSON, George Taylor, B.COMM. LL.D.; Canadian business executive; b. 22 Sept. 1924, Winnipeg, Manitoba; s. of late James A. Richardson and Muriel (née Sprague) Richardson; m. Tannis Maree Thorlakson 1948; two s. one d.; ed. Grosvenor and Ravenscourt Schools, Winnipeg, and Univ. of Manitoba; joined family firm of James Richardson & Sons, Ltd., Winnipeg 1946, Vice-Pres. 1954, Pres. 1966–93, Chair. 1993–; Dir. subsidiaries of James Richardson and Sons, Ltd.; mem. Winnipeg Commodity Exchange, Chicago Bd. of Trade; Hon. LL.D. (Manitoba, Winnipeg). *Leisure interests:* hunting, helicopter flying. *Address:* James Richardson & Sons Ltd., Richardson Building, 1 Lombard Place, Winnipeg, Manitoba, R3B 0Y1 (Office); Briarmeade, P.O. Box 158, St. Germain, Manitoba, R0G 2A0, Canada (Home). *Telephone:* 934-5811 (Office); 253-4221 (Home).

RICHARDSON, Graham; Australian politician, broadcaster and journalist; b. 27 Sept. 1949, Kogarah, Sydney; m. Cheryl Gardener 1973; one s. one d.; ed. Marist Brothers Coll., Kogarah; state organiser Australian Labor Party, N.S.W. 1971–76, Gen. Sec. 1976–94, State Campaign Dir. 1976; Vice-Pres. Nat. Labor Party 1976, Del. to Nat. Conf. 1977–94, convenor Nat. Industrial Platform Cttee.; Senator for N.S.W. March 1983–94; Minister for the Environment and the Arts 1987–90, for Sports, Tourism and Territories 1988–90, for Social Security 1990, of Transport and Communications 1991–92, of Health 1993–94; political commentator on election coverage and journalist, The Nine Network 1994–; journalist, The Bulletin 1994–; fmr. Chair. Senate Estimates Cttee. 1986, Senate Select Cttee. on TV Equalisation; mem. several senate cttees. and three ministerial cttees.; mem. Bd. Sydney Organizing Cttee. for the Olympic Games 1996–. *Leisure interests:* golf, reading, skiing. *Address:* 24 Artarmon Road, Willoughby, N.S.W. 2028, Australia.

RICHARDSON, Ian William, C.B.E., F.R.S.A.M.D.; British actor; b. 7 April 1934, Edinburgh; s. of John Richardson and Margaret (Drummond) Richardson; m. Maroussia Frank 1961; two s.; ed. Tynecastle, Edinburgh, Royal Scottish Acad. of Music and Drama, Glasgow Univ.; joined Birmingham Repertory Theatre Co. 1958, playing leading parts including Hamlet; joined R.S.C., Stratford and Aldwych 1960–75, tours with R.S.C. to Europe, U.S.A., U.S.S.R., Japan; James Bridie Gold Medal (R.S.A.M.D.); Tony Nomination, New York; Drama Desk Award, New York, Royal Television Soc. Award 1981/82, 1991, Broadcasting Press Guild Award 1990; B.A.F.T.A. Award 1991. *Stage appearances include:* Arragon (Merchant of Venice), Sir Andrew Aguecheek (Twelfth Night) 1960, Malatesti (Duchess of Malfi) 1960, Oberon (A Midsummer Night's Dream) 1961, Tranio (Taming of the Shrew) 1961, The Doctor (The Representative) 1963, Edmund (King Lear) 1964, Antipholus of Ephesus (Comedy of Errors) 1964, Herald and Marat (Marat/Sade) 1964, 1965, Ithamore (The Jew of Malta) 1964, Ford (Merry Wives of Windsor) 1964, 1966, 1969, Antipholus of Syracuse (Comedy of Errors) 1965, Chorus (Henry V) 1965, Vindice (The Revengers Tragedy) 1965, 1969, Coriolanus 1966, Bertram (All's Well That Ends Well) 1966, Malcolm (Macbeth) 1966, Cassius (Julius Caesar) 1968, Pericles 1969, Angelo (Measure for Measure) 1970, Buckingham (Richard III) 1970, Proteus (Two Gentlemen of Verona) 1970, Prospero (The Tempest) 1970, Tom Wrench (Trelawny), Sadler's Wells 1971–72, Richard II/Bolingbroke (Richard II) 1973, Berowne (Love's Labour's Lost) 1973, Iachimo (Cymbeline) 1974, Shalimov (Summer Folk) 1974, Henry Higgins (My Fair Lady), Broadway 1974, Ford (Merry Wives of Windsor) 1975, Richard III 1975, Jack Tanner (Man and Superman), Shaw Festival Theatre, Niagara-on-the Lake, Canada, The Government Inspector, Romeo and Juliet, Old Vic 1979, Lolita (New York) 1981, The Miser (Chichester) 1995, The Magistrate (Chichester and London) 1997. *Film appearances include:* The Darwin Adventure 1971, Man of la Mancha 1972, Marat/Sade, Hound of the Baskervilles 1982, The Sign of Four 1982, Whoops Apocalypse 1986, The Fourth Protocol 1986, Asking for Trouble 1986, Burning Secret 1988, Rosencrantz and Guildenstern are Dead 1990, The Year of the Comet 1991, Words Upon the Window Pane 1993, Baps 1996, Dark City 1996. *TV appearances include:* Anthony Beavis (Eyeless in Gaza) 1971, Voyage Round My Father, Canterbury Tales, Danton's Death (BBC) 1977, Sorry (BBC) 1978, Ike—The War Years (ABC TV, U.S.A.) 1978, Tinker, Tailor, Soldier, Spy (BBC) 1979, Churchill and His Generals (BBC) 1979, Private Schulz (BBC) 1980, A Cotswold Death (BBC) 1981, The Woman in White (BBC serial) 1982, Underdog 1982, Salad Days 1982, Brass 1983, Mistral's Daughter, The Master of Ballantrae 1984, Six Centuries of Verse 1984, Nehru (Mountbatten—the Last Viceroy) 1985, Monsieur Quixote 1985, Star Quality 1985, Blunt 1986, Porterhouse Blue 1986, Devil's Disciple 1986, Troubles 1988, Pursuit (TV mini-series) 1988, Burning Secret 1988, The Winslow Boy 1989, Under a Dark Angel's Eye (HTV), Phantom of the Opera (TV mini-series), The Plot to Kill Hitler (TV mini-series), The Gravy Train (TV mini-series), King of the Wind 1989, House of Cards (BBC), The Gravy Train Goes East (TV mini-series) 1991, An Ungentlemanly Act 1992, To Play the King (BBC TV mini-series) 1993, Remember (U.S. TV mini-series) 1993, Catherine the Great (mini-series) 1994, Savage Play (mini-series) 1994, The Final Cut (TV mini-series) 1995; The Canterville Ghost (Carlton TV) 1997. *Publications:* Preface to Cymbeline 1976, Preface to The Merry Wives of Windsor 1988. *Leisure interests:* archaeology, music, books, cinematography, travel. *Address:* c/o London Management, 2–4 Noel Street, London, W1V 3RB, England. *Telephone:* 0171-237 9000.

RICHARDSON, Joanna, M.A., F.R.S.L.; British author; b. London; d. of late Frederick Richardson and Charlotte Richardson (née Benjamin); ed. The Downs School, Seaford, Sussex, St. Anne's Coll., Oxford; mem. Council, R.S.L. 1961–86; Prix Goncourt de la Biographie 1989 (for Judith Gautier; first time award was made to a non-French author); Chevalier, Ordre des Arts et des Lettres. *Publications:* Fanny Brawne: a biography 1952, Théophile Gautier: his Life and Times 1958, Edward FitzGerald 1960, The Pre-Eminent Victorian: A Study of Tennyson 1962, The Everlasting Spell: A Study of Keats and his Friends 1963, Introduction to Victor Hugo: Choses Vues 1964, Edward Lear 1965, George IV: A Portrait 1966, Creevey and Greville 1967, Princess Mathilde 1969, Verlaine 1971, Enid Starkie 1973, Stendhal: a critical biography 1974, Victor Hugo 1976, Zola 1978, Keats and his Circle: an album of portraits 1980, The Life and Letters of John Keats 1981, Letters from Lambeth: the Correspondence of the Reynolds Family with John Freeman Milward Dovaston 1808–1815, 1981, Colette 1983, Judith Gautier 1987, Portrait of a Bonaparte: The Life and Times of Joseph-Napoleon Primoli 1851–1927 1987, Baudelaire 1994; FitzGerald: Selected Works 1962 (ed.), Essays by Divers Hands (ed. and trans.) 1964, Verlaine Poems (ed. and trans.) 1974, Baudelaire Poems (ed. and trans.) 1975, Gautier, Mademoiselle de Maupin (trans.) 1981; has contributed to The Times, The Times Literary Supplement, Sunday Times, Spectator, New Statesman, New York Times Book Review, The Washington Post, French Studies, French Studies Bulletin, Modern Language Review, Keats-Shelley Memorial Bulletin, etc. *Leisure interest:* antique collecting. *Address:* c/o Curtis Brown Group, Haymarket House, 28–29 Haymarket, London, SW1Y 4SP, England. *Telephone:* 0171-396 6600.

RICHARDSON, Joely; British actress; b. 1958, Lancs.; d. of the late Tony Richardson and of Vanessa Redgrave (q.v.); m. Tim Bevan; one d.; ed. Lycée, St Paul's Girls' School, London, Pinellas Park High School, Fla., The Thacher School, Ojai, Calif. and Royal Acad. of Dramatic Art; television appearances in Body Contact, Behaving Badly 1989; London stage debut in Steel Magnolias 1989. *Films:* Wetherby 1985, Drowning by Numbers 1988, Shining Through 1991, Rebecca's Daughters 1992, Lady Chatterley's Lover (TV) 1993, Lochness 1994, Sister, My Sister 1995, 101 Dalmatians 1995, Believe Me 1995, Hollow Reed 1996, Event Horizon 1996.

RICHARDSON, Keith, M.A.; British writer, administrator and fmr. journalist; b. 14 June 1936, Wakefield, Yorks.; s. of Gilbert Richardson and Ellen Richardson; m. Sheila Carter 1958; three d.; ed. Wakefield Grammar School, Univ. Coll. Oxford; feature writer, The Financial Times 1960–63; Industrial Ed. and European Corresp. The Sunday Times 1964–68, 1970–83; Production Man. GKN 1969–70; Head of Group Public Affairs, B.A.T. Industries 1983–88; Sec.-Gen. The European Round Table of Industrialists 1988–98. *Publications:* Monopolies and Mergers 1963, Do it the Hard Way 1971,

Daggers in the Forum 1978, Reshaping Europe 1991, Beating the Crisis 1993, Europe Made Simple 1998. *Leisure interest:* mountaineering. *Address:* European Round Table, Avenue Jaspar 113, 1060 Brussels, Belgium. *Telephone:* (2) 534 31 00. *Fax:* (2) 534 73 48.

RICHARDSON, Sir Michael (John de Rougemont), Kt.; British banker; b. 9 April 1925; s. of Arthur Richardson and Audrey de Rougemont; m. Octavia Mayhew 1949; one s. two d.; ed. Harrow School and Kent School, Conn., U.S.A.; Capt. Irish Guards 1943–49; Drayton Group 1949–52; partner, Panmure Gordon & Co. 1952–71, Cazenove & Co. 1971–81; Man. Dir. N. M. Rothschild & Sons Ltd. 1981–90, Vice-Chair. 1990–95; Chair. Smith New Court PLC 1990–94, Consultant 1995–97; Vice-Chair. J.O. Hambro Magan & Co. 1995–97, NatWest Markets Corp. Advisory (now Hawkpoint Partners) Ltd. 1997–. *Leisure interests:* fox hunting, sailing. *Address:* 4 Great St. Helen's, London, EC3A 6HA; 32 Queen Anne's Gate, London, SW1H 9AB, England.

RICHARDSON, Miranda; British actress; b. 3 March 1958, Southport; d. of William Alan Richardson and Marian Georgina (née Townsend) Richardson; ed. Old Vic Theatre School, Bristol. *Theatre appearances include:* Moving 1980–81, All My Sons, Who's Afraid of Virginia Woolf?, The Life of Einstein, A Lie of the Mind 1987, The Changeling, Mountain Language 1988, Etta Jenks, The Designated Mourner 1996. *Film appearances:* Dance with a Stranger (debut 1985; Best Actress Award, Evening Standard), The Innocent, Empire of the Sun, The Mad Monkey, Eat the Rich, Twisted Obsession, The Bachelor 1992, Enchanted April 1992 (Golden Globe Award for Best Comedy Actress 1993), The Crying Game 1992, Damage (B.A.F.T.A. Award for Best Supporting Actress 1993), Tom and Viv 1994, La Nuit et Le Moment 1994, Kansas City, Swann 1995, Evening Star 1996, The Designated Mourner 1996, Apostle 1996, All For Love, Jacob Two Two and the Hooded Fang 1998, The Big Brass Ring 1998, Sleepy Hollow 1998. *Television appearances include:* The Hard Word, Sorrel and Son, A Woman of Substance, After Pilkington, Underworld, Death of the Heart, Blackadder II and III, Die Kinder (mini-series) 1990, Sweet as You Are (Royal TV Soc.'s Best Actress Award), Fatherland (Golden Globe Award), Saint X 1995, Magic Animals, Dance to the Music of Time 1997, The Scold's Bridle, Merlin 1997, Alice 1998, Ted and Ralph 1998. *Leisure interests:* gardening, junkshops, music, occasional art, reading, softball, walking. *Address:* c/o Kerry Gardner Management, 7 St. George's Square, London, SW1V 2HX, England.

RICHARDSON, Natasha Jane; British actress; b. 11 May 1963; d. of the late Tony Richardson and of Vanessa Redgrave (q.v.); m. 1st Robert Fox 1990 (divorced 1994); m. 2nd Liam Neeson (q.v.) 1994; two s.; ed. Lycée Française de Londres, St. Paul's Girls' School, Cen. School of Speech and Drama; Most Promising Newcomer Award 1986; Plays and Players Award 1986, 1990; Best Actress, Evening Standard Film Awards 1900; London Theatre Critics Award 1990. *Stage appearances include:* A Midsummer Night's Dream, Hamlet, The Seagull 1985, China 1986, High Society 1986, Anna Christie 1990, 1992. *Film appearances include:* Every Picture Tells a Story 1985, Gothic 1987, A Month in the Country 1987, Patty Hearst 1988, Fat Man and Little Boy 1989, The Handmaid's Tale 1990. The Comfort of Strangers 1990, The Favour, The Watch and The Very Big Fish 1992, Past Midnight 1994, Widows Peak 1994, Nell 1994. *Television appearances include:* In a Secret State 1985, Ghosts 1986, Hostages 1992, Suddenly Last Summer 1993, Zelda 1993, Tales from the Crypt 1996. *Address:* ICM Limited, Oxford House, 76 Oxford Street, London, W1N 0AX, England.

RICHARDSON, Peter Damian, PH.D., F.R.S., A.C.G.I., D.I.C.; British mechanical engineer; b. 22 Aug. 1935, West Wickham; s. of Reginald W. Richardson and the late Marie S. Richardson; one d.; ed. Imperial Coll. London; demonstrator Dept. of Mechanical Eng., Imperial Coll. 1955–58; went to U.S.A. 1958; Visiting Lecturer Brown Univ. 1958–59, Research Assoc. 1959–60, Asst. Prof. of Eng. 1960–65, Assoc. Prof. 1965–68, Prof. 1968–84, Prof. of Eng. and Physiology 1984–, Chair. Univ. Faculty 1987–; Chair. Exec. Cttee. Center Biomedical Eng. 1972–; Consultant to Industry U.S. Govt. Agencies; recipient of Sr. Scientist Award Alexander Von Humboldt Foundation 1976, Laureate in Medicine, Ernst Jung Foundation 1987; mem. American Soc. of Mechanical Eng., American Soc. of Artificial Internal Organs, European Soc. of Artificial Organs, Biomedical Eng. Soc. *Publications:* Principles of Cell Adhesion 1995, contribs. to many professional journals. *Address:* Box D, Brown Univ., Providence, RI 02912, U.S.A. *Telephone:* (401) 8632687.

RICHARDSON, Robert Coleman, PH.D.; American professor of physics and researcher; b. 26 June 1937, Washington, D.C.; s. of Robert Franklin Richardson and Lois (Price) Richardson; m. Betty Marilyn McCarthy 1962; two d.; ed. Virginia Polytechnic Inst. and State Univ., Duke Univ.; served in U.S. Army 1959–60; Research Assoc. Cornell Univ., Ithaca, N.Y. 1966–67, Asst. Prof. 1968–71, Assoc. Prof. 1972–74, Prof. 1975–; Chair. Int. Union Pure and Applied Physics Comm. (C-5) 1981–84; mem. Bd. Assessment Nat. Bureau of Standards 1983–; mem. Editorial Bd. Journal of Low Temperature Physics 1984–; Fellow A.A.A.S., American Physical Soc.; mem. N.A.S.; Guggenheim Fellow 1975, 1983; Simon Memorial Prize, British Physical Soc. 1976, Oliver E. Buckley Prize, American Physical Soc. 1981, shared Nobel Prize for Physics 1966. *Leisure interests:* photography, gardening. *Address:* Department of Physics, Cornell University, Clark Hall, Ithaca, NY 14853, U.S.A.

RICHARDSON, Ruth; New Zealand politician; fmr. Legal Adviser, Federated Farmers; Nat. Party M.P. for Selwyn 1981–94; Shadow Minister for Finance 1987; Minister of Finance 1990–93; consultant Ruth Richardson (N.Z.) Ltd. 1994–. *Address:* RD5, Christchurch, New Zealand. *Telephone:* (3) 347-9146.

RICHARDSON, William Blaine, M.A.; American diplomatist and politician; b. 15 Nov. 1947, Pasadena, Calif.; m. Barbara Flavin 1972; ed. Tufts Univ., Fletcher School of Law and Diplomacy; staff mem. U.S. House of Reps. 1971–72, Dept. of State 1973–75, U.S. Senate Foreign Relations Cttee. 1975–78; Exec. Dir. N.M. State Democratic Cttee. 1978, Bernalillo Co. Democratic Cttee. 1978; business exec. Santa Fe 1978–82; mem. (Democrat) 98th-103rd Congresses from 3rd Dist. N.M. 1982–97; Perm. Rep. to UN 1997–98; Sec. of State for Energy 1998–. *Address:* c/o Department of Energy, Forrestal Building, 1000 Independence Avenue Southwest, Washington, DC 20585, U.S.A. *Telephone:* (202) 586-4670.

RICHARDSON, William Chase, M.B.A., PH.D.; American university administrator; b. 11 May 1940, Passaic, N.J.; s. of Henry B. and Frances (Chase) Richardson; m. Nancy Freeland 1966; two d.; ed. Trinity Coll., Hartford, Conn. and Univ. of Chicago; Research Assoc., Instr. Univ. of Chicago 1967–70; Asst. Prof. Univ. of Washington, School of Public Health and Community Medicine 1971–73, Assoc. Prof. 1973–76, Prof. of Health Services 1976–84, Chair. Dept. of Health Services 1973–76, Graduate Dean, Vice-Provost for Research, 1981–84; Exec. Vice-Pres., Provost, and Prof. Dept. of Family and Community Medicine, Pennsylvania State Univ. 1984–90; Pres. Johns Hopkins Univ. 1990–95; Prof. Dept. of Health Policy Man. 1990–95, Prof. Emer. 1995–; Pres. C.E.O. W.K. Kellogg Foundation Battle Creek, Mich. 1995–; mem. Inst. of Medicine, N.A.S.; Fellow American Public Health Asscn.; Trinity Whitlock Award; Mary H. Bachmeyer Award (Univ. of Chicago); Kellogg Fellow. *Publications:* articles in professional journals. *Address:* W.K. Kellogg Foundation, 1 Michigan Avenue E., Battle Creek, MI 49017, U.S.A.

RICHARDSON OF DUNTISBOURNE, Baron (Life Peer), cr. 1983; **Gordon William Humphreys Richardson,** K.G., P.C., M.B.E.; British banker; b. 25 Nov. 1915, London; s. of John Robert and Nellie Richardson (née Humphreys); m. Margaret Alison Sheppard 1941; one s. one d.; ed. Nottingham High School, and Gonville and Caius Coll., Cambridge; S. Notts. Hussars Yeomanry 1939, Staff Coll., Camberley 1941; called to the Bar, Gray's Inn 1947; mem. Bar Council 1951–55; Industrial and Commercial Finance Corpn. Ltd. 1955–57; Dir. J. Henry Schroder and Co. 1957–62; Chair. J. Henry Schroder Wagg and Co. Ltd. 1962–72; Chair. Schroders Ltd. 1965–73, J. Henry Schroder Banking Corpn. (U.S.A.) 1967–69, Schroders AG (Switzerland) 1967, Schroders Inc. (U.S.A.) 1969–73; Dir. Bank of England 1967–73, Gov. 1973–83; Dir. BIS 1973–93, Vice-Chair. 1985–88, 1991–93; Chair. Cttee. on Turnover Taxation 1963–64; Vice-Chair. Legal and Gen. Assurance Soc. Ltd. 1959–70, Lloyds Bank Ltd. 1962–66; Vice-Chair. Chase Manhattan Int. Advisory Council 1996–; Dir. Rolls-Royce (1971) Ltd. 1971–73, ICI 1972–73; mem. Int. Advisory Bd. Chemical Bank 1986–96, Chair. 1986–96; Chair. Morgan Stanley Int. Inc. 1986–96; mem. Co. Law Amendment Cttee. 1959–62; mem. Court, London Univ. 1962–65; mem. Nat. Econ. Devt. Council 1971–73, 1980–83; Chair. Industrial Devt. Advisory Bd. 1972–73, "Group of Ten" 1982–83, "Group of 30" 1985–91; Hon. Chair. "Group of Thirty" 1991–; Dir. Glyndebourne Arts Trust 1982–88, Royal Opera House 1983–88; Chair. Pilgrim Trust 1984–89; Hon. Master of Bench of Gray's Inn 1973; one of H.M. Lieuts. for City of London 1974–; High Steward of Westminster 1985–89; Deputy High Steward, Univ. of Cambridge 1982–; Deputy Lieut. for Glos. 1983; Hon. Fellow, Wolfson Coll., and Gonville and Caius Coll., Cambridge Univ.; Hon. D.Sc. (The City Univ.) 1975, (Univ. of Aston in Birmingham) 1979, Hon. LL.D. (Cambridge) 1979, Hon. D.C.L. (East Anglia) 1984; Benjamin Franklin Medal (Royal Soc. of Arts) 1984. *Leisure interests:* reading, walking. *Address:* c/o Morgan Stanley, 25 Cabot Square, Canary Wharf, London, E14 4QA, England. *Telephone:* 0171-425 8004.

RICHLER, Mordecai; Canadian writer; b. 1931, Montreal; s. of Moses Isaac Richler and Lily Rosenberg; m. Florence Wood 1960; three s. two d.; ed. Montreal Hebrew Acad., Baron Byng High School and Sir George Williams Univ.; Canada Council Junior Arts Fellowship 1959, 1960; Fellowship in Creative Writing, Guggenheim Foundation, New York 1961, Canada Council, Sr. Arts Fellowship 1967; Writer-in-residence, Sir George Williams Univ. 1968–69; Visiting Prof. Carleton Univ., Ottawa 1972–74; Editorial Bd., Book-of-the-Month Club, New York 1976; Paris Review Humour Prize 1968, Canadian Gov.-Gen.'s Award for Fiction 1969, 1972, Golden Bear, Berlin Film Festival 1974, Commonwealth Writers Prize 1990, Giller Prize for best work of fiction (Canada) 1997, Leacock Hamow Award (Canada) 1998. *Publications:* (novels) The Acrobats 1954, Son of a Smaller Hero 1955, A Choice of Enemies 1957, The Apprenticeship of Duddy Kravitz 1959, The Incomparable Atuk 1963, Cocksure 1968, St. Urbain's Horseman 1971, Images of Spain 1978, Joshua Then and Now 1980, Solomon Gursky Was Here 1990; (stories) The Street 1972, Barney's Version 1997; (film scripts) No Love for Johnnie, Life at the Top, The Apprenticeship of Duddy Kravitz, etc.; (TV plays) The Trouble with Benny, etc.; (essays) Hunting Tigers under Glass 1969, Shovelling Trouble 1973, Home Sweet Home 1984; (for children) Jacob Two-Two Meets the Hooded Fang 1975, The Best of Modern Humour (Ed.) 1983, Jacob Two-Two and the Dinosaur 1987, This Year in Jerusalem 1994; (non-fiction) Canadian Writing Today (ed.) 1970, Writers on World War II (ed.) 1991, Oh Canada! Oh Quebec! Lament for a Divided Nation 1992. *Leisure interest:* poker. *Address:* Appartment 80c, 1321 Sherbrooke

Street West, Montreal, Quebec; c/o McClelland and Stewart, 481 University Avenue, Toronto, Ont., M5G 2E9, Canada. *Telephone:* 514-288-2008.

RICHMOND, Julius B., M.D.; American physician; b. 26 Sept. 1916, Chicago, Ill.; s. of Jacob Richmond and Anna (Dayno) Richmond; m. 1st Rhee Chidekel 1937 (died 1985); three s. (one deceased); m. 2nd Jean Rabow 1987; ed. Univ. of Illinois; Intern, Cook County Hosp. Chicago 1939–41; Resident, Municipal Contagious Diseases Hosp. Chicago 1941–42, 1946; mem. Faculty, Univ. of Ill. Medical School 1946–53, Prof. of Paediatrics 1950–53, Dir. Inst. of Juvenile Research 1952–53; Prof., Chair. Dept. of Paediatrics, Coll. of Medicine, State Univ. of New York at Syracuse 1953–65, Dean, Medical Faculty and Chair. Dept. of Paediatrics 1965–70; Prof. of Child Psychiatry and Human Devt., Prof., Chair. Dept. of Preventive and Social Medicine, Harvard Medical School 1971–77, Prof. of Health Policy Harvard Medical School and Harvard School of Public Health 1981–88, John D. MacArthur Emer. Prof. of Health Policy. 1988–; Psychiatrist-in-Chief, Children's Hosp. Medical Center, Boston 1971–77, Adviser on Child Health Policy 1981–, Dir. Div. of Health Policy, Research and Educ. 1981–88; Dir. Judge Baker Guidance Center, Boston 1971–77; Asst. Sec. Health and Surgeon-Gen. Dept. of Health and Social Services 1977–81; mem. N.A.S. (Inst. of Medicine) several awards and hon. degrees. *Publications:* seven books on paediatrics. *Address:* Harvard Medical School, Department of Social Medicine, 641 Huntington Avenue, Room 314, Boston, MA 02115 (Office); 79 Beverly Road, Chestnut Hill, MA 02167, U.S.A. (Home). *Telephone:* (617) 432-1410 (Office); (617) 277-4830 (Home).

RICHMOND, Sir Mark Henry, Kt., SC.D., F.R.S.; British academic; b. 1 Feb. 1931, Sydney, Australia; s. of Harold Sylvester Richmond and Dorothy Plaistowe Tegg; m. Shirley Jean Townrow 1958; one s. one d. (and one d. deceased); ed. Epsom Coll., Clare Coll., Univ. of Cambridge; mem. scientific staff, Medical Research Council 1958–65; Reader in Molecular Biology, Univ. of Edinburgh 1965–68; Prof. of Bacteriology, Univ. of Bristol 1968–81; Vice-Chancellor and Prof. of Molecular Bacteriology, Victoria Univ. of Manchester 1981–90; mem. Public Health Laboratory Service Bd. 1976–85; Chair. Cttee. of Vice-Chancellors and Prins. of the U.K. 1987–89, Microbiological Food Safety Cttee. 1989–90, Science and Eng. Research Council 1990–94; Group Head of Research, Glaxo 1993–95, Science Adviser 1995–96; mem. staff School of Public Policy, Univ. Coll. London 1996–; mem. Int. Science Advisory Cttee., UNESCO 1996–; mem. and fmr. mem. numerous bds.; Robert Koch Award 1977. *Publications:* numerous scientific articles. *Leisure interests:* gardening, hill walking, opera. *Address:* School of Public Policy, University College London, 29-30 Tavistock Square, London, WC1H 9EZ, England. *Telephone:* 0171-209 6593.

RICHTER, Burton, PH.D.; American physicist; b. 22 March 1931, Brooklyn, New York; s. of Abraham Richter and Fannie (Pollack) Richter; m. Laurose Becker 1960; one s. one d.; ed. Mass. Inst. of Technology; joined Stanford Univ. 1956–, Research Assoc. in Physics, High Energy Physics Lab., Stanford Univ. 1956–59; mem. group building first electron storage ring and conducting a colliding beam experiment extending validity of quantum electrodynamics; Asst. Prof., Stanford Univ. 1959–63, Assoc. Prof. 1963–67, Prof. 1967–, Paul Pigott Prof. in Physical Sciences 1980–; worked at Stanford Linear Accelerator Center 1963–, Tech. Dir. 1982–84, Dir. 1984–; set up a group which built a high energy electron positron machine (SPEAR) and has continued to develop new accelerator and detector techniques including most recently the SLAC linear collider; Pres. (desig.), IUPAP; mem. Bd. of Dirs. Varian Assocs., Litel Instruments; sabbatical year at European Org. for Nuclear Research (CERN), Geneva 1975–76; Loeb Lecturer, Harvard Univ. 1974, DeShalit Lecturer, Weizmann Inst. 1975; mem. N.A.S. 1977; Fellow, American Acad. of Arts and Sciences 1989, American Physical Soc. (Pres. 1994), A.A.A.S.; E. O. Lawrence Medal 1976, Nobel Prize for Physics (jointly with Samuel Ting, q.v.) for discovery of the heavy, long-lived "psi" particle 1976. *Publications:* over 300 articles in various scientific journals 1963–89. *Address:* Stanford Linear Accelerator Center, P.O. Box 4349, Stanford University, Stanford, CA 94309, U.S.A.

RICHTER, Gerhard; German artist; b. 9 Feb. 1932, Dresden; s. of Horst and Hildegard Richter; m. 1st Marianne (née Eufinger); m. 2nd Isa (née Genzken) 1982; m. 3rd Sabine (née Moritz) 1995; one s. two d.; ed. Staatliche Kunstakademien Dresden and Düsseldorf; emigrated to West Germany 1961; Visiting Prof. Kunstakademie Hamburg 1967, Coll. of Art, Halifax, Canada 1978; Prof. Staatliche Kunstakademie Düsseldorf 1971–94; mem. Akad. der Künste, Berlin; one-man shows in galleries and museums all over world 1964–; paintings in public collections in Berlin, Cologne, Basle, Paris, New York, Chicago, Toronto, London, etc.; mem. Acad. of Arts, Berlin; Kunstpreis Junger Westen 1966, Arnold Bode Preis 1982, Kokoschka Prize (Austria) 1985, Wolf Prize 1994–95. *Address:* Bismarckstrasse 50, 50996 Cologne, Germany.

RICHTER, Horst-Eberhard, M.D., D.PHIL.; German professor of psychological medicine; b. 28 April 1923, Berlin; s. of Otto and Charlotte Richter; m. Bergrun Luckow 1947; one s. two d.; ed. Berlin Univ.; Dir. Advisory and Research Centre for Childhood Emotional Disturbances, Wedding Children's Hosp., Berlin 1952–62; Physician, Psychiatric Clinic, W. Berlin Free Univ. 1955–62; Dir. Berlin Psychoanalytic Inst. 1959–62; Chief of Dept. of Psychosomatic Medicine, Univ. of Giessen, Fed. Repub. of Germany 1962–, Dir. Centre for Psychosomatics 1973, now Hon. Dir.; Dir. Sigmund-Freud Inst Frankfurt am Main 1992–; mem. PEN, Germany; Research Prize, Swiss Soc. of Psychosomatic Medicine 1970; Theodor-Heuss Prize 1980. *Publications:* Eltern, Kind und Neurose 1963, Herzneurose (with D. Beckmann) 1969, Patient Familie 1970, Giessen-Test (with D. Beckmann) 1972, Die Gruppe 1972, Lernziel Solidarität 1974, The Family as Patient 1974, Flüchten oder Standhalten 1976, Der Gotteskomplex 1979, Alle redeten vom Frieden 1981, Sich der Krise stellen 1981, Zur Psychologie des Friedens 1982, Die Chance des Gewissens 1986, Leben statt Machen 1987, Die hohe Kunst der Korruption 1989, Russen und Deutsche 1990, Umgang mit Angst 1992, Wer nicht leiden will, muss hassen 1993, Psychoanalyse und Politik 1995. *Address:* Friedrichstrasse 28, 35392 Giessen, Germany. *Telephone:* (0641) 994-5626. *Fax:* (0641) 74350.

RICHTER PRADA, Gen. Pedro; Peruvian politician and army officer; fmr. Chief of Staff of the Army, fmr. Minister of the Interior; Chair. Jt. Chiefs of Staff 1978–81; Prime Minister, Minister of War and C.-in-C. of Armed Forces of Peru 1978–80; Pres. Mokichi Okada Foundation, Peru 1981–. *Address:* c/o Oficina del Primer Ministro, Lima, Peru.

RICHTHOFEN, Hermann, Freiherr von, DR.JUR.; German diplomatist; b. 20 Nov. 1933, Breslau; s. of Herbert Freiherr von Richthofen and Gisela Freifrau von Richthofen (née Schoeller); m. Christa Gräfin von Schwerin 1966; one s. two d.; joined diplomatic service 1963; served Saigon and Djakarta; Head of Dept. Perm. Rep. Office of Fed. Repub. of Germany for G.D.R. 1975–78; Dir. German and Berlin Dept. Ministry of Foreign Affairs 1978–80; Dir. Working Party on German Policy, Fed. Chancellery 1980–86; Dir. Gen. Legal Dept. Ministry of Foreign Affairs 1986, Political Dept. 1986–88; Amb. to U.K. 1988–93; Perm. Rep. to NATO 1993–98; Chair. Deutsch-Englische Gesellschaft, Berlin; Trustee 21st Century Trust, London. *Leisure interests:* skiing, walking, swimming, literature, history, arts, music. *Address:* Beckerstr. 6A, 12157 Berlin, Germany.

RICK, Charles Madeira, Jr., PH.D.; American geneticist; b. 30 April 1915, Reading, Pa.; s. of late Charles M. Rick and Miriam C. (Yeager) Rick; m. Martha Elizabeth Overholts 1938 (died 1983); one s. one d.; ed. Pennsylvania State and Harvard Univs.; Asst. Plant Breeder, W. Atlee Burpee Co., Lompoc, Calif. 1936, 1937; Instructor and Asst. Geneticist, Univ. of Calif. at Davis 1940, other academic ranks, then Prof. and Geneticist 1955–; mem. Genetics Study Section of Nat. Insts. of Health 1958–62; Co-ordinator Tomato Genetics Co-operative 1950–82; Visiting Lecturer, N. C. State Univ. 1956, Univ. de São Paulo, Brazil 1965; Faculty Research Lecturer, Univ. of Calif. 1961; Carnegie Visiting Prof., Univ. of Hawaii 1963; Visiting Scientist, Univ. of Puerto Rico 1968; Visiting Prof. Univ. de Rosario, Argentina 1980; Univ. Lecturer, Cornell Univ. 1987; mem. Panel in Genetic Biology, Nat. Science Foundation 1971–72; Nat. Plant Genetics Resources Board, U.S. Dept. of Agric. 1975–82; mem. N.A.S.; Guggenheim Fellow 1948, 1950; Hon. Fellow Indian Soc. Genetics and Plant Breeding 1990; Penn. State Alumni Fellow 1991; Fellow American Soc. for Horticultural Science 1992; Centennial Lecturer Ontario Agricultural Coll., Univ. of Guelph 1974; Filippo Maseri Florio World Prize for Distinguished Research in Agriculture 1997; Vaughan Research Award of American Soc. for Horticultural Science 1946, Campbell Award of A.A.A.S. 1959, M. A. Blake Award, American Soc. Horticultural Science 1974, Merit Award, Botanical Soc. of America 1976, Frank N. Meyer Memorial Medal, American Genetics Asscn. 1982, Thomas Roland Medal, Mass. Horticultural Soc. 1983, Distinguished Econ. Botanist, Soc. for Econ. Botany 1987, Genetic and Plant Breeding Award, Nat. Council of Commercial Plant Breeders 1987, Award of Distinction, Coll. of Agric., Univ. of Calif. (Davis) 1991, Distinguished Service Award, Calif. League of Food Processors 1993, Alexander von Humboldt Award 1993, Hall of Fame, American Soc. for Horticultural Research 1998. *Publications:* 160 papers in research journals, and 154 research notes in Reports of Tomato Genetics Co-operative. *Leisure interests:* gardening, photography. *Address:* Department of Vegetable Crops, University of California, Davis, CA 95616 (Office); 8 Parkside Drive, Davis, CA 95616, U.S.A. (Home). *Telephone:* (530) 752-1737 (Office); (530) 756-1387 (Home). *Fax:* (530) 752-9659.

RICKMAN, Alan; British actor; ed. Chelsea Coll. of Art, Royal Coll. of Art and Royal Acad. of Dramatic Art (RADA); spent three years with RSC at Stratford; later appeared at Bush Theatre, Hampstead and Royal Court Theatre. *Stage appearances include:* Les Liaisons Dangereuses (London and Broadway), The Lucky Chance (Royal Court), Tango at the End of Winter (Piccadilly) 1991, Hamlet 1992, Antony and Cleopatra (Nat. Theatre) 1998. *Television appearances include:* role of Obadiah Slope in The Barchester Chronicles 1982, Pity in History 1984, Revolutionary Witness, Spirit of Man 1989, Rasputin 1995. *Films include:* The January Man, Close My Eyes, Truly, Madly, Deeply, Die Hard, Robin Hood: Prince of Thieves, Bob Roberts 1992, Mesmer 1993, An Awfully Big Adventure 1994, Sense and Sensibility 1995, Michael Collins 1996, Rasputin 1996, Mesmer, Dark Harbour 1997, The Judas Kiss 1997, Dogma 1998; dir. The Winter Guest 1997. *Address:* c/o ICM, Oxford House, 76 Oxford Street, London, W1N 0AX, England.

RICKS, Christopher Bruce, F.B.A.; British professor of English literature; b. 18 Sept. 1933; s. of James Bruce Ricks and Gabrielle Roszak; m. 1st Kirsten Jensen 1956 (dissolved); two s. two d.; m. 2nd Judith Aronson 1977; one s. two d.; ed. King Alfred's School, Wantage, Oxon., Balliol Coll., Univ. of Oxford; 2nd Lieut. Green Howards 1952; Andrew Bradley Jr. Research Fellow Balliol Coll. Univ. of Oxford 1957, Fellow Worcester Coll. 1958–68; Prof. of English Bristol Univ. 1968–75; Fellow Christ's Coll., Prof. of English

Univ. of Cambridge 1975–86, King Edward VII Prof. of English Literature 1982–86; Prof. Boston Univ. 1986–; Visiting Prof. at Univs. of Berkeley and Stanford 1965, Smith Coll. 1967, Harvard Univ. 1971, Wesleyan 1974, Brandeis 1977, 1981, 1984, U.S.A.; Vice-Pres. Tennyson Soc.; Fellow American Acad. of Arts and Sciences 1991; Hon. Fellow, Balliol Coll. 1989, Worcester Coll. 1990, Christ's Coll. Cambridge 1993; Hon. D.Litt. (Oxford) 1998; George Orwell Memorial Prize 1979; Beefeater Club Prize for Literature 1980. *Publications:* Milton's Grand Style 1963, The Poems of Tennyson (Ed.) 1969 (revised 1987), Tennyson 1972, Keats and Embarrassment 1974, The State of the Language (Ed. with Leonard Michaels) 1980, 1990, The Force of Poetry 1984, The New Oxford Book of Victorian Verse 1987 (Ed.), Collected Poems and Selected Prose of A. E. Housman (Ed.) 1988, T.S. Eliot and Prejudice 1988, Ed. (with William Vance) The Faber Book of America 1992, Beckett's Dying Words (Clarendon Lectures) 1993, Essays in Appreciation 1996, Inventions of the March Hare: Poems 1909–1917 by T.S. Eliot (Ed.) 1996. *Address:* 39 Martin Street, Cambridge, MA 02138, U.S.A.; Lasborough Park, near Tetbury, Glos., GL8 8UF, England. *Telephone:* (617) 354-7887 (U.S.A.); (01666) 890252 (England).

RICO, Francisco, PH.D.; Spanish professor of medieval literature; b. 28 April 1942, Barcelona; s. of late Cipriano Rico and María Manrique; m. Victoria Camps 1966; three s.; ed. Univ. of Barcelona; Prof. of Medieval Literature, Autonomous Univ. of Barcelona 1971; Visiting Prof. The Johns Hopkins Univ. 1966–67, Princeton Univ. 1981, Scuola Normale Superiore 1987; Gen. Dir. Centre of Spanish Letters, Ministry of Culture 1985–86; Ed. Book Series: Letras e ideas, Filología, Biblioteca clásica; mem. Royal Spanish Acad. 1986–; Foreign mem. British Acad. 1992. *Publications:* El pequeño mundo del hombre 1970, The Spanish Picaresque Novel and the Point of View 1970, Vida u obra de Petrarca (Vol. 1) 1974, Historia y crítica de la literatura española (8 vols.) 1980–84, Breve biblioteca de autores españoles 1990, El sueño del humanismo (De Petrarca a Erasmo) 1993, Critical Edition of Cervantes' Don Quixote 1998. *Leisure interest:* contemporary literature. *Address:* Santa Teresa 38, 08190 St. Cugat del Vallès, Barcelona; Apartado 1, Universidad Autónoma de Barcelona, 08193 Bellaterra-Barcelona, Spain. *Telephone:* 674 07 08; 581 15 26.

RICUPERO, Rubens; Brazilian international civil servant and fmr. diplomatist and politician; b. 1 March 1937, São Paulo; fmr. Amb. to U.S.A.; Minister of the Environment and Amazonian Affairs 1993–94, of Finance March–Sept. 1994; Sec.-Gen. of UNCTAD Sept. 1995–. *Address:* Office of the Secretary-General, UNCTAD, Palais des Nations, 1211 Geneva 10, Switzerland. *Fax:* (22) 907-0042.

RIDDICK, Frank Adams, Jr., M.D.; American physician; b. 14 June 1929, Memphis; s. of Frank Adams Riddick Sr. and Falba Crawford Riddick; m. Mary Belle Alston 1952; two s. one d.; ed. Vanderbilt and Washington Univs.; Staff Physician, Ochsner Clinic, New Orleans 1961–, Asst. Medical Dir. 1969–73, Assoc. Medical Dir. 1973–75, Medical Dir. 1975–92, Trustee, Alton Ochsner Medical Foundation 1973–, C.E.O. 1991–; Clinical Prof. of Medicine, Tulane Univ., New Orleans 1977–; Chair. Council on Medical Educ., American Medical Assen. 1982–84, Council on Judicial and Ethical Affairs 1995–; mem. N.A.S. Inst. of Medicine; Distinguished Physician Award, American Soc. of Internal Medicine 1980; Physician Exec. Award, American Coll. of Medical Group Admins. 1984; Distinguished Alumnus Award, Vanderbilt Univ. School of Medicine 1988. *Publications:* 56 scientific papers. *Leisure interest:* travel. *Address:* Ochsner Clinic, 1516 Jefferson Highway, New Orleans, LA 70121; 1923 Octavia Street, New Orleans, LA 70115, U.S.A. (Home) *Telephone:* (504) 838-4001 (Office); (504) 897-1737 (Home).

RIDE, Sally, PH.D.; American astronaut and professor of physics; b. 26 May 1951, Los Angeles; d. of Dale Ride and Joyce Ride; m. Steven Hawley (divorced); no c.; ed. Westlake High School, Los Angeles and Stanford Univ.; astronaut trainee, NASA 1978–79, astronaut 1979–87; on-orbit capsule communicator STS-2 mission, Johnson Space Center, NASA, Houston; on-orbit capsule communicator STS-3 mission NASA, mission specialist STS-7 1983; Scientific Fellow, Stanford Univ. 1987–89; Dir. Calif. Space Inst. and Prof. of Physics, Univ. of Calif. at San Diego 1989–96; mem. Presidential Comm. on Space Shuttle 1986, Presidential Comm. of Advisers on Science and Tech. 1994–; mem. Bd. of Dirs. Apple Computer Inc. 1988–90. *Publications:* To Space and Back (jtly.) 1986, The Third Planet: Exploring the Earth from Space (jtly.) 1994. *Address:* California Space Institute, 0426, University of California at San Diego, La Jolla, CA 92093, U.S.A. *Telephone:* (619) 534-5827. *Fax:* (619) 822-1277.

RIDGE, Thomas Joseph, J.D.; American politician and lawyer; b. 26 Aug. 1945, Munhall, Pa.; m. Michele Moore 1979; one s. one d.; ed. Harvard Univ. and Dickinson School of Law, Carlisle, Pa.; admitted Pa. Bar 1972; practising lawyer, Erie, Pa. 1972–82; Asst. Dist. Attorney, Erie, Pa. 1979–82; mem. U.S. House of Reps. 1983–95; Gov. of Pennsylvania Jan. 1995–; mem. numerous cttees.; Republican. *Address:* Office of the Governor, Room 225, Harrisburg, PA 17120, U.S.A. *Telephone:* (717) 787 2500. *Fax:* (717) 783-1396.

RIEBER-MOHN, Georg Fredrik; Norwegian lawyer; b. 13 Aug. 1945, Lillehammer; m. Kari Nergaard 1967; two s. one d.; ed. Univ. of Oslo; Deputy Gov. Western Prison Dist. 1971–74; Asst. Judge, Magistrates' Court of Stavanger 1975–76; Dist. Attorney (Regional Head of Prosecutions) 1976–80; Gen. Dir. Prison and Probation Service 1980–85; Judge, Appeal Court 1985–86; Gen. Dir. of Public Prosecutions 1986–. *Leisure interest:* salmon fishing. *Address:* Karl Johans Gate 12, Postbox 8002 DEP, 0030 Oslo 1 (Office); Nedre Hval Gård, 3525 Hallingby, Norway (Home). *Telephone:* 22-33-02-70 (Office).

RIEDLBAUCH, Václav; Czech composer; b. 1 April 1947, Dýšina; m.; two s.; ed. Prague Conservatoire; lecturer, Prague Acad. of Performing Arts, Sr. Lecturer, Sec. Dept. of Composition 1984–; Chief Composer Nat. Theatre Opera 1987–89; Chair. Young Composers Section, Czech Composers' and Performing Artists' Union 1982–; Artist of Merit 1987; compositions include Macbeth (for ballet), quartet for four saxophones, Vision (symphonic poem). *Address:* Academy of Performing Arts, Malostranské nám., 110 00 Prague 1 (Office); Revoluční 6, 110 00 Prague 1, Czech Republic (Home). *Telephone:* 530046 (Office); 2310710 (Home).

RIEFENSTAHL, Leni; German film director, photographer and writer; b. 22 Aug. 1902; d. of Alfred and Bertha Riefenstahl; ed. Kunstakademie, Berlin; solo dancer 1920s; acted in films 1920s and 1930s; directed first film 1932; Silver Medal Venice Biennale (for The Blue Light) 1932, Gold Medal 1937, 1938. *Films include:* The White Hell of Pitz Palu (actor) 1929, The Blue Light (actor/dir.) 1932, S.O.S. Iceberg (actor) 1933, Triumph of the Will (dir., documentary of Nuremberg Rally) 1934, Olympische Spiele (dir., documentary of Berlin Olympic Games) 1936, Tiefland 1945. *Publications:* The Last of the Nuba 1974, People of the Kau 1976, Coral Gardens 1978, Mein Afrika (photographs) 1982, Memoiren 1987, Wonders Under Water 1991, The Sieve of Time (autobiog.) 1992, Leni Riefenstahl: A Memoir 1994. *Address:* 82343 Pöcking, Germany.

RIEGLE, Donald W., Jr., M.B.A.; American politician; b. 4 Feb. 1938, Flint, Mich.; s. of Donald Wayne and Dorothy (née Fitchett) Riegle; m. 3rd Lori L. Hansen 1978; five c.; ed. Flint Cen. High School, Flint Jr. Coll., Western Michigan Univ., Univ. of Michigan, Michigan State Univ., Harvard; Sr. Pricing Analyst, IBM Corpn. 1961–64; mem. faculty, Mich. State Univ., Boston Univ., Harvard Univ., Univ. of Southern Calif.; mem. U.S. House of Reps. 1967–76, mem. House Cttee. on Appropriations 1967–73; changed party affiliation from Republican to Democrat Feb. 1973; mem. Special Task Force of House of Reps. on Energy and Econ. 1975–95, Senate Budget Cttee. 1977–95, Senate Finance Cttee. 1987–95, House Cttee. on Int. Relations, Sub-Cttee. on Int. Political and Mil. Affairs, Sub-Cttee. on Int. Security and Scientific Affairs; Chair. Cttee. on Housing, Banking and Urban Affairs 1989–95, Sub-Cttee. on Health, Families and the Uninsured 1989–95; U.S. Senator from Mich. 1977–95; Hon. LL.D. (Defiance Coll., Ohio, St. Benedict's Coll., Kan., Schoolcraft Coll. Mich.). *Publication:* O Congress (with T. Armbrister) 1972.

RIESCO, Germán, B.S.; Chilean diplomatist, politician and business executive; b. 17 Aug. 1941, Santiago; s. of Ignacio Riesco and Eliana Zanartu; m. Jacqueline Cassel van Doorn 1974; one d. four step s. one step d.; ed. Colegio San Ignacio, Santiago, Univ. of Calif. (Davis and Berkeley); mem. Parl. 1969–73; Dir. Agricultural Planning Office 1976–78; Pres. Nat. Agricultural Soc. 1979–81, 1981–83; Vice-Pres. Nat. Party 1983–88; Pres. PAC-Center Alliance Party 1988–90; mem. Bd. Fundación Chile 1983–90; mem. Chilean Comm. for Int. Political Studies; Amb. to U.K. 1990–93 (also accred. to Ireland 1992–93); del. to numerous int. confs. etc. *Leisure interests:* reading, horse-riding, travel. *Address:* 5308 Agustín Denegri, Vitacura, Santiago, Chile (Home). *Telephone:* (56-2) 2182799 (Home).

RIESENHUBER, Heinz Friedrich, DR.RER.NAT.; German politician; b. 1 Dec. 1935, Frankfurt; s. of Karl and Elisabeth (née Birkner) Riesenhuber; m. Beatrix Walter 1968; two s. two d.; ed. Gymnasium in Frankfurt and Univs. of Frankfurt and Munich; with Erzgesellschaft mbH, c/o Metallgesellschaft, Frankfurt 1966–71; Tech. Man. Synthomer-Chemie GmbH, Frankfurt 1971–82; joined CDU 1961, Chair. Frankfurt Branch 1973–78; mem. Bundestag 1976–; Fed. Minister for Research and Technology 1982–93; Dr. h.c. (Weizmann Inst., Israel, Berg Acad., Poland, Surrey, Göttingen); Distinguished Service Cross, Commdr. Légion d'honneur, and numerous other decorations. *Publications:* articles in specialist journals. *Leisure interest:* reading. *Address:* c/o Bundeshaus, Charles-de-Gaulle-Str. 6, 53113 Bonn, Germany.

RIESTER, Walter; German politician and trade unionist; b. 27 Sept. 1943, Kaufbeuren; ed. Labour Acad. Frankfurt; apprentice tiler 1957–60; tiler 1960–68; youth training officer German TU Fed. Baden-Württemberg Region 1970, Departmental Gen. Sec. for Youth Questions Stuttgart Region 1970–77; Admin. Sec. IG Metall Geislingen 1977–78, Second Deputy 1978–79, Sec. Dist. HQ IG Metall Stuttgart 1980–88, Dist. Man. 1988–93, Second Chair. IG Metall Germany 1993–98; Fed. Minister of Labour and Social Affairs 1998–; mem. SPD. *Address:* Ministry of Labour and Social Affairs, Rochusstrasse 1, 53123 Bonn, Germany.

RIFA'I, Zaid al-, M.A.; Jordanian diplomatist; b. 27 Nov. 1936, Amman; s. of Samir Pasha al-Rifa'i and Alia Shukry; m. Muna Talhouni 1965; one s. one d.; ed. Victoria Coll., Cairo, and Harvard and Columbia Univs.; joined diplomatic service 1957; Attaché, Ministry of Foreign Affairs 1957; Sec., Embassy, Cairo 1957; Sec. Jordanian Del. to UN 1957–59; Chief of Royal Protocol 1965; Sec.-Gen. of Royal Court and Private Sec. to H.M. King Hussein 1967; Chief of Royal Court 1969; Amb. to U.K. 1970–72; Political Adviser to King Hussein 1972–73; Prime Minister of Jordan 1973–76, 1985–89; Minister for Foreign Affairs and Defence 1973–76, of Defence 1985–89; Medal of Independence, Order of the Jordanian Star, Order of the

Renaissance (Egypt). *Leisure interests:* music, reading, bridge, water-skiing, sailing, tennis. *Address:* Jabal Amman, Amman, Jordan. *Telephone:* 44565.

RIFBJERG, Klaus; Danish author; b. 15 Dec. 1931, Copenhagen; s. of Thorvald Rifbjerg and Lilly Nielsen; m. Inge Merete Gerner 1955; one s. two d.; ed. Princeton Univ., U.S.A., and Univ. of Copenhagen; Literary critic, Information 1955–57, Politiken 1959–65 (Copenhagen daily newspapers); Literary Dir. Gyldendal Publrs. 1984–92, mem. Bd. of Dirs. 1992–; Prof. of Aesthetics, Laererhøjskole, Copenhagen 1986; Dr. h.c. (Lund) 1991, (Odense) 1996; Aarestrup Medal 1964, Danish Critics' Award 1965, Grant of Honour from the Danish Dramatists 1966, Danish Acad. Award 1966, Golden Laurels 1967, Soren Gyldendal Award 1969, Nordic Council Award 1970, Grant of Honour from the Danish Writers' Guild 1973, PH Prize 1979, Holberg Medal 1979, H.C. Andersen Prize 1988. *Publications include:* novels: Den Kroniske Uskyld 1958, Operaelsken 1966, Arkivet 1967, Lonni Og Karl 1968, Anna (Jeg) Anna 1970, Marts 1970 1970, Leif den Lykkelige JR. 1971, Til Spanien 1971, Lena Jorgensen, Klintevej 4, 2650 Hvidovre 1971, Brevet til Gerda 1972, R.R. 1972, Spinatfuglene 1973, Dilettanterne 1973, Du skal ikke vaere ked af det Amalia 1974, En hugorm i solen 1974, Vejen ad hvilken 1975, Tak for turen 1975, Kiks 1976, Twist 1976, Et Bortvendt Ansigt 1977, Tango 1978, Dobbeltgœnger 1978, Drengene 1978, Joker 1979, Voksdugshjertet 1979, Det sorte hul 1980, De hellige aber 1981, Maend og Kvinder 1982, Jus 1982, En omvej til Klostret 1983, Falsk Forår 1984, Borte tit 1986, Engel 1987, Rapsodi i blåt 1991; short stories: Og Andre Historier 1964, Rejsende 1969, Den Syende Jomfru 1972, Sommer 1974, Det. Svage Køn 1989; non-fiction: I Medgang Og Modgang 1970, Deres Majestæt! 1977; plays: Gris Pa Gaflen 1962, Hva's Skal Vi Lave 1963, Udviklinger 1965, Hvad en Mand Har Brug For 1966, Voks 1968, Ar 1970, Narrene 1971, Svaret Blaeser i Vinden 1971, Det Korte af det lange 1976; poems: Livsfrisen 1979 and several other vols. of poetry; twenty radio plays, essays, several film and TV scripts. *Address:* c/o Gyldendal Publishers, 3 Klareboderne, 1001 Copenhagen, Denmark.

RIFKIN, Joshua, B.S., M.F.A.; American musician; b. 22 April 1944, New York; s. of Harry H. Rifkin and Dorothy Helsh; m. Helen Palmer 1995; one d.; ed. Juilliard School and New York, Göttingen and Princeton Univs.; Musical Adviser, Assoc. Dir. Nonesuch Records 1963–75; Asst., Assoc. Prof. of Music, Brandeis Univ. 1970–82; Dir. The Bach Ensemble 1978–; Visiting Prof. Yale Univ. 1982–83, Princeton Univ. 1988, Stanford Univ. 1989, King's Coll. London 1991, Univ. Basel 1993, Ohio State Univ. 1994; Fellow, Inst. for Advanced Study, Berlin 1984–86; guest conductor English Chamber Orchestra, Los Angeles Chamber Orchestra, St. Louis Symphony Orchestra, St. Paul Chamber Orchestra, Scottish Chamber Orchestra, BBC Symphony Orchestra, numerous others; made several recordings of Rags by Scott Joplin, Bach's Mass in B minor 1982, Bach's Magnificat 1983, numerous Bach cantatas 1986–90, Rags and Tangos 1990, Haydn Symphonies 1994; Gramophone Award 1983. *Publications:* articles in musical journals and the New Grove Dictionary of Music and Musicians. *Leisure interests:* food and wine, cinema, daughter. *Address:* c/o Clarion/Seven Muses, 47 Whitehall Park, London N19 3TW, England.

RIFKIND, Rt. Hon. Sir Malcolm Leslie, Kt., P.C., Q.C., M.P., LL.B., M.SC.; British politician; b. 21 June 1946; s. of E. Rifkind; m. Edith Steinberg 1970; one s. one d.; ed. George Watson's Coll. and Univ. of Edinburgh; lecturer, Univ. of Rhodesia 1967–68; called to Scottish Bar 1970; mem. Parl. for Edinburgh, Pentlands 1974–97; Parl. Under-Sec. of State, Scottish Office 1979–82, FCO 1982–83; Minister of State, FCO 1983–86; Sec. of State for Scotland 1986–90, for Transport 1990–92, for Defence 1992–95, for Foreign and Commonwealth Affairs 1995–97; Pres. Scottish Conservative and Unionist Party 1998–; Hon. Col. 162 Movement Control Regt., Royal Logistic Corps (V); mem. Queen's Bodyguard for Scotland, Royal Co. of Archers; Commdr. Order of Merit (Poland). Conservative. *Address:* c/o House of Commons, London, SW1A 0AA, England.

RIGBY, Jean Prescott, A.R.A.M., A.R.C.M.; British opera singer; b. Fleetwood, Lancs.; d. of Thomas Boulton Rigby and Margaret Annie Rigby; m. James Hayes 1987; three s.; ed. Elmslie Girls' School, Blackpool, Birmingham School of Music, R.A.M. and Opera Studio; studied piano and viola at Birmingham then singing at R.A.M. with Patricia Clark, with whom she continues to study; Prin. Mezzo-Soprano, English Nat. Opera 1982–90, roles include Mercedes, Marina, Lucretia, Dorabella, Octavian, Penelope, Jocasta, Helen (King Priam), Rosina; début Covent Garden 1983, roles have included Tebaldo, Mercedes, Hippolyta, second Lady, Magic Flute and Olga, Eugene Onegin, Cenerentola, Nicklausse (Hoffman); Glyndebourne début 1984, sang Nancy in Albert Herring and Mercedes in Carmen 1985; American début 1993; TV appearances in Così fan Tutte and film on Handel; videos of Xerxes, Rigoletto, Lucretia, Carmen, Albert Herring; also sings concert repertoire and has made recordings with Giuseppe Sinopoli; numerous prizes and scholarships at R.A.M. including Countess of Munster, Leverhulme, Peter Stuyvesant, R.S.A. scholarships and the Prin.'s Prize; Royal Overseas League and Young Artists' Competition 1981; Hon. F.R.A.M. 1989; Hon. Assoc. Birmingham Conservatoire 1996. *Leisure interests:* theatre, sport, British heritage. *Address:* c/o Harold Holt Ltd., 31 Sinclair Road, London, W14 0NS, England.

RIGBY, Peter William Jack, M.A., PH.D.; British medical research scientist; b. 7 July 1947, Savernake; s. of Jack Rigby and Lorna Rigby; m. 1st Paula Webb 1971 (divorced 1983); m. 2nd Julia Maidment 1985; one s.; ed. Lower School of John Lyon, Harrow and Jesus Coll. Cambridge; mem. scientific staff, MRC Lab. of Molecular Biology, Cambridge 1971–73; Helen Hay Whitney Foundation Research Fellow, Stanford Univ. Medical School 1973–76; lecturer, Sr. lecturer in Biochem. Imperial Coll. London 1976–83; Reader in Tumour Virology, Univ. of London 1983–86; Head, Genes and Cellular Controls Group and Div. of Eukaryotic Molecular Genetics, MRC Nat. Inst. for Medical Research 1986–; mem. Science Council, Celltech Therapeutics 1982–; European Ed. Cell 1984–97; mem. Scientific Advisory Bd. Somatix Therapy Corpn. 1989–97; Scientific Cttee. Cancer Research Campaign 1983–88, 1996–; Chair. Scientific Advisory Bd.: Proflix 1996–, Hexagen Tech. Ltd. 1996–; Carter Medal, Clinical Genetics Soc. 1994. *Publications:* papers on molecular biology in scientific journals. *Leisure interests:* narrow boats, listening to music, sport. *Address:* Division of Eurkaryotic Molecular Genetics, MRC National Institute for Medical Research, The Ridgeway, Mill Hill, London, NW7 1AA, England. *Telephone:* 0181-913 8533. *Fax:* 0181-913 8527.

RIGG, Dame (Enid) Diana (Elizabeth), D.B.E.; British actress; b. 20 July 1938, Doncaster, Yorks.; d. of Louis Rigg and Beryl (Helliwell) Rigg; m. 1st Menahem Gueffen 1973 (divorced 1976); m. 2nd Archibald Hugh Stirling 1982 (divorced 1993); one d.; ed. Fulneck Girls' School, Pudsey, Yorks, R.A.D.A.; Professional début as Natella Abashwilli (The Caucasian Chalk Circle), York Festival 1957; repertory Chesterfield and Scarborough 1958; Chair. MacRobert Arts Centre, Univ. of Stirling, Chancellor Univ. of Stirling 1997–; Prof. of Theatre Studies, Oxford Univ. 1998–; Dir. United British Artists 1982–; a Vice-Pres. Baby Life Support Systems (BLISS) 1984–; mem. Arts Council Cttee. 1986; mem. British Museum Devt. Fund, Asscn. for Business Sponsorship of the Arts; Assoc. Artist of R.S.C., Stratford and Aldwych 1962–79; Vice-Pres. BLISS; Dr. h.c. (Stirling Univ.) 1988; Hon. D.Litt. (Leeds) 1992, (South Bank) 1996; Plays and Players Award for Best Actress (Phaedra Britannica 1975, Night and Day 1978), BAFTA Award for Best Actress in Mother Love 1990, Evening Standard Award for Best Actress (Medea 1993, Mother Courage and Her Children 1996, Who's Afraid of Virginia Woolf? 1996), Tony Award for Best Actress in Medea 1994. *Roles with R.S.C. include:* Andromache (Troilus and Cressida), 2nd Ondine, Violanta and Princess Bertha (Ondine), Philippe Trincant (The Devils), Gwendolen (Becket), Bianca (The Taming of the Shrew), Madame de Tourvel (The Art of Seduction), Helena (A Midsummer Night's Dream), Adriana (Comedy of Errors), Cordelia (King Lear), Nurse Monika Stettler (The Physicists), Lady Macduff (Macbeth); toured Eastern Europe, U.S.S.R., U.S.A. in King Lear, Comedy of Errors 1964; Viola (Twelfth Night), Stratford 1966; mem. Nat. Theatre 1972. *Roles there included:* Dottie Moore (Jumpers) 1972, Hippolita ('Tis Pity She's A Whore) 1972, Lady Macbeth (Macbeth) 1972, Célimène (The Misanthrope), Washington and New York 1973, 1975, The Governor's Wife (Phaedra Britannica) 1975, rejoined Nat. Theatre at the Lyttelton to play Ilona in The Guardsman 1978. *Other stage appearances include:* Heloise (Abelard and Heloise) London 1970, Los Angeles, New York 1971, Eliza Doolittle (Pygmalion) London 1974, Ruth Carson (Night and Day) London 1978, Colette, Seattle and Denver 1982, Hesione Hushabye (Heartbreak House) London 1983, Rita in Little Eyolf, London 1985, Cleopatra in Antony and Cleopatra, Chichester 1985, Wildfire, London 1986, Phyllis in Follies 1987, Love Letters, San Francisco 1990, Cleopatra in All for Love, London 1991, Berlin Bertie 1992, Medea 1993 (London and Broadway), Mother Courage and Her Children, London, 1995, Who's Afraid of Virginia Woolf?, London 1996–97. *TV appearances include:* Sentimental Agent 1963, A Comedy of Errors 1964, The Hothouse 1964, Emma Peel (The Avengers) 1965–67, Women Beware Women 1965, Married Alive 1970, Diana (U.S. series) 1973, In This House of Brede 1975, Three Piece Suite 1977, Clytemnestra in The Serpent Son 1979, The Marquise 1980, Hedda Gabler 1981, Rita Allmers in Little Eyolf 1982, Regan in King Lear 1983, Witness for the Prosecution 1983, Bleak House 1984, Host, Held in Trust, A Hazard of Hearts 1987, Worst Witch 1987, Unexplained Laughter 1989, Mother Love 1989, Host, Mystery! 1989 (U.S.A.), Zoya 1995, The Haunting of Helen Walker 1995, Moll Flanders 1996, Samson & Delilah 1996, Rebecca 1996 (Emmy Award for Best Supporting Actress 1997). *Films include:* A Midsummer Night's Dream 1969, The Assassination Bureau 1969, On Her Majesty's Secret Service 1969, Julius Caesar 1970, The Hospital 1971, Theatre of Blood 1973, A Little Night Music 1977, The Great Muppet Caper 1981, Evil under the Sun 1982, A Good Man in Africa 1993. *Publications:* No Turn Unstoned 1982, So To The Land 1994. *Leisure interests:* reading, writing, cooking, travel. *Address:* c/o Duncan Heath, ICM, Oxford House, 76 Oxford Street, London, W1N 0AX, England.

RIGGIO, Leonard; American business executive; b. 1941, N.Y.; m. (divorced); two d.; ed. Brooklyn Tech. High School, New York Univ.; fmrly. with New York Univ. campus bookstore; opened Waverly Student Book Exchange 1965; acquired Barnes & Noble Bookstore 1971, now Chair., C.E.O. Barnes & Noble Inc. *Address:* c/o Barnes & Noble Inc., 122 5th Avenue, New York, NY 10011, U.S.A.

RIGGS, Lorrin Andrews, A.B., M.A., PH.D.; American psychologist; b. 11 June 1912, Harput, Turkey; s. of Ernest Wilson Riggs and Alice (Shepard) Riggs; m. 1st Doris Robinson 1937 (died 1993); two s.; m. 2nd Caroline Cressman 1994; ed. Dartmouth Coll. and Clark Univ.; N.R.C. Fellow, Biological Sciences, Univ. of Pa. 1936–37; Instructor Univ. of Vermont 1937–38, 1939–41; with Brown Univ. 1938–39, 1941–, Research Assoc., Research Psychologist Nat. Defence Research Cttee., Asst. Prof., Assoc. Prof. 1938–51,

Prof. of Psychology 1951–, L. Herbert Ballou Foundation Prof. of Psychology 1960–68, Edgar J. Marston Univ. Prof. of Psychology 1968–77, Prof. Emer. 1977–; Guggenheim Fellow, Univ. of Cambridge 1971–72; mem. American Psychological Asscn. (Div. Pres. 1962–63), Eastern Psychological Asscn. (Pres. 1975–76), A.A.A.S. (Chair. and Vice-Pres. Section 1 1964), Optical Soc. of America, N.A.S., American Physiological Soc., Int. Brain Research Org., Soc. for Neuroscience, Soc. of Experimental Psychologists, American Acad. of Arts and Sciences, Asscn. for Research in Vision and Ophthalmology (Pres. 1977); Howard Crosby Warren Medal, Soc. of Experimental Psychologists 1957, Jonas S. Friedenwald Award, Asscn. for Research in Ophthalmology 1966, Edgar D. Tillyer Award, Optical Soc. of America 1969, Charles F. Prentice Award, American Acad. of Optometry 1973, Distinguished Scientific Contribution Award, American Psychological Asscn. 1974, Kenneth Craik Award, Cambridge Univ. 1979, Frederick Ives Medal, Optical Soc. of America 1982, William James Fellow, American Psychological Soc. 1989. *Publications:* numerous scientific articles on vision and physiological psychology. *Address:* 80 Lyme Road, Hanover, NH 03755, U.S.A. *Telephone;* (603) 643-2342.

RIGHI-LAMBERTINI, H.E. Cardinal Egano; Italian ecclesiastic; b. 22 Feb. 1906, Casalecchio di Reno, Bologna; ordained priest 1929; Titular Archbishop of Doclea 1960–79; cr. Cardinal 1979; fmr. mem. Council for the Public Affairs of the Church, Sacred Congregation for the Bishops, Secr. for Non-Christians; Hon. Pres. Cen. Comm. for Sacred Art in Italy; Hon. mem. Pontifical Acad.; Deacon of S. Giovanni Bosco in Via Tuscolana. *Address:* Piazza della Città Leonina 9, 00193 Rome, Italy. *Telephone:* 687.94.63.

RIIS, Povl, M.D.; Danish physician; b. 28 Dec. 1925, Copenhagen; s. of Lars Otto Riis and Eva Elisabeth (née Erdmann) Riis; m. Else Harne 1954; one s. three d.; ed. Univ. of Copenhagen; Specialist in internal medicine 1960, gastroenterology 1963; Head of Medical Dept. B, Gentofte Univ. Hosp. 1963–76; Prof. of Internal Medicine, Univ. of Copenhagen 1974–; Head of Gastroenterological Dept. C, Herlev Co. Hosp. 1976–96; Asst. Ed. Journal of the Danish Medical Asscn. 1957–67, Chief Ed. 1967–90; Ed. Bibliothek for Laeger 1965–90, Danish Medical Bulletin 1968–90, Nordic Medicine 1984–91; mem. Bd., Danish Soc. for Internal Medicine 1962–67, Danish Anti-Cancer League 1970–75, Danish Soc. for Theoretical and Applied Therapy 1972–77, Int. Union against Cancer 1978–86; mem. Danish Medical Research Council 1968–74, Chair. 1972–74; mem. Danish Science Advisory Bd. 1972–74, Co-Chair. 1974; mem. Nordic Scientific Co-ordination Cttee. for Medicine 1968–72, Chair. 1970–72; Chair. Nordic Medical Publs. Cttee. 1970–72; Vice-Pres. European Science Foundation (ESF) 1974–77, mem. Exec. Council 1977–83; Chair. ESF Cttee. on Genetic Manipulation 1975–77, Chair. ESF Liaison Cttee. on Genetic Manipulation 1977–83; mem. Council for Int. Org. of Medical Sciences Advisory Cttee. 1977; mem. Trustees Foundation of 1870 1976, Trier-Hansen Foundation 1977, Hartmann Prize Cttee. 1986, Buhl Olesen Foundation 1982, Madsen Foundation 1978, Jakobsen Foundation 1989, Brinch Foundation 1990–96; Chair. Danish Central Scientific-Ethical Cttee. 1979–98, Nat. Medical Bd. Danish Red Cross 1985–94, Int. Org. of Inflammatory Bowel Diseases 1986–89; mem. Nat. Cttee. on Scientific Misconduct 1992–; Danish Foreign Office del. Helsinki negotiations, Hamburg 1980; mem. Bd. Danish Helsinki Cttee.; mem. Int. Cttee. of Medical Journal Eds. 1980–90, Editorial Bd., Acta med. Scand., Journal Int. Medicine 1980, Ethics Bd., Danish Medical Asscn. 1980–82, WHO European Advisory Cttee. for Medical Research 1980–85, Scientific Bd., Danish Nat. Encyclopaedia 1991–, Editorial Bd. JAMA 1994–; Vice-Dean Faculty of Medicine, Univ. of Copenhagen 1979–82; Chair. Nat. Medical Bd. of Danish Red Cross; Chair. Nat. Center for First Aid and Health Promotion -1991, AgeForum 1996–; Hon. mem. Icelandic Medical Asscn. 1978, Danish Soc. of Gastroenterology 1995; Hon. M.R.C.P. (U.K.) 1991; Hon. D.Med. (Univ. of Odense) 1996; Alfred Benzon Prize, August Krogh Prize 1974, Christensen-Ceson Prize 1976, Klein-Prize 1980, Barfred-Pedersen Prize 1980, Hagedorn Prize 1983, Nordic Gastro Prize 1983, Nordic Language Prize in Medicine 1993. *Publications:* Contributor: Handbook of Scientific Methodology (in Danish) 1971–, World Medical Asscn. Helsinki Declaration 1975, We Shall All Die—but how? (in Danish) 1977; Author: Handbook of Internal Medicine (in Danish) 1968, Grenzen der Forschung 1980; Community and Ethics (in Danish) 1984, Medical Ethics (in Danish) 1985, Ethical Issues in Preventive Medicine 1985, Medical Science and the Advancement of World Health 1985, Bearing and Perspective 1988, The Appleton Consensus 1988, Face Death 1989, Ethics in Health Education 1990, The Future of Medical Journals 1991, Research on Man: Ethics and Law 1991, Scientific Misconduct—Good Scientific Practice 1992, Health Care in Europe after 1992 1992, A Better Health Service–but how? (in Danish), The Culture of General Education 1996; many articles in medical journals; lyrics to contemporary Danish compositions. *Leisure interests:* tennis, music, mountain walking. *Address:* Nerievej 7, 2900 Hellerup, Denmark (Home). *Telephone:* 39629688. *Fax:* 39629588.

RIKLIS, Meshulam; American business executive; b. 2 Dec. 1923, Istanbul, Turkey; s. of Pinhas and Betty (Guberer) Riklis; m. 1st Judith Stern 1944; one s. two d.; m. 2nd Pia Zadora 1977; one s. one d.; ed. High School, Israel, Univ. of Mexico and Ohio State Univ.; Co-Dir. Youth Activities and Mil. Training, Hertzlia High School, Tel-Aviv 1942; went to U.S. 1947, naturalized 1955; Teacher of Hebrew, Talmud Torah School, Minneapolis 1951; Research Dept., Piper, Jaffray and Hopwood 1951–53, Sales Rep. 1953–56; Chair., C.E.O. Rapid Electrotype Co., American Color-type Co. 1956–57; Pres. Rapid-American Corpn. 1957–73, C.E.O. 1957, Chair. 1958, Pres., C.E.O. 1957–73, Chair., C.E.O. 1973–76, Chair., Pres., C.E.O. 1976–; Vice-Chair. McCrory Corpn. 1960–69, Vice-Chair. Exec. Cttee. and Dir. 1970–, Chair. 1975–85; owner Riviera Hotel, Las Vegas. *Address:* Riklis Family Corporation, 2901 Las Vegas Blvd, Las Vegas, NV 89109; McCrory Corpn., 1700 Broadway, Suite 1403, New York, NY 10019, U.S.A.

RILEY, Bridget Louise, C.H., C.B.E., A.R.C.A.; British artist; b. 24 April 1931, London; d. of John Fisher and the late Bessie Louise (née Gladstone) Riley; ed. Cheltenham Ladies' Coll., Goldsmiths Coll. of Art and Royal Coll. of Art, London; first one-woman exhbn. in London at Gallery One 1962, followed by others in England, America, Switzerland, Australia and Japan; has exhibited in group shows in Australia, Italy, France, Holland, Germany, Israel, America, Japan and Argentina; represented Great Britain at Biennale des Jeunes, Paris 1965, at Venice Biennale 1968; retrospective exhbn. Europe and U.K. 1970–72; second retrospective exhbn. touring America, Australia and Japan 1978–80; Arts Council Touring Exhbn. 1984–85; paintings, drawings, and prints in public collections in England, Ireland, Switzerland, Netherlands, Austria, Germany, Japan, Israel, America, Australia and New Zealand; founder mem. and fmr. Dir. S.P.A.C.E. Ltd.; mem. R.S.A.; Trustee, Nat. Gallery 1981–88; Hon. Dr. of Letters (Manchester Univ.) 1976, (Exeter) 1997, Dr. h.c. (Ulster) 1986, (Oxford) 1993, (Cambridge) 1995, (De Montfort) 1996. Hon. D.Litt (Cambridge) 1995; AICA Critics Prize 1963; Prize in Open Section, John Moores Liverpool Exhbn. 1963; Peter Stuyvesant Foundation Travel Bursary to U.S.A. 1964; Major Painting Prize, Venice Biennale 1968; Prize at Tokyo Print Biennale 1971; Gold Medal at Grafikk-bienniale, Fredrikstad, Norway 1980; *Address:* c/o Karsten Schubert Ltd., 41-42 Foley Street, London, W1P 7LD, England.

RILEY, Sir Ralph, Kt., M.A., PH.D., D.SC., F.R.S.; British scientist; b. 23 Oct. 1924, Scarborough; s. of Ralph and Clara Riley; m. Joan Elizabeth Norrington 1949; two d.; ed. Univ. of Sheffield; Demonstrator, Dept. of Botany, Univ. of Sheffield 1951–52, with Plant Breeding Inst., Cambridge 1952–78, Head, Cytogenetics Dept. 1955–71, Dir. of Inst. 1971–78; Sec. and Deputy Chair., Agricultural and Food Research Council, London 1978–85; Fellow of Wolfson Coll. 1967–92, Emer. Fellow 1992–; Chair. Bd. Rothamsted Experimental Station 1990–; mem. Bd. Int. Rice Research Inst. (IRRI) 1973–78; mem. Bd. Int. Centre Agric. Research in Dry Areas (ICARDA) 1989–93, Tech. Advisory Cttee. of Consultative Group for Int. Agricultural Research 1993–; Pres. Int. Congress on Genetics 1993; Fellow Indian Nat. Acad. of Agricultural Sciences; mem. Indian Science Acad., Agric. Acad. of France; Foreign Assoc. mem. N.A.S.; Trustee Lawes Agricultural Trust; Royal Medal (Royal Soc.) 1981; Wolf Prize in Agric. (shared) 1986. *Publications:* scientific papers and reviews on plant breeding and the cytology and genetics of crop plants. *Leisure interest:* village life. *Address:* 16 Gog Magog Way, Stapleford, Cambridge, CB2 5BQ, England. *Telephone:* (01223) 843845. *Fax:* (01223) 845825.

RILEY, Richard Wilson, LL.B.; American politician; b. 2 Jan. 1933, Greenville, South Carolina; s. of E. P. and Martha Dixon Riley; m. Ann Yarborough 1957; three s. one d.; ed. Greenville Sr. High School, Furman Univ. and South Carolina School of Law; Lieut. in U.S. Navy; Legal Counsel to U.S. Senate Cttee. of Olin D. Johnston 1960; with family law firm 1961–62; mem. S.C. House of Reps. 1962–66, S.C. Senate 1966–76; S.C. State Chair. for Jimmy Carter's Presidential Election Campaign 1976; Gov. of South Carolina 1979–87; Personnel Dir. for Bill Clinton's Transition Team 1991–92; Sec. of Educ. Jan. 1993–. *Address:* Department of Education, 600 Independence Avenue, S.W., Washington, DC 20202, U.S.A.

RILEY, Terry Mitchell, M.A.; American composer, pianist and raga singer; b. 24 June 1935, Colfax, Calif.; s. of Wilma Ridlofi and Charles Riley; m. Ann Yvonne Smith 1958; three c.; ed. San Francisco State Univ. and Univ. of California, and pvt. studies with Duane Hampton, Adolf Baller and Pandit Pran Nath; taught music composition and N. Indian Raga at Mills Coll. 1971–83; freelance composer and performer 1961–; launched Minimal Music movt. with composition and first performance of In C 1964; John Simon Guggenheim Prize 1980. *Compositions include:* The Harp of New Albion for Solo Piano in Just Intonation, Salome Dances for Peace (string quartet), Cadenza on the Night Plain, Sunrise of the Planetary Dream Collector, Sri Camel, a Rainbow in Curved Air, In C, The Ten Voices of the Two Prophets, Persian Surgery Dervishes, Jade Palace (for large orchestra) 1989, June Buddhas 1991, The Sounds (concerto for string quartet and orchestra) 1991, The Saint Adolf Ring (chamber opera) 1992, Ritmos and Melos 1993, El Hombe (piano quintet) 1993, Ascension (solo guitar) 1993, The Heaven Ladder. *Leisure interests:* music, gardens and orchards. *Address:* 13699 Moonshine Road, Camptonville, CA 95922, U.S.A. *Telephone:* (916) 288-3522. *Fax:* (916) 288-3468.

RILLING, Helmuth, D.PHIL., D.THEOL.; German conductor, professor of music and church music director; b. 29 May 1933, Stuttgart; s. of Eugen Rilling and Hildegard Plieninger; m. Martina Greiner 1967; two d.; ed. protestant theological seminars of Schöntal and Urach, Staatliche Hochschule für Musik, Stuttgart, studied organ with Fernando Germani, Conservatorio di Santa Cecilia, Rome and conducting with Leonard Bernstein, New York; organist and choirmaster, Gedächtniskirche, Stuttgart 1957–98; taught organ and conducting, Berliner Kirchenmusikschule, Berlin-Spandau and Dir., Spandauer Kantorei 1963–66; Prof. of Conducting, Staatliche Hochschule für Musik, Frankfurt 1966–85; taught at Ind. Univ., Bloomington, U.S.A. 1976–77; Dir. Frankfurter Kantorei 1969–81; f. Summer

Festival (now Oregon Bach Festival), Eugene, U.S.A. 1970–; Founder and Dir. Gächinger Kantorei, Stuttgart 1954–, Figuralchor of the Gedächtniskirche, Stuttgart 1957–80, Bach-Collegium Stuttgart 1965–, Sommer Acad. Johann Sebastian Bach Stuttgart 1979–, Int. Bach Acad. Stuttgart 1981–, Bach Acad. Tokyo, Buenos Aires 1983, Real Filharmonía de Galicia, Santiago de Compostela, Spain 1996–, Prague, Cracow, Moscow, Budapest, Caracas; world-wide int. appearances with own ensembles and as guest conductor and guest prof.; regular co-operation with Israel Philharmonic Orchestra, The Cleveland Orchestra, Boston Symphony Orchestra, Toronto Symphony Orchestra, New York Philharmonic, Vienna Philharmonic Orchestra, Münchner Philharmoniker, Radio-Sinfonie-Orchester Munich; mem. Kungl. Musikaliska Akad. Stockholm 1993; Hon. Dr. Fine Arts (Concordia Coll., U.S.A.) 1990; Distinguished Service Award (Univ. of Oregon) 1985, Harvard Glee Club Medal 1989; UNESCO/IMC Music Prize 1994; Theodor-Heuss Prize 1995. *Publications:* Johann Sebastian Bach, Matthäus-Passion, Einführung und Studienanleitung 1975, Johann Sebastian Bach's H-moll-Messe 1975. *Recordings:* all the sacred cantatas and oratorios of J. S. Bach, complete recording of J. S. Bach's work 1998–(2000) and many others. *Address:* Internationale Bachakadermie, Johann-Sebastian-Bach-Platz, Hasenbergsteige 3, 70178 Stuttgart, Germany. *Telephone:* 0711 61921-0. *Fax:* 0711 619212-3.

RIMAWI, Fahad Namr al-, B.A.; Jordanian journalist; b. 1942, Palestine; m.; two s. one d.; ed. Cairo Univ., Egypt; Ed. Difa (newspaper) 1965–67; Ed. in Chief, Jordan News Agency 1968–70; Sec. Editorial Bd. of Afkar (magazine) 1970–73; Dir. Investigating Dept. of Al-Raie (newspaper) 1975–76; writer Al-Destour (newspaper) 1978–81; Political writer, Al-Raiue (newspaper) 1981–85; Corresp. al Talie'ah (magazine) Paris 1982–85; political writer 1985–94; Publr. and Ed.-in-Chief Al Majd (weekly). *Publications:* Mawaweel Fi al Layl Al Taweel, short stories in Arabic 1982. *Address:* P.O. Box 926856, Amman 1110 Jordan. *Telephone:* (9626) 553 0553 (Office); (9626) 5160615 (Home). *Fax:* (9626) 553 0552.

RIMINGTON, Dame Stella, D.C.B., M.A.; British civil servant; b. 1935; m. John Rimington 1963; two d.; ed. Nottingham High School for Girls, Edin. Univ.; Dir.-Gen. Security Service 1992–96; Dir. (non-exec.) Marks and Spencer 1997–, BG PLC 1997–, G.K.R. Group 1997–; Chair. Inst. of Cancer Research 1997–; Hon. LL.B. (Nottingham) 1995, (Exeter) 1996; Hon. Air Commodore 7006 (VR) Squadron Royal Auxiliary Air Force 1997–. *Address:* P.O. Box 1604, London, SW1P 1XB, England.

RINDLER, Wolfgang, PH.D.; British university professor; b. 18 May 1924, Vienna; s. of Dr. Ernst Rindler; m. 1st Phyllis Berla 1959 (died 1966); m. 2nd Linda Veret 1977; two s. one d.; ed. Ruthin Grammar School, Liverpool Univ., Imperial Coll., London; asst. lecturer Univ. of Liverpool 1947–49; lecturer Sir John Cass Coll., London 1949–56; Asst. Prof. Cornell Univ., U.S.A. 1956–63; Assoc. and Full Prof. Southwest Center for Advanced Studies, Dallas, Texas 1963–69, Prof. Univ. of Texas at Dallas 1969–; Visiting Prof. Univ. of Vienna, Univ. of Rome, Max-Planck Inst. at Munich and Potsdam, King's Coll. London; Visiting Fellow Churchill Coll., Cambridge 1990; mem. Foreign Editorial Bd. Rendiconti di Matematica 1984–; Hon. mem. Austrian Acad. of Sciences 1998; Assoc. Ed. American Journal of Physics 1988–91; Gold Medal of Honour, City of Vienna 1996. *Publications:* Special Relativity 1960, Essential Relativity 1969, Introduction to Special Relativity 1982, Spinors and Space-Time (with R. Penrose) Vol. I 1984, Vol. II 1986, numerous research and encyclopedia articles on special and gen. relativity and cosmology. *Address:* Physics Department, University of Texas at Dallas, Richardson, TX 75083 (Office); 7110 Spring Valley Road, Dallas, TX 75240, U.S.A. (Home). *Telephone:* (972) 883-2880 (Office); (972) 387-9768 (Home).

RING, Wolfhard, DR.RER.NAT.; German business executive; b. 15 April 1930, Cologne; m. Karina Hellmann 1968; two s.; ed. Univs. of Göttingen and Karlsruhe; Research Asst. Univ. of S. Carolina; Chemie-Konzern Hüls AG, Marl 1960, Dir. of Research and Devt. 1981, Exec. Vice-Pres. and mem. Bd. Dirs. Hüls America Inc. 1985; mem. Bd. Rütgerswerke AG 1989, Chair. Bd. 1989–95; Visiting Prof. Univ. of Münster 1977–. *Leisure interests:* music, history, modern art. *Address:* Rütgerswerke AG, Mainzer Landstrasse 217, 60326 Frankfurt am Main, Germany. *Telephone:* (069) 7592-544. *Fax:* (069) 7592-400.

RINGADOO, Sir Veerasamy, Kt., G.C.M.G., BAR.-AT-LAW; Mauritian politician; b. 1920, Port Louis; s. of Nagaya Ringadoo; m. Lydie Vadamootoo 1954; one s. one d.; ed. Port Louis Grammar School and London School of Econs., England; called to the Bar 1949; elected Municipal Councillor 1956; elected mem. Legis. Council for Moka-Flacq 1951–67; Minister for Labour and Social Security 1959–64, for Educ. 1964–67, of Agric. and Natural Resources 1967–68, of Finance 1968–82; Gov.-Gen. of Mauritius 1986–92; First Pres. of Mauritius March–June 1992; attended London Constitutional Conf. 1965; First mem., Legis. Assembly (M.L.A.) for Quartier Militaire and Moka 1967–86 (Lab); Gov. IMF; Chair. African Devt. Bank and African Devt. Fund 1977–78; Officer, Ordre National Malgache 1969, Médaille de l'Assemblée Nat. Française 1971; Hon. Fellow L.S.E. 1976; Hon. LL.D. (Mauritius) 1975, Hon. D.Litt. (Andhra Univ., India) 1978. *Address:* Cnr. Antelme and Farquhar Streets, Quatre Bornes, Mauritius.

RINSER, Luise; German author; b. 30 April 1911, Pitzling/Oberbayern; d. of Joseph Rinser and Luise Rinser; m. 1st Horst-Guenther Schnell 1939 (deceased); two s.; m. 2nd Carl Orff (died 1982); School teacher 1935–39; works banned 1941; imprisoned 1944–45; after World War II became literary critic of Neue Zeitung, Munich; now free-lance writer; mem. Akad. der Künste, PEN Centre of Germany; most of her books translated into 24 languages; Hon. Citizen Rocca di Papa, Italy, many literary prizes. *Publications:* novels: Die gläsernen Ringe 1940, Mitte des Lebens 1950, Daniela 1953, Abenteuer der Tugend 1957, Ich Bin Tobias 1968, Der schwarze Esel 1974, Mirjam 1983, Silberschuld 1987, Abaelards Liebe 1991; short stories: Ein Bündel weisser Narzissen 1956, Geschichten aus der Loewengrube 1986; essays: Schwerpunkt, Über die Hoffnung, Vom Sinn der Traurigkeit, Unterentwickeltes Land Frau, Wie, wenn wir ärmer würden 1974, Dem Tode geweiht 1974; letters: Hochzeit der Widersprüche 1973, Reinheit und Ekstase: Briefe über die Liebe 1997; diaries: Gefängnis/Tagebuch 1946, Baustelle 1970, Grenz-Übergänge 1972, Kriegsspielzeug 1978, Winterfruehling 1982, Im Dunkeln Singen 1984, Wachsender Mond 1988; plays: Philemon, Leo und Sonja Tolstoi 1991; travel: Wenn die Wale kämpfen 1976, Khomeini und der islamische Gottesstaat 1979, Nordkoreanisches Reise-Tagebuch 1981; autobiography: Den Wolf umarmen 1981, Das Geheimnis des Brunnens; children's books: Bruder Feuer 1975, Das Squirrel, Drei Kinder und ein Stern 1988; autobiog. *Leisure interests:* politics, theology, music. *Address:* I-00040 Rocca di Papa, Rome, Italy.

RINTZLER, Marius Adrian; German opera and concert singer; b. 14 March 1932, Bucharest, Romania; m. Sanda Dragomir 1964; ed. Acad. of Music, Bucharest; soloist with Bucharest Philharmonic 1959; début in opera in Bucharest as Don Basilio in Il Barbiere di Siviglia 1964; went to Germany 1966; leading bass at Düsseldorf's Deutsche Oper am Rhein 1968–; guest singer with major opera cos., including Metropolitan, San Francisco, Glyndebourne, Paris, Brussels, Munich; repertoire includes various roles in Richard Strauss' Rosenkavalier (Ochs), Capriccio (La Roche), Schweigsame Frau (Morosus), in Rossini's La Cenerentola (Don Magnifico), Il Barbiere (Bartolo), in Richard Wagner's Ring (Alberich), in Mozart's Don Giovanni (Leporello), Die Entführung (Osmin); appears with major symphony orchestras in Europe and U.S.A., including Philharmonia (London), Berlin Philharmonic, Cleveland Symphony; also gives recitals, TV appearances in England, Germany and France; Kammersänger. *Address:* Friedingstrasse 18, 40625 Düsseldorf, Germany. *Telephone:* (0211) 297083.

RIORDAN, Richard; American politician and business executive; b. 1930, Flushing, N.Y.; m. 1st Eugenia Riordan; six c. (two deceased); m. 2nd Jill Riordan; Mayor of Los Angeles 1993–; Co-founder LEARN 1991; mem. Republican Party. *Address:* Los Angeles City Hall, 200 N. Spring Street, Suite 305, Los Angeles, CA 90012, U.S.A.

RÍOS, Juan; Peruvian poet, dramatist, journalist and critic; b. 28 Sept. 1914, Barranco, Lima; s. of Rogelio Ríos and Victoria Rey (de Ríos); m. Rosa Saco 1946; one d.; National Prize for Playwriting 1946, 1950, 1952, 1954, 1960; Nat. Poetry Prize 1948, 1953; Writers' Fellowship, UNESCO, Europe and Egypt 1960–61; mem. Academia Peruana de la Lengua Correspondiente a la Española. *Publications:* Canción de Siempre 1941, Malstrom 1941, La Pintura Contemporánea en el Perú 1946, Teatro (I) 1961, Ayar Manko 1963, Primera Antología Poética 1982. *Address:* Bajada de Baños 109, Barranco, Lima 04, Peru. *Telephone:* 671799 (Lima).

RÍOS MONTT, Gen. Efraín; Guatemalan politician and army officer; b. 1927; joined army 1943; defence posting, Washington, D.C. 1973; contested presidential election for Christian Democratic coalition 1974; Mil. Attaché, Madrid; fmr. Commdr. Honour Guard Brigade; Dir. Mil. Acad.; installed as leader of mil. junta after coup March 1982; Minister of Nat. Defence March–Sept. 1982; Pres. of Guatemala, also C.-in-C. of the Army 1982–83; overthrown Aug. 1983; leader Frente Republicano Guatemalteco; Pres. of Guatemalan Congress 1995–96. *Address:* Frente Republicano Guatemalteco, 6a Avenida A 3-18 Zona 1, Guatemala City, Guatemala. *Telephone:* 250-1778.

RIPA DI MEANA, Carlo; Italian politician and journalist; b. 15 Aug. 1929, Marina di Pietrasanta, Lucca; m. Marina Punturieri; journalist on Il Lavoro (weekly journal of the Confederazione Generale Italiana del Lavoro) and on L'Unità (Italian daily) 1950–53; co-f. and ran weekly Nuova Generazione 1953–56; co-f. and Ed. magazine Passato e Presente 1957; publisher's ed. for Feltrinelli and Rizzoli 1958–66; resgnd. from Italian CP 1957, joined Italian Socialist Party 1958; Sec.-Gen. Club Turati, Milan 1967–76; Regional Councillor, Lombardy, Leader, Socialist Party group in the Council 1970–82; mem. bd. La Scala Theatre, Milan 1970–74; Chair. Venice Biennale 1974–79; head of int. relations, Italian Socialist Party 1979–80; mem. European Parl. 1979–; mem. Comm. of the European Communities (responsible for Citizen's Europe, information, culture and tourism) 1985–89, (responsible for communication) 1986–89, (responsible for environment, nuclear safety and civil protection) 1989–93; Minister for the Environment 1992–93, leader Green Party 1993–98 (left PSI); Chair. Istituto per la Cooperazione economica internazionale e i problemi dello sviluppo 1983–. *Publications:* Un viaggio in Viet Nam 1956, Dedicato a Raymond Roussel e alle sue impressioni d'Africa 1965, Il governo audiovisivo 1973. *Address:* European Parliament, Centre Européen, Plateau du Kirchberg, 2929 Luxembourg.

RIPKEN, Calvin Edward (Cal), Jr.; American professional baseball player; b. 24 Aug. 1960, Havre de Grace, Md.; player minor league teams in Bluefield, Miami, Charlotte, Rochester 1978–81; player Baltimore Orioles 1978–; highest single season fielding percentage 1990; maj. league record for consecutive games played (breaking Lou Gehrig's record of 2,131 in 1995), 2,632 ending in 1998; Rookie of the Year, Int. League 1981; Rookie of the Year, Baseball Writers Asscn., American League 1982; Silver Slugger Award 1983–86, 1989, 1991, 1993—94; Golden Glove Award 1991–92; Sportsman of the Year, Sports Illustrated 1995; numerous other awards. *Address:* c/o Baltimore Orioles, Oriole Park at Camden Yards, 333 West Camden Street, Baltimore, MD 21201, U.S.A.

RIPPON, Angela; British broadcaster and journalist; b. 12 Oct. 1944, Plymouth, Devon; d. of John Rippon and Edna Rippon; m. Christopher Dare 1967; ed. Plymouth Grammar School; Ed., Producer and Presenter, Westward Television (ITV) 1967–73; Presenter and Reporter, BBC TV Plymouth 1966–69; Reporter, BBC TV Nat. News 1973–75, Newsreader 1975–81; Presenter TV-am Feb.–April 1983, LBC–1994; Arts and Entertainment Corresp. for WNEV-TV, Boston, 1984–85; Vice-Pres. Int. Club for Women in TV 1979–; Dir. Nirex. 1986–; Newsreader of the Year 1975, 1976, 1977; TV Personality of the Year 1977. *TV appearances include:* Angela Rippon Reporting (documentary), Antiques Roadshow, In the Country, Compere, Eurovision Song Contest 1976, Royal Wedding 1981, Masterteam (BBC) 1985, 1986, 1987, Come Dancing 1988–, What's My Line? 1988–. *Radio series include:* Angela Rippon's Morning Report for LBC 1992, Angela Rippon's Drive Time Show, LBC 1993. *Publications:* Riding, In the Country, Victoria Plum (children's stories), Mark Phillips—The Man and his Horses 1982, Angela Rippon's West Country 1982, Badminton: A Celebration 1987. *Leisure interests:* cooking, gardening, riding. *Address:* c/o I.M.G., Media House, 3 Burlington Lane, Chiswick, London, W4 2TH, England. *Telephone:* 0181-747 9977.

RIS, Hans, PH.D.; American professor of zoology; b. 15 June 1914, Bern, Switzerland; s. of August Ris and Martha Ris; m. 1st Hania W. Wislicka 1947 (divorced 1971); one s. one d.; m. 2nd Theron Caldwell 1980; ed. Univs. of Bern, Switzerland, Rochester and New York and Columbia and Yale Univs.; Lecturer in Zoology, Col. Univ. 1941–42; Asst. Prof. of Biology, Johns Hopkins Univ. 1942–44; Asst. then Assoc. Prof. of Physiology, Rockefeller Inst., New York 1944–49; Assoc. Prof. of Zoology, Univ. of Wis., Madison 1949–53, Prof. 1953–84, Prof. Emer. 1984–, Dir. Madison High Voltage Electron Microscope Facility 1969–86; Hon. Prof. Beijing Univ. 1995–; mem. N.A.S.; Fellow American Acad. of Arts and Sciences. *Publications:* 100 publs. of original research results in scientific journals 1938–. *Leisure interests:* reading, photography, hiking, camping, skiing. *Address:* Zoology Research, University of Wisconsin, 1117 W. Johnson, Madison, WI 53706; 5542 Riverview Drive, Waunakee, WI 53597, U.S.A. (Home). *Telephone:* (608) 262-2694 (Office); (608) 849-7341 (Home). *Fax:* (608) 265-3083.

RISCHEL, Jørgen, M.A., D.PHIL.; Danish professor of linguistics and phonetics; b. 10 Aug. 1934, Kullerup; s. of Ejner Rischel and Gunnild Rischel; m. Anna-Grethe Rischel 1961; three d.; ed. Univs. of Copenhagen, Iceland and Oslo; lecturer in Danish, Univ. of Bergen, Norway 1960–61; Assoc. Ed. Norwegian-English Dictionary Project, Univ. of Wis. 1961–62; Asst. Prof., later Assoc. Prof. Univ. of Copenhagen 1963–78, Prof. of Linguistics 1978–81, Prof. of Phonetics 1981–98; Visiting Prof. Univ. of Calif. 1978; research work in S.E. Asia 1982–, full-time 1997–; Co-Ed. Acta Linguistica Hafniensia to 1996, Folia Linguistica, and Int. Journal of American Linguistics; Dir. Int. Critical Pali Dictionary project 1996; mem. Royal Danish Acad. of Sciences and Letters 1978–, Acad. Europaea 1989; mem. Danish Research Council for the Humanities 1988–90, Comm. for Scientific Research in Greenland 1990–, Comité Int. Permanent de Linguistes 1990–; Kt., Order of Dannebrog. *Publications:* The Lepchas (with Halfdan Siiger) Vol. II 1967, Topics in West Greenlandic Phonology (Essay) 1974, Pioneers of Eskimo Grammar (with Knut Bergsland) 1987, Minor Mlabri — A Hunter-Gatherer Language of Northern Indochina 1995, Aspects of Danish Prosody (with Hans Basbøll) 1995, co-author of dictionaries of various languages and ed. of works on the Faroe Islands. *Address:* Institute of General and Applied Linguistics, University of Copenhagen, 80 Njalsgade, 2300 Copenhagen S (Univ.); 57 Stenhøjgaardsvej, 3460 Birkerød, Denmark (Home). *Telephone:* 35-328660 (Univ.); 42-816803 (Home). *Fax:* 35-328635.

RISK, Sir Thomas Neilson, Kt., LL.D., F.R.S.E.; British banker; b. 13 Sept. 1922, Glasgow; s. of late Ralph Risk, C.B.E., M.C., and Margaret N. Risk; m. Suzanne Eiloart 1949; four s. (one deceased); ed. Kelvinside Acad. and Glasgow Univ.; Partner, Maclay, Murray & Spens (Solicitors), Glasgow and Edin. 1950–81; Gov. Bank of Scotland 1981–91; Dir. Standard Life Assurance Co. 1965–88, Chair. 1969–77; Dir. The British Linen Bank Ltd. 1968–91, Gov. 1977–86; Dir. Scottish Financial Enterprise 1986–90, Chair. 1986–89; Chair. Univ. of Glasgow Trust 1992–; Dir. Barclays Bank PLC 1983–85, Howden Group PLC 1971–87, Merchants Trust PLC 1973–94, MSA (Britain) Ltd., Shell U.K. Ltd. 1982–92, Bank of Wales PLC 1986–91; Hon. LL.D. (Glasgow) 1985, Dr. h.c. (Edin.) 1990. *Leisure interests:* golf, reading. *Address:* 10 Belford Place, Edinburgh, EH4 3DH, Scotland. *Telephone:* (0131) 332-9425.

RISTE, Olav, D.PHIL.; Norwegian historian; b. 11 April 1933, Volda; s. of Olav Riste and Bergliot Meidell; m. Ruth Pittman 1964; ed. Univs. of Oslo and Oxford; lecturer, Volda Gymnas 1963–64; Historian, Office of Mil. History (with leaves of absence) 1964–79, Dir. 1979–80; Research Fellow, Charles Warren Center, Harvard Univ. 1967–68; Visiting Scholar, L.S.E. 1971, 1986; Visiting Prof. Freie Univ. Berlin 1972–73; Dir. Research Centre for Defence History (with leaves of absence) 1980–87; Adjunct Prof. of History, Univ. of Bergen 1980–98, Univ. of Oslo 1998–; Guest Scholar, Woodrow Wilson Center, Washington, D.C. 1982; Dir. Norwegian Inst. for Defence Studies 1988–95, Research Dir. 1996–; Fellow, Norwegian Acad. of Science and Letters. *Publications:* The Neutral Ally 1965, Norway and the Second World War (ed.) 1966, Norway 1940–45: The Resistance Movement 1970, London-regjeringa: Norge i krigsalliansen 1940–45 I-II 1973–79, Western Security: The Formative Years (ed.) 1985, Norge i Krig: Utefront 1987, Otto Ruge: Felttoget (ed.) 1989, Fredsgeneralen (ed.) 1995, "Strengt hemmelig." Norsk etterretningsteneste 1945–70 (with A. Moland) 1997, "Top Secret". The Norwegian Intelligence Service 1945–1970 (with A. Moland) 1999. *Leisure interests:* classical music, skiing. *Address:* Husarveien 18, 1362 Billingstad, Norway. *Telephone:* 66-84-63-05.

RITBLAT, John Henry, F.S.V.A.; British business executive; b. 3 Oct. 1935; m. 1st Isabel Paja 1960 (died 1979); two s. one d.; m. 2nd Jill Rosemary (née Slotover) Zilkha 1986; ed. Dulwich Coll., Coll. of Estate Management, London Univ.; Chair. and Man. Dir. The British Land Co. PLC 1970–, Chair. and Chief Exec. The British Land Corpn. 1991–; Founder and Chair. Conrad Ritblat & Co., Consultant Surveyors and Valuers 1958, Man. Dir. 1970, Chair. Conrad Ritblat Group PLC 1993–; Chair. Milner Estates PLC; Man. Dir. Union Property Holdings (London) Ltd. 1969, Crown Estates Paving Commn. 1969–; mem. Bd. of Govs. Weizmann Inst. 1991–; Gov. London Business School 1991–; Dir. and Gov. R.A.M. 1998–; mem. Council, Business in the Community 1987–, Prince of Wales' Royal Parks Tree Appeal Cttee. 1987–, Patrons of British Art (Tate Gallery), Nat. Art. Collections Fund, British Library Bd. 1995–; Pres. British Ski Fed. 1994–; Life Fellow Royal Soc. of Arts; Life mem. Royal Inst. of G.B. *Leisure interests:* golf, skiing, Real tennis, books, architecture. *Address:* 10 Cornwall Terrace, Regent's Park, London, NW1 4QP, England. *Telephone:* 0171-486 4466. *Fax:* 0171-935 5552.

RITCHIE, Cedric E., O.C.; Canadian banker; b. 22 Aug. 1927, Upper Kent, N.B.; s. of E. Thomas Ritchie and Marion (née Henderson) Ritchie; m. Barbara Binnington 1956; ed. Bath High School, N.B.; joined The Bank of Nova Scotia, Bath N.B. 1945, served various branches in the Maritime Provs. and Montreal, Asst. Insp. 1954–56, Chief Accountant 1960–63, Asst. Gen. Man. Admin. 1963–66, Jt. Gen. Man. 1966–68, Chief Gen. Man. Int. 1968–70, Chief Gen. Man. 1970–72, Dir. 1972–, Pres. 1972–79, C.E.O. 1972–93, Chair. of Bd. 1974–95; Chair. and Dir. numerous other banks and trust cos. *Leisure interests:* golf, skiing, curling. *Address:* Scotia Plaza, 44 King Street W., Toronto, Ont. M5H 1H1, Canada.

RITCHIE, Ian, DIPL. ARCH. (DIST.), R.A., R.I.B.A., F.R.S.A.; British architect; b. 24 June 1947, Hove; s. of Christopher Ritchie and Mabel Long; m. Jocelyne van den Bossche 1972; one s.; ed. Polytechnic of Central London; project architect Foster Assocs. 1972–79; in pvt. practice, France 1976–78; ind. consultant 1979–81; founder partner Chrysalis Architects 1979–81; co-founder Rice Francis Ritchie 1981, Dir. 1981–87, Consultant 1987–89; Prin. Ian Ritchie Architects 1981–; comms. include: Eagle Rock House, Sussex, several projects for the Louvre, Paris, including work on the Louvre Pyramid, space-age pharmacy at Boves, France, cultural centre, Albert, France, planetarium, Greenwich, Ecology Gallery, Natural History Museum, London, office block, Stockley Business Park, three all-glass towers facing Reina Sofía Museum of Modern Art, Madrid, glass hall, Leipzig Int. Exhbn. Centre, Bermondsey Station, London Underground, railway station canopy, Würzburg, electricity pylons, France, Royal Opera House Theatre, Tower Bridge, London, work on Nat. Museum of Science, Tech. and Ind., La Villette, Paris, Crystal Palace Concert Platform, White City redevt., Crystal Palace redevt., Odyssey Belfast, Theatre Royal Production Centre, Plymouth, Scotland's Home of Tomorrow, Glasgow, West Pier, Brighton, 21st Century Monument, Dublin; numerous exhbns.; Chair. Touch the Earth 1988–; Visiting Prof. Tech. Univ. Vienna 1994–95; mem. Advisory Bd. London Docklands Devt. Corpn. 1990–96, Council Steel Construction Inst. 1994–97, Advisory Bd. City journal 1994–, Research Cttee. Nat. Maritime Museum 1995–97, Royal Fine Art Comm. 1995–(2001), UK Construction Foresight Panel 1996–98; Adviser, Natural History Museum 1991–95; numerous awards, including Iritecna Prize for Europe (Italy) 1991, Eric Lyons Memorial Award for Housing in Europe 1992, Commonwealth Asscn. of Architects Robert Matthews Award 1994, AIA Award 1997, Civic Trust Award 1997, RIBA Award, Stephen Lawrence Award 1998, RFAC Arts Building of the Year 1998. *Publications:* (Well) Connected Architecture 1994, The Biggest Glass Palace in the World 1997, Ian Ritchie. Tecnoecologie. *Leisure interests:* art, swimming, reading, writing, film-making. *Address:* 110 Three Colt Street, London, E14 8A2, England. *Telephone:* 0171-338 1100. *Fax:* 0171-338 1199.

RITCHIE, Ian Russell, M.A.; British television executive; b. 27 Nov. 1953, Leeds; s. of Hugh Ritchie and Sheelah Ritchie; m. Jill Middleton-Walker 1982; two s.; ed. Leeds Grammar School, Trinity Coll. Oxford; Barrister 1976-77; Industrial Relations Adviser, Eng. Employers' Fed. 1978–79; joined Granada TV 1980, Head Production Services 1987–88; Dir. of Resources, Tyne-Tees TV 1988–91, Man. Dir. 1991–, Group Deputy Chief Exec. Yorkshire Tyne-Tees TV PLC 1993; Man. Dir. Nottingham Studios, Cen. TV 1993–94; Man. Dir. London News Network 1994–96; C.E.O., subsequently C.O.O. Channel 5 Broadcasting 1996–97; Man. Dir. Russell Reynolds Assocs. 1997–. *Leisure interests:* golf, tennis, theatre. *Address:* Russell Reynolds Associates, 24 St. James's Square, London, SW1Y 4HZ, England. *Telephone:* 0171-830 8066. *Fax:* 0171-873 0069.

RITCHIE, J. Murdoch, PH.D., D.SC., F.R.S.; British professor of pharmacology; b. 10 June 1925, Aberdeen, Scotland; s. of Alexander Farquharson and

Agnes Jane Bremner; m. Brenda Rachel Bigland 1951; one s. one d.; ed. Univs. of Aberdeen and London; Research Physicist in Radar at Telecommunications Research Establishment, Malvern 1944–46; Jr. Lecturer in Physiology, Univ. Coll. London 1949–51; mem. of staff, Inst. for Medical Research, Mill Hill 1951–56; Asst. Prof. of Pharmacology, Albert Einstein Coll. of Medicine, New York, U.S.A. 1956–57, Assoc. Prof. 1958–63, Prof. 1963–68; Prof. and Chair. Dept. of Pharmacology, Yale Univ. School of Medicine, U.S.A. 1968–74, Dir. Div. of Biological Sciences 1975–78, Eugene Higgins Prof. of Pharmacology 1968–; Fellow Univ. Coll. London; Hon. M.A. (Yale) 1968; Hon. D. Sc. (Aberdeen) 1987; Van Dyke Memorial Award 1983. *Publications:* numerous scientific articles in Journal of Physiology, Proceedings of Royal Soc., Nature, Proceedings of N.A.S., U.S.A. *Leisure interests:* chess, skiing and squash. *Address:* 47 Deepwood Drive, Hamden, CT 06517, U.S.A. *Telephone:* (203) 785-4567 (Office); (203) 777-0420 (Home).

RITCHIE, John Hindle, PH.D., M.B.E.; British architect; b. 4 June 1937, Delaval, Northumberland; s. of Charles Ritchie and Bertha Ritchie; m. Anne Leyland 1963; two d.; ed. Univs. of Liverpool and Sheffield; research and devt. architect 1963–74; environmental planner, Merseyside 1974–81; Devt. Dir. Merseyside Devt. Corpn. 1981–85, Chief Exec. and mem. Bd. 1985–91, maj. projects included Liverpool Waterfront Redevelt. 1981–91, Albert Dock Conservation (Civic Trust Jubilee Award 1981, European Gold Medal 1986), Liverpool Int. Garden Festival 1984; devt. consultant 1991–; with Lord Chancellor's panel of inspectors 1994–. *Leisure interests:* urban and rural conservation. *Address:* The Mount, Heswall, Wirral, L60 4RD, England. *Telephone:* (0151) 342–4943. *Fax:* (0151) 342–4943.

RITHAUDDEEN AL-HAJ BIN TENGKU ISMAIL, Y.M. Tengku Ahmad; Malaysian politician and barrister; b. 24 Jan. 1932, Kota Bharu; s. of Y. M. Tengku Ismail and Y. M. Besar Zabidah Tengku abd Kadir; m. Y. M. Tengku Puan Sri Datin Noor Aini 1957; three s. two d.; mem. of Royal family of Kelantan; ed. Nottingham Univ. and Lincoln's Inn, U.K.; Circuit Magistrate in Ipoh 1956–58, Pres. of Sessions Court 1958–60; Deputy Public Prosecutor and Fed. Counsel 1960–62; mem. Council of Advisers to Ruler of State of Kelantan (MPR), resgnd. to enter pvt. practice; Chair. East Coast Bar Cttee. of Malaya; Chair. Sri Nilam Co-operative Soc., Malaysia; mem. Malayan Council 1967, 1968, 1969, 1970; Sponsor, Adabi Foundation; Sponsor, Kelantan Youth; Adviser, Kesatria; Chair. Farmers' Org. Authority; Minister with Special Functions Assisting Prime Minister on Foreign Affairs 1973–75; mem. Supreme Council, United Malays' Nat. Org. 1975–; Minister for Foreign Affairs 1975–81, 1984–86, for Trade and Industry 1981–83, for Information 1986, of Defence 1986–90; Jt. Chair. Malaysia-Thailand Devt. Authority (Gas and Oil); Chair. Kinta Kellas Investments PLC 1990–, Idris Hydraulic (Malaysia) Berhad 1991–, Concrete Eng. Products Berhad, Road Builder (Malaysia) Holdings Berhad; Adviser, KPMG Peat Marwick Malaysia; Pro-Chancellor Nat. Univ. of Malaysia; Deputy Pres. Football Asscn. of Malaysia. *Leisure interest:* golf. *Address:* Road Builder (M) Holdings Bhd., 5th Floor, 38 Jalan Dang Wangi, Kuala Lumpur, Malaysia. *Telephone:* (03) 2916888. *Fax:* (03) 2550230.

RITTER, Gerhard A., DR.PHIL.; German professor of modern history; b. 29 March 1929, Berlin; s. of Wilhelm Ritter and Martha (née Wietasch) Ritter; m. Gisela Kleinschmidt 1955; two s.; ed. Arndt.-Oberschule, Berlin, Univ. of Tübingen, Free Univ., Berlin; research, Univ. of Oxford, England 1952–54; Asst. Free Univ., Berlin 1954–61, Prof. of Political Science 1962–65; Prof. of Modern History, Univ. of Münster 1965–74; Prof. of Modern History, Univ. of Munich 1974–94, Prof. Emer. 1994–; fmr. Guest Prof., Washington Univ., St. Louis, Mo., Univ. of Oxford, Univ. of Calif. (Berkeley), Tel-Aviv Univ.; mem. Senate and Main Cttee., Deutsche Forschungsgemeinschaft (German Research Soc.), Bonn 1973–76; Chair. Asscn. of Historians of Germany 1976–80; mem. Bavarian Acad. of Sciences, Munich, Comm. for History of Parliamentarism and Political Parties, Historische Kommission, Berlin; Hon. Fellow St. Antony's Coll., Oxford; Dr. h.c. (Univ. Bielefeld) 1994. *Publications:* Die Arbeiterbewegung im Wilhelminischen Reich 1959, Parlament und Demokratie in Grossbritannien 1972, Deutsche Sozialgeschichte 1870–1914 (with Jürgen Kocka) 1982, Arbeiterbewegung, Parteien und Parlamentarismus 1976, Die II Internationale 1918/19. Protokolle, Memoranden, Berichte und Korrespondenzen 1980, Staat, Arbeiterschaft und Arbeiterbewegung in Deutschland 1980, Die deutschen Parteien 1830–1914 1985, Social Welfare in Germany and Britain 1986, Der Sozialstaat 1991, Wahlen in Deutschland 1946–91 (with M. Niehuss) 1991, Das Deutsche Kaiserreich 1871–1914 1992, Arbeiter im Deutschen Kaiserreich 1871–1914 (with Klaus Tenfelde) 1992, Grossforschung und Staat in Deutschland 1992, Der Umbruch von 1989/91 und die Geschichtswissenschaft 1995, Arbeiter, Arbeiterbewegung und soziale Ideen in Deutschland 1996, Soziale Lage und Sozialpolitik in Deutschland seit Beginn des 19. Jahrhunderts 1998, Über Deutschland, Die Bundesrepublik in der deutschen Geschichte 1998. *Leisure interests:* sailing, tennis. *Address:* Bismarckweg 3, Allmannshausen, 82335 Berg/Starnberger See, Germany (Home). *Telephone:* (8151) 51466.

RITTER, Jorge Eduardo, PH.D.; Panamanian politician and diplomatist; b. 1950; m.; two c.; ed. Pontificia Univ., Colombia; Clerk to Legis. Comm. 1973–77; Lecturer in Constitutional and Civil Law Univ. of Panama; fmr. mem. Governing Council Inst. for Human Resources Training and Devt.; Vice-Minister of Labour and Social Welfare 1977-78; Pvt. Sec. and Adviser to Pres. of Panama 1978-81; Minister of Foreign Affairs (desig.) 1981; teacher Nat. Political Training Coll. of the Guardia Nacional 1981; Minister of Interior and Justice 1981–82; Amb. to Colombia 1982–86; Perm. Rep. to UN 1986–88; Minister of Foreign Affairs 1988–89; Chair. Exec. Council Nat. Telecommunications Inst. 1981; Chair. Bd. Civil Aviation Authority 1981–82; mem. Bd. Banco Ganadero 1980–, Ritter, Diás y Asociados 1982–, Banco Interocéanico de Panamá 1985–. *Address:* c/o Ministry of Foreign Affairs, Panamá 4, Panama.

RITTERMAN, Janet Elizabeth, PH.D., M.MUS., F.R.N.C.M.; music college director; b. 1 Dec. 1941 Sydney, Australia; d. of Charles Eric Palmer and Laurie Helen Palmer; m. Gerrard Peter Ritterman 1970; ed. North Sydney Girls' High School and New South Wales State Conservatorium of Music, Australia, Univ. of Durham and King's Coll. London, U.K.; pianist; accompanist, chamber music player; Sr. Lecturer in Music, Middx. Polytechnic 1975–79, Goldsmiths' Coll. Univ. of London 1980–87; Head of Music, Dartington Coll. of Arts 1987–90, Dean Academic Affairs 1988–90, Acting Prin. 1990–91, Prin. 1991–93; Visiting Prof. of Music Educ., Univ. of Plymouth 1993–; Dir. Royal Coll. of Music 1993–; Chair. Assoc. Bd. Royal Schools of Music (Publishing) Ltd. 1993–, The Mendelssohn and Boise Foundations 1996–97, Advisory Panel, Arts Research Ltd. 1997–; Vice-Pres. Nat. Asscn. of Youth Orchestras 1993–; mem. Music Panel, Arts Council of England 1992–98, Council Royal Musical Asscn. 1994– (Vice-Pres. 1998–), Bd. English Nat. Opera 1996–, Exec. Cttee. Inc. Soc. of Musicians 1996–, Panel, Arts and Humanities Research Bd. 1998–; Trustee, Countess of Munster Musical Trust 1993–, Prince Consort Foundation 1993–; Fellow Nene Coll., Northampton 1997, Dartington Coll. of Arts 1997; Gov. Associated Bd. Royal Schools of Music 1993–; Hon. R.A.M.; Hon. D.Univ. (Univ. of Cen. England) 1996. *Publications:* articles in learned journals, France, Germany and U.K. *Leisure interests:* reading, theatre-going, country walking. *Address:* Royal College of Music, Prince Consort Road, London, SW7 2BS, England. *Telephone:* 0171-591 4363. *Fax:* 0171-589 7740.

RITTNER, Luke Philip Hardwick; British arts administrator; b. 24 May 1947, Bath; s. of Stephen Rittner and Joane Rittner; m. Corinna Frances Edholm 1974; one d.; ed. Blackfriars School, Laxton, City of Bath Tech. Coll., Dartington Coll. of Arts and London Acad. of Music and Dramatic Art; Asst. Admin. Bath Festival 1968–71, Jt. Admin. 1971–74, Admin. Dir. 1974–76; Founder and Dir. Asscn. for Business Sponsorship of the Arts 1976–83; Sec.-Gen. Arts Council of Great Britain 1983–90; U.K. Cultural Dir. Expo '92 1990–92; Chair. English Shakespeare Co. 1990–94; Dir. Marketing and Communications, Sotheby's Europe 1992–; Chair. London Choral Soc. 1994–, Exec. Bd. London Acad. of Music and Dramatic Art 1994–; Artistic Adviser to Spanish Arts Festival, London 1991–94; Gov. Urchfont Manor, Wiltshire Adult Educ. Centre 1982–83; mem. Music Panel, British Council 1979–83, Council Victoria and Albert Museum 1980–83, J. Sainsbury Arts Sponsorship Panel 1990, Olivier Awards Theatre Panel 1992; non-exec. mem. Bd. Carlton Television 1991–93; Trustee Bath Preservation Trust 1968–73, Theatre Royal, Bath 1979–82; Foundation Trustee Holburne Museum, Bath 1981–. *Leisure interests:* the arts. *Address:* 29 Kelso Place, London, W8 5QG, England.

RITTS, Herb; American photographer; fmr. salesman; photographic work appears in maj. int. fashion magazines including Vogue, Harpers Bazaar; celebrity photographs include portraits of Nancy Reagan, Mikhail Gorbachev, Dalai Lama, Tina Turner, Madonna and Naomi Campbell; also engaged in fine art work and in directing videos and commercials; work has been exhibited in galleries. *Publications include:* Notorious 1993.

RITZEN, Jo, D. ECON.; Netherlands politician and economist; b. 3 Oct. 1945, Heerlen, Limburg Prov.; ed. Univ. of Delft; Prof. of Educ. Econs., Nijmegen Univ. 1981–83; Prof. of Public Sector Econs., Erasmus Univ., Rotterdam 1983–89; sometime adviser to Minister of Social Affairs; Minister of Educ., Culture and Science 1989–. *Address:* Ministry of Education, Culture and Science, Europaweg 4, P.O.B. 25000, 2700 Zoetermeer, The Netherlands. *Telephone:* (79) 531911. *Fax:* (79) 531953.

RIVAS-MIJARES, Gustavo, M.SC., DR.ING.; Venezuelan environmental engineer; b. 7 Nov. 1922, Valencia; s. of J. A. Rivas-Montenegro and Amparo Mijares de Rivas; m. Ligia Cardenas 1946; four c.; ed. Liceo Pedro Gual, Valencia, Univ. Central de Venezuela, Caracas and Univ. of Michigan; Prof. of Sanitary Eng., Faculty of Eng., Univ. Central de Venezuela 1945–85, Dean, Grad. School 1973–76; Pres. Nat. Acad. of Physics, Mathematics and Natural Science 1981–85; Dir. Nat. Council of Scientific and Tech. Research 1968–72; fmr. Dir. Venezuela Inst. of Scientific Research; Pres. Superior Council, Universidad Simón Bolívar Caracas, Venezuela 1988–89; Fellow mem. Third World Acad. of Sciences 1988; Foreign Assoc. Nat. Acad. of Eng., U.S.A., Mexico, Spain; Nat. Science Prize, Venezuela 1986; several awards. *Publications:* author and co-author of several books and 116 research papers. *Address:* Urb. Santa Rosa de Lima, Calle C, Res. Jarama, Apt. 7–A, Caracas, Venezuela. *Telephone:* 917156.

RIVERA CARRERA, Cardinal Norberto, D.D.; Mexican ecclesiastic; b. 6 June 1942, La Purísima; s. of Ramón Rivera Cháidez and Soledad Carrera de Rivera; ed. Conciliary Seminary, Durango, Gregorian Univ., Rome; ordained priest 1966; Prof. of Ecclesiology, Univ. Pontificia de Mexico 1982; Bishop of Tehuacán 1985, Archbishop Primate of Mexico 1995–; cr. Cardinal Feb. 1998; mem. Cttee. of Presidency of Papal Council for the Family 1993–; Apostolic Visitor for Diocesan and Religious Seminaries 1993–. *Address:* Curia Arzobispal, Aptdo. Postal 24-4-33, Durango #90, Col. Roma, C.P. 06700 Mexico, D.F., Mexico. *Telephone:* (5) 208-3200. *Fax:* (5) 208-5350.

RIVERS, Larry; American artist; b. 1923, New York; m. 1st Augusta Berger 1945 (divorced); two s.; m. 2nd Clarice Price 1961; two c.; ed. New York Univ.; studied with Hans Hofmann; one-man exhbns. New York galleries 1949–; exhibited in group shows, Vanguard Gallery, Paris 1953, American Fed. of Arts travelling exhbn. 1954–55, Museum of Modern Art, New York 1956, Museum de Arte Moderne, São Paulo, Brazil 1957, Art Inst., Chicago, Minneapolis Inst. of Arts, special exhbn. sponsored by Museum of Modern Art, Japan, Museum Mexico City, Hirshhorn Gallery, Washington, Los Angeles Co. Museum, Museum Caracas, Venezuela 1979–80, Hanover Museum, Fed. Repub. of Germany 1980; works in perm. collections, William Rockhill Nelson Gallery of Art, Kansas City, Minneapolis Inst. of Arts, State Univ. Coll. of Educ., New Paltz, New York, Brooklyn Museum of Art, Metropolitan Museum of Art, Museum of Modern Art, Whitney Museum of American Art, New York, R.I. School of Design, Providence, N.C. Museum of Art, Raleigh, Corcoran Gallery of Art, Washington; works in pvt. collections; Stage Designer The Toilet (play); appeared in film Pull My Daisy; mural History of the Russian Revolution; special awards Corcoran Gallery of Art 1954, Arts Festival, Spoleto, Italy, Newport, R.I. 1958. *Publications:* Drawings and Digressions 1979, What Did I Do? The Unauthorized Autobiography of Larry Rivers 1992.

RIVETTE, Jacques; French film director; b. 1 March 1928, Rouen; s. of André and Andrée (née Amiard) Rivette; ed. Lycée Corneille, Rouen; journalist and critic on Cahiers du Cinéma 1953–82; Asst. to Jacques Becker and Jean Renoir 1954; Dir. of Films 1956–; Chevalier, Ordre nat. du Mérite; Grand Prix nat. 1981. *Films:* Le coup du berger (director) 1956, Paris nous appartient (author and director) 1958–60, Suzanne Simenon, La Religieuse de Diderot 1966, L'Amour fou 1968, Out One: Spectre 1973, Céline et Julie vont en bateau 1974, Le vengeur, Duelle 1976, Le pont du Nord 1982, Merry-go-round 1983, Wuthering Heights 1984, L'amour par terre 1984, The Gang of Four (Berlin Film Award 1989) 1988, La Belle Noiseuse 1991, Jeanne La Pucelle 1993, Haut, Bas, Fragile 1994; Dir. La religieuse (theatre) 1963. *Address:* 20 boulevard de la Bastille, 75012 Paris, France.

RIVLIN, Alice Mitchell, M.A., PH.D.; American economist and government official; b. 4 March 1931, Philadelphia; d. of Allan Mitchell and Georgianna Fales; m. 1st Lewis A. Rivlin 1955 (divorced 1977); two s. one d.; m. 2nd Sidney G. Winter 1989; ed. Bryn Mawr Coll. and Radcliffe Coll.; mem. staff, Brookings Inst. Washington, D.C. 1957–66, 1969–75, 1983–93, Dir. of Econ. Studies 1983–87; Dir. Congressional Budget Office 1975–83; Prof. of Public Policy, George Mason Univ. 1992; Deputy Dir. U.S. Office of Man. and Budget 1993–94, Dir. 1994–96; Vice-Chair Fed. Reserve Bd. 1996–; mem. American Econ. Asscn. (Nat. Pres. 1986); MacArthur Fellow 1983–88. *Publications:* The Role of the Federal Government in Financing Higher Education 1961, Microanalysis of Socioeconomic Systems (with others) 1961, Systematic Thinking for Social Action 1971, Economic Choices (with others) 1986, The Swedish Economy (with others) 1987, Caring for the Disabled Elderly: Who Will Pay? 1988, Reviving the American Dream 1992. *Address:* Federal Reserve System, 20th Street and C Street N.W., Washington, D.C. 20551, U.S.A.

RIVLIN, Moshe; Israeli executive; b. 16 Jan. 1925, Jerusalem; s. of Yitzhak and Esther Rivlin; m. Ruth Moav (Horbaty) 1960; two d.; ed. Teachers' Seminary, Graduate Aluma Inst. for Jewish Studies, Mizrachi Teacher's Coll. and School for Political Science, Hebrew Univ., Jerusalem; Major in ZAHAL 1948–49; Consul in U.S.A. 1952–58; Dir., Information Dept., The Jewish Agency 1958–60, Sec.-Gen. 1960–66, Dir.-Gen. and Head of Admin. and Public Relations Dept. 1966–71; elected Dir.-Gen. of reconstituted Jewish Agency 1971–77; Assoc. mem. Exec., World Zionist Org. 1971; Chair. Keren Kayemeth Le Israel 1977–; mem. Bd. of Govs. Ben-Gurion Univ., Coll. for Public Admin., Jewish Telegraphic Agency; mem. Exec. Cttee. Yad Ben-Zvi, mem. Council Yad Ben-Gurion; mem. Bd. of Dirs. Jerusalem Post, Beit Hatfutzot, Hebrew Univ. *Address:* Keren Kayemeth Le Israel, P.O. Box 283, Jerusalem; 34 Hapalmach Street, Jerusalem, Israel (Home). *Telephone:* 02/6244023 (Office); 02/5635173 (Home).

RIVOYRE, Christine Berthe Claude Denis de, L. ÈS L.; French author and journalist; b. 29 Nov. 1921, Tarbes; d. of François Denis de Rivoyre and Madeleine née Ballande; ed. Inst. du Sacré Coeur, Bordeaux and Poitiers, Faculté des lettres, Paris and Univ. of Syracuse, U.S.A.; journalist Le Monde (daily) 1950–55; Literary Dir. Marie-Claire (monthly magazine) 1955–65; mem. Haut Comité de la Langue française, Conseil Supérieur des Lettres, Prix Medicis Jury; Chevalier, Légion d'honneur, Chevalier des Arts et des Lettres; Prix Paul Morand (Académie française) 1984. and other awards. *Publications:* L'alouette au miroir 1956, La mandarine 1957, La tête en fleurs 1960, La glace à l'ananas 1962, Les sultans 1964, Le petit matin 1968, Le seigneur des chevaux (with A. Kalda) 1969, Fleur d'agonie 1970, Boy 1973, Le voyage à l'envers 1977, Belle alliance 1982, Reine-Mère 1985, Crépuscule taille unique 1989, Racontez-moi les flamboyants 1995. *Address:* Dichats Ha, Onesse-Laharie, 40110 Morcenx, France.

RIX, Timothy John, C.B.E., B.A., C.I.MGT., F.R.S.A.; British publisher; b. 4 Jan. 1934, Maidenhead, Berks.; s. of late Howard T. Rix and of Marguerite Selman Rix; m. 1st Wendy E. Wright 1960 (dissolved 1967); m. 2nd Gillian Greenwood 1968; one s. two d.; ed. Radley Coll., Clare Coll., Cambridge and Yale Univ.; joined Longman Green & Co. Ltd. 1958, Overseas Educ. Publr. 1958–61, Publishing Man. Far East and S.E. Asia 1961–63, Head, English Language Teaching Publishing 1964–68, Div. Man. Dir. 1968–72, Jt. Man. Dir. 1972–76, Chief Exec. Longman Group Ltd. 1976–90, Chair. 1984–90; Chair. Addison-Wesley-Longman Group Ltd. 1988–89; Chair. Pitman Examinations Inst. 1987–90; Dir. Pearson Longman Ltd. (now Pearson PLC) 1979–83, Goldcrest Television 1981–83, Yale Univ. Press Ltd., London 1984–, ECIC (Man.) Ltd. 1990–92, Blackie & Son Ltd. 1990–93, B.H. Blackwell Ltd. 1991–95, Geddes and Grosset Ltd. 1996–98, Jessica Kingsley Publrs. Ltd. 1997–, Frances Lincoln Ltd. 1997–, Meditech Media Ltd. 1997–; Pres. Publishers Asscn. 1981–83; mem. British Library Bd. 1986–96, British Council Bd. 1988–97, Health Educ. Authority Bd. 1995–; Chair. Book Trust 1986–88, British Library Centre for the Book 1989–95, Book Marketing Ltd. 1990–, Soc. of Bookmen 1990–92, British Library Publishing 1992–, Book Aid Int. 1994–, Bell Educational Trust 1994–, Nat. Book Cttee. 1997–; mem. Oxford Brookes Univ. Devt. Cttee. 1991–96, Finance Cttee., Oxford Univ. Press 1992–, Council, Ranfurly Library Services 1992–94; Hon. Pres. Independent Publishers' Guild 1993–; other professional appointments. *Publications:* articles on publishing in trade journals. *Leisure interests:* reading, landscape, wine. *Address:* Top Flat, 27 Wolseley Road, London, N8 8RS, England. *Telephone:* 0181-341 4160. *Fax:* 0181-341 4160.

RIZA, Iqbal, M.A.; Pakistani international civil servant; b. 20 May 1934, India; s. of Sharif Alijan; m. 1959; two s.; ed. Pakistan and U.S.A.; Pakistan Foreign Service 1958–77; served Spain, Germany, Sudan, U.K., U.S.A.; Dir. Foreign Service Acad. Lahore 1968–71; Deputy Chief of Mission, Washington, D.C. 1972–76; Chargé d'Affaires, Paris 1977; joined UN 1978; assigned to negotiations in Iran-Iraq war 1981–87; Dir. UN Gen. Ass. 1988; Chief, UN Electoral Mission, Nicaragua 1988–90; Special Rep. of UN Sec.-Gen. in El Salvador 1991–93; Asst. Sec.-Gen. for Peace-keeping Operations 1993–97, Under-Sec.-Gen., Chief of Staff in Exec. Office of Sec.-Gen. 1997–. *Leisure interests:* reading, music, riding. *Address:* United Nations, New York, NY 10017, U.S.A.

RIZAYEV, Ramiz Gasangulu ogly, DR. CHEM. SC.; Azerbaijani diplomatist and chemist; b. 2 Nov. 1939, Nakhichevan; m.; one s. one d.; ed. Azerbaijan State Univ.; Corresp. mem. Azerbaijan Acad. of Sciences 1983; Dir. Inst. of Inorganic and Physical Chem. Azerbaijan Acad. of Sciences 1985–93; Plenipotentiary Rep., then Amb. of Azerbaijan to Russian Fed. 1993–; numerous inventions in the field of oil extraction and oil processing, of 36 patents in various countries; mem. Scientific Council on Catalysis Russian Acad. of Sciences; mem. Ed. Bd. Neftekhimiya (journal); 250 scientific articles on problems of oil chem. and chemical catalysis. *Address:* Azerbaijan Embassy, Leontyevsky per. 16, 103009 Moscow, Russia. *Telephone:* (095) 229 1649 (Office).

RIZZOLI, Angelo; Italian publisher; b. 12 Nov. 1943, Como; s. of Andrea and Lucia (née Solmi) Rizzoli; m. Eleonora Giorgi 1979; one c.; ed. univ.; Pres. and Man. Ed. Rizzoli Editore 1978–; Pres. Cineriz Distributori Associati 1978–, Rizzoli Film 1978–. *Address:* Via Angelo Rizzoli 2, 20132 Milan, Italy (Office). *Telephone:* 02-25-841.

RO JAI-BONG; Korean politician; b. Masan, S. Kyongsang Prov. fmr. political adviser to Pres.; Chief Presidential Sec. March–Dec. 1990; Prime Minister Repub. of Korea 1990–91. *Address:* c/o Office of the Prime Minister, 77 Sejong-no, Chongno-ku, Seoul, Republic of Korea.

ROA BASTOS, Augusto; Paraguayan writer and journalist; b. 1917; ed. Asunción; returned to Paraguay after 40 years in exile March 1989; awarded John Simon Guggenheim Memorial Foundation 1971. *Publications:* Poetry: El Ruiseñor y la Aurora 1936, El Naranjal Ardiente 1947–49; Novels: El Trueno entre las Hojas 1953, Hijo de Hombre 1960, El Baldío 1966, Los Pies sobre el Agua 1967, Madera Quemada 1967, Moriencia 1969, Cuerpo Presente y otros cuentos 1971, Yo el Supremo 1974, Los Congresos 1974, El Somnámbulo 1976; Screenplays: El Trueno entre las Hojas 1955, Hijo de Hombre 1960, Shunko 1960, Alias Gardelito 1963, Castigo al Traidor 1966, El Señor Presidente 1966, Don Segundo Sombra 1968. *Address:* Berutti 2828, Martínez, Buenos Aires, Argentina.

ROA-KOURI, Raúl; Cuban diplomatist; b. 9 July 1936, Havana; s. of Raúl Roa and Ada Kouri; m. 1st (dissolved); two d.; m. 2nd María Rodríguez de Roa-Kouri 1976 (dissolved); one d.; m. 3rd Lillian Martin de Roa-Kouri 1996; ed. Univ. of Havana, Columbia Univ. in New York, U.S.A.; Deputy Perm. Rep. to UN 1959–60; Amb. to Czechoslovakia 1961–63, to Brazil 1963–64; Dir. of Trade Policy, Ministry of Foreign Trade 1964–66; Dir.-Gen. of Int. Dept. Ministry for Food Industries 1967–70; Dir.-Gen. of Nat. Cttee. for Econ., Scientific and Tech. Co-operation 1971–72; Perm. Sec. CMEA Nat. Cttee. for Econ. Scientific and Tech. Co-operation 1972–76; Sr. Political Adviser to Vice-Pres. of Council of State in charge of Foreign Affairs 1976–78; Perm. Rep. to UN 1978–84; Vice-Minister of Foreign Affairs 1984; Amb. to UNESCO 1993–94; Amb. to France 1994–; mem. Scientific Council, Center for Int. Econ. Research, Havana Univ. 1986–. *Leisure interests:* music, literature, tennis, writing. *Address:* Cuban Embassy, 16 rue de Presles, 75015 Paris, France. *Telephone:* 1-45-67-55-35. *Fax:* 1-45-66-80-92.

ROACH, Maxwell Lemuel; American jazz musician; b. 10 Jan. 1924, Elizabeth City, N.C.; s. of Alphonzo Roach and Cressie (née Saunders) Roach; m. 1st Mildred Wilkinson 1949 (divorced); one s. one d.; m. 2nd Abbey Lincoln 1962 (divorced); ed. Manhattan School of Music, New England Conservatory of Music; Prof. of Music, Univ. of Massachusetts 1973–; specialized in percussion instruments, with Charlie Parker 1946–48, later with Thelonius Monk, Bud Powell, Dizzy Gillespie, etc.; Co-leader Max Roach-

Clifford Brown Quintet 1954–56; appearances at Paris Jazz Festival 1949, Newport Jazz Festival 1972; composer and choreographer Freedom Now suite; Officier des Arts et des Lettres 1989; Hon. mem. American Acad. and Inst. of Arts and Letters; received Best Record of Year Award, Down Beat magazine 1956, and other awards; mem. Jazz Artists Guild Inc.

ROBAINA GONZÁLEZ, Roberto, B.ED.; Cuban politician; b. 18 March 1956, Pinar del Río; m.; one s.; ed. Pinar del Río Higher Pedagogical Inst.; Prof. of Mathematics 1978; Pres. Fed. of Univ. Students 1979; First Sec. Young Communist League, Plaza Municipality 1983, mem. Nat. Bureau of Young Communist League 1984–85, Second Sec. 1985–86, First Sec. 1986–93; Deputy for Consolación del Sur municipality Nat. Ass. of People's Power 1986–92, Deputy for Cerro municipality 1992–; mem. Council of State 1986–98; mem. Cen. Cttee. of Communist Party of Cuba, Politburo of Cen. Cttee. 1990; Minister of Foreign Affairs 1993–; mem. Cuban Internationalist Mil. Contingent to Angola 1998. *Address:* Ministry of Foreign Affairs, Calzada 360, esq. a G. Plaza de la Revolución, Havana, Cuba. *Telephone:* 31-3151. *Fax:* 33-3085.

ROBARDS, Jason Nelson, Jr.; American actor; b. 26 July 1922, Chicago; s. of Jason Nelson Robards and Hope Robards (née Glanville); m. 1st Eleanor Pitman 1948; two s. one d.; m. 3rd Lauren Bacall (q.v.) 1961 (divorced); one s.; m. 4th Lois O'Connor 1970; one s. one d.; ed. American Academy of Dramatic Arts; served with U.S. Navy 1939–46; *plays include:* Stalag 17 1951–53, The Chase 1952, The Iceman Cometh 1956, Long Day's Journey into Night 1956–58, 1976, Henry IVth Part 1 1958, Macbeth, The Disenchanted 1958–59, Toys in the Attic 1960, Big Fish, Little Fish 1961, A Thousand Clowns 1962, After the Fall 1964, But for Whom, Charlie 1964, Hughie 1964, The Devils 1965, We Bombed in New Haven 1968, The Country Girl 1972, A Moon for the Misbegotten 1973, A Touch of the Poet 1977–78, You Can't Take it with You 1983, Love Letters 1989, Park Your Car in Harvard Yard 1991, No Man's Land 1993, Moonlight 1995, Molly Sweeney 1996, Moonlight 1997; *films include:* The Journey 1959, By Love Possessed 1961, A Thousand Clowns, Big Hand for the Little Lady 1966, Any Wednesday 1966, St. Valentine's Day Massacre 1967, The Night They Raided Minsky's 1968, The Loves of Isadora 1969, Once Upon a Time in the West 1969, Ballad of Cable Hogue 1970, Johnny Got His Gun 1971, Murder in the Rue Morgue 1971, The War Between Men and Women 1972, Pat Garrett and Billy the Kid 1973, All the President's Men 1976, Julia 1977, Comes a Horseman 1978, Hurricane 1979, Melvin and Howard 1979, Max Dugan Returns 1982, Something Wicked This Way Comes 1983, Square Dance 1987, The Good Mother 1988, Black Rainbow 1989, Parenthood 1989, Reunion 1989, Quick Change 1989, Storyville, Philadelphia 1994, Little Big League 1994, The Paper 1994, Crimson Tide 1995, Thousand Acres 1997; *television films include:* For Whom the Bell Tolls 1959, The Iceman Cometh 1961, One Day in the Life of Ivan Denisovitch 1963, Washington Behind Closed Doors 1977, FDR: The Last Year 1980, The Day After 1983, Sakharov 1984, Johnny Bull 1986, Inherit the Wind 1988, The Christmas Wife 1988, Chernobyl: The Final Warning 1991; mem. Bd. Dirs. American Academy of Dramatic Arts 1957–; ANTA Award for Outstanding Contribution to Living Theater 1959, Perry Award as Best Actor 1959, Academy Awards for Best Supporting Actor 1976, 1977, New York Film Critics Circle Award for Best Supporting Actor 1976, Emmy 1988, American Council for the Arts Lifetime Achievement Award 1996, Drama League Lifetime Contrib. to Theatre 1997, Nat. Medal of Arts 1997, First Claiborne Pell Award for Lifetime Contrib. to the Arts 1997. *Address:* c/o Paradigm Talent Agency, 200 West 57th Street, Suite 900, New York, NY 10019, U.S.A.

ROBB, Charles Spittal, B.B.A., J.D.; American politician and lawyer; b. 26 June 1939, Phoenix, Ariz.; s. of James Spittal Robb and Frances Howard (née Woolley) Robb; m. Lynda Bird Johnson (d. of late Pres. Lyndon B. Johnson) 1967; three d.; ed. Cornell Univ., Univ. of Wisconsin and Univ. of Virginia; admitted to Va. Bar 1973; law clerk to John D. Butzner, Jr., U.S. Court of Appeals 1973–74; admitted to U.S. Supreme Court Bar 1976; Attorney, Williams, Connolly and Califano 1974–77; Lieut.-Gov. of Virginia 1978–82, Gov. 1982–86; Senator from Virginia 1989–; Chair. Democratic Govs. Asscn. 1984–85, Democratic Leadership Council 1986–88; Chair Educ. Comm. of the States, Educ. Sub-Cttee. of the Nat. Govs. Asscn's. Standing Cttee. on Human Resources; Chair. Southern Govs. Asscn. 1984–85; Pres. Council of State Govts. 1985–86; Partner, Hunton and Williams 1986–; mem. Bd. various educational insts.; mem. American, Va. Bar Asscns., Va. Trial Lawyers' Asscn.; Bronze Star, Viet Nam Service Medal with four stars, Vietnamese Cross of Gallantry with Silver Star; Raven Award 1973; Seven Socs. Org. Award, Univ. of Va. *Address:* U.S. Senate, 154 Russell Senate Office Building, Washington, DC 20510, U.S.A.

ROBB, John Weddell; British business executive; b. 27 April 1936; s. of John Robb and Isabella Robb; m. Janet Teanby 1965; two s. one d.; ed. Daniel Stewart's Coll. Edin.; Market Research Exec. H.J. Heinz 1952; Product Man. Assoc. Fisheries 1960; Marketing Exec. Young & Rubicam 1965; joined Beecham Group 1966, Man. Dir. Beecham (Far East), Kuala Lumpur 1971, Vice-Pres. W. Hemisphere Div. Beecham Products, U.S.A. 1974, Man. Dir. Food and Drink Div., Beecham Products 1976, mem. Bd. Beecham Group 1980, Chair. Food and Drink Div. 1980, Chair. Beecham Products 1984–85, Group Man. Dir. 1985–88; Dir. (non-exec.) Nat. Freight Corpn. 1983– (Deputy Chair. (non-exec.) 1990–), Allied-Lyons PLC 1991–, Del La Rue Co. 1993–, Unigate 1996–; Deputy Chief Exec. Wellcome PLC 1989–90, Chief Exec. 1990–95, Chair. 1994–95; Deputy Chair. Horserace Betting Levy Bd. 1993–; Chair. British Energy PLC 1995, Logitron Holdings PLC 1996–, Chair. Hewden Stuart PLC 1999–; Trustee Royal Botanic Garden, Edin. 1997–. *Leisure interests:* golf, gardening, racing.

ROBBE-GRILLET, Alain; French writer, film-maker and agronomist; b. 18 Aug. 1922, Brest; s. of Gaston Robbe-Grillet and Yvonne Canu; m. Catherine Rstakian 1957; ed. Lycée Buffon, Lycée St. Louis and Inst. Nat. Agronomique, Paris; Chargé de Mission, Inst. Nat. de la Statistique 1945–48; Engineer Inst. des Fruits Tropicaux (Guinea, Morocco, Martinique and Guadeloupe) 1949–51; Literary Adviser Editions de Minuit 1955–85; Dir. Centre for the Sociology of Literature, Univ. of Brussels 1980–; Prix Louis Delluc 1963; Chevalier, Légion d'honneur; Officier Ordre nat. du mérite, des Arts et des Lettres. *Publications:* Novels: Les gommes 1953, Le voyeur 1955, La jalousie 1957, Dans le labyrinthe 1959, La maison de rendez-vous 1965, Projet pour une révolution à New York 1970, Topologie d'une cité fantôme 1976, La belle captive 1977, Un régicide 1978, Souvenirs du triangle d'or 1978, Djinn 1981, Le miroir qui revient 1984, Angélique ou l'enchantement 1988, Les derniers jours de Corinthe 1994; short stories: Instantanés 1962; essay: Pour un nouveau roman 1964. *Films:* L'année dernière à Marienbad 1961; films directed: L'immortelle 1963, Trans-Europ-Express 1967, L'homme qui ment 1968, L'Eden et après 1970, Glissements progressifs du plaisir 1974, Le jeu avec le feu 1975, La belle captive 1983, Un bruit qui rend fou 1995. *Leisure interest:* collection of cacti. *Address:* 7 rue Bernard-Palissy, 75006 Paris (Office); 18 boulevard Maillot, 92200 Neuilly-sur-Seine, France (Home). *Telephone:* 47-22-31-22 (Home).

RÖBBELEN, Gerhard Paul Karl, DR.RER.NAT.; German professor of plant breeding; b. 10 May 1929, Bremen; s. of Ernst Röbbelen and Henny Röbbelen; m. Christa Scherz 1957; two s. one d.; ed. Univs. of Göttingen and Freiburg Br.; Asst. Prof. Inst. of Agronomy and Plant Breeding, Univ. of Göttingen 1957–67, Prof. and Head Div. of Cytogenetics 1967–70, Dir. of Inst. 1970–94, Dean Faculty of Agric. 1971–72, Prof. Emer. 1994–; Visiting Prof. Univ. of Mo., U.S.A. 1966–67; Ed. Plant Breeding 1976–; mem. German Soc. for Genetics (Pres. 1969–70, 1977–79), European Asscn. for Research in Plant Breeding—EUCARPIA (Chair. Section for Oil and Protein Crops 1978–86, Pres. 1986–89), German Botanical Soc., Asscn. for Applied Botany, Genetics Soc. of Canada, German Soc. Fat Research (Pres. 1989–92), German Soc. of Plant Breeding (Pres. 1991–96), Acad. of Sciences, Göttingen 1981, Acad. Leopoldina 1990; Hon. Drs. Agric. (Kiel) 1976, (Halle/Saale) 1997. *Publications:* over 300 articles on research into plant genetics and breeding. *Leisure interests:* music, mountain climbing, gardening. *Address:* 8 Von Siebold-strasse, 37075 Göttingen (Office); 9 Tuckermannweg, 37085 Göttingen, Germany.

ROBBINS, Frederick Chapman, A.B., B.S., M.D.; American physician; b. 25 Aug. 1916, Auburn, Ala.; s. of William J. Robbins and Christine (Chapman) Robbins; m. Alice Havemeyer Northrop 1948; two d.; ed. Univ. of Missouri and Harvard Medical School; served U.S. Army 1942–46; Senior Fellow, Nat. Research Council 1948–50; Research Fellow, Harvard Medical School 1948–50; Instructor, Harvard Medical School 1950–51, Assoc. (Pediatrics) 1951–52; Assoc., Research Div. of Infectious Disease, Children's Medical Center, Boston 1950–52; Assoc. Physician and Assoc. Dir. of Isolation Services, Children's Hospital, Boston 1950–52; Research Fellow, Boston Lying-in Hospital 1950–52; Asst. Children's Medical Service, Mass. Gen. Hospital, Boston 1950–52; Dir. Dept. of Pediatrics and Contagious Diseases, Cleveland Metropolitan Gen. Hospital 1952–66; Prof. of Pediatrics, Case Western Reserve Univ. School of Medicine, Cleveland 1950–80, Dean 1966–80, Dean Emer. 1980–, Prof. Emer. 1987–; now Dir. Center Adolescent Health, School of Medicine; Assoc. Pediatrician Univ. Hospitals, Cleveland 1952–66; Pres. Inst. of Medicine, N.A.S. 1980–85; mem. Nat. Acad. of Sciences 1972, American Philosophical Soc. 1972, American Acad. of Arts and Sciences; Hon. D.Sc. (John Carroll and Mo. Univs.); Hon. LL.D. (New Mexico) 1968; Bronze Star 1945; First Mead Johnson Award (jointly) 1953; Nobel Prize for Physiology and Medicine (jointly) 1954; Medical Mutual Honor Award for 1969. *Publications:* various scientific papers related to virus and rickettsial diseases, especially 'Q' fever in the Mediterranean area and cultivation of poliomyelitis viruses in tissue culture. *Address:* Case Western Reserve University, School of Medicine, 10900 Euclid Avenue, Cleveland, OH 44106 (Office); 2626 West Park Boulevard, Shaker Heights, OH 44120, U.S.A. (Home).

ROBBINS, Keith Gilbert, D.PHIL., D.LITT., F.R.S.E.; British historian and university college principal; b. 9 April 1940, Bristol; s. of Gilbert Henry John Robbins and Edith Mary Robbins; m. Janet Carey Thomson 1963; three s. one d.; ed. Bristol Grammar School, Magdalen Coll. Oxford, St. Antony's Coll. Oxford; lecturer, Univ. of York 1963–71; Prof. of History Univ. Coll. of N. Wales, Bangor 1971–79; Prof. of Modern History, Univ. of Glasgow 1980–91; Prin. Univ. of Wales, Lampeter 1991–; Pres. Historical Asscn. 1988–91; Winston Churchill Travelling Fellow 1990. *Publications:* Munich 1938, 1968, Sir Edward Grey 1971, The Abolition of War . . . 1976, John Bright 1979, The Eclipse of a Great Power: Modern Britain 1870–1975 1983, 1870–1992 (2nd edn.) 1994, The First World War 1984, Nineteenth-Century Britain: Integration and Diversity 1988, Appeasement 1988, Blackwell Dictionary of Twentieth-Century British Political Life (ed.) 1990, Churchill 1992, History, Religion and Identity in Modern Britain 1993, Politicians, Diplomacy and War in Modern British History 1994, Bibliography of British History 1914–1989 1996, Great Britain: Identities, Institutions and the Idea of Britishness 1997, The World Since 1945: a Concise History 1998. *Leisure* *interests:* walking, music. *Address:* University of Wales, Lampeter, Ceredigion, SA48 7ED, Wales. *Telephone:* (01570) 422351. *Fax:* (01570) 423423.

ROBBINS, Kenneth L.; American advertising executive; Exec. Vice-Pres. SSC & B (now Lintas Worldwide), New York; now Chair. and C.E.O. Int. Div. Lintas Worldwide, New York. *Address:* Lintas Worldwide, 1 Dag Hammarskjold Plaza, New York, NY 10017, U.S.A.

ROBBINS, Tim; American actor, director and screen writer; b. 1958, New York; one s. with Susan Sarandon (q.v.); ed. Univ. Coll. of Los Angeles; began career as mem. Theatre for the New City; Founder and Artistic Dir. The Actors' Gang. *Theatre:* (actor) Ubu Roi 1981; (Dir.) A Midsummer Night's Dream 1984, The Good Woman of Setzuan 1990; (co-writer with Adam Simon) Alagazam, After the Dog Wars, Violence: The Misadventures of Spike Spangle, Farmer, Carnage—A Comedy (rep. U.S.A. at Edin. Int. Festival, Scotland). *Films:* Bull Durham 1988, Cadillac Man, Jacob's Ladder, Five Corners, Tapeheads, Miss Firecracker, Eric the Viking, Jungle Fever, The Player, The Shawshank Redemption, Short Cuts, The Hudsucker Proxy, I.Q.; (actor, writer, dir.) Bob Roberts; Dead Man Walking (writer, dir.), Nothing to Lose (dir., actor), The Moviegoer, Arlington Road, The Cradle Will Rock. *Address:* c/o ICM, 8942 Wilshire Blvd, Beverly Hills, CA 90211, U.S.A.

ROBBINS, Tom, B.A.; American author; b. 22 July 1936, Blowing Rock, N.C.; s. of George T. Robbins and Katherine d'Avalon Robbins; m. Terrie Lunden 1967 (divorced 1972); one s.; ed. Virginia Commonwealth Univ. and Univ. of Washington; operated black market ring in S. Korea 1956–57; int. news ed. Times-Dispatch, Richmond, Va. 1959–62; art critic, The Seattle Times and contrib. to Artforum and Art in America etc. 1962–65; art critic, Seattle Magazine 1965–67. *Publications:* novels: Another Roadside Attraction 1971, Even Cowgirls Get the Blues 1976, Still Life With Woodpecker 1980, Jitterbug Perfume 1984, Skinny Legs and All 1990, Half Asleep in Frog Pajamas 1994. *Leisure interests:* volleyball, white magick, psychedelic plants, art, pop culture and religions. *Address:* P.O. Box 338, La Conner, WA 98257, U.S.A.

ROBENS OF WOLDINGHAM, Baron (Life Peer), cr. 1961, of Woldingham in the County of Surrey; **Alfred Robens,** P.C., D.C.L., LL.D.; British politician; b. 18 Dec. 1910, Manchester; s. of George and Edith Robens; m. Eva Powell 1937; ed. council school; Official of Union of Distributive and Allied Workers 1935–45; Manchester City Councillor 1942–45; Labour M.P. for Wansbeck Div. of Northumberland 1945–50, Blyth 1950–60; Parl. Pvt. Sec. to Minister of Transport 1945–47; Parl. Sec. Minister of Fuel and Power 1947–51; Minister of Labour April-Oct. 1951; Labour Relations Consultant, Atomic Power Construction Ltd. 1960; Deputy Chair. Nat. Coal Bd. 1960–61, Chair. 1961–71; Chair. Johnson Matthey and Co. Ltd. 1971–83, Hon. Pres. 1983–86; Chair. Vickers Ltd. 1971–79, St. Regis Newspapers 1975–80, Alfred Robens Assocs. 1984–; Chair. Snamprogetti 1980–88, Pres. 1988–; Dir. American Medical (Europe) Ltd. 1981–; mem. NEDC 1962–71; Pres. Advertising Asscn. 1963–67; Chair. Foundation on Automation and Employment 1970; Chair. Council of the Manchester Business School 1970–79; mem. Royal Comm. on Trade Unions and Employers' Asscns. 1965–68; Chair. Govt. Enquiry into Safety and Health of People at Work 1970–72; Chair. Eng. Industries Council 1976–80; Gov. Queen Elizabeth's Training Coll. for the Disabled 1951–80; Chair. of Govs. Guy's Hosp. 1965–74; Dir. J. H. Sankey and Son Ltd., Bank of England 1966–81, St. Regis Paper Co. (U.K.) 1971–81, St. Regis Int. (U.K.) 1976–81, Trust-house-Forte 1971–85, Times Newspapers Holdings Ltd. 1980–83; Chair. Jt. Econ. Mission to Malta 1967; Chancellor, Univ. of Surrey 1966–77; Fellow, Manchester Coll. of Science and Tech. 1965–; Hon. D.C.L. (Newcastle, Manchester), Hon. LL.D. (Leicester, London and Manchester Univs.); Mackintosh Medal, Advertising Asscn. 1970, Albert Medal of R.S.A. 1977. *Publications:* Human Engineering 1970, Ten Year Stint 1971. *Leisure interest:* gardening. *Address:* House of Lords, London, SW1A 0PW; 3 Dockett Moorings, Mead Lane, Chertsey, Surrey, KT16 8LS, England. *Telephone:* (01932) 566620.

ROBERT, Jacques Frédéric, D. EN D.; French professor of law; b. 29 Sept. 1928, Algiers, Algeria; s. of Frédéric Robert and Fanny Robert; m. Marie-Caroline de Bary 1958; two s. two d.; ed. Lycée E. F. Gautier, Algiers, Univs. of Algiers and Paris, C.N.R.S.; Prof. of Law, Univs. of Algiers 1956–60, Rabat, Morocco 1960–62, Grenoble 1962–65; Dir. Maison franco-japonaise, Tokyo 1965–68; Prof. of Law, Univ. of Nanterre 1968–69, Univ. of Paris II 1969–; Contributor, Le Monde and La Croix 1970–; Dir. Revue de droit public 1977–; Pres. Univ. of Paris II (Panthéon) 1979–85; Pres. of Centre français de Droit comparé 1985–; mem. Conseil Constitutionnel 1989–98; Prix Paul Deschanel 1954; Officier, Légion d'honneur; Order of the Sacred Treasure (Japan); Officier des Palmes académiques; Officier, Ordre nat. du Mérite; Commdr., Order of Honour (Austria). *Publications:* Les violations de la liberté individuelle 1954, La monarchie marocaine 1963, Le Japon 1970, Introduction à l'Esprit des Lois 1973, Libertés publiques 1988; L'Esprit de défense 1988. *Leisure interests:* music, photography, tennis. *Address:* Conseil Constitutionnel, 2 rue de Montpensier, 75001 Paris (Office); 14 Villa Saint-Georges, 92160 Antony, France (Home). *Telephone:* 40.15.30.00 (Office); 46.66.12.32 (Home).

ROBERTO, Holden (see Holden, Roberto).

ROBERTS, Barbara; American politician; b. 21 Dec. 1936, Corvallis, Ore.; m. Frank Roberts 1974; two s.; mem. Multnomah County Bd. of Commrs., Ore. 1978; mem. Ore. House of Reps. 1981–85; Sec. of State of Ore. 1985–91; Gov. of Oregon 1990–95; Democrat.

ROBERTS, Bernard, F.R.C.M.; British concert pianist; b. 23 July 1933, Manchester; s. of William Wright Roberts and Elsie Alberta Ingham; m. 1st Patricia May Russell 1955 (dissolved 1987); two s.; m. 2nd Caroline Ireland 1992; ed. William Hulme's Grammar School, Manchester, Royal Coll. of Music, London; won Scholarship to R.C.M. 1949; début as concert pianist, Wigmore Hall, London 1957; Piano Prof., R.C.M. 1962–99; numerous solo recitals and concerto performances, chamber music player; Hon. D. Univ. (Brunel). *Leisure interests:* philosophy, religion, model railways. *Address:* Uwchlaw'r Coed, Llanbedr, Gwynedd, LL45 2NA, Wales. *Telephone:* (01341) 241532.

ROBERTS, Bert; British business executive; b. 1942; trained as electrical eng.; joined MCI 1972, C.E.O. 1991, Chair. 1992–. *Address:* MCI Communications, 1801 Pennsylvania Avenue N.W., Washington, DC 20006, U.S.A. *Telephone:* (202) 872-1600.

ROBERTS, Brian Leon; American communications executive; b. 28 June 1959, Philadelphia; s. of Ralph J. Roberts and Suzanne F. Roberts; m. Aileen Kennedy 1985; one s. two d.; ed. Univ. of Pennsylvania; Vice-Pres. Operations Comcast Cable Communications Inc. 1985–86, Exec. Vice-Pres. Comcast Corpn. 1986–. also mem. Bd. Dirs., now Pres.; Vice-Chair. Walter Katz Foundation; mem. Bd. Dirs. Turner Broadcasting System, QVC Network, Viewer's Choice, Cable Labs., Cable TV Asscn. *Address:* Comcast Corporation, 1500 Market Street, Philadelphia, PA 19102, U.S.A.

ROBERTS, Chalmers McGeagh, A.B.; American journalist; b. 18 Nov. 1910; m. Lois Hall 1941; two s. one d.; ed. Amherst Coll.; Reporter Washington Post, D.C. 1933–34, Associated Press, Pittsburgh Bureau 1934–35, Toledo News-Bee 1936–38, Japan Times, Tokyo 1938–39; Asst. Man. Ed. Washington Daily News 1939–41; Sunday Ed. Washington Times-Herald 1941; Office of War Information, London and Washington 1941–43; U.S. Army Air Force 1943–46; Life magazine 1946–47; Washington Star 1947–49; Washington Post 1949–71, Chief Diplomatic corresp. 1954–71, contrib. columnist 1971–, San Diego Union contrib. columnist 1971–86; mem. American Newspaper Guild; Hon. Dr. of Humane Letters 1963; Order of Merit, Fed. Repub. of Germany. *Publications:* Washington Past and Present 1950, Can We Meet the Russians Half Way? 1958, The Nuclear Years: the Arms Race and Arms Control, 1945–70 1970, First Rough Draft: a Journalist's Journal of Our Times 1973, In the Shadow of Power: The Story of the Washington Post 1989, How Did I Get Here So Fast? 1991. *Address:* 6699 MacArthur Boulevard, Bethesda, MD 20816, U.S.A. (Office and Home). *Telephone:* 301-229-2471.

ROBERTS, (Charles) Patrick; American politician; b. 20 April 1936, Topeka, Kan.; m. Franki Fann 1970; two s. one d.; ed. Kansas State Univ.; Publr. Litchfield Park, Arizona 1962–67; Admin. asst. to U.S. Senator F. Carlson 1967–68, U.S. Congressman Keith Sebelius 1968–70; mem. 97th to 104th Congresses 1980–97; Senator from Kansas Jan. 1997–; Republican. *Address:* United States Senate, 302 Hart Senate Office Building, Washington, DC 20510, U.S.A.

ROBERTS, Sir Denys Tudor Emil, K.B.E., Q.C., M.A., B.C.L.; British judge and administrator; b. 19 Jan. 1923, London; s. of William David Roberts and Dorothy Eliza Morrison; m. 1st B. Marsh 1949; one s. one d.; m. 2nd Fiona Alexander 1985; one s.; ed. Aldenham School, Wadham Coll., Oxford and Lincoln's Inn; Captain, Royal Artillery 1943–46; English Bar 1950–53; Crown Counsel, Nyasaland (now Malawi) 1953–59; Attorney-Gen., Gibraltar 1960–62; Solicitor-Gen., Hong Kong 1962–66, Attorney-Gen. 1966–73, Colonial Sec. 1973–76, Chief Sec. 1976–78, Chief Justice Hong Kong and Brunei 1979–88, of Brunei 1988–; Pres. Court of Appeal for Bermuda 1988–94; Pres. MCC 1989–90; Seri Paduka Makhuta Brunei; Hon. Fellow Wadham Coll.; Hon. Bencher Lincoln's Inn. *Publications:* eight books (including four novels) 1955–. *Leisure interests:* writing, cricket, tennis, walking. *Address:* Supreme Court, Bandar Seri Begawan, Brunei; Leithen Lodge, Innerleithen, Peeblesshire, EH44 6NW, Scotland. *Telephone:* (01896) 830 297 (Scotland). *Fax:* (01896) 830 726.

ROBERTS, Sir Derek Harry, Kt., C.B.E., B.SC., F.R.S., F.ENG.; British physicist and business executive; b. 28 March 1932, Manchester; s. of Harry Roberts and Alice Roberts (née Storey); m. Winifred Short 1958; one s. one d.; ed. Manchester Cen. High School and Manchester Univ.; Research Scientist, Plessey Co. 1953–67; Gen. Man. Plessey Semiconductors 1967–69; Dir. Plessey Allen Clark Research Centre 1969–73; Man. Dir. Plessey Microsystems Div. 1973–79; Dir. of Research, The General Electric Co. PLC 1979–83, Tech. Dir. 1983–85, Jt. Deputy Man. Dir. (Tech.) 1985–88, Dir. 1988–; Provost Univ. Coll., London 1989–99; Pres. B.A.A.S. 1996–97; Visiting Prof., Univ. Coll. London 1979; Hon. D.Sc. (Bath) 1982, (Loughborough) 1984, (City) 1985, (Lancaster) 1986, (Manchester) 1987, (Queens Univ., Belfast) 1990, D.Univ. (Open) 1984, (Salford), (Essex), (London) 1988. *Publications:* about 25–30 tech. papers in learned soc. journals. *Leisure interest:* gardening. *Address:* University College London, Gower Street, London, WC1E 6BT; The Old Rectory, Maids Moreton, Buckingham, England. *Telephone:* 0171-380 7234; (01280) 813470.

ROBERTS, Sir Gareth Gwyn, Kt., PH.D., F.R.S.; British university vice-chancellor; b. 16 May 1940, Wales; s. of Edwin Roberts and Meri Roberts; m. 1st Charlotte Standen 1962; two s. one d.; m. 2nd Carolyn Rich 1993; two step-d.; ed. Univ. Coll. of N. Wales, Bangor; lecturer in Physics, Univ. of Wales 1963–66; research physicist, Xerox Corpn. U.S.A. 1966–68; Sr.

lecturer, Reader and Prof. of Physics, Univ. of Ulster 1968–76; Prof. of Applied Physics and Head, Dept. of Applied Physics and Electronics, Univ. of Durham 1976–85; Visiting Prof. of Electronic Eng., Dept. of Eng. Science and Fellow, Brasenose Coll. Oxford 1985–93; Chief Scientist and Dir. of Research, Thorn EMI PLC; Vice-Chancellor, Univ. of Sheffield 1991–; Chair. Defence Scientific Advisory Council 1993–97, CVCP 1995–97; Pres. Inst. of Physics 1998–; Dir. Sheffield Health Authority 1996–, Univs. Superannuation Scheme 1997; mem. HEFCE 1997–, USS Bd. 1997–; Fellow Brasenose Coll. Oxford 1985–95, Hon. Fellow 1995; Holweck Gold Medal and Prize, Inst. of Physics 1986. *Publications:* Insulating Films on Semiconductors 1979, Langmuir-Blodgett Films 1990; many publs. and patents on physics of semiconductor devices and molecular electronics. *Leisure interests:* watching soccer, classical music, organizing 'town and gown' functions. *Address:* University of Sheffield, Firth Court, Western Bank, Sheffield S10 2TN (Office); The Croft, Snaithing Lane, Sheffield, S10 3LF, England (Home). *Telephone:* (0114) 222 1007 (Office); (0114) 282 4305 (Home). *Fax:* (0114) 272 7407.

ROBERTS, Ivor Anthony, C.M.G., M.A.; British diplomatist; b. 24 Sept. 1946; s. of the late Leonard Moore Roberts and of Rosa Maria Roberts (née Fusco); m. Elizabeth Bray Bernard Smith 1974; two s. one d.; ed. St. Mary's Coll., Crosby, Keble Coll., Oxford; entered diplomatic service 1968, with Middle East Centre for Arab Studies 1969, Third, then Second Sec. Paris 1970–73, Second, then First Sec. FCO 1973–78, First Sec. Canberra 1978–82, Deputy Head of News Dept. FCO 1982–86, Head Security Co-ordination Dept. FCO 1986–88, Minister and Deputy Head of Mission, Madrid 1989–93, Chargé d'affaires Belgrade 1994–96; Amb. to Yugoslavia 1996–97, to Ireland 1998–; Fellow Inst. of Linguists 1991; Sr. Assoc. Mem. St. Antony's Coll., Oxford 1997–. *Leisure interests:* opera, skiing, golf, photography. *Address:* British Embassy, 29 Merrion Road, Dublin 4, Ireland. *Telephone:* (1) 2053700. *Fax:* (1) 2053885.

ROBERTS, John D., PH.D.; American chemist and educator; b. 8 June 1918, Los Angeles, Calif.; s. of Allen Andrew Roberts and Flora Dombrowski; m. Edith M. Johnson 1942; three s. one d.; ed. Univ. of California at Los Angeles; Instructor Univ. of Calif. at Los Angeles; Nat. Research Fellow in Chem., Harvard Univ. 1945–46, Instructor 1946; Instructor M.I.T. 1946–47, Asst. Prof. 1947–50, Assoc. Prof. 1950–53; Guggenheim Fellow, Calif. Inst. of Technology 1952–53, Prof. of Organic Chem. 1953–72, Inst. Prof. of Chem. 1972–88, Prof. Emer. 1988–, lecturer 1988–, Chair. Div. of Chem. and Chemical Eng. 1963–68, Acting Chair. 1972–73, Dean of the Faculty 1980–83, Vice-Pres. and Provost 1980–83; Visiting Prof. Ohio State Univ. 1952, Harvard Univ. 1959–60, Univ. of Munich 1962; Distinguished Visiting Prof. Univ. of Iowa 1967; Visiting Prof. Stanford Univ. 1973; Distinguished Grad. Lecturer Scripps Research Inst. 1996; mem. N.A.S., Chair. Section of Chem. 1968–71, of Math. and Physical Sciences 1976–78, Class I 1977–79, Counsellor 1980–83; mem. American Philosophical Society 1974, Counsellor, Class I 1983–86; Dr. h.c. (Munich); Hon. D.Sc. (Temple Univ., Wales, Scripps Research Inst.); numerous awards, including Nat. Medal of Science 1990, Welch Award 1990, Arthur C. Cope Award 1994. *Publications:* Nuclear Magnetic Resonance 1958, Spin-Spin Splitting in High Resolution Nuclear Magnetic Resonance Spectra 1961, Molecular Orbital Calculations 1961, Basic Principles of Organic Chemistry 1965, Modern Organic Chemistry 1967, Organic Chemistry, Methane to Macromolecules 1971, At the Right Place at the Right Time 1990; and numerous articles 1940–. *Leisure interests:* tennis, skiing, sailing, classical music, colour photography. *Address:* California Institute of Technology, Crellin Laboratory, Pasadena, CA 91125, U.S.A. *Telephone:* (626) 395-6036.

ROBERTS, John Morris, C.B.E., D.PHIL.; British historian; b. 14 April 1928, Bath, Somerset; s. of late Edward Henry Roberts and Dorothy Julia Hallett; m. Judith Armitage 1964; one s. two d.; ed. Taunton School, Keble Coll., Univ. of Oxford; nat. service 1949–50; Prize Fellow Magdalen Coll., Univ. of Oxford 1951–53, Tutorial Fellow Merton Coll. 1954–79, Warden 1984–94, Hon. Fellow 1994–; Vice-Chancellor Univ. of Southampton 1979–85; mem. Bd. of Govs. BBC 1988–93; mem. Bd. British Council 1991–98; Trustee Nat. Portrait Gallery 1984–98; Writer and Presenter BBC TV Series, The Triumph of the West 1985; Hon. Fellow, Merton and Keble Colls., Univ. of Oxford; Hon. D.Litt. (Southampton) 1987. *Publications:* The History of the World 1997 and other historical books and articles. *Leisure interest:* music. *Address:* c/o Merton College, Oxford, OX1 4JD, England.

ROBERTS, Julia; American actress; b. 1967, Smyrna, Ga.; m. Lyle Lovett 1993 (divorced 1995); ed. high school; appeared in TV movie Baja Oklahoma; Golden Globe Award for performance in Steel Magnolias 1990; UNICEF Goodwill Amb. 1995. *Films:* Blood Red, Satisfaction, Mystic Pizza, Steel Magnolias, 3000, Flatliners, Pretty Woman, Sleeping with the Enemy, Dying Young, Batman, Hook, The Player, The Pelican Brief 1993, I Love Trouble 1994, Prêt à Porter 1994, Mary Reilly 1994, Something to Talk About 1996, Michael Collins 1996, Everyone Says I Love You 1996, My Best Friend's Wedding 1997, Conspiracy Theory 1997, Notting Hill 1998, Stepmom 1998, Runaway Bride 1999. *Address:* ICM, 8942 Wilshire Boulevard, Beverly Hills, CA 90211, U.S.A.

ROBERTS, Lewis Edward John, C.B.E., M.A., D.PHIL., F.R.S.; British research scientist; b. 31 Jan. 1922, Cardiff; s. of Rev. W.E. Roberts and L.L. Roberts; m. Eleanor M. Luscombe 1947; one s.; ed. Swansea Grammar School, Jesus Coll., Oxford and Clarendon Lab., Oxford; Scientific Officer, Chalk River Labs., Ont. 1946–47; Scientist, A.E.R.E., Harwell 1947–67, Asst. Dir. 1967–75, Dir. 1975–86; Commonwealth Fund Fellow, Univ. of Calif. (Berkeley) 1954–55; mem. UKAEA 1979–86; Wolfson Prof. of Environmental Risk Assessment, Univ. of E. Anglia 1986–90, Emer. Prof. 1990–. *Publications:* Nuclear Power and Public Responsibility 1984, Power Generation and the Environment 1990; papers in scientific journals on solid state chemistry and thermodynamics, radioactive waste man., risk analysis. *Leisure interests:* reading, gardening. *Address:* Penfold Wick, Chilton, Didcot, Oxon., OX11 0SH, England. *Telephone:* (01235) 834309.

ROBERTS, Michèle (Brigitte), M.A. (OXON); British novelist and poet; b. 20 May 1949, Herts.; d. of Reginald Roberts and Monique Caulle; m. Jim Latter 1991; two step-s.; ed. Convent Grammar School, Somerville Coll., Oxford and University Coll. London; Visiting Fellow Univ. of E. Anglia 1992, Univ. of Nottingham Trent 1994, 1996–; W.H. Smith Literary Award 1993. *Publications:* novels: A Piece of the Night 1978, The Visitation 1983, The Wild Girl 1984, The Book of Mrs. Noah 1987, In the Red Kitchen 1990, Daughters of the House 1992, Flesh and Blood 1994, Fair Exchange 1999; (ed. jtly.) Mind Readings 1996, Impossible Saints 1997; Stories: During Mother's Absence 1993; essays: Food, Sex and God 1998; poetry: The Mirror of the Mother 1986, Psyche and the Hurricane 1991, All the Selves I Was 1995; Plays: The Journeywoman 1988, Child-Lover 1995. Film: The Heavenly Twins 1993. *Address:* c/o Gillon Aitken, Aitken & Stone, 29 Fernshaw Road, London, SW10 0TG, England.

ROBERTS, Richard, PH.D.; British scientist; b. 6 Sept. 1943, Derby; s. of John Walter Roberts and Edna Wilhelmina Roberts; m. 1st Elizabeth Dyson 1965 (deceased); one s. one d.; m. 2nd Jean Tagliabue 1986; one s. one d.; ed. Sheffield Univ.; researcher Harvard Univ., Cold Spring Harbour Lab. Research Inst., Long Island; Research Dir. New England Biolabs 1992–; mem. Scientific Advisory Bd. Genex 1994–; Hon. D.Sc. (Sheffield) 1994; Nobel Prize in Physiology or Medicine (for the discovery of 'split genes') 1993. *Address:* New England Bio-Laboratories, 32 Tozer Road, Beverly, Massachussetts 01915, U.S.A.

ROBERTSON, Geoffrey R., Q.C., B.A., LL.B., B.C.L.; Australian lawyer; b. 30 Sept. 1946, Sydney; s. of Francis Robertson and Bernice Beattie; m. Kathy Lette 1990 (q.v.); one s. one d.; ed. Epping Boys' High School and Univs. of Sydney and Oxford; Rhodes scholar; solicitor, Allen, Allen & Hemsley 1970; called to bar, Middle Temple, London 1973; Q.C. 1988; Visiting Prof. Univ. of N.S.W. 1979, Univ. of Warwick 1981; leader, Amnesty missions to S. Africa 1983–90; consultant on Human Rights to Govt. of Australia 1984; Head, Doughty St. Chambers 1990–; Counsel to Royal Comm. on gun-running to Colombian drug cartels 1991; Asst. Recorder 1993–; mem. Exec. Council, Charter 88, Justice, ICA; Freedom of Information Award 1992. *Publications:* Reluctant Judas 1976, Obscenity 1979, People Against the Press 1983, Geoffrey Robertson's Hypotheticals 1986, Does Dracula Have Aids? 1987, Freedom, The Individual and The Law 1989, Media Law (with A. Nicol) 1992, The Justice Game 1998, Crimes Against Humanity 1999. *Leisure interests:* tennis, opera, fishing. *Address:* Doughty Street Chambers, 11 Doughty Street, London, WC1N 2PG, England. *Telephone:* 0171-404 1313. *Fax:* 0171-404 2283.

ROBERTSON, Rt. Hon. George Islay Macneill, P.C., M.A.; British politician; b. 12 April 1946; s. of George Robertson and Marion Robertson; m. Sandra Wallace 1970; two s. one d.; ed. Dunoon Grammar School and Univ. of Dundee; Research Asst. Tayside Study 1968–69; Scottish Research Officer, Gen. & Municipal Workers' Union 1969–70, Scottish Organizer 1970–78; M.P. for Hamilton 1978–97, for Hamilton South 1997–; Parl. Pvt. Sec. to Sec. of State for Social Services 1979; Opposition Spokesman on Scottish Affairs 1979–80, on Defence 1980–81, on Foreign and Commonwealth Affairs 1981; Prin. Spokesman on European Affairs 1984–94; Shadow Spokesman for Scotland 1994–97; Sec. of State for Defence May 1997–; Chair. British-German Parl. Group 1992–93, Hon. Pres. 1993–; Chair. Scottish Council of Labour Party 1977–78; Vice-Chair. Bd. British Council 1985–94, Prince's Trust Community Venture, Blantyre 1990–; Vice-Pres. Operation Raleigh 1982–; mem. Bd. Scottish Devt. Agency 1975–78, Scottish Tourist Bd. 1974–76; mem. Council, Nat. Trust for Scotland 1976–82, 1983–85; mem. Steering Cttee. Königswinter Conf. 1983–92; mem. Council, British Atlantic Cttee. 1981–; mem. Council, Royal Inst. of Int. Affairs 1984–91; mem. Council, G.B./Russia Centre 1986–97; Gov. Ditchley Foundation 1989–; many other appts.; Commdr's. Cross, Order of Merit (Germany). *Leisure interests:* photography, golf. *Address:* House of Commons, London, SW1A 0AA (Office); 3 Argyle Park, Dunblane, FK15 9DZ, Scotland (Home). *Telephone:* 0171-219 3000 (Office).

ROBERTSON, Sir Lewis, Kt., C.B.E., F.R.S.E.; British industrialist and administrator; b. 28 Nov. 1922, Dundee, Scotland; s. of John Robertson and Margaret Robertson (née Arthur); m. Elspeth Badenoch 1950; two s. (and one s. deceased) one d.; ed. Trinity Coll., Glenalmond, and trained as accountant; R.A.F. Intelligence 1942–46; worked in textile industry, Chair. and Man. Dir. Scott & Robertson PLC 1946–70; Chief Exec. and Deputy Chair. Grampian Holdings PLC 1971–76; Deputy Chair. and Chief Exec. Scottish Devt. Agency 1976–81; Dir. Scottish & Newcastle Breweries PLC 1975–87, Whitman Int., S.A., Geneva 1987–90, Edinburgh Income Trust 1989–, Berkeley Hotel Co. 1995–97, Advanced Man. Programme Scotland 1996–; Chair. F.H. Lloyd Holdings PLC 1982–87, Triplex PLC 1983–87, Triplex Lloyd PLC 1987–90, Girobank Scotland 1984–90, Borthwicks PLC

1985–89, Lilley PLC 1986–93, Havelock Europa PLC 1989–92, Stakis PLC 1991–95, Postern Exec. Group Ltd. 1991–96; Trustee (Exec. Cttee.), Carnegie Trust for the Univs. of Scotland 1963– (Chair. 1990–); mem. Monopolies and Mergers Comm. 1969–76, British Council (Chair. Scottish Advisory Cttee.) 1978–87, Restrictive Practices Court 1983–96; mem. Council Royal Soc. of Edin. 1992, Treas. 1994–; Hon. LL.D. (Dundee) 1971; Hon. D.B.A. (Napier) 1992; Hon. D.Univ. (Stirling) 1993. *Leisure interests:* work, computer use, list-making, things Italian, music, literature. *Address:* 32 Saxe Coburg Place, Edinburgh, EH3 5BP, Scotland (Office). *Telephone:* 0131-332 5221. *Fax:* 0131-343 1840.

ROBERTSON, Sir Rutherford Ness, Kt., A.C., C.M.G., D.SC., PH.D., F.R.S.; Australian botanist; b. 29 Sept. 1913, Melbourne; s. of Rev. J. Robertson and Mrs. J. Robertson; m. Mary Rogerson 1937; one s.; ed. St. Andrew's Coll., Christchurch, New Zealand, Sydney Univ., and St. John's Coll., Cambridge; Asst. Lecturer, later Lecturer in Botany, Sydney Univ. 1939–46; Sr. Research Officer, later Chief Research Officer, Commonwealth Scientific and Industrial Research Org. (CSIRO), Div. of Food Preservation 1946–59, mem. Exec. of CSIRO 1959–62; Visiting Prof. Univ. of Calif. 1958–59; Prof. of Botany, Univ. of Adelaide 1962–69; Chair. Australian Research Grants Cttee. 1965–69; Master, Univ. House, Australian Nat. Univ., Canberra 1969–72, Pro-Chancellor 1984–86; Dir. Research School of Biological Sciences 1972–78; Hon. Visitor Sydney Univ. 1979–86; Deputy Chair. Australian Science and Tech. Council 1977–81; Fellow, Australian Acad. of Science 1954, Pres. 1970–74; Pres. Australian and New Zealand Asscn. for the Advancement of Science 1965; Pres. 13th Int. Botanical Congress 1981; Patron Australian Cttee. Cambridge Commonwealth Trust 1993–97; Foreign Assoc. U.S. Acad. of Sciences 1962; Foreign mem. American Philosophical Soc. 1971; Hon. mem. Royal Soc. of New Zealand 1971; Hon. Foreign mem. A.A.A.S. 1973; Hon. Fellow, St. John's Coll. Cambridge 1973, Royal Soc., Edin. 1983; Hon. D.Sc. (Tasmania) 1965, (Monash) 1970, (Australian Nat. Univ.) 1979; Hon. Sc.D. (Cambridge) 1969; Clarke Memorial Medal, Royal Soc. of N.S.W. 1954, Farrer Memorial Medal 1963, A.N.Z.A.A.S. Medal 1968, Mueller Medal 1970, Burnet Medal 1975. *Publications:* Electrolytes in Plant Cells (co-author) 1961, Protons, Electrons Phosphorylation and Active Transport 1968, The Lively Membranes 1983. *Leisure interest:* reading. *Address:* Unit 12, Linton Retirement Village, Glebe Street, Yass, N.S.W. 2582, Australia. *Telephone:* (06) 226 3093.

ROBICHAUD, Hon. Louis Joseph, C.C., P.C., Q.C., B.A.; Canadian politician; b. 21 Oct. 1925, St. Anthony, Kent County, N.B.; s. of Amédée Robichaud and Annie (née Richard) Robichaud; m. 1st Lorraine Savoie 1951 (died 1986); three s. one d.; m. 2nd Jacqueline Grignon 1998; ed. Sacred Heart and Laval Univs.; pvt. law practice 1951–60; mem. N.B. Legislature 1952–71, Leader of Opposition 1958–60, 1970–71; Premier of N.B. 1960–70, Attorney-Gen. 1960–65, Minister of Youth 1968–70; mem. Senate Dec. 1973–; numerous hon. degrees; Liberal. *Address:* 1501–400 Stewart Street, Ottawa, Ont., K1N 6L2, Canada.

ROBINS, Lee Nelken, M.A., PH.D.; American professor of social science; b. 29 Aug. 1922, New Orleans, La.; m. Eli Robins 1946; four s.; ed. Radcliffe Coll. and Harvard Univ.; Research Assoc. Inst. for Urban and Regional Studies, Washington Univ., St. Louis, Mo. 1962–63, Research Assoc. Prof. Dept. of Psychiatry 1962–66, Research Prof. of Sociology in Psychiatry 1966–68, Prof. of Sociology in Psychiatry 1968–91, Prof. Dept. of Sociology 1969–91, Univ. Prof. of Social Science, Prof. of Social Science in Psychiatry 1991–; NIMH Special Research Fellowship, Washington Univ. 1968–70; mem. Inst. of Medicine (N.A.S.); Research Scientist Award 1970. *Publications include:* Deviant Children Grown Up: A Sociological and Psychiatric Study of Sociopathic Personality 1966, Studying Drug Abuse 1985, Psychiatric Disorders in America 1991. *Address:* Washington University School of Medicine, Department of Psychiatry, St. Louis, MO 63110, U.S.A. *Telephone:* (314) 362-2469.

ROBINS, Sir Ralph (Harry), Kt., B.SC., F.ENG., F.R.AE.S.; British business executive; b. 16 June 1932, Heanor; s. of Leonard Haddon and Maud Lillian Robins; m. Patricia Maureen Grimes 1962; two d.; ed. Imperial Coll., Univ. of London; Devt. Engineer, Rolls-Royce 1955–66, Exec. Vice-Pres. Rolls-Royce Inc. 1971, Man. Dir. Rolls-Royce Industrial and Marine Div. 1973, Commercial Dir. Rolls-Royce Ltd. 1978, Man. Dir. Rolls-Royce PLC 1984–89, Deputy Chair. 1989–92, and Chief Exec. 1990–92, Chair. Rolls Royce 1992–; Chair. Defence Industries Council 1986–; Pres. Soc. of British Aerospace Cos. 1986–87, Deputy Pres. 1987–88; Dir. (non-exec.) Standard Chartered 1988–, Schroders 1990–, Marks & Spencer 1992–, Cable & Wireless 1994–; mem. Council for Science and Tech. 1993–98; Fellow of Imperial Coll.; Hon. F.I. Mech. E. 1996, Hon. D.B.A. (Strathclyde) 1996; Commdr. Order of Merit (Germany) 1996. *Leisure interests:* tennis, golf, music, classic cars. *Address:* Rolls-Royce PLC, 65 Buckingham Gate, London, SW1E 6AT, England. *Telephone:* 0171-222 9020. *Fax:* 0171-227 9185.

ROBINS, Robert Henry, M.A., D.LIT., F.B.A.; British professor of general linguistics; b. 1 July 1921, Broadstairs; s. of Dr. J. N. Robins and Muriel W. Robins; m. Sheila M. Fynn 1953 (died 1983); ed. Tonbridge School and New Coll. Oxford; lecturer in Linguistics, S.O.A.S. Univ. of London 1948–55; Reader in Gen. Linguistics, Univ. of London 1955–65, Prof. 1966–86, Prof. Emer. 1986–; Visiting Prof. Univs. of Washington, Hawaii, Minn., S. Fla. and Salzburg 1963–79; Hon. Sec. Philological Soc. 1961–88, Pres. 1988–92; Pres. Perm. Int. Cttee. of Linguistics 1977–97; Hon. mem. Linguistic Soc. of America. *Publications:* nine books on linguistics. *Leisure interests:* travel, gardening. *Address:* 65 Dome Hill, Caterham, Surrey, CR3 6EF, England. *Telephone:* (01883) 343778.

ROBINSON, Sir Albert Edward Phineas, Kt., M.A.; business executive (retd.); b. 30 Dec. 1915, Durban; s. of Charles Phineas Robinson and Mabel Victoria Robinson; m. 1st Mary J. Bertish 1944 (died 1973); four d.; m. 2nd Mrs. M. L. Royston-Pigott (née Barrett) 1975; ed. Durban High School and Stellenbosch, L.S.E., Trinity Coll., Cambridge and Leiden Univs.; Barrister-at-Law, Lincoln's Inn; Imperial Light Horse, N. Africa 1940–43; mem. Johannesburg City Council and Leader United Party in Council 1945–48; United Party M.P., South African Parl. 1947–53; perm. resident in S. Rhodesia (now Zimbabwe) 1953; Dir. banks, building socs., several financial and industrial cos. 1953–61; Chair. Cen. African Airways Corpn. 1957–61; mem. Monckton Comm. 1960; High Commr., Fed. of Rhodesia and Nyasaland in the U.K. 1961–63; Deputy Chair. Gen. Mining and Finance Co. Ltd. 1963–71; Chair. Johannesburg Consolidated Investment Corpn. Ltd. 1971–80, Rustenburg Platinum Mines Ltd. 1971–80; Dir. Anglo-American Corpn. of South Africa Ltd. 1965–88; Chancellor, Univ. of Bophuthatswana 1980–91; Hon. D.Com. *Address:* 43 St. Mary Abbots Court, Warwick Gardens, London, W14 8RB, England.

ROBINSON, Arthur Howard, M.A., PH.D.; American cartographer and geographer; b. 5 Jan. 1915, Montreal, Canada; s. of James Howard Robinson and Elizabeth Peavey Robinson; m. 1st Mary Elizabeth Coffin 1938 (died 1992); one s. one d.; m. 2nd Martha Elizabeth Rodabaugh 1993; ed. Saffron Walden Friends School, England, McGuffey High School, Oxford, Ohio., Miami, Wisconsin and Ohio State Univs.; Sec. to a Dir. Ohio Bd. of Liquor Control 1936; Teaching Asst. Geography, Univ. of Wis. 1936–38, Ohio State Univ. 1938–41; Chief Map Officer, Map Div., Office of Strategic Services 1941–45 (mem. U.S. Del. Cairo and Quebec Allied Confs. during Second World War); mil. service 1944–45 (promoted to major); Asst. Prof., later Prof., Univ. of Wis. 1945–80, Prof. Emer. 1980–; Dir. Univ. of Wis. Cartographic Laboratory 1966–73; Lawrence Martin Prof. of Cartography 1967–; mem. Bd. of dirs. American Congress on Surveying and Mapping 1952–54, Bd. of dirs. Cartography Div. 1966–69, 1970, Vice-Chair. 1970, Chair. 1971–72, Ed. American Cartographer 1973–76; mem. Council Asscn. of American Geographers 1960–64, Vice-Pres. 1962–63, Pres. 1963–64; Corresp. mem. Comm. II (Tech. Terms), Int. Cartographic Asscn. 1964–72, mem. Comm. on the History of Cartography 1976–, Chair. Cttee. on Statutes 1976–84, Pres. 1972–76, Past Pres. 1976–80; Chair. Cttee. on State Cartography 1974–79, 1981–82; mem. Gov.'s Cttee. on State Mapping (Wis.) 1961–63; Co-Ed. Int. Yearbook of Cartography 1961–73; Fellow British Cartographic Soc. 1998; Hon. D. Litt. (Miami) 1966, Hon. D. Sc. (Ohio State) 1984; numerous awards including Citation for Meritorious contribs. to Geography (Cartography), Asscn. American Geographers 1953, American Congress on Surveying and Mapping (ACSM) Award for Meritorious Service to the Discipline of Cartography 1979, Carl Mannerfelt Medal, Int. Cartographic Asscn. 1981, Presidential Citation for Outstanding Services to ACSM 1988, Silver Medal, British Cartographic Soc. 1991, O. M. Miller Medal, American Geographical Soc. 1998. *Publications:* numerous books and monographs and over 100 professional papers on maps and cartography including The Look of Maps 1952, Elements of Cartography 1953, Robinson Map Projection 1963, The Atlas of Wisconsin (with J.B. Culver) 1974, The Nature of Maps: Essays Toward and Understanding of Maps and Mapping (with B. Petchenik) 1976, Early Thematic Mapping in the History of Cartography 1982, Which Map is Best? 1986, Cartographical Innovations: An Historical International Handbook of Mapping Terms to 1900 (Co-Ed. with H. Wallis) 1987, Choosing a World Map 1988. *Address:* 7802 Courtyard Drive, Madison, WI 53719, U.S.A. *Telephone:* (608) 833-5145.

ROBINSON, (Arthur Napoleon) Raymond, M.A., LL.B., S.C.; Trinidad and Tobago head of state, barrister and economist; b. 16 Dec. 1926, Calder Hall; s. of James Andrew Robinson and Emily Isabella Robinson; m. Patricia Jean Rawlins 1961; one s. one d.; ed. Bishop's High School, Tobago, St. John's Coll., Oxford and Inner Temple, London; M.P. West Indies 1958–61; Rep. of Trinidad and Tobago Council of Univ. of West Indies 1959–61; Minister of Finance and Gov. for Trinidad Bd. of Govs. of IMF and IBRD 1961–67; Deputy Leader, People's Nat. Movement 1967–70; Minister of External Affairs 1967–68; Consultant to the Foundation for the Establishment of an Int. Criminal Court 1971; Chair. Democratic Action Congress 1971–86; Rep. for Tobago East, House of Reps. 1976–80; Chair. Tobago House of Ass. 1980–86; Leader Nat. Alliance for Reconstruction 1986–91; Prime Minister of Trinidad and Tobago 1986–91, also Minister of the Economy; Minister Extraordinaire for Tobago, the UN and Int. Orgs., Adviser to the Prime Minister 1995–97; Expert Consultant to UN Secr. on Crime Prevention 1979; Vice-Chair. Parliamentarians for Global Action 1993, Pres. 1995–96, Hon. Patron 1997–; Visiting Scholar, Harvard Univ. 1971; Hon. Fellow St. John's Coll., Oxford 1989; Studentship Prize, Inner Temple; Distinguished Int. Criminal Law Award 1977; Chief of Ile Ife 1991; K. St. J. 1992. *Publications:* The New Frontier and the New Africa 1961, Fiscal Reform in Trinidad and Tobago 1966, The Path of Progress 1967, The Teacher and Nationalism 1967, The Mechanics of Independence 1971, Caribbean Man 1986 and contributions to Encyclopaedia Britannica. *Leisure interests:* walking, swimming, travel, reading, modern music. *Address:* The President's House, St. Ann's; 21 Ellerslie Park, Maraval, Trinidad; Robinson Street,

Scarborough, Tobago, Trinidad and Tobago. *Telephone:* 624-1261 (Pres.'s House); 622-7785 (Port of Spain); 639-4558 (Tobago).

ROBINSON, Basil William, B.LITT., M.A., F.B.A., F.S.A.; British museum curator (retd.); b. 20 June 1912, London; s. of William Robinson and Rebecca Frances Mabel (née Gilbanks) Robinson; m. 1st Ailsa Mary Stewart 1945 (died 1954); m. 2nd Oriel Hermione Steel 1958; one s. one d.; ed. Winton House, Winchester, Winchester Coll., Corpus Christi Coll., Oxford; taught at Holyrood School, Bognor Regis 1936–39; Asst. Keeper Victoria & Albert Museum 1939; war service 1940–46; Deputy Keeper, Dept. of Metalwork, Victoria & Albert Museum 1954–66, Keeper 1966–72, Keeper Emer. 1972–76; Consultant Sotheby's 1976–91; Uchiyama Memorial Prize (Japan) 1983; Pres. Royal Asiatic Soc. 1970–73. *Publications include:* Descriptive Catalogue of the Persian Paintings in the Bodleian Library 1958, Kuniyoshi 1961, Arts of the Japanese Sword 1961, Persian Miniature Paintings 1967, Persian Paintings in the India Office Library 1976, Persian Paintings in the John Rylands Library 1980, Kuniyoshi: The Warrior Prints 1982, The Aldrich Book of Catches 1989, Fifteenth-Century Persian Painting: Problems and Issues 1991, Collection Jean Pozzi 1992. *Leisure interests:* singing catches, cats. *Address:* 41 Redcliffe Gardens, London, SW10 9JH, England. *Telephone:* 0171-352 1290.

ROBINSON, Derek Charles, PH.D., F.R.S.; British research scientist; b. 27 May 1941, Isle of Man; s. of Alexander Robinson and Grace Kitchen; m. Marion Quarmby 1968; one d.; ed. Queen Elizabeth School, Kirkby Lonsdale, Manchester Univ.; with A.E.R.E., Harwell 1965–68; visiting scientist I. V. Kurchatov Inst. of Atomic Energy, Moscow 1968–69, also to Tokyo Nagoya and S. Australia 1978–79; researcher UKAEA, Culham Lab. 1970–78, group leader 1979–86, Div. Head 1986–92, Research Dir. 1993–96, Dir. Culham Div. 1996–; Chair. Scientific Advisory Bd. Max Planck Inst. for Plasma Physics 1996–; mem. Tech. Advisory Cttee., Int. Thermonuclear Experiment Reactor 1991–, Consultative Cttee. for Fusion Programme 1996–, also Fusion Tech. Steering Cttee., IAEA Int. Fusion Research Council, Int. Energy Agency Fusion Power Co-ordinating Cttee.; C. V. Boys Prize, Inst. of Physics 1979, also Guthrie Prize and Medal 1998. *Publications:* papers in learned journals. *Leisure interests:* gardening, photography, hill-walking. *Address:* Thatched Cottage, Church Street, Appleford, Abingdon, Oxon., OX14 4PA, England. *Telephone:* (01235) 848500.

ROBINSON, Rt. Rev. Donald William Bradley, A.O., M.A.; Australian ecclesiastic; b. 9 Nov. 1922, Australia; s. of late Ven. R. B. Robinson and Gertrude Ross; m. Marie E. Taubman 1949; three s. one d.; ed. Sydney Church of England Grammar School, Univ. of Sydney and Queens' Coll. Cambridge; curate, St. Matthew's, Manly 1950–51, St. Philip's, Sydney 1952–53; lecturer, Moore Theological Coll. 1952–53, Sr. Lecturer 1954–59, Vice-Prin. 1959–72, Acting Prin. 1968; Visiting Lecturer, Union Biblical Seminary, Yeotmal, India 1969; consecrated Asst. Bishop of Sydney 1973; Bishop in Parramatta 1973–82; Archbishop of Sydney 1982–93; Dr. h.c. (Australian Coll. of Theol.). *Address:* 1 Jubilee Avenue, Pymble, NSW 2073, Australia. *Telephone:* (2) 9449 3033.

ROBINSON, (Francis) Alastair Lavie; British banker; b. 19 Sept. 1937, London; s. of late Stephen Robinson; m. Lavinia Napier 1961; two d.; ed. Eton Coll.; Gen. Man. Mercantile Credit Co. 1971–78; Chair. Exec. Cttee. then C.E.O. and Pres. Barclays America Corpn., U.S.A. 1981–83; Regional Gen. Man. Barclays Bank Int. 1983–87; Dir. Personnel, Barclays Bank PLC 1987–90, Exec. Dir. 1990–96, Group Vice-Chair. 1992–96; Dir. RMC PLC 1996–; Dir. Marshall of Cambridge (Holdings) Ltd. 1996–, Portman Building Soc. 1998–. *Leisure interests:* music, country pursuits, golf. *Address:* 24 Clarendon Street, London, SW1V 4RF, England.

ROBINSON, Geoffrey; British politician; b. 25 May 1938, s. of Robert Norman Robinson and Dorothy Jane Robinson (née Skelly); m. Marie Elena Giorgio 1967; one s. one d.; ed. Emanuel School, Univ. of Cambridge, Yale Univ.; research asst. Labour Party 1965–68; sr. exec. Industrial Reorganisation Corpn. 1968–70; Financial Controller British Leyland 1971–72; Man. Dir. Leyland Innocenti, Milan 1972–73; Chief Exec. Jaguar Cars 1973–75, Meriden Motor Cycle Workers' Co-operative 1978–80 (Dir. 1980–82); M.P. for Coventry N.W. 1976–; H.M. Paymaster General 1997–98; Opposition Spokesman on Science 1982–83, on Regional Affairs and Industry 1983–86. Chair. TransTec PLC 1986–97; Dir. W. Midlands Enterprise Bd. 1980–84; Labour. *Leisure interests:* reading, architecture, gardens. *Address:* c/o House of Commons, London, SW1A 0AA, England.

ROBINSON, Gerrard Jude, F.C.M.A.; British business executive; b. 23 Oct. 1948; s. of Antony Robinson and Elizabeth Ann Robinson; m. 1st Maria Ann Borg 1970 (divorced 1990); one s. one d.; m. 2nd Heather Peta Leaman 1990; one s. one d.; ed. St. Mary's Coll., Castlehead; started work aged 16 as a cost clerk in a Matchbox toy factory; Works Accountant, Lesney Products 1970–74; Financial Controller, Lex Industrial Distribution and Hire 1974–80; Finance Dir. Coca-Cola 1980–81, Sales and Marketing Dir. 1981–83, Man. Dir. 1983–84; Man. Dir. Grand Metropolitan (GrandMet) Contract Services 1984–87; led a man. buy-out of GrandMet catering div. 1987; Chief Exec. Compass GP PLC 1987–91, Granada Group PLC 1991–95, Chair. 1995–; Chair. Arts Council May 1998–; Hon. D. Litt. (Ulster); London Weekend Television 1994–96, ITN 1995–97, BSkyB 1995–98. *Leisure interests:* golf, opera, chess, skiing, reading, music. *Address:* Stornoway House, 13 Cleveland Row, London, SW1A 1GG, England. *Telephone:* 0171-451 3000.

ROBINSON, James D., III, M.B.A.; American business executive; b. 19 Nov. 1935, Atlanta, Ga.; s. of James D. Robinson Jr. and Josephine Crawford; m. 1st Bettye Bradley (divorced); one s. one d.; m. 2nd Linda Gosden 1984; ed. Georgia Inst. of Tech., Harvard Graduate School of Business Admin.; Officer, U.S. Naval Supply Corps 1957–59; various depts. of Morgan Guaranty Trust Co. 1961–66, Asst. Vice-Pres. and Staff Asst. to Chair. and Pres. 1967–68; Gen. Partner, White, Weld & Co. 1968–70; Exec. Vice-Pres. American Express Co. 1970–75, Dir. 1975–93, Pres. 1975–77, 1989–93, Chair. of Bd. and C.E.O. 1977–93, C.O.O. 1989–93; Pres. and C.E.O. (Banking), American Express Int. Banking Corpn. 1970–73, Vice-Chair. 1973–75, Dir. 1973–93, Chair., C.E.O. American Express Int. Banking Corpn. 1983–84; Chair. American Express Credit Corpn. 1973–75; also Dir. various subsidiaries; Chair. N.Y. State Savings Bond Cttee. 1980–81; Pres. J. D. Robinson Inc. 1993–; Chair. and C.E.O. RRE Investors 1994–; Chair. Bd. of Overseers and Mans., Memorial Sloan-Kettering Cancer Center; Dir. of numerous cos. and orgs., including The Coca-Cola Co., Union Pacific Corp., New York City Partnership and Chamber of Commerce Inc., Nat. Acad. Foundation; Sr. Advisor Salomon Smith Barney 1997–; mem. of numerous orgs., including The Business Council and Inter-American Devt. Bank; Hon. mem. Bd. of Trustees The Brookings Inst. *Address:* J.D. Robinson, Inc., 126 E. 56th Street, 22nd Floor, New York, NY 10022, U.S.A.

ROBINSON, Kenneth Ernest, C.B.E., D.LITT., LL.D., F.R.HIST.S.; British historian and university administrator; b. 9 March 1914, London; s. of late Ernest Robinson and Isabel Robinson; m. Stephanie Christine S. Wilson 1938 (died 1994); one s. one d.; ed. Monoux Grammar School, Walthamstow, Hertford Coll., Oxford, and London School of Econs.; entered Colonial Office 1936; Asst. Sec. 1946–48, resigned; Fellow of Nuffield Coll. 1948–57, Hon. Fellow 1984–; Reader in Commonwealth Govt., Oxford 1948–57; Leverhulme Research Fellow 1952–53; Reid Lecturer, Acadia Univ. 1963; part-time mem., Directing Staff, Civil Service Selection Bd. 1951–56, Chair. Panel 1972–77; Prof. of Commonwealth Affairs and Dir. of Inst. of Commonwealth Studies, Univ. of London 1957–65, Hon. Life mem. 1980–; Vice-Chancellor, Univ. of Hong Kong 1965–72; mem. Colonial Econ. Research Cttee. 1949–62, Colonial Social Science Research Council 1958–62, Councils of Overseas Devt. Inst. 1960–65, Int. African Inst. 1960–65, Royal Inst. of Int. Affairs 1962–65, African Studies Asscn. of U.K. 1963–65, 1978–81, Asscn. of Commonwealth Univs. 1967–69, Royal Asiatic Soc. Hong Kong Branch 1965–69, Hong Kong Man. Asscn. 1966–72, Univ. of Cape Coast 1972–74, Inter-Univ. Council for Higher Educ. Overseas 1973–79, Royal Commonwealth Soc. 1974–87 (Vice-Pres. 1983), Royal African Soc. 1983–, (Pres. 1989–95); Gov. L.S.E. 1959–65; Ed. Journal of Commonwealth Political Studies 1961–65; Hallsworth Research Fellow, Manchester Univ. 1972–74; Callander Lecturer, Aberdeen Univ. 1979; Dir. Survey of Resources for Commonwealth Studies, Univ. of London 1974–75; J.P. Hong Kong 1967–72; Corresp. mem. Acad. des Sciences d'Outre-Mer, Paris; Hon. LL.D. (Chinese Univ. of Hong Kong) 1969; Hon. Dr. (Open Univ.) 1978; Special Commonwealth Award, Ministry of Overseas Devt. 1965. *Publications:* Africa Today (co-author) 1955, Africa in the Modern World (co-author) 1955, Five Elections in Africa (with W. J. M. Mackenzie) 1960, Essays in Imperial Government (with A. F. Madden) 1963, The Dilemmas of Trusteeship 1965, A Decade of the Commonwealth (with W. B. Hamilton and C. Goodwin) 1966, University Co-operation and Asian Development (co-author) 1967, L'Europe au XIXe et XXe siècles, Vol. VII (co-author) 1967, Experts in Africa (co-author) 1980, Perspectives in Imperialism and Decolonisation (Festschrift; ed. M. Twaddle) 1984. *Address:* 52 The Cloisters, Pegasus Grange, Whitehouse Road, Oxford, OX1 4QQ, England. *Telephone:* (01865) 725517.

ROBINSON, Mary, LL.M.; Irish international civil servant and fmr. head of state; b. 21 May 1944, Ballina, Co. Mayo; d. of Dr. Aubrey Bourke and Tessa O'Donnell; m. Nicholas Robinson 1970; two s. one d.; ed. Mount Anville, Trinity Coll. Dublin, King's Inns, Dublin and Harvard Univ., U.S.A.; Barrister 1967, Sr. Counsel 1980; called to English Bar (Middle Temple) 1973; Reid Prof. of Consitutional and Criminal Law, Trinity Coll. Dublin 1969–75, lecturer in European Community Law 1975–90; Founder and Dir. Irish Centre for European Law 1988–90; Senator 1969–89; Pres. of Ireland 1990–97; UN High Commr. for Human Rights 1997–; mem. Dublin City Council 1979–83; mem. New Ireland Forum 1983–84; mem. Irish Parl. Jt. Cttee. on EC Secondary Legislation 1973–89; mem. Vedel Cttee. on Enlargement of European Parl., EC 1971–72, Saint-Geours Cttee. on Energy Efficiency, EC 1978–79, Advisory Bd. of Common Market Law Review 1976–90, Irish Parl. Jt. Cttee. on Marital Breakdown 1983–85, Editorial Bd. of Irish Current Law Statutes Annoted 1984–90, Advisory Cttee. of Interights, London 1984–90, Int. Comm. of Jurists, Geneva 1987–90, Cttee. of Man., European Air Law Asscn. 1989–90, Scientific Council of European Review of Public Law 1989–90, Euro Avocats, Brussels 1989–90; Gen. Rapporteur, Human Rights at the Dawn of the 21st Century, Council of Europe, Strasbourg 1993; Pres. Cherish (Irish Asscn. of Single Parents) 1973–90; mem. Royal Irish Acad.; Hon. Bencher King's Inns, Dublin, Middle Temple, London; Hon. Prof. of Law, Manchester Univ.; Hon. Fellow Trinity Coll. Dublin, Inst. of Engineers of Ireland, Royal Coll. of Physicians in Ireland, Hertford Coll. Oxford, Royal Coll. of Psychiatrists, London, Royal Coll. of Surgeons, Ireland, Royal Coll. of Obstetricians and Gynaecologists, London; Hon. mem. N.Y. Bar Asscn., Bar of Tanzania; LL.D. h.c. (Nat. Univ. of Ireland, Cambridge, Brown, Liverpool, Dublin, Montpellier, St. Andrews, Melbourne, Columbia, Nat. Univ. of Wales, Poznań, Toronto, Fordham, Queens Univ. Belfast); Dr. h.c. of Public Services (Northeastern Univ.); Hon.

Doctorat en Sciences Humaines (Rennes) 1996, Hon. LL.D. (Coventry) 1996; Berkeley Medal, Univ. of Calif., Medal of Honour, Univ. of Coimbra, Medal of Honour, Ordem dos Advogados, Portugal, Gold Medal of Honour, Univ. of Salamanca, Andrés Bello Medal, Univ. of Chile, New Zealand Suffrage Centennial Medal, Freedom Prize, Max Schmidheiny Foundation (Switzerland), UNIFEM Award, Noel Foundation, Los Angeles, Marisa Bellisario Prize, Italy 1991, European Media Prize, The Netherlands 1991, Special Humanitarian Award, CARE, Washington, D.C. 1993, Int. Human Rights Award, Int. League of Human Rights, New York 1993, Liberal Int. Prize for Freedom 1993, Stephen P. Duggan Award (U.S.A.) 1994; Freedom of the City of Cork; Hon. A.O. *Address:* Palais des Nations, United Nations, 1211 Geneva 10, Switzerland.

ROBINSON, Peter David, M.P.; British politician; b. 29 Dec. 1948; s. of David McCrea Robinson and Sheliah Robinson; m. Iris Collins 1970; two s. one d.; ed. Annadale Grammar School, Castlereagh Further Educ. Coll.; Gen. Sec. Ulster Democratic Unionist Party 1975–79, Deputy Leader 1980–87; M.P. for Belfast E., Northern Ireland Ass. 1982–86; M.P. for Belfast E., House of Commons 1979–; (resigned seat Dec. 1985 in protest against Anglo-Irish Agreement; re-elected Jan. 1986); mem. Castlereagh Borough Council 1977, Deputy Mayor 1978, Mayor 1986; mem. Northern Ireland Forum 1996–; mem. Belfast East, N.I. Ass. 1998–; Democratic Unionist. *Publications:* Ulster—the facts 1982 (jtly.); booklets: The North Answers Back 1970, Capital Punishment for Capital Crime 1978, Self Inflicted 1981, Ulster in Peril 1981, Savagery and Suffering 1981, Their Cry Was "No Surrender" 1989, The Union Under Fire 1995. *Address:* House of Commons, London, SW1A 0AA, England; 51 Gransha Road, Dundonald, BT16 0HB; Strandtown Hall, 96 Belmont Avenue, Belfast, BT4 3DE, Northern Ireland.

ROBINSON, Raymond (see Robinson, Arthur Napoleon Raymond).

ROBLES, Marisa, H.R.C.M., F.R.C.M.; British concert harpist; b. 4 May 1937, Madrid, Spain; m. 3rd David W. Bean 1985; two s. one d. from previous marriages; ed. Madrid Royal Conservatoire of Music; Prof. of the Harp, Madrid Conservatoire 1958–; Harp Tutor to Nat. Youth Orchestra of G.B. 1964–69; Prof. of Harp Royal Coll. of Music, London 1969–; Artistic Dir. World Harp Festival, Cardiff, Wales 1991, World Harp Festival II 1994; soloist with James Galway (q.v.) Albert Hall, London 1978; played with major orchestras including New York Philharmonic 1984; tours in Europe, U.S.A., Australia, Japan, S. America, Canada; made various records and appeared in many musical programmes on television. *Publications:* several harp pieces and arrangements. *Leisure interests:* theatre, indoor plants, nature in general, cooking, spending private time with family. *Address:* 38 Luttrell Avenue, London, SW15 6PE, England. *Telephone:* 0181-785 2204.

ROBOZ, Zsuzsi; British artist; b. 15 Aug. 1939, Budapest, Hungary; d. of Imre Roboz and Edith Grosz; m. A. T. (Teddy) Smith 1964; ed. Royal Acad. of Arts, London; also studied with Pietro Annigoni, Florence; various commissions 1956–, including scenes back-stage at Windmill Theatre, London 1964, theatre card of ballet movements for Theatre Museum 1979, portrait of H.R.H. Alice, Duchess of Gloucester 1981; has exhibited at numerous galleries including Walker Galleries, London 1958, André Weil Gallery, Paris 1960, 1968, O'Hana Gallery, London 1967, 1970, 1973, Hong Kong Arts Festival 1976, Curwen Gallery, London 1977, Hamilton Gallery, London 1979, L'Horizon Gallery, Brussels 1980, Piccadilly Festival of Arts 1981, Vigado Gallery, Budapest 1988, Amsterdam Gallery, Lincoln Center, New York 1989, Business Design Centre, London 1993, Mall Galleries 1993, Roy Miles Gallery 1994, David Messum Gallery 1995; portraits painted include Dame Ninette de Valois, Lord Olivier and Lucian Freud; rep. in perm. public collections at Tate Gallery, London, Nat. Portrait Gallery, London, Theatre Museum, London, Museum of Fine Arts, Budapest, Graves Art Gallery, Sheffield, Bradford Museum and City Art Galleries, St. Andrews Convent, London, Barnwell Church, Northants, New Scotland Yard, London, Durham Univ., St. John's Coll., Cambridge, Royal Festival Hall, London, Pablo Casals Museum, Jamaica; also rep. in various pvt. collections; guest of honour Spring Festival, Budapest 1984. *Publications include:* Women and Men's Daughters 1970, Chichester 10, Portrait of a Decade 1975, British Ballet Today (with James Monahan) 1980, British Art Now (with Edward Lucie-Smith (q.v.)) 1993, Twentieth Century Illusions 1998. *Leisure interests:* classical music, reading, swimming. *Address:* 6 Bryanston Court, George Street, London, W1H 7HA, England. *Telephone:* 0171-723 6540.

ROBSON, Bryan, O.B.E., M.A.; British footballer; b. 11 Jan. 1957, Chester-le-Street; s. of Brian Robson and Maureen Lowther; m. Denise Robson 1979; one s. two d.; ed. Birtley Lord Lawson Comprehensive; professional footballer with Manchester United, F.A. Cup winners 1983, 1985, 1990; Euro Cup Winners' Cup 1991; player, Man. Middlesbrough FC 1994–; asst. coach English Nat. Team 1994–; winner of League Championship 1992–93; Hon. M.A. (Salford) 1992, (Manchester) 1992. *Leisure interests:* golf, horse racing. *Address:* Middlesbrough FC, Cellnet Riverside Stadium, Middlesbrough, Cleveland, TS3 6RS, England. *Telephone:* (01642) 227227.

ROBSON, Sir James Gordon, Kt., C.B.E., M.B., CH.B., F.R.C.A., F.R.C.S., D.SC.; British professor of anaesthetics; b. 18 March 1921, Stirling, Scotland; s. of James C. Robson and Freda E. Howard; m. 1st Martha G. Kennedy 1945 (died 1975); one s.; m. 2nd Jennifer Kilpatrick 1984; ed. High School of Stirling and Univ. of Glasgow; Wellcome Research Prof. of Anaesthetics, McGill Univ., Montreal 1956–64; Dir. and Prof. of Anaesthetics, Royal Postgraduate Medical School, Univ. of London 1964–86; Dean, Faculty of Anaesthetists, Royal Coll. of Surgeons 1973–76; Vice-Pres. Royal Coll. of Surgeons 1977–79; Master, Hunterian Inst. 1982–88; Consultant Adviser in Anaesthetics to Dept. of Health and Social Security 1975–84; Chair. Medical and Survival Cttee. Royal Nat. Lifeboat Inst. 1988–91, mem. Cttee. Man. 1988–, Vice-Pres. 1992–96, Life Vice-Pres. 1996–; Civilian Consultant to the Army in Anaesthetics 1982–88; Chair. Advisory Cttee. on Distinction Awards 1984–94; Pres. Scottish Soc. of Anaesthetists 1985–86, Royal Soc. of Medicine 1986–88; Hon. F.R.C.P. (Canada) 1988; Hon. F.R.C.P.S. (Glasgow) 1993; Hon. D.Sc. (McGill) 1984, (Glasgow) 1991. *Publications:* numerous articles in learned journals on neurophysiology, anaesthesia, pain and central nervous system mechanisms of respiration. *Leisure interests:* golf, wet fly fishing. *Address:* Brendon, Lyndale, London, NW2 2NY, England.

ROBUCHON, Joël; French chef and restaurateur; b. 7 April 1945, Poitiers; s. of Henri Robuchon and Julienne Douteau; m. Janine Pallix 1966; one s. one d.; Apprenti 1960–63, Commis 1963–64, Chef de Partie 1965–69, Chef 1970–78, Dir. Hotel Nikko de Paris 1978–81, Proprietor and Chef Restaurant Jamin, Paris 1981–94, Restaurant Joël Robuchon 1994–96, announced retirement 1996; Man. Relais du Parc 1992; numerous demonstrations overseas; Officier du Mérite Agricole; Chevalier des arts et des Lettres; Chevalier, Ordre National du Mérite; Chevalier de la courtoisie de France; Chevalier, Légion d'honneur; professional awards include: Trophée National de l'Académie Culinaire de France 1972, Meilleur Ouvrier de France 1976, Lauréat du Prix Hachette 1985, chef de l'Année 1987, Chef of the Century, Gault Millan Guidebook; also some 15 gold, silver and bronze medals. *Publications:* Ma cuisine pour vous 1986, Simply French 1991, Le Meilleur et le plus simple de Robuchon 1992, les Dimanches de Joël Robuchon 1993, Le Meilleur et le plus simple de la pomme de terre, Recettes du terroir d'hier et d'aujourd'hui, Le carnet de route d'un compagnon cuisinier 1995, L'Atelier de Joël Robuchon 1996, Le Meilleur de la France 1996, Cuisinez comme un grand chef 1997, le Meilleur et le plus simple pour maigrir 1998. *Address:* Société de gestion culinaire, 67 boulevard du Général Martial Valin, 75015 Paris, France.

ROCARD, Michel Louis Léon, L. ÈS L.; French politician; b. 23 Aug. 1930, Courbevoie; s. of Yves Rocard and Renée Favre; m. 2nd Michèle Legendre 1972 (divorced); two s.; one s. one d. from 1st marriage; ed. Lycée Louis-le-Grand, Paris, Univ. of Paris, Ecole Nat. d'Admin.; Nat. Sec. Asscn. des Etudiants socialistes, French Section of Workers' Int. (Socialist Party) 1955–56; Insp. des Finances 1958, Econ. and Financial Studies Service 1962, Head of Budget Div., Forecasting Office 1965, Insp. Gen. des Finances 1985; Sec.-Gen. Nat. Accounts and Budget Comm. 1965; Nat. Sec. Parti Socialiste Unifié (PSU) 1967–73; Cand. in first round of elections for presidency of French Repub. 1969; Deputy (Yvelines) to Nat. Assembly 1969–73, 1978–81; left PSU to join Parti Socialiste (PS) 1974, mem. Exec. Bureau 1975–81, 1986–, Nat. Sec. in charge of public sector 1975–79, First Sec. 1993–94; Mayor of Conflans-Sainte-Honorine 1977–94; Minister of State, Minister of Planning and Regional Devt. 1981–83, of Agric. 1983–85; Prime Minister of France 1988–91; M.P. for Yvelines 1986–88; mem. European Parl. 1994–; mem. Senate 1995–97; Grand Cross, ordre nat. du Mérite, Commdr. du Mérite agricole, Grand Cross, Order of Christ (Portugal), Grand Officer, Order of the Tunisian Repub., and numerous other decorations. *Publications:* Le PSU et l'avenir socialiste de la France 1969, Des militants du PSU présentés par Michel Rocard 1971, Questions à l'Etat socialiste 1972, Un député, pourquoi faire? 1973, Le marché commun contre Europe (with B. Jaumont and D. Lenègre) 1973, L'inflation au coeur (with Jacques Gallus) 1975, Parler vrai 1979, A l'épreuve des faits: textes politiques (1979–85) 1986, Le coeur à l'ouvrage 1987, Un pays comme le nôtre, textes politiques 1986–89 1989, Les Moyens d'en sortir 1996, L'art de la paix (essay) 1998. *Leisure interests:* skiing, sailing, gliding. *Address:* European Parliament, 97-113 rue Belliard, B1047 Brussels, Belgium; Hôtel de Ville, 63 rue Maurice Berteaux, 78700 Conflans-Sainte-Honorine, France.

ROCCA, Costantino; Italian golfer; b. 4 Dec. 1956, Bergamo; m.; one s. one d.; fmr. factory worker and caddie; turned professional 1981; qualified for PGA European Tour through 1989 Challenge Tour; won Open V33 Da Grand Lyon and Peugeot Open de France, first Italian golfer to be mem. European Ryder Cup team 1993; mem. winning European Ryder Cup team 1995. *Leisure interests:* fishing, football. *Address:* Bergamo, Italy.

ROCHA VIEIRA, Lieut.-Gen. Vasco Joaquim, M.A.; Portuguese administrator and army officer; b. 16 Aug. 1939, Lagoa; s. of João da Silva Vieira and Maria Vieira Rocha e Vieira; m. Maria Leonor de Andrada Soares de Albergaria 1976; three s.; ed. Tech. Univ. of Lisbon; Prof. Mil. Acad. Lisbon 1968–69; Army Staff course 1969–72; engineer Urbanization Dept. Urban Council, Lisbon 1969–73; Sec. for Public Works and Communications, Govt. of Macau 1974–75; Dir. Engineers Branch, Portuguese Army 1975–76; Army Chief-of-Staff 1976–78; Mil. Rep. of Portugal, SHAPE, Mons, Belgium 1978–82; Army War Coll. course 1982–83; Nat. Defence course 1983–84; Prof. Army War Coll. Lisbon 1983–84; Deputy Dir. Nat. Defence Inst. Lisbon 1984–86; Minister for Portuguese Autonomous Region of the Azores 1986–91; Gov. of Macau 1991–; Grand Cross, Order of Prince Henry; Knight Commdr. Mil. Order of Aviz; service medals; decorations from Brazil, France, Belgium, U.S.A. and Japan. *Leisure interests:* tennis, golf. *Address:* Palácio do Governo, Rua da Praia Grande, Macau. *Telephone:* 565555. *Fax:* 972746.

ROCHAS DA COSTA, Celestino; São Tomé e Príncipe politician; fmrly. Minister of Labour, Educ. and Social Security; Prime Minister of São Tomé and Príncipe 1988–91; mem. Movimento de Libertação de São Tomé e Príncipe (MLSTP). *Address:* c/o Prime Minister's Office, São Tomé, São Tomé and Príncipe.

ROCHAT, Philippe H.P., LL.D.; Swiss civil aviation executive; m.; three c.; ed. Univ. of Lausanne; journalist and reporter, Swiss Radio-TV 1967–74; Asst. to Deputy Dir. Fed. Office for Civil Aviation, Berne 1975–77; Admin. and Commercial Dir. Geneva Airport 1977–85; Alt. Rep. of Belgium on ICAO Council within ABS (Austria-Benelux-Switzerland) Group 1985–86; Rep. of Switzerland, ICAO Council 1986–89; Dir. Marketing and Environment, Geneva Airport 1989–91; Sec.-Gen. ICAO 1991–97. *Publications:* articles, reports and lectures. *Leisure interests:* skiiing, hiking, tennis, various cultural activities. *Address:* c/o International Civil Aviation Organization, 999 University Street, Montreal, Quebec, H3C 5H7, Canada. *Telephone:* (514) 954-8221. *Fax:* (514) 954-6376.

ROCHE, (Eamonn) Kevin; American architect; b. 14 June 1922, Dublin, Ireland; s. of Eamon and Alice (Harding) Roche; m. Jane Tuohy 1963; two s. three d.; ed. Nat. Univ. of Ireland and Illinois Inst. of Tech.; with Eero Saarinen & Assocs. 1950–66, Chief Designer 1954–66; Partner, Kevin Roche, John Dinkeloo and Assocs. 1966–; Pres. American Acad. of Arts and Letters 1994–97; Academician Nat. Inst. of Arts and Letters, American Acad. in Rome 1968–71; mem. Fine Arts Comm., Washington, D.C., Acad. d'Architecture; Academician Nat. Acad. of Design; mem. Bd. of Trustees, Woodrow Wilson Int. Center for Scholars, Smithsonian Inst. Accad. Nazionale Di San Luca 1984; LL.D. h.c. (Ireland Nat. Council for Educational Awards); Brunner Award, Nat. Acad. of Arts and Letters 1965, Brandeis Univ. Creative Arts Award 1967, ASID 1976 Total Design Award, Académie d'Architecture 1977 Grand Gold Medal, Pritzker Architecture Prize 1982, Gold Medal A.I.A. 1993, A.I.A. Twenty-five Year Award 1995 and other awards. *Major works include:* IBM World Fair Pavilion, New York; Oakland Museum; Rochester Inst. of Tech.; Ford Foundation Headquarters, New York; Fine Arts Center, Univ. of Mass.; Power Center for the Performing Arts, Univ. of Mich.; Creative Arts Center, Wesleyan Univ., Middletown, Conn.; Coll. Life Insurance Co. of America Headquarters, Indianapolis; Six new wings, Master Plan, Metropolitan Museum of Art, New York; Office Complex, UN Devt. Corpn., New York; Denver Center for the Performing Arts, Denver, Colo.; John Deere & Co., West Office Bldg., Moline, Ill.; Union Carbide Corpn. World HQ, Conn.; General Foods Corpn. HQ, Rye, N.Y.; John Deere Insurance Co. Headquarters, Moline, Ill.; Bell Telephone Labs., Holmdel, N.J., Morgan Bank Headquarters, New York; Northern Telecom HQ, Atlanta, Ga.; E. F. Hutton Headquarters, New York; Bouygues HQ, Paris, IBM Hudson Hills Computer Research Lab., New York 1984, UNICEF HQ, New York 1984, Leo Burnett Company HQ, Chicago 1985, Corning Glass Works HQ, Corning, N.Y. 1986, Merck and Co. HQ, Readington, N.J. 1987, The Jewish Museum 1988, Museum of Jewish Heritage Holocaust Memorial, New York, 1993, Nations Bank Plaza, Atlanta, Ga. 1996, Tata Cummins, India 1996, Ampang Tower, Kuala Lumpur, Malaysia 1996, Millennia, Singapore 1996, Total System Services Corpn. HQ, Columbus, Ga 1997. *Address:* 20 Davis Street, P.O. Box 6127, Hamden, CT 06517, U.S.A.

ROCHEFORT, Jean; French actor; b. 29 April 1930, Paris; s. of Celestin Rochefort and Fernande Guillot; m. 3rd Françoise Vidal 1989; one s. one d.; two s. one d. from previous marriages; ed. Conservatoire nat. d'art dramatique. *Films include:* 20,000 Leagues Under the Sea 1960, La Porteuse de pain 1964, Qui êtes-vous Polly Magoo? 1967, Les Dimanches de la vie 1967, Le Temps de mourir 1970, Céleste 1970, l'Oeuf 1971, l'Héritier 1972, Le Fantôme de la liberté 1974, Un divorce heureux 1975, Isabelle devant le désir 1975, Que la fête commence 1975, Les Magiciens 1976, Un éléphant ça trompe énormément 1976, Le Crabe-tambour 1977, Chère inconnue 1980, Un étrange voyage 1981, l'Indiscrétion 1982, Le Grand frère 1982, Un dimanche de flic 1983, l'Ami de Vincent 1983, Réveillon chez Bob, Frankenstein 90 1984, La Galette du roi 1986, Tandem 1987, Le Moustachu 1987, Je suis le seigneur du château 1989, Le Mari de la coiffeuse 1990, Le Château de ma mère 1990, Le Bal des casse-pieds 1992, La Prochaine fois le feu 1993, Tombés du ciel 1994, Tom est tout seul 1995, Les Grands ducs 1996, Ridicule 1996. *Television:* Le Scénario défendu 1984, l'Enigme blanche 1985, Eleveur de chevaux; Trophée Dussane 1970, César 1975 (for Que la fête commence), 1978 (for Best Actor of the Year, in Le Crabe-tambour), best actor awards Montreal 1982, Brussels 1982, Locarno 1984; Chevalier Légion d'honneur, Officier des Arts et des Lettres. *Leisure interest:* riding. *Address:* c/o Artmédia, 10 avenue George-V, 75008 Paris, France.

ROCHER, Guy, C.C., O.Q., PH.D., F.R.S.C.; Canadian professor of sociology; b. 20 April 1924, Berthierville, P.Q.; s. of late Barthélemy Rocher and late Jeanne Magnan; m. 1st Suzanne Cloutier 1949; m. 2nd Claire-Emmanuèle Depocas 1985; four d.; ed. Univ. of Montreal, Univ. Laval and Harvard Univ.; Asst. Prof. Univ. Laval 1952–57, Assoc. Prof. 1957–60; Prof. of Sociology, Univ. of Montreal 1960–; Deputy Minister of Cultural Devt. Govt. of Quebec 1977–79, of Social Devt. 1981–82; mem. Royal Comm. on Educ. in Quebec 1961–66; Vice-Pres. Canada Council of Arts 1969–74, Cttee. on Univ. Research, Royal Soc. of Canada 1989–90; Pres. Radio-Quebec 1979–81; mem. American Acad. of Arts and Sciences; Hon.LL.D. (Laval) 1996; Dr. h.c. Sociology (Moncton) 1997; Prix Marcel-Vincent (ACFAS) 1989, Prix Léon-Gérin (Quebec Govt.) 1995, Prix Molson 1997, Prix Esdras-Minville 1998; Outstanding Contribution Award (Canadian Asscn. Sociology and Anthropology) 1988, Médaille Pierre Chauveau (Royal Soc. of Canada) 1991. *Publications:* Introduction à la sociologie générale 1969, Talcott Parsons et la sociologie américaine, Le Québec en mutation 1973, Ecole et société au Québec 1975, Entre les rêves et l'histoire 1989, Le Québec en jeu 1992, Entre droit et technique 1994, Etudes de sociologie du droit et de l'éthique 1996, Théorie et emergence du droit 1998, and numerous articles on sociology, on sociology of law, of education and of health, and on the evolution of Quebec society. *Leisure interests:* tai-chi, skiing, swimming, concerts, reading. *Address:* Faculté de Droit, Université de Montréal, C.P. 6128, Succursale Centre-Ville, Montreal, P.Q., H3C 3J7 (Office); 5610 Avenue Decelles, Apt. 16, Montreal, P.Q., H3T 1W5, Canada (Home). *Telephone:* (514) 343-5993 (Office); (514) 344-0882 (Home). *Fax:* (514) 343-7508.

ROCHESTER, George Dixon, PH.D., F.R.S., F.INST.P.; British professor of physics; b. 4 Feb. 1908, Wallsend; s. of Thomas and Ellen Rochester; m. Idaline Bayliffe 1938; one s. one d.; ed. Wallsend Secondary School, Univs. of Durham, Stockholm and California; Earl Grey Scholar, Durham Univ. 1926–29; Earl Grey Fellow, Stockholm Univ. 1934–35; Commonwealth Fund Fellow Univ. of Calif. 1935–37; Asst. Lecturer, Manchester Univ. 1937–46, Lecturer 1946–49, Sr. Lecturer 1949–53, Reader 1953–55; Prof. of Physics, Durham Univ. 1955–73, Emer. 1973–, Second Pro-Vice-Chancellor 1967–69, Pro-Vice-Chancellor 1969–70; Scientific Adviser in Civil Defence, N.W. Region 1952–55; mem. Council of Council for Nat. Academic Awards (CNAA) 1964–74; Hon D.Sc. (Newcastle) 1973, (CNAA) 1975, Hon. Fellowship (Newcastle upon Tyne Polytechnic) 1977; C.V. Boys Prizeman 1956; Symons Memorial Lecturer, Meteorological Soc. 1962. *Publications:* (with J. G. Wilson) Cloud Chamber Photographs of the Cosmic Radiation 1952; also scientific papers on elementary particles, cosmic rays, spectroscopy and the history of science. *Leisure interests:* reading, walking, television, church. *Address:* 18 Dryburn Road, Durham, DH1 5AJ, England. *Telephone:* (0191) 386 4796.

ROCKBURNE, Dorothea; American artist; b. Montreal, P.Q., Canada; m. 1951 (divorced); one d.; ed. Black Mountain Coll., N.C.; numerous one-person exhbns. including Bykert Gallery, New York 1970, 1972, 1973, Sonnabend Gallery, Paris 1971, Galleria Toselli, Milan 1972, 1974, 1983, Lisson Gallery, London 1973, Galleria Schema, Florence 1973, 1975, 1992, John Weber Gallery, New York 1976, 1978, Texas Gallery, Houston 1979, 1980, Museum of Modern Art, New York 1980, Xavier Fourcade, New York 1980, 1985, 1986, Arts Club of Chicago 1987, André Emmerich Gallery, New York 1988, 1989, 1991, 1992, 1994, Rose Museum, Brandeis Univ. (retrospective) 1989, Guild Hall Museum, East Hampton, N.Y. 1995, Portland Museum of Art, Portland, Maine 1996, Rockefeller Foundation Center, Bellagio, Italy 1997; participant in numerous group shows; work in many public collections including Whitney Museum, Museum of Modern Art, Metropolitan Museum of Art, artist-in-residence, American Acad. in Rome 1991; Guggenheim Museum, New York and Corcoran Gallery, Washington, D.C.; frescoes at Hilton Hotel, San Jose, Calif. 1992, Sony HQ, New York 1993, Edward T. Grignoux U.S. Courthouse, Portland, Maine 1996, Brooklyn Courthouse, New York 1996, UOFM, Mich. 1997; Guggenheim Fellow 1972; Art Inst. of Chicago Painting Award 1972; Nat. Endowment for the Arts 1974; Visiting Artist, Skowhegan School of Painting and Sculpture 1984; Creative Arts Award, Brandeis Univ. 1985; Avery Distinguished Prof. Bard Coll. Annandale-on-Hudson, N.Y. 1986. *Leisure interests:* music, mathematics. *Address:* 140 Grand Street, New York, NY 10013, U.S.A. *Telephone:* (212) 226-4471. *Fax:* (212) 226-4471.

ROCKEFELLER, David, B.S., PH.D.; American banker; b. 12 June 1915, New York; s. of John Davison Rockefeller Jr. and Abby Greene (née Aldrich) Rockefeller; brother of Laurance (q.v.); m. Margaret McGrath 1940; two s. four d.; ed. Harvard Coll., London School of Econs., Univ. of Chicago; Sec. to Mayor Fiorello H. La Guardia, New York 1940–41; Asst. Regional Dir. U.S. Office of Defense, Health and Welfare Services 1941–42; served in U.S. Army (Capt.) 1942–45; Foreign Dept. Chase Nat. Bank 1946–48, Second Vice-Pres. 1948–49, Vice-Pres. 1949–51, Sr. Vice-Pres. 1951–55; Exec. Vice-Pres. Chase Manhattan Bank 1955–57, Vice-Chair. Bd. 1957–61, Pres and Chair. Exec. Cttee. 1961–69, C.E.O. 1969–80, Chair. of Bd. 1969–81, Chair. Chase Int. Investment Corpn. 1961–81, Chase Int. Advisory Cttee. 1980–; Chair. Bd. Rockefeller Group Inc. 1981–95, Rockefeller Center Properties, Inc. 1996–, Rockefeller Center Properties Inc. Trust; Chair. Rockefeller Univ. 1950–75, Chair Exec. Cttee. 1975–, Council on Foreign Relations 1970–85, Americas Soc. 1981–92, Rockefeller Brothers Fund Inc. 1981–87, and numerous other chairmanships; Trustee Rockefeller Family Fund, Carnegie Endowment for Int. Peace, Museum of Modern Art, Chicago Univ., etc.; Hon. LL.D. from 13 univs.; Hon. D.Eng. (Colorado School of Mines) 1974, (Notre Dame Univ.) 1987; Hadrian Award (World Mathematics Fund) 1994, U.S. Presidential Medal of Freedom 1998; Grand Officier, Légion d'honneur; numerous American and foreign awards. *Publications:* Unused Resources and Economic Waste 1940, Creative Management in Banking 1964. *Leisure interest:* sailing. *Address:* 30 Rockefeller Plaza, New York, NY 10112, U.S.A.

ROCKEFELLER, James S.; American businessman; b. 8 June 1902, New York; s. of William G. and Elsie (Stillman) Rockefeller; m. Nancy Carnegie 1925; two s. two d.; ed. Yale Univ.; worked with Brown Brothers & Co. 1924–30; joined Nat. City Bank of New York (now Citibank) 1930, Asst. Cashier 1931, Asst. Vice-Pres. 1933, Vice-Pres. 1940, Sr. Vice-Pres. 1948, Exec. Vice-Pres. 1952, Pres. and Dir. 1952–59, Chair. and Dir. 1959–67; served with U.S. Army 1942–46; Pres. and Dir. Indian Spring Land Co.; Vice-Pres. and Dir. Indian Rock Corpn.; mem. Bd. of Overseers, Memorial

Hosp. for Cancer and Allied Diseases, New York; Trustee of Estate of William Rockefeller, American Museum of Natural History; Hon. Dir. NCR Corpn. *Leisure interests:* farming, shooting, fishing. *Address:* 425 Park Avenue, New York, N.Y. 10022, U.S.A.

ROCKEFELLER, John Davison, IV, B.A.; American politician; b. 18 June 1937, New York; s. of John Davison III and Blanchette F. (Hooker) Rockefeller; m. Sharon Percy 1967; three s. one d.; ed. Harvard and Yale Univs. and Int. Christian Univ., Tokyo; mem. Nat. Advisory Council, Peace Corps 1961, Special Adviser to Dir. 1962, Operations Officer in Charge of work in Philippines until 1963; Bureau of Far Eastern Affairs, U.S. State Dept. 1963, later Asst. to Asst. Sec. of State for Far Eastern Affairs; consultant, President's Comm. on Juvenile Delinquency and Youth Crime 1964, White House Conf. on Balanced Growth and Econ. Devt. 1978, Pres.'s Comm. on Coal 1978–80; field worker, Action for Appalachian Youth Program 1964; mem. W. Va. House of Dels. 1966–68; Sec. of State, W. Va. 1968–72; Pres. W. Va. Wesleyan Coll., Buckhannon 1973–75; Gov. of W. Va. 1977–85, Senator from W. Va. Jan. 1985–, Chair. Senate Steel Caucus, Bipartisan Cttee. on Comprehensive Health Care; Republican. *Publications:* articles in magazines. *Address:* US Senate, 531 Hart Senate Building, Washington, DC 20510, U.S.A.

ROCKEFELLER, Laurance Spelman, A.B.; American conservationist and business executive; b. 26 May 1910, New York; s. of John Davison Jr. and Abby Greene (née Aldrich) Rockefeller; m. Mary French 1934; one s. three d.; ed. Princeton Univ., Harvard Law School; served in U.S.N.R. 1942–45; Dir. Eastern Airlines 1938–60, 1977–81, Advisory Dir. 1981–87; Chair. Rockefeller Center 1953–56, 1958–66, Hudson River Valley Comm. 1965–66, New York Zoological Soc. 1970–75 (Hon. Chair. 1975–), Rockefeller Brothers Fund 1958–80 (Vice-Chair. 1980–82, Advisory Trustee 1982–85), Citizens' Advisory Cttee. on Environmental Quality 1969–73 (mem. 1973–79); Pres. American Conservation Asscn. 1958–80 (Chair. 1980–85, Hon. Chair. 1985–), Pres. Jackson Hole Preserve Inc. 1940–87, Chair. 1987–96, Chair. Emer. and Trustee 1997, Palisades Interstate Park Comm. 1970–77 (Commr. Emer. 1978–); Dir. Reader's Digest Asscn. 1973–93; Trustee Emer., Princeton Univ.; Trustee Alfred P. Sloan Foundation 1960–82; Trustee Emer. Nat. Geographical Soc.; mem. Nat. Cancer Advisory Bd. 1972–79, Memorial Sloan-Kettering Cancer Center (Chair. 1975–82, Hon. Chair. 1982–); Commdr., Ordre Royal du Lion (Belgium) 1950, Hon. O.B.E., Congressional Gold Medal and several American awards. *Address:* Room 5600, 30 Rockefeller Plaza, New York, NY 10112, U.S.A.

ROCKLEY, 3rd Baron, **James Hugh Cecil;** British merchant banker; b. 5 April 1934, London; m. Sarah Cadogan 1958; one s. two d.; ed. Eton Coll. and New Coll. Oxford; with Wood Gundy & Co., Canada 1957–62; joined Kleinwort Benson Ltd. 1962, apptd. to Bd. 1970, Head, Corp. Finance Div. 1983, Vice-Chair. 1985–93, Chair. 1993, Vice-Chair. Kleinwort Benson Group PLC 1988–93, Chair. 1993–96; Chair. Dartford River Crossing 1988–93, Kleinwort Devt. Fund 1991–93, Midland Expressway 1992–93; Dir., Equity and Law 1980–92, Christies Int. 1989–, Cobham (fmrly. FR Group) 1990–, Abbey Nat. 1990–, Foreign and Colonial Investment Trust 1991–, Cadogan Group 1996–, Dusco (UK) 1996. *Address:* Lytchett Heath, Poole, Dorset, BH16 6AE, England.

ROCKWELL, John Sargent, PH.D.; American journalist and arts administrator, music critic and author; b. 16 Sept. 1940, Washington, D.C.; s. of Alvin John and Anne Hayward; m. Linda Mevorach; one d.; ed. Harvard Univ., Univ. of Munich and Univ. of Calif. Berkeley; music and dance critic, Oakland (Calif.) Tribune 1969; asst. music and dance critic, Los Angeles Times 1970–72; freelance music critic, New York Times 1972–74, staff music critic 1974–91, Ed. Arts and Leisure section 1998–; European cultural corresp. and prin. classical recordings critic, New York Times, Paris 1992–94; Dir. Lincoln Center Festival, Lincoln Center for the Performing Arts, New York 1994–98. *Publications:* All American Music: Composition in the Late 20th Century 1983, Sinatra: An American Classic 1984. *Address:* New York Times, 229 West 43rd Street, New York, NY 10036, U.S.A.

RODDICK, Anita Lucia, O.B.E.; British business executive; b. 23 Oct. 1942, Littlehampton; d. of Henry Perilli and Gilda De Vita; m. Gordon Roddick 1970; two d.; ed. Maude Allen Secondary Modern School for Girls, Newton Park Coll. of Educ., Bath; teacher of English and History, worked in library of Int. Herald Tribune, Paris, and Women's Rights Dept. of ILO, based at UN, Geneva, then owned and managed restaurant and hotel; opened first branch of The Body Shop, Brighton, Sussex 1976; The Body Shop Int. floated on Unlisted Securities Market 1984; Group Man. Dir. The Body Shop Int. PLC –1994, C.E.O. 1994–98, Jt. Chair. 1998–; Trustee The Body Shop Foundation 1990–, New Acad. of Business 1996; Patron of various orgs.; Hon. Fellow, Bath Coll. of Higher Educ. 1994; Hon. D. Univ. (Sussex) 1988, (Open Univ.) 1995, Hon. LL.D. (Nottingham) 1990, (New England Coll.) 1991, (Victoria, Canada) 1995; Hon. D.Sc. (Portsmouth) 1994; Hon. D.B.A. (Kingston) 1996; Veuve Clicquot Business Woman of the Year 1984, British Asscn. of Industrial Eds. Communicator of the Year 1988, Co. NatWest Retailer of the Year Award 1988, UN "Global 500" Environment Award 1989, Business Leader of Year, Nat. Asscn. of Women Business Owners (U.S.A.) 1992, Botwinick Prize in Business Ethics 1994, Business Leadership Award, Univ. of Michigan 1994, First Annual Womanpower Award, Women's Business Devt. Center 1995, U.S.A. Women's Center Leadership Award 1996, American Dream Award, Hunter Coll. 1996, Philanthropist of the Year, Inst. of Fundraising Managers 1996. *Leisure interests:* theatre, arts. *Publication:* Body and Soul (autobiog.) 1991. *Address:* The Body Shop International, Watersmead, Littlehampton, West Sussex, BN17 6LS, England. *Telephone:* (01903) 731500. *Fax:* (01903) 726250.

RODDIE, Ian Campbell, C.B.E., T.D., D.SC., M.D., F.R.C.P.I.; British professor of physiology; b. 1 Dec. 1928, N. Ireland; s. of late Rev. J. R. W. Roddie and of Mary H. (Wilson) Roddie; m. 1st Elizabeth A. G. Honeyman 1958 (deceased); one s. three d.; m. 2nd Katherine O'Hara 1974 (divorced); one s. one d.; m. 3rd Janet Doreen Saville 1987; ed. Methodist Coll. Belfast and Queen's Univ. Belfast; Resident Medical Officer, Royal Victoria Hosp., Belfast 1953–54; Lecturer in Physiology, Queen's Univ. of Belfast 1957–60, Sr. Lecturer 1960–62, Reader 1962–64, Dunville Prof. of Physiology 1964–87, Prof. Emer., Dean of Medicine 1976–82, Pro-Vice-Chancellor 1984–87; Visiting Prof., Chinese Univ. of Hong Kong 1987–90; Staff Consultant, Asian Devt. Bank, Manila 1987–88; Deputy Medical Dir. and Head Medical Educ., King Khalid Nat. Guard Hosp., Jeddah, Saudi Arabia 1990–94; Consultant, Int. Finance Corpn. World Bank 1993–; mem. Royal Irish Acad.; Harkness Fellowship 1960; Conway Bronze Medal 1977. *Publications:* Physiology for Practitioners 1971, Multiple Choice Questions in Human Physiology 1971, The Physiology of Disease 1975. *Leisure interests:* travel, writing. *Address:* Calle San Bernabé 3, Lomas del Marbella Club-Pueblo, 29600 Marbella (Málaga), Spain. *Telephone:* (95) 277 2596. *Fax:* (95) 277 8641.

RODGERS, Joan, B.A.; British soprano opera and concert singer; b. 4 Nov. 1956, Whitehaven, Cumbria; d. of Thomas Rodgers and Julia Rodgers; m. Paul Daniel (q.v.) 1988; two d.; ed. Whitehaven Grammar School, Univ. of Liverpool and Royal Northern Coll. of Music, Manchester; first maj. professional engagement as Pamina (The Magic Flute), Aix-en-Provence Festival 1982; début at Metropolitan Opera House, New York, in same role 1995; other appearances include title role (Theodora) at Glyndebourne, The Governess (Turn of the Screw) for Royal Opera House, Blanche (Dialogues des Carmélites) for English Nat. Opera and in Amsterdam, Marschallin (Der Rosenkavalier) for Scottish Opera and title role (Alcina) for English Nat. Opera; regular appearances at Royal Opera House, English Nat. Opera, Glyndebourne, Promenade Concerts and with leading British and European cos.; recent concert engagements in London, Europe and U.S.A. with conductors including Solti, Barenboim, Mehta, Rattle, Harnoncourt and Salonen; Kathleen Ferrier Memorial Scholarship 1981; Royal Philharmonic Soc. Award as Singer of the Year 1997, Evening Standard Award for Outstanding Individual Performance in Opera 1997. *Leisure interests:* walking, cooking, talking. *Address:* c/o Ingpen and Williams Ltd., 26 Wadham Road, London, SW15 2LR, England.

RODGERS, John, M.S., PH.D.; American professor of geology; b. 11 July 1914, Albany, N.Y.; s. of Henry D. Rodgers and Louise W. (Allen) Rodgers; ed. Albany Acad., Cornell and Yale Univs.; Dept. of Geology, Cornell Univ. 1935–36, Instructor 1936–37; Field Geologist, U.S. Geological Survey 1938–, in full time employment 1940–46; Scientific Consultant, U.S. Army Corps. of Engineers 1944–46; Instructor, Yale Univ. 1946–47, Asst. Prof. 1947–52, Assoc. Prof. 1952–59, Prof. 1959–62, Silliman Prof. of Geol. 1962–85, Emer. 1985–; Gen. Sec. Int. Comm. on Stratigraphy 1952–60; Sr. Fellow, Nat. Science Foundation 1959–60; Commr. Conn. Geol. and Nat. History Survey 1960–71; Visiting Lecturer, Coll. de France 1960; Exchange scholar Soviet Union 1967; Asst. Ed. American Journal of Science 1948–54, Ed. 1954–; mem. N.A.S., American Philosophical Soc.; Hon. mem. Geol. Soc. of London 1970; Pres. Conn. Acad. of Arts and Sciences 1969, Geol. Soc. of America 1970; Hon. mem. Soc. Géologique de France 1973; Foreign mem., U.S.S.R. (now Russian) Acad. of Sciences 1976; Foreign Corresp. mem. Acad. real de Ciencias y Artes, Barcelona 1976; John Simon Guggenheim Fellow (Australia) 1973–74; Medal of Freedom, U.S. Army 1946, Penrose Medal (Geological Soc. of America) 1981, James Hall Medal (N.Y. State Geological Survey) 1986, Prix Gaudry, Société géologique de France 1987, Médaille Paul Fourmarier, Acad. Royale des Sciences, Lettres et Beaux Arts de Belgique 1987, Career Contrib. Award (Geological Soc. of America) 1989, William Clude DeVane Medal 1990. *Publications:* Principles of Stratigraphy (with C. Dunbar) 1957, The Tectonics of the Appalachians 1970, The Harmony of the World (record, with W. Ruff) 1979; many articles on geology. *Leisure interests:* music (piano), travel, reading (history, philosophy). *Address:* Department of Geology, Yale University, P.O. Box 208109, New Haven, CT 06520, U.S.A. *Telephone:* (203) 432-3128.

RODGERS, Patricia Elaine Joan, M.A., D.POL.SC.; Bahamian diplomatist; b. Nassau; ed. School of St. Helen & St. Catherine, Abingdon, Univ. of Aberdeen, Graduate Inst. of Int. Relations, St. Augustine, Trinidad, Inst. Universitaire des Hautes Etudes Int., Univ. of Geneva; Counsellor and Consul, Washington, D.C. 1978–83; Alt. Rep. to OAS 1982–83; Deputy High Commr. (Acting High Commr.) in Canada 1983–86, High Commr. 1986–88; High Commr. in U.K. (also accred. to France, Belgium and Germany) 1988–92; mem. Bahamas Del. to UN Conf. on Law of the Sea 1974, 1975, OAS Gen. Ass. 1982, Caribbean Co-ordinating Meeting (Head of Del.), OAS 1983, Canada/Commonwealth Caribbean Heads of Govt. Meeting 1985, Commonwealth Heads of Govt. Meeting Nassau 1985, Vancouver 1987; Adviser to Bahamas Del., Annual Gen. Meetings of World Bank and IMF 1978–82; mem. Commonwealth Observer Group, Gen. Elections Lesotho 1993; Perm. Sec., Ministry of Tourism 1995–. *Publications:* Mid-Ocean Archipelagos and International Law; A Study of the Progressive Development of International Law 1981. *Leisure interests:* folk art, theatre, gourmet cooking. *Address:* c/o Ministry of Tourism, P.O.B. N-3701, Market Plaza, Bay Street, Nassau, Bahamas. *Telephone:* 322-7500. *Fax:* 328-0945.

RODGERS OF QUARRY BANK, Baron (Life Peer), cr. 1992, of Kentish Town in the London Borough of Camden, **William Thomas Rodgers,** P.C., M.A.; British politician and administrator; b. 28 Oct. 1928, Liverpool; s. of William Arthur and Gertrude Helen Rodgers; m. Silvia Schulman 1955; three d.; ed. Sudley Road Council School, Quarry Bank High School, Liverpool and Magdalen Coll., Oxford; Gen. Sec. Fabian Soc. 1953–60; Labour Cand. for Bristol West 1957; Borough Councillor, St. Marylebone 1958–62; M.P. for Stockton-on-Tees 1962–74, for Stockton Div. of Teeside 1974–83; Parl. Under-Sec. of State, Dept. of Econ. Affairs 1964–67, Foreign Office 1967–68; Leader, U.K. del. to Council of Europe and Ass. of WEU 1967–68; Minister of State, Bd. of Trade 1968–69, Treasury 1969–70; Chair. Expenditure Cttee. on Trade and Industry 1971–74; Minister of State, Ministry of Defence 1974–76; Sec. of State for Transport 1976–79; Opposition Spokesman for Defence 1979–80; left Labour Party March 1981; Co-founder Social Democratic Party March 1981, mem. Nat. Cttee. 1982–87, Vice-Pres. 1982–87; Dir.-Gen. R.I.B.A. 1987–94; Chair. Advertising Standards Authority 1995–; Liberal Democrat. *Publications:* Hugh Gaitskell 1906–1963 (Ed.) 1964, The People Into Parliament (co-author) 1966, The Politics of Change 1982, Ed. and co-author Government and Industry 1986. *Leisure interests:* reading, walking, cinema. *Address:* House of Lords, London, SW1A 0PW; 43 North Road, London, N6 4BE, England.

RODIER, Jean-Pierre; French business executive and mining engineer; b. 4 May 1947; s. of Pierre Rodier and Gabrielle Sayen; m. Michèle Foz 1969; ed. Lycée de Saumur, Lycée de Pamiers, Lycée de Pierre-en-Fermat, Toulouse; Asst. Sec.-Gen. Mines Directorate, Ministry of Industry 1975–78, Sec.-Gen. 1978; Head of Econs. and Budget mission of Dir.-Gen. of Energy and Raw Materials 1979; Head of Raw Material and Subsoil Dept. 1981–83; tech. adviser to Prime Minister's Office 1983–84; Dir. of Gen. Man. Penarroya mining and metallurgy Co. 1984–85, Asst. Dir.-Gen. 1985–86, Pres. and Dir. Gen. 1986–88; Pres. Bd. Dirs. Metaleurop 1988–91; Deputy Administrator Mining Union 1991–94; Pres. and Dir.-Gen. Pechiney 1994–; Pres. Bd. Dirs. Ecole nat. supérieure des techniques industrielles et des mines d'Alès 1992–95. *Address:* Société Pechiney, Pechiney-Balzac, Tour Pascal "A", 6 Place des Degrés, La Defense 7, 92048 Paris-La Défense, Cedex 68, France.

RODIN, Judith, PH.D.; American physician; b. 9 Sept. 1944, Philadelphia, Pa.; d. of Morris Rodin and Sally (Winson) Seitz; m. 1st 1978; one s.; m. 2nd Paul Verkuil 1994; ed. Univ. of Pennsylvania and Columbia Univ.; Nat. Science Foundation Postdoctoral Fellow, Univ. of Calif. 1971; Asst. Prof. of Psychology, New York Univ. 1970–72; Asst. Prof. Yale Univ. 1972–75, Assoc. Prof. 1975–79, Prof. of Psychology 1979–83, Dir. of Grad. Studies 1982–89, Philip R. Allen Prof. of Psychology 1984–94, Prof. of Medicine and Psychiatry 1985–94, Chair. Dept. of Psychology 1989–91, Dean Grad. School of Arts and Sciences 1991–92, Provost 1992–94; Prof. of Psychology, Medicine and Psychiatry, Univ. of Pa. 1994–, Pres. Univ. of Pa. 1994–; Chair. John D. & Catherine T. MacArthur Foundation Research Network on Determinants and Consequences of Health-Promoting and Health-Damaging Behavior 1983–93; Chair. Council of Pres.'s, Univs. Research Asscn. 1995–96; has served on numerous Bds. of Dirs., including Int. Life Sciences Inst. 1993–, Aetna Life & Casualty Co. 1995–; has served as mem. of numerous professional cttees., including Pres. Clinton's Cttee. of Advisors on Science and Tech. 1994–, Pa. Women's Forum 1995–; chief ed. Appetite 1979–92; has served on numerous editorial bds.; mem. Bd. of Trustees, Brookings Inst. 1995–; Fellow A.A.A.S., American Acad. of Arts and Sciences; Hon. D.Hum.-Litt. (New Haven) 1994, (Medical Coll. of Pa. and Hahnemann Univ.) 1995; numerous awards and prizes, including 21st Century Award, Int. Alliance, Glass Ceiling Award, American Red Cross. *Publications:* author or co-author of 10 books on the relationship between psychological and biological processes in human health and behaviour; 100 articles in academic journals. *Leisure interests:* tennis, travel, reading. *Address:* University of Pennsylvania, Office of the President, 100 College Hall, Philadelphia, PA 19104, U.S.A. *Telephone:* (215) 898-7221 (Office). *Fax:* (215) 898-9659.

RODINO, Peter Wallace, Jr.; American politician; b. 7 June 1909, Newark, N.J.; s. of Peter and Margaret (Gerard) Rodino; m. Marianna Stango 1941; one s. one d.; ed. New Jersey Law School; admitted to N.J. Bar 1938; mem. House of Reps. for N.J. 1948–74; Chair. House Judiciary Cttee. 1973; Del. N. Atlantic Assembly 1962–, Intergovernmental Cttee. for European Migration 1962–72 (Chair. 1971–72); partner Rodino & Rodino, East Hanover, N.J. 1989–; mem. Pres. Select Comm. on Western Hemisphere Immigration; Chair. Impeachment investigation of Pres. Richard Nixon 1973–74; 13 hon. degrees; Bronze Star, Kt., Order of the Crown (Italy), Grand Kt., Order of Merit (Italy), and numerous other awards and decorations.

RODIONOV, Gen. Igor Nikolayevich; Russian army officer (retd.); b. 1 Dec. 1936, Kurakino, Penza Region; m.; one s.; ed. Orel Tank Higher Mil. School, Mil. Acad. of Armoured Units, Mil. Acad. of Gen. Staff; asst. of commdr., master sgt.'s student's co. Orel Tank Higher School 1965–67; in Group of Soviet Troops in Germany 1957–64; commdr. tank co., deputy commdr. tank bn. 1964–67; deputy commdr. tank regt., commdr. regt., deputy commdr., commdr. div. Carpathy Mil. Command 1970–78; commdr. Army corps Cen. Group of Troops 1980–83; commdr. 5th Army Far E. Mil. Command 1983–85; commdr. Army of Turkestan Mil. Command, participant of war in Afghanistan 1985–86; First Deputy Commdr. Moscow Mil. Command 1986–88; commdr. Caucasian Mil. Command, involved in dispersal of demonstration in Tbilisi 1989; Chief Mil. Acad. of Gen. Staff 1989–96; Minister of Defence of Russian Fed., mem. Security Council and Defence Council 1996–97; discharged by Pres. Yeltsin. *Address:* c/o Ministry of Defence, Myasnitskaya 37, 103175 Moscow, Russia.

RODIONOV, Piotr Ivanovich; Russian politician; b. 26 Jan. 1951, Przhevalsk, Kyrgyz S.S.R.; m.; three c.; ed. Leningrad Inst. of Vessel Construction, Leningrad Inst. of Finance and Econs., Higher School of Commerce, Acad. of Nat. Econs.; with U.S.S.R. Ministry of Gas Industry; chief technologist, Head of Div., with Lentransgas 1984–88; Dir-Gen. Lentransgas 1989–96; mem. Bd. Dirs. Russian Jt. Gazprom 1996–; rep. of Russian Govt. to Gazprom 1996–, to United Emergy System of Russia 1996–; mem. Govt. Comm. for Operational Problems 1996–; Hon. Worker of Gas Industry. *Address:* Gazprom, Nametkina str. 16, 117884 Moscow, Russia.

RODMAN, Dennis Keith; American basketball player; b. 13 May 1961, Trenton, N.J.; ed. Cooke County Jr. Coll., Southeastern Oklahoma State Univ.; with Detroit Pistons 1986–93; forward San Antonio Spurs 1993–95, Chicago Bulls 1995–; N.B.A. Defensive Player of the Year 1990, 1991; N.B.A. Championship Team 1989–90, 1996, All-Defensive First Team 1989–93, All-Defense Second Team 1994; All-Star team 1990, 1992. *Address:* Chicago Bulls United Center, 1901 West Madison Street, Chicago, IL 60612, U.S.A.

RODRIGUES, Christopher, M.B.A.; British business executive; b. 24 Oct. 1949; s. of Alfred John Rodrigues and Joyce Margaret Rodrigues (née Farron-Smith); m. Priscilla Purcell Young 1976; one s. one d.; ed. Univ. of Cambridge, Harvard Univ.; fmr. man. trainee Spillers; fmrly. with McKinsey, American Express; fmr. C.O.O., fmr. Chief Exec. Thomas Cook; Chief Exec. Bradford & Bingley Bldg. Soc. 1996–; Dir. (non-exec.) Energis PLC 1997–, Financial Services Authority 1997–. *Leisure interests:* cooking, rowing, opera. *Address:* Bradford & Bingley Building Society, Croft Road, Crossflatts, Bingley, W. Yorks., BD16 2UA, England. *Telephone:* (01274) 554426. *Fax:* (01273) 569116.

RODRIGUEZ IGLESIAS, Gil Carlos, PH.D.; Spanish judge and professor of law; b. 26 May 1946, Gijón; m. Teresa Diez Gutiérrez 1972; two d.; ed. Oviedo Univ. and Univ. Autónoma of Madrid; Asst. Univs. of Oviedo, Freiburg, Autónoma of Madrid and Complutense of Madrid 1969–77; lecturer, Univ. Complutense of Madrid 1977–82, Prof. 1982–83; Prof. Univ. of Granada 1983–, Dir. Dept. of Int. Law 1983–86; Judge, Court of Justice of European Communities 1986–, Pres. 1994–; Orden de Isabel la Católica; Orden de San Raimundo de Peñafort; Hon. Bencher Gray's Inn 1995; Dr. h.c. (Turin) 1996, (Babes-Bolyai' Cluj-Napoca, Romania) 1996. *Publications:* El régimen jurídico de los monopolios de Estado en la Comunidad Económica Europea 1976; articles and studies on EC law and int. law. *Address:* Court of Justice of the European Communities, Plateau du Kirchberg, 2925 Luxembourg. *Telephone:* 4303-2265. *Fax:* 4303-2777.

RODRÍGUEZ LARA, Maj.-Gen. Guillermo; Ecuadorean army officer; b. 4 Nov. 1923; ed. Quito Mil. Acad. and studies abroad; C.-in-C. of Army 1971; President of Ecuador (following coup d'état) 1972–76.

ROEG, Nicolas Jack, C.B.E.; British film director; b. 15 Aug. 1928, London; s. of Jack Nicolas Roeg and Mabel Roeg; m. 1st Susan Rennie Stephen 1957 (divorced); four s.; m. 2nd Theresa Russell; two s.; ed. Mercers School; started in film industry as clapper-boy; B.F.I. Fellow 1994; Hon. D.Litt. (Hull) 1995. *Principal films:* as cinematographer: The Caretaker 1963, The Masque of the Red Death, Nothing but the Best 1964, Fahrenheit 451 1966, Far from the Madding Crowd 1967, Petulia 1968; Dir: Performance (with Donald Cammell) 1968, Walkabout 1970, Don't Look Now 1972, The Man who Fell to Earth 1975, Bad Timing 1979, Eureka 1983, Insignificance 1984, Castaway 1985, Track 29 1987, Aria (Sequence) 1988, Cold Heaven 1989, The Witches 1989, Sweet Bird of Youth 1989, Without You I'm Nothing (exec. producer) 1990, Young Indy—Paris 1916 1991, Cold Heaven 1991, Heart of Darkness 1993, Two Deaths 1994, Full Body Massage 1995, Hotel Paradise 1995, Samson and Delilah 1996. *Address:* c/o I.C.M. Oxford House, 76 Oxford Street, London, W1R 1RB, England; c/o Robert Littman, 9454 Lloydcrest Drive, Beverly Hills, Los Angeles, CA 90210, U.S.A.

ROEHM, Carolyne, B.F.A.; American fashion designer; b. 7 May 1951, Kirksville, Mo.; d. of Kenneth Smith and Elaine (Beaty) Bresee; m. 1st Axel Roehm 1978 (divorced 1981); m. 2nd Henry R. Kravis 1985; ed. Washington Univ. St. Louis; designed sportswear for Kellwood Co. New York; apprentice, Oscar de la Renta, Rome 1975–84; Pres. Carolyne Roehm Inc. (fashion design house) 1984–; Pres. Council of Fashion Designers of America 1989. *Leisure interests:* gardening, skiing, tennis, opera, playing the piano.

ROEM, Mohammad; Indonesian politician; b. 16 May 1908, Parakan, Kedu Central Java; s. of Dzoelkarnain Djojosasmito and Siti Tarbiyah; m. Markisah Dahlia 1932; one s. one d.; ed. Law School, Batavia (now Jakarta); Solicitor in pvt. practice, Jakarta 1940–67; fmr. leader of Islamic Youth Movement; Indonesian Minister of the Interior 1946–48; mem. del. in Dutch-Indonesian talks leading to Agreement Linggajati 1947, Renville Agreement 1948; Chair. Indonesian del. leading to Van Roijem-Roem Statements 1949; Deputy Chair. Round Table Conf. with Netherlands Govt. 1949; first High Commr. of Indonesia to the Netherlands 1950; Minister of Foreign Affairs 1950–51, of Home Affairs 1952–53; First Vice-Premier 1956–57; mem. Exec. Cttee. Masjumi Party 1945–62, Third Deputy Chair. 1959; Pres. Islamic Univ., Medan 1953–62; detained 1962–66; founder-mem. Partai Muslimin

Indonesia 1967, Chair. 1968–72; mem. World Muslim Congress 1975–; mem. Bd. Dirs. Asian Conf. for Religion and Peace; Vice-Chair. Bd. of Curators, Islamic Medical Faculty, Jakarta. *Publications:* Bunga Rampai Sejarah I (1972), II (1977). *Leisure interests:* swimming, horse-riding. *Address:* c/o Jalan Teuku Cik Ditiro 58, Jakarta-Pusat, Indonesia. *Telephone:* 343393.

ROEMER, John E., PH.D.; American professor of economics; b. 1 Feb. 1945, Washington, D.C.; s. of Milton I. Roemer and Ruth Rosenbaum Roemer; m. Carla Natasha Muldavin 1968; two c.; ed. Harvard Univ., Univ. of California, Berkeley; Asst. Prof., Univ. of Calif., Davis 1974, Prof. of Econs. 1981–, Dir. Program on Economy, Justice and Society 1988; Guggenheim Fellow; Fellow Econometric Soc. *Publications:* A General Theory of Exploitation and Class 1982, Free to Lose 1988, Egalitarian Perspectives 1994, A Future for Socialism 1994, Theories of Distributive Justice 1996, Equality of Opportunity 1998. *Address:* Department of Economics, University of California, Davis, CA 95616, U.S.A. *Telephone:* (916) 752-3226. *Fax:* (916) 752-9382.

ROESKY, Herbert Walter, DR. SC.; German professor of inorganic chemistry; b. 6 Nov. 1935, Laukischken; s. of Otto Roesky and Lina Roesky; m. Christel Roesky 1964; two s.; ed. Univ. of Göttingen; lecturer 1970, Prof. of Inorganic Chem., Univ. of Frankfurt 1971–80; Dir. Inst. of Inorganic Chem., Univ. of Göttingen 1980–, Dean Dept. of Chem. 1985–87; Visiting Prof. Univ. of Auburn, U.S.A. 1984, Tokyo Inst. of Tech. 1987; mem. Gesellschaft Deutscher Chemiker (Vice-Pres. 1995), American Chemical Soc., Chemical Soc., London, Gesellschaft Deutscher Naturforscher und Ärzte, Deutsche Bunsen-Gesellschaft für Physikalische Chemie, Göttinger Akad., Akad. Leopoldina, Austrian Acad. of Sciences; mem. Selection Bd., Alexander von Humboldt-Stiftung 1973–84, numerous editorial bds.; Wöhler Prize 1960, French Alexander von Humboldt Prize 1986, Leibniz Prize 1987; Alfred-Stock-Gedächtnispreis 1990, Georg Ernst Stahl Medal 1990; Manfred and Wolfgang Flad Prize 1994, Grand Prix Fondation de la maison de la chimie, Carus Prize 1998. *Publications: c.* 700 learned papers and articles. *Leisure interest:* antique collecting. *Address:* Institute of Inorganic Chemistry, University of Göttingen, Tammannstrasse 4, 37077 Göttingen, Germany. *Telephone:* (0551) 393001. *Fax:* (0551) 393373.

ROESTAM, Soepardjo; Indonesian politician; b. 12 Aug. 1926, Sokoraja, Cen. Java; ed. Jr. High School, Purwokerto, Army Staff and Command Coll., Bandung and Infantry School, Fort Benning, U.S.A.; Mil. attaché, Netherlands 1952, Malaysia 1952–62; Head, Asia-Pacific Directorate, Dept. of Foreign Affairs 1967–71; Amb. to Yugoslavia 1971–72, to Malaysia 1972–74; Gov. of Cen. Java 1974–83; Minister of Home Affairs 1983–88, Minister Co-ordinator for Public Welfare 1988–93. *Address:* c/o Office of the Co-ordinating Minister for Public Welfare, Jln. Merdeka Barat 3, Jakarta 10110, Indonesia.

ROGACHEV, Igor Alekseevich, PH.D.; Russian diplomatist; b. 1 March 1932, Moscow; s. of Aleksey Petrovich Rogachev; m. Dulber Rogacheva; one s. one d. (adopted); ed. Moscow Inst. of Int. Relations 1955; worked as interpreter in China 1956–58; joined diplomatic service 1958; Attaché, Embassy in China 1959–61; mem. Cen. Admin. U.S.S.R Ministry of Foreign Affairs 1961–65; First Sec. Embassy, U.S.A. 1965–69; Counsellor Embassy, China 1969–72; Deputy Head, Far Eastern Dept., Ministry of Foreign Affairs 1972–75, Head Asian Section, Dept. of Planning of int. policies 1975–78, Head of South-East Asia Dept. 1978–83, Head First Far East Div. 1983–86, Dept. of Socialist Countries June–Aug. 1986, Deputy-Minister of Foreign Affairs 1986–91; Russian Amb. to China 1992–; Order of People's Friendship 1971, Honour Sign Order 1982, Order of Friendship 1996, and several medals. *Publications:* numerous articles and essays on Asian Pacific countries and region. *Leisure interests:* playing the piano, tennis, reading. *Address:* Russian Embassy, 4 Dongzhimennei Beizhong Street, Beijing 100600, China. *Telephone:* (10) 532-20-51; (10) 532-13-81. *Fax:* (10) 532-48-53.

ROGÉ, Pascal; French pianist; b. 6 April 1951, Paris; ed. Paris Conservatoire; début Paris 1969, London 1969; two s.; First Prize, Marguérite Long-Jacques Thibaud Int. Competition 1971; specialist in Ravel, Poulenc, Debussy, Satie; soloist with leading orchestras; exclusive recording contract with Decca, London. *Leisure interests:* reading, tennis, riding. *Address:* Lorentz Concerts, 3 rue de la Boétie, 75008 Paris, France; 17 avenue des Cavaliers, 1224 Geneva, Switzerland.

ROGER OF TAIZÉ, Brother (Roger Louis Schutz-Marsauche); French/Swiss monk; b. 12 May 1915, Provence, Switzerland; s. of Charles Schutz and Amélie Marsauche; ed. theological studies in Lausanne and Strasbourg; founder and Prior of Taizé (int. ecumenical, monastic community) 1940–; arrived in Taizé 1940; lived there alone for two years sheltering Jews and political refugees; joined by the first brothers in 1942; there are now small fraternities of brothers living among the poor on every continent; attended Second Vatican Council 1962–65; launched Pilgrimage of Trust on Earth 1982; Templeton Prize for Religion 1974; Dr. h.c. (Catholic Theological Acad. of Warsaw) 1986; Hon. D.D. (Glasgow) 1991; UNESCO Prize for Peace Educ. 1988, Robert Schuman Prize for his participation in construction of Europe 1992. *Publications:* Sources of Taizé, No Greater Love, Peace of Heart in All Things, The Wonder of a Love, with Mother Teresa of Calcutta: The Way of the Cross, Mary Mother of Reconciliations, Prayer: Seeking the Heart of God. *Address:* The Taizé Community, 71250 Cluny, France. *Telephone:* (3) 85.50.30.30. *Fax:* (3) 85.50.30.20.

ROGERS, Gen. Bernard William, M.A.; American army officer; b. 16 July 1921, Fairview, Kan.; s. of late W. H. Rogers and Mrs. Rogers; m. Ann Ellen Jones 1944; one s. two d.; ed. Kansas State Coll., U.S. Mil. Acad., Univ. of Oxford, U.S. Army Command and Gen. Staff Coll., U.S. Army War Coll.; Commdg. Officer, Third Bn., Ninth Infantry Regt., Second Infantry Div., Korea 1952–53; Commdr., First Battle Group, 19th Infantry, 24th Infantry Div., Augsburg, Fed. Repub. of Germany 1960–61; Exec. Officer to the Chair., Joint Chiefs of Staff, the Pentagon 1962–66; Asst. Div. Commdr., First Infantry Div., Repub. of Viet Nam 1966–67; Commdt. of Cadets, U.S. Mil. Acad. 1967–69; Commdg. Gen., Fifth Infantry Div., Fort Carson, Colo. 1969–70; Chief of Legis. Liaison, Office of the U.S. Sec. of the Army 1971–72; Deputy Chief of Staff for Personnel 1972–74; Commdg. Gen., U.S. Army Forces Command, Fort McPherson, Ga. 1974–76; Chief of Staff, U.S. Army 1976–79, Supreme Allied Commdr. Europe, NATO 1979–87; Rhodes Scholar 1947–50; Hon. Fellow Univ. Coll., Oxford; Hon. LL.D. (Akron, Boston), Hon. D.C.L. (Oxford) 1983; Distinguished Grad. Award, U.S. Mil. Acad. 1995; D.S.C., D.D.S.M., D.S.M. of Army, Navy and Air Force, Silver Star, Legion of Merit, Bronze Star, Air Medal. *Publications:* Cedar Falls-Junction City: a Turning Point 1974, NATO's Strategy: An Undervalued Currency 1985, The Realities of NATO Strategy 1985, NATO's Conventional Defense Improvements Initiative: A New Approach to an Old Challenge, NATO's 16 Nations 1986, Western Security and European Defence RUSI 1986, NATO and U.S. National Security: Misperception Versus Reality 1987, Soldat und Technik 1987, Arms Control and NATO, The Council for Arms Control 1987, Arms Control: for NATO, the Name of the Game is Deterrence, Global Affairs 1987; contribs. to Atlantic Community Quarterly 1979, Foreign Affairs 1982, NATO Review 1982, 1984, RUSI 1982, Strategic Review, Nato's 16 Nations 1983, Géopolitique 1983, Europa Archiv 1984, Leaders Magazine 1984. *Leisure interests:* golf, reading. *Address:* 1467 Hampton Ridge Drive, McLean, VA 22101, U.S.A. *Telephone:* (703) 448-0188.

ROGERS, David, B.A.; British business executive; b. 29 Nov. 1946; m.; two s.; ed. Grimsby Grammar School and Lanchester Coll.; GEC British Domestic Appliances 1964–71; Black & Decker 1972–77; Plessey Office Systems 1977–86; Philips Electronics 1986–94, C.E.O. Philips Advanced Telecommunications Enterprises 1993–94; fmr. C.E.O. Amstrad PLC and Amstrad Consumer Electronics.

ROGERS, Sir Frank Jarvis, Kt.; British newspaper publisher; b. 24 Feb. 1920, Lawton, Cheshire; s. of Percy Rogers and Elsie Rogers; m. Esma Sophia Holland 1949 (died 1998); two d.; ed. Wolstanton Grammar School; journalist 1937–49; mil. service 1940–46; Gen. Man. Nigerian Daily Times 1949–52; Man. Argus, Melbourne 1952–55; Man. Dir. Overseas Newspapers 1958–60; Dir. Daily Mirror 1960–65; Man. Dir. IPC 1965–70; Vice-Chair. Newspaper Publrs. Assn. 1968–69, Dir. 1971–73, Chair. 1990–98; Chair. Nat. Newspapers Steering Group 1970–72; Dir. EMAP (fmrly. East Midland Allied Press) 1971–91, Chair. 1973–90; Adviser on Corp. Affairs The Plessey Co. Ltd. 1973–81; Deputy Chair. Argyll Investments Ltd. 1982–90; Exec. Dir. 1986–, Deputy Chair. Daily Telegraph PLC 1986–95; Trustee Reuters Founders Share Co. 1989–, Chair. 1998–. *Leisure interests:* golf, motoring. *Address:* Greensleeves, Loudwater Drive, Loudwater, Rickmansworth, Herts., WD3 4HJ, England.

ROGERS, George Ernest, PH.D., F.A.A.; Australian professor of biochemistry; b. 27 Oct. 1927, Melbourne; s. of Percy Rogers and Bertha Beatrice (née Baxter) Rogers; m. Racheline Aladjem 1972; two d.; ed. Caulfield Grammar School, Univ. of Melbourne and Trinity Coll., Cambridge, England; Research Scientist, Wool Research Unit, CSIRO 1951–53, Sr. Research Scientist Div. of Protein Chem. 1957–62; Research Scientist, Univ. of Cambridge, England 1954–56; Reader in Biochem., Univ. of Adelaide 1963–77, Prof. of Biochem. 1978–92 and Chair. Dept. of Biochem. 1988–92, Emer. Prof. of Biochemistry, Hon. Visiting Research Fellow 1992–; Visiting Fellow, Clare Hall, Cambridge, England 1970; Visiting Scientist, Univ. de Grenoble, France 1977; Guest Scientist, N.I.H., Bethesda, U.S.A. 1985; CSIRO studentship 1954–56; Bourse Scientifique de Haut Niveau 1977; mem. Australian Soc. of Biochemistry and Molecular Biology, New York Acad. of Sciences; Eleanor Roosevelt Int. Cancer Research Fellow 1985; Lemberg Medal, Australian Biochemical Soc. 1976. *Publications include:* The Keratins (jtly.) 1972, The Biology of Wool and Hair (jtly.) 1989; 120 publs. in scientific journals on wool and hair growth. *Leisure interests:* family activities, swimming, golf, gardening. *Address:* Department of Animal Science, University of Adelaide, Waite Campus, Adelaide, S.A. 5064 (Office); 1 Gandys Gully Road, Stonyfell, S.A. 5066, Australia (Home). *Telephone:* (08) 8303 6543 (Office); (08) 8332 4143 (Home). *Fax:* (08) 8303 7114.

ROGERS, Paul; British actor; b. 22 March 1917, Plympton, Devon; s. of Edwin and Dulcie Myrtle Rogers; m. 1st Jocelyn Wynne 1939 (divorced 1955); two s.; m. 2nd Rosalind Boxall 1955; two d.; ed. Newton Abbot Grammar School, Devon and Michael Chekhov Theatre Studio; first stage appearance at Scala Theatre 1938; Stratford-on-Avon Shakespeare Memorial Theatre 1939; Royal Navy 1940–46; with Bristol Old Vic Co. 1947–49, London Old Vic 1949–53, 1955–56. *Plays include:* The Merchant of Venice 1952, The Confidential Clerk 1953, Macbeth 1954, The Taming of the Shrew; toured Australia as Hamlet 1957; The Elder Statesman 1958, King Lear 1958, Mr. Fox of Venice 1959, The Merry Wives of Windsor 1959, A Winter's Tale 1959, One More River 1959, JB 61, Photo Finish 1962, The Seagull 1964, Season of Goodwill 1964, The Homecoming 1965, 1968, Timon of Athens (Stratford) 1965, The Government Inspector 1966, Henry IV (Stratford) 1966, Plaza Suite 1969, The Happy Apple 1970, Sleuth (London 1970, New York 1971), Othello (Old Vic) 1974, Heartbreak House (Nat. Theatre) 1975, The Marrying of Ann Leete (Aldwych) 1975, The Return of A. J. Raffles (Aldwych) 1975, The Zykovs (Aldwych) 1976, Volpone, The Madras House (Nat. Theatre) 1977, Half Life (Nat. Theatre), Eclipse (Royal Court Theatre) 1978, Merchant of Venice (Birmingham Repertory Co.) 1979, You Never Can Tell (Lyric, Hammersmith) 1979, The Dresser (New York) 1981–82, The Importance of Being Earnest (Nat. Theatre) 1982, A Kind of Alaska (Nat. Theatre) 1982, The Applecart (Haymarket) 1986, Danger: Memory! 1986, King Lear 1989, Other People's Money (Lyric) 1990. *Films include:* A Midsummer Night's Dream 1968, The Looking-Glass War 1969, The Reckoning 1969, The Homecoming 1973, The Abdication 1975, Mr. Quilp 1975. *TV films:* Porterhouse Blue 1986, Return of the Native 1993. *Address:* 9 Hillside Gardens, Highgate, London, N6 5SU, England. *Telephone:* 0181-340 2656.

ROGERS, William P., LL.B.; American government official and lawyer; b. 23 June 1913, Norfolk, N.Y.; s. of Harrison Alexander and Myra (Beswick) Rogers; m. 1936; three s. one d.; ed. Canton High School, New York, Colgate Univ. and Cornell Univ. Law School; joined law firm of Cadwalader, Wickersham and Taft, New York 1937; Asst. Dist. Attorney, County 1938–42, 1946–47; officer in U.S. Navy 1942–46; Chief Counsel, Senate War Investigating Cttee. 1947–48, Senate Perm. Investigating Cttee. 1948–50; mem. law firm of Dwight, Royall, Harris, Koegel and Caskey 1950–53; Deputy Attorney Gen. of the U.S. 1953–57, Attorney Gen. 1957–61; U.S. Rep., Gen. Ass. UN 1965; U.S. Rep., UN Ad Hoc Cttee. on S.W. Africa 1967; mem. Pres. Comm. on Law Enforcement and Admin. of Justice 1965–67; with Royall, Koegel, Rogers and Wells 1961–69; U.S. Sec. of State 1969–73; partner law firm of Rogers and Wells 1973–; Head Comm. to Investigate Challenger Disaster 1986; Chair. Advisory Bd. Merrill Lynch. *Address:* Rogers & Wells, 200 Park Avenue, New York, NY 10166, U.S.A.

ROGERS OF RIVERSIDE, Baron (Life Peer), cr. 1996, of Chelsea in the Royal Borough of Kensington and Chelsea; **Richard George Rogers,** Kt., A.A.DIPL., M. ARCH., R.A.; British architect; b. 23 July 1933, Florence, Italy; s. of Nino Rogers and Dada Geiringer; m. 1st Su Brumwell 1961; three s.; m. 2nd Ruth Elias 1973; two s.; ed. Architectural Asscn., London, Yale Univ.; Fulbright, Edward D. Stone and Yale Scholar; Chair. Richard Rogers Architects Ltd., London and Berlin, Richard Rogers Japan KK, Tokyo, Architecture Foundation, Nat. Tenants Resource Centre, Govt. Urban Task Force; Dir. River Café Ltd.; numerous exhbns., including Museum of Modern Art, N.Y., and Royal Acad., London; Saarinen Prof. Yale Univ. 1985; has also taught at Architectural Asscn., London, at Cambridge, Princeton, Columbia, Harvard, Cornell, McGill and Aachen Univs. and at UCLA; Vice-Chair. Arts Council of England 1994–97; mem. UN Architects' Cttee.; Hon. F.R.I.B.A., F.A.I.A. 1986; Trustee Tate Gallery 1981–89 (Chair. 1984–88), London First 1993–98, U.K. Bd. Médecins du Monde; Reith Lecturer 1995; Dr. h.c. (Westminster) 1993, (R.C.A.) 1994, (Bath) 1994, (South Bank) 1996; Hon. D.Litt. (Univ. Coll., London) 1997; winner of numerous int. competitions including Centre Pompidou, Paris 1971–77, Lloyd's HQ, London 1978; Constructa Prize 1986, 1992, Eternit Int. Prize 1988; eleven R.I.B.A. awards 1969–, Royal Gold Medal R.I.B.A. 1985, Civic Trust Award 1987, and many other awards; Chevalier Légion d'honneur 1986; major int. work includes: masterplanning: Royal Docks, London 1984–86, Potsdamer Platz, Berlin 1991, Shanghai Pu Dong Financial Dist. 1992, Greenwich Peninsula Masterplan 1997–98; airports and HQ bldgs.: PA Tech., Cambridge 1975–83, PA Tech., Princeton, NJ, U.S.A. 1984, European Court of Human Rights, Strasbourg 1990–95, Marseille Airport 1992, Law Courts, Bordeaux, France 1992–98, VR Techno offices and lab., Gifu, Japan 1993–98, Channel 4 HQ 1994; current projects include: masterplanning of Heathrow Airport Terminal 5 1989–, Montevetro Housing, Battersea, London 1994–, ParcBIT devt., Majorca 1994–, Lloyd's Register of Shipping HQ, London 1995–99, Daiwa Europe HQ, London 1995–, New Millennium Experience, Greenwich, London 1996–99, masterplanning of Piana di Castello, Florence 1997–, new terminal for Barajas Airport, Madrid 1997–, Tribunal de Grand Instance 1998–, Nat. Ass. for Wales 1998–. *Publications:* Richard Rogers and Architects 1985, A+U: Richard Rogers 1978–88 1988, Architecture: A Modern View 1990, A New London (with Mark Fisher) 1992, Reith Lecturer 1995, Cities for a Small Planet 1997, Richard Rogers The Complete Works (Vol. 1) 1999. *Leisure interests:* friends, food, travel, art, architecture. *Address:* Thames Wharf, Rainville Road, London, W6 9HA, England. *Telephone:* 0171-385 1235. *Fax:* 0171-385 8409.

ROGERSON, Philip Graham; British business executive; b. 1 Jan. 1945, Manchester; s. of Henry Rogerson and Florence Rogerson; m. Susan Janet Kershaw 1968; one s. two d.; ed. William Hulme's Grammar School, Manchester; with Dearden Harper, Miller & Co. Chartered Accountants 1962–67; with Hill Samuel & Co. Ltd. 1967–69; with Thomas Tilling Ltd. 1969–71; with Steetly Ltd. 1971–72; with J.W. Chafer Ltd. 1972–78; joined ICI 1978, Gen. Man. Finance 1989–92; Man. Dir. Finance British Gas PLC 1992–94, Exec. Dir. 1994–96, Deputy Chair. 1996–98; Deputy Chair. (non-exec.) Aggreko PLC 1997–; Dir. (non-exec.) Halifax Bldg. Soc. (now Halifax PLC) 1995–. Shandwick Int. PLC 1997–, LIMIT PLC 1997, Int. Public Relations 1997–, Wates City of London Properties 1998–; Chair. (non-exec.) Pipeline Integrity Int. 1998–; Chair. Viridian Group PLC 1999– (Deputy Chair. 1998), Trustee Changing Faces 1997–, School for Social Entrepreneurs 1997–. *Leisure interests:* golf, theatre, opera, ballet.

ROGOFF, Ilan; Israeli concert pianist and conductor; b. 26 July 1943, Israel; s. of Boris Rogoff and Sofija Rogoff; m. Vesna Zorka Mimiça 1985; two d.; ed. Israel Acad. of Music, Royal Conservatoire, Brussels, Mannes Coll., Juilliard School, New York; has played all over Israel, Europe, N. America, Latin America, Japan and Far East with Israel Philharmonic Orchestra and many other orchestras; recordings include works by Bach–Busoni, César Franck, Schumann, Schubert, Chopin, Beethoven and Liszt; has performed twentieth-century and contemporary works including world premiere of concerti by John McCabe and by Ivan Erod; conducting début 1985, with Israel Philharmonic Dec. 1988; Music and Artistic Dir. Sociedad Filarmónica de Mallorca 1992–93; lectures and recital/lectures, master classes; Trustee Tel Aviv Museum, Misgav Ladach Hosp., Jerusalem; f. Ilan Rogoff Foundation, Colombia to provide medical care to children of poor families; various int. awards. *Leisure interests:* water sports, reading, visual arts, theatre, cinema and music research. *Address:* Apdo. 1098, 07080 Palma de Mallorca, Spain. *Telephone:* (71) 677654. *Fax:* (71) 677252.

ROH TAE WOO; Korean politician; b. 4 Dec. 1932, Taegu; m. Roh (née Kim) Ok Sook 1959; one s. one d.; ed. Taegu Tech. School, Kyongbuk High School, Korean Mil. Acad., U.S. Special Warfare School, Repub. of Korea War Coll.; served in Korean War 1950; Commanding Gen. 9th Special Forces Brigade 1974–79, 9th Infantry Div. Jan.–Dec. 1979, Commdr. Capital Security Command 1979–80, Defence Security Command 1980–81, Four-Star Gen. 1981, retd. from army July 1981; Minister of State for Nat. Security and Foreign Affairs 1981–82, Minister of Sports 1982, of Home Affairs 1982; Pres. Repub. of Korea 1988–93; mem. Nat. Ass. 1985; Chair. Democratic Justice Party 1985–87, Pres. 1987–90, Jt. Pres. Democratic Liberal Party (DLP) 1990–92 (had to quit the ruling party by agreement); Pres. Seoul Olympic Organising Cttee. 1983, Korean Amateur Sports Asscn. 1984, Korean Olympic Cttee. 1984; arrested Nov. 1995, charged with aiding Dec. 1979 Coup Dec. 1995; also charged with taking bribes; convicted of mutiny and treason, sentenced to 22½ years imprisonment Aug. 1996; numerous decorations. *Publications:* Widaehan pot'ougsaram ui shidae 1987, Korea: A Nation Transformed 1990. *Leisure interests:* tennis, swimming, golf, music, reading.

ROHATYN, Felix George; American investment banker; b. 29 May 1928, Vienna; s. of Alexander Rohatyn and Edith Knoll; m. 1st Jeannette Streit 1956; three s.; m. 2nd Elizabeth Fly 1979; ed. Middlebury Coll., Vt.; moved to U.S.A. 1942; joined Lazard Freres & Co. (investment bankers) 1948, Gen. Partner 1960–97; Amb. to France 1997–; mem. Bd. of Dirs. Pfizer Co., General Instrument Crown Cork and Seal; eight hon. degrees. *Address:* American Embassy, 2 avenue Gabriel, 75382 Paris, cedex 08, France. *Telephone:* (1) 43-12-22-22. *Fax:* (1) 43-12-97-63.

ROHDE, Helmut; German politician and journalist; b. 9 Nov. 1925, Hanover; m. 1st Hanna Müller 1950; one s.; m. 2nd Ruth Basenaü 1983; ed. Acad. for Labour, Political Studies and Econs.; journalist, German Press Agency; Press Officer, Ministry for Social Affairs, Lower Saxony; mem. Parl. (Bundestag) 1957–87; mem. European Parl. 1964–; Parl. State Sec. Fed. Ministry of Labour and Social Affairs 1969–74; Chair. SPD Working Group for Issues Concerning Employees 1973–84; Fed. Minister for Educ. and Science 1974–78; Deputy Chair. SPD, Bundestag 1979; Prof. Univ. of Hanover 1985–; Hon. Prof. (Univ. Bremen) 1994; Paul Klinger Prize 1974, Gold Medal, Asscn. of War-Blinded. *Publications:* Sozialplanung—Theorie und Praxis der deutschen Sozialdemokratie, Gesellschaftspolitische Planung und Praxis, Für eine soziale Zukunft, and numerous articles on social and education policy. *Leisure interests:* modern art, music, modern jazz. *Address:* Sanddornweg 3, 53757 Sankt Augustin, Germany. *Telephone:* (2241) 333593.

ROHMER, Eric (pseudonym of Maurice Henri Joseph Schérer); French film director; b. 21 March 1920, Tulle, Corrèze; s. of Désiré Schérer and Jeanne Monzat; m. Thérèse Barbet 1957; ed. in Paris; School teacher and journalist until 1955; film critic of Revue du cinéma, Arts, Temps modernes, La Parisienne 1949–63; founder (with others) and fmr. co-editor of La Gazette du cinéma (review); fmr. co-editor of Cahiers du cinéma; co-dir. Soc. des Films du Losange 1964–; made educational films for French TV 1964–70; Officier des Arts et des Lettres; Prix Max-Ophuls 1970 (for Ma nuit chez Maud); Prix Louis-Delluc 1971, Prix du Meilleur Film du Festival de Saint-Sébastien 1971, Prix Méliès 1971 (all for Le genou de Claire), Prix Speciale Soc. des Auteurs et Compositeurs 1982, Best Dir. Award, Berlin Film Festival 1983, Officier, Légion d'honneur. *Wrote and directed:* Présentation ou Charlotte et son steak 1951, Véronique et son cancre 1958, Le signe du lion (first feature) 1959, La boulangère de Monceau 1962, La carrière de Suzanne 1963, La collectionneuse 1966, Ma nuit chez Maud 1969, Le genou de Claire 1970, L'amour l'après-midi 1972, La Marquise d'O 1976, Percival le Gallois 1978, La Femme de l'Aviateur, Le Beau Mariage 1982, Pauline à la Plage 1982, Les Nuits de la pleine Lune 1984, Le Rayon Vert 1985, Four Adventures of Reinette and Mirabelle 1987, My Girlfriend's Boyfriend 1988, A Tale of Springtime 1990, A Winter's Tale 1992, Tous les Matins du Monde 1992, L'Arbre, Le Maire et la Mediathèque 1993, Les Rendez-vous de Paris 1995, Conte d'été 1996, A Summer's Tale 1996. *Publications:* Alfred Hitchcock, Charlie Chaplin 1973, Six contes moraux 1974, L'organisation de l'espace dans le "Faust" de Murnau 1977, The Taste for Beauty 1991. *Address:* Les Films du Losange, 22 avenue Pierre 1er de Serbie, 75116 Paris, France.

ROHNER, Georges; French artist; b. 20 July 1913, Paris; m. Suzanne Guy 1943; two s.; ed. Atelier Lucien Simon; mil. service and painting, Guadeloupe

1934; prisoner-of-war 1940; exhbns. in Philadelphia 1949, Galerie Framond, Paris 1951, 1953, 1956; Prof. Ecole Nat. Supérieure des Arts Décoratifs 1963–; mem. Inst. de France (Acad. des Beaux Arts, Chair. of Ingres) 1963; exhbns. in London 1973, New York 1974, 1990, Galerie Framond, Paris 1983–84, 1988; Retrospectives, Musée de Quimper 1987, Galerie Framond 1991; Chevalier, Légion d'honneur; Officier des Arts et des Lettres. *Address:* c/o Galerie Framond, 3 rue des Saints Pères, 75006 Paris, France. *Telephone:* 42.60.74.77.

ROHR, Hans Christoph von, PH.D.; German business executive; b. 1 July 1938, Stettin; s. of Hansjoachim von Rohr; m.; two c.; ed. Univs. of Heidelberg, Vienna, Bonn and Kiel and Princeton Univ.; joined Klöckner-Werke AG, Bremen; subsequently held leading position with Klöckner subsidiary in Argentina; worked for Fisser & von Doornum, Einden; mem. Bd. Klöckner & Co. Duisburg 1984; Chair. Exec. Bd. Klöckner-Werke AG 1991–95; Man. Chair. Industrial Investment Council GmbH 1997; Chair. (non-exec.) Baring Brothers (Germany) GmbH. *Address:* Huyssenallee 100, 45128 Essen, Germany.

ROHRER, Heinrich, PH.D.; Swiss physicist; b. 6 June 1933, Buchs, St. Gallen; m. Rose-Marie Egger 1961; two d.; ed. Swiss Federal Inst. of Technology; post-doctoral research, Rutgers Univ., N.J.; with IBM Research Lab., Rüschlikon 1963–, Man. Physics Dept.; sabbatical, Univ. of Calif. Santa Barbara 1974–75; Nobel Prize for Physics (with Ernst Ruska and Gerd Binnig) for work in pioneering devt. of electronic microscope 1986; IBM Fellow 1986; Dir. Swiss Inst. of Tech. 1993; mem. European Acad. 1998–; Hon. D.Sc. (Rutgers Univ.) 1987; named to Nat. Inventors Hall of Fame 1994. *Address:* IBM Research Laboratory, Säumerstrasse 4, 8803 Rüschlikon, Zürich, Switzerland. *Telephone:* 41-1-72 48 111.

ROIZMAN, Bernard, SC.D.; American professor of virology; b. 17 April 1929, Romania; m. Betty Cohen 1950; two s.; ed. Temple Univ., Phila., The Johns Hopkins Univ., Baltimore; Instructor of Microbiology, Johns Hopkins Univ. 1956–57, Research Assoc. 1957–58, Asst. Prof. 1958–65; Assoc. Prof. of Microbiology, Univ. of Chicago 1965–69, Prof. 1969–84, Prof. of Biophysics 1970–, Chair. Interdepartmental Cttee. on Virology 1969–85, 1988–, Joseph Regenstein Prof. of Virology 1981–83, Joseph Regenstein Distinguished Service Prof. of Virology 1984–; Chair. Dept. of Molecular Genetics and Cell Biology 1985–88; fmr. ed. of numerous specialist scientific publs. and mem. Editorial Bd. Journal of Virology 1970–, Intervirology 1972–85, Virology 1976–78, 1983–; Ed.-in-Chief Infectious Agents and Diseases 1992–96; mem. or fmr. mem. numerous grant review panels, int. panels, including Chair. Herpesvirus Study Group, Int. Cttee. for Taxonomy of Viruses 1971–94, Chair. Bd. of Dirs. 1991–; Scientific Advisory Bd., Teikeo-Showa Univs. Center 1983–; mem. Int. Microbial Genetics Comm., Int. Asscn. of Microbiological Sciences 1979–86; numerous nat. panels on vaccines, cancers; Scholar in Cancer Research at American Cancer Soc., Inst. Pasteur (with Andre Lwoff), Paris 1961–62; Travelling Fellow Int. Agency for Research Against Cancer (with Dr. Klein), Stockholm, Sweden 1970; Fellow Japanese Soc. for Promotion of Science, American Acad. of Arts and Sciences, American Acad. of Microbiology; mem. N.A.S., American Asscn. of Immunologists, Soc. for Experimental Biology and Medicine, American Soc. for Microbiology, for Biological Chemists, Soc. for Gen. Microbiology (U.K.), American Soc. for Virology; Hon. D.Sc. (Paris) 1997; numerous awards. *Publications:* author or co-author of approx. 400 papers in scientific journals and books, Ed. or Co-Ed. of 12 books. *Address:* Viral Oncology Laboratories, University of Chicago, Marjorie B. Kouler Viral Oncology Laboratories, 910 East 58th Street, Chicago, IL 60637 (Office); 5555 South Everett Avenue, Chicago, IL 60637, U.S.A. (Home). *Telephone:* (773) 702-1898 (Office).

ROJAS DE MORENO DÍAZ, María Eugenia; Colombian politician; b. 1934; d. of the late Gen. Gustavo Rojas Pinilla (Pres. of Colombia 1953–57); m. Samuel Moreno Díaz; two s.; fmr. mem. of the Senate; Majority Leader, Bogotá City Council; Leader, Alianza Nacional Popular (ANAPO) 1975–. *Address:* Alianza Nacional Popular (ANAPO), Santa Fe de Bogotá, DC, Colombia.

ROJO, Luis Angel, PH.D.; Spanish economist; b. 6 May 1934, Madrid; s. of Luis Rojo and Luisa Duque de Rojo; m. Concepción de Castro 1958; two s. one d.; ed. Univ. of Madrid and London School of Econs.; economist, Research Dept. Ministry of Commerce 1959–68; Asst. Prof. Dept. of Econ. Analysis, Faculty of Econs., Univ. of Madrid, 1959–65, Prof. of Econ. Analysis 1966–84; Gen. Dir. of Research and Studies, Bank of Spain 1971–88, Deputy Gov. 1988, Gov. (–2000); mem. Royal Acad. of Moral and Political Sciences; First Int. Prize "Rey Juan Carlos I" for Econs. 1986. *Publications:* Keynes y el pensamiento macroeconómico actual 1965, El Nuevo Monetarismo 1971, Renta, precios y balanza de pagos 1975, Marx: Economía y sociedad (with V. Pérez Díaz) 1984, Keynes: su tiempo y el nuestro 1984. *Leisure interests:* San Agustín, 9 28014 Madrid, Spain. *Telephone:* 532 49 47.

ROKITA, Jan Maria, LL.M.; Polish politician and lawyer; b. 18 June 1959, Cracow; s. of Tadeusz Rokita and Adela Rokita; m. Nelli Arnold 1994; one d.; ed. Jagellonian Univ., Cracow, Pontifical Acad. of Theology, Cracow; fmr. active mem. of Independent Students' Union (NZS), Chair. NZS Acad. Comm., Jagellonian Univ. 1980–81; interned 1982; banned from practising law 1983–89; co-founder and participant Freedom and Peace Movt. 1985–88; founder and mem. Intervention and Law-abidingness Comm. of Solidarity Trade Union 1986–89; mem. Civic Cttee. attached to Lech Wałęsa 1988–90; organizer and Chair. Int. Conf. on Human Rights, Cracow 1988; political commentator in illegal bi-weekly Świat 1989–90; participant Round Table debates 1989; Deputy to Sejm (Parl.) 1989–, Deputy Chair. Civic Parl. Club 1989–90, Deputy Chair. Democratic Union Parl. Club 1991–96, Deputy Chair. Freedom Union Parl. Club 1996–97, mem. Solidarity Election Action Parl. Club 1997–, Chair. Parl. Comm. for Admin. and Internal Affairs 1997, mem. Extraordinary Parl. Comm. for Examining Laws Determining Competences of Organs of Public Admin. 1997–; Minister-Chief of Office of Council of Ministers 1992–93; POLCUL Foundation Award (Australia) 1988; mem. Conservative Peasant Party (SKL) 1997–. *Publications:* political and historical journalism. *Leisure interest:* politics, music, architecture. *Address:* Sejm RP, ul. Wiejska 4/6/8, 00-902 Warsaw, Poland. *Telephone:* (22) 694 18 44, 694 19 38. *Fax:* (22) 628 62 16.

ROLANDIS, Nicos A.; Cypriot politician, company executive and barrister; b. 10 Dec. 1934, Limassol; m. Lelia Aivaliotis; one s. two d.; ed. Pancyprian Gymnasium Nicosia, Middle Temple, London; called to the bar, Middle Temple 1956; practised law in Cyprus for a short time then entered business; owner of industrial and commercial cos.; active in politics 1976–, founding mem. Democratic Group (now Democratic Party), f. Liberal Party 1986, Pres. 1986–98; Minister of Foreign Affairs 1978–83; mem. House of Reps. 1991–96; Vice-Pres. Liberal Int. 1994–99; Minister of Commerce, Industry and Tourism 1998–. *Address:* P.O. Box 1414, Nicosia (Office); 13 Ayias Agapis, Strovolos, Nicosia, Cyprus (Home). *Telephone:* 867111. *Fax:* 375323.

ROLFE JOHNSON, Anthony, C.B.E.; British singer; b. 5 Nov. 1940, Tackley, Oxon; m. Elisabeth Jones Evans; one s. two d., and two s. from previous marriage; has appeared with all major U.K. opera cos. and with Netherlands Opera, Hamburg State Opera, Zürich Opera, at the Monnaie Theatre, Brussels, La Scala Milan, Metropolitan Opera New York and at Aix-en-Provence and Salzburg Festivals; roles include Fenton (Falstaff), Albert Herring, Don Ottavio (Don Giovanni), Tamino (Magic Flute), Essex (Gloriana), Ferrando (Così fan tutte), Male Chorus (Rape of Lucretia), Orfeo (Monteverdi's Orfeo), Jupiter (Semele) and Aschenbach (Death in Venice); concerts with all major U.K. orchestras and with Chicago Symphony, Boston Symphony, New York Philharmonic and Cleveland orchestras in U.S.A.; recordings include Acis and Galatea, Saul, Hercules, Jephtha, Alexander's Feast, Esther, Solomon, Semele, Messiah, J. S. Bach's St. Matthew Passion and St. John Passion, Peter Grimes, Samson, Oedipus Rex, Orfeo, War Requiem. *Address:* c/o Lies Askonas Ltd., 6 Henrietta Street, London, WC2E 8LA, England. *Telephone:* 0171-495 1808.

ROLL OF IPSDEN, Baron (Life Peer), cr. 1977, of Ipsden in the County of Oxford; **Eric Roll,** K.C.M.G., C.B., PH.D., B.COM.; British banker and former civil servant; b. 1 Dec. 1907, Austria; s. of Mathias Roll and Fany (Frendel) Roll; m. Winifred Taylor 1934 (died 1998); two d.; ed. Univ. of Birmingham; Asst. Lecturer, Univ. Coll., Hull 1930, Prof. of Econs. and Commerce 1935–39; Special Fellow, Rockefeller Foundation 1939–41; Deputy mem., Combined Food Bd. 1941–46; Asst. Sec. Ministry of Food 1946–47, The Treasury 1947, Under-Sec. 1948–53; Chair. Econ. Cttee., OEEC 1948–53; Minister, U.K. del. to NATO 1952–53; Under-Sec. Ministry of Agric., Fisheries and Food 1953–57; Exec. Dir. Int. Sugar Council 1957–59; Deputy Sec. Ministry of Agric., Fisheries and Food 1960–61; Deputy Leader, U.K. del. to EEC Brussels Conf. 1961–63; Econ. Minister and Head of U.K. Treasury del., Washington; Exec. Dir. for U.K., IMF, IBRD 1963–65; Perm. Under-Sec. of State, Dept. of Econ. Affairs 1964–66; Chair. S. G. Warburg & Co. Ltd. 1974–84, Jt. Chair. 1984–87, Pres. S. G. Warburg Group PLC 1987–95; Sr. Adviser, Warburg Dillon Read 1995–; Chair. Mercury Securities 1974–84, Pres. 1984–87; Dir. Bank of England 1968–77, Peugeot Talbot Motor Co. Ltd. 1967–87; Chair. NEDC Cttee. on Finance for Industry 1975–80; Hon. Chair. Book Devt. Council; Chancellor, Southampton Univ. 1974–84; Hon. Fellow L.S.E. 1997; Hon. D.Sc. (Hull, Birmingham), Hon. LL.D. (Southampton). *Publications:* An Early Experiment in Industrial Organization 1930, Spotlight on Germany 1933, About Money 1934, Elements of Economic Theory 1935, Organized Labour (co-author) 1938, The British Commonwealth at War (co-author) 1943, The Combined Food Board 1957, The World after Keynes 1968, Uses and Abuses of Economics 1977, Crowded Hours 1985, A History of Economic Thought 1992, Where Did We Go Wrong? 1995. *Leisure interests:* reading, music. *Address:* c/o Warburg Dillon Read, 1 Finsbury Avenue, London, EC2M 2PP, England.

RÖLLER, Wolfgang, DR. RER. POL.; German bank executive; b. 20 Oct. 1929, Uelsen, Lower Saxony; m.; three s.; ed. Univs. of Berlin and Frankfurt; joined Dresdner Bank AG, Frankfurt/Main, Deputy mem. Bd. of Man. Dirs. 1971–73, Full mem. 1973–85, Chair. Man. Bd. 1985–93, Chair. Supervisory Bd. May 1993–; Chair. Supervisory Bd. ABD Securities Corpn., New York, Metallgesellschaft AG, Deutscher Investment-Trust Gesellschaft für Wertpapieranlagen m.b.H., Frankfurt, Dresdnerbank Investment Man. Kapitalanlageges. m.b.H., Frankfurt, Heidelberger Zementwerke AG; mem. Supervisory Bd. Allianz AG Holding, Munich, Daimler-Benz AG, Stuttgart, Degussa AG, Frankfurt, Henkel KGaA, Düsseldorf, Hoechst AG, Frankfurt; Fried. Krupp GmbH, Essen; Rheinisch-Westfälisches Elektrizitätswerk AG (fmr. Chair. Supervisory Bd.), Essen; fmrly. Chair. Deutsche Lufthansa AG, Cologne; mem other supervisory, advisory and man. bds. *Address:* Dresdner Bank AG, Jürgen-Ponto-Platz 1, 60329 Frankfurt/Main, Germany.

ROLLINS, Ed; American politician; b. 1943, Vallejo, Calif.; ed. Chico State Coll.; intern for Speaker of Calif. Ass.; Dean, Washington Univ. St. Louis 1970; worked on numerous presidential election campaigns 1972; Republican. *Publication:* Bare Knuckles and Back Rooms: My Life in American Politics (with Tom DeFrank) 1996. *Address:* c/o Republican National Committee, 310 First Street, SE, Washington, DC 20003, U.S.A.

ROLLINS, Reed Clark, B.A., M.S., PH.D.; American botanist; b. 7 Dec. 1911, Lyman, Wyoming; s. of William Clarence Rollins and Clara Rachel Slade Rollins; m. 1st Alberta Fitz-Gerald 1939 (divorced 1975); m. 2nd Kathryn W. Roby 1978; one s. one d.; ed. Univ. of Wyoming, State Coll. of Washington, Harvard Univ.; Teaching Fellow, State Coll. of Washington 1934–36; teaching asst., summer school Univ. of Wyoming 1935, in biology, Harvard 1936–37; instructor biology, asst. curator, Dudley Herbarium, Stanford 1940–41; Asst. Prof., Curator 1941–47, Assoc. Prof., Curator 1947–48; Assoc. geneticist, Guayule Research Project, Dept. of Agric. 1943–45; Principal Geneticist, Stanford Research Inst. 1946–47; geneticist div. rubber plant investigations, Dept. of Agric. 1947–48; Assoc. Prof., Botany 1948–54 and Dir., Gray Herbarium, Harvard Univ. 1948–78; Asa Gray Prof. of Systematic Botany, Harvard Univ. 1954–82, Emer. 1982–; Supervisor, Bussey Inst., Harvard Univ. 1967–78; Fellow, Soc. of Fellows, Harvard Univ. 1937–40; mem. N.A.S., American Soc. of Naturalists (Vice-Pres. 1960, Pres. 1966), A.A.A.S., American Inst. of Biological Sciences, Genetics Soc. of America; Chair. Inst. of Plant Sciences, Harvard Univ. 1965–69; Chair. Admin. Cttee. Farlow Library and Herbarium, Harvard Univ. 1974–78; Chair. Botany Section, N.A.S. 1977–80; Pres. Section of Nomenclature, XIII Int. Botanical Congress, Sydney 1981; Centenary Medal, French Botanical Soc., Certificate of Merit, Botanical Soc. of America, Congress Medals XI and XII Int. Botanical Congress, Gold Seal, Nat. Council of State Garden Clubs 1981. *Publications:* Revised edn. of Fernald and Kinsey's Edible Wild Plants of Eastern North America, The Genus Lesquerella (Cruciferae) in North America (with E. Shaw), The Cruciferae of North America 1993; articles and technical papers in professional journals. *Address:* Gray Herbarium, 22 Divinity Avenue, Cambridge, MA 02138 (Office); 19 Chauncy Street, Cambridge, MA 02138, U.S.A. (Home). *Telephone:* (617) 495-2364 (Office); (617) 876-5442 (Home).

ROLLINS, (Theodore Walter) Sonny; American jazz musician; b. 7 Sept. 1930, New York; s. of Walter Rollins and Valborg Solomon; m. 1st Dawn Finney 1956 (divorced); m. 2nd Lucille Pearson 1959; ed. High School, New York; began rehearsing while in high school with Thelonious Monk; recorded with Bud Powell 1949; wrote standards "Airegin" and "Oleo" recorded with Miles Davis 1953; played and recorded with Clifford Brown/Max Roach 1955; recorded album Saxophone Colossus 1957, wrote and recorded Freedom Suite 1958; took sabbatical playing on a N.Y. bridge 1959–61; scored and played music for film Alfie 1966; has appeared in Jazz Heritage series, Smithsonian Inst. and at Newport Jazz Festival; numerous concert tours in Europe, Far East; Dr. h.c. (Bard Coll.) 1993, (Long Island Univ.) 1998, (Wesleyan Univ.) 1998; Guggenheim Fellow 1972; recipient of numerous awards for instrumental playing 1950s–. *Address:* P.O. Box 175, Germantown, NY 12526, U.S.A.

ROLOFF-MOMIN, Ulrich; German lawyer; b. 29 April 1939, Osnabrück; m. Christine Fischer-Defoy 1993; two s. from previous marriage; fmr. Head West Berlin Univ. of the Arts; mem. Berlin Parl., Head Cttee. of the Arts 1975–77; Pres. Neue Gesellschaft für Bildende Kunst 1975–91; Berlin Senator for Cultural Affairs 1991–1995.

ROMAHI, Seif al-Wady, PH.D.; professor and diplomatist; b. 28 Dec. 1938, Muzeira'a, Palestine; s. of Ahmed al-Hajj Abdul-Nabi; m. Zaka al-Masri 1971; one s. two d.; ed. Lebanese State Univ., Univ. Coll. London, Southern Illinois Univ., U.S.A. and Univ. of Birmingham, U.K.; Area Educ. Supt., Ministry of Educ., Qatar 1960–64; Vice-Pres. Office of the Ruler of Abu Dhabi, Pres. U.A.E. 1968–73; Rep. League of Arab States in U.S.A. 1970–72; Assoc. Prof. of Middle East Studies and Political Science, Southern Ill. Univ., U.S.A. 1971–72; Minister Plenipotentiary, Foreign Ministry, U.A.E., set up U.A.E. Embassies Beijing, Tripoli, Tokyo and Seoul 1973–91; Founder and Prof., Diplomatic Training Centre, U.A.E. 1980–82; Co-founder and Chief Rep. Nat. Bank of Abu Dhabi in Japan 1982–86; Prof. of Int. Law, Diplomacy and Islamic Civilization, Int. Univ. of Japan, Sophia Univ., Tokyo; founder, Gen. Man. Arab Int. Co. for Investment and Educ. (A.I.C.I.E.) 1988–91, Chair. 1990–94; founder Applied Science Univ., Amman, Jordan, Pres. Bd., Prof. of Diplomacy and Int. Law 1990–95; co-founder Islamic-American Univ. Coll., Chicago; planner Jordan Women's Univ., Zaitouneh Jordanian Univ., American Univ. of the Middle East in Jordan, Graduate Studies Univ. in Jordan; co-author Abu Dhabi Public Service Code; mem. Acad. of Islamic Research (India), Japanese Acad. of Middle East Studies, Middle East Studies Asscn. of U.S.A. and Canada, Middle East Inst., Washington, D.C., British Soc. for Middle East Studies, Japanese Assoc. for Middle Eastern Studies; Mayor of Muzeira'a; Hon. Ph.D. (World Univ.) 1985; Order of Independence (Jordan). *Publications:* Economics and Political Evolution in Arabian Gulf States 1973, The Palestinian Question and International Law 1979, Studies in International Law and Diplomatic Practice 1980, Arab Customs and Manners 1984; contribs. to professional and scientific journals. *Leisure interests:* calligraphy, travel, poetry, listening to music, painting, reading and research. *Address:* P.O. Box 35087, Amman, Jordan. *Telephone:* (6) 552-5480 (Office); 551-3274 (Home). *Fax:* (6) 552-8328.

ROMAN, Petre, D.TECH., PH.D.; Romanian university professor and politician; b. 22 July 1946, Bucharest; s. of Valter Roman and Hortensia Roman; m. Mioara Georgescu; two d.; ed. Petru Groza High School, Bucharest, Bucharest Polytechnic Inst. and Nat. Polytechnic Inst. of Toulouse; fmrly. Prof. and Head of Dept. Hydraulics Dept., Faculty of Hydroenergy, Bucharest Polytechnic Inst.; Prime Minister 1989–91; Pres. Democratic Party (fmrly. Nat. Salvation Front) 1990–; mem. Parl. 1992–, Chair. Defence, Public Order and Nat. Security Cttee, Chamber of Deputies; Pres. of Senate; Special Rapporteur of North Atlantic Ass.; Traian Vuia Award, Romanian Acad. 1990, Great Cross of Merit, France; Star of Repub. of Ecuador; High Award of Repub. of Colombia. *Publications:* Introduction to the Physics of Fluid Pollution 1980, Fluid Mechanics 1989, Dynamic Hydrology 1990, Le Devoir de Liberté 1992, Romania incotro? 1995. *Leisure interests:* sports, hunting, reading, hiking. *Address:* The Senate, Piata Revolutiei, 71243, Bucharest, Romania.

ROMANI, Roger; French politician; b. 25 Aug. 1934, Tunis, Tunisia; s. of Dominique Romani and Madeleine Santelli; m. Joelle Fortier 1971; began career with ORTF; various positions in pvt. offices of govt. Ministers 1967–71; Conseiller de Paris 1971–; Adviser, Office of Jacques Chirac (Minister of Agric. 1973, of Interior 1974, Prime Minister 1974–76); Deputy to Mayor of Paris 1977–; mem. Conseil Régional, Ile-de-France 1977; Senator for Paris 1977–93, Pres. RPR Group in Senate 1986–93; Adviser to fmr. Prime Minister Chirac 1986–88; Minister-Del. for Relations with Senate 1993–95; Minister for Relations with Parl. 1995–97; adviser to Pres. Chirac 1997–. *Address:* Présidence de la République, 55-57 rue du Faubourg Saint Honoré, 75008 Paris; Hôtel de Ville, 75196 Paris, France.

ROMANO, Sergio, LL.D.; Italian diplomatist and historian; b. 7 July 1929, Vicenza; s. of Romano Romano and Egle Bazzolo; m. Mary Anne Heinze 1954; two s. one d.; ed. Liceo C. Beccaria, Milan, Univ. of Milan, Univ. of Chicago; foreign corresp. and film critic for Italian radio and newspapers, Paris, London and Vienna 1948–52; entered Italian Foreign Service 1954; Vice-Consul, Innsbruck, Austria 1955; Sec., Italian Embassy, London 1958–64; Private Sec. to Minister of Foreign Affairs 1964; mem. Diplomatic Staff of the Pres. of the Repub. 1965–68; Counsellor (later Minister), Italian Embassy, Paris 1968–77; Dir.-Gen. of Cultural Relations, Ministry of Foreign Affairs 1977–83; Guest Prof. Faculty of Political Sciences, Univ. of Florence 1981–83; Italian Perm. Rep. Atlantic Council, Brussels 1983–85, Amb. to U.S.S.R. 1985–89; mem. Ateneo Veneto, Venice, Accad. Olimpica, Vicenza; Dr. h.c. (Inst. d'Etudes Politiques, Paris); Grand' Ufficiale of the Italian Order of Merit, Commdr. Légion d'honneur, other European and Latin-American honours. *Publications:* Crispi, Progetto per una Dittatura 1973, 1986, La Quarta Sponda 1977, Histoire de l'Italie du Risorgimento à nos jours 1977, Italie 1979, Giuseppe Volpi, Industria e Finanza tra Giolitti e Mussolini 1979, La Francia dal 1870 ai nostri giorni 1981, Benedetto Croce, La Philosophie comme histoire de la Liberté (Ed.) 1983, La Lingua e il Tempo 1983, Giovanni Gentile, La Filosofia al Potere 1984, Florence, Toscane 1988, Giolitti, Lo Stile del Potere 1989, Disegni per una Esposizione 1989.

ROMANOV, Piotr Vasilyevich, DR.TECH.SC.; Russian politician; b. 21 July 1943, Kansk, Krasnoyarsk territory; ed. Siberia Inst. of Tech.; engineer, then chief of workshop, Chief Engineer, Dir.-Gen. Krasnoyarsky Production Unit of Mil. Chemical Enterprise Enisey 1967–96; mem. Russian Council of Fed. 1993; Co-Chair. Russian Nat. Sobor 1992–93, mem. Org. Cttee. All-Russia Congress of Russian Communists, Co-Chair. Co-ordination Council All-Russia Congress of Russian Communists 1994–; mem. State Duma 1995–; Sec. Cen. Cttee. CP of Russian Fed. 1997–; Hero of Socialist Labour. *Address:* Communist Party of Russian Federation, Bolshoy Komsomolsky per. 8/7, 101000 Moscow, Russia, PO Krasnoyarsky, Krasnoyarsk, Russia (Office). *Telephone:* 206 8789 (Moscow) (Office).

ROMANUS, Sven Einar; Swedish judge; b. 19 Jan. 1906, Karlstad; s. of Anton and Reidunn (Lindboe) Romanus; m. Alfhild Sandfaerhus 1932 (died 1996); one s. two d.; ed. Univ. of Stockholm; Justice, Supreme Court 1951–69, Chief Justice 1969–73; Minister of Justice 1976–79; Chair. Swedish Nat. Council for Radioactive Waste 1980–81, Swedish Nat. Bd. for Spent Nuclear Fuel 1981–84; Commdr. Grand Cross, Order of North Star, King's Medal of the Seraphim. *Address:* Hoegalidsgatan 26, 11730 Stockholm, Sweden. *Telephone:* (08) 669 5104.

ROMASHIN, Anatoliy Vladimirovich; Russian actor; b. 1 Jan. 1931, Leningrad; m. Yuliana Borisovna Ivanova; ed. Moscow Arts Theatre School; actor with Mayakovsky Theatre, Moscow 1959–85; Prof. All-Union (now Russian) Inst. of Cinematography 1985–; over 120 films including Remember, Caspar! (Prize for best male role, Berlin Festival 1963), The Red Tent 1969, Agony 1973, Unfinished Piece for Mechanical Piano 1977, Birthday 1982, Darling of the Public 1983, The Key 1991, Sin 1992, Shadows of Faberget 1993; stage roles in many classical and contemporary plays; one of founders of Theatre of Moon 1992; dir. and actor in The Dreams of Adult Robinson, Byzantia; U.S.S.R State Prize 1977; R.S.F.S.R. People's Artist 1982. *Address:* Theatre of Moon, Bolshoi Kozikhinsk per. 30 (Office); Vspolny per. 16 korp. 1, Apt. 60, 103101 Moscow, Russia (Home). *Telephone:* 299-44-92 (Theatre); 299-05-08 (Home).

ROMER, Roy R., B.S., LL.B.; American politician; b. 31 Oct. 1928, Garden City, Kan.; s. of Irving Rudolph and Margaret Elizabeth (née Snyder) Romer; m. Beatrice Miller 1952; five s. two d.; ed. Colorado State Univ., Univ. of Colorado, Yale Univ.; farmed in Colo. 1942–52; admitted to Colo. Bar 1952; independent practice, Denver 1955–66; mem. Colo. House of Reps. 1958–62, Colo. Senate 1962–66; Commr. for Agric. for Colo. 1975; State Treas. 1977–86; Gov. of Colorado 1987–98; owner Arapahoe Aviation Co., Colo.

Flying Acad., Geneva Basin Ski Area, Chain Farm Implement and Industrial Equipment Stores in Colo., Fla. and Va.; Gov. Small Business Council; mem. Agric. Advisory Cttee., Colo. Bd. of Agric., Colo. Bar Asscn.; Chair. Nat. Educ. Goals Panel, Democratic Govs.' Asscn. 1991, Democratic Nat. Cttee. 1997–; Democrat. *Address:* c/o Office of the Governor, State Capital Building, Denver, CO 80203, U.S.A.

ROMERO, Pepe; American (naturalized) classical guitarist; b. 3 Aug. 1944, Málaga, Spain; s. of Celedonio Romero and Angelita (née Gallego) Romero; m. 1st Kristine Eddy 1965; m. 2nd Carissa Sugg 1987; one s. three d.; ed. various music acads. in U.S.A., including Music Acad. of the West; began career in Seville, Spain, as part of Romero Quartet 1951, re-formed in U.S.A. 1960; averages 200–250 concerts a year world-wide; recordings number more than 50 solos, plus others with the Romero Quartet and various orchestras; artist-in-residence Univ. of Southern Calif. 1972, Univ. of Calif., San Diego 1984. *Publications:* Guitar Method, Guitar Transcriptions for 1, 2 and 4 guitars. *Leisure interests:* photography, chess.

ROMERO-BARCELÓ, Carlos Antonio, B.A., LL.B., J.D.; Puerto Rican politician and lawyer; b. 4 Sept. 1932, San Juan, Puerto Rico, s. of Antonio Romero-Moreno and Josefina Barceló-Bird; m. 1st; two s.; m. 2nd Kathleen Donnelly 1966; one s., one d.; ed. Phillips Exeter Acad., N.H., Yale Univ., Univ. of Puerto Rico; admitted to bar, San Juan, Puerto Rico 1956; Pres. Citizens for State 51 1965–67; Mayor of San Juan 1969–77; Pres. New Progressive Party 1974–86, Chair. 1989; Pres. Nat. League of Cities 1974–75; Gov. of Puerto Rico 1977–85; Chair. Southern Govs. Conf. 1980–81; Resident Commr. in Washington, D.C. 1991–; mem. Council on Foreign Affairs 1985–, Int. Platform Asscn. 1985–; Hon. LL.D. (Univ. of Bridgeport, Conn.) 1977; James J. and Jane Hoey Award for Interracial Justice, Catholic Interracial Council of N.Y. 1977; Special Gold Medal Award, Spanish Inst., New York 1979; U.S. Attorney-General's Medal 1981. *Publications:* Statehood is for the Poor 1973, Statehood for Puerto Rico, Vital Speeches of the Day 1979, Puerto Rico, U.S.A.: The Case for Statehood, Foreign Affairs 1980, The Soviet Threat to the Americas, Vital Speeches of the Day 1981. *Leisure interests:* reading, horse riding, tennis, swimming, water sports, golf. *Address:* 428 Cannon House Office Bldg., Washington, D.C. 20515, U.S.A.

ROMERO KOLBECK, Gustavo, M.A.; Mexican economist and public official; b. 3 July 1923, Mexico City; s. of Gustavo and Ana María (de Romero) Kolbeck; m. Leonor Martínez 1950; one s. two d.; ed. Nat. Univ. of Mexico, George Washington Univ. and Chicago Univ.; Prof. at Nat. School of Econs. 1949, Nat. Univ. of Mexico 1966; Dir. School of Econs. Anahuac Univ. 1967–70; Economist Bank of Mexico 1944–45; Research Dept. of Banco de Comercio 1946; Head of Dept. of Econ. Studies, Banco Nacional de México 1949–54; Deputy Dir. and Dir. of Public Investments, Ministry of Programming and Budget 1954–62; Founder and Dir., Centre for Econ. Study of Private Sector 1963–65; mem. Bd. of Govs. CONCANACO 1967; Dir. and Founder of journals Business Trends and Expansión 1967–69; Amb. to Japan 1971–73, to U.S.S.R. 1982–83; Dir.-Gen. Financiera Nacional Azucarera S.A. 1973, Nacional Financiera, S.A. 1974–76, Bank of Mexico 1976–82; Alt. Gov. World Bank 1974–76, IMF and IADB 1976–82; Dir.-Gen. Banco Obrero, S.A. 1983; decorations from Japan, France, Fed. Repub. of Germany, Brazil and other countries. *Leisure interests:* swimming, reading. *Address:* Rubén Darío 45-2, Cd. Rincón del Bosque 11580, México D.F., Mexico (Home).

ROMERO MENA, Gen. Carlos Humberto; Salvadorean army officer and politician; b. Chalatenango; s. of late José María Romero and of Victoria Mena de Romero; m. Gloria Guerrero de Romero; two s. two d.; ed. Capitán General Gerardo Barrios Mil. School, Escuela de Armas y Servicios, Escuela de Comando y Estado Mayor Manuel Enrique Araujo; Section Commd., Adjutant, and Paymaster, Capt.-Gen. Gerardo Barrios Mil. School and other mil. bodies; Regt. Commdr. Cavalry; Second Officer 1st Infantry Regt.; Sub-Dir. Escuela de Armas y Servicios and Head Dept. Personnel, Gen. Staff Armed Forces; Mil. Attaché to Embassy, Mexico; Head of Staff of Presidency of Repub.; Minister Defence and Public Security; Pres. Cen. American Defense Council 1973–77; Pres. of Repub. of El Salvador 1977–79 (overthrown in coup); del. 7th Conf. of American Armies 1966, 2nd Conf. of Cen. American Defense Council 1960, 6th Conf. of American Intelligence Officials 1967; Partido de Conciliación Nacional.

ROMITI, Cesare, B.ECON.; Italian industrial executive; b. 24 June 1923, Rome; m. Luigina Gastaldi; two s.; jonied Bombrini Parodi Delfino (BPD) Group 1947; Gen. Man. Finance and Co-ordination SNIA Viscosa 1968–70; Man. Dir. and Gen. Man. Alitalia Airlines 1970–73, Italstat (IRI group) 1973–74; Head Corp. Finance Planning and Control Dept., Fiat S.p.A. 1974–76, Man. Dir. Fiat S.p.A. and Vice-Chair. I.H.F. 1976–96, Chair. 1996–98, Man. Dir. Fiat Auto S.p.A. 1989–90; Dir. Mediobanca 1991; Chair. Rizzoli Corriere della sera newspaper and publishing group 1998; Head RSC Editori 1998–; mem. Exec. Cttee. Italian Stock Cos. Asscn., Bd. Turin Industrial Asscn., Confindustria, Aspen Inst. Italia, Advisory Bd. Deutsche Bank, Alcatel Alsthom, Council of Int. Advisers, Swiss Bank, Bd. Int. Advisers, Westinghouse Electric S.A.; received 18-month suspended sentence and banned from holding corporate office April 1997, case on appeal; indicted on charges of corruption and bribery June 1998. *Address:* Fiat S.p.A., Corso Marconi 10, 10125 Turin, Italy. *Telephone:* (11) 6565.1.

RONAY, Egon, LL.D.; British publisher and journalist; b. Pozsony, Hungary; m. 2nd Barbara Greenslade 1967; one s. (and two d. by previous marriage); ed. School of Piarist Order, Budapest, Univ. of Budapest and Acad. of Commerce, Budapest; trained in kitchens of family catering firm and abroad; managed 5 restaurants within family firm; emigrated from Hungary 1946; Gen. Man. 2 restaurant complexes in London before opening own restaurant The Marquee 1952–55; gastronomic and good living columnist, Sunday Times 1986–91 and Sunday Express 1991, weekly columnist on eating out, food, wine and tourism, Daily Telegraph and later Sunday Telegraph 1954–60; weekly column, The Evening News 1968–74; Ed.-in-Chief Egon Ronay Recommends (Heathrow Airport Magazine) 1992–94; mem. Acad. des Gastronomes (France) 1979; Founding Vice-Pres. Int. Acad. of Gastronomy; founder and Pres. British Acad. of Gastronomes; founder the Egon Ronay Guides 1957, publr. 1957–85; Médaille de la Ville de Paris 1983, Chevalier de l'Ordre du Mérite Agricole 1987. *Publication:* The Unforgettable Dishes of My Life 1989. *Address:* 37 Walton Street, London, SW3 2HT, England. *Telephone:* 0171-584 1384.

RONG GAOTANG; Chinese sports official; b. May 1912, Bazhou Co., Hebei Prov.; ed. Tsinghua Univ.; joined CCP 1936; Sec. Communist Youth League Beijing Mun. Cttee. 1949; Sec. Secr. Communist Youth League Cen. Cttee.; Sec.-Gen. then Vice-Dir. State Physical Culture and Sports Comm.; Vice-Pres. All-China Sports Fed; mem., Sec.-Gen. CCP Cen. Consultative Cttee.; Vice-Pres. Soong Ching Ling foundation 1983–; Head Chinese Celebrities Asscn 1994–; mem. 5th CPPCC Standing Cttee. *Address:* All-China Sports Federation, Beijing, People's Republic of China.

RONG YIREN; Chinese financial company executive and government official; b. 1 May 1916, Wuxi, Jiangsu; s. of Rong Deshen; m. Yang Jinaqing 1936; five c.; ed. St. John's Univ., Shanghai; Man. Mow Sing Flour Mills, Wuxi 1937–55; Vice-Pres. Foh Sing Flour Mills, Shanghai 1947–55; Pres. Sung Sing Textile Printing and Dyeing Co., Shanghai 1950–55; Chair. and Pres. China Int. Trust and Investment Corpn. (CITIC), Beijing 1979–82, Chair. 1983–93; Vice-Mayor Shanghai 1957–66; Vice-Minister, Ministry of Textile Industry 1959–66; mem. 2nd, 3rd, 4th, 5th Nat. Cttees. of CPPCC; Vice-Chair. 7th Nat. Cttee.; mem. 1st, 2nd, 3rd, 4th, 5th, 6th NPC; Vice-Chair. Nat. Cttee. CPPCC 1978–83, Standing Cttee. 6th, 7th NPC; Vice-Pres. of People's Repub. of China March 1993–98; Vice-Chair. Soong Ching Ling Foundation, Beijing 1982–; Vice-Chair. then Chair. All-China Asscn. of Industry and Commerce 1953–93; Hon. Chair. China Football Asscn. 1984; Chair. Bd. of Trustees Jinan Univ. Guangzhou 1985–; Chair. Bd. of Dirs. Jinan Univ. 1986–; Hon. Chair. Bd. CITIC Industrial Bank 1987–; a Pres. China Council for Promoting Peaceful Reunification 1988–; Hon. Adviser, China Confucius Foundation 1992–. *Publications:* articles and speeches on China's devt. and related matters. *Leisure interests:* walking, rose-gardening, spectator sports, including soccer. *Address:* Office of the Vice-President, Great Hall of the People, Beijing, People's Republic of China. *Telephone:* 309-97-58. *Fax:* 309-96-33.

RONNEBURGER, Uwe; German politician and farmer; b. 23 Nov. 1920, Kiel; s. of Ernst-Erich Ronneburger and Anneliese Ronneburger; m.; five c.; pvt. farmer 1948–73; active in local govt. and church affairs in Schleswig-Holstein; mem. FDP 1957–; Deputy Chair. 1976–82, now Fed. Cen. Cttee.; Deputy Chair. of FDP Parl. Group 1973–75, 1983–90; mem. Landtag of Schleswig-Holstein 1975–80; mem. Bundestag 1972–75, 1980–90; Chair. Defence Cttee. 1990; fmr. Chair. Cttee. for Interior German Relations; mem. Synod, Evangelical Church of Germany 1972–80. *Address:* Staatshof, 25882 Tetenbüll, Germany. *Telephone:* 04864/844. *Fax:* 04864/283.

RONSON, Gerald Maurice; British business executive; b. 26 May 1939; s. of Henry Ronson and Sarah Ronson; m. Gail Ronson 1967; four d.; Chief Exec. Heron Corpn. PLC 1976–, Chair. 1978–83; Chair. Heron Int. PLC 1983–93, Chief Exec. 1983–; Chair., Chief. Exec. Snax 24 Corpn. Ltd.; found guilty of one charge of conspiracy, two of false accounting and one of theft Aug. 1990; sentenced to one year's imprisonment and fined £5 million; released Feb. 1991; case referred back to Court of Appeal Dec. 1994, appeal rejected Nov. 1995. *Leisure interests:* yachting, shooting. *Address:* Heron House, 19 Marylebone Road, London, NW1 5JL, England (Office). *Telephone:* 0171-486 4477.

RONTÓ, Györgyi; Hungarian biophysicist; b. 13 July 1934, Budapest; d. of György Rontó and Erzsébet Lanczkor; m. Dr. Dezső Holnapy 1961; two s.; ed. Semmelweis Univ. of Medicine, Budapest; Prof. Semmelweis Univ. 1980, Dir. Semmelweis Univ. Inst. of Biophysics 1982–, including Research Group for Biophysics of the Hungarian Acad. of Sciences; Gen. Sec. Hungarian Biophysical Soc. 1969–90, Vice-Pres. 1990–98; Vice-Pres. Asscn. Int. de Photobiologie 1988–92; officer European Soc. for Photobiology; specialises in effects of environmental physical and chemical agents on nucleo-proteins; special interest in biological dosimetry of environmental and artificial UV radiations. *Leisure interests:* arts, architecture, gardening. *Publications:* A biofizika alapjai (An Introduction to Biophysics) 1987 (also English and German editions), Light in Biology and Medicine (Vol. 2) 1991; about 100 articles. *Address:* c/o Institute of Biophysics, 1088 Budapest, Puskin u. 9, Hungary. *Telephone:* (36 1) 266-6656.

ROOCROFT, Amanda; British opera singer; b. 9 Feb. 1966, Coppull; d. of Roger Roocroft and Valerie Roocroft (née Metcalfe); m. Manfred Hemm 1995; one s.; ed. Royal Northern Coll. of Music; appearances include Sophie in Der Rosenkavalier, Welsh Nat. Opera 1990, Pamina in The Magic Flute, Covent Garden 1991, 1993, Fiordiligi in Cosí Fan Tutte, Glyndebourne 1991, European tour with John Eliot Gardiner 1992, Bavarian State Opera 1993, 1994, Covent Garden 1995, Giulietta in I Capuleti e I Montecchi, Covent Garden

1993, Ginevra in Ariodante, English Nat. Opera 1993, Donna Elvira in Don Giovanni, Glyndebourne 1994, Amelia in Simon Boccanegra, Bavarian State Opera 1995; début at BBC Promenade Concert and Edin. Festival 1993; regular concert engagements and recitals; Kathleen Ferrier Prize 1988; Silver Medal, Worshipful Co. of Musicians 1988; Royal Philharmonic Soc./Charles Heidsieck Award 1990. *Recordings include:* Amanda Roocroft (solo album) 1994, Mozart and his Contemporaries 1996. *Leisure interests:* theatre, cinema, reading, cooking. *Address:* c/o Ingpen & Williams Ltd., 26 Wadham Road, London, SW15 2LR, England. *Telephone:* 0181-874 3222. *Fax:* 0181-877 3113.

ROOD, Johannes (Jon) Joseph Van, PH.D., M.D.; Netherlands immunologist; b. 7 April 1926, The Hague; s. of Albert van Rood and Rientje Röell; m. Sacha Bsse. van Tuyll van Serooskerken 1957; one s. two d.; ed. Univ. of Leiden; worked in bloodbanking 1952–; in charge of Bloodbank and foundation of Dept. of Immunohaematology, Univ. Hosp., Leiden 1957; work in tissue typing 1958–; worked on antibody synthesis in Public Health Research Inst., New York 1962; lecturer in Immunohaematology, Univ. of Leiden 1965–, Prof. in Internal Medicine 1969–; Founder Eurotransplant 1967, Europdonor 1970. *Publications:* Leukocyte Antibodies in Sera of Pregnant Women 1958, Platelet Survival 1959, Erythrocyte Survival with DFP 32 1961, Leukocyte Groups, the Normal Lymphocyte Transfer Test and Homograft Sensitivity 1965, Platelet Transfusion 1965, The Relevance of Leukocyte Antigens 1967, A Proposal for International Co-operation: EUROTRANSPLANT 1967, Transplantation of Bone-marrow cells and Fetal Thymus in an Infant with Lymphonenic Immunological Deficiency 1969, The 4a and 4b Antigens: Do They or Don't They? 1970, Anti HL-A 2 Inhibitor in Normal Human Serum 1970, HL-A Identical Phenotypes and Genotypes in Unrelated Individuals 1970, HL-A and the Group Five System in Hodgkin's Disease 1971, The (Relative) Importance of HL-A Matching in Kidney Transplantation 1971, Simultaneous Detection of Two Cell Populations by Two Colour Fluorescence and Application to the Recognition of B Cell Determinants 1976, HLA-linked Control of Susceptibility to Tuberculoid Leprosy and Association with HLA-DR types 1978. *Leisure interest:* sailing. *Address:* Department of Immunohaematology, University Hospital, Leiden 2333AA, Netherlands. *Telephone:* (71) 5226187. *Fax:* (71) 5210457.

ROOKE, Sir Denis Eric, Kt., O.M., C.B.E., B.SC.(ENG.), F.R.S., F.ENG.; British engineer and business executive; b. 2 April 1924, London; s. of F. G. Rooke; m. Elizabeth Brenda Evans 1949; one d.; ed. Westminster City School, Addey and Stanhope School, Univ. Coll., London; served with Royal Electrical and Mechanical Engineers in U.K. and India 1944–49; joined S.E. Gas Bd. 1949, Asst. Mechanical Engineer 1949, Deputy Man. of Works 1954, Devt. Engineer 1959; seconded to N. Thames Gas Bd. 1957; mem. tech. team aboard Methane Pioneer 1959; Devt. Engineer, Gas Council 1960 (name changed to British Gas Corpn. 1973, and to British Gas PLC 1986), mem. for Production and Supply 1966–71, Deputy Chair. 1972–76, Chair. 1976–89; mem. Offshore Energy Tech. Bd. 1975–78; mem. Nat. Econ. Devt. Council (NEDC) 1976–80, U.K. Energy Comm. 1977–79; part-time mem. British Nat. Oil Corpn. (BNOC) 1976–82; Pres. Welding Inst. 1981–83; Chair. Council for Nat. Academic Awards 1978–83; Trustee Science Museum 1988–95 (Chair. 1995); Commr. Royal Comm. for the Exhbn. of 1851 1984–; Pres. Royal Acad. of Eng. 1986–91; Chancellor Loughborough Univ. of Tech. 1989–; Fellow, Univ. Coll. London 1972; Hon. Fellow, Inst. of Chemical Engineers, Inst. of Gas Engineers (Pres. 1975–76), Inst. of Mechanical Engineers, Inst. of Energy, Inst. of Civil Engineers 1988, Inst. of Electrical Engineers 1988; Master Worshipful Co. of Eng. 1985–86; Hon. Fellow City & Guilds of London Inst., Humberside Coll. of Higher Educ., Univ. of Plymouth 1991; Hon. Sr. Fellow R.C.A. 1991; Hon. D.Sc. (Salford) 1978, (Leeds) 1980, (City Univ.) 1985, (Durham) 1986, (Cranfield Inst. of Tech.) 1987, (London) 1991, (Loughborough) 1994; Hon. D. Tech. (Council for Nat. Acad. Awards) 1986; Hon. LL.D. (Bath) 1987; Hon. D. Eng. (Bradford) 1989, (Liverpool) 1994; Hon. D.Univ. (Surrey) 1990. *Publications:* numerous papers to learned socs. and professional asscns. *Leisure interests:* photography, listening to music. *Address:* 1 Great Cumberland Place, London, W1H 7AL (Office); 23 Hardy Road, Blackheath, London, SE3 7NS, England (Home). *Telephone:* 0171-723 5173 (Office).

ROONEY, Mickey; (Joe Yule, Jr.); American actor; b. 23 Sept. 1920, Brooklyn; s. of Joe Yule and Nell Carter; m. 1st Ava Gardner 1942 (divorced 1943); m. 2nd Betty J. Rase 1944 (divorced 1949); two s.; m. 3rd Martha Vickers 1949 (divorced); m. 4th Elaine Mahnken (divorced 1958); m. 5th Barbara Thomason 1958; four c.; m. 6th Margie Lang 1966 (divorced 1967); m. 7th Carolyn Hockett (divorced); one s. and one adopted s.; m. 8th Jan Chamberlin 1978; two step s.; ed. in Dayton Heights, Vine Street Grammar School and Pacific Mil. Acad.; served AUS, World War II; first appeared in vaudeville with parents; later appeared with Sid Gould; numerous TV programmes including series The Mickey Rooney Show; stage appearances in Sugar Babies 1979, The Will Rogers Follies 1993; Special Acad. Award 1940; Tony Award for Best Musical Actor 1980. *Films include:* Judge Hardy's Children, Hold That Kiss, Lord Jeff, Love Finds Andy Hardy, Boys Town, Stablemates, Out West With the Hardys, Huckleberry Finn, Andy Hardy Gets Spring Fever, Babes in Arms, Young Tom Edison, Judge Hardy and Son, Andy Hardy Meets Debutante, Strike Up the Band, Andy Hardy's Private Secretary, Men of Boystown, Life Begins for Andy Hardy, Babes on Broadway, A Yank at Eton, The Human Comedy, Andy Hardy's Blonde Trouble, Girl Crazy, Thousands Cheer, National Velvet, Ziegfeld Follies, The Strip, Sound Off, Off Limits, All Ashore, Light Case of Larceny, Drive a Crooked Road, Bridges at Toko-Ri, The Bold and Brave, Eddie, Private Lives of Adam and Eve, Comedian, The Grabbers, St. Joseph Plays the Horses, Breakfast at Tiffany's, Somebody's Waiting, Requiem for a Heavyweight, Richard, Pulp, It's a Mad, Mad, Mad, Mad World, Everything's Ducky, The Secret Invasion, The Extraordinary Seaman, The Comic, The Cockeyed Cowboys of Calico County, Skidoo, B.J. Presents, That's Entertainment, The Domino Principle, Pete's Dragon, The Magic of Lassie, Black Stallion, Arabian Adventure, Erik the Viking, My Heroes Have Always Been Cowboys 1991, Little Nimo: Adventures in Slumberland (voice) 1992, Silent Night Deadly Night 5: The Toymaker, The Milky Life, Revenge of the Red Baron, That's Entertainment III, The Legend of O.B. Taggart 1995. *Publications:* I.E. An Autobiography 1965, Life Is Too Short 1991, Search for Sunny Skies 1994, Sinbad: The Battle of the Dark Knights 1998, The First Day of May 1998, The Face on the Barroom Floor 1998, Babe: Pig in the City 1999. *Address:* P.O. Box 3186, Thousand Oaks, CA 91359, U.S.A.

ROOTS, Ott, PH.D.; Estonian environmental scientist; b. 9 May 1946, Tallinn; ed. Tallinn Tech. Univ., Inst. of Chem., Estonian Acad. of Sciences; scientist Inst. of Zoology and Botany, Estonian Acad. of Sciences 1971–74, Baltic Sea Dept., Inst. of Thermo-physics and Electro-physics 1974–84; Chief Researcher Baltic Br., Inst. of Applied Geophysics 1984–90; Chief Researcher Water Protection Lab., Tallinn Tech. Univ. 1990–92; Sr. Scientist Dept. of Environmental Carcinogenesis, Inst. of Experimental and Clinical Medicine 1992–94; Monitoring Councillor, Environment Information Centre, Ministry of the Environment 1993–; Del. Helsinki Comm. (HELCOM) (expert on persistent organic contaminants) 1974–, UN ECE ICP (expert on monitoring) 1994–; Coordinator Finnish-Estonian Training Project (environmental monitoring) 1996–; mem. Nat. Geographic Soc., Washington 1996, New York Acad. of Sciences 1997; Bronze Medal, Environmental Protection Exhbn. (Russia) 1982, honoured by Ministry of the Environment, Estonia for work in environmental protection 1996. *Publications include:* Polychlorinated Piphenyls and Chlororganic Pesticides in the Ecosystem of the Baltic Sea 1992, Toxic Chlororganic Compounds in the Ecosystem of the Baltic Sea 1996 and contrib. to publs. for Estonian Environment Information Centre. *Address:* Environment Information Centre, Ministry of Environment, Mustamäe tee 33, Tallinn 0006, Estonia. *Telephone:* 656-5373. *Fax:* 656-4071.

ROPER, Warren Richard, M.SC., PH.D., F.R.S., F.R.S.N.Z., F.N.Z.I.C.; New Zealand professor of chemistry; b. 27 Nov. 1938, Nelson; s. of Robert J. Roper and Nancy L. Robinson; m. Judith D. C. Miller 1961; two s. one d.; ed. Nelson Coll., Univ. of Canterbury and Univ. of N. Carolina; lecturer, Univ. of Auckland 1966, Prof. of Chem. 1984–; Visiting Lecturer, Univ. of Bristol 1972; Visiting Prof. Univ. of Leeds 1983, Univ. of Rennes 1984, 1985, Stanford Univ. 1988; Centenary Lecturer, Royal Soc. of Chem. 1988; G.T. Seaborg Lecturer, Univ. of Calif., Berkeley 1995; Fellow Japan Soc. for Promotion of Science 1992; Royal Soc. of Chem. Award in Organometallic Chem. 1983, I.C.I. Medal (N.Z. Inst. of Chem.) 1984, Hector Medal, Royal Soc. of N.Z. 1991, Inorganic Chem. Award, Royal Australian Chemical Inst. 1992. *Publications:* over 150 original papers and reviews in scientific journals. *Leisure interests:* listening to music (especially opera), walking. *Address:* Department of Chemistry, The University of Auckland, Private Bag, Auckland (Office); 26 Beulah Road, Auckland 10, New Zealand (Home). *Telephone:* (09) 373-7999 (Ext. 8320) (Office); (09) 478-6940 (Home).

RORTY, Richard McKay, PH.D.; American professor of humanities; b. 4 Oct. 1931, New York; s. of James Hancock Rorty and Winifred Raushenbush Rorty; m. 1st Amelie Oksenberg 1954 (divorced 1972); one s.; m. 2nd Mary Varney 1972; one s. one d.; ed. Univ. of Chicago, Yale Univ.; taught at Yale and Wellesley Coll. 1954–61 (army service 1957–58); taught at Princeton, latterly as Stuart Prof. of Philosophy 1961–82; Prof. Univ. of Va. 1982–; Pres., Eastern Div., American Philsophical Asscn.; Fellow American Acad. of Arts and Sciences; MacArthur Fellow. *Publications:* Philosophy and the Mirror of Nature 1980, Consequences of Pragmatism 1982, Contingency, Irony and Solidarity 1989, Objectivity, Relativism and Truth 1991, Essays on Heidegger and Others 1991, Truth and Progress: Philosophical Papers 1998, Achieving our Country: Leftist Thought in Twentieth Century America 1998. *Leisure interest:* bird watching. *Address:* 412 Cabell Hall, University of Virginia, Charlottesville, VA 22903 (Office); 402 Peacock Drive, Charlottesville, VA 22903, U.S.A. (Home). *Telephone:* (804) 979-4152 (Home).

ROS, Enrique Jorge, LL.D.; Argentine diplomatist; b. 16 July 1927; ed. Univs. Buenos Aires and Paris; practised as lawyer 1949–54; joined Diplomatic Service 1954; Perm. Mission to OAS 1956–58, to UN 1959–63; Chargé d'Affaires, The Hague 1965–67; Embassy, London 1967–71; Head of Mission, Beijing 1973–75; Amb. to Israel 1976–77, to UN 1977–80; Dir.-Gen. Foreign Policy Bureau, Ministry of Foreign Affairs 1980, Under-Sec. for Foreign Affairs 1980–82; Amb. to Spain 1982–84, to Japan 1984–89, to Viet Nam (non-resident) 1985–89; mem. Higher Council of Ambs. of Ministry of Foreign Affairs 1990–; Chair. Bilateral Admin. Comm. of River Plate 1991; decorations from Bolivia, Brazil, Chile, Colombia, Ecuador, Paraguay, Peru, Venezuela, Japan. *Leisure interests:* reading, gardening. *Address:* Ministry of Foreign Affairs, Arenales 761, Buenos Aires, Argentina.

ROSATI, Dariusz Kajetan, D.ECON.; Polish professor of economics; b. 8 Aug. 1946, Radom; s. of Angelo Rosati and Wanda Pleszczyńska; m. Teresa Nowińska 1971; one s. one d.; ed. Main School of Planning and Statistics; scientific researcher Main School of Planning and Statistics (now Main

School of Commerce), Warsaw 1969–, Asst. Prof. 1978, Prof. 1990–; with Citibank, New York 1978–79, Princeton Univ., NJ 1986–87; Dir. Inst. of Econ. Situation and Foreign Trade Prices, Warsaw 1988–91; Head UN Section for Cen. and E. Europe, Geneva 1991–95; Minister of Foreign Affairs 1995–97; mem. Council of Monetary Policy of Nat. Bank of Poland 1998–. *Publications:* Decision-Making 1977, Inflation 1989, Export Policies 1990, Polish Way to Market 1998; about 200 scientific articles. *Leisure interests:* sports, reading. *Address:* ul. Świgtokrzyska 12, 00-919 Warsaw, Poland. *Telephone:* (22) 653 28 88.

ROSE, Sir Clive (Martin), G.C.M.G., M.A., F.R.S.A.; British diplomatist (retd.); b. 15 Sept. 1921, Banstead, Surrey; s. of the late Bishop Alfred Rose; m. Elisabeth MacKenzie Lewis 1946; two s. three d.; ed. Marlborough Coll. and Christ Church, Oxford; Rifle Brigade (rank of Maj., mentioned in despatches), Europe, India, Iraq 1941–46; Commonwealth Relations Office 1948; High Comm. Madras 1948–49; Foreign Office 1950; served in Bonn, Montevideo, Paris, Washington and London 1950–73; Imperial Defence Coll. 1968; Amb. and Head of UK Del. to Mutual and Balanced Force Reduction talks, Vienna 1973–76; Deputy Sec. to Cabinet Office 1976–79; U.K. Perm. Rep. on N. Atlantic Council 1979–82; Consultant to Control Risks Group Ltd. 1983–95; Chair. Control Risks Information Services Ltd. 1991–93 (Dir. 1986–93); Pres. Emergency Planning Asscn. 1987–93; mem. Advisory Bd. Royal Coll. for Defence Studies 1985–92; Chair. Council Royal United Services Inst. 1983–86, Vice-Pres. 1986–93, Vice-Patron 1993–; Hon. F.I.C.D. *Publications:* Campaigns Against Western Defence: NATO's Adversaries and Critics 1985, The Soviet Propaganda Network: a Directory of Organisations Serving Soviet Foreign Policy 1988. *Leisure interests:* gardening, genealogy. *Address:* Chimney House, Lavenham, Suffolk, CO10 9QT, England.

ROSE, Eliot Joseph Benn, C.B.E.; British publisher; b. 7 June 1909, London; s. of Col. E. A. Rose and Julia E. Rose; m. Pamela Gibson 1946; one s. one d.; ed. Rugby, and New Coll., Oxford; served R.A.F. 1939–45; Literary Ed. The Observer 1948–51; Dir. Int. Press Inst., Zürich 1952–62; Dir. Survey of Race Relations in Britain 1963–69; Editorial Dir., Westminster Press 1970–74; Chair. Penguin Books Ltd. 1973–80; Dir. Pearson Longman 1974–81; Chair. InterAction Trust 1968–84, Runnymede Trust 1978–90; Consultant to UNICEF 1981. *Publication:* Colour and Citizenship 1969. *Leisure interest:* music. *Address:* 37 Pembroke Square, London, W.8; Rocks Farm, Groombridge, Tunbridge Wells, Kent, England. *Telephone:* 0171-937 3772; (01892) 864223.

ROSE, Comte François Jean-Baptiste Hubert Edouard Marie de Tricornot de; French diplomatist (retd.); b. 3 Nov. 1910; s. of Henri Tricot and Marie-Thérèse Hugonnet; m. Yvonne Daday 1933; two d.; ed. Ecole Libre des Sciences Politiques, Paris; Sec. Embassy to U.K. 1937, Italy 1945–46; mem. French del. to UN 1946–50; Minister-Counsellor, Spain 1952–56; Ministry of Foreign Affairs, Paris 1956–60; mem. Atomic Energy Comm. (Paris) 1950–64; Pres. European Nuclear Research Org. (CERN) 1958–60; Asst. to Chief of Staff, Nat. Defence 1961–62; Amb. to Portugal 1964–69; Amb. and Perm. Rep. to N. Atlantic Council 1970–75; Amb. de France 1974; Vice-Pres. Council of Int. Inst. Strategic Studies (London); Pres. Comité des prix de revient des fabrications d'armement au ministère de la Defense; mem. Trilateral Comm. (European Group); Officier, Légion d'honneur, Commdr. Ordre nat. du Mérite, Croix de guerre. *Publications:* La France et la défense de l'Europe 1976, European Security and France 1984, La paix. Pourquoi pas? (with J. D. Remond and Chantal Ruiz-Barthélémy) 1986, Defendre de la Défense 1989, La Troisième Guerre Mondiale n'a pas eu lieu, L'Alliance Atlantique et la Paix 1995. *Leisure interests:* golf, skiing, shooting. *Address:* 10 rue de la Cuve, 75016, Paris, France (Home).

ROSE, Gen. Sir (Hugh) Michael, K.C.B., C.B.E., D.S.O., Q.G.M.; British army officer; b. 5 Jan. 1940; s. of late Lieut.-Col. Hugh Rose and of Barbara Allcard; m. Angela Shaw 1968; two s.; ed. Cheltenham Coll., St. Edmund Hall, Oxford and Royal Coll. of Defence Studies; commissioned, Gloucestershire Regt. Territorial Army Volunteer Reserve 1959; R.A.F. Volunteer Reserve 1962; Coldstream Guards 1964; served Germany, Aden, Malaysia, Gulf States, Dhofar, N. Ireland, Falkland Islands; Brigade Major, 16 Para. Brigade 1973–75; C.O. 22 SAS Regt. 1979–82; Command, 39 Infantry Brigade 1983–85; Commdt. School of Infantry 1987–88; Dir. Special Forces 1988–89; G.O.C. N.E. Dist. and Commdr. 2nd Infantry Div. 1989–91; Commdt. Staff Coll. 1991–93; Commdr. U.K. Field Army and Insp.-Gen. of Territorial Army 1993–94; Commdr. (UN Forces in) Bosnia-Herzegovina 1994–95; Adjutant Gen. 1995–97; Aide de Camp Gen. to the Queen 1995–97; Hon. Col. Oxford Univ.'s Officer's Training Corps 1995–. *Publication:* Fighting for Peace 1998. *Leisure interests:* sailing, skiing. *Address:* c/o Regimental H.Q. Coldstream Guards, Wellington Barracks, Birdcage Walk, London, SW1E 6HQ; P.O. Box 17, Crewkerne, Somerset, TA18 7YR, England. *Fax:* (01308) 867119.

ROSE, Richard, B.A., D.PHIL., F.B.A.; author and professor of public policy; b. 9 April 1933, St. Louis, Mo.; s. of Charles Imse Rose and Mary Conely Rose; m. Rosemary J. Kenny 1956; two s. one d.; ed. Clayton High School, Mo., Johns Hopkins Univ., L.S.E., Oxford; worked in political public relations, Miss. Valley 1954–55; Reporter St. Louis Post-Dispatch 1955–57; lecturer in Govt., Univ. of Manchester 1961–66; Prof. of Politics Strathclyde Univ. 1966–82, Prof. of Public Policy and Dir., Centre of Public Policy 1976–; Consultant Psephologist, The Times, Ind. Television, Daily Telegraph, etc. 1964–; Sec. Cttee. on Political Sociology, Int. Sociology Asscn. 1970–85; Founding Mem. European Consortium for Political Research 1970; mem. U.S./U.K. Fulbright Comm. 1971–75; Guggenheim Fellow 1974; Visiting scholar at various insts., Europe, U.S.A.; mem. Home Office Working Party on Electoral Register 1975–77; Co-Founder British Politics Group 1974–; Convenor Work Group on U.K. Politics, Political Studies Asscn. 1976–88; mem. Council Int. Political Science Asscn. 1976–82; Tech. Consultant OECD, UNDP, World Bank; Dir. S.S.R.C. Research Programme, Growth of Govt. 1982–86; Ed. Journal of Public Policy 1985–, Chair. 1981–85; Scientific Adviser, New Democracies Barometer, Paul Lazarsfeld Soc., Vienna 1991–; Hon. Vice-Pres. U.K. Political Studies Asscn.; Hon. Fellow American Acad. of Arts and Sciences, Finnish Acad. of Science and Letters; AMEX Prize in Int. Econs. 1992. *Publications:* numerous books on politics and public policy including What is Europe?, Politics in England, Public Employment in Western Nations, Taxation by Political Inertia, Understanding Big Government, Do Parties Make a Difference?, Presidents and Prime Ministers, The Postmodern President, Voters Begin to Choose: Loyalties of Voters, International Almanac of Electoral History, Northern Ireland: Time of Choice, Ordinary People in Public Policy, Lesson-Drawing in Public Policy: Inheritance in Public Policy, How Russia Votes, Democracy and Its Alternatives, Understanding Post-Communist Societies, A Society Transformed: Hungary in Time-Space Perspective; many papers in academic journals. *Leisure interests:* architecture, music, writing. *Address:* Centre for the Study of Public Policy, University of Strathclyde, Livingstone Tower, Richmond Street, Glasgow, G1 1XH (Office); Bennochy, 1 East Abercromby Street, Helensburgh, G84 7SP, Scotland (Home). *Telephone:* (0141) 548-3217 (Office); (01436) 672164 (Home); *Fax:* (0141) 552-4711. (Office); (01436) 673125 (Home).

ROSEANNE; American actress; b. 3 Nov. 1952, Salt Lake City; d. of Jerry Barr and Helen Barr; m. 1st Bill Pentland 1974 (divorced 1989); m. 2nd Tom Arnold 1990 (divorced 1994); three c. (from previous marriage); m. 3rd Ben Thomas 1994; one s.; fmr. window dresser, cocktail waitress; worked as comic in bars and church coffeehouse, Denver; produced forum for women performers Take Back the Mike, Univ. of Boulder, Colo; performer, The Comedy Store, Los Angeles; featured on TV special Funny and The Tonight Show; TV special, On Location: The Roseanne Barr Show 1987; star of TV series, Roseanne ABC 1988–97; Emmy award (Outstanding Leading Actress in a Comedy Series) 1993. *Film:* She Devil 1989, Freddy's Dead 1991, Even Cowgirls Get the Blues 1994, Blue in the Face 1995, Unzipped 1995, Meet Wally Sparks 1997. *Publications:* My Life as a Woman 1989, Roseanne: My Lives 1994. *Address:* Full Moon and High Tide Productions, 4024 Radford Avenue, # 916917 Studio City, CA 91604, U.S.A.

ROSEAU, Maurice Edmond Adolphe, PH.D.; French professor of science; b. 3 Nov. 1925, Asnières; s. of Marcel Roseau and Cécile Roseau; m. Marie-Françoise Louët 1960; one s. two d.; ed. Lycée Condorcet, Paris, École Normale Supérieure and Univ. of Paris; French army N. Africa 1944–45; teacher in maths. in Lycée, Le Mans 1948–49; Research Fellow Nat. Centre for Scientific Research 1949–52; Assoc. Prof. at Univ. of Caen 1952–54, Univ. of Poitiers 1954–57; temp. mem. at Inst. of Math. Sciences, Univ. of New York 1957–58; Prof. at Univ. of Lille 1958–62, Univ. of Paris 1963–; Visiting Prof. Univ. Of Calif., Berkeley 1967, 1978, Catholic Univ. of Rio de Janeiro 1971, Univ. of Louvain 1974; mem. of Acad. des Sciences 1982; Scientific Adviser at Nat. Inst. for Research in Transportation and Safety 1983–92; mem. Higher Council for Research and Tech. 1987–, Scientific Cttee. Fondation de France; Chevalier, Légion d'honneur. *Publications:* Vibrations non linéaires et théorie de la stabilité 1966, Solutions périodiques ou presque périodiques de la mécanique non linéaire 1970, Equations différentielles 1976, Asymptotic Wave Theory 1976, Vibrations des systèmes mécaniques 1984, and numerous papers on waves and vibrations. *Address:* 144 bis Avenue du Général Leclerc, 92330 Sceaux, France (Home). *Telephone:* (1) 43 50 77 64 (Home).

ROSELLE, David, PH.D.; American mathematician and university president; b. 30 May 1939, Vandergrift, Pa.; s. of William Roselle and Suzanne Clever; m. Louise H. Dowling 1967; one s. one d.; ed. West Chester State Coll. and Duke Univ.; Asst. Prof. Univ. of Md. 1965–68; Assoc. Prof., Prof. La. State Univ. 1968–74; Prof. Va. Polytechnic Inst. and State Univ. 1974–87, Dean, Graduate School 1979–81, Dean of Research and Grad. Studies 1981–83, Univ. Provost 1983–87; Pres. Univ. of Ky. 1987–90, Univ. of Del. 1990–; numerous grants and honours. *Publications:* numerous mathematics articles in graph theory and combinatorics. *Leisure interests:* golf, reading, jogging. *Address:* Office of the President, University of Delaware, Newark, DE 19716; 47 Kent Way, Newark, DE 19711, U.S.A. *Telephone:* (302) 831-2111 (Office); (302) 831-2721 (Home).

ROSEMAN, Saul, M.S. PH.D.; American biochemist; b. 9 March 1921, Brooklyn, N.Y.; s. of Emil Roseman and Rose (née Markowitz) Roseman; m. Martha Ozrowitz 1941; one s. two d.; ed. City Coll. of New York and Univ. of Wisconsin; Instructor to Asst. Prof., Univ. of Chicago 1948–53; Asst. Prof. to Prof. of Biological Chem. and Chemist, Rackham Arthritis Research Unit, Univ. of Mich. 1953–65; Prof. of Biology, Johns Hopkins Univ. 1965–, Chair. Dept. of Biology 1969–73, 1988–90, Dir., McCollum-Pratt Inst. 1969–73, 1988–90; Ralph S. O'Connor Prof. of Biology; Consultant, Nat. Cystic Fibrosis Research Foundation. Nat. Science Foundation, American Cancer Soc., Hosp. for Sick Children, Toronto; Scientific Counsellor to Nat. Cancer Inst.; Counsellor to American Soc. of Biological Chemists; mem. Editorial Bd. Journal of Biological Chemistry 1962–75, Journal of Lipid Research 1967–73,

Journal of Membrane Biology 1969–80, Biochimica et Biophysica Acta 1971–75, Biochemistry 1976–80; Fellow American Acad. of Microbiology 1992; mem. American Soc. of Biological Chemists, American Acad. of Arts and Sciences, American Chemical Soc., Nat. Acad. of Sciences., A.A.A.S., Biophysical Soc., American Asscn. of Univ. Profs.; Hon. mem. Biochemical Soc. of Japan; Lynch Lecturer, Univ. of Notre Dame 1989; Van Niel Lecturer, Stanford Univ. 1992; Hon. M.D. (Univ. of Lund, Sweden) 1984; Sesquicentennial Award (Univ. of Mich.) 1967, 15th Annual T. Duckett Jones Memorial Award, Helen Hay Whitney Foundation 1973, Rosensteihl Award (Brandeis Univ.) 1974, Gairdner Foundation Int. Award 1981, Townsend Harris Medal, City Coll. of New York 1987, Special Award, 11th Int. Symposium on Glycoconjugates, Toronto, Canada 1991, Karl Meyer Award, Soc. of Complex Carbohydrates 1993. *Publications:* c. 200 original articles in scientific journals. *Leisure interests:* sailing, music, reading, athletics. *Address:* Department of Biology and McCollum-Pratt Institute, The Johns Hopkins University, MD 21218 (Office); 8206 Cranwood Court, Baltimore, MD 21208, U.S.A. (Home). *Telephone:* (410) 516-7333 (Office); (410) 486-7439 (Home).

ROSEN, Charles, PH.D.; American pianist; b. 5 May 1927, New York City; s. of Irwin Rosen and Anita Gerber; ed. Juilliard School of Music, Princeton Univ.; studied piano with Moriz Rosenthal and Hedwig Kanner-Rosenthal 1938–45; recital début, New York 1951; first complete recording of Debussy Etudes 1951; première of Double Concerto by Elliott Carter, New York 1961; has played recitals and as soloist with orchestras throughout America and Europe; has made over 35 recordings including Stravinsky: Movements with composer conducting 1962, Bach: Art of Fugue, Two Ricercars, Goldberg Variations 1971, Beethoven: Last Six Sonatas 1972, Boulez: Piano Music, Vol. I, Diabelli Variations, Beethoven Concerto No. 4, 1979, Schumann: The Revolutionary Masterpieces, Chopin: 24 Mazurkas 1991; Prof. of Music, State Univ. of N.Y. 1972–90; Nat. Book Award 1972; Edison Prize, Netherlands 1974; Guggenheim Fellowship 1974; Messenger Lectures, Cornell Univ. 1975, Bloch Lectures, Univ. of Calif., Berkeley 1977, Gauss Seminars, Princeton Univ. 1978; Norton Prof. of Poetry, Harvard Univ. 1980–81; George Eastman Prof., Balliol Coll., Oxford 1987–88, Prof. of Music and Social Thought, Univ. of Chicago 1988–96; Dr. Mus. h.c. (Trinity Coll., Dublin 1976, Leeds Univ. 1976, Durham Univ.), Dr. h.c (Cambridge) 1992. *Publications:* The Classical Style: Haydn, Mozart, Beethoven 1971, Schoenberg 1975, Sonata Forms 1980, Romanticism and Realism (with Henri Zerner) 1984, The Musical Language of Elliott Carter 1985, Frontiers of Meaning 1994, The Romantic Generation 1995, and several articles.

ROSÉN, Haiim B., PH.D.; Israeli professor of linguistics and classics; b. 4 March 1922, Vienna, Austria; s. of late Georg Rosenrauch and Olga Gerstl; m. Hannah Steinitz 1953; one s.; ed. schools in Vienna, Hebrew Univ., Jerusalem, Ecole Pratique des Hautes Etudes and Coll. de France, Paris; went to Palestine 1938; school-teacher, Tel Aviv 1944–49; mem. Faculty, Hebrew Univ. Jerusalem 1949–, Prof. of Gen. and Indo-European Linguistics 1968–, Head, Dept. of Linguistics 1973–86; Prof. of Classics and Hebrew Linguistics, Tel Aviv Univ. 1961–91, Emer. Prof. 1991–; mem. Israeli Nat. Acad. of Sciences and Humanities; Rep. of Israel, Perm. Int. Cttee. of Linguists; visiting professorships at Univ. of Chicago, Univ. of Paris, Coll. de France, Univ. of Tübingen etc.; Israel State Prize in the Humanities 1978, Humboldt Research Award 1993. *Publications:* about 25 books including Ha-Ivrit Shelanu (Our Hebrew Language) 1955, East and West–Selected writings in linguistics, 3 vols. 1982–94, Herodoti Historiae edition in the Bibliotheca Teubneriana, 2 vols. 1987–97; about 200 articles on classical philology, general, Indo-European and Hebrew linguistics. *Address:* 13, Bruria, Jerusalem 93184, Israel. *Telephone:* (2) 6784-236.

ROSEN, Milton William, B.S.; American engineer and physicist; b. 25 July 1915, Philadelphia, Pa.; s. of Abraham Rosen and Regina (Weiss) Rosen; m. Josephine Haar 1948; three d.; ed. Univ. of Pennsylvania, Univ. of Pittsburgh, and California Inst. of Tech.; Engineer Westinghouse Electric and Mfg. Co. 1937–38; Engineer-physicist Naval Research Lab., Washington 1940–58, Scientific Officer Viking Rocket 1947–55, Head Rocket Devt. Branch 1953–55, Tech. Dir. Project Vanguard (earth satellite) 1955–58; Engineer NASA 1958–74; Chief Rocket Vehicle Devt. Programs 1958–59, Asst. Dir. Launch Vehicle Programs 1960–61, Dir. Launch Vehicles and Propulsion 1961–63; Sr. Scientist, Office of DOD and Interagency Affairs, NASA 1963–72; Deputy Assoc. Admin. for Space Science (Eng.) 1972–74; Exec. Sec. Space Science Bd. 1974–78; Exec. Sec. Cttee. on Impacts of Stratospheric Change, Nat. Acad. of Sciences 1978–80, Cttee. on Underground Coal Mine Safety 1980–83; Exec. Dir. Space Applications Board 1983–85; Chair. Greater Washington Asscn. of Unitarian Churches 1966–68; Study Leader, Inst. for Learning in Retirement, American Univ., Washington, D.C. *Publication:* The Viking Rocket Story 1955. *Leisure interests:* music, art collecting, rug making. *Address:* 5610 Alta Vista Road, Bethesda, MD 20817, U.S.A. *Telephone:* (301) 530-1497.

ROSENBERG, Pierre Max; French curator; b. 13 April 1936, Paris; s. of Charles Rosenberg and Gertrude Rosenberg; m. 2nd Béatrice de Rothschild 1981; one d.; ed. Lycée Charlemagne, Faculté de droit de Paris and Ecole du Louvre; Chief Curator Dept. des Peintures, Musée du Louvre 1983, Inspecteur gén. des musées 1988, Conservateur gén. du Patrimoine 1990–94, Pres. 1994–; Curator Musée Nat. de l'Amitié et des Relations franco-américaines de Blérancourt 1981–93; Chevalier des Arts et des Lettres, Ordre nat. du Mérite; elected to Acad. Française 1995. *Publications:* numerous works on 17th and 18th centuries. *Address:* Musée du Louvre, 34–36 quai du Louvre, 75058 Paris cedex 01 (Office); 35 rue de Vaugirard, 75006 Paris, France (Home).

ROSENBERG, Richard Morris; American banker; b. 21 April 1930, Fall River, Mass.; s. of Charles Rosenberg and Betty Peck; m. Barbara K. Cohen 1956; two s.; ed. Suffolk and Golden Gate Univs.; publicity asst. Crocker-Anglo Bank, San Francisco 1959–62; Banking Services Officer, Wells Fargo Bank 1962–65, Asst. Vice-Pres. 1965–68, Vice-Pres. Marketing Dept. 1968, Vice-Pres. Dir. of Marketing 1969, Sr. Vice-Pres. Marketing and Advertising Div. 1970–75, Exec. Vice-Pres. 1975, Vice-Chair. 1980–83; Vice-Chair. Crocker Nat. Corpn. 1983–85; Pres. and C.O.O. Seafirst Corpn. 1986–87; Dir., Pres. and C.O.O. Seattle-First Nat. Bank 1985–87; Vice-Chair. Bd. Bank America Corpn. San Francisco 1987–90; Chair. and C.E.O. BankAmerica Corpn./Bank of America 1990–91, of Bank America Corpn. (merged with Security Pacific Corpn.) 1990–96, also Pres.; Dir. Airborne Express, Potlatch Corp., Pacific Telesis Group, Northrop Grumman Corp., Pacific Mutual Life Insurance Co., San Francisco Symphony, United Way; mem. State Bar of Calif.; Trustee, Univ. of Southern Calif., Calif. Inst. of Tech. *Leisure interests:* tennis, avid reader, history. *Address:* Bank America Corporation, Dept. 3001, Box 37000, San Francisco, CA 94137, U.S.A.

ROSENBERG, Steven A., M.D., PH.D.; American physician and immunologist; b. 2 Aug. 1940, New York; s. of Abraham Rosenberg and Harriet Wendroff; m. Alice R. O'Connell 1968; three d.; ed. Bronx High School of Science and Johns Hopkins Univ.; Intern, Peter Bent Brigham Hosp. Boston 1963–64, Surgical Resident 1968–69, further surgical training 1972–74; Fellow in Immunology, Harvard Medical School 1969–70, Nat. Insts. of Health 1970–72; Chief of Surgery, Nat. Cancer Inst. Bethesda, Md. 1974–; Prof. of Surgery, Uniformed Services Univ. of Health Sciences; mem. numerous professional socs.; Public Health Service Medal 1981; Armand Hammer Cancer Prize 1985. *Publications:* thirteen books and hundreds of articles in medical journals. *Address:* National Cancer Institute, 31 Center Drive, Building 10, Bethesda, MD 20892, U.S.A.

ROSENBLITH, Walter Alter; American scientist and university professor; b. 21 Sept. 1913, Vienna, Austria; s. of David A. and Gabriele (Roth) Rosenblith; m. Judy O. Francis 1941; one s. one d.; ed. Berlin, Lausanne, Paris, Bordeaux Univs.; Research Engineer, France 1937–39, N.Y. Univ. 1939–40; Teaching Fellow in Physics, Univ. Calif. (Los Angeles) 1940–43; Asst. Prof., Assoc. Prof., Acting Head, Dept. of Physics, S. Dak. School of Mines and Tech. 1943–47; Research Fellow, Harvard Univ., Psycho-Acoustic Laboratory 1947–51, lecturer otology and laryngology 1969–; Assoc. Prof., Communications Biophysics, M.I.T. 1951–57, Prof. 1957–84, Inst. Prof. 1975–84, Rosenblith Prof. 1995–; Research Assoc. in Otology, Harvard Medical School and Massachusetts Eye and Ear Infirmary 1957–; Chair. M.I.T. Faculty 1967–69; Assoc. Provost M.I.T. 1969–71, Provost 1971–80; Dir. Kaiser Industries 1968–76, SofTech. Inc. 1981–87; Fellow, Acoustical Soc. of America, World Acad. of Art and Science, American Asscn. for the Advancement of Science, Soc. of Experimental Psychologists, Inst. of Electrical and Electronic Engineers; mem. Nat. Acad. of Eng., Nat. Acad. of Sciences (Foreign Sec. 1982–86), Inst. of Medicine (also Council mem. 1970–76), American Acad. of Arts and Sciences, Biophysical Soc., Soc. for Neuroscience, American Otological Soc., Life Science Panel, Pres.'s Science Advisory Cttee. 1961–66; Cen. Council, Exec. cttee. and Hon. Treas. Int. Brain Research Org. (UNESCO) 1960–68, Council Int. Union for Pure and Applied Biophysics 1961–69; Inaugural Lecturer, Tata Inst. for Fundamental Research 1962; Weizmann Memorial Lectures 1962; Consultant, WHO 1964–65, Carnegie Corpn. of New York 1986–, Carnegie Comm. on Science, Tech. and Govt. 1988–; mem. Nat. Acad. of Sciences, Nat. Research Council Brain Science Cttee. 1965–68, Pres.'s Cttee. on Urban Housing 1967–68, Bd. Foreign Scholarships 1978–81 (Chair. 1980–81), Bd. of Trustees, Brandeis Univ. 1979–; Chair. Science Advisory Council, Callier Center for Communication Disorders 1968–86, mem. Bd. of Govs. Weizmann Inst. of Science 1973–86, Advisory Cttee. to Dir. Nat. Inst. of Health 1970–74, Nat. Research Council Gov. Bd. 1974–76; mem. Selection Cttee. Tyler Prize for Environmental Achievement 1973–; USIA Advisory Panel on Int. Educational Exchange 1982–86; Chair. Research Cttee., Health Effects Inst. 1981–89, mem. Bd. of Dirs. 1989–; U.S. Co-ordinator, U.S.-France Science and Tech. Program 1979-82; mem. Council on Foreign Relations 1983–92; Vice-Pres. Int. Council of Scientific Unions 1984–88; Chair. Int. Advisory Panel of Chinese Univ. Devt. Project II 1986–91; mem. Governing Council, Int. Centre of Insect Physiology and Ecology (Kenya) 1987–90; Fellow A.A.A.S., American Acad. of Arts and Sciences; Hon. Sc.D. (Univ. of Pa.) 1976, (S. Dak. School of Mines and Tech.) 1980, (Brandeis Univ.) 1988, Dr. h.c. (Fed. Univ. of Rio de Janeiro) 1976, Chevalier Légion d'honneur 1982. *Publications:* Noise and Man (with K. N. Stevens) 1953, Processing Neuroelectric Data (Editor) 1959, Sensory Communication (Editor) 1961, and contributor of numerous articles and chapters to professional publications. *Address:* Massachusetts Institute of Technology, 77 Massachusetts Avenue, Cambridge, MA 02139, U.S.A.

ROSENKRANZ, Franklin Daniel; British business executive; b. 28 May 1945, Nakuru, Kenya; s. of Manfred Rosenkranz and Hendel Rosenkranz; m. Catherine Eisenklam 1990; ed. Univ. of Manchester Inst. of Science & Tech. (UMIST), Univ. of Waterloo, Canada and Manchester Business School; Plessey Radar 1970–73; joined BOC PLC, Hammersmith 1973–74; Business Man. Sparklets 1974–76; U.K. Man. BOC Sub Ocean Services 1976–78, Gen. Man. 1978–81; Business Devt. Dir. Edwards High Vacuum 1982–83, Man. Dir. 1983–90; Chief Exec. Vacuum Tech. and Distribution Services, BOC

H.Q.,Windlesham 1990–94; Man. Dir. and mem. Bd. Dirs. BOC Group PLC 1994, Chief Exec. 1996–. *Leisure interests:* reading, music, theatre, sport, gardening. *Address:* The BOC Group PLC, Chertsey Road, Windlesham, Surrey, GU20 6HJ, England. *Telephone:* (01276) 477222. *Fax:* (01276) 477693.

ROSENNE, Shabtai, LL.B.. PH.D.; Israeli lawyer and diplomatist (retd.); b. 24 Nov. 1917, London, England; s. of Harry Rowson and Vera Rowson; m. Esther Schultz 1940; two s.; ed. London Univ. and Hebrew Univ. of Jerusalem; Advocate (Israel), Political Dept., Jewish Agency for Palestine 1946–48; Legal Adviser, Ministry of Foreign Affairs 1948–66; Deputy Perm. Rep. to UN 1967–71; Perm. Rep. to UN, Geneva 1971–74; Ministry of Foreign Affairs 1974–82; mem. Israeli del. to UN Gen. Assemblies 1948–83, Vice-Chair. Legal Cttee. Gen. Assembly 1960; mem. Israeli del. to Armistice Negotiations with Egypt, Jordan, Lebanon and Syria 1949; mem. Israel del. to UN Conf. on Law of the Sea 1958, 1960, Chair. 1973, 1978–82; Chair. Israel del. to UN Conf. on Law of Treaties 1968, 1969, mem. other UN confs.; Govt. Rep. before Int. Court of Justice in several cases; mem. Int. Law Comm. 1962–71, UN Comm. on Human Rights 1968–70; Visiting Prof., Bar Ilan Univ. 1976–; Arthur Goodhart Visiting Prof. of Legal Science, Cambridge 1985–86; Belle van Zuylen Visiting Prof., State Univ. of Utrecht 1986–87, Univ. of Amsterdam 1987; Visiting Scholar, Univ. of Va. 1988–92; mem. Inst. of Int. Law 1963–, Rapporteur, Termination and Modification of Treaties 1965; Fellow Jewish Acad. of Arts and Sciences 1981; Hon. mem. American Soc. of Int. Law 1976; Israel Prize 1960; Certificate of Merit, American Soc. of Int. Law 1968. *Publications:* International Court of Justice 1957, The Time Factor in Jurisdiction of the International Court of Justice 1960, The Law of Treaties: Guide to the Vienna Convention 1970, Procedure in the International Court 1983, Practice and Methods of International Law 1984, Developments in the Law of Treaties 1945–86 1989, Documents on the International Court of Justice 1991, An International Law Miscellany 1993, The World Court: What It Is And How It Works 1995, The Law and Practice of the International Court 1920–1996 (4 vols.) 1997; numerous articles, mainly on law. *Address:* P.O. Box 3313, Jerusalem 91033, Israel. *Telephone:* 02-652 4339. *Fax:* 02-652 6401.

ROSENSHINE, Allen Gilbert, B.A.; American advertising executive; b. 14 March 1939; s. of Aaron Rosenshine and Anna Zuckerman; m. Suzan Weston-Webb 1979; two s.; ed. Columbia Coll.; copywriter, J.B. Rundle, New York 1962–65; copywriter, Batten, Barton, Durstine & Osborn, New York 1965, copy supervisor 1967, Vice-Pres. 1968, Assoc. Creative Dir. 1970, Sr. Vice-Pres. and Creative Dir. 1975–77, Exec. Vice-Pres. 1977–80, Pres. 1980–82, C.E.O. 1981–86, Chair. 1983–86; Pres. and C.E.O. BBDO Int. New York 1984–86; Pres. and C.O.O. Omnicom Group, New York 1986–88; Chair. and C.E.O. BBDO Worldwide, New York 1989–. *Address:* BBDO Worldwide, 1285 Avenue of the Americas, New York, NY 10019, U.S.A.

ROSENTHAL, Abraham Michael; American journalist; b. 2 May 1922, Sault St. Marie, Ont., Canada; s. of Harry and Sarah (née Dickstein) Rosenthal; m. 1st Ann Marie Burke 1949; three s.; m. 2nd Shirley Lord 1987; with New York Times 1944–, UN Bureau 1946–54, New Delhi 1954–58, Warsaw 1958–59, Geneva 1959–61, Tokyo 1961–63, Metropolitan Ed. 1963–66, Asst. Man. Ed. 1966–68, Assoc. Man. Ed. 1968–69, Man. Ed. 1969–77, Exec. Ed. 1977–86, Assoc. Ed. and columnist 1986–87, columnist 1986–; Ed. at large, Ed. Consultant G.P. Putnam 1988–; Pulitzer Prize 1960, Nat. Press Foundation Award 1986, Light of Truth Award 1994. *Publications:* 38 Witnesses, One More Victim (co-author). *Address:* New York Times, 229 West 43rd Street, New York, NY 10036, U.S.A.

ROSENTHAL, Gert, M.A.; Guatemalan economist; b. 11 Sept. 1935, Amsterdam; s. of Ludwig Rosenthal and Florence Rosenthal (née Koenigsberger); m. Margit Uhlmann Rosenthal 1959; four d.; ed. Univ. of Calif., Berkeley, U.S.A.; economist Nat. Planning Office, Guatemala 1960–65, Sr. Official Ministry of Finance 1966–67, Sr. Economist Secr. of the Cen. American Common Market 1967–68, Minister of Planning, Nat. Planning Office 1969–70; Fellow Adlai Stevenson Inst. for Int. Affairs, Chicago, U.S.A. 1971; Project Coordinator UNCTAD, Geneva 1972; Dir. Mexico Office ECLAC, Mexico City 1975–85; Deputy Exec. Sec. ECLAC Santiago, Chile 1986–87, Exec. Sec. 1988–. *Publications:* numerous articles on devt. econs. especially relating to Cen. America from 1965 to the present. *Address:* Av. Dag Hammarskjold s/n, Santiago, Chile (Office). *Telephone:* (562) 210 2554 (Office).

ROSENTHAL, Jean, L. ÈS L.; French publisher; b. 2 Aug. 1923, Paris; s. of Marcel Rosenthal and Yvonne La Touche; m. Françoise Moreau 1975; ed. Lycée Condorcet, Sorbonne Univ.; entered journalism 1946, translations field 1949; Dir. Overseas Rights, Edns. Robert Laffont, Paris 1962; Pres. Edns. Stock, Paris 1981–88, Ed. Dir. 1988–91; Chevalier des Arts et des Lettres, Chevalier Ordre de la Croix du Sud (Brazil). *Publications:* trans. of Saul Bellow, John Le Carré, Herman Wouk, Henry Miller, Philip Roth, Norman Mailer, Ken Follett, etc. *Address:* 30 rue de Varenne, 75007 Paris; Chaumes, 89500 Villeneuve-sur-Yonne, France.

ROSENTHAL, Norman Leon, B.A.; British art curator; b. 8 Nov. 1944; s. of Paul Rosenthal and Kate Zucker; m. Manuela Beatriz Mena Marques 1989; two d.; ed. Westminster City Grammar School, Univ of Leicester; librarian Thomas Agnew & Sons 1966–68; Exhbns. Officer, Brighton Museum and Art Gallery 1970–71, Exhbn. Organiser Inst. Contemporary Arts 1974–76, Exhbns. Sec. R.A. 1977–; organiser of many exhbns. including: Art into Society, I.C.A. 1974, A New Spirit in Painting, 1981, Zeitgeist, W. Berlin 1982, German Art of the Twentieth Century, and Staatsgalerie, Stuttgart 1985–86, Italian Art of the Twentieth Century, Royal Acad 1989, Metropolis, Berlin 1991, American Art in the Twentieth Century, and Martin-Gropius Bau, Berlin 1993, Sensation, 1997; TV and radio broadcasts on contemporary art; mem. Opera Bd., Royal Opera House 1995–, Bd. Palazzo Grassi, Venice 1995–; Hon. Fellow R.C.A. 1987; Chevalier, Ordre des Arts et des Lettres 1987, Cavaliere Ufficiale, Order of Merit (Italy) 1992, Cross, Order of Merit (Germany) 1993. *Leisure interest:* music, especially opera. *Address:* The Royal Academy of Arts, Burlington House, Piccadilly, London, W1V 0DS, England. *Telephone:* 0171-439 7438.

ROSENTHAL, Philip, M.A.; German ceramics and glass executive and politician; b. 23 Oct. 1916, Berlin; s. of Dr. Philipp and Maria (née Frank) Rosenthal; m. 4th Lavinia McLeod Day; m. 5th; two s. three d.; ed. Wittelsbacher Gymnasium, Munich, St. Laurence Coll., Ramsgate, and Exeter Coll., Oxford; Advertising Man. Rosenthal AG 1950–58, Chair. Bd. 1958–82, Chair. Advisory Bd. 1982–89, Hon. Chair. 1998–; adviser on design and marketing; SPD mem. of Parl. 1969–83; Parl. Sec of State at Ministry of Econs. and Finance 1970–71; Chair. SPD comm. on workers' capital sharing; SPD Spokesman on Communications 1983–; Pres. Bauhaus Museum and Archive 1965–84; Hon. Prof. of Design, Bremer Hochschule für Künste; Hon. Lecturer Exeter Coll.; mem. German Design Council, Darmstadt; Hermann Lindrath Prize 1980, Gläserne Letter, Economic Press Club of Munich Prize 1981; Grosses Bundesverdienstkreuz 1982; Hon. Citizen Selb 1989. *Publications:* Einmal Legionär, publications on design, co-determination and capital sharing. *Leisure interests:* mountaineering, walking, rowing. *Address:* Schloss Erkesreuth, 95100 Selb, Germany. *Telephone:* Selb 720.

ROSENTHAL, Thomas Gabriel, M.A.; British publisher, critic and broadcaster; b. 16 July 1935; s. of Erwin I. J. Rosenthal; m. Ann Judith Warnford-Davis; two s.; ed. Perse School, Cambridge and Pembroke Coll., Cambridge; served R.A. 1954–56; joined Thames and Hudson Ltd 1959, Man. Dir. Thames and Hudson Int. 1966; joined Martin Secker and Warburg Ltd. as Man. Dir. 1971, Dir. Heinemann Group of Publrs. 1972–84, Man. Dir. William Heinemann Int. Ltd. 1979–84, Chair. World's Work Ltd. 1979–84, Heinemann Zsolnay Ltd. 1979–84, Kaye and Ward Ltd. 1980–84, William Heinemann, Australia and S.A. 1981–82, Pres. Heinemann Inc. 1981–84; Jt. Man. Dir. and Jt. Chair. André Deutsch Ltd. 1984, C.E.O. 1987–96, Sole Man. Dir. and Chair. 1987, Chair. 1984–98; Chair. Frew McKenzie (Antiquarian Booksellers) 1985–93, Bridgewater Press 1997–; Art Critic The Listener 1963–66; Chair. Soc. of Young Publrs. 1961–62; mem. Cambridge Univ. Appointments Bd. 1967–71, Exec. Cttee. Nat. Book League 1971–74, Cttee. of Man. Amateur Dramatic Club, Cambridge (also Trustee), Council R.C.A. 1982–87, Exec. Council Inst. of Contemporary Arts 1987– (Chair. 1996–); Trustee Phoenix Trust; mem. Editorial Bd. Logos 1989–93. *Publications:* Monograph on Jack B. Yeats 1964, Monograph on Ivon Hitchens (with Alan Bowness) 1973; A Reader's Guide to European Art History 1962, A Reader's Guide to Modern American Fiction 1963, Monograph on Arthur Boyd (with Ursula Hoff) 1986, The Art of Jack B. Yeats 1993; articles in journals and newspapers. *Leisure interests:* opera, pictures, bibliomania. *Address:* Flat 7, Huguenot House, 19 Oxendon Street, London, SW1Y 4EH, England. *Telephone:* 0171-839 3589. *Fax:* 0171-839 0651.

ROSENZWEIG, Mark Richard, PH.D.; American physiological psychologist and neuroscientist; b. 12 Sept. 1922, Rochester, New York; s. of Jacob Rosenzweig and Pearl Grossman Rosenzweig; m. Janine S. A. Chappat 1947; one s. two d.; ed. Univ. of Rochester and Harvard Univ.; served U.S. Navy 1944–46; Asst. Prof., Univ. of Calif., Berkeley 1951–56, Assoc. Prof. 1956–60, Prof. 1960–91, Emer. Prof. 1991–, Prof. in the Grad. School 1994–; main area of interest: neural mechanisms of learning and memory formation; main findings: plastic anatomical and neurochemical responses of the nervous system of vertebrates to training and differential experience, specific neurochemical processes required for formation of the successive stages of memory, requirement of protein synthesis in brain for formation of long-term memory; Fellow A.A.A.S., American Psychological Soc., American Psychological Asscn.; Charter mem. Int. Brain Research Org., Soc. for Neuroscience; mem. N.A.S., American Physiological Soc., Société Française de Psychologie; mem. Exec. Cttee., Int. Union of Psychological Science, Vice-Pres. 1980–84, Pres. 1988–92, Past Pres. 1992–96, mem. U.S. Nat. Cttee. 1985–96, Chair. 1985–88; mem. Int. Cttee. on Social Science Information and Documentation 1972–80 (Pres. 1976–78); mem. Advisory Cttee. for Int. Council of Scientific Unions (N.A.S.—N.R.C.) 1985–88; Ed. Annual Review of Psychology 1968–94; Dr. h.c. (Université René Descartes, Sorbonne, Paris) 1980, (Université Louis Pasteur, Strasbourg); Distinguished Scientific Contrib. Award (American Psychological Asscn.) 1982, Award for Distinguished Contributions to Int. Psychology (American Psychological Asscn.) 1997. *Publications:* Psychology: An introduction (with P. H. Mussen) 1973, 1977, 1979, Biologie de la Mémoire 1976, Neural mechanisms of learning and memory (Co-Ed. with E. L. Bennett) 1976, Physiological Psychology (with A. L. Leiman) 1982, 1989, Psychophysiology: Memory, motivation and event-related potentials in mental operations (Co-Ed. with R. Sinz) 1983, International Psychological Science: Progress, Problems and Prospects 1992, Biological Psychology (with A.L. Leiman and S.M. Breedlove) 1996; book chapters and articles in scientific journals. *Leisure interests:* travel, photography. *Address:* Department of Psychology, 3210 Tolman Hall, University of California, Berkeley, CA 94720-1650, U.S.A. *Telephone:* (510) 642-5292. *Fax:* (510) 642-5293.

ROSHAL, Leonid Mikhailovich, M.D., D.SC.; Russian paediatrician; b. 27 April 1933, Livnya, Orel Region; s. of Mikhail Filippovich Roshal and Emilia Lazarevna Roshal; m. 2nd Veda Zuponcic; one s.; ed. Moscow Medical Inst.; paediatrician and specialist, paediatric surgeon Moscow hosps. 1957–61; jr., sr. researcher, then sr. research paediatric surgeon MONIKI Inst. 1961–81; Chief Urgent Surgery Clinic of Research Inst. of Paediatrics, U.S.S.R. (now Russian) Acad. of Medical Sciences 1982–; Chair. Int. Task Force Cttee. on Paediatric Disaster Medicine; mem. Exec. Cttee. World Asscn. for Emergency and Disaster Medicine; Pres. Int. Charitable Fund for Children in Disasters and Wars; mem. Bd. of Dirs. Asscn. of Paediatric Surgery, Russia, British Asscn. of Paediatric Surgeons. *Publications:* 6 books and more than 150 scientific articles on surgery and problems of children in catastrophes and wars. *Leisure interest:* music. *Address:* Children's Hospital, B. Polyanka str. 20, Moscow, Russia. *Telephone:* 238 30 00 (Office). *Fax:* 230 29 98.

ROSHCHEVSKY, Mikhail Pavlovich; Russian physiologist; b. 5 March 1933; m.; two d.; ed. Ural State Univ.; jr., sr. researcher, scientific sec. Ural Research Inst. of Agric. 1958–60; sr. researcher Inst. of Biol Komi A.S.S.R. 1960–70; Deputy Chair. Presidium Scientific Cen. Komi A.S.S.R. 1970–83, Chair. 1983–; Dir. Inst. of Physiology Komi Scientific Cen. Ural br. U.S.S.R. Acad. of Sciences 1983–; Corresp. mem. U.S.S.R. (now Russian) Acad. of Sciences 1987, mem. 1990; studies of ecological-physiological aspects of blood circulation, electrophysiology of heart, electrocardiology; mem. Dept. of Physiology Russian Acad. of Sciences. *Publications:* books and scientific works. *Address:* Presidium of Komi Scientific Centre, Kommunisticheskaya str. 24, 167610 Syktyvkar, Komi Republic, Russia. *Telephone:* (82122) 42-16-08 (Office), 42-25-11 (Home).

ROSHOLT, (Aanon) Michael; South African chartered accountant and business executive; b. 1920, Johannesburg; m. Beatrice Ash 1948; three s.; ed. Michaelhouse School; commissioned as Lieut., Natal Field Artillery, World War II, prisoner-of-war 1942–45; joined firm of C.A.s Goldby, Panchaud and Webber, and later became Sr. Partner; non-exec. mem. Bd., Thos. Barlow and Sons Ltd. 1961–63, Joint Deputy Chair. 1963–68, Jt. Deputy Chair. and Man. Dir. 1968–72; Vice-Chair. and Chief Exec., Barlow Rand Ltd. 1972–79, Chair. 1979 (retd.); Deputy Chair. Standard Bank of S.A. Ltd.; Deputy Chair. Standard Bank Investment Corpn. Ltd; Dir. S.A. Breweries, S.A. Mutual Life Assurance Soc., ASA Ltd.; Chair. Ash Bros; Chancellor Univ. of Witwatersrand 1982–96; Chair. S.A. Urban Foundation, Residential Devt. and Construction Div. of Urban Foundation, Michaelhouse School Trust, African Children's Feeding Scheme, Nat. Business Initiative, IDT Finance Corpn.; Patron Natal Univ. Devt. Foundation; Trustee S.A. Foundation; Dir. Family Housing Asscn.; Patron S.A. Soc. for Co-operative Educ.; Nat. Fund-Raising Chair. New Era Schools Trust; Vice-Chair. Job Creation S.A.; Patron Free Market Foundation; Hon. Fellow and Trustee Coll. of Medicine of S.A.; Hon. D.Econ. (Natal); Paul Harris Fellowship (Rotary). *Leisure interests:* squash, golf, fishing, photography, ornithology, reading. *Address:* P.O. Box 782248, Sandton, 2146 South Africa.

ROSI, Francesco; Italian film director; b. 1922, Naples; apprenticed as asst. to Antonioni and Visconti; dir. first feature, La Sfida (The Challenge) 1958. *Films:* Salvatore Giuiliano, Hands Over the City, More than a Miracle, Just Another War, Lucky Luciano, The Mattei Affair, Three Brothers, Chronicle of a Death Foretold, To Forget Palermo.

ROSNAY, Joël, D. ÈS SC.; French biologist; b. 12 June 1937, Mauritius; m. Stella Jebb 1959; one s. two d.; ed. Mass. Inst. of Tech.; Dir. of Applied Research, Inst. Pasteur 1975–84; Dir. of Devt. and Int. Relations, Cité des sciences et de l'industrie de La Villette 1988–, Dir. of Strategy 1996–; Columnist Europe 1 1987–95; Prix de l'Information Scientifique, Acad. des Sciences 1990. *Publications:* Les Origines de la Vie 1965, Le Macroscope 1975, La Révolution biologique 1982, Branchez-vous 1985, L'Avenir du vivant 1988, L'Avenir en direct 1989, les Rendez-vous du futur 1991, L'homme symbiotique 1995. *Leisure interests:* skiing, surfing. *Address:* Cité des Sciences et de l'Industrie de la Villette, 30 avenue Corentin Cariou, 75019 Paris; 146 rue de l'Université, 75007 Paris, France.

ROSOMAN, Leonard Henry, O.B.E., R.A., F.S.A.; British artist and teacher; b. 27 Oct. 1913, London; s. of Henry Edward Rosoman and Lillian Blanche Rosoman (née Spencer); m. 1st Jocelyn Rickards 1963 (divorced 1968); m. 2nd Roxanne Wruble Levy 1994; ed. Deacons School, Peterborough, Durham Univ., R.A. Schools and Cen. School of Art and Design, London; taught Reimann School, London 1937–39; Official War Artist to Admiralty 1943–45; taught Camberwell School of Art, London 1946–47; taught Edin. Coll. of Art 1947–56, Chelsea School of Art, London 1956–57, R.C.A., London 1957–78; freelance artist 1978–; designed and painted vaulted ceiling in Lambeth Palace Chapel, London; exhbns. at Rowland Browse & Delbanco and Fine Art Soc., London, Lincoln Center and Touchstone Gallery, New York, State Univ. of New York at Albany, Oldham Art Gallery, David Paul Gallery, Chichester and Royal Acad. of Art; Winston Churchill Fellow 1966–67; Hon. A.R.C.A.; Hon. mem. Royal Scottish Soc. of Painters in Water Colours, Royal W. of England Acad. *Leisure interest:* travel, bicycling. *Address:* 7 Pembroke Studios, Pembroke Gardens, London, W8 6HX, England. *Telephone:* 0171-603 3638.

ROSS, André Louis Henry, L. EN D.; French diplomatist; b. 13 March 1922, Calais; s. of René Ross and Yvonne Alexander; m. Thérèse Anne Guéroult 1951; ed. Univ. of Paris and Ecole nat. d'admin.; First Counsellor, Bangkok 1964–66; Amb. to Laos 1968–72, Zaire 1972–78, India 1979–83, Japan 1983–85; Sec.-Gen. Ministry of Foreign Affairs 1985–87; Amb. of France 1985; Sr. Adviser Indosuez Bank 1987–; mem. Council of French Museums 1988–96; mem. Comm. des archives diplomatiques 1988–; Pres. France-Amérique, Paris 1993–98; Chair. Foundation for Japanese Civilization, Tanaka Foundation 1998–; Commdr., Légion d'honneur, Ordre nat. du Mérite. *Leisure interests:* the arts, history and mathematics *Address:* Indosuez, 96 boulevard Haussmann, 75008 Paris (Office); 1 rue de Fleurus, 75006 Paris, France (Home). *Telephone:* (1) 45 48 55 60.

ROSS, Dennis B.; American diplomatist; involved in American policy in Middle East since 1986, now Special Middle East Co-ordinator. *Address:* Department of State, 2201 C Street NW, Washington, DC 20520, U.S.A. *Telephone:* 202-647-6575. *Fax:* 202-647-6575.

ROSS, Diana; American singer and actress; b. 26 March 1944, Detroit; d. of Fred and Ernestine Ross; m. 1st Robert Ellis Silberstein 1971 (divorced 1976); three d.; m. 2nd Arne Naess 1985; one s.; fmr. lead singer Diana Ross and the Supremes; solo singer 1970–; numerous records with Supremes and solo; TV specials. *Films include:* Lady Sings the Blues 1972, Mahogany 1975, The Wiz 1978; citation from Vice-Pres. Humphrey for efforts on behalf of Pres. Johnson's Youth Opportunity Programme; from Mrs. Martin Luther King and Rev. Abernathy for contribution to Southern Christian Leadership Conf. cause; Billboard, Cash Box and Record World magazine awards as world's outstanding female singer; Grammy Award 1970; Female Entertainer of the Year, Nat. Asscn. for the Advancement of Colored People 1970; Cue Award as Entertainer of the Year 1972; Golden Apple Award 1972; Gold Medal Award, Photoplay 1972; Antoinette Perry Award 1977; Golden Globe Award 1972. *Albums include:* I'm Still Waiting 1971, Touch Me In The Morning 1973, Why Do Fools Fall in Love? 1981, Eaten Alive 1984, Chain Reaction 1986, Workin' Overtime 1989, Surrender 1989, Ain't No Mountain High Enough 1989, The Forces Behind the Power 1991, The Remixes 1994, Diana 1981, Out of Darkness (TV) 1994. *Publication:* Secrets of a Sparrow (autobiog.) 1993.

ROSS, Rt. Hon. Lord; Donald MacArthur Ross, P.C., M.A., LL.B., F.R.S.E.; British judge (retd.); b. 29 March 1927, Dundee; s. of John Ross and Jessie MacArthur Thomson; m. Dorothy M. Annand 1958; two d.; ed. High School of Dundee and Univ. of Edinburgh; nat. service with Black Watch 1947–49; T.A. rank of Capt. 1949–58; Advocate 1952; Q.C. (Scotland) 1964; Vice-Dean, Faculty of Advocates 1967–73, Dean 1973–76; Sheriff Prin. of Ayr and Bute 1972–73; Senator, Coll. of Justice, Scotland and Lord of Session 1977–97; Lord Justice Clerk of Scotland and Pres. of Second Div. of the Court of Session 1985–97; Chair. Judicial Studies Cttee. for Scotland 1997–; mem. Parole Bd. for Scotland 1997–; Deputy Chair. Boundary Comm. for Scotland 1977–85; mem. Scottish Cttee. of Council on Tribunals 1970–76, Cttee. on Privacy 1970; mem. Court of Heriot Watt Univ. 1978–90 (Chair. 1984–90); Lord High Commr. to Gen. Ass. of Church of Scotland 1990, 1991; Hon. LL.D. (Edin.) 1987, (Dundee) 1991, (Abertay, Dundee) 1994, (Aberdeen) 1998; Hon. D.Univ. (Heriot Watt) 1988. *Publication:* contrib. to Stair Memorial Encyclopaedia of Scots Law. *Leisure interests:* gardening, walking, travelling. *Address:* 33 Lauder Road, Edin, EH9 2JG, Scotland. *Telephone:* (0131) 667 5731.

ROSS, Ian Gordon, A.O., M.SC., PH.D., F.A.A.; Australian professor of chemistry; b. 5 July 1926, Sydney; s. of Gordon R. Ross and Isabella M. Jenkins; m. Viola Bartlett 1975; ed. Univs. of Sydney and London; Research Assoc., Fla. State Univ. 1953; lecturer, then Reader in Physical Chem., Univ. of Sydney 1954–67, Prof. of Chem. 1968–90; Pro-Vice-Chancellor Australian Nat. Univ. 1975, 1989–90, Deputy Vice-Chancellor 1977–88; Chair. Australian Research Grants Cttee. 1977–79, Inquiry into Govt. Labs. 1982–83, Australian & New Zealand Asscn. for the Advancement of Science 1984–86, Communication Research Inst. of Australia 1994–; Sec. for Science Policy, Australian Acad. of Science 1989–93; Dir. Anutech Pty. Ltd. 1979–87; Hon. LL.D.; H. G. Smith Medal, Royal Australian Chem. Inst. 1972. *Publications:* scientific papers on theoretical chemistry and molecular spectroscopy. *Address:* 3 Highland Close, Queanbeyan, N.S.W. 2620, Australia. *Telephone:* (02) 6297-3510. *Fax:* (02) 6299-6324.

ROSS, Ian Munro, PH.D., F.I.E.E.E.; American electrical engineer; b. 15 Aug. 1927, Southport, England; m. Christina Leinberg 1955; one s. two d.; ed. Gonville and Caius Coll. Cambridge, England; went to U.S.A. 1952, naturalized 1960; with AT&T Bell Labs. (and affiliates) 1952–92, Exec. Dir., Network Planning Div. 1971–73, Vice-Pres., Network Planning and Customer Services 1973–76, Exec. Vice-Pres., Systems Eng. and Devt. 1976–79, Pres. 1979–91, Pres. Emer. 1991–; Dir., Thomas & Betts Corpn., B. F. Goodrich Co.; Liebmann Memorial Prize, I.E.E.E. 1963; Public Service Award, NASA 1969, 1975, I.E.E.E. Medal of Honour 1988; Fellow, American Acad. of Arts and Sciences; mem. Nat. Acad. of Eng. *Address:* Lucent Technologies, 101 Crawfords Corner Road, Holmdel, NJ 07733-1988; 5 Blackpoint Road, Horseshoe, Rumson, NJ 07760, U.S.A. (Home). *Telephone:* (201) 949-3242.

ROSS, James Hood, B.A.; British business executive; b. 13 Sept. 1938, London; s. of Capt. T. D. Ross R.N. and Lettice Ferrier Hood; m. Sara B. V. Purcell 1964; one s. two d.; ed. Sherborne School, Jesus Coll. Oxford and Manchester Business School; British Petroleum Co. PLC 1959–92, Gen. Man. BP Zaïre, Burundi and Rwanda, Gen. Man. BP Tanker Co., Gen. Man. Stolt-Nielsen (U.S.A.), Gen. Man. Corp. Planning BP, Chief Exec. BP Oil

Int., Chair. and Chief Exec. BP America; Chief Exec. Cable & Wireless PLC 1992–96; Chair. Littlewoods Org. 1996–; Dir. (non-exec.) McGraw Hill Inc. 1988–; Trustee, The Cleveland Orchestra 1988–; Chair. Bd. Manchester Business School 1993–. *Leisure interests:* music, gardening, sailing. *Address:* Sir John Moores Building, 100 Old Hall Street, Liverpool, L70 1AB, England. *Telephone:* 0151-235 2807.

ROSS, Steven J.; American communications executive; b. 1927, New York; m.; ed. Paul Smith's Coll.; Pres. Dir. Kinney Services Inc. 1961–72; Pres. Warner Communications Inc. New York 1972–, Chair. Bd. and C.E.O. 1972–; Co-Chair., Co-C.E.O. Time Warner Inc. New York 1989–90, Chair. Co-C.E.O. 1990. *Address:* c/o Time Warner Inc., 75 Rockefeller Plaza, New York, NY 10019, U.S.A.

ROSS GOOBEY, Alastair; British business executive; b. 6 Dec. 1945; s. of George Henry Ross Goobey and Gladys Edith Menzies; m. Sarah Georgina Mary Stille; one s. one d.; ed. Marlborough Coll., Trinity Coll. Cambridge; with Kleinwort Benson 1968–1972; with Hume Holdings Ltd. 1972–77; Investment Man. Pension Fund, Courtaulds Ltd. 1977–81; Dir. Geoffrey Morley & Partners Ltd. 1981–85; Special Adviser to Chancellor of Exchequer, HM Treasury 1986–87 and 1991–92; Chief Investment Strategist, James Capel & Co. 1987–93; Chief Exec., Hermes Pensions Man. Ltd. 1993–; Pres. Investment Property Forum 1995–; Chair. HM Treasury Pvt. Finance Panel 1996–97; Dir. Scottish Life 1978–1986, Cheltenham and Gloucester PLC 1989–91, 1992–97, TR Property Investment Trust PLC 1994–, John Wainwright & Co. Ltd. 1994–; mem. Pensions Law Review Cttee. (Goode Cttee.) 1992–93; nominated mem. Council of Lloyd's 1997–; Liveryman Gold and Silver Wyre Drawers' Co. *Publications:* The Money Moguls 1987, Bricks and Mortals 1992, Kluwer Handbook on Pensions (Jt. Ed.). *Leisure interests:* music, cricket, writing, broadcasting (The Board Game, BBC Radio 4). *Address:* Standon House, 21 Mansell Street, London, E1 8AA, England. *Telephone:* 0171-702 0888.

ROSSEL, Eduard Ergartovich, CAND.ECON.SC; Russian politician; b. 8 Oct. 1937, Bor, Gorki region; m.; one d.; ed. Sverdlovsk Ore Inst.; master construction site, head of construction trust Sreduralstroi; supervised construction of Krasnouralsk superphosphate factory, Nevyansk cement factory, Nizhny Tagil metallurgy plant; head Sverdlovsk regional exec. cttee., then Gov. Sverdlovsk Region 1991–93, 1995–; mem. Russian Council of Fed. 1993–; Chair. Sverdlovsk regional Duma 1994–; f. and Chair. Org. Preobrazhenie Otechestva; Pres. Asscn. for Econ. Co-operation of Ural Region 1995–; mem. Bd. Union of Russian Govs. 1996; mem. Int. Acad. of Regional Devt. and Co-operation. *Address:* Governor's Office, Oktyabrskaya pl. 1, 620031 Yekaterinburg, Russia. *Telephone:* (343) 270-54-73, 270-54-68. *Fax:* 270-54-72.

ROSSELLINI, Isabella; American actress and model; b. 18 June 1952, Rome; d. of Roberto Rossellini and Ingrid Bergman; m. 1st Martin Scorsese (q.v.) 1979 (divorced 1982); m. 2nd Jonathan Wiedemann (divorced); one d.; ed. Acad. of Fashion and Costume, Rome; and New School for Social Research, New York; worked briefly as costume designer for father's films; went to New York 1972; worked as journalist for Italian TV; cover-girl for Vogue 1980; contract to model Lancôme cosmetics 1982–95; Vice-Pres. Lancaster Cosmetics GPs Marketing Dept. 1995–. *Films include:* A Matter of Time 1976, White Nights 1985, Blue Velvet 1986, Tough Guys Don't Dance 1987, Siesta 1987, Zelly and Me, Cousins 1989, Wild at Heart 1990, The Siege of Venice 1991, Death Becomes Her, The Pickle, The Innocent, Fearless 1994, Wyatt Earp 1994, Immortal Beloved 1994, The Innocent 1995, The Funeral 1996, Big Night 1996, Crime of the Century 1996, Left Luggage 1998. *Address:* c/o United Talent Agency, 9560 Wilshire Boulevard, Floor 5, Beverly Hills, CA 90212, U.S.A.

ROSSELLÓ, Pedro, B.S., M.D.; Puerto Rican politician and surgeon; b. 5 April 1944, San Juan; m. Irma Margarita Nevares; three s.; ed. Notre Dame Univ., Yale Univ., Harvard Univ., Univ. of Puerto Rico; fmr. pediatric surgeon, Prof. of Medicine; Dir. of Health, City of San Juan 1985–88; cand. elections to Congress 1988; Chair. New Progressive Party 1991; Gov. of Puerto Rico 1993–; Pres. Council of State Govts. 1998–; Chair. Govs.' Asscn., Southern Govs.' Asscn. 1998–, Southern Int. Trade Council, Southern Tech. Council; mem. Advisory Council Welfare to Work Partnership, U.S.A., Democratic Nat. Cttee., Nat. Advisory Bd. of Initiative and Referendum Inst., Bd. of Dirs. U.S.-Spain Council and other bodies; five times men's singles tennis champion, Puerto Rico; Hon. LL.D (Notre Dame) 1995, (Mass.) 1995; Pres.'s Award, U.S. Hispanic Chamber of Commerce 1999, LULAC 1998. *Address:* Office of the Governor, La Fortaleza, San Juan, 00901, Puerto Rico.

ROSSI, Guido, LL.M.; Italian business executive and professor of law; b. 16 March 1931, Milan; ed. Univ. of Pavia and Harvard Law School; fmr. Prof. of Commercial Law, Univs. of Trieste, Venice and Pavia; fmr. Prof. of Law, State Univ. of Milan; Chair. CONSOB (Italian cos. and stock exchange regulatory body 1981–82; Senator, Repub. of Italy (tenth legislature); Chair. Montedison S.p.A., Milan 1993–95, Ferruzzi Finanziaria S.p.A. 1993; Dir. Eridiana Beghin-Say 1993–. *Publications include:* Trasparenza e Vergogna, La Società e La Borsa 1982, La Scalata del mercato 1986; several other books and numerous studies on subjects of corp. enterprises, the securities market and antitrust legislation.

ROSSI, José Lucien André, D. EN D.; French politician and lawyer; b. 18 June 1944, Ajaccio, Corsica; s. of Pierre Rossi and Emilie Leca; m. Denise Ferri 1968; two d.; ed. Ecoles Sainte-Lucie and Castelvecchio, Lycée Fesch, Ajaccio, Faculté de Droit and Inst. d'Etudes Politiques, Paris; Asst. Faculté de Droit, Paris 1969–73; served in pvt. office of Minister of Labour 1972, Minister of Educ. 1972–74; Press Officer to Minister of Health 1974–75; Parl. Relations Officer to Minister of Labour 1975–78, to Minister of Educ. 1978; pvt. office of Pres. of Senate 1981–82; mem. Conseil Général, Corsica 1973–, Pres. 1985–98; Conseiller Régional, Corsica 1975–85; Deputy Mayor of Ajaccio 1983–90, 1995–; Pres. Corsica Tourism and Leisure Agency 1983–84; Pres. Regional Information Centre 1979–85; Deputy to Nat. Ass. 1988–94; Sec.-Gen. Parti Républicain 1989–91; Mayor of Grosseto-Prugna 1990–95; Vice-Pres. Union pour la Démocratie Française (UDF) group in Nat. Ass. 1993–94; Minister of Industry, Posts and Telecommunications and Foreign Trade 1994–95; Deputy to Nat. Ass. 1995–; Deputy Sec.-Gen. U.D.F. 1996–97; Titular Judge Higher Court of Justice 1997–; Pres. Démocratie liberalé Group, Nat. Ass. 1998–. *Publication:* Les Maires de grandes villes en France 1972. *Address:* Assemblée Nationale, 75355 Paris (Office); Assemblée de Corse, 22 cours Grandval, BP 277, 20187 Ajaccio cedex (Office); 461 boulevard Rive Sud, 20166 Porticcio, France (Home).

ROSSIER, William; American diplomatist; fmrly. involved in negotiations with GATT, OECD, UNCTAD; fmr. Chair. EFTA, ECE, UNCTAD Trade and Devt. Bd.; Chair. World Trade Org. Gen. Council 1996. *Address:* c/o World Trade Organization, Centre William Rappard, rue de Lausanne 154, 1211 Geneva, Switzerland.

ROSSINOT, André, D. EN MED.; French politician and doctor; b. 22 May 1939, Briey, Meurthe-et-Moselle; s. of Lucien Rossinot and Jeanne Fondeur; m. 3rd Françoise Cordelier 1985; one s. one d.; three c. from previous marriages; ed. Lycée Poincaré and Faculty of Medicine, Nancy; ear, nose and throat specialist in private practice; Town Councillor, Nancy 1969–71; Mayor of Nancy 1983–; Vice-Pres. Greater Nancy Urban Council 1996–; Deputy to Nat. Ass. (UDF) 1978–86, 1995–97; Pres. Parti Radical 1983–88, 1994–97, Hon. Pres. 1997–; Minister for Relations with Parliament 1986–88, of Civil Service 1993–95; Vice-Pres. Nat. Ass. 1988–89; Pres. Conf. Permanente des caisses de crédit municipal 1987–93; Nat. Vice-Pres. UDF 1983–90, 1994–; mem. Political Bureau Union pour la France 1990–, UDF 1991–; Pres. Centre d'étude et de recherche sur les collectivités locales européennes 1991; Vice-Pres. Asscn. des Eco Maires 1990–; Pres. Nouveau Contrat Social 1992–, TGV 1994–, Inst. nat. du génie urbain 1996–. *Address:* Hôtel de Ville, place Stanislas, 54000 Nancy, France.

ROST, Andrea; Hungarian operatic soprano; b. 1962, Budapest; d. of Ferenc Rost and Erzsébet Privoda; m. Miklós Harazdy 1985; one s. one d.; ed. Ferenc Liszt Acad. of Music, Budapest; operatic début, Budapest 1989; First Prize, Helsinki Competition 1989; La Scala début as Gilda in Rigoletto 1994; début, Metropolitan Opera, New York as Adina 1996; took part in Superconcert with José Carreras and Placido Domingo, Budapest 1996; appeared as Elisabeth in Donizetti's opera, London 1997; début, Tokyo Opera, as Violetta 1998; took part in concert in memory of Lehar with José Carreras and Placido Domingo, Bad Ischl, Austria 1998; has also appeared at Staatsoper, Vienna, Salzburg Festival, Opéra Bastille, Paris, Royal Opera House, Covent Garden and Chicago Opera. *Address:* Budaörs, Stefánia u. 12, 2040 Hungary. *Telephone:* (23) 416-583.

ROSTOW, Eugene Victor, LL.D.; American lawyer, economist and government official; b. 25 Aug. 1913, Brooklyn, N.Y.; s. of Victor A. and Lillian Rostow; brother of Walt Whitman Rostow (q.v.); m. Edna B. Greenberg 1933; two s. one d.; ed. Yale Coll., King's Coll., Cambridge, and Yale Law School; admitted to N.Y. Bar 1938, practised in New York City 1937–38; mem. Faculty, Law School, Yale 1938–, Prof. of Law 1944–84, Sterling Prof. of Law and Public Affairs 1964–84, Dean 1955–65 (on leave 1966–69), Prof. Emer., Sr. Research Scholar 1984–; Visiting Prof., Univ. of Chicago 1941; Pitt Prof. of American History and Insts., Professorial Fellow, King's Coll., Cambridge 1959–60; Guggenheim Fellow 1959–60; Adviser to Dept. of State 1942–44, 1961–66; Asst. Exec. Sec. Econ. Comm. for Europe, UN 1949–50; Under-Sec. of State for Political Affairs, Dept. of State 1966–69; Eastman Visiting Prof. and Fellow of Balliol Coll., Oxford 1970–71; Visiting Research Prof. of Law and Diplomacy Nat. Defense Univ., Washington 1984–90, 1992–; Distinguished Fellow, U.S. Inst. of Peace 1990–92; Pres. Atlantic Treaty Asscn. 1973–76; Dir. Arms Control and Disarmament Agency 1981–83; Fellow, A.A.A.S.; Hon. LL.D. (Cambridge); Kt. Commdr., Order of the Crown, Belgium, Chevalier, Légion d'honneur. *Publications:* Planning for Freedom 1959, The Sovereign Prerogative 1962, Law, Power and the Pursuit of Peace 1968, Peace in the Balance 1972, Is Law Dead? (Ed.)1971, The Ideal in Law 1978, Toward Managed Peace 1993, A Breakfast for Bonaparte 1994. *Address:* National Defence University, Washington, DC 20319; School of Law, Yale University, New Haven, CT 06520 (Office); 1315 4th Street, S.W., Washington, DC 20024, U.S.A. (Home).

ROSTOW, Walt Whitman, PH.D.; American economist; b. 7 Oct. 1916, New York, N.Y.; s. of Victor A. Rostow and Lillian H. Rostow; brother of Eugene Victor Rostow (q.v.); m. Elspeth Vaughan Davies 1947; one s. one d.; ed. Yale and Oxford Univs.; Instructor in Econs. Columbia Univ. 1940–41; Maj., U.S. Army 1942–45; Asst. Chief German-Austrian Econ. Div. State Dept. 1945–46; Harmsworth Prof. of American History, Oxford Univ. 1946–47; Asst. to Exec. Sec. UN Econ. Comm. for Europe 1947–49; Pitt Prof. of American History Cambridge Univ. 1949–50; Prof. of Econ. History M.I.T. and Staff mem. M.I.T. Center for Int. Studies 1951–60; Deputy Special Asst.

to the Pres. for Nat. Security Affairs Jan.-Nov. 1961; Counsellor and Chair. Policy Planning Council, Dept. of State 1961–66; Special Asst. to the Pres., The White House 1966–69; currently Prof. of Econs. and History, Univ. of Texas; Chair. Bd. and C.E.O. The Austin Project 1992–; Presidential Medal of Freedom (with distinction) 1969, Asscn. of American Publrs. Award for outstanding book on Social Sciences 1990, Legion of Merit, Hon. O.B.E. (U.K.). *Publications:* The American Diplomatic Revolution 1947, Essays on the British Economy of the XIX century 1948, The Process of Economic Growth 1952, The Growth and Fluctuation of the British Economy 1790-1850 (with A. D. Gayer and A. J. Schwartz) 1953, The Dynamics of Soviet Society (with A. Levin and others) 1953, The Prospects for Communist China (with others) 1954, An American Policy in Asia (with R. W. Hatch) 1955, A Proposal: Key to an Effective Foreign Policy (with Max F. Millikan) 1957, The United States in the World Arena 1960, The Stages of Economic Growth 1960, View from the Seventh Floor 1964, A Design for Asian Development 1965, East-West Relations: Is Detente Possible? (with William E. Griffith) 1969, Politics and the Stages of Growth 1971, The Diffusion of Power 1972, How it All Began 1975, The World Economy: History and Prospect 1978, Getting from Here to There 1978, Why the Poor Get Richer and the Rich Slow Down 1980, British Trade Fluctuations 1868–1896 1981, Pre-Invasion Bombing Strategy: General Eisenhower's Decision of March 25th, 1944 1981, The Division of Europe after World War II: 1946 1981, Europe after Stalin: Eisenhower's Three Decisions of March 11th, 1953 1982, Open Skies: Eisenhower's Proposal of July 21st, 1955 1982, The Barbaric Counter-Revolution: Cause and Cure 1983, Eisenhower, Kennedy and Foreign Aid 1985, The United States and the Regional Organization of Asia and the Pacific: 1965–85 1986, Rich Countries and Poor Countries: Reflections from the Past, Lessons for the Future 1987, Essays on a Half Century: Ideas, Politics, and Action 1988, History, Policy and Economic Theory 1989, Theorists of Economic Growth from David Hume to the Present 1990, The Great Spike and Afterwards: Reflections on the 21st Century 1997. *Leisure interest:* tennis. *Address:* 1 Wildwind Point, Austin, TX 78746, U.S.A. *Fax:* (512) 478-9104.

ROSTROPOVICH, Mstislav Leopoldovich; Russian 'cellist, conductor and pianist; b. 27 March 1927, Baku, Azerbaijan; s. of Leopold Rostropovich and Sofia Fedotova; m. Galina Vishnevskaya (q.v.) 1955; two d.; ed. Moscow Conservatoire; 'cello début (U.S.S.R.) 1940; numerous concert tours in U.S.S.R. and abroad as soloist and 'cellist in trio with Emil Gilels and Leonid Kogan, and later with David Oistrakh and Sviatoslav Richter, and as pianist with Galina Vishnevskaya; début in U.S.A. as 'cellist 1955, as conductor 1975; Music Dir. Nat. Symphony Orchestra (Washington, D.C.) 1977–94; Conductor Laureate 1991–; deprived of Soviet citizenship 1978, citizenship restored 1990; Joint Artistic Dir. Aldeburgh Festival (U.K.) 1977–; founder and Pres. Rencontres Musicales d'Evian festival (France); mem. Union of Soviet Composers 1950–78, 1989–; Prof. Moscow and Leningrad Conservatoires 1960–78; among composers who have written works for him are Prokofiev, Shostakovich, Miaskovsky, Khachaturian, Kabalevsky, Britten, Piston, Shchedrin, Schnittke, Bernstein; f. Int. Competition for young 'cellists; Hon. mem. Acad. of St. Cecilia (Rome), Guildhall School of Music and Drama 1991, A.A.A.S.; Hon. F.R.A.M.; Hon. K.B.E. 1987; Hon. D.Mus. (Oxford) 1980; hon. degrees (including Humanities, Law, Letters, Music) from over 20 univs.; First Prize at All-Union Competition of Musicians 1945, Int. 'Cellist Competitions, Prague 1947, 1950, Budapest 1949, U.S.S.R. State Prize 1951, People's Artist of the U.S.S.R., Lenin Prize 1964, Gold Medal, Royal Philharmonic Soc. (U.K.), Siemens Prize (Fed. Repub. of Germany), Sonning Prize (Denmark), Albert Schweitzer Music Award 1985; Commdr., Ordre des Arts et des Lettres (France), Légion d'honneur, Presidential Medal of Freedom 1987, Four Freedoms Award 1992, Kennedy Center Honor 1992, Freedom of Speech and Expression Award (Franklin Delano Roosevelt) 1992, Imperial Award 1993. *Address:* c/o National Symphony Orchestra, John F. Kennedy Center for the Performing Arts, Washington, DC 20566, U.S.A.; Gazetny per. 13, Apt. 79, 103009 Moscow, Russia. *Telephone:* (202) 785-8100 (U.S.A.); (095) 229.04.96 (Home, Russia).

RØSTVIG, Maren-Sofie, PH.D.; Norwegian professor of English literature; b. 27 March 1920, Melbo; d. of Olaf Røstvig and Sigrid Røstvig; ed. Univ. of Oslo and Univ. of Calif. Los Angeles; imprisoned by Nazi regime 1943, subsequently released; joined Resistance Movt. and published underground newspaper until end of World War II 1944–45; Reader in English Literature, Univ. of Oslo 1955–67, Prof. 1968–87, Sr. Research Fellow 1988, retd. 1990; mem. Norwegian Acad. of Science and Letters; Mil. Medal of Participation. *Publications:* The Happy Man. Studies in the Metamorphoses of a Classical Ideal 1600–1760 (two vols.) 1954–58, The Hidden Sense and Other Essays 1963, Fair Forms 1975, Configurations. A Topomorphical Approach to Renaissance Poetry 1994; contribs. to learned journals and collections of scholarly essays on English literature. *Address:* Huk Avenue 59H, 0287 Oslo, Norway. *Telephone:* 22 43 72 94.

ROTA, Gian-Carlo, PH.D.; American (b. Italian) professor of applied mathematics and philosophy; b. 27 April 1932, Vigevano (Prov. of Pavia); s. of Dr. Giovanni Rota and Gina Facoetti Rota; m. Teresa Rondon-Tarchetti 1956 (divorced 1979); ed. Princeton Univ., Yale Univ.; early years in Italy and Quito, Ecuador, arrived in U.S.A. 1950, naturalized U.S. Citizen 1961; Benjamin Peirce Instructor, Harvard Univ. 1957–59, Asst. Prof., then. Assoc. Prof., then Prof. of Math. M.I.T. 1967–74, Prof. of Applied Math. and Philosophy 1975–; Prof. Rockefeller Univ. 1965–67; Fellow Los Alamos Lab. 1966–; Consultant Brookhaven Nat. Lab. 1971–76; mem. N.A.S. (Chair. Maths. Section 1994–97), American Acad. of Arts and Sciences, Academia Argentina de Ciencias, Univ. of Bologna, Istituto Lombardo; Dr. h.c. (Strasbourg) 1984, (Università dell'Aquila) 1990, (Polytechnic Univ.) 1997; Steele Prize, American Math. Soc. 1990; Killian Faculty Achievement Award, M.I.T. 1996. *Publications:* Chief Ed. Encyclopaedia of Mathematics (70 vols. to date), Ed. Advances in Mathematics, about 250 papers in specialized journals. *Leisure interests:* philosophy, phenomenology. *Address:* 1105 Massachusetts Avenue, Apt. 8F, Cambridge MA, 02138, U.S.A. *Telephone:* (617) 547-3588.

ROTAS, Nikiphoros Giorgos; Greek composer; b. 14 May 1929, Athens; s. of Vasilis Rotas and Katherini Giannakopoulos; m. Maria Paschalis 1956; one s. two d.; ed. Theatriko Spoudastirio, Conservatory of Athens and Music Acad. of Vienna; took part in nat. resistance against German Occupation 1941–44; since 1962 composer, teacher of music, lecturer, broadcaster and dir. of music educ. in professional dance schools; mem. Greek Composers' Asscn., Greek Play Writers' and Composers' Asscn., Theatre Museum; compositions include more than 60 works for all kinds of instrumental and/or vocal ensembles: oratorios, cantatas, large symphonic works, electronic music, works for string orchestra, ballets, chamber music, songs; about 40 works for theatre and music for cinema and TV; award for The Song of the Creation, Vienna 1960, Abgangspreiz (Music Acad. of Vienna) 1961. *Publications:* The Way We Listen to Music 1986; articles in newspapers. *Address:* 15 Astydamantos Street, Athens 116 34, Greece (Home). *Telephone:* 7211.730 (Home).

ROTBLAT, Sir Joseph, K.C.M.G., C.B.E., M.A., D.SC., PH.D., F.INST.P., F.R.S.; British (b. Polish) physicist; b. 4 Nov. 1908, Warsaw; s. of the late Z. Rotblat; ed. Univ. of Warsaw; Research Fellow, Radiological Lab. of Scientific Soc. of Warsaw 1933–39; Asst. Dir. of Atomic Physics, Inst. of Free Univ. of Poland 1937–39; Oliver Lodge Fellow, Univ. of Liverpool 1939–40, Lecturer, later Sr. Lecturer, Dept. of Physics 1940–49, Dir. of Research in Nuclear Physics 1945–49; Prof. of Physics, Univ. of London, at St. Bartholomew's Hosp. Medical Coll. 1950–76, Emer. 1976–; Sec.-Gen. Pugwash Confs. 1957–73, Pres. 1988–97; mem. WHO Man. Group; Ed. Physics in Medicine and Biology; Pres. Hosp. Physicists' Asscn., British Inst. of Radiology; Pres. Int. Youth Science Fortnight; mem. Polish Acad. of Sciences, A.A.A.S.; Foreign Hon. mem. American Acad. of Arts and Sciences; Foreign mem. Czechoslovak Acad. of Sciences; Hon. Fellow UMIST, Queen Mary and Westfield Coll. 1996, Royal Soc. of Edin. 1998; Hon. D.Sc. (Bradford) 1973, (Liverpool) 1989, (City Univ.) 1996, (Slovak Acad. of Sciences) 1996; Dr. h.c. (Univ. of Moscow); Bertrand Russell Soc. Award 1983, Albert Einstein Peace Prize 1992, Nobel Peace Prize 1995; Order of Merit (Poland); Kt. Commdr. Order of Merit (Fed. Repub. of Germany); Copernicus Medal of Polish Acad. of Sciences 1996; Hon. Freeman, London Borough of Camden 1997. *Publications:* Atomic Energy, a Survey 1954, Atoms and the Universe 1956, 1973, Science and World Affairs 1962, Aspects of Medical Physics 1966, Pugwash 1967, Scientists in the Quest for Peace 1972, Nuclear Reactors: To Breed or Not to Breed? 1977, Nuclear Energy and Nuclear Weapon Proliferation 1979, Nuclear Radiation in Warfare 1981, Scientists, the Arms Race and Disarmament 1982, The Arms Race at a Time of Decision 1984, Nuclear Strategy and World Security 1985, World Peace and the Developing Countries 1986, Strategic Defence and the Future of the Arms Race 1987, Coexistence, Co-operation and Common Security 1988, Verification of Arms Reductions 1989, Global Problems and Common Security 1989, Nuclear Proliferation: Technical and Economic Aspects 1990, Building Global Security through Co-operation 1990, Towards a Secure World in the 21st Century 1991, Striving for Peace, Security and Development in the World 1992, A Nuclear-Weapon-Free World: Desirable? Feasible? 1993, A World at the Crossroads 1994, World Citizenship: Allegiance to Humanity 1996, Nuclear Weapons: The Road to Zero 1998. *Leisure interests:* travel, music. *Address:* 8 Asmara Road, London, NW2 3ST, England. *Telephone:* 0171-435 1471.

ROTH, Joe; American film executive and producer; b. 1948; fmrly. production asst. various commercials and films; fmrly. lighting dir. Pitched Players, also producer; co-f. Morgan Creek Productions 1987–89; Chair. Twentieth Century Fox Film Corpn. 1989–92; f. Caravan Pictures 1992–94; Chair. Walt Disney Motion Pictures Group 1994–. *Films produced include:* Tunnelvision, Cracking Up, Americathon, Our Winning Season, The Final Terror, The Stone Boy, Where the River Runs Black, Bachelor Party, Off Beat, Streets of Gold (also dir.), Revenge of the Nerds (also dir.), Young Guns, Dead Ringers, Skin Deep, Major League, Renegades, Coupe de Ville (also dir.), Enemies: A Love Story; films for Caravan Pictures include Walt Disney's The Three Musketeers, Angie, Angels in the Outfield, I Love Trouble, A Low Down Dirty Shame, Houseguest, The Jerky Boys, Heavyweights, Tall Tale, While You Were Sleeping. *Address:* Walt Disney Studio, 500 South Buena Vista Street, Burbank, CA 91521, U.S.A.

ROTH, John, M.Eng.; Canadian communications executive; b. Alberta; ed. McGill Univ., Montreal; with RCA 1964–69; joined Nortel 1969, Head Wireless Div. 1991–93, Pres. Nortel North America 1993–95, Group C.O.O. 1995–97, Chief Exec. 1997–. *Leisure interest:* making stained-glass windows. *Address:* Northern Telecom Limited, 3 Robert Speck Parkway, Mississauga, Ont., Canada.

ROTH, Klaus Friedrich, B.A., M.SC., PH.D., F.R.S.; British mathematician; b. 29 Oct. 1925, Breslau, Germany; s. of the late Dr. Franz Roth and Mathilde

Roth (née Liebrecht); m. Dr. Melek Khairy 1955; ed. St. Paul's School, London, Peterhouse, Cambridge, and Univ. Coll., London; Asst. Master Gordonstoun School 1945–46; postgraduate student Univ. Coll., London 1946–48; mem. Mathematics Dept. Univ. Coll., London 1948–66 (title of Prof. in Univ. of London conferred 1961); Prof. of Pure Mathematics (Theory of Numbers), Imperial Coll., London 1966–88, Visiting Prof. 1988–96, Hon. Research Fellow Dept. of Mathematics, Univ. Coll., London 1996–; Visiting Lecturer, M.I.T. 1956–57, Visiting Prof. 1965–66; Fellow Univ. Coll. London 1979; Foreign Hon. mem. A.A.A.S. 1966; Hon. Fellow Peterhouse, Cambridge 1989; Hon. F.R.S.E. 1993; Fields Medal (Int. Congress of Mathematicians) 1958, De Morgan Medal (London Mathematical Soc.) 1983, Sylvester Medal (Royal Soc.) 1991. *Publications:* papers in journals of learned societies. *Leisure interests:* chess, cinema, ballroom dancing. *Address:* Colbost, 16A Drummond Road, Inverness IV2 4NB, Scotland (Home); 24 Burnsall Street, London, SW3 3ST, England (Home). *Telephone:* (01463) 712595 (Inverness); 0171-352 1363 (London).

ROTH, Sir Martin, Kt., M.D., F.R.C.P., F.R.C. PSYCH., F.R.S.; British professor of psychiatry; b. 6 Nov. 1917, Budapest, Hungary; s. of late Samuel Simon Roth and Regina Roth; m. Constance Heller 1945; three d.; ed. St. Mary's Hospital Medical School, London and McGill Univs.; Dir. of Clinical Research, Graylingwell Hosp. 1950–55; Visiting Asst. Prof. McGill Univ. 1954; Prof. of Psychological Medicine, Univ. of Newcastle upon Tyne (fmrly. Durham Univ.) 1956–77; Prof. of Psychiatry, Univ. of Cambridge 1977–85, Prof. Emer. 1985–; Fellow Trinity Coll., Cambridge 1977–; Hon. Physician Royal Victoria Infirmary, Newcastle upon Tyne 1956–77; mem. Medical Research Council 1964–68; mem. Clinical Research Bd. 1964–70, Chair. Grants Cttee. 1968–70; Co-Ed. British Journal of Psychiatry 1968, Psychiatric Developments 1983–; mem. Cen. Health Services Council, Standing Medical Advisory Cttee., Dept. of Health and Social Security 1968–75; Visiting Prof. Swedish univs. 1967; Mayne Guest Prof. Univ. of Queensland 1968; Visiting Prof. Univ. of Iowa 1976, Univ. of Indianapolis 1976; Pres. Section of Psychiatry, Royal Soc. of Medicine 1968–69; First Pres. Royal Coll. of Psychiatrists 1971–75; Hon. mem. Soc. Royale de Médecine Mentale de Belgique 1970, Canadian Psychiatric Asscn. 1972; Corresp. mem. Deutsche Gesellschaft für Psychiatrie und Nervenheilkunde 1970; Adolf Meyer Lecturer, American Psychiatric Asscn. 1971; Distinguished Fellow American Psychiatric Asscn. 1972, Linacre Lecturer St. John's Coll. Cambridge 1984; Hon. Fellow Australian and New Zealand Coll. of Psychiatrists 1974, Royal Coll. of Psychiatrists 1975; Hon. Sc.D. (Dublin) 1977; Hon. D.Sc. (Indiana) 1993; Anna Monika Award 1977, Paul Hoch Award 1979, Gold Medal, Soc. of Biological Psychiatry 1980, Golden Florin, City of Venice 1979, Leonard Cammer Memorial Award 1981, Kesten Award (Univ. of S. Calif.) 1983, Sandoz Prize, Int. Gerontological Asscn. 1985, Kraepelin Medal 1985, Max-Planck Inst., Munich, Salmon Medal, N.Y. Acad. of Medicine, Gold Medal, Int. Alzheimer's Soc. 1992, Camillo Golgi Award in Neuroscience, Italian Acad. of Neuroscience 1993, Lifetime Achievement Award, Soc. of Biological Psychiatry 1996. *Publications:* Clinical Psychiatry (with W. Mayer-Gross and Eliot Slater) 1954, Clinical Psychiatry (with E. Slater) 1977; Editor: Psychiatry, Genetics and Pathography: A Tribute to Eliot Slater 1979, Psychiatry, Human Rights and the Law 1985, Alzheimer's Disease and Related Disorders (with Iversen), Reality of Mental Illness (with J. Kroll), CAMDEX-Cambridge Examination for Mental Disorders of the Elderly (with Mountjoy, Huppert and Tym) 1988, Handbook of Anxiety Vols. I–V (Jt. ed.). *Leisure interests:* literature, music, swimming. *Address:* Trinity College, Cambridge, CB2 1TQ, England. *Telephone:* (01223) 338400.

ROTH, Philip, M.A.; American writer; b. 19 March 1933, Newark, N.J.; s. of Bess Finkel Roth and the late Herman Roth; m. 1st Margaret Martinson 1959 (died 1968); m. 2nd Claire Bloom (q.v.) 1990; ed. Bucknell Univ. and Univ. of Chicago; in U.S. Army 1955–56; Lecturer in English, Univ. of Chicago 1956–58; Visiting Lecturer, Univ. of Iowa Writers' Workshop 1960–62; Writer-in-Residence, Princeton Univ. 1962–64, Univ. of Pa. 1967–80; Distinguished Prof. of Literature, Hunter Coll. 1989–92; Visiting Lecturer, State Univ. of N.Y., Stony Brook 1967, 1968; Houghton Mifflin Literary Fellow 1959; Guggenheim Fellowship Grant 1959–60, Rockefeller Grant 1965, Ford Foundation Grant 1966; mem. Nat. Inst. of Arts and Letters 1970–; Daroff Award of Jewish Book Council of America 1959, Award of Nat. Inst. of Arts and Letters 1959, Nat. Book Award for Fiction 1960, Nat. Book Critics' Circle Award (for The Counterlife) 1987, (for Patrimony) 1992, Nat. Arts Club's Medal of Honor for Literature 1991, PEN/Faulkner Fiction Award (for Operation Shylock) 1993, shared Karel Capek Prize 1994, Nat. Book Award for Fiction (for Sabbath's Theater) 1995, Pulitzer Prize (for American Pastoral) 1998. *Publications:* Goodbye Columbus (novella and stories) 1959; novels: Letting Go 1962, When She Was Good 1967, Portnoy's Complaint 1969, Our Gang 1971, The Breast 1972, The Great American Novel 1973, My Life as a Man 1974, Reading Myself and Others (essays) 1975, The Professor of Desire 1977, The Ghost Writer 1979, A Philip Roth Reader 1980, Zuckerman Unbound 1981, The Anatomy Lesson 1983, The Prague Orgy 1985, Zuckerman Bound 1985, The Counterlife 1986, The Facts: A Novelists Autobiography 1988, Deception 1990, Patrimony 1991, Operation Shylock 1993, Sabbath's Theater 1995, American Pastoral 1997, I Married a Communist 1998. *Address:* c/o Wylie Agency, Inc., 250 W. 57th Street, Suite 2114, New York, NY 10107, U.S.A.

ROTH, Tim; British actor; b. 1961, Dulwich; ed. Dick Sheppard Comprehensive School, Brixton and Camberwell Coll. of Art; began acting career with fringe groups including Glasgow Citizens Theatre, The Oval House and the Royal Court; appeared on London stage in Metamorphosis; numerous TV appearances. *Films:* The Hit, A World Apart, The Cook the Thief His Wife and Her Lover, Vincent & Theo, Rosencrantz and Guildenstern are Dead, Jumpin at the Boneyard, Reservoir Dogs, Bodies Rest and Motion, Pulp Fiction, Little Odessa, Rob Roy, Captives, Four Rooms, Hoodlums, Everyone Says I Love You, Liar, The War Zone (dir.).

ROTH, William V., Jr.; American politician; b. 22 July 1921, Great Falls, Mont.; s. of William V. and Clara Nelson Roth; m. Jane K. Richards 1965; one s. one d.; ed. Univ. of Oregon and Harvard Univ.; admitted to Del. Bar and U.S. Supreme Court; fmr. Congressman from Delaware; mem. Republican Nat. Cttee. 1961–64; Senator from Delaware 1971–; Chair. Senate Govt. Affairs Cttee. 1981. *Address:* U.S. Senate, 104 Hart Senate Office Building, Washington, DC 20510, U.S.A.

ROTHENBERG, Alan I., J.D.; American lawyer; b. 10 April 1939; m. Georgina Rothenberg; three c.; ed. Univ. of Mich.; admitted Calif. Bar 1964; partner Manatt Phelps Rothenberg & Phillips, Los Angeles 1968–90, Latham & Watkins, LA 1990–; Instr. in Sports Law, Univ. of S. Calif. 1969, 1976, 1984, Whittier Coll. of Law 1980, 1984; Pres. Los Angeles Clippers Basketball Team 1982–89, US Soccer Fed., Chicago 1990–; mem. Soccer Comm. 1984 Olympic Games; mem. Equal Educ. Opportunities Comm. State of Calif. Bd. of Educ. 1972–75; mem. Bd. of Govs. Nat. Basketball Asscn.; Pres. Constitutional Rights Foundation 1987–90; Chair. Pres. C.E.O. 1994 World Cup Organizing Cttee. 1990. *Address:* Latham & Watkins, 633 W. 5th Street, Suite 4000, Los Angeles, CA 90071; Office of the President, US Soccer Federation, 1801-1811 South Prairie Avenue, Chicago, IL 60616, U.S.A.

ROTHENBERG, Susan, B.F.A.; American artist; b. 20 Jan. 1945, Buffalo, New York; d. of Leonard Rothenberg and Adele Cohen; m. George Trakas 1971 (divorced 1976); one d.; ed. Cornell and George Washington Univs. and Corcoran Museum School; one-woman exhbns. include Akron Art Museum 1981–82, Stedelijk Museum, Amsterdam 1982, San Francisco Museum of Art 1983, Carnegie Inst. Museum of Art, Pittsburg 1984, Los Angeles County Museum of Art 1983, Inst. of Contemporary Art, Boston 1984, Aspen Center for the Visual Arts 1984, Willard Gallery 1976, 1977, 1979, 1981, 1983; has participated in numerous group exhbns. at Museum of Modern Art, Whitney Museum of American Art, Venice Biennale and galleries in Germany, Denmark, Spain, Finland etc.; work exhibited in several public collections in U.S.A. and Netherlands; Guggenheim Fellow 1980. *Address:* c/o Sperone Westwater, 142 Greene Street, New York, NY 10012, U.S.A.

ROTHENBERGER, Anneliese; German opera singer (soprano) and painter; b. 19 June 1926, Salenstein; d. of Josef Rothenberger and Sophie Häffner; m. Gerd W. Dieberitz 1954; ed. Real- und Musikhochschule, Mannheim; début, Coblenz Theatre 1947; with State Opera Hamburg, Munich, Vienna 1958–70; guest singer at La Scala, Milan, Metropolitan Opera, New York, and Salzburg, Glyndebourne and Munich Festivals, etc.; TV Special 1969–; several exhbns. as painter, Germany and Switzerland; Distinguished Service Cross 1st Class, Great Cross. *Films:* Die Fledermaus 1955, Der Rosenkavalier. *Publication:* Melody of My Life 1973. *Leisure interests:* driving, books, painting, modelling. *Address:* Quellenhof, 8268 Salenstein am Untersee, Switzerland.

ROTHERMERE, 4th Viscount, cr. 1919, of Hemsted; **Jonathan Harold Esmond Vere Harmsworth;** British newspaper proprietor; b. 3 Dec. 1967, London; s. of the late 3rd Viscount Rothermere and Patricia Evelyn Beverley Brooks; m. Claudia Clemence 1993; one s. one d.; ed. Gordonstoun School, Scotland, Duke Univ., U.S.A.; joined Mirror Group 1993; joined Northcliffe Newspapers Group Ltd. 1995; Deputy Man. Dir., then Man. Dir. Evening Standard 1997; Deputy Chair. Assoc. Newspapers Ltd. 1998–, Teletext (subsidiary of Harmsworth Media) 1998–; Chair. Assoc. New Media 1998, Daily Mail and Gen. Trust PLC 1998–; Pres. Newspaper Press Fund 1999–. *Address:* Daily Mail and General Trust PLC, Room 602, Northcliffe House, 2 Derry Street, London, W8 5TT, England. *Telephone:* 0171-938 6610. *Fax:* 0171-937 0043.

ROTHSCHILD, 4th Baron, cr. 1885; **(Nathaniel Charles) Jacob Rothschild,** G.B.E., B.A.; British banker; b. 29 April 1936; s. of late 3rd Baron Rothschild; m. Serena Dunn 1961; one s. three d.; ed. Eton Coll. and Christ Church, Oxford; Chair. St James's Place Capital PLC (fmrly. J. Rothschild Holdings) 1971–96, Five Arrows 1980–, RIT Capital Partners, Bd. of Trustees, Nat. Gallery 1985–91; Chair. Bd. of Trustees Nat. Heritage Memorial Fund 1992–98; Pres. Inst. of Jewish Affairs 1992–; Chair. RIT Capital Partners; mem. Council, Royal Coll. of Art 1986–92 (Sr. Fellow 1992); Commdr. Order of Henry the Navigator (Portugal). *Address:* 14 St. James's Place, London, SW1A 1NP, England. *Telephone:* 0171-493 8111.

ROTHSCHILD, Baron David René James de; French banker; b. 15 Dec. 1942, New York; s. of Baron Guy de Rothschild (q.v.) and Baroness Alix Schey de Koromla; m. Olimpia Aldobrandini 1974; ed. Lycée Carnot, Paris and Inst. d'Etudes Politiques, Paris; Dir. Société Le Nickel 1970–73; Dir.-Gen. Cie. du Nord 1973–78; Chair. Man. Bd. Banque Rothschild 1978–82; Pres.-Dir.-Gen. Paris-Orléans Man. 1982–84, Paris-Orléans Banque 1984–86; Chair. Rothschild & Cie Banque 1986–, Rothschild NA Inc. 1986–, Rothschild Canada 1990–; Chair. Man. Bd. Saint-Honoré-Matignon (investment co.) 1986; Pres.-Dir.-Gen. Francarep; Pres. Financière Viticole S.A., Rothschild Europe; Dir. Cie. Financière Martin-Maurel, Imetal, Asscn. française des entreprises privées (Afep), Rothschilds Continuation Ltd., etc.; Vice-Pres. Incolder 1990; Deputy Chair. N.M. Rothschild, London 1992–; Chair. N.M. Rothschild Corporate Finance 1996–; Pres. Fondation Rothschild. *Leisure interests:* golf, skiing, tennis. *Address:* 17 avenue Matignon, 75008 Paris (Office); 6 rue de Tournon, 75006 Paris, France (Home).

ROTHSCHILD, Edmund Leopold de, C.B.E., T.D.; British merchant banker; b. 2 Jan. 1916, London; s. of Lionel N. de Rothschild and Marie Louise Beer; m. 1st Elizabeth E. Lentner 1948 (died 1980); two s. two d.; m. 2nd Anne Evelyn Harrison, J.P. 1982; Deputy Chair. British Newfoundland Corpn. Ltd. 1963–69, Churchill Falls (Labrador) Corpn. Ltd. 1966–69; Dir. N. M. Rothschild & Sons Ltd. 1975–94, Rothschild Continuation Holdings, AUR Hydropower Ltd. 1980–, Exbury Enterprises Ltd.; Pres. Asscn. of Jewish Ex-Servicemen and Women; Vice-Chair. Cen. British Fund for Jewish Relief and Rehabilitation; Vice-Pres. Queen's Nursing Inst., Trustee British Freedom from Hunger Campaign; Vice-Pres. Council of Christians and Jews; Pres. Research Into Ageing, Inst. of Jewish Affairs 1992–; Hon. LL.D. (Memorial Univ. of Newfoundland) 1961; Hon. D.Sc. (Salford) 1983; Order of the Sacred Treasure, 1st Class (Japan) 1973. *Publications:* Window on the World 1949, A Gilt-Edged Life – Memoir (autobiog.) 1998. *Leisure interests:* gardening, fishing, photography. *Address:* N. M. Rothschild & Sons Ltd., New Court, St. Swithins Lane, London, EC4P 4DU; Exbury House, Exbury, Nr. Southampton, SO4 1AF, England. *Telephone:* 0171-280 5000; (01703) 893-145.

ROTHSCHILD, Baron Elie Robert de, F.R.S.M.; French banker; b. 29 May 1917, Paris; s. of Baron Robert and Nelly (née Beer) de Rothschild; m. Liliane Fould-Springer 1942; one s. two d.; ed. Lycée Louis le Grand, Faculty of Law, Univ. de Paris; Pres. Rothschild Bank, Zürich, Assicurazioni Generali, Trieste and Venice; Officier, Légion d'honneur, Croix de guerre, Ufficiale Ordine al Merito della Repubblica Italiana. *Leisure interests:* breeding, gardening. *Address:* 32 Ormonde Gate, London, SW3 4HA, England.

ROTHSCHILD, Sir Evelyn de, Kt.; British banker; b. 29 Aug. 1931; s. of the late Anthony Gustav de Rothschild; m. Victoria Schott 1972; two s. one d.; ed. Harrow, Trinity Coll., Cambridge; Chair. Economist Newspaper 1972–89, United Racecourses Ltd. 1977–94, British Merchant Banking and Securities Houses Asscn. (fmrly. Accepting Houses Cttee.) 1985–89; now Chair. N. M. Rothschild & Sons Ltd. *Leisure interests:* art, racing. *Address:* N. M. Rothschild & Sons Ltd., New Court, St. Swithin's Lane, London, E.C.4, England.

ROTHSCHILD, Baron Guy Edouard Alphonse Paul de; French banker; b. 21 May 1909, Paris; s. of the late Baron Edouard and Germaine (née Halphen) de Rothschild; m. 1st Alix Schey de Koromla 1937 (dissolved 1956); one s.; m. 2nd Baronne Marie-Hélène de Zuylen de Nyevelt van de Haar 1957 (deceased); one s.; ed. Lycées Condorcet and Louis-le-Grand, Univ. de Paris; Pres. Compagnie du Nord (fmr. Cie. du chemin de fer du Nord) 1949, Dir., Exec. Pres. 1968; Pres., Dir.-Gen. Soc. minière et métallurgique de Penarroya 1964–71; Pres., Dir.-Gen. Banque Rothschild-Paris 1968–78; Pres., Dir.-Gen. Imetal (fmr. Soc. Le Nickel) 1971–79; Pres. Fonds juif unifié 1950–82; Officier, Légion d'honneur, Croix de guerre, Chevalier du mérite agricole. *Publications:* Contre Bonne Fortune (The Whims of Fortune, autobiog.) 1985, Mon ombre siamoise 1993, Le Fantôme de Léa 1998. *Leisure interests:* breeding and racing horses. *Address:* 17 avenue Matignon, 75008 Paris; Hôtel Lambert, 2 rue St. Louis en l'Ile 75004, Paris, France.

ROUCH, Jean, PH.D.; French anthropologist and film-maker; b. 31 May 1917, Paris; s. of Jules Rouch and Lucienne (née Gain); m. Jane Margaret George 1952 (deceased); started career as civil engineer, Head of Public Works Dept., Niger 1942; C.O., Reconnaissance Section, Engineer Corps, First French Army 1944–45; made first ever canoe journey down Niger River from source to sea (with Jean Sauvy and Pierre Ponty) 1946–47; studied Songhay people of Niger and the Dogon of Mali; has made over 100 films, including Circoncision (Grand Prix, Festival du film maudit, Biarritz 1949), Les Maîtres Fous (Grand Prix, Venice Int. Film Festival 1957), Moi, un Noir (Prix Louis Delluc 1958), Chronique d'un Eté (with Edgar Morin; Prix internationale de la Critique, Cannes 1961) La Chasse au Lion à l'Arc (prizewinner, Venice Documentary Film Festival 1965), Le Vieil Anaï (Int. Critics' Prize, Venice 1980), Dionysos (Official choice, Venice Festival 1984), Boulevard d'Afrique (Official choice, Venice Festival 1987), Enigma 1986, Bac ou mariage 1988, Liberté, égalité, fraternité . . . et puis après 1990, Madame L'eau 1992, la Vache merveilleuse 1995, Moi fatigué debout, moi couché 1997; Dir. of Research, Cen. Nat. de la Recherche Scientifique, Paris 1966–86; Head of Int. Anthropological Film Cttee. 1953–86; Gen. Sec. Cinémathèque Française 1985–86, Pres. 1987–91; Pres. C.I.C.T. (UNESCO) 1991; Visiting Prof., Harvard Univ., U.S.A. (summer school) 1980–86; Hon. Ph.D. (Leyden) 1980, (U.S.C., Los Angeles) 1991; Officier, Légion d'honneur, Officier des Arts et des Lettres; Croix de guerre. *Publications:* four major vols. about the Songhay people of the Niger river 1954–57. *Leisure interests:* swimming, bicycling, canoeing on African rivers, drawing and painting. *Address:* Musée de l'Homme, place du Trocadéro, 75116 Paris (Office); 168 boulevard du Montparnasse, 75014 Paris, France (Home). *Telephone:* 47043820 (Office); 43354862 (Home).

ROUCO VARELA, Cardinal Antonio María, LIC.EN.D., D.C.L.; Spanish ecclesiastic; b. 20 Aug. 1936, Villalba; s. of Vicente Rouco and María Eugenia Varela; ordained priest 1959; taught at Mondoñedo Seminary, Lugo 1964–66, Univ. of Munich 1966–69, Univ. Pontificia de Salamanca 1969–76 (Vice-Rector 1972–76); Auxiliary Bishop of Santiago de Compostela 1976–84, Archbishop of Santiago de Compostela 1984–94, of Madrid 1994–; cr. Cardinal Feb. 1998; Gran. Canciller San Dámaso Faculty of Theology. *Publications:* Staat und Kirche im Spanien des XVI Jahrunderts 1965, Sacramento e diritto: antinomia nella Chiesa (with E. Corecco) 1972. *Leisure interests:* music, reading. *Address:* Arzobispado, Calle San Justo 2, 28071 Madrid, Spain. *Telephone:* (91) 366 56 01. *Fax:* (91) 366 77 39.

ROUILLY, Jean, L. EN D.; French television executive; b. 21 Dec. 1943, Villennes-sur-Seine; s. of Roger Rouilly and Nicole Antigna; m. Annyck Graton 1987; one s.; ed. Lycées Jules Verne and Georges Clémenceau, Faculté de Droit, Bordeaux and Inst. d'Etudes Politiques, Bordeaux; Asst. to the Dir., Office de Radiodiffusion-Télévision Francaise, 1966–70, Admin. Documentary Programmes 1970–72, Gen. Man. to Del. Gen. of TV Production 1972–74; Sec.-Gen. Production, Antenne 2 1975–81, Asst. Dir. Finance 1981–85, Production Man. 1985–87, Dir.-Gen. Programme Production 1987–90; Asst. Dir.-Gen. Antenne 2 1987–90; Dir. Films A2 1981–87, Dir.-Gen. 1987–90; Sec.-Gen. TV5 1983–85; Dir.-Gen. Hachette Int. T.V. (now Europe Images Int.) 1990–. *Address:* Europe Images International, 25 rue François 1er, 75008 Paris (Office); 7 rue Edouard Laferrière, 92190 Meudon, France (Home). *Telephone:* 42 99 41 23 (Office).

ROULEAU, Joseph-Alfred, O.C.; Canadian bass singer; b. 28 Feb. 1929, Matane, Quebec; s. of Joseph-Alfred Rouleau and Florence Bouchard; m. 1st Barbara Whittaker 1952; one d.; m. 2nd Jill Renée Moreau; one s. one d.; ed. Coll. Jean De Brebeuf, Montreal, Univ. of Montreal, Conservatoire of Music, Province of Quebec; three years in Milan for singing studies; début in Montreal 1955, at Royal Opera House, Covent Garden 1957–, has sung over 40 roles at Covent Garden; guest artist at principal Opera Houses all over the world; tours of Canada 1960, Australia (with Joan Sutherland) 1965, Russia 1966, 1969, Romania, S. Africa 1974, 1975, 1976; Paris Opera 1975, Metropolitan Opera, New York 1984, 1985, 1986, San Francisco 1986, 1987; Prof. of Voice, Univ. of Quebec (U.Q.A.M.) 1980, mem. Admin. Bd.; mem. Bd. Corpn. of Montréal Opéra Co. 1980–; recordings include: Scenes from Anna Bolena, Ruddigore, Romeo et Juliette (Gounod); L'enfance du Christ (Berlioz), Semiramide, Boris Godunov, Renard (Stravinsky), F. Leclerc's Songs, Les habitués du rêve de Jacques Hêtu (song cycle), and recording of French operatic arias with Royal Opera House Orchestra; several awards including Prix Calixa-Lavallée 1967 (La Société St. Jean Baptiste, Montreal), Silver Medal (Royal Opera House, Covent Garden) 1983, Felix Award for Best Classical Artist of the Year 1989, Prix du Québec pour les Arts d'interprétation 1990. *Major roles include:* Boris Godunov (Boris Godunov), Philip II (Don Carlo), Basilio (Barber of Seville), Mephisto (Faust), Dosifei (Khovanschina), Don Quixote (Don Quixote), Inquisitore (Don Carlo), Ramfis (Aida), Prince Gremin (Onegin), Father Lawrence (Roméo et Juliette). *Leisure interests:* tennis, golf, reading. *Address:* 32 Lakeshore Road, Beaconsfield, Que. H9W 4H3, Canada (Home). *Telephone:* (514) 697 9266.

ROUMI, Khalfan bin Mohamad al-, B.A.; United Arab Emirates politician; b. 1945, Sharjah; m.; three d.; ed. Coll. of Educ. Baghdad, Iraq and Univ. of Southampton, U.K.; Deputy Dir. of Educ. 1970–72; Sec. of State, Ministry of Educ. 1972–77; Minister of Health 1977; Minister of Work and Public Affairs 1983, also fmr. Minister of Information and Culture; mem. Constituent Cttee. *Leisure interests:* reading, history, poetry and sociology. *Address:* c/o Ministry of Information and Culture, P.O. Box 17, Abu Dhabi, United Arab Emirates.

ROURKE, Mickey (Philip Andre); American actor and boxer; b. 1956, New York; m. 1st Debra Feuer (divorced); m. 2nd Carre Otis; ed. Actors' Studio, New York. *Film appearances include:* Fade to Black, 1941 1979, Heaven's Gate 1980, Body Heat 1981, Diner 1982, Eureka 1983, Rumblefish 1983, Rusty James 1983, The Pope of Greenwich Village 1984, 9½ Weeks 1984, Year of the Dragon 1985, Angel Heart 1986, A Prayer for the Dying 1986, Barfly 1987, Johnny Handsome 1989, Homeboy 1989, Francesco 1989, The Crew 1989, The Desperate Hours 1990, Wild Orchid 1990, On the Sport 1990, Harley Davidson and the Marlboro Man 1991, White Sands 1992, F.T.W., Fall Time, Double Time, Another 9½ Weeks, The Rainmaker 1997, Love in Paris 1997, Double Team 1997, Buffalo '66 1997, Thursday 1998.

ROUSE, Irving, B.S., PH.D., D.F.L.; American professor of anthropology; b. 29 Aug. 1913, Rochester, N.Y.; s. of B. Irving Rouse and Louise Bohachek; m. Mary Mikami 1939; two s.; Asst., then Assoc. Curator, Peabody Museum of Natural History, Yale Univ. 1938–62, Curator 1977–85, Curator Emer. 1985–, Instructor to Assoc. Prof. 1939–54, Prof. of Anthropology 1954–69, Charles J. MacCurdy Prof. of Anthropology, Yale Univ. 1969–84, Prof. Emer. 1984–, fmr. Chair. Dept. of Anthropology; Pres. Soc. for American Archaeology 1952–53, American Anthopology Asscn. 1967–68, Asscn. for Field Archaeology 1977–79; mem. American Acad. of Arts and Sciences, Nat. Acad. of Sciences, Royal Anthropological Inst., Soc. of Antiquaries of London; A. Cressy Morrison Prize in Natural Sciences, Viking Fund Medal in Anthropology, Distinguished Service Award, American Anthropological Asscn. *Publications:* Prehistory in Haiti 1939, Culture of the Ft. Liberté Region, Haiti 1941, Archaeology of the Maniabón Hills, Cuba 1942, A Survey of Indian River Archaeology, Florida 1951, Porto Rican Prehistory 1952, An Archaeological Chronology of Venezuela (with J. M. Cruxent) 1958, Venezuelan Archaeology (with J. M. Cruxent) 1963, Introduction to Prehistory 1972,

Migrations in Prehistory 1986, The Tainos 1992. *Leisure interests:* singing, swimming. *Address:* Department of Anthropology, Yale University, Box 208277, New Haven, CT 06520-8277 (Office); 12 Ridgewood Terrace, North Haven, CT 06473, U.S.A. (Home). *Telephone:* (203) 432-3690 (Office); (203) 288-1485 (Home). *Fax:* (203) 432-3669.

ROUSSEL, Paul Henri Michel; French business executive; b. 3 March 1954, Bayeux; s. of Jacques Roussel and Janine Piton; m. Jacqueline Claire Roussel 1975; one s. one d.; ed. Lycée Malherbe, Caen; Head of Group, Havas Conseil 1976–80; Consumer Dir. SNIP 4 1981–83; Consumer Dir. Robert & Partners 1984–86; Commercial and Marketing Dir. L'Equipe magazine 1986–89, Deputy Dir.-Gen. 1990–92, Dir.-Gen. 1993–; Deputy Dir.-Gen. Groupe Amaury 1995–. *Leisure interests:* tennis, football, skiing. *Address:* L'Equipe, 4 rue Rouget de l'Isle, 92137 Issy-les-Moulineaux, France. *Telephone:* 40.93.20.20. *Fax:* 40.93.20.08.

ROUSSELET, André Claude Lucien, L.EN D.; French business executive; b. 1 Oct. 1922, Nancy; s. of Marcel and Yvonne (née Brongniart) Rousselet; m. Catherine Roge (divorced); two s. one d.; ed. Lycée Claude Bernard, Paris, Faculte de Droit, Paris and Ecole Libre des Sciences Politiques; Chef de Cabinet, Prefects of Ariege and L'Aube 1944; Sub-prefect of Condom 1946, Pointe-à-Pitre 1948, Issoudun 1935; Chef de Cabinet, Minister of the Interior 1954; Special Asst. Office of Minister of Posts and Telecommunications 1955; Chef de Cabinet, Minister of Justice 1956; Dept. of External Relations, Simca 1958; Pres.-Dir.-Gen. Société nouvelles des autoplaces G7 1962–67, 1972–; Deputé for Haute-Garonne 1967–68; Man. Galérie de France and Dir. du Cabinet, Pres. of Repub. 1981–82; Pres.-Dir.-Gen. Agence Havas 1982–86 (now Dir.); mem. Comité stratégique de Havas 1987; Pres.-Dir.-Gen. Canal Plus 1984–94; Pres. société éditrice de InfoMatin (Sodepresse) 1994–; Pres. Advisory Council Tonna Electronique 1990, Sodepresse 1995; Dir Information; Pres. Editorial Soc. Sodepresse; Dir. Télévision le mensuel (publication). *Leisure interests:* golf, tennis, painting. *Address:* 44 avenue George V, 75008 Paris; 28 rue Henri Barbusse, 92110 Clichy, France.

ROUSSELLE, Régis; French stockbroker; b. 25 Jan. 1948, Rheims; ed. Ecole des Arts et Manufactures and Faculté des Sciences Econs.; Chair. Finance Eng. 1974–81; Stockbroker Meeschaert-Rousselle 1981–87, Chair. 1988–89; Chair. Soc. des Bourses Françaises 1988–90, Conseil des Bourses de Valeurs 1988–90; Coll. mem. Comm. des Opérations de Bourse 1988–90; Pres. Economics and Finance Professionals Group of Fmr. Students of Ecole centrale de Paris 1988–. *Address:* Commission des operations de bourse, 17 place de Bourse, 75082 Paris, France.

ROUSSELY, François; French industrial executive; b. 9 Jan. 1945, Dordogne; ed. Paris Inst. of Political Science, French Nat. School of Admin.; auditor, State Accounting Office 1978; sr. civil servant, Ministry of Interior, Prin. Pvt. Sec. 1981–84; assigned to chair. of a parl. cttee., Assemblée Nat. 1986–89; Dir.-Gen. Nat. Police (Ministry of Interior) 1989–91; Gen. Sec. for Admin. of Ministry of Defence 1991–96; Sec.-Gen. and mem. Exec. Cttee. Soc. Nat. des Chemins de Fer (SNCF) 1997; Prin. Pvt. Sec. Ministry of Defence 1998; Chair. Electricité de France (EDF) 1998–; mem. Comité de l'Energie Atomique; Officier Légion d'honneur, Officier Ordre nat. du Mérite. *Address:* Electricité de France (EDF), 32 rue de Monceau, 75008 Paris, France. *Telephone:* (01) 40.42.50.00. *Fax:* (01) 40.42.89.00.

ROUSSIN, Michel, D.LITT.; French politician, civil servant and police officer; b. 3 May 1939, Rabat, Morocco; s. of Gabriel Roussin and Sylvia Tonieti; m. Annick Dussud 1966; two s.; ed. St. Joseph Coll., Avignon, Paris Univ.; artillery officer 1960–63; police officer 1963–90; responsible for Press Relations Directorate of Police and Mil. Justice 1969–72; Mil. Commdr. Hotel Mâtignon 1972–76; Pvt. Sec. to Indre-et-Loire Prefect 1976–77, to Dir.-Gen. of Foreign Documentation and Counter-Espionage (SDECE) 1977–81, to Mayor of Paris 1984–86, 1989, to Prime Minister 1986; with Ministry of Defence 1980–81; with Compagnie Gen. des Eaux 1981–83; Tech. Adviser at Mayor's Office 1983–84; Minister of Co-operation 1993–94; Deputy Mayor of Paris 1994–; Chair. SAE Int. 1995–; Bd. Dirs. Eiffage Group 1996–; Saga Group 1997–; Défense nationale (journal) 1998–. *Address:* c/o Hôtel de Ville, 75004 Paris; SAE International, 2 rue Laborde, 75008 Paris, France.

ROUTTI, Jorma Tapio, PH.D.; Finnish civil servant and scientist; b. 17 Dec. 1938, Jyväskylä; s. of Olli Routti and Rauha Kuusalo; m. Irmeli Saurama 1964; two d.; ed. Helsinki Univ. of Tech. and Univ. of Calif. at Berkeley; researcher Univ. of Calif. at Berkeley 1964–69; Visiting Scientist C.E.R.N., Geneva 1970–72; Prof. Helsinki Univ. of Tech. 1973–90; Pres. SITRA Finland 1986–95; Dir.-Gen. Science, Research and Devt., European Comm. 1996–; Fulbright Fellow, American Scandinavian Foundation Fellow, Eisenhower Exchange Fellow; Hon. Ph.D. (Univ. of Jyväskylä), Hon. D.Tech. (Helsinki Univ. of Tech.). *Publications:* about 200 publs. in physics, computer science, energy studies, science policy. *Leisure interests:* tennis, skiing. *Address:* European Commission, Directorate-General XII, rue de la Loi 200, B-1049 Brussels, Belgium. *Telephone:* 295 27 53. *Fax:* 295 76 29.

ROUVILLOIS, Philippe André Marie, L. EN D.; French government official; b. 29 Jan. 1935, Saumur; s. of Gen. Jean Rouvillois and Suzanne Hulot; m. Madeleine Brigol 1960; four s.; ed. Lycée Fustel-de-Coulanges, Strasbourg, Lycée Louis-le-Grand, Faculté de Droit, Paris and Inst. d'Etudes Politiques, Paris; Insp. of Finance 1959; Office of Revenue 1964; Adviser, Pvt. Office of Minister of Econ. and Finance 1966–68; Deputy Dir. Office of Revenue, Ministry of Econ. and Finance 1967, Head of Service 1969; Deputy Dir.-Gen. of Revenue 1973, Dir.-Gen. 1976; Insp.-Gen. of Finance 1982; Deputy Dir.-Gen. SNCF 1983–87, Dir.-Gen. 1987–88, Pres. Admin. Bd. 1988; Gen. Man. and Pres. Admin. Council, Atomic Energy Comm. (CEA) 1989–95; Pres. CEA-Industrie 1989–92, 1993–; Pasteur Inst. 1997–; Commdr. Légion d'honneur, Croix de Valeur militaire. *Address:* CEA-Industrie, 31–33 rue de la Fédération, 75752 Paris cedex 15, France.

ROUX, Albert Henri; French chef and restaurateur; brother of Michel André Roux (q.v.); b. 8 Oct. 1935, Semur-en-Brionnais; s. of the late Henri Roux and of Germaine Roux (née Triger); m. Monique Merle 1959; one s. one d.; ed. Ecole Primaire, St. Mandé; mil. service, Algeria; founder (with brother Michel Roux), Le Gavroche Restaurant, London 1967 (now owned jtly. with his son Michel Jr.), The Waterside Inn, Bray 1972 (now owned solely by Michel Roux); opened 47 Park Street Hotel 1981; opened Le Poulbot, Le Gamin, Gavvers, Les Trois Plats and Rouxl Britannia (all as part of Roux Restaurants Ltd.) 1969–87; commenced consultancy practice 1989; founder-mem. Acad. Culinaire de Grande Bretagne, Maître Cuisinier de France 1968; Hon. Prof. Bournemouth Univ. 1995–; Chevalier du Mérite Agricole; Hon. D.Sc. (Council for Nat. Academic Awards) 1987. *Publications:* with Michel Roux: New Classic Cuisine 1983, The Roux Brothers on Pâtisserie 1986, The Roux Brothers on French Country Cooking 1989, Cooking for Two 1991. *Leisure interests:* fishing, racing. *Address:* Le Gavroche, 43 Upper Brook Street, London, W1Y 1PF, England (Office). *Telephone:* 0171-408 0881 (Restaurant). *Fax:* 0171-491 4387 (Restaurant).

ROUX, Bernard Georges Marie; French business executive; b. 15 Aug. 1934, St. Raphaël (Var); s. of Edouard Roux and Juliette Boyer; m. 3rd Roselyne Mainfroy 1983; three s. (two s. two d. from fmr. marriages); ed. École de Commerce, Faculté de Droit de Lyon: Commercial Dir. Meunier Textiles 1959; Dir.-Gen. Centrale voile ameublement (Groupe Rhodiaceta) 1963; joined Axe Publicité 1965, Dir 1967; f. Roux Séguéla agency with Jacques Séguéla 1969; Pres. Roux, Séguéla, Cayzac et Goudard 1991; f. RLC 1992– (changed to Opera-RLC 1993); Pres. and Dir.-Gen. Gymnase Club 1997–. *Leisure interests:* tennis, reading, cinema. *Address:* Opera RLC, 20 rue Troyon, 75017 Paris; 8 square Chezy, 92200 Neuilly-sur-Seine, France.

ROUX, Jean-Louis, C.C.; Canadian official, theatre director, actor, author and senator; b. 18 May 1923, Montreal; s. of Louis Roux and Berthe Leclerc; m. Monique Oligny 1950; one s.; ed. Coll. Sainte-Marie and Univ. de Montréal; mem. Les Compagnons de Saint Laurent theatrical co. 1939–42, Ludmilla Pitoëff theatrical co. 1942–46; mil. training 1942–46; founder, Théâtre d'Essai, Montreal 1951; Sec.-Gen., Théâtre du Nouveau Monde 1953–63 (co-founder 1950), Artistic Dir. 1966–82; Dir.-Gen. Nat. Theatre School of Canada 1982–87; has appeared in more than 200 roles (in both French and English) on stage (Montreal, Stratford, Paris), TV, cinema, and radio and directed more than 50 theatrical productions; apptd. to Senate 1994; Lieut. Gov. of Quebec 1996; Chair. Canada Council for the Arts 1998; mem. Royal Soc. of Canada 1982–; Life Gov. Nat. Theatre School of Canada; Dr. h.c. (Laval Univ.) 1988, (Univ. of Ottawa) 1995; Hon. LL.D. (Concordia Univ.) 1993; numerous awards and medals including Molson Award 1977, World Theatre Award 1985, Ordre de la Pléiade 1995, Kt. of Grace Order of St. John of Jerusalem 1996; Chevalier, Ordre Nat. du Québec 1989. *Leisure interests:* reading, chess, swimming, walking. *Address:* 4145 Blueridge Crescent, Apt. 2, Montreal, Quebec, H3H 1S7, Canada. *Telephone:* (514) 937-2505.

ROUX, Michel André; French chef and restaurateur; brother of Albert Henri Roux (q.v.); b. 19 April 1941; s. of late Henri Roux and of Germaine Roux (née Triger); m. 1st Françoise Marcelle Becquet (divorced 1979); one s. two d.; m. 2nd Robyn Margaret Joyce 1984; ed. Ecole Primaire St. Mandé, Brevet de Maîtrise; commis pâtissier and cuisinier British Embassy, Paris 1955–57; commis cook to Cécile de Rothschild 1957–59, Chef 1962–67; mil. service 1960–62; propr. Le Gavroche 1967, The Waterside Inn 1972, Le Gavroche (Mayfair) 1981; mem. Acad. Culinaire de France (UK br.), Asscn. Relais et Desserts, Asscn. Relais et Châteaux; numerous culinary awards include: Gold Medal Cuisiniers Français (Paris) 1972, Laureate Restaurateur of the Year 1985; Chevalier, Ordre Nat. du Mérite 1987, Ordre des Arts et des Lettres 1990 and numerous other awards and decorations. *Publications:* New Classic Cuisine 1983, Roux Brothers on Pâtisserie 1986, At Home with the Roux Brothers 1987, French Traditional Country Cooking 1989, Cooking for Two 1991, Desserts, a Lifelong Passion 1994, Sauces 1996. *Leisure interests:* shooting, skiing, walking. *Address:* The Waterside Inn, Ferry Road, Bray, Berks., SL6 2AT, England. *Telephone:* (01628) 771966. *Fax:* (01628) 789182.

ROWE-HAM, Sir David (Kenneth), G.B.E., F.C.A.; British accountant; b. 19 Dec. 1935; s. of late Kenneth Henry Rowe-Ham and of Muriel Phyllis Rowe-Ham; m. Sandra Celia Glover (née Nicholls); three s.; ed. Dragon School, Charterhouse; mem. Stock Exchange 1964–84; Sr. Partner, Smith Keen Cutler 1972–82; Dir. W. Canning PLC 1981–86, Savoy Theatre Ltd. 1986–98, Williams PLC 1992–, CLS Holdings PLC 1994–99; Regional Dir. (London) Lloyds Bank PLC 1985–91; Pres. The Crown Agents Foundation 1996–; Chair. Advisory Panel, Guinness Flight Unit Trust Managers Ltd. 1987–; Consultant, Touche Ross & Co. 1984–93; Chair. Birmingham Municipal Bank 1970–72, Olayan Europe Ltd. 1989–, Asset Trust PLC 1982–89, Brewin Dolphin Holdings PLC 1992–, Apta Healthcare PLC 1994–96, Coral Products PLC 1995–, Gradus Group PLC (Joint Chair.) 1995–97; Lord Mayor of London 1986–87; Chair. Political Council, Jr. Carlton Club 1977, Deputy Chair. Carlton Political Cttee. 1977–79; Gov. Royal Shakespeare Co.;

Trustee, Friends of D'Oyly Carte; Gov., Christ's Hosp.; Hon. D.Litt. (City Univ.) 1986; Pedro Ernesto Medal, Rio de Janeiro 1987; K.St.J. 1986; Commdr. de l'Ordre du mérite 1984; Commdr. Order of the Lion, Malawi 1985; Order of the Aztec Eagle (Class II), Mexico 1985; Order of King Abdul Aziz (Class I) 1987; Grand Officier du Wissam Alouite 1987, Order of Diego Losada of Caracas 1987. *Leisure interest:* theatre. *Address:* 140 Piccadilly, London, W1V 9FH, England. *Telephone:* 0171-235 4802.

ROWLAND, Frank Sherwood, PH.D.; American professor of chemistry; b. 28 June 1927, Delaware, Ohio; s. of Sidney A. Rowland and Margaret Lois Drake Rowland; m. Joan Lundberg 1952; one s. one d.; ed. Chicago and Ohio Wesleyan Univs.; Instructor in Chemistry, Princeton Univ. 1952–56; Asst. to Prof., Kansas Univ. 1956–64; Prof., Univ. of Calif. Irvine 1964–, Daniel G. Aldrich Endowed Prof. of Chemistry 1985–89, Bren Prof. of Chemistry 1989–94, Bren Research Prof. 1994–; Guggenheim Fellow 1962, 1974; mem. American Acad. of Arts and Sciences 1977, N.A.S. 1978– (Foreign Sec. 1994–), American Philosophical Soc. 1995; Fellow A.A.A.S. (Chair. Bd. Dirs. 1993); Tyler Prize in Ecology and Energy (now called World Prize for Environmental Achievement), Japan Prize in Environmental Science and Tech. 1989; Nobel Prize for Chemistry 1995, Nevada Medal 1997; Hon. Sc.D. (E. Anglia) 1996; numerous other awards, lectureships and cttee. memberships. *Publications:* articles in scientific journals. *Leisure interests:* athletics, opera. *Address:* University of California, Department of Chemistry, 571 PS1, Irvine, CA 92697; 4807 Dorchester Road, Corona del Mar, CA 92625, U.S.A. (Home). *Telephone:* (714) 760-1333.

ROWLAND, Air Marshal Sir James Anthony, A.C., K.B.E., D.F.C., A.F.C., B.E., C.ENG., F.R.AE.S., F.I.E. (Aust.), F.T.S.E.; Australian air force officer (retd.); b. 1 Nov. 1922, Armidale, N.S.W.; s. of Commdr. Louis Claude Rowland and Elsie Jean Wright; m. Faye Alison Doughton 1955; one d.; ed. Univ. of Sydney; Master Bomber, Pathfinder Force, Bomber Command R.A.F. 1944; with R.A.A.F.; Chief Test Pilot, Aircraft Research and Devt. Unit 1951–54; Officer Commanding Research and Devt. 1958–60; Chief Tech. Officer, No. 82 Wing 1957, Mirage Mission, Paris 1961–64; Commanding No. 3 Aircraft Depot, Amberley 1967–68; Sr. Eng. Staff Officer, HQ Operational Command 1969–70; with Dept. of Air: Dir.-Gen. of Aircraft Eng. 1972, Air Mem. for Tech. Services 1973–74; Chief of Air Staff, R.A.A.F. 1975–79; mem. Admin. Appeals Tribunal 1979–80; Gov. N.S.W. 1981–89; mem. Police Bd. N.S.W. 1989–92; Chair. Air Transport Council N.S.W. 1989–; Dir. Angus and Coote Ltd. 1989–, Focus Books Pty. Ltd. 1990–97, Thomson CSF Pacific Holdings PLC 1994–98; Chair. The Preston Group 1991–95; Pres. Royal Humane Soc. N.S.W. 1989–; Chancellor Univ. of Sydney 1990–91; Chair. Airsys ATM 1997–, Zylotech Ltd. 1997–; Consultant Office Française d'Exportation de Matériel Aéronautique (OFEMA), Australia 1980; Councillor, Royal Aeronautical Soc., Australian Branch 1973–75; Hon. D. Eng. (Sydney Univ.) 1983; K.St.J. *Publications:* official reports, contributions to journals. *Leisure interests:* carpentry, history, surfing. *Address:* 17 Pindari Avenue, Mosman 2088, Australia. *Telephone:* (02) 9960-2345.

ROWLAND, Sir John David, Kt., M.A.; British business executive; b. 10 Aug. 1933; s. of Cyril Arthur Rowland and Eileen Mary Rowland; m. 1st Giulia Powell 1957 (divorced 1991); one s. one d.; m. 2nd Diana L. Matthews 1991; ed. Trinity College, Cambridge Univ.; joined Matthews Wrightson and Co. 1956, Dir. 1965; Dir. Matthews Wrightson Holdings 1972; Dir. Project Fullemploy 1973–88; Deputy Chair. Stewart Wrightson Holdings PLC 1978–81, Chair. 1981–87; Vice-Pres. British Insurance and Investment Brokers Asscn. 1980–; Chair. Westminster Insurance Agencies 1981–88; Dir. Royal London Mutual Insurance Soc. 1985–86; Deputy Chair. Willis Faber PLC 1987–88; Dir. Fullemploy Group Ltd. 1989–90; Chair. Sedgwick Group PLC 1989–92; Pres. Templeton Coll., Oxford 1998–; mem. Council, Lloyd's 1987–90, Chair. 1993–97; Dir. Somerset House Ltd. 1997–, NatWest Group 1998–; Chair. NatWest April 1999– (Jt. Deputy Chair. 1998–99); mem. Pres.'s Cttee., Business in the Community; mem. of council Industrial Soc., Contemporary Applied Arts, Templeton Coll.; Gov. Coll. of Insurance 1983–85, Chair. 1985; Hon. M.A. (Oxford) 1993, Hon. D.Phil. (London Guildhall) 1996, Hon. D.Sc. (City) 1997. *Leisure interests:* golf, running slowly. *Address:* National Westminster Bank, 41 Lothbury, London, EC2P 2BP; 105 Barnsbury Street, London, N1 1EP; Giffords Hall, Wickhambrook, Newmarket, Suffolk, CB8 8PQ, England.

ROWLAND, John Grosvenor; American politician; b. 24 May 1957, Waterbury, Conn.; s. of Sherwood L. Rowland and Florence M. Jackson; m. Deborah Nebhan 1982; one s. two d.; ed. Villanova Univ.; mem. Conn. House of Reps. 1980–84; mem. U.S. House of Reps. 1985–91; Gov. of Connecticut Jan. 1995–; Pres. Rowland Asscns.; Bd. Dirs. American Cancer Soc.; Republican. *Address:* Office of the Governor, State Capitol, 210 Capitol Avenue, Hartford, CT 06106 (Office); 990 Prospect Avenue, Hartford, CT 06105, U.S.A. (Home).

ROWLANDS, Christopher John, M.A., F.C.A., C.B.I.M., F.R.S.A.; British business executive; b. 29 August 1951, Leeds; s. of late Wilfred John Rowlands and of Margaretta Rowlands (née Roberts); m. Alison Mary Kelly 1978; two d.; ed. Roundhay School, Leeds, Gonville and Caius Coll., Cambridge; articled clerk Peat Marwick Mitchell 1973–75, Man. 1981, seconded as partner, Zambia 1981–83, Sr. Man., London 1983–85; Controller Business Planning Asda Group PLC 1985–86, Div. Dir. Group Finance 1986–88, Deputy Man. Dir. and Finance Dir. Property Devt. and Investment 1988–92; Group Finance Dir. HTV 1992–93, Chief Exec. 1993–97; Chief Exec. The TV Corpn. 1998–; Dir. (non-exec.) Access Plus PLC; mem. Council, Ind. TV Asscn. Co. 1993–97. *Leisure interests:* family, theatre, church, reading, skiing, tennis, travel. *Address:* The Television Corporation PLC, 30 Sackville Street, London, W1X 1DB (Office); Buchan House, Northumberland Road, Bristol, BS6 7BB, England (Home). *Telephone:* 0171-478 7400 (Office); (0117) 924 3528 (Home). *Fax:* 0171-478 7407 (Office).

ROWLINSON, John Shipley, F.ENG., F.R.S.; British scientist and university professor; b. 12 May 1926, Handforth, Cheshire; s. of Frank Rowlinson and Winifred Jones; m. Nancy Gaskell 1952; one s. one d.; ed. Trinity Coll., Univ. of Oxford; Research Assoc., Univ. of Wis. 1950–51; Research Fellow, then Lecturer, then Sr. Lecturer in Chem., Univ. of Manchester 1951–60; Prof. of Chemical Tech., Univ. of London 1961–73; Dr. Lee's Prof. of Chem., Univ. of Oxford 1974–93; Fellow Exeter Coll., Oxford 1974–; A.D. White Prof.-at-Large, Cornell Univ. 1990–96; Hoffman Lecturer, Gesellschaft Deutscher Chemiker 1980, Faraday Lecturer 1983, Lennard-Jones Lecturer 1985, Royal Soc. of Chem., Mary Upson Prof. of Eng., Cornell Univ. 1988; Physical Sec. and Vice-Pres. Royal Soc. 1994–99; Meldola Medal, Royal Inst. of Chem. 1954; Marlow Medal, Faraday Soc. 1956, Leverhulme Medal, Royal Soc. 1993. *Publications:* Liquids and Liquid Mixtures (jtly.) 1982 (3rd edition), The Perfect Gas 1963, Thermodynamics for Chemical Engineers (jtly.) 1975, Molecular Theory of Capillarity (jtly.) 1982, J. D. van der Waals: On the Continuity of the Gaseous and Liquid States (ed.) 1988, Record of the Royal Society 1940–89 (jtly.) 1992, Van der Waals and Molecular Science (jtly.) 1996. *Leisure interest:* mountaineering. *Address:* Physical and Theoretical Chemistry Laboratory, South Parks Road, Oxford, OX1 3QZ (Office); 12 Pullens Field, Headington, Oxford, OX3 0BU, England (Home). *Telephone:* (01865) 275973 (Office); (01865) 767507 (Home). *Fax:* (01865) 275410.

ROWNY, Lieut.-Gen., The Hon. Edward Leon, B.C.E., M.A., M.S., PH.D.; American army officer; b. 3 April 1917, Baltimore, Md.; s. of Gracyan J. and Mary Ann (née Rodgers) Rowny; m. Mary Rita Leyko 1941; four s. one d.; 2nd Lieut. U.S. Army 1941; eventually Lieut.-Gen. 1970; in African campaign 1942, European and Middle Eastern Campaigns 1944–45; Korea 1950–52; Viet Nam 1962–63; Special Asst. Tactical Mobility Dept. of army 1963–75; Commdg. Gen. 24th Infantry Div., Europe 1965–66; Deputy Chief of Staff Logistics, Europe 1968–69; Deputy Chief of Research and Devt. 1969–70; Commdg. Gen. Intelligence Corps, Korea, 1970–71; Deputy Chair. Mil. Comm. NATO 1971–73; Joint Chiefs of Staff rep. to SALT del., Geneva 1973–79; Chief Arms Control Negotiator 1981–85; Special Adviser to Pres. 1985–89; Special Counsellor to State Dept. 1989–90; Pres. Nat. War Coll. Alumni Asscn. 1987–88; D.S.M., Silver Star with two oak leaf clusters, Legion of Merit with four oak clusters, Combat Infantry Badge with star. *Publication:* It Takes One to Tango 1992. *Address:* 1105 S. 23rd Road, Arlington, VA 22202, U.S.A.

ROY, Jules, D.F.C.; French writer and fmr. air force officer; b. 22 Oct. 1907, Rovigo, Algeria; s. of Henri Dematons and Mathilde Roy (née Paris); m. 1st Mirande Grimal 1929; one s. one d.; m. 2nd Sonia Lescaut 1965; ed. Algiers seminary; infantry officer 1928–35, air force officer 1935–53; served with airborne forces, Algeria 1940, with R.A.F. (night bombers), U.K. 1944–45; served in Indochina 1952–53; resgnd. on grounds of conscience; Grand Croix Légion d'honneur, Croix de guerre 1939–45, Commdr. des Arts et des Lettres. *Publications:* La vallée heureuse 1946, Prières pour des pilotes, Le métier des armes 1948, La guerre d'Algérie 1960, La bataille de Dien Bien Phu 1963, Les chevaux du soleil 1980, Une affaire d'honneur 1984, Guynemer, l'ange de la mort 1986, Mémoires barbares 1989, Citoyen Bolis, tambour de village 1990, Vézelay ou l'amour fou 1990, Rostropovitch, Gainsbourg et Dieu 1992, Amours barbares 1993, Un après-guerre amoureux 1995, Adieu ma mère, adieu mon coeur 1996. *Address:* Editions Albin Michel, 22 rue Huyghens, 75014 Paris; Clos du Couvent, 89450 Vézelay, France.

ROYAL, H.R.H. The Princess; Anne Elizabeth Alice Louise, L.G., G.C.V.O.; b. 15 Aug. 1950; d. of Queen Elizabeth II and Prince Philip, Duke of Edinburgh; m. 1st Capt. Mark Anthony Peter Phillips 1973 (divorced 1992); one s., Peter Mark Andrew, b. 15 Nov. 1977, one d., Zara Anne Elizabeth, b. 15 May 1981; m. 2nd Commander Timothy Laurence, R.N., M.V.O., 1992; ed. Benenden School, Kent; Col.-in-Chief, 14th/20th King's Hussars, Worcs. and Sherwood Foresters Regt. (29th/45th Foot), Royal Regina Rifles, 8th Canadian Hussars (Princess Louise's), Royal Corps of Signals, The Canadian Armed Forces Communications and Electronics Branch, The Royal Australian Corps of Signals, The Royal Scots, Royal New Zealand Corps of Signals, King's Royal Hussars, Royal Logistics Corps; Royal New Zealand Nursing Corps, The Grey and Simcoe Foresters Militia; Chief Commdt., W.R.N.S.; Hon. Air Commodore, R.A.F. Lyneham; Pres. W.R.N.S. Benevolent Trust, British Acad. of Film and Television Arts, Hunters' Improvement and Light Horse Breeding Soc., Save the Children Fund, Windsor Horse Trials, The Royal School for Daughters of Officers of the Royal Navy and Royal Marines (Haslemere), British Olympic Asscn., Council for Nat. Acad. Awards; Patron, Asscn. of Wrens, Riding for the Disabled Asscn., Jersey Wildlife Preservation Fund, The Royal Corps of Signals Asscn., The Royal Corps of Signals Inst., Missions to Seamen, British Knitting and Clothing Export Council, The Army and Royal Artillery Hunter Trials, Gloucs. and North Avon Fed. of Young Farmers' Clubs, Royal Lymington Yacht Club, Royal Port Moresby Soc. for the Prevention of Cruelty to Animals, Horse of the Year Ball, Benenden Ball, British School of Osteopathy, the Royal Tournament, Communications and Electronics Branch Inst., All England Women's Lacrosse Asscn., Home Farm Trust; Vice-Patron, British Show Jumping Asscn.; Commdt.-in-Chief, St. John Ambulance and

Nursing Cadets, Women's Transport Service; Freeman of the City of London, of the Fishmongers' Co., Master Warden Farriers' Co., Master and Hon. Liveryman, Carmen's Co., Hon. Liveryman Farriers' Co.; Hon. Freeman, Farmers' Co., Loriners' Co.; Yeoman, Saddlers' Co.; Hon. mem., British Equine Veterinary Asscn., Royal Yacht Squadron, Royal Thames Yacht Club, Minchinhampton Golf Club, Lloyds of London; Hon. Life mem. RNVR Officers' Asscn.; Life mem. Royal British Legion Women's Section, Royal Naval Saddle Club; mem. Island Sailing Club; Visitor, Felixstowe Coll.; official visits abroad to the 14th/20th King's Hussars in Fed. Repub of Germany 1969, 1975, to see the work of the Save the Children Fund in Kenya 1971, to the 2,500th anniversary celebrations of the Iranian monarchy 1971, to 14th/20th King's Hussars and to see the work of the Save the Children Fund, Hong Kong 1971, to S.E. Asia 1972, Munich 1972, Yugoslavia 1972, Ethiopia and the Sudan 1973, to visit Worcs. and Sherwood Foresters Regt. in Berlin 1973, in Hereford, Fed. Repub. of Germany 1974, to Canada 1974, to Australia 1975, to U.S.A. 1977, to Fed. Repub. of Germany, and Norway 1978, to Portugal, Fed. Repub. of Germany, Thailand, Gilbert Islands, New Zealand, Australia and the Bahamas, Canada 1979, to Royal Corps of Signals in Cyprus, France, Belgium and Fiji 1980, Royal Corps of Signals in Berlin, Nepal, Worcestershire and Sherwood Foresters Regiment and 14th/20th King's Hussars in Fed. Repub. of Germany; U.S.A., Canada and tour of Africa, North Yemen and Lebanon 1982, to France, Japan, Hong Kong, Singapore, Pakistan, Australia, Netherlands and B.A.O.R. 1983, U.S.A., Africa, India, Bangladesh, Fed. Repub. of Germany, U.A.E. 1984; Chancellor, Univ. of London 1981–; has accompanied the Queen and the Duke of Edinburgh on several State Visits; has taken part in numerous equestrian competitions including Montreal Olympics 1976, Horse of the Year Show, Wembley and Badminton Horse Trials; winner of Raleigh Trophy 1971 and Silver Medal in 1975 in Individual European Three Day Event; Sportswoman of the Year, Sports Writers' Asscn., Daily Express, World of Sport, BBC Sports Personality 1971, Special B.A.F.T.A. Award 1993. *Publication:* Riding Through My Life 1991. *Address:* Buckingham Palace, London, S.W.1, England.

ROYAL, Ségolène; French politician; b. 22 Sept. 1953, Dakar, Senegal; d. of Jacques Royal and Hélène Dehaye; m.; two s. two d.; ed. Univs. of Nancy and Paris; Conseillère Gen. La Mothe Saint Héray (Deux-Sèvres); Deputy to Nat. Ass. 1988–92; Sec. Comm. for Production and Exchange, Nat. Ass.; mem. Nat. Cttee. on Tourism; adviser on environment, town planning and social affairs to Pres. of Repub. 1982–88; Minister of the Environment 1992–93; Deputy to Nat. Ass. from Deux-Sèvres 1993–; practised law in Paris; Pres. Nat. Council of Socialist Group 1994–95; Deputy Minister of Educ. 1997–. *Publications:* Le Printemps des Grands Parents, Le Ras-le-bol des Bébés Zappeurs 1989, Pays, Paysans, Paysages 1993, la Vérité d'une femme 1996. *Address:* Ministère de l'Enseignement scolaire, 110 rue de Grenelle, 75007 Paris; Assemblée Nationale, 75355 Paris; Parti socialiste, 10 rue de Solférino, 75333 Paris, France.

ROYER, Jean; French politician; b. 31 Oct. 1920, Nevers; s. of Léon-Antoine Royer and Odette Bourgoin: m. Lucienne Leux 1944; two s. two d.; ed. Ecole primaire supérieure Paul-Louis-Courier, Tours and Univ. de Poitiers; teacher at Langeais 1945–48, at Sainte-Maure 1950–54, at Tours 1954–58; del. of RPF (Rassemblement du Peuple Français) 1947–51; Ind. Deputy to Nat. Ass. 1958–73, 1976–97; Mayor of Tours 1959–95; Councillor for Tours-ouest Dist. 1961; Minister of Commerce, Trades and Crafts 1973–74, of Posts and Telecommunications March–May 1974; Presidential cand. 1974; Pres. Loire Basin Devt. Org. 1984–95; Pres. 'République et Liberté' group, Assemblée Nationale.

ROYO SÁNCHEZ, Arístides, PH.D.; Panamanian politician and lawyer; b. 14 Aug. 1940, La Chorrera; s. of Roberto Royas and Gilma Sánchez; m. Adele Ruíz 1963; one s. two d.; ed. Nat. Institute, Panama City, Univs. of Salamanca and Bologna; Gen. Sec. of the Gen. Solicitorship of the Repub. of Panama 1965–68; Prof. of Consular, Notariate and Mercantile Law, Univ. of Panama 1966–69, then Prof. of Criminal Law, research 1967–71; mem. Law Codification Comm. 1969; mem. drafting comms. for Penal Code 1970, Constitution 1972; mem. Legis. Comm. of Nat. Council of Legislation 1972–73; Gen. Sec. School of Lawyers of Panama 1973; mem. Morgan & Morgan (lawyers) 1968–; a negotiator of Torrijos-Carter Canal Treaties between Panama and U.S.A. 1977; mem. Org. Comm. of Democratic Revolutionary Party; Minister of Educ. 1973–78; Pres. of Panama 1978–82; Amb. to Spain 1982–85; Grand Cross, Alfonso X the Wise (Spain) 1977, Extraordinary Grand Cross, Vasco Núñez de Balboa (Panama) 1978; Grand Collar, Order of Manuel Amador Guerrero (Panama) 1978; Grand Collar, Order of Isabel la Católica (Spain) 1979; Grand Cross, Légion d'honneur 1979; Extraordinary Grand Cross, Order of Boyaca (Colombia) 1979; Dr. h.c. Univ. San Martín de Porres, Lima, Peru 1979; hon. mem. Spanish Law Soc. 1979. *Publications:* Philosophy of Law in Cathrein and Del Vecchio 1963, History of Spanish Commercial Code 1964, The Responsibility of the Vettore in Sea Shipping 1965, Extraterritoriality of the Panamanian Criminal Law 1967, Project of Criminal Code of Panama, The Participation of Labourers in the Utilities of Enterprises, Revolution or De Facto Government, Manager in the Enterprise 1970, Commentaries to the Law on Retiring Funds for Journalists 1971, The Technician and the Politician in Public Administration 1973, Popular Consultation of the Law 1972. *Leisure interests:* reading, writing, skiing, jogging. *Address:* Morgan and Morgan, P.O. Box 1824, Panama City 1, Panama. *Telephone:* (507) 63-8822 (Office).

ROZANOV, Yevgeny Grigoryevich; Russian architect; b. 8 Nov. 1925, Moscow; s. of Grigory Alexandrovich Rozanov and Anastasiya Nikolaevna Rozanova; m. Aida Iljenkova 1952; one s.; ed. Moscow Inst. of Architecture; mem. CPSU 1964–91; Dir. of Mezentsev Inst. of Standard and Experimental Design of Culture and Sports Activities 1970–85; major bldgs. designed in Essentuki, Vladivostok, Tashkent, Moscow (notably Dinamo Sports Centre); teacher of architecture at Moscow Architectural Inst. 1960–85, Prof. 1953–85; Chair. State Cttee. on Architecture and Town Planning 1987–91; Sec. U.S.S.R. Union of Architects 1981–92; People's Deputy of the U.S.S.R. 1989–91; mem. U.S.S.R. (now Russian) Acad. of Arts 1979; Pres. Int. Acad. of Architecture (Moscow br.) 1991–; Khamza Uzbek State Prize 1969, 1970, U.S.S.R. State Prize 1975, 1980; People's Architect of U.S.S.R. 1983. *Leisure interests:* painting, drawing, sculpture, music. *Address:* International Academy of Architecture, Bolshaya Dmitrovka 24, 103824 Moscow (Office); Kosygina Str. 9, Apt. 74, Moscow, Russia (Home). *Telephone:* (095) 229-72-61 (Office); 137-56-09 (Home). *Fax:* (095) 229-72-61.

ROZES, Simone, L. EN D.; French lawyer; b. 29 March 1920, Paris; d. of Léon Ludwig and Marcelle Cetre; m. Gabriel Rozes 1942; one s. one d.; ed. Lycée de Sèvres, Lycée de St.-Germain-en-Laye, Univ. of Paris, Ecole Libre des Sciences Politiques; trainee lawyer, Paris 1947–49; Surrogate Judge, Bourges 1949–50; attaché, Justice Dept. 1951–58; Admin. Chief, Cabinet of the Minister of Justice 1958–62, Judge 1962, Vice-Pres. Tribunal de Grande Instance de Paris 1969–73, Pres. 1976–81; Dir. Reformatory Educ. 1973–76; mem. UN Crime Prevention and Control Cttee. 1977; Advocate-Gen. European Court of Justice 1981–82; First Advocate Gen. 1982–84; Hon. Pres. Cour de Cassation 1984–88; Pres. Int. Soc. of Social Defence, Soc. of Comparative Law, Inst. Frederik R. Bull; mem. Bd. Alliance Française, AXA-UAP; mem. French section, French-British Council; Hon. LL.D. (Edin.), Grand Croix, Légion d'honneur; Officier, Ordre nat. du Mérite; Médaille de l'Educ. Surveillée, Médaille de l'Admin. Pénitentiaire, Commdr. Cross, Order of Merit (Fed. Repub. of Germany). *Leisure interest:* travelling. *Publication:* Le Juge et l'avocat (jtly.) 1992. *Address:* 2 Rue Villaret de Joyeuse, 75017 Paris, France. *Telephone:* (1) 43 80 16 67. *Fax:* (1) 47 63 42 90.

RÓŻEWICZ, Tadeusz; Polish poet and playwright; b. 9 Oct. 1921, Radomsko; ed. Jagiellonian Univ., Cracow; fmr. factory worker and teacher; mem. Art Acad. of Leipzig; Corresp. mem. Bavarian Acad. of Fine Arts 1982–, Acad. of Arts (G.D.R.); Dr. h.c. (Wrocław) 1991; State Prize for Poetry 1955, 1956, Literary Prize, City of Cracow 1959, Prize of Minister of Culture and Art 1962, State Prize 1st Class 1966, Austrian Nat. Prize for European Literature 1982, Prize of Minister of Foreign Affairs 1974, 1987, Golden Wreath Prize for poetry (Yugoslavia) 1987; Home Army Cross, London 1956, Alfred Jurzykowski Foundation Award, New York 1966, Medal of 30th Anniversary of People's Poland 1974, Order of Banner of Labour (2nd class) 1977, Great Cross of Order Polonia Restituta 1996. *Publications:* 15 vols. of poetry including Niepokój (Faces of Anxiety), Czerwona rękawiczka (The Red Glove), Czas który idzie (The Time Which Goes On), Równina (The Plain), Srebrny kłos (The Silver Ear), Rozmowa z księciem (Conversation with the Prince), Zielona róża (The Green Rose), Nic w płaszczu Prospera (Nothing in Prosper's Overcoat), Twarz (The Face), Duszyczka (A Little Soul), Poezje (Poetry) 1987, Słowo po słowie (Word by Word) 1994, Zawsze fragment (Always the Fragment) 1996. *Plays include:* Kartoteka (The Card Index), Grupa Laokoona (Laocoön's Group), Świadkowie albo nasza mała stabilizacja (The Witnesses), Akt przerywany (The Interrupted Act), Śmieszny staruszek (The Funny Man), Wyszedł z domu (Gone Out), Spaghetti i miecz (Spaghetti and the Sword), Maja córeczka (My Little Daughter), Stara kobieta wysiaduje (The Old Woman Broods), Na czworakach (On All Fours), Do piachu (Down to Sand), Białe małżeństwo (White Marriage), Odejście Głodomora (Starveling's Departure), Na powierzchni poematu i w środku: nowy wybór wierszy, Pułapka (The Trap), Próba rekonstrukcji. *Prose includes:* Tarcza z pajęczyny, Opowiadania wybrane (Selected Stories), Na powierzchni poematu (They Came to See a Poet) 1991, Płaskorzeźba (Bas-Relief) 1991, Nasz starszy brat 1992, Historia pięciu wierszy 1993. *Address:* ul. Januszewicka 13 m. 14, 53-136 Wrocław, Poland. *Telephone:* 67 71 38.

ROZHDESTVENSKY, Gennadiy Nikolayevich; Russian conductor; b. 4 May 1931, Moscow; s. of Nikolai Anosov and Natalia Rozhdestvenskaya; m. Viktoria Postnikova; one s.; ed. Moscow State Conservatoire; Asst. Conductor, Bolshoi Theatre 1951, Conductor 1956–60, Prin. Conductor 1965–70; Chief Conductor of U.S.S.R. Radio and TV Symphony Orchestra 1961–74; Chief Conductor Stockholm Philharmonia 1974–77, 1992–95, Moscow Chamber Opera 1974–83; Founder, Artistic Dir., Chief Conductor, State Symphony Orchestra of Ministry of Culture 1983–92; Prin. Conductor BBC Symphony Orchestra 1978–82, Vienna Symphony Orchestra 1980–83; has been guest conductor of numerous orchestras throughout Europe, America and Asia; Prof. of Conducting, Moscow State Conservatoire 1965–; Hon. mem. Swedish Royal Acad. 1975; Merited and People's Artist of the R.S.F.S.R. 1966, People's Artist of the U.S.S.R. 1976, Hero of Socialist Labour 1991, Lenin Prize 1970 and other decorations. *Publications:* The Fingering of Conducting 1974, Thoughts about Music 1975; numerous articles. *Leisure interest:* music. *Address:* c/o Victor Hochhauser Ltd., 4 Oak Hill Way, London N.W.3, England. *Telephone:* (095) 299-58-71 (Moscow).

ROZOV, Viktor Sergeevich; Russian dramatist; b. 21 Aug. 1913, Yaroslavl; s. of Sergey Rozov and Ekaterina Rozova; m. Nadezda Kozlova 1945; one s. one d.; ed. M. Gorki Literary Inst.; worked initially as actor in Kostroma and Moscow; served in Red Army 1941–45; Prof. Literary Inst.

1967–; U.S.S.R. State Prize 1967. *Works include:* plays: Her Friends 1949, Pages from Life 1953, In Search of Joy 1957, Uneven Fight 1960, Before Supper 1962, The Immortals (made into film The Cranes are Flying) 1957, A Traditional Meeting 1967, From Evening till Noon 1970, How Things Stand 1973, The Little Hog 1978 (banned, then performed Moscow 1979), The Capercaillie's Nest 1979, The Hidden Spring 1989, At Home 1989, The Journey in Different Directions (memoirs) 1987, Examining the Old Photographs (memoirs, vol. 2) 1995, Gofman 1996. *Leisure interest:* philately. *Address:* Chernyachovskogo Str. 4, Apt. 28, 125319 Moscow, Russia. *Telephone:* (095) 151-15-28.

ROZOVSKY, Mark Grigorievich; Russian theatre director and scriptwriter; b. 3 April 1937, Petropavlovsk; ed. Moscow Univ. Higher Scriptwriters' School; f. and managed 'Our Home' (amateur studio theatre) with fellow students of Moscow Univ. 1958–70; theatre officially disbanded 1970, revived in 1987 as professional co. U Nikitskikh Vorot; wrote 3 books on theatre, dir. versions of Karamzin, Kafka, Dostoevsky and others in Leningrad, Moscow and Riga 1970–87; Chief Dir. Moscow State Music Hall 1974–79; dir. Orpheus and Eurydice (rock-opera) 1975, and a musical adaptation of 'Strider' jointly with Georgii Tovstonogov (q.v.), by L. N. Tolstoy for Gorky Theatre, Leningrad; Theatre of Nations Prize Hamburg and Avignon 1979. *Other productions include:* Amadeus (P. Shaffer) for Moscow Arts Theatre; libretto for opera about Mayakovsky; work for TV including documentary on Meyerhold, Triumphal Square 1984; works for Gorky Theatre Leningrad and Theatre of Russian Drama, Riga, Latvia, and his own Studio Theatre, Moscow; Romances with Oblomov, Alexandrinsky Theatre, St. Petersburg 1992. *Address:* Theatre-Studio U Nikitskikh Vorot, Bolshaya Nikitskaya Str. 23/9, 103009 Moscow, Russia. *Telephone:* (095) 291-84-19.

RU XIN; Chinese philosopher; b. 1932, Wujiang Co., Jiangsu Prov.; joined CCP 1948; Deputy Dir. of Philosophy Inst., Acad. of Social Sciences 1979–; Exec. Vice-Pres. Acad. of Social Sciences 1984–; alt. mem. 14th CCP Cen. Cttee. 1992–; Vice-Chair. Academic Degrees Cttee., State Council 1995–; Pres. ROK Study Centre. *Address:* Academy of Social Sciences, 5 Jianguomen Nei Da Jie, Beijing 100732, People's Republic of China.

RUAN CHONGWU; Chinese politician; b. 1933, Huai'an Co., Hebei Prov.; ed. Moscow Auto-Eng. Inst.; Deputy Dir. Shanghai Materials Research Inst.; joined CCP 1952; Deputy Sec. Shanghai Municipal Scientific Workers' Asscn.; Science and Tech. Counsellor, Chinese Embassy in Bonn 1978; Vice-Mayor Shanghai 1983–85; Sec. CCP, Shanghai Municipality 1983–85; mem. 12th CCP Cen. Cttee. 1985–87, 13th Cen. Cttee. 1987–92, 14th Cen. Cttee. 1992–; Minister of Public Security 1985–87; Vice-Minister Science and Tech. Comm., State Council 1987–89, of Labour 1989–93; Sec. CPC 2nd Hainan Provincial Cttee. 1993–; Gov. of Hainan 1993. *Address:* c/o Office of the Governor, Haikou City, Hainan Province, 570003, People's Republic of China.

RUBBIA, Carlo; Italian professor of physics; b. 31 March 1934, Gorizia; s. of Silvio Rubbia and Bice Rubbia; m. Marisa Rubbia; one s. one d.; ed. high school, Pisa and Columbia and Rome Univs.; research physicist. CERN 1960, mem. Cttee. CERN 1985, Dir.-Gen. 1989; Prof. of Physics, Harvard Univ. 1972–88; mem. Papal Acad. of Science 1986–; Foreign mem. U.S.S.R. Acad. of Sciences; mem. American Acad. of Arts and Sciences, Accademia dei Lincei, European Acad. of Sciences; Nobel Prize for Physics 1984, Leslie Prize for exceptional achievements 1985, Jesolo d'Oro 1986. *Address:* c/o Organisation Européenne pour la Recherche Nucléaire (CERN), EP Division, 1211 Geneva 23, Switzerland.

RUBENS, Bernice Ruth, B.A.; British author; b. 26 July 1928, Cardiff; d. of Eli Reuben and Dorothy Reuben; m. Rudi Nassauer 1947; two d.; ed. Cardiff High School for Girls and Univ. of Wales, Cardiff; author and dir. of documentary films on Third World subjects; Fellow Univ. Coll., Cardiff; Hon. D.Lit. (Wales) 1991; Booker Prize 1970; American Blue Ribbon (documentary film) 1972. *Publications:* Set on Edge 1960, Madame Sontsatzka 1962, Mate in Three 1964, The Elected Member 1968, Sunday Best 1970, Go Tell the Lemming 1972, I Sent a Letter to my Love 1974, Ponsonby Post 1976, A Five-year Sentence 1978, Spring Sonata 1979, Birds of Passage 1980, Brothers 1982, Mr. Wakefield's Crusade 1985, Our Father 1987, Kingdom Come 1990, A Solitary Grief 1991, Mother Russia 1992, Autobiopsy 1993, Yesterday in the Back Lane (novel) 1995, The Waiting Game (novel) 1997, I, Dreyfus (novel) 1999. *Leisure interest:* playing 'cello. *Address:* 111 Canfield Gardens, London, NW6 3DY, England. *Telephone:* 0171-625 4845.

RUBENSTEIN, Edward, M.D.; American professor of medicine; b. 5 Dec. 1924, Cincinnati; s. of Louis Rubenstein and Nettie Nathan; m. Nancy Ellen Millman 1954; three s.; ed. Cincinnati Univ. Coll. of Medicine; Laboratory Asst., Dept. of Physiology, Cincinnati Univ. 1947; Intern, then Jr. Asst., then Sr. Asst. Resident in Medicine, Cincinnati Gen. Hosp. 1947–50, Medical Chief, Psychosomatic Service 1953–54; Research Fellow, May Inst., Cincinnati 1950; Chief of Medicine, U.S.A.F. Hosp., March Airforce Base 1950–52; Sr. Asst. Resident in Medicine, Barnes Hosp., St. Louis 1952–53; Chief, Clinical Physiology Unit, San Mateo Co. Gen. Hosp. 1955–63, Chief of Medicine 1960–70; Prof. of Medicine and Assoc. Dean of Postgraduate Medical Educ., Stanford Univ. School of Medicine 1971, now Emer; Ed.-in-Chief Scientific American 1978–94; mem. Inst. of Medicine of N.A.S.; Master, American Coll. of Physicians; T.V. documentary Being Human 1979; research in synchrotron radiation; Fellow A.A.A.S., Royal Soc. of Medicine; Kaiser Award, Albion Walter Hewlett Award 1993. *Publications:* Intensive Medical Care 1971, Handbook on Synchrotron Radiation Vol. 4 (Ed.), Introduction to Molecular Medicine (Ed.), Synchrotron Radiation in the Life Sciences (Ed.); numerous scientific papers. *Address:* Department of Medicine, Stanford Medical Centre, Stanford, CA 94305, U.S.A. *Telephone:* (415) 723 7188.

RUBENSTEIN, Howard Joseph, LL.B.; American public relations executive; b. 3 Feb. 1932, New York; s. of Samuel Rubenstein and Ada Sall; m. Amy Forman 1959; three s.; ed. Univ. of Pa., Harvard Univ. and St. John's Law School; admitted New York State Bar 1960; Pres. Howard J. Rubenstein Assocs. Inc. (public relations consultants), New York 1954–; numerous civic and other public appts. including Co-Chair. Holocaust Comm. 1993–; Bd. Dirs. Albert Einstein Coll. of Medicine 1997–; mem. Mayor's Business Advisory Council, New York 1996–, communications adviser Gov.'s Jerusalem 3000 Cttee. 1996–; Hon. LL.D. (St. John's Law School) 1990. *Address:* Howard J. Rubenstein Associates Inc., 1345 Avenue of the Americas, New York, NY 10105; 993 Fifth Ave, New York, NY 10028, U.S.A.

RUBIK, Ernő; Hungarian inventor, architect and designer; b. 13 July 1944, Budapest; s. of Ernő Rubik Sr. and Magdolna Szántó; m.; one s. two d.; ed. Technical Univ. and Acad. of Applied Arts, Budapest; consecutively Asst. Prof., then Assoc. Prof., Acad. of Applied Arts, Dir. of Postgraduate Studies 1983–86; Hon. Prof. Acad. of Crafts and Design, Budapest 1987; Inventor Rubik's Cube and other games and puzzles; Pres. Rubik Studio; Labour Order of Merit Gold Medal of the Hungarian People's Repub., Toy of the Year award 1981–82 of United Kingdom, Fed. Repub. of Germany, Italy, Sweden, Finland, France, U.S.A.; State Prize 1983; Pres. Hungarian Acad. of Eng. 1990–96. *Publications:* co-author and editor of A bűvös kocka (The Magic Cube) 1981, Rubik's Magic 1986, Rubik's Cubic Compendium 1987. *Leisure interests:* swimming, skiing, sailing. *Address:* Rubik Studio, 1122 Budapest, Városmajor u. 74, Hungary. *Telephone:* 1569–533.

RUBIKS, Alfreds; Latvian politician; b. 1935, Daugavpils, Latvia; ed. Riga Polytechnic; mem. CPSU 1958–91; started work as engineer at Riga Electro-Machinery Plant 1959–; komsomol and party work; Sec. Latvian Komsomol Cen. Cttee.; First Sec. of Leningradsky Region of Riga Regional CP Cttee. 1976–82; Minister of Local Industry for Latvian S.S.R. 1982–84; Chair. Exec. Cttee. Riga City Council of People's Deputies 1984–90; First Sec. Cen. Cttee. Latvian CP 1990–91; U.S.S.R. People's Deputy 1989–91; mem. CPSU Cen. Cttee. 1990–91; mem. CPSU Politburo July 1990–91; arrested by Latvian authorities Aug. 1991, accused of high treason; elected to Saeima (Parl.) 1993; sentenced to 8 years' imprisonment 1995; released 1997; mem. Saeima 1998–. *Address:* Saeima, Ecaba str. 11, 226-811 Riga, Latvia.

RUBIN, James P., B.A., M.I.A.; American politician; b. 1960, New York; m. Christiane Amanpour (q.v.) 1998; ed. Columbia Univ.; Research Dir. Arms Control Asscn., Washington D.C. 1985–89, also consultant to Senate Foreign Relations Cttee. on nuclear arms control issues; fmrly. staff mem. U.S. Senate Foreign Relations Cttee., Sr. Foreign Policy Adviser to Joseph R. Biden, Jr. (q.v.); Sr. Adviser and spokesman for U.S. Rep. to UN, Madeleine Albright (q.v.) 1993–96; Dir. of Foreign Policy and spokesman Clinton/Gore presidential campaign Aug.–Nov. 1996; Sr. Adviser to Sec. of State 1996–97; Asst. Sec. of State for Public Affairs 1997–; Democrat. *Address:* Department of State, Washington, DC 20038, U.S.A.

RUBIN, Louis Decimus, Jr., PH.D.; American writer, professor of English and publisher; b. 19 Nov. 1923, Charleston, S.C.; s. of Louis Decimus Rubin, Sr. and Janet Weinstein Rubin; m. Eva Maryette Redfield 1951; two s.; ed. High School of Charleston, Coll. of Charleston, Univ. of Richmond and Johns Hopkins Univ.; U.S. Army 1943–46; instructor in English Johns Hopkins Univ. 1948–54; Exec. Sec. American Studies Asscn. 1954–56 (also fmr. Vice-Pres.); Assoc. Ed. News Leader, Richmond, Va. 1956–57; Assoc. Prof. of English, Hollins Coll., Prof., Chair. of Dept. 1960–67, Prof. of English Univ. of N.C. 1967–73, Univ. Distinguished Prof. 1973-89, Prof. Emer. 1989–; Visiting Prof. La. State Univ., Univ. of Calif. at Santa Barbara, Harvard Univ.; lecturer, Aix-Marseille at Nice, Kyoto Summer American Studies Seminars; USICA, Austria, Germany; Ed. Southern Literary Studies Series, Louisiana State Univ. Press 1965; Co-Ed. Southern Literary Journal 1968–89; Editorial Dir. Algonquin Books, Chapel Hill 1982–91, Advisor 1991–; fmr. Pres. Soc. for Study of Southern Literature; fmr. Chair. American Literature Section, Modern Language Asscn.; mem. S.C. Acad. of Authors, Fellowship of Southern Writers; Hon. D.Litt. (Richmond, Clemson, Coll. of Charleston, Univ. of the South). *Publications:* author: Thomas Wolfe: The Weather of His Youth 1955, No Place on Earth 1959, The Faraway Country 1964, The Golden Weather (novel) 1961, The Curious Death of the Novel 1967, The Teller in the Tale 1967, George W. Cable 1969, The Writer in the South 1972, William Elliott Shoots a Bear 1975, The Wary Fugitives 1978, Surfaces of a Diamond (novel) 1981, A Gallery of Southerners 1982, The Even-Tempered Angler 1984; editor: Southern Renascence 1953, Idea of an American Novel 1961, South 1961, Comic Imagination in American Literature 1973, The Literary South 1979, American South 1980, The History of Southern Literature 1985, An Apple for My Teacher 1986, The Edge of the Swamp: a study in the Literature and Society of the Old South 1989, Algonquin Literary Quiz Book 1990, The Mockingbird in the Gum Tree 1991, Small Craft Advisory 1991, The Heat of the Sun 1995, Babe Ruth's Ghost 1996. *Leisure interests:* baseball, classical music, reading. *Address:* 702 Gimghoul Road, Chapel Hill, NC 27514, U.S.A. (Home).

RUBIN, Robert; American business executive, lawyer and government official; b. 29 Aug. 1938, New York; s. of Alexander Rubin and Sylvia (née Seiderman) Rubin; m. Judith L. Oxenberg 1963; two s.; ed. Harvard Univ.,

London School of Econs., Yale Law School; lawyer Cleary, Gottlieb, Steen & Hamilton New York 1964–66; joined Goldman, Sachs 1966, Vice-Chair. & Co-C.O.O. 1987–90, Co-Chair. 1990–92; Chair. New York Host Cttee. 1992 Democratic Convention; Asst. to Pres. Clinton (q.v.) for Econ. Policy 1993–95; Sec. of Treasury Jan. 1995–99; Hon. D.Hum.Litt. (Yeshiva Univ.) 1996; Nat. Asscn. of Christians and Jews Award 1977, Columbia Business School Award 1996, Euromoney Magazine's Finance Minister of the Year Award 1996, Medal for High Civic Service, Citizens' Budget Comm. 1997, Foreign Policy Asscn. Medal 1998, Jefferson Award, American Inst. for Public Service 1998, Award of Merit, Yale Univ. 1998, Paul Tsongas Award 1998, Global Leadership Award, UN Asscn. 1998. *Leisure interest:* fly fishing. *Address:* c/o Department of the Treasury, 1500 Pennsylvania Avenue, NW, Washington, DC 20220, U.S.A.

RUBIN, Vera Cooper, PH.D.; American astronomer; b. 23 July 1928, Philadelphia; d. of Philip Cooper and Rose Applebaum Cooper; m. Robert J. Rubin 1948; three s. one d.; ed. Vassar Coll., Cornell Univ., Georgetown Univ.; Research Assoc. to Asst. Prof. Georgetown Univ. 1955–65; mem. Staff Dept. of Terrestrial Magnetism, Carnegie Inst., Wash. 1965–; Distinguished Visiting Astronomer, Cerro Tololo Inter-American Observatory 1978, Chancellor's Distinguished Prof. Astronomy Univ. of Calif., Berkeley 1981; Pres.'s Distinguished Visitor, Vassar Coll. 1987; B. Tinsley Visiting Prof., Univ. of Texas 1988; Oort Visiting Prof., Univ. of Leiden 1995; has observed at Kitt Peak Nat. Observatory, Lowell, Palomar, McDonald, Las Campanas, Chile observatories; Assoc. Ed. Astronomical Journal 1972–77, Astrophysical Journal of Letters 1977–82; mem. Council American Astronomical Soc. 1977–80; mem. Editorial Bd. Science Magazine 1979–87; mem. Council Smithsonian Inst. 1979–85, Space Telescope Science Inst. 1990–92; Pres. Galaxy Comm. Int. Astronomical Union 1982–85; mem. N.A.S., American Acad. of Arts and Sciences, American Philosophical Soc., Pres's Cttee. to select recipients of Nat. Medal of Science; Weizmann Women and Science Award 1996; Gold Medal Royal Astronomical Soc., London 1996, Helen Hogg Prize, Canadian Astronomical Soc. 1997; Hon. D.Sc. (Creighton Univ.) 1978, (Harvard Univ.) 1988, (Yale Univ.) 1990, (Williams Coll.) 1993. *Publications:* over 150 scientific papers on the dynamics of galaxies in specialist journals. *Leisure interests:* family, garden, hiking, travel. *Address:* Department of Terrestrial Magnetism, Carnegie Institution of Washington, 5241 Broad Branch Road, N.W., Washington, DC 20015, U.S.A.

RUBIN, William, PH.D.; American art historian and curator; b. 11 Aug. 1927, New York; ed. Univ. of Paris, Columbia Univ.; Prof. of Art History Sarah Lawrence Coll. 1952–67, City Univ. of New York 1960–68; Adjunct Prof. Art History, Inst. of Fine Arts, New York Univ. 1968–; Chief Curator Painting and Sculpture, Museum of Modern Art, New York 1968, Dir. Painting and Sculpture 1973–88, Dir. Emer. 1988–; exhbns. arranged include: Dada, Surrealism and their Heritage 1968, New American Painting and Sculpture 1969, Stella 1970, Miro 1973, Picasso: A Retrospective 1980, Giorgio DeChirico 1982, Primitivism in 20th Century Art 1984, Frank Stella 1970–87 1987, Picasso and Braque: Pioneering Cubism 1989, Ad Reinhardt 1991; American Ed. Art Int. Magazine 1959–64; Trustee Sarah Lawrence Coll. 1980–86; Officier Légion d'honneur 1991, Officier des Arts et Lettres (Paris) 1979. *Publications:* Matta 1957, Modern Sacred Art and the Church of Assy 1961, Dada, Surrealism and their Heritage 1966, Dada and Surrealist Art 1969, Frank Stella 1970, Picasso in the Collection of the Museum of Modern Art 1973, The Paintings of Gerald Murphy 1974, Anthony Caro 1975, (with Carolyn Lanchner) André Masson 1976, Paris-New York: Situation de l'Art 1978; ed. (with Carolyn Lanchner) Cézanne: The Late Work 1977, Picasso: A Retrospective 1980, Giorgio DeChirico 1982, Picasso and Portraiture: Representation and Transformation 1996.

RUBINSTEIN, Amnon, PH.D.; Israeli politician, author and professor of law; b. 5 Sept. 1931, Tel. Aviv; s. of Aaron Rubinstein and Rachel (Vitozny) Rubinstein; m. Ronny Havatgeleth 1959; one s. one d.; ed. Hebrew Univ., London School of Econs.; mil. service Israeli Defence Forces; fmr. Dean Faculty of Law and Prof. of Law, Tel Aviv Univ.; mem. Knesset (Parl.) 1977–; mem. Constitution Cttee.; Minister of Communications 1984–87, of Energy and Infrastructure and Science and Tech. 1992–93, of Educ. and Culture 1993–96; fmr. Chair. Shinui Party. *Publications:* Jurisdiction and Illegality 1965, The Zionist Dream Revisited 1985 (French trans. Le Rêve et l'histoire), The Constitutional Law of Israel (4th edn.) 1991. *Leisure interests:* music, drama, swimming. *Address:* Shinui, 19 Rehov Levontin, Tel Aviv 65112 (Office); 13 Yacov Street, Tel Aviv 69015, Israel. *Telephone:* (03) 495454 (Home).

RUCKELSHAUS, William Doyle; American government official; b. 24 July 1932, Indianapolis, Ind.; s. of John K. and Marion (Doyle) Covington Ruckelshaus; m. Jill E. Strickland 1962; one s. four d.; ed. Portsmouth Priory School, R.I. and Princeton and Harvard Univs.; served with U.S. Army 1953–55; admitted to Indiana Bar 1960; attorney with Ruckelshaus, Bobbit & O'Connor 1960–68; Partner Ruckelshaus, Beveridge, Fairbanks & Diamond (fmrly. Ruckelshaus, Beveridge & Fairbanks), Sr. Partner 1974–76; Deputy Attorney-Gen. Ind. 1960–65; Minority Attorney, Ind. State Senate 1965–67; mem. Ind. House of Reps. 1967–69; Asst. Attorney-Gen., U.S. Civil Div., Dept. of Justice 1969–70; Dir. Environmental Protection Agency 1970–73; Acting Dir. FBI 1973; Deputy Attorney-Gen. 1973; Sr. Vice-Pres. Weyerhaeuser Co. 1976–83; Dir. Environmental Protection Agency 1983–84; mem. firm Perkins Coie, Seattle 1985–88; Chair. C.E.O. Browning-Ferris Industries Inc., Houston 1988–95; f., Prin. Madrone Investment Group 1996–; fmr. mem. Bd. Dirs. Cummins Engine Co., Inc., Peabody Int. Corpn., Church and Dwight Co. Inc., Nordstrom, Inc.; fmr. Chair. Bd. Geothermal Kinetics Inc., Trustees of Urban Inst.; mem. Bd. American Paper Inst., Council on Foreign Relations, Twentieth Century Fund; Trustee, Pacific Science Center Foundation, Seattle Chamber of Commerce, The Conservation Foundation, Seattle Art Museum; mem. Public Interest Advisory Cttee. Harvard Univ. Medical Project, Bd. of Overseers, Harvard J.F.K. School of Govt., Bd. of Regents, Seattle, Univ.; mem. several U.S. bar asscns. *Publication:* Reapportionment—A Continuing Problem 1963. *Leisure interests:* tennis, fishing, reading. *Address:* Madrone Investment Group, 1000 2nd Avenue, Suite 3700, Seattle, WA 98104, U.S.A.

RUDDEN, Bernard (Anthony), LL.D., D.C.L., F.B.A.; British professor of law; b. 21 Aug. 1933, Carlisle; s. of John Rudden and Kathleen Rudden; m. Nancy Campbell 1957; three s. one d.; ed. City of Norwich School and St. John's Coll. Cambridge; Fellow and Tutor, Oriel Coll. Oxford 1965–79; Prof. of Comparative Law, Univ. of Oxford and Fellow, Brasenose Coll. Oxford 1979–; Hon. LL.D. (McGill) 1979. *Publications:* Soviet Insurance Law 1966, Law of Property (co-author) 1982, The New River 1985, Basic Community Cases 1987, Source-Book on French Law (co-author) 1991, Basic Community Law (co-author) 1996. *Address:* Brasenose College, Oxford, OX1 4AJ, England. *Telephone:* (01865) 277865. *Fax:* (01865) 277822.

RUDDLE, Francis Hugh, PH.D.; American professor of biology and human genetics; b. 19 Aug. 1929, West New York, N.J.; s. of Thomas Hugh Ruddle and Mary Henley (Rodda); m. Nancy Marion Hartman 1964; two d.; ed. Wayne State Univ., Detroit and Univ. of California, Berkeley; Research Assoc., Child Research Center of Mich., Detroit 1953–56; Nat. Insts. of Health Postdoctoral Fellow, Dept. of Biochemistry, Univ. of Glasgow, Scotland 1960–61; Asst. Prof., Yale Univ. 1961–67, Assoc. Prof. 1967–72, Prof. of Biology and Human Genetics 1972–, Chair. Dept. of Biology 1977–83, 1988–, Ross Granville Harrison Prof. of Biology 1983–88, Sterling Prof. of Biology 1988–; Pres. American Soc. of Human Genetics 1985; Pres. American Soc. of Cell Biology 1986; Fellow A.A.A.S; mem. N.A.S., American Genetic Asscn., American Soc. of Biological Chemists, American Soc. of Zoologists, Genetics Soc. of America. *Leisure interest:* boating. *Address:* Department of Biology, Yale University, Kline Biology Tower, P.O. Box 6666, New Haven, CT 06511-8112, U.S.A. *Telephone:* (203) 436-0418.

RUDDOCK, Joan Mary, M.P., B.SC., A.R.C.S.; British politician; b. 28 Dec. 1943; d. of Ken Anthony and Eileen Anthony; m. Dr. Keith Ruddock 1963 (died 1996); ed. Pontypool Grammar School for Girls and Imperial Coll. London; worked for Shelter (nat. campaign for the homeless) 1968–73; Dir. Oxford Housing Aid Centre 1973–77; Special Programmes Officer with unemployed young people, Manpower Services Comm. 1977–79; Man., Reading Citizens Advice Bureau 1979–87; Chair. Campaign for Nuclear Disarmament (CND) 1981–85, Vice-Chair. 1985–86; M.P. for Deptford 1987–97, for Lewisham Deptford 1997–; mem. Select Cttee. on Televising House of Commons; mem. British Del., Council of Europe 1988–89; Shadow Spokesperson on Transport 1989–92, on Home Affairs 1992–94, on Environmental Protection 1994–; Parl. Under Sec. of State for Women 1997–98; Hon. Fellow Goldsmith's Coll., Univ. of London 1996; Frank Cousins Peace Award 1984; Labour. *Publications:* CND Scrapbook 1987, The CND Story (contrib.) 1983, Voices for One World (contrib.) 1988. *Address:* House of Commons, Westminster, London, SW1A 0AA, England. *Telephone:* 0171-219 4513. *Fax:* 0171-219 6045.

RUDENSTINE, Neil Leon, PH.D.; American university administrator; b. 21 Jan. 1935, Ossining, New York; s. of Harry Rudenstine and Mae Rudenstine; m. Angelica Zander 1960; one s. two d.; ed. Princeton Univ., Oxford Univ., Harvard Univ.; instructor. English Dept., Harvard Univ. 1964–66, Asst. Prof. 1966–68, Prof. of English, Pres. Harvard Univ. 1991–; Assoc. Prof. of English, Princeton Univ. 1968–73, Dean of Students 1968–72, Prof. of English 1973–88, Dean of Coll. 1972–77, Provost 1977–88; Exec. Vice-Pres. Andrew W. Mellon Foundation, New York 1988–91; Hon. Fellow New Coll., Oxford Univ.; Fellow American Acad. of Arts and Sciences. *Publications:* Sidney's Poetic Development 1967, English Poetic Satire: Wyatt to Byron (with George Rousseau) 1972, In Pursuit of the PhD (with William G. Bowen) 1992. *Address:* Office of the President, Harvard University, Cambridge, MA 02138; 33 Elmwood Avenue, Cambridge, MA 02138, U.S.A. (Home).

RUDHOLM, Sten, LL.B.; Swedish lawyer; b. 27 April 1918, Karlstad; s. of Henning Rudholm and Lajla Nystrom; m. Eva Adler-Anderson 1944; three d.; ed. legal studies; Asst. Judge, Svea Court of Appeal 1954, Judge 1961, Attorney-Gen. 1962–67, Pres. Svea Court of Appeal 1967–83; Marshal of the Realm 1983–86; Chancellor, Royal Swedish Order 1982–96; mem. Swedish Acad.; LL.D. h.c. *Leisure interests:* literature, tennis, skiing. *Address:* Udden Pl. 2510, 76294 Rimbo, Sweden. *Telephone:* 08-51294035.

RUDIN, Scott; American film and theatre producer; b. 14 July 1958, New York; production asst., Asst. to theatre producers Kermit Bloomgarden and Robert Whitehead; Casting Dir., Producer with Edgar Scherick; Exec. Vice-Pres. Production 20th Century Fox 1984–86, Pres. Production 1986–87; f. Scott Rudin Productions 1990. *Films:* He Makes Me Feel Like Dancing 1982 (Outstanding Children's Program Emmy award 1982, Feature Documentary Acad. Award 1982), Mrs Soffel 1984, Flatliners 1990, Pacific Heights 1990, Regarding Henry 1991, Little Man Tate 1991, The Addams Family 1991,

Sister Act 1992, Jennifer Eight 1992, Life With Mikey 1993, The Firm 1993, Searching for Bobby Fischer 1993, Sister Act 2 1993, Addams Family Values 1993, I.Q. 1994, Nobody's Fool 1994, Sabrina 1995, Clueless 1995, Up Close and Personal 1996, Ransom 1996, Marvin's Room 1996, The First Wives' Club 1996, In and Out 1997, Twilight 1998, The Truman Show 1998, A Civil Action 1998. *Theatre:* Passion 1994 (Tony Award Best Musical 1994), Indiscretions 1995, Hamlet 1995, Seven Guitars 1995, A Funny Thing Happened on the Way to the Forum 1996, Skylight 1997, On the Town (New York Shakespeare Festival) 1997, The Chairs 1998, The Judas Kiss 1998, Closer (London) 1998. *Address:* Scott Rudin Production, 120 West 45th Street, New York, NY 10036; c/o William Morris Agency, 151 El Camino Drive, Beverly Hills, CA 90212, U.S.A.

RUDINI, Gen.; Indonesian army officer; b. 15 Dec. 1929, Malang, E. Java; s. of R. I. Poespohandojo and R. A. Koesbandijah; m. Oddyana Rudini 1959; one s. two d.; ed. Breda Mil. Acad., Netherlands, reaching rank of Second Lieut.; Commdr. Kostrad Infantry/Airborne Brigade 1972–73; Commdr. Indonesian contingent of UN Peace-keeping Force in Middle East 1973–76; Commdr. Kostrad Airborne Combat 1976–81; Commdr. N. and Cen. Sulawesi Mil. Region, Manado 1981, later Commdr. of Kostrad; Chief of Staff, Indonesian Army 1983–88; Minister of Home Affairs 1988–93, concurrently Chair. of the Election Cttee. *Leisure interests:* sport, music. *Address:* c/o Ministry of Home Affairs, Jalan Merdeka Utara 7, Jakarta Pusat, Indonesia.

RUDMAN, Michael P.; American publishing executive; b. 1950, New York; ed. Michigan and New York Univs.; Pres. Nat. Learning Corpn., also C.E.O., Dir.; Pres. Delaney Books Inc., also C.E.O., Dir.; Pres. Frank Merriwell Inc., also C.E.O., Dir.; mem. Asscn. of American Publrs. *Address:* National Learning Corporation, 212 Michael Drive, Syosset, NY 11791, U.S.A.

RUDMAN, Warren Bruce, LL.B.; American politician and lawyer; b. 18 May 1930, Boston, Mass.; s. of Edward G. and Theresa (née Levenson) Rudman; m. Shirley Wahl 1952; one s. two d.; ed. Valley Forge Mil. Acad., Syracuse Univ., Boston Coll. Law School; rank of Capt. U.S. Army 1952–54; admitted to N.H. Bar, mem. law firm Stein, Rudman and Gormley 1960–69; Attorney-Gen. N.H., Concord 1970–76; Partner Sheehan, Phinney, Bass and Green 1976–80; Fiscal Agent Gov. Walter Peterson's campaign 1968, Special Counsel to Gov. Peterson 1969–70; Republican Senator from N.H. 1980–92; co-founder Concord Coalition 1992–; Deputy Chair. Fed. Reserve Bank of Boston 1993; partner Paul, Weiss, Rifkind, Wharton and Garrison 1993–; Founder, Chair. Bd. Trustees Daniel Webster Jr. Coll., New England Aeronautical Inst. 1965–81; Sr. Advisory Cttee., John F. Kennedy School of Govt., Harvard Univ.; dir. Chubb Corpn. 1993–, Raytheon Corpn. 1993–, Dreyfus Corpn. 1993–; mem. American Legion, Sub-Cttee. on Defence Co-operation of the North Atlantic Ass., Sec. of State's Advisory Panel on Overseas Security; Bronze Star. *Address:* Paul Weiss Rifkind Wharton & Garrison, 1615 L Street, N.W., Suite 1300, Washington, DC 20036, U.S.A. (Office).

RUDOWSKI, Witold Janusz; Polish professor of surgery; b. 17 July 1918, Piotrków Trybunalski; s. of Maksymilian Rudowski and Stefania Rudowska; m. Irena Rudowska 1940; two s. one d.; ed. Clandestine Univ., Warsaw 1943; Assoc. Prof. of Surgery, Warsaw Univ. 1954–61, Extraordinary Prof. 1961–70, Ordinary Prof. 1971–; Consultant Surgeon and Sr. Research Worker, Madame M. Curie Cancer Insts. in Warsaw 1948–64; Dir. and Head, Dept. of Surgery, Inst. of Haematology and Blood Transfusion, Warsaw 1964–88; Deputy Head Dept. of Medical Sciences of Polish Acad. of Sciences (PAN) 1973–90; Chair. Scientific Council to Minister of Health and Social Welfare 1970–75, mem. Presidium 1979–87; Expert WHO 1965–, mem. and First Vice-Chair. Exec. Bd. 1985–88; Vice-Pres. Int. Fed. of Surgical Colls., Pres. 1975–78; Deputy Chair. Polish Haematological Soc. 1966–88; Pres. Polish Surgeons' Soc. 1980–83; Corresp. mem. Polish Acad. of Sciences 1973–83, mem. 1983–; Hon. mem. N. Pacific Surgical Asscn. 1974, Italian Soc. of Surgical Research 1975, W. African Coll. of Surgeons 1975, Czechoslovakian Soc. of Physicians, Surgical Section; Hon. Fellow, American Coll. of Surgeons 1971, Royal Coll. of Surgeons of Edin. 1972, Royal Coll. of Surgeons of England 1973, Royal Coll. of Physicians and Surgeons of Canada 1974, Coll. of Dutch Surgeons, Swedish Surgical Soc., Royal Coll. of Surgeons in Ireland 1978, Royal Australasian Coll. of Surgeons 1979, Swiss Surgical Soc. 1983, German Surgical Asscn. 1984, Italian Surgical Asscn. 1983, Coll. of Medicine of S.A. 1990, Int. Soc. of Surgeons 1993; Dr. h.c. (Poznań Medical Acad.) 1975, (Warsaw Medical Acad.) 1979, (Łódź Medical Acad.) 1980, (Wrocław Medical Acad.) 1982, (Edin. Univ.) 1983, (Jagiellonian Medical Acad.) 1989, (Białystok Medical Acad.) 1990, (Lublin Medical Acad.) 1993, State Prize (2nd class) 1972, State Prize (2nd class, collective) 1978, Hon. Meritorious Physician of People's Poland 1980, Award of Int. Surgeons' Soc., Toronto, Canada 1989; Silver Cross of Virtuti Militari 1944, Gold Cross of Merit 1956, Commdr. Cross Order of Polonia Restituta 1979, with Star 1994, Medal for Warsaw 1970, Krzyż Armii Krajowej (Home Army Cross). *Publications:* Burn-Therapy and Research 1976, Disorders of Hemostasis in Surgery 1978, Surgery of the Spleen 1987; and 500 papers in Polish and other languages on cancer, clinical pathophysiology, burns and blood transfusion. *Leisure interests:* literature, music, photography. *Address:* al. Armii Ludowej 17 m. 1, 00-632 Warsaw, Poland. *Telephone:* (22) 625 44 39.

RUDZIŃSKI, Witold; Polish composer and musicologist; b. 14 March 1913, Siebież (now in Russia); s. of Henryk Rudziński and Maria Rudzińska; m. Nina Rewieńska 1958; one s. three d.; ed. Wilno Univ. and Wilno Conservatoire and Paris; Prof. Wilno Conservatoire 1939–42, Łódź Conservatoire 1945–47, Extraordinary Prof. 1964, Ordinary Prof. 1983; Dir. Dept. of Music, Ministry of Culture 1947–48; Ed. Muzyka 1951–54; Prof. State Higher School of Music, Warsaw 1957–83; Chief Dept. of Theory of Music; Pres. Warsaw Branch of Polish Composers Union 1963–69, 1977–83; Dr. h.c. (Acad. of Music, Warsaw) 1998; Officer and Commdr., Cross of Polonia Restituta; Special Award, Monaco 1963, First Prize, Edward Grieg Competition, 1965, Minister of Culture and Art Prize, 1st Class 1976, 1978, 1981, Prize of Chair. Council of Ministers 1984, etc. *Works include:* Piano Concerto, two Symphonies, Symphonic Suite, two String Quartets, two Sonatas for piano and violin, cantata, flute quartet, song cycle, chamber works for piano, flute, 'cello, woodwind and percussion instruments; Operas: Janko Muzykant, Komendant Paryża (Commander of Paris), Odprawa posłów greckich (Dismissal of the Greek Envoys), Sulamita (Sulamith), Chłopi (The Peasants); opera for children: The Ring and the Rose; music poem Dach świata (Roof of the World) for recitative and orchestra; Gaude Mater Polonia for solo voice, choir, recitative and orchestra; Lipce (oratorio), Hebraic songs, Litany for Holy Mother of Ostra Brama (Wilno), In the Circle of Psalms (oratorio), Kaszuby wedding songs for mixed choir, Passacaglia for violin, Divertimento rustico for orchestra and violin, Triple Concerto for Trumpet, Two Cors, percussion and string orchestra 1998. *Publications:* Muzyka dla wszystkich (Music for Everybody), monographs on Moniuszko and Bartok, studies in musical rhythm, Music of Our Century. *Leisure interests:* history, biography, linguistics. *Address:* ul. Narbutta 50 m. 6, 02-541 Warsaw, Poland. *Telephone:* (22) 49 34 77.

RUELLE, David Pierre, PH.D.; French (b. Belgian) research mathematician and physicist; b. 20 Aug. 1935, Ghent, Belgium; s. of Pierre Ruelle and Marguerite de Jonge; m. Janine Lardinois 1960; one s. two d.; ed. high school at Mons and Free Univ. of Brussels; Research Asst. and Privatdozent, Eidgenössische Technische Hochschule, Zürich 1960–62; mem. Inst. for Advanced Study, Princeton 1962–64; Prof. Inst. des Hautes Etudes Scientifiques, Bures-sur-Yvette 1964–; mem. Acad. des Sciences 1985; Foreign Hon. mem. American Acad. of Arts and Sciences 1992; mem. Acad. Europaea 1993; Dannie Heineman Prize 1985; Boltzmann Medal 1986; Chevalier, Légion d'honneur 1989. *Publications:* Statistical Mechanics: Rigorous Results 1969, Thermodynamic Formalism 1978, Elements of Differentiable Dynamics and Bifurcation Theory 1989, Chance and Chaos 1991. *Address:* I.H.E.S., 91440 Bures-sur-Yvette (Office); 1 avenue Charles-Comar, 91440 Bures-sur-Yvette, France (Home). *Telephone:* (1) 60-92-66-37 (Office).

RÚFUS, Milan; Slovak poet, literary historian and essayist; b. 10 Dec. 1928, Závazná Poruba; m.; one d.; ed. Comenius Univ., Bratislava; at Inst. of Slovak Language and Literature Faculty of Philosophy Comenius Univ. 1952–89; Assoc. Prof., lecturer in Slovak Language and Literature Inst. Universitario, Naples 1971–72; State Prize 1970, Slovak Nat. Prize 1982; Tomáš Garrigue Masaryk Order 1990; Hon. Litt.D. (Bratislava); L'udovít Štúr Order (1st Class) 1993; World Congress of Slovaks Nat. Prize; Nat. Literature Prize 1996; mem. Club of Ind. Writers of Slovakia. *Publications:* Until We Have Matured 1956, Bells 1968, A Triptych 1969, People of the Mountains 1969, The Table of the Poor 1972, The Cradle 1972; A Boy is Drawing a Rainbow 1974, Music of Forms (accompanied by paintings of L. Fulla) 1977, Forest (accompanied by photographs of M. Martincek) 1978, Ode to Joy 1981, Severe Bread 1987, A Late Self-Portrait 1993, Reading from Destiny 1996, Dragonfly 1998; for children: Book of Fairy Tales 1975, Saturday Evenings 1979, A Small Well 1985, Silent Fern 1990, Small Prayers 1990, Small Prayers for a Child 1995; essays: Man, Time and Work 1968, Four Epistles to People 1969, On Literature 1974, And What is a Poem 1978, Epistles Old and New 1997. *Address:* Fialkové údolie 31, 811 01 Bratislava, Slovakia.

RUGARLI, Giampaolo; Italian author; b. 5 Dec. 1932, Naples; s. of Mirko Rugarli and Rubina De Marco; m. Maria Pulci 1985; three c.; ed. legal studies; bank dir. since 1972; a dir. of Cariplo 1981–85; contrib. Messaggero and Corriere della Sera and other reviews; Premio Bagutta Opera Prima 1987; Premio Capri 1990. *Publications:* Il Superlativo assoluto, La troga, Il nido di ghiaccio, Diario di un uomo a disagio, Andromeda e la notte, L'orrore che mi hai dato 1987, Una montagna australiana 1992, Per i pesci non è un problema 1992, I camini delle fate 1993, Il manuale del romanziere (The Novelist's Handbook) 1993, L'infinito, forse 1995. *Leisure interest:* gardening. *Address:* Via Colle di Giano 62, Olevano Romano 00035, Italy. *Telephone:* 06/9564518.

RUGGIERO, Renato; Italian diplomatist and politician; b. 9 April 1930, Naples; ed. Univ. of Naples; entered Diplomatic Service 1955; served São Paulo, Moscow, Washington; Counsellor, Belgrade 1966; Counsellor for Social Affairs, Perm. Mission to European Communities 1969; Chef de Cabinet Pres. of Comm. of European Communities 1970–73, Dir.-Gen. of Regional Policy 1973–77, Comm. Spokesperson 1977; Co-ordinator EEC Dept., Ministry of Foreign Affairs 1978; Diplomatic Counsellor of Pres. of Council 1979; Chef de Cabinet of Minister of Foreign Affairs 1979; Perm. Rep. to European Communities 1980–84; Dir.-Gen. for Econ. Affairs, Ministry of Foreign Affairs 1984–85; Sec.-Gen. Ministry of Foreign Affairs 1985–87, Minister of Foreign Trade 1987–91; Dir.-Gen. World Trade Org. 1995–99; Personal Rep. of Pres. of Council, Econ. Summits Bonn 1978, Tokyo 1979, Venice 1980, London 1984, Bonn 1985, Tokyo 1986, Venice 1987; Pres. Exec. Cttee. OECD; Kt., Grand Cross, Order of Merit. *Address:* c/o World Trade

Organization, Centre William Rappard, 154 rue de Lausanne, 1211 Geneva, Switzerland.

RÜHE, Volker; German politician; b. 25 Sept. 1942, Hamburg; m. Anne Rühe 1968; two s. one d.; ed. Univ. of Hamburg; fmr. teacher; mem. Hamburg City Council 1970–76; mem. Bundestag 1976–; Deputy Chair. CDU/CSU Parl. Group 1982–89; Sec. Gen. CDU 1989–92; Minister of Defence 1992–98. *Address:* c/o Ministry of Defence, Hardthöhe, Postfach 1328, Germany.

RUIJGH, Cornelis Jord, D.PHIL.; Netherlands professor of Greek; b. 28 Nov. 1930, Amsterdam; s. of Jord Ruijgh and Trijntje Swart; ed. Univ. of Amsterdam and Ecole Pratique des Hautes Etudes, Paris; Asst. in Greek Philology, Univ. of Amsterdam 1954–66, lecturer, Ancient Greek Language 1966–69, Prof. of Ancient Greek Language, Dialectology and Mycenology 1969–95; mem. Royal Netherlands Acad.; mem. Int. Perm. Cttee. of Mycenaean Studies 1970–; Prix Zographos; Michael Ventris Memorial Award. *Publications:* L'élément achéen dans la langue épique, 1957, Etudes sur la grammaire et le vocabulaire du grec mycénien 1967, Autour de *'te* épique' 1971, Scripta Minora I 1991, Scripta Minora II 1996 etc. *Leisure interest:* music. *Address:* Keizersgracht 800, 1017 ED Amsterdam, Netherlands. *Telephone:* (020) 6247995.

RUITENBERG, Elis Joost, PH.D.; Netherlands professor of immunology; b. 24 May 1937, Amersfoort; s. of E. J. Ruitenberg and D. H. van Mechelen; m. Christiane Friederike Ambagtsheer 1963; three d.; ed. Univ. of Utrecht; veterinarian, Lab. Zoonoses, Nat. Inst. of Public Health, Bilthoven 1964–, Head Pathology Lab. 1970, Dir. Div. of Immunology 1979, Vaccine Production 1980; Dir. Div. of Microbiology and Immunology, Nat. Inst. of Public and Environmental Protection, Bilthoven 1984, Deputy Dir.-Gen. 1986; Prof. of Veterinary Immunology, Univ. of Utrecht 1984–; Gen. and Scientific Dir. Sanquin Blood Supply Foundation (CLB) 1989–; Chair. Netherlands-Vietnam Medical Cttee. 1998–; Visiting Prof., Nat. School of Public Health, Madrid, Spain 1987; mem. numerous advisory cttees. including Advisory Council for Devt. Research; mem. Royal Netherlands Acad. of Arts and Sciences; Schimmel Viruly Award 1976, Annual Award, Nat. Journal of Veterinary Medicine 1977, Award Medical Acad., Poznan, Poland, Kt., Order of Netherlands Lion 1988, Schornagel Award 1996. *Publications include:* Anisakiasis, Pathogenesis, diagnosis and prevention 1970, Preventive Screening of Adults (with D.A.T. Griffiths) 1987, Statistical Analysis and Mathematical Modelling of AIDS (with J. C. Jager) 1988, AIDS Impact Assessment Modelling and Scenario Analysis (with J. C. Jager) 1992; numerous articles on immunology, vaccinology, pathology and parasitology. *Leisure interests:* European languages, history, cycling. *Address:* Plesmanlaan 125, 1066 CX Amsterdam, Netherlands. *Telephone:* (020) 5123224. *Fax:* (020) 5123252.

RUKEYSER, Louis Richard, A.B.; American broadcaster, lecturer, columnist and author; b. 30 Jan. 1933, New York; s. of Merryle Stanley Rukeyser and Berenice Helene Simon; m. Alexandra Gill 1962; three d.; ed. Princeton Univ.; reporter, Baltimore Sun Newspapers 1954–65, Chief Political Corresp. Evening Sun 1957–59, Chief London Bureau of The Sun 1959–63, Chief Asian Corresp. 1963–65; Sr. Corresp. and Commentator ABC News 1965–73, Paris Corresp. 1965–66, Chief London Bureau 1966–68, Econ. Ed. and Commentator 1968–73; Presenter Wall St. Week (PBS-TV programme) 1970–; nationally syndicated econ. columnist McNaught Syndicate 1976–86, Tribune Media Services 1986–93; also lecturer; Ed.-in-Chief Louis Rukeyser's Wall Street 1992–, Louis Rukeyser's Mutual Funds 1994–; Hon. Litt. D. (N.H. Coll.) 1975; Hon. LL.D. (Moravian Coll.) 1978, (Mercy Coll.) 1984; Hon. D.B.A. (Southeastern Mass. Univ.) 1979; Hon. L.H.D. (Loyola Coll.) 1982, (Johns Hopkins Univ.) 1986, (American Univ.) 1991, Hon. D. of Finance (Roger Williams Univ.) 1997; Overseas Press Club Award 1963, G. M. Loeb Award (Univ. of Conn.) 1972, George Washington Honor Medal Freedoms Foundation 1972, 1978, Janus Award for Excellence in Financial News Programming 1975, New York Financial Writers Assen. Award 1980, Free Enterprise Man of the Year Award, Texas A. and M. Univ. Centre for Educ. and Research in Free Enterprise 1987, Hero of Wall Street Award, Museum of American Financial History 1998. *Publications:* How to Make Money in Wall Street 1974, What's Ahead for the Economy: The Challenge and the Chance 1983, Louis Rukeyser's Business Almanac 1988, Louis Rukeyser's Book of Lists 1997. *Address:* 586 Round Hill Road, Greenwich, CT 06831, U.S.A.

RUML, Jan; Czech politician; b. 5 March 1953, Prague; m. Marie Ruml; two s.; ed. grammar school, Prague; stoker, woodcutter, worker with Shipping Dept., engineer, cattle-minder; signed Charter 77, Feb. 1977; freelance journalist 1977–79; mem. Cttee. for Protection of the Unjustly Persecuted 1979–; ed. of "Information on Charter 77" (samizdat periodical) 1979–; in custody, indicted for subversive activities 1981–82; co-f. of Lidové noviny (monthly samizdat) 1988–90; spokesman of Charter 77 1990; First Deputy Minister of Interior of C.S.F.R. 1990–91; Deputy Minister of Interior 1991–92; mem. Civic Democratic Party (CDP) 1992–97; founder and Chair. Unie Svobody 1998–; Deputy to House of Nations, Fed. Ass. June–Dec. 1992; Minister of Interior of Czech Repub. 1992–97; mem. State Defence Council, Czech Repub. Nov. 1992–; Chair. Interdepartmental Anti-drug Comm. 1993–95 (Vice-Chair. 1996–), Comm. for Prevention of Crime 1994–; mem. of Parl. 1996–98, Senator 1998–; Hon. Medal of the French Nat. Police 1992. *Publication:* (with Jana Klusáková) What Was, Is and Will Be (in Czech). *Address:* Parliament of the Czech Republic, Sněmovní 4, 118 26 Prague 1, Czech Republic. *Telephone:* 24 59 2111 (Office).

RUMMEL, Reinhard Franz, DR.ING.; German professor of physical geodesy; b. 3 Dec. 1945, Landshut; m. Renate Schophaus 1970; one s. one d.; ed. Hans Leinberger Gymnasium, Technische Univ. Munich and Technische Hochschule, Darmstadt; Research Assoc. Dept. of Geodetic Science, Ohio State Univ., Columbus, Ohio 1974–76; scientist, German Geodetic Research Inst. and Bavarian Acad. of Science, Munich 1976–80; Prof. of Physical Geodesy, Faculty of Geodetic Eng. Delft Univ. of Tech. 1980–; mem. Netherlands Acad. of Science; Speuerwerkpreis, KIVI, Netherlands 1987. *Publications:* Zur Behandlung von Zufallsfunktionen und -folgen in der physikalischen Geodäsie 1975, Geodesy's Contribution to Geophysics 1984, Satellite Gradiometry 1986, Encyclopedia of Earth System Science, Vol. II (on geodesy) 1992. *Address:* Delft University of Technology, Faculty of Geodesy, Thijsseweg 11, 2629 JA Delft, Netherlands. *Telephone:* (015) 785100. *Fax:* (015) 782348.

RUMSFELD, Donald H., A.B.; American fmr. government official; b. 9 July 1932, Chicago; s. of George and Jeannette (née Husted) Rumsfeld; m. Joyce Pierson 1954; one s. two d.; ed. Princeton Univ.; mem. 88th-91st Congresses; Republican; Asst. to Pres. and Dir. Office of Econ. Opportunity 1969–70; Dir. Cost of Living Council, Counsellor to Pres. 1971–73; Amb. to NATO 1973–74; White House Chief of Staff 1974–75; Sec. of Defense 1975–77; mem. Cabinet 1969–73, 1974–77; Pres. and C.E.O. G. D. Searle and Co., Skokie, Ill. 1977–85; Sr. Adviser, William Blair and Co. 1985–90; Chair. and C.E.O. General Instrument Corpn. 1990–93; Chair. Gilead Sciences, Inc. 1997–; Pres. Special M.E. Envoy 1983–84; Chair. Eisenhower Exchange Fellowships 1986–93, U.S. Ballistic Missile Threat Comm. 1998; mem. Presidential Advisory Cttee. on Arms Control 1982–86, Nat. Econ. Comm. 1988–89; mem. Bd. of Dirs. ABB, Kellogg Co., Tribune Co.; mem. Bd. of Trustees, RAND Corpn. 1977–98; 11 hon. degrees; Presidential Medal of Freedom, Woodrow Wilson Award. *Leisure interests:* sports, reading. *Address:* 400 North Michigan Avenue, Suite 405, Chicago, IL 60611, U.S.A. *Telephone:* (312) 645-0251. *Fax:* (312) 645-0258.

RUNCIE, Baron (Life Peer) cr. 1991, of Cuddesdon in the County of Oxfordshire; **Rt. Rev. and Rt. Hon. Robert Alexander Kennedy Runcie,** P.C., M.C., M.A.; British ecclesiastic; b. 2 Oct. 1921; s. of Robert Dalziel and Anne Runcie; m. Angela Rosalind Turner 1957; one s. one d.; ed. Merchant Taylors', Crosby, Brasenose Coll., Oxford, and Westcott House, Cambridge; served in Scots Guards, World War II; Deacon 1950; Priest 1951; Curate, All Saints, Gosforth 1950–52; Chaplain, Westcott House, Cambridge 1953–54, Vice-Prin. 1954–56; Fellow, Dean and Asst. Tutor, Trinity Hall, Cambridge 1956–60; Vicar of Cuddesdon and Prin. of Cuddesdon Theological Coll. 1960–70; Canon and Prebendary of Lincoln 1969; Bishop of St. Albans 1973–80; Archbishop of Canterbury 1980–91; Hon. Asst. Bishop of St. Albans 1991–; High Steward of Univ. of Cambridge 1991–; Chair. BBC and IBA Cen. Religious Advisory Cttee. 1973–80; Anglican Chair., Anglican-Orthodox Joint Doctrinal Comm. 1973–80; Select Preacher, Cambridge 1957, 1975 and Oxford 1959, 1973; Hon. Fellow, Trinity Hall, Cambridge 1975, Brasenose Coll., Oxford 1978, Merton Coll. Oxford 1991; Teape Lecturer, St. Stephen's Coll., Delhi 1962; Visitor of King's Coll., Pres. Royal School of Church Music 1980; Hon. D.D. (Oxford) 1980, (Cambridge) 1981, (Univ. of South Sewanee) 1981, (Durham) 1982, (St. Andrews) 1989, Hon. D.C.L. (Univ. of Kent) 1982, (Univ. of West Indies) 1984, (Berkeley Divinity School) 1986, (Yale) 1986; Hon. D.Litt. (Univ. of Keele) 1981, (Univ. of Liverpool) 1983; Freedom of St. Albans, of the City of London, of Canterbury; Hon. Master of the Bench of Grays Inn 1980; Patron of Christian Unity Award, Council of Christian Unity, Yale Univ. 1986; Cross of the Order of the Holy Sepulchre, Greek Orthodox Church 1986, Franklin D. Roosevelt Four Freedoms Medal 1996. *Publications:* Cathedral and City: St. Albans Ancient and Modern (Ed.) 1977, Windows unto God 1983, Seasons of the Spirit 1983, One Light for One World 1988, The Unity We Seek 1989. *Leisure interests:* travel, reading novels. *Address:* 26A Jennings Road, St. Albans, Herts., AL1 4PD, England. *Telephone:* (01727) 848021. *Fax:* (01727) 842319.

RUNCIMAN, The Hon. Sir Steven (James Cochran Stevenson), Kt., C.H., M.A., F.B.A.; British historian; b. 7 July 1903, Northumberland; s. of 1st Viscount Runciman and Hilda Stevenson; ed. Eton Coll., and Trinity Coll., Cambridge; Fellow Trinity Coll., Cambridge 1927–38; Lecturer Cambridge Univ. 1931–38; Press Attaché, British Legation, Sofia 1940–41; Prof. of Byzantine Studies, Istanbul Univ. 1942–45; Rep. of British Council, Greece 1945–47; Chair. Anglo-Hellenic League 1951–67; Trustee, British Museum 1960–67; Councillor Emer. Nat. Trust for Scotland 1985–; Fellow British Acad. 1957; Hon. Fellow Trinity Coll., Cambridge; Foreign mem. American Philosophical Soc. 1965; Hon. Litt.D. (Cambridge, Chicago, Durham, London, Oxford, St. Andrews, New York); Hon. LL.D. (Glasgow); Hon. D. Phil. (Salonika, Sofia); Hon. D.D. (Wabash, U.S.A.); Hon. D. Litt. Hum. (Ball State, U.S.A.); Companion of Literature (R.S.L.) 1987; Silver PEN award 1969, Wolfson Literary Award for History 1982, Gold Medal, City of Athens 1991, Int. Award for Culture, Onassis Foundation 1997; Kt., Commdr. Order of the Phoenix (Greece), Order of the Madara Horseman, 1st Class (Bulgaria); apptd. by Oecumenical Patriarch, Grand Orator of the Great Church 1970. *Publications:* The Emperor Romanus Lecapenus 1929, The First Bulgarian Empire 1930, Byzantine Civilisation 1933, The Medieval Manichee 1947, History of the Crusades (3 vols.) 1951–54, The Eastern Schism 1955, The Sicilian Vespers 1958, The White Rajahs 1960, The Fall of Constantinople 1453 1965, The Great Church in Captivity 1968, The Last Byzantine Renaissance 1970, The Orthodox Churches and the Secular State 1972, Byzantine

Style and Civilization 1975, The Byzantine Theocracy 1977, Mistra 1979, A Traveller's Alphabet 1991. *Address:* Elshieshields, Lockerbie, Dumfriesshire, DG11 1LY, Scotland. *Telephone:* (01387) 810-280.

RUNDQUIST, Dmitri Vasilyevich; Russian geologist and mineralogist; b. 10 Aug. 1930; m.; two d.; ed. Leningrad Inst. of Mines; jr., sr. researcher, Deputy Dir. All-Union Research Inst. of Geology 1954–84; Dir. Inst. of Geology and Geochronology Russian Acad. of Sciences 1984–90, Head of Lab. 1990–; Corresp. mem. U.S.S.R. (now Russian) Acad. of Sciences 1984, mem. 1990, Acad.-Sec. Dept. of Geology, Geophysics, Geochemistry and Mining Sciences 1996–; research in mineralogy, petrography, developed theory on laws of mineral deposit location; U.S.S.R. State Prize; Merited Geologist of Russian Fed. *Publications include:* Greisen Deposits 1971, Zones of Endogenic Mineral Deposits 1975, Precambrian Geology 1988. *Address:* State Geological Museum, Morkhovaya 11, 103009 Moscow; Department of Geology, Geophysics, Geochemistry and Mining Sciences, Leninsky Prosp. 32A, 117993 Moscow, Russia. *Telephone:* (095) 203-53-87 (Museum); 938-55-44 (Acad.).

RUNYON, Marvin T., B.S.; American civil servant and business executive; b. 16 Sept. 1924, Fort Worth, Tex.; s. of Marvin Runyon and Lora Whittington; three s. one d.; ed. Texas A & M Univ.; war service 1943–45; various positions with Ford Motor Co. 1945–80; Pres. and C.E.O. Nissan Motor Mfg. Corpn. U.S.A., Smyrna, Tenn. 1980–87; Chair. Bd. of Dirs. Tenn. Valley Authority 1987–92; Postmaster-Gen. U.S. Postal Service 1992–98; mem. numerous cttees., public bodies etc. *Address:* c/o U.S. Postal Service, Room 10022, 475 L'Enfant Plaza, S.W., Washington, DC 20260, U.S.A.

RUPEL, Dimitrij, PH.D.; Slovenian politician and sociologist; b. 7 April 1946, Ljubljana; m.; ed. Ljubljana Univ., Univ. of Essex, Brandeis Univ. (Mass., U.S.A.); worked as journalist in Yugoslav newspapers and magazines; was considered as dissident for criticism of Yugoslav Communist regime; Asst. Prof. Ljubljana Univ. 1982–89, Prof. 1989–; lectured in Queen's Univ. (Canada) 1985, Cleveland State Univ. 1989; one of founders of Cultural-Political journal Nova Revija 1987; founder and first Chair. Opposition Slovenian Democratic Party 1989; Minister of Foreign Affairs, mem. first elected Govt. of Slovenia 1990, Chair. Cttee. for Culture, Educ. and Sports; elected Mayor of Ljubljana 1992–97; Amb. to U.S.A. 1997–. *Publications include:* Secret of the State 1992, The disenchanted Slovenia 1993, plays for radio. *Address:* Embassy of the Republic of Slovenia, 1525 New Hampshire Avenue, N.W., Washington, DC 20036, U.S.A.

RUPERT, Anthony Edward, M.SC., F.I.A.M.; South African business executive; b. 4 Oct. 1916, Graaff Reinet; s. of late John P. Rupert and Hester A. van Eeden; m. H. Goote 1941; two s. one d.; ed. Volks High School, Graaff Reinet, Pretoria Univ. and Univ. of S.A.; Lecturer in Chem., Pretoria Univ. 1939–41; Founder Rembrandt Group of Cos. (tobacco) 1948–, Chair. Advisory Council 1997–; Chair. Tech. and Industrial Investments Ltd. 1950–; Chair. Rembrandt Controlling Investments 1990–; Founder and Pres. World Wide Fund for Nature, S.A.; Chair. Historical Homes of S.A. Ltd.; Chair. Peace Parks Foundation 1997–; Fellow of the Int. Acad. of Man.; Life mem. South African Chemical Inst., South African Inst. of Man., South African Acad. for Arts and Science; mem. of Honour World Wild Fund for Nature; Hon. Prof. in Business Admin. at Univ. of Pretoria 1964–83; Hon. D.Sc. (Pretoria), Hon. D.Comm. (Stellenbosch), Hon. LL.D. (Univ. of Cape Town), Hon. D.Lit. (Univ. of Natal); Decoration for Meritorious Service 1980, Commdr. Order of Golden Ark. *Publications:* Progress through Partnership, Leaders on Leadership, Inflation—How to Curb Public Enemy Number One, Priorities for Coexistence. *Leisure interests:* research, conservation, art. *Address:* 34 Alexander Street, P.O. Box 456, Stellenbosch (Office); 13 Thibault Street, Mostertsdrift, Stellenbosch, South Africa (Home). *Telephone:* (21) 888 3320 (Office).

RUSBRIDGER, Alan, M.A.; British journalist; b. 29 Dec. 1953, Lusaka, Zambia; s. of G.H. Rusbridger and B.E. (née Wickham) Rusbridger; m. Lindsay Mackie 1982; two d.; ed. Magdalene Coll., Cambridge Univ.; reporter Cambridge Evening News 1976–79; reporter, columnist The Guardian 1979–86, Features Ed. 1989–93, Deputy Ed. 1993–95, Ed. 1995–; TV Critic The Observer 1986–87; Washington Corresp. London Daily News 1987; Ed. of the Year, Granada TV What the Papers Say Awards 1996, Newspaper Focus Awards 1996. *Leisure interests:* cricket, golf, playing music. *Address:* The Guardian, 119 Farringdon Road, London, EC1R 3ER, England. *Telephone:* 0171-278 2332. *Fax:* 0171-239 9997.

RUSCHA, Edward Joseph; American artist; b. 16 Dec. 1937, Omaha, Neb.; s. of Edward Joseph Ruscha and Dorothy Driscoll; m. Danna Knego 1967; one s.; ed. Chouinard Art Inst., Los Angeles; first one-man exhbn. Los Angeles 1963; produced films Premium 1970, Miracle 1975; major exhbns., San Francisco Museum of Modern Art 1982, Musée St. Pierre, Lyons, France 1985, Museum of Contemporary Art, Chicago 1988, Centre Georges Pompidou, Paris 1989, Serpentine Gallery, London 1990, Museum of Contemporary Art, Los Angeles 1990, Robert Miller Gallery, New York 1992, Thaddaeus Ropac, Salzburg, Austria 1992; first public comm., for Miami Dade Cultural Center's Main Library, Miami, Fla. 1985; represented in numerous perm. collections; Guggenheim Foundation Fellowship 1971. *Publications:* 12 books, including Twenty-six Gasoline Stations 1963, The Sunset Strip 1966. *Address:* c/o Leo Castelli, 420 W Broadway, New York, NY 10012, U.S.A.

RUSH, Geoffrey; Australian actor; b. 6 July 1951, Toowoomba, Queensland; s. of Roy Baden Rush and Merle Kiehne; m. Jane Menelaus 1988; one s. one d.; studied at Jacques Lecoq School of Mime, Paris, began professional career with Queensland Theatre Co. *Films include:* The Wedding 1980, Starstruck 1982, Twelfth Night 1986, Midday Crisis 1994, Dad and Dave on our Selection 1995, Shine (Acad. Award, BAFTA Award, Australian Film Inst. Award, Golden Globe Award, numerous other awards), Children of the Revolution 1996, Elizabeth 1998, Shakespeare in Love (BAFTA Award for Best Supporting Actor) 1998. *Address:* c/o Shanahan Management, P.O. Box 478, Kings Cross, NSW 2011, Australia.

RUSHDIE, (Ahmed) Salman, M.A., F.R.S.L.; British writer; b. 19 June 1947, Bombay, India; s. of Anis Ahmed and Negin (née Butt) Rushdie; m. 1st Clarissa Luard 1976 (divorced 1987); one s.; m. 2nd Marianne Wiggins 1988 (divorced 1993); one step-d.; m. 3rd Elizabeth West 1997; ed. Cathedral and John Connon Boys' High School, Bombay, Rugby School, England, King's Coll., Cambridge; British citizen 1964; mem. Footlights revue, Univ. of Cambridge 1965–68; actor, fringe theatre, London 1968–69; advertising copy-writer 1969–73; wrote first published novel Grimus 1973–74; part-time advertising copy-writer while writing second novel 1976–80; mem. Int. PEN 1981–, Soc. of Authors 1983–, Exec. Cttee. Nat. Book League 1983–, Council Inst. of Contemporary Arts 1985–, British Film Inst. Production Bd. 1986–; Hon. Prof. M.I.T. 1993; Hon. D.Litt (Bard Coll.) 1995; Hon. Spokesman Charter 88 1989; Exec. mem. Camden Cttee. for Community Relations 1977–83; Booker McConnell Prize for Fiction 1981, Colette Prize 1993, Booker of Bookers Award 1993; Arts Council Literature Bursary 1981, English Speaking Union Literary Award 1981, James Tait Black Memorial Book Prize 1981, Prix du Meilleur Livre Etranger for Shame 1984; Kurt Tucholsky Prize Sweden 1992, Prix Colette Switzerland 1993, Austrian State Prize for European Literature 1994, Whitbread Fiction Award 1996, British Book Awards Author of the Year 1996. *Publications:* Grimus 1975, Midnight's Children 1981, Shame 1983, The Jaguar Smile: A Nicaraguan Journey 1987, The Satanic Verses 1988, Is Nothing Sacred (lecture) 1990, Haroun and the Sea of Stories (novel) 1990, Imaginary Homelands: Essays and Criticism 1981–91 1991, The Wizard of Oz 1992, East, West (short stories) 1994, The Moor's Last Sigh (novel) 1995, The Vintage Book of Indian Writing 1947–97 1997, The Ground Beneath Her Feet 1999, and has written articles for New York Times, Washington Post, The Times and Sunday Times, etc. *Leisure interests:* films, chess, table tennis, involvement in politics, especially race relations. *Address:* c/o Wylie Agency Ltd., 36 Parkside, 42 Knightsbridge, London, SW1X 7JR, England.

RUSSELL, Sir George, Kt., C.B.E., B.A., F.R.S.A., C.B.I.M., F.I.D.; British business executive; b. 25 Oct. 1935; s. of William H. and Frances A. Russell; m. Dorothy Brown 1959; three d.; ed. Gateshead Grammar School, Durham Univ.; Vice-Pres. and Gen. Man. Welland Chemical Co. of Canada Ltd. 1968, St. Clair Chemical Co. Ltd. 1968; Man. Dir. Alcan UK Ltd. 1976; Asst. Man. Dir. Alcan Aluminium (UK) Ltd. 1977–81, Man. Dir. 1981–82; Man. Dir. and C.E.O. British Alcan Aluminium 1982–86; Dir. Alcan Aluminiumwerke GmbH, Frankfurt 1982–86, Alcan Aluminium Ltd. 1987–; Group Chief Exec. Marley PLC 1986–89, Chair. 1989–93, C.E.O. 1989–92, Chair. (non-exec.) 1993–97; Deputy Chair. Channel Four TV 1987–88; Chair. Ind. TV News (I.T.N.) 1988; Chair. Independent Broadcasting Authority (IBA) 1989–90, Independent Television Comm. (ITC) 1991–96; Chair. Camelot Group PLC 1995–; Chair. Luxfer Holdings Ltd. 1976; Dir. Northern Rock Building Soc. 1985–, 3i Group PLC 1992– (Chair. non-exec. 1993–), Taylor Woodrow PLC 1992–; Chair. Northern Devt. Co. 1994–; Visiting Prof. Univ. of Newcastle upon Tyne 1978; mem. Northern Industrial Devt. Bd. 1977–80, Washington Devt. Corpn. 1978–80, IBA 1979–86, Civil Service Pay Research Unit 1980–81, Council CBI 1984–85, Widdicombe Cttee. of Inquiry into Conduct of Local Authority Business 1985; Fellow Inst. of Industrial Mans.; Hon. Fellow R.I.B.A., Royal Television Soc.; Trustee Beamish Devt. Trust 1985–90, Thomas Bewick Birthplace Trust; Hon. D. Eng. (Newcastle upon Tyne) 1985; Hon. D.B.A. (Northumbria) 1992; Hon. LL.D. (Sunderland) 1995, (Durham) 1997. *Leisure interests:* tennis, badminton, bird watching. *Address:* 3i Group PLC, 91 Waterloo Road, London, SE1 8XP, England.

RUSSELL, John, C.B.E., B.A.; British art critic; b. 22 Jan. 1919, Fleet, Hants.; s. of Isaac J. Russell and Harriet E. (née Atkins) Russell; m. 1st Alexandrine Apponyi 1945 (divorced 1950); one d.; m. 2nd Vera Poliakoff 1956 (divorced 1971, died 1992); m. 3rd Rosamund Bernier 1975; ed. Magdalen Coll., Oxford; Hon. attaché Tate Gallery, London 1940; with Ministry of Information 1941, Intelligence Div. Admiralty 1942–46; mem. editorial staff Sunday Times 1946–74; moved to U.S. 1974; Art Critic New York Times 1974–, Chief Art Critic 1982–90; Fellow R.A. 1989; awarded Empire Grand Medal of Honour, Austria, Officier des Arts et Lettres, France, Order of Merit, Fed. Repub. of Germany. *Publications include:* Shakespeare's Country 1942, Switzerland 1950, Braque 1959, Erich Kleiber: A Memoir 1956, Paris 1960, Max Ernst 1967, Vuillard 1971, Francis Bacon 1971, Seurat 1965, Henry Moore 1968, The Meanings of Modern Art 1981, (revised 1990), Reading Russell 1989, London 1994, Matisse: Father and Son 1999; contrib. to numerous books. *Address:* 166 East 61st Street, New York, NY 10021, U.S.A.

RUSSELL, Ken; British film director; b. 3 July 1927, Southampton; s. of Henry Russell and Ethel Smith; m. 1st Shirley Russell; four s. one d.; m. 2nd Vivian Jolly 1984; one s. one d.; m. 3rd Hetty Baines 1992; one s.; ed. Nautical Coll., Pangbourne; fmr. actor and freelance magazine photographer;

has directed many television documentaries for BBC which have been shown all over the world; Hon. D.Litt. (Univ. Coll., Salford) 1994; has directed the following television documentaries: Elgar, Bartok, Debussy, Henri Rousseau, Isadora Duncan, Delius, Richard Strauss, Clouds of Glory, The Mystery of Dr. Martini, The Secret Life of Arnold Bax; television series: Lady Chatterley's Lover; films: French Dressing 1964, Billion Dollar Brain 1967, Women in Love 1969, The Music Lovers 1970, The Devils 1971, The Boyfriend 1971, Savage Messiah 1972, Mahler 1973, Tommy 1974, Lisztomania 1975, Valentino 1977, Altered States 1981, Gothic 1986, Aria (segment) 1987, Salome's Last Dance 1988, The Lair of the White Worm 1988, The Rainbow 1989, Whore 1990, Prisoners of Honour 1991; acted in film The Russia House 1990; theatre: Rake's Progress (Stravinsky) 1982, Die Soldaten (Zimmerman) 1983; opera: Princess Ida 1992, Salome, Bonn 1993. *Publications:* A British Picture: an Autobiography 1989, Altered States: The Autobiography of Ken Russell 1991, Fire Over England 1993. *Leisure interest:* music. *Address:* c/o Peter Rawley, ICM, 8942 Wilshire Boulevard, Beverly Hills, CA 90021, U.S.A.; 16 Salisbury Place, London, W1H 1FH, England.

RUSSELL, Kurt von Vogel; American actor; b. 17 March 1951, Springfield, Mass.; s. of Bing Oliver and Louise Julia (Crone) Russell; m. Season Hubley 1979 (divorced); one s.; one s. by Goldie Hawn; lead role in TV series The Travels of Jamie McPheeters 1963–64; child actor in many Disney shows and films; professional baseball player 1971–73. *Films include:* It Happened at the World's Fair 1963, Unlawful Entry 1992, Captain Ron 1992, Tombstone 1993, Stargate 1994, Executive Decision 1996, Escape from L.A. 1996, Breakdown 1997, Soldier 1998. *TV series include:* Travels with Jamie McPheeters 1963–64, The New Land 1974, The Quest 1976. *TV films include:* Search for the Gods 1975, The Deadly Tower 1975, Christmas Miracle in Caulfield USA 1977, Elvis 1979, Amber Waves 1988; numerous TV guest appearances; recipient 5 acting awards, 10 baseball awards, 1 golf championship; mem. Professional Baseball Players' Asscn., Stuntman's Asscn. *Address:* Creative Artists' Agency, 9830 Wilshire Boulevard, Beverly Hills, CA 90212-1825, U.S.A.

RUSSELL, Paul; British music industry executive; b. London; ed. L.S.E.; fmrly. band mem. Red Diamond; fmrly. with law firm Balin & Co.; joined CBS 1973, fmrly. Man. Dir., Pres. Sony Music Europe 1993–. *Address:* Sony Music Europe, 10 Great Marlborough Street, London, W.1., England.

RUSSELL, Sir Peter (Edward Lionel) Russell, Kt., D.LITT., F.B.A., F.R.HIST.S.; British professor of Spanish; b. 24 Oct. 1913, Christchurch, New Zealand; s. of Hugh B. Wheeler and Rita M. Russell; ed. Cheltenham Coll. and Queen's Coll. Oxford; lecturer, St. John's Coll. Oxford 1937–53, Queen's Coll. 1938–45; war service (Intelligence Corps) 1940–46; Fellow, Queen's Coll. Oxford and univ. lecturer in Spanish Studies 1946–53; King Alfonso XIII Prof. of Spanish Studies, Oxford Univ. 1953–81; Fellow, Exeter Coll. Oxford 1953–81, Emer. 1981; Taylorian special lecturer, Oxford 1983; Visiting Prof. Univ. of Va. 1982, Univ. of Tex. 1983, 1987, Johns Hopkins Univ. 1986, Vanderbilt Univ. 1987; Hon. Fellow Queen's Coll., Oxford 1990; mem. Portuguese Acad. of History, Real Acad. de Buenas Letras, Barcelona; Commdr. Order of Isabel the Catholic (Spain), Order of Prince Henry the Navigator (Portugal). *Publications include:* As Fontes de Fernão Lopes 1941, The English Intervention in Spain and Portugal in the Time of Edward III and Richard II 1955, Prince Henry the Navigator 1960, Temas de la Celestina y otros estudios 1978, Prince Henry the Navigator: the rise and fall of a culture hero 1984, Cervantes 1985, Comedia o Tragicomedia de Calisto y Melibea (La Celestina) 1992, Portugal, Spain and the African Atlantic 1343–1490 1995; articles and reviews in professional journals etc. *Leisure interest:* travel. *Address:* 23 Belsyre Court, Woodstock Road, Oxford, OX2 6HU, England. *Telephone:* (01865) 556086. *Fax:* (01865) 556086.

RUSSELL, William Martin (Willy); British author; b. 23 Aug. 1947; s. of William Russell and Margery Russell; m. Ann Seagroatt 1969; one s. two d.; ed. St. Katharine's Coll. of Educ., Liverpool; ladies hairdresser 1963–69; teacher 1973–74; Fellow in Creative Writing, Manchester Polytechnic 1977–78; founder mem. and Dir. Quintet Films; Hon. Dir. Liverpool, Playhouse; work for theatre includes: Blind Scouse (3 short plays) 1971, When the Reds (adaptation) 1972, John, Paul, George, Ringo and Bert (musical) 1974, Breezeblock Park 1975, One for the Road 1976, Stags and Hens 1978, Educating Rita 1979, Blood Brothers (musical) 1983, Our Day Out (musical) 1983, Shirley Valentine 1986; screenplays include: Educating Rita 1981, Shirley Valentine 1988, Dancing through the Dark 1989; TV and radio plays. *Publications:* Breezeblock Park 1978, One for the Road 1980, Educating Rita 1981, Our Day Out 1984, Stags and Hens 1985, Blood Brothers 1985, Shirley Valentine 1989; songs and poetry. *Leisure interests:* playing the guitar, composing songs, gardening, cooking. *Address:* c/o Casarotto Ramsay Ltd., National House, 60–66 Wardour Street, London, W1V 3HP, England. *Telephone:* 0171-287 4450.

RUSSELL BEALE, Simon; British actor; b. 12 Jan. 1961, Penang, Malaya; s. of Lieut.-Gen. Sir Peter Beale and Lady Beale; Assoc. Artist of R.S.C. 1986. *Theatre:* (Traverse Theatre, Edin.): Die House, Sandra/Manon, Points of Departure, The Death of Elias Sawney; (Lyceum, Edin.): Hamlet (Royal Court, London): Women Beware Women, The Duchess of Malfi, Volpone, Rosencranz and Guildenstern are Dead. *RSC productions include:* The Winter's Tale, The Art of Success, Everyman in his Humour, The Fair Maid of the West, The Storm, Speculators, The Constant Couple, The Man of Mode, Restoration, Mary and Lizzie, Some Americans Abroad, Playing with Trains, Troilus and Cressida, Edward II (title role), Love's Labours Lost, The Seagull, Richard III (title role), The Tempest, King Lear, Ghosts, Othello. *TV includes:* A Very Peculiar Practice, Down Town Lagos, The Mushroom Picker, Dance to the Music of Time (Royal TV Soc. Award for Best Actor 1997, BAFTA Award for Best Actor 1998), The Double Life of Franz Schubert. *Film:* Orlando. *Leisure interests:* medieval history, music. *Address:* c/o Richard Stone Partnership, 25 Whitehall, London, SW1A 2BS, England. *Telephone:* 0171-839 6421.

RUSSO, Carlo; Italian judge; b. 19 March 1920, Savona; s. of Giovanni Russo and Nilde Volta; m. Elena Neviani 1945; one d.; Deputy to Italian Parl. 1948–79; fmr. Pres. Parl. Comm. of Chamber of Deputies; Pres. Italian Comm. for Security and Cooperation in Europe 1980–; Judge, European Court of Human Rights 1981–; Cavaliere di Gran Croce della Repubblica Italiana, Ordine di S. Gregorio di San Silvestro del Vaticano, Hon. G.C.M.G., Grand Officier, Légion d'honneur; decorations from Germany and Malta. *Publications:* numerous articles on int. law in Italian and foreign reviews. *Leisure interest:* yachting. *Address:* Corso Italia 13, 17100 Savona, Italy. *Telephone:* (019) 829784.

RUSSO, René; American actress; b. 1955, Calif.; fmrly. model Eileen Ford Agency. *Film appearances include:* Major League 1989, Mr Destiny, One Good Cop, Freejack, Lethal Weapon 3, In the Line of Fire, Outbreak, Get Shorty, Tin Cup, Ransom, Buddy, Lethal Weapon 4 1998. *Television appearance:* Sable (Series). *Address:* c/o Progressive Artists Agency, 400 South Beverly Drive, Suite 216, Beverly Hills, CA 90212, U.S.A.

RUSSO JERVOLINO, Rosa; Italian politician; b. 1936, Naples; ed. Univ. of Rome; worked in Research Dept. CNEL 1961–68; joined Legis. Div. Ministry of the Budget 1969; mem. staff, subsequently Nat. Vice-Pres. Centro Italiano femminile 1969–78; mem. Nat. Exec. Women's Movement of Christian Democrat (DC) Party 1968–78, Pres. Oct. 1992–; Nat. Organizer DC Family Div. 1974–; Senator 1979–; Minister for Social Affairs 1989–92, of Educ. 1992–94; Chair. Parl. Supervisory Comm. of RAI (nat. TV and radio corpn.) 1985–. *Address:* Senato, Palazzio Madama, 00186 Rome, Italy.

RUSTIN, Jean; French artist; b. 3 March 1928, Moselle; s. of Georges Rustin and Andrée Carrat; m. Elsa Courand 1949; two s. (one deceased); ed. Ecole Nationale Supérieure des Beaux Arts, Paris; one-man exhbns. Galerie La Roue, Paris 1959–68, ARC (Musée Art Moderne, Ville de Paris) 1971, Galerie 9, Paris 1972–75, Tsuchya Gallery, Japan 1973, Maison des Arts, Creteil 1982, Galerie Isy Brachot 1981–86, European Fine Art Gallery, Maastricht 1991, Cooling Gallery, London 1992, Oberhausen, Germany 1994, Bergen Op Zoom, Netherlands 1994; numerous group exhbns. including Foire Devand-Lineart, Belgium 1990, Galerie Marnia Neerman, Bruges, Belgium 1986–; works displayed at Musée d'Art Moderne, Paris and numerous other museums and centres in Europe and the U.S.A.; subject of books including Rustin by Edward Lucie-Smith 1991. *Leisure interest:* the violin. *Address:* 167 avenue Gambetta, 75020 Paris, France; Fondation Rustin, 57 Sanderusstraat, 2018 Antwerp, Belgium. *Telephone:* (1) 43-61-08-98 (Paris); (3) 216.43.29 (Antwerp).

RUTHVEN, Kenneth Knowles, PH.D., F.A.H.A.; British professor of English; b. 26 May 1936; ed. Univ. of Manchester; Asst. Lecturer, Lecturer, Sr. Lecturer Univ. of Canterbury, Christchurch, N.Z. 1961–72, Prof. of English 1972–79; Prof. of English, Univ. of Adelaide 1980–85, Univ. of Melbourne, Vic., Australia 1985–. *Publications:* A Guide to Ezra Pound's Personae 1969, The Conceit 1969, Myth 1976, Critical Assumptions 1979, Feminist Literary Studies: An Introduction 1984, Ezra Pound as Literary Critic 1990, Beyond the Disciplines: The New Humanities (ed.) 1992, Nuclear Criticism 1993; Southern Review (Adelaide) (ed.) 1981–85, Interpretations series (gen. ed.) 1993–96 (19 vols.). *Address:* English Department, University of Melbourne, Parkville, Vic. 3052, Australia. *Telephone:* (3) 9344-5506. *Fax:* (3) 9349-3043.

RUTKIEWICZ, Ignacy; Polish journalist; b. 15 April 1929, Vilna; s. of Józef Rutkiewicz and Maria Rutkiewicz (née Turkułł); m. Wilma Helena Koller 1961; two s.; ed. Poznań Univ.; journalist Wrocławski Tygodnik Katolicki (weekly) 1953–55; journalist, Zachodnia Agencja Prasowa (ZAP) 1957–66, Polska Agencja Interpress 1967–70; Ed. Odra (monthly) 1961–, Ed.-in-Chief 1982–90; Co-founder, mem. Editorial Council Więź (monthly), Warsaw 1958–; Pres.-Ed.-in-Chief Polish Press Agency (PAP), Warsaw 1990–92, 1992–94; Adviser to Prime Minister, Warsaw 1994–95; TV journalist TV Centre of Educ. and Press Analysis 1994–; Sec. TV Comm. for Ethics 1996–98; Ed.-in-Chief Antena (weekly) 1998; Adviser to Minister of Culture and Arts 1998–; Co-founder and Vice-Pres. Polish-German Soc., Warsaw 1990–; Vice-Pres. Alliance Européenne des Agences de Presse, Zürich 1991–92; mem. Bd., Polish Journalists' Asscn. 1980–82, 1998, Pres. 1993–95; mem. Council on Media and Information, Pres.'s Office 1993–95; mem. Euroatlantic Asscn. 1995–; mem. Bd. Press Centre for Central and Eastern Europe Foundation 1996–, Programme Bd. Nat. Club of Admirers of Lithuania 1996–, Programme Bd. Polish Press Agency 1998–; City of Wrocław Award 1963, B. Prus Award of SDP 1990, Phil epistémoni Award, Jagiellonian Univ., Kraków 1991. *Publications:* author and co-author of more than 10 books. *Leisure interests:* literature, recent history, foreign languages, mountain trips, skiing. *Address:* Telewizyjna Agencja Informacyjna S.A., pl. Powstańców Warszawy 7, 00-999 Warsaw (Office); Al. Jerozolimskie 42/55, 00-024 Warsaw, Poland (Home). *Telephone:* (22) 827 58 13 (Home).

RUTSKOY, Maj.-Gen. Aleksandr Vladimirovich, CAND.ECON.SC.; Russian politician and military officer; b. 16 Sept. 1947, Proskurov, Kamenets Podolsk Region (now Khmelnitsky, Ukraine); s. of Vladimir Alexandrovich Rutskoy and Zinaida Iosifovna Rutskaya; m. Lyudmila Rutskaya; two s. one d.; ed. Higher Air Force Coll., Barnaul, Y. Gagarin Higher Air Force Acad., Acad. of Gen. Staff; fmr. mem. CPSU (expelled 1991); Regimental Commdr., Afghan War 1985–86; Deputy Commdr. Army Air Force 1988; R.S.F.S.R. People's Deputy, mem. Supreme Soviet, mem. Presidium of Supreme Soviet 1990–91; Leader Communists for Democracy (renamed People's Party of Free Russia Oct. 1991, renamed Russian Social Democratic Party 1994); Vice-Pres. R.S.F.S.R. (now Russia) 1991–93; Head Centre for the Operational Supervision of the Progress of Reforms 1991–93; Leader Civic Union coalition 1992–93; declared Acting Pres. of Russia by Parl. Sept. 1993; arrested as one of organizers of failed coup d'état Oct. 1993; freed on amnesty Feb. 1994; Chair. Social-Patriotic movt. Derzhava 1994; Gov. of Kursk Region 1996–; mem. Council Europe Parl. 1996–; Hero of Soviet Union 1988; eight Russian and Afghan orders. *Publications include:* March Records 1995, Bloody Autumn 1995, Liberal Reforms—Strong Power 1996, Agrarian Reform in Russia 1996. *Leisure interests:* painting, gardening, designing, fishing. *Address:* Parliament House, Red Square, 305002 Kursk; Council of the Federal Assembly of the Russian Federation, 26 Bolshaya Dimitrovka Street, 103426 Moscow, Russia. *Telephone:* (07122) 2-62-62 (Kursk); (095) 292-6698 (Moscow). *Fax:* (07122) 2-65-62 (Kursk).

RUTT, Rev. Cecil Richard, C.B.E., M.A., D.LITT.; British ecclesiastic; b. 27 Aug. 1925, Langford, Beds.; s. of Cecil Rutt and Mary Hare Turner; m. Joan M. Ford 1969; ed. Huntingdon Grammar School, Kelham Theological Coll. and Pembroke Coll., Cambridge; RNVR 1943–46; ordained 1951; curate St. George's, Cambridge 1951–54; Church of England Mission to Korea 1954–74, consecrated Bishop 1966, Bishop of Taejon, Repub. of Korea 1968–74; Bishop of St. Germans, Cornwall 1974–79; Bishop of Leicester 1979–90; Chair. Advisory Council for Relations of Bishops and Religious Communities 1980–90; joined Roman Catholic Church as a layman Sept. 1994; became priest 1995; mem. Anglican/Orthodox Jt. Doctrinal Discussions 1983–89; Hon. Fellow Northumbrian Univs. East Asia Centre 1990–; Bard of the Gorseth of Cornwall 1976, Chaplain 1993; Chaplain, Order of St. John of Jerusalem 1978; Hon. D.Litt. (Confucian Univ., Seoul) 1974; Tasan Cultural Award (for writings on Korea) 1964, Order of Civil Merit, Peony Class (Korea) 1974. *Publications:* Korean Anglican Hymnal (ed.) 1961, Korean Works and Days 1964, P'ungnyu Han'guk (in Korean) 1965, An Anthology of Korean Sijo 1970, The Bamboo Grove 1971, James Scarth Gale and His History of the Korean People 1972, Virtuous Women 1974, A History of Hand Knitting 1987, The Book of Changes (Zhouyi): A Bronze Age Document 1996, Korea: A Cultural and Historical Dictionary (with Keith Pratt) 1999; contributions to various Korean and liturgical publications. *Address:* 3 Marlborough Court, Falmouth, Cornwall, TR11 2QU, England. *Telephone:* (01326) 312276.

RUTTER, John Milford, D.MUS., M.A.; British composer and conductor; b. 24 Sept. 1945, London; m. JoAnne Redden 1980; two s. one step-d. ; ed. Highgate School and Clare Coll., Cambridge; Dir. of Music Clare Coll., Cambridge 1975–79, part-time lecturer in Music, Open Univ. 1975–87; Founder and Dir. The Cambridge Singers 1981–; Hon. Fellow Westminster Choir Coll., Princeton. *Compositions include:* choral: The Falcon 1969, Gloria 1974, Bang! (opera for young people) 1975, The Piper of Hamelin (opera for young people) 1980, Requiem 1985, Magnificat 1990, numerous carols, anthems and songs; orchestral works and music for TV; ed. and recorded original version of Fauré Requiem 1984. *Address:* Old Laceys, St. John's Street, Duxford, Cambridge, CB2 4RA, England. *Telephone:* (01223) 832474. *Fax:* (01223) 836723.

RUTTER, Sir Michael Llewellyn, Kt., C.B.E., M.D., F.R.C.P., F.R.C.PSYCH., F.R.S.; British professor of child psychiatry; b. 15 Aug. 1933; s. of Llewellyn Charles Rutter and Winifred Olive Rutter; m. Marjorie Heys 1958; one s. two d.; ed. Birmingham Univ. Medical School, training in paediatrics, neurology and internal medicine 1955–58; practised at Maudsley Hosp. 1958–61; Nuffield Medical Travelling Fellow, Albert Einstein Coll. of Medicine, New York 1961–62; scientist with MRC Social Psychology Research Unit 1962–65; Sr. Lecturer, then Reader, Univ. of London Inst. of Psychiatry 1966–73, Prof. of Child Psychiatry 1973–98, Research Prof. 1998–, Dir. MRC Research Centre for Social, Genetic and Developmental Psychiatry 1994–98; Hon. Dir. MRC Child Psychiatry Unit 1984–98; Fellow Center for Advanced Study in Behavioral Sciences, Stanford Univ. 1979–80; guest lecturer at many insts. in Britain and America; Pres. Soc. for Research in Child Devt. April 1999– (Pres. elect 1997–99); Hon. Fellow British Psychological Soc. 1978, Hon. Fellow American Acad. of Pediatrics 1981, Royal Soc. of Medicine 1996; Hon. doctorates (Leiden) 1985, (Catholic Univ. of Leuven) 1990, (Birmingham) 1990, (Edin.) 1990, (Chicago) 1991, (Minnesota) 1993, (Jyväskylä) 1996; numerous awards U.K. and U.S.A. *Publications:* Children of Sick Parents 1966, jtly. A Neuropsychiatric Study in Childhood 1970, ed. jtly. Education, Health and Behaviour 1970, ed. Infantile Autism 1971, Maternal Deprivation Reassessed 1981, ed. jtly. The Child with Delayed Speech 1972, Helping Troubled Children 1975, jtly. Cycles of Disadvantage 1976, ed. jtly. Child Psychiatry 1977, (2nd edn. as Child and Adolescent Psychiatry 1985), ed. jtly. Autism 1978, Changing Youth in a Changing Society 1979, jtly. Fifteen Thousand Hours: Secondary Schools and Their Effect on Children 1979, ed. Scientific Foundations of Developmental Psychiatry 1981, A Measure of Our Values: Goals and Dilemmas in the Upbringing of Children 1983, jtly. Lead versus Health 1983, jtly. Juvenile Delinquency 1983, ed. Developmental Neuropsychiatry 1983, ed. jtly. Stress, Coping and Development 1983, ed. jtly. Depression and Young People 1986, Studies of Psychosocial Risk: The Power of Longitudinal Data (Ed.) 1988, Parenting Breakdown: The Making and Breaking of Inter-generational Links (jtly.) 1988, Straight and Devious Pathways from Childhood to Adulthood (Ed. jtly.) 1990, Biological Risk Factors for Psychosocial Disorders (Ed. jtly.) 1991, Developing Minds (jtly.) 1993, Development Through Life: a handbook for clinicians (Ed. jtly.) 1994, Stress, Risk and Resilience in Children and Adolescents (Ed. jtly.) 1994, Psychological Disorders in Young People 1995, Antisocial Behaviour by Young People (jtly.) 1998. *Leisure interests:* fell walking, tennis, wine tasting, theatre. *Address:* 190 Court Lane, Dulwich, London, SE21 7ED, England.

RÜÜTEL, Arnold, PH.D., DR. AGR. SC.; Estonian politician and agronomist; b. 10 May 1928, Saaremaa; s. of Feodor Rüütel and Juulia Rüütel; m. Ingrid Rüütel 1958; two d.; ed. Estonian Agric. Acad.; sr. agronomist, Saaremaa Dist., Estonian S.S.R. 1949–50; Deputy Dir. Estonian Inst. of Livestock-breeding and Veterinary Sciences 1957–63; mem. CPSU 1964–90; Dir. of Tartu State Research Farm 1963–69; Rector Estonian Agric. Acad. 1969–77; Sec. of Cen. Cttee. of Estonian CP on Agric. Problems 1977–79; First Deputy Chair. Council of Ministers of Estonia 1979–83; Chair. Supreme Council of Estonian S.S.R. 1983–90, of Republic of Estonia 1990–92; Deputy Pres. of U.S.S.R. Presidium of Supreme Soviet 1984–91; founder, Chair. Inst. of Nat. Devt. and Cooperation 1992–; founder and Chair. Estonian Rural People's Party (Maarava) 1994–; Deputy Speaker of State Ass. (Riigikogu) March 1995–; Presidential Cand. 1996; mem. Tallinn City Council 1993–. *Leisure interests:* nature protection, sports. *Address:* Riigikogu, Lossi Plats 1A, 0100 Tallinn (Office); Koidula Str. 3–5, 0010 Tallinn, Estonia (Home). *Telephone:* (2) 316-311 (Office); (2) 432-888 (Home).

RUZIMATOV, Farukh Sadullovich; Russian ballet dancer; b. 26 June 1963, Tashkent; ed. Vaganova Acad. of Russian Ballet; with Mariinsky Theatre 1981–, soloist 1986–; guest dancer Bolshoi Theatre, Moscow; with American Ballet Theatre 1990–91; toured abroad; main roles include Albert in Giselle, Siegfried in Swan Lake, Basil in Don Quixote, The Prince in The Nutcracker; prize-winner int. competitions in Varna 1983, Paris 1984, Merited Artist of Russia and Tatarstan, Benoit de la Dance Prize. *Address:* Mariinsky Theatre, Teatralnaya pl. 1, St. Petersburg, Russia (Office). *Telephone:* (812) 315 5742 (Office).

RWIGYEMA, Pierre Célestin; Rwandan politician; fmrly. Minister of Primary and Secondary Educ.; Prime Minister of Rwanda 1995–; mem. Democratic Republican Movt. (MDR). *Address:* Office of the Prime Minister, Kigali, Rwanda.

RYABOV, Nikolai Timofeyevich; Russian politician and lawyer; b. 9 Dec. 1946, Salsk, Rostov Region; ed. Rostov Univ.; mem. CPSU 1968–91; worked as tractor driver, engineer Salsk Agricultural Machine Factory 1966–72; taught in higher educ. school of Rostov Region 1973–90; People's Deputy of Russia 1990–93; mem. Supreme Soviet 1990–92, Chair. Sub-Cttee. for legis. 1990–91; Chair. Council of Repubs. 1991–92, Deputy Chair. Supreme Soviet 1992–93; Deputy Chair. Constitutional Comm. 1991–93, Chair. Cen. Election Comm. of Russian Fed. 1993–96; Amb. to Czech Repub. 1996–. *Address:* Russian Embassy, Pod Kaštany str. 1, 16000 Prague 6, Bulenec, Czech Republic. *Telephone:* (2) 381-943. *Fax:* (2) 373-800.

RYABOV, Vladimir Vladimirovich; Russian composer and pianist; Chelyabinsk; m. 1st; one d.; m. 4th Ellen Levine; ed. Moscow State Conservatory (expelled twice for non-conformist attitudes), Gnessin Pedagogical Inst. of Music (under Aram Khachaturyan), Leningrad State Conservatory; taught composition in Leningrad and Sverdlovsk conservatories 1977–81; toured as pianist in Russia, Finland, U.S.A. performing standard repertoire and own compositions; winner First S. Prokofiev Int. Composers' Competition 1991; Merited Artist of Russia. *Compositions include:* 4 symphonies (Nine Northern Tunes 1977, Pushkin 1980, Listen 1981, In Memoriam of J. Brahms 1983, 5 string quintets, works for full and chamber orchestras, sonatas and other compositions for piano, violin, viola, organ, choir, song cycles on Russian and German poetry, transcriptions and paraphrases of classical music. *Address:* Novoyasenevsky pr. 14, kor. 2 Apt. 48, Moscow, Russia; Orisaarentie 6, E00840 Helsinki, Finland. *Telephone:* (095) 421 7767 (Moscow).

RYAN, Alan James, M.A., F.B.A.; British professor of politics and author; b. 9 May 1940, London; s. of James W. Ryan and Ivy Ryan; m. Kathleen Alyson Lane 1971; one d.; ed. Christ's Hospital and Balliol Coll. Oxford; Fellow, New Coll. Oxford 1969–; Reader in Politics, Univ. of Oxford 1978–88; Prof. of Politics, Princeton Univ. 1988–96, Mellon Fellow, Inst. for Advanced Study 1991–92; Warden, New Coll. Oxford 1996–; Visiting Prof., City Univ. of New York, Univs. of Texas, Calif., Witwatersrand Univ., Univ. of Cape Town; Visiting Fellow, Australian Nat. Univ.; de Carle Lecturer, Univ. of Otago; del. Oxford Univ. Press 1982–87. *Publications:* The Philosophy of John Stuart Mill 1970, The Philosophy of the Social Sciences 1970, J. S. Mill 1974, Property and Political Theory 1984, Property 1987, Russell: A Political Life 1988, John Dewey and the High Tide of American Liberalism 1995, Liberal Anxieties and Liberal Education 1988. *Leisure interest:* dinghy sailing. *Address:* New College, Oxford, OX1 3BN, England.

RYAN, Arthur Frederick; American financial executive; b. 14 Sept. 1942, Brooklyn; s. of Arthur Ryan and Gertrude Wingert; m. Patricia Kelly; two s. two d.; ed. Providence Coll.; Area Man. Data Corpn. Washington, D.C. 1965–72; Project Man. Chase Manhattan Corpn. and Bank, New York 1972–73, Second Vice-Pres. 1973–74, Vice-Pres. 1974–75, Operations Exec. 1978, Exec. Vice-Pres. 1982, later Vice-Chair., Pres. 1990–94; Chair. and C.E.O. Prudential Insurance Co. of America Dec. 1994–; mem. American Bankers Asscn. *Address:* Prudential Insurance Company, 751 Broad Street, Newark, NJ 07102, U.S.A.

RYAN, George H., B.S.; American politician; b. 24 Feb. 1934, Maquoketa, Iowa; s. of Thomas J. Ryan and Jeanette (née Bowman) Ryan; m. Lura Lynn Lowe 1956; one s. five d.; ed. Ferris State Coll.; fmrly. with U.S. Army, Korea; mem. Ill. House of Reps. 1973–82, minority leader 1977–80, Speaker 1981–82, Lieut.-Gov. of Ill. 1983–91, State Sec. 1991–99; Gov. of Illinois Jan. 1999–; numerous awards; Republican. *Address:* Governor's Office, 207 State House, Springfield, IL 62706, U.S.A.

RYAN, Meg; American actress; b. 19 Nov. 1961, Fairfield, Conn.; m. Dennis Quaid (q.v.) 1991; one s.; ed. Bethel High School and New York Univ.; fmrly. appeared in TV commercials; TV appearances in As the World Turns, One of the Boys, Amy and the Angel, The Wild Side, Charles in Charge; owner of Prufrock Pictures. *Films:* Rich and Famous 1981, Amityville III-D, Top Gun, Armed and Dangerous, Innerspace, D.O.A., Promised Land, The Presidio, When Harry Met Sally, Joe Versus the Volcano, The Doors, Prelude to a Kiss, Sleepless in Seattle, Flesh and Bone, Significant Other, When a Man Loves a Woman, I.Q., Paris Match, Restoration, French Kiss 1995, Two for the Road 1996, Courage Under Fire 1996, Addicted to Love 1997, City of Angels 1998, You've Got Mail 1998. *Address:* c/o ICM, 8942 Wilshire Boulevard, Beverly Hills, CA 90211, U.S.A.

RYAN, Peter Allen, B.A., M.M.; Australian author and publisher; b. 4 Sept. 1923, Melbourne; s. of Emmett F. Ryan and Alice D. Ryan; m. Gladys A. Davidson 1947; one s. one d.; ed. Malvern Grammar School, Melbourne and Univ. of Melbourne; mil. service 1942–45; Dir. United Service Publicity Pty. Ltd. 1953–57; Public Relations Man., Imperial Chemical Industries of Australia and New Zealand Ltd. 1957–61; Asst. to Vice-Chancellor, Univ. of Melbourne 1962; Dir. Melbourne Univ. Press 1962–88; mem. Solicitors Disciplinary Tribunal 1984–88; Sec. Bd. of Examiners for Barristers and Solicitors 1988–; Exec. Officer Vic. Council of Legal Educ. and Admin. Officer Vic. Council of Law Reporting 1989–. *Publications:* Fear Drive My Feet 1959, The Preparation of Manuscripts 1966, Encyclopedia of Papua and New Guinea (Gen. Ed.) 1972, Redmond Barry 1973, William Macmahon Ball: A Memoir 1989, Black Bonanza, A Landslide of Gold 1991, Lines of Fire: Manning Clark and Other Writings 1997. *Leisure interests:* reading, writing, riding. *Address:* Supreme Court, William Street, Melbourne, Vic. 3000, Australia. *Telephone:* 603-4388.

RYAN, Richie, B.A.; Irish fmr. politician and lawyer; b. 1929, Dublin; s. of James R. Ryan and Irene Boyle; m. Mairéad King 1956; three s. two d.; ed. Synge St. Christian Brothers' School, Dublin, Univ. Coll., Dublin, Inc. Law Soc. of Ireland Law School; Personal Asst. to Minister for Justice 1954–57; mem. Dáil (House of Reps.) 1959–82; mem. Dublin Health Authority (Chair. 1967–68), mem. Eastern Health Bd. 1967–73; mem. Dublin City Council 1960–73; Commr. of Irish Lighthouses Authority 1960–; Del. to Consultative Assembly, Council of Europe 1968–73; Amnesty Int. Rep. in Middle East 1969–70; mem. of European Parl. 1973, 1977–86, Vice-Pres. Budget Cttee.; fmr. Trustee of Fine Gael Party and Spokesman on Foreign Affairs; Minister for Finance, Minister for the Public Service 1973–77; Chair. Bd. Govs. IMF, World Bank and IDA 1976–77; Gov. IMF, World Bank and European Investment Bank 1973–77; Pres. EEC Council of Ministers of Finance and Economy 1975; Rep. EEC in U.S.A., Saudi Arabia, Kuwait, U.A.E., Iran and Bahrain 1975, 1976; Del. to Inter-Parl. Union, Iran 1966; mem. Jt. Ass. European Parl. and ACP States 1979–86; fmr. mem. of Court of Auditors of European Communities; fmr. Vice-Pres. European Union of Christian Democrats; mem. Inc. Law Soc. of Ireland, Inst. of Taxation in Ireland, Amnesty Int. (Irish Section). *Leisure interests:* reading, theatre, music. *Address:* European Court of Auditors, 12 Rue Alcide de Gasperi, 1615 Luxembourg. *Telephone:* Luxembourg (352) 4398-370.

RYAN, Thomas Anthony (Tony), LL.D.; Irish business executive; b. 2 Feb. 1936, Co. Tipperary; m.; three s.; ed. Christian Brothers School, Thurles, Co. Tipperary, N. Western Univ., Chicago; Aer Lingus 1956–75; f. GPA Group with Aer Lingus and Guinness Peat Group, Chair., CEO 1975–93; Chair. and C.E.O. GE Capital Aviation Services 1994–, GE Aviation Services 1994–; Chair. (non-exec.) Ryanair 1995–; Dir. (non-exec.) Bank of Ireland 1988, Trafalgar House 1989–; Consul for Mexico in Ireland; mem. Bd. Govs. Nat. Gallery of Ireland, Europe Round Table, Nat. Univ. of Ireland 1987, Hon. mem. Limerick Univ. 1986; Hon. LL.D. (Trinity Coll., Dublin). *Leisure interests:* farming, the arts.

RYAZANOV, Eldar Aleksandrovich; Russian film director; b. 18 Nov. 1927, Moscow; studied at VGIK under Pyriev, Kozintsev and Eisenstein; writes most of his own scripts (often together with playwright Emil Braginsky); People's Artist of the U.S.S.R. 1974. *Films include:* Voices of Spring 1955, Carnival Night 1956, The Girl without an Address 1957, How Robinson was Created 1961, The Hussar Ballad 1962, Let Me Make a Complaint 1964, Look out for the Cars 1966, The Zigzag of Success 1968, The Old Rascals 1971, The Amazing Adventures of Italians in Russia 1973, The Irony of Fate 1975, An Official Romance 1978, Garage 1979, Put in a Word for the Poor Hussar 1981, Railway Station for Two 1983, A Cruel Romance 1984, Forgotten Melody for Flute 1988, Dear Elena Sergeevna 1988, The Promised Heaven 1991 (Nika Prize 1992), The Prediction 1993, Hey, Fools! 1996; numerous TV productions, including interviews with Boris Yeltsin and Naina Yeltsin 1993. *Publication:* Not Summarizing (memoirs). *Address:* Bolshoi Tishinski per. 12, Apt. 70, 123557 Moscow, Russia. *Telephone:* 253-56-11; 549-57-75.

RYBAKOV, Boris Aleksandrovich; Russian historian; b. 3 June 1908; m.; one s.; ed. Moscow State Univ.; researcher Aleksandrov Museum 1930; on staff State Museum of History 1931–36; sr. researcher, head of div. Inst. of History of Material Culture U.S.S.R. Acad. of Sciences 1956–87; Hon. Dir. Inst. of Archaeology U.S.S.R. Acad. of Sciences; corresp. mem. U.S.S.R. (now Russian) Acad. of Sciences 1953, mem. 1958; research in history, archaeology and culture of Old Russia, its political, trade and cultural relations in Middle Ages; Foreign mem. Bulgarian Acad. of Sciences; Hero of Socialist Labour; Lenin Prize, U.S.S.R. State Prize, Gold Medal of Slovak Acad. of Sciences. *Publications include:* Craftsmanship 9th–13th centuries 1938, History of Culture of Old Russia 1948, Herodot's Skiphia 1979, Kiev Rus and Russian principalities 12th–13th Centuries 1982, numerous articles. *Address:* Institute of Archaeology, Russian Academy of Sciences, D. Ulyanov str. 19, 117036 Moscow, Russia. *Telephone:* (095) 126 9494 (Office); (095) 237-48-53 (Home).

RYBKIN, Ivan Petrovich, DR.POLIT.SCH., CAND. TECH. SC.; Russian politician; b. 20 Oct. 1946, Semigorovka, Voronezh Region; m.; two d.; ed. Volgograd Inst. of Agric. Acad. of Social Sciences at Cen. Cttee. CPSU; sr. engineer Kolkhoz Zavety Ilyicha Volgograd Region 1968–69; lecturer, Prof., Head of Chair, Deputy Dean, Volgograd Inst. of Agric. 1970–87; Sec. Party Cttee. 1983–87, First Sec. CPSU Dist. Cttee. in Volgograd, Second Sec. Volgograd Regional Cttee. CPSU 1987–91; Head of Div. Cen. Cttee. CP of R.S.F.S.R. 1991; People's Deputy of Russia 1990–93; one of founders and Co-Chair. faction Communists of Russia 1990–91; mem. Agrarian Party, concurrently one of founders Socialist Party of Workers 1991–93; deputy to State Duma (Parl.) 1993–96, Chair. 1994–95; mem. Council on Personnel Policy of Pres. Yeltsin 1994–95, mem. Security Council 1994–96, Sec. 1996–98; head of group negotiating with Chechen leaders 1996–98; Deputy Prime Minister 1998; Plenipotentiary Rep. of Russian Pres. to C.I.S. states May 1998–; Chair. Political Union Regions of Russia, concurrently of Election Block 1995; Prize for Contribution to Peace with Chechnya (Ichkeria) 1996. *Publications:* State Duma; Fifth Attempt, We are Doomed to Consensus, numerous articles. *Address:* Office of the President, Kremlin korp 1, Moscow, Russia. *Telephone:* (095) 206-43-75.

RYCKMANS, Pierre, PH.D.; Belgian professor of Chinese studies and writer; b. 28 Sept. 1935, Brussels; m. Chang Han-fang; three s. one d.; ed. Univ. of Louvain; fmr. Prof. of Chinese Studies, Univ. of Sydney; mem. Académie Royale de Littérature Française (Brussels) 1991; Prix Stanislas-Julien (Institut de France), Prix Jean Walter (Acad. Française), The Independent (U.K.) Foreign Fiction Award 1992, Christina Stead Prize for Fiction (N.S.W.) 1992, etc.; Officer Ordre de Léopold. *Publications:* (under pen-name Simon Leys) The Chairman's New Clothes: Mao and the Cultural Revolution 1977, Chinese Shadows 1977, The Burning Forest 1985, La Mort de Napoléon 1986 (English trans. 1991), Les Entretiens de Confucius 1989, L'humeur, l'honneur, l'horreur 1991, The Analects of Confucius 1996, The View from the Bridge 1996, The Angel and the Octopus 1999. *Address:* 6 Bonwick Place, Garran, A.C.T. 2605, Australia. *Fax:* (2) 62 81 48 87.

RYDER, Winona; American actress; b. 29 Oct. 1971, Winona, Minn.; d. of Michael Horowitz and Cynthia Istas; ed. Petaluma Jr. High School, San Francisco and acting classes at American Conservatory Theatre, San Francisco. *Films include:* Lucas 1986, Square Dance, Beetlejuice 1969, Heathers, Great Balls of Fire, Welcome Home Roxy, Carmichael, Edward Scissorhands, Mermaids, The Age of Innocence, Reality Bites, House of Spirits, Boys, Little Women, How to Make an American Quilt, The Crucible, Looking for Richard, Boys, Alien Resurrection. *Address:* c/o Carole Obie Arts Entertainment, 9460 Wilshire Boulevard, 7th Floor, Beverly Hills, CA 90210, U.S.A.

RYDER OF EATON HASTINGS, Baron (Life Peer), cr. 1975, of Eaton Hastings, Oxfordshire; **Sydney Thomas Franklin (Don) Ryder,** Kt.; British business executive; b. 16 Sept. 1916, Ealing, London; s. of John Ryder; m. Eileen Winifred Dodds 1950; one s. one d.; Ed. Stock Exchange Gazette 1950–60; Jt. Man. Dir. Kelly Iliffe Holdings and Assoc. Iliffe Press 1960–61, Sole Man. Dir. 1961–63; Dir. Int. Publishing Corpn. 1963–70; Man. Dir. Reed Paper Group 1963–68, Chair., Chief Exec. Reed Int. 1968–74; Industrial Adviser, Cabinet Office 1974; Chair. Nat. Enterprise Bd. 1975–77; Dir. Metropolitan Estate Property Corpn. Ltd. 1972–75; part-time mem. British Gas Corpn. 1973–78; mem. of Council and Bd. of Fellows, B.I.M. 1970, Cranfield Inst. of Tech. 1970–74, Industrial Soc. 1971, N.E.D.C. 1975–77; Pres. Nat. Materials Handling Centre 1970–77; Vice-Pres. Royal Soc. for Prevention of Accidents 1973–. *Leisure interests:* sailing, squash, chess. *Address:* House of Lords, London, S.W.1, England.

RYDER OF WARSAW, Baroness (Life Peer), cr. 1979, of Warsaw in Poland; **Susan Ryder,** C.M.G., O.B.E.; British social worker; b. 3 July 1923, Leeds; d. of Charles Ryder and Elizabeth Ryder; m. Group Capt. Leonard Cheshire (Lord Cheshire) 1959 (died 1992); one s. one d.; ed. Benenden School, Cranbrook, Kent; served World War II with First Aid Nursing Yeomanry and Polish Section of Special Operations Exec. 1939–45; Founder, Sue Ryder Foundation for the Sick & Disabled of all age groups; Co-founder and Trustee Ryder-Cheshire Foundation; Pres. Leonard Cheshire Foundation; Hon. Fellow Liverpool John Moores Univ. 1998; Hon. LL.D. (Liverpool) 1973, (Exeter) 1980, (London) 1981, (Leeds) 1984, (Cambridge) 1989; Hon. D.Litt. (Reading) 1982, Hon. D.C.L. (Kent) 1986; Dr. h.c. (Essex) 1993; Officer's Cross, Order of Polonia Restituta 1965, Medal of Yugoslav Flag with Gold Wreath and Diploma 1971, Golden Order of Merit (Poland) 1976, Order of Smile (Poland) 1981, Commdr.'s Cross of Order of Polonia Restituta 1992, Silver Cross, Czech Parachutists 1996, Humanitarian Award (Poland) 1996, Ecclesiae Populoque Servitium Praestanti (Poland) 1996. *Publications:* And the Morrow is Theirs (autobiog.) 1975, Child of My Love (autobiog.) 1986; Remembrance (annual magazine of Sue Ryder Foundation). *Leisure interests:* music, architecture, building. *Address:* Sue Ryder Foundation, Cavendish, Sudbury, Suffolk, CO10 8AY, England. *Telephone:* (01787) 280653. *Fax:* (01787) 280548.

RYDER OF WENSUM, Baron (Life Peer), cr. 1997, of Wensum in the County of Norfolk; **Richard Andrew Ryder,** O.B.E., P.C., B.A.; British politician; b. 4 Feb. 1949; m. Caroline Mary Stephens 1981; one s. (deceased) one d.; ed. Radley Coll., Magdalene Coll., Cambridge; Political Sec. to Margaret Thatcher, Leader of the Opposition and Prime Minister 1975–81; M.P. for Mid-Norfolk 1983–97; Parl. Pvt. Sec. to Financial Sec. to the Treasury 1984, Parl. Pvt. Sec. to Foreign Sec. 1984–86; Govt. Whip 1986–88; Parl. Sec. Ministry of Agric. 1988–89; Econ. Sec. to Treasury 1989–90; Paymaster Gen. 1990; Parl. Sec. to Treasury and Govt. Chief Whip 1990–95; Chair. Easter Counties Radio; partner in family farming business. *Address:* c/o House of Lords, Westminster, London SW1A 0PW, England.

RYDIN, Bo, B.SC.; Swedish business executive; b. 7 May 1932; s. of Gunnar Rydin and Signe (née Höög) Rydin; m. 1st Monika Avréus 1955 (died 1992); m. 2nd Françoise You 1997; with Stockholms Enskilda Bank 1956–57; Marma-Långrör AB 1957–60; A.B. Gullhögens Bruk 1960, Pres. 1965–71; Pres. and C.E.O. Svenska Cellulosa AB 1972–88, Chair. and C.E.O. 1988–90, Chair. 1990–; Chair. Svenska Cellulosa AB, SCA, AB Industrivärden, Graningeverken, Skanska AB; Vice-Chair. Svenska Handelsbanken, Sransra; mem. Bd. IBM, Emea, SAS Ass. of Reps., Scancem; Chair. Fed. of Swedish Industries 1993–94; mem. Royal Swedish Acad. of Eng. Sciences, Royal Swedish Acad. of Agric. and Forestry; D.Econs. h.c.; D.Tech. h.c.; King's Medal 12th Dimension of Order of the Seraphim. *Leisure interests:* golf, hunting, opera. *Address:* AB Industrivärden, Storgatan 10, Box 5403, 114 84 Stockholm (Office); Karlavägen 3, 114 24 Stockholm, Sweden (Home).

RYE, C. Richard, B.COM.; Australian civil servant; b. 13 Aug. 1935, Manly, N.S.W.; s. of Rev. Leslie Howard Rye and Gladys Rye; m. Blanca Luz Rye 1963; one d.; ed. Univ. of Melbourne; joined Australian Bureau of Statistics 1953; transferred to Treasury 1968, Asst. Sec., Econ. Branch 1970; Minister for Financial Affairs, Embassy, Washington D.C. 1975–76; First Asst. Sec. Gen. Financial and Econ. Policy Div., Treasury 1976–79; Deputy Sec. for Econ. Affairs 1979–1983; Deputy Sec. of the Treasury 1983–85; Exec. Dir. IMF 1985–89; Chair. Commonwealth Grants Comm. 1989–. *Address:* 59 Pandanus Street, Fisher, A.C.T. 2611, Canberra, Australia.

RYKIEL, Sonia (b. Flis); French fashion designer; b. 25 May 1930, Paris; m.; one s. one d.; began designing rabbit-hair sweaters which established her reputation 1963; opened own boutique, Paris 1968; opened further boutiques specializing in men's knitwear and household linens 1976, 1981; launched first perfume 7e Sens 1979; supervised renovation of Hotel Crillon, Paris 1982; first boutique opened New York 1983; launched first children's collection 1984; Vice-Pres. Chambre Syndicale du Prêt-à-Porter des Couturiers et des Créateurs de Mode, Paris 1982; launched Sonia Rykiel perfume 1997; Hon. Prof. China Textile Univ., Shanghai 1998; Officier Ordre des Arts et des Lettres 1993, Award for Design Excellence (Costume Cttee., Chicago Historical Soc.); Officier, Légion d'honneur 1996. *Publications:* Et je la voudrais nue 1979, Célébration 1988, La collection 1989, Colette et la mode 1991, Collection terminée, collection interminable 1993, Tatiana Acacia (jtly.) 1993, Les lèvres rouges 1996, Sonia Rykiel (memoirs) 1997. *Address:* 175 boulevard Saint Germain, 75006 Paris, France. *Telephone:* (1) 49.54.60.00. *Fax:* (1) 49.54.60.96.

RYLANCE, Mark; British actor and director; b. 1960, Ashford, Kent; ed. Royal Acad. of Dramatic Art and Chrysalis Theatre School, Balham; joined The Citizen's Theatre, Glasgow 1980; has since worked with RSC, Royal Nat. Theatre, Royal Opera House, Scottish Ballet, Shared Experience, Bush Theatre, Tricycle Theatre, London Theatre of Imagination, Contact Theatre, Oxford Playhouse, Project Theatre, Dublin, Mermaid Theatre, Royal Court, American Repertory Theatre, Boston, Theatre for a New Audience, New York, Pittsburgh Playhouse, Thelma Holte; now Assoc. actor, RSC; Artistic Dir. Shakespeare's Globe, Phoebus Cart; recent work includes title role in Phoebus Cart's production of Macbeth (also dir.) and Proteus in The Two Gentlemen of Verona, Shakespeare's Globe's Prologue Season 1996; title role in Henry V in Shakespeare's Globe's opening season 1997, Bassanio in The Merchant of Venice and Hippolito in The Honest Whore, Shakespeare's Globe 1998; TV appearances include The Grass Arena, Love Lies Bleeding, In Lambeth, Incident in Judea; Olivier Award for Best Actor 1994. *Films:* Prospero's Books, Angels and Insects, Institute Benjamenta, Hearts of Fire. *Address:* c/o Shakespeare's Globe, Southwark, London S.E.1, England.

RYNNE, Etienne Andrew, M.A., M.R.I.A., F.S.A.; Irish professor of archaeology; b. 11 Sept. 1932, Dublin; s. of Dr. Michael Rynne and Nathalie Fournier; m. Aideen Lucas 1967; four s. one d.; ed. Terenure Coll., Dublin, Ecole des Roches, Verneuil-sur-Avre, France, Clongowes Wood Coll., Clane, Co. Kildare and Univ. Coll. Dublin; part-time Archaeological Asst., Nat. Museum of Ireland 1954–56, Asst., Irish Antiquities Div. 1957–66, Asst.-Keeper 1966–67; lecturer in Celtic Archaeology, Univ. Coll., Galway 1967–78, Prof. of Archaeology 1978–; Hon. Curator Galway City Museum 1972–86; Pres. Royal Soc. of Antiquaries of Ireland 1985–89, Galway Archaeological & Historical Soc. 1989–95; Ed. North Munster Antiquarian Journal 1964–; mem. Royal Irish Acad.; Travelling Studentship Prize, Nat. Univ. of Ireland 1956. *Publications:* Ed. North Munster Studies 1967, Figures from the Past 1987; about 200 articles in learned journals. *Leisure interests:* archaeology (visiting ancient sites, museums etc.), art history, sport (boxing, athletics). *Address:* Department of Archaeology, University College, Galway, Ireland. *Telephone:* 091-524411 (Office). *Fax:* 091-525700 (Office).

RYRIE, Sir William Sinclair, K.C.B., M.A., F.R.S.A.; British merchant banker and fmr. civil servant; b. 10 Nov. 1928, Calcutta, India; s. of Rev. Dr. Frank Ryrie and Mabel M. Ryrie; m. 1st Dorrit Klein 1953 (dissolved 1969); two s. one d.; m. 2nd Christine G. Thomson 1969; one s.; ed. Heriot's School, Edinburgh, Edinburgh Univ.; army service, Lieut. Intelligence Corps in Malaya 1951–53 (despatches 1953); joined Colonial Office as Asst. Prin. 1953; seconded to Govt. of Uganda 1956–58; Prin., UN Affairs, Colonial Office 1959–63; Prin., Balance of Payments Div. of H.M. Treasury 1963–66, Asst. Sec. for Int. Monetary Affairs 1966–69; Prin. Pvt. Sec. to Chancellor of the Exchequer 1969–71; Under-Sec., Public Sector Group in Treasury 1971–75; Econ. Minister, Embassy in U.S.A. and Exec. Dir. of IMF, IBRD, IDA, IFC 1975–79; Second Perm. Sec., Domestic Economy Sector, H.M. Treasury 1980–82; Perm. Sec. Overseas Devt. Admin. 1982–84; Exec. Vice-Pres. and Chief Exec. Int. Finance Corpn., World Bank Group 1984–93; Exec. Dir. Barings PLC 1994–95, Vice-Chair. ING Barings Holding Co. Ltd. 1995–98; Chair. Baring Emerging Europe Trust 1994–; Deputy Chair. Commonwealth Devt. Corpn. 1994–98; Dir. W. S. Atkins Ltd. 1994–, First NIS Regional Fund 1994–, Ashanti Goldfields Co. 1995–; mem. Group of Thirty 1992–; Council mem. Overseas Devt. Inst. 1994–; Pres. Edin. Univ. Devt. Trust 1994–; Dir. CARE UK 1993–. *Publication:* First World, Third World 1995. *Leisure interests:* walking, photography. *Address:* Hawkwood, Hawkwood Lane, Chislehurst, Kent, BR7 5PW, England.

RYTKHEU, Yuriy Sergeyevich; Russian/Chukchi writer; b. 8 March 1930, Uellen, Chukotka N.O., Magadan Region; m. Galina Vinogradova 1949; two s. one d.; ed. Leningrad Univ.; foremost Chukchi writer; works have been translated into Russian; started writing for the newspaper Soviet Chukotka 1947; mem. CPSU 1967–91. *Publications:* Short stories: Friends and Comrades, People of our Coast 1953, When the Snow Melts (novel) 1960, The Sorceress of Konerga 1960, The Saga of Chukotka 1960, Farewell to the Gods (short stories) 1961, Nunivak (tales) 1963, The Magic Gauntlet (novel) 1963, In the Vale of the Little Sunbeams (novel) 1963, The Walrus of Dissent (stories) 1964, Blue Foxes (stories) 1964, Wings Are Becoming Stronger in Flight (novel) 1964, Bear Stew (verses) 1965, The Finest Ships 1967, Dream at the Onset of Mist 1969, Frost on the Threshold 1971, The Harpoon Thrower 1971, White Snows (novel) 1975, When the Whales Depart 1976, Contemporary Legends 1980, The Magic Numbers (novel) 1985, Island of Hope (novel) 1987, The Dream in the Beginning of Mist (novel) 1988, Intercontinental Bridge 1989, The Journey to Youth or The Time of Red Cloudberries 1991, Unter dem Sternbild der Trauer 1997, Unna 1998. *Address:* Suvorovsky Prosp. 56, Apt. 84, 193015 St. Petersburg, Russia. *Telephone:* (812) 274-85-26. *Fax:* (812) 274-85-26.

RYTTER, Jakob, LL.D.; Danish diplomatist; b. 17 Dec. 1932, Aarhus; s. of the late Ejnar I. J. Rytter and Ingeborg J. Rytter; m. Suzanne Engelsen 1963 (died 1986); two d.; ed. Marselisborg Gymnasium, Aarhus, Lycée de Fontainebleau, Univ. of Aarhus, Institut d'Etudes Politiques, Paris; mil. service 1960; entered Danish Foreign Office 1961, Sec. of Embassy, Bonn 1963–66, Del. to UN Gen. Ass., New York 1966, 1968, First Sec. Tel Aviv 1969–72, Counsellor Danish EC Representation, Brussels 1973–78, Dir. EC Affairs, Danish Foreign Ministry 1978–83, Deputy Perm. Rep., Danish EC Representation 1983–86; Amb. to Israel 1986–89, 1992–96, Amb., Perm. Rep. to the EC, Brussels 1989–92; Amb. to the Netherlands 1996– and Perm. Rep. to OPCW, The Hague 1998–; Chair. Admin. and Financial Council, European Schools 1977–78; Commdr. (First Class) of Dannebrog. *Address:* Royal Danish Embassy, Koninginnegracht 30, Postbus 85654, 2508 CJ The Hague, Netherlands; Esplanaden 28, DK-1263 Copenhagen K., Denmark. *Telephone:* (70) 302 59 59 (Netherlands); 33 339798 (Denmark).

RYZHKOV, Nikolai Ivanovich; Russian politician; b. 28 Sept. 1929, Donetz; m. Lyudmila Sergeyevna Ryzhkova; one d.; ed. S.M. Kirov Ural Polytechnic Inst.; mem. CPSU 1956–91; Chief Engineer 1965–70, Deputy Dir., later Dir. S. Ordhonskidze Ural Factory of Heavy Machine Bldg. 1970; Gen. Dir. of Production Uralmash Factory 1971–75; First Deputy Minister of Heavy and Transport Machine Bldg. 1975–79; mem. Cen. Cttee. CPSU in charge of Heavy Industry 1981–90; mem. Politburo 1985–90; Chair. Council of Ministers 1985–90; First Deputy Chair. of Gosplan 1979–82; Head Econ. Affairs 1982–85; Deputy of the U.S.S.R. Supreme Soviet 1974–89; People's Deputy of the U.S.S.R. 1989–91; cand. for Pres. of Russia 1991; Chair. Bd. Tveruniversalbank; 1993–95, Pres. Int. Public Union; leader pre-election bloc "Power to People"; mem State Duma Dec. 1995–, Chair. deputies bloc Narodovlastiye; U.S.S.R. State Prizes 1969, 1979; Order of Lenin (twice), Order of Red Banner of Labour (twice) and other decorations. *Publication:* Perestroika: a series of betrayals. *Address:* State Duma, Okhotny Ryad 1, 103009, Moscow, Russia. *Telephone:* (095) 292-88-40. *Fax:* (095) 292-73-41.

RYZHKOV, Vladimir Aleksandrovich; Russian politician; b. 3 Sept. 1966, Altai Territory; ed. Altai State Univ.; Deputy Head Altai Territory Soc. of Encouraging Perestroika 1988–90; Deputy Chair. Altai Territory Movt. Democratic Russia 1990–91; Sec. to Head of Altai Territory Admin., mem. State Duma 1993–; mem. Cttee. on Fed. and Regional Policy 1994–95; Deputy Chair. faction Russia Our Home 1996–97, First Deputy Chair. State Duma (Parl.) 1997–. *Publications:* over 40 articles on contemporary policy. *Address:* State Duma, Okhotny Ryad 1, 103265 Moscow, Russia (Office). *Telephone:* (095) 292 9725 (Office). *Fax:* (095) 292 1785 (Office).

RYZHOV, Yuri Alexeevich, D.TECH.; Russian politician and scientist; b. 28 Oct. 1930, Moscow; m.; two d.; ed. Moscow Physical Tech. Inst.; mem. CPSU 1961–90; engineer 1954–60; sr. researcher Moscow Inst. of Aviation 1960–, Prof. 1970–, Prorector 1972–86, Rector 1986–91; mem. U.S.S.R (now Russian) Acad. of Sciences 1987; author of works on aerodynamics of high velocities; political activities since late 1980s; mem. of the Supreme Soviet of the U.S.S.R. 1989–91; mem. Interregional Group of Deputies 1989–; Russian Amb. to France 1992–98. *Leisure interest:* music. *Address:* Moscow State Aviation Inst., Volokolamskoye shosse, 125871 Moscow, Russia. *Telephone:* (095) 158-13-78 (Office); (095) 135-12-44 (Home).

RZEMYKOWSKI, Tadeusz; Polish politician and economist; b. 8 July 1946; Jastrowie, Pila Prov.; m.; two s.; ed. Higher School of Economics, Poznań; with Piła branch of the Oil and Gas Exploration Plant; mem. Polish Econ. Soc.; mem. Polish United Workers' Party (PZPR) 1965–90; mem. Voivodship Council and Supervisory Bd. of Social Democracy of Poland (SdRP); Senator 1993–; mem. Democratic Left Alliance Parl. Club, vice-leader Nat. Economy Cttee. 1993–97; Vice-Marshal of the Senate 1997. *Address:* Kancelaria Senatu RP, ul. Wiejska 6, 00-902 Warsaw, Poland. *Telephone:* (22) 694 14 47, 694 20 03.

S

SÁ, Angelo Calmon de; Brazilian politician and banker; b. 1 Nov. 1935, Salvador-Bahia; s. of Francisco de Sá and Maria dos Prazeres Calmon de Sá; m. Ana Maria Carvalho 1962; two s. two d.; ed. Univ. Federal da Bahia; Sec. of Industry and Commerce, Bahia State 1967–70, Sec. of Finance 1970–71; Minister of Industry and Commerce 1977–79; Minister of Regional Devt. 1992–93; Pres. Banco do Brasil S.A. 1974–77, mem. Bd. of Dirs. 1987–; mem. Bd. of Dirs. Banco Econômico S.A. 1977–, Pres. and C.E.O. 1979–92, Chair. of Bd. 1992–; Chair. Brazilian Cocoa Trade Comm. (Comcauba) 1980–; Dir. Nordeste Química S.A. 1980–, American Express Int. Bank Ltd., New York 1982–, Associação de Exportadores Brasileiros 1982–; mem. Int. Advisory Council Wells Fargo Bank, San Francisco 1979–; mem. Nat. Monetary Council, representing pvt. sector 1979–86; Vice-Pres. Bahia Chamber of Commerce 1981–; Dir. Brazilian Exporters' Asscn. 1982–; Pres. Brazil section, Brazil-U.S. Business Council 1984–87, mem. Exec. Cttee. 1987–; mem. Bd. of Trustees, Eisenhower Exchange Fellowships Inc.; several Brazilian honours. *Publication:* study on the Bank of Brazil as an agent of development and a factor of national integration. *Leisure interests:* riding, tennis, golf. *Address:* Banco Econômico S.A., Rua Miguel Calmon, 285, Edf. Goes Calmon, 11° andar, 40015 Salvador-Bahia, Brazil.

SAADAWI, Nawal al-, M.D.; Egyptian writer and medical practitioner; b. 27 Oct. 1931; m. Sherif Hetata 1964; one s. one d.; ed. Cairo Univ.; novelist and writer 1956–; Dir.-Gen. Ministry of Health 1965–72; psychiatrist 1974–; Pres. Arab Women's Solidarity Asscn.; with UN(O) Beirut, Lebanon and Ethiopia; Hon. D. Univ. (York) 1994; Short Story Award (Cairo) 1974, Franco-Arab Literary Award (Paris) 1982 and many other literary prizes. *Publications:* 30 books (novels, collections of short stories, memoirs, plays, and studies on women in the Arab World), including Women and Sex 1971, The Hidden Face of Eve: Women in the Arab World, Woman at Point Zero, God Dies by the Nile, The Circling Song, The Fall of the Imam 1987, My Travels Around the World; 16 of her books trans. into many languages. *Leisure interests:* swimming, walking.

SAATCHI, Baron (Life Peer), cr. 1996, of Staplefield in the County of West Sussex; **Maurice Saatchi,** B.SC.; British advertising executive; b. 21 June 1946; s. of Nathan Saatchi and Daisy Saatchi; brother of Charles Saatchi (q.v.); m. Josephine Hart 1984; one s.; one step-s.; ed. London School of Econs.; co-founder Saatchi & Saatchi Co. 1970; Chair. Saatchi & Saatchi Co. PLC 1984–94, Dir.–1994; co-f. and partner M&C Saatchi Agency 1995–; Chair. Megalomedia PLC 1995–; Dir. (non-exec.) Loot 1998–; Gov. L.S.E., Trustee Victoria and Albert Museum 1988–; mem. Council Royal Coll. of Art 1997–. *Address:* 36 Golden Square, London, W1R 4EE, England (Office). *Telephone:* 0171-543 4500.

SAATCHI, Charles; British advertising executive; b. 9 June 1943; s. of Nathan Saatchi and Daisy Saatchi; brother of Maurice Saatchi (q.v.); m. 1st Doris Lockhart 1973 (divorced 1990); m. 2nd Kay Saatchi 1990; one d.; ed. Christ's Coll. Finchley; fmr. jr. copywriter, Benton & Bowles (U.S. advertising agency), London; Assc. Dir. Collett Dickenson Pearce 1966–68; with Ross Cramer formed freelance consultancy, Cramer Saatchi, Dir. 1968–70; co-founder (with Maurice Saatchi q.v.), of Saatchi and Saatchi (advertising agency) 1970, (Saatchi & Saatchi PLC 1984), Dir. 1970–93, Pres. 1993–95; co-f. and partner M&C Saatchi Agency 1995–. *Leisure interest:* collecting contemporary art. *Address:* 36 Golden Square, London, W1R 4EE, England (Office). *Telephone:* 0171-543 4500.

SABA, Elias, B.LITT.; Lebanese politician and economist; b. 1932, Lebanon; s. of Shukri Saba and Guilnar Abou Haidar; m. Hind Sabri Shurbagi 1960; five d.; ed. American Univ. of Beirut and Univ. of Oxford; Econ. Adviser to Ministry of Finance and Petroleum, Kuwait and Kuwait Fund for Arab Econ. Devt. 1961–62; Chair. Dept. of Econs., American Univ. of Beirut 1963–67; Assoc. Prof. of Econs., American Univ. of Beirut 1967–69; Deputy Prime Minister of the Lebanon, Minister of Finance and of Defence 1970–72; Econ. and Financial Adviser to the Pres. 1972–73; Chair., Gen. Man. St. Charles City Centre S.A.R.L. 1974–; Vice-Chair. Banque du Crédit Populaire, Chair. Allied Bank, Beirut 1983; Chair., C.E.O. The Associates, S.A.R.L. 1981–; mem. Nat. Dialogue Cttee. 1975. *Publication:* Postwar Developments in the Foreign Exchange Systems of Lebanon and Syria 1962. *Leisure interests:* hunting, vintage and classic cars. *Address:* P.O. Box 5292, Ayoub Centre, Ashrafieh, Beirut, Lebanon.

SABA, Shoichi, B.ENG., F.I.E.E.E.; Japanese business executive; b. 28 Feb. 1919; s. of Wataru Saba and Sumie Saba; m. Fujiko Saito 1945 (deceased); two s. (one deceased) one d.; ed. Tokyo Imperial Univ.; Pres. Toshiba Corpn. 1980–86, Chair. 1986–87, Adviser 1987–; Dir. ICI (U.K.) 1985–91 and numerous other bodies; Vice-Chair. Keidanren 1986–92, Vice-Chair. Bd. of Councillors 1992–94, Advisor 1994–; Chair. Electronic Industries Asscn. of Japan 1986–87, The Japan Inst. of Industrial Eng. 1982–88, Japan Int. Devt. Org. Ltd. (JAIDO) 1989–94, Nat. Bd. of Govs., Nat. Asscn., Boy Scouts of Nippon 1994–; Pres. Japanese Ind. Standards Cttee. 1994–; mem. Public Review Bd., Arthur Andersen and Co. (U.S.A.) 1991–; Progress Prize (Inst. of Electrical Engineers of Japan) 1958; Blue Ribbon Medal (Govt. of Japan) 1980, Commdr.'s Cross, Order of Merit (Fed. Repub. of Germany) 1988, Hon. C.B.E. (U.K.) 1989, Order of the Sacred Treasure (1st Class) 1990, Hon. K.B.E. (U.K.) 1993. *Leisure interests:* golf, yachting. *Address:* c/o Toshiba Corpn., 1-1 Shibaura 1-chome, Minato-ku, Tokyo 105, Japan.

SABAH, Sheikh Jaber al-Ahmad al-Jaber al-; Amir of Kuwait; b. 1928, Kuwait; ed. Almubarakiyyah School, Kuwait, and private tutors; Gov. of Ahmadi and Oil areas 1949–59; Pres. Dept. of Finance and Economy 1959; Minister of Finance, Industry and Commerce 1963, 1965; Prime Minister 1965–67; Crown Prince 1966–77; Amir Dec. 1977–, succeeding his uncle. *Address:* Sief Palace, Amiry Diwan, Kuwait (official residence).

SABAH, Sheikh Jaber al-Ali al-Salem al–; Kuwaiti politician; b. 20 Oct. 1928; Pres. Dept. of Electricity, Water and Gas 1952–63; mem. High Exec. Cttee. to organize establishments and depts. 1954; mem. Defence High Council; Minister of Information 1964–71, 1975–81; Deputy Prime Minister 1975–81; Chair. Kuwait Int. Petroleum Investment Co. 1981. *Address:* c/o Council of Ministers, Kuwait City, Kuwait.

SABAH, Sheikh Saad al-Abdullah al-Salim al-; Kuwaiti Crown Prince and politician; b. 1930, Kuwait; m. Sheikha Latifah Fahad al-Sabah; one s. four d.; ed. Kuwait govt. schools and Hendon Coll., U.K.; Deputy Chief, Police and Public Security Dept. 1959, Chief 1961; Minister of Interior 1961, and of Defence 1965; Crown Prince Jan. 1978–; Prime Minister Feb. 1978–; Ex-officio Chair. Supreme Defence Council, Supreme Petroleum Council, Civil Service Council, Supreme Housing Council. *Leisure interests:* fishing, gardening, photography. *Address:* Diwan of H.H. The Crown Prince and Prime Minister, P.O. Box 4, Safat, 13001, Kuwait.

SABAH, Sheikh Sabah al-Ahmad al-Jaber al-; Kuwaiti politician; b. 1929; ed. Mubarakiyyah Nat. School, Kuwait and privately; mem. Supreme Cttee. 1955–62; Minister of Public Information and Guidance and of Social Affairs 1962–63, of Foreign Affairs 1963–91, acting Minister of Finance and Oil 1965, Minister of the Interior 1978; Deputy Prime Minister 1978–91; acting Minister of Information 1981–84; now First Deputy Prime Minister and Minister of Foreign Affairs. *Address:* c/o Ministry of Foreign Affairs, P.O. Box 3, Safat, Gulf Street, Kuwait.

SABAH, Sheikh Salim al-Sabah al-Salim al-; Kuwaiti diplomatist; b. 18 June 1937; s. of the late Sheikh Sabah al-Salim al-Sabah, Amir of Kuwait; ed. Secondary School Kuwait, Gray's Inn, London, and Christ Church, Oxford; joined Foreign Service 1963; fmr. Head Political Dept. Ministry of Foreign Affairs; Amb. to the U.K. 1965–70; also to Norway, Denmark and Sweden 1968–70; Amb. to U.S.A. 1970–75, also accred. to Canada; Minister of Social Affairs and Labour 1975–78, of Defence 1978–87, of the Interior 1987–91; Deputy Prime Minister and Minister of Foreign Affairs 1991 then Deputy Prime Minister and Minister of Defence. *Address:* Ministry of Defence, P.O. Box 1170, 13012 Safat, Kuwait City, Kuwait.

SABATIER, Robert; French writer; b. 17 Aug. 1923, Paris; s. of Pierre Sabatier and Marie Exbrayat; m. Christiane Lesparre 1957; fmr. manual worker and factory exec.; produced journal La Cassette; Commdr., Légion d'honneur; Commdr. Ordre nat. du Mérite, des Arts et des Lettres; Officier du Mérite agricole; Lauréat de la Soc. des gens de lettres 1961; Grand Prix de Poésie de l'Académie française 1969 for Les châteaux de millions d'années; Antonin-Artaud Prize and Prix Apollinaire for poems Les fêtes solaires; mem. l'Académie Goncourt. *Publications:* Alain et le nègre 1953, Le marchand de sable 1954, Le goût de la cendre 1955, Les fêtes solaires 1955, Boulevard 1956, Canard au sang 1958, Saint Vincent de Paul, Dédicace d'un navire 1959, La Sainte-Farce 1960, La mort du figuier 1962, Dessin sur un trottoir 1964, Les poisons délectables (poems) 1965, Le Chinois d'Afrique 1966, Dictionnaire de la mort 1967, Les châteaux de millions d'années (poems) 1969, Les allumettes suédoises 1969, Trois sucettes à la menthe 1972, Noisettes sauvages 1974, Histoire de la poésie française des origines à nos jours (8 vols.) 1975, Icare et autres poèmes 1976, Les enfants de l'été 1978, Les fillettes chantantes 1980, L'oiseau de demain 1981, Les années secrètes de la vie d'un homme 1984, David et Olivier 1986, Lecture (poetry) 1987, La Souris Verte 1990, Le Livre de la déraison souriante 1991, Olivier et ses amis 1993, Ecriture (poems) 1993, Le Cygne Noir 1995, Le Lit de la merveille 1997, Les Masques et le miroir 1998. *Address:* 64 boulevard Exelmans, 75016 Paris, France.

SABATINI, Gabriela; Argentinian tennis player; b. 16 May 1970, Buenos Aires; coached by Angel Gimenez; won French and Italian Jr. and Orange Bowl 18s 1984; reached semi-finals French Open, won Japan Open 1985; reached semi-finals Wimbledon, runner-up French Open 1986; reached semi-finals French Open, runner-up Italian Open, winner Tokyo and Brighton, runner-up French Open doubles (with Steffi Graf) 1987, finalist German Open 1989, Winner U.S. Open 1990, reached finals Wimbledon 1991; winner Italian Open 1992; retd. 1996.

SÁBATO, Ernesto; Argentinian writer; b. 24 June 1911, Rojas; m. Matilde Kusminsky-Richter; two s.; ed. Univ. Nacional de la Plata; fmr. Dir. of Cultural Relations, Argentina; has lectured in following Univs.: Paris, Columbia, Berkeley, Madrid, Warsaw, Bucharest, Bonn, Milan, Pavia, Florence, etc.; Pres. Comisión Nacional sobre Desaparición de Personas (CONADEP) 1984; mem. the Club of Rome, Ribbon of Honour, Argentine Soc. of Letters;

Prize of the Inst. of Foreign Relations (Stuttgart) 1973, Grand Prize of Argentine Writers' Soc. 1974, Prix Meilleur Livre Etranger for Abaddon el Exterminador (Paris) 1977; Chevalier, Ordre des Arts et des Lettres (France), Chevalier, Légion d'honneur 1978, Gran Cruz de la República Española, Gabriela Mistral Prize 1984, Cervantes Prize, Madrid 1984, Jerusalem Literary Prize 1989. *Publications:* Uno y el Universo 1945, Hombres y Engranajes 1951, Heterodoxia 1953, El escritor y sus fantasmas 1963, Tres Aproximaciones a la Literatura de Nuestro Tiempo 1969 (essays); El Túnel 1947, Sobre Héroes y Tumbas 1961, Abaddon el Exterminador 1976 (novel). *Address:* Langeri 3135, Santos Lugares, Argentina. *Telephone:* 757-1373.

SÁBATO, Jorge Federico, D.JUR.; Argentinian politician; b. 25 May 1938, La Plata; ed. Univ. de Buenos Aires, Univ. of Paris; researcher, C.N.R.S., Paris; researcher in Political Science; Prof. Faculties of Econs. and Eng., Univ. de Buenos Aires; Expert UN and OAS projects in Brazil, Peru, Ecuador, Colombia and Venezuela; Sec. of State and Adviser to Pres. 1983–84; Sec. of State for Foreign Affairs 1984–85, Int. Relations and Culture 1985–87; Minister of Educ. and Justice 1987–89; holds numerous decorations, including Gran Cruz de la Orden del Mérito Civil (Spain) 1985, Gran Cruz, Orden de la República Italiana 1985, Gran Cruz, Orden del Mérito (Fed. Repub. of Germany) 1987. *Publications:* various books and articles on science of politics. *Address:* c/o Ministerio de Educación y Justicia de la Nación, Buenos Aires, Argentina.

SABATTANI, H.E. Cardinal Aurelio; Italian ecclesiastic; b. 18 Oct. 1912, Imola; ordained priest 1935; fmr. Prelate of Loreto –1971; Prefect of Holy See's Supreme Tribunal 1983; cr. Cardinal 1983; fmr. Archpriest Vatican Basilica, fmr. Vicar-Gen. of His Holiness for the Vatican City, hon. mem. Pontifical Acad. *Address:* Palazzo del Tribunale, Piazza S. Marta, 00120 Vatican City, Italy. *Telephone:* (06) 69884615.

SABBAH, Michel; Palestinian ecclesiastic; b. 1933, Nazareth; ed. Patriarchate Seminary of Beit-Jala and in Beirut and Paris; ordained priest 1955; fmr. Dir. Gen. of Schools, Patriarchate of Jerusalem; priest, Misdar, nr. Amman; Pres. Frères Univ. Bethlehem; Latin (Roman Catholic) Patriarch of Jerusalem 1988; Pres. Bishop's Conf. for Arab Countries. *Address:* Office of the Latin Patriarch, P.O. Box 14152, Jerusalem, Israel. *Telephone:* 2-292323.

SABHAVASU, Pramual; Thai politician; b. 29 Nov. 1927, Muang Dist., Ayutthaya; ed. Ayutthaya Wittyalai and Wat Bovornnives Schools; Chat-Thai Party MP 1975–76, 1979–; Premier's Adviser 1976; Minister of Industry 1986, 1990–91; of Finance 1988–90; Deputy Prime Minister Sept.–Dec. 1990. *Address:* c/o Office of the Deputy Prime Minister, Bangkok, Thailand.

SABISTON, David Coston, Jr., M.D.; American professor of surgery; b. 4 Oct. 1924, Onslow County, N.C.; s. of David Coston and Marie (Jackson) Sabiston; m. Agnes Barden 1955; three d.; ed. Univ. of N.C. and Johns Hopkins Univ. School of Medicine; Intern, Asst. Resident, Chief Resident in Surgery, Johns Hopkins Hospital 1947–53; Asst. Prof., Assoc. Prof., Prof. of Surgery, Johns Hopkins Univ. School of Medicine 1953–64; Howard Hughes Investigator 1955–61; James Buchanan Duke Prof. of Surgery and Chair. of Dept., Duke Univ. Medical Center 1964–94, Chief of Staff 1994–96, Dir. of Int. Programs 1996–; Fulbright Research Scholar, Univ. of Oxford 1961; Research Assoc. Hosp. for Sick Children, London 1961; mem. or fellow of numerous professional orgs.; Hon. mem. Colombian Surgical Soc., German Soc. for Surgery, Japanese Coll. of Surgeons; Hon. F.R.C.S.; Hon. F.R.C.S.E., F.R.A.C.S.; Hon. Fellow, Asociación de Cirugía del Litoral Argentino, Brazilian Coll. of Surgeons, Royal Coll. of Physicians and Surgeons of Canada; several achievement awards. *Publications:* Gibbon's Surgery of the Chest (Co-Ed.) 1969, Textbook of Surgery (Ed.) 1972, Essentials of Surgery (Ed.). *Address:* Duke University Medical Center, P.O. Box 2600 MSRB, Durham, NC 27710 (Office); 1528 Pinecrest Road, Durham, NC 27705, U.S.A. (Home). *Telephone:* 919-684-2831 (Office).

SABOURET, Yves Marie Georges; French civil servant; b. 15 April 1936, Paris; s. of Henri and Colette (née Anthoine) Sabouret; m. 1st Anne de Caumont la Force 1965 (divorced); one s. two d.; m. 2nd Laurence Vilaine 1991; one d.; ed. Ecole Nat. d'Admin.; Inspecteur des finances 1964–81; technical counsellor, Office of Minister of Supply and Housing 1968–69; Dir. Office of Minister of Labour, Employment and Population 1969–72; Counsellor for Social and Cultural Affairs to Prime Minister Pierre Messmer 1972–74; Conseiller gén., Côtes du Nord (Canton de Matignon) 1973–92; Pres. Société de développement régional de la Bretagne 1977–; Vice-Pres., Société Matra 1979; Dir.-Gen. Hachette 1981–90, Vice-Pres. 1981–90; Pres. Atlas Copco France 1984–; Co-Dir.-Gen. La Cinq 1990; Dir.-Gen. NMPP 1994–; Chevalier Légion d'honneur, Officier Ordre nat. du Mérite, Croix de la Valeur militaire. *Address:* NMPP, 52 rue Jacques Hillairet, 75012 Paris; 12 Ave Pierre Ier de Serbie, 75016 Paris, France.

SABOURIN, Louis, LL.L., PH.D., F.R.S.C.; Canadian academic; b. 1 Dec. 1935, Quebec City; s. of Rolland Sabourin and Valeda Caza; m. Agathe Lacerte 1959; one s. two d.; ed. Univ. of Ottawa, Univ. of Paris, France, Institut d'Etudes Politiques de Paris, France, Columbia Univ., U.S.A.; Prof. Dir. Dept. of Political Science, Univ. of Ottawa, Dean of Faculty of Social Science; Founder and Dir. Inst. of Int. Co-operation and Devt., Visiting Sr. Research Fellow Jesus Coll., Oxford, and Queen Elizabeth House, England 1974–75; Pres. OECD Devt. Centre, Paris 1977–82; Prof. Int. Econ. Orgs., Ecole Nationale d'Admin. Publique, Univ. of Quebec 1983–, Dir. Groupe d'Etude de Recherche et de Formation Internationales 1983–; Visiting Prof. University of Paris (Sorbonne) 1982, Univ. of Notre Dame and Stanford Univ. 1992; founding mem. Asia-Pacific Foundation, Montreal Council of Foreign Relations; Pontifical Comm. on Justice and Peace; Pres. Soc. de Droit Int. Economique 1988; Legal Counselor Hudon, Gendron, Harris, Thomas 1989–; Ford Int. Fellow 1962, Canada Council Scholar 1963; mem. Pontifical Acad. of Social Sciences, Rome 1994; Dr. h.c. (Sorbonne, Paris) 1998; Chevalier Pléiade de la Francophonie 1988; Chevalier Légion d'honneur 1989. *Publications:* Le système politique du Canada 1969, Dualité culturelle dans les activités internationales du Canada 1970, Canadian Federalism and International Organizations 1971, Le Canada et le développement international 1972, Allier la théorie à la pratique: le développement de la Chine nouvelle 1973, International Economic Development: Theories, Methods and Prospects 1973, The Challenge of the Less Developed Countries 1981, La crise économique: contraintes et effets de l'interdépendance pour le Canada 1984, Passion d'être, désir d'avoir, le dilemme Québec-Canada dans un univers en mutation 1992, Les organisations économiques internationales 1994; numerous articles. *Leisure interests:* music, travel, wine-tasting (Grand officier du Tastevin), skiing, tennis, cycling. *Address:* GERFI-ENAP, 1001 rue Sherbrooke East, Suite 300, Montreal, Quebec H2L 4Z1, Canada. *Fax:* (514) 522-8222.

SABUROV, Yevgeny Fedorovich, C.ECON.SC.; Russian economist; b. 13 Feb. 1946, Crimea; m. Tatiana Petrovna; three d.; ed. Moscow State Univ.; researcher econ. inst. in Moscow –1990; Deputy Minister of Educ. of Russian Fed. 1990–91; project leader Programme of Econ. Reform in Russia April–Aug. 1991; Deputy Prime Minister, Minister of Econ. Aug.–Nov. 1991; Dir. Cen. for Information and Social Tech. of Russian Govt. 1991–94; Head of Govt. of Repub. of Crimea Feb.–Oct. 1994; Prof. Acad. of Econs.; Dir. Investment Research Inst. 1995–; Chief Consultant, Menatep Bank 1995–; Chair. Bd. of Guardians, Inst. for Urban Econs. 1996–; mem. Acad. of Information, Acad. of Social Sciences. *Publications:* over 100 articles on problems of econ. reform in Russia. *Address:* Menatep Bank, 5 Zagorodnoye Schosse, Moscow, 113152 Russia. *Telephone:* (095) 958-24-26. *Fax:* (095) 958-24-28.

SACHER, Paul; Swiss musician; b. 28 April 1906, Basel; m. Maja Stehlin 1934; ed. Univ. and Conservatoire of Basel; founder of Basel Chamber Orchestra 1926, with Chamber Choir 1928; founder of Schola Cantorum Basiliensis 1933; conductor of Collegium Musicum Zürich 1941–; Dir. Basel Acad. of Music 1954–69; constituted Paul Sacher Foundation 1973, containing musical autographs and archives; has conducted in almost all European countries; has been responsible for more than 250 first performances of musical works and commissioned works by Bartók, Britten, Henze, Hindemith, Honegger, Martín, Martinu, Strauss and Stravinsky; Hon. Pres. Asscn. of Swiss Musicians; Hon. mem. Int. Soc. for Contemporary Music, Hungarian Kodaly Soc. (Budapest), Royal Philharmonic Soc. (London); Corresp. mem. Bayerische Akad. der Schönen Künste; Hon. Fellow Hebrew Univ. of Jerusalem 1987; Hon. Prof. Bundesministerium für Unterricht, Kunst und Sport (Vienna) 1987; Dr. Phil. h.c. (Basle) 1951; Hon. D.Mus. (Oxford) 1988, (Rochester, U.S.A.) 1990, (McGill) 1994; Dr. h.c. in Medicine and Surgery (Genoa) 1992; Schönberg Medal 1953, Mozart Medal (Salzburg) 1956, Hans-Georg Nägeli Medal (Zürich) 1966, Litteris et artibus Medal 1st Class (Vienna) 1972, Kunstpreis der Stadt Basel 1972, Béla Bartók Memorial Medal (Hungary) 1981, Gold Medal for Cultural Merit, Canton of Zürich 1981, Pro Cultura Hungarica Award 1991, Silver Medal Charles Univ. Prague 1992, and other prizes and awards; Officier de l'Ordre des Arts et des Lettres, Commendatore, Ordine al Merito (Italy), Officier, Légion d'honneur 1985, Grosse Verdienstkreuz mit Stern des Verdienstordens, Germany. *Publications:* Articles in reports of Basel Chamber Orchestra, and book on Adolf Hamm (organist). *Leisure interests:* trees, gardening, books. *Address:* Schönenberg, 4133 Pratteln BL, Basel, Switzerland. *Telephone:* 061-8215100.

SACHS, Jeffrey David, PH.D.; American professor of international trade; b. 5 Nov. 1954; s. of Theodore Sachs and Joan Sachs; m. Sonia Ehrlich; one s. two d.; ed. Harvard Univ.; Research Assoc. Nat. Bureau of Econ. Research, Cambridge, Mass. 1980–85; Asst. Prof. of Econs. Harvard Univ. 1980–82, Assoc. Prof. 1982–83, Galen L. Stone Prof. of Int. Trade 1984–; Dir. Harvard Inst. for Int. Devt. 1995–; Adviser, Brookings Inst. Washington, D.C. 1982–; Founder and Chair. Exec. Cttee. Inst. of Econ. Analysis, Moscow 1993–; econ. adviser to various govts. in Latin America, Eastern Europe and fmr. Soviet Union 1991–94; Fellow, World Econometric Soc.; Frank E. Seidman Award in Political Econ. 1991; Hon. PH.D. (St. Gallen). *Publications:* Macroeconomics in the Global Economy (with F. Larrain) 1993, Poland's Jump to the Market Economy 1993, The Transition in Eastern Europe (with O. Blanchard and K. Froot) 1994, Economic Reform and the Process of Global Integration (with A. Warner) 1995, The Collapse of the Mexican Peso; What Have We Learned (jtly.) 1995, Natural Resource Abundance and Economic Growth (with A. Warner) 1996; articles, papers and lectures. *Leisure interests:* skiing, biking, watching ballet. *Address:* Harvard Institute for International Development, One Eliot Street, Cambridge, MA 02138, U.S.A. *Telephone:* (617) 495-4112. *Fax:* (617) 495-8685.

SACHS, Leo, PH.D., F.R.S.; British/Israeli professor of biology; b. 14 Oct. 1924, Leipzig, Germany; s. of Elias Sachs and Louise Sachs; m. Pnina Salkind 1970; one s. three d.; ed. City of London School, Univ. of Wales, Bangor, Trinity Coll., Cambridge; research scientist in genetics, John Innes Inst. 1951–52; research scientist Weizmann Inst. of Science, Rehovot, Israel 1952–, Assoc. Prof. 1960, est. Dept. of Genetics and Virology 1960, Prof. 1962, Head Dept. of Genetics 1962–89, Dean Faculty of Biology 1974–79, now Otto Meyerhof Prof. of Biology; mem. European Molecular Biology Org. 1965, Israel Acad. of Sciences and Humanities 1975; Foreign mem. European Acad. 1998; Dr. h.c. (Bordeaux) 1985, Hon. D.Med. (Lund) 1997; Israel Prize for Natural Sciences 1972, Rothschild Prize in Biological Sciences 1977, Wolf Prize in Medicine 1980, Royal Soc. Wellcome Foundation Prize 1986, Warren Alpert Foundation Prize, Harvard Medical School, Mass. 1997, Bristol-Myers Award for Distinguished Achievement in Cancer Research 1983. *Publications:* papers in various scientific journals on blood cell devt., cancer research and control of growth and differentiation. *Leisure interests:* music, museums. *Address:* Department of Molecular Genetics, Weizmann Institute of Science, Rehovot 76100, Israel. *Telephone:* (8) 934-3970. *Fax:* (8) 934-4108.

SACHTOURIS, Miltos; Greek poet; b. 1919, Athens; Greek National Literary Award 1962, 1987. *Publications include:* I Lismonimeni 1945, O Peripatos 1960, Ta Stigmata 1962, Poems 1945–71 1977, Ektoplasmata 1986. *Address:* 14 Mithimnis Street, 112 57 Athens, Greece.

SACIRBEY, Muhamed, J.D., M.B.A.; Bosnian and Herzegovinian politician; b. 20 July 1956, Sarajevo; s. of Nedzib Sacirbey and Aziza Sacirbey; m. Susan Walter; ed. Tulane Univ. and Columbia Univ. New York; admitted New York Bar 1981; attorney, Booth & Baron New York 1981–83; Financial Analyst, Vice-Pres. Standard Poor's Corpn. New York 1983–85; Financial Investment Banking, Trepp & Co. New York 1985–87; Sr. Vice-Pres. and Man. Dept. of Investment, security Pacific Merchant Bank, New York 1987–91; partner, consultant, Princeton Finance, New York 1991–92; Perm. Mission of Repub. of Bosnia-Herzegovina to the UN, New York 1992–95; Minister of Foreign Affairs of Bosnia-Herzegovina 1995–96; Amb. to UN 1996–. *Leisure interests:* athletic activities, reading. *Address:* Permanent Mission of Bosnia-Herzegovina, 866 UN Plaza, Suite 580, New York, NY 10017, U.S.A. *Telephone:* (212) 751-9015; (212) 751-9019.

SACKS, David G.; American business executive and lawyer; b. 6 Jan. 1924, New York; s. of Irving Sacks and Jeannette Greenhoot; m. Naomi Gostin 1947; two s. two d.; ed. Columbia Univ.; partner, Simpson Thacher & Bartlett, New York 1961–67, Sr. Partner 1967–76, Counsel 1981–83; Chief Admin. Officer, Lehman Bros. Inc. New York 1976–81; Exec. Vice-Pres. (financial admin.) The Seagram Co. Ltd., Montreal 1983–86, Pres. and C.O.O. 1986–89; Exec. Vice-Pres. (financial admin.) Joseph E. Seagram & Sons, New York 1983–86, Pres. and C.O.O. 1986–89; Vice-Chair. The Seagram Co. Ltd. and Joseph E. Seagram & Sons Inc., Montreal and New York 1989–91; Pres. United Jewish Appeal, Fed. of Jewish Philanthropies 1989–92. *Address:* Joseph E. Seagram & Sons, 375 Park Avenue, Basement 4, New York, NY 10152, U.S.A.

SACKS, Jonathan Henry, PH.D.; British rabbi; b. 8 March 1948, London; s. of late Louis Sacks and of Louisa (née Frumkin) Sacks; m. Elaine Taylor 1970; one s. two d.; ed. Christ's Coll. Finchley, Gonville & Caius Coll., Cambridge, New Coll., Oxford, London Univ., Jews' Coll., London and Yeshivat Etz Hayyim, London; lecturer in Moral Philosophy, Middx. Poly. 1971–73; lecturer in Jewish Philosophy, Jews' Coll., London 1973–76, in Talmud and Jewish Philosophy 1976–82, Chief Rabbi Lord Jakobovits Prof. (first incumbent) in Modern Jewish Thought 1982–, Dir. Rabbinic Faculty 1983–90, Prin. 1984–90, Chief Rabbi of the United Hebrew Congregations of the Commonwealth 1991–; Visiting Prof. of Philosophy Univ. of Essex 1989–90; currently Visiting Prof. of Philosophy Hebrew Univ., Jerusalem, and of Theology and Religious Studies King's Coll., London; rabbi Golders Green Synagogue, London 1978–82, Marble Arch Synagogue, London 1983–90; Ed. Le'ela (journal) 1985–90; mem. CRAC; Presentation Fellow King's Coll., London 1993; Hon. Fellow Gonville and Caius Coll., Cambridge 1993; Sherman Lecturer, Manchester Univ. 1989, Reith Lecturer 1990, Cook Lecturer 1997; Hon. D.D. (Cantab.) 1993; Dr. h.c. (Middx. Univ.) 1993, (Haifa Univ., Israel) 1996, (Yeshiva Univ., N.Y.) 1997, (St. Andrews Univ.) 1998; Hon. LL.D. (Univ. of Liverpool) 1997; Jerusalem Prize 1995. *Publications:* Torah Studies 1986, Tradition and Transition (essays) 1986, Traditional Alternatives 1989, Tradition in an Untraditional Age 1990, The Persistence of Faith (Reith Lecture) 1991, Orthodoxy Confronts Modernity (Ed.) 1991, Crisis and Covenant 1992, One People?: Tradition, Modernity and Jewish Unity 1993, Will We Have Jewish Grandchildren? 1994, Faith in the Future 1995, Community of Faith 1995, The Politics of Hope 1997. *Leisure interests:* walking, music. *Address:* 735 High Road, London, N12 0US, England (Office). *Telephone:* 0181-343 6301 (Office). *Fax:* 0181-343 6310 (Office).

SACKS, Oliver Wolf, B.M., B.CH.; British neurologist and writer; b. 9 July 1933, London; s. of Dr. Samuel Sacks and Dr. Muriel Elsie (Landau) Sacks; ed. St. Paul's School, London and Queen's Coll., Oxford; Resident, Univ. of Calif., L.A. 1962–65; Consultant Neurologist, Bronx State Hosp., New York 1965–91, Beth Abraham Hosp., Bronx 1965–, Headache Unit, Montefiore Hosp., Bronx 1966–68, several clinics and homes for the aged and chronically ill, New York 1966–; Consultant Neurologist and mem. Medical Advisory Bd., Gilles de la Tourette Syndrome Asscn., New York 1974–; Instructor in Neurology, Albert Einstein Coll. of Medicine, Bronx, New York 1966–75, Asst. Clinical Prof. of Neurology 1975–78, Assoc. Clinical Prof. 1978–85, Clinical Prof. 1985–; Fellow American Acad. of Arts and Letters 1996; Hawthornden Prize (for Awakenings) 1974. *Publications:* Migraine 1970, Awakenings 1973, A Leg to Stand On 1984, The Man Who Mistook His Wife For A Hat 1985, Seeing Voices: A Journey Into The World of the Deaf 1989, An Anthropologist on Mars 1995, The Island of the Colourblind 1996, Cycad Island 1996. *Address:* 2 Horatio Street, New York, NY 10014, U.S.A. *Telephone:* (212) 633-8373.

SADANAGA, Ryoichi, D.SC.; Japanese mineralogist and crystallographer; b. 25 June 1920, Osaka; m. Sakiko Iwata 1945; two d.; ed. Univ. of Tokyo; Prof. of Mineralogy, Univ. of Tokyo 1959–81, Prof. Emer. 1981–; mem. Japan Acad. 1981–. *Publication:* Introduction to Crystallography 1986. *Address:* 4-1-4, Suimeidai, Kawanishi-shi, Hyogo-ken, 666-0116 Japan. *Telephone:* (0727) 92 5100. *Fax:* (0727) 92 5200.

SADDAM HUSSEIN, LL.B.; Iraqi politician; b. 1937, Tikrit, nr. Baghdad; m. Sajida Khairalla 1963; two s. two d.; ed. al-Karkh Secondary School, Baghdad, al-Qasr al-Aini Secondary School, Cairo, Cairo Univ. and al-Mustanseriya Univ., Baghdad; joined Arab Baath Socialist Party 1957; sentenced to death for attempted execution of Gen. Abdul Karim Qassim 1959; joined leadership of Cairo branch of Baath Party 1962; returned to Iraq following revolution 1963; mem. 4th Regional Congress and 6th Nat. Congress of Baath Party 1963; mem. Regional Leadership of Baath Party in Iraq following overthrow of Party rule 1963; mem. 7th Nat. Congress, Syria 1964; arrested for plotting overthrow of Abdul Salam Aref 1964; elected mem. Leadership by 8th Nat. Congress while still in prison 1965; Deputy Sec. Regional Leadership of Baath Party 1966–79, Sec. 1979–; played prominent role in July 1968 revolution; Act. Deputy Chair. Revolutionary Command Council 1968–69; Deputy Chair. Revolutionary Command Council 1969–79, Chair. 1979–; Pres. of Iraq July 1979– also Prime Minister May 1994–; Deputy Sec. Regional Leadership in 7th Regional Congress 1968; mem. Nat. Leadership of Party in 10th National Congress 1970; rank of Gen. 1976; forces invaded Iran Sept. 1980 initiating 1980–88 Iran-Iraq War; illegally invaded and annexed Kuwait Aug. 1990, forces defeated and forced to withdraw by UN-backed Allied Force under command of Gen. Norman Schwarzkopf (q.v.) Feb. 1991; Order of Rafidain, 1st Class 1976. *Publication:* One Trench or Two. *Address:* Presidential Palace, Karradat Mariam, Baghdad, Iraq.

SADIE, Stanley John, C.B.E., M.A., PH.D., MUS.B.; British writer on music; b. 30 Oct. 1930, Wembley; s. of David Sadie and Deborah Sadie (née Simons); m. 1st Adèle Bloom 1953 (died 1978); two s. one d.; m. 2nd Julie Anne McCornack Vertrees; one s. one d.; ed. St. Paul's School, London, Gonville and Caius Coll., Cambridge; Prof. Trinity Coll. of Music 1957–65; Music Critic, The Times 1964–81; Ed., The Musical Times 1967–87, New Grove Dictionary of Music and Musicians 1970–, Master Musicians series 1976–; Music Consultant to Man and Music (Granada TV series) 1984–90; broadcaster on musical subjects; Ed. of 18th-century music; Pres. Int. Musicological Soc. 1992–97; Chair. The Handel House Trust 1994–96, Pres. 1996–; mem. Critics' Circle, American Musicological Soc., Royal Musical Asscn. (Pres. 1989–94); Hon. R.A.M. 1982; Hon. F.R.C.M. 1994; Hon. D.Litt. (Leicester) 1982. *Publications:* Handel 1962, The Pan Book of Opera/The Opera Guide (with A. Jacobs) 1964, Mozart 1966, Beethoven 1967, Handel 1968, Handel Concertos 1972, The New Grove Dictionary of Music and Musicians, 20 vols. (Ed.) 1980, Mozart (The New Grove) 1982, The New Grove Dictionary of Musical Instruments, 3 Vols. (Ed.) 1984, The Cambridge Music Guide (with A. Latham) 1985, Mozart Symphonies 1986, The New Grove Dictionary of American Music, 4 Vols. (Co-Ed.) 1986, Handel Tercentenary Collection (Co-Ed.) 1987, The Grove Concise Dictionary of Music (Ed.) 1988, History of Opera (Ed.) 1989, Performance Practice, 2 vols. (Co-Ed.) 1989, Man and Music, A Social History, 8 vols. (Gen. Ed.) 1989–93, Music Printing and Publishing (Co-Ed.) 1990, The New Grove Dictionary of Opera, 4 vols. (Ed.) 1992, Wolfgang Amadè Mozart: Essays on his Life and Work (Ed.) 1995, New Grove Book of Operas 1996; and contribs. to various music periodicals and journals. *Leisure interests:* watching cricket, drinking (coffee, wine), family. *Address:* 12 Lyndhurst Road, London, NW3 5NL, England. *Telephone:* 0171-435 2482. *Fax:* 0171-435 6481.

SADIK, Nafis, M.D.; Pakistani international official and physician; b. 18 Aug. 1929, Jaunpur, India; d. of Iffat Ara and Mohammad Shoaib; m. Azhar Sadik 1954; one s. two d. and two adopted d.; ed. Loretto Coll. Calcutta, Calcutta Medical Coll., Dow Medical Coll. Karachi and Johns Hopkins Univ.; Intern, Gynaecology and Obstetrics, City Hosp., Baltimore, Md. 1952–54; civilian medical officer in charge of women's and children's wards in various Pakistani armed forces hosps. 1954–63; Resident, Physiology, Queens Univ., Kingston, Ont. 1958; Head, Health Section, Planning Comm., on Health and Family Planning, Pakistan 1964; Dir. of Planning and Training, Pakistan Cen. Family Planning Council 1966–68, Deputy Dir.-Gen. 1968–70, Dir.-Gen. 1970–71; Tech. Adviser, UN Population Fund (UNFPA) 1971–72, Chief, Programme Div. 1973–77, Asst. Exec. Dir. 1977–87, Exec. Dir. UNFPA 1987–; Sec.-Gen. Int. Conf. on Population and Devt. 1994; Pres. Soc. for Int. Devt. 1994–; Fellow ad eundem, Royal Coll. of Obstetricians and Gynaecologists; Hon. D.Hum.Litt. (Johns Hopkins) 1989, (Brown) 1993, (Duke) 1995; Hon. LL.D. (Wilfrid Laurier) 1995; Hon. D.Sc. (Mich.) 1996, (Claremont) 1996; Bruno H. Schubert-Stiftung Prize 1995; Hugh Moore Award 1976, Women's Global Leadership Award 1994, Peace Award (UNA) 1994, Prince Mahidol Award 1995; Order of Merit, First Class (Egypt) 1994. *Publications:* Population: National Family Planning Programme in Pakistan 1968, Population: the UNFPA Experience (ed.) 1984, Population Policies and Programmes: Lessons learned from Two Decades of Experience 1991, Making a Difference: Twenty-five Years of UNFPA Experience 1994; articles in professional journals. *Leisure interests:* bridge, reading, theatre, travel.

Address: United Nations Population Fund, 220 East 42nd Street, 19th Floor, New York, NY 10017, U.S.A. *Telephone:* (212) 297-5111. *Fax:* (212) 297-4911.

SADOVNICHY, Victor Antonovich, D.PHYSICAL-MATH.SC.; Russian physicist; b. 3 April 1939, Krasnopavlovka, Kharkov Region; m.; three c.; ed. Moscow Univ.; asst., docent, Deputy Dean Chair of Mechanics and Math., Moscow Univ. 1972–78, Prof., Prorector 1982–84, Head Chair of Math. Analysis, First Prorector 1982–92, Rector 1992–; Corresp. mem. Russian Acad. of Sciences 1994, mem. 1997; mem. Russian Acad. of Tech. Sciences; Sec.-Gen. Asscn. of U.S.S.R. Univs. 1987–91; Vice-Pres. Int. Acad. of Higher School 1992–; mem. Perm. Cttee., Conf. of Rectors of Europe; State and Lomonosov Prizes. *Address:* Moscow State University, 119899 Moscow, Russia. *Telephone:* 939-27-29.

SADOWSKI, Wiesław; Polish economist and professor of statistics; b. 2 Jan. 1922, Warsaw; m. Stefania Sadowska 1947; one d.; ed. Main School of Planning and Statistics, Warsaw; scientific worker at Main School of Planning and Statistics (now Main School of Commerce), Warsaw 1945–92, Prof. 1960–, Rector 1965–78; Corresp. mem. Polish Acad. of Sciences (PAN) 1969–, Hon. Chair. Cttee. of Statistics and Econometrics 1993–; mem. numerous Polish and foreign scientific asscns., incl. Int. Statistical Inst.; Deputy to Sejm (Parl.) 1969–80; Pres. Cen. Statistical Office (GUS) 1980–89, of Scientific Bd. 1989–; Chair. Polish-Finnish Friendship Soc. 1984–91; Dr. h.c. (Łódź Univ.) 1997; Order of Banner of Labour (1st Class), Commdr.'s and Officer's Cross, Order of Polonia Restituta, Meritorious Teacher of Polish Repub., Commdr.'s Cross, Order of Finnish Lion and other decorations. *Publications:* numerous works on statistics and econometrics. *Leisure interest:* music. *Address:* al. Na Skarpie 19 m. 3, 00-488 Warsaw, Poland. *Telephone:* (22) 621 56 94.

SÆBØ, Magne, D.THEOL.; Norwegian professor of Old Testament theology; b. 23 Jan. 1929, Fjelberg; s. of Samson Saebø and Malla Ølfaernes; m. Mona Uni Bjørnstad 1953; three s.; ed. Free Faculty of Theology, Oslo and Univ. of Oslo; studied Old Testament and Semitic languages in Jerusalem, Kiel and Heidelberg; teacher of Biblical Hebrew, Univ. of Oslo 1961–70; lecturer in Old Testament, Free Faculty of Theology (Church of Norway) 1969–70, Prof. 1970–, Dean 1975–77, 1988–90; Ed.-in-Chief int. project on Hebrew Bible/Old Testament: The History, and Its Interpretation I-III; Ed.-in-Chief Tidsskrift for Teologi og Kirke (Univ. Press), Oslo 1977–94; mem. Bd. Norwegian Bible Soc. 1965–91, Chair. O.T. Trans. Cttee. 1968–78, Gen. Trans. Cttee. 1978–91; Chair. Norwegian Israel Mission 1978–87; mem. WCC Consultation on the Church and the Jewish People 1976–81; Chair. Lutheran European Comm. on the Church and the Jewish People, Hanover 1979–82; Pres. Int. Org. for the Study of Old Testament 1995–98; mem. Royal Soc. of Science and Letters, Trondheim, Norwegian Acad. of Science and Letters, Oslo, Nathan Söderblom Soc., Uppsala; received on 65th birthday Festschrift Text and Theology 1994; Kt. 1st Class of Royal Norwegian Order of St. Olav 1994, Fridtjof Nansen Award for Eminent Research 1995. *Publications:* Sacharja 9-14. Untersuchungen von Text und Form 1969, Gjennom alle tider 1978, Ordene og Ordet. Gammeltestamentlige studier 1979, Salomos ordsprǎk, Forkynneren, Høysangen, Klagesangene (Commentary) 1986; articles in int. journals and theology books. *Leisure interests:* biographies, stamp collecting, mountain walking. *Address:* The Free Faculty of Theology, P.O. Box 5144, Majorstua, N-0302 Oslo (Office); Lars Muhles vei 34, N-1300 Sandvika, Norway (Home). *Telephone:* 22590586 (Office); 67543806 (Home). *Fax:* 22691890.

SAEMALA, Francis Joseph, B.A.; Solomon Islands diplomatist and civil servant; b. 23 June 1944; m. Eve Mercy 1974; four s. one d.; ed. Victoria Univ., Wellington, N.Z.; Head of Planning, Cen. Planning Office 1976; Sec. to Independence Timetable Talks del. and Jt. Sec. to Constitutional Conf. in London 1977; Special Sec. to Chief Minister 1976, to Prime Minister 1978–81; Sec. to Leader of the Opposition 1981–82; Perm. Sec. Ministry of Foreign Affairs and Int. Trade 1982–83; Perm. Rep. to UN 1983–90; M.P. 1989–; Chair. Parl. Foreign Relations Cttee. 1992–93, 1995; Chair. Solomon Islands Ports Auth. Bd. 1991–93; Deputy Prime Minister, Minister of Foreign Affairs 1993–94. *Publications:* Our Independent Solomon Islands, Solomon Islands in Politics in Melanesia. *Address:* Auki, Malaita Province, Solomon Islands.

SÁENZ ABAD, Alfredo; Spanish banker; b. Nov. 1942, Las Arenas, Basque Country; ed. Univ. of Valladolid and Deusto Univ. Bilbao; mem. Bd. Tubacex (Basque steel pipe producer) 1965–80; Dir. of Planning, Banco de Vizcaya 1981; Man. Dir. Banca Catalana 1983; Man. Dir. Banco Bilbao Vizcaya 1988, First Vice-Pres. 1990; Pres. Banco Español de Crédito 1993–. *Address:* Banco Español de Crédito, Alcalá 14, 20814 Madrid, Spain. *Telephone:* (91) 3382263. *Fax:* (91) 3381883.

SAFDIE, Moshe, O.C., B.ARCH., F.R.A.I.C.; Canadian architect; b. 14 July 1938, Haifa; s. of Leon Safdie and Rachael Esses; m. 1st Nina Nusynowicz 1959 (divorced 1981); one s. one d.; m. 2nd Michal Ronnen 1981; two d.; ed. McGill Univ. Montreal, Canada; with VanGinkel & Assocs., Montreal 1961–62; Louis I. Kahn, Philadelphia 1962–63; architect, planner Canadian Corpn. for 1967 World Exhbn. 1963–64; Moshe Safdie & Assocs., Montreal 1964–, Jerusalem 1970–, Moshe Safdie and Assocs. Inc., Boston 1978–, Toronto 1985–; Visiting Prof. McGill Univ. 1970–71; Davenport Prof. of Architecture, Yale Univ. 1971–72; Prof. of Architecture and Dir. Desert Research Inst., Ben Gurion Univ., Israel 1975–78; Dir. Urban Design Program of Harvard Univ. 1978–84; Ian Woodner (Studio) Prof. of Architecture and Urban Design, Grad. School of Design 1984–89; mem. Israel Inst. of Architects and Engineers, Royal Canadian Acad. of Arts; Fellow Royal Architectural Inst. Canada, mem. American Inst. of Architects, Order of Architects of Que., Ont. Asscn. Architects; *projects include:* Habitat '67, Montreal; Coldspring New Town, Baltimore; Mamilla Business District, Jerusalem; Musée de la Civilisation, Quebec City; Hosh Dist. Restoration, Jerusalem; Colegio Hebreo Maguen David, Mexico City; National Gallery of Canada, Ottawa; Ardmore Habitat Apartments, Singapore; Ottawa City Hall, Ford Center for the Performing Arts, Vancouver; Library Square, Vancouver; The Esplanade, Cambridge, Mass.; Musée des beaux arts de Montréal, Quebec; Harvard Business School master plan and Morgan Hall, Boston; Hebrew Union Coll., Jerusalem; Skirball Museum and Cultural Center, L.A., Calif.; Hon. Fellow, American Inst. of Architects 1996; Hon. LL.D. (McGill Univ.) 1982, Dr. h.c. (Laval Univ.) 1988; Hon. D.F.A. (Univ. of Vic.) 1989; Hon. D.Eng. (Tech. Univ. of Nova Scotia) 1996; Lieut.-Gov. Gold Medal (Canada) 1961, Massey Medal for Architecture (Canada) 1967, Urban Design Concept Award (U.S.A.) 1980, Int. Design Award in Urban Design (U.S.A.) 1980, Rechter Prize for Architecture 1982, Mt. Scopius Award for Humanitarianism (Israel) 1987, Prix d'excellence in Architecture, Canada 1988, Gov. Gen.'s Medal for Architecture (Canada) 1992, Nentra Award for Professional Excellence 1995, Gold Medal (Australia) 1995. *Publications:* Beyond Habitat 1970, The Japan Architect 1970, The Coldspring Presentation 1972, Horizon 1973, For Everyone a Garden 1974, Habitat Bill of Rights 1976, Form and Purpose 1982, The Harvard Jerusalem Studio: Urban Design for the Holy City 1986, Beyond Habitat by 20 years 1987, The Language and Medium of Architecture 1989, Jerusalem: The Future of the Past 1989, Moshe Safdie: Buildings and Projects 1967–1992 1996, The City After the Automobile 1997. *Address:* 100 Properzi Way, Somerville, MA 02143-3798, U.S.A.; 165 Avenue Road, Suite 301, Toronto, Ont., M5R 3S4, Canada; 4 Ha'emek, 7 Schlomo Street, Hamelech, Jerusalem 94106, Israel. *Telephone:* (617) 629-2100 (U.S.A.).

SAFFAR, Salman Mohamed al-, PH.D.; Bahraini diplomatist; b. 1931, Bahrain; m.; ed. Baghdad Univ., Iraq and Sorbonne, Paris; Primary School teacher, Bahrain 1949–54, Secondary school teacher 1959–60; with Ministry of Foreign Affairs 1970–; Permanent Rep. to UN 1971–81; Amb. to France 1982–88; Dir. of Econ. Affairs, Ministry of Foreign Affairs 1988–91; Amb. to Russia 1992–94. *Address:* Ministry of Foreign Affairs, P.O. Box 547, Manama, Bahrain.

SAFIRE, William; American journalist and author; b. 17 Dec. 1929, New York; s. of Oliver C. Safir and Ida Panish; m. Helene Belmar Julius 1962; one s. one d.; ed. Syracuse Univ.; journalist, New York Herald Tribune Syndicate 1949–51; Corresp. WNBC-WNBT, Europe and Middle East 1951, Radio and TV Producer, WNBC, New York 1954–55; Vice-Pres. Tex McCrary Inc. 1955–60; Pres. Safire Public Relations Inc. 1960–68; Special Asst. to Pres. Nixon, Washington 1968–73; Columnist, New York Times, Washington 1973–; mem. American Acad. of Arts and Sciences, Pulitzer Bd.; Trustee Syracuse Univ.; Pulitzer Prize for Distinguished Commentary 1978. *Publications:* The Relations Explosion 1963, Plunging into Politics 1964, Safire's Political Dictionary 1968, Before the Fall 1975, Full Disclosure 1977, Safire's Washington 1980, On Language 1980, What's the Good Word? 1982, Good Advice (with Leonard Safir) 1982, I Stand Corrected 1984, Take My Word for It 1986, Freedom (novel) 1987, You Could Look It Up 1988, Words of Wisdom 1989, Language Maven Strikes Again 1990, Leadership (with Leonard Safir) 1990, Coming To Terms 1991, The First Dissident 1992, Good Advice on Writing (with Leonard Safir) 1992, Lend Me Your Ears 1992, Safire's New Political Dictionary 1993, Quote the Maven 1993, In Love With Norma Loquendi 1994, Sleeper Spy 1995, Watching My Language 1997. *Address:* c/o New York Times, 1627 I Street, N.W., Washington, DC 20006, U.S.A.

SAGALAYEV, Eduard Mikhailovich; Russian journalist; b. 3 Oct. 1946, Samarkand; m.; one s. one d.; ed. Samarkand Univ., Acad. of Social Sciences Cen. Cttee. CPSU; Dir., Sr. Ed. Cttee. on TV and Radio Samarkand; on staff, Deputy Exec. Sec. Leninsky Put 1969–72; Exec. Sec. Komsomolets Uzbekistana Tashkent 1972–73; instructor Propaganda Div. Cen. Comsomol Cttee. Moscow 1973–75; Deputy Ed.-in-Chief programs for youth, U.S.S.R. Cen. TV 1975–80, Ed.-in-Chief 1980–88; Ed.-in-Chief Information section of Cen. TV 1988–90; Dir. Gen. Studio Channel IY 1990; First Deputy Chair. All-Union State Radio and TV Corpn. 1991–92; Dir. Gen. TV Ostankino Jan.–July 1992; f. and Pres. TV-6, Moscow's first independent broadcasting co. 1992–96, 1997–; Chair. Russian TV and Broadcasting co. (RTR) 1996–97; Chair. Bd. of U.S.S.R. Journalists' Union 1990–91; Chair. Confed. of Journalists of CIS 1991–96, Ind. Asscn. of TV Broadcasters 1995; mem. Acad. of Russian TV; U.S.S.R. State Prize 1978. *Address:* TV-6, Ilyinka str. 15 bldg. 1, 103070 Moscow, Russia. *Telephone:* (095) 206-03-02. *Fax:* 206-08-86.

SAGAN, Françoise (pseudonym of Françoise Quoirez); French writer; b. 21 June 1935, Cajarc; d. of Pierre and Marie (née Laubard) Quoirez; m. 1st Guy Schoeller 1958 (divorced); m. 2nd Robert Westhoff 1962 (divorced); one s.; ed. Couvent des Oiseaux and Couvent du Sacré Coeur, Paris; Prix des Critiques for Bonjour tristesse 1954. *Publications:* Bonjour tristesse 1954, Un certain sourire 1956, Dans un mois, dans un an 1957, Aimez-vous Brahms . . . 1959, La chamade 1965, Le garde du coeur 1968, Un peu de soleil dans l'eau froide 1969, Des bleus à l'âme 1972, Il est des parfums (with Guillaume Hanoteau) 1973, Les merveilleux nuages 1973, Un profil perdu 1974, Réponses 1975, Des yeux de soie 1976, La femme fardée, Musique de scène 1981, De guerre lasse 1985, Un sang d'aquarelle 1987,

Dear Sarah Bernhardt 1988, Les Faux-Fuyants 1991, Répliques 1992 ... Et toute ma sympathie 1993, Evasion (novel) 1993, Un Chagrin de Passage 1994, le Miroir égaré 1996; scenario for the ballet Le rendez-vous manqué (with Michel Magne); own film adaption of Dans un mois, dans un an; Dir. Les fougères bleues (film) 1976; *Plays:* Château en Suède 1959, Les violons parfois ... 1961, La robe mauve de valentine 1963, Bonheur, impair et passe 1964, Le cheval évanoui 1966, L'écharde 1966, Un piano dans l'herbe 1970, Zaphorie 1973, Le lit défait 1977, Pol Vandromme 1978, Il fait beau jour et nuit 1978, Le chien couchant 1980, Un orage immobile 1983, l'Excès contraire 1987. *Address:* 14600 Honfleur, France.

SAGARRA, Eda, M.A., DR.PHIL., LITT.D., M.R.I.A.; Irish professor of Germanic languages; b. 15 Aug. 1933, Dublin; d. of Kevin O'Shiel and Cecil Smiddy; m. Albert Sagarra i Zacarini 1961; one d.; ed. Loreto Convents, Bray and Foxrock, Univ. Coll. Dublin and Univs. of Freiburg, Zürich and Vienna; Jr. Lecturer, lecturer, Univ. of Manchester 1958–68; Special Lecturer in German History 1968–75; Prof. of German, Trinity Coll. Dublin 1975–, Dean of Visiting Students 1979–86; Registrar of Dublin Univ. 1981–86; mem. Council, Royal Irish Acad. (Sec. 1993–), Nat. Council for Educational Awards 1991–96; mem. Germanistische Kommission of German Research Council 1982–90; mem. Bd. Inst. of Germanic Studies of Univ. of London 1983–87; mem. Academia Europaea 1991–, Quality Review Group 1998–, Max Planck Inst.; Bundesverdienstkreuz (Austria); Bundesverdienstkreuz (Fed. Germany); Goethe Medal 1990, Jakob and Wilhelm Grimm Prize 1995. *Publications:* Tradition and Revolution 1971, A Social History of Germany 1648–1914 1977, Theodor Fontane: Der Stechlin 1986, Literatur und Anthropologie um 1800 (Ed. with Jürgen Barkhoff) 1992, Companion to German Literature 1494 to the Present (with Peter Skrine) 1997; scientific bibliographies/review essays on German women writers; articles on legal, social and literary history of servants in Germany. *Leisure interests:* golf (county golfer 1969–75), ornithology, cooking, European politics. *Address:* 5066 Arts Building, Trinity College, Dublin 2 (Office); 30 Garville Avenue, Rathgar, Dublin 6, Ireland (Home). *Telephone:* (1) 608 1589 (Office); (1) 4975967. *Fax:* (1) 677 2694.

SAGDEEV, Roald Zinnurovich, D.SC.; Russian physicist; b. 26 Dec. 1932, Moscow; m. Susan Eisenhower (grand-d. of late Pres. Eisenhower) 1990; ed. Moscow State Univ.; Research Worker, Inst. of Atomic Energy, U.S.S.R. Acad. of Sciences 1956–61; Head of Lab., Inst. of Nuclear Physics, Siberian Dept., Acad. of Sciences 1961–70, Inst. of High Temperature Physics of U.S.S.R. Acad. of Sciences 1970–73; Prof. Novosibirsk State Univ. 1964–73; Dir. Inst. of Space Research 1973–88, Sr. Researcher 1988–; Distinguished Prof. Univ. of Md., U.S.A. 1990–, founder and Dir. East-West Space Science Center 1992–; Corresp. mem. U.S.S.R. (now Russian) Acad. of Sciences 1964, mem. 1968–; specialist on global warming, plasma physics, controllable thermonuclear synthesis, cosmic ray physics; mem. Council of Dirs. Int. Fund for Survival and Devt. of Mankind 1988–; Head Scientific-Methodical Centre for Analytical Research, Inst. of Space Research 1988–; mem. N.A.S. Swedish Royal Acad., Max Planck Soc.; U.S.S.R. People's Deputy 1989–91; Hon. Dr. (Tech. Univ. Graz, Austria) 1984; Hero of Socialist Labour 1986; Lenin Prize 1984; Order of October Revolution, Order of Red Banner, and other decorations. *Address:* Institute of Space Research, Russian Academy of Sciences, Profsoyuznaya Str. 84/32, 117810 Moscow B-485, Russia; University of Maryland, College Park, MD 20742, U.S.A. *Telephone:* (095) 333-14-66 (Moscow); (301) 985-7000 (U.S.A.).

SAGER, Dirk; German journalist; b. 13 Aug. 1940, Hamburg; m. Irene Dasbach-Sager; one s. one d.; fmrly. with Radio R.I.A.S. Berlin; fmr. corresp. Z.D.F. TV, East Berlin, Washington D.C., Chief of Moscow Office 1990–97, 1998– of Brandenburg Office 1997–98. *Leisure interest:* reading. *Publication:* Betrogenes Rubland 1996. *Address:* Zweites Deutsches Fernsehen, August-Bebel-Strasse 15-16, 14482 Potsdam, Germany.

SAGET, Louis Joseph Edouard; French government official (retd.); b. 27 April 1915, Paris; s. of Pierre Saget and Jeanne (née Barbare) Saget; m. Anne Vincens 1940; five c.; ed. Lycée Janson-de-Sailly, Paris; Mayor of Tananarive 1954–56; First Counsellor, French Embassy, Madagascar 1959–60; High Commr. in Comoro Islands 1960–62; Commissaire aux Comptes, European Launcher Devt. Org. 1963–66; Gov. of French Somaliland 1966–67; High Commr. in Djibouti 1967–69; Conseiller maître à la Cour des Comptes 1970–84; Pres. Agence nat. pour l'amélioration de l'habitat 1971–78, Comm. de terminologie du ministère de la Défense 1973–87; Investigator, Comité central d'enquête sur le coût et le rendement des services publics 1974–84; mem. Electoral Comm. for French living abroad 1977–88, Cttee. for Fiscal Matters, Customs and Exchange 1987–93; mem. town council of Méréville 1969–95; Officier Légion d'honneur, Commdr. Nat. du Mérite, Croix de guerre, Commdr. de l'Etoile noire, Commdr. de l'Ordre nat. Malgache, Grand Commdr. of the Order of the Star of Ethiopia, Commdr. de l'Etoile equatoriale de Gabon, Nat. Order of Upper Volta, Order of the Leopard of Zaire, Grand Officier Ordre du Croissant Vert des Comores. *Leisure interest:* nature. *Address:* 13 rue Cambon 75001 Paris (Office); 1 rue de Laborde, 91660 Méréville, France (Home).

SAGLIO, Jean-François; French mining engineer; b. 29 July 1936, Toulon; s. of Georges Saglio; m. Odile Bertrand 1968; two s. one d.; ed. Ecole Polytechnique and Ecole Supérieure des Mines, Paris; Engineer, Govt. Del. Algiers 1960–61; Mining Engineer, Mines de Metz 1961–66; founder/Dir. Agence de Bassin Rhin-Meuse, Metz 1966–69; Adviser, Cabinet of Pres. of France 1969–73; Head, Perm. Secr. for Study of Water Problems of Paris 1971–73; Dir. in charge of Pollution and Nuisance, Ministry of Environment 1973–78; Pres. Dir.-Gen. Agence Foncière et Technique de la Région Parisienne 1979–81; Dir. of Innovation and Valorization of Research, Elf Aquitaine, also Dir. of New Projects 1981–84; Pres. Dir.-Gen. INOVELF 1981–84; Asst. Dir.-Gen. Société Elf-France 1984; Asst. Dir.-Gen. Refineries and Distribution, Société Nat. Elf Aquitaine 1984; Dir.-Gen. of Industry, Ministry of Industry, Posts & Telecommunications and Tourism 1987–88; Dir. Soc. Roussel-Uclaf 1989–91; Pres. Admin. Council Rhin-Meuse 1992–97; Dir.-Gen. CEA Industrie 1992–94; Pres. Dexter SA 1992, Inst. français de l'environnement 1995; mem. Conseil Général des Mines 1991–; Officier, Légion d'honneur, Ordre nat. du Mérite; Croix de la Valeur militaire. *Address:* 143 rue de la Pompe, 75116 Paris, France (Home). *Telephone:* 45.53.05.44 (Home).

SAHABDEEN, Desamanya Abdul Majeed Mohamed, PH.D.; Sri Lankan foundation administrator, entrepreneur, fmr. civil servant and scholar; b. 19 May 1926; s. of Abdul Majeed and Shaharwan Majeed; m. Ruchia Halida 1959; one s. one d.; ed. Univ. of Ceylon; joined Ceylon Civil Service 1950, served as Sec., Dir., Commr., Chair. several maj. govt. orgs. until 1973; Visiting Head Dept. of Western Philosophy, Univ. of Sri Lanka, Vidyodaya (now Sri Jayawardanapura) 1957–59; Chair. Majeedsons Group of Cos. 1973–, Muslim Law (Amendments) Cttee. 1990; f. A.M.M. Sahabdeen Trust Foundation 1991, for Educ. and Social Devt.; Mohamed Sahabdeen Int. Awards for science, literature and human devt. est. by Act. of Parl. 1991; f. Mohamed Sahabdeen Inst. for advanced studies and research in Pahamune 1997; mem. Presidential Comms. on Delimitation of Electoral Dists. 1988, Taxation 1989, Finance and Banking 1990, Industrialization 1990, Public Service Comm. 1989; mem. Press Council 1998; Vice-Patron Sri Lanka-India Friendship Soc. 1998; received Desamanya (highest civilian honour) 1992. *Publications:* several articles and books on philosophy and allied subjects, including Sufi Doctrine in Tamil Literature 1986, God and the Universe 1995, The Circle of Life. *Leisure interests:* philosophy, classical music. *Address:* A.M.M. Sahabdeen Trust Foundation, 10 Ward Place, Colombo 07, Sri Lanka. *Telephone:* (1) 684405; (1) 684406. *Fax:* (1) 683043; (1) 683050.

SAHADE, Jorge, PH.D.; Argentinian astrophysicist; b. 23 Feb. 1915, Alta Gracia; s. of Nallib Jorge Sahade and María Cassab; m. 1st Myriam Stella Elkin Font 1948 (died 1974); one s. one d.; m. 2nd Adela Emilia Ringuelet 1975; ed. Colegio de Monserrat, Córdoba, Univ. of Córdoba, Univ. of La Plata; Fellow Univ. of La Plata at Univ. of Chicago (Yerkes Observatory) 1943–46; Prof. Univ. of Córdoba 1948–55, Dir. Córdoba Observatory 1953–55; Guggenheim Fellow Univ. of Calif., Berkeley 1955–57, Research Astronomer 1957–58, 1960; Prof. and Head Div., Univ. of La Plata Observatory 1958–71, in charge of two-m. telescope project 1958–69, Dir. Observatory 1968–69, Dean Faculty of Exact Sciences 1969; Dir. Inst. of Astronomy and Space Physics, Buenos Aires 1971–74; Pres. Argentine Astronomical Asscn. 1963–69; Pres. Comm. 29, Int. Astronomical Union (IAU) 1964–67, Vice-Pres. Exec. Cttee. IAU 1967–73, Pres. 1985–88, Adviser 1988–91, Vice-Pres. Comm. 38 1988–91, Pres. 1991–94; Pres. Argentine Space Agency (CONAE) 1991–94; Emer. Researcher, CONICET 1995; Scientific Co-ordinator of Argentinian participation, Gemini Project 1996–; Chair. COSPAR Advisory Panel on Space Research in Developing Countries 1973–79, Pres. 1979–82; mem. Bd. Dirs. Nat. Research Council 1969–73, 1996, Exec. Bd. ICSU 1972–76, Gen. Cttee. 1972–80, COSTED 1973–79; Visiting Prof. at numerous univs.: Indiana, Sussex, Mons, Collège de France, Int. School for Advanced Study (Trieste), San Marcos (Peru), Porto Alegre (Brazil); Visiting Astronomer Dominion Astrophysical Observatory, Victoria, B.C., later Visiting Research Officer; Visiting Scientist Max-Planck Institut-für-Astrophysik, Fed. Repub. of Germany, Cerro Tololo Interamerican Observatory, Chile, Trieste Observatory; Guest Investigator at numerous observatories; Hon. Prof. Univ. of San Marcos, Peru 1987; Hon. mem. Argentine Asscn. of Friends of Astronomy 1970, Argentine Astronomical Asscn. 1985; founder-mem. Argentine Acad. of Aeronautical and Space Sciences 1989; foreign, corresp. mem. numerous acads.; Dr. h.c. (Córdoba) 1987, (San Juan) 1996; Golden Planetarium Award 1973, Konex Award 1983, Diploma of Recognition, World Cultural Council 1987; Asteroid (2605)=1974 QA named Sahade at the proposal of the discoverer 1986, Consagración Científica Medal 1988; IAU Symposium No. 151 dedicated to J. Sahade; CASLEO's 2.15m telescope named Jorge Sahade 1996. *Publications:* 180 research papers in int. journals. *Leisure interests:* music, travel, walking. *Address:* C.C. 677, Observatorio Astronómico, FCAG, Universidad Nacional de La Plata, 1900 La Plata (Office); 53-448 (p. 11 # 1), 1900 La Plata, Argentina (Home). *Telephone:* (221) 4217308, 4838810 (Office). *Fax:* (221) 4211761.

SAHE AL KAFAJE, Galib Nahe; Iraqi artist; b. 1932, Emara; m. 1967; three d.; ed. Inst. of Fine Arts, Baghdad and Acad. of Fine Arts, Rome; Instructor Inst. of Fine Arts, Baghdad 1966, Acad. of Fine Arts, Baghdad 1969; work includes mural at Saddam Airport 1987, 130 graphics at Rashed Hotel, Baghdad; works in collection at Saddam Art Center and have been widely exhibited in European cities, New Delhi, Cairo etc.; several awards. *Leisure interest:* handicrafts in gold. *Address:* College of Fine Arts, University of Baghdad, P.O. Box 17635, Jadiriya, Baghdad (Office); Dawoody, Street 15 No 102, Baghdad, Iraq (Home). *Telephone:* 5423690.

SAHEL, El Mostafa, L. EN D.; Moroccan politician; b. 5 May 1946, El Jadida; s. of Maati Sahel and Hajja Ghita; m. Farida Benmansour Nejjai 1972; two s.; ed. Lycée Mohamed V, Casablanca, Univ. Mohamed V, Rabat and Univ. de

Sorbonne, Paris; Insp. des Finances 1968–70; Financial Controller 1970–74; Head of Service of Working Budget 1974–81, Equipment Budget 1981–86; Dir. of Budget 1986–91; Sec.-Gen. Ministry of Finance 1992–93; Dir.-Gen. of Communal Equipment Funds 1993–; Minister of Ocean Fisheries, Admin. Affairs and Parl. Relations 1993–98; Ordre de Mérite, Ordre du Trône. *Leisure interest:* golf. *Address:* Ministère des Pêches Maritimes et de la Marine Marchande, Nouveau Quartier Administratif B.P. 476, Agdal, Rabat; Fonds d'Equipement Communal, 1 rue Baht, Agdal, Rabat, Morocco. *Telephone:* (212-7) 77 05 48/29; (212-7) 77 80 52 – 77 05 74. *Fax:* (212-7) 77 67 24; (212-7) 77 80 95.

SAHGAL, Nayantara; Indian writer; b. 10 May 1927, Allahabad; d. of Ranjit Sitaram Pandit and Vijaya Lakshmi Pandit; m. 1st Gautam Sahgal 1949 (divorced 1967); one s. two d.; m. 2nd E. N. Mangat Rai 1979; ed. Wellesley Coll., U.S.A.; Scholar-in-Residence, holding creative writing seminar, Southern Methodist Univ., Dallas, Texas 1973, 1977; Adviser English Language Bd., Sahitya Akademi (Nat. Acad. of Letters), New Delhi; mem. Indian Del. to UN Gen. Ass. 1978; mem. Nat. Exec., People's Union for Civil Liberties; Fellow, Radcliffe Inst. (Harvard Univ.) 1976, Wilson Int. Centre for Scholars, Washington, D.C. 1981–82, Nat. Humanities Center, N.C. 1983–84; mem. jury Commonwealth Writers' Prize 1990, Chair. Eurasia Region 1991; Annie Besant Memorial Lecture (Banares Hindu Univ.) 1992; Arthur Ravenscroft Memorial Lecture (Univ. of Leeds) 1993; foreign hon. Mem. American Acad. Arts and Sciences 1990; Hon. D. Litt. (Leeds) 1997. *Publications:* Prison and Chocolate Cake 1954, A Time to be Happy 1958, From Fear Set Free 1962, This Time of Morning 1965, Storm in Chandigarh 1969, History of the Freedom Movement 1970, The Day in Shadow 1972, A Situation in New Delhi 1977, A Voice for Freedom 1977, Indira Gandhi's Emergence and Style 1978, Indira Gandhi: Her Road to Power 1982, Rich Like Us (awarded Sinclair Prize 1985; Sahitya Akad. Award 1987) 1985, Plans for Departure 1985 (awarded Commonwealth Writers' Prize 1987), Mistaken Identity 1988, Relationship: Extracts from a Correspondence 1994, Point of View 1997. *Leisure interests:* walking, reading, music. *Address:* 181B Rajpur Road, Dehra Dun, 248009 Uttar Pradesh, India. *Telephone:* (0135) 684-278.

SAHL, Mort(on) Lyon, B.S.; American comedian; b. 11 May 1927, Montreal, Canada; s. of Harry Sahl; m. 1st Sue Babior 1955 (divorced 1957); m. 2nd China Lee; one c.; ed. Compton Jr. Coll., Univ. of Southern California; Ed. Poop from the Group; magazine writing; many night club engagements; radio and TV performances, including Comedy News TV show, Steve Allen Show, Jack Paar Show, Eddie Fisher Show, Nightline, Wide Wide World; monologues on long-playing records; in Broadway revue, The Next President 1958; one-man show Broadway 1987; films include: In Love and War 1958, All the Young Men 1960, Doctor, You've Got to be Kidding 1967, Nothing Lasts Forever 1984; TV film: Inside the Third Reich 1982. *Publication:* Heartland 1976.

SAHLIN, Mona; Swedish politician; b. 9 March 1957, Sollefteа; m. Bo Sahlin; three c.; ed. Correspondence School, Swedish Cooperative Movt. 1978–80; Sec. State Employees' Union 1980–82; M.P. 1982–; Minister of Employment 1990–91; Gen. Sec. Swedish Social Democratic Party 1992–94; Govt. Rep. Bd. of Swedish Sports Confed. 1983–90; Chair. Cttee. on Working Hours; mem. Bd. Centre for Working Life 1982–90; Deputy Prime Minister and Minister with Special Responsibility for Equality Issues 1994–95; Minister, Ministry of Industry and Commerce Oct. 1998–. *Address:* Riksdag, 10012 Stockholm, Sweden. *Telephone:* (8) 786 4000. *Fax:* (8) 211524.

SAIBOU, Brig. Ali; Niger politician and army officer; fmr. Chief of Staff of Armed Forces; fmr. Acting Head of State; Pres. Mouvement nat. pour une Société de développement (MNSD); Chair. of the Higher Council for Nat. Orientation (fmrly Conseil militaire Suprême) 1987; Pres. of the Council of Ministers 1987, Minister of Nat. Defence 1987–91, of Interior 1987–89 (stripped of exec. power Aug. 1991).

SAID, Edward W., M.A., PH.D.; American university professor; b. Nov. 1935, Jerusalem; m. Mariam Cortas 1970; one s. one d.; ed. Victoria Coll., Cairo, Mt. Hermon School, Mass., Princeton and Harvard Univs.; instructor in English, Columbia Univ. 1963–65, Asst. Prof. of English and Comparative Literature 1967–69, Prof. 1969–77, Parr Prof. 1977–89; Old Dominion Foundation Prof. in Humanities, Columbia Univ. 1989–, Univ. Prof. 1992–; Visiting Prof. of Comparative Literature, Harvard Univ. 1974, of Humanities, Johns Hopkins Univ. 1979; Editor, Arab Studies Quarterly; Chair. Bd. of Trustees, Inst. of Arab Studies; mem. Palestine Nat. Council, Council on Foreign Relations, New York, Acad. of Literary Studies, PEN Club, New York, American Acad. of Arts and Sciences; Fellow, Center for Advanced Study in Behavioral Science, Stanford 1975–76; Bowdoin Prize (Harvard Univ.); Lionel Trilling Award 1976. *Publications:* Joseph Conrad and the Fiction of Autobiography, Beginnings: Intention and Method, Orientalism, The Question of Palestine, Literature and Society, Covering Islam 1981, The World, the Text and the Critic 1983, After the Last Sky 1986, Blaming the Victims 1988 (ed.), Musical Elaborations 1991, Culture and Imperialism 1993, Representations of the Intellectual 1994, Politics of Dispossession 1994, Ghazzah-Arihah: Salam Amriki 1994. *Address:* Columbia University, Department of English, 602 Philosophy Hall, New York, NY 10027, U.S.A.

SAID, Hakim Mohammed; Pakistani physician; b. 9 Jan. 1920; s. of late Hakim Abdul Majeed and Rabia Begum; m. Nemat Begum 1943 (deceased); one d.; ed. Ayurvedic and Unani Tibbi (Medical) Coll., Delhi; Founder, Sec.-Gen. Soc. for Promotion of Eastern Medicine 1956; Founder, Pres. Coll. of Eastern Medicine, Karachi 1958; Pres. Inst. of Health and Medical Research, Hamdard Foundation, Soc. for the Promotion and Improvement of Libraries, Hamdard Acad., Pakistan Historical Soc., Ibn-i-Khaldun Educ. Soc., Inst. of Cen. and West Asian Studies Karachi Univ.; Chair. Hamdard Waqf Labs.; organized Health of the Nation Conf., Karachi 1971, formed Nat. Health Cttee.; mem. Exec. Cttee. Union Int. d'Education pour la Santé, Paris until 1976; Adviser to Pres. of Pakistan on Tibb (Traditional Medicine) 1979–82; Founder-Pres. Madinat al-Hikmat; Pres. Hamdard Foundation; mem. numerous socs.; participant, organizer many int. confs. and congresses; mem. New York Acad. of Sciences, British Soc. for the History of Science; Assoc. mem. Royal Soc. of Health, U.K.; Fellow Royal Acad. of Islamic Civilization Research, Jordan; Hon. D.Sc. (Medicine Alternativa Internazional) 1984; Sitara-i-Imtiaz (Award for Social and Educ. Service, Govt. of Pakistan) 1966, Sadiq Dost (Award from people of Bahawalpur), Islamic Medicine Prize from Kuwait Foundation for the Advancement of Sciences 1982. *Publications include:* numerous essays, Medicine in China, Europe Nama, Germany Nama, Wonders of the Human Body, Health of the Nation, The Employer and Employee, Tazkàr-i-Muhammad, Pharmacopoeia of Eastern Medicine, Main Currents of Contemporary Thought in Pakistan (2 vols.), Maqalat-i-Sham-i-Hamdard, Maqalat-i Ibn al-Haitham, Pharmacographia Indica, Al-Biruni Commemorative Volume, Greco-Arab Medicine and Modern Western Medicine—Conflict or Symbiosis, Ek Musafir Char Mulk, Al-Biruni, His Times, Life and Works, Safar Nama Roos, Switzerland Men Merey Chand Shab-O-Roz, Diseases of the Liver—Greco-Arab Concepts, Proceedings of the International Symposium on New Researches in Biology and Genetics: Problems of Science and Ethics, Proceedings of the Int. Conf. on History and Philosophy of Science, Greco-Arab Concepts on Cardiovascular Diseases, Korea Kahani. *Leisure interest:* tennis. *Address:* Hamdard Foundation Pakistan, Hamdard Centre, Nazimabad, Karachi 74600 (Office); 58/1 Upper Sind Colony, Karachi 5, Pakistan (Home). *Telephone:* 6616001 (Office); 410612 (Home).

SAID, Sayed Faisal bin Ali al-; Omani diplomatist and politician; b. 1927, Muscat; attached to Ministry of Foreign Affairs, Muscat 1953–57; lived abroad 1957–70; Perm. Under-Sec. Ministry of Educ. 1970–72; Minister of Econ. Affairs 1972; Perm. Rep. to UN, Amb. to U.S.A. 1972–73; Minister of Educ. 1973–76, of Omani Heritage 1976–, of Culture 1979–. *Address:* Ministry of National Heritage and Culture, P.O. Box 668, Muscat 113, Oman. *Telephone:* 602555.

SAID, Wafic; Saudi Arabian (b. Syrian) financier; b. 1939, Damascus; s. of Rida Said; m. Rosemary Buchanan; three c. (one s. deceased); ed. in Lebanon and at Inst. of Banking, London; began banking career in Geneva; returned to London, opened several kebab restaurants 1967; moved to Saudi Arabia and entered construction business; became Saudi Arabian citizen 1981; Gov. R.S.C., London. *Leisure interests:* horse racing, collecting art and antiques. *Address:* c/o Royal Shakespeare Company, Barbican Theatre, London, E.C.2, England.

SAIER, Oskar, DR.JUR.CAN.; German ecclesiastic; b. 12 Aug. 1932, Wagensteig; s. of Adolf Saier and Berta Saier; ed. Univs. of Freiburg and Tübingen; curate 1957; Asst. Kanonist. Inst. Univ. of Munich 1963; Auxiliary Bishop in Freiburg 1972, Archbishop 1978–; Chair. Pastoral Comm. of German Conf. of Bishops 1979–98; mem. Vatican Congregation for the Clergy 1984; Second Chair. of German Conf. of Bishops 1987; Freeman of Buchenbach 1972, of St. Peter, Black Forest 1977, and of Bethlehem, Israel 1984; Order El Sol del Peru 1990, Grosses Bundesverdienstkreuz 1992, Verdienstmedaille des Landes Baden-Württemberg 1997. *Publication:* Communio in der Lehre des Zweiten Vatikanischen Konzils 1973. *Address:* Herrenstrasse 35, 79098 Freiburg, Germany. *Telephone:* 21881. *Fax:* 0761/34663.

SAIF, Abdulla Hassan; Bahrain banker; b. 10 March 1945, Muharraq; ed. Inst. of Cost and Man. Accountants, U.K., IMF Inst. and other int. forums; apprentice, Bahrain Petroleum Co. 1957, served in all depts. until 1971; Head of Finance and Admin. Civil Aviation Directorate 1971–74; Deputy Dir.-Gen. Bahrain Monetary Agency 1974–77, Dir.-Gen. 1977, now Gov.; Chair. Gulf Int. Bank B.S.C.; Chair. Specific Council for Training of Banking Sector; mem. Bd. of Dirs. Gulf Air Co., Org. for Social Insurance, Civil Service Pension Bd.; Alt. Gov. IMF. *Address:* c/o Gulf International Bank B.S.C., Al-Dowali Building, 3 Palace Avenue, P.O. Box 1017, Manama, Bahrain. *Telephone:* 534000.

SAIF AL-ISLAM, Mohamed al-Badr, H.R.H.; fmr. Imam of the Yemen; b. 1927; ed. Coll. for Higher Education, Sana'a (Yemen); Minister for Foreign Affairs 1955–61, and Minister of Defence and C.-in-C. 1955–62; succeeded to Imamate on the death of his father, Imam Ahmed Sept. 1962; in hills, Yemen, leading Royalist Forces in civil war 1962–68; replaced by Imamate Council May 1968; in exile in Saudi Arabia 1968. *Address:* Jeddah, Saudi Arabia.

SAIFUDIN (see Seypidin).

SAIGH, Nassir M. Al-, D.B.A.; Saudi Arabian business administrator; b. 10 Oct. 1942, Riyadh; s. of Mohammed Al-Saigh and Noura Al-Saigh; m. Azza J. Hammad 1989; ed. Univ. of Kentucky, Lexington, Univ. of Indiana, Bloomington, King Saud Univ., Riyadh; Chair. Business Admin. Dept., King Saud Univ. 1980–83, Asst. Prof., Faculty of Admin. Sciences 1979–80; Chief Ed., Arab Journal of Admin. 1983–; Dir.-Gen. Arab Admin. Devt. Org. 1983–.

Publications: Administrative Reform in the Arab World: Readings 1986, Public Administration and Administrative Reform in the Arab World 1986. *Leisure interest:* reading. *Telephone:* 687327 (Home).

SAINSBURY, (Richard) Mark, D.PHIL.; British professor of philosophy; b. 2 July 1943, London; m. Gillian McNeill Rind 1969 (separated 1982); one s. one d.; ed. Sherborne School, Corpus Christi Coll., Oxford; Radcliffe Lecturer in Philosophy, Magdalen Coll., Oxford 1968–70; lecturer in Philosophy, St. Hilda's Coll., Oxford 1970–73, Radcliffe Lecturer in Philosophy, Brasenose Coll., Oxford 1973–75; lecturer in Philosophy, Univ. of Essex 1975–78, Bedford Coll., Univ. of London 1978–84, King's Coll., London 1984–87, Reader 1987–89, Stebbing Prof. of Philosophy 1991–; Ed. Mind 1991; Radcliffe Fellow 1987–88; Fellow King's Coll., London 1994, British Acad. 1998. *Publications:* Russell 1979, Paradoxes 1988, Logical Forms 1991. *Address:* Department of Philosophy, King's College, London, London, WC2R 2LS, England. *Telephone:* 0171-873 2553. *Fax:* 0171-873 2270.

SAINSBURY OF PRESTON CANDOVER, Baron (Life Peer), cr. 1989, of Preston Candover in the County of Hampshire; **John Davan Sainsbury,** K.G., M.A.; British business executive; b. 2 Nov. 1927, London; s. of the late A. J. (later Baron) Sainsbury; m. Anya Linden 1963; two s. one d.; ed. Stowe School and Worcester Coll., Oxford; Dir. J Sainsbury Ltd. 1958–92, Vice-Chair. 1967–69, Chair., C.E.O. 1969–92, Pres. 1992–; Dir. Royal Opera House, Covent Garden 1969–85 (Chair. 1987–91), The Economist 1972–80, Royal Opera House Trust 1974–84, 1987–97; Chair. Friends of Covent Garden 1969–81, Benesh Inst. of Chorology 1986–87, Dulwich Picture Gallery 1994–; Vice-Pres. Contemporary Arts Soc. 1984–; mem. Council, Retail Consortium 1975–79, Pres. 1993–97; mem. Nat. Cttee. for Electoral Reform 1976–85; Jt. Hon. Treas. European Movement 1972–75; Fellow, Inst. of Grocery Distribution 1973; Hon. Fellow Worcester Coll. Oxford 1982; Gov. Royal Ballet School 1965–76, 1987–91, Royal Ballet 1987– (Chair. 1995–); Trustee Nat. Gallery 1976–83, Westminster Abbey Trust 1977–83, Tate Gallery 1982–83, Rhodes Trust 1984–98, Prince of Wales Inst. of Architecture 1992–96; Hon. Bencher, Inner Temple 1985; Hon. D.Sc. (London) 1985, Hon. D.Litt. (South Bank) 1992; Albert Medal (R.S.A.) 1989. *Address:* c/o J Sainsbury PLC, Stamford House, Stamford Street, London, SE1 9LL, England.

SAINSBURY OF TURVILLE, Baron (Life Peer), cr. 1997, in the County of Buckinghamshire; **David John Sainsbury,** M.B.A.; British business executive; b. 24 Oct. 1940; s. of Sir Robert Sainsbury; m. Susan C. Reid 1973; three d.; ed. King's Coll. Cambridge and Columbia Univ. N.Y.; joined J Sainsbury 1963, Finance Dir. 1973–90, Deputy Chair. J Sainsbury PLC 1988–92, Chair. and C.E.O. 1992–98, Dir. J. Sainsbury U.S.A. Inc.; Parl. Under-Sec. of State for Science 1998–; mem.. Cttee. of Review of Post Office (Carter Cttee.) 1975–77; fmr. Trustee, Social Democratic Party (SDP); mem. Gov. Body, London Business School 1985– (Chair. 1991–98); Visiting Fellow, Nuffield Coll. Oxford 1987–95; Hon. I.Eng. 1994. *Publications:* Government and Industry: A New Partnership 1981, Wealth Creation and Jobs (with C. Smallwood) 1987. *Address:* 4 Charterhouse Mews, Charterhouse Square, London, EC1M 6BB, England. *Telephone:* 0171-253 6812. *Fax:* 0171-253 6813.

ST. AUBIN de TERAN, Lisa Gioconda; British author; b. 2 Oct. 1953, London; d. of Jan Rynveld Carew and Joan Mary St. Aubin; m. 1st Jaime Terán 1970 (divorced 1981); one d.; m. 2nd George Macbeth 1981 (divorced 1989; deceased); one s.; m. 3rd Robbie Duff-Scott 1989; one d.; ed. James Allen's Girls' School, Dulwich; travelled widely in France and Italy 1969–71; managed sugar plantation in Venezuelan Andes 1971–78; moved to Italy 1983; appeared in BBC-TV documentary Santos to Santa Cruz in Great Railway Journeys series 1994; Somerset Maugham Award; John Llewelyn Rhys Award; Eric Gregory Award for Poetry. *Publications:* novels: Keepers of the House 1982, The Slow Train to Milan 1983, The Tiger 1984, The Bay of Silence 1986, Black Idol 1987, Joanna 1990, Nocturne 1993, The Palace 1998; The High Place (poetry) 1985; The Marble Mountain (short stories) 1989; Distant Landscapes (novella) 1995; Off the Rails—A Memoir 1989, Venice: The Four Seasons 1992, A Valley in Italy 1994, The Hacienda; My Venezuelan Years 1997, ed. The Virago Book of Wanderlust and Dreams 1998. *Leisure interests:* travelling, medicinal plants, gardening, architecture, bric-a-brac, antiques, reading. *Address:* c/o Maggie Phillips, Ed Victor Ltd., 6 Bayley Street, Bedford Square, London, WC1B 3HB, England. *Telephone:* 0171-304 4100.

ST. JOHN, (Harold) Bernard, Q.C.; Barbadian politician and lawyer (retd.); b. 16 Aug. 1931, Christ Church; m. Stella Hope; one s. two d.; ed. Boys' Foundation, Harrison Coll., Univ. of London, Inner Temple; called to Bar 1954; pvt. legal practice, Barbados and Eastern Caribbean 1954–; Q.C. 1969; Legal Adviser to Southern Dist. Council; Pres. Barbados Bar Asscn.; mem. Senate 1964–66, 1971–76; mem. House of Ass. 1966–71, 1976–; Chair. Barbados Labour Party 1966–71; Leader of the Opposition 1970–71; Minister of Trade, Tourism and Industry 1976–86, also Deputy Prime Minister, Prime Minister and Minister of Finance 1985–86; Trustee, Barbados Labour Party 1986–; Chair. Caribbean Tourism Research Cen. 1977–79; Pres. ACP (African, Caribbean and Pacific) Council of Ministers 1979; Pres. Latin American Council of Ministers 1980. *Leisure interest:* fishing. *Address:* 3 Enterprise, Christchurch, Barbados (Home).

ST. JOHN OF FAWSLEY, Baron (Life Peer), cr. 1987, of Preston in the County of Northampton; **Norman Antony Francis St. John-Stevas,** P.C., M.A., B.C.L., PH.D., F.R.S.L.; British politician, barrister, author and journalist; b. 18 May 1929; s. of the late Stephen Stevas and Kitty St. John O'Connor; ed. Ratcliffe, Fitzwilliam Coll., Cambridge, Christ Church, Oxford, and Yale; Barrister, Middle Temple 1952; Lecturer, King's Coll., London 1953–56; Tutor in Jurisprudence, Christ Church, Oxford 1953–55, Merton Coll., Oxford 1955–57; Founder mem. Inst. of Higher European Studies, Bolzano 1955; Legal Adviser to Sir Alan Herbert's Cttee. on Book Censorship 1954–59; Legal and Political Corresp., The Economist 1959–64; Conservative M.P. for Chelmsford 1964–87; Sec. Conservative Party Home Affairs Cttee. 1969–72; mem. Fulbright Comm. 1961; Parl. Select Cttee. Race Relations and Immigration 1970–72; Parl. Under-Sec. for Educ. and Science 1972–73; Minister of State for the Arts 1973–74; mem. Parl. Select Cttee. on Race Relations and Immigration 1970–72, on Civil List 1971–83, on Foreign Affairs 1983–87; mem. Shadow Cabinet 1974–79, Shadow Leader of the House of Commons 1978–79, Opposition Spokesman on Educ. 1974–78, Science 1974–78 and the Arts 1974–79; Chancellor of the Duchy of Lancaster 1979–81; Leader of the House of Commons 1979–81; Minister for the Arts 1979–81; Vice-Chair. Cons. Parl. N. Ireland Cttee. 1972–87; Vice-Chair. Cons. Group for Europe 1972–75; Chair. Royal Fine Art Comm. 1985–; Master Emmanuel Coll., Cambridge 1991–96, Life Fellow 1996; Vice-Pres. Theatres Advisory Council 1983; founder mem. Christian-Social Inst. of Culture, Rome 1969; mem. Council RADA 1983–88, Nat. Soc. for Dance 1983–, Nat. Youth Theatre 1983– (Patron 1984–), Royal Coll. of Art 1985–; Trustee Royal Philharmonic Orch. 1985–88, Decorative Arts Soc. 1984–; Hon. Sec. Fed. of Conservative Students 1971–73; Ed. The Dublin (Wiseman Review) 1961; Romanes Lecturer, Oxford 1987; Hon. F.R.I.B.A.; Hon. D.D. (Susquehanna, Pa) 1983, Hon. D.Litt. (Schiller) 1985, (Bristol) 1988, Hon. LL.D. (Leicester) 1991, Hon. D.Arts (De Montfort) 1996; Hon. LL.D. (Leicester) 1991; Silver Jubilee Medal 1977; Kt. Grand Cross, St. Lazarus of Jerusalem 1963; Cavaliere Ordine al Merito della Repubblica (Italy) 1965, Commendatore 1978. *Publications:* Obscenity and the Law 1956, Walter Bagehot 1959, Life, Death and the Law 1961, The Right to Life 1963, Law and Morals 1964, The Literary Essays of Walter Bagehot 1965, The Historical Essays of Walter Bagehot 1968, The Agonising Choice 1971, The Political Essays of Walter Bagehot 1974, The Economic Works of Walter Bagehot 1978, Pope John Paul, His Travels and Mission 1982, The Two Cities 1984. *Leisure interests:* reading, talking, listening to music, travelling, walking, appearing on television. *Address:* 7 Upper Harley Street, Regent's Park, London, NW1 4PS; The Old Rectory, Preston Capes, Daventry, Northants., NN11 6TE, England.

SAINT LAURENT, Yves (Henri Donat); French couturier; b. 1 Aug. 1936, Oran, Algeria; s. of Charles Mathieu Saint Laurent and Lucienne-Andrée Wilbaux; ed. Lycée d'Oran; worked with Christian Dior 1954–57, successor to Christian Dior 1957–60; Shareholder Société Yves Saint Laurent 1962–; consultant to Chinese govt. 1987–; designed costumes for: (ballets) Cyrano de Bergerac 1959, Adage et Variations, Notre-Dame de Paris 1965, Sheherezade 1973, Delicate Balance 1967; (films) The Pink Panther 1962, Belle de Jour 1967, La Chamade 1968, La Sirène du Mississippi 1969, L'Affaire Stavisky 1974; designed stage sets and costumes for: Les Chants de Maldoror 1962, Spectacle Zizi Jeanmaire 1961, 1963, 1968; exhbns.: Metropolitan Museum of Art, New York 1983, Beijing Museum of Fine Arts 1985, Musée des Arts de la Mode, Paris 1986; House of Painters of U.S.S.R. 1986, Hermitage Museum Leningrad (now St. Petersburg) 1987, Art Gallery of N.S.W. Sydney 1987, Sezon Museum, Tokyo 1990, Espace Mode Méditerranée, Marseille 1993; Neiman-Marcus Award for fashions 1958, Oscar, Harper's Bazaar 1966, Int. Award of Council of Fashion Designers of America 1982, Best Fashion Designer Oscar 1985. Chevalier Légion d'honneur. *Address:* 5 avenue Marceau, 75116 Paris, France.

SAINT-PHALLE, Niki de; French artist; b. 29 Oct. 1930, Neuilly-sur-Seine; m. Harry Mathews 1948 (separated 1960); two d.; lived with artist Jean Tinguely since 1960; ed. Convent of Sacré Coeur, New York; numerous one-woman shows in Paris, New York, London, Amsterdam, Brussels, Munich, Zürich, Geneva, Tokyo etc. since 1961; retrospective exhbns. Kunstverein, Düsseldorf 1968, Kunstverein, Hannover 1969, Kunstmuseum, Lucerne 1969, Centre Georges Pompidou, Paris (and touring) 1980; participant in group exhbns. including Paris Biennale 1963, Dada, Surrealism and Their Heritage, Museum of Modern Art, New York 1968, The Figurative Tradition, Whitney Museum, New York 1980; public collections include Centre Georges Pompidou, Paris, Stedelijk Museum, Amsterdam, Whitney Museum and Moderna Museet, Stockholm; work includes paintings, 'Nana' sculptures, object-reliefs and assemblages, theatre sets, films and outdoor sculptures. *Address:* c/o Gimpel Fils, 30 Davies Street, London, W1Y 1LG, England; L'Auberge du Cheval-Blance, 91840 Soisy-sur-Ecole, Essones, France (Home).

SAITO, Eishiro; Japanese steel industry executive; b. 22 Nov. 1911, Niigata City; s. of Tooru and Tome Saito; m. Toshiko Kato 1939; one s. one d.; ed. Tokyo Imperial Univ.; joined Japan Iron and Steel Co. Ltd. 1941; Dir. Yawata Iron and Steel Co. Ltd. 1961, Man. Dir. 1962, Sr. Man. Dir. 1969; Sr. Man. Dir. Nippon Steel Corpn. 1970, Exec. Vice-Pres. 1973, Rep. Dir. and Pres. 1977–, Rep. Dir. and Chair. 1981–87, Hon. Chair. and Sr. Adviser 1987–; Chair. Keidanren (Japan Fed. of Econ. Orgs.) 1986; Hon. Chair. Kozai Club (Steel Materials Club), Japan Iron and Steel Exporters' Asscn., Japan Iron and Steel Fed.; Chair. Int. Iron and Steel Inst. 1977–79; Blue Ribbon Medal, First Class Order of the Rising Sun, Ordem de Rio Branco,

Order of Bernard O'Higgins, Grossen Stern der Völkerfreundschaft, Orden de Mayo Gran Cruz. *Leisure interests:* golf, "Go", reading. *Address:* 1-18-808, Hiroo 4-chome, Shibuya-ku, Tokyo 150, Japan (Home).

SAITO, Gunzi, PH.D.; Japanese professor of chemistry; b. 10 March 1945, Hokkaido; m. Atsuko Nishikawa 1971; three s.; ed. Otaru Choryo High School, Hokkaido Univ.; Postdoctoral Fellow, Emory Univ., Atlanta, Ga., U.S.A. 1973–74, Guelph Univ., Ont., Canada 1975–76; Welch Fellow Univ. of Tex., Dallas, U.S.A. 1977–78; Research Assoc., Inst. for Molecular Science, Okazaki 1979–84; Assoc. Prof., Inst. for Solid State Physics, Tokyo Univ. 1984–89; Prof., Dept. of Chem., Faculty of Science, Kyoto Univ. 1989–; mem. Science Council, Ministry of Educ., Sport and Culture 1996–; Inoue Award 1988, Nishina Award 1988, Japan Surface Science Award 1991. *Publications:* The Physics and Chemistry of Organic Superconductors (Co-Ed.) 1990; more than 500 scientific articles on organic superconductors, organic metals and other organic functional materials. *Address:* Chemistry Division, Graduate School of Science, Kyoto University, Sakyo-ku, Kitashirakawa, Kyoto 606-01, Japan. *Telephone:* (75) 753-4035. *Fax:* (75) 753-4000.

SAITO, Nobufusa, D.SC.; Japanese nuclear chemist; b. 28 Sept. 1916, Tokyo; m. Haruko Umeda 1944; one s. two d.; ed. Tokyo Imperial Univ.; fmr. Asst. Prof., Kyushu and Seoul Univs., Prof. of Inorganic Chem., Tokyo Univ. 1956–65; Chief Researcher, Inst. of Physical and Chemical Research 1959–76; fmr. Consultant to Int. Atomic Energy Agency (I.A.E.A.), Dir. of Isotopes Div. 1963–65; Prof. Inorganic and Nuclear Chem., Tokyo Univ. 1965–77, Dir. Radioisotope Centre 1970–77; Prof. Inorganic and Analytical Chem. Toho Univ. 1978–87, Dean, Faculty of Science 1979–82; Pres. Japan Chemical Analysis Centre 1990–; Dir. Japan Radioisotopes Asscn. 1967–; Tech. Adviser, Japan Atomic Energy Research Inst. 1966–; mem. Chemical Soc. of Japan (Vice-Pres. 1976–78, Pres. 1981–82, Hon. mem. 1987–), American Chemical Soc., Atomic Energy Soc. of Japan, Japan Soc. for Analytical Chem., Pres. 1979–80, Hon. mem. 1980–; Chem. Soc. of Japan Award 1974; Nat. Purple Ribbon Medal for Chemistry 1979; Royal Decoration of Second Order of Sacred Treasure 1987. *Leisure interests:* music, travel. *Address:* 5-12-9, Koshigoe, Kamakura 248, Japan. *Telephone:* 0467-31-3178.

SAITOTI, George, PH.D.; Kenyan politician; ed. Univ. of Warwick, U.K.; fmr. Prof. of Math. and Chair. Dept. of Math., Univ. of Nairobi; mem. E. African Legis. Ass. 1974–77; Dir. and Exec. Chair. Kenya Commercial Bank 1977–82; nominated M.P. 1983; Minister of Finance and Planning 1983–85, of Finance 1986–93, of Planning and Nat. Devt. 1993–; Vice-Pres. of Kenya 1989–97; Chair. Annual Meetings Bd. of Govs., IMF and World Bank Group 1990. *Address:* Treasury Building, Harambee Avenue, POB 30007, Nairobi, Kenya. *Telephone:* 338111.

SAKAGUCHI, Chikara; Japanese politician; mem. House of Reps.; fmr. Dir. Finance Cttee.; Chair. Komeito Policy Bd.; Minister of Labour Aug. 1993–94. *Address:* House of Representatives, Tokyo, Japan.

SAKAIYA, Taichi (pseudonym of Kotaro Ikeguchi); Japanese politician, author and fmr. civil servant; b. 1935; fmr. civil servant at Ministry of Int. Trade and Industry; became full-time writer 1978; Dir.-Gen. Econ. Planning Agency 1998–. *Publications include:* Yudan 1975. *Address:* Economic Planning Agency, 3-1-1, Kasumigaseki, Chiyoda-ku, Tokyo 100, Japan. *Telephone:* (03) 3581-0261. *Fax:* (03) 3581-3907.

SAKAKI, Hiroyuki, M.S., PH.D.; Japanese university professor; b. 6 Oct. 1944, Aichi; s. of Yone-ichiro Sakaki and Fumiko Sakaki; m. Mutsuko Sakaki 1973; one s. four d.; ed. Univ. of Tokyo; Assoc. Prof. Inst. of Industrial Science, Univ. of Tokyo 1973; Visiting Scientist, IBM T.J. Watson Research Center (group of Dr. Leo Esaki) 1976–77; Prof. Inst. of Industrial Science, Univ. of Tokyo 1987–; Prof. Research Center for Advanced Science and Tech. Univ. of Tokyo 1988–; Dir. for Quantum Wave Project (Japan's governmental project for Exploratory Research for Advanced Tech. (ERATO)) 1988–93; Dir. for Japan-U.S. Jt. Research Project on Quantum Transition 1994–(98); IBM Science Prize 1989; Hattori-Hokokai Prize 1990; Japan Applied Physics Soc. Prize 1983, 1990, Shimazu Science Prize. *Leisure interests:* listening to classical music, museum stroll for paintings. *Address:* Research Center for Advanced Science and Technology, University of Tokyo, 4-6-1 Komaba, Tokyo 153; Institute of Industrial Science, University of Tokyo, 7-22-1 Roppongi, Tokyo 106 (Offices); 1–41–5 Kagahara, Tsuzukiku, Yokohama 224, Japan (Home). *Telephone:* (3) 3401-7429; (3) 3481-4464 (Offices); (45) 943-1539 (Home).

SAKAKIBARA, Eisuke, PH.D.; Japanese politician; ed. Univs. of Tokyo and Michigan; fmrly. lecturer Harvard Univ. and in Japan; with Ministry of Finance; Vice-Minister for Int. Affairs 1997–99; sentenced to a suspended two-year prison term for accepting bribes. *Publication:* Beyond Capitalism 1990. *Address:* c/o Ministry of Finance, 3-1-1, Kasumigaseki, Chiyoda-ku, Tokyo 100, Japan.

SAKAMOTO, Ryoichi; Japanese composer; b. 1952, Tokyo; m. Akiko Yano 1979; ed. Shinjuku High School, Composition Dept., Tokyo Fine Arts Univ.; began composing at age of ten; mem. group Yellow Magic Orchestra 1978–83; solo albums include Thousand Knives 1978, Musical Encyclopaedia 1984; composed soundtrack for, and starred in film Merry Christmas Mr. Laurence 1982, soundtrack for Wuthering Heights 1992.

SAKER, Ahmad, D.ECON.; Syrian diplomatist; b. 17 May 1938; s. of late Mahmoud Saker and Hasina Saker; m. Layla Hassan; three s. one d.; ed. Damascus Univ., Government Univ. of Moscow; postings in Czechoslovakia, Iran, India, Turkey, U.S.S.R. 1966–75; Minister Plenipotentiary, Ministry of Foreign Affairs, Damascus; lecturer in Political Economy, Damascus Higher Planning Inst. 1976–79, Perm. Mission to UN, Geneva 1980–85; Dir. Americas Div., Ministry of Foreign Affairs 1985–88; Amb. Plenipotentiary and Extraordinary to Poland 1988–93; Dir. Africa Dept., then Asia Dept., Ministry of Foreign Affairs 1993–95, Asia, Australia Dept. 1995–. *Publications:* numerous articles on econ. and political affairs and human rights. *Leisure interests:* reading, sports (especially swimming), painting. *Address:* Adawi Inshaat Building 101, Apt. 10, Damascus, Syria. *Telephone:* 4442070; 4455848.

SAKMANN, Bert, B.A., M.D.; German physician; b. 12 June 1942, Stuttgart; s. of Berthold Sakmann and Annemarie Schaeffer Sakmann; m. Dr. Christiane Wulfert 1970; two s. one d.; ed. Univ. of Tübingen, Univ. of Munich, Univ. Hosp., Munich, Univ. of Göttingen; Research Asst. Max-Planck-Institut für Psychiatrie, Munich 1969–70; British Council Fellow Dept. of Biophysics, Univ. Coll., London 1971–73; Research Asst. Max-Planck-Institut für biophysikalische Chemie, Univ. of Göttingen 1974–79, Research Assoc. Membrane Biology Group 1979–82, Head Membrane Physiology Unit 1983–85, Dir. 1985–87, Prof. Dept. of Cell Physiology 1987–89; Dir. Dept. of Cell Physiology Max-Planck-Institut für medizinische Forschung, Heidelberg 1989–; Prof. of Physiology, Univ. of Heidelberg 1990–; Foreign mem. Nat. Acad., U.S.A. 1993, Royal Soc., U.K. 1994; shared Nobel Prize for Medicine and Physiology 1991 for discoveries about single ion channels in cells; numerous other awards, prizes and guest lectures. *Publications:* The Visual System: Neurophysiology, biophysics and their clinical applications 1972 (contrib.), Advances in Pharmacology and Therapeutics 1978 (contrib.), Single Channel Recording 1983 (jt. ed.), Membrane Control of Cellular Activity 1986 (contrib.), Calcium and Ion Channel Modulation 1988 (contrib.), Neuromuscular Junction 1989 (contrib.), numerous articles. *Leisure interests:* music, reading, tennis, skiing. *Address:* Max-Planck-Institut für medizinische Forschung, Jahnstrasse 29, 69120 Heidelberg, Germany. *Telephone:* (6221) 486460.

SAKO, Soumana, PH.D.; Malian politician and civil servant; b. 23 Dec. 1950, Nyamina; s. of Sayan Sako and Djeneba Traore; m. Cisse Toure; two s. two d.; ed. Univ. of Pittsburgh, Pa., U.S.A.; Advisor Ministry of Foreign Affairs and Int. Co-operation 1981–82; Sr. Advisor Ministry of Planning and Econ. Man. 1982–84; Dir. of Sr. Staff, Ministry of State-Owned Enterprises 1985–87; Minister of Finance and Commerce Feb.-Aug. 1987; Deputy Controller-Gen. Office of the Pres. 1988–89; UNDP official serving in Cen. African Repub. –1991, Sr. Economist for Madagascar and Comoros Is. 1993–97; Prime Minister of Mali 1991–92; Prof. of Devt. Econs. and Public Finance, Univ. of Mali 1998–; int. consultant 1998–. *Leisure interests:* soccer, chess, gardening. *Address:* BP 433, Bamako, Mali. *Telephone:* 236196. *Fax:* 229748.

SAKS, Gene; American actor and director; b. 8 Nov. 1921, New York; m. Beatrice Arthur (divorced); two s. one d.; ed. Cornell Univ.; began acting career off-Broadway at Provincetown Playhouse and the Cherry Lane Theatre; appeared in Dog Beneath the Skin (Auden), Him (e. e. cummings), The Bourgeois Gentilhomme (Molière); Broadway appearances in Mr Roberts, South Pacific, Middle of the Night, The Tenth Man, A Shot in the Dark, Love and Libel, A Thousand Clowns; début as dir. on Broadway with Enter Laughing 1963; later dir. plays: Nobody Loves an Albatross, Half a Sixpence, Generation, Mame, Same Time, Next Year, California Suite, I Love My Wife (Tony award), Brighton Beach (Tony award), Biloxi Blues 1985 (Tony award), Broadway Bound 1986, A Month of Sundays 1987, Rumours 1988, Jake's Woman 1992, Lost in Yonkers (original Broadway stage production). *Films directed:* Barefoot in the Park, The Odd Couple, Cactus Flower, Last of the Red Hot Lovers, Brighton Beach Memoirs, Mame. *Film appearances:* A Thousand Clowns, Prisoner of Second Avenue, Lovesick, The One and Only, The Goodbye People 1986, Brighton Beach Memoirs, Nobody's Fool 1994, IQ 1994. *Address:* c/o ICM, 40 West 57th Street, New York, NY 10036, U.S.A.

SAKURAUCHI, Yoshio; Japanese politician; b. 1912; ed. Keio Univ.; returned to House of Reps. twelve times, House of Councillors once; fmr. Pres. Japanese Electro-Chemical Asscn.; Parl. Vice-Minister of Justice; Minister of Int. Trade and Industry 1964–65; Chair. House of Reps. Foreign Affairs Cttee. 1971; Minister of Agric. and Forestry 1972–73; Chair. Policy Research Council, Liberal-Democratic Party (LDP) Sept.–Dec. 1976; Minister of Construction and Dir.-Gen. Nat. Land Agency 1977–78; Sec.-Gen. LDP 1979–81; Minister of Foreign Affairs 1981–82, House of Reps. Speaker (–1993) and LDP Advisor. *Address:* c/o Liberal-Democratic Party, 7, 2-chome, Hirakawacho, Chiyoda-ku, Tokyo, Japan.

SALA, Marius, PH.D.; Romanian linguist; b. 8 Sept. 1932, Vaşcău, Bihor Co.; s. of Sabin Sala and Eleonora Tocoianu; m. Florica Sala 1958; one d.; ed. Coll. of Philology, Bucharest Univ.; researcher, Inst. of Linguistics, Bucharest 1955–90, Deputy Dir. 1990–94, Dir. 1994–; Visiting Prof. Heidelberg 1971, Málaga 1968, 1970, 1973, 1979, Madrid 1978, 1981, 1987, Mexico City 1981, Cologne 1984, Frankfurt 1992, Oviedo 1994; Corresp. mem. Royal Acad. Spain 1978, Mexican Inst. of Culture 1981, Romanian Acad. 1993, Acad. Nacional de Letras, Montevideo 1994–, Int. Cttee. of Onomastic Studies 1969; mem. Int. Cttee. of the Mediterranean Linguistic Atlas 1960; mem. Man. Junta of the Int. Asscn. of Hispanists 1974–80; mem. Cttee. Soc. of Romance Linguistics 1974–80, 1989–; mem. Perm. Int. Cttee. of Linguists

1987–92; Prize of Romanian Acad. 1970; Prize of Mexican Acad. Centennial 1976. *Publications:* Contribuţii la fonetica istorică a limbii române (Contributions to the Historical Phonetics of the Romanian Language) 1970, Estudios sobre el judeo-español de Bucarest, Mexico City 1970, Phonétique et Phonologie du Judéo-Espagnol de Bucarest, The Hague 1971, Le judéo-espagnol, The Hague 1976, Contributions à la phonétique historique du roumain, Paris 1976, El léxico indígena del español americano, Apreciaciones sobre su vitalidad (co-author), Mexico–Bucharest 1977, El español de América, (Vol. 1), Léxico (co-author), Bogotá 1982, Limbile lumii. Mică enciclopedie (The Languages of the World: A concise encyclopaedia) (co-author), 1981, Les langues du monde (Petite Encyclopédie) (co-author), Paris 1984, Etimologia şi Limba Română (Etymology and the Romanian Language) (co-author) 1987, Vocabularul Reprezentativ Al Limbilor Romanice (The Representative Vocabulary of the Romance Languages) (co-author) 1988, El problema de las lenguas en contacto, Mexico City 1988, Enciclopedia Limbilor Romanice (Encyclopaedia of the Romance languages) (co-author) 1989, Unité des langues romanes 1996, Limba română, limbă romanică (Romanian Language, Romance Language) 1997, Limbi în contact (Languages in Contact) 1997, De la latină la română (From Latin to Romanian) 1998. *Leisure interests:* philately, cooking. *Address:* Institutul de Lingvistică, Calea 13 Septembrie 13, 79515 Bucharest, B.O. 42-37, Romania.

SALA-I-MARTÍN, Xavier, PH.D.; Spanish professor of economics; b. 17 June 1963, Barcelona; ed. Univ. Autònoma, Barcelona, Harvard Univ.; Assoc. Prof. Yale Univ. 1990–95; fmrly. Prof. Univ. Pompeu Fabra, Barcelona, Research Assoc. Nat. Bureau of Econ. Research, Cambridge, Mass.; Prof. of Econs. Columbia Univ. 1996–; consultant IMF 1992–, World Bank 1996–; Nat. Science Foundation Award 1998; King Juan Carlos I Prize for Social Sciences 1998. *Publications include:* Apuntes de Crecimiento Economica 1994, Economic Growth 1995, over 40 scientific articles. *Address:* 420 West 118th Street, New York, NY 10027, U.S.A.

SALAKHITDINOV, Makhmud, D.SC.; Uzbekistan mathematician; b. 23 Nov. 1933, Namangan, Uzbek S.S.R.; s. of Salahiddin Shamsuddinov and Zuhra Shamsuddinova; m. Muharram Rasulova 1955; three s. one d.; ed. Cen. Asian State Univ.; Asst. Tashkent State Univ. 1958–59; Scientific Fellow, Chief of Section, Deputy Dir., Dir. Inst. of Math. Uzbek S.S.R. Acad. of Sciences 1959–85, Chief, Differential Equation Section 1974–; Vice-Pres. Uzbek S.S.R. Acad. of Sciences 1984–85, Pres. 1988–94, Chair. Dept. of Physical and Math. Sciences 1994–; Chief of Chair. (jt.), Tashkent State Univ. 1980–85; Minister of Higher and Secondary Specialized Educ. of Uzbek S.S.R. 1985–88; Uzbekistan People's Deputy 1990–; Ed. papers of Uzbekistan Acad. of Sciences; Honoured Scientist of Uzbek S.S.R.; Badge of Honour; Uzbek State Prize. *Publications:* Mixed-complex Type Equation 1974, Ordinary Differential Equation 1982; contribs. to professional publs. *Leisure interests:* walking, reading fiction. *Address:* 70 Gogol Street, Tashkent, Uzbekistan. *Telephone:* (3712) 337281. *Fax:* (3712) 334901.

SALAKHOV, Tayir Teimur ogly; Azerbaijani painter; b. 29 Nov. 1928, Baku, Azerbaijan; m. Varvara Salakhova; three d.; ed. Azerbaijan Azimzade Higher School of Fine Arts, Moscow State Inst. of Fine Arts; docent, Prof. Azerbaijan State Inst. of Arts 1963–74; Chair. Exec. Bd. Azerbaijan Union of Artists 1972–74; Head of studio Moscow State Inst. of Fine Arts 1974–; Hon. Pres. Int. Asscn. of Art, Paris; First Sec. Exec. Bd. U.S.S.R. Union of Artists 1973–; mem. Exec. Bd. U.S.S.R. Acad. of Fine Arts, Sec. 1986–; author of numerous portraits, landscapes, theatre decorations; Hon. mem. Austrian Soc. of Fine Arts 1975, Acad. of Fine Arts, Kazakhstan, Acad. of Fine Arts, Kyrgyzstan; corresp. mem. French Acad. of Fine Arts 1986–; Hon. citizen Trenton, NJ, Santa Fe, NM, and Billings, Mont.; Prize of Cen. Komsomol Cttee. 1959, Akhundov Prize of Azerbaijan S.S.R. 1964, U.S.S.R. State Prize 1968, State Prize of Azerbaijan 1970 (for picture New Sea), Grekov's Gold Medal 1977, hero of Socialist Labour 1989, People's Painter of Russia 1996–, Order of Istiglal of Azerbaijan 1998, Order of Za Zaslugi pered Otechestvom (3rd class) (Russia) 1998. *Address:* Russian Academy of Fine Arts, Prechistenka str. 21, 119034, Moscow, Russia (Office). *Telephone:* (095) 201-39-71. *Fax:* (095) 290-20-88.

SALAMÉH, Riad, B.A.ECON.; Lebanese banker; b. 17 July 1950, Beirut; s. of Toufic Salamé and Renée Salamé; ed. Coll. Notre Dame, American Univ. of Beirut; Merrill Lynch, Beirut 1973–76, 1978–85, Paris 1976–78, Sr. Vice-Pres. and Financial Counsellor, Paris 1985–93; Gov. Banque du Liban 1993–. *Address:* Banque du Liban, Hamra, Masraf Loubnan Street, P.O. Box 11-5544, Beirut, Lebanon. *Telephone:* 01 341230/9. *Fax:* 001-212-4-782-740 (routed via New York).

SALÁNKI, János, M.D.; Hungarian physician and biologist; b. 11 May 1929, Debrecen; m. Katalin Rózsa; two d.; ed. Medical Univ. Debrecen., Lomonosov Univ. Moscow 1959; Dir. Balaton Limnological Research Inst., Hungarian Acad. of Sciences, Tihany 1962–90, Research Prof. 1991–; Research Prof. Univ. of Veszprém 1998–; Titular Prof. Eötvös Loránd Univ. Budapest; Pres. Int. Union of Biological Sciences (IUBS) 1988–91, Hungarian National IUBS Cttee., Int. Soc. for Invertebrate Neurobiology (ISIN) 1989–95, Interdisciplinary Cttee. for Bioindicators (IUBS); Chief Ed. Acta Biologica; mem. Ed. Bd., Acta Physiologica Hungarica, Journal of Aquatic Ecosystem Stress and Recovery, Gen. Physiology and Biophysics, Lakes and Reservoirs: Research and Management; mem. Int. Lake Environment Cttee. 1987–95; corresp. mem. Hungarian Acad. of Sciences 1976, mem. 1987–; Labour Order of Merit, Order of Merit for Hungary. *Publications:* Ed. 9 vols. on Invertebrate Neurobiology, 10 vols. on Environmental Biology and Hydrobiology, 234 papers. *Address:* 8237 Tihany, Váralja utca 18, Hungary. *Telephone:* 36 (87) 448-244 (Office). *Fax:* (36) 87-448-006.

SALAS COLLANTES, Javier; Spanish business executive; b. 1949; ed. Faculty of Econs. Univ. of Madrid; joined Instituto Nacional de Industria (INI) 1973, Chair. Oct. 1990–; Chair. Iberia 1993–95. *Leisure interest:* hill-trekking.

SALAYEV, Eldar Unis ogly, D.PHYSICAL-MATH.SC.; Azerbaijani scientist and politician; b. 31 Dec. 1933, Nakhichevan City; s. of Yunis Sala oglu Salayev and Telly Tahir kizi Salayeva; m. Dilara Ashraf Guseynova; two s.; ed. Azerbaijan Univ.; mem. CPSU 1963–91; jr. researcher, Deputy Dir. Inst. of Physics, Azerbaijan Acad. of Sciences 1956–73, Dir. 1973–83; Corresp. mem. Acad. of Sciences of Azerbaijan 1980, mem. 1983, Pres. 1983–; mem. Council on coordination of scientific activities of Acads. of Sciences, Presidium of U.S.S.R. Acad. of Sciences 1985–91; Chair. Repub. Council, Presidium of Acad. of Sciences of Azerbaijan; Ed.-in-Chief Doklady Akademii Nauk Azerbaijana; Deputy to U.S.S.R. Supreme Soviet 1985–89; U.S.S.R. People's Deputy 1989–91; Merited Worker of Arts of Azerbaijan. *Publications:* Dynamics and statistics, non-linear effects on layer crystals, type of selenite-gallium 1993; more than 200 scientific publs. in numerous journals. *Leisure interest:* sport. *Address:* Azerbaijan Academy of Sciences, İstiglaliyat str. 10, 370001 Baku, Azerbaijan. *Telephone:* 923529. *Fax:* 925699.

SALCEDO-BASTARDO, José Luis; Venezuelan diplomatist and writer; b. 15 March 1926, Carúpano, Sucre; s. of Joaquín Salcedo-Arocha and Catalina (née Bastardo) Salcedo-Arocha; m. María Cecilia Avila 1968; four s.; ed. Universidad Central de Venezuela, Univ. de Paris and L.S.E.; Teacher of Social Sciences 1945; Chief Ed. Revista Nacional de Cultura 1948–50; Asst. lecturer, Universidad Central de Venezuela 1949; Founder Rector, Univ. of Santa María, Caracas 1953; Senator for State of Sucre mem. Senate Foreign Relations Cttee. 1958; Amb. to Ecuador 1959–61, to Brazil 1961–63; Prof. of Sociology, Univ. Central de Venezuela 1964; Pres. Nat. Inst. of Culture and Fine Arts 1965–67; Vice-Pres., Supreme Electoral Council 1970–74; Amb. to France 1974–76, to U.K. 1984–87, to G.D.R. 1987–90; Sec.-Gen. to Presidency 1976–77; Minister of State for Science, Tech. and Culture 1977–79; mem. Exec. Cttee. Centre for Higher Int. Studies, Andean Univ. of Bolivia 1992–, Centre for Diplomatic and Strategic Studies, Paris 1992–, Comm. V (Educ., Culture, Science and Tech.) of Andean Parl. 1993–; Pres. Nat. Comm. for Bicentenary of Antonio José de Sucre 1993. *Publications:* Por el Mundo Sociológico de Cecilio Acosta 1945, En Fuga hacia la Gloria 1947, Visión y Revisión de Bolívar 1957, Biografía de Don Egidio Montesinos 1957, Tesis para la Unión 1963, Bases de una Acción Cultural 1965, Historia Fundamental de Venezuela 1970, La Conciencia del Presente 1971, Carabobo: Nacionalidad e Historia 1972, Bolívar: Un Continente y un Destino 1972, El Primer Deber 1973, Despolitizar la Historia: una tarea para el desarrollo 1973, De la Historia y los Deberes 1975, Bolívar y San Martín 1975, Un Hombre Diáfano 1976, Crucible of Americanism (Miranda's London House) 1979, Concordancias Ideológicos y Literarias en Bolívar 1981, Andrés Bello Americano 1982, Reiteración Bolivariana 1983, Andrés Eloy Blanco para jóvenes 1983, Simón Bolívar, L'unico scopo e la libertá 1983, Simón Bolívar: La Esperanza del Universo 1983, Bolívar, el Nacer Constante 1986, Bolívar: las ideas y los pueblos 1994, El Hombre y los hombres 1994. *Leisure interest:* travelling abroad. *Address:* Apartado Postal 2777, Caracas, Venezuela (Home).

SALEH, Lt.-Col. Ali Abdullah; Yemeni politician and army officer; b. c. 1942; participated in 1974 coup; Mil. Gov., Taiz Province until June 1978; mem. Provisional Presidential Council, Deputy C.-in-C. of Armed Forces June-July 1978; Pres. of Yemen Arab Repub. 1978–90, 1990–94; of Presidential Council of Repub. of Yemen 1990–94, of Repub. of Yemen 1994–; C.-in-C. of Armed Forces July 1978–90. *Address:* Office of the President, Sana'a, Republic of Yemen.

SALEH, Ali Saleh Abdulla al-, B.COM.; Bahraini politician and official; b. 28 Dec. 1942; s. of Abdulla Al Saleh; m. Afaf Radhi Salman Almousawi 1970; one s. two d.; ed. Ain Shams Univ., Cairo; Dir. of several public cos. 1975–95; now Minister of Commerce; Chair. Bahrain Promotions and Marketing Bd., Bahrain Int. Exhbn. Centre, Bahrain Stock Exchange; Deputy Chair. Bahrain Chamber of Commerce and Industry 1975–93, Shura (Consultative Council) 1993–95; mem. Bd. of Trustees Univ. of Bahrain 1985–95, Bahrain Centre for Studies and Research. *Leisure interests:* reading, music, travel. *Address:* Ministry of Commerce, P.O. Box 5479, Manama, Bahrain. *Telephone:* 532121. *Fax:* 530469.

SALEH, Jaime Marcelino; Netherlands Antilles government official and judge; b. 21 April 1941, Bonaire, Netherlands Antilles; m. Marguerite Marie Halabi; two s. two d.; ed. State Univ. of Utrecht; prosecutor, Netherlands 1967–68, Curaçao 1968–71; attorney-at-law, Curaçao 1971–74; Judge, High Court of the Netherlands Antilles and Aruba 1974–79, Chief Justice 1979–89, Chief Judge, Mil. Court of Justice 1979–89; Gov.-Gen. of Netherlands Antilles 1990–; Order of Merit of Corps Consulaire 1989, Order of Libertador en el grado de Gran Cordon 1996; Almirate Luis Brion Naval Medal 1994. *Publications:* various works on law and politics, with particular reference to the Netherlands Antilles. *Address:* Fort Amsterdam 1, Curaçao, Netherlands Antilles. *Telephone:* (9) 461-1289. *Fax:* (9) 461-1412.

SALEK, Lieut.-Col. Mustapha Ould; Mauritanian army officer and politician; ed. Saumur Mil. Acad., France; Chief of Staff of Armed Forces 1968–69,

March 1978; fmr. Dir. Société Nat. d'Import/Export (SONIMEX); Commdr. Third Mil. Region 1977; Head of State and Chair. Mil. Cttee. for Nat. Recovery (later for Nat. Salvation) 1978–79; sentenced to 10 years' imprisonment for plotting against Pres. Haidalla March 1982.

SALEM, Elie Adib, PH.D.; Lebanese politician and academic; b. 5 March 1930, Bterram Kurah; s. of Adib Salem and Lamia (née Malik) Salem; m. Phyllis Sell; two s. two d.; ed. American Univ. of Beirut, Univ. of Cincinatti, U.S.A., Johns Hopkins Univ., U.S.A.; Instructor in Public Admin., American Univ. of Beirut 1954–56, Assoc. Prof. of Political Studies and Public Admin. 1962–68, Asst. Dean of Arts and Sciences 1966–68, Chair. Middle East Area Program and Prof. of Political Studies and Public Admin. 1969–74, Chair. Dept. of Political Studies and Public Admin. 1972–74, Dean of Arts and Sciences 1974–82; Asst. Prof. of Middle East Politics, School of Advanced Int. Studies, Johns Hopkins Univ. 1956–62; Visiting Prof. Dept. of Govt. and Research Scholar Int. Devt. Research Center, Ind. Univ. 1968–69; Deputy Prime Minister and Minister of Foreign Affairs 1982–84; Adviser to Pres. on Foreign Affairs 1984–88; Founder and Pres. Lebanese Centre of Policy Studies 1988–; Pres. Univ. of Balamand 1993–. *Publications include:* The Arab Public Administrative Conference 1954, Political Theory and Institutions of the Khawarij 1956, Modernization without Revolution: Lebanon's Experience 1973, "Rusum Dar al-Khilafah al Abbasiyah" manuscript by Hlal al Sab' (translator) 1977, Violence and Diplomacy in Lebanon 1982–88 1994; articles in professional journals. *Leisure interests:* tennis, swimming, table tennis. *Address:* Sibnai, Baabda, Villa Salem, Beirut, Lebanon. *Telephone:* (1) 468887.

SALGADO, Sebastião Ribeiro, Jr., PH.D.; Brazilian photographer; b. 8 Feb. 1944, Aimorés, Minas Gerais; m. Lélia Deluiz Wanick 1967; two s.; ed. São Paulo Univ., Vanderbilt Univ., U.S.A., Univ. of Paris; with Brazilian Ministry of Finance 1968–69; with Investment Dept., Int. Coffee Org., London 1971–73; photo-reporter, working in Europe, Africa (particularly covering drought in Sahel) and Latin America 1973–, with Sygma News Agency of Paris 1974, with Gamma agency 1975–79, mem. Magnum Photos 1979–; numerous one-person exhbns. Europe, Brazil, Israel, China, Canada, Cuba, including L'Afrique des Colères 1977–78, Sahel – L'Homme en Détresse 1986, Other Americas 1986–90; many prizes, including Kodak/City of Paris award for book Autres Amériques 1984, Oskar Barnack Prize, World Press Photos, the Netherlands, for work in Sahel 1985, Int. Center of Photography Photojournalist of the Year Award, New York 1986, 1988, Photographer of the Year Award, American Soc. of Magazine Photographers 1987, Olivier Rebbot Award, Overseas Press Club, New York 1987, King of Spain Award 1988, Erich Salomon Award, Germany 1988, Erna and Victor Hasselblad Award, Sweden 1989, Grand Prix Nationaux 1995. *Publications:* several books of photographs and exhbn. catalogues, including Autres Amériques 1986, Sahel: L'Homme en Détresse 1986, Les Cheminots 1988, Sahel: El Fin del Camino 1988, Workers: an archaeology of the industrial age 1993.

SALIM, Salim Ahmed; Tanzanian diplomatist; b. 23 Jan. 1942, Pemba Island, Zanzibar; m. Amne Salim; three c.; ed. Lumumba Coll., Zanzibar, Univ. of Delhi and Columbia Univ., New York; Publicity Sec. of UMMA Party and Chief Ed. of its official organ Sauti ya UMMA 1963; Exec. Sec. United Front of Opposition Parties and Chief Ed. of its newspaper; Sec. Gen. All-Zanzibar Journalists Union 1963; Amb. to United Arab Repub. 1964–65; High Commr. to India 1965–68; Dir. African and Middle East Affairs Div., Ministry of Foreign Affairs 1968–69; Amb. to People's Repub. of China and Democratic People's Repub. of Korea June-Dec. 1969; Perm. Rep. to UN 1970–80 (Pres. of Gen. Ass. 1979), also High Commr. to Jamaica, accred. to Guyana, Trinidad and Tobago, Barbados, and Amb. to Cuba 1971–80; Chair. UN Special Cttee. on Decolonization 1972–80; Minister of Foreign Affairs 1980–84, Prime Minister of Tanzania 1984–85, Deputy Prime Minister, Minister of Defence and Nat. Service 1986–89; Sec.-Gen. OAU 1989–; a fmr. Vice-Pres. of Tanzania; Chair. UN Security Council Cttee. on Sanctions against Rhodesia Jan.–Dec. 1975; fmr. del. of Tanzania at UN Gen. Ass. and other int. confs; Hon. LL.D. (Univ. of Philippines); Hon. D.H. (Univ. of Maiduguri, Nigeria) 1983; Hon. D.C.L. (Univ. of Mauritius) 1991; Hon. Dr. of Arts (Univ. of Khartoum, Sudan) 1995; Hon. Ph.D. (Univ. of Bologna, Italy) 1996. *Address:* Organization of African Unity, P.O.B. 3243, Addis Ababa, Ethiopia.

SALINAS DE GORTARI, Carlos, PH.D.; Mexican politician; b. 1948, Mexico City; ed. Nat. Univ. of Mexico and Harvard Univ.; Asst. Prof. of Statistics, Nat. Univ. of Mexico 1970; Research Asst. Harvard Univ. 1974; taught Public Finance and Fiscal Policy in Mexico 1976, 1978; Asst. Dir. of Public Finance, Ministry of Finance 1971–74, Head of Econ. Studies 1974–76, Asst. Dir. of Financial Planning 1978, Dir.-Gen. 1978–79; Dir.-Gen. of Econ. and Social Policy, Ministry of Programming and Budget 1979–81; Dir.-Gen. Inst. of Political, Social and Econ. Studies 1981–82; Minister of Planning and Fed. Budget 1982–87; named as Pres. Cand. by Partido Revolucionario Institucional (PRI) 1987; Pres. of Mexico 1988–94. *Publications:* numerous articles and essays. *Address:* c/o Office of the President, Los Pinos, Puerta 1, Col. San Miguel, Chapultepec, 11850 México, D.F., Mexico.

SALINAS IZAGUIRRE, Abel; Peruvian politician, engineer and economist; b. 12 May 1930, Puerto Supe; Dir. Nat. Housing Corpn. 1961; Prof. of Econ. Planning, Latin American Inst. of Econ. and Social Planning, Chile 1965; Prof. of Project Preparation and Evaluation, Faculty of Econs., Universidad Nacional Federico Villareal 1966; Chair. Lima Public Works Bd. 1970; mem. Higher Council of Nat. Econ. Devt. Fund 1971; Lima Prov. Councillor 1983; Minister of the Interior 1985–87, of Energy and Mines 1987–88, of Economy and Finance 1988–89; mem. Colegio de Ingenieros del Perú, Colegio de Economistas del Perú, Asociación Electrotécnica Peruana, Instituto de Desarrollo Económico y Social de Argentina, Centro de Estudios de Desarrollo Económico del Paraguay. *Address:* Plaza 30 de Agosto 150, San Isidro, Lima, Peru. *Telephone:* 416990.

SALINGER, J(erome) D(avid); American author; b. 1 Jan. 1919, New York; s. of Sol and Miriam (née Jillich) Salinger; m. Claire Douglas 1953 (divorced 1976); one s. one d.; ed. Manhattan public schools and a military coll.; travelled in Europe 1937–38; army service with 4th Infantry Div. (Staff Sergeant) 1942–46; mem. Légion d'honneur. *Publications include:* The Catcher in the Rye 1951, Franny and Zooey, Raise High the Roof Beam, Carpenters and Seymour—An Introduction 1963 (novels), For Esme with Love and Squalor 1953 (stories); numerous stories, mostly in the New Yorker 1948–, Hapworth 16, 1924 1997. *Address:* c/o Harold Ober Associates Inc., 425 Madison Avenue, New York, NY 10017, U.S.A.

SALINGER, Pierre Emil George, B.S.; American journalist and politician; b. 14 June 1925, San Francisco; s. of the late Herbert Edgar Salinger and of Jehanne Bietry Carlson; m. 3rd Nicole Helene Gillmann 1965 (divorced 1988); one s.; m. 4th Nicole Christine Beauvillain 1989; two s. (one deceased) one d. from 1st marriage; ed. Univ. of San Francisco; San Francisco Chronicle 1942–55; U.S. Navy Second World War; Press Officer, Calif., Stevenson for Pres. Campaign 1952, Richard Graves for Gov. (Calif.) 1954; West Coast Ed., Contributing Ed. Collier's Magazine 1955–56; Investigator, Senate Labor Rackets Cttee. 1957–59; Press Sec. to Senator John F. Kennedy 1959–61, to Pres. John F. Kennedy 1961–63, to Pres. Lyndon Johnson 1963–64; U.S. Senator from Calif. 1964–65; Dir. Nat. Gen. Productions 1965; Vice-Pres. Nat. Gen. Corpn. 1965, Continental Airlines 1965–68; Chair. Great America Man. and Research Co. Int. (Gramco) 1968–, Deputy Chair. Gramco (U.K.) Ltd. 1970–71; Sr. Vice-Pres. Amprop Inc. 1969; Roving Ed. L'Express, Paris 1973–78; Roving reporter in Europe for ABC (TV) 1977–87 (Adviser on Foreign Affairs 1987–93); Bureau Chief, ABC News, Paris 1977–87; Chief Foreign Corresp. ABC News 1983–93; Sr. Ed. Europe ABC News 1988–93, Int. Consultant to ABC News 1993–; Vice-Chair. Burson-Marsteller 1993–96; Dir. Global Teleworks Corpn. 1993–; now ind. public relations consultant; lecturer at over 60 U.S. univs. and colls. 1965–69; Trustee, Robert F. Kennedy Memorial Foundation, American Coll. in Paris (now American Univ. in Paris) 1973–88; Officier Légion d'honneur 1978; Democrat. *Publications:* A Tribute to John F. Kennedy 1964, With Kennedy 1966, A Tribute to Robert F. Kennedy 1968, On Instructions of my Government (novel) 1971, Je suis un américain 1975, La France et le nouveau monde 1976, Venezuelan Notebooks 1978, America Held Hostage: The Secret Negotiations 1981, The Dossier (novel, with Leonard Gross) 1984, Above Paris (with Robert Cameron) 1984, Mortal Games (novel, with Leonard Gross) 1988, La Guerre du Golfe—Le Dossier Secret (with Eric Laurent) 1990, P.S. A Memoir 1995, John F. Kennedy, Commander in Chief 1997. *Address:* 3904 Hillandale Court, N.W., Washington, DC 20007, U.S.A. *Telephone:* (202) 337-6744. *Fax:* (202) 337-6746.

SALISBURY, David Murray, M.A.; British financial executive; b. 18 Feb. 1952; s. of Norman Salisbury and Isobel Sutherland Murray; m. Lynneth Mary Jones 1977; two d.; ed. Harrow School, Trinity Coll., Oxford; joined J. Henry Schroder Wagg & Co. Ltd. 1974, Chief Exec. Schroder Capital Man. Int. Inc. 1986–, Jt. Chief Exec. Schroder Investment Man. Ltd. 1995–97, Chair. 1997–; Dir. Dimensional Fund Advisers Inc. 1991–96; Gov. Harrow School 1996–. *Leisure interests:* tennis, skiing. *Address:* 33 Gutter Lane, London, EC2V 8AS, England (Office).

SALKIND, Ilya; film producer; b. 1947, Mexico; s. of Alexander Salkind; ed. Univ. of London; Assoc. Producer, Cervantes, The Light at the Edge of the World, Spain, 1974. *Films with Alexander Salkind include:* Bluebeard, The Three Musketeers, The Four Musketeers, The Twist, The Prince and the Pauper, Superman, Superman 2, Superman 3, Supergirl, Santa Claus: The Movie, Christopher Columbus: The Discovery.

SALLAH, Ousman Ahmadou, B.A.; Gambian diplomatist; b. 26 July 1938, Kudang; s. of Ahmadou Jabel Sallah and Haddy Sallah; m. Ramou Sallah 1966; two s. two d.; ed. Trinity Coll., Hartford, Conn., School of Int. Affairs, Columbia Univ., New York; Asst. Sec., Prime Minister's Office 1967; Asst. Sec. Ministry of External Affairs 1967–68, Deputy Perm. Sec. 1973–74; First Sec., Head of Chancery and Acting High Commr., London 1971; Amb. to Saudi Arabia (also accred. to Egypt, Iran, Kuwait, Qatar and U.A.E.) 1974–79, to U.S.A. 1979–83; Perm. Rep. to UN 1979–83, 1987–94; Perm. Sec. Ministry of External Affairs and Head of Gambian Diplomatic Service 1982–; Hon. LL.D. (Trinity Coll., Hartford); Diploma in Int. Relations and Diplomacy from UNITAR. *Leisure interest:* tennis. *Address:* P.O. Box 667, Banjul, The Gambia. *Telephone:* 39-23-63 (Home).

SALLE, David, M.F.A.; American artist; b. 1952, Okla.; s. of Alvin S. Salle and Tillie D. (née Brown) Salle; ed. California Inst. of Arts; one-man shows include: Project Inc., Cambridge, Mass. 1975, Foundation Corps de Garde, Groningen, Holland 1976, 1978, Artists Space, New York 1976, Foundation de Appel, Amsterdam 1977, The Kitchen, New York 1977, 1979, Mary Boone Gallery, New York 1981–83, Lucio Amelio Gallery, Naples 1981, Mario Diacono, Rome 1982, Anthony D'Offay Gallery, London 1982, Akira Ikeda

Gallery, Tokyo 1983, Castelli Graphics, New York 1984, Gagosian Gallery, Los Angeles 1984, 1991, Tel Aviv Museum of Art 1989, Maria Diacono Gallery, Boston 1990, Castelli Graphics, N.Y.C. 1990, Gagosian Gallery, New York 1991; retrospective exhbn. Museum of Contemporary Art, Chicago 1987; group shows include: Serial Gallerie, Amsterdam 1977, Studio Cannaviello, Milan 1979, Grand Palais, Paris 1980, Nigel Greenwood Gallery, London 1981, Kunsthallen, Göteborg, Sweden 1981, New York Public Library 1982, Whitney Museum of American Art, New York 1982–83, Kassel 1982, Venice 1982, Stockholm 1983, Madrid 1983, São Paulo 1983, London (Tate Gallery) 1983, Pace Gallery 1983, Museo de Arte Contemporaneo de Monterrey, Mexico 1991; Guggenheim Fellow 1986. *Address:* c/o Leo Castelli Gallery, 420 W. Broadway, New York, NY 10012, U.S.A.

SALLEH, M. Nor, PH.D.; Malaysian forester; b. 20 Oct. 1940, Kuala Pilah; s. of Mohammed Nor and Nyonya Nor; m. Habiba Alias 1966; two s. one d.; ed. Univ. of Adelaide, Australia, Australian Forestry School, Canberra, ITC Delft, Netherlands; Deputy Conservator of Forests, Forest Dept. Peninsular Malaysia 1965, Dir. Forest Inventory 1971; Dir. Forestry Research Inst., Kepong 1977–85; Dir. Gen. Forest Resarch Inst. of Malaysia (FRIM) 1985–; Vice-Pres. Int. Union of Forest Research Orgs. (IUFRO) 1986–90, Pres. 1991; Pres. Malaysian Nature Soc. 1978–; Dr. h.c. (Nat. Univ. of Malaysia) 1992, (Aberdeen) 1993; K.M.N. 1981, D.S.N.S. 1989, Award of Third World Network of Scientific Orgs. (TWNSO) for Public Understanding of Science 1991; Langkawi Environmental Award 1991, Nat. Science Award 1993. *Publications:* The Tropical Garden City 1990, The Malaysian Marine Heritage 1991, over 100 articles and contributions to seminars, books and journals. *Leisure interests:* squash, badminton, reading, nature oriented activities. *Address:* Forest Research Institute Malaysia, Kepong, 52109 Kuala Lumpur, Malaysia. *Telephone:* (3) 634-2152. *Fax:* (3) 634-2825.

SALLINEN, Aulis Heikki; Finnish composer and professor of arts; b. 9 April, 1935, Salmi; s. of Armas Rudolf Sallinen and Anna Malanen; m. Pirkko Holvisola 1955; four s.; ed. Sibelius Acad.; primary school teacher 1958–60; Man. Finnish Radio Orchestra 1960–69; Prof. of Arts 1979–; composer of seven symphonies, five operas, violin concerto, cello concerto, flute concerto and other orchestral music, five string quartets and other chamber music; film score for The Iron Age 1983; mem. Swedish Royal Music Acad. 1979; Dr.Phil.h.c. (Turku) 1991, (Helsinki) 1994; Nordic Council Music Prize 1978, Wihuri Int. Sibelius Prize 1983.

SALLOUM, Nasir Muhammad, PH.D.; Saudi Arabian engineer; b. 4 Nov. 1936, Medina, Saudi Arabia; resident engineer, Ministry of Communications 1965; Head of Study Dept., Ministry of Communications 1965–68; Deputy Minister of Communications 1976–96; Minister of Transport Aug. 1996–; mem. Bd. of Saudi Arabian Railways Authority. *Leisure interests:* reading, travel. *Address:* Ministry of Transport, Airport Road, Riyadh, Saudi Arabia. *Telephone:* (1) 404-3000. *Fax:* (1) 403-1401.

SALMAN IBN ABDUL AZIZ, H.R.H. Prince; Saudi Arabian politician; b. 13 Dec. 1936; s. of the late King Abdul Aziz ibn Saud; m.; brother of H.R.H. King Fahd (q.v.); Gov. of Riyadh 1962–; Chair. Bd. Riyadh Water and Sanitary Drainage Authority, and numerous other orgs.; active in Abdul Aziz Foundation. *Leisure interest:* reading. *Address:* Office of the Governor, Riyadh, Saudi Arabia.

SALMERÓN, Fernando; Mexican philosopher; b. 30 Oct. 1925, Córdoba, Veracruz; s. of Prof. Fernando A. Salmerón and Ana María Roíz de Salmerón; m. Alicia Castro V. 1952; four s. two d.; ed. University of Veracruz, Nat. Autonomous Univ. of Mexico (UNAM), Albert Ludwig Univ., Fed. Repub. of Germany; Dir. Faculty of Philosophy, Univ. of Veracruz 1956–58, Rector 1961–63; Dir. Inst. of Philosophical Investigations (UNAM) 1966–78, Investigator of Complete Time 1981–93, Investigator Emer. 1993–; Rector Iztapalapa Section, Metropolitan Autonomous Univ. 1978–79, Gen. Rector 1979–81; mem. El Colegio Nacional 1972–; Hon. Dr. Univ. of Veracruz, Investigador Nacional 1984, Prize of Nat. Univ. 1993, Nat. Prize for Social Sciences, History and Philosophy 1993. *Publications include:* Las Mocedades de Ortega y Gasset 1959, Cuestiones educativas y páginas sobre México 1962, La Filosofía y las actitudes morales 1971, Etica y análisis (ed.) 1985, Ortega y Gasset (ed.) 1984, Ensayos filosóficos 1988, Philosophie und Rechtstheorie in Mexico (co-ed.) 1989, Enseñanza y Filosofía 1991, Concepciones de la ética (co-ed.) 1992, Epistemología y cultura (co-ed.) 1993, La identidad personal y la colectiva (co-ed.) 1994, Los estudios cervantinos de José Gaos 1994. *Address:* El Colegio Nacional, Luis González Obregón 23, México 1, D.F. (Office); Congreso 70, Tlalpan, 1400 México D.F., Mexico (Home). *Telephone:* 573 21 65 (Home).

SALMON, Robert; French journalist; b. 6 April 1918, Marseille; s. of Pierre Salmon and Madeleine Blum; m. Anne-Marie Jeanprost 1942; five c.; ed. Lycée Louis le Grand, Ecole Normale Supérieure and at the Sorbonne; Founder Mouvement de Résistance Défense de la France; mem. Comité Parisien de Libération; Leader Paris Div., Mouvement de Libération Nationale; mem. Provisional Consultative Ass. 1944, First Constituent Ass. 1945; Founder Pres. and Dir. Gen. France-Soir 1944; fmr. Pres. Soc. France-Editions (Elle, Le Journal de Dimanche, Paris-Presse, etc.), Hon. Pres. 1976–; fmr. Pres. Soc. de Publications Economiques (Réalités, Connaissance des Arts, Entreprise, etc.); Sec.-Gen. Féd. Nat. de la Presse 1951–77; Hon. Pres. French Cttee. Int. Press Inst. 1973; mem. Admin. Council Fondation Nat. des Sciences Politiques 1973–93; Prof. Inst. d'Etudes Politiques, Univ. of Paris, and Ecole Nat. d'Admin. 1967–88; mem. Haut Conseil de l'audiovisuel 1973–82; mem. Comm. de la République Française pour l'UNESCO 1979–; Commdr., Légion d'honneur, Croix de guerre, Rosette de la Résistance, Médaille des évadés. *Publications:* Le sentiment de l'existence chez Maine de Biran 1943, Notions élémentaires de psychologie 1947, L'organisation actuelle de la presse française 1955, Information et publicité 1956, L'information économique, clé de la prospérité 1963. *Leisure interests:* yachting, skiing, gardening. *Address:* 4 rue Berlioz, 75116 Paris, France.

SALMOND, Rt. Hon. Alexander Elliot Anderson, M.A.; Scottish politician; b. 31 Dec. 1954, Linlithgow; s. of Robert F. Salmond and Mary S. Milne; m. Moira McGlashan; ed. Linlithgow Acad., St. Andrews Univ.; Vice-Pres. Fed. of Student Nationalists 1974–77, St. Andrews Univ. Students' Rep. Council 1977–78, f. mem. Scottish Nationalists' Party (SNP) 79 Group 1979; Asst. Agricultural and Fisheries Economist Dept. of Agric. and Fisheries 1978–80; Economist Bank of Scotland 1980–87, M.P. for Banff and Buchan 1987–; mem. SNP Nat. Exec. Cttee. 1981–82, 1983–, SNP Exec. Vice Convener for Publicity 1985–87, SNP Nat. Convener (Leader) 1990–; SNP Parl. Spokesperson on Constitution and Fishing 1997–; Hon. Vice-Pres. Scottish Centre for Econ. and Social Research. *Leisure interests:* golf, reading. *Address:* 17 Maiden Street, Peterhead, Aberdeenshire, AB42 6EE, Scotland; House of Commons, London S.W.1, England. *Telephone:* (01779) 470444 (Constituency Office); 0171-219 3494 (House of Commons).

SALOLAINEN, Pertti Edvard, M.SC. (ECON.); Finnish politician; b. 19 Oct. 1940, Helsinki; s. of Ella Elisabeth Salolainen and Edvard Paavali Salolainen; m. Anja Sonninen 1964; one s. one d.; ed. Helsinki School of Econs.; TV journalist, Finnish Broadcasting Co. 1962–65, producer 1965–66, corresp. in London 1966–69, mem. Working Cttee., Supervisory Bd. 1970–87; journalist, BBC, London 1966; Head of Dept. Finnish Employers' Confed. 1969–89; mem. Parl. 1970–96; Minister for Foreign Trade 1987–95; Deputy Prime Minister 1991–95; Head, negotiating team for entry of Finland into EU 1993–95; Amb. to U.K. 1996–; Chair. Finance Cttee. IPU 1982–87; Hon. Founder Worldwide Fund for Nature Finland 1972, Vice-Pres. and mem. Supervisory Bd. 1972–89; mem. Supervisory Bd.'s Working Cttee. Outokumpu Mining Co. 1979–91; mem. Supervisory Bd. Suomi-Salama Insurance Co. 1980–91, Finnair 1995–; mem. Legal Cttee. Nordic Council 1982–87; Freeman of City of London 1998; several one-man exhbns. of art and photographs in Finland, Germany and U.K.; Grand Cross of the Lion of Finland 1994, Grand Cross of the Nordstjerna Order (Sweden) 1996, Grand Cross of the Fed. Repub. of Germany, Grand Cross of Hungary, Grand Cross of Austria, Medal of Merit, Finnish Defence Force 1997, Int. Conservation Award, Worldwide Fund for Nature, Gold Medal of Merit, Finnish Asscn. for Nature Conservation; Nat. Coalition Party (Leader 1991–94). *Leisure interests:* nature conservation, photography, sports. *Address:* Finnish Embassy, 38 Chesham Place, London, SW1X 8HW, London, England. *Telephone:* 0171-838 6200. *Fax:* 0171-838 9500.

SALOMONS, Jean-Pierre (see Aumont, Jean-Pierre).

SALONEN, Esa-Pekka, F.R.C.M.; Finnish conductor and composer; b. 30 June 1958, Helsinki; ed. Sibelius Acad., Helsinki; studied composition with Rautavaara and conducting with Panula; studied in Italy 1979–81; Prin. Guest Conductor, Philharmonia Orchestra 1984, Oslo Philharmonic Orchestra 1985–; Music Dir., L.A. Philharmonic Orchestra 1992–; Prin. Conductor Swedish Radio Symphony Orchestra 1985; Artistic Adviser New Stockholm Chamber Orchestra 1986; Artistic Dir. Helsinki Festival 1995–96; Royal Philharmonic Soc. Opera Award 1995; Litteris et Artibus Medal (Sweden) 1996. *Compositions:* orchestral: Concerto (for Alto Saxophone and Orchestra) 1980–81, Giro 1981; Chamber Music: YTA 1 (for Alto flute), YTA II (for Piano) 1985, YTA III (for Cello) 1987, FLOOF (for Soprano and Chamber Ensemble) 1988; radiophonic music: Baalal 1982. *Address:* c/o Van Walsum Management, 26 Wadham Road, London, SW15 2LR, England.

SALPETER, Edwin E., M.SC., PH.D.; American physicist and professor; b. 3 Dec. 1924, Vienna, Austria; s. of Jakob L. and Friedericke Salpeter; m. Miriam M. Mark 1950; two d.; ed. Sydney Boys' High School, Australia and Univ. of Birmingham, England; Dept. of Scientific and Industrial Research Fellow, Univ. of Birmingham, England 1948–49; Research Assoc., then Assoc. Prof., Cornell Univ., U.S. 1949–56, Prof. of Physics and Astrophysics 1956–71, J. G. White Distinguished Prof. of Physical Sciences 1971–; mem. Nat. Science Bd. 1978–84; Visiting Prof. A.N.U. 1954, Sydney Univ. 1960, Cambridge Univ. 1968; mem. N.A.S., American Acad. of Arts and Sciences, American Philosophical Soc., Deutsche Akad. Leopoldina; foreign mem. Australian Acad. of Sciences, Royal Soc. (London); Hon. D.Sc. (Sydney, Chicago, N.S.W. and Case Western Reserve Univs.); Crafoord Laureate 1997. *Publications:* One book and over 300 scientific papers on quantum mechanics, plasma physics and theoretical astrophysics. *Leisure interests:* tennis, skiing, photography. *Address:* 612 Space Sciences, Cornell Univ., Ithaca, NY 14853 (Office); 116 Westbourne Lane, Ithaca, NY 14850, U.S.A. (Home). *Telephone:* 607-255-4937.

SALTER, John Rotherham, M.A., F.R.S.A., F.R.G.S., F.I. MGT., M.INST.W.M., A.C.I.ARB.; British international business lawyer and solicitor; b. 2 May 1932, London; s. of Herbert Salter and Nora Salter; m. Cynthia Brewer 1961; one s. two d.; ed. Queen Elizabeth's School, Ashridge Coll., Lincoln Coll., Oxford and King's Coll. London; Lieut. R.A. 1951–53; partner, Denton Hall 1961–94, consultant 1994–; Chair. Environmental Law Group 1994–98, Chair. Maj. Projects Group 1994–98; Vice-Chair. IBA Cttee. of Energy and Natural Resources Law 1976–79, IBA Cttee. on Int. Environmental Law 1979–82;

Chair. North Sea Gas Gathering Consortium 1979–80; Chair. Section on Business Law, Int. Bar Asscn. 1986–88; Chair. ABA Cttee. on Int. Law 1993–95, Legal Issues Group of ISWA 1994–; Treas. Anglo-American Real Property Inst. 1985–86; Trustee, Petroleum Law Educ. Trust 1980–98, IBA Educ. Trust 1983–95; consultant, UNIDO 1983–84; Vice-Chair. ABA Cttee. on Comparative Govt. Law 1988–91; Chair. IBA Cttee. on Oil and Gas Construction Law 1989–93; mem. Bd. Int. Capital Markets Group 1987–89; mem. Law Soc.'s Planning Panel 1991–97; Legal Assoc., Royal Town Planning Inst. 1992–98; Chair. The Silver Soc. 1986–87, The Care Foundation 1994–, Hospice in the Weald 1994–, IBA Standing Cttee. on UN and World Orgs. (UNWOC) 1995–, Murray Soc. 1996–98; mem. Soc. of Chemical Industry, London Chapter of Lamda Alpha Int., Advisory Cttee. on Integrated Environmental Man. by Distance Learning, Bath Univ., Scientific and Tech. Cttee., ISWA 1994–; Visiting Fellow Cranfield Univ. 1993–, mem. of Court 1995–, Visiting Prof. of Law 1997–; Hon. mem. Bar of Madrid 1987–; mem. Sr. Common Room, Lincoln Coll., Oxford 1991–; mem. of Court Worshipful Co. of Fan-Makers 1997–; Freeman of London and of Glasgow; Hon. Fellow Centre for Petroleum and Mineral Law and Policy, Univ. of Dundee. *Publications:* Planning Law for Industry (jt. ed.) 1981, U.K. Onshore Oil and Gas Law 1986, Corporate Environmental Responsibility—Law and Practice 1992; contrib. to U.K. Oil and Gas Law 1984, Halsbury's Laws of England (Vol. 58) 1986, Law of the European Communities 1986, Vaughan's Law of the European Communities Service 1990, Environment and Planning Law 1991, Frontiers of Environmental Law 1991, Directors' Guide to Environmental Issues 1992, European Community Energy Law 1994, European Environmental Law 1994, How to Understand an Act of Parliament (with D. J. Gifford) 1996, Understanding the English Legal System (with D. J. Gifford) 1997; numerous articles in professional journals. *Leisure interests:* the arts, archaeology, sailing, tennis. *Address:* Denton Hall, 5 Chancery Lane, Clifford's Inn, London, EC4A 1BU, England. *Telephone:* 0171-242 1212. *Fax:* 0171-320 6651.

SALTER, Lionel Paul, M.A., MUS.B., L.R.A.M.; British musicologist; b. 8 Sept. 1914, London; s. of Morris Salter; m. Christine Fraser 1939; three s.; ed. Owen's School, London Acad. of Music, Royal Coll. of Music, St. John's Coll., Cambridge; Music Asst. in films 1936–38, and in TV 1937–39; during army service, Guest Conductor for Radio France Symphony Orchestra 1943–44; then various BBC posts as Asst. Conductor with Theatre Orchestra 1945–46, Producer, Gramophone Dept. 1946–48, European Music Supervisor 1948–53, Artists' Man. 1953–55, Head of Overseas Music 1956, of TV Music 1956–63, of Opera 1963–67, Asst. Controller, Music 1967–74; Chair. Radio Music Group, European Broadcasting Union 1965–74; Programme Ed., Edinburgh Int. Festival 1951–55, and for BBC Promenade Concerts 1968–74; Ed. BBC Music Guides 1967–75; Ed. Associated Bd. of Royal Schools of Music 1977–95; Vice-Chair. British Fed. of Music Festivals 1984–87, Iberian and Latin-American Music Soc. 1997–98. *Publications:* numerous musical works; books and articles on music; opera translations. *Address:* 26 Woodstock Road, London, NW11 8ER, England. *Telephone:* 0181-458 3568. *Fax:* 0181-458 3568.

SALTYKOV, Boris Georgievich, C.ECON.SC.; Russian politician and economist; b. 27 Dec. 1940, Moscow; s. of Georgy Saltykov and Evdokia M. Saltykova (née Pukaleva); m. Lubov N. Klochkova 1972; two d.; ed. Moscow Inst. of Physics and Tech.; researcher, Head of lab., Head of Div. Cen. Inst. of Econ. and Math. U.S.S.R. (now Russian) Acad. of Sciences 1967–86; Head of Div. Inst. of Econ. and Forecasting of Progress in Science and Tech. (now Forecasting of Econ.) U.S.S.R. Acad. of Sciences 1986–91; Deputy Dir. Analytical Centre U.S.S.R. Acad. of Sciences 1991; Minister of Science, Higher School and Tech. Policy of Russian Fed. 1991–92; Deputy Prime Minister of Russian Fed. 1992–93; Minister of Science and Tech. Policy 1993–96; Pres. Russian House of Int. Scientific-Tech. Co-operation 1996–; mem. State Duma (Parl.) 1993–95; Chair. Russian Comm. for UNESCO 1992–. *Leisure interest:* cars. *Address:* Bryusov per. 11, 103009 Moscow, Russia. *Telephone:* (095) 229-58-40. *Fax:* (095) 200-32-77.

SALVATICI, Nilo; Italian banker; b. 10 March 1922, Monticiano; s. of Arturo Salvatici and Serafina Mugelli; m. Dina Branconi 1946; two c.; served for 43 years with Bank Monte dei Paschi di Siena, retiring with title of Cen. Man.; fmr. Chair. Monte Paschi Belgio, Brussels; fmr. Dir. Istituto Nazionale di Credito Agrario, Florence; Dir. Istituto dell'Enciclopedia Italiana Treccani, Rome, Banksiel, Milan; Chair. Cassa di Risparmio di Prato; Grande Ufficiale della Repubblica Italiana. *Leisure interests:* numismatics, philately. *Address:* 93 Strada Terrensano e Belcaro, 53100 Siena, Italy. *Telephone:* 0577/ 47 074.

SALVETTI, Carlo; Italian physicist; b. 30 Dec. 1918, Milan; s. of Adriano Salvetti; m. Piera Pinto 1951; two d.; ed. Univ. of Milan; fmr. Prof. of Theoretical Physics, Univ. of Bari; Dir.-Gen. Nuclear Study Centre, Ispra 1957–59; Dir. Int. Atomic Energy Agency (IAEA) Research Div. 1959–62; Gov. for Italy to IAEA 1962–64, 1968–70, Chair. Bd. of Govs. IAEA 1963–64; Chair. European Atomic Energy Soc. 1967–68, mem. EAES Council 1963–72; Chair. Euratom Scientific and Technical Cttee. 1969–70, mem. 1967–73; Chair. ENEA-OECD Steering Cttee. 1969–73; Chair. ANS, Italian Section 1971–75; Prof. of Gen. Physics, Univ. of Milan; Vice Pres., Italian Nat. Cttee. for Nuclear Energy (C.N.E.N.) 1964–81; Chair. Italian Forum for Nuclear Energy (FIEN) 1965–; Consultant to ENEA 1981–; mem. Bd. of Moscow Int. Energy Club (MIEC); Chair. Italian Nuclear Soc. (SNI) 1975–79, 1991–; mem. Bd. European Nuclear Soc. (ENS) 1975–, Chair. 1979–81, Hon. Fellow 1986–; mem. Consultative Cttee. on Fusion (CCF) within Comm. of European Communities 1976–81; Fellow, American Nuclear Soc. 1970–. *Publications:* over 120 scientific and technical articles on nuclear physics, reactor theories and energy problems. *Leisure interests:* golf, painting. *Address:* Via Gramsci 38, 00197 Rome, Italy. *Telephone:* (06) 3200960.

SALZMAN, Pnina; Israeli pianist; b. 1923, Tel-Aviv; m. Igal Weissmann 1947; one d.; ed. Ecole normale de musique and Conservatoire national de musique, Paris; gave first concert in Paris at age of twelve; since then has given concerts in Israel, Japan, U.S.S.R., S. Africa, Australia, New Zealand, France, Britain, Belgium, Denmark, Sweden, Norway, Finland, U.S.A., etc., under baton of Sir Malcolm Sargent, Charles Munch, Koussevitsky, etc.; over 300 concerts with Israeli orchestras and regular performances with orchestras all over the world; fmr. Prof. of Piano, Tel-Aviv Univ. *Leisure interests:* gardening, painting, graphology. *Address:* 20 Dubnov Street, Tel-Aviv, Israel. *Telephone:* 261993.

SAMARAKIS, Antonis; Greek author; b. 16 Aug. 1919, Athens; s. of Evripidis Samarakis and Adriani Pantelopoulos; m. Eleni Kourebanas 1963; ed. Univ. of Athens; Chief of Emigration, Refugees and Technical Assistance Depts., Ministry of Labour 1935–40, 1944–63; active in resistance movt. during second World War; has served on many humanitarian missions in many parts of the world for ILO, UNHCR, ICEM and Council of Europe; Expert on social and labour problems (many African countries, chiefly Guinea) ILO 1968–69; denied a passport Oct. 1970; mem. PEN, Nat. Soc. of Authors; Officier, Ordre de Léopold II (Belgium); hon. citizen of San Francisco and New Orleans; Greek Nat. Book Award 1962, Greek Prize of the Twelve 1966, Grand Prix de la Littérature policière (France) 1970, Europalia Prize for Literature 1982. *Publications:* short stories: Wanted: Hope 1954, I Refuse 1961, The Jungle 1966, The Passport (in Nea Kimina 2) 1971; novels: Danger Signal 1959, The Flaw 1965; contributor to The Child's Song (anthology of poems for children); works have been translated into 16 languages and frequently adapted for cinema and television. *Leisure interest:* travel. *Address:* 59 Anagnostopoulou Street, 106 72 Athens, Greece. *Telephone:* 01-3647.444.

SAMARANCH TORELLO, Juan Antonio, Marqués de Samaranch; Spanish international sports official and diplomatist; b. 17 July 1920, Barcelona; s. of Francisco Samaranch and Juana Torello; m. María Teresa Salisachs Rowe 1955; one s. one d.; ed. German Coll., Higher Inst. of Business Studies, Barcelona; mem. Spanish Olympic Cttee. 1954–, Pres. 1967–70; mem. Int. Olympic Cttee. 1966, Vice-Pres. 1974–78, Pres. 1980–; Amb. to U.S.S.R. (also accred. to Mongolia) 1977–80; fmr. Chair. La Caixa (Savings Bank); Pres. Int. Boat Show; Dr.h.c.; Seoul Peace Prize 1990, numerous decorations from many countries. *Leisure interests:* philately, art. *Address:* International Olympic Committee, Château de Vidy, 1007 Lausanne, Switzerland; Avda. Pau Casals, 24, 08021 Barcelona, Spain (Home). *Telephone:* (3) 268 3288 (Spain). *Fax:* (3) 268 1149 (Spain).

SAMARAS, Andonis C., B.A.(ECONS.), M.B.A.; Greek politician; b. 23 May 1951, Athens; s. of Constantinos Samaras and Eleni Samaras; m. Georgia Kritikou 1990; one s. one d.; ed. Amherst Coll., Harvard Business School, U.S.A.; M.P. for Messinia 1977–; Minister of Finance 1989, of Foreign Affairs 1989–90, 1990–92; Founder-Pres. Politiki Anixi Party 1993–. *Leisure interests:* tennis, swimming, music, poetry, reading. *Address:* 11 Aiolou Street, Athens 10555, Greece. *Telephone:* 3254355-9. *Fax:* 3249429.

SAMARSKY, Aleksandre Andreyevich; Russian mathematician; b. 19 Feb. 1919; m.; two d.; ed. Moscow State Univ.; asst., teacher, docent Moscow State Univ.; head of lab. Inst. of Applied Math; Dir. Centre of Mathematical Modelling; corresp. mem. U.S.S.R. (now Russian) Acad. of Sciences 1966, mem. 1976; research in math. physics, theory of differential equations, theory of nonlinear processes, computational math., math. modelling; Chair. Nat. Council on Mathematical Modelling; Deputy Pres. Scientific Council on Mathematical Modelling; Ed. Mathematical Modelling journal; Hon. Dir. Hemnitz Tech. Univ. (Germany); Hero of Socialist Labour, Lenin Prize, U.S.S.R. State Prize. *Publications include:* 3 books and numerous articles in scientific journals. *Leisure interests:* geography, fiction. *Address:* Institute of Applied Mathematics, Russian Academy of Sciences, Miusskaya pl. 4, 125047 Moscow, Russia. *Telephone:* (095) 250 7986 (Office).

SAMIOS, Nicholas Peter, PH.D.; American physicist; b. 15 March 1932, New York; s. of Peter Samios and Niki Samios; m. Mary Linakis 1958; two s. one d.; ed. Columbia Coll., Columbia Univ., New York; Instructor, Dept. of Physics, Columbia Univ. 1956–59, Adjunct Prof. 1970–; Asst. Physicist Brookhaven Nat. Lab. Dept. of Physics 1959–62, Assoc. Physicist 1962–64, Physicist 1964–68, Group Leader 1965–75, Sr. Physicist 1968–, Chair. Div. of Particles and Fields 1975–76, Chair. PEP Experimental Program Cttee. (of SLAC & LBL) 1976–78, Adjunct Prof., Stevens Inst. of Tech. 1969–75, Chair. Dept. of Physics 1975–81, Deputy Dir. 1981, Acting Dir. 1982, Dir. 1982–97; mem. Bd. of Dirs. Stony Brook Foundation 1989, Adelphi 1989–97, Long Island Asscn. 1990–97; mem., fmr. mem. or fmr. chair. numerous specialist cttees. and bds.; Corresp. mem. Akademia Athenon 1994–; Fellow American Physical Soc. 1964, mem. Exec. Cttee. 1976–77; Fellow American Acad. of Arts and Sciences; mem. N.A.S.; E. O. Lawrence Memorial Award 1980, New York Acad. of Sciences Award in Physical and Math. Sciences 1980, AUI Distinguished Scientist 1992, W.K.H. Panofsky Prize 1993. *Address:* Brookhaven National Laboratory, Upton, New York, NY 11973-5000, U.S.A. *Telephone:* (516) 344-4545.

SAMOILOV, Vladimir Yakovlevich; Russian actor; b. 15 March 1924, Odessa; s. of Yakov Ivanovich Samoilov and Evdokiya Dmitrievna Samoïlova; m. Nadezhda Fedorovna 1948; one s.; ed. Odessa Theatre School; active service in World War II; acted at theatres in Ivanovo, Odessa, Kemerovo and Gorky 1948–69, Mayakovsky Theatre 1969–; U.S.S.R. State Prize 1976, 1986, R.S.F.S.R. State Prize 1972, People's Artist of U.S.S.R. 1984. *Roles include:* Richard III (Shakespeare), Satin, Suslov in Gorky's plays Lower Depths and Summer Folk, Velikatov in Ostrovsky's Actors and Admirers, Korzukhin in Bulgakov's Flight, Yermolayev in Galin's Birds of Passage are Flying, etc. *Films include:* The 26 Commissars of Baku, The Stars Won't Stop Shining, The Prize (State Prize 1976), An Especially Important Mission, Sibiriada 1979, White Snow of Russia 1981, Marriage in Malinovka, Zimorodok, Liberation. *Address:* Kooperativnaya Str. 9, Apt. 12, 119045 Moscow, Russia. *Telephone:* 245-47-06.

SAMOILOVA, Tatyana Yevgeniyevna; Russian film actress; b. 4 May 1934, Leningrad; d. of Eugeniy V. Samoilov and Zinaida I. Levina-Samoilova; one s.; ed. Shchukin Theatre School; Cannes Festival Palm Award for The Cranes are Flying 1958 and Special Prize for personal creative achievements in cinematography 1990; Merited Artist of the R.S.F.S.R.; Order of the Badge of Honour; *Roles include:* Maria (The Mexican) 1955, Veronika (The Cranes Are Flying) 1957, Tanya (The Unsent Letter) 1960, Natasha (Leon Garros Looks for a Friend) 1960, Alba (Alba Regia) 1961, Sonia (They Went East) 1964, Anna (Anna Karenina) 1968; Ykaterina (A Long Way to a Short Day) 1972, Masha (Ocean) 1974, Maria (Jewels for the Dictatorship of the Proletariat) 1976. *Address:* Spiridonyevsky per. 8/11, 103104 Moscow, Russia. *Telephone:* (095) 202-78-18.

SAMPAIO, Jorge; Portuguese politician; b. 18 Sept. 1939; m. Maria José Ritta; one s. one d.; fmr. Sec.-Gen. Socialist Party (PS); Mayor of Lisbon; Pres. of Portugal March 1996–. *Leisure interests:* music, golf. *Address:* Presidência da República, Palácio de Belém, 1300 Lisbon, Portugal. *Telephone:* 3637141. *Fax:* 3636603.

SAMPEDRO, José Luis; Spanish economist and novelist; b. 1 Feb. 1917, Barcelona; s. of Luis Sampedro and Matilde Saez; m. Isabel Pellicer Iturrioz 1944; one d.; ed. Madrid Univ.; Civil Service, Ministry of Finance 1935–50, 1957–62; Asst. Prof. of Econ. Structure, Madrid Univ. 1947–55, Prof. 1955–69; Economist, Ministry of Commerce 1951–57; Adviser to Spanish Del. to UN 1956–58; Special Prof. of Econ. Sociology, Madrid Univ. 1962–65; Asst. Gen. Dir. Banco Exterior de España 1962–69; Visiting Prof. Univ. of Salford 1969–70, Univ. of Liverpool 1970–71; Econ. Adviser Customs Bureau, Ministry of Finance 1971–79; nominated mem. Senate 1977–79; Econ. Adviser Banco Exterior de España 1979–81; Vice-Pres. Fundacion Banco Exterior de España 1981–84; Spanish Nat. Award for new playwrights 1950; Real Academia Española 1990. *Publications:* Economics: Principles of Industrial Location 1954, Effects of European Economic Integration 1957, Economic Reality and Structural Analysis 1958, The European Future of Spain 1960, Regional Profiles of Spain 1964, Decisive Forces in World Economics 1967, Economic Structure 1969, Conscience of Underdevelopment 1973, Inflation Unabridged 1976; Fiction: Congreso en Estocolmo 1952, El Río que nos lleva 1962, El Caballo Desnudo 1970, Octubre, Octubre 1981, La Sonrisa Etrusca 1985, La Vieja Sirena 1990, Mar al Fondo 1993, Mientras la Tierra Gira 1993, Real Sitio 1993, La Estatua de Adolfo Espejo 1994, La Sombra de los Días 1994, Fronteras 1995; plays: La Paloma de Cartón 1950, Un sitio para vivir 1956. *Leisure interests:* human communication. *Address:* Cea Bermúdez 51, 28003 Madrid, Spain. *Telephone:* 544-2860.

SAMPER, Armando; Colombian agricultural economist; b. 9 April 1920, Bogotá; s. of late Daniel Samper Ortega and of Mayita Gnecco de Samper; m. Jean K. de Samper 1945; two s. two d.; ed. Cornell Univ., U.S.A.; research and teaching posts in agricultural econs., Colombia 1943–49; Inter-American Inst. of Agricultural Sciences of OAS, Turrialba, Costa Rica 1949–69, Head of Scientific Communications Service 1949–54, Dir. of Regional Services 1955–60, Dir. of Inst. 1960–69, Dir. Emer. 1969–; Visiting Prof. Univ. of Chicago 1954–55; Minister of Agric. 1966–67, 1969–70; Agricultural Adviser, Banco de la República, Bogotá 1970–72; Chancellor Univ. de Bogotá 1971; FAO Asst. Dir.-Gen. for Latin American Affairs, Santiago, Chile 1972–74; Pres. Nat. Corpn. for Forestry Research and Devt. (CONIF), Bogotá 1975–77, Consultant Delsa Ltd. 1978–92; Dir.-Gen. Colombian Sugar Cane Research Centre 1978–90, Dir. Emer. 1990–; consultant COLCIENCIAS 1990–91; mem. Bd. Int. Centre of Tropical Agriculture 1967–76 (Chair. 1973–76, Chair. Emer. 1976–), Foundation for Higher Educ. 1978–95 (Chair. 1984–89), UN Science and Tech. Cttee. 1981–83, Nat. Council of Science and Tech. 1982–86, Gimnasio Moderno 1989–, Oil Palm Research Center 1991–, Aquaculture Research Centre 1993–; Chair. Emer., Colombian Program for the Admin. of Agric. Research 1990–; Vice-Chair. Bd. Colombian Corpn. for Agric. Research 1993–94; mem. Nat. Acad. Econ. Sciences 1984–. *Publications:* Importancia del Café en el Comercio Exterior de Colombia 1948, A Case Study of Cooperation in Secondary Education in Chile 1957, Política de Transformación Rural 1967, Memoria del Ministro de Agricultura al Congreso Nacional 1966–67, Desarrollo Institucional y Desarrollo Agrícola (3 vols.) 1969, El Cuatrenio de la Transformación Rural 1966–70, Los Estudios Microeconómicos en Colombia 1988. *Address:* Apartado Aéreo 100-286, Santa Fe de Bogotá, Colombia. *Telephone:* (1) 611 09 41 (Office). *Fax:* (1) 616 48 13.

SAMPERMANS, Françoise, L. ÈS L.; French business executive; b. 10 July 1947, Paris; d. of Jacques Durand and Jeannine Behot; one s. one d.; joined CIT-TRANSAC 1974; est. public relations service, Chapelle Darblay 1978; Head of Public Relations, Entreprise et Crédit 1981; Dir. of Communications, Transmission, Group Thomson 1982; subsequently Deputy Dir., Dir. of Communications, Alcatel CIT; Dir. of Communications, Alcatel N.V. 1987, Alcatel Alsthom 1987; Dir.-Gen. Générale Occidentale 1991–95; Dir. in charge of communications section and assoc. services, Alcatel Alsthom; Pres. Dir.-Gen. Groupe Express 1992–95; Vice-Pres. Quebecor-Europe 1996–; Vice-Pres. Baroque Music Centre, Versailles. *Address:* 18 rue Charles Silvestri, 94300 Vincennes, France.

SAMPHAN, Khieu (see Khieu Samphan).

SAMPRAS, Pete; American tennis player; b. 12 Aug. 1971, Washington; s. of Sam Sampras and Georgia Sampras; U.S Open Champion 1990, 1993, 1995, 1996; Grand Slam Cup Winner 1990; IBM/ATP Tour World Championship—Frankfurt Winner 1991; U.S. Pro-Indoor Winner 1992; Wimbledon Singles Champion 1993, 1994, 1995, 1997, 1998; European Community Championships Winner 1993, 1994; ranked No. 1 1993; Winner Australian Open 1994; RCA Championships 1996, ATP Tour World Championships, 1996, Australian Open 1997; Winner San José Open 1997, Philadelphia Open 1997, Cincinnatti Open 1997; Munich Open 1997, Paris Open 1997, Hanover Open 1997; mem. U.S. Davis Cup Team 1991, 1995.

SAMPSON, Anthony (Terrell Seward), M.A.; British writer and journalist; b. 3 Aug. 1926, Billingham, Durham; s. of Michael Sampson and Phyllis (née Seward) Sampson; m. Sally Bentlif 1965; one s. one d.; ed. Westminster School and Christ Church, Oxford; served with Royal Navy 1944–47; Sub Lieut. R.N.V.R. 1946; Ed. Drum magazine, Johannesburg 1951–55; Editorial Staff, The Observer 1955–66, Chief American Corresp. 1973–74, Ed. The Observer Colour Magazine 1965–66; Assoc. Prof. Univ. of Vincennes, Paris 1968–70; Contributing Ed. Newsweek 1977–; Chair. Soc. of Authors 1992–94; Editorial Adviser, Brandt Comm. 1979; Dir. The New Statesman 1979–83; Ed. The Sampson Letter 1984–86; awarded Prix Int. de la Presse for The Seven Sisters 1976. *Publications:* Drum, a Venture into the New Africa 1956, The Treason Cage 1958, Commonsense about Africa 1960, (with S. Pienaar), Anatomy of Britain 1962, Anatomy of Britain Today 1965, South Africa: Two Views of Separate Development 1966, Macmillan: a Study in Ambiguity 1968, The New Anatomy of Britain 1971, The Sovereign State: the Secret History of ITT 1973, The Seven Sisters 1975, The Arms Bazaar 1977, The Money Lenders 1981, The Changing Anatomy of Britain 1982, Empires of the Sky 1984, The Oxford Book of Ages (with Sally Sampson) 1985, Black and Gold: Tycoons, Revolutionaries and Apartheid 1987, The Midas Touch 1989, The Essential Anatomy of Britain 1992, Company Man 1995, The Scholar Gypsy 1997. *Leisure interest:* gardening. *Address:* 27 Ladbroke Grove, London W11 3AY; Quarry Garden, Wardour, nr. Tisbury, Wiltshire, SP3 6HR, England. *Telephone:* 0171-727 4188 (London); (01747) 870407 (Wiltshire).

SAMSONOV, Gen. Viktor Nikolayevich; Russian military officer; b. 10 Nov. 1941, Dukhovnitsky, Saratov Region; m.; two c.; ed. Far E. Higher Commdg. School of Gen. Troops, M. Frunze Mil. Acad., Mil. Acad. of Gen. Staff; commdr. of platoon, of marines co. Pacific Ocean Navy 1964–72; chief of staff, tank div., commdr. Caucasian Mil. Command; head of staff 7th Army, Commdr. 1972–87; head of staff Caucasian Mil. Command, concurrently mil. commdt. of Yerevan 1987–90; commdr. of troops of Leningrad Mil. Command 1990–91; head Gen. Staff of Armed Forces, First Deputy U.S.S.R. Minister of Defence 1991–92; head Gen. HQ of United Armed Forces of C.I.S. 1992–93; Co-ordinator of mil. co-operation of C.I.S. countries 1993–96; Head Gen. Staff of Armed Forces of Russian Fed. Oct. 1996–97. *Leisure interests:* flower-growing, hunting, fishing, opera, ballet. *Address:* Ministry of Defence, Myasnitskaya str. 37, 101000 Moscow, Russia.

SAMSONOWICZ, Henryk, HH.D.; Polish politician and historian; b. 23 Jan. 1930, Warsaw; m.; one s. one d.; ed. Warsaw Univ.; Staff mem. Warsaw Univ. 1950–, Asst., Sr. Asst., Lecturer 1950–60, Asst. Prof. 1960–71, Prof., History Inst. 1971–, Rector 1980–82; mem. Civic Cttee. attached to Lech Wałęsa, (q.v.), Chair. of Solidarity Trade Union, Chair. Science and Educ. Comm. 1988–89; participant Round Table plenary debates, mem. group for political reforms and team for science, educ. and tech. progress Feb.–April 1989; Minister of Nat. Educ. 1989–91; Deputy Head Scientific Research Cttee. 1994–97; mem. Polish Historical Soc., Chair. Gen. Bd. 1977–82, Soc. for Advancement and Propagation of Sciences 1980–, Acad. Europaea 1992–, Polish Acad. of Sciences 1994–; Dr. h.c. (Duquesne Univ., U.S.A.), (High School of Educ., Cracow), (Nicolaus Copernicus Univ., Toruń); Commdr.'s Cross of Order of Polonia Restituta, Gold Cross of Merit, Nat. Educ. Comm. Medal, Officier Légion d'honneur. *Publications:* books include: Złota jesień polskiego Średniowiecza (Golden Autumn of the Polish Middle Ages) 1971, Dziedzictwo Średniowiecza (Heritages of the Middle Ages) 1994, Miejsce Polski w Europie (Poland's Place in Europe) 1996; numerous articles. *Address:* Instytut Historyczny Uniwersytetu Warszawskiego, ul. Krakowskie Przedmieście 26/28, 00-325 Warsaw, Poland. *Telephone:* (22) 826 19 88.

SAMUELSON, Paul Anthony, PH.D., LL.D., D.LITT., D.SC.; American economist; b. 15 May 1915, Gary, Ind.; s. of Frank Samuelson and Ella Lipton; m. 1st Marion E. Crawford 1938 (died 1978); four s. (including triplets) two d.; m. 2nd Risha Eckaus 1981; ed. Hyde Park High School Chicago, Univ. of Chicago and Harvard Univ.; Prof. of Econs. at M.I.T. 1940–65, Inst. Prof. 1966–85, Inst. Prof. Emer. June 1986–, Gordon Y. Billard Fellow 1986, mem. Radiation Lab. Staff 1944–45; Visiting Prof. of Political Economy, New York

Univ. 1987–; Consultant to Nat. Resources Planning Bd. 1941–43, to War Production Bd. 1945, to U.S. Treasury 1945–52, 1961–74, to Rand Corpn. 1949–75, to Council of Econ. Advisers 1960–68, to Fed. Reserve Bd. 1965–, to Finance Cttee., N.A.S. 1977–, to Loomis, Sayles & Co. Boston and to Burden Investors Services Inc.; Research Advisory Bd. Cttee. for Econ. Devt. 1960; Advisory Bd. to Pres. Eisenhower's Comm. on Nat. Goals 1960; Nat. Task Force on Econ. Educ. 1960–61; Special Comm. on Social Sciences of Nat. Science Foundation 1967–68; Comm. on Money and Credit; Econ. Adviser to Pres. Kennedy during election campaign; author of report to Pres. Kennedy on State of American Economy 1961; Assoc. Ed. Journal of Public Econs., Journal of Int. Econs., Journal of Nonlinear Analysis; N.A.S. Guggenheim Fellow 1948–49; mem. American Acad. of Arts and Sciences, American Economic Asscn. (Pres. 1961), Int. Econ. Asscn. (Pres. 1965–68, lifetime hon. Pres.); Fellow A.A.A.S., American Philosophical Soc., Econometric Soc. (Council mem., Vice-Pres. 1950, Pres. 1951); Corresp. Fellow British Acad.; Corresp. mem. Leibniz-Akademie der Wissenschaften und der Literatur; numerous hon. degrees; numerous awards including Nobel Prize for Economic Science 1970, Albert Einstein Commemorative Award 1971, Alumni Medal, Univ. of Chicago 1983, Britannica Award 1989, Gold Scanno Prize, Naples 1990, Medal of Science 1996; M.I.T. est. Paul A. Samuelson Professorship in Econs. 1991. *Publications:* Foundations of Economic Analysis 1947, Economics 11 edns. 1948–1980, 12th–16th edns. (with William D. Norhaus) 1985–98 (trans. into 30 languages), Readings in Economics (Ed.), 7 edns. 1955–73, Linear Programming and Economic Analysis (jtly.) 1958, 1987, Collected Scientific Papers, I and II 1966, III 1972, IV 1979, V 1986, Collected Scientific Papers of Paul A. Samuelson (vols. I–V) 1966–87; author and jt. author of numerous articles on economics. *Leisure interest:* tennis. *Address:* Massachusetts Institute of Technology, Department of Economics, Cambridge, MA 02139; 94 Somerset Street, Belmont, MA 02178, U.S.A. (Home). *Telephone:* (617) 253-3368 (M.I.T.). *Fax:* (617) 253-0560.

SAMUELSON, Sir Sydney Wylie, Kt., C.B.E.; British film commissioner; b. 7 Dec. 1925; s. of G.B. Samuelson and Marjorie Samuelson; m. Doris Magen 1949; three s.; ed. Irene Avenue Council School, Lancing, Sussex; served R.A.F. 1943–47; from age 14 career devoted to various aspects of British film industry; cinema projectionist 1939–42; asst. film ed. 1943; asst. film cameraman, cameraman and dir. of documentary films 1947–59; f. co. to service film, TV etc. supplying technical equipment 1954; continued filming as technician on locations throughout the world until 1959; Chair. Samuelson Group PLC 1966–90, Pres. 1990–95; first British Film Commr. 1991–97; Perm. Trustee, BAFTA 1973–, Chair. Bd. Man. 1976–, Fellow 1993; Chair. BAFTA-Shell UK Venture Cttee. 1988-91; Hon. Pres. Brighton Jewish Film Festival; mem. Exec. Cttee. Cinema and TV Veterans (Pres. 1980–81); mem. Council and Exec. Cttee. Cinema & TV Benevolent Fund 1969–92 (Trustee 1982–90); Fellow B.F.I. 1997; Gov. British Soc. of Cinematographers 1969–79; Patron Moving Image Soc. (BKSTS); many other professional appts.; Michael Balcon Award, BAFTA 1985; Award of Merit, Guild of Film Production Execs. 1986; Dr. h.c. (Sheffield Hallam) 1996. *Leisure interests:* collecting recorded film music, vintage motoring, veteran jogging. *Address:* 31 West Heath Avenue, London, NW11 7QJ, England. *Telephone:* 0181-455 6696. *Fax:* 0181-458 1957.

SAMUELSSON, Bengt Ingemar, D.M.S., M.D.; Swedish medical chemist; b. 21 May 1934, Halmstad; s. of Anders Samuelsson and Stina Nilsson; m. Inga Bergstein 1958; three c.; ed. Karolinska Inst. Stockholm; Asst. Prof. Karolinska Inst. 1961–66, Prof. of Medicine and Physiological Chemistry 1972, Chair. Dept. of Physiological Chem. 1973–83, Dean, Faculty of Medicine 1978–83, Rector 1983–95; Research Fellow, Harvard Univ. 1961–62; Prof. of Medical Chem. Royal Veterinary Coll. Stockholm 1967–72; mem. Nobel Cttee. of Physiology or Medicine 1984–89, Chair. 1987–89; Chair. Nobel Foundation 1993–; mem. Research Advisory Bd. Swedish Govt. 1985–88, Nat. Comm. on Health Policy 1987–90, European Science and Tech. Ass. 1994–; Special Advisor to Commr. for Research and Educ., EC 1995–; mem. Royal Swedish Acad. of Sciences; Hon. mem. Asscn. of American Physicians, A.A.A.S., Swedish Medical Asscn., American Soc. of Biological Chemists, Italian Pharmacology Soc., Acad. Nat. Medicina de Buenos Aires, Int. Soc. of Haematology; Foreign Assoc. N.A.S.; Foreign mem. Royal Soc. (London), Mediterranean Acad. of Sciences, Acad. Europaea, French Acad. of Sciences, Spanish Soc. of Allergology and Clinical Immunology, Royal Nat. Acad. of Medicine (Spain), Int. Acad. of Sciences; Hon. Prof. Bethune Univ. of Medical Sciences, Changchun, China 1986; Hon. D.Sc. (Chicago) 1978, (Illinois) 1983, (Louisiana State Univ.) 1993; Dr. h.c. (Rio de Janeiro) 1986, (Complutense Univ., Madrid) 1991, (Milan) 1993; Hon. D. Univ. (Buenos Aires) 1986; recipient of numerous honours and awards including Louisa Gross Horwitz Award 1975, Lasker Award 1977, Gairdner Foundation Award 1981, Nobel Prize in Physiology or Medicine 1982, Abraham White Science Achievement Award 1991, City of Medicine Award 1992, Maria Theresa Medal 1996. *Publications:* articles in professional journals. *Address:* Karolinska Institute, Department of Medical Biochemistry and Biophysics, Solnavagen 1, 17177 Stockholm, Sweden.

SAN GIACOMO, Laura; American actress; b. 1962, New Jersey; m. Cameron Dye; ed. Carnegie Mellon Univ., Pennsylvania; started career in regional theatre productions. *Theatre includes:* North Shore Fish, Beirut, The Love Talker, Italian American Reconciliation. *Films:* Sex, Lies and Videotape (New Generation Award, L.A. Film Critics' Asscn.) 1989, Pretty Woman, Vital Signs, Quigley Down Under, Once Around, Under Suspicion, Where the Day Takes You, Nina Takes a Lover, Stuart Saves His Family, Eat Your Heart Out 1997, Suicide Kings 1997, Apocalypse 1997, With Friends Like These . . . 1998. *Television:* Miami Vice, Crime Story, Spenser: For Hire, The Equalizer, Just Shoot Me. *Address:* More Medavoy Management, 7920 West Sunset Boulevard, Suite 401, Los Angeles, CA 90046, U.S.A.

SANBAR, Samir H., B.B.A.; Lebanese international civil servant; b. 9 March 1934, Haifa; ed. American Univ. of Beirut; Deputy Ed. Al Howadeth, Al-Sayyad (Arab weeklies) and journalist with various Lebanese, Arab and int. media; Political Ed. Al-Usbu Al Araby (pan-Arab weekly), Beirut 1954–65; Information Officer of Special Rep. of Sec.-Gen. for UNYOM 1964; Special Asst. to Personal Rep. of Sec.-Gen. of UNITAR 1965–70; Special Asst. to Exec. Dir. UNITAR 1970–73; accompanied UN Secs.-Gen. on all visits to Middle East 1973–87; Dir. UN Information Centre, Beirut, Chief, Information Services of ECWA and Co-ordinator of UN public information activities in Gulf countries 1975–82; special assignment to assist Office of Sec.-Gen. in liaison and media functions during establishment of UNIFIL 1978–82; Chief UN Centres Services 1982–87; Dir. UN Information Centres, Dept. of Public Information 1987–93; Special Rep. of UN Sec.-Gen. to head UN mission to verify Referendum in Eritrea 1993; Asst. Sec.-Gen. UN Dept. of Public Information 1994–. *Address:* 240 East 47th Street, New York, NY 10017, U.S.A. *Telephone:* (212) 963-6830. *Fax:* (212) 963-4361.

SANBERK, H. E. Özdem; Turkish diplomatist; b. 1 Aug. 1938, Istanbul; s. of Halil Turgut Sanberk and Nimet Sanberk; m. Sumru Sanberk; one d.; ed. Univ. of Istanbul; fmrly. at Embassies in Bonn, Paris, Madrid; fmr. Foreign Policy Adviser to Prime Minister Turgut Ozal; fmr. Under-Sec. to Ministry of Foreign Affairs; fmr. Amb. to EU; Amb. to London June 1995–. *Address:* Turkish Embassy, 43 Belgrave Square, London, SW1X 8PA; 69 Portland Place, London, W.1, England. *Telephone:* 0171-393 0202. *Fax:* 0171-396 6666.

SANCAR, M. Sitki, M.SC.; Turkish petroleum executive; b. 8 Oct. 1941, Gemlik; m. Ayse Sancar 1968; one s. one d.; ed. Univs. of Istanbul and Tulsa, Okla.; well site geologist, Turkish Petroleum Co. (TPAO) 1967–70, research geologist and Dist. Man. 1974–79; Gen. Dir. MTA-Mineral Research & Exploration Inst. of Turkey 1979–88; Deputy Under-Sec. Ministry of Energy 1988–93; Chair. and Gen. Man. TPAO 1993–; hon. mem. Chamber of Petroleum Engineers of Turkey. *Publications:* several scientific papers. *Address:* TPAO, M. Kemal Mah. 2 Cad. 86, 06520 Ankara (Office); Binses Sitesi, 4 Cad. 21, Ümitköy, 06530 Ankara, Turkey (Home). *Telephone:* (312) 286-9100 (Office). *Fax:* (312) 286-9000 (Office).

SÁNCHEZ DE LOZADA, Gonzálo; Bolivian politician; b. 1 July 1930; m. Ximena Iturralde Monje; one s. one d.; ed. Univ. of Chicago; Founder and Man. Telecine Ltda. (documentary and commercial film production) 1953–57; Founder and Gen. Man. Andean Geo-Services Ltd. 1957–62; Founder and Pres. Compañía Minera del Sur 1962–79; Pres. COMSUR 1980–82; mem. Parl. 1979–80, 1982–85; Senator for Cochabamba and Pres. Senate 1985–86; Minister for Planning and Coordination 1986–88; Presidential cand. 1989; Leader, Movimiento Nacionalista Revolucionario (MNR) 1988–; Pres. of Bolivia 1993–97. *Address:* c/o Genaro Sanjines 541, Pasaje Kuljis, La Paz, Bolivia.

SÁNCHEZ HERNÁNDEZ, Col. Fidel; Salvadorean politician and army officer; b. 7 July 1917; Mil. Attaché, Washington 1960–62; Minister of Interior 1962–66; Pres. of El Salvador 1967–72; fmr. Leader of Partido de Conciliación Nacional (PCN). *Address:* Partido de Conciliación Nacional, Calle Arce 1128, San Salvador, El Salvador.

SANCHEZ-VICARIO, Arantxa; Spanish tennis player; b. 18 Dec. 1971, Barcelona; d. of Emilio and Marisa Vicario; coached by Juan Núñez; won first professional title at Brussels 1988; winner, French Open Women's title 1989, 1994, 1998, Int. Championships of Spain 1989, 1990, Virginia Slims Tournaments Newport 1991, Washington 1991, winner Canadian Open 1992, Australian Open 1992, 1993, U.S. Open 1994, named Int. Tennis Fed. World Champion 1994; Silver Medal (doubles), Bronze Medal (singles) 1992 Olympics, Silver Medal (singles); Bronze Medal (doubles) 1996 Olympics.

SÁNCHEZ-VILELLA, Roberto; Puerto Rican politician; b. 19 Feb. 1913, Mayaguez; s. of Luis Sánchez-Frasqueri and Angela Vilella-Vélez; one s. three d.; ed. Ohio State Univ.; Sub-Commr. of the Interior 1941–42; Dir. Transportation Authority of Puerto Rico 1942–45; Special Asst. to Pres. of Senate 1946–47; Resident Engineer Caribe Hilton Hotel 1947–48; Exec. Sec. to Govt. 1949–51; Sec. of State 1952–64; Gov. Puerto Rico 1965–69; Prof. School of Public Admin. 1974–94, School of Laws, Univ. of Puerto Rico 1987–94; fmr. Pres. People's Party; mem. Puerto Rico Coll. of Engineers, American Soc. of Public Administrators; Hon. LL.D. (Ohio State Univ.) 1966; Hon. D.Eng. (Mayagüez Campus, Univ. of Puerto Rico) 1996; Hon. D.Jur. (Rio Piedras Campus, Univ. of Puerto Rico) 1996. *Leisure interests:* reading, dominoes. *Address:* 414 Muñoz Rivera Avenue, Suite 7-A, Stop 31-1/2, Hato Rey, Puerto Rico 00918. *Telephone:* 753-9156.

SANCHO-ROF, Juan, D.CHEM.ENG.; Spanish businessman; b. 9 Feb. 1940, Madrid; m. Paloma Suils; two s. three d.; ed. Universidad Complutense de Madrid and Instituto de Estudios Superiores de la Empresa, Barcelona; Technical–Commercial post Petronor S.A. (Petróleos del Norte) 1970–76, Deputy Gen. Man. 1976–85; Chair. and C.E.O. Repsol Petróleo S.A. 1985, Pres. 1995–; now Pres. Petronor. *Publications:* several technical works.

Address: Petronoz, Apdo 1418, Plaza de Carlos VII, Bilbao 9; José Abascal 4, 28003 Madrid, Spain. *Telephone:* 446-52 00 (Office); 446-60 70 (Home).

SANDAGE, Allan Rex, PH.D., D.SC.; American astronomer; b. 18 June 1926, Iowa City; s. of Charles H. Sandage and Dorothy M. Briggs; m. Mary L. Connelly 1959; two s.; ed. Univ. of Illinois and California Inst. of Tech.; staff mem. Mount Wilson and Palomar Observatories 1952–; Asst. Astronomer Hale Observatories, Calif. 1952–56, Astronomer 1956–; Sr. Research Astronomer Space Telescope Scientific Inst. 1986–; Homewood Prof. of Physics, Johns Hopkins Univ., Baltimore 1987–88; Assoc. Ed. annual reviews of astronomy and astrophysics; Visiting Astronomer, Univ. of Hawaii 1986; Visiting Lecturer, Harvard Univ. 1957; Consultant, Nat. Science Foundation 1961–63; mem. Cttee. on Science and Public Policy 1965; Philips Lecturer, Haverford Coll. 1968; Research Assoc. Australian Nat. Univ. 1968–69; Fulbright-Hayes Scholar 1972; Grubb-Parson Lecturer, Royal Astronomical Soc. 1992; mem. Royal and American Astronomical Socs.; numerous hon. degrees; Helen Warner Prize of American Astronomical Soc. 1960, Russell Prize 1973; Eddington Medal, Royal Astronomical Soc. (U.K.) 1963; Pope Pius XI Gold Medal, Pontifical Acad. of Sciences 1966; Gold Medal, Royal Astronomical Soc. (U.K.) 1967, Rittenhouse Medal 1968, Nat. Medal of Scientific Merit 1971, Elliott Gresson Medal, Franklin Inst. 1973, Gold Medal of Pacific Astronomical Soc. 1975, Crafoord Prize, Swedish Acad. of Science 1991, Adion Medal, Observatoire de Nice 1991, Tomalla Gravity Prize, Swiss Physical Soc. 1992. *Publications:* numerous scientific papers and Hubble Atlas of Galaxies. *Leisure interests:* bread-making, gardening. *Address:* Carnegie Observatories, 813 Santa Barbara Street, Pasadena, CA 91101 (Office); 8319 Josard Road, San Gabriel, CA 91775, U.S.A. (Home). *Telephone:* (818) 285-5086 (Home).

SANDBERG, Baron (Life Peer), cr. 1997, of Passfield in the County of Hampshire; **Michael Graham Ruddock Sandberg,** Kt., C.B.E., F.C.I.B., F.R.S.A.; British banker; b. 31 May 1927, Thames Ditton, Surrey; s. of late Gerald Arthur Clifford Sandberg and Ethel Marion (née Ruddock) Sandberg; m. Carmel Mary Roseleen Donnelly 1954; two s. two d.; ed. St. Edward's School, Oxford; mil. service 1945–48, commissioned into 6th DCO Lancers, Indian Army, later 1st King's Dragoon Guards; joined Hongkong and Shanghai Banking Corpn. 1949, Deputy Chair. 1973–77, Chair. 1977–86; Chair. British Bank of the Middle East 1980–86; Pres. Surrey County Cricket Club 1987–88; Vice-Pres. Chartered Inst. of Bankers 1984–87; J.P. Hong Kong 1972–86; Dir. Int. Totalizator Systems Inc., New World Devt. Ltd., Winsor Ind. Corpn.; mem. of Exec. Council of Hong Kong 1978–86; Treasurer Univ. of Hong Kong 1977–86; Chair. of Stewards, Royal Hong Kong Jockey Club 1981–86, Hon. Steward 1986; Hon. LL.D. (Hong Kong) 1984, (Pepperdine) 1986; Freeman City of London, Liveryman Worshipful Co. of Clockmakers. *Leisure interests:* horse racing, cricket, bridge, horology. *Address:* Suite 9, 100 Piccadilly, London, W1V 9FN, England; Domaine de la Haute Germaine, Ste Marguerite, Le Broc, Alpes Maritimes, France. *Telephone:* 0171-629 2204 (London).

SANDBLOM, (John) Philip, M.D., PH.D.; Swedish professor of surgery and university administrator; b. 29 Oct. 1903, Chicago, Ill., U.S.A.; s. of Dr. John N. Sandblom and Ellen Chinlund; m. Grace Schaefer 1932; three s. two d.; ed. Northwestern Univ. and Karolinska Institutet, Stockholm; Assoc. Prof. of Surgery, Karolinska Institutet, Stockholm 1944; Surgeon-in-Chief, Crown Princess Louise's Children's Hospital 1945–50; Prof. of Surgery and Head of Dept. of Surgery, Lund Univ. 1950–70, Vice-Chancellor of Lund Univ. 1957–68; Visiting Prof. Univ. of Calif., San Diego 1972–73, Univ. of Lausanne 1973–80, Univ. of Taipei 1982; mem. of Board, Soc. for Modern Art 1936–46, Gen. Art Soc. 1943–70; Treas. Swedish Surgical Soc. 1946–52, Pres. 1957–58, 1970; mem. Insurance Advisory Bd. 1947–50; Pres. Soc. Int. de Chirurgie 1967; Hon. Fellow, American Coll. of Surgeons, Royal Coll. of Surgeons of England, Edin., and in Ireland; Hon. mem. American Surgical Asscn., Southern Surgical Asscn., Soc. Int. de Chirurgie, Asscn. of Surgeons of Great Britain and Ireland, Swedish, Danish, French, Italian, Northern, Swiss and Finnish Surgical Socs.; Corresp. mem. Deutsche Gesellschaft für Chirurgie and Norwegian Surgical Soc.; Ph.D. h.c. and many hon. degrees. *Publications:* Function of the Human Gall Bladder 1932, Function of the Sphincter Oddi., Tensile Strength of Healing Wounds 1944, Hemobilia 1972, The Responsibility of Society to Surgery, The Role of the University in the World of Violence, The Difference in Men, Portal Hypertension, 100 Years of Surgical Research, Creativity and Disease, 11th edn. 1999; teaching film: Atraumatic Surgical Technique 1976, and various papers. *Leisure interests:* collecting works of modern art, sailing, skiing. *Address:* 2 chemin des Bluets, 1009 Pully Lausanne, Switzerland. *Telephone:* (21) 729 6877.

SANDER, Michael Arthur, B.SC.; South African business executive; b. 2 Oct. 1941, Germiston; s. of Norman William Henry Sander and Nora McLaverty; m. Pamela Wendy Mills 1968; one s. one d.; ed. Durban High School, Univ. of Natal; joined AECI Ltd. as Overseas Industrial Bursar, and seconded to ICI Heavy Organic Chemicals Div., Teeside, U.K. 1963–65; then returned to AECI Devt. Dept. and became involved in new project devt.; apptd. Gen. Man., Anikem (Pty.) Ltd. 1970; moved to subsidiary Co. Rand Carbide as Devt. Man. 1977; Man. Dir. AECI Chlor-Alkali and Plastics Ltd. 1982, Chair. 1984; Exec. Dir. AECI Ltd. 1984, Man. Dir. 1985–95, Chair. (non-exec.) 1994–97; Chair. Daewood Electronics; Deputy Chair. Amic (Pty.) Ltd., currently Dir. of a number of AECI group subsidiary and assoc. cos. *Leisure interests:* shooting, fishing, photography, music. *Address:* P.O. Box 61587, Marshalltown 2107, South Africa.

SANDERLING, Kurt; German conductor; b. 19 Sept. 1912, Arys; m. 1st Nina Bobath 1941; m. 2nd Barbara Wagner 1963; three s.; Conductor Leningrad Philharmonic 1941–60, Chief Conductor Berlin Symphony Orchestra 1960–77; Guest Conductor (mainly in Europe and N. America); many awards and prizes (U.S.S.R. and G.D.R.). *Address:* Am Iderfenngraben 47, 13156 Berlin, Germany. *Telephone:* 916 75 58. *Fax:* 916 75 58.

SANDERS, Donald Neil, A.O., C.B., B.ECON.; Australian banker; b. 21 June 1927, Sydney; s. of L. G. and R. M. Sanders; m. Betty Elaine Constance 1952; four s. one d.; ed. Wollongong High School, Univ. of Sydney; Commonwealth Bank of Australia 1943–60; Australian Treasury 1956; Bank of England 1960–61; with Reserve Bank of Australia 1961–87, Supt., Credit Policy Div. of Banking Dept. 1964–66, Deputy Man. of Banking Dept. 1966–67, of Research Dept. 1967–70; Australian Embassy, Washington D.C. 1968; Chief Man. of Securities Markets Dept. 1970–72, of Banking and Finance Dept. 1972–74, Adviser and Chief Man. 1974–75, Deputy Gov. and Deputy Chair. of Bd. 1975–87; Man. Dir. Commonwealth Banking Corpn. 1987–91; Man. Dir., C.E.O. Commonwealth Bank of Australia 1991–92; Chair. H-G Ventures Ltd. 1995–; Dir. Lend Lease Corpn. Ltd., MLC Ltd., Queensland Investment Corpn., Australian Chamber Orchestra Pty. Ltd. *Leisure interests:* golf, music. *Address:* "Somerset", Taralga Road, via Goulburn, N.S.W. 2580, Australia. *Telephone:* (02) 48402095.

SANDERS, Jeremy Keith Morris, PH.D., F.R.S.; British professor of chemistry; b. 3 May 1948, London; s. of Sidney Sanders and Sylvia Sanders (née Rutman); m. Louise Elliott 1972; one s. one d.; ed Wandsworth School, Imperial Coll., London, Univ. of Cambridge; research asst. in Pharmacology Stanford Univ. 1972–73; demonstrator in Chemistry Univ. of Cambridge 1973–78, lecturer 1978–92, Reader 1992–96, Prof. 1996–; Fellow Selwyn Coll., Cambridge 1976–; Pedler Lecturer, Royal Soc. of Chemistry 1996. *Publication:* Modern NMR Spectroscopy (with B. K. Hunter). *Address:* University Chemical Laboratory, Lensfield Road, Cambridge, CB2 1EW, England. *Telephone:* (01223) 336411. *Fax:* (01223) 336017.

SANDERS, Ronald, C.M.G.; diplomatist and international relations consultant; b. 26 Jan. 1948, Guyana; m. Susan Ramphal 1975; ed. Sacred Heart R.C. School, Guyana, and Boston Univ., U.S.A., Univ. of Sussex; Man. Dir. Guyana Broadcasting Service, Public Affairs Adviser to Prime Minister of Guyana 1973–76; Lecturer in Communications, Univ. of Guyana 1975–76; Consultant to Pres. of Caribbean Devt. Bank, Barbados 1977–78; Special Adviser to the Minister of Foreign Affairs of Antigua and Barbuda 1978–82; Deputy Perm. Rep. of Antigua and Barbuda to the UN, New York 1982–83; Antigua and Barbuda Amb. Extraordinary and Plenipotentiary accred. to UNESCO 1983–87; Antigua and Barbuda High Commr. in U.K. 1984–87, 1995– (also accred to Fed. Repub. of Germany 1986–87, 1996–, to France 1996–); Pres. Caribbean Broadcasting Union 1975–76; Chair. Caribbean Sub-Group at UNESCO 1983–85; mem. Bd. of Dirs. of Caribbean News Agency 1976–77; mem. Inter-Governmental Council of the Int. Programme for the Devt. of Communications at UNESCO 1983–87; mem. Exec. Bd. UNESCO 1985–87; Visiting Fellow, Oxford Univ. 1987–89; freelance broadcaster with BBC World Service 1987–89; Consultant (Int. Rels.) Atlantic Tele-Network, U.S. Virgin Is. 1989–97; mem. Bd. Dirs. Swiss American Nat. Bank of Antigua 1990–97, Guyana Telephone and Telegraph Co. 1991–97, Emerging Communications Inc., U.S. Virgin Is. 1998–. *Publications:* Broadcasting in Guyana 1978, Antigua and Barbuda: Transition, Trial, Triumph 1984, Inseparable Humanity: Anthology of Reflections of the Commonwealth Secretary-General (Ed.) 1988, Crumbled Small: The Caribbean in World Politics 1999, numerous articles on media ownership and control, communication and development and Antarctica. *Leisure interests:* reading, West Indian history, cinema. *Address:* 24 Chelmsford Square, London, NW10 3AR, England.

SANDERSON, Tessa, O.B.E.; British athlete; b. 14 March 1956; ed. Bilston Coll. of Further Educ.; Silver Medal for javelin Euro Championships 1978; Gold Medal for javelin (Olympic record), Olympic Games, Los Angeles 1984; Gold Medal World Cup 1992; competed Olympic Games, Atlanta 1996; sports presenter Sky News 1989–92; Patron Disabled Olympics; Hon. Fellow Wolverhampton Polytechnic; Hon. B.Sc. (Birmingham Univ.). *Publication:* My Life in Athletics (autobiog.) 1985. *Leisure interest:* cardiofunk (low impact aerobic exercise workout). *Address:* c/o Derek Evans, 68 Meadowbank Road, Kingsbury, London, N.W.9., England.

SANDIFORD, Rt. Hon. Lloyd Erskine, P.C., M.A.(ECON.); Barbadian politician; b. 24 March 1937; s. of Cyril G. Sandiford and Eunice Sandiford; m. Angelita P. Ricketts 1963; one s. two d.; ed. Harrison Coll., Barbados, Univ. Coll. of the W. Indies, Jamaica and Univ. of Manchester; Asst. Master, Modern High School, Barbados 1956–57, Kingston Coll., Jamaica 1960–61; part-time Tutor and Lecturer, Univ. of W. Indies, Barbados 1963–65; Sr. Grad. Master, Harrison Coll. 1964–66; Asst. Tutor, Barbados Community Coll. 1976–86; mem. Barbados Senate 1967–71, House of Ass. for St. Michael South 1971–; Personal Asst. to Prime Minister 1966–67; Minister of Educ. 1967–71, of Educ., Youth Affairs, Community Devt. and Sport 1971–75, of Health and Welfare 1975–76; Deputy Prime Minister and Minister of Educ. and Culture 1986–87; Prime Minister and Minister of Econ. Affairs June–July 1987, Econ. Affairs and the Civil Service 1987–94, also of Home Affairs, fmrly. of Finance; mem. Democratic Labour Party, Pres. 1974–75; founder, Acad of Politics. *Leisure interests:* choral singing, reading. *Address:* Hillvista, Porters, St James, Barbados.

SANDLE, Michael Leonard, F.R.B.S., D.F.A.; British artist; b. 18 May 1936, Weymouth, Dorset; s. of Charles E. Sandle and Dorothy G. (née Vernon) Sandle; m. 1st Cynthia D. Koppel 1971 (divorced 1974); m. 2nd Demelza Spargo 1988; one s. one d.; ed. Douglas High School, Isle of Man, Douglas School of Art and Tech. and Slade School of Fine Art; studied lithography, Atelier Patris, Paris 1960; began sculpture 1962; held various teaching posts in U.K. 1961–70 including Leicester and Coventry Colls. of Art; resident in Canada 1970–73; Visiting Prof. Univ. of Calgary 1970–71; Visiting Assoc. Prof. Univ. of Victoria, B.C. 1972–73; Lecturer in Sculpture, Fachhochschule für Gestaltung, Pforzheim, Fed. Germany 1973–77, Prof. 1977–80; Prof. Akad. der Bildenden Künste, Karlsruhe 1980–; resgnd. from R.A. 1997; various exhbns. in U.K. and internationally since 1957 including V. Biennale, Paris 1966, Documenta IV, Kassel 1968, Documenta VI 1977, Whitechapel Art Gallery, London 1988, Württembergischer Kunstverein, Stuttgart 1989, Ernst Múzeum, Budapest 1990, Henry Hering Memorial Medal, Nat. Sculpture Soc. of America 1995; works in many public collections in U.K., Germany, Australia, U.S.A. etc. *Address:* Schloss Scheibenhardt, 76135 Karlsruhe, Germany. *Telephone:* Karlsruhe 86 86 33.

SANDLER, Adam; American actor and screenwriter; b. 1964; ed. New York Univ. *Films include:* Shakes the Clown, Coneheads, Mixed Nuts, Airheads, Billy Madison, Happy Gilmore, Bullet Proof, Guy Gets Kid 1998, The Wedding Singer 1998, The Water Boy 1998; actor, writer Saturday Night Live. *Television appearances include:* Saturday Night Live Mother's Day Special 1992, MTV Music Video Awards 1994, Saturday Night Live Presents Pres. Bill Clinton's All-Time Favorites 1994, The 37th Annual Grammy Awards 1995, The ESPY Awards 1996. *Screenplays:* (co-writer) Billy Madison, Happy Gilmore, The Water Boy; recorded album They're All Gonna Laugh at You! 1993. *Address:* c/o Ballstein-Grey, 9150 Wilshire Boulevard, Suite 350, Beverly Hills, CA 90212, U.S.A.

SANDLER, Ron, M.B.A.; South African financial executive; b. 5 March 1952, Durban, South Africa; s. of Bernard M. Sandler and Carla Sandler; m. Susan Lee 1977; two s.; ed. Queens' Coll. Cambridge, Stanford Univ., U.S.A.; ran L.A. office of Boston Consulting, U.S.A., then London office of Booz Allen; f. own man. consultancy firm 1988; apptd. Chair. Quadrex Holdings 1990; joined Lloyd's of London 1994, Chief Exec. 1995–. *Address:* 5 Southside, Wimbledon, London, SW19 4TG, England. *Telephone:* 0181-946 1179.

SANDMO, Agnar, DR.OECON.; Norwegian economist; b. 9 Jan. 1938, Tønsberg; m. Tone Sverdrup 1959; two s. one d.; ed. Tønsberg Gymnasium and Norwegian School of Econs. and Business Admin.; Grad. Fellow, Norwegian School of Econs. and Business Admin. 1963–66, Asst. Prof. of Econs. 1966–71, Prof. 1971–, Vice-Rector 1985–87; Visiting Fellow, Catholic Univ. of Louvain 1969–70; Visiting Prof. Univ. of Essex 1975–76; mem. Petroleum Price Bd. 1976–80 and several Govt. bds. and cttees. on social science and gen. research policy; Fellow, Econometric Soc.; mem. Norwegian and Swedish Acads. of Science; Pres. European Econ. Asscn. 1990; Dr. h.c. (Univ. of Oslo) 1997; Order of St. Olav 1997. *Publications:* articles and books on econs. and econ. policy. *Address:* Norwegian School of Economics and Business Administration, Helleveien 30, 5035 Bergen-Sandviken (Office); Øyjordsbotten 28a, 5035 Bergen-Sandviken, Norway (Home). *Telephone:* 55-959000 (Office); 55-256586 (Home).

SANDOVAL, Arturo; Cuban jazz trumpeter; b. 1949, Artemisa; m. Marianela Sandoval; one s.; ed. Nat. School of Art; began trumpet playing aged 12 and made first public appearances in Cuba aged 13; played in group with Chucho Valdez until 1981; formed own group in 1981 and now undertakes annual maj. world tour; festival appearances at Tokyo, Newport, Montreux, Antibes, Chicago, the Hague and the Hollywood Bowl; several record albums.

SANDOVAL IÑIGUEZ, H. E. Cardinal Juan; Mexican ecclesiastic; b. 28 March 1933, Yahualica, Jalisco; s. of Esteban Sandoval and María Guadalupe Iñiguez; ed. Seminario Diocesano de Guadalajara, Pontifica Universidad Gregoriana; ordained as a Catholic priest 1957; teacher Seminario de Guadalajara 1961, Prof. of Philosophy, Vice-Rector 1971, Rector 1980; Bishop's Coadjutor, Juarez 1988, Bishop of Juarez 1992; Archbishop of Guadalajara 1994; cr. Cardinal 1994; mem. IV Latin American Archbishop's Conference, Santo Domingo 1992. *Address:* Arzobispado, Liceo 17, Apdo. 1-331, 44100 Guadalajara, México. *Telephone:* (3) 614-5504. *Fax:* (3) 658-2300.

SANDRE, Didier (Didier de Maffre); French actor; b. 17 Aug. 1946, Paris; s. of Pierre Maffre and Geneviève Gevril; one d.; m. 2nd Nada Stranlar 1990; ed. Lycée d'Enghien-les-Bains, Collège Estienne, Paris; stage roles include: Lulu, Dom Juan, La Tempête, Le Conte d'hiver, Phèdre, L'Ecole des Femmes, Le Misanthrope, Tartuffe, Les Paravents, Fausse Suivante, Terre Etrangère, L'Illusion comique, Martyr de Saint-Sébastien, Madame de Sade, Le Mariage de Figaro, Le Soulier de Satin, Ivanov, Le Chemin Solitaire, Partage de midi. *Films include:* Mensonge 1993, Train d'enfer, La Femme de ma vie, Petits arrangements avec les morts 1995; Chevalier des Arts et des Lettres; Prix du Syndicat de la Critique 1987, Moliere Prize for Best Actor in An Ideal Husband 1996. *Leisure interests:* piano, skiing, climbing. *Address:* c/o Agents Associe's Guy Bonnet, 201 rue Faubourg St. Honoré, 75008 Paris, France. *Telephone:* 42.56.04.57.

SANDURA, Wilson Runyararo, LL.B.; Zimbabwean barrister; b. 29 July 1941, Shamva; s. of late Fore Sandura and Gilliet Sandura; m. 1st Joyce Alexis Sandura 1972 (divorced 1976); m. 2nd Caroline Elizabeth Sandura 1985; two s.; ed. Mavuradonha Mission, Goromonzhi High School, Morehouse Coll., U.S.A., London Univ., England; joined the Bar, Lincoln's Inn, England; pvt. practice as barrister 1973–80; Regional Magistrate 1980–82; Perm. Sec., Ministry of Justice 1982–83; Judge, High Court 1983–84, Judge Pres. 1984–97, Judge, Supreme Court 1998–. Chair. several comms. 1985, 1989. *Leisure interest:* gardening. *Address:* Supreme Court, P.B. 870, Causeway, Harare, Zimbabwe. *Telephone:* 736 951, 726 314.

SANDVED, Arthur Olav, D.PHIL.; Norwegian professor of English; b. 2 Feb. 1931, New York; s. of Ole Sandved and Ane Aarsland; m. Ruth Øgaard 1953; three d.; ed. Univ. of Oslo; lecturer in English Language, Univ. of Trondheim 1959–63, Univ. of Oslo 1963–71; Reader in English Philology, Univ. of Oslo 1971–74, Prof. of English Language 1974–96; mem. Norwegian Acad, Royal Norwegian Acad. Trondheim. *Publications:* Studies in the Language of Caxton's Malory and that of the Winchester Manuscript 1968, An Advanced English Grammar (with P. Christophersen) 1969, Introduction to Chaucerian English 1985, Vers fra Vest (anthology of Old English verse translated into Norwegian) 1987, Peter Plogmann (extracts from Piers Plowman translated into Norwegian) 1990, Paradise Lost (translated into Norwegian) 1993, trans. King Lear into Norwegian 1995, trans. the three parts of King Henry VI into Norwegian 1996, trans. Henry VIII into Norwegian 1997, Fra "Kremmersprog" til Verdensspråk (history of English studies in Norway 1850–1943) 1998. *Address:* I. F. Gjerdrums vei 74, 1362 Billingstad, Norway. *Telephone:* (66) 84 57 77.

SANÉ, Pierre Gabriel Michel, M.SC.; Senegalese administrator; b. 7 May 1948, Dakar; s. of Nicolas Sané and Thérèse Carvalho; m. Ndeye Coumba Sow, 1981; one s. one d.; ed. Lycée Van Vollenhoven, Dakar, Ecole Supérieure de Commerce de Bordeaux, France, Ecole Nouvelle d'Organisation Economique et Sociale, Paris, London School of Econs., U.K., Carleton Univ., Ottawa, Canada; Vice-Pres. Fédération des Etudiants d'Afrique Noire en France 1971–72; auditor with audit firms in France 1973–77; Deputy Gen. Man. Société Sénégalaise Pharmaceutique (Senepharma) 1977–78; joined Int. Devt. Research Centre (IDRC) 1978, various positions Ottawa, Nairobi and Dakar, to Regional Dir. E. and Southern Africa, Nairobi April–Oct. 1992; Sec.-Gen. Amnesty Int., London Oct. 1992–; mem. Amnesty Int. 1988–; Pres. PANAF 92 1991–92, Founding mem. Int. Cttee.; winner, Concours Nat. de Commercialisation, France 1972. *Publications:* papers and reports on African devt., science and tech. and research man. for IDRC. *Leisure interests:* reading, travelling, music, museums, arts. *Address:* Amnesty International, 1 Easton Street, London, WC1X 8DJ, England. *Telephone:* 0171-413 5500. *Fax:* 0171-956 1157.

SANEJOUAND, Jean Michel, D. EN L.; French painter; b. 18 July 1934, Lyon; s. of Henri Felix Sanejouand and Angêle Fardel; m. Michelle Bourgeois 1957; two s.; ed. Institut d'études politiques, Faculté de Droit, Lyon; self-taught in art; worked as artist, Lyon 1955–59, Paris 1959–93, Vaulandry 1993–; 'charges-objets' (assemblage works) 1963–67, 'organisations d'espaces' (environmental works) 1967–75, 'calligraphies d'humeurs' (calligraphic works on canvas) 1968–77, 'espaces-peintures' (painted and drawn works) 1978–86, black and white paintings 1987–93, sculptures 1988–, colour paintings 1993–96; 'sculptures-peintures' (paintings of sculptures) 1997–; retrospective exhbn. Centre Georges Pompidou, Paris, 1995. *Address:* Belle-Ville, 49150 Vaulandry, France. *Telephone:* 02.41.82.88.71.

SANGER, David John, F.R.A.M., F.R.C.O., A.R.C.M.; British organist; b. 17 April 1947, London; s. of Stanley C. Sanger and Ethel L. F. Sanger; ed. Eltham Coll., London and Royal Acad. of Music; studied organ in Paris with Marie-Claire Alain and later with Susi Jeans 1966–68; First Prize, Int. Organ Competition, St. Albans 1969, since when has been freelance soloist and teacher of organ; has performed throughout Europe and in U.S.A. and Canada; Prof. of Organ, Royal Acad. of Music 1983–; First Prize, Int. Organ Competition, Kiel 1972; has recorded six organ symphonies of Louis Vierne and complete organ works of César Franck. *Publication:* Play the Organ (organ tutor for beginners) 1990. *Leisure interests:* fell-walking, tennis, swimming, photography, choir-training, singing. *Address:* Old Wesleyan Chapel, Embleton, Nr. Cockermouth, Cumbria, CA13 9YA, England. *Telephone:* (017687) 76628. *Fax:* (017687) 76628.

SANGER, Frederick, O.M., C.H., C.B.E., PH.D., F.R.S.; British research biochemist; b. 13 Aug. 1918, Rendcomb, Glos.; s. of Frederick Sanger and Cicely Crewdson; m. Joan Howe 1940; two s. one d.; ed. Bryanston School and St. John's Coll., Cambridge; biochemical research at Cambridge 1940–; Beit Memorial Fellowship 1944–51; mem. Scientific Staff, Medical Research Council 1951–83; retd., Fellow, King's Coll., Cambridge 1954, Hon. Fellow 1983; Hon. Foreign mem. American Acad. of Arts and Sciences 1958; hon. mem. American Soc. of Biological Chemists, Japanese Biochemical Soc.; corresp. mem. Asociación Química de Argentina; mem. Acad. of Science of Argentina and Brazil, World Acad. of Arts and Science, Russell Cttee. against Chemical Weapons 1981–; Foreign Assoc. N.A.S., French Acad. of Sciences; Corday-Morgan Medal and Prize, Chemical Soc. 1951, Nobel Prize for Chemistry 1958 and (jointly) 1980, Alfred Benzon Prize 1966; Royal Medal (Royal Soc.) 1969; Hopkins Memorial Medal 1971; Gairdner Foundation Annual Award 1971, 1979, Hanbury Memorial Medal 1976, William Bate Hardy Prize 1976, Copley Medal 1977, G. W. Wheland Award 1978, Louisa Gross Horwitz Prize 1979, Albert Lasker Basic Medical Research Award, Columbia Univ. (with W. Gilbert, q.v.) 1979, Gold Medal, Royal Soc. of Medicine 1983; Hon. D.Sc. (Leicester, Oxford, Strasbourg, Cambridge 1983). *Publications:* various papers on protein and nucleic acid structure and metabolism in scientific journals. *Leisure interests:* boating, gardening. *Address:* Far Leys, Fen Lane, Swaffham Bulbeck, Cambridge, CB5 0NJ, England (Home). *Telephone:* (01223) 811610.

SANGER, Ruth Ann, PH.D., F.R.S.; British medical research scientist; b. 6 June 1918, Southport, Queensland; d. of Hubert Sanger and Katharine M. Ross (Cameron); m. Robert Russell Race, C.B.E., F.R.C.P., F.R.S. 1956 (died 1984); ed. Abbotsleigh, Sydney and Sydney and London Univs.; mem. of scientific staff, Red Cross Blood Transfusion Service, Sydney 1941–46, Medical Research Council Blood Group Unit, Lister Inst., London 1946–83, Dir. 1973–83; Hon. M.D. (Helsinki) 1990; Karl Landsteiner Award, American Asscn. of Blood Banks (with Dr. R. R. Race) 1957, Philip Levine Award, American Soc. of Clinical Pathologists (with Dr. R. R. Race) 1970, Gairdner Award, Toronto 1972, Oliver Memorial Award 1973. *Publications:* Blood Groups in Man (with Dr. R. R. Race) 1950; many papers on blood groups in medical and scientific journals. *Address:* 22 Vicarage Road, East Sheen, London, SW14 8RU, England. *Telephone:* 0181-876 1508.

SANGHELI, Andrei; Moldovan politician; b. 20 July 1944, Grinautsy, Moldova; m.; one s.; ed. Kishinev Agric. Inst., Kishinev Higher CP School; mem. CPSU 1967–91; agronomist, Deputy Dir., Dir. of collective farms, Moldova 1971–75, Sec. Kamenka Regional CP Cttee. 1975–79, Vice-Chair. Council of Collective Farms of Moldova 1979–80; Chair. Dondushansk Regional Exec. Cttee.; First Sec. Regional CP Cttee. 1980–86; First Deputy-Chair. Council of Ministers, Chair. State Agric.-Industrial Cttee. 1986–89, First Deputy Prime Minister of Moldova; Minister of Agric. and Food 1990–92; Prime Minister of Moldova 1992–96; Chair. Union of Agrarians; now works in agribusiness. *Address:* House of Parliament, Prosp. 105, 277073, Chişinău, Moldova. *Telephone:* (3732) 23 30 92. *Fax:* (3732) 24 26 96.

SANGMA, Shri P.A., M.A., LL.B.; Indian politician and lawyer; b. 1 Sept. 1947, Chapahati Village, West Garo Hills Dist.; m. Soradini K. Sangma 1973; two s. two d.; ed. Dalu High School, St. Anthony's Coll. Shillong and Dibrugarh Univ.; mem. Lok Sabha 1977–79, 1980–84, 1985–89, 1991–; Deputy Minister, Ministry of Industry 1980–82, Ministry of Commerce 1982–85; Minister of State for Commerce 1985–86, for Home Affairs 1986; Minister of State (Independent Charge) for Labour 1986–88; Chief Minister, Meghalaya State 1988–90; Minister of State (Independent Charge) for Coal 1991–95, also for Labour 1993–95; Minister of Information and Broadcasting 1995–96; Speaker Lok Sabha 1996–98; del. to various int. confs.; mem. Congress (I). *Leisure interests:* reading, discussion, music, indoor games. *Address:* Lok Sabha, New Delhi 110001 (Office); Dakopgeri, New Tura P.O., West Garo Hills, Meghalaya, India (Home).

SANGSTER, Robert Edmund; British racehorse owner; b. 23 May 1936; s. of late Vernon Sangster; m. Susan Mary Dean; five s. one d.; ed. Repton Coll.; Chair. Vernons Org. 1980–88, Sangster Group Ltd. 1988–; owner of Derby winners The Minstrel 1977, Golden Fleece 1982; other winners include 2,000 Guineas: Lomond 1983, El Gran Señor 1984, Rodrigo de Triano 1992; 1,000 Guineas: Las Meninas 1994; King George and Queen Elizabeth Stakes: The Minstrel 1977; Ascot Gold Cup: Gildoran 1984, 1985; Irish Derby: The Minstrel 1977, Assert 1982, El Gran Señor 1984, Law Society 1985; Irish 2,000 Guineas: Jaazeiro 1978, King's Lake 1981, Sadlers Wells 1984, Prince of Birds 1988, Rodrigo de Triano 1992, Turtle Island 1994; Irish 1,000 Guineas: Lady Capulet 1977, Godetia 1979; Irish Oaks: Godetia 1979; Irish St. Leger: Transworld 1997, Gonzales 1980, Leading Council 1985, Dark Lomond 1988; French Derby: Assert 1982, Caerleon 1983; French 2,000 Guineas: River Lady 1982; French 1,000 Guineas: Turncoat 1984; Prix de l'Arc de Triomphe: Alleged 1977, 1978, Detroit 1980; Breeder's Cup Mile: Royal Heroine 1984, Royal Academy 1990; Hollywood Derby: Royal Heroine 1983; Melbourne Cup: Beldale Ball 1980; Golden Slipper Stakes: Marauding 1987; Sydney Cup: Marooned 1986. *Leisure interests:* golf, boxing. *Address:* Manton House, Manton House Estate, Marlborough, Wiltshire, SN8 1PN, England.

SANGUINETI, Edoardo; Italian writer; b. 9 Dec. 1930, Genoa; s. of Giovanni Sanguineti and Giuseppina Cocchi; m. Luciana Garabello 1954; three s. one d.; ed. Univ. degli Studi, Turin; Prof. of Italian Literature, Univ. of Salerno 1968–74, Genoa 1974; Town Councillor of Genoa 1976–81; mem. Chamber of Deputies 1979–83. *Publications:* Laborintus 1956, Opus metricum 1960, Interpretazione di Malebolge 1961, Tre studi danteschi 1961, Tra liberty e crepuscolarismo 1961, Alberto Moravia 1962, K. e altre cose 1962, Passaggio 1963, Capriccio italiano 1963, Triperuno 1964, Ideologia e linguaggio 1965, Il realismo di Dante 1966, Guido Gozzano 1966, Il Giuoco dell' Oca 1967, Le Baccanti di Euripide (trans.) 1968, Fedra di Seneca (trans.) 1969, T.A.T. 1969, Teatro 1969, Poesia Italiana del Novecento 1969, Il Giuoco del Satyricon 1970, Orlando Furioso (with L. Ronconi) 1970, Renga (with O. Paz, J. Roubaud, C. Tomlinson) 1971, Storie Naturali 1971, Wirrwarr 1972, Catamerone 1974, Le Troiane di Euripide (trans.) 1974, Giornalino 1976, Postkarten 1978, Le Coefore di Eschilo (trans.) 1978, Giornalino secondo 1979, Stracciafoglio 1980, Edipo tiranno di Sofocle (trans.) 1980, Scartabello 1981, Segnalibro 1982, Alfabeto apocalittico 1984, Scribilli 1985, Faust, un travestimento 1985, Novissimum Testamentum 1986, Smorfie 1986, La missione del critico 1987, Bisbidis 1987, Ghirigori 1988, Commedia dell'Inferno 1989, Lettura del Decameron 1989, Senzatitolo 1992, I Sette contro Tebe di Eschilo (trans.) 1992, Dante reazionario 1992, Gazzettini 1993, Per musica 1993, Satyricon di Petronio (trans.) 1993, Opere e introduzione critica 1993, Malebolge (with E. Baj) 1995, Libretto 1995, Per una critica dell'avanguardia poetica (with J. Burgos) 1995, Tracce (with M. Lucchesi) 1995, Minitarjetas 1996, Orlando Furioso, un travestimento ariostesco 1996, Corollario 1997, Il mio amore è come una febbra (with S. Liberovici) 1998. *Address:* Via Pergolesi 20, 16159 Genoa, Italy. *Telephone:* 010-7452050.

SANGUINETTI, Julio María; Uruguayan politician and lawyer; b. 1936; m. Marta Canessa; one s. one d.; mem. Gen. Ass. 1962–73; Minister of Industry and Labour 1969–72, of Educ. and Culture 1972–73; then Pres. Comisión Nacional de Artes Plásticas and Pres. of UNESCO Comm. for promotion of books in Latin America; Pres. of Uruguay 1985–89, 1995–; Leader (Foro Batllista) Colorado Party 1989–94; Pres. Nat. Fine Arts Council. *Address:* Office of the President, Casa de Gobierno, Edif. Libertad, Avda. Luis Alberto de Herrera 3350, esq. Avda José Pedro Varela, Montevideo, Uruguay. *Telephone:* (2) 472110. *Fax:* (2) 809397.

SANKEY, John Anthony, C.M.G., M.A.; British diplomatist (retd.); b. 8 June 1930, London; m. Gwendoline Putman 1958; two s. two d.; ed. Cardinal Vaughan School, Kensington, Peterhouse, Cambridge, NATO Defence Coll., Rome; Colonial Office 1953, U.K. Mission to UN, New York 1961, First Sec. FCO 1964, Guyana 1968, Singapore 1971, Malta 1973, The Hague 1975, Special Counsellor for African Affairs, FCO 1980–82; High Commr. in Tanzania 1982–85; Perm. Rep. to the UN in Geneva and to GATT 1985–90; Chair. GATT Working Group on trade in domestically prohibited goods 1990; Sec.-Gen. Soc. of London Art Dealers 1991–96; Dir. Int. Art and Antiques Loss Register 1993–96. *Leisure interest:* Victorian sculpture. *Address:* 108 Lancaster Gate, London, W2 3NW, England. *Telephone:* 0171-723 2256.

SANT, Alfred, M.SC., D.B.A.; Maltese politician; b. 28 Feb. 1948; ed. Univ. of Malta, Inst. Int. d'Admin. Publique, Paris, Boston Univ. and Harvard Business School; Second Sec., First Sec. Malta Mission to European Communities, Brussels 1970–75; adviser on gen. and financial man. Ministry of Parastatal and People's Industries, Valletta 1977–78; Man. Dir. Medina Consulting Group 1978–80; Exec. Deputy Chair. Malta Devt. Corpn. 1980–82; consultant to pvt. and public sectors 1982–; Chair. Metal Fond Ltd., Bottex Clothing 1982–84, First Clothing Cooperative 1983–87; lecturer, Man. Faculty, Univ. of Malta 1984–87; Adviser to Prime Minister on econ. and diplomatic affairs 1985–87; Chair. Dept. of Information, Malta Labour Party 1982–92; Pres. Malta Labour Party 1984–88, Leader 1992–; mem. Parl. 1987–; Prime Minister of Malta 1996–98; Leader of the Opposition 1998–. *Publications:* articles in the press and professional publs. *Address:* National Labour Centre, Mile End Road, Hamrun, Malta. *Telephone:* 235312. *Fax:* 240717.

SANTANDER, Teresa, PH.D.; Spanish librarian; b. 11 June 1925, Salamanca; ed. Univ. of Salamanca, PH.D; Instructor in Greek Language, Instituto Nacional de Enseñanza Media "Lucia de Medrano", Salamanca 1949–50; Asst., Archives, Libraries and Museums, Univ. of Salamanca 1955; then mem. of Corps of Professional Archivists, Librarians and Archaeologists 1958; Dir. León Public Library and León Libraries Prov. Co-ordinating Centre 1958–60; Librarian, Univ. of Salamanca 1960–74, Dir. of Library and Archives 1974–90; mem. Centro de Estudios Salmantinos. *Publications:* Indice de médicos españoles (with Luis S. Granjel) 1957, La creación de la cátedra de Cirugía en la Universidad de Salamanca 1965, Cristóbal de Vega en la Universidad de Salamanca 1968, Un manuscrito desconocido de Plotino en Salamanca 1969, Hipócrates en España (16th century) 1971, Nebrija y la imprenta salamantina del Renacimiento 1981, La iglesia de San Nicolás y el antiguo teatro anatómico de la Universidad de Salamanca 1983, Escolares médicos en Salamanca 1984, Reseña sobre la Biblioteca y Archivo Universitarios de Salamanca 1986, Publicaciones periódicas salmantinas existentes en la Biblioteca Universitaria (1793–1981) 1986, Un autógrafo del doctor Francisco López de Villalobos 1987, Incunables de la Biblioteca Universitaria de Salamanca 1990, Antonio Tovar: Bibliografía y recuerdos (1911–1985) 1990, Fuentes para una historia de la Universidad de Salamanca 1990, Aproximación a la biblioteca de don Diego de Covarrubias 1992, El Hospital del Estudio (Asistencia y hospitalidad de la Universidad de Salamanca, 1413–1810) 1993, La imprenta en el siglo XVI 1994. *Address:* Calle de Zamora 44, 1°, 37002 Salamanca, Spain.

SANTELLI, Claude Jean Xavier, L. ÈS L.; French playwright, television director and producer; b. 17 June 1923, Metz, Moselle; s. of late César Santelli and of Elisa Franceschi; m. 1st Olympe Collet 1949 (deceased); m. 2nd Prune Delons 1994; ed. Lycées Montaigne, Louis-le-Grand, Paris, Univ. de Paris; actor in occupied Germany 1944–49; French teacher École pratique de l'Alliance française, Conf. Organizer Union des sciences politiques 1949–55; playwright 1954–, for TV 1956–; producer and presenter, Livre, mon Ami 1958–68, producer Théâtre de la Jeunesse 1960–66; mem. controlling Cttee. Organization de la Radiodiffusion-Télévision Française (O.R.T.F.) 1965–74, Controller of New Year programmes 1964, 1968; mem. Council of Cultural Devt. 1971–73; Pres. Soc. des auteurs et compositeurs dramatiques 1982–84, 1986–88, 1990–92. *Plays include:* le Fantôme (after Plautus) 1954, la Famille Arlequin (prix Molière) 1955, Lope de Vega 1958; producer of first French TV serial le Tour de France par deux enfants 1957–58; Writer and Dir. Lancelot du lac, Producer TV programmes les Cent livres des hommes 1970, la Porte ouverte 1971, la Légende du siècle 1972, Screenplay and Dir. Histoire vraie, Histoire d'une fille de ferme 1973, Madame Baptiste, la Confession d'un enfant du siècle 1974, le Père Amable, Première Neige 1975, Author and Dir. la Vérité de Madame Langlois 1977, la Chaine 1979, le Neveu de Rameau 1980, Jacques le fataliste et son maître

1984; Dir. theatrical production of La tour de Nesle 1986, Les Rideaux 1989; numerous adaptations for children's drama programmes; Officier, Légion d'honneur, Officier, ordre nat. du Mérite, Médaille de la Résistance, Officier, Arts et Lettres. *Address:* 110 boulevard Saint-Germain, 75006 Paris, France (Home).

SANTER, Jacques, D. EN D; Luxembourg politician; b. 18 May 1937, Wasserbillig; m. Danièle Binot; two s.; ed. Athénée de Luxembourg, Univs. of Paris and Strasbourg and Inst. d'Etudes Politiques, Paris; advocate, Luxembourg Court of Appeal 1961–65; attaché, Office of Minister of Labour and Social Security 1963–65; Govt. attaché 1965–66; Parl. Sec. Parti Chrétien-Social 1966–72, Sec.-Gen. 1972–74, Pres. 1974–82; Sec. of State for Cultural and Social Affairs 1972–74; mem. Chamber of Deputies 1974–79; mem. European Parl. 1975–79, Vice-Pres. 1975–77; Municipal Magistrate, City of Luxembourg 1976–79; Minister of Finance, of Labour and of Social Security 1979–84; Prime Minister, Minister of State and Minister of Finance July 1984–89, Prime Minister, Minister of State, of Cultural Affairs and of the Treasury and Financial Affairs 1989–94; Pres. European Comm. 1994–99; has responsibility for common foreign and security policy, monetary matters, institutional questions and inter-governmental conf.; Hon. LL.D. (Wales) 1998. *Leisure interests:* walking, swimming. *Address:* 69 rue J.-P. Huberty, 1742 Luxembourg (Home).

SANTER, Rt. Rev. Mark, M.A.; British ecclesiastic; b. 29 Dec. 1936, Bristol; s. of Rev. Canon E. A. R. Santer and Phyllis C. Barlow; m. 1st Henriette Cornelia Weststrate 1964 (died 1994); m. 2nd Sabine Böhmig Bird 1997; one s. two d.; ed. Marlborough Coll., Queens' Coll. and Westcott House, Cambridge; Curate All Saints Cuddesdon 1963–67; Tutor Cuddesdon Coll., Oxford 1963–67; Dean and Fellow Clare Coll., Cambridge 1967–72; Asst. Lecturer in Divinity, Univ. of Cambridge 1968–72; Principal Westcott House 1973–81; Area Bishop of Kensington 1981–87; Bishop of Birmingham 1987–; Co-Chair. Anglican/R.C. Int. Comm. 1983–99; Hon. Fellow Clare Coll. 1987, Queens' Coll. 1991; Hon. D.D. (Birmingham) 1998. *Publications:* Documents in Early Christian Thought (with M. F. Wiles) 1975, Their Lord and Ours (Ed.) 1982. *Address:* Bishop's Croft, Old Church Road, Harborne, Birmingham, B17 0BG, England. *Telephone:* (0121) 427 1163. *Fax:* (0121) 426 1322.

SANTO CARVALHO, Evaristo do Spirito; São Tomé e Príncipe fmr. politician; Prime Minister of São Tomé and Príncipe July–Oct. 1994; mem. Partido de Convergência Democrática-Grupo de Reflexão (PCD-GR) (expelled from party July 1994). *Address:* c/o Office of the Prime Minister, São Tomé, São Tomé and Príncipe.

SANTORUM, Rick, M.B.A., J.D.; American politician; b. 10 May 1958, Winchester, Va.; s. of Aldo Santorum and Catherine Dughi; m. Karen Garver 1990; two s. two d.; ed. Pennsylvania State Univ., Pennsylvania State Coll., Univ. of Pittsburgh and Dickinson Law School; mem. Bar of Pa. 1986; Admin. Asst. to State Senator Doyle Corman, Harrisburg, Pa. 1981–86; Exec. Dir. Local Govt. Cttee. Pa. State Senate 1981–84, Transport Cttee. 1984–86; Assoc. Attorney, Kirkpatrick and Lockhart, Pittsburgh 1986–90; mem. 102–103rd Congresses from 18th Pa. Dist. 1991–95; Senator from Pennsylvania Jan. 1995–; Republican. *Leisure interests:* golf, cross country skiing, racquet sports. *Address:* U.S. Senate, 120 Russell Senate Office Bldg., Washington 20510; 127 Seminole Drive, Pittsburgh, Pa. 15228, U.S.A. (Home).

SANTOS, Corentino Virgilio; Cape Verde banker and diplomatist; b. 12 Dec. 1946, São Vicente; s. of Virgilio Santos and Joseph Ana Ramos; one s. one d.; ed. Technical Univ. of Lisbon, Portugal; served as Sr. Technician on Industrial Economy, Office of Sec. of State for Industry; apptd. Under-Sec. for Finance during transition to independence of Cape Verde 1974; Gov. Bank of Cape Verde 1975–84; Perm. Rep. to UN 1984–87; Econ. Dir. IMF 1990–95. *Publication:* study on financial structures of Portuguese industry (co-author) 1973. *Leisure interests:* reading, sport. *Address:* c/o Ministry of Foreign Affairs, Praça Dr Lorena, Praia, Santiago, Cape Verde.

SAOUMA, Edouard; Lebanese international official and agricultural engineer; b. 6 Nov. 1926, Beirut; m. Inès Forero; one s. two d.; ed. St. Joseph's Univ. School of Eng., Beirut, Ecole nat. Supérieure d'Agronomie, Montpellier, France; Dir. Tel Amara Agricultural School 1952–53, Nat. Centre for Farm Mechanization 1954–55; Sec.-Gen. Nat. Fed. of Lebanese Agronomists 1955; Dir.-Gen. Nat. Inst. for Agricultural Research 1957–62; mem. Governing Board, Nat. Grains Office 1960–62; Lebanese del. to FAO 1955–62, Deputy Regional Rep. for Asia and Far East 1962–65, mem. of Secr. 1963–, Dir. Land and Water Devt. Div. 1965–75, Dir.-Gen. of FAO 1976–93; Minister of Agric., Fisheries and Forestry Oct.–Nov. 1970; Hon. Prof. of Agronomy, Agric. Univ. of Beijing; Accademico Corrispondente dell' Accademia Nazionale di Agricoltura (Italy); Dr. h.c. from 16 univs.; Order of the Cedar (Lebanon), Said Akl Prize (Lebanon); Chevalier du Mérite agricole (France), Grand Croix, Ordre nat. du Tchad, du Ghana, de la Haute Volta (Burkina Faso), Gran Cruz al Mérito Agrícola (Spain), Kt. Commdr. Order of Merit (Greece), Orden del Mérito Agrícola (Colombia), Gran Oficial del Orden de Vasco Núñez de Balboa (Panama), Orden al Mérito Agrícola (Peru), Order of Merit (Egypt, Mauritania), Grand Officier, Ordre de la République (Tunisia), Grand Officier, Ordre Nat. (Madagascar). *Publications:* technical publs. in agriculture. *Address:* P.O. Box H0210, Baabda, Lebanon.

SAPIN, Michel; French politician; b. 9 April 1952, Boulogne-Billancourt; m. Yolande Millan 1982; three c.; ed. Inst. d'Etudes Politiques, Paris and Ecole Nat. d'Admin.; joined Parti Socialiste 1975; elected Deputy to Nat. Ass. 1981, Vice-Pres. 1984, Pres. Legal Comm. 1988; town councillor, Nanterre 1989–94; Minister Del. and Keeper of the Seals, Ministry of Justice 1991; Minister of Finance 1992–93; regional councillor lle de France 1992–94; mem. Council Banque de France 1994–95; Mayor of Argenton-sur-Creuse 1995–; Gen. Councillor l'lndre 1998–; Pres. Centre Regional Council 1998–. *Address:* Mairie, 69 rue Auclert Descottes, 36200 Argenton-sur-Creuse; Conseil régional du Centre, 5 rue Saint-Pierre Lentin, 45041 Orléans cedex 01 (Office); 7 rue Dupertuis, 36200 Argenton-sur-Creuse, France (Home).

SAPORTA, Marc, LL.D.; French writer; b. 20 March 1923; s. of Jaime Saporta and Simone Nahmias; m. 1st Denise Kleman 1949 (died 1966); m. 2nd Michèle Truchan; three d.; ed. Univs. of Paris and Madrid; worked in Dept. of Cultural Activities UNESCO 1948–53, Asst. Ed. Informations et Documents 1954–71, Ed. 1971–78; Ed.-in-Chief Dept. of Publs. U.S. Information Agency (Paris) 1978–84; Literary Critic L'Express 1954–71, La Quinzaine Littéraire 1966–71. *Publications:* Les lois de l'air 1953, La convention universelle du droit d'auteur de l'UNESCO 1952, Le grand défi: U.S.A.-U.R.S.S., I 1967, II 1968 (Ed. and Co-Author), Histoire du roman américain 1970, La vie quotidienne contemporaine aux U.S.A. 1972, Go West 1976, William Faulkner (Ed. and jt. author) 1983, Henry James (Ed. and jt. author) 1983, I. B. Singer (Ed. and jt. author) 1984, Nathalie Sarraute (Ed. and jt. author) 1984, Marguerite Duras (Ed. and jt. author) 1985, Vivre aux Etats-Unis 1986, André Breton ou le Surréalisme Même (Ed. and Co-Author) 1988, Israel 1988, Les Erres du Faucon, une Psychobiographie de William Faulkner 1989, Le Roman américain 1997; novels: Le furet 1959, La distribution 1961, La quête 1961, Composition numéro un 1962, Les invités 1964. *Leisure interest:* ice-skating. *Address:* 9 rue Saint-Didier, 75116 Paris, France.

SARABHAI, Mrinalini; Indian dancer and choreographer; b. 11 May 1918, Madras; d. of Shri Swaminadhan and Smt. Ammu Swaminadhan; m. Dr. Vikram A. Sarabhai; one s. one d.; studied under Meenakshi Sundaram Pillai; founder/Dir. Darpana Acad. of Performing Arts, Ahmedabad 1949; Chair. Handicrafts & Handloom Devt. Corpn. of Gujarat State; Chair. Friends of Trees, Gujarat State; mem. Sangeet Natak Acad., New Delhi; Hon. Consultant, Nat. Centre for Performing Arts, Bombay; Pres. Alliance Française; Exec. Cttee. Int. Dance Council 1990; adviser to many arts and cultural insts. in India; Fellow Sangeet Natak Akademi 1994; Vishwa Gurjari Award 1984; Deshikothama Award (Vishwa Bharati Univ. Shantiniketan) 1987, Fellowship Award Kerala Acad. of Arts 1990, Honor Summus Award (Watumull Foundation) 1991, First Hall of Fame Award for lifelong service to dance 1991, Vijay Shri Award (Int. Friendship Soc. of India) 1991, Pandit Omkarnath Thakur Award (Gujarat Govt.) 1991, Pres.'s Award of Padmabhushan 1992, Raseshwar Award 1992, Scroll of Honour for her work in dance and choreography 1995, Kalidas Samman Award 1996, Kerala Kalamandalam Fellowship 1995. *Leisure interests:* reading, watching TV, writing, dancing, social work. *Publications:* Staging a Sanskrit Classic—Bhasa's Vision of Vasavadatta (with John D. Mitchell) 1992, one novel, textbook on Bharata Natyam, a book on various classical dance-dramas, children's books and articles in newspapers and journals. *Address:* Darpana Academy of Performing Arts, Usmanpura, Ahmedabad 380013, Gujarat, India. *Telephone:* 445189.

SARAH, Peter John, O.A.M., M.PHIL., L.R.A.M., A.R.C.M., A.MUS.A., F.R.S.A.; Australian arts administrator; b. 7 Aug. 1946, W. Australia; s. of Rimmington V. Sarah and Jean Ada Price Sarah; ed. Scotch Coll. Perth, Univ. of W. Australia and Univ. of London; Asst. Dir. (Touring and Devt.), Western Australian Arts Council 1977–81; Gen. Man. Arts Council of S. Australia 1981–85; Dir. Arts and Entertainment, Australian Bicentennial Authority 1985–89; Chief Exec. Contemporary Dance Trust 1990–94; Chief Exec. The Year of Opera and Music Theatre 1995–97; Gen. Man. Theatre Royal, Newcastle upon Tyne 1998–; Trustee Acad. of Indian Dance. *Leisure interests:* sailing, architecture. *Address:* 10 Mall Chambers, Kensington Mall, London, W8 4DY, England.

SARAIVA GUERREIRO, Ramiro Elysio; Brazilian diplomatist; b. Salvador; s. of José Affonso Guerreiro and Esther Saraiva Guerreiro; m. Gloria Vallim Guerreiro 1947; one s. one d.; ed. Univ. of Brazil and Rio Branco Inst. (Diplomatic Acad.); Foreign Service 1945; Brazilian Mission to UN 1946–69; Embassies, La Paz 1950–51, Washington 1956–58; Minister-Counsellor, Montevideo 1966–67, deputy del. to Meeting of Chiefs of American States 1967; del. Emergency Special Session of UN Gen. Ass. 1967; Asst. Sec.-Gen. of Int. Orgs., Ministry of Foreign Affairs 1967–79; mem. del. to numerous UN Gen. Assemblies; Under Sec.-Gen. of External Policy 1969; Rep. at meetings of Comm. of Sea Bed and Ocean Floor 1969–72; Chief of del. UN Conf. on Law of the Sea 1968–77, 26th Session of GATT 1970, Geneva 1970–74, Disarmament Cttee. 1970–74, Chief of Section of Brazilian-German Cttee. on Econ. Co-operation and Science and Tech. 1974, 1975, 1977; Amb. to France 1978–79; Minister of Foreign Affairs 1979–85; Chief of Dels. to 24th–28th UN Gen. Assemblies 1979–83; mem. Geographical Soc. (Rio de Janeiro), American Soc. of Int. Law, Brazilian Soc. of Air Law, Argentine Council for Int. Relations. *Leisure interests:* reading, golf. *Address:* c/o Ministério das Relações Exteriores, Esplanada dos Ministérios 70170, Brasília, DF, Brazil.

SARAMAGO, José; Portuguese author and poet; b. 16 Nov. 1922, Azinhaga; m. Pilar del Rio; one c.; Grinzane Cavour Prize, Mondello Prize, Flaiano

Prize, Ind. Prize, Luís de Camões Prize, Nobel Prize for Literature 1998. *Publications include:* (novels) Manual de pintura e caligrafia 1976, Objecto quase 1978, Levantado do chão 1980, Memorial do convento 1982, O ano da morte de Ricardo Reis 1984, A jangada de pedra 1986, História do Cerco de Lisboa 1989, O Evangelho Segundo Jesus Cristo 1991, Eusaio sobre a Cegueira 1995; (poetry) Os poemas possíveis 1966, Provavelmente Alegria 1970, O ano de 1993 1975; (plays) A noite 1979, Que farei com este livro? 1980, A segunda vida de Francisco de Assisi 1987, In Nomine Dei 1993; (opera libretto) Blimunda 1990, Divara 1993; (other writing) Deste mundo e do outro 1971, A bagagem do viajante 1973, O embargo 1973, Os opiniões que o D.L. teve 1974, Os apontamentos 1976, Viagem a Portugal 1981, Cadernos de Lanzarote 1994–96, O poeta perguntador (ed.) 1979. *Address:* Los Topes 3, 35572 Tias Lanzarote, Canaries, Spain; Ray-Güde Mertin, 1 Friedrichstrasse, 61348 Bad Hamburg 1, Germany.

SARANDON, Susan Abigail; American actress; b. 4 Oct. 1946, New York; d. of Philip Tomalin and Lenora Criscione; m. Chris Sarandon 1967 (divorced 1979); one d. with Franco Amurri; two s. with Tim Robbins (q.v.); ed. Catholic Univ. of America; stage appearances include A Coupla White Chicks Sittin' Around Talkin', An Evening with Richard Nixon, A Stroll in the Air, Albert's Bridge, Private Ear, Public Eye, Extremities, numerous TV appearances. *Films include:* Joe 1970, Lady Liberty 1971, The Rocky Horror Picture Show 1974, Lovin' Molly 1974, The Great Waldo Pepper 1975, The Front Page 1976, Dragon Fly 1976, Walk Away Madden, The Other Side of Midnight 1977, The Last of the Cowboys 1977, Pretty Baby 1978, King of the Gypsies 1978, Loving Couples 1980, Atlantic City 1981, Tempest 1982, The Hunger 1983, Buddy System 1984, Compromising Positions 1985, The Witches of Eastwick 1987, Bull Durham 1988, Sweet Hearts Dance 1988, Married to the Mob, A Dry White Season 1989, The January Man 1989, White Palace, Thelma and Louise 1991, Light Sleeper 1991, Lorenzo's Oil, The Client, Little Women 1995, Safe Passage 1995, Dead Man Walking (Acad. Award for Best Actress 1996) 1996, James and the Giant Peach 1996, Illuminata 1998, Twilight 1998, Stepmom 1999. *Address:* c/o ICM, Martha Luttrell, 8942 Wilshire Boulevard, Beverly Hills, CA 90211, U.S.A.

SARASIN, Arsa; Thai diplomatist; b. 1936; s. of Pote Sarasin (former Prime Minister of Thailand, q.v.); ed. Boston Univ.; Perm. Sec. Ministry of Foreign Affairs until 1986; Amb. to U.S.A. 1986–88; Minister of Foreign Affairs 1991–92. *Address:* c/o Ministry of Foreign Affairs, Saranrom Palace, Bangkok 10200, Thailand.

SARASIN, Pote; Thai politician, lawyer and international administrator; b. 25 March 1907, Bangkok; m.; five s. one d.; ed. Wilbraham Acad., Mass., and Middle Temple, London; practised law in Thailand 1933–45; mem. Senate 1948–50; Deputy Minister of Foreign Affairs 1948, Minister of Foreign Affairs 1948–50; rep. Thailand on UN Korea Comm. 1950; Amb. to U.S.A. 1952–57; Del. to UN 1952–55; Prime Minister 1957–58; Sec.-Gen. SEATO 1957–63; Minister of Econ. Affairs and Nat. Devt., Thailand 1963–68; Minister of Econ. Affairs 1968–69; Vice-Chair. United Thai People's Party 1968; Deputy Prime Minister and Minister of Nat. Devt. 1969–71; mem. Nat. Exec. Council and Dir. Econ., Finance and Industry Affairs 1971–72; mem. Thai Bar Assn. *Address:* Saha-Pracha-Thai, 1/226, Sri Ayudhya, Dusit, Bangkok, Thailand.

SARASTE, Jukka-Pekka; Finnish conductor; b. 22 April 1956, Heinola; m. Marja-Lisa Ollila; three s. one d.; Prin. Conductor Finnish Radio Symphony Orchestra 1987–; Music Dir. Toronto Symphony Orchestra Sept. 1994–; has been guest conductor with Boston Symphony Orchestra, Cleveland Orchestra, San Francisco Orchestra, Frankfurt Radio Orchestra, N.Y. Philharmonic Orchestra; has toured Japan, Hong Kong, Taiwan, Germany, U.S.A., Canary Islands Festival; Artistic Adviser Finnish Chamber Orchestra. *Recordings include:* complete Sibelius symphonies 1995 (with Finnish Radio Symphony Orchestra) Mussorgsky (with Toronto Symphony Orchestra), Nielsen Symphonies 4 and 5 (with Finnish Radio Symphony Orchestra). *Address:* c/o Van Walsum Management Ltd., 26 Wadham Road, London, SW15 2LR, England. *Telephone:* 0181-874 6344. *Fax:* 0181-877 0077.

SARBANES, Paul Spyros, B.A., LL.B.; American politician and lawyer; b. 3 Feb. 1933, Salisbury, Md.; s. of Spyros P. and Matina (née Tsigounis) Sarbanes; m. Christine Dunbar 1960; two s. one d.; ed. Princeton Univ., Balliol Coll., Oxford, Harvard Law School; Rhodes Scholar, Balliol Coll., Oxford 1954–57; admitted to Maryland Bar 1960; Law Clerk to Circuit Judge 1960–61; Assoc., Piper and Marbury, Baltimore 1961–62; Admin. Asst. to Chair. Council of Econ. Advisers 1962–63; Exec. Dir. Charter Revision Comm., Baltimore 1963–64; Assoc., Venable, Baetjer & Howard, Baltimore 1965–70; mem. Md. House of Dels. 1967–71, U.S. House of Reps. 1971–76, Senator from Maryland Jan. 1977–; Democrat. *Address:* United States Senate, 309 Hart Senate Building, Washington, DC 20510; Tower 1, Suite 1010, 100 South Charles Street, Baltimore, MD 21201, U.S.A.

SARCINELLI, Mario; Italian banker and economist; b. 9 March 1934, Foggia; ed. Univ. of Pavia, Univ. of Cambridge; joined Bank of Italy 1957, fmr. Head Data Processing and Information Systems Dept., Cen. Man. for Banking Supervision 1976, Deputy Dir.-Gen. 1976; Econ. Adviser to Italian Del. to UN 1960; Dir.-Gen. Treasury 1982-91; Minister of Foreign Trade April–July 1987; Vice-Pres. EBRD 1991–94; Chair. Monetary Cttee. 1989–90, Banca Nazionale del Lavoro S.p.A. 1994–98; fmr. Chair., numerous public orgs.; alt. mem. EEC Cttee. of Govs. of Cen. Banks 1978–81, Bd. Dirs. BIS 1978–81; fmr. bd. mem. numerous orgs. *Address:* c/o Banca Nazionale del Lavoro S.p.A., Via V. Veneto 119, Rome, Italy.

SARDANIS, Andreas Sotiris; Zambian company director; b. 13 March 1931, Cyprus; m. Danae Gavas 1962; two s.; ed. in Cyprus; emigrated to Zambia 1950; managerial posts in trading and transport undertakings 1950–65; Chair. and Man. Dir. Industrial Devt. Corpn. 1965–70; Perm. Sec. Ministry of Commerce, Industry and Foreign Trade 1968; later Perm. Sec. Ministry of Trade, Industry and Mines, and Perm. Sec. Ministry of Devt. and Finance; Man. Dir. Zambia Industrial and Mining Corpn. Ltd. (ZIMCO) and Chair. of its subsidiaries, Indeco Ltd, and Mindeco Ltd. 1970–71; Perm. Sec., Ministry of State Participation April–Dec. 1970; Man. Dir. Sardanis Assocs. 1971–76; Chair. ITM Int. S.A. 1976–. *Address:* Chaminuka, P.O. Box 32946, Lusaka, Zambia. *Telephone:* 261661.

SARDENBERG, Ronaldo Mota; Brazilian diplomatist; b. 8 Oct. 1940, São Paulo; m.; four c.; ed. Univ. of Brazil Law School; joined External Relations Ministry 1964, Adviser, Econ., Tech. and Commodities Div. 1964–67, mem. staff Embassy in Washington, D.C. 1967–70, mem. staff Perm. Mission to UN, New York 1970–74, Political Adviser in Multilateral and Afro-Asian Affairs 1974–76, Co-ordinator of Policy Planning 1976–78, Special Sec. for Political and Econ. Affairs, Int. Bilateral Area then Head Policy Planning team 1978–82, apptd. Chargé d'Affaires, Embassy in Moscow 1982, rank of Amb. 1983, Amb. to U.S.S.R. 1985–89, to Spain 1989–90; Perm. Rep. to UN 1990–95. *Address:* c/o Ministry of Foreign Affairs, Palácio de Itamaraty, Esplanada dos Ministérios, 70170 Brasília, DF, Brazil.

SAREI, Sir Alexis Holyweek, Kt., C.B.E., J.C.D.; Papua New Guinea diplomatist and ecclesiastic; b. 25 March 1934, Buka, N. Solomons; s. of Joseph Nambong and Antonina Mota; m. Claire Dionne 1972; three s. four d. (all adopted); ed. Univ.; Roman Catholic Priest 1966–71; Pvt. Sec. to Chief Minister 1972–73; Dist. Commr. 1973–75; Warden, Univ. of Papua New Guinea 1972; Premier, N. Solomons Prov. Govt. 1976–80, 1984–87; High Commr. in U.K. (also Amb. to other European and Middle Eastern countries) 1980–83; started village co-operative 1984; Chair. of Peit Community Govt. 1988–90; Papua New Guinea Independence Medal; succeeded uncle as Chief of Petisuun Clan. *Publication:* The Practice of Marriage Among the Solos 1974. *Leisure interests:* golf, psychology, painting. *Address:* 8039 Adoree Street, Downey, CA 90242-4263, U.S.A. *Telephone:* 562-869-1264. *Fax:* 562-869-1684.

SARFATI, Alain; French architect and town-planner; b. 23 March 1937, Meknès, Morocco; s. of Maurice Sarfati and Sarah Levy de Valencia; two d.; ed. Lycée Poeymirau, Meknès, Lycée Laknal, Sceaux, Ecole des Beaux Arts, Paris and Inst. d'Urbanisme, Univ. de Paris; town planner, Inst. d'Urbanisme, Paris region 1966; founder of review A.M.C. and Atelier de Recherche et d'Etudes d'Amènagement (AREA) 1967; Prof. of Architecture, Nancy 1969; Prof. and Head of Dept. Ecole des Beaux Arts, Paris-Conflans 1979–; architectural adviser, Ministère de l'Equipement, de l'Urbanisme, du Logement et des Transports 1985–; Vice-Pres. of Construction Planning, Ministère de l'Equipement, du Logement des Transports et de la Mer 1988; mem. consultative cttee. Centre Scientifique et Technique du Bâtiment 1990–; Vice-Pres. Ordre Nat. des Architectes 1992; work includes housing, schools, hospitals, leisure centres and Centre des Archives du Monde du Travail, Roubaix 1993; Chevalier, Ordre du Mérite, Officier des Arts et des Lettres. *Address:* 28 rue Barbet de Jouy, 75007 Paris (Office); 79 rue du Cherche-Midi, 75006 Paris, France (Home). *Telephone:* 45.50.34.10 (Office); 45.44.44.38 (Home).

SARGENT, John Turner; American publisher; b. 26 June 1924; m. 1st Neltje Doubleday 1953 (divorced); one s. one d.; m. 2nd Elizabeth Nichols Kelly 1985; Doubleday and Co. Inc., Ed. 1949–50, Advertising and Publicity, Trade Sales man. 1950–60, Vice-Pres. and Dir. 1960–61, Pres. 1961–78, Chair. Bd. 1978; Dir. Grumman Corpn., Atlantic Mutual Cos.; Trustee East River Savings Bank, New York Public Library, New York Zoological Soc., American Acad. in Rome, Kips Bay Boys Club, Alger Fund, Castle Convertible Fund. *Address:* Halsey Lane, Watermill, NY 11976, U.S.A. (Home).

SARGENT, Wallace Leslie William, PH.D., F.R.S.; British astronomer; b. 15 Feb. 1935, Elsham, Lincs.; s. of Leslie and Eleanor Sargent; m. Anneila I. Cassells 1964; two d.; ed. Scunthorpe Tech. High School and Manchester Univ.; Research Fellow in Astronomy, Calif. Inst. of Tech. 1959–62; Senior Research Fellow, Royal Greenwich Observatory 1962–64; Asst. Prof. of Physics, Univ. of Calif., San Diego 1964-66; Asst. Prof. of Astronomy, Calif. Inst. of Tech. 1966–68, Assoc. Prof. 1968—71. Prof. 1971–81, Exec. Officer for Astronomy 1975–81, Ira S. Bowen Prof. of Astronomy 1981–, Dir. Palomar Observatory 1997–; Fellow, American Acad. of Arts and Sciences; Alfred P. Sloan Foundation Fellow 1968–70; George Darwin Lecturer, Royal Astronomical Soc. 1987; Assoc. Royal Astronomical Soc. 1998; Thomas Gold Lecturer, Cornell Univ. 1995; Sackler Lecturer, Harvard Univ. 1995; Sackler Lecturer, Univ. of Calif. Berkeley 1996; Helen B. Warner Prize, American Astronomical Soc. 1969, Dannie Heineman Prize, American Astronomical Soc. 1991, Bruce Gold Medal, Astronomical Soc. of the Pacific 1994. *Publications:* numerous papers in scientific journals. *Leisure interests:* reading, gardening, watching sports, oriental rugs. *Address:* Department of Astronomy 105–24, California Institute of Technology, Pasadena, CA 91125 (Office); 400 South Berkeley Avenue, Pasadena, CA 91107, U.S.A. (Home). *Telephone:* (626) 356-4055 (Office); (626) 795-6345 (Home). *Fax:* (626) 568-9352.

SARGESON, Alan McLeod, PH.D., F.A.A., F.R.S.; Australian professor of inorganic chemistry; b. 13 Oct. 1930, Armidale, N.S.W.; s. of Herbert L. Sargeson and Alice McLeod; m. Marietta Anders 1959; two s. two d.; ed. Maitland Boys' High School and Univ. of Sydney; Lecturer, Dept. of Chem., Univ. of Adelaide 1956–57; Research Fellow, John Curtin School of Medical Research, A.N.U. 1958; Fellow, A.N.U. 1960, Sr. Fellow, Research School of Chem. 1967, Professorial Fellow 1968–78, Prof. 1978–96, Dean 1986–88, Prof. Emer. 1996–; Foreign mem. Royal Danish Acad. of Arts and Sciences, American Acad. of Arts and Sciences; Foreign Assoc. N.A.S.; Hon. D.Sc. (Sydney, Copenhagen, Bordeaux). *Leisure interests:* swimming, music, cycling, walking, literature. *Address:* Department of Chemistry, The Faculties, Australian National University, Canberra, A.C.T. 0200, Australia. *Telephone:* (6) 249 3160. *Fax:* (6) 249 0760.

ŠARINIĆ, Hrvoje; Croatian politician; b. 17 Feb. 1935, Rijeka; ed. Inst. of Civil Eng., Zagreb Univ.; worked in France as head of construction co.; gen. rep. of French nuclear industry in France; Gen. Man. Yugoslav Co. CITRAM in Morocco; Head of Admin. to Pres. of Croatia 1991–92, 1993–; Prime Minister 1992; mem. Croatian Democratic Union (CDU). *Address:* c/o Office of the President, Nazorova 59, 41000 Zagreb, Croatia.

SARKISIAN, Sos Artashesovich; Armenian actor; b. 24 Oct. 1929, Armenia; ed. Yerevan Theatre Inst.; acted with Sundukian Theatre 1954–; acted in films 1960–; People's Artist of Armenian S.S.R. 1972, Armenian State Prize for work in the theatre 1979, People's Artist of U.S.S.R. 1985; U.S.S.R. People's Deputy 1989–91. *Roles include:* Mkrtych in The Triangle (Armenian State Prize 1975), Gibaryanin, Solaris 1973, Amboin, Gikor 1982. *Address:* Sundukian Theatre, Abovyan Str. 35, Yerevan, Armenia.

SARKISOV, Aleksander Aleksandrovich, DR. TECH. SC.; Russian aviation engineer, b. 19 May 1936; ed. Ufa Inst. of Aviation; engineer, Ufa Experimental Construction Bureau SOYUZ, U.S.S.R. Ministry of Aviation 1959–72; Deputy Chief Constructor, Deputy Dir. 1972–83; Deputy Head, chief engineer, First Deputy Head, Dept. of Experimental Construction of Aircraft Engines, Ministry of Aviation Industry 1984–86; Gen. Constructor, Dir. Klimov factory 1988–91; Chair. Bd. Dirs. MTA Corpn.; Pres. Klimov Corpn.; Chair. Jt. Venture Pratt-Whitney-Klimov 1991–; sr. mem., American Inst. of Aviation and Astronautics; mem. Russian Acad. of Transport, Acad of Eng., Acad. of Aviation; Lenin Prize, Lawrence Prize, Prize of Zhukovsky Acad. of Transport 1994. *Leisure interests:* history, art, architecture.

SARKISOV, Ashot Arakelovich; Russian nuclear energy specialist; b. 30 Jan. 1924, Tashkent, U.S.S.R.; s. of Arakel A. Sarkisov and Evgeniya B. Grigoryan; m. Nelli G. Sarkisov 1951; two s.; ed. F. Dzerzhinsky Higher Marine Eng. School, Leningrad Univ.; worked as engineer Baltic fleet; Chair. Higher Marine School, Sevastopol; Deputy Dir. Naval Acad.; Chair. Scientific-Tech. Council of the Navy; Head of Dept., Inst. for Nuclear Safety; corresp. mem. U.S.S.R. (now Russian) Acad. of Sciences 1981, mem. 1994, Counsellor 1996; research in theory of dynamic processes and automatic protection of nuclear plants, problems of safety and security in nuclear energy. *Publications include:* Dynamics of Nuclear Power Plants of Submarines 1964, Nuclear Propulsion Power Plants 1968, Dynamic Regimes in the Operation of Nuclear Propulsion Power Plants 1971, Physics of Transitional Processes in Nuclear Reactors 1983, Nuclear Propulsion Power Plants and Steam Generators 1985, Thermo-Electric Generators with Nuclear Sources of Heat 1987, Physical Principles of Nuclear Steam-Productive Plants 1989. *Leisure interests:* tennis, history of the Navy. *Address:* Institute for Nuclear Safety, B. Tulskaya str. 52, 113191 Moscow, Russia. *Telephone:* (095) 958-1459 (Office). *Fax:* (095) 958 0040.

SARKISOV, Donat Semenovich, DR. MED. SC.; Russian physician; b. 6 Sept. 1924, Moscow; m.; one d.; ed. Mil. Navy Acad. of Medicine; Head Div. of Pathological Anatomy, Vishnevsky Inst. of Surgery 1958–; mem. Presidium Russian Acad. of Medical Sciences, Chief Scientific Sec. 1995–; Merited Worker of Science of Russian Fed.; State Prizes 1991, 1996; mem. Int. Acad. of Pathology. *Publications:* over 300 scientific works and over 20 books including monographs: Electron-Microscopic Radioautography of Cell 1980, Essays on History of General Pathology 1992, New Ways of Using Cultured Fibroblasts to Restore Skin in Patients with Severe Burns 1995, General Pathology of Man 1996. *Address:* Russian Academy of Medical Sciences, Solyanka str. 14, 109801 Moscow, Russia. *Telephone:* (095) 298 21 44 (Office). *Fax:* (095) 298 21 64.

SARKISYAN, Armen, CAND. PHYSICAL-MATH. SC.; Armenian politician; b. 1953, Yerevan; m.; two s.; ed. Yerevan State Univ.; docent Yerevan State Univ. 1979–84; researcher Cambridge Univ. U.K. 1984–85; lecturer Yerevan State Univ. 1985–90, Head Dept. of Math. Modelling; Prof. London Univ. 1992–; apptd. Chargé d'affairs, then Amb. Repub. of Armenia to U.K. 1992–; Amb., doyen of Armenian Diplomatic Corps to Europe (also accred. to Belgium, Netherlands, Vatican, Luxembourg) 1993–96; mem. London Int. Inst. of Strategic Studies; Hon. Mem. Royal Soc. of Int. Relations and Cen. of Strategic Studies, Oxford Univ.; author of numerous articles on politology, theoretical physics, astronomy and math. modelling. *Leisure interests:* playing violin, piano, tennis. *Address:* Embassy of Armenia, 25A Cheniston Gardens, London, W8 6TG, England. *Telephone:* 0171-938 5435. *Fax:* 0171-938 2595.

SARKISYAN, Fadey Tachatovich; Armenian politician and scientist; b. 18 Sept. 1923, Yerevan; s. of Tachat Sarkisyan and Maria Sarkisyan; m. Tatiana Roubenovna; one d.; ed. Mil. Acad. of St. Petersburg; mem. CPSU 1945–91; responsible for new techniques in devt. and Scientific Centres of U.S.S.R. Ministry of Defence 1945–63; Gen. Dir. Yerevan Computer Research Inst. 1963–77; Chair. Council of Ministers of Armenian S.S.R. 1977–89; Deputy to U.S.S.R. Supreme Soviet 1979–89; Academician–Sec. Nat. Acad. of Sciences 1989–93, Pres. 1993–. *Address:* Armenian Academy of Sciences, 24 Marshal Bagramian, Yerevan, 375019, Armenia. *Telephone:* (2) 527031 (Office); (2) 527419 (Home). *Fax:* (2) 506407.

SARKÖZY de NAGY BOSCA, Nicholas Paul Stéphane; French politician, barrister and civil servant; b. 28 Jan. 1955, Paris; s. of Paul Sarkozy de Nagy Bosca and Andrée Mallah; m. Marie-Dominique Culioli 1982; two s.; ed. Inst. of Political Studies, Paris, Paris Univ.; barrister Paris 1981–87; Assoc. Leibovici Claude Sarkozy 1987; mem RPR Cen. Cttee. 1977–, Nat. Del. 1978–79, Nat. Sec. 1988–90, Asst. Sec.-Gen. 1990–93; Town Councillor Neuilly-sur-Seine 1977–83, Mayor 1983–; Pres. Nat. Cttee. Jacques Chirac's Presidential Campaign 1981; Regional Councillor Ile-de-France 1983–88; (RPR) Deputy to Nat. Ass. from Hauts-de-Seine 1988–93, 1993–95, 1997–; Chief Spokesman R.P.R. 1997–; Minister of the Budget 1993–94, of Communications 1994–95; mem. RPR Political Office 1995–; Sec.-Gen. R.P.R. 1998–. *Publications:* Georges Mandel, moine de la politique 1994, Au bout de la passion, l'équilibre (co- author) 1995. *Leisure interests:* tennis, cycling. *Address:* Mairie, 96 Ave A. Peretti, 92200 Neuilly-sur-Seine; Assemblée Nationale, 75355 Paris; 52 Blvd Malesherbes, 75008 Paris, France.

SARNE, Tanya, B.A.; British fashion designer; b. London; m.; one s. one d.; ed. Sussex Univ.; worked as a model then as a teacher, then briefly in film production; travelled extensively throughout S. America and Europe; returned to England and set up co. importing Alpaca wool knitted garments influenced by traditional Inca designs which launched career in 1970s; introduced Scandinavian labels In Wear and Laize Adzer to U.K.; est. successful labels Miz 1978 and Ghost 1984; British Apparel Export Award for Womenswear 1993, 1995. *Address:* Ghost, The Chapel, 263 Kensal Road, London, W10 5DB, England. *Telephone:* 0181-960 3121. *Fax:* 0181-960 8374.

SARNEY, José; Brazilian politician; b. 1930; Asst. to Maranhão State Gov. 1950; Maranhão State Rep. 1956, re-elected 1958, 1962; elected Gov. of Maranhão 1965; state senator (Arena Party, now Partido Democrático Social (PDS)) 1970; Nat. Pres. Arena 1970; fmr. Chair. PDS; mem. Partido Frente Liberal 1984, PMDD; acting Pres. of Brazil March–April 1985, Pres. 1985–90; fmr. Pres. of Senate; mem. Brazilian Acad. of Letters. *Publication:* Tales of Rain and Sunlight 1986. *Leisure interests:* literature, painting. *Address:* Senado Federal, Brasília; c/o Oficio do Presidente, Palácio do Planalto, Praça dos Tres Podêres, 70.150 Brasília, D.F., Brazil.

SARPANEVA, Timo Tapani; Finnish artist and designer; b. 31 Oct. 1926, Helsinki; s. of Akseli Johannes Sarpaneva and Martta Sofia Karimo; m. 1st Ann-Mari Holmberg (divorced); m. 2nd Marfatta Svennerig; three s. one d.; ed. Industrial Art Inst., Helsinki; Designer for A. Ahlström Oy, Iittala Glassworks 1950–; Teacher in Textile Printing and Design, Industrial Art Inst. Helsinki 1953–57; Artistic Dir. Porin Puuvilla Cotton Mill 1955–66; AB Kinnasand Textile Mill, Sweden 1964–; Designer for Juhava Oy, Jughans AG, Fed. Repub. of Germany, Opa Oy, Primo Oy, Rosenlew Oy, Roserthal AG, Fed. Repub. of Germany, Villayhnymä; invited by Brazilian Govt. to lecture on and exhibit Finnish art glass 1958; exhbn. architect for Finnish industrial art exhbns. in most European countries, Japan and U.S.A.; architect for Finnish Section, Expo 1967, Montreal; pvt. exhbns. in Finland, Sweden, Norway, Denmark, Iceland, Netherlands, England, Germany, France, Italy, U.S.A., Brazil, U.S.S.R., Australia; mem. Bd. of Dirs. Asscn. of Arts and Crafts, State Cttee. of Design, Bd. of Inst. of Industrial Design; numerous awards, including three Grand Prix at Milan Triennali; Hon. Dr. of Design, Royal Coll. of Art, London 1967; Commdr., Order of Lion of Finland. *Address:* Via Navegna 7, Minusio, Locarno, Switzerland.

SARRAUTE, Nathalie, L. ÈS L., L. EN D.; French writer; b. 18 July 1900, Ivanovo, Russia; d. of Ilya Tcherniak and Pauline Chatounovski; m. Raymond Sarraute 1925; three d.; ed. Univs. of Paris and Oxford; books have been trans. into 27 languages; Prix International de Littérature 1964, Grand Prix national 1982; Prix Cavour 1984; Dr. h.c. (Dublin) 1976, (Canterbury) 1980, (Oxford) 1991. *Publications:* Tropismes 1939, Portrait d'un inconnu 1948, Martereau 1953, L'ère du soupçon 1956, Le Planétarium 1959, Les fruits d'or 1963, Le silence 1965, Le mensonge 1966, Entre la vie et la mort 1968, Isma 1970, Vous les entendez? 1972, C'est beau 1975, disent les imbéciles 1976, Elle est là 1978, L'usage de la parole 1980, Pour un oui ou pour un non 1982, Enfance 1983, Paul Valéry et l'enfant d'éléphant 1985, Tu ne t'aimes pas 1989, Ici 1995, La Pléiade 1996, Ouvrez 1997. *Address:* 12 avenue Pierre 1er de Serbie, 75116 Paris, France.

SARRAZIN, Jürgen; German banker; b. 21 March 1936, Freiberg; ed. Univ. of Heidelberg; joined Dresdner Bank AG 1960, Sr. Gen. Man. 1975, Man. Dir. 1983, Chair. Bd. Man. Dirs. 1993; Chair. Supervisory Bds./ Bd. Dirs. Deutsch-Südamerikanische Bank AG, Hamburg, Dresdner Bank Luxembourg S.A., Dresdner Bank (Switzerland) Ltd., Zürich, Banque pour l'Europe S.A. Europa Bank AG, Luxembourg, United European Bank S.A., Geneva; Deputy Chair. Supervisory Bd. Deutsche Hypothekenbank Frankfurt, Frankfurt-am-Main; mem. Bd. Dirs. Kleinwort Benson Group PLC, London; Chair. Supervisory Bd. Bilfinger & Berger Bauaktiengesellschaft; mem. Supervisory Bd. Daimler Benz AG, Degussa AG, Fried. Krupp AG Hoesch-Krupp, Henkel KGaA, Hoechst AG, Lahmeyer AG, Nestlé Deutschland AG; mem. Bd. Dirs. Banque Nat. de Paris. *Address:* c/o Dresdner Bank AG, 60301 Frankfurt-am-Main, Germany.

SARRE, Claude-Alain, DR. ÈS L.; French industrialist; b. 10 April 1928, Douai; s. of Henri Sarre and Claudine Vau; m. Simone Allien 1952; two s. one d.; ed. Inst. d'Etudes Politiques, Paris, Univ. d'Aix-Marseille; with Cie. Air France; joined Soc. André Citroën 1955, Commercial Dir. 1968, Chair., Man. Dir. Soc. Automobiles Citroën and Soc. Commerciale Citroën 1968–70; joined Lainière de Roubaix-Prouvost Masurel S.A. 1970, Pres., Dir.-Gen. 1972–77; Chair. Inst. de Devt. industriel 1975–77; Dir. Soc. Sommer-Allibert 1976; Pres. and Dir. Gen. Nobel-Bozel 1978–82; Dir. gen. Conseil national du patronat français 1983–88; Pres. Council of Improvement, Magni; Chevalier, Légion d'honneur. *Publication:* Vivre sa soumission 1997. *Address:* Le grand pin, La Crémade Nord, 13100 Le Tholonet, France.

SARRE, Massamba, L. EN. D.; Senegalese diplomatist; b. 6 Oct. 1935, St. Louis; m.; four c.; ed. Law Colls. Dakar, Senegal and Grenoble, France; Asst. Coll. of Law and Econ. Sciences, Dakar 1959; Asst. Sec.-Gen. to Minister of Foreign Affairs 1960–62, Sec.-Gen. 1962–64, Cabinet Dir. 1964–68; Amb. to Morocco 1968–72, to Iran accred. to Turkey, Pakistan, Afghanistan, Bahrain and Qatar 1972–79, to Tunisia 1979–80; Perm. Rep. to UN 1980–88; Amb. to France, accred. to Spain and Portugal 1988–96; del. at numerous confs. of UN, OAU, Non-Aligned Countries and Islamic Conf. *Address:* c/o Embassy of Senegal, 14 avenue Robert Schuman, 75007 Paris, France.

SARTON, May, M.A.; American writer; b. 3 May 1912, Wondelgem, Belgium; d. of George Alfred Leon and Eleanor (née Elwes) Sarton; ed. Shady Hill School, Cambridge, Inst. Belge de culture française, Brussels; Briggs-Copeland Instructor of Composition Harvard Univ. 1950–52; Fellow American Acad. of Arts and Sciences; mem. Poetry Soc. of America; Bryn Mawr Fellow in Poetry 1953–54; Guggenheim Foundation Fellow 1954–55; recipient Nat. Foundation for Arts and Humanities grant 1967; several hon. degrees; numerous awards including Golden Rose Award for Poetry 1945, Alexandrine Medal (Coll. St. Catherine) 1975, Human Rights Award 1985, N.E. Author Award (Booksellers' Asscn.) 1990. *Publications include:* Encounter in April 1937, The Single Hound 1938, Inner Landscape 1939, The Bridge of Years 1946, The Leaves of the Tree 1950, Shower of Summer Days 1952, Faithful are the Wounds 1955, I Knew a Phoenix 1959, Joanna and Ulysses 1963, Mrs Stevens Hears the Mermaids Singing 1961, As Does New Hampshire 1967, Plant Dreaming Deep 1968, A Grain of Mustard Seed 1971, Punch's Secret 1974, Crucial Conversations 1975, A Walk Through the Woods 1976, A Reckoning 1978, Recovering 1980, A Winter Garland 1982, At Seventy, A Journal 1984 (reissued 1996), Letters from Maine 1984, The Magnificent Spinster 1985, May Sarton: A Self Portrait 1986, After the Stroke 1988, Honey in the Hive 1988, As We Are Now (autobiog.), Coming into Eighty and Earlier Poems, At Eighty-two: A Journal, The Education of Harriet Hatfield, Encore, Endgame, Halfway to Silence, The House by the Sea, Journal of a Solitude, Kinds of Love, A Shower of Summer Days, The Single Hound, The Small Room, A World of Light Portraits and Celebrations, Writings on Writing. *Address:* c/o The Women's Press Ltd., 34 Great Sutton Street, London, EC1V 0DX, England. *Telephone:* 0171-251 3007.

SARTORIUS, Norman, M.D., PH.D., F.R.C. PSYCH.; psychiatrist and psychologist; b. 28 Jan. 1935, Münster, Germany; m. Vera Pezikozič 1963; one d.; ed. Univ. of Zagreb, Univ. of London; Consultant, Dept. of Psychiatry, Univ. of Zagreb 1959–64; Research Fellow, Inst. of Psychiatry, Univ. of London 1964–65; WHO Consultant in psychiatric epidemiology 1967–68; Medical Officer in charge of Epidemiological and Social Psychiatry and Standardization of Psychiatric Diagnosis, Classification and Statistics, WHO 1969–73, Chief, Office of Mental Health 1974–76, Dir. Div. of Mental Health 1976–93; Prof. Univ. of Zagreb, Univ. of Geneva, Univ. of Prague; Hon. Fellow Royal Coll. of Psychiatrists, U.K., Royal Australian and New Zealand Coll. of Psychiatrists; Corresp. mem. Royal Spanish Acad. of Medicine; Hon. mem. of numerous professional and scientific orgs.; Hon. Dr. Med. (Umea); Hon. D.Sc. (Bath); Rema Lapouse medal. *Publications:* more than 250 articles, several books (author or Ed.) on schizophrenia, transcultural psychiatry, mental health policy, scientific methodology. *Leisure interests:* chess, reading. *Address:* Department of Psychiatry, University of Geneva, 16-18 blvd. de St. Georges, 1205 Geneva, Switzerland. *Telephone:* (022) 327 7581. *Fax:* (022) 327 7575.

SARTZETAKIS, Christos A., LL.D.; Greek fmr. Head of State and lawyer; b. 6 April 1929, Salonika; m. Efi Argyriou; one d.; ed. Salonika Univ. and Law Faculty, Paris (Sorbonne); called to Bar 1954; apptd. J.P. 1955, Judge of 1st Instance 1956; Investigating Magistrate in Lambrakis affair (which inspired Vasilis Vasilikos' novel Z, later made into film) 1963–64; postgraduate studies Paris 1965–67; mem. Société de Législation Comparée, Paris 1966–; fmr. mem. Admin. Council Hellenic Humanistic Soc. recalled by junta and posted to Volos Court of Misdemeanours 1967–69; arrested and detained for 50 days on unspecified charges 1969; reinstated as an Appeal Judge 1974; Sr. Appeal Judge, Nauplion 1981, Justice of Supreme Court 1982–85; Pres. of Greece 1985–90; mem. Société de Législation Comparée, Paris 1966–; fmr. mem. Admin. Council Hellenic Humanistic Soc. *Address:* c/o Office of the President, Athens, Greece.

SARY IENG (see Ieng Sary).

SASSER, James Ralph, J.D.; American politician; b. 30 Sept. 1936, Memphis, Tenn.; s. of Joseph Ralph and Mary Nell (née Gray) Sasser; m. Mary Ballantine Gorman 1962; one s. one d.; ed. Vanderbilt Univ.; served U.S. Marine Corps Reserve 1958–65; partner Goodpasture, Carpenter, Woods and Sasser, Nashville 1961–76; Chair. Tennessee Democratic State Cttee. 1973–76; Senator from Tennessee 1977–95; Amb. to People's Repub. of China Feb. 1996–; mem. A.B.A., UN Asscn. *Address:* American Embassy, 3 Xiu Shui Bei Jie, Beijing 100600, People's Republic of China.

SASSMANNSHAUSEN, Günther, DIP.GEOLOGY; German businessman; b. 3 June 1930, Weidenau; joined Preussag AG, Hanover 1955, Tech. Dir. 1960, Asst. Dir. 1965, mem. Bd. of Dirs. 1968, fmr. Pres. and Chief Exec. Dir.; Chair. Amalgamated Metal Corpn. Ltd., London; Pres. Wirtschaftsvereinigung Metalle, Düsseldorf; mem. Supervisory Bd., Salzgitter AG 1983–; Hon. Dr.Ing. *Address:* P.O. Box 4827, 3000 Hanover 1, Germany.

SASSOON, David; British fashion designer; b. 5 Oct. 1932, London; s. of George Sassoon and Victoria Gurgi; ed. Chelsea Coll. of Art and Royal Coll. of Art; designer, Belinda Bellville 1958; first ready-to-wear collection 1963; Dir. Belinda Bellville 1964; Licensee Vogue Butterick U.S.A. 1966 (became Bellville Sassoon 1970); Dir. and sole shareholder Bellville Sassoon 1983–; Licencee, Japan 1988. *Leisure interests:* theatre, ballet. *Address:* Bellville Sassoon, 18 Culford Gardens, London, SW3 2ST, England.

SASSOON, Vidal; hair stylist; b. 17 Jan. 1928, London; s. of Nathan and Betty (Bellin) Sassoon; m. (divorced 1980); two s. two d.; ed. New York Univ.; served with Palmach Israeli Army; cr. a form of hairstyling based on Bahaus and geometric forms; Founder and Chair. Vidal Sassoon Inc.; Pres. Vidal Sassoon Foundation; f. Vidal Sassoon Centre for the Study of Anti-Semitism and Related Bigotries at Hebrew Univ., Jerusalem; awards include French Ministry of Culture award, award for services rendered, Harvard Business School, Intercoiffure Award, Cartier, London 1978; Fellow Hair Artists Int.

SASSOU-NGUESSO, Col. Denis; Republic of the Congo politician and army officer; b. 1943; mem. Council of State 1976–77; First Vice-Pres., Mil. Cttee. of the Parti Congolais du Travail (PCT), co-ordinator of PCT activities 1977–79, concurrently Minister of Nat. Defence; President of the Congo People's Republic 1979–92, Oct. 1997–, also fmr. Minister of Defence and Security; Cand. Pres. Elections 1992; Pres. Cen. Cttee. PCT; Leader Forces Démocratiques Unies (alliance of six parties including PCT) 1994–95. *Address:* Palais du Peuple, Brazzaville, Republic of the Congo.

SATARAWALA, Kershasp Tehmurasp, M.A.; Indian administrator and diplomatist; b. 15 Feb. 1916, Satara, Maharashtra; s. of Tehmurasp P. Satarawala and Meherbai H. Chhiber; m. Frainy Bilimoria 1947; three d.; ed. Bilimoria High School, Panchagani, Wadia Coll., Poona and Govt. Coll., Lahore; Fellow, Nuffield Foundation, London; in Indian Army during Second World War; Indian Admin. Service 1947–75; with Indian Airlines 1967–71, Man. Dir., later Chair.; Adviser to Govs. of Gujarat, Orissa, Jammu and Kashmir 1971–80; Special Sec. Foreign Trade Ministry, later Sec. Steel and Mines Ministry 1972–73; Sec.-Gen. Family Planning Asscn. of India 1976–81; Chair. Gujarat Aromatics Ltd. 1977–83; mem. Indian Wild Life Bd. 1976–81, Nat. Cttee. on Environmental Planning 1980–83, Minorities Comm. 1981–83; Vice-Chair. Organizing Cttee. and Co-ordinator IX Asian Games, New Delhi 1982; Co-ordinator Non-aligned Summit Meeting, New Delhi 1983; Lieut.-Gov. of Goa, Daman and Diu and Admin., Dadra and Nagar Haveli 1983–84; Gov. of Punjab 1984–85; Amb. to Mexico, Guatemala and El Salvador 1985–88; Padma Bhushan 1983. *Publications:* Plan on Tourism and Civil Aviation for Gujarat 1972, Gir Lion Sanctuary 1972, Perspective Plan of Gujarat 1974–84; articles on industrial devt., environment, etc. *Leisure interests:* classical music, trekking, golf. *Address:* 423 Kriti Apartments, Narangi Bagh Road, Pune 411001, India. *Telephone:* (020) 623213.

SATAROV, Georgy Aleksandrovich, CAND. TECH. SC.; Russian psephologist; b. 22 Aug. 1947, Moscow; m. Yelena Veniaminovna Satarova; two d.; ed. Moscow State Univ.; teacher Moscow Pedagogical Inst. 1973–90; one of founders and Dir. Cen. of Applied Political Studies (INDEM) 1990; Dir. Russian Social-Politican Cen.; mem. Pres. Council 1993–96; Asst. to Pres. on relations with Fed. Council, political parties and public orgs. 1994–96; mem. Expert-Analytical Council 1994–97; Chair. INDEM Fund 1997–. *Publications include:* Computer Discovers America, Mathematical Methods of Computation and Historical-Topological Studies; works on theory of management and politology. *Leisure interests:* writing verses and songs.

SATHE, Vasant P., B.A., LL.B.; Indian politician; b. 5 March 1925, Nasik, Maharashtra; s. of Purushottam Sathe and Shrimati Indira; m. Jayashree Sathe 1949; one s. two d.; ed. Bhonsale Mil. School, Nagpur Univ.; took part in Quit India Movement and was imprisoned 1942; associated with Socialist Party and PSP until 1964; joined Congress Party 1964; Pres. Madhya Pradesh Textile Workers' Fed. 1956–60, Vidarbha Textile Workers' Fed. 1960–65; mem. Lok Sabha 1972–; Minister of Information and Broadcasting, Govt. of India 1980–82, of Chemicals and Fertilizers 1982–85, of Steel, Mines and Coal 1985–86, of Energy 1986–89, of Mines and Steel (Acting) 1987–88, of Communications Feb.–June 1988; Sr. adviser, Indian del. to 25th UN Gen. Ass.; Pres. ICCR 1993–96; mem. inter-parl. del. to Tokyo 1964; Vice-Pres. Maharashtra Congress (I) Cttee.; mem. All India Congress Cttee.; mem. Maharashtra State Congress (I) Parl. Bd. *Publications:* Towards Social Revolution: A Case for Economic Democracy 1985, Restructuring of Public Sector in India 1988, The Challenge of Change 1989, Two Swords in one Scabbard 1989, Tax Without Tears 1994. *Leisure interests:* music, folk dances, economics. *Address:* 2 Krishna Menon Marg, New Delhi 110 011; 7

Pandit Pant Marg, New Delhi 110 001; 7 Pandit Pant Marg, New Delhi 110 001, India. *Telephone:* 3016948.

SATO, Humitaka, PH.D.; Japanese astrophysicist; b. 23 March 1939, Yamagata; s. of Mokichi Sato and Kane Sato; m. Keiko Okazaki 1965; one s. one d.; ed. Kyoto Univ.; Prof. of Astrophysics and Relativity, Kyoto Univ. 1974–, Dean Faculty of Sciences 1993; Dir. Yukawa Inst. for Theoretical Physics 1976–80; Nishina Prize 1973. *Publications:* Black Holes 1976, Discovery of Big Bang 1983, Invitation to Cosmology 1988. *Address:* Department of Physics, Kyoto University, Yoshida-Honmachi, Sakyo-ku, Kyoto 606-01, Japan. *Telephone:* 81-75-753-3886.

SATO, Kazuo, PH.D.; Japanese/American professor of economics; b. 5 Jan. 1927, Sapporo, Japan; s. of Kinzo Sato and Naka Sato; m. Midori Sasayama 1961; one s. two d.; ed. Hokkaido Univ., Yale Univ.; Research Asst. Yale Univ. 1956–59, Asst. Prof. Osaka Univ., Japan 1959–65; Econ. Affairs Officer, UN (New York) 1962–70; Prof. State Univ. of New York at Buffalo 1970–83, Leading Prof. 1978–83; Prof. Rutgers Univ. 1984–; Visiting Prof. M.I.T. 1969–70, Univ. of Pittsburgh 1976, State Univ. of New York at Albany 1978, Columbia Univ. 1981–83, Yale Univ. 1985; Visiting Fellow Osaka Univ. 1987, Netherlands Inst. for Advanced Studies in the Humanities and Social Sciences 1988, Nagoya City Univ., Japan 1990. *Publications:* Production Functions and Aggregation 1975, Industry and Business in Japan 1980, The Anatomy of Japanese Business 1984, Macroeconomics 1989, The Japanese Economy: Primer 1996, The Transformation of the Japanese Economy 1996, Ed. Japanese Economic Studies 1972–. *Address:* Rutgers University, New Brunswick, NJ 08903 (Office); 300 E 71, 15H, New York, NY 10021-5245, U.S.A. (Home). *Telephone:* (732) 932-7077 (Office); (212) 737-9407 (Home). *Fax:* (732) 932-7416.

SATO, Megumu; Japanese politician; b. 28 Feb. 1924; ed. Kyoto Univ.; joined Ministry of Posts and Telecommunications; mem. House of Reps. 1969–; Parl. Vice-Minister for Home Affairs 1974–75, for Post and Telecommunications 1976, Minister 1984–85; Minister of Justice 1990–91; Dir.-Gen. Nat. Land Agency May-June 1994; Liberal Democratic Party. *Publication:* Ohshu Zakki Sekai no Tabi kara. *Leisure interests:* Go, sport. *Address:* House of Representatives, Tokyo, Japan.

SATO, Mitsuo; Japanese banker; b. 1 Feb. 1933, Gunma; m. (wife deceased); two s.; ed. Univ. of Tokyo and Harvard Law School; entered Ministry of Finance 1955; Sr. Deputy Dir. Int. Taxation and Div. Tax Bureau, Ministry of Finance 1968–70; Sr. Economist, Tax Policy Div. Fiscal Affairs Dept, IMF 1970–73; Dir. Research Div. Tax Bureau, Ministry of Finance 1976–78; Dir. Securities Cos. Div., Securities Bureau, Ministry of Finance 1978–79; Dir.-Gen. Fukuoka Regional Tax Bureau, Nat. Tax Admin. Agency 1980–81; Deputy Dir.-Gen. Customs and Tariff Bureau, Ministry of Finance 1981–83, Deputy Dir.-Gen. Int. Finance Bureau 1983–84; mem. Policy Bd. Bank of Japan 1984–85; Dir.-Gen. Customs and Tariff Bureau, Ministry of Finance 1985–86; Man. Dir. Tokyo Stock Exchange 1986–88, Sr. Man. Dir. 1988–91, Deputy Pres. 1991–93; Pres. and Chair. Bd. of Dirs. Asian Devt. Bank 1993–98. *Address:* c/o Asian Development Bank, 6 ADB Avenue, Mandaluyong City 0401, Metro Manila, Philippines. *Telephone:* (2) 632-4444. *Fax:* (2) 636-2444.

SATO, Moriyoshi; Japanese politician; b. 28 March 1922; ed. Chuo Univ.; Private Sec. to two Govt. Ministers; mem. of House of Reps. 1969–; Parl. Vice-Minister for Transport 1975–76, for Nat. Land Agency 1976–77; Deputy Sec.-Gen. Liberal Democratic Party 1977–78, Vice-Chair. Policy Affairs Research Council; Minister of Agric. Forestry and Fisheries 1984–85; Dir-Gen. Nat. Land Agency, Minister of State Feb.–Dec. 1990; Dir.-Gen. Hokkaido Devt. Agency and Okinawa Devt. Agency May-June 1994. *Leisure interest:* reading.

SATO, Ryuzo, PH.D., DR.ECON.; Japanese professor of economics; b. 5 July 1931, Akita-ken; m. Kishie Hayashi 1959; one s. one d.; ed. Hitotsubashi Univ., Tokyo; Fulbright Scholar, Johns Hopkins Univ. 1957–62; Prof. of Econs. Brown Univ. 1967–85; C.V. Starr Prof. of Econs. New York Univ. 1985–, also Dir. Japan-U.S. Center, New York Univ. Stern School of Business; Adjunct Prof. of Public Policy, John F. Kennedy School of Govt. Harvard Univ. 1983; Guggenheim Fellow; Ford Foundation Fellow. *Publications:* Theory of Technical Change and Economic Invariance 1981, Research and Productivity (with G. Suzawa) 1983, Growth Theory and Technical Change 1996, Production, Stability and Dynamic Invariance 1999. *Address:* The Center for Japan-U.S. Business and Economic Studies, 44 West Fourth Street, Suite 7-190, New York, NY 10012, U.S.A. *Telephone:* (212) 998-0750. *Fax:* (212) 995-4219.

SATO, Shinji; Japanese politician; mem. House of Reps.; fmr. Minister of Transport; Minister for Int. Trade and Industry 1996.

SAUD, H.R.H. Prince Sultan Bin Abdulaziz Al; Saudi Arabian politician; b. 1930; s. of late King Abdulaziz; ed. at court and abroad; Gov. of Riyadh 1947; Minister of Agric. 1954, of Transportation 1955; Vice-Pres. Supreme Cttee. for Educ. Policy; Minister of Defence and Civil Aviation and Insp. Gen. 1963, 1982–; Chair. Bd. Saudia Airlines 1963; Chair. Bd. General Enterprise of Mil. Industries; Chair. Council of Manpower 1980; Second Deputy Prime Minister 1982–; Chair Supreme Council for Islamic Affairs 1994; Order of Merit (First Class) from many countries. *Address:* Ministry of Defence and Civil Aviation, P.O. Box 26731, Airport Road, Riyadh 11165, Saudi Arabia. *Telephone:* (1) 476-9000. *Fax:* (1) 405-5500.

SAUD AL-FAISAL, H.R.H. Prince, B.A.(ECONS.); Saudi Arabian politician and diplomatist; b. 1941, Riyadh; s. of late King Faisal; ed. Princeton Univ., U.S.A.; fmr. Deputy Minister of Petroleum and Mineral Resources 1971–74; Minister of State for Foreign Affairs March–Oct. 1975, Minister of Foreign Affairs Oct. 1975–; leader del. to UN Gen. Ass. 1976; Special Envoy of H.M. King Khaled in diplomatic efforts to resolve Algerian-Moroccan conflict over Western Sahara, and the civil war in Lebanon; mem. Saudi Arabian del. to Arab restricted Summit, Riyadh, Oct. 1976 and to full Summit Conf. of Arab League, Oct. 1976; Founding mem. King Faisal's Int. Charity Soc. *Leisure interest:* reading. *Address:* Ministry of Foreign Affairs, Nasseriya Street, Riyadh 11124, Saudi Arabia. *Telephone:* (1) 406-7777.

SAUDARGAS, Algirdas; Lithuanian politician and biophysicist; b. 17 April 1948, Kaunas; m. Laima Saudargene; one s. one d.; ed. Kaunas Inst. of Medicine; research asst. Inst. of Math. and Information Tech. Lithuanian Acad. of Sciences 1972–77; sr. lecturer Lithuanian Acad. of Agric. 1977–82; researcher Kaunas Inst. of Medicine (now Acad.) 1982–90; founder mem. Sąjūdis Movt., Chair. Sąjūdis Seimas (Parl.) Political Cttee. 1988–90; elected to Supreme Soviet Repub. of Lithuania 1990; Minister of Foreign Affairs 1990–92, Nov. 1996–; mem. official del. Repub. of Lithuania to negotiations with Soviet Union; mem. Seimas, Cttee. on Foreign Affairs, mem. Seimas del. to European Parl. Dec. 1992–, Chair. Subcttee. on European Affairs 1995–; Chair. Lithuanian Christian Democratic Party 1995– (mem. 1989–). *Leisure interest:* reading. *Address:* Ministry of Foreign Affairs, J. Tumo-Vaižganto str. 2, Vilnius 2600, Lithuania. *Telephone:* (2) 61 85 37 (Office). *Fax:* (2) 61 85 37.

SAUDEK, Jan; Czech photographer; b. 13 May 1935, Prague; s. of Gustav Saudek and Pavla Saudeková; m. 1st Marie Geislerová 1958 (divorced 1973); m. 2nd Marie Šrámková 1974 (died 1993); two s. three d.; studied reproduction photography at graphic school; factory worker 1953–83; over 400 solo exhbns. world-wide, over 300 jt. exhbns.; works include Man Holding New Born Child 1966, Artist's Father of the Cemetery 1972, Mother and Daughter 1979, Walkman 1984; exhbn. of paintings, Prague 1997, 1998; Ordre des arts et des lettres 1990. *Publications include:* Il Teatro de la Vita 1980, Life, Love, Death and Such Other Trifles 1992, Theatre of the Life 1992, The Letter 1995, Jubilations and Obsessions 1995, Album 1997. *Leisure interests:* women, running long distances, painting. *Address:* Blodkova 6, 130 00 Prague 3, Czech Republic. *Fax:* (2) 627 4695; 61216219.

SAUDI ARABIA, King of (see Fahd ibn Abdul Aziz).

SAUER, Fernand Edmond; French international official, pharmacist and lawyer; b. 14 Dec. 1947, St. Avold, Moselle; m. Pamela Sheppard; one s. two d.; ed. Univs. of Strasbourg and Paris II; fmr. hosp. pharmacist and pharmaceutical insp. Ministry of Health; joined European Comm. Brussels, Head of Pharmaceuticals 1985; Exec. Dir. European Agency for Evaluation of Medicinal Products (EMEA), London 1995–. *Address:* European Agency for the Evaluation of Medicinal Products, 7 Westferry Circus, Canary Wharf, London, E14 4HB, England. *Telephone:* 0171-418 8400. *Fax:* 0171-418 8416.

SAUER, Louis; American architect and urban planner; b. 15 June 1928, Forest Park, Ill.; s. of Frank J. Sauer and Jeanne LaFazia; m. 1st Elizabeth Mason 1956; two c.; m. 2nd Perla Serfaty 1990; ed. Univ. of Pennsylvania, Int. School of City Planning, Venice, Italy, Illinois Inst. of Tech.; Prin. Louis Sauer Assoc. Architects, Phila., Pa. 1961–79; Prof. of Architecture, Univ. of Pa. 1974–79, Carnegie-Mellon Univ., Pittsburgh, Pa. 1979–85, Univ. of Colo. 1985–89; Commr., Ville de Montréal Jacques Viger Comm. 1991–; Partner Archiris Inc., Pittsburgh 1981–84; Prin. Louis Sauer Architect, Boulder, Colo. 1985–89; Dir. of Urban Design, Daniel Arbour and Assocs., Montreal, Canada 1989–. *Work includes:* Water Plaza and high-rise housing, Cincinnati, renewal plan for Fells Point waterfront, public open-space landscape, pvt. housing and housing for the elderly, Baltimore, new town devt. for Golf Course Island, Reston, Va., Oaklands Mills Village Center, Columbia, Md., housing at Society Hill, Phila.; work in Canada includes master-plans for Verdun Nuns Island 1991, Bois-Franc St.-Laurent New Town 1992, Ville de Laval 1993, Angus C. P. Rail Rosemont Community 1993, Gatineu City Town Centre 1993, Ile Bizard Town Centre 1993; fmr. Consultant to U.S.A.I.D. to advise govts. of Lebanon, Egypt and Portugal on low-income housing devt.; Fellow American Inst. of Architects; Nat. Endowment for the Arts Design Fellowships 1978; over 50 design and public service awards. *Leisure interests:* gardening, fishing. *Address:* 3472 Marlowe Street, Montreal, Quebec, H4A 3L7, Canada. *Telephone:* (514) 485-4616. *Fax:* (514) 939-1814.

SAUERLÄNDER, Willibald, DR.PHIL.; German art historian; b. 29 Feb. 1924, Waldsee; s. of Wilhelm Sauerländer and Anita Sauerländer-Busch; m. Brigitte Rückoldt 1957; one s.; ed. Univ. of Munich; Visiting mem. Inst. for Advanced Study, Princeton 1961–62, 1973; Prof. of History of Art, Univ. of Freiburg/Br. 1962–70; Dir. Zentralinst. für Kunstgeschichte, Munich 1970–89; Visiting Prof. Inst. of Fine Arts, New York Univ. 1964–65, Collège de France, Paris 1981, Madison/Wis. Univ. 1982, Harvard 1984–85, Berkeley 1989; Mellon Lectures, Washington 1991, New York Univ. 1992; mem. Bayerische Akad. der Wissenschaften, Medieval Acad. of America, British Acad., Soc. Nat. des Antiquaires de France, Royal Soc. of Antiquaries, London, Kon. Acad. Voor Wetenschappen, Letteren en Schone Kunsten van Belgie, Acad. Europaea, Acad. des Inscriptions et Belles-Lettres, American Acad. of Art and Sciences; Dr. h.c. *Publications:* Die Kathedrale von Chartres 1954, Jean-Antoine Houdon: Voltaire 1963, Gotische Skulptur in Frankreich 1140-1270 1970, Das Königsportal in Chartres 1984, Das Jahrhundert der grossen Kathedralen 1990, Initiälen 1996. *Leisure interests:* reading, travelling. *Address:* c/o Zentralinstitut für Kunstgeschichte, Meiserstrasse 10, 80333 Munich, Germany. *Telephone:* 089/5591-546.

SAUL, David, PH.D., J.P.; Bermudian politician; b. 27 Nov. 1939, Bermuda; s. of John A. Saul and Sarah Elizabeth Saul; m. Christine Hall 1963; one s. one d.; ed. Mt. St. Agnes Acad., Saltus Grammar School, Loughborough Coll. U.K., Queen's and Toronto Univs. Canada; teacher 1962–67; consultant to Ont. Educ. Communications Authority 1970–72, to Bermuda Dept. of Educ. 1972–73, Visiting Prof. Univ. of Toronto 1972; Perm. Sec. Ministry of Educ. 1972–76; Financial Sec. Ministry of Finance 1976–81; Chief Admin. Officer, Gibbons Co. 1981–84; Pres. Fidelity Int. Bermuda Ltd. 1984–95, Bermuda Defence Bd. 1997–, Bermuda Audubon Soc. 1998, Bermuda Debating Soc. 1998; Chair. Bermuda Council on Int. Affairs 1983–85; Dir. Bermuda Monetary Authority 1986–88 (Pres. 1997–), London Bermuda Reins Co. Ltd., Bermuda Track and Field Asscn. 1987–, Fidelity Investments 1997; Trustee Bermuda Underwater Exploration Inst. 1992–; mem. House of Ass. 1989–; Minister of Finance 1989–95; Prime Minister of Bermuda 1995–97; United Bermuda Party. *Leisure interests:* scuba diving, fishing, canoeing, oil painting. *Address:* Rocky Ledge, 18 Devonshire Bay Road, DV 07, Bermuda. *Telephone:* 236-7338. *Fax:* 236-5087.

SAUL, Ralph Southey, B.A., LL.B.; American stock exchange official, lawyer and insurance executive; b. 21 May 1922, Brooklyn, N.Y.; s. of Walter Emerson and Helen Douglas; m. Bette Jane Bertschinger 1956; one s. one d.; ed. Univ. of Chicago and Yale Law School; war service, U.S.N.R. 1943–46; attached to American Embassy, Prague 1947–48; admitted to D.C. Bar 1951, to New York Bar 1952; Assoc., firm of Lyeth and Voorhees, New York City 1951–52; Asst. Counsel to Gov. of New York State 1952–54; Staff Attorney, Radio Corpn. of America 1954–58; with Securities and Exchange Comm. 1958–65, Dir. Div. of Trading and Markets 1963–65; Vice-Pres. for Corporate Devt., Investors Diversified Services, Inc. 1965–66; Pres. American Stock Exchange 1966–71; Vice-Chair. First Boston Corpn. 1971–74; Chair., C.E.O. INA Corpn., Phila., 1975–81; Chair. CIGNA Corpn. (formerly Connecticut Gen. and INA Corpn.) 1982–84, Peers and Co. 1985, mem., Bd. of Dirs. Sun Co. 1976, Certain Teed Corpn. 1983, Drexel Burnham 1989–; mem. A.B.A., N.Y. Stock Exchange (regulatory advisory cttee.). *Address:* c/o Cigna Corporation, 1 Logan Square, P.O. Box 7716, 18th and Cherry Streets, Philadelphia, PA 19192, U.S.A.

SAULNIER, Air Chief Marshal Jean-Michel; French air force officer; b. 15 Nov. 1930, Parcé-sur-Sarthe; s. of Emile Saulnier and Eugénie Gilois; m. Claudie Reynaud 1954; two s. one d.; ed. Ecole de l'air; served in Far East 1952–54; subsequently at various French bases as fighter pilot; Ecole d'application militaire de l'énergie atomique, Cherbourg 1961–65; C.O. Dijon base 1965; Gen. Staff post, then C.O. Luxeuil nuclear air base 1971; Chef de cabinet to Air Force Chief of Staff 1973–76; C.O. Air Force Officers' School, Salon-de-Provence 1976–79; Commdr. Strategic Air Force squadrons 1979–81; Special Chief of Staff, Defence Cabinet 1981–85; Chief of Defence Staff 1985–87; Conseiller maître, Cour des comptes 1988, Hon. Conseiller maître 1996–; Adviser to Minister of Defence 1989–91; Grand Officier, Légion d'honneur, Grand Croix ordre nat. du Mérite, Médaille de l'Aéronautique. *Address:* 34 Les Maguanarelles, 84160 Lourmarin, France (Home).

SAUNDERS, Ernest Walter, M.A., F.INST.M.; British business executive; b. 21 Oct. 1935, Vienna, Austria; m. Carole A. Stephings 1963; two s. one d.; ed. St. Paul's School, London, and Emmanuel Coll., Cambridge; Man. Dir. Beecham Products Int., Dir. Beecham Products 1966–73; Chair. European Div. Great Universal Stores 1973–77; Pres. Nestlé Nutrition SA and mem. Man. Cttee., Nestlé SA, Vevey, Switzerland 1977–81; Chief Exec. and Deputy Chair. Guinness PLC 1981–86, Chief Exec. and Chair. 1986–87; Chair. Arthur Guinness Son & Co. (G.B.) Ltd., 1982–87, Guinness Brewing Worldwide 1982–87, Guinness-Harp Corpn. 1983–86, Martin Retail Group 1984–86, Distillers Co. Ltd. 1986–87; charged with fraud in connection with illegal share dealings Oct. 1987, found guilty on 12 charges of conspiracy, theft and false accounting Aug. 1990, sentenced to five years' imprisonment on charges of conspiracy and theft Aug. 1990; sentence halved by Appeal Court May 1991; released from prison June 1991; case referred back to Court of Appeal Dec. 1994, appeal rejected Nov. 1995; European Court of Human Rights ruled trial was unfair, Dec. 1996; now marketing consultant, lecturer; Pres. Stambridge Assocs. (now Stambridge Man.) 1992–; Dir. Queens Park Rangers Football & Athletic Club 1983, Brewers' Soc. 1983; fmr. Chair, C.E.O. Arthur Bell & Sons PLC. *Leisure interests:* skiing, tennis, football.

SAUNDERS, Jennifer; British actress and writer; b. 1 July 1958; m. Adrian Edmondson; three d.; ed. Cen. School of Speech and Drama, London. *Theatre:* An Evening with French and Saunders (nat. tour) 1989, Me and Mamie O'Rourke 1993. *Television series:* The Comic Strip Presents . . . 1990, Girls on Top, French and Saunders (5 series), Absolutely Fabulous 1993, 1994, 1995 (Emmy Award 1993). *Publications:* A Feast of French and Saunders (with Dawn French) 1992, Absolutely Fabulous: the scripts 1993. *Address:* c/o Peters, Fraser & Dunlop, The Chambers, Chelsea Harbour, London, SW10 0XF, England.

SAUNDERS, Stuart John, M.D., F.R.C.P., F.C.P.S.A.; South African physician; b. 28 Aug. 1931, Cape Town; s. of Lilian Emily and the late Albert Frederick Saunders; m. 1st Noreen Merle Harrison 1956 (died 1983); one s. one d.; m. 2nd Anita Louw 1984; ed. Christian Brothers Coll. and Univ. of Cape Town; Registrar in Pathology and Medicine, Groote Schuur Hosp. and Univ. of Cape Town 1955–58; Research Asst. Royal Postgraduate Medical School, London 1959–60; Lecturer and Sr. Lecturer, Groote Schuur Hosp. and Univ. of Cape Town 1961–70; Fellow in Medicine Harvard Medical School and Mass. Gen. Hosp. 1963–64; Prof. and Head of Medicine Dept. Groote Schuur Hosp. and Univ. of Cape Town 1971–80; Deputy Principal for Planning, Univ. of Cape Town 1978–80, Vice-Chancellor and Prin. Univ. of Cape Town 1981–96; Past Pres. S.A. Inst. of Race Relations; Adams Fellowship; Oppenheimer Memorial Trust Advanced Study Grant; Life Fellow (Univ. of Cape Town); Hon. D.SC., Hon. F.C.M.; Hon. LL.D. (Aberdeen), (Sheffield), (Princeton); Hon. D.Sc. (Toronto). *Publications:* Access to and Quality in Higher Education: A Comparative Study 1992; numerous scientific publications particularly in the field of liver diseases. *Leisure interests:* reading, fishing. *Address:* 45 Belvedere Avenue, Oranjezicht, 8001 Cape Town, South Africa. *Telephone:* 453035. *Fax:* 4620047.

SAUNIER-SEÏTÉ, Alice Louise, D. ÈS L.; French politician and educator; b. 26 April 1925, Saint-Jean-le-Centenier; d. of Daniel-René and Marie-Louise (Lascombe) Saunier; m. 1st Elie-Jacques Picard 1947 (divorced); two s.; m. 2nd Jérôme Seïté (deceased); ed. Lycée de Tournon, Facultés des Lettres et des Sciences de Paris, Ecole nat. des langues orientales vivantes; Attachée, then Chargée de recherche, Nat. Centre for Scientific Research (C.N.R.S.) 1958–63; lecturer in geography, faculté des lettres, Rennes 1963–65, Prof. 1965–69; mem. Nat. Cttee. for Scientific Research 1963–70; mem. Perm. Section C.N.R.S. 1967–70; Dir. Collège littéraire universitaire, Brest 1966–68, Dean of faculté des lettres et sciences sociales 1968–69; Dir. Inst. universitaire de technologie, Sceaux 1970–73; Prof. Univ. of Paris XI 1969–73, Vice-Pres. 1970–71; Rector, Acad. of Reims 1973–76; Sec. of State for Univs. 1976–77, Minister of Univs. 1978–81, of the Family and Women's Affairs 1981; Prof. of Geographic Organization of Space, Hon. Chair. Dept. of Econs. and Man., Conservatoire Nat. des Arts et Metiers 1981–94; Municipal Councillor, Manso 1971–83, Deputy Mayor 1977–83; mem. political bureau, Parti Républicain 1978–; Councillor, Paris 1983–; Vice-Pres. Nat. Movt. of Local Reps. 1983–90, Pres. 1990–98, Founder-Pres. Fondation de la Mutuelle des élus Loceaux 1991–; Dir.-Treas., Inst. Océanographique (Pres. 1996–); Dir. then Vice-Pres. Inst. de barrages-réservoirs du Bassin de la Seine; Dir. Vieux Paris Comm.; mem. Jury, Prix Mémorial, French Inst. 1995–; Conseiller de Paris; Pres. Club des Explorateurs français; mem. Acad. des Sciences Morales et Politiques; Assoc. mem. Institut d'Egypte, Acad. of Sciences, Iceland; Commdr. Légion d'honneur; Commdr. des Palmes académiques; Commdr. Ordre des Arts et Lettres; Medaille d'or de la jeunesse et des sports; Medal of C.N.R.S.; Medal of Société de géographie de Paris; decorations from Burkina Faso, Cameroon, Ivory Coast, Egypt, Gabon, Greece, Indonesia, Iceland, Luxembourg, Portugal and Sweden. *Publications:* Les vallées septentrionales du Massif de l'Oetztal 1963, Südföhn d'Innsbruck (contrib.) 1965, En première ligne 1982, Remettre l'état à sa place 1984, Une Europe à la carte 1985, Le cardinal de Tournon, le Richelieu de François 1er (1997). *Leisure interest:* fencing. *Address:* 9 Place de l'Hôtel-de-Ville, 75004 Paris; Institut de France, 23 quai de Conti, 75006 Paris, France. *Telephone:* 42.76.50.74.

SAUR, Klaus Gerhard; German publisher; b. 27 July 1941, Pullach; s. of Karl-Otto Saur and Veronika Saur; m. Lilo Stangel 1977; one s. one d.; ed. High School, Icking and Commercial High School, Munich; Marketing Man. Vulkan-Verlag, Essen 1962; Publishing Man. K.G. Saur, Munich 1963, Publishing Dir. 1966; Pres. K.G. Saur New York and K.G. Saur, London 1977; Man. Dir. K.G. Saur Munich 1988–; founder World Guide to Libraries, Publrs. Int. Directory; Sr. Vice-Pres. Reed Reference Publishing, New Providence; Chair. Bd. Frankfurt Book Fair; mem. Bd. F.A. Brockhaus Bibliographical Inst. (Mannheim); Chair. Bd. Deutsche Bibliothek (German Nat. Library); Hon. Prof. Univ. of Glasgow, Humboldt-Univ. Berlin; Hon. Fellow, Tech. Univ. of Graz; Senator h.c. (Ludwig Maximilians Univ., Munich) 1992; Dr. Phil. h.c. (Marburg) 1985, (Ishevsk, Russia) 1997, (Pisa, Italy) 1998; D.Hum.Litt. (Simmons Univ. Coll., Boston) 1991; Hon. Medal City of Munich 1988, Hon. Bene Merenti Medal, Bavarian Acad. of Sciences 1997; Bundesverdienstkreuz der Bundesrepublik Deutschland, Officier Ordre des Arts et Lettres (France). *Leisure interests:* special German exile literature 1933–45, int. politics, history of publishing and book trade. *Address:* Ortlerstrasse 8, 81373 Munich, Germany. *Telephone:* 089 53 56 88.

SAURA, Carlos; Spanish film director; b. 4 Jan. 1932, Huesca; m.; two c.; ed. film school in Madrid. *Films include:* La Prima Angelica, La Caza (Silver Bear, Berlin Film Festival), Blood Wedding, Carmen (flamenco version), El Amor Brujo, El Dorado 1987, The Dark Night 1989, Dispara! 1993, Ay Carmela!.

SAUTET, Claude; French writer and film director; b. 23 Feb. 1924, Montrouge (Seine); s. of Jean Sautet and Marguerite Parant; m. Graziella Escojido 1953; one s.; ed. Lycée de Coutances, Ecole nat. supérieure des arts décoratifs; head of a centre for juvenile delinquents 1944; music critic Combat 1947–49; asst. dir. several films 1953–58; co-writer or dir. Nous n'irons plus au bois (short) 1951, Bonjour sourire 1955, Classes tous risques 1959, L'Arme à gauche 1965, Les Choses de la vie (Prix Louis-Delluc 1969), César et Rosalie 1972 (Grand Prix du Cinéma français 1973 and Prix Jean le Duc, Acad. française 1973), Vincent, François, Paul . . . et les autres 1974 (Prix Jean Cocteau 1974), Le Fauve est lâché 1958, Les Yeux sans visage 1960, Symphonie pour un massacre 1963, Le Vie de château 1964, Le Diable par la queue 1966, La Chamade 1967, Borsalino 1970, Les Mariés de l'An

II 1971, Mado 1976, Une Histoire simple 1978 (Acad. Award for best foreign film 1980), Garçon 1983, Quelques jours avec moi 1988 (Grand Prix Soc. des auteurs et compositeurs dramatiques 1988 and Prix Georges de Beauregard for best dir. 1988), Un coeur en hiver 1992 (Grand prix Acad. nat. du cinéma 1993, César for best dir. 1993), Nelly et M. Arnaud 1995 (Grand Prix France cinéma 1995, Prix Louis-Delluc 1995, César for Best Actor 1996, Pierre Bellan Prize for Best Dir. 1996). *Leisure interests:* 17th and 18th century music, jazz. *Address:* 15 avenue des Gobelins, 75005 Paris, France.

SAUTTER, Christian; French economist and politician; b. 9 April 1940, Autun; s. of Yves Sautter and Huguette Duval; m. 1st Gisèle Jacquet (deceased); two d.; m. 2nd Catherine Cadou 1996; ed. Ecole Polytechnique, Ecole nat. de la Statistique et de l'Administration Economique, Institut d'Etudes Politiques, Paris; economist, Inst. Nat. de la Statistique et des Etudes Economiques (INSEE) 1965–71; researcher, Japanese Planning Agency's Econ. Research Inst., Tokyo 1971–72; Head, Business Research Div., INSEE 1973–76, planning research dept. 1976–78; Dir. Centre d'études prospectives et d'informations internationales (CEPII) 1979–81; Adviser on int. econ. questions to Presidency of Repub. 1981–82, Deputy Sec.-Gen. of Presidency 1982–85, 1988–91; Insp.-Gen. of Finance, Ministry of Finance 1985–88, 1993–; Prefect of Paris and Ile-de-France Region 1991–93; Minister of State attached to Minister for the Economy, Finance and Industry, with responsibility for the budget 1997–; Dir. of Studies on Japanese Economy, Ecole des Hautes Etudes en Sciences Sociales 1975–; Chevalier Légion d'honneur, Officier Ordre nat. du Mérite. *Publications:* several publs. on Japanese economy. *Address:* Ministry of the Budget, 139 rue de Bercy, Télédoc 146, 75572 Paris cédex 12 (Office); 1 rue de Turbigo, 75001 Paris, France. *Telephone:* (1) 40.04.04.04. *Fax:* (1) 43.41.22.03 (Office).

SAUVAGNARGUES, Jean Victor; French diplomatist and politician; b. 2 April 1915, Paris; s. of Edmond Sauvagnargues and Alice Caplan; m. Lise Marie L'Evesque 1948; two s. two d.; ed. Ecole Normale Supérieure; entered Ministry of Foreign Affairs 1941, attached to French Embassy, Bucharest, later on staff of Gen. de Gaulle 1945–46; Head of Political Service for German Affairs 1946–49, Deputy Dir. for Central Europe 1949–54; in office of Antoine Pinay, Minister of Foreign Affairs 1955–56; Dir. Gen. for Moroccan and Tunisian Affairs Jan.–March 1956; Amb. to Ethiopia 1956–60; Dir. for Middle Eastern Affairs and African Affairs; Amb. to Tunisia 1962–70, to Fed. Repub. of Germany 1970–74, to U.K. 1978–81; Minister of Foreign Affairs 1974–76; Commdr., Légion d'honneur, Commdr., Ordre nat. du Mérite, Croix de guerre 1939–45; Hon. G.C.M.G. *Address:* 14 avenue Pierre 1er de Serbie, 75116 Paris, France.

SAVARY, Jérôme; French theatre director and actor; b. 27 June 1942, Buenos Aires, Argentina; s. of Jacques Savary and Claire Hovelaque; one s. two d.; moved to France 1947; ed. Collège Cévenol, Haute-Loire; studied music Paris; became jazz musician New York 1961; returned to France; f. Compagnie Jérôme Savary 1965, subsequently called Grand Magic Circus, then Grand Magic Circus et ses animaux tristes 1968–; theatre dir. 1969–; Dir. Centre Dramatique Nat. du Languedoc-Roussillon, Béziers and Montpellier 1982–85; Dir. Carrefour Européen, Théâtre-du 8e 1985–; Dir. Théâtre Nat. de Chaillot 1988–; dir. about 80 plays and shows in Europe, Brazil, Canada, U.S.A., Israel; several TV films of plays and operas, and three films for cinema; Prix Dominique for Cyrano de Bergerac; Molière award for best musical and 6 nominations 1987, Victoire de la Musique 1987 for best musical, for Cabaret; Chevalier Ordre des Arts et des Lettres; Grand Badge of Hon., Austria. *Publications:* La Vie privée d'un magicien ordinaire 1985, Ma vie commence à 20h30 1991, Magic Circus 1966–96, 30 ans d'aventures et d'amour 1996. *Address:* Théâtre National de Chaillot, 1 place du Trocadéro, 75116 Paris, France. *Telephone:* (1) 53.65.31.02. *Fax:* (1) 47.55.08.00.

SAVCHENKO, Arkadiy Markovich; Belarus opera singer (baritone); b. 6 April 1936, Vitebsk, Byelorussia; s. of Mark Iosifovich Savchenko and Marfa Stratonovna Savchenko; m. Glasova Serafima Semienovna 1977; two s.; ed. Moscow Conservatoire; soloist with Byelorussian (now Belarus) Bolshoi Theatre 1960–; Faculty mem., Prof., Vocal Dept., Belarus Acad. of Music 1987–; People's Artist of U.S.S.R. 1985. *Roles include:* Yevgeny in Tchaikovsky's Yevgeny Onegin, Kizgaylo in Smolsky's Ancient Legend, Telramud in Wagner's Lohengrin, Malatesta in Donizetti's Don Pasquale, Jermon in Verdi's Traviata, Valentin in Gounod's Faust, Rigoletto in Verdi's Rigoletto, Renato in Verdi's A Masked Ball, Zurga in Bizet's Pearl Fishers, Almaviva in Mozart's The Marriage of Figaro, Tomsky, Eletsky in Tchaikovsky's Queen of Spades, Gryaznoy in Rimsky-Korsakov's The Tsar's Bride, Don Giovanni in Mozart's Don Giovanni, Amonasro in Verdi's Aida, Rodrigo in Verdi's Don Carlos, Sharpless in Puccini's Madame Butterfly, Escamillo in Bizet's Carmen, Figaro in Rossini's The Barber of Seville, Prince Igor in Borodin's Prince Igor, Alfio in Mascagni's Cavalleria Rusticana etc. *Leisure interests:* gardening, fishing, reading. *Address:* Bolshoi Teatr, 1 Parizhskaya Kommuna Square, 220029 Minsk (Theatre); 8–358 Storozhovskaya Str., 220002 Minsk, Belarus (Home). *Telephone:* (17) 341133 (Theatre); (17) 391551 (Home). *Fax:* (17) 340584.

SAVELYEVA, Lyudmila Mikhailovna; Russian actress; b. 24 Jan. 1942, Leningrad (now St. Petersburg); ed. Vaganova Ballet School, Leningrad; People's Artist of the R.S.F.S.R. 1985. *Films include:* War and Peace (Natasha), by Bondarchuk 1966–67, The Sunflowers (de Sica) 1971, Flight 1971, The Headless Horseman 1973, The Seagull 1973, Yulia Vrevskaya 1978, The Hat 1982, The Fourth Year of War 1983, Success 1985, Another's Belaya and Ryaboy 1986, White Rose–Emblem of Grief, Red Rose–Emblem of Love 1989. *Theatre productions include:* The Price (Miller), M. Rozovsky theatre. *Address:* Tverskaya Str. 19, Apt. 76, 103050 Moscow, Russia. *Telephone:* 299-99-34.

SAVI, Toomas; Estonian politician and physician; b. 30 Dec. 1942, Tartu, Estonia; m. Kirsi Savi; two d.; ed. Tartu State Univ.; chief physician U.S.S.R. light athletics team, concurrently sr. researcher Tartu State Univ. 1970–80; Chief physician Tartu Physical Culture Dispensary 1979; Head Scientific Research Medical Centre, Tartu 1982–90; worked as Asst. Doctor Cen. Hosp. Kuopio Univ. and Kajaani Cen. Hosp., Finland 1991–92; mem. Tartu Town Council 1991–; Deputy Mayor of Tartu 1993; Chair. Riigikogu (Parl.) 1995–; mem. Estonian Olympic Team, Pres. Estonian Sports Medicine Fed. *Address:* Riigikogu, Lossi plats 1a, EE0100 Tallinn, Estonia (Office). *Telephone:* (2) 31-63-01.

SAVILL, Rosalind Joy, B.A., F.S.A., F.R.S.A.; British curator; b. 12 May 1951, Hants.; d. of Dr. Guy Savill and Lorna Williams; one d.; ed. Wycombe Abbey School, Chatelard School, Montreux and Univ. of Leeds; Museum Asst., Ceramics Dept., Victoria & Albert Museum 1973–74; Museum Asst. and Sr. Asst., The Wallace Collection 1974–78, Asst. to Dir. 1978–92, Dir. 1992–; mem. Arts Panel, Nat. Trust 1995–; Gov. Camden School for Girls 1996–; Leverhulme Scholar 1975; Getty Scholar 1985; Nat. Art Collections Fund Prize 1990. *Publications:* The Wallace Collection Catalogue of Sèvres Porcelain, 3 Vols. 1988; articles, reviews, contribs. to exhbn. catalogues etc. *Leisure interests:* music, the countryside and gardens. *Address:* The Wallace Collection, Hertford House, Manchester Square, London, W1M 6BN, England. *Telephone:* 0171-935 0687. *Fax:* 0171-224 2155.

SAVIMBI, Jonas; Angolan nationalist leader; b. 1934; m. Vinona Savimbi; ed. Univ. of Lausanne; fmr. Sec.-Gen. União das Populações de Angola (UPA); Foreign Minister of Governo Revolucionário de Angola no Exilio (GRAE) 1962–64; resgnd. from GRAE at OAU meeting, Cairo July 1964; studied at Univ. of Lausanne 1964–65; moved to Lusaka; founded União Nacional para a Independência Total de Angola (UNITA) near Luso, March 1966; Pres. UNITA March 1966–; Leader UNITA forces in guerrilla war against the Portuguese and in Angolan civil war against MPLA forces after Portuguese withdrawal in Nov. 1975; proclaimed Pres. of People's Democratic Repub. of Angola Nov. 1975 (rival MPLA regime is recognized internationally); engaged in guerrilla activities against MPLA 1976–91; returned to Luanda Sept. 1991; participated in elections as UNITA cand. 1992; claimed elections were rigged and resumed guerrilla activities Nov. 1992–.

SAVIN, Anatoliy Ivanovich, D.TECH.SC.; Russian specialist in radio analysis and systems analysis; b. 6 April 1920; ed. Bauman Tech. Inst., Moscow; mem. CPSU 1944–91; fmrly. employed as engineer and constructor; constructor with machine-bldg. plant 1944–51; positions of responsibility on eng. side of radio-tech. industry 1951–; Gen. Dir. Scientific and Production Asscn. Kometa 1973–; corresp. mem. Acad. of Sciences 1979, mem. 1984–, Prof. 1984; main research has been on complex radio-tech. automatized informational systems; inventor of cosmic radio-telescope KRT-10; Acad. of Sciences Raspletin Prize 1972, Lenin Prize 1972, Hero of Socialist Labour 1976, State Prizes 1946, 1949, 1951, 1981. *Address:* TsNII Kometa, Velozavodskaya Str. 5, 109280 Moscow, Russia. *Telephone:* 275-15-33.

SAVOLA, Kai Kari; Finnish freelance theatre director; b. 30 Sept. 1931, Helsinki; s. of Tauno Savola and Hilppa Korpinen; m. Terttu Byckling 1958; two s. one d.; ed. Helsinki Univ.; Admin. Dir. Helsinki Student Theatre 1959–62; Man. Dir. Finnish Drama Agency 1962–65; Literary Man. Helsinki City Theatre 1965–68; Dir.-Gen. Tampere Workers' Theatre 1968–73; Dir. Finnish Nat. Theatre 1973, Dir.-Gen. 1974–92; stage direction of Finnish, English, Russian and Japanese drama; designed the two experimental stages of the Finnish Nat. Theatre (with Prof. Heikki Siren) 1976, 1987; Prof. h.c.; Commdr. Order of White Rose of Finland. *Publications:* translations of English and German plays into Finnish. *Address:* Laivurinkatu 39 A 12, 00150 Helsinki, Finland. *Telephone:* (9) 636 939. *Fax:* (9) 636 939.

SAVOSTYANOV, Maj.-Gen., Yevgeny Vadimovich, CAND. TECH. SC.; Russian politician; b. 28 Feb. 1952, Moscow; m.; two s.; ed. Moscow Mining Inst.; jr. researcher Inst. of Physics of the Earth U.S.S.R. Acad. of Sciences 1975–77; researcher Inst. for Problems of Complex Use of Mineral Wealth U.S.S.R. Acad. of Sciences 1975–90; f. and Co-Chair. Club of Voters of Acad. of Sciences for election of Andrey Sakharov and other scientists as people's deputies from Acad. of Sciences; Asst. to Chair. Moscow City Soviet, then Dir.-Gen. Dept. Moscow Mayor's Office 1990–91; mem. Co-ordination Council Movt. Democratic Russia; mem. Org. Cttee. of Democratic Reforms 1991; Deputy Dir. Russian Fed. Service of Counterespionage, Head of Dept. Moscow and Moscow Region 1991–94; Adviser to Chair. Russian Fed. of Ind. Trade Unions 1995–96; Deputy Head Admin. of Russian Presidency 1996–. *Address:* Office of the President, Staraya pl. 4, entr. 1, Moscow, Russia (Office). *Telephone:* (095) 206 2433 (Office).

SAVOY, Guy; French chef and restaurateur; b. 24 July 1953, Nevers; m. Marie Danielle Amann 1975; one s. one d.; for three years Chef at La Barrière de Clichy, Paris; Proprietor Restaurant Guy Savoy, Paris 1980–, Restaurant Le Bistrot de l'Etoile Troyon 1989–, Restaurant Le Bistrot de l'Etoile-Niel 1989–, Restaurant Le Bistrot l'Etoile-Lauriston 1991, Restaurant La Butte Chaillot 1992, Les Bookinistes 1994, Le Cap Vernet, Paris 1995. *Publications:* Les Légumes gourmands 1985, La Gourmandise apprivoisée 1987. *Leisure interest:* modern painting. *Address:* Restaurant Guy Savoy, 18 rue Troyon, 75017 Paris; 101 boulevard Pereire, 75017 Paris, France. *Telephone:* (Guy Savoy) 43.80.40.61, 43.80.35.22; (Bistrot de l'Étoile) 42.67.25.95.

SAVVINA, Iya Sergeyevna; Russian actress; b. 2 March 1936, Voronezh; ed. Moscow State Univ.; played leading role in adaptation of Chekhov's The Lady with the Lap-dog 1960; acts in cinema, and on stage with Mossovet Theatre, Moscow 1960–78, with Moscow Arts Theatre 1978–; U.S.S.R. State Prize 1983; U.S.S.R. People's Artist 1990. *Films include:* Lady with a Lapdog 1960, A Gentle Woman 1960, Asya's Happiness 1967 (State Prize 1990), Anna Karenina 1968, A Day in the Life of Dr. Kalinnikova 1974, A Lovers' Romance 1975, An Open Book, 1980, Garage 1980, Private Life 1983, Last, Last the Fascination . . . 1985, Mother and Son 1990, Lev Trotsky 1993; numerous stage roles in classical and contemporary works. *Address:* Bolshaya Gruzinskaya Str. 12, Apt. 43, 123242 Moscow, Russia. *Telephone:* 254-97-39.

SAWA, Metropolitan Michał Hrycuniak, TH.D.; Polish ecclesiastic; b. 15 April 1938, Sniatycze; ed. Christian Acad. of Theology, Warsaw, Univ. of Belgrade; teacher Orthodox Seminary, Warsaw 1962–, Rector Int. Section 1964–65; Rector Orthodox Theological Seminary, Jabłeczna 1970–79; Assoc. Prof. and Prof. Christian Acad. of Theology, Warsaw 1966–, Prof. of Theological Sciences 1990–; ordained deacon 1964; ordained priest 1966; Dir. Chancellery of Metropolitan of Warsaw and all Poland 1966–70; Superior Monastery of St. Onufrey at Jabłeczna 1970–79; ordained Bishop 1979, Bishop of Łódź and Poznań 1979–81, of Białystok and Gdańsk 1981–89; Archbishop 1987; Metropolitan of Warsaw and all Poland, Primate of the Polish Autocephalous Orthodox Church May 1998–; Orthodox Ordinary of the Polish Armed Forces 1994–98, rank of Brig.-Gen. 1996; f. quarterly publs. of Diocese of Białystok and Gdańsk and of Orthodox Ordinate of Polish Armed Forces. *Publication:* Prawosławne Pojmowanie Małżeństwa (The Orthodox Understanding of Marriage) 1994. *Address:* al. Solidarności 52, 03-402 Warsaw, Poland. *Telephone:* (22) 619-08-86. *Fax:* (22) 619-08-86.

SAWALLISCH, Wolfgang; German conductor; b. 26 Aug 1923, Munich; m. Mechthild Schmid; ed. Wittelsbacher Gymnasium, Munich; studied under Profs. Ruoff, Haas and Sachsse; mil. service 1942–46, P.O.W. in Italy; conductor Augsburg 1947–53; Musical Dir. Aachen 1953–58, Wiesbaden 1958–60, Cologne Opera 1960–63; Conductor Hamburg Philharmonic Orchestra 1960–73, Hon. mem. 1973–; Prin. Conductor Vienna Symphony Orchestra 1960–70, Hon. mem. and hon. conductor 1980; Prof. Staatliche Hochschule für Musik, Cologne 1960–63; Musical Dir. Bayerische Staatsoper Munich 1971–92; Prin. Conductor Bayerisches Staatsorchester; Perm. Conductor Teatro alla Scala, Milan; conducted at many Festivals; recordings in Germany, U.S.A. and Britain; Hon. Conductor NHK Symphony Orchestra, Tokyo 1967; Artistic Dir. Suisse Romande Orchestra, Geneva 1973–80; Dir. Bayerische Staatsoper, Munich 1982–92; Music Dir. Philadelphia Orchestra 1993–; Accademico Onorario Santa Cecilia; Österreichisches Ehrenkreuz für Kunst und Wissenschaft, Bayerischer Verdienstorden, Bruckner-Ring of Vienna Symphony Orchestra 1980, Grosses Bundesverdienstkreuz (mit Stern), Bayerische Maximiliansorden für Wissenschaft und Kunst 1984, Orden der aúfgehenden sonne am Halsband, Japan, Robert-Schumann-Preis 1994, Chevalier Légion d'honneur, Commdr. des Arts et des Lettres, Cavaliere di Gran Croce (Italy). *Publications:* Im Interesse der Deutlichkeit—Mein Leben mit der Musik 1988, Kontrapunkte 1993. *Address:* Hinterm Bichl 2, 83224 Grassau/Chiemsee, Germany. *Telephone:* 2315.

SAWCHUK, Arthur R., B.SC.; Canadian business executive; m. Mary Sawchuk; one s. one d.; ed. Univ. of Manitoba; joined DuPont eng. group, Kingston, Ont. 1958; transferred to Montreal, holding managerial positions in fibres marketing 1967; Div. Man. Home Furnishings, Toronto 1974; Man. Corp. Planning and Devt. 1981; Div. Man. Packaging 1984; Vice-Pres. and Gen. Man. Fibres and Intermediate Chemicals 1985; Sr. Vice-Pres. and mem. Corp. Policy Advisory Council 1988; Pres., C.E.O., Dir. DuPont Canada Inc. 1992–97, Chair. 1995–97; mem. Bd. Dirs. Canadian Chemical Producers' Asscn., Avenor Inc., Mfrs. Life Insurance Co., Ontario Hydro. *Address:* c/o DuPont Canada Inc., P.O. Box 2200, Streetsville, Mississauga, Ont. L5M 2H3, Canada.

SAWDY, Peter Bryan; British company executive; b. 17 Sept. 1931, London; s. of Alfred Eustace Leon and Beatrice (Lang) Sawdy; m. 1st Anne Stonor 1955 (divorced 1989, died 1995); two d.; m. 2nd Judith Mary Bowen 1989; ed. Ampleforth Coll., London School of Econs. (external); nat. service, commissioned Queen's Regt., also served Parachute Regt. Egypt and Iraq 1951–53; Exec. Trainee, Brooke Bond Group 1953; Buying Exec., Brooke Bond Ceylon Ltd. 1956, Chair. 1964; Dir. Brooke Bond Group 1965; Dir. Brooke Bond Liebig Ltd. 1968, Man. Dir. 1975–77; Group Chief Exec. Brooke Bond Group 1977–81, Deputy Chair., Group Chief Exec. 1981–85; Deputy Chair. Hogg Group 1992–94 (Dir. 1986–); Dir. Griffin Int. Ltd. 1988–, Yule Catto PLC 1990–, Lazard Birla Indian Investment Fund PLC 1994–; Dir. Costain Group 1979–, Chair. 1990–93; Deputy Chair. and Chief Exec. Brooke Bond Group 1981–85. *Leisure interests:* squash, golf, 20th-century Literature. *Address:* 13 Clarendon Street, London, SW1V 2EN, England.

SAWYER, Amos; Liberian politician; fmrly. installed as leader of interim Govt. of Nat. Unity (by leaders of combined guerrilla forces which overthrew regime of fmr. Pres. Samuel Doe 1990) Aug. 1990, inaugurated Nov. 1990; fmr. leader Liberian People's Party (LPP).

SAWYER, Charles Henry, PH.D.; American anatomist and educator; b. 24 Jan. 1915, Ludlow, Vt.; s. of John Guy Sawyer and Edith Mabel (Morgan) Sawyer; m. Ruth Eleanor Shaeffer 1941; one d.; ed. Middlebury Coll., Cambridge Univ., England and Yale Univ.; Instructor in Anatomy, Stanford Univ. 1941–44; Assoc., Asst. Prof., Assoc. Prof., Prof. of Anatomy, Duke Univ. 1944–51; Prof. of Anatomy, U.C.L.A. 1951–85, Chair. Dept. 1955–63, Acting Chair. 1968–69, Emer. Prof. of Anatomy 1985–; Fellow American Acad. of Arts and Sciences; mem. N.A.S.; Hon. mem. Hungarian Soc. of Endocrinology and Metabolism, Japan Endocrine Soc.; Koch Award (Endocrine Soc.) 1973, Hartman Award (Soc. for Study of Reproduction) 1977, Henry Gray Award (American Asscn. of Anatomists) 1983. *Publications:* over 300 major scientific publs., principally on neuroendocrinology of reproduction; (Sr. Ed.) Steroid Hormones and Brain Function 1971. *Leisure interests:* music (symphonic, chamber and piano). *Address:* Department of Neurobiology, University of California at Los Angeles School of Medicine, Los Angeles, CA 90095-1763; 466 Tuallitan Road, Los Angeles, CA 90049, U.S.A. (Home). *Telephone:* (310) 825-9569 (University). *Fax:* (310) 825-2224.

SAXENA, Surrendra Kumar, PH.D.; Canadian international co-operative official; b. 3 April 1926, Aligarh, India; m. Ingalill Gunnel Amanda Friberg 1961; one s. two d.; ed. Univ. of Agra, Inst. of Social Studies, The Hague, Municipal Univ., Amsterdam; Asst. Prof, Dept. of Econs., Birla Coll. 1949–52; Research Fellow, Inst. of Social Studies, The Hague 1955–56; with ICA Regional Office and Educ. Centre for S.E. Asia 1959–61, Regional Officer 1961–68; Dir. Int. Co-operative Alliance (ICA) 1968–81; Sr. Consultant to Swedish Co-operative Centre, Stockholm 1981–83; Consultant on Co-operatives and Rural Devt.; Consultant to the World Bank, Asian Devt. Bank, CIDA, Canadian Cooperative Asscn.; Dr. h.c. Univ. of Sherbrooke, Canada; Severin Jorgensen Prize (Copenhagen) 1978, Indian Co-operative Movement Medal 1979, Highest Medal of Yugoslavia Co-operative Union 1980. *Publications:* Nationalisation and Industrial Conflict: Example of British Coal Mining 1955, Global Review of Co-operative Food Processing from the Perspective of Developing Countries 1983, Organisation of Technical Assistance in Co-operative Movements in Canada, Sweden and the United States—Some Lessons for other Movements 1985, Co-operatives and Peace 1986, Co-operatives in Developing Countries 1986, A State Movement Partnership Model 1986, Co-operatives in India and Pakistan: Some Aspects, Co-operatives and Environment: An International Perspective 1995, Ends of a Circle. *Leisure interests:* golf, music. *Address:* 56 Raymerville Drive, Markham, Ont. L3P 4J5, Canada. *Telephone:* (905) 294-9747. *Fax:* (905) 294 7208.

SAY, Rt. Rev. Richard David, K.C.V.O., D.D.; British ecclesiastic; b. 4 Oct. 1914, London; s. of Commdr. Richard Say, O.B.E., R.N.V.R., and Kathleen Mary Wildy; m. Irene Frances Rayner, O.B.E., J.P., 1943; two s. (one deceased) two d.; ed. Univ. Coll. School, Christ's Coll., Cambridge and Ridley Hall, Cambridge; Curate Croydon Parish Church 1939–43, St. Martin-in-the-Fields 1943–50, Gen. Sec., Church of England Youth Council 1944–47; Gen. Sec., British Council of Churches 1947–55; Rector of Hatfield and Domestic Chaplain to Marquess of Salisbury, K.G. 1955–61; Hon. Canon of St. Albans 1957–61; Bishop of Rochester 1961–88; Asst. Bishop of Canterbury 1988–; Church of England del. to World Council of Churches 1948, 1954, and 1961; Sub-Prelate of the Order of St. John of Jerusalem; Chaplain to the Pilgrims of G.B. 1968–; mem. House of Lords 1969–88; High Almoner to H.M. the Queen 1970–88; Deputy Pro-Chancellor, Univ. of Kent 1977–83, Pro-Chancellor 1983–93; Court of Ecclesiastical Causes Reserved 1984–92; Chair. Age Concern England 1986–89, Patron 1992–; Vice-Pres. UNA, G.B. and Northern Ireland 1986–; Pres. Friends of Kent Churches 1988–; Hon. D.C.L. (Kent) 1987; Hon. mem. Inst. of Royal Engineers 1986; Hon. Freeman Borough of Tonbridge and Malling 1987, Borough of Rochester Upon Medway 1988–. *Leisure interests:* history, travel. *Address:* 23 Chequers Park, Wye, Ashford, Kent, TN25 5BB, England. *Telephone:* (01233) 812720.

SAYED, Mostafa Amr El-, PH.D.; American professor of chemistry; b. 8 May 1933, Zifta, Egypt; s. of Amr El-Sayed and Zakia Ahmed; m. Janice Jones 1957; three s. two d.; ed. Ein Shams Univ., Cairo, Egypt, Florida State, Yale and Harvard Univs., Calif. Inst. of Tech.; Asst. Prof., Univ. of Calif., Los Angeles 1961–64, Assoc. Prof. 1964–67, Prof. 1967–; Consultant to Space Tech. Lab. on Laser Tech. 1962–63, Electro-Optical Systems on Laser Tech. 1963–66, N. American Aviation on the Minuteman Program 1964–65, Navy Electronics Labs. on Dye and Liquid Lasers 1969–73, Ford Research Labs. 1970, Northrop Corpn. on Molecular Energy Transfer 1979–81; Vice-Pres. Egyptian American Scholars 1977–; Pres. Arab Physical Soc. 1979–; Ed. Journal of Physical Chem., American Chemical Soc. 1980–; Jt. Ed. Int. Reviews in Physical Chem. 1984–; mem. Physical Chem. Div., IUPAC 1985–; fmr. mem. N.A.S.; mem. American Acad. of Arts and Sciences; Trustee Bd. of Trustees of Associated Univs. Inc. 1988–; Alfred P. Sloan Fellow 1965–71; John Simon Guggenheim Memorial Foundation Fellow 1967-68; Fresenius Nat. Award in Pure and Applied Chem. 1967, Alexander von Humboldt Sr. U.S. Scientist Award, West German Govt. 1982. *Publications:* many articles in scientific journals. *Address:* Department of Chemistry and Biochemistry, University of California, Los Angeles, CA 90024 (Office); 3325 Colbert Avenue, Los Angeles, CA 90066, U.S.A. (Home). *Telephone:* (213) 825-1352 (Office); (213) 391-2272 (Home).

SAYEGH, Bishop Selim Wahban, PH.D.; Jordanian ecclesiastic; b. 1935, Jordan; s. of Wahban Sayigh; ed. Lateran Univ., Rome; Pres. of the Latin Patriarchal Court, Jerusalem 1967–79; Rector of the Latin Patriarichal

Seminary 1976–81; Titular Bishop of Aquae in Proconsulari, Vicar Gen. for Transjordan 1982–; Commdr. of the Equestrian Order of the Holy Sepulchre of Jerusalem. *Publications:* Le Statu Quo des Lieux-Saints 1971, The Christian Family's Guidebook. *Leisure interests:* chess, table tennis, volley-ball, history, ecclesiastical law. *Address:* Latin Vicariate, P.O. Box 1317, Amman, Jordan. *Telephone:* (6) 563-7740.

SAYLES, John Thomas, B.S.; American writer, film director, actor and scriptwriter; b. 28 Sept. 1950, Schenectady; s. of Donald John Sayles and Mary (née Rausch) Sayles; ed. Williams Coll. *Screenwriter for:* Piranha 1978, The Lady in Red 1979, Battle Beyond the Stars 1980, The Howling 1981, Alligator 1981, The Challenge 1982, The Perfect Match 1980. *Films include:* Baby It's You 1983, Return of the Secaucus Seven 1980 (L.A. Film Critics Award), Lianna 1983, The Brother from Another Planet 1984, Matewan (also screenwriter and acted in) 1987, Eight Men Out 1989, City of Hope 1991, Malcolm X, Passion Fish (dir., screenwriter and acted in), Matinee, My Life's in Turnaround 1994, The Secret of Roan Inish (dir., screenwriter, ed.), Lone Star (dir., screenwriter), Men With Guns (dir., screenwriter, ed.). *Publications:* Pride of the Bimbos 1975, Union Dues 1979, Thinking in Pictures 1987, I-80 Nebraska, M.490-M.205 (O Henry Award) 1975, Breed, Golden State (O Henry Award) 1977, Hoop, The Anarchists' Convention 1979, New Hope for the Dead (play) 1981, Turnbuckle (play), Los Gusanos 1991. *Address:* Paramount Pictures, 5555 Melrose Avenue, Los Angeles, CA 90038; Paradigm, 10100 Santa Monica Boulevard, Los Angeles, CA 90067, U.S.A.

SCACCHI, Greta; actress; b. Milan, Italy; one d.; ed. Bristol Old Vic Drama School. *Films:* Second Sight, Heat and Dust, Defence of the Realm, The Coca-Cola Kid, A Man in Love, Good Morning Babylon, White Mischief, Paura e Amore (Three Sisters), La Donna dell Luna, Woman in the Moon, Schoolmates, Presumed Innocent, Shattered, Fires Within, Turtle Beach, Salt on our Skin, The Browning Version, Jefferson in Paris 1994, Country Life 1995, Emma 1996, Cosi, The Serpent's Kiss 1997, Tom's Midnight Garden 1998, The Red Violin 1998, Cotton Mary 1998. *Television:* The Ebony Tower, Dr. Fischer of Geneva, Waterfront (series), Rasputin (Emmy Award 1996), The Odyssey (series) 1996, Macbeth 1998. *Theatre:* Cider with Rosie, In Times like These, Airbase, Uncle Vanya. *Address:* c/o Susan Smith & Associates, 121 North San Vicente Boulevard, Beverly Hills, CA 90211, U.S.A.

SCAIFE, Brendan (Kevin Patrick), D.SC.ENG., PH.D., M.R.I.A.; Irish electrical engineer; b. 19 May 1928, London; s. of James Scaife and Mary Kavanagh; m. Mary Manahan 1961; three s. one d.; ed. Cardinal Vaughan Memorial School, London, Chelsea Polytechnic and Queen Mary Coll. London; G.E.C. Research Labs, Wembley 1953–54; Scholar, School of Theoretical Physics, Dublin Inst. for Advanced Studies 1954–55; Inst. for Industrial Research and Standards, Dublin 1955–56; Electricity Supply Bd. Dublin 1956; Coll. of Tech., Dublin 1956–61; lecturer in Electronic Eng., Trinity Coll. Dublin 1961–66, Fellow 1964, Reader 1966, Assoc. Prof. 1967–72, Prof. of Eng. Science 1972–86, Prof. of Electromagnetics 1986–88, Sr. Fellow 1987–88, Fellow Emer. 1988–; Visiting Prof. Univ. of Salford 1969–82; mem. Royal Irish Acad.; Boyle Medal (Royal Dublin Soc.) 1992. *Publications:* Complex Permittivity (compiler) 1971, Studies in Numerical Analysis (ed.) 1974, Principles of Dielectrics (revised edn.) 1998. *Address:* Department of Electronic and Electrical Engineering, Trinity College, Dublin 2 (Office); 6 Trimleston Avenue, Booterstown, Blackrock, Co. Dublin, Ireland (Home). *Telephone:* 01-608 1580 (Office); 01-269 3867 (Home). *Fax:* 01-677 2442 (Office).

SCALES, John Tracey, O.B.E., L.R.C.P., F.R.C.S., C.I.MECH.E.; British professor and medical practitioner; b. 2 July 1920, Colchester; s. of W.L. Scales; m. Cecilia May Sparrow 1945 (deceased 1992); two d.; ed. Haberdashers' Aske's School, London, King's Coll., London, Univs. of Glasgow and Birmingham, Charing Cross Hosp. Medical School; Capt. R.A.M.C. 1945–47; House Surgeon Royal Nat. Orthopaedic Hosp., Stanmore 1947, M.O. Plastics Unit 1949, Hon. Sr. Registrar 1952, Hon. Consultant in Orthopaedic Prosthetics 1958; lecturer Inst. of Orthopaedics, Univ. of London 1951, Sr. Lecturer 1952, Reader Biomedical Eng. 1968, Prof. 1974–87, Emer. Prof. 1987–; Visiting Prof. Biomedical Centre, Cranfield Univ. 1997–; Hon. Consultant Royal Nat. Orthopaedic Hosp., Stanmore, Royal Orthopaedic Hosp., Birmingham, Mount Vernon Hosp., Middx.; Hon. Dir. R.A.F.T. Inst. of Plastic Surgery, Mount Vernon Hosp. 1988–93, Dir. of Pressure Sore Prevention 1994–97; Hon. mem. British Asscn. Plastic Surgeons 1993; Sr. Companion Fellow British Orthopaedic Asscn. 1993; Hon. Fellow Biological Eng. Soc. 1994; Thomas Henry Green Prize in Surgery, Robert Danis Prize, S.G. Brown Award (Royal Soc.), James Berrie Prize, Jackson Burrows Medal, Donald Julius Groen Prize (Inst. of Mech. Eng.), A.A. Griffith Silver Medal. 1974, Clemson Award (Clemson Univ., U.S.A.) 1974, Commissioned Kentucky Col. for contribs. to surgery, U.S.A. 1994. *Publications:* numerous articles and scientific papers. *Leisure interests:* dogs, Goss china. *Address:* Fairbanks, Riverview Road, Pangbourne, Berks., RG8 7AU, England (Home). *Telephone:* (0118) 984 3568 (Home). *Fax:* (0118) 9844945.

SCALES, Prunella Margaret Rumney West, C.B.E.; British actress; d. of John Richardson Illingworth and Catherine Scales; m. Timothy West (q.v.) 1963; two s.; ed. Moira House, Eastbourne, Old Vic Theatre School, London, Herbert Berghof Studio, New York; in repertory, Huddersfield, Salisbury, Oxford, Bristol Old Vic etc.; seasons at Stratford and Chichester 1967–68. *Plays include:* The Promise 1967, Hay Fever 1968, The Wolf 1975, Make and Break 1980, An Evening with Queen Victoria 1980, The Merchant of Venice 1981, Quartermaine's Terms 1981, When We Are Married 1986, Single Spies (double bill) 1988, School for Scandal, Long Day's Journey into Night (Nat. Theatre), Happy Days 1993, Staying On 1996, Some Singing Blood (Royal Court), The Mother Tongue, The Editing Process 1994. *Television includes:* Fawlty Towers (series) 1975, 1978, Mapp and Lucia (series) 1985–86, Absurd Person Singular 1985, What the Butler Saw 1987, After Henry (series) 1988–92, A Question of Attribution 1991, Signs and Wonders 1995, Breaking the Code 1995, Lord of Misrule 1995, Dalziel & Pascoe 1996, Signs and Wonders, Lord of Misrule, Breaking the Code 1997. *Films include:* An Awfully Big Adventure 1994, Stiff Upper Lips 1997; numerous radio broadcasts, readings, poetry recitals, fringe productions; has directed plays at numerous theatres including Bristol Old Vic, Arts Theatre, Cambridge, Nottingham Playhouse, W. Yorkshire Playhouse (Getting On); Pres. Council for the Protection of Rural England 1997–; Freeman of City of London 1990; Hon. D.Litt. (Bradford) 1995, (East Anglia) 1996. *Leisure interest:* gardening, crosswords. *Address:* c/o Jeremy Conway,18–21 Jermyn Street, London, SW1Y 6HP, England.

SCALFARI, Eugenio, D.IUR.; Italian editor; b. 6 April 1924, Civitavecchia; m. Simonetta de Benedetti 1959; two d.; contrib. Il Mondo, L'Europeo 1950–; Promoter Partito Radicale 1958, L'Espresso 1955–, Ed.-in-Chief 1963–68, Man. Dir. 1970–75; Promoter La Repubblica 1976–, Ed.-in-Chief 1976–96, Dir. 1988–; Deputy to Parl. 1968–72; Siena Award 1985, Journalist of the Year Award 1986. *Publications:* Rapporto sul Neocapitalismo Italiano, Il Potere Economico in URSS, L'Autunno della Repubblica, Razza Padrona, Interviste ai Potenti, L'Anno di Craxi, La Sera Andavamo in Via Veneto, Incontro con Io, La Morale Perduta. *Address:* c/o La Repubblica, Piazza dell'Indipendenza 11/B, 00185 Roma, Italy. *Telephone:* (06) 49821.

SCALFARO, Oscar Luigi; Italian politician and lawyer; b. 9 Sept. 1918, Novara; ed. Università Cattolica del Sacro Cuore, Milan; elected Christian Democrat (D.C.) M.P. for Turin-Novara-Vercelli 1948; Sec. then Vice-Chair. Parl. Group and mem. Nat. Council of D.C., mem. of D.C. Cen. Office during De Gasperi's leadership, Under-Sec. of State at Ministry of Labour and Social Security in Fanfani Govt., Under-Sec. in Ministry of Justice, Under-Sec. in Ministry of Interior 1959–62; Minister of Transport and Civil Aviation in Moro, Leone and Andreotti Govts. Minister of Educ. in second Andreotti Govt.; Vice-Chair. House of Deputies; Minister of the Interior 1983–87; mem. House of Deputies Comm. for Foreign and Community Affairs; Pres. of Italy May 1992–. *Address:* Palazzo del Quirinale, 00187 Rome, Italy. *Telephone:* (06) 46991.

SCALIA, Antonin, A.B., LL.B.; American judge; b. 11 March 1936, Trenton, N.J.; s. of S. Eugene and Catherine L. (Panaro) Scalia; m. Maureen McCarthy 1960; five s. four d.; ed. Univ. of Fribourg, Switzerland and Harvard Univ.; called to Bar, Ohio 1962, Virginia 1970; Assoc. Jones, Day, Cockley & Reavis, Cleveland 1961–67; Assoc. Prof. Univ. of Va. Law School 1967–70, Prof. 1970–74; Gen. Counsel Office of Telecommunications Policy, Exec. Office of President 1971–72; Chair. Admin. Conf. U.S., Washington 1972–74; Asst. Attorney Gen., U.S. Office of Legal Counsel, Justice Dept. 1974–77; Prof. Law School, Univ. of Chicago 1977–82; Visiting Prof. Georgetown Law Center 1977, Stanford Law School 1980–81; Judge, U.S. Court of Appeals (D.C. Circuit) 1982–86; Judge, U.S. Supreme Court 1986–; Hon Master of the Bench, Inner Temple, London 1986; mem. numerous advisory councils etc. *Address:* U.S. Supreme Court, 1 First Street, N.E., Washington, DC 20543, U.S.A.

SCAMMON, Richard M.; American psephologist; b. 17 July 1915, Minneapolis, Minn.; s. of Dr. Richard E. and Julia (Simms) Scammon; m. Mary Stark Allen 1952; one d.; ed. Univ. of Minnesota, London School of Econs., Univ. of London and Univ. of Michigan; Research Sec., Radio Office, Univ. of Chicago 1939–41; Army Service 1941–46; Chief, Political Activities Branch, Civil Admin. Div., Office of Military Govt. U.S. (Germany) 1946–48; Chief, Div. of Research for Western Europe, Dept. of State 1948–55; Dir. Elections Research Center, Washington 1955–61, 1965–95; Dir. of the Census 1961–65; Chair. U.S. Del. to Observe Elections in U.S.S.R. 1958, Chair. Pres.'s Comm. on Registration and Voting Participation 1963, OAS Electoral Mission to the Dominican Repub. 1966; Pres. Nat. Council on Public Polls 1969–70; Chair. Select Comm. on Western Hemisphere Immigration 1966–68; mem. U.S. Del. to UN Gen. Ass. 1973; Consultant, State Dept. (West Bank autonomy) 1979–80, (El Salvador) 1981–82; Bilderberg Lecturer 1985; Chantauqua Lecturer 1989; mem. Nat. Bipartisan Comm. on Cen. America 1983–84; mem. Editorial Bd. Public Opinion, World Affairs, Electoral Studies; mem. Bd. of Dirs. Int. Foundation for Electoral Systems 1987. *Publications:* Editor, America Votes Vol. 1 1956, Vol. 2 1958, Vol. 3 1960, Vol. 4 1962, Vol. 5 1964, Vol. 6 1966, Vol. 7 1968, Vol. 8 1970, Vol. 9 1972, Vol. 10 1973, Vol. 11 1975, Vol. 12 1977, Vol. 13 1979, Vol. 14 1981, Vol. 15 1983, Vol. 16 1985, Vol. 17 1987, Vol. 18 1989, Vol. 19 1991; Ed. America at the Polls 1965, (1988), Co-Author This U.S.A. 1965, The Real Majority 1970. *Address:* c/o Mrs. Mary Scammon, 333 Russell Avenue, Apt. 304, Gaithersburg, MD 20877, U.S.A. *Telephone:* (301) 216-5878.

SCANLAN, John Oliver, M.ENG., PH.D., M.R.I.A., F.I.E.E., F.I.E.E.E.; Irish professor of electronic engineering; b. 20 Sept. 1937, Dublin; s. of John and Hannah Scanlan; m. Ann Weadock 1961; ed. St. Mary's Coll., Dundalk, Univ. Coll. Dublin; Research Engineer, Mullard Research Labs., Surrey,

U.K. 1959–63; lecturer, Univ. of Leeds, U.K. 1963–68, Prof. of Electronic Eng. 1968–73; Prof. of Electronic Eng., Univ. Coll. Dublin 1973–; Sec. Royal Irish Acad. 1981–89, Pres. 1993–96; Dir. Bord Telecom Eireann 1984–97. *Publications:* Analysis and Synthesis of Tunnel Diode Circuits 1966, Circuit Theory (Vols. 1 and 2) 1970. *Leisure interests:* music, golf. *Address:* Department of Electronic and Electrical Engineering, Engineering Building, University College Dublin, Belfield, Dublin 4, Ireland. *Telephone:* 2693244.

SCANLON, Baron (Life Peer), cr. 1979, of Davyhulme in the County of Greater Manchester; **Hugh Parr Scanlon;** British trade unionist; b. 26 Oct. 1913, Australia; m. Nora Markey 1943; two d.; ed. Stretford Elementary School, Nat. Council of Labour Colls.; apprentice; instrument maker; Shop Steward, Convener Associated Electrical Industries, Trafford Park; Div. Organizer Amalgamated Eng. Union, Manchester 1947–63, mem. Exec. Council AEU London 1963–67; Pres. Amalgamated Union of Engineering Workers (AUEW) 1967–78; fmr. Vice-Pres., mem. Exec. Cttee. Int. Metalworkers' Fed.; fmr. mem. Nat. Econ. Devt. Council (NEDC); fmr. mem. Metrication Bd.; fmr. Pres. European Metalworkers' Fed.; Chair., Chief Exec. Eng. Industry Training Bd. 1975–82; mem. Advisory Council for Applied Research and Devt. 1982–; mem. British Gas Corpn. 1976–82, Govt. Cttee. of Inquiry into Teaching of Maths in Primary and Secondary Schools in England and Wales 1978–; Hon. D.C.L. (Kent) 1988. *Leisure interests:* golf, swimming, gardening. *Address:* 23 Seven Stones Drive, Broadstairs, Kent, England.

SCANNELL, Vernon, F.R.S.L.; British poet, author and broadcaster; b. 23 Jan. 1922; ed. Leeds Univ.; served with Gordon Highlanders 1940–45; various jobs including teacher, Hazelwood Prep. School 1955–62; Southern Arts Asscn. Writing Fellowship 1975–76; Visiting Poet, Shrewsbury School 1978–79; Resident Poet, King's School, Canterbury 1979. *Publications:* several novels including The Fight 1953, A Lonely Game (for younger readers) 1979 and Ring of Truth 1983; volumes of poetry including The Masks of Love 1960 (Heinemann Award), A Sense of Danger (Ed., with Ted Hughes and Patricia Beer) 1962; New Poems, a PEN anthology 1962; Walking Wounded: poems 1962–65, 1968, Epithets of War: poems 1965–69, 1969; Mastering the Craft (Poets Today Series) 1970, Pergamon Poets, No. 8 (with J. Silkin) 1970, Selected Poems 1971, The Winter Man: new poems 1973, The Apple Raid and other poems 1974 (Cholmondeley Poetry Prize), The Loving Game 1975, New and Collected Poems 1950–80, 1980, Winterlude and other poems 1982, Funeral Games 1987, A Time for Fires 1991, The Black and White Days (poems) 1996; (*criticism*) Not Without Glory: poets of World War II 1976, How to Enjoy Poetry 1982, How to Enjoy Novels 1984; (*autobiography*) The Tiger and the Rose 1971, A Proper Gentleman 1977, Argument of Kings (autobiog.) 1987, The Drums of Morning: Growing Up in the Thirties 1992; Sporting Literature: an Anthology 1987, The Clever Potato, Poems for Children 1988, Soldiering On, Poems of Military Life 1989, Love Shouts and Whispers (poems for children) 1990, Travelling Light (for children) 1991, Collected Poems 1950–1993 1994, The Black and White Days 1996. *Leisure interests:* listening to radio (mainly music), drink, boxing (as a spectator), films, reading. *Address:* 51 North Street, Otley, W. Yorks., LS21 1AH, England. *Telephone:* (01943) 467176.

SCARAMUZZI, Franco; Italian agricultural scientist; b. 26 Dec. 1926, Ferrara; s. of Donato Scaramuzzi and Alberta Rovida; m. Maria Bianca Cancellieri 1955; one s. one d.; Prof. of Pomology, Univ. of Pisa 1959, Univ. of Florence 1969–; Rector Magnificus, Univ. of Florence 1979–91; Past Pres. Int. Soc. of Horticultural Science; Hon. Pres. Italian Horticultural Soc., Italian Acad. of Vine and Wine; Pres. Accademia dei Georgofili; mem. Soviet (now Russian) Acad. of Agricultural Sciences; Hon. mem. Rotary. *Address:* Via Donizetti 6, 50144 Florence (Office); Viale Amendola 38, 50121 Florence, Italy (Home). *Telephone:* (055) 333462 (Office); (055) 2342825 (Home).

SCARDINO, Marjorie Morris, J.D., B.A.; American business executive; b. 25 Jan. 1947, Arizona; d. of Robert Weldon Morris and Beth Lamb Morris; m. Albert James Scardino 1974; two s. one d.; ed. Baylor Univ., Univ. of San Francisco; partner Brannen, Wessels and Searcy law firm 1975–85; publr. The Ga. Gazette Co. 1978–85; Pres. The Economist Newspaper Group Inc. 1985–93, Man. Dir. Economist Intelligence Unit 1992–93, Chief Exec. The Economist Group 1993–97; Chief Exec., Dir. Pearson PLC 1997–; Dir. W. H. Smith Group PLC 1994–, Con Agra Inc. 1994–; Fellow London Business School. *Address:* Pearson PLC, 3 Burlington Gardens, London, W1X 1LE, England. *Telephone:* 0171-411 2300. *Fax:* 0171-411 2399.

SCARF, Herbert Eli, PH.D.; American economist; b. 25 July 1930, Philadelphia, Pa.; s. of Louis H. Scarf and Lena Elkman; m. Margaret Klein 1953; three d.; ed. Temple Univ. and Princeton Univ.; employee of Rand Corpn., Santa Monica, Calif. 1954–57; Asst. and Assoc. Prof., Dept. of Statistics, Stanford Univ., Calif. 1957–63; Fellow, Center for Advanced Study in the Behavioral Sciences, Stanford, Calif. 1962–63; Prof. of Econs., Yale Univ. 1963–70, Stanley Resor Prof. of Econs. 1970–78, Sterling Prof. of Econs. 1979–; Dir. Cowles Foundation for Research in Econs. 1967–71, 1981–84, Dir. Div. of Social Sciences 1971–72, 1973–74; Visiting Prof., Stanford Univ., Calif. 1977–78, Mathematical Sciences Research Inst. Spring 1986; Ford Foundation Sr. Faculty Fellowship 1969–70; Fellow Econometric Soc., Pres. 1983; Fellow American Acad. of Arts and Sciences; mem. N.A.S., American Philosophical Soc.; Distinguished Fellow American Econ. Asscn. 1991; Hon. L.H.D. (Chicago) 1978; Lanchester Prize, (Operations Research Soc. of America) 1974, Von Neumann Medal 1983. *Publications:* Studies in the Mathematical Theory of Inventory and Production (with K. Arrow and S. Karlin) 1958, The Optimality of (S, s) Policies in the Dynamic Inventory Problem 1960, The Computation of Economic Equilibria (with Terje Hansen) 1973, Applied General Equilibrium Analysis (with John Shoven, eds.) 1984; articles in learned journals. *Leisure interests:* music, reading, hiking. *Address:* Yale University, Cowles Foundation for Research in Economics, P.O. Box 208281, New Haven, CT 06520-8281; 88 Blake Road, Hamden, CT 06517, U.S.A. (Home). *Telephone:* (203) 432-3693 (Office); (203) 776–9197 (Home).

SCARFE, Gerald A.; British cartoonist; b. 1 June 1936, London; m. Jane Asher; two s. one d.; has contributed cartoons to Punch 1960–, Private Eye 1961–, Daily Mail 1966–, The Sunday Times 1967–, Time 1967–; exhibited at Grosvenor Gallery (group exhbns.) 1969, 1970, Pavillion d'Humour, Montreal 1969, Expo 1970, Osaka 1970; one-man exhbns. Waddell Gallery, New York 1968, 1970, Vincent Price Gallery, Chicago 1969, Grosvenor Gallery 1969, Nat. Portrait Gallery 1971, Royal Festival Hall 1983, Langton Gallery 1986, Chris Beetles Gallery 1989, Nat. Portrait Gallery 1998–99, Comic Art Gallery, Melbourne; animation and film directing BBC 1969–; consultant designer and character design for film Hercules 1997; Zagreb Prize for BBC film Long Drawn Out Trip 1973; *Theatre design:* Ubu Roi (Traverse Theatre) 1957, What the Butler Saw (Oxford Playhouse) 1980, No End of Blame (Royal Court, London) 1981, Orpheus in the Underworld (English Nat. Opera, Coliseum) 1985, Who's a Lucky Boy (Royal Exchange, Manchester) 1985, Born Again 1990, The Magic Flute (L.A. Opera) 1992, An Absolute Turkey 1993, Mind Millie for Me (Haymarket, London) 1996, Fantastic Mr. Fox (L.A. Opera) 1998. *Publications:* Gerald Scarfe's People 1966, Indecent Exposure 1973, Expletive Deleted: The Life and Times of Richard Nixon 1974, Gerald Scarfe 1982, Father Kissmass and Mother Claus 1985, Scarfe by Scarfe (autobiog.) 1986, Gerald Scarfe's Seven Deadly Sins 1987, Line of Attack 1988, Scarfeland 1989, Scarfe on Stage 1992, Scarfe Face 1993, Hades: the truth at last 1997. *Leisure interests:* drawing, painting, sculpting. *Address:* c/o ICM, Oxford House, 76 Oxford Street, London, W1N 0AX, England.

SCARGILL, Arthur; British trade unionist; b. 11 Jan. 1938, Worsborough, Yorks.; s. of the late Harold Scargill and of Alice Scargill; m. Anne Harper 1961; one d.; ed. White Cross Secondary School; worked first in a factory, then Woolley Colliery 1955; mem. Barnsley Young Communist League 1955–62; mem. Nat. Union of Mineworkers (N.U.M.) 1955–, N.U.M. Branch Cttee. 1960, Branch del. to N.U.M. Yorks. Area Council 1964, mem. N.U.M. Nat. Exec. 1972–, Pres. Yorks. N.U.M. 1973–82, Pres. N.U.M. 1981–; Chair. N.U.M. Int. Cttee.; Pres. Int. Miners Org. Sept. 1985–; mem. Labour Party 1966–95; mem. T.U.C. Gen. Council 1986–88; f. Socialist Labour Party 1996; contested Newport East 1997. *Address:* National Union of Mineworkers, 2 Huddersfield Road, Barnsley, S. Yorks., S70 2LS, England.

SCARMAN, Baron (Life Peer), cr. 1977, of Quatt in the County of Salop (Shropshire); **Leslie George Scarman,** Kt., P.C., O.B.E., Q.C.; British judge; b. 29 July 1911, London; s. of George Charles and Ida Irene Scarman; m. Ruth Clement Wright 1947; one s.; ed. Radley Coll. and Oxford Univ.; Harmsworth Law Scholar, Middle Temple 1936; R.A.F. (Volunteer Reserve) 1940–45; Q.C. 1957; Judge, High Court of Justice, England 1961; Chair. Law Comm. for England and Wales 1965–72; Lord Justice of Appeal 1973–77, Lord of Appeal in Ordinary 1977–86 (retd.); Chancellor of Univ. of Warwick 1981–89; Pres. Royal Inst. of Public Admin. 1981–89, Constitutional Reform Centre 1984–, Citizen Action Compensation Campaign 1988–; numerous hon. degrees include Hon. LL.D. (London, Warwick, Kent, Exeter, City of London, Cambridge, Wales); Hon. D.C.L. (Oxford, Freiburg); Hon. D. Univ. (Brunel) 1987. *Publications:* Pattern of Law Reform 1967, English Law—the New Dimension 1974, Scarman Report on the Brixton Riots 1981. *Leisure interests:* music, walking, gardening, history. *Address:* House of Lords, London, SW1A 0PW, England. *Telephone:* 0171-219 3000.

SCAZZIERI, Roberto, DR.SC.POL., M.LITT., D.PHIL.; Italian professor of economics; b. 1 May 1950, Bologna; s. of Guerrino Scazzieri and Fosca Lambertini; m. Maria Cristina Bacchi 1983; one s.; ed. Liceo Minghetti, Bologna, Univ. of Bologna, Univ. of Oxford, U.K.; Asst. Lecturer, Univ. of Bologna 1974–79, lecturer in Theory and Policy of Econ. Growth 1980–83, in Econ. Principles 1983–86, in Advanced Econ. Analysis 1985–87, Assoc. Prof. of Econs., Faculty of Political Sciences 1986–87, Full Prof. of Econs., Faculty of Econ. and Commerce and Dept. of Econs. 1990–; Prof. of Econs., Faculty of Statistics, Univ. of Padua 1987–90; Visiting Scholar, Dept. of Applied Econs., Cambridge Univ. 1987, 1989, Research Assoc. 1992–93; Visiting Fellow Clare Hall 1992, Life mem. 1992; Visiting Fellow Gonville and Caius Coll. 1999; Resident Fellow Bologna Inst. for Advanced Study 1997; Visiting Prof. Univ. of Lugano, Switzerland 1997; Man. Ed. and Review Ed. Structural Change and Economic Dynamics; Dir. of Research Ministry of Univ. and Science and Nat. Research Council; mem. Steering Cttee. Bologna-Cambridge-Harvard Sr. Seminars Network; mem. Steering Cttee. Bologna Inst. for Advanced Study, Int. Inst. of Econ. Analysis; mem. Man. Bd. European Summer School in Structural Change and Econ. Dynamics (Selwyn Coll., Cambridge Univ.) 1995–; mem. Scientific Cttee. Int. Centre for the History of Univs. and Science 1994; Foundation Fellow Kyoto Univ.; Rector's Del., Bologna-Clare Hall Fellowship 1993–; mem. Bologna Acad. of Sciences 1994; Bonaldo Stringher Prize Scholarship (Bank of Italy) 1974, St. Vincent Prize for Econs. 1984. *Publications:* Efficienza produttiva e livelli di attività 1981, Protagonisti del pensiero economico (co-author) 1977–82, Sui momenti costitutivi dell'economia politica 1983 (co-author), Foundations of Economics: Structures of Inquiry and Economic Theory 1986, The Economic Theory of Structure and Change 1990, A Theory of Production: Tasks, Processes and Technical Practices 1993, Production and Economic Dynamics (with M. Landesmann) 1996, Incommensurability and Translation. Kuhnian Perspectives on Scientific Communication and Theory Change (jtly.), Edward Elgar 1999; numerous articles. *Leisure interests:* reading and conversation, art, walking. *Address:* Università degli Studi di Bologna, Piazza Scaravilli 2, 40126 Bologna (Office); Via Garibaldi 5, 40124 Bologna, Italy (Home). *Telephone:* (51) 258146 (Office); (51) 582789 (Home).

SCHABRAM, Hans, DR.PHIL.; German professor of medieval English; b. 27 Sept. 1928, Berlin; s. of Paul Schabram and Lucia Schabram; m. Candida Larisch 1956; two s. one d.; ed. Univs. of Berlin and Cologne; Asst. English Dept. Univ. of Heidelberg 1957–63; Prof. of Medieval English Language and Literature Univ. of Giessen 1964–67, Univ. of Göttingen 1968–; mem. Akad. der Wissenschaften, Göttingen. *Publications:* 55 publs. on English Philology since 1956. *Address:* Seminar für Englische Philologie der Universität, Humboldtallee 13, 37073 Göttingen (Office); Heinz-Hilpert-Str. 6, 37085 Göttingen, Germany. *Telephone:* 0551-397571 (Office); 0551-55444 (Home).

SCHACHMAN, Howard Kapnek, PH.D.; American biochemist and educator; b. 5 Dec. 1918, Philadelphia, Pa.; s. of Morris H. and Rose Kapnek Schachman; m. Ethel H. Lazarus 1945; two s.; ed. Mass. Inst. of Technology and Princeton Univ.; Fellow, Nat. Inst. of Health 1946–48; Instructor (Biochem.), Univ. of Calif., Berkeley 1948–50, Asst. Prof. 1950–54, Assoc. Prof. 1955–59, Prof. of Biochem. and Molecular Biology 1959–91, Prof. Emer. 1991–94, Prof. of Grad. School 1994–, Chair. Dept. of Molecular Biology, Dir. Virus Lab. 1969–76, N.I.H. Ombudsman in Basic Sciences 1994–; Carl and Gerty Cori Lecturer, Washington Univ. School of Medicine, St. Louis 1993; Faculty Research Lecturer, Univ. of Calif. at Berkeley 1994; Pres. American Soc. for Biochemistry and Molecular Biology 1987–88, Chair. Public Affairs Cttee. 1989–; mem. N.A.S. (Chair. Biochemistry Section 1990–93), A.A.A.S., American Acad. of Arts and Sciences; Foreign mem. Accad. Nazionale dei Lincei, Rome 1996; Scholar-in-Residence Fogarty Int. Center, NIH 1977–78; Pres. Fed. of American Socs. for Experimental Biology 1988–89; mem. Scientific Council and Scientific Advisory Bd. of Stazione Zoologica Naples, Italy 1988–, Bd. of Scientific Consultants of Memorial Sloan-Kettering Cancer Center 1988–97, Bd. of Scientific Counselors Nat. Cancer Inst., Div. of Cancer Biology and Diagnosis 1989–92; Special Adviser to Dir. of N.I.H. 1994–; Hon. D.Sc. (Northwestern Univ.) 1974; Hon. M.D. (Naples) 1990; Calif. Section Award, American Chemical Soc. 1958, E. H. Sargent & Co. Award for Chemical Instrumentation, American Chemical Soc. 1962, John Scott Award, City of Philadelphia 1964, Warren Triennial Prize, Mass. Gen. Hosp. 1965, Merck Award, American Soc. of Biological Chemists 1986, Alexander von Humboldt Award 1990, Alberta Heritage Foundation for Medical Research Visiting Professorship, Univ. of Alberta 1996, Theodor Svedberg Award 1998. *Publications:* Ultracentrifugation in Biochemistry 1959; articles. *Leisure interest:* sports. *Address:* Department of Molecular and Cell Biology, 229 Stanley Hall #3206, University of California, Berkeley, CA 94720-3206, U.S.A. *Telephone:* (510) 642-7046.

SCHACHT, Henry Brewer, M.B.A.; American business executive; b. 16 Oct. 1934, Erie, Pa.; s. of Henry Schacht and Virginia Schacht; m. Nancy Godfrey 1960; one s. three d.; ed. Yale and Harvard Univs.; Investment Man. Irwin Man. Co. 1962–64; Vice-Pres. Finance, Subsidiaries and Int. Areas, Cummins Engine Co., Inc. 1964–69; Pres. Cummins Engine Co., Inc. 1969–77, Chair. 1977–95, C.E.O. 1977–94; Chair., C.E.O. Lucent Techs., Murray Hill, N.J. 1995–; Dir. AT&T, Chase Manhattan Corpn., Chase Manhattan Bank N.A.; mem. Business Council and Council of Foreign Relations; Trustee, Ford Foundation, Brookings Inst., Yale Univ., Business Enterprise Trust, Calver Educ. Foundation; Sr. Mem. The Conf. Bd. *Address:* Lucent Technologies, 600 Mountain Avenue, New Providence, NJ 07974, U.S.A.

SCHADEWALDT, Hans, DR. MED.; German professor of medical history; b. 7 May 1923, Kottbus; s. of Johannes Schadewaldt and Hedwig Schadewaldt; m. Lotte Schadewaldt 1943; four s.; ed. Univs. of Tübingen, Würzburg and Königsberg; lecturer Univ. of Freiburg 1961–63; Prof. History of Medicine, Univ. of Düsseldorf 1963–, Dean, Faculty of Medicine 1976–77; mem. numerous int. medical socs.; mem. Rhine-Westfalian Acad. Arts and Sciences (Pres. 1990); Hon. Fellow Royal Soc. of Medicine; Officier Ordre du Mérite Culturel, Monaco; Officier Ordre des Palmes Académiques, Paris; Bundesverdienstkreuz, Commdr.'s Cross, Order of Merit. *Publications:* Michelangelo und die Medizin seiner Zeit 1965, Die berühmten Ärzte 1966, Kunst und Medizin 1967, Der Medizinmann bei den Naturvölkern 1968, Geschichte der Allergie 1979–83, Die Chirurgie in der Kunst 1983, Das Herz, ein Rätsel für die antike und mittelalterliche Welt 1989, Betrachtungen zur Medizin in der bildenden Kunst 1990, 100 Jahre Pharmakologie bei Bayer 1890–1990 1990, Totentanz und Heilberufe 1993, Chronik der Medizin 1993, Die Seuchen kehren zurück 1994. *Address:* Brehmstrasse 82, 40239 Düsseldorf, Germany. *Telephone:* 0211 623163; 0211 3114053. *Fax:* 0211 3113949.

SCHAEFER, Henry Frederick, III, PH.D.; American professor of chemistry and researcher; b. 8 June 1944, Grand Rapids, Mich.; s. of Henry Frederick Schaefer, Jr. and Janice Christine Trost Schaefer; m. Karen Regine Rasmussen; three s. two d.; ed. Massachusetts Inst. of Tech., Stanford Univ.; Prof. of Chem., Univ. of Calif., Berkeley 1969–87; Wilfred T. Doherty Prof. and Dir. Inst. for Theoretical Chem., Univ. of Tex. 1979–80; Graham Perdue Prof. and Dir. Center for Computational Quantum Chem., Univ. of Ga. 1987–; Ed. Molecular Physics 1991–, Encyclopedia of Computational Chem. 1995–(98); Pres. World Asscn. of Theoretically Oriented Chemists 1996–; Alfred P. Sloan Research Fellow 1972–74; John Simon Guggenheim Fellow 1976–77; mem. Int. Acad. of Quantum Molecular Sciences; numerous lectureships including Albert Einstein Centennial Lecturer, Nat. Univ. of Mexico 1979, Lester P. Kuhn Lecturer, Johns Hopkins Univ. 1982, John Howard Appleton Lecturer, Brown Univ. 1985, J. A. Erskine Lecturer, Univ. of Canterbury, Christchurch, N.Z. 1986, John Lee Pratt Lecturer, Univ. of Va. 1988, Guelph-Waterloo Distinguished Lecturer, Univ. of Guelph and Univ. of Waterloo, Ont., Canada 1991, John M. Templeton Lecturer, Case Western Reserve Univ. 1992, Herbert H. King Lecturer, Kansas State Univ. 1993, Francis A. Schaeffer Lectures, Washington Univ., St. Louis 1994, Mary E. Kapp Lecture, Va. Commonwealth Univ. 1996, Abbott Lectures, Univ. of N.D. 1997, C. S. Lewis Lecture, Univ. of Tenn. 1997, Joseph Frank McGregory Lecture, Colgate Univ. 1997, Kenneth S. Pitzer Lecture, Univ. of Calif. at Berkeley 1998; three hon. degrees; American Chemical Soc. Award in Pure Chem. 1979, Leo Hendrik Baekeland Award (American Chem. Soc.) 1983; Annual Medal, World Asscn. of Theoretical Organic Chemists 1990, Centenary Medal, Royal Soc. of Chem., London 1992. *Publications:* The Electronic Structure of Atoms and Molecules 1972, Modern Theoretical Chemistry 1977, Quantum Chemistry 1984, A New Dimension to Quantum Chemistry 1994; 800 publs. in scientific journals. *Leisure interests:* Bible study, running, hiking. *Address:* Center for Computational Quantum Chemistry, University of Georgia, Athens, GA 30602, U.S.A. *Telephone:* (706) 542-2067. *Fax:* (706) 542-0406.

SCHAEFER, William Donald, LL.M., J.D.; American politician; b. 2 Nov. 1921, Baltimore; s. of William Henry Schaefer and Tululu Skipper; ed. Baltimore Univ.; law practice, Baltimore 1943–; mem. Baltimore City Council 1955–67, Pres. 1967–71, Mayor 1971–86; Gov. of Maryland 1986–95, Comptroller 1999–; professional lecturer and William Donald Schaefer Chair, School of Public Affairs, Univ. of Md., and Inst. for Policy Studies, Johns Hopkins Univ. 1996–; fmr. Counsel Gordon, Feinblatt, Rothman, Hoffberger & Hollander; numerous hon. degrees; numerous awards including: Jefferson Award 1979, Michael A. DiNunzio Award 1981, Distinguished Mayor Award, Nat. Urban Coalition 1982, Best Mayor in America, Esquire Magazine 1984, Commendation, Pres.'s Council on Physical Fitness and Sports 1988, Making Marylanders Safe Award, Marylanders Against Handgun Abuse 1991; Democrat. *Address:* Louis L. Goldstein Treasures Building, Annapolis, MD 21404, U.S.A. *Telephone:* (410) 240-7827. *Fax:* (410) 974-3808.

SCHAEFERS, Wolfgang Friedrich Wilhelm, DR.ING.; German business executive and engineer; b. 11 Dec. 1930, Oberhausen; s. of Friedrich and Adele (née Verhufen) Schaefers; m. Christel Weingarten 1954; two s.; ed. Rheinisch-Westfälische Technische Hochschule, Aachen; Works Man. with Mannesmann AG 1961–62; mem. Man. Bd. Verein Deutscher Eisenhüttenleute 1962–64 (also currently); Technical Works Man. Rheinstahl Hüttenwerke AG 1964–69; mem. Man. Bd. Rheinstahl AG (Thyssen Industrie AG from April 1976) 1969–75, Spokesman 1975–76, Chair. 1976–80; Chair. Supervisory Bd. Thyssen Nordseewerke GmbH, Thyssen Schalker Verein GmbH, Thyssen Giesserei AG, Österreichische Salen-Kunststoffwerk Gesellschaft mbH; Chair. Advisory Bd. Thyssen Industrie AG Henschel; Vice-Chair. Supervisory Bd. Henschel Flugzeug-werke AG; mem. Supervisory Bd., Messerschmitt-Bölkow-Blohm GmbH, München; mem. Max-Planck-Gesellschaft zur Förderung der Wissenschaften e.V. Deutsch-Türkische Gesellschaft für Kultur, Wirtschaft und Handel e.V. and other socs.; Special mem. South African Inst. of Foundrymen; Cttee. or Bd. positions with nine firms and asscns. in steel and other sectors. *Publications:* numerous publs. on technical subjects, including steel production. *Leisure interests:* sailing, hunting.

SCHAEFFER, Bogusław, D.PHIL; Polish composer and playwright; b. 6 June 1929, Lwów (now Lviv, Ukraine); s. of Władysław and Julia Schaeffer; m. Mieczysława Hanuszewska 1953; one s.; ed. State Higher School of Music (student of A. Malawski), Jagiellonian Univ., Cracow; wrote first dodecaphonic music for orchestra, Music for Strings: Nocturne 1953; Assoc. Prof. State Higher School of Music, Cracow 1963–, Extraordinary Prof. of Composition, Higher School of Music, Mozarteum, Salzburg 1986–89, Prof. 1989–; Chief Ed. Forum Musicum 1967–; leads Int. Summer Courses for New Composition in Salzburg and Schwaz (Austria) 1976–; Hon. mem. Int. Soc. for Contemporary Music in Warsaw; G. Fitelberg Prize 1959, 1960, 1964, A. Malawski Prize 1962, Minister of Culture and Arts Prize 1971, 1980, Union of Polish Composers Prize 1977; Kt.'s Cross of Polonia Restituta Order, Gold Cross of Merit. *Publications:* Nowa Muzyka. Problemy współczesnej techniki kompozytorskiej (New music. Problems of contemporary technique in composing) 1958, Klasycy dodekafonii (Classics of dodecaphonic music) 1964, Leksykon kompozytorów XX wieku (Lexicon of 20th century composers) 1965, W kręgu nowej muzyki (In the sphere of new music) 1967, Mały informator muzyki XX wieku 1975, Introduction to Composition (in English) 1975, Historia muzyki (Story of Music) 1980, Kompozytorzy XX wieku (20th century composers) 1990, Trzy rozmowy (kompozytor, dramaturg, filozof) (Three Conversations: Composer, Playwright and Philosopher) 1992. *Main compositions:* Extrema, Tertium datur, Scultura, S'alto for alto saxophone, Collage and form, Electronic music, Visual music, Heraclitiana, Missa elettronica, Jangwa, Missa Sinfonica, Piano Concerto, Maah, Sinfonia, opera Liebesblicke, Mini opera, also film and theatre music, Miserere, Organ Concerto, 8 string quartets, Orchestral and Electronic Changes, Concerto for Violin, Piano and Orchestra, Symphony/Concerto for 15 solo instrumentalists and orchestra, Heideggerriana, Winter Musik for horn and piano, Concerto for percussion, electronic media and orchestra. *Plays:* Darknesses, Dawn, Paradise of the Eskimo, Sins of Old Age, The Actor, Rehearsals, Séance, Tutam, Rondo, Wot-if, Together, Revenge, Toast, Harvest, Promotion, Blockheads, Daybreak, Multi, Largo (trans. into 17 languages). *Leisure interests:* literature, theatre. *Address:* Osiedle Kolorowe 4, m. 6, 31-938 Cracow, Poland; Plainstr. 85, A-5020, Salzburg, Austria. *Telephone:* 644-19-60 (Poland); 456012 (Austria).

SCHAFER, Edward, M.B.A.; American state governor; b. 8 Aug. 1946, Bismarck, N.D.; s. of Harold Schafer and Marian Schafer; m. Nancy Jones; four c.; ed. Univ. of N. Dakota and Denver Univ.; quality control insp. Gold Seal 1971–73, Vice-Pres. 1974, Chair. Man. Cttee. 1975–78, Pres. 1978–85; Owner/Dir. H & S Distribution 1976–; Pres. Dakota Classics 1986–, TRIESCO Properties 1986–, Fish 'N Dakota 1990–94; Gov. of North Dakota 1992–; Republican. *Address:* Office of the Governor, 600 E. Boulevard Avenue, Bismarck, ND 58505, U.S.A.

SCHÄFER, Walter; German banker; b. 19 Dec. 1936, Lohra, Marburg; m. Edelgard Schäfer; two c.; ed. Municipal Savings Banks and Banking System Training Inst., Bonn; qualified as Savings Banks Customer Counsellor; bank Branch Man. 1966; Deputy Exec. Pres. Hessian Savings Bank and Giro Asscn., Frankfurt 1974; mem. Bd. of Man. Dirs. Hessische Landesbank Girozentrale, Frankfurt 1980; Chair. Man. Bd. Landesbank Schleswig-Holstein, Kiel 1993, Landesbank Hessen-Thüringen Girozentrale, Frankfurt 1996–. *Address:* Vorstandvors, Landesbank Hessen-Thüringen, Junghofstr. 18-26, 60311 Frankfurt (Office); Mannenweg 14, 6397 Karbenl, Germany (Home). *Telephone:* (69) 19132-2213 (Office).

SCHAFF, Adam, PH.D.; Polish philosopher and sociologist; b. 10 March 1913, Lvov (now Lviv, Ukraine); s. of Maks Schaff and Ernestina Schaff de domo Felix; m. 1st Anna Schaff 1935 (died 1975); one d.; m. 2nd Teresa Schaff 1976; ed. Lvov Univ. and Ecole des Sciences Politiques et Economiques, Paris; scientific work in U.S.S.R. 1940–45; Prof. Łódź Univ. 1945–48; Prof. of Philosophy, Warsaw Univ. 1948–70; Dir. Polish United Workers' Party Inst. of Social Sciences 1950–57; mem. Polish Acad. of Sciences (Chair. Philosophy Cttee. 1951–68, Dir. Inst. of Philosophy and Sociology 1957–68); Visiting Prof., Univ. of Vienna 1969–72, Hon. Prof. of Philosophy 1972–88; mem. Bulgarian Acad. of Sciences; mem. Polish Workers' Party 1944–48, Polish United Workers' Party (PZPR) 1948–84, 1989–90, (mem. Cen. Cttee. 1959–68); mem. Exec. Cttee. Int. Fed. of Philosophical Asscns.; mem. of Int. Inst. of Philosophy, Paris; mem. Royal Acad. of Political and Moral Sciences, Madrid; Hon. Pres. Bd. of Dirs. of the European Centre for Social Sciences in Vienna; mem. Exec. Cttee., Club of Rome; Ed. Myśl Współczesna (Contemporary Thought) 1946–51, Myśl Filozoficzna (Philosophical Thought) 1951–56; Dr. h.c. (Mich. Univ., Ann Arbor) 1967; Dr. h.c. (Sorbonne) 1975, (Univ. de Nancy) 1982; State Prizes, 1st and 2nd Class, Commdr. Cross of Polonia Restituta Order, Order of Banner of Labour (First Class), Nicolaus Copernicus Medal, Polish Acad. of Sciences. *Publications:* Pojęcie i słowo (Concept and Word) 1946, Wstęp do teorii marksizmu (Introduction to the Theory of Marxism) 1947, Narodziny i rozwój filozofii marksistowskiej (Birth and Development of Marxist Philosophy) 1949, Z zagadnień marksistowskiej teorii prawdy (Some Problems of the Marxist Theory of Truth) 1951, Obiektywny charakter praw historii (The Objective Character of Historical Laws) 1955, Wstęp do semantyki (Introduction to Semantics) 1960, Filozofia człowieka (A Philosophy of Man) 1962, Język i poznanie (Language and Cognition) 1963, Marksizm a jednostka ludzka (Marxism and the Human Individual) 1965, Szkice z filozofii języka (Essays in the Philosophy of Language) 1967, Historia i prawda (History and Truth) 1970, Gramatyka generatywna a koncepcja wrodzonych idei (Generative Grammar and Conception of Innate Ideas) 1972, Strukturalizm i marksizm (Structuralism and Marxism) 1975, Entfremdung als soziales Phänomen (Alienation as a Social Phenomenon) 1977, Stereotypen und das menschliche Handeln 1980, Die Kommunistische Bewegung am Scheideweg 1982, Polen Heute 1983, Wohin führt der Weg? 1985, Perspektiven des modernen Sozialismus 1988, Ökumenischer Humanismus 1992, Mi Siglo XX 1993, Noticias de un hombre con dudas 1997, Meditaciones sobre el socialismo 1997. *Leisure interest:* tennis. *Address:* al. J. Ch. Szucha 2/4 m. 24, 00-582 Warsaw, Poland; Flossgasse 2/28, A-1020 Vienna, Austria. *Telephone:* (22) 628 18 32 (Warsaw); (1) 212 9239 (Vienna).

SCHAFFSTEIN, Friedrich, DR. JUR.; German professor of law; b. 28 July 1905, Göttingen; s. of Dr. Karl Schaffstein; ed. Univs. of Innsbruck and Göttingen; teacher in criminal law Univ. of Göttingen 1927–33, Prof. of Criminal Law, Leipzig 1933–35, Univ. of Kiel 1935–41, Univ. of Strasbourg 1941–45, Verwaltungs-akademie Lüneburg 1946–50; Prof. of Law (Criminal and Criminology) Univ. of Göttingen 1953–70, Prof. Emer. 1970–; mem. Akademie der Wissenschaften, Göttingen. *Publications:* Die Entwicklung der allgemeiner Lehren vom Verbrechen im gemeinen Strafrecht 1930, Wilhelm von Humboldt 1952, Die Strafrechtswissenschaft im Zeitalter des Humanismus 1954, Jugendstrafrecht (9th edn.) 1987, Abhandlungen zur Strafrechtsgeschichte und Wissenschaftsgeschichte 1987. *Address:* Stift am Klausberg, Habichtsweg 55, 37075 Göttingen, Germany. *Telephone:* 0551-2098529.

SCHAIRER, George Swift, M.S.; American aircraft and missile design engineer; b. 19 May 1913, Wilkinsburg, Pa.; s. of Otto Sorg and Elizabeth Blanch Swift Schairer; m. Mary Pauline Tarbox 1935; two s. two d.; ed. Oakmont Public School, Oakmont, Pa., Summit New Jersey High School, Swarthmore Coll., Mass. Inst. of Tech., and Advanced Management Program, Hawaii Univ.; Automotive Engineer, Bendix Aviation Corpn., South Bend, Ind. 1935–37; Engineer, Consolidated Vultee Aircraft Corpn., San Diego 1937–39; Chief Aerodynamist, Boeing Co. 1939–46, Staff Engineer (Aerodynamics and Power Plant) 1946–51, Chief of Technical Staff 1951–56, Asst. Chief Engineer 1956–57, Dir. of Research 1957–59, Vice-Pres. (Research and Devt.) 1959–71, Vice-Pres. Research 1971–78 (retd.); consultant The Boeing Co. 1978–88; mem. N.A.S. 1968–, Nat. Acad. of Eng., Int. Acad. of Astronautics; Hon. Fellow, A.I.A.A.; official of numerous other orgs.; Sylvanus Albert Reed Award, Inst. of Aeronautical Sciences 1949; Daniel Guggenheim Medal 1967; Hon. D.Eng. (Swarthmore Coll.) 1958. *Publications:* numerous papers on aeronautics and related subjects. *Leisure interests:* sailing, model airplane building, photography, fine arts. *Address:* 4242 Hunts Point Road, Bellevue, WA 98004, U.S.A. (Home). *Telephone:* (206) 454-3602 (Home).

SCHALLER, George Beals, PH.D.; American zoologist; b. 26 May 1933, Berlin, Germany; s. of George Ludwig Schaller and Bettina (Byrd) Iwersen; m. Kay Suzanne Morgan 1957; two s.; ed. Univ. of Alaska, Univ. of Wisconsin; Research Assoc., Johns Hopkins Univ., Baltimore 1963–66; research zoologist New York Zoological Soc. 1966–, Dir. Int. Conservation Programme 1979–; Adjunct Assoc. Prof., Rockefeller Univ., New York 1966–; Research Assoc. American Museum of Natural History; Fellow Guggenheim Foundation 1971; Hon. Dir. Explorers' Club 1991; Int. Cosmos Prize, Japan 1996, Tyler Environmental Prize 1997; Gold Medal, World Wildlife Fund 1980; Order of Golden Ark, Netherlands 1978, Cosmos Prize, Japan 1996, Tyler Environmental Prize 1997. *Publications:* The Mountain Gorilla 1963, The Year of the Gorilla 1964, The Deer and the Tiger 1967, The Serengeti Lion 1972 (Nat. Book Award 1973), Stones of Silence 1980, The Giant Pandas of Wolong 1985, The Last Panda 1993, Tibet's Hidden Wilderness 1997, Wildlife of the Tibetan Steppes 1998. *Address:* The Wildlife Conservation Society, Bronx Park, Bronx, New York, NY 10460, U.S.A.

SCHALLY, Andrew Victor, PH.D.; American medical researcher; b. 30 Nov. 1926, Wilno, Poland (now Vilnius, Lithuania); s. of Casimir Peter and Maria (Lacka) Schally; m. 1st Margaret Rachel White; one s. one d.; m. 2nd Ana Maria de Medeiros-Comaru 1976; ed. Bridge of Allen, Scotland, London Univ., McGill Univ., Montreal, Canada; Asst. Prof. of Physiology and Asst. Prof. of Biochem., Baylor Univ. Coll. of Medicine, Houston, Tex. 1960–62; Chief, Endocrine and Polypeptide Labs., Veterans Admin. Hosp., New Orleans, La. 1962–; Sr. Medical Investigator, Veterans Admin. 1973–; Assoc. Prof. of Medicine, Tulane Univ. School of Medicine, New Orleans, La. 1962–67, Prof. of Medicine 1967–; mem. N.A.S., A.A.A.S.; Charles Mickle Award 1974, Gairdner Foundation Award 1974, Edward T. Tyler Award 1975, Borden Award in the Medical Sciences (Asscn. of American Medical Colls.) 1975, Lasker Award 1975, shared Nobel Prize for Physiology or Medicine with Roger Guillemin (q.v.) for discoveries concerning peptide hormones 1977. *Publications:* numerous scientific papers, particularly concerning hormones and cancer. *Leisure interest:* swimming. *Address:* Veterans Administration Hospital, 1601 Perdido Street, New Orleans, LA 70112 (Office); 5025 Kawanee Avenue, Metairie, LA 70006, U.S.A. (Home). *Telephone:* (504) 589-5230 (Office).

SCHAMA, Simon Michael, M.A.; British historian and author; b. 13 Feb. 1945, London; s. of late Arthur Schama and of Gertrude Steinberg; m. Virginia Papaioannou 1983; one s. one d.; ed. Christ's Coll. Cambridge; Fellow and Dir. of Studies in History, Christ's Coll. Cambridge 1966–76; Fellow and Tutor in Modern History, Brasenose Coll. Oxford 1976–80; Prof. of History (Mellon Prof. of the Social Sciences), Harvard Univ. 1980; Prof. Columbia Univ. 1997–; art critic, New Yorker 1995–; Wolfson Prize 1977; Leo Gershoy Prize (American Historical Asscn.) 1978; Nat. Cash Register Book Prize for non-fiction (for Citizens) 1990. *Television film:* Rembrandt: The Public Eye and the Private Gaze (for BBC) 1992. *Publications:* Patriots and Liberators: Revolution in the Netherlands 1780–1813 1977, Two Rothschilds and the Land of Israel 1978–79, The Embarrassment of Riches: An Interpretation of Dutch Culture in the Golden Age 1987, Citizens: A Chronicle of the French Revolution 1989, Dead Certainties (Unwarranted Speculations) 1991, Landscape and Memory 1995. *Leisure interests:* wine, Dutch bulbs, children's fiction. *Address:* Center for European Studies, 27 Kirkland Street, Cambridge, MA 02138; Department of History, Fayerweather Hall, Columbia University, New York, NY 10027, U.S.A. *Telephone:* (617) 495-4303 (Cambridge).

SCHANBERG, Sydney Hillel, B.A.; American journalist; b. 17 Jan. 1934, Clinton, Mass.; s. of Louis and Freda (née Feinberg) Schanberg; two d.; ed. Harvard Univ.; joined New York Times 1959, reporter 1960, Bureau Chief, Albany, New York 1967–69, New Delhi, India 1969–73, S.E. Asia Corresp., Singapore 1973–75, City Ed. 1977–80, Columnist 1981–85; Assoc. Ed., Columnist Newsday newspaper, New York 1986–; numerous awards, including Page One Award for Reporting 1972, George Polk Memorial Award 1972, Overseas Press Club Award 1972, Bob Considine Memorial Award 1975, Pulitzer Prize 1975. *Address:* Newsday Inc., 2 Park Avenue, New York, NY 10016; 164 West 79th Street, Apt. 12-D, New York, NY 10024, U.S.A.

SCHARANSKY, Natan (b. Anatoly); Israeli (b. Soviet) politician, human rights activist and computer scientist; b. 20 Jan. 1948, Donetsk, U.S.S.R.

(now Ukraine); m. Natalya (now Avital) Stiglitz 1974; a leading spokesman for Jewish emigration movt. in U.S.S.R.; arrested by Soviet authorities for dissident activities 1977; received 13-year prison sentence on charges of treason 1978; following worldwide campaign, Soviet authorities released him in exchange for eastern spies held in West and he took up residence in Israel Feb. 1986; Visiting Prof. Brandeis Univ., Waltham, Mass.; Leader Israel B'Aliyah Party; Minister of Trade and Industry. 1996–. *Publication:* Fear No Evil 1988. *Address:* Ministry of Trade and Industry, P.O. Box 229, 30 Rehov Agron, Jerusalem 91002, Israel. *Telephone:* 2-6220339. *Fax:* 2-6259274.

SCHARP, Anders; Swedish business executive; b. 8 June 1934; ed. Royal Inst. of Tech. Stockholm; joined AB Electrohelios 1960 (merged with AB Electrolux 1963), Exec. Vice-Pres. (Production and Research & Devt.) 1974; Pres. AB Electrolux 1981, C.E.O. 1986; Chair. SAAB-Scania 1990–95; Chair. Saab AB 1995–; Chair., C.E.O. AB SKF April 1992–; Chair. Incentive AB 1992–98; Chair. White Consolidated Industries 1993–98, fmrly. C.E.O.; mem. Bd. Swedish Asscn. of Metalworking Industries, Swedish Metal Trades Employers' Asscn., Swedish Employers' Confed., AB Investor. *Address:* SAAB AB, S-581 88 Linköping, Sweden.

SCHARPING, Rudolf; German politician; b. 2 Dec. 1947, Niederelbert, Westerwald; m.; three c.; ed. Univ. of Bonn; joined Social Democratic Party (SPD) 1966; State Chair. and Nat. Deputy Chair. Jusos (Young Socialists) 1966; mem. State Parl. of Rhineland-Palatinate 1975; Party Leader of SPD in Rhineland-Palatinate 1985; Leader of Opposition in Rhineland-Palatinate 1987; Minister-Pres. of Rhineland-Palatinate 1991–94; Leader, SPD 1993–95, Deputy Chair. 1995, Chair. SPD Parl. Group, Leader of the Opposition 1994; Chair. Social Democratic Party of Europe 1995; Minister of Defence Oct. 1998–. *Address:* Ministry of Defence, 53003 Bonn, Hardthöhe, Postfach 1328, Germany.

SCHATZ, Gottfried, PH.D.; Austrian professor of biochemistry; b. 18 Aug. 1936, Strem; s. of Andreas Schatz and Anna Schatz; m. Merete Bjorn Petersen 1962; three c.; ed. Univ. of Graz; Asst. Prof. Univ. of Vienna 1961–64; Postdoctoral Fellow, Public Health Research Inst. City of New York 1964–66; Assoc. Prof., Prof. Cornell Univ. 1968–74; Prof. of Biochemistry, Univ. of Basle 1974–; Innitzer Prize 1967; Hansen Gold Medal 1983; Sir Hans Krebs Medal 1985; Otto Warburg Medal 1988, etc. *Publications:* about 140 scientific publs. in biochemical journals. *Leisure interests:* music, jogging. *Address:* Biocenter, University of Basle, Petersplatz 1, 4003 Basle (Office); Unterer Rebbergweg 33, CH-4153 Reinach, Switzerland (Home). *Telephone:* (61) 267 2150 (Office); (61) 711 2795 (Home).

SCHATZMAN, Evry; French research scientist; b. 16 Sept. 1920, Neuilly; s. of Benjamin Schatzman and Cécile Kahn; four c.; ed. Ecole Normale Supérieure; Research Assoc. Centre Nat. de la Recherche Scientifique (C.N.R.S.) 1945, Head of Research 1948; Prof. Univ. of Paris 1954; Dir. of Research, C.N.R.S. 1976–89; mem. Acad. of Sciences 1985–; Prix Holweck 1976, Médaille d'Or, C.N.R.S. 1983; Chevalier, Légion d'honneur, Officier, Ordre nat. du Mérite. *Publications:* Astrophysique Générale 1957, Structure de l'Univers 1968, Science et Société 1971, Les enfants d'Uranie 1986, Le message du photon voyageur 1987, La science menacée 1989, L'expansion de l'Univers 1989, Les Etoiles 1990, L'outil théorie 1992, The Stars 1993; more than 200 research papers, mainly on physical processes in astrophysics. *Address:* 11 rue de l'Eglise, Dompierre, 60420 Maignelay-Montigny, France. *Telephone:* (16) 44.51.24.14 (Dompierre); 42.09.20.97 (Paris); 45.07.78.73 (Office).

SCHAUB, Alexander, D.J.; German civil servant; b. 14 June 1941, Duisburg; s. of Franz Schaub and Gertrud Stockert; m. Nicole Van der Meulen 1974; one s. two d.; ed. Univs. of Freiburg, Lausanne, Cologne and Bonn and Coll. of Europe, Bruges; with Fed. Ministry of Econ. Affairs 1971; mem. Secr. of Ralf Dahrendorf 1973; mem. Secr. and Deputy Chef de Cabinet of Guido Brunner 1974–78; Deputy Chef de Cabinet Messrs Davignon and Burke 1980, of Pres. Gaston Thorn 1981; Chef de Cabinet of Willy de Clercq 1985–89; Dir. DG External Relations and Trade Policy, European Comm. 1989–90, Deputy Dir. Gen. DG Internal Market and Industrial Affairs 1990–93, Deputy Dir.-Gen. DG Industry 1993–95, Dir.-Gen. DG IV Competition 1995–; Grosses Silbernes Ehrenzeichen mit Stern (Austria). *Publications:* Die Anhörung des Europäischen Parlaments in Rechtsetzungsverfahren der EWG 1971, Food Quality in the Internal Market of 1993 1993, Gentechnik im Lebensmittelbereich—Die Politik der EG-Kommission 1994 and numerous contribs. to legal and professional journals, articles in newspapers etc. *Leisure interests:* tennis, skiing. *Address:* European Commission, 150 avenue de Cortenberg, 1000 Brussels, Belgium. *Telephone:* 32-2-295.23.87. *Fax:* 32-2-295.01.28.

SCHÄUBLE, Wolfgang, DR.IUR.; German politician and lawyer; b. 18 Sept. 1942, Freiburg; s. of Karl Schäuble and Gertrud (née Göhring) Schäuble; m. Ingeborg Hensle 1969; one s. three d.; ed. Univs. of Freiburg and Hamburg; Regional Pres., Junge Union, S. Baden 1969–72; worked in admin. of taxes, Baden-Württemberg 1971–72; mem. Bundestag 1972–, Exec. Sec. CDU/CSU Parl. group 1981–84; mem. parl., European Council 1975–84; Chair. CDU Cttee. on Sport 1976–84; Regional Vice-Pres., CDU, S. Baden 1982–95, mem. Federal Exec. Cttee. CDU; Minister with special responsibility and Head of Chancellery 1984–89, of Interior 1989–91; CDU Parl. Leader Nov. 1991–, Leader 1998–; legal practice in Offenburg 1978–84; Chair. Arbeitsgemeinschaft Europäischer Grenzregionen (AGEG) 1979–82; Grosses Bundesverdienstkreuz; Commdr., Ordre nat. du Mérite. *Leisure interests:* chess, music. *Address:* The Bundestag, Görresstr. 15, 53113 Bonn, Germany.

SCHAWLOW, Arthur Leonard, PH.D., LL.D., D.SC.; American professor of physics; b. 5 May 1921, Mount Vernon, N.Y.; s. of Arthur and Helen (Mason) Schawlow; m. Aurelia Keith Townes 1951; one s. two d.; ed. Univ. of Toronto; Postdoctoral Fellow and Research Assoc., Columbia Univ. 1949–51; Research Physicist, Bell Telephone Labs. 1951–61; Visiting Assoc. Prof., Columbia Univ. 1960; J. G. Jackson—C. J. Wood Prof. of Physics, Stanford Univ. 1961–91, Prof. Emer. 1991–, Chair. Dept. of Physics 1966–70; Dir. Optical Soc. of America 1966–69, Pres. 1975, Hon. Mem. 1983; mem. Council, American Physical Soc. 1966–70, Chair. Div. of Electron and Atomic Physics 1974, Vice-Pres. 1980, Pres. 1981; mem. N.A.S.; Fellow, American Acad. of Arts and Sciences; Hon. mem. Royal Irish Acad. 1991; hon. doctorates from Univs. of Ghent, Toronto, Bradford, Alabama, Trinity Coll. Dublin, Lund, Victoria Univ., Toronto; mem. U.S. Nat. Inventors Hall of Fame 1996; Thomas Young Medal and Prize (Inst. of Physics and Physical Soc. U.K.), Ballantine Medal (Franklin Inst.), Liebmann Prize (Inst. of Electrical and Electronic Engineers), Calif. Scientist of the Year 1973; Geoffrey Frew Fellowship (Australian Acad. of Sciences) 1973, Frederic Ives Medal (Optical Soc. of America) 1976, Marconi Int. Fellowship 1977, shared Nobel Prize in Physics for devt. of laser spectroscopy 1981, Schawlow Medal (Laser Inst. of America) 1982, Nat. Medal of Science 1991, Yoshiaki Arata Award, (High Temperature Soc. of Japan) 1995, Ronald H. Brown American Innovator Award (U.S. Dept. of Commerce) 1996. *Publications:* Microwave Spectroscopy (with C. H. Townes) 1955, and over 200 scientific papers. *Leisure interest:* jazz music. *Address:* Department of Physics, Stanford University, Stanford, CA 94305; 850 Webster Street, Apt. 117, Palo Alto, CA 94301, U.S.A. (Home).

SCHECKTER, Jody David; South African racing driver and business executive; b. 21 Jan. 1950, East London, nr. Durban; m. Pam Bailey; one s.; raced karts from age of 11, graduated to motorcycles and racing cars; won S.A. Formula Ford Sunshine Series in 1970, competed in Britain from 1971; World Champion 1979, runner-up 1977, third 1974 and 1976. *Grand Prix wins:* 1974 Swedish (Tyrrell-Ford), 1974 British (Tyrrell-Ford), 1975 South African (Tyrrell-Ford), 1976 Swedish (Tyrrell-Ford), 1977 Argentine (Wolf-Ford), 1977 Monaco (Wolf-Ford), 1977 Canadian (Wolf-Ford), 1979 Belgian (Ferrari), 1979 Monaco (Ferrari), 1979 Italian (Ferrari); retd. 1980, running a business in Atlanta, Ga. *Leisure interest:* keeping fit.

SCHEEL, Walter; German politician; b. 8 July 1919, Solingen; m. 1st Eva Kronenberg 1942 (died 1966); one s.; m. 2nd Dr. Mildred Wirtz 1969 (died 1985); one s. two d.; m. 3rd Barbara Wiese 1988; ed. Reform-Gymnasium, Solingen; served German Air Force, World War II; fmr. head of market research org.; mem. Landtag North Rhine-Westphalia 1950–53; mem. Bundestag 1953–74, Vice-Pres. 1967–69; Fed. Minister for Econ. Co-operation 1961–66; Chair. of Free Democrats 1968–74 (Hon. Chair. 1979); Vice-Chancellor, Minister of Foreign Affairs 1969–74; Pres. Fed. Repub. of Germany 1974–79; mem. European Parl. 1958–61; Pres. Bilderberg Conf. –1985; Chair. German Council of European Movt. 1980–85; Chair. Bd. of Trustees, Friedrich Naumann Foundation 1979–90; Chair. Admin. Council, Germanic Nat. Museum, Nuremberg 1978, Cttee. European Music Year 1983–86, Supervisory Bd., DEG-German Investment and Devt. Co. 1980–, Directory for Thoroughbreds and Races 1981; Pres. Europa-Union Deutschland 1980–89; mem. Supervisory Bd. ROBECO Group 1982–89, Supervisory Bd. Thyssen AG 1980–, Supervisory Bd. Thyssen Stahl AG 1983–; Hon. Pres. German Fed. of Artists; Theodor Heuss Prize 1971, Peace Prize (Kajima Inst., Tokyo) 1973; numerous hon. degrees and awards from Germany and abroad; Fondation du Mérite Européen 1984. Grosses Bundesverdienstkreuz (special class). *Publications:* Konturen einer neuen Welt 1965, Schwierigkeiten, Ernüchterung und Chancen der Industrieländer 1965, Formeln deutscher Politik 1968, Warum Mitbestimmung und wie 1970, Die Freiburger Thesen der Liberalen (with K.-H. Flach and W. Maihofer) 1972, Bundestagreden 1972, Reden und Interviews 1974–79, Vom Recht des anderen—Gedanken zur Freiheit 1977, Die Zukunft der Freiheit 1979, Nach 30 Jahren; Die Bundesrepublik Deutschland, Vergangenheit, Gegenwart, Zukunft 1979, Die andere deutsche Frage 1981, Wen Schmerzt noch Deutschlands Teilung? 1986. *Leisure interest:* modern art. *Address:* Flemingstrasse 107, 81925 Munich, Germany.

SCHEER, François, D.E.S.; French diplomatist; b. 13 March 1934, Strasbourg; s. of Alfred Scheer and Edmée Lechten; m. 2nd Nicole Roubaud 1985; one s. one d.; one s. three d. from 1st marriage; ed. Faculty of Law, Univ. of Paris, Inst. d'Etudes Politiques de Paris, Ecole Nat. d'Admin. Second Sec. Embassy, Algiers 1962–64; Direction des Affaires Economiques et Financières, Admin. Cen. 1964–67; Cultural Attaché Embassy, Tokyo 1967–71; Deputy Dir. for Budget 1971, also for Financial Affairs 1972–76; Amb. to Mozambique and Swaziland 1976–77; Deputy Perm. Rep. to European Community 1977–79, Dir. of Cabinet to the Pres. of the European Parl. 1979–81; Dir. of Cabinet of Minister of Foreign Affairs 1981–84; Amb. to Algeria 1984–86; Amb. and Perm. Rep. for France to the EC 1986–88; Sec. Gen. Ministry of Foreign Affairs 1988–92; Amb. Perm. Rep. to the EC (now EU) 1992–93; Amb. to Fed. Repub. of Germany 1993–99; mem. Cttee. for Atomic Energy 1988–92; Admin. Cie. générale des matières nucléaires (Cogema) 1989–93; mem. Conseil d'Admin. Ecole Nat. d'Admin. 1991–95; Officier Légion d'honneur; Commdr. Ordre Nat. du Mérite. *Address:* 22, rue Bobillot, 75013 Paris, France. *Telephone:* (1) 45 81 35 84. *Fax:* (1) 45 80 76 43.

SCHEFFLER, Israel, PH.D.; American philosopher and educator; b. 25 Nov. 1923, New York; s. of Leon Scheffler and Ethel Grünberg Scheffler; m. Rosalind Zuckerbrod 1949; one s. one d.; ed. Brooklyn Coll., Jewish Theological Seminary and Univ. of Pennsylvania; mem. Faculty, Harvard Univ. 1952–, Prof. of Educ. 1961–62, Prof. of Educ. and Philosophy 1962–64, Victor S. Thomas Prof. of Educ. and Philosophy 1964–92, Prof. Emer. 1992–, Hon. Research Fellow in Cognitive Studies 1965–66, Co-Dir. Research Center for Philosophy of Educ. 1983–; Fellow Center for Advanced Study in Behavioral Sciences, Palo Alto, Calif. 1972–73; Guggenheim Fellow 1958–59, 1972–73; mem. American Acad. of Arts and Sciences. *Publications:* Philosophy and Education 1958, The Language of Education 1960, The Anatomy of Inquiry 1963, Conditions of Knowledge 1965, Science and Subjectivity 1967, Logic and Art (co-ed.) 1972, Reason and Teaching 1973, Four Pragmatists 1974, Beyond the Letter 1979, Of Human Potential 1985, Inquiries 1986, In Praise of the Cognitive Emotions 1991, Work, Education and Leadership (co-author) 1995, Teachers of my Youth 1995, Symbolic Worlds 1997. *Leisure interest:* reading. *Address:* Larsen Hall, Harvard University, Cambridge, MA 02138, U.S.A. *Telephone:* (617) 495-3569. *Fax:* (617) 495-0540.

SCHEIBE, Erhard A.K., DR. RER. NAT.; German professor of philosophy; b. 24 Sept. 1927, Berlin; s. of Albert Scheibe and Maria (née Heidenreich) Scheibe; m. Maria Elgert-Eggers 1958; two s. one d.; ed. Berlin and Singen High Schools, Univ. of Göttingen; Asst. Max Planck Inst. of Physics, Göttingen 1956–57; Asst. and lecturer Univ. of Hamburg 1957–64; Prof. of Philosophy, Univ. of Göttingen 1964–83, Univ. of Heidelberg 1983–92; mem. Acad. of Sciences, Göttingen, Acad. of Sciences and Literature, Mainz, Int. Acad. of Philosophy of Science, Brussels. *Publications:* Die kontingenten Aussagen in der Physik 1964, The Logical Analysis of Quantum Mechanics 1973, Die Reduktion physikalischer Theorien (Vol. 1) 1997, (Vol. 2) 1999. *Leisure interests:* music, art, literature. *Address:* Moorbirkenkamp 2A, 22391 Hamburg, Germany. *Telephone:* 040-5368107.

SCHEIDER, Roy; American actor; b. 10 Nov. 1932, Orange, NJ.; ed. Franklin and Marshall Coll.; mem. Lincoln Center Repertory Co., American Repertory Co.; stage appearances in 1960s at McCann Theater, Princeton, Boston Fine Art Festival, American Shakespeare Festival, Arena Stadium, Washington, D.C.; off-Broadway appearances in Sergeant Musgrave's Dance, The Alchemist; Obie Award for Performance in Stephen D 1968; League of New York Award for Most Distinguished Stage Performance for Pinter's Betrayal 1980; TV appearances include: As Short a Name, Cell without a Number, Assignment Munich, Jacobo Timerman, Tiger Town, Somebody has to Shoot the Pictures. *Films include:* Paper Lion, Star, Stilleto, Puzzle of a Downfall Child, Klute 1971, The French Connection 1971, The Outside Man, The Seven-Ups, Sheila Levine is Dean and Living in New York, Jaws, Marathon Man, L'Attentat, Sorcerer, Last Embrace, Jaws II 1979, All that Jazz 1979, Still of the Night, Blue Thunder, 2010, The Men's Club, 52 Pick Up, Cohen and Tate, Night Game, The Crew, The Fourth Man, The Russia House, The Naked Lunch, 2010, Romeo is Bleeding, Covert Assassin.

SCHELL, Jonathan, B.A.; American journalist; b. 21 Aug. 1943, New York; s. of Orville Hickock Schell Jr. and Marjorie Bertha; m. Elspeth Schell; two s. one d.; ed. Putney School, Vt., Harvard Univ. and Int. Christian Univ., Tokyo; articles describing Operation Cedar Falls, one of largest U.S. mil. exercises of Vietnam War and other experiences in Vietnam appeared in New Yorker 1967; mem. staff, New Yorker 1968–87; Fellow, Inst. of Politics, Kennedy School of Govt. 1987; Visiting Prof. Inst. of Liberal Arts, Emory Univ. Atlanta, Ga. 1987, New York Univ. School of Journalism 1988; Ferris Prof. Princeton Univ. 1989; columnist, Newsday and New York Newsday 1990; mem. New York Inst. for the Humanities, New York Univ. 1991–; Melcher Book Award for The Fate of the Earth 1982. *Publications:* The Village of Ben Suc 1967, The Military Half: An Account of Destruction in Quang Ngai and Quang Tin 1968, The Time of Illusion 1976, The Fate of the Earth 1982, The Abolition, History in Sherman Park 1987, Observing the Nixon Years: Notes & Comment from the New Yorker on the Vietnam War and the Watergate Crisis 1969–75 1989.

SCHELL, Jozef Stephaan, PH.D.; Belgian professor of genetics; b. 20 July 1935, Antwerp; m. Elizabeth Frederick 1968; two s.; Prof. Inst. of Genetics, Rijksuniversteit Ghent 1967–95; Prof. Collège de France, Paris 1994–; Dir. Max-Planck-Inst. für Züchtungsforschung, Cologne 1978; mem. numerous scientific advisory councils etc.; mem. N.A.S., Deutsche Akad. der Naturforscher Leopoldina, Rheinisch-Westfälisch Akad. etc.; Foreign mem. Royal Swedish Acad.; Foreign Fellow, Indian Nat. Science Acad.; Dr. h.c. (Univ. Louis Pasteur) 1992, (Hebrew Univ.) 1994; numerous awards and prizes including Prix Francqui 1979, Mendel Medal (Akad. Leopoldina) 1985, Otto Bayer Prize 1985, Humboldt Prize 1985, Rank Prize for Nutrition 1987, IBM Prize 1987, Wolf Prize in Agriculture 1990, Australia Prize for Agric. and Environment 1990, Charles L. Mayer Prize (French Acad.) 1990, Hansen Gold Medal 1991, Max Planck Prize 1992, Wilhelm-Exner-Médaille 1995, Japan Prize 1996. *Publications:* articles in professional journals, book chapters. *Leisure interests:* tennis, sailing. *Address:* Collège de France, 11 place Marcelin-Berthelot, 75231 Paris Cedex 05, France.

SCHELL, Maximilian; Swiss actor; b. 8 Dec. 1930, Vienna; s. of Hermann Ferdinand Schell and Margarete Noe von Nordberg; m. Natalya Andreichenko 1985; one d.; ed. Humanistisches Gymnasium, Basel, Freies Gymnasium, Zürich, and Univs. of Zürich, Basel and Munich; Corporal, Swiss Army 1948–49; various appearances on stage in Switzerland and Germany 1952–55; German début in Children, Mothers and a General 1955; American film début in Young Lions 1958, on Broadway stage in Interlock 1958; Critics Award (Broadway) 1958; New York Critics Award 1961, 1978; Golden Globe Award 1961, 1974; Acad. Award 1961, 1970, 1971, 1978, 1985; Silver Award San Sebastian 1970, 1975; German Fed. Award 1971, 1979, 1980; Film Critics' Award, Chicago 1973; Golden Cup 1974; Bavarian Film Prize 1984. *Principal films acted in:* Judgment at Nuremberg 1961, Five Finger Exercise 1961, Reluctant Saint 1962, Condemned of Altona 1962, Topkapi 1964, Return from the Ashes 1965, Beyond the Mountains 1966, The Deadly Affair 1966, Counterpoint 1966, Krakatoa, East of Java 1967, The Castle 1968, First Love 1969, Pope Joan 1971, Paulina 1880 1971, The Pedestrian 1973, The Odessa File 1974, The Man in the Glass Booth 1975, Assassination 1975, Cross of Iron 1977, Julia 1977, Avalanche Express 1978, The Black Hole 1979, The Diary of Anne Frank 1980, The Chosen 1980, Les îles 1983, Phantom of the Opera 1983, Man Under Suspicion 1983, The Assisi Underground 1984, Peter the Great (TV mini-series) 1985, The Rosegarden 1989, The Freshman, Stalin (TV) 1992, Miss Rose White (TV), Labyrinth 1990, A Far Off Place 1993, Little Odessa 1995; Producer, Dir. First Love 1969, Tales from the Vienna Woods 1979, Dir. and wrote screenplay End of the Game 1975; Dir. Volkstheater, Munich 1981–. *Principal plays acted in:* Hamlet, Prince of Homburg, Mannerhouse, Don Carlos, Sappho (Durrell), A Patriot for Me, The Twins of Venice, Old Times, Everyman 1978/79/80; Dir. All for the Best, A Patriot for Me, Hamlet, Pygmalion, La Traviata 1975, Tales from the Vienna Woods, Nat. Theatre 1977, The Undiscovered Country, Salzburg Festival 1979/80, Der Seidene Schuh, Salzburg Festival 1985. *Address:* Keplerstrasse 2, 8000 Munich 80, Germany. *Telephone:* 089-478577.

SCHELLING, Friedrich Wilhelm Eugen Eberhard von; German banker; b. 3 May 1906, Berlin; s. of Ulrich and Lina (von Jagemann) von Schelling, great-grandson of F. W. J. von Schelling, philosopher (1775-1854); m. Hildegard Oelkers 1932; one s. one d.; ed. Kaiserin Augusta Gymnasium, Berlin and Univs. of Heidelberg and Berlin; Judge, Berlin 1931–32; Reichsbank, Berlin 1932–45; Reichsbankdirektor, Hamburg 1946–48; Bank deutscher Länder, Frankfurt (Main) 1948–57; Pres. of Landeszentralbank of Free and Hanseatic City of Hamburg 1957–74; Grosses Bundesverdienstkreuz mit Stern. *Publication:* Die Bundesbank in der Inflation 1975, Wir brauchen Grundlagenforschung zum neuen Weltwährungsystem (article) 1979. *Leisure interests:* history, philosophy. *Address:* Kaspar-Ohm-Weg 16, 22391 Hamburg, Germany. *Telephone:* 5-36-11-90 (Home).

SCHELLING, Thomas Crombie, PH.D.; American university professor; b. 14 April 1921, Oakland, Calif.; s. of John M. Schelling and Zelda M. Ayres Schelling; m. 1st Corinne Tigay Saposs 1947 (divorced 1991); four s.; m. 2nd Alice M. Coleman 1991; ed. Univ. of California at Berkeley and Harvard Univ.; Fiscal Analyst, U.S. Bureau of the Budget 1945–46; Econ. Econs. Cooperation Admin., Copenhagen and Paris 1948–50, Exec. Office of the Pres. 1951–53; Assoc. Prof. and Prof. of Econs., Yale Univ. 1953–58; Lucius N. Littauer Prof. of Political Economy, Harvard Univ. 1958–; Distinguished Prof. of Econs. and Public Affairs Univ. of Md. 1990–; Sr. Staff mem. The Rand Corpn. 1958–59; Pres. American Econ. Asscn. 1991; Fellow American Acad. of Arts and Sciences; mem. N.A.S., Inst. of Medicine. *Publications:* National Income Behavior 1951, International Economics 1958, Strategy of Conflict 1960, Strategy and Arms Control (with Morton H. Halperin) 1961, Arms and Influence 1967, Micromotives and Macrobehavior 1978, Choice and Consequence 1984. *Leisure interests:* running, hiking. *Address:* Department of Economics, University of Maryland, College Park, MD 20742, U.S.A. *Telephone:* (301) 405-3494. *Fax:* (301) 403-4675.

SCHENCK, Michael U. R. von, DR. IUR.; Swiss diplomatist; b. 21 April 1931, Basel; s. of Dr. Ernst von Schenck and Selma Oettinger; ed. Humanistisches Gymnasium and Univ., Basel, and in Lausanne; Swiss Trade Fair 1950–55; Die Woche 1950–55; Swiss Foreign Ministry 1957–67, 1973–93, Del. to OECD 1958, Del. to UN 1959–61, UN Narcotics Conf. 1961, Swiss Tech. Assistance Authority 1961–67; Founder and Dir. Swiss Volunteers for Devt. 1962–67; Sec.-Gen. Int. Sec. for Volunteer Service (ISVS) 1967–71; Harvard Univ. 1972–73; Rep. to IAEA and UNIDO, Swiss Embassy, Vienna 1973–77; Head Econ. Dept., Swiss Embassy, Bonn 1977–79; Amb. to Ghana (also accred. to Liberia, Sierra Leone and Togo) 1979–83, to Finland 1983–86, to Bulgaria 1987–89, to N.Z., (also accred. Samoa, Tonga and Fiji) 1989–93. *Publications:* Der Statutenwechsel im internationalen Obligationenrecht 1955, Volunteer Manpower for Development 1967, Conferencia Regional sobre Servicio Voluntario 1968, An International Peace Corps 1968, Youth Today 1968, Youth's Role in Development 1968, International Volunteer Service 1969. *Leisure interests:* skiing, hiking. *Address:* P.O. Box 641, 4010 Basel 10, Switzerland.

SCHENK, Juraj; PH.D.; Slovak politician and academic; b. 6 May 1948, Bratislava; ed. Komenský Univ., Bratislava; lecturer, reader, Prof. Dept. of Sociology, Komenský Univ., Bratislava, Czechoslovakia 1972–94; Chair. Slovak Sociological Soc. Slovak Acad. of Sciences; mem. int. sociological socs. rep. of Slovakia to World Sociological Asscn.; Minister of Foreign Affairs of Slovak Repub. 1994–96. *Publications:* numerous monographs, scientific studies and essays on self-regulation and auto-control of social systems. *Address:* Comenius University, Šafárikovo nám. 6, 818 06 Bratislava, Slovakia.

SCHENKER, Joseph G., M.D.; Israeli physician; b. 20 Nov. 1933, Cracow, Poland; s. of the late Itzhak Schenker; m. Ekaterina Idels 1959; two s.; ed.

Herzlia High School, Tel Aviv and the Hebrew Univ. of Jerusalem; Exec. Chief of Teaching Obstetrics and Gynaecology, Hebrew Univ. Medical School 1977–84; Chair. Dept. of Obstetrics and Gynaecology, Hadassah Univ. Hosp. 1978; Prof. Obstetrics and Gynaecology, Hebrew Univ. Jerusalem 1979–; Chair. Dept. of Obstetrics and Gynaecology, Hadassah Univ. Hosp., Jerusalem.; Pres. Israel Soc. of Obstetrics and Gynaecology 1984–92; Pres. Israel Medical Asscn., Jerusalem br. 1984–; Chair. of Directory, Bd. Examination in Obstetrics and Gynaecology, State of Israel 1979–83, of Advisory Cttee. 1979–86; Acting Chair. of Hadassah Org. of Heads of Depts. 1983–; Chair. Residency Programme, Medical Council 1987, of Cttee. Licensing Physicians, Ministry of Health 1987; Pres. of Int. Soc. for Study of Pathophysiology 1983; Chair. European Residency Exchange Programme, Extended European Bd. of Gynaecology and Obstetrics 1993– (Pres. of Bd. 1994–), Cttee. for European Examination for Excellence in Gynaecology and Obstetrics 1993–, FIGO (Int. Fed. of Gynaecology and Obstetrics) Cttee. for Study of Ethical Aspects of Human Reproduction 1994–; Pres. Int. Acad. of Human Reproduction 1996–; mem. Exec. Bd. FIGO 1991–; Deputy Pres. and Sec. Israeli Soc. of Obstetrics and Gynaecology 1993–, Israel Medical Council 1985–, European Asscn. of Gynaecology and Obstetrics; Founder mem. European Soc. of Human Reproduction, Int. Soc. of Gynaecological Endocrinology, Int. Soc. of Study of Pathophysiology of Pregnancy and other orgs.; mem. exec. bds. and cttees., hon. mem. or mem. numerous int. professional orgs.; Hon. Fellow American Coll. of Obstetricians and Gynaecologists, Royal Coll. of Obstetricians and Gynaecologists and other int. orgs.; mem. Editorial Bd. Human Reproduction (Oxford), Int. Journal of Gynaecology and Obstetrics (U.S.A.), Int. Journal of Foeto-Maternal Medicine (Germany), European Journal of Obstetrics, Gynaecology and Reproductive Biology, and several other journals. *Publications:* Ed. Recent Advances in Pathophysiological Conditions in Pregnancy 1984, The Intrauterine Life-Management and Therapy 1986; more than 500 articles in medical journals on obstetrics and gynaecology, new tech. in reproduction, ethical and legal aspects of IVF etc. *Leisure interests:* history, chess. *Address:* Department 03-64N, Hadassah Hospital, P.O. Box 12000, Jerusalem 91120; 5 Mendele Street, Jerusalem 91147, Israel (Home). *Telephone:* (2) 6776424 (Office); (2) 637775 (Home). *Fax:* (2) 6432445.

SCHEPISI, Frederic Alan; Australian film writer, director and producer; b. 26 Dec. 1939, Melbourne; s. of Frederic Thomas and Loretto Ellen (née Hare) Schepisi; m. 1st Joan Mary Ford 1960; m. 2nd Rhonda Elizabeth Finlayson 1973 (divorced 1983); m. 3rd Mary Rubin 1984; three s. four d.; ed. Assumption Coll., Kilmore, Vic., Marist Brothers' Juniorate, Macedon, Vic., Marcellin Coll., Melbourne; Carden Advertising, Melbourne, Press TV Production; Paton Advisory Service, Melbourne 1961–64; Victorian Man. Cinesound Productions, Melbourne 1964–66; Man. Dir., The Film House, Melbourne 1966–79, Chair. 1979–; Australian Film Inst. Award Best Film (for Evil Angels) 1989, Longford Award 1991 (for A Cry in the Dark), Chauvel Award 1994. *Films:* A Devil's Playground 1975, The Chant of Jimmie Blacksmith 1978, Barbarosa 1981, Iceman 1983, Plenty 1985, Roxanne 1986, Evil Angels 1990, (also known as A Cry in the Dark), The Russia House 1990, Mr. Baseball 1991, Six Degrees of Separation 1993, IQ 1994. *Leisure interests:* tennis, swimming. *Address:* c/o Schoenfeld and Partners, 616 St. Kilda Road, Melbourne, Vic. 3004, Australia.

SCHERAGA, Harold A., PH.D.; American professor of chemistry; b. 18 Oct. 1921, Brooklyn, New York; s. of Samuel and Etta Scheraga; m. Miriam Kurnow 1943; one s. two d.; ed. City Coll. of New York and Duke Univ.; American Chemical Soc. Postdoctoral Fellow Harvard Medical School 1946–47; Instructor of Chem. Cornell Univ. 1947–50, Asst. Prof. 1950–53, Assoc. Prof. 1953–58, Prof. 1958–92, Todd Prof. 1965–92, Todd Prof. Emer. 1992–; Chair. Chem. Dept. 1960–67; Guggenheim Fellow and Fulbright Research Scholar Carlsberg Lab., Copenhagen 1956–57, Weizmann Inst., Rehovoth, Israel 1963; Nat. Inst. of Health Special Fellow Weizman Inst., Rehovoth, Israel 1970; Visiting Lecturer Wool Research Labs. C.S.I.R.O., Australia Dec. 1959; Visiting Prof. Weizmann Inst., Rehovoth, Israel 1972–78, Japan Soc. for the Promotion of Science 1977; Regional Dir. Nat. Foundation for Cancer Research 1982–; mem. N.A.S., American Acad. of Arts and Sciences; Vice-Chair. Cornell Section American Chemical Soc. 1954–55, Chair. 1955–56, Councillor 1959–62; mem. Advisory Panel in Molecular Biology Nat. Science Foundation 1960–62; mem. Ed. Bd. numerous scientific journals; mem. Biochem. Training Cttee., Nat. Insts. of Health 1963–65, Fogarty Scholar 1984, 1986, 1988, 1989, 1990, 1991; mem. Comm. on Molecular Biophysics Int. Union for Pure and Applied Biophysics 1967–69; mem. Comm. on Macromolecular Biophysics, Int. Union for Pure and Applied Biophysics 1969–75, Pres. 1972–75; mem. Comm. on Subcellular and Macromolecular Biophysics, Int. Union for Pure and Applied Biophysics 1975–81; mem. Exec. Comm. Div. of Biological Chem. American Chemical Soc. 1966–69; Vice-Chair. Div. of Biological Chem. American Chemical Soc. 1970, Chair. 1971; mem. Council Biophysical Soc. 1967–70; mem. Research Career Award Cttee. Nat. Inst. of Health 1967–71; mem. Bd. of Governors Weizmann Inst., Rehovoth, Israel 1970–97; hon. life mem. New York Acad. of Sciences 1985; hon. mem. Hungarian Biophysical Soc. 1989; American Chemical Soc. Eli Lilly Award in Biochem. 1957; Welch Foundation Lecturer 1962; Harvey Lecturer 1968; Gallagher Lecturer 1968–69, Lemieux Lecturer 1973, Hill Lecturer 1976, Venable Lecturer 1981; Hon. Sc.D. (Duke Univ.) 1961, (Univ. of Rochester) 1988, (Univ. of San Luis) 1992, (Technion) 1993; Townsend Harris Medal C.C.N.Y. 1970; Nichols Medal, N.Y. Section, American Chem. Soc. 1974; City Coll. Chem. Alumni Scientific Achievement Award Medal 1977; American Chem. Soc. Kendall Award in colloid chem. 1978; Linderstrøm-Lang Medal 1983, Kowalski Medal 1983, Pauling Medal, American Chemical Soc. 1985, Mobil Award, American Chem. Soc. 1990, Repligen Award, American Chem. Soc. 1990, Stein and Moore Award, Protein Soc. 1995, American Chemical Soc. Award for Computers in Chemical and Pharmaceutical Research 1997. *Publications:* Protein Structure 1961, Theory of Helix-Coil Transitions in Biopolymers 1970; 1,000 articles; research on physical chem. of proteins and other macromolecules; structure of water; chemistry of blood clotting and growth factors. *Leisure interests:* golf, skiing. *Address:* 212 Homestead Terrace, Ithaca, NY 14850, U.S.A. *Telephone:* (607) 272-5155.

SCHERER, Peter Julian; New Zealand journalist; b. 15 Aug. 1937, Stratford; s. of Arnold F. Scherer and Constance M. White; m. Gaelyn P. Morgan 1964; one s. one d.; ed. Browns Bay School and Takapuna Grammar School; joined New Zealand Herald 1955; mem. later Chief, Wellington Bureau 1960–71; Chair. Parl. Press Gallery 1965; leader-writer, Duty Ed., Business News Ed. 1973–76, Editorial Man. 1977–83, Asst. Ed. 1977–85; Ed. New Zealand Herald 1985–96; Dir. Community Newspapers Ltd. 1972–73, Wilson & Horton group 1989–96, N.Z. Press Asscn. 1991–96; Chair. N.Z. Associated Press 1985–90, N.Z. section, Commonwealth Press Union (CPU) 1989–94; Chair. planning cttee., North Health medical workforce 1996–97; Councillor, CPU, London 1989–94; mem. N.Z. Press Council 1988–97, Communications and Media Law Asscn. 1990–97; mem. Communications Advisory Council N.Z. Comm. for UNESCO 1989–94; mem. Bd. of Control, Newspaper Publishers Asscn. of N.Z. 1991–96; mem. N.Z. Nat. Cttee. for Security Co-operation in Asia-Pacific 1994–96, N.Z. Div., Inst. of Dirs. 1989–96; other professional appts.; CPU Fellowship 1963; Cowan Prize 1959. *Leisure interests:* reading, tennis, gardening, fishing. *Address:* Apartment C, 25 Ring Terrace, St. Mary's Bay, Auckland 1001; 267 School Road, Tomarata, RD4 Wellsford 1242, New Zealand. *Telephone:* (09) 378-9184 (Auckland); (09) 431-5244 (Wellsford). *Fax:* (09) 378-9184 (Auckland).

SCHERMERS, Henry G., LL.D; Netherlands professor of law; b. 27 Sept. 1928, Epe; s. of Petrus Schermers and Amelia M. Schermers Gooszen; m. Hotsche A.C. Tans 1957; one s. two d.; mil. service 1948–50; Int. Org. Dept., Ministry of Foreign Affairs 1953–56, Office of Legal Adviser 1956–63; Prof. of Law, Univ. of Amsterdam 1963–78, Univ. of Leiden 1978–; Dir. Int. Course in European Integration 1965–81; Pres. Acad. Council Asser Inst., The Hague 1977–90; Ed. Common Market Law Review 1978–93; Visiting Prof. Univ. of Mich. 1968–69, 1994, Queen Mary Coll., London 1988; Dean Leiden Law School 1985–87; Jacques Delors Prof. of European Community Law, Univ. of Oxford 1996–97; mem. European Comm. of Human Rights 1981–96; mem. Inst. of Int. Law; Corresp. Fellow British Acad.; Hon. Dr. (Edin., Osnabrück); Commdr. Order of Orange-Nassau; Kt. Order of the Netherlands Lion, Officer, Crown of Belgium, Officier, Ordres des Palmes Académiques (France). *Publications:* International Institutional Law 1972, Judicial Protection in the European Communities 1976; articles collected in Opera Patris (7 vols.), (3rd edn.) 1995. *Leisure interests:* sports, youth, carpentry. *Address:* Hugo de Grootstraat 27, Leiden (Office); Herengracht 15, 2312 LA, Leiden, Netherlands (Home). *Telephone:* 071-5277746 (Office); 071-5124294 (Home).

SCHERPENHUIJSEN ROM, Willem; Netherlands banker; b. 1936; fmr. Chair. NMB Postbank; Chair. International Nederlande (formed by merger of NMB Postbank and Internationale Nederlande Groep in 1991) 1992–94. *Address:* c/o ING Bank NV, P.O. Box 1800, 1000 BV Amsterdam, Netherlands.

SCHEUCH, Erwin K., DR.RER.POL.; German sociologist; b. 9 June 1928, Cologne; s. of Otto Wilhelm Scheuch and Cecilie Bauschert; m. Dr. Ute Pulm 1985; two s.; ed. Univ. of Conn., U.S.A., Univs. of Frankfurt and Cologne; Research Asst. UNESCO Inst. for Social Research, Cologne 1951–53, Inst. for Social Research, Univ. of Cologne 1953–58; Instructor Univ. of Cologne 1961; Lecturer in Social Relations, Harvard Univ. 1962–64; Prof. of Sociology, Univ. of Cologne 1965–93, Prof. Emer. 1993–; Visiting Prof. of Sociology, Berlin 1965, Inst. for Advanced Studies, Princeton 1973–74, Auckland Univ. 1977, Univ. of Penn. 1975, Stockholm Univ. 1979, Paris 1981; Dir. Cen. Archive for Empirical Social Research 1964–93, Inst. of Applied Social Research 1965–93 (Pres.); Chair. Kölner Gesellschaft für Sozialforschung 1990–; Past Pres. Inst. Int. de Sociology; mem. Int. Acad. for Tourism Research, Academia Scientarium et Artium Europaea, P.E.N.; Counsellor to Nestle, The Social Affairs Unit (London), Visions in Leisure; Rockefeller Foundation Fellow, Columbia Univ., Univ. of Mich., Univ of Calif., Berkeley, Univ. of Chicago 1959–60; Bundesverdienstkreuz (First Class). *Publications:* Soziologie der Wahl 1965, Wiedertäufer der Wohlstandsgesellschaft 1969, Die alte Rechte und die Neue Linke 1970, Haschisch und LSD als Modedrogen 1973, Grundbegriffe der Soziologie (2nd edn.) 1975, Kulturintelligenz als Machtfaktor 1976, Wird die Bundesrepublik unregierbar? 1976, Das Forschungsinstitut 1978, Historical Social Research 1979, Datenzugang und Datenschutz 1981, Gesundheitspolitik zwischen Staat und Selbstverwaltung 1982, Empirische Sozialforschung in der modernen Gesellschaft 1983, Zwischen Wohlstand und Bankrott 1984, (with Ute Scheuch) China und Indien 1987 (with Gräf and Kühnel), Volkszählung, Volkszählungsprotest u. Bürgerverhalten 1989, Wie Deutsch Sind die Deutschen? (with Ute Scheuch) 1991, Perspectives des sciences sociales en Allemagne aujourd'hui 1991, Muss Sozialismus misslingen? 1991, Cliquen, Klüngel und Karrieren (with Ute Scheuch) 1992, Empirische Sozialforschung über Entwicklungsländer 1992, USA—ein maroder Gigant? Amerika besser verstehen (with Ute Scheuch) 1992, Bürokraten auf den Chefetagen (with Ute Scheuch) 1995, Quantitative Social Research in Germany and Japan (with Ch. Hayashi) 1996. *Leisure interests:* modern literature, jazz, tennis. *Address:* Kölner Gesellschaft für Sozialforschung e. V., Liliencronstr. 6, 50931 Cologne-Lindenthal (Office); Hauptstr. 39c, 51143 Cologne, Germany (Home). *Telephone:* (0221) 47694-62 (Office); (02203) 87638 (Home). *Fax:* (0221) 47694-98 (Office); (02203) 87753 (Home).

SCHEVILL, James, B.S.; American professor of English (retd.), poet and playwright; b. 10 June 1920, Berkeley, Calif.; s. of Rudolph Schevill and Margaret Erwin Schevill; m. 1st Helen Shaner 1942; two d.; m. 2nd Margot Blum 1966; ed. Harvard and Brown Univs.; with U.S. Army 1942–46, rank of Capt.; teacher, Calif. Coll. of Arts and Crafts 1951–58, Pres. of Faculty Ass. 1956; San Francisco State Univ. 1959–68, Prof. of English 1968; Prof. of English, Brown Univ. 1969–85, Prof. Emer. 1985–; Pres. Rhode Island Playwrights' Theatre 1984; Co.-Dir., Dir. Creative Writing Program, Brown Univ. 1972–75; Dir. The Poetry Centre, San Francisco State Univ. 1961–68; adaptor and translator (with A. Hall) of Bertolt Brecht's Galileo 1983; mem. Bd. Trinity Square Repertory Co., Providence, Rhode Island 1975–82; Hon. M.A. (Browns) 1970; Hon. L.H.D. (Rhode Island Coll.) 1986; numerous awards including Ford Foundation grant in theatre to work with Joan Littlewood's Theatre Workshop in London 1960–61, William Carlos Williams Award for The Stalingrad Elegies 1965, Guggenheim Fellowship in Poetry 1981, McKnight Fellowship in Playwriting 1984, Literary Award for Plays, American Acad. of Arts and Letters, New York 1991. *Publications: poetry:* Tensions 1947, The American Fantasies 1951, The Right To Greet 1955, Selected Poems 1945–59 1959, Private Dooms and Public Destinations: Poems 1945–62 1962, The Stalingrad Elegies 1964, Release 1968, Violence and Glory: Poems 1962–68 1969, The Buddhist Car and Other Characters 1973, Pursuing Elegy 1974, The Mayan Poems 1978, Fire of Eyes: A Guatemalan Sequence 1979, The American Fantasies: Collected Poems 1945–81 1983, Performance Poems 1984, The Invisible Volcano 1985, Collected Poems, Vol. II, 1945–1986, Ambiguous Dancers of Fame 1987, Winter Channels 1994. *Plays:* High Sinners, Low Angels 1953, The Bloody Tenet 1957, Voices of Mass and Capital A 1962, The Black President and Other Plays 1965, Lovecraft's Follies 1969, Cathedral of Ice 1975, Wastepaper Theatre Anthology (Co.-Ed.) 1978, Collected Short Plays 1986, Oppenheimer's Chair 1985, Time of the Hand and the Eye 1986, Shadows of Memory 1989, Mother O or the Last American Mother 1990, The Garden on F Street (with Mary Gail) 1992, The Phantom of Life: A Melville Play 1993, 5 Plays 5 (collection of plays) 1993, The Complete American Fantasies 1996, Myth of the Docile Woman 1997. *Other publications:* Sherwood Anderson: His Life and Work (biog.) 1951, The Roaring Market and the Silent Tomb (biog.) 1956, The Cid (trans.) 1961, Breakout: In Search of New Theatrical Environments 1973, The Arena of Ants (novel) 1976, Six Historians by Ferdinand Schevill (Ed.) 1956, numerous readings 1960–, Bern Porter (A Personal Biography) 1993. *Address:* Brown University, Providence, RI 02912; 1309 Oxford Street, Berkeley, CA 94709, U.S.A. (Home). *Telephone:* (401) 863-1000 (Office); (510) 845-2802 (Home).

SCHICKEL, Richard, B.S.; American writer; b. 10 Feb. 1933, Milwaukee; s. of Edward J. Schickel and Helen (née Hendricks) Schickel; two d.; ed. Univ. of Wisconsin; St. Ed. Look Magazine 1957–60, Show Magazine 1960–63; self-employed 1963–; Film Critic Life Magazine 1965–72, Time Magazine 1973–; Pres. Lorac Productions 1986–; Consultant Rockefeller Foundation 1965; Lecturer in History of Art, Yale Univ. 1972, 1976; Guggenheim Fellow 1964; mem. Nat. Soc. of Film Critics, N.Y. Film Critics. *Publications:* The World of Carnegie Hall 1960, The Stars 1962, Movies: The History of an Art and an Institution 1964, The Gentle Knight 1964, The Disney Version 1968, The World of Goya 1968, Second Sight: Notes on Some Movies 1972, His Pictures in the Papers 1974, Harold Lloyd: The Shape of Laughter 1974, The Men Who Made the Movies 1975, The World of Tennis 1975, The Fairbanks Album 1975, Another I, Another You 1978, Singled Out 1981, Cary Grant: A Celebration 1984, D. W. Griffith: An American Life 1984, Intimate Strangers: The Culture of Celebrity 1985, James Cagney, A Celebration 1985, Striking Poses 1987, Schickel on Film 1989, Brando: A Life in Our Times 1991, Double Indemnity 1992; Co-Ed. Film 1967–68; Producer, Dir., Writer: (TV Specials) The Man Who Made the Movies 1973, Funny Business 1978, Into the Morning: Willa Cather's America 1978, The Horror Show 1979, James Cagney: That Yankee Doodle Dandy 1981, From Star Wars to Jedi: The Making of a Saga 1983, Minnelli on Minnelli: Liza Remembers Vincent 1987, Gary Cooper: American Life, American Legend 1989, Myrna Loy: So Nice to Come Home To 1990, Barbara Stanwyck: Fire and Desire 1991, Eastwood & Co: Making Unforgiven 1992, Hollywood on Hollywood 1993, Elia Kazan: A Director's Journey 1995, Clint Eastwood: A Biography 1996, The Moviemakers 1996, Eastwood on Eastwood 1997, The Harryhausen Chronicles 1998; Producer, Writer: TV Life Goes to the Movies 1976, SPFX 1980, Cary Grant, A Celebration 1989.

SCHIEFFER, Bob, B.A.; American broadcaster; b. Austin, Tex.; m. Patricia Penrose; two d.; ed. Texas Christian Univ.; reporter Fort Worth Star-Telegram; news anchorman WBAP-TV, Dallas, with CBS 1969–, Pentagon Corresp. 1970–74, White House Corresp. 1974–79, Chief Washington Corresp. 1982–, anchorman CBS Sunday Night News 1973–74, Sunday Ed. CBS Evening News, then Sun. Ed. 1976–; now Moderator Face the Nation, CBS News; co-anchorman CBS Morning News 1985–; participant CBS special reports including Peace and the Pentagon 1974, Watergate: The White House Transcripts 1974, The Mysterious Alert 1974, Ground Zero 1981; various awards. *Publication:* The Acting President (with Gary P. Gates) 1989. *Address:* c/o Face the Nation, CBS News, 2020 M Street, N.W., Washington, DC 20036; c/o CBS News Weekend/Sunday News, 524 W. 57th Street, New York, NY 10019, U.S.A.

SCHIEFFER, Rudolf; German professor of history; b. 31 Jan. 1947, Mainz; s. of Theodor Schieffer and Annelise Schreibmayr; Research Assoc. DFG project, Spätantike Reichskonzilien 1971–75; Research Assoc. Monumenta Germaniae Historica, Munich 1975–80; Prof. of Medieval and Modern History, Univ. of Bonn 1980–94; Prof. of Medieval History, Univ. of Munich; Pres. Monumenta Germaniae Historica, Munich 1994–; Corresp. mem. Nordrhein-Westfäl. Acad. of Sciences, Austrian Acad.; mem. Bavarian Acad.; Corresp. Fellow Royal Historical Soc., Medieval Acad. of America. *Publications:* Die Entstehung von Domkapiteln in Deutschland 1976, Hinkmar v. Reims, De ordine palatii (with T. Gross) 1980, Die Entstehung des päpstlichen Investiturverbots für den deutschen König 1981, Die Karolinger 1992. *Address:* Monumenta Germaniae Historica, Postfach 340223, 80099 Munich, Germany. *Telephone:* 089-28638383.

SCHIFF, Andras; Hungarian concert pianist; b. 21 Dec. 1953, Budapest; s. of Odon Schiff and Klara Schiff (Csengeri); m. Yuuko Shiokawa 1987; ed. Franz Liszt Acad. of Music, Budapest, with Prof. Pal Kadosa Gyorgy Kurtag and Ferenc Rados, and privately with George Malcolm; recitals in London, New York, Paris, Vienna, Munich, Florence; concerts with New York Philharmonic, Chicago Symphony, Vienna Philharmonic, Concertgebouw, Orchestre de Paris, London Philharmonic, London Symphony, Royal Philharmonic, Israel Philharmonic, Philadelphia, Washington Nat. Symphony; played at Salzburg, Edin., Aldeburgh, Feldkirch Schubertiade, Lucerne, and Tanglewood Festivals; recordings include Bach Goldberg Variations, Bach Partitas, Bach Piano Concertos, Mendelssohn Concertos 1 and 2, all the Schubert Sonatas, Schubert Trout Quintet, Schumann and Chopin 2, all the Mozart Concertos, Bach Two- and Three-part Inventions, Bach Well-Tempered Clavier, Beethoven Violin and Piano Sonatas with Sandor Vegh, Beethoven Piano Concertos, Bartok Piano Concertos, Tchaikovsky Piano Concerto, Bach English Suites, Bach French Suites, Lieder with Peter Schreier (q.v.), Robert Holl and Cecilia Bartoli, etc.; f. Musiktage Mondsee Festival 1989 (Artistic Dir. 1989–98); Prizewinner at 1974 Tchaikovsky Competition in Moscow and Leeds Piano Competition 1975; Liszt Prize 1977, Premio della Accademia Chigiana, Siena 1987, Wiener Flotenuhr 1989, Bartok Prize 1991, Instrumentalist of the Year 1993, Royal Philharmonic Soc.'s Instrumentalist of the Year 1994, Claudio Arrau Memorial Medal 1994, Kossuth Prize 1996, Soning Prize (Copenhagen 1997). *Leisure interests:* literature, languages and soccer. *Address:* c/o Terry Harrison Artists Management, The Orchard, Market Street, Charlbury, Oxon., OX7 3PJ, England. *Telephone:* (01608) 810330. *Fax:* (01608) 811331.

SCHIFF, Heinrich; Austrian cellist and conductor; b. 18 Nov. 1951, Gruunden; studied cello in Vienna with Tobias Kühne and André Navarra; London and Vienna debuts 1973; subsequently undertook extensive concert tours in Europe, Japan and U.S.A. appearing with maj. orchestras; interpreter of contemporary music including work of Lutosławski, Henze, Krenek and Penderecki and has given first performances of many new works; Artistic Dir. Northern Sinfonia 1990–91; Prin. Guest Conductor, Deutsche Kammerphilharmonie 1990–92; Prin. Conductor, Musikkollegium, Winterthur and Copenhagen Philharmonic Orchestra 1995–; guest conductor of many int. orchestras. *Address:* Künstlersekretariat Astrid Schoerke, Mönckebergallee 41, 30453 Hannover, Germany. *Telephone:* (511) 401048. *Fax:* (511) 407435.

SCHIFFER, Claudia; German fmr. fashion model; b. 1971, Düsseldorf; fashion model for Karl Lagerfeld 1990, model for Revlon 1992–96, Chanel –1997; has appeared on numerous covers for magazines and journals; designs calendars; appears on TV specials; created exercise video; appeared in films Richie Rich, The Blackout 1997; has share in Fashion Café, New York; announced retirement from modelling 1998. *Publication:* Memories 1995. *Address:* c/o United Talent Agency, 9560 Wilshire Boulevard, Beverly Hills, CA 90212, U.S.A.

SCHIFFRIN, Andre, M.A.; American publisher; b. 12 June 1935, Paris; s. of Jacques Schiffrin and Simone Heymann; m. Maria Elena de la Iglesia 1961; two d.; ed. Yale Univ. and Univ. of Cambridge; with New American Library 1959–63; with Pantheon Books, New York 1962–90, Ed., Ed.-in-Chief, Man. Dir. 1969–90; Publr. Schocken Books (subsidiary of Pantheon Books Inc.) 1987–90; Pres. Fund for Ind. Publishing 1990–; Dir., Ed.-in-Chief The New Press, New York City 1990–; Visiting Fellow, Davenport Coll. 1977–79; Visiting Lecturer, Yale Univ. 1977, 1979; mem. Council Smithsonian Inst.; mem. Bd. of Dirs. New York Council for Humanities; mem. Special Cttee. American Centre, Paris 1994–; mem. Visting Cttee. of Grad. Faculty The New York School 1995–; other professional appts. and affiliations; Hon. Fellow, Trumbull Coll. Yale Univ. *Publications:* contribs. to professional journals. *Address:* The New Press, 450 West 41st Street, New York, NY 10036 (Office); 250 West 94th Street, New York, NY 10025, U.S.A. (Home).

SCHIFRES, Michel Maurice René; French journalist; b. 1 May 1946, Orleans; s. of Jacques Schifres and Paulette Mauduit; m. (divorced); two c.; ed. Lycée du Mans, Lycée de Caen, Faculté des Lettres de Caen; journalist with Combat 1970–72, with Monde 1972–74; Head of political affairs Quotidien de Paris 1974–76; Asst. Head of political affairs France-Soir 1976, Head of political affairs Journal du Dimanche 1977, Editorial Dir. Journal du Dimanche 1985–89; mem. Comm. on quality of radio and TV broadcasts 1977–79; Editorial Dir. France-Soir 1989–92, Asst. Dir.-Gen. 1992; Asst. Editorial Dir. Figaro 1992–; Chevalier, ordre nat. du Mérite. *Publications include:* La CFDT des militants 1972, D'une France à l'autre 1974, L'Elysée de Mitterand 1987, Villes de Chiens 1988. *Leisure interest:* antiques. *Address:* Le Figaro, 37 rue du Louvre, 75002, Paris (Office); 150 avenue Emile Zola, 75015 Paris, France (Home).

SCHILY, Otto; German politician and lawyer; b. 20 July 1932, Bochum; s. of Frans Schily; m. (divorced); two c.; ed. Munich, Hamburg and Berlin Univs.; mem. Bundestag 1983–86, 1987–89, 1990–, SPD 1990–; Deputy Chair. SPD 1994–; Minister of the Interior Oct. 1998–; mem. Presidium Neue Gesellschaft für bildende Kunst; Adviser, Humanist Union. *Address:* Ministry of the Interior, 53117 Bonn, Graurheindorfer Str. 198; Oberanger 38, 80331 Munich, Germany. *Telephone:* (228) 6811 (Bonn); 0228-161 (Munich). *Fax:* (228) 6814665 (Bonn).

SCHIMBERNI, Mario, B.ECON.; Italian industrial executive; b. 10 March 1923, Rome; s. of Tommaso Schimberni and Lina Ludovici; m. Angela Peppicelli; ed. Rome Univ.; lecturer in Industrial and Commercial Techniques, Rome Univ. 1946–54; various admin., financial and managerial posts with Bomprini Parodi Delfino 1954–64, Gen. Man. 1964–70, SNIA Viscosa 1970–72, Man. Dir. 1972–75; Pres. Montefibre 1975–77; Deputy Chair. Montedison 1977–80, Chair. 1980–87; Chair. CEFIC 1982–84, META 1984–88, Erbamont; 1983–88, Ausimont 1985–88; Deputy Chair. Himont 1983–88, Confindustria 1983–88; Special Commr. Nat. Railway Authority 1988; Chair. Fincentro 1988–, Armando Curcio Ed. 1988–. *Address:* Armando Curcio Editore S.p. A., Via IV Novembre, 00187, Rome, Italy. *Telephone:* (06) 699971. *Fax:* (6) 6999 7247.

SCHINDLER, Alexander Moshe; American rabbi; b. 4 Oct. 1925, Munich, Germany; s. of Eliezer Schindler and Sali Hoyda; m. Rhea Rosenblum 1956; two s. three d.; ed. Coll. of City of New York, Hebrew Union Coll.; Asst. Rabbi, Temple Emanuel, Worcester, Mass. 1953–56, Assoc. Rabbi 1956–59; Dir. New England Council, Union of American Hebrew Congregations 1959–63, Nat. Dir. of Educ. 1963–67, Vice-Pres. 1967–72, Pres. 1973–96, Pres. Emer. 1996–; mem. Exec. Bd. Conf. of Pres. of Maj. Jewish American Orgs. 1967–96, Chair. 1976–78; mem. Exec. Bd. Hebrew Union Coll., Jewish Inst. of Religion 1967–96; Vice-Pres. Memorial Foundation of Jewish Culture 1967–96, Chair. Exec. Cttee. 1994–96, Pres. 1996–; World Jewish Congress; mem. Exec. Cttee. American Section, World Zionist Org. 1973–96, Bd. of Dirs. of United Israel Appeal, American Jt. Distribution Comm. of United Jewish Appeal (Sec. 1992–94); Vice-Pres. World Union for Progressive Judaism; founding ed. Dimensions; Townsend Harris Medal, Coll. of City of New York 1979; Hon. D.D.; Bronze Star, Purple Heart. *Publication:* From Discrimination to Extermination 1950. *Address:* Union of American Hebrew Congregations, 838 Fifth Avenue, New York, NY 10021; 6 River Lane, Westport, CT 06880, U.S.A.

SCHINTGEN, Romain, D. EN D.; Luxembourg judge; b. 22 March 1939, Luxembourg; m. Lucie Dui 1974; one d.; ed. Athénée Grand-Ducal de Luxembourg and Facultés de Droit, Montpellier and Paris; advocate, Luxembourg Bar 1964, attorney-at-law 1967; Asst. Ministry of Labour 1967, Counsellor 1974, Admin.-Gen. 1987; Pres. Conseil Economique et Social 1988–89; Judge, Tribunal of First Instance of EC 1989–96, fmr. Pres. of Fifth Chamber; Commdr. Ordre de la Couronne de Chêne; decorations from Germany, Portugal, Spain. *Publications:* Le Droit du Travail au Grand-Duché de Luxembourg, Droit des pays de la CEE, Droit du Travail-Luxembourg. *Address:* c/o Tribunal de première instance des Communautés européennes, rue du Fort Niedergrünewald, 2925 Luxembourg.

SCHINZLER, Hans-Jürgen, DR. JUR.; German insurance executive; b. 12 Oct. 1940, Madrid, Spain; mem. Admin. Bd. Münchener Rückversicherungsgesellschaft, Munich, Chair. Bd. 1993–; Deputy Chair. Allgemeine Kreditversicherung AG, Mainz, Allianzversicherung AG, Munich. *Address:* Königinstrasse 107, 80802 Munich, Germany. *Telephone:* 089 38913534.

SCHIRMBECK, Heinrich; German author, cultural and natural philosopher; b. 23 Feb. 1915, Recklinghausen; s. of Heinrich Schirmbeck and Elise Graebe; m. 1st Ursula Possekel 1940 (divorced); m. 2nd Ilse Weber 1955 (divorced); m. 3rd Evelyne Rossberg 1966 (divorced); three s. two d.; ed. Recklinghausen Gymnasium; former bookseller and later newspaper ed., freelance radio contrib. 1950–80; mem. Deutsche Akad. für Sprache und Dichtung, Darmstadt, Akad. der Wissenschaften und der Literatur, Mainz (Literaturpreis 1950); mem. German PEN centre; Förderpreis zum Immermann-Preis der Stadt Düsseldorf 1962, Goethe-Plakette der Stadt Frankfurt am Main 1995. *Publications include:* Ärgert Dich Dein Rechtes Auge 1957, Der Junge Leutnant Nikolai 1958, Bausteine zu einer Poetik im Atomzeitalter 1964, Ihr werdet sein wie Götter 1966, Die Pirouette des Elektrons 1980, Für eine Welt der Hoffnung 1988, Ein Leben für die Zukunft: Der Grenzgänger 1995, Die Angst des Ödipus—Zum sozial-ethischen Defizit der Moderne 1996 and many other novels, novellas, short stories, essays etc. *Leisure interests:* classical music, literature, philosophy, ecology. *Address:* Park Rosenhöhe 13, 64287 Darmstadt, Germany. *Telephone:* 06151/712583.

SCHIRNER, Jochen; German business executive; b. 27 Feb. 1939; s. of Karl Schirner and Inge Schirner; m. Marietheres Schirner 1962; two s. one d.; joined Rheinische Blattmetall AG (now VAW-Leichtmetall GmbH) 1963–, Head Business Man. Dept. 1969, Dir. 1974, Chair. Bd. of Dirs. 1986–98; mem. bd. dirs. of numerous cos. *Address:* Kiefernweg 16, 53639 Königswinter, Germany (Home).

SCHLAGMAN, Richard Edward, F.R.S.A.; British publisher; b. 11 Nov. 1953; s. of Jack Schlagman and the late Shirley Schlagman (née Goldston); ed. Univ. Coll. School, Hampstead, Brunel Univ.; co-f., Jt. Chair., Man. Dir. Interstate Electronics Ltd. 1973–86; purchased Bush from Rank Org., renamed IEL Bush Radio Ltd. 1981, floated on London Stock Exchange 1984, sold as Bush Radio PLC 1986; acquired Phaidon Press Ltd. 1990, Chair. and Man. Dir. 1990–; mem. Exec. Cttee. Patrons of New Art, Tate Gallery, Royal Opera House Trust, Glyndebourne Festival Soc., Designers and Arts Dirs. Asscn. of U.K.; patron Bayreuth, Salzburger Festspiele. *Leisure interests:* music, art. *Address:* Phaidon Press Limited, Regent's Wharf, All Saints Street, London, N1 9PA, England. *Telephone:* 0171-843 1000. *Fax:* 0171-843-1010.

SCHLESINGER, Arthur, Jr., A.B.; American writer and educator; b. 15 Oct. 1917, Columbus, Ohio; s. of the late Arthur Meier and Elizabeth Bancroft Schlesinger; m. 1st Marian Cannon 1940 (divorced 1970); two s. two d.; m. 2nd Alexandra Emmet 1971; one s.; ed. Phillips Exeter Acad., Harvard Univ. and Peterhouse, Cambridge, England; Soc. of Fellows Harvard 1939–42; with Office of War Information 1942–43; Office of Strategic Services 1943–45; U.S. Army 1945; Assoc. Prof. of History, Harvard Univ. 1946–54, Prof. 1954–61; Special Asst. to Pres. of U.S.A. 1961–64; Schweitzer Prof. of the Humanities, City Univ. of New York 1966–94; Consultant, Econ. Co-operation Admin. 1948, Mutual Security Admin. 1951–52; mem. Adlai Stevenson campaign staff 1952 and 1956; mem. American Historical Asscn., American Inst. of Arts and Letters (Pres. 1981–84, Chancellor 1984–87), Jury Cannes Film Festival 1964; numerous hon. doctorates including Hon. D.Litt. (Oxon.) 1987; Parkman Prize 1957, Pulitzer Prize for History 1946, for Biography 1966, Nat. Book Award 1966, Gold Medal, Nat. Inst. of Arts and Letters 1967, Fregene Prize for Literature 1983, U Thant Award for Int. Understanding 1998. *Publications:* Orestes A. Brownson: A Pilgrim's Progress 1939, The Age of Jackson 1945, The Vital Center (English title The Politics of Freedom) 1949, The General and the President (with R. H. Rovere) 1951, The Age of Roosevelt: Vol. I The Crisis of the Old Order 1957, Vol. II The Coming of the New Deal 1958, Vol. III The Politics of Upheaval 1960, Kennedy or Nixon 1960, The Politics of Hope 1963, Paths of American Thought (ed. with Morton White) 1963, A Thousand Days: John F. Kennedy in the White House, 1965, The Bitter Heritage: Vietnam and American Democracy 1941–1966 1967, The Crisis of Confidence 1969, History of American Presidential Elections (ed. with F. L. Israel) 1971, The Imperial Presidency 1973, Robert Kennedy and His Times 1978, Cycles of American History 1986, The Disuniting of America 1991, Running for President (ed.) 1994, The Vital Center 1997; articles in various magazines and newspapers. *Leisure interests:* tennis, movies. *Address:* 455 E. 51st Street, New York, NY 10022, U.S.A. (Office). *Telephone:* (212) 751-6898.

SCHLESINGER, Helmut, DR.OEC.(PUBL.); German banker (retd.); b. 4 Sept. 1924, Penzberg; s. of Franz Schlesinger and Maria Schlesinger; m. Carola Mager 1949; one s. three d.; ed. Univ. of Munich; Ifo Inst. for Econ. Research, Munich 1949–52; joined Deutsche Bundesbank 1952, Head, Research and Statistics Dept. 1964, mem. Directorate and Cen. Bank Council 1972, Deputy Gov. 1980–91, Pres. 1991–93; mem. Supervisory Bd. BIZ, Basel, Kaufhof Holding AG, Cologne, METRO AG; mem. Advisory Bd. BHF-Bank, Frankfurt, IDEA Ltd. 1995–; Hon. Prof. Post-Grad. School of Admin. Sciences, Speyer; Ludwig Erhard Prize for econ. journalism; Dr. h.c. (Frankfurt, Göttingen, St. Gallen); Grand Cross of Merit, Germany and decorations from Sweden, Hungary, Luxembourg, Austria. *Publications:* Public Debt – Without End? (in German), and numerous publs. in professional journals. *Leisure interests:* mountaineering, skiing, literature. *Address:* 14 Epsteinstrasse, 60431 Frankfurt, Germany.

SCHLESINGER, John Richard, C.B.E.; British film and theatre director; b. 16 Feb. 1926, London; s. of Dr. Bernard Schlesinger, O.B.E., F.R.C.P., and Winifred Henrietta Regensburg; ed. Uppingham School and Balliol Coll. Oxford; early career as actor on television and in films Singlehanded, Battle of the River Plate, Brothers in Law and numerous others; directed shorts for Tonight and Monitor (BBC); made films for BBC Television including part of The Valiant Years; joined Sapphire Films for Four Just Men; Assoc. Dir. Nat. Theatre 1973–88; Shakespeare Prize (FVS Found., Hamburg) 1981. *Major films:* Terminus 1961 (Venice Golden Lion), A Kind of Loving 1962 (Berlin Golden Bear), Billy Liar 1963, Darling 1965 (New York Film Critics' Award), Far From the Madding Crowd 1967, Midnight Cowboy 1968 (Dirs. Guild of America Award, Acad. Award for best Dir. and British Film Acad. Award), Sunday Bloody Sunday 1970 (David Donatello Award, British Film Acad. Award), Olympic Marathon in Visions of Eight 1973, The Day of the Locust 1974, Marathon Man 1976, Yanks 1978, Honky Tonk Freeway 1980, The Falcon and the Snowman 1985, The Believers 1986, Madame Sousatzka 1988, Pacific Heights 1990, The Innocent 1992, Cold Comfort Farm 1994, Eye for an Eye 1995, Sweeney Todd 1997. *Plays and television drama:* No Why (John Whiting), Aldwych Theatre 1964, Timon of Athens, Royal Shakespeare Theatre, Stratford 1965, Days in the Trees, Aldwych 1966, I and Albert, Piccadilly Theatre 1972, Heartbreak House, Nat. Theatre 1975, Julius Caesar, Nat. Theatre 1977, True West, Nat. Theatre 1980, Separate Tables (for TV) 1982, An Englishman Abroad (BBC) 1983 (British

Acad. Award, Barcelona Film Festival and Broadcasting Press Guild Award), A Question of Attribution (BBC TV) (British Acad. Award) 1991, Cold Comfort Farm (BBC TV) 1994. *Operas directed:* Les Contes d'Hoffmann, Royal Opera House, Covent Garden (Soc. of West End Theatres Award 1980), Der Rosenkavalier, Covent Garden 1984, Un Ballo in Maschera, Salzburg Festival 1989. *Leisure interests:* gardening, travel, music, antiques. *Address:* c/o Duncan Heath, ICM, Oxford House, 76 Oxford Street, London, W1R 1RB, England (agent). *Telephone:* 0171-636 6565 (agent).

SCHLÖNDORFF, Volker; German film director; b. 1939, Wiesbaden; m. Margarethe von Trotta (q.v.); has directed numerous cinema and television films; mem. German PEN Centre; Prize of the Int. Film Critics, Cannes 1966, Konrad-Wolf-Prize 1997. *Films include:* Der junge Törless, Mord und Totschlag, Michael Kohlhaas, Der plötzliche Reichtum der armen Leute von Kombach, Baal, Die Moral der Ruth Halbfass, Strohfeuer, Die Ehegattin, Übernachtung in Tirol, Die verlorene Ehre der Katharina Blum, Die Blechtrommel (The Tin Drum) (Golden Palm of Cannes) 1979, Die Fälschung 1981, Circle of Deceit 1982, Eine Liebe von Swann (Swann in Love) 1984, Death of a Salesman 1985, The Handmaid's Tale 1989, Voyager 1991, The Ogre 1996.

SCHLUMPF, Leon; Swiss politician; b. 3 Feb. 1925, Felsberg, Canton Grisons; m. Trudi Rupp; three d.; ed. Univ. of Zürich; private practice as lawyer and notary, Chur 1951–65; mem. Grisons Cantonal Parl. 1955–74, Pres. 1964–65, Head, Cantonal Dept. of Interior and Public Econ. 1966–74; mem. Nat. Council 1966–74; mem. Council of States 1974–; Controller of Prices, Swiss Confed. 1974–78; mem. Fed. Council 1979–87; Head of Fed. Dept. of Transport, Communications and Energy 1979–87; Pres. of Switzerland Jan.-Dec. 1984; Swiss People's Party. *Address:* c/o Department of Transport, Communications and Energy, Berne, Switzerland.

SCHLÜTER, Poul Holmskov, LL.B.; Danish politician and lawyer; b. 3 April 1929, Tønder; s. of Johannes Schlüter; m. 1st Lisbeth Schlüter 1979 (died 1988); two s. one d.; m. 2nd Anne Marie Vessel Schlüter 1989; ed. Univs. of Aarhus and Copenhagen; barrister and Supreme Court Attorney; Leader of Conservative Youth Movement (KU) 1944, nat. leader 1951; del. to Int. Congress of World Asscn. of Youth 1951, 1954; Chair. Young Conservatives, mem. Exec. Cttee. Conservative Party 1952–55, 1971, Nat. Chair. Jr. Chamber 1961, Vice-Pres. Jr. Chamber Int. 1962; mem. Folketing (Parl.) 1964–; Chair. Jt. Danish Consultative Council on UN 1966–68; M.P. Foreign Affairs Cttee. 1968, Chair. 1982; mem. Council of Europe 1971–74; fmr. Chair. Conservative Party 1974; Chair. Danish del. to Nordic Council and mem. presiding cttee. 1978–79; Prime Minister of Denmark 1982–93; Dir. Nat. Cleaning Group 1993–, Int. Service System (ISS). *Address:* c/o Prime Minister's Office, Christiansborg, Prins Jørgens Gaard 11, 1218 Copenhagen K, Denmark.

SCHMALENBACH, Werner, DR.PHIL.; German art museum director; b. 13 Sept. 1920, Göttingen; s. of Dr. Herman Schmalenbach and Sala (née Müntz); m. Esther Grey; two d.; ed. Basle Grammar School and Univ. of Basle; organiser of exhbns., Gewerbemuseum, Basle 1945–55; Dir. Kestner Gesellschaft, Hannover 1955–62; mem. working cttee., "Documenta II", Kassel 1959, 1964, 1968; German Commr., Venice Biennale 1960, São Paulo Biennale 1961, 1963, 1965; Dir. Kunstsammlung Nordrhein-Westfalen, Düsseldorf (Museum of Modern Art) 1962–90; Grosses Bundesverdienstkreuz; Officer, Nat. Order of Southern Cross (Brazil). *Publications:* Der Film 1947, Die Kunst Afrikas 1956, Julius Bissier 1963, Kurt Schwitters 1967, Antoni Tàpies 1974, Fernand Léger 1976, Eduardo Chillida 1977, Marc Chagall 1979, Emil Schumacher 1981, Joan Miró 1982, Paul Klee 1986, African Art from the Barbier-Mueller Collection (ed.) 1989, Amedeo Modigliani 1990, Die Lust auf das Bild 1996, Henri Rousseau 1997. *Address:* Poststrasse 17, 40667 Meerbusch, Germany. *Telephone:* 77802.

SCHMID, Hans Heinrich, DR.THEOL.; Swiss university rector; b. 22 Oct. 1937, Zürich; s. of Gotthard Schmid and Erika Hug; m. Christa Nievergelt 1962; two s. two d.; ed. Zürich and Göttingen Univs.; Asst. Prof. Univ. of Zürich 1967–69; Prof. for Old Testament, Kirchliche Hochschule Bethel/Bielefeld 1969–76, Univ. of Zürich 1976–88; Rector, Univ. of Zürich 1988–; Dr. theol. h.c. (Leipzig) 1991. *Publications include:* Altorientalische Welt in der alttestamentlichen Theologie (essays) 1974, Der sogennante Jahwist. Beobachtungen und Fragen zur Pentateuchforschung 1976. *Leisure interest:* conducting a chamber orchestra. *Address:* Künstlergasse 15, 8001 Zürich (Office); In der Halden 11, 8603 Schwerzenbach, Switzerland (Home). *Telephone:* (01) 634 2210 (Office); (01) 825 25 33 (Home). *Fax:* (01) 634 2212.

SCHMID, Rudi, M.D., PH.D.; American (b. Swiss) professor of medicine; b. 2 May 1922, Glarus, Switzerland; s. of Rudolf Schmid and Bertha Schiesser; m. Sonja D. Wild 1949; one s. one d.; ed. gymnasium, Zurich, Univ. of Zurich, Univ. of Minnesota; intern in internal medicine Univ. of Calif., San Francisco 1948–49, Prof. of Medicine and Chief Gastroenterology Unit and Dir. of Liver Center 1966–83, Dean School of Medicine 1983–89, Assoc. Dean for Int. Relations 1989–95, Emer. Prof. of Medicine 1991–; Resident Internal Medicine, Univ. of Minn. 1949–52, Instructor in Medicine 1952–54; Research Fellow in Biochem. Columbia Univ. Coll. of Physicians and Surgeons 1954–55; Sr. Investigator Nat. Insts. of Health, Bethesda, Md. 1955–57; Assoc. in Medicine Harvard Medical School, Thorndike Memorial Lab., Boston City Hosp. 1957–59, Asst. Prof. of Medicine Harvard Medical School 1959–62; Prof. of Medicine Univ. of Chicago 1962–66; mem. numerous editorial bds.; Hon. Ed.-in-chief World Journal of Digestion 1996–; mem. Acad. Leopoldina (German Acad. of Sciences) 1965, N.A.S. 1974–, American Acad. of Arts and Sciences 1982–, Swiss Acad. of Medical Science 1994–, German American Acad. Council 1994–. *Publications:* over 200 scientific publs. in the field of porphyrin, heme and bile pigment metabolism, liver function, liver disease, muscle and blood diseases. *Leisure interests:* travel, reading, music, skiing, mountain climbing, tennis. *Address:* 211 Woodland Road, Kentfield, CA 94904, U.S.A. (Home).

SCHMIDBAUR, Hubert, D.RER.NAT.; German professor of chemistry; b. 31 Dec. 1934, Landsberg/L; s. of Johann B. Schmidbaur and Katharina S. Ehelechner; m. Rose-Marie Fukas; one s. one d.; ed. Univ. of Munich; Asst. Prof., Univ. of Munich 1960–64; Assoc. Prof., Univ. of Marburg 1964–69; Prof., Univ. of Würzburg 1969–73; Prof. and Head of Dept., Tech. Univ. of Munich 1973–, Dean Faculty of Science 1983–; mem. Göttingen, Leopoldina, Bavarian and Finnish Acads., Senate, German Science Foundation; A. Stock Prize, German Chemical Soc., F. Kipping Award, American Chemical Soc., Leibniz Award, German Science Foundation, Dwyer Medal, Bailar Medal, Bundesverdienstkreuz. *Publications:* about 700, including books, monographs and scientific papers on inorganic, metalorganic and analytical chemistry. *Address:* Konigsberger Str. 36, 85748 Garching, Germany. *Telephone:* (0049) 089-28913130. *Fax:* (0049) 089-28913125.

SCHMIDHUBER, Peter M.; German international official; b. 15 Dec. 1931, Munich; one d.; ed. Univ. of Munich; mem. Bavarian Christian Social Union Party (CSU) 1952–; served in Bavarian State Ministries of Finance and of Econ. Affairs and Transport 1961–72; lawyer in Munich 1972–; Hon. Munich City Councillor 1960–66; mem. Bundestag 1965–69, 1972–78; mem. Bavarian Landtag, Bavarian State Minister for Fed. Affairs and Proxy for Free State of Bavaria to Fed. Govt. 1978–87; mem. Bundesrat 1978–87; mem. N. Atlantic Ass. 1978–87; mem. European Comm. 1987–, EC Commr. for Budget and Financial Control 1989–95, for the Cohesion Fund 1993–95; Dir. Bundesbank 1995–; Bundesverdienstkreuz. *Address:* Wehnerstr. 12, 81243 Munich, Germany (Home). *Telephone:* 835031 (Home).

SCHMIDT, Andreas; German singer; b. 30 June 1960, Düsseldorf; m. Eva Grundhoff 1989; one s. one d.; studied piano, organ, conducting in Düsseldorf, singing in Düsseldorf and Berlin; youngest mem. of Deutsche Oper Berlin 1983; debut Hamburg State Opera 1985, Munich State Opera 1985, Covent Garden London 1986, Vienna State Opera 1988, Geneva Opera 1989, Salzburg Festival 1989, Aix-en-Provence Festival 1991, Metropolitan New York 1991, Edin. Festival 1991, Paris Bastille 1992, Paris Garnier 1993, Glyndebourne Festival 1994, State Opera Berlin 1995, Amsterdam Opera 1995, Bayreuth Festival 1996; has sung with maj. orchestras including Berlin, Geneva, Vienna, Munich, London, New York, Israel Philharmonic orchestras, Cincinnati, Cleveland Symphony orchestras, La Scala, Milan; 1st Prize Deutscher Musikwettbewerb, several German and int. awards and prizes. *Leisure interests:* fly-fishing, golf, literature, art. *Address:* c/o IMG Artists, Media House, 3 Burlington Lane, London, W4 2TH, England; Fossredder 51, 22359 Hamburg, Germany.

SCHMIDT, Benno C., Jr.; American university president; b. 20 March 1942, Washington; s. of Benno Charles Schmidt Sr. and Martha Chastain; m. 2nd Helen Cutting Whitney 1980; one d. (one s. one d. by previous marriage); ed. Yale Coll. and Yale Law School; Clerk to Chief Justice Earl Warren 1966–67; Dept. of Justice 1967–69; mem. Faculty, Columbia Univ. Law School 1969–86, Dean 1984–86; Pres. and Prof. of Law, Yale Univ. 1986–92; Pres., C.E.O. The Edison Project 1992–; Dir. Nat. Humanities Center, Chapel Hill, N.C. 1985–; Hon. Master of Bench, Gray's Inn 1988. *Publications:* Freedom of the Press versus Public Access 1976, The Judiciary and Responsible Government 1910–1921 (with A. M. Bickel) 1984; papers on constitutional law, freedom of the press and first amendment issues.

SCHMIDT, Chauncey Everett, B.S., M.B.A.; American banker; b. 7 June 1931, Oxford, Ia.; s. of Walter F. Schmidt and Vilda Saxton; m. Anne Garrett McWilliams 1954; one s. two d.; ed. U.S. Naval Acad., Harvard Graduate School of Business Admin.; with First Nat. Bank of Chicago 1959–75, Vice-Pres. 1965, Gen. Man., London 1966, Gen. Man. for Europe, Middle East and Africa 1968, Sr. Vice-Pres. 1969–72, Exec. Vice-Pres. 1972, Vice-Chair. 1973, Pres. 1974–75; Chair. and C.E.O., Bank of Calif. 1976–; Chair., Pres., C.E.O. BanCal Tri-State Corpn. 1976–; Dir. Amfac Ltd., Calif. Bankers Clearing House Asscn., Calif. Roundtable, Bay Area Council; Exec. Bd. San Francisco Bay Area Council of Boy Scouts of America; Bd. of Govs. San Francisco Symphony; mem. Fed. Advisory Council of Fed. Res. System, Advisory Council of Japan-U.S. Econ. Relations, SRI Int. Council, Int. Monetary Conf., American Bankers Asscn. *Address:* 525 Middlefield Road, Suite 140, Menlo Park, CA 94025 (Office); 40 Why Worry Lane, Woodside, CA 94062, U.S.A. (Home). *Telephone:* (650) 322-3000 (Office).

SCHMIDT, Christian, PH.D., D.SC.ECON.; French university professor; b. 20 July 1938, Neuilly-sur-Seine; s. of Paul Schmidt and Jeanne Loriot; m. Marie-Pierre de Cossè Brissac 1988; ed. Facultés de Lettres, Droit, Sciences, Inst. d'Etudes Politiques, Paris, Inst. des Hautes Etudes de Défence Nationale, Acad. of Int. Law, The Hague; Research Asst. Inst. of Applied Econ. Sciences Laboratoire Coll. de France 1964–67; Asst. La Sorbonne 1967–70; Chargé de Mission Forecasting Admin. Ministry of Finances 1970–72; f. Dir. Econ. Perspectives 1969–86; Asst. Dir. French Inst. of War Studies 1980–82; Pres. Charles Gide Asscn. for the Study of Econ. Thought 1981–90; Consultant on Econ. Aspects of Disarmament UN 1980; Prof. Univ. of Paris IX 1983–; Pres., Founder Asscn. française des économistes de défense 1981–, Int. Defence Econ. Asscn. 1985–; Dir. Econ. and Sociology Lab., Defence Org. (LES.OD.) 1984–; Co-Dir. (Research Group) CNRS 1990–; mem. various editorial bds; Prix de L'institut (Acad. des Sciences Morales et Politiques) 1986, 1993; Croix de Chevalier, Légion d'honneur. *Publications:* Conséquences Economiques et Sociales de la Course aux Armaments 1983, Essai sur l'Economie Ricardienne 1984, La Semantique Economique en Question 1985, Peace, Defence and Economic Analysis 1987, Penser la Guerre, Penser l'Economie 1991, Game Theory and International Relations 1994, Uncertainty and Economic Thought 1996, Game Theory and Economic Analysis 1996, The Rational Foundations of Economic Behaviour (co-Ed.) 1996, Economic Essays (gen. ed.) 1997, De la Théorie des Jeux: Essai d'Interprétation 1999; numerous articles in learned journals. *Leisure interests:* theatre, opera. *Address:* Université de Paris-IX Dauphine, Place du Maréchal de Lattre de Tassigny, 75775 Paris cedex 16; 7 rue de Saint-Simon, 75007 Paris, France. *Telephone:* (1) 44.05.96.86 (Home). *Fax:* (1) 44.05.46.87 (Office); (1) 42.84.35.89 (Home).

SCHMIDT, Helmut, German politician and economist; b. 23 Dec. 1918, Hamburg; s. of Gustav and Ludovica Schmidt; m. Hannelore Glaser 1942; one d.; ed. Lichtwarkschule and Univ. Hamburg; Man. Transport Admin. of State of Hamburg 1949–53; mem. Social Democrat Party 1946–; mem. Bundestag 1953–61, 1965–87; Chair. Social Democrat (SPD) Parl. Party in Bundestag 1967–69; Vice-Chair. SPD 1968–84; Senator (Minister) for Domestic Affairs in Hamburg 1961–65; Minister of Defence 1969–72, for Econ. and Finance July-Dec. 1972, of Finance 1972–74; Fed. Chancellor 1974–82; Sr. Ed. Die Zeit 1983–, Publr. 1985–89; Adviser, Daiwa Securities Research Inst. 1986–; Dr. h.c. (Newberry Coll.) 1973, (Johns Hopkins Univ.) 1976, (Harvard Univ.) 1979, Hon. D.C.L. (Oxford) 1979, Hon. Dr. (Sorbonne Univ.) 1981, (Louvain) 1984, (Georgetown) 1986, (Bergamo) 1989, (Tokyo) 1991; European Prize for Statesmanship (F.U.S. Foundation) 1979; Richard Dimbleby Lecturer 1990; Nahum Goldmann Silver Medal 1980; Athinai Prize 1986. *Publications:* Defence or Retaliation 1962, Beiträge 1967, Strategie des Gleichgewichts 1969 (English edition "Balance of Power" 1970), Auf dem Fundament des Godesberger Programms 1973, Bundestagsreden (2nd edition) 1975, Kontinuität und Konzentration (2nd edition) 1976, Als Christ in der politischen Entscheidung 1976, Deutschland 1976—Zwei Sozialdemokraten im Gespräch (with Willy Brandt) 1976, Der Kurs heisst Frieden 1979, Pflicht zur Menschlichkeit 1981, Freiheit verantworten 1983, Weltwirtschaft ist unser Schicksal 1983, Eine Strategie für den Westen, (English ed.) A Grand Strategy for the West, (Adolphe Bentinck Prize 1986) 1985, Vom deutschen Stolz: Bekenntnisse zur Erfahrung von Kunst 1986, Menschen und Mächten 1987, (English ed.) Men and Powers 1988, Die Deutschen und ihre Nachbarn 1990, Handeln für Deutschland 1993, Das Jahr der Entscheidung 1994, Weggefährten 1996, Jahrhundertwende 1998, Allgemeine Erklärung der Menschenpflichten 1998, Globalisierung 1998, Auf der Suche nach einer öffentlichen Moral 1998. *Address:* c/o Bundeshaus, Görresstrasse 15, 53113 Bonn, Germany. *Telephone:* (228) 16 87880. *Fax:* (228) 16 80591.

SCHMIDT, Maarten, PH.D., SC.D.; Netherlands astronomer; b. 28 Dec. 1929, Groningen; s. of W. Schmidt and A. W. Haringhuizen; m. Cornelia J. Tom 1955; three d.; ed. Univs. of Groningen and Leiden; Scientific Officer Univ. of Leiden Observatory 1949–59; Carnegie Fellow Mt. Wilson Observatory, Pasadena 1956–58; Assoc. Prof. Calif. Inst. of Tech. 1959–64, Prof. of Astronomy 1964–96; discovered large red shifts in spectra of quasi-stellar radio sources (quasars); Rumford Award, American Acad. of Arts and Sciences 1968. *Leisure interest:* classical music. *Address:* California Institute of Technology, 105 24 Robinson Laboratory, 1201 E. California Boulevard, Pasadena, CA 91125, U.S.A. *Telephone:* (213) 356-6811.

SCHMIDT, Ole; Danish conductor and composer; b. 14 July 1928, Copenhagen; s. of Hugo Schmidt and Erna S. P. Schmidt; m. Lizzie Rode Schmidt 1960; two d.; ed. Royal Danish Acad. of Music, Copenhagen; conducting debut 1955; Conductor, Royal Theatre, Copenhagen 1959–65; Chief Conductor, Hamburg Symphony 1969–70; Conductor Danish Radio Concert Orchestra 1971–73; Chief Conductor and Artistic Dir. Aarhus Symphony 1978–84; Perm. Guest Conductor, Royal Northern Coll. of Music, Manchester 1986–; Chief Conductor and Artistic Dir. The Toledo Symphony, Ohio 1989–; Carl Nielsen Legat 1975; Gramex Award 1975, H. C. Lumbye Award 1988. *Leisure interests:* writing, painting, gardening. *Address:* Puggaardsgade 17, 1573 Copenhagen V, Denmark (Home).

SCHMIDT, Werner P., DR.RER.POL.; German business executive; b. 5 July 1932, Borken, Westphalia; m. Annely Bresser 1957; one s. one d.; ed. Univ. of Münster, Kalamazoo Coll., Michigan, Univ. of Cologne; Sales Planning Man., Marketing Man., Domestic Sales Man., Ford Werke AG 1956–67; Export Man., Volkswagen Werk AG 1967–71; Pres. Volkswagen do Brasil 1971–73; Chair. Man. Bd., Audi NSU Auto Union AG 1973–75, mem. Man. Bd., Volkswagen AG 1975–94; Pres. AUDI AG, Ingolstadt Neckarsulm. *Address:* Unterer Kamp 4, 38444 Wolfsburg, Germany.

SCHMIDT-JORTZIG, Edzard; DR. IUR.; German politician; b. 8 Oct. 1941, Berlin; s. of Rear Adm. Friedrich-Traugott Schmidt and Carla Freiin von Frydag; m. Marion von Arnim 1968; two d. two s.; academic counsellor and Prof., Münster 1977; Prof. and Head Law Dept., Kiel Univ. 1982; Higher Admin. and Constitutional Court Judge, Lüneburg 1983–91, 1993–94; mem. Bundestag Oct. 1994–; Fed. Minister of Justice 1996–98; mem. FDP. *Publications:* Zur Verfassungsmässigkeit von Kreisumlagesätzen 1977, Kommunale Organisationshoheit 1979, Die Einrichtungsgarantien der Verfassung 1979, Kommunalrecht 1982, Gemeindliches Eigentum an Meereshäfen 1985, Reformüberlegungen für die Landessatzung Schleswig-Holstein 1988, Handbuch des Kommunalen Finanz-und Haushaltsrechts (with J. Makswit) 1991. *Address:* c/o Federal Ministry of Justice, Heinemannstrasse 6, 53175 Bonn, Germany.

SCHMIDT-NIELSEN, Knut, DR. PHIL.; American professor of physiology; b. 24 Sept. 1915, Norway; s. of Sigval and Signe Torborg (Sturzen-Becker) Schmidt-Nielsen; ed. Oslo and Copenhagen Univs.; Research Fellow Carlsberg Labs., Copenhagen 1941–44; Research Fellow, Univ. of Copenhagen 1944–46; Research Assoc. Swarthmore Coll. Dept. of Zoology 1946–48; Research Assoc. Stanford Univ. Dept. of Physiology 1948–49; Docent Univ. of Oslo 1947–49; Asst. Prof. Univ. of Cincinnati Coll. of Medicine 1949–52; Prof. of Physiology, Dept. of Zoology, Duke Univ. 1952–, James B. Duke Prof. of Physiology 1963–; Guggenheim Fellow, Algeria 1953–54; Brody Memorial Lecturer Univ. of Mo. 1962; Harvey Soc. Lecturer 1962 (Hon. mem. 1962); Regents' Lecturer Univ. of Calif. (Davis) 1963; Hans Gadow Lecturer Cambridge Univ. 1971; Visiting Agassiz Prof. Harvard Univ. 1972; Wellcome Prof. in Basic Medical Sciences, Univ. of S.D. 1988; mem. numerous scientific Cttees., including Advisory Bd. to the Physiological Research Lab., Scripps Inst. of Oceanography 1963–69, Chair. 1968–69; U.S. Nat. Cttee. for Int. Union of Physiological Sciences 1966–78, Vice-Chair. 1969–78; Biomedical Engineering Advisory Cttee., Duke Univ. 1968; Animal Resources Advisory Cttee., Nat. Inst. of Health 1968; mem. Organizing Cttee., First Int. Conf. Comparative Physiology 1972, Pres. 1972–80; mem. Advisory Bd., Bio-Medical Sciences, Inc. 1973–74; Chair. Interunion Comm. on Comparative Physiology 1976–80; Pres. Int. Union of Physiological Sciences 1980–86; mem. Editorial Bd. several scientific journals; mem. N.A.S., Royal Norwegian Soc. of Arts and Science 1973, Royal Danish Acad. 1975; Foreign mem. Royal Soc., London 1986; Hon. mem. Deutsche Ornitologen–Gesellschaft 1988, American Soc. of Zoologists 1990; Fellow, American Acad. of Arts and Sciences, N.Y. Acad. of Science, A.A.A.S.; Hon. Fellow Zoological Soc. of London 1990; Int. Prize for Biology, Japan Soc. for Promotion of Science 1992; Foreign Assoc. Acad. des Sciences (France) 1968; Hon. D.Med. (Univ. of Lund, Sweden) 1986, Hon. Dr.Phil. (Univ. of Trondheim, Norway) 1993. *Publications:* Animal Physiology 1960 (trans. in several languages), Desert Animals, Physiological Problems of Heat and Water 1964, How Animals Work 1972, Animal Physiology, Adaptation and Environment 1975, Scaling: Why is Animal Size so Important? 1984, The Camel's Nose: Memoirs of a Curious Scientist 1998; numerous articles. *Address:* Department of Zoology, Duke University, Box 90325, Durham, NC 27708-0325, U.S.A. *Telephone:* (919) 684-2687. *Fax:* (919) 684-6168.

SCHMIDT-ROHR, Ulrich, DR.RER.NAT.; German physicist; b. 25 May 1926, Frankfurt an der Oder; s. of Georg and Ruth Schmidt-Rohr; m. Helma Wernery 1963; four s. one d.; ed. Friedrichsgymnasium, Frankfurt an der Oder, Technische Hochschule, Berlin and Brunswick, and Univ. of Heidelberg; research Lab., OSRAM 1948–49; Asst., Univ. of Heidelberg 1950–53; F.S.S.P. Fellow, M.I.T. 1954; Asst. Max Planck Inst. for Medical Research 1955–58, Max Planck Inst. for Nuclear Physics 1958–61; Dir. Inst. for Nuclear Physics, Kernforschungsanlage, Jülich 1962–65; Dir. Max Planck Inst. for Nuclear Physics 1966–. *Publications:* papers on nuclear physics and accelerators. *Address:* Max Planck Institut für Kernphysik, Postfach 10 39 80, 69029 Heidelberg, Germany. *Telephone:* (06221) 516 202-204.

SCHMIED, Wieland; Austrian professor of art history; b. 5 Feb. 1929, Frankfurt-am-Main; m. Erika Schmied 1966; two d.; ed. Univ. of Vienna; Dir. Kestner-Gesellschaft, Hannover 1963–74; Dir. Berliner Künstlerprogramm DAAD (artists-in-residence programme) 1978–86; Prof. of Art History and Rector Acad. of Fine Arts, Munich 1986–94; Pres. Int. Summer Acad. of Fine Arts, Salzburg 1980–; mem. Bayerische Akademie der Schönen Künste 1988– (Pres. 1995–); Vienna City Prize for Essays 1984, Staatspreis for Essays, Vienna 1992, Friedrich Märker Award for Essays, Munich 1994, Theo Wormland Award, Munich 1997. *Publications:* monographs on Alfred Kubin 1967, Caspar David Friedrich 1975, Giorgio de Chirico 1982, Francis Bacon 1985, Ezra Pound 1994, Edward Hopper 1995, Thomas Bernhards Häuser 1995; maj. catalogues on modern art. *Address:* Bayerische Akademie der Schönen Künste, Max Joseph Platz 3, 80539 Munich, Germany.

SCHMITT, Harrison H., PH.D.; American fmr. astronaut, politician and businessman; b. 3 July 1935, Santa Rita, N.M.; s. of Harrison A. and Ethel Hagan Schmitt; m. Teresa Fitzgibbons 1985; ed. Calif. Inst. of Technology, Univ. of Oslo, Norway, and Harvard Univ.; Fulbright Fellowship 1957–58, Kennecott Fellowship in Geology 1958–59, Harvard Fellowship 1959–60, Harvard Travelling Fellowship 1960, Parker Travelling Fellowship 1961–62, Nat. Science Foundation Postdoctoral Fellowship, Dept. of Geological Sciences, Harvard 1963–64; has done geological work for Norwegian Geological Survey, Oslo, for U.S. Geological Survey, N.M. and Montana, and in Alaska 1955–56; with U.S. Geological Survey Astrogeology Dept. until 1965; Project Chief on photo and telescopic mapping of moon and planets; selected as scientist-astronaut by NASA June 1965; completed flight training 1966; Lunar Module pilot Apollo XVII Dec. 1972; Chief, Astronaut Office, Science and Applications, Johnson Space Center 1974; Asst. Admin., Energy Programs, NASA, Washington, D.C. 1974–76; Senator from New Mexico 1977–83; Consultant 1983–; mem. Pres.'s Foreign Intelligence Advisory Bd. 1984–85, Army Sciences Bd. 1985–89, Army Research Lab. Tech. Review Bd. 1993–; co.-leader group to monitor Romanian Elections 1990; Chair., Pres. Annapolis Center 1994–; Adjunct Prof. Univ. of Wis. 1995–; Lovelace Award, NASA 1989, Gilbert Award, GSA 1989; Republican. *Address:* P.O. Box 14338, Albuquerque, NM 87191, U.S.A.

SCHMUDE, Dr. Jürgen; German politician and lawyer; b. 9 June 1936, Insterburg; m.; two c.; ed. Göttingen, Berlin, Bonn, Cologne Univs.; practised law, Essen; mem. Social Democratic Party 1957–; various local party functions 1957–; mem. town council and del. district council, Moers 1964–71; mem. Bundestag 1969–94; Sec. of State to Fed. Minister of the Interior 1974–78; Fed. Minister of Educ. and Science 1978–81, of Justice 1981–82; Pres. Synod of Evangelical Churches (Fed. Repub. of Germany) 1985–. *Address:* Am Jostenhof 2, 47441 Moers, Germany.

SCHNABEL, Julian, B.F.A.; American painter; b. 1951; ed. Univ. of Houston; solo exhbns. Houston, New York, San Francisco, Los Angeles, Chicago, Düsseldorf, Zürich, Amsterdam, London, Paris, Rome, Tokyo etc.; numerous group exhbns. including Venice Biennale 1980, 1982, Royal Acad. London 1981, 64th Whitney Biennial 1987; Dir. and wrote screenplay for film Build a Fort and Set It on Fire 1995, Dir. film Basquiat 1996. *Publication:* Nicknames of Maître D's and Other Excerpts From Life 1988. *Address:* Pace Gallery New York, 32 East 57th Street, New York, NY 10022, U.S.A.

SCHNEBLI, Dolf, M.ARCH.; Swiss architect; b. 27 Dec. 1928, Baden; s. of Robert Schnebli and Margret Heer; m. Jamileh Jahanguiri; one s. two d.; ed. Swiss Fed. Inst. of Tech. (ETH), Zürich and Harvard Grad. School of Design; own architectural office 1958; partner, Ryser, Engeler, Meier 1970; Prof. ETH Zürich 1972; Partner, Schnebli Ammann Ruchat 1989; Pres. Schnebli Ammann Ruchat & Assocs. Architecture, Planning, Urban Design 1994; Hon. Prof. South China Univ. 1983; numerous first prizes in architecture competitions and other awards. *Address:* Südstrasse 45, 8008 Zürich, Switzerland. *Telephone:* 01-383-14 30. *Fax:* 01-383 27 37.

SCHNEEBELI, Christian; French oil executive; b. 1 Oct. 1938, Zürich, Switzerland; s. of Walter Schneebeli and Gertrud Maria Witschi; m. Elisabeth Duval 1966; one s. one d.; ed. Ecole Polytechnique, Paris; joined Mobil Group 1962; man. positions in Benelux 1971–73, Japan 1973–77, Sweden 1977–80, France 1980–88; Area Exec. Europe 1988–92; Pres.-Dir-Gen. Mobil Oil Française 1993–. *Address:* Mobil Oil Française, Tour Septentrion, 92976 Paris La Défense cedex (Office); 46 rue Spontini, Paris 75116, France (Home). *Telephone:* (1) 41.45.45.22 (Office).

SCHNEIDER, Dieter, DR. RER. POL.; German professor of business administration; b. 2 April 1935, Striegau, Silesia; s. of Walter Schneider and Lina Schneider, née Wolff; m. Marlene Jakobs 1971; ed. Univs. of Frankfurt and Nuremberg; Prof., Univ. of Münster 1965, Univ. of Frankfurt am Main 1970, Univ. of Bochum 1973–; Dr. h.c. (Duisburg, Würzburg, Bayreuth) 1992, (Göttingen) 1995. *Publications:* Steuerbilanzen 1978, Grundzüge der Unternehmensbesteuerung 1990, Allgemeine Betriebswirtschaftslehre 1987, Investition, Finanzierung und Besteuerung 1992, Betriebswirtschaftslehre (Vol. 1) 1993, (Vol. 2) 1994, (Vol. 3) 1997. *Leisure interests:* classical and chamber music. *Address:* Ruhr-Universität Bochum, Fakultät für Wirtschaftswissenschaft, Seminar für Angewandte Wirtschaftslehre V, Universitäts-strasse 150, 44801 Bochum, Germany. *Telephone:* 0234/700 2906.

SCHNEIDER, Manfred; German business executive; b. 21 Dec. 1938, Bremerhaven; m.; one d.; ed. Univs. of Freiburg, Hamburg and Cologne; joined Bayer AG, Leverkusen 1966, Head Finance and Accounting Dept. of subsidiary co. Duisburger Kupferhütte, then Chair. of Bd. 1971–81, returned to Bayer AG 1981, apptd. Head Regional Co-ordination, Corp. Auditing and Control 1984, mem. Bd. of Man. 1987–, Chair. 1992–; mem. Supervisory Bd. Daimler-Benz AG, Stuttgart, RWE Aktiengesellschaft, Essen, Varta AG, Bad Homburg, Allianz Lebensversicherungs-AG, Stuttgart, Metro AG, Cologne; Vice-Pres. Chemical Industry Asscn. (VCI). *Address:* Bayer AG, D-51368 Leverkusen, Germany. *Telephone:* 214 30-81886.

SCHNEIDER, Oscar, DR.JUR.UTR.; German politician; b. 3 June 1927, Altenheideck, Bavaria; s. of Josef Schneider; m. Josefine Kampfer 1961; two d.; ed. Univs. of Erlangen and Würzburg; mem. Nuremberg City Council 1956; mem. Bundestag 1969–94; Chair. Bundestag Cttee. on Regional Planning, Building and Urban Devt. 1972-82; Minister for Regional Planning, Building and Urban Devt. 1982–89; Pres. Curatorial Cttee. German Historical Museum 1990–; CSU. *Address:* c/o Bundeshaus, NH 1117, 53113 Bonn, Germany.

SCHNEIDER, William George, O.C., PH.D., F.R.C.S., F.R.S.; Canadian physical chemist; b. 1 June 1915, Wolseley, Saskatchewan; s. of Michael Schneider and Phillipina Kraushaar; m. Jean Purves 1940; two d.; ed. Saskatchewan, McGill and Harvard Univs.; Research Physicist Oceanographic Inst., Woods Hole, Mass., U.S. 1943–46; Research Chemist Div. of Pure Chem. Nat. Research Council of Canada, Ottawa 1946, Dir. Div. of Pure Chem. 1963–66, Vice-Pres. (Scientific) 1965–67, Pres. 1967–80; Pres. Int. Union of Pure and Applied Chemistry 1983–85; Hon. LL.D. (Alberta, Laurentian); Hon. D.Sc. (Memorial, Saskatchewan, Moncton, McMaster, Laval, York, New Brunswick, Montreal, McGill, Acadia, Regina, Ottawa); Henry Marshall Tory Medal of the Royal Soc. of Canada; Chemical Inst. of Canada Medal, Montreal Medal 1973. *Publications:* High Resolution Nuclear Magnetic Resonance (with J. A. Pople and H. J. Bernstein) 1959; over 120 scientific papers. *Leisure interests:* skiing, tennis. *Address:* 65 Whitemarl Drive, Unit 2, Ottawa, Ont., K1L 8J9, Canada. *Telephone:* (613) 748-9742.

SCHNEIDERHAN, Wolfgang; Austrian violinist; b. 28 May 1915; m. Irmgard Seefried 1948; three d.; studied under Prof. Julius Winkler and Prof. Ottokar Sevcik; solo debut in Copenhagen 1926; leader Vienna Symphonic Orchestra 1933–37, Vienna Philarmonic Orchestra 1937–49; mem. Schneiderhan Quartet 1937–51; Prof. Mozarteum, Salzburg 1936–56; Prof. Staatsakademie, Vienna 1939–50; Prof. Musik-Hochschule, Vienna 1975–; formed trio with Edwin Fischer and Enrico Mainardi 1949–55; Leader of master classes, Lucerne 1949–; f. Festival Strings, Lucerne 1956; Conductor 1965–; f. Int. Fritz Kreisler Violin Competition, Vienna 1979; f. trio with Boris Pergamenschikow and Paul Badura-Skoda 1981; mem. Royal Acad. of Music, Stockholm; Hon. mem. Verein des Beethoven-Hauses, Bonn 1964–, Österreichen-Deutschen Kulturgesellschaft 1980; Schubert Medal 1927, Musikpreis Stadt Berlin 1940, Mozart Medal 1941, 1953, Nicolai Medal (Vienna Philharmonic) 1942, Grosses Ehrenkreuz (1st class) 1961, Grosses Verdienstorden (Fed. Repub. of Germany) 1965, Ritterkreuz Daneborg-Orden (Denmark) 1963, Ehrennadel (Luzern) 1980, Grosses Silbernes Ehrenzeichen (Austria) 1980, Honour Medal of Vienna in Gold 1986, Title of Hofrat 1986. *Musical arrangements:* Beethoven Violin Concerto 1968, works by Brahms, Mozart, Haydn, Tartini, Viotti 1977. *Leisure interest:* painting. *Address:* Kaasgrabengasse 98 A, 1190 Vienna, Austria.

SCHNITZER, Moshe, M.A.; Israeli diamond exporter; b. 21 Jan. 1921; m. Varda Reich 1946; one s. two d.; ed. Balfour High School, Tel-Aviv, Hebrew Univ. of Jerusalem; Chair. Asscn. of Diamond Instructors 1943–46; Vice-Pres. Israel Diamond Exchange 1951–66, Pres. 1966–93, Hon. Pres. 1993–; Pres. Israel Exporters' Asscn. of Diamonds 1962–; World Pres. Int. Fed. of Diamond Exchanges 1968–72, Hon. World Pres. 1993–; partner Diamond Export Enterprise 1953–; mem. Consulting Cttee. to Minister of Commerce and Industry 1968–; Ed. The Diamond; Most Distinguished Exporter of Israel 1964. *Publication:* Diamond Book (in Hebrew) 1946. *Address:* Israel Diamond Exchange, 1 Jabotinsky Road, Ramat Gan 52520, P.O. Box 3025 (Office); Uri 4, Tel-Aviv 64954, Israel (Home). *Telephone:* (3) 575 1188. *Fax:* (3) 575-2479.

SCHOCKEMÖHLE, Alwin; German show jumper (retd.); b. 29 May 1937, Osterbrock, Kreis Meppen; s. of Aloys and Josefa (née Borgerding) Schockemöhle; m. 2nd Rita Wiltfang; two s. one d.; two d. from previous marriage; began riding 1946, in public events 1948–; trained in Mil. riding 1954–55; reserve for Mil. and Showjumping, Melbourne Olympics 1956; specialized in showjumping 1956–77; first Derby win, riding "Bachus", Hamburg 1957; continually in int. showjumping events 1960–77; Showjumping Champion Fed. Repub. of Germany (four times); second in European Championship (three times); European Champion riding "Warwick" 1975, 1976; Gold Medal (Team Award) Rome Olympics 1960; Gold Medal (Individual Award) and Silver Medal (Team Award) riding "Warwick" Montreal Olympics 1976. *Publication:* Sportkamerad Pferd (A Horse for sports companion). *Address:* 49453 Mühlen, Kreis Diepholz/Niedersachsen, Germany.

SCHOELLER, François; French engineer; b. 25 March 1934, Nancy; s. of Gustave Schoeller and Suzanne Woeflin; m. Colette Canonge 1960; three c.; ed. Ecole Polytechnique and Ecole Nat. Supérieure des Télécommunications; eng. equatorial office of P.T.T., Brazzaville 1960–63; Chief Eng., regional man., Télécommunications de Strasbourg 1963–73; Operational Dir. Télécommunications de Marseille 1973–75, Regional Dir. Montpellier 1975–80, Regional Dir. with grade of engineer-general 1980; Chair. TéléDiffusion de France 1983–86; Dir. Higher Educ. in telecommunication 1987–94; Pres. France Cables et Radio de México 1994–97; Project Man. France Telecom 1997–; Commdr. Ordre nat. du Mérite; Officier, Légion d'honneur. *Address:* 6 rue Marietta Martin, 75016 Paris, France.

SCHOELLER, Franz Joachim Philipp; German diplomatist; b. 24 July 1926, Düsseldorf; s. of Franz and Therese Schoeller; m. Helga Ingetraud Neul 1956; one s. one d.; ed. Univs. of Paris and Cologne; Attaché Foreign Service, Bonn 1955; Third Sec., Foreign Office, Bonn 1957–59, Second Sec. 1963–66, Minister and Deputy Chief of Protocol, 1973–75, Amb. and Chief of Protocol 1975–80; served Paris 1956–57, Rome 1959–61; Consul and chargé d'affaires, Dar-es-Salaam 1961–63; First Sec., Madrid 1966–69; Counsellor, Teheran 1971–73; Amb. to Brazil 1980–83, Amb. to France 1983–87, Amb. to Poland 1987–89; Order of Merit of Fed. Repub. of Germany; Commdr. Légion d'honneur; Hon. K.C.V.O. *Leisure interests:* archaeology, history, skiing, mountain climbing. *Address:* Adalbert-Stifter-Strasse 7, 53113 Bonn, Germany.

SCHOENDOERFFER, Pierre; French writer, scriptwriter and film director; b. 5 May 1928; m. Patricia Chauvel 1957; two s. one d.; served as able seaman on Swedish ship S.S. Anita Hans 1947–48; combat cameraman in French Expeditionary Corps, Indochina 1952–55, taken prisoner by Viet Minh. *Films:* La Passe du Diable (Pellman Award 1958, Award of City of Berlin 1958) 1957, Ramuntcho 1958, Pêcheurs d'Islande 1959, La 317ème Section (Platoon 317) (Award for Best Script, Cannes 1965) 1964, Objectif: 500 Millions 1966, Le Crabe Tambour (Grand Prix du Cinéma Français 1977, Prix Femina Belge 1978, 3 Césars 1978) 1977, L'Honneur d'un Capitaine (Grand Prix du Cinéma de l'Académie Française, Prix Leduc, Grand Prix de l'Académie du Cinéma) 1982, Dien Bien Phu 1992. *Documentaries:* Attention Hélicoptère (Gold Sun, Mil. Film Festival, Versailles) 1963, The Anderson Platoon (Oscar, U.S.A. 1968, Int. Emmy Award, U.S.A. 1968, Prix Italia 1967, Merit Award of Guild of TV Dirs. and Producers, U.K. 1967 and other awards) 1967, La Sentinelle du Matin 1976, Reminiscence (sequel to

Anderson Platoon) 1989; mem. Institut de France; Prix Vauban for literary and cinematographic work 1984; Officier, Légion d'honneur; Médaille militaire; Officier, Ordre Nat. du Mérite; Croix de guerre (6 mentions); Officier des Arts et Lettres. *Publications:* La 317ème Section (Prix de l'Académie de Bretagne) 1963, L'Adieu au Roi (Farewell to the King) (Prix Interallié) 1969, Le Crabe Tambour (The Paths of the Sea) (Grand Prix du Roman de l'Académie Française) 1976, Là Haut 1981, Dien Bien Phu, De la Bataille au Film 1992. *Address:* 3 bis rue de l'Alboni, 75016 Paris, France. *Telephone:* (1) 40-50-06-41 (Paris).

SCHOLES, Gordon Glen Denton, A.O.; Australian politician and fmr. engine driver; b. 7 June 1931; s. of Glen Scholes and Mary Scholes; m. Della Kathleen Robinson 1957; two d.; mem. House of Reps. 1967–93; Councillor, Geelong City 1965–67; Pres. Geelong Trades Hall Council 1965–67, Deputy Chair. of Cttees. House of Reps. 1969–72, 1990–93, Deputy Speaker and Chair. Cttees. 1973–75, Speaker 1975–76; Opposition Spokesman on Postal and Telecommunications Comms. 1976–77, on Primary Industry June–Dec. 1977, on Defence 1977–83, on A.C.T. 1980–83; Minister for Defence 1983–84, for Territories 1984–87. *Leisure interests:* golf, stamp-collecting. *Address:* 20 Stephen Street, Newtown, Vic. 3220, Australia.

SCHOLES, Myron S., M.B.A., PH.D.; American professor of law and finance; b. 1941; ed. McMaster Univ., Univ. of Chicago; instructor Univ. of Chicago Business School 1967–68; Asst. Prof. M.I.T. Man. School 1968–72, Assoc. Prof. 1972–73; Assoc. Prof. Univ. of Chicago 1973–75, Prof. 1975–79, Edward Eagle Brown Prof. of Finance 1979–82; Prof. of Law, Stanford Univ. 1983–, also Peter E. Buck Prof. of Finance; Man. Dir. Salomon Bros. 1991–93; Dir. Centre for Research in Security Prices, Univ. of Chicago 1975–81; Sr. Research Fellow Hoover Inst, Stanford Univ. 1988–; Prin. Long-Term Capital Man. 1994–; shared Nobel Prize for Econs. 1997 for devising Black-Scholes Model for determining value of derivatives. *Address:* Graduate School of Business, Stanford University, Stanford, CA 94305, U.S.A.

SCHOLEY, Sir David Gerald, Kt., F.R.S.A., C.B.E.; British banker; b. 28 June 1935, Kingswood, Surrey; s. of Dudley and Lois Scholey; m. Alexandra Drew 1960; one s. one d.; ed. Wellington Coll. and Christ Church, Oxford; joined S. G. Warburg & Co. Ltd. 1965, Dir. 1967–, Deputy Chair. 1977–80, Joint Chair. 1980–87; Dir. Mercury Securities PLC 1969, Deputy Chair. Mercury Securities PLC 1980–84, Chair. 1984–86; Chair. S. G. Warburg (now Warburg Dillon Read) Group PLC 1985–95, fmr. C.E.O., C.E.O. July–Nov. 1995, Sr. adviser 1995–; Chair. Swiss Bank Corp. Int. Advisory Council 1995–97; Dir. Orion Insurance Co. PLC 1963–67, Stewart Wrightson Holdings PLC 1972–81, Union Discount Co. of London Ltd. 1976–81, Bank of England 1981–98, British Telecom PLC 1985–94, Chubb Corpn., U.S.A. 1991–, Gen. Electric Co. 1992–95, J. Sainsbury PLC 1996–, Inst. européen d'admin. des affaires (INSEAD) (Chair. U.K. Council 1992–97, Int. Council 1995–),Vodafone Group PLC 1998–; Sr. adviser Int. Finance Corpn. 1996–; mem. Export Guarantees Advisory Council 1970–75, Deputy Chair. 1974–75; Chair. Construction Exports Advisory Bd. 1975–78; mem. Cttee. on Finance for Industry, Nat. Econ. Devt. Office 1980–87; Gov. Wellington Coll. 1977–89, 1996– (Vice-Pres. 1998–), BBC 1994–; Hon. Treasurer I.I.S.S. 1984–90; Trustee Glyndebourne Arts Trust 1989–, Nat. Portrait Gallery 1992–. *Address:* Warburg Dillon Read, 1 Finsbury Avenue, London, EC2M 2PA, England. *Telephone:* 0171-568 2400. *Fax:* 0171-568 4225.

SCHOLEY, Sir Robert, Kt., C.B.E., D.ENG., F.ENG., F.I.M.; British company executive and engineer; b. 8 Oct. 1921, Sheffield; s. of Harold and Eveline Scholey; m. Joan Methley 1946; two d.; ed. King Edward VII School, Sheffield Univ.; joined United Steel Co. 1947, holding various eng. and production posts within the organization until the nationalization of the steel industry; Dir. Rotherham Div., Midland Group (British Steel Corpn.) 1968, Dir. Special Steels Div., Steelworks Group 1970, Man. Dir. Operations 1972, Man. Dir. Strip Mills Div. 1972–73, Chief Exec., mem. of Bd. 1973–76, Deputy Chair. and Chief Exec. 1976–86, Chair. 1986–92; Pres. Eurofer 1985–90; Dir. Eurotunnel 1987–94; Chair. Int. Iron and Steel Inst. 1989–90; Non-Exec. Dir. Nat. Health Service Policy Bd. 1989–92; mem. Higher Educ. Funding Council for England 1992–95; Pres. Inst. of Metals 1989–90; Chair. Close Bros. 1999–; British Inst. of Man. Gold Medal Award 1988, City Personality of the Year Award 1989. *Leisure interests:* history of the arts, reading, photography, caravanning, gardening. *Address:* c/o British Steel PLC, 9 Albert Embankment, London, SE1 7SN, England.

SCHÖLLKOPF, Ulrich, PH.D.; German professor of chemistry; b. 11 Oct. 1927, Ebersbach; m. Edith Jennewein 1957; two s. one d.; ed. Univ. of Tübingen, Univ. of Calif., Los Angeles; lecturer in Chem., Univ. of Heidelberg 1961–63; Assoc. Prof. Univ. of Göttingen 1964–68, Prof. 1968–; Ed. Liebigs Annalen der Chemie; mem. Cttee. for the Dr. Paul-Janssen Prize, Akad. der Wissenschaften, Göttingen, Liebigs Denkmünze der GDCh; Award of the Japanese Soc. for the Promotion of Science. *Publications:* 250 articles in scientific journals. *Address:* Eichenweg 5, 37120 Bovenden, Germany (Home). *Telephone:* Göttingen 8925 (Home).

SCHOLTEN, Willem, B.L.; Netherlands politician; b. 1 June 1927, Deventer; s. of G. and W. H. (née Berends) Scholten; m. C. M. van der Eijk 1954; one s. one d.; ed. Rijksbelastingacademie, Univ. of Amsterdam; Insp. of Taxes 1950–63; mem. Second Chamber, States-Gen. (Parl.) 1963–71; Sec. of State for Finance 1971–73; mem. European Parl. 1973–76; mem. Council of State 1976–78; Minister of Defence 1978–80; Vice-Pres. Council of State 1980–97; Minister of State 1997–. *Address:* Koningsspil 87, 2265 VJ Leidschendam, Netherlands (Home). *Telephone:* 070-3276785 (Home).

SCHOLZ, Rupert, DR. JUR.; German politician and fmr. academic; b. 23 May 1937, Berlin; m.; ed. Free Univ. of Berlin and Univ. of Heidelberg; taught law, Berlin and Munich 1972–81; Senator for Justice, W. Berlin 1981–88, for Fed. Affairs 1983–88; Minister of Defence 1988–90; mem. CDU 1983–; mem. Bundestag 1990–. *Address:* Bundeshaus, 53113 Bonn, Germany.

SCHÖNBERG, Claude-Michel; French composer; b. 6 July 1944, France; s. of Adolphe Schönberg and Julie Nadás; m. Béatrice Szabo 1979; one s. one d.; started in business as producer for EMI France and as pop song writer 1967–72; recording his own songs in France 1974–77; composed musicals La Révolution Française 1973, Les Misérables 1980–84, Miss Saigon 1985–86, Martin Guerre; recipient of Tony, Grammy, Evening Standard and Laurence Olivier Awards for musicals. *Address:* c/o Cameron Mackintosh Limited, 1 Bedford Square, London, WC1B 3RA, England. *Telephone:* 0171-637 8866.

SCHONBERG, Harold C.; American music critic; b. 29 Nov. 1915, New York, N.Y.; s. of David and Minnie Schonberg; m. 1st Rosalyn Krokover 1942 (died 1973); m. 2nd Helene Cornell 1975; ed. Brooklyn Coll. and New York Univ.; Assoc. Ed. American Music Lover 1938–42; Music Critic New York Sun 1946–50; Contributing Ed. and Record Columnist Musical Courier 1948–52; Music and Record Critic New York Times 1950–60, Sr. Music Critic 1960–80, Cultural Correspondent 1980–85; columnist for The Gramophone (London) 1948–60; Contributing Ed. Int. Encyclopaedia of Music and Musicians; U.S. Army service 1942–46; Pulitzer Prize for Criticism 1971. *Publications:* The Guide to Long-Playing Records: Chamber and Solo Instrument Music 1955, The Collector's Chopin and Schumann 1959, The Great Pianists 1963, The Great Conductors 1967, Lives of the Great Composers 1970, Grandmasters of Chess 1973, Facing the Music 1981, The Glorious Ones: Classical Music's Legendary Performers 1985, Horowitz: His Life and Music 1992. *Leisure interests:* chess, golf, poker, backgammon. *Address:* 160 Riverside Drive, New York, NY 10024, U.S.A.

SCHÖNBORN, H.E. Cardinal Christoph, O.P.; Austrian ecclesiastic; b. 22 Jan. 1945; ordained priest 1970; Bishop 1991; Coadjutor 1995; Archbishop of Vienna 1995; cr. Cardinal Feb. 1998. *Address:* Wollzeile 2, 1010 Vienna, Austria. *Telephone:* (0222) 51 5520. *Fax:* (0222) 51 552 3728.

SCHÖNE, Albrecht, DR.PHIL.; German philologist; b. 17 July 1925, Barby; s. of Friedrich Schöne and Agnes Moeller; m. Dagmar Haver 1952; one s. one d.; ed. Univs. of Freiburg, Basle, Göttingen and Münster; Extraordinary Prof. of German Literature, Univ. of Münster 1958; Prof. of German Philology, Univ. of Göttingen 1960–90, Prof. Emer. 1990–; Pres. Int. Asscn. for Germanic Studies 1980–85; mem. Akad. der Wissenschaften, Göttingen, Deutsche Akad. für Sprache und Dichtung, Bayerische, Nordrhein-Westfäl. Akad. der Wissenschaften, Austrian and Netherlands Acads.; Hon. mem. Modern Language Asscn. of America; Foreign Hon. mem. American Acad. of Arts and Sciences; Hon. Dr. phil., Hon. Dr. theol.; several prizes; Ordre Pour le Mérite. *Publications:* numerous books and articles on German literature and philology. *Leisure interests:* riding, hunting, painting. *Address:* University of Göttingen, Humboldtallee 13, 37073 Göttingen (Office); Grotefendstrasse 26, 37075 Göttingen, Germany (Home). *Telephone:* 0551-56449 (Home).

SCHOTT, Rüdiger, D.PHIL.; German professor of ethnology; b. 10 Dec. 1927, Bonn; s. of Albert Schott and Beatrice von Kryger; m. Helga Schott 1958; four d.; ed. Univs. of Bonn, Göttingen and London, U.K.; Asst. in research project on Early History of Property 1954–58; Deutsche Forschungsgemeinschaft Scholar 1958–60; Asst., Arnold-Bergstraesser-Inst. for Cultural Research, Freiburg, Lecturer in Social Anthropology, Univ. of Freiburg/Br. 1961–64; apptd. Univ. Lecturer, Univ. of Bonn 1964; Prof. of Ethnology, Univ. of Münster, Westphalia 1965–93, Prof. Emer. 1993–; mem. Acad. of Sciences of North Rhine-Westphalia. *Publications:* Anfänge der Privat- und Planwirtschaft 1955, Aus Leben und Dichtung eines westafrikanischen Bauernvolkes 1970, Afrikanische Erzählungen als religionsethnologische Quellen 1990, Bulsa Sunsuelima: Folktales of the Bulsa in Northern Ghana (Vol. 1 Part I) 1993, (Vol. 1 Parts II–III) 1996, Orakel und Opferkulte bei Völkern der westafrikanische Savanne 1997; more than 90 articles in scientific journals. *Address:* Nachtigallenweg 56, 53115 Bonn, Germany (Home). *Telephone:* (0288) 26 48 60 (Home).

SCHOTTE, H.E. Cardinal Jan; Belgian ecclesiastic; b. 29 April 1928, Beveren-Waregem; s. of Marcel Schotte and Rhea Duhou; ed. Sacred Heart Diocesan Coll., Waregem, Belgium, C.I.C.M. Scholasticate, Scheut-Brussels and Katholieke Universiteit, Leuven; Asst. Prof. Canon Law Catholic Univ., Leuven 1955–62; Rector I.H.M. Seminary, Catholic Univ. of America, Washington D.C. 1963–66; Sec. Gen. Congregation Immaculate Heart of Mary, Rome 1967–72; Attaché for Int. Orgs. Secr. of State, Vatican 1972–80; Vice-Pres. Pontifical Comm. for Justice and Peace 1980–85; Sec. Gen. Synod of Bishops 1985–; Titular Bishop of Silli 1984, Titular Archbishop 1985; cr. Cardinal 1994; mem. Pontifical Comm. for the Catechism of the Catholic Church 1986–92; Pres. Labour Office of Apostolic See, Vatican 1989–; mem. Pontifical Comm. for Latin America, Vatican 1989–, Congregation for Bishops 1985–; mem. Jt. Working Group Holy See-WCC 1983–; mem. Interdicasterial Comm. on the Universal Catechism 1993–; mem. Congregation for

Evangelization of Peoples 1994–; mem. Supreme Court Signature Apostolica 1998–; mem. Final Court of Appeal, Vatican City State 1998; Special Envoy of the Pope, Taiwan 1996; Officier, Légion d'honneur, Ordre Leopold II (Belgium), Kt. Commdr. Grand Cross, Order of Holy Sepulchre (U.S.A.). *Address:* Sinodo dei Vescovi, 00120 Vatican City State, Italy. *Telephone:* 0039-6-69884821. *Fax:* 0039-6-69883392.

SCHRADER, Paul Joseph, M.A.; American screenwriter and director; b. 22 July 1946, Grand Rapids, Mich.; m. 1st Jeannine Oppewall (divorced); m. 2nd Mary Beth Hurt 1983; ed. Calvin Coll. and Univ. of Calif. at Los Angeles; film critic for L.A. Free Press magazine 1970–71; Ed. Cinema magazine 1970–; screenplays: Taxi Driver 1976, Obsession 1976, Raging Bull 1981, The Mosquito Coast 1986; co-author of screenplays; The Yazuka 1974, Rolling Thunder 1977, Old Boyfriends 1979, directed: Bluecollar (also Co-writer) 1978, Hardcore 1978, American Gigolo (also Co-writer) 1979, Cat People 1982, Mishima (also Co-writer) 1985, Patty Hearst 1989, The Comfort of Strangers 1990, Light Sleeper 1991 (also writer), Witch-hunt 1994, Touch 1997. *Publication:* Transcendental Style in Film: Ozu, Bresson, Dreyer 1972. *Address:* 9696 Culva Blvd., Ste 203, Culver City, CA 90232, U.S.A.

SCHREIER, Peter; German tenor and conductor; b. 29 July 1935, Meissen; ed. Dresden Hochschule für Musik; sang with Dresden State Opera 1959–63; joined Berlin Staatsoper 1963; has appeared at Vienna State Opera, Salzburg Festival, La Scala, Milan, Sadler's Wells, London, Metropolitan Opera, New York and Teatro Colón, Buenos Aires; recital début London 1978; début as conductor 1969; has conducted recordings of several choral works by J. S. Bach and Mozart. *Address:* Calberlastr. 13, 01326 Dresden, Germany.

SCHREMPP, Jürgen E., DIPL.-ING.; German businessman and engineer; b. 15 Sept. 1944, Freiburg; joined Daimler-Benz AG 1967; mem. Bd. of Man. Mercedes-Benz of S. Africa (then UCDD) 1974–82, mem. Bd. of Man. 1980–82, Vice-Pres. 1984–87, Chair. Bd. of Man. 1985–87; Pres. Euclid Inc., Cleveland, Ohio, U.S.A (wholly owned subsidiary of Daimler-Benz AG) 1982–84; Daimler-Benz AG 1987–89, mem. Bd. of Man. 1989, Chair. 1994–; Chair. Bd. of Man. Deutsche Aerospace AG 1989–95; Chair. Supervisory Bd. Messerschmidt-Bölkow-Blohm GmbH (now inc. in Deutsche Aerospace AG) 1990–92, Dornier GmbH 1990–, Telefunken Systemtechnik GmbH 1990–; Chair. Man. Bd. Daimler-Benz AG May 1995–; mem. Supervisory Bd. Airbus Industrie, France 1990–, MTU Motoren- und Turbinen-Union München GmbH 1990–, MTU Motoren- und Turbinen-Union Friedrichshafen GmbH 1990–, Deutsche Aerospace Airbus GmbH 1992– (Chair. 1992–), Bayerische Vereinsbank AG, South African Coal, Oil and Gas Corpn. Ltd.; mem. Advisory Bd. Allianz Versicherung AG; mem. Int. Council J. P. Morgan; numerous other commercial appointments. *Address:* 70546 Stuttgart, Germany. *Telephone:* 3 81 99-2 35.

SCHREYER, Rt. Hon. Edward Richard, P.C., C.C., C.M.M., C.D., M.A. LL.D.; Canadian politician and diplomatist; b. 21 Dec. 1935, Beausejour, Manitoba; s. of John J. Schreyer and Elizabeth Gottfried; m. Lily Schulz 1960; two s. two d.; ed. Cromwell Public School, Beausejour Collegiate, United Coll., St. John's Coll. and Univ. of Manitoba; mem. for Brokenhead, Manitoba Legislature 1958, re-elected 1959, 1962; Prof. Political Science and Int. Relations, Univ. of Manitoba 1962–65; M.P. for Springfield Constituency 1965–68, for Selkirk 1968; Leader, Manitoba New Democratic Party 1969–78; Premier of Manitoba, Minister of Dominion-Provincial Relations 1969–77, Minister of Hydro 1971–77, of Finance 1972–74; Leader of the Opposition 1977–78; Gov.-Gen. of Canada 1979–84; High Commr. to Australia, also accred. to Papua New Guinea and Solomon Islands 1984–88; Amb. to Vanuatu 1984–88; Distinguished Visiting Prof. Univ. of Winnipeg 1989–90, Simon Fraser Univ. 1991; Distinguished Fellow, Inst. of Integrated Energy Systems, Univ. of Victoria 1992–94, Dept. of Geography, Univ. of B.C. 1995–, Chair. Canadian Shield Foundation 1984–; Dir. Perfect Pacific Investments 1989–, China Int. Trust and Investment Corpn. (Canada) Ltd. 1991–, Swan-E-Set Bay Resort and Country Club 1991–, Habitat for Humanity Canada 1992–, Sask. Energy Conservation and Devt. Authority 1993–, Alt. Fuel Systems Inc. (Calgary) 1994–, Cephalon Oil and Gas Resource Corp. (Calgary) 1994–; Hon. Dir. Sierra Legal Defence Fund 1991–; mem. Int. Asscn. of Energy Econs., Churchill Econ. Advisory Cttee., Pacific Inst. of Deep Sea Tech.; Counsellor Canada West Foundation 1989–; Sr. Adviser Summit Council for World Peace (World Peace Fed.), Washington DC 1991–; Hon. Adviser Canadian Foundation for the Preservation of Chinese Cultural and Historical Treasures 1994–; Hon. Patron John Diefenbaker Soc. 1991–; Gov.-Gen. Vanier Award 1975. *Leisure interests:* reading, golf, sculpting, woodworking. *Address:* 250 Wellington Center, Unit 401, Winnipeg, Man. R3M 0B3, Canada. *Telephone:* (204) 989-7580. *Fax:* (204) 989-7581.

SCHREYER, William Allen, B.A.; American business executive; b. 13 Jan. 1928, Williamsport, Pa.; s. of late William Schreyer and Elizabeth Engel; m. Joan Legg 1953; one d.; ed. Pennsylvania State Univ.; with Merrill Lynch, Pierce, Fenner & Smith, Inc. 1948–93, Vice-Pres. 1965–78, Sales Dir., New York 1969–72, Regional Dir. 1972–73, now Chair., Pres. and C.E.O.; Chair. Merrill Lynch Govt. Securities, Inc. 1973–76, 1981–; Exec. Vice-Pres. Capital Markets Activities 1976–78, fmr. Pres. and C.E.O.; Pres., C.E.O. Merrill Lynch & Co. 1984–92, Chair. 1985–93, Chair. Emer. 1993–; Dir. Merrill Lynch & Co. Trustee Medical Center, Princeton 1974–80; Bd. Dirs. Schering-Plough Corpn., Deere and Co.; Trustee American Man. Asscns. 1979–; mem. Securities Industry Asscn., Gov. 1979–; Hon. D.H.; Distinguished Alumnus Award (Pa. State Univ.). *Leisure interests:* tennis, reading, swimming. *Address:* Merrill Lynch & Co., Inc., 800 Scudders Mill Road, Plainsboro, N.J. 08536 (Office); 117 Mercer Street, Princeton, NJ 08540, U.S.A. (Home).

SCHRIEFFER, John Robert, PH.D.; American professor of physics; b. 31 May 1931, Oak Park, Ill.; m. Anne Grete Thomson 1960; one s. two d.; ed. Mass. Inst. of Technology and Univ. of Illinois; Nat. Science Foundation Fellow, Univ. of Birmingham, U.K., and Univ. Inst. for Theoretical Physics, Copenhagen 1957–58; Asst. Prof., Univ. of Chicago 1957–60, Univ. of Ill. 1959–60; Assoc. Prof., Univ. of Ill. 1960–62; Prof., Univ. of Pa. 1962, Mary Amanda Wood Prof. of Physics 1964–79; Prof. of Physics, Univ. of Calif., Santa Barbara 1980–91, Essan Khashoggi Prof. of Physics 1985; Prof. Fla. State Univ., Tallahassee 1992–; Chief Scientist Nat. High Magnetic Field Lab. 1992–; Vice-Pres. American Physical Soc. 1994–96, Pres. 1996; Univ. Eminent Scholar, Fla. State Univ. System 1996; Dir. Inst. for Theoretical Physics, Santa Barbara 1984–89; Andrew D. White Prof. Cornell Univ. 1969–75; mem. N.A.S., American Acad. Arts and Sciences, mem. American Philosophical Soc. 1974, mem. Royal Danish Acad. of Science and Letters; mem. Nat. Medal of Science Cttee.; Guggenheim Fellow 1967–68; Fellow American Physical Soc. (Pres. 1997); hon. doctorates (Geneva, Technische Hochschule, Munich, Univs. of Pa., Ill., Cincinatti and Tel Aviv); Buckley Prize 1968; Comstock Prize (N.A.S.) 1968; Nobel Prize for Physics (with J. Bardeen (q.v.) and L. N. Cooper) 1972; John Ericsson Medal (American Soc. of Swedish Engineers) 1976, Alumni Achievement Award, Univ. of Ill. 1979, Nat. Medal of Science 1985, Superconductivity Award of Excellence (World Congress of Superconductivity) 1996. *Publication:* Theory of Superconductivity 1964. *Address:* NHMFL, Florida State University, 1800 E. Paul Dirac Drive, Tallahassee, FL 32306, U.S.A.

SCHROCK, Richard R., PH.D.; American professor of chemistry; b. 4 Jan. 1945, Berne, Indiana; m. Nancy F. Carlson 1971; two s.; ed. Univ. of California, Riverside, Harvard Univ., Cambridge Univ., U.K.; Research Chemist, Cen. Research and Devt. Dept., E.I. du Pont de Nemours & Co. 1972–75; Asst. Prof. of Chem., M.I.T. 1975–78, Assoc. Prof. 1978–80, Prof. 1980–89, Frederick G. Keyes Prof. of Chem. 1989–; Sherman T. Fairchild Scholar, Calif. Inst. of Tech. 1986, SERC Visiting Fellow, Cambridge, U.K. 1991; American Chemical Soc. (A.C.S.) Award in Organometallic Chem. 1985 and Harrison Howe Award 1990, Inorganic Chem. Award 1996, Bailar Medal, Univ. of Ill. 1998. *Publications:* papers in scientific journals. *Address:* Department of Chemistry, 6-331, Massachusetts Institute of Technology, 77 Massachusetts Avenue, Cambridge, MA 02139, U.S.A. *Telephone:* (617) 253-1596.

SCHRODER, Baron Bruno Lionel, M.B.A.; British business executive; b. 17 Jan. 1933; s. of the late Baron Bruno Schroder and Margaret Eleanor Phyllis (née Darell) Schroder; m. Patricia Leonie Mary Holt 1969; one d.; ed. Eton, Univ. Coll., Oxford, Harvard Business School; Second Lieut. Life Guards 1951–53; joined Schroders PLC 1960, Dir. 1963–, J. Henry Schroder & Co. Ltd. 1966–, Schroders Inc. 1984–; Gov. English Nat. Ballet; mem. Exec. Cttee. Air Squadron, Court of Assts. Worshipful Co. of Goldsmiths, Liveryman Guild of Air Pilots and Air Navigators; Queen Beatrix of Netherlands Wedding Medal. *Leisure interests:* flying, stalking, shooting. *Address:* Schroders PLC, 120 Cheapside, London, EC2V 6DS, England. *Telephone:* 0171-382 6000. *Fax:* 0171-288 2006.

SCHRÖDER, Gerhard; German public servant; b. 3 March 1921; ed. Marburg Univ.; Officer, Radio, Film and Press Affairs, Ministry of Culture and Education, Lower Saxony 1952–59; Head of Arts Dept., Ministry of Culture and Education, Lower Saxony 1960–61; mem. Admin. Council, North German Radio 1955–61; Dir.-Gen. Norddeutscher Rundfunk (North German Radio and TV) 1961–73; Chair. ARD (Asscn. of German Broadcasting Orgs.) 1970–71; Dir.-Gen. Radio Bremen (Radio and TV) 1974–85, Chair. Bd. of Dirs. and Dir.-Gen. 1980–86; media consultant 1986–. *Address:* Rondeel 5, 22301 Hamburg, Germany.

SCHRÖDER, Gerhard; German politician; b. 7 April 1944, Mossenberg, Detmold Dist.; m. Hiltrud Hensen 1984; two d.; ed. Univ. of Göttingen; apprentice as shop asst. 1961; joined Social Democratic Party (SDP) 1963, Chair. 1999–; lawyer, Hanover 1976; Nat. Chair. of Young Socialists 1978–80; mem. Bundestag 1980–86; Leader of Opposition in State Parl. of Lower Saxony 1986; Minister-Pres. of Lower Saxony 1990–98; Chancellor of Germany Oct. 1998–. *Address:* Bundeskanzlevamt, Adenauerallee 139–141, 53113 Bonn, Germany.

SCHRÖDER, Werner Hermann, DR. PHIL.; German professor of philology; b. 13 March 1914, Vaethen; s. of Hermann Schröder and Hedwig Eikemeier; m. 1st Ursula Nehm 1949; m. 2nd Anne-Ilse Radke 1973; three s. three d.; ed. Universität Halle; archivist, Landeshauptarchiv Sachsen-Anhalt, Magdeburg 1948–52; Dozent, Martin Luther Univ. Halle-Wittenberg 1953–56, Prof. of German Philology 1956–59; Prof. of Germanic and German Philology, Univ. of Marburg 1960–82, Prof. Emer. 1982–; mem. Mainz Acad. *Publications:* fifteen books and numerous articles. *Address:* 35037 Marburg, Roter Hof 10, Germany.

SCHROEDER, Barbet; French film producer and director; b. 26 April 1941, Teheran, Iran; ed. Sorbonne, Paris; worked as jazz tour operator Europe, photojournalist India, critic for Cahiers du Cinéma and L'Air de Paris 1958–63; Asst. to Jean-Luc Godard on Les Carabiniers 1963; f. own production co. Les Films du Losange 1964; worked as actor and producer.

Films produced include: The Collector, My Night at Maud's, Claire's Knee, Chloe in the Afternoon, Céline and Julie go Boating, The Rites of Death, Perceval Le Gallois, Le Navire Night, Le Pont du Nord, Mauvaise Conduite, Une Sale Historie. *Films directed include:* More, Sing-Song (documentary), La Vallée, General Idi Amin Dada (documentary), Maîtresse, Koko, the Talking Gorilla (documentary), Charles Bukowski (50 four-minute videos), Tricheurs, Barfly, Reversal of Fortune, Single White Female, Kiss of Death, Before and After (also producer), Desperate Measures.

SCHROEDER, Manfred Robert, DR.RER.NAT.; American physicist; b. 12 July 1926, Ahlen, North Rhine-Westphalia; s. of Karl and Hertha Schroeder; m. Anny Menschik 1956; two s. one d.; Head of Acoustics Research Dept., Bell Labs., U.S.A. 1958–63, Dir. of Acoustics, Speech and Mechanics Research 1963–69; Dir. Drittes Physikalisches Inst., Univ. of Göttingen 1969–91; mem. Nat. Acad. of Eng. Washington, Göttingen Acad. of Sciences, Max-Planck Soc.; Fellow American Acad. of Arts and Sciences 1986, New York Acad. of Sciences 1993; 45 U.S. patents in various fields; Gold Medal, Audio Eng. Soc. 1972; Baker Prize Award, Inst. of Electrical and Electronics Engineers, New York 1977, Sr. Award, Acoustics, Speech and Signal Processing Soc. 1979, Lord Rayleigh Gold Medal, British Inst. of Acoustics, Gold Medal, Acoustical Soc. of America 1991,Niedersachsenpreis 1992, Helmholtz Médaille, German Acoustical Soc. 1995. *Publications:* Speech and Speaker Recognition 1985, Number Theory in Science and Communication 1986, Fractals, Chaos, Power Laws 1991, and about 130 articles on acoustics, speech, hearing, microwaves, computer graphics. *Leisure interests:* skiing, sailing, bicycling, photography, graphics. *Address:* Drittes Physikalisches Institut, Universität Göttingen, Bürgerstrasse 42-44, 37073 Göttingen; Rieswartenweg 8, 37077 Göttingen, Germany (Home). *Telephone:* (49-551) 397713. *Fax:* (49-551) 397720.

SCHROEDER, Paul W., PH.D.; American professor of history; b. 23 Feb. 1927, Cleveland, Ohio; s. of Rupert H. Schroeder and Elfrieda Koch; m. Violet Doolin 1950; two d.; ed. Concordia Seminary, Texas Christian Univ. and Univ. of Tex.; Asst. Prof., Assoc. Prof. of History, Concordia Sr. Coll. 1958–63; Prof. of History, Univ. of Ill. 1963; Beveridge Prize, American Historical Asscn. 1956; Webb Memorial Prize 1962; Sr. Univ. Scholar, Univ. of Ill. 1989; British Int. Studies Asscn. Award 1990. *Publications:* The Axis Alliance and Japanese-American Relations 1941 1958, Metternich's Diplomacy at its Zenith 1820–23 1962, Austria, Great Britain and the Crimean War: The Destruction of the European Concert 1972, The Transformation of European Politics 1763–1848 1994. *Leisure interests:* tennis, music, woodworking. *Address:* Department of History, University of Illinois, 810 S. Wright Street, Urbana, IL 61801 (Office); 708 S. Elm, Champaign, IL 61820, U.S.A. (Home). *Telephone:* (217) 333-3835 (Office); (217) 352-6307 (Home).

SCHROEDER, Steven Alfred, M.D.; American professor of medicine; b. 26 July 1939, New York; s. of Arthur E. Schroeder; m. Sally Ross Schroeder 1967; two s.; ed. El Cerrito High School, Stanford Univ., Harvard Univ.; Fellow, Harvard Community Health and Medical Care and Instructor Harvard Medical School 1970–71; Asst. Prof. of Medicine and Health Care Sciences, later Assoc. Prof., The George Washington Univ. Medical Center 1971–76; Medical Dir. The George Washington Univ. Health Plan 1971–76; Assoc. Prof. of Medicine, Univ. of Calif., San Francisco 1976–80, Prof. 1980–90, Chief, Div. of Gen. Internal Medicine 1980–90; Clinical Prof., Univ. of Medicine and Dentistry of N.J., Robert Wood Johnson Medical School 1991–; Pres. Robert Wood Johnson Foundation 1990–; Visiting Prof. Dept. of Community Medicine, St. Thomas's Hosp. Medical School, London 1982–83; Ed. Current Medical Diagnosis and Treatment 1987–94; mem. Asscn. of American Physicians, Inst. of Medicine. *Publications:* more than 190 articles. *Leisure interests:* climbing, hiking, tennis, gardening, literature, history. *Address:* Robert Wood Johnson Foundation, College Road, P.O. Box 2316, Princeton, NJ 08543; 49 W. Shore Drive, Pennington, NJ 08534, U.S.A.

SCHULBERG, Budd, LL.D.; American novelist and scriptwriter; b. 27 March 1914, New York, N.Y.; s. of Benjamin P. and Adeline (Jaffe) Schulberg; m. 1st Virginia Ray 1936 (divorced 1942); one d.; m. 2nd Victoria Anderson 1943 (divorced 1964); two s.; m. 3rd Geraldine Brooks 1964 (died 1977); m. 4th Betsy Langman 1979; one s. one d.; ed. Deerfield Acad. and Dartmouth Coll.; short-story writer and novelist 1936–; Screenwriter for Samuel Goldwyn, David O. Selznick and Walter Wanger, Hollywood, Calif. 1936–40; Lieut. U.S. Navy 1943–46, assigned to Office of Strategic Service; taught writing courses and conducted workshops at various institutes in the U.S.; mem. Authors Guild, Dramatists Guild, American Civil Liberties Union, American Soc. Composers Authors and Publishers, Sphinx, Writers Guild of America East, Bd. of Trustees, Humanitas Prize, Advisory Cttee. on Black Participation John F. Kennedy Center for the Performing Arts; Founder Watts Writers Workshop, Frederick Douglass Creative Arts Center, New York; numerous awards for writings, numerous humanitarian awards. *Publications:* novels: What Makes Sammy Run? 1941, The Harder They Fall 1947 (screen adaptation 1955), The Disenchanted 1950, Waterfront 1955, Sanctuary V 1969, Some Faces in the Crowd (short stories) 1953, From the Ashes: Voices of Watts (Ed. and author of introduction) 1967, Loser and Still Champion: Muhammad Ali 1972, The Four Seasons of Success 1972, Swan Watch (with Geraldine Brooks) 1975, Everything That Moves 1980, Moving Pictures: Memories of a Hollywood Prince 1981, Writers in America 1983, Love, Action, Laughter and Other Sad Tales (short stories) 1990, Sparring with Hemingway: And Other Legends of the Fight Game 1995; plays, films: Winter Carnival (with F. Scott Fitzgerald) 1939, The Pharmacist's Mate 1951, On the Waterfront (Acad. Award and Screen Writers Guild Award for the screenplay) 1954, A Face in the Crowd (German Film Critics Award) 1957, Wind Across the Everglades 1958, The Disenchanted 1958, What Makes Sammy Run? (television play 1959, stage 1964), Senor Discretion Himself (musical) 1985, A Table at Ciru's 1987; Joe Louis: For All Time (film documentary) 1988; stories and articles in numerous anthologies; contrib. to Newsday Syndicate, Esquire, Saturday Review, Life, Harper's, Playboy, Intellectual Digest, The New Republic, The New Yorker, The New York Times. *Leisure interests:* bird watching, boxing, fishing, Mexican archaeology, Black Arts movement. *Address:* Miriam Altshuler Literary Agency, RR # 1, Box 5, Old Post Road, Red Hook, NY 12571; c/o Mickey Freiberg, 10 000 Santa Monica Boulevard, Suite 300, Los Angeles, CA 90067, U.S.A.

SCHULLER, Gunther; American composer and conductor; b. 22 Nov. 1925, New York; s. of Arthur E. and Elsie (Bernartz) Schuller; m. Marjorie Black 1948; two s.; ed. St. Thomas Choir School, New York, N.Y. and Manhattan School of Music; Principal French horn, Cincinnati, Symphony Orchestra 1943–45, Metropolitan Opera Orchestra 1945–59; teacher, Manhattan School of Music 1950–63; Head Composition Dept., Tanglewood 1963–84; Music Dir. First Int. Jazz Festival, Washington 1962; active as conductor since mid-1960s with major orchestras in Europe and U.S.A.; reconstructed and orchestrated 1912 opera Der Gelbe Klang by De Hartmann/Kandinsky; Pres. New England Conservatory of Music 1967–77; Pres. Nat. Music Council 1979–81; Artistic Dir. Summer Activities, Boston Symphony Orchestra, Tanglewood, Berkshire Music Center 1969–84, Festival at Sandpoint 1985–; f. and Pres. Margun Music Inc. 1975, G.M. Records 1980; mem. American Acad. of Arts and Sciences, Nat. Inst. of Arts and Letters; Creative Arts Award, Brandeis Univ. 1960; Nat. Inst. Arts and Letters Award 1960; Guggenheim Grant 1962, 1963; ASCAP Deems Taylor Award 1970; Rogers and Hammerstein Award 1971; William Schuman Award, Columbia Univ. 1989; Max Rudolf Award 1998; Gold Medal American Acad. of Arts and Letters 1996, Order of Merit, Germany 1997; Hon. D.Mus. (Ill. Univ.) 1966; (Northeastern Univ.) 1967, (Colby Coll.) 1969, (Ill. Univ.) 1970, (Williams Coll.) 1975, (Rutgers Univ.) 1980, (Oberlin Coll.) 1989, (Fla. State Univ.) 1991. *Compositions include:* Symphony for Brass and Percussion 1950, Fantasy for Unaccompanied Cello 1951, Recitative and Rondo for Violin and Piano 1953, Dramatic Overture 1951, Music for Violin, Piano and Percussion 1957, String Quartet No. 1 1957, Woodwind Quintet 1958, Spectra 1958, Concertino for Jazz Quartet and Orchestra 1959, Seven Studies on Themes of Paul Klee 1959, Conversations 1960, Variants (ballet with choreography by Balanchine) 1961, Music for Brass Quintet 1961, String Quartet No. 2 1965, Symphony 1965, Sacred Cantata 1966, Gala Music (Concerto for Orchestra) 1966, The Visitation (opera commissioned by Hamburg State Opera) 1966, Movements for Flute and Strings, Six Renaissance Lyrics, Triplum I 1967, Shapes and Designs 1968, Fisherman and his Wife (opera) 1970, Capriccio Stravagante 1972, Tre Invenzioni 1972, Three Nocturnes 1973, Four Soundscapes 1974, Triplum II 1975, Violin Concerto 1976, Concerto No. 2 for Horn and Orchestra 1976, Diptych (for organ) 1976, Concerto No. 2 for Orchestra 1977, Concerto for Contrabasson and Orchestra 1978, Deaï (for three orchestras) 1978, Concerto for Trumpet and Orchestra 1979, Eine Kleine Posaunenmusik 1980, In Praise of Winds (symphony for large wind orchestra) 1981, Concerto No. 2 for Piano and Orchestra 1981, Symphony for Organ 1981, Concerto Quarternio 1983, On Light Wings (piano quartet) 1984, Farbenspiel (Concerto No. 3 for Orchestra) 1985, String Quartet No. 3 1986, Chimeric Images 1988, Concerto for String Quartet and Orchestra 1988, Concerto Flute and Orchestra 1988, Horn Sonata 1988, On Winged Flight: a Divertimento for Band 1989, Chamber Symphony 1989, Impromptus and Cadenzas for Chamber Sextet 1990, Violin Concert No. 2 1991, Brass Quintet No. 2 1993, The Past is the Present for orchestra 1994, Sextet for left hand piano and woodwind quintet 1994, Concerto for organ and orchestra 1994, Mondrian's Vision 1994, Blue Dawn into White Heat (concert band) 1995, An Ave Ascending 1996, etc. *Publications:* Horn Technique 1962, Early Jazz, Its Roots and Musical Development, Vol. I 1968, Musings: The Musical Worlds of Gunther Schuller 1985, The Swing Era: The Development of Jazz 1930–45 1989. *Address:* c/o Margun Music Inc., 167 Dudley Road, Newton Center, MA 02159; Festival at Sandpoint, P.O. Box 695, Sandpoint, ID 83864, U.S.A. *Telephone:* 617-332-6398 (MA).

SCHULTE, Dieter; German trades unionist; b. 13 Jan. 1940; m; two c.; began career as blast furnace bricklayer, Thyssen; became active in trades union movement; now head of Deutscher Gewerkschaftsbund (Fed. of German Unions). *Address:* Deutscher Gewerkschaftsbund, Hans-Böckler-Str. 39, 40476 Düsseldorf, Germany.

SCHULTES, Richard Evans, PH.D., F.L.S.; American botanist, plant explorer, professor and museum director; b. 12 Jan. 1915, Boston, Mass.; s. of Otto Richard Schultes and Maude Beatrice (Bagley) Schultes; m. Dorothy McNeil 1959; two s. one d.; ed. Harvard Univ.; Research Fellow, Harvard Botanical Museum 1942–53, Curator, Ames Orchid Herbarium 1953–58, Curator, Econ. Botany 1958–85, Dir. Harvard Botanical Museum 1967–85; Prof. of Biology Harvard Univ. 1970–72, Mangelsdorf Prof. of Natural Sciences 1973–81, Jeffrey Prof. of Biology 1981–85, Prof. Emer. 1985–; NRC Fellow, Exploration Amazon 1941–42, Collaborator U.S. Dept. of Agriculture, Amazon 1942–43, Plant Explorer 1944–54; Adjunct Prof. of Pharmacognosy, Univ. of Ill. 1975–; mem. Scientific Advisory Bd., Palm Oil Research Inst.

of Malaysia 1980–89; Consultant, Rubber Research Inst., Malaysia 1988; Guggenheim Fellow 1942; mem. numerous acads., socs.; Hon. D.Sc. (Massachusetts Coll. of Pharmacy); Orden Victoria Regia (Colombia) 1969, Cruz de Boyacá 1986; Gold Medal for Conservation (Duke of Edin. Award for World Wildlife Fund, Int.) 1984, Tyler Prize for Environmental Achievement 1987, Certificate of Merit, Botanical Soc. of America 1988, Lindbergh Award 1991, Harvard Univ. Medal 1992, Annual Linnean Gold Medal 1992, Janaki-Ammal Medal (India) 1992, George Sobert Unite Medal of Honor 1995. *Publications:* Economic Botany of the Kiowa Indians (with Vestal) 1941, Native Orchids of Trinidad and Tobago, Plants and Human Affairs (with Hill) 1960, Generic Names of Orchids: their origin and meaning (with Pease) 1963, The Botany and Chemistry of Hallucinogens (with Hofmann) 1973, Plants of the Gods (with Hofmann) 1979, Hallucinogenic Plants 1976, The Glass Flowers at Harvard (with Davis) 1982, Where the Gods Reign 1988, El Reino de los Dioses 1988, The Healing Forest 1990, Vine of the Soul 1992. *Leisure interests:* gardening, photography, listening to classical music.

SCHULTZE, Charles Louis, PH.D.; American economist and government official; b. 12 Dec. 1924, Alexandria, Va.; s. of Richard Lee and Nora Woolls (née Baggett) Schultze; m. Rita Irene Hertzog 1947; one s. five d.; ed. Georgetown Univ. and Univ. of Maryland; U.S. Army 1943–46; Admin. Asst. Democratic Nat. Cttee. 1948; Research Specialist, Army Security Agency 1948–49; Instructor, Coll. of St. Thomas (St. Paul, Minn.) 1949–51; Economist, Office of Price Stabilization 1951–52, Council of Econ. Advisers 1952–53, 1955–59, Machine and Allied Products Inst. 1953–54; Assoc. Prof. of Econs., Indiana Univ. 1959–61; Prof. of Econs., Univ. of Md. 1961–87; Asst. Dir., Bureau of the Budget 1962–65, Dir. 1965–68; Sr. Fellow, Brookings Inst., Washington 1968–76, 1981–87, 1991–96, Emer. 1997–; Dir. Econ. Studies, Brookings Inst., Washington 1987–90; Chair. Council of Econ. Advisers to Pres. 1977–81. *Publications:* National Income Analysis 1964, The Politics and Economics of Public Spending 1969 (co-author), Setting National Priorities: The 1974 Budget, The Public Use of Private Interest 1977, Other Times, Other Places 1986, American Living Standards (Co-Ed. and Co-Author) 1988, Barriers to European Growth (Co-Ed. and Co-Author) 1989, An American Trade Strategy: Options for the 1990s (Co-Ed.) 1990, Memos to the President 1992. *Address:* Brookings Institution, 1775 Massachusetts Avenue, N.W., Washington, DC 20036; 5520 33rd Street, N.W., Washington, DC 20015, U.S.A. (Home).

SCHULZ, Charles Monroe; American cartoonist; b. 26 Nov. 1922, Minneapolis, Minn.; s. of Carl and Dena (née Halverson) Schulz; m. 1st Joyce Halverson 1949 (divorced 1972); two s. three d.; m. 2nd Jean Clyde 1973; Cartoonist for St. Paul Pioneer Press, St. Paul, Minn., Saturday Evening Post 1948–49; created syndicated comic strip Peanuts 1950–; Hon. L.H.D. (Anderson Coll., Ind.) 1963; Outstanding Cartoonist award (Nat. Cartoonist Soc.) 1956; Emmy Award (CBS children's programme A Charlie Brown Christmas 1966); Commdr. des Arts et des Lettres 1990. *Publications include:* collected cartoons published in book form: Peanuts 1952, More Peanuts 1954, Good Grief, More Peanuts 1956, Good Ol' Charlie Brown, Snoopy, You're Out of Your Mind Charlie Brown, But We Love You Charlie Brown, Peanuts Revisited, Go Fly a Kite Charlie Brown, Peanuts Every Sunday, You Can Do It Charlie Brown, Happiness is a Warm Puppy 1962, Love is Walking Hand in Hand 1965, A Charlie Brown Christmas 1965, You Need Help, Charlie Brown 1969, Charlie Brown's All-Stars 1966, You've Had It Charlie Brown 1969, The Snoopy Festival 1974, Its Your Turn Snoopy 1978, Dogs Don't Eat Dessert 1987, By Supper Possessed 1988, Talk is Cheep, Charlie Brown 1988, Peanuts 1996; author and illustrator of Snoopy and the Red Baron 1966, Snoopy and His Sopwith Camel 1969, The Snoopy Come Home Movie Book 1972, The Charlie Brown Dictionary and others. *Address:* United Media, 200 Madison Avenue, Floor 4, New York, NY 10016; No. 1, Snoopy Place, Santa Rosa, CA 95401, U.S.A.

SCHULZ, Peter; German lawyer; b. 25 April 1930, Rostock; s. of Albert Schulz and Emmi Munck; m. Dr. Sonja Planeth 1955; one s. one d.; ed. Univ. of Hamburg; practising lawyer, Hamburg 1959–; mem. Hamburg City Council 1961–, Senator for Justice 1966–71; fmr. Deputy Regional Chair. Social Democratic Party, Hamburg-North; Second Burgomaster of Hamburg and Deputy Pres. of the Senate and Dept. of Educ. 1970–71; Chief Burgomaster of Hamburg and Pres. of Senate 1971–74; Pres. of Hamburg City Council 1978–82, Vice-Pres. 1982–83, Pres. 1983–87. *Address:* Mönckebergstrasse 7, 18055 Rostock, Germany.

SCHUMACHER, Joel; American film director; b. 29 Aug. 1939, N.Y.; ed. Parson School of Design, New York; began to work in fashion industry aged 15; later opened own boutique Paraphenalia; costume designer for Revlon in 1970s; also set and production designer; wrote screenplays Sparkle, Car Wash, The Wiz; also wrote and directed for TV. *Films include:* The Incredible Shrinking Woman, DC Cab (also screenplay), St. Elmo's Fire (also screenplay), The Lost Boys, Cousins, Flatliners, Dying Young, Falling Down, The Client, Batman Forever, A Time to Kill, Batman and Robin, Eight Millimeter.

SCHUMACHER, Michael; German motor racing driver; b. 3 Jan. 1969; m. Corinna Betsch 1995; one d.; began professional career 1983; 2nd place, Int. German Formula 3 Championship 1989; driver for Mercedes 1990; Int. German Champion, Formula 3 Championship 1990; European Formula 3 Champion 1990; World Champion, Formula 3, Macau and Fiji 1990; Formula 1 contestant since 1991; First Formula 1 victory, Spa 1992; other Grand Prix wins: Estoril 1993, Brasília 1994, 1995, Pacific (Aida) 1994, Imola 1994, Monaco 1994, 1995, Montreal 1994, Magny Cours 1994, 1995, Budapest 1994, European (Jerez) 1994, (Nürburgring) 1995, Barcelona 1995; Third Place, World Motor Racing Championship 1992, Fourth Place 1993; Formula One World Champion 1994, 1995; Italian Grand Prix 1996; Japan Grand Prix 1997; Canada Grand Prix 1998; Hungarian Grand Prix 1998. *Publication:* Formula For Success (with Derick Allsop) 1996. *Address:* c/o Weber Management GmbH, Tränkestr. 11, 70597 Stuttgart, Germany. *Telephone:* (711) 726460. *Fax:* (711) 7264633, 7264684.

SCHUMER, Charles Ellis, J.D., B.A.; American politician; b. 23 Nov. 1950, Brooklyn, N.Y.; s. of Abraham Schumer and Selma (née Rosen) Schumer; m. Iris Weinshall 1980; one d.; ed. Harvard Univ.; called to Bar N.Y. 1975; mem. staff U.S. senator Claiborne Pell 1973; Assoc. Paul, Weiss, Rifking, Wharton and Garrison 1974; mem. N.Y. State Ass. 1975–80, Chair. Subcttee. on City Man. and Governance 1977, Cttee. on Oversight and Investigation 1979; mem. 97th–98th Congresses from 16th N.Y. Dist. 1981–85, 99th–105th Congresses from 10th (now 9th) N.Y. Dist. 1985–99, Senator from New York Jan. 1999–; Democrat. *Address:* U.S. Senate, Washington, DC 20510, U.S.A.

SCHÜSSEL, Wolfgang; Austrian politician; b. 7 June 1945, Vienna; m.; two c.; ed. Vienna Univ.; Sec. Parl. Austrian People's Party (ÖVP) 1968, Chair. 1995–; Sec.-Gen. Austrian Econ. Fed. 1975–89; M.P. 1979; Leader ÖVP group of Econ. Fed. Parl. Dels. 1987; Minister of Econ. Affairs 1989–95; Vice-Chancellor of Austria and Minister of Foreign Affairs March 1996–; Deputy Chair. Parl. Finance Cttee. *Publications:* several books on issues relating to democracy and economics. *Address:* Ministry of Foreign Affairs, 1014 Vienna, Ballhausplatz 2, Austria. *Telephone:* (1) 531150. *Fax:* (1) 5352547.

SCHUSTER, Hans-Günter, D.SC.; German scientist and civil servant; b. 17 Dec. 1918, Bonn; s. of Rudolf Schuster and Sophie Schuster-Leinen; m. Helga Schuster-Kleffmann 1944; one s. one d; ed. Univs. of Göttingen and Bonn; Asst. Bonn Univ. 1948–50, Scientific Asst. Inst. of Applied Physics 1950–55, Head of Physical Studies 1956–65; Adviser, Ministry of Scientific Research 1965–67; Dir. Nuclear Research and Technical Div., Ministry of Educ. and Science 1968–71; Deputy Dir.-Gen. of Industrial, Tech. and Scientific Affairs Comm. of the European Communities 1971–73, Dir.-Gen. of Research, Science and Educ. 1973–81, Co-ordinator for bilateral co-operation, Fed. Ministry for Research and Tech., in particular for India 1981–83; Special Adviser to Senate of Berlin 1984–88; Grosses Bundesverdienstkreuz 1983, Officier, Ordre nat. du Mérite 1987. *Address:* Höhenweg 32, 53127 Bonn, Germany. *Telephone:* (0228) 28-33-43 (Home).

SCHÜTZ, Klaus; German politician and diplomatist; b. 17 Sept. 1926; m. Heide Seeberger 1953; two s. one d.; ed. Paulsen-Realgymnasium, Humboldt Univ. zu Berlin and Harvard Univ., U.S.A.; war service, seriously wounded 1944–45; Asst., Inst. für Politische Wissenschaften, Freie Univ., Berlin 1951–61; mem. City Ass. 1954–57, 1963–77; mem. Bundestag 1957–61; Liaison Senator between Berlin Senate and Bonn Govt. 1961–66; mem. Bundesrat 1961–77, Pres. 1967–68; Under-Sec. Ministry of Foreign Affairs 1966–67; Governing Mayor of West Berlin 1967–77; Chair. Berlin Social Democratic Party 1968–77; Amb. to Israel 1977–81; Dir.-Gen. Deutsche Welle 1981–87; Dir. Landesanstaltung für Rundfunk NRW, Düsseldorf 1987–93; Pres. Landesverband Berlin des Deutschen Roten Kreuzes 1996–. *Address:* 9 Konstanzerstrasse, 10707 Berlin, Germany.

SCHÜTZEICHEL, Rudolf, DR. PHIL.; German professor of philology; b. 20 May 1927, Rahms; s. of Matthias Schützeichel and Gertrud Schützeichel; m. Margrit Britten 1955; two d.; ed. Univ. of Mainz; Docent Univ. of Cologne 1960–63; Prof. of German Philology, Univ. of Groningen 1963–64, Univ. of Bonn 1964–69, Univ. of Münster 1969–; mem. Akad. Wissenschaften, Göttingen, Kgl. Akademie, Göteborg; Dr. phil. h.c. (Leipzig) 1992; Festschrift 1987 (Althochdeutsch 2 Bände Heidelberg); Officer Orders of Orange-Nassau. *Publications:* Mundart, Urkundensprache und Schriftsprache 1974, Grundlagen d.w. Mitteldeutsch 1976, Das alem. Memento Mori 1967, Codex. Pal. lat. 52 1982, Mittelrh. Passionsspiel 1978, Gottschald Namenkunde 1982, Addenda und Corrigenda (I) 1982, (II) 1985, (III) 1991, Textgebundenheit 1981, Althochdeutsch. Wörterb. (5th edn.) 1995; Ed. various publs. including BNF.NF. 1966–, Sprachwissenschaft 1976–, NOWELE 1983–. *Address:* Potstiege 16, 48161 Münster, Germany. *Telephone:* 0251 861345.

SCHWAB, John Joseph, M.D., M.S.; American professor of psychiatry; b. 10 Feb. 1923, Cumberland, Md.; s. of Joseph L. Schwab and Eleanor A. Cadden; m. Ruby E. Baxter 1945; one d.; ed. Univs. of Kentucky, Louisville and Illinois; Fellow in Psychosomatic Medicine, Duke Univ.; Resident in Medicine, Univ. of Louisville; Fellow in Cardio-Renal Physiology, Univ. of Ill.; Resident in Psychiatry, Univ. of Fla.; Capt., U.S. Army 1949–54; Educ. Officer, Yokohama Medical Coll. 1953–54; Internist/psychosomaticist, Holzer Clinic, Galipolis, Ohio 1954–59; Nat. Inst. of Mental Health career teacher, Univ. of Fla. 1962–64; Psychiatrist and mem. Faculty, Univ. of Fla. 1961–73; Prof. of Psychiatry and Medicine, Gainesville 1967–73; Prof., Chair. Dept. of Psychiatry and Behavioral Sciences, School of Medicine, Univ. of Louisville 1974–91, Prof. of Psychiatry 1991–93, Prof. Emer. 1993–, Assoc. Dir. of Clinical Psychopharmacological Research 1991–; Visiting Lecturer numerous univs. and medical schools 1964–; Visiting Prof., Univ. of Würzburg 1985–91, El Azar Univ. (Cairo) 1991; Chair. Epidemiologic Studies Review Comm., Center for Epidemiologic Studies, Nat. Inst. of Medical Health 1973–75, Consultant, Psychiatry Br. 1975–; Pres. Acad. of Psychosomatic Medicine 1969–71; First Pres. American Asscn. of Social Psychiatry 1970–73;

mem. Bd. of Regents American Coll. of Psychiatry 1979–82; Pres. Psychiatrists for Better Psychiatry 1990–96; Hon. Faculty mem. Kolleg Psychotherapeutische, Würzburg 1992–; Distinguished Lecturer, Howard Univ. 1992; Univ. of Louisville Affirmative Action Award 1980, Caduceus Award 1998; Ky. Mental Health Award 1998. *Publications:* author or co-author of nine books and 200 articles on psychiatry, epidemiology, and evaluating family mental health. *Leisure interests:* music, poetry, philosophy. *Address:* Department of Psychiatry and Behavioral Sciences, School of Medicine, University of Louisville, Louisville, KY 40292 (Office); 6217 Innes Trace Road, Louisville, KY 40222, U.S.A. (Home). *Telephone:* (502) 852-5391 (Office); (502) 426-6015 (Home).

SCHWAETZER, Irmgard; German politician; b. 5 April 1942, Münster; m. Udo Philipp; ed. Univs. of Passau, Münster and Bonn; worked in pharmaceutical industry in Germany and abroad 1971–80; mem. FDP 1975–, Gen. Sec. 1982–84, mem. Presidium 1982–, Deputy Chair. 1988–94; mem. Bundestag 1980–; mem. Landesvorstand Nordrhein-Westfalen 1980–; Minister of State, Ministry of Foreign Affairs 1987–91; Chair., Nat. Union of Liberal Women 1990–95; Minister for Planning and Construction 1991–94; Regional Pres., Aachen 1997–. *Address:* c/o Bundesministerium für Raumordnung, Bauwesen und Städtebau, Deichmanns Aue, D-5300 Bonn 2, Germany.

SCHWALB LÓPEZ ALDANA, Fernando; Peruvian politician; b. 26 Aug. 1916, Lima; m. Carmen Rosa Tola de Schwalb 1950; two s. one d.; ed. Pontifica Univ. Católica del Perú; entered Ministry of Foreign Affairs 1933; entered diplomatic service 1939; Second Sec., Washington, D.C. 1944–45, First Sec. 1945–48, Minister Counsellor 1948; pvt. law practice 1949–50, 1950–53, 1968–69; Alt. Exec. Dir. IBRD 1950; Senator from Lima 1962 (prevented from taking office by coup d'état); Minister of Foreign Affairs 1963–65; Chair. Council of Ministers 1963–65; Chair. Peruvian Del. to Gen. Ass. of UN 1963; First Vice-Pres. 1980–84, Prime Minister of Peru 1983–84, Minister of Foreign Affairs 1983–84; Amb. to U.S.A. 1980–82; Pres. Banco Central de Reserva del Perú 1966–68; Rep. of Pres. to Bogotá Meeting of Presidents 1966; Banco de la República, Bogotá 1969; Consultant, Cen. Banking Service, IMF 1969–82; mem. Partido Acción Popular. *Publication:* El Contrato de la Florgreen y el Pago a la I.P.C. *Address:* c/o Oficina del Primer Ministro, Lima, Peru.

SCHWAN, Gesine Marianne, DR.RER.POL.; German university professor; b. 22 May 1943, Berlin; d. of Hildegard Schneider (née Olejak) and Hans R. Schneider; m. Alexander Schwan 1969; one s. one d.; ed. Lycée Français de Berlin, Free University of Berlin; Asst. Prof. Dept. of Political Sciences, Free Univ. of Berlin 1971–77, Prof. 1977–; Fellow Woodrow Wilson Int. Center for Scholars 1980–81; By-Fellow Robinson Coll. Cambridge, U.K. 1984; Verdienstkreuz (1st class). *Publications:* Leszek Kolakowski, Eine Philosophie der Freiheit nach Marx 1971, Die Gesellschaftskritik von Karl Marx 1974, Sozialdemokratie u. Marxismus (with Alexander Schwan) 1974, Sozialismus in der Demokratie; Eine Theorie Konsequent sozialdemokratischen Politik 1982, Der normative Horizont moderner Politik I und II (with Alexander Schwan) 1985, Politik und Schuld: Die zerstörerische Macht des Schweigens 1997; Jahrbuch für Politik (co-ed.) 1991–. *Leisure interests:* music, theatre, travelling. *Address:* Department of Political Science, Free University of Berlin, Ihnestrasse 21, 1000 Berlin 33 (Office); Teutonenstrasse 6, 14129 Berlin, Germany (Home). *Telephone:* (030) 838 2340 (Office); (030) 803 83 66 (Home).

SCHWARTZ, Jacob T., PH.D.; American computer scientist; b. 9 Jan. 1930, New York; s. of Harry and Hazel Schwartz; m. 1st Frances E. Allen 1972; two d.; m. 2nd Diana Robinson 1989; ed. City Coll. of New York, Yale Univ.; Instructor, Computer Science Dept., Yale Univ. 1951–53, Asst. Prof. 1953–56; Assoc. Prof. of Math. and Computer Science, New York Univ. 1957–58, Prof. 1958–; Chair. Computer Science Dept., Courant Inst. of Mathematical Sciences, New York Univ. 1969–77, now Dir.; Assoc. Ed. Journal of Programming Languages; mem. Editorial Bd., Journal of Computer and System Sciences, Communications on Pure and Applied Math., Advances in Applied Math.; mem. N.A.S.; mem. (fmr. Chair.) Computer Science Bd., Nat. Research Council; Sloane Fellow 1961–62; Distinguished Lecturer, Univ. of Calif., Santa Barbara 1978, M.I.T. 1980; Wilbur Cross Medal (Yale Univ.), Townsend Harris Medal (City Univ. of New York), Steele Prize (American Mathematical Soc.) 1981. *Publications:* numerous scientific papers; Linear Operators (3 vols.) 1958–70, Matrices and Vectors for High Schools and Colleges 1961, Relativity in Illustrations 1962, Lectures on the Mathematical Method in Analytical Economics (2 vols.) 1962, W*Algebras 1967, Lie Groups; Lie Algebras 1967, Lectures on Nonlinear Functional Analysis 1968, Lectures on Differential Geometry and Topology 1969, Programming Languages and their Compilers 1969, On Programming: an Interim Report on the SETL Project 1973, Higher Level Programming 1981. *Leisure interests:* history, music. *Address:* New York University, Courant Institute of Mathematical Sciences, 251 Mercer Street, New York, NY 10012, U.S.A. *Telephone:* (212) 998-3375.

SCHWARTZ, Maxime; French administrator and scientist; b. 1 June 1940, Blois; ed. Ecole Polytechnique; entered Inst. Pasteur 1963, Deputy Dir. 1985–87, Dir.-Gen. 1987–; also mem. of the Scientific Council of the Inst. Pasteur and Head of the Dept. of Molecular Biology. *Address:* L'Institut Pasteur, 25–28 rue du Dr Roux, 75015 Paris, France.

SCHWARTZENBERG, Roger-Gérard, D. EN D.; French politician and professor of law; b. 17 April 1943, Pau, Pyrénées-Atlantiques; s. of André Schwartzenberg and Simone Gutelman; ed. Inst. d'Etudes Politiques, Paris; Prof. Univ. de droit, d'économie et de sciences sociales de Paris II 1969–, Inst. d'Etudes Politiques 1972–83; Pres. Mouvement des Radicaux de Gauche 1981–83, Hon. Pres. 1983–; mem. European Parl. 1979–83; Sec. of State, Ministry of Educ. 1983–84; Sec. of State responsible for univs., Ministry of Educ. 1984–86; Deputy for Val de Marne to Nat. Ass. 1986–; Sec. to Nat. Ass. 1988–92, 1993–97, Vice-Pres. Foreign Affairs Comm. 1992–; Mayor of Villeneuve-Saint-Georges 1989–95; Deputy Judge High Court of Justice and Court of Justice of the Repub. 1993–97; Deputy Pres. Radical 1996–. *Publications:* books on political and legal topics. *Leisure interest:* tennis. *Address:* Assemblée Nationale, 75355 Paris; Université de Droit de Paris, 12 Place du Panthéon, 75005 Paris, France.

SCHWARZ, Antoine, L. EN D.; French administrator and business executive; b. 9 Aug. 1943, Paris; s. of Willy Schwarz and Elisabeth du Brusle de Rouvroy; m. Christine Coudreau 1974; two s. one d.; ed. Inst. d'Etudes Politiques de Paris, Ecole Nat. d'Admin.; Admin. to the Treasury, Ministry of the Economy and Finance 1971–74; Prin. Inst. d'Études Politiques 1972–74; Head Service Juridique et Technique de l'Information 1974; Head of Cabinet André Rossi 1975–76, Raymond Barre 1977; Dir. Radio Monte-Carlo 1978–81, Editions Mondiales 1982–83; Counsellor Centre Nat. de la Cinématographie 1984–85; Pres. and Dir.-Gen. Société Financière de Radiodiffusion (SOFIRAD) 1986–89; Pres. Sofica-valor 1988–89, Consultant 1990; Founder, Pres. Radiofina 1993; Pres. SFP-Productions 1994–; Chevalier Ordre du Mérite. *Address:* SFP-Productions, 2 Ave de L'Europe, 94366 Bry-Sur-Marne cedex; 20 square de la Motte-Piquet, 75015 Paris, France (Home).

SCHWARZ, Gerard; American conductor; b. 19 Aug. 1947, Weehawken, N.J.; m. Jody Greitzer 1984; two s. two d.; ed. Professional Children's School, Juilliard School; joined American Brass Quintet 1965; Music Dir. Erick Hawkins Dance Co. 1966, Eliot Feld Dance Co. 1972; Co-Prin. Trumpet, New York Philharmonic 1973–74; founding Music Dir. Waterloo Festival 1975; Music Dir. New York Chamber Symphony 1977–, L.A. Chamber Orchestra 1978–86; est. Music Today series, Merkin Concert Hall, New York 1981 (Music Dir. 1988–89); Music Adviser Mostly Mozart Festival, Lincoln Center, New York 1982–84, Music Dir. 1984–; Music Adviser Seattle Symphony 1983–84, Prin. Conductor 1984–85, Music Dir. 1985–; Artistic Adviser Tokyu Bunkamura's Orchard Hall, Japan 1994–; Guest Conductor, Cosmopolitan Symphony, Aspen Festival Chamber, Tokyo Philharmonic, Residentie, The Hague, St. Louis Symphony, Kirov, St. Petersburg, Royal Liverpool Philharmonic and Vancouver Symphony Orchestras, City of London Symphonia and London Mozart Players; has conducted many U.S. orchestras, and the Hong Kong Philharmonic, Jerusalem Symphony, Israeli Chamber and English Chamber, London Symphony, Helsinki Philharmonic, and Monte Carlo Philharmonic Orchestras, Ensemble Contemporain, Paris and Nat. Orchestra of Spain; operatic conducting début, Washington Opera 1982; has also conducted Seattle Opera 1986 and San Francisco Opera 1991; numerous recordings for Delos, Nonesuch, Angel and RCA labels; numerous TV appearances; Hon. D.F.A. (Fairleigh Dickinson Univ., Seattle Univ.), Hon. D.Mus. (Univ. of Puget Sound); named Conductor of the Year 1994 by Musical America Int. Directory of the Performing Arts; Ditson Conductor's Award, Columbia Univ. 1989; has received two Record of the Year Awards, one Mumms Ovation Award. *Address:* Seattle Symphony, 305 Harrison Street, Seattle, WA 98109–4645, U.S.A. *Telephone:* (206) 443-4740. *Fax:* (206) 443-2551.

SCHWARZ, Harry Heinz, B.A., LL.B.; South African politician and lawyer, diplomatist; b. 13 May 1924, Cologne, Germany; s. of Fritz Schwarz and Alma Schwarz; m. Annette Louise Rudolph 1952; three s.; ed. Univ. of Witwatersrand; with S.A. Air Force (seconded to R.A.F.) during World War II; mem. Middle Temple; practised as attorney and advocate 1949–; Chief Exec. Merchant Bank 1969–74; mem. Johannesburg City Council 1951–57; mem. Transvaal Prov. Council 1958–74, Leader of Opposition 1960–74; M.P. 1974–91; Amb. to U.S.A. 1991–94; Sr. Advisor to Akin Gump Strauss Hauer & Feld, U.S.A., Hofmeyr Inc., Johannesburg fmr. columnist Sunday Star; Hon. Col. 15 Squadron (S.A. Air Force); several Dr. h.c.; Order of Meritorious Service. *Publications:* Poverty Erodes Freedom, and articles and book chapters on politics, law and economics. *Leisure interest:* writing. *Address:* P.O. Box 3089, Parklands, 2121, South Africa. *Telephone:* (11) 286 1115. *Fax:* (11) 784 9976.

SCHWARZENBERK, Karel Jan; Czech/Swiss human rights worker, businessman and consultant; b. 10 Dec. 1937, Prague; m. Countess of Hardegg (divorced 1994); two s. one d.; family moved to Vienna 1953; ed. Law Faculty, Vienna, Graz, Coll. of Forestry, Munich; owner of a timber processing plant, two farms and two travel agencies in Austria; Chair. Int. Helsinki Federation for Human Rights 1990–, Council of Consultants to the Pres. of Czechoslovakia 1990; Head Pres.'s Office 1990–91; Chancellor to Pres. of Czechoslovakia 1991–92; withdrew from politics 1992; Council of Europe Prize for Human Rights 1991. *Address:* Schwarzenberkská kancelář, Bělohorská 165, 160 00 Prague 6, Czech Republic. *Telephone:* 205 13 667, 35 15 00.

SCHWARZENEGGER, Arnold Alois, B.A.; American (b. Austrian) actor, author, businessman and fmr. bodybuilder; b. 30 July 1947, Graz, Austria; s. of Gustav Schwarzenegger and Aurelia Schwarzenegger; m. Maria Owings Shriver 1985; two s. two d.; ed. Univ. of Wisconsin-Superior; went to U.S.A. 1968, naturalized 1983; film appearances include: Stay Hungry 1976 (Golden Globe Award), Pumping Iron 1977, The Jayne Mansfield Story 1980, Conan, the Barbarian 1982, The Destroyer 1983, The Terminator 1984, Commando 1985, Raw Deal 1986, Predator 1987, Running Man 1987, Red Heat 1988, Twins 1989, Total Recall 1990, Kindergarten Cop 1990, Terminator II 1991, Last Action Hero 1993, Dave (cameo) 1993, True Lies 1994, Junior 1994, Eraser 1996, Single All the Way 1996, Batman and Robin 1997, With Wings of Eagles 1997; Nat. Weight Training Coach Special Olympics; Bodybuilding Champion 1965–80; Jr. Mr. Europe 1965, Best Built Man of Europe 1966, Mr. Europe 1966, Mr. International 1968, Mr. Universe (amateur) 1969 and numerous other prizes; volunteer, prison rehabilitation programmes; Chair. Pres.'s Council on Physical Fitness and Sport 1990. *Publications:* Arnold: The Education of a Bodybuilder 1977, Arnold's Bodyshaping for Women 1979, Arnold's Bodybuilding for Men 1981, Arnold's Encyclopedia of Modern Bodybuilding 1985, Arnold's Fitness for Kids (jtly.) 1993. *Address:* PMK, Suite 200, 955 South Carillo Drive, Los Angeles, CA 90048, U.S.A.

SCHWARZKOPF, Dame Elisabeth Legge-, D.B.E.; German-born singer (now Austrian/British nationality); b. 9 Dec. 1915, Jarotschin; d. of Friedrich and Elisabeth (née Fröhlich) Schwarzkopf; m. Walter Legge 1953 (died 1979); ed. Berlin Hochschule für Musik; debut at Deutsches Opernhaus, Berlin; sang at inauguration of post-war Bayreuth Festival 1951; appeared at Vienna State Opera, La Scala Milan, Covent Garden, San Francisco; Metropolitan Opera, New York 1964–66; guest singer, Salzburg Festival 1947–64; created Anne Trulove in Stravinsky's Rake's Progress; prin. roles include Contessa (Le Nozze di Figaro), Marschallin (Rosenkavalier), Fiordiligi (Così fan Tutte), Eva (Meistersinger), Donna Elvira (Don Giovanni), Gräfin (Capriccio), etc.; producer Der Rosenkavalier, Brussels 1981; recordings include 16 complete operas, 6 complete operettas, songs, arias and lieder; Hon. mem. Acad. di Santa Cecilia, Rome, Acad. of Arts and Letters, Stockholm, R.A.M.; Corresp. mem. Bayerische Akad. der Künste; Hon. D.Mus. (Cambridge) 1976, American Univ. of Washington D.C.; Hon. D.Lit. (Glasgow) 1990; Prof. (Baden-Württemberg) 1990; Lilli Lehmann Medal, Salzburg 1950, Preis Diapason d'Or 1984, Premio Viotti 1991, Medaille Mozart, UNESCO 1991, etc., Grosses Verdienstkreuz 1974, Order of Dannebrog (1st Class) (Denmark), mem. Ordre pour le Mérite (Fed. Repub. of Germany) 1983; Commdr. Ordre des Arts et des Lettres 1985, Grosses Bundesverdienstkreuz mit Stern 1995. *Publication:* Walter Legge: On and Off the Record, A Memoir of Walter Legge 1982. *Leisure interests:* photography, mountain walking. *Address:* Kammersängerin, Rebhusstrasse 29, 8126 Zumikon, Switzerland.

SCHWARZKOPF, Gen. H. Norman, B.S.; American army officer; b. 22 Aug. 1934, Trenton, N.J.; s. of H. Norman Schwarzkopf and Ruth Bowman; m. Brenda Holsinger 1968; one s. two d.; ed. U.S. Mil. Acad. and Univ. of Southern Calif.; 2nd Lieut. U.S. Army 1956; Deputy Commdr. 172nd Infantry Brigade, Fort Richardson, Alaska 1974–76; Commdr. 1st Brigade, 9th Infantry Div. Fort Lewis, Wash. 1976–78; Deputy Dir. Plans, U.S. Pacific Command, Camp Smith, Hawaii 1978–80; Asst. Div. Commdr. 8th Infantry Div. (mechanized), U.S. Army Europe, Fed. Repub. of Germany 1980–82; Dir. Mil. Personnel Man. Office of Deputy Chief of Staff for Personnel, Washington, D.C. 1982–83; Commdg. Gen. 24th Infantry Div. (mechanized), Fort Stewart, Ga. 1983–85; Deputy Commdr. U.S. forces in Grenada Operation 1983; Asst. Deputy Chief of Staff Operations, H.Q., Dept. of Army, Washington, D.C. 1985–86; Commdg. Gen. I Corps., Fort Lewis, Wash. 1986–87; Deputy Chief of Staff for Operations and Plans, H.Q., Dept. of Army, Washington, D.C. 1987–88; C.-in-C. U.S. Cen. Command, MacDill Air Force Base, Fla. 1988–91; retd. 1992; contrib. and analyst NBC News 1995–; Chair. Starbright Foundation 1995–; Commdr. Allied Forces in War to liberate Kuwait after illegal invasion and annexation by Iraq (Operation Desert Storm) 1990–91; D.S.M., D.F.C., Silver Star with two oak leaf clusters, Legion of Merit, Bronze Star with three oak leaf clusters, Purple Heart with oak leaf cluster, Grand Officier Légion d'honneur 1991, Hon. Private French Foreign Legion 1991, Distinguished Order of Kuwait 1991, Hon. K.C.B. (U.K.) 1991. *Publication:* It Doesn't Take A Hero (autobiog.) (with Peter Petre) 1992. *Leisure interests:* hunting, fishing, skeet and trap-shooting. *Address:* c/o International Creative Management, 40 West 57th Street, New York, NY 10019, U.S.A.

SCHWARZ-SCHILLING, Christian, DR.PHIL.; German politician; b. 19 Nov. 1930, Innsbruck, Austria; s. of Prof. Rheinhard Schwarz-Schilling and Duzsa Schwarz-Schilling; m. Marie Luise Jonen 1957; two d.; ed. Univs. of Berlin and Munich; mem. Landtag, Hesse, Fed. Repub. of Germany 1966–76; Sec.-Gen. Hesse CDU 1967–80, Deputy Chair. 1967–96; mem. Bundestag 1976–; Minister of Posts and Telecommunications 1982–92; Deputy Chair. CDU/CSU Fed. Medium and Small Business Asscn. 1977–97; Pres. Exec. Cttee. European Medium and Small Business Union 1979–82; Chair. Inquiries Cttee. Bundestag New Information and Communication Technologies 1981–82; Pres. Dr. Schwarz-Schilling and Partner GmbH 1993–97; Chair. Bundestag Subcttee. on Human Rights and Humanitarian Aid 1995–; Int. Mediator-Arbitrator for Fed. of Bosnia and Hercegovina 1995–; Chair. Bd. Aquila Beteiligungen GmbH 1996–; Hon. D.Univ. (Bryant Coll., U.S.A.) 1997; Grosses Bundesverdienstkreuz mit Stern. *Leisure interests:* swimming, skiing, piano. *Address:* Dr. Schwarz-Schilling & Partner GmbH, Industriestrasse 35, 63654 Büdingen; Am Dohlberg 10,63654 Büdingen, Germany. *Telephone:* (6042) 9644-0. *Fax:* (6042) 9644-32.

SCHWEBEL, Stephen M., B.A., LL.B.; American judge and lawyer; b. 10 March 1929, New York; s. of Victor Schwebel and Pauline Pfeffer Schwebel; m. Louise I. N. Killander 1972; two d.; ed. Harvard Coll., Univ. of Cambridge and Yale Law School; Attorney 1954–59; Asst. Prof. of Law, Harvard Univ. 1959–61; Asst. Legal Adviser, then Special Asst. to Asst. Sec. of State for Int. Org. Affairs 1961–67; Exec. Vice-Pres. and Exec. Dir. American Soc. of Int. Law 1967–73; Consultant, then Counsellor on Int. Law, Dept. of State 1967–74, Deputy Legal Adviser 1974–81; Prof. of Int. Law, then Edward B. Burling Prof. of Int. Law and Org., Johns Hopkins Univ., Washington 1967–81; Legal Adviser to U.S. Del. and Alt. Rep. in 6th Cttee., UN Gen. Ass. 1961–65; visiting lecturer or professor at Cambridge Univ. 1957, 1983, Australian Nat. Univ. 1969, Hague Acad. of Int. Law 1972, Inst. Univ. de hautes études int., Geneva 1980, and various American univs. 1987–; Rep. in various Cttees. UN 1962–74; Assoc. Rep., Rep., Counsel or Deputy Agent in cases before Int. Court of Justice 1962–80; Judge Int. Court of Justice 1981–, Vice-Pres. 1994–97; Pres. 1997–; mem. Int. Law Comm. 1977–81; arbitrator or chair. in int. commercial arbitrations 1982–; mem. Tribunal in Eritrea–Yemen Arbitration 1997–; Pres. Admin. Tribunal, IMF 1994–; Hon. Bencher, Gray's Inn 1998–; mem. Bd. of Eds., American Journal of Int. Law 1967–97; mem. Council on Foreign Relations; mem. Inst. of Int. Law. *Publications:* The Secretary-General of the United Nations 1952, The Effectiveness of International Decisions (ed.) 1971, International Arbitration: Three Salient Problems 1987, Justice in International Law 1994; author of some 100 articles in legal periodicals and the press on problems of international law and relations. *Leisure interests:* music, cycling. *Address:* International Court of Justice, Peace Palace, 2517 KJ, The Hague, Netherlands.

SCHWEIGER, Til; German actor; m. Dana Schweiger; ed. acting acad., Cologne; fmrly. worked providing voice-overs for foreign films. *Films include:* Manta Manta 1991, Ebbie's Bluff (Max Ophuls Prize for Best Actor) 1992, Der Bewegte Mann 1994, Maennerpension, Das Superweib, Brute 1996, Knocking on Heaven's Door 1996 (also producer and co-writer).

SCHWEIKER, Richard Schultz, B.A.; American fmr. politician and businessman; b. 1 June 1926, Norristown, Pa.; s. of Malcolm A. Schweiker and Blanche Schultz; m. Claire Joan Coleman 1955; two s. three d.; ed. Pennsylvania State Univ.; Business exec. 1950–60; mem. U.S. House of Reps. 1960–68; U.S. Senator from Pa. 1969–80; Sec. of Health and Human Services 1981–83; Pres. American Council of Life Insurance 1983–94; Chair. Partnership for Prevention 1991–97; mem. Bd. of Dirs. Tenet Healthcare Corpn. 1984–, LabOne Inc. 1994–; ten hon. degrees and numerous awards; Republican. *Address:* 904 Lynton Place, McLean, VA 22102-2113, U.S.A. (Office).

SCHWEITZER, Louis, L. EN D.; French administrative official; b. 8 July 1942, Geneva, Switzerland; m. Agnes Schmitz 1972; two d.; ed. Inst. d'Etudes Politiques, Paris, Faculté de Droit, Paris and Ecole Nat. d'Administration; Insp. of Finance 1970–; special assignment, later Deputy Dir., Ministry of the Budget 1974–81; Dir. du Cabinet to Minister of Budget 1981–83, of Industry and Research 1983, to Prime Minister 1984–86; Prof. Inst. d'Etudes Politiques de Paris 1982–86; Vice-Pres. for Finance and Planning Régie Renault 1986–90, Chief Finance Officer 1988–90, Exec. Vice-Pres. 1989–90, Pres. and C.O.O. 1990, Chair. and C.E.O. 1992–; Admin., Soc. Générale 1989–93, UAP 1988–94, Inst. Pasteur 1988–94, Péchiney 1989–, I.F.R.I. 1989–, Réunion des Musées Nat. 1990–96, Renault Véhicules Industriels 1992–, B.N.P. 1993–, Roussel UCLAF 1994–97, Crédit Nat. 1995–, Philips 1997–. *Address:* Renault, 34 quai du Point du Jour, 92100 Boulogne-Billancourt; 1 rue Dauphine, 75006 Paris, France.

SCHWERY, H.E. Cardinal Henri; Swiss ecclesiastic; b. 14 June 1932, St. Léonard, Valais; s. of late Camille Schwery and Marguerite Terroux; ed. Lycée-Coll. de Sion, Valais, Grand Séminaire de Sion and Pontificia Università Gregoriana, Rome; ordained priest 1957; teacher of science, math. and religious studies, Lycée-Coll. de Sion 1961–, Rector 1972–77; Dir. Pensionnat de la Sitterie (Petit Séminaire) de Sion 1968–72; Diocesan Chaplain, Action Catholique de Jeunesse Etudiante 1958–66; Mil. Chaplain 1958–77; Bishop of Sion 1977–95, Bishop Emer. 1995–; cr. Cardinal 1991. *Publications:* Un Synode extraordinaire 1986, Chemin de Croix, chemin de lumière, L'Année Mariale dans le diocèse de Sion 1987, Sentiers Pastoraux 1988, Sentiers épiscopaux – Regards sur nos familles (2 Vols.) 1992, Magnificat (in collaboration) 1992. *Leisure interest:* spirituality. *Address:* Case postale 2334, CH 1950 Sion 2, Switzerland. *Telephone:* 027/323 26 32. *Fax:* 027/323 26 32.

SCHWYZER, Robert, DR. PHIL.; Swiss molecular biologist; b. 8 Dec. 1920, Zürich; s. of Robert Schwyzer and Rose Schätzle; m. Rose Nägeli 1948; two s. one d.; ed. primary school, Nathan Hale, Minneapolis, U.S.A., Canton High School (A), Zürich, and Dept. of Chemistry, Univ. of Zürich; Privatdozent, Univ. of Zürich 1951–59, Asst. Prof. 1960–63; initiation of Polypeptide Research, Head of Polypeptide Research Group, Ciba Ltd., Basel 1952–63, Asst. Man. 1960–63; Prof. and Head of (new) Dept. of Molecular Biology, Swiss Fed. Inst. of Tech., Zürich 1963–; Prof.-in-Res., Clinical Research Inst. of Montreal 1991–; Werner Award, Swiss Chemical Soc. 1957; Ruzicka Prize, Swiss Fed. Inst. of Tech. 1959; Otto Nägeli Award, Switzerland 1964; Vernon Stouffer Award, American Heart Asscn., Cleveland 1968; Ernesto Scoffone Award 1982; Alan E. Pierce Award, American Peptide Symposia 1985; Rudinger Gold Medal, European Peptide Symposia 1988. *Publications:* Scientific papers on syntheses of biologically active polypeptides; structure activity relationships; relationships between structure and biophysical interactions with lipid-bilayer membranes; molecular mechanisms of opioid receptor selection by peptides, new principles governing receptor specificity. *Leisure interests:* mountain climbing, skiing, literature. *Address:* Institut für

Molekularbiologie und Biophysik, Eidgenössische Technische Hochschule, 8093 Zürich; 8180 Bülach, Switzerland (Home). *Telephone:* 01-860-7111.

SCHYGULLA, Hanna; German actress; b. 1943; has made nearly 40 films; *stage appearances include:* Mother Courage 1979; *films include:* Die Ehe der Maria Braun (Silberner Bär Berlinale) 1979, Die Dritte Generation 1979, Lili Marleen 1980, Die Fälschung 1981, La Nuit de Varennes 1982, Eine Liebe in Deutschland 1983, The Story of Piera 1983, Miss Arizona 1987, The Summer of Mr. Forbes, Dead Again 1991, The Merchant of Four Seasons 1998; *television appearances include:* 8 Stunden sind kein Tag (series) 1972. *Leisure interests:* travel, painting.

SCIAMA, Dennis William, PH.D., F.R.S.; British scientist; b. 18 Nov. 1926, Manchester; s. of Abraham Sciama and Nelly Ades; m. Lidia Dina 1959; two d.; ed. Malvern Coll. and Trinity Coll. Cambridge; Prize Fellow, Trinity Coll. Cambridge 1952–56; Lecturer in Math., Cambridge Univ. 1961–70; Fellow Peterhouse, Cambridge 1963–70; Sr. Research Fellow, All Souls Coll. Oxford 1970–85, Emer. Fellow 1985–; Prof. of Astrophysics, Int. School of Advanced Studies, Trieste, Italy 1983–; Consultant, Int. Centre for Theoretical Physics, Trieste 1983–; Extraordinary Fellow, Churchill Coll., Cambridge 1986–94; Foreign mem. American Philosophical Soc., American Acad. of Arts and Sciences, Accademia dei Lincei. *Publications:* The Unity of the Universe 1959, The Physical Foundations of General Relativity 1966, Modern Cosmology 1971, Modern Cosmology and the Dark Matter Problem 1993, Questo Bizzarro Universo 1998. *Address:* International School of Advanced Studies, Strada Costiera 11, 34014 Trieste, Italy. *Telephone:* (040) 3787 475. *Fax:* (040) 3787-528.

SCITOVSKY, Anne A., M.A.; American economist; b. 17 April 1915, Ludwigshafen, Germany; d. of H. W. Aickelin and Gertrude M. Aickelin; m. Tibor Scitovsky 1942 (divorced 1966); one d.; ed. Barnard Coll., New York, L.S.E., Columbia Univ.; Economist Legis. Reference Service, Library of Congress 1941–44; Economist Bureau of Research and Statistics, Social Security Bd. 1944–46; Sr. Research Assoc. Palo Alto Medical Research Foundation 1963–73, Chief, Health Econs. Dept. 1973–91, sr. staff scientist 1992–; Lecturer Inst. for Health Policy Studies, School of Medicine, Univ. of Calif., San Francisco 1975–91; mem. Nat. Cttee. on Vital Health Statistics 1975–79, mem. Pres.'s Comm. for the Study of Ethical Problems in Medicine and Biomedical and Behavioral Research 1979–82, Inst. of Medicine Council on Health Care Tech. Assessment 1986–90, Health Resources and Services Admin., AIDS Advisory Comm. 1990–94; mem. N.A.S. Inst. of Medicine 1980–. *Publications:* articles in official documents and professional journals. *Leisure interests:* reading, photography, swimming. *Address:* Research Institute, Palo Alto Medical Foundation, 860 Bryant Street, Palo Alto, CA 94301 (Office); 161 Erica Way, Menlo Park, CA 94028, U.S.A. (Home). *Telephone:* (650) 854-5727 (Home).

SCLATER, John G., PH.D., F.R.S.; British professor of geophysics; b. 17 June 1940, Edinburgh, Scotland; s. of John G. Sclater and Margaret Bennett Glen; m. 1st Fredrica R. Sclater 1968 (divorced 1985), two s.; m. 2nd Paula Ann Edwards 1985 (divorced 1991); m. 3rd Naila G. Burchett 1992; ed. Stonyhurst Coll., Edinburgh Univ. and Cambridge Univ.; Postdoctoral Research Geophysicist, Scripps Inst. of Oceanography 1965–67, Asst. Research Geophysicist 1967–72; Assoc. Prof. M.I.T. 1972–77, Prof. 1977–83; M.I.T. Dir., Jt. Program in Oceanography with the Woods Hole Oceanographic Inst. 1981–83; Assoc. Dir. Inst. for Geophysics, Univ. of Texas at Austin, Prof., Dept. of Geological Sciences and Shell Distinguished Chair. in Geophysics 1983–91; Prof. of Geophysics, Scripps Inst. of Oceanography, Univ. of Calif. (San Diego) 1991–; Fellow Geological Soc. of America, American Geophysical Union; mem. N.A.S.; Rosenstiel Award 1978; Bucher Medal, American Geophysical Union 1985. *Leisure interests:* running, swimming, golf. *Address:* GRD 0215, Scripps Institution of Oceanography, University of California at San Diego, La Jolla, CA 92093, U.S.A. *Telephone:* (619) 534-8653.

SCLATER, John Richard, C.V.O., M.A., M.B.A.; British business executive; b. 14 July 1940; s. of Arthur Sclater and Alice Sclater (née Collett); m. 1st Nicola Cropper 1967 (divorced); one s. one d. (deceased); m. 2nd Grizel Dawson 1985; ed. Charterhouse, Gonville & Caius Coll. Cambridge and Yale and Harvard Univs.; Glyn, Mills & Co. 1964–70; Dir. Williams, Glyn & Co. 1970–76; Man. Dir. Nordic Bank 1976–85, Chair. 1985; Dir. Guinness Peat Group PLC 1985–87, Jt. Deputy Chair. 1987; Dir. and Deputy Chair. Guinness Mahon & Co. Ltd. 1985–87, Chair. 1987; Dir. Foreign and Colonial Investment Trust PLC 1981–, Chair. 1985–; Chair. Foreign & Colonial Enterprise Trust PLC 1986–, Foreign & Colonial Ventures Advisers Ltd. 1988–, Foreign & Colonial Ventures Ltd. 1990–98, Berisford PLC 1990– (Dir. 1986–), County Catering & Leisure Ltd. 1990–, Hill Samuel Bank Ltd. 1992–96, (Dir. 1990–), IBIS (201) Ltd. 1992–, Foreign & Colonial Pvt. Equity Trust 1996–, Reabourne Merlin Life Sciences Investment Trust PLC 1997–, Argent Group Europe Ltd. 1998–; Pres. Equitable Life Assurance Soc. 1994– (Dir. 1985–); Deputy Chair. Yamaichi Int. (Europe) Ltd. 1988–97, Union PLC 1986–96, (Dir. 1981–, Chair. 1996), Millennium & Copthorne Hotels PLC 1996–; Dir. James Cropper PLC, Holker Estates Co. Ltd., Grosvenor Estate Holdings, Fuel Tech (Europe) Ltd., Berner Nicol & Co. Ltd., Hypo Foreign & Colonial Man. (Holdings) Ltd.; Dir. and Gov. Brambletye School 1976–; Trustee The Grosvenor Estate 1973–, Coll. of Arms Trust 1994–; mem. Council of Duchy of Lancaster 1987–, CBI City Advisory Group 1988–; Freeman City of London, Liveryman Goldsmiths' Co.; Gov. Int. Students Trust 1976–. *Leisure interests:* country pursuits. *Address:* 117 Eaton Square, London, SW1W 9AA, England. *Telephone:* 0171-235 2223. *Fax:* 0171-235 1228.

SCOFIELD, Paul, C.B.E.; British actor; b. 21 Jan. 1922, Hurstpierpoint, Sussex; s. of Harry Scofield and Mary Scofield; m. Joy Parker 1943; one s. one d.; trained London Mask Theatre Drama School; Birmingham Repertory Theatre 1941 and 1943–46; Stratford-upon-Avon Shakespeare Memorial Theatre 1946–48; Arts Theatre 1946; Phoenix Theatre 1947; with H. M. Tennent 1949–56; Assoc. Dir. Nat. Theatre 1970–71; Hon. LL.D. (Glasgow Univ.), Hon. D.Lit. (Kent) 1973, (Sussex) 1985; Shakespeare Prize, Hamburg 1972; Danish Film Acad. Award; Tony Award, Evening Standard Drama Award for John Gabriel Borkman 1996; Life Achievement Award American Film Inst. 1996. *Has appeared in:* Chekhov's Seagull, Anouilh's Ring Round the Moon, Charles Morgan's The River Line; Richard II, Time Remembered, A Question of Fact, Hamlet (also in Moscow), Power and the Glory, Family Reunion, A Dead Secret, Expresso Bongo, The Complaisant Lover, A Man for all Seasons, Stratford Festival, Ont., Canada 1961, Coriolanus, Don Armado New York 1961–62, A Man for All Seasons London 1962–63, King Lear 1963 (E. Europe, Helsinki, Moscow, New York 1964), Timon of Athens 1965, The Government Inspector London 1966, Staircase 1967, Macbeth 1968, The Hotel in Amsterdam 1968, Uncle Vanya 1970, The Captain of Köpenik 1971, Rules of the Game 1971, Savages 1973, The Tempest 1974, 1975, Dimetos 1976, Volpone 1977, The Madras House 1977, The Family 1978, Amadeus 1979, Othello 1980, Don Quixote 1982, A Midsummer Night's Dream 1982, I'm Not Rappaport 1986, Exclusive 1989, Heartbreak House 1992, John Gabriel Borkman (Royal Nat. Theatre) 1996. *Films:* The Train 1963, A Man for All Seasons 1967 (Oscar and New York Film Critics Award, Moscow Film Festival and British Film Acad. Awards), King Lear 1970, Scorpio 1972, A Delicate Balance 1972, '1919', Anna Karenina 1984, When the Whales Came 1988, Henry V 1989, Hamlet 1991, Quiz Show 1993, The Little Riders 1995, The Crucible 1995. *Television:* The Ambassadors 1977, The Potting Shed 1981, If Winter Comes 1981, Song at Twilight 1982, Come into the Garden Maud 1982, A Kind of Alaska 1984, Summer Lightning 1985, Only Yesterday 1986, The Attic 1988, Utz 1991, Martin Chuzzlewit 1994. *Address:* The Gables, Balcombe, Sussex, RH17 6ND, England.

SCOGNAMIGLIO, Carlo, D.ECON.; Italian politician, economist and business consultant; b. 27 Nov. 1944, Varese; s. of Luigi Scognamiglio and Esther (née Pasini) Scognamiglio; m. Delfina Rattazzi 1980; one s. one d.; ed. L. Bocconi Univ., Milan, London School of Econs.; Asst. Lecturer L. Bocconi Univ.; Asst. Prof. of Finance, Univ. of Padua 1973–79; Asst. Prof. of Industrial Econs. Univ. L. Bocconi, Milan 1975–84; Prof. of Econs. and Industrial Policy, Libera Universita Int. degli Studi Sociali, Rome 1979–, Dean and Rector 1984; Liberal Party cand. in Milan constituency, elected to Senate 1992, Chair. European Affairs Cttee., mem. Budget Cttee., re-elected to Senate 1994 as Liberal Party mem. of Polo delle Libertà alliance, Pres. of Senate 1994–; Pres. Rizzoli-Corriere della Sera 1983–84, Vice-Pres. 1984–; Bulkitalia 1984; Minister of Defence Oct. 1998–; a founder, Bocconi School of Business Admin. 1979; Acad. of France award for economics 1988. *Publications include:* The White Book on PPSS 1981, The White Book on the Italian Financial Market 1982, Theory and Policy of Finance 1987, Industrial Economics 1987, Report to Minister of Treasury of Commission for Privatization of Industry 1990. *Leisure interests:* economics, history. *Address:* Libera Università Int. degli Studi Sociali, Viale Pola 12, 00198 Rome; Ministry of Defence, Via XX Settembre 8, 00187 Rome; 2 Via Carducci, 20123 Milan, Italy.

SCOLA, Ettore; Italian director and screen writer; b. 10 May 1931, Trevico (Avellino); m. Gigliola Fantoni 1956; two d.; studied law, then worked in journalism and radio; started scriptwriting 1952–; directed: Se permettete parliamo di donne 1964, La Congiuntura 1965, Thrilling 1965, L'arcidiavolo 1966, Riusciranno i nostri eroi a ritrovare l'amico misteriosamente scomparso in Africa? 1968, Il commissario Pepe 1969, Dramma della gelosia (tutti i particolari in cronaca) (Jealousy, Italian Style) 1970, Permette? Rocco Papaleo 1971, La più bella serata della mia vita 1972, Trevico—Torino . . . viaggio nel Fiat-nam 1973, C'eravamo tanto amati 1974, Brutti, sporchi e cattivi 1976 (Best Dir., Cannes Film Festival), Signore e signori buonanotte 1976, Una giornata particolare (A Special Day) 1977 (Special Jury Prizes, Cannes Film Festival), I nuovi mostri 1977, La terrazza 1979, Passione d'amore 1980, Il mondo nuovo 1982, Le bal 1983, Maccheroni 1985, La Famiglia (The Family) 1987, Splendor 1988, Che Orà È? 1989, Il Viaggio di Capitan Fracassa 1990, Mario, Maria e Mario 1992, Romanzo di un giovane povero 1995.

ŠCOLČ, Jožef; Slovenian politician; b. 19 Aug. 1960, Breginje; ed. Ljubljana Univ.; active in Socialist Youth League of Slovenia (ZSMS) 1979–84; mem. of Pres. Republican Conf. of Socialist Youth League (RKZSMS) 1984–, Pres. 1988–92; leader of movt. for pluralism and democratization; Chair. Cttee. for Constitution 1990; mem. first elected Parl. and leader of ZSMS Deputies' Club (later Liberal Democratic Party) 1990–94; co-ordinator of Liberal Democracy of Slovenia; Pres. Nat. Ass. of Slovenian Repub. 1994–96; Minister of Culture 1997–. *Address:* Ministry of Culture, Cankarjeva str. 5, 1000 Ljubljana, Slovenia. *Telephone:* (61) 178 5915 (Office).

SCOON, Sir Paul, G.C.M.G., G.C.V.O., O.B.E.; Grenadian public administrator; b. 4 July 1935; m. Esmai Monica Lumsden 1970; two step-s. one step-d.; ed. Inst. of Educ., Leeds, Toronto Univ.; teacher Grenada Boys' Secondary

School 1953–67, Chief Ed. Officer 1967–68; with Civil Service 1968, Vice-Pres. Civil Service Asscn. 1968, Perm. Sec. 1969, Sec. to Cabinet 1970–72, Deputy Dir, Commonwealth Foundation 1973–78, Gov. Centre for Int. Briefing, Farnham Castle 1973–78, Gov.-Gen. of Grenada 1978–92; now Chair. Grenada Tourism Bd. *Address:* P.O. Box 180, St George's, Grenada.

SCORSESE, Martin, M.A.; American film director and writer; b. 17 Nov. 1942, Flushing, N.Y.; s. of Charles Scorsese and Catherine (née Cappa) Scorsese; m. 1st Laraine Marie Brennan 1965; one d.; m. 2nd Julia Cameron (divorced); one d.; m. 3rd Isabella Rossellini (q.v.) 1979 (divorced 1983); m. 4th Barbara DeFina 1985; ed. New York Univ.; faculty asst. and instructor, Film Dept., New York Univ. 1963–66; instructor 1968–70; dir. and writer of films: What's a Nice Girl Like You Doing in a Place Like This? 1963, It's Not Just You, Murray 1964, Who's That Knocking At My Door? 1968, The Big Shave 1968; dir. play The Act 1977–78; dir. and writer of documentaries; supervising ed. and asst. dir. Woodstock 1970; assoc. producer and post-production supervisor Medicine Ball Caravan 1971, Box Car Bertha 1972; dir. films: Mean Streets 1973, Alice Doesn't Live Here Any More 1974, Taxi Driver 1976, New York, New York 1977, King of Comedy 1981; actor and dir. The Last Waltz 1978; dir. Raging Bull 1980, After Hours 1985, The Color of Money 1986; dir. The Last Temptation of Christ 1988 (Courage in Filmmaking Award, Los Angeles Film Teachers Asscn. 1989), Good Fellas 1989, Cape Fear 1991, The Age of Innocence 1993, Clockers 1994, Casino 1995, Kundun 1997; exec. producer: The Crew 1989, Naked in New York 1994, Grace of my Heart 1996; producer: The Grifters 1989; co-producer Mad Dog and Glory 1993; acted in Cannonball 1976, Triple Play 1981, Dreams 1990; Edward J. Kingsley Foundation Award 1963, 1964; first prize, Rosenthal Foundation Awards of Soc. of Cinematologists 1964; named Best Dir., Cannes Film Festival 1986; first prize, Screen Producer's Guild 1965, Brown Univ. Film Festival 1965, shared Rosellini Prize 1990, Award American Museum of Moving Image 1996, etc. *Publications:* Scorsese on Scorsese 1989, The Age of Innocence: the shooting script (with Jay Cocks) 1996, Casino (with Nicholas Pileggi) 1996. *Address:* Jeff Doolly Starr & Co., 350 Park Avenue, 9th Floor, New York, NY 10022; c/o CAA, 9830 Wilshire Boulevard, Beverly Hills, CA 90212, U.S.A.

SCOTT, Alastair Ian, PH.D., F.R.S.E., F.R.S.; British professor of chemistry; b. 10 April 1928, Glasgow, Scotland; s. of William and Nell (Newton) Scott; m. Elizabeth W. Walters 1950; one s. one d.; ed. Univ. of Glasgow; Lecturer in Organic Chem. Univ. of Glasgow 1957–62; Prof. Univ. of British Columbia, Vancouver 1962–65, Univ. of Sussex 1965–68, Yale Univ. 1968–77; Distinguished Prof. Texas A & M Univ. 1977–80, Davidson Prof. of Chemistry and Biochemistry 1982–; Prof. Dept. of Chem. Univ. of Edin. 1980–82; mem. American Chem. Soc., Royal Soc. of Chem., Biochem. Soc.; Hon. mem. Pharmaceutical Soc. of Japan 1984; Hon. M.A. (Yale) 1968; Hon. D.Sc. (Coimbra) 1990, (Univ. Pierre et Marie Curie, Paris) 1992; Corday Morgan Medal, Royal Soc. of Chem. 1964, Guenther Award, American Chem. Soc. 1975, A.C. Cope Scholar Award, American Chem. Soc. 1992, Centenary Lecturer (Royal Soc. of Chem.) 1994, Tetrahedron Prize 1995, Royal Soc. of Chem. Award in Natural Product Chem. 1995, and other awards. *Publications:* Interpretation of Ultraviolet Spectra of Natural Products 1964, Handbook of Naturally Occurring Compounds (co-author) 1972; articles in professional journals. *Address:* Department of Chemistry, Texas A & M University, College Station, TX 77843, U.S.A. *Telephone:* (409) 845-3243. *Fax:* (409) 845-5992.

SCOTT, Alexander Brian, D.PHIL., M.R.I.A.; British academic; b. 1 Dec. 1933, Bangor, N. Ireland; s. of John Scott and Lil Scott; m. Margaret Byrne 1997; ed. Foyle Coll. Londonderry, Queen's Univ. Belfast and Merton Coll. Oxford; Temporary Lecturer, Magee Univ. Coll. Londonderry 1957–58; Asst. Dept. of Western Manuscripts, Bodleian Library, Oxford 1958–62; lecturer, Dept. of Humanity, Aberdeen Univ. 1963–64; lecturer, Dept. of Latin, Queen's Univ. Belfast 1964, Reader in Late Latin 1971–92, Prof. of Late Latin 1992–94, Emer. Prof. 1995–; mem. Royal Irish Acad. *Publications:* Hildeberti Cenomanensis Carmina Minora 1969, Malachy, a life 1976, Expugnatio Hibernica, The Conquest of Ireland by Gerald of Wales 1978, Medieval Literary Theory and Criticism c.1100–1375 1988, Liudprand of Cremona 1992. *Leisure interest:* travelling by train, preferably in France. *Address:* School of Greek, Roman and Byzantine Studies, Queen's University of Belfast, University Road, Belfast, BT7 1NN, Northern Ireland (Office); 31 Valentia Road, Drumcondra, Dublin 9, Ireland (Home). *Telephone:* (01232) 245133 (Office); (01) 8372924 (Home).

SCOTT, Charles Thomas; British advertising executive; b. 22 Feb. 1949; with Binder Hamlyn 1967–72; Chief Accountant, ITEL Int. Corpn. 1972–77; Controller, IMS Int. Inc. 1978–84, Chief Financial Officer 1985–89; Chief Financial Officer, Saatchi & Saatchi Co. (now Cordiant PLC) PLC 1990–91, C.O.O. 1991–92, C.E.O. 1993–95, Chair. 1995–97, Saatchi & Saatchi (non-exec.) 1997–, Bates Worldwide 1997. *Address:* Cordiant PLC, 83/89 Whitfield Street, London, W1A 4XA, England. *Telephone:* 0171-436 4000. *Fax:* 0171-436 1998.

SCOTT, George C(ampbell); American actor, producer and director; b. 18 Oct. 1927, Wise, Va.; s. of George C. Scott and late Helena Scott; m. 1st Patricia Reed (divorced); m. 2nd Colleen Dewhurst 1960 (divorced); m. 3rd Trish Van Devere 1972; six c. from previous marriages; ed. Redford High School and Univ. of Missouri; appeared in Richard III, New York Shakespeare Festival 1957; subsequent theatrical appearances included As You Like It, Children of Darkness 1957–58; Broadway appearances in Comes a Day 1958, The Andersonville Trial 1959, The Wall 1960; co-founder Theater of Mich. Company 1961; produced, directed and appeared in General Seeger 1962 and produced Great Day in the Morning 1962; Dir. Death of a Salesman, New York 1975, All God's Chillun Got Wings 1975; Dir. and acted in Present Laughter 1982, On Borrowed Time 1991. *Films include:* The Hanging Tree 1958, Anatomy of a Murder 1959, The Hustler 1962, Dr. Strangelove 1963, The List of Adrian Messenger 1963, The Yellow Rolls-Royce 1964, The Bible 1966, The Flim-Flam Man 1967, Petulia 1969, Patton: Lust for Glory 1970, Jane Eyre 1971, They Might be Giants 1971, The Hospital 1972, Precinct 1945, Oklahoma Crude, Rage (also dir.), Day of the Dolphin 1973, Bank Shot (also dir.), The Savage is Loose (also dir.), The Hindenberg, Sly Fox 1976, The Prince and The Pauper 1976, Islands in the Stream 1977, Movie Movie 1978, Hard Core 1979, The Changeling 1980, The Formula 1980, Taps 1981, Il Duce 1985, Dick Tracy 1989, The Exorcist III 1990, The Rescuers Down Under (voice) 1990, Malice 1993, Angus; refused Acad. Award (Oscar) for Patton: Lust for Glory 1971; *TV series:* East Side, West Side 1963–64. *Address:* 11755 Wilshire Boulevard, # 2320, Los Angeles, CA 90025, U.S.A.

SCOTT, James, M.SC., F.R.C.P.; British physician; b. 13 Sept. 1946, Ashby de la Zouch; s. of Robert B. Scott and Iris O. (née Hill) Scott; m. Diane M. Lowe 1976; two s. one d.; ed. London Univ., London Hosp. Medical Coll.; house surgeon London Hosp. 1971–72; house physician Hereford Co. Hosp. July-Dec. 1972; Sr. House Officer Queen Elizabeth Hosp., Midland Centre for Neurosurgery and Neurology, Birmingham Jan.-Dec. 1973; Registrar Gen. Hosp., Birmingham Jan.-Dec. 1974, Royal Free Hosp., Academic Dept. of Medicine 1975–76; Hon. Sr. Registrar, MRC Research Fellow Hammersmith Hosp., Dept. of Medicine 1976–80; Postdoctoral Fellow Univ. of Calif., Dept. of Biochemistry and Biophysics 1980–83; Clinical Scientist; Head Div. of Molecular Medicine, MRC Research Centre 1983–91; Hon. Consultant Physician Northwick Park Hosp., Harrow 1983–91, Hammersmith Hosp. 1992–97; Prof., Chair. of Medicine Royal Postgrad. Medical School 1992–97; Hon. Dir. MRC Molecular Medicine Group 1992–; Dir. of Medicine Hammersmith Hosps. NHS Trust, Dir. Div. of Medical Cardiology 1994–97; Prof of Medicine Imperial Coll. School of Medicine 1997–, Deputy Vice-Prin. for Research 1997–; European Ed. Arteriosclerosis, Thrombosis and Vascular Biology (Journal of American Heart Asscn.); several prizes and awards include Graham Bull Prize (Royal Coll. of Physicians) 1989, Squibb Bristol Myers Award for Cardiovascular Research 1993, etc. *Publications:* numerous articles on molecular medicine, molecular genetics, atherosclerosis, RNA modification, RNA editing and gene expression. *Leisure interests:* family and friends, the twentieth-century novel, British impressionist and modern painting, long distance running, swimming. *Address:* Department of Molecular Medicine, Imperial College School of Medicine, Hammersmith Hospital, Du Cane Road, W12 0NN, England.

SCOTT, Peter, M.A., Q.C.; British lawyer; b. 19 April 1935; ed. Monroe High School, Rochester, New York, U.S.A., Balliol Coll. Oxford; called to Bar 1960, Q.C. 1978; Chair. of Bar 1987 (Vice-Chair. 1985–86); Standing Counsel to Dir.-Gen. of Fair Trading 1974–78, to Dept. of Employment 1973–78; mem. Interception of Communications Tribunal 1986–, Lord Chancellor's Advisory Cttee. on Legal Educ. and Conduct 1991–94; Chair. Inst. of Actuaries Appeal Bd. 1995–; Judicial Chair. City Disputes Panel 1997–; Harmsworth Scholar of Middle Temple; Bencher of Middle Temple. *Address:* Fountain Court, Temple, London, EC4Y 9DH (Office); 4 Eldon Road, London, W8 5PU, England (Home). *Telephone:* 0171-583 3335 (Office).

SCOTT, Rt. Hon. Sir Richard Rashleigh Folliott, Kt., B.A., LL.B.; British judge; b. 2 Oct. 1934, Dehra Dun, India; s. of late Lieut. Col. C. W. F. Scott and Katharine Scott (née Rashleigh); m. Rima E. Ripoll 1959; two s. two d.; ed. Michaelhouse Coll. Natal, Univ. of Cape Town and Trinity Coll. Cambridge; called to Bar, Inner Temple 1959; practising barrister, Chancery Bar 1960–83; Q.C. 1975; Attorney-Gen. to Duchy of Lancaster 1980–83; Bencher, Inner Temple 1981; Chair. of the Bar 1982–83 (Vice-Chair. 1981–82); High Court Judge, Chancery Div. 1983; Vice-Chancellor, County Palatine of Lancaster 1987–91; a Lord Justice of Appeal 1991–94; Vice-Chancellor of the Supreme Court of Justice 1994–; Head of Civil Justice 1995–; conducted inquiry into the sale of arms to Iraq 1992–96; Ed.-in-Chief Supreme Court Practice 1996–; Hon. mem. American Bar Assoc., Canadian Bar Assoc; Hon. LLD. (Birmingham) 1996. *Publications:* Report of the Inquiry into the Export of Defence Equipment and Dual-Use Goods to Iraq and the Related Prosecutions; articles in legal journals. *Leisure interests:* equestrian activities, tennis, bridge. *Address:* Royal Courts of Justice, Strand, London, WC2A 2LL, England. *Telephone:* 0171-936 6412.

SCOTT, Ridley; British film director; b. 30 Nov. 1937, South Shields; ed. Royal Coll. of Art; dir. of numerous award-winning TV commercials since 1970; débût as feature film dir. with The Duellists 1978; Hon. D.Litt. (Sunderland) 1998. *Other films include:* Alien, Blade Runner, Legend, Someone to Watch Over Me, Black Rain, Thelma and Louise, 1492: Conquest of Paradise 1992, White Squall 1995, G. I. Jane 1997, Gladiators 1999; co-producer The Browning Version 1994. *Address:* Scott Free, 42/44 Beak Street, London, W1R 3DA, England. *Telephone:* 0171-437 3163. *Fax:* 0171-734 4978.

SCOTT, Timothy; British sculptor; b. 18 April 1937, Richmond, Surrey; s. of A. C. Scott and Dorothea Scott; m. Malkanthi Wirekoon 1958; two s. three d.; ed. Lycée Jaccard, Lausanne, Architectural Asscn. and St. Martin's School of Art, London; worked at Atelier Le Corbusier-Wogenscky and others, Paris 1959–61; Sr. Lecturer Canterbury Coll. of Art 1975–76; Head of Fine Art Dept., Birmingham Polytechnic 1976–78; Head Dept. of Sculpture, St. Martin's School of Art 1980–86; Prof. of Sculpture, Akad. der Bildenden Künste Nürnberg 1993–; numerous visiting lectureships in U.S.A., Canada, Australia, Germany, U.K., Chile. *One-man exhbns.* (since 1964): Waddington, Kasmin Galleries, London, Rubin, Emmerich, Tibor de Nagy, Meredith Long Galleries, New York, Galerie Wentzel, Hamburg, David Mirvish, Toronto, Klonaridis, Toronto, Galerie Biederman, Munich, Galerie Ziegler, Zurich, Deutschland Funk, Cologne, Galerie In Fonte, Berlin, Galerie Tiergarten, Hanover, Deutsche Bank, Colombo, Galerie Winkelmann, Düsseldorf, Galerie Appel & Fertsch, Frankfurt, Galerie Fahlbusch, Mannheim. *Retrospectives*: Whitechapel, London 1967, Museum of Modern Art, Oxford 1969, Corcoran Gallery of Art, Washington 1973, Museum of Fine Arts, Boston, U.S.A. 1972, Edmonton Art Gallery, Alberta 1976 (touring: Regina, Windsor, Toronto), Kunsthalle Bielefeld 1979–80 (touring: Lübeck, Duisburg, Ludwigshafen, Munich), Kettles Yard, Cambridge, Kunstverein Braunschweig 1988–89 (touring: Münster, Saarbrücken, Leverkusen, Regensburg). *Leisure interests:* music, architecture, travel, Sri Lanka, Indian culture, food. *Address:* 50 Clare Court, Judd Street, London, WC1H 9QW; Keeper's Cottage, Troutsdale, N. York Moors, N. Yorks., England; Albrecht Dürer Strasse 10, Nurenberg 90403, Germany. *Telephone:* 0171-837 7157 (London).

SCOTT, Tony; British film director; b. 21 June 1944, Newcastle; ed. Sunderland Coll. of Art, Leeds Coll. of Art, Royal Coll. of Art Film and TV Dept.; dir. One of the Missing 1989 (Grand Prix, Mar Del Plata Festival, Argentina, Prix de la Télévision Suisse, Nyon, Second Prize, Esquire Film Festival, U.S.A., Diploma of Merit, Melbourne); Asst. Dir. Dream Weaver 1967, The Movement Movement 1967; cameraman The Visit, Untitled, Compromise, Milian, Fat Man; worked for Derrick Knight & Alan King Assocs., Visual Dir. and Cameraman, pop promotional films, Now Films Ltd., TV Cameraman, Seven Sisters 1968, Co-producer and actor, Don't Walk (promotional film), Asst. Cameraman, Gulliver; Writer, Dir., Ed. Loving Memory 1969–70; Visual Dir. and Cameraman, publicity film for Joe Egg; other films include Revenge, Top Gun, Beverley Hills Cop II, Days of Thunder, The Last Boy Scout, True Romance, Crimson Tide, The Fan, Enemy of the State; Dir. Scott Free Enterprises Ltd.; Dir. of TV and cinema commercials for Ridley Scott and Assocs. *Address:* c/o Bill Unger, 752 26th Street, Santa Monica, CA 90402, U.S.A.

SCOTT, W. (William) Richard, PH.D.; American sociologist and educator; b. 18 Dec. 1932, Parsons, Kan.; s. of Charles H. Scott and Hildegarde Hewit; m. Joy Lee Whitney 1955; three c.; ed. Parsons Jr. Coll., Kan., Univ. of Kansas, Univ. of Chicago; Asst. Prof., Dept. of Sociology, Stanford Univ. 1960–65, Assoc. Prof. 1965–69, Prof. 1969–, Chair. Dept. of Sociology 1972–75, Dir. Orgs. Research Training Program 1972–89; Dir. Stanford Center for Orgs. Research 1988–96; Prof. by courtesy, Dept. of Health Research and Policy, School of Medicine 1972–, and of Educ., School of Educ., and of Organizational Behaviour, Graduate School of Business, Stanford Univ. 1977–; Sr. Researcher, Nat. Center for Health Services Research, Dept. of Health, Educ. and Welfare, Washington, D.C. 1975–76; Visiting Prof. Kellogg Grad. School of Man., Northwestern Univ. 1997; Ed. Annual Review of Sociology 1986–91; mem. Gov. Bd., Comm. on Social and Behavioral Sciences and Educ., N.A.S. 1990–96; Woodrow Wilson Fellow 1954–55; Social Science Research Council Fellow 1958–59, Fellow Center for Advanced Study in the Behavioral Sciences 1989–90; mem. Inst. of Medicine; Distinguished Scholar Award, Acad. of Man. 1988; Richard D. Irwin Award 1996. *Publications:* Metropolis and Region (with others) 1960, Formal Organizations (with P. M. Blau) 1962, Social Processes and Social Structures 1970, Evaluation and the Exercise of Authority (with S. M. Dornbusch) 1975, Organizations: Rational, Natural and Open Systems 1981, Organizational Environments (with J. W. Meyer) 1983, Hospital Structure and Performance (with A. Flood) 1987, Institutional Environments and Organizations: Structural Complexity and Individualism (with J. W. Meyer) 1994, Institutions and Organizations 1995, Institutional Change and Organizations: Transformation of a Healthcare Field (with others) 1999. *Leisure interests:* reading, tennis, cross-country skiing. *Address:* Stanford University Department of Sociology, Building 120, Stanford, CA 94305 (Office); 940 Lathrop Place, Stanford, CA 94305, U.S.A. (Home). *Telephone:* (415) 723-3959 (Office); (415) 857-1834 (Home).

SCOTT BROWN, Denise, R.I.B.A. M.ARCH., M.C.P.; American architect and urban planner; b. 3 Oct. 1931, Nkana, Zambia; d. of Simon Lakofski and Phyllis Hepker; m. 1st Robert Scott Brown 1955 (died 1959); m. 2nd Robert Venturi (q.v.) 1967; one s.; ed. Kingsmead Coll. Johannesburg, Univ. of Witwatersrand, Architectural Assn. London and Univ. of Pennsylvania; Asst. Prof. Univ. of Pa. School of Fine Arts 1960–65; Assoc. Prof. Univ. of Calif. Los Angeles 1965–68; Venturi, Scott Brown & Assocs. Inc., Philadelphia 1967–, partner 1969–89, Prin. 1989–; Visiting Prof. Univ. of Calif. (Berkeley) 1965, Yale Univ. 1967–71, Univ. of Pa. 1982–83; Eero Saarinen Visiting Critic, Yale Univ. 1987, Eliot Noyes Visiting Critic, Harvard Univ. 1990; mem. Advisory Bd., Carnegie Mellon Univ. Dept. of Architecture 1992–, Bd. of Overseers for Univ. Libraries, Univ. of Pa. 1995–; numerous other academic and professional appts.; Hon. D.Eng. (Tech. Univ. of Nova Scotia) 1991; Hon. D.Hum.Litt. (Pratt Inst.) 1992; Hon. D.F.A. (Univ. of Pa.) 1994; Hon. D.Lit. (Univ. of Nev.) 1998; President's Medal, Architectural League of N.Y. 1986; Chicago Architecture Award 1987; Nat. Medal of Arts 1992, Philadelphia Award 1992, Benjamin Franklin Medal Award (R.S.A.) 1993, numerous other awards and distinctions; Commendatore, Repub. of Italy 1987. *Publications:* Learning from Las Vegas (with R. Venturi and S. Izenour) 1977, A View from the Campidoglio: Selected Essays, 1953–84 (with R. Venturi) 1984, Urban Concepts 1990; articles in professional journals. *Leisure interests:* travelling, writing, teaching, lecturing. *Address:* Venturi, Scott Brown & Associates Inc., 4236 Main Street, Philadelphia, PA 19127, U.S.A. *Telephone:* (215) 487-0400.

SCOTT-JOYNT, Rt. Rev. Michael, M.A.; British ecclesiastic; b. 1943; m. Louise White 1965; two s. one d.; ed. King's Coll. Cambridge and Cuddesdon Theological Coll.; ordained deacon 1967, priest 1968; Curate, Cuddesdon 1967–70; Tutor, Cuddesdon Coll. 1967–71, Chaplain 1971–72; Team Vicar, Newbury 1972–75; Priest-in-charge, Caversfield 1975–79, Bicester 1975–79, Bucknell 1976–79; Rector, Bicester Area Team Ministry 1979–81; Rural Dean of Bicester and Islip 1976–81; Canon Residentiary of St. Albans 1982–87; Dir. of Ordinands and In-Service Training, Diocese of St. Albans 1982–87; Bishop Suffragan of Stafford 1987–95; Bishop of Winchester 1995–. *Address:* Wolvesey, Winchester, Hants., SO23 9ND, England. *Telephone:* (01962) 854050. *Fax:* (01962) 842376.

SCOTTO, Renata; Italian soprano; b. 24 Feb. 1935, Savona; m. Lorenzo Anselmi; ed. under Ghirardini at Milan; joined La Scala Opera Company after début in La Traviata at Teatro Nuovo, Milan 1953; then studied under Merlino and Mercedes Llopart; roles in La Sonnambula, I Puritani, L'Elisir d'amore, Lucia di Lammermoor, Falstaff, La Bohème, Turandot, I Capuleti, Madame Butterfly, Tosca, Manon Lescaut, Otello, Rosenkavalier (Marschallin) 1992, La Voix Humaine 1993, Pirata 1993, etc. *Address:* c/o Robert Lombardo Associates, 61 W. 62nd Street, Apt. 6F, New York, NY 10023, U.S.A.

SCOTT-THOMAS, Kristin; British actress; b. Redruth; m.; one s. one d.; ed. Cen. School of Speech and Drama and Ecole Nat. des Arts et Technique de Théâtre, Paris; stage debut in Schnitzler's La Lune Déclinante Sur 4 ou 5 Personnes Qui Danse while student in Paris; has lived in France since age of 18; stage appearances include La Terre Etrangère, Naive Hirondelles and Yes Peut-Etre; appearances on French, German, Australian, U.S. and British television include L'Ami d'Enfance de Maigret, Blockhaus, Chameleon La Tricheuse, Sentimental Journey, The Tenth Man, Endless Game, Framed, Titmuss Regained, Look at it this Way, Body and Soul. *Films:* Djamel et Juliette, L'Agent Troubé, La Méridienne, Under the Cherry Moon, A Handful of Dust, Force Majeure, Bille en tête, The Bachelor, Bitter Moon, Four Weddings and a Funeral (B.A.F.T.A. Award), Angels and Insects (Evening Standard Film Award), Richard III, The English Patient, Amour et Confusions, The Horse Whisperer.

SCOWCROFT, Lieut.-Gen. Brent, PH.D.; American government official and air force officer; b. 19 March 1925, Odgen, Utah; s. of James Scowcroft and Lucile Balantyne Scowcroft; m. Marian Horner 1951 (died 1995); one d.; ed. U.S. Mil. Acad., West Point, and Columbia Univ.; Operational and Admin. positions in U.S. Air Force 1948–53; taught Russian history as Asst. Prof., Dept. of Social Sciences, U.S. Mil. Acad., W. Point 1953–57; Asst. Air Attaché, U.S. Embassy, Belgrade 1959–61; Assoc. Prof., Political Science Dept., U.S. Air Force Acad., Colorado 1962–63, Prof., Head of Dept. 1963–64; Plans and Operations Section, Air Force HQ, Washington 1964–66; various Nat. Security posts with Dept. of Defense 1968–72; Mil. Asst. to Pres., The White House 1972, Deputy Asst. to Pres. for Nat. Security Affairs 1973–75, Asst. to Pres. for Nat. Security Affairs 1975–77, 1989–93; Pres. Forum for Int. Policy 1993–; Pres. The Scowcroft Group 1994–; mem. Pres.' Gen. Advisory Cttee. on Arms Control 1977–81; Dir. Atlantic Council, U.S. Bd. of Visitors U.S. Air Force Acad. 1977–79, Council on Foreign Relations, Rand Corpn., Mitre Corpn.; Vice-Chair. UNA/U.S.A.; Chair. Presidential Comm. on Strategic Forces 1983–89; mem. Cttee. to Advise Dir. of CIA 1995–; mem. Cttee. of Enquiry into Nat. Security Council 1986–87; Defense D.S.M., Air Force D.S.M. (with two oak leaf clusters), Legion of Merit (with oak leaf cluster), Air Force Commendation Medal, Nat. Security Medal, Hon. K.B.E. 1993. *Publication:* A World Transformed (with George Bush) 1998. *Address:* 1750 K Street, NW, Suite 800, Washington, DC 20006, U.S.A.

SCRANTON, William Warren, A.B., LL.B.; American politician and lawyer; b. 19 July 1917, Madison, Conn.; s. of Worthington Scranton and Marion Margery Warren Scranton; m. Mary Lowe Chamberlin 1942; three s. one d.; ed. Hotchkiss School, Yale Univ. and Yale Univ. Law School; U.S. Army Air Force 1941–45; Pa. bar 1946; Assoc. O'Malley, Harris, Harris and Warren 1946–47; Vice-Pres. Int. Textbook Co., Scranton, Pa. 1947–52, later Dir. and mem. Exec. Cttee.; Pres. Scranton-Lackawanna Trust Co. 1954–56; Chair. Bd. and Dir. Northeastern Pennsylvania Broadcasting Co. 1957–61; Special Asst. to U.S. Sec. of State 1959–60; mem. U.S. House of Reps. 1961–63; Gov. of Pennsylvania 1963–67; Special Envoy to Middle East on behalf of Pres.-elect Nixon Dec. 1968; Chair. President's Commission on Campus Unrest 1970; Special Consultant to the Pres. 1974; Perm. Rep. to UN 1976–77; Chair of Bd. Northeastern Bank of Pa. 1974–76; Chair. UNA; official judge S.E. Wisconsin Scientific Fair, Milwaukee 1988–; Dir. Cummins Engines Co., IBM Corpn., New York Times Co., Mobil Oil; numerous hon. degrees; Republican. *Leisure interests:* tennis, swimming, hiking. *Address:* Marquette University School of Dentistry, 604 N. 16th Street, Milwaukee, Wis. 53233, U.S.A.

SCREECH, Michael Andrew, M.A., D.LITT., F.B.A., F.R.S.L.; British clergyman and academic; b. 2 May 1926, Plymouth; s. of Richard John Screech M.M. and Nellie Screech (née Maunder); m. Anne Reeve 1956; three s.; ed. Sutton High School, Plymouth and Univ. Coll. London; served Intelligence Corps, mainly Far East; Lecturer then Sr. Lecturer, Birmingham Univ. 1951–60; Reader, then Prof. of French, Univ. of London 1960–71, Fielden Prof. of French Language and Literature 1971–84; Sr. Research Fellow, All Souls Coll. Oxford 1984–93, Emer. 1993–; Extraordinary Fellow, Wolfson Coll. Oxford 1993–; ordained deacon 1993, priest 1994; Visiting Prof. London, Ont. 1964, Albany, N.Y. 1969; Johnson Prof. Madison, Wis. 1979; Edmund Campion Lecturer, Regina, Sask. 1985, Dorothy Ford Wiley Prof. of Renaissance Culture, Chapel Hill, N.C. 1986; Prof. Collège de France 1989; Visiting Prof. Sorbonne 1990; Comité de Publ. d'Humanisme et Renaissance 1965–; Corresp. mem. Soc. Historique et Archéologique de Genève 1988; Fellow Univ. Coll. London; Hon. D.Litt. (Exeter) 1993, Hon. D.D. (Geneva) 1998; Médaille de la Ville de Tours; Ordre National du Mérite 1983, Chevalier, Légion d'honneur 1992. *Publications:* The Rabelaisian Marriage 1958, L'Evangélisme de Rabelais 1959, Le Tiers Livre de Pantagruel 1964, Les 52 Semaines de Lefèvre d'Etaples 1965, Les Regrets et Antiquités de Du Bellay 1966, Gargantua 1967, Marot Evangélique 1967, La Pantagrueline Prognostication 1975, Rabelais 1979, Ecstasy and the Praise of Folly 1981, 1988, Montaigne and Melancholy 1983, Erasmus' Annotations on the New Testament (with Anne Reeve) Vol. 1 1986, Vol. 2 1989, Vol. 3 1993, A New Rabelais Bibliography (with Stephen Rawles) 1987, Montaigne: An Apology for Raymond Sebond 1987, Montaigne: The Complete Essays 1991, Some Renaissance Studies 1992, Rabelais and the Challenge of the Gospel 1992, Clément Marot: A Renaissance Poet Discovers the Gospel 1993, The Doctrina et Politia Ecclesiae Anglicanae of Warden Mocket (ed.) 1995, Monumental Inscriptions in All Souls College, Oxford 1997, Laughter at the Foot of the Cross 1998, Montaigne's Copy of Lucretius 1998. *Leisure interest:* walking. *Address:* 5 Swanston-field, Whitchurch-on-Thames, Reading, RG8 7HP, England. *Telephone:* (01865) 274134 (Study); (0118) 984 2513 (Home). *Fax:* (0118) 984 2513 (Home).

SCRIMSHAW, Nevin Stewart, PH.D., M.D., M.P.H.; American professor of nutrition; b. 20 Jan. 1918, Milwaukee, Wis.; s. of Stewart and Harriet (née Smith) Scrimshaw; m. Mary Ware Goodrich 1941; four s. one d.; ed. Ohio Wesleyan Univ., Harvard Univ. and Univ. of Rochester; Consultant in Nutrition, Pan American Sanitary Bureau, Regional Office of the Americas, WHO 1948–49, Regional Adviser in Nutrition 1949–53; Dir. Inst. of Nutrition of Cen. America and Panama (INCAP), Guatemala 1949–61, Consulting Dir. 1961–65, Consultant 1965–; Adjunct Prof., Public Health Nutrition, Columbia Univ. 1959–61, Visiting Lecturer 1961–66; Visiting Lecturer on Tropical Public Health, Harvard Univ. 1968–85; Head, Dept. of Nutrition and Food Science, M.I.T. 1961–79, Inst. Prof. 1976–88, Inst. Prof. Emer. 1988–, Dir. Clinical Research Centre 1962–66, 1979–85, Principal Investigator 1962–86; Visiting Prof. Tufts Univ. 1987; Dir. M.I.T./Harvard Int. Food and Nutrition Program 1979–88; Dir. Int. Food and Nutrition Programme, UN Univ. 1976–97, Dir. Devt. Studies Div. 1986–87, Sr. Adviser UN Univ. Food and Nutrition Programme 1998–; Pres. Int. Union of Nutritional Scientists 1978–81; Fellow, A.A.A.S. American Acad. of Arts and Sciences; mem. N.A.S., Inst. of Medicine, American Acad. of Arts and Sciences and numerous other nat. and foreign scientific socs. and asscns.; mem. numerous cttees. and advisory panels to UN agencies and other orgs.; Int. Award, Inst. of Food Technologists 1969, Goldberger Award in Clinical Nutrition, American Medical Asscn. 1969, First James R. Killian Jr. Faculty Achievement Award, M.I.T. 1972, McCollum Award, American Soc. for Clinical Nutrition 1975, Conrad A. Elvehjem Award, American Inst. of Nutrition 1976, 1st Bolton L. Corson Medal, Franklin Inst. 1976, Medal of Honor, Fundación F. Cuenca Villoro 1978, Bristol Meyers Award 1988, World Food Prize 1991, etc. *Publications:* over 600 scientific articles and 20 books on various aspects of human and animal nutrition, nutrition and infection, agricultural and food chemistry, and public health. *Address:* Charles Street Station, P.O. Box 500, Boston, MA 02114 (Office); Sandwich MT Farm, PO Box 330, Campton, NH 03223, U.S.A. (Home). *Telephone:* (617) 227-8747 (Office). *Fax:* (617) 227-9405.

SCRIPPS, Charles Edward; American newspaper publisher; b. 27 Jan. 1920, San Diego; s. of Robert Paine and Margaret Lou (née Culbertson) Scripps; m. 1st Louann Copeland 1941 (divorced 1947); m. 2nd Lois Anne MacKay 1949 (died 1990); two s. two d.; m. 3rd Mary Elizabeth Breslin 1993; ed. William and Mary Coll. and Pomona Coll.; Reporter, Cleveland Press, Ohio 1941; Successor-Trustee, Edward W. Scripps Trust 1945, Chair. Bd. of Trustees 1948–; Vice Pres., Dir. E.W. Scripps Co. 1946–, Chair. of Bd. 1953–, Chair. Exec. Cttee. 1994–; Chair. Bd. Scripps Howard, Inc. 1987–. *Address:* Scripps Howard, 312 Walnut Street, 28th Floor, Cincinnati, OH 45202 U.S.A, (Office).

SCRIVENER, Christiane; French international official; b. 1 Sept. 1925, Mulhouse; d. of Pierre Fries and Louise Fries; m. Pierre Scrivener 1944; one s. (deceased); ed. Harvard Business School and Univ. of Paris; business manager involved since 1958 in org. of French tech. co-operation with more than 100 countries, devt. of int. tech. and industrial exchanges and promotion of French tech. abroad; State Sec. for Consumer Affairs 1976–78; mem. European Parl. 1979–89; mem. Union pour la Démocratie (UDF); EEC Commr. for Taxation and Customs Union and Social Security 1989–94; Pres. Europe-Avenir, Ombudsman Société Générale 1996–, Plan Int. France 1997–; mem. Bd., Alliance Française 1995–97; Officier, Légion d'honneur. *Publications:* Le rôle et la responsabilité à l'égard du public 1978, L'Europe, une bataille pour l'avenir 1984, Histoires du petit Troll 1986. *Leisure interests:* skiing, music. *Address:* 21 Avenue Robert-Schuman, 92100 Boulogne-Billancourt, France.

SCRIVER, Charles Robert, C.C., G.O.Q., M.D., C.M., F.R.S., F.R.S.C.; Canadian professor of pediatrics, human genetics and biology; b. 7 Nov. 1930, Montreal; s. of Walter DeMoulpied and Jessie Marion Boyd; m. Esther Peirce 1956; two s. two d.; intern Royal Victoria Hosp. Montreal 1955–56, Resident 1956–57, Resident Montreal Children's Hosp. 1956–57, Chief Resident (Pediatrics) 1960–61, physician 1961–; Children's Medical Center, Boston, U.S.A. 1957–58; McLaughlin Travelling Fellow Univ. Coll. London, U.K. 1958–60; Asst. Prof. of Pediatrics McGill Univ. 1961, Markle Scholar 1961–66, Assoc. Prof. 1965–69, Prof. of Pediatrics, Genetics and Biology 1969–, Co-Dir. MRC Genetics Group 1972–95, Alva Prof. of Human Genetics 1994–; Assoc. Dir. Canadian Genetic Diseases Network 1989–98; Pres. Canadian Soc. for Clinical Investigation 1974–75, Soc. for Pediatric Research 1975–76, American Soc. Human Genetics 1986, American Pediatric Soc. 1994–95; mem. Medical Advisory Bd./Scientific Advisory Bd. Howard Hughes Medical Inst. 1981–88; Fellow A.A.A.S. 1992; Hon. D.Sc. (Manitoba) 1992, (Glasgow, Montreal) 1993; numerous awards and prizes including Allen Award, American Soc. of Human Genetics 1978, Gairdner Foundation Int. Award 1979, McLaughlin Medal, Royal Soc. of Canada 1981, Canadian Rutherford Lectureship, Royal Soc., London 1983, Ross Award, Canadian Pediatric Soc. 1990, Award of Excellence (Genetic Soc. of Canada) 1992, Prix du Québec 1995. *Publications:* Amino Acid Metabolism and its Disorders (co-author) 1973, Garrod's Inborn Factors in Disease (co-author) 1989, Metabolic Basis of Inherited Disease (6th, 7th edns., Sr. Ed.) (co-author) 1989–; author or co-author of more than 500 scientific articles. *Leisure interests:* literature, music, photography. *Address:* Montreal Children's Hospital, 2300 Tupper Street, Montreal, Que. H3H 1P3 (Office); 232 Strathearn Avenue, Montreal, Que. H4X 1Y2, Canada (Home). *Telephone:* 934-4417 (Office). *Fax:* (514) 934-4329.

SCRUTON, Roger; British philosopher; b. 27 Feb. 1944, Buslingthorpe; s. of John Scruton and Beryl C. Haines; m. 1st Danielle Laffitte 1975 (divorced 1983); m. 2nd Sophie Jeffreys 1996; ed. High Wycombe Royal Grammar School, Jesus Coll. Cambridge and Inner Temple, London; Fellow, Peterhouse, Cambridge 1969–71; lecturer in Philosophy, Birkbeck Coll. London 1971–79, Reader 1979–86, Prof. of Aesthetics 1986–92; Prof. of Philosophy, Boston Univ. 1992–95; f. and Dir. The Claridge Press 1987–; Ed. The Salisbury Review 1982–. *Publications:* Art and Imagination 1974, The Aesthetics of Architecture 1979, The Meaning of Conservatism 1980, Fortnight's Anger 1981, A Dictionary of Political Thought 1982, Sexual Desire 1986, Francesca 1991, A Dove Descending 1991, Conservative Texts: An Anthology 1991, The Xanthippic Dialogues 1993, Modern Philosophy 1993, The Classical Vernacular 1994, Modern Philosophy 1996, An Intelligent Person's Guide to Philosophy 1997, The Aesthetics of Music 1997, Town and Country (co-ed.) 1998. *Leisure interests:* music, literature, hunting. *Address:* Sunday Hill Farm, Brinkworth, Wilts. SN15 5AS, England.

SCUDAMORE, Peter, M.B.E.; British jockey; b. 13 June 1958, Hereford; s. of Michael Scudamore and Mary Scudamore; m. Marilyn Scudamore 1980; two s.; fmr. point-to-point and amateur jockey; worked in estate agency; professional Nat. Hunt jockey 1979–93; 1,677 winners (retd. April 1993); seven times champion Nat. Hunt jockey inc. 1988–89 when he rode record 221 winners; Dir. Chasing Promotions 1989–; racing journalist Daily Mail 1993–; Jt. Pres. Jockeys' Asscn.; in partnership with trainer Nigel Twiston-Davies. *Publications:* A Share of Success (jtly.) 1983, Scudamore on Steeplechasing (jtly.), Scu; The Autobiography 1993. *Leisure interests:* cricket, music, watching sport. *Fax:* (01451) 850569.

SCULLY, Sean Paul, B.A.; American artist; b. 30 June 1945, Dublin; s. of John Anthony and Holly Scully; m. Catherine Lee; ed. Croydon Coll. of Art; with Fine Art Dept., Newcastle Univ. 1967–71; lecturer Harvard Univ. 1972–73; lecturer Chelsea School of Art and Goldsmiths School of Art, London 1973–75; lecturer Princeton Univ. 1978–83; lecturer in Painting Parsons School of Design, New York 1983–; one-man exhbns. in London, Los Angeles, New York, Berlin, Washington, etc. 1973–; exhibited at Carnegie Inst., Pittsburgh, Boston Museum of Fine Arts, Chicago Art Inst. 1987, Univ. Art Museum, Berkeley, Calif. 1987, Whitechapel Art Gallery, London 1989, Lenbachhaus, Munich 1989, Palacio Velázquez, Madrid 1989, Mary Boone Gallery, New York 1993, Fort Worth Museum of Modern Art 1993; works in public collections in U.K., U.S.A., Australia, Germany, Ireland; Stuyvesant Foundation Prize 1970, 1972 Prize, John Moore's Liverpool Exhbn. 8, 1974 Prize John Moore's Liverpool Exhbn. 9; Guggenheim Fellowship 1983. *Address:* c/o Timothy Taylor Gallery, 1 Bruton Place, London, W1, England.

SCULTHORPE, Peter Joshua, A.O., O.B.E.; Australian composer; b. 29 April 1929, Launceston, Tasmania; s. of Joshua Sculthorpe and Edna Moorhouse; ed. Launceston Grammar School, Univ. of Melbourne and Wadham Coll., Oxford; lecturer, Sr. lecturer in Music, Univ. of Sydney 1963–68; Visiting Fellow, Yale Univ. 1965–67; Reader in Music, Univ of Sydney 1968–91, Prof. in Musical Composition and Sydney Moss lecturer in Music 1992–; Visiting Prof. of Music, Univ. of Sussex 1971–72; comms. from bodies including Australian Broadcasting Comm., Birmingham Chamber Music

Soc., Australian Elizabethan Theatre Trust, Australian Ballet, Musica Viva Australia, Australian Chamber Orchestra; Hon. D.Litt. (Tasmania, Sussex), Hon. D.Mus. (Melbourne); Australian Council Composers' Award 1975–77, Australian Film Inst. Award 1980, Ted Albert Award 1993, Sir Bernard Heinze Award 1994, ABC Classic FM Listeners' Choice Award 1998, and numerous other awards. *Compositions published include:* The Loneliness of Bunjil 1954, Sonatina 1954, Irkanda I 1955, II 1959, III 1960, IV 1961, Ulterior Motifs, a musical farce and music for various revues 1957–59, Sonata for Viola and Percussion 1960, Theme and Journey's End (from film They Found a Cave) 1962, The Fifth Continent 1963, String Quartet No. 6 1965, No. 7 1966, No. 8 1969, No. 9 1975, No. 10 1983, No. 11 1990, Sun Music I 1965, Sun Music for Voices and Percussion 1966, Sun Music III 1967, IV 1967, Morning Song for the Christ Child 1966, Red Landscape 1966, Tabuh Tabuhan 1968, Autumn Song 1968, Sea Chant 1968, Sun Music II 1969, Orchestral Suite (from film The Age of Consent) 1968, Sun Music Ballet 1968, Love 200 for pop group and orchestra 1970, The Stars Turn 1970, Music for Japan 1970, Dream 1970, Night Pieces 1971, Landscape 1971, How The Stars Were Made 1971, Ketjak 1972, Koto Music I 1973, II 1976, Rites of Passage 1973, The Song of Tailitnama 1974, Postcard from Nourlangie to Clapham Common 1993, From Saibai 1993, Memento Mori for orchestra 1993, From Ubirr for string quartet and didgeridoo 1994; various works for radio, television, theatre and film. *Leisure interests:* gardening, collecting Sung ceramics. *Address:* 91 Holdsworth Street, Woollahra, N.S.W. 2025, Australia.

SCUTT, Der, F.A.I.A.; American architect and interior designer; b. 17 Oct. 1934, Reading, Pa.; s. of George W. Scutt and Hazel Smith; m. Leena Liukkonen 1967; two c.; ed. Pennsylvania State Univ., Yale Univ.; design partner Swanke Hayden Connell & Partners 1975–81; Prin. Der Scutt Architect, New York 1981–; projects include One Astor Plaza and Minskoff Theatre, New York 1973, Equitable Life Assurance Data Center, Easton, Pa 1973, Creative Perfumery Center, Teaneck, N.J. 1973, Grand Hyatt Hotel, New York 1980, 520 Madison Ave., N.Y. 1983, Continental Center Office Tower N.Y. 1983, Trump Tower, N.Y. 1983, U.S. H.Q. Hong Kong Bank, N.Y. 1985, office bldg. 625 Madison Avenue, N.Y. 1988, IFF World HQ, N.Y.C. 1994, and other office bldgs. N.Y.; mem. American Inst. of Architects, Bd. of Govs. N.Y. Bldg. Congress 1984–92 (Treasurer 1988), Bd. of Trustees Chapin Soc. 1984–, Nat Maritime Historical Soc. 1991–, Ocean Liner Museum, New York 1994; numerous design awards. *Address:* 44 West 28th Street, New York, NY 10001, U.S.A.

SEAGA, Rt. Hon. Edward Philip George, B.A., P.C.; Jamaican politician; b. 28 May 1930, Boston, Mass., U.S.A.; s. of Philip and Erna (née Maxwell) Seaga; m. Marie Elizabeth Constantine 1965 (divorced 1995); two s. one d.; ed. Wolmers Boys' School, Kingston, and Harvard Univ.; Field Researcher with Inst. of Social and Econ. Research (Univ. of West Indies) on devt. of child and revival spirit cults; nominated to Upper House, Legis. Council 1959; Asst. Sec. to Jamaican Labour Party 1960, Sec. 1962; M.P. for Western Kingston 1962–; Minister of Devt. and Social Welfare 1962–67, of Finance and Planning 1967–72; Leader of Jamaican Labour Party Nov. 1974–; Leader of Opposition 1974–80; Prime Minister 1980–89; Minister of Finance and Planning, Information and Culture 1980–89, of Defence 1987–89; fmr. Man.Dir. Consulting Service Ltd., Capital Finance Co. Ltd., Chair. Premium Group 1989–. *Publications:* Development of the Child, Revival Spirit Cults. *Leisure interests:* classical music, reading, shooting, hockey, football, cricket, tennis, swimming. *Address:* 24–26 Grenada Crescent, New Kingston, Kingston 5, Jamaica, West Indies (Home).

SEAGAL, Steven; American film actor and martial arts expert; b. 10 April 1951, Lansing, Mich.; m. 1st Miyako Fujitoni; one s. one d.; m. 2nd Kelly Le Brock; one s. two d.; moved to Japan aged 17 remaining there for 15 years; established martial arts acads. (dojo) in Japan and L.A. *Films:* Above the Law 1988, Hard to Kill 1990, Marked for Death 1990, Out for Justice, The Deadly Ground (Dir.) 1994, Under Siege 2 1995, The Glimmer Man, Executive Decision, Fire Down Below. *Address:* ICM, 8942 Wilshire Boulevard, Beverly Hills, CA 90211, U.S.A.

SEALY, Leonard Sedgwick; British professor of law; b. 22 July 1930, Putaruru, New Zealand; s. of Desmond Sealy and Mary Mark; m. Beryl Edwards 1960; one s. two d.; ed. Stratford High School, N.Z., Auckland Univ. and Gonville & Caius Coll. Cambridge; barrister and solicitor (N.Z.) 1953–; Fellow, Gonville & Caius Coll. Cambridge 1959–, Tutor 1960–76, Sr. Tutor 1970–75; Asst. Lecturer, Univ. of Cambridge 1959–61, Lecturer 1961–91, S. J. Berwin Prof. of Corporate Law 1991–97. *Publications:* several books on commercial and corp. law. *Address:* Gonville & Caius College, Cambridge, CB2 1TA, England. *Telephone:* (01223) 332471. *Fax:* (01223) 332456.

SEAMAN, Christopher, M.A., A.R.C.M.; British conductor; b. 7 March 1942, Faversham; s. of Albert Edward Seaman and Ethel Margery (née Chambers) Seaman; ed. Canterbury Cathedral Choir School, The King's School, Canterbury, King's Coll., Cambridge; prin. timpanist London Philharmonic Orchestra 1964–68; Asst. Conductor BBC Scottish Symphony Orchestra 1968–70, Chief Conductor 1971–77; Chief Conductor Northern Sinfonia Orchestra 1973–79; Prin. Conductor BBC Robert Mayer Concerts 1978–87; Conductor-in-Residence Baltimore Symphony Orchestra 1987–; Chief Guest Conductor Utrecht Symphony Orchestra 1979–83; Music Dir, Naples Philharmonic Orchestra Florida 1993–; appears as Guest Conductor worldwide, and has appeared in U.S.A., Germany, France, Holland, Belgium, Italy, Spain, Australia, and all parts of the U.K.; Hon. F.G.S.M. *Leisure interests:* people, reading, shopping, theology. *Address:* 25 Westfield Drive, Glasgow, G52 2SG, Scotland.

SEAMAN, Rev. Sir Keith Douglas, K.C.V.O., K.ST.J., O.B.E., M.A., LL.B., DIP.HUM.; Australian state governor and ecclesiastic; b. 11 June 1920, McLaren Vale; s. of late Eli Semmens Seaman and Ethel Maud Seaman; m. Joan Isabel Birbeck 1946; one s. one d.; ed. Unley High School and Univ. of Adelaide; South Australia (S.A.) Public Service 1937–54; entered Methodist ministry 1954; Minister, Renmark 1954–58; Cen. Methodist Mission 1958–77; Dir. 5KA, 5AU, 5RM Broadcasting Cos. 1960–77 (Chair. 1971–77); Sec. Christian TV Asscn. S.A. 1959–73; mem. Exec. World Asscn. of Christian Broadcasting 1963–70; R.A.A.F. Overseas HQ, London 1941–45, Flt. Lieut.; Supt. Adelaide Cen. Methodist Mission 1971–77; mem. Australian Govt. Social Welfare Comm. 1973–76; Gov. of S. Australia 1977–82. *Leisure interests:* gardening, reading. *Address:* 93 Rosetta Village, Victor Harbor, South Australia 5211, Australia. *Telephone:* (085) 523535.

SEAMANS, Robert Channing, Jr.; American engineer, educator and government official; b. 30 Oct. 1918, Salem, Mass.; s. of Robert Channing Seamans and Pauline (Bosson) Seamans; m. Eugenia Merrill 1942; three s. two d.; ed. Harvard and Massachusetts Institute of Technology; M.I.T. 1941–55, teaching and project management positions, successively Assoc. Prof. Dept. of Aeronautical Eng., Chief Engineer Project Meteor 1950–53, Dir. Flight Control Lab. 1953–55; Radio Corpn. of America 1955–60, successively Man. Airborne Systems Lab., Chief Systems Engineer Airborne Systems Dept., Chief Engineer Missile Electronics and Control Div.; Assoc. Admin. and later Deputy Admin. Nat. Aeronautics and Space Admin. (NASA) 1960–68; Consultant to Admin. (NASA) 1968–69; Sec. of Air Force 1969–73; Visiting Prof. of Aeronautics and Astronautics and of Management, M.I.T. 1968, Jerome Clarke Hunsaker Prof. 1968–69, Henry R. Luce Prof. of Environment and Public Policy 1977–84, Dean of Eng. 1978–81, Sr. Lecturer Dept. of Aeronautics and Astronautics 1984–; mem. Nat. Acad. of Eng. 1968–, Pres. 1973–74; Admin., Energy Research and Devt. Admin. 1974–77; mem. Scientific Advisory Board, U.S. Air Force 1957–62, Assoc. Adviser 1962–67; Nat. Del. to Advisory Group for Aerospace Research and Devt. (NATO) 1966–69; Dir. Nat. Geographic Soc. (and fmr. Trustee); fmr. Dir. Charles Stark Draper Lab. Inc., Combustion Eng. Inc., Eli Lilly and Co., Johnny Appleseed's Inc., Aerospace Corpn., Putnam Funds; mem. numerous scientific and other orgs.; Hon. D.Sc. (Rollins Coll.) 1962, (New York Univ.) 1967; Hon. D. Eng. (Norwich Acad.) 1971, (Notre Dame) 1974, (Rensselaer Polytech. Inst.) 1974; Hon. LL.D. (Univ. of Wyoming) 1975, Thomas Coll. 1980; Dr. of Public Service (George Washington Univ.) 1975; Naval Ordnance Devt. Award 1945; Lawrence Sperry Award, American Inst. of Aeronautics and Astronautics 1951; NASA Distinguished Service Medal 1965, 1969; General Thomas D. White U.S. Air Force Space Trophy 1973; Dept. of Defense Distinguished Public Service Medal 1973; Dept. of Air Force Exceptional Civilian Award 1973, Nat. Soc. of Professional Engineers Achievement Award, Thomas D. White Nat. Defence Award 1980, Daniel Guggenheim Award 1995. *Leisure interests:* tennis, sailing, skiing. *Address:* 675 Hale Street, Beverly Farms, MA 01915, U.S.A.

SEARLE, John; American professor of philosophy; b. 1932, Denver, Colo.; s. of George W. Searle and Hester Beck Searle; m. Dagmar Carboch 1958; two s.; ed. Univ. of Wisconsin, Oxford Univ.; Prof. of Philosophy Univ. of California, Berkeley 1959–; Chair. Educ. TV series in Calif. 1960–74; involved with student radical movt. 1964; Advisor to Nixon Admin. on student unrest in Univs. 1971, Reith Lecturer 1984; Rhodes Scholar 1952. *Publications:* Speech Acts 1969, The Campus War 1972, Expression and Meaning 1979, Intentionality 1983, Minds, Brains and Science 1984, The Foundations of Illocutionary Logic (with D. Vanderveken) 1985, The Rediscovery of the Mind 1992, (On) Searle on Conversation 1992, The Construction of Social Reality 1995, Mystery of Consciousness 1997, Mind, Language and Society 1998; contrib. to John Searle and his Critics; articles on artificial intelligence and philosophy. *Address:* Department of Philosophy, University of California, Berkeley, CA 94720, U.S.A. *Telephone:* (510) 642 3173. *Fax:* (510) 642-5160.

SEARLE, Ronald, R.D.I., A.G.I.; British artist; b. 3 March 1920, Cambridge; s. of late William James and of Nellie (Hunt) Searle; m. 1st Kaye Webb (dissolved 1967, died 1996); one s. one d.; m. 2nd Monica Koenig 1967; ed. Central School, Cambridge and Cambridge School of Art; first drawings published 1935–39; served with Royal Engineers 1939–46; prisoner-of-war in Japanese camps 1942–45; contributor to nat. publs. 1946; mem. Punch 'Table' 1956; special features artist Life magazine 1955; Holiday 1957, The New Yorker 1966–; Designer of medals for the French Mint 1975–, British Art Medal Soc. 1983–; One-Man Exhbns. Leicester Galleries (London) 1950, 1954, 1957, Kraushaar Gallery (New York) 1959, Bianchini Gallery (New York) 1963, Kunsthalle (Bremen) 1965, in Paris 1966, 1967, 1968, 1969, 1970, 1971, Bibliothèque Nationale 1973, in Munich 1967, 1968, 1969, 1970, 1971, 1973, 1976, 1981, in London 1968, Neue Galerie Wien, Vienna 1985, 1988, Imperial War Museum 1986, Fitzwilliam Museum, Cambridge 1987, Wilhelm Busch Museum, Hanover 1996, Stadtmuseum, Munich 1996, etc.; work rep. in Victoria and Albert Museum, Imperial War Museum, and British Museum (London), Bibliothèque Nationale, Paris and in several German and American museums; designer of several films including John Gilpin, On the Twelfth Day, Energetically Yours (awards at Venice, Edinburgh, San Francisco and other film festivals), Germany 1960, Toulouse-Lautrec, Dick Deadeye, or Duty Done 1975; Royal Designer for Industry 1988; designed animation sequences for films Those Magnificent Men in their Flying Machines 1965, Monte-Carlo or Bust! 1969, Scrooge 1970, Dick Deadeye 1975; Los Angeles Art Dirs. Club Medal 1959, Philadelphia Art Dirs. Club Medal 1959, Nat. Cartoonists' Soc. Award 1959, 1960, Gold Medal, III Biennale, Tolentino, Italy 1965, Prix de la Critique Belge 1968, Grand Prix de l'Humour noir (France) 1971, Prix d'Humour, Festival d'Avignon 1971, Medal of French Circus 1971, Prix International "Charles Huard" 1972, La Monnaie de Paris Medal 1974, Bundesrechtsanwaltskammer Award (Germany) 1998. *Publications:* Forty drawings 1946, John Gilpin 1952, Souls in Torment 1953, Rake's Progress 1955, Merry England 1956, Paris Sketchbook 1957, The St. Trinian's Story (with Kaye Webb) 1959, U.S.A. For Beginners 1959, Russia for Beginners 1960, The Big City 1958 (all with Alex Atkinson), Refugees 1960 1960, Which Way did he Go? 1961, Escape from the Amazon 1963, From Frozen North to Filthy Lucre 1964, Those Magnificent Men in their Flying Machines 1965, Haven't We Met Before Somewhere? (with Heinz Huber) 1966, Searle's Cats 1967, The Square Egg 1968, Hello—Where did all the People Go? 1969, Secret Sketchbook 1970, The Second Coming of Toulouse-Lautrec 1970, The Addict 1971, More Cats 1975, Designs for Gilbert and Sullivan 1975, Paris! Paris! (with Irwin Shaw) 1977, Searle's Zoodiac 1977, Ronald Searle (monograph) 1978, The King of Beasts 1980, The Big Fat Cat Book 1982, Illustrated Winespeak 1983, Ronald Searle in Perspective (monograph) 1984, Ronald Searle's Golden Oldies: 1941–1961, 1985, Something in the Cellar 1986, To the Kwai—and Back 1986, Ah Yes, I Remember It Well . . .: Paris 1961–1975 1987, Non-Sexist Dictionary 1988, Slightly Foxed—but still Desirable 1989, Carnet de Croquis 1992, The Curse of St. Trinian's 1993, Marquis de Sade Meets Goody Two-Shoes 1994, Ronald Searle dans le Monde 1998, etc. *Address:* c/o Tessa Sayle Agency, 11 Jubilee Place, London, SW3 3TE, England; Eileen McMahon Agency, P.O. Box 1062, Bayonne, N.J. 07002, U.S.A. *Telephone:* 0171-823 3883 (London); (201) 436 4362 (New York). *Fax:* 0171-823 3363 (London); (201) 436 4363 (New York).

SEATON, Michael John, PH.D., F.R.S; British professor of physics; b. 16 Jan. 1923, Bristol; s. of Arthur William Robert and Helen Amelia (née Stone) Seaton; m. 1st Olive May Singleton 1943 (died 1959); one s. one d.; m. 2nd Joy Clarice Balchin 1960; one s.; ed. Wallington County School, Surrey, Univ. Coll., London; Asst. Chemist British Industrial Solvents 1940–42; Navigator R.A.F. 1942–46; student Univ. Coll., London 1946–50, Asst. lecturer 1950–52, lecturer 1952–59, Reader 1959–63, Prof. 1963–88, Prof. Emer. 1988–; Chargé de Recherche, Inst. d'Astrophysique, Paris 1954–55; Fellow-Adjoint, Jt. Inst. Lab. Astrophysics, Boulder, Colo. 1963–; Sr. Research Fellow, Science and Eng. Research Council 1984–88; Pres. Royal Astronomical Soc. 1979–81; Hon. mem. American Astronomical Soc. 1983; Foreign Assoc. N.A.S. 1986; Gold Medal, Royal Astronomical Soc. 1983, Guthrie Medal and Prize, Inst. of Physics 1984, Hughes Medal, Royal Soc. 1992. *Publications:* 260 papers in various journals on theoretical atomic physics and astronomy. *Address:* Chutsworth, Bwlch, Powys, LD3 7RQ, Wales. *Telephone:* (01874) 730-652.

SECOMBE, Sir Harry Donald, Kt., C.B.E., F.R.S.A.; British comedian, actor and singer; b. 8 Sept. 1921; m. Myra J. Atherton 1948; two s. two d.; ed. Dynevor School, Swansea; served R.A. 1939–46; Windmill Theatre 1947–48; gen. variety 1948–; appearances at London Palladium 1956, 1958–61, 1966; Royal Command Performances 1951, 1955, 1957, 1958, 1963, 1966, 1969, 1975, 1978, 1987; appeared in musicals Pickwick 1963, 1993, The Four Musketeers 1967, The Plumber's Progress 1975; appeared in The Goon Show, BBC Radio 1949–60 and in special performance for 50th anniversary of BBC 1972; TV appearances 1950–; TV presenter: Highway, Tyne Tees TV 1983–93, Sunday Morning with Secombe, STV 1994, Songs of Praise, BBC TV 1995–; Hon. D.Mus. (Wales). *Films:* Davy 1957, Jetstorm 1959, Bed-Sitting Room 1968, Oliver 1968, Song of Norway 1969, Rhubarb 1969, Doctor in Trouble 1970, The Magnificent Seven Deadly Sins 1971, Sunstruck 1972. *Publications:* Twice Brightly 1974, Goon for Lunch 1975, Katy and the Nurgla 1978, Welsh Fargo 1981, Goon Abroad 1982, The Harry Secombe Diet Book 1983, Harry Secombe's Highway 1984, The Highway Companion 1987, Arias and Raspberries (autobiog.) 1989, The Nurgla's Magic Tear 1990, Strawberries and Cheam: An Autobiography 1996. *Leisure interests:* film photography, literature, travel, golf, cricket. *Address:* c/o 12 Sylvaways Close, Cranleigh, Surrey, GU6 7HG; 46 St. James's Place, London, SW1A 1NS, England. *Telephone:* 0171-629 2768.

SEDAKA, Neil; American singer and composer; b. 13 March 1939; s. of Mac Sedaka and Eleanor Appel; m. Leba M. Strassberg 1962; one s. one d.; ed. Juilliard School of Music; solo perfomer worldwide 1959–; composer of numerous popular songs including: Breaking Up Is Hard to Do, Stupid Cupid, Calendar Girl, Oh! Carol, Stairway to Heaven, Happy Birthday Sweet Sixteen, Laughter in the Rain, Bad Blood, Love Will Keep Us Together, Lonely Night (Angel Face); recipient of numerous gold records and recording industry awards. *Recordings include:* In the Pocket, Sedaka's Back, The Hungry Years, Steppin' Out, A Song, All You Need Is The Music, Come See About Me, Greatest Hits 1988, Oh! Carol and Other Hits 1990, Timeless 1992. *Address:* c/o Neil Sedaka Music, 201 East 66th Street, Ste. 3N, New York, NY 10021, U.S.A.

SEDGWICK, (Ian) Peter; British business executive; b. 14 Oct. 1935; m. Verna Mary Sedgwick 1956; one s. one d.; with Nat. Provincial Bank 1952–59, Ottoman Bank Africa and Middle East 1959–69, J. Henry Schroder Wagg & Co. Ltd. 1969–90; Dir. Schroders Nominees Ltd. 1981–95, C.E.O. Schroder Investment Man. Ltd. 1985–94, Dir. Schroder Unit Trusts Ltd. 1987–95, Group Man. Dir. Investment Man. Schroders PLC 1987–95, Deputy Chair. 1995–, Dir. (non-exec.) Schroder & Co. Inc. 1991–, Chair. 1996–, Pres., C.E.O. Schroders Inc. New York 1996–; Chair. Schroder Asian Growth Fund 1991–, Schroder UK Growth Fund 1994–; Dir. (non-exec.) Equitable Life Assurance Soc. 1991–, INVESCO Blue Chip Trust PLC 1991–, INVESCO City & Commercial Investment Trust PLC (fmrly. New City & Commercial Trust PLC) 1992–. *Leisure interest:* golf. *Address:* Schroders PLC, 120 Cheapside, London, EC2V 6DS, England. *Telephone:* 0171-658 6476. *Fax:* 0171-658 2211.

ŠEDIVÝ, Jaroslav, D.PHIL., C.SC.; Czech politician; b. 12 Nov. 1929, Prague; s. of Jaroslav Šedivý and Marie Šedivý; m. Marie Poslušná 1962; one s. one d.; ed. Charles Univ., Prague; with Czech Acad. of Sciences 1954–57; scientist Inst. of Int. Policy and Econ. 1957–70; imprisoned on charges of subversion of the state 1970–71; worker, driver, window cleaner 1972–88; researcher Prognostic Inst., Prague 1989; adviser to Minister for Foreign Affairs 1989–90; Amb. to France 1990–95, to Belgium, Luxembourg and NATO 1995–97; Perm. Rep. to UNESCO 1993–95; Minister for Foreign Affairs 1997, Jan.–July 1998; Amb. to Switzerland 1998–; Dr. h.c. (J. F. Kennedy Univ., Buenos Aires) 1998. *Publications:* Policy and Relations 1969, Humiliated Revolution (published under pseudonym Y. Heřtová) 1978, Metternich contra Napoleon (published under pseudonym Jan Halada) 1985, Palace Černín in the Year Zero 1997, Mystery and Sins of the Templars 1999. *Address:* Ministerstvo Zahraničních vecí, Prague 1, Loretánské nam. č. 5, Czech Republic. *Telephone:* 24-18-11-11.

ŠEDIVÝ, Maj.-Gen. Jiří; Czech army officer; b. 3 Jan. 1953, Príbram; m.; two d.; ed. Mil. High School, Mil. Univ. for Land Army, Mil. Acad., Brno; mem. CP 1975–89; various commands Czech Army 1975–96, including Commdr., Czech Unit, Implementation Force (IFOR), Bosnia 1996; Commdr. Czech Land Army 1997–98, Chief of Gen. Staff 1998–; four Mil. Merit Awards; two Memorial Badges. *Leisure interests:* sport, music. *Address:* c/o Ministry of Defence, Tychonova 1, 160 00 Prague 6, Czech Republic. *Telephone:* 330-4-1111.

SEDKI, Atef, D.ECON.; Egyptian politician; b. 1930; ed. law school and the Sorbonne, Paris; Prof. of Gen. Finance, Cairo Univ. 1958–73; Cultural Attaché, Egyptian Embassy, Paris 1973–80; Pres. Govt. Advisory Council Comm. for Economic and Financial Affairs 1980–85; Pres. Govt. Audit Office 1985–86; Prime Minister of Egypt 1986–95; Minister of Int. Co-operation 1987–95. *Address:* c/o Office of the Prime Minister, Cairo, Egypt.

SEDNEY, Jules; Suriname politician; b. 28 Sept. 1922, Paramaribo; s. of Eugene Eowin Leonard Sedney and Marie Julia Linger; m. Ina Francis Waaldyk 1951 (divorced 1985); two s. three d.; one d. by A. Calor; ed. Graaf van Zinzendorfschool, Mulo, and Univ. of Amsterdam; fmr. teacher; held sr. post with Cen. Bank of Suriname 1956–58, Pres. 1980; Minister of Finance 1958–63; Dir. Industrial Devt. Corpn. of Suriname and Nat. Devt. Bank 1963; left Nationale Partij Suriname (NPS) and joined Progressieve Nationale Partij (PNP) 1967; Prime Minister and Minister of Gen. Affairs 1970–73; Prof. of Econs., Univ. of Suriname 1976–80; Chair. Nat. Planning Council 1980; fmr. Dir. Suriname Trade and Industry Asscn. 1990–92; Chair. Monitoring Group Suriname Structural Adjustment Programme 1992–96, Tripartite Advisory Bd. to Govt. of Suriname 1994–98, Seniority Bd. of Econ. Advisers to Pres. of the Repub. 1998–. *Leisure interests:* bridge, golf. *Address:* Maysteet 24, Paramaribo, Suriname. *Telephone:* (692) 421029. *Fax:* (692) 421029.

SEDOV, Leonid Ivanovich; Russian scientist; b. 14 Nov. 1907, Rostov-on-Don; s. of Ivan and Raisa Sedov; m. Galia Tolstova 1931; one s. one d.; ed. Moscow Univ.; at the Aero-hydro-dynamics Inst. 1930–47; Prof. at Moscow Univ. 1937–, Chief, Dept. of Hydrodynamics 1941–; at V. I. Steklov Math. Inst. 1945–; at the Cen. Aircraft Engine Designing Inst. 1947–53; Chair. Scientific Council for Mechanics of Liquid and Gas 1965–; mem. U.S.S.R. (now Russian) Acad. of Sciences 1953–; Chief Ed. Cosmic Research 1953–; Pres. Int. Astronautical Fed. 1959–61, Vice-Pres. 1962–80; Vice-Pres. Int. Astronautical Acad. 1980–; Hon. mem. several acads.; Chaplygin Prize 1946, State Prize 1952, Lomonosov Prize 1954, Hero of Socialist Labour 1967, Belsch Prize 1968, Légion d'honneur 1971; Liapounov Medal 1974, H. Obert Gold Ring 1976, D. and F. Guggenheim Int. Astronautics Award 1977, A. D. Emil Prize 1981. *Publications:* Extension of Powerful Blasts, Two-Dimensional Problems in Hydrodynamics and Aerodynamics 1950, 1980, Similarity and Dimensional Methods in Mechanics 1944, Some Unsteady Movements in Compressible Liquid 1945, Introduction to Continuous Mechanics 1962, Nonlinear Mechanics of Continuous Media 1969, Mechanics of Continuous Media, Vols. I and II 1973, 1976, 1983, 1994, Thoughts about Science and Scientists 1980, Gravity and Electromagnetics Fundamentals 1990. *Address:* Institute of Mechanics, MGU, Michurinsky prosp. 1, 117192 Moscow B-192 (Office); Leninskie Gory, MGU, Zona II, Apt. 84, Moscow, Russia (Home). *Telephone:* 939-32-10 (Office). *Fax:* 939-01-65.

SEDYKH, Yuriy Georgievich; Russian athlete; b. 11 May 1955, Novocherkassk, North Caucasus; m.; one s.; ed. secondary school and Kiev Inst. of Physical Culture; hammer thrower; mem. U.S.S.R. athletics team 1973; European Junior Champion 1973; European Champion, Prague 1978; gold medallist Olympic Games, Montreal 1976, Moscow 1980; world hammer throwing record 81.80 m., Moscow 1980 (record broken 1982). *Address:* c/o Russian Light Athletics Federation, Luzhnetskaya Nab. 8, Moscow, Russia. *Telephone:* 201-01-50.

SEEFELDER, Matthias, DR.RER.NAT.; German industrial executive; b. 1920, Boos, Kreis Memmingen, Bavaria; ed. Humanistisches Gymnasium, Univ. of Munich; joined BASF AG 1951, Deputy mem. Man. Bd. 1971, mem. Man. Bd. 1973, Chair. Man. Bd. 1974–83, Chair. Supervisory Bd. 1983–90, Hon. Chair. 1990–; Hon. Prof., Faculty of Chem., Univ. of Heidelberg 1974; Chair. Supervisory Bd. MAN Aktiengesellschaft 1983–92; mem. Bd. of Trustees, Soc. of the Friends of the Haus der Kunst, Munich; Corresp. mem. Acad. of Sciences, Mainz; Hon. mem. Court of the Tech. Univ. of Munich, Univ. of Mannheim and Univ. of Heidelberg; Chair. Deutsch-Französische Gesellschaft für Wissenschaft und Tech. (DFGWT), e.V., Bonn; Officier, Légion d'honneur, Cross of Outstanding Merit, Grand Cross with Star, Order of Merit (Fed. Repub. of Germany), Gran Cruz de la Orden del Mérito Civil (Spain) 1982. *Address:* BASF Aktiengesellschaft, 67056 Ludwigshafen, Germany. *Telephone:* 0621-604 3261.

SEELERT, Bob; American business executive; fmr. Gen. Man. Gen. Foods, Pres. coffee and int. foods div. –1989; fmrly. with Kayser-Roth (hosiery group), Topco American (grocery co.); Chief Exec. Cordiant PLC (frmly. Saatchi & Saatchi) 1995–97; C.E.O. Saatchi & Saatchi 1997–. *Address:* Cordiant PLC, 83 Whitfield Street, London W.1, England. *Telephone:* 0171-436 4000.

SEGAL, Anthony Walter, M.D., PH.D., D.SC., F.R.S., F.R.C.P. (U.K.); British medical scientist; b. 24 Feb. 1944, Johannesburg, South Africa; s. of Cyril Segal and Doreen Segal (née Hayden); m. Barbara Miller 1966; three d.; ed. Univs. of Cape Town and London; Sr. Clinical Fellow, Wellcome Trust 1979–86; Charles Dent Prof. of Medicine, Univ. Coll. London 1986–. *Leisure interests:* golf, sculpture, theatre, art. *Address:* Department of Medicine, University College London, 2nd Floor, Rayne Institute, 5 University Street, London, WC1E 6JJ (Office); 48B Regents Park Road, London, NW1 7SX, England (Home). *Telephone:* 0171-209 6175 (Office); 0171-586 8745 (Home). *Fax:* 0171-209 6211 (Office).

SEGAL, George, B.A.; American film actor and producer; b. 13 Feb. 1934, New York, N.Y.; s. of George and Fanny (Bodkin) Segal; m. 1st Marion Sobol 1956 (divorced 1983); two d.; m. 2nd Linda Rogoff 1983; ed. Manhasset Bay High School, Great Neck Junior High School, The George School, Haverford Coll., Columbia Coll. *Films include:* The Young Doctors 1961, Act One 1962, The Longest Day 1962, Invitation to a Gunfighter 1964, The New Interns 1964, Ship of Fools 1965, King Rat 1965, Who's Afraid of Virginia Woolf? 1966, The Quiller Memorandum 1966, Bye Bye Braverman 1968, No Way to Treat a Lady 1968, The Bridge at Remagen 1969, She Couldn't Say No 1969, The Southern Star 1969, Loving 1970, Where's Poppa? 1970, The Owl and the Pussy Cat 1970, Born to Win 1972, The Hot Rock 1972, A Touch of Class 1972, Blume in Love 1972, The Terminal Man 1973, California Split 1973, Blackbird 1974, Russian Roulette 1975, The Duchess and the Dirtwater Fox 1976, Fun with Dick and Jane 1976, Rollercoaster 1977, Who is Killing the Great Chefs of Europe? 1978, Lost and Found 1979, The Last Married Couple in America 1980, Stick 1983, The Endless Game (TV) 1989, Look Who's Talking 1990, The Clearing, For The Boys 1991, The Mirror has Two Faces 1996, Flirting with Disaster 1996. *Address:* c/o Starr & Co., 350 Park Avenue, New York, NY 10022, U.S.A.

SEGAL, Judah Benzion, M.C., D.PHIL., F.B.A.; British university professor of Semitic Languages; b. 21 June 1912, Newcastle upon Tyne; s. of Prof. Moses Hirsch Segal and Hanna Leah; m. Leah Seidemann 1946; two d.; ed. Magdalen Coll. School, Oxford, St. Catharine's Coll., Cambridge and St. John's Coll., Oxford; Deputy Asst. Dir., Public Security, Anglo-Egyptian Sudan 1939–41; served in army in Middle East 1942–44; in charge of Arab Educ., Tripolitania, Libya 1945–46; Lecturer in Hebrew, Reader in Aramaic and Syriac, S.O.A.S., Univ. of London 1947–60; Prof. of Semitic Languages, Univ. of London 1961–79, Prof. Emer. 1979–; Pres. Leo Baeck Coll., London (fmrly. Prin.); Hon. Fellow S.O.A.S.; Freeman of City of Urfa, Turkey. *Publications:* The Diacritical Point and the Accents in Syriac 1953, The Hebrew Passover 1963, Edessa, the Blessed City 1970, Aramaic Texts from North Saqqara 1983, A History of the Jews of Cochin 1993, Aramaic and Mandaic Incantation Bowls in the British Museum 1999. *Leisure interests:* walking, meditation. *Address:* 17 Hillersdon Avenue, Edgware, Middx. HA8 7SG, England (Home). *Telephone:* 0181-958 4993.

SEGAL, Ronald Michael, B.A.; South African author; b. 14 July 1932, Cape Town; s. of Leon and Mary Segal; m. Susan Wolff 1962; one s. two d.; ed. Univ. of Cape Town and Trinity Coll., Cambridge; Dir. Faculty and Cultural Studies Nat. Union of S. African Students 1951–52; Pres. Univ. of Cape Town Council of Univ. Socs. 1951; won Philip Francis du Pont Fellowship to Univ. of Virginia (U.S.A.) 1955 but returned to S. Africa to found Africa South (quarterly) 1956; helped launch economic boycott April 1959; banned by S. African Govt. from all meetings July 1959; in England with Africa South in Exile, April 1960–61; Gen. Ed. Penguin African Library 1961–84; Pluto Crime Fiction 1983–86; Hon. Sec. S. African Freedom Asscn. 1960–61; Convenor, Int. Conf. on Econ. Sanctions against S. Africa 1964, Int. Conf. on S.W. Africa 1966; Visiting Fellow, Center for Study of Democratic Insts., Santa Barbara 1973; Founding Chair. The Walton Soc. 1975–79, Pres. 1979–; Chair. Ruth First Memorial Trust 1983–. *Publications:* The Tokolosh (a fantasy) 1960, Political Africa: A Who's Who of Personalities and Parties 1961, African Profiles 1962, Into Exile 1963, Sanctions Against South Africa (Ed.) 1964, The Crisis of India 1965, The Race War 1966, South West Africa: Travesty of Trust (Ed.) 1967, America's Receding Future 1968, The Struggle against History 1971, Whose Jerusalem? The Conflicts of Israel 1973, The Decline and Fall of the American Dollar 1974, The Tragedy of Leon Trotsky 1979, The State of the World Atlas 1981, The New State of the World Atlas 1984, The Book of Business, Money and Power 1987, The Black Diaspora 1995. *Leisure interest:* day-dreaming. *Address:* The Old Manor House, Manor Road, Walton-on-Thames, Surrey, England. *Telephone:* (01932) 227766.

SEGAL, Uri; Israeli orchestral conductor; b. 7 March 1944, Jerusalem; s. of Alexander and Nehama Segal; m. Ilana Finkelstein 1966; one s. three d.; ed. Rubin Acad., Jerusalem and Guildhall School of Music, London; Prin. Conductor Bournemouth Symphony Orchestra 1980–82, Philharmonia Hungarica 1981–85; Music Dir. Chautauqua Festival (New York) 1990–; Founder/Chief Conductor Century Orchestra (Osaka) 1990–; orchestras conducted include Berlin Philharmonic, Stockholm Philharmonic, Concertgebouw, Orchestre de Paris, Vienna Symphony, Israel Philharmonic, London Symphony, London Philharmonic, Pittsburgh Symphony, Chicago Symphony and Houston Symphony; tours have included Austria, Switzerland, Spain, Italy, France, U.K., Scandinavia and the Far East; recordings include Mahler Symphony No. 4 (with N.Z. Symphony Orchestra), music by Britten (Bournemouth Symphony), music by Stravinsky (Suisse Romande), concertos with Lupu, De Larrocha, Firkušný and Ashkenazy; First Prize Dimitri Mitropoulos Int. Competition, New York 1969. *Leisure interests:* reading, photography, cooking. *Address:* c/o Olivia M.A. Artists' Management, 28 Sheffield Terrace, London, W8 7NA, England. *Telephone:* 0171-221 3606. *Fax:* 0171-221 3607.

SEGNI, Mario; Italian politician; f., fmr. leader Democratic Alliance; fmr. mem. Christian Democrat Party; mem. Camera dei Deputati. *Address:* Camera dei Deputati, Rome, Italy.

SEGUELA, Jacques Louis; French advertising executive; b. 23 Feb. 1934, Paris; s. of Louis Seguela and Simone Le Forestier; m. Sophie Vinson 1978; one s. two d.; ed. Lycée de Perpignan, Faculté de Pharmacie de Montpellier; reporter, Paris Match 1960; with France Soir group's leisure magazines 1962; produced several TV programmes; joined Delpire 1964, then Axe; f. Roux Seguela Agency; f. Roux Seguela Cayzac & Goudard with Alain Cayzac and Jean Michel Goudard 1978, Vice-Pres. (Euro-RSCG) 1991–96, Havas Advertising 1996–; César winner; Chevalier, Légion d'honneur, Chevalier des Arts et des Lettres. *Publications:* Terre en rond 1961 (Prix littérature sportive), Ne dites pas à ma mère que je suis dans la publicité, elle me croit pianiste dans un bordel 1979, Hollywood lave plus blanc 1982, Fils de pub 1984, Cache Cache Pub, Demain il sera tros star 1989, C'est gai la pub 1990, Vote au-dessus d'un nid de cocos 1992, Pub Story 1994, La parole de Dieu 1995, le Futur a de l'avenir 1996. *Address:* Havas Advertising, 84 rue de Villiers, 92300 Levallois-Perret, France.

SÉGUIN, Philippe Daniel Alain, L. ÈS L.; French politician; b. 21 April 1943, Tunis, Tunisia; s. of Robert Séguin and Denyse Danielle; m. 2nd Béatrice Bernascon; one d.; two s. one d. by first m.; ed. Lycée Carnot, Tunis, Lycée de Draguignan, Ecole Normale d'Instituteurs, Var, Faculté des Lettres, Aix-en-Provence and Ecole Nationale d'Administration; Auditor, Cour des Comptes 1970, Conseiller Référendaire 1977; Acad. de Nice 1971; Dir. of Studies, Inst. d'Etudes Politiques, Aix-en-Provence 1970–74; Maître de Conferences, Inst. d'Etudes Politiques, Paris 1971–77; Prof. Centre de Formation Professionelle et de Perfectionnement 1971–73; Secr.-Gen. Presidency of the Repub. 1973–74; Asst. to Dir. of Physical Educ. and Sport 1974–75; Dir. Office of Sec. of State responsible for relations with Parl. 1977; Chargé de mission, Office of Prime Minister 1977–78; Deputy to Nat. Ass. 1978–86, Vice-Pres. 1981–86; Mayor of Epinal 1983–97; Nat. Sec. RPR 1984–86, Pres. 1997–99; Minister of Social Affairs and Employment 1986–88; Deputy for Les Vosges June 1988–; Pres. Nat. Ass. April 1993–97, Parl. Floor Leader 1997–; Pres. nat. tripartite comm., French Fed. of Football; Hon. D.Litt. (Loughborough Univ. of Tech.) 1987; Chevalier du Mérite Agricole. *Publications:* Réussir l'alternance 1985, La force de convaincre 1990, Louis Napoléon le Grand 1990, De l'Europe en général et de la France en particulier (jtly.) 1992, Discours pour la France 1992, Demain, la France: tome I: la Priorité sociale (jty.), Tome II: La Reconquête du Territoire 1993, Ce que j'ai dit 1993, Discours encore et toujours républicains 1994, Deux France (jtly.) 1994, 240 dans un fauteuil 1995. *Address:* Assemblée nationale, 75355 Paris, France.

SEGUY, Georges; French trade unionist; b. 16 March 1927, Toulouse; s. of André Seguy and Gabrielle Monfouga; m. Cécile Sédeillan 1949; two s. one d.; ed. Armand-Leygues school, Toulouse; apprentice typographer 1942; mem. French C.P. 1942–, mem. Cen. Cttee. 1954–, Political Bureau 1956–82; arrested by Gestapo and deported to Mauthausen Concentration Camp 1944; electrician, S.N.C.F. (French Railways) 1946; mem. Railway Workers' Union, Toulouse 1946–49; Sec. Fédération des cheminots C.G.T. (Confédération Générale du Travail) 1949, Sec.-Gen. 1961–65; Sec. C.G.T. 1965–67, Sec.-Gen. 1967–82; Pres. Inst. C.G.T. d'Histoire Sociale 1982–; mem. Exec. Cttee. Fédération syndicale mondiale 1970–83; Officier, Légion d'honneur; Order of the October Revolution 1982. *Publications:* Le mai de la C.G.T. 1972, Lutter (autobiog.) 1975, Le 1er Mai les 100 printemps 1989, la Grève 1993. *Leisure interests:* shooting, fishing. *Address:* 263 rue de Paris, 93516 Montreuil Cedex, France (Office).

SEHGAL, Amar Nath, M.A.; Indian sculptor; b. 5 Feb. 1922, Campbellpur, West Pakistan; s. of Ram Asra Mal and Parmeshwari Devi; m. Shukla Dhawan 1954; two s.; ed. Punjab Univ., Govt. Coll., Lahore, and New York Univ.; one-man exhbns. New York 1950–51, Paris 1952, East Africa and India; Hon. Art Consultant to Ministry of Community Devt., Govt. of India 1955–66; organized sculpture exhbns. in Belgrade 1964, Musée d'Art Moderne, Paris 1965, Pauls-kirche Frankfurt 1965, Haus am Lutzoplatz West Berlin 1966, Musées Royaux D'Art et Histoire, Brussels 1966, Musée Etat Luxembourg 1966, Wiener Secession, Vienna 1966, Flemish Acad. Arts 1967, Tokyo Int. Fair 1973, etc.; retrospective exhbn. Nat. Gallery of Modern Art, New Delhi 1972, City Hall, Ottawa 1975, Aerogolf, Luxembourg 1975, India House, New York 1976, Rathaus, Fransheim, Fed. Repub. of Germany 1977, Frankfurt Airport 1977, Neustadt 1978, Brenners Park, Baden-Baden 1979, Luxembourg 1980; exhbns., Dubai, Abu Dhabi 1980, Jeddah 1981, Chaux de Fond (Switzerland) 1982, Cercle Munster, Luxembourg 1987, Berne 1988, New York 1991, London 1991, New Delhi 1992; participated in Sculpture Biennale, Musée Rodin, Paris 1966 and UNESCO Conf. on role of art in contemporary soc. 1974; org. Int. Children Art Workshop UNESCO, Paris 1979; est. The Creative Fund, charitable org.; Sculpture Award, Lalit Kala Acad. 1957; President's Award, Lalit Kala Acad. 1958 (donated to Prime Minister Nehru during Chinese invasion). *Major works:* Voice of Africa (Ghana) 1959, A Cricketer 1961, Mahatma Gandhi, Amritsar, To Space Unknown (bronze; Moscow) 1963; commissioned to decorate Vigyan Bhawan (India's Int. Conferences Building) with bronze sculptural mural depicting rural life of India; bronze work Conquest of the Moon, White House Collection 1969; Anguished Cries (bronze) monument, W. Berlin 1971; Gandhi monument, Luxembourg 1971; Monument to Aviation, New Delhi Airport, 1972; Rising Spirit, White House Collection 1978; The Crushing Burden, inaugurated 2nd World Population Conf., Mexico 1984; Victims of Torture, designed for U.N.; monument to Freedom Fighters of Namibia, Vienna 1986; Bust of Sam Nujoma (q.v.), Nat. Gallery of Modern Art, New Delhi 1993; Int. Year of Peace sculpture, Head with Horns 1986; Captive, inaugurated at UN Conf. on sanctions against South Africa, Paris 1986; Nari, monument to Women, Int. Women's Day 1986; Flute Player (gift of children of India to UNICEF) 1986; monument to Nehru 1989; exhbn. of gold sculptures Luxembourg 1990; works in Jerusalem, Vienna, Paris, West Berlin, Antwerp, Luxembourg, Connecticut, New Delhi; UN Peace Medal 1985; Fellow Lalit Kala Akad. 1992. *Publications:* Arts and Aesthetics, Organising Exhibitions in Rural Areas, Der Innere Rhythmus (poems) 1975, Folio of Graphics 1981; folios of graphics with poetry in English, French, Arabic 1981–84, Folio on Ganesha 1991, Lonesome Journey, A Collection of Poems 1996, Awaiting a New Dawn 1997. *Leisure interests:* writing poetry, photography. *Address:* J-23 Jangpura Extension, New Delhi 14, India; The Creative Fund, 1 Montée de Clausen, 1343 Luxembourg. *Telephone:* 699206 (India); (352) 47 02 20 (Luxembourg).

SEIDELMAN, Susan, M.F.A.; American film director; b. 11 Dec. 1952, nr. Philadelphia, Pa.; ed. Drexel Univ. and New York Univ. Film School; worked at a UHF TV station in Philadelphia; directing debut with And You Act Like One Too (Student Acad. Award, Acad. of Motion Picture Arts and Sciences); then dir. Deficit (short film funded by American Film Inst.) and Yours Truly, Andrea G. Stern). The Dutch Master. *Films:* Smithereens (dir., producer, co-scriptwriter), Desperately Seeking Susan, Making Mr Right, Cookie, She-Devil, The Dutch Master 1994, The Barefoot Executive 1995. *Address:* c/o William Morris Agency, 151 El Camino Drive, Los Angeles, CA 90048, U.S.A.

SEIDENFADEN, Gunnar, D.PH. & SC.; Danish diplomatist and scientist; b. 24 Feb. 1908, Varde; s. of Aage Seidenfaden and Annalise Teilmann Harck; m. Alix Arnstedt 1939 (died 1993); one s. four d.; ed. Copenhagen Univ.; expeditions to Greenland 1928–34, Thailand 1934–35, Spitsbergen 1938; U.S.A., Canada, Alaska 1947–49, S. America 1950, Far East 1955–57, China and Japan 1958, Thailand 1964–92; Danish Foreign Service 1940–73, Washington 1945–50, Ministry of Foreign Affairs, Copenhagen 1950–55, Amb. S.E. Asia 1955–59, to U.S.S.R. 1959–61; Deputy Under-Sec. of State 1961–67; Chair. Nat. Security Cttee. 1968–70; Amb. for Environment Problems 1970–78; mem. Royal Danish Acad. of Sciences and Letters; Danish and foreign awards. *Publications:* Modern Arctic Exploration 1938, The Orchids of Thailand (with Tem Smitinand) 1959–65; numerous scientific papers on orchids. *Leisure interest:* East-Asiatic orchids. *Address:* Borsholmgård pr. 3100 Hornbak, Denmark. *Telephone:* 49 75 01 06. *Fax:* 49 75 02 48.

SEIDLER, Harry, A.C., O.B.E., M.ARCH.; Australian architect; b. 25 June 1923, Vienna, Austria; s. of Max and Rose Seidler; m. Penelope Evatt 1958; one s. one d.; ed. Wasagymnasium, Vienna, Austria, Cambridge Tech. School, U.K., Univ. of Manitoba, Canada, Harvard Univ. and Black Mountain Coll., U.S.A.; postgraduate work under Walter Gropius, Harvard Univ. 1946; study with painter Josef Albers, Black Mountain Coll. 1946; Chief Asst. with Marcel Breuer, New York 1946–48; Prin. Architect, Harry Seidler and Assocs., Sydney, Australia 1948–; Thomas Jefferson Prof. of Architecture, Univ. of Va. 1978; Visiting Prof. Harvard Univ. 1976–77, Univ. of N.S.W. 1980; Visiting Prof., Univ. of Sydney 1984, Univ. of Tech., Sydney 1993–96, ETH, Zürich 1993; mem. Acad. d'Architecture, Paris 1982, Int Acad. of Architects, Sofia 1987; Hon. F.A.I.A. 1966; Life Fellow, Royal Australian Inst. of Architects 1970; Fellow Australia Acad. of Tech. Sciences 1979; Hon. LL.D. (Manitoba) 1988, (Univ. of Tech., Sydney) 1991; Wilkinson Award 1965, 1966, 1967; Sir John Sulman Medal 1951, 1967, 1981, 1983, 1991, Civic Design Award 1967, 1981, 1992, Pan Pacific Citation of the A.I.A. 1968, numerous R.A.I.A. awards including Gold Medal 1976, Gold Medal, City of Vienna 1990, Royal Gold Medal, R.I.B.A. 1996; Cross of Honour (1st Class) for Art and Science, Austria. *Major works:* Rose Seidler House 1949–51 (made a Historic Houses Trust museum 1988), flats and housing units in Australia, urban redevelopment projects for McMahons Point 1957, city centre redevelopment "Australia Square", Sydney 1962–66, Commonwealth Trade Office Complex, Canberra 1970–72, High Rise Apartments, Acapulco 1970, M.L.C. Center, Martin Place, Sydney 1972–75, Australian Embassy, Paris 1974–76, Hong Kong Club and Offices 1980–84, Grosvenor Place, Sydney 1982–88, Riverside Centre, Brisbane 1984–86, Capita Tower, Sydney 1984–89, Hilton Hotel, Brisbane 1984–86, Shell House, Melbourne 1985–89, Waverley Art Gallery, Melbourne 1988, QVI Tower, Perth 1987–91, Wohnpark Neue Donau (housing devt., Vienna) 1993–(98). *Publications:* Houses, Interiors and Projects 1949–1954, Harry Seidler 1955–63, Architecture in the New World 1974, Australian Embassy, Paris 1979, Two Towers, Sydney 1980, Interment: The Diaries of Harry Seidler 1940–41 1986, Riverside Centre 1988, Harry Seidler: Four Decades of Architecture 1992, Harry Seidler—The Master Architect Series III 1997. *Leisure interests:* photography, architecture, skiing. *Address:* 2 Glen Street, Milsons Point, N.S.W. 2061, Australia. *Telephone:* (02) 9922 1388 (Office); (02) 9498 5986 (Home). *Fax:* (02) 9957 2947.

SEIDMAN, L(ewis) William, LL.B., M.B.A.; American government official; b. 29 April 1921, Grand Rapids, Mich.; s. of Frank Seidman and Esther Lubetsky; m. Sarah Berry 1944; one s. five d.; ed. Dartmouth Coll., Harvard Univ. and Univ. of Mich.; army service 1942–46; mem. Mich. Bar 1949, D.C. Bar 1977; Special Asst. for Financial Affairs to Gov. of Mich. 1963–66; Nat. Man. Partner, Seidman & Seidman (certified public accountants) New York 1969–74; Asst. for Econ. Affairs to Pres. Gerald Ford 1974–77; Dir. Phelps Dodge Corpn. New York 1977–82, Vice-Chair. 1980–82; Dean, Coll. of Business Admin. Ariz. State Univ. 1982–85; Chair. Fed. Deposit Insurance Corpn. (FDIC) 1985–91; Chair. Detroit Fed. Reserve Bank, Chicago 1970; Co-Chair. White House Conf. on Productivity 1983–84; Chair. Resolution Trust Corpn. 1989–91; Chief Commentator CNBC-TV 1991–; Publr. Bank Director (magazine); Bronze Star Medal. *Address:* CNBC, 1825 K Street, NW, Washington, DC 20007 (Office); 1694 31st Street, N.W., Washington, DC 20007, U.S.A. (Home).

SEIFART, Angel Roberto; Paraguayan politician and lawyer; b. 12 Sept. 1941, Asunción; ed. Nat. Univ. of Asunción; fiscal agent in commercial and civil law 1966–67; Judge of the First Instance 1968–74; mem. Court of Appeal (First Chamber) 1974–77; Pres. Judicial Magistrates Asscn. 1974–75; Nat. Rep. Asociación Nacional Republicana (Partido Colorado) 1978–93, interim mem. Governing Bd. 1981–87, titular mem. 1989–; Minister of State, Educ. and Culture 1990–91; Vice-Pres. of Paraguay 1993–98; mem. Man. Comm. of Rural Asscn. of Paraguay 1983–89. *Address:* Office of the Vice-President, Gral. Díaz, Calle Alberdi, Asunción, Paraguay.

SEIFERT, Robin (Richard), J.P., F.R.I.B.A., F.R.S.A., DIP.ARCH.; British architect; b. 25 Nov. 1910, Switzerland; s. of William Seifert; m. Josephine Jeannette Harding 1939; two s. one d.; ed. Cen. Foundation School, London and Univ. Coll., London; commenced architectural practice 1934; Prin., R. Seifert and Partners, Architects 1934–; Corps of Royal Engineers 1940–44; Indian Army 1944–46; Hon. Lt.-Col. 1946; pvt. practice 1948–; fmr. mem. British Waterways Bd. 1971–74, Home Office Cttee. of Man. for Homeless Discharged Prisoners; fmr. mem. Council R.I.B.A. 1971–74; R.I.B.A. Architectural Exhbn. (depicting 50 years of practice) Heinz Gallery 1984; Fellow, Univ. Coll. London 1971; Liveryman, City of London. *Principal works include:* Centre Point, St. Giles Circus; Drapers Gardens; Nat. Provincial Bank H.Q.; Royal Garden Hotel, Kensington; Tolworth Towers, Surbiton; Woolworth House, Marylebone Rd.; I.C.T.H.Q., Putney; Kellogg House, Baker Street, The Times Newspaper Bldg., Printing House Square, Guinness Mahon Bank, Gracechurch Street, Dunlop House, King Street, St. James's, B.S.C. Research Labs., Middlesbrough, Britannia Hotel, Park Tower Hotel, London, Heathrow Hotel, Sobell Sports Centre, A.T.V. Centre Birmingham, Int. Press Centre, Metropolitan Police H.Q., Putney, Wembley Conference Centre, Princess Grace Hospital, Marylebone Road, BR Offices, Euston Station. *Leisure interests:* chess, violin. *Address:* Eleventrees, Milespit Hill, Mill Hill, London, NW7 2RS, England (Home). *Telephone:* 0181-959 3397 (Home).

SEIGNORET, Sir Clarence (Henry Augustus), G.C.B., O.B.E.; Dominican fmr. Head of State; b. 25 Feb. 1919, Roseau; s. of Clarence A. Seignoret and Violet Seignoret, née Riviere; m. Judith Laronde 1950; two s.; ed. Convent High School and Dominica Grammar School, Roseau and Balliol Coll., Oxford; Perm. Sec. 1956–67; Sec. to the Cabinet 1967–77; apptd. Admin.'s Deputy, Gov.'s Deputy and Acting Pres. on six occasions 1966–83; apptd. Acting Pres. on two occasions 1981–83; Exec. Sec. Dominica Asscn. of Industry and Commerce 1980–83; Pres. of Dominica 1983–93; Patron of numerous orgs.; The Collar of the Order of the Liberator Simón Bolívar (Venezuela) 1987, Medal of Honour (Dominica) 1993. *Leisure interests:* agriculture, horticulture. *Address:* 24 Cork Street, Roseau, Commonwealth of Dominica, West Indies. *Telephone:* 4482108.

SEILLIÈRE de LABORDE, Ernest-Antoine; French business executive and civil servant; b. 20 Dec. 1937, Neuilly-sur-Seine; s. of Jean Seillière de

Laborde and Renée de Wendel; m. Antoinette Barbey 1971; two s. three d.; ed. Ladycross Coll., Lycée Janson-de-Sailly, Faculty of Law, Paris, Nat. School of Admin.; attaché High Comm. of Algeria 1962; with Ministry of Information 1963, Sec. for Foreign Affairs 1966, mem. French del. at negotiations for EEC, Brussels and Gen. Agreement on Tariffs and Trade, Geneva 1966–69, adviser on foreign affairs 1969, attached to the Prime Minister 1969–72, tech. adviser to Minister for Foreign Affairs 1972–73, Minister of Armed Forces 1973–74; with Centre for Int. Affairs Harvard Univ. 1975, Jt. Dir.-Gen. of Industrial Politics 1976; joined Wendel Group 1978, Gen. Dir., Admin. CGIP 1978–87, Pres., Dir.-Gen. 1987–, fmrly. Vice-Pres. Marine-Wendel, Pres. 1992–; Vice-Pres. Carnaud SA (later CMB Packaging) 1984–91; Pres. surveillance cttee. CarnaudMetalbox 1991–, Regnault Reynolds SA; Vice-Pres. Fed. of Mechanical Industries 1985; fmrly. Vice-Pres. Nat. Council of French Employers (CNPF), Pres. 1997–; Chevalier Légion d'honneur, Officier Ordre nat. du Mérite. *Address:* Compagnie générale d'industrie et de participations, 89 rue Taitbout, 75009 Paris, France.

SEIN WIN, U; Myanmar politician; s. of U Ba Lwin; cousin of Aung San Suu Kyi (q.v.); leader New Democracy Party, banned by ruling State Law and Order Restoration Council (SLORC); Pres. of outlawed Nat. Coalition Govt. of Union of Burma 1990.

SEINFELD, Jerry; American comedian; b. 29 April 1955, Brooklyn; s. of Kal Seinfeld and Betty Seinfeld; ed. Queens Coll., N.Y.; fmrly. salesman; stand-up comedian 1976–; joke-writer Benson (TV series) 1980; actor Seinfeld (TV series) 1989–, also co-writer, producer; Emmy Award Outstanding Comedy Series (for Seinfeld) 1993; two American Comedy Awards. *Publication:* Sein Language 1993. *Address:* c/o Lori Jonas Public Relations, 417 South Beverly Drive, Suite 201, Beverly Hills, CA 90212, U.S.A.

SEIP, Anne-Lise, D.PHIL.; Norwegian professor of modern history; b. 6 Nov. 1933; d. of Edvin Thomassen and Birgit Thomassen; m. Jens Arup Seip 1960; one s. one d.; ed. Univ. of Oslo; Sr. Lecturer Inst. of Criminology and Penal Law, Univ. of Oslo 1974–75, Dept. of History 1975–85, Prof. of Modern History Aug. 1985–; mem. Norwegian Acad. of Science. *Publications include:* Eilert Sundt. 1983, Sosialhjelpstaten blir til 1984, Veier til velferdsstaten 1994; numerous articles. *Leisure interests:* books, music, gardening. *Address:* Department of History, University of Oslo, P.O. Box 1072, Blindern, 0316 Oslo, Norway.

SEIPP, Walter, DR.JUR.; German banker and business executive; b. 13 Dec. 1925, Langen; m. 1954; two s.; ed. Univ. of Frankfurt am Main; Jr. Barrister 1950–53; with Deutsche Bank AG 1951–74 (Exec. Vice-Pres. 1970–74); mem. Man. Bd., Westdeutsche Landesbank Girozentrale 1974–77, Vice-Chair. 1978–81; Chair. Man. Bd., Commerzbank AG 1981–91, now Chair. Supervisory Bd.; Chair. Supervisory Bd., Berliner Commerzbank AG, Rheinische Hypothekenbank AG, Frankfurt, Essen; Chair. Admin. Bd., Commerzbank Int. S.A., Luxembourg, Commerzbank (Schweiz) AG, Zürich; Chair. Supervisory Bd. Commerz Int. Capital Man. GmbH, Frankfurt; Chair. Bd. of Dirs., Commerzbank Capital Markets Corpn., N.Y., Commerz-Securities (Japan) Co. Ltd., Commerzbank, S.E. Asia Ltd., Singapore; mem. Bd. of Dirs., Int. Monetary Conf., Wash. (Pres. 1987–88), mem. Supervisory Bd., Bayer AG, Leverkusen, Daimler Benz AG, Stuttgart, Deutsche Shell AG, Hamburg, Vereinigte Industrie-Unternehmungen AG, Bonn, Linde AG Wiesbaden, Allianz Versicherungs AG, Munich, Hochtief AG, Essen, MAN AG, Munich, Thyssen AG, Duisburg; mem. Bd. of Man. Dirs. Bundesverband deutscher Banken e.V., Cologne; mem. advisory cttee. of three cos.

SEITE, Berndt; German politician and veterinary surgeon; b. 22 April 1940, Hahnswalde, Silesia; m. Annemarie Seite 1964; two c.; ed. Humboldt Univ. Berlin; mem. Synod of Lutheran Church in Mecklenburg and mem. Protestant WCC 1975; initiated autumn anti-govt. demonstrations in fmr. G.D.R. (with Gottfried Timm) 1989; co-founder, New Forum 1989; joined Christian Democratic Union (CDU) 1990; Chair. Röbel Dist. Council 1990; Gen. Sec. CDU Asscn. in Mecklenburg-Western Pomerania 1991–92; Minister-Pres. of Mecklenburg-Western Pomerania 1992–; mem. Landtag of Mecklenburg-Western Pomerania 1994–. *Address:* Staatskanzlei, Schlossstrasse 2-4, 19053 Schwerin, Germany. *Telephone:* (0385) 5880.

SEITERS, Rudolf; German politician; b. 13 Oct. 1937, Osnabrück; s. of Adolf Seiters and Josefine Gördel; m. Brigitte Kolata; three c.; qualified as lawyer; joined Junge Union and Christian Democratic Party (CDU) 1958, Regional Chair. Junge Union, Osnabrück-Emsland 1963–65, Chair. CDU Land Asscn. Hanover 1965–68, mem. Junge Union Fed. Exec. Cttee. 1967–71, Sr. Chair. CDU Land Asscn. Lower Saxony 1968–70; Head Econ. and Housing Dept., Office of Regierungspräsident (Regional Gov.), Osnabrück 1967–69; mem. Deutscher Bundestag 1969–; mem. CDU Fed. Exec. Cttee. 1971–73; Parl. Party Man. CDU/CSU Parl. Party in Bundestag 1971–76, Sr. Parl. Man. 1984–89; Parl. Party Man. 1982–84; Fed. Minister for Special Tasks and Head of Fed. Chancellery 1989–91, of the Interior 1991–93; Chair. CDU/Christian Social Union in Bundestag 1994–; Grosses Bundesverdienstkreuz. *Address:* Spiekerooger Strasse 6, 26871 Papenburg, Germany.

SEITZ, Frederick, A.B., PH.D.; American physicist; b. 4 July 1911, San Francisco; s. of Frederick and Emily Seitz; m. Elizabeth K. Marshall 1935 (died 1992); ed. Stanford and Princeton Univs.; Instructor of Physics, Univ. of Rochester 1935–36, Asst. Prof. 1936–37; on staff of Research Laboratory of Gen. Electric Co. 1937–39; Asst. Prof., Univ. of Pa. 1939–41; Assoc. Prof. 1941–42, Prof. and Head of Dept. of Physics, Carnegie Inst. of Tech. 1942–49; Prof. Physics Univ. of Ill. 1949–57, Head of Dept. 1957–64, Dean Graduate Coll. and Vice-Pres. of Research 1964–65; NATO Science Adviser 1959–60; Pres. Rockefeller Univ. 1968–78, Pres. Emer. 1978–; mem. American Philosophical Soc., N.A.S. (full-time Pres. 1962–69), American Physics Soc. 1961, American Acad. of Arts and Sciences, American Inst. of Physics; mem. numerous advisory cttees., incl. Advisory Group on Anticipated Advances in Science and Tech. (White House) 1970–76, Nat. Aeronautics and Space Admin. (SPAC) 1973– (Chair. 1976–77), Nat. Cancer Advisory Bd. 1976–82; Chair. of Bd., John Simon Guggenheim Foundation 1976–83; Dir. Texas Instruments 1971–82, Akzona Corpn. 1973–82, Ogden Corpn. 1977–; mem. Bd. of Trustees, Rockefeller Univ., Univ. Corpn. for Atmospheric Research (UCAR) 1975–82, American Museum of Natural History 1975–; Nat. Medal of Science 1973, Joseph Henry Medal, Smithsonian Inst. 1997; Vannevar Bush Award 1983; numerous hon. degrees. *Publications:* The Modern Theory of Solids 1940, The Physics of Metals 1943, Solid State Physics 1955, The Science Matrix 1992, On the Frontier: My Life in Science 1994, Stalin's Captive: Nikolaus Riehl and the Soviet Race for the Bomb 1995. *Address:* Rockefeller University, 1230 York Avenue, New York, NY 10021, U.S.A. *Telephone:* (212) 327-8423.

SEITZ, Konrad, M.A., DR.PHIL.; German diplomatist; b. 18 Jan. 1934, Munich; m. Eva Kautz 1965; Prof. of Classics, Univs. of Marburg and Munich 1956–64; entered Foreign Office 1965; served New Delhi 1968–72, UN Mission, New York 1972–75; main speech writer for Minister of Foreign Affairs 1975; Head, Policy Planning Staff, Foreign Office 1980–87; Amb. to India 1987–90; Co-Chair. Comm. Economy 2000, Baden-Württemberg 1992–93; Amb. to Italy 1992–95, to China 1995–; Chair. Zukunftskommission 2000, Baden-Württemberg; Grosses Bundesverdienstkreuz. *Publications:* The Japanese-American Challenge: Germany's Hi-tech Industries Fight for Survival 1990, The Aimless Elites—Are the Germans Losing the Future? (with others), Europa—una Colonia Tecnológica? 1995, America and Japan: the Battle for Technological Supremacy 1998; contribs. to foreign and econ. journals and newspapers. *Leisure interests:* history of ideas, literature, art. *Address:* German Embassy, 5 Dong Zhi Men Wai Dajie, Beijing 100600, People's Republic of China. *Telephone:* 6532 2161. *Fax:* 6532 4932.

SEITZ, Raymond G. H.; American diplomatist and business executive; b. 8 Dec. 1940, Hawaii; m. Caroline Gordon Richardson; two s. one d.; ed. Yale Univ.; joined Foreign Service 1966; served Montreal, Political Officer, Nairobi, Vice-Consul, Seychelles 1966–70; Prin. Officer, Bukavu, Zaire 1970–72; Secretariat Staff Washington 1972 then Dir. of Staff; Special Asst. to Dir.-Gen. Foreign Service 1974; Political Officer, London 1975–79; Deputy Exec. Sec., Dept. of State 1979–81, Sr. Deputy Asst. Sec. for Public Affairs 1981–82, Exec. Asst. to Sec. Shultz 1982–84; Minister, U.S. Embassy London 1984–89; Asst. Sec. of State for European and Canadian Affairs 1989–91; Amb. to U.K. 1991–94; Vice-Chair. Lehman Bros. (Europe) 1995–; Dir. The Telegraph 1994–, GEC 1994–, Cable and Wireless 1995–, B.A. 1995–, Rio Tinto 1996–, Hong Kong Telecom 1997–; Trustee Nat. Gallery, London, Royal Acad., London; Hon. D. Univ. (Herriot-Watt) 1994; Dr. h.c. (Open Univ.) 1997. *Address:* Lehman Brothers International, (Europe), 1 Broadgate, London, EC2M 7HA, England.

SEKIYA, Katsutsugu; Japanese politician; ed. Chuo Univ., Univ. of British Columbia, Canada; joined Japan Airlines 1963; sec. to a mem. of House of Reps. 1966; mem. LDP; mem. for Ehime, House of Reps. 1976; fmr. Minister of Posts and Telecommunications, Chair. House of Reps. Transport Cttee.; Minister of Construction 1998–. *Address:* Ministry of Construction, 2-1-3, Kasumigaseki, Chiyoda-ku, Tokyo 100, Japan. *Telephone:* (03) 3580-4311. *Fax:* (03) 5251-1922.

SEKIZAWA, Tadashi, B.ENG.; Japanese businessman; b. 6 Nov. 1931, Tokyo; m. Misako Sekizawa; two s.; joined Fujitsu Ltd. 1954, Gen. Man. Switching Systems Group 1982–84, Bd. Dir. 1984–, Man. Dir. 1986–88, Exec. Dir. 1988–90, Pres. and Rep. Dir. 1990–; Vice-Chair. Communication Industry Asscn. of Japan 1990–98, Chair. 1998–, Japan Electronic Industry Devt. Asscn. 1990–. *Leisure interests:* literature, travel, motoring. *Address:* Fujitsu Ltd., 1-6-1 Marunouchi 1-chome, Chiyoda-ku, Tokyo 100, Japan. *Telephone:* (813) 3216 3211.

SELA, Michael, PH.D.; Israeli immunologist and chemist; b. 6 March 1924, Tomaszow, Poland; s. of Jakob and Roza Salomonowicz; m. 1st Margalit Liebman 1948 (died 1975); two d.; m. 2nd Sara Kika 1976; one d.; ed. Hebrew Univ., Jerusalem and Geneva Univ.; joined Weizmann Inst. of Science 1950, Head Dept. of Chemical Immunology 1963–75, Vice-Pres. 1970–71, Dean Faculty of Biology 1970–73, mem. Bd. of Govs. 1970–, Pres. 1975–85, Deputy Chair. 1985–; W. Garfield Weston Prof. of Immunology 1966; Visiting Scientist, N.I.H., Bethesda 1956–57, 1960–61; Visiting Prof. Molecular Biology, Univ. of Calif., Berkeley 1967–68; Visiting Prof., Dept. of Medicine, Tufts Univ. School of Medicine, Boston 1986–87; Inst. Prof. 1985; Fogarty Scholar-in-Residence, Fogarty Int. Center, Bethesda, Md. 1973–74; mem. WHO Expert Advisory Panel of Immunology 1962–; Chair. Council, European Molecular Biology Org. 1975–79; Pres. Int. Union Immunological Socs. 1977–80; Chair. Scientific Advisory Cttee. European Molecular Biology Lab. Heidelberg 1978–81; WHO Advisory Cttee. on Medical Research 1979–82, WHO Special Programme for Research and Training in Tropical Diseases 1979–81; mem. Council Paul Ehrlich Foundation (Frankfurt) 1980–97; mem.

Advisory Bd. UCLAF, France 1980–92; Founding mem. Bd. Dir. Int. Foundation for Survival and Devt. of Humanity, Moscow and Washington 1988–92; Nat. mem. Gen. Cttee. Int. Council of Scientific Unions 1984–93; mem. Scientific Advisory Group of Experts, Programme for Vaccine Devt., WHO 1987–92; mem. Int. Guidance Panel, Israel Arts and Science Acad. 1987–; Vice-Pres. Asscn. Franco-Israélienne pour Recherche Scientifique et Technologique 1992–98; mem. Exec. Bd. Int. Council of Human Duties, Trieste 1995–; mem. other int. bodies; serves on many editorial bds., including Exec. Advisory Bd. of Dictionary for Science and Tech. 1989–, European Journal of Immunology, Cambridge Encyclopedia of the Life Sciences, Handbook of Biochemistry and Molecular Biology, Experimental and Clinical Immunogenetics, Receptor Biology Reviews, The FASEB Journal, Encyclopedia of Human Biology, Encyclopedia of the Life Sciences, Vaccine; mem. Israel Acad. of Sciences and Humanities 1971, Pontifical Acad. of Sciences 1975, Deutsche Akad. der Naturforscher Leopoldina 1989; Hon. mem. American Soc. Biological Chemists 1968, American Asscn. of Immunologists 1973, Scandinavian Soc. for Immunology 1971, Harvey Soc. 1972, French Soc. for Immunology 1979, Chilean Soc. for Immunology 1981, Romanian Acad. 1991, Romanian Acad. of Medical Sciences 1991, Romanian Soc. for Immunology; Foreign mem. Max-Planck Soc., Freiburg 1967, Russian Acad. of Sciences 1994, French Acad. of Sciences 1995; Foreign Assoc. N.A.S. 1976, Italian Acad. of Sciences 1995, American Philosophical Soc. 1995; Foreign Hon. mem. American Acad. Arts and Sciences 1971; Fellow A.A.A.S. 1989; Dr. h.c. (Bordeaux II) 1985, (Nat. Autonomous Univ. of Mexico) 1985, (Tufts Univ.) 1989, Colby Coll. 1989, (Univ. Louis Pasteur) 1990, (Hebrew Univ. of Jerusalem) 1995; awarded N.I.H. Lectureship 1973; Israel Prize Natural Sciences 1959, Rothschild Prize for Chem. 1968, Otto Warburg Medal, German Soc. of Biological Chem. 1968, Emil von Behring Prize, Phillipps Univ. 1973, Gairdner Int. Award, Toronto 1980, Prize, Inst. de la Vie Fondation Electricité de France, Lille 1984, Prix Jaubert, Faculty of Science, Univ. of Geneva 1986, Interbrew-Baillet Latour Health Prize 1997, Karl Landsteiner Medal, Toronto 1986, Albert Einstein Gold Medal 1995, Harnak Medal, Max-Planck-Soc. 1996, Wolf Prize in Medicine 1998; Commdr.'s Cross of Order of Merit Award, Fed. Repub. of Germany 1986; Officier, Légion d'honneur, 1987; Caballero, Order of San Carlos (Colombia) 1997. *Publications:* over 700 in immunology, biochemistry and molecular biology; Ed. The Antigens (7 vols. published). *Address:* Weizmann Institute of Science, Rehovot, 76100 Israel. *Telephone:* (8) 9466969. *Fax:* (8) 9469713.

SELANGOR, H.R.H. the Sultan of; Sultan Salahuddin Abdul Aziz Shah ibni Al-Marhum Sultan Hisamuddin Alam Shah Haji, D.K., D.M.N., S.P.M.S., S.P.D.K., D.P.; Malaysian ruler; b. 8 March 1926; ed. Sekolah Melayu Pengkalan Batu, Kelang, Malay Coll., Kuala Kangsar, London Univ.; Tengku Laksamana Selangor 1946; Regent of Selangor during father's absence 1960; succeeded his late father as Ruler of Selangor Sept. 1960; installed as eleventh Yang-di Pertuan Agong (Supreme Head of State) 26 April 1999; Maj. Royal Malay Regt.; Hon. Group Capt. Royal Malaysia Air Force; Chancellor Univ. of Agric., Malaysia. *Address:* Shah Alam, Selangor, Malaysia.

SELBORNE, 4th Earl cr. 1882; **John Roundell Palmer,** K.B.E., F.R.S.; British farmer; b. 24 March 1940; s. of late Viscount Wolmer; m. Joanna van Antwerp James 1969; three s. one d.; ed. Eton Coll., Christ Church Oxford; Man. Dir. Blackmoor Estate Ltd. 1962–; Chair. Hops Marketing Bd. 1978–82, Agricultural and Food Research Council 1983–89; Pres. Royal Agricultural Soc. of England 1987–88; Chair. Jt. Nature Conservation Cttee. 1991–97; Chair. House of Lords Select Cttee. on Science and Tech. 1993–97; mem. Govt. Panel on Sustainable Devt. 1994–97; Chair. AMC 1994–; Dir. Lloyds TSB Group 1995–; Chancellor Univ. of Southampton 1996–; Pres. Royal Geographical Soc. (with Inst. of British Geographers) 1997–; Hon. LL.D. (Bristol) 1988; Hon. D.Sc. (Cranfield) 1991; Massey-Ferguson Nat. Award for Services to U.K. Agric. 1990. *Address:* Temple Manor, Selborne, Alton, Hants, GU34 3LR, England.

SELBY, Philip; British composer; b. 6 Feb. 1948; s. of George Selby and Sarah (née Knott) Selby; m. Rosanna Burrai 1974; one s.; ed. Manor Park Grammar School, Nuneaton, Royal Manchester Coll. of Music; composition studies with G. Petrassi and Karlheinz Stockhausen; appeared as guitar soloist, Birmingham Town Hall 1966, Royal Albert Hall, London 1970, All-India Radio and TV, Pakistani TV, Youth Palace, Teheran, Istanbul Univ.; début as composer with first performance of From the Fountain of Youth (for guitar and chamber orch.), Leamington 1975; mem. Composers' Guild of G.B., Performing Rights Soc.; Chevalier Ordre Souverain et Militaire de la Milice du Saint Sépulcre 1988. *Compositions include:* Suite for guitar 1965–67, Symphonic Dance for orchestra 1973, Fantasia for guitar 1974, Rhapsody for piano and orchestra 1975, A Nature Meditation for violin and small orch., Guitar Concerto 1976–77, Sonatina for piano 1978, Spirit of the Earth for flute 1978, Branch Touches Branch, pastorale 1979, Isa Upanishad (cantata sacra for double chorus and orch.) 1979–87, Sonata for timpani 1980, Siddhartha (dance symphony) 1981–84, Logos for trumpet 1982, Ring Out Ye Bells (carol) 1988, Symphony of Sacred Images (for soprano and bass soli, double chorus and orchestra) 1992, Anthem for Gibraltar (unison voices and organ) 1994, Beatus Vir (motet) 1995, String Quartet No. 1 (Non Potho Reposare, Amore Coro) 1996–97, Autoritratto Vittorio Alfieri (for soprano, violin and guitar) 1998; various songs. *Leisure interests:* reading, travel. *Address:* Hill Cottage, Via 1 Maggio 93, 00068 Rignano Flaminio, Rome, Italy. *Telephone:* (0761) 507945.

SELECMAN, Charles E.; American business executive; b. 17 Sept. 1928, Dallas, Tex.; s. of Frank A. and Eloise (née Olive) Selecman; m. 1st Nan Harton Nash 1951 (divorced 1975); three d.; m. 2nd Judith Wallace Pollard 1976 (divorced 1984); m. 3rd Barbara Ann Calvert 1985; ed. Southern Methodist Univ.; fmrly. employed by Gen. Motors Corpn. and Chance Vought Aircraft; Divisional Personnel Man., Axelson Div., U.S. Industries Inc. 1956, Exec. Vice-Pres., Axelson Div. 1966; Vice-Pres. U.S. Industries Inc. 1967, Exec. Vice-Pres. and Dir. 1968, Pres. 1970–73, Vice-Chair. and Chief Exec. 1973–74; owner Charles E. Selecman and Assocs. 1974–75; Pres., C.E.O. E. T. Barwick Industries Inc. 1975–78, Marshalsea Industries Inc. 1980–83, Spinks Industries Inc. 1980; partner Marshalsea Texas Partners, Dallas 1978–86; Chair., Pres., C.E.O. Input Output Inc., Houston 1984–93, Chair. 1993–. *Address:* Input/Output Inc., 12300 Parc Crest Drive, Stafford, TX 77477, U.S.A.

SELEŠ, Monica; American tennis player; b. 2 Dec. 1973, Novi Sad, Yugoslavia; d. of the late Karol Seleš and of Esther Seleš; moved to U.S.A. 1986; became U.S. citizen March 1994; semi-finalist, French Open 1989, won French Open 1990, 1991, 1992, Virginia Slims Championships 1990, 1991, 1992, Australian Open 1991, U.S. Open 1991, 1992, Australian Open 1991, 1992, 1993, 1996, Canadian Open 1995, 1996; winner L.A. Open 1997, Canadian Open 1997, Tokyo Open 1997; quarter-finalist, Wimbledon Championships 1990; named youngest No. 1 ranked player in tennis history for women and men, at 17 years 3 months 9 days. *Publication:* Monica: From Fear to Victory 1996. *Address:* c/o International Management Group, 1 Erieview Plaza, Cleveland, OH 44114; Sarasota, FL, U.S.A.

SELEZNEV, Gennadiy Nikolaevich; Russian politician; b. 6 Nov. 1947, Serov, Sverdlovsk Region; m. Irina Borisovna 1978; one d.; ed. Leningrad Univ. (by correspondence); mem. CPSU 1970–91, CP of Russian Fed. 1992–; work in komsomol 1968–74; Ed.-in-Chief Smena 1974–80, Komsomolskaya pravda 1980–88, Uchitelskaya gazeta (newspaper for teachers) 1988–91; First Deputy Ed., Ed.-in-Chief, Pravda 1991–93, dismissed 1993; Ed.-in-Chief Pravda Rossii 1995–96; mem. State Duma (Parl.) 1993–, Deputy Chair. 1995–96, Chair. 1996–; Chair. Parl. Union of Russia and Belarus 1997. *Address:* State Duma, Okhotny Ryad 1, Moscow, Russia. *Telephone:* 292-66-41; 292-33-49.

SELF, Colin Ernest, D.F.A.; British artist; b. 17 July 1941, Rackheath; s. of Ernest Walter Self and Kathleen Augustine (née Bellamy) Self; m. 1st Margaret Ann Murrell 1963; m. 2nd Jessica Prendergast 1978; one s. two d.; ed. Norwich Art School, Slade School of Fine Art, London Univ.; various one-man and group exhbns.; Drawing Prize Biennale de Paris 1967, Giles Bequest Prize Bradford Biennale 1969, Tolly Cobbold Prize 1979. *Leisure interests:* nature study: in a constant perennial dreamy but acute way, unacademically, all music. *Address:* 31 St. Andrews Avenue, Thorpe, Norwich, Norfolk, NR7 0RG, England.

SELF, Will, M.A.; British author and cartoonist; b. 26 Sept. 1961; s. of Peter John Otter Self and Elaine Rosenbloom; m. 1st Katharine Sylvia Anthony Chancellor 1989 (divorced 1996); one s. one d.; m. 2nd Deborah Jane Orr 1997; one s.; ed. Christ's Coll., Exeter Coll., Oxford; cartoon illustrations appeared in New Statesman and City Limits; columnist The Observer 1995–97, The Times 1997–. *Publications:* short stories: Quantity Theory of Insanity 1991, Grey Area 1994, Tough Tough Toys for Tough Tough Boys 1998; novellas: Cock and Bull 1992, The Sweet Smell of Psychosis 1996; novels: My Idea of Fun 1993, Great Apes 1997; Junk Mail (selected journalism) 1995; collected cartoons 1985. *Address:* c/o David Godwin, 14A Goodwins Court, London, W.C.2, England. *Telephone:* 0171-240 9992.

SELINGER, Benjamin Klaas, DR.RER.NAT., D.SC., F.T.S., F.T.S.E., F.R.A.C.I.; Australian professor of chemistry and management consultant; b. 23 Jan. 1939, Sydney; s. of Herbert Selinger and Hilde Wittner; m. Veronica Hollander 1967; two s.; ed. Sydney Boys High School, Univ. of Sydney, Tech. Univ. Stuttgart and Australian Nat. Univ. (ANU); Lecturer in Physical Chem. ANU 1966–71, Sr. Lecturer 1971–78, Head, Dept. of Chem. 1988–91, Prof. of Chemistry 1992–, Prof. Emer.; Chair. Bd. of Nat. Registration Authority for Agric. and Veterinary Chemicals 1993–97; mem. numerous govt. bodies, advisory cttees., etc.; various academic posts overseas; Deputy Chair ANZAAS 1994–; Fellow, Royal Australian Chem. Inst., Royal Inst. of G.B., Australian Acad. of Tech. Sciences and Engs., Australian Acad. of Forensic Sciences; Archibald Olle Prize 1979; Special Eureka Prize for Science Communication (ABC/Australian Museum) 1991; Alexander von Humboldt Fellow; ANZAAS Medallist 1993; many other awards and distinctions. *Publications:* Chemistry in the Market Place 1975–98 (5th edn.), Thinking with Fourier 1992, Expert Evidence 1992. *Leisure interests:* bushwalking, science museums, forensic chemistry. *Address:* Department of Chemistry, Australian National University, Canberra, A.C.T. 0200 (Office); 56 Brereton Street, Garran, Canberra, A.C.T. 2605, Australia (Home). *Telephone:* 06 249 2929 (Office). *Fax:* 06 249 0602 (Office); 06 285 2832 (Home).

SELLA, George John, Jr., B.S., M.B.A.; American business executive; b. 29 Sept. 1928, West New York, N.J.; s. of George John Sella and Angelina Dominoni; m. Janet May Auf-der Heide 1955; two s. three d.; ed. Princeton and Harvard Univs.; joined American Cyanamid Co. 1954, Pres. Europe/Mideast/Africa Div. 1976–77, Corp. Vice-Pres. 1977, Vice-Chair. 1978, Pres. 1979–90, C.E.O. 1983–, Chair. 1984–; mem. NAM, Soc. of Chem. Industry, Pharmaceutical Manufacturers Asscn. *Address:* American Cyanamid Co., One Cyanamid Plaza, Wayne, NJ 07470, U.S.A. *Telephone:* (201) 831-2000.

SELLARS, Peter, B.A.; American theatre and opera director; b. 27 Sept. 1957; ed. Harvard Univ.; Dir. Boston Shakespeare Co. 1983–84; Dir. and Man. American Nat. Theater at J. F. Kennedy Center, Washington 1984–; Fellow MacArthur Foundation, Chicago 1983. *Productions include:* Nixon in China, The Mikado, Orlando, The Marriage of Figaro, Don Giovanni, Così fan tutte, Die Zauberflöte, Ajax, Zangezi, Merchant of Venice (London), The Rake's Progress 1996. *Address:* American National Theater, Kennedy Center, Washington, DC 20566, U.S.A.

SELLECK, Tom; American actor; b. 29 Jan. 1945, Detroit, Mich.; ed. Univ. of Southern Calif.; m. 1st Jackie Ray (divorced 1982); one step-s.; m. 2nd Julie Mack 1987; one d.; *Films include:* Myra Breckenridge, Midway, Coma, Seven Minutes, High Road to China, Runaway, Lassiter, Three Men and a Baby, Her Alibi 1988, Quigley Down Under, An Innocent Man 1989, Three Men and a Little Lady 1991, Folks 1991, Mr. Baseball 1991, Christopher Columbus: The Discovery 1992, Folks! 1992, Mr Baseball, In & Out. *Television includes:* Returning Home, Bracken's World, The Young and the Restless, The Rockford Files, The Sacketts, played Thomas Magnum in Magnum P.I., Divorce Wars, Countdown at the Super Bowl, Gypsy Warriors, Boston and Kilbride, The Concrete Cowboys, Murder She Wrote, The Silver Fox, The Closer (series) 1998, Last Stand at Saber River, Friends, Ruby, Jean and Joe, Broken Trust. *Leisure interests:* volleyball (Hon. Capt. U.S. Men's Volleyball Team for 1984 Olympic Games), outrigger canoe specialist. *Address:* c/o Esme Chandlee, 2967 Hollyridge Drive, Los Angeles, CA 90068, U.S.A.

SELLERT, Wolfgang, DR. JUR.; German professor of law; b. 3 Nov. 1935, Berlin; s. of Else Horst-Günther; m. Dr. Urte Wenger 1962; two d.; Asst. in Dept. for History of German Law, Univ. of Frankfurt 1965–72, Prof. 1972–77; Prof. History of German Law and Civil Law Georg-August Univ., Göttingen 1977–; Dir. German-Chinese Inst. of Econ. Law, Univ. of Nanjing 1995–; mem. Akademie der Wissenschaften, Göttingen 1984–. *Publications:* Über die Zuständigkeitsabgrenzung von Reichshofrat und Reichskammergericht 1965, Prozessgrundsätze über Stilus Curiae am Reichshofrat 1973, Die Ordnungen des Reichshofrats 1980, Studien- u. Quellenbuch zur Geschichte der dt. Strafrechtspflege 1989, Recht u. Gerechtigkeit in der Kunst 1991. *Leisure interests:* collecting old manuscripts and baroque literature. *Address:* Konrad-Adenauer-Strasse 25, 37075 Göttingen, Germany. *Telephone:* 0551/23771. *Fax:* 0551/23771.

SELLICK, Phyllis, O.B.E., F.R.A.M., F.R.C.M.; British concert pianist; b. 16 June 1911, Newbury Park, Essex; m. Cyril Smith 1937 (died 1974); one s. (deceased) one d.; ed. Glenarm Coll., Ilford, Royal Acad. of Music and in Paris; Prof. Royal Coll. of Music, London; Vice-Pres. Inc. Soc. of Musicians Centenary Year 1982–83; Malcolm Arnold, Bliss, Gordon Jacob, Tippett and Vaughan Williams have dedicated works to her. *Leisure interests:* reading, Scrabble, bridge. *Address:* Beverley House, 29A Ranelagh Avenue, Barnes, London, SW13 0BN, England.

SELLSCHOP, Jacques Pierre Friedrich, PH.D., F.INST.P.; South African professor of nuclear physics; b. 8 June 1930, S.W. Africa (now Namibia); s. of Jacques Pierre François Sellschop and Millicent Emily Sellschop (née Sehnert); m. 2nd Susan Tucker 1968; two s. two d.; ed. Christian Brothers' Coll., Pretoria, Univs. of Pretoria and Stellenbosch, Cambridge Univ., U.K.; Founding Dir. Nuclear Physics Research Unit, Univ. of Witwatersrand, Johannesburg 1958, Dean Faculty of Science 1979–83, Deputy Vice-Chancellor (Research) 1984; Co-Chair. Advisory Cttee., Ministry of Arts, Culture, Science and Tech. 1994–; Pres. Jt. Council of Scientific Socs. 1994–; mem. numerous Univ. Councils; mem. Bd. Faculty of Eng. 1958–, Faculty of Science 1958–; mem. Univ. Senate 1958, Senate mem. of Council 1980–84, ex-officio mem. of Council 1984–87, 1988–92; Fellow A.A.A.S., Inst. Nuclear Eng., Geological Soc. of S.A.; Heraeus Foundation Fellowship 1993; Dr. h.c. (Frankfurt); Hon. D.Sc. (Cape Town) 1995; South African Medal of South African Asscn. of the Advancement of Science, Percy Fox Foundation Annual Award, John F. W. Herschel Award, De Beers Medal of S. African Inst. of Physics 1990, Max Planck Research Award 1992, Asscn. Scientific and Tech. Socs. Nat. Award 1993. *Publications:* 125 scientific publs. *Leisure interest:* woodwork. *Address:* University of the Witwatersrand, Private Bag 3, WITS 2050, South Africa. *Telephone:* (011) 716-1111.

SELMER, Knut S., D.JUR.; Norwegian professor of law; b. 7 Nov. 1924, Oslo; m. Elisabeth Schweigaard (Elisabeth Schweigaard Selmer) 1950; one s. one d.; ed. Univ. of Oslo; Research Fellow, Univ. of Oslo 1953–58, Prof. of Insurance Law 1959–89; Sec. for revision of Norwegian Marine Insurance Conditions 1957–67; Chair. Public Comm. for revision of Norwegian Insurance Contracts Act 1973–87; Founder and Chair. Norwegian Research Center for Computers and Law 1970–86; Chair. Bd. Norwegian Data Inspectorate 1980–96; Shakespeare Chair., European Acad. 1998–; Chair. Bd. Norwegian Legal Information System, Lovdata 1980–89. *Publications:* The Survival of General Average 1958, A Decade of Computers and Law (with J. Bing) 1980, Forsikringsrett 1982; numerous articles on insurance law, tort law and computer law. *Address:* Krusesgate 11, 0263 Oslo 2, Norway.

SELTEN, Reinhard, DR. PHIL. NAT.; German economist; b. 5 Oct. 1930, Breslau; s. of Adolf Selten and Käthe Luther; m. Elisabeth Langreiner 1959; ed. Univ. of Frankfurt-am-Main; Prof. Freie Univ. Berlin 1969; Prof. Univ. of Bielefeld; Prof. of Econ. Theory, Univ. of Bonn 1984–96, Prof. Emer. 1996–; mem. Rheinisch-Westfalen Akad. der Wissenschaften; Fellow, Econometric Soc.; Foreign Hon. mem. American Acad. of Arts and Sciences; shared Nobel Prize for Econs. 1994; Dr. h.c. (Bielefeld) 1989, (Frankfurt) 1991, (Graz) 1996, (E. Anglia) 1996. *Publications:* Preispolitik der Mehrproduktenunternehmung in der stat. Theorie 1970, General Equilibrium with Price Making Firms (with T. Marschak) 1974, Models of Strategic Rationality 1988, A General Theory of Equilibrium Selection in Games (with J. Harsanyi) 1988. *Address:* Laboratorium für Experimentelle Wirtschaftsforschung, Universität Bonn, 53113 Bonn, Germany. *Telephone:* (0228) 739190. *Fax:* (0228) 739493.

SEMAGO, Vladimir Vladimirovich; Russian politician; b. 10 Jan. 1947; m.; one s.; ed. Moscow Inst. of Construction Eng., All-Union Acad. of Foreign Trade; with Mosoblstroi 1973–77; Deputy Dir.-Gen., Solnechny 1977–81; accountant, tourist co., commerce dept., State Cttee. of Tourism 1981–83; Deputy Chair., Domodedovo Dist. Consumers' Union 1983–86; chief engineer, State Cttee. of Science and Tech. of U.S.S.R. Council of Ministers 1986–87; f. Jt. Venture Moscow Commercial Club; co-f. Ecology and Energy Resources 1992; mem. CP of Russian Fed. 1993–; mem. State Duma 1993–; mem. Cttee. on Problems of Women, Family and Youth; Chair. Bd. Dirs. Rosebusinessbank; mem. Presidium, Co-ordination Council Round Table of Russian Business; mem. People's Patriotic Union of Russia. *Leisure interests:* travelling, collecting modern paintings. *Address:* State Duma, Okhotny ryad 1, 103265 Moscow, Russia. *Telephone:* (095) 292 8000 (Office).

SEMEL, Terry, B.S.; American film company executive; b. 24 Feb. 1943, New York; s. of Ben Semel and Mildred (Wenig) Semel; m. Jane Bovingdon 1977; one s. two d.; ed. Long Island Univ., City Coll. of New York; Domestic Sales Man. CBS Cinema Center Films, Studio City, Calif. 1970–72; Vice-Pres., Gen. Man. Walt Disney's Buena Vista, Burbank, Calif. 1972–75; Pres. W.B. Distribution Corpn., Burbank 1975–78; Exec. Vice-Pres., C.O.O. Warner Bros. Inc., Burbank 1979–80, Pres., C.O.O. 1980–96, Chair. C.E.O. 1994–; Chair., Co-C.E.O. Warner Music Group Inc. 1995–; Vice-Chair. San Diego Host Cttee. for Republican Nat. Convention 1996; mem. Bd. Dirs. Revlon. *Address:* Warner Music Group Inc., 30th Floor, 75 Rockefeller Plaza, New York, NY 10019, U.S.A.

SEMENOV, Victor Aleksandrovich; Russian politician, b. 14 Jan. 1958, Novokuzyanovo, Moscow Region; m.; one s. one d.; ed. Moscow K. Timiryazev Acad. of Agric.; on state farm, later Agric. Co. Belaya Dacha 1980–85; instructor Agric. Dept., Lyubertsy Town CP Cttee. 1987–88; Dir.-Gen. Belaya Dacha 1989–98; Minister of Agric. and Food of Russian Fed. April 1998–. *Leisure interests:* gardening, fishing, hunting. *Address:* Ministry of Agriculture and Food, Orlikov per. 1/11, 107139 Moscow, Russia. *Telephone:* (095) 207 4243; (095) 975 4368 (Office).

SEMENOV, Gen. Vladimir Magomedovich; Russian army officer; b. 8 June 1940, Karachaevo-Cherkessk; ed. Baku Higher All-Troops School, Frunze Mil. Acad., General Staff Acad.; mem. CPSU 1963–91; mem. Cen. Cttee. 1990–91; commdr. of mil. units 1958–70, Head of staff, Commdr. of regt. 1973, Head of staff, Deputy Commdr. of Div. 1975, Commdr. 1979, Commdr. of army corps 1982–84, Commdr. of army 1984–86, First Deputy Commdr., Commdr. of troops of Baikal Command 1986–91; Deputy Minister of Defence of U.S.S.R., C.-in-C. of Land Troops 1991–92; Commdr. of Land Troops of Russia 1992–97; U.S.S.R. People's Deputy 1989–91. *Address:* Ministry of Defence, Novy Arbat 19, Moscow, Russia. *Telephone:* 293-39-19 (Office).

SEMENOV, Yuri Pavlovich; Russian aviation engineer; b. 20 April 1935; m.; two d.; ed. Dnipropetrovsk State Univ.; worked in aviation industry as engineer, Head of constructors' group, leading constructor 1967–72, chief constructor, 1972–77; First Deputy Constructor-Gen. 1977–89; Dir.-Gen. Research-Production Union Energiya 1989–; corresp. mem. U.S.S.R. (now Russian) Acad. of Sciences 1987–; mem. Int. Acad. of Astronautics; main research in universal space complexes, heavy carrier rockets, integrated information systems based on heavy universal space platforms; took part in devt. and construction of spaceships Progress, Soyuz, Buran, orbit stations Salut, Mir; Lenin Prize 1978, U.S.S.R. State Prize 1985; K. Tsyolkovsky Gold Medal, Hero of Socialist Labour. *Leisure interests:* sports. *Address:* RKK Energiya, Lenina str. 4A, 141070 Korolev, Moscow Region, Russia. *Telephone:* (095) 513 7248 (Office).

SEMENYAKA, Lyudmila Ivanova; Russian ballerina; b. 16 Jan. 1952, Leningrad (St. Petersburg); m. (divorced); one s.; ed. Leningrad Choreographic School; danced with Kirov Ballet 1970–72; and Bolshoi Theatre Co., Moscow 1972–96; Anna Pavlova Prize, Paris 1976, U.S.S.R. State Prize 1977, U.S.S.R. People's Artist 1986, Evening Standard Prize 1986. *Roles include:* Aurore (Eshpai's Angara), Giselle, Odette/Odile (Swan Lake), Anastasia (Ivan the Terrible), Katerina (Stone Flower). *Address:* Bolshoi Theatre, Teatralnaya ploshchad 1, Moscow, Russia. *Telephone:* 253-87-42 (Home).

SEMENZA, Giorgio, DR. MED.; Swiss professor of biochemistry; b. 23 June 1928, Milan, Italy; s. of Prof. Carlo Semenza and Clementina Gerli; m. Berit Andersson 1958; three c.; ed. Univ. of Milan; post-doctoral studies, Univ. of Uppsala 1955–56; Asst. lecturer, lecturer, Dept. of Biochem. Univ. of Zürich 1956–64, Asst. Prof. 1964–69; Prof. of Biochem. Swiss Fed. Inst. of Tech., Zürich 1969–95, Chair. or Co.-Chair., Dean of School of Natural Sciences 1980–82; Prof. of Biochemistry, Univ. of Milan 1995–; Visiting Prof. at numerous foreign univs.; Hon. mem. Spanish Soc. of Biochemistry 1997; Corresp. mem. Istituto Lombardo di Scienze a. Lettere, Milan 1997; Purkine Gold Medal, Prague 1988; Dr. h.c. (Madrid) 1985. *Publications:* some 250 publs. in journals; Ed. 12 books. *Leisure interests:* literature, films, theatre. *Address:* Dipartimento di Chimica e Biochimica Medica, Università di Milano, Via Saldini 50, 20133 Milan, Italy.

SEMERDZHIEV, Col.-Gen. Atanas; Bulgarian politician; b. 21 May 1924, Velingrad; ed. Soviet mil. acads.; mem. Bulgarian Communist Party 1943–90, Bulgarian Socialist Party 1990–; fmr. guerrilla fighter and served in Patriotic War 1944–45; Chief of Gen. Staff of Bulgarian People's Army 1962–89; First Deputy Minister of Nat. Defence 1966–89; Minister of the Interior 1989–90; Vice-Pres. of Bulgaria 1990–91. *Address:* c/o Office of the Vice-President, Sofia, Bulgaria.

SEMIGIN, Gennady Yuryevich, DR. RER. POL.; Russian businessman; b. 23 March 1961; ed. Riga Higher Mil. Political School, Moscow Juridical Inst., Acad. of Finance; army service 1985–90; f. Centre of Econs. and Russian AKROS 1990; f. Russian Group of Finance and Industry 1991; mem. Council on Business, Russian Presidency 1992–; mem. Exec. Bd. Russian Union of Businessmen, Pres. Russian Group of Finance and Industry 1991–; f. Nat. Public Scientific Fund 1996; Pres. Congress of Russian Business Circles; mem. Comm. on Regulation of Labour and Social Relations, Russian Acad. of Social Sciences, Acad. of Political Sciences; corresp. mem. Acad. of Natural Sciences. *Leisure interests:* swimming, tennis, running, classical music, boxing, history, philosophy, art, econs. *Address:* R.K.K. Energiya, Lenina str. 4, 141070 Korolev, Moscow Region, Russia. *Telephone:* (095) 513 7248; (095) 583 0404 (Office).

SEMIKHVATOV, Mikhail Alexandrovich; Russian geologist; b. 21 Feb. 1932; m.; one s.; ed. Moscow State Univ.; jr., sr. researcher, head of lab. Inst. of Geology 1954–; corresp. mem. U.S.S.R. (now Russian) Acad. of Sciences 1990, mem. 1994; research in stratigraphy, paleontology; N. Shatsky Prize. *Publications include:* General Problems of the Proterozoic Stratigraphy in the U.S.S.R. *Leisure interest:* expeditions to Siberia. *Address:* Institute of Geology, Russian Academy of Sciences, Pyzhevsky per. 7, 109017 Moscow, Russia. *Telephone:* (095) 230-81-32 (Office).

SEMIZOROVA, Nina Lvovna; Russian ballerina; b. 15 Oct. 1956, Krivoi Rog; d. of Lev Alexandrovich Semizorov and Larisa Dmitrievna Semizorova; m. 1st Maris Liepa 1980; m. 2nd Mark Peretokine 1988; one d.; ed. Kiev Choreographic School; danced with Shevchenko Theatre of Opera and Ballet, Kiev 1975–78, with Bolshoi, Moscow 1978–; many appearances abroad. First Prize, Int. Ballet Competition, Moscow 1977, Artist of Merit of Ukrainian S.S.R. 1977; Honoured Artist of Russia 1987; Laureate of Moscow Komsomol 1987. *Roles include:* Odile/Odette, Lady Macbeth, Giselle, Don Quixote, Sleeping Beauty, La Bayadère, Spartacus, The Golden Age, Paquita, Raymonda, Les Sylphides. *Leisure interest:* reading. *Address:* 2 Zhukovskaya Street, Apt. 8, Moscow, Russia. *Telephone:* 923-40-84 (Home). *Fax:* 923-40-84.

SEMKOW, Jerzy (Georg), M.A.(MUS.); Polish conductor; b. 12 Oct. 1928, Radomsko; s. of Aleksander and Waleria Sienczak Semkow; ed. Jagiellonian Univ., Cracow, State Higher School of Music (student of A. Malawski), Cracow and Leningrad Music Conservatoire; Asst. Conductor, Leningrad Philharmonic Orch. 1954–56; Conductor, Bolshoi Opera and Ballet Theatre, Moscow 1956–58; Artistic Dir. and Prin. Conductor, Warsaw Nat. Opera 1960–62; Perm. Conductor, Danish Royal Opera, Copenhagen 1965–68; Prin. Conductor Italian Radio and TV (RAI) Orchestra, Rome 1969–73; Conductor Cleveland Symphony Orchestra 1970–71; Musical Dir. and Prin. Conductor St. Louis Symphony Orchestra 1975–; Artistic Dir and Prin. Conductor, Rochester Philharmonic Orchestra, New York 1986–; guest conductor of London Philharmonic, New York Philharmonic, Chicago Symphony, Boston Symphony and many other leading European and American orchestras; engagements at Covent Garden, La Scala, Berlin, Vienna, Madrid, Paris, Rome, etc.; Commdr. Cross of Polonia Restituta. *Leisure interests:* reading, yachting. *Address:* c/o ICM Artists, 40 West 57th Street, New York, NY 10019, U.S.A.

SEMPÉ, Jean-Jacques; French cartoonist; b. 1932, Bordeaux; s. of Ulysse Sempé and Juliette Marson; one s. one d.; work appears in L'Express magazine; has produced an album annually for 30 years; retrospective exhbn. Pavillon des Arts, Les Halles, Paris 1991; Officier des Arts et des Lettres. *Publications include:* Par Avion, L'Histoire de Monsieur Sommer (with Patrick Süsskind), Ames Soeurs 1991, Insondables Mystères 1993, Raoul Taburin 1995, Les Musiciens 1996, Grands rêves. *Address:* c/o Paris-Match, 63 avenue des Champs-Elysées, 75008 Paris; c/o Editions Denoël, 9 rue du Cherche-Midi, 75006 Paris, France.

SEMPLE, John Laughlin, C.B., B.A.; British civil servant; b. 10 Aug. 1940, Belfast; s. of the late J. E. Semple and of Violet E. G. Semple; m. Maureen Anne Kerr 1970; two s. one d.; ed. Campbell Coll., Belfast and Corpus Christi Coll., Cambridge; joined Home Civil Service, Ministry of Aviation 1961, transferred to Northern Ireland Civil Service 1962, succession of posts relating to industrial training, financial planning, community relations, physical planning, Belfast devt. and housing policy, Perm. Sec. Northern Ireland Dept. of Finance and Personnel 1988–97, Head. Northern Ireland Civil Service 1997–, also Second Perm. Sec. Northern Ireland Office 1998–. *Leisure interests:* golf, tennis, skiing. *Address:* Parliament Buildings, Stormont, Belfast, BT4 3SS, Northern Ireland.

SEMPRÚN, Jorge; Spanish politician and writer; in exile in France following Spanish Civil War; fought in the French Resistance in World War II, captured by Nazis and sent to Buchenwald concentration camp; became leader of proscribed Spanish Communist Party, expelled as deviationist; Minister of Culture 1988–91; mem. Acad. Goncourt; Jerusalem Prize 1997; Dr. h.c. (Turin) 1990. *Publications:* Le Grand Voyage (novel, in French), The Autobiography of Federico Sánchez (under pseudonym), Literature or Life 1998; screenplays for films: Z, La Guerre est finie.

SEN, Amartya Kumar, PH.D., F.B.A.; Indian economist; b. 3 Nov. 1933, Santiniketan, Bengal; s. of Ashutosh and Amita Sen; m. 1st Nabaneeta Dev 1960 (divorced 1975); two d.; m. 2nd Eva Colorni 1978 (died 1985); one s. one d.; m. 3rd Emma Rothschild; ed. Presidency Coll., Calcutta and Trinity Coll., Cambridge; Prof. of Econs., Jadavpur Univ., Calcutta 1956–58; Fellow, Trinity Coll., Cambridge 1957–63; Prof. of Econs., Univ. of Delhi 1963–71, Chair. Dept. of Econs. 1966–68; Hon. Dir. Agricultural Econs. Research Centre, Delhi 1966–68, 1969–71; Prof. of Econs. L.S.E. 1971–77, Oxford Univ. 1977–80; Drummond Prof. of Political Economy 1980–88; Lamont Univ. Prof., Harvard Univ. 1987–98; Master Trinity Coll., Cambridge 1998–; Visiting Prof., Univ. of Calif., Berkeley 1964–65, Harvard Univ. 1968–69; Andrew D. White Prof.-at-Large Cornell Univ 1978–84; Pres. Int. Econ. Asscn. 1986–89; Fellow, Econometric Soc., Pres. 1984; Hon. Prof. Delhi Univ.; Foreign hon. mem. American Acad. of Arts and Sciences; Hon. Fellow, Inst. of Social Studies, The Hague, Hon. Fellow L.S.E., Inst. of Devt. Studies; Hon. D.Litt. (Univ. of Saskatchewan, Canada) 1979 (Visva-Bharati Univ., India) 1983 (Oxford) 1996; Hon. D.Univ. (Essex) 1984, (Caen) 1987; Dr. h.c. (Caen) 1987, (Bologna) 1988, (Univ. Catholique de Louvain) 1989; Hon. D.Sc. (Bath) 1984, (Bologna) 1988; Senator Giovanni Agnelli Inst. Prize for Ethics 1989, Nobel Prize for Econs. 1998. *Publications:* Choice of Techniques: An Aspect of Planned Economic Development 1960, Growth Economics 1970, Collective Choice and Social Welfare 1970, On Economic Inequality 1973, Employment, Technology and Development 1975, Poverty and Famines 1981, Utilitarianism and Beyond (jointly with Bernard Williams) 1982, Choice, Welfare and Measurement 1982, Resources, Values and Development 1984, Commodities and Capabilities 1985, On Ethics and Economics 1987, The Standard of Living 1988, Hunger and Public Action (with Jean Drèze) 1989, Social Security in Developing Countries (with others) 1991, Inequality Reexamined 1992, The Quality of Life (jtly.) 1993; articles in various journals in econs., philosophy and political science. *Address:* Trinity College, Cambridge, CB2 1TQ, England.

SEN, Mrinal; Indian film director; b. 14 May 1923, Faridpur (now Bangladesh); s. of late Dinesh Chandra Sen and Saraju Sen; m. Gita Shome 1953; one s.; started making films 1956, directed 24 feature films; mem. jury numerous int. film festivals; Chair. Gov. Council Film & TV Inst. of India 1983–85; Chair. Indian People's Human Rights Comm. 1987–90; Vice-Chair. Fed. of Film Socs. of India 1980–92, Cinéma et Liberté (Paris) 1992; Pres. Int. Fed. of Film Socs. 1991–; Padma Bhushan 1981; Hon. D.Litt. (Burdwan Univ.) 1981; Commdr. Ordre des Arts et des Lettres 1985; numerous awards. *Films include:* The Dawn 1956, Wedding Day 1960, Up in the Clouds 1965, Two Brothers 1966, Bhuvan Shome 1968, Calcutta trilogy—The Interview, Calcutta 71 and Guerrilla Fighter (Calcutta Trilogy 1971–73), Royal Hunt 1976, The Outsiders 1977, Man with an Axe 1978, And Quiet Rolls and Dawn 1979, In Search of Famine 1980, The Kaleidoscope 1982, The Case is Closed 1983, The Ruins 1984, Genesis 1986, Suddenly One Day 1989, World Within, World Without 1991. *Leisure interests:* reading, travelling, loafing about. *Address:* 4E, Motilal Nehru Road, Calcutta 700029, India. *Telephone:* 478899.

SEN, Samar R., PH.D.; Indian economist; b. 29 June 1916, Noakhali; s. of late Satya R. Sen and of Ashalata Sen; m. Anita Sen 1948; two s.; ed. Calcutta Univ., Univ. of Dhaka and London School of Econs.; taught econs., Univ. of Dacca 1940–48; Deputy Econ. Adviser, Govt. of India 1948–51; Econ. and Statistical Adviser, Ministry of Food and Agric., Govt. of India 1951–58; Leader of Indian Agricultural Del. to U.S.S.R. 1954; Chair. FAO Comm. on Commodity Problems 1956; mem. and sec. Indian Agricultural Del. to People's Repub. of China 1957; Jt. Sec. (Plan Co-ordination and Admin.), Planning Comm. 1959–63; mem. UN Cttee. on Int. Trade 1963; Adviser (Programme Admin.) and Additional Sec., Govt. of India 1963–69; Adviser (Indicative World Plan) FAO 1967–68; Vice-Chair. Irrigation Comm., Govt. of India 1969–70; mem. UN Cttee. on Social Devt. 1968, Advisory Bd., UNCTAD 1969–77; Pres. Int. Asscn. of Agricultural Economists 1970–76; Amb. and Exec. Dir. IBRD, IFC and IDA 1970–78; Chair. Int. Food Policy Research Inst., Washington, D.C. 1979, Govt. of India Comm. on Cost of Production 1979, Cttee. of Chairmen of Int. Agric. Research Centres of World Bank Group 1981–; Chair. Northern Bd., Reserve Bank of India 1982; Dir. Reserve Bank of India 1983–; Dir. Nat. Bank of Agric. and Rural Devt. 1982–; mem. Comm. on Centre-State Relations, Govt. of India 1983–87; has taken part in and led numerous Indian and int. agric. and devt. comms., and delegations; active participant in Gandhian non-violent movt.; mem. Int. Policy Council for Agric. and Trade 1989–; Hon. Fellow London School of Econs., American Agricultural Econs. Asscn.; First Prize, Asia, World Essay Competition on Disarmament. *Publications:* Strategy for Agricultural Development, Economics of Sir James Stewart, Population and Food Supply, Planning Machinery in India, Growth and Instability in Indian Agriculture, Politics of Indian Economy, Decision Making and Agriculture, International Monetary and Financial System and Institutions, Restrictionism during the Great Depression in Indian Tea, Jute and Sugar Industries, Price Policy for the Plan, Economics of Oligopoly in Oligarchy, India's Political System:

What is to be done. *Leisure interests:* golf, travel, photography. *Address:* 41 Poorvi Marg, Vasant Vihar, New Delhi, 11057, India. *Telephone:* 6145861.

SENDAK, Maurice Bernard; American illustrator and writer; b. 10 June 1928, New York; s. of Philip and Sadie (Schindler) Sendak; ed. Art Students League, New York; writer and illustrator of children's books 1951–; co-founder, Artistic Dir. The Night Kitchen 1990–; one-man show Gallery School of Visual Arts, New York 1964, Ashmolean Museum, Oxford 1975, American Cultural Center, Paris 1978; Hans Christian Andersen Illustrators Award 1970; Nat. Medal of Arts 1997. *Publications (writer and illustrator):* Kenny's Window 1956, Very Far Away 1957, The Sign on Rosie's Door 1960, The Nutshell Library 1963, Where the Wild Things Are (Caldecott Medal 1964) 1963, On Books and Pictures 1986, Caldecott and Co. (collection of reviews and articles) 1989, We Are All in the Dumps with Jack and Guy 1993. *Illustrator:* A Hole is to Dig 1952, A Very Special House 1954, I'll Be You and You Be Me 1954, Charlotte and the White Horse 1955, What Do You Say, Dear? 1959, The Moonjumpers 1960, Little Bear's Visit 1962, Schoolmaster Whackwell's Wonderful Sons 1962, Mr. Rabbit and the Lovely Present 1963, The Griffin and the Minor Canon 1963, Nikolenka's Childhood 1963, The Bat-Poet 1964, Lullabies and Night Songs 1965, Hector Protector and As I Went Over the Water 1965, Zlateh the Goat 1966, Higgelty Pigglety Pop, Or There Must Be More To Life 1967, In the Night Kitchen 1970, The Animal Family 1965, In The Night Kitchen Coloring Book 1971, Pictures by Maurice Sendak 1971, The Juniper Tree and Other Tales from Grimm 1973, Outside Over There 1981, The Love for Three Oranges (with Frank Corsaro) 1984, Nutcracker (with Ralph Manheim) 1984, The Cunning Little Vixen 1985, Dear Mili 1988, I Saw Esau 1992, The Ubiquitous Pig 1992; writer, dir. and lyricist for TV animated special Really Rosie 1975. *Stage designs:* The Magic Flute 1980, The Love for Three Oranges 1984, L'enfant et les sortilèges 1987, The Cunning Little Vixen (for N.Y. Opera) 1989, Idomeneo (opera) 1990. *Address:* c/o HarperCollins, 10 East 53rd Street, New York, NY 10022, U.S.A.

SENDERENS, Alain; French chef; b. 2 Dec. 1939, Hyeres; s. of René Senderens and Lucette (née Azan) Senderens; m. Eventhia (née Pappadinas) Senderens 1974; one s.; ed. Lycée de Vic-en Bigorre; Apprentice Chef Hôtel des Ambassadeurs, Lourdes 1957–61, La Tour d'Argent, Paris 1963; Sauce Cook Lucas Carton Restaurant 1963–65, Man. 1985–; Chief Sauce Cook Orly Hilton Hotel, Paris 1966–68; Gen. Man. l'Archestrate, Paris 1968–85; Chair. Bd. of Dirs., Auberge Franc Comtoise, Lucas Carton; Pres. Chambre Syndicale de la Haute Cuisine Française, Conseil Nat. des Arts Culinaires 1990–; Chevalier, Légion d'honneur, Officier des Arts et des Lettres, ordre nat. du Mérite, Chevalier du Mérite Agricole. *Publications:* La Cuisine Réussie 1981, La Grande Cuisine à Petits Prix 1984, la Cuisine réussie, Figues sans barbarie 1991, Proust, la Cuisine retrouvée (jtly.) 1991, Manger, c'est la santé (jtly.) 1993. *Leisure interests:* reading, jogging, classical music. *Address:* Restaurant Lucas Carton, 9 place de la Madeleine, 75008 Paris (Office); 11 place de la Madeleine, 75008 Paris (Home), France. *Telephone:* 42 65 22 90.

SENDOV, Blagovest Hristov, D.SC., PH.D.; Bulgarian mathematician; b. 8 Feb. 1932, Assenovgrad; s. of Christo and Marushka Sendov; m. 1st Lilia Georgieva 1958 (divorced 1982), two d.; m. 2nd Anna Marinova 1982; one s.; ed. gymnasium in Assenovgrad, Sofia Univ., Moscow State Univ., and Imperial Coll., London; cleaner in Sofia 1949–52; teacher in Boboshevo and Elin Pelin 1956–58; Asst., Dept. of Algebra, Univ. of Sofia 1958–60, Asst. in numerical analysis and computer science 1960-63, Asst. Prof. of Computer Sciences 1963–67, Prof. of Computer Science 1967, Dean, Faculty of Math. 1970–73, Rector 1973-79; mem. Parl. 1976–90, 1994–, Pres. of Parl. 1995–97, Vice-Pres. 1997–; Vice-Pres. Bulgarian Acad. of Sciences 1980–82, Vice-Pres. and Scientific Sec.-Gen. 1982–88, Dir. Centre for Informatics and Computer Tech. 1985–90; Pres. 1988–91; Pres. Comm. of Science 1986–88; Hon. Pres. Int. Asscn. of Univs. 1985–; Vice-Pres. Int. Fed. for Information Processing 1985–88, Pres. 1989–91; Vice-Pres. World Peace Council 1983–86, IIP—UNESCO 1986–90; Extraordinary Vice-Pres. ICSU 1990–93; mem. Exec. Cttee. and Bd. of Dirs., Int. Foundation for Survival and Devt. of Humanity 1988–; awards and decorations include Dimitrov Prize for science, Honoured Scientist 1984 and two Orders of People's Repub. of Bulgaria. *Publications:* Numerical Analysis, Old and New 1973, Hausdorff Approximation 1979, Averaged Moduli of Smoothness (monograph); textbooks and articles in learned journals. *Leisure interests:* tennis, travelling. *Address:* Centre for Informatics and Computer Technology, Bulgarian Academy of Sciences, G. Bonchev Str. bl. 25A, 1113 Sofia, Bulgaria. *Telephone:* 708494. *Fax:* 707273.

SENGHAAS, Dieter, DR.PHIL.; German professor of social science; b. 27 Aug. 1940, Geislingen; m. Eva Knobloch 1968; one d.; ed Univs. of Tübingen, Michigan and Frankfurt, and Amherst Coll.; Research Fellow, Center for Int. Affairs, Harvard Univ. 1968–70; Research Dir., Peace Research Inst., Frankfurt (PRIF) 1971–78; Prof. of Int. Relations, Univ. of Frankfurt 1972–78; Prof. of Social Science, Univ. of Bremen 1978–; mem. several nat. and int. scientific orgs.; Lentz Int. Peace Research Award 1987. *Publications:* Aggressivität und kollektive Gewalt 1972, Aufrüstung durch Rüstungskontrolle 1972, Gewalt-Konflikt-Frieden 1974, Weltwirtschaftsordnung und Entwicklungspolitik (5th edn.) 1987, Abschreckung und Frieden (3rd edn.) 1981, Rüstung und Militarismus (2nd edn.) 1982, Von Europa lernen 1982, The European Experience 1985, Die Zukunft Europas 1986, Europas Entwicklung und die Dritte Welt 1986, Konfliktformationen im internationalen System 1988, Europa 2000: Ein Friedensplan 1990, Friedensprojekt Europa 1992, Wohin driftet die Welt 1994, Zivilisierung wider Willen 1998; Ed. and co-Ed. of 27 books related to political science, int. affairs, etc. *Leisure interest:* music. *Address:* Freiligrathstrasse 6, 28211 Bremen, Germany. *Telephone:* (0421) 23 04 36. *Fax:* (0421) 249169.

SENGHOR, Léopold Sédar; Senegalese former Head of State and writer; b. 9 Oct. 1906; m. 2nd Colette Hubert 1957; three s. (two deceased); ed. Lycée de Dakar, Lycée Louis-le-Grand, Paris and Univ. de Paris; Classics Teacher, Lycée Descartes, Tours 1935–44, Lycée Marcelin Berthelot, Paris 1944–48; mem. Constituent Assemblies 1945–46; Deputy from Senegal to Nat. Assembly 1946–58; Prof., Ecole Nat. de la France d'Outre-Mer 1948–58; Sec. of State, Présidence du Conseil 1955–56; mem. Consultative Ass., Council of Europe; Pres. Fed. Ass., Mali Fed. of Senegal and Sudan 1959–60, Pres. Senegal Repub. 1960–80, also Minister of Defence 1968–69; Chair. OCAM 1972–74; fmr. Sec.-Gen. Union Progressiste Sénégalaise (from 1977 Parti Socialiste Sénégalais), nat. party of Parti Féderaliste Africain (PFA); Chair. ECONAS 1978–79; Vice-Pres. Socialist Int.; Vice-Pres. Haut conseil de la francaphonie 1985–; Chair. Exec. Bureau, Socialist Inter-African Feb. 1981–; fmr. Pres. Int. Confed. of Socs. of Authors and Composers; mem. Inst. Français: Acad. des Sciences morales et politiques 1969, Acad. Française 1983 (mem. Comm. du dictionnaire 1986–), American Acad. of Arts and Letters; numerous hon. degrees; Dag Hammarskjöld Prize 1965; Peace Prize of German Book Trade, Frankfurt; Haile Sellassie African Research Prize 1973; Apollinaire Prize for Poetry 1974, Alfred de Vigny Prize, Aasan World Prize 1981, Jawaharlal Nehru Award 1984, Athinai Prize 1985; Grand-croix, Légion d'honneur, Commdr. Ordre des Palmes académiques, Commdr. des Arts et des Lettres. *Publications:* Chants d'ombres (poems) 1945, Hosties noires (poems) 1948, Chants pour Naëtt (poems) 1949, Ethiopiques (poems) 1956, Nocturnes (poems) 1961, Langage et poésie négro-africaine 1954, L'apport de la poésie nègre 1953, Esthéthique négro-africain 1956, Collected Poems 1977, Liberté IV: Socialisme et planification 1983, Poèmes 1984. *Address:* Corniche Ouest, Dakar, Senegal; 150 rue du Général Leclerc, 14790 Verson, France.

SENKO, Vladimir Leonovich; Belarus diplomatist; b. 5 Aug. 1946; ed. Moscow State Inst. of Int. Relations, Diplomatic Acad.; diplomatic service 1973–; with U.S.S.R. Embassy, Poland 1973–79, Second Sec. 1981–85, First Sec. 1988–91; Third Sec. Fourth European Div. U.S.S.R. Ministry of Foreign Affairs 1979–81; First Sec. Dept. of Socialist Countries, U.S.S.R. Ministry of Foreign Affairs 1987–88: Deputy Minister of Foreign Affairs Belarus Repub. 1991–92; Belarus Amb. to U.K. 1994; Minister of Foreign Affairs of Belarus 1994–97. *Address:* Ministry of Foreign Affairs, Leninsky prospect 19, 220030 Minsk, Belarus. *Telephone:* (17) 24-47-05. *Fax:* (17) 27-45-21.

SENSI, H.E. Cardinal Giuseppe Maria, D.CN.L.; Italian ecclesiastic; b. 27 May 1907, Cosenza; s. of Francesco Sensi and Melania Sensi Andreotti Loria; ed. Lateran Univ., Rome; ordained 1929; diplomatic service for the Holy See 1934–76; cr. Cardinal 1976; hon. mem. Acad. Cosentina 1976. *Address:* 16 Piazza S. Callisto, 00153 Rome, Italy.

SEOW, Yit Kin; British-Singaporean concert pianist; b. 28 March 1955, Singapore; ed. Yehudi Menuhin School and Royal Coll. of Music, England; went to U.K. 1967; toured U.S.A. 1972; Promenade Concerts, Royal Albert Hall and Royal Festival Hall (with Philharmonia Orchestra), London 1975; appeared Beethovenfest, Bonn 1977, Hong Kong Arts Festival (with Berlin Radio Symphony Orchestra) 1977, Promenade Concerts (with Royal Philharmonic Orchestra) 1982, Poland 1984, Hongkong Asian Arts Festival 1984; toured Russia for BBC 1988; recordings of Satie, Schubert 1989; Gold Disc of Yellow River Concerto 1984; winner BBC Piano Competition 1974, Rubinstein Prize 1977. *Leisure interests:* gardening, theatre, cinema. *Address:* 8 North Terrace, London, SW3 2BA, England. *Telephone:* 0171-584 5393.

SEPÚLVEDA, Bernardo, LL.B.; Mexican politician; b. 14 Dec. 1941, Mexico City; s. of Bernardo and Margarita Sepulveda; m. Ana Yturbe 1970; three s.; ed. Nat. Univ. of Mexico and Queens' Coll., Cambridge; fmrly. taught int. law, El Colegio de México and Faculty of Political Science, Univ. of Mexico; Asst. Dir. of Juridical Affairs, Ministry of Presidency 1968–70; Dir.-Gen. of Int. Financial Affairs, Ministry of Finance 1976–81; Int. Adviser, Minister of Programming and Budget 1981; Amb. to U.S.A. March–Dec. 1982; Sec. of Foreign Affairs 1982–88; Amb. to U.K. 1989–93; Foreign Affairs Advisor to Pres. of Mexico 1993–; Sec. Int. Affairs Institutional Revolutionary Party (PRI) 1981–82; Pres. to UN Sixth Comm. on Transnat. Corpns. 1977–80; Hon. Fellow Queen's Coll. Cambridge 1991; Hon. G.C.M.G. *Publications:* Foreign Investment in Mexico 1973, Transnational Corporations in Mexico 1974, A View of Contemporary Mexico 1979, Planning for Development 1981. *Address:* Rocas 185, México, D.F. 01900, Mexico. *Telephone:* (5) 6520641. *Fax:* (525) 6529739.

SEQUEIRA, Luis, PH.D.; American professor of plant pathology; b. 1 Sept. 1927, San José, Costa Rica; s. of Raul Sequeira and the late Dora Jenkins; m. Elisabeth Steinvorth 1954; one s. three d.; ed. Harvard Univ.; Teaching Fellow, Harvard Univ. 1949–52; Parker Fellow, Harvard and Instituto Biológico, São Paulo, Brazil 1952–53; Plant Pathologist, Asst. Dir., then Dir. Coto Research Station, United Fruit Co., Costa Rica 1953–60; Research Assoc., N.C. State Univ., Raleigh, N.C. 1960–61; Assoc. Prof., then Prof., Dept. of Plant Pathology, Univ. of Wis., Madison 1961–78, Prof., Depts. of Bacteriology and Plant Pathology 1978–82, J. C. Walker Prof. 1982–; Consultant Agracetus, Madison 1982–93; Chief Scientist, Competitive Grants

Office, USDA, Washington, D.C. 1987–88; research interests include physiology and biochemistry of plant-parasite interactions, identification of genes for virulence in pathogens, particularly bacteria, and breeding plants for disease resistance; Fellow American Phytopathological Soc. (Pres. 1985–86, Award of Distinction 1994), American Acad. of Microbiology; mem. N.A.S., Linnean Soc. of London; E. M. Stakman Award. *Publications:* approximately 250 publs. in journals and covering plant pathology, bacteriology, biochemistry and genetics. *Leisure interests:* classical music, cross-country skiing. *Address:* Department of Plant Pathology, University of Wisconsin, 1630 Linden Drive, Madison, WI 53706; 10 Appomattox Court, Madison, WI 53705, U.S.A. (Home). *Telephone:* (608) 262-3456 (Office); (608) 833-3440 (Home).

SERAPHIN, Oliver; Dominican politician; b. 2 Aug. 1943; s. of Perry and Theotil Seraphin; m. Virginia Rabess 1978; three s.; Prime Minister of Dominica and Minister for Foreign Affairs 1979–80; Leader Democratic Labour Party 1979–85, Deputy Leader Labour Party of Dominica 1985. *Leisure interests:* table-tennis, reading, music. *Address:* 44 Green's Lane, Goodwill, Dominica.

ŞERBAN, Andrei; Romanian stage director; b. 21 June 1943; s. of Gheorghe Şerban and Elpis Şerban; m.; two c.; ed. Bucharest Theatrical and Cinematographic Art Inst.; int. scholarships: Ford 1970, Guggenheim 1976, Rockefeller 1980; Obie Awards; Tony Award, prizes at the Avignon, Belgrade and Shiraz festivals; has delivered numerous lectures; Gen. Man. Nat. Theatre of Romania 1990–93; productions in Romania include Ubu Roi 1966, Julius Caesar 1968, Jonah 1969, An Ancient Trilogy (Medea, The Trojan Women, Elektra) 1990; American productions include: Medea (Euripides) 1970, The Cherry Orchard 1972, Fragments of a Trilogy (Medea, Elektra, The Trojan Women) 1974, As You Like It 1976, Uncle Vanya 1979, The Umbrellas of Cherbourg 1980, The Seagull 1981, The Three Sisters 1983, The Miser 1988, Twelfth Night 1989; opera productions: Eugene Onegin 1980, Turandot 1984, Norma 1985, Fidelio (Covent Garden) 1986, The Puritans (Paris Opera). *Address:* Teatrul Naţional, Bd. N. Bălcescu 2, Bucharest, Romania. *Telephone:* 614.56.92.

SEREBRIER, José; American conductor and composer; b. 3 Dec. 1938, Montevideo; s. of David Serebrier and Frida Serebrier (née Wasser); m. Carole Farley 1969; one d.; started conducting at age of 12; went to U.S.A. 1956; studied composition with Vittorio Giannini, Curtis Inst., Phila. 1956–58, and conducting with Antal Dorati; guest conductor in U.S.A., S. America and Europe; Assoc. Conductor American Symphony Orchestra, with Leopold Stokowski 1962–68; conducted alongisde Leopold Stokowski world première of Charles Ives' Fourth Symphony, Carnegie Hall, New York; conducted first performance in Poland of Charles Ives' Fourth Symphony; Composer-in-Residence with Cleveland Orchestra 1968–70; Music Dir. Cleveland Philharmonic Orchestra 1968–71; Artistic Dir. Int. Festival of Americas, Miami 1984–, Miami Festival 1985–; numerous recordings; Deutsche Schallplatten Critics' Award 1991, U.K. Music Retailers' Asscn. Award for Best Symphony Recording (Mendelssohn symphonies) 1991, Diapason d'Or recording award, France. *Compositions:* Quartet for Saxophones 1955, Pequeña música (wind quintet) 1955, Symphony No. 1 1956, Momento psicológico (string orchestra) 1957, Suite canina (wind trio) 1957, Symphony for Percussion 1960, The Star Wagon (chamber orchestra) 1967, Nueve (double bass and orchestra) 1970, Colores mágicos (variations for harp and chamber orchestra) 1971, At Dusk, in Shadows (solo flute), Andante Cantabile (strings), Night Cry (brass), Dorothy and Carmine (flute and strings), George and Muriel (contrabass), Winter (violin concerto). *Publication:* orchestration of 14 songs by Edvard Grieg. *Leisure interest:* reading. *Address:* 20 Queensgate Gardens, London, SW7 5LZ, England.

SERGEYEV, Marshal Igor Dmitrievich; Russian army officer; b. 20 April 1938, Verkhny, Voroshilovgrad Region; m.; one s.; ed. Nakhimov Black Sea Higher Navigation School, Military Eng. Acad., Gen. Staff Acad.; with rocket troops since 1960, Head of staff of regt. 1971, Commdr. of regt. 1973, Head of staff, Commdr. of Div. 1975–80, Head of staff of Rocket Army 1980–83, Chief of operation div., Deputy-Head of General Staff of Rocket Troops 1983–85, First Deputy then Deputy C.-in-C. of Rocket Troops 1989–92, C.-in-C. of strategic Rocket Troops 1992–97; Minister of Defence May 1997–. *Address:* Ministry of Defence, Znamenka 19, 103160 Moscow, Russia. *Telephone:* 296-39-66, 293-27-32 (Office).

SERGEYEV, Ivan Ivanovich; Russian civil servant and politician; b. 7 Sept. 1941, Electrostal, Moscow Region; Deputy, First Deputy Chair., Exec. Cttee. Moscow Regional Soviet 1976–83; Deputy, First Deputy Head, Dept. on Problems of Diplomatic Corps U.S.S.R. (now Russian) Ministry of Foreign Affairs 1983–97; Deputy Minister of Foreign Affairs 1997–. *Address:* Ministry of Foreign Affairs, Smolenskaya-Sennaya 32/34, Moscow, Russia. *Telephone:* (095) 244 9520 (Office).

SERICHE DOUGAN, Angel Serafin; Equatorial Guinean politician; Prime Minister of Equatorial Guinea March 1996–. *Address:* Office of the Prime Minister, Malabo, Equatorial Guinea.

SERJEANT, Graham Roger, C.M.G., M.D., F.R.C.P.; British medical research scientist; b. 26 Oct. 1938, Bristol; s. of Ewart E. Serjeant and Violet E. Serjeant; m. Beryl E. King 1965; ed. Sibford School, Banbury, Bootham School, York, Clare Coll. Cambridge, London Hosp. Medical School and Makerere Coll. Kampala; House Physician, London Hosp. 1963–64; Royal United Hosp. Bath 1965–66; Royal Postgraduate Medical School 1966; Medical Registrar, Univ. Hosp. of the West Indies 1966–67; Wellcome Research Fellow, Dept. of Medicine, Univ. Hosp. of the West Indies 1967–71; mem. scientific staff, MRC Abnormal Haemoglobin Unit, Cambridge 1971–72, Epidemiology Research Unit, Jamaica 1972–74; Dir. MRC Labs., Jamaica 1974–; Hon. Commdr. Order of Distinction (Jamaica) 1996. *Publications:* The Clinical Features of Sickle Cell Disease 1974, Sickle Cell Disease 1992 (2nd edn.); numerous papers on sickle cell disease in medical journals. *Leisure interest:* squash. *Address:* Medical Research Council Laboratories, University of the West Indies, Mona, Kingston 7, Jamaica. *Telephone:* 927 2471; 927 2984.

SERKIN, Peter Adolf; American concert pianist; b. 24 July 1947, New York; s. of Rudolf Serkin and Irene Busch; ed. Curtis Inst. of Music; début, New York 1959; concert appearances in recital and with orchestras worldwide including Philadelphia, Cleveland, New York, Chicago, Berlin, London, Zürich, Paris and Japan; has premiered works composed for him by Knussen, Takemitsu, Lieberson, Berio; has given benefit performances to aid hunger and war victims; records for RCA, ProArte, CBS, New World; Premio Accademia Musicale Chigian Siena 1983. *Address:* 711 West End Avenue, New York, NY 10025, U.S.A.

SEROTA, Sir Nicholas Andrew, Kt., M.A.; British art gallery director; b. 27 April 1946; s. of Stanley Serota and Baroness Serota; m. 1st Angela M. Beveridge 1973 (divorced 1995); two d.; m. 2nd Teresa Gleadowe 1997; ed. Haberdashers' Aske's School, Hampstead and Elstree, Christ's Coll. Cambridge and Courtauld Inst. of Art; Regional Art Officer and Exhbn. Organizer, Arts Council of G.B. 1970–73; Dir. Museum of Modern Art, Oxford 1973–76; Dir. Whitechapel Art Gallery 1976–88; Dir. The Tate Gallery, London 1988–; Chair. British Council Visual Arts Advisory Cttee. 1992– (mem. 1976–); Sr. Fellow Royal Coll. of Art 1996; Trustee Public Art Devt. Trust 1983–87, Architecture Foundation 1991–, The Little Sparta Trust 1995–; Hon. Fellow, Queen Mary and Westfield Coll., Univ. of London, R.I.B.A., Goldsmiths' Coll. Univ. of London; Hon. D. Arts. (City of London Polytechnic) 1990; Hon. D. Litt. (Plymouth) 1993, (Keele) 1994, (South Bank) 1996, (Surrey) 1997. *Publication:* Experience or Interpretation: The Dilemma of Museums of Modern Art 1997. *Address:* The Tate Gallery, Millbank, London, SW1P 4RG, England. *Telephone:* 0171-887 8000.

SERRA, Richard, M.F.A.; American sculptor; b. 2 Nov. 1939, San Francisco, Calif.; ed. Univ. of Calif. (Berkeley and Santa Barbara) and Yale Univ.; one-man shows include: Richard Hines Gallery, Seattle 1979, Venice Biennale 1981, Akira Ikeda Gallery, Nagoya, Japan 1982, Margo Levin Gallery 1984, Visual Arts Museum 1985, Bonnefantenmuseum, Maastricht 1990, Pace Gallery 1992; frequent exhbns. at Leo Castelli Gallery, New York since 1970; works in many perm. collections including Whitney Museum of Modern Art, Guggenheim Museum, Museum of Modern Art (New York), Art Gallery of Ontario, Stedelijk Museum Amsterdam; Skohegan School Medal 1975. *Publications:* Weight and Measure 1992, Writings/Interviews 1994. *Address:* 173 Duane Street, New York, NY 10013, U.S.A.

SERRA PUCHE, Jaime, PH.D.; Mexican economist; b. 11 Jan. 1951, Mexico City; s. of Jorge Serra and Carmen Puche; m. Joanna Wright 1987; three s.; ed. Univ. Nacional Autónoma de México, El Colegio de México and Yale Univ.; Deputy Minister of Revenues, SHCP 1986–88; Minister of Trade and Industry and Head NAFTA negotiations 1988–94; Minister of Finance 1994; Sr. Partner, SAI (Law and Econs.). *Leisure interest:* jogging. *Address:* SAI Consultores, S.C., Prol. Paseo de la Reforma 600-103, Col. Santa Fe, México, D.F. 01210, México. *Telephone:* (05) 259 66 18. *Fax:* (05) 259 39 28.

SERRA RAMONEDA, Antoni, PH.D.; Spanish fmr. university rector and economist; b. 20 July 1933, Barcelona; s. of Antoni Serra Riera and Enriqueta Ramoneda Ruis; m. Margarita de la Figuera Buñuel 1958; one s. two d.; ed. Lycée Français, Barcelona and Univ. Complutense de Madrid; Sec. Faculty of Econ. Sciences, Univ. of Barcelona 1960–64; Sec.-Gen. Univ. Autónoma de Barcelona 1960–72, Dir. Inst. of Educ. Sciences 1977–78, Rector 1980–85; Pres. Comisión de Control Caja de Pensiones para la Vejez y de Ahorros 1979–82, Sec.-Gen. 1982–84; Pres. Caja de Ahorros de Cataluña 1984. *Publications:* Libro Blanco sobre los efectos para Cataluña del ingreso de España en la CEE, La industria textil algodonera y el Mercado Común Europeo, Sistema Económico y Empresa. *Address:* Pl. Bonanova 5, Barcelona 08022, Spain (Home). *Telephone:* (93) 2478101 (Home).

SERRA SERRA, Narcís, DR.ECON.; Spanish politician; b. 30 May 1943, Barcelona; ed. Barcelona Univ. and London School of Econs.; worked in Chamber of Commerce, Industry and Shipping, Barcelona; mem. Moviment Febrer del 62, linked to Catalan br. of Frente de Liberación Popular; Asst. Prof. of Econ. Theory, Barcelona Univ.; opened econ. research bureau, Barcelona; mem. Convergència Socialista de Catalunya 1974, mem. Exec.; joined Office of Territorial Policy and Town Planning, Generalitat (Catalan autonomous govt.) 1977–79; Mayor of Barcelona 1979; Minister of Defence 1982–91; Deputy Prime Minister 1991–95; First Sec. Partit dels Socialistes de Catalunya. *Address:* c/o PSC/PSOE, Calle Nicaragua 75, 08029 Barcelona, Spain. *Telephone:* (93) 3210100. *Fax:* (93) 4397811.

SERRANO ELIAS, Jorge; Guatemalan politician and businessman; fmr. Pres. Advisory Council of State 1982–83; Pres. of Guatemala 1991–93.

SERRAULT, Michel Lucien; French actor and singer; b. 24 Jan. 1928, Brunoy, Seine-et-Oise; s. of Robert Serrault and Adeline Foulon; m. Juanita Peyron 1958; two d. (one deceased); ed. Petit Séminaire de Conflans and

Centre du Spectacle de la rue Blanche, Paris; stage appearances include: L'Ami de la famille, Pour avoir Adrienne, Le Train pour Venise, Sacré Léonard, Quand épousez-vous ma femme?, Monsieur Dodd 1965, Opération Lagrelèche 1966, Gugusse 1968, Le Vision voyageur et les Bonshommes 1970, Le Tombeur 1972, La Cage aux folles 1973, L'Avare 1986, Knock 1992; numerous film and TV appearances; Officier, Légion d'honneur, Cmmdr. des Arts et des Lettres. *Recent films include:* On ne meurt que deux fois (Prix George Chamara 1986), La Cage aux Folles III, Mon beau-frère a tué ma soeur 1985, Le Miraculé 1987, Ennemis intimes 1988, En toute innocence 1988, Bonjour l'angoisse 1988, Ne réveillez pas un flic qui dort 1988, Comédie d'amour 1989, Le Docteur Petiot 1989, Joyeux Noël, Bonne année 1989, Docteur Petiot 1990, la Vieille qui marchait dans la mer 1991, Ville à vendre 1992, Vieille Canaille 1992, Bonsoir 1994, Le Bonheur est dans le pré 1995, Nelly et M. Arnand 1995 (César Award for Best Actor, Pierre Belan Prize for Best Male Leading Role), Artemisia 1997, Rien ne va plus 1997, Le Comédien 1997. *Publication:* Le Cri de la Carotte 1995. *Leisure interest:* trumpet. *Address:* MS Productions, 12 rue Greuze, 75116 Paris (Office); 34 boulevard de Château, 92200 Neuilly-sur-Seine, France (Home).

SERRE, Jean-Pierre, D. ÈS SC.; French mathematician; b. 15 Sept, 1926, Bages; s. of Jean Serre and Adèle Serre; m. Josiane Heulot 1948; one d.; ed. Lycée de Nîmes and Ecole Normale Supérieure; Prof. of Algebra and Geometry, Coll. de France 1956–, now Hon. Prof.; mem. Acads. of Sciences of France, Sweden, U.S.A., Netherlands; Hon. F.R.S. (U.K.); Commdr., Légion d'honneur, Grand Officier, Ordre nat. du Mérite; Fields Medal, Int. Congress of Math. 1954; Prix Balzan 1985, Médaille d'or, C.N.R.S. *Publications:* Homologie singulière des espaces fibrés 1951, Faisceaux algébriques cohérents 1955, Groupes algébriques et corps de classes 1959, Corps Locaux 1962, Cohomologie galoisienne 1964, Abelian *l*-adic representations 1968, Cours d'arithmétique 1970, Représentations linéaires des groupes finis 1971, Arbres, amalgames, SL2 1977, Lectures on the Mordell-Weil Theorem 1989, Topics in Galois Theory 1992. *Address:* 6 avenue de Montespan, 75116 Paris, France (Home). *Telephone:* 01 45 53 35 63 (Home).

SERREAU, Coline; French film director; d. of Jean-Marie Serreau; has acted in several stage plays including Lapin, lapin in Paris; wrote and acted in Bertuccelli's On s'est trompé d'histoire d'amour 1973; directed Oedipus the King for Italian TV; f. trapeze school in Canada; directed: Mais qu'est-ce qu'elles veulent? (documentary) 1975, Pourquoi pas! 1976, Qu'est-ce qu'on attend pour être heureux! 1982, Trois hommes et un couffin (Three Men and a Cradle) 1985, Romuald et Juliette 1989.

SERRIN, James B., PH.D.; American professor of mathematics; b. 1 Nov. 1926, Chicago, Ill.; s. of Helen Wingate Serrin and James B. Serrin; m. Barbara West 1952; three d.; ed. Western Michigan Coll. and Indiana Univ.; M.I.T. 1952–54; Univ. of Minn. 1955–, Chair. 1964–65, Regents Prof. of Math. 1968–; Fellow A.A.A.S., American Acad. of Arts and Sciences; mem. N.A.S., Finnish Acad. of Science; Hon. D.Sc. (Sussex, Ferrara, Padua); G. D. Birkhoff Award, American Math. Soc. *Publications:* Mathematical Principles of Fluid Dynamics 1958, New Perspectives on Thermodynamics 1985, The Problem of Dirichlet for Quasilinear Elliptic Differential Equations 1969. *Address:* Department of Mathematics, University of Minnesota, Minneapolis, MN 55455 (Office); 4422 Dupont Avenue South, Minneapolis, MN 55409, U.S.A. (Home). *Telephone:* (612) 624-9530 (Office). *Fax:* (612) 626-2017.

SERVAN-SCHREIBER, Jean-Claude, L. EN D.; French media executive; newspaperman; b. 11 April 1918, Paris; s. of late Robert Servan-Schreiber and Suzanne Grémieux; m. 1st Christiane Laroche 1947 (divorced); m. 2nd Jacqueline Guix de Pinos 1955 (divorced); two s. three d.; m. 3rd Paule Guinet 1983 (divorced); ed. Exeter Coll., Oxford and Sorbonne; served World War II in Flanders 1940, in Resistance 1941–42, in N. Africa 1943, France 1944, Germany 1945; with Les Echos 1946–65, Gen. Man. 1957, Dir. 1963–65; Deputy for Paris, Nat. Ass. 1965–67; Asst. Sec.-Gen. U.N.R.-U.D.T. 1965; Pres. Rassemblement français pour Israël May 1967; Dir.-Gen. Régie française de publicité 1968–78; mem. Haut Conseil de l'audiovisuel 1973–81; Pres. Groupe Européen des Régisseurs de Publicité Télévisée 1975–78; mem. Conseil politique, R.P.R. 1977–81; Conseiller du Groupe de Presse L'Expansion 1980–93; Special Adviser Mitsubishi Electric (Europe) 1992–; Pres. Inst. Arthur Vernes 1993–; Commdr., Légion d'honneur, Ordre nat. du Mérite, Médaille mil., Croix de guerre, Croix du Combattant volontaire de la Résistance, Legion of Merit (U.S.A.), etc. *Address:* 147 bis rue d'Alésia, 75014 Paris, France. *Telephone:* (01) 45.39.96.11. *Fax:* (01) 45.39.48.96.

SERVAN-SCHREIBER, Jean-Jacques; French politician, economist and writer; b. 13 Feb. 1924, Paris; s. of Emile and Denise (née Bresard) Servan-Schreiber; four s.; ed. Ecole Polytechnique, Paris; joined the Free French Forces of Gen. de Gaulle as fighter pilot 1943 (trained U.S. Air Force); Foreign Affairs Ed. Le Monde 1948–53; founder L'Express 1953, Ed. 1953–70; elected and re-elected Pres. Radical Party 1970–79; elected and re-elected Deputy for Nancy 1970–79, and Pres. Region of Lorraine 1975–78; Minister of Reform 1974; Pres. World Centre for Computer Literacy 1981–85; Prof. of Strategic Thinking, Chair. Int. Cttee. Carnegie Mellon Univ. 1985–; Croix de la Valeur mil. *Publications:* Lieutenant en Algérie 1957, Le défi Américain 1967, Le manifeste radical 1970, Le pouvoir régional 1971, Le défi mondial 1981, Le choix des juifs 1988, Passions 1991, Les Fossoyeurs 1993. *Address:* 37 avenue du Roule, 92200 Neuilly-sur-Seine, France.

SERVATIUS, Bernhard, DR.JUR.; German lawyer; b. 14 April 1932, Magdeburg; s. of Rudolf Servatius and Maria Servatius; m. Ingeborg Servatius 1985; ed. Univs. of Fribourg, Hamburg and other univs.; lawyer 1959–, now Sr. Partner, Dr. Servatius & Partner (legal firm); Sole Partner, Treubesitz GmbH, Hamburg (trust co.); legal adviser to Axel Springer and Springer Publishing Group 1970; Chair. Supervisory Bd. Rheinische Merkur GmbH; Chief Rep. of Axel Springer and Acting Chair. of Man. Admin. Verlagshaus Axel Springer 1984; Chair. Supervisory Bd. Axel Springer Verlag July 1985–; Prof. 1985–; many other professional and public appts; Bundesverdienstkreuz Erste Klasse. *Address:* Axel Springer Verlag AG, Axel-Springer Strasse 65, 10888 Berlin, Germany.

SERVOLINI, Luigi, D.LIT., D.F.A.; Italian xylographer, writer and art critic; b. 1 March 1906, Leghorn (Livorno), Tuscany; s. of Carlo Servolini; m. Odetta Andreoni 1930; one s. one d.; ed. Pisa Univ., Acad. of Fine Arts, Carrara; Prof. of Xylography and Lithography, R. Istituto del Libro di Urbino, and Dir. of Library, Urbino Univ. 1930–39; Dir. artistic and cultural insts. at Forlì 1939–53; First Gen. Dir. Istituto Rizzoli per l'Insegnamento delle arti grafiche, Milan 1953–56; Prof. History of Art; Headmaster; Prof. Special School for Art Historians, Istituto Storia d'Arte, Univ. of Pisa 1969–72; Pres. "Incisori d'Italia" Asscn. 1955–; also painter and lithographer and has since 1923 taken part in many important exhbns.; works represented in 80 European and American Public Galleries; has won several prizes; Hon. mem. Accademico Disegno, Florence; Ed. "Comanducci" Dictionary; mem. Ordine dei Giornalisti (Rome) 1935; Ed. La Voce degli IDIT (fortnightly); Pres. of Engraving Art Acad., Rome 1974–, Nat. Asscn. of Art Critics (ANCA-ECSA), Rome 1980–; Grand Officer Italian Repub. *Publications:* Ugo da Carpi 1929, La Xilografia a chiaroscuro italiana nei secoli XVI, XVII e XVIII 1930, Tecnica della Xilografia 1935, A. Bosse 1937, Problemi e aspetti dell'Incisione 1939, J. de Barbari 1943, Pittura gotica romagnola 1944, Xilografia giapponese 1949, La Xilografia 1950, Incisione italiana di cinque secoli 1951, Incidere 1952, 1961, Dizionario Incisori ital. moderni e contemporanei 1955, Mosaico di Romagna 1957, Autobiografia di Bodoni 1958, I procedimenti artistici e industriali della Grafica 1959–63, Gli Incisori d'Italia 1960, Il Comanducci: Dizionario dei Pittori (5 vols.) 4th edn. 1971–73, Acqueforti di Giovanni Fattori 1966, Athena: Storia dell' Arte classica e italiana (3 vols.) 1966–68, Dalla pietra litografica alla stampa offset 1968, L'Arte di Incidere 3rd edn. 1971, La Serigrafia Originale 1973, Gli Incisori d'Italia, Vol. II, 1974, Tecnica della Xilografia giapponese 1975, La storia e le tecniche dell' Incisione 1977, Ugo da Carpi: i chiaroscuri e le altre opere 1977. *Leisure interests:* ancient and modern prints, ex libris, hypnotism. *Address:* 00195 Rome, Via Simone de Saint Bon 25, Italy. *Telephone:* 06-3720378.

ŠEŠELJ, Vojislav, DR. JUR.; Serbian politician; b. 11 Nov. 1954, Sarajevo; s. of Nicola Šešelj and Danica Šešelj (née Misita); m. Jadranka Pavlovic; two s.; ed. Sarajevo Univ.; docent Sarajevo Univ. 1981–84; Prof. Pristina Univ. 1991–, was persecuted by authorities for nationalistic activities, arrested and sentenced to 8 years' imprisonment 1984, released after 22 months; later was arrested twice 1990, 1994–95; Head of Cetniks (royalists) Movt. 1989; f. and leader Serbian Radical Party 1990; supported war against Croatia 1991; cand. for presidency of Serbia 1997; Deputy Prime Minister 1997–; worked and lectured in European countries, U.S.A., Canada. *Publications:* over 50 books including Political Essence of Militarism and Fascism 1979, Dusk of Illusions 1986, Democracy and Dogma 1987, Debrozovisation of Public Mentality 1990, Destruction of Serbian National Being 1992, Actual Political Challenges 1993, Are we Theatened with Slobotomia 1994, Selected Works 1994. *Address:* Serbian Radical Party, Ohridska str. 1, 11000 Belgrade, Yugoslavia. *Telephone:* (11) 45 77 45 (Home).

SESSIONS, William S., J.D.; American government official and judge; b. 27 May 1930, Fort Smith, Ark.; s. of Will A. Sessions and Edith A. Steele; m. Alice June Lewis 1952; three s. one d.; ed. Baylor Univ.; called to Texas Bar 1959; Partner, McGregor & Sessions, Waco, Tex. 1959–61; Assoc. Tirey, McLaughlin, Gorin & Tirey, Waco 1961–63; Partner, Haley, Fulbright, Winniford, Sessions & Bice, Waco 1963–69; Chief, Govt. Operations Section, Criminal Div. Dept. of Justice 1969–71; U.S. Attorney, U.S. Dist. Court (Western Dist.) Texas, San Antonio 1971–74, U.S. Dist. Judge 1974–80, Chief U.S. Dist. Judge 1980–87; Dir. Fed. Bureau of Investigation (FBI) 1987–93; Partner, Sessions & Sessions, L.C.; Hon. Dir. Martin Luther King Jr. Fed. Holiday Comm. 1991–93, 1994–; mem. numerous cttees. and subcttees.; mem. A.B.A.; numerous awards. *Publications:* articles in professional journals. *Address:* 112 East Pecan, 29th Floor, San Antonio, TX 78205, U.S.A. *Telephone:* (210) 229-3000. *Fax:* (210) 229-1194.

SETCH, Terry, D.F.A.; British artist and teacher; b. 11 March 1936, Lewisham, London; s. of Frank Setch and Florence Skeggs; m. Dianne Shaw 1967; one d.; ed. Sutton School of Art and Slade School of Fine Art; Lecturer, Foundation Dept., Leicester Coll. of Art 1960–64; Sr. Lecturer in Fine Art, Cardiff Coll. of Art 1964–, in Art History Hayward Gallery, London 1987; exhbns: Artist in Nat. Parks, Victoria and Albert Museum, London 1988–89, Images of Paradise, Survival Int. 1989, Tree of Life, South Bank Centre, London 1989–90, Shared Earth (Anglo-Soviet landscapes) (tour) 1991–92, Innovation and Tradition, Tate Gallery, London 1993, Royal Acad. of Arts Summer Exhbn. 1993, 1995, 1996, Disclosures, tour Wales 1995, Nat. Museum of Wales, Cardiff, and Barcelona 1996; solo exhbns. Cardiff, Penarth, London 1992, Edin. 1993, Fishguard, London, 1995, Penarth 1997, works in Tate Gallery and other collections; comm.: mural for restaurant, Nat. Museum of Wales 1993; broadcasts: (BBC TV) Statements 1990, (BBC

TV) Wales Arts Awards 1993, (HTV) A Word in Your Eye 1997, (BBC TV) Catalyst 1997, (BBC Radio) Culture Vultures 1997; John Moores Exhbn. (Third Prize) 1985, Athena Awards (shortlist prizewinner) 1988. *Address:* 111 Plymouth Road, Penarth, Vale of Glamorgan, CF64 5DF, Wales. *Telephone:* (01222) 712113.

SETCHELL, David Lloyd, M.A.; British chartered accountant; b. 16 April 1937, Anston, Yorks.; s. of Raymond Setchell and Phyllis Jane Lloyd; m. Muriel Mary Davies 1962; one s. one d.; ed. Woodhouse Grammar School and Jesus Coll. Cambridge; Peat Marwick 1960–64; Shawinigan Ltd. 1964–71; Vice-Pres. Gulf Oil Chemicals (Europe) 1971–82; Man. Dir. Gulf Oil (G.B.) Ltd. 1982–98; Pres. Inst. of Petroleum 1996–98, Oil Industries Club 1993–95; Council mem. Cheltenham and Gloucester Coll. of Higher Educ. 1994–; Gov. Cheltenham Coll. 1998–; Dir. Cheltenham Arts Festivals 1994–. *Leisure interests:* golf, music, theatre. *Address:* South Hayes, Sandy Lane Road, Cheltenham, Glos., GL53 9DE, England. *Telephone:* (01242) 571390.

SETH, Vikram, PH.D.; Indian author; b. 1952, Calcutta; s. of Premnath Seth and Leila Seth; ed. Doon School, India, Tonbridge School, U.K., Corpus Christi Coll., Oxford, Stanford Univ., U.S.A.; W.H. Smith Literary Prize 1994, Commonwealth Writers' Prize 1994; Hon. Fellow Corpus Christi Coll., Oxford 1994. *Publications:* The Golden Gate: A Novel in Verse, From Heaven Lake: Travels Through Sinkiang and Tibet, A Suitable Boy (novel) 1993, Arion and the Dolphin (libretto) 1994, Beastly Tales (animal fables) 1994, An Equal Music (novel) 1999; several vols. of poetry. *Address:* c/o Shiel Land Associates, 43 Doughty Street, London, WC1N 2LF, England.

SETHNESS, Charles Olin, A.B., M.B.A.; American government official, financial executive and university administrator; b. 24 Feb. 1941, Evanston, Ill.; s. of C. Olin Sethness and Alison Louise Burge; m. 2nd Geraldine Greene 1977; one s. one step.-s. two step.-d.; ed. New Trier High School, Princeton Univ. and Harvard Business School; Sr. Credit Analyst, American Nat. Bank and Trust Co. of Chicago 1963–64; Research Asst. Harvard Business School 1966–67; with Morgan Stanley & Co. 1967–73, 1975–81; Vice-Pres. 1972–73, Man. Dir. 1975–81; Man. Morgan & Cie. Int. S.A., Paris 1971–73; Exec. Dir. World Bank Group and Special Asst. to Sec. of Treasury 1973–75; Assoc. Dean for External Relations, Harvard Business School, Boston 1981–85; Asst. Sec. of the Treasury for Domestic Finance 1985–88; Dir. Capital Markets Dept. Int. Finance Corpn. 1988–89; Chief Financial Officer Inter-American Devt. Bank 1990–. *Address:* 6219 Garnett Drive, Chevy Chase, MD 20815, U.S.A.

SEVERIN, (Giles) Timothy, M.A., D.LITT.; British traveller and author; b. 25 Sept. 1940; s. of Maurice Watkins and Inge Severin; m. Dorothy Virginia Sherman 1966 (divorced 1979); one d.; ed. Tonbridge School, Keble Coll., Oxford; Commonwealth Fellow, U.S.A. 1964–66; expeditions: led motorcycle team along Marco Polo's route 1961, canoe and launch down River Mississippi 1965, Brendan Voyage from W. Ireland to N. America 1977, Sindbad Voyage from Oman to China 1980–81, Jason Voyage from Greece to Soviet Georgia 1984, Ulysses Voyage, Troy to Ithaca 1985, Crusade: on horseback from Belgium to Jerusalem 1987–88, Travels on horseback in Mongolia 1990, China Voyage: bamboo sailing raft Hong Kong-Japan-Pacific 1993, Spice Islands Voyage in Moluccas, E. Indonesia 1996; Hon. D.Litt. (Dublin) 1997. *Publications:* Tracking Marco Polo 1964, Explorers of the Mississippi 1967, The Golden Antilles 1970, The African Adventure 1973, Vanishing Primitive Man 1973, The Oriental Adventure 1976, The Brendan Voyage 1978, The Sindbad Voyage 1982, The Jason Voyage 1984, The Ulysses Voyage 1987, Crusader 1989, In Search of Genghis Khan 1991, The China Voyage 1994, The Spice Islands Voyage 1997. *Address:* Inchy Bridge, Timoleague, Co. Cork, Ireland. *Telephone:* (023) 46127. *Fax:* (023) 46233.

SEVERINO, Rodolfo Certeza, Jr., M.A.; Philippine diplomatist; m. Rowena V. Romero; ed. Ateneo de Manila Univ., Johns Hopkins Univ. School of Advanced Int. Studies, Washington, D.C.; Assoc. Ed. Manor Press Inc. 1956–59, Philippine Int. 1957–59, Marketing Horizons 1961–64; with Operation Brotherhood, Laos 1959–61; special asst. to Senator Raul S. Manglapus (q.v.), Philippine Senate 1961–64; information asst. UN Information Centre, Manila 1964–65; Third, then Second and First Sec. Embassy, Washington, D.C. 1967–74; special asst. to Under-Sec. of Foreign Affairs 1974–76, Under-Sec. 1992–97; Chargé d'Affaires Embassy, Beijing 1976–78; Consul-Gen., Houston, Texas 1979–86; Asst. Sec. for Asian and Pacific Affairs 1986–88; Amb. to Malaysia 1988–92; Sec.-Gen. Asscn. of S.E. Asian Nations (ASEAN) 1997–. *Address:* Association of South East Asian Nations, 70A Jalan Sisingamangaraja, P.O. Box 2072, Jakarta 12110, Indonesia. *Telephone:* (21) 726-2410. *Fax:* (21) 739-8234.

SEVON, Leif, LL.M.; Finnish judge; b. 31 Oct. 1941, Helsingfors; s. of Ensio Sevon and Ulla Sevon; m. (divorced); one s. one d.; ed. Univ. of Helsinki; Asst. Univ. of Helsinki 1966–71, Asst. Prof. 1971–74; Counsellor of Legislation, Ministry of Justice 1973–78; Sr. Judge, Chamber Pres. City Court of Helsinki 1979–80; Dir. of Legislation, Ministry of Justice 1980–86, Dir.-Gen. Dept. of Legislation 1986–91; Judge, Supreme Court of Justice 1991; Counsellor, Dept. of Trade, Ministry of Foreign Affairs 1991–92; Pres. EFTA Court 1994; Judge, Court of Justice of European Communities Jan. 1995–. *Publications:* books, articles and translations. *Address:* Cour de Justice des Communautés Européennes, Palais 103, 2925 Luxembourg. *Telephone:* (352) 4303-2830. *Fax:* (352) 4303-2828.

SEVOSTYANOV, Grigory Nikolayevich; Russian historian; b. 5 April 1916; m.; one s.; ed. Novocherkassk Polytech. Inst.; teacher Novocherkassk Polytech. Inst. 1940–41; Asst. Deputy Chair. Govt. Belorussian S.S.R. 1944–45; Attaché Ministry of Foreign Affairs 1947; jr., sr. researcher, head of div. Inst. of History U.S.S.R. Acad. of Sciences 1950–68; head of div., head of dept. Inst. of Comprehensive History U.S.S.R. Acad. of Sciences 1968–88; chief researcher 1988–; mem. U.S.S.R. (now Russian) Acad. of Sciences 1987; research in history of America and int. relations, problems of history of World War II, workers' movt. in USA; U.S.S.R. State Prize. *Publications:* Policy of Great States in the Far East on the eve of World War II 1961, U.S.A. and France in wartime 1939–45: History of International Relations 1974, History of USA 1983–87 and other books and articles. *Address:* Institute of Comprehensive History, Russian Academy of Sciences, Leninsky pr. 32a, 117334 Moscow, Russia. *Telephone:* (095) 938-19-11 (Office); (095) 928-86-07 (Home).

SEWARD, George Chester, LL.B.; American lawyer; b. 4 Aug. 1910, Omaha, Neb.; s. of George F. Seward and Ada L. Rugh; m. Carroll F. McKay 1936 (died 1991); two s. two d.; ed. Male High School, Louisville, Ky. and Univ. of Virginia; with Shearman & Sterling, New York 1936–53, Seward & Kissel, New York, Washington D.C. and Budapest, Hungary 1953–; Dir. Witherbee Sherman Corpn. 1952–66 (Pres. 1964–66), Howmet Corpn. 1955–75, Clas. P. Young Co. 1965–72; Trustee Benson Iron Ore Trust 1969–80; Founder and Hon. Life Pres. Business Law Section of Int. Bar Asscn.; Hon. Life Pres. and life mem. Council of Int. Bar Asscn.; Founder, Chair. (1988–91) and Hon. Chair. Int. Capital Markets Group of Féd. Int. des Bourses de Valeurs, Int. Fed. of Accountants and Int. Bar Asscn.; Chair. Cttee. on Corporate Laws of A.B.A. 1952–58, American Bar Foundation Cttee. on Model Business Corpn. Acts 1956–65, Banking Cttee. of A.B.A. 1960–61; life mem. Council of Section of Business Law of A.B.A. (Chair. 1958–59); mem. House of Dels., A.B.A. 1959, 1963–74, Jt. Cttee. on Continuing Legal Educ. of the American Law Inst. and A.B.A. 1965–76, Univ. of Va. Arts and Sciences Council 1984–93 (Pres. 1991–93), N.Y. Stock Exchange Legal Advisory Cttee. 1984–87; Fellow American Law Inst., American Asscn. of Bar of City of New York, N.Y. State, Ky., Va. and D.C. Bar Asscns.; Trustee Edwin Gould Foundation for Children 1955–96, The Nature Conservancy Eastern Long Island, N.Y. 1975-88, N.Y. Genealogical and Biographical Soc.; George Seward Lecture series sponsored by Int. Bar Asscn. *Publications:* Basic Corporate Practice, Seward and Related Families, co-author Model Business Corporation Act Annotated, ed. We Remember Carroll. *Address:* Seward & Kissel, 1 Battery Park Plaza, New York, NY 10004 (Office); 48 Greenacres Avenue, Scarsdale, NY 10583, U.S.A. (Home).

SEWELL, Brian; British art historian and critic; art critic for Evening Standard; British Press Awards Critic of the Year 1988, Arts Journalist of the Year 1994, Hawthornden Prize for Art Criticism 1995. *Publications:* South from Ephesus 1988, The Reviews that Caused the Rumpus 1994, An Alphabet of Villains 1995. *Address:* The Evening Standard, Northcliffe House, 2 Derry Street, London, W8 5EE, England. *Telephone:* 0171-938 6000. *Fax:* 0171-937 2648.

SEWELL, Rufus Frederick; British actor; b. 29 Oct. 1967; s. of the late Bill Sewell; m. Yasmin Abdallah 1999. *Stage appearances include:* Royal Hunt of the Sun, Comedians, The Lost Domain, Peter and the Captain, Pride and Prejudice, The Government Inspector, The Seagull, As You Like It, Making it Better, Arcadia, Translations, Rat in the Skull, Macbeth. *Television appearances include:* The Last Romantics, Gone to Seed, Middlemarch, Dirty Something, Citizen Locke, Cold Comfort Farm, Henry IV. *Film appearances include:* Twenty-One, Dirty Weekend, A Man of No Importance, Carrington, Victory, Hamlet, The Woodlanders, The Honest Courtesan, Martha Meet Frank, Daniel and Laurence, Illuminata, Dark City. *Address:* c/o Julian Belfrage Associates, 46 Albemarle Street, London, W1X 4PP, England. *Telephone:* 0171-491 4400. *Fax:* 0171-493 5460.

SEWERYN, Andrzej; Polish actor; b. 25 April 1946, Heilbronn; m.; one s. one d.; ed. State Higher School of Drama, Warsaw; actor Athenaeum Theatre, Warsaw 1968–82, Peter Brooks Group 1984–88, perm. mem. Comédie Française, Paris 1993–; co-operation with film, TV and radio; mem. SPATiF (Asscn. of Polish Theatre and Film Actors) 1969–82; Prize Le Syndicat professionnel de la Critique dramatique et musicale de France 1996; leading roles in Don Carlos, Peer Gynt, Don Juan; films: Kliefhorn in Polish Roads (TV series) 1977, Marek in On the Silver Globe 1976–79 (TV series), Zenon in The Border 1977, Rukacki in Połanieck Family 1977 (TV series), Rościszewski in Without Anaesthetic 1978, Ksiadz in The Brute 1979, Roman in Roman and Magda 1979 (TV series), Kung-fu 1979, Conductor 1979 (Prize Int. Film Festival in Berlin), Mahabharata 1988, French Revolution 1989, Schindler's List 1994; numerous roles on TV. *Address:* Comédie Française, Place Colette, 75001 Paris, France. *Telephone:* 01.44.58.14.00. *Fax:* 01.44.58.14.50.

SEXWALE, (Gabriel) Tokyo; South African politician; b. 5 March 1953; s. of Frank Sexwale; m. Judy Sexwale; three c.; imprisoned for 13 years on Robben Island for guerrilla activities; mem. ANC Mil. Wing; Chair. ANC, Witwatersrand Region, Transvaal Prov.; Premier Pretoria - Witwatersrand - Vereeniging Prov. (now Gauteng), May 1994–; mem ANC Nat. Exec. Cttee. 1991–. *Address:* Private Bag X61, Marshalltown 2107, South Africa.

SEYBOU, Brig. Ali; Niger fmr. Head of State and army officer; fmr. army chief of staff; mem. Supreme Mil. Council; Pres. of Niger 1987–93. *Address:* c/o Office of the President, Niamey, Niger.

SEYDOUX FORNIER de CLAUSONNE, Jérôme; French business executive; b. 21 Sept. 1934, Paris; s. of René Seydoux Fornier de Clausonne and Geneviève Schlumberger; m. 1st (divorced); three s. one d.; m. 2nd Sophie Desserteaux-Bessis 1988; one s.; ed. Lycées Montaigne, Louis-le-Grand and Buffon; financial analyst Istel, Lepercq and Co. Inc. N.Y. 1962–63; sleeping partner Bank of Neuflize, Schlumberger, Mallet 1964, partner 1966, mem. Bd. Dirs. 1969–70; admin. Schlumberger Ltd. 1969, Exec. Vice Pres. 1970, Dir. Gen. 1975–76; admin. Compagnie Deutsch 1964–, Danone (fmrly. BSN) 1973–; Pres. Pricel 1976; Pres. Chargeurs 1980–96, now Vice-Pres., Dir.-Gen.; Pres. Admin. Council of France 5 1986; Pres., Dir.-Gen. Pathé Palace (fmrly. Pathé Cinema) 1991–, now Pres., Dir.-Gen. Pathé; Chair. BSkyB 1998–; owner Libération newspaper. *Leisure interests:* skiing, golf. *Address:* Pathé, 5 boulevard Malesherbes, 75008 Paris, France.

SEYDOUX FORNIER de CLAUSONNE, Nicolas Pierre, L. EN D., L. EN SC.ECON.; French business executive; b. 16 July 1939, Paris; s. of René Seydoux Fornier de Clausonne and Geneviève Schlumberger; m. Anne-Marie Cahen-Salvador 1964; two c.; ed. Lycée Buffon, Faculté de Droit, Paris, New York Business School and Inst. d'Etudes Politiques, Paris; Head of legal service, Cie. Int. pour l'Informatique, Paris 1967–70; financial analyst, Morgan, Stanley & Co. Inc. New York 1970–71, Morgan & Cie. Int. S.A. Paris 1971–74; Vice-Pres.-Dir.-Gen. Société Gaumont 1974, Pres.-Dir.-Gen. 1975–; Pres. Féd. Nat. des Distributeurs de Films 1988–; Chevalier, Légion d'honneur. *Leisure interests:* vintage cars, skiing. *Address:* Gaumont, 30 avenue Charles de Gaulle, 92200 Neuilly-sur-Seine (Office); 5 place du Palais-Bourbon, 75007 Paris, France (Home).

SEYMOUR, Lynn, C.B.E.; Canadian ballet dancer; b. 8 March 1939, Wainwright, Alberta; d. of E. V. Springett; m. 1st Colin Jones 1963 (divorced 1974); three s.; m. 2nd Philip Pace 1974; m. 3rd Vanya Hackel 1983 (divorced 1988); ed. Royal Ballet School; Graduated into Royal Ballet 1957; promoted to Soloist rank 1958, to Prin. 1958; joined Deutsche Oper, Berlin 1966; Guest Artist, Royal Ballet 1970–78; Artistic Dir. of Ballet Bayerische Staatsoper 1979–80; Guest Artist with other cos. incl. Alvin Ailey; Evening Standard Drama Award 1977. *Ballets:* The Burrow 1958, Swan Lake 1958, Giselle 1958, The Invitation 1960, The Two Pigeons 1961, Symphony 1963, Romeo and Juliet 1964, Anastasia 1966, Dances at a Gathering, The Concert, The Seven Deadly Sins, Flowers 1972, Shukumei, The Four Seasons 1975, Side Show, Rituals 1975, Manon Lescaut 1976, A Month in the Country 1976, Mayerling 1978, Manon 1978, Choreography for Rashomon 1976, The Court of Love 1977, Intimate Letters 1978, Mae and Polly, Boreas, Tattooed Lady, Wolfy, the Ballet Rambert 1987. *Publication:* Lynn: leaps and boundaries (autobiog. with Paul Gardner) 1984. *Address:* c/o Artistes in Action, 16 Balderton Street, London, W1Y 1TF, England.

SEYPIDIN AZE; Chinese politician; b. 1916, Artush, Xinjiang; ed. Cen. Asia Univ., Moscow; Leader of Uighur Uprisings 1933, 1944; participant in armed rebellion and establishment of E. Turkestan Repub. 1944; Minister of Educ., E. Turkistan Repub. 1945; Deputy Chair. Xinjiang Uighur People's Govt. 1949–54, Chair. 1955–68; Deputy Commdr. Xinjiang Uighur Mil. Region, PLA 1949; Second Sec. CCP Xinjiang Uighur 1956–68; Alt. mem. 8th Cen. Cttee. of CCP 1956; Pres. Xinjiang Uighur Univ. 1964; Vice-Chair. Xinjiang Uighur Revolutionary Cttee. 1968, Chair. 1972–78; mem. 9th Cen. Cttee. of CCP 1969; Second Sec. CCP Xinjiang Uighur 1971, First Sec. 1973–78; Alt. mem. Politburo, 10th Cen. Cttee. of CCP 1973, 1975–78; First Political Commissar Xinjiang Uighur Mil. Region, PLA 1974–78; Chair. Presidium Nat. People's Congress 1975; Alt. mem. Politburo, 11th Cen. Cttee. of CCP 1976; Exec. Chair. Presidium 5th Nat. People's Congress; Vice-Chair. Cttee. 5th Nat. People's Congress 1978–83; Vice-Chair. Standing Cttee. 6th NPC 1983–88, 7th NPC 1988; Exec. Chair. Presidium 6th NPC 1986–88, 7th NPC 1988; Pres. China-Pakistan Friendship Asscn.; Hon. Chair. China Society for Study of Uygur History and Culture; Hon. Pres. Minority Writers' Soc. 1985–, Minority Literature Foundation Dec. 1986; mem. 12th CCP Cen. Cttee. 1982–87, 13th Cen. Cttee. 1987–92, Presidium of 14th CCP Nat. Congress 1992–97; Vice-Chair. 8th Nat. Cttee. CPPCC 1993–98. *Address:* 19 Xi Jiaomin Xiang, Xicheng District, People's Republic of China.

SEZGIN; Ismet; Turkish politician; b. 1928, Aydln; m.; two c.; ed. Izmir School of Economy and Trade; Founder-mem. True Path Party (DYP); deputy from Aydın 1961–80; fmr. Minister of Youth and Sports, and of Finance; Minister of the Interior 1991–93, of Nat. Defence and Deputy Prime Minister June 1997–. *Address:* Milli Savunma Bakanliği, 06100 Ankara, Turkey. *Telephone:* (312) 425-4596. *Fax:* (312) 418-4737.

SFAR, Rachid; Tunisian politician; b. 11 Sept. 1933, Mahdia; ed. Lycée des Garçons, Sfax, Inst. de Hautes Etudes, Tunis and Ecole Nat. des Impôts, Paris; Inspector of Taxes 1960; Dir.-Gen. Régie Nat. des Tabacs et Allumettes (RNTA) 1965; Dir. of Taxation, Ministry of Finance 1969; Sec.-Gen. Ministry of Educ. 1971–73, Ministry of Finance 1973–77; Minister of Mines and Energy 1977–78, of Defence 1978–80, of Health 1980–83, of Nat. Economy 1983–86, of Finance and Economy April–July 1986; Prime Minister 1986–87; Deputy to Nat. Ass. 1979–; Pres. Chamber of Deputies 1988; mem. Cen. Cttee. and Politburo, Parti Socialiste Destourien 1979–; Amb. to EEC 1989–92; Grand Cordon, Ordre de l'Indépendence; Grand Officier, Ordre de la République. *Address:* 278 avenue de Tervuren, 1150 Brussels, Belgium. *Telephone:* (02) 771-73-95.

SGORLON, Carlo Pietro Antonio, PH.D.; Italian novelist and journalist; b. 27 July 1930, Cassacco, Udine; s. of Antonio Sgorlon and Livia Sgorlon; m. Edda Agarinis 1961; ed. Liceo Classico di Udine, Univs. of Pisa and Munich; secondary school teacher 1953–79; journalist 1969–; Enna Prize 1968, Rapallo Prize 1968, Supercampiello Prizes 1973 and 1983, Vallombrosa Prize 1983, Soroptomist Prize 1983, Strega Prize 1985, Hemingway Prize 1987, Palme D'Oro Prize 1988, Nonino Prize 1989, Campano D'Oro Prize 1989, Fiuggi Prize 1989, Un Libro per L'Avvenire Prize 1989, Tascabile S. Benedetto del Tronto Prize 1989, Napoli Prize 1989, Latina Prize 1989, Isola d'Elba Prize 1997, Ennio Flaiano Prize 1997, Rhegium Prize 1997. *Publications:* Kafka narratore 1961, La Poltrona 1968, Elsa Morante 1972, Il Trono di Legno 1973, Regina di Saba 1975, Gli dei torneranno 1977, La Luna Color Ametista 1978, La Carrozza di Rame 1979, La Contrada 1981, La Conchiglia di Anataj 1983, L'Armata dei Fiumi Perduti 1985, Sette Veli 1986, L'Ultima Valle 1987, Il Caldèras 1988, I Racconti della Terra di Canaan 1989, La Fontana di Lorena 1990, Il Patriarcato della Luna 1991, La Foiba Grande 1992, Il Guaritore 1993, Il Regno dell'Uomo 1994. Il Costruttore 1995, La Malga di Sîr 1997, Il Processo di Tolosa 1998. *Leisure interests:* painting, carpentry, walking. *Address:* Via Micesio 15, Udine CAP 33100, Italy. *Telephone:* 0432 294140.

SGOUROS, Dimitris; Greek concert pianist; b. 30 Aug. 1969, Athens; s. of Sotirios Sgouros and Marianthi Sgouros; ed. Univ. of Athens, Athens Conservatory of Music, Univ. of Maryland, U.S.A. and Royal Acad. of Music, London; debut (aged 7) Piraeus 1977; numerous concerts in Europe since 1981; first U.S. appearance (aged 12), with NSO of Washington, Carnegie Hall, New York 1982; appeared at Prague Spring Festival 1986; played twelve different piano concertos on six nights with Singapore Symphony Orchestra, Sgouros Festival, Singapore 1990; has also played in Australia, New Zealand, Korea, Hong Kong, Romania and Russia; recordings of works by Schumann, Brahms, Rachmaninov, Tchaikovsky, Liszt, Mozart, Chopin; Int. Competition, Acad. of Athens 1982, Los Angeles 1984, Leonardo da Vinci Int. Prize and other prizes. *Leisure interests:* mathematics, conducting opera. *Address:* Tompazi 28 Str., Piraeus 18537, Greece. *Telephone:* 3-01-8959778. *Fax:* 3-01-4538737.

SHABANGU, Albert H. N., M.A.; Swazi politician and teacher; b. 23 March 1944, Hlathikhulu; s. of Lovela Shabangu and Mlambile Alice Shabangu (née Mamba); m. Minah Nomsa Dlamini 1976; two s. two d.; ed. Univ. of Leeds, William Pitcher Coll.; teacher, then head teacher 1971–91; M.P. 1991–, also Minister, fmrly. responsible for Transport and Communications, Labour and Public Service, Econ. Planning and Devt., Minister for Foreign Affairs April 1998–; Pres. Swaziland Nat. Asscn. of Teachers 1972–91; Chief Counsellor Order of King Sobhuza II. *Leisure interests:* athletics, soccer, boxing, choral music. *Address:* Ministry of Foreign Affairs, P.O. Box 518, Mbabane, Swaziland. *Telephone:* 42661. *Fax:* 42669.

SHABDURASULOV, Igor Vladimirovich; Russian civil servant; b. 3 Oct. 1957, Tashkent; m.; three c.; ed. Moscow State Univ.; Head, UNESCO Project Great Silk Way, Russian Acad. of Sciences 1983–86; on staff Div. of Science, Culture and Educ., Russian Govt.; mem., Admin. of Russian Presidency, then Head, Dept. of Culture, Russian Govt. 1993–94; Head, Dept. of Culture and Information, Russian Govt. 1994–98; Deputy Head, Admin. of Russian Presidency, Head Group of speech writers April–Sept. 1998; Dir.-Gen. Russian Public TV Sept. 1998–. *Address:* Russian Public TV, Akademika Koroleva str. 12, 127000 Moscow, Russia. *Telephone:* (095) 217 6330 (Office).

SHACK, William Alfred, PH.D.; American professor of anthropology; b. 19 April 1923, Chicago, Ill.; s. of William Shack and Emma McAvoy Shack; m. Dorothy C. Nash 1960; one s.; ed. School of Art, Inst. of Chicago, Univ. of Chicago, L.S.E., Univ. of London; Asst. Prof. of Sociology and Anthropology, N.E. Ill. State Coll. 1961–62; Asst. Prof. of Sociology, Haile Selassie I Univ., Ethiopia 1962–65; Research Assoc., Dept. of Anthropology, Univ. of Chicago 1965–66; Assoc. Prof. of Anthropology, Univ. of Ill., Chicago 1966–70; Prof. of Anthropology, Univ. of Calif., Berkeley 1970–94, Prof. Emer. 1994–, Dean, Grad. Div. 1979–85, Pres. Faculty Club 1989–95; Chair., N. American Cttee., Royal Anthropological Inst., London 1983–86; Visiting Prof. M. I. B. Ecole Nat. des Ponts et Chaussées, Paris 1991–, Univ. of Bristol 1994–; Fellow A.A.A.S., Calif. Acad. Sciences (Trustee, Vice-Pres. 1992–96, Vice-Chair. 1992–96), American Anthropological Asscn., Int. African Inst. (Exec. Council 1984, Vice-Chair. 1985–87, Chair. 1987–97); Trustee, Bd. Dirs. World Affairs Council of N. Calif.; Chevalier, Ordre nat. du Mérite 1987. *Publications:* The Gurage 1966, The Central Ethiopians 1974, Gods and Heroes (co-author) 1974, Strangers in African Societies (co-ed.) 1979, Politics in Leadership (co-ed.) 1979, The Kula 1985. *Leisure interest:* vintage motor racing. *Address:* Department of Anthropology, University of California, 232 Kroeber Hall, Berkeley, CA 94720; 2597 Hilgard Avenue, Berkeley, CA 94709, U.S.A. (Home). *Telephone:* (415) 642-3391 (Office).

SHACKLETON, Robert Millner, PH.D., F.R.S.; British geologist; b. 30 Dec. 1909, Purley, Surrey; s. of John Milner Shackleton and Agnes Mitford Shackleton; m. 1st Gwen Isabel Harland 1933 (divorced); m. 2nd Judith Wyndham Jeffreys 1948 (divorced); m. 3rd Peigi Wallace 1983; two s. three d.; ed. Sidcot School, Somerset, Univ. of Liverpool and Imperial Coll., London; Chief Geologist, Whitehall Explorations Ltd., Fiji 1933–34; Lecturer,

Imperial Coll. 1934–40; Geologist, Geological Survey, Kenya 1940–45; Lecturer, Imperial Coll. 1945–48; Herdman Prof. of Geology, Univ. of Liverpool 1948–63; Prof. of Geology, Univ. of Leeds 1963–76, Dir. Research Inst. of African Geology 1966–76; Hon. Sr. Research Fellow, Open Univ. 1977–; Visiting Prof., Imperial Coll. 1985–89; Silver Medal, Liverpool Geological Soc.; Murchison Medal, Geological Soc. of London; Clough Medal, Edinburgh Geological Soc. *Publications:* numerous papers in geological journals. *Leisure interests:* gardening, painting, travel. *Address:* The Croft Barn, Church Street, East Hendred, Oxfordshire, OX12 8LA, England. *Telephone:* (01235) 834802.

SHAER, Ali Hassan ash-; Saudi Arabian politician; b. 1927, Medina; ed. Mil. Acad., King Saud Univ.; Chief Instructor Mil. School Taif; Dir. Topography Div. Mil. Operations Dept.; Commdr. Medina Mil. School, King Abdulaziz Mil. Acad; Mil. Attaché, Embassy Pakistan; Amb. to Lebanon 1975–83; Minister of Information 1983–95; King Abdulaziz Medal (First Class), several foreign decorations. *Address:* c/o Ministry of Information, P.O. Box 570, Nasseriya Street, Riyadh 11161, Saudi Arabia.

SHAFAREVICH, Igor Rostislavovich, DR.PHYS.-MATH.SC.; Russian mathematician; b. 3 June 1923, Zhitomir; m.; two c.; ed. Moscow Univ.; Research Officer Moscow Math. Inst. 1943–44; staff mem. Faculty of Mechanics and Math., Moscow Univ. 1944–52; Prof. Moscow Univ. 1953–75 (dismissed for dissident activities); lecturer, Head of Dept., V. Steklov Math. Inst. 1960–; corresp. mem. U.S.S.R. (now Russian) Acad. of Sciences 1958, mem. 1991; mem. Bd. Moscow Math. Soc. 1964, Pres. 1970–74; mem. U.S.S.R. Human Rights Cttee.; mem. Political Council, Nat. Salvation Front 1992; Hon. mem. U.S. Acad. of Sciences, Acad. Leopoldina, American Acad. of Arts and Sciences, Royal Soc., London; Dr. h.c. (Paris); Lenin Prize 1959, Heinemann Prize, Göttingen Acad. of Sciences 1975. *Publications include:* Has Russia a Future? and "Socialism" in Solzhenitsyn's From Under the Rubble, Socialism as a Phenomenon in Global History 1977, Russophobia 1990. *Address:* c/o V. Steklov Mathematical Institute, Vavilova Street 42, 117966 Moscow, Russia. *Telephone:* 135-25-49 (Office); 930-18-02 (Home).

SHAFEI, Col. Hussein Mahmoud El-; Egyptian politician and army officer; b. 8 Feb. 1918, Tanta; s. of Mahmoud El-Shafei; m. Magda Gabr 1948; two s. one d.; ed. Mil. Coll., Cairo; commissioned as 2nd Lieut. 1938; took part in Palestine hostilities 1948; graduated from Staff Officers' Coll. 1953 and apptd. Officer-in-Charge Cavalry Corps; Minister of War and Marine 1954, of Social Affairs (Egypt) 1954–58; Minister of Labour and Social Affairs, U.A.R. 1958–61; Vice-Pres. of U.A.R. and Minister of Social Affairs and Waqfs 1961–62; mem. Presidency Council 1962–64; Vice-Pres. of U.A.R. (Egypt) 1964–67, 1970–75; Vice-Pres. and Minister of Religious Institutions (Waqfs) 1967–70; Pres. Egyptian del. to OAU Summit Conf. 1973–74; participated in preparing constitution of federation between Egypt, Syria and Libya. *Leisure interests:* riding, tennis, swimming, drawing.

SHAFFER, Peter Levin, C.B.E., F.R.S.L.; British playwright; b. 15 May 1926, Liverpool; s. of Jack Shaffer and Reka (née Fredman) Shaffer; ed. St. Paul's School, London, and Trinity Coll., Cambridge; with Acquisitions Dept. New York Library 1951; returned to England 1954; with Publicity Dept. Boosey and Hawkes 1954; Literary Critic, Truth 1956–57; playwright 1957–; Cameron Mackintosh Prof. of Contemporary Theatre, St. Catherine's Coll. Oxford 1994–95; mem. European Acad. 1998–; Evening Standard Drama Award 1958; New York Drama Critics Circle Award 1959–60; Antoinette Perry Award for Best Play and N.Y. Drama Critics Circle Award 1975 (Equus) and 1981 (Amadeus); Evening Standard Drama Award 1957 (Five Finger Exercise) and 1980, London Drama Critics Award; Acad. Award for Best Screenplay (Amadeus) 1984; Hon. D. Litt. (Buckingham) 1989, (Bath) 1992; apptd. mem. European Acad. at Yuste 1998. *Plays:* Five Finger Exercise, London 1958, New York 1939 (film 1962), The Private Ear and The Public Eye, London 1962, U.S.A. 1963, The Royal Hunt of the Sun London 1964, New York 1964 (film 1965, opera adaptation, London 1977), Black Comedy, London 1965, New York 1967, White Lies, New York 1967 (revised as The White Liars, London 1968, and as White Liars, London 1976), The Battle of Shrivings 1970, Equus, London 1973, New York 1974 (film 1977), Amadeus, London 1979, New York 1980 (film 1984), Yonadab 1985, Lettice and Lovage, London 1987, New York 1990 (Evening Standard Award for Best Comedy 1988), The Gift of the Gorgon 1992; Whom Do I Have The Honour of Addressing? 1989 (radio play); also performed on stage, Chichester, Guildford, Malvern 1996; also television plays. *Leisure interests:* architecture, walking, music. *Address:* c/o McNaughton-Lowe Representation, Douglas House, 16–18 Douglas Street, London, SW1P 4PB, England. *Telephone:* 0171-834 4646.

SHAFFER, Richard Forrest, M.F.A.; American artist; b. 17 March 1947, Calif.; s. of Kendall C. Shaffer, Sr. and Marjorie Cockcroft; m. Camilla Mardon 1994; two s. one d.; ed. Univ. of California, New York School for Social Research, Stanford Univ.; artist in residence Roswell Museum and Art Center 1976, MacDowell Colony N.Y. 1977; Assoc. Prof. of Art Univ. of Texas at Arlington 1979–85; Rockefeller Fellow, Bellagio, Italy 1983; Visiting Artist Univ. of Calif. at Santa Barbara 1992–94, Univ. of Calif. at Santa Cruz 1994–96; Awards in Visual Arts; Nat. Endowment Award 1981. *Publications:* Selected Work: Richard Shaffer 1984, Kein Licht (catalogue) 1990, Paintings and Prints (catalogue) 1993. *Leisure interests:* surfing, phenomenology. *Address:* 1200 El Rancho Drive, Santa Cruz, CA 95060, U.S.A. *Telephone:* (408) 469-0838. *Fax:* (408) 662-9827.

SHAFIE, Tan Sri Haji Mohammed Ghazali, P.M.N., S.S.A.P., S.I.M.P., S.P.D.K.: Malaysian politician; b. 22 March 1922, Kuala Lipis; m. Puan Sri Khatijah binti Abdul Majid; two s.; ed. Raffles Coll., Singapore, Univ. Coll. of Wales; fmr. civil servant; assigned to Office of Commr. for Malaya, London; later Commr. for Fed. of Malaya, New Delhi; Deputy Sec. for External Affairs 1957, Acting Perm. Sec. 1959; Senator 1970–72; Minister with Special Functions 1970–72, also of Information 1971–72; mem. Parl. 1972–; Minister of Home Affairs 1973–81, of Foreign Affairs 1981–84; Govt. Special Envoy 1984; Chair. Paremba; Visiting Prof., Nat. Univ. of Singapore. *Address:* 15 Jalan Ampang Hilir, 55000 Kuala Lumpur, Malaysia. *Telephone:* 456 24 63.

SHAFIQ, Mohammad Musa, M.A.; Afghanistan politician; b. 1924, Kabul; ed. Ghazi High School, Al Azhar Univ., Cairo and Columbia Univ., U.S.A.; joined Ministry of Justice 1957, later became Dir. Legis. Dept.; also taught at Faculty of Law and Political Science, Kabul Univ.; Partner, pvt. law firm, Kabul 1961; Deputy Minister of Justice 1963–66; Adviser, Ministry of Foreign Affairs 1966–68; Amb. to Egypt, also accred. to Lebanon, Sudan and Ghana 1968–71; Minister of Foreign Affairs 1971–73; Prime Minister 1972–73 (deposed by mil. coup); in detention 1973–75.

SHAGARI, Alhaji Shehu Usman Aliu; Nigerian fmr. Head of State and educationist; b. 25 Feb. 1925, Shagari; m.; eight s. ten d.; ed. Middle School, Sokoto, Barewa Coll., Kaduna, Teacher Training Coll., Zaria; Science Teacher, Sokoto Middle School 1945–50; Headmaster, Argungu Sr. Primary School 1951–52; Sr. Visiting Teacher, Sokoto Prov. 1953–58; mem. Fed. Parl. 1954–58; Parl. Sec. to the Prime Minister 1958–59; Fed. Minister of Econ. Devt. 1959–60, of Establishments 1960–62, of Internal Affairs 1962–65, of Works 1965–66; Sec. Sokoto Prov. Educ. Devt. Fund 1966–68; State Commr. for Educ., Sokoto Prov. 1968–70; Fed. Commr. for Econ. Devt. and Reconstruction 1970–71, for Finance 1971–75; fmr. Chair. Peugeot Automobile Nigeria Ltd.; mem. Constituent Assembly 1977–83; Presidential candidate for the Nat. Party of Nigeria (NPN) 1979; Pres. of Nigeria and C.-in-C. of the Armed Forces 1979–83 (deposed by mil. coup), also Minister of Defence 1982–83; under house arrest 1983–86, banned from holding public office and from political activity Aug. 1986; confined to Shagari Village 1986–88; granted unrestricted freedom 1988; Proprietor 1995–96; Hon. LL.D. (Ahmadu Bello Univ.) 1976; Grand Commdr. Order of the Niger 1993. *Publications:* Wakar Nigeria (poem), Shehu Usman Dan-Fodio: Ideas and Ideals of his Leadership. *Address:* 6A Okoll'e Eboh Street, Ikoyi, Lagos, Nigeria.

SHAH, Eddy (Selim Jehane); British newspaper publisher; b. 1944, Cambridge; s. of Moochool Shah and Hazel Strange; m. Jennifer Shah; two s. one d.; ed. several schools including Gordonstoun; worked as Asst. Stage Man. in Repertory Theatre; also worked in TV, and later as space salesman for free newspaper once published by Manchester Evening News; launched Sale and Altrincham Messenger freesheet in 1974, Stockport Messenger 1977, also propr. of Bury Messenger; launched Today newspaper 1986, Chair., CEO 1986–88; launched The Post Oct. 1988 (folded Dec. 1988). *Publications:* Ring of Red Roses (novel) 1991, The Lucy Ghosts 1992, Manchester Blue (novel) 1992, Fallen Angels (novel) 1994. *Leisure interest:* golf.

SHAH, Prakash, LL.B., M.COM.; Indian diplomatist; b. 4 July 1939, Bombay; s. of H. Patel; m. Veenu Lall; two d.; joined Indian Foreign Service 1961; Third Sec. EEC 1962–64; Second Sec. Washington, D.C. 1964–67; Ministry of External Affairs 1967–69; Ministry of Finance 1969–71; First Sec., Petroleum Counsellor, Embassies, Iran and Gulf States 1971–75; Dir. Ministry of Petroleum 1975–77; Dir. Indian Petrochemicals Ltd., Petrofils Co-operatives Ltd. 1976–77; Dir./Jt. Sec. Ministry of External Affairs 1977–78; Jt. Sec. to Prime Minister 1978–80; High Commr. in Malaysia and Brunei 1980–83; Amb. to Venezuela and Consul-Gen. to Netherlands Antilles 1983–85; Jt. Sec. Ministry of External Affairs 1985–88, Additional Sec. 1989–90; Dir. Kudremakh Iron Ore Ltd. 1986; Amb. and Perm. Rep. to UN, Geneva 1991–92; Amb. to Japan 1992–95; Perm. Rep. to UN, New York 1995–97; del. to numerous int. confs. etc. *Publications:* articles in professional journals. *Leisure interests:* cricket, tennis, golf, bridge. *Address:* c/o Ministry of External Affairs, S. Block, New Delhi, 110 011, India.

SHAHA, Rishikesh; Nepalese politician and diplomatist; b. 1925, Tansen, Palpain Prov.; s. of Raja Tarak Bahadur Shaha and Madan Dibeshwari; m. Siddhanta Rajyalakshmi 1946; one s.; ed. Patna Univ. and Allahabad Univ., India; Lecturer in English and Nepalese Literature, Tri-Chandra Coll. 1945–48; Opposition Leader, First Advisory Assembly 1952; Gen. Sec., Nepalese Congress 1953–55; Perm. Rep. (with rank of Amb.) to UN 1956–60; Amb. to U.S.A. 1958–60; Chair. UN Int. Comm. investigating death of Dag Hammarskjöld 1961; Minister of Finance, Planning and Economic Affairs 1961–62, of Foreign Affairs July-Sept. 1962; Amb.-at-large 1962–63; Chair. Standing Cttee., Council of State 1963–64; Visiting Prof. East-West Center, Univ. of Hawaii 1965–66; M.P. 1967–70; solitary confinement 1969–70; Visiting Prof., School of Int. Studies of Jawaharlal Nehru Univ. 1971; Regent's Prof., Univ. of Calif., Berkeley 1971–72; returned to Nepal, arrested Dec. 1974; Fellow, Woodrow Wilson Int. Center for Scholars, Washington, D.C. 1976–77; returned to Nepal, arrested May 1977, released 1989; campaigned for restoration of multi-party democracy before 1980 referendum; Alumni Fellow, East-West Centre 1984; Pres. Human Rights Org. of Nepal 1988–; honoured by Human Rights Watch and Asia Watch for work as Human Rights Monitor 1989. *Publications:* Nepal and the World 1954, Heroes and Builders of Nepal (in U.K.) 1965, An Introduction to Nepal 1975,

Nepali Politics—Retrospect and Prospect (in U.K.) 1975, Essays in the Practice of Government in Nepal (in India) 1982, Future of South Asia (in India) 1986, Modern Nepal: A Political History (1769–1955) 1990, Politics in Nepal 1980–1990 1990, Three Decades and Two Kings—End of Nepal's Partyless Monarchic Rule 1990, Ancient and Medieval Nepal 1991. *Leisure interests:* reading, writing, big game hunting. *Address:* Shri Nivas, Chandol, Kathmandu, Nepal. *Telephone:* 411766.

SHAHABUDDEEN, Mohamed, PH.D., LL.D., S.C.; Guyanese international judge; b. 7 Oct. 1931; m. 1955; two s. one d.; ed. Univ. of London and Hague Acad. of Int. Law; called to the Bar, Middle Temple, London 1954; pvt. legal practice 1954–59; magistrate 1959; Crown Counsel 1959–62; Solicitor-Gen. (with rank of Justice of Appeal from 1971) 1962–73; Attorney-Gen. 1973–88; Minister of Justice and sometimes Acting Foreign Minister 1978–88; Vice-Pres. of Guyana 1983–88; Judge, Int. Court of Justice 1988–97; Chair. Legal Practitioners' Disciplinary Cttee., Advisory Council on the Prerogative of Mercy; mem. Guyana del. to numerous int. confs.; hon. Bencher of the Middle Temple; HQ mem. Int. Law Asscn.; mem. Soc. Française pour le droit int., American Soc. of Int. Law, Advisory Bd. European Journal of Int. Law, Bd. of Electors of Whewell Professorship of Int. Law of Cambridge Univ.; Assoc. mem. Inst. de droit int., Int. Acad. of Comparative Law; Order of Excellence, Order of Roraima, Cacique's Crown of Honour. *Publications:* several books and articles. *Address:* International Court of Justice, Peace Palace, 2517 KJ The Hague, Netherlands. *Telephone:* (70) 302-2-323. *Fax:* (70) 364-99-28.

SHAHAL, Moshe; Israeli politician and lawyer; b. 1934, Iraq; m.; two c.; ed. Haifa Univ., Tel Aviv Univ.; mil. service Israeli Defence Forces; mem. Seventh Knesset (Parl.) –1974, mem. Finance Cttee., mem. Econ. Cttee., mem. Labour Cttee.; mem. Eighth Knesset 1974–77, mem. Finance Cttee., mem. Constitution, Law and Justice Cttee.; mem. Tenth Knesset 1983–; Deputy Speaker, mem. Knesset Cttee., mem. Constitution, Law and Justice Cttee.; Minister of Energy and Infrastructure 1984–90, 1993–94; of Police and Communications 1992–93, of Internal Security 1993–96; fmr. Chair. Israeli Consumers' Council; fmr. Perm. Observer to European Council; fmr. Perm. Rep. to Inter-Parl. Union; Labour Party. *Address:* c/o The Knesset, Jerusalem, Israel.

SHAHEEN, C. Jeanne, B.A., M.SC.; American politician; b. 28 Jan. 1947, St. Charles, Mo.; m. William H. Shaheen; three c.; ed. Univs. of Shippensburg and Mississippi; mem. N.H. Senate; Gov. of New Hampshire 1997–; Democrat. *Address:* Office of the Governor, 107 N. Main Street, Room 208, Concord, NH 03301, U.S.A.

SHAIMIEV, Mintimer Sharipovich; Tatar politician; b. 20 Dec. 1937, Anyakovo, Aktanyshski Region, Tatarstan; s. of Sharip Shaimiev and Naghima Safioullina; m. Sakina Shaimieva; two s.; ed. Kazan Inst. of Agric.; Engineer, Chief Engineer Service and Repair Station, Mouslyumovski Dist., Tatar A.S.S.R. 1959–62; Man. Selkhoztekhnika Regional Asscn., Tatar A.S.S.R. 1962–67; Instructor, Deputy Chief of Agricultural Dept., Tatar Regional Cttee. of CPSU, City of Kazan 1967–69; Minister of Land Improvement and Water Man., Kazan 1969–83; First Deputy Chair. Council of Ministers, Tatar A.S.S.R. 1983, Chair. 1983–85, First Sec. 1989–90; Sec. Tatar Regional Cttee. of CPSU 1983–85, First Sec. 1989–90; Chair. Supreme Soviet, Tatar A.S.S.R. 1990–91; Pres. Tatarstan 1991–. *Leisure interests:* chess, gardening, skiing. *Address:* Office of the President, Kremlin, Kazan. 420014, Tatarstan, Russia. *Telephone:* (8432) 327 466, 327 001. *Fax:* (8432) 367 088.

SHAKAA, Riyadh al, B.A.; Jordanian politician and lawyer; b. 1941, Nablus; ed. Univ. of Cairo; Lawyer and mem. Jordanian Bar Asscn.; mem. Lower House of Parl. for Nablus 1985–; Minister of Justice 1985–89 and –1998. *Address:* c/o Ministry of Justice, P.O.Box 6040, Amman, Jordan.

SHAKAR, Karim Ebrahim al-, B.A.; Bahraini diplomatist; b. 23 Dec. 1945, Manama; m. Fatima Al-Mansouri 1979; three d.; ed. Univ. of New Delhi; joined Ministry of Foreign Affairs 1970; mem. Perm. Mission to the UN, rising to rank of 1st Sec.. 1972–76; Apptd. Chief Foreign Affairs and Int. Org., Bahrain 1977; Perm. Rep. to the UN Office, Geneva, and Consul-Gen., Switzerland 1982–87; Amb. (non-resident) to Fed. Repub. of Germany and Austria 1984–; Perm Rep. to the UN Office, Vienna 1982, Perm. Rep. (non-resident) 1984–; Perm Rep. to the UN 1987–90; Amb. to U.K. 1990–95, Amb. (non-resident) to Ireland, Denmark and the Netherlands 1992–95; Dir. Int. Directorate at Ministry of Foreign Affairs, Bahrain 1995–. *Leisure interests:* reading, travelling. *Address:* c/o Ministry of Foreign Affairs, P.O. Box 547, Government House, Government Road, Manama, Bahrain. *Telephone:* 211 715: *Fax:* 224006; 622309.

SHAKED, Shaul, PH.D.; Israeli professor of Iranian studies and comparative religion; b. 8 Feb. 1933, Debrecen, Hungary; m. Miriam Schächter 1960; one s. two d.; ed. Hebrew Univ. Jerusalem and S.O.A.S., Univ. of London; Asst. Lecturer, S.O.A.S. 1964–65, Lecturer 1964–65; Lecturer, Assoc. Prof., Prof. Hebrew Univ. Jerusalem 1965–, Chair. Dept. of Indian, Iranian and Armenian Studies 1971–72, 1974–75, Chair. Dept. of Comparative Religion 1972–74, 1977–79; Chair. Ben Zvi Inst. for Study of Jewish Communities in the East 1975–79, Inst. of Asian and African Studies 1981–85; Fellow, Israel Acad. of Sciences and Humanities; Visiting Prof. Univ. of Calif. Berkeley 1969–70, Columbia and New York Univs. 1980–81, Univ. of Heidelberg 1987–88; Visiting Fellow Wolfson Coll., Cambridge, NIAS, The Netherlands. *Publications include:* A tentative bibliography of Geniza documents 1964, Amulets and Magic Bowls (with J. Naveh) 1985, Dualism in Transformation 1994, From Zoroastrian Iran to Islam 1995; articles and book chapters. *Address:* Institute of Asian and African Studies, The Hebrew University, Mount Scopus, Jerusalem 91905, Israel (Office). *Telephone:* (02) 883675 (Office); (02) 416005 (Home).

SHAKER, Mohamed Ibrahim, LL.B., D. ÈS SC. POL.; Egyptian diplomatist; b. 16 Oct. 1933, Cairo; m. Mona El Kony 1960; one s. one d.; ed. Cairo Univ., Inst. of Int. Studies, Univ. of Geneva, Switzerland; Rep. of Dir.-Gen. of IAEA to UN, New York 1982–83; Deputy Perm. Rep. of Egypt to UN, New York 1984–86; Amb. to Austria, Perm. Rep. to UN in Vienna, Gov. on IAEA Bd. of Govs., Perm. Rep. to UNIDO 1986–88; Amb. to U.K. 1988–97; mem. Core Group, Programme for Promoting Nuclear Non-proliferation (PPNN) 1987–, UN Sec.-Gen.'s Advisory Bd. on Disarmament Matters Jan. 1993– (Chair. 1995); Order of the Republic (Second Grade) 1976, Order of Merit (First Grade) 1983. *Publications:* The Nuclear Non-Proliferation Treaty: Origin and Implementation, 1959–1979 1980; several articles and contribs. to books on nuclear energy and nuclear non-proliferation. *Leisure interests:* tennis, music. *Address:* 9 Aziz Osman Street, Zamalek, Cairo, Egypt (Home). *Telephone:* 340 9593 (Cairo).

SHAKER, Field Marshal Sharif Zaid ibn; Jordanian politician and army officer; b. 4 Sept. 1934, Amman; s. of Amir Shaker; m.; one s. one d.; ed. Vic. Coll., Alexandria, Sandhurst Mil. Coll., U.K., Long Armour Course and Staff Coll., Leavenworth, U.S.A.; Asst. Mil. Attache, Embassy, U.K. 1957–58; Commdr. 1st Infantry Regt. 1963; Asst. Chief of Staff for Operations 1970, Chief of Staff 1972; C.-in-C. Jordan Armed Forces 1976–88; Minister of State, Chief of the Royal Court, Mil. Adviser to King Hussein (q.v.) on Armed Forces Affairs 1988–89, 1989–91; Prime Minister of Jordan April–Dec. 1989, 1991–93; Chief of Royal Court 1993, 1995–96; numerous decorations, including Order of the Star of Jordan (First Class). *Address:* c/o Office of the Prime Minister, P.O. Box 80, 35216 Amman, Jordan.

SHAKESPEARE, Frank; American diplomatist and fmr. radio and television executive; b. 9 April 1925, New York; s. of Frank J. Shakespeare Sr. and Frances Hughes Shakespeare; m. Deborah Ann Spaeth Shakespeare 1954; one s. two d.; ed. Holy Cross Coll., Worcester, Mass.; Liberty Mutual Insurance Co., Washington, D.C. 1947–49; Procter and Gamble Co. 1949–50; Radio Station WOR, New York 1950, CBS 1950; Gen. Man. WXIX-TV, Milwaukee, Wis. 1957–59; Vice-Pres. and Gen. Man. WCBS-TV, New York 1959–63; Vice-Pres and Asst. to Pres. CBS-TV Network 1963–65; Exec. Vice-Pres. CBS-TV Stations 1965–67; Pres. CBS Television Service Div. 1967–69; Dir. U.S. Information Agency 1969–73; Exec. Vice-Pres. Westinghouse Electric Co. 1973–75; Pres. RKO Gen. 1975–83, Vice-Chair. 1983–85; Chair. Bd. Radio Free Europe/Radio Liberty Inc. 1982–85; Amb. to Portugal 1985–86, to the Holy See 1986–89; Dir. Heritage Foundation 1989–, Bradley Foundation 1989–; Young Man of Year, New York 1960. *Address:* 303 Coast Boulevard, La Jolla, CA 92037, U.S.A. *Telephone:* (619) 459-8640.

SHAKHNAZAROV, Georgiy Khosroevich, DR. LEGAL SC.; Russian political scientist and politician; b. 4 October 1924, Baku; s. of Hosrov Shakhnazarov and Rosalia Shakhnazarov; m. Anna Shaskina 1952; one s.; active service in World War II; ed. Azerbaijan Univ.; consultant, Socialist Countries Dept. of CPSU Cen. Cttee. 1967–69; on staff of Prague journal World Marxist Review 1970–72; Pres. Soviet (now Russian) Asscn. of Political Sciences 1974–95; Vice-Pres. Int. Political Science Asscn. 1974–88; Deputy Head, 1982–86, First Deputy Head of Socialist Countries Dept. 1986–88; full-time aide to Mikhail Gorbachev (q.v.) 1988–91, Chancellor to Pres. of U.S.S.R. 1991; People's Deputy of Russia 1989–91; mem. Supreme Soviet 1989–91; Dir. Centre of Global Problems, Int. Fund for Social, Economic and Political Research (Gorbachev Fund) 1991–; corresp. mem. Acad. of Sciences 1987; U.S.S.R. State Prize 1980. *Publications include:* Preis der Freiheit, ein Bilanz von Corbatschows Berater 1996; several science-fiction novels and stories; numerous articles. *Address:* International Fund for Social, Economic and Political Research, Leningradsky Prosp. 49, 125468 Moscow, Russia. *Telephone:* 943-95-45.

SHAKHRAY, Sergey Mikhailovich, LL.D.; Russian politician; b. 30 April 1956, Simferopol; s. of Mikhail A. Shakray and Zoya A. Shakray; m. Tatyana Shakhray 1985; two s. one d.; ed. Rostov State Univ.; Head of Law. Moscow State Univ.; People's Deputy of Russia 1990–92; Chair. of the Legis. Cttee. of Russian Supreme Soviet 1990; State Councillor on legal issues of Russian Fed. 1991–92; Vice-Prime Minister of Russia Dec. 1991–April 1992, 1993, 1994–95; Chair. State Cttee. for nat. problems; f. and Chair. Party of Russian Unity and Consent (PRES) 1993–; Head interim admin. in zone of emergency situation in N. Ossetia and Ingushetia 1992–93; mem. State Duma (Parl.) 1993–; Minister for Nationalities and Nat. Problems 1994–95; Deputy Head of Pres. Yeltsin's Admin., Pres.'s Rep. at Constitutional Court 1996–98; Deputy Chair. Political Consultative Council of Pres. Yeltsin; adviser to Prime Minister 1998–. *Leisure interests:* fishing, bicycling, badminton, Russian baths. *Address:* House of Government, Krasnopresnenskaya Emb. 2, 103 274 Moscow, Russia. *Telephone:* (095) 925-35-81.

SHAKUROV, Sergey Kayumovich; Russian actor; b. 1 Jan. 1942, Moscow; ed. Theatre School of Cen. Children's Theatre; with K. Stanislavsky Drama Theatre 1978–88; acted in several other theatres. *Stage roles include:* Ivanov (Chekhov), Hamlet and others. *Films include:* Their Own Among Strangers, A Stranger Among His Own 1974, 100 Days after Childhood 1975, The Taste of Bread 1979, Portrait of the Artist's Wife 1982, Recipe of Her Youthfulness 1984, Visit to Minotaurus 1987, Dogs' Feast 1991, Squadron 1992, Hagy-Trager 1993, Declaration of Love 1995, Cranberries in Sugar 1995; U.S.S.R. State Prize 1980; prizes of All-Union Film Festivals for Best Actor 1988, 1991; People's Actor of Russia 1991. *Address:* Bibliotechnaya str. 27, Apt. 94, 109544 Moscow, Russia (Home). *Telephone:* 270- 15-32 (Home).

SHALALA, Donna Edna, PH.D.; American professor of political science; b. 14 Feb. 1941, Cleveland, O.; d. of James A. Shalala and Edna Smith; ed. Western Coll. and Syracuse Univ.; Volunteer, Peace Corps, Iran 1962–64; Asst. to Dir. Metropolitan Studies Program, Syracuse Univ. 1965–69; Instr., Asst. to Dean, Maxwell Grad. School, Syracuse Univ. 1969–70; Asst. Prof. of Political Science, Bernard Baruch Coll., City Univ. New York 1970–72; Assoc. Prof. of Politics and Educ. Teachers' Coll. Columbia Univ. 1972–79; Asst. Sec. for Policy Devt. and Research, Dept. of Housing and Urban Devt. Washington 1977–80; Prof. of Political Science and Pres. Hunter Coll. City Univ. New York 1980–88; Prof. of Political Science, Chancellor, Univ. of Wis. Madison 1988–92; Sec. of Health and Human Services Jan. 1993–; Dir. Inst. of Int. Econs. 1981–93, Ditchley Foundation 1981–93; mem. Nat. Acad. of Arts and Sciences, American Soc. for Public Admin.; 24 hon. degrees. *Publications:* Neighborhood Governance 1971, The City and the Constitution 1972, The Property Tax and the Voters 1973, The Decentralization Approach 1974. *Leisure interests:* tennis, mountain-climbing, reading, spectator sports. *Address:* Department of Health and Human Services, 200 Independence Avenue S.W., Room 615F, Washington, DC 20201, U.S.A.

SHALIKASHVILI, Gen. John; American army officer; b. 27 June, 1936, Warsaw, Poland; s. of Dimitri Shalikashvili and Maria (Ruediger) Shalikashvili; m. 1st Gunhild Bartsch 1963 (died 1965); m. 2nd Joan Zimpelman 1966; one s.; ed. Bradley Univ., Naval War Coll., U.S. Army War Coll., George Washington Univ.; entered U.S. army active duty 1958; various troop and staff assignments Alaska, U.S.A., Fed. Repub. of Germany, Viet Nam, Repub. of Korea 1959–75; Commdr. 1st Bn., 84th Field Artillery, 9th Infantry Div., Fort Lewis, Washington 1975–77; Deputy Chief of Staff for Operations, S. European Task Force, Vicenza, Italy 1978–79; Commdr. Div. Artillery 1st Armored Div. U.S. Army, Nürnberg, Fed. Repub. of Germany 1979–81; Chief, Politico-Mil. Div., later Deputy Dir., Strategy, Plans and Policy, ODCSOPS, the Army Staff, Washington D.C. 1981–84; rank of Brig. Gen. 1983; Asst. Div. Commdr. 1st Armored Div. U.S. Army, Nürnberg, Fed. Repub. of Germany 1984–86; Dir. of Strategy, Plans, Policy, ODCSOPS, the Army Staff, Washington D.C. 1986–87; rank of Maj.-Gen. 1986; Commdg. Gen. 9th Infantry Div. Fort Lewis, Washington 1987–89; rank of Lieut. Gen. 1989; Deputy C.-in-C. U.S. Army Europe, Heidelberg, Fed. Repub. of Germany 1989–91; Asst. to Chair. Jt. Chiefs of Staff, Washington, D.C. 1991–92; rank of Gen. 1992; Supreme Allied Commdr. Europe and C.-in-C. U.S. European Command 1992–93; Chair. Jt. Chiefs of Staff 1993–97; mem. Bd. Govs. of American Red Cross, Asscn. of U.S. Army, Field Artillery Asscn., Retd. Officers Asscn., Council on Foreign Relations, American Acad. of Achievement, Bradley Univ. Bd. of Trustees; Hon. LL.D. (Univ. of Md., Bradley Univ.); numerous awards and decorations, including Mil. Order of the Carabao. *Address:* 9302 76th Street, S.W., Tacoma, WA 98498, U.S.A.

SHAMASK, Ronaldus; Netherlands fashion designer; b. 24 Nov. 1945, Amsterdam; self-educated in design; window-dresser for dept. store in Melbourne, Australia 1959; fashion illustrator, The Times and The Observer newspapers, London 1967–68; set and costume designer, Company of Man (multi-media artists' org.) Buffalo, N.Y. 1968–71; subsequently undertook design and clothing comms. for private clients in New York; founder-partner with Murrray Moss, Moss Shamask, New York 1978–; opened Moss boutique, Madison Avenue, New York and presented first collection 1979; costume designer, Lucinda Childs Dance Co. premiere of Available Light, Next Wave Fall Festival, Brooklyn Acad. of Music 1983; work exhibited at Hayden Gallery, M.I.T. 1982 and in perm. collection of Smithsonian Inst.; Coty Fashion Award 1981; Fil d'Or, Conf. Int. du Lin 1982.

SHAMGAR, Meir; Israeli judge; b. 13 Aug. 1925, Danzig (now Gdańsk, Poland); s. of Eliezer Shamgar and Dina Shamgar; m. Geula Shamgar 1955 (deceased); two s. one d.; ed. Balfour Coll. Tel Aviv, Hebrew Univ. Jerusalem, Govt. Law School and London Univ.; Mil. Advocate-Gen. 1961–68; Legal Adviser, Ministry of Defence April–Aug. 1968; Attorney-Gen. of Israel 1968–75; Justice, Supreme Court 1975, Deputy Chief. Justice 1982, Pres. of Supreme Court (Chief Justice of Israel) 1983–95; Hon. Fellow Open Univ. of Israel; Dr. h.c. (Weizman Inst., Hebrew Univ. Jerusalem, Ben Gurion Univ., Beer-Sheva, Tel-Aviv Univ.) 1997, (Bar Ilan Univ.) 1998; Israel Prize for Special Service to Society and State 1996. *Publications:* The Military Government of the Territories Administered by Israel 1967–80: The Legal Aspects 1982; numerous articles and essays in legal publs. *Address:* Kiriat Ben Gurion, Rehov Shaare Mishpat, Jerusalem 91909 (Office); 12 Shahar Street, Jerusalem 96263, Israel (Home). *Telephone:* 02-759666 (Office); 02-6526130 (Home).

SHAMIR, Shimon, PH.D.; Israeli diplomatist and historian; b. 15 Dec. 1933, Romania; m. Daniela (née Levin) Shamir 1958; one s. two d.; ed. Hebrew Univ. of Jerusalem and Princeton Univ.; Lecturer in Modern History, Hebrew Univ. of Jerusalem 1960–66; Prof. of Modern History, Tel–Aviv Univ. 1966–, Dir. Shiloah Center 1966–73, Head Graduate School of History 1973–76, Kaplan Chair in the History of Egypt and Israel 1980–; Dir. Israeli Acad. Center, Cairo 1982–84; Amb. to Egypt 1988–90. *Publications:* A Modern History of the Arabs in the Middle East, 1798–1918 1965, Egypt under Sadat: The Search for a New Orientation 1978, Self-Views in Historial Perspective in Egypt and Israel 1981, The Jews of Egypt: A Mediterranean Society in Modern Times 1987. *Address:* Department of History, Tel–Aviv University, Ramat–Aviv, 69 978 Tel–Aviv, Israel.

SHAMIR, Yitzhak; Israeli politician; b. (as Yitzhak Yernitsky) 15 Oct. 1915, Ruzinoy, Poland; m.; one s. one d.; ed. Hebrew Secondary School, Białystok, Warsaw Univ. and Hebrew Univ. of Jerusalem; emigrated to Palestine 1935; mem. Irgun Zvai Leumi (Jewish Mil. Org.) 1937, then a founder and leader of Lohamei Herut Yisrael 1940–48; arrested by British Mandatory Authority 1941, 1946 (exiled to Eritrea); given political asylum in France, returned to Israel 1948; retd. from political activity until 1955; Sr. post Civil Service 1955–65; Man. Dir. several business concerns 1965–; mem. Herut Movt. 1970–, Chair. Exec. Cttee. 1975–; mem. Knesset 1973–96, Speaker 1977–80; Minister of Foreign Affairs 1980–83, Prime Minister of Israel 1983–84, 1986–92; also fmr. Minister of Labour and Social Affairs; Deputy Prime Minister Sept. 1984–86, Minister of Foreign Affairs 1984–86; Acting Minister of the Interior 1987–88; Dr. h.c. (Hebrew Union Coll., L.A. Jewish Inst. of Religion) 1991. *Publication:* Summing Up (memoirs) 1992. *Address:* Beit Amot Mishpat, 8 Shaul Hamelech Boulevard, Tel Aviv 64733, Israel.

SHAN KUO-HSI, H.E. Cardinal Paul, S.J.; Taiwanese ecclesiastic; b. 2 Dec. 1923, Puyang; s. of John Shan Cheng-Yin and Maria Teresa Shan Tsung Auo; ordained priest 1955; Bishop 1980; transferred to Kaohsiung 1991; cr. Cardinal Feb. 1998. *Address:* Bishop's House, 125 Szu-wei 3rd Road, Kaohsiung 80203, Taiwan.

SHANGE, Ntozake, M.A.; American playwright and poet; b. 18 Oct. 1948, Trenton, N.J.; d. of Paul Williams and Eloise Williams; m. David Murray 1977 (divorced); one c.; ed. Barnard Coll. and Univ. of S. Calif.; mem. Faculty, Sonoma State Univ. 1973–75, Mills Coll. 1975, City Coll. of New York 1975, Douglass Coll. 1978; author and actress in For Colored Girls Who Have Considered Suicide/When the Rainbow is Enuf (play) 1976, Where the Mississippi Meets the Amazon (play) 1977; author and Dir. A Photograph: A Study in Cruelty 1979; Dir. The Mighty Gents 1979; performing mem. Sounds in Motion Dance Co.; author, An Evening with Diana Ross: The Big Event 1977; Guggenheim Fellow 1981; mem. Nat. Acad. of TV Arts and Sciences, Acad. of American Poets, PEN America etc.; recipient of numerous drama and poetry awards. *Publications include:* plays: Melissa and Smith 1976, From Okra to Greens 1978, Spell #7 1979, Black and White Two Dimensional Planes 1979, Boogie Woogie Landscapes 1980, Mouths 1981, A Photograph: Lovers in Motion 1981, Three Views of Mt. Fuji 1987; novels: Sassafrass, Cypress and Indigo 1976, Betsey Brown 1985, The Love Space Demands 1991, I Live in Music 1994; poetry: Natural Disasters and Other Festive Occasions 1977, Nappy Edges 1978, Three Pieces 1981, A Daughter's Geography 1983, From Okra to Greens 1984; essays, short stories, non-fiction, adaptations; contribs. to magazines and anthologies. *Address:* c/o St. Martin's Press, 175 Fifth Avenue, New York, NY 10010, U.S.A.

SHANKAR, Ramsewak; Suriname fmr. Head of State and economist; fmr. Agric. Minister; Pres. of Suriname 1988–90 (overthrown in coup); fmr. Head of Armed Forces, fmr. Chair. Council of State and Security Comm.

SHANKAR, Ravi; Indian sitar player and composer; b. 7 April 1920; m. Sukanya Rajan 1989; two d. (one s. deceased); pupil of Ustad Allauddin Khan 1938; fmr. Dir. of Music All-India Radio and founder of the Nat. Orchestra; Founder Kinnara School of Music, Bombay 1962, Kinnara School of Music, Los Angeles 1967; many recordings of traditional and experimental variety in India, U.K. and the U.S.A.; Concert tours in Europe, U.S.A. and the East; Visiting Lecturer Univ. of Calif. 1965; appeared in film, Raga 1974; elected to Rajya Sabha (Upper House) 1986; Fellow Sangeet Natak Akademi 1977; numerous hon. degrees; Silver Bear of Berlin 1966; Award of Indian Nat. Acad. for Music, Dance and Drama 1962; Award of Padma Bhushan 1967, Padma Vibhushan 1981, Deshikottam 1981, Int. Music Council UNESCO Award 1975, Ramon Magsaysay Award 1992, Praemium Imperiale 1997, Polar Music Prize 1998. *Film Scores:* Pather Panchali, The Flute and the Arrow, Nava Rasa Ranga, Charly, Gandhi, etc. and many musical compositions including Concerto for Sitar No. 1 1971, No. 2 1981, Raga Jogeshwari 1981, Homage to Mahatma Gandhi 1981, Ghanashyam (opera) 1989. *Publications:* My Music, My Life 1968, Rag Anurag (Bengali), Ravi: The Autobiography of Ravi Shankar (with others) 1995. *Address:* c/o Christopher Tennant Artists' Management, Unit 2, 39 Tadema Road, London, SW10 0PY, England.

SHANKARANAND, B., B.A., L.L.B.; Indian politician; b. 19 Oct. 1925, Chikodi, Belgaum Dist., Karnataka; s. of Buburao Talwar; m. Kamaladevi Shankaranand; two s. six d.; ed. Govt. Law Coll., Bombay and R.L. Law Coll., Belgaum; fmrly. associated with Republican Party of India and PSP; mem. Lok Sabha 1967–70, 1971–79, 1980–96; Gen. Sec. Congress Party in Parl. 1969–71, mem. Exec. Cttee.; Deputy Minister of Parl. Affairs 1971–77; Minister of Health, Educ. and Family Welfare Jan.–Oct. 1980, of Health and Family Welfare 1980–84, of Irrigation and Power Jan.–Sept. 1985, of Law and Justice and Water Resources 1988–89, of Law and Justice July–Nov. 1989, of Petroleum and Natural Gas 1991–93, of Health and Family Welfare 1993–94; mem. numerous cttees.; Del. to UNCTAD 1968, UN Gen. Ass. 1969. *Leisure interests:* cricket, football. *Address:* 8 Tees January Marg, New Delhi 110001, India. *Telephone:* 3011307.

SHANKARDASS, Raghuvansh Kumar Prithvinath, M.A., LL.M.; Indian lawyer; b. 9 June 1930, Nairobi, Kenya; s. of P. N. Shankardass and Pushpavati Shankardass; m. Ramma Handoo 1955; ed. Trinity Coll., Cambridge, Lincoln's Inn, London; Gen. Sec. Bar Asscn. of India 1975–85, Vice-Pres. 1985–; Asst. Sec.-Gen. Int. Bar Asscn. 1980–82, Vice-Pres. 1984–86, Pres. 1986–88; Gen. Sec. Indian Law Foundation 1975–, Pres. 1991–; Chair. Panel of Commrs. UN Compensation Comm. 1996–; Fellow American Bar Foundation 1997; Ed. The Indian Advocate 1990–; Pres. Cambridge Univ. Majlis 1953; Trustee India Foundation for the Arts 1994–; Hon. O.B.E. 1996. *Leisure interests:* golf, badminton, music, reading, travel. *Address:* 87 Lawyer's Chambers, Supreme Court of India, New Delhi 110 001, India (Office); B-12 Maharani Bagh, New Delhi 110 065 (Home). *Telephone:* (11) 3383703, (11) 3381041 (Office), (11) 6830636 (Home). *Fax:* 6848104.

SHANKS, Ian Alexander, PH.D., F.ENG., F.I.E.E., F.R.S., F.R.S.A.; British scientist; b. 22 June 1948, Glasgow; s. of Alexander Shanks and Isabella A. Beaton; m. Janice Coulter 1971; one d.; ed. Dumbarton Acad., Univ. of Glasgow, and Portsmouth Polytechnic; Projects Man. Scottish Colorfoto Labs. Ltd. Alexandria 1970–72; Jr. Research Fellow, Royal Signals and Radar Establishment (RSRE), Malvern, later Sr. Scientific Officer, Prin. Scientific Officer 1973–82; Sr. Scientist, later Prin. Scientist/Sr. Man. Unilever Research, Sharnbrook, Beds. 1982–86, Divisional Science Adviser 1994–; Chief Scientist, Thorn EMI PLC 1986; Visiting Prof. of Electrical and Electronic Eng. Univ. of Glasgow 1985–; mem. Optoelectronics Cttee. The Rank Prize Fund.; fmr. mem. Science Consultative Group, BBC; fmr. mem. Council and Vice-Pres. Royal Soc.; fmr. mem. Advisory Bd. for Research Councils, Office of Public Service and Science; Chair. Inter-Agency Cttee. for Marine Science and Technology; Paterson Medal and Prize, Inst. of Physics 1984. *Publications:* 40 research papers and over 75 patents mainly on liquid crystals, displays and biosensors. *Leisure interests:* music, collecting antique pocket watches. *Address:* Unilever Research & Engineering Division, Colworth House, Sharnbrook, Bedford, MK44 1LQ (Office); Kings Close, 11 Main Road, Biddenham, Bedford, MK40 4BB, England (Home). *Telephone:* (01234) 328773 (Home).

SHANNON, Claude Elwood, PH.D.; American applied mathematician; b. 30 April 1916; s. of Claude Elwood and Mabel Catherine Wolf; m. Mary Elizabeth Moore 1949; two s. one d.; ed. Univ. of Michigan and M.I.T.; Research mathematician Bell Telephone Laboratories 1941–56, Consultant 1957–72; Visiting Prof. of Communication Sciences M.I.T. 1956, Prof. of Communication Sciences and Math. 1957–58, Donner Prof. of Science 1958–78, Prof. Emer. 1978–; Fellow Center for Advanced Study in the Behavioral Sciences, Stanford, Calif. 1957–58, Inst. of Radio Engineers; Visiting Fellow, All Souls Coll., Oxford 1978; mem. N.A.S., American Acad. of Arts and Sciences, I.R.E., American Mathematical Soc.; Hon. D.Sc. (Oxford) 1978, (East Anglia) 1982; Alfred Noble Prize A.I.E.E., Morris Liebman Award I.R.E., Stuart Ballantine Medal, Franklin Soc., Research Corpn. Award, Harvey Prize, Technion, Haifa, Israel; Kyoto Prize 1985. *Publications:* Mathematical Theory of Communication 1949; numerous technical papers; Ed. (with J. McCarthy) Automata Studies 1956. *Address:* 5 Cambridge Street, Winchester, MA 01890, U.S.A.

SHANNON, Richard Thomas, PH.D.; New Zealand/British professor of modern history; b. 10 June 1931, Suva, Fiji; s. of Edward Arthur Shannon and Grace Shannon (née McLeod); ed. Mount Albert Grammar School, Auckland, N.Z., Auckland Univ. Coll., Gonville and Caius Coll. Cambridge; Lecturer and Sr. Lecturer in History, Univ. Coll. Auckland 1955–57, 1961–62; lecturer in English History, Univ. of E. Anglia, Norwich, U.K. 1963–65, Sr. Lecturer 1965–71, Reader 1971–79; Prof. of Modern History, Univ. of Wales Swansea 1979–97, Head History Dept. 1982–88, Dean Faculty of Arts 1985–88, Prof. Emer. 1997–; Visiting Fellow Peterhouse, Cambridge 1988–89; Leverhulme Sr. Research Fellowship 1988–90. *Publications:* Gladstone and the Bulgarian Agitation, 1876 1963, The Crisis of Imperialism, 1865–1915 1974, Gladstone, Vol. I 1809–1865 1982, The Age of Disraeli 1868–1881 1992, The Age of Salisbury, 1881–1902 1996, Gladstone Vol. II 1865–1898 1999. *Leisure interests:* mid-Wales Borders. *Address:* Flat A, 86 Portland Place, London, W1N 3HA, England; Old School House, Cascob, Presteigne, Powys, LD8 2NT, Wales. *Telephone:* 0171-436 0214 (London); 0547 560 377 (Cascob).

SHANNON, Robert William Ernest, PH.D.; British engineer; b. 10 Oct. 1937, Belfast, Northern Ireland; s. of Robert Albert Ernest Shannon and Letitia Shannon; m. Annabelle McWatters 1959; one s. one d.; ed. Belfast Tech. High School, The Queen's Univ. Belfast; Research Fellow The Queen's Univ. Belfast 1966–70; Research and Devt., British Gas 1970–83, Dir. On Line Inspection Centre 1983–89, H.Q. Dir. of Eng. Research 1989–91, Group Dir. of Devt. 1991–93, Dir. of Special Projects, British Gas Global 1993–95; Consultant 1995–; Bd. mem. Industrial Research and Tech. Unit, Northern Ireland 1995–; mem. Exec. Bd. The European Prize Charitable Trust; Pres. The Institution of Mechanical Engineers 1996–; Chair. N.I.G.C./I.R.T.U. Foresight Steering Cttee. 1996–, Cen. TC54 Harmonization Cttee. 1997–, I.Mech.E. Research and Tech. Cttee. 1998–, Royal Acad. of Eng. Int. Cttee., Inst. of Gas Engineers Research and Tech. Cttee. 1998–; Dir. ERA Technology 1997–; Fellow Royal Acad. of Eng., Professorial Fellowship 1996; two hon. degrees; MacRobert Award, Inst. of Gas Engineers Gold Medal, Royal Soc. Mullard Medal. *Publications:* Experience with On-Line Inspection 1981; over 50 scientific publs. *Leisure interests:* reading, gardening, walking. *Address:* Lindisfarne, 16 Friths Drive, Reigate, Surrey, RH2 0DS, England. *Telephone:* (01737) 223559. *Fax:* (01737) 223559.

SHANTSEV, Valery Pavlinovich; Russian politician; b. 1947, Susanovo Kostroma Region; m.; one s. one d.; ed. Moscow Aviation School, Moscow Inst. of Radiotech., Electronics and Automation, Acad. of Nat. Econs.; master factory Salut 1968–75; party service, instructor Perov Dist. CP Cttee., deputy head Machine Construction Dept. Moscow City CP Cttee. 1975–85; Chair. Exec. Cttee. Perov Dist. Soviet, First Sec. Perov Dist. CP Cttee., Chair. Perov Dist. Soviet of People's Deputies 1985–90; Sec. Moscow City CP Cttee., deputy of Moscow Soviet 1990–91; Commercial Dir. Hockey Club Dynamo 1993–94; Prefect of S. Admin. dist. of Moscow 1994; mem. Cen. Exec. Cttee. CP of Russian Fed. 1993–95; Deputy Mayor of Moscow 1996–, concurrently First Deputy Prime Minister Moscow Govt. *Address:* Office of the Mayor, Tverskaya str. 13, 103032 Moscow, Russia (Office). *Telephone:* (095) 290 7735, 290 7374 (Office).

SHAO DADI: Chinese artist; b. 16 Jan. 1938, Beijing; s. of Shao Wen-Gang and Song Junmei; m. Jiang Ruizhang 1968; one s. one d.; ed. Middle School attached to Cen. Art Inst., teacher training, Dept. of History of Arts and Crafts at Cen. Inst. of Arts and Crafts; Lecturer, Beijing Arts and Crafts School; Sr. Lecturer, Nat. Educ. Dept. of China 1988; mem. Beijing Branch, Chinese Asscn. of Artists, Beijing Inst. of Arts and Crafts. *Works include:* Portrait of Characters (sketch), Comers from the North of Shaanxi Province (oil painting), Scenery Sketch of Xinjiang Uygur Autonomous Region, Bronze Decorative Patterns, Electrical Appliance for Family Use (book jacket design), The Great Wall (painting) 1987, Suzhou Gardens (frescoes) 1987, The Grove from Trees (pottery design) 1988. *Publications include:* The Aesthetics of Floating 1989, The Great Wall, Sketches and Portraits 1991, The Anthology of Chinese Minority Nationality Bronze Ornaments 1993. *Leisure interests:* literature, music. *Address:* National Education Department of China, c/o State Education Commission, 37 Damucang Hutong, Xicheng Qu, Beijing 100816, People's Republic of China.

SHAO HUAZE: Chinese journalist, army officer and government official; b. June 1933, Chun'an Co., Zhejiang Prov.; ed. PLA Political Cadres' School No 2, Chinese People's Univ.; joined PLA 1951; joined CCP 1957; Ed. Jiefangjun Ribao (PLA Daily) 1964; Vice-Dir. Jiefangjun Ribao 1981; Dir. Propaganda Dept. PLA Gen. Political Dept. 1985; rank of Maj. Gen. 1988; Ed.-in-Chief Renmin Ribao (People's Daily) 1989, Dir. 1992–, mem. 14th CCP Cen. Cttee. 1992; mem. 15th CCP Cen. Cttee. 1997–. *Address:* People's Daily, 2 Jin Tai Xi Lu, Beijing, People's Republic of China.

SHAO QIHUI; Chinese administrator and engineer; b. 1934, Wuxi City, Jiangsu Prov.; joined CCP 1953; Gov. of Heilongjiang Prov. 1989–93; mem. 14th CCP Cen. Cttee. 1992–; a Vice-Minister, Ministry of Machine-Bldg. Industry 1994–98; Dir. State Admin. of Machine Bldg. Industry 1998–. *Address:* State Administration of Machine Building Industry, 46 Sanlihe Lu, Xichen Qu, Beijing, People's Republic of China.

SHAO YANXIANG: Chinese poet; b. 10 June 1933, Beijing; s. of Shao Ji and Cheng Ying; m. Xie Wenxiu 1957; one s. one d.; attached to Radio Beijing as editor and corresp. 1949; detained in labour camp during "Cultural Revolution" 1966–77; rehabilitated 1978; Deputy Ed.-in-Chief Shikan magazine 1978. *Publications:* Singing of the City of Beijing 1951, Going to the Faraway Place 1955, To My Comrades 1956, The Campfire in August 1956, A Reed-Pipe 1957, Love Songs to History 1980, At the Faraway Place 1981, In Full Blossom Lake Flowers 1983, Flower Late in Blossom 1984, Collection of Long Lyrics 1985, Essays Written at Mornings and Evenings 1986, 100 Articles with Sorrows and Joys 1986, There's Joy, there's Sorrow 1988, Selected Poems 1992, Written in Little Honeycomb 1993, Catch that Butterfly 1993, Idle Talk 1993, Rewriting the Bible 1993, One's Own Cup 1993, Essay Workshop 1994, Genuine Absurdity and Sham Absurdity 1994, Multum in Parvo 1994, Selected Poems of Shao Yanxiang 1995, Collection of Works by Shao Yanxiang (3 vols.). *Leisure interests:* enjoying music, Chinese calligraphy. *Address:* A15-3-401 Hufang Road, Beijing 100052, People's Republic of China. *Telephone:* (010) 63536604.

SHAPAR, Howard Kamber, B.A., J.D.; American international official; b. 6 Nov. 1923, Boston, Mass.; m. Henriette Albertine Emilie van Gerrevink 1977; two s. one d.; ed. Amherst Coll., Yale Univ.; Chief Counsel U.S. Atomic Energy Comm.'s Idaho Operations Office 1956–62; Asst. Gen. Counsel for Licensing and Regulation, U.S. Atomic Energy Comm. 1962–76; Exec. Legal Dir. U.S. Nuclear Regulatory Comm. 1976–82; Dir.-Gen. OECD Nuclear Energy Agency, Paris 1982–88; Counsel to Shaw, Pittman, Potts and Trowbridge 1988–; Past Pres. Int. Nuclear Law Asscn.; mem. Bars of State of New Mexico, Court of Appeals for Dist. of Columbia, Dist. of Columbia Bar Asscn., U.S. Supreme Court; Distinguished Service Award, U.S. Nuclear Regulatory Comm. 1980; Presidential Award of Meritorious Exec. 1981. *Publications:* articles in legal journals and periodicals; papers on atomic energy law. *Address:* 4610 Langdrum Lane, Chevy Chase, MD 20815, U.S.A. *Telephone:* (301) 986-5217.

SHAPIRO, Ascher H(erman), S.B., SC.D.; American mechanical engineering educator and consultant; b. 20 May 1916, New York City; s. of Bernard Shapiro and Jennie (Kaplan) Shapiro; m. 1st Sylvia Helen Charm 1939; m. 2nd Regina Julia Lee 1961; m. 3rd Kathleen Larke Crawford 1985; one s. two d.; ed. Massachusetts Inst. of Tech.; mem. Teaching Faculty M.I.T. 1938–, Ford Prof. of Eng. 1962–75, Chair. of Faculty 1964–65, Head of Dept.

of Mechanical Eng. 1965–74, Inst. Prof. 1975–86, Inst. Prof. Sr. Lecturer 1986–; Visiting Prof., Cambridge Univ. 1955–56; Founder and Chair. Nat. Cttee. for Fluid Mechanics Films 1962–; mem. U.S.A.F. Scientific Advisory Bd. 1964–66; Councillor, American Acad. of Arts and Sciences 1966–69; mem. Editorial Bd. Journal Applied Mech. 1955–56, Editorial Cttee. Annual Review of Fluid Mech. 1967–71, Editorial Bd. M.I.T. Press 1977–87, Chair. 1982–87; Consultant to Govt. and Industry in propulsion, compressors and turbines, fluid dynamics, bioengineering, fluid machinery, industrial centrifuges; Patentee: fluid metering equipment, combustion chamber, propulsion apparatus and gas turbines, magnetic disc storage devices, vacuum pump, low density wind tunnels, recipe-conversion calculator, centrifuge apparatus (ten); mem. Bd. of Govs., Israel Inst. of Tech.; Fellow, American Acad. of Arts and Sciences, A.S.M.E., A.I.A.A., American Inst. of Medical and Biomedical Eng.; mem. N.A.S., Nat. Acad. of Eng.; Hon.mem. A.S.M.E. Int.; Dr. Sc. h.c. (Salford, U.K.) 1978, (Technion-Israel Inst. of Tech.) 1985; Naval Ordnance Devt. Award 1945, Joint Certificate for Outstanding Contribution, War and Navy Depts. 1947, Richards Memorial Award of A.S.M.E. 1960, Worcester Reed Warner Medal of A.S.M.E. 1965, Lamme Medal of American Soc. for Eng. Educ. 1977, Townsend Harris Medal (Coll. of the City of New York) 1978, Fluids Eng. Award (A.S.M.E.) 1981, J. P. Den Hartog Distinguished Educator Award of M.I.T. 1984. *Publications:* The Dynamics and Thermodynamics of Compressible Fluid Flow Vol. I 1953, Vol. II 1954, Physical Measurements in Gas Dynamics and Combustion (Contrib. to) 1954, Shape and Flow: The Fluid Dynamics of Drag 1961, Handbook of Fluid Dynamics (Contrib. to) 1961; and numerous tech. articles in fields of thermodynamics, propulsion, gas dynamics, fluid mechanics, biomedical engineering; educational films (The Fluid Dynamics of Drag 1958, Vorticity 1961, Pressure Fields and Fluid Acceleration 1964); 39 videotape lecture series, Fluid Dynamics (with text notes) 1984. *Address:* Mechanical Engineering Department, Massachusetts Institute of Technology, 77 Massachusetts Avenue, Cambridge, MA 02139; 111 Perkins Street, Jamaica Plain, MA 02174, U.S.A. (Home). *Telephone:* (617) 253-4337 (Office); (617) 522-4418 (Home).

SHAPIRO, Bernard; Canadian academic administrator and public servant; b. Montreal; ed. McGill Univ.; fmr. Deputy Minister of Educ. Ont. Prov.; Prin. and Vice-Chancellor McGill Univ. 1994–. *Address:* McGill University, James Administration Building, Room 506, 845 Sherbrooke Street West, Montreal, Qué. H3A 2T5, Canada. *Telephone:* (514) 398-4180. *Fax:* (514) 398-4768.

SHAPIRO, Harold Tafler, PH.D.; American university president and professor of economics; b. 8 June 1935, Montreal, Canada; s. of Maxwell Tafler and Mary Taffler; m. Vivian Shapiro; four d.; ed. McGill Univ. and Princeton Univ. Grad. School; Asst. Prof. of Econs. Univ. of Mich. 1964, Assoc. Prof. 1967, Prof. 1970, Vice-Pres. for Academic Affairs 1977, Pres. 1980–88; Pres. Princeton Univ. 1988–, Prof. of Econs. and Public Affairs 1988–; mem. Conf. Bd. Inc., Bretton Woods Cttee.; mem. Pres.'s Council of Advisors on Science and Tech. 1990–92; Chair. Nat. Bioethics Advisory Comm. 1996–; Dir. Dow Chemical Co., Nat. Bureau of Econ. Research; mem. N.A.S. (Inst. of Medicine); Fellow American Acad. of Arts and Sciences; Trustee, Alfred P. Sloan Foundation, Univ. of Pa. Medical Center, Univs. Research Asscn., Educational Testing Service; mem. Inst. of Medicine of N.A.S., American Philosophical Soc. *Address:* Office of the President, Princeton University, 1 Nassau Hall, Princeton, NJ 08544, U.S.A.

SHAPIRO, Irwin I., PH.D.; American physicist; b. 29 Oct. 1929, New York; s. of Esther Feinberg and Samuel Shapiro; m. Marian Helen Kaplun 1959; one s. one d.; ed. Cornell and Harvard Univs.; mem. staff., M.I.T. Lincoln Lab. 1954–70, Prof. of Geophysics and Physics 1967–80; Redman Lecturer, McMaster Univ. 1969; Sherman Fairchild Distinguished Scholar, Calif. Inst. of Tech. 1974; Schlumberger Prof., M.I.T. 1980–86, Prof. Emer. 1986–; Sr. Scientist Smithsonian Astrophysical Observatory 1982–; Paine Prof. of Practical Astronomy and Prof. of Physics, Harvard Univ. 1982–97; Dir. Harvard-Smithsonian Center for Astrophysics 1983–; John C. Lindsay Lecturer, NASA Goddard Space Flight Center 1986; Prof., Harvard Univ., Timken 1997–; current research is on radio and radar techniques, applications to astrometry, astrophysics, geophysics, planetary physics and tests of theories of gravitation; mem. Editorial Bd. Celestial Mechanics 1969–75, Annals of Physics 1977–82; Assoc. Ed. Icarus 1969–75; Fellow A.A.A.S., American Geophysical Union, American Physical Soc.; mem. Int. Astronomical Union, N.A.S.; mem. Radio Science Teams, Mariner Venus-Mercury, Viking, and Pioneer Venus Missions 1970–79, Space Science Bd. (N.A.S.) 1977–82, NSF Astronomy Advisory Cttee. 1983–86, Task Group on Astronomy and Astrophysics of Nat. Research Council Space Science Bd. Study "Major Directions for Space Science: 1995–2015" 1984–86, Tech. Oversight Cttee. of Nat. Earth Orientation Service 1986–, NASA Astrophysics Subcttee. 1992–; Albert A. Michelson Medal of Franklin Inst. 1975, Benjamin Apthorp Gould Prize of N.A.S. 1979, John Simon Guggenheim Fellowship 1982, New York Acad. of Sciences Award in Physical and Math. Sciences 1982, Dannie Heineman Award of American Astronomical Soc. 1983, Bowie Medal (American Geophysical Union) 1993, Einstein Medal 1994, Gerard Kuiper Award 1997. *Publications:* Prediction of Ballistic Missile Trajectories from Radar Observations 1958; Ed. of trans. of Mathematical Foundations of Quantum Statistics (Khinchin) 1960; numerous scientific articles and tech. reports. *Address:* Harvard-Smithsonian Centre for Astrophysics, 60 Garden Street, Cambridge, MA 02138 (Office); 17 Lantern Lane, Lexington, MA 02173, U.S.A. (Home). *Telephone:* (617) 495-7100.

SHAPIRO, Joel, M.A.; American sculptor; b. 27 Sept. 1941, New York; s. of Dr. Joseph Shapiro and Dr. Anna Shapiro; m. Ellen Phelan; one d.; ed. N.Y. Univ.; teacher Princeton Univ. 1974–75, 1975–76, School of Visual Arts 1977–82; One-man exhbns. include Paula Cooper Gallery, N.Y. 1970–89, Whitney Museum of Art, New York Stedelijk Museum, Amsterdam 1985, Hirshorn Museum and Sculpture Garden, Washington, D.C. 1987, Hans Strelow, Dusseldorf 1988, Toledo Museum of Art 1989, Waddington Gallery, London 1989, Baltimore Art Museum 1990, Center for Fine Arts, Miami 1991, Des Moines Art Center 1991, Gallery Seomi, Seoul 1994, Glerie Aronowitsch, Stockholm 1995, Karsten Greve, Paris 1995, Pace Gallery, New York 1995, Walker Art Centre/Minneapolis Sculpture Garden 1995, Nelson-Atkins Museum of Art/Kansas City Sculpture Park 1996, Pace Wildenstein Gallery 1996, Addison Gallery, Mass. 1997, Haus der Kunst, Munich 1997, Galerie Jamileh Weber, Zurich 1997; Group exhbns. England, U.S.A., Australia, Germany, Holland 1969–89; Nat. Endowment for the Arts 1975; mem. American Acad. of Arts and Letters, Swedish Royal Acad. of Art; Brandeis Award 1984; Skowhegan Medal for Sculpture 1986. *Publications:* Chicago Museum of Contemporary Art 1976, The Whitney Museum of American Art 1982. *Address:* c/o Pace Gallery, 33 Bleecker Street, New York, NY 10012, U.S.A.

SHAPIRO, Karl Jay; American poet and fmr. university teacher; b. 10 Nov. 1913, Baltimore, Md.; s. of Joseph and Sara Shapiro; m. 1st Evalyn Katz 1945 (divorced 1967); one s. two d.; m. 2nd Teri Kovach 1967 (died 1982); m. 3rd Sophie Wilkins 1985; ed. Johns Hopkins Univ.; served with U.S. Army 1941–45; Consultant in poetry, Library of Congress 1946–47; Assoc. Prof. of Writing, Johns Hopkins Univ. 1947–50; Ed. Poetry 1950–55; Prof. of Writing, Univ. of Neb. 1956–66; Prof. of English, Univ. of Ill. at Chicago Circle 1966–68; Prof. of English Univ. of Calif. at Davis 1955–56, 1968–85; Ed. Prairie Schooner 1956–63; Guggenheim Fellowship 1945–46, 1953–54; mem. Nat. Inst. of Arts and Letters, American Acad. of Arts and Sciences, PEN; Fellow in American Letters, Library of Congress; Hon. D.H.L. (Wayne State) 1960, Hon. D.Litt. (Bucknell) 1972; Jeanette S. Davis Prize 1942; Levinson Prize 1943; Contemporary Poetry Prize 1943; American Acad. of Arts and Letters Grant 1944; Pulitzer Prize (Poetry) 1945; Shelley Memorial Prize 1945; Bollingen Prize for Poetry 1969, Robert Kirsch Award, L.A. Times 1989, Charity Randall Citation (from Int. Poetry Forum) 1990. *Publications:* Poems 1935, Person, Place and Thing 1942, The Place of Love 1942, V-Letter and Other Poems 1944, Essay on Rime 1945, Trial of a Poet 1947, Bibliography of Modern Prosody 1948, Poems 1942–53 1953, Beyond Criticism 1953, Poems of a Jew 1958; Ed. Newberry Library Bulletin 1953–, In Defence of Ignorance 1960, American Poetry Anthology 1960, The Bourgeois Poet 1964, A Prosody Handbook (with Robert Beum) 1965, To Abolish Children 1968, White-haired Lover 1968, Selected Poems 1968, Edsel (novel) 1971, The Poetry Wreck (selected essays) 1975, Adult Bookstore (poems) 1976, Collected Poems 1940–1978, Love and War, Art and God 1984, New and Selected Poems 1940–86, The Younger Son (autobiog., vol. 1) 1988, Reports of my Death (autobiog., vol. 2) 1990, The Old Horsefly (poems) 1993, The Wild Card 1998. *Leisure interest:* painting. *Address:* 211 West 106th Street 11c, New York, NY 10025, U.S.A. *Telephone:* (212) 222-3560 (Home).

SHAPIRO, Robert Leslie, B.S., J.D.; American lawyer; b. 2 Sept. 1942, Plainfield, N.J.; ed. Univ. Coll. of Los Angeles, Loyola Univ.; called to bar Calif. 1969, U.S. Court of Appeals 1972, U.S. Dist. Court Calif. 1982; Deputy Dist. Attorney L.A. 1969–72; sole practice 1972–87; counsel Bushkin, Gaims, Gaines, Jonas 1987–88; with Christensen, White, Miller, Fink & Jacobs 1988–95; partner Christensen, Miller, Fink, Jacobs, Glaser, Weil & Shapiro 1995–; American Jurisprudence Award, Bancroft Whitney 1969; Best Criminal Defence Lawyer, Bar Asscn. 1993; f. Trial Lawyers for Public Justice 1982; mem. Nat. Asscn. of Criminal Defence Lawyers, Calif. Attorneys for Criminal Justice, Bar Asscn. *Publication:* Search for Justice 1996. *Address:* 2121 Avenue of the Stars, Floor 19, Los Angeles, CA 90067, U.S.A.

SHAPLEY, Lloyd Stowell, PH.D.; American professor of mathematics and economics; b. 2 June 1923, Cambridge, Mass.; s. of Harlow Shapley and Martha Betz; m. Marian Ludolph 1955; two s.; ed. Belmont Hill School, Phillips Exeter Acad., Harvard and Princeton Univs.; served in U.S. Army Air Corps in meteorology and cryptanalysis 1943–45; research mathematician, Rand Corpn. 1948–49, 1954–81; visiting appointments at Calif. Inst. of Tech. 1955–56, Indian Statistical Inst. 1979, Hebrew Univ. of Jerusalem 1979–80, Catholic Univ. of Louvain, Belgium 1982, Nat. Univ. of Defence Tech., China 1987; intermittent teaching, Rand Graduate Inst. 1970; Prof. of Math. and Econs. U.C.L.A. 1981–; main research interest: theory of games; Fellow, Econometric Soc., American Acad. of Arts and Sciences; mem. N.A.S.; Hon. Ph.D. (Hebrew Univ. of Jerusalem) 1986; Bronze Star, U.S. Army 1943; Von Neumann Theory Prize, ORSA/TIMS 1981. *Publications:* Geometry of Moment Spaces (with S. Karlin) 1953, Values of Non-Atomic Games (with R. Aumann) 1974. *Leisure interest:* Kriegsspiel. *Address:* Department of Mathematics and Department of Economics, University of California at Los Angeles, Los Angeles, CA 90024, U.S.A. *Telephone:* (213) 825-4418.

SHAPOSHNIKOV, Air Marshal Yevgeny Ivanovich; Russian air force officer and politician; b. 3 Feb. 1942, Bolshoy Log, Rostov region; s. of Ivan Sevastinovich Shaposhnikov and Klavdia Stepanova Shaposhnikova; m. Zemfira Nikolayevna Shaposhnikova 1980; one s. two d.; ed. Kharkov Higher

Aviation School, Y. Gagarin Aviation Acad., Gen. Staff Acad.; served Soviet Army 1959–; Head Soviet Air Force in Germany 1987–88; First Deputy Commdr. All-Union Soviet Air Force 1988–, Commdr. 1990–91; Minister of Defence and Head Soviet Armed Forces Aug.–Dec. 1991; C.-in-C. of the Armed Forces of the C.I.S. 1991–93; Sec. of Security Council, resgnd. 1993; rep. of Pres. Yeltsin in Rosvooruzhenie (state-owned armaments co.); Gen. Dir. Aeroflot 1995–97; Adviser to Pres. Yeltsin 1997–; mem. Bd. Democratic Reforms Movt. 1993–. *Leisure interests:* literature, theatre, tennis. *Address:* Office of the President, Kremlin, Moscow, Russia. *Telephone:* (095) 910 12 46. *Fax:* (095) 206 89 01.

SHAPOVALYANTS, Andrei Georgiyevich; Russian economist; b. 23 Feb. 1952, Moscow; m.; two d.; ed. Moscow Plekhanov Inst. of Nat. Econs.; researcher, Inst. Elektronika, Main Computation Centre, U.S.S.R. State Planning Cttee., Head of Div., U.S.S.R. State Planning Cttee. 1969–90; Head, Div. of Financial-Credit Policy, U.S.S.R. Ministry of Econs. and Prognosis 1991; Deputy, First Deputy Minister of Econs. and Finance of Russian Fed. 1991–93; Acting Minister of Econs. and Finance, First Deputy Minister 1993–98, Minister Sept. 1998–; mem. Presidium, Russian Govt. 1998–. *Address:* Ministry of Economics and Finance, 1st Tverskaya-Yamskaya str. 1–3, 125818 Moscow, Russia. *Telephone:* (095) 251 8226 (Office).

SHARIF, Omar (Michael Chalhoub); Egyptian actor; b. 10 April 1932, Cairo; s. of Claire and Joseph Chalhoub; m. 1st Faten Hamama 1955 (divorced 1967); one s.; m. 2nd 1973; ed. Victoria Coll., Cairo; Salesman, lumber-import firm; made first film The Blazing Sun 1953; starred in 24 Egyptian films and two French co-production films during following five years; commenced int. film career with Lawrence of Arabia; appeared in play The Sleeping Prince, England 1983. *Films include:* Lawrence of Arabia, The Fall of the Roman Empire, Behold a Pale Horse, Genghis Khan, The Yellow Rolls-Royce, Doctor Zhivago, Night of the Generals, Mackenna's Gold, Funny Girl, Cinderella-Italian Style, Mayerling, The Appointment, Che, The Last Valley, The Horsemen, The Burglars, The Island, The Tamarind Seed, Juggernaut, Funny Lady, Ace Up My Sleeve, Crime and Passion, Bloodline, Green Ice, Top Secret, Peter the Great (TV), The Possessed, Mountains of the Moon, Michaelangelo and Me, Drums of Fire, Le Guignol, The Puppet, The Rainbow Thief, 588 rue Paradis, Gulliver's Travels (TV), Heaven Before I Die, The 13th Warrior. *Publication:* The Eternal Male (autobiog.) 1978. *Leisure interests:* bridge and horse racing. *Address:* c/o William Morris Agency, 151 El Camino Drive, Beverly Hills, CA 90212, U.S.A.

SHARIF, Safwat ash-; Egyptian politician; b. 1933, Cairo, Egypt; ed. Mil. Acad., Inst. of Strategic Studies; with Presidency of the Republic 1957–74; Dir. Gen., local information, State Information Dept. 1975, Dir. of Foreign Information Service, State Information Dept.; mem. Arab Information Cttee. 1975; Sec. Ministry of Information 1977; Chair. Information Au-thority 1978; mem. of the Media Cttee. 1979; mem. constituent cttee. Nat. Democratic Party; Chief, Council of TV and Radio Trustees 1980; Minister of Information Jan. 1982–. *Address:* Ministry of Information, Radio and TV Bldg., Corniche en Nil, Cairo, Egypt. *Telephone:* (2) 5748984. *Fax:* (2) 5748981.

SHARIR, Abraham; Israeli politician and lawyer; b. 1932, Tel Aviv; m.; four c.; ed. law faculty, Hebrew Univ., Jerusalem; mil. service with Israeli Air Force; mem. Ninth Knesset (Parl.) –1981, mem. Finance Cttee., Chair. Likud Faction; mem. Tenth Knesset; Minister of Tourism 1981, 1984–86, of Tourism and Justice 1986–88; mem. High Court of Labour Relations, of Govt. Cttee. on Pensions; Likud Party. *Address:* c/o Ministry of Tourism, P.O. Box 1018, Jerusalem, Israel.

SHARMA, Arun Kumar, D.SC., F.N.A., F.A.SC., F.N.A.SC.; Indian botanist; b. 31 Dec. 1924, Calcutta; s. of late Charu Chandra Sharma and of Shovamoyee Sharma; m. Archana Mookerjea 1955; ed. Univ. of Calcutta; Research Scholar, Botanical Survey of India 1946–48; Asst. Lecturer, Univ. of Calcutta 1948–52, Lecturer 1952–62, Reader 1962–69, Prof. and Head, Dept. of Botany 1969–80, Programme Coordinator, Centre of Advanced Study, Dept. of Botany 1980–90; Pres. Indian Nat. Science Acad. 1983–84, Golden Jubilee Prof. 1985–90, Hon. Prof. 1990–; Gen. Pres. Indian Science Congress Asscn. 1981; Founding Pres. Fed. of Asian Scientific Acads. and Socs. 1984–; Fellow Third World Acad. of Sciences; Padma Bhushan, Om Prakash Bhasin Foundation Award 1993, First J. C. Bose Memorial Prize 1994, G. M. Modi Research Award 1994 and numerous other awards. *Publications:* Chromosome Techniques: Theory and Practice (with Archana Sharma) 1980, Chromosome in Evolution of Eukaryotic Groups, Vols. I and II (with Archana Sharma) 1983, Chromosome Techniques—a manual (with Archana Sharma) 1994; book chapters, articles in journals etc. *Leisure interests:* photography, bird-watching. *Address:* Centre of Advanced Study (Cell & Chromosome Research), Department of Botany, University of Calcutta, 35 Ballygunge Circular Road, Calcutta 700 019 (Office); Flat No. 2F2, 18/3 Gariahat Road, Calcutta, 700 019, India (Home). *Telephone:* (33) 475-3682 (Office); (33) 440-5802 (Home). *Fax:* (33) 473-2805.

SHARMA, Dwarka Prasad, M.COM., LL.B., PH.D.; Indian university vice-chancellor (retd.); b. 28 Oct. 1933, Umreth; s. of Shri B. L. Sharma; m. Chandra Prabha Sharma 1963; three c.; Chair. and Dean Faculty of Commerce and Man. Sri Krishnadevaraya Univ., Anantapur 1974–89, Bhopal Univ. (renamed Barkatullah Univ.) 1989–91; Rector (Pro-Vice-Chancellor) Barkatullah Univ. 1991–93; Dir. C. Rajagopalachari Inst. of Man. 1989–93; Regional Co-ordinator AIMS; Chair., Bhopal Br., IIMM; Visiting Prof. at several Indian and foreign univs.; Best Teacher Award Govt. of Andhra Pradesh 1982. *Publications:* Rural Economy of India 1976, Rural Banking in India 1981, Company Law and Secretarial Practice 1984, numerous research publs. *Leisure interests:* reading, writing. *Address:* 4/9B, Saket-nagar, Bhopal, M.P., 462024, India. *Telephone:* (0755) 582802.

SHARMA, Shanker Dayal, M.A., LL.M., PH.D.; Indian politician and barrister; b. 19 Aug. 1918, Bhopal; s. of Khushi Lal Sharma and Subhadra Sharma; m. Vimala Sharma; two s. one d.; ed. Lucknow Univ., Cambridge Univ. and Lincoln's Inn; lawyer 1942–; mem. All India Congress Cttee. 1950–; Pres. Bhopal State Congress Cttee. 1950–52; Chief Minister of Bhopal 1952–56; mem. Cen. Advisory Bd. of Educ. 1952–64; mem. Consultative Cttees. on Legislation, Bhopal and Madhya Pradesh Legis. Assemblies 1952–64; Minister, Madhya Pradesh Govt. 1956–67; Gen. Sec. Indian Nat. Congress 1968–72; Pres. All India Congress Cttee. 1972–74; mem. Lok Sabha (Parl.) 1971–77; Minister of Communications 1974–77; fmr. Gov. of Andhra Pradesh –1985, Gov. of Punjab 1985–86; Vice-Pres. of India 1987–92; Pres. of India 1992–97; served as Chair. and mem. of numerous parl. cttees.; suspended from Congress (I) Party 1986; Ed.-in-Chief Light and Learning, Ilm-au-Noor; Ed. Lucknow Law Journal; Hon. D.P.A. (London), LL.D. (Vikram and Bhopal Univs.), LL.D. (Cambridge) 1993. *Publications:* Congress Approach to International Affairs, Secularism in Indian Ethos, Towards a New India, Aspects of Indian Thought, Our Heritage of Humanism. *Leisure interests:* travel, reading, swimming. *Address:* 23 Safdarjang Road, New Delhi 110 011, India.

SHAROEV, Ioakim Georgiyevich; Russian theatre and film director; b. 19 Aug. 1930, Baku; s. of Georgi Georgiyevich Sharoev and Valentina Nikolaevna (née Rizkova) Sharoeva; m. Irene Nikolaevna Agafonova 1965; one s. one d.; ed. Lunacharsky State Inst. of Dramatic Art; Dir. of State Academic Bolshoi Theatre 1954–59; Artistic Dir. of Kremlin Theatre 1959–60; Prin. Dir. All-Russian Visiting Concert Admin. and Moscow Variety Theatre 1960–64; artistic dir. of musical film org. Ekran 1969–73; teacher Lunacharsky State Inst. of Dramatic Art 1964–, Prof. 1977–; Prin. Dir. Cultural Programmes 'Olympic Games—80'; Prin. Dir. of Moscow Stanislavsky and Nemirovich-Danchenko Musical Theatre 1982–87; Dir. of Studies, Russian Acad. of Theatre Art 1987–; Art Dir. Youth Moscow Studio School 1989–; a founder of Int. Union of Variety Artists (Vice-Pres. 1992–); Artistic Dir. Vivat Russia Festival 1992; Prin. Dir. Inauguration Ceremony 800 Years Moscow 1997; Artistic Dir. Fire of World Youth Olympic Games, Moscow 1998; mem. Russian Acad. of Creative Art 1992, Russian Acad. of Essential Sciences 1998; U.S.S.R. People's Artist 1984. *Opera productions include:* La Battaglia di Legnano (Verdi), The Queen of Spades, Iolanta (Tchaikovsky), Orpheus in Hiroshima (Akutagava), Cavalleria Rusticana (Mascagni), Orpheus and Euridice (Haydn), Golden Calf, Dorotea (Khrennikov). *Leisure interest:* collecting semi-precious stones. *Address:* c/o Russian Academy of Theatre Art, Maly Kislovski pereulok 6, Moscow, Russia. *Telephone:* 915-74-17.

SHARON, Major-Gen. Ariel; Israeli politician and army officer (retd.); b. 1928; m.; two s.; active in Hagana since early youth; Instructor, Jewish Police units 1947; Platoon Commdr. Alexandroni Brigade; Regimental Intelligence Officer 1948; Co. Commdr. 1949; Commdr. Brigade Reconnaissance Unit 1949–50; Intelligence Officer, Cen. Command and Northern Command 1951–52; studies at Hebrew Univ. 1952–53; in charge of Unit 101, on numerous reprisal operations until 1957, Commdr. Paratroopers Brigade, Sinai Campaign 1956; studies Staff Coll., Camberley, U.K. 1957–58; Training Commdr., Gen. Staff 1958; Commdr. Infantry School 1958–69; Commdr. Armoured Brigade 1962; Head of Staff, Northern Command 1964; Head, Training Dept. of Defence Forces 1966; Head Brigade Group during Six-Day War 1967; resigned from Army July 1973; recalled as Commdr. Cen. Section of Sinai Front during Yom Kippur War Oct. 1973, forged bridgehead across Suez Canal; founder mem. Likud Front Sept. 1973; mem. Knesset (Parl.) 1973–74, 1977–; Adviser to Prime Minister 1975–77; Minister of Agric. in charge of Settlements 1977–81, of Defence 1981–83, without Portfolio 1983–84, of Trade and Industry 1984–90, of Construction and Housing 1990–92, of Foreign Affairs and Nat. Infrastructure 1996–; mem. Ministerial Defence Cttee. 1990–92; Chair. Cabinet Cttee. to oversee Jewish immigration from U.S.S.R. 1991–96. *Publication:* Warrior (autobiog.) 1989. *Address:* Ministry of National Infrastructure, 48 Petah Tikva Tol, Tel-Aviv 61171, Israel. *Telephone:* 3-6388127. *Fax:* 3-6388130.

SHARP, John Randall; Australian politician (retd.); b. 15 Dec. 1954; s. of J.K. Sharp; m. Victoria Sharp 1986; two s. one d.; ed. The King's School, N.S.W., Orange Agricultural Coll.; farmer; mem. House of Reps. for Gilmore, N.S.W. 1984–93; M.P. (Nat. Party of Australia) for Hume, N.S.W. 1993–; Shadow Minister for Tourism and Sport 1988, for Tourism, Sport and Youth Affairs 1988–89, for Land Transport and Shipping 1989–90, for Shipping and Waterfront Reform 1990–93, for Transport 1993–96; Minister for Transport and Regional Devt. 1996–97; Deputy Man. of Opposition Business in the House 1990–94; Exec. Dir. Lincox 1999–. *Leisure interests:* rugby union, scuba diving, skiing, tennis. *Address:* 6 Greenaway Place, Goulburn, N.S.W. 2580, Australia.

SHARP, Phillip Allen, PH.D. ; American professor of biology and academic administrator; b. 6 June 1944; s. of Joseph W. Sharp and Katherin A. Sharp; m. Ann H. Holcombe 1964; three d.; ed. Union Coll., Ky., Univ. o f Illinois, California Inst. of Tech. and Cold Spring Harbor, New York; Research Asst., Dept. of Chem., Univ. of Ill. 1966–69; Postdoctoral Fellow, Lab. of

Prof. Norman Davidson, Calif. Inst. of Tech. 1969–71, Cold Spring Harbor Lab. 1971–72, Sr. Research Investigator 1972–74; Assoc. Prof., Center for Cancer Research and Dept. of Biology, M.I.T. 1974–79, Prof. 1979–, Assoc. Dir. Center for Cancer Research 1982–85, Dir. 1985–91, Head of Dept. of Biology 1991–; Co-founder, Chair. Scientific Bd., mem. Bd. of Dirs. Biogen, Inc.; Chair. Gen. Motors Cancer Research Foundation Awards Ass. 1994–, Scientific and Med. Advisory Bd. Huntsman Cancer Foundation 1995, Scientific Advisory Cttee. Dana-Farber Cancer Inst. 1996; mem. Cttee. on Science, Eng., and Public Policy 1992–95, Gen. Motors Cancer Research Foundation Advisory Council 1993–, Pres.'s Advisory Council on Science and Tech. 1991–97, Nat. Cancer Advisory Bd., N.I.H. (Presidential appointment) 1996; mem. and Trustee Alfred P. Sloan Foundation 1995–; mem. N.A.S., N.A.S. Inst. of Medicine, American Acad. of Arts and Sciences, American Philosophical Soc.; Fellow A.A.A.S.; Dr. h.c. (Union Coll., Ky.); Hon. D.Sc. (Univ. of Ky., Univ. of Tel-Aviv); Howard Ricketts Award, Eli Lilly Award, N.A.S. U.S. Steel Foundation Award, Gen. Motors Research Foundation Alfred P. Sloan, Jr. Prize for Cancer Research, Gairdner Foundation Int. Award, New York Acad. of Sciences Award in Biological and Medical Sciences, Louisa Gross Horwitz Prize, Albert Lasker Basic Medical Research Award, Dickson Prize (Univ. of Pittsburgh), shared Nobel Prize for Medicine 1993. *Publications:* numerous papers in scientific journals. *Leisure interests:* family, reading, sports. *Address:* Center for Cancer Research, Room E17-529B, Massachusetts Institute of Technology, 40 Ames Street, Cambridge, MA 02138 (Office); 36 Fairmont Avenue, Newton, MA 02158, U.S.A. (Home). *Telephone:* (617) 253-6421.

SHARP, Robert Phillip, PH.D.; American geologist; b. 24 June 1911, Calif.; s. of Julian Hebner Sharp and Alice Darling; m. Jean Prescott Todd 1938; one s. one d. (both adopted); ed. Oxnard Union High School, Calif., California Inst. of Tech., Harvard Univ.; Asst. Prof., Univ. of Ill. 1938–43; Capt., U.S.A.A.F. 1943–46; Prof. of Univ. of Minn. 1946–47; Prof., Calif. Inst. of Tech. 1947–79, Robert P. Sharp Emer. Prof. of Geology 1979–, Chair. Div. of Geological Sciences 1952–68; mem. N.A.S.; Kirk Bryan Award, Penrose Medal, Geological Soc. of America, NASA Exceptional Scientific Achievement Medal, Nat. Medal of Science 1989, Charles P. Daly Medal, American Geographical Soc. 1990, G.K. Gilbert Award and Distinguished Career Award, Geological Soc. of America 1996. *Publications:* Living Ice: understanding glaciers and glaciation 1989, 100 papers on geomorphology, glaciers, glaciation, dunes and related subjects in scientific journals, and several books. *Leisure interests:* fly fishing, snorkelling, skiing. *Address:* Division of Geological and Planetary Sciences, California Institute of Technology, Pasadena, 1200 E. California Blvd., CA 91106; 1901 Gibraltar Road, Santa Barbara, CA 93105, U.S.A. (Home). *Telephone:* (626) 395-6124 (Office); (805) 962-6675 (Home). *Fax:* (818) 568-0935.

SHARPE, Kevin Michael, M.A., D.PHIL., F.R.HIST.S.; British historian; b. 26 Jan. 1949, Kent; s. of Thomas H. Sharpe and Nell D. Sharpe; ed. Sir Joseph Williamson's Mathematical School, Rochester and St. Catherine's Coll. Oxford; Sr. Scholar, St. Catherine's Coll. Oxford 1971–74; Fellow, Oriel Coll. Oxford 1974–78; Lecturer, Christ Church, Oxford 1976–78; Lecturer in Early Modern History, Univ. of Southampton 1978–89, Reader 1989–, Prof. of Modern History seconded to Research School 1994; Visiting Fellow, Inst. for Advanced Study, Princeton 1981, Huntington Library, San Marino, Calif. 1982; Visiting Prof. Stanford Univ. Humanities Center 1985–86; Visiting Fellow, Humanities Centre, A.N.U. 1990; Visiting Prof., Calif. Inst. of Tech. 1992–93; Visiting Fellow St. Catherine's Coll. Oxford 1996; Wolfson Award 1980; Fulbright Fellow 1981; Royal Historical Soc. Whitfield Prize 1987. *Publications:* Faction and Parliament 1978, Sir Robert Cotton: History and Politics in Early Modern England 1979, Criticism and Compliment: The Politics of Literature in the England of Charles I 1987, Politics of Discourse 1987, Politics and Ideas in Early Stuart England 1989, The Personal Rule of Charles I 1993, Culture and Politics in Early Stuart England (ed.) 1994, Refiguring Revolution (Ed.) 1998; articles and reviews in The Sunday Times, The Independent, Times Literary Supplement, Spectator, History Today and other journals. *Leisure interests:* cycling, travel, conversation. *Address:* Department of History, University of Southampton, SO9 5NH (Office); 97 Livingstone Road, Portswood, Southampton, SO2 1DG, England. *Telephone:* (01703) 592231 (Office); (01703) 553303 (Home).

SHARPE, Tom (Thomas Ridley), M.A.; British novelist; b. 30 March 1928, London; s. of Rev. George Coverdale Sharpe and Grace Egerton Sharpe; m. Nancy Anne Looper 1969; three d.; ed. Lancing Coll., Pembroke Coll., Univ. of Cambridge; Social Worker 1952; Teacher 1952–56; Photographer 1956–61; Lecturer in History at Cambridge Coll. of Arts and Tech. 1963–71; full-time novelist 1971–. *Publications:* Riotous Assembly 1971, Indecent Exposure 1973, Porterhouse Blue 1974, Blott on the Landscape 1975, Wilt 1976, The Great Pursuit 1977, The Throwback 1978, The Wilt Alternative 1979, Ancestral Vices 1980, Vintage Stuff 1982, Wilt on High 1984, Grantchester Grind 1995, The Midden 1996. *Leisure interests:* photography, gardening. *Address:* 38 Tunwells Lane, Great Shelford, Cambridge, CB2 5LJ, England.

SHARPE, William Forsyth, PH.D.; American economist; b. 16 June 1934, Cambridge, Mass.; s. of Russell Thornley Sharpe and Evelyn Forsyth (Jillson) Maloy; m. 1st Roberta Ruth Branton 1954 (divorced 1986); one s. one d.; m. 2nd Kathryn Dorothy Peck 1986; one step-s. one step-d.; ed. Univ. of California, Los Angeles; economist, Rand Corpn. 1957–61; Asst. Prof. of Econs., Univ. of Washington 1961–63, Assoc. Prof. 1963–67, Prof. 1967–68; Prof., Univ. of Calif., Irvine 1968–70; Timken Prof. of Finance, Stanford Univ. 1970–89, Prof. Emer. 1989–92; Pres. William F. Sharpe Assocs. 1986–92; Prof. of Finance Stanford Univ. 1993–95, STANCO 25 Prof. of Finance 1995–; Graham and Dodd Award 1972, 1973, 1986, 1988, Nicholas Molodovsky Award 1989, Nobel Prize for Econ. Sciences 1990. *Publications:* Economics of Computers 1969, Portfolio Theory and Capital Markets 1970, Fundamentals of Investments 1989, Investments 4th edn. 1989. *Leisure interests:* sailing, peran and all kinds of music. *Address:* Department of Business, Stanford University, Stanford, CA 94305, U.S.A.

SHARQI, H.H. Sheikh Hamad bin Mohammed al-; ruler of Fujairah; b. 25 Sept. 1948; ed. Mons Mil. Acad., Hendon Police Coll.; Minister of Agric. and Fisheries, U.A.E. Fed. Cabinet 1971; Ruler of Fujairah 1974–; mem. Supreme Council 1974–. *Address:* Emiri Court, P.O. Box 1, Fujairah, United Arab Emirates.

SHATKIN, Aaron Jeffrey, PH.D.; American scientist; b. 18 July 1934, R.I.; s. of Morris and Doris Shatkin; m. Joan Arlene Lynch 1957; one s.; ed. Bowdoin Coll. and Rockefeller Univ.; Research Chemist N.I.H., Bethesda, Md. 1961–68; Visiting Scientist Salk Inst., La Jolla, Calif. 1968–69; mem. Roche Inst. of Molecular Biology, Nutley, N.J. 1968–86, Head Lab. of Molecular Biology 1977–83, Head Dept. of Cell Biology 1983–86; Univ. Prof. of Molecular Biology, Rutgers Univ. 1986–; Prof. of Molecular Genetics and Microbiology, R. W. Johnson Medical School 1986–; Adjunct Prof. Rockefeller Univ. 1978–87, N.J. Univ. of Medicine 1981, Princeton Univ. 1984–87; Dir. and Prof., N. J. Center for Advanced Biotechnology and Medicine 1986–; Visiting Prof. Georgetown Univ. Medical School, Washington, D.C. 1968; Instructor Cold Spring Harbor Lab. 1972, 1973, 1974, Univ. of Puerto Rico 1978, 1980; Ed.-in-Chief Molecular and Cellular Biology 1980–90; mem. N.A.S. 1981–, American Acad. of Arts and Sciences 1997, several editorial bds; Fellow American Acad. of Microbiology 1992; Hon. D.Sc. (Bowdoin Coll.) 1979; U.S. Steel Award in Molecular Biology 1977, N.J. Pride Award in Science 1989, Thomas Alva Edison Science Award 1991. *Publications:* more than 200 publs. in scientific journals including original reports and review articles. *Leisure interests:* travel, birds, running. *Address:* Center for Advanced Biotechnology and Medicine, 679 Hoes Lane, Piscataway, NJ 08854-5638, U.S.A. (Office). *Telephone:* (732) 235-5311 (Office). *Fax:* (732) 235-5318.

SHATNER, William, B.A.; American actor; b. 22 March 1931, Montréal, P.Q., Canada; s. of Joseph Shatner and Anne Shatner; m. 1st Gloria Rand 1956 (divorced 1969); m. 2nd Marcy Lafferty 1973 (divorced 1996); m. 3rd Nerine Kidd 1997; three d.; ed. McGill Univ.; appeared, Montréal Playhouse 1952, 1953; juvenile roles, Canadian Repertory Theatre, Ottawa 1952–53, 1953–54; appeared Shakespeare Festival, Stratford, Ont. 1954–56; Broadway appearances include: Tamburlaine the Great 1956, The World of Suzie Wong 1958, A Shot in the Dark 1961; numerous television appearances. *Films include:* The Brothers Karamazov 1958, The Explosive Generation 1961, Judgement at Nuremberg 1961, The Intruder 1962, The Outrage 1964, Dead of Night 1974, The Devil's Rain 1975, Star Trek 1979, The Kidnapping of the President 1979, Star Trek: The Wrath of Khan 1982, Star Trek III, The Search for Spock 1984, Star Trek IV: The Voyage Home 1986, Star Trek V: The Final Frontier 1989, Star Trek VI: The Undiscovered Country 1991, National Lampoon's Loaded Weapon 1993, Star Trek: Generations 1994, Ashes of Eden 1995, Star Trek: Avenger 1997, Tek Net 1997. *Publications:* Man O' War 1996, Tek Kill 1996, The Return 1996, Avenger 1997, Delta Search: Quest For Tomorrow 1997. *Address:* c/o Lemli Productions, 760 North La Cienega Boulevard, Los Angeles, CA 90069, U.S.A.

SHATROV (Marshak), Mikhail Filippovich; Russian dramatist and scriptwriter; b. 3 April 1932; s. of Filipp Semenovich and Cecilia Alexandrovna Marshak; m. Julia Vladimirovna Chernyshova; one d.; ed. Moscow Mining Inst.; Pres. and Chair. of Bd. of Dirs. Zao Moskva-Krasnye Kholmy Co. 1994–; began writing plays in 1955; U.S.S.R. State Prize 1983. *Plays include:* In the Name of Revolution 1957, The Peace of Brest Litovsk 1962, The Sixth of July 1963, Przevalsky's Horse 1972, The Dictatorship of Conscience 1986, Further . . . Further . . . Further 1988; Scripts for films include: Two Lines of Tiny Handwriting 1981, Tehran -43 1981, February (novel) 1988, Maybe 1993. *Address:* Serafimovich str. 2, Apt. 349, 109072 Moscow, Russia. *Telephone:* (095) 959-31-68.

SHAW, Bernard Leslie, PH.D., F.R.S.; British professor of chemistry; b. 28 March 1930, Springhead, Yorks.; s. of Tom Shaw and Vera Shaw; m. Mary Elizabeth Neild 1951; two s.; ed. Hulme Grammar School, Oldham and Manchester Univ.; Sr. DSIR Fellow, Torry Research Station, Aberdeen 1953–55; Research Scientist, ICI Ltd. 1956–61; Lecturer, School of Chem., Univ. of Leeds 1962–65, Reader 1965–71, Prof. 1971–94, Research Prof. 1995–; Visiting Prof. Univ. of Western Ont., Carnegie Mellon Univ. 1969, ANU 1983, Univ. of Auckland 1986, Univ. of Strasbourg 1993; mem. Science and Eng. Research Council Chemistry Cttee. 1975–78, 1981–84;Chemical Soc. Award in Transition Metal Chem. 1975, Tilden Lecturer, Chemical Soc. 1975, Liversidge Lecturer Royal Soc. of Chem. 1987–88, Ludwig Mond Lecturer and Prizewinner Royal Soc. of Chem. 1992–93, Sir Edward Frankland Lecturer and Prizewinner 1995. *Publications:* Inorganic Hydrides, Organo-Transition Metal Compounds and Related Aspects of Homogeneous Catalysis and about 400 research papers. *Leisure interests:* walking, pottery, gardening, tennis. *Address:* School of Chemistry, University of Leeds, Leeds, LS2 9JT (Office); 14 Monkbridge Road, Leeds, West Yorks., LS6 4DX, England (Home). *Telephone:* (0113) 233 6402 (Office); (0113) 275 5895 (Home). *Fax:* (0113) 233 6565 (Office).

SHAW, Colin Don, C.B.E., M.A.; British fmr. broadcasting executive, writer and lecturer; b. 2 Nov. 1928, Liverpool; s. of Rupert M. Shaw and Enid F. Shaw (née Smith); m. Elizabeth A. Bowker 1955; one s. two d.; ed. Liverpool Coll., St. Peter's Hall, Oxford, Inner Temple; served with R.A.F. 1947–49; joined BBC as radio drama producer 1953–57, variety of posts 1957–69, Sec. to Bd. 1969–71, Chief Sec. 1972–77; Dir. of TV Ind. Broadcasting Authority 1977–83; Dir. Programme Planning Secr. Ind. Cos. TV Asscn. 1983–87; Dir. Broadcasting Standards Council 1988–96; mem. Arts Council of G.B. 1978–80; Gov. English Speaking Union of G.B. 1976–83; Trustee Int. Inst. of Communications 1983–89; Hon. Visiting Prof. Univ. of Manchester 1996. *Publications:* Deciding What We Watch 1999, several radio plays and a stage play for children. *Leisure interests:* travel, reading, theatre. *Address:* Lesters, Little Ickford, Aylesbury, Bucks., HP18 9HS, England. *Telephone:* (01844) 339225. *Fax:* (01844) 338351.

SHAW, Fiona; actress; b. Fiona Wilson 1959; ed. Royal Acad. of Dramatic Art; debut in Love's Labours Lost; stage appearances include Julia in The Rivals, Nat. Theatre, Mary Shelley in Howard Brenton's Bloody Poetry, Hampstead; joined Royal Shakespeare Co. (RSC) 1985; appeared with RSC as Celia in As You Like It, Tatyana in Gorky's Philistines, Madame des Volonges in Les Liaisons Dangereuses, Beatrice in Much Ado About Nothing, Portia in The Merchant of Venice, Kate in The Taming of the Shrew, Mistress Carol in James Shirley's Hyde Park, and as Sophocles's Electra; appeared as Rosalind in As You Like It, Old Vic 1990, as Shen Te/Shui Ta in Brecht's The Good Person of Sichuan, Nat. Theatre 1990 (Olivier Award for Best Actress 1990, London Critics' Award for Best Actress 1990), as Richard II in Richard II, and in The Waste Land 1996, The Prime of Miss Jean Brodie, Royal Nat. Theatre 1998; B.A.F.T.A. Award for Machinal 1994; Bancroft Gold Medal (R.A.D.A.). *Films include:* My Left Foot, Mountains of the Moon, Three Men and a Little Lady 1990, Super Mario Brothers 1992, Undercover Blues 1993, Jane Eyre 1996, The Avengers 1997, The Butcher's Boy 1997. *Address:* c/o ICM, Oxford House, 76 Oxford Street, London, W1N 0AX, England; Eglantine, Montenotte, Cork, Ireland.

SHAW, Sir Neil McGowan, Kt.; Canadian business executive; b. 31 May 1929, Montréal; s. of Harold LeRoy Shaw and Fabiola Shaw (née McGowan); m. 1st Frances Audrey Robinson 1952 (divorced 1980); two s. three d.; m. 2nd Elizabeth Fern Mudge 1985; ed. Knowlton High School, Lower Canada Coll.; Trust Officer Crown Trust Co. 1947–54; with Canada Dominion Sugar (now Redpath Industries) 1954–, Merchandising Man. 1954–66, Vice-Pres. 1967–72, Pres. 1972–80, Vice-Chair. 1981–98; Group Man. Dir. Tate and Lyle PLC, England 1980–86, Chair. 1986–93, C.E.O. 1986–92, Exec. Chair. 1992–94, Redpath Industries Ltd. 1972–; fmrly. Chair. Tate and Lyle Holdings Ltd., England, Tate and Lyle Industries Ltd., England, Tate and Lyle Inc., New York; Dir. Tunnel Refineries Ltd., England, United Biscuits (Holdings) PLC 1988–97, G. R. Amylum N.V., Brussels, Americare Corpn. Alcantara, Lisbon, Canadian Imperial Bank of Commerce, Toronto 1986–, A. E. Staley Manufacturing Co., Ill. 1991, M & G Investment Income Trust PLC 1991–95; Dir. Inst. of Dirs. 1986–; Chair. World Sugar Research Org. 1994– (Dir. 1982–), Foundation and Friends of Royal Botanic Gardens, Kew 1994– (Trustee 1990–), Anglo-Canadian Support Group CARE 1989–, Business in the Community 1991–95; Gov. Montréal Gen. Hospital, Reddy Memorial Hospital, World Food and Agro Forum 1988; mem. Canadian Memorial Foundation 1989–, Council of Advisers to Premier of Quebec 1987–, Advisory Council Prince's Youth Business Trust 1990–, London Enterprise Agency 1986–, Food Asscn. 1989–, Listed Cos. Advisory Cttee. 1991–, British N. American Cttee. 1991–; Chair. and Dir. CAPOCO Ltd. (Theatre Royal Windsor) 1991–, The Atkins Restaurant Co. Ltd. 1993–; Dir. United World Coll. of Atlantic 1997. *Leisure interests:* sailing, skiing, golf. *Address:* Titness Park, Mill Lane, Sunninghill, Ascot, Berks., SL5 7RU, England (Home).

SHAW, Sir Run Run, Kt., C.B.E.; British business executive; b. 14 Oct. 1907, Shanghai, China; s. of the late Shao Hang-yin and Wang Shun-xiang; m. 1st Lily Wang Mee-chun 1932 (deceased); two s. two d.; m. 2nd Lee Manglan 1997; ed. in China; Founder and Chair. Shaw Group of Cos. 1959–; Chair. Shaw Foundation HK Ltd. 1973–; Pres. Hong Kong Red Cross Soc. 1972–, Hong Kong Arts Festival 1974–88, Bd. of Govs. Hong Kong Arts Centre 1978–88, Television Broadcasts Ltd., TVE (Holdings) Ltd. 1980–; mem. Council, The Chinese Univ. of Hong Kong 1977–92; Chair. Bd. of Trustees, United Coll., Chinese Univ. of Hong Kong 1983–92; Local Adviser on Hong Kong for People's Repub. of China 1992–; mem. Preparatory Cttee., Hong Kong Special Admin. Region (SAR) 1995–98; Founder, Shaw Coll. Chinese Univ. of Hong Kong 1986; Queen's Badge, Red Cross 1982; hon. degrees from Univ. of Hong Kong, Chinese Univ. of Hong Kong, Univs. of E. Asia (Macau), Sussex, New York at Stony Brook, City Polytechnic of Hong Kong, Hong Kong Baptist Coll., Hong Kong Polytechnic, Pepperdine Univ.; Commdr. Order of Crown of Belgium. *Leisure interests:* shadow-boxing, golf. *Address:* Shaw House, Lot 220, Clear Water Bay Road, Kowloon, Hong Kong. *Telephone:* 2719-8371.

SHAW YU-MING, PH.D.; Taiwanese public servant and academic; b. 3 Nov. 1938, Harbin; m. Shirley Shiow-jyu Lu; one s. one d.; ed. Nat. Chengchi Univ., Tufts Univ. and Univ. of Chicago, U.S.A.; Asst. Prof. of History, Newberry Coll., S.C. 1967–68, 1972–73; Assoc. Prof. of History, Univ. of Notre Dame, Ind. 1973–82; held various research posts in Asian studies in U.S.A.; Dir. Asia and World Inst., Taiwan 1983–84; Dean, Graduate School of Int. Law and Diplomacy, Nat. Chengchi Univ. 1984–, Dir. Inst. of Int. Relations 1984–87, 1994–; Dir.-Gen. Govt. Information Office and Govt. spokesman 1987–91; Prof. of History, Nat. Chengchi Univ. 1991–; Pres. Cultural Foundation of the United Daily News Group 1992–; awards from American Council of Learned Socs., Asia Foundation, Inst. of Chinese Culture, U.S.A. and others. *Publications include:* China and Christianity 1979, Problems in Twentieth Century Chinese Christianity 1980, Twentieth Century Sino-American Relations 1980, History and Politics in Modern China 1982, International Politics and China's Future 1987, Beyond the Economic Miracle 1988, An American Missionary in China: John Leighton Stuart and Chinese-American Relations 1993. *Address:* 64 Wan Shou Road, Taipei, Taiwan.

SHAWA, Lol Mohammed; Chadian politician and fmr. resistance leader; b. 15 June 1939, Mao (Kanem); s. of Mohammed Shawa and Amy Shawa; m. Fatimé Adouly Lol 1970; four s. two d.; ed. Int. Inst. of Public Admin. and Inst. for the Study of Int. Relations, Paris; Leader of Mouvement populaire pour la libération du Tchad (the Third Army) 1979; Prime Minister and Head of State April–Aug. 1979; studied in Paris 1979–82; Minister of Transport 1982–85. *Address:* B.P. 1104, N'Djamena, Chad.

SHAWCROSS, Baron (Life Peer), cr. 1959, of Friston; **Hartley William Shawcross,** Kt., P.C., G.B.E., Q.C., LL.D.; British jurist, politician and businessman; b. 4 Feb. 1902, Giessen, Germany; s. of John and Hilda Shawcross; m. 1st Rosita Alberta Shyvers 1924; m. 2nd Joan Winifred Mather (died 1974); two s. one d.; ed. Dulwich Coll. and abroad; called to Bar 1925; Sr. Law Lecturer Liverpool Univ. 1927–34; Deputy Regional Commr. S.E. Region 1941; Regional Commr. N.W. Region 1942–45; Recorder of Salford 1941–45; Chair. Catering Wages Comm. 1943–45; Asst. Chair. E. Sussex Quarter Sessions 1941; Labour M.P. for St. Helens 1945–58; Attorney-Gen. 1945–51; Pres. Bd. of Trade April-Nov. 1951; Judge of Int. Court of Arbitration, The Hague; Chair. Royal Comm. on the Press 1961–62; Chair. British Medical Research Council 1962–65; Chair. "Justice" (British branch of Int. Comm. of Jurists) 1956–73; Chief Prosecutor, Nuremberg Trials 1945–46; U.K. del. UN 1945–49; withdrew from Labour Party 1958, joined SDP 1983; mem. Monckton Comm. 1959–60 (resgnd.); Pres. Rainer Foundation until 1972; Chair. Int. Chamber of Commerce Special Comm. of Eminent Persons on Ethical Practices; Chair. Dominion Lincoln Assurance Co. Ltd., Thames Television Co. Ltd. 1969–74, Upjohn and Co. Ltd. to 1977, City of London Panel on Takeovers and Mergers 1969–80, Press Council 1974–78, London and Continental Bankers 1974–80; Dir. Shell Transport and Trading Co. Ltd. until 1973, EMI Ltd. until 1980, European Enterprises Devt. Co. S.A. (Luxembourg), Times Newspapers Ltd. 1967–74, Ranks, Hovis Macdougall Ltd. until 1977 (consultant 1977–94), Caffyns Ltd. (Deputy Chair., until 1994), Morgan et Cie. S.A., Morgan et Cie. International S.A. until 1976, The Observer 1981–93; Special Adviser to J. P. Morgan 1968–94; mem. Court of London Univ. until 1978; Sussex Univ. Exec. Council, Pro-Chancellor 1962–65, Chancellor 1965–85; mem. Int. Cttee. of Jurists, Bd. of Trustees, American Univ. of Beirut until 1975, Council of Int. Chambers of Commerce; Hon. mem. New York and American Bar Asscns.; Hon. F.R.C.O.G. 1979, Royal Coll. of Surgeons 1981; Hon. D.Litt.(Loughborough) 1980; Hon. LL.D. (Columbia, Bristol, Michigan, Lehigh, Liverpool, Hull Univs.); Hon. D.C.L. (New Brunswick Univ. and London). *Publication:* Life Sentence: The Memoirs of Hartley Shawcross 1995. *Leisure interest:* yachting. *Address:* J. P. Morgan, 60 Victoria Embankment, London, EC4Y 0JP (Office); Friston Place, East Dean, Nr. Eastbourne, E. Sussex, BN20 0AH, England. *Telephone:* 0171-325 5127 (Office).

SHAWCROSS, William; British journalist; b. 28 May 1946; s. of Baron Shawcross (q.v.); m. 1st Marina Warner 1972 (divorced 1980); one s.; m. 2nd Michal Levin 1981 (divorced); one d.; m. Olga Forte 1993; ed. Eton, Univ. Coll. Oxford; freelance journalist in Czechoslovakia 1968–69; Corresp. for The Sunday Times, London, 1969–72; Chair. Article 19, Int. Centre on Censorship. *Publications:* Dubcek 1970, Crime and Compromise: Janos Kadar and the Politics of Hungary since Revolution 1974, Sideshow: Kissinger, Nixon and the Destruction of Cambodia 1979, Quality of Mercy: Cambodia, The Holocaust and the Modern Conscience 1985, The Shah's Last Ride 1989, Murdoch 1992, Cambodia's New Deal 1994. *Address:* c/o Green & Heaton Ltd., 37 Goldhawk Row, London, W.12; Friston Place, East Dean, E. Sussex, BN20 0AH, England. *Telephone:* 0171-289 8089 (London).

SHAWN, Wallace; American actor; b. 12 Nov. 1943, New York; s. of William Shawn; ed. Harvard Univ., Magdalen Coll., Oxford Univ. *Films include:* My Dinner with André, Manhattan 1979, The Princess Bride, The Moderns, Scenes from the Class Struggle in Beverly Hills, We're No Angels, Shadows and Fog, Mom and Dad Save the World, Nickel and Dime, The Cemetery Club, Unbecoming Age, The Meteor Man, Vanya on 42nd Street, Mrs Parker and the Vicious Circle, Clueless, Canadian Bacon, Toy Story (voice), The Wife, House Arrest, All Dogs Go To Heaven II (voice). *Stage appearances include:* My Dinner with André, A Thought in Three Parts, Marie and Bruce 1979, Aunt Dan and Lemon 1985, The Fever 1991. *Address:* William Morris Agency, 151 El Camino Drive, Beverly Hills, CA 90212, U.S.A.

SHAYE, Robert; American cinema executive; b. 4 March 1939, Detroit, Mich.; ed. Univ. of Michigan, Columbia Univ.; first prize Soc. of Cinematologists' Rosenthal Competition for best film directed by American under 25; wrote, produced, directed and ed. short films and TV commercials, including award-winning shorts, Image and On Fighting Witches; f. New Line Cinema 1967, Chair. and C.E.O. *Films:* (producer and exec. producer) Stunts, XTRO,

Alone in the Dark, The First Time, Polyester, Critters, Quiet Cool, My Demon Lover, A Nightmare on Elm Street (parts 1-6), The Hidden, Stranded, Critters 2, Hairspray, Heart Condition, Book of Love (dir.), Wes Craven's New Nightmare (also actor). *Television:* Freddy's Nightmare: the Series (exec. producer). *Address:* New Line Cinema, 116 North Robertson Boulevard, Suite 200, Los Angeles, CA 90046, U.S.A.

SHAZLY, Lieut.-Gen. Saad Mohamed el-Husseiny el-, M.POL.SC.; Egyptian army officer and diplomatist; b. 1 April 1922, Cairo; s. of Mohamed el-Husseiny el-Shazly and Tafida Ibrahim el-Shazly; m. Zeinat Mohamed Metwally 1942; ed. Khedive Ismail Secondary School, Cairo, Cairo Univ., Mil. Coll., and in U.S.S.R; Officer of the Guards 1943–48; Platoon Commdr. Arab-Israeli War 1948; Commdr. of Parachute School 1954–56; Commdr. of Parachute Battalion 1956–58; Commdr. United Arab Repub. Contingent, UN, Congo 1960–61; Defence Attaché, London 1961–63; Brigade Commdr. in Yemen Civil War 1965–66; Commdr. Shazly Task Force Group, Egyptian-Israeli War 1967; Commdr. of Special Forces, Paratroopers and Rangers 1967–69; Commdr. Red Sea District 1970–71; Chief of Staff of Egyptian Armed Forces 1971–73; Amb. to U.K. 1974–75, to Portugal 1975–78; founder and Sec.-Gen. Nat. Front Party 1980; Chief Ed. Algabha, Alger 1980–; mem. Int. Inst. for Strategic Studies; mem. Bd. of Dirs. Islamic Inst. of Defence Tech.; holder of 23 decorations including Mil. Medal of Courage 1949, Médaille de Congo 1961, Medal of Yemen 1966, Medal of Distinguished Mil. Duty 1972, Order of the Repub. (1st Class) 1974, Honour Star 1974, Syrian Honour Star (Knight) 1974, Palestinian Honour Star 1974. *Publications:* How an Infantry Division can Cross a Water Barrier 1973, Fonética Arabe Com Letras Portuguesas 1978, Kuraanunn Kariim 1978, The Crossing of the Suez 1980, Four Years in the Diplomatic Service 1983, Arab Military Option 1984, The Eighth Crusade 1990; contributes to numerous journals. *Leisure interests:* gliding, shooting, fencing, golf, camping, chess.

SHCHAPOV, Yaroslav Nikolayevich; Russian historian and university professor; b. 6 May 1928, Moscow; s. of Nikolai Mikhailovich Shchapov and Eugenia Nikolayevna Shchapova; m. Yulia Leonidovna Sinelnikova 1954; one s.; ed. Moscow State Univ.; sr., chief librarian V. Lenin State Library 1952–57; jr., sr., leading, chief researcher Inst. of History of U.S.S.R., U.S.S.R. Acad. of Sciences 1957–90; Head Centre of Church and Religious History, Inst. of Russian History Russian Acad. of Sciences 1990–; corresp. mem. U.S.S.R. (now Russian) Acad. of Sciences 1987; Pres. Russian Soc. of Historians and Archivists 1990–96; Dir. Manor Schapovo Mun. Museum, Podolsk 1998–; Chair. Scientific Council Role of Religion in History; Hon. Mem. Russian Palestine Soc.; mem. Russian Ass. of the Nobility, Russian Manor Shchapovo Soc.; research in history of old Russia, law, social relations, religion, culture, old Russian manuscripts, Russian-Byzantine relations, Russian Orthodox Church; B. Grekov Prize; Order of Friendship of the Peoples 1988, Church Order St. Sergius of Radonezh (Second Class) 1997, Order of Honour 1998. *Publications:* Byzantine and South Slavic Legal Heritage in Russia of 11th–13th Centuries 1978, State and Church in Early Russia 10th–13th Centuries 1989 (publ. U.S.A. 1993), Russian Orthodox Church and the Communist State (Documents from Secret Archives) 1996, Reference Books for the Researcher in Russian History 1998; numerous articles. *Leisure interests:* genealogy, family history. *Address:* Institute of Russian History, Russian Academy of Sciences, D. Ulyanov str. 19, 117036 Moscow, Russia. *Telephone:* (095) 126-26-65 (Office); (095) 438-22-89 (Home). *Fax:* (095) 126-39-55 (Office).

SHCHARANSKY, Anatoly (see Scharansky, Natan).

SHCHEDRIN, Rodion Konstantinovich; Russian composer; b. 16 Dec. 1932, Moscow; s. of Konstantin Mikhailovich Shchedrin and Konkordia Ivanovna Shchedrin; m. Maya Plisetskaya 1958; ed. Moscow Conservatoire; Chair. R.S.F.S.R. (now Russian) Union of Composers 1973–90; U.S.S.R. People's Deputy 1989–91; mem. Acad. of Fine Arts, Berlin, Bavarian Acad. of Fine Arts; Hon. mem. American Liszt Soc., Int. Music Council; Lenin Prize, U.S.S.R. and Russian State Prizes, Russian Union of Composers Prize, Beethoven Soc. Prize, U.S.S.R. and Russian People's Artist. *Compositions include:* operas: Not Only Love 1961, Dead Souls (operatic scenes in three acts) 1976, Lolita (after V. Nabokov) 1994; ballets: Humpbacked Horse 1960, Carmen Suite 1967, Anna Karenina 1972, The Seagull 1980, Lady with a Lapdog 1985; for orchestra: two symphonies 1958, 1965, 5 concertos for orchestra 1963, 1968, 1988, 1989, 1998; Self-Portrait 1984, Stykhisa 1988, Old Russian Circus Music 1989; 4 concertos for piano and orchestra 1954, 1966, 1973, 1992, concerto for cello and orchestra 1994, concerto for trumpet and orchestra 1995, concerto dolce for viola and chamber orchestra 1997; Chamber Suite 1961, Poetoria 1974, The Sealed Angel (Slavonic Mass) 1988, Nina and the Twelve Months (musical) 1988, Piano Terzelto 1996, Concerto Cantabile (for violin and strings) 1997, works for chamber orchestra, string trio, piano, violin, organ and cello, and song cycles, music for theatre and cinema. *Leisure interests:* jogging, fishing, water-skiing, wind surfing. *Address:* Theresienstrasse 23, 80333 München, Germany; 25/9, Tverskaya St., apt. 31, 103050 Moscow, Russia (Homes). *Telephone:* (089) 285834 (Munich); (7-095) 299-72-39 (Moscow). *Fax:* (089) 282057 (Munich).

SHCHERBAKOV, Vladimir Ivanovich, DR. ECON. SC.; Russian politician; b. 5 Dec. 1949, Primorsky krai; s. of Ivan Shcherbakov and Elena Shcherbakova; m. Natalia Hesnokova; one s.; ed. Togliatti Polytech. Inst.; engineer-mechanic; mem. CPSU 1970–91; party work in Togliatti 1971–74; engineer, controller, Chief Planning and Econ. Dept., Volga Motor Car Plant 1970–82; Deputy Dir.-Gen., Dir. Econ. and Planning Dept., Kama Big Lorries Plant 1982–85; Chief Machine Bldg. and Metal Trade Plant Dept., U.S.S.R. State Cttee. for Labour and Social Affairs 1985–88; First Deputy Chief Nat. Economy Man. Dept., U.S.S.R. Council of Ministers 1988–89; Minister of Labour and Social Affairs 1989–91; Deputy Prime Minister, later First Deputy Minister of Economy and Planning of the U.S.S.R. March-Aug. 1991; Pres. Interprivatization Fund 1991–; Chair. Russian United Industrial Party 1995–; mem Presidium, All-Union Soc. Znanie, Bureau, All-Union Econ. Soc. *Publications include:* about 50 monographs and articles, including Big Economic Complexes: Mechanism of Management, Industrial Labour and its Remuneration, New Mechanisms of Labour Remuneration, etc. *Leisure interests:* hunting, sports. *Address:* Interprivatization Fund, Solyanka 3, bldg. 3, 109028 Moscow, Russia. *Telephone:* 924-60-61. *Fax:* 923-14-11.

SHEARER, Alan; British footballer; b. 1970, Gosforth, Newcastle upon Tyne; coached as a child at Wallsend Boys' Club; striker; played for Southampton 1987–92, Blackburn Rovers 1992–96; signed by Newcastle United for world record transfer fee of £15 million 1996, now Capt.; first played for England 1992, Capt. 1996–. *Address:* Newcastle United Football Club, St. James Park, Newcastle upon Tyne, NE1 4ST England. *Telephone:* (0191) 201 8400.

SHEARER, Rt. Hon. Hugh Lawson; Jamaican politician; b. 18 May 1923, Martha Brae, Trelawny; ed. St. Simon's Coll.; journalist Jamaica Worker 1941–47; mem. Kingston and St. Andrew Corpn. 1947–51; mem. House of Reps. 1955–59; mem. Legis. Council (now Senate) 1961–66; Minister without Portfolio and Leader of Govt. Business in the Senate 1962–67; Deputy Leader Jamaica Labour Party 1967–74; Jamaican del. to UN 1962–72; Prime Minister, Minister of Defence and Minister of External Affairs 1967–72; Leader of the Opposition 1972–74; M.P. for South-East Clarendon 1976–; Deputy Prime Minister and Minister of Foreign Affairs 1980–89, Minister of Foreign Trade 1980–86, of Industry 1986–89; Island Supervisor, Bustamante Industrial Trade Union 1953, Vice-Pres. 1960–79, Pres. 1979–; Chair. Jt. Trade Unions Research Devt. Centre 1992–; Pres. Jamaica Confed. of Trade Unions 1994–; Hon. LL.D. (Howard Univ.) 1968, (Univ. College of the West Indies, Jamaica) 1994; Order of Jamaica 1990. *Address:* c/o Bustamante Industrial Trade Union, 98 Duke Street, Kingston, Jamaica.

SHEARER, Moira; British ballet dancer, actress and writer; b. 17 Jan. 1926, Dunfermline; d. of Harold King; m. Ludovic Kennedy (q.v.) 1950; one s. three d.; trained Mayfair School; debut with Int. Ballet 1941; joined Sadler's Wells 1942; fmrly. performed with Old Vic Theatre, Bristol Old Vic Theatre; Dir. Border TV 1977–82; mem. BBC Gen. Advisory Council 1970–77, Scottish Arts Council 1971–73; fmrly. touring lecturer on ballet. *Stage performances (ballet and plays) include:* Sleeping Beauty 1946, Cinderella 1948, Carmen 1950, Ballet Imperial 1950, A Midsummer Night's Dream 1954, I Am a Camera 1955, Man of Distinction 1957, The Cherry Orchard 1977, Hay Fever 1978, A Simple Man 1987, The Aspern Papers 1994. *Film appearances include:* The Red Shoes 1948, Tales of Hoffman 1950, Story of Three Loves 1952, The Man Who Loved Redheads 1954, Peeping Tom 1960, Black Tights 1961. *Publications include:* Balletmaster: A Dancer's View of George Balanchine 1986, Ellen Terry (biography) 1998.

SHEARING, George Albert, O.B.E.; jazz pianist and composer; b. 13 Aug. 1919; s. of James Philip Shearing and Ellen Amelia Shearing (née Brightman); m. 1st Beatrice Bayes 1941 (divorced); one d.; m. 2nd Eleanor Geffert 1984; ed. Linden Lodge School for the Blind, London; founded and performed with George Shearing Quintet 1949–67; has also led other jazz ensembles; composed many popular songs, including Lullaby of Birdland 1952; many recordings 1939–; mem. Bd. Guide Dogs for the Blind, Hadley School for the Blind; Golden Plate Award, American Acad. of Achievement 1968, Helen Keller Achievement Award 1995. *Address:* c/o Joan Shulman, 103 Avenue Road, Suite 301, Toronto, Ont., M5R 2GR, Canada.

SHEARMAN, John Kinder Gowran, M.A., PH.D., F.B.A.; British professor of history of art; b. 24 June 1931, Aldershot; s. of Brig. C. E. G. Shearman and Evelyn W. Shearman; m. 1st Jane D. Smith 1957 (deceased); one s. three d.; m. 2nd Deirdre Roskill 1983; ed. Felsted School, Courtauld Inst.; Lecturer to Prof., Courtauld Inst., Univ. of London 1957–79, Deputy Dir. 1974–78; Dept. of Art and Archaeology, Princeton Univ., U.S.A. 1979–87, Chair. 1979–85, Class of 1926 Prof. 1986–87; Prof. of Fine Art, Harvard Univ. 1987–93, Chair. 1990–93, William Dorr Boardman Prof. 1988–94, Adams Univ. Prof. 1994–; mem. Accademia del Disegno, Florence, Accademia di San Luca, Rome, American Acad. of Arts and Sciences; Serena Medal, British Acad. *Publications:* Andrea del Sarto 1965, Mannerism 1967, Raphael's Cartoons 1972, Catalogue, Earlier Italian Paintings in the Royal Collection 1983, Funzione e Illusione 1983, Only Connect . . . 1992. *Leisure interests:* sailing, music, travel. *Address:* 3 Clement Circle, Cambridge, MA 02138, U.S.A. *Telephone:* (617) 876-9548.

SHEBBEARE, Thomas Andrew (Tom), C.V.O., B.A.; British charity administrator; b. 25 Jan. 1952; s. of the late Robert Austin Shebbeare and Frances Dare Graham; m. Cynthia Jane Cottrell 1976; one s. one d.; ed. Malvern Coll., Univ. of Exeter; with World Univ. Service 1973–75; Gen. Sec. British Youth Council 1975–80; Admin. Council of Europe 1980–85; Exec. Dir. European Youth Foundation 1985–88; Exec. Dir. Prince's Trust and Royal Jubilee Trust 1988–; Dir. Inst. for Citizenship Studies 1991–; Trustee Nations Trust (S.A.) 1995–. *Leisure interests:* family, cooking, food and drink.

Address: 18 Park Square East, London, NW1 4LH, England. *Telephone:* 0171-543 1234.

SHEED, Wilfrid John Joseph, M.A.; American author; b. 27 Dec. 1930, London, England; s. of Francis Joseph and Maisie (Ward) Sheed; m. 1st Maria Bullitt Dartington 1957 (divorced); three c.; m. 2nd Miriam Ungerer; one s. two d.; ed. Lincoln Coll., Oxford Univ.; film reviewer Jubilee magazine 1959–61, Assoc. Ed. 1959–66; drama critic and fmr. book ed. Commonweal magazine, New York; film critic Esquire magazine 1967–69; Visiting Prof. Princeton Univ. 1970–71; columnist N.Y. Times 1971–; judge and mem. editorial bd. Book of the Month Club 1972–88; Guggenheim Fellow 1971–72; mem. P.E.N. Club. *Publications include:* A Middle Class Education 1961, The Hack 1963, Square's Progress 1965, Office Politics 1966, The Blacking Factory 1968, Max Jamison 1970, The Morning After 1971, People Will Always Be Kind 1973, Three Mobs: Labor, Church, and Mafia 1974, Transatlantic Blues 1978, The Good Word 1979, Clare Boothe Luce 1982, Frank and Maisie 1985, The Boys of Winter 1987, Baseball and Lesser Sports 1991, My Life as a Fan 1993, In Love with Daylight 1995; ed. of G. K. Chesterton's Essays and Poems 1957, 16 Short Novels 1986; contributes articles to popular magazines. *Address:* Sag Harbor, New York, NY 11963, U.S.A.

SHEEHAN, Neil, A.B.; American journalist; b. 27 Oct. 1936, Holyoke, Mass.; s. of Cornelius Sheehan and Mary O'Shea; m. Susan Margulies 1965; two d.; ed. Harvard Univ.; Viet Nam Bureau Chief, UPI Saigon 1962–64; reporter, New York Times, New York, Jakarta, Saigon, Washington, D.C. 1964–72; Guggenheim Fellow 1973–74; Adlai Stevenson Fellow 1973–75; Fellow, Lehrman Inst. 1975–76; Rockefeller Foundation Fellow 1976–77; Fellow, Woodrow Wilson Center for Int. Scholars 1979–80; mem. Soc. of American Historians; Hon. Litt.D. (Columbia Coll., Chicago) 1972; Hon. L.H.D. (American Int. Coll.) 1990, (Lowell Univ.) 1991; recipient of numerous awards for journalism; Nat. Book Award 1988, J. F. Kennedy Award 1989, Pulitzer Prize for non-fiction 1989. *Publications:* The Arnheiter Affair 1972, A Bright Shining Lie: John Paul Vann and America in Viet Nam 1988, After the War Was Over: Hanoi and Saigon 1992; contrib. to The Pentagon Papers 1971; articles and book reviews for popular magazines. *Address:* 4505 Klingle Street, N.W., Washington, DC 20016, U.S.A. (Home).

SHEEHY, Sir Patrick, Kt.; British business executive; b. 2 Sept. 1930; s. of Sir John Francis Sheehy and Jean (née Newton) Sheehy; m. Jill Patricia Tindall 1964; one s. one d.; ed. Ampleforth Coll., Yorks; Irish Guards 1948–50; joined British-American Tobacco Co. 1950, first appointment, Nigeria, Ghana 1951, Regional Sales Man., Nigeria 1953, Ethiopian Tobacco Monopoly 1954, Marketing Dir., Jamaica 1957, Gen. Man., Barbados 1961, Netherlands 1967; Dir. British-American Tobacco 1970–82, mem. Chair.'s Policy Cttee. and Chair. Tobacco Div. Bd. 1975; Deputy Chair. BAT Industries 1976–81, Vice-Chair. 1981–82, Chair. 1982–95; Chair. British-American Tobacco Co. 1976–81, BAT Financial Services 1985–90, Barder Marsh (now Marlborough) 1995–; Dir. Eagle Star Holdings 1984–87, British Petroleum 1984–, The Spectator (1828) Ltd. 1988–, Cluff Resources 1992–96, Celtic Football Club 1996–; Dir. (non-exec.) Pvt. Bank and Trust Co. 1996–; Chair. Council of Int. Advisors Swiss Bank Corpn. 1985–, U.K. Home Office Inquiry into Police Responsibilities and Rewards 1992–93; C.E.O. Rainbow 1993–; Dir. Asda Property Holdings 1994–; mem. Pres.'s Cttee., CBI 1986–; mem. Trade Policy Research Centre 1984–89, Action Cttee. for Europe 1985–; mem. CBI Task Force on Urban Regeneration; Chevalier, Légion d'honneur. *Leisure interests:* golf, reading. *Address:* 11 Eldon Road, London, W8 5PU, England. *Telephone:* 0171-937 6250.

SHEEN, Charlie; American actor; b. 3 Sept. 1965, New York; s. of Martin Sheen (q.v.) and Janet Sheen; m. Donna Peele 1995; ed. Santa Monica High School; TV debut in The Execution of Private Slovik; cinema debut in Apocalypse Now; pleaded no contest to charge of assault on girlfriend, given one year's suspended sentence, two years' probation, 300 hours' community service and fined 1997; TV films include Silence of the Heart, The Boys Next Door; cinema includes Grizzly II: The Predator, The Red Dawn, Lucas, Platoon, The Wraith, Day Off, Young Guns, Wall Street, Eight Men Out, Major League, Backtrack, Men at Work, Courage Mountain, Navy Seals, The Rookie, Stockade (dir.), Secret Society, Hot Shots, Dead Fall, The Three Musketeers, The Chase, Major League II 1994, Terminal Velocity 1994, The Shadow Conspiracy 1995, Shockwave 1995, All Dogs Go To Heaven II (voice), The Arrival 1996, Money Talks 1997, No Code of Conduct 1998, Free Money 1998, Letter From Death Row 1998. *Leisure interests:* baseball, music, film-making. *Address:* c/o Jeffrey Ballard Public Relations, 4814 Lemara Avenue, Sherman Oaks, CA 91403, U.S.A.

SHEEN, Martin (b. Ramon Estevez); American actor; b. 3 Aug. 1940, Dayton, Ohio; m. Janet Sheen 1961; three s. one d.; worked as shipping clerk, American Express Co., New York; Hon. Mayor of Malibu 1989–. *Stage appearances:* The Connection (début, New York and European tour), Never Live Over A Pretzel Factory, The Subject Was Roses, The Crucible. *Films:* The Incident, Catch-22, Rage, Badlands, Apocalypse Now, Enigma, Gandhi, The King of Prussia, That Championship Season, Man, Woman and Child, The Dead Zone, Final Countdown, Loophole, Wall Street, Nightbreaker, Da 1988, Personal Choice 1989, Cadence (also Dir.) 1990, Judgement in Berlin 1990, Limited Time, The Maid 1990, Cadence (also dir.), Hear No Evil, Hot Shots Part Deux (cameo), Gettysburg 1993, Trigger Fast, Hits!, Fortunes of War, Sacred Cargo, The Break, Dillinger & Capone, Captain Nuke and the Bomber Boys, Ghost Brigade, The Cradle Will Rock, Dead Presidents, Dorothy Day, Gospa, The American President, The War At Home, Spawn. *TV appearances include:* The Defenders, East Side/West Side, My Three Sons, Mod Squad, Cannon, That Certain Summer, Missiles of October, The Last Survivors, Blind Ambition, Shattered Spirits, Nightbreaker, The Last P.O.W.?, Roswell. *Address:* c/o Jeff Ballard, 4814 Lemara Avenue, Sherman Oaks, CA 91403, U.S.A.

SHEIKH, Abdulla ibn Muhammad ibn Ibrahim al-, PH.D.; Saudi Arabian politician; b. 1949; ed. Shari'ah College, Imam Muhammad bin Saud Univ. and Al-Azhar Univ., Cairo; Dean, Imam Muhammad bin Saud Univ., 1975; Asst. Prof., 1988; Minister of Justice 1992–. *Address:* Ministry of Justice, University Street, Riyadh 11137, Saudi Arabia. *Telephone:* (1) 405-7777. *Telex:* 4054443.

SHELBY, Richard Craig, A.B., LL.B.; American politician; b. 6 May 1934, Birmingham, Ala.; s. of O. H. Shelby and Alice L. Skinner; m. Annette Nevin 1960; two s.; ed. Alabama Univ.; Law Clerk, Supreme Court of Ala. 1961–62; law practice, Tuscaloosa, Ala. 1963–79; Prosecutor, City of Tuscaloosa 1964–70; U.S. Magistrate, Northern Dist. of Ala. 1966–70; Special Asst. Attorney-Gen., State of Ala. 1969–70; Pres. Tuscaloosa Co. Mental Health Asscn. 1969–70; mem. Ala. State Senate 1970–78; mem. 96th–99th Congresses, 7th Ala. Dist. 1979–87; Senator from Alabama Jan. 1987–; fmr. mem. Exec. Cttee. Ala. State Democratic Party; joined Republican Party Nov. 1994; mem. American Bar Asscn.; Democrat. *Address:* U.S. Senate, 110 Hart Senate Building, Washington, DC 20510 (Office); 1414 High Forest Drive, North Tuscaloosa, AL 35406, U.S.A. (Home).

SHELDON, Sidney; American author; b. 11 Feb. 1917, Chicago, Ill.; s. of Otto Sheldon and Natalie Marcus; m. 1st Jorja Curtright 1951 (died 1985); one d.; m. 2nd Alexandra Kostoff 1989; ed. Northwestern Univ.; served U.S. A.A.F. World War II; fmr. reader, Universal and 20th Century Fox Studios; creator, writer and producer, Nancy, The Patty Duke Show, I Dream of Jeannie; creator, Hart to Hart (TV) show); Acad. Award (Oscar) for screenplay, The Bachelor and the Bobby Soxer 1947; Writers Guild of America Screen awards for Easter Parade 1948, Annie Get Your Gun 1950; Tony Award for Redhead 1959. *Publications:* screenplays including: Billy Rose's Jumbo, The Bachelor and the Bobby Soxer 1947, Easter Parade, Annie Get Your Gun, Dream Wife (also dir.), Buster Keaton Story (also dir.); plays including: Roman Candle, Jackpot, Dream with Music, Alice in Arms, Redhead; novels: The Naked Face 1970, The Other Side of Midnight 1975, A Stranger in the Mirror 1976, Bloodline 1977, Rage of Angels 1980, Master of the Game 1982, If Tomorrow Comes 1985, Windmills of the Gods 1987, Memories of Midnight 1991, The Doomsday Conspiracy 1991, The Stars Shine Down 1992, Nothing Lasts Forever 1994, Morning, Moon and Night 1995, The Best Laid Plans 1997, Tell Me Your Dreams 1998. *Address:* c/o William Morrow & Co., 1350 Avenue of the Americas, New York, NY 10019, U.S.A.

SHELDRICK, George Michael, M.A., PH.D.; British professor of chemistry; b. 17 Nov. 1942, Huddersfield; s. of George Sheldrick and Elizabeth Sheldrick; m. Katherine E. Herford 1968; two s. two d.; ed. Huddersfield New Coll. and Jesus Coll. Cambridge; Fellow, Jesus Coll. Cambridge and Univ. Demonstrator/Lecturer, Cambridge Univ. 1966–78; Prof. of Inorganic Chem., Univ. of Göttingen 1978–; author of widely used computer programme for crystal structure determination (SHELX); Meldola and Corday-Morgan Medals, Royal Soc. of Chem., Leibniz Prize (Deutsche Forschungsgemeinschaft), Patterson Award (American Crystallographic Asscn.). *Publications:* around 700 scientific papers. *Leisure interests:* chess, tennis. *Address:* c/o Department of Inorganic Chemistry, University of Göttingen, Tammannstr. 4, 37077 Göttingen, Germany. *Fax:* 551-392582.

SHELLEY, Howard Gordon; British concert pianist and conductor; b. 9 March 1950, London; s. of Frederick Gordon Shelley and Anne Taylor; m. Hilary MacNamara 1975; one s. one step-s.; professional début Wigmore Hall, London 1971; regular soloist with all London and provincial British orchestras; regular tours to U.S.A. and Canada, Australia, Hong Kong, fmr. U.S.S.R. and Europe; repertoire from Mozart through Liszt to Gershwin; three piano concertos written for him (Cowie, Chapple, Dickinson); recordings include Rachmaninov's piano concertos and complete piano music, Vaughan Williams Piano Concerto, Schubert Sonatas, Chopin Preludes and Scherzi, Mozart Piano Concertos 9, 12, 13, 14, 17, 19, 20, 21, 22, 23, 24 and 27 (as pianist/conductor), Peter Dickinson's Piano Concerto and Howard Ferguson Piano Concerto and Sonata, Gershwin Piano Concerto, Rhapsody in Blue and Second Rhapsody, Hindemith "Four Temperaments", Alwyn Piano Concertos, Szymanowski Sinfonia Concertante, Mendelssohn Piano Concertos 1 and 2, Korngold Left Hand Concerto, Mozart Symphonies 32, 35, 38, Schubert Symphonies 3, 5, Hummel piano concertos; conducting début with London Symphony Orchestra 1985; Assoc. Conductor, London Mozart Players 1990–92, Prin. Guest Conductor 1992–; Hon. F.R.C.M. 1993; Dannreuther Concerto Prize 1971. *Address:* c/o Intermusica, 16 Duncan Terrace, London, N1 8BZ; 38 Cholmeley Park, London, N6 5ER, England. *Telephone:* 0171-278 5455 (Intermusica).

SHELOV-KOVEDYAYEV, Fedor Vadimovich; Russian politician; b. 15 June 1956, Moscow; m.; two c.; ed. Moscow State Univ.; researcher Inst. of History of U.S.S.R. (now Russian) Acad. of Sciences; mem. Club of Moscow Intellectuals Moskovskaya Tribuna 1989–91; R.S.F.S.R. People's Deputy; mem. Cttee. on Human Rights, Supreme Soviet 1990–93; mem. State Duma

1993–95; mem. Constitutional Comm. on Regional Policy and Co-operation; mem. Parl. Block Coalition of Reforms; First Deputy Minister of Foreign Affairs 1991–92; mem. Political Council, Democratic Choice of Russia Party 1993–96; Co-Chair., Int. Russian Club. *Publications:* History of the Bosphorus from 6th to 14th Century BC and over 90 scientific works. *Address:* Democratic Choice of Russia Party, Ogareva str. 5, 103009 Moscow, Russia.

SHELTON, Gen. Hugh, M.SC.; American army officer; b. 2 Jan. 1942, Tarboro, N.C.; m. Carolyn L. Johnson; three s.; ed. N.C. State Univ., Auburn Univ., Air Command and Staff Coll., Nat. War Coll.; commissioned into Infantry 1963; served in mainland U.S.A., Hawaii, 2 tours of Vietnam; fmrly. Commdr. 3rd Bn. 60th Infantry Div., Fort Lewis, Wash., Asst. Chief of Staff for Operations 9th Infantry Div., Commdr. 1st Brigade 82nd Airborne Div., Fort Bragg, N.C., Chief of Staff 10th Mountain Div., Fort Drum, N.Y.; rank of Brig. Gen. 1987; Jt. Staff Operations Directorate 1987–89; Asst. Div. Cmmdr. for Operations 101st Airborne Div. (Air Assault) (including during Operations Desert Shield and Desert Storm 1990–91) 1989–91; rank of Maj.-Gen. 1991; Commdr. 82nd Airborne Div., Fort Bragg, N.C. 1991–93; rank of Lieut.-Gen. 1993; Commdr. 23rd Airborne Corps. 1993, Commander Jt. Task Force for Operation Restore Democracy, Haiti 1994; rank of Gen. March 1996; Commdr. in Chief U.S. Special Operations Command 1996–97; Chair. Jt. Chiefs of Staff Oct. 1997–; recipient Defense D.S.M. (with 2 oak leaf clusters), D.S.M., Legion of Merit (with oak leaf cluster), Bronze Star Medal (with V device, 3 oak leaf clusters), Purple Heart, numerous other decorations. *Address:* The Pentagon, Washington, D.C., 20318, U.S.A.

SHELTON, William E., ED.D.; American university president; b. 6 Sept. 1944, Batesville, Miss.; s. of Loyd Shelton and Merle Shelton; m. Sharon Nordengreen Shelton 1965; one s.; ed. Univ. of Mississippi, and Memphis State Univ., Tenn.; high school teacher, Olive Br., Miss. 1967–68; elementary school Prin., Oakland, Tenn. 1968–70; Admin./Instr. N.W. Miss. Jr. Coll. Senatobia 1970–75; Vice-Pres. Henderson State Univ. Arkadelphia, Ark. 1975–83; Vice-Pres. Kent State Univ., Ohio 1983–89; Pres. Eastern Mich. Univ. 1989–. *Leisure interests:* golf, flying. *Address:* Office of the President, Eastern Michigan University, 202 Welch Hall, Ypsilanti, MI 48197, U.S.A. *Telephone:* (313) 487-2211.

SHEMYAKIN, Mikhail Mikhailovich (b. Kardanov); Russian sculptor and painter; b. 1943, Moscow; ed. Inst. of Painting, Sculpture and Architecture, Leningrad (now St. Petersburg); one-man exhbn. Leningrad 1962; arrested for dissident activities, interned in lunatic asylums; emigrated in 1971; lived in Paris 1971–81; living in U.S.A. 1981–; f. Foundation for Helping Soviet Veterans of the War in Afghanistan 1989; visited Russia frequently after citizenship was restored 1990; created Peter the Great Memorial in St. Petersburg; one man exhbns. in America, Europe and Russia; mem. European Acad. of Arts, Paris, New York Acad. of Sciences and Arts; Dr. h.c. (San Francisco); State Prize 1993, Pres. of Russia Prize 1995.

SHEMYAKIN, Yevgeniy Ivanovich, DR. TECH. SC.; Russian mining specialist; b. 9 Dec. 1929, Novosibirsk; s. of I. Shemyakin and Ella Shemyakina; m. L.T. Petrova 1952; one s. one d.; ed. Leningrad Univ.; sr. research asst. at U.S.S.R. Acad. of Sciences Inst. of Chemico-Physics 1955–60; head of lab. of U.S.S.R. Acad. of Sciences Inst. of Theoretical and Applied Mechanics 1960–70; Prof. Novosibirsk State Univ. 1963–87, Chair. of Elasticity 1967–87; Acting Dir. of U.S.S.R. Acad. of Sciences Inst. of Mining (Siberian Div.) 1970–72, Dir. 1972–87; Chair. Supreme State Cttee. of Attestation, Moscow, 1987–92; Prin. Consultant, Russian Acad. of Sciences Inst. of Dynamics of Geospheres 1987–92; Prof. Moscow State Univ. 1987–, Chair. of Wave and Gas Dynamics 1988–; Vice-Pres. of Presidium of Siberian Div. of Acad. of Sciences 1980–85; Chair. Russian Acad. of Sciences Scientific Council on Underground Space and Underground Construction 1994–; mem. of U.S.S.R. (now Russian) Acad. of Sciences 1984, Royal Swedish Soc. of Engineers 1987, Czech Acad. of Science, Slovak Acad. of Science, Int. Soc. for Rock Mechanics (Vice-Pres. 1988–92), Int. Mining Congress; mem. CPSU 1963–91; mem. of several scientific editorial bds. U.S.S.R. State Prize 1984. *Publications:* author and co-author of more than 200 scientific and technical papers. *Leisure interests:* ancient history, old underground constructions. *Address:* Department of Mechanics and Mathematics, Moscow Lomonosov State University, Vorobyevy Gory, 119899 Moscow, Russia, (Office). *Telephone:* 939-37-54 (Office); (095) 332-62-63 (Home). *Fax:* 939-49-95.

SHEN, James C.H., M.A.; Taiwanese diplomatist; b. 15 June 1909; m. Winifred Wei; one s. two d.; ed. Yenching Univ., Beijing, Univ. of Missouri, U.S.A.; Ed. Cen. News Agency, Nanjing 1936–37; Chief Editorial Section, Int. Dept., Ministry of Information, Chongqing 1938–43; Dir. Pacific Coast Bureau, Ministry of Information 1943–47; Dir. of Int. Dept., Govt. Information Office 1947–48, Sec. to Pres. of Repub. of China, Taipei 1956–59; Dir. of Information Dept., Ministry of Foreign Affairs, Taipei 1959–61, Dir.-Gen. 1961–66; Amb. to Australia 1966–68; Vice-Minister of Foreign Affairs 1968–71; Amb. to U.S.A. 1971–79; Nat. Policy Adviser to the Pres. 1979–; Ed. China News, Taipei 1983–85, Asian Cultural Quarterly; Faculty-Alumni Gold Medal (Univ. of Missouri) 1972. *Publication:* The US and Free China—How the US Sold Out Its Ally, My Earlier Years. *Address:* 7th Floor, 11 Lansui Bldg., Garden City, Hsintien, Taipei Co., Taiwan.

SHEN BEIZHANG; Chinese businessman; b. Jan. 1929; Cixi Co., Zhejiang Prov.; ed. Jiaotong Univ. Shanghai; Chair. Shanghai Overseas Corpn. 1990–; Chair. and Gen. Man., Shanghai Int. Group Corpn. 1991–; mem. 8th CPPCC 1993–.

SHEN DALI; Chinese writer, historian and translator; b. 4 Sept. 1938, Yanan; s. of late Shen Xu and Song Ying; m. Dong Chun 1993; one s. one d.; ed. Beijing Foreign Languages Univ.; Prof. titulaire, French Dept. Beijing Foreign Languages Univ. 1957–; translator at UNESCO, Paris 1979–81, réviseur 1985–; visiting scholar in France 1990–91; Prof. Univ. of Montreal, Canada 1994; Prof. INALCO, Paris 1995; Prés. du Jury "Grands Reportages," FIPA 1996; del. to Cultural Comm. CIO, Lausanne, Switzerland 1997; mem. Chinese Writers' Asscn.; awarded title "Membre d'honneur" by L'Association des Amis de la Commune de Paris, 1981; Chevalier, Ordre des Arts et des Lettres 1991, Croix de vermeil du Mérite et Dévouement français 1996. *Publications:* The Children of Yenan (novel, also in French and Italian) 1985, Les Fleurs du rêve (poetry) 1986, Les Lys rouges (novel) 1987, La Flûte des Titans 1987, The Humble Violet, The Meteor, Le rêve dans le pavillon d'azur, Le temps des cigales, Le Tableau de Paris (prose) 1989, L'Etoile filante (novel) 1993, (augmented edn.) 1995, Voyage en Europe et en Amérique du Nord 1996, Les Amants du lac 1996 (film). *Translations include:* Le Temps des cerises, Montserrat, Selected Poems of Eugene Pottier (additional transls.): Les Fleurs jumelles (play) 1982, L'Epreuve (novel) 1985, Les Trésors de la cité interdite 1986, Poésies choisies de la Commune de Paris 1986, l'Internationale, la Marseillaise, Le Chant du départ, N'a qu'un oeil, La paix du ménage, Le Vésuve, Les Couteaux, Les Yeux de demain, La Vraie Dame au camélias. *Leisure interest:* music. *Address:* French Department, Beijing Foreign Languages University, Beijing 100081; Bat N 49-1-4, Dongdaqiaolu, Beijing 100020, People's Republic of China (Home). *Telephone:* 65007458. *Fax:* (10) 6841 4003.

SHEN DAREN; Chinese party official; b. 1928, Wuxian Co., Jiangsu Prov.; joined CCP 1954; Deputy Sec. Jiangsu Prov. CCP Cttee. 1983–86; Sec. Changzhou Municipal CCP Cttee.; Sec. Ningxia Hui Autonomous Regional Cttee. 1987–89; Sec. Jiangsu Prov. CP 1989, NPC Deputy, Chair. Standing Cttee. of 8th People's Congress 1993–; mem. CCP 13th Cen. Cttee. 1987–92, 14th Cen. Cttee. 1992–. *Address:* Jiangsu Provincial Communist Party, Nanjing City, Jiangsu, People's Republic of China.

SHEN RONG; Chinese writer; b. Oct. 1936, Hubei; perm. mem. Chinese Writers' Asscn. 1985–; Perm. mem. China PEN 1986–; mem. Chinese Int. Exchange Asscn. 1990–. *Publications:* Forever Green (novel), No Way Out, Light and Dark, A Middle-aged Woman. *Address:* Chinese Writers' Association, 15 Nongzhanguan Nanli, Chaoyang District, Beijing, People's Republic of China.

SHEN ZULUN; Chinese party and government official; b. 1931, Ningbo Co., Zhejiang Prov.; joined CCP 1948; Vice-Gov. Zhejiang Prov. 1983–86, NPC Deputy; Gov. Zheijiang Prov. People's Govt. 1988; Deputy Sec. CPC 8th Zhejiang Prov. Cttee. 1987; mem. CCP Cen. Cttee. 1987; Standing Cttee. CPPCC 8th Nat. Cttee. 1993–.

SHENG HUAREN; Chinese politician; b. 1935, Xieyang Co., Jiangsu Prov.; joined CCP 1954; Dir. Planning Dept. of Ministry of Chemical Industry; Vice-Gen. Man. China Petrochemical Works Corp. 1983, then Gen. Man.; mem. 15th CCP Cen. Cttee. 1997–; Minister of State Econ. and Trade Comm. 1998–. *Address:* State Economy and Trade Commission, Beijing, People's Republic of China.

SHENGELAIA, Eldar Nikolayevich; Georgian film director; b. 26 Jan. 1933, Georgia (brother of Georgiy Nikolayevich Shengelaia, q.v.); s. of Nikolai Shengelaia and Nato Vachnadze; m. 1st Ariadna Shengelaia (Shprink) 1957 (divorced 1980); two d.; m. 2nd Nelly Davlianidze 1981; one d.; ed. Moscow Inst. of Cinematography; dir. at Mosfilm 1958–59, at Kartuli Pilmi film studio, Georgia 1960–; mem. CPSU 1966–90; Chair. Georgian Film-makers' Union 1976–; fmr. sec. U.S.S.R. Film-makers' Union; teacher, Tbilisi Theatre Inst., Tbilisi State Univ., Head of Film and TV Dept.; Deputy, Supreme Soviet of Georgian S.S.R. 1980–85, 1986–90, mem. Presidium 1989–90; elected to Supreme Soviet of Georgian Repub. (representing Democratic Centre) 1990–91; People's Deputy of U.S.S.R., U.S.S.R. Supreme Soviet 1989–91; mem. State Council, Ga., Parl. Repub. of Ga. 1992–; mem. Georgian Parl. 1995–, now Deputy Chair.; Chair. Cultural Comm.; People's Artist of Georgia 1979, U.S.S.R. Prize 1985, People's Artist of U.S.S.R. 1987; numerous other prizes. *Films include:* The Legend of the Ice Heart 1957, The Snow Fairy Tale 1958, White Caravan 1963, Mikela 1965, An Extraordinary Exhibition 1968, The Screwballs 1974, Stepmother of Samanishvili 1978, Blue Mountains or an Improbable Event 1984, Tbilisi 9 April Chronicles 1989, Express Information 1994. *Address:* c/o Georgian Film-makers' Union, Kakabadze Street 2, 380008 Tbilisi (Office); Ioseliani Street 37, Flat 58, 380091 Tbilisi, Georgia (Home). *Telephone:* 99-75-18 (Office); 99-80-80 (Home).

SHENGELAIA, Georgiy Nikolayevich; Georgian film director and actor; b. 11 May 1937, Tbilisi (brother of Eldar Nikolayevich Shengelaia, q.v.); s. of Nicolai Shengelaia and Nato Vachnadze; m. 1st Sofiko Chiaureli 1957 (dissolved); m. 2nd Ketevan Ninya 1985; three s.; ed. Moscow Inst. of Cinematography; Georgian State Prize 1980. *Films include:* Alaverdoba 1966, Pirosmani 1969, Melodies of Veriysky Suburb 1973, Come into the Grape Valley 1977, The Girl with the Sewing-Machine 1980, Journey of the Young Composer 1985, Kchareba An Gogi 1987, Death of Orpheus 1996. *Roles include:* Dato (Our Yard), Georgi (Otar's Widow), Gela (The Tale about a Girl). *Address:* Kekelidze Street 16, Apt. 12, 380009 Tbilisi, Georgia. *Telephone:* (32) 22-64-11. *Fax:* (32) 99-07-54, 93-50-97.

SHENIN, Oleg Semyonovich; Russian politician; b. 22 July 1937, Vladimirskaya, Volgograd Dist.; s. of Semyon Sidorovich Shenin and Angelina Nikolaevna Shenina; m. Tamara Aleksandrovna Shenina 1955; one s. two d.; ed. Krasnoyarsk Tech. College for Mining, Tomsk Eng. Inst. and CPSU Cen. Cttee. Acad. of Social Sciences; mem. CPSU 1962–91; from works foreman to trust man. at construction sites in Krasnoyarsk Dist. 1955–74; party work 1974–91; First Sec. Achinsk City Cttee., Second Sec. Khakassk Dist. Cttee. (obkom), Sec. Krasnoyarsk Dist. Cttee., First Sec. Khakassk Dist. Cttee. (obkom) 1974–87; First Sec. Krasnoyarsk Dist. Cttee. 1987–90; elected U.S.S.R. People's Deputy 1989; Chair. Krasnoyarsk Dist. Council of People's Deputies 1990–91; fmr. mem. CPSU Cen. Cttee.; mem. Political Bureau, Sec. Cen. Cttee. 1990–91; arrested Aug. 1991 for alleged participation in attempted coup d'état; charged with conspiracy Jan. 1992, released Oct. 1992; on trial 1993, released on amnesty 1994; leader Union of Communist Parties (SCP-CPSU) 1994–, Int. Comm. for Union and Brotherhood of Peoples 1997–. *Leisure interest:* sport. *Address:* Union of Communist Parties, Novaya sq. 14, 103132 Moscow, Russia. *Telephone:* (095) 278-31-39. *Fax:* (095) 278-31-39.

SHENNAN, Joseph Hugh, PH.D., F.R.HIST.S.; British professor of history; b. 13 March 1933, Liverpool; s. of Hugh Cringle Shennan and Mary Catherine Jones; m. Margaret King Price 1958; three s.; ed. St. Edward's Coll. Liverpool, Univ. of Liverpool and Corpus Christi Coll. Cambridge; Asst. Lecturer, Lecturer in History, Univ. of Liverpool 1960–65; Lecturer, Sr. Lecturer, Reader in History, Lancaster Univ. 1965–74, Prof. of European Studies 1974–79, Prof. of European History 1979–, Pro-Vice-Chancellor (Academic) 1985–93, Deputy Vice-Chancellor 1993–98; Sr. Research Scholar (Visiting Fellow) Corpus Christi Coll. Cambridge 1984–85; founding Ed. European Studies Review (now European History Quarterly) 1970–79. *Publications:* The Parlement of Paris 1968, Government and Society in France 1461–1661 1969, The Origins of the Modern European State 1450–1725 1974, Philippe, Duke of Orleans: Regent of France, 1715–1723 1979, France Before the Revolution 1983, Liberty and Order in Early Modern Europe: The Subject and the State, 1650–1800 1986, Louis XIV 1986, International Relations in Europe, 1689–1789 1995. *Leisure interests:* golf, the 18th century, watching Liverpool Football Club. *Address:* Bull Beck House, Four Acres, Brookhouse, Lancaster, LA2 9JW, England (Home). *Telephone:* (01524) 770517.

SHENOUDA III, Anba, B.A., B.D.; Egyptian ecclesiastic; b. 3 Aug. 1923; ed. Cairo Univ. and Coptic Orthodox Theological Coll.; theological teacher and writer; fmr. Bishop and Prof. of Theology, Orthodox Clerical Coll., Cairo; 1st Chair., Asscn. of Theological Colls. in the Near East; 117th Pope of Alexandria and Patriarch of the See of St. Mark of Egypt, the Near East and All Africa (Coptic Orthodox Church) 1971–81, 1985; removed from post by Pres. Sadat and banished to desert monastery Wadi Natroun Sept. 1981, released Jan. 1985. *Address:* Coptic Orthodox Patriarchate, St Mark Cathedral, P.O. Box 9035, Anba Ruess, 222 Ramses Street, Abbasiya, Cairo, Egypt.

SHEPARD, Roger Newland, M.S., PH.D.; American professor of psychology; b. 30 Jan. 1929, Palo Alto, Calif.; s. of Orson C. Shepard and Grace N. Shepard; m. Barbaranne Bradley 1952; two s. one d.; ed. Stanford and Yale Univs.; N.A.S.-N.R.C. Postdoctoral Research Assoc. Naval Research Lab. Washington, D.C. 1955–56; Research Fellow, Harvard Univ. 1956–58; mem. tech. staff, Bell Telephone Labs. 1958–66, Head of Dept. 1963–66; Prof. of Psychology, Harvard Univ. 1966–68, Dir. Psychological Labs. 1967–68; Prof. of Psychology, Stanford Univ. 1968–98; Pres. Psychometric Soc. 1973–74, Div. of Experimental Psychology, American Psychological Asscn. 1980–81; Ray Lyman Wilbur Prof. of Social Science 1989–98, Prof. Emer. 1998–; Guggenheim Fellow 1971–72; Fowler Hamilton Fellow, Christ Church, Oxford 1987; mem. N.A.S., American Acad. of Arts and Sciences; Distinguished Scientific Contribution Award, American Psychological Asscn. 1976; Howard Crosby Warren Medal, Soc. of Experimental Psychologists 1981, Nat. Medal of Sciences 1995. *Publications:* Multidimensional Scaling: Theory and Applications in the Behavioral Sciences (with A. K. Romney and S. B. Nerlove) 1972, Mental Images and their Transformations (with L. A. Cooper) 1982. *Leisure interests:* art, music, theoretical physics. *Address:* c/o Building 420, Room 356, Stanford University, Stanford, CA 94305, U.S.A.

SHEPARD, Sam; American playwright and actor; b. 5 Nov. 1943, Fort Sheriden, Ill.; s. of Samuel Shepard Rogers and Jane Schook Rogers; m. O-Lan Johnson Dark 1969 (divorced); one s.; one s. one d. with Jessica Lange (q.v.); ed. Duarte High School, Mount San Antonio Jr. Coll. *Plays include:* Cowboys—Rock Garden (double bill), Chicago—Icarus' Mother—Red Cross (triple bill; 1966, Obie Award), La Turista (1967 Obie Award), Forensic and the Navigators (1968 Obie Award), Melodrama Play, Tooth of Crime (1973 Obie Award), Back Dog Beast Bait, Operation Sidewinder, 4-H Club, The Unseen Hand, Mad Dog Blues, Shaved Splits, Rock Garden (included in Oh! Calcutta!), Curse of the Starving Class (1978 Obie Award), True West, Fool for Love, A Lie of the Mind, Simpatico. *Film appearances include:* Days of Heaven, Frances, The Right Stuff, Country, Crimes of the Heart, Baby Boom, Defenceless 1989, Voyager, Thunderheart 1992, The Pelican Brief 1994, Safe Passage 1995, The Good Old Boys 1995, Curtain Call 1997, The Only Thrill 1997. *Screenplay:* Paris, Texas (Palme d'Or, Cannes Film Festival 1984), Far North (also dir.) 1989, Silent Tongue (also dir.), *Publications:* A Murder of Crows 1996 (novel), Cruising Paradise (short stories) 1996. *Address:* ICM, 8942 Wilshire Boulevard, Beverly Hills CA 90211, U.S.A.

SHEPARD, Stephen Benjamin; American journalist; b. 20 July 1939, New York; s. of William Shepard and Ruth Shepard (née Tanner); m. Lynn Povich 1979; one s. one d.; ed. City Coll., N.Y., Columbia Univ.; reporter, ed., writer Business Week 1966–75, Exec. Ed. 1982–84, Ed.-in-Chief 1984–; Asst. Prof., Dir. Walter Bagehot Fellowship Program in econs. and business journalism, Columbia Univ. 1975–76; Sr. Ed. Newsweek 1976–81; Ed. Saturday Review 1981–82; mem. American Soc. of Magazine Eds. (Vice-Pres. 1990–92, Pres. 1992–94), Council on Foreign Relations, Century Asscn. *Address:* Business Week, McGraw Hill Inc., 39th Floor, 1221 Avenue of the Americas, New York, NY 10020 (Office); 322 Central Park West, New York, NY 10025, U.S.A. (Home).

SHEPHARD, Rt. Hon. Gillian Patricia, P.C., M.A.; British politician; b. 22 Jan. 1940; d. of Reginald Watts and Bertha Watts; m. Thomas Shephard 1975; two step-s.; ed. North Walsham High School for Girls, St. Hilda's Coll., Oxford; Educ. Officer and Schools Inspector 1963–75; lecturer Cambridge Univ. Extra-Mural Bd. 1965–87; Councillor Norfolk County Council 1977–89 (Chair. Social Services Cttee. 1978–83, Educ. Cttee. 1983–85); Chair. W. Norfolk and Wisbech Health Authority 1981–85, Norwich Health Authority 1985–87; M.P. for South West Norfolk 1987–97, for Norfolk South West 1997–; Co-Chair. Women's Nat. Comm. 1990–91; Parl. Pvt. Sec. to Econ. Sec. to the Treasury 1988–89; Parl. Under-Sec. of State Dept. of Social Security 1989–90; Minister of State (Treasury) 1990–92; Sec. of State for Employment 1992–93, for Agric., Fisheries and Food 1993–94, for Educ. 1994–95, for Educ. and Employment 1995–97; Shadow Leader of House of Commons and Shadow Chancellor of Duchy of Lancaster 1997–; Opposition Spokesman on Environment, Transport and the Regions 1998–; Deputy Chair. Conservative Party 1991–92; Hon. Fellow St. Hilda's Coll. 1991. *Leisure interests:* music, gardening, France. *Address:* House of Commons, London, SW1A 0AA, England.

SHEPHEARD, Sir Peter Faulkner, Kt., C.B.E., B.ARCH., F.R.T.P.I.; British architect, town planner and landscape architect; b. 11 Nov. 1913, Birkenhead; s. of Thomas Faulkner Shepheard and Catherine Emily Shepheard; m. Mary Bailey 1943; one s. one d.; ed. Birkenhead School, Liverpool School of Architecture; Asst. to Derek Bridgwater 1937–40; Royal Ordnance Factories, Ministry of Supply 1940–43; Tech. Officer on Greater London Plan, later on Research and Master Plan, Stevenage New Town, Ministry of Town and Country Planning 1943–47; Deputy Chief Architect and Planner, Stevenage Devt. Corpn. 1947–48; pvt. practice (Shepheard Epstein & Hunter) 1948–89, now solo; Visiting Prof. of Landscape Architecture, Graduate School of Fine Arts, Univ. of Pennsylvania 1959–70, Prof. of Architecture and Environmental Design 1971–, Dean 1971–78, Dean Emer. 1979–; Pres. R.I.B.A. 1969–71, Architectural Asscn. 1954–55, Inst. of Landscape Architects 1965–66; Master, Art Workers Guild 1984; mem. Royal Fine Art Comm. 1968–71, Countryside Comm. 1968–71; Artistic Adviser, Commonwealth War Graves Comm. 1977–; RIBA Distinction in Town Planning 1956; Hon. Fellow, Royal Architectural Inst. of Canada 1972, A.I.A. 1973; Hon. D.Litt. (Liverpool) 1994. *Publications:* Modern Gardens 1953, Gardens 1969, Illustrator A Book of Ducks and Woodland Birds. *Leisure interests:* music, poetry, drawing, gardening. *Address:* 21 Well Road, London, NW3 1LH, England; Graduate School of Fine Arts, University of Pennsylvania, Philadelphia, PA 19104-6311, U.S.A.

SHEPHERD, 2nd Baron, cr. 1946, of Spalding; **Malcolm Newton Shepherd,** P.C.; British politician; b. 27 Sept. 1918, Blackburn; s. of George Robert and Ada Shepherd; m. Allison Redmond 1941 (died 1998); two s.; ed. Friends' School, Saffron Walden; Opposition Chief Whip, House of Lords 1963–64, Govt. Chief Whip 1964–67, Minister of State, Commonwealth Office 1967–68, FCO 1968–70; Deputy Leader of House of Lords 1967–70, Deputy Leader of the Opposition, House of Lords 1970–74; Lord Privy Seal, Leader of House of Lords 1974–76 (resgnd.); Deputy Chair. Sterling Group of Cos. 1976–86; Chair. Packaging Council, Civil Service Pay Research Unit 1978–81, Nat. Bus Co. 1979–84; Chair. Medical Research Council 1978–82; Chair. Chequepoint Int. 1989–; Adviser, Sun Hung Kai Securities, Hong Kong 1978–; Pres., Centre Européen de l'Entreprise Publique 1985–, Inst. of Road Transport Engineers 1987–; mem. House of Lords Select Cttee. on European Community, European Policy Forum. *Leisure interest:* golf. *Address:* 29 Kennington Palace Court, Sancroft Street, London, SE11 5UL, England. *Telephone:* 0171-582 6772.

SHEPHERD, Cybill; American actress; b. 1950, Memphis, Tenn.; m. 1st David Ford 1978 (divorced); one d.; m. 2nd Bruce Oppenheim 1987; twin s.; fmr. magazine cover girl; eight years of commercials for L'Oréal Préférence; film debut in The Last Picture Show 1971; Emmy Award for series Moonlighting 1985. *Films include:* The Heartbreak Kid 1973, Daisy Miller 1974, At Long Last Love 1975, Taxi Driver 1976, Special Delivery 1976, Silver Bears 1977, The Lady Vanishes 1978, Earthright 1980, The Return 1986, Chances Are 1988, Texasville 1990, Alice 1990, Once Upon A Crime 1992, Married to It 1993; TV series include The Yellow Rose 1983–84, Moonlighting 1985–89, Cybill 1994–98; numerous TV films.

SHEPPARD OF DIDGEMERE, Baron (Life Peer), cr. 1994, of Roydon in the County of Essex; **Allen John George Sheppard,** K.C.V.O., B.SC.; British company director; b. 25 Dec. 1932, London; s. of John Baggott Sheppard and Lily Sheppard (née Palmer); m. 1st Peggy Damaris (née Jones) 1959 (divorced 1980); m. 2nd Mary Stewart 1980; ed. Ilford Co. School, London School of Econs.; with Ford 1958–68, Chrysler 1968–71, British Leyland 1971–75, Grand Metropolitan 1975–96, C.E.O. 1986–93, Chair. 1987–96; Chair. London First 1992–, Group Trust PLC 1994–, McBride PLC 1995–, GB

Railways PLC 1996–, Unipart 1996–; Vice-Pres. Brewers' Soc. 1987–; Chair. Bd. of Trustees, Prince's Youth Business Trust 1990–94, Advisory Bd., British American Chamber of Commerce 1991–94; Chair. Business in the Community 1994–97; Gov. L.S.E. 1989–; Dir. High Point Rendel 1997–; Dir. (non-exec.) Bowater PLC 1994–95; Hon. LL.D. (South Bank Univ.) 1994. *Publications:* Your Business Matters 1958, Maximum Leadership 1995, various articles in professional journals. *Leisure interests:* reading, gardens, red setter dogs. *Address:* House of Lords, London, SW1A 0PW, England.

SHEPPARD OF LIVERPOOL, Baron (Life Peer), cr. 1998, of West Kirby in the County of Merseyside; **Rt. Rev. David Stuart Sheppard,** M.A.; British ecclesiastic and fmr. test cricketer; b. 6 March 1929, Reigate, Surrey; s. of Stuart Sheppard and Barbara Sheppard; m. Grace Isaac 1957; one d.; ed. Sherborne School, Trinity Hall, Cambridge and Ridley Hall Theological Coll. Cambridge; Asst. Curate, St. Mary's Islington 1955–57; Warden, Mayflower Family Centre, Canning Town 1957–69; Bishop Suffragan of Woolwich 1969–75; Bishop of Liverpool 1975–97; Vice-Chair. Archbishop of Canterbury's Comm. on Urban Priority Areas 1983–85; Chair. BBC and IBA Cen. Religious Advisory Cttee. 1989–92, Gen. Synod Bd. for Social Responsibility 1991–96, Churches' Enquiry into Unemployment and the Future of Work 1995–97; played cricket for Cambridge 1950–52 (Capt. 1952), Sussex 1947–62 (Capt. 1953), England 22 times 1950–63 (Capt. 1954); Hon. LL.D. (Liverpool Univ.) 1983, Hon. D.Tech. (Liverpool Polytechnic) 1987, Hon. D.D. (Cambridge Univ.) 1990, (Univ. of Wales) 1998, Hon. D.D. (Exeter) 1998. *Publications:* Parson's Pitch 1964, Built as a City 1974, Bias to the Poor 1983, The Other Britain (Dimbleby Lecture) 1984, Better Together (with Archbishop Worlock, q.v.) 1988, With Christ in the Wilderness 1990, With Hope in Our Hearts (with Archbishop Worlock) 1994. *Leisure interests:* relaxing at home, following cricket, painting, gardening, cooking, birdwatching. *Address:* 11 Melloncroft Drive, West Kirby, Wirral, L48 2JA, England.

SHEPPERD, Sir Alfred Joseph, Kt., B.SC. (ECON.); British business executive; b. 19 Dec. 1925, London; s. of Alfred C. Shepperd and Mary A. Williams; m. Gabrielle Bouloux 1950; two d.; ed. Archbishop Tenison's School and Univ. Coll., London; with Rank Org. 1949, Selincourt & Sons, Ltd. 1963, Chamberlain Group 1965; Man. Dir. Keyser Ullmann Industries, Ltd. 1967; Finance Dir. Wellcome Foundation, Ltd. 1972, Chair. and C.E.O. 1977–90; Chair. and C.E.O. Wellcome PLC 1986–90; Chair. Burroughs Wellcome Co. 1986–90, St. Bartholomew's NHS Trust 1992–93; Dir. Keyser Ullman Ltd. 1967, Laporte Industries, Ltd. 1971, Anglia Maltings (Holdings) Ltd. 1972–97, Mercury Asset Man. Group PLC 1987–96 (fmrly. Mercury Asset Man. Holdings Ltd.), Isososcele PLC 1991–93, Oxford Instruments PLC 1991–95, Nat. Transcommunications 1992–95; Commendatore della Repubblica, Italy 1983, Encomienda al Mérito de Sanidad, Spain 1988, Order of Leopold II, Belgium 1989. *Address:* Courtmead, 6 Guildown Avenue, Guildford, Surrey, GU2 5HB, England.

SHER, Antony; British actor, artist and author; b. 14 June 1949, Cape Town, South Africa; ed. Webber Douglas School; numerous appearances at Liverpool Playhouse, Nottingham Playhouse, Royal Court Theatre, Nat. Theatre, R.S.C. (R.S.C. Assoc. Artist 1982–) etc.; Best Actor Awards from Drama Magazine and The London Standard Awards, for performance as Richard III (R.S.C.) 1985, Olivier Award for Best Actor, Soc. of West End Theatres, for performances as Richard III, as Arnold in Torch Song Trilogy 1985, for Stanley 1997, Best Actor Award, Martini TMA Awards, for performance as Titus Andronicus 1996, Peter Sellers Evening Standard Film Award for performance as Disraeli in Mrs. Brown 1998. *Plays include:* John, Paul, Ringo and Bert (Lyric Theatre), Teeth n' Smiles, Cloud Nine, A Prayer for My Daughter (Royal Court Theatre), Goosepimples (Hampstead and Garrick Theatres), King Lear, Tartuffe, Richard III, Merchant of Venice, The Revenger's Tragedy, Hello and Goodbye, Singer, Tamburlaine the Great, Travesties, Cyrano de Bergerac, The Winter's Tale (R.S.C.), Torch Song Trilogy (Albery Theatre), True West, Arturo Ui, Uncle Vanya, Titus Andronicus (Royal Nat. Theatre), Stanley (Royal Nat. Theatre, Circle in the Square Theater, New York). *Films:* Shadey, The Young Poisoner's Handbook, Alive and Kicking, Mrs. Brown. *Television appearances include:* The History Man, Collision Course, The Land of Dreams, Genghis Cohn, The Moon Stone. *Publications:* Year of the King 1986, Middlepost 1988, Characters 1989, Changing Steps (screenplay) 1989, The Indoor Boy 1991, Cheap Lives 1995, Woza Shakespeare! (co-written with Gregory Doran) 1996, The Feast 1998; Hon. D.Litt. (Liverpool) 1998. *Address:* c/o Conway Van Gelder Robinson Ltd., 18–21 Jermyn Street, London, SW1Y 6HP, England. *Telephone:* 0171-287 0077.

SHERIF, Osama El-, B.A.; Jordanian publisher; b. June 1960, Jerusalem; s. of Mahmoud El-Sherif and Aida El-Sherif; m. Ghada Yasser Amr 1984; one s. one d.; ed. Univ. of Missouri; Chief Ed. The Jerusalem Star 1985–88; Pres. Info-Media, Jordan 1989–; Publr., Chief Ed. and weekly columnist, The Star, Jordan 1990–; Publr. Arabian Communications & Publishing (ACP) 1994–, BYTE Middle East 1994–, Al Tiqaniyyah Wal 'Amal 1995–. *Leisure interests:* novel and short-story writing, travel, photography, horse riding. *Address:* P.O. Box 9313, Amman 11191, Jordan. *Telephone:* (6) 5648298.

SHERIMKULOV, Medetkan; Kyrgyzstan politician; b. 17 Nov. 1939, Tchapaevo (Kyrgyzia); m.; three d.; ed. Kyrgyz Univ., Moscow Univ.; mem. CPSU 1962–91; lecturer Kyrgyz Univ.; instructor Div. of Science, Cen. Cttee. CP of Kyrgyzia 1971–73; Sec. Party Cttee., Kyrgyz Univ. 1973–76; Sec. Issyk-Kul Regional CP Cttee. 1976–80; Head Div. of Propaganda, Cen. Cttee. CP, Kyrgyz S.S.R. 1986–90; Chair. Supreme Soviet (now Uluk Kenesh) of Repub. of Kyrgyzstan 1990–94; cand. for Presidency of Kyrgyzstan 1995.

SHERLOCK, Alexander, C.B.E., F.R.S.A., M.B., B.S.; British doctor and politician; b. 14 Feb. 1922, Coventry; s. of Thomas Sherlock and Evelyn Alexander; m. 1st Clarice C. Scarff 1945; one s. two d.; m. 2nd Eileen Hall 1976; one step-d.; ed. Magdalen Coll. School, Oxford, Stowmarket Grammar School, London Hosp. Medical School and Gray's Inn; House Physician, House Surgeon, London Hosp. 1945; R.A.F. 1946–48; Asst. Deputy Coroner, St. Pancras 1960–62; medical practitioner 1948–79; mem. European Parl. 1979–89 (Spokesman on Environment, Health and Consumer Protection); Vice-Pres. Inst. of Trading Officers 1981–, Asscn. of Environmental Health Officers 1981–, Soc. of District Councils 1981–; Officer, Order of St. John of Jerusalem. *Leisure interest:* gardening. *Address:* 16 Victoria Road, Felixstowe, Suffolk, IP11 7PT, England. *Telephone:* (01394) 284503.

SHERMAN, Sir Alfred, Kt., B.SC., F.R.S.A.; British journalist and public affairs adviser; b. 11 Nov. 1919; s. of Jacob Vladimir Sherman and Eva Sherman (née Goldental); m. Zahava Levin 1958 (died 1993); one s.; ed. Hackney Downs County Secondary School, London and L.S.E.; served in Int. Brigade, Spanish Civil War 1937–38 and in field security and occupied enemy territory admin., war of 1939–45; leader writer, Jewish Chronicle; various positions on Daily Telegraph 1965–86, leader writer 1977–86; Public Affairs Adviser in private practice as Interthought; Co-Founder Centre for Policy Studies 1974, Dir. of Studies –1984; Adviser to Radovan Karadžić 1993–94; Consultant, Nat. Bus Co.; mem. economic advisory staff, Israeli Govt. in 1950s; Councillor, RBK&C 1971–78; Chair. Lord Byron Foundation for Balkan Studies. *Publications:* Local Government Reorganisation and Industry 1970, Councils, Councillors and Public Relations 1973, Local Government Reorganization and the Salary Bill 1974, Waste in Wandsworth (with D. Mallam) 1976, Crisis Calls for a Minister for Denationalization 1980, The Scott Report 1981, Communism and Arab Nationalism: a reappraisal, Capitalism and Liberty, Our Complacent Satirists, Political Violence in Britain; contribs. to newspapers and periodicals, including The Guardian, The Independent and the Spectator. *Address:* 14 Malvern Court, Onslow Square, London, SW7 3HU, England (Home). *Telephone:* 0171-581 4075 (Home).

SHERMAN, Cindy, B.A.; American artist; b. 1954, Glen Ridge, N.J.; ed. State Univ. Coll., Buffalo; numerous solo exhbns. Buffalo, Houston, New York, Genoa, Paris, Amsterdam, Tokyo etc.; numerous group exhbns. Buffalo, New York, Chicago, Washington, London, Paris, Venice Biennale 1982, Documenta 7, Kassel 1982 etc.; work in perm. collections including Museum of Fine Arts, Houston, Museum Boymans-van Beuningen, Rotterdam, Museum of Modern Art, New York, Tate Gallery, London, Centre Pompidou, Paris, Stedelijk Museum, Amsterdam, Metropolitan Museum of Art, New York, San Francisco Museum of Modern Art. *Address:* c/o Metro Pictures, 519 W. 24th Street, New York, NY 10011, U.S.A.

SHERMAN, Martin; American playwright; b. New Jersey; ed. Boston Univ. *Plays include:* Cracks, Bent, A Madhouse in Goa, When She Danced, Some Sunny Day. *Films include:* The Clothes in the Wardrobe (The Summer House in U.S.A.), Indian Summer.

SHERRIN, Edward George (Ned), C.B.E., M.A.; British director, writer and presenter; b. 18 Feb. 1931, Low Ham, Somerset; s. of Thomas Adam Sherrin and Dorothy Finch (née Drewett) Sherrin; ed. Sexey's School, Bruton, Exeter Coll., Oxford, Gray's Inn; Producer ATV 1956–58, BBC 1958–65; created That Was the Week That Was (satire programme) 1961; Film producer 1965–75, The Virgin Soldiers 1968, The National Health 1972; theatre producer 1972–; directed and narrated Side by Side by Sondheim, London 1976–77, N.Y. 1977–78; directed and co-adapted The Ratepayers' Iolanthe, London 1984 (Olivier Award); directed Mr. and Mrs. Nobody 1987, Jeffrey Bernard is Unwell 1989 (Australia 1992), Same Old Moon, Bookends 1990, Our Song 1992, A Passionate Woman 1994, Salad Days (revival tour) 1995, (Vaudeville Theatre) 1996, Good Grief 1998. *Publications:* (with Caryl Brahms) Cindy-Ella or I Gotta Shoe 1962, Rappel 1910 1964, Benbow was his Name 1967, Ooh la! la! 1973, After you M. Feydeau 1975; A Small Thing Like an Earthquake 1983, Cutting Edge 1984, Too Dirty for the Windmill 1985; (with Neil Shand) 1956 and All That 1986, Loose Neds 1990; Ned Sherrin's Theatrical Anecdotes 1991, Ned Sherrin in His Anecdotage 1993, The Oxford Book of Humorous Quotations 1994, Scratch an Actor (novel) 1996, Sherrin's Year (diary) 1996. *Leisure interests:* theatre, cricket. *Address:* 4 Cornwall Mansions, Ashburnham Road, London, SW10 0PE. *Telephone:* 0171-352 7662.

SHERRINGTON, David, M.A., PH.D., F. INST. P., F.R.S.; British professor of physics; b. 29 Oct. 1941, Blackpool; s. of late James A. Sherrington and Elfreda Cameron; m. Margaret Gee-Clough 1966; one s. one d.; ed. St. Mary's Coll. Middlesbrough and Univ. of Manchester; Asst. Lecturer in Theoretical Physics, Univ. of Manchester 1964–67, Lecturer (on leave) 1967–69; Asst. Research Physicist, Univ. of Calif. San Diego 1967–69; Lecturer in Solid State Physics, Imperial Coll. London 1969–74, Reader 1974–83, Prof. of Physics 1983–89; Cadre Supérieur, Inst. Laue Langevin, Grenoble 1977–79; Wykeham Prof. of Physics, Univ. of Oxford 1989–; Ulam Scholar, Los Alamos Nat. Lab., U.S.A. 1995–96; Fellow, Royal Soc., Inst. of Physics, American Physical Soc., New Coll. Oxford 1989–. *Publications:* articles in scientific journals, co-ed. of 7 books. *Leisure interests:* travel, wine. *Address:* Theoretical Physics, 1 Keble Road, Oxford, OX1 3NP (Office); 53 Cumnor Hill, Oxford, OX2 9EY, England (Home). *Telephone:* (01865) 273952 (Office); (01865) 862057 (Home). *Fax:* (01865) 273947.

SHERWOOD, David J.; American business executive; b. 1922; ed. Rutgers Univ., Boston Univ., Stanford Univ.; served with U.S. army 1942–46; Vice-Pres. Fireman's Fund and Insurance Co. 1946–70; with Prudential Insurance Co. of America 1970–, Exec. Vice-Pres. 1977–78, Pres. and Dir. 1978–84; Gov. New York Insurance Corpn. 1984–. *Address:* c/o Prudential Insurance Co., Prudential Plaza, Newark, NJ 07101, U.S.A.

SHESHINSKI, Eytan, PH.D.; Israeli university professor; b. 29 June 1937, Haifa; s. of Alice Sheshinski and Baruch Sheshinski; m. Ruth H. Sheshinski 1960; four d.; ed. Hebrew Univ. Jerusalem, M.I.T., U.S.A.; Asst. Prof. Harvard Univ. 1966–67; Lecturer, then Assoc. Prof., later Prof. Hebrew Univ., Jerusalem 1967–; Visiting Prof. Harvard Univ., Stanford Univ., M.I.T., Columbia Univ.; Chair. Bd. Koor Industries 1990–, Khevrat Ha'Ovdim 1989–92; Sir Isaac Wolfson Prof. of Public Finance; Fellow Econometric Soc., mem. Royal Swedish Acad. of Sciences, American Acad. of Arts and Sciences. *Publications:* The Optimal Linear Income Tax (Review of Econ. Studies 1972), Inflation and Costs of Price Adjustment (Review of Econ. Studies 1977), Optimum Pricing, Inflation and the Costs of Price Adjustments (ed.) 1993. *Leisure interests:* tennis, hiking. *Address:* 4 Kaufman Street, Tel Aviv 68012, Israel. *Telephone:* 5105681. *Fax:* 5195353.

SHESTAKOV, Sergey Vasilyevich; Russian biologist; b. 23 Nov. 1934, Leningrad; s. of Vasily Ivanovich Shestakov and Ludmila Shestakova; m. Galina A. Grigorieva 1964; one s.; ed. Moscow State Univ.; on staff Moscow State Univ. 1957–; Dir. Int. Biotech. Centre; Dir. N. Vavilov Inst. of Gen. Genetics, Russian Acad. of Sciences 1988–91; Corresp. mem. Russian Acad. of Sciences 1987, Chair. Scientific Council on Genetics; mem. Russian Biotech. Acad., Int. Acad. of Science, New York Acad. of Sciences; Visiting Prof. Mich. State Univ., U.S.A. 1992; Fulbright-Hays Fellowship 1975; UNESCO Fellowship Award 1985; U.S.S.R. State Prize 1988, Lomonosov Prize 1995, Hon. Distinguished Scientist of Russian Fed. 1995, N. Vavilov Gold Medal; research in molecular biology and genetics of microorganisms, radiation genetics; discovery of genetic transformation in cyanobacteria; 7 patented inventions. *Publications:* on molecular genetics of DNA repair and recombination, photosynthesis, nitrogen-fixation, resistance to stresses. *Leisure interest:* sports. *Address:* Department of Genetics, Moscow State University, 119899 Moscow, Russia. *Telephone:* (095) 939-35-12. *Fax:* (095) 939-50-22.

SHESTAKOVA, Tatyana Borisovna; Russian actress; b. 23 Oct. 1948, Leningrad; d. of Boris Shestakov and Aleksandra Shestakova; m. Lev Dodin 1972; ed. Leningrad Theatre Inst.; Leningrad Theatre for Children 1972–75; Leningrad Comedy Theatre 1975–80; Bolshoi Drama Theatre 1980–83; Maly Drama Theatre 1983–; has also played for Moscow Arts Theatre; toured abroad 1983, 1987, 1992; U.S.S.R. State Prize 1986, R.S.F.S.R. Merited Artist 1987, National "Triumph" Prize 1992. *Roles include:* Liza (The House) 1980, Sonya (Uncle Vanya) 1982, She (The Meek One) 1985, Anfisa (Brothers and Sisters) 1986, Anna (Stars of the Morning Sky) 1987, Lebyadkina (The Possessed), Lubov Andreevna (The Cherry Orchard) 1994, Dame Elegant (Roberto Zucco) 1994, Katya and Ivanova (Claustrophobia) 1994, Anna Petrovna (Play Without a Name) 1997. *Leisure interests:* travelling, books, music. *Address:* Maly Drama Theatre, Rubinstein Str. 18, St. Petersburg, Russia. *Telephone:* 113-21-08. *Fax:* 113-33-66.

SHETREET, Shimon; Israeli politician; b. 1946, Morocco; ed. Hebrew Univ., Chicago Univ.; Sec. Council for Public Justice; Chair. Cttee. on Broadcasting Authority Law; Chair. Int. Conf. on Legal Matters; Chair. Bd. Dirs. Afro-Asian Inst. of the Histadrut; Minister of Economy, Science and Tech. 1992–95, of Religious Affairs 1995–96; mem. Knesset 1988; served on numerous cttees. 1988–92, including the Landau Comm. on the Israeli Court System, the Council for Admin. Courts, plenum of the Israel Broadcasting Authority 1984–87; Dir. Leumi Bank; Labour. *Publications:* numerous books and articles on legal matters. *Address:* c/o Hebrew University of Jerusalem, Mount Scopus, Jerusalem 91905, Israel.

SHEVARDNADZE, Eduard Amvrosiyevich; Georgian politician; b. 25 Jan. 1928, Mamati Lanchkhutsky Dist., Georgia; s. of Ambrosi Shevardnadze and Sophio Pateishvili; m. Nanuli Tsagareishvili 1950; one s. one d.; ed. Party School of the Cen. Cttee., CP of Georgia, and Kutaisi Pedagogical Inst.; mem. CPSU 1948–91; Komsomol and party work 1946–56; Second Sec. 1956–57, First Sec. Komsomol in Georgia 1957–61; First Sec. Mtskheti raion 1961–63, Pervomaisky raion, Tbilisi, CP of Georgia 1963–64; First Deputy Minister 1964–65, Minister of Public Order (renamed Ministry of Internal Affairs 1968) 1965–72; First Sec. Tbilisi City Cttee. of Cen. Cttee., CP of Georgia 1972; mem. Cen. Cttee., CP of Georgia 1958–64, 1966–91, mem. Politburo 1972–91, First Sec. 1972–85; mem. Cen. Cttee. of CPSU 1976–91, Cand. mem. Politburo 1978–85, mem. 1985–90; Deputy to U.S.S.R. Supreme Soviet 1978–; mem. Political Consultative Council 1991; Minister of Foreign Affairs 1985–90, Nov.–Dec. 1991; Head Soviet Foreign Policy Assen. 1991–92; mem. Presidential Council 1990–91; founder mem. Bd. Democratic Reform Movt. 1991; Chair. Georgian State Council March–Oct. 1992; Chair. Supreme Soviet of Georgia and Head of State 1992–95, elected Pres. of Georgia Nov. 1995–; Dr. h.c. numerous univs.; various decorations. *Publications:* My Choice 1991, The Future Belongs to Freedom 1991. *Address:* Chancellery of the President, Rustaveli prospect 29, 380008 Tbilisi, Georgia. *Telephone:* (32) 999069, 999292, 997985.

SHEYNIS, Viktor Leonidovich, DR.SC.; Russian politician and economist; b. 16 Feb. 1931, Kiev; s. of Leonid M. Sheynis and Liah O. Kimelfeld; m. Alla K. Nazimova 1953; ed. Leningrad Univ.; history teacher in secondary school 1953–56; manual worker Kirov factory, Leningrad 1958–64; teacher at Leningrad Univ. 1966–75; on staff as researcher at Inst. of World Economy and Int. Relations (IMEMO) 1975–92; one of the authors of Russian Constitution and electoral laws 1993–99; People's Deputy 1990–93; mem. Supreme Soviet of Russia 1991–93; co-founder faction Consent in Name of Progress 1992–93; mem. Council of Reps. of Movt. "Democratic Russia" 1990–93, Yabloko movement 1993–97, Yabloko Party 1998–; mem. State Duma (Parl.) 1993–, mem. Cttee. on Legislation and Reform of the Judicial System. *Publications:* over 200 including Developing Nations at the Turn of the Millennium 1987. *Leisure interests:* tourism, cinematography, reading. *Address:* State Duma, Okhotny Ryad 1, 103265 Moscow, Russia. *Telephone:* 292-45-62. *Fax:* 292-96-83.

SHI DAZHEN; Chinese government official and engineer; b. 1932, Wuxi City, Jiangsu Prov.; ed. Shandong Inst. of Tech. 1955; joined CCP 1978; alt. mem. 13th Cen. Cttee. CCP 1988–92, 14th Cen. Cttee. CCP 1992–97; Vice-Minister of Energy and Resources 1988–93, Minister of Electric Power Industry 1993–98; Vice-Chair. Econ. Cttee. 9th Nat. Cttee. of CPPCC 1998–. *Address:* National Committee of Chinese People's Political Consultative Conference, 23 Taipingqiao Street, Beijing, People's Republic of China.

SHI FU; (b. Guo Shifu); Chinese composer; b. Sept. 1929, Xiangtan, Hu'nan Prov.; ed. Cen. China Advanced Arts Teachers Training Coll.; joined PLA 1950; joined CCP 1983. *Publications:* Uygur Folk Songs, Kazakh Folk Songs. *Address:* c/o General Political Department of the People's Liberation Army, Beijing, People's Republic of China.

SHI GUANGSHENG; Chinese politician; b. Sept. 1939, Changli, Hebei Prov.; ed. Beijing Foreign Trade Inst.; joined CCP 1965; clerk, Deputy Section Dir. then Vice-Gen. Man. of China Metals and Minerals Import and Export Corpn.; Dir. Import and Export Dept. of Ministry of Foreign Trade, then Asst. Minister of Foreign Trade 1965–93; Vice-Minister of Foreign Trade and Econ. Co-operation 1993–98, Minister 1998–. *Address:* Ministry of Foreign Trade and Economic Co-operation, 2 Dongchangan Jie, Dongcheng Qu, Beijing 100732, People's Republic of China.

SHI JILIANG; Chinese banker; Pres. Agricultural Bank of China. *Address:* Agricultural Bank of China, 23 Fuxing Lu, Beijing 100036, People's Republic of China. *Telephone:* (1) 8216807. *Fax:* (1) 68297160.

SHI JIUYONG, M.A.; Chinese lawyer; b. 9 Oct. 1926, Zhejiang; m. Zhang Guoying 1956; one s.; ed. St. John's Univ. Shanghai and Columbia Univ. New York; Asst. Research Fellow, Inst. of Int. Relations, Beijing 1956–58; Sr. lecturer, Assoc. Prof. of Int. Law, Foreign Affairs Coll. Beijing 1958–64; Research Fellow in Int. Law, Inst. of Int. Law, Beijing 1964–73, Inst. of Int. Studies, Beijing 1973–80; Prof. of Int. Law, Foreign Affairs Coll. Beijing 1984–93, Foreign Econ. Law Training Centre of Ministry of Justice; Legal Adviser, Ministry of Foreign Affairs 1980–93, Chinese Centre of Legal Consultancy, Office of Chinese Sr. Rep. Sino-British Jt. Liaison Group (on question of Hong Kong) 1985–93; Adviser to Chinese Soc. of Int. Law, Inst. of Hong Kong Law of Chinese Law Soc.; mem. American Soc. of Int. Law, mem. Standing Cttee. Beijing Cttee. of CPCC 1988–93, mem. 8th Nat. Cttee. 1993; mem. Int. Law Comm. (ILC) 1987–93, Chair. 1990; a Judge, Int. Court of Justice 1994–; legal adviser to Chinese dels. at numerous int. confs. etc. *Publications:* numerous publs. on int. law. *Leisure interest:* classical music. *Address:* International Court of Justice, Peace Palace, Carnegieplein 2, 2517 KJ The Hague, Netherlands.

SHI LIMING; Chinese biologist; b. 18 Dec. 1939, Leqing County, Zhejiang Prov.; s. of Shi Zhihou and Li Yueya; m. Zhou Guie 1970; two d.; ed. Fudan Univ., Shanghai; Dir. Kunming Inst. of Zoology; mem. Biological Div., Chinese Acad. of Sciences. *Leisure interest:* classical music.*Address:* Kunming Institute of Zoology, Kunming, Yunnan Province, People's Republic of China. *Telephone:* (0871) 5140930. *Fax:* (0871) 5151823.

SHI MING; Taiwanese political activist; m. (divorced); ed. Waseda Univ., Tokyo; guerrilla fighter in N.E. China after graduation; joined Communist Party and worked in underground movt.; resigned 1949; returned to Taiwan but fled following his involvement in unsuccessful plot to assassinate Gen. Chiang Kai-shek; lived in Japan 1952–93; returned to Taiwan 1993. *Publication:* 400 Years of Taiwan History 1962.

SHI SHENGRONG; Chinese Inner Mongolia politician; b. 1929, Shenmu; Chair. of CPPCC Inner Mongolia Autonomous Region Cttee. 1989–. *Address:* Committee of People's Political Consultative Conference, Inner Mongolia Autonomous Region, Hohhot City, People's Republic of China.

SHI WANPENG; Chinese administrator; b. Dec. 1936, Tianjin; ed. Beijing Railway Inst.; joined CCP 1971; Vice-Minister in charge of State Econ. and Trade Comm. 1993–. *Address:* State Economic and Trade Commission, Beijing, People's Republic of China.

SHI YUNSHEN, Vice-Adm.; Chinese naval officer; b. Jan. 1940, Fushun City, Liaoning Prov.; ed. PLA Air Force Aviation School and PLA Navy Acad.; joined PLA 1956; mem. CCP 1960–; pilot, squadron leader, deputy group commdr. and deputy regt. commdr. Naval Aviation 1962–70; Deputy Commdr. Naval Fleet Aviation 1976–81; Div. Commdr. Naval Aviation 1981–83; Commdr. Naval Fleet Aviation 1983–90; Deputy Commdr. PLA Naval Aviation Dept. 1990–92; Deputy Commdr. PLA Navy 1992–97, Commdr. 1997–; rep. 13th Nat. Congress of CCP 1987; mem. 15th CCP Cen. Cttee. 1997–. *Address:* c/o Ministry of National Defence, Jingshanqian Jie, Beijing, People's Republic of China. *Telephone:* (1) 6370000.

SHI ZHONGCI; Chinese computer scientist; b. Dec. 1933, Ningpo Co., Zhejiang Prov.; Dir. Computer Centre, Acad. of Sciences 1988–; mem. Chinese Sciences Acad. 1992–. *Address:* Computer Centre, Zhong Guan Cun, Beijing 100080, People's Republic of China.

SHIEH, Samuel C.; Taiwanese banker and academic; ed. Univ. of Minnesota; fmr. Prof.; Gov. Cen. Bank of China 1989–94; Nat. Policy Adviser to Pres. 1994–. *Address:* c/o Office of the Governor, Central Bank of China, 2 Roosevelt Road, Sec. 1, Taipei 10757, Taiwan.

SHIELDS, Brooke Christa Camille, B.A.; American actress and model; b. 31 May 1965, New York; d. of Francis Shields and Teri Schmon; m. Andre Agassi (q.v.) 1997; began modelling of Ivory Soap commercials 1966, later for Calvin Klein jeans and Colgate toothpaste commercials; TV appearances include: The Tonight Show, Bob Hope specials, The Diamond Trap 1988, Friends; TV films: The Prince of Central Park 1977, After the Fall, Wet Gold; appeared on Broadway in Grease 1994–95. *Films:* Alice, Sweet Alice 1975, Pretty Baby 1977, King of the Gypsies 1978, Wanda Nevada 1978, Just You and Me Kid 1978, Blue Lagoon 1979, Endless Love 1980, Sahara 1983, Brenda Starr 1986, Backstreet Strays 1989, Brenda Starr, An American Love, Seventh Floor 1993, Running Wild 1993, Freaked 1993, Freeway 1997. *Address:* Christa Inc., Suite 630, 2300 West Sahara, Box 18, Las Vegas, NV 89102, U.S.A.

SHIELDS, Carol Ann, O.C., M.A.; Canadian author and university professor; b. 2 June 1935, Oak Park, Ill., U.S.A.; d. of Robert Warner and Inez Warner; m. Donald Hugh Shields 1957; one s. four d.; ed. Hanover Coll. and Univ. of Ottawa; Lecturer Univ. of Ottawa 1976–77, Writer-in-Residence 1989; Lecturer Univ. of B.C. 1978–79; Prof. Univ. of Man. 1980–; Writer-in-Residence, Univ. of Winnipeg 1987; Chancellor Univ. of Winnipeg 1996–; mem. Canada Council, Royal Soc. of Canada; hon. degrees Univs. of Ottawa, Winnipeg, B.C., Toronto and Western Ont., Queen's Univ., Hanover Coll.; prizes and awards include Marian Engel Award 1990, Gov.-Gen.'s Award 1993, Pulitzer Prize 1995, Orange Prize 1998. *Publications:* Others 1972, Intersect 1974, Small Ceremonies 1976, The Box Garden 1977, Happenstance 1980, A Fairly Conventional Woman 1982, Various Miracles (short stories) 1985, Swann: A Mystery 1987, The Orange Fish 1989, Departure and Arrivals 1990, Coming to Canada 1992, The Republic of Love 1992, Thirteen Hands 1993, The Stone Diaries 1993, Various Miracles 1994, Small Ceremonies 1994, The Box Garden 1995, Larry's Party 1997; contribs. to numerous Canadian magazines and journals. *Leisure interests:* theatre, France. *Address:* 701-237 Wellington Crescent, Winnipeg, Man., R3M 0A1, Canada.

SHIELDS, Margaret Kerslake, Q.S.O., B.A., M.P.; New Zealand politician; b. 18 Dec. 1941, Wellington; d. of Ernest Blake Porter and Dorothy Bessie Porter, née Levy; m. Patrick John Shields 1960; two d.; ed. Victoria Univ., Wellington; researcher Consumers' Inst. and Dept. of Statistics; M.P. for Kapiti 1981–; Minister of Customs and of Consumer Affairs 1984–87, of Women's Affairs, Consumer Affairs and Statistics 1987–88, 1989–90, of Customs 1988–89, Assoc. Minister of Educ. 1989–90; mem. Wellington Regional Council 1995–, Deputy Chair. 1998–; co-founder, Pres. and Nat. Sec. of Soc. for Research on Women; Dir. UN Int. Research and Training Inst. for the Advancement of Women (INSTRAW) 1991–94; co-convenor of Second UN Women's Convention 1975; mem. Wellington Hosp. Bd. 1977–80, Complaints Review Tribunal of N.Z. Human Rights Comm. 1994–, Council of Vic. Univ. of Wellington 1996–; Govt. Del. to UN Int. Women's Year Conf. Mexico 1975, participated in IPU Conf. Seoul 1983, speaker IPU Conf. Geneva 1989; Labour. *Leisure interests:* tennis, hiking, gardening, music, drama. *Address:* 23 Haunui Road, Pukera Bay, Porirua, New Zealand. *Telephone:* (04) 239 9949. *Fax:* (04) 239 9084.

SHIELDS, Sir Robert, Kt., M.D., CH.B., F.R.C.S., F.R.C.S. (E.); British surgeon and professor of surgery; b. 8 Nov. 1930, Paisley, Scotland; s. of Robert Alexander Shields and Isobel Dougall Shields (née Reid); m. Grace Marianne Swinburn 1957; one s. two d; ed. John Neilson Inst., Paisley, Univ. of Glasgow; House Officer posts at Western Infirmary, Glasgow 1953–54; served R.A.M.C. 1954–56, R.A.M.C. (T.A.), Surgeon Specialist 1956–61; Lecturer, Univ. of Glasgow 1960–63; Sr. Lecturer, then Reader in Surgery, Welsh Nat. School of Medicine 1963–69; Prof. of Surgery, Univ. of Liverpool 1969–96, Hon. Consultant Surgeon, Liverpool Health Authority 1969–96; Dean Faculty of Medicine, Univ. of Liverpool 1980–84; Pres. Royal Coll. of Surgeons, Edin. 1994–97; mem. Gen. Medical Council 1982, MRC 1987–91; Deputy Lieut. of Merseyside 1991; Hon. Fellow American Coll. of Surgeons 1990; Hon. F.C.S. (S.A.); Hon. F.H.K.C.S.; Hon. F.R.C.S.I.; Hon. F.R.C.P.(E); Hon. F.R.A.C.S.; Hon. Fellow Acad. of Medicine Singapore; Hon. D.Sc. (Wales) 1990; Moynihan Medal, Assen. of Surgeons of G.B. and Ireland 1965, Bellahouston Medal (Univ. of Glasgow) 1966. *Publications:* Surgical Emergencies II 1979, Textbook of Surgery 1983, Gastro-Intestinal Emergencies 1991. *Leisure interests:* sailing, walking. *Address:* c/o Royal College of Surgeons of Edinburgh, Nicolson Street, Edinburgh, EH8 9DW, Scotland; Strathmore, 81 Meols Drive, West Kirby, Merseyside, L48 5DF, England.

SHIGEHARA, Kumiharu, B.L.; Japanese economist; b. 5 Feb. 1939, Maebashi; s. of Seizaburo Shigehara and Rutsu Tanabe; m. Akiko Yoshizawa 1965; one s. one d.; ed. Maebashi High School and Univ. of Tokyo; economist, Bank of Japan 1962–70; admin. OECD 1970–71, Prin. Admin. 1971–72, Head, Monetary Div. 1972–74; Councillor for Policy Planning, Bank of Japan 1974–76, Man. Int. Affairs 1976–80; Deputy Dir. Gen. Econs. Branch, OECD 1980–82; Gen. Man. Bank of Japan 1983–87; Dir. Gen. Econs. Branch, OECD 1987–89; Dir.-Gen. Inst. for Monetary and Econ. Studies and Chief Economist, Bank of Japan 1989–92; Head, Econs. Dept. and Chief Economist, OECD 1992–97, Deputy Sec.-Gen. 1997–; Hon. Ph.D. *Publications:* The Role of Monetary Policy in Demand Management (co-author) 1975, Europe After 1992 1991, The Problems of Inflation in the 1990s (ed.) 1992, Evolving International Trade and Monetary Regimes 1992, Causes of Declining Growth in Industrialised Countries 1992, Price Stabilization in the 1990s 1993, Long-term Tendencies in Budget Deficits and Debt 1995, The Options regarding the Concept of a Monetary Policy Strategy 1996. *Leisure interests:* golf, tennis. *Address:* 2 rue André Pascal, 75775 Paris, Cedex 16, France. *Telephone:* (01) 45.24.80.30. *Fax:* (01) 45.24.79.31.

SHIH, Stan; Taiwanese business executive; b. 18 Dec. 1944, Taiwan; m. Carolyn Yeh; two s. one d.; ed. Nat. Chiao Tung Univ.; with Unitron Industrial Corpn. 1971–72, Qualitron Industrial Corpn. 1972–76; Chair. and C.E.O. The Acer Group; title of Dato (Malaysia) 1994. *Publications:* more than 100 articles on man., marketing etc.

SHIH CHI-YANG, LL.M., D.JUR.; Chinese politician; b. 5 May 1935, Taichung City; m. Jeanne Tchong-Koei Li 1968; ed. Nat. Taiwan Univ. and Univ. of Heidelberg; Asst. Dept. of Law, Nat. Taiwan Univ. 1959–62, Assoc. Prof. 1967–71, Prof. (part-time) 1971–84; Research Asst. Inst. of Int. Relations, Nat. Chengchi Univ. 1967–69, Research Fellow 1969–71; Deputy Dir. 5th Section, Cen. Cttee., Kuomintang 1969–72, Deputy Dir. Dept. of Youth Activities 1972–76; Admin. Vice-Minister, Ministry of Educ. 1976–79; Political Vice-Minister, Ministry of Educ. 1979–80, Ministry of Justice 1980–84; Minister of Justice 1984–88; Vice-Premier 1988–93; Sec.-Gen. Nat. Security Council 1993–94; Pres. Judicial Yuan 1994–. *Address:* Judicial Yuan, 124 Chungching S. Road, Sec. 1, Taipei, Taiwan. *Telephone:* 02-3618577.

SHIH MING-TEH; Taiwanese politician; m. Linda Gail Arrigo; fmr. political prisoner in Taiwan; Leader, Taiwan Democratic Progressive Party (DPP) 1993–; mem. Taiwan Legis. Council. *Address:* Room 601, 10 Tsingtao E. Road, Taipei, Taiwan.

SHIHATA, Ibrahim F. I., L. EN D., S.J.D.; Egyptian administrator and lawyer; b. 19 Aug. 1937, Damietta; s. of Ibrahim Shihata and Neamat El Ashmawy; m. Samia S. Farid 1967; one s. two d.; ed. Cairo Univ., Harvard Univ., U.S.A.; mem. of the Council of State of Egypt 1957–60; lecturer, Faculty of Law, Ain Shams Univ. 1964–66, Assoc. Prof. 1970–72; Legal Adviser to Kuwait Fund for Arab Econ. Devt. 1966–70, Gen. Counsel 1972–76; also adviser and consultant to Arab Govts. and Int. Orgs. 1965–; Dir.-Gen. OPEC Fund for Int. Devt. (fmrly. OPEC Special Fund) 1976–83; mem. Exec. Bd., IFAD 1977–83; Vice-Pres. and Gen. Counsel, IBRD 1983; Sec.-Gen. Int. Centre for Settlement of Investment Disputes (ICSID) 1983; Chair. of Bd. Int. Devt. Law Inst. 1983; mem. Exec. Council, American Soc. Int. Law 1986–; Founding Advisory Dir. Inst. of Transnat. Arbitration 1986–; mem. Advisory Cttee. Research Centre for Int. Law 1985–. *Publications:* The World Bank in a Changing World 1991, Legal Treatment of Foreign Investment 1993, 16 other books; more than 150 essays on different aspects of international law and finance. *Address:* The World Bank, 1818 H Street, N.W., Washington, DC 20433, U.S.A. *Telephone:* (202) 458-1601. *Fax:* (202) 477-5828.

SHIKHMURADOV, Boris Orazovich; Turkmenistan politician and diplomatist; b. 1949 Ashkhabad; ed. Moscow State Univ., Diplomatic Acad.; journalist, diplomatist Press Agency Novosti and U.S.S.R. Ministry of Foreign Affairs 1971–72; responsible positions in missions abroad, then on staff U.S.S.R. Ministry of Foreign Affairs 1983–86; worked in U.S.S.R. Embs. to Pakistan, India, missions to Turkey, Afghanistan, U.S.A., China, Singapore; apptd. Deputy, then First Deputy Minister of Foreign Affairs of Turkmenistan May 1992; Deputy Chair. Cabinet of Ministers of Turkmenistan 1992–; Minister of Foreign Affairs 1995–. *Address:* Ministry of Foreign Affairs, Ashgabat, Turkmenistan. *Telephone:* (3632) 35 66 88 (Office). *Fax:* (3632) 25 35 83 (Office).

SHIKIN, Gennadi Serafimovich; Russian diplomatist; b. 30 Aug. 1938, Leningrad; m.; one s.; ed. Moscow Inst. of Int. Relations; fmr. mem. CPSU; diplomatic service 1962–; Attaché, U.S.S.R. Embassy to Yugoslavia 1964–66; Third, Second Sec., Dept. of Press, U.S.S.R. Ministry of Foreign Affairs 1966–68; Second Sec., First Sec., U.S.S.R. Embassy, German Fed. Repub. 1968–74; Counsellor, 1974–76, Deputy Head, of Third European Dept., Ministry of Foreign Affairs 1978–86; Amb. to Austria 1986–90, to G.D.R. April–Dec. 1990, to Yugoslavia 1991–96; Amb.-at-Large 1996–. *Address:* Ministry of Foreign Affairs, Sadovaya-Sennaya 32/34, Moscow, Russia.

SHILOV, Aleksandr Maksovich; Russian artist; b. 6 Oct. 1943, Moscow; m. Anna Yuryevna Yalpah 1979; one s. one d. (deceased); ed. Surikov Inst. of Arts, Moscow; painted series of portraits of Soviet celebrities including cosmonauts, actors (Irina Arkhipova, M. Ulyanov), cycle Soldiers' Mothers;

exhbns. in Moscow, St. Petersburg; f. Moscow State A. Shilov Picture Gallery 1997; Lenin Komsomol Prize 1977; People's Artist of U.S.S.R. 1985. *Address:* Romanov per. 3, Apt. 71, 103009 Moscow, Russia. *Telephone:* 203-24-20.

SHILOV, Igor Aleksandrovich; Russian zoologist; b. 9 April 1921; m. 1st Svetlana Alexandrovna Krasova 1951, 2nd Anna Nikolaevna Soldatova 1961; one s.; ed. Moscow State Univ.; jr., sr. researcher, asst., docent, Prof. Moscow State Univ. 1950–; corresp. mem. U.S.S.R. (now Russian) Acad. of Sciences 1984, mem. 1994; research in gen. problems of ecology, population and physiological ecology of animals; Vice Pres. All-Russian Teriological Soc.; U.S.S.R. State Prize. *Publications include:* Physiological Ecology of Animals 1985. *Leisure interest:* photography. *Address:* Moscow State University, Vorobyevy gory, 119899 Moscow, Russia. *Telephone:* (095) 939 2797 (Office).

SHILTON, Peter, M.B.E.; British footballer; b. 18 Sept. 1949, Leicester; s. of Les Shilton and May Shilton; m. Sue Shilton 1970; played for English Youth side; played for Leicester City 1965–74, Stoke City 1974–77, Nottingham Forest 1977–82, Southampton 1982–87, Derby Co. 1987–92, Bolton 1995, Leyton Orient 1996; Man. Plymouth Argyle F.C. 1992–95; became first England goalkeeper to win more than 100 caps at European Championships 1988; record English league appearances (1,004); record English cap holder (125). *Address:* Hubbards Cottage, Bentley Lane, Maxstoke, nr. Coleshill, B46 2QR, England.

SHIMADA, Masao, LL.D.; Japanese university chancellor (retd.); b. 29 Sept. 1915, Tokyo; m. Tsumae Shimada 1945; ed. Univs. of Tokyo and Beijing; mem. Inst. of Oriental Culture, Tokyo Univ. 1941–47; Prof. Meiji Univ. 1947–84, Chancellor 1984–92, Prof. Emer. 1992–. *Publications:* Study on Social History of Liao 1951, Study on the Constitution of Liao 1954, Study of Official Systems of Liao 1978, Study on the History of Liao Dynasty 1979, Compilation of Modern Codes at the Late Ch'ing Period 1980, Study of the Northern Eurasian Legal System 1981, Study of the Special Laws for Mongolia in the Ch'ing Dynasty 1982, Studies on the Mongolian Laws 1986, History of Liao 1991, Studies in the Effectiveness of the Ch'ing Mongol Laws 1992, North Asian Legal History 1995. *Address:* No. 601, Mansion-Ichigaya, 82, Ichigaya Yakuoji, Shinjuku, Tokyo, Japan. *Telephone:* 03-3268-0290.

SHIMAMURA, Yoshinobu; Japanese politician; fmr. Parl. Vice-Minister of Agric., Forestry and Fisheries; mem. House of Reps., fmr. Chair. Cttee. on Transport; Minister of Educ. 1995–96; mem. LDP; fmr. Chair. LDP Diet Affairs Cttee. *Address:* c/o Ministry of Education, 3-2-2, Kasumigaseki, Chiyoda-ku, Tokyo 100, Japan.

SHIMELL, William; British opera singer; b. 23 Sept. 1952, Ilford, Essex; s. of W. Shimell and F. E. Shimell; m. Olga Slavka 1996; ed. Westminster Abbey Choir School, St. Edward's School, Oxford, Guildhall School of Music and Drama, Nat. Opera Studio, London; best known for interpretations of Don Giovanni, Conte Almaviva (Marriage of Figaro) and Don Alfonso (Così fan Tutte), which he has sung in opera houses worldwide including La Scala, Milan, Metropolitan Opera House, New York, Paris Opéra, Rome Opera, Vienna Staatsoper, Covent Garden; Assoc. Guildhall School of Music and Drama. *Leisure interests:* sailing, cooking. *Address:* c/o IMG Artists, Media House, 3 Burlington Lane, London, W4 2TH, England. *Telephone:* 0181-233 5800.

SHIMOGAICHI, Yoichi; Japanese business executive; b. 26 Aug. 1934; two s.; ed. Univ. of Tokyo; joined NKK Corpn. 1958, Gen. Man. Sales Coordination, Export and Corp. Planning Depts. 1981–86, mem. Bd. of Dirs., Gen. Man. Corp. Planning Dept. 1987, Man. Dir. 1989, Sr. Man. Dir., Deputy Dir. Steel Div. 1991, Exec. Vice-Pres., Exec. Dir. Steel Div. 1994–, Exec. Vice-Pres. April 1997, Pres. 1997–; exec. mem. Bd. of Dirs. Japan Fed. of Econ. Orgs. 1997–; mem. Export and Import Transaction Council 1996–, Coal Mining Council 1997–; Dir. Japan Iron and Steel Fed. 1997–. *Leisure interest:* bird watching. *Address:* NKK Corporation, 1-1-2 Marunouchi, Chiyoda-ku, Tokyo 100-8202, Japan.

SHINEFIELD, Henry Robert, B.A., M.D.; American pediatrician; b. 11 Oct. 1925, Paterson, N.J.; s. of Louis Shinefield and Sarah (Kaplan) Shinefield; m. Jacqueline Walker 1983; one s. three d.; ed. Columbia Univ.; Asst. Resident Pediatrician New York Hosp. (Cornell) 1950–51, Pediatrician Outpatients 1953–59, Instructor in Pediatrics 1959–60, Asst. Prof. 1960–64, Assoc. Prof. 1964–65; Chief of Pediatrics, Kaiser-Permanente Medical Center, San Francisco 1965–89; Co-Dir. Kaiser Permanente Pediatric Vaccine Study Center, Calif.; Assoc. Clinical Prof. of Pediatrics, Univ. of Calif. 1966–68, Clinical Prof. of Pediatrics 1968–, Clinical Prof. of Dermatology 1970–; mem. Inst. of Medicine, N.A.S., American Bd. of Pediatrics; Fellow American Acad. of Pediatrics. *Leisure interests:* skiing, tennis, travel. *Address:* 2200 O'Farrell Street, San Francisco, CA 94115 (Office); 2705 Larkin Street, San Francisco, CA 94109, U.S.A. (Home). *Telephone:* (415) 202-3597 (Office); (415) 771-5372 (Home).

SHINGU, Yasuo; Japanese business executive; b. 1 Feb. 1926, Hyogo Pref.; s. of Rokutaro Shingu and Sawa Shingu; m. 1955; one s. one d.; ed. Univ. of Tokyo; Gen. Man. Treasury Dept. Sumitomo Metal Industries Ltd. 1971, Gen. Man. Controlling Dept. 1974, Dir. 1977, Man. Dir. 1981, Sr. Man. Dir. 1983, Exec. Vice-Pres. 1984, Pres. and C.E.O. 1986–92, Hon. Chair. 1992–, fmrly. C.E.O.; Chair. Bd. of Dirs. Iron and Steel Educ. Inst.; Exec. Dir. Japan Fed. of Econ. Orgs., Japan Fed. of Employers' Asscns., Kansai Econ. Fed.; Man. Dir. Kansai Cttee. for Econ. Devt.; Dir. Int. Iron and Steel Inst., Japan Iron and Steel Fed. *Leisure interests:* golf, visiting historic sites. *Address:* 5-23 Ise-Cho, Ashiya City, Hyogo Prefecture 659, Japan. *Telephone:* 0797-22-7466.

SHINOZAKI, Akihiko, LL.B.; Japanese business executive; b. 8 Nov. 1927, Hokkaido; s. of Hikoshiro Shinozaki and Katsuno Shinozaki; m. Tetsuko Inoue 1954; one s. two d.; ed. Tokyo Univ.; joined Sumitomo Metal Mining Co., Ltd. 1952, Dir. 1979–83, Man. Dir. 1983–87, Sr. Man. Dir. 1987–88, Pres. 1988–95, Chair. 1995, Exec. Adviser 1998–; Exec. Dir. Japan Fed. of Employers' Asscns. 1989–; Trustee, Japan Asscn. of Corporate Execs. 1988–, Japan Mining Industry Asscn. 1990– (Pres. 1993–94); Chair. Keidanren Cttee. on Energy and Resources 1996–; Blue Ribbon Medal 1992. *Leisure interests:* appreciating paintings, golf. *Address:* Sumitomo Metal Mining Co. Ltd., 11-3 Shimbashi 5-chome, Minato-ku, Tokyo 105, Japan. *Telephone:* 03-3436-7744.

SHIPLEY, Jenny; New Zealand politician; b. 1952; m.; two c.; fmr. primary school teacher; farmer 1973–88; joined Nat. Party 1975; fmr. Malvern Co. Councillor; M.P. for Ashburton (now Rakaia) 1987–; Minister of Social Welfare 1990–93 and of Women's Affairs 1990–98, of Health 1993–96, of State Services 1996–97, also of State Owned Enterprises, of Transport, of Accident Rehabilitation and Compensation Insurance, Minister Responsible for Radio New Zealand; Minister in Charge of N.Z. Security Intelligence Service 1997–; Prime Minister of N.Z. Dec. 1997–. *Address:* Parliament Buildings, Wellington, New Zealand. *Telephone:* (4) 471-9700. *Fax:* (4) 473-2508.

SHIPLEY, Walter Vincent, B.S.; American banker; b. 2 Nov. 1935, Newark, N.J.; s. of L. Parks and Emily (née Herzog) Shipley; m. Judith Ann Lyman 1957; one s. four d.; ed. Williams Coll., New York Univ.; with Chemical Bank 1956–96, Exec. Vice-Pres. Int. Div., New York 1978–79, Sr. Exec. Vice-Pres. –1981, Pres. 1982–83, Chair. Bd. 1983–92, Pres., C.O.O. 1992–93, Chair., C.E.O. 1994–96; Chair. Chase Manhattan Banking Co. 1996–, C.E.O. 1996–99 (created after merger of Chomzal Banking Corpn. with Chase Manhattan Corpn.); Dir. Champion Int. Corpn., NYNEX Corpn., Atlantic Corpn., Exxon Corpn.; mem. Bd. Dirs. Japan Soc., Lincoln Center for the Performing Arts Inc., N.Y. City Partnership Inc., N.Y. Chamber of Commerce and Industry, Goodwill Industries of Greater N.Y. Inc., United Way of Tri-State; mem. The Business Council, Business Roundtable, Council for Foreign Relations, Pilgrims of U.S., English-Speaking Union; mem. Bd. of Trustees, Cen. Park Conservancy. *Address:* Chase Manhattan Corporation, 270 Park Avenue, New York, NY 10017, U.S.A.

SHIPUK, Pavel Vladimirovich; Belarus politician; b. 1949, Opol, Brest Region; ed. Belarus Polytech. Inst.; Sr. Engineer, Dir. Gomel Lomonosov Glass factory 1966–88; Dir., Pres. Gomelsteklo 1988–94; Chair. Gomel Exec. Cttee. 1994–97; after dissolution of Parl. elected Chair. Nat. Ass. 1997–. *Address:* Parliament Buildings, 220010 Minsk, Belarus. *Telephone:* 22 66 94.

SHIRAISHI, Takashi, PH.D.; Japanese professor of economics; b. 1921, Tokyo; m. Toshiko Shiraishi; one d.; ed. Keio Univ., Harvard Business School; Lecturer Keio Univ. 1947–49, Asst. Prof. 1949–58, Prof. 1958–86, Vice-Pres. 1965–77, Dean, Faculty of Business and Commerce 1975–77, Prof. Emer. 1986–; Prin. Keio High School 1964–65; Dean Faculty of Social Sciences, Kyorin Univ. 1984–92; Dir. Japan Soc. of Int. Econs. 1974–; Dir. and Pres. Union of Nat. Econ. Asscns. in Japan 1975–90; mem. Int. Exchange Program Cttee. of Japan Soc. for the Promotion of Science 1982–84; mem. Exec. Cttee., Int. Econ. Asscn. 1984–89. *Publications:* Economic Development and Direct Investment 1978, History of Economic Growth and Policy of Japan since the Second World War 1983, Japan's Trade Policies 1989, Reformation of World Economy and Japan 1991, History of Japan's Machine Export 1992, New Age of Asia and Japan 1993, Foreign Exchange Rates and the Japanese Economy 1996. *Address:* 1-19-10, Jiyugaoka, Meguroku, Tokyo, Japan. *Telephone:* 03-3717-7118.

SHIRAYANAGI, H.E. Cardinal Peter Seiichi, D.CN.L.; Japanese ecclesiastic; b. 17 June 1928, Tokyo; s. of Peter Hisazo Shirayanagi and Maria Kura Shirayanagi; ed. Gyosei Stella Maris School, Major Seminary, Tokyo and Urban Univ., Rome; ordained priest 1954; Sec. Archbishop's House 1954–66, in Rome 1957–60; Auxiliary Bishop of Tokyo 1966; Coadjutor with right of succession 1969; Archbishop of Tokyo 1970–; cr. Cardinal 1994; Vice-Pres. Bishops' Conf. of Japan 1975, Pres. 1983–92; Pres. Episcopal Comm. for Social Action 1975. *Leisure interest:* piano. *Address:* Archbishop's House, 3-16-15 Sekiguchi, Bunkyo-ku, Tokyo 112, Japan. *Telephone:* (03) 3943-2301. *Fax:* (03) 3944-8511.

SHIRIASHI, Kazuko; Japanese poet; b. 1931, Vancouver, B.C.; m.; one d.; mem. VOU avant-garde literary group 1948–53; with Kazuo Ono has mounted series of poetry/dance productions. *Publications:* poetic works include Seasons of Sacred Lust (in English) 1978.

SHIRKOV, Dmitrii Vasilevich, PH.D.; Russian physicist; b. 3 March 1928, Moscow; s. of Vasili Shirkov and Elizaveta Makushina; m. Svetlana Rastopchina 1950; two s. one d.; ed. Moscow State Univ.; attached to Steklov Math. Inst. of Acad. of Sciences, in Moscow 1950–58 and Jt. Inst. for Nuclear Research, Dubna 1958–60, 1971–; worked at Inst. of Math., Siberian Div. of Acad. of Sciences, Novosibirsk 1960–70; Prof., Univ. of Novosibirsk 1963–69; Nobel Guest Prof., Lund Univ., Sweden 1970–71; Prof., Moscow State Univ. 1972–; Corresp. mem. U.S.S.R. (now Russian) Acad. of Sciences 1960, mem. 1994; Foreign mem. Saxonian Acad. of Sciences; Lenin and State Prize.

Publications: Co-author: Introduction to the Theory of Quantized Fields 1957, A New Method in the Theory of Superconductivity 1958, Dispersion Theories of Strong Interactions at Low Energies 1967, Quantum Fields 1980, Theory of Particle Interactions 1986; numerous published papers mainly on the theory of elementary particles. *Leisure interests:* tourism, skiing. *Address:* Laboratory of Theoretical Physics, Joint Institute for Nuclear Research, Joliot Curie str. 6, 141980 Dubna, Moscow Region, Russia. *Telephone:* (0221) 65088 (Inst.); (095) 926-22-95 (Office); (095) 137-65-46 (Home).

SHIRLEY, George; American tenor; b. 18 April 1934, Indianapolis, Ind.; s. of Irving E. and Daisy (née Bell) Shirley; m. Gladys Lee Ishop 1956; one s. one d.; ed. Wayne State Univ.; debuts with Metropolitan Opera, New York Opera, Festival of Two Worlds (Spoleto, Italy), Santa Fé Opera 1961, Teatro Colón, Buenos Aires 1965, La Scala, Milan 1965, Glyndebourne Festival 1966, Royal Opera, Covent Garden, Scottish Opera 1967, Vienna Festival 1972, San Francisco Opera 1977, Chicago Lyric Opera 1977, Théâtre Municipal d'Angers 1979, Edinburgh Festival 1979, Nat. Opera Ebony, Philadelphia 1980, Spoleto Festival, Charleston, S.C. 1980, Tulsa Opera, Okla. 1980, Ottawa Festival 1981, Deutsche Oper 1983, Guelph Spring Festival 1983, Bregenz Festival, Austria 1998; Prof. of Voice, Univ. of Md. 1980–87; Prof. of Music, Univ. of Mich. 1987–, Joseph Edgar Maddy Distinguished Univ. Prof. of Music 1992–; Hon. H.D.H. (Wilberforce Univ.); Hon. LL.D. (Montclair State Coll.); Hon. D.F.A. (Lake Forest Coll.); Hon. D.Hum.Litt. (Northern Iowa) 1997; Nat. Arts Club Award 1960, Concorso di Musica e Danza (Italy) 1960; Distinguished Scholar-Teacher Award, Univ. of Md. 1985–86. *Leisure interests:* tennis, sketching and cartoons, writing. *Address:* c/o Ann Summers International, Box 188, Station A, Toronto M5W 1B2, Canada; University of Michigan School of Music, Ann Arbor, MI 48109, U.S.A. *Telephone:* (416) 362-1422 (Canada); (734) 665-7821 (Mich.).

SHIRLEY-QUIRK, John, C.B.E., B.SC.; British concert and opera singer; b. 28 Aug. 1931, Liverpool; s. of Joseph Stanley and Amelia Shirley-Quirk; m. 1st Dr. Patricia Hastie 1952 (died 1981); one s. one d.; m. 2nd Sara Watkins 1981 (died 1997); one s. two d.; ed. Holt School, Liverpool, and Liverpool Univ.; Flying Officer, R.A.F. (Educ. Branch) 1952–55; Asst. Lecturer, Acton Tech. Coll. 1956–60; Vicar Choral, St. Paul's Cathedral 1960–61; professional singer 1961–; mem. Voice Faculty, Peabody Conservatory, Baltimore, U.S.A. 1992–; mem. Voice Dept., Coll. of Fine Arts, Carnegie-Mellon Univ., Pittsburgh, Pa. 1994–98; Hon. R.A.M. 1972; D.Mus. h.c. (Liverpool) 1976; Hon. D.Univ. (Brunel) 1981; many recordings and first performances, particularly works of Benjamin Britten. *Leisure interests:* clocks, canals, trees. *Address:* 6062 Red Clover Lane, Clarksville, MD 21029, U.S.A.

SHIVAS, Mark, M.A.; British film and television producer; b. 24 April 1938; s. of James Dallas Shivas and Winifred Alice Lighton Shivas (née Bristow); ed. Whitgift School, Merton Coll. Oxford; Asst. Ed. Movie Magazine 1962–64; freelance journalist; joined Granada TV 1964, Dir., Producer 1965–68; Producer of Drama, BBC TV 1969–88, Head of Drama 1988–93, Head of Films 1993–97; Creative Dir. Southern Pictures 1979–81. *Productions include:* The Six Wives of Henry VIII (BAFTA awards, Prix Italia), The Evacuees (BAFTA and Emmy awards), Casanova, The Glittering Prizes, Rogue Male, Professional Foul (BAFTA Award), Telford's Change, On Giant's Shoulders (Emmy Award); for Channel 4: The Price, What if it's Raining?, The Storyteller (Emmy Award), Talking Heads 2. *Feature films include:* Moonlighting 1982, A Private Function 1984, The Witches 1988, Truly, Madly, Deeply 1991, Enchanted April 1991, The Snapper 1993, Priest 1995, Small Faces 1996, Jude 1996, Regeneration 1997, Hideous Kinky 1998. *Publications:* articles in art journals. *Leisure interests:* Italy, gardens, swimming, cycling, moviegoing. *Address:* 38 Gloucester Mews, London, W2 3HE, England. *Telephone:* 0171-723 4678. *Fax:* 0171-262 1415.

SHKOLNIK, Vladimir Sergeyevich; Kazakhstan politician and scientist; b. 17 Feb. 1949, Serpukhov, Moscow Region; m.; two c.; ed. Moscow Inst. of Physics and Math.; mem. Kazakhstan Acad. of Sciences; various posts from engineer to Deputy Dir. Mangistauz Energy Complex 1973–92; Dir.-Gen. Agency of Atomic Energy Repub. of Kazakhstan 1992–94; Minister of Science and New Tech. 1994–96; Minister of Science 1996–; Pres. Kazakhstan Acad. of Sciences March 1996–. *Address:* Shchevchenko str. 28, Almaty, Kazakhstan (Office). *Telephone:* (3272) 62-93-85; 62-38-01 (Office).

SHLAUDEMAN, Harry Walter, B.A.; American diplomatist (retd.); b. 17 May 1926, Los Angeles, Calif.; s. of Karl Whitman and Florence Pixley Shlaudeman; m. Carol Jean Dickey 1948; two s. one d.; ed. Stanford Univ., Calif.; served U.S. Marine Corps. 1944–46; joined U.S. Foreign Service 1955; Vice-Consul, Barranquilla, Colombia 1955–56; Political Officer, Bogotá, Colombia 1956–58; assigned language training, Washington, D.C. 1958–59; Consul, Sofia, Bulgaria 1960–62; Chief of Political Section, Santo Domingo, Dominican Repub. 1962–64; Officer in Charge of Dominican Affairs, Dept. of State, Washington, D.C. 1964–65, Asst. Dir. Office of Caribbean Affairs 1965–66, Sr. Seminar Foreign Policy 1966–67, Special Asst. to Sec. of State 1967–69, Dir. INR RAR, Dept. of State 1969; Deputy Chief of Mission, Counsellor of Embassy, Santiago, Chile 1969–73; Deputy Asst. Sec. of State for Inter-American Affairs 1973–75; Amb. to Venezuela 1975–76; Asst. Sec. of State for Inter-American Affairs 1976–77; Amb. to Peru 1977–80, to Argentina 1980–83; Exec. Dir. Nat. Bipartisan Cttee. on Cen. America 1983–84; Pres.'s Special Amb. to Cen. America 1984–86; Amb. to Brazil 1986–89, to Nicaragua 1990–92; Presidential Medal of Freedom 1992. *Leisure interest:* golf. *Address:* 7006 Pebble Beach Way, San Luis Obispo, CA 93401, U.S.A. (Home). *Telephone:* (805) 787-0858.

SHMAKOV, Mikhail Viktorovich; Russian trade union leader; b. 12 Aug. 1949, Moscow; m.; one s.; ed. Bauman Moscow Higher Tech. School; engineer in defence industry factories 1972–75, 1977–86; army service 1975–77; Head Moscow Trade Union of Workers of Defence Industry 1986–90; Chair. Moscow City Council of Trade Unions later transformed into Moscow Fed. of Trade Unions 1990–93; Chair. Fed. of Ind. Trade Unions (FNPR) Oct. 1993–. *Leisure interest:* sports. *Address:* Federation of Independent Trade Unions, Leninsky pr. 42, 117119 Moscow, Russia. *Telephone:* (095) 938-86-52 (Office).

SHMAROV, Valery Nikolayevich; Ukrainian politician; b. 1945; m.; one s.; ed. Kiev School of Electrotechnology, Kiev State Univ.; radio equipment mechanic, Head of lab. Production Union, Kiev Radiozavod 1966–72; head of lab., chief of div., chief of workshop, chief of dept. 1973–87, Dir. Zhulyany Machine Construction Factory 1987–92; First Deputy Dir.-Gen. Nat. Space Agency of Ukraine 1992–93; Deputy Prime Minister on problems of mil.-industrial complex 1993–94; Deputy Prime Minister and Minister of Defence 1994–96. *Address:* Ministry of Defence, Bankova vul. 6, 252005 Kiev, Ukraine. *Telephone:* (044) 226-26-56.

SHMELEV, Geliy Ivanovich; Russian economist; b. 11 June 1927; m. (wife deceased); ed. Rostov State Univ.; head of div. Rostov Inst. of Railway Eng. 1952–54; sr. teacher Black Sea Inst. of Mechanization and Electrification of Agric. 1954–59; sr. teacher, docent Lipetsk br. Moscow Inst. of Steel and Alloys 1962–70; sr. researcher Inst. of Econ. U.S.S.R. Acad. of Sciences 1970–72; head of div. Inst. of Int. Econ. and Political Studies U.S.S.R. Acad. of Sciences; Sr. researcher Inst. of Econs. Russian Acad. of Sciences 1998; corresp. mem. U.S.S.R. (now Russian) Acad. of Sciences and Russian Acad. of Agric. Sciences 1990; research in agrarian policy and econ., social problems of the village. *Publications:* Distribution and Usage of Labour in the Collective Farms 1964, Subsidiary Smallholding and its relations with Public Production 1971, Subsidiary Smallholding: Possibilities and Prospects 1983, Social and Economic Problems to Develop Agriculture in Socialist European Countries 1996, A Reform in American and Russian Scientists' Eyes 1996. *Address:* Institute of Economies, Russian Academy of Sciences, Nakhimovsky prosp. 32, 117 28 Moscow, Russia. *Telephone:* (095) 332-45-54 (Office).

SHMELYEV, Nikolai Petrovich, DR.ECON. SC.; Russian economist and author; b. 18 June 1936, Moscow; s. of Petr Shmelyev and Maria Shmelyeva; m. Gulia Shmelyeva 1965; one d.; ed. Moscow Univ.; mem. CPSU 1962–91; researcher Inst. Econ. U.S.S.R. Acad. of Sciences 1958–61; Prof., Head of Dept., Inst. of Econ. of World Socialist System (IEMSS), U.S.S.R. Acad. of Sciences 1961–68, 1970–82; sr. scientific researcher, Inst. of U.S.A. and Canada 1982–92; sr. researcher, Russian Acad. of Sciences Inst. of Europe 1992–; researcher, Slavic Research Centre, Hokkaido Univ., Japan 1995; U.S.S.R. People's Deputy 1989–91; Corresp. mem. Russian Acad. of Sciences 1994–; lecturer, Stockholm Inst. of Econ. of East European Countries; lecturer, Middlebury Coll. Vt., U.S.A. *Publications:* books and articles on econ. problems, World Economic Tendencies, Progress and Contradictions 1987, Advances and Debts 1989, The Turning Point 1990; novels and stories include Pashkov House 1987, Performance for Mr. Prime Minister 1988, Pirosmani 1988, Silvestr 1991, V Puti Ya Zanemog 1995, Bezumnaya Greta 1995. *Leisure interests:* books, travelling. *Address:* Institute of Europe, Mokhovaya 8/3, 103873 Moscow; 3-d Frunzenkaya 7, Apt. 61, 119270 Moscow, Russia (Home). *Telephone:* 203-72-37 (Office); 242-13-06 (Home). *Fax:* (095) 200-42-98.

SHOCHAT, Avraham; Israeli politician and construction engineer; b. 1936, Tel Aviv; paratrooper Israel Defence Forces; Br. Dir. Solel Boneh (Histadrut construction company); co-f. city of Arad; Mayor of Arad 1967–89; Chair. Citizens' Cttee. Arad, Devt. Towns Council, Econ. Cttee., Finance Cttee.; Deputy Chair. Union of Local Authorities; Minister of Finance 1992–96, also of Energy; mem. Knesset 1988–; Dir. Israel Aircraft Industries; Labour. *Address:* c/o The Knesset, Jerusalem, Israel.

SHOCK, Sir Maurice, Kt., M.A.; British academic; b. 15 April 1926; s. of Alfred Shock and Ellen Shock; m. Dorothy Donald 1947 (died 1998); one s. three d.; ed. King Edward's School, Birmingham and Balliol and St. Antony's Colls. Oxford; served Intelligence Corps. 1945–48; Lecturer in Politics, Christ Church and Trinity Coll. Oxford 1955–56; Fellow and Praelector in Politics, Univ. Coll. Oxford 1956–77; Estates Bursar 1959–74; Vice-Chancellor, Univ. of Leicester 1977–87; Rector, Lincoln Coll. Oxford 1987–94, Hon. Fellow 1995; Chair. Nuffield Provincial Hosps. Trust 1988–; mem. Franks Comm. of Inquiry into Univ. of Oxford 1964–66; Hebdomadal Council, Oxford Univ. 1969–75; Chair. Univ. Authorities Panel 1980–85. *Publications:* The Liberal Tradition; articles on politics and recent history. *Leisure interests:* gardening, theatre. *Address:* 4 Cunliffe Close, Oxford, OX2 7BL, England.

SHOEMAKER, Sydney, PH.D.; American professor of philosophy; b. 29 Sept. 1931, Boise, Idaho; s. of Roy Hopkins Shoemaker and Sarah Anderson Shoemaker; m. Molly McDonald 1960; one s.; ed. Reed Coll., Edinburgh Univ., Cornell Univ.; instructor, Ohio State Univ. 1957–60; Santayana Fellow, Harvard Univ. 1960–61; Asst. then Assoc. Prof., Cornell Univ. 1961–67, Prof. 1970–, Susan Linn Sage Prof. 1978–; Assoc. Prof. Rockefeller Univ. 1967–70; ed. The Philosophical Review, many terms 1964–; Gen. Ed. Cambridge Studies in Philosophy 1982–90; Vice-Pres. Eastern Div. American

Philosophical Asscn. 1992–93, Pres. 1993–94; John Locke Lecturer, Oxford Univ. 1972; Josiah Royce Lecturer, Brown Univ. 1993; Fulbright Scholar 1953–54, Fellow Center for Advanced Study in Behavioral Sciences 1973–74, Nat. Endowment for the Humanities Fellowship 1980–81, Guggenheim Fellow and Fellow at Nat. Humanities Center 1987–88; mem. American Acad. of Arts and Sciences, American Philosophical Asscn. *Publications:* Self-Knowledge and Self-Identity 1963, Identity, Cause and Mind 1984, Personal Identity (with Richard Swinburne) 1984, The First Person Perspective 1996. *Leisure interests:* music, reading, gardening. *Address:* The Sage School of Philosophy, 218 Goldwin Smith Hall, Cornell University, Ithaca, NY 14850 (Office); 104 Northway Road, Ithaca, NY 14850, U.S.A. (Home). *Telephone:* (609) 2577382 (Office); (607) 2577382 (Home). *Fax:* (609) 2558177 (Office).

SHOEMAKER, Willie (William Lee); American jockey; b. 19 Aug. 1931, Fabens, Tex.; s. of Bebe and Ruby (Call) Shoemaker; m. Cynthia Barnes 1978; one d.; jockey since 1949; Winner Ky. Derby 1955, 1959, 1965, 1986, Belmont Stakes 1957, 1959, 1962, 1967, 1985, Preakness Stakes 1963, 1967; has won more than 810 Stakes races; first jockey to have 8,000 wins; retd. 1990 with 8,833 wins. *Address:* c/o Vincent Andrews Management, 315 South Beverly Drive, Suite 216, Beverly Hills, CA 90212, U.S.A.

SHOEMATE, C. Richard, M.B.A.; American business executive; b. 10 Dec. 1939, LaHarpe, Ill.; s. of Richard Osborne Shoemate and Mary Jane (née Gillette) Shoemate; m. Nancy Lee Gordon 1962; three s.; ed. Western Ill. Univ. and Univ. of Chicago; Comptroller Corn Products Unit, CPC Int. 1972–74, Plant Man. 1974–76, Vice-Pres. Operations 1976–81; Corpn. Vice-Pres. CPC Int. 1983–88, Pres. 1988–98, Chair., C.E.O. 1990–98; Chair., Pres., C.E.O. Bestfoods (fmrly. CPC Int.) 1998–; Pres. Canada Starch Co. 1981–83, mem., Bd. of Dirs. 1981–88; Bd. of Dirs. Corn Refiners Asscn. 1985–88. *Address:* Bestfoods, 700 Sylvan Avenue, Englewood Cliffs, NJ 07632, U.S.A. (Office).

SHOENBERG, David, M.B.E., F.R.S., PH.D.; British physicist (retd.); b. 4 Jan. 1911, St. Petersburg, Russia; s. of Sir Isaac Shoenberg and Esther Shoenberg (née Aisenstein); m. Catherine Félicitée Fischmann 1940; one s. two d.; ed. Latymer Upper School, London and Trinity Coll. Cambridge; Exhbn. of 1851 Sr. Student 1936–39; Research in Low Temperature Physics 1932–; in charge of Royal Soc. Mond. Lab. 1947–73; Lecturer in Physics 1944–52, Reader 1952–73, UNESCO Adviser on Low Temperature Physics, Nat. Physical Lab. of India 1953–54; Prof. of Physics Cambridge Univ. and Head of Low Temperature Physics Group, Cavendish Lab. 1973–78, Prof. Emer. 1978–; Life Fellow Gonville and Caius Coll. Cambridge; Hon. Foreign mem. American Acad. of Arts and Sciences; Guthrie Lecturer 1966, Rutherford Memorial Lecturer (India and Sri Lanka) 1980, Krishnan Memorial Lecturer 1988; Dr. h.c. (Lausanne) 1973; Fritz London Award for Low Temperature Physics 1964, Royal Soc. Hughes Medal 1995. *Publications:* Superconductivity 1938, 1952, Magnetism 1949, Magnetic Oscillations in Metals 1984, Kapitza in Cambridge and Moscow (co-ed.) 1990; scientific papers on low temperature physics and magnetism. *Address:* c/o Cavendish Laboratory, Madingley Road, Cambridge, CB3 0HE (Office); 2 Long Road, Cambridge, CB2 2PS, England (Home). *Telephone:* (01223) 337389 (Office).

SHOGO, Watanabe; Japanese executive; b. 31 Aug. 1915; m. Murako Tajima 1943; two s. one d.; ed. Tokyo Univ.; with the Industrial Bank of Japan Ltd. 1938–62; Man. Dir. Nikko Securities Co. 1962, Sr. Man. Dir. 1963, Vice-Pres. 1966, Pres. 1970–91, Chair. 1973–; Pres. Nikko Research Centre Ltd. 1970–88, Japan Fund Inc. 1973– (Vice-Chair. 1974–), Dir. Pvt. Investment Co. for Asia (PICA) 1975–, Tokyo Stock Exchange 1973–; Exec. Dir. Japan Fed. of Employers' Asscn. 1970; Trustee, Japan Cttee. for Econ. Devt. 1971–; Man. Dir. Fed. of Econ. Orgs. (Keidanren) 1970–; Pres. Bond Underwriters Asscn. of Japan 1972–73; mem. Trilateral Comm. 1973–; Chair. Securities Dealers Asscn. of Japan 1975–; mem. Securities and Exchange Council 1976–, Financial System Council 1976–, Taxation System Council of Govt. *Leisure interest:* oil painting. *Address:* Nikko Securities Company Ltd., 3-1, Marunouchi 3-chome, Chiyoda-ku, Tokyo (Office); 6-2, Eifuku 3-chome, Suginami-ku, Tokyo, Japan (Home). *Telephone:* (03) 283-2211 (Office); (03) 328-4205 (Home).

SHOIGU, Lieut.-Gen., Sergey Kuzhugetovich; Russian politician; b. 21 May 1955, Chadan, Tuva A.S.S.R., Russia; m.; two d.; ed. Krasnoyarsk Polytech. Inst.; engineer, sr. master construction trust in Krasnoyarsk 1977–78; man. construction trusts Achinskamulinstroi, Cayantyazhstroi, Abakanvagonstroi 1979–88; Second Sec. Abakan City CP Cttee., insp. CP Cttee. Krasnoyarsk Territory 1989–90; Deputy Chair. State Cttee. on Architecture and Construction R.S.F.S.R. 1990–91; Chair. State Cttee. of Russian Fed. on Civil Defence, Emergencies and Natural Disasters 1991–94; Minister of Civil Defence, Emergencies and Natural Disasters 1994–. *Leisure interests:* singing, playing guitar. *Address:* Ministry of Civil Defence, Emergencies and Natural Disasters, Teatralny proezd 3, 103012, Moscow, Russia (Office). *Telephone:* (095) 925-07-50; (095) 926-35-00 (Office).

SHOKHIN, Aleksandr Nikolayevich, DR.EC.SC.; Russian politician; b. 25 Nov. 1951, Savinskoye, Arkhangelsk Region; m. Tatyana Valentinovna Shokhina; one s. one d.; ed. Moscow Univ.; on staff Inst. of Econ., State Planning Cttee., Inst. of Labour, State Cttee. of Labour 1974–82; researcher, Cen. Econ.-Math. Inst. and Inst. for Industrial Prognostics, U.S.S.R. Acad. of Sciences 1982–87; adviser, Head of Dept. of Int. Econ. Relations, Ministry of Foreign Affairs 1987–91; Dir. Inst. of Employment Problems May–Aug. 1991; Russian Minister of Labour Aug.–Nov. 1991; Deputy Chair. of Russian Govt. 1991–94; Minister of Labour and Employment 1991–92, of Foreign Econ. Relations 1992–93, of Econs. 1994; Man. for Russia, IMF and IBRD 1992–94; mem. Bd. State Specialized Export-Import Bank 1995–; Pres. Higher School of Econs. 1995–; mem. Bd. Russian Party of Unity and Consent 1993–95; Co-ordinator pre-election Union "Our Home Russia" 1995, Chair. 1997–98; mem. State Duma (parl.) 1993–, First Deputy Chair. 1996–97; Deputy Prime Minister Sept. 1998 (resgnd.) *Publications:* several books including Social Problems of Perestroika 1989, Consumer's Market 1989, Interactive of Powers in the Legislative Process 1997; over 100 scientific articles. *Address:* State Duma, Okhotny Ryad 1, 103009 Moscow, Russia. *Telephone:* 292-83-01. *Fax:* 292-83-00.

SHOKIN, Yuri Ivanovich; Russian mathematician; b. 9 July 1943, Kansk; m. 1968; two d.; ed. Novosibirsk State Univ.; sr. researcher, head of lab. Computers Cen. Siberian branch U.S.S.R. Acad. of Sciences 1969–76, head of lab. Inst. Theoretical and Applied Mechanics Siberian branch 1976–83, Dir. Computers Cen. Siberian branch in Krasnoyarsk 1983–90; Dir. Inst. of Computational Tech. Siberian branch Russian Acad. of Sciences 1990–, Gen. Scientific Sec. Siberian br. 1992–97, Gen. Dir. United Inst. of Informatics 1997–; Dir. Technopark Novosibirsk 1998–; corresp. mem. U.S.S.R. (now Russian) Acad. of Sciences 1984, mem. 1994; research in computational math., numerical methods of mech., applied math. *Publications:* Interval Analysis 1981, Numerical Modelling of Tsunami Waves 1983, Method of Differential Approximation: Application in Gas Dynamics 1985, Methods of Interval Analysis 1986, numerous scientific articles. *Address:* Institute of Computational Technologies, Siberian Branch of Russian Academy of Sciences, akademik Lavrentyev Prosp. 6, 630090 Novosibirsk, Russia. *Telephone:* (3832) 34-11-50. *Fax:* (3832) 34-13-42.

SHOMAN, Issa, B.A.; Jordanian banker; b. 1934, Jerusalem; m. 1968; two s. one d.; ed. American Univ. of Beirut; Sr. Man. Arab Bank Ltd., Dubai. *Leisure interest:* tennis. *Address:* P.O. Box 11364, Jordan (Home). *Telephone:* 227-012.

SHONEKAN, Chief Ernest Adegunle Oladeinde, LL.B.; Nigerian administrative official and lawyer; b. 9 May 1936, Lagos; m. Beatrice Oyelayo Oyebola 1965; two s. three d.; ed. Church Missionary Soc. (CMS) Boys' School, Lagos, CMS Grammar School, Lagos and Univ. of London; legal asst. UAC of Nigeria Ltd. 1964–67, asst. legal adviser 1967–73, deputy legal adviser 1974–75, legal adviser 1975–78, Dir. 1976, Chair. 1980–; Gen. Man. Bordpak Premier Packaging Co. 1978–79; Chair. Transitional Council of Nigeria Jan.–Aug. 1993; Pres. of Nigeria and Head of Interim Govt. Aug.–Nov. 1993. *Address:* UAC of Nigeria Ltd., P.O. Box 9, Lagos (Office); 12 Alexander Avenue, Ikoyi, Lagos, Nigeria (Home). *Telephone:* 661091 (Office); 681437 (Home).

SHOOMBE, Pachukoni; Namibian politician; b. 12 Dec. 1936, Okadiva, Oshana Region; m.; five c.; ed. Okahao Training Coll., UN Inst. for Namibia, Lusaka, Zambia; teacher 1958–74; Prin. Oshigambo Girls' School 1960–63; mem. SWAPO 1963–, joined mil. arm abroad 1974, elected mem. SWAPO Women's Council Cen. Cttee. and Exec. Cttee. 1980, SWAPO Cen. Cttee. 1982, 1991; rep. SWAPO as Exec. Sec. for Information and Publicity, Pan-African Women's Org., Algeria and Angola 1985–89; apptd. Election Deputy Commr. for Northern Region, Oshakati 1989; mem. Constitutional Ass. 1989, Nat. Ass. 1990–; Chair. Nat. Ass. Select Cttee. on Human Resources; mem. Cttee. on Standing Rules and Orders, Public Accounts Cttee.; SWAPO Sec. for Finance 1991–; mem. nat. group of IPU; UNESCO Int. Award for work in SWAPO refugee camps 1980–85. *Leisure interests:* fighting against the oppression of women, reading, cooking, baking. *Address:* P.O. Box 1971, Windhoek, Namibia. *Fax:* 232368.

SHORE OF STEPNEY, Baron (Life Peer) cr. 1997, of Stepney in the London Borough of Tower Hamlets, **Peter (David) Shore,** P.C., M.P.; British politician; b. 20 May 1924; m. Elizabeth Catherine Wrong 1948; two s. (one deceased) two d.; ed. Quarry Bank High School, Liverpool, and King's Coll., Cambridge; mem. Labour Party 1948–; Head of Research Dept., Labour Party 1959–64; M.P. for Stepney 1964–74, for Tower Hamlets, Stepney and Poplar 1974–83, Bethnal Green and Stepney 1983–97; Parl. Pvt. Sec. to Prime Minister 1965–66; Joint Parl. Sec. Ministry of Tech. 1966–67; Sec. of State for Econ. Affairs 1967–69; Minister without Portfolio 1969–70; Labour Party Spokesman on European Affairs 1971–74; Sec. of State for Trade 1974–76, for the Environment 1976–79; Pres. British Overseas Trade Bd. 1974–76; Opposition Spokesman for Foreign Affairs 1979–80, for Treasury and Econ. Affairs Dec. 1980–83, for Trade and Industry 1983–84; Shadow Leader of the House of Commons 1983–87; mem. Select Cttee. On Foreign Affairs 1987–97, Cttee. on Standards in Public Life 1994–; Hon. Fellow, Queen Mary Coll., London. *Publications:* Entitled to Know 1966, Leading the Left 1993. *Leisure interest:* swimming. *Address:* House of Lords, Westminster, London, SW1A 0AA; 23 Dryburgh Road, London, S.W.15, England.

SHORT, Rt. Hon. Clare, P.C., B.A.; British politician; b. 15 Feb. 1946, Birmingham; d. of Frank Short and Joan Short; m. 1st 1964 (divorced 1974); one s.; m. 2nd Alex Lyon 1981 (died 1993); ed. Keele and Leeds Univs.; with Home Office 1970–75; Dir. All Faith for One Race 1976–78, Youthaid 1979–83; M.P. for Birmingham Ladywood 1983–; Shadow Employment Spokesperson 1985–89, Social Security Spokesperson 1989–91, Environment Protection Spokesperson 1992–93, Spokesperson for Women 1993–95;

Shadow Sec. of State for Transport 1995–96, for Overseas Devt. 1996–97; Sec. of State for Int. Devt. 1997–; Chair. All Party Group on Race Relations 1985–86, Nat. Exec. Cttee. (NEC) Women's Cttee. 1993–97; Vice-Pres. Socialist Int. Women 1992–97; mem. Select Cttee. on Home Affairs 1983–95, NEC of Labour Party 1988–98; mem. Nat. Union of Public Employees (NUPE). *Leisure interests:* books, family, swimming. *Address:* House of Commons, London, SW1A 0AA, England.

SHORT, Rt. Hon. Edward Watson (see Glenamara, Baron).

SHORT, Nigel; British chess player; b. 1 June 1965, Leigh, Lancs.; s. of David Short and Jean Gaskill; m. Rea Karageorgiou 1987; one d.; at age of 12 beat Jonathan Penrose in British championship; Int. Master 1980, Grand Master 1984; British Champion 1984, 1987, English Champion 1991; Pres. Grand Masters' Assen. 1992; defeated Anatoly Karpov 1992; defeated by Kasparov 1993; ranked seventh player in world; chess columnist, The Daily Telegraph 1991; stripped of int. ratings by World Chess Fed. June 1993; resgnd. from FIDE and formed Professional Chess Assen. with Gary Kasparov (q.v.) 1993. *Publication:* Learn Chess with Nigel Short 1993. *Leisure interests:* politics, guitar playing. *Address:* c/o The Daily Telegraph, 1 Canada Square, London, E14 5DT, England.

SHORT, Roger Valentine, SC.D., F.A.A., F.R.S., F.R.S.E., F.R.C.V.S., F.R.C.O.G.; British professor of reproductive biology; b. 31 July 1930, Weybridge; s. of F. A. Short and M. C. Short; m. 1st Dr. Mary Bowen Wilson 1958 (divorced 1981); one s. three d.; m. 2nd Dr. Marilyn Bernice Renfree 1982; two d.; ed. Sherborne School, Univs. of Bristol, Wisconsin and Cambridge; mem. ARC Unit of Reproductive Physiology and Biochem., Cambridge 1956–72; Lecturer, then Reader Dept. of Veterinary Clinical Studies, Cambridge 1961–72; Dir. MRC Unit of Reproductive Biology, Edin., Scotland 1972–82; Prof. of Reproductive Biology, Monash Univ., Australia 1982–95; Professorial Fellow, Dept. of Perinatal Medicine, Univ. of Melbourne 1996–; holder of patents for use of melatonin to control jet lag 1983, 1986, 1987; Hon. Prof., Univ. of Edin. 1976–82; Fellow, Magdalene Coll., Cambridge 1961–72; Fellow American Acad. of Arts and Sciences; Hon. D.Sc. (Guelph, Bristol). *Publications include:* Reproduction in Mammals, vols. 1–8 (ed. with C. R. Austin) 1972–86, Contraceptives of the Future (ed. with D. T. Baird) 1976; contrib. to numerous scientific journals. *Leisure interests:* gardening, wildlife, history of biology. *Address:* Department of Perinatal Medicine, Royal Women's Hospital, University of Melbourne, Vic. 3053, Australia. *Telephone:* (3) 93442635. *Fax:* (3) 93472472.

SHORTER, Wayne, B.A.; American musician; b. 25 Aug. 1933, Newark; ed. New York Univ.; played saxophone with Art Blakey 1959–63, Miles Davis 1964–70, Weather Report 1970–86, Miles Davis Tribute Band 1992; served U.S. Army 1956–58; winner numerous Down Beat Magazine Awards, Best Soprano Sax 1984, 1985. *Solo albums include:* Native Dancer, Soothsayer, Etcetera 1981, Atlantis 1986, Phantom Navigator 1987, Joy Rider 1988, Native Dancer 1990, The All Seeing Eye 1994. *Address:* c/o Blue Note Records, 1750 Vine Street, Los Angeles, CA 90028, U.S.A.

SHOSTAKOVICH, Maksim Dmitriyevich; American conductor; b. 10 May 1938, Leningrad, U.S.S.R. (now St. Petersburg, Russia); s. of the late Dmitriy Shostakovich; m. 1st; one s.; m. 2nd Marina Tisie 1989; one s. one d.; ed. Cen. Music School, Moscow Conservatory; studied conducting under Rabinovich, Gauk, Rozhdestvensky (q.v.); Asst. Conductor, Moscow Symphony Orchestra; Conductor, State Academic Symphony Orchestra; piano debut age 19 in father's Second Piano Concerto; Prin. Conductor and Artistic Dir. U.S.S.R. Radio and TV Symphony Orchestra, touring Western Europe, Japan, U.S.A. 1971–81; requested and granted political asylum in U.S.A. while on tour with U.S.S.R. Radio and TV Symphony Orchestra, Nuremberg April 1981; conducted Nat. Symphony Orchestra, Capitol steps, Washington, D.C., U.S.A. May 1981; Prin. Guest Conductor Hong Kong Philharmonic 1982–; Music Dir. New Orleans Symphony 1987–91; Music Dir. New Orleans Symphony Orchestra 1986–91; Hon. Music Dir. La. Philharmonic Orchestra 1993–94; has conducted all maj. North American orchestras and many in Europe, Asia, South America; conducted premiere of father's 15th Symphony and recorded virtually all father's symphonies in U.S.S.R.; has performed with leading soloists, incl. Emil Gilels, Oistrakh, Rostropovich. *Address:* c/o Columbia Artists Management, Inc., 165 West 57th Street, New York, NY 10019 (Office); P.O. Box 273, Jordanville, NY 13361, U.S.A. (Home).

SHPEK, Roman Vasilyevich; Ukrainian economist; b. 1954; m.; one s. one d.; ed. Lvov Inst. of Wood Tech.; engineer, chief of warehouse Wood Enterprise Osmoloda Ivano-Frankovsk Region 1976–78; Chief Engineer, Dir. Verkhovinsk Wood Enterprise 1978–85; Dir. Vorokhta Wood Enterprise 1985–89; Deputy Minister of Wood Industry Ukrainian S.S.R. 1989–91; Deputy Chair. Ukrainian State Cttee. on Wood Processing Industry 1991–92; Minister of Property Privatization and Production Demonopolization March–Nov. 1992; First Deputy Minister of Econs. of Ukraine 1992–94, Minister 1994–96; Chair. Nat. Agency for Reconstruction and Devt.; mem. Verkhovna Rada 1996–. *Address:* Verkhovna Rada, M. Hrushevskoho str. 5, 252019 Kiev, Ukraine.

SHRESTHA, Surya Prasad, M.A.; Nepalese diplomatist; b. 1 March 1937, Taplejung; s. of late L. P. Shrestha and G. K. Shrestha; m. Ginni Baba Shrestha 1958; two s. two d.; ed. Tribhuvan Univ. and London School of Econs. and Political Science; joined H.M. Govt. Service 1958; Parl. Secr. and Ministry of Devt. 1958–63; Under-Sec. Ministry of Home and Panchayat 1963–65; Election Comm. 1965–66; Jt. Zonal Commr. 1970–74; Zonal Commr. Bagmati Zone 1974–78; Acting Sec. Ministry of Home and Panchayat 1978–79; Sec. of Industry and Commerce 1979–83; Jt. mem. Nat. Planning Comm. 1983–85; Chief Election Commr. 1985–92; Amb. to U.K. 1992–97; several honours and awards. *Publication:* Democracy Prevails: General Election in Nepal 1991. *Leisure interests:* reading, gardening. *Address:* c/o Ministry of Foreign Affairs, Shital Niwas, Maharajganj, Kathmandu, Nepal.

SHREVE, Susan Richards, M.A.; American author; b. 2 May 1939, Toledo, Ohio; d. of Robert Richards and Helen Richards; m. 1st Porter Shreve (divorced 1987); m. 2nd Timothy Seldes 1987; two s. two d.; ed. Univs. of Pennsylvania and Virginia; Prof. of English Literature, George Mason Univ., Fairfax, Va. 1976–; Visiting Prof., Columbia Univ., New York 1982–, Princeton Univ., N.J. 1991, 1992, 1993; Pres. PEN/Faulkner Foundation 1985–; producer The American Voice for TV 1986–; Essayist, MacNeil/Lehrer Newshour; Guggenheim Fellowship; NEA Fellowship in Fiction. *Publications:* novels: A Fortunate Madness 1974, A Woman Like That 1977, Children of Power 1979, Miracle Play 1981, Dreaming of Heroes 1984, Queen of Hearts 1987, A Country of Strangers 1989, Daughters of the New World 1992, The Train Home 1993, Skin Deep, Women and Race 1995, The Visiting Physician 1995; also several children's books. *Address:* 3319 Newark Street, N.W., Washington, DC 20008, U.S.A.

SHRIVER, Duward F., PH.D.; American professor of chemistry; b. 20 Nov. 1934, Glendale, Calif.; s. of D.L. Shriver and J.S. Shriver; m. Shirley A. Clark 1957; two s.; ed. Univ. of California, Berkeley, Univ. of Michigan; instructor, Northwestern Univ., Evanston, Ill. 1961–62, Asst. Prof. 1962–67, Assoc. Prof. 1967–71, Prof. 1971–78, Morrison Prof. of Chem. 1988–, Chair. Chemistry Dept. 1992–95; Alfred P. Sloan Research Fellow 1967–69; Guggenheim Fellow 1983–84; American Chemical Soc. Award for Distinguished Service in Inorganic Chem. 1987, Materials Research Soc. Medal 1990. *Publications:* five books, including Inorganic Chemistry (jtly.) 1990; 295 scientific papers. *Address:* Department of Chemistry, Northwestern University, 2145 Sheridan Road, Evanston, IL 60208, U.S.A. *Telephone:* (847) 491-5655. *Fax:* (847) 491-7713.

SHRIVER, (Robert) Sargent, Jr., A.B., LL.D.; American public servant and politician; b. 9 Nov. 1915, Westminster, Md.; s. of Robert Sargent and Hilda Shriver; m. Eunice Kennedy 1953; four s. one d.; ed. Yale Univ.; admitted to N.Y. Bar 1941; served U.S.N. (Lieut. Commdr.) 1941–45; Asst. Ed. Newsweek 1945–46; Adviser The Joseph P. Kennedy, Jr. Foundation 1955–; Asst. Gen. Man. The Merchandise Mart 1948–61; mem. Chicago Bd. of Educ. 1955–60, Pres. 1956–60; Dir. The Peace Corps 1961–66, Office of Econ. Opportunity 1964–68; Special Asst. to the Pres. 1964–68; Amb. to France 1968–70; Democratic Vice-Presidential Cand. 1972; Partner, Fried, Frank, Harris, Shriver & Jacobson 1971–86, of counsel 1986–; mem. American Comm. on East-West Accord 1978–, Americans for SALT 1979–; Dir. The Arms Control Assen. 1983–; mem. Bd. of Arms Control Assen.; Pres. Special Olympics Int. 1984–, C.E.O. and Chair. 1990–; official of numerous educational bodies; Hon. LL.D., Hon. L.H.D., Hon. D.C.L., etc. from numerous univs.; Golden Heart Presidential Award (Philippines), Médaille de Vermeil (City of Paris), U.S. Presidential Medal of Freedom 1994 and many other national awards. *Publication:* Point of the Lance 1964. *Address:* Special Olympics International, 1325 "G" Street, N.W., Suite 500, Washington, DC 20005, U.S.A. *Telephone:* (202) 628-3630. *Fax:* (202) 347-3460.

SHRONTZ, Frank Anderson, LL.B., M.B.A.; American business executive; b. 14 Dec. 1931, Boise, Ida.; s. of Thurlyn Howard Shrontz and Florence Elizabeth Anderson; m. Harriet Ann Houghton 1954; three s.; ed. Univ. of Idaho, Harvard Graduate School and Stanford Graduate School (Sloan Fellow); Asst. Sec. of the Air Force 1973–75; Asst. Sec. of Defense 1976; Corpn. Vice-Pres., Contract Admin. and Planning 1977; Vice-Pres., Gen. Man. Boeing Commercial Airplane Co. 1978–82, Vice-Pres., Sales, Boeing Commercial Airplane Co. (Div. of Boeing Co.) 1982–84, Pres. 1984–85, Pres., C.E.O. 1986–96 and mem. of Bd. of Dirs., The Boeing Co. 1985–97, Chair. 1988–97, C.E.O. 1988–96, Chair. Emer. 1997–; mem. Bd. of Dirs. Citicorp 1986–, 3M Co., Chevron; Distinguished Service Award, Dept. of Defense. *Leisure interests:* hunting, skiing, golf. *Address:* c/o The Boeing Company, P.O. Box 3707, Seattle, WA 98124, U.S.A. (Office).

SHU HUIGUO; Chinese politician and agronomist; b. July 1938, Jing'an Co., Jiangxi Prov.; ed. Zhejiang Agricultural Coll.; joined CCP 1980; Dir. Dept. of Agric., Animal Husbandry and Fishery, Jiangxi Prov.; Vice-Gov. Jiangxi Prov. 1991–; Vice-Sec. CCP Jiangxi Provincial Cttee. 1995, Sec. 1997–; mem. 15th CCP Cen. Cttee. 1997–. *Address:* Chinese Communist Party Jiangxi Provincial Committee, Nanchang City, Jiangxi Province, People's Republic of China.

SHU SHENGYOU; Chinese politician; b. Dec. 1936, Yushan Co., Jiangxi Prov.; joined CCP 1959; Mayor Jingdezhen City; Vice-Gov. Jiangxi Prov. 1991, Gov. 1996–; Vice-Sec. CCP Jiangxi Provincial Cttee. 1995–; mem. 15th CCP Cen. Cttee. 1997–. *Address:* Jiangxi Provincial Government, Nanchang, Jiangxi Province, People's Republic of China.

SHU TING (GONG SHUTING); Chinese poet; b. (as Gong Peiyu) 18 May 1952, Shima, Zhangzhou City, Fujian Prov.; m. Chen Zhongyi; mem. Writers' Assen. Fujian 1983–, Vice-Chair. 1985–, Council of Writers' Assen. of China 1985–. *Publications:* Shuangweichuan 1982, Shu Ting Shuqing Shixuan 1984, Poesiealbum Shu Ting 1989, Selected Poems of Seven Chinese Poets

1993. *Address:* 13 Zhonghua Road, Gulangyu, Xiamen City, Fujian Province, 361002, People's Republic of China.

SHUE, Elisabeth; American actress; b. 6 Oct. 1963; m. Davis Guggenheim; ed. Wellesley Coll., Harvard Univ.; studied with Sylvie Leigh, Showcase Theater; appeared in Broadway plays including Some Americans Abroad, Birth and After Birth. *Films include:* The Karate Kid 1984, Link 1986, Adventures in Babysitting 1987, Cocktail 1988, Body Wars 1989, Back to the Future Part II 1989, Part III 1990, Soapdish 1991, The Marrying Man 1991, Twenty Bucks 1993, Heart and Souls 1993, Radio Inside 1994, Blind Justice 1994, The Underneath 1995, Leaving Las Vegas 1995, The Trigger Effect 1996, The Saint 1996, Palmetto 1997, Deconstructing Harry 1997, Cousin Bette 1997. *TV films include:* Charles and Diana, Double Switch 1987, Hale the Hero 1992, Blind Justice. *TV series:* Call to Glory 1984. *Address:* c/o Creative Arts Agency, 9830 Wilshire Boulevard, Beverly Hills, CA 90212, U.S.A.

SHUKLA, Vidya Charan, B.A.; Indian politician; b. 2 Aug. 1929, Raipur; s. of Ravi Shanker and Bhawani Shukla; m. Sarala Shukla 1951; three d.; ed. Morris Coll., and Univ. Coll. of Law, Nagpur; mem., Lok Sabha 1957–62, 1962–67, 1967–70, 1971–77; Deputy Minister of Communications and Parl. Affairs Jan.-Feb. 1966; Deputy Minister for Home Affairs 1966–67; Minister of State in Ministry of Home Affairs 1967–70; Minister of Revenue and Expenditure in Ministry of Finance 1970–71, Minister of Defence Production 1971–74, Minister of Planning 1974–75, for Information and Broadcasting 1975–77, for Civil Supplies 1980–81, for Foreign Affairs 1990–91, for Water Resources and Parl. Affairs 1991–96; Pres. Special Organising Cttee., 9th Asian Games, Delhi; Pres. All-India Council of Sports 1981–83; Chair. Nat. Insts. of Physical Educ. and Sports 1981–85; Pres. Indian Olympic Asscn. 1984–88; expelled from Congress (I) Party 1987; f. Jan Monha (People's Front) Oct. 1987. *Leisure interests:* hunting, tracking and photography. *Address:* Labhandi, Raipur District, Madhya Pradesh; B-103, M. S. Flats, Baba Kharak, Singh Marg, New Delhi 110001, India. *Telephone:* 3016463. (Madhya Pradesh).

SHUKRI, Ibrahim; Egyptian politician; b. 22 Sept. 1916; joined Misr al-Fatat (Young Egypt) party 1935; shot in Cairo strike 1935; managed family estate, Sharbeen; Sec.-Gen. Misr al-Fatat 1946; elected Vice-Pres., then Pres. Socialist Party (fmrly. Misr al-Fatat) 1947–53; mem. for Kahaliyya, People's Ass. 1949–52; imprisoned for opposing the monarchy 1952, released after revolution 1952; returned to estate; joined Arab Socialist Union on its formation 1962, elected to Exec. Cttee. 1964; re-elected mem. for Kahaliyya 1964–68; Pres. Farmers' Union and Sec. Professional Asscn. 1965–66; Gov. Wadi al-Gadeed 1968–76; elected to People's Ass. 1976; Minister of Agric. and Agrarian Reform 1977–98, of Land Improvement May-Oct. 1978; Chair. Socialist Labour Party Oct. 1978–; fmrly. Man. Ed. Al-Sha'b (party newspaper); Leader of the Opposition, People's Assembly 1979–86. *Address:* Socialist Labour Party, 12 Sharia Awali el-Ahd, Cairo, Egypt.

SHULL, Clifford Glenwood, PH.D.; American professor of physics; b. 23 Sept. 1915, Pittsburg; s. of David Shull and Daisy Bistline; m. Martha-Nuel Summer 1941; three s.; ed. Carnegie Inst. of Tech. and New York Univ.; research physicist, Texas Co. 1941–46; Chief Physicist, Oak Ridge Nat. Lab. 1946–55; Prof. of Physics, M.I.T. 1955–86, Prof. Emer. 1986–; Fellow, N.A.S., American Physics Soc., A.A.A.S., American Acad. of Arts and Sciences, New York Acad. of Sciences, etc.; Humboldt Sr. U.S. Scientist Award 1979; Gregori Aminoff Prize 1993; shared Nobel Prize for Physics 1994. *Address:* 4 Wingate Road, Lexington, MA 02421, U.S.A. (Home).

SHULL, Harrison, PH.D.; American professor of chemistry; b. 17 Aug. 1923, Princeton, N.J.; s. of Prof. George H. Shull and Mary J. Nicholl; m. 1st Jeanne L. Johnson 1948 (dissolved 1962); two s. two d.; m. 2nd Wil J. Bentley 1962; three s. one d.; ed. Princeton Univ. and Univ. of California, Berkeley; Nat. Research Council post-doctoral Fellow, Univ. of Chicago 1948–49; Asst. Prof., Iowa State Univ. 1949–54; Assoc. Prof., Indiana Univ. 1955–58, Prof. 1958–61, Research Prof. 1961–79, Dir. Research Computing Center 1959–63, Dean Grad. School 1965–72; founder, supervisory Quantum Chem. Program Exchange 1962–87; Vice-Chancellor for Research and Devt., Indiana Univ. 1972–76; Chair. Naval Studies Bd. 1974–79, 1996–; Provost, Rensselaer Polytechnic Inst. 1979–82; Chancellor, Univ. of Colo. at Boulder 1982–85, Prof. of Chem. 1985–88; Provost Naval Postgrad. School 1988–95; Nat. Science Foundation Sr. post-doctoral Fellow 1968–69; Guggenheim Fellow 1954–55; Alfred P. Sloan Research Fellow 1956–58; mem. N.A.S.; Fellow, American Acad. of Arts and Sciences. *Publications:* numerous articles in Journal of Chemical Physics, Physical Review, Journal of Physical Chemistry etc. *Address:* Naval Postgraduate School, Code 09/hs, Monterey, CA 93940, U.S.A.

SHULMAN, Alexandra; British journalist; b. 13 Nov. 1957, London; d. of Milton Shulman and Drusilla Beyfuss; m. Paul Spike 1994; one s.; ed. St. Paul's Girls' School and Univ. of Sussex; Sec. Over-21 magazine; Writer and Commissioning Ed., later Features Ed. Tatler 1982–87; Ed. Women's Page, Sunday Telegraph 1987, later Deputy Ed. 7 Days current affairs photo/reportage; Features Ed. Vogue 1988; Ed. GQ 1990; Ed. Vogue 1992–. *Address:* Condé Nast Publications, Vogue House, Hanover Square, London, W1R 0AD, England. *Telephone:* 0171-499 9080.

SHULMAN, Lawrence Edward, M.D., PH.D., F.A.C.P.; American biomedical research administrator and rheumatologist; b. 25 July 1919, Boston, Mass.; s. of David Herman Shulman and Belle (Tishler) Shulman; m. 1st Pauline K. Flint 1946, 2nd Reni Trudinger 1959; one s. two d.; ed. Harvard and Yale Univs.; Research Assoc. John B. Pierce Foundation, New Haven, Conn. 1942–45; Intern, Resident and Fellow in Internal Medicine, Johns Hopkins Hospital and Univ. 1949–53; Dir. Connective Tissue Div. Johns Hopkins Univ. Medical School 1955–75; Assoc. Prof. of Medicine, Johns Hopkins Univ. 1964–; Assoc. Dir. for Arthritis, Musculosceletal and Skin Diseases, N.I.H. 1976–82, Dir. 1982–86; Dir. Nat. Inst. of Arthritis and Musculoskeletal and Skin Diseases 1986–94, Dir. Emer. 1994–; N.I.H. Emissary for Clinical Research 1994–; several awards. *Publications:* over 100 scientific publications. *Leisure interests:* music, politics. *Address:* 6302 Swords Way, Bethesda, MD 20817, U.S.A.

SHULMAN, Robert Gerson, M.A., PH.D.; American biophysicist; b. 3 March 1924, New York; s. of Joshua S. Shulman and Freda (Lipshay) Shulman; m. 1st Saralee Deutsch 1952 (died 1983); three s.; m. 2nd Stephanie S. Spangler 1986; ed. Columbia Univ.; Research Assoc. Columbia Univ. Radiation Lab., New York 1949; AEC Fellow in Chem. Calif. Inst. of Tech. 1949–50; Head, Semiconductor Research Section, Hughes Aircraft Co. Culver City, Calif. 1950–53; mem. tech. staff, Bell Labs., Murray Hill, N.J. 1953–66, Head, Biophysics Research Dept. 1966–79; Prof. of Molecular Biophysics and Biochemistry, Yale Univ. 1979–, Dir. Div. of Biological Sciences 1979–94, Sterling Prof. of Biophysics and Biochemistry 1994–, Emissary for Clinical Research 1995–; numerous visiting professorships, lectureships etc.; mem. N.A.S., Inst. of Medicine; Guggenheim Fellow, Cambridge 1961–62. *Address:* Yale University MR Center, Department of Molecular Biophysics and Biochemistry, P.O. Box 208024, New Haven, CT 06520, U.S.A. (Office).

SHULTZ, George Pratt, B.A., PH.D.; American politician, economist and educator; b. 13 Dec. 1920, New York; s. of Birl E. and Margaret Lennox Pratt Shultz; m. 1st Helena M. O'Brien 1946; two s. three d.; m. 2nd Charlotte Mailliard Swig 1997; ed. Princeton Univ. and M.I.T.; Assoc. Prof. of Industrial Relations, M.I.T. 1955–57; Sr. Staff Economist, President's Council of Econ. Advisers 1955–56; Prof. of Industrial Relations, Grad. School of Business, Univ. of Chicago 1957–68, Dean, Grad. School of Business 1962–68; Pres. Industrial Research Asscn. 1968; U.S. Sec. of Labor 1969–70; Dir. Office of Man. and Budget, Exec. Office of the Pres. 1970–72; U.S. Sec. of Treasury 1972–74; Chair. Council on Econ. Policy 1973–74; Sec. of State 1982–89; Exec. Vice-Pres. Bechtel Corpn. 1974–75, Pres. 1975–77, Vice-Chair. 1977–81, Pres. Bechtel Group Inc. 1981–82; Prof. of Man. and Public Policy, Grad. School of Business, Stanford Univ. 1974–82, of Int. Economy 1989–91, Prof. Emer. 1991–; Chair. J.P. Morgan Int. Council, Advisory Council Inst. of Int. Studies, Stanford, Gov's. Econ. Policy Advisory Bd., Calif.; mem. Bd. GM Corpn. Advisory Council, Gulfstream Aerospace Corpn., AirTouch Communications, Bechtel Group Inc., Charles Schwab & Co.; Chair. Pres. Reagan's Econ. Policy Advisory Bd. 1981–82; mem. Bd. of Trustees, Center for Advancement of Study in the Behavioral Sciences, Stanford, Calif.; mem. Gilead Sciences Bd.; Distinguished Fellow, Hoover Inst., Stanford Univ. 1989–; Jefferson Award 1986; Grand Cordon, Order of the Rising Sun 1989, Seoul Peace Prize 1992. *Publications include:* Pressures on Wage Decisions, Labor Problems,The Dynamics of a Labor Market, Management Organization and the Computer, Strategies for the Displaced Worker, Guidelines, Informal Controls and the Market Place, Workers and Wages in the Urban Labor Market, Leaders and Followers in an Age of Ambiguity, Economic Policy beyond the Headlines (co-author), Turmoil and Triumph: My Years as Secretary of State 1993. *Leisure interests:* golf, tennis. *Address:* Hoover Institution, Stanford, CA 94305-6010, U.S.A. *Telephone:* (650) 725-3492. *Fax:* (650) 723-5441.

SHULTZ, Mikhail Mikhailovich, PH.D.; Russian chemist; b. 1 July 1919, Petrograd; m. Nina Dimitrievna Paromova 1944; m.; two s.; ed. Leningrad State Univ.; served in Second World War 1941–45; Asst. Prof. Leningrad State Univ. 1950–53, Assoc. Prof. 1953–65, Full Prof. 1965, Head of Lab. Research Inst. of Chem. 1965–72, Dean Chem. Dept. 1967–72; Dir. I. Grebenshchikov Inst. of Silicate Chem. U.S.S.R (now Russian). Acad. of Sciences 1972–; mem. U.S.S.R. (now Russian) Acad. of Sciences 1979–; research in physical chem., thermodynamics of heterogeneous systems, chem. and electrochem. of glass; Chair. Scientific Council for New Non-Metallic Inorganic Materials 1990–; Vice-Pres. Soc. of Ceramics 1991–; Deputy Academician-Sec. Dept. of Physics, Chem. and Tech. of Inorganic Materials, Russian Acad. of Science 1991–; Ed. Soviet Journal of Glass Physics and Chem. 1975–90; mem. editorial bds. Cement and Concrete Research 1976–94, Revue de Chimie Minérale 1981–87; U.S.S.R. State Prizes 1973, 1986; Hammer and Sickle Gold Medal 1991; Hero of Socialist Labour 1991; Patriotic War Orders (2nd Class) 1945, 1995; Orders of Labour, Red Banner 1971, 1975; Order of Lenin 1979, 1991. *Publications include:* Dependence of Electrode Properties of Glass on their Structure 1963, Contemporary Ideas concerning the Structure of Glasses and their Properties 1988, numerous articles in scientific journals. *Leisure interests:* painting, photography, gardening. *Address:* I. Grebenshchikov Institute of Silicate Chemistry, Russian Academy of Sciences, Odoevskogo str., 24 Korp. 2, St. Petersburg 199155, Russia. *Telephone:* (812) 350 6516. *Fax:* (812) 218 5401 (Office); 553-72-72 (Home).

SHUMAKOV, Valery Ivanovich, M.D., PH.D.; Russian surgeon and transplantologist; b. 9 Nov. 1931, Moscow; s. of Ivan Shumakov and Nataly Shumakova; m. Nataly Shumakova 1960; one s. one d.; ed. Sechenov First Medical Inst.; worked as surgeon, Head of Lab. of Assisted Circulation and

Artificial Heart, Head of Dept. of Transplantology and Artificial Organs, Inst. of Clinical and Experimental Surgery of U.S.S.R. (now Russian) Ministry of Public Health 1956–74; Dir. Russian Research Inst. of transplantology and artificial organs 1974–; Head Dept. of Physics of Living Systems, Moscow Inst. of Physics and Tech.; carried out the first heart, liver, pancreas and spleen transplants in clinical practice in Russia; carried out the first implantations of artificial cardiac ventricle and artificial heart in Russia; mem. Russian Acad. of Medical Sciences 1988, Russian Acad. of Sciences 1993, Russian Acad. of Medical and Tech. Sciences 1993; Chair. Scientific Council on Transplantology and Artificial Organs, Presidium of Acad. of Medical Sciences; Ed. journal Transplantology and Artificial Organs; mem. admin. of Russian Soc. of Cardiovascular Surgeons; mem. of numerous European and int. scientific socs; U.S.S.R. State Prize, 1971; Meritorious Inventor of Russian Fed. 1978; Hero of Socialist Labour 1990. *Publications:* 18 monographs, 70 patents and more than 350 scientific works in the field of surgery. *Leisure interests:* swimming, literature. *Address:* Research Institute of Transplantology and Artificial Organs, Shchukinskaya ul. 1, 123436 Moscow, Russia. *Telephone:* (095) 196-18-03. *Fax:* (095) 943-00-08.

SHUMEIKO, Vladimir Filippovich, C.TECH.SC.; Russian politician, economist and manager; b. 10 Feb. 1945, Rostov-Don; m.; two d.; ed. Rostov Polytech. Inst.; worked in factories as foreman, engineer, chief engineer, Dir.-Gen. Concern Krasnodar Factory of Measuring Instruments –1991; People's Deputy of Russia 1990–92; Vice-Chair. Supreme Soviet of Russia 1991–92, First Deputy Prime Minister of Russia 1992–93; Pres. Confed. of Entrepreneurs' Unions of Russia 1992–93; mem. Council of Fed. (Upper House of Parl.) 1993–96, Chair. 1994–96; Founder and Chair. Reform–New Course Movt. 1996–. *Publication:* Russian Reforms and Federalism 1995. *Leisure interests:* fishing, woodworking, collecting small bells. *Address:* Novi Arbat 19, Moscow, Russia. *Telephone:* (095) 203-47-47.

SHUMWAY, Norman Edward, M.D., PH.D.; American surgeon; b. 1923, Kalamazoo, Mich.; m. Mary Lou Sturman; one s. three d.; ed. Vanderbilt Univ. and Univ. of Minnesota; Intern, Univ. of Minnesota Hospitals 1949–50, Medical Fellow in Surgery 1950–51, 1953, 1954; Nat. Heart Inst. Research Fellow 1954–56, Special Trainee 1956–57; mem. Surgical Staff, Stanford Univ. Hospitals 1958–, Asst. Prof. of Surgery 1959–61, Assoc. Prof. 1961–65, Head of Div. of Cardiovascular Surgery 1964–74, Prof. of Surgery 1965–96, Prof. Cardiovascular Surgery 1974–96, Francis and Charles D. Field Prof. 1976–96; Chair. Dept. of Cardiovascular Surgery, Stanford Univ. Medical Center 1974–96; has performed heart transplant operations. *Address:* c/o Department of Cardiovascular Surgery, Stanford University Medical Center, 300 Pasteur Drive, Palo Alto, CA 94304, U.S.A.

SHUSHKEVICH, Stanislau Stanislavavich, D.SC.; Belarus politician; b. 15 Dec. 1934, Minsk; m. Irina Kuzminichna Shushkevich; one s. one d.;. ed. Belarus Univ.; mem. CPSU 1967–91; researcher, Inst. of Physics, Belarus Acad. of Sciences 1959–60; eng. Minsk Radio Plant 1960–61; Chief eng., Head of Section Belarus Univ. 1961–67; Prof. Minsk Radiotechnical Inst. 1967–69; Head of Chair., Belarus Univ. 1969–86, Pro-Rector 1986–90; involvement in politics 1989– (as critic of govt. negligence in aftermath of Chernobyl accident); mem. Supreme Soviet (backed by opposition Belarus Popular Front) 1990–91; Chair. Supreme Soviet 1991–94; mem. –1996; mem. Civil Action faction; Cand. in presidential elections 1994; Corresp. mem. Belarus Acad. of Sciences; Belarus State Prize; Council of Ministers Prize.

SHVYDKOY, Mikhail Yefimovich, D.F.A.; Russian theatre scholar and politician; b. 5 Sept. 1940, Kyrgyzia; m.; two d.; ed. Moscow Lunacharsky Inst. of Theatre Art; reviewer Radio Co., Ed.-in-Chief magazine Theatr 1973–90; Ed.-in-Chief Publrs. Co. Kultura, Russian Fed. Ministry of Culture 1990–93; Deputy Minister of Culture 1993–97; Deputy Chair. Russian TV and Radio Co., Ed.-in-Chief TV Channel Kultura 1997–98; Chair. All-Russian State Radio and TV Holding 1998–; Chair. Nat. Comm. World Decade of Culture at UNESCO, Vice Pres. Cttee. on Communications Int. Inst. of Theatre at UNESCO. *Publications:* Dramatic Composition: Theatre and Life, Secrets of Lonely Comedians, Sketches on Foreign Theatre of the Late 20th Century; numerous articles on history and contemporary state of theatre in Russian and foreign periodicals. *Address:* VGTRK, 5th Yamskogo polya str. 19/21, 127124 Moscow, Russia (Office). *Telephone:* (095) 251-40-50 (Office).

SIAGURU, Sir Anthony, K.B.E.; Papua New Guinea fmr. government minister and international public servant; b. 4 Nov. 1946, Wewak, East Sepik Prov.; s. of Anthony Khaisir and Maria Krakemoine; m. Mina Isikini 1972; three s.; ed. Papua New Guinea and Harvard Univs.; Sec. Dept. of Foreign Affairs and Trade 1975–80; M.P. 1982–87, Minister of Public Service, of Youth and Devt.; Foundation Chair. S. Pacific Games 1988–90; Deputy Sec.-Gen. (Political) Commonwealth Secr. 1990–95; Chair. Port Moresby Stock Exchange, Pacific Reinsurance Corpn., PNG Centre for Commercial Disputes, PNG Chapter of Transparency Int.; Dir. Kula Fund, Lihir Gold, Steamships Trading, PEACE Foundation of Melanesia and Red Shield Appeal; columnist PNG Post Courier; fmr. mem. Bd. of Man. Inst. of Commonwealth Studies; Hon. Corresp. Sec. Royal Over-Seas League, fmr. mem. Cen. Council; mem. Royal Commonwealth Soc. *Publications include:* The United States' Dilemma, Ethics of Public Decision-making; numerous articles on nat. and int. affairs. *Leisure interests:* tennis, fishing, gardening. *Address:* P.O. Box 850, Port Moresby, NCD, Papua New Guinea. *Telephone:* 3092000. *Fax:* 3092099.

SIALE BILEKA, Silvestre; Equatorial Guinean politician; fmr. Minister of Justice and Religion; Prime Minister and Head of Govt. of Equatorial Guinea 1991–93, 1993–95; Minister of Foreign Affairs and Francophone Affairs 1991–92; mem. Partido Democrático de Guinea Ecuatorial (PDGE). *Address:* c/o Office of the Prime Minister, Malabo, Equatorial Guinea.

SIAZON, Domingo L., B.A., B.SC., M.P.A.; Philippine politician and international civil servant; b. 1939, Aparri, Cagayan; m.; ed. Ateneo de Manila Univ., Tokyo Univ., Japan, Harvard Univ., U.S.A.; interpreter and translator, then Attaché, and Third Sec. and Vice-Consul, Embassy in Tokyo 1964–68; Acting Resident Rep. to IAEA, Alt. Perm. Rep. to UNIDO, Third, Second, then First Sec., Embassy in Berne 1968–73; First Sec. and Consul-Gen., Embassy in Vienna, then Amb. to Austria, also Perm. Rep. to IAEA, UNIDO and UN at Vienna 1973–85; Dir.-Gen. UNIDO 1985–93; Minister of Foreign Affairs May 1995–. *Address:* Department of Foreign Affairs, 2330 Roxas Blvd., Pasay City, Metro Manila, Philippines.

SIBLEY, Dame Antoinette, D.B.E.; British ballerina; b. 27 Feb. 1939, Bromley, Kent; d. of Edward G. Sibley and Winifred Smith; m. 1st Michael Somes 1964 (divorced 1973, died 1994); m. 2nd Panton Corbett 1974; one s. one d.; joined the Royal Ballet 1956, Soloist 1959, Prin. Ballerina 1960–; dances leading roles in: Swan Lake, Sleeping Beauty, Coppelia, The Nutcracker, La Fille Mal Gardée, Romeo and Juliet, Jabez and the Devil (cr. role of Mary), The Dream (cr. Titania), Jazz Calendar (cr. Friday's Child), Enigma Variations (cr. Dorabella), Thais (cr. Thais), Triad (cr. the Girl), Manon (cr. Manon), Soupirs (cr. pas de deux), Symphonic Variations, Daphnis and Chloe, Varii Capricci, The Good-Humoured Ladies, A Month in the Country, etc.; L'Invitation au Voyage; made film The Turning Point 1978; Vice-Pres. Royal Acad. of Dancing 1989–91, Pres. 1991–. *Publications:* Sibley and Dowell 1976, Antoinette Sibley 1981, Reflections of a Ballerina 1985. *Leisure interests:* doing nothing, opera, cinema, reading. *Address:* c/o Royal Academy of Dancing, 36 Battersea Square, London, SW11 3RA; c/o Royal Academy of Dancing, 36 Battersea Square, London, SW11 3LT, England.

SIBOMANA, Adrien; Burundian politician; fmr. Deputy Speaker Nat. Ass.; fmr. Gov. Muramvya Prov.; Vice-Pres. Comm. on Nat. Unity; Prime Minister 1988–94, also fmr. Minister of Planning.

SICILIANO, Enzo, PH.D.; Italian novelist, playwright and journalist; b. 27 May 1934, Rome; s. of Natale Siciliano and Giuseppina Jenzi; m. Flaminia Petrucci 1963; two s.; literary critic, La Stampa, Turin 1969–77; Jt. Ed., with Alberto Moravia and Francesca Sanvitale, Nuovi Argomenti 1972–; Literary Critic, Corriere della Sera, Milan 1977–; Theatre Critic, Epoca, Milan 1982–85; Literary Critic, L'Espresso, Rome 1985–; Premio Viareggio 1981. *Publications:* Racconti ambigui 1963, Autobiografia letteraria 1971, Rosa (pazza e disperata) 1973, La notte matrigna 1975, Puccini 1977, Vita di Pasolini 1978, La voce di Otello 1982, Diamante 1984, La Letteratura Italiana (Vols. 1, 2, 3) 1986, 1987, 1988, Cuore e fantasmi 1990, Carta Blu 1992. *Address:* Nuovi Argomenti, via Sicilia 136, 00187 Rome (Office); via Caroncini 53, 00197 Rome, Italy (Home). *Telephone:* 06 47497376 (Office).

SICKINGHE, Jonkheer Feyo Onno Joost, LL.D.; Netherlands business executive (retd.); b. 1 May 1926, The Hague; s. of Jonkheer D. W. Sickinghe and Jonkvrouwe W. J. M. E. Radermacher Schorer; m. M. C. van Eeghen 1952; two s. two d.; ed. Univ. of Utrecht; Solicitor 1952–55; various functions within Stork N.V. 1955–63; Man. Dir. Koninklijke Machinefabriek Stork N.V. 1963–69; Pres. Bd. of Man. and C.E.O. Stork N.V. 1969–89; fmr. Chair. Foundation Amsterdam Promotion, French Chamber of Commerce and Ind. in the Netherlands; mem. numerous Supervisory Bds. including Stork N.V. and FMO; Commdr. Order of Oranje Nassau; Officier Légion d'honneur. *Leisure interests:* sailing, theatre. *Address:* Oud Blaricummerweg 7, Naarden, Netherlands. *Telephone:* 02159-43728.

SIDDALL, Sir Norman, Kt., C.B.E., B.ENG., D.SC., F.ENG., F.I.MIN.E., C.B.I.M., F.R.S.A.; British mining engineer; b. 4 May 1918; m. Pauline Arthur 1943; two s. one d.; ed. King Edward VII School, Sheffield, Sheffield Univ.; with B.A. Collieries Ltd. as Undermanager, then Asst. Man. of Gedling Colliery, later as Man. of Bestwood Colliery, Nottingham 1936–47; Area Gen. Man. of No. 5 Area in East Midlands Div.; Area Gen. Man. of No. 1 (Bolsover) Area 1957; Chief Mining Eng., H.Q. Production Dept. 1966; Dir.-Gen. of Production 1967; mem. Nat. Coal Bd. 1971–83, Deputy Chair. 1973–82, Chair. 1982–83; Vice-Chair. Int. Organizing Cttee. World Mining Congress 1977; Dir. British Mining Consultants Ltd., CIN Management Ltd.; D.L. (Notts.); Hon. D.Sc. (Nottingham) 1982; Krupinski Medal 1982. *Address:* Brentwood, High Oakham Road, Mansfield, Notts, NG18 5AJ, England.

SIDDHI SAVETSILA, Air Chief Marshal; Thai politician and air force officer; b. 7 Jan. 1919, Bangkok; s. of Phraya Wanapruksapijarn and Khunying Wanapruksapijarn; m. Khunying Thida Savetsila 1952; two s. two d.; ed. Chulalongkorn Univ. and M.I.T.; fmr. pilot officer, Royal Thai Air Force and Adviser to Royal Thai Air Force; mem. Nat. Ass. 1973, Nat. Reform Council 1976; Minister, Prime Minister's Office 1979–80, Second Kriangsak Govt.; Sec.-Gen. Nat. Security Council 1975–80; Minister of Foreign Affairs 1980–90; M.P. 1983–90; Leader Social Action Party 1986–90; Deputy Prime Minister 1986; Special ADC to H.M. the King 1986; Hon. LL.D. (Philippines) 1983, (Nat. Univ. Singapore) 1985; numerous decorations. *Leisure interests:* reading, exercise. *Address:* c/o Ministry of Foreign Affairs, Saranrom Palace, Bangkok 10200, Thailand. *Telephone:* 225-6312.

SIDDIKY, B. A., B.L.; Bangladeshi diplomatist; b. 4 Jan. 1915, Dhaka; m. (wife deceased); nine c.; ed. Calcutta and Dhaka Univs.; Advocate, Calcutta High Court 1946, Advocate-Gen. of E. Pakistan 1957–60, served on Bench of Dhaka High Court 1960–67, Chief Justice of E. Pakistan 1967–72; mem. Exec. Cttee. of World Judges Conf., Geneva and ex-officio mem. Supreme Judicial Council of Pakistan; past Chair. of Pakistan and Bangladesh Red Cross Socs.; past Pres. of Bangladesh Muslim League; Cabinet Minister and Adviser to Pres. of Bangladesh 1985–86; Perm. Rep. of Bangladesh to the UN 1986–89. *Address:* c/o Ministry of Foreign Affairs, Topkhana Road, Dhaka, Bangladesh.

SIDKI, Aziz, B.ENG., M.A., PH.D.; Egyptian politician; b. 1 July 1920, Cairo; ed. Cairo Univ., Univ. of Oregon and Harvard Univ.; taught Cairo Univ.; Tech. Counsellor to the President 1953; Ministry for Industry 1956–63, Deputy Prime Minister and Minister for Industry and Mineral Wealth 1964–65; Minister for Industry, Petroleum and Mineral Wealth 1968–71; Deputy Prime Minister 1971–72; Prime Minister 1972–73; Acting Gen. Sec. Arab Socialist Union 1971–73; Personal Asst. to Pres. Sadat 1973–75; fmr. Amb. to France; has participated in various int. confs. on industrial affairs. *Address:* c/o The Presidency, Cairo, Egypt.

SIDLIN, Murry, M.M.; American conductor; b. 6 May 1940, Baltimore, Md.; ed. Academia Chigiana, Siena, Cornell Univ.; Asst. Conductor, Baltimore Symphony Orchestra 1971–73; Dir. of Md. Ballet Co. 1971–73; Prin. Conductor Baltimore Chamber Players 1971–73; Resident Conductor Nat. Symphony Orchestra under Dorati 1973–77, Wolf Trap American Univ. Music Acad. 1974; Host and Conductor Children's TV series Music is . . . . 1977; Music Dir. Tulsa Philharmonic Orchestra 1978–80; Music Dir. Hew Haven Symphony 1977–, Long Beach Symphony 1980–, Resident Conductor Aspen Music Festival 1978–; Guest Conductor with numerous orchestras in N. America, also performances in Europe and at the Festival Casals in Puerto Rico; Carnegie Hall début 1975; winner of Baltimore Symphony Orchestra Young Conductor's Competition 1962. *Address:* Shaw Concerts Inc., 3436 Springhill Road, Lafayette, CA 94549, U.S.A.

SIDOROV, Vasily Sergeyevich; Russian diplomatist; b. 2 Jan. 1945, Moscow; m.; two c.; ed. Moscow Inst. of Int. Relations; on staff Ministry of Foreign Affairs 1967–; Amb. to Greece; Deputy Head Dept. of int. orgs. 1990–91; Deputy Perm. Rep. of Russia to UN 1991–94, First Deputy, Minister of Foreign Affairs 1994–95, Deputy Minister 1995–98; Perm. Rep. to UN in Geneva 1998–. *Address:* Permanent Mission of Russia to the United Nations, Avenue de la Paix 5, 1201 Geneva, Switzerland. *Telephone:* (022) 733 1870.

SIDOROV, Veniamin Aleksandrovich; Russian physicist; b. 19 Oct. 1930, Babarino, Suzdal Dist., Vladimir Region; s. of Alexandr Mikhailovich Sidorov and Maria Vasilievna Sidorova; m. 1st Gendlina Larisa Semenovna 1962; one s. one d.; m. 2nd Lupashina Irina Sergeevna 1975; one s.; ed. Moscow State Univ.; attached to Inst. of Atomic Energy, then Budker Inst. of Nuclear Physics, Siberian Div. of U.S.S.R. (now Russian) Acad. of Sciences 1962–, Deputy Dir. of Inst. 1977–; Corresp. mem. U.S.S.R. (now Russian) Acad. of Sciences 1968–; Lenin Prize 1967, U.S.S.R. Council of Ministers Prize 1985, U.S.S.R. State Prize 1989. *Publications:* numerous works, mainly on colliding beam experiments in elementary particle physics. *Address:* Institute of Nuclear Physics, Siberian Division of Russian Academy of Sciences, Lavrentiev prospect 11, 630090 Novosibirsk, Russia. *Telephone:* (03832) 34-10-31 (Office); 35-09-10 (Home). *Fax:* (03832) 35-21-63.

SIDOROV, Yevgeniy Yurievich; Russian literary critic and essayist; b. 11 Feb. 1938, Sverdlovsk (now Ekaterinburg); s. of Yuri Sidorov and Natalia Sidorova; m. Vera Indurskaya 1972; two s.; ed. Moscow State Univ., Acad. of Social Sciences of the Cen. Cttee. of CPSU; mem. CPSU 1962–92; Ed. Moskovski Komsomolets 1962–65, Literaturnaya Gazeta 1965–67, Yunost 1967–72; maj. works devoted to the analysis of Russian contemporary literature; Pro-rector of Moscow Gorky Literary Inst. 1978, Rector 1987–92; Minister of Culture of Russia 1992–97; mem. State Duma (Parl.) 1993–95; Perm. Rep. to UNESCO 1998–; several nat. and int. literary prizes including Mediterranium Golden Oliva (Palermo, Italy) 1991. *Publications:* On the Stylistic Variety of Soviet Prose, Time to Write, On the Way to Synthesis, Yevgeniy Yevtushenko, The Flow of Poetry Days, Pages and Fates; articles on cinema and theatre. *Leisure interests:* chess, friends, travelling. *Address:* Permanent Mission of Russia to UNESCO, 1 rue Miollis, 75015 Paris; 135 rue de la Tour, 75116 Paris, France. *Telephone:* (01) 45.04.37.52; (01) 42.12.84.48. *Fax:* (01) 42.67.51.99.

SIDQI, Atif; Egyptian politician and fmr. professor of law; fmr. Prof. Cairo Univ. Law School; fmr. adviser on econ. affairs; to Vice-Pres. Mubarak; mem. Shura; fmr. Cultural Attaché, Embassy, Paris; Head Cen. Auditing Agency 1981–86; Prime Minister of Egypt 1986–96, also fmr. Minister of Int. Co-operation; mem. Nat. Democratic Party. *Address:* c/o Office of the Prime Minister, Cairo, Egypt.

SIEBERT, Horst, PH.D.; German economist; b. 20 March 1938, Neuwied; ed. Univ. of Cologne, Wesleyan Univ., Conn., Univ. of Münster; Asst. Prof. of Econs. Texas A & M Univ.; tenured position Univ. of Münster; Prof. of Econs. and Chair. of Econs. and Int. Trade, Univ. of Mannheim 1969–84; Prof. of Econs. and Chair. of Int. Econs. Univ. of Konstanz 1984–89; Chair. of Theoretical Econs. and Pres. Inst. of World Econs. Univ. of Kiel 1989–; mem. Council of Govt. Econ. Advisers 1990–. *Publications:* The New Economic Landscape in Europe 1991, Aussenwirtschaft 1994, Economics of the Environment: Theory and Policy 1998, Arbeitslos ohne Ende? Strategien für mehr Beschäftigung 1998, The World Economy 1999. *Address:* Kiel Institute of World Economics, Düsternbrooker Weg 120, 24105 Kiel, Germany. *Telephone:* (431) 8814-236. *Fax:* (431) 8814-501.

SIEFF, Jeanloup; French photographer; b. 30 Nov. 1933, Paris; m. Barbara Willms-Rix 1979; one s. one d.; ed. coll. Paris and Photography School, Vevey, Switzerland; photo-journalist and fashion photographer, Paris 1954–58; Magnum Agency 1958–59; worked in New York for magazines including Harper's Bazaar, Esquire 1961–66; returned to work in Paris on magazines, books, TV; exhbns. at Hamilton Gallery, London 1983, 1986, Museum of Modern Art, Paris 1986, Beijing and Guangdong 1992, Osaka 1993, Tokyo 1994, Berlin 1997, Warsaw 1997, Paris 1997, Brussels 1999, New York 1999; Prix Niepce 1959, Grand Prix National de Photographie 1992; Chevalier des arts et des lettres, Chevalier, Légion d'honneur. *Publications:* La Photo 1976, Death Valley 1978, Portraits de dames assises 1982, Sicily 1984, Torses nus 1986, Demain le temps sera plus vieux 1990, Derrières 1994, Danse 1997, Portraits 1999. *Leisure interests:* writing, reading, tap dance, tennis, bicycles, children. *Address:* 87 rue Ampère, 75017 Paris, France. *Telephone:* (1) 42-67-13-48. *Fax:* (1) 40-53-04-18.

SIEFF OF BRIMPTON, Baron (Life Peer), cr. 1980, of Brimpton in the Royal County of Berkshire; **Marcus Joseph Sieff,** Kt., O.B.E., M.A.; British business executive (retd.); b. 2 July 1913; s. of late Lord Sieff; m. 1st Rosalie Fromson 1937 (divorced 1947); one s.; m. 2nd Elsa Gosen 1951 (divorced 1953); m. 3rd Brenda Beith 1956 (divorced 1962); one d; m. 4th Mrs. Pauline L. Moretzki (née Spatz) 1963; one d.; ed. Manchester Grammar School, St. Paul's, and Corpus Christi Coll., Cambridge; served War 1939–45, R.A.; joined Marks and Spencer Ltd., 1935, Dir. 1954, Asst. Man.-Dir. 1963, Vice-Chair. 1965, Jt. Man. Dir 1967–83, Deputy Chair. 1971, Chair, Marks and Spencer PLC 1972–84, Pres. 1984–85; Hon. Pres. 1985–; mem. British Nat. Export Council 1965–71 (Chair. Export Cttee. for Israel 1965–68); Hon. Pres., Jt. Israel Appeal; Vice Pres., Policy Studies Inst., mem. Exec. 1975–; Hon. Pres. Anglo-Israeli Chamber of Commerce, 1975–; Chair. First Int. Bank of Israel Trust 1983–94; Dir. N. M. Rothschild & Sons 1983–; Chair. (non-exec.) The Independent 1986–92; Chair. Newspaper Publishing Oct. 1986–; Trustee, Nat. Portrait Gallery 1986–93; Hon. F.R.C.S. 1984; Hon. LL.D. (St. Andrews) 1983, (Reading) 1985, (Leicester) 1988, Hon. Dr. (Babson Coll., Mass.) 1984; Hambro Award, Businessman of the Year, 1977; Hon. Master of Bench of Inner Temple 1987; Aims Nat. Free Enterprise Award, 1978; B'nai B'rith Int. Gold Medallion for Humanitarianism 1982; Retailer of the Year Award, Nat. Retail Merchants' Asscn. 1982, British Inst. of Management Gold Medal 1983. *Publications:* Don't Ask the Price (autobiog.) 1987, Marcus Sieff on Management 1990. *Address:* c/o House of Lords, London, SW1A 0PW, England.

SIEGBAHN, Kai Manne Börje, B.SC., D.PHIL.; Swedish physicist; b. 20 April 1918, Lund; s. of Dr. Manne Siegbahn (winner of 1924 Nobel Prize for Physics) and of Karin (née Högbom) Siegbahn; m. Anna-Brita Rhedin 1944; three s.; Prof. of Physics, Royal Inst. of Tech., Stockholm 1951–54, Univ. of Uppsala 1954–84; mem. Royal Swedish Acad. of Science, Royal Swedish Acad. of Eng. Sciences, Royal Soc. of Science, Royal Acad. of Arts and Science of Uppsala, Royal Physiographical Soc. of Lund, Societas Scientiarum Fennica, Norwegian Acad. of Science, Royal Norwegian Soc. of Sciences and Letters, Papal Acad. of Science 1986–; Hon. mem. American Acad. of Arts and Sciences, Comité Int. des Poids et Mesures, Paris; Pres. Int. Union of Pure and Applied Physics; Hon. D.Sc. (Univ. of Durham) 1972, (Univ. of Basel) 1980, (Univ. of Liège) 1980, (Upsala Coll., N.J.) 1982, (Sussex) 1983; Lindblom Prize 1945, Björkén Prize 1955, 1977, half-share of Nobel Prize for Physics 1981 for work on atomic spectroscopy; Celsius Medal 1962, Sixten Heyman Award 1971, Harrison Howe Award 1973, Maurice F. Hasler Award 1975, Charles Frederick Chandler Medal 1976, Torbern Bergman Medal 1979, Pittsburgh Award of Spectroscopy 1982, Röntgen Medal 1985, Finggi Award 1986, Humboldt Award 1986, Premo Castiglione Di Sicilia 1990. *Publications:* Beta- and Gamma-Ray Spectroscopy 1955, Alpha-, Beta- and Gamma-Ray Spectroscopy 1965, ESCA-Atomic Molecular and Solid Structure Studied by Means of Electron Spectroscopy 1967, ESCA Applied to Free Molecules 1969 and 450 scientific papers. *Address:* c/o Institute of Physics, University of Uppsala, Box 530, 751 21 Uppsala, Sweden (Office).

SIEGEL, Ira Theodore, M.B.A.; American publishing executive; b. 23 Sept. 1944; s. of David A. Siegel and Rose Minsky; m. Sharon R. Sacks 1965; three d.; ed. New York and Long Island Univs.; Business Man. Buttenheim Publishing Co., New York 1965–72; Corp. Vice-Pres. (research) Cahners Publishing Co. (Div. Reed Publishing Co. U.S.A., Boston) 1972–86; Pres. R. R. Bowker Publishing Co. (Div. Reed Publishing, U.S.A., New York) 1986–91, Martindale-Hubbell Div. NJ 1990–91, Reed Reference Publishing 1991–95, Pres., C.E.O. 1993–95; Pres., C.E.O. Lexis-Nexis 1995–97; Vice-Chair., C.O.O., Pres. Advanstar Holdings, New York 1998–; mem. Bd. Reed Elsevier, U.S.A. *Address:* 8 Brentwood Drive, North Caldwell, NJ 07006, U.S.A.

SIEGELMAN, Don Eugene, J.D.; American politician; b. 24 Feb. 1946, Mobile, Ala.; m. Lori Allen; one s. one d.; ed. Univs. of Alabama, Georgetown and Oxford; called to bar Ala. 1972; Sec. of State of Ala. 1979–87, Attorney-Gen. 1987–94, Lieut.-Gov. 1996–99, Gov. of Alabama Jan. 1999–; Democrat. *Address:* Governor's Mansion, 1142 S. Perry Street, Montgomery, AL 36104, U.S.A.

SIEMIĄTKOWSKI, Zbigniew, Polish politician; b. 8 Oct. 1957, Ciechanów; m.; one d.; ed. Warsaw Univ.; Sr. Asst. Warsaw Univ. 1982–89; Deputy to Sejm (Parl.) 1991–; mem. Comm. for Nat. and Ethnic Minorities; mem. Comm. of Justice; mem. Polish United Workers' Party (PZPR) 1978–90; mem. Social Democracy of Polish Repub. (SdRP) 1990–; Minister of Internal Affairs 1996; mem. Council of Ministers 1997. *Leisure interest:* family, tourism. *Address:* Sejm R.P., ul. Wiejska 4/6/8, 00-902 Warsaw, Poland. *Telephone:* (22) 625 37 82; 694 22 26.

SIEPMANN, Mary Aline (Mary Wesley), C.B.E.; British writer; b. 24 June 1912; d. of Col. Harold Mynors Farmar and Violet Hyacinth (née Dalby); m. 1st 2nd Baron Swinfen 1937 (divorced 1945); two s.; m. 2nd Eric Siepmann (died 1970) 1952; one s.; ed. pvtly., L.S.E. *Publications:* for children: Speaking Terms 1968, The Sixth Seal 1968, Haphazard House 1983; for adults: Jumping the Queue 1983, The Camomile Lawn 1984, Harnessing Peacocks 1985, The Vacillations of Poppy Carew 1986, Not That Sort of Girl 1987, Second Fiddle 1988, A Sensible Life 1990, A Dubious Legacy 1992, An Imaginative Experience, Part of the Furniture 1997. *Leisure interest:* reading. *Address:* c/o Transworld Publishers, 61–63 Uxbridge Road, London, W5 5SA, England.

SIEVERS WICKE, Hugo K.; Chilean veterinary physician and politician; b. 1903, Rengo; m. Elena Kutz Schroer 1931; ed. Colegio Alemán, Santiago and Univs. de Chile, Buenos Aires, La Plata, Rio de Janeiro, Inst. Pasteur and Inst. Curie, Paris, Inst. of Tropical Medicine, Hamburg; Asst. at Inst. for Veterinary Research 1924–27; Prof. School of Agric. 1927–28; Mil. Veterinary Physician 1926–32; Dir. Inst. of Veterinary Research, Ministry of Agriculture 1930–42; Dean School Veterinary Medicine, Univ. de Chile 1936–61; Vice-Rector Univ. de Chile 1953–61, now Prof. Emer.; Minister of Agric., Lands and Colonization 1955; Perm. Del. Int. Congress of Veterinary Medicine 1936–59; Pres. Chilean Soc. of Sciences 1964; Founder mem. Soc. of Veterinary Physicians of Chile (and fmr. Pres.), Chilean Natural History Soc., Anatomical Soc.; mem. Chilean Acad. Natural Sciences; Hon. mem. Soc. of Veterinary Science, Peru; Hon. Prof. Cen. Univ. de Quito, and Univ. Nacional de San Marcos, Lima; Dr. h.c. Univ. Austral de Chile; Decoration of the Rising Sun, Japan 1959; Decoration Eloy Alfaro Int. Foundation, Gold Medal Camara di Commercio, Industria e Agricultura, Trento, Italy. *Publications:* La vuelta del Mundo con 10 Estudiantes, Rutas Patagónicas, Chilenos en la Amazonia, Max Westenhöfer 1871–1951 (biography), Domingo Amunátegui Solar (biography), Teliatría, Nosotros y la Comunidad, Proteinas y Alimentación.

SIEVERTS, Thomas C. W., DIPL.ING.; German architect and town planner; b. 8 June 1934, Hamburg; s. of Rudolf Sieverts and Elisabeth Sieverts (née Ronnefeldt); m. Heide Pawelzick 1966; one s. two d.; ed. in Stuttgart, Liverpool and Berlin; with Kossak and Zimmermann founded Freie Plannungsgruppe Berlin 1965; Prof. of Town Planning Dept. of Architecture, Hochschule der Künste, Berlin 1967–70; Guest Prof., Grad. School of Design, Harvard Univ. 1970–71; Prof. of Town Planning, Dept. of Architecture, Tech. Hochschule, Darmstadt 1971–99; Special Prof. of Urban Design, Inst. of Planning Studies, Univ. of Nottingham 1978–88; in practice as architect and town planner, Bonn 1978–; town planning consultant to the City of Vienna, planning Danubia area 1973–78, the Gürtel area 1984–88; Dir. of Int. Bldg. Exhbn. Emscher Park (Ruhr) 1989–94; Fellow Inst. for Advanced Study, Berlin 1995–96; mem. Scientific Advisory Council World Exhbn., 'Expo 2000', Hanover 1989–99; Deubau Prize (Essen) 1969, Verdienstzeichen in Gold (Vienna) 1988, Bauherren Prize 1992, Deutsche Städtebau Prize 1993. *Publications:* Zwischenstadt 1997, many contribs. to periodicals and books. *Leisure interest:* drawing. *Address:* Buschstrasse 20, 53113 Bonn, Germany. *Telephone:* 0228/218706 (Office). *Fax:* (0228) 217101.

SIEW, Vincent C.; Taiwanese politician; b. 3 Jan. 1939, Chiayi City, Taiwan; m.; three d.; ed. Nat. Chengchi Univ., Georgetown Univ.; Vice-Consul, Kuala Lumpur, Malaysia 1966-69, Consul 1969–72; Section Chief Asia Pacific Affairs Dept., Ministry of Foreign Affairs 1972; Deputy Dir. 4th Dept. Bd. of Foreign Trade, Ministry of Econ. Affairs 1972–74, Dir. 1974-77, Deputy Dir.-Gen. Bd. of Foreign Trade 1977–82, Dir.-Gen. 1982–88; Vice-Chair. Council for Econ. Planning and Devt., Exec. Yuan 1988–89; Dir.-Gen. Dept. of Organizational Affairs, Kuomintang Cen. Cttee.; Minister of Econ. Affairs 1990–93; Minister of State, Chair. Council for Econ. Planning and Devt., Exec. Yuan 1993–94; Minister of State, Chair. Mainland Affairs Council, Exec. Yuan 1994–95; legislator 1996–97; Premier of Taiwan 1997–; Eisenhower Fellow, U.S.A. 1985. *Address:* Office of the Premier, Taipei, Taiwan.

SIFIC, Mokdad; Algerian politician; fmr. civil servant; fmr. Minister of Public Works; Prime Minister of Algeria 1994–96. *Address:* c/o Office of the Prime Minister, rue Docteur Sâddune, Algiers, Algeria.

SIGCAU, Princess Stella, B.A.; South African politician; b. 1937; d. of Botha Sigcau (fmr. Pres. of Transkei); m. Ronald Tshabalala 1962 (deceased); two c.; ed. Univ. of Fort Hare; M.P. for Lusikisiki, Transkei Parl. 1968; Minister of the Interior, Public Works and Energy, Educ. and Post and Telecommunications –1976, of Interior Affairs 1976–81, Post and Telecommunications, Transkei 1981–87; Leader Transkei Nat. Independence Party 1987; Prime Minister of Transkei 1987 (ousted in a coup); Del. for Cape Traditional Leaders at Multiparty Negotiation Process, World Trade Centre 1994; Chair. ANC Women's League, Transkei; mem. ANC Women's League Nat. Exec. Council; Minister for Public Enterprises, Govt. of Nat. Unity 1994–. *Leisure interests:* reading, farming. *Address:* Private Bag X15, Hatfield 0028, South Africa.

SIGOGNE, Philippe; French economist; b. 1943; formerly Dir. of Diagnostics, Observatoire Français des Conjonctures Economiques (OFCE); Pres. Asscn. des Instituts Européens des Conjonctures Economiques (AIECE) 1990–. *Address:* Association des Instituts Européens des Conjonctures Economiques, 3 place Montesquieu, B.P.4, 1348 Louvain-la-Neuve, Belgium. *Telephone:* (10) 47-41-52. *Fax:* (10) 47-39-45.

SIGRIST, Helmut, DR. RER. POL.; German diplomatist; b. 8 Sept. 1919, Frankfurt/Main; s. of Friedrich and Gertrude (née Oslender) Sigrist; m. Berthild Klein 1951; two s. two d.; ed. Humanistisches Gymnasium, Leipzig, Erfurt, Gelsenkirchen-Schalke, Philosophisch-theologische Hochschule, Bamberg, and Univs. of Heidelberg and Denver, Colo., U.S.A.; Nat. Labour Service 1937; Mil. Service and P.O.W. 1937–45; univ. studies 1945–50; entered Diplomatic Service 1951; Second Sec., later Sec., Washington 1953–55, Sec., Rome 1957–62, New Delhi 1962–64; Dir. Training Centre for Senior Foreign Service Officials, Bonn 1955–57; Deputy Exec. Sec. EEC Comm. 1964–67; Deputy Sec.-Gen. Comm. of European Communities, Brussels 1967; Dir.-Gen. External Relations, Comm. of European Communities 1968–72; in charge of Int. Trade Negotiations for the Fed. Repub. of Germany 1973–75; Asst. Dir. Foreign Trade Policy, Devt. Policy and European Econ. Integration 1974–77; Perm. Rep. (Amb.) of the Fed. Repub. of Germany with the European Communities 1977; Amb. to Greece 1979–84. *Address:* Donatusstr. 21, 53175 Bonn, Germany. *Telephone:* 0228-374495.

SIGUA, Tengiz Ippolitovich, D.TECH.S.; Georgian politician; b. 9 Nov. 1934, Lentekhi; s. of Ipolite Sigua and Lidia Schavdia; m. Nina Iwania 1975; one d.; ed. Georgian Polytechnical Inst.; engineer and Dir. Metallurgy Inst. Georgian Acad. of Sciences 1962–90; fmr. Leading mem. Round Table—Free Georgia Alliance, Chair. All-Georgia Rustaveli Soc.; apptd. Head of Govt. by Zviad Gamsakhurdia, Nov. 1990; resigned Aug. 1991 and joined the opposition; mem. State Council March–Oct. 1992; mem. Supreme Soviet 1992–95; apptd. Prime Minister by Mil. Council 1992–93 (resgnd.), now in parl. opposition; Vice-Pres. Georgian Rustaveli Soc. 1989, Pres. 1992–93. *Leisure interests:* sport, art. *Address:* Phanaskerteli str. 16, Apt. 31, 380094 Tbilisi, Georgia (Home).

SIGURDSSON, Jón, M.SC.ECON.; Icelandic politician and economist; b. 17 April 1941, Ísafjördur; m. Laufey Thorbjarnardóttir; four c.; ed. Akureyri Coll., Univ. of Stockholm and L. S. E.; Econ. Inst. of Iceland 1964–71 (Dir. Econ. Research 1970–71); Chief Econ. Research Div. Econ. Devt. Inst. 1972–74; Man. Dir. Nat. Econ. Inst. and Econ. Adviser to govt. 1974–80, 1983–86; Exec. Dir. for Nordic countries IMF 1980–83, Alt. Gov. IMF for Iceland 1974–87; Assoc. jt. IBRD/IMF Devt. Cttee. 1974–; IBRD Gov. for Iceland 1987–; EBRD Gov. for Iceland 1991–; mem. Althing (SDP) 1987–; Minister of Justice and Ecclesiastical Affairs 1987–88, of Commerce 1987–93, of Industry 1988–93, of Nordic Co-operation 1988–89; Chair. OECD Council of Ministers 1989, Nordic Council of Ministers 1989; mem. Salaries Arbitration Court 1970–80; Rep. for Iceland Econ. and Devt. Review Cttee. OECD 1970–80, 1983–86; Gov. and Chair. Bd. of Dirs., Cen. Bank of Iceland 1993–94; Pres. and C.E.O. Nordic Investment Bank 1994– (mem. Bd. 1976–87, Chair. 1984–86). *Address:* c/o Nordic Investment Bank, Fabianinkatu 34, P.O. Box 249, 00171-Helsinki, Finland. *Telephone:* (9) 18001. *Fax:* (9) 1800210.

SIGURDSSON, Niels P.; Icelandic diplomatist (retd.); b. 1926, Reykjavík; s. of Sigurdur B. Sigurdsson and Karitas Einarsdóttir; m. Olafia Rafnsdóttir; two s. one d.; ed. Univ. of Iceland; joined Diplomatic Service 1952; First Sec. Paris Embassy 1956–60; Deputy Perm. Rep. to NATO and OECD 1957–60; Dir. Int. Policy Div. Ministry of Foreign Affairs, Reykjavík 1961; Del. to the UN Gen. Ass. 1965; Amb. and Perm. Rep. of Iceland to N. Atlantic Council; Amb. to Belgium and the EEC 1968; Amb. to UK. 1971–76, to Fed. Repub. of Germany 1976–78, to Holy See 1977–95, Amb.-at-Large 1979–84, to Norway 1985–89; Chair. Icelandic Del. to Madrid Conf. 1980–83; with Ministry of Foreign Affairs 1990–96. *Leisure interests:* swimming, riding. *Address:* Sólheimar 15, 104 Reykjavík, Iceland.

SIHANOUK, King (Norodom) (see (Norodom) Sihanouk, King).

SIIG, Arvi; Estonian poet; b. 8 Nov. 1938, Tallinn, Estonia; s. of Karl Siig and Helene Siig; m. Valentine Siig; one s. one d.; ed. Tallinn Teacher Training College, and Tartu Univ.; first works published 1958; author of at least ten books of poetry, translated into several foreign languages. *Publications include:* The Trumpet Solo 1962, Reporter with a Camera of Poetry 1966, A Broken Poem 1971, A Constellation of Silence 1973, The Time of Turning-Point 1976, Radius of Audibility 1978, Epigrammophone 1980, Yes! 1982; The Sacred Everyday Life (translations of Russian poetry). *Leisure interests:* travelling, gardening. *Address:* Kingisepp Street 59, Apt. 20, 0010 Tallinn, Estonia. *Telephone:* (3726) 43-85-20.

SIILASVUO, Gen. Ensio; Finnish army officer; b. 1 Jan. 1922, Helsinki; s. of Lieut.-Gen. Hjalmar Siilasvuo and Salli Kolsi; m. Salli Paldanius 1947; three s.; ed. Lycée of Oulu, Finnish Mil. Acad., Finnish Command and Staff Coll.; Platoon Commdr., Infantry Co. Commdr. and Chief of Staff, Infantry Regiment 11 1941–44; Co. Commdr., Infantry Regt. 1 1945–50; attended Command and Staff Coll. 1951–52; various staff appointments in mil. districts of N. Finland 1953–57; Commdr. Finnish Contingent, UN Emergency Force 1957; Mil. Observer, UN Observation Group in Lebanon 1958; Finnish

Defence Attaché in Warsaw 1959–61; Staff Officer Third Div. 1962–64; Commdr. Finnish Contingent, UN Force in Cyprus 1964–65; Instructor, Nat. Defence Coll. 1965–67; Chief, Foreign Dept. GHQ 1967; Sr. Staff Officer, UN Truce Supervision Org. in Palestine 1967–70; Chief of Staff, UN Truce Supervision Org. in Palestine 1970–73, Commdr. UN Emergency Force 1973–75; Chief Co-ordinator of UN Peace-Keeping Missions in Middle East 1975–80, retd. from UN Service 1980; rank of Gen. 1998; Chair. Bd. Suomen Michelin Ltd. 1980–; mem. Bd. Finnish Nat. Theatre 1980–; hon. doctorate (Helsinki) 1990; Grand Cross of the Order of the Lion of Finland, Finnish Cross of Freedom 3rd and 4th Class, Knight of the Order of the White Rose of Finland 1st Class, Grand Cross of the Egyptian Order of Merit, Grand Cross of the Belgian Order of Leopold II, Commdr., Légion d'honneur, Commdr., Lebanese Order of the Cedar, Commdr., U.S. Legion of Merit, Grand Cross of the Order of the Pole Star (Sweden). *Publication:* In the Service of Peace in the Middle East 1992. *Leisure interests:* UN peace-keeping affairs, history of the Middle East. *Address:* Castréninkatu 6 A 17, 00530 Helsinki, Finland. *Telephone:* (09) 766-783.

SIIMANN, Mart; Estonian politician; b. 1946, Killingi-Nomme, Estonia; ed. Tartu State Univ.; m.; two c.; psychologist, Deputy Head Lab. of Scientific Org. of Work and Man. 1971–75; sr. research asst. Tartu State Univ. 1975–82; broadcaster, Deputy Dir.-Gen., Ed.-in-Chief Estonian TV 1982–87; Dir.-Gen. Estonian Radio 1987–89; Dir.-General Estonian TV 1989–92; Man. Dir. commercial TV station ReklamTV 1992–95; mem. Riigikogu (Parl.), Chair. Coalition Party Faction, mem. Constitutional Cttee. 1995–98; Chair. Coalition Party 1997–; Prime Minister of Estonia 1997–. *Leisure interests:* sport, literature, fishing, philosophy. *Address:* Office of the Prime Minister, Lossi Plats 1A, Tallinn 0100, Estonia. *Telephone:* (06) 316-701. *Fax:* (06) 316-707.

SIJTHOFF, Hendrik Albert Henri; Netherlands publisher; b. 1915; ed. Univs. of Leipzig and Lausanne; Chair. Bd. of Het Financieele Dagblad; C.E.O. Sijthoff Holding N.V. *Address:* Weesperstraat 85, 1018 VN, Amsterdam, Netherlands (Office); Ch. de Cyrano, 1009 Pully, Switzerland (Home).

SILAJDŽIĆ, Haris, PH.D.; Bosnia and Herzegovina politician; b. 1945, Sarajevo; m.; one s.; ed. Benghazi Univ., Libya; teacher, Prof. Priština Univ. –1990; Minister of Foreign Affairs Repub. of Bosnia and Herzegovina 1990–93; Prime Minister 1993–96; Chair. Movt. for Bosnia and Herzegovina; Co-Chair. newly formed Govt. of Bosnia and Herzegovina Nov. 1996–. *Publications:* several books and papers on int. relations, including relations between U.S.A. and Albania, 6 books and over 100 papers on eng. in U.S.A., mainly on thermal and fluid eng.; ed. three scientific journals. *Address:* c/o Council of Ministers, 71000 Sarajevo, Bosnia and Herzegovina (Office).

SILAPA-ARCHA, Banharn, LL.M.; Thai politician; b. 20 July 1932; s. of Sengkim and Sai-eng sae Ba; ed. Ramkhamhaeng Univ.; elected to Suphan Buri Municipal Council 1973; co-founder Chart Thai Party 1975, Sec.-Gen. 1976, Party Leader 1994–; mem. Legis. Ass. 1973–; Deputy Minister of Industry 1976; Minister of Agric. 1980; Senator 1986; Minister of Communications 1986, of Industry 1989, of Finance 1990, of Interior 1990–91, of Communications 1992; Leader of Opposition 1992–95; Prime Minister 1995–96, also Minister of the Interior. *Address:* c/o Office of the Prime Minister, Bangkok 10300, Thailand.

SILAS, Cecil Jesse, B.S.; American business executive; b. 15 April 1932, Miami; s. of David Edward and Hilda Videll (née Carver) Silas; m. Theodosea Hejda 1965; three s. one d.; ed. Miami Sr. High School, Georgia Inst. of Tech.; joined Phillips Petroleum Co. 1953–; Pres. Phillips Petroleum Co. Europe-Africa, Brussels and London 1968–74; Man. Dir. NRG Europe-Africa, London 1974–76; Vice-Pres. Gas and Gas Liquids, NRG, Bartlesville, Okla. 1976–78; Sr. Vice-Pres. Natural Resources Group, Bartlesville 1978–80, Exec. Vice-Pres. 1980–82; Pres. and C.O.O. (also Dir. and Chair. Exec. Cttee.) Phillips Petroleum Co. 1982–85, Chair. and C.E.O. 1985–94; Chair. Bd. American Petroleum Inst. –1993, Bd. U.S. Chamber of Commerce; mem. Bd. of Dirs. Halliburton Co.; Dir. Ethics Resource Centre; Commdr., Royal Order of St. Olav, Norway 1976. *Leisure interests:* golf, fishing, hunting. *Address:* 2400 Terrace Drive, Bartlesville, OK 74004, U.S.A. (Home). *Telephone:* (918) 333-8577 (Home).

SILAYEV, Ivan Stepanovich; Russian politician; b. 21 Oct. 1930; m.; two c.; ed. Kazan Aviation Inst.; mem. CPSU 1959–91; foreman, shop supt., deputy chief engineer, chief engineer, plant dir. in Gorky 1954–74; Deputy Minister of Aircraft Industry of U.S.S.R. 1974–77, First Deputy Minister 1977–80, Minister 1981–85; Minister of Machine Tool and Instrument-Making Industry of U.S.S.R. 1980–81; mem. of CPSU Cen. Cttee. 1981–91; Deputy Pres. Council of Ministers of the U.S.S.R. 1985–89; Pres. Council of Ministers of the R.S.F.S.R. 1989–91; Pres. Inter-Republican Econ. Cttee. of the U.S.S.R. 1991; Russian Perm. Rep. to EC (now EU) 1992–94; Pres. Bd. of Dirs. Ecology of Russia Consortium 1995–; Chair. Bd. Moscow Interregional Commercial Bank 1996–, Int. Union of Mechanical Engineers 1997–; Hero of Socialist Labour 1975; Lenin Prize 1972; Deputy to U.S.S.R. Supreme Soviet 1981–89. *Address:* International Union of Mechanical Engineers, Bolskaya Dmitrovka 5, Moscow, Russia. *Telephone:* (095) 203-06-08.

SILBER, John Robert, PH.D., L.H.D., LL.D. ED.D., LITT.D., F.R.S.A.; American professor of philosophy and university administrator; b. 15 Aug. 1926, San Antonio, Tex.; s. of Paul G. Silber and Jewell Joslin; m. Kathryn Underwood 1947; one s. six d.; ed. Trinity, Northwestern and Yale Univs.; Instructor in Philosophy, Yale Univ. 1952–55; Asst. Prof., Univ. of Texas 1955–59, Assoc. Prof. 1959–62, Prof. of Philosophy 1962–70, Chair. Dept. of Philosophy 1962–67, Chair. Comparative Studies Program 1967, Univ. Prof. of Arts and Letters 1967–70, Dean, Coll. of Arts and Sciences 1967–70; Prof. of Philosophy and Law, Boston Univ. 1971–, Prof. of Int. Relations 1996–, Pres. 1971–96, Chancellor 1996–; mem. Bd. of Dirs. Americans for Medical Progress 1992–, Chair. 1994–95, mem. Exec. Cttee. 1995–; mem. Bd. of Dirs. Northeast Savings Bank 1988–95, U.S. Surgical Corpn. 1994–98, Mutual of American Institutional Funds Inc. 1996–; Vice-Chair. U.S. Strategic Inst.; Chair. Mass. Bd. of Educ. 1996–; mem. Bd. of Dirs. Nat. Humanities Faculty 1968–72, Exec. Bd., Nat. Humanities Inst. 1975–78, Bd. of Dirs. New England Holocaust Memorial Cttee.; mem. Bd. of Trustees Boston Univ. 1971–, Coll. of St. Scholastica 1973–85, Univ. of Denver 1985–89, Adelphi Univ. 1989–97; mem. Pres.'s Advisory Bd., Radio Broadcasting to Cuba 1985–92; Pres. Southwestern Philosophy Soc. 1966–67; Fulbright Research Fellow 1959–60; Guggenheim Fellow 1963–64; Wilbur Lucius Cross Medal, Yale Univ. 1971, Ehrenmedaille, Univ. of Heidelberg 1986. *Publications:* The Ethical Significance of Kant's "Religion" 1960, Democracy: Its Counterfeits and Its Promise 1967, The Tuition Dilemma 1978, Straight Shooting: What's Wrong with America and How to Fix It 1989, Ist Amerika zu Retten? 1992; Ed. Kant's Religion Within the Limits of Reason Alone 1960, Works in Continental Philosophy 1967; Assoc. Ed. Kant-Studien 1968–. *Address:* Office of the Chancellor, Boston University, 147 Bay State Road, Boston, MA 02215; 132 Carlton Street, Brookline, MA 02446-4009, U.S.A. *Telephone:* (617) 353-2208 (Office). *Fax:* (617) 353-9674.

SILBERMAN, Laurence Hirsch, LL.B.; American lawyer, banker and diplomatist; b. 12 Oct. 1935, York, Pa.; s. of William and Anna Hirsch; m. Rosalie Gaull 1957; one s. two d.; ed. Dartmouth Coll., Harvard Law School; with Moore, Torkildson & Rice, Quinn & Moore, law firm 1961–64; partner Moore, Silberman & Schulze 1964–67; lawyer Nat. Labor Relations Bd. 1967–69; solicitor, Labor Dept. 1969–70, Under-Sec. for Labor Affairs 1970–73; Partner Steptoe & Johnson 1973–74; Deputy Attorney-Gen., Dept. of Justice 1974–75; Amb. to Yugoslavia 1975–77 (withdrawn); Man. Partner Morrison and Foerster (Washington, D.C.) 1978–79, 1983–85; Exec. Vice-Pres. Legal and Govt. Affairs Div., Crocker Nat. Bank 1979–83; Sr. Fellow, American Enterprise Inst. for Public Policy Research, Washington, D.C. 1977–78, Visiting Fellow 1978–85; Vice-Chair. Advisory Council on Gen. Govt., Republican Nat. Comm. 1977–80; mem. U.S. Gen. Advisory Cttee. on Arms Control and Disarmament 1981–85; Assoc. Prof. of Admin. Law Georgetown Univ., Washington 1987–94, 1999–, New York Univ. 1995–96, Harvard 1998–; U.S. Circuit Judge 1985–. *Address:* U.S. Court of Appeals, D.C. Circuit, U.S. Courthouse, Washington, DC 20001, U.S.A.

SILBERSTON, (Zangwill) Aubrey, C.B.E., M.A.; British professor of economics; b. 26 Jan. 1922, London; s. of Louis Silberston and Polly Silberston (née Kern); m. 1st Dorothy Marion Nicholls 1945 (divorced); m. 2nd Michèle Ledić 1985; one s. (one d. deceased); ed. Hackney Downs School, London, Jesus Coll. Cambridge; Economist, Courtaulds Ltd. 1946–50; Research Fellow St. Catharine's Coll. Cambridge 1950–53, Univ. Lecturer in Econs., Cambridge 1953–71, Fellow St. John's Coll. 1958–71, Chair. Faculty Bd. of Econs. and Politics 1966–70; Official Fellow in Econs., Nuffield Coll. Oxford 1971–78, Dean 1972–78; Prof. of Econs. Imperial Coll. London 1978–87, Sr. Research Fellow, Man. School 1987–; mem. Monopolies Comm. 1965–68, Bd. British Steel Corpn. 1967–76, Royal Comm. on the Press 1974–77, Restrictive Practices Court 1986–92, Royal Comm. on Environmental Pollution 1986–96; Sec.-Gen. Royal Econ. Soc. 1979–92, Vice-Pres. 1992–; Pres. Confed. of European Econ. Asscns. 1988–90, Vice-Pres. 1990–92; Dir. Brussels Office, London Economics 1992–. *Publications:* Education and Training for Industrial Management 1955, The Motor Industry 1959, Economic Impact of the Patent System 1973, The Multi-Fibre Arrangement and the UK Economy 1984, The Future of the Multi-Fibre Arrangement 1989, Technology and Economic Progress (Ed.) 1989, Environmental Economics (Ed.) 1995, Beyond the Multifibre Arrangement 1995, The Changing Industrial Map of Europe 1996; articles in Economic Journal, Oxford Economic Papers etc. *Leisure interests:* opera, ballet. *Address:* 53 Prince's Gate, London, SW7 2PG, England. *Telephone:* 0171-594 9354. *Fax:* 0171-594 9353.

SILGUY, Yves-Thibault Christian Marie de; French diplomatist; b. 22 July 1948, Rennes; s. of Raymond de Silguy and Claude de Pompery; m. Jacqueline de Montillet de Grenaud; one s. one d.; ed. Inst. Saint-Martin, Faculté de Droit et des Sciences Economiques, Rennes, Univ. de Paris I, Inst. d'Etudes Politiques de Paris and Ecole Nat. d'Admin.; entered Ministry of Foreign Affairs 1976; Deputy Chef de Cabinet to François-Xavier Ortoli, Vice-Pres. of EC Comm. 1981–85; Second Counsellor,Washington, D.C. 1985–86; Adviser on European Questions and Int. Econs., Office of Prime Minister Chirac 1986–88; Dir. of Int. Affairs, Usinor-Sacilor 1990–93; Adviser on European Affairs to Prime Minister Balladur 1993–94; Commr. for Economic and Monetary Union, EC 1995–; Chevalier, Légion d'honneur. *Publications:* Le Syndrome du diplodocus 1996, L'Euro 1998. *Leisure interests:* sailing, hunting, tennis. *Address:* Commission of the European Communities, 200 rue de la Loi, 1049 Brussels, Belgium.

SILJA, Anja; German opera singer; b. 17 April 1940, Berlin; m. Christoph von Dohnanyi (q.v.); one s. two d.; appearances in Salome, Lulu, Fidelio, Elektra, and the complete Wagner repertoire, also as Marie (Wozzeck), Hana Glawari (The Merry Widow), Carmen, Tosca, Katya Kabanová, Die Frau

(Erwartung), Elena (The Makropoulos Case), Minnie (The Girl of the Golden West), Luise (Kabale und Liebe), Jenny (Rise and Fall of the City of Mahagonny), Katerina (Lady Macbeth of Mtsensk); guest appearances in Vienna, New York, San Francisco, Chicago, Salzburg Festivals, Stuttgart, Cologne, Budapest, Brussels, London, Tokyo, Geneva, Paris, Rome, Barcelona, Copenhagen, Hamburg, Frankfurt, Bayreuth. *Leisure interests:* driving, decorating, tennis, ice-skating, gardening. *Address:* c/o Severence Hall, Cleveland, OH 44106, U.S.A.

SILLARD, Yves; French aerospace engineer; b. 5 Jan. 1936, Coutances, Manche; s. of Roger Sillard and Madeleine (Guerrand) Sillard; m. 1st Annick Legrand 1966 (divorced); m. 2nd Hélène Benech-Badiou 1982; ed. Ecole Massillon, Ecole Polytechnique, Ecole nat. Supérieure de l'Aéronautique; Test. Eng. and then Head of Colomb-Béchard unit of Centre d'Essais en Vol 1960–62, Tech. Dir. of Cazeaux annex 1963–64; Head of Concorde Programme at Secrétariat général à l'Aviation civile 1965; Head of Div. setting up French Guiana Space Centre, Kourou 1966–68; Tech. Dir. and then Dir. Space Centre, Kourou 1968–72; Dir. of Launchers, Centre Nat. des Etudes Spatiales 1973–76, Man. Dir. 1976–82; Chair. and Man. Dir. Centre nat. pour l'exploitation des océans 1982–; Chair. Conseil d'administration de l'institut français de recherche pour l'exploitation de la mer 1985–89; French Nat. Co-ordinator for EUREKA Programme 1986–89; Gen. Del., Armaments 1989–93; mem. Atomic Energy Cttee. 1989–93; Chair., Man. Dir. Cogepag 1993–, Défence conseil international (DCI) 1993–97; Asst. Sec. Gen. for Scientific Affairs and Environment, NATO 1998; Commdr., Légion d'honneur, Chevalier, Ordre nat. du Mérite, Médaille de l'Aéronautique, Commdr. Merit (Fed. Repub. of Germany). *Address:* c/o NATO, B1110 Brussels, Belgium; 11 avenue de Ségur, 75007 Paris, France.

SILLITOE, Alan; British author; b. 4 March 1928, Nottingham; s. of Christopher Sillitoe and Sabina Burton; m. Ruth Fainlight 1959; one s. one d.; ed. elementary school, Radford, Nottingham; worked in various factories, Nottingham 1942–45; air traffic control asst. 1945–46; served as wireless operator, R.A.F., Malaya 1946–49; lived six years in France and Spain; Visiting Prof. of English, DeMontfort Univ., Leicester 1993–97; Fellow, Royal Geographical Soc., Royal Inst. of Navigation; Hon. Fellow, Manchester Polytechnic; Hon. doctorate (Nottingham Polytechnic) 1990; Dr. h.c. (Nottingham Univ.) 1994; Hawthornden Prize 1960. *Publications:* (novels) Saturday Night and Sunday Morning 1958, The General 1960, Key to the Door 1961, The Death of William Posters 1965, A Tree on Fire 1967, A Start in Life 1970, Travels in Nihilon 1971, Raw Material 1972, The Flame of Life 1974, The Widower's Son 1976, The Storyteller 1979, Her Victory 1982, The Lost Flying Boat 1983, Down From The Hill 1984, Life Goes On 1985, Out of the Whirlpool 1987, The Open Door 1989, Last Loves 1990, Leonard's War: A Love Story 1991, Snowstop 1993, Alligator Playground 1997, The Broken Chariot 1998; (stories) The Loneliness of the Long Distance Runner 1959, The Ragman's Daughter 1963, Guzman, Go Home 1968, Men, Women and Children 1973, The Second Chance 1981, The Far Side of the Street 1988, Collected Stories 1995; (essays) Mountains and Caverns 1975, The Mentality of the Picaresque Hero 1993; (poems) The Rats and Other Poems 1960, A Falling Out of Love 1964, Love in the Environs of Voronezh 1968, Barbarians and Other Poems 1974, Storm and Other Poems 1974, Snow on the North Side of Lucifer 1979, Sun Before Departure 1984, Tides and Stone Walls (with Victor Bowley) 1986, Collected Poems 1993; (travel) Road to Volgograd 1964, Leading the Blind: A Century of guide book travel 1815–1914 1995, The Saxon Shore Way (with Fay Godwin) 1983, Nottinghamshire (with David Sillitoe) 1986; (plays) Three Plays 1978; All Citizens are Soldiers 1969 (trans. of Lope de Vega play Fuenteovejuna, with Ruth Fainlight); (children's books) The City Adventures of Marmalade Jim 1967, Big John and the Stars 1977, The Incredible Fencing Fleas 1978, Marmalade Jim on the Farm 1980, Marmalade Jim and the Fox 1985; Alligator Playground 1998; (autobiog.) Life without Armour 1995. *Leisure interests:* geography, navigation, radio communications, travel. *Address:* 14 Ladbroke Terrace, London, W11 3PG, England.

SILLS, Beverly; American coloratura soprano; b. (as Belle Silverman) 25 May 1929, Brooklyn, New York; d. of the late Morris Silverman and of Sonia Bahn; m. Peter Bulkeley Greenough 1956; one s. one d. three step-c.; ed. pupil of Estelle Liebling; debut at San Francisco Opera as Helen of Troy in Mefistofele 1953, at New York City Opera as Rosalinda in Die Fledermaus 1955; with New York City Opera 1955–80, Gen. Dir. 1979–88, Pres. New York City Opera Bd. 1989–90, Man. Dir. Metropolitan Opera, New York 1991–94; Chair. Lincoln Center 1994–; debut at the Vienna State Opera as Queen of the Night (The Magic Flute) 1967, at La Scala, Milan in The Siege of Corinth 1969, at Royal Opera House, Covent Garden in title role of Lucia di Lammermoor 1970, Metropolitan Opera, New York as Pamira in Siege of Corinth 1975; other best known roles include Cleopatra (Julius Caesar), Queen Elizabeth I (Roberto Devereux), all three heroines in The Tales of Hoffmann, Manon (Manon), Violetta (La Traviata), Marie (Daughter of the Regiment), Rosina (Barber of Seville); title roles in Anna Bolena and Maria Stuarda, Norma, Lucrezia Borgia; recordings for Columbia, RCA, Angel, ABC—Audio Treasury; has appeared at most of the major opera houses of Europe and Latin America and given numerous recitals with leading orchestras throughout U.S.A.; retd. 1980; Dir. Warner Communications Inc., New York 1982–, American Express, Macy's; host Live from Lincoln Center (TV series) 1998; Presidential Medal of Freedom, other awards. *Publications:* Bubbles: a self-portrait 1976, Beverly (autobiog.) 1987. *Address:* c/o Vincent and Farrell Associates, 157 West 57th Street, Suite 502, New York, NY 10019, U.S.A.

SILUNGWE, Annel Musenga, LL.M.; Zambian lawyer; b. 10 Jan. 1936, Mbala, Zambia; s. of Solo Musenga Silungwe and Janet Nakafunda Silungwe; m. Abigail Nanyangwe Silungwe 1960; two s. four d.; ed. Univ. of Zambia, Inner Temple, London; Resident Magistrate 1967, Sr. Resident Magistrate (Class II) 1968, (Class I) 1970; Judge of the High Court 1971; nominated M.P. and apptd. Minister of Legal Affairs and Attorney-Gen. 1973; State Counsel 1974; Chief Justice 1975–92; Judge, Court of Appeal, Seychelles 1992–; Judge of High Court and Supreme Court, Dir. Justice Training Centre, Ministry of Justice, Namibia; Chair. Judicial Services Comm. 1975, Council of Legal Educ. 1975, Council of Law Reporting 1975. *Leisure interests:* music, golf, photography. *Address:* Ministry of Justice, Private Bag 13302, Windhoek, Namibia. *Telephone:* (61) 2063893. *Fax:* (61) 2063988.

SILVEIRA GODINHO, José António da; Portuguese fmr. politician, economist and business executive; b. 16 Oct. 1943, Lisbon; s. of Raul Catarino Godinho and Angela da Silveira Godinho; m. Isabel Maria Canhoto Segura de Faria 1972; three s.; ed. Lisbon Tech. Univ.; Sr. Vice-Pres. Banco de Portugal 1975–79; mem. Man. Bd. Banco Pinto & Sotto Mayor 1979–82; Sec. of State for Finance 1980–81; Exec. mem. Bd. Banco Espírito Santo 1982–93; Sec. of State for Nat. Defence 1986–87; Minister of Internal Affairs 1987–90; Amb. to OECD 1993–96; mem. Bd. of Dirs. (Economist) Espírito Santo, Ca. de Seguros S.A. 1996–. *Leisure interests:* reading, travelling, music, sport. *Address:* Rua de Buenos Aires, 43-3°, 1200 Lisbon, Portugal. *Telephone:* (1) 395 6282.

SILVER, Casey; American film company executive; began career as screenwriter; asst. to Adrian Lyne (q.v.); fmr. Vice-Pres. Production, Sr. Vice-Pres. Production TriStar Pictures, Dir. of Devt. and Production Simpson-Bruckheimer; joined Universal Pictures as Exec. Vice-Pres. Production 1987, Pres. 1989, Pres. Universal Pictures 1994, Chair. 1995–. *Address:* Universal Pictures, 100 Universal City Plaza, Universal City, CA 91608, U.S.A.

SILVER, Joan Micklin; American film and theatre director and scriptwriter; b. 24 May 1935, Omaha, Neb.; d. of Maurice Micklin and Doris Shoshone; m. Raphael Silver 1956; three d.; ed Sarah Lawrence Coll.; began career as writer for educational films; original screenplay for Limbo purchased by Universal Pictures; commissioned by Learning Corpn. of America to write and direct short narrative film The Immigrant Experience 1972 and wrote and dir. two children's films for same co.; dir. plays: Album and Maybe I'm Doing it Wrong; also dir. for television. *Films include:* Hester Street (dir. and screenplay), Bernice Bobs Her Hair (dir. and screenplay), Between the Lines (dir.), On the Yard (producer), Head Over Heels (dir. and screenplay, retitled Chilly Scenes of Winter), Crossing Delancey (dir.), Loverboy (dir.), Big Girls Don't Cry . . . They Get Even (dir.), In the Presence of Mine Enemies (dir.) 1996, Invisible Child (dir.) 1998. *Radio:* Great Jewish Short Stories from Eastern Europe and Beyond (dir.) 1995. *Address:* Silverfilm Productions Inc., 510 Park Avenue, Suite 9B, New York, NY 10022-1105, U.S.A. *Telephone:* (212) 355-0282. *Fax:* (212) 421-8254.

SILVER, Joel; American film producer; b. 14 July 1952, South Orange, N.J.; ed. New York Univ.; fmrly. asst. to Lawrence Gordon, Pres. Lawrence Gordon Productions; producer, Vice-Pres. Universal Pictures; appeared in film Who Framed Roger Rabbit 1988. *Films:* The Warrior 1979, Xanadu 1980, 48 Hours 1982, Jekyll & Hyde . . . Together Again 1982, Streets of Fire 1984, Brewster's Millions 1985, Weird Science 1985, Commando 1985, Jumpin' Jack Flash 1986, Lethal Weapon 1986, Predator 1987, Action Jackson 1988, Die Hard 1988, Lethal Weapon 2 1989, Roadhouse 1989, Ford Fairlane 1990, Die Hard 2 1990, Predator 2 1990, Hudson Hawk 1991, Richochet 1991, The Last Boy Scout 1991, Lethal Weapon 3 1992, Demolition Man 1993, The Hudsucker Proxy, Richie Rich 1994, Demon Knight 1994, Assassins 1995, Fair Game 1995, Executive Decision 1996, Conspiracy Theory, Father's Day. *Television:* Tales from the Crypt, Two Fisted Tales, Parker Can, W.E.I.R.D. World. *Address:* Silver Pictures, 4000 Warner Boulevard, Burbank, CA 91522-0001, U.S.A.

SILVERMAN, Bernard Walter, M.A., PH.D., F.R.S.; British professor of statistics; b. 22 Feb. 1952; s. of Elias Silverman and Helen Silverman; m. Rowena Fowler 1985; one s.; ed. City of London School, Jesus Coll., Cambridge; Research Fellow Jesus Coll., Cambridge 1975–77; Calculator Devt. Man. Sinclair Radionics 1976–77; Weir Fellow Univ. Coll., Oxford 1977–78, also jr. lecturer Oxford Univ.; lecturer, then Reader, Prof. of Statistics Univ. of Bath 1978–93, Head School of Mathematical Sciences 1988–91; Prof. of Statistics Univ. of Bristol 1993–; Chartered Statistician; various awards from U.K. and U.S.A. *Publications include:* Density Estimation for Statistics and Data Analysis 1986, Nonparametric Regression and Generalized Linear Models (with P. J. Green) 1994, Functional Data Analysis (with J. O. Ramsay) 1997; numerous papers in learned journals. *Leisure interests:* church, opera, theatre, family, talking. *Address:* School of Mathematics, University of Bristol, University Walk, Bristol, BS8 1TW, England. *Telephone:* (0117) 928 7968.

SILVERMAN, Fred, M.A.; American broadcasting executive; b. 13 Sept. 1937, New York; m. Cathy Kihn; one s. one d.; ed. Syracuse Univ., Ohio State Univ.; with WGN-TV Chicago; exec. position WP1X-TV New York; Dir. Daytime Programmes CBS-TV New York, Vice-Pres. Programmes 1970–75; Pres. ABC Entertainment 1975–78; Pres. NBC 1978–81; ind. film producer 1981–; Pres.

The Fred Silverman Co. 1986–. *Address:* Fred Silverman Production, 12400 Wilshire Boulevard, Suite 920, Los Angeles, CA 90025, U.S.A.

SILVERMAN, Henry Richard, LL.B.; American business executive and lawyer; b. 2 Aug. 1940, New York; s. of Herbert Silverman and Roslyn (née Moskowitz) Silverman; m. 1st Susan H. Herson 1965 (divorced 1977); two d.; m. 2nd Nancy Ann Kraner 1978; one d.; ed. Hackley School, Tarrytown, N.Y., Williams Coll., Philadelphia and New York Univs.; with U.S.N.R. 1965–73; called to Bar N.Y. 1965; with U.S. Tax Court 1965; with U.S. Court of Appeals 1965; practice law 1965–66; with White, Weld & Co. 1966; gen. partner Oppenheimer & Co. 1966–70; Pres., C.E.O. ITI Corpn. 1970–72; f., Pres. Trans-York Securities Corpn. 1972; C.E.O. Vavasseur America Ltd. 1974–75; gen. partner Brisbane Partners 1976–77; Prin. various investment groups 1977–, Silverman Energy Co. 1977–, NBC Channel 20 1977–83, ABC Channel 9 1977–81, Delta Queen Steamboat 1977–86, also dir.; Pres., C.E.O. Reliance Capital Corpn. (subsidiary Reliance Group Holdings Inc.) 1982–, Sr. Vice-Pres. Business Devt. Reliance Group Holdings Inc. 1982–90; gen. partner Blackstone Group 1990–91; Chair., C.E.O. HFS Inc. 1990–; Dir. N.Y. Univ. Hosp. 1987–. *Address:* 712 5th Avenue, Floor 41, New York, NY 10019, U.S.A.

SILVERSTONE, Alicia; American actress; b. 4 Oct. 1976, Calif.; stage debut in play Carol's Eve at Met Theatre, Los Angeles; starred in three Aerosmith videos including Cryin'; formed own production co. First Kiss Productions. *Films:* The Crush 1993, The Babysitter 1995, True Crime 1995, Le Nouveau Monde 1995, Hideaway 1995, Clueless 1995, Batman and Robin 1997, Excess Baggage (also producer) 1997, Free Money 1998. *TV:* Torch Song 1993, Shattered Dreams 1993, The Cool and the Crazy 1994, The Wonder Years 1997. *Address:* c/o Premiere Artists Agency, Suite 510, 8899 Beverly Boulevard, Los Angeles, CA 90048; First Kiss Productions, c/o Columbia Pictures, 10202 Washington Boulevard, Culver City, CA 90232, U.S.A.

SILVESTRINI, H.E. Cardinal Achille; Italian ecclesiastic; b. 25 Oct. 1923, Brisighella; ordained Catholic priest 1946, elected Archbishop of Novaliciana, Mauritania 1979, consecrated bishop 1979; Sec. Council for Public Affairs of the Church 1979; cr. Cardinal 1988 with title of St. Benedict outside the Gate of St. Paul; Prefect of the Supreme Tribunal of the Apostolic Signatura 1988–91; Prefect of the Congregation for the Eastern Churches 1991–, and Grand Chancellor of the Pontifical Eastern Inst.; mem. Congregations for the Doctrine of the Faith, for the Oriental Churches, for the Causes of the Saints, for the Bishops, for the Evangelization of Peoples, for Catholic Educ.; mem. Pontificial Councils for the Interpretation of Legislative Texts, for Inter-Religious Dialogue. *Address:* Congregation for the Eastern Churches, Palazzo del Bramante, Via della Conciliazione 34, 00193 Rome, Italy. *Telephone:* (6) 6988-4282. *Fax:* (6) 6988-4300.

SILVESTROV, Valentin Vasilyevich; Ukrainian composer; b. 30 Sept. 1937, Kiev; ed. Kiev State Conservatory (pupil of B. Lyatoshinsky); author of compositions performed in U.S.S.R. and many countries of Europe and U.S.A. including 5 symphonies for large symphony orchestra 1963–82, Symphony for baritone with orchestra Echo Momentum on verses of A. Pushkin 1987, string quartets 1978, 1988, Dedication—symphony for violin and orchestra 1991, Mertamusica for piano and orchestra 1992, numerous chamber ensembles, piano pieces, vocal cycles, choruses; S. Koussevitsky Prize (U.S.A.) 1967, Prize of Gaudeamus Soc. (Netherlands) 1970. *Address:* Entuziastov str. 35/1, Apt. 49, 252147 Kiev, Ukraine (Home). *Telephone:* (044) 517-04-47 (Home).

SIMAI, Mihály; Hungarian economist; b. 4 April 1930, Budapest; s. of Mátyás Simai and Jolán Rosenberg; m. Vera Bence 1953; one d.; Prof. of Int. Econs. and Nat. Business, Univ. of Econs., Budapest 1971–, Dir. of Grad. Studies in Int. Bus. and Strategy 1987–, in Int. Relations 1991–; Deputy Dir. Research Inst. of World Econs., Budapest 1973–87; mem. Hungarian Acad. of Sciences 1979–; Pres. Hungarian UN Ass., Hungarian Nat. Cttee. for UNICEF 1981–; Hon. Pres. World Fed. of UN ASS. 1982–; Chair. Council UN Univ. 1990–92; Vice-Pres. Int. Studies Asscn. 1988–; fmr. Pres. Ed. Cttee. Acta Oeconomica; Dir. Hungarian Acad. of Sciences Inst. of World Econs. 1987–91; Dir. UN Univ. World Inst. for Devt. Econs. Research 1993–96; mem. Governing Council, Nat. Studies Asscn. 1984–, Governing Bd. Karl Polanyi Inst. 1988–, Advisory Bd. for UN TNCs 1990–, Editorial Bd. Environmental Econs. 1991–, Advisory Bd. Global Governance 1993–; Peace Fellow U.S. Inst. for Peace 1991–92; Labour Order of Merit (Golden Degree), Order of the Star of Hungary (Golden Degree), Order of the Flag of the Hungarian Repub. 1990. *Publications:* Capital Export in the Contemporary Capitalist System 1962, The World Economic System of Capitalism, 1965, View from the 26th Floor 1969, Joint Ventures with Foreign Partners 1971, The United States before the 200th Anniversary 1974, Planning and Plan Implementation in the Developing Countries 1975, The United Nations and the Global Problems 1977, Interdependence and Conflicts in the World Economy 1981, Economic Decolonization and the Developing Countries 1981, The United Nations Today and Tomorrow 1985, Power, Technology and the World Economy of the 1990s 1990, Foreign Direct Investments in Hungary 1991, The Future of Global Governance: Managing Risk and Change in the International System 1994, International Business Policy 1997; numerous articles on int. econ. and political issues. *Leisure interests:* hiking, skiing. *Address:* Institute of World Economics, Hungarian Academy of Sciences, 1123 Budapest, Kálló esperes utca 15, Hungary. *Telephone:* 361 319 9375. *Fax:* 361 319 9385.

SIMATUPANG, Lieut.-Gen. Tahi Bonar; Indonesian international church official and retd. army officer; b. 28 Jan. 1920, Sidikalang; s. of late Simon Mangaraja Soaduon and of Mina Boru Sibuea; m. Sumarti Budiardjo 1949; two s. one d.; ed. Mil. Acad.; Dir. of Org., Gen. Staff of Indonesian Nat. Army 1945–48; Deputy Chief of Staff, Armed Forces of Repub. of Indonesia 1948–49, Acting Chief of Staff 1949–51, Chief of Staff 1951–54; Mil. Adviser to Govt. of Indonesia 1954–59; retd. from mil. service 1959; Pres. Council of Churches in Indonesia 1967, Christian Conf. in Asia 1973–77; mem. Presidium World Council of Churches 1975–83; mem. Supreme Advisory Council, Republic of Indonesia 1973–78; D.Hum. Litt. (Tulsa) 1969. *Publications:* Pioneer in War, Pioneer in Peace (Role of the Armed Forces in Indonesia) 1954, Report from Banaran—Experiences during the People's War 1959, Christian Task in Revolution 1966, National Resilience in the New Situation in Southeast Asia 1980, From Revolution to Development 1984, Christian Faith and Pancasile (the Indonesian State Ideology) 1984, Hope, Fear and Determination 1985, Christian Presence in War, Revolution and Development 1986, Indonesia: Leadership and National Security Perceptions 1987. *Leisure interest:* reading. *Address:* Jalan Diponegoro 55, Jakarta, Indonesia. *Telephone:* 337800.

SIMBOMANA, Adrien; Burundian politician; fmr. Deputy Speaker Nat. Ass.; Gov. of Muramvya Prov. –1988; fmr. Vice-Pres. of Comm. on Nat. Unity; Prime Minister of Burundi 1988–92, fmr. Minister of Planning. *Address:* c/o Office of the Prime Minister, Bujumbura, Burundi.

SIMEON II, H.R.H., Simeon Borisov Saxe-Coburg-Gotha; former King of Bulgaria; b. 1937; s. of the late King Boris and of Queen Joanna; m. Margarita Gomez y Acebo 1962; five c.; ed. in England, Victoria Coll., Alexandria and Valley Forge Mil. Acad. Pa.; proclaimed King of Bulgaria 1943; deposed 1946; sought refuge in Egypt in 1947; has since lived mainly in Spain; Constitutional Court ruled in 1998 that confiscation of royal property by Communist regime had been illegal; returned to Bulgaria 1996. *Address:* Madrid, Spain.

SIMEÓN NEGRÍN, Rosa Elena; Cuban politician and virologist; b. 17 June 1943, Havana; m.; one d.; ed. Marianao High School and Univ. of Havana; Chief, Dept. of Virology, Nat. Center of Scientific Research (CENIC) 1968–73, Chief, Microbiological Div. 1974–76; Prof. School of Veterinary Medicine 1969–73, Nat. Hosp. and Nat. Center of Scientific Investigations 1975, Nat. Inst. of Veterinary Medicine 1977–78, 1981; Dir. Nat. Center of Agric. Health (CENSA) 1985; Pres. Acad. of Sciences of Cuba 1985–94; Minister of Science, Tech. and Environment 1994–; many other professional appts.; awards and decorations from Cuba, Czechoslovakia and France. *Publications:* articles in professional journals. *Address:* Ministry of Science, Technology and Environment, Capitolio Nacional, 10200 Havana, Cuba. *Telephone:* (07) 62-8631. *Fax:* (07) 93-8654.

SIMIC, Charles; American poet; b. 1938, Belgrade, Yugoslavia; s. of George Simic and Helen Matijevich; m. Helen Dubin; one s. one d.; ed. Oak Park High School, Chicago, Univ. of Chicago and New York Univ.; arrived in U.S.A. 1954; army service 1961–64; worked for Chicago Sun-Times as proofreader; later business Man. Aperture Magazine 1966–69; Prof. of English, Calif. State Univ., Hayward 1970–73; lecturer in American Literature Univ. of N.H. 1973–; first vol. of poems published 1967; Pulitzer Prize for Poetry for The World Doesn't End (prose poems) 1990. *Publications include:* poems: What the Grass Says 1967, White 1972, Biography and a Lament 1976, Austerities 1982, Selected Poems 1985, Unending Blues 1986, The World Doesn't End 1989, The Book of Gods and Devils 1990, Hotel Insomnia 1992, A Wedding in Hell 1994, Walking the Black Cat; prose: The Uncertain Certainty 1985, Wonderful Words, Silent Truth 1990, The Unemployed Fortune Teller. *Address:* Department of English, University of New Hampshire, P.O. Box 192, Strafford, NH 03884, U.S.A.

SIMION, Eugen Ioan, PH.D.; Romanian literary critic; b. 25 May 1933, Chiojdeanca, Prahova County; s. of Dragomir Simion and Sultana Simion; m. Adriana Manea 1957; one d.; ed. Coll. of Philology, Bucharest Univ.; researcher Romanian Acad. 1957–62; Ed. Gazeta literară 1962–68; Asst. Lecturer, Bucharest Univ. 1964, Assoc. Prof. 1971, Prof. of Romanian Literature 1990–; Visiting Prof. Sorbonne, Paris 1970–73; Dir. Caiete critice (cultural review) 1991–; mem. Bd. Romanian Writers' Union; mem. Romanian Acad. 1991 (Vice-Pres. 1994), Academia Europaea, London 1992; Vice-Pres. Intergovernmental Cttee. for the World Decade for Cultural Devt.-UNESCO 1992; mem. Int. Union of Literary Critics; prizes of the Romanian Writers' Union; Prize of the Romanian Acad. *Publications include:* Eminescu's Fiction 1964, Trends in Today's Literature 1965, E. Lovinescu the Sceptic Saved 1971, The Romanian Writers Today (Vol. I) 1974, (Vol. II) 1976, (Vol. III) 1983, (Vol. IV) 1989; A Time to Live, a Time to Confess (Paris Diary), The Morning of Poets 1980, Defying Rhetoric 1985, Mercutio's Death 1993, Talking to Petru Dumitriu 1994, Mircea Eliade, A Spirit Amplitude 1995, The Return of the Author 1996. *Address:* Apolodor 13-15, Bucharest, Romania.

SIMITIS, Konstantinos, DR.JUR.; Greek politician and lawyer; b. 23 June 1936, Athens; s. of George Simitis and Fani Cristopoulou; m. Daphne Arkadiou; two c.; ed. Univ. of Marburg and London School of Econs.; Supreme Court lawyer 1961–; taught in W. German univs. 1971–75; Prof. of Commercial Law, Univ. of Athens 1977; active in politics 1965–, mem. Nat. Council of Panhellenic Liberation Movt. (PAK) during colonels' dictatorship, mem. Pasok 1974–, mem. Cen. Cttee. of Pasok, Pres. 1996–; mem. Parl. 1985–;

Minister of Agric. 1981–85, of Nat. Economy 1985–87, of Educ. and Religious Affairs 1989–90, of Industry, Energy, Tech. and Trade 1993–95; Prime Minister of Greece Jan. 1996–. *Publications:* several books and numerous articles in Greek and German on legal and econ. matters. *Address:* Ministry of the Prime Minister, Leoforos Vassilissis Sophias 15, 10674 Athens; Herodou Atticou 19, Maximos Mansion, 10674 Athens, Greece. *Telephone:* 6717071. *Fax:* 6715799.

SIMMEN, Jeannot, DR.PHIL.HABIL.; Swiss art critic and curator; b. 14 Sept. 1946, Zürich; s. of Georg Simmen and Claere Bráugger; m. Brigit Blass 1988; two d.; ed. Univ. of Zürich, Free Univ. of Berlin; exhbn. projects include: Licht: Objekt/Medium, Grau Absolut; Guest Prof., Univs. of Wuppertal, Kassel, Essen 1990–; Curator Schwerelos (exhbn.), Grosse Orangerie, Charlottenburg Palace, Berlin 1991–92, Die Macht des Alters—Strategien der Meisterschaft, Kronprinzen-Palais, Berlin 1998; Dir. media future project Ars Digitalis, Acad. of Fine Arts, Berlin 1996. *Publications:* Schwerelos 1990, Vertikal 1994, Malewitsch 1998, 1999. *Leisure interests:* art and the media. *Address:* Goethe-Strasse 45, 14163 Berlin, Germany. *Telephone:* (030) 809071-45. *Fax:* (030) 809071-46.

SIMMONDS, Rt. Hon. Dr. Kennedy Alphonse, P.C.; Saint Christopher and Nevis politician; b. 12 April 1936; s. of the late Arthur Simmonds and of Bronte Clarke; m. Mary Camella Matthew 1976; three s. two d.; ed. Basseterre Boys' School, St. Kitts-Nevis Grammar School and Univ. of the West Indies; Intern, Kingston Public Hosp., Jamaica 1963; Registrar in Internal Medicine, Princess Margaret Hosp., Bahamas 1966–68; Resident in Anaesthesiology, Pittsburgh 1968–69; medical practice in St. Kitts and Anguilla 1964–66, in St. Kitts 1969–80; founder mem. People's Action Movt. 1965, Pres. 1976, unsuccessfully contested elections 1966, 1971, 1975; elected to Parl. 1979; Premier 1980–83; Minister of Home and External Affairs, Trade, Devt. and Industry 1980–84, of Finance, Home and Foreign Affairs 1984–95; Prime Minister 1983–95; Fellow American Coll. of Anaesthesiologists. *Address:* P.O. Box 167, Earle Morne Development, Basseterre, St. Kitts, West Indies.

SIMMONS, David, B.A.; Australian politician; b. 7 Nov. 1947, Broken Hill, N.S.W.; m. Kaye Simmons; one s. one d.; ed. Univ. of New England, N.S.W.; Head Social Science Dept., Bathurst High School, N.S.W.; Alderman, Bathurst City Council 1978–83; M.P. for Calare, N.S.W. 1983–96; mem. House of Reps. Cttee. on Finance and Public Admin. 1985–89; Minister for Defence, Science and Personnel 1989–90, for Arts, Tourism and Territories 1990–91, for Local Govt. and Family Support 1991–93; Chair. House of Reps. Cttee. on Banking, Fin. and Public Admin. 1994; Exec. Dir. Hunter Regional Tourism Org. 1996–97; Gen. Man. Newcastle Regional Chamber of Commerce 1997–. *Leisure interests:* golf, stamp collecting. *Address:* Newcastle Regional Chamber of Commerce, 51 King Street, Newcastle, N.S.W. 2300, Australia.

SIMMONS, Jean; British actress; b. 31 Jan. 1929, London; d. of Charles Simmons and Winifred Ada (née Loveland) Simmons; m. 1st Stewart Granger 1950 (divorced 1960); one d.; m. 2nd Richard Brooks (q.v.) 1960 (divorced 1977, died 1992); one d.; ed. Orange Hill School, Burnt Oak, London; in films from 1943; stage appearance, Philadelphia, and on tour in A Little Night Music 1974–75; appeared in TV series The Dain Curse 1978, Down at the Hydro 1982; Homage Award (Cannes Film Festival) 1988, Lake Como Italian Film Award 1989; Commdr. des Arts et Lettres 1990, BFI Fellowship 1994. *Films include:* Great Expectations 1946, Black Narcissus 1946, Hamlet 1948, Adam and Evelyne 1949, So Long at the Fair 1950, Young Bess 1953, The Robe 1953, The Actress 1953, Guys and Dolls 1956, The Big Country 1958, Home Before Dark 1958, Elmer Gantry 1960, Spartacus 1960, The Grass is Greener 1961, All the Way Home 1963, Life at the Top 1965, Tough Night in Jericho 1967, Divorce American Style 1967, The Happy Ending 1969, Dominique 1979, The Thornbirds (TV) 1982 (Emmy Award), The Dawning 1988, Great Expectations (TV) 1989, People Like Us (TV) 1990, December Flower (TV), How To Make an American Quilt. *Address:* c/o A. Morgan Maree, Jr. and Assoc., 4727 Wilshire Boulevard, Suite 600, Los Angeles, CA 90010, U.S.A.

SIMMONS, Richard D., A.B., LL.B.; American newspaper publisher; b. 30 Dec. 1934, Cambridge, Mass.; m. Mary DeWitt Bleecker 1961; two s.; ed. Harvard and Columbia Univs.; admitted to New York bar; Assoc. Satterlee, Warfield & Stephens 1958–62; Gen. Counsel Giannini Science Corpn. 1962–64; Vice-Pres. and Gen. Counsel Southeastern Publishing Service Corpn. 1964–69; Counsel Dun & Bradstreet Inc., New York 1969–70, Vice-Pres. and Gen. Counsel 1970–72; Pres. Moody's Investors Service 1973–76, Dun & Bradstreet Inc. 1975–76; Exec. Vice-Pres. Dun & Bradstreet Corpn., New York 1976–78, Dir. and Vice-Chair. Bd. 1979–81; Pres. and C.O.O. The Washington Post Co. 1981–91, now Dir.; Pres. Int. Herald Tribune 1989–96; Dir. Union Pacific Corpn., Washington Post Co., J. P. Morgan & Co. Inc., Morgan Guaranty Trust Co., Inc., Yankee Publishing, Inc.; Trustee The Children's Aid Soc., Int. House, Rockefeller Univ. Council, Cttee. for Econ. Devt. *Address:* 105 N. Washington Street, Suite 202, Alexandria, VA 22314, U.S.A.

SIMMONS, Robert Malcolm, PH.D., F.R.S.; British professor of biophysics; b. 23 Jan. 1938, London; s. of Stanley Laurence Simmons and Marjorie Simmons (née Amys); m. Mary Ann (Anna) Ross 1967; one s. one d.; ed. King's Coll. London, Royal Inst., Univ. Coll. London; lecturer Univ. Coll., London Univ. 1967–81; MRC Staff Scientist King's Coll., Univ. of London 1981–83, Prof. of Biophysics 1983–. *Publication:* Muscular Contraction 1992. *Leisure interests:* music, fishing. *Address:* Randall Institute, King's College London, 26–29 Drury Lane, London, WC2B 5RL, England. *Telephone:* 0171-465 5362. *Fax:* 0171-497 9078.

SIMMS, David John, PH.D.; Irish professor of mathematics; b. 13 Jan. 1933, Sankeshwar, India; s. of John Gerald Simms and Eileen Mary (née Goold-Verschoyle) Simms; m. Anngret Erichson 1965; three s.; ed. Berkhamstead School, Trinity Coll., Dublin and Peterhouse, Cambridge, England; Asst. in Math., Univ. of Glasgow 1958–60, Lecturer in Math. 1960–64; Instructor in Math., Princeton Univ., N.J. 1962–63; Lecturer in Math., Univ. of Dublin 1964–73, Assoc. Prof. 1973–; Visiting Prof. Univ. of Bonn 1966–67, 1972–73, 1978–80; Fellow, Trinity Coll., Dublin; mem. Royal Irish Acad. 1978–, Vice-Pres. 1983–84, 1987–88, 1995–96; Gold Medal in Math., Univ. of Dublin 1955. *Publications include:* Lie Groups and Quantum Mechanics 1968, Lectures on Geometric Quantization (with N. M. Woodhouse) 1974. *Address:* Trinity College, Dublin 2, Ireland. *Telephone:* (01) 608 1944.

SIMMS, Sir Neville Ian, Kt., B.SC., M.ENG., F.I.C.E.; British business executive and civil engineer; b. 11 Sept. 1944, Glasgow; ed. Queen Elizabeth Grammar School, Crediton, Univs. of Newcastle upon Tyne and Glasgow; joined Tarmac group 1970, Operations Dir. Tarmac Construction Industrial Div. 1980–82, Tarmac Nat. Construction 1982–84, Jt. Man. Dir. Tarmac Construction Int. 1984–85, Man. Dir. Tarmac Construction Regions 1985–88, Chief Exec. Tarmac Construction Ltd. 1988–92, Exec. Dir. Tarmac PLC 1988–, Group Chief Exec. 1992–, Deputy Chair. 1994–; mem. Members' Ass., TransManche Link 1988–, Co-Chair. 1993–; Pres. du Conseil de Surveillance d'Entreprise Nicoletti, Nice 1992–; Dir. (non-exec.) Ruberoid PLC 1993–94, Courtaulds PLC 1994–, Bank of England 1995–; Chair. Nat. Contractors Group 1989; mem. Overseas Project Bd. of Dept. of Trade and Industry 1988–90, Environment Task Force, Bldg. Employers' Confed. 1991–92, Better Made in Britain Cttee. for Construction 1989–, H.M. Treasury's Pvt. Finance Panel 1993–, Midlands Industrial Council 1994–, Construction Procurement Group 1994–; Hon. D.Tech. (Wolverhampton) 1997; Fellow Chartered Inst. of Bldg., Pres.'s Medal 1995. *Publications:* Building Towards 2001; numerous speeches and articles on industry-related topics. *Address:* Tarmac PLC, Hilton Hall, Hilton Lane, Essington, Wolverhampton, WV11 2BQ, England. *Telephone:* (01902) 307407. *Fax:* (01902) 307408.

SIMON, Claude; French writer; b. 10 Oct. 1913, Tananarive, Madagascar; s. of Antoine Simon and Suzanne (née Denamiel) Simon; ed. Collège Stanislas, Paris; Prix de l'Express for La Route des Flandres 1960; Prix Médicis for Histoire 1967, Nobel Prize for Literature 1985; Grand Croix, Ordre nat. du Mérite. *Publications:* Le tricheur 1945, La corde raide 1947, Gulliver 1952, Le sacre du printemps 1954, Le vent 1957, L'herbe 1958, La route des Flandres 1960, Le palace 1962, Femmes 1966, Histoire 1967, La bataille de Pharsale 1969, Orion aveugle 1970, Les corps conducteurs 1971, Tryptyque 1973, Leçon de choses 1975, Les Géorgiques 1981, La chevelure de Bérénice 1985, Discours de Stockholm 1986, L'invitation 1988, Album d'un amateur 1988, L'acacia 1989, Photographies 1992, Le jardin des plantes 1997. *Address:* Editions de Minuit, 7 rue Bernard-Palissy, 75006 Paris; place Vieille, Salses, 66600 Rivesaltes, France.

SIMON, Herbert A., PH.D.; American social scientist; b. 15 June 1916, Milwaukee, Wis.; s. of Arthur Simon and Edna Merkel Simon; m. Dorothea Pye 1937; one s. two d.; ed. Univ. of Chicago; Research Asst., Univ. of Chicago 1936–38; Staff mem. Int. City Managers' Asscn. 1938–39; Dir. of Admin. Measurement Studies, Bureau of Public Admin. Univ. of Calif. at Berkeley 1939–42; Asst. Prof., later Prof., Ill. Inst. of Tech. 1942–49, Chair. of Dept. 1946–49; Prof. of Admin., Carnegie-Mellon Univ. 1949–65, Richard King Mellon Prof. of Computer Sciences and Psychology 1965–; Chair. Bd. of Dirs. Social Science Research Council 1961–66, Div. of Behavioral Sciences of Nat. Research Council 1968–70; Ford Lecturer, New York Univ. 1960, Vanuxem Lecturer, Princeton Univ. 1961, William James Lecturer, Harvard Univ. 1963, Harris Lecturer, Northwestern Univ. 1967, Compton Lecturer, M.I.T. 1968, Katz-Newcomb Lecturer, Univ. of Michigan 1976, Hovland Lecturer, Yale Univ. 1976, Gaither Lecturer, Univ. of Calif. (Berkeley) 1980, Camp Lecturer, Stanford Univ. 1982, Lecturer, Univ. of Calif. (Los Angeles) 1983, Univ. of Michigan 1983; mem. President's Science Advisory Cttee. 1968–72, Nat. Acad. of Sciences, American Philosophical Soc., Bd. of Trustees, Carnegie-Mellon Univ. 1972–93, Emer. Trustee 1993–; Distinguished Fellow, American Econ. Asscn. 1976; Foreign mem. Yugoslav Acad. of Sciences; Hon. Prof., Tianjin Univ., Beijing Univ.; Hon. mem. Inst. of Electrical and Electronic Engineers, Inst. of Psychology, Chinese Acad. of Sciences; Hon. D.Sc. (Yale, Case Inst. of Tech., Marquette, Columbia, Gustavus Adolphus, Duquesne, Mich. Technological, Carnegie Mellon), Hon. LL.D. (Chicago, McGill, Mich., Pittsburgh, Harvard), Hon. Fil.D. (Lund), Hon. D.Phil. (Paul Valery Univ. of Montpellier) 1984; Hon. Dr. Econ.Sc. (Erasmus), Hon. D.Hum.Litt., Hon. D.Sc. (Illinois Inst. Tech.), Hon. D.rer.Pol. (Pavia), Dr. h.c. (Univ. of Rome); Distinguished Scientific Contributions Award, American Psychological Asscn. 1969, A. M. Turing Award, Asscn. for Computing Machinery 1975, Nobel Prize for Econs. 1978, Procter Prize 1980, James Madison Award, American Political Science Asscn. 1984, Nat. Medal of Science 1986, Von Neumann Theory Prize 1988. *Publications:* Administrative Behavior 1947, 1957, 1976, Public Administration 1950, Models of Man 1957, Organizations 1958, The Shape of Automation 1960, 1965, The Sciences of the Artificial 1969, 1981, Human Problem-Solving 1972, Models of Discovery 1977, Models of Thought, Vol. I 1979, Vol. II 1989, Models of

Bounded Rationality (2 vols.) 1982, Reason in Human Affairs 1983, Protocol Analysis 1984, Scientific Discovery 1986, Models of my Life 1991. *Leisure interests:* hiking, music. *Address:* Department of Psychology, Carnegie-Mellon University, Schenley Park, Pittsburgh, PA 15213, U.S.A. *Telephone:* (412) 268-2787.

SIMON, Josette; British actress; d. of Charles Simon and Eileen Petty; m. Mark Padmore 1996; ed. Cen. School of Speech Training and Dramatic Art; appeared in TV series Blake's 7; joined RSC; Hon. M.A. (Leicester) 1995; appeared as Isabella in Measure for Measure 1988, as Maggie in Arthur Miller's After the Fall, Nat. Theatre, in The White Devil, Nat. Theatre 1991, as Ellida Wangel in Ibsen's The Lady from the Sea, Lyric Theatre, Hammersmith 1994, The Taming of the Shrew, Leicester 1995, The Maids, Donmar Warehouse 1997, Titania in A Midsummer Night's Dream 1999, several concert performances. *Films include:* Cry Freedom, Milk and Honey (Best Actress Atlantic Film Festival 1988, Paris Film Festival 1990), A Child From the South, Bitter Harvest, Bridge of Time. *TV includes:* Henry IV, Parts 1 and 2, Bodyguards, Kavanagh Q.C. *Address:* c/o Conway van Gelder Ltd., 18–21 Jermyn Street, London, SW1Y 6HP, England. *Telephone:* 0171-287 0077. *Fax:* 0171-287 1940.

SIMON, Neil; American playwright; b. 4 July 1927, New York; s. of Irving Simon and Mamie Simon; m. 1st. Joan Baim 1953 (deceased); two d.; m. 2nd Marsha Mason 1973 (divorced); m. 3rd Diane Lander 1987; one d.; ed. New York Univ.; wrote for various television programmes, including The Tallulah Bankhead Show 1951, The Phil Silvers Show 1958–59, NBC Special, The Trouble with People 1972. *Plays:* Come Blow Your Horn 1961, Little Me (musical) 1962, Barefoot in the Park 1963, The Odd Couple 1965, Sweet Charity (musical) 1966, The Star-Spangled Girl 1966, Plaza Suite 1968, Promises, Promises (musical) 1968, Last of the Red Hot Lovers 1969, The Gingerbread Lady 1970, The Prisoner of Second Avenue 1971, The Sunshine Boys 1972, The Good Doctor 1973, God's Favorite 1974, California Suite 1976, Chapter Two 1977, They're Playing Our Song 1979, I Ought to be in Pictures 1980, Fools 1981, Little Me (revised version) 1982, Brighton Beach Memoirs 1983, Biloxi Blues 1985, The Odd Couple Female Version 1985, Broadway Bound 1986, Rumors 1988, Lost in Yonkers 1991, Jake's Women 1992, The Goodbye Girl (musical) 1993, Laughter on the 23rd Floor 1993, London Suite 1995. *Screenplays:* After the Fox 1966, Barefoot in the Park 1967, The Odd Couple 1968, The Out-of-Towners 1970, Plaza Suite 1971, The Last of the Red Hot Lovers 1972, The Heartbreak Kid 1973, The Prisoner of Second Avenue 1975, The Sunshine Boys 1975, Murder By Death 1976, The Goodbye Girl 1977, The Cheap Detective 1978, California Suite 1978, Chapter Two 1979, Seems Like Old Times 1980, Only When I Laugh 1981, I Ought to Be in Pictures 1982, Max Dugan Returns 1983, Lonely Guy (adaptation) 1984, The Slugger's Wife 1984, Brighton Beach Memoirs 1986, Biloxi Blues 1988, The Marrying Man 1991, Broadway Bound (TV film) 1992, Lost in Yonkers 1993, Jake's Women (TV film) 1996, London Suite (TV film) 1996; other motion pictures adapted from stage plays: Come Blow Your Horn 1963, Sweet Charity 1969, The Star-Spangled Girl 1971; mem. Dramatists Guild, Writers' Guild of America; many awards and nominations including Emmy Award 1957, 1959; Antoinette Perry (Tony) Awards for The Odd Couple 1965, Biloxi Blues 1985 (Best Play), Lost in Yonkers 1991 (Best Play), Evening Standard Award 1967, 10 Tony award nominations, Oscar nomination for The Odd Couple 1969, Writers' Guild Screen Award for The Odd Couple 1969, Writers' Guild Laurel Award 1979, American Comedy Award for Lifetime Achievement 1989, Pulitzer Prize for Lost in Yonkers 1991; Hon. D.Hum.Litt. (Hofstra Univ.) 1981, (Williams Coll.) 1984. *Publications:* Rewrites: A Memoir 1996; individual plays. *Address:* c/o A. DaSilva, 502 Park Avenue, New York, NY 10022, U.S.A.

SIMON, Paul; American politician, educationalist, and writer; b. 29 Nov. 1928, Eugene, Ore.; s. of Martin Paul Simon and Ruth (née Troemel) Simon; m. Jeanne Hurley 1960; one s. one d.; ed. Univ. of Oregon, Dana Coll., Blair, Neb.; publisher Troy (Ill.) Tribune 1948–66, and weeklies; mem. Ill. House of Reps. 1955–63, Ill. Senate 1963–69, Lieut. Gov. Ill. 1969–73; Fellow John F. Kennedy Inst. of Politics, Harvard 1972–73; Prof. of Public Affairs Reporting Sangamon State Univ., Springfield 1973; mem. 94th–98th Congresses, Ill.; U.S. Senator from Illinois 1985–97; Dir. of Public Policy, Southern Ill. Univ. 1996–; mem. Bd. of Dirs. Dana Coll.; recipient American Political Science Asscn. Award 1957; holds 27 hon. degrees; Democrat. *Publications:* Lovejoy: Martyr to Freedom 1964, Lincoln's Preparation for Greatness 1965, a Hungry World 1966, Protestant-Catholic Marriages Can Succeed (with Jeanne Hurley Simon) 1967, (with Arthur Simon) The Politics of World Hunger 1973, You Want to Change the World, So Change It 1971, The Tongue-Tied American 1980, The Once and Future Democrats 1982, The Glass House, Politics and Morality in the Nation's Capitol 1984, Beginnings 1986, Let's Put America Back to Work 1986, Winners and Losers 1989, Advice and Consent 1992, Freedom's Champion: Elijah Lovejoy 1994, All Tapped Out 1998, P.S.: The Autobiography of Paul Simon. *Address:* Southern Illinois University, Public Policy Institute, Carbondale, IL 62901, U.S.A.

SIMON, Paul, B.A.; American composer and musician; b. 13 Oct. 1942, Newark; s. of Louis and Belle Simon; m. 1st Peggy Harper; one s.; m. 2nd Carrie Fisher 1983 (divorced); m. 3rd Edie Brickell 1992; one s.; ed. Queens Coll., Brooklyn Law School; fmrly. mem. singing duo Simon and Garfunkel (q.v.) 1964–71; solo performer 1972–. *songs with Garfunkel include:* The Sounds of Silence, Dangling Conversation, Homeward Bound, I Am a Rock, At the Zoo, 7 O'Clock News, 59th Street Bridge Song, Scarborough Fair, Mrs. Robinson, The Boxer, Bridge Over Troubled Water; *albums with Garfunkel:* Wednesday Morning 3 A.M. 1964, Sounds of Silence 1966, Parsley, Sage, Rosemary and Thyme 1966, The Graduate 1968. Bookends 1968, Bridge Over Troubled Water 1970, Concert in Central Park 1982; *solo albums:* Paul Simon 1972, There goes Rhymin' Simon 1973, Live Rhymin' 1975, Still Crazy After All These Years 1975, Greatest Hits, etc. 1977, One-Trick Pony 1980, Hearts and Bones 1983; Graceland 1986; Paul Simon: Solo 1990, Rhythm of the Saints 1990, 1964–93 1993; wrote score, author screenplay One-Trick Pony; wrote musical The Capeman 1997; appeared in film Annie Hall 1977; Grammy Award for Mrs Robinson (song), Bridge Over Troubled Water (album), The Graduate (soundtrack), Still Crazy After All These Years (album), Graceland (album) 1986; Emmy Award for NBC Paul Simon Special, Born at the Right Time tour, S. Africa 1992; series with Art Garfunkel, Paramount 1993. *Address:* c/o Warner Bros. Records, 28 Kensington Church Street, London, W8 4ET, England.

SIMON, William Edward, B.A.; American politician and financier; b. 27 Nov. 1927, Paterson, N.J.; s. of Charles Simon and Eleanor Kearns; m. 1st Carol Girard 1950 (died 1995); two s. five d.; m. 2nd Tonia Adams Donnelly 1996; ed. Lafayette Coll., Easton, Pennsylvania; joined Union Securities, N.Y. 1952, Asst. Vice-Pres., Man. Municipal Trading Dept. 1955; Vice-Pres. Weedon & Co. 1957–64; joined Salomon Bros. 1964, later Partner; Deputy Sec. U.S. Treasury Dept. 1973–74, Head of Federal Energy Office 1973–74; Sec. of the Treasury 1974–77; Chair. Econ. Policy Bd. 1974–77; Chair. Council on Wage and Price Stability 1975–77; Chair. William E. Simon & Sons Inc., Morristown, N.J.; Chair. Wesray Corpn., Morristown 1981–86 (now Chair. Emer.), Wesray Capital Corpn. 1984–86, William E. Simon Foundation Inc., John M. Olin Foundation; Co-Chair. WSGP Int. Inc.; mem. Bd. of Dirs., Exec. Cttee. Securities Industry Asscn. 1972; Chair. Public Finance Council; Founder, Past Pres. Asscn. of Primary Dealers in U.S. Govt. Securities; mem. Cttee. to Fight Inflation 1980, Bretton Woods Cttee., Econ. Policy Advisory Bd. 1981–; Nat. Chair. Fund Raising, U.S. Olympic Cttee. (Jesse Owens Int. Award 1990); Chair. Debt Man. Cttee. of N.Y.; Trustee, Lafayette Coll., Mannes Coll. of Music, Newark Acad.; mem., Trustee etc. numerous other bodies; Hon. LL.D. (Lafayette Coll.) 1973, (Pepperdine Univ.) 1975, Hon. D.C.L. (Jacksonville Univ.) 1976, Hon. D.Sc. (New England Coll.) 1977, Hon. Dr. Phil. (Tel Aviv Univ.) 1976; numerous awards and medals, including Pres.'s Award for Outstanding Achievement 1976. *Publications:* A Time for Truth 1978, A Time for Action 1980. *Address:* William E. Simon and Sons Inc., P.O. Box 1913, Morristown, NJ 07960-1913 (Office); T-Bill Ranch, 4000 Highway 154, Santa Barbara, CA 93105, U.S.A. (Home).

SIMON OF GLAISDALE, Baron (Life Peer), cr. 1970; **Jocelyn Edward Salis Simon,** Kt., P.C.; British judge; b. 15 Jan. 1911, London; s. of Frank Cecil Simon and Claire Evelyn Simon, M.B.E.; m. 1st Gwendolen Helen Evans 1934 (died 1937); m. 2nd Fay Elizabeth Leicester Pearson 1948; three s.; ed. Gresham's School, Holt and Trinity Hall, Cambridge; M.P. (Conservative) 1951–62; Joint Parl. Under-Sec. of State, Home Office 1957–58; Financial Sec. to Treasury 1958–59; Solicitor-Gen. 1959–62; Pres. of Probate, Divorce and Admiralty Div. of High Court 1962–71; Lord of Appeal in Ordinary 1971–77; Hon. Fellow Trinity Hall, Cambridge 1963; Dr. h.c. (Cambridge) 1994; Elder Brother Trinity House. *Publications:* Co-author of Change is Our Ally 1954, Rule of Law 1955, The Church and the Law of Nullity 1955. *Address:* House of Lords, London, SW1A 0PW, England.

SIMON OF HIGHBURY, Baron (Life Peer), cr 1997, of Canonbury in the London Borough of Islington, **David Alec Gwyn Simon,** Kt., C.B.E., M.A., M.B.A.; British business executive; b. 24 July 1939, London; s. of late Roger Simon and of Barbara Hudd; m. 1st Hanne Mohn 1964; two s.; m. 2nd Sarah Smith 1992; ed. Gonville and Caius Coll., Cambridge; joined B.P. 1961, Marketing Dir., Holland 1972–75, Marketing Co-ordinator, European Region 1975–80, Marketing Dir., Oil U.K. 1980–82, Man. Dir., Oil Int. Ltd. 1982–85, Man. Dir. B.P. Co. PLC 1986–95, Deputy Chair. 1990–95, Group Chief Exec. 1992–95, Chair. 1995–97; Non-Exec. Dir. Grand Metropolitan PLC 1990–96; Dir. Bank of England 1995–97; Minister Responsible for Trade and Competitiveness in Europe (attached to Dept. of Trade and Industry) May 1997–; Dir. (non-exec.) The RTZ Corpn. PLC 1995–97; mem. Supervisory Bd. Allianz AG 1996–97; mem. Advisory Bd. Deutsche Bank 1992–97; mem. Int. Advisory Council, Allianz A.G. Holding 1993–97. *Leisure interests:* golf, books, music. *Address:* House of Lords, Westminster, London, SW1A 0PW, England.

SIMONDS-GOODING, Anthony James Joseph; British broadcasting executive; b. 10 Sept. 1937; s. of Maj. and Mrs Hamilton Simonds-Gooding; m. 1st Fiona Menzies 1961 (divorced 1982); three s. two d. (one s. deceased); m. 2nd Marjorie A. Pennock 1982, one step-s.; ed. Ampleforth Coll. and Britannia Royal Naval Coll. Dartmouth; served Royal Navy 1953–59; with Unilever 1960–73; Marketing Dir. Whitbread & Co., PLC 1973, subsequently Man. Dir. (U.K.), latterly Group Man. Dir. until 1985; Chair. and Chief Exec. Saatchi PLC 1985–87; Chief Exec. British Satellite Broadcasting 1987–90, Chair. 1993–; Chair. S. P. Lintas 1994–95, Ammivati Puris Lintas 1994–96; Chair. Designers and Art Dirs. Asscn. 1992–; Dir. ICA Devt. Cttee. 1992–94, Cancer Relief Macmillan Fund 1992–, Robinsons PLC 1993–, Brixton Prison 1994–97, Community Hosps. Group PLC 1995–, Interbrand Newell & Sorrell 1996–, Clark & Taylor 1996–, Blick PLC 1997–, Kunick PLC 1997–. *Address:* Burchetts Brook, Holmbury St. Mary, Surrey, RH5 6NA, England.

SIMONE, Nina (b. Eunice Wayman); American singer; b. 21 Feb. 1933, Tryon, N.C.; ed. Juilliard School of Music, N.Y.; sang in clubs in Philadelphia; signed contract with Bethlehem Records 1959, Colpix 1960, Phillips 1965, RCA 1967; active in civil rights movt. in early 60's; moved to Paris, now lives in the Netherlands; *recordings include:* I Loves You Porgy, Don't Let Me Be Misunderstood, I Put a Spell on You, Ain't Got No . . . I Got Life, Young, Gifted and Black, Baltimore, My Baby Just Cares For Me, etc.; Dr. h.c. (Chicago, Univ. of Mass., Amherst).

SIMONET, Henri François, D. EN D., D. ÈS SC.; Belgian politician; b. 10 May 1931, Brussels; m. Marie-Louise Angenent 1960; one s. one d.; ed. Univ. Libre de Bruxelles and Columbia Univ., U.S.A.; Asst., Univ. Libre de Bruxelles 1956–58, now Prof.; Financial Adviser, Inst. National d'Etudes pour le Développement du Bas-Congo 1958–59; Legal Adviser, Comm. of Brussels Stock Exchange 1959–60; Deputy Dir. Office of Econ. Programming 1961; Dir. of Cabinet of Ministry of Econ. Affairs and Power 1961–65; Dir. of Cabinet of Deputy Prime Minister responsible for Co-ordination of Econ. Policy 1965; Mayor of Anderlecht 1966–84; M.P. for Brussels 1966–84, 1985–92; Minister of Econ. Affairs 1972–73; mem., Vice-Pres. Comm. of the European Communities 1973–77; Minister of Foreign Affairs 1977–80; Sec. of State for Brussels Econ. Affairs 1977–79; Financial Consultant and Corp. Dir. *Publications:* various books and articles on economics, financial and political topics. *Address:* 34 avenue Franklin Roosevelt, 1050 Brussels, Belgium.

SIMONETTA; Italian fashion designer; b. Duchess Colonna di Cesarò; d. of Duke Giovanni Colonna di Cesarò and Countess Barbara Antonelli; m. 1st Count Galeazzo Visconti di Modrone 1944; one d.; m. 2nd Alberto Fabiani (fashion designer) 1952; one s.; separated Feb. 1970 and has taken back her maiden name of Duchess Colonna di Cesarò; opened fashion Atelier, Rome 1946; transferred fashion business to Paris 1962; Philadelphia Fashion Group Award 1953, Davison Paxon Award, Atlanta 1959, Fashion Oscar from Filene's of Boston 1960; after five consecutive years in list of world's best dressed women is in "Hall of Fame"; Hon. citizen of Austin, New Orleans and Las Vegas. *Publication:* A Snob in the Kitchen 1967.

SIMONIA, Nodari Aleksandrovich; Russian political economist; b. 30 Jan. 1930; m.; one d.; ed. Moscow Inst. of Int. Relations; corresp. mem., Russian Acad. of Sciences 1990, mem. 1997–, jr. researcher, sr. researcher, head of sector, head of div., Deputy Dir., Inst. of Oriental Studies 1955–86; Deputy Dir., Inst. of World Econs. and Int. Relations 1986–; main research in social-econ. and political problems of developing countries. *Address:* IMEMO, Profsoyuznaya str. 23, 117859 Moscow, Russia. *Telephone:* (095) 120 8450 (Office); (095) 434 1563 (Home).

SIMONIS, H.E. Cardinal Adrianus J.; Netherlands ecclesiastic; b. 26 Nov. 1931, Lisse, Rotterdam; ordained 1957; consecrated Bishop of Rotterdam 1971; Archbishop of Utrecht 1983–; cr. Cardinal 1985; Pres. Netherlands Bishops' Conf.; mem. Congregations for Insts. of Consecrated Life and for Societies of Apostolic Life, for Catholic Educ., Pontifical Council for the Promotion of Christian Unity. *Address:* Aartsbisdom, B.P. 14019, Maliebaan 40, 3508 SB Utrecht, Netherlands. *Telephone:* (030) 2316956. *Fax:* (030) 2311962.

SIMONIS, Heide, M.A.; German politician; b. 4 July 1943, Bonn; d. of Dr. Horst Steinhardt and Sophia Brück; m. Prof. Udo E. Simonis 1967; tutor in German, Univ. of Zambia 1967–69, Goethe Inst. and Nat. TV and Radio Service, Tokyo 1970–72; mem. Bundestag 1976–88; Minister of Finance, Schleswig-Holstein 1988–93, Minister-Pres. 1993–; Social Democratic Party (SPD). *Address:* Klosterufer 2, 24582 Bordesholm, Germany.

SIMONOV, Aleksey Kirillovich; Russian film director and human rights activist; b. 8 Aug. 1939, Moscow; s. of Konstantin Simonov; m.; two s.; ed. Inst. of Oriental Languages at Moscow State Univ., All-Union Inst. of Cinematography; lab., Inst. of Permafrost Studies 1952–56; translator, U.S.S.R. State Cttee. for Int. Econ. Relations in Indonesia 1963–64; Ed., Khudozhestennaya Literatura 1964–67; film dir. EKRAN TV Studio 1970–91; lecturer All-Russian Inst. of Cinematography 1991–93; Sec. U.S.S.R. Union of Cinematographists 1991; f. Konf 1991; Co.-Chair. Licence Cttee. of Russian Fed. 1992–93; mem. Movt. of Democratic Reforms 1991–93; mem. Public Chamber of Russian Presidency; a founder Movt. for Mil. Reform 1995; directed over 20 feature films and documentaries including Team 1985; mem. Editorial Bd., Sovyetsky Ekran (magazine) 1988–92, Rossia (weekly) 1992–96. *Publications:* numerous articles in newspapers and magazines Yunost, Ogonyok, Moskva; translator of English, Myanma and African plays. *Address:* Krasnoarmeiskaya str. 27, apt. 3, 125319 Moscow, Russia (Home). *Telephone:* (095) 151 3718 (Home).

SIMONOV, Pavel Vasilyevich; Russian neurophysiologist and psychophysiologist; b. 20 April 1926, Leningrad (now St. Petersburg); s. of Vasily Simonov and Maria Stankevich; m. Olga Simonova 1948; one s. one d.; ed. Mil. Medical Acad., Leningrad; Scientific Worker, subsequently Head, Experimental Lab., Cen. Mil. Hosp., Moscow 1951–61; Sr. Scientific Worker, subsequently Dir., Inst. of Higher Nervous Activity and Neurophysiology, U.S.S.R. (now Russian) Acad. of Sciences 1961–; corresp. mem. U.S.S.R. (now Russian) Acad. of Sciences 1981, mem. 1987, Academician-Sec. Dept. of Physiology 1988–96; Pavlov Prize, U.S.S.R. Acad. of Sciences 1981, U.S.S.R. State Prize 1987. *Publications:* Higher Nervous Activity of Man: Motivational-Emotional Aspects 1975, The Emotional Brain 1986, The Motivated Brain 1991, Temperament, Character, Personality 1991, The Creative Brain 1993. *Leisure interests:* neurophysiology and psychophysiology of motivations and emotions. *Address:* Russian Academy of Sciences, Institute of Higher Nervous Activity and Neurophysiology, Butlerov Street 5A, 117865 Moscow, Russia. *Telephone:* (095) 334-70-00 (Office); 332-68-86 (Home). *Fax:* (095) 338-85-00.

SIMONS, Elwyn LaVerne, M.A., PH.D., D.PHIL.; American professor of anthropology and anatomy; b. 14 July 1930, Lawrence, Kan.; s. of Verne Franklin Simons and Verna Irene (Cuddeback) Simons; m. 1st Mary Hoyt Fitch 1964; one s.; m. 2nd Friderun A. Ankel 1972; one s. one d.; ed. Rice, Princeton and Oxford Univs.; Lecturer in Geology, Princeton Univ. 1958–59; Asst. Prof. of Zoology, Univ. of Pennsylvania 1959–61; Visiting Assoc. Prof. of Geology and Curator of Vertebrate Paleontology, Yale Univ. 1960–61, Assoc. Prof. and Head Curator 1961–65; Prof. of Geology and Curator in charge, Div. of Vertebrate Paleontology, Peabody Museum 1965–77; Prof. of Anthropology and Anatomy, Duke Univ., 1977–, James B. Duke Prof. 1982–, Prof. of Zoology and Dir. Duke Primate Center 1977–91, Scientific Dir. 1991–; mem. Exec. Cttee., Center for Tropical Conservation 1991–; mem. Steering Cttee., Madagascar Fauna Group 1990–; has directed over 70 expeditions to Wyoming, Iran, India and Madagascar, and 29 to the Egyptian Fayum in search of fossil primates and associated fauna; discovered Gigantopithecus in India, discovered and named Aegyptopithecus, Catapithecus, Arsinoea and Proteopithecus in Egypt; mem. N.A.S., American Philosophical Soc.; Hon. M.A. (Yale) 1967; Hon. D.Sc. (Oxford) 1996; numerous awards including Annandale Medal, Asiatic Soc. of Calcutta, Hon. Citizen Fayum Prov., Egypt; Chevalier Ordre. Nat., Madagascar. *Publications:* 262 scientific articles, abstracts and books. *Leisure interests:* drawing and painting, folk singing, genealogy. *Address:* Duke University Primate Center, 3705 Erwin Road, Durham, NC 27706 U.S.A. (Office). *Telephone:* (919) 684-2535 (Office). *Fax:* (919) 490-5394.

SIMPSON, Alan Kooi, B.S., J.D.; American politician; b. 2 Sept. 1931, Cody, Wyo.; s. of Milward Lee Simpson and Lorna (née Kooi) Simpson; m. Ann Schroll 1954; two s. one d.; ed. Univ. of Wyoming; called to Wyo. Bar 1958, U.S. Supreme Court 1964; Asst. Attorney Gen. Wyo. State 1959; Attorney for Cody 1959–69; Partner Simpson, Kepler, Simpson & Cozzens, Cody 1959–78; mem. Wyo. House of Reps. 1964–77, U.S. Senate from Wyoming 1978–97, Asst. Majority Leader 1985–87, Asst. Minority Leader 1987–97; Trustee Buffalo Bill Historical Center, Cody, Gottsche Foundation Rehabilitation Center; mem. Wyo. Bar Asscn., American Bar Asscn., Asscn. of Trial Lawyers of America; Hon. LL.D. (Calif. Western School of Law) 1983, (Colo. Coll.) 1986, (Notre Dame Univ.) 1987; recipient Centennial Alum Award (Wyoming Univ.) 1987, Thomas Jefferson Award in Law, Univ. of Virginia 1998.

SIMPSON, (Alfred William) Brian, J.P., M.A., D.C.L., F.B.A.; British professor of law; b. 17 August 1931, Kendal; s. of Rev. B. W. Simpson and M. E. Simpson; m. 1st Kathleen Seston 1954 (divorced 1968); one s. one d.; m. 2nd Caroline E. A. Brown 1969; one s. two d.; ed. Oakham School, Rutland and Queen's Coll., Oxford; Jr. Research Fellow, St. Edmund Hall, Oxford 1954–55; Fellow Lincoln Coll., Oxford 1955–73, Jr. Proctor 1967–68; Dean Faculty of Law, Univ. of Ghana 1968–69; Prof. of Law, Univ. of Kent 1973–85, Prof. Emer. 1985–; Prof. of Law, Univ. of Chicago, U.S.A. 1983–86; Prof. of Law, Univ. of Mich. 1987–; Goodhart Visiting Prof., Univ. of Cambridge, U.K. 1993–94; Fellow American Acad. of Arts and Sciences, British Acad; Barrister-at-law, Gray's Inn. *Publications:* A History of the Common Law of Contract 1975, Cannibalism and the Common Law 1984, A Biographical Dictionary of the Common Law (Ed.) 1984, A History of the Land Law 1986, Legal Theory and Legal History 1987, Invitation to Law 1988, In the Highest Degree Odious: Detention Without Trial in Wartime Britain 1992, Leading Cases in the Common Law 1995. *Leisure interests:* sailing, flying. *Address:* University of Michigan Law School, Hutchins Hall, Ann Arbor, MI 48109, U.S.A.; 36 High Street, Wingham, Kent, CT3 1AB, England. *Telephone:* (734) 763-0413 (U.S.A.); (01227) 720 979 (Kent, England). *Fax:* (734) 763-9375 (U.S.A.).

SIMPSON, Joanne (Gerould), PH.D.; American meteorologist; b. 23 March 1923, Boston, Mass.; d. of Russell Gerould and Virginia Vaughan; m. 1st Victor Starr 1944; m. 2nd William Malkus 1948; two s. one d.; m. 3rd Robert Simpson 1965; ed. Univ. of Chicago; instructor, later Asst. Prof., New York Univ., Univ. of Chicago, Ill. Inst. of Tech. 1943–51; meteorologist, Woods Hole Oceanographic Inst. 1951–60; Prof. of Meteorology, Univ. of Calif. at L.A. 1960–64; Dir. Experimental Meteorology Lab., NOAA, Coral Gables, Fla. 1965–74; Prof. of Environmental Sciences, Univ. of Va. 1974–76, William W. Corcoran Prof. 1976–81; Affiliate Prof. of Atmospheric Science, Colo. State Univ. 1980–; Head, Severe Storms Branch, Goddard Lab. for Atmospheres, Goddard Space Flight Center, NASA 1979–88, Chief Scientist for Meteorology 1988–; Goddard Sr. Fellow, NASA 1989–94; Study Scientist for Tropical Rainfall Measuring Mission, Goddard Space Flight Center 1986–89, Project Scientist 1986–98; mem. Bd. on Geophysics and Environmental Data 1993–, on Atmospheric Sciences and Climate 1997–; Guggenheim Fellow 1954; Fellow American Meteorological Soc. (Pres. 1989, Hon. mem. 1995); mem. Nat. Acad. of Eng., American Geophysical Union (Fellow 1994), The Oceanography Soc.; Hon. D.Sc. (State Univ. of New York) 1991; NASA Exceptional Scientific Achievement Medal 1982, Meisinger Award 1962 and Rossby Research Medal 1983, American Meteorological Soc., NASA Nordberg Award 1994 and numerous other prizes and awards. *Publications:* more than

150 papers on tropical meteorology, tropical cloud systems and modelling, tropical storms and tropical rain measurement from space. *Leisure interests:* sailing, reading, travel. *Address:* NASA/GSFC, Centre for Earth Sciences, Greenbelt, MD 20771, U.S.A. *Telephone:* (301) 286-8569. *Fax:* (301) 286-1762.

SIMPSON, John Cody Fidler-, C.B.E., M.A., F.R.G.S.; British broadcaster and writer; b. 9 Aug. 1944, Cleveleys; s. of Roy Fidler-Simpson and Joyce Leila Vivien Cody; m. 1st Diane Petteys 1965 (divorced 1996); two d.; m. 2nd Adèle Krüger 1996; ed. St. Paul's School, London, Magdalene Coll. Cambridge; joined BBC 1966, Foreign Corresp. in Dublin, Brussels, Johannesburg 1972–78, Diplomatic Corresp., BBC TV 1978–80, Political Ed. 1980–81, Diplomatic Ed. 1982–88, Foreign Affairs Ed. (now World Affairs Ed.) 1988–; Contributing Ed. The Spectator 1991–95; columnist, Sunday Telegraph 1995–; Hon. D.Litt. (De Montfort) 1995. *Publications:* Despatches from the Barricades 1990, From the House of War 1991, The Darkness Crumbles 1992, In the Forests of the Night 1993, Lifting the Veil: Life in Revolutionary Iran 1995, The Oxford Book of Exile 1995, Strange Places, Questionable People (autobiog.) 1998. *Leisure interests:* travel, scuba diving, book collecting. *Address:* c/o BBC World Affairs Unit, Television Centre, Wood Lane, London, W12 7RJ, England. *Telephone:* 0181-743 8000. *Fax:* 0181-745 7591.

SIMPSON, Louis Aston Marantz, PH.D.; American writer and teacher; b. 27 March 1923, Jamaica, West Indies; s. of Aston and Rosalind (Marantz) Simpson; m. 1st Jeanne Rogers 1949 (divorced 1954); one s.; m. 2nd Dorothy Roochvarg 1955 (divorced 1979); one s. one d.; m. 3rd Miriam Bachner (née Butensky) 1985; ed. Munro Coll., Jamaica, Columbia Univ., New York; Assoc. Ed. Bobbs-Merrill Publishing Co., New York 1950–55; Instructor, Asst. Prof. Columbia Univ. 1955–59; Prof. Univ. of Calif. at Berkeley 1959–67; Prof. State Univ. of New York at Stony Brook 1967–91, Distinguished Prof. 1991–; Hon. D.H.L. (Eastern Mich. Univ.) 1977; Hon. D.L. (Hampden-Sydney Coll.) 1991; Pulitzer Prize for Poetry 1964, Columbia Univ. Medal for Excellence 1965, Elmer Holmes Bobst Award for poetry 1987. *Publications:* poetry: The Arrivistes: Poems 1940–49 1949, Good News of Death and other Poems 1955, The New Poets of England and America (Ed.) 1957, A Dream of Governors 1959, At the End of the Open Road 1963, Selected Poems 1965, Adventures of the Letter I 1971, Searching for the Ox 1976, Caviare at the Funeral 1980, People Live Here: Selected Poems 1949–83; The Best Hour of the Night 1983; Collected Poems 1988, In the Room We Share 1990, There You Are 1995, Nombres et poussière 1996; prose: James Hogg: a Critical Study 1962, Riverside Drive 1962, An Introduction to Poetry (Ed.) 1967, North of Jamaica 1971, Three on the Tower: the Lives and Works of Ezra Pound, T. S. Eliot and William Carlos Williams 1975, A Revolution in Taste 1978, A Company of Poets 1981, The Character of the Poet 1986, Selected Prose 1989, Ships Going into the Blue 1994, The King My Father's Wreck 1995. *Leisure interests:* dogs, fishing. *Address:* 186 Old Field Road, Setauket, NY 11733, U.S.A. *Telephone:* (516) 751-2727. *Fax:* (516) 751-2727.

SIMPSON, Norman Frederick; British playwright; b. 29 Jan. 1919, London; s. of George Frederick Simpson; m. Joyce Bartlett 1944; one d.; ed. Emanuel School, London, and Birkbeck Coll., Univ. of London; teacher in adult educ. until 1963; full-time playwright 1963–. *Publications:* plays: A Resounding Tinkle 1958, The Hole 1958, One Way Pendulum (also film) 1959, The Form 1961, The Cresta Run 1965, Some Tall Tinkles 1968; Co-Author Diamonds for Breakfast (film) 1968, Was He Anyone? 1973; novel: Harry Bleachbaker 1976. *Leisure interests:* reading, walking.

SIMPSON, O. J. (Orenthal James); American fmr. professional football player, actor and sports commentator; b. 9 July 1947, San Francisco; s. of Jimmie Simpson and Eunice Durton; m. 1st Marguerite Whitley 1967 (divorced); one s. one d.; m. 2nd Nicole Brown 1985 (divorced 1992, died 1994); two s.; ed. Univ. of S. Calif. and City Coll. San Francisco; mem. world record 440 yard relay team (38.6 sec.) 1967; Downtown Athletic Club 1968; Halfback, Buffalo Bills 1969–78, San Francisco 49'ers 1978–79; American Football League All-Star Team 1970, ProBowl Team 1972–76; sports commentator, ABC Sports 1979–86; analyst, ABC Monday Night Football broadcasts 1984–85; co-host, NFL Live on NBC 1990; has appeared in several TV films; recipient of various football awards; acquitted of two charges of murder Oct. 1995; civil suit trial began Sept. 1996, found responsible for deaths of Nicole Brown Simpson and Ronald Goldman by a civil jury Feb. 1997, ordered to pay $8.5 million in compensatory damages, and to pay $25 million in punitive damages to victims' familes, case on appeal. *Films include:* The Towering Inferno 1974, Killer Force 1976, The Cassandra Crossing 1977, Capricorn One 1978, Firepower 1979, Hambone & Hillie 1984, The Naked Gun 1988, The Naked Gun 2½: The Smell of Fear 1991, The Naked Gun 33⅓: The Final Insult 1994. *Publication:* I Want to Tell You 1995.

SIMS, Geoffrey Donald, O.B.E., PH.D., A.R.C.S., D.I.C., F.I.E.E., F.C.G.I., F.ENG.; British fmr. university vice-chancellor; b. 13 Dec. 1926, London; s. of Albert Sims and Jessie Sims; m. Pamela Richings 1949; one s. two d.; ed. Wembley County Grammar School and Imperial Coll. London; Research Physicist, G.E.C., Wembley 1948–54; Sr. Scientific Officer, UKAEA, Harwell 1954–56; Lecturer, Sr. Lecturer, Dept. of Electrical Eng. Univ. Coll. London 1956–63; Prof. and Head of Dept. of Electronics, Univ. of Southampton 1963–74, Dean of Faculty 1967–70, Sr. Deputy Vice-Chancellor 1970–72; Vice-Chancellor, Univ. of Sheffield 1974–90; Chair. Council for Educ. in the Commonwealth 1991–96; Hon. D.Sc. 1979; Hon. Sc.D. 1989; Hon. D.Sc.Eng. 1990; Hon. LL.D. (Dundee) 1990, (Sheffield) 1991; Symons Medal (Asscn. of Commonwealth Univs.) 1991. *Publications:* Microwave Tubes and Semiconductor Devices (with I. M. Stephenson) 1963, Variational Techniques in Electromagnetism (translation) 1965; numerous papers on microwaves, electronics and education. *Leisure interests:* golf, music, travel. *Address:* Ingleside, 70 Whirlow Lane, Sheffield, S11 9QF, England. *Telephone:* (0114) 236 6196. *Fax:* (0114) 236 6196.

SIMUTIS, Anicetas, M.A.; Lithuanian diplomatist; b. 11 Feb. 1909, Tirkšliai; s. of Anicetas Simutis and Janina Simutis; m. Janina Čiurlys 1936; two c.; ed. Univ. of Vytautas Magnus, Kaunas and Columbia Univ., New York; joined Lithuanian Ministry of Foreign Affairs 1931; Sec. Consulate-Gen. of Lithuania 1936, Consular Attaché 1939, Vice-Consul 1951, Consul-Gen. 1967; Amb. and Perm. Rep. of Lithuania to UN 1991–93. *Publications:* The Economic Reconstruction of Lithuania after 1918 1942, Lithuanian World Directory 1953; articles in periodicals. *Address:* 160 Garfield Place, East Rockaway, NY 11518, U.S.A. (Home). *Telephone:* (516) 599-6376 (Home). *Fax:* (212) 595-8301.

SIN, H.E. Cardinal Jaime L., B.SC.ED., D.D.; Philippine ecclesiastic; b. 31 Aug. 1928, New Washington, Aklan; s. of Juan Sin and Maxima Reyes Lachica de Sin; ed. New Washington Elementary School, St. Vincent Ferrer Seminary; ordained Roman Catholic Priest 1954; Missionary Priest 1954–57; First Rector, St. Pius X Seminary, Roxas City 1957–67; Domestic Prelate to Pope John XXIII 1960; Auxiliary Bishop of Jaro, Iloilo 1967; Archbishop of Jaro 1972, of Manila 1974–; cr. Cardinal 1976; Chair. Comm. on Seminaries and Priestly Vocations 1969–73, Comm. on Clergy 1974–77; mem. Pontifical Comm. on Social Communications 1975–; mem. Admin. Council, Catholic Bishops' Conf. of the Philippines (CBCP) 1968–72, Vice-Pres. CBCP 1970–74; Perm. mem. of the Synod of Bishops in Rome 1977–; mem. Pontifical Comm. on the Evangelization of Peoples 1978; mem. Sacred Congregation for Catholic Educ. 1978; mem. Secr. for Non-Christians 1978; now mem. Congregations for the Clergy, for Divine Worship and the Discipline of the Sacraments, for Insts. of Consecrated Life and for Socs. of Apostolic Life; Royal Acad. of Spanish Language 1978; Pres. Catholic Bishops' Conf. of the Philippines 1978, 1980; Hon. LL.D. 1975, Hon. D.H.L. 1975, Hon. D.S.T. (Santo Tomas Univ. Manila) 1977, Hon. LL.D. (Angeles Univ.) 1978, Hon. D.Hum.Litt. (Univ. of Iloilo City) 1980, Hon. D.Phil. (Manila) 1980, Hon. D.Phil. (Fu Jen Univ. Taipei) 1980, Dr. h.c. (Yale) 1986; over 100 citations; Distinguished Son of Iloilo Award 1974, Honoured Don of Capiz Award 1976, Outstanding Aklanon Award 1979, Grand Cross, Knights of the Holy Sepulchre of Jerusalem 1976, Distinguished Son of Manila 1976, Rajah Soliman Award for Distinguished Citizenry 1976, Gran Cruz de Isabel la Catolica of the King of Spain 1977, Outstanding Citizen Award for Religion, Manila 1979, Bailiff Grand Cross of Honour and Devotion, Sovereign Military Order of Malta, Rome 1979. *Publications:* Ratio Fundamentalis for Philippine Seminaries 1972, The Revolution of Love 1972, The Church Above Political Systems 1973, A Song of Salvation 1974, Unity in Diversity 1974, La Iglesia Renueva Sus Medios de Evangelicación y Adapta a la Idiosincracia de los Pueblos 1978, The Future of Catholicism in Asia 1978, Christian Basis of Human Rights 1978, Separation, Not Isolation 1978, Slaughter of the Innocents '79, 1979, Discipline, Discipleship and Discerning Service, The Making of "Men for Others" 1980; over 200 papers, articles in periodicals. *Leisure interests:* music: Bach, Chopin, Wagner, Strauss; reading, writing. *Address:* Arzobispado, 121 Arzobispo Street, Intramuros, P.O. Box 132, 1099 Metro Manila, Philippines. *Telephone:* (02) 481867. *Fax:* (02) 481548.

SINANI, Musaid bin Muhammad al-, M.B.A.; Saudi Arabian politician; b. 1946; ed. King Saud Univ. and Univ. of Ariz.; with the Gen. Org. for Social Insurance (GOSI) 1970, Deputy Gov. 1980–1981, Gov. 1982; Minister of Labour and Social Affairs 1995–. *Address:* Ministry of Labour and Social Affairs, Omar bin al-Khatab Street, Riyadh 11157, Saudi Arabia. *Telephone:* (1) 477-8888. *Fax:* (1) 478-9175.

SINAY, Yakov Grigoryevich; Russian physicist; b. 21 Sept. 1935; m.; one s.; ed. Moscow State Univ.; jr., sr. researcher Moscow State Univ. 1960–71; sr., chief of research L. Landau Inst. for Theoretical Physics U.S.S.R. Acad. of Sciences; mem. U.S.S.R. (now Russian) Acad. of Sciences 1991; research in ergodic theory of dynamic systems, math. problems of statistical physics and probability theory; mem. Ed. Bd. Uspekhi Matematicheskyh nauk, mem. Ed. Bd. Theoretical and Math. Physics; Hon. mem. American Acad. of Science and Art in Boston, shared Wolf Prize 1997. *Publications include:* Dynamic Systems with Elastic Mappings 1970, Math. Theory of Phase Transitions 1981, numerous articles in scientific journals. *Address:* L. Landau Institute for Theoretical Physics, Russian Academy of Sciences, Kosygin str. 2, 117940 Moscow, Russia. *Telephone:* (095) 137-32-44 (Office).

SINCLAIR, Charles James Francis, B.A., F.C.A.; British business executive; b. 4 April 1948; s. of Sir George Sinclair and late Lady Jane Sinclair; m. Nicola Bayliss 1974; two s.; ed. Winchester Coll. and Magdalen Coll. Oxford; Voluntary Service Overseas, Zambia 1966–67; Deardon Farrow, chartered accountants 1970–75; Associated Newspapers Holdings Ltd. 1975, Man. Dir. 1988; Group Chief Exec. Daily Mail and Gen. Trust PLC 1988–; Dir. (non-exec.) Euromoney Publs. PLC 1985–, Schroders PLC 1990–, Reuters Holdings PLC 1994–. *Leisure interests:* opera, fishing, skiing. *Address:* Daily Mail and General Trust PLC, Northcliffe House, 2 Derry Street, London, W8 5TT, England. *Telephone:* 0171-938 6000. *Fax:* 0171-938 4626.

SINCLAIR, Sir Clive Marles, Kt.; British inventor and business executive; b. 30 July 1940, London; s. of George William Carter Sinclair and Thora Edith Ella (née Marles) Sinclair; m. Ann Trevor-Briscoe 1962 (divorced 1985); two s. one d.; ed. St. George's Coll., Weybridge; Ed. Bernards Publrs. Ltd. 1958–61; Chair. Sinclair Radionics Ltd. 1962–79, Sinclair Research Ltd. 1979–, Sinclair Browne Ltd. 1981–85, Cambridge Computer 1986–90; Chair. British Mensa 1980–98; Visiting Fellow, Robinson Coll., Cambridge 1982–85; Visiting Prof. Imperial Coll., London 1984–92; Dir. Shaye Communications Ltd. 1986–91, Anamartic Ltd.; Hon. D.Sc. (Bath Univ.) 1983, (Warwick Univ., Heriot Watt) 1983, (UMIST) 1984; Hon. Fellow, Imperial Coll., London 1984; Royal Soc. Mullard Award 1984. *Publications:* Practical Transistor Receivers 1959, British Semiconductor Survey 1963. *Leisure interests:* music, poetry, mathematics, science, poker. *Address:* Sinclair Research Ltd., 7 York Central, 70 York Way, London, N1 9AG, England. *Telephone:* 0171-837 6150 (Office); 0171-837 6316 (Home). *Fax:* 0171-278 3101.

SINCLAIR, Rt. Hon. Ian McCahon, P.C., B.A., LL.B.; Australian politician; b. June 1929, Sydney; s. of George and Hazel Sinclair; m. 1st Margaret Tarrant 1956 (died 1967); one s. two d.; m. 2nd Rosemary Edna Fenton 1970; one s.; ed. Knox Grammar School, Wahroonga and Sydney Univ.; barrister 1952–; mem. Legis. Council in N.S.W. Parl. 1961–63, House of Reps. 1963–; Minister for Social Services 1965–68; Minister Assisting Minister for Trade and Industry 1966–71; Minister for Shipping and Transport 1968–71, for Primary Industry 1971–72; Deputy Leader Country Party (now Nat. Party) 1971–84, Fed. Parl. Leader 1984–89, Party Spokesman on Defence, Foreign Affairs, Law and Agric. 1973–75, Opposition Spokesman on Agric., Leader of Opposition in House of Reps. 1974–75; Minister for Agric. and Northern Australia Nov.-Dec. 1975, for Primary Industry 1975–79, for Communications 1980–82, for Defence 1982–83; Leader of Govt. in House of Reps. 1975–82; Leader of Opposition in House of Reps. 1983–87, Opposition Spokesman for Defence 1983–87, for Trade and Resources 1987–89; Shadow Special Minister of State 1994; mem. Jt. Cttee. of Foreign Affairs, Defence and Trade 1991–, Chair. 1996–98; Speaker, House of Reps., Fed. Parl. 1998–; Man. Dir. Sinclair Pastoral Co. 1953–, Grazier 1953–; Dir. Farmers' and Graziers' Co-operative Co. Ltd. 1962–65; Nat. Party; Hon. D. Univ. *Leisure interests:* squash, sailing, surfing. *Address:* Parliament House, Canberra, A.C.T. 2600; Glenclair, Bendemeer, N.S.W. 2355, Australia (Home).

SINCLAIR, Keith Val, A.O., M.A., LIT.D., D.PHIL., D.LITT.; Australian and New Zealand professor of French; b. 8 Nov. 1926, Auckland N.Z.; s. of late Valentine L. Sinclair and Coral D. Keith; ed. Univ. of N.Z., Victoria Univ. of Wellington, Univs. of Paris and Oxford; part-time tutor, Univ. of Oxford 1952–55; Lecturer, Sr. Lecturer, Australian Nat. Univ. 1955–62; Assoc. Prof. Univ. of Calif. (Davis) 1963–64; Sr. Lecturer, Assoc. Prof. Univ. of Sydney 1964–71; Visiting Prof. Northwestern Univ. Evanston, Ill. 1971; Prof. of French, Univ. of Conn., Storrs 1972–79; Prof. of French and Head, Dept. of Modern Languages, James Cook Univ., Townsville 1979–91, Prof. Emer., Dir. Inst. of Modern Languages 1982–91, mem. Council 1982–85, Chair. Academic Bd.; Foundation Sec. Australian Acad. of the Humanities 1969–72; mem. various professional socs. etc.; Hon. D.Litt. (James Cook Univ.) 1993, (Sydney Univ.) 1994; K.C.St.J.; decorations from Belgium, France, Italy, Luxembourg, Australia. *Publications:* The Melbourne Livy 1961, Anglo-Norman: The Last Twenty Years 1965, Descriptive Catalogue: Medieval Manuscripts in Australia 1969, Tristan de Nanteuil 1971, Prières en ancien français 1978, French Devotional Texts of the Middle Ages 1979, Hospitallers' Riwle 1984, Rober le Chapelain: Corset, a Rhymed Commentary on the Seven Sacraments 1996, Laplace in New Zealand 1998, numerous articles. *Leisure interests:* swimming, tennis. *Address:* 156 Bertels Crescent, Chapman, A.C.T., Australia.

SINCLAIR OYANEDER, Lieut.-Gen. Santiago; Chilean army officer and politician; b. 29 Dec. 1927, Santiago; m. Doris Manley Ramirez; three s. one d.; ed. Cavalry School, Acad. of War; Sec. of Studies, Mil. School 1963; Adjutant, Army C.-in-C. 1966; Head of Army Public Relations 1967; mem. UN Observers Group, Suez Canal 1968; Lecturer, Acad. of War 1970, Vice-Dir. 1973; Commdr. 2nd Cazadores Cavalry Regt. 1973; Mil. Attaché, Chilean Embassy, Repub. of Korea 1975; Sec., Deputy C.-in-C. of Army 1976; Dir. of Army Operations 1977; Chief Min. of Presidential Staff 1979; Head Pres.'s Consultative Cttee. 1982–; Deputy C.-in-C. of Army 1985; Senator, Nat. Congress 1990–(98); numerous mil. decorations. *Address:* P.O. Box 1732, Santiago, Chile. *Telephone:* 232-5148. *Fax:* 232-5148.

SINDEN, Sir Donald Alfred, Kt., C.B.E., F.R.S.A.; British actor and author; b. 9 Oct. 1923, Plymouth; s. of Alfred E. and Mabel A. (née Fuller) Sinden; m. Diana Mahony 1948; two s.; entered theatrical profession with Charles F. Smith's Co., Mobile Entertainments Southern Area 1942; with Leicester Repertory Co. 1945; with Memorial Theatre Co., Stratford-upon-Avon 1946–47; with Old Vic and Bristol Old Vic 1948; appeared in The Heiress 1949–50; with Bristol Old Vic 1950; Red Letter Day 1951; appeared in 23 films including The Cruel Sea, Doctor in the House 1952–60; returned to theatre, appearing in Odd Man In 1957, Peter Pan 1960, Guilty Party 1961, as Richard Plantagenet in Henry VI (The Wars of the Roses), as Price in Eh!, etc. (R.S.C.) 1963–64, British Council tour of S. America in Dear Liar and Happy Days 1965, There's a Girl in my Soup 1966, as Lord Foppington in The Relapse (R.S.C.) 1967, Not Now Darling 1968, as Malvolio, Henry VIII, as Sir Harcourt Courtly in London Assurance 1972 (toured U.S.A. 1974), In Praise of Love 1973, as Stockmann in An Enemy of the People 1975, Habeas Corpus (U.S.A.) 1975, as Benedick in Much Ado About Nothing, King Lear (R.S.C.) 1976–77, Shut Your Eyes and Think of England 1977, Othello (R.S.C.) 1979–80, Present Laughter 1981, Uncle Vanya 1982, The School for Scandal 1983 (European tour 1984), Ariadne auf Naxos 1983, Two into One 1984, The Scarlet Pimpernel 1985, Major Barbara 1988, Over My Dead Body 1989, Oscar Wilde 1990, Out of Order 1990 (Australian tour 1992), Venus Observed 1991, She Stoops to Conquer 1993, Hamlet 1994, That Good Night 1996; Dir. The Importance of Being Earnest 1987. *Television series include:* Our Man from St. Marks, Two's Company, Discovering English Churches, Never the Twain; Chair. British Theatre Museum Asscn. 1971–77, Theatre Museum Advisory Council 1973–80; Pres. Fed. of Playgoers Socs. 1968–93, Royal Theatrical Fund 1983–; Vice-Pres. London Appreciation Soc. 1960–; Assoc. Artist, R.S.C. 1967–; mem. Council, British Actors Equity Asscn. 1966–77 (Trustee 1988–), Council, R.S.A. 1972, Advisory Council, V. & A. Museum 1973–80, Arts Council Drama Panel 1973–77, Leicestershire Educ. Arts Cttee. 1974–, BBC Archives Advisory Cttee. 1975–78, Council, London Acad. of Music and Dramatic Art 1976–, Kent and E. Sussex Regional Cttee., Nat. Trust 1978–82, Arts Council 1982–86; Drama Desk Award (for London Assurance) 1974, Variety Club of G.B. Stage Actor of 1976 (for King Lear), Evening Standard Drama Award Best Actor (for King Lear) 1977. *Publications:* A Touch of the Memoirs 1982, Laughter in the Second Act 1985, The Everyman Book of Theatrical Anecdotes (ed.) 1987, The English Country Church 1988, Famous Last Words (ed.) 1994. *Leisure interests:* theatrical history, architecture, ecclesiology, genealogy, serendipity, London. *Address:* Rats Castle, Isle of Oxney, Kent, TN30 7HX, England.

SINDIKUBWABO, Théodore; Rwandan politician; fmr. Speaker of Nat. Devt. Council; Pres. of Rwanda April–July 1994 (after death of fmr. Pres. Habyarimana which led to civil war); accused by UN Tribunal of participation in genocide 1995.

SINFELT, John Henry, PH.D.; American chemist; b. 18 Feb. 1931, Munson, Pa; s. of Henry Gustave Sinfelt and June Lillian McDonald; m. Muriel Jean Vadersen 1956; one s.; ed. Pennsylvania State Univ. and Univ. of Illinois; Scientist Exxon Research and Eng. Co. 1954–, Sr. Research Assoc. 1968–72, Scientific Adviser 1972–79, Sr. Scientific Adviser 1979–96, Sr. Scientific Adviser Emer. 1996–; Consultant Prof. Dept. of Chemical Eng., Stanford Univ. 1996–; active in catalysis research, formulated and developed the concept of bimetallic clusters as catalysts, applied the concept in petroleum refining for production of lead-free petrol; mem. N.A.S., American Philosophical Soc., Nat. Acad. of Eng.; Fellow American Acad. of Arts and Sciences; Hon. Sc.D. (Univ. of Ill.) 1981; Nat. Medal of Science 1979, Perkin Medal in Chem. 1984, N.A.S. Award for the Industrial Application of Science 1996, and many other awards and prizes. *Publications:* Bimetallic Catalysts: Discoveries, Concepts and Applications 1983; 170 articles in scientific journals; 45 patents. *Address:* Exxon Research and Engineering Company, Clinton Township, Route 22 East, Annandale, NJ 08801, U.S.A.

SINGER, Sir Hans Wolfgang, Kt., PH.D.; British development economist; b. 29 Nov. 1910, Elberfeld, Germany; s. of Heinrich Singer and Antonia Spier; m. Ilse Lina Plaut 1934; one s. (and one s. deceased); ed. Univs. of Bonn and Cambridge; researcher, Pilgrim Trust Unemployment Enquiry 1936–38; Asst. lecturer, Univ. of Manchester 1938–44; economist, Ministry of Town and Country Planning 1945–46; lecturer, Univ. of Glasgow 1946–47; UN Secr. New York 1947–69; Professorial Fellow, Inst. of Devt. Studies, Univ. of Sussex 1969–, Prof. Emer. 1980–; consultant to developing countries and int. orgs. etc.; Frances Wood Memorial Prize; Hon. D.Litt. (Univ. Nacional del Litoral Santa Fe, Argentina), (Sussex), (Glasgow), (Lisbon), (Innsbruck). *Publications include:* International Development: Growth and Change 1964, Food Aid: The Challenge and the Opportunity (with Jennings and Wood), 1987, Rich and Poor Countries (with J. Ansari), The Foreign Aid Business (with K. Raffer) 1996; articles in professional journals. *Leisure interests:* chess, music. *Address:* The Institute of Development Studies, University of Sussex, Brighton, East Sussex, BN1 9RE (Office); 18 The Vale, Ovingdean, Brighton, East Sussex, BN2 7AB, England (Home). *Telephone:* (01273) 678279 (Office). *Fax:* (01273) 621202.

SINGER, Isadore Manuel, PH.D.; American mathematician; b. 3 May 1924, Detroit, Mich.; s. of Simon Singer and Freda Rose; m. Sheila Ruff 1961; five c.; ed. Univs. of Michigan and Chicago; C.L.E. Moore Instructor at M.I.T. 1950–52; Asst. Prof. Univ. of Calif. (Los Angeles) 1952–54; Visiting Asst. Prof. Columbia Univ. 1954–55; Visiting mem. Inst. for Advanced Study, Princeton 1955–56; Asst. Prof. M.I.T. 1956, Assoc. Prof. 1958, Prof. of Math. 1959, Norbert Wiener Prof. of Math. 1970–79; Visiting Prof. of Math., Univ. of Calif., Berkeley 1977–79, Prof. 1979–83; Miller Prof. Univ. of Calif., Berkeley 1982–83; John D. MacArthur Prof. of Math., M.I.T. 1983–, Inst. Prof. 1987–; mem. N.A.S., American Math. Soc., Math. Asscn. of America, American Acad. of Arts and Sciences, American Philosophical Soc., American Physical Soc.; Sloan Fellow 1959–62, Guggenheim Fellow 1968–69, 1975–76; Bôcher Memorial Prize 1969, 1975–76; Nat. Medal of Science 1985, Wigner Prize, Int. Congress of Mathematicians 1989. *Publications:* Lecture Notes on Elementary Topology and Geometry; author of research articles in functional analysis, differential geometry and topology. *Leisure interests:* literature, hiking, tennis. *Address:* Department of Mathematics, Massachusetts Institute of Technology, Room 2-387, 77 Massachusetts Avenue, Cambridge, MA 02139, U.S.A.

SINGER, Maxine, PH.D.; American biochemist; b. 15 Feb. 1931, New York; d. of Hyman Frank and Henrietta Perlowitz Frank; m. Daniel M. Singer

1952; one s. three d.; ed. Swarthmore Coll. and Yale Univ.; Research Chemist, Enzymes and Cellular Biochemistry Section, Nat. Inst. of Arthritis and Metabolic Diseases, N.I.H., Bethesda, Md. 1958–74, Chief, Nucleic Acid Enzymology Section, Lab. of Biochemistry, Div. of Cancer Biology and Diagnosis, Nat. Cancer Inst. 1974–79, Chief, Lab. of Biochemistry 1979–87, research chemist 1987–88, Scientist Emer. 1988–; Pres. Carnegie Inst., Wash. 1988–; Visiting Scientist, Dept. of Genetics, Weizmann Inst. of Science, Rehovot, Israel 1971–72; Dir. Foundation for Advanced Educ. in Sciences 1972–78, 1985–86; mem. Yale Corpn. 1975–90; Chair. Smithsonian Council 1992–94 (mem. 1990–94); Chair. Comm. on the Future of the Smithsonian 1994–96; mem. editorial bd. Journal of Biological Chem. 1968–74, Science 1972–82; Chair. editorial bd. Proceedings of N.A.S. 1985–88; Scientific Council Int. Inst. of Genetics and Biophysics, Naples 1982–86, Bd. of Govs. of Weizmann Inst., Human Genome Org. 1989–, Cttee. on Science, Eng. and Public Policy, N.A.S. 1989–91, Int. Advisory Bd., Chulabhorn Research Inst. 1990–; mem. Bd. Dirs. Johnson & Johnson; mem. N.A.S., American Soc. of Biological Chemists, American Soc. of Microbiologists, American Chemical Soc., American Acad. of Arts and Sciences, Inst. of Medicine of N.A.S., American Philosophical Soc., New York Acad. of Sciences; Trustee Wesleyan Univ., Middletown, Conn. 1972–75, Whitehead Inst. 1985–94; Hon. D.Sc. (Wesleyan Univ.) 1977, (Swarthmore Coll.) 1978, (Univ. of Md.) 1985, (Brandeis Univ.) 1988, (Radcliffe Coll.) 1990, (Williams Coll.) 1990, (Franklin and Marshall Coll.) 1991, (George Washington Univ.) 1992, (New York Univ.) 1992, (Lehigh Univ.) 1992, (Dartmouth) 1993, (Yale) 1994, (Harvard) 1994; Dir.'s Award, Nat. Insts. of Health 1977, Nat. Medal of Science 1992 and other awards. *Publications:* molecular biology textbooks (with Paul Beig), Why Aren't Black Holes Black? (with Robert Hazen) and numerous articles in major scientific journals. *Leisure interests:* scuba diving, cooking, literature. *Address:* Carnegie Institution of Washington, 1530 P St., N.W., Washington, DC 20005 (Office); 5410 39th Street, N.W., Washington, DC 20015, U.S.A. (Home). *Telephone:* (202) 387-6404.

SINGER, Peter Albert David, M.A., B.PHIL.; Australian philosopher and author; b. 6 July 1946, Melbourne; s. of Ernest Singer and Cora Oppenheim; m. Renata Diamond 1968; three d.; ed. Scotch Coll., Univ. of Melbourne and Univ. Coll. Oxford.; Radcliffe Lecturer, Univ. Coll. Oxford 1971–73; Visiting Asst. Prof. Dept. of Philosophy, New York Univ. 1973–74; Sr. Lecturer, Dept. of Philosophy, La Trobe Univ. 1975–76; Prof. Dept. of Philosophy, Monash Univ. 1977–99, Dir. Centre for Human Bioethics 1987–91, Deputy Dir. 1992–99; Decamp Prof. of Bioethics, Princeton Univ., N.J., U.S.A. 1999–; various visiting positions in U.S.A., Canada and Italy. *Publications:* numerous books and articles, including Animal Liberation 1975, Practical Ethics 1979, How Are We to Live? 1993, Rethinking Life and Death 1994, Ethics into Action 1998. *Leisure interests:* bushwalking, gardening, swimming. *Address:* University Center for Human Values, Princeton, NJ 08544, U.S.A.

SINGH, Bhishma Narain, B.A.; Indian politician; b. 13 July 1933, Palamau, Bihar; m. Ram Kumari Devi 1950; two s. two d.; ed. Takeya High School, Sasaram, Bihar and Banaras Hindu Univ.; active Congress worker 1953–; mem. All Indian Congress Cttee.; mem. Bihar Legis. Assembly 1967–69, 1969–72, 1972–76; Minister, State Gov. of Bihar 1971, 1972–73, 1973–74; mem. Rajya Sabha 1976, 1982, Deputy Chief Whip, Congress Parl. Party 1977, later Chief Whip; Minister of Parl. Affairs 1980–83, of Communications Jan.–March 1980, of Works and Housing, Labour, Supply and Food and Civil Supplies 1980–83; Gov. of Assam and Meghalaya 1983–89, of Sikkim 1985–86, of Arunachal Pradesh 1987, of Tamil Nadu 1991–93; Deputy Chair. Cen. Cooperative Bank, Daltonganj 1964; Dir. Bihar State Co-operative Mktg. Union 1967; Chair. Bihar State Co-operative Housing Construction Finance Soc. 1974–75, Bihar State Credit and Investment Corpn. 1974. *Leisure interests:* horse riding, marksman, music, dance and drama, especially tribal folk dances. *Address:* Hamid Ganj, P.O. Daitonganj, Palamau District, Bihar, India.

SINGH, Bipin; Indian dancer and choreographer; b. 23 Aug. 1918, Vill-Singari-Cachar; s. of Laikhomsana Singha and Indubala Devi; m. 1st Manorama Sinha; m. 2nd Kalavati Devi; five s. three d.; Manipuri dance teacher, Calcutta 1936; joined Madam Menaka Troup 1938, toured India and abroad; dir. dance dramas, Bombay 1943; collected and recorded the oral traditions of Manipuri dance and music; toured world with routines; founded Manipuri Nartanalaya in Bombay, Manipur and Calcutta 1972. *Publications:* Vaisnav Sangeet Damodar (Ed.) 1985, Panchamsarsanhita and Sangeet Damodar (Ed.) 1986. *Leisure interests:* walking, listening to news. *Address:* Manipuri Nartanalaya, 15A Bipin Pal Road, Calcutta 700026, India. *Telephone:* 465 922.

SINGH, Buta; Indian politician; b. 21 March 1934, Jalandhar Punjab; s. of Sardar Bir Singh; ed. Lyallpur Khalsa Coll., Jalandhar and Guru Nanak Khalsa Coll., Bombay; elected to Lok Sabha 1962, 1967, 1971, 1980, 1984; Union Deputy Minister for Railways 1974–76, for Commerce 1976–77; Minister of State in Ministry of Shipping and Transport 1980–81; Minister of Supply and Rehabilitation 1981–82, of Sport 1982–83, Cabinet Minister in charge of several ministries 1983–84, Minister of Agric. 1984–86, of Home Affairs 1986–89, of Civil Supplies, Consumer Affairs and Public Distribution 1995–96, of Communications 1998; mem. Planning Comm. 1985, Gen. Sec. Indian Nat. Congress 1978–80; Pres. Amateur Athletic Fed. of India 1976–84. *Address:* c/o Ministry of Communications, Sanchar Bhavan, 20 Asoka Road, New Delhi 110 001, India.

SINGH, Chaudhary Randhir, M.A., LL.B.; Indian politician; b. 1 July 1924, Bayanpur, Haryana; s. of late Chaudhary Chandgi Ram and Chhoti Devi; m. Vijay Lakshmi Chaudhary 1939; four s. three d.; ed. St. Stephen's Coll., Delhi, Univ. of Delhi; fmr. mem. Parl. (Lok Sabha), All India Congress Cttee., several Parl. Cttees., Exec. Congress Party in Parl.; mem. Nat. Comm. on Agric. 1970–76; Chair. Agric. Prices Comm., Govt. of India 1976–79, 1980–83, 1987–89; Gov. Sikkim 1996–; Chair. or mem. numerous Govt. working groups on land reform and agricultural devt. issues; fmrly. Chair. Punjab Praja Socialist Party, mem. Nat. Exec. of Punjab Praha Socialist Party of India, Sec.-Gen. United Front of Opposition Parties Punjab, Chair. AICC Land Reforms Panel, Sr. Vice-Chair. and Sec.-Gen. Farmers' Parl. Forum of India; active in social work in Haryana; recipient of numerous awards for work on behalf of peasant families and minority groups. *Publications:* 18 books on agricultural devt. and problems of rural peoples. *Leisure interests:* listening to and reading Urdu poetry, especially by Md. Iqbal and Ghalib, folk songs and dances. *Address:* Office of Governor, Raj Bhavan, Gangtok, Sikkim, India. *Telephone:* (03592) 22400. *Fax:* (03592) 22742.

SINGH, Gopal, PH.D.; Indian politician, poet and writer; b. 29 Nov. 1919, Serai Niamat Khan, N.W. Frontier Prov.; s. of Atma Singh and Nanaki Devi; m. 1950; one d.; nominated M.P. 1962–68; Amb. to Bulgaria and Caribbean countries 1970–76; Chair. High Power Comm. of Minorities, Scheduled Castes, Scheduled Tribes and other Weaker Sections 1980–84; Gov. Goa, Daman and Diu 1984, of Nagaland 1989; has lectured at univs. in U.K., U.S.A., Thailand, Egypt, Iran and India; fmr. Sec.-Gen. Indian Council for Africa; Chair. Presidium, World Punjabi Congress; many awards and decorations. *Publications:* first free-verse English translation of the Sikh Scripture; five books of Punjabi verse; A History of the Sikh People 1469–1978, The Religion of the Sikhs, A History of Punjabi Literature; The Unstruck Melody (poetry), The Man Who Never Died (poetry); collection of short stories, children's books, an English-Punjabi lexicon, several biographies and books of literary criticism. *Leisure interests:* reading, walking. *Address:* Raj Bhavan, Kohima, India. *Telephone:* 3445.

SINGH, Karan, M.A., PH.D.; Indian politician; b. 9 March 1931, Cannes, France; s. of Lieut.-Gen. H.H. Maharaja Sir Hari Singh, G.C.S.I., G.C.I.E., G.C.V.O., and Maharani Tara Devi, C.I.; m. Princess Yasho Rajya Lakshmi of Nepal 1950; two s. one d.; ed. Doon School, Univ. of Jammu and Kashmir, and Delhi Univ.; appointed Regent of Jammu and Kashmir 1949; elected Sadar-i-Riyasat (Head of State) by Jammu and Kashmir Legis. Ass. Nov. 1952, recognized by Pres. of India and assumed office 17 Nov. 1952, re-elected 1957 and 1962, Gov. 1965–67; Union Minister for Tourism and Civil Aviation 1967–73, for Health and Family Planning 1973–75, 1976–77, for Educ. 1979–80; re-elected mem. of Parl. 1977, 1980; mem. Upper House of Parl.; Amb. to U.S.A. 1989–91; Vice-Pres. Indian Council for Cultural Relations; Pres. Delhi Music Soc.; led Indian Del. to World Population Conf., Bucharest; Vice-Pres. World Health Assembly 1975–76; fmr. Chancellor Jammu and Kashmir Univ., Banaras Hindu Univ.; fmr. Sec. Jawaharlal Nehru Memorial Fund; fmr. Chair. Indian Bd. for Wild Life, Life Trustee of the India Int. Centre; Hon. Maj.-Gen. Indian Army; Hon. Col. Jammu and Kashmir Regt. 1962; Dr. h.c. (Aligarh Muslim Univ.) 1963. *Publications:* Prophet of Indian Nationalism: The Political Thought of Sri Aurobindo Ghosh 1893–1910 1963, Heir Apparent 1983, One Man's World 1986, Religions of India, Humanity at the Crossroads 1988, and several books on political science, philosophical essays, travelogues, translations of Dogra-Pahari folk-songs and poems in English. *Leisure interests:* reading, writing, music. *Address:* 3 Nyaya Marg, Chanakyapuri, New Delhi 110021, India. *Telephone:* (011) 301 5291. *Fax:* (011) 379 4911.

SINGH, Khushwant, LL.B.; Indian author; b. Feb. 1915; m. Kaval Malik; one s. one d.; ed. Government Coll., Lahore, King's Coll. and Inner Temple, London; practised, High Court, Lahore 1939–47; joined Indian Ministry of External Affairs 1947; Press Attaché, Canada and then Public Relations Officer, London 1948–51; Ministry of Information and Broadcasting; edited Yojana; Dept. of Mass Communication, UNESCO 1954–56; commissioned by Rockefeller Foundation and Muslim Univ., Aligarh, to write a history of the Sikhs 1958; M.P. 1980–; Ed.-in-Chief The Hindustan Times, New Delhi 1980–83; Visiting lecturer Hawaii, Oxford, Princeton, Rochester, Swarthmore; numerous TV and radio appearances; Grove Press Award; Mohan Singh award; Padma Bhushan 1974; Ed. The Illustrated Weekly of India 1969–78. *Publications:* Mark of Vishnu 1949, The Sikhs 1951, Train to Pakistan 1954, Sacred Writings of the Sikhs 1960, I shall not hear the Nightingale 1961, Umrao Jan Ada—Courtesan of Lucknow (trans.) 1961, History of the Sikhs (1769-1839) Vol. I 1962, Ranjit Singh: Maharaja of the Punjab 1962, Fall of the Sikh Kingdom 1962, The Skeleton (trans.) 1963, Land of the Five Rivers (trans.) 1964, History of the Sikhs (1839-Present Day) Vol. II 1965, Khushwant Singh's India 1969, Indira Gandhi Returns 1979, Editor's Page 1980, Iqbal's Dialogue with Allah (trans.) 1981, Punjab Tragedy (with Kuldip Noyar) 1984, Roots of Dissent 1992, and others. *Address:* 49E Sujan Singh Park, New Delhi 110003, India. *Telephone:* 690159.

SINGH, Manmohan, PH.D.; Indian politician; b. 26 Sept. 1932, Gah, Punjab; s. of Gurumukh Singh and Amrit Kaur; ed. Univ. of Cambridge; econ. adviser, Ministry of Finance 1972; Gov. Reserve Bank of India 1982; Sec.-Gen. South Comm. 1987; econ. adviser to Prime Minister 1990; Minister of Finance 1991–96. *Address:* c/o Ministry of Finance, North Block, New Delhi 110001, India.

SINGH, Sukhmander, M.S., PH.D.; American professor of civil engineering; b. 15 Sept. 1939, Lambi; s. of Mahla Singh and Jangir Kaur; m. Charanjit Kaur 1967; one s. one d.; ed. Punjabi Univ., Patiala, Punjab, Indian Inst. of Tech., Delhi, Univ. of Ottawa and Carleton Univ., Ottawa, Canada, Rice Univ., Houston, Tex., Univ. of Calif., Berkeley; Assoc. lecturer, Indian Inst. of Tech., Delhi, India 1966–67; Teaching Asst., Univ. of Ottawa 1967–68; Visiting lecturer, Univ. of Alaska, Anchorage 1975, San Jose State Univ., Calif. 1978; Assoc. Prof. of Civil Eng., Calif. State Univ., L.A., Calif. 1983–86; Assoc. Prof. of Civil Eng., Santa Clara Univ., Calif. 1986–90, Chair. Dept. of Civil Eng. and Chair. Eng. Mechanics 1990–; professional work as engineer with John V. Lowney & Assocs., Palo Alto, Calif. 1969, Dames & Moore, San Francisco, London, Houston, Anchorage and Seattle offices 1969–83, as Consultant 1983–; Consultant with Purcell, Rhoades and Assocs., Hayward, Calif. 1987–, with Calpine/Kaiser 1989–; mem. numerous cttees. on soil dynamics and geotechnical eng.; research on liquefaction of silts and geotechnology of cold regions. *Publications:* numerous scientific papers. *Leisure interests:* reading, hiking, volleyball playing. *Address:* Department of Civil Engineering, Santa Clara University, Santa Clara, CA 95053, U.S.A. *Telephone:* (408) 554-6869.

SINGH, Vishwanath Pratap, LL.B.; Indian politician; b. 25 June 1931, Allahabad; s. of Raja Bahadur Ram Gopal Singh; m. Sita Kumari 1955; two s.; ed. Poona and Allahabad Univs.; Pres. Students Union, Udai Pratap Coll., Varanasi 1947–48; mem. Exec. Body, Allahabad Univ. 1969–71; mem. Legis. Ass., Uttar Pradesh 1969–71; Whip, Congress Legis. Party 1970–71; mem. Lok Sabha 1971–77, 1988–94, Rajya Sabha 1983–94; Union Deputy Minister for Commerce 1974–76, Union State Minister for Commerce 1976–77, 1983; Minister of Finance 1984–86, of Defence 1986–87; Prime Minister of India 1989–90; Chief Minister of Uttar Pradesh 1980–82, mem. Legis. Council 1980–81, Legis. Ass. 1981–83, Pres. Uttar Pradesh 1980–82, mem. Legis. Council 1980–81, Legis. Ass. 1981–83, Pres. Uttar Pradesh Congress Cttee. 1984; Additional Charge of Dept. of Supply 1983; expelled from Congress (1) Party 1987; f. and Leader Jan Morcha Party 1987; Leader Janata Dal Party 1988–91 (resgnd.); Pres. Samajwadi Janata Dal (Coalition) 1988–90. *Leisure interests:* painting, photography. *Address:* 1 Teen Murti Marg, New Delhi 110001; 4 Ashok Road, Allahabad, India.

SINGHVI, Laxmi Mall, LL.D., S.J.D.; Indian diplomatist and jurist; b. 9 Nov. 1931, Jodhpur; s. of Dashrathmal Singhvi and Akal Kaur Singhvi; m. Kamla Singhvi 1957; one s. one d.; ed. Jodhpur, Allahabad, Harvard and Cornell Univs.; Dir. Indian Law Inst. 1957–58; Sr. Standing Counsel for Govt. of India and State of Uttar Pradesh; Sr. Advocate, Supreme Court of India 1967–; independent mem. for Jodhpur, Lok Sabha 1962–67; Tagore Law Prof.; Dir. Benett Coleman & Co. Ltd. (owners of the Times of India Publications) and Punjab Nat. Bank Ltd.; Founder and Chair. Inst. of Constitutional and Parl. Studies 1964; Chair. Commonwealth Legal Educ. Asscn. 1972–77; Chair. Nat. Legal Aid Asscn. of India; Chair. Nat. Fed. of UNESCO Asscns. in India 1974–; Chair. Indian Nat. Cttee. for Abolition of Death Penalty 1977–, Govt. of India Cttee. on Local Self Govt. 1986–87; fmr. Pres., now Pres. Emer. Supreme Court of India Bar Asscn., Pres. Asian Human Rights Conf. 1985, Indian Human Rights Trust, Indian Centre for the Independence of Judges and Lawyers; mem. UN Sub-Comm. on Protection of Minorities, UN Working Group for Protection of All Persons under any Form of Imprisonment or Detention; Chair. Samachar Bharati news agency; Life Trustee India Int. Centre, Pres. 1988–; Chair. Nat. Task Force on Child Labour 1989; Pres. Indian Centre for the Rights of the Child; Chief Justice Mehrchant Centennial Oration 1989; Pres. Authors Guild of India; High Commr. in U.K. 1991–97; Trustee Jnanpith Awards; Hon. Bencher and Master, Middle Temple, London 1987–; Award for Humanism Jury G. D. Birle Int. Centre 1988; delivered C. D. Deshmukh Memorial Oration 1988; Jawaharlal Nehru Memorial Centennial Oration; Hon. Prof. of Law (Delhi, Andhra), Calcutta); Hon. LL.D. (Jabalpur Univ.) 1983, (Banaras Hindu Univ.) 1984, (Westminster) 1996, (London) 1997, (Luton) 1997; Hon. Patron, Commonwealth Legal Educ. Assoc., London. *Leisure interests:* performing arts, poetry, gardening. *Address:* Flat 4F, White House, 10 Bhagwan Das Road, New Delhi 110001, India.

SINGLETON, William Dean; American newspaper proprietor; b. 1 Aug. 1951, Tex.; s. of late William Hyde Singleton and of Florence E. Myrick Singleton; m. Adrienne Casale 1983; two s. one d.; Pres. Gloucester Co. Times, N. J.; Vice-Chair., Pres., C.E.O. MediaNews Group, Inc. 1988–; Pres., Chair. The Houston Post 1988–95, The Denver Post; Vice-Chair. 27 daily newspapers and 55 non-daily publications including Houston Post, Denver Post, with daily circulation in excess of 1.1 million in 10 states. *Leisure interest:* skiing. *Address:* Media News Group, 1560 Broadway, Suite 1450, Denver, CO 80202, U.S.A.

SINGSON, Gabriel, LL.M.; Philippine banker; b. 18 March 1929, Lingayen, Pangasinan; m. Moonyeen Retizos; two s. one d.; ed. Pangasinan Provincial High School, Ateneo de Manila and Univ. of Michigan Law School, Ann Arbor; Assoc. Attorney, Law Office of Justice Jose Bengzon 1952–55; Prof. of Commercial Law and Civil Law, Ateneo de Manila Law School 1956–72; Legal and Evaluation Officer, Cen. Bank 1955–60, Tech. Asst. Monetary Bd. 1960–62, Asst. to Deputy Gov. 1963–66, 1968–70; Legal Officer, Asian Devt. Bank 1967–68; Asst. to Gov. (with rank of Dir.), Cen. Bank 1970–73, Special Asst. to Gov. 1973–74, Gen. Counsel 1974–75, Deputy Gov. and Gen. Counsel 1975–80, Sr. Deputy Gov. 1980–92; Pres. Philippine Nat. Bank 1992–93; Chair. Monetary Bd. and Gov. Bangko Sentral ng Pilipinas 1993–; Chair. PR Holdings Inc. (holding co. of Philippine Air Lines); Vice-Chair. Philippine Air Lines. *Publications:* articles on Asian Devt. Bank, foreign loans, foreign investments and foreign exchange regulations. *Leisure interests:* golf. *Address:* Bangko Sentral ng Pilipinas, A. Mabini corner Vito Cruz Streets, Malate, 1004 Metro Manila; 28 Polk Street, Greenhills, San Juan, Metro Manila, Philippines (Home). *Telephone:* (2) 524-7011 (Office). *Fax:* 522-3987 (Office).

SINN, Hans-Werner; German economist; b. 7 March 1948, Brake, Westphalia; m. Gerlinde Sinn (née Zoubek) 1971; two s. one d.; ed. Helmsholtz-Gymnasium, Bielefeld, Univ. of Münster, Univ. of Mannheim; lecturer Univ. of Münster 1972–74, Univ. of Mannheim 1974–78, Sr. Lecturer 1979–83, Assoc. Prof. 1983–84; Visiting Asst. Prof. Univ. of Western Ont. 1978–79; Prof. of Econs. and Insurance Univ. of Munich 1984–94; Dir. Centre for Econ. Studies 1991–; Prof. of Econs. and Public Finance 1994–; Chair. Verein für Socialpolitik (German Econ. Asscn.) 1997–; Medal of Univ. of Helsinki. *Publications:* Economic Decisions under Certainty 1980, Capital Income Taxation and Resource Allocation 1985, Jumpstart: the Economic Unification of Germany 1991, Making Sense of Subsidiarity: How Much Centralization for Europe? 1993, Wohnungspolitik auf dem Prüfstand 1995, Wohnungspolitik für die neuen Länder 1995, Der Staat im Bankwesen: Zur Rolle der Landesbanken in Deutschland 1997, numerous articles on public finance and other subjects. *Leisure interest:* photography. *Address:* Schackstr. 4, 80539 Munich, Germany. *Telephone:* 89 2180-2748. *Fax:* 89 397303.

SINOPOLI, Giuseppe; Italian conductor and composer; b. 2 Nov. 1946, Venice; s. of late Giovanni Sinopoli and of Maria Sinopoli; m. Silvia Cappellini 1979; two s.; ed. Benedetto Marcello Conservatoire, Venice and Medical School of Univ. of Padua; qualified as surgeon and psychiatrist; studied conducting with Swarowsky, Vienna 1972; f. Bruno Maderna Ensemble, Venice, to play contemporary music 1975; début Covent Garden, London (Puccini's Manon Lescaut) 1983; U.S. début with New York Philharmonic Orchestra 1983; Prin. Conductor Philharmonia Orchestra, London 1983–87, Music Dir. 1987–92; Chief Conductor Staatskapelle Dresden 1992–97; Direttore Musicale, Festival Taormina Arte 1990–93. *Compositions include:* 25 studi su tre parametri 1969, Musica per calcolatori analogici 1969, Numquid et unum (cembalo and flute) 1970, Opus Ghimal (orchestra) 1971, Sunyata (string quintet and soprano) 1972, Piano Sonata 1974, String Quartet 1977, Lou Salome (opera) 1981. *Leisure interests:* reading, studying archaeology, collecting antique objects. *Address:* c/o Hannelore Tschöpe, Künstlersekretariat, Zehetmeierstr. 10, 80939 Munich 40, Germany. *Telephone:* 089-32 46 49 53. *Fax:* 089-32 45 01 56.

SINOWATZ, Fred; Austrian politician, b. 5 Feb. 1929, Neufeld an der Leitha, Burgenland; m. Hermine Sinowatz 1954; one s. one d.; ed. Univ. of Vienna; joined Burgenland provincial govt. service 1953; mem. Burgenland Prov. Legis. 1961–71, Pres. 1964; Party Sec. Burgenland Austrian Socialist Party (SPÖ) Org. 1961–78, Deputy Chair. 1978, Chair. –1988; mem. Nat. Exec. SPÖ 1981, Chair. 1983–88; mem. Nationalrat 1971; Fed. Minister of Educ. and Arts 1971–83; Fed. Vice-Chancellor 1981, Chancellor 1983–86. *Address:* Loewelstrasse 18, 1010 Vienna, Austria.

SINSHEIMER, Robert Louis, S.B., S.M., PH.D.; American biologist; b. 5 Feb. 1920, Washington, D.C.; s. of Allen and Rose Davidson Sinsheimer; m. 1st Flora Joan Hirsch 1943 (divorced 1972); one s. two d.; m. 2nd Kathleen Mae Reynolds 1972 (divorced 1980); m. 3rd Karen B. Keeton 1981; ed. M.I.T.; Research Assoc., Biology, M.I.T. 1948–49; Assoc. Prof. of Biophysics, Iowa State Coll. 1949–55, Prof. 1955–57; Prof. of Biophysics, Calif. Inst. of Tech. 1957–77, Chair. Div. of Biology 1968–77, Visiting Prof. of Biology 1987–88; Prof. Dept. of Biological Sciences, Univ. of Calif. at Santa Barbara 1988–90, Emer. Prof. 1990–; Chancellor, Univ. of Calif. at Santa Cruz 1977–87; mem. N.A.S., mem. Council 1970–73; Pres. Biophysical Soc. 1970–71; Chair. Bd. of Editors, N.A.S. Proceedings 1972–80; Calif. Scientist of the Year Award 1968, Beijerinck Medal of the Royal Netherlands Acad. of Sciences 1969. *Publications:* The Strands of Life (memoirs) 1994; more than 250 scientific papers 1946–. *Leisure interests:* travel, hiking and photography. *Address:* Department of Biological Sciences, University of California at Santa Barbara, Santa Barbara, CA 93106 (Office); 4606 Via Cavente, Santa Barbara, CA 931110, U.S.A. (Home). *Telephone:* (805) 893-8038 (Office); (805) 683-2247 (Home).

SINT, Marjanne; Netherlands public servant; b. 24 July 1949, Amsterdam; ed. Univ. of Amsterdam and IMEDE Business School; mem. staff, Ministry of Econ. Affairs 1974–77, Ministry of Culture, Health and Social Affairs 1977–79; Econ. Ed., Intermediair 1979–80, Chief Ed. 1980–81; Publisher, VNU Business Publs. 1981–87; Pres. Dutch Labour Party (PvdA) 1987, Chair. 1988; mem. staff Ministry of Interior 1991–95; Chief Exec. City of Amsterdam 1995–. *Publications:* Tussen wal en schip, etnische minderheden in Nederland 1980, Economen over crisis 1982. *Leisure interests:* literature, poetry, music, modern art and architecture. *Address:* c/o Partij van de Arbeid, Nic. Witsenkade 30, 1017 ZT Amsterdam, Netherlands. *Telephone:* (31)–020 55.121.55.

SINYAVSKAYA, Tamara Ilyinichna; Russian opera singer (mezzo-soprano); b. 6 July 1943, Moscow; m. Muslim Magovaev 1974; ed. Moscow Music Coll. and State Theatre Art Inst.; soloist with Bolshoi Theatre 1964–; studied at La Scala, Milan 1973–74. *Roles include:* Olga in Tchaikovsky's Eugene Onegin; Carmen; Blanche and Frosya in Prokofiev's Gambler and Semyon Kotko, Vanya in Glinka's Life of the Tsar, Ratmir in Glinka's Ruslan and

Lyudmila, Lyubasha in Rimsky-Korsakov's The Tsar's Bride, Varvara in Not Love Alone; First Prize Int. Singing Competition, Sofia 1968, Grand Prix Singing Competition, Belgium 1969, First Prize at Int. Tchaikovsky Competition, Moscow 1970, People's Artist of R.S.F.S.R. 1976, People's Artist of U.S.S.R. 1982. *Address:* c/o Bolshoi Theatre, Teatralnaya Pl. 1, Moscow, Russia.

SIPHANDONE, Gen. Khamtay; Laotian politician and army officer; b. 8 Feb. 1924, Houa Khong Village, Champassak Prov.; mil. officer 1947–48, rep. of Lao Itsala 1948, mem. Front Cen. Cttee. 1950–52, Chair. Control Cttee. 1952–54; Gen. staff mem. Pathet Lao 1955–56, head Cen. Cttee. 1957–59, propaganda and training officer 1959–60, mem. Cen. Cttee. 1957, C.-in-C. 1960, mem. Politburo 1972; mem. Lao People's Revolutionary Party (LPRP) 1972, leader Nov. 1992–; mem. Secr. LPRP 1982; Deputy Prime Minister and Minister of Nat. Defence 1975–91; Prime Minister of Laos 1991–98; fmr. Supreme Commdr. Lao People's Army; Pres. of Laos Feb. 1998–. *Address:* Office of the President, Vientiane, Laos.

SIPINEN, Arto Kalevi; Finnish architect; b. 20 April 1936, Helsinki; s. of Veikko Emil Sipinen and Tuovi Maria Heino; m. 2nd Sinikka Rossi 1986; one s. one d.; ed. Helsinki Univ. of Tech.; worked with Alvar Aalto 1959–61, Viljo Revell 1961–63; own architectural practice 1963–; lecturer, Helsinki Univ. of Tech. 1964–67, Acting Prof. of Architecture 1991–92; mem. SAFA community planning dept. bd. 1964–66; Chair. SAFA competition cttee. 1964–66; SAFA competition judge 1965–; work includes Imatra City Hall 1970, Jyväskylä Univ. Library and Admin. Bldg. 1974, Music and Art Bldg. 1976, Raisio City Hall 1981, Imatra Cultural Centre 1986, Mikkeli Concert Hall 1988, Espoo Cultural Centre 1989, Lahti Main Library 1990, Tammela Town Hall 1991, Mäntsälä Town Hall 1992, Kuusamo Cultural Centre 1995 and planning projects in Helsinki city centre; more than 40 prizes in architectural competitions; other awards include SL Pro Finlandia Medal 1990, Concrete Structure of the Year Prize 1990. *Address:* Arkkitehtitoimisto Arto Sipinen Oy, Ahertajantie 3, 02100 Espoo, Finland. *Telephone:* 358-0-4552011. *Fax:* 358-0-4552513.

SIPPEL, Heinz, DR.RER.POL.; German banker; b. 7 Nov. 1922, Leverkusen; m. Christa Dausel 1953; one d.; ed. Carl Duisberg Gymnasium, Leverkusen, Cologne Univ.; Kreditanstalt für Wiederaufbau 1951–56; Man. Regional Credit Dept., Commerzbank AG, Düsseldorf 1957–61; Head of Credit Dept., Bankhaus Friedrich Simon, Düsseldorf 1961–62; joined Rheinische Girozentrale und Provinzialbank as Head of Essen Branch 1962, Alt. mem. Man. Bd. 1967, mem. Man. Bd. 1968; mem. Man. Bd., Westdeutsche Landesbank Girozentrale 1969; Chair. Man. Bd., Hessische Landesbank Girozentrale 1975–85; Dir. LHB Internationale Handelsbank AG, Frankfurt (AR-Vors); Bundesverdienstkreuz 1982. *Leisure interests:* hiking, gardening, classical music. *Address:* 61476 Kronberg, Parkstrasse 38, Germany.

SIRAT, René-Samuel; French rabbi; b. 13 Nov. 1930, Bône (now Annaba), Algeria; s. of Ichoua Sirat and Oureida Atlan; m. 1st Colette Salamon 1952; one s. two d.; m. 2nd Nicole Holzman 1978; ed. Lycée St. Augustin, Bône, Univs. of Strasbourg, Paris (Sorbonne) and Jerusalem, Ecole Nat. des Langues Orientales (ENLOV); Rabbi, Toulouse 1952–55; Chaplain, Jeunesse juive 1955–63; Prof. Emer., Institut Nat. des Langues et Civilisations orientales (INALCO, fmrly. ENLOV) Dir. of Hebrew Studies 1965–96; Prof., Ecole Rabbinique de France 1965–70, 1977–80; Insp.-Gen. of Hebrew, Ministry of Educ. 1972–80; Pres. Hebrew Examining Bd., Certificate of Professional Aptitude and Higher Studies 1973–78; Dir. Centre de Documentation et Recherches des Etudes Juives modernes et contemporaines 1974–; Pres. Hebrew Examining Bd., Agrégation 1978–80; Dir. Ecole Hautes Etudes de Judaïsme 1985–; Pres. Centre Universitaire Rachi, Troyes 1989; Chief Rabbi of France 1981–87; Chief Rabbi, Consistoire Central 1988; Pres. Conseil Permanent de la Conférence des Rabbins européens 1989–; Pres. Académie Hillel 1989–, Inst. des connaissances des religions du livre 1996–; Dr. h.c. (Yeshiva Univ., U.S.A.) 1985; Chevalier, Légion d'honneur, Commdr., Ordre nat. du Mérite, Officier des Palmes Académiques, Prix de Jérusalem, Commdr. des Arts et des Lettres. *Publications:* Omer Hasikha (co-ed.) 1973, Mélanges A. Neher (co-ed.) 1974, Mélanges Vajda 1974–80 (co-ed.), La joie austère 1990, La tendresse de Dieu 1996. *Address:* Académie Hillel, 52 rue des Vignes, 75016 Paris, France.

SIREN, Heikki; Finnish architect; b. 5 Oct. 1918, Helsinki; s. of Prof. J. S. and Sirkka Siren; m. Kaija Siren (q.v.) 1944; two s. two d.; started private practice with Kaija Siren, Siren Architects Ltd. 1949–; mem. Finnish Acad. of Tech. Sciences 1971–; Foreign mem. Académie d'Architecture, Paris 1983; Hon. F.A.I.A.; Hon. mem. Finnish Architects' Asscn. (SAFA) 1992; Hon. Citation and Medal São Paulo Biennal 1957, Medal São Paulo Biennal 1961, Hon. Citation "Auguste Perret", Union Int. des Architectes 1965; Prof. h.c. 1970, Hon. D.Tech. 1982; Camillo Sitte Prize, Vienna 1979, Grande Médaille d'Or d'Académie d'Architecture, Paris 1980, Architectural Prize of the State of Finland 1980, Grand Golden Order of the City of Vienna 1982, Prize of Finnish Cultural Foundation 1984, Cultural Prize of City of Helsinki 1988; Officier Ordre nat. du Mérite 1971, SLK (Finland) 1974, Grand Silver Order of Austria 1977. *Major works include:* Little Stage of Nat. Theatre, Helsinki 1954, Concert House, Lahti 1954, Chapel in Otaniemi 1957, Church in Orivesi 1960, Office Buildings, Helsinki 1965, Housing Area in Boussy St. Antoine, Paris 1970, "Round Bank" Kop, Helsinki, schools, sports centres, offices, industrial bldgs., housing, holiday centres, etc., Brucknerhaus Concert Hall, Linz, Austria 1974, Golf complex, Karuizawa, Japan 1974, Golf Club, Onuma, Hokkaido, Japan 1976, Reichsbrücke, Vienna, Austria, Conference Palace, Baghdad, Iraq. *Publications:* Kaija and Heikki Siren, Architects 1978. *Leisure interests:* boat planning, theatre. *Address:* Tiirasaarentie 35, 00200 Helsinki, Finland. *Telephone:* (0) 673032 (Office).

SIREN, Katri (Kaija) Anna-Maija Helena; Finnish architect; b. 23 Oct. 1920, Kotka; d. of Gottlieb and Lydia Tuominen; m. Heikki Siren (q.v.) 1944; two s. two d.; private practice in partnership with Heikki Siren, Siren Architects Ltd. 1949–; Hon. F.A.I.A.; Hon. mem. Finnish Architects' Asscn. (SAFA) 1992; Foreign mem. Académie d'Architecture, Paris 1983; Hon. Citation and Medal São Paulo Biennal 1957, Medal São Paulo Biennal 1961, Hon. Citation "Auguste Perret", Union Int. des Architectes 1965; Grande Médaille d'Or d'Académie d'Architecture, Paris 1980, Architectural Prize of the State of Finland 1980, Prize of Finnish Cultural Foundation 1984; Grand Silver Order of Austria (with star) 1977, SVR 1 rit. (Finland) 1981. *Publications:* selected works published in Kaija and Heikki Siren, Architects 1976. *Leisure interests:* fine arts and nature. *Address:* Tiirasaarentie 35, Helsinki 20, Finland. *Telephone:* 673032 (Office).

SISCO, Joseph John, PH.D.; American government official; b. 31 Oct. 1919; m. Jean Churchill Head 1946; two d.; ed. Knox Coll. and Univ. of Chicago; U.S. Army 1941–45; CIA 1950–51; Dept. of State 1951–76, Officer-in-Charge, UN Political Affairs 1951–58; Deputy Dir. Office of UN Political and Security Affairs 1958–60, Dir. 1960–62; Deputy Asst. Sec. 1962–65; Asst. Sec. of State for Int. Org. Affairs, Dept. of State July 1965–69; Asst. Sec. State, Middle East-S. Asia 1969–74; Under-Sec. of State for Political Affairs 1974–76; mem. U.S. dels. to UN Gen. Ass. 1952–68; Pres. American Univ. in Washington 1976–80, Chancellor 1980–81; Foreign Affairs Analyst, Castle TV news; partner Sisco Assocs., Man. Consultants, Washington 1981–; Dir. Geico, Raytheon, Gilette, Tenneco, InterPublic Group Inc.; Rockefeller Public Service Award 1971. *Address:* 1250 24th Street, N.W., Washington, DC 20037 (Office); 2517 Massachusetts Avenue, N.W., Washington, DC 20008, U.S.A (Home).

SISSON, Charles Hubert, C.H., D.LITT., F.R.S.L.; British writer; b. 22 April 1914, Bristol; s. of R. P. and E. M. (née Worlock) Sisson; m. Nora Gilbertson 1937; two d.; ed. Univ. of Bristol, postgraduate studies in Berlin and Paris; various posts in Ministry of Labour, later Dept. of Employment 1936–, Under-Sec. 1962–73; served in army, in the ranks 1942–45; Simon Senior Research Fellow, Univ. of Manchester 1956–57; Joint Ed. PN Review (fmrly. Poetry Nation) 1976–84; Hon. D.Litt. (Bristol) 1980. *Publications:* An Asiatic Romance 1953, Versions and Perversions of Heine 1955, The Spirit of British Administration 1959, The London Zoo (poems) 1961, Christopher Homm 1965, Art and Action 1965, Numbers (poems) 1965, Catullus (trans.) 1966, Metamorphoses (poems) 1968, English Poetry 1900-1950 1971, The Case of Walter Bagehot 1972, In the Trojan Ditch (collected poems and selected trans.) 1974, The Poetic Art 1975, Lucretius (trans.) 1976, Anchises (poems) 1976, David Hume 1976, The Avoidance of Literature (collected essays) 1978, Some Tales of La Fontaine (trans.) 1979, Exactions (poems) 1980, The Divine Comedy of Dante (trans.) 1980, Philip Mairet: Autobiographical and Other Papers (ed.) 1981, Selected Poems 1981, Anglican Essays 1983, The Song of Roland (trans.) 1983, The Regrets of Joachim du Bellay (trans.) 1984, Collected Poems 1984, The Aeneid (trans.) 1986, Britannicus, Phaedra, Athalia of Racine (trans.) 1987, God Bless Karl Marx (poems) 1987, On the Look-Out (autobiog.) 1989, In Two Minds: Guesses at Other Writers 1990, Antidotes (poems) 1991, English Perspectives: Essays on Liberty and Government 1992, Is There a Church of England? 1993, What and Who (poems) 1994, Poems: Selected 1995, Collected Translations 1996, Collected Poems 1998. *Leisure interests:* gardening and washing-up. *Address:* Moorfield Cottage, The Hill, Langport, Somerset, TA10 9PU, England. *Telephone:* (01458) 250845.

SISSONS, Peter George, M.A.; British television presenter; b. 17 July 1942; s. of George Sissons and Elsie Evans; m. Sylvia Bennett 1965; two s. one d.; ed. Liverpool Inst. High School for Boys and Univ. Coll. Oxford; grad. trainee, Independent TV News 1964, gen. reporter 1967, industrial corresp. 1970, industrial ed. 1972–78; presenter, News at One 1978–82, Channel Four News 1982–89; presenter, BBC TV news (9 O'Clock News 1994–) 1989–, Chair. BBC TV Question Time 1989–93; Broadcasting Press Guild Award 1984; Royal Television Soc. Judges' Award 1988. *Address:* BBC Television Centre, Wood Lane, London, W12 7RJ, England. *Telephone:* 0181-743 8000.

SISULU, Albertina Nontsikelelo; South African politician; b. 1919, Tsomo, Transkei; m. Walter Max Ulyate Sisulu (q.v.) 1944; five c.; trained as a nurse, Johannesburg N.E. Hosp.; joined Fed. of S. African Women 1954, Pres. 1984; mem. Women's League, African Nat. Congress (ANC) 1948, Deputy Pres. 1991, mem. Nat. Exec. Cttee. of ANC 1991–; ANC M.P. 1994–; participated in women's protest against introduction of Women's Pass; under continual banning orders (including house arrest) 1964–82; Transvaal Pres. United Democratic Front (UDF) 1983–91; tried and sentenced to 4 years' imprisonment for furthering aims of ANC 1984, successful appeal 1987; elected to Nat. Council, Women's Congress, UDF 1987; Leader UDF Del. to U.S.A. and to England July 1989; Pres. World Peace Council 1993. *Address:* P.O. Box 61884, Marshalltown 2107, South Africa.

SISULU, Walter Max Ulyate; South African politician; b. 18 May 1912, Transkei; m. Albertina Notsikelelo (q.v.) 1944; three s. two d. three adopted c.; ed. Mission School, Transkei; fmr. miner, factory worker, baker; joined

ANC 1940, becoming Sec.-Gen.; f., Treas. ANC Youth League; Org. Defiance Campaign 1952; banned from attending public meetings 1952; arrested Dec. 1956, charged with treason, acquitted March 1961, arrested Nov. 1962 for breach of house-arrest provisions, sentenced to six years' imprisonment for incitement to strike March 1963, freed on bail pending appeal; went underground, rearrested July 1963, sentenced to life imprisonment, Rivonia Trial June 1964, released Oct. 1989, mem. ANC Nat. Exec. Cttee 1991–, Deputy Pres. ANC 1991–94; Chancellor Univ. of Venda 1992; hon. degrees U.S.S.R. Acad. of Sciences, Univ. of Durban Westville, Lincoln Univ., Pennsylvania, York Univ. Toronto; Freeman City of Stoke-on-Trent, U.K.; Catherine A. Dumfrey Award (jtly. with Albertina Sisulu), Boston, Mass. 1991. *Leisure interrests:* reading, music. *Address:* African National Congress, 10th Floor, 51 Plein Street, Johannesburg 2001; P.O. Box 61884, Marshalltown 2107, South Africa.

SITEK, Ján; Slovak politician; b. 19 June 1956, Trstená, Dolný Kubín Dist.; m.; four d.; ed. Transport and Communication Univ. of Žilina; engineer with Tesla Orava 1975–80; researcher with ZŤS Martin 1980–81; Head Construction Unit of construction co. Pozemné stavby Žilina 1981–92; f. Orava branch of Slovak Nat. Party 1990; Chair. local org. of Slovak Nat. Party, Dolný Kubín 1990–; Minister of Defence 1994–98. *Address:* Slovenská Národná Strane (SNS), Mierova 60, Bratislava, Slovakia.

SITHOLE, Rev. Ndabaningi; Zimbabwean politician and clergyman; b. 1920; m. Vesta Sithole; ed. Waddilove Inst., Marandellas and Newton Theological Coll., U.S.A.; teacher 1941–55; U.S.A. 1955–58; ordained at Mount Silinda Congregationalist Church 1958; Principal, Chikore Cen. Primary School; Pres. African Teachers Asscn. 1959–60; Treas. Nat. Dem. Party (NDP) 1960; Del. to Fed. Review Conf. London Dec. 1960; fmr. Chair. Zimbabwe African People's Union (ZAPU) S. Rhodesia, Pres. July-Aug. 1963; Leader Zimbabwe African Nat. Union (ZANU) Rhodesia 1963, incorporated in African Nat. Council Dec. 1974, formed ANC (Sithole), contested March 1980 elections as leader of ZANU (Sithole) Party;, now leader ZANV-Ndonga; sentenced to 12 months' imprisonment Dec. 1963, sent to Wha Wha Restriction Camp May 1965; tried and sentenced to six years' hard labour for incitement to murder Ian Smith Feb. 1969, released Dec. 1974; then in exile in Zambia with section of the African Nat. Council (ANC) led by Bishop Muzorewa; withdrew faction of ZANU from ANC Sept. 1976; attended Rhodesian Constitutional Conf., Geneva 1976; mem. Transitional Exec. Council to prepare for transfer of power in Rhodesia 1978–79; M.P. 1979; seeking political asylum in U.S.A. 1987, in self-imposed exile, returned to Zimbabwe 1991; mem. Nat. Ass. 1995–96; arrested Oct. 1995; found guilty of treason 1997, sentenced to two years' imprisonment for conspiracy Dec. 1997, case on appeal to Supreme Court. *Publications:* African Nationalism 1969, 1967, The Polygamist 1973, Roots of a Revolution: Scenes from Zimbabwe's Struggle 1977. *Address:* c/o ZANU-Ndonga, P.O.Box UA 525, Union Avenue, Harare, Zimbabwe.

SITKOVETSKY, Dmitry; American violinist; b. 27 Sept. 1954, Baku, U.S.S.R. (now Azerbaijan); son of Julian Sitkovetsky and Bella Davidovich; m. Susan Roberts; ed. Moscow Conservatory, The Juilliard School of Music; début with Berlin Philharmonic 1980; appearances with Vienna Symphony, Orchestre de Paris, and the Amsterdam, Rotterdam, Munich and Royal Philharmonics in Europe and the Chicago, Cincinnati, Detroit, Montreal and Toronto Symphonies in North America, Carnegie Hall début 1986; Artistic Dir. Kuhmo Festival, Finland 1983–; First Prize Fritz Kreisler Competition, Vienna 1979, Avery Fisher Career Grant 1983.

SITRUK, Jo; French rabbi; b. 16 Oct. 1944, Tunis; m. Danielle Azoulay 1965; nine c.; ed. Seminary rue Vauquelin, Paris; Asst. to Rabbi Max Warsharski, Lower Rhine region 1970–75; Rabbi, Marseilles 1975–87; Chief Rabbi of France 1987–. *Address:* Consistoire Central Union des Communautés Juives de France, 19 rue Saint Georges, 75009 Paris, France. *Telephone:* 49408800.

SIVAN, Amiram; Israeli business executive; b. 1938, Israel; m. Aliza Sivan 1960; two s. one d.; ed. Hebrew Univ., Jerusalem; Econ. Research Dept. of State Revenue Authority 1962–65, Co-ordinator of social budgets, Budget Dept. 1965–69, Deputy Dir. of Budgets 1969–73; Dir. Gen. of Nat. Insurance Inst. 1974–76; Dir. Gen. of Ministry of Finance 1976–79; Chair. Bd. of Dirs. and C.E.O. of TEUS (Devt. Areas Industrialization Ltd.) 1980–86; Chair. Bd. of Man. of Bank Hapoalim B.M. 1986–. *Leisure interest:* music. *Address:* P.O. Box 27, 50 Rothschild Blvd., Tel-Aviv 66883 (Office); 33 Mishol Ha'ya'ara, Ramot 02, Jerusalem, Israel (Home). *Telephone:* (3) 567-3333. *Fax:* (3) 560-7028 (Office).

SIVARAMAN, Madras Ramanathan, M.A.; Indian civil servant and international official; b. 31 March 1940, Manjeri, Kerala; s. of M.S. Ramanathan; m. Nalini Sivaraman; one s. one d.; Sec. of Finance, Govt. of Madhya Pradesh 1982–87; Jt. and Additional Sec., Ministry of Commerce, Delhi 1987–90; Dir.-Gen. of Civil Aviation 1990–93; Sec. (Revenue) Ministry of Finance 1993–96; Exec. Dir. IMF Aug. 1996–. *Publications:* papers on taxation and public enterprises. *Leisure interests:* flying, trekking, jogging, reading. *Address:* 700 19th Street, N.W., Room 13-304, Washington, DC 20431, U.S.A. *Telephone:* (202) 623-7431. *Fax:* (202) 623-4961.

SIVASITHAMPARAM, Murgugesu; Sri Lankan politician and lawyer; b. 20 July 1923, Jaffna; s. of Cittampalam and Maheswari Murugesu; m. Sarathadevi (Sivasithamparan) 1949; one s. one d.; ed. Vigresmara Coll., St. Joseph's Coll., Univ. Coll., Law Coll.; Sec. of Union Soc., Univ. Coll. 1947–48; Pres. Law Students' Union, Law Coll. 1949–50; mem. House of Reps. for Udduppiddi 1960–70; Gen. Sec. All Ceylon Tamil Congress 1966–77, then Pres.; Joint Sec.-Gen. Tamil United Liberation Front (TULF) 1976–78, Pres. 1978–; M.P. for Nallur 1977–83. *Address:* Head Office, Tamil United Liberation Front, 146/19 Havelock Road, Colombo 5 (Office); 100 Norris Canal Road, Colombo 10, Sri Lanka (Home). *Telephone:* 503831 (Office); 91017 (Home). *Fax:* 595192 (Office).

SIWIEC, Marek Maciej; Polish politician and journalist; b. 13 March 1955, Piekary Śląskie; m.; one s. one d.; ed. Acad. of Mining and Metallurgy, Cracow; asst. Acad. of Mining and Metallurgy 1980–83; Ed.-in-Chief, Student Weekly 1983–87, ITD (weekly) 1987–90, Trybune (daily) 1990–91; mem. Nat. Council of Radio and TV 1993–96; Minister of State in Chancellery of Pres. of Poland, Head Nat. Security Office and Sec. Cttee. for the Protection of the Country 1996–; Deputy to Sejm (Parl.) 1991–97; mem. Polish del. to Parl. Ass., Council of Europe; mem. Polish United Workers' Party (PZPR), Social Democracy of Polish Repub. (SdRP) 1990–, presidium of Head Council 1991–93. *Leisure interests:* jogging, travelling. *Address:* Biuro Bezpieczeństwa Narodowego, Al. Ujazdowskie 5, 00-902 Warsaw, Poland. *Telephone:* (22) 694 68 00. *Fax:* (22) 694 71 04.

SIZOVA, Alla Ivanovna; Russian ballet dancer; b. 22 Sept. 1939, Moscow; d. of Ivan Sizov and Ekaterina Sizova; m. Mikhail Serebrennikov 1965; one s.; ed. Leningrad School of Ballet; joined Leningrad Kirov Theatre of Opera and Ballet 1958–; a frequent partner of Mikhail Baryshnikov (q.v.); teacher A. Vagnova Choreography School 1987–91, Universal Ballet School 1991–; People's artist of the R.S.F.S.R. 1983. *Major roles:* Masha (Nutcracker), Mirta (Giselle), Pas de trois (Le Corsaire), Katerina (Stone Flower), Waltz and Mazurka (Chopiniana), Pas de trois (Swan Lake), Aurora (Sleeping Beauty), Maria (Fountain of Bakhchisarai), Juliet (Romeo and Juliet), Cinderella (Cinderella), Kitri (Don Quixote), Girl (Leningrad Symphony); Gold Medals Youth Festival, Vienna 1959, 1st Int. Ballet Contest, Varna; Anna Pavlova Diploma, Paris 1964. *Address:* Universal Ballet School, 4301 Harewood Road, N.E., Washington, DC 20017, U.S.A.

SJAASTAD, Anders Christian, PH.D.; Norwegian politician; b. 21 Feb. 1942, Oslo; s. of Andreas and Ingrid Sjaastad; m. Torill Oftedal Sjaastad 1969; one d.; ed. Univ. of Oslo; Pres. Norwegian Students' Asscn., Univ. of Oslo 1967; Research Asst., Inst. of Political Science, Univ. of Oslo 1968–70; research at Norwegian Inst. of Int. Affairs 1970–, Dir. of Information 1973–; mem. Høyre (Conservative Party), Vice-Chair. Oslo Høyre 1977–88, Chair. 1996; Deputy mem. Storting (Parl.) 1981–85, 1997–; mem. Storting (Parl.) 1985–97; Minister of Defence 1981–86; Pres. European Movt. in Norway 1989–92; Chair. Defence and Security Cttee. (North Atlantic Ass.) 1994–97; Vice-Chair. Standing Cttee. on Justice (Stortinget) 1993–97; mem. Norwegian Nat. Defence Comm. 1974–78, Norwegian Cttee. on Arms Control and Disarmament 1976–81, N. Atlantic Ass. 1989–. *Publications:* Departmental Decision Making (Co-author) 1972, Politikk og Sikkerhet i Norskehavsområdet (with J. K. Skogan) 1975, Norsk Utenrikspolitisk Arbok (Ed.) 1975, Deterrence and Defence in the North (Co-Ed. and contrib.) 1985, Arms Control in a Multipolar World (contrib.) 1996. *Address:* Norwegian Institute of International Affairs, P.O. Box 8159, Oslo, Norway.

SKALICKÝ, Jiří; Czech politician; b. 26 April 1956, Kolín; m.; three s. one d.; ed. Coll. of Advanced Chemical Tech., Prague; research worker with Astrid (state enterprise), Prague 1981–90; mem. Civic Democratic Alliance (CDA) 1990–98, Deputy Chair. 1990–92; Deputy to House of Nations, Fed. Ass. of Č.S.F.R. 1990–92; mem. Plan and Budget Cttee., House of Nations, Fed. Ass. 1990–92; Minister for Nat. Property Admin. and Privatization 1992–96, for the Environment 1996–98; Chair. Presidium of Nat. Property Fund 1992–96; Deputy Chair. Civic Democratic Alliance 1995–97, Chair. 1997–98, Vice-Premier 1997; Senator 1998—. *Address:* Unie Svobody, Legerova 72, 120 00 Prague 2; Senate of the Czech Republic, Valdštejnské nám. 10/65, 11800 Prague 1, Czech Republic. *Telephone:* 24 22 12 15; (02) 27 93 51. *Fax:* 24 22 12 15.

SKÅNLAND, Hermod, M.A.; Norwegian banker; b. 15 June 1925, Tromsø; s. of Peder Skånland and Margit (née Maurstad) Skånland; m. Jorid Henden 1972; one d.; ed. Univ. of Oslo; Asst. Bureau of Statistics 1949–52, Consultant 1952–58, Head of Section 1958–60; Dir.-Gen. Ministry of Finance 1960–71; Deputy Gov. Bank of Norway 1971–85, Gov. 1985–93; Prof. Norwegian School of Man. 1994; Commdr. Order of St. Olav 1987, Finnish Lion with Star 1988, Icelandic Falcon with Star 1988, Order of Merit (Luxembourg) 1990. *Publications:* The Norwegian Credit Market since 1900, 1967, The Dilemma of Income Policies 1981, The Central Bank and Political Authorities 1984. *Address:* Solvegen 1B, 1177 Oslo 11, Norway (Home).

SKARSGÅRD, J. Stellan; Swedish actor; b. 13 June 1951, Göteborg; s. of J. Skarsgård and Gudrun Skarsgård; m. My Günther 1976; five s. one d.; with Royal Dramatic Theatre, Stockholm 1972–87; Best Actor, Berlin Film Festival 1982; twice Best Film Actor in Sweden; Best Actor, Rouen Film Festival 1988, 1992, Best Actor, Chicago Film Festival 1991, Jury's Special Prize, San Sebastián Film Festival 1995, European Film Award. *Films include:* Simple Minded Murderer 1982, Serpent's Way 1986, Hip Hip Hurrah 1987, The Unbearable Lightness of Being 1988, Good Evening Mr Wallenberg 1990, The Ox 1992, Wind 1992, The Slingshot 1993, Zero Kelvin 1994, Breaking the Waves 1995, Insomia 1997, Amistad 1997, Good Will

Hunting 1997, Ronin 1998, Deep Blue Sea 1998, Passion of Mind 1999; for television: Hamlet 1984.

SKATE, William (Bill) Jack; Papua New Guinea politician; b. 1953, Baimuru Dist., Gulf Prov.; m.; three c.; ed. Univ. of Tech., Lae; fmr. Gen. Man. P.S.A. Savings and Loans Soc., Nat. Capital Dist. Comm.; fmr. govt. adviser; M.P. 1992–95, 1997–; Speaker of Parl. 1992-94; Deputy Leader of Opposition 1994–95; Gov., Nat. Capital Dist. 1995–97; Prime Minister of Papua New Guinea July 1997–; Pres. and founder PNG First Party 1998–. *Address:* Office of the Prime Minister, P.O. Box 6605, Boroko, N.C.D., Papua New Guinea. *Telephone:* 276715. *Fax:* 276629.

SKATOV, Nikolai Nikolayevich, D.LIT.; Russian linguist; b. 2 May 1931; m.; one d.; ed. Kostroma State Pedagogical Inst.; sr. teacher, Acting Head, Chair of Literature, Kostroma State Pedagogical Inst. 1956–62; sr. teacher, sr. researcher, docent, Prof., Head Dept. of Literature, Leningrad State Pedagogical Inst. 1962–; Chair., Comm. on Literature and Educ., Russian Acad. of Sciences; Deputy Head, Comm. on Russian Literature, Presidium Russian Acad. of Sciences; Ed.-in-Chief Russkaya Literature (magazine); corresp. mem. Russian Acad. of Sciences 1997–; Dir. Inst. of Russian Literature. *Publications:* 12 books and over 200 scientific works. *Address:* Institute of Russian Literature, Makarova nab. 4, 199034 St. Petersburg, Russia (Office). *Telephone:* (812) 218 1901 (Office); (812) 311 4958 (Home).

SKAUGE, Arne; Norwegian politician; b. 27 Jan. 1948, Bergen; m.; two c.; ed. Norwegian School of Econs. and Business Admin; auditing dept., municipality of Bergen 1966–67; consultant, private consulting firm for social planning 1971–76; Dir. of personnel, Bergen municipality 1976; proxy mem. Storting 1973–77, mem. 1977–78; Minister of Trade and Shipping 1981–83, of Finance 1989–90; State Sec. Office of the Prime Minister 1984–86; mem. Nordic Council 1983–84, 1988–89; Conservative Party. *Address:* c/o Storting, Akersgt. 42, 0030 Oslo 1, Norway.

SKEAT, Theodore Cressy, B.A.; British papyrologist; b. 15 Feb. 1907, St. Albans, Herts.; s. of Walter William Skeat and Theodora Duckworth; m. Olive Martin 1942 (died 1992); one s.; ed. Whitgift School, Christ's Coll., Cambridge, and British School of Archaeology, Athens; Assistant Keeper, Dept. of Manuscripts, British Museum 1931–48, Deputy Keeper 1948–61, Keeper 1961–72; Cromer Greek Prize 1932. *Publications:* Fragments of an Unknown Gospel (with H. I. Bell) 1935, Scribes and Correctors of the Codex Sinaiticus (with H. J. M. Milne) 1938, The Reigns of the Ptolemies 1954, Papyri from Panopolis 1964, Catalogue of Greek Papyri in the British Museum, Vol. VII 1974, The Birth of the Codex (with C. H. Roberts) 1983, The Reign of Augustus in Egypt 1993. *Address:* 12 Berkeley Court, 31/33 Gordon Road, London, W5 2AE, England. *Telephone:* 0181-998 9174.

SKEHEL, Sir John James, Kt., PH.D., F.R.S.; British research scientist; b. 27 Jan. 1941, Blackburn, Lancs.; s. of Joseph Skehel and Ann Skehel; m. Anita Varley 1962; two s.; ed. St. Mary's Coll. Blackburn, Univ. Coll. of Wales, Aberystwyth and UMIST; Postdoctoral Fellow, Marischal Coll. Aberdeen 1965–68; Fellow, Helen Hay Whitney Foundation 1968–71; mem. Scientific Staff, Nat. Inst. for Medical Research 1971–, Dir. 1987–; Dir. World Influenza Centre 1975–93; Hon. Prof. of Virology, Glasgow Univ. 1997–; Feldberg Prize 1986; Koch Prize 1987; Prix Louis Jeantet de Médecine 1988; ICN Int. Prize in Virology 1993. *Publications:* articles in scientific journals. *Address:* The National Institute for Medical Research, The Ridgeway, Mill Hill, London, NW7 1AA (Office); 49 Homewood Road, St. Albans, Herts., AL1 4BG, England (Home). *Telephone:* 0181-959 3666 (Office); (01727) 860603 (Home).

ŠKELE, Andris; Latvian politician; b. 16 Jan. 1958; m. Dzintra Škele; two c.; ed. Latvian Acad. of Agric.; Head of Sector, sr. research asst., Deputy Dir. Latvian Scientific Research Inst. of Mechanization and Electricity 1981–90; First Deputy Minister of Agric. 1990–93; Chair. of Exec. Bd. several corps. incl. Rigas Miesnicks (Riga Butchers), Rigas Venu (Riga Wines), Rigas Alus (Riga Beer), Kaija (Seagull) and state corp. Latvijas Kagnicciba (Latvian Shipping); mem. Saeima (Parl.), Prime Minister 1995–97. *Address:* c/o Office of the Prime Minister, Brivibas Blvd. 36, 1520 Riga, Latvia.

SKEMPTON, Alec Westley, D.SC., F.I.C.E., F.G.S., F.R.S.; British professor of engineering; b. 4 June 1914, Northampton; s. of A. W. Skempton and Beatrice Edridge Payne; m. Mary Wood 1940 (died 1993); two d.; ed. Northampton Grammar School and Univ. of London; at Building Research Station 1936–46; Univ. Reader in Soil Mechanics, Imperial Coll., Univ. of London 1946–54, Prof. of Soil Mechanics 1955–57, Prof. of Civil Eng. 1957–81, Prof. Emer. 1981–, Sr. Research Fellow 1981–; Lecturer in Copenhagen, Paris, Harvard Univ., Univs. of Illinois, Stockholm, Madrid, Florence, Tokyo, Berkeley; Special Lecturer, Architectural Asscn. 1948–57; Visiting Lecturer, Cambridge Univ. School of Architecture 1962–66, Edinburgh Univ. School of Architecture 1968; Hitchcock Foundation Prof. at Univ. of Calif., Berkeley 1978; Chair. Joint Cttee. on Soils, Ministry of Supply and Road Research Bd. 1954–59; Pres. Int. Soc. Soil Mechanics and Foundation Eng. 1957–61; mem. Council Inst. of Civil Eng. 1949–54, Vice-Pres. Inst. of Civil Eng. 1974–76; mem. Cathedrals Advisory Cttee. 1964–69, Council N.E.R.C. 1973–76; Consultant to Binnie & Partners, John Mowlem & Co. Ltd.; Pres. Newcomen Soc. 1977–79, Pres. Smeatonian Soc. 1981; Fellow, Royal Soc. 1961; Foreign Assoc. U.S. Nat. Acad. of Eng. 1976; Hon. M.R.I.A. 1991; Hon. D.Sc. (Durham) 1968, (Aston) 1980, (Chalmers, Gothenburg) 1982; James Alfred Ewing Medal 1968, Lyell Medal 1972, Dickinson Medal 1974, Inst. Structural Eng. Gold Medal 1981. *Publications:* Over 100 papers on soil mechanics, geology and history of civil engineering; William Jessop, Engineer (Co-author) 1979, John Smeaton, F.R.S. 1981, Selected Papers on Soil Mechanics 1984, British Civil Engineering Literature (1640–1840) 1987, Civil Engineers and Engineering in Britain 1600–1830 1996. *Address:* Department of Civil Engineering, Imperial College, London, SW7 2AZ; 16 The Boltons, London, SW10 9SU, England. *Telephone:* 0171-589 5111 (Office); 0171-370 3457 (Home).

SKHIRI, Neji; Tunisian banker; b. 15 Feb. 1934, Monastir; m. Slimane Nebiha 1962; one s. three d.; ed. Univ. of Tunis, Centre for Educ. of Bankers, Paris; Gen. Man. Cen. Bank of Tunisia 1958–80; Deputy Chair., Chair. Banque du Sud 1980–84; Deputy Chair. Union of Arab Banks 1980–89, Chair. 1989–92; Chair. Soc. Tunisienne de banque 1984–87, Union Int. de Banques 1987–89, Banque du Maghreb Arab 1989–91, Banque Tunisio-Quatari d'investissement 1991–95, NSK Finances 1996–, Tunisian-Italian Chamber of Commerce and Industry; Mayor of Monastir 1985–90; Officer Order of the Repub., Kt. Order of Independence. *Leisure interests:* science and literature. *Address:* 3 rue Hamidi, Menzah I, 1004 Tunis, Tunisia. *Telephone:* 751-584. *Fax:* 232-363.

SKIDELSKY, Baron (Life Peer), cr. 1991, of Tilton in the County of East Sussex; **Robert Jacob Alexander Skidelsky,** M.A., D.PHIL., F.B.A., F.R.HIST.S., F.R.S.L.; British professor of political economy; b. 25 April 1939; s. of late Boris Skidelsky and Galia Sapelkin; m. Augusta Hope 1970; two s. one d.; ed. Brighton Coll. and Jesus Coll. Oxford; Research Fellow, Nuffield Coll. Oxford 1965; Assoc. Prof. Johns Hopkins Univ., U.S.A. 1970; Prof. of Political Economy Univ. of Warwick 1990–; Chair. Social Market Foundation; Chair. Hands Off Reading Campaign 1994–97; Conservative Front Bench Spokesman on Culture, Media and Sport 1997–; mem. Lord Chancellor's Advisory Council on Public Records 1988–93; mem. Schools Examination and Assessment Council 1992–93; Gov. Brighton Coll. 1998–; Hon. D.Litt. (Buckingham) 1997. *Publications:* Politicians and the Slump 1967, English Progressive Schools 1970, Oswald Mosley 1975, John Maynard Keynes, (Vol. 1) 1983, (Vol. 2) 1992, Interests and Obsessions 1993, The World After Communism 1995, The Politics of Economic Reform 1998. *Leisure interests:* tennis, opera. *Address:* Tilton House, Firle, East Sussex, BN8 6LL, England. *Telephone:* (01323) 811570, 811017. *Fax:* (01323) 811017.

SKILBECK, Malcolm, M.A., PH.D., F.A.A.S.S.; Australian educational researcher and consultant; b. 22 Sept. 1932, Northam, W.A.; s. of Charles Harrison Skilbeck and Elsie Muriel Nash Skilbeck; m. Dr. Helen Connell 1984; one s. four d.; ed. Sydney Univ., Univ. of Ill. and Univ. of London; Prof. and Dean of Educ., Univ. of Ulster 1971–75; Foundation Dir., Australian Curriculum Devt. Centre 1975–81; Dir. of Studies, Schools Council for Curriculum and Examinations for England and Wales 1981–83; Prof. of Curriculum Studies, Univ. of London, Inst. of Educ. 1981–85; Vice-Chancellor and Prin. Deakin Univ. 1986–91; Deputy Dir. for Educ., Directorate of Educ., Employment, Labour and Social Affairs, OECD 1991–97; Consultant to OECD, UNESCO, nat. govts., British Council, Australian Int. Devt. Assistance Bureau. *Publications:* Culture and the Classroom 1976, A Core Curriculum for the Common School 1982, School Based Curriculum Development 1984, Evaluating the Curriculum for the Eighties 1984, Curriculum Reform 1990, The Vocational Quest 1994, Redefining Tertiary Education 1998. *Leisure interests:* gardens, books, art, travel. *Address:* P.O. Box 278, Drysdale, Vic. 3222, Australia.

SKINNER, Hon. James John, Q.C.; Irish-born lawyer; b. 24 July 1923; s. of late William Skinner; m. Regina Brigitte Reiss 1950; three s. two d.; ed. Trinity Coll., Dublin and King's Inns, Dublin; called to the Irish Bar 1946, joined Leinster Circuit; called to the English Bar, Gray's Inn 1950, to the Northern Rhodesia Bar 1951; Q.C., N. Rhodesia 1964, M.P. for Lusaka E. 1964–68; Minister of Justice, Lusaka 1964–65; Attorney-Gen. 1965–69; Minister of Legal Affairs 1967–68; Chief Justice of Zambia March–Sept. 1969; Chief Justice of Malawi 1970–85; Social Security Commr. 1986–96, a Child Support Commr. 1993–96; Grand Commdr., Order of Menelik II (Ethiopia) 1965. *Address:* 12A Ashley Court, Ashley Road, Epsom, Surrey, KT18 5AJ, England.

SKINNER, Quentin Robert Duthie, M.A., F.B.A.; British professor of modern history; b. 26 Nov. 1940, Oldham; s. of Alexander Skinner and Winifred (née Duthie) Skinner; m. 2nd Susan James 1979; one s. one d.; ed. Bedford School, Gonville and Caius Coll., Cambridge; Fellow Christ's Coll., Cambridge 1962–, Vice-Master 1997–; Lecturer in History, Univ. of Cambridge 1967–78, Prof. of Political Science 1978–96; Regius Prof. of Modern History, Univ. of Cambridge 1996–, Pro-Vice-Chancellor 1999–; mem. Inst. of Advanced Study, Princeton, N.J. 1974–75, 1976–79; Foreign mem. American Philosophical Soc. 1997; Hon. Fellow Gonville and Caius Coll., Cambridge 1997; Hon. Foreign mem. American Acad. of Arts and Sciences 1986; mem. Academia Europaea 1989; Hon. D.Litt. (Chicago, E. Anglia) 1992, (Helsinki) 1997; Wolfson Literary Award 1979. *Publications:* The Foundations of Modern Political Thought, Vol. I The Renaissance 1978, Vol. II The Age of Reformation 1978, Machiavelli 1981, Philosophy in History (ed. jtly. and contrib.) 1984, The Return of Grand Theory in the Human Sciences (ed. and contrib.) 1985, The Cambridge History of Renaissance Philosophy (ed. jtly. and contrib.) 1988, Machiavelli: The Prince (ed. and introduction) 1988, Meaning and Context: Quentin Skinner and His Critics (ed. James Tully) 1988, Machiavelli and Republicanism (ed. jtly. and contrib.) 1990, Political

Discourse in Early-modern Britain (ed. jtly. and contrib.) 1993, Milton and Republicanism (ed. jtly.) 1995, Reason and Rhetoric in the Philosophy of Hobbes 1996, Liberty before Liberalism 1998. *Address:* Christ's College, Cambridge, CB2 3BU, England. *Telephone:* (01223) 334 974.

SKINNER, Samuel, LL.B.; American politician and lawyer; b. 10 June 1938; m. Mary Jacobs 1989; two s. one d.; ed. Univ. of Ill. and DePaul Univ.; with IBM Corpn. 1961–68; Asst. U.S. Attorney, Northern District of Ill. 1968–74, First Asst. U.S. Attorney 1974–75, U.S. Attorney 1975–77; private law practice, Chicago 1977–84; Chair. Regional Transportation Authority of Northeastern Ill. 1984–88; U.S. Sec. of Transportation 1989–91, White House Chief of Staff 1991–93; Pres. Commonwealth Edison Co. 1993–98. *Address:* c/o Commonwealth Edison Co., P.O. Box 767, Chicago, IL 60690, U.S.A..

SKOK, Vladimir Ivanovich; Ukrainian physiologist; b. 4 June 1932; m.; one d.; ed. Kiev State Univ.; sr. researcher Kiev State Univ., Inst. of Physiology 1956–62; Head of div. A. Bogomolets Inst. of Physiology 1962–; Prof. of Physiology 1977; mem. Ukrainian Acad. of Sciences 1979, Acad.-Sec. Dept. of Biochem., Physiology and Theoretical Med. 1974–78, 1981–88, Vice-Pres. 1988–93; mem. U.S.S.R. (now Russian) Acad. of Sciences 1987, Ukrainian Pedagogic Acad. 1992 and Polish Acad. of Sciences 1994; main research in physiology, biophysics and pharmacology of automatic nervous system; Vice-Pres. I. Pavlov Physiological Soc.; U.S.S.R. State Prize 1981, I. Sechenov Prize. *Publications include:* Physiology of Autonomic Ganglia 1973, Neuro-Muscular Physiology 1986, Neuronal Acetylcholine Receptors, London 1989, Natural Activity of Autonomic Ganglia 1989 and numerous articles. *Leisure interests:* hunting, fishing. *Address:* Institute of Physiology, Bogomoletz str. 4, 252024 Kiev, Ukraine. *Telephone:* (04) 293-0158 (Office); 225 2368 (Home).

SKOKOV, Yuri Vladimirovich, C.TECH.SC.; Russian politician; b. 16 June 1938, Vladivostok; ed. Leningrad Electrotech. Inst.; mem. CPSU 1967–91; researcher, Deputy Dir. Kalinin Research Inst. of Electric Sources U.S.S.R. Ministry of Defence 1969–75, Dir. 1975–76; Deputy Dir.-Gen. Research Production Union Quant 1977–86, Dir. 1986–90; U.S.S.R. People's Deputy 1989–91; People's Deputy of Russian Fed. 1990–; Chair. Bd. of Concern Quantemp 1988–90, First Deputy Chair. Council of Ministers of R.S.F.S.R. 1990–91; Econ. Counsellor to Pres. of Russia 1990–91; Sec. Council on Problems of Fed. and Territories 1991–92; Sec. Security Council 1992–93; Head Fed. of Community Producers of Russian Fed. 1994–; Chair. Bd. Centre for Int. and Inter-regional Econ. Problems 1994; Chair. Bd. Congress of Russian Communities 1995–. *Address:* Federation of Commodity Producers, Novy Arbat 15, 121019 Moscow; Congress of Russian Communities, Arbat str. 15, 121019 Moscow, Russia. *Telephone:* 203-06-08 (Federation); 242-00-17 (Congress).

SKOL, Michael, B.A.; American diplomatist; b. 15 Oct. 1942, Chicago, Ill.; s. of Ted Skol and Rebecca Skol; m. Claudia Serwer 1973; ed. Yale Univ., Univ. of the Americas, Mexico City; joined U.S. Foreign Service 1965; served in Buenos Aires, Saigon, Santo Domingo, Naples, Rome, San José and Bogotá (Deputy Chief of Mission), and as Desk Officer for Costa Rica, Paraguay and Uruguay; Deputy Dir. for Policy Planning, and Dir. Andean Affairs, State Dept. Bureau of Inter-American Affairs; Deputy Asst. Sec. of State for S. America, 1988–90; Amb. to Venezuela 1990–93; Prin. Deputy Asst. Sec. Latin American/Caribbean Dept. of State 1993–95; Sr. Vice-Pres. Diplomatic Resolutions Inc., Washington 1996–97; Pres. Skol and Assocs. Inc., Washington 1998–. *Address:* Skol and Associates Inc., Suite 650, 1133 Connecticut Avenue, Washington, DC 20036 (Office); 3033 Cleveland Avenue, N.W., Washington, DC 20008 (Home), U.S.A.

SKOLIMOWSKI, Jerzy; Polish film director; b. 5 May 1938, Warsaw; m. Joanna Szczerbic; ed. Warsaw Univ. and State Superior Film School, Łódź; wrote scripts for Wajda's Innocent Sorcerers, Polanski's Knife in the Water and Łomnicki's Poślizg; dir., designer, author, ed., actor Rysopis 1964, author, dir., actor, Walkover 1965; author, dir., Barrier 1966; dir. Le Départ 1967; author, dir., actor Hands Up 1967; dir. Adventures of Gerard 1969; Grand Prix for Barrier Int. Film Festival, Bergamo 1966, Silver Palm for Scream, Cannes Film Festival 1978, British Film Award (for Moonlighting) 1982, Special Prize, Venice Film Festival 1985. *Films:* Rysopis (Identification Marks: None) 1964, Walkover 1965, Bariera (Barrier) 1966, Le Départ 1967, Ręce do góry (Hands Up) 1967, Dialogue 20-40-60 1968, Adventures of Gerard 1969, The Deep End 1971, King, Queen, Knave 1972, Lady Frankenstein (or Terminus) 1976, The Shout 1978, Moonlighting 1982, Success is the Best Revenge 1984, The Lightship 1985, Torrents of Spring 1988, Before and After Death 1990, 30 Door Key, The Hollow Men. *Publications:* Poetry: Gdzieś blisko siebie (Somewhere Close to Oneself); Play: Ktoś się utopił (Somebody Got Drowned). *Address:* c/o Film Polski, ul. Mazowiecka 6/8, 00-048 Warsaw, Poland.

SKOOG, Folke (Karl), PH.D.; American plant physiologist; b. 15 July 1908, Sweden; s. of Karl (G.) Skoog and Sigrid (Person) Skoog; m. Birgit Anna Lisa Bergner 1947; one d.; ed. California Inst. of Technology and Univ. of California; Instructor and Research Assoc., Harvard Univ. 1937–41; Asst. Prof., Assoc. Prof. of Biology, Johns Hopkins Univ. 1941–44; Tech. Rep. (Chemist), U.S. Army 1944–46; Assoc. Prof. of Botany, Univ. of Wis. 1947–49, Prof. of Botany 1949, now Emer.; mem. American Soc. of Plant Physiologists (Vice-Pres. 1956–57, Pres. 1957–58), Botanical Soc. of America (Chair. Physiology Section 1954–55), N.A.S., American Acad. of Arts and Sciences, Soc. of Gen. Physiologists (Pres. 1957–58), Soc. of Devt. Biology (Pres. 1970–71), Int. Plant Growth Substances Asscn. (Vice-Pres. 1976–79, Pres. 1979–82), Royal Soc. of Sciences, Sweden, Royal Acad. of Sciences, Sweden, Akad. Leopoldina, Germany; Hon. mem. Russian Soc. of Plant Physiologists; mem. of editorial bd. Journal of Plant Growth Regulation 1982, Plant Cell Reports 1981, Archives of Biochem. and Biophysics 1980–85; Hon. Ph.D. (Lund, Sweden); Hon. D.Sc. (Univ. of Ill.), (Pisa) 1991; Hon. D. Agrarie (Swedish Univ. of Agricultural Sciences) 1991; Stephen Hales Medal of American Soc. of Plant Physiologists 1955, Certificate of Merit of Botanical Soc. of America 1956, Reid Barnes Award, American Soc. of Plant Physiologists 1970, Nat. Medal of Science 1991, Cosimo Ridolfi Medal, Univ. of Pisa 1991, John Ericsson Medal, American Soc. of Swedish Engineers 1992, Distinguished Life Achievement Award, World Congress of Cell and Tissue Culture 1992, Chailakhyan Medal 1994. *Publications:* Plant Growth Substances (Editor) 1951 and 1980; author and co-author of many scientific articles on plant growth, auxins and cytokinins 1933–87. *Leisure interests:* farming, sport. *Address:* Department of Botany, University of Wisconsin, Madison, WI 53706-1381 (Office); 2820 Marshall Court, Madison, WI 53705, U.S.A. (Home). *Telephone:* (608) 262-2790 (Office); (608) 233-3372 (Home).

SKOTHEIM, Robert Allen, PH.D.; American administrator; b. 31 Jan. 1933, Seattle, Wash.; s. of Sivert O. Skotheim and Marjorie F. (née Allen) Skotheim; m. Nadine Vail 1953; one s. two d.; ed. Wash. Univ.; instructor to Prof. of History, Wash. Univ., Wayne State Univ., UCLA, Colo. Univ. 1962–72; Provost, Faculty Dean Hobart and William Smith Colls. 1972–75; Pres. Whitman Coll. 1975–88; Dir. Huntington Library, Art Collections, Botanical Gardens 1988–90, Pres. 1990–; Guggenheim Memorial Fellowship 1967–68; numerous hon. degrees. *Publications:* American Intellectual Histories and Historians 1966, co-ed. Historical Scholarship in the United States and Other Essays 1967, ed. The Historian and the Climate of Opinion 1969, Totalitarianism and American Social Thought 1971, co-ed. American Social Thought: Sources and Interpretations (two vols.) 1972. *Address:* The Huntington Library, Art Collections and Botanical Gardens, 1151 Oxford Road, San Marino, CA 91108 (Office); 1650 Orlando Road, San Marino, CA 91108; 2120 Place Road, Port Angeles, WA 98362, U.S.A. (Homes). *Telephone:* (626) 405-2115 (Office). *Fax:* (626) 405-2289.

SKOU, Jens Christian, M.D.; Danish professor of biophysics; b. 8 Oct. 1918, Lemvig; s. of Magnus Martinus Skou and Ane Margrethe Skou; m. Ellen Margrethe Nielsen 1948; two d.; ed. Univ. of Copenhagen; Asst. Prof. Inst. of Physiology, Univ. of Aarhus 1947, Assoc. Prof. 1954, Prof. and Chair. of Dept. 1963, Prof. of Biophysics 1978–88; mem. Royal Danish Acad. of Sciences, Deutsche Akad. der Naturforscher, Leopoldina, European Molecular Biology Org.; Foreign Assoc. N.A.S. (U.S.A.); Hon. mem. Japanese Biochemical Soc., American Physiological Soc.; Dr. medicinae h.c. (Copenhagen) 1986; Leo Prize 1959, Novo Prize 1964, Consul Carlsen Prize 1973, Anders Retzius Gold Medal 1977, Erik K. Fernström's Nordic Prize 1985, shared Nobel Prize for Chemistry 1997 (for study of energy consumption in cells). *Publications:* scientific papers on the mechanism of action of local anaesthetics 1946–57; scientific publs. on structure and function of the Na, K-pump, the transport system in the cell membrane responsible for the exchange of cations across membranes 1957–. *Leisure interests:* classical music, yachting, skiing. *Address:* Rislundvej 9, Risskov, 8240, Denmark. *Telephone:* 86.17.79.18. *Fax:* 86.12.95.99.

SKOULARIKIS, Ioannis P.; Greek politician and lawyer; b. 1929, Smyla, Ileia Pref.; m. Koula Poulos; one s. one d.; ed. Athens Univ. Law School; specialist in labour law; former Counsel, Supreme Court and State Council; Legal Counsel, Greek Gen. Confed. of Labour 1964–65; active in dissident politics from student days and helped set up several anti-regime orgs. including Panhellenic Liberation Movt. (PAK) during colonel's dictatorship; M.P. 1974–; Minister of Public Order 1981–85, of Justice 1989, of Labour 1994–95. *Address:* 162 Papadiamantopoulou Street, 157 73 Zografou, Athens, Greece. *Telephone:* (01) 7713-555.

SKOURAS, Thanos, PH.D.; Greek professor of economics; b. 21 Dec. 1943, Athens; s. of Spyros D. Skouras and Ismini Xanthopoulos; m. 1st Gella Varnava 1966 (divorced 1987); two s.; m. 2nd Savina Ioannides 1998; ed. Athens Coll., King's Coll. Durham Univ., and London School of Econs., U.K.; Asst. Lecturer, Lecturer, Sr. Lecturer, Middlesex Polytechnic at Enfield, U.K. 1967–73; Prin. Lecturer and Head Econs. Div., Thames Polytechnic 1974–77; Head Dept. of Applied Econ. Studies, N.E. London Polytechnic (now Univ. of E. London) 1978–86; Prof., Athens Univ. of Econs. and Business 1986–, Deputy Chair. Econs. Dept. 1987–89, Vice-Rector 1989–92, Pres. Research Centre 1989–92; fmr. Visiting Lecturer, Architectural Asscn. School, London, Cambridge Univ., CEMI, Beijing, Fudan Univ., Shanghai, Katholieke Univ. Leuven; Adviser to Deputy Minister of Nat. Economy, Athens; mem. Council of Econ. Advisers 1986–88; Ed. The Thames Papers in Political Economy 1974–86, The British Review of Econ. Issues 1976–85; Assoc. Ed. Greek Econ. Review 1985–; mem. Editorial Bd. Int. Review of Applied Econs. 1993–; Councillor Royal Econ. Soc., London 1982–86; mem. Governing Council Greek Centre of Planning and Econ. Research 1987–88; Chair. Cttee. for Financing of Major Infrastructure Projects 1988; Council mem. Euro-China Research Asscn. for Man. 1989–92; mem. Supreme Disciplinary Council, Econ. Chamber of Greece 1990–92; Consultant European Comm. DG XVI 1992–; Chair. Bd. Abax Stockbroking 1991–94; mem. Bd. Ergose 1996–97, Commercial Bank 1997, Greek Econ. Soc. 1999–; Hon. Research Fellow Polytech. of E. London 1986–91. *Publications:* Land and its Taxation in Recent Economic Theory 1977, Post-Keynesian Economic

Theory (Co-Ed.) 1985, The Greek Economy: Economic Policy for the 1990s (Ed.) 1991; about 40 articles in professional journals. *Address:* 8 Chlois Street, 145 62 Athens, Greece. *Telephone:* 820 3353. *Fax:* 808 2543.

SKOVHUS, Bo; Danish opera singer; b. 22 May 1962, Aarhus; s. of Freddy Jorgensen and Birthe Skovhus; one d.; ed. Music Acad., Aarhus Royal Music Acad. and Opera School, Copenhagen; début in Don Giovanni, Vienna Volksoper 1988, début as Silvio, Pagliacci Vienna Staatsoper 1991; regular guest singer with all maj. opera cos. including Metropolitan, New York, San Francisco, Houston, Munich State Opera, Hamburg State Opera, Berlin, Cologne, Covent Garden, Dresden, etc.; many recitals in Europe, U.S.A. and Japan; recordings of Don Giovanni, Le Nozze di Figaro, The Merry Widow, Britten's War Requiem, Carmina Burana, Fidelio, Zemlinsky's Lyric Symphony, various works by Schubert, Schumann, Wolf and recordings of arias; Kammersänger (Austria) 1997. *Address:* Balmer und Dixon Management, Granitweg 2, CH-8006, Zurich, Switzerland. *Telephone:* (01) 361 93 55. *Fax:* (01) 362 62 80.

SKRINSKY, Aleksandr Nikolayevich, D.SC.; Russian physicist; b. 15 Jan. 1936, Orenburg; s. of Nikolay Alexandrovich Skrinsky and Galina Stepanovna Skrinskaya; m. Lydia Borisovna Golovanova; one s. one d.; ed. Moscow State Univ.; Research Worker, Inst. of Nuclear Physics, Siberian Dept., U.S.S.R. (now Russian) Acad. of Sciences, Head of Laboratory 1959–, Deputy Dir. 1971–77, Dir. of Inst. 1977–; Prof. Novosibirsk Univ. 1967–85; corresp. mem. U.S.S.R. (now Russian) Acad. of Sciences 1968–70, mem. 1970, Academician-Sec. Nuclear Physics Dept. 1988–; mem. Int. Cttee. for Future Accelerators (ICFA) 1983–90 (Chair. 1990–93), CERN Scientific Policy Cttee. 1985–91; Lenin Prize 1967, U.S.S.R. State Prize 1989. *Publications:* more than 200 scientific works in the field of accelerator physics and technology, elementary particle physics. *Leisure interests:* ski-running, swimming, music. *Address:* Russian Academy of Sciences, Nuclear Physics Department, Leninsky prosp. 32A, 117334 Moscow, Russia. *Telephone:* (095) 938-07-53. *Fax:* (095) 938-17-35.

SKROWACZEWSKI, Stanisław; Polish conductor and composer; b. 3 Oct. 1923, Lwów (now Ukraine); s. of Paweł Skrowaczewski and Zofia (Karszniewicz) Skrowaczewska; m. Krystyna Jarosz 1956; two s. one d.; ed. Lwów Conservatoire and State Higher School of Music, Cracow; Conductor, Wrocław Philharmonic Orchestra 1946–47; further composition studies with Nadia Boulanger and P. Klecki, Paris 1947–49; Artistic Dir. and First Conductor, Silesian Philharmonic Orch., Katowice 1949–54; First Conductor, Cracow Philharmonic Orch. 1955–56; Dir. Nat. Philharmonic Orch., Warsaw 1957–59; Musical Dir. Minnesota Orchestra 1960–79; tours in Europe, N. and S. America, Israel; Prin. Conductor and Musical Adviser, Hallé Orchestra 1984–(91); Musical Adviser St. Paul Chamber Orchestra 1986–; D.H.L. h.c. (Hamline Univ., St. Paul, Minnesota) 1961; D.Mus. h.c. (Macalester Coll., St. Paul, Minn.) 1977; Dr. h.c. (Univ. of Minnesota) 1979; State Prize (3rd class) 1956, First Prize, Int. Conductor's Competition, Rome 1956, Conductor's Award of Columbia Univ., New York 1973, Third Prize, Kennedy Center Friedheim Award Competition (for Ricercari Notturni) 1978; 5 ASCAP Awards for imagination programming with Minneapolis Symphony 1961–74, Gold Medal, Bruckner-Mahler Soc. 1979; Commdr. Cross of Order Polonia Restituta. *Compositions include:* Symphony for String Orchestra, three other symphonies, Muzyka Nocą (Music by Night, suite of nocturnes), four string quartets, two overtures, Cantique des Cantiques (voice and orch.), Prelude, Fugue, Post-Ludium (orch.), English Horn Concerto 1969, Ricercari Notturni (orchestral), Clarinet Concerto, Violin Concerto 1985, Concerto for Orchestra 1985, Fanfare for Orchestra 1987, Sextet 1988, String Trio 1990, Triple Concerto 1992, Chamber Concerto 1993, Passacaglia Fantasiosa 1995, Trio for piano, clarinet and bassoon, six piano sonatas; also music for opera, ballet, film and theatre. *Leisure interests:* alpinism, skiing, books, film, theatre. *Address:* P.O. Box 700, 1120 Terndale Road North, Wayzata, MN 55391, U.S.A. (Home). *Fax:* (612) 473-7384.

SKUBISZEWSKI, Krzysztof, LL.D.; Polish politician and lawyer; b. 8 Oct. 1926, Poznań; s. of Ludwik Skubiszewski and Aniela Skubiszewska (née Leitgeber); ed. Poznań Univ., Univ. de Nancy and Harvard Univ.; mem. Staff, Poznań Univ. (renamed Adam Mickiewicz Univ.) 1948–73, Voluntary Asst., Jr. Asst., Lecturer 1948–56, Asst. Prof. 1956–61, Dozent, Dept. of Int. Law 1961–73, Pro-Dean Law Faculty 1961–63; Prof. Inst. of State and Law, Polish Acad. of Sciences, Warsaw 1973–96; Minister of Foreign Affairs 1989–93; mem. Iran-U.S. Claims Tribunal, The Hague 1993–, Pres. 1994–; Judge ad hoc Int. Court of Justice 1994–; mem. Bureau, Court of Conciliation and Arbitration, OSCE, Geneva 1995–; Chair., Council for Foreign Policy 1996–; Visiting Scholar, School of Int. Affairs, Columbia Univ., New York 1963–64, Prof. invité, Univ. de Genève 1971, 1979; Visiting Fellow, All Souls College, Oxford 1971–72; Curator, Student Asscn. of UN Friends, Poznań 1960–73; mem. Poznań Friends of Learning Soc., West Inst. in Poznań, Inst. de Droit Int. 1971–, Polish Group of Int. Law Asscn. 1971–, American Soc. of Int. Law, Oxford Soc., Soc. Française pour le Droit Int.; mem. Legal Sciences Cttee., Polish Acad. of Sciences 1981–; corresp. mem. Polish Acad. of Sciences 1989–, Inst. de France; mem. Primatial Social Council 1981–84, Consultative Council attached to Chair. of Council of State 1986–89; Dr. h.c. (Ghent, Turin, Liège, Mainz, Geneva); Hon. Bencher, Gray's Inn 1990; Alexander von Humboldt Foundation Award 1984; numerous decorations. *Publications:* Pieniądz na terytorium okupowanym 1960, Uchwały prawotwórcze organizacji międzynarodowych 1965, Zachodnia granica Polski 1969, Individual Rights and the State in Foreign Affairs (co-author) 1977, Resolutions of the General Assembly of the United Nations 1985, Polityka zagraniczna i odzyskanie niepodległości 1997; over 90 articles on int. law. *Address:* Iran-United States Claims Tribunal, Parkweg 13, 2585 JH The Hague, Netherlands (Office); ul. Lewicka 13/15, m. 8, 02-547 Warsaw, Poland (Home). *Telephone:* (70) 352 00 64 (Office); (22) 49 38 76 (Home). *Fax:* (70) 350 24 56 (Office).

SKULACHEV, Vladimir Petrovich; Russian biologist; b. 21 Feb. 1935, Moscow; s. of Petr Stepanovich Skulachev and Nadezhda Aronovna Skulacheva; m. Severina Inna Isaakovna; four s. one d.; ed. Moscow State Univ., jr. researcher, head of div., head of lab. Moscow State Univ.; Dir. A. Belozersky Inst. of Physico-Chem. Biol.; corresp. mem. U.S.S.R. (now Russian) Acad. of Sciences 1974, mem. 1990; research in biochem., bioenergetics, investigation of molecular mechanisms of energy transformation in membranes of bacteria, mitochondria and chloroplasts; U.S.S.R. State Prize. *Publications:* Energy Accumulation in Cells 1969, Energy Transformation in Biomembranes 1972, Membranes Bioenergies 1988, numerous other books and articles. *Leisure interests:* badminton, skiing. *Address:* A. N. Belozersky Institute of Physico-Chemical Biology, Moscow State University, 119899 Moscow, Russia. *Telephone:* (095) 939-55-30 (Office); (095) 939-01-47 (Home). *Fax:* (095) 939-03-38.

SKURATOV, Yuri Ilyich, DR. JUR.; Russian lawyer and civil servant; b. 1952, Ulan-Ude; s. of Ilya I. Skuratov and Raisa G. Skuratova; m. Elena D. Besedina 1976; one s. one d.; ed. Sverdlovsk Inst. of Law; teacher, Dean Sverdlovsk Inst. of Law 1977–89; Deputy Head Div. on legis. initiatives and legal issues, CPSU Cen. Cttee. 1989–91; sr. consultant Russian Ministry of Security 1991–92; Dir. Research Inst. of Problems of Justice, Gen. Prosecutor's Office of Russia 1993–95; Gen. Prosecutor 1995–. *Publications:* over 90 scientific works on problems of civil and criminal law. *Leisure interests:* chess, swimming. *Address:* General Prosecutor's Office, Bolshaya Dmitrovka str. 15A, 103793 Moscow, Russia. *Telephone:* (095) 292-88-69.

ŠKVORECKÝ, Josef, PH.D.; Czech/Canadian writer and translator; b. 29 Sept. 1924, Náchod; m. Zdena Salivarová; ed. Charles Univ., Prague; worked as teacher, Secondary Social School; ed. World Literature (journal); Chair. Editorial Bd. of journal The Flame –1968; emigrated to Canada 1968; Co-founder (with Zdena Škvorecky) of Sixty-Eight Publishers, Toronto, which, up to 1990, published 216 titles by authors banned in Czechoslovakia; Professor of English and American Literature, Toronto Univ. 1969–90, Prof. Emer. 1990–; mem. of Board of Consultants to President Havel (q.v.) Feb. 1990–June 1991; Dr. h.c. (Masaryk Univ., Brno) 1991; Hon. Citizen of Prague 1990, Order of the White Lion (3rd Grade) Czechoslovakia 1990. *Publications:* Cowards (novel) 1958, The Legend of Emoeke (story) 1963, Bass-saxophone (story) 1965, Ideas of a Reader of Detective Stories, The Seven-Armed Candlestick, End of the Nylon Age (story) 1968, The Little Lion (novel), The Tank Battalion (novel) 1969, The Miracle Game (novel) 1972, Priest Knox's Sins, The Clean Season, A Stop to Lieutenant Borůvka (novel) 1972, Lieutenant Borůvka Is Coming Back, Tale of An Engineer of Human Souls (novel) 1977, Scherzo Capriccioso (novel) 1984, Sadness of Lieutenant Borůvka (novel) 1988, Voice from America, Bitter Jazz (dramatized stories) 1990, Texas Bride (novel) 1993, Two Murders in My Double Life (novel) 1996, 5 full-length film screenplays.

SKWEYIYA, Zola Sidney Themba, LL.D.; South African politician and civil servant; b. 14 April 1942, Cape Town; s. of Winnie Skweyiya; one c.; ed. Lovedale High School, Univ. of Fort Hare; mem. ANC 1956, mil. training, Lusaka 1965; Chief ANC Rep. at OAU, Addis Ababa 1980–85, ANC Rep. UN Comm. on Human Rights 1984–93; f. ANC legal and constitutional dept. 1985, Head 1985–94; mem. ANC Nat. Exec. Cttee. 1991–; Minister of Public Services and Admin., Govt. of Nat. Unity 1994–; Chair., Trustee Nat. Children's Rights Comm. 1990–; Trustee S.A. Legal Defence Fund 1991–. *Leisure interests:* listening to jazz and classical music, reading. *Address:* Private Bag X884, Pretoria 0001, South Africa.

SKYRMS, Brian, PH.D.; American professor of philosophy; b. 11 March 1938, Pittsburgh, Pa.; s. of Frederick John Skyrms and Marie Margaret (Schlipf) Skyrms; m. Pauline Jenkins 1972; two s.; ed. Lehigh Univ., Univ. of Pittsburgh; Asst. Prof., Calif. State Univ., Northridge 1964–65, Univ. of Del. 1965–66; Visiting Asst. Prof., Univ. of Mich. 1966–67; Asst. Prof. then Assoc. Prof., Univ. of Ill., Chicago 1967–70, Prof. 1970–80; Prof. of Philosophy, Univ. of Calif., Irvine 1980–97, Distinguished Prof. of Philosophy and Prof. of Econs. 1997–, Dir. Program in History and Philosophy of Science; mem. Governing Bd. American Philosophical Asscn. 1987–90, Philosophy of Science Asscn. 1990–91; mem. several editorial bds. including American Philosophical Quarterly, and Philosophy of Science; Ed. Cambridge Studies in Probability, Induction and Decision Theory; Fellow American Acad. of Arts and Sciences 1994; Guggenheim Fellow 1987–88, Fellow, Center for Advanced Study in the Behavioral Sciences 1993–94, numerous science fellowships; Univ. of Calif. Pres.'s Research in the Humanities 1993–94. *Publications:* Choice and Chance: An Introduction to Inductive Logic 1966, Causal Necessity 1980, Pragmatics and Empiricism 1984, The Dynamics of Rational Deliberation 1990, Evolution of the Social Contract 1996; Ed. or Co-Ed. seven books; numerous articles in learned journals. *Address:* School of Social Sciences, University of California at Irvine, Irvine, CA 92697-5100, U.S.A. *Telephone:* (949) 824-6495.

SLABBERT, Frederik van Zyl, D.PHIL.; South African politician; b. 2 March 1940, Pretoria; m. 1st Mana Jordaan; one s. one d.; m. 2nd Jane

Stephens 1984; ed. Pietersburg High School, Univs. of Witwatersrand and Stellenbosch; Lecturer in Sociology, Univ. of Stellenbosch 1964–68, Sr. Lecturer 1970–71; Sr. Lecturer and Acting Head, Dept. of Sociology, Rhodes Univ., Grahamstown 1969, Univ. of Cape Town 1972–73; Prof. and Head Dept. of Sociology, Univ. of Witwatersrand 1973–74; Visiting Prof. WBS Business School 1988–; M.P. for Rondebosch 1974–86; Nat. Leader Progressive Fed. Party and Leader of the Opposition 1979–86; Chair. Cen. Witwatersrand Metropolitan Chamber 1991–94; Co-Chair. Task Group for Local Govt. Elections 1994–; co-f. Inst. for Democratic Alternatives 1988–; Dir. Adcorp Holdings 1996–. *Publications:* South Africa's Options; Strategies for Sharing Power (with David Welsh) 1979, The Last White Parliament 1986, The System and The Struggle 1989, The Quest for Democracy: South Africa in Transition 1992, and various articles on S.A. politics. *Leisure interests:* squash, tennis, swimming. *Address:* P.O. Box 98, Witwatersrand 2050, South Africa. *Telephone:* (011) 6436641.

SLACK, Paul Alexander, D.PHIL., F.B.A.; British historian; b. 23 Jan. 1943, Bradford; s. of Isaac Slack and Helen Slack (née Firth); m. Diana Gillian Manby 1965; two d.; ed. Bradford Grammar School, St. John's Coll., Oxford; Jr. Research Fellow Balliol Coll., Oxford 1966–69, Fellow and Tutor in Modern History, Exeter Coll. 1973–96, Reader in Modern History, Univ. of Oxford 1990–96, Chair. Gen. Bd. of Faculties 1995–96, Prin. Linacre Coll. 1996–, Pro-Vice-Chancellor 1997–; Lecturer in History, York Univ. 1969–72. *Publications:* The Impact of Plague in Tudor and Stuart England 1985, Poverty and Policy in Tudor and Stuart England 1988, The English Poor Law 1531–1782 1990, From Reformation to Improvement: Public Welfare in Early Modern England 1999. *Leisure interests:* opera, fell-walking. *Address:* Linacre College, Oxford, OX1 3JA, England. *Telephone:* (01865) 271650. *Fax:* (01865) 271668.

SLADE, Rt. Hon. Sir Christopher John; British judge (retd.); b. 2 June 1927, London; s. of late George Penkivil Slade, K.C., and Mary A. A. Slade; m. Jane G. A. Buckley 1958; one s. three d.; ed. Eton Coll. and New Coll., Oxford; called to Bar 1951, Q.C. 1965; in practice at Chancery Bar 1951–75; Judge, High Court of Justice, Chancery Div. 1975–82; Judge of Restrictive Practices Court 1980–82, Pres. 1981–82; Lord Justice of Appeal 1982–91; mem. Gen. Council of Bar 1958–62, 1965–69; mem. Senate of Four Inns of Court 1966–69; Bencher, Lincoln's Inn 1973; mem. Lord Chancellor's Legal Educ. Cttee. 1969–71; Treas., Lincoln's Inn 1994. *Leisure interests:* multifarious. *Address:* 16 Elthiron Road, London, SW6 4BN, England. *Telephone:* 0171-731 0938.

SLADKEVIČIUS, H.E. Cardinal Vincentas; Lithuanian ecclesiastic; b. 20 Aug. 1920, Kaišiadorys; ordained 1944; teacher at Kaunas seminary 1952–57; elected bishop of Abora 1957, consecrated 1957; priest in Birzai region (banned from moving elsewhere) 1957–82; cr. Cardinal 1988; Bishop of Kaunas 1989–; Apostolic Admin. Metropolitan See of Kaunas. *Address:* M. Valančiaus 6, 3000 Kaunas, Lithuania. *Telephone:* (07) 206486.

SLANEY, Sir Geoffrey, K.B.E., M.SC., CH.M., F.R.C.S.; British professor of surgery; b. 19 Sept. 1922, West Hallam; s. of Richard and Gladys L. Slaney; m. Josephine M. Davy 1956; one s. two d.; ed. Univs. of Birmingham, London and Illinois; House Surgeon and Surgical Registrar, Gen. Hosp., Birmingham 1947–48; Capt. R.A.M.C. 1948–50; Surgical Registrar, Coventry, London and Hackney Hosps. 1950–53; Surgical Registrar, Lecturer in Surgery and Surgical Research Fellow, Queen Elizabeth Hosp., Birmingham 1953–59; Hunterian Prof. Royal Coll. of Surgeons 1961–62; Prof. of Surgery, Univ. of Birmingham 1966–87; Barling Prof., Head Dept. of Surgery, Queen Elizabeth Hosp., Birmingham 1971–86, now Emer.; Pres. Royal Coll. of Surgeons of England 1982–86, James IV Asscn. Surgeons 1984–87, Int. Surgical Group 1985–86, Vascular Surgical Soc. 1974–75; Chair. Asscn. Profs. of Surgery 1979–81, Confed. of Royal Colls. and Faculties in the U.K. 1984–86; Hon. Consulting Surgeon United Birmingham Hosps. and Regional Hosp. Bd. 1959–, Royal Prince Alfred Hosp., Sydney 1981–; Hon. Consulting Surgeon Emer. City of London and Hackney Health Authority 1983–; Fellow, Asscn. of Surgeons of G.B. and Ireland, American Surgical Asscn.; Hon. F.R.C.S.I., F.R.A.C.S., F.C.S.S.L., F.A.C.S., F.R.C.S.C., F.C.S.S.A.; F.R.C.Anaes; Jacksonian Prize and Medal (Royal Coll. of Surgeons) 1959, Pybus Memorial Medal 1978, Miles Memorial Medal 1984, Vanderbilt Univ. Medal 1987, Brooke Medal, Ileostomy Asscn. of G.B. and Ireland 1990. *Publications:* Metabolic derangements in gastrointestinal surgery (with B. N. Brooke) 1967, Cancer of the Large Bowel (co-author) 1991; numerous contributions to medical and surgical journals. *Leisure interests:* family, fishing. *Address:* 23 Aston Bury, Edgbaston, Birmingham, B15 3QB, England. *Telephone:* 0121-454 0261.

SLAOUI, Driss; Moroccan diplomatist, professor and business executive; b. 12 Dec. 1926; m.; two c.; studied law in Grenoble and Paris; Under-Sec. of State for the Interior 1958; Sec. of State for Commerce, Industry and the Merchant Marine 1959; various ministerial posts 1960–68; Dir.-Gen. Royal Cabinet 1962 and 1969–71; Counsellor to King of Morocco Oct. 1977–; Perm. Rep. to the UN 1974–76, 1986–90; Sec.-Gen. Org. of Countries Signatories of the Charter of Casablanca 1961; Gov. of Bank of Morocco 1964; Dir.-Gen. Nat. Investment Soc. Oct. 1978–; Prof. in Faculty of Law at Rabat 1971–. *Address:* c/o Ministry of Foreign Affairs, Avenue Franklin Roosevelt, Rabat, Morocco.

SLATER, Christian; American actor; b. 18 Aug. 1969, New York; s. of Michael Hawkins and Mary Jo Slater; appeared at age of seven in TV series One Life to Live; professional stage début at age of nine in touring production of The Music Man; sentenced to 90 days imprisonment for two counts of battery and one of being under the influence of cocaine 1998. *Stage appearances include:* Macbeth, David Copperfield, Merlin, Landscape of the Body, Side Man. *Films include:* The Name of the Rose, Tucker: The Man and his Dream, Heathers, The Legend of Billie Jean, Cry Wolf, Tales from the Darkside: The Movie, Gleaming the Cube, The Wizard, Pump up the Volume, Young Guns II, Robin Hood: Prince of Thieves, Kuffs, Mobsters, Where the Day Takes You, Untamed Heart, True Romance, Murder in the First, Untitled, True Romance, Jimmy Hollywood, Interview with a Vampire, Bed of Roses, Hard Rain, Broken Arrow, Austin Powers: International Man of Mystery, The Flood, Very Bad Things (also exec.-producer). *Address:* c/o CAA, 9830 Wilshire Boulevard, Beverly Hills, CA 90212, U.S.A.

SLATER, Edward Charles, F.R.S., M.SC., PH.D., SC.D.; Australian professor of physiological chemistry; b. 16 Jan. 1917, Melbourne; s. of Edward Brunton Slater and Violet Podmore; m. Marion Winifred Hutley 1940; one d.; ed. Univs. of Melbourne and Cambridge, U.K.; Biochemist, Australian Inst. of Anatomy, Canberra 1939–46; Research Fellow, Molteno Inst., Cambridge Univ. 1946–55; Prof. of Physiological Chem., Dir. Lab. of Biochem., Univ. of Amsterdam, Netherlands 1955–85; Hon. Prof. Univ. of Southampton 1985–; mem. Royal Netherlands Acad. of Science and Letters, Hollandsche Maatschappij van Wetenschappen; Corresp. mem. Australian Acad. of Science; Hon. mem. American Soc. of Biological Chemists, Acad. Nacional de Ciencias Exactas, Físicas y Naturales, Argentina, Japanese Biochem. Soc., Biochemical Soc. (U.K.), Netherlands Biochemical Soc.; Foreign mem. Acad. Royale de Médecine, Belgium, Royal Swedish Acad. of Sciences; Hon. D.Sc. (Southampton, Bari); Kt. Order of the Netherlands Lion. *Publications:* about 450 contributions to learned journals. *Leisure interest:* yachting. *Address:* 9 Oaklands, Lymington, Hants., SO41 3TH, England. *Telephone:* (01590) 679455. *Fax:* (01590) 680791.

SLATER, James Derrick, F.C.A.; British company director and author; b. 13 March 1929, Wirral, Cheshire; s. of Hubert and Jessica Slater; m. Helen Wyndham Goodwyn 1965; two s. two d.; ed. Preston Manor County School; Dir. A.E.C. Ltd. 1959; Deputy Sales Dir. Leyland Motor Corpn. 1963; acquired with associates, H. Lotery and Co., Ltd., which was then renamed Slater, Walker Securities Ltd., and appointed Chair. and Man. Dir. 1964–72, Chair., C.E.O. 1972–75; Dir. BLMC 1969–75; Chair. Salar Properties Ltd. 1983–, Parentcare 1988–. *Publications:* Return to Go (autobiog.) 1977; on investment: The Zulu Principle 1992, Investment Made Easy 1994, Pep Up Your Wealth 1994, Beyond the Zulu Principle 1996; childrens books: Goldenrod, Goldenrod and the Kidnappers, Grasshopper and the Unwise Owl, The Boy Who Saved Earth, A. Mazing Monsters, Grasshopper and the Pickle Factory 1979, Roger the Robot Series 1980. *Leisure interests:* chess, backgammon, bridge, salmon fishing.

SLATER, Sir Jock (John) Cunningham Kirkwood, G.C.B., L.V.O.; British naval officer; b. 27 March 1938, Edin., Scotland; s. of James K. Slater and M. C. B. (née Bramwell) Slater; m. Ann Frances Scott 1972; two s.; ed. Edinburgh Acad., Sedbergh School, Royal Naval Coll. Dartmouth; Lieut. H.M.S. Soberton 1965; Lieut. Commdr., Equerry to H.M. The Queen 1968–71; Commdr. H.M.S. Jupiter 1972–73; Capt. H.M.S. Kent 1976–77; with Royal Coll. of Defence Studies 1978; Capt. H.M.S. Illustrious 1981–83; Capt. School of Maritime Operations, H.M.S. Dryad 1983–85; Rear Adm., Asst. Chief of Defence Staff 1985–87; Flag Officer Scotland, Northern Ireland, Naval Base Commdr. Rosyth 1987–89; Vice-Adm., Chief of Fleet Support 1989–91; Adm., C.-in-C. of Fleet, Allied C.-in-C. Channel and Eastern Atlantic 1991–92; Vice-Chief of Defence Staff 1993–95, Chief of Naval Staff and First Sea Lord 1995–98; Hon. mem. Highland Soc. of London; Gov. Sedbergh School 1997–; awarded Sword of Honour and The Queen's Telescope (B.R.N.C. Dartmouth) 1958, Cheetham Hill Memorial Prize (H.M.S. Dryad) 1966; Freeman of the City of London; Liveryman of the Shipwrights Co.; Elder Brother, Trinity House; Hon. D.Sc. (Cranfield) 1998; Commdr. Legion of Merit (U.S.A.), Grande Ufficiale, Order of Merit of Italian Repub. *Leisure interests:* outdoor. *Address:* c/o Naval Secretary, Victory Building, H.M. Naval Base, Portsmouth, PO1 3LS, England.

SLATER, Joseph Elliott; American administrator; b. 17 Aug. 1922, Salt Lake City, Utah; m. Annelore Kremser 1947; two d.; ed. Univ. of California; Naval Reserve Officer, Mil. Govt. Planning Officer, Berlin, London and Paris 1943–46; U.S. Sec. of Econ. Directorate, Allied Control Comm. for Germany; Asst. U.S. Sec. of Allied Control Council Econ. and Financial Affairs 1945–48; mem. UN Affairs Planning Staff, Dept. of State, Washington 1949; Sec.-Gen. Allied High Comm. for Germany, Bonn 1949–52; Exec. Sec. Office of U.S. Special Rep. in Europe, U.S. Sec. to NATO and mem. U.S. Del. to OEEC 1952; Chief Economist, Creole Petroleum Corpn., Caracas 1954–57; Sec. to President's Comm. on Foreign Assistance 1959; Assoc. Dir., Int. Affairs Program, Program Officer (Office of Int. Relations), Ford Foundation 1957–67; Asst. Man. Dir. Devt. Loan Fund 1960–61, and Deputy Asst. Sec. of State for Educ. and Cultural Affairs 1961–62; Pres. Salk Inst. 1967–72; Pres. Aspen Inst. for Humanistic Studies 1969–86; Pres. Emer., Trustee, Sr. Fellow 1986–; Pres. Anderson Foundation 1969–72; Pres. Emer. Salk Inst.; Chair. John J. McCloy Int. Center 1986–; mem. Council on Foreign Relations, New York, UN Policy Studies Group, Dir. AMIDEAST, Centre for Public Resources; Trustee, Acad. for Educ. Devt., Int. Inst. for Environmental Affairs, American Council on Germany, Carnegie Hall, Eisenhower Exchange Fellowships, Trustee and Special Fellow, Salk Inst.; Trustee Lovelace

Medical Foundation 1993–; mem. of bd. Volvo N. America; Hon. LL.D. (Univ. of Denver, Colorado Coll., Kyung Hee Univ., Korea, Univ. of N.H.); Commander's Cross, German Order of Merit. *Address:* 870 UN Plaza, New York, NY 10017, U.S.A. (Home).

SLATER, Rodney E., B.S., J.D.; American politician and administrator; b. 23 Feb. 1955, Tutwyler, Miss.; m. Cassandra Wilkins; one c.; ed. Eastern Michigan Univ., Univ. of Arkansas; Asst. Attorney-Gen., Ark. 1980–82; Special Asst. to Gov. of Ark. for community and minority affairs 1983–85, Exec. Asst. for econ. and community programs 1985–87, Dir. Intergovernmental Relations Ark. State Univ. 1987–93; Admin. Fed. Highway Admin. Dept. of Transportation, Washington D.C. 1993–97; Sec. of Transportation 1997–; Ark. Liaison Martin Luther King Jr. Fed. Holiday Comm. 1983–87; mem. Ark. Sesquicentennial Comm. 1986, Ark. State Highway and Transportation Comm. 1987–93, Chair. 1992–93; Pres. W. Harold Flowers Law Soc. 1985–92; Sec., Treasurer Ark. Bar Asscn. 1989–93; Deputy Campaign Man., Sr. Travelling Adviser Clinton for President Campaign 1992; deputy to Chair. Clinton/Gore Transition Team 1992–93. *Address:* Federal Highway Administration, 400 7th Street SW, Room 4218, Washington, D.C. 20590, U.S.A.

SLATKIN, Leonard; American conductor; b. 1 Sept. 1944, L.A.; s. of Felix Slatkin and Eleanor Aller; m. Linda Hohenfeld 1986; studied violin, piano, viola, composition, conducting; ed. Indiana Univ., Los Angeles City Coll., Juilliard School; Founder, Music Dir. and Conductor St. Louis Symphony Youth Orchestra 1979–80, 1980–81; Guest Conductor, orchestras in most countries; Asst. Conductor Youth Symphony of New York, Carnegie Hall 1966, Juilliard Opera, Theatre and Dance Dept. 1967, St. Louis Symphony Orchestra 1968–71, Assoc. Conductor 1971–74, Music dir. and Conductor 1979–96; Music Dir. Nat. Symphony Orchestra, Washington D.C. 1996–; Prin. Guest Conductor Minn. Orchestra 1974–, summer artistic dir. 1979–80; Music Dir. New Orleans Philharmonic Symphony Orchestra 1977–78. *Address:* National Symphony Orchestra, Kennedy Center for the Performing Arts, Washington, DC 20566, U.S.A. *Fax:* (202) 416-8105.

SLATYER, Ralph Owen, A.C., A.O., D.SC., F.R.S.; Australian research scientist; b. 29 April 1929, Melbourne; s. of Thomas H. Slatyer and Jean Slatyer; m. June H. Wade 1953; one s. two d.; ed. Univ. of Western Australia; Research Scientist, later Chief Research Scientist, CSIRO Div. of Land Research 1951–67; Prof. of Biology Research School of Biological Sciences, Australian Nat. Univ. 1967, Dir. Research School of Biological Sciences 1984–89; Amb. to UNESCO, Paris 1978–81; Chair. (part-time), Australian Science and Tech. Council, Canberra 1982–87; Chief Scientist, Dept. of Prime Minister and Cabinet, Canberra 1989–92; Chair. Australian Foundation for Science 1992–94; Visiting Fellow, Inst. of Advanced Studies, Australian Nat. Univ. 1994–; Foreign mem. Korea Acad. of Science and Tech. 1996; Edgeworth David Medal, Royal Soc. of N.S.W. 1968; Australian Medal of Agric. Science 1968, Medal of Australia and N.Z. Asscn. for the Advancement of Science 1991. *Publications include:* Plant-Water Relationships 1967, Man and the New Biology 1970; ed. of several books and author of numerous scientific publs. *Leisure interests:* bush-walking, cycling. *Address:* Research School of Biological Sciences, Australian National University, Canberra, A.C.T. 0200 (Office); 54 Musgrave Street, Yarralumla, A.C.T. 2600, Australia (Home). *Telephone:* (06) 285.1728.

SLAVITT, David Rytman, M.A.; American author; b. 23 March 1935, White Plains, N.Y.; s. of Samuel Slavitt and Adele Slavitt; m. 1st Lynn Meyer 1956 (divorced 1977); two s. one d.; m. 2nd Janet Lee Abrahm 1978; ed. Yale and Columbia Univs.; writer, assoc. ed., movie ed. Newsweek 1958–65; Visiting Lecturer, Univ. of Md. 1977; Visiting Assoc. Prof. Temple Univ. 1978–80; Lecturer in English and Comparative Literature, Columbia Univ. 1985–86; teacher of creative writing, Rutgers Univ. 1987; Lecturer in English, Univ. of Pa. 1991–97; Assoc. Fellow, Trumbull Coll. Yale Univ.; has lectured widely at U.S. univs. and other academic insts.; Nat. Endowment for Arts Fellowship in Translation 1988; Nat. Acad. and Insts. of Arts and Letters Award 1989; Rockefeller Foundation Artist's Residence, Bellagio 1989. *Publications:* novels: Rochelle, or Virtue Rewarded 1967, Feel Free 1968, Anagrams 1970, ABCD 1972, The Outer Mongolian 1973, The Killing of the King 1974, King of Hearts 1976, Jo Stern 1978, Cold Comfort 1980, Ringer 1982, Alice at 80 1984, The Agent 1986, The Hussar 1987, Salazar Blinks 1988, Lives of the Saints 1990, Turkish Delights 1993, The Cliff 1994, Get Thee to a Nunnery 1999; seven novels under pseudonyms; short stories: Short Stories Are Not Real Life 1991; poetry: Suits for the Dead 1961, The Carnivore 1965, Day Sailing 1968, Child's Play 1972, Vital Signs: New and Selected Poems 1975, Rounding the Horn 1978, Dozens 1981, Big Nose 1983, The Walls of Thebes 1986, Equinox 1989, Eight Longer Poems 1990, Crossroads 1994, A Gift 1996, Epic and Epigram 1997, PS3569.L3 1998; non-fiction: Understanding Social Psychology 1976, Physicians Observed 1987, Virgil 1991; plays: King Saul 1967, The Cardinal Sins 1969; screenplays, translations, book reviews, articles in journals and magazines etc. *Address:* 523 South 41st Street, Philadelphia, PA 19104, U.S.A. *Telephone:* (215) 382-3994.

SLEEP, Wayne, O.B.E.; British dancer, actor, choreographer; b. 17 July 1948, Plymouth; ed. Royal Ballet School (Leverhulme Scholar); joined Royal Ballet 1966, Soloist 1970, Prin. 1973; roles in: Giselle, Dancers at a Gathering, The Nutcracker, Romeo and Juliet, The Grand Tour, Elite Syncopations, Swan Lake, The Four Seasons, Les Patineurs, Petroushka (title role), Cinderella, The Dream, Pineapple Poll, Mam'zelle Angot, 4th Symphony, La Fille Mal Gardée, A Month in the Country, A Good Night's Sleep, Coppelia; also roles in operas: A Midsummer Night's Dream, Aida; theatre roles: Ariel in the Tempest, title role in Pinocchio, Genie in Aladdin, Soldier in The Soldier's Tale, Truffaldino in the Servant of Two Masters, Mr Mistoffelees in Cats: choreography and lead role, The Point: co-starred in Song and Dance 1982, 1990, Cabaret 1986; f. own co., DASH 1980; dancer and jt. choreographer, Bits and Pieces 1989; films: The Virgin Soldiers, The First Great Train Robbery, The Tales of Beatrix Potter; numerous TV appearances including series The Hot Shoe Show 1983, 1984; Show Business Personality of the Year 1983. *Publications:* Variations on Wayne Sleep 1983, Precious Little Sleep (autobiog.) 1996. *Leisure interest:* entertaining. *Address:* c/o Nick Thomas Artists, Event House, Queen Margaret's Road, Scarborough, YO11 2SA; 22 Queensberry Mews West, London, SW7 2DY, England. *Telephone:* (01723) 500038.

ŠLEŽEVIČIUS, Adolfas; Lithuanian politician; b. 1948, Mirziskes, Šiauliai Region; ed. Acad. of Nat. Econ., U.S.S.R. Council of Ministers; sr. engineer-constructor, chief mechanic, chief engineer Kaunas dairy factory 1971–77; Vice-Minister of Dairy and Meat Industry of Lithuania 1977–81; Chair. dairy production enterprise Pienocentras 1989–90; Vice-Minister of Agric. 1990–91; Pres. Lithuanian-Norwegian Joint Venture C. Olsen-Baltic 1991–93; Pres. Lithuanian Dairy Producers Asscn. 1992–; Prime Minister of Lithuania 1993–96; consultant to pvt. cos.

SLICHTER, Charles Pence, B.A., M.A., PH.D.; American professor of physics; b. 21 Jan. 1924, Ithaca, N.Y.; s. of Sumner Huber Slichter and Ada Pence Slichter; m. 1st Gertrude Thayer Almy 1952 (divorced 1977); three s. one d.; m. 2nd Anne FitzGerald 1980; two s.; ed. Browne and Nichols School, Cambridge, Mass. and Harvard Univ.; Instructor, Univ. of Ill. 1949–51, Asst. Prof. of Physics 1951–54, Assoc. Prof. 1954–55, Prof. of Physics 1955–97, mem. Center for Advanced Study, Univ. of Ill. 1968–, Prof. of Chemistry 1986–97, Center for Advanced Study Prof. Emer. of Physics and Chem. 1997–, Research Prof. of Physics 1997–; mem. Bd. of Dirs. Polaroid Corpn. 1975–; Morris Loeb Lecturer, Harvard Univ. 1961; mem. President's Science Advisory Cttee. 1965–69, Cttee. on the Nat. Medal of Science 1969–74, President's Cttee. on Science and Tech. 1976; Alfred Sloan Fellow 1957–63; mem. Corpn. of Harvard Univ. 1970–95; mem. Comm. on Physical Sciences, Math. and Applications, Nat. Research Council 1993–96; Fellow American Physical Soc., A.A.A.S.; mem. N.A.S., American Acad. of Arts and Sciences, American Philosophical Soc., Nat. Science Bd. 1975–84; mem. Int. Soc. of Magnetic Resonance (ISMAR), Vice-Pres. 1983–86, Pres. 1987–90; Hon. mem. Corpn., Woods Hole Oceanographic Inst.; Hon. D.Sc. (Univ. of Waterloo) 1993; Hon. LL.D. (Harvard) 1996; Langmuir Prize of American Physical Soc. 1969, ISMAR Award 1986, Comstock Prize (N.A.S.) 1993, Buckley Prize of Americal Physical Soc. 1996, and other awards. *Publications:* Principles of Magnetic Resonance 1963, 1978, 1989; articles on solid state physics, chemical physics and magnetic resonance. *Address:* Dept. of Physics, Univ. of Illinois at Urbana-Champaign, 1110 W. Green Street, Urbana, IL 61801 (Office); 61 Chestnut Court, Champaign, IL 61821, U.S.A. (Home). *Telephone:* (217) 333-3834 (Office); (217) 352-8255 (Home).

SLIGER, Bernard Francis, PH.D.; American university administrator; b. 30 Sept. 1924, Chassell, Mich.; s. of Paul F. Sliger and Hazel MacLauchlin; m. Greta Taube 1945; two s. two d.; ed. Michigan State Univ. and Univ. of Minnesota; faculty mem. La. State Univ. 1953, Prof. of Econs. 1961, Head Dept. 1961–65, Vice-Chancellor, Dean Acad. Affairs 1965–68; Sec. Admin., Chief Budget Officer, State of La. 1968–69; Sec.-Treas. La. Office Bldg. Corpn. 1969–72; Organizer, Exec. Dir. La. Co-ordinating Council of Higher Educ. 1969–72; Prof. of Econs., Fla. State Univ., Tallahassee 1973–, Exec. Vice-Pres. 1972–76, Acting Pres. 1976–77, Pres. 1977; Pres. Fla. State Univ. 1977–91, Interim Pres. 1993–94, Pres. Emer. and Dir. Gus A. Stavros Center for the Advancement of Free Enterprise and Econ. Educ. 1992–; mem. Bd. of Dirs., Fed. Reserve Bank of Atlanta 1983–88; mem. Bd. of Trustees STI Bank of Atlanta 1992–; mem. Bd. of Trustees and Treas. The Claude Pepper Foundation 1993–; mem. Tallahassee Community Advisory Bd. AvMed Health Plan 1998–; consultant on econ. theory and public finance to pvt. and public comms.; mem. numerous asscns. *Publications include:* Public Finance 1964; contribs. to numerous professional publs. *Address:* Stavros Center for the Advancement of Free Enterprise and Economic Education, The Florida State University, Tallahassee, FL 32306-4035 (Office); 3341 East Lakeshore Drive, Tallahassee, FL 32312, U.S.A. (Home). *Telephone:* (904) 644-4772 (Office). *Fax:* (904) 644-9866.

SLIPMAN, Sue, O.B.E.; British consumer representative; b. 3 Aug. 1949; d. of Mark Slipman and Doris Barham; one s.; ed. Stockwell Manor Comprehensive School, Univs. of Wales, Leeds and London; Sec. and Nat. Pres. Nat. Union of Students 1975–78; mem. Advisory Council for Adult and Continuing Educ. 1978–79; area officer Nat. Union of Public Employees 1979–85; Dir. Nat. Council for One Parent Families 1985–95; Dir. London Training and Enterprise Council 1995–96; Dir. Gas Consumer's Council 1996–; contested (SDP/Alliance) Hayes and Harlington 1987; Chair. Women for Social Democracy 1983–86, Advice Guidance and Counselling Lead Body 1992–, Better Regulation Task Force 1997; Vice-Chair. British Youth Council 1977–78; Dir. Social Market Foundation 1992–93; Trustee Full Employment UK 1990–95; mem. various groups and councils. *Publications include:* Helping Ourselves to Power: A Handbook for Women on the Skills of Public Life 1986, Helping One Parent Families to Work 1988, Maintenance: A System to Benefit Children 1989, Making Maintenance Pay 1990. *Leisure interest:*

swimming. *Address:* Gas Consumer's Council, 15 Wilton Road, London, SW1V 1LT, England. *Telephone:* 0171-931 0977.

ŚLISZ, Józef; Polish politician, union leader and farmer; b. 20 March 1934, Łukawiec; s. of Jan Ślisz and Stefania Ślisz; m. Stanisława Szuberla 1961; one s. two d.; ed. secondary school; pvt. farmer, on father's farm until 1961, runs own hog-raising farm in Łąka 1961–; mem. Agric. Solidarity Ind. Self-governing Trade Union 1980–81; co-organizer and participant agric. strike, Rzeszów Jan.–Feb. 1981, co-signatory agreements in Ustrzyki and Rzeszów; mem. Solidarity of Pvt. Farmers Trade Union March 1981–, Chair. Provisional Nat. Farmers' Council Solidarity 1987–89; mem. Civic Cttee. attached to Lech Wałęsa (q.v.) 1988–91, Chair. of Solidarity Trade Union 1988; participant Round Table plenary debates, mem. group for union pluralism, Co-Chair. team for agric. matters Feb.–April 1989; Senator 1989–93, Vice-Marshal of the Senate 1989–93; f. and leader, Agrarian Christian Party 1992–, Polish Peasant Party Solidarity (PSL Solidarność) 1989. *Leisure interest:* historical books. *Address:* Łąka 328, 36-004 Łąka, Woj. Rzeszowskie, Poland. *Telephone:* (017) 72 10 18.

SLIVA, Anatoly Yakovlevich, CAND. JUR.; Russian politician; b. 10 Feb. 1940; Slavgorod, Belarus; m.; ed. Moscow State Univ.; teacher, dean All-Union Juridical Inst. by correspondence; sr. scientific consultant, Deputy Head of Div. of local soviets, U.S.S.R. Supreme Soviet 1988–92; Deputy Head State Law Dept. at Russian Presidency, concurrently Head Div. on Interaction with Organs of Representative and Exec. Power 1992–94; Official Rep. of Russian Pres. on legal problems to Supreme Soviet Russian Fed. 1992; mem. State Duma, Chair. Cttee. on problems of local man. 1993–95; Rep. of Russian Pres. to Council of Fed. 1996–98; mem. Constitutional Court of Russian Fed. 1998. *Address:* Constitutional Court, Ilyinka str. 21, 103132, Moscow, Russia. *Telephone:* (095) 206-92-25.

SLOMAN, Sir Albert Edward, Kt., C.B.E., M.A., D.PHIL.; British university administrator; b. 14 Feb. 1921, Launceston, Cornwall; s. of Albert Sloman, C.C. and L. F. Brewer; m. Marie B. Bergeron 1948; three d.; ed. Launceston Coll. and Wadham Coll., Oxford; lecturer, Univ. of Calif. (Berkeley) 1946–47; Reader in Spanish, Univ. of Dublin 1947–53; Fellow, Trinity Coll., Dublin 1950–53; Prof. of Spanish, Univ. of Liverpool 1953–62; Vice-Chancellor, Univ. of Essex 1962–87; Pres. Conf. of European Rectors and Vice-Chancellors 1969–74; Vice-Pres. Int. Asscn. of Univs. 1970–75; Chair. Cttee. of Vice-Chancellors and Principals 1981–83; Chair. Bd. of Govs. Centre for Information on Language Teaching and Research 1979–86; Chair. British Acad. Studentship Selection Cttee. (Humanities) 1965–87, Overseas Research Students Fees Support Scheme 1980–87, Univs. Council for Adult and Continuing Educ. 1984–87, Selection Cttee. Commonwealth Scholarships Comm. 1986–94; Chair. Int. Bd. United World Colls. 1988–93; Vice-Chair. Council of Asscn. of Commonwealth Univs. 1984–87; mem. Econ. and Social Cttee. EEC 1973–82, Cttee. for Int. Co-operation in Higher Educ. 1981–88 (Chair. 1985–88), Cttee. of Man., British Inst. in Paris 1982–96, Bd. of Govs. Univ. of Guyana 1966–92; Inspection of Ruskin Coll., Oxford 1986–87; Pres. Penzance Library 1990–96; Dir. Close Bros. Bessa Cos. 1992–98; Dr. h.c. (Nice) 1974, (Essex) 1988, (Liverpool) 1989. *Publications:* The Sources of Calderón's El Príncipe Constante 1950, The Dramatic Craftsmanship of Calderón 1958, Calderón, La Vida Es Sueño (Editor) 1960, Bulletin of Hispanic Studies (Editor) 1953–62, A University in the Making 1964. *Leisure interest:* travel. *Address:* 19 Inglis Road, Colchester, Essex, CO3 3HU, England.

SLONIMSKI, Piotr, D.SC., M.D.; French biologist; b. 9 Nov. 1922, Warsaw; s. of Piotr Slonimski; m. Hanna Kulagowska 1951 (deceased); one d.; ed. Lycée Stephane Batory, underground Univ. of Warsaw, Jagiellonian Univ. of Cracow and Faculté des Sciences, Paris; Polish underground army 1939–45; Asst. Univ. of Cracow 1945–47; Attaché, CNRS 1947, Chargé 1952, Maître 1956, Dir. 1962; Prof. of Genetics, Faculté des Sciences and Univ. P. et M. Curie 1965–91, Prof. Emer. 1992–; Dir. Centre de Génétique Moléculaire, CNRS 1971–91, Hon. Dir. CNRS, Gif-sur-Yvette br. 1992–; Dir.-Gen. Groupement de Recherches et d'Etudes sur les Genomes (GREG) 1993–96; Visiting Prof. Univs. of Calif., Chicago and Louvain; mem. Acad. des Sciences (Inst. de France), Bavarian, Polish and Belgian Acads., Academia Europaea, American Acad. of Arts and Sciences etc.; Dr. h.c. (Wrocław, Louvain, Warsaw); CNRS Gold Medal 1985, Hansen Gold Medal 1987 and other awards; Chevalier, Légion d'honneur, Mil. Cross (Poland), Officier, Ordre Nat. du Mérite, Commdr. with Star of Merit of the Repub. (Poland). *Publications:* scientific publs. on cellular respiration, genetics and biogenesis of mitochondria, structure and function of genes. *Leisure interest:* mushroom hunting. *Address:* Centre de Génétique Moléculaire du CNRS, avenue de la Terrasse, 91190 Gif-sur-Yvette Cedex, France.

SLONIMSKY, Sergey Mikhailovich; Russian composer and pianist; b. 12 Aug. 1932, Leningrad (now St. Petersburg); s. of Mikhail Slonimsky and Ida Kaplan; m. Raisa Zankisova; one s. one d.; ed. Leningrad Conservatoire; teacher of composition at Leningrad (now St. Petersburg) Conservatoire 1958–, Prof. 1976–; R.S.F.S.R. People's Artist 1987; R.S.F.S.R. State (Glinka) Prize 1983. *Works include:* Virineya (opera) 1967, The Master and Margarita (opera) 1970–72, Icarus (ballet) 1975, Mary Stuart (opera) 1980, Hamlet (opera) 1991, Ivan the Terrible (opera) 1994, 10 symphonies 1958–95, 24 preludes and figures for piano 1993–94. *Publication:* musicological study of Prokofiev's symphonies 1964. *Leisure interest:* telling funny stories. *Address:* St. Petersburg Conservatoire of Music, Teatralnaya ploshchad, St. Petersburg; 9 Kanal Griboedova, Apt. 97, 191186 St. Petersburg, Russia. *Telephone:* 311-85-85.

SLOVES, Marvin, B.A.; American advertising agency executive; b. 22 April 1933, New York; s. of John H. Sloves and Evelyn S. (Wishan) Sloves; ed. Brandeis Univ. and Oriental Inst., Univ. of Chicago; Staff Researcher, Leo Burnett Co., Chicago 1962; Dir. of Research, Earle Ludgin Co., Chicago 1963–64; Account Exec. Ted Bates Co., New York 1965–67; Pres. and C.E.O., Scali, McCabe, Sloves, Inc., New York 1967–81, Chair. and C.E.O. 1981–93; Vice-Chair. The Lowe Group 1993–95; Co-Chair. Lowe & Partners/Scali, McCabe, Sloves 1995–. *Leisure interests:* boxing, memorabilia collecting. *Address:* Bogtown House, P.O. Box 50, North Salem, NY 10560, U.S.A. (Home).

SLYNN OF HADLEY, Baron (Life Peer), cr. 1992, of Egginton in the County of Bedfordshire; **Gordon Slynn,** Kt., P.C., M.A., LL.B.; British lawyer; b. 17 Feb. 1930; s. of John and Edith Slynn; m. Odile M. H. Boutin 1962; ed. Sandbach School, Goldsmith's Coll. and Trinity Coll., Cambridge; called to bar, Gray's Inn 1956, Bencher 1970, Vice-Treas. 1987, Treas. 1988; Q.C. 1974; Junior Counsel, Ministry of Labour 1967–68, Treasury (Common Law) 1968–74; Leading Counsel to Treasury 1974–76; Recorder of Hereford 1971, a Recorder and Hon. Recorder 1972–76; Judge, High Court of Justice, Queen's Bench Div. 1976–81; Pres. Employment Appeal Tribunal 1978–81; Chief Steward of Hereford 1978– (Freedom of the City 1996); Advocate-Gen., Court of Justice of the European Communities 1981–88, Judge 1988–92, a Lord of Appeal in Ordinary 1992–; Lecturer in Air Law, London School of Econs. 1958–61; Visiting Prof. in Law, Univ. of Durham 1981–88, Cornell 1983 (Irvine Lecturer 1984), Kings Coll. London 1985–90, Univ. of Tech., Sydney 1990–, Nat. Univ. of India, Bangalore 1992–; Hon. Vice-Pres. Union Int. des Avocats 1976–; Vice-Chair. Exec. Council Int. Law Asscn. 1986–88, Chair. 1988–; Gov. Sadlers Wells 1988–95; Chair. Govs. Mill Hill School 1989–95; Chair. Bd. Acad. of Ancient Music; hon. mem. Canadian Bar Asscn., Georgia Trial Lawyers' Asscn., Fla. Defense Lawyers Asscn., Indian Soc. of Int. Law, Fellow Int. Soc. of Barristers (U.S.A.); Hon. Fellow, Univ. Coll. at Buckingham 1981; Hon. LL.D. (Birmingham) 1983, (Buckingham) 1983, (Exeter) 1985, (Univ. of Tech., Sydney) 1991, (Staffordshire) 1994, (City Univ.) 1995, (Pondicherry) 1997, (Kingston) 1997; Hon. Decanus legis (Mercer) 1986, Hon. D.C.L. (Durham) 1989. *Publications:* contributions to Halsbury's Laws of England and Atkins' Court Forms. *Leisure interests:* music, travel. *Address:* House of Lords, Westminster, London, SW1A 0PW, England.

SMALE, John G., B.S.; American business executive; b. 1 Aug. 1927, Listowel, Ont., Canada; s. of Vera G. and Peter J. Smale; m. Phyllis Anne Weaver 1950; two s. two d.; ed. Miami Univ. (Ohio); worked for Vick Chemical Co., New York 1949–50; with Bio-Research Inc., New York 1950–52; with Procter and Gamble Co. 1952, Dir. 1972, Pres. 1974–86, C.E.O. 1981–90, Chair. 1986–90; Dir. Gen. Motors Corpn., Detroit 1992–95, Chair. Exec. Comm. of Bd. 1996–, Exec. Cttee. Gen. Motors Corpn. Detroit 1996– (also Bd. Dirs.); Hon. LL.D. (Kenyon Coll.) 1974, (Miami Univ.) 1979, Hon. D.Sc. (DePauw Univ.) 1983, Hon. D.Iur (St. Augustine's Coll.) 1985. *Address:* c/o General Motors Corporation, P.O. Box 599, Cincinnati, OH 45201, U.S.A.

SMALLMAN, Raymond Edward, C.B.E., PH.D., D.SC., F.R.S., F.ENG.; British professor of metallurgy and materials science; b. 4 Aug. 1929, Wolverhampton; s. of David Smallman and Edith French; m. Joan D. Faulkner 1952; one s. one d.; ed. Rugeley Grammar School and Univ. of Birmingham; Sr. Scientific Officer, A.E.R.E. Harwell 1953–58; Lecturer, Dept. of Physical Metallurgy, Univ. of Birmingham 1958–63, Sr. Lecturer 1963–64, Prof. of Physical Metallurgy 1964–69, Head, Dept. of Physical Metallurgy and Science of Materials 1969–81, Feeney Prof. and Head, Dept. of Metallurgy and Materials 1969–, Deputy Dean, Faculty of Science and Eng. 1981–84, Dean 1984–85, Dean of Eng. 1985–87, Vice-Prin. Univ. of Birmingham 1987–92; Pres. Birmingham Metallurgical Asscn. 1972–73; Vice-Pres. Metals Soc. 1980–84; Vice-Pres. Fed. of European Materials Socs. 1992–94, Pres. 1994–96; Council mem., Science & Eng. Research Council 1992–94, (Materials Comm. 1988–91); mem. Council Inst. of Materials (Chair. Int. Affairs Cttee. 1993–97), Vice-Pres. 1995–; Visiting Prof. Stanford Univ. 1962, N.S.W. 1974, Cape Town 1976, Hong Kong 1990–; Van Horn Distinguished Lecturer, CASE Western Reserve Univ. 1978; Warden Birmingham Assay Office 1994–98, Guardian 1997–; mem. Lunar Soc. 1991–; Hon. Foreign mem. China Ordnance Soc., Metal Science Soc. Czech Repub.; Hon. D.Sc. (Wales) 1990, (Novi Sad) 1990; Sir George Beilby Gold Medal, Inst. of Metals and Chem Soc. 1969, Rosenhain Medal Inst. of Metals 1972, Elegant Work Prize, Metals Soc. 1979, Platinum Medal, Inst. of Metals 1989. *Publications:* Modern Metallography (jtly.) 1968, Structure of Metals and Alloys (jtly.) 1969, Defect Analysis in Electron Microscopy (jtly.) 1975, Modern Physical Metallurgy, 4th edn. 1985, Metals and Materials: science, processes and applications 1994; scientific papers on relationship of microstructure of materials and properties in learned journals. *Leisure interests:* writing, travel, friendly golf, bridge. *Address:* School of Metallurgy and Materials, University of Birmingham, Edgbaston, Birmingham, B15 2TT (Office); 59 Woodthorne Road South, Tettenhall, Wolverhampton, WV6 8SN, England (Home). *Telephone:* (0121) 414-5223 (Office); (01902) 752545 (Home). *Fax:* (0121) 414-5247.

SMART, John Jamieson Carswell, A.C., M.A., B.PHIL., F.A.H.A.; Australian professor of philosophy; b. 16 Sept. 1920, Cambridge, England; s. of William

M. Smart and Isabel M. Carswell; m. 1st Janet Paine 1956 (died 1967); one s. one d.; m. 2nd Elizabeth Warner 1968; ed. King's Coll. Choir School, Cambridge, The Leys School, Cambridge, Univ. of Glasgow and Queen's Coll. Oxford; served Royal Signals 1940–45; Jr. Research Fellow, Corpus Christi Coll. Oxford 1948–50; Hughes Prof. of Philosophy, Univ. of Adelaide 1950–72, Prof. Emer. 1972–; Reader in Philosophy, La Trobe Univ. 1972–76; Prof. of Philosophy, Research School of Social Sciences, A.N.U. 1976–85, Prof. Emer. 1986–; Fellow, Center for Advanced Study in the Behavioral Sciences, Stanford, U.S.A. 1979; Visiting Prof. Princeton 1957, Harvard 1963, Yale 1964, Stanford 1982, Univ. of Ala. at Birmingham 1990; G.D. Young Lecturer, Univ. of Adelaide 1987; Hon. Fellow Corpus Christi Coll. Oxford 1991; Hon. D.Litt. (St. Andrews) 1983, (La Trobe) 1992. *Publications:* An Outline of a System of Utilitarian Ethics 1961, Philosophy and Scientific Realism 1963, Between Science and Philosophy 1968, Ethics, Persuasion and Truth 1984, Essays Metaphysical and Moral 1987, Our Place In the Universe 1989, Atheism and Theism (with J.J. Haldane) 1996. *Leisure interest:* walking. *Address:* 74 Mackenzie Street, Hackett, A.C.T. 2602, Australia. *Telephone:* (02) 62488171.

SMART, (Roderick) Ninian, M.A., B.PHIL.; British professor of religious studies; b. 6 May 1927, Cambridge; s. of William Marshall Smart and Isabel Macquarrie Carswell; m. Libushka Bariffaldi 1954; two s. two d.; ed. Glasgow Acad. and Oxford Univ.; army service, Intelligence Corps. 1945–48, rank of Capt. 1947; Lecturer in Philosophy Univ. Coll., Wales 1952–56, in History and Philosophy of Religion King's Coll., London 1956–61; H.G. Wood Prof. of Theology Birmingham Univ. 1961–67; founding Prof. of Religious Studies Lancaster Univ. 1967–82, Hon. Prof. 1982–86; Prof. of Religious Studies Univ. of Calif., Santa Barbara 1976–, J.F. Rowny Prof. of Religious Studies 1988–; editorial consultant BBC TV series The Long Search 1974–77; Vice-Pres. American Acad. of Religion 1998, Pres. (elect) 1999; Visiting Lecturer Yale Univ. 1955–56, Banaras Hindu Univ. 1960; Visiting Prof. in Philosophy and History, Univ. of Wis. 1965, of Religious Studies, Princeton Univ. 1971, Univ. of Otago 1971, Univ. of Qd. 1980, 1985, Univ. of Cape Town 1982, Harvard Univ. 1983, Univ. of Hong Kong 1989; Gifford Lecturer Edin. Univ. 1979–80; Hon. D.H.L. (Loyola Chicago) 1968, Hon. D.Litt. (Glasgow) 1984, (Kelaniya Univ., Sri Lanka) 1990, (Lancaster) 1995, (Middx.) 1996; Hon. D.Univ. (Stirling) 1986, (Middx.). *Publications:* Reasons and Faiths 1958, Doctrine and Argument in Indian Philosophy 1964, Philosophers and Religious Truth 1964, The Philosophy of Religion 1968, The Religious Experience of Mankind 1969, The Phenomenon of Religion 1973, The Science of Religion and the Sociology of Knowledge 1974, Beyond Ideology 1981, Concept and Empathy 1986, Religion and the Western Mind 1987, World Religions 1989, Christian Systematic Theology in a World Context (with Steven Konstantine) 1991, Buddhism and Christianity: Rivals and Allies 1993, The Religions of Asia 1993, Religions of the West 1993, Religion and Nationalism 1994, Choosing a Faith 1995, The Dimensions of the Sacred 1996, Lights of Asia: The Buddha and Christ 1997, Reflections in the Mirror of Religion 1997, World Philosophies 1999. *Leisure interests:* painting, poetry, cricket and tennis. *Address:* Department of Religious Studies, Univ. of California at Santa Barbara, CA 93106, U.S.A.; Religious Studies, University of Lancaster, LA1 4YG, England. *Telephone:* (01524) 65201.

SMART, Stephen Bruce, Jr., A.B., S.M.; American fmr. government official and business executive; b. 7 Feb. 1923, New York; s. of Stephen Bruce Smart and Beatrice Cobb; m. Edith Minturn Merrill 1949; one s. three d.; ed. Harvard Coll., and Mass. Inst. of Tech.; U.S. Army 1943–46, 1951–53; Sales Engineer, Permutit Co., New York 1947–51; joined Continental Group (fmrly. Continental Can Co.) 1951, various sales and gen. man. posts 1951–62, Vice-Pres. Cen. Div. 1962–65, Marketing and Corpn. Planning 1965–68, Exec. Vice-Pres. Paper Operations 1969–73, Vice-Chair. 1973–75, Pres. and C.O.O. 1975–81; Chair. and C.E.O. Continental Group 1981–85; Under-Sec. for Int. Trade U.S. Dept. of Commerce 1985–88; Consultant, Dept. of State, Washington 1988; Sr. Fellow, World Resources Inst. 1989–95; Dir. World Resources Inst. 1993–, League of Conservation Voters 1995. *Publication:* Ed. Beyond Compliance: A New Industry View of the Environment 1992. *Leisure interests:* fishing, sailing, American decorative arts. *Address:* 20561 Trappe Road, Upperville, VA 20184, U.S.A. (Home). *Telephone:* (540) 554-8302 (Home).

SMARTH, Rosny; Haitian politician and agricultural economist; Prime Minister of Haiti 1996–97. *Address:* c/o Office of the Prime Minister, Palais National, Port-au-Prince, Haiti.

SMIDT, Kristian, PH.D.; Norwegian professor of English Literature; b. 20 Nov. 1916, Sandefjord; s. of Bishop Johannes Smidt and Jofrid Smidt (née Grimstvedt); m. 1st Aagot Karner 1940 (divorced 1973); m. 2nd Anne Oulie-Hansen 1973; one s. two d.; ed. Aske's Hatcham, London, Univ. of Oslo; Reader in English Literature Univ. of Oslo 1953–55, Prof. 1955–85, Prof. Emer. 1985–, Dir. British Inst. 1955–73; Prof. of English Literature (temporary) Univ. of Tromsø 1973–76; Rockefeller Fellowship, Princeton Univ. 1951–52; Folger Shakespeare Library Fellowship, Washington D.C. 1960–61; Visiting Fellowship Clare College, Cambridge Univ. 1984; mem. Norwegian Acad. of Science and Letters, Vetenskaps-societen, Lund, Sweden, Norwegian Acad. of Language and Literature; Hon. O.B.E. 1985, Nansen Award 1994. *Publications:* James Joyce and the Cultic Use of Fiction 1959, Poetry and Belief in the Work of T.S. Eliot 1961, Unconformities in Shakespeare's Plays 1982–93, Shakespeare i norsk oversettelse 1994; Ed. Shakespeare's Richard III: Parallel Texts 1969. *Address:* Solveien 137, 1169 Oslo, Norway. *Telephone:* 22-28-86-42.

SMILEY, Jane Graves, M.F.A., PH.D.; American writer and university professor; b. 26 Sept. 1949, Los Angeles; d. of James La Verne Smiley and Frances (Graves) Nuelle; m. 1st John Whiston 1970 (divorced); m. 2nd William Silag 1978 (divorced); two d.; m. 3rd Stephen M. Mortensen 1987; one s.; ed. Vassar Coll. and Univ. of Iowa; Asst. Prof. Iowa State Univ. Ames 1981–84, Assoc. Prof. 1984–89, Prof. 1989–90, Distinguished Prof. 1992–; Visiting Prof. Univ. of Iowa 1981, 1987; Pulitzer Prize for Fiction 1992; Nat. Book Critics Circle Award 1992 and other awards and prizes. *Publications:* Barn Blind 1980, At Paradise Gate 1981, Duplicate Keys 1984, The Age of Grief 1987, The Greenlanders 1988, Ordinary Love and Goodwill 1989, A Thousand Acres 1991, Moo: A Novel 1995. *Leisure interests:* cooking, swimming, playing piano, quilting. *Address:* Department of English, Iowa State University, 201 Ross Ames, IA 50011, U.S.A.

SMIRNOV, Igor Nikolaevich; Russian politician; b. 1941, Petropavlovsk-Kamchatsky; m.; two s.; ed. Zaporozhie Machine Construction Inst.; mem. CPSU 1963–90; engineer, chief engineer, chief of shop; Dir. Zaporozhie Factory Electromash 1959–87; Dir. Tiraspol Jt. Trade Union 1989–91, Chair. Tiraspol City Exec. Cttee. 1990–91; Pres. Self-Declared Pridniestrovskaya Repub. (expelled from CPSU for separatism 1990) 1991–; People's Deputy of Moldova 1990–92 (deprived of the authority by Parl.). *Address:* House of Government, Tiraspol, Pridnestrovskaya Republic, Moldova.

SMIRNOV, Igor Pavlovich, DR.PHIL.SC.; Russian literary scholar; b. 19 May 1941, Leningrad (now St. Petersburg); s. of Valentina Lomakina and Pavel Smirnov; m. Johanna Renate Döring 1979; ed. Leningrad Univ.; Research Assoc. Leningrad Inst. of Russian Literature; left U.S.S.R. 1981; Prof. Univ. of Konstanz, Fed. Germany. *Publications include:* Meaning in Art and the Evolution of Poetic Systems 1977, Diachronic Transformations of Literary Genres and Motifs 1981, Essays on the History of the Typology of Culture (with Johanna Smirnov) 1982, The Emergence of the Inter-text 1985, Towards a Theory of Literature 1987, Being and Creating 1990, On Old Russian Culture, Russian National Specifity, and the Logic of History 1991, Psychohistory of Russian Literature from Romanticism to the Present Day 1995, A Novel of Secrets—Dr. Zhivago 1996. *Address:* Department of Russian, University of Konstanz, 78457 Konstanz, D-159; Guerickestr. 35, 80805 Munich, Germany. *Telephone:* (089) 361 21 82 (Home).

SMIRNOV, Stanislav Alekseyevich, DR. ECON. SC.; Russian business executive; b. 18 April 1954, Mashok, Vladimir Region; m.; two c.; ed. Moscow Inst. of Motor Car Transport; Sec. Moscow City Comsomol Cttee. 1982–85, First Sec. 1985–89; Sec., Second Sec. Cen. Comsomol Cttee. 1989–90; Peoples' Deputy of Russian Fed.; mem. Supreme Soviet; Chair. Comm. on Problems of Youth 1990–93; expelled from CPSU 1991; mem. of Presidium, Fed. of Mfrs. of Russia; mem. Council on Industrial Policy and Business of Russian Presidency; mem. Co-ordination Council Round Table of Russian Business 1994; corresp. mem. Russian Acad. of Sciences 1997–; Dir. Russian Chamber of Commerce and Industry of Russian Fed. 1991–. *Publications:* over 100 scientific works. *Address:* Chamber of Commerce and Industry, Ilyinka str. 6, 103684 Moscow, Russia. *Telephone:* (095) 929 0001 (Office).

SMIRNOV, Vitaly Georgiyevich; Russian sports official; b. 14 Feb. 1935, Khabarovsk; m. Smirnova Irina Aleksandrovna; three s.; ed. Cen. State Inst. of Physical Culture; instructor, Head Div. of Sports Moscow Comsomol Cttee. 1958–60; First Sec. Kuntzevo Regional Comsomol Cttee.; Moscow Region 1960; Chair. Moscow Regional Council, Union of Sports Socs. and Orgs. 1960–62; Second Sec., First Sec. Moscow Regional Comsomol Cttee. 1962–68; First Sec. City Cttee. of CPSU 1968–70; Deputy Chair., First Deputy Chair. U.S.S.R. Cttee. of Sports and Physical Culture 1970–75; First Deputy Chair. Org. Cttee. of Olympic Games 1980 in Moscow 1975–81; Chair. State Cttee. on Sports and Physical Culture of Russian Fed. 1981–90; Chair. U.S.S.R. Olympic Cttee. 1990–92; Pres. Olympic Cttee. of Russia 1992–; mem. Int. Olympic Cttee. 1971–; mem. Acad. of Creativity 1994–. *Leisure interests:* hunting, fishing, tennis. *Address:* Luzhnetskaya nab. 8, 119871 Moscow, Russia. *Telephone:* (095) 201 1850 (Office). *Fax:* (095) 248 3611 (Office).

SMIRNOV, Vladimir Nikolaevich; Russian biochemist; b. 17 May 1937, Cheliabinsk; ed. Leningrad Univ.; m. 1st Valeriana Kreier 1956 (divorced 1973), 2nd Galina Chernonsova 1976; one s.; mem. CPSU 1976–91; post-graduate 1959–64; Jr., Sr. Research Fellow at U.S.S.R. Acad. of Med. Science Inst. of Medical Radiology 1964–68; Head of Biochemical Section, Ministry of Health 1968–72; Corresp. mem. of U.S.S.R. (now Russian) Acad. of Sciences 1981; Prof. of Biological Science 1977; Head of Lab. at All-Union Scientific Centre for Cardiology (br. of U.S.S.R. (now Russian) Acad. of Medical Science) 1973–76, Dir. 1976–82; Dir. of Inst. of Experimental Cardiography of Acad. of Medical Sciences 1982–; corresp. mem., then mem. Acad. of Medical Sciences 1984–; U.S.S.R. State Prize 1978. *Publications:* works on molecular biology, biochemistry of the heart, cellular and molecular athero- and trombogenesis. *Leisure interests:* hunting, fishing. *Address:* Institute of Experimental Cardiology, Cardiology Research Centre, 3rd Cherepkovskaya 15A, 112552 Moscow, Russia. *Telephone:* (095) 415-00-35 (Office); 203-84-83 (Home). *Fax:* (095) 415-29-62.

SMITH, Albert Charles, PH.D.; American biologist; b. 5 April 1906, Springfield, Mass.; s. of Henry J. and Jeanette R. (Machol) Smith; m. 1st Nina Grönstrand 1935, one s. one d.; m. 2nd Emma van Ginneken 1966; ed.

Columbia Univ.; Asst. Curator, N.Y. Botanical Garden 1928–31, Assoc. Curator 1931–40; Curator, Herbarium Arnold Arboretum, Harvard Univ. 1940–48; Curator, Div. of phanerogams, U.S. Nat. Museum, Smithsonian Inst. 1948–56; Program Dir. Systematic Biology, Nat. Science Foundation 1956–58; Dir. Museum of Nat. History, Smithsonian Inst. 1958–62, Asst. Sec. 1962–63; Prof. of Botany and Dir. of Research, Univ. of Hawaii 1963–65, Gerrit Parmile Wilder Prof. of Botany 1965–70, Prof. Emer. 1970–; Ray Ethan Torrey Prof. of Botany, Univ. of Mass. 1970–76, Prof. Emer. 1976–; Editorial Consultant, Nat. Tropical Botanical Garden 1977–91; mem. N.A.S.; Fellow, American Acad. of Arts and Sciences, etc.; Robert Allerton Award for excellence in Tropical Botany 1979; Asa Gray Award 1992; Charles Reed Bishop Medal 1995. *Publications:* Flora Vitiensis Nova: A New Flora of Fiji (5 vols.) 1979–91; and articles on plant taxonomy, evolutionary biology and phytogeography. *Address:* Department of Botany, University of Hawaii, Honolulu, HI 96822 (Office); 5113 Maunalani Circle, Honolulu, HI 96816, U.S.A. (Home). *Telephone:* (808) 732-0057.

SMITH, Andrew David; British politician; b. 1 Feb. 1951; m.; one step-s.; ed. Reading Grammar School and St. John's Coll. Oxford; joined Labour Party 1973; mem. Oxford City Council 1976–87; M.P. for Oxford East 1987–; Opposition Spokesman on Higher Educ. 1988–92, on Treasury and Econ. Affairs 1992–94; Shadow Chief Sec. to H.M. Treasury 1994–96; Shadow Transport Sec. 1996–97; Minister of State, Dept. for Educ. and Employment May 1997–; Chair. Bd. Oxford Brookes Univ. (formerly Oxford Polytechnic) 1987–93. *Address:* House of Commons, London, SW1A 0AA (Office); 4 Flaxfield Road, Blackbird Leys, Oxford, OX4 5QD, England (Home).

SMITH, Anthony David, C.B.E., M.A.; British administrator; b. 14 March 1938; s. of Henry and Esther Smith; ed. Brasenose Coll., Oxford; Current Affairs Producer, B.B.C. 1960–71; Fellow, St. Antony's Coll., Oxford 1971–76; Dir. British Film Inst. 1979–88; Pres. Magdalen Coll., Oxford 1988–; mem. Bd. of Dirs. Channel Four TV 1980–84; mem. Acton Soc. Trust 1978–; Chair. Writers and Scholars Educational Trust (Index on Censorship) 1989–; mem. Arts Council 1990–94; Hon. Fellow Brasenose Coll. 1994. *Publications:* The Shadow in the Cave: the broadcaster, the audience and the state 1973, British Broadcasting 1974, The British Press since the War 1976, Subsidies and the Press in Europe 1977, The Politics of Information 1978, Television and Political Life 1979, The Newspaper: an international history 1979, Newspapers and Democracy 1980, Goodbye Gutenberg—the newspaper revolution of the 1980s, The Geopolitics of Information 1980, The Age of the Behemoths 1991, From Books to Bytes 1993, The Oxford Illustrated History of Television 1995, Software for the Self: culture and technology 1996. *Address:* Magdalen College, Oxford, OX1 4AU; Albany, Piccadilly, London, W1V 9RP, England. *Telephone:* (01865) 276000 (Oxford); 0171-734 5494 (London).

SMITH, Anthony Felstead, LL.B.; Australian lawyer; b. 12 April 1936, Newcastle, N.S.W.; s. of late Thomas W. F. Smith and Zara M. Wells; m. Beverley J. Green 1960; three s.; ed. Newcastle and Melbourne High Schools and Univ. of Melbourne; practising solicitor 1960–; partner Gillotts 1966; Sr. Partner, Minter Ellison, Melbourne –1989; mem. Int. Bar Asscn. 1976–, Sec.-Gen. 1988–90, Moderator Judges' Forum 1990–94; Judge Co. Court of Vic. 1990–; Pres. Admin. Appeals Tribunal April 1990–92; Vice-Pres. Anti-Cancer Council of Vic. 1993–95; mem. Council La Trobe Univ. 1991–97. *Publication:* Defamation in Civil Precedents and Pleadings (co-author) 1989. *Leisure interests:* tennis, golf, swimming. *Address:* Judges' Chambers, County Court, William Street, Melbourne, Vic. 3000 (Office); 30 Ferdinand Avenue, North Balwyn, Vic. 3104, Australia (Home). *Telephone:* (03) 603 6535 (Office); (03) 857 7110.

SMITH, Bernard William, PH.D.; Australian academic; b. 3 Oct. 1916, Sydney; s. of Charles Smith and Rose Anne Tierney; m. 1st Kate Challis 1941 (died 1989); one s. one d.; m. 2nd Margaret Forster 1995; ed. Univ. of Sydney, Warburg Inst., London and A.N.U., Canberra; school teacher N.S.W. 1935–44, Educ. Officer, Art Gallery, N.S.W. 1944–52; lecturer, Sr. Lecturer Univ. of Melbourne 1955–63, Reader 1964–66; Art critic The Age, Melbourne 1963–66; Prof. of Contemporary Art and Dir. Power Inst. of Fine Arts, Univ. of Sydney 1967–77, Sr. Assoc., Dept. of Fine Arts 1977–; Pres. Australian Acad of Fine Arts 1977–80; Chevalier, Ordre des Arts et des Lettres. *Publications:* Place, Taste and Tradition 1945, European Vision and the South Pacific 1960, Australian Painting 1962, The Boy Adeodatus 1985, The Art of Captain Cook's Voyages (jt. author) 1985–87, The Death of the Artist as Hero 1988, The Critic as advocate 1989, Imagining the Pacific 1992, Noel Counihan 1994, Poems 1938–1993 1996. *Leisure interests:* swimming, walking, reading. *Address:* 168 Nicholson Street, Fitzroy, Vic. 3065, Australia. *Telephone:* (03) 9419-7470. *Fax:* (03) 9419-8092.

SMITH, Brian (see Smith, E. Brian).

SMITH, Brian (see Smith, Sir Norman Brian).

SMITH, Carsten, D.JUR.; Norwegian judge; b. 13 July 1932, Oslo; s. of Oscar Smith and Julie Høyer; m. Lucy Dahl 1958; three d.; ed. Univ. of Oslo; attorney 1956; Deputy Judge 1960; Asst. Prof. Univ. of Oslo 1957, Assoc. Prof. 1960, Prof. of Law 1964–91, Dir. Inst. of Pvt. Law 1972–73, Dean, Faculty of Law 1977–79; Temporary Supreme Court Justice 1987, 1989–90; Chief Justice, Supreme Court of Norway 1991–; mem. Norwegian Acad. of Science and Letters, Pres. 1991; mem. and chair. numerous public cttees. for preparation of legislation and org. of research and educ. etc.; recipient of several orders, hon. degrees and awards. *Publications include:* Law of Torts and Social Security (co-author) 1953, Law of Guarantees (Vols. I–III) 1963–81, State Practice and Legal Theory 1978, Banking Law and State Regulations 1980, Contemporary Legal Reasoning 1992, The Law and the Life 1996; other books and articles in fields of int. law, constitutional law, admin. law and pvt. law. *Address:* Justitiarius i Høyesterett, P.O. Box 8016 Dep, 0030 Oslo, Norway. *Telephone:* 22035901. *Fax:* 22428554.

SMITH, Rt. Hon. Chris(topher) Robert, P.C., M.P., PH.D.; British politician; b. 24 July 1951; s. of Colin Smith and Gladys Smith (née Luscombe); ed. George Watson's Coll., Edin., Pembroke Coll., Cambridge, Harvard Univ. (Kennedy Scholar 1975–76); Devt. Sec. Shaftesbury Soc. Housing Asscn. 1977–80; Devt. Co-ordinator Soc. for Co-operative Dwellings 1980–83; Councillor London Borough of Islington 1978–83, Chief Whip 1978–79, Chair. Housing Cttee. 1981–83; Labour M.P. for Islington S. and Finsbury 1983–; Opposition Spokesman on Treasury and Econ. Affairs 1987–92; Principal Opposition Spokesman on Environmental Protection 1992–94, on Nat. Heritage 1994–95, on Social Security 1995–96, on Health 1996–97; Sec. of State for Culture, Media and Sport May 1997–; Chair. Labour Campaign for Criminal Justice 1985–88, Tribune Group of M.P.s 1988–89; Pres. Socialist Environment and Resources Asscn. 1992–97; mem. Exec. Fabian Soc. 1990–97; mem. Bd. Shelter 1986–92; has held positions in several other orgs. *Publication:* Creative Britain 1998. *Leisure interests:* mountaineering, literature, theatre, music. *Address:* House of Commons, London, SW1A 0AA, England.

SMITH, Sir David Cecil, Kt., F.R.S., F.R.S.E.; British academic; b. 21 May 1930, Port Talbot; s. of William Smith and Elva Smith; m. Lesley Mutch 1965; two s. one d.; ed. Colston's School, Bristol, St. Paul's School, London and Queen's Coll. Oxford; Browne Research Fellow, Queen's Coll. Oxford 1956–59; Harkness Fellow, Univ. of Calif. Berkeley 1959–60; Univ. Lecturer, Dept. of Agric. Science, Univ. of Oxford 1960–74; Fellow and Tutor, Wadham Coll. Oxford 1964–74; Melville Wills Prof. of Botany, Univ. of Bristol 1974–80; Sibthorpian Prof. of Rural Econ. Univ. of Oxford 1980–87; Prin. and Vice-Chancellor, Univ. of Edin. 1987–94; Pres. Wolfson Coll., Oxford 1994–; Hon. D.Sc. (Aberdeen) 1990, (Edin.) 1994 and numerous hon. degrees; Commdr. Order of Merit (Italy), Commdr. Order of Merit (Poland). *Publication:* Biology of Symbiosis (with A. E. Douglas) 1987. *Leisure interest:* writing. *Address:* Wolfson College, Oxford, OX2 6UD, England. *Telephone:* (01865) 274101.

SMITH, David Collville; Zimbabwe politician and farmer; b. 1922, Argyllshire, U.K.; came to S. Rhodesia as farm asst. 1946; later set up farming partnership in Mazoe Valley; appointed to various agricultural cttees.; Minister of Agric. 1968–76, Deputy Prime Minister and Minister of Finance 1976–79; Minister of Commerce and Industry 1980–81; fmr. mem. Rhodesian Front.

SMITH, Delia, O.B.E., F.R.T.S.; British cookery writer and broadcaster; m. Michael Wynn Jones; creator and presenter of several TV series; cookery writer Evening Standard newspaper 1972–85; columnist Radio Times; consultant food ed. Sainsbury's Magazine; Dir. Norwich Football Club; Dr. h.c. (Nottingham Univ.) 1996; Special Award, Andre Simon Memorial Fund 1994. *Publications:* How to Cheat at Cooking 1971, Country Fare 1973, Recipes from Country Inns and Restaurants 1973, Family Fare: Book 1 1973, Book 2 1974, Evening Standard Cookbook 1974, Country Recipes from Look East (regional TV programme) 1975, More Country Recipes from Look East 1976, Frugal Food 1976, Book of Cakes 1977, Recipes from Look East 1977, Food for Our Times 1978, Cookery Course: Part 1 1978, Part 2 1979, Part 3 1981, The Complete Cookery Course 1982, A Feast for Lent 1983, A Feast for Advent 1983, One is Fun 1985, Food Aid Cookery Book (ed.) 1986. A Journey into God 1988, Delia Smith's Christmas 1990, Delia Smith's Summer Collection 1993, Delia Smith's Winter Collection 1995, How to Cook: Book 1 1998. *Address:* c/o Deborah Owen Limited, 78 Narrow Street, Limehouse, London, E14 8BP, England. *Telephone:* 0171-987 5119. *Fax:* 0171-538 4004.

SMITH, E. Brian, M.A., D.SC., F.R.S.C.; British scientist and university vice-chancellor; b. 10 Oct. 1933, Mold, North Wales; s. of S. Eric Smith and Dilys Olwen Hughes; m. 1st Margaret Barr 1957 (divorced 1978); two s. one d.; m. 2nd Regina Arvidson Ball 1983; two step-d.; ed. Alun Grammar School, Mold, Wirral Grammar School, Univ. of Liverpool; Fellow St. Catherine's Coll. Oxford and Lecturer in Physical Chem., Oxford Univ. 1960–88; Master St. Catherine's Coll. 1988–93; Vice-Chancellor Cardiff Univ. 1993–. *Publications:* Virial Coefficients of Pure Gases and Mixtures 1969, Basic Chemical Themodynamics 1973, Intermolecular Forces 1981, Forces Between Molecules 1986; papers in scientific journals. *Leisure interest:* mountaineering. *Address:* P.O. Box 920, Cardiff, CF1 3XP, Wales.

SMITH, Elizabeth Jean, M.A., F.R.S.A.; British broadcasting executive; b. 15 Aug. 1936, Ajmer, India; d. of Sir Robert and Lady Hay; m. Geoffrey Smith 1960; one s. one d.; ed. Univ. of Edinburgh; producer, Radio News, BBC 1960; Asst. Head, Cen. Talks and Features, BBC World Service 1980, Head, Current Affairs 1984, Controller, English Programmes 1987–94; Sec.-Gen. Commonwealth Broadcasting Asscn. 1994–; Fellow, Radio Acad. *Address:* Commonwealth Broadcasting Association, 17 Fleet Street, London, EC4Y 1AA, England. *Telephone:* 0171-583 5550. *Fax:* 0171-583 5549.

SMITH, Emil L., B.S., PH.D.; American biochemist and biophysicist; b. 5 July 1911, New York City; s. of Abraham and Esther Smith; m. Esther Press

1934; two s.; ed. Columbia, Cambridge and Yale Univs.; Instructor, Columbia Univ. 1936–38; Fellow, Rockefeller Inst. 1940–42; Sr. Biochemist and Biophysicist, E. R. Squibb & Sons 1942–46; Assoc. Prof. and Prof., Univ. of Utah 1946–63; Prof. and Chair. Dept. of Biological Chem., Univ. of Calif., L.A. 1963–79; Prof. Emer. 1979–; Foreign mem. Russian Acad. of Sciences; mem. N.A.S., American Acad. of Arts and Sciences, American Philosophical Soc., etc.; Guggenheim Fellow (Cambridge and Yale) 1938–40; Stein-Moore Award (Protein Soc.) 1987. *Publications:* Principles of Biochemistry (co-author) 1954; many articles on biochemistry and biophysics. *Leisure interests:* music, literature, art. *Address:* Department of Biological Chemistry, University of California, School of Medicine, Los Angeles, CA 90095, U.S.A. *Telephone:* (310) 825-6494. *Fax:* (310) 206-5272.

SMITH, Francis Barrymore, PH.D., F.A.H.A.; Australian historian; b. 16 May 1932, Hughesdale; s. of Francis John Smith and Bertha Smith; m. Ann Stokes 1965; two s. two d.; ed. Univ. of Melbourne and Cambridge Univ.; Lecturer in History, Univ. of Melbourne 1962–66; Prof. Fellow in History, Inst. of Advanced Studies, A.N.U. 1974–94, Hancock Prof. of History 1995–98; Ed. Historical Studies 1963–67; Pres. Australian Historical Assn. 1978–80. *Publications:* Making of the Second Reform Bill 1966, Radical Artisan: William James Linton 1973, The People's Health 1830–1910 1979, 1990, Florence Nightingale: Reputation and Power 1982, Retreat of Tuberculosis 1987, 'Agent Orange': The Australian Aftermath 1994. *Address:* Division of Historical Studies, Institute of Advanced Studies, Australian National University, Canberra 0200, Australia. *Telephone:* (02) 6249 2354. *Fax:* (02) 6249 3969.

SMITH, Sir Francis Graham (See Graham-Smith, Sir Francis).

SMITH, Frank Thomas, D.PHIL., F.R.S.; British professor of applied mathematics; b. 24 Feb. 1948, Bournemouth; s. of Leslie Maxwell Smith and Catherine Matilda Smith; m. Valerie Sheila Hearn 1972; three d.; ed. Bournemouth Grammar School, Jesus Coll. Oxford, Univ. Coll. London; Research Fellow, Southampton Univ. 1972–73; Lecturer in Math., Reader then Prof., Imperial Coll. London 1973–84; Golsmid Prof. of Applied Math., Univ. Coll. London 1984–; Visiting Prof. Univ. of Western Ont., Canada 1978–79. *Publications:* Boundary-Layer Separation (Co-Ed.); scientific papers, mostly on theoretical and computational fluid dynamics. *Address:* Mathematics Department, University College, Gower Street, London, WC1E 6BT (Office); 9 Woodham Park Road, Woodham, Weybridge, Surrey, KT15 3ST, England (Home). *Telephone:* 0171-387 7050 (Office); (01932) 352394 (Home).

SMITH, Gordon Scott, PH.D.; Canadian diplomatist, professor and consultant; b. 19 July 1941, Montreal, P.Q.; s. of G. Meredith Smith and late Helen Scott; m. Lise G. Lacroix; three s. one d.; ed. Lower Canada Coll. Montreal, McGill Univ., Univ. of Chicago and M.I.T.; joined Defence Research Bd. 1966; transferred to Dept. of External Affairs 1967; mem. Canadian Del. to NATO 1968–70; Special Adviser to Minister of Nat. Defence 1970–72; joined Privy Council Office 1972; Deputy Sec. to Cabinet (Plans) 1978–79; Deputy Under-Sec. Dept. of External Affairs 1979; Assoc. Sec. to Cabinet, Privy Council Office 1980–81; Sec. Ministry of State for Social Devt. 1981–84; Assoc. Sec. to Cabinet and Deputy Clerk of Privy Council 1984; Deputy Minister for Political Affairs, Dept. of External Affairs 1985; Amb. and Perm. Rep. of Canada to NATO 1985–90; Sec. to the Cabinet for Fed.-Provincial Relations, Govt. of Canada 1990–91; Amb. to the EC 1991–94; Deputy Minister of Foreign Affairs 1994–97; Chair. Int. Devt. Research Centre; Sr. Advisor to Pres.; Prof. Victoria Univ.; Sr. Fellow and Prof. Univs. of B.C. and Westminster (London); Pres. investment banking and political risk consultancy. *Leisure interests:* squash, tennis, sailing, skiing, antiques. *Address:* 2027 Runnymede Avenue, Victoria, BC V8S 2V5, Canada. *Telephone:* (250) 595 8622. *Fax:* (250) 595 8682.

SMITH, Hamilton O., M.D.; American university professor and research scientist; b. 23 Aug. 1931, New York; s. of Tommie Harkey and Bunnie Othanel Smith; m. Elizabeth Anne Bolton 1957; four s. one d.; ed. Univ. of Illinois, Univ. of California at Berkeley, Johns Hopkins Univ. School of Medicine, Baltimore, Md.; Internship, Barnes Hosp., St. Louis, Mo. 1956–57; Lieut. in U.S.N.R., Sr. Medical Officer 1957–59; Resident, Henry Ford Hosp., Detroit, Mich. 1960–62; Postdoctoral Fellow, Dept. of Human Genetics, Univ. of Mich. 1962–64, Research Assoc. 1964–67; Asst. Prof. of Microbiology, Johns Hopkins Univ. School of Medicine 1967–69, Assoc. Prof. 1969–73, Prof. of Microbiology 1973–81, Prof. of Molecular Biology & Genetics 1981–; sabbatical year with Inst. für Molekular-Biologie, Zürich Univ. 1975–76; Guggenheim Fellow 1975–76; shared Nobel Prize for Physiology and Medicine 1978 with Prof. Werner Arber and Dr. Daniel Nathans (qq.v.) for work on restriction enzymes; mem. N.A.S. 1980, A.A.A.S. *Leisure interests:* piano, classical music. *Address:* Department of Molecular Biology, Johns Hopkins University School of Medicine, 720 Rutland Avenue, Baltimore, MD 21205 (Office); 8222 Carrbridge Circle, Baltimore, MD 21204, U.S.A. (Home). *Telephone:* (301) 955-3650 (Office); (301) 821-5409 (Home).

SMITH, Hans J., B.SC., S.M.P.; South African business executive; b. 15 Jan. 1941, Krugersdorp; s. of Hendrik C. Smith and late Johanna Smith; m. Lydia Minnaar 1969; two d; ed. Kensington High School, Univ. of Pretoria and Harvard Univ.; with Gold Fields of S. Africa 1965–70; Sr. Investment Analyst, Gencor 1970, Asst. Gen. Man. Buffalo Fluorspar Mine 1972, Gen. Man. Msuali Asbestos 1973, Operations Man. Chrome Div. Corp. H.Q. 1974, Man. Dir. Zululand Titanium 1978; Tech. Dir. Octha Diamonds 1981; rejoined Gencor as Man. Strategic Planning, Corporate Mining Div. 1985, Sr. Man. Marketing, Coal Div. 1985; Chief Consultant, Safety and Health, Genmin 1988; Man. Dir. Trans-Natal Coal Corpn. Ltd. 1988; Man. Dir. Samancor Ltd. 1989; Chief Exec. New Business, Group Co. Gencor 1993; Chief Exec. and Man. Dir. Iscor Ltd. 1993, Exec. Chair. 1995–. *Leisure interests:* tennis, golf, jogging, scuba diving, underwater photography. *Address:* Iscor Ltd., P.O. Box 450, Pretoria 0001, South Africa. *Telephone:* (012) 307 300. *Fax:* (012) 326 4721.

SMITH, Harvey (see Smith, Robert Harvey).

SMITH, Henry Sidney, M.A., F.B.A., D.LIT.; British professor of Egyptology; b. 14 June 1928, London; s. of Sidney Smith and Mary W. Smith (née Parker); m. Hazel Flory Leeper 1961 (died 1991); ed. Merchant Taylors School, Sandy Lodge, Middx. and Christ's Coll., Cambridge; Asst. Lecturer in Egyptology, Faculty of Oriental Studies, Cambridge 1954–59, Lecturer 1959–63; Wallis Budge Fellow in Egyptology, Christ's Coll., Cambridge 1955–63; Field Dir. Egypt Exploration Soc. Archaeological Survey of Nubia, Epigraphist at Nubian sites 1959–65; Reader in Egyptian Archaeology, Univ. Coll. London 1963–70, Edwards Prof. of Egyptology 1970–86, Emer. Prof. 1986–; Prin. Epigraphist and Site Supervisor, Egypt Exploration Soc., Saqqara, Egypt 1964–70, Field Dir., Sacred Animal Necropolis 1971–76, Anubieion 1976–81, Dir. Memphis Project in Egypt 1981–88; Corresp. mem. Deutsches Archäologisches Institut; Medallist, Collège de France, Paris 1984. *Publications:* Preliminary Reports of the EES Archaeological Survey of Egyptian Nubia 1961, A Visit to Ancient Egypt: Memphis and Saqqara, c. 600–30 B.C. 1974, The Fortress of Buhen, II: The Inscriptions 1976, I: The Archaeological Report (with W. B. Emery and A. Millard) 1979, Saqqara Demotic Papyri I (with W. J. Tait) 1984, The Anubieton at Saqqara, Vols. I and II (with D. G. Jeffreys and Lisa L. Giddy) 1988, 1992, The Sculpture from the Sacred Animal Necropolis at North Saqqara 1964–76 (with Elizabeth Anne Hastings) 1997; excavation reports, text publications and historical articles in int. journals. *Leisure interests:* varied. *Address:* Ailwyn House, High Street, Upwood, Huntingdon, Cambridgeshire, PE17 1QE, England (Home). *Telephone:* (01487) 812196 (Home).

SMITH, Ian Douglas; Zimbabwean politician; b. 8 April 1919; m. Janet Watt (died 1994); two s. one d.; ed. Chaplin School, Gwelo, S. Rhodesia (now Gweru, Zimbabwe), and Rhodes Univ., Grahamstown, S. Africa; R.A.F. 1941–46; farmer; M.P. S. Rhodesia Legis. Ass. 1948–53, Parl. of Fed. of Rhodesia and Nyasaland 1953–61; fmr. Chief Whip United Fed. Party, resgnd. 1961; foundation mem. and Vice-Pres. Rhodesian Front (renamed Republican Front 1981) 1962, Pres. 1964–87; Deputy Prime Minister and Minister of Treasury S. Rhodesia 1962–64; Prime Minister of Rhodesia 1964–79, proclaimed Rhodesia's Unilateral Declaration of Independence, Nov. 1965; Minister without Portfolio in Bishop Muzorewa's Govt. 1979; mem. Transitional Exec. Council to prepare for transfer of power in Rhodesia 1978–79; M.P. for Republican Front (now Conservative Alliance of Zimbabwe) 1980–88, suspended from Parl. 1987–88; Independence Decoration 1970, Grand Commdr., Order of the Legion of Merit 1979. *Address:* Gwenoro Farm, Shurugwi; 3 Phillips Avenue, Belgravia, Harare, Zimbabwe.

SMITH, Ian William Murison, PH.D., F.R.S.; British professor of chemistry; b. 15 June 1937, Leeds; s. of William Murison Smith and Margaret Moir Smith; m. Susan Morrish 1961; two s. two d.; ed. Giggleswick School, Christ's Coll., Cambridge; Fellow Christ's Coll., Cambridge 1963–85, demonstrator in Physical Chem., Cambridge Univ., 1966–71, lecturer Physical Chem. 1971–85, tutor Christ's Coll., Cambridge 1968–76, Dir. of Studies 1972–85; Prof. of Chemistry, Univ. of Birmingham 1985–91, Head School of Chemistry 1989–93, Mason Prof. of Chemistry 1991–; Tilden Medal, Royal Soc. of Chem., Special Award for Reaction Kinetics, Royal Soc. of Chem., Polanyi Medal. *Publications:* Kinetic and Dynamics of Elementary Gas Reactions 1980; (ed.) Modern Gas Kinetics 1987; over 200 contribs. to scientific journals. *Leisure interests:* occasional golf, even more occasional tennis, theatre, walking, gardening under supervision. *Address:* School of Chemistry, University of Birmingham, Edgbaston, Birmingham, B15 2TT; 21 St. Bernards Road, Olton, Solihull, West Midlands, B92 7AU, England (Home). *Telephone:* (0121) 414 4422 (Office). *Fax:* (0121) 414 4426 (Office).

SMITH, Ivor, M.A.; British architect; b. 27 Jan. 1926, Leigh-on-Sea, Essex; s. of H.S. Smith and F.E. Smith; m. Audrey Lawrence 1947; one s. three d.; ed. Bartlett School of Architecture, Univ. Coll. London, Cambridge Univ. School of Architecture, Architectural Assn. School of Architecture, London; City Architects Dept., Sheffield 1951–61; in pvt. architectural practice 1961–87; Prof., Univ. Coll. Dublin 1969–73, Bristol Univ. 1975–82, Heriot Watt Univ. 1982–90; Educational Consultant, The Caribbean School of Architecture. *Leisure interests:* walking, drawing. *Address:* The Station Officer's House, Prawle Point, Kingsbridge, Devon, TQ7 2BX, England. *Telephone:* (01548) 511432.

SMITH, Jack; British artist; b. 18 June 1928, Sheffield; s. of John Edward Smith and Laura Smith; m. Susan Craigie Halkett 1956; ed. Sheffield Coll. of Art, St. Martin's School of Art and Royal Coll. of Art; one-man exhbns. Beaux Arts Gallery 1952–54, 1956, 1958, Catherine Viviano, New York 1958, 1962–63, Whitechapel Gallery, London 1959, Matthiesen Gallery, London 1960–63, Midland Group Gallery, Nottingham 1961, Grosvenor Gallery, London 1965, Marlborough Fine Art, London 1968, Gothenberg Museum, Sweden 1968, Whitechapel Gallery, London 1971, Redfern Gallery, London 1974, 1976, 1977, Fischer Fine Art, London 1981–83, Angela Flowers

Gallery, London 1990, 1991, 1992, 1996; sets and costumes for Ballet Rambert's Carmen Arcadiae Mechanicae Perpetuum 1985, Royal Ballet's Pursuit 1987; 1st Prize, John Moores, Liverpool 1957; Nat. Prize, Guggenheim Int. 1960. *Address:* 29 Seafield Road, Hove, Sussex, BN3 2TP, England. *Telephone:* (01273) 738312.

SMITH, James Herbert, M.A.(ECON.); Bahamian banker; b. 26 Oct. 1947, Nassau; s. of late Bertram A. Smith and of Rosalie B. Smith; m. Portia M. Campbell 1973; two s. one d.; ed. Ryerson Polytechnical Coll., Toronto and Univs. of Windsor and Alberta, Canada; Deputy Perm. Sec. Ministry of Econ. Affairs 1977–79; Under-Sec. Cabinet Office 1980–84; Sec. for Revenue, Ministry of Finance 1984–85, Perm. Sec. 1985–86; fmr. Chair. Bahamas Devt. Bank; Gov. Cen. Bank of the Bahamas 1987–97; Deputy Chair. Bahamas Mortgage Corpn. 1990–; Chair. Paradise Island Bridge Authority 1991–. *Leisure interests:* reading, golf. *Address:* P.O. Box CB 10973, Nassau, Bahamas (Home). *Telephone:* (809) 327-3213 (Home).

SMITH, Jean Kennedy; American diplomatist and foundation executive; b. 20 Feb. 1928, Massachusetts; d. of Rose (Fitzgerald) Kennedy and Joseph P. Kennedy; m. Stephen E. Smith 1956 (died 1990); two s. two d.; ed. Manhattanville Coll., Purchase, N.Y.; mem. Bd. trustees Joseph P. Kennedy Jr. Foundation 1964–, John F. Kennedy Center for the Performing Arts 1964– (Chair. Educ. Cttee. 1964–74 and f. center's children's programmes); fmr. mem. Bd. Carnegie Endowment for Int. Peace; f. Very Special Arts (int. programme for people with disabilities) 1974; Amb. to Ireland 1993–98; Hon. Irish Citizen; several hon. degrees; Jefferson Award for Outstanding Public Service, American Inst. for Public Service, Margaret Mead Humanitarian Award, Council of Cerebral Palsy Auxiliaries, Irish American of the Year Award, Irish America Magazine 1995, Rotary One Int. Award, Rotary Club of Chicago 1997, Terence Cardinal Cooke Humanitarian Award 1997. *Publication:* Chronicles of Courage: Very Special Artists 1993. *Leisure interests:* the arts, tennis, golf, sailing, reading. *Address:* 4 Sutton Place, New York, NY 10022, U.S.A. *Telephone:* (212) 758-3610. *Fax:* (212) 813-1871.

SMITH, Jennifer M.; Bermudian politician; b. 14 Oct. 1947, Bermuda; began career as journalist; reporter Bermuda Recorder 1970–74, Ed. 1974; on staff of Fame magazine, later Ed.; joined ZBM Radio and TV; art teacher at Sr. Training School (attached to Bermuda Prison Service) for eight years; contested St. George's N. seat for Progressive Labour Party (PLP) in House of Ass. elections 1972, 1976, 1980; mem Senate 1980–; Shadow Minister for Educ.; mem. House of Ass. (PLP) 1989, 1993, 1998–; Leader of PLP 1996–; Prime Minister of Bermuda Nov. 1998–. *Leisure interests:* painting, dancing, reading, working with young people, writing, collecting match-book covers and first day stamp covers. *Address:* Office of the Prime Minister, St. George's, Bermuda.

SMITH, John Francis, Jr. (Jack), M.B.A.; American business executive; b. 6 April 1938, Worcester, Mass.; s. of John Francis Smith Sr. and Eleanor C. Sullivan; m. 1st Marie Roberta Halloway 1962 (divorced); two s.; m. 2nd Lydia G. Sigrist 1988; one step-d.; ed. Boston and Massachusetts Univs.; Divisional Man., Gen. Motors Corpn., Framingham, Mass. 1961–73, Asst. Treas., New York 1973–80, Comptroller, Detroit 1980–81, Dir. Worldwide Planning 1981–84, Pres. and Gen. Man., Gen. Motors Canada, Oshawa 1984–86, Vice-Pres. Gen. Motors Corpn. and Pres. Gen. Motors Europe 1986–88, Exec. Vice-Pres. Int. Operations, Gen. Motors Corpn., Detroit 1988–90, Vice-Chair. 1990, Pres. Gen. Motors 1992–, C.O.O. April–Nov. 1992; Chair. Jan. 1996–; bd. dirs., mem. Finance Cttee. 1990–; mem. Bd. Govs. Jr. Achievement Canada, Ltd. 1984; Bd. Dirs. Procter & Gamble; mem. Bd. of Detroit Renaissance. *Address:* c/o General Motors Corporation, 3044 Grand Boulevard, Detroit, MI 48202; Globe Headquarters, Renaissance, P.O. Box 100, 100 Renaissance Center, Detroit, MI 48625, U.S.A.

SMITH, Ley, B.A.; American business executive; b. 1934; ed. Univ. of Western Ont.; joined Upjohn Co. 1958, now Pres. and C.O.O.

SMITH, Dame Maggie Natalie, D.B.E.; British actress; b. 28 Dec. 1934, Ilford, Essex; d. of Nathaniel Smith and Margaret Little; m. 1st Robert Stephens 1967 (divorced 1975); two s.; m. 2nd Beverley Cross 1975; ed. Oxford High School for Girls; first appeared with Oxford Univ. Dramatic Soc. (O.U.D.S.) in Twelfth Night 1952; appeared in revue New Faces N.Y. 1956, Share My Lettuce 1957, The Stepmother 1958; with Old Vic Co. 1959–60 playing in The Double Dealer, As You Like It, Richard II, The Merry Wives of Windsor, What Every Woman Knows; other appearances include Rhinoceros 1960, Strip the Willow 1960, The Rehearsal 1961, The Private Ear and The Public Eye 1962, Mary, Mary 1963; with Nat. Theatre played in The Recruiting Officer 1963, Othello (Desdemona) 1964, The Master Builder 1964, Hay Fever 1964, Much Ado About Nothing 1965, Miss Julie 1965, A Bond Honoured 1966, The Beaux' Stratagem 1970, Hedda Gabler 1970, Three Sisters, Design for Living (Los Angeles) 1971, Private Lives London 1972, U.S.A. 1974–75, Peter Pan 1973, Snap 1974; played 1976, 1977, 1978 and 1980 seasons, Stratford, Ont., Canada, Night and Day 1979, Virginia, London 1981, The Way of the World, Chichester Festival and London 1984–85, Interpreters, London 1985, The Infernal Machine 1986, Coming in to Land 1987, Lettice and Lovage, London 1987, New York 1990, The Importance of Being Earnest 1993, Three Tall Women 1994–95, Talking Heads 1996, A Delicate Balance 1997. *Films include:* The V.I.P.s 1963, The Pumpkin Eater 1964, Young Cassidy 1965, Othello 1966, The Honey Pot 1967, Hot Millions 1968, The Prime of Miss Jean Brodie 1969, Travels with My Aunt 1972, Love and Pain and the Whole Damn Thing 1973, Murder by Death 1975, Death on the Nile 1978, California Suite 1978, Quartet 1980, Clash of the Titans 1981, Evil under the Sun 1982, Ménage à Trois 1982, The Missionary 1982, A Private Function 1984, A Room with a View 1986, The Lonely Passion of Judith Hearn 1987, Paris by Night 1988, Hook 1991, The Secret Garden 1993, Richard III 1995, First Wives Club 1996, Washington Square 1998, Tea with Mussolini 1999; Dir. United British Artists 1982–; Hon. D.Lit. (St. Andrews, Leicester) 1982, (Cambridge) 1993; Hon. D.Litt. (Bath) 1986. Awards: Evening Standard Best Actress Award 1962, 1970, 1982, 1985, 1994; Variety Club Actress of the Year 1963; L.A. Critics Award Best Actress 1970; Variety Club Award Best Stage Actress 1972 (plays); Acad. Award for Best Actress 1969, for Best Supporting Actress 1979; Best Actress Award from Soc. of Film and Television Arts (U.K.) 1969; Best Actress Award from Film Critics' Guild (U.S.A.) 1969 (films), BAFTA Award for Best Actress 1984, 1987, 1989, BAFTA Award for Lifetime Achievement 1992; Tony Award 1990; Shakespeare Prize, FVS Foundation, Hamburg 1991. *Leisure interest:* reading. *Address:* c/o Write on Cue, 29 Whitcomb Street, London, WC2H 7EP, England.

SMITH, Martin Cruz; American writer; b. 11 March 1942, Reading, Pa.; s. of John Smith and Louise Lopez; m. Emily Arnold 1968; one s. two d.; ed. Univ. of Pennsylvania; Golden Dagger Award, Crime Writers' Asscn. 1981. *Publications:* Gorky Park 1981, Stallion Gate 1986, Polar Star 1989, Red Square 1992, Rose 1996.

SMITH, Michael, C.C., O.B.C., PH.D., F.R.S., F.R.S.C.; Canadian professor of biochemistry; b. 26 April 1932, Blackpool, England; s. of Rowland Smith and Mary Agnes Smith (née Armstead); m. Helen Wood Christie 1960; two s. one d.; ed. Arnold School, Blackpool, Univ. of Manchester; Postdoctoral Fellow, B.C. Research Council, Univ. of B.C., Vancouver, B.C., Canada 1956–60; Research Assoc., Inst. for Enzyme Research, Univ. of Wis., U.S.A. 1960–61; Head, Chem. Div., Vancouver Lab., Fisheries Research Bd. of Canada, Vancouver 1961–66; Assoc. Prof., Dept. of Biochemistry, Univ. of B.C., Vancouver 1966–70, Prof., Dept. of Biochemistry 1971–97; Career Investigator (fmrly. entitled Research Assoc.), M.R.C. of Canada 1966–; Peter Wall Distinguished Prof. of Biotech. 1994–; Dir. Genome Sequence Centre, B.C. Cancer Research Centre 1998–; 25 hon. degrees; Boehringer-Mannheim Prize, Canadian Biochemical Soc. 1981, Gold Medal, Science Council of B.C. 1984, Gairdner Foundation Int. Award 1986, Flavelle Medal, R.S.C. 1992, Nobel Prize for Chem. 1993, Prin. Award, Ernest C. Manning Awards Foundation 1994; Order of B.C. *Publications:* numerous publs. in scientific literature. *Leisure interests:* classical music, sailing, skiing. *Address:* Biotechnology Laboratory, University of British Columbia, Room 237, Wesbrook Building, 6174 University Boulevard, Vancouver, B.C. V6T 1Z3 (Office); 2618 Point Grey Road, Vancouver, B.C., V6K 1A5, Canada (Home). *Telephone:* (604) 822-0863 (Office). *Fax:* (604) 822-9127.

SMITH, Michael, T.D.; Irish politician and fmr. farmer; b. Nov. 1940, Roscrea, Co. Tipperary; m. Mary T. Ryan; one s. six d.; ed. Univ. Coll. Cork; fmr. farmer; mem. Irish Farmers' Asscn. 1969–; mem. Tipperary North Riding County Council 1967–88, Chair. 1986–87; mem. Dáil 1969–73, 1977–82; Minister of State, Dept. of Agric. 1980–81; Senator, Agric. Panel 1982–83, Culture and Educ. Panel 1983–87; Minister of State, Dept. of Energy 1987–88; Minister for Energy 1988–89; Minister of State, Dept. of Industry and Commerce 1989–91; Minister for the Environment 1992–94; Fianna Fáil. *Address:* Lismackin, Roscrea, Co. Tipperary, Ireland (Home). *Telephone:* (0505) 43157 (Home).

SMITH, Michelle; Irish swimmer; b. 15 Dec. 1960; 1996 Olympic champion, 400m individual medley, 400m freestyle and 200m individual medal; banned from swimming for four years after being found guilty of tampering with urine sample.

SMITH, Sir (Norman) Brian, Kt., C.B.E., PH.D., M.SC., C.INST.M., F.C.I.M.; British business executive; b. 10 Sept. 1928, Monton; s. of Vincent Smith and Louise Smith; m. Phyllis Crossley 1955; one s. one d. (and one s. deceased); ed. Sir John Deanes Grammar School, Northwich and Univ. of Manchester; joined ICI 1954, Deputy Chair. Fibres Div. 1972, Chair. Fibres Div. 1975–78, Dir. ICI 1978–85, Chair. ICI Americas 1981–85; Deputy Chair. Metal Box PLC (now MB Group PLC) 1985–86, Chair. 1986–89; Dir. Lister & Co. 1985–94 (Deputy Chair. 1990–91, Chair. 1991–94), Davy Corpn. 1986–91; Pres. British Textile Confed. 1977–79; mem. British Overseas Trade Bd. 1980–81, 1983–87; Chair. Priorities Bd. for R and D into Agric. and Food 1987–92; Dir. Cable and Wireless PLC 1988–95 (Chair. 1995–98), Yorkshire Chemicals 1990–91, Mercury Communications 1990–93, Berisford Int. PLC 1990–96, Oxford Diocesan Bd. of Finance 1990–, John Cabot CTC Bristol Trust 1997–98; Chair. BAA PLC 1991–98, Heatherwood & Wexham Park Hosps. Trust 1991–97, Standing Conf. on Schools' Science and Tech. 1992–96, Hydron Ltd. 1994–, Hong Kong Telecommunications 1995–97, Dir. (non-exec.) 1997–; Fellow Textile Inst. *Leisure interests:* sailing, tennis, gardening. *Address:* c/o BAA PLC, 130 Wilton Road, London, SW1V 1LQ, England.

SMITH, Paul B., C.B.E.; British menswear designer and retailer; b. 5 July 1946, Nottingham; s. of late Harold B. Smith and Marjorie Smith; ed. Beeston Fields School, Nottingham; first Paul Smith Shop opened, Nottingham 1970, others in London 1979, 1982, 1983, 1987, 1998, New York 1987, first Paul Smith franchise shop in Hong Kong 1990, flagship store Tokyo, Japan 1991 (now over 200 shops in Japan); first Paul Smith Collection Show, Paris 1976; launched childrenswear collection 1991, toiletries range 1986, Paul Smith for Women 1994; designed limited edn. Mini 1998; Royal Designer for Industry R.C.A. 1991; Hon. M. Des. (Nottingham Polytechnic) 1991, Queen's Award for Industry 1995. *Address:* Paul Smith Ltd., 40/44 Floral Street, Covent Garden, London, WC2E 9DG, England. *Telephone:* 0171-836 7828. *Fax:* 0171-379 0241.

SMITH, Richard, C.B.E.; British artist; b. 1931, Letchworth, Herts.; m. Betsy Scherman; two s.; ed. Luton School of Art, St. Albans School of Art and Royal Coll. of Art; lived in New York 1959–61, 1963–65; teacher St. Martin's School of Art, London 1961–63; Artist-in-Residence, Univ. of Virginia 1967; Grand Prix São Paulo Bienal 1967; one-man exhbns. at the Kasmin Gallery 1963, 1967, Whitechapel Gallery 1966; participated in the Pittsburgh Int. 1961, New Shapes in Colour, Amsterdam, Berne and Stuttgart 1966–67 and in exhbns. at Guggenheim Museum, Tate Gallery, etc.; works represented in Tate Gallery, Stuyvesant Foundation, Contemporary Art Soc., the Ulster Museum, Belfast, the Walker Art Centre, etc.

SMITH, Richard John, A.M., B.A., LL.B.; Australian diplomatist; b. 14 Dec. 1934, Tamworth, N.S.W.; s. of C.A. Smith and T.A. O'Halloran; m. Janet Campbell 1958; two s. two d.; ed. Sydney High School, Sydney Univ.; teacher, London 1958–59; solicitor N.S.W. 1959–61; Foreign Affairs trainee 1961, First Sec., Washington 1967–70, Deputy Perm. Rep. Australian Mission to the U.N., Geneva 1972–74, Asst. Sec. Int. Legal Branch 1974–75; Amb. to Israel 1975–77; First Asst. Sec. Legal and Treaties Div. 1977–81, Man. and Foreign Service Div. 1981–83, Acting Deputy Sec. Dept. of Foreign Affairs 1983–85; Amb. to Thailand 1985–88; Deputy Sec. Dept. of Foreign Affairs and Trade, Canberra 1988–90; High Commr. in U.K. 1991–94; Amb. to the Philippines 1994–96; Dir. Gen. Office of Nat. Assessments, Canberra 1996–. *Leisure interests:* walking, reading, travel. *Address:* Office of National Assessments, P.O. Box E436, Queen Victoria Terrace, Canberra, ACT 2600, Australia.

SMITH, Robert Clinton, B.A.; American politician; b. 30 March 1941; s. of Donald Smith and Margaret Eldridge; m. Mary Jo Hutchinson 1966; two s. one d.; ed. Lafayette Coll. and Long Beach State Univ.; owner/Man. Yankee Pedlar Realtors, Wolfeboro, N.H. 1975–85; mem. 99th Congress from 1st District of N.H. 1985–91; Senator from New Hampshire 1990–; mem. Cttee. on Small Business, Cttee. on Science and Tech.; mem. Small Business Task Force, Congressional Leaders United for Balanced Budget; Republican. *Address:* U.S. Senate, 307 Dirksen Senate Office, Washington, DC 20510, U.S.A.

SMITH, Sir Robert Courtney, Kt., C.B.E., F.R.S.E., M.A., C.A.; British business executive; b. 10 Sept. 1927; s. of late John Smith and Agnes Smith; m. Moira R. Macdougall 1954; one s. two d. (and one s. deceased); ed. Kelvinside Acad. Glasgow, Sedbergh School and Trinity Coll. Cambridge; served Royal Marines 1945–47, Royal Marine Forces Volunteer Reserve 1951–57, Hon. Col. Royal Marine Reserve Scotland 1992–96; Partner, Arthur Young McClelland Moores & Co. (chartered accountants) 1957–78; Dir. Sidlaw Group (Chair. 1980–88), Standard Life Assurance (Chair. 1982–88), Volvo Trucks (GB), Edinburgh Investment Trust 1983–98, British Alcan Aluminium 1983–, Bank of Scotland 1985–97; Chair. Alliance and Second Alliance Trust 1984–96; fmr. Dir. William Collins (Vice-Chair. 1979–89); Chair. Scottish Industrial Devt. Bd. 1982–88; Chancellor's Assessor, Glasgow Univ. 1984–96; Hon. Col. H.M. Reserves, Scotland 1992–96; Hon. LL.D. (Glasgow) 1978 (Aberdeen) 1991; mem. Order of St. John. *Leisure interests:* racing, gardening. *Address:* 64 Reform Street, Dundee, DD1 1TJ, Scotland.

SMITH, (Robert) Harvey; British show jumper and farmer; b. 29 Dec. 1938; m. 1st Irene Shuttleworth (divorced 1986); two s.; m. 2nd Susan Dye 1987; winner of numerous int. show jumping competitions including John Player Trophy (7 times), King George V Gold Cup, British Jumping Derby (4 times); Grand Prix and Prix des Nations wins in UK, Ireland, Europe and U.S.A.; participated in Olympic Games 1968, 1972; BBC TV commentator, Olympic Games, Los Angeles 1984. *Publications:* Show Jumping with Harvey Smith 1979, Bedside Jumping 1985.

SMITH, Robert Howard, J.D.; American banker; b. 3 Sept. 1935, Glendale, Calif.; s. of James H. Smith and Marie V. Jenkins; m. Loretta M. Gesell 1958; three s. (one deceased), one d.; ed. Univ. of S. Calif. and Van Norman Univ. Los Angeles; various positions, Security Pacific Bank, Los Angeles 1961–66, Man. 1969–71, Regional Vice-Pres. 1971–74, Sr. Vice-Pres. 1974–80, Exec. Vice-Pres. 1980–84, Vice-Chair. 1984, Pres. and C.E.O. 1987–; Vice-Chair. Security Pacific Bank & Security Pacific Corpn. (now Bank America Corpn.) 1984–92; C.E.O. Security Pacific Corpn. 1990–92. *Address:* c/o Bank America Corporation, 555 California Street, San Francisco, CA 94104, U.S.A.

SMITH, Roger B., M.B.A.; American business executive (retd.); b. 12 July 1925, Columbus, Ohio; s. of Emmet Quimby and Bess (née Obetz) Smith; m. Barbara Ann Rasch 1954; two s. two d.; ed. Detroit Univ. School and Univ. of Mich.; served in U.S. Navy 1944–46; with Gen. Motors, Detroit 1949–90, Dir. Financial Analysis Section, Asst. Treas., New York 1960–68, Gen. Asst. Treas., Detroit 1968, Treas. 1970–71, Vice-Pres. Financial Staff 1971–72, Vice-Pres. and Group Exec., Nonautomotive and Defense Group 1972–74, Dir. 1974–90, Exec. Vice-Pres. 1974–81, Vice-Chair. Finance Cttee. 1975–80, Chair. and C.E.O. Gen. Motors 1981–90; Vice-Chair. Gen. Motors Cancer Research Foundation 1978–; mem. U.S. Corp. Council on S. Africa 1985–; Chair. Business Roundtable 1986–; Trustee Cranbrook Schools and Michigan Colls. Foundation; mem. Bd. of Dirs. Johnson and Johnson, Citicorp., Pepsi Co., Int. Paper Co., Council for Financial Aid to Educ., Motor Vehicle Mfrs. Asscn.; Dr. h.c. (DePauw Univ.) 1979. *Address:* c/o GM Corporation 31 East Judson Street, Pontiac, MI 48342 (Office); Bloomfield Hills, MI 48013, U.S.A. (Home).

SMITH, Sir Roland, Kt., B.A., PH.D.(ECON.); British business executive and professor; b. 1 Oct. 1928; s. of late Joshua Smith and of Hannah Smith; m. Joan Shaw 1954; ed. Univs. of Birmingham and Manchester; flying officer R.A.F. 1953; Asst. Dir. Footwear Mfrs. Fed. 1955; lecturer in Econs., Univ. of Liverpool 1960, Dir. Business School 1963; part-time Prof. of Marketing, Univ. of Manchester 1966–88, Prof. Emer. 1988–; Chair. Temple Bar Investment Trust Ltd. 1980–, House of Fraser 1981–86 (Deputy Chair. 1980–81), Readicut Int. 1984–96 (Deputy Chair. 1982–84), Hepworth PLC 1986–97, Phoenix Properties and Finance 1986–87, Kingston Oil and Gas 1987–91, British Aerospace 1987–92, P & P PLC 1988–97; Chair. Manchester United Football Club 1991–; Hon. Visiting Prof. UMIST 1988–, Chancellor Jan. 1996–; non-exec. Chair. Sr. Eng. Ltd. 1973–92; Dir. (non-exec.) Bank of England 1991–96; Hon. D.Sc. (Cranfield Inst. of Tech.) 1989. *Leisure interest:* walking.

SMITH, Wilbur Addison, B.COMM.; British author; b. 9 Jan. 1933, Zambia; m. Danielle Antoinette Smith 1971; two s. one d.; ed. Michaelhouse, Natal and Rhodes Univ.; business exec. 1954–58; factory owner 1958–64; professional author 1961–. *Publications:* When the Lion Feeds 1964, The Dark of the Sun 1965, The Sound of Thunder 1966, Shout at the Devil 1968, Gold Mine 1970, The Diamond Hunters 1971, The Sunbird 1972, Eagle in the Sky 1974, The Eye of the Tiger 1975, Cry Wolf 1976, A Sparrow Falls 1977, Hungry as the Sea 1978, Wild Justice 1979, A Falcon Flies 1980, Men of Men 1981, The Angels Weep 1982, The Leopard Hunts in Darkness 1984, The Burning Shore 1985, Power of the Sword 1986, Rage 1987, The Courtneys 1987, The Courtneys in Africa 1988, A Time to Die 1989, Golden Fox 1990, Elephant Song 1991, River God 1993, The Seventh Scroll 1995, Birds of Prey 1997. *Leisure interests:* fishing, wildlife. *Address:* c/o Charles Pick Consultancy, Flat 3, 3 Bryanston Place, London, W1H 7FN, England.

SMITH, Wilfred Cantwell, M.A., PH.D., D.D., LL.D., D.LITT., D.H.L.; Canadian university professor; b. 21 July 1916, Toronto; s. of Victor Arnold Smith and Sarah Cantwell; m. Dr. Muriel Struthers 1939; three s. two d.; ed. Upper Canada Coll., Univ. of Grenoble, Univ. of Madrid, American Univ., Cairo, Univ. of Toronto, Cambridge and Princeton Univs.; served as rep. among Muslims of the Canadian Overseas Missions Council, chiefly in Lahore 1940–49; lecturer in Indian and Islamic History, Forman Christian Coll., Lahore 1941–45; Prof. of Comparative Religion 1949–63, and Dir. Inst. of Islamic Studies, McGill Univ. 1951–63; Visiting Prof., London Univ. 1960, Princeton Univ. 1965, Univ. of Toronto 1968, Univ. of Washington 1978; Prof. of World Religions and Dir. Center for the Study of World Religions, Harvard Univ. 1964–73; McCulloch Prof. of Religion, Dalhousie Univ., Halifax, Canada 1973–78; Prof. of Comparative History of Religion and Chair., The Study of Religion, Harvard Univ. 1978–84, Prof. Emer. 1984–; Sr. Killam Fellow, Univ. of Toronto, Visiting Prof. of Religion, Trinity Coll., Toronto 1985–86; Pres. American Soc. for the Study of Religion 1966–69; Fellow, Royal Soc. of Canada (Pres. Humanities and Social Sciences Section 1972–73), American Acad. of Arts and Sciences; Pres. Middle East Studies Asscn. of N. America 1977–78, Pres. Canadian Theological Soc. 1979–80, Pres. American Acad. of Religion 1982–83; Chauveau Medal, Royal Soc. of Canada 1974. *Publications:* Modern Islam in India 1943, Islam in Modern History 1957, Meaning and End of Religion 1963, Faith of Other Men 1963, Questions of Religious Truth 1967, Religious Diversity 1976, Belief and History 1977, Faith and Belief 1979, Towards a World Theology 1981, On Understanding Islam 1981, What is Scripture? – a comparative approach 1993; works have been translated into 10 languages. *Address:* 877 Yonge Street, Toronto, Ont., M4W 3M2, Canada.

SMITH, Will; American actor and singer; b. 25 Sept. 1968, Philadelphia; m. 1st Sheree Smith; one s.; partner Jada Pinkett. *Television series:* The Fresh Prince of Bel Air 1990–. *Film appearances include:* Where the Day Takes You 1992, Made in America 1993, Six Degrees of Separation 1993, Bad Boys 1995, Independence Day 1996, Men in Black 1997, Enemy of the State 1998. *Albums include:* (as The Fresh Prince with DJ Jazzy Jeff) And in This Corner . . . 1989, Homebase 1991, Rock the House 1991, He's the DJ, I'm the Rapper 1988, Code Red 1993, Big Willie Style 1997. *Singles include:* Just One of Those Days 1987, Girls Ain't Nothing But Trouble 1988, Brand New Funk 1988, A Nightmare On My Street 1988, Jazzy's Groove 1989, I Think I Can Beat Mike Tyson 1989, The Things That U Do 1991, Summertime 1991, Ring My Bell 1991, I'm Looking for the One 1993, Boom! Shake the Room 1993. *Address:* c/o Creative Artists Agency, 9830 Wilshire Boulevard, Beverly Hills, CA 90212, U.S.A.

SMITH OF CLIFTON, Baron (Life Peer), cr. 1997, of Mountsandel in the County of Londonderry; **Trevor Arthur Smith,** Kt., B.SC.(ECON.), LL.D., F.R.HIST.S., F.R.S.A., C.I.MGT.; British university vice-chancellor; b. 14 June 1937, London; s. of the late Arthur J. Smith and Vera G. Cross; m. 1st Brenda Eustace 1960 (divorced 1973); two s.; m. 2nd Julia Bullock 1979; one d.; ed. London School of Econs.; schoolteacher, London 1958–59; Asst. Lecturer in Politics, Univ. of Exeter 1959–60; Research Officer, Acton Soc. Trust 1960–62; Lecturer in Politics, Univ. of Hull 1962–67; Lecturer, Queen Mary Coll. London 1967, Sr. Lecturer, Head Dept. 1972–85, Dean of Social

Studies 1979–82, Prof. of Politics 1983–91, Pro-Prin. 1985–87, Sr. Pro-Prin. 1987–89, Sr. Vice-Prin., Queen Mary & Westfield Coll. 1989–91; Vice-Chancellor and Hon Prof., Univ. of Ulster 1991–; Chair. Joseph Rowntree Reform Trust Ltd. 1987–, Political Studies Asscn. of U.K. 1988–89, Vice-Pres. 1989–91, Pres. 1991–93; Dir. Job Ownership Ltd. 1978–85, New Society Ltd. 1986–88, Statesman and Nation Publishing Co. Ltd. 1988–90, Bell Educ. Trust Ltd. 1988–93, Gerald Duckworth Ltd. 1990–95; Deputy Pres. Inst. for Citizenship Studies 1991–; Dir. Irish Peace Inst. 1992–; Pres. Belfast Civic Trust 1995–; mem. Admin. Bd. Int. Asscn. of Univs. 1995–96, Editorial Bd. Government and Opposition journal 1995–, Bd. A Taste of Ulster 1996–; Hon. LL.D. (Dublin) 1992, (Hull) 1993, (Belfast) 1995, (Nat. Univ. of Ireland) 1996; Hon. mem. of Senate (Fachhochschule Augsburg) 1994. *Publications:* Training Managers (with M. Argyle) 1962, Town Councillors (with A. M. Rees) 1964, Town and County Hall 1966, Anti-Politics 1972, The Fixers (with Alison Young) 1996; contributed to numerous other publs. *Leisure interest:* water-colour painting. *Address:* University House, University of Ulster, Coleraine, Co. Londonderry, BT52 1SA, Northern Ireland. *Telephone:* (01265) 324329. *Fax:* (01265) 324901.

SMITHERS, Sir Peter Henry Berry Otway, Kt., D.PHIL.; British politician and international civil servant; b. 9 Dec. 1913, Moor Allerton, Yorks.; s. of the late Lt.-Col. H. Otway Smithers, J.P. and Ethel M. M. Berry; m. Dorothy Jean Sayman 1943; two d.; ed. Harrow School and Magdalen Coll., Oxford; called to Bar, Inner Temple 1936, joined Lincoln's Inn 1937; Naval Service 1939–45; M.P. 1950–64; Parl. Pvt. Sec. to Minister of State for Colonies 1952–56, to Sec. of State for Colonies 1956–59; Vice-Chair. Conservative Parl. Foreign Affairs Cttee. 1958–62; Parl. Under-Sec. of State, Foreign Office 1962–64; mem. U.K. Del. to UN Gen. Ass. 1960–63, Consultative Ass., Council of Europe 1952–56, 1960; Vice-Pres. European Ass. of Local Authorities 1959–62; Sec.-Gen. Council of Europe 1964–69; Sr. Fellow UNITAR, New York 1969–73; Gen. Rapporteur, European Conf. of Parliamentarians and Scientists 1971–76; 22 one-man exhbns. of photography in U.S.A., U.K., France and Italy 1984–; Hon. Fellow Royal Horticultural Soc. 1996; Hon. Citizen of Vico Morcote 1994; Hon. Dr. jur. (Zürich) 1970; Humboldt Gold Medal (for int. work on conservation of nature and natural resources) 1970; Veitch Memorial Medal (Royal Horticultural Soc.) 1994 and 8 Royal Horticultural Soc. Gold Medals for Photography of Plants 1981–92; Medal of Honour of the Parl. Ass., Strasbourg 1984; Herbert Medal, Int. Bulb Soc. 1997; Chevalier, Légion d'honneur; Orden Mexicana de la Aguila Azteca. *Publications:* Life of Joseph Addison 1954, Adventures of a Gardener 1995, Gardening Book of the Year Award 1995. *Leisure interests:* horticulture, on line. *Address:* 6921 Vico Morcote, Switzerland. *Telephone:* 996-1973.

SMITHSON, Peter Denham; British architect; b. 18 Sept. 1923, Stockton-on-Tees; s. of William Blenkiron Smithson and Elizabeth Denham; m. Alison Margaret Gill (Smithson) 1949 (died 1993); one s. two d.; ed. Stockton-on-Tees Grammar School, Univ. of Durham and Royal Acad. Schools, London; Asst. of L.C.C. 1949–50; in private practice as architect with Alison Smithson 1950–; Visiting Prof. of Architecture, Bath Univ. 1978–89, Univ. of Delft 1982–83, Univ. of Munich 1984–85, Univ. of Barcelona 1985–86. *Principal works:* Hunstanton School; Economist Bldg., London; Robin Hood Gardens, G.L.C. Housing in Tower Hamlets; Garden Bldg. St. Hilda's Coll., Oxford; Amenity Building, Univ. of Bath; Second Arts Building, Univ. of Bath; 6E, Univ. of Bath; works at Tecta, Lauenforde, Germany 1986–97; works at The Hexenhaus, Bad Kaulshafen, Germany 1986–97. *Exhibitions:* Milan Triennale 1968, Venice Biennale 1976, Toy-Town, Canadian Centre for Architecture, Montreal 1997–98, On the Floor, Off the Floor, Cologne 1998, The Lattice, Cologne 1999. *Publications:* Urban Structuring Studies, Euston Arch, Ordinariness and Light, Without Rhetoric, The Heroic Period of Modern Architecture, The Shift: Monograph (all with A. Smithson), Walks Within the Walls, Bath, Oxford and Cambridge Walks, The 1930s (with A. Smithson), Changing the Art of Inhabitation. *Address:* Cato Lodge, 24 Gilston Road, London SW10 9SR, England. *Telephone:* 0171-373 7423; 0171-373 3838.

SMOLDEREN, Luc Hippolyte Marie, LL.D., PH.D.; Belgian diplomatist; b. 7 Feb. 1924, Antwerp; m. Baroness Fiorella de Vinck de Winnezeele 1954; one s. three d.; ed. Catholic Univ., Louvain; Attorney, Brussels 1950–53; joined Ministry of Foreign Affairs 1953; mem. Del. to UN, New York 1956–58, to NATO, Paris 1959–64; Inspector of Diplomatic Posts, Ministry of Foreign Affairs, Brussels 1965–71; Amb. to Syria 1971–76; Perm. Rep. to IAEA, Vienna 1976–80; Amb. to Morocco 1981–85, to France 1986–89; mem. Soc. Royale de Numismatique de Belgique (Pres.), Acad. Royale d'Archéologie de Belgique; Grand Officer Ordre de la Couronne de Belgique, de la Couronne de Chêne (Luxembourg), Commdr. Ordre de Léopold, de Léopold II, Ordine al Merito (Italy), Grand Cordon Order of Merit (Syria). *Publications:* Jonghelinck waradin de la Monnaie d'Anvers 1969, Quentin Metsys médailleur d'Erasme 1969, La Statue du duc d'Albe à Anvers 1972, Le Tombeau de Charles le Téméraire 1980, Jacques Jonghelinck, Sculpteur, Médailleur et Graveur de Sceaux (1530–1606) 1996; more than 20 studies on Flemish sculpture and medals in the 16th century. *Address:* 9 avenue de l'Observatoire, 1180 Uccle-Brussels, Belgium.

SMOLENSKY, Aleksander Pavlovich; Russian businessman and banker; b. 6 July 1954; m.; one s.; worked on enterprises of Moscow communal econ. 1974–87; many times persecuted by authorities for pvt. enterprising activities, was arrested 1981–82; deprived of the right to take responsible posts 1987; leader Construction-Assembly Co-operative, Moscow 1987–89; f. and Pres. Stolychny Bank (now Stolychny Savings Bank) 1991–; Chair. Bd. Agroprombank 1996–, United SSB-Agro Bank 1997; Order of Friendship of Peoples 1994. *Address:* SSB-Agro Bank, Pyatnitskaya str. 70, 113095 Moscow, Russia. *Telephone:* (095) 236-42-11.

SMOUT, Thomas Christopher, M.A., PH.D., F.R.S.E., F.B.A.; British historian; b. 19 Dec. 1933, Birmingham; s. of Sir Arthur J. G. Smout and Lady Smout (Hilda Smout, née Follows); m. Anne-Marie Schøning 1959; one s. one d.; ed. Leys School, Cambridge, Clare Coll. Cambridge; joined staff Edin. Univ. 1959, Prof. of Econ. History 1970–79; Prof. of Scottish History, Univ. of St. Andrews 1980–91, Dir. St. John's House Inst. for Advanced Historical Studies, Univ. of St. Andrews 1992–97, Inst. for Environmental History, Univ. of St. Andrews 1992–; Visiting Prof. Strathclyde Univ. 1991–, Dundee Univ. 1993–; Deputy Chair. Scottish Nat. Heritage 1992–97, mem. Bd. 1992–; Historiographer to the Queen in Scotland 1993–; mem. Bd. NCC (Scotland) 1991–92; Dr. h.c. (Queen's Univ., Belfast) 1995, (Edin.) 1996. *Publications:* Scottish Trade on the Eve of the Union 1963, History of the Scottish People, 1560–1830 1969, State of the Scottish Working Class in 1843 (with Ian Levitt) 1979, Scottish Population History from the 17th Century to the 1930s (with M. W. Flinn) 1976, Century of the Scottish People, 1830–1950 1986, Scottish Voices (with S. Wood) 1990, Prices, Food and Wages in Scotland (with A. Gibson) 1995. *Leisure interests:* birdwatching, conservation. *Address:* Chesterhill, Shore Road, Anstruther, Fife, KY10 3DZ, Scotland. *Telephone:* (01333) 310330.

SMURFIT, Anthony; Irish business executive; s. of Michael Smurfit (q.v.); mem. Bd., Jefferson Smurfit Group, Chief Exec. Smurfit France 1996–. *Address:* Smurfit France, 2 rue Goethe, 75116 Paris, France. *Telephone:* 1-4952-3200. *Fax:* 1-4952-3221.

SMURFIT, Michael, Jr., M.B.A.; Irish business executive; s. of Michael Smurfit (q.v.); ed. Michael Smurfit Grad. School of Business, Univ. Coll. Dublin; fmr. Vice-Pres. World Purchasing, Jefferson Smurfit Group, Pres. and Chief Exec., Smurfit Packaging Corpn. and Smurfit Paperboard Inc. 1996–. *Address:* Smurfit Packaging Corporation, 8182 Maryland, Clayton, MO 63105, U.S.A. *Telephone:* (314) 746-1203.

SMURFIT, Michael William Joseph; Irish business executive; b. 1936; m. 1st Norma Treisman (divorced); two s. two d.; m. 2nd Birgitta Beimark; two s.; joined Jefferson Smurfit & Sons Ltd. 1955; f. Jefferson Smurfit Packaging Ltd. (Lancashire) 1961; rejoined Jefferson Smurfit Group, Dir. 1964, Jt. Man. Dir. 1967, Deputy Chair. 1979; Chair. and C.E.O. Jefferson Smurfit Group PLC, Dublin 1977–; Chair. Jefferson Smurfit Corpn. & Container Corpn. of America, Dir. numerous Jefferson Smurfit subsidiaries and assocs.; fmr. Chair. Telecom Eireann; Hon. LL.D. (Trinity Coll., Dublin), (Univ. of Scranton, Pa.). *Address:* Jefferson Smurfit Group PLC, Beech Hill, Clonskeagh, Dublin 4, Ireland. *Telephone:* (01) 269 6622. *Fax:* (01) 269 4481.

SMYTH, Craig Hugh, A.B., M.F.A., PH.D.; American art historian and educationist; b. 28 July 1915, New York; s. of George Hugh Smyth and Lucy Salome Humeston; m. Barbara Linforth 1941; one s. one d.; ed. Hotchkiss School, Princeton Univ.; Research Asst. Nat. Gallery of Art, Wash., D.C. 1941–42; served in U.S. N.R. 1942–46; Officer-in-Charge, Dir. Cen. Art Collecting Point, Munich 1945–46; lecturer Frick Collection, New York 1946–50; Asst. Prof. of Fine Arts, Inst. of Fine Arts, New York Univ. 1950–53, Assoc. Prof. 1953–57, Prof. 1957–73, Acting Dir. 1951–53, Dir. 1953–73; Visiting Scholar, Inst. for Advanced Study, Princeton 1971, 1983, 1985, Bibliotheca Hertziana, Rome 1972, 1973; Prof. of Fine Arts, Harvard Univ. 1973–85, Prof. Emer. 1985–; Kress Prof. Center for Advanced Study in the Visual Arts, Nat. Gallery of Art, Washington 1987-88; Dir. Harvard Univ. Center of Italian Renaissance Studies, Florence 1973–85; mem. American Acad. of Arts and Sciences 1978, Inst. for Advanced Study, Princeton 1978, American Philosophical Soc. 1979; Chair. Advisory Cttee. for the Getty Center for Advanced Study 1982–, Comm. for the Conf. celebrating the 400th Anniversary of the Uffizi Gallery 1981–82; mem. Accad. Fiorentina delle Arti del Disegno 1978; Accad. di San Luca 1995; Alt. mem. Comité Int. d'Histoire d'Art 1970–83, mem. 1985–88; Trustee, The Burlington Magazine 1987–; Hon. Trustee, Metropolitan Museum of Art; Chevalier Légion d'honneur. *Publications:* Mannerism and Maniera 1963, revised edn. 1992, Bronzino as Draughtsman 1971, Michelangelo Architect (with H.A. Milton) 1988, Repatriation of Art from the Collecting Point in Munich after World War II 1988, ed. Michaelangelo Drawings Nat. Gallery of Art 1992, series of articles on Michelangelo and St. Peter's (with H. A. Millon) 1969–, articles on relations between Venice and Florence in painting and sculpture during 15th and 16th centuries 1979, ed. and contrib. to The Early Years of Art History in the United States: Notes and Essays on Departments, Teaching and Scholars 1993, The Early Years of Art History in The United States (with Peter M. Lukehart) 1994. *Leisure interests:* reading the classics, music. *Address:* P.O. Box 39, Cresskill, NJ 07626, U.S.A. *Telephone:* 201-568-5262.

SNEAD, Samuel Jackson; American golfer; b. 27 May 1912, Hot Springs, Va.; m. Audrey Snead; two s.; professional 1935–; Canadian Open Champion 1938, 1940, 1941; U.S. P.G.A. Champion 1942, 1949, 1951; British Open Champion 1946; four times runner-up U.S. Open; World Sr. Professional Champion 1964, 1965, 1970, 1972, 1973; played in seven Ryder Cup matches, twice as capt.; eight times in World Cup, four times in winning team; oldest professional to win a major tournament 1965; at age 62 tied for third place in U.S. P.G.A. Championship; 135 tournament wins (164 unofficially, with 84 official U.S. P.G.A. tournaments); U.S. P.G.A. Player of the Year 1949.

Publications: How to Hit a Golf Ball 1940, How to Play Golf 1946, Education of a Golfer (with Al Stump) 1962, The Driver 1974, Golf begins at Forty 1978. *Address:* c/o PGA, 100 Avenue of the Champions, Palm Beach Gardens, FL 33418, U.S.A.

SNEDDON, Ian Naismith, M.A., D.SC., F.R.S.E., F.R.S., F.I.M.A.; British professor of mathematics (retd.); b. 8 Dec. 1919, Glasgow; s. of Naismith and Mary Sneddon; m. Mary C. Macgregor 1943; two s. one d.; ed. Hyndland School, Glasgow, Univ. of Glasgow and Trinity Coll., Cambridge; Jr. Scientific Officer, Ministry of Supply 1942–45; Bryce Fellow in Math. Univ. of Glasgow 1945–46, lecturer in Natural Philosophy 1946–50, Simson Prof. of Math. 1956–85, Prof. Emer. 1985–; Prof. of Math. Univ. Coll. of North Staffs. (now Univ. of Keele) 1950–56; Visiting Prof. of Math., Univ. of Strathclyde 1985–91; Foreign mem. Polish Acad. of Sciences, Accad. delle Scienze di Torino; Eringen Prize (Soc. of Eng. Science, U.S.A.). *Publications:* Wave Mechanics and its Applications (with N. F. Mott) 1947, The Elements of Partial Differential Equations 1957, Mixed Boundary Value Problems in Potential Theory 1966, Crack Problems in the Mathematical Theory of Elasticity (with M. Lowengrub) 1969, An Introduction to the Use of Integral Transforms 1972, The Linear Theory of Themoelasticity 1974, The Solution of Ordinary Differential Equations (with E. L. Ince) 1987. *Leisure interests:* music, painting in oils. *Address:* 19 Crown Terrace, Glasgow, G12 9ES, Scotland. *Telephone:* 0141-339 4114.

SNEGUR, Mircea, DR.AGRI.SC.; Moldovan politician; b. 17 Jan. 1940, V. Trifăneşti, Floreşti Dist.; s. of Ion Snegur and Ana Snegur; m. Georgeta Snegur 1960; one s. one d.; ed. Kishinev Inst. of Agric.; mem. CPSU 1964–90; work as agronomist, man. state and collective farms 1967–71, with Ministry of Agric. 1971–78; Dir.-Gen. Research Production Asscn. "Selektsia", Kishinev 1978–81; Sec. C.P. Cttee., Yedinetsky Dist. 1981–85; Sec. Cen. Cttee. of CP of Moldavia 1985–89, Chair. Presidium of Supreme Soviet of Moldavia 1989–90; Chair. Supreme Soviet April–Sept. 1990; Pres. of Moldova 1990–96; Chair. Party of Resurrection and Accord and Leader of the Opposition 1996–. *Leisure interests:* billiards, history and detective fiction, sports programmes. *Address:* House of Parliament, Stefan Cel Mare Prosp. 105, Chişinău, Moldova.

SNELL, Esmond Emerson, B.A., M.A., PH.D.; American professor of biochemistry (retd.); b. 22 Sept. 1914, Salt Lake City, Utah; s. of Heber C. Snell and Hedwig Ludwig; m. Mary Caroline Terrill 1941; two s. one d. (and one s. deceased); ed. Brigham Young Univ. and Univ. of Wis.; Asst. Prof. of Chem., Univ. of Texas 1941–42, Assoc. Prof. 1943–45, Prof. 1951–56, Assoc. Dir. Clayton Foundation, Biochemical Inst. of Univ. of Texas 1954–56; Assoc. Prof. of Biochem., Univ. of Wis. 1945–47, Prof. 1947–51; Prof. of Biochem., Univ. of Calif. at Berkeley 1956–76, Chair. Dept. of Biochem. 1956–62; Prof. and Chair. Dept. of Microbiology, Univ. of Texas at Austin 1976–80, Ashbel Smith Prof. of Chemistry and Microbiology 1980–90, Emer. Prof. 1990–; Ed. Annual Review of Biochemistry 1962–64, 1968–83; Walker-Ames Visiting Prof. of Biochem., Univ. of Wash., Seattle 1953; Guggenheim Fellow, Univs. of Cambridge, Copenhagen and Zürich 1954–55, Max-Planck Inst. für Zellchemie, Munich 1962–63, Rockefeller Univ., New York, Hebrew Univ., Jerusalem, and Univs. of Freiburg and Würzburg 1970; mem. Editorial Bd., American Chemical Soc. 1948–58, Biological Chem. 1949–59, Biochemical and Biophysical Research Communications 1970–85, Biofactors 1988–91; mem. N.A.S., American Soc. of Biological Chemists (Pres. 1961–62), American Acad. of Arts and Sciences; Hon. D.Sc. (Wisconsin) 1982; Eli Lilly Award in Bacteriology and Immunology 1945, Meade-Johnson Vitamin B Complex Award 1946, Osborn Mendel Award 1951, Kenneth A. Spencer Award in Agricultural Chem. (American Chemical Soc.) 1973, U.S. Sr. Scientist Award, Humboldt Fund 1978, W. C. Rose Award (American Soc. of Biological Chemists) 1985. *Publications:* over 300 research papers in scientific journals, including Journal of Biological Chemistry, Journal of Bacteriology, Biochemistry, Proc. of N.A.S., Journal of American Chemical Soc.; Biochemical Preparations, Vol. III (Ed.) 1953, Methods in Enzymology (Contrib.) 1957, 1967, Comprehensive Biochemistry (Contrib.) 1963, 1964, 1971, International Union of Biochemistry Symposium Series, Vol. 30 1963, Vol. 35 1968 (Co-Ed.), Annual Review of Biochemistry (vols. 38 to 52) (Ed.). *Leisure interests:* travel, gardening. *Address:* Department of Microbiology, University of Texas at Austin, Austin, TX 78712; 5001 Greystone Drive, Austin, TX 78731, U.S.A. *Telephone:* (512) 471-5543. *Fax:* (512) 471-7088.

SNELLGROVE, David Llewelyn, LITT.D., PH.D., F.B.A.; British professor of Tibetan and author; b. 29 June 1920, Portsmouth; s. of Lieut.-Commdr. Clifford Snellgrove, R.N. and Eleanor M. Snellgrove; ed. Christ's Hospital, Horsham, Southampton Univ. and Queen's Coll., Cambridge; war service in India until 1946; Lecturer in Tibetan, S.O.A.S., Univ. of London 1950–60, Reader in Tibetan, Univ. of London 1960–74, Prof. of Tibetan 1974–82, Prof. Emer. 1982–; has undertaken numerous expeditions to India and the Himalayas; co-founder, Inst. of Tibetan Studies (now Inst. of Buddhist Studies), Tring, Herts. 1966, fmr. Chair. of Trustees; numerous overseas visits as visiting Prof. or consultant; expeditions in Indonesia 1987–94, in Cambodia 1995–; Rockefeller Grant 1961–64; Leverhulme Grant 1978–81. *Publications:* Buddhist Himalaya 1957, Himalayan Pilgrimage 1961, The Hevajra Tantra (2 vols.) 1959, The Nine Ways of Bon 1967, Four Lamas of Dolpo (2 vols.) 1967, A Cultural History of Tibet (with H. E. Richardson) 1968, The Cultural Heritage of Ladakh (with T. Skorupski) (2 vols.) 1979–80, Indo-Tibetan Buddhism, Indian Buddhists and their Tibetan successors 1986; gen. ed. and maj. contrib. The Image of the Buddha 1978. *Address:* Via Matteo Gay 26/7, 10066 Torre Pellice, Italy; Villa Bantay Chah, Krom 11, no. 0718, Siem Reap, Cambodia.

SNIJDERS, Wouter, LL.D.; Netherlands lawyer; b. 26 May 1928, Hilversum; s. of Emilius Paulus Snijders and Aleida Augustus Berendina Eskes; four c.; ed. Gymnasium Hilversum and Univ. of Amsterdam; lawyer Rotterdam 1954–58, Court's Clerk 1958–61, Judge Dist. Court 1961–70; Judge Raadsheer Supreme Court 1970–86, Vice-Pres. 1986–; Govt. Commr. New Civil Code 1971–; Hon. Dr. (Univ. of Leiden); mem. Koninklijke Med. Akad. van Wetenschappen. *Address:* Odijokstraat 6, II, 2596 AG Nassau, The Netherlands. *Telephone:* (070) 3248650.

SNIPES, Wesley; American actor; one s.; ed. High School for the Performing Arts, New York and State Univ. of New York, Purchase; fmr. telephone repair man, New York; Broadway appearances include Boys of Winter, Execution of Justice, Death and King's Horsemen, Waterdance; appeared in Martin Scorsese's video Bad 1987; ACE Award for Best Actor for Vietnam War Stories (TV) 1989. *Films:* Wildcats, Streets of Gold, Major League, Mo Better Blues 1990, Jungle Fever 1991, New Jack City, White Men Can't Jump, Demolition Man., Boiling Point, Sugar Hill, Drop Zone, To Wong Foo, Thanks for Everything, Julie Newmar 1995, The Money Train, Waiting to Exhale, The Fan 1996, One Night Stand, Murder at 1600, Blade 1997, The Vampire Slayer 1997, U.S. Marshals 1998, Down in the Delta (also co-producer) 1998; co-founder Struttin Street Stuff puppet theatre mid-1980s. *Address:* Amen RA Films, 9460 Wilshire Boulevard, Beverly Hills, CA 90212, U.S.A.

SNODGRASS, Anthony McElrea, D.PHIL, F.B.A., F.S.A.; British professor of archaeology; b. 7 July 1934, London; s. of Maj. W. M. Snodgrass and Kathleen M. Snodgrass; m. 1st Ann Vaughan 1959 (divorced 1978); three d.; m. 2nd Annemarie Künzl 1983; one s.; ed. Marlborough Coll. and Worcester Coll., Oxford; nat. service R.A.F. 1953–55; Lecturer in Classical Archaeology, Univ. of Edin. 1961–68, Reader 1968–75, Prof. 1975–76; Laurence Prof. of Classical Archaeology, Univ. of Cambridge 1976–; Sather Prof. in Classics, Univ. of Calif. at Berkeley 1984–85; Geddes-Harrower Prof. Univ. of Aberdeen 1995–96; Fellow, Clare Coll., Cambridge 1977–; Vice-Pres. British Acad. 1990–92; mem. Humanities Research Bd. 1994–95. *Publications:* Early Greek Armour and Weapons 1964, Arms and Armour of the Greeks 1967, The Dark Age of Greece 1971, Archaeology and the Rise of the Greek State 1977, Archaic Greece: the Age of Experiment 1980, An Archaeology of Greece 1987, Homer and the Artists 1998. *Leisure interests:* mountaineering, skiing. *Address:* Museum of Classical Archaeology, Sidgwick Avenue, Cambridge, CB3 9DA; Clare College, Cambridge, CB2 1TL, England. *Telephone:* (01223) 335960 (Museum).

SNODGRASS, W. D., M.A., M.F.A.; American poet, critic and teacher; b. 5 Jan. 1926, Wilkinsburg, Pa.; s. of Bruce DeWitt Snodgrass and Helen J. Murchie; m. 1st Lila Jean Hank 1946 (divorced 1953); one d.; m. 2nd Janice Marie Wilson 1954 (divorced 1966); one s. one step-d.; m. 3rd Camille Rykowski 1967 (divorced 1977); m. 4th Kathleen Brown 1985; ed. State Univ. of Iowa; Instructor, English Dept., Cornell Univ., Ithaca 1955–57, Univ. of Rochester 1957–58; Prof. English Dept., Wayne State Univ. 1959–68; Prof. English and Speech, Syracuse Univ. 1968–76; Distinguished Prof. of Creative Writing and Contemporary Poetry, Univ. of Delaware 1979–94; Visiting Prof., Old Dominion Univ., Norfolk, Va. 1978; Leader, Poetry Workshop, Morehead, Kentucky 1955, Yellow Springs, Ohio 1958, 1959; mem. Nat. Inst. of Arts and Letters 1972, Acad. American Poets 1973; Guggenheim Fellow 1972–73; Pulitzer Prize for Poetry 1960, Guinness Prize for Poetry 1961, Coll. of William and Mary Bicentennial Medal 1976, and other awards. *Publications:* Heart's Needle 1959, After Experience 1968, In Radical Pursuit (critical essays) 1975, The Führer Bunker (poems) 1977, Six Troubadour Songs (trans. with music), Traditional Hungarian Songs (trans. with music) 1978, If Birds Build with your Hair 1979, The Boy Made of Meat 1983, Six Minnesinger Songs (trans. with music) 1983, Magda Goebbels (poems) 1983, D.D. Byrde Callyng Jennie Wrenn (poem) 1984, The Four Seasons 1984, Remains 1985, The Death of Cock Robin 1987, Selected Poems, 1957–1987 1987, W. D.'s Midnight Carnival 1989, Autumn Variations 1990, Snow Songs 1992, Each in His Season 1993, The Führer Bunker: The Complete Cycle 1995, Selected Translations (poems and songs) 1998, After-Images (autobiographical sketches) 1999. *Leisure interests:* translating medieval music to be sung, playing the lute, woodcarving, owl-watching. *Address:* R.D.1, Box 51, Erieville, NY 13061, U.S.A. (Home).

SNOUSSI, Ahmed, PH.D.; Moroccan diplomatist; b. 22 April 1929, Meknes; m. Farida Snoussi; three c.; ed. Faculté de Droit, Univ. de Paris and Inst. des Hautes Etudes Politiques; Dir. of Public Information, Govt. of Morocco and ed. various publs. on foreign affairs 1958–60; Sec.-Gen. Ministry of Tourism, Information and Fine Arts 1963; Minister of Information 1967–71 (Moroccan Commr.-Gen. Expo 67, Montreal); Amb. of Kingdom of Morocco to Nigeria 1965, to Cameroon 1966, to Tunisia 1971, to Algeria 1973, to Mauritania and Envoy of the King to Heads of State 1978–79; Head Moroccan del. UN Security Council 1992–94; Amb. and Perm. Rep. of Morocco to UN 1997–; fmr. Chair. Exec. Bd. Somathon Tuna Fishing and Packing Corpn., Lafarge Maroc Group; fmr. Pres. Cinouca Corpn., Asscn. of Deep Sea Fishing Fleets, Nat. Producers Asscn. *Address:* Permanent Mission of the Kingdom of Morocco to the United Nations, 767 Third Avenue, 30th Floor, New York, NY 10017, U.S.A. *Telephone:* (212) 421-1580. *Fax:* (212) 980 1512.

SNOW, Jonathan George (Jon); British television journalist; b. 28 Sept. 1947; s. of late Rt. Rev. George Snow and Joan Snow; partner, Madeleine Colvin; two d.; ed. St. Edward's School, Oxford, Univ. of Liverpool; Voluntary Service Overseas, Uganda 1967–68; Co-ordinator New Horizon Youth Centre, London 1970–73 (Chair. 1986–); journalist, Independent Radio News, LBC 1973–76; reporter, ITN 1977–83, Washington Corresp. 1983–86, Diplomatic Ed. 1986–89; presenter, Channel Four News 1989–; Visiting Prof. of Broadcast Journalism, Nottingham Trent Univ. 1992–; Chair. Prison Reform Trust 1992–96, Media Trust 1995–, Single Homeless Action 1998–, Trustee Noel Buxton Trust 1992–, Stephen Lawrence Trust; Hon. D. Litt. (Nottingham Trent) 1994; Monte Carlo Golden Nymph Award, for Eritrea air attack reporting 1979, TV Reporter of the Year, for Afghanistan, Iran and Iraq reporting, Royal Television Soc. (RTS) 1980, Valiant for Truth Award, for El Salvador reporting 1982, Int. Award, for El Salvador reporting, RTS 1982, Home News Award, for Kegworth air crash reporting, RTS 1989, RTS Presenter of the Year 1994. *Publications:* Atlas of Today 1987, Sons and Mothers 1996. *Address:* Channel Four News, ITN, 200 Gray's Inn Road, London, WC1X 8HB, England. *Telephone:* 0171-430 4237. *Fax:* 0171-430 4607.

SNOW, Peter John, British television presenter, reporter and author; b. 20 April 1938, Dublin, Ireland; s. of Brig. John F. Snow, C.B.E. and Peggy Pringle; m. 1st Alison Carter 1964 (divorced 1975); one s. one d.; m. 2nd Ann Macmillan 1976; one s. two d.; ed. Wellington Coll. and Balliol Coll. Oxford; Second Lieut. Somerset Light Infantry 1956–58; newscaster and reporter, ITN 1962–79, diplomatic and defence corresp. 1966–79; presenter, BBC Newsnight 1979–97, Tomorrow's World 1997–, BBC Election Programmes 1983–, BBC Radio 4 Mastermind 1998–; Judges' Award, Royal TV Soc. 1998. *Publications:* Leila's Hijack War (jointly) 1970, Hussein: a biography 1972. *Leisure interests:* sailing, skiing, model railways, photography. *Address:* c/o BBC TV Centre, Wood Lane, London, W12 7RJ, England. *Telephone:* 0181-752 4646.

SNOWDON, 1st Earl of, cr. 1961; **Antony Charles Robert Armstrong-Jones,** G.C.V.O., F.R.S.A., R.D.I.; British photographer; b. 7 March 1930, London; s. of late Ronald Owen Lloyd Armstrong-Jones, M.B.E., Q.C., D.L., and the Countess of Rosse; m. 1st H.R.H. The Princess Margaret (q.v.) 1960 (divorced 1978); one s. one d.; m. 2nd Lucy Lindsay-Hogg 1979; one d.; ed. Eton Coll. and Jesus Coll., Cambridge; Consultant, Council of Industrial Design 1962–89; in charge of design of Investiture of H.R.H. the Prince of Wales, Caernarfon 1969; Editorial Adviser, Design Magazine 1961–87; Artistic Adviser to The Sunday Times and Sunday Times Publs. Ltd. 1962–90; photographer Telegraph Magazine 1990–96; Constable of Caernarfon Castle 1963–; Pres. Civic Trust for Wales, Contemporary Art Soc. for Wales, Welsh Theatre Co.; Vice-Pres. Univ. of Bristol Photographic Soc.; Sr. Fellow, Royal Coll. of Art 1986, Provost 1995–; Fellow, Inst. of British Photographers, British Inst. of Professional Photography, Chartered Soc. of Designers, Royal Photographic Soc., Royal Soc. of Arts, Manchester Coll. of Art and Design; mem. Faculty Royal Designers for Industry; Hon. mem. North Wales Soc. of Architects, South Wales Inst. of Architects; Chair. Snowdon Report on Integrating the Disabled 1972; mem. Council, Nat. Fund for Research for the Crippled Child; Founder Snowdon Award Scheme for Disabled Students 1980; Pres. (England) Int. Year of Disabled People 1981; Patron British Disabled Water Ski Asscn.; mem. The Prince of Wales Advisory Group on Disability 1983; Metropolitan Union of YMCAs, British Water Ski Fed., Welsh Nat. Rowing Club, Circle of Guide Dog Owners; designed Snowdon Aviary, London Zoo 1965 (Listed Grade II 1998), Chairmobile 1972; Dr. h.c. (Bradford) 1989; LL.D. (Bath) 1989; Dr. h.c. (Portsmouth) 1993; Art Dirs. Club of New York Certificate of Merit 1969, Soc. of Publication Designers Certificate of Merit 1970, The Wilson Hicks Certificate of Merit for Photocommunication 1971, Soc. of Publication Designers' Award of Excellence 1973, Design and Art Dirs. Award 1978, Royal Photographic Soc. Hood Award 1979, Silver Progress Medal, Royal Photographic Soc. 1986. *Television documentaries:* Don't Count the Candles (six awards, including two Emmys) 1968, Love of a Kind 1970, Born to be Small 1971, Happy being Happy 1973, Mary Kingsley 1975, Burke and Wills 1975, Peter, Tina and Steve 1977, Snowdon on Camera (presenter) 1981. *Exhibitions:* Photocall, London 1958, Assignments, Cologne, London, Brussels 1974, U.S.A., Canada, Japan, Australia, Denmark, France, Holland, Serendipity, Brighton, Bradford 1989, Bath 1990, Snowdon on Stage 1996. *Publications:* London 1958, Malta (in collaboration with Sacheverell Sitwell) 1958, Private View (with John Russell and Bryan Robertson) 1965, Assignments 1972, A View of Venice (with Derek Hart) 1972, Inchcape Review 1977, Pride of the Shires (jointly) 1979, Personal View 1979, Tasmania Essay 1981, Sittings: 1979–83 1983, Israel: A First View 1986, My Wales (with Viscount Tonypandy) 1986, Stills 1983–87, 1987, Public Appearances 1987–1991 1991, Wild Flowers 1995, Snowdon on Stage 1996, Wild Fruit 1997. *Leisure interest:* photography. *Address:* 22 Launceston Place, London, W8 5RL, England. *Telephone:* 0171-937 1524.

SNOWE, Olympia J., B.A.; American politician; b. 21 Feb. 1947, Augusta, Maine; d. of George Bouchles and Georgia Bouchles; m. John McKernan (q.v.) 1969; ed. Univ. of Maine; mem. Maine House of Reps. 1973–76, Maine Senate 1976–78; mem. 96th–103rd Congresses from 2nd Maine Dist. 1979–95; Deputy Republican Whip; Senator from Maine Jan. 1995–; Hon. LL.D. (Husson Coll.) 1981, (Maine) 1982, (Bowdoin Coll.) 1985. *Address:* U.S. Senate, 250 Russell Senate Building, Washington, DC 20510, U.S.A.

SNOWMAN, A. Kenneth; C.B.E., F.S.A.; British antique dealer; b. 26 July 1919, London; s. of Emanuel Snowman, M.V.O., O.B.E. and Harriette Snowman (née Wartski); m. Sallie Moghilevkine 1942 (died 1995); one s.; ed. University College School, London, St. Martin's School of Art, Byam Shaw School of Art (under F. Ernest Jackson); War Painter, mem. Civil Defence during Second World War; exhibited frequently at Royal Acad.; also exhibited at Salon, Paris, Leicester Galleries, London; has illustrated several children's books; joined family firm Wartski 1940, now Chair.; organized Fabergé Exhbn., Victoria and Albert Museum, London 1977; Guest Curator, Cooper Hewitt Museum, New York 1983; Pres. British Antique Dealers Asscn. 1976–77; Chair. Burlington House Fair, Royal Acad. (original Antique Dealers' Fair); Liveryman, Goldsmiths Co. and Painter Stainers Co. *Publications:* The Art of Carl Fabergé 1953, Eighteenth Century Gold Boxes of Europe 1966, Eighteenth Century Gold Boxes of Paris 1974, Carl Fabergé, goldsmith to the Imperial Court of Russia 1979; catalogue Fabergé Exhbn., Victoria and Albert Museum 1977, Fabergé Exhbn., Cooper Hewitt Museum 1983; contrib. to catalogue Munich Fabergé Exhbn. 1986–87, Helsinki Fabergé Exhbn. 1980, Connoisseur Dictionary of Antiques 1955, Great Houses of Europe 1961, Great Private Collections 1963, Masterpieces from the House of Fabergé 1984, Fabergé, Lost and Found 1993; introduction to Fabergé, Imperial Jeweller (exhbn. 1993–94); contrib. for many years to Connoisseur, Apollo and Antique Collector magazines and to Antiques Magazine, New York. *Leisure interests:* painting, writing. *Address:* 14 Grafton Street, London, W1X 4DE, England (Office). *Telephone:* 0171-493 1141 (Office). *Fax:* 0171-409 7448.

SNOWMAN, (Michael) Nicholas, M.A.; British music administrator; b. 18 March 1944, London; s. of Kenneth Snowman and the late Sallie Snowman (née Moghilevkine); m. Margo Michelle Rouard 1983; one s.; ed. Hall School and Highgate School, London, Magdalene Coll. Cambridge; Asst. to Head of Music Staff, Glyndebourne Festival 1967–69; Co-founder and Gen. Man. London Sinfonietta 1968–72; Admin. Music Theatre Ensemble 1968–71; Artistic Dir. Institut de Recherche et de Coordination Acoustique/Musique (IRCAM), Centre d'Art et de la Culture Georges Pompidou 1972–86; Co-founder and Artistic Adviser Ensemble InterContemporain 1975–92, mem. Bd. 1992–, Vice-Chair. 1998–; mem. Music Cttee. Venice Biennale 1979–86; Artistic Dir. Projects in 1980, 1981, 1983, Festival d'Automne de Paris; Programme Consultant Cité de la Musique, La Villette, Paris 1991–92; Gen. Dir. (Arts) South Bank Centre, London 1986–92, Chief Exec. 1992–98; Gen. Dir. Glyndebourne Opera 1998–; mem. British Section, Franco-British Council 1995–; Trustee New Berlioz Edn. 1996–; Gov. Royal Acad. of Music 1998–, Nat. Opera Studio 1998–; Chevalier Ordre Nat. du Mérite, Officier Ordre des Arts et des Lettres, Polish Order of Cultural Merit. *Publications:* The Best of Granta (Co-Ed.) 1967, The Contemporary Composers (Series Ed.) 1982–; papers and articles on music, cultural policy and France. *Leisure interests:* films, eating, spy novels. *Address:* Glyndebourne, Lewes, East Sussex, BN8 5UU, England. *Telephone:* (01273) 812321. *Fax:* (01273) 814088.

SNYDER, Allan Whitenack, D.SC., F.A.A., F.T.S., F.R.S.; American/Australian optical scientist; b. 28 Nov. 1940; s. of E. H. Snyder and Zelda Cotton; ed. Cen. High School, Pa. State Univ., M.I.T., Harvard Univ. and Univ. Coll., London Univ.; Greenland Ice Cap Communications Project 1961; Consultant, Gen. Telecommunications and Electricity Research Lab. 1963–67, British Post Office and Standard Telecommunications Lab. 1968–70; Sr. Research Fellow, later Prof. Fellow, A.N.U. 1971–79, Chair. Optical Physics and Visual Sciences Inst. for Advanced Studies 1978–, Head Applied Math. 1979–82, Founder and Head Optical Sciences Centre 1983–, Foundation Dir. Centre for the Mind 1997, Peter Karmel Professorial Chair of Science and the Mind 1997; Nat. Science Foundation Fellowship, Dept. of Applied Physics, Yale Univ. Medical School, U.S.A. 1970–71; Guggenheim Fellow 1977, Foundation Fellow, Nat. Vision Research Inst. of Australia 1983, Royal Soc. Quest Research Fellow, Cambridge Univ., England 1987; Assoc. Ed. Journal of Optical Soc. of America 1981–83; Research Medal, Royal Soc. of Vic. 1974, Thomas Rankin Lyle Medal, Australian Acad. of Science 1985, Edgeworth David Medal, Royal Soc. of N.S.W., Sutherland Memorial Medal, Australian Acad. of Technological Sciences 1991, CSIRO Research Medal 1995, Harrie Massey Medal and Prize, British Inst. of Physics 1996, Arthur E. Mills Oration and Medal, R.A.C.P. 1966, Int. Australia Prize 1997. *Publications include:* Photoreceptors Optics (jtly.) 1975, Optical Waveguide Sciences (jtly.) 1983, Optical Waveguide Theory (jtly.) 1983. *Leisure interests:* art, thought and mind. *Address:* Optical Sciences Centre, Research School of Physical Sciences and Engineering, Australian National University, Canberra, A.C.T. 2601, Australia (Office). *Telephone:* (6) 2492626 (Office). *Fax:* (6) 249 5184.

SNYDER, Richard E.; American publisher; b. 6 April 1933, New York; s. of Jack Snyder and Molly Rothman; m. 1st Otilie Freund 1963 (divorced); one s. one d.; m. 2nd Laura Yorke 1992; ed. Tufts Univ., Medford; sales rep. Simon & Schuster 1961, Vice-Pres. Marketing 1966–69, Vice-Pres. Trade Books 1969–73, Exec. Vice-Pres. Trade and Educ. Admin. 1973–75, Pres. and C.O.O. 1975–78, Pres. and C.E.O. 1978–86, Chair. and C.E.O. 1986–94, consultant 1994–95; Chair., C.E.O. Golden Books Family Entertainment 1996–; Chair. PEN, N.Y. Area 1988; Dir. Reliance Group Holdings, Children's Blood Foundation; f. mem. Nat. Book Foundation, Nat. Book Awards; mem. Council on Foreign Relations, N.Y. Zoological Soc. business cttee., other appointments. *Address:* Golden Books Family Entertainment Inc., 850 3rd Avenue, New York, NY 10022, U.S.A.

SOARES, Mário Alberto Nobre Lopes, L. ÈS L., D. EN D.; Portuguese politician, lawyer and historian; b. 7 Dec. 1924, Lisbon; s. of João Lopes Soares and Elisa Nobre Soares; m. Maria Barroso Soares 1949; one s. one d.; ed. Univ. of Lisbon, Faculty of Law, Sorbonne, Paris; active opponent to Salazar's dictatorship; deported to São Tomé March–Nov. 1968; rep. of Portuguese socialists at various European socialist congresses and 11th Congress of Socialist Int., Eastbourne, U.K. 1969; Portuguese rep. Int. League of Human Rights; imprisoned 12 times on political grounds; in exile in Paris 1970–74, returned to Portugal after coup April 1974; f. Partido Socialista 1973, Sec.-Gen. 1973–86; Vice-Pres. Socialist Int. 1976–86, Hon. Pres. 1986–; Minister of Foreign Affairs 1974–75; in charge of negotiations leading to independence of Portuguese colonies; Minister without Portfolio March-Aug. 1975; Deputy, Constituent Ass. 1975, Legis. Ass. 1976; mem. Council of State; Prime Minister of Portugal for three periods 1976–85; initiated negotiations in 1977 leading to Portugal joining the European Community, as Prime Minister signed Treaty of Accession June 1985; Pres. of Portugal 1986–96; Pres. Ind. World Comm. on the Oceans 1995–, Portugal Africa Foundation 1997–, European Movt. 1997, Steering Cttee. World Water Contract, Cttee. of Experts; fmr. Pres. Council of Europe; State Councillor; Corresp. mem. Academia Brasileira de Letras; Dr. h.c. (Rennes, Hankuk, Lancaster, São Paulo, Brown, Salamanca, Princeton, Bologna, Turin, Sorbonne, Univ. Libre Bruxelles, Oxon., Leicester); Joseph Lemaire Prize 1975, Int. Prize of Human Rights 1977, Robert Schuman Prize 1987; numerous Portuguese and foreign decorations. *Publications:* As ideias político-sociais de Teófilo Braga 1950, Escritos Políticos 1969, Portugal's Struggle for Liberty 1972, Destruir o Sistema, Construir uma Vida Nova 1973, Caminho Difícil, do Salazarismo ao Caetanismo 1973, Escritos do Exílio 1975, Liberdade para Portugal (with Willy Brandt and Bruno Kreisky) 1975, Portugal, quelle Révolution? 1976, O Futuro será o Socialismo Democrático 1979, Resposta Socialista para o Mundo em Crise 1983, Persistir 1983, A Árvore e a Floresta 1985, Intervenções I–VI 1987–92, Vols. VII–VIII 1994, Moderador e Árbitro 1995; contribs. to República, Seara Nova, Ibéria (New York) etc. *Leisure interests:* books, and collecting contemporary Portuguese paintings. *Address:* Rua Dr. João Soares, 2-3, 1600 Lisbon, Portugal (Home).

SOARES ALVES, Francisco José, M.A.; Portuguese archaeologist; b. 18 April 1942, Lisbon; s. of José Augusto Ferreira Alves and Margaret Hellen Libbie Mason Soares; m. (divorced); ed. D. João de Castro High School, Lisbon, Univ. of Paris, DEA—Inst. d'Art et d'Archéologie, Paris; Dir. archaeological campus, Braga (Bracara Augusta) 1976–80; Dir. Portuguese Dept. of Archaeology 1980–82; Dir. Nat. Museum of Archaeology 1980–96; Dir. of underwater archaeology on the site of "L'Océan" (French flagship sunk in 1759) 1984–. *Leisure interest:* diving. *Address:* c/o Museu Nacional de Arqueologia e Etnologia, Praça do Império, 1400 Lisbon, Portugal.

SOBCHAK, Anatoliy Aleksandrovich, D.JUR.; Russian politician and academic lawyer; b. 1937, Chita; m. Lyudmila Borisovna Naroussova; one d. (and one d. by previous m.); ed. Leningrad Univ.; mem. CPSU 1988–90; lawyer in Stavropol, lecturer, Leningrad School of Militia, then Inst. of Tech.; head of Law Faculty, Leningrad Univ.; People's Deputy 1989–91, mem. U.S.S.R. Supreme Soviet 1989–91; mem. Political Consultative Council Sept. 1991–; Chair. of Comm. established by Congress of People's deputies to investigate killing of participants in April 1989 Tbilisi riots; mem. of Supreme Soviet Cttee. for Questions of Legislation, Legality and Law and Order; founder-mem. of Inter-Regional group of deputies within the Soviet Parliament; Chair. City Soviet of Leningrad 1990–91, Mayor of St. Petersburg 1991–96; living in Paris 1997–. *Publications:* Khozdeniye vo Vlast (Pilgrimage into Power) 1991, For A New Russia 1992, Tbilisi Breakdown: Bloody Sunday 1993. *Address:* c/o Naberezhnaya Moyki 31, Apt. 8, St. Petersburg, Russia. *Telephone:* (812) 110-63-72.

SOBERS, Sir Garfield (Gary) St. Aubrun, Kt.; Barbadian cricketer; b. 28 July 1936, Bridgetown; s. of Thelma and John Sobers; m. Prudence Kirby 1969; two s. one d.; ed. Bay St. School, Barbados; left-hand batsman, left-arm bowler, using all kinds of bowling; outstanding all-rounder; teams: Barbados 1952–74 (Capt. 1965–71), S. Australia 1961–64, Notts. 1968–74 (Capt. 1968–71, 1973); 93 Tests for W. Indies 1953–74, 39 as Capt., scoring 8,032 runs (average 57.7) with 26 hundreds, including record 365 not out (record 1958–94), taking 235 wickets (average 34.0) and holding 109 catches; scored 28,315 runs (86 hundreds), took 1,043 wickets and held 407 catches in first-class cricket; hit 6 sixes in an over, Notts. v. Glamorgan at Swansea 1968; toured England 1957, 1963, 1966, 1969, 1973; Hon. Life mem. M.C.C. 1981. *Publications:* Cricket Advance 1965, Cricket Crusader 1966, King Cricket 1967 (with J. S. Barker), Cricket in the Sun (with J. S. Barker) 1967, Bonaventure and the Flashing Blade 1967, Sobers: Twenty Years at the Top 1988, Sobers: The Changing Face of Cricket (with Peter Simmonds) 1995. *Address:* c/o West Indies Cricket Board, P.O. Box 616, St. John's, Antigua, West Indies.

SOBOLEV, Viktor Viktorovich; Russian astronomer; b. 2 Sept. 1915, Petrograd; ed. Univ. of Leningrad (now St. Petersburg); Chair. of Dept. of Astrophysics, Univ. of Leningrad 1948–, Prof. 1949–; corresp. mem. U.S.S.R. (now Russian) Acad. of Sciences 1958–81, mem. 1981–; Dir. Leningrad (now St. Petersburg) Univ. Observatory 1961–62, Chief scientific researcher 1962–; Hero of Socialist Labour 1985, Order of Lenin. *Publications:* Moving Envelopes of Stars 1960, A Treatise on Radative Transfer 1963, Light Scattering in Planetary Atmospheres 1975, etc. *Leisure interests:* chess, poetry, tennis. *Address:* St. Petersburg State University, 10-ya Liniya 33, 199178 St. Petersburg, Russia. *Telephone:* (812) 218-44-38 (Office); 114-51-23 (Home).

SODANO, H.E. Cardinal Angelo, S.T.D., J.C.D.; Italian ecclesiastic; b. 23 Nov. 1927, Isola d'Asti; s. of Hon. Giovanni Sodano and Delfina Brignolo; ed. Pontifical Gregorian Univ. Rome, Pontifical Lateran Univ. Rome and Pontifical Ecclesiastical Acad. Rome; Sec. Apostolic Nunciatures in Ecuador, Uruguay and Chile 1961–68; official, Council for Public Affairs of Church, Vatican City State 1968–77; Apostolic Nuncio, Chile 1978–88; Sec. Council for Public Affairs of the Church 1988–89; Sec. for Relations with States of Secr. of State 1989–90; Pro-Sec. of State of His Holiness Pope John Paul II 1990–91; cr. Cardinal 1991, Sec. of State 1991–; Titular Bishop of Albano; mem. Congregations for the Doctrine of the Faith, for the Bishops; other appointments; numerous honours and awards. *Address:* Office of the Secretary of State, 00120 Vatican City State. *Telephone:* (396) 698-83913. *Fax:* (396) 698-85255.

SÖDER, Karin Anne-Marie; Swedish politician; b. 30 Nov. 1928, Frykerud; d. of Yngve and Lilly Bergenfur; m. Gunnar Söder 1952; two s. one d.; elementary school teacher 1950–64; vocational guidance teacher 1965–70; mem. Stockholm Co. Council 1968–73; mem. Riksdag (Parl.) 1971–91; Minister for Foreign Affairs 1976–78, for Social Affairs and Nordic Affairs 1979–82; Second Vice-Chair. Centre Party 1971–79, First Vice-Chair. 1979–85, Chair. 1986–87; mem. Swedish Social Welfare Bd. 1972–76, Nat. Courts Admin. Bd. 1975–76; Chair. Governing Bd. Stockholm Peace Research Inst. 1978–79, Swedish Del. to Nordic Council 1984–91, Middle Parties group of reps. to Nordic Council 1984–90; Pres. Swedish Save the Children Asscn. 1983–95; Vice-Chair. Stockholm Int. Environmental Inst. 1989–93, Chair. 1993–97; mem. Bd. Royal Inst. of Tech., Stockholm 1988–97, Vice-Chair. 1994–97; Chair. The Letterstedt Soc. 1991, Selma Lagerlöf Soc. 1998; mem. China Council for Int. Co-operation on Environment and Devt. 1992–96; mem. Bd. Skandia 1987–, Wermlandsbanken 1988–92; Dr. Tech. h.c. 1995. *Leisure interests:* music, nature, mountain trekking. *Address:* Näsbydalsvägen 10, 183 63 Täby, Sweden.

SÖDERBERG, Erik Axel Olof R:son, M.SC.; Swedish business executive; b. 17 Nov. 1926, Stockholm; s. of Ragnar O. Söderberg and Ingegerd A. Wallenberg; m. 1st Helene M. Schultz 1948; two s. two d.; m. 2nd Sonja Blichfeldt 1980; ed. Univ. of Commerce, Göteborg and Columbia Univ., New York; Dir. Söderberg & Haak AB, Stockholm 1952, Vice-Pres. 1954–66; Man. Dir. Förvaltnings AB Ratos, Stockholm (investment co.) 1958–69, Chair. 1974–95; Man. Dir. AB Nordiska Kompaniet 1966–76; Hon. R.V.O., Hon. C.B.E. 1969. *Leisure interests:* golf, yachting, skiing, reading, racehorse owner. *Address:* Box 1661, S-111 96 Stockholm, Sweden. *Telephone:* (8) 700 1700 (Office).

SODERBERG, Nancy E., B.A.; American government official; b. 13 March 1958, San Turce, Puerto Rico; d. of Lars Olof Soderberg and Nancy (MacGilvrey) Soderberg; ed. Vanderbilt Univ., Georgetown Univ.; budget and reports analyst, Bank of New England, Boston 1980–82; Research Asst. Brookings Inst., Washington, D.C. 1982–83; Research Asst., U.S. Agency for Int. Devt., Washington 1983; Del. Selection Asst., Mondale-Ferraro Cttee., Washington 1983, Foreign Policy Adviser 1984; Deputy Issues Dir., Foreign Policy, Dukakis for Pres. Cttee., Boston 1988; Foreign Policy Adviser to Senator Edward Kennedy, Washington 1985–88, 1989–92; Foreign Policy Dir. Clinton/Gore Transition, Little Rock 1992–93; Special Asst. to Pres. for Nat. Security Affairs, Staff Dir. Nat. Security Council, Washington 1993–95, Deputy Asst. to Pres. for Nat. Security Affairs 1995–; mem. Council for Foreign Relations. *Address:* National Security Council, The White House, 1600 Pennsylvania Avenue, N.W., Washington, DC 20500, U.S.A.

SODERBERGH, Steven; American film director; b. 14 Jan. 1963, Atlanta; s. of Peter Andrew Soderbergh and Mary Ann Bernard; m. Elizabeth Jeanne Brantley 1989 (divorced 1994); ed. high school and animation course at Louisiana State Univ.; aged 15 made short film Janitor; briefly ed. Games People Play (TV show); made short film Rapid Eye Movement while working as coin-changer in video arcade; produced video for Showtime for their album 90125 (Grammy nomination); author, screenplay for Sex, Lies and Videotape. *Films:* Sex, Lies and Videotape 1989 (Cannes Palme d'Or 1989), Kafka 1991, The Last Ship 1991, King of the Hill 1993, The Underneath 1996, Schizopolis 1996, Out of Sight 1998; exec. producer Suture 1994, The Daytrippers 1996, writer Mimic 1997, Nightwatch 1998. *Address:* P.O. Box 2000, Orange, VA 22960, U.S.A.

SÖDERSTROM, Elisabeth Anna, C.B.E.; Swedish soprano opera singer; b. 7 May 1927; m. Sverker Olow 1950; three s.; studied singing under Andrejewa de Skilonz and Opera School, Stockholm; engaged at Royal Opera, Stockholm 1950–; appearances at Salzburg 1955, Glyndebourne 1957, 1959, 1961, 1963, 1964, 1979, Metropolitan Opera, New York 1959, 1960, 1962, 1963, 1983, 1984, 1986, 1987; frequent concert and TV appearances in Europe and U.S.A.; toured U.S.S.R. 1966; Artistic Dir. Drottningholm Court Theatre 1993–97; mem. Royal Acad. of Music, Hon. R.A.M.; Singer of the Court (Sweden) 1959; Prize for Best Acting, Royal Swedish Acad. 1965, "Literis et Artibus" award 1969; Order of Vasa, Stelle della Solidarietà dell'Italia, Commdr. of the Order of Vasa 1973, Commandeur des Arts et des Lettres 1986. *Roles include:* Fiordiligi (Così fan Tutte), Countess and Susanna (Figaro), Countess (Capriccio), Christine (Intermezzo); sang three leading roles in Der Rosenkavalier 1959. *Publications:* I Min Tonart 1978, Sjung ut Elisabeth 1986. *Leisure interests:* sailing, literature, embroidery.

Address: Drottningholms Teatermuseum, Box 27050, 10251, Stockholm 27, Sweden. *Telephone:* (8) 665 1452. *Fax:* (8) 665 1473.

SODNOM, Dumaagiyn; Mongolian politician; b. 1933; ed. School of Finance and Econs., Ulaanbaatar, Higher School of Finance and Econs., U.S.S.R.; Expert, Ministry of Finance 1950–54, Dir. of Dept. in Ministry 1958–63; Minister of Finance 1963–69; First Deputy Chair. State Planning Comm. with rank of Minister 1969–72, Chair. State Planning Comm. 1972–74; Deputy Chair. Council of Ministers 1974–84, Chair. 1984–90 (resgnd.); mem. Cen. Cttee. Mongolian People's Revolutionary Party (MPRP) 1966, mem. Political Bureau 1984–90; Deputy, Great People's Hural (Assembly) 1966–90; Dir. State Oil Co. 1990–92; Counsellor to the Prime Minister 1992–. *Address:* Office of the Prime Minister, Ulan Bator, Mongolia.

SOEHARTO (see **SUHARTO**).

SOFAER, Abraham David, LL.D.; American lawyer; b. 6 May 1938, Bombay, India; m. Marian Bea Scheuer 1977; five s. one d.; ed. Yeshiva Coll. and New York Univ.; called to New York Bar 1965; law clerk, U.S. Court of Appeals 1965–66, to Hon. William J. Brennan, Jr., U.S. Supreme Court 1966–67; Asst. U.S. Attorney, South Dist., New York 1967–69; Prof. of Law, Columbia Univ. 1969–79; Judge, U.S. Dist. Court for South Dist., New York 1979–85; Legal Adviser, State Dept., Washington, D.C. 1985–90; partner Hughes Hubbard and Reed 1991–94; George P. Shultz Distinguished Scholar, Sr. Fellow, Hoover Inst. 1994–; Prof. of Law, Stanford Univ., Calif. 1996–. *Publications:* War, Foreign Affairs and Constitutional Power: The Origins 1976; articles in legal journals. *Address:* The Hoover Institution, Stanford University, Stanford, CA 94305 (Office); 1200 Bryant Street, Pala Alto, CA 94301, U.S.A (Home). *Telephone:* (650) 725-3763 (Office). *Fax:* (650) 723-2103 (Office).

SOFOLA, Chief Idowu, Bobagunwa of Remo, Balogun of Idotun-Ikenne Remo, Aare Maiyegun of Owu-Abeokuta; Nigerian lawyer; b. 29 Sept. 1934, Ikenne, Ogun State; s. of late Chief Sanni Sofola and Chief Salamotu Sofola; m. Olusola Sofola 1963; four s. one d.; ed. Eko Boys High School, Lagos, Westminster Coll. of Commerce and Holborn Coll. of Law, London; Gen. Sec. Nigerian Bar Asscn. 1979–81; Asst. Sec.-Gen. Int. Bar. Asscn. 1980–82, Deputy Sec.-Gen. 1982–86, Sec.-Gen. 1986–88, Nigerian Rep., and mem. several cttees.; mem. Gen. Council of the Bar 1978–83; mem. Body of Benchers 1983–; admitted to Inner Bar, Sr. Advocate of Nigeria June 1989; mem. Comm. Boy Scouts; Distinguished Citizen of Ogun State. *Leisure interest:* table tennis. *Address:* 132 Broad Street, P.O. Box 5854, Lagos, Nigeria. *Telephone:* 2664245 (Office); 4973913 (Home, Lagos); 037-630087 (Home, Ikenne). *Fax:* (01) 2664449/2619436.

SOGLO, Nicéphore, B.A.; Benin politician; b. 29 Nov. 1934, Lomé, Togo; ed. Univ. of Paris-Sorbonne and Ecole nat. d'admin., Paris, France; fmr. inspector-gen. of finances, tech. adviser, Finance Ministry; Head Finance Dept. 1963; fmr. Chair. Nat. Monetary Comm., other financial insts.; Gov. IMF 1964; Prime Minister of Benin 1990–91, Pres. of Benin 1991–96; leader Parti de la Renaissance de Benin. *Address:* c/o Office of the President, P.O. Box 1288, Cotonou, Benin.

SOHLMAN, Staffan A.R., B.A.; Swedish diplomatist; b. 21 Jan. 1937, Rome, Italy; s. of Rolf R. Sohlman and Zinaida Jarotskaja; m. Åsa Maria Carnerud 1961; one s. one d.; ed. Sigtuna Humanistiska Laroverk, Washington and Lee Univ., Stockholm and Lund Univs.; Nat. Inst. for Econ. Research 1962–65; Ministry of Finance 1965–68; mem. Swedish Del. to OECD 1968–70; Ministry for Foreign Affairs, Dept. for Devt. Co-operation 1970–75, Head Multilateral Dept. 1972, Project Leader Secr. for Futures Studies 1975–77, Head Transport Div. 1977–78; Deputy Dir.-Gen. Nat. Bd. of Trade 1978–84; Head Multilateral Dept. of Ministry for Foreign Affairs Trade Dept. 1984–88; Co-ordinator for Econ. Co-operation with Cen. and Eastern Europe, Ministry for Foreign Affairs 1989–90; Dir. Cen. Bank 1989; Amb., Perm. Rep. Swedish Del. to OECD 1991–95, Acting Sec.-Gen. OECD Oct.–Nov. 1994; Chair OECD Steel Cttee. 1986–88, OECD Liaison Cttee. with Council of Europe 1992, OECD Council Working Party on Shipbldg. 1993–95, Wassenaar Arrangement on Export Control for Conventional Arms and Dual-Use Goods and Technolgies 1996–99; Amb. and Insp. Gen. of Mil. Equipment, Ministry for Foreign Affairs 1995, Amb. and Insp. Gen., Head Nat. Inspectorate of Strategic Products 1996. *Publications:* Swedish Exports and Imports 1965–70, Resources, Society and the Future 1980. *Leisure interests:* music, art, architecture, literature. *Address:* Hornsgatan 5, 118 49 Stockholm, Sweden.

SOISSON, Jean-Pierre Henri Robert, L. EN D.; French politician; b. 9 Nov. 1934, Auxerre; s. of Jacques and Denise (Silve) Soisson; m. Catherine Lacaisse 1961; two s.; ed. Lycée Jacques-Amyot, Auxerre, Faculté de Droit, Paris, Ecole nationale d'administration; Auditor, Audit Office 1961; with del. to Algeria 1961–62; lecturer, Institute d'études politiques de Paris 1962–68; tech. adviser to Sec.-Gen. of Merchant Navy 1964–65, to Sec. of State for Information, later for Foreign Affairs 1966–67, to Minister of Agric. 1967–68; Conseiller referendaire, Audit Office 1968–; Deputy to Nat. Assembly for Yonne 1968–78; Deputy Sec.-Gen. Fédération nationale des républicains indépendants 1969–75, Vice-Pres. 1975–78; fmr. Sec.-Gen. Parti Republicain; Co. Councillor, Auxerre sud-ouest 1970–76, Mayor 1971–98, Deputy Mayor 1998–; Pres. Caisse d'Aide à l'équipement des collectivités locales 1973–74; fmr. Pres. parl. group for rural devt.; Sec. of State for Univs. 1974–76, for Professional Training 1976, to Minister of the Quality of Life (Youth and Sport) 1976–78; Minister for Youth, Sport and Leisure 1978–81, of Labour, Employment and Professional Training 1988–91, of State for the Civil Service and Admin. Reform 1991–92, of Agric. and Forests 1992–93; Conseiller Général for Canton of Auxerre Sud-Ouest 1982–88; Vice-Pres. Regional Council for Bourgogne 1983–92; 1st Vice-Pres., Yonne 1982–88 (Deputy 1993–); Pres. (Council for Bourgogne) 1992–93, 1998–; Pres. Comm. de surveillance de La Caisse des dépots et consignations; Sec.-Gen. United France 1991, Mouvement des Réformateurs 1992–; Deputy (Ind. then République et Liberté group) to Nat. Ass. for Yonne 1993–; Pres. Communauté des communes de l'auxerrois 1998–; Croix de la valeur militaire, Chevalier du Mérite agricole, Officier de l'ordre nat. (Madagascar), Chevalier de l'ordre nat. (Senegal, Benin and Niger); Commdr. Arts et Lettres. *Publications:* Le Piège (with Bernard Stasi and Olivier Stirn) 1973, La victoire sur l'hiver 1978, L'enjeu de la formation professionnelle 1987, Mémoires d'ouverture 1990, Politique en jachère 1992, #3, Voyage en Norvège 1995, Charles le Téméraire 1997. *Leisure interests:* tennis, skiing. *Address:* Assemblée Nationale, 75355 Paris; Mairie, 89000 Auxerre (Office); Mouvement des réformateurs, 7 rue de Villersexel, 75007 Paris (Office); 22 rue Philibert Roux, 89000 Auxerre, France (Home).

SOKOLOFF, Louis, M.D.; American research scientist; b. 14 Oct. 1921, Philadelphia; s. of Morris and Goldie Sokoloff; m. Betty Jane Kaiser 1947; one s. one d.; ed. Univ. of Pennsylvania; Research Fellow, Instructor and Assoc. in Physiology and Pharmacology, Graduate School of Medicine, Univ. of Pa. 1949–53; Assoc. Chief, Section on Cerebral Metabolism, Lab. of Neurochemistry, Nat. Inst. of Mental Health, Bethesda, Md. 1953–56, Chief, Section on Cerebral Metabolism, Lab. of Clinical Science 1956–57, Chief 1957–68, Chief Lab. of Cerebral Metabolism 1968–; Sr. mem. Inst. of Medicine, N.A.S. 1997–; Hon. D.Sc. (Glasgow) 1989; Dr. h.c. (Philipps Univ. of Marburg) 1990; Hon. Sc.D. (Georgetown) 1992, (Mich. State) 1993; Hon. M.D. (Rome) 1992; F. O. Schmitt Medal in Neuroscience 1980, Albert Lasker Clinical Medical Research Award 1981, Karl Spencer Lashley Award 1987, Distinguished Grad. Award, Univ. of Pa. 1987, N.A.S. Award in Neuroscience 1988, Cerebrovascular Disorder Research Promotion Award, Georg Charles de Hevesy Nuclear Medicine Pioneer Award 1988, Mihara 1988, Ralph Gerard Award of Soc. of Neuroscience 1996. *Publications:* The Action of Drugs on the Cerebral Circulation (Pharmacological Review 11) 1959, The Relationship Between Function and Energy Metabolism: Its Use in the Localization of Functional Activity in the Nervous System (Neurosciences Research Program Bulletin 19 (2)) 1981, Metabolic Probes of Central Nervous System Activity in Experimental Animals and Man (Magnes Lecture Series, Vol. I) 1984. *Leisure interests:* music, tennis, literature, history. *Address:* Laboratory of Cerebral Metabolism, National Institute of Mental Health, Building 36, Room 1A05, 9000 Rockville Pike, Bethesda, MD 20892, U.S.A. *Telephone:* (301) 496-1371. *Fax:* (301) 480-1668.

SOKOLOV, Aleksandr (Sasha) Vsevolodovich; Russian writer; b. 6 Nov. 1943, Ottawa, Canada; s. of Vsevolod Sokolov and Lidia Sokolova; m. 2nd Johanna Steindl 1975; one s.; one d. from previous m.; ed. Moscow Univ.; left U.S.S.R. 1975 for Austria, U.S.A., Canada, France, Greece; returned to U.S.S.R. 1989 (first emigré writer to do so); now lives in Moscow, retaining Canadian citizenship; works published in U.S.S.R. 1989–. *Publications include:* School for Fools 1976, Entre Chien et Loup 1979, Palisandriia 1985. *Address:* c/o Ardis Publishers, Ann Arbor, MI, U.S.A.

SOKOLOV, Boris Sergeyevich; Russian palaeontologist and geologist; b. 9 April 1914, Vyshny Volochek, Tver Region; ed. Leningrad State Univ.; Laboratory State Asst., Asst. Lecturer, Leningrad (now St. Petersburg) State Univ. 1937–41, Lecturer 1945–60, Prof. 1964–; Chief of Geological search party, Sr. Research Worker, Head of Dept., All-Union Oil Research Geological Inst. 1943–60; Head of Dept., Inst. of Geology and Geophysics, Siberian Dept. of U.S.S.R. (now Russian) Acad. of Sciences 1960–78; Scientific Head of Lab., Moscow Palaeontological Inst. 1979–; Vice-Pres. Int. Palaeontological Asscn. 1972–; Pres. All-Union Palaeontological Soc. of U.S.S.R. (now Russian) Acad. of Sciences 1974–; Acad. Sec., section of Geology, Geophysics and Geochemistry and mem. of Presidium of U.S.S.R. (now Russian) Acad. of Sciences 1975–91; Councillor to Pres. 1991–; mem. French, Bulgarian and Chinese Geological Socs.; Corresp. mem. U.S.S.R. (now Russian) Acad. of Sciences 1958–68, mem. 1968–; Hon. mem. Swedish Geological Soc. 1968–, Czechoslovak Acad. of Sciences; Lenin Prize 1967; Hero of Socialist Labour 1984; Order of Lenin (twice) and other decorations. *Publications:* works on biosphere of the Earth etc. *Address:* Palaeontological Institute, Profsoyuznaya str. 113, 117 647 Moscow, Russia. *Telephone:* (095) 339-95-66 (Office); (095) 146-84-44 (Home).

SOKOLOV, Grigory Lipmanovich; Russian pianist; b. 18 April 1950, Leningrad; ed. Leningrad Conservatory (pupil of Moisey Halfin); Second Prize, All-Union Competition of Musicians 1965, First Prize, Int. Tchaikovsky Competition 1966; numerous concert appearances in Europe since late 1960s; Prof. Leningrad Conservatory 1975; People's Artist of Russia 1988. *Address:* World Management for the Arts, 253 Fifth Avenue, Fifth Floor, New York, NY 10016, U.S.A. *Telephone:* (812) 296-44-09 (St. Petersburg, Russia).

SOKOLOV, Maksim Yur'yevich; Russian journalist; b. 1959, Moscow; m.; ed. Moscow State Univ.; worked as programmer in All-Union Centre of Transport, U.S.S.R. State Cttee. on Science and Tech. 1981–83; All-Union Research Inst. of Patent Information 1983–84; All-Union Research Inst. for

Man. of Coal Industry 1985–87; Research Inst. of Gen. Plan of Moscow 1988–89; journalist since late 1980s; contrib. Commersant (weekly) 1989–97; political observer, Izvestiya 1998–; publs. in newspapers Nezavisimaya Gazeta, Atmoda, Segodnya, magazines Vek XX i Mir, Oktyabr, Soviet Analyst (U.K.); commentator, TV programmes; special corresp., Gong-94 (weekly). *Leisure interests:* travelling, cooking, reading fiction, mushroom hunting. *Address:* Izvestiya, Tverskaya str. 18, 103791 Moscow, Russia. *Telephone:* (095) 299 2122 (Office).

SOKOMANU, George (b. George Kalkoa); Ni-Vanuatu politician; b. 13 Jan. 1937, Vanuatu; m. Leitak Matautava 1960; four s. one d.; fmr. Deputy Chief Minister and Minister of the Interior of New Hebrides; Pres. of Vanuatu 1980–88; arrested Dec. 1988; sentenced to six years imprisonment March 1989, released April 1989; Sec.-Gen. South Pacific Comm. 1992–95; Deputy Prime Minister, Minister of Home Affairs, Local Govt., Police and Defence 1994–95. *Address:* Mele Village, P.O. Box 1319, Port Vila, Vanuatu.

SOKORSKI, Włodzimierz; Polish writer, journalist and politician; b. 2 July 1908, Aleksandrowsk; m.; four c.; ed. Univ. of Warsaw; General Sec. Polish Socialist Party "Left Wing" 1929–31; Col., Polish Army Second World War; Vice-Minister 1948–53, Minister of Culture and Art 1953–56; Pres., Cttee. for Radio and Television 1956–72; Ed.-in-Chief monthly Miesięcznik Literacki 1966–90; Vice-Pres. Polish UNESCO Cttee.; fmr. mem. Bd. Warsaw Branch, Polish Writers' Asscn., Deputy Chair. 1979–80; mem. Nat. Council of Culture 1982–90; Deputy mem. Cen. Cttee. Polish United Workers' Party 1948–75; Deputy to Seym 1947–55, 1965–76; Chair. Gen. Bd. of Union of Fighters for Freedom and Democracy (ZBoWiD) 1981–82, Presidium mem. 1983–90; mem. Union Veterans of the Polish Republic and of Former Political Prisoners 1990–; numerous Govt. and Army awards including Virtuti Militari, Order of Lenin (U.S.S.R.), Order of Banner of Labour, 1st Class, Commdr. Cross and Commdr. Cross with Star of Order of Polonia Restituta, Order of Builders of People's Poland 1979. *Publications:* Rozdarty bruk (The Torn Pavement—novel) 1936, Problemy polityki kulturalnej (Problems of Cultural Policy) 1947, Sztuka w walce o socjalizm (Arts for Socialism) 1950, Dziennik podróży (The Journey Diary) 1954, Grubą kreską (Drawing Thick Lines—essay) 1958, Zakręty (Curves—essay) 1959, Okruchy (Crumbs—short stories) 1961, Escapes (play) 1961, Współczesność i młodzież (The Present Day and Youth) 1963, Współczesna kultura masowa (The Modern Mass Culture) 1967, Spotkania (The Meeting—play), Milczenie (Silence—play), Polacy pod Lenino (Poles of Lenino—war memoirs) 1971, Notatki (Notes—Memoirs) 1975, Nie ma powrotów tych samych (Returning is Never the Same—play) 1975, Piotr (Peter—novel) 1976, Ludzie i sprawy (People and Affairs—memoirs) 1977, Ludzie stamtąd (history) 1978, Leon Schiller, Xawery Dunikowski 1978; Kroki (novel) 1978, Tamte lata 1979, Refleksje o kulturze: literatura i sztuka trzydziestopięciolecia 1980, Czas, który nie mija (memoirs) 1980, Umarli przychodzą nad ranem 1980, Zostać sobą 1982, Każda rzeka ma swój nurt 1983, Nie można powtórzyć 1984, Skazani na siebie (novel) 1986, Znaki zapytania (novel) 1987, Uwikłania (novel) 1990, Nic nie jest proste (novel) 1990; Wspomnienia (Reminiscences) in Miesięcznik Literacki 1984–90; numerous radio and television plays. *Leisure interests:* swimming, skiing, flowers. *Address:* al. Róż 6 m.5, 00-556 Warsaw, Poland. *Telephone:* (22) 29 55 20.

SOKUROV, Alexander Nikolayevich; Russian film director; b. 14 June 1951, Irkutsk; ed. Gorky (now Nizhny Novgorod) Univ., All-Union Inst. of Cinematography; worked in Gorky (now Nizhny Novgorod) TV, Lenfilm Studio, directed feature and documentary films; Founder and Dir. Experimental School of Young Cinema Vanguard. *Films include:* A Solitary Voice of a Man (Bronze Leopard, Locarno Int. Festival 1978), Mournful Callousness, Days of Eclipse (FIPRESSI Prize—Montreal Int. Festival), A Sonata for Hitler, Second Round, Elegy (about F. Shalyapin), Moscow Elegy (dedicated to A. Tarkovsky) Soviet Elegy, Russian Elegy, The Quiet Pages, The Spiritual Voices (Sony Prize, Locarno Int. Festival 1995), Oriental Elegy (Grand Prix Oberhausen Festival 1996), Mother and Son (prizes at Int. Festivals of Berlin, Moscow 1997), The Knot: Solzhenitsyn 1998. *Address:* Smolenskaya nab. 4, Apt. 222, 199048 St. Petersburg, Russia.

SOLANA MADARIAGA, Javier (brother of Luis Solana Madariaga, q.v.); Spanish politician; b. 1942, Madrid; m. Concepción Jiménez; two c.; ed. Colegio del Pilar, Universidad Complutense de Madrid; won Fulbright scholarship to study physical sciences in U.S.A. until 1968; Asst. to Prof. Nicolas Cabrera, Univ. of Va. 1968–71, then at Universidad Autónoma de Madrid (where contract was cancelled for political reasons); mem. Exec., Federación Socialista Madrileña and Federación de Trabajadores de la Enseñanza, Unión General de Trabajadores; Prof. of Physical Sciences, Universidad Complutense de Madrid; mem. Congress of Deputies for Madrid; mem. Fed. Exec. Comm., Partido Socialista Obrero Español, former Press Sec. and Sec. for Research and Programmes; Minister of Culture and Govt. Spokesman 1982–88; Minister of Educ. and Science 1988–92, of Foreign Affairs 1992–95; Sec.-Gen. NATO Dec. 1995–. *Address:* NATO, Boulevard Léopold III, 1050 Brussels, Belgium.

SOLANA MADARIAGA, Luis (brother of Javier Solana Madariaga, q.v.); Spanish business executive; b. 1935, Madrid; m. Leonor Pérez Pita; two c.; ed. Univ. of Madrid; joined Banco Urquijo, rising to Gen. Deputy Dir.; opened pvt. law office; Deputy for Segovia 1977; Pres. Nat. Telephone Co. of Spain 1982–89; Chair. R.T.V.E. 1989–90; mem. Bd. of Dirs. C.E.O.E., Regional Cttee., Madrid Socialist Fed.; Vice-Pres. Spanish Mastiff Asscn. *Publications:* Rota ha entrado en guerra (novel), numerous articles in newspapers and magazines.

SOLBES MIRA, Pedro, D.POL.SCI.; Spanish politician; b. Pinoso, Alicante 1942; m.; two c.; ed. Univ. of Madrid, Inst. of European Studies of Free Univ., Brussels; Sub-Del. and Regional Del. of Commerce in Valencia 1968–73, Commercial Counsellor to Spain's Perm. Representation to the EC 1973–78, Advisor to Minister of Relations with the EC 1978–79; Dir. Gen. Commercial Policy, Ministry of Economy and Commerce 1982, Tech. Sec. Gen. 1982–; Sec. of State for the EC; Minister of Agric., Fishing and Food 1991–93, of Economy and Finance 1993–96; Chair. Bd. EBRD 1994. *Address:* c/o Partido Socialista Obrero Español, Ferraz 68 y 70, 28008 Madrid, Spain.

SOLBRIG, Otto Thomas, PH.D.; American professor of biology; b. 21 Dec. 1930, Buenos Aires, Argentina; s. of Hans Solbrig and Rose Muggleworth; m. Dorothy Crosswhite 1969; one s. one d.; ed. Colegio Nacional de Mar de La Plata, Univ. Nacional de La Plata and Univ. of Calif. Berkeley; Research Asst. Univ. of La Plata 1951–54; Teaching Fellow, Univ. of Calif. Berkeley 1956–58; Asst. then Assoc. Curator, Gray Herbarium, Harvard Univ. 1960–66, Dir. 1963–78; Assoc. Prof., Prof. Univ. of Mich. Ann Arbor 1966–69; Bussey Prof. of Biology Harvard Univ. 1969–; numerous professional appts. and affiliations etc.; Fellow, American Acad. of Arts and Sciences; Fellow, A.A.A.S.; Guggenheim Fellow 1975–76; Cooley Prize 1961; Congressional Antarctic Medal 1967; Willdenow Medal, Berlin Botanical Gardens 1979; Extraordinary Prof. h.c. Univ. of La Plata 1991; Distinguished Prof. h.c. (Univ. of Buenos Aires) 1994; Hon. M.A. (Harvard) 1969. *Publications:* author or co-author of 16 books and more than 210 articles and chapters in books on plant population biology, cytology, ecology, evolution and taxonomy. *Leisure interest:* sailing. *Address:* Department of Organismic and Evolutionary Biology, Harvard University, 22 Divinity Avenue, Cambridge, MA 02138, U.S.A. *Telephone:* (617) 495-4302. *Fax:* (617) 495-9484.

SOLE TURA, Jordi, D.LAW.; Spanish politician; b. 23 May 1930, Mollet del Vallés, Barcelona; ed. Cen. Univ. of Barcelona; Prof. of Political Law Cen. Univ. of Barcelona 1982; mem. United Catalonian Socialist Party (PSUC) 1956–64; founder Bandera Roja 1970 (rejoined PSUC 1974); mem. Central Cttee. Spanish CP; Deputy PSUC for Barcelona and spokesman and Vice-Pres. Parl. Communist Group 1977–, mem. Perm. Deputation of Congress and Statutory Cttees., Mixed Constitution-Regulation Body, Territorial Admin. Body, Constitutional Body, Justice Body; Deputy PSC-PSOE for Barcelona and Pres. Constitutional Comm. of Congress 1989–; Minister of Culture 1991–93; mem. group of Deputies who drafted the Spanish Constitution of 1978. *Publications:* several books including Introduction to the Spanish Political Regime. *Address:* Partido Socialista Obrero Español, Ferraz 68 y 70, 28008 Madrid, Spain.

SOLERI, Paolo, D.ARCH.; American architect and urban planner; b. 21 June 1919, Turin, Italy; m. Corolyn Woods 1949 (died 1982); two d.; ed. Turin Polytechnic Frank Lloyd Wright Fellowship, Taliesin, Ariz.; went to U.S.A. 1947 to study; returned to Italy 1949; commissioned to design and build ceramics factory, Ceramica Artistica Solimene; resident in U.S.A 1955–; Pres. Cosanti Foundation (for research into urban planning); Prin. Paolo Soleri Assocs. Inc., Architects; since 1970 developing Arcosanti as an Urban Lab. in Cen. Ariz.; exbhns. of work have appeared in over 70 public and private museums, colls. and univs., U.S.A.; exhbn. at N.Y. Acad. of Sciences 1989–90; Distinguished Visiting Lecturer, Coll. of Architecture, Ariz. State Univ.; Gold Medal, World Biennale of Architecture, Sofia, Bulgaria 1981; Gold Medal, American Inst. of Architects; Hon. Dr. (Dickinson Coll., Carlisle, Pa., Moore Coll. of Art, Phila., Ariz. State Univ.); Utopis Award 1989. *Publications:* Sketchbooks of Paolo Soleri 1970, Arcology: City in the Image of Man 1970, Matter becoming Spirit 1971, Fragments 1981, Omega Seed 1981, Arcosanti: an Urban Laboratory? 1983, Paolo Soleri's Earth Casting (with Scott M. Davis) 1984, Space for Peace 1984, Technology and Cosmogenesis 1986. *Address:* Cosanti Foundation, 6433 Doubletree Road, Scottsdale, AZ 85253, U.S.A. *Telephone:* (602) 948-6145.

SOLH, Rashid; Lebanese politician and lawyer; b. 1926, Beirut; ed. Coll. des Frères des Ecoles Chrétiennes, Coll. Al Makassed, Faculty of Law; Beirut; successively Judge, Pres. of the Labour Arbitration Council, Examining Magistrate, Attorney-Gen. of the Charéi Tribunal; Ind. mem. Chamber of Deputies for Beirut 1964, 1972; Prime Minister 1974–75, May–Oct. 1992. *Address:* Chambre des Députés, Place de l'Etoile, Beirut, Lebanon.

SOLIMAN, Mohammed Sidky; Egyptian politician and engineer; b. 1919; ed. Fuad I Univ., Cairo; studied eng. and mil. science; Col. in Egyptian Army -1962; Minister of Aswan High Dam 1962–66; Prime Minister 1966–67; Deputy Prime Minister and Minister of Industry, Electricity and the Aswan Dam June 1967–70, 1971; Order of Lenin. *Address:* Cairo, Egypt.

SOLIMAN, Soliman Metwalli; Egyptian politician; b. 25 Oct. 1927, Menofia; one s. three d.; ed. Cairo Univ.; Engineer, Ministry of Irrigation; Engineer, Corps of Engineers; Gov. Bani-Suef 1976, Menofia 1977; Minister of State for Parl. Affairs, Minister for Local Govenorates 1978; Minister of Transport, Communications and Maritime Transportation 1980, now Minister of Transport and Communications. *Address:* Ministry of Transport, Sharia Qasr el-Eini, Cairo, Egypt. *Telephone:* (2) 355 5566. *Fax:* (2) 355 5564.

SOLIS PALMA, Manuel; Panamanian politician; Minister of Educ. 1984–88; Prime Minister of Panama 1988–89; First Vice-Pres. of Panama 1988–89; Minister in Charge of the Presidency of the Repub. 1988–89.

SOLLERS, Philippe (pseudonym of Philippe Joyaux); French author; b. 28 Nov. 1936, Bordeaux; s. of Octave Joyaux and Marcelle Molinié; m. Julia Kristeva 1967; one s.; ed. Lycées Montesquieu and Montaigne, Bordeaux and Ecole Sainte-Geneviève, Versailles; Dir. L'Infini (review) 1983–; mem. reading cttee. Editions Gallimard 1990–, Ass. of French Museums 1998–; Prix Médicis 1961, Grand Prix du Roman de la Ville de Paris 1988, Prix Paul-Morand (Académie française) 1992, Chevalier Légion d'honneur, Officier, Ordre nat. du Mérite, des Arts et des Lettres. *Publications:* Une Curieuse Solitude 1958, Le Parc 1961, Drame 1965, Nombres, Logiques 1968, Lois 1972, H 1973, Paradis, Vision à New York 1981, Femmes 1983, Portrait du joueur 1985, Théorie des exceptions 1986, Paradis 2 1986, Le Coeur absolu 1987, Les Surprises de Fragonard 1987, Les Folies françaises 1988, De Kooning, vite 1988, Le Lys d'or 1989, Carnet de nuit 1989, la Fête à Venise 1991, Improvisations 1991, Le Secret 1993, Venise Éternelle 1993, La Guerre du Goût 1994, Femmes, Mythologies (jtly.) 1994, Les Passions de Francis Bacon 1996, Sade contre l'Etre Suprême 1996, Picasso, le héros 1996, Studio 1997. *Address:* L'Infini, 5 rue Sébastien-Bottin, 75007 Paris, France (Office).

SOLOMIN, Vitaly Mefodievich; Russian actor and theatre director; b. 12 Dec. 1941, Chita; m.; two d.; ed. Shchepkin Drama School; with Moscow Maly Drama Theatre 1963–68, actor Mossoviet Theatre 1986–88, Free Cause 1988–; cinema debut 1963. *Film roles include:* Elder Sister 1967, Kingdom of Women 1968, Salut, Maria 1971, Dauria 1972, A Jump from the Roof 1978, Sibiriada 1979, Adventures of Sherlock Holmes and Dr. Watson 1979–83, Winter Cherries 1985, Winter Cherries II 1990; Minister of Culture of Russian Fed. 1990–91; A. Popov Gold Medal; People's Artist of Russia.

SOLOMON, Anthony Morton, M.A., PH.D.; American economist and banker; b. 27 Dec. 1919, Arlington, N.J.; s. of Jacob and Edna (née Yudin) Solomon; m. Constance Beverly Kaufman 1950; one s. one d.; ed. Univ. of Chicago, Harvard Univ.; mem. American Financial Mission to Iran 1942–46; Securities Analyst, Bache & Co. 1950–51; Publr. Nat. Industrial Directory, Mexico 1951–53; Pres. Rosa Blanca Products Corpn., Mexico 1953–61; Lecturer, Harvard Business School 1961–63; Chair. AID Mission to Bolivia 1963; Chair., as Special Consultant to Pres. Kennedy on Mission of U.S. Trust Territory, Pacific Islands 1963; Deputy Asst. Sec. of State for Latin America and Deputy Asst., Agency for Int. Devt. (AID) 1963–65; Asst. Sec. of State for Econ. Affairs 1965–69; Pres. Int. Investment Corpn. for Yugoslavia, London 1969–72; Adviser to Chair., Ways and Means Cttee., House of Reps. 1972–73; Under-Sec. for Monetary Affairs, Treasury Dept. 1977–80; Pres. and C.E.O. New York Federal Reserve Bank 1980–84; Adviser The Blackstone Group, Toyota; Chair. U.K. Fund, Europe Fund, Andy Warhol Foundation for the Visual Arts, Exec. Cttee. Inst. for Int. Econs.; Dir. Alexandria Real Estate Equities, Urban America. *Leisure interest:* sculpture. *Address:* 535 Park Avenue, New York, NY 10021, U.S.A. (Office).

SOLOMON, Arthur Kaskel, PH.D., D.PHIL., SC.D.; American professor of biophysics; b. 26 Nov. 1912, Pittsburgh, Pa.; s. of Mark K. Solomon and Hortense Nattans; m. Mariot Fraser Matthews 1972; one s. one d. from previous m.; ed. Univs. of Princeton, Harvard and Cambridge; Research Fellow, Cavendish Lab., Cambridge 1937–39; Research Assoc., Physics and Chem., Harvard Univ. 1939–41; Research Fellow, Biological Chem., Harvard Medical School 1940–42, Asst. Prof. of Physiological Chem. 1946–57, Assoc. Prof. Biophysics 1957–68, Prof. Biophysics 1968–82, Prof. Emer. 1982–; Chair. Comm. on Higher Degrees in Biophysics, Harvard 1959–80, Council on the Arts, Harvard 1973–76; Sec.-Gen. Int. Union for Pure and Applied Biophysics 1961–72; mem. Exec. Cttee., Int. Council of Scientific Unions (ICSU) 1966–72; mem. U.S. Nat. Comm. for UNESCO 1969–74; Science Policy Adviser to Thai Govt. 1969–72; mem. Editorial Bd. Journal of General Physiology 1958–88; mem. Bd. of Int. Orgs. and Programs, N.A.S. 1973–80; Chair. ICSU-UNESCO Distinguished Fellowship Cttee. 1982–85; Chair. 1977–79; mem. American Chem. Soc., American Physiol. Soc., Biophysics Soc., Soc. Gen. Physiology; Pres. Read's Inc. 1961–77; mem. U.S. Del to Gen. Ass. of UNESCO, Paris 1978; U.S. Del. to 17th Gen. Ass. ICSU Athens 1978; Fellow American Acad. of Arts and Sciences, A.A.A.S.; Trustee, Inst. of Contemporary Art, Boston 1946–76, Pres. 1965–71; Overseer, Museum of Fine Arts, Boston 1978–84; mem. Collectors Cttee., Nat. Gallery of Art, Washington, D.C. 1985–87; Order Andres Bello, Venezuela 1974. *Publications:* Why Smash Atoms 1940, and over four hundred scientific articles. *Leisure interests:* art, travel. *Address:* Biophysical Laboratory, Harvard Medical School, 221 Longwood Avenue, Boston, MA 02115 (Office); 27 Craigie Street, Cambridge, MA 02138, U.S.A. (Home). *Telephone:* (617) 432-5488 (Office); (617) 876-0149 (Home).

SOLOMON, David H., M.D.; American professor of medicine; b. 7 March 1923, Cambridge, Mass.; s. of Frank Solomon and Rose Roud Solomon; m. Ronda Markson 1946; two d.; ed. Brown Univ. and Harvard Medical School; Medical House Officer, Peter Bent Brigham Hospital 1946–47; Research Fellow in Medicine, Peter Bent Brigham Hospital and Harvard Medical School 1947–48; Sr. Asst. Surgeon, U.S. Public Health Service and Investigator, Gerontology Section, Nat. Heart Inst. 1948–50; Sr. Asst. Resident Physician, Peter Bent Brigham Hospital 1950–51; Fellow in Endocrinology, New England Center Hospital 1951–52; Instr. School of Medicine, Univ. of Calif. Los Angeles (UCLA) 1952–54, Asst. Prof. 1954–60, Assoc. Prof. 1960–66, Prof. of Medicine 1966, Chief of Medicine (Harbor-UCLA Medical Center) 1966–71, Chair. Dept. of Medicine 1971–81, Assoc. Dir. Multicampus Div. of Geriatric Medicine 1982–89, Dir. UCLA Center on Aging 1991–96, Prof. Emer. UCLA 1993–; Consultant, Wadsworth Hosp., Los Angeles 1952–, Sepulveda Hosp. 1971–; several awards. *Publications:* co-author of three books, author of 202 scientific papers, 44 book chapters, 11 review articles and 122 published abstracts. *Leisure interests:* golf, running, reading, hiking, bridge. *Address:* UCLA Center on Aging, 10945 Le Conte Avenue, P.O. Box 956980, Los Angeles, CA 90095-6980 (Office); 2103 Ridge Drive, Los Angeles, CA 90049, U.S.A. (Home). *Telephone:* (310) 794-0676 (Office). *Fax:* (310) 794-0681.

SOLOMON, David Henry, A.M., D.SC., PH.D., F.A.A., F.R.A.C.I., F.T.S.; Australian chemist; b. 19 Nov. 1929, Adelaide; s. of H. J. Solomon and M. Mead; m. Harriet Newport 1954; three d.; ed. N.S.W. Univ. of Tech. and Univ. of N.S.W.; Balm Paints Pty. Ltd. (now Dulux Australia Ltd.), Sydney 1946–53, 1955–63; demonstrator/teacher Fellow, N.S.W. Univ. of Tech. 1953–55; seconded to ICI Paints Div., Slough 1959–60; Sr. Research Scientist, Sr. Prin. Research Scientist, CSIRO Div. of Applied Mineralogy 1963–70; at Georgia Kaolin Co., Elizabeth, N.J., U.S.A. 1968–69; Chief Research Scientist/Chief of Div. CSIRO Div. of Applied Organic Chem. 1970–86; Acting Dir. CSIRO Inst. of Industrial Technology 1986–87; Deputy Dir. CSIRO Inst. of Industrial Technologies 1989–90; Head of School and ICI Aust.-Masson Prof. of Chem., Univ. of Melbourne 1990–94, Professorial Fellow 1996–; Fellow, Australian Acad. of Technological Sciences and Eng.; David Syme Research Prize 1976, Polymer Medal, Royal Australian Chemical Inst. 1978, Leighton Memorial Medal 1985, CSIRO Medal 1987, 1990, Clunies Ross Nat. Science & Tech. Award 1994 and other awards. *Publications:* six books, 180 scientific papers and 23 patents. *Leisure interest:* farming. *Address:* Department of Chemical Engineering, University of Melbourne, Parkville, Vic. 3052, Australia. *Telephone:* (03) 9344 6511. *Fax:* (03) 9347 5180.

SOLOMON, Edward I., PH.D.; American chemist; b. 20 Oct. 1946, New York; s. of Mordecai L. Solomon and Sally S. Solomon; m. Darlene J. Spira 1984; one s. one d.; ed. Rensselaer Polytechnic Inst., Tory, New York, Princeton Univ.; Research Assoc., Princeton Univ., N.J. 1972–73; Postdoctoral Fellow H.C. Ørsted Inst. 1973–74, Calif. Inst. of Tech. 1974–75; Asst. Prof. M.I.T. 1975–79, Assoc. Prof. 1979–81, Prof. 1981–82; Prof., Stanford Univ. 1982–, Spaght Prof. of Chem. 1991–; First Glen Seaborg and other lectureships; Fellow A.A.A.S., American Acad. of Arts and Sciences; Sloan Fellowship, N.I.H. Merit Award., Japan Soc. for Promotion of Science Invitation Fellow, Dean's Award for Distinguished Teaching, Westinghouse Foundation Nat. Talent Search award, Remsen Award 1994. *Publications:* 285 papers in scientific journals. *Leisure interests:* tennis, running, gourmet dining, int. travel. *Address:* Department of Chemistry, Stanford University, Roth Way, Stanford, CA 94305, U.S.A. *Telephone:* (650) 723-4694. *Fax:* (650) 725-0259.

SOLOMON, Sir Harry, Kt.; British business executive; b. 20 March 1937, Middlesbrough; s. of Jacob Solomon and Belle Solomon; m. Judith D. Manuel 1962; one s. two d.; ed. St. Alban's School and Law Soc. School of Law; qualified solicitor 1960; in pvt. practice 1960–75; Man. Dir. Hillsdown Holdings PLC 1975–84, Jt. Chair. 1984–87, Chair. 1987–93, Dir. (non-exec.) 1993–97; Chair. Harveys Holdings PLC 1994–; Dir. Princedale Group PLC 1993–; Dir. (non-exec.) Charterhouse European Holding Ltd., Frogmore Estates PLC, U.S. Industries Inc.; fmr. Dir. Maple Leaf Foods Inc.; Hon. F.R.C.P. *Leisure interests:* jogging, tennis, theatre, collector of historical autographed letters. *Address:* 3 Coach House Yard, Hampstead High Street, London, NW3 1QB, England.

SOLOMON, Hollis, B.A.; American gallery owner and film producer; d. of Nathan Dworken and Ethel Goldman; m. Horace Solomon 1954 (separated 1985); two s.; ed. Vassar and Sarah Lawrence Colls.; opened alternative space called 28 Greene Street 1969–72, Holly Solomon Gallery, 392 W. Broadway 1975–84, Holly Solomon Gallery at 724 Fifth Avenue 1985–. *Leisure interests:* reading, television, Scrabble. *Address:* 444 East 57 Street, New York, NY 10022, U.S.A. (Home). *Telephone:* (212) 758-1887.

SOLOMON, Ionel; French physicist; b. 1 Jan. 1929, Bucharest, Romania; m. Solange Suganas 1960; one s. one d.; ed. Ecole Polytechnique and Univ. of Liverpool; Ingénieur Commissariat à l'Energie Atomique, Saclay 1953; Research Fellow, Harvard Univ. 1956; Dir. of PMC Lab. Ecole Polytechnique 1962; Research Dir. Centre Nat. de la Recherche Scientifique (CNRS) 1968; Pres. Physics Dept. Ecole Polytechnique 1973; Visiting Prof. Tokyo Univ. 1980; Pres. French Physical Soc. 1971; mem. Acad. des Sciences; six prizes and medals from Ministry of Educ., French Physical Soc., Inst. of Physics (U.K.) and Acad. des Sciences. *Publications:* many scientific publs. on magnetic resonance (1955–65), on semiconductor physics (1965–76), on amorphous silicon and solar energy (1976–87) and recently on material research and applications. *Address:* Ecole Polytechnique, Laboratoire PMC, 91128 Palaiseau, France. *Telephone:* (01) 69.33.46.61. *Fax:* (01) 69.33.30.04.

SOLOMON, Yonty, B.MUS., F.R.C.M.; British/South African concert pianist; b. 6 May 1938, Cape Town, South Africa; s. of David and Chaze Riva Solomon; ed. Univ. of Cape Town; studied with Dame Myra Hess in London, Guido Agosti in Rome, Charles Rosen (q.v.) in U.S.A.; Concert début in Wigmore Hall, London 1963; recitals and concertos in U.K., Netherlands, U.S.A., Canada, Romania, South Africa; gave first performances of works dedicated to him by Richard Rodney Bennett (q.v.), Wilfred Mellers, Merilaainen, Wilfred Josephs; given solo performing rights by composer Kaikhosru Sorabji 1976–77 for all his works; panel of judges of Royal Overseas

League Commonwealth Music Competition 1974–; many TV and radio engagements; many recitals devoted to Charles Ives, J. S. Bach (The Well-Tempered Klavier and Klavierübung), Janáček, Boulez, Granados, Albéniz and much rarely performed piano music; first performance of unpublished scores by K. S. Sorabji 1978; Prof. of Piano, Royal Coll. of Music, London 1978–; Visiting Artist-in-Res., Nottingham Univ. 1980–; Hon. mem. Royal Philharmonic Soc.; Hon. R.C.M. (London) 1982; Master classes in piano and chamber music at Int. Musicians Seminar (Cornwall) 1982; Scholarships from Univ. of Cape Town; Harriet Cohen Beethoven Medal 1962, Commonwealth Award. *Publications:* Schumann Symposium 1973, Bach's "48", Analysis and Historical Survey 1972. *Leisure interests:* collecting botanical books, growing camellias. *Address:* 56 Canonbury Park North, London, N1 2JT, England. *Telephone:* 0171-226 8123. *Fax:* 0171-226 8123.

SOLOMOS, Alexis; Greek stage director and author; b. 9 Aug. 1918, Athens; s. of John Solomos and Aspasia Eliopoulos; m. Catherine Spathis 1953; two d.; ed. Athens Univ., Athens Nat. Theatre Dramatic School, London Royal Acad. of Dramatic Art, Yale Univ., Piscator New School; stage dir. in U.S.A. and U.K.; stage dir. Athens Nat. Theatre 1950–80; Founder and Dir. Proscinio Theatre 1964; Dir. Festival of Greek Classical Theatre, Ypsilanti, Mich., U.S.A. 1965–66; Prof. Athens Nat. Dramatic School; Asst. Man. Dir. Hellenic Broadcasting Foundation; Dir. Athens Nat. Theatre 1980, 1991. *Publications include:* Living Aristophanes 1961, Saint Bacchus 1964, The Age of Theatre 1973, My Good Thalia 1984, Theatrical Dictionary 1989, Euripides 1995; trans. of more than 30 foreign plays into Greek. *Leisure interests:* travel, crosswords, dogs and cats. *Address:* 13 Fokilidou Street, 106 73 Athens, Greece. *Telephone:* 3626.730; 3626.677.

SOLOVEY, Yelena Yakovlevna; Russian actress; b. 24 Feb. 1947; m.; one s. one d.; ed. VGIK; worked in cinema 1970–83; with Lensovet Theatre, Leningrad (now St. Petersburg) 1983–90; over 40 films; emigrated to U.S.A. 1991 (lives in New York); U.S.S.R. People's Artist 1990. *Roles include:* Klarich in King Stag 1970, Rimma in The Seven Brides of Zbruyev 1971, Dostigaeva in Yegor Bulychov and Others 1973, Lyuba in An Old-Style Drama 1972, Lenochka in Vanyushin's Kids 1974, Olga Voznesenskaya in Slave of Love 1976, Sofia in An Unfinished Piece for Mechanical Piano 1977, Olga Ilyinskaya in A Few Days in the Life of I. I. Oblomov 1980 (1st Prize for best female actor, Oxford Int. Festival 1980), Nadezhda Antonovna in Crazy Money 1982, The Fact 1982 (1981 Cannes Prize), There Was No Sorrow 1983, Helena's husband in On the Eve 1985, Life of Klim Samgin 1988.

SOLOVYEV, Gleb Mikhailovich, PH.D., D.M.S.; Russian surgeon; b. 9 Sept. 1928, Moscow; m. Albine Dmetrevne 1951; one d.; ed. First Medical Inst. Moscow; mem. CPSU 1950–91; postgraduate studies 1952–55; attached to Acad. of Medical Sciences 1955–60; Dir. Cardiac Surgery Lab., Research Inst. of Clinical and Experimental Surgery 1960–69, Deputy Dir. 1963–69; Dir. of Inst. for Organ and Tissue Transplants, Acad. of Medical Sciences 1969–74; Dir. Clinic of Cardiac Surgery, Sechenov Moscow Medical Acad. 1974–80, Head of Dept. of Cardiovascular Surgery 1980–, of Surgery 1990–; mem. Russian Acad. of Medical Sciences 1995; State Prize (for part in developing kidney transplants) 1971 and numerous other prizes. *Address:* Medical Academy City Hospital, Kolomensky pr. 4, 115487 Moscow, Russia.

SOLOVYEV, Sergey Aleksandrovich; Russian film director and scriptwriter; b. 25 Aug. 1944, Kem, Karelia; m. Tatyana Drubich; ed. All-Union Inst. of Cinematography with Leningrad TV 1960–69; film dir. Mosfilm Studio 1969–, artistic dir. Krug Film Union 1987–; Sec. U.S.S.R. Union of Cinematographers 1986–90; Chair. Moscow Union of Cinematographers 1990–97; Co-Chair. Russian Union of Cinematographers 1990–92; Prof. All-Russian Inst. of Cinematography; debut as scriptwriter Look into the Face 1966, as film dir. Family Happiness. *Films include:* Yegor Bulychev and Others 1971, Station Inspector 1972, A Hundred Days After Childhood 1975 (Silver Bear, Berlin, Prize of All-Union Festival, Tunes of A White Night 1977), Rescuer 1980, Direct Heir 1982, Strange, White and Speckled 1986, Assa 1987, Black Rose: an Emblem of Sadness, Red Rose: an Emblem of Love 1989, The House Under the Starry Sky 1991, Three Sisters 1994. *Address:* Akademika Pilyugina str. 8, korp. 1, Apt. 330, 117393 Moscow, Russia (Home). *Telephone:* 132 3695 (Home).

SOLOW, Robert Merton, PH.D.; American economist; b. 23 Aug. 1924, Brooklyn, N.Y.; s. of Milton and Hannah Solow; m. Barbara Lewis 1945; two s. one d.; ed. Harvard Univ.; Asst. Prof. of Statistics, Massachusetts Inst. of Technology 1950–53, Assoc. Prof. of Econs. 1954–57, Prof. of Econs. 1958–73, Inst. Prof. 1973–95, Inst. Prof. Emer. 1995–; W. Edwards Deming Prof., New York Univ. 1996; Sr. Economist, Council of Econ. Advisers 1961–62; Marshall Lecturer, Cambridge Univ. 1963–64; De Vries Lecturer, Rotterdam 1963, Wicksell Lecturer, Stockholm 1964; Eastman Visiting Prof., Oxford Univ. 1968–69; Killian Prize Lecturer, M.I.T. 1978; Geary Lecturer, Dublin 1980; Overseas Fellow, Churchill Coll., Cambridge 1984; Mitsui Lecturer, Birmingham 1985; Nobel Memorial Lecture, Stockholm 1987 and numerous others in int. academic insts.; mem. Nat. Comm. on Tech., Automation and Econ. Progress 1964–65, Presidential Comm. on Income Maintenance 1968–69; mem. Bd. of Dirs. Fed. Reserve Bank of Boston 1975–81, Chair. 1979–81; Fellow, Center for Advanced Study in Behavioral Sciences 1957–58, Trustee 1982–95; Vice-Pres. American Econ. Asscn. 1968, Pres. 1979, Vice-Pres. A.A.A.S. 1970; Pres. Econometric Soc. 1964; Trustee Woods Hold Oceanographic Inst. 1988–, Alfred P. Sloan Foundation 1992–, Resources for the Future 1994–96, Urban Inst. 1994–, German Marshall Fund of U.S. 1994–; mem. Nat. Science Bd. 1995–; Fellow American Acad. of Arts and Sciences, mem. of Council, N.A.S. 1977–80, mem. 1972–; corresp. mem. British Acad., mem. American Philosophical Soc.; Fellow Acad. dei Lincei (Rome); Hon. LL.D. (Chicago) 1967, (Lehigh) 1977, (Brown) 1972, (Wesleyan) 1982; Hon. Litt.D. (Williams Coll.) 1974; Dr. h.c. (Paris) 1975, (Geneva) 1982, (Conservatoire Nat. des Arts et Métiers, Paris) 1994; Hon. D.Litt. (Warwick) 1976, (Colgate) 1990, (Glasgow) 1992, (Harvard) 1992; Hon. Sc.D. (Tulane) 1983; Hon. Dr. Soc. Sc. (Yale) 1986, (Univ. of Mass., Boston) 1989, (Helsinki) 1990, (Boston Coll.) 1990, (Chile) 1992, (Rutgers Univ.) 1994; Hon. D.Sc. in Business Admin. (Bryant Coll.) 1988; Hon. D.Eng. (Colorado School of Mines) 1996; David A. Wells Prize, Harvard Univ. 1951, John Bates Clark Medal, American Econ. Asscn. 1961, Killian Award, M.I.T. 1977, Seidman Award in Political Econ. 1983, Nobel Prize for Econs. 1987, Orden pour le mérite, Germany 1995. *Publications:* Linear Programming and Economic Analysis 1958, Capital Theory and the Rate of Return 1963, Sources of Unemployment in the United States 1964, Price Expectations and the Behavior of the Price Level 1970, Growth Theory: An Exposition 1970, The Labor Market as a Social Institution 1989, A Critical Essay On Modern Macroeconomic Theory (with Frank Hahn) 1995. *Leisure interest:* sailing. *Address:* Department of Economics, Massachusetts Institute of Technology, Cambridge, MA 02139; 528 Lewis Wharf, Boston, MA 02110, U.S.A. (Home). *Telephone:* (617) 253-5268; (617) 227-4436.

SOLVAY, Jacques Ernest; Belgian business executive; b. 4 Dec. 1920, Ixelles; s. of Ernest-John Solvay and Marie Graux; m. Marie-Claude Boulin 1949; one s. three d.; ed. Univ. of Brussels; joined Solvay Cie. 1950, mem. Bd. 1955, Chair. 1971; Dir. Société Générale de Banque 1965–; Chair. Soltex Polymer Corpn. 1974–; Hon. Pres. Fédération des Industries Chimiques de Belgique; Pres. Belgo-British Union; mem. European Advisory Council, Tenneco Inc. 1986–; Chevalier de l'Ordre de Leopold; Hon. K.B.E. *Leisure interest:* orchid growing. *Address:* c/o Solvay Cie. S.A., rue de Prince Albert 33, B-1050 Brussels.

SOLYMAR, László, M.A., PH.D., F.R.S.; British engineer; b. 24 Jan. 1930, Budapest, Hungary; s. of Pál Solymar and Aranka Gold; m. Marianne Klopfer 1955; two d.; ed. Tech. Univ., Budapest, Hungarian Acad. of Sciences; lecturer Tech. Univ., Budapest 1952–53; research engineer Research Inst. for Telecommunications, Budapest 1953–56, Standard Telecommunications Labs. Ltd., Harlow, Essex 1956–65; lecturer Dept. of Eng. Science, Univ. of Oxford 1966–86, Fellow Brasenose Coll. 1966–86, Donald Pollock Reader in Eng. Science 1986–92, Fellow Hertford Coll. 1986–, Prof. of Applied Electromagnetism 1992–97, Leverhulme Emer. Fellow 1997–; Visiting Prof. Physics Lab., Ecole Normale Superieure, Univ. of Paris 1965–66, Tech. Univ. of Denmark 1972–73, Dept. of Physics, Univ. of Osnabrück 1987, Optical Inst., Tech. Univ., Berlin 1990, Dept. of Materials, Autonomous Univ. of Madrid 1993, 1995, Tech. Univ., Budapest 1994; Faraday Medal, I.E.E. 1992. *Publications:* various research and text books, and papers in learned journals; also three radio plays. *Leisure interests:* history, bridge, chess, swimming. *Address:* Department of Engineering Science, University of Oxford, Parks Road, Oxford, OX1 3PJ, England. *Telephone:* (01865) 273110. *Fax:* (01865) 273905.

SOLYMOSI, Zoltan; Hungarian ballet dancer; b. 1967, Budapest; ed. Ballet Acad. Budapest; joined Dutch Nat. Ballet as Prin. Dancer 1986, Munich Staatsoper 1989, La Scala Milan 1990; int. guest appearances; first appearance with Royal Ballet, London in Swan Lake, Metropolitan Opera House, New York 1991; full-time Artist of the Royal Ballet 1992–96, of English Nat. Ballet 1996; Resident Guest, London City Ballet 1996; repertoire includes prin. roles in maj. classical ballets, various works by Balanchine, works by Hungarian and Dutch choreographers, MacMillan and Ashton.

SOLYOM, Janos Paul; Hungarian/Swedish concert pianist and conductor; b. 26 Oct. 1938, Budapest; s. of Dr. I. Solyom and M. Weill; m. Camilla Lundberg 1987; ed. Franz Liszt Acad. of Music, Budapest; int. concert career 1958–; mem. Royal Swedish Acad. of Music; Royal Swedish Medal for Outstanding Artistic Merit 'Litteris et Artibus'. *Leisure interests:* architecture, parapsychology. *Address:* Norr Mälarstrand 54, VII S-112 20 Stockholm, Sweden. *Telephone:* 8-652 4272. *Fax:* 8-652 4272.

SÓLYOM, László, LL.D.; Hungarian judge; b. 3 Jan. 1942, Pécs; m. Erzsébet Nagy; one s. one d.; ed. Univ. of Pécs, Friedrich Schiller Univ., Jena, Hungarian Acad. of Sciences; lecturer in civil law Univ. of Jena 1966–69; research fellow Hungarian Acad. of Sciences 1969–82; Prof. of Law Univ. of Budapest 1982–, Catholic Univ. of Budapest 1996–, Univ. of Cologne 1999–; Pres. Constitutional Court 1990–98; legal adviser to environmental groups and other civic movts. 1982–89; mem. Int. Comm. of Jurists, Geneva, scientific council, Wissenschaftskolleg zu Berlin Inst. for Advanced Study, Berlin. *Publications:* The Decline of Civil Law Liability 1980, Die Persönlichkeitsrechte: Eine vergleichend-historische Studie über ihre Grundlagen 1984, Verfassungsgerichtsbarkeit in Ungarn: Analysen und Entscheidungssammlung 1990–93 (with Georg Brunner) 1995. *Address:* Magyar Köztársassag Alkotmánybírosága, Constitutional Court, 1015 Budapest, Donati u. 35–45, Hungary.

SOLZHENITSYN, Aleksandr Isayevich; Russian writer; b. 11 Dec. 1918, Kislovodsk; m. 1st Natalya Reshetovskaya (separated 1970); m. 2nd Natalya Svetlova; three s.; ed. Rostov Univ. and Correspondence Course in Literature, Moscow History and Literature Inst.; joined Army 1941, attended artillery school, commissioned 1942, served at front as Commdr. of Artillery Battery, and twice decorated for bravery; sentenced to eight years in a forced labour camp 1945–53; contracted, later cured of cancer; in exile in Siberia 1953–57; officially rehabilitated 1957; taught mathematics at secondary school, Ryazan; expelled from Writers' Union of U.S.S.R. Nov. 1969; expelled from U.S.S.R. Feb. 1974, lived in Vt., U.S.A.; ended exile as treason charges dropped 1991; returned to Russia, citizenship restored 1994; hosted A Meeting with Solzhenitsyn 1995; mem. American Acad. of Arts and Sciences 1969–, Russian Acad. of Sciences 1997–; Hon. Fellow, Hoover Inst. on War, Revolution and Peace 1975; Prix du Meilleur Livre Etranger (France) for The First Circle and Cancer Ward 1969, Nobel Prize for Literature 1970, Templeton Prize 1983; Hon. U.S. Citizen 1974. *Publications:* One Day in the Life of Ivan Denisovich 1962 (film 1971), Matryona's Home and An Incident at Krechetovka Station 1963 (short stories), For the Good of the Cause 1964 (short story), The First Circle (publ. U.S.A. and U.K. 1968), Cancer Ward (U.S.A. and U.K. 1968), The Easter Procession (short story), The Love Girl and the Innocent (play, U.K.) 1969, Collected Works (6 vols.) 1969, 1970, Stories and Prose Poems 1971, August 1914 1971, The Gulag Archipelago Vol. I 1973, Vol. II 1974, Vol. III 1976, Letter to Soviet Leaders 1974, Peace and Aggression 1974, Quiet Flows the Don: The Enigma of a Novel 1974, Candle in the Wind (play), The Oak and the Calf: Sketches of Literary Life in the Soviet Union 1975, The Nobel Prize Lecture 1975, Lenin in Zürich 1975, Détente (with others) 1976, Prussian Nights (poem trans. by Robert Conquest) 1977, Collected Works 1978–, Victory Celebrations, Prisoners (play) 1983, October 1916 1985, The Red Wheel, Live Not by Lies (essay) 1988, August 1914 (second version) 1989, Rebuilding Russia 1990, The Russian Question at the End of the 20th Century 1994, Invisible Allies (addendum to The Oak and the Calf) 1995, November 1916, Russia is Falling 1998. *Address:* P.O. Box 121, Cavendish, VT 05142, U.S.A.

SOMARE, Rt. Hon. Sir Michael Thomas, P.C., C.H., G.C.M.G.; Papua New Guinea politician; b. 9 April 1936, Rabaul, East New Britain Prov.; s. of Sana Ludwig Somare and Painari Betha; m. Veronica Bula Kaiap 1965; three s. two d.; ed. Sogeri Secondary School, Admin. Coll.; Teacher various schools 1956–64; Asst. Area Educ. Officer, Madang 1962–63; Broadcasts Officer, Dept. of Information and Extension Services, Wewak 1963–66, radio broadcaster and journalist 1966–67; mem. House of Assembly for East Sepik Regional 1968–; Parl. Leader Pangu Party 1968–88; Deputy Chair. Exec. Council 1972–73, Chair. 1973–75; Chief Minister Papua New Guinea 1974–75, Prime Minister 1975–80, 1982–85; Minister for Nat. Resources 1976–77, for Public Service Comm. and Nat. Planning 1977–80; Acting Minister for Police 1978–80; Leader of the Opposition 1980–82; Minister of Foreign Affairs 1988–94; Gov. E. Sepik Prov. 1995; Chair. Bd. of Trustees, P.N.G.; mem. Second Select Cttee. on Constitutional Devt. 1968–72, Australian Broadcasting Comm. Advisory Cttee.; six hon. degrees; Ancient Order of Sikatuna, Title of Rajah (Philippines) 1976, Queen's Silver Jubilee Medal 1977; Pacific Man of the Year Award 1983, Grand Cross of Equestrian Order of St. Gregory the Great 1993. *Leisure interests:* reading, golf, soccer, cricket, fishing. *Address:* House of Assembly, Port Moresby; Karan, Murik Lakes, East Sepik, Papua New Guinea.

SOMAVIA, Juan O.; Chilean diplomatist; m.; two c.; ed. Catholic Univ. of Chile, Univ. of Paris; various posts in Ministry of Foreign Relations; Founder and Exec. Dir. Latin American Inst. for Transnat. Studies, Mexico; Co-ordinator Third World Forum; mem. Bd. of Dirs. and Vice-Pres. for Latin America of Inter-Press Service 1976–87; Sec.-Gen. South American Peace Comm. 1987; Pres. Int. Comm. of Chilean opposition No Campaign for Referendum 1988–89; Perm. Rep. to UN, New York 1990–98; Dir. Gen. ILO 1998–; fmr. consultant to GATT and UNDP; mem. Bd. of Dirs. Int. Foundation for Devt. Alternatives, mem. MacBride Comm. on communication problems; Leonidas Proaño Prize, Latin American Human Rights Asscn. for contrib. to peace and regional security. *Address:* International Labour Organization, 4 route des Morillons, 1211 Geneva 22, Switzerland.

SOMERS, Daryl; Australian broadcaster; m. Julie da Costa 1985; professional vocalist and drummer; first TV appearance on New Faces, GTV 9, Melbourne 1968; debut as TV host on weekday children's show Cartoon Corner 1971 (ran till 1977), later same year became co-host (with P. McKenna) of Hey Hey It's Saturday (continues as host); Chief Exec. Somers Carroll Pty. Ltd., owners of Hey Hey 1979–. *TV appearances:* (host) Daryl Somers Show, own Tonight show, Bandstand, Ossie Ostrich Video Show, Family Feud (game show), Blankety Blanks (game show), the King of Pop Awards; numerous other Tonight and variety shows; live singing performances with Melbourne Symphony Orchestra, concerts, pantomimes and sporting events. *Address:* c/o GTV 9, 22 Bendigo Street, Richmond 3121, Australia.

SOMLYÓ, György; Hungarian poet, novelist, critic and translator of poetry; b. 28 Nov. 1920, Balatonboglár; s. of Zoltán Somlyó and Margit Bolgár; m. (divorced 1986); one s.; ed. Budapest Univ. and the Sorbonne, Paris; Lecturer in Modern Poetry Budapest Univ. 1975–78; Ed. Arion 1966–87; organizer Int. Meeting of Poets, Budapest 1966, 1970; corresp. PO&SIE poetry magazine, Paris 1976–; mem. Széchenyi Hungarian Acad. of Arts and Letters; corresp. mem. Académie Mallarmé, Paris 1977–; József Attila prize (four times), Tibor Déry Prize 1987, Kassák Prize, Soros Foundation 1991, Gabriela Mistral Memorial Medal (Chile) 1996, Kossuth Prize 1997; Officier, Ordre des Arts et Lettres (France) 1984, Order of Flag of Hungarian Repub. 1990. *Publications include:* Collected Works: Vol. 1: A költészet vérszerződése (The Blood Covenant of Poetry) 1977, Vols 2, 3: Collected Poems 1978, Vol. 4: Másutt (Elsewhere) 1979, Vol. 5: Szerelöszönyeg (Catwalk) 1981, Vol. 6: Megiratlan könyvek (Unwritten Books) 1982, Vol. 7: Miért hal meg az ember? (Why the Man Dies?) 1984, Philoktetész sebe (Philoctetes' Wound) 1980, Árnyjáték (Shadow Play) 1977, Rámpa (Ramp) 1984, Picasso 1981, Parisiens (poems in French) 1987, A Költészet ötödik évada (The Fifth Season of Poetry) 1988, Ami rajtam tul van (What's Beyond Me) 1988, Városok (Cities: essays) 1990, Nom titok (No Secret: poems) 1992, Az elvitathatatlan hely (The Evident Place, essays) 1994; Ed. 1001 Sonnets of World Literature (anthology) 1991; *translations:* Szélrózsa I/III (Compass Card) 1973, Az utazás (The Journey), French Poetry from Baudelaire to our days 1984, Palimpszeszt (poems) 1990, Párizsi Kettös (Duo in Paris) 1991, A Negyedik Szoba (The Fourth Room) (poems) 1994, Énekek Éneke (Song of Songs) 1994, Töresvonlak (Breaklines) (poems) 1997, Paul Valéry: Füretele (notebooks) 1997, SEB ÉS KES (Wound and Knife) (Selected poems 1976–97) 1998. *Address:* Irinyi J. u. 39, H-1111 Budapest, Hungary. *Telephone:* (1) 186-09-54.

SOMMARUGA, Cornelio, LL.D.; Swiss diplomatist; b. 29 Dec. 1932, Rome, Italy; s. of Carlo Sommaruga and Anna-Maria Valagussa; m. Ornella Marzorati 1957; two s. four d.; ed. Rome, Paris, Univ. of Zürich; bank trainee, Zürich 1957–59; joined Diplomatic Service 1960; Attaché, Swiss Embassy, The Hague 1961; Sec. Swiss Embassy, Bonn 1962–64, Rome 1965–68; Deputy Head of Del. to EFTA, GATT and UNCTAD, Geneva 1969–73; Asst. Sec.-Gen. EFTA July 1973–75; Minister plenipotentiary, Div. of Commerce, Fed. Dept. of Public Economy, Berne 1976, Amb. 1977; del. Fed. Council for Trade Agreements 1980–84; State Sec. for External Econ. Affairs 1984–87; Pres. Int. Cttee. Red Cross 1987–98; Pres., UN Econ. Comm. for Europe 1977–78; Presidential Award, Tel-Aviv Univ.; Dr. h.c. (Fribourg) 1985, (Braga) 1990, (Nice-Sophia Antipolis, Seoul Nat. Univ.) 1992; M.D. h.c. (Bologna) 1991. *Publications:* La posizione costituzionale del Capo dello Stato nelle Costituzioni francese ed italiana del dopoguerra 1957, and numerous articles in journals and periodicals. *Address:* c/o International Committee of the Red Cross, 19 avenue de la Paix, 1202 Geneva, Switzerland (Office).

SOMMER, Elke; German actress; b. 5 Nov. 1940, Berlin; d. of Friedrich Schletz and Renate Schletz; m. Joe Hyams (twice); Wolf Walther 1993; first film, L'Amico del Giaguaro 1958; since then has made more than 70 films including The Prize, The Victors, Shot in the Dark, The Oscar; own TV show (PBS), Painting with Elke 1985; Golden Globe Award 1965, Jefferson Award, Merit of Achievement Award 1990. *Leisure interests:* riding, art. *Address:* 91080 Marloffstein, Germany; 540 N. Beverly Glen Boulevard W., Los Angeles, CA 90024, U.S.A. *Telephone:* 09131-5366-0 (Germany); (310) 724-8990 (U.S.A). *Fax:* 09131-5366-99 (Germany); (310) 724-8993 (U.S.A.).

SOMMER, Theo, DR.PHIL.; German journalist; b. 10 June 1930, Constance; s. of Theo and Else Sommer; m. 1st Elda Tsilenis 1952; four s. one d.; m. 2nd Heide Grenz 1976; m. 3rd Sabine Grewe 1989; ed. Schwäbisch-Gmünd, Tübingen, Chicago and Harvard Univs.; Local Ed. Schwäbisch-Gmünd 1952–54; Political Ed. Die Zeit 1958, Deputy Ed.-in-Chief 1968, Ed.-in-Chief and Joint Publr. 1973–92, Publr. 1993–; Lecturer in Int. Relations, Univ. of Hamburg 1967–70; Head of Planning Staff, Ministry of Defence 1969–70; mem. Deutsche Gesellschaft für Auswärtige Politik, mem. Council Int. Inst. for Strategic Studies; Contrib. Ed. Newsweek; Commentator German TV, Radio; Theodor-Wolff-Preis 1966; Hon. Dr. Univ. of Md., U.S.A. *Publications:* Deutschland und Japan zwischen den Mächten 1935–40, Vom Antikominternpakt zum Dreimächtepakt 1962, Reise in ein fernes Land 1964, Ed. Denken an Deutschland 1966, Ed. Schweden-Report 1974, Die chinesische Karte 1979, Allianz in Umbruch 1982, Blick zurück in die Zukunft 1984, Reise ins andere Deutschland 1986. *Address:* Die Zeit, Pressehaus, Speersort 1, 20095 Hamburg, Germany. *Telephone:* 603-73-00.

SOMORJAI, Gabor Arpad, PH.D.; American professor of chemistry; b. 4 May 1935, Budapest; s. of Charles Somorjai and Livia Ormos; m. Judith Kaldor 1957; one s. one d.; ed. Univ. of Tech. Sciences, Budapest, Univ. of Calif., Berkeley; mem. Research Staff IBM, New York 1960–64; at Faculty of Dept. of Chem., Univ. of Calif., Berkeley 1964–, Asst. Prof. 1964–67, Assoc. Prof. 1967–72, Prof. 1972–; Faculty Sr. Scientist, Materials Science Div. and Dir. Surface Science and Catalysis Program, Lawrence Berkeley Lab., Berkeley, Calif. 1964–; numerous awards and visiting professorships in U.S.A. and U.K. including Visiting Fellow Emmanuel Coll., Univ. of Cambridge 1969; Centenary Lecturer Royal Soc. of Chem., U.K. 1983; Hinshelwood Lecturer, Univ. of Oxford 1994; Linnett Lecturer, Univ. of Cambridge 1994; mem. N.A.S. 1979–, Fellow A.A.A.S. 1982–, American Physical Soc., mem. American Acad. of Arts and Sciences 1983, American Chem. Soc.; Hon. mem. Hungarian Acad. of Sciences 1990; Dr. h.c. (Sorbonne) 1990, (Univ. Libre de Bruxelles) 1992; Emmett Award American Catalysis Soc. 1977, Colloid and Surface Chem. Award American Chem. Soc. 1981, Peter Debye Award, American Chem. Soc. 1989, Adamson Surface Chemistry Award/American Chem. Soc. 1994, Von Hippel Award, Materials Research Soc. 1997. *Publications:* Principles of Surface Chemistry 1972, Chemistry in Two Dimensions 1981, Introduction to Surface Chemistry and Catalysis 1994, serves editorial bds. of numerous scientific publs., nearly 600 publs. in major scientific journals. *Leisure interest:* swimming. *Address:* Department of Chemistry, University of California, D58, Hildebrand Hall, Berkeley, CA 94720; 665 San Luis Road, Berkeley, CA 94707, U.S.A. (Home). *Telephone:* (510) 642-4053.

SON, Masayoshi; Japanese business executive; ed. Univ. of California; started by importing used video games from Japan (to U.S.A.); co-developed pocket electronic translator bought by Sharp; f. Softbank (Japan's largest software distributor); retailer of personal computer games, Japan.

SON SANN; Cambodian politician and financial administrator; b. 5 Oct. 1911, Phnom-Penh; m. Nema Machhwa 1940; five s. two d.; ed. Ecole des Hautes Etudes Commerciales de Paris; Deputy Gov. Provinces of Battambang and Prey-Veng 1935–39; Head of Yuvan Kampuchearath (Youth Movement); Minister of Finance 1946–47; Vice-Pres. Council of Ministers 1949; Minister of Foreign Affairs 1950; Mem. of Parl. for Phnom-Penh and Pres. Cambodian Nat. Assembly 1951–52; Gov. of Nat. Bank of Cambodia 1954–68; Minister of State (Finance and Nat. Economy) 1961–62; Vice-Pres., in charge of Economy, Finance and Planning 1965–67, Pres. Council of Ministers May-Dec. 1967; First Vice-Pres. in charge of Econ. and Financial Affairs 1968; Leader Khmer People's Nat. Front 1986; involved in help for Khmer refugees 1979; involved in anti-Vietnamese guerrilla war 1979–91; Prime Minister, Coalition Govt. of Democratic Kampuchea 1982–91; mem. Supreme Nat. Council of Cambodia 1991–93; Chair. Constituent Ass. 1993; High Counsellor to H.M. the King; Grand Croix de l'Ordre Royal du Cambodge, Séna yaya-sedth, Commdr. du Sowathara (Mérite économique), Grand Officier Légion d'honneur, Commdr. du Monisaraphon, Médaille d'or du Règne, Grand Officier du Million d'Eléphants (Laos), Mil. Medal with Golden Palm 1993, Grand Cross (Yugoslavia), Grand Cross of Order of the Nile, Grand Cross (Belgium). *Leisure interest:* Buddhist books.

SONDECKIS, Saulius; Lithuanian conductor; b. 11 Oct. 1928, Šiauliai, Lithuania; s. of Jackus Sondeckis and Rozalija Sondeckienė; m. Silvija Sondeckienė; three s.; ed. Lithuanian Conservatory as violinist, Moscow State Conservatory; f., conductor and artistic dir. Lithuanian Chamber orchestra; tours fmr. U.S.S.R. and Europe 1960–; teacher Vilnius M. Čiurlionis School of Arts 1955–85, f. Youth Orchestra; winner of Gold Medal at Herbert von Karajan Stiftung Competition in Berlin 1976; f. and Artistic Dir. St. Petersburg Camerata Chamber Orchestra (now Orchestra of Hermitage Museum) 1989–; Prof. Vilnius Conservatory 1957–, Chair. Strings Dept. 1959–87; Prof. St. Petersburg Conservatory 1989–91; f. (with G. Kremer) Kremerata Baltica Chamber Orchestra 1996; conducted various European, U.S. and Japanese orchestras; worked together with Rostropovich and many other distinguished soloists; first performance of chamber music by Alfred Schnittke, Sergey Slonimsky, Arvo Pärt, contemporary Lithuanian composers: U.S.S.R. People's Artist 1980, Lithuanian State Prize 1971, U.S.S.R. State Prize 1987, State Prize of Lithuanian Govt. 1998; Lithuanian Grand Duke First and Fifth Order of Gediminas Cavalier. *Address:* Čiurlionio 28, Vilnius, Lithuania. *Telephone:* (02) 33-15-57; 33-27-68 (Home). *Fax:* (02) 62-36-46 (Home).

SONDHEIM, Stephen Joshua; American song writer; b. 22 March 1930, New York City; s. of Herbert Sondheim and Janet Fox; ed. George School, Newtown, Pa., Williams Coll., Williamstown, Mass., private instruction; Pres. Dramatists' Guild 1973–81, Council mem. 1981–; Visiting Prof. of Drama and Musical Theatre, Oxford Univ. Jan.–June 1990; mem. American Acad. and Inst. of Arts and Letters 1983–; Antoinette Perry Award for Company 1971, Follies 1972, A Little Night Music 1973, Sweeney Todd 1979; Drama Critics' Award 1971, 1972, 1973, 1976, 1979; Evening Standard Drama Award 1996; Grammy Award 1984, 1986; television: Topper (co-author) 1953, Evening Primrose (music and lyrics) 1967; lyrics: West Side Story 1957, Gypsy 1959, Do I Hear a Waltz? 1965, Candide 1974; music and lyrics: A Funny Thing Happened on the Way to the Forum 1962, Anyone Can Whistle 1964, Company 1970, Follies 1971, A Little Night Music 1973, The Frogs 1974, Pacific Overtures 1976, Sweeney Todd 1978, Merrily We Roll Along 1981, Sunday in the Park with George 1984, Into the Woods (Drama Critic's Circle Award 1988) 1986, Follies 1987, Assassins 1989, Passion 1994; anthologies: Side by Side by Sondheim 1977, Marry Me a Little 1980, You're Gonna Love Tomorrow 1983, Putting It Together 1993; screenplay: (with Anthony Perkins) The Last of Sheila 1973; film scores: Stavisky 1975, Reds 1981, Dick Tracy 1989.

SONG BAORUI; Chinese politician; b. Dec. 1937, Shunyi Co., Beijing; ed. Qinghua Univ.; joined CCP 1958; fmr. Deputy Dir., Chief Engineer China Welding Rod Plant, Dir. China Welding Rod Plant Inst. 1975–82; Man. China Welding Materials Manufacture Co. 1982–83; Deputy Sec. then Sec. CCP Zigong City Cttee. 1983–86; fmr. mem. Standing Cttee. CCP Sichuan Prov. Cttee; Chair. Sichuan Prov. Comm. for Restructuring the Economy 1986–89, Exec. Deputy Sec. CCP Sichuan Prov. Cttee. 1989–; Gov. of Sichuan Prov. 1996–; alt. mem. 14th CCP Cen. Cttee.; Deputy 8th NPC; mem. 15th CCP Cen. Cttee. 1997–. *Address:* c/o People's Government of Sichuan, Chengdu, Sichuan Province, People's Republic of China.

SONG DEFU; Chinese party and government official; b. 1946, Yanshan Co., Hebei Prov.; joined PLA and CCP 1965; First Sec. of Secr. Communist Youth League of China 1985–93; Minister of Personnel 1993–; Party Group Sec., Ministry of Personnel; Head Nat. Leading Group for Placement of Demobilized Army Officers 1993–; mem. 13th CCP Cen. Cttee. 1987–92, 14th CCP Cen. Cttee. 1992–97, 15th CCP Cen. Cttee. 1997–. *Address:* 12 Hepingli Zhongjie Street, East District, Beijing 100716, People's Republic of China.

SONG DEMIN; Chinese politician; b. 1930, Dongfeng Co., Jilin Prov.; Sec.-Gen. 8th Nat. Cttee. CPPCC 1993; mem. CCP 1948. *Address:* National Committee of Chinese People's Political Consultative Council, 23 Taiping Qiao Street, Beijing, People's Republic of China.

SONG HANLIANG; Chinese politician and geologist; b. 1934, Shaoxing Co., Zhejiang Prov.; ed. Xibei Univ.; joined CCP 1960; geologist, head of geological prospecting team and Dir. of Prospecting Research Inst., Xinjiang Petroleum Admin. Bureau; Vice-Chair. Xinjiang Autonomous Region CCP Cttee. 1983–85, Sec. 1985–94; mem. Standing Cttee. of Xinjiang Prov. CCP Cttee. 1985, Sec. 1985–86; First Political Commissar, Xinjiang Production and Construction Corps 1987–96; mem. 13th Cen. Cttee. CCP 1987–92, 14th Cen. Cttee. 1992–, 8th NPC 1993–. *Address:* Dangwei Office of Xinjiang Autonomous Region, Urumqi, Xinjiang, People's Republic of China.

SONG HONG-ZHAO, B.S., M.D., F.R.C.O.G.; Chinese obstetrician and gynaecologist; b. 13 Aug. 1915, Suzhou, Jiangsu Prov.; m.; three s. one d.; ed. Suzhou Univ., Peiping Union Medical Coll.; Prof. of Obstetrics and Gynaecology, Chinese Union Medical Univ., Chinese Acad. of Medical Sciences, Beijing; Hon. Prof., Chi-nan Univ. School of Medicine, Guangdong, W. China Medical Univ., Sichuan, Xian Medical Univ., Shaanxi; consultant Shenzhen People's Hosp., Chang-zhan Hosp. of Obstetrics and Gynaecology, Guangzhou Hosp. of Maternity and Child Health, Guangdong Prov.; Visiting Prof., Univ. of Hong Kong 1987, 1994; mem. CPPCC Nat. Standing Cttee.; Vice-Chair. Science, Educ., Culture, Medicine and Athletics Sub-cttee.; special interests: gynaecological oncology, especially trophoblastic diseases; Hon. Chair. Soc. of Obstetrics and Gynaecology; Hon. Chief Ed. Chinese Journal of Obstetrics and Gynaecology; Adviser to Journal of Practical Obstetrics and Gynaecology, Journal of Recent Advances in Obstetrics and Gynaecology; Past Pres. Int. Soc. on Study of Trophoblastic Diseases; Academician, Chinese Acad. of Eng. (Medicine Div.); mem. Int. Soc. of Gynaecological Oncology; Fellow ad eundem Royal Coll. of Obstetricians and Gynaecologists (U.K.) 1995; First Grade Prize for Study of Trophoblastic Diseases, State Comm. of Science and Tech. 1985, Tan Kah-Kee Prize 1989, "Advanced Worker" honour 1990, Ho-Leung-Ho-Lee Foundation (Hong Kong) Prize for Promotion of Sciences and Tech. 1995. *Publications:* Trophoblastic Neoplasms: Diagnosis and Treatment (in Chinese) 1981, Studies of Trophoblastic Diseases in China 1988, Basic Knowledge of Obstetrics and Gynaecology 1993; 160 papers in Chinese and foreign scientific journals. *Leisure interest:* philately. *Address:* Department of Obstetrics and Gynaecology, Beijing Union Medical College Hospital, Beijing 100730, People's Republic of China. *Telephone:* 6529-6201 (Office); 6513-0127 (Home). *Fax:* 6512-4875.

SONG JIAN, D.SC.; Chinese state official; b. 29 Dec. 1931, Rongcheng Co., Shandong Prov.; s. of Song Zengjin and late Jiang Yuxian; m. Wang Yusheng 1961; one s. one d.; ed. Moscow Univ.; joined CCP 1947; Head, Lab. of Cybernetics, Inst. of Math., Acad. Sinica 1960–70; Dir. Guided Missile Control Lab., 7th Ministry of Machine Bldg. Industry 1962–70; Head, Chief Scientist, Space Science Div., Acad. of Space Tech. 1971–78, Vice-Pres., Deputy Science Dir., Acad. of Space Tech. 1978–81; Vice-Minister and Chief Eng. Scientist, Ministry of Astronautics 1981–84; Research Prof., Beijing Inst. of Information and Control 1983–; Chair. State Science & Tech. Comm. 1984–98; mem. Chinese Acad. of Sciences 1991–; State Councillor 1986–98; Visiting Prof. M.I.T., Harvard, Univ. of Minn. 1980; Vice-Pres. China Soc. of Demographic Science 1982–86; Assoc. Chief Ed. System & Control Letters 1983–85; Chief Ed. Automatic Control & System Eng., Encyclopaedia of China 1983–; mem. Ed. Bd. Encyclopaedia of China 1984–; Council mem. Int. Fed. of Automatic Control 1984–87; Vice-Pres. China System Eng. Soc. 1985–87; mem. Chinese Acad. of Eng. 1994–, Pres. 1998–; Foreign mem. Russian Acad. of Sciences 1994, Royal Swedish Acad. of Eng. Sciences 1994; Corresp. mem. Nat. Acad. of Eng. of Mexico 1985; Prof. Qinghua Univ., Fudan Univ., Harbin Univ. of Tech. 1986–; Hon. Distinguished Visiting Prof. Washington Univ. 1986–; mem. 13th Cen. Cttee. CCP 1987–92, 14th Cen. Cttee. 1992–97, 15th Cen. Cttee. 1997–; Vice-Chair. 9th Nat. Cttee. CPPCL 1998–; Hon. D. Hum. Litt. (Houston) 1996; numerous nat. and int. awards. *Publications:* Reference Frames in Space Flight 1963, Engineering Cybernetics (co-author) 1980, China's Population: Problems and Prospects 1981, Recent Development in Control Theory and its Applications 1984, Population Projections and Control 1981, Population Control Theory 1985, Population Control in China: Theory and Applications 1985, Population System Control 1988, Science and Technology and Social System 1988; numerous articles. *Leisure interest:* swimming. *Address:* National Committee of Chinese People's Political Consultative Conference, 23 Taipingqiao Street, Beijing, People's Republic of China.

SONG MUWEN; Chinese publishing executive; b. 1929, Yushu Co., Jilin; Chair. Publrs'. Asscn. of China 1993–; Pres. Copyright Research Society; mem. NPC Educ., Science, Culture and Public Health Cttee. *Address:* Publishers' Association of China, 85 Dongsi Nan Dajie, Beijing 100703, People's Republic of China. *Telephone:* (010) 65228632. *Fax:* (010) 65228632.

SONG PING; Chinese party official; b. 1917, Juxian Co., Shandong Prov.; ed. Inst. Marxism-Leninism, Yan'an; joined CCP 1937; Vice-Minister, Labour 1953; Vice-Chair. State Planning Comm. 1957–63; Sec. CCP Gansu, and Vice-Chair. Gansu Revolutionary Cttee. 1972, First Sec. CCP Gansu, Chair. Gansu Revolutionary Cttee., Second Political Commissar, PLA Lanzhou Mil. Region and First Political Commissar Gansu Mil. District, PLA 1977–80; mem. 11th Cen. Cttee. CCP 1977; First Vice-Chair. State Planning Comm. 1981–83; Minister in charge of State Planning Comm. 1983–87; mem. 12th Cen. Cttee. CCP 1982–87, Political Bureau 1987–92, 13th Cen. Cttee., mem. Standing Cttee. 1989–92; Chair. Family Planning Asscn. 1990–; Hon. Pres. Chinese Asscn. for Promotion of the Population Culture; Deputy Sec.-Gen., First Session of the 7th NPC March 1988; Deputy Dir. Leading Group for

Co-ordinating Nat. Scientific Work 1983; State Councillor 1983–88; Vice-Chair. Environmental Protection Cttee. State Council 1984–87, Nat. Agric. Zoning Cttee. 1983–; Deputy Head Leading Group for Scientific Work, State Council 1983–92; Head Leading Group for Econ. Information Man., State Council 1986–92; Head Org. Dept. Cen. Cttee. CCP 1988–90; visited Pakistan 1991; mem. Presidium 14th CCP Nat. Congress Oct. 1992; Hon. Dir.-in-Chief China Welfare Fund for Handicapped; Hon. Adviser "Happiness Project" Org. *Address:* Central Committee of CCP, Zhang Nan Hai, Beijing, People's Republic of China.

SONG QINGWEI, Gen.; Chinese army officer and party official; b. 1929, Lingxian Co., Shandong Prov.; joined CCP 1945; Political Commissar of PLA Jinan Mil. Area Command 1987–95; rank of Lieut.-Gen. 1988, of Gen. 1994; mem. 14th CCP Cen. Cttee. 1992–97; Vice-Chair. Foreign Affairs Cttee. 9th NPC 1998–. *Address:* c/o Standing Committee of National People's Congress, Beijing, People's Republic of China.

SONG RENQIONG; Chinese politician; b. 1903, Hunan Prov.; m.; two s. four d.; ed. Huangpu Mil. Acad.; joined CCP 1926, on Long March 1934–35; Alt. mem. 7th Cen. Cttee. CCP 1945; Cadre in S.W. China 1949–54; Minister of 3rd Ministry of Machine Building 1954, 2nd Ministry of Machine Building 1959–60, 7th Ministry of Machine Building 1977–79; mem. 8th Cen. Cttee. CCP 1956, First Sec. N.E. Bureau 1961–67; Dir. Org. Dept. CCP 1979–; Chair. Credentials Cttee. 5th NPC 1980–83; mem. Secr. 11th Cen. Cttee. CCP; mem. Politburo 12th Cen. Cttee. CCP 1982–85, Chair. Credentials Cttee. 1982; Vice-Chair. Cen. Advisory Comm. 1985, 1987; Adviser Cen. Party Consolidation Guidance Comm. 1983–92; mem. Presidium 14th CCP Nat. Congress Oct. 1992; Hon. Pres. Volleyball Asscn. *Address:* Zhongnandai, Beijing, People's Republic of China.

SONG RUIXIANG; Chinese politician; b. 1939, Jintan Co., Jiangsu Prov.; joined CCP 1959; Gov. of Qinghai Prov. 1988–93; Minister of Geology and Mineral Resources 1993–98, Party Group Sec. Ministry of Geology and Mineral Resources; Chair. Nat. Mineral Reserves Comm. 1995–96; Vice-Chair. Nat. Mineral Resources Cttee. 1996–98; Vice-Dir. State Gen. Admin. of Environment Protection 1998–; mem. 15th CCP Cen. Cttee. 1997–. *Address:* State General Administration of Environment Protection, Beijing, People's Republic of China.

SONG ZHAOSU; Chinese politician; b. March 1941, Nanyang, He'nan Prov.; ed. Zhengzhou Univ.; joined CCP 1965; Vice-Sec. CCP He'nan Prov. Cttee. 1993–98; Deputy Gov. then Gov. Gansu Prov. 1998–; alt. mem. CCP 15th Cen. Cttee. 1997–. *Address:* Gansu Provincial People's Government, Lanzhou, Gansu Province, People's Republic of China.

SONN, Franklin Abraham; South African diplomatist; b. 11 Oct. 1939, Vosburg Dist.; s. of Pieter (Pat) Sonn and Magdalene Klein; m.; two c.; ed. UNISA and Univ. of W. Cape; fmr. Rector, Peninsula Technikon; fmr. Chair. Comm. of Technikon Prins., Chair. W. Cape Foundation for Community Work, Mobil Foundation of S. Africa, Inst. for Distance Educ.; Chair. Bd. Trustees, Die Suid-Afrikaan Magazine, Nat. Educ. and Training Forum 1994–; Vice-Chair. Urban Found.; Dir. Metropolitan M-Net 1994–; mem. Bd. Corp. Africa; Vice-Pres. Jt. Council of Teachers Asscn. of S. Africa; numerous other public appts.; Amb. to U.S.A. 1995–. *Publications include:* A Decade of Struggle 1986; numerous papers and official documents. *Leisure interests:* reading, walking, mountaineering, squash. *Address:* South African Embassy, 3051 Massachusetts Avenue, N.W., Washington, DC 20008, U.S.A. *Telephone:* (202) 232-4400. *Fax:* (202) 232-3402.

SONNENFELD, Barry; American cinematographer and film director; *cinematographer (films):* Blood Simple 1984, Compromising Positions 1985, Three O'Clock High 1987, Raising Arizona 1987, Throw Momma from the Train 1987, Big 1988, When Harry Met Sally . . . 1989, Miller's Crossing 1990, Misery 1990. *Television:* Out of Step 1984 (Emmy Award for best cinematography 1984); director (films): The Addams Family 1991, Addams Family Values 1993, Get Shorty 1995, Men in Black 1997; dir. and co-producer: For Love or Money 1993. *Address:* c/o Gersh Agency, 232 North Canon Drive, Beverly Hills, CA 90210; United Talent Agency, 9560 Wilshire Boulevard, Beverly Hills, CA 90212, U.S.A.

SONNENFELDT, Helmut, M.A.; American international business consultant and fmr. government official; b. 13 Sept. 1926, Berlin, Germany; s. of Dr. Walther H. Sonnenfeldt and Dr. Gertrud L. Sonnenfeldt; m. Marjorie Hecht 1953; two s. one d.; ed. Univ. of Manchester, Johns Hopkins Univ.; went to U.S.A. 1944; mem. Counterintelligence Corps, U.S. Army, Pacific and European Theaters; with Dept. of State 1952–69, Policy Officer, U.S. Disarmament Admin. 1960–61, Director Office of Research and Analysis for the U.S.S.R. and E. Europe 1966–69; Senior Staff mem. for Europe and East-West Relations, Nat. Security Council 1969–74; Counsellor of Dept. of State 1974–77; Trustee, Johns Hopkins Univ. 1974–, Visiting Scholar, School of Advanced Int. Studies, Johns Hopkins Univ. 1977–78; Guest Scholar, Brookings Inst. 1978–; Lecturer on Soviet Affairs, Johns Hopkins Univ. School of Advanced Int. Studies; Consultant Washington Center for Foreign Policy Research; Gov. and Dir. UN Asscn. of U.S.A. 1980; Dir. Atlantic Council of U.S.A. 1978; mem. Int. Inst. of Strategic Studies, London 1977–, (mem. Exec. Cttee. 1986–), Council of Foreign Relations, Royal Inst. of Int. Affairs, London, Int. Advisory Council, Credit-Anstalt-Bankverein, Vienna 1983–; Editorial Bd. Politique Internationale (Paris) 1978–, Foreign Policy 1980–; govt. rep. to numerous confs. and meetings abroad; Consultant to int. investments firms and banks. *Publications:* Soviet Policy in the 1980s 1985, articles on int. issues in American and European journals. *Leisure interests:* tennis, music, reading biography. *Address:* Brookings Institution, 1775 Massachusetts Ave, N.W., Washington, DC 20036; 5600 Wisconsin Avenue, #1505, Chevy Chase, MD 20815, U.S.A. *Telephone:* (202) 797-6028. *Fax:* (202) 797-6004.

SONTAG, Susan, M.A.; American author and film director; b. 16 Jan. 1933; m. Philip Rieff 1950 (divorced 1958); one s.; ed. Univ. of Chicago and Harvard Univ.; mem. American Inst. of Arts and Letters, American Acad. of Arts and Sciences, PEN (Pres. American Centre 1987–89); Officier, Ordre des Arts et des Lettres (France); Guggenheim Fellow 1966, 1975, Rockefeller Foundation Fellow 1965, 1974; recipient Ingram Merrill Foundation Award in Literature in the Field of American Letters 1976, Creative Arts Award, Brandeis Univ. 1976, Arts and Letters Award, American Acad. of Arts and Letters 1976, Nat. Book Critics Circle Prize 1978, MacArthur Fellowship 1990–95, Elmer Holmes Bobst Award 1991. *Films include:* Duet for Cannibals 1969, Brother Carl 1971, Promised Lands 1974, Unguided Tour 1983; Dir. Waiting for Godot, Sarajevo 1993. *Publications:* The Benefactor (novel) 1963, Death Kit (novel) 1967, Against Interpretation (essays) 1966, Styles of Radical Will 1969, On Photography 1977, Illness as Metaphor 1978, I, Etcetera (stories) 1978, Under the Sign of Saturn 1980, A Susan Sontag Reader (anthology) 1982, A Barthes Reader (introduction) 1982, AIDS and Its Metaphors 1989, The Way We Live Now 1991, The Volcano Lover (novel) 1992, Alice in Bed (play) 1993, Under the Sign of Saturn (poetry) 1996. *Address:* 470 W. 24th Street, New York, NY 10011, U.S.A.

SOONG, James Chu-yul, PH.D.; Taiwanese politician; b. 16 March 1942, Hunan; m. Viola Chen; one s. one d.; ed. Nat. Chengchi Univ., Taipei, Univ. of California, Berkeley, Catholic Univ. of America, Georgetown Univ., Washington D.C.; Sec. Exec. Yuan, Taiwan 1974–77; Deputy Dir.-Gen. Govt. Information Office 1977–79; Assoc. Prof., Nat. Taiwan Univ. 1975–79; Research Fellow, Inst. of Int. Relations, Nat. Chengchi Univ. 1974–; Personal Sec. to the Pres. 1978–89; Dir.-Gen. Govt. Information Office, Govt. Spokesman 1979–84; mem. Cen. Cttee. Kuomintang 1981–, Dir.-Gen. Dept. of Cultural Affairs, Kuomintang 1984–87; Deputy Sec.-Gen., Cen. Cttee. Kuomintang 1987–89, Sec.-Gen. 1989–93; mem. Cen. Standing Cttee. 1988–; Gov., Taiwan Provincial Govt. 1993–; Man. Dir. China TV Co. 1984–93, Taiwan TV Enterprise 1984–93; Chair. Hua-hsia Investment Corpn.; Eisenhower Fellowship 1982, and several decorations. *Publications:* A Manual for Academic Writers, How to Write Academic Papers, Politics and Public Opinions in the United States, Keep Free China Free. *Address:* 1 Sheng-Fu Road, Chung-Hsin New Village, Nantou, Taiwan. *Telephone:* (049) 332201. *Fax:* (049) 329224.

SOPHUSSON, Fridrik; Icelandic politician; b. 18 Oct. 1943, Reykjavík; m. Dr. Sigridur Duna Kristmundsdottir 1990; one d. and five c. from first m.; ed. Reykjavík Higher Secondary Grammar School and Univ. of Iceland; lawyer, part-time teacher Hlídaskóli School, Reykjavík 1963–67; Man. Icelandic Man. Asscn. 1972–78; mem. Radio Council Icelandic State Broadcasting Service 1975–78; Nat. Research Council and Exec. Cttee. of State Hosps. 1984–87; Cen. Cttee. Independence Party 1969–77, 1981–, Vice-Chair. 1981–89, 1991–; Pres. Independence Party's Youth Fed. 1973–77; M.P. for Reykjavík 1978–; Minister of Industry and Energy 1987–88, of Finance 1991–98; mem. Bd. of Dirs. Nat. Bank of Iceland 1990–92, Icelandic Church Aid 1990–92. *Address:* c/o Ministry of Finance, Avnarhvali, 150 Reykjavík, Iceland.

SOPRANI, Luciano; Italian fashion designer; b. 12 April 1946, Reggiolo, Reggio Emilia; ed. secondary and agric. schools, Guastalla; asst. Achille Maramotti's Max Mara fashion co., Reggio Emilia and Milan 1967–70, designer 1970–74; freelance designer working for Dorian, Heylett, Pim's, Gruppo Finanziario Tessile etc. in Milan and Reggio Emilia 1975–81; founder-dir. Luciano Soprani S.R.L., Milan 1981–; design collections including Basile Women 1981–, Basile Men 1982–, Luciano Soprani Women 1982–, Gucci for Men and Women 1983–, Luciano Soprani Shoes for Women 1984–.

SORABJI, Richard Rustom Kharsedji, C.B.E., B.PHIL., M.A., F.B.A.; British professor of philosophy; b. 8 Nov. 1934, Brighton; s. of late Prof. Richard Kakushru Sorabji and Mary Katherine Sorabji (née Monkhouse); m. Margaret Anne Catherine Taster 1958; one s. two d.; ed. Charterhouse, Pembroke Coll., Oxford Univ.; Assoc. Prof. Sage School of Philosophy, Cornell Univ. 1962–69; Prof. King's Coll. 1970–, Prof. of Ancient Philosophy 1981–, British Acad./Wolfson Research Prof. 1996–, Designer, First Dir. King's Coll. Centre for Philosophical Studies 1989–91; Supernumerary Fellow, Wolfson Coll., Oxford 1996–; Pres. Aristotelian Soc. 1985–86; founder, organizer int. project to translate the ancient commentators on Aristotle in 50 vols. 1985–; Dir. Inst. of Classical Studies, London Univ. 1991–96; Foreign Hon. mem. American Acad. of Arts and Sciences 1997. *Publications:* Aristotle on Memory 1972, Necessity, Cause and Blame 1980, Time, Creation and the Continuum 1983, Matter, Space and Motion 1988, Animal Minds and Human Morals 1993; ed. numerous vols. on Aristotle. *Leisure interests:* archaeology, architecture. *Address:* Department of Philosophy, King's College, Strand, London, WC2R 2LS, England. *Telephone:* 0171-873 2231. *Fax:* 0171-876 1797.

SORATO, Bruno, D.ECON.; Italian business executive; b. 7 May 1922, Venice; m. Giovanna Coin 1949; one d.; ed. in Rome; Exec. SAVA, Venice 1947–64; Exec. AISA São Paulo 1965–66; Man. Dir. NABALCO Pty. Ltd.,

Sydney 1967–72; mem. Exec. Cttee. Swiss Aluminium Ltd. 1972–74, Deputy Chair. Exec. Cttee. 1975–83, Pres. and C.E.O. 1983–85; Dir. Union Bank of Switzerland 1981.

SØRENSEN, Bengt Algot, DR.PHIL.; Danish professor of German literature; b. 24 Nov. 1927, Aarhus; s. of Christian Sørensen and Selma Mellquist; m. Agnes M. Pedersen 1954; one s. two d.; ed. Aarhus, Hamburg and Tübingen Univs.; Lecturer in Scandinavian Languages and Literature, Bonn, Germany 1955–60; Lecturer in German Literature, Aarhus Univ. 1962–66; Prof. of German Literature, Odense Univ. 1966–; Visiting Prof. Univ. of Calif. at Irvine 1980, Univ. of Kiel 1983; Pres. Danish Research Council for the Humanities 1971–73; mem. Exec. Council European Science Foundation 1983–89; Vice-Pres. IVG (Int. Vereinigung der Germanistik) 1995; mem. Royal Danish Acad.; Gold Medal, Univ. of Aarhus 1953. *Publications:* Symbol und Symbolismus 1963, Allegorie und Symbol 1972, Herrschaft und Zärtlichkeit 1984, Jens Peter Jacobsen 1990, Geschichte der deutschen Literatur Bd. I, II 1997, Funde und Forschungen. Ausgewählte Essays 1997; numerous articles about Danish and German literature. *Leisure interests:* fishing, gardening. *Address:* University of Odense, 5230 Odense (Office); Heliosvaenget 28, Lejl. 109, 5250 Odense SV, Denmark (Home). *Telephone:* 66 15 86 00 (Office). *Fax:* 65 93 16 64.

SØRENSEN, John Kousgård, M.A., DR.PHIL.; Danish academic; b. 6 Dec. 1925, Copenhagen; s. of Erik Sørensen and Astrid Sørensen; m. Solveig Baastrup 1951; one s.; ed. Univ. of Copenhagen; Asst. Prof. Inst. for Name-Research, Univ. of Copenhagen 1951, Assoc. Prof. 1965, Prof. of Danish Language 1969–94; Hon. Vice-Pres. English Place-Name Soc. 1969; mem. Royal Danish Acad.; Sahlgren Prize 1981; Dr. h.c. (Uppsala) 1981; Jancke Prize 1992, Språk och Kulturs Umeå Prize 1997. *Publications:* Danske bebyggelsesnavne på sted 1958, Svendborg amts bebyggelsesnavne 1958, Danske sø- og ånavne 1-8 1968–96, Odense amts bebyggelsesnavne 1969, Stednavneforskning 1-2 (with V. Dalberg) 1972–79, Danmarks gamle Ordsprog 2, 6, 7 1977–88, Patronymer i Danmark 1–2 1984–97; articles on onomastics, lexicography, proverbs etc. *Leisure interest:* music. *Address:* Nivåvaenge 12-3, 2990 Nivå, Denmark. *Telephone:* 49 14 75 43.

SÓRENSEN, Jórgen Haugen; Danish sculptor; ed. Coll. of Art and Design, Copenhagen; began as apprentice plasterer and potter; exhbns. at Museum of Modern Art New York, Yorks. Sculpture Park; works in collections in Denmark, England, Italy, Slovenia, Turkey, Olympic Sculpture Park, Seoul; dir. film JHS late 1960s; Prix de la Critique for JHS (Paris Biennale) 1963.

SØRENSEN, Knud, D.PHIL.; Danish professor of philology; b. 2 Feb. 1928, Aarhus; s. of late Oscar Sørensen and Ingeborg Petersen; m. 1st Gerda Riisberg 1955 (died 1973); m. 2nd Margit Riisberg 1975; two s. one d.; ed. Copenhagen Univ.; Lecturer, Handelshøjskolen i Kobenhavn 1955–62; Prof. Danmarks Laererhøjskole 1962–67; Prof. of English Philology, Aarhus Univ. 1967–92; Assoc. Ed. English Studies 1970–; Visiting Prof. State Univ. of New York, Binghamton; mem. Vetenskapssocieteten i Lund, Royal Danish Acad. *Publications:* Thomas Lodge's Translation of Seneca's De Beneficiis 1960, Engelsk grammatik (with P. Steller) 1966, Engelske lån i dansk 1973, Aspects of Modern English Prose Style 1975, English Influence on Contemporary Danish 1982, Charles Dickens: Linguistic Innovator 1985, English Past and Present 1988, English and Danish Contrasted 1991, Engelsk i Dansk 1995, A Dictionary of Anglicisms in Danish 1997. *Leisure interest:* classical music. *Address:* Råhøj Allé 12, 8270 Højbjerg, Denmark (Home). *Telephone:* 86 27 21 06.

SORENSEN, Theodore Chaikin, B.S.L., LL.B.; American government official and lawyer; b. 8 May 1928, Lincoln, Nebraska; s. of Christian A. Sorensen and Annis Chaikin; m. Gillian Martin 1969; one d.; three s. from previous marriage; ed. Univ. of Nebraska; Attorney, Fed. Security Agency 1951–52; Staff Researcher, Joint Cttee. on Railroad Retirement 1952–53; Asst. to Senator John F. Kennedy 1953–61; Special Counsel to Presidents Kennedy and Johnson 1961–64; with law firm Paul, Weiss, Rifkind, Wharton & Garrison, New York 1966–; Ed.-at-Large Saturday Review 1966–69; mem. Advisory Cttee. for Trade Negotiations March 1979–81; Chair. Task Force on Political Action Cttees.; mem. Task Force on Foreign Policy 1986, Int. Trade Round Table 1986, Democratic Nat. Cttee. 1981–82, Comm. on White House Fellows 1996–; Dir. The Twentieth-Century Fund 1984– (Chair. 1994–), Council on Foreign Relations 1993–, Nat. Democratic Inst. for Int. Affairs 1993–, Cen. Asian-American Enterprise Fund 1995–; Chair. U.S.-Japanese Program Cttee. of Japan Soc. 1990; Trustee The New York Acad. of Medicine 1991–97; Democrat. *Publications:* Decision-Making in The White House 1963, Kennedy 1964, The Kennedy Legacy 1970, Watchmen in the Night: Presidential Accountability After Watergate 1975, A Different Kind of Presidency 1984, A Widening Atlantic? Domestic Change and Foreign Policy (co-author Ralf Dahrendorf) 1986, Let the World go Forth: The Speeches, Statements and Writings of John F. Kennedy (Ed.) 1988, Why I Am a Democrat 1996. *Address:* c/o Paul, Weiss, Rifkind, Wharton and Garrison, 1285 Avenue of the Americas, New York, NY 10019, U.S.A. (Office). *Telephone:* (212) 373-3000.

SORENSTAM, Annika; Swedish golfer; b. 1970; ed. Univ. of Arizona, U.S.A.; winner Australian tournament 1994; champion in U.S.A. (three wins including U.S. Women's Open) and Europe (two wins) 1995; winner World Championship, Repub. of Korea, Australian Masters 1995; Rookie of the Year 1993; Sports Personality of the Year, Sweden 1995; lives in Nevada, U.S.A.

SORHAINDO, Crispin; Dominican politician; b. 23 May 1931, Vieille Case; s. of Clive Sorhaindo and Rosa Frederick; m. Ruby Etheldreda Allport 1956; two s. four d.; Speaker House of Ass. –1993; fmr. Sr. Official Caribbean Devt. Bank (CDB); Pres. of Dominica 1993–98. *Leisure interests:* reading, gardening. *Address:* Morne Prosper, P.O. Box 572, Roseau, Dominica. *Telephone:* 448.8787. *Fax:* 449.8920.

SOROKIN, Vladimir Gregoriyevich; Russian writer and painter; b. 7 Aug. 1955, Bykovo, Moscow Region; m. Sorokina Irina Igorevna; two d.; ed. Moscow Gubkin Inst. of Oil and Gas Industry; worked as artistic ed. Smena 1979–80; freelance 1980–; was not published in U.S.S.R. until 1987. *Publications include:* The Queue (novel) 1985, Thirteenth Love of Marina (novel) 1993, Obelisk (short stories) 1994, The Hearts of the Four 1994 (novel), The Norm (selected texts) 1994, A Novel 1994; mem. Union of Russian Writers, Union of Graphic Artists of Russia, Russian PEN Centre; scholarship of Deutsche Akademische Austauschung Dienst 1992. *Leisure interests:* chess, cooking. *Address:* Proyezd Odoyevskogo 7, korp. 5, Apt. 621, Moscow, Russia (Home). *Telephone:* 422- 67-39 (Home).

SOROS, George; Hungarian investment banker and philanthropist; b. 1930, Budapest; ed. London School of Econs.; with Singer & Friedlander (merchant bankers), London; moved to Wall Street 1956; set up pvt. mutual fund, Quantum fund, registered in Curaçao 1969; since 1991 has created other funds, Quasar Int., Quota, Quantum Emerging Growth, Quantum Realty Trust; Pres. Soros Fund Man., New York 1973–; set up Open Society Fund, Soros Foundations, Cen. European Univ. since 1979; f. Global Power Investments 1994; Dr. h.c. (Oxford). *Publication:* The Alchemy of Finance 1987, Opening the Soviet System 1990, Underwriting Democracy 1991, Soros on Soros: Staying Ahead of the Curve (jtly.) 1995, The Crisis of Global Capitalism 1998. *Address:* Soros Fund Management, 888 7th Avenue, 3300 New York, NY 10106, U.S.A.

SOROUR, Ahmed Fathy, M.L., PH.D.; Egyptian politician and professor of criminal law; b. 9 July 1932, Cairo; s. of Mostafa Kamel Sorour and Fatma Ali Hassan; m. Zeinab El-Housseiny; one s. two d.; ed. Cairo Univ., Univ. of Michigan, U.S.A.; Prof. of Criminal Law, Cairo Univ. 1959–, Head of Criminal Law Dept. 1978–83, Dean, Faculty of Law 1983–85, Vice-Rector Cairo Univ. 1985–86; Minister of Educ. 1986–90; Chair. Supreme Council of Univs. 1986–90; Speaker of the Egyptian People's Ass. 1990–; Pres. IPU Council 1994–; Science and Arts Medal (Class A), Highest Distinction Award 1993; Ordre de la Pléiade, France. *Publications:* Theory of Nullity 1959, Offences against Public Interest 1963, Penal Law (Part I and II) 1980, Criminal Procedures Law 1993, Constitutional Legality and Human Rights 1995, Probation. *Address:* 11583 Majlis Al-Shaab, Cairo, Egypt. *Telephone:* (02) 3543130. *Fax:* (02) 3543116.

SORRELL, John William, C.B.E., F.C.S.D., F.R.S.A.; British designer; b. 28 Feb. 1945, London; s. of late John William Sorrell and of Elizabeth Jane Sorrell (née Taylor); m. Frances Mary Newell (q.v.) 1974; two s. one d.; ed. Hornsey Coll. of Art; designer, Maine Wolff & Partners 1964; partner Goodwin Sorrell 1964–71; Design Man. Wolff Olins 1971–76; founder and Co-Chair. Newell and Sorrell 1976–97, Chair. Interbrand Newell and Sorrell 1997–; Vice-Pres. Chartered Soc. of Designers 1989–92; Chair. DBA 1990–92, Design Council 1994–; mem. British Rail Architecture and Design Panel 1991–93, R.S.A. Design Advisory Group 1991–93, D & AD Strategic Planning Soc., Inst. of Design, New Millennium Experience Co. Creative Review Group 1998– (and 'Godparent' for Identity Zone), Panel 2000, Dept. of Trade & Industry's Encouraging Competitiveness Working Party 1998; Gov. Design Dimension 1991–93; Hon. mem. Romanian Design Centre; Hon. D. Design (De Montfort) 1997; R.S.A.'s Bicentenary Medal 1998. *Publications:* Secret of Design Effectiveness 1995, Utopian Nights 1996, Utopian Papers 1996–. *Leisure interests:* arboriculture, Arsenal Football Club, art, film.

SORRELL, Martin Stuart, M.A., M.B.A.; British business executive; b. 14 Feb. 1945, London; s. of Jack and Sally Sorrell; m. Sandra Finestone 1971; three s.; ed. Haberdashers' Aske's School, Christ's Coll., Cambridge and Harvard Business School; Consultant, Glendinning Assocs. 1968–69; Vice-Pres. Mark McCormack Org. 1970–74; Dir. James Gulliver Assocs. 1975–77; Group Financial Dir. Saatchi and Saatchi Co. PLC 1977–86; Group Chief Exec. WPP Group PLC 1986–; Dir. Storehouse PLC 1994–97; Dir. (non-exec.) Colefax and Fowler Group PLC 1997–; mem. Advisory Bd. Int. Grad. School of Man., Univ. of Navarra 1989–, Judge Inst. for Man. Studies, Univ. of Cambridge 1990–, IBM 1997–; Bd. Dirs. of Assocs., Harvard Business School 1998–; mem. Panel 2000 1998; Gov. London Business School 1990–, other appointments. *Leisure interests:* family, skiing, cricket. *Address:* WPP Group PLC, 27 Farm Street, London, W1X 6RD, England. *Telephone:* 0171-408 2204 (Office).

SORSA, (Taisto) Kalevi; Finnish politician and business executive; b. 21 Dec. 1930, Keuruu; s. of Kaarlo O. Sorsa and Elsa S. Sorsa (née Leinonen); m. Elli Irene Lääkäri 1953; ed. School of Social Science (now Univ. of Tampere); Chief Ed., Vihuri 1954–56; Literary Ed. Tammi (publishing house) 1956–59; Programme Asst. Specialist UNESCO 1959–65; Sec.-Gen. of Finnish UNESCO Cttee. 1965–69; Deputy Dir. Ministry of Educ. 1967–69; Sec.-Gen. Social Democratic Party 1969–75, Pres. 1970–91; mem. Parl. 1975–87; Minister Foreign Affairs Feb.–Sept. 1972, 1975–76, 1979–82; Prime Minister 1972–75, 1977–79, 1982–87; Deputy Prime Minister and Minister of Foreign Affairs 1987–89; Speaker of Parl. 1989–91; mem. Man. Bd., Bank of Finland 1991–; Chair. Foreign Affairs Cttee. 1970–72, 1977, 1979–82,

Socialist Int. Study Group on Disarmament 1978–80, Chair. Socialist Int. Advisory Council 1980–96, Vice-Pres. 1980–96; Chair. Bd. of Admin. Finnair 1981–94, Chair. Bd. of Finnair 1994–97; Nat. Defence Council 1982–87, Soviet-Finnish Comm. on Econ. Co-operation 1983–89; Dir. Bank of Finland until 1996 (retd.); Dr. h.c. (Tampere); Commdr. Grand Cross, Order of the White Rose of Finland, Grand Cross, Order of Orange-Nassau, Grand Cross, Order of the Icelandic Falcon, Great Golden Decoration with Ribbon, Order of Merit of Austria, Grand Cross of the Order of Merit, People's Repub. of Poland, Grand Cross, Order of the North Star of Sweden, Grand Star, Order of the Star of Friendship between Peoples (G.D.R.), Grand Cross, Order of San Marino, Grand Cross, Order of Merit of the Repub. of Senegal, Grand Cross, Order of Dannebrog (Denmark), Order of the Banner of Hungary (Second Class), Grand Cross of the Order of Merit (Federal Repub. of Germany), Grand Cross, Order of the Southern Cross (Brazil), Grand Cross, Order of the Star (Jordan), Grand Cross, Order of Isabella The Catholic (Spain), Order of Trishakti-Patta (First Class, Nepal); Hon. K.C.M.G. *Leisure interests:* the arts, social and international questions, outdoor life. *Address:* Hakaniemenranta 16D, 00530 Helsinki, Finland. *Telephone:* 773 43 63. *Fax:* 753 61 18.

SORVINO, Mira, A.B.; American actress; b. 1968; d. of Paul Sorvino; ed. Harvard Univ.; Acad. Award Best Supporting Actress (for Mighty Aphrodite). *Film appearances include:* Amongst Friends 1993 (also assoc. producer), The Second Greatest Story Ever Told 1993, Quiz Show 1994, Parallel Lives 1994, Barcelona 1994, Tarantella 1995, Sweet Nothing 1995, Mighty Aphrodite 1995, The Dutch Master 1995, Blue in the Face 1995, Beautiful Girls 1996, Norma Jean and Marilyn 1996, Jake's Women 1996, Romy and Michele's High School Reunion 1997, The Replacement Killers 1997, Mimic 1997. *Address:* c/o The William Morris Agency, 151 South El Camino Drive, Beverly Hills, CA 90212, U.S.A.

SOSA PIETRI, Andrés; Venezuelan business executive; b. 1943, Caracas; ed. Univ. Catolica Andrés Bello and Harvard Univ.; fmr. legal consultant, petrochemical sector; later ran group of cos. manufacturing valves and other specialized products for petroleum industry; served briefly as indep. Senator representing MAS (Venezuela's Socialist Party) in 1970s; Chair. Petróleos de Venezuela, S.A. (PDVSA) 1991. *Address:* c/o Petróleos de Venezuela S.A., Torre Este, Avda Liberator, La Campiña, Apdo 169, Caracas 1010-A, Venezuela.

SOSKOVETS, Oleg Nikolayevich; Russian politician; b. 11 May 1949, Taldy-Kurgan, Kazakh S.S.R.; m. Evgenia Valentinovna Soskovets; one s. one d.; ed. High School of Karaganda Metallurgic Plant; mem. CPSU 1972–91; rolling mill operator, foreman, chief of workshop Karaganda Metallurgic plant 1971–84; chief engineer, Deputy Dir. 1984–87, Dir. 1987–88, Dir. Gen. 1988–91; U.S.S.R. People's Deputy 1989–91; U.S.S.R. Minister of Metallurgy April–Nov. 1991; Pres. Roschermet 1992; First Deputy Prime Minister of Kazakhstan, Minister of Industry 1992; Chair. Cttee. on Metallurgy of Russian Fed. 1992–96; First Deputy Prime Minister of Russia 1993–96; Pres. Asscn. of Finance-Industrial Groups 1996–. *Publications:* more than 100 works on problems of metallurgic production.

SOTIN, Hans; German opera and concert singer; b. 10 Sept. 1939, Dortmund; m. Regina Elsner 1964; three c.; with Opera House, Essen 1962–64; State Opera, Hamburg 1964–, State Opera, Vienna 1970–; perm. mem. Bayreuth Festival 1971–; guest appearances worldwide; private singing teacher. *Address:* 2106 Bendestorf, Schulheide 10, Germany. *Telephone:* 04183/6614.

SOTIRHOS, Michael; American diplomatist; b. 12 Nov. 1928, New York; m. Estelle Manos 1968; two c.; ed. Bernard M. Baruch School of Business and Civic Admin., City Coll. of New York; partner Ariston Sales Co. Ltd. 1948, founder Chair. 1958–; founder and Chair. Ariston Interior Designers, Inc. New York 1948–85; partner, Cortina Valley Assocs., Haines Valley, New York, Marla Realty, New York, Hampton Properties, Hampton, Va.; mem. Bd. of Dirs. The Rainbow Fund; active service in Republican Party since 1960; Nat. Chair. Ethnic Voters for Reagan-Bush '84; fmr. Nat. Chair. Nat. Republican Heritage Groups Council; fmr. mem. Exec. Cttee. Republican Nat. Cttee.; has held numerous Govt. and public appts.; Amb. to Jamaica 1985–89, to Greece 1989–93; awards include Dwight D. Eisenhower Award (Republican Nat. Cttee.) 1985; Order of St. Mark (Patriarchate of Jerusalem), Order of St. Andrew (Greek Orthodox Church).

SOTKILAVA, Zurab Lavrentievich; Georgian tenor; b. 12 March 1937, Sukhumi; m.; two d.; ed. Tbilisi Polytech. Inst., Tbilisi Conservatory; professional football-player in Dynamo, Tbilisi; soloist Tbilisi Opera Theatre 1965–74; Prof. Tbilisi Conservatory 1976–88; with Bolshoi Theatre 1974–; toured with Bolshoi and independently in Europe and America, opera parts include Vodemon (Iolanthe), Absalom (Absalom and Eteri), Cavaradossi (Tosca), Richard (Un Ballo in Maschera), Manrico (Il Trovatore), Radames (Aida), José (Carmen), Otello and others; Grand Priz Gold Orpheus Festival (Bulgaria) 1986, Second Prize Int. Tchaikovsky Competition (1970), Grand Priz Barcelona Competition 1970; Hon. Academician Boston Acad. of Arts; People's Artist of U.S.S.R. and Georgia. *Address:* Bolshoi Theatre, Teatralnaya pl. 1, Moscow, Russia. *Telephone:* (095) 244-07-31 (Home).

SOTO, Jesús-Rafael; Venezuelan artist; b. 5 June 1923, Ciudad Bolívar; ed. School of Fine Arts, Caracas; Dir., School of Fine Arts, Maracaibo, Venezuela 1947–50; in Paris since 1950; early exponent of "optical art"; various films made on works in field of kinetic art and vibrations since 1958; one-man exhbns. at Caracas 1949, 1957, 1961, Paris 1956, 1959, 1962, 1965, 1967, 1969, 1970, 1979, Brussels 1957, Essen 1961, Antwerp 1962, Stuttgart 1964, New York 1965, 1966, 1971, 1974, 1996, Retrospective Exhbn., Signals, London 1965, Galerie Hermanns, Munich 1989, Galeria Theo, Madrid 1990, 1992 and others; represented in perm. collections including: Tate Gallery, London, Museum of Fine Arts, Caracas, Albright-Knox Art Gallery, Buffalo, Cali Inst. of Fine Arts, Cali, Colombia, Stedelijk Museum, Amsterdam, Museum of Contemporary Arts, São Paulo, Moderna Museet, Stockholm, Kaiser Foundation, Córdoba, Argentina, Palace of Fine Arts, Brussels, Kröller-Müller Museum, Otterloo, Holland, Museum of Modern Art, Jerusalem; numerous prizes including Wolf Prize, São Paulo Bienal 1963, David Bright Foundation Prize, Venice Biennale 1964, Picasso Medal 1981, 1990, other awards and prizes, several hon. degrees. *Major works include:* sculpture for garden of School of Architecture, Univ. City of Caracas, two murals and sculpture for Venezuelan pavilion, Brussels Exhbn. 1958. *Address:* 10 rue Villehardouin, 75003 Paris, France.

SOTOMAYOR, Antonio; Bolivian painter; b. 1904, Chulumani; s. of Carmen Celina Meza and Juan Sotomayor; m. Grace La Mora Andrews 1926; ed. La Paz School of Applied Arts; awarded first prize of Nat. Exposition of Painting 1921; F.R.S.A. *Works include:* El Crucifijo, Copacabana, Lavanderas, Funeral Aimara, Alacitas, Madre, Rezando Reposo, Historical Murals Palace Hotel and Sharon Building, San Francisco, Murals at Sonoma Mission Inn, Calif., Mural El Tigero, Hillsborough, Calif.; murals Peruvian Pavilion and terra cotta fountain Pacific Area, Theme Building, Golden Gate, Int. Exposition 1939–40, Murals, San Francisco; Art Faculty, Mills Coll. and Calif. School of Fine Arts; Mural Altarpiece, St. Augustine Church, Pleasanton, Calif., Glass Mosaic Façade, Hillsdale Methodist Church, Calif.; Mural, Matson Navigation Co., San Francisco, Calif.; Murals, Grace Cathedral, San Francisco, Calif.; backdrop for San Francisco Civic Auditorium Concerts; Altarpiece, Church of St. Francis, Nuevo Progresso, Guatemala; Mural, Peruvian Embassy, Washington, D.C.; Chapel Altarpiece, La Casa de los Pobres, Tihuana, Mexico; Award of Honor (City and County of San Francisco) 1978. *Publications:* Pinturas interpretativas de indígenas de Bolivia 1929, Pinturas con motivos mejicanos 1930, Khasa Goes to the Fiesta 1967, Balloons 1972. *Leisure interests:* music, travel. *Address:* 3 Le Roy Place, San Francisco, CA 94109, U.S.A. *Telephone:* (415) 673-6193.

SOULAGES, Pierre; French painter; b. 24 Dec. 1919, Rodez; m. Colette Llaurens 1942; ed. Lycée de Rodez; exhibited abstract painting since 1947 in Salon des Surindépendants, Salon de Mai et Réalités Nouvelles; one-man exhbn., Lydia Conti Gallery, Paris 1949, Birch Gallery, Copenhagen 1951, Stangl Gallery, Munich 1952, Kootz Gallery, New York 1954–65, Gimpel Gallery, London 1955, Galerie de France, Paris 1956–92, Knoedler Gallery 1968; exhibited in int. festivals including Biennales of Venice and São Paulo, and the itinerary of the Guggenheim Collection, the Carnegie Inst., Pittsburgh, The New Decade at the Museum of Modern Art, New York, Tate Gallery, London, etc.; also décors for theatres and ballet; and lithographs and engravings. Works in Museums of Modern Art, Paris, and N.Y., Tate Gallery, London, Guggenheim Museum, N.Y., Phillips Gallery, Washington, Museum of Modern Art, Rio de Janeiro, museums in many American cities, in Europe, Australia and Japan; retrospective exhbns. Hanover, Essen, The Hague, Zürich 1960–61, Ljubljana 1961, Massachusetts Inst. of Tech. 1962, Copenhagen Glyptothek 1963, Fine Arts Museum, Houston 1966, Musée Nat. d'Art Moderne, Paris 1967; Carnegie Inst., Pittsburgh, Albright Knox Art Gallery, Buffalo, Musée de Québec, Musée d'Art Contemporain, Montreal 1968, Oslo, Aalborg, Neuchâtel, Charleroi 1973, Musée Dynamique, Dakar 1974, Gulbenkian Foundation, Lisbon, Museo de arte contemporáneo, Madrid, Musée Fabre, Montpellier, Museo de Arte Moderno, Mexico City 1975, Museu de Arte Moderna, Rio de Janeiro, Museo de Arte Moderno, Caracas 1976, Museu de Arte Contemporâneo, São Paulo 1976, Centre Georges Pompidou, Paris 1979, Museé du Parc de la Boverie, Liège 1980, Kunstlerhaus, Salzburg 1980, Kunstbygning, Århus; Kunstpavillon, Esbjerg; Palais de Charlottenborg, Copenhagen 1982; Musée d'Unterlinden, Colmar 1983; Museum Seibu, Tokyo 1984; Pulchri Studio, The Hague 1985, Galerie de France 1986, Museum Fridecianum, Kassel, I.V.A.M., Valencia, Musée des Beaux-Arts, Nantes 1989, Galleries Tollarno, Melbourne 1989, Galerie Fandos, Valencia, Galerie Pauli, Lausanne 1990, Museum Moderner Kunst, Vienna 1991, Nat. Museum of Contemporary Art, Seoul, Nat. Palace of Fine Arts, Beijing, Nat. Museum of Fine Arts, Taiwan 1993, Musée d'art moderne de la Ville de Paris 1996, Fine Arts Museum, Montréal 1996, Museu de Arte, São Paulo 1996, Deichtorhallen, Hamburg 1997; Hon. mem. American Acad. of Arts and Letters; Commdr. Légion d'honneur, des Arts et des Lettres, Grand Officier, Ordre nat. du Mérite; Grand Prix, Tokyo Biennale 1957, Carnegie Prize, Pittsburgh, U.S.A. 1964, Grand Prix des Arts de la Ville de Paris 1975, Rembrandt Prize, Germany, 1976, Prix Nat. de Peinture, Paris 1986, Proemium Imperiale, Tokyo 1992. *Address:* 18 rue des Trois-Portes, 75005 Paris, France.

SOULIOTI, Stella; Cypriot politician and lawyer; b. 13 Feb. 1920, Limassol; sister of Michael Cacoyannis (q.v.); d. of Panayiotis and Angeliki Cacoyannis; m. Demetrios Souliotis 1949; one d.; ed. Cyprus, Egypt and Gray's Inn, London; joined Women's Auxiliary Air Force, Nicosia and served in Middle East 1943–46; called to the Bar, London 1951; law practice, Limassol 1952–60; Minister of Justice 1960–70, concurrently Minister of Health 1964–66; Law Commr. 1971–84; Attorney-Gen. 1984–88; Co-ordinator of

Foreign Aid to Cyprus Refugees 1974–; Adviser to Pres. of Cyprus on Cyprus Problem 1976–; Chair. Cyprus Overseas Relief Fund 1977–82; Visiting Fellow Wolfson Coll., Cambridge 1982–83; Pres. Cyprus Red Cross 1961–, Cyprus Scholarship Board 1962–; Chair. Cyprus Town and Country Planning Cttee. 1967–70; Vice-Pres. Cyprus Anti-Cancer Soc. 1971–; Hon. Vice-Pres. Int. Fed. of Women Lawyers 1967–; Trustee Cambridge Commonwealth Scholarship Trust for Cyprus 1983–; mem. Exec. Bd. UNESCO 1987–91; LL.D. h.c. (Nottingham) 1972. *Leisure interests:* reading, writing, music, theatre. *Address:* P.O. Box 24102, 1703 Nicosia, Cyprus. *Telephone:* 666955.

SOUMAKIS, Stavros Aristidi; Greek politician and medical practitioner; b. 18 Sept. 1951, Piraeus; m. Alexandra Papadopoulou; ed. Athens Univ. Medical School; practised as doctor in various hosps., Piraeus 1979–86, as obstetrician and gynaecologist, Helena maternity clinic –1993; Founder-mem. Panhellenic Socialist Students' Movt., Panhellenic Fighting Movt. 1969; mem. Panhellenic Socialist Movt. (PASOK) 1974–; elected Town Councillor, Piraeus 1982, 1986; elected an M.P. for Piraeus 1993; Minister of Merchant Marine 1996–; mem. Cen. Cttee. PASOK, Sec. Econ. Section, mem. Health Cttee.; Chair. Admin. Bd. Metaxa Hosp., Piraeus 1983–87; Sec. Doctors' Professional Syndicate. *Address:* Ministry of Merchant Marine, Odos Gregoriou Lambraki 150, Piraeus, Greece. *Telephone:* (01) 4121211. *Fax:* (01) 4134286.

SOUSA FRANCO, António L. P. de, PH.D.; Portuguese politician and professor of law; b. 21 Sept. 1942, Lisbon; s. of António de Sousa Franco and Maria de Jesus Pacheco; m. Maria Matilde Pessoa Figueiredo de Sousa Franco 1983; one d.; ed. Univ. of Lisbon; Univ. Prof. Schools of Law, Lisbon, Coimbra and Portuguese Catholic Univ.; Dean, Schools of Law, Univ. of Lisbon 1979–85, Portuguese Catholic Univ. 1989–95; Man. SACOR (oil-refining enterprise) 1968–72, Nat. Petrochemical Co. 1972–74, Caixa Geral Depósitos e Previdência 1974–75; mem. Parl. 1976–79, 1980–81; mem. Parl. Ass. for NATO 1978–79; Sec. of State for Treasury 1976; Minister of Finance 1979, 1995–; Pres. Portuguese Court of Auditors 1986–95; Pres. PSD-Social Democratic Party 1977–78; mem. Acad. of Sciences; numerous professional appointments and affiliations; Grã Cruz da Ordem Militar de Cristo; decorations from Italy and Brazil; five academic awards. *Publications:* over 1,000 publs. on politics, econs., finance etc. *Leisure interests:* history studies, travel, reading, tennis. *Address:* Ministry of Finance, Avenida Infante D. Henrique 5, 1100 Lisbon; Rua de S. Bernardo 38, R/c Dtọ, 1200 Lisbon, Portugal (Home).

SOUTER, Brian; British business executive; fmrly. trainee accountant; f. Stagecoach Selkent bus co. with sister Ann Gloag (q.v.); now Chair. Stagecoach Holdings. *Address:* Stagecoach Holdings, Charlotte House, 20 Charlotte Street, Perth, PH1 5LL, Scotland.

SOUTER, David Hackett; American judge; b. 17 Sept. 1939, Melrose, Mass.; s. of Joseph A. Souter and Helen A. Hackett; ed. Harvard Univ. and Univ. of Oxford; admitted N.H. Bar; Assoc. Orr & Reno, Concord 1966–68; Asst. Attorney-Gen. N.H. 1968–71, Deputy Attorney-Gen. 1971–76, Attorney-Gen. 1976–78; Assoc. Justice, N.H. Superior Court 1978–83, N.H. Supreme Court 1983–90; Assoc. Justice U.S. Supreme Court Oct. 1990–; mem. American Bar Assen., N.H. Bar Assen. *Address:* U.S. Supreme Court, Supreme Court Building, 1 First Street, N.E., Washington, DC 20543, U.S.A.

SOUTHALL, Ivan Francis, A.M., D.F.C.; Australian author; b. 8 June 1921, Melbourne; s. of Francis and Rachel (née Voutier) Southall; m. 1st Joyce Blackburn 1945 (divorced); one s. three d.; m. 2nd Susan W. Stanton 1976; ed. Box Hill Grammar School; RAAF 1942–47; self-employed writer 1947–; Whitall Poetry and Literature Lecturer, Library of Congress 1973; May Hill Arbuthnot Honor Lecturer 1974; Emer. Fellowship, Australia Council 1993; State Library of Vic. Retrospective Exhbn., "Southall A to Z" 1998; Australian Children's Book of the Year Award 1966, 1968, 1971, 1976, Australian Picture Book of the Year Award 1969, Carnegie Medal 1972, Nat. Children's Book Award 1986. *Publications:* over 60 works translated into 22 languages including They Shall Not Pass Unseen 1956, Softly Tread the Brave 1960, Hills End 1962, Ash Road 1965, To the Wild Sky 1967, The Fox Hole 1967, Let the Balloon Go 1968, Bread and Honey 1970, Josh 1971, Fly West 1974, Matt and Jo 1974, What About Tomorrow 1976, King of the Sticks 1979, The Golden Goose 1981, The Long Night Watch 1983, A City out of Sight 1984, Christmas in the Tree 1985, Rachel 1986, Blackbird 1988, The Mysterious World of Marcus Leadbeater 1990, Ziggurat 1997. *Leisure interests:* house and garden. *Address:* P.O. Box 25, Healesville, Vic. 3777, Australia.

SOUTHAM, Gordon Hamilton, O.C.; Canadian civil servant (retd.); b. 19 Dec. 1916, Ottawa; s. of Wilson Mills Southam and Henrietta Alberta (née Cargill); m. 1st Jacqueline Lambert-David 1940 (divorced 1968); three s. one d.; m. 2nd Gro Mortensen 1968 (divorced 1978); one s. one d.; m. 3rd Marion Tantot 1981; ed. Ashbury Coll., Trinity Coll., Toronto and Christ Church, Oxford; Officer, Second World War, British and Canadian Armies; Reporter The Times, London 1945–46; Editorial Writer Ottawa Citizen 1946–47; joined Dept. of External Affairs 1948; Second Sec., Stockholm 1949–53, Ottawa 1953–59; Chargé d'affaires, Warsaw 1959–60, Amb. 1960–62; Head Information Div., Dept. of External Affairs 1962–64; Dir. Southam Inc. 1964–87; Co-ordinator, Nat. Arts Centre 1964–67, Dir.-Gen. 1967–77; Chair. Festival Canada Cttee. 1978–79, Nat. Theatre School, Montreal 1979–81; Pres. Canadian Mediterranean Inst. 1980–86, Chair. 1986–92, Hon. Fellow 1992–; Chair. Rideau Canal Museum, Smiths Falls 1984–92, Hon. Chair. 1992–; Chair. Official Residences Council 1985–93; Chancellor Univ. of King's Coll. 1988–96; Co-Chair. Task Force on Mil. History Museums 1990–91; Vice-Pres. (France) Canadian Battle of Normandy Foundation 1991–98, Vice-Pres. 1998–; Hon. LL.D. (Univ. of Trent, Carleton Univ.) 1978, Hon. D.C.L. (King's Coll.)., Hon. D. Univ. (Ottawa). *Leisure interests:* the arts, reading, walking. *Address:* 280 Thorold Road, Ottawa, Ont., K1M 0K2 (winter); P.O. Box 126, Portland, Ont. K0G 1V0, Canada (summer). *Telephone:* (613) 272-3606 (summer).

SOUTHERN, Sir Richard (William), Kt., F.B.A.; British historian; b. 8 Feb. 1912; s. of Matthew Henry Southern; m. Sheila Cobley 1944; two s.; ed. Royal Grammar School, Newcastle upon Tyne and Balliol Coll., Oxford; Jr. Research Fellow, Exeter Coll., Oxford 1933–37; studied in Paris 1933–34 and Munich 1935; Fellow and Tutor, Balliol Coll. 1937–61; served with Oxford and Bucks. Light Infantry 1940, Second Lieut. Durham Light Infantry 1941, 155th Regiment R.A.C. 1942, rank of Capt. 1943, Maj. 1944; Political Intelligence Dept. Foreign Office 1943–45; Jr. Proctor Oxford Univ. 1948–49; Birkbeck Lecturer in Ecclesiastical History Trinity Coll., Cambridge 1959–60; Chichele Prof. of Modern History, Oxford 1961–69; Pres. Royal Historical Soc. 1968–72, Selden Soc. 1973–76, St. John's Coll., Oxford 1969–81 (Hon. Fellow 1981–); Raleigh Lecture, British Acad. 1962, David Murray Lecture, Glasgow Univ. 1963, Gifford Lecture, Glasgow Univ. 1970–72, G. M. Trevelyan Lecture Cambridge Univ. 1980–81; Corresponding Fellow Medieval Acad. of America 1965, Monumenta Germaniae Historica 1982; Foreign Hon. mem. American Acad. of Arts and Sciences 1972; Hon. Fellow, Balliol Coll., Oxford 1968, Sidney Sussex Coll., Cambridge 1971, St. John's Coll., Oxford 1981; Hon. D.Litt. (Glasgow) 1964, (Durham) 1969, (Cantab) 1971, (Bristol) 1974, (Newcastle) 1977, (Warwick) 1978, (St. Anselm's Coll.) 1981, (Columbia) 1982, (Univ. of the South) 1985; Hon. LL.D. (Harvard) 1977; Int. Balzan Foundation Prize 1987. *Publications:* The Making of the Middle Ages 1953, Western Views of Islam in the Middle Ages 1962, Eadmer's Vita Anselmi (ed.) 1963, St Anselm and his Biographer 1963, Memorials of St. Anselm (co-ed.) 1969, Medieval Humanism and other studies 1970 (R.S.L. award), Western Society and the Church in the Middle Ages 1970, Robert Grosseteste 1986, St. Anselm: a portrait in a landscape 1990, Scholastic Humanism and the Unification of Europe (Vol. 1) 1995; articles in English Historical Review, Medieval and Renaissance Studies, etc. *Address:* 40 St. John Street, Oxford, 0X1 2LH, England.

SOUTHGATE, Sir Colin, Kt.; British business executive; b. 24 July 1938, New Malden, Surrey; s. of Cyril Alfred Southgate and Edith Isabelle Southgate; m. Sally Southgate 1962; two s. two d.; ed. City of London School; began career with NPI; later worked in computers with ICT then ICL; launched own firm Software Sciences 1970; business sold to Thorn EMI 1982; Dir. Thorn EMI 1984, Man. Dir. 1985, Chief Exec. 1987, Chair. 1989–; Chair. Thorn PLC 1996–, Royal Opera House 1998–; Dir. (non-exec.) Bank of England 1991–, PowerGen 1990–96 (Chair. 1993–96), Dir. Terence Chapman Group 1997–; Deputy Pres. CBI 1995–96; Trustee Nat. Gallery 1998–; Gov. The Man. Coll., Henley 1991–97; mem. World Business Council for Sustainable Devt. 1994–96. *Address:* EMI Group PLC, 4 Tenterden Street, Hanover Square, London, W1A 2AY, England. *Telephone:* 0171-355 4848.

SOUTHWOOD, Sir (Thomas) Richard Edmund, Kt., D.SC., PH.D., A.R.C.S., F.R.S.; British academic; b. 20 June 1931, Kent; s. of Edmund W. Southwood and Ada Mary (née Regg) Southwood; m. Alison Langley (Harden) 1955; two s.; ed. Gravesend Grammar School and Imperial Coll., Univ. of London; ARC Research Scholar, Rothamsted Experimental Station 1952–55; Research Asst. and Lecturer, Zoology Dept., Imperial Coll. 1955–64; Visiting Prof., Escuela Nacional de Agricultura, Mexico 1964; Visiting Prof., Dept. of Entomology, Univ. of Calif. at Berkeley 1964–65; Reader in Insect Ecology, Univ. of London 1964–67, Prof. of Zoology and Applied Entomology 1967–79; Linacre Prof. of Zoology, Univ. of Oxford 1979–93; Fellow of Merton Coll. Oxford 1979–; Pro-Vice-Chancellor Univ. of Oxford 1987–89, 1993–98, Vice-Chancellor 1989–93; A. D. White Prof.-at-Large, Cornell Univ., U.S.A. 1985–91; Chair. Environmental Sciences Policy Dept., Central European Univ. (Budapest) 1991–95; Fellow of Imperial Coll., London 1984; Fellow of Eton Coll. 1993–; Dean of Royal Coll. of Science 1971-72; Trustee British Museum (Natural History) 1974–83, Chair. 1980–83; Mem. Royal Comm. on Environmental Pollution 1974–85, Chair. 1981–85; Pres. British Ecological Soc. 1976–78, Hon. mem. 1988; Vice Pres. Royal Soc. 1982–84; Chair. Nat. Radiological Protection Bd. 1985–94; Dir. (non-exec.) Glaxo-Wellcome PLC 1992–; Chair. U.K. Round Table on Sustainable Devt. 1995–99; Rhodes Trustee 1985–; East Malling Trustee 1986–; Lawes Trustee 1987–; mem. Acad. Europaea, Pontifical Acad. of Sciences; Hon. Foreign mem. American Acad. of Arts and Sciences; Foreign mem. Norwegian Acad. of Science and Letters, Royal Netherlands Acad. of Arts and Sciences, Hungarian Acad. of Sciences; Foreign Assoc. N.A.S. (U.S.A.); Hon. mem. Ecological Soc. of America; Fellow Entomological Soc. of America; Hon. Fellow Westminster Coll. 1995, Royal Coll. of Radiologists; Hon. F.R.C.P., Hon. D.Sc. (Griffith Univ., East Anglia, McGill, Warwick, Liverpool, Durham, Sussex, Vic.); Hon. LL.D. (London), (Brookes, Bristol); Fil. Dr. h.c. (Lund, Sweden); Scientific Medal, Zoological Soc., Linnean Medal; Cavaliere Ufficiale (Italy), Ordem Merito (II) (Portugal); D.L. (Oxfordshire) *Publications:* Land and Water Bugs of the British Isles 1959, Life of the Wayside and Woodland 1963, Ecological Methods 1966, 1999, Insects on Plants (with D. R. Strong and J. H. Lawton) 1984, Insects and the Plant Surfaces (with B. Juniper) 1986, Radiation and Health (with R. R. Jones) 1987, The Treatment and Handling of Wastes (with A. D. Bradshaw and F. Warner) 1992. *Leisure interests:* natural history, gardening, reading. *Address:* Merton College, Oxford, OX1 4JD, England.

SOUZA, Francis Newton; Indian painter; b. 12 April 1924, Goa; s. of Joseph Newton Souza and Lily Mary Antunes; m. 1st Maria Figueredo 1947 (divorced 1964); one d.; m. 2nd Liselotte Kristian (in common law); three d.; m. 3rd Barbara Zinkant 1965 (divorced 1977); one s.; ed. St. Xavier's Coll. and Sir Jamsetjee Jeejeebhoy School of Art, Bombay, Central School of Art, London, École des Beaux Arts, Paris; f. Progressive Artists' Group; one-man exhbns. in London (including Hartnell Gallery 1996) and major cities of England, in Paris, Stockholm, Copenhagen, Johannesburg and principal cities of Germany and U.S.A., Switzerland and U.A.E.; retrospective exhbns. in London 1951, New Delhi (Kumar Gallery) 1962, 1965, Leicester 1967, Detroit 1968, Minneapolis Int. Art Festival 1972, New Delhi and Bombay 1987; festival of Indian exhibits, Museum of Modern Art, Oxford and R.A. 1982; East-West Visual Arts Encounter 1985 (organized by Fed. Repub. of Germany), Bombay; represented in Baroda Museum, Nat. Gallery, New Delhi, British Museum, Tate Gallery, London, Wakefield Gallery, Haifa Museum, Nat. Gallery, Melbourne, Victoria & Albert Museum, London, Glenbarra Art Museum, Himeji, Japan, etc.; several awards. *Publications:* Nirvana of a Maggot in Encounter, Words and Lines (autobiog.) 1959, Statements 1977, The White Flag Revolution 1982, New Poems 1985. *Address:* 148 West 67 Street, New York City, NY 10023, U.S.A. *Telephone:* (212) 874-1343. *Fax:* (212) 874-1343.

SOVERN, Michael Ira, B.A., LL.B.; American professor of law and university president; b. 1 Dec. 1931, New York; m. 2nd Eleanor Lean 1963 (divorced 1974); m. 3rd Joan Wit 1974 (died 1993); m. 4th Patricia Walsh 1995; two s. one d. from first marriage; one d. from second marriage; ed. Columbia Coll., Columbia School of Law; called to the Bar 1956; mem. Faculty, Columbia Law School 1957–, Prof. of Law 1960–, Dean, Law School 1970–79, Chancellor Kent Prof. in Law 1977–, Univ. Provost 1979–80, Pres. 1980–93; Chair. Japan Soc. 1993–, American Acad., Rome 1993–, nat. advisory council Freedom Forum Media Studies Center 1993–; Pres. Schubert Foundation 1996–; Dir. Chemical Bank 1981–96, AT & T, GNY Insurance Group, Orion Pictures Corpn., Asian Cultural Corpn., other appointments; Fellow, American Acad. of Arts and Sciences; mem. American Law Inst.; Hon. D.Phil (Tel Aviv), Hon. LL.D (Columbia) 1980. *Publications:* Legal Restraints on Racial Discrimination in Employment 1966, Law and Poverty 1969. *Address:* School of Law, Columbia University, 435 W 116th Street, New York, NY 10027, U.S.A.

SOW, Abdoulaye Sékou; Malian politician; b. 1931; fmr. Dir. Nat. Admin. School (ENA), Bamako; arrested by regime of Pres. Traore during 1970s; later Dir. of Nat. Tourism Office; tech. adviser to various govt. ministeries; contributed to drafting of Mali's new constitution; Minister of State responsible for Defence until 1993; Prime Minister 1993. *Address:* c/o Office of the Prime Minister, Bamako, Mali.

SOWRY, Roger; New Zealand politician; b. 1958, Palmerston North; m.; three c.; ed. Victoria Univ. of Wellington; fmr. Distribution Man., R. Hannah & Co.; Nat. Party M.P. 1990–; apptd. Jr. Whip, then Sr. Govt. Whip 1993–96; Minister of Social Welfare, Minister in Charge of War Pensions, Assoc. Minister of Health 1996–98, and Minister in Charge of Social Services, Work, Income, Welfare, Housing, Employment, and Leader of the House 1998–; Deputy Divisional Chair. Wellington Young Nationals 1979–80, Electorate Chair. Pencarrow 1982–86, Divisional Councillor 1985–96, Deputy Chair. Wellington Div. 1988–90, Wellington Rep. on N.Z. Nat. Exec. 1989–90. *Address:* Department of Social Welfare, Private Bag 21, Wellington 1, New Zealand. *Telephone:* (04) 916-3860. *Fax:* (04) 916-3913.

SOYINKA, Wole, B.A.; Nigerian playwright and lecturer; b. 13 July 1934, Abeokuta; s. of Ayo and Eniola Soyinka; m.; c.; ed. Univ. of Ibadan, Nigeria, and Univ. of Leeds, England; worked at Royal Court Theatre, London; Research Fellow in Drama, Univ. of Ibadan 1960–61; Lecturer in English, Univ. of Ife 1962–63; Sr. Lecturer in English, Univ. of Lagos 1965–67; political prisoner 1967–69; Artistic Dir. and Head Dept of Theatre Arts, Univ. of Ibadan 1969–72; Research Prof. in Dramatic Literature, Univ. of Ife 1972, Prof. of Comparative Literature and Head of Dept. of Dramatic Arts 1976–; passport seized Sept. 1994, living in France; charged with treason March 1997 in absentia; Ed. Ch'Indaba (fmrly. Transition) Accra; Artistic Dir. Orisun Theatre, 1960 Masks; Literary Ed. Orisun Acting Editions; Pres. Int. Theatre Inst. 1986–; Fellow, Churchill Coll., Cambridge 1973–74; mem. American Acad. of Arts and Letters; Fellow, Ghana Asscn. of Writers, Pan-African Writers Asscn.; Chair. Nigeria Road Safety Comm. 1988–91; Writers Guild Lifetime Achievement Award 1996; Hon. D.Litt. (Leeds) 1973, (Yale) 1981, (Morehouse), (Paul Valéry), (Bayreuth), (Ibadan), (Harvard); Hon. D.Sc.S. (Edin.) 1977; Prisoner of Conscience Award, Amnesty Int., Jock Campbell-New Statesman Literary Award 1969; Nobel Prize for Literature 1986; George Benson Medal, R.S.L. 1990, and numerous other awards; Commdr. Légion d'honneur; Commdr. Fed. Republic of Nigeria 1986; Commdr. Order of Merit (Italy) 1990. *Publications:* plays: The Lion and the Jewel 1959, The Swamp Dwellers 1959, A Dance of the Forests 1960, The Trials of Brother Jero 1961, The Strong Breed 1962, The Road 1964, Kongi's Harvest 1965, Madmen and Specialists 1971, Before the Blackout 1971, Jero's Metamorphosis 1973, Camwood on the Leaves 1973, The Bacchae of Euripides 1974, Death and the King's Horsemen 1975, Opera Wonyosi 1978, From Zia, with Love 1991, A Scourge of Hyacinths (radio play) 1992, The Beatification of Area Boy 1995; novels: The Interpreters 1964, The Forest of a Thousand Daemons (trans.), Season of Anomy 1973; non-fiction: The Man Died (prison memoirs) 1972, Isara: A voyage round Essay 1990, Continuity and Amnesia 1991; poetry: Idanre and Other Poems 1967, A Shuttle in the Crypt 1972, Poems of Black Africa (ed.) 1975, Ogun Abibman 1977, Mandela's Earth and Other Poems 1988; lectures: Myth, Literature and the African World 1972; Aké, The Years of Childhood (autobiog.) 1982, Art, Dialogue and Outrage 1988, Ibadan: The Pentelemes Years (memoir) 1994, The Open Sore of a Continent, A Personal Narrative of the Nigerian Crisis 1996. *Address:* c/o P.O. Box 935, Abeokuta, Ogun State, Nigeria.

SPACEK, Mary Elizabeth (Sissy); American actress; b. 25 Dec. 1949, Quitman, Tex.; d. of Edwin A. and Virginia Spacek; m. Jack Fisk 1974; two d.; ed. Lee Strasberg Theater Inst. *Films:* Prime Cut 1972, Ginger in the Morning 1972, Badlands 1974, Carrie 1976, Three Women 1977, Welcome to L.A. 1977, Heart Beat 1980, Coal Miner's Daughter 1980, Raggedy Man 1981, Missing 1982, The River 1984, Marie 1985, Violets are Blue 1986, Crimes of the Heart 1986, 'night Mother 1986, JFK 1991, The Long Walk Home, The Plastic Nightmare, Hard Promises 1992, Trading Mom 1994, The Grass Harp 1995, Streets of Laredo 1995, If These Walls Could Talk 1996, Affliction 1998, Blast From the Past 1999. *TV films:* The Girls of Huntington House 1973, The Migrants 1973, Katherine 1975, Verna, USO Girl 1978, A Private Matter 1992, A Place for Annie 1994, The Good Old Boys 1995; Best Actress (Nat. Soc. Film Critics) for Carrie 1976, Best Supporting Actress (New York Film Critics) for Three Women 1977, Best Actress (New York and Los Angeles Film Critics, Foreign Press Asscn., Nat. Soc. Film Critics) 1980; Album of the Year Award (Country Music Asscn.) for Coal Miner's Daughter 1980. *Address:* c/o Steve Tellez, CAA, 9830 Wilshire Boulevard, Beverly Hills, CA 90212, U.S.A.

SPACEY, Kevin; American actor; b. 26 July 1959, S. Orange, N.J.; ed. Chatsworth High School, L.A., Juillard Drama School, N.Y.; stage début in Henry IV, Part I; Broadway début in Ghosts 1982; other theatre appearances include: Hurlyburly 1985, Long Day's Journey into Night, London 1986, Yonkers, N.Y. (received Tony award), The Iceman Cometh, London 1998. *Films:* Working Girl 1988, See No Evil, Hear No Evil 1989, Dad 1989, Henry and June 1990, Glengarry Glen Ross 1992, Consenting Adults 1992, Hostile Hostages 1994, Outbreak 1995, The Usual Suspects 1995, Seven 1995, Looking for Richard 1996, A Time to Kill 1996, LA Confidential 1997, Midnight in the Garden of Good and Evil 1997; Dir. Albino Alligator 1997.

SPADER, James; American actor; b. 7 Feb. 1960, Boston; ed. Phillips Acad. *Films include:* Endless Love 1981, The New Kids 1985, Pretty in Pink 1986, Baby Boom 1987, Less Than Zero 1987, Mannequin 1987, Jack's Back 1988, The Rachel Papers 1989, Sex, Lies and Videotape 1989, Bad Influence 1990, The Music of Chance 1993, Dream Lover 1994, Wolf 1994, Stargate 1994, Two Days in the Valley 1996, Crash 1997, Keys to Tulsa 1997, Critical Care 1997, Curtain Call 1998, Supernova 1998. *Address:* c/o ICM, 8942 Wilshire Boulevard, Beverly Hills, CA 90211, U.S.A.

SPAHR, Charles Eugene, B.S.; American oil executive; b. 8 Oct. 1913, Kansas City; s. of Charles T. Spahr and Imogene (Hedrick) Spahr; m. Mary Jane Bruckmiller 1937; one s. four d.; ed. Univ. of Kansas and Harvard Univ. Business School; joined Standard Oil Co. (Ohio) 1939, Vice-Pres. (Transportation) 1951, Exec. Vice-Pres. and Dir. 1955, Pres. 1957–69, Chair. 1970–78; Major in Army Corps of Engineers 1942–45; Dir. Supply and Transportation Div. Petroleum Admin. for Defense 1952; fmr. Dir. Air Products and Chemicals Inc., Ohio Bell, Lincoln Inst. of Land Policy, Repub. Steel Corpn., Harco Corpn., TRW Inc., Cleveland Electric Illuminating Co. (now part of Centerior Energy); Hon. Dir. and fmr. Chair. American Petroleum Inst.; mem. Bd. of Trustees Kan. Univ. Endowment Asscn.; Hon. Trustee Lutheran Hospital; Hon. Trustee Colgate Rochester Divinity School; Emer. mem. Bd. of Trustees Baldwin-Wallace Coll., Chair. 1964–78; Emer. mem. Bd. of Trustees and First Chair., Int. Center for Artificial Organs and Transplantation; fmr. mem. Nat. Petroleum Council; fmr. Chair. Plans for Progress Advisory Council; Hon. Dr. Eng. (Cleveland State Univ.), Hon. LL.D. (Baldwin-Wallace Coll.), Citation for Distinguished Service (Univ. of Kansas), Gold Medal for Distinguished Achievement, American Petroleum Inst. 1980, NERO Distinguished Service Award 1984, Rufus Putnam Distinguished Service Award 1987, Gourgas Medal 1990. *Leisure interests:* fishing, golfing. *Address:* 24075 Lyman Boulevard, Shaker Heights, OH 44122, U.S.A. *Telephone:* (216) 464-0599; (216) 464-9973.

SPAIN, James W., M.A., PH.D.; American diplomatist, writer and investment manager; b. 22 July 1926, Chicago; s. of Patrick Spain and Mary Ellen Forristal; m. Edith Burke James 1951 (deceased); three s. one d. (deceased); ed. Univ. of Chicago, Columbia Univ.; Consultant to Sec. of the Army, Tokyo 1949–50; Cultural Officer, Dept. of State, Karachi, Pakistan 1951–53; Research Fellow, Ford Foundation 1953–55; Research Lecturer, Columbia Univ. 1955–63; mem. Policy Planning Staff, Dept. of State 1963–64; Dir. Office of Research and Analysis for Near E.-S. Asian Affairs 1964–66; Country Dir. for Pakistan and Afghanistan 1966–69; Chargé d'affaires, Islamabad 1969; Consul-Gen., Istanbul 1970–72; Deputy Chief of Mission, Ankara 1972–74; Diplomat in Residence, Florida State Univ., Tallahassee 1974–75, Amb. to Tanzania 1975–79, to UN 1979, to Turkey 1980–81, to Sri Lanka 1985–89; Foreign Affairs Fellow, Carnegie Endowment for Int. Peace and Rand Corpn., Washington 1982–84; Chair. Joseph Fraser Memorial

Hosp., Lanka Infrastructures Ltd.; Dir. Mountain Hawk Federal Express, Rainbow Foundation. *Publications:* The Way of the Pathans 1962, The Pathan Borderland 1963, American Diplomacy in Turkey 1984, Pathans of the Latter Day 1995, In Those Days: A Diplomat Remembers 1998. *Address:* 42 Galle Face Court II, Colombo 3, Sri Lanka. *Telephone:* 437179.

SPALDING, D. Brian, SC.D., PH.D., F.I.MECH.E., F.INST.F., F.R.S., F.ENG.; British professor of heat transfer and business executive; b. 9 Jan. 1923, New Malden, Surrey; s. of Harold and Kathleen Spalding; m. 1st Eda Ilse-Lotte Goericke; two s. two d.; m. 2nd Colleen King; two s.; ed. King's Coll. School, Wimbledon, The Queen's Coll. Oxford and Pembroke Coll. Cambridge; Bataafsche Petroleum Matschapij 1944–45; Ministry of Supply 1945–47; ICI Research Fellow at Cambridge Univ. 1948–50, Demonstrator in Eng. 1950–54; Reader in Applied Heat, Imperial Coll. of Science and Tech., London 1954–58, Prof. of Heat Transfer 1958–88, Prof. Emer. 1988–, Head of Computational Fluid Dynamics Unit 1981–88; Man. Dir. Conduction Heat and Mass Transfer Ltd. 1970–75, Concentration, Heat and Momentum Ltd. 1975–; Chair. CHAM of N. America Ltd. 1977–91; mem. Royal Norwegian Soc.; Bernard Lewis Combustion Medal 1982, Medaille d'Or 1980. *Publications:* Numerical Prediction of Flow, Heat Transfer Turbulence and Combustion (selected works) 1983, Heat Exchanger Design Handbook (jtly.) 1982, Combustion and Mass Transfer 1979, GENMIX: A General Computer Program 1978, Mathematical Models of Turbulence (jtly.) 1972, Heat and Mass Transfer in Recirculating Flows (Co-Author) 1967, Convective Mass Transfer (Co-Author) 1963, Engineering Thermodynamics (Co-Author) 1958, Some Fundamentals of Combustion 1955, Innocents of the Latter Day (fiction) 1996; numerous scientific papers. *Leisure interests:* poetry and reading. *Address:* Concentration, Heat and Momentum Ltd. (CHAM), Bakery House, 40 High Street, Wimbledon, SW19 5AU, England. *Telephone:* 0181-947 7651. *Fax:* 0181-879 3497.

SPANG-HANSSEN, Ebbe, D.PHIL.; Danish professor of Romance philology (retd.); b. 14 Sept. 1928, Copenhagen; m. Gerda Friese Jensen 1952; two s. one d.; ed. Univ. of Copenhagen and Paris-Sorbonne; lecturer Paris-Sorbonne 1961–64; Prof. of Romance Philology, Univ. of Copenhagen 1966–95; mem. Royal Danish Acad. of Sciences. *Publications:* Les Prépositions incolores du Français moderne 1963, La Segmentation automatique du Français écrit (with Bente Maegaard) 1978, Grammaire Française (ed. and co-author with Knud Togeby) (5 vols.) 1980–85; books on European humanism. *Leisure interest:* music. *Address:* Åsletten 6, 3500 Vaerlose, Denmark. *Telephone:* 44-98-10-10.

SPANGENBERG, Christa; German publisher; b. 1928, Munich; d. of Edgar J. Jung and Minni Jung; m. Berthold Spangenberg 1946 (died 1986); two s.; ed. music and language studies; honorary work for Börsenverein des Deutschen Buchhandels; lecturer, Univ. of Munich 1987–; Founder Int. Youth Library Foundation, Munich 1996–. *Publications:* Elly Petersens praktisches Gartenlexikon, Praktisches Balkon- und Zimmerpflanzen-lexikon, Grüne Uhr, Garten Uhr, ABC für Kleine Gärtner. *Leisure interests:* gardening, music. *Address:* Bäumlstrasse 6, 80638 Munich, Germany. *Telephone:* 17 14 23. *Fax:* 17 14 23.

SPARGO, Peter Ernest, F.R.S.S.A.F.; South African educator; b. 7 June 1937, Johannesburg; s. of Alfred Hugh Spargo and Lilias (née Fisher) McCall Spargo; m. Celia Rosamunde Key 1964; four d.; ed. Jeppe High School, Univ. of Witwatersrand, Johannesburg and Magdalene Coll., Cambridge; Science Teacher Jeppe High School 1961–63; Lecturer in Science Educ. Johannesburg Coll. of Educ. 1964–71; Science Educ. Planner, Pretoria 1972–75; School of Educ., Univ. of Cape Town 1976–97, Dir. Science Educ. Unit 1980–97, Hon. Research Assoc., Dept. of Chem. 1999–; Nat. Chair. S.A. Asscn. of Teachers of Physical Science 1975–82; Trustee and Dir. S. African Science Educ. Project 1977–; Educ. Consultant to Shell Oil Co. (U.S.A.) 1977–89, Rössing Uranium Co. (Namibia) 1982–90; Nat. Pres. Fed. of Science and Math. Teachers Asscns. of S.A. 1977–79, 1984–85; Gen. Sec. Royal Soc. of S. Africa 1986–89; Hon. Nat. Pres. S. African Spelaeological Asscn. 1996–; Medal of Honour (Fed. of Science and Math. Teachers Asscns. of S.A.) 1981. *Publications:* numerous publs. in the fields of science education, history of science and history of physics and chemistry, author of science textbooks. *Leisure interests:* walking, reading, gardening. *Address:* P.O. Box 211, Rondebosch 7701, South Africa. *Telephone:* (21) 686 4289.

SPARK, Dame Muriel Sarah, D.B.E., C.LIT., F.R.S.E.; British author; b. Edinburgh; d. of Bernard Camberg and Sarah Elizabeth Maud Uezzell; m. S. O. Spark 1937 (divorced); one s.; ed. James Gillespie's High School for Girls, Edinburgh, Heriot-Watt Coll.; Foreign Office 1944–45; Ed. The Poetry Review 1947–49; Gen. Sec. Poetry Soc., London; Hon. mem. American Acad. of Arts and Letters 1978; Hon. D.Litt. (Strathclyde) 1971, (Edin.) 1989, (Aberdeen) 1995, (St. Andrews) 1998; D. Univ. (Heriot-Watt) 1995; The Observer Story Prize 1951, Italia Prize 1962, James Tait Black Memorial Prize 1965, Ingersoll Prize (U.S.A.), T.S. Eliot Award 1992, David Cohen British Literature Prize 1997, Int. PEN Gold Pen Award 1998; Commdr. Ordre des Arts et des Lettres. *Publications:* Mary Shelley 1951, The Fanfarlo and Other Verse 1952, John Masefield (a critical study) 1953, The Comforters 1957, Robinson 1958, The Go-Away Bird and Other Stories 1958, Memento Mori 1959 (play 1964; BBC TV 1992), The Bachelors 1960, The Ballad of Peckham Rye 1960, The Prime of Miss Jean Brodie 1961 (play 1966, film 1969, TV 1978), Voices at Play 1961, Doctors of Philosophy (play) 1963, The Girls of Slender Means 1963, The Mandelbaum Gate 1965, Collected Stories I. 1967, Collected Poems I. 1967, The Public Image 1968, The Very Fine Clock (juvenile) 1968, The Driver's Seat 1970 (film 1974), Not to Disturb 1971, The Hothouse by The East River 1973, The Abbess of Crewe 1974 (film 1977), The Takeover 1976, Territorial Rights 1979, Loitering with Intent 1981, Bang-Bang You're Dead (stories) 1982, Going Up to Sotheby's (poems) 1982, The Only Problem 1984, The Stories of Muriel Spark 1985, Mary Shelley 1987, 1992, A Far Cry from Kensington 1988, Symposium 1990, Curriculum Vitae (autobiog.) 1992, The Essence of the Brontës 1993, The French Window and The Small Telephone (juvenile) 1993, Omnibus I 1993, Omnibus II 1994, The Portobello Road (stories) 1995, The Hanging Judge (stories) 1995, Reality and Dreams 1996, Omnibus III 1996, Harper and Wilton 1996, Omnibus IV 1997. *Address:* c/o David Higham Assocs. Ltd., 5–8 Lower John Street, Golden Square, London, W1R 4HA, England.

SPARKS, Robert Stephen John, PH.D., F.R.S.; British professor of geology and volcanologist; b. 15 May 1949, Harpenden, Herts.; s. of Kenneth Grenfell Sparks and Ruth Joan Rugman; m. Ann Elizabeth Talbot 1971; two s.; ed. Imperial Coll. London; Fellow of Royal Comm. of Exhbn. of 1851, Lancaster Univ. 1974–76; NATO Post-doctoral Fellow, Univ. of Rhode Island, U.S.A. 1976–78; lecturer, Univ. of Cambridge 1978–89, Fellow Trinity Hall, Cambridge 1980–89; Prof. of Geology, Bristol Univ. 1989–, Channing Willis Prof. of Geology 1990–; Chief Scientist Montserrat Volcano Observatory 1997–; Prof. of Earth Sciences, Nat. Environment Research Council 1998–; Pres. Geological Soc. of London 1994–96; Fellow American Geophysics Union 1998; Bigsby Medal, Geological Soc. of London. *Publications:* Volcanic Plumes 1997 and 170 scientific articles and papers on volcanology (especially physics of volcanic eruptions), fluid mechanics, petrology and other geological topics. *Leisure interests:* music, tennis, football, squash, travel, family. *Address:* Walnut Cottage, Brinsea Road, Congresbury, Bristol, BS19 5JF, England.

SPASSKIY, Nikolai Nikolayevich; Russian diplomatist; b. 1961, Moscow; ed. Moscow Inst. of Int. Relations; with U.S.S.R. (later Russian) Ministry of Foreign Affairs 1983–; Deputy Head, First Deputy, Dept. of N. America 1992–94; Dir. 1994–97; mem. Collegium, Ministry of Foreign Affairs 1995; Amb. to Italy 1997–. *Address:* Russian Embassy, Via Gacta 5, 00186 Rome, Italy. *Telephone:* (06) 494 1680 (Office). *Fax:* (3906) 49 10 31 (Office).

SPASSKY, Boris Vasiliyevich; French/Russian chess-player and journalist; b. 30 Jan. 1937, Leningrad (now St. Petersburg); m. 1st Marina Shcherbacheva 1975; m. 2nd; ed. Faculty of Journalism, Leningrad State Univ.; in Leningrad Section of Voluntary Sport Soc., Trud 1959–61; Trainer, Leningrad Section of Voluntary Sport Soc., Locomotiv 1964–79; played in numerous individual and command int. chess tournaments; U.S.S.R. Grand Master, Int. Grand Master and World Chess Student Champion 1956, U.S.S.R. Chess Champion 1962, World Chess Champion 1969–72 (when lost to Bobby Fischer); left U.S.S.R. 1976, lost against Bobby Fischer in Yugoslavia 1992; several decorations; now lives in Paris.

SPÄTH, Lothar; German politician; b. 16 Nov. 1937, Sigmaringen; s. of Friedrich and Helene (née Lillich) Späth; m. Ursula Heinle 1962; one s. one d.; ed. Gymnasium, Heilbronn, State School of Man., Stuttgart; mem. Landtag 1968–91; Chair. CDU group in Stuttgart Landtag 1972–78, Hon. Leader 1991–; Rep. of CDU for Baden-Württemberg 1977–91; Sec. of Interior Feb.–Aug. 1978, Minister-Pres. of Baden-Württemberg 1978–91; Pres. Bundesrat 1985–86; Chair. Jenoptik AG, Jena 1991–; Royal Norwegian Consul-Gen. of Thuringia and Saxony-Anhalt 1992–; Dr. h.c. (Karlsruhe) 1984, (Pecs). *Publications:* Wende in die Zukunft 1985, 1992– Der Traum von Europa 1989, Natur und Wirtschaft 1992, Sind die Deutschen noch zu retten? 1993, Countdown für Deutschland 1995, Blühende Phantasien und harte Realitäten 1997, Die zweite Wende 1998. *Leisure interests:* modern painting and graphics, card games, tennis. *Address:* Carl-Zeiss-Str. 1, 07743 Jena, Germany. *Telephone:* (03641) 650. *Fax:* (03641) 652483.

SPAULDING, Winston, Q.C.; Jamaican fmr. politician and lawyer; b. 26 Aug. 1939; m.; five c.; called to the Bar, Inner Temple, London 1966; worked briefly in Jamaican and British civil service, and practised law in the Bahamas; subsequently established legal practice in Jamaica; fmr. mem. Nat. Exec. People's Nat. Party; Deputy Leader Jamaica Labour Party 1977–83; Senator and Opposition Spokesman on Security and Justice 1977–80; M.P. for Cen. St. James 1980–83 and for S.E. St. Andrew 1983–89; Minister of Nat. Security and Justice and Attorney-Gen. 1980–86; Chair. Defence Bd. 1980–86, Legislation Cttee. 1980–86, Statute Law Commrs. under the Law Revision Act 1980–86; mem. Council of Legal Educ. 1980–86; Founder mem. Jamaica Council for Human Rights; Founder and First Chair. Human Rights Bureau of Jamaica Labour Party; as Minister of Justice initiated review of Gun Court Act which included abolition of mandatory life sentence; as Minister of Security initiated establishment of Police Staff Coll. *Address:* 21 Balmoral Avenue, Kingston 10, Jamaica (Office). *Telephone:* 92-98601. *Fax:* 92-96196.

SPAVENTA, Luigi; Italian professor of economics; b. 5 March 1934, Rome; s. of Renato Spaventa and Lydia De Novellis; m. Margaret Royce 1962; three c.; ed. Univ. of Rome and King's Coll. Cambridge; Prof. of Econ. Policy, Univ. of Palermo 1963–64; Prof. of Econs. Univ. of Perugia 1964–70, Univ. of Rome 1970–; mem. Italian Parl. (on leave from univ.) 1976–83; Visiting Fellow, All Souls Coll. Oxford 1968–69; Visiting scholar, IMF 1984; Luigi Einaudi Prof. Cornell Univ. 1989; Minister of the Budget 1993–94; Chair. of Bd. Finanza & Futuro S.p.A., Banca Monte dei Paschi di Siena S.p.A. 1997–98; Chair. Consob (Securities Comm.) 1998–; Fellow, Centre for Econ. Policy

Research; Research Dir. Centro Europa Ricerche; Kt. Grand Cross Order of Merit (Italy). *Publications:* essays and articles in specialized journals. *Address:* Consob, Via Isonzo 19/d, 00198 Rome (Office); Via G.B. De Rossi, 29-00161 Rome, Italy (Home). *Telephone:* (06) 8477216 (Office); (06) 44238191 (Home). *Fax:* (06) 8477212 (Office); (06) 4404572 (Home).

SPEAKES, Larry Melvin; American public relations executive; b. 13 Sept. 1939, Cleveland, Miss.; s. of Harry Speakes and Ethlyn Fincher; m. Laura Crawford 1968; two s. one d.; ed. Univ. of Mississippi; news ed. Oxford (Miss.) Eagle 1961–62, Bolivar Commercial, Cleveland 1962–63; Man. Ed. Bolivar Commercial 1965–66; Gen. Man. Progress Publs. Leland, Miss. 1966–68; Ed. Leland Progress, Hollandale Herald, Bolivar Co. Democrat, Sunflower Co. News; Press Sec. to Senator for Mississippi 1968–74; Staff Asst. Exec. Office of Pres. of U.S.A. March–May 1974, Press Asst. to Special Counsel to Pres. May–Aug. 1974; Asst. to White House Press Sec. 1974–76, Asst. Press Sec. to Pres. 1976–77; Press Sec. to Gerald R. Ford 1977; Vice-Pres. Hill & Knowlton, Inc., Washington 1977–81; Prin. Deputy Press Sec. and Asst. to Pres. of U.S.A. 1981–87; Sr. Vice-Pres. Merrill Lynch & Co., Inc., New York 1987–88; corp. communications consultant and lecturer on politics and the presidency 1988–91; Vice-Pres., Communications, Northern Telecom Ltd., Washington and Toronto 1991–93; Senior Vice-Pres. Corp. and Legis. Affairs, U.S. Postal Service 1994–98; Sr. Advisor to Postmaster Gen. 1998–; Litt.D. h.c. (Ind. Cen. Univ.); several achievement awards. *Address:* 4800 Thiban Terrace, Annandale, VA 22003, U.S.A.

SPEAR, Laurinda Hope, M.A., F.A.I.A.; American architect; b. 23 Aug. 1951, Rochester, Minn.; d. of Harold Spear; m. Bernardo Fort-Brescia 1976; five s. one d.; ed. Columbia and Brown Univs.; founding prin., Arquitectonica; projects include low-income housing, high-rise condominiums, residential additions and renovations, office towers, medical office bldgs., retail complexes and hotels in U.S.A., France, Luxembourg and Peru; faculty mem. in charge of design studio, Univ. of Miami School of Architecture; lecturer to professional, civil and academic groups; numerous exhbns. throughout U.S.A. and Europe including Paris Biennale 1982, Inst. of Contemporary Art, Philadelphia 1986, Buenos Aires Biennale 1987, Inst. Français d'Architecture, Paris 1988, Centrum voor Architectuur en Stedebouw, Brussels 1991, Gallery MA, Tokyo 1993; various architectural awards. *Address:* FAIA, 550 Brickell Avenue, Suite 200, Miami, FL 33131, U.S.A.

SPEAR, Walter Eric, PH.D., D.SC., F.R.S., F.R.S.E., F.INST.P.; British physicist; b. 20 Jan. 1921, Frankfurt/Main, Germany; s. of David and Eva (née Reineck) Spear; m. Hilda D. King 1952; two d.; ed. Univ. of London; Lecturer in Physics, Univ. of Leicester 1953, Reader 1967; Visiting Prof., Univ. of Purdue and Univ. of N.C. 1957–58, 1965–66; Prof. of Physics, Univ. of Dundee 1968–90; Max Born Prize 1977, Europhysics Prize 1977, MakDougal-Brisbane Medal (R.S.E.) 1981, Rank Prize for Optoelectronics 1988, Mott Award 1989, Rumford Medal (Royal Soc.) 1989. *Publications:* numerous papers in scientific journals and contributions to books on electronic, optical and transport properties in crystalline and amorphous solids and liquids. *Leisure interests:* music, languages, literature. *Address:* 20 Kelso Place, Dundee, DD2 1SL, Scotland. *Telephone:* (01382) 667649.

SPEARMAN, Thomas David, PH.D., M.R.I.A.; Irish professor of natural philosophy and university vice-provost; b. 25 March 1937, Dublin; s. of Thomas Spearman and Elizabeth Leadbeater; m. Juanita Smale 1961; one s. two d.; ed. Greenlanes and Mountjoy Schools, Dublin, Trinity Coll., Dublin and St. John's Coll., Cambridge; Research Fellow, Univ. Coll. London 1960–61; Research Assoc. Univ. of Ill. 1962–64; Lecturer in Theoretical Physics, Univ. of Durham 1964–66; Univ. Prof. of Natural Philosophy, Trinity Coll. Dublin 1966–97, Fellow 1969–94, Senior Fellow 1994–97, Bursar 1974–77, Vice-Provost 1991–97; Prof. Associé, Univ. of Montpellier 1985–; Chair. Trustee Savings Bank, Dublin 1989–92; mem. Council, European Physical Soc. 1979–82; mem. European Space Science Cttee. 1984–89; Vice-Pres. European Science Foundation 1983–89; Treas. Royal Irish Acad. 1980–88; Treas. Academia Europaea 1989–; mem. European Science and Tech. Ass. 1994–. *Publications:* Elementary Particle Theory (with A. D. Martin) 1970; numerous papers and articles on aspects of elementary particle physics, inverse problems and history of science. *Leisure interests:* walking, gardening, reading, listening to music, looking at pictures. *Address:* House no. 25, Trinity College, Dublin 2 (Office); St. Elmo, Marlborough Road, Glenageary, Co. Dublin, Ireland (Home). *Telephone:* 1-608 2360 (Office).

SPECTER, Arlen; American politician; b. 12 Feb. 1930, Wichita, Kan.; s. of Harry and Lillie Shanin Specter; m. Joan Lois Levy 1953; two s.; ed. Univ. of Oklahoma, Univ. of Pennsylvania, Yale Univ.; served U.S.A.F. 1951–53; Asst. Dist. Attorney, Phila., Pa. 1959–63, Dist. Attorney 1966–74; Asst. Counsel, Warren Comm., Washington, D.C. 1964; Special Asst. Attorney-Gen., Pa. Dept. of Justice 1964–65; Del. Republican Nat. Convention 1968, 1972, Alt. Del. 1976; Senator from Pennsylvania (Republican) 1981–, Chair. Select Cttee. on Intelligence, Special Cttee. on Ageing and Veterans Affairs; mem. Nat. Advisory Cttee. on Peace Corps 1969–; Lecturer in Law, Univ. of Pa. Law School 1969–72, Temple Univ. Law School 1972–76; mem. White House Conf. on Youth 1971, Gov. Justice Comm., Regional Planning Council, Nat. Advisory Comm. on Criminal Justice Standards and Goals, Criminal Rules Cttee. of Pa. Supreme Court and Judicial Council of Phila.; mem. American, Pa. and Phila. Bar Asscns., Nat. Council on Alcoholism; Hon. LL.B (Phila. Coll. of Textiles and Science) 1968; Sons of Italy Award, Alessandroni Lodge. *Publications:* articles in law reviews. *Address:* U.S. Senate, 711 Senate Hart Building, Washington, DC 20510, U.S.A.

SPEDDING, Sir Colin Raymond William, Kt., C.B.E., M.SC., PH.D., D.SC., C.BIOL., F.I.HORT., F.R.A.S.E., F.R.AG.S.; British university professor; b. 22 March 1925, Cannock; s. of Robert Spedding and Ilynn Spedding; m. Betty N. George 1952 (died 1988); two s. (one deceased) one d.; ed. London Univ. (external); Allen & Hanbury 1947; Grassland Research Inst. 1949–75, Deputy Dir. 1972–75; Visiting, then part-time Prof. of Agric. Systems, Univ. of Reading 1970–75, Prof. 1975–90, Head, Dept. of Agric. and Horticulture 1975–83, Dean, Faculty of Agric. and Food 1983–86, Dir. Centre for Agricultural Strategy 1981–90, Pro-Vice-Chancellor 1986–90; Pres. Inst. of Biology 1992–94; Chair. UK Register of Organic Food Standards 1987–, Farm Animal Welfare Council 1988–98, Apple and Pear Research Council 1989–97, Council of Science and Tech. Insts. 1994–; Deputy Chair. People's Dispensary for Sick Animals (PDSA) 1996–; Vice-Pres. Inst. of Biology 1997–; Advisory Dir. World Soc. for the Protection of Animals 1998–; numerous other professional and public appts.; Hon. Assoc. Royal Coll. of Veterinary Surgeons; Hon. F.I. Biol.; Hon. D.Sc. (Reading); George Hedley Memorial Award 1971; Hawkesbury Centenary Medal of Honour, Univ. of W. Sydney, and other honours and distinctions. *Publications:* ten books and about 200 scientific papers. *Address:* Vine Cottage, Orchard Road, Hurst, Reading, RG10 0SD, England. *Telephone:* (0118) 9341771.

SPEKREIJSE, Henk; Netherlands professor of visual systems analysis; b. 4 Nov. 1940, Rijssen; m. Y.J.M. van der Heijden; two d.; ed. Tech. Univ. Delft and Univ. of Amsterdam; Prof. of Visual Systems Analysis, Netherlands Ophthalmic Research Inst., Lab. of Medical Physics and Informatics 1977–; Dir. of Neuroresearch Netherlands Ophthalmic Research Inst. 1985–95; mem. Royal Netherlands Acad. of Arts and Sciences 1985–; AKZO Award 1985. *Publications:* Analysis of EEG responses in man, evoked by sine wave modulated light 1966, Spatial Contrast (with L. H. van der Tweel) 1977, Visual Pathways, Electrophysiology and Pathology (with P. A. Apkarian) 1981, Systems Approach in Vision (with D. Regan and D. M. Shapley) 1986, Brain Topography, Vol. 5, No. 2 (with B. W. van Dijk and F. H. Lopes da Vega) 1992. *Address:* The Netherlands Ophthalmic Research Institute and the Laboratory of Medical Physics, P.O. Box 12141, 1100 AC Amsterdam-Zuidoost (Office); Voorstraat 11, 1394 CS Nederhorst den Berg, Netherlands (Home). *Telephone:* (20) 5664584. *Fax:* (20) 6916521.

SPELLING, Aaron, B.A.; American television producer and writer; b. 22 April 1923, Dallas, Tex.; s. of David Spelling and Pearl Wall; m. Carole Gene Marer 1968; one s. one d.; ed. Univ. de Paris (Sorbonne), Southern Methodist Univ.; served U.S.A.A.F. 1942–45; Co-owner Thomas-Spelling Productions 1969–72; Co-Pres. Spelling-Goldberg Productions 1972–76; Pres. Aaron Spelling Productions Inc., Los Angeles 1977–86, Chair. and C.E.O. 1986–; mem. Bd. of Dirs. American Film Inst.; mem. Writers' Guild of America, Producers' Guild of America, The Caucus, Hollywood Radio and TV Soc., Hollywood TV Acad. of Arts and Sciences; Bronze Star Medal; Purple Heart with oak leaf cluster; Eugene O'Neill Award 1947, 1948; Nat. Asscn. for Advancement of Colored People Image Award 1970, 1971, 1973, 1975; Man of the Year Award (Publicists' Guild of America) 1971; B'nai B'rith Man of the Year Award 1985, N.A.A.C.P. Humanitarian of the Year 1983; producer of numerous TV programmes, including Dynasty, The Colbys, Love Boat, Hotel, Beverley Hills 90210, Melrose Place, Sunset Beach, Pacific Palisades and over 110 Movies of the Week for American Broadcasting Corpn.; films produced include Mr. Mom, 'Night, Mother, Surrender, Cross My Heart, Soapdish; author of numerous TV plays and films. *Publication:* Aaron Spelling: A Prime Time Life 1996. *Address:* Spelling TV Inc., 5700 Wilshire Boulevard, Suite 575, Los Angeles, CA 90036, U.S.A.

SPENCE, Jonathan Dermot, PH.D.; American professor of history; b. 11 Aug. 1936, Surrey, England; s. of Dermot Spence and Muriel Crailsham; m. 1st Helen Alexander 1962 (divorced 1993); two s.; m. 2nd Chin Annping 1993; ed. Univ. of Cambridge and Yale Univ.; Asst. Prof. of History, Yale Univ. 1966–71, Prof. 1971–; Visiting Prof. Univ. of Beijing 1987; mem. Bd. of Govs. Yale Univ. Press 1988–; mem. American Acad. of Arts and Sciences, American Philosophical Soc.; Guggenheim Fellow 1979–80; MacArthur Fellow 1987–92; Vursell Prize, American Acad. and Inst. of Arts and Letters 1983; Hon. L.H.D. (Knox Coll.) 1984, (New Haven) 1989; Hon. Litt. D. (Wheeling Coll.) 1985, (Chinese Univ. of Hong Kong) 1996, (Gettysburg) Coll. 1996; Comisso Prize (Italy) 1987; Gelber Literary Prize (Canada) 1991; other honours and distinctions. *Publications:* Ts'Ao Yin and The K'Ang-Hsi Emperor 1966, To Change China 1969, Emperor of China 1974, The Death of Woman Wang 1978, The Gate of Heavenly Peace 1981, The Memory Palace of Matteo Ricci 1984, The Question of Hu 1988, The Search for Modern China 1990, Chinese Roundabout 1992, God's Chinese Son 1996. *Address:* Department of History, Yale University, P.O. Box 208324, New Haven, CT 06520; 691 Forest Road, New Haven, CT 06515, U.S.A.

SPENCER, Anthony James Merrill, M.A., PH.D., SC.D., F.R.S.; British applied mathematician and professor; b. 23 Aug. 1929, Birmingham; s. of James L. Spencer and Gladys Merrill; m. Margaret Bosker 1955; three s.; ed. Queen Mary's Grammar School, Walsall and Queens' Coll. Cambridge, Univs. of Keele and Birmingham; Research Assoc., Div. of Applied Math., Brown Univ., U.S.A. 1955–57; Sr. Scientific Officer UKAEA 1957–60; Lecturer Dept. of Theoretical Mechanics Nottingham Univ. 1960–63, Reader 1963–65, Prof. 1965–94, Prof. Emer. 1994–; Visiting Prof. Brown Univ. 1966, 1971, Lehigh Univ. 1978, Univ. of Queensland 1982; Erskine Fellow, Univ. of Canterbury 1995. *Publications:* Deformation of Fibre-Reinforced Materials 1972, Engineering Mathematics (2 vols.) 1975, Continuum Mechanics 1980,

Ed.: Continuum Theory of the Mechanics of Fibre-Reinforced Composites 1984, Continuum Models of Discrete Systems 1987. *Address:* School of Mathematical Sciences, University of Nottingham, Nottingham, NG7 2RD (Office); 43 Stanton Lane, Stanton-on-the-Wolds, Keyworth, Nottingham, NG12 5BE, England (Home). *Telephone:* (0115) 951 3838 (Office); (0115) 937 3134 (Home). *Fax:* (0115) 951 3837 (Office).

SPENCER, Sir Derek Harold, Kt., Q.C., M.A., B.C.L.; British politician; b. 31 March 1936, Gisburn, Yorks.; s. of late Thomas Spencer and Gladys Heslop; m. 1st Joan Nutter 1960 (divorced); two s. one d.; m. 2nd Caroline Pärn 1988; one s.; ed. Clitheroe Royal Grammar School and Keble Coll. Oxford; part-time tutor in Law, Keble Coll. Oxford 1960–64; called to the Bar, Gray's Inn, London 1961, Q.C. 1980, Bencher 1991; Recorder, Crown Court 1979–92, 1998–; mem. Parl. for Leicester South 1983–87, for Brighton Pavilion 1992–97; Parl. Private Sec. to Home Office Ministers 1986, to Attorney-Gen. 1987; Solicitor-Gen. 1992–97; Conservative. *Leisure interests:* reading, swimming, walking. *Address:* 18 Red Lion Court, London, EC4A 3EB, England.

SPENCER, Elizabeth, M.A.; American author; b. 1921, Carollton, Miss.; d. of James L. Spencer and Mary James McCain; m. John A. B. Rusher 1956; ed. Belhaven Coll. and Vanderbilt Univ.; Writer-in-residence, Univ. of N. Carolina 1969, Hollins Coll. 1973, Concordia Univ. 1977–78, Adjunct Prof. 1981–86; Visiting Prof. Univ. of N.C., Chapel Hill 1986–92; Vice-Chancellor Fellowship of Southern Writers 1993–97; mem. American Acad. of Arts and Letters; Guggenheim Foundation Fellow 1953; Rosenthal Foundation Award, American Acad. of Arts and Letters 1957; McGraw-Hill Fiction Award 1960, Award of Merit for short story, American Acad. of Arts and Letters 1983, Salem Award for Literature 1992, Dos Passos Award for Fiction 1992, N.C. Gov.'s Award for Literature 1994, and other awards; Hon. Litt. D. (Southwestern Univ., Memphis) 1968, (Concordia Univ.) 1987, (Univ. of the South) 1992, (Univ. of N.C.) 1998. *Publications:* Fire in the Morning 1948, This Crooked Way 1952, The Voice at the Back Door 1956, The Light in the Piazza 1960, Knights and Dragons 1965, No Place for an Angel 1967, Ship Island and other stories 1968, The Snare 1972, The Stories of Elizabeth Spencer 1981, Marilee 1981, The Salt Line 1984, Jack of Diamonds and Other Stories 1988, For Lease or Sale (play) 1989, On the Gulf 1991, The Night Travellers 1991, Landscapes of the Heart (memoir) 1998; short stories in magazines and collections. *Address:* 402 Longleaf Drive, Chapel Hill, NC 27514, U.S.A. (Home). *Telephone:* (919) 929 2115.

SPENCER, John; British snooker player; b. 15 Sept. 1935, Radcliffe, Lancs.; s. of William Spencer and Anne (née Bleakley) Spencer; m. Margot Anni Sawbridge 1969; ed. Stand Grammar School; Chair. World Professional Billiards and Snooker Asscn. Ltd.; World Professional Snooker Champion in 1969, 1971, 1977. *Publication:* Spencer on Snooker. *Leisure interest:* golf. *Address:* 17 Knowles Street, Radcliffe, Lancs., M26 4DN, England. *Telephone:* (0161) 725 9656. *Fax:* (0161) 725 9650.

SPERBER, Dan; French social sciences researcher; b. 20 June 1942, Cagnes; s. of late Manes Sperber; ed. Sorbonne, Oxford Univ.; researcher CNRS 1965–, Dir. 1983–; Rivers Memorial Medal (Royal Anthropological Inst.) 1991. *Publications:* Rethinking Symbolism 1975, On Anthropological Knowledge 1982, Relevance: Communication and Cognition (with Deirdre Wilson) 1986, Explaining Culture 1996. *Address:* CREA, 1 rue Descartes, 75005, Paris, France.

SPERLICH, Peter Werner, P.H.D.; American political scientist; b. 27 June 1934, Breslau, Germany (now Wrocław, Poland); s. of Max Otto and Anneliese Gertrud (née Greulich) Sperlich; arrived in U.S.A. 1956, naturalized 1961; ed. Mankato State Univ., Univ. of Mich.; faculty mem. Univ. of Calif., Berkeley 1963–, Prof. of Political Science 1980–, Prof. Law School 1963–; consultant, court and law firms; Social Science Research Council Fellow 1966, Ford Foundation Fellow 1968; mem. American Legal Studies Asscn., Law and Soc. Asscn., Nat. Asscn. for Dispute Resolution, Int. Soc. of Political Psychology, Soc. for Psychological Study of Social Issues, American, Int. and Western Political Science Asscns., Conf. Group on German Politics; research on law and politics in U.S., Germany, Austria, Denmark, the Netherlands, Switzerland, the U.K., Canada, the U.S.S.R., Japan. *Publications:* Conflict and Harmony in Human Affairs 1971, Single Family Defaults and Foreclosures 1975, Trade Rules and Industry Practices 1976, Over-the-Counter Drug Advertisements 1977, Residing in a Mobile Home 1977, An Evaluation of the Emergency School Aid Act Nonprofit Organisation 1978, also numerous articles. *Address:* University of California, 210 Barrows Hall, Berkeley, CA 94720 (Office); 39 Adeline Drive, Walnut Creek, CA 94596, U.S.A. (Home).

SPERO, Nancy, B.F.A.; American artist; b. 24 Aug. 1926, Cleveland, Ohio; d. of Henry Spero and Polly Spero; m. Leon Golub 1951; three s.; ed. Chicago Art Inst., Atelier André l'Hôte, École des Beaux Arts, Paris. *Solo exhibitions include:* Everson Museum of Art (Syracuse, N.Y.) 1987, Rhona Hoffman Gallery (Chicago) 1988, Museum of Contemporary Art (Los Angeles) 1988, Le Grand Halle de la Villette (Paris) 1989, S. L. Simpson Gallery (Toronto) 1989, Josh Baer Gallery (New York) 1989, 1991, Haus am Walsee (Berlin) 1990, Honolulu Acad. of Arts 1990, Gallery Hibell (Tokyo) 1990, Anthony Reynolds Gallery (London) 1990, Galleria Stefani Miscetti (Rome) 1991, Künstlerhaus Salzburg 1991, Barbara Gross Galerie (Munich) 1991, Galerie Raymond Bollag (Zurich) 1991, Jürgen Becker Galerie (Hamburg) 1991, Museum of Modern Art (New York) 1992. *Joint exhibitions include:* (with Georgina Starr) Ikon Gallery (Birmingham, U.K.) 1998. *Permanent installations include:* R. C. Harris Water Filtration Plant (Toronto) 1988, Well Woman Centre and exterior mural (Londonderry) 1990, Inst. of Contemporary Art (Philadelphia) 1991, Von der Heydt Museum (Wuppertal) 1991, Circulo de Bellas Artes (Madrid) 1991; also rep. in perm. collections including Art Gallery of Ont. (Toronto), Australian Nat. Gallery, Centro Cultural (Mexico), Museum of Fine Arts (Hanoi), Ulmer Museum (Germany), Musée des Beaux-Arts de Montréal; CAPS Fellow N.Y. State Council on the Arts 1976–77; Hon. D.F.A. (Chicago) 1991. *Address:* 530 La Guardia Place, New York, NY 10012, U.S.A.

SPETH, James Gustave, B.A., B.LITT., LL.B.; American international organization administrator; b. 3 March 1942, Orangeburg, S.C.; m. Caroline Cameron Council 1964; two s. one d.; ed. Yale Univ. and Oxford Univ.; barrister, Washington 1969, Clerk, Supreme Court 1969–70; Sr. Staff Attorney Nat. Resources Defence Council, Washington 1977–79, mem. Bd. dirs. 1981–82; Chair. Council for Environmental Quality 1977–79; Prof. of Law Georgetown Univ. 1981–82; Pres. and f. World Resources Inst. 1982–93; joined UNDP 1982, Admin. 1993–. *Address:* UNDP, One UN Plaza, New York, NY 10017, U.S.A. *Telephone:* (212) 906 5000. *Fax:* (212) 826 2057.

SPIELBERG, Steven, B.A.; American film director; b. 18 Dec. 1947, Cincinnati, Ohio; s. of Arnold and Leah (née Posner) Spielberg; m. 1st Amy Irving (q.v.) 1985 (divorced 1989); two s.; m. 2nd Kate Capshaw; two d. (one adopted); ed. Calif. State Coll., Long Beach; won film contest with war film Escape to Nowhere 1961; dir. episodes of TV series, including Night Gallery, Marcus Welby, M.D., Columbo; directed 20-minute short Amblin'; Dir. TV films Duel 1971, Something Evil 1972; Dirs. Guild of America Award Fellowship 1986; Co-f. Dreamworks SKG 1995–; f. Starbright Foundation; Irving G. Thalberg Award 1987, Golden Lion Award (Venice Film Festival) 1993, B.A.F.T.A. Award 1994, Acad. Award for Schindler's List 1994, David Lean (B.A.F.T.A.); John Huston Award for Artists Rights 1995, Grosses Bundesverdienstkreuz 1998; Dr. h.c. (Univ. of S. Calif.) 1994; Hon. D.Litt. (Sussex) 1997; John Huston Award 1995. *Films directed:* The Sugarland Express 1974, Jaws 1975, Close Encounters of the Third Kind 1977, 1941 1979, Raiders of the Lost Ark 1981, E.T. (The Extra Terrestrial) 1982, Indiana Jones and the Temple of Doom 1984, The Color Purple (also produced) 1985, Empire of the Sun 1988; I Wanna Hold Your Hand (produced) 1978, Poltergeist (co-wrote and produced) 1982, Gremlins (produced) 1984, Young Sherlock Holmes 1985 (exec. producer), Back to the Future (co-exec. producer), The Goonies (writer and exec. producer) 1986, Batteries Not Included (exec. producer) 1986, The Money Pit (co-produced) 1986, An American Tail (co-exec. producer) 1986, Always 1989, Gremlins II (exec. producer), Dad (exec. producer), Joe versus the Volcano (exec. producer), Hook 1991, Cape Fear (co-exec. producer) 1992, Jurassic Park 1992, Schindler's List 1993, Casper (producer) 1995, Some Mother's Son 1996, Twister 1996 (exec. producer); The Lost World: Jurassic Park 1997, Amistad 1997, Deep Impact 1998, Saving Private Ryan 1998 (Acad. Award for Best Dir.). *Publication:* Close Encounters of the Third Kind (with Patrick Mann). *Address:* CAA, 9830 Wilshire Boulevard, Beverly Hills, CA 90212, U.S.A.

SPIELMANN, Alphonse, D. EN D.; Luxembourg judge; b. 23 May 1931, Brattert; m. Catherine Hildgen 1961; three s.; ed. Faculté de Droit and Inst. de Criminologie, Univ. of Paris and Centre Universitaire de Luxembourg; Attorney-Gen., Grand Duchy of Luxembourg; Judge, European Court of Human Rights 1985–; numerous int. activities. *Publications:* Liberté d'expression ou censure? 1982, La Convention européenne des droits de l'homme et le droit luxembourgeois 1991. *Leisure interest:* history of Second World War. *Address:* 12 Côte d'Eich, L-1450 (Office); 108 rue des Muguets, 2167 Luxembourg (Home). *Telephone:* 47 59 81/1.

SPIELVOGEL, Carl, B.A.; American advertising executive; b. 27 Dec. 1928, New York City; s. of Joseph Spielvogel and Sadie (née Tellerman) Spielvogel; m. Barbara Lee Diamonstein 1981; two s. one d.; ed. Baruch Coll.; reporter, columnist, New York Times 1950–60; with McCann Erickson, Inc., Interpublic Group of Cos., Inc., New York City 1960–74; Vice-Chair., Chair. Exec. Cttee. and Dir. Interpublic Group of Cos., Inc. 1974–80; Chair. and C.E.O. Backer & Spielvogel, Inc. 1980–87, Backer Spielvogel Bates Worldwide Inc. New York 1987–94; Chair., C.E.O. United Auto Group 1994–; Dir. Manhattan Industries, Franklin Corpn., N.Y. Philharmonic, numerous other orgs.; Chair. Cttee. Div., WNET-Public Broadcasting, Business Cttee., Metropolitan Museum of Art. *Address:* United Auto Group Inc., 375 Park Avenue, Suite 2201, New York, NY 10152, U.S.A.

SPIERS, Ronald Ian, B.A., M.A.; American diplomatist; b. 9 July 1925, Orange, N.J.; s. of Thomas Hoskins and Blanca (née De Ponthier) Spiers; m. Patience Baker 1949; one s. three d.; ed. Dartmouth Coll., Princeton Univ.; U.S.N. 1943–46; mem. U.S. Del. to UN 1955–58; Dir. Disarmament Affairs, State Dept., Washington 1958–62, NATO Affairs 1962–66; Political Counsellor, U.S. Embassy in London 1966–69, Minister 1974–77; Asst. Sec. of State for Political-Mil. Affairs 1969–73; Amb. to the Bahamas 1973–74, to Turkey 1977–80; Asst. Sec. for Intelligence and Research, Dept. of State 1980–81; Amb. to Pakistan 1981–83; Under-Sec. for Man., Dept. of State 1983–89; Under-Sec.-Gen. for Political and Gen. Ass. Affairs and Secr. Services, UN, New York 1989–92; consultant to State Dept. 1992–; mem. Council on Foreign Relations; Fellow Nat. Acad. of Public Admin. *Leisure interests:* gardening, furniture making, classical music. *Address:* RR1, Box 54A, S. Londonderry, VT 05155, U.S.A.

SPIES von BÜLLESHEIM, Freiherr Adolf Wilhelm, DR.JUR.; German business executive, politician, lawyer and farmer; b. 4 June 1929, Hückelhoven; s. of Egon Freiherr von Büllesheim and Maria Freiin von Oer; m. Maria Gräfin von Mirbach-Harff 1961; one s. four d.; ed. Univs. of Bonn and Munich; solicitor, Düsseldorf and Mönchengladbach 1960–; farmer on family estate in Hückelhoven 1961–; Mayor of Hückelhoven 1969–73; mem. Bundestag 1972–87; mem. WEU 1977–87, Council of Europe 1977–87; Chair. Eschweiler Bergwerks Verein AG, Herzogenrath 1987–; mem. bd. of several cos.; Bundesverdienstkreuz, Commdr. Ordre de Mérite (Luxembourg) 1989. *Leisure interests:* hunting, skiing. *Address:* Haus Hall bei Ratheim, 41836 Hückelhoven, Germany. *Telephone:* 02433-5066.

SPINETTA, Jean-Cyril, LL.B., B.SC.; French airline executive; b. 4 Oct. 1943, Paris; s. of Adrien Spinetta and Antoinette Brignole; m. Nicole Spinetta (née Ricquebourg); two s. two d.; ed. Institut d'études politiques and Ecole Nationale d'administration, Paris; entered French civil service 1972, Head Investments and Planning Dept., Ministry of Educ. 1972–76; Head Information Dept., Office of the Prime Minister 1981–83, Chief of Staff for Michel Delebarre 1984–90; successively Minister of Labour and Vocational Training, Minister of Social Affairs and Employment and Minister of Planning and Devt., Housing and Transport; joined Air Inter 1990, Pres. and C.E.O. 1990–93; advisory posts to Pres. of France (including industrial matters) 1993–95; Admin. in charge of Public Service 1995–96; joined staff of Edith Cresson, European Commr. for Science, Research and Educ. 1996–97; Chair. and C.E.O. Air France 1997–; Chevalier Légion d'honneur, Ordre nat. du Mérite, Officier des Palmes Académiques. *Address:* Groupe Air France, 45 rue de Paris, 95747 Roissy CDG Cedex (Office); 7 rue Pierre-Nicole, 75005 Paris, France. *Telephone:* 41 56 78 00 (Office). *Fax:* 41 56 61 59 (Office). *Telephone:* 43 25 01 95 (Home).

SPIRIDONOV, Yury Alekseyevich, CAND. TECH. SC.; Russian politician; b. 1938; ed. Sverdlovsk Mining Inst., Higher CP School at Cen. Cttee. CPSU; engineer mine, Gorny Magadan Region 1961–69; master, head of section, chief engineer, Dir. Yager oil mine Komi Autonomous Repub. 1969–75; party functionary different posts in Ukhta City CP Cttee. 1975–85; Second Sec., First Sec. Komi Regional CP Cttee. 1985–89; U.S.S.R. Peoples' Deputy 1989–92; Chair. Supreme Soviet Komi Autonomous Repub. 1990–94; Chair. of Komi Repub. Govt., Head of Repub. 1994–; mem. Russian Council of Fed. 1993–; Peoples' Deputy of Komi Autonomous Repub. *Address:* House of Government, Kommunisticheskaya str. 9, 167010 Syktyvkar, Komi Republic, Russia (Office). *Telephone:* (08212) 42 07 80 (Office). *Fax:* (08212) 42 37 70 (Office).

SPIRIN, Aleksandr Sergeyevich; Russian biochemist; b. 4 Sept. 1931, Kaliningrad, Moscow Region; m. Lydia Pavlovna Gavrilova; one s.; ed. Moscow State Univ.; mem. Staff, Bakh Inst. of Biochem. 1958–62, Head of Lab. 1962–73; Prof. Moscow State Univ. 1964–, Head of Chair. of Molecular Biology 1973–; Head of Lab. and Dir. Inst. of Protein Research 1967–; discovered informosomes, predicted the discovery of informational (metrical) RNC 1976; Corresp. mem. U.S.S.R. (now Russian) Acad. of Sciences 1966–70, mem. 1970–, mem. Presidium 1988–91; Chair. Bd. Pushchino Scientific Centre 1990–; mem. Deutsche Akad. der Naturforscher Leopoldina 1974; mem. Czechoslovak Acad. of Sciences 1988; Dr. h.c. (Univ. of Granada) 1972; Lenin Prize 1976; Sir Hans Krebs Medal 1969; Order of Lenin and other decorations. *Publications:* Macromolecular Structure of Ribonucleic Acids 1964, The Ribosome 1969, Ribosome Structure and Protein Biosynthesis 1986. *Leisure interest:* hunting. *Address:* Institute of Protein Research, Russian Academy of Sciences, 142292 Pushchino, Moscow Region, Russia. *Telephone:* (095) 924-04-93; (08277) 73-08-30.

SPIROIU, Lieut.-Gen. Niculae; Romanian politician; b. 6 July 1936, Bucharest; s. of Constantin Spiroiu and Paulina Spiroiu; m. 1963 (wife died 1991); one s. one d.; ed. Tech. Mil. Acad.; scientific researcher with the Centre of Studies and Tests for Tanks and Autos Deputy Chief and Tech. Dept. Chief; State Sec. and Head of the Army Supply Dept.; Minister of Nat. Defence 1992–94; Counsellor Minister to UN 1994–. *Leisure interests:* reading, symphonic music, motor cycling, motoring. *Address:* c/o Ministry of Foreign Affairs, 71274 Bucharest, Al. Modrogan 14, Romania.

SPITAELS, Guy; Belgian politician; ed. Catholic Univ. of Louvain; Prof. of Econs. Univ. of Brussels; joined Socialist Party (French-speaking) 1961; Chef de Cabinet to Prime Minister Edmond Leburton 1973; Vice-Premier 1979–81; Leader of Socialist Party (French-speaking) 1981–92, Wallonia Regional Govt. (PS-PSC coalition) 1992–94; Chair. Confed. of European Socialist Parties 1989. *Address:* Parti Socialiste, Maison du PS, 13 blvd. de l'Empereur, 1000 Brussels, Belgium.

SPITAL, Hermann Josef Silvester, DR.THEOL.; German ecclesiastic; b. 31 Dec. 1925, Münster; ed. Gymnasium Paulinum, Münster, and theological studies in Münster; ordained 1952; Generalvikar, Münster 1973; consecrated bishop 1980; Bishop of Trier 1981–. *Address:* Liebfrauenstrasse 1, 54290 Trier, Germany. *Telephone:* 0651-7105209.

SPITERI, Lino, M.A.; Maltese politician and journalist (retd.); b. 21 Sept. 1938, Qormi; s. of late Emanuel Spiteri and of Pauline Spiteri (née Calleja); m. Vivienne Azzopardi 1964; two s. two d.; ed. Lyceum, Plater Coll. and St. Peter's Coll., Oxford; teacher 1956–57; Clerk U.K. Mil. Establishment 1957–62; Deputy Ed. Il-Helsien (daily) 1962–64, It-Torca (weekly) 1964–66; Ed. Malta News 1967–68; Research Officer Malta Chamber of Commerce 1968–70; with Cen. Bank of Malta as Sr. Research Officer, then Asst. Head of Research 1971, Head of Research 1972, Deputy Gov. and Chair. Bd. of Dirs. 1974–81; Minister of Finance 1981–83, of Econ. Planning and Trade 1983–87; Opposition Spokesman on Econs. and Finance 1989–96; Chair. Public Accounts Cttee. 1995–96, co-Chair, Malta-EU Jt. Parl. Cttee. 1996–; Minister for Econ. Affairs and Finance 1996–97; mem. Malta Labour Party Gen. Exec. 1958–66; Gen. Sec. Labour League of Youth 1961–62; M.P. 1962–66; Malta Corresp. for Observer, Observer Foreign News Service, Guardian 1967–71; mem. Malta Broadcasting Authority 1968–70; mem. Comm. on Higher Educ. 1977–79; Chair. Students Selection Bd. 1978–79; Pres. Qormi Football Club 1977–79; columnist, Sunday Times of Malta, and others. *Publications:* Studies: The Development of Tourism in Malta 1968, The Development of Industry in Malta 1969; *fiction:* Tad-Demm u L-Laham (short stories) 1968, Hala taz-Zghozija (short stories) 1970, Anatomija (short stories) 1978, Iz-Zewgt Ihbieb (short stories) 1979, Stqarrija (verses) 1979, Rivoluzzjoni do minore (novel), Il-Halliel (short stories), Jien Nimxi Wahdi (verses), Mal-Hmura tas-silla (short stories), Fejn Jixrob il-Qasab fis-sajf (short stories), Stejjer ghal Valenlina (short stories), Ghaliex ix-Xewk (verses), Moods and Angles (collected articles). *Leisure interests:* listening to other people's views, reading, writing. *Address:* Dar iz-Zerniq, Notary Zarb Street, Attard, BZN 03, Malta. *Telephone:* 356 435089.

SPIVAKOV, Vladimir Teodorovich; Russian violinist and conductor; b. 12 Sept. 1944, Ufa; m. Satinik Saakyants; three d.; studied violin since six years old with B. Kroger in Leningrad; ed. Moscow State Conservatory, postgrad. with Yury Yankelevich; prize winner several int. competitions including Tchaikovsky, Moscow; founder and conductor Chamber Orchestra Virtuosi of Moscow 1979 (since 1988 resides in Spain); f. and Artistic Dir. Music Festival in Colmar, France 1988–; U.S.S.R. State Prize 1989, U.S.S.R. People's Artist 1990. *Leisure interests:* collector of paintings. *Address:* Columbia Artists Management, 165 West 57th Street, New York, NY 10019, U.S.A.; Vspolny per. 17 Apt. 14, Moscow, Russia. *Telephone:* 290-23-24 (Moscow); (01) 46.04.77.85 (Paris).

SPOHR, Arnold Theodore, O.C.; Canadian ballet director, teacher and choreographer; b. 26 Dec. 1927, Rhein, Canada; ed. St. John's High School and Winnipeg Teachers' Coll.; Piano Teacher 1946–51; Prin. Dancer Royal Winnipeg Ballet 1947–54; CBC Television Choreographer and performer 1955–57; Choreographer Rainbow Stage 1957–60; Artistic Dir. Royal Winnipeg Ballet 1958–88; Dir.-Teacher Royal Winnipeg Ballet School 1958–88, Artistic Dir. Emer. 1988–; Dir. Nelson School of Fine Arts Dance Dept. 1964–67; Artistic Dir. Dance Dept. Banff School of Fine Arts 1967–81; mem. Bd. of Dirs. Canadian Theatre Centre; Hon. LL.D. (Univ. of Manitoba) 1970, many awards including Molson Prize, Canada Council 1970, Centennial Medal, Gov. of Canada 1967, Molson Prize 1970, Royal Bank Award 1987. *Choreography:* Ballet Premier 1950, Intermed 1951, E Minor 1959, Hansel and Gretel 1960, and 18 musicals for Rainbow State. *Leisure interests:* sports, piano, travel-research for study of every type of dancing. *Address:* Canada's Royal Winnipeg Ballet, 380 Graham Avenue, Winnipeg, Man., R3C 4K2, Canada.

SPONG, Rt. Rev. John Shelby, A.B., D.D.; American ecclesiastic; b. 16 June 1931, Charlotte, N.C.; s. of John Shelby Spong and Doolie Griffith Spong; m. 1st Joan Lydia Ketner 1952 (died 1988); three d.; m. 2nd Christine Mary Bridger 1990; ed. Univ. of North Carolina, Chapel Hill, Virginia Theological Seminary, Alexandria, Va. and St. Paul's Coll.; Rector St. Joseph's, Durham, N.C. 1955–57, Calvary Church, Tarboro, N.C. 1957–65, St. John's Church, Lynchburg, Va. 1965–69, St. Paul's Church, Richmond, Va. 1969–76, Bishop, Diocese of Newark, N.J. 1976–; Pres. N.J. Council of Churches; Quatercentenary Fellow, Emmanuel Coll., Cambridge 1992; Roger Baldwin Award. *Publications:* Honest Prayer 1973, This Hebrew Lord 1974, 1988, Dialogue: In Search of Jewish-Christian Understanding 1975, Christpower 1975, Life Approaches Death. A Dialogue on Medical Ethics 1976, The Living Commandments 1977, The Easter Moment 1980, Into the Whirlwind 1983, Beyond Moralism 1986, Consciousness and Survival 1987, Living in Sin? 1988, Rescuing the Bible from Fundamentalism 1991, Born of a Woman 1992, Resurrection: Myth or Reality? 1994, Liberating the Gospels. Reading the Bible with Jewish Eyes 1996, Why Christianity Must Change or Die: A Bishop Speaks to Believers in Exile 1998. *Address:* 31 Mulberry Street, Newark, NJ 07102; 43 Ogden Place, Morristown, NJ 07960, U.S.A. *Telephone:* (973) 430-9973 (Newark); (973) 538-9825 (Morristown). *Fax:* (973) 622-3503 (Office); (973) 540-9584 (Home).

SPONHEIM, Lars, M.SC.; Norwegian politician; b. 23 May 1957; m.; three c.; Consultant 1981–84; teacher Statens Gartnerskule Hjeltnes 1984–88, Prin. 1992–; mem. local council Ulvik Municipality 1984–, Mayor 1988–91; mem. County Council, Hordalund Co. 1992–93; Dir. of Agric., Ulvik and Granvin Municipalities 1993; M.P. for Hordalund Co. to Storting (Parl.) 1993–; mem. Parl. Finance Cttee.; Leader Liberal Party 1996–; Minister of Trade and Industry 1997–. *Address:* Venstre, Møllergt 16, 0179 Oslo, Norway. *Telephone:* 22-42-73-20.

SPOONER, Sir James Douglas, Kt.; British business executive and accountant; b. 11 July 1932, London; s. of the late Vice-Adm. E. J. Spooner, D.S.O., and Megan (née Foster) Spooner; m. Jane A. Glover 1958; two s. one d.; ed. Eton Coll. and Christ Church, Oxford; served in R.N.V.R. 1951–52; with Shell Int. Petroleum 1955–59; Deloitte Plender Griffiths & Co. 1959–62; Partner, Dixon Wilson & Co. (chartered accountants) 1963–72; Chair. Coats

Viyella PLC 1969–89, Morgan Crucible Co. PLC 1983–97, Council, King's Coll., London 1986–98, Trustees, British Telecom Pension Scheme 1982–98; Dir. John Swire & Sons Ltd. 1970–, J. Sainsbury PLC 1981–94, Barclays Bank PLC 1983–94. *Leisure interests:* music, reading, shooting. *Address:* Swire House, 59 Buckingham Gate, London, SW1E 6AJ, England. *Telephone:* 0171-834 7717. *Fax:* 0171-630 0380.

SPORBORG, Christopher Henry; British banker; b. 17 April 1939; s. of the late Henry Nathan Sporborg and of Mary Rowlands; m. Lucinda Jane Hanbury 1961; two s. two d.; ed. Rugby School, Emmanuel Coll., Cambridge; served as officer, Coldstream Guards; joined Hambros Bank 1962, Dir. 1970, Exec. Dir. Corp. Finance Dept. 1975, Deputy Chair. 1983–95; Chair. Hambro Countrywide 1986–; Vice-Chair. Hambros PLC 1986–90, Deputy Chair. 1990–; Dir. various Hambro Group Cos.; Chair. Atlas Copco (U.K.) Holdings Ltd., Hambros Insurance Services Group 1993–; mem. Horserace Totalisator Bd. 1993; Finance Steward, Jockey Club. *Leisure interests:* riding, racing. *Address:* Brooms Farm, Upwick Green, Albury, Ware, Herts., England. *Telephone:* (01279) 771444.

SPOTSWOOD, Marshal of the R.A.F. Sir Denis, G.C.B., C.B.E., D.S.O., D.F.C., F.R.AE.S.; British air force officer; b. 26 Sept. 1916; s. of F. H. and M. C. Spotswood; m. Ann Child 1942; one s.; joined R.A.F. 1936; service in Squadrons U.K. and N. Africa 1937–43; Dir. of Plans, H.Q. Supreme Allied Commdr., S.E. Asia 1944–46; Stations (Fighter) 1948–50, 1954–56; Commdt. and Air Officer Commdg. (A.O.C.) R.A.F. Coll. Cranwell, 1958–61; Asst. Chief of Staff (Air Defence) SHAPE 1961–63; C.-in-C. R.A.F. Germany and Commdr. 2nd Allied Tactical Air Force 1965–68; C.-in-C. Strike Command 1968–71; Chief of Air Staff 1971–74; Vice-Chair. Rolls-Royce Ltd. 1974–81; Chair. Rolls-Royce (India) 1979–80; Pres. Soc. of British Aerospace Cos. 1978–79; Chair. Smiths Industries Int. Aerospace and Defence Cos. 1980–82, Dir. 1982–91; Chair. Turbo Union Ltd.; Dir. Rolls Royce/Turbomeca Ltd.; Dir. Dowty Group 1980–87; Chair. Trustees, Royal Air Force Museum 1974–80; Chair. Royal Star and Garter Home 1979–84; A.D.C. to H.M. The Queen 1957–61, Air A.D.C. to H.M. The Queen 1970–74; U.S. Legion of Merit. *Leisure interests:* bridge, rugby (spectator), golf. *Address:* Coombe Cottage, Hambleden, Oxon, RG9 6SD, England.

SPOTTISWOODE, Clare Mary Joan, C.B.E., M.A., M.PHIL.; British business executive; b. 20 March 1953, Lancs.; d. of Robert Spottiswoode and Charlotte Nuttall; m. Oliver Richards 1977; one s. three d.; ed. Cheltenham Ladies' Coll., Clare Coll. Cambridge and Yale Univ.; economist, H.M. Treasury 1977–80; sole proprietor, import business, Spottiswoode Trading 1980–84; Chair. and Man. Dir. Spottiswoode & Spottiswoode Ltd. (micro-computer software house) 1984–90; also held several non-exec. directorships, taught at London Business School and acted as software consultant; Dir.-Gen. of Gas Supply (Ofgas) 1993–98; Sr. Vice-Pres. European Water 1998–; Dir. (non-exec.) Booker PLC; Gov. Nat. Inst. of Econ. and Social Research; mem. Inst. of Man. Bd. of Companions; Hon. Dr. Soc. Sci. (Brunel) 1997. *Publications:* Quill 1984, Abacus 1984. *Leisure interests:* children, theatre, gardening. *Address:* European Water, Azurix, 34 Park Street, London, England.

SPRANGER, Carl-Dieter; German politician and lawyer; b. 28 March 1939, Leipzig; s. of Rudolf Spranger and Hertha Spranger; m. Gudrun Spranger 1968; one s. two d.; Asst. lecturer, Univ. of Erlangen 1964–67; public prosecutor 1968; dist. court judge, Ansbach 1969; called to Bar 1977; mem. Bundestag; Parl. State Sec. Ministry of Interior 1982–91; Minister for Econ. Cooperation and Devt. 1991–98; Grosses Bundesverdienstkreuz, Bayerischer Verdienstorden; Christian Social Union (CSU). *Leisure interests:* reading, travel, walking, music, sport. *Address:* c/o Bundesministerium für wirtschaftliche Zusammenarbeit, Friedrich-Ebert-Allee 40, 53113 Bonn (Office); Urlasstrasse 18, 8800 Ansbach, Germany (Home). *Telephone:* 0981-85-095 (Home).

SPRATT, Sir Greville Douglas, G.B.E., T.D., D.LITT., J.P., D.L., F.R.S.A.; British business executive; b. 1 May 1927, Westcliff-on-Sea; s. of Hugh D. Spratt and Sheelah I. Stace; m. Sheila F. Wade 1954; three d.; ed. Leighton Park, Charterhouse and Sandhurst; served Coldstream Guards 1945–46; Commissioned Oxfordshire and Bucks Light Infantry 1946; seconded to Arab Legion 1946–48; joined HAC Infantry Bn. 1950, C.O. 1962–65, Regimental Col. 1966–70, mem. Court of Assistants 1960–70, 1978–95; ADC to H.M. The Queen 1973–78; Lloyd's of London 1948–61, Underwriting Mem. 1950–; Man. Dir. J. & N. Wade group 1972–76; Liveryman, Ironmongers' Co. 1977–, Master 1995–96; Alderman, Castle Baynard Ward 1978–95; Sheriff of City of London 1984–85; Lord Mayor of London 1987–88; Chancellor, City Univ. 1987–88; Dir. Williams Lea Group, Craigie Taylor Int. Ltd.; Chair. Forest Mere Ltd., Charterhouse Enterprises Ltd.1992–95, Action Research for the Crippled Child 1989–; Claremont and Kingsmead Underwriting Agency 1994–97; Regional Chair. Nat. Westminster Bank 1992–93; Vice-Pres. British Red Cross 1993–, Greater London Taura 1994–; holder of numerous civic, educational and charitable positions; Trustee Chichester Theatre and Cathedral; Hon. Col. London Army Cadet Force 1983–, Queen's Fusiliers 1988–92, London Regt. 1992–95; Hon. D.Litt. (City Univ.) 1988; Légion d'honneur, Ordre Nat. du Mérite (France); Commdr. Order of Lion (Malawi), Order of Aztec Eagle (Mexico), Order of Olav (Norway), Order of Merit (Senegal), K.St.J. *Leisure interests:* tennis, music, mil. history, stamp, coin and bank-note collecting. *Address:* W. Kingsley Place, Kingsley Green, W. Sussex, GU27 3LR, England. *Telephone:* (01428) 644367.

SPRIGGE, Timothy Lauro Squire, PH.D. F.R.S.E.; British university professor; b. 14 Jan. 1932, London; s. of Cecil Sprigge and Katriona Sprigge; m. Giglia Gordon 1959; one s. two d.; ed. Gonville and Caius Coll. Cambridge; lecturer in Philosophy, Univ. Coll. London 1961–63, Univ. of Sussex 1963–70, Reader in Philosophy 1970–79; Prof. of Logic and Metaphysics, Univ. of Edin. 1979–89, Endowment Fellow and Prof. Emer. 1989–. *Publications:* Correspondence of Jeremy Bentham, Vols. 1 and 2 (Ed.) 1968, Facts, Words and Beliefs 1968, Santayana: An Examination of his Philosophy 1974, The Vindication of Absolute Idealism 1983, Theories of Existence 1984, The Rational Foundations of Ethics 1987, James and Bradley: American Truth and British Reality 1993. *Leisure interests:* Five Hundred, Pinochle, Skat, Victorian novels. *Address:* Philosophy Department, David Hume Tower, University of Edinburgh, George Square, Edinburgh, EH8 9JX (Office); 31A Raeburn Place, Edinburgh, EH4 1HU, Scotland (Home). *Telephone:* (0131) 667 1011 (Office); (0131) 315 2443 (Home).

SPRING, Richard (Dick), B.A., B.L.; Irish politician; b. 29 Aug. 1950, Tralee, Co. Kerry; s. of Dan Spring and Anna Laide; m. Kristi Lee Hutcheson 1977; two s. one d.; ed. Mount St. Joseph Coll., Roscrea, Co. Tipperary, Trinity Coll., Dublin, King's Inns, Dublin; mem. Dáil Éireann (House of Reps.) for Kerry North 1981–; Leader of Labour Party 1982–97; Tanaiste (Deputy Prime Minister) 1982–87, and Minister for the Environment 1982–83, for Energy 1983–87, Tanaiste and Minister for Foreign Affairs 1993–97; fmr. Irish rugby union int. *Leisure interests:* sport, reading, golf, swimming. *Address:* Leinster House, Dublin 2; Cloonanorig, Tralee, Co. Kerry, Ireland (Home).

SPRINGS, Alice (pseudonym of June Browne); Australian photographer; b. June 1923, Melbourne; m. Helmut Newton (q.v.) 1948; fmrly. professional actress; professional photographer 1970–; clients have included Jean-Louis David, Fashion Magazine Dépêche Mode, Elle, Marie-Claire, Vogue, Vogue Homme, Nova, Mode Int., Absolu, London Cosmoplitan; contrib. to Egoiste, Vanity Fair, Interview, Passion, Stern, Decoration Internationale, Tatler, Photo, Les Cahiers de l'Energumène. *Solo exhbns:* Canon Gallery, Amsterdam 1978, Canon Gallery, Geneva 1980, Duc et Camroux, Paris 1980, David Heath Gallery, Atlanta 1982, Yuen Lui Gallery, Seattle 1982, Olympus Gallery, London 1983, Galerie de France, Paris 1983, Musée Cheret, Nice 1984, Musée de Sainte Croix, Poitiers 1985, Documenta Gallery, Turin 1985, Centre Culturel, Orleans 1985, Centre Culturel et Artistique, Arbusson 1986, Espace Photographie de la Ville de Paris/Paris Audiovisuel 1986, Fotoform, Frankfurt/Main 1987, Gerfiollet, Amsterdam 1988, Olympus Galerie, Hamburg 1988, Nat. Portrait Gallery London 1988, Musée d'Art Moderne, Paris 1988, Museo Contemporaneo, Mexico City 1990, Rheinisches Landesmuseum, Bonn 1991/92, 'Arrêt sur l'image', Bordeaux 1993, Galerie im alten Rathaus am Markt, Wittlich 1993, Hochschule für Graphik und Buchkunst, Leipzig 1993, FORUM, Bremen 1993. *Group exhbns. include:* Photokina, Cologne 1976, Photographers' Gallery, London 1979, G. Ray Hawkins, L.A. 1981, Grey Art Gallery, N.Y. 1981, Paris Audiovisuel, French Photographers, Museum of Modern Art, Bratislava 1991, Teatro Circo (courtesy of Paris Audiovisuel), Braga 1992. *Catalogues:* Alice Springs Portraits, Musée Saint Croix, Poitiers 1985, Espace Photo, Paris 1986, Musée d'Art Moderne de la Ville de Paris 1988, Centro Cultural Arte Contemporaneo, Mexico City 1991, Rheinisches Landesmuseum, Bonn 1991/92. *Publications:* Alice Springs Portraits 1983, 1986, 1991. *Film:* TV documentary "Helmut by June" for Canal Plus 1995.

SPRINGSTEEN, Bruce; American singer and songwriter; b. 23 Sept. 1949, Freehold, N.J.; s. of Douglas and Adele Springsteen; m. 1st Julianne Phillips 1985 (divorced 1988); m. 2nd Patti Scialfa; one s. one d.; attended community coll.; performed in New York and N.J. nightclubs; signed with Columbia Records 1972; first LP record Greetings from Asbury Park, New Jersey 1973; tours of U.S.A. and Europe with E-Street Band 1974–92; Golden Record Award 1975 (for Born to Run), Acad. Award for Best Original Song in a Film 1994, MTV Best Video from a Film Award 1994 (for Philadelphia). *Albums include:* The Wild, The Innocent and the E-Street Shuffle 1974, Born to Run 1975, Darkness on the Edge of Town 1978, The River 1981, Nebraska 1982, Born in the U.S.A. (25 million copies sold 1992) 1984, Bruce Springsteen and the E. Street Band Live 1975–85 1986, Tunnel of Love 1987, Chimes of Freedom 1988, Human Touch 1992, Lucky Town 1992, Bruce Springsteen Greatest Hits 1995, The Ghost of Tom Joad 1995; Grammy Award, Best Male Vocalist 1984, 1987. *Address:* c/o Premier Talent Agency, 3 E. 54th Street, New York, NY 10022, U.S.A.

SPRINKEL, Beryl Wayne, PH.D.; American economist and fmr. government official; b. 20 Nov. 1923, Richmond, Mo.; s. of Clarence and Emma (née Schooley) Sprinkel; m. 1st Esther Pollard (deceased); m. 2nd Barbara Angus Pipher (deceased); two s.; m. 3rd Lory Reid (née Kiefer) 1993; ed. N.W. Missouri State Univ., Univs. of Missouri, Oregon and Chicago; served with U.S. army 1943–45; Instructor in Econs. and Finance, Univ. of Missouri, Columbia 1948–49, Univ. of Chicago 1950–52; with Harris Trust and Savings Bank, Chicago 1952–81, Vice-Pres., economist 1960–68, Dir. Research 1968–81, Exec. Vice-Pres. 1974–81; Under-Sec. for Monetary Affairs, Dept. of the Treasury 1981–85; Chair. Pres.'s Council of Econ. Advisors 1985–89; mem. Pres.'s Cabinet 1987–89; Consulting Economist 1989–; mem. Bd. Duff and Phelps Utilities Income Inc. Fund; Pres. Homewood-Flossmoor (Ill.) Community High School 1959–60; seven hon. degrees; Distinguished Alumnus Award (Chicago Univ.), Distinguished Service Award (Northwest Mo. State Univ.). *Publications:* Money and Stock Prices 1964, Money and

Markets—A Monetarist View 1971, Winning with Money (co-author) 1977. *Leisure interests:* reading, writing, golf, tennis, fishing, travel. *Address:* 20140 St. Andrews Drive, Olympia Fields, IL 60461; 16625 Waters Edge, CT 101, Ft. Myers, FL 33908, U.S.A. *Telephone:* (708) 481-9384 (Ill.); (941) 482-7593 (Fla.).

SPYCHALSKA, Ewa; Polish politician and trade union activist; b. 17 Aug. 1949, Warsaw; m.; one s. one d.; ed. Acad. of Social Sciences, Warsaw; teacher 1969–78; office worker 1978–85; mem. and activist of trade unions 1969–; Chair. All-Poland Trade Unions Agreement (OPZZ) 1991–96; Deputy to Sejm (Parl.) 1991–96; Vice-Chair. Democratic Left Alliance Parl. Club (SLD); Amb. to Belarus 1996–98; Adviser, Chancellery of the Pres. 1998–. *Leisure interests:* tourism, literature. *Address:* Kancelaria Presidenta R.P., ul. Wiejslia 10, 00 902 Warsaw, Poland. *Telephone:* (22) 695 26 91.

SRB, Adrian Morris, M.S., PH.D.; American professor of genetics; b. 4 March 1917, Howells, Neb.; s. of Jerome Ve. Srb and Viola Morris; m. Jozetta Marie Helfrich 1940; one s. two d.; ed. Howells High School, Univ. of Nebraska, Stanford Univ. and California Inst. of Tech.; Civilian, Office of Scientific Research and Devt. 1944; Asst. Prof. of Biology, Stanford Univ. and Research Fellow, Calif. Inst. of Tech. 1946–47; Assoc. Prof. Plant Breeding, Cornell Univ. 1947–51; Research Assoc., Calif. Inst. of Technology 1949; Prof. of Plant Breeding, Cornell Univ. 1951–63, Prof. of Genetics, Devt. and Physiology, Biological Sciences 1965; Jacob Gould Schurman Prof. 1976; Fulbright Research Scholar and Guggenheim Fellow, Univ. of Paris 1953–54; Nat. Science Foundation Sr. Post-doctoral Research Fellow, Centre Nat. de la Recherche Scientifique, Gif-sur-Yvette, France 1960–61, Univ. of Edinburgh, Scotland 1967–68; Emer. mem. N.A.S.; Educ. Advisory Bd., John Simon Guggenheim Memorial Foundation; Hon. mem. Chilean Genetics Soc.; Fellow, American Acad. of Arts and Sciences; Hon. Foreign Fellow, Edinburgh Botanical Soc.; Fellow, New York Acad. of Sciences, A.A.A.S.; Trustee, Cornell Univ. 1975–; Hon. D.Sc. (Univ. of Nebraska) 1969; Distinguished Teacher Award 1967. *Publications:* General Genetics (with R. D. Owen) 1952, Pathways to the Understanding of Genetics 1953, Adaptation (with B. Wallace) 1961, 1964, General Genetics (with R. D. Owen and R. S. Edgar) 1965, Ed. Genes, Enzymes, and Population 1973; over 100 research papers in scientific journals. *Leisure interests:* music, collecting juvenile books, gardening. *Address:* 411 Cayuga Heights Road, Ithaca, NY 14850, U.S.A. (Home). *Telephone:* 272-8492 (Home).

SREDIN, Vasily Dmitriyevich; Russian diplomatist; b. 1948; ed. Moscow State Inst. of Int. Relations; with U.S.S.R. Ministry of Foreign Affairs, diplomatic posts abroad 1972–; Counsellor-Envoy, Embassy of U.S.S.R. (now Russia), Canada 1990–96; Deputy Head, N. America Dept., Ministry of Foreign Affairs 1996–97, Acting Dir. 1997–; State-Sec. Deputy Minister of Foreign Affairs 1998–. *Address:* Ministry of Foreign Affairs, Smolenskaya-Sennaya pl. 32/34, 121200 Moscow, Russia. *Telephone:* (095) 244 3448 (Office).

SSEMOGERERE, Paul Kawanga; Ugandan politician; Leader Democratic Party (DP); fmr. leader of Opposition in Nat. Ass.; Minister of Internal Affairs 1986–88, Second Deputy Prime Minister and Minister of Foreign Affairs 1988–94, of the Public Service 1994, of Regional Co-operation 1989; Pres. Democratic Party; Cand. in 1996 Presidential elections. *Address:* Democratic Party, P.O. Box 7098, Kampala, Uganda. *Telephone:* (41) 230244.

STAAB, Heinz A., DR.RER.NAT., DR.MED.; German professor of chemistry; b. 26 March 1926, Darmstadt; m. Dr. Ruth Müller 1953; one s. one d.; ed. Univs. of Marburg, Tübingen and Heidelberg; research assoc., Max Planck Inst., Heidelberg 1953–59; Asst. Prof. of Chem., Univ. of Heidelberg 1956–61, Assoc. Prof. 1961–62, Prof. 1963–; Dir. Inst. of Organic Chem., Univ. of Heidelberg 1964–74; Dir. Max Planck Inst. for Medical Research 1974–; Pres. Max Planck Soc. for the Advancement of Science, Munich 1984–90; mem. German Science Council 1976–79; Senator, Deutsche Forschungsgemeinschaft 1976–82 and 1984–90; mem. Bd. of Govs. Weizmann Inst. of Science, Israel 1977–; Pres. Gesellschaft Deutscher Naturforscher und Ärzte 1981–82; Pres. German Chem. Soc. 1984–85; mem. Heidelberg Acad. of Sciences (Pres. 1994–96), Acad. Leopoldina, Academia Europaea; Hon. mem. Senate Max-Planck Soc. 1990, corresp. mem. Austrian Acad. 1988, Bavarian Acad. 1991; Hon. Fellow Indian Acad. of Sciences 1988; Hon. Prof. Chinese Acad. of Sciences 1992; Foreign mem. Russian Acad. of Sciences 1994; Ph.D. h.c. (Weizmann Inst. of Science) 1984; Adolf von Baeyer Award (German Chem. Soc.) 1979. *Publications:* Einführung in die theoretische organische Chemie 1959 (translations) and about 350 publications in professional journals. *Leisure interests:* travel, history, classical music. *Address:* Schlosswolfsbrunnenweg 43, 69118 Heidelberg, Germany (Home). *Telephone:* 486421 (Office); (06221) 803330 (Home). *Fax:* 486219.

STAATS, Elmer Boyd, PH.D.; American economist and government official; b. 6 June 1914, Richfield, Kansas; s. of Wesley F. and Maude (Goodall) Staats; m. Margaret S. Rich 1940; one s. two d.; ed. McPherson Coll., and Univs. of Kansas and Minnesota; Research Asst., Kansas Legis. Council 1936; mem. Staff, Public Admin. Service, Chicago 1937–38; Fellow, Brookings Inst. 1938–39; Staff mem. Bureau of the Budget 1939–47, Asst. to Dir. 1947, Asst. Dir. (Legis. Reference) 1947–49, Exec. Asst. Dir. 1949–50, Asst. Dir. 1958–59, Deputy Dir. 1950–53, 1959–66; Research Dir., Marshall Field & Co., Chicago 1953; Exec. Officer Operations Co-ordinating Bd., Nat. Security Council 1953–58; Comptroller Gen. of the United States 1966–81; mem. Bd. of Dirs. of several corpns.; mem. numerous public orgs. including Pres. American Soc. for Public Admin. 1961–62; Pres. Harry S. Truman Scholarship Foundation 1981–84, Chair. Bd. of Trustees 1984–; Chair. Govt. Procurement Round Table 1984–; mem. Bd. of Dirs. of American Acad. of Political and Social Science 1966, Bd. of Govs. Int. Org. of Supreme Audit Insts. 1969–81, Visiting Cttee. John F. Kennedy School of Govt., Harvard Univ. 1974–80, Visiting Cttee., Graduate School of Man., Univ. of Calif. at Los Angeles 1976–85, Visiting Cttee. to the Cttee. in Public Policy Studies, Univ. of Chicago 1976–; President's Comm. on Budget Concepts 1967–68; mem. Bd. of Govs. Int. Center on Election Law and Admin. 1985–87; Dir. George C. Marshall Foundation 1984–; mem. Bd. of Visitors, Nat. Defense Univ. 1981–90; Hon. mem. Soc. of Mfg. Engineers 1978–; Hon. Life mem. Municipal Finance Officers Asscn. of U.S.A. and Canada 1980; Trustee, Cttee. for Econ. Devt. 1981–, Nat. Planning Asscn. 1981–; Dr. Publ. Service (George Washington Univ.) 1971, Dr. Admin. (Univ. of S. Dak.) 1973, Hon. Certified Internal Auditor (Inst. of Internal Auditors) 1973; Hon. LL.D. (McPherson Coll.) 1966, (Duke Univ.) 1975, (Nova Univ.) 1976, (Lycoming Coll.) 1982, (Univ. of Penn.); Hon. D.Hum.Litt. (Ohio State Univ.) 1982; Rockefeller Public Service Award 1961; Productivity Award, American Productivity Cen. 1980; Medal of Honor AICPA 1980, Presidential Citizens Medal 1981, Accounting Hall of Fame 1981, Inst. of Internal Auditors Thurston Award 1988, and other medals and awards. *Publication:* Personnel Standards in the Social Security Program 1939. *Address:* Harry S. Truman Scholarship Foundation, 712 Jackson Place, N.W., Washington, DC 20006; 5011 Overlook Road, N.W., Washington, DC 20016, U.S.A. *Telephone:* (202) 395-3530/4831 (Office).

STABREIT, Immo Friedrich Helmut, DR. JUR.; German diplomatist; b. 24 Jan. 1933, Rathenow/Havel; s. of Kurt Stabreit and Johanna Maria née Groeger; m. Barbara Philippi 1962; two s. one d.; ed. Princeton Univ., Free Univ. of Berlin and Univ. of Heidelberg; jr. law clerk 1957–61; Financial Dept. ECSC, Luxembourg 1959; entered foreign service 1962; served Moscow 1962–63, 1966–71; Fellow, Center for Int. Affairs, Harvard Univ. 1974–75; Head, Consumer Producer Relations Div. Int. Energy Agency, Paris 1975–78; Ministry of Foreign Affairs 1978–83; Fed. Chancellery 1983–87; Amb. to South Africa 1987–92, to U.S.A. 1992–95, to France 1995–98; Exec. Vice-Pres. German Soc. for Foreign Politics. *Leisure interests:* sport, reading. *Address:* Petersbergstr. 8, 53604 Bad Honnef, Germany.

STADEN, Berndt von; German diplomatist; b. 24 June 1919, Rostock; s. of Richard von Staden and Camille von Voigt; m. Wendelgard von Neurath 1961; two s. one d.; ed. Bonn and Hamburg Univs.; mil. service 1940–45; Jr. Barrister 1948–51; with Foreign Ministry 1951–86; served Brussels 1953–55; Dir. Soviet Affairs Desk, Bonn 1955–58; Staff mem. EEC Comm., Brussels, Head of Office of Pres. of Comm. 1958–63; Counsellor, Embassy, Washington 1963–68; Deputy Asst. State Sec., Foreign Office 1968–70, Asst. State Sec., Head of Political Dept. 1970–73; Amb. to U.S.A. 1973–79; Head of Dept. for Foreign Relations and Security, Fed. Chancery 1979–81; State Sec. Foreign Office 1981–83; Co-ordinator for German-American Co-operation 1982–86; Prof. of Diplomacy, Georgetown Univ., Washington, D.C. 1985, 1988, 1990; Order of Merit (Fed. Repub. of Germany). *Leisure interests:* music, horseback riding. *Address:* Leinfelderhof, 71665 Vaihingen, Germany. *Telephone:* (0049) 7042-5440.

STADLER, Sergey Valentinovich; Russian violinist and conductor; b. 20 May 1962, Leningrad; s. of Valentin Raumundovich Stadler and Margarita Petrovna Stadler; m. Ilse Liepa; ed. Leningrad State Conservatory, studied with Mikhail Vaiman, Boris Gutnikov in Leningrad Conservatory, with Leonid Kogan, Viktor Tretyakov in Moscow State Conservatory; prize winner several int. competitions; tours Europe and U.S.A. since 1976; first performed music by Russian composers Rodion Shchedrin, Sergey Slonimsky, Boris Tishchenko and others; taught in Leningrad State Conservatory 1984–88; began conducting 1996. *Address:* Kaiserstrasse 43, Munich, Germany. *Telephone:* 89/337 005 (Munich); (812) 164-34-51 (St. Petersburg); (095) 2073833 (Moscow).

STADTMAN, Earl R., PH.D.; American biochemist; b. 15 Nov. 1919, Carrizozo, N.M.; s. of Walter W. Stadtman and Minnie Ethyl Stadtman; m. Thressa Campbell Stadtman (q.v.) 1943; ed. Univ. of California; Research Asst. Dept. of Food Technology, Univ. of Calif. 1943–46, Research Asst., Div. of Plant Nutrition 1948–49; Atomic Energy Comm. Fellow, Biochemical Research Lab., Mass. Gen. Hospital 1949–50; Chemist (Biochem.) GS-15-Lab. for Cellular Physiology and Metabolism Nat. Insts. of Health (NIH) 1950–58, Chief of Enzyme Section, Lab. of Cellular Physiology and Metabolis, NIH 1958–62, Chief, Lab. of Biochem., Nat. Heart Inst., NIH 1962–; mem. N.A.S., American Acad. of Arts and Sciences, U.S. Cttee. for Int. Union of Biochemistry (mem. Council 1977–80), Exec. Cttee. 1982–85, Council of American Soc. of Biological Chemists (Pres. 1983–); Hon. D.Sc. (Mich.) 1987; Hon. Ph.D. (Weizmann Inst. of Science, Rehovot, Israel) 1988; Paul Lewis Award in Enzyme Chem. 1952, Washington Acad. of Sciences Annual Award in Biological Chem. 1957, Superior Service Award of Dept. of Health, Educ. and Welfare 1968, Distinguished Service Award 1970, Hillebrand Award of American Chemical Soc. 1969, Award in Microbiology, N.A.S. 1970, Nat. Medal of Science 1980, Meritorious Rank Award, Sr. Exec. Service 1981, Presidential Rank Award, Distinguished Sr. Exec. 1982, ASBC-Merck Award in Biochemistry 1983, Welch Foundation Award in Chem. 1991, Research Award American Aging Asscn. 1992, Paul Glen Award American Gerontology Soc. 1993. *Publications:* numerous scientific articles 1953–. *Leisure interests:* gardening, bowling, badminton, travelling. *Address:* National Heart and

Lung Institute, 9000 Rockville Pike, Bethesda, MD 20814 (Office); 16907 Redland Road, Derwood, MD 20855, U.S.A. (Home). *Telephone:* (301) 869-1747.

STADTMAN, Thressa Campbell, PH.D.; American biochemist; b. 12 Feb. 1920, Sterling, New York; d. of Earl and Bessie (Waldron) Campbell; m. Earl R. Stadtman (q.v.) 1943; ed. Cornell Univ. and Univ. of California (Berkeley); Research Assoc., Univ. of Calif. (Berkeley) 1942–47; Research Assoc., Harvard Medical School, Boston 1949–50; Biochemist, Nat. Heart, Lung and Blood Inst., Nat. Insts. of Health 1950–, Section Head, Lab. of Biochemistry 1974–; Ed.-in-Chief Bio Factors (IUB-sponsored journal) 1987–; Senior Exec. Service 1988–; Pres. (elect) Int. Soc. of Vitamins and Related Bio Factors 1995; Helen Haye Whitney Fellow, Oxford Univ., England 1954–55; Rockefeller Foundation Grantee, Univ. of Munich, Fed. Repub. of Germany 1959–60; mem. N.A.S., American Acad. of Arts and Sciences, Burroughs-Welcome Fund Toxicology Advisory Cttee. 1994–; Hillebrand Award, Chemical Soc. of Washington 1979, Rose Award, American Soc. of Biological Chemists 1987, Klaus Schwarz Medal 1988, Public Health Service Special Recognition Award 1991. *Publications:* original research papers in fields of Methane Biosynthesis, Amino Acid Metabolism, Vitamin B12 biochemistry, selenium biochemistry. *Leisure interests:* travel, gardening, skiing. *Address:* 16907 Redland Road, Derwood, MD 20855, U.S.A. (Home).

STAFFORD, Godfrey Harry, C.B.E., M.A., M.SC., PH.D., F.R.S.; British physicist; b. 15 April 1920, Sheffield; s. of Henry and Sarah Stafford; m. Helen Goldthorp 1950; one s. twin d.; ed. Rondebosch Boys' High School, Univ. of Cape Town, Gonville and Caius Coll., Cambridge; South African Naval Forces 1941–46; A.E.R.E., Harwell 1949–51; Head of Biophysics Subdivision, Council for Scientific and Industrial Research, Pretoria 1951–54; Cyclotron Group, AERE 1954–57; Head of Proton Linear Accelerator Group, Rutherford Laboratory 1957, Head of High Energy Physics Div. 1963, Deputy Dir. 1966, Dir. 1969–79; Dir. of Atlas and Rutherford Laboratory 1975–79, Dir.-Gen. 1979–81; U.K. del. IUPAP Comm. on Particles and Fields 1975–81; Vice-Pres. Inst. of Physics Meetings Cttee. 1976–79; Chair. CERN Scientific Policy Cttee. 1978–81; Master of St. Cross Coll., Oxford 1979–87; Pres. European Physical Soc. 1984–86, Inst. of Physics 1986–88; Visiting Fellow St. Cross Coll. 1971–79, Hon. Fellow 1987; Vice-Pres. European Physical Soc. 1982; Gov. Westminster Coll.; Ebden Scholar, Univ. of Cape Town; Hon. Scientist Rutherford Appleton Lab. 1986; Hon. D.Sc. (Birmingham) 1980; Glazebrook Prize and Medal, Inst. of Physics 1981. *Publications:* papers and articles in learned journals on biophysics, nuclear physics and high energy physics. *Leisure interests:* music, foreign travel, walking. *Address:* Ferry Cottage, North Hinksey Village, Oxford, OX2 0NA, England. *Telephone:* (01865) 247621 (Home).

STAFFORD, H.E. Cardinal James Francis; American ecclesiastic; b. 26 July 1932, Baltimore; s. of F. Emmett Stafford and Mary Dorothy Stafford; ordained priest 1957; Bishop 1976; Archbishop Emer. of Denver 1996; Pres. Pontifical Council for the Laity; cr. Cardinal Feb. 1998. *Address:* 200 Josephine Street, P.O. Box 1620, Denver, CO 80206, U.S.A. *Telephone:* (303) 388-4411. *Fax:* (303) 388-0517.

STAFFORD, John Rogers, A.B., J.D.; American business executive and lawyer; b. 24 Oct. 1937, Harrisburg, Pa.; s. of Paul Henry Stafford and Gladys Lee Sharp; m. Inge Paul 1959; four d.; ed. Montgomery Blair High School, Dickinson Coll., George Washington Univ. Law School; Assoc., Steptoe and Johnson 1962–66; Gen. Attorney, Hoffman-LaRoche 1966–67, Group Attorney 1967–70; Gen. Counsel, American Home Products Corpn. 1970–74, Vice-Pres. 1974–77, Sr. Vice-Pres. 1977–80, Exec. Vice-Pres. 1980–81, Pres. 1981–, Chair., Pres. and C.E.O. 1986–; Dir. Mfrs. Hanover Corpn., Metropolitan Life Insurance Co., Cen. Park Conservancy, Pharmaceutical Mfrs. Asscn., Project Hope, American Paralysis Asscn., numerous other orgs.; mem. Bd. of Trustees U.S. Council for Int. Business; mem. American Bar Asscn., Dist. of Columbia Bar Asscn.; Order of the Coif; Outstanding Achievement Alumnus Award 1981. *Leisure interests:* boating, golf. *Address:* American Home Products Corporation, 5 Giralda Farms, Madison, NJ 07940, U.S.A.

STAFFORD-CLARK, Max; British theatre director; b. 17 March 1941; s. of David Stafford-Clark and Dorothy Stafford-Clark; m. 1st Carole Hayman 1971; m. 2nd Ann Pennington 1981; one d.; ed. Felsted School, Riverdale Country Day School, New York and Trinity Coll. Dublin; Artistic Dir. Traverse Theatre, Edin. 1968–70; Dir. Traverse Workshop Co. 1970–74; Artistic Dir. Joint Stock 1974–79, English Stage Co. at Royal Court Theatre 1979–93, Out of Joint 1993–; Visiting Prof. Royal Holloway and Bedford Coll., Univ. of London 1993–94; Maisie Glass Prof. Univ. of Sheffield 1995–96; Visiting Prof. Univ. of Herts. 1999–. *Principal productions:* Fanshen, Top Girls, Tom and Viv, Rat in the Skull, Serious Money, Our Country's Good, The Libertine, The Steward of Christendom, Shopping And Fucking. *Publication:* Letters to George 1989. *Address:* 7 Gloucester Crescent, London, NW1 7DS, England.

STALLKAMP, Thomas; American business executive; b. 1946; fmrly. Vice-Pres. for Procurement and Supply Chrysler Corpn., Pres. 1998–. *Address:* Chrysler Corporation, 1200 Chrysler Drive, 415-03-05 Highland Park, Michigan, MI 48288, U.S.A.

STALLONE, Sylvester Enzio; American actor and film director; b. 6 July 1946, New York; s. of Frank Stallone and Jacqueline Labofish; m. 1st Sasha Czach 1974 (divorced); two s.; m. 2nd Brigitte Nielsen 1985 (divorced 1987); m. 3rd Jennifer Flavin 1997; two d.; ed. American Coll. of Switzerland, Univ. of Miami; has had many jobs including usher, bouncer, horse trainer, store detective, physical education teacher; now actor, and producer and dir. of own films; f. White Eagle Co.; Oscar for best film 1976, Golden Circle Award for best film 1976, Donatello Award 1976, Christopher Religious Award 1976; Dir. Carolco Pictures Inc. 1987–; mem. Screen Actors Guild, Writers Guild, Dirs. Guild; Hon. mem. Stuntmans' Asscn.; Officier Ordre des Arts et des Lettres. *Film appearances include:* Lords of Flatbush 1973, Capone 1974, Rocky 1976, F.I.S.T. 1978, Paradise Alley 1978, Rocky II 1979, Nighthawks 1980, Escape to Victory 1980, Rocky III 1981, First Blood, Rambo 1984, Rocky IV 1985, Cobra 1986, Over the Top 1986, Rambo II 1986, Rambo III 1988, Lock Up 1989, Set Up 1990, Tango and Cash 1990, Rocky V 1990, Isobar 1991, Stop or My Mom Will Shoot 1991, Oscar 1991, Cliffhanger 1992, Demolition Man 1993, Judge Dredd 1994, The Specialist 1994, Assassins 1995, Firestorm 1996, Daylight 1996, Cop Land 1997, An Alan Smithee Film: Burn Hollywood Burn 1998; producer, dir. film Staying Alive 1983. *Address:* William Morris Agency, 151 El Camino Drive, Beverly Hills, CA 90212, U.S.A.

STALS, Christian Lodewyk, D.COMM.; South African central banker; b. 13 March 1935; s. of Petrus J. Stals and Lilian Barnard; m. Hester Barnard 1958; three s. one d.; ed. Afrikaans Hoër, Germiston and Univ. of Pretoria Extramural Div.; joined South African Reserve Bank 1955, Gen. Man. 1975, Deputy Gov. 1976, Sr. Deputy Gov. 1981; Dir.-Gen. Dept. of Finance 1985; Special Econ. Adviser to Minister of Finance 1989; Gov. South African Reserve Bank 1989–99; Chancellor, Univ. of Pretoria 1997–; State President's Decoration for Distinguished Service. *Leisure interest:* golf. *Address:* c/o South African Reserve Bank, P.O. Box 427, Pretoria, 0001, South Africa.

STAMBOLIĆ, Petar; Yugoslav politician (retd.); b. 12 July 1912; ed. Univ. of Belgrade; mem. Young Communist League 1933, CP of Yugoslavia 1935–; organized resistance in Serbia 1941; Sec. Cen. Cttee. of Nat. Liberation Army and partisan units for Serbia 1943; Deputy and mem. Presidium Antifascist Council of Nat. Liberation of Yugoslavia 1943; mem. Cen. Cttee. of CP of Serbia 1945, Sec. 1948–57; First Vice-Chair. Council of Ministers, Serbia 1945–47; Pres. Exec. Council, Serbia 1948–53, Pres. Serbian Ass. 1953–57; Minister of Agric. and Forests, Yugoslavia 1947–48; Pres. Fed. People's Ass. 1957–63; Pres. Fed. Exec. Council 1963–67; mem. Collective Presidency of Yugoslavia 1974–84, Vice-Pres. 1974–75, 1981–82, Pres. 1982–83; mem. Cen. Cttee. of CP of Yugoslavia 1948–, mem. Politbureau 1951–68, and Exec. Cttee. 1952–68, Cen. Cttee. League of Communists of Yugoslavia, Chair. Ideological Comm. 1948–63; mem. Presidium of Cen. Cttee. of League of Communists of Yugoslavia 1966; mem. Council of Fed. 1963; Pres. Cen. Cttee. League of Communists of Serbia 1968–88; Order of Hero of the People and other decorations.

STAMP, Gavin Mark, PH.D., F.S.A.; British architectural historian and writer; b. 15 March 1948, Bromley, Kent; s. of Barry Hartnell Stamp and Norah Clare Stamp (née Rich); m. Alexandra Artley 1982; two d.; ed. Dulwich Coll., London, Gonville and Caius Coll., Cambridge; freelance writer and teacher until 1990; lecturer, Mackintosh School of Architecture, Glasgow School of Art 1990–; Chair. The Twentieth Century Soc. (fmrly. The Thirties Soc.) 1983–; Founder and Chair. Alexander Thomson Soc. 1991–; Hon. F.R.I.A.S. 1994; Hon. F.R.I.B.A. 1998. *Publications:* Robert Weir Schultz and his work for Marquesses of Bute 1981, The Great Perspectivists 1982, The Changing Metropolis 1984, The English House 1860–1914 1986, Telephone Boxes 1989, Greek Thomson (co-ed) 1994. *Address:* 1 Moray Place, Strathbungo, Glasgow, G41 2AQ, Scotland.

STAMP, Terence; British actor; b. 22 July 1938, London; s. of Thomas Stamp and Ethel Esther Perrott; theatre work before film debut in Billy Budd 1962; Hon. Dr. of Arts (Univ. of East London) 1993. *Other films include:* Term of Trial 1962, The Collector 1965, Modesty Blaise 1966, Far From the Madding Crowd 1967, Poor Cow 1967, Blue 1968, Theorem 1968, Tales of Mystery 1968, The Mind of Mr. Soames 1969, A Season in Hell 1971, Hu-man 1975, The Divine Creature 1976, Striptease 1977, Meetings With Remarkable Men 1978, Superman 1978, Superman II 1979, Death in the Vatican 1980, The Bloody Chamber 1982, The Hit 1984, Link 1985, Legal Eagles 1986, The Sicilian 1986, Wall Street 1988, Alien Nation 1988, Young Guns 1988, Prince of Shadows 1991, The Real McCoy 1992, The Adventures of Priscilla Queen of the Desert 1994, Bliss 1995, Limited Edition 1995, Mindbender, Love Walked In 1996, Kiss the Sky 1997. *Theatre:* Dracula, The Lady from the Sea. *Publications:* Stamp Album (memoirs, Vol. 1) 1988, Coming Attractions (memoirs, Vol. 2) 1988, Double Feature (memoirs, Vol. 3) 1989, The Night (novel) 1992, Stamp Collection (jtly.) 1997. *Address:* c/o Markham and Froggatt, 4 Windmill Street, London, W1P 1HF, England.

STANBURY, Hon. Robert Douglas George, P.C., Q.C., B.A., LL.B., F.I.D.; Canadian executive, lawyer and fmr. politician; b. 26 Oct. 1929, Exeter, Ont.; s. of James George Stuart Stanbury and Elizabeth Jean (Hardy); m. Miriam Voelker 1952; two s. two d.; ed. Exeter and St. Catharines public schools, St. Catharines Coll. Inst., Univ. of Western Ontario and Osgoode Hall Law School; Pres. Canadian Univ. Liberal Fed. 1954; Partner Hollingworth & Stanbury, Barristers and Solicitors, Toronto 1955–65; mem. North York Bd. of Educ. 1961–64, Vice-Chair. 1962, Chair. 1963–64; mem. Metropolitan School Bd., Toronto 1963–64 and Metropolitan Toronto Planning Bd.

1963; M.P. 1965–77; Chair. House of Commons Standing Cttee. on Broadcasting, Films and Assistance to the Arts 1966–68; Parl. Sec. to Sec. of State of Canada 1968–69; Minister without Portfolio responsible for Citizenship 1969–71, for Information Canada 1970–71; Minister of Communications 1971–72, of Nat. Revenue 1972–74; Queen's Counsel 1974–; Del. to UN Gen. Assembly 1974, 1975, 1976, to UNESCO Conf., Paris 1969, UN Conf. on Crime, Kyoto 1970, UN Conf. on Apartheid, Lagos 1977, Inter-American Devt. Bank meeting, Kingston 1977; Chair. Canadian Group IPU 1974–77; Founding Chair. Canadian Parl. Helsinki Group 1977; Pres. Hamilton Foundation 1982–83; Vice-Pres. Gen. Counsel and Dir., Firestone Canada Inc. 1977–83, Chair. and C.E.O. 1983–85; Counsel Inch Easterbrook & Shaker 1986–; Dir. Art Gallery of Hamilton (Vice-Pres. 1982–86, Pres. 1986–87), mem. Bd. of Govs. 1988–, Dir. Art Gallery of Hamilton Foundation 1996–; Dir. Hamilton and Dist. Chamber of Commerce 1980–85 (Pres. 1983–84), Dayton Tire Canada Ltd. 1977–85, Canadian Chamber of Commerce 1982–86, Chedoke-McMaster Hospitals 1983–92, (Vice-Chair. 1987–89), Workers' Compensation Bd. of Ont. 1985–88, 1991–94 (Vice-Chair. 1991–94); mem. Canadian Broadcast Standards Council (Ont.) 1990– (Vice-Chair. 1996–), Nunavut Arbitration Bd. 1994–, Advisory Council, Grad. School of Journalism, Univ. of W. Ont. 1994–97; Pres. Inst. of Corporate Dirs. in Canada 1987–88; Chair. McMaster Univ. Business Advisory Council 1987–88, Employers' Council on Workers' Compensation 1996; Pres. and C.E.O. Canadian Council for Native Business 1989–91; mem. Law Soc. of Upper Canada, Canadian Council of Administrative Tribunals, Int. Comm. of Jurists, UNA in Canada; Fellow Inst. of Dirs. 1985–; Canadian Centennial Medal 1967, Queen's Silver Jubilee Medal 1977. *Address:* 1 King Street W., Suite 1500, Hamilton, Ont., L8P 4X8 (Office); 607 Edgewater Crescent, Burlington, Ont., L7T 3L8, Canada (Home). *Telephone:* (905) 525-4481 (Office). *Fax:* (905) 525-0031 (Office).

STANCLIFFE, Rt. Rev. David Staffurth, M.A.; British ecclesiastic; b. 1 Oct. 1942, Devizes, Wilts.; s. of late Very Rev. Michael Stancliffe and Barbara Tatlow; m. Sarah Smith 1965; one s. two d.; ed. Westminster School, Trinity Coll. Oxford and Cuddesdon Theological Coll.; ordained deacon 1967, priest 1968; Asst. Curate, St. Bartholomew's, Armley, Leeds 1967–70; Chaplain, Clifton Coll. Bristol 1970–77; Canon Residentiary, Portsmouth Cathedral 1977–82, also Dir. of Ordinands and Lay Ministry Adviser, Diocese of Portsmouth 1977–82; Vicar, St. Thomas of Canterbury, Portsmouth and Provost of Portsmouth 1982–93; Bishop of Salisbury 1993–; mem. Gen. Synod 1985–, Liturgical Comm. 1986– (Chair. 1993–), Cathedral's Fabric Comm. 1991–; Pres. Council, Marlborough Coll. 1994–; D.Litt. h.c. (Portsmouth) 1993. *Publications include:* Liturgy for a New Century 1990 (contrib.), The Identity of Anglican Worship 1991, Enriching the Christian Year 1992, Celebrating Common Prayer—Pocket Version 1994, The Sense of the Sacramental 1995. *Leisure interests:* old music, travel, Italy. *Address:* South Canonry, 71 The Close, Salisbury, Wilts., SP1 2ER, England. *Telephone:* (01722) 334031.

STANFIELD, Hon. Robert Lorne, B.A., LL.B., Q.C., LL.D.; Canadian politician; b. 11 April 1914, Truro, Nova Scotia; s. of Frank Stanfield and Sarah Emma (Thomas) Stanfield; m. 1st Nora Joyce Stanfield 1940 (died 1954); one s. three d.; m. 2nd Mary Stanfield 1957 (died 1977); m. 3rd Anne Stanfield 1978; ed. Ashbury Coll., Ottawa, Dalhousie and Harvard Univs.; Gov. Dalhousie Univ. 1949–56; Premier, Minister of Educ., Nova Scotia 1956–67; M.P. for Halifax, Nova Scotia 1968–79; fmr. Leader Progressive Conservatives Nova Scotia; Leader of Opposition, Leader Nat. Progressive Conservative Party of Canada 1967–76; Leader Govt. Mission to Middle East 1979–80; Chair. Inst. for Research on Public Policy 1981–87; Chair. Commonwealth Foundation 1987–91; Hon. LL.D. (New Brunswick) 1958, (McGill) 1967, (St. Dunstan's) 1967, (St. Mary's) 1968, (Dalhousie), (McMaster) 1985. *Leisure interest:* gardening. *Address:* 136 Acacia Avenue, Rockcliffe Park, Ottawa, Ont., K1M 0R1, Canada.

STANIER, Field Marshal Sir John Wilfred, G.C.B., M.B.E., D.L.; British army officer; b. 6 Oct. 1925, Essex; s. of the late Harold Allan and Penelope Rose (née Price) Stanier; m. Cicely Constance Lambert 1955; four d.; ed. Marlborough Coll., Merton Coll., Oxford, Imperial Defence Coll., Staff Coll.; commissioned into 7th Queen's Own Hussars 1946; served N. Italy, Germany and Hong Kong; commanded Royal Scots Greys 1966–68, 20 Armoured Brigade 1969–70; G.O.C. 1st Armoured Div. 1973–75; Commdt. Staff Coll., Camberley 1975–78; Vice-Chief of Gen. Staff 1978–80; C.-in-C. U.K. Land Forces 1981–82; Chief of Gen. Staff 1982–85; rank of Field Marshal 1985; ADC to the Queen 1981–85; Chair. Royal United Services Inst. for Defence Studies 1986–89; Col. Royal Scots Dragoon Guards 1979–85; Col. Commdt. Royal Armoured Corps 1982–85; Constable of the Tower of London 1990–96; Chair. Control Risks (GS) Ltd. 1985–96; mem. Council Marlborough Coll. 1984–96; D.L. of Hampshire 1986. *Publication:* War and the Media (with Miles Hudson) 1997. *Leisure interests:* fishing, sailing. *Address:* c/o Coutts & Co., 440 The Strand, London, WC2R 0QS, England. *Telephone:* (01252) 842341. *Fax:* (01252) 844141.

STANISZEWSKI, Stefan, M.A.; Polish diplomatist; b. 11 Feb. 1931, Bukowa; s. of Andrzej Staniszewski and Katarzyna Staniszewska; m. Wanda Szuszkiewicz 1953; one d.; ed. Warsaw Univ. and Jagellonian Univ., Cracow; fmr. active mem. of student and social org. 1951–58; Head of Dept., Iskry Publrs., Warsaw 1958–60; in Ministry of Foreign Affairs 1960–95; official, Office of Minister 1960–63, Second Sec., then First Sec. and Counsellor, Polish Embassy, Paris 1963–69; Dir. Dept. for West Europe, Ministry of Foreign Affairs; mem. Governing Council of Ministry 1969–72; Amb. to Sweden 1972–77, to U.K. 1981–86; Dir. Dept. of Press, Cultural and Scientific Co-operation, Ministry of Foreign Affairs 1977–81, Dir. Dept. of Press and Information 1987–90, Press Spokesman of Ministry 1988–90; Amb. to Libya 1990–95; Commdr.'s Cross, Order of Polonia Restituta, Légion d'honneur, First Class, Order of Polar Star (Sweden), Aztec Eagle Order (Mexico). *Leisure interests:* swimming, modern painting. *Address:* ul. Okrąg 1 m. 51, 00-415 Warsaw, Poland. *Telephone:* (22) 621 27 55.

STANKEVIČIUS, Česlovas Vytautas; Lithuanian politician and biophysicist; b. 27 Feb. 1937, Vilkaviskis Region; s. of Jonas Stankevičius and Uršula Dubickaite; m. Jadvyga Litvinaite 1962; two s.; ed. Kaunas Polytech. Coll., Kaunas Polytech. Inst.; engineer, sr. engineer Kaunas City Construction Design Inst. 1965–94; Chair. Bd. Sajudis Movt.; elected Deputy to Supreme Soviet Repub. of Lithuania; signatory to March 11th Act on Re-establishment of Independence; Head official dels. in negotiations with Russia 1990; Head Lithuanian Parl. del. to N. Atlantic Ass. 1991–92; co-author project on nat. security and defence concept of Lithuania; mem. Seimas, Parl. Group of Christian Democrats 1996–; Minister of Defence 1996–. *Leisure interests:* literature, theatre, museums. *Address:* Ministry of Defence, Totoriu 25/3, Vilnius 2001, (Office); Latvių str. 54, Apt. 1, 2000 Vilnius, Lithuania (Home). *Telephone:* (02) 62 48 21 (Office); (02) 61 08 52 (Home). *Fax:* (02) 623443.

STANLEY, Eric Gerald, PH.D., F.B.A.; British academic; b. 19 Oct. 1923; m. Mary Bateman, M.D., F.R.C.P. 1959; one d.; ed. Queen Elizabeth's Grammar School, Blackburn, Univ. Coll., Oxford; Lecturer in English Language and Literature, Univ. of Birmingham 1951–62; Reader in English Language and Literature, Univ. of London, Queen Mary Coll. 1962–64, Prof. 1964–75; Prof. of English, Yale Univ. 1975–76; Rawlinson and Bosworth Prof. of Anglo-Saxon, Univ. of Oxford, and Fellow Pembroke Coll. Oxford 1977–91, Prof. Emer. 1991–; mem. Mediaeval Acad. of America 1975–; Corresp. mem. Fryske Akad. 1991–, Bavarian Acad. of Sciences 1994–; Sir Israel Gollancz Memorial Lecturer, The British Acad. 1984. *Publications:* books and academic articles, some of them in A Collection of Papers with Emphasis on Old English Literature 1987, In the Foreground: Beowulf 1994. *Leisure interest:* travel. *Address:* Pembroke College, Oxford, OX1 1DW, England.

STANLEY, Julian Cecil, Jr., B.S., ED.D.; American professor of psychology; b. 9 July 1918, Macon, Ga.; s. of Julian C. Stanley and Ethel May Cheney Stanley; m. 1st Rose Roberta Sanders 1946 (died 1978); m. 2nd Barbara Sprague Kerr 1980; one d. one step-s. one step-d.; ed. Georgia Southern Univ. and Harvard Univ.; postdoctoral studies at Univs. of Mich., Chicago, six N.Z. univs. (Fulbright Lecturer), Catholic Univ. of Louvain, Belgium (Fulbright Act Research Scholar), Center for Advanced Study in the Behavioral Sciences, Stanford Univ., Calif.; taught science and math. in high school, Atlanta, Ga. 1937–42; Instructor in Psychology, Newton (Mass.) Jr. Coll. 1946–48; Instructor in Educ., Harvard Univ. 1948–49; Assoc. Prof. of Educational Psychology, George Peabody Coll. for Teachers 1949–53; Assoc. Prof. of Educ., Univ. of Wis. 1953–57, Prof. 1957–62, Prof. of Educational Psychology 1962–67, Chair. Dept. 1962–64, Dir. Lab. of Experimental Design 1961–67; Prof. of Educ. and Psychology, Johns Hopkins Univ. 1967–71, Prof. of Psychology 1971–, Dir. of Study of Mathematically Precocious Youth 1971–; Fellow A.A.A.S., American Statistical Asscn., American Psychological Asscn., American Psychological Soc.; Hon. D.E.E. (Univ. of N. Texas), Hon. D.Hum.Litt. (State Univ. of W. Ga.). *Publications:* author, co-author or ed. of 13 books and approx. 400 articles, book chapters and reviews; books (co-author) include Experimental and Quasi-Experimental Designs for Research 1966, Mathematical Talent 1974, The Gifted and the Creative 1977, Educating the Gifted 1979, Academic Precocity 1983. *Leisure interests:* cinema, hiking, travelling. *Address:* Study of Mathematically Precocious Youth (SMPY), Bloomberg Center, Johns Hopkins University, Baltimore, MD 21218, U.S.A. *Telephone:* (410) 516-6179, 7087. *Fax:* (410) 516-7239.

STANNARD, Robert William, C.M.G., B.COM.(N.Z.), F.C.A.(N.Z.); New Zealand business executive; b. 16 Sept. 1926, Gisborne; s. of William C. Stannard and Clara Stannard; m. Shirley M. Sparkes 1956; one s. (deceased) two d.; ed. Horowhenua Coll., Levin and Victoria Univ., Wellington; J. L. Arcus & Sons (chartered accountants), Wellington 1944–49; Peat, Marwick, Mitchell & Co. (chartered accountants), London and Singapore 1949–53; partner, Bowden, Bass & Cox (now KPMG), Wellington 1954–87; Statutory Man. Cornish Group 1974–90, Public Service Investment Soc. 1979–87; mem. Nat. Parks Centennial Comm. 1983–88; Chair. Databank Systems Ltd. 1985–93, N.Z. Fishing Industry Bd. 1988–93, Nat. Australia Bank (N.Z.) Ltd. 1991–92, Overseas Investment Comm. 1978–97, Milburn N.Z. Ltd. 1987–97, Trustees Executors 1991–, Bank of N.Z. 1993–96; Dir. Fiordland Travel Ltd. 1973–97, Commercial Fisheries Services Ltd. 1998–; Trustee Chatham Islands Enterprise Trust 1991–94; N.Z. 1990 Medal. *Leisure interests:* lawn bowls, mountain tramping. *Address:* c/o KPMG, 135 Victoria Street, Wellington; P.O. Box 996, Wellington, New Zealand. *Telephone:* (04) 382-8800. *Fax:* (04) 802-1225.

STANSFIELD SMITH, Sir Colin, Kt., C.B.E., M.A., DIP.ARCH., A.R.I.B.A.; British architect; b. 1 Oct. 1932, Manchester; s. of Stansfield Smith and Mary Simpson; m. Angela Jean Earnshaw 1961; one s. one d.; ed. William Hulmes Grammar School, Manchester and Cambridge Univ. School of Architecture; London County Council (Schools Div.) 1958–60; Sr. Asst. then Assoc. Partner, Emberton Frank & Tardrew (architects) 1960–65; partner, Emberton Tardrew & Partners 1965–71; Deputy County Architect, Cheshire

County Council 1971–73; County Architect, Hampshire County Council 1973–92, Consultant Co. Architect 1992–; Prof. of Architectural Design Studies, Portsmouth Univ. (fmrly. Polytech.) School of Architecture 1990–; R.I.B.A. Gold Medal 1991. *Publications:* Hampshire Architecture 1974–84 1985, Schools of Thought, Hampshire Architecture 1974–91; articles in Architects' Journal and Architectural Review. *Leisure interests:* golf, painting. *Address:* Three Minsters House, 76 High Street, Winchester, Hants., SO23 8UL (Office); 8 Christchurch Road, Winchester, Hants., SO23 9SR, England (Home). *Telephone:* (01962) 847800 (Office); (01962) 851970.

STANTON, Frank (Nicholas), PH.D.; American administrator; b. 20 March 1908, Muskegon, Mich.; s. of Frank Cooper Stanton and Helen Josephine Schmidt; m. Ruth Stephenson 1931 (died 1992); ed. Ohio Wesleyan Univ., Ohio State Univ.; Dir. CBS Inc. 1945–78, Pres. 1946–71, Vice-Chair. 1971–73; Chair. American Red Cross 1973–79, Vice-Pres. League of Red Cross Socs., Geneva; Licensed Psychologist, N.Y.; Diplomate, American Bd. of Professional Psychology; Dir. New York Life Insurance Co. 1956–81, Atlantic Richfield Co. 1973–81, Pan American World Airways Inc. 1967–81, American Electric Power Co. Inc. 1969–80, New Perspective Fund, Inc., Interpublic Group of Cos. Inc., EuroPacific Growth Fund, Capital Income Builder Fund, Capital World Growth and Income Fund, Sony Music Entertainment Inc., Museum of TV and Radio; Chair. Broadcast Int.; Trustee American Crafts Council 1957–75, Inst. for Architecture and Urban Studies 1970–75, Rockefeller Foundation 1961–73, The Rand Corpn. 1956–78, The Observer (London) 1976–85, Int. Herald Tribune 1983–91; Chair. Carnegie Inst. of Washington; Founding Chair. and Trustee, Center for Advanced Study in the Behavioural Sciences 1953–71; Chair. U.S. Advisory Comm. on Information 1964–73; Co-Founder, Office of Radio Research, Princeton Univ. 1937; Chair., Panel on Int. Information, Educ. and Cultural Relations, Georgetown Univ. 1974–75; Dir.-Trustee, Educational Broadcasting Corpn., Int. Design Conf. in Aspen, Lincoln Center Inst., etc.; Dir. Recorded Anthology of American Music Inc., Lincoln Center for the Performing Arts 1960, Business Cttee. for the Arts 1967–77, Chair. 1972–74, Municipal Art Soc. of New York 1974–77; mem. The Business Council 1956–, N.Y. Council on the Arts 1965–70, Nat. Portrait Gallery Comm. 1977–, Bd. of Overseers Harvard 1978–84, Pres.'s Cttee. on the Arts and the Humanities 1983–91; Fellow, A.A.A.S., American Psychological Asscn., American Acad. of Arts and Sciences, New York Acad. of Science; mem. Architectural League of N.Y., Council on Foreign Relations Inc., Inst. of Electrical and Electronic Engineers, Nat. Acad. of Television Arts and Sciences (elected to Hall of Fame 1986), Radio-Television News Dirs. Asscn., Int. Radio and Television Soc.; numerous medals, awards, and hon. degrees. *Publications:* Students' Guide—The Study of Psychology (co-author) 1935, Radio Research 1941, Radio Research 1942–43, Communications Research 1948–49 (co-ed.), International Information, Education and Cultural Relations—Recommendations for the Future 1975. *Address:* 25 West 52nd Street, New York, NY 10019, U.S.A. (Office). *Fax:* (212) 765-4620.

STANZEL, Franz Karl, D.PHIL.; Austrian professor of English; b. 4 Aug. 1923, Molln; s. of Franz and Luise Stanzel; m. Ina v. Navarini 1962; one d.; ed. Univ. of Graz and Harvard Univ.; lecturer in English, Univ. of Graz 1949–50, 1951–57; Asst. Prof. Univ. of Göttingen 1957–59; Prof. Univ. of Erlangen 1959–62; Prof. of English, Univ. of Graz 1962–96, Prof. Emer. 1996–, Dean, Faculty of Arts and Sciences 1967–68, Head Dept. of English 1962–78; mem. Austrian Acad.; Dr. h.c. (Fribourg). *Publications include:* Typische Erzählsituationen im Roman 1955, Typische Formen des Romans 1964, Narrative Situations in the Novel 1969, Der literarische Aspekt unserer Vorstellungen vom Charakter fremder Völker 1974, Theorie des Erzählens 1979, A Theory of Narrative 1984, Englische und deutsche Kriegsdichtung, Sprachkunst 1987, Intimate Enemies (ed.) 1993, Europäer: Ein imagologischer Essay 1997, Europäischer Völkerspiegel (ed.) 1998. *Leisure interests:* cross-country skiing, gardening, travel. *Address:* Karl-Franzens-Universität Graz, Universitäts-platz 3, 8010 Graz; Am Blumenhang 31/5, 8010 Graz, Austria. *Telephone:* (316) 47 55 56. *Fax:* (316) 380-9765.

STAPLE, George Warren, C.B., Q.C.; British lawyer; b. 13 Sept. 1940, Bristol; s. of Kenneth Staple and Betty Staple; m. Olivia Lowry 1968; two s. two d.; ed. Haileybury; Assoc. Condon & Forsyth, New York 1963; admitted solicitor 1964; partner, Clifford-Turner, later Clifford Chance 1967–92, 1997–; Dir. Serious Fraud Office 1992–97; Legal Assessor, Disciplinary Cttee. Stock Exchange 1978–92; Dept. of Trade & Industry Insp. Consolidated Goldfields 1986, Aldermanbury Trust 1988; a Chair. Authorization and Disciplinary Tribunals of Securities Asscn. 1987–91, Securities and Futures Authority 1991–92; mem. Commercial Court Cttee. 1977–92; mem. Council, Law Soc. 1986–; mem. Law Advisory Cttee. of British Council 1998–; Gov. London Guildhall Univ. 1982–94; Fellow Chartered Inst. of Arbitrators 1986, Soc. for Advanced Legal Studies 1997. *Leisure interests:* cricket, hill walking. *Address:* Clifford Chance, 200 Aldersgate Street, London, EC1A 4JJ, England. *Telephone:* 0171-600 1000. *Fax:* 0171-600 5555.

STAPLETON, Nigel John, M.A.; British business executive; b. 1 Nov. 1946, London; s. of Frederick E. J. Stapleton and Katie M. Tyson; m. Johanna Molhoek 1982; one s.; ed. Univ. of Cambridge; internal auditor, Unilever Ltd. 1968–70; Group Man. Internal Audit, Unilever Ltd. 1970–73, Sr. Auditor 1973–75; Corp. Planning Man. BOCM Silcock 1975–77, Devt. Dir. 1977–80; Commercial mem. N. American office, Unilever PLC 1980–83; Vice-Pres. Finance, Unilever US Inc. 1983–86; Finance Dir. Reed Int. PLC, London 1986–96, Deputy Chair. 1994–97, Chair. 1997–; Deputy Chair., Chief Financial Officer, Reed Elsevier 1994–, Co-Chair. 1996–; Dir. (non-exec.) GEC 1997–. *Address:* Reed Elsevier, Head Office, 25 Victoria Street, London, S.W.1., England.

STAPP, Col. John Paul, PH.D., M.D., SC.D.; American fmr. air force officer and aerospace scientist; b. 11 July 1910, Bahia, Brazil; s. of late Rev. Charles F. and Mary Louise (née Shannon) Stapp; m. Lillian Lanese 1957; ed. Baylor Univ. (Texas), Univs. of Texas and Minnesota and School of Aviation Medicine; joined U.S.A.F. Medical Corps 1944; pioneer of research on effects of mechanical force on living tissues, especially with regard to high-speed flight and space flight; conducted rocket sled deceleration tests on himself; planned and directed high-altitude (102,000 feet) manned balloon flights 1957; organized Aeromedical Facility (Edwards Air Force Base, Calif.) and Aeromedical Field Lab. (Holloman Air Force Base, N.M.); Chief Aerospace Medical Lab., Wright Air Devt. Div. (Wright-Patterson Air Force Base, Ohio) 1958–60; Special Asst. Advanced Studies, Aerospace Medical Center (Brooks Air Force Base, Tex.) 1960–61, Chief Scientist 1961–65; Chief of Impact Injury, Armed Forces Inst. of Pathology 1965–67; retd from U.S.A.F. 1970; Chief Scientist (Medicine) Nat. Highway Safety Traffic Admin. 1967–70; Consultant Dept. of Transport 1970–, Science Lab., New Mexico State Univ. 1972; Adjunct Prof. Univ. Southern Calif. Systems Man. Center 1972–; Adviser Los Angeles Safety and Systems Man. Center 1973–; Vice-Pres. Int. Astronautical Fed. 1960; Perm. Chair. Annual Stapp Car Crash Conf. 1955; Pres. Civil Aviation Medical Asscn. 1968, American Rocket 1978–79, New Mexico Research Inst. 1986–; Chair. Gov.'s Comm., Int. Space Hall of Fame 1986–91; Hon. Chair. Stapp Foundation, Soc. of Automotive Engineers 1996–; Fellow, American Inst. Aeronautics and Astronautics, British Interplanetary Soc., Soc. of Automotive Engineers 1983; mem. Int. Acad. Astronautics, Int. Acad. Aviation and Space Medicine, American Medical Asscn., Nat. Research Council Int. Acad. Aviation Medicine, etc.; annual John Paul Stapp Biomechanics Award est. by Aerospace Medical Asscn. 1992; many awards include: John Jefferies Award 1953, Cheney Award 1955, Liljenkrantz Award 1957, Gorgas Medal 1957, Distinguished Service Medal (U.S.A.F.) 1971, Elliot Cresson Medal of Franklin Inst. 1973, Excalibur Award, Nat. Motor Vehicle Safety Council 1975, Certificate of Achievement, Nat. Space Club 1976, elected to Int. Space Hall of Fame 1979, Lovelace Award (NASA Asscn. of Flight Surgeons) 1982, Outstanding Award (Aviation and Service), Honda Medal, American Soc. of Mechanical Engineers 1984, Nat. Aviation Hall of Fame 1985, Harold S. Diehl Award (Univ. Minn.) 1990, Nat. Medal of Tech. 1991, Distinguished Public Service Award, Nat. Aviation and Space Asscn. 1993, induction 1st Flight Soc. 1998; Commdr. Legion of Merit. *Publications:* Human Exposure to Linear Deceleration (Journal of Aviation Medicine) 1950, Crash Protection in Air Force Transports (Aeronautical Engineering Review) 1953, Effects of Mechanical Force on Living Tissue (Journal of Aviation Medicine) 1955, 1956 and 1958, Space Cabin Landing Impact Vector Effects on Human Physiology 1964, Biomechanics of Injury in the Prevention of Highway Injury 1967, Voluntary Human Tolerance Levels in Impact Injury and Crash Protection 1970, Biodynamics of Deceleration, Impact and Blast in Aerospace Medicine 1971. *Leisure interests:* travel, writing, music, teaching. *Address:* P.O. Box 553, Alamogordo, NM 88310, U.S.A. (Home). *Telephone:* (505) 437-3645 (Home).

STARCK, Christian, DR.IUR.; German professor of law; b. 9 Jan. 1937, Breslau; s. of Walter Starck and Ruth Hubrich; m. Brigitte Edelmann 1965; one s. two d.; ed. Univs. of Kiel, Freiburg and Würzburg; clerk, Fed. Constitutional Court 1964–67; govt. official 1968–69; lecturer, Univ. of Würzburg 1969–71; Prof. of Public Law, Univ. of Göttingen 1971–; Rector, Univ. of Göttingen 1976–77; Judge, Constitutional Court of Lower Saxony 1991–; Ed. Studien und Materialen zur Verfassungsgerichtsbarkeit 1973–; co-ed. Juristenzeitung 1978–, Staatswissenschaften und Staatspraxis 1990–; mem. TV Bd. Zweites Deutsches Fernsehen 1978–92; mem. Asscn. of German Profs. of Public Law 1969– (Exec. Cttee. 1988, 1989, Pres. 1998, 1999), Exec. Cttee. Int. Asscn. of Constitutional Law 1981–, Exec. Cttee. German Asscn. of Comparative Law 1985–; Visiting Prof. Paris I (Panthéon-Sorbonne) 1987; mem. Acad. of Sciences of Göttingen 1982–; Fellow Inst. for Advanced Study, Berlin 1990–91. *Publications include:* Der Gesetzesbegriff des Grundgesetzes 1970, Rundfunkfreiheit als Organisationsproblem 1973, Das Bundesverfassungsgericht im politischen Prozess 1976, ed. Bundesverfassungsgericht und Grundgesetz (2 vols.) 1976, Vom Grund des Grundgesetzes 1979, La Constitution, cadre et mesure du droit 1994, Praxis der Verfassungsauslegung 1994, Die Verfassungen der neuen deutschen Länder 1994, Der demokratische Verfassungsstaat 1995, Das Bonner Grundgesetz Kommentar, vol. I, 4th edn. 1999. *Leisure interests:* architecture, literature, walking. *Address:* Platz der Göttinger Sieben 6, 37073 Göttingen (Office); Schlegelweg 10, 37075 Göttingen, Germany (Home). *Telephone:* 0551/397412 (Office).

STARCK, Philippe-Patrick; French designer; b. 18 Jan. 1949, Paris; s. of André Starck and Jacqueline Lanourisse; m. Brigitte Laurent 1977 (deceased); two c.; ed. Institution Notre-Dame de Sainte-Croix, Neuilly-sur-Seine, Ecole Nissim de Camondo, Paris; f. Starck Product 1979; Interior architecture: La Main-Bleue 1976, Les Bains-Douches 1978, pvt. apartments in Elysée Palace 1982, Le Café Costes 1984, La Cigale, Paris 1987, restaurants, housing and offices in Tokyo 1986–88, Royalton Hotel, New York 1988, Paramount Hotel, New York 1990, Teatriz Restaurant, Madrid 1990, Groningen Museum 1994, Peninsula Restaurant, Hong Kong 1994, Delano Hotel, Miami 1995, Theatron Restaurant, Mexico 1995, Mondrian Hotel, L.A. 1996, Asia de Cuba Restaurant, New York 1997; architecture includes factory, Laguiole 1988, Nani Nani bldg., Tokyo 1989, bldgs. in U.S.A., Japan, France, Spain, Ecole Nat. des Arts Décoratifs, Paris 1995, air traffic control tower for Bordeaux Airport 1997; created furniture for Pres. of the Repub. 1982, for French, Italian, Spanish, Japanese and Swiss cos.; designed boats for Bénéteau, vases for Daum, luggage for Vuitton, toothbrush for Fluocaril, urban furniture for Jean-Claude Decaux, Olympic Flame 1992, children's toys, Aprilia scooters, etc.; Worldwide Artistic Dir. Thomson Consumer Electronics Group 1993–96; Prof., Domus Acad., Milan, Italy, Ecole des Arts Décoratifs de Paris; Artistic Dir. Int. Design Yearbook; exhbns. at Georges Pompidou Museum and Decorative Arts Museum, Paris, Villa Medici, Italy, Deutsches Museum, Munich, Kunstmuseum, Düsseldorf, Museum of Modern Art, Kyoto, Japan, Design Museum, London and in Switzerland and U.S.A.; numerous prizes, including Oscar du Luminaire 1980, three 1st prizes at Neocon, Chicago 1986, Delta de Plata, Barcelona 1986, Platinum Circle Award, Chicago 1987, Grand prix nat. de la Création Industrielle 1988; three awards for hotels in U.S.A. 1990, 1991, one for Hotel Paramount 1992, Disseny Barcelona 1995, Design-Zentrum Nordrhein Westfalen Award (Germany) for Duraint bathroom design 1995, Harvard Excellence in Design Award 1997; Officier des arts et des lettres. *Leisure interest:* sailing. *Address:* Starck-Ubik, 27 rue Pierre Poli, 92130 Issy les Moulineaux, France. *Telephone:* 41.08.82.82. *Fax:* 41.08.96.65.

STARFIELD, Barbara, M.D., M.PH.; American physician; b. 18 Dec. 1932; d. of Martin and Eva (née Illions) Starfield; m. Neil A. Holtzman 1955; three s. one d.; ed. Swarthmore Coll., State Univ. of New York, The Johns Hopkins Univ.; teaching asst. (anatomy), Downstate Med. Center, New York 1955–57; intern. and resident in Pediatrics, Johns Hopkins Univ. Hosp. 1959–62, Dir., Pediatric Medical Care Clinic 1963–66; Dir. Pediatric Clinical Scholars Program, Johns Hopkins Univ. 1971–76, Asst. Prof., Assoc. Prof. 1967–76, Prof. and Div. Head, Health Policy, The Johns Hopkins Univ. School of Hygiene and Public Health 1976–; Univ. Distinguished Prof., Johns Hopkins Univ. 1994–; mem. Nat. Advisory Council for Health Care Policy, Research and Evaluation, U.S. Dept. of Health and Human Services 1990–93, Nat. Cttee. Vital and Health Statistics (USDHHS) 1994–; mem. Inst. of Medicine, N.A.S.; Dave Luckman Memorial Award 1958, Career Devt. Award 1970–75, Armstrong Award (Ambulatory Pediatric Asscn.) 1983, Annual Research Award (Ambulatory Pediatric Asscn.) 1990, Pew Primary Care Achievement Award 1994, Martha May Eliot Award (APHA) 1994. *Publications:* Effectiveness of Medical Care 1985, Primary Care: Concept, Evaluation and Policy 1992, Primary Care: Balancing Health Needs, Services and Technology 1998; over 150 scientific articles. *Address:* The Johns Hopkins Univ. School of Hygiene and Public Health, 624 N. Broadway, Baltimore, MD 21205, U.S.A. *Telephone:* (410) 955-9725. *Fax:* (410) 614-9046.

STARK, Sir Andrew Alexander Steel, K.C.M.G., C.V.O., M.A., D.L.; British diplomatist (retd.); b. 30 Dec. 1916, Fauldhouse, Scotland; s. of Thomas Bow Stark, and Barbara Black Stark; m. Rosemary Helen Oxley Parker 1944; three s. (one deceased); ed. Bathgate Acad. and Univ. of Edinburgh; British Army 1940–46; entered Diplomatic Service 1948, First Sec., British Embassy, Vienna 1951–53; Asst. Pvt. Sec. to Sec. of State 1953–56; First Sec., British Embassy, Belgrade 1956–58, Rome 1958–60; Counsellor, Foreign Office 1960–63; Counsellor British Embassy, Bonn 1964–68; Amb. British Mission to UN 1968; UN Under-Sec.-Gen. 1968–71; Amb. to Denmark 1971–76; Deputy Under-Sec. of State, FCO 1976–78; Dir. Maersk Co. Ltd. 1978–90 (Chair. 1978–87), Scandinavian Bank Ltd. 1978–88, Carlsberg Brewery Ltd. 1980–87; Adviser on European Affairs to Soc. of Motor Manufacturers and Traders Ltd. 1978–88; Chair. Cttee. The Festival of Scandinavian Arts 1992; Chair. Anglo-Danish Trade Advisory Bd. 1983–93, Anglo-Danish Soc. 1983–95, Hon. Pres. 1995–; Pro-Chancellor Univ. of Essex 1983–95, Chair. Council 1983–89, mem. 1978–; Hon. D. Univ. (Essex) 1990; Grosses Verdienstkreuz, Fed. Repub. of Germany 1965, Kt. Grand Cross, Order of the Dannebrog 1974. *Leisure interests:* reading, music, shooting, golf. *Address:* Fambridge Hall, White Notley, Witham, Essex, England. *Telephone:* (01376) 583117.

STARK, Nathan J., B.S., J.D.; American lawyer; b. 9 Nov. 1920, Minn.; s. of Harold and Anna Stark; m. Lucile Seidler 1943; three s. one d.; ed. U.S. Merchant Marine Acad. and Illinois Inst. of Tech., Chicago Kent Coll. of Law; Man., Vice-Pres. Rival Mfg. Co. 1952–58; Partner, Downey, Abrams, Stark & Sullivan, law firm 1958–59; Sr. Vice-Pres. Hallmark Cards Inc. 1959–74; Pres., Chair. of Bd., Crown Center Redevt. Corpn. 1970–74; Sr. Vice-Chancellor, Health Sciences, Univ. of Pittsburgh, also Prof. of Health Services Admin. 1974–84; Under-Sec., U.S. Dept. of Health and Human Services 1979–80; Sr. Vice-Chancellor Emer., Univ. of Pittsburgh 1984–, Vice-Pres. Univ. Health Center 1981–; partner, law firm of Kominers, Fort, Schlefer & Boyer 1984–; mem. Bd. Dirs., Alleghaney Foundation 1980–, Curry Foundation 1986–, Health Enterprise Int. 1990–, Accreditation Council for Continual Medical Educ. 1991; Pres. Nat. Acad. of Social Insurance, C.E.O. 1992–95; mem. Nat. Bd. of Medical Examiners, N.A.S. Inst. of Medicine; Hon. mem. American Hosp. Asscn.; Hon. Fellow, American Coll. of Hosp. Admins., American Acad. of Pediatrics; numerous awards including Citation of a Layman for Distinguished Service, American Medical Asscn.; Hon. LL.D. (Park Coll.) (Univ. of Missouri); Hon. D.Hum.Litt. (Scholl Coll. of Podiatric Medicine, Hahneman Univ.). *Publications:* numerous papers on health admin. and contribs. to professional journals. *Address:* 4343 Westover Place, NW, Washington, DC 20016, U.S.A.

STARK, Ray; American film producer; m. Fran Stark; ed. Rutgers Univ.; talent agent, Famous Artist Agency until 1957; co-founder, Seven Arts Production Co. 1957; independent film producer 1966–; Thalberg Award, Acad. of Motion Picture Arts and Sciences 1980. *Films include:* The World of Suzie Wong 1960, The Night of the Iguana 1964, Reflections in a Golden Eye 1967, Funny Girl 1968, The Owl and the Pussycat 1970, Fat City 1972, The Way We Were 1973, Funny Lady 1975, The Sunshine Boys 1975, Murder By Death 1976, Smokey and the Bandit 1977, The Goodbye Girl 1978, The Cheap Detective 1978, California Suite 1978, Chapter Two 1979, The Electric Horseman 1979, Seems Like Old Times 1980, Annie 1981, Nothing in Common 1986, Peggy Sue Got Married 1986, The Secret of My Success 1987, Biloxi Blues 1988, Steel Magnolias 1989, Barbarians at the Gate 1993 (TV), Mr Jones, Dr Jekyll and Ms. Hyde 1995, Mariette in Ecstasy 1996, The Gillian on Her 37th Birthday 1996, Harriet the Spy 1996, Random Hearts 1998. *Address:* Rastar Productions, Hepburn Building West, Sony Studios, 10202 W. Washington Blvd., Culver City, CA 90232, U.S.A.

STARKE, Heinz, DR.JUR.; German politician; b. 27 Feb. 1911, Schweidnitz; s. of Fritz Starke and Margarete Dorn; m. Madeleine Nuel 1958; ed. Univs. of Berlin, Breslau and Jena; worked for Econ. Admin. Body of British Zone of Occupation; fmr. Dir. Bayreuth Chamber of Commerce; mem. European Ass. 1958–79; mem. Bundestag 1953–80; Minister of Finance 1961–62; mem. Free Democratic Party until 1970, Christian Social Union 1970–. *Leisure interests:* history and history of the arts. *Address:* Europastrasse 6, 53175 Bonn, Germany. *Telephone:* Bonn 375049.

STARKER, Janos; American cellist and educator; b. 5 July 1924, Budapest, Hungary; s. of Margit and Sandor Starker; m. 1st Eva Uranyi 1944 (divorced); one d.; m. 2nd Rae Busch 1960; two d.; ed. Franz Liszt Acad. of Music, Budapest; solo cellist, Budapest Opera House and Philharmonic Orchestra 1945–46; solo cellist Dallas Symphony Orchestra 1948–49, Metropolitan Opera Orchestra 1949–53, Chicago Symphony Orchestra 1953–58; Resident cellist, Indiana Univ. 1958–, Prof. of Music 1961, now Distinguished Prof. of Cello; inventor of Starker bridge for orchestral string instruments; worldwide concert tours; mem. American Fed. of Musicians; Hon. mem. Royal Acad. of London; Hon. D.Mus. (Chicago Conservatory) 1961, (Cornell Coll.) 1978, (East West Univ.) 1982, (Williams Coll.) 1983, (Lawrence Univ.); Grand Prix du Disque 1948, George Washington Award 1972, Sanford Fellowship Award, Yale 1974, Herzl Award 1978, Ed Press Award 1983, Kodály Commemorative Medallion, New York 1983, Arturo Toscanini Award 1986, Indiana Univ. Tracy Sonneborn Award 1986, Indiana Govs. Award 1995, Medal of Paris 1995, Grammy Award 1998; Chevalier Ordre des Arts et des Lettres. *Publications:* Method 1964, Bach Suites 1971, Concerto Cadenzas, Schubert-Starker Sonatina, Bottermund-Starker Variations, Beethoven Sonatas, Beethoven Variations, Dvořák Concerto; numerous magazine articles. *Leisure interests:* writing, swimming and staying alive. *Address:* Department of Music, Indiana University, Bloomington, IN 47405, U.S.A.

STARKEY, David, PH.D., F.S.A., F.R.HIST.S.; British historian; b. 3 Jan. 1945, Kendal; s. of Robert Starkey and Elsie Lyon; ed. Kendal Grammar School, Fitzwilliam Coll, Cambridge; Research Fellow Fitzwilliam Coll., Cambridge 1970–72, Visiting Fellow 1998–; Lecturer in History, Dept. of Int. History, L.S.E. 1972–98; Visiting Vernon Prof. of Biography, Dartmouth Coll., N.H., U.S.A. 1987, 1989; British Council Specialist Visitor Australia 1989; contribs. to various newspapers; panellist Moral Maze (BBC Radio 4), presenter weekend show Talk Radio 1995–98; presenter/writer This Land of England (Channel 4 TV) 1985, Henry VIII (Channel 4 TV) 1998; mem. Editorial Bd. History Today 1980–, Commemorative Plaques Working Group, English Heritage 1993–; Pres. Soc. for Court Studies 1996–; Patron Tory Group for Homosexual Equality 1994–; Historical Adviser to Henry VIII Exhbn.; Nat. Maritime Museum, Greenwich 1991; Hon. Assoc. Rationalist Press Asscn. 1995–; Freeman Worshipful Co. of Barbers 1992. *Publications:* This Land of England (with David Souden) 1985, The Reign of Henry VIII: Personalities and Politics 1985, Revolution Reassessed: Revisions in the History of Tudor Government and Administration (ed. with Christopher Coleman) 1986, The English Court from the Wars of the Roses to the Civil War (ed.) 1987, Rivals in Power: the Lives and Letters of the Great Tudor Dynasties (ed.) 1990, Henry VIII: A European Court in England 1991, The Inventory of Henry VIII, vol. 1 (with Philip Ward) 1998; numerous articles in learned journals. *Leisure interests:* decorating, gardening. *Address:* c/o Speakers for Business, 1–2 Pudding Lane, London, EC3R 8AB, England. *Telephone:* 0171-929 5559. *Fax:* 0171-929 5558.

STARKOV, Vladislav Andreyevich; Russian journalist; b. 28 Feb. 1940, Tomsk; s. of Andrei Nikolayevich Starkov and Maria Mikhailovna Starkova; m. Yulia Fedorovna Kuznetsova; one d.; ed. Rostov State Univ.; researcher and computer engineer U.S.S.R. Meteorology Centre 1962–73; corresp. Radio Moscow 1973–76; ed. Znaniye Publishing House 1976–79, ed. Mezhdunarodnye Otnosheniya (journal) 1979–80; Ed.-in-Chief Argumenty i Fakty (weekly) 1980–95; Argumenty i Fakty Publrs. 1995–; R.S.F.S.R. People's Deputy 1990–93. *Leisure interests:* reading fiction, swimming. *Address:* AiF, Myasnitskaya str. 42, 101000 Moscow, Russia. *Telephone:* (095) 921 02 34 (Office).

STAROBINSKI, Jean, PH.D., M.D.; Swiss academic; b. 17 Nov. 1920, Geneva; s. of Aron Starobinski and Szayndla Frydman; m. Jacqueline H. Sirman 1954; three s.; ed. Univs. of Geneva and Lausanne; Asst. Prof. Johns Hopkins Univ. 1953–56, Prof. of French Literature, History of Ideas 1958–85; Pres.

Rencontres Int. de Genève 1965–; mem. Acad. Lincei, British Acad., American Acad. of Arts and Sciences, Deutsche Akad.; Assoc. mem. Acad. des Sciences Morales et Politiques (France); Hon. degrees from Univs. of Lille 1973, Brussels, Lausanne 1979, Chicago 1986, Columbia (New York) 1987, Montreal 1988, Strasbourg 1988, Neuchâtel 1990, Nantes 1992, Oslo 1994, Urbino 1995, Cluj 1995, ETH, Zürich 1998; Balzan Prize 1984, Monaco Prize 1988; Officier, Légion d'honneur. *Publications:* Rousseau 1958, The Invention of Liberty 1964, Words Upon Words 1971, 1789: The Emblems of Reason 1973, Montaigne In Motion 1983, Le Remède dans le Mal 1989, La Mélancolie au Miroir 1989, Largesse 1994. *Leisure interest:* music. *Address:* 12, Rue de Candolle, 1205 Geneva, Switzerland. *Telephone:* (22) 3209864.

STARODUBOV, Vladimir Ivanovich; Russian politician and surgeon; b. 17 May 1950, Kosobrodsk, Kurgan Region; ed. Sverdlovsk State Medical Inst.; surgeon, Head, Surgery Dept., Nizhny Tagil Hosp., Sverdlovsk Region 1973–77; asst., Chair of Surgery, Sverdlovsk State Inst. of Medicine 1977–80; Chief, Sverdlovsk town clinic 1980–81; instructor, Sverdlovsk Regional CP Cttee. 1981–87; Deputy Head, Sverdlovsk Regional Dept. of Public Health 1987–88; First Deputy Head, Main Dept. of Public Health, Sverdlovsk, Regional Soviet 1988–89; Head, Main Dept. of Treatment and Prophylactics, Ministry of Public Health R.S.F.S.R. 1989–90; Deputy Minister of Public Health Russian Fed. 1990–94; Head, Chair of Econs. of Man., Russian Medical Univ. 1994–96; Deputy Minister of Public Health and Medical Industry 1996–98, Minister of Public Health 1998–. *Address:* Ministry of Public Health, Rakhmanovsky per. 3, Neglinnaya str. 25, 101431 Moscow, Russia. *Telephone:* (095) 923 8404; (095) 927 2744 (Office).

STARODUBTSEV, Vasily Aleksandrovich; Russian politician; b. 25 Dec. 1931, Volovchik, Lipetsk Region; m.; one s. one d.; ed. All-Union Inst. of Agric.; Chair. Lenina Kolkhoz 1964–; Chair. Council of Kolkhozes Russian Fed., then Chair. U.S.S.R. Council of Agric. Workers 1966–; U.S.S.R. Peoples' Deputy 1989–; Chair. U.S.S.R. Farmers' Union 1990–; mem. State Cttee. for the State of Emergency coup d'état 1991; arrested, then released on amnesty; Dir. Agrarian Party; mem. Int. Acad. of Information Processes and Tech.; mem. Cen. Cttee. of CP of Russian Fed. 1997–; mem. Presidium, Co-ordination Council, People's Patriotic Union of Russia; Gov. of Tula Region; mem. Council of Feds. 1996; Hero of Socialist Labour, U.S.S.R. State Prize. *Leisure interest:* yoga. *Address:* Administrative Buildings, Tula, Russia. *Telephone:* (0872) 27 84 36 (Office).

STAROVOITOV, Gen. Aleksander Vladimirovich; Russian communications engineer; b. 18 Oct. 1940; m.; one s.; ed. Penza Polytech. Inst.; engineer, deputy head of workshop, sr. engineer, Head of lab., Head of div., Deputy Dir., Dir.-Gen., Kristall, Dir. Penza Research Electrotech. Inst. 1962–86; Deputy Head, Dept. of Govt. Telecommunications 1986–91; Chair. Cttee. on Govt. Telecommunications of Pres. Gorbachev 1991; Dir.-Gen. Fed. Agency of Govt. Telecommunications and Information of Pres. Yeltsin 1991–98; Chair. Co-ordination Council of C.I.S. on Security of System of Govt. Telecommunications; Constructor-Gen. of Integrated State System of Confidential Telecommunications of Russia; mem. Acad. of Eng. Sciences; mem. Acad. of Cryptography. *Address:* c/o FAPSI, Bolshoi Kiselny per. 4, 103031 Moscow, Russia.

STAROWIEYSKI, Franciszek; Polish surrealist painter and poster designer; b. 8 July 1930, Cracow; ed. Acad. of Fine Arts, Cracow and Warsaw; many one-man exhbns. including Museum of Modern Art, Houston, Tex. 1975, Museum of Modern Art, Seibul, Tokyo 1976, Museum of Modern Art, New York 1985, and in Poland, France, Italy and Switzerland; works shown at São Paulo Biennale 1973; Venice Biennale 1986; prizewinner all main int. poster festivals; works in many museums and pvt. collections in Poland and abroad; Visiting Prof. Berliner Hochschule der Künste, W. Berlin 1980; about 300 film and theatre posters; presenter own TV shows on art. *Leisure interest:* collecting Baroque art. *Address:* ul. Bernardyńska 23 m. 75, 02-901 Warsaw, Poland. *Telephone:* (22) 840 38 84.

STARR, Kenneth Winston, M.A.; American lawyer; b. 21 July 1946, Vernon, Texas; s. of W.D. Starr and Vannie M. (née Trimble) Starr; m. Alice J. Mendell 1970; one s. two d.; ed. George Washington, Brown and Duke Univs.; law clerk Court of Appeals (5th Circuit), Miami 1973–74, Supreme Court 1975–77; assoc. Gibson, Dunn & Crutcher, L.A. 1974–75, assoc. partner 1977–81; counsellor to Attorney-Gen. Justice Dept., Washington DC 1981–83, Solicitor Gen, 1989–93; judge Court of Appeals (D.C. Circuit) 1983; partner Kirkland & Ellis, Washington DC 1993–94; ind. counsel for Whitewater Investigation as well as any collateral matters arising out of any investigation of such matters including obstruction of justice or false statements 1994–; mem. several law orgs. *Publications:* contrib. articles to legal journals. *Address:* Kirkland and Ellis, 655 15th Street, Suite 1200, Washington, DC 2005, U.S.A.

STARR, Ringo (Richard Starkey), M.B.E.; British entertainer; b. 7 July 1940, Dingle, Liverpool; m. 1st Maureen Cox 1965 (divorced 1975); two s. one d.; m. 2nd Barbara Bach 1981; ed. Dingle Vale Secondary Modern School; plays drums; formerly an apprentice engineer; played with Rory Storme's Hurricanes 1959–62; joined The Beatles Aug. 1962; appeared with The Beatles in the following activities: performances in Hamburg 1962; toured Scotland, Sweden, U.K. 1963, Paris, Denmark, Hong Kong, Australia, New Zealand, U.S.A., Canada 1964, France, Italy, Spain, U.S.A. 1965, Canada, Spain, Philippines, U.S.A. 1966; attended Transcendental Meditation Course at Maharishi's Acad., Rishikesh, India Feb. 1968; formed Apple Corps Ltd., parent org. of The Beatles Group of Companies 1968; following break-up of group, now records solo. *Recordings by the Beatles include:* Please, Please Me 1963, With the Beatles 1963, A Hard Day's Night 1964, Beatles for Sale 1965, Help! 1965, Rubber Soul 1966, Revolver 1966, Sergeant Pepper's Lonely Hearts Club Band 1967, The Beatles (White Album) 1968, Yellow Submarine 1969, Abbey Road 1969, Let It Be 1970, Anthology I 1995, Anthology II 1996. *Films by The Beatles:* A Hard Day's Night 1964, Help! 1965, Yellow Submarine (animated colour cartoon film) 1968, Let it Be 1970; TV film Magical Mystery Tour 1967. *Individual appearances in films:* Candy 1968, The Magic Christian 1969, 200 Motels 1971, Blindman 1971, That'll be the Day 1973, Born to Boogie (also directed and produced) 1974, Son of Dracula (also produced) 1975, Lisztomania 1975, Ringo Stars 1976, Caveman 1981, The Cooler 1982, Give My Regards to Broad Street 1984.

STARZEWSKI, Tomasz; Polish fashion designer; b. 1961; ed. St. Martin's School of Art, London; collections shown around the world as part of the British Collections, a group he founded in 1987; opened House of Tomasz Starzewski, London 1991. *Address:* Tomasz Starzewski, 15–17 Pont Street, London, SW1X 9EH, England. *Telephone:* 0171-235 4526.

STASI, Bernard, L. EN D.; French politician; b. 4 July 1930, Reims; s. of Mario and Mercédès (née Camps) Stasi; m. Danielle Beaugier 1979; ed. Institut d'Etudes Politiques, Paris and Ecole Nat. d'Admin.; attached to the Cabinet of the Pres. of the Nat. Assembly 1955; served in army 1955–57; Civil Admin., Ministry of Interior 1959; Chef de Cabinet to the Prefect of Algiers 1959–60; Head of Section, Directorate-Gen. of Political Affairs and Territorial Admin., Ministry of Interior 1960–62; Tech. Adviser, Cabinet of the Sec. of State for Youth and Sports 1963–65; Directeur de Cabinet to the Sec. of Overseas Depts. 1966–68; Deputy for Marne, Nat. Ass. 1968–93; mem. European Parl. 1994–98; charged with missions to Israel, G.B., Cuba and Chile; Mayor of Epernay 1970–77, 1983–; Médiateur de la République (Ombudsman) 1998–; Vice-Pres. Centre Démocratie et Progrès 1969–75, Centre des Démocrates Sociaux 1976–84 (first Vice-Pres. 1984); Minister for Overseas Depts. and Territories 1973–74; Fed. Sec. Féd. des Réformateurs 1975–; mem. Regional Council of Champagne-Ardenne 1976–88, Pres. 1981–88; Pres. Fédération française de course d'orientation 1970–88; Pres. Nat. Council for Regional Econs. and Productivity 1986–88; Founder, Groupe d'études parlementaires pour l'aménagement rural 1970; Vice-Pres. Co-operative and Devt. Comm., Christian Democrat Int. 1993–; mem. Bd. of Dirs. Association des Maires de France; mem. various municipal orgs.; Chevalier, Légion d'honneur, Officier de Réserve, Chevalier Ordre nat. du Mérite, Officier du Mérite sportif, Grand' Croix de l'Ordre du Croissant vert (Comoros), Grand' Croix de l'Ordre de l'Etoile d'Anjouan. *Publication:* Le Piège (with J. P. Soisson and O. Stirn) 1973, Vie associative et démocratie nouvelle 1979, l'Immigration: une chance pour la France 1984, La Politique au coeur 1993. *Leisure interests:* football, tennis, skiing, sailing. *Address:* Hôtel de Ville, 51200 Epernay; 53 avenue d'Iéna, 75016 Paris, France. *Telephone:* 01.45.02.72.72 (Paris).

STASSE, François; French civil servant and economist; b. 11 Jan. 1948, Neuilly-sur-Seine; s. of Roger Stasse and Christiane (née Deveaux) Stasse; m. Nathalie Duhamel 1978; ed. Inst. of Political Studies, Paris; with Ministry of Industry 1972–73; joined Gen. Bd. of Planning 1974, Dir. Commr.'s Office 1979–81; Tech. Adviser to Pres. of Rep. on Econs. and Finance 1981–84; Counsel Council of State 1984, Sr. mem. 1996; Dir. State Hosp. Paris 1989–93; mem. consultative cttee. on future of state medical provision 1998–; Dir.-Gen. Bibliothèque nationale de France 1998–. *Publications include:* La Morale de l'histoire 1994. *Address:* Conseil d'État, place du Palais Royal, 75100 Paris; Bibliothèque nationale de France, 11 quai François Mauriac, 75013 Paris, France.

STASSINOPOULOS, Michael; Greek politician, university professor and judge; b. 27 July 1903, Calamata; s. of Demetrios Stassinopoulos and Catherine Scopetou; m. Stamatia Ritsoni 1942; one d.; ed. Athens Univ.; Lecturer in Admin. Law, Athens Univ. 1937–68; Prof. Admin. Law, High School of Political Sciences, Athens 1939–68, Dean 1951–58; State Council Adviser 1943–58; Political Adviser to Dodecanese Gov. 1947; Chair. Cttee. for the Civil Servants Code 1948; Minister of the Press and subsequently Minister of Labour 1952; Chair. Hellenic Nat. Broadcasting Inst. Admin. Bd. 1953; Chair. Nat. Opera Admin. Bd. 1953–63; Minister of the Press 1958; Vice-Pres. State Council 1963, Pres. 1966–69; M.P. Nov.–Dec. 1974; Pres. of Greece Dec. 1974–June 1975; Judge ad hoc, Int. Court of Justice, The Hague 1976–78; mem. Acad. of Athens 1968, Pres. 1978; Chief Justice until 1974; Dr. h.c. (Univ. of Bordeaux) 1957, (Univ. of Paris) 1974, Order of St. George (First Class). *Publications:* The States' Civil Responsibility 1949, Administrative Acts Law 1950 (in French), Civil Service Laws 1951, Administrative Disputes Laws 1953, Principles of Administrative Law 1954, Principles of Public Finance 1956, Traité des actes administratifs (in French), Poems 1949, The Land of the Blue Lakes 1950, Harmonia (poems) 1956, Thought and Life (essays) 1970, The Wolf's Law (essays) 1972, Le droit de la défense (in French) 1977, Political History of Greece 1978, Two Seasons (poems) 1979. *Leisure interests:* poetry, cinema, gardening. *Address:* Taygetou Street 7, 154 52 Psichicon, Athens, Greece. *Telephone:* 6713-197.

STAUDINGER, Ulrich; German publisher; b. 30 May 1935, Berlin; s. of Wilhelm Staudinger and Elfriede Poth; m. Irmengard Ehrenwirth 1960 (died 1989); one s. two d.; ed. Volksschule and Realgymnasium; publishing training 1954–57; Lingenbrinck Barsortiment, Hamburg 1957–58; Publicity and

Sales, Ensslin & Laiblin, Jugendbuchverlag, Reutlingen 1958–59; Production, Carl Hanser Verlag, Munich 1959–60; Dawson & Sons, London 1960; Franz Ehrenwirth Verlag, Munich 1960; partner, Ehrenwirth Verlag, Munich 1964; responsible for purchase of Franz Schneekluth Verlag KG, Darmstadt by Ehrenwirth Verlag 1967 and following purchase of all parts of Franz Schneekluth Verlag the cos. were amalgamated into a single firm in 1976; purchased parts of Philosophia Verlag G.m.b.H., Düsseldorf 1978; various professional appts. *Address:* Franz Schneekluth Verlag, Widenmayerstrasse 34, 80538 Munich (Office); Asgardstrasse 34, 8000 Munich 81, Germany (Home). *Telephone:* 089/22 13 91 (Office); 089/98 63 67 (Home).

STAUNTON, Imelda Mary Philomena Bernadette; British actress; b. 9 Jan. 1956; d. of Joseph Staunton and Bridie McNicholas; m. Jim Carter 1983; one d.; ed. La Sainte Union Convent, Highgate, London, R.A.D.A.; repertory Exeter, Nottingham, York 1976–81. *Stage appearances include:* Guys and Dolls 1982, 1996, Beggar's Opera 1985, She Stoops to Conquer, Chorus of Disapproval 1985 (Olivier Award, Best Supporting Actress), The Corn is Green 1985, Fair Maid of the West 1986, Wizard of Oz 1986, Comrades 1987, Uncle Vanya 1988, Into the Woods 1990, Phoenix 1990 (Olivier Award, Best Actress in a Musical). *Television appearances include:* The Singing Detective 1986, Yellowbacks 1990, Sleeping Life, Roots, Up the Garden Path 1990, Antonia and Jane. *Film appearances include:* Peter's Friends 1992, Much Ado About Nothing 1993, Deadly Advice 1994, Sense and Sensibility, Twelfth Night, Remember Me 1996, Shakespeare in Love 1998. *Address:* c/o Peters Fraser and Dunlop, 503/4 The Chambers, Chelsea Harbour, London, SW10 0XF, England.

STAVROPOULOS, William S., PH.D.; American chemical company executive; m. Linda Stavropoulos; one s. one d.; ed. Fordham Univ., Univ. of Washington; research chemist, Pharmaceutical Research Div., Dow Chemical Co. 1967, Diagnostics Product Research Div. 1970, Research Man. 1973, Diagnostic Products Business Man. 1976, Business Man. for polyolefins 1977, Dir. of Marketing, Dow U.S.A. Plastics Dept. 1979, Commercial Vice-Pres. Dow Latin America 1980, Pres. 1984, Commercial Vice-Pres. Dow U.S.A., Basics and Hydrocarbons 1985, Group Vice-Pres. 1987, Pres. Dow U.S.A. 1990, Vice-Pres. The Dow Chemical Co. 1990, Sr. Vice-Pres. 1991, Pres., C.O.O. 1993–, C.E.O. 1995–; mem. Bd. of Dirs. Dow Corning Corpn. 1991, Marion Merrell Dow Inc. 1992, Dowell Schlumberger 1992, Chemical Bank; Trustees Midland Community Center, and other bodies. *Address:* The Dow Chemical Company, 2030 Willard H, Dow Centre, Midland, MI 48674, U.S.A.

STCHIN GOWA; Chinese actress; b. 2 Nov. 1949, Guangzhou City; with Inner Mongolia Song and Dance Ensemble 1965–79; film actress, First August Film Studio 1981–; winner Golden Rooster Award, Hundred Flowers. *Films include:* Luotuo Xiangzi 1981 (Best Actress Award in China 1982), Fleeting Time 1984 (Best Actress Award in Hong Kong), Xianghun Girl 1992 (Best Film in Berlin Film Festival). *Address:* Room 307, Building 2, Panjiapo Hutong, Beijing 100020, People's Republic of China.

STEAD, Christian Karlson (C.K.), C.B.E., PH.D., LITT.D., F.R.S.L.; New Zealand writer and professor of English (retd.); b. 17 Oct. 1932, Auckland; s. of James Walter Ambrose Stead and Olive Ethel Stead (née Karlson); m. Kathleen Elizabeth Roberts 1955; one s. two d.; ed. Mt. Albert Grammar School, Auckland Univ. Coll. and Auckland Teachers' Coll.; lecturer in English Univ. of New England, N.S.W., Australia 1956–57; Michael Hiatt Baker Scholar Univ. of Bristol 1957–59; lecturer, Sr. Lecturer, Assoc. Prof. Univ. of Auckland 1960–67, Prof. of English 1967–86, Prof. Emer. 1986–; prof., writer 1986–; Nuffield Fellow, Univ. of London 1965, Hon. Fellow 1977, Sr. Visiting Fellow St. John's Coll., Oxford 1996–97; Katherine Mansfield Prize 1960, New Zealand Book Award for Poetry 1972, 1986, New Zealand Book Award for Fiction 1985, 1995. *Publications:* seven novels including All Visitors Ashore, The Death of the Body, The Singing Whahapapa, nine collections of poems including Straw into Gold: Poems New and Selected, two collections of short stories, four works of literary criticism including The New Poetic: Yeats and Eliot, In the Glass Case: Essays on New Zealand Literature, (Ed.) Letters and Journals of Katherine Mansfield, (Ed.) The Faber Book of Contemporary South Pacific Stories. *Address:* 37 Tohunga Crescent, Parnell, Auckland, 1001, New Zealand. *Telephone:* (649) 3799420. *Fax:* (649) 3799420.

STEAD, Rev. (George) Christopher, LITT.D., F.B.A.; British professor of divinity (retd.); b. 9 April 1913, Wimbledon; s. of Francis B. Stead and Rachel E. Stead (née Bell); m. D. Elizabeth Odom 1958; two s. one d.; ed. Marlborough Coll., King's Coll., Cambridge, New Coll., Oxford and Cuddesdon Coll., Oxford; ordained 1938; Curate, St. John's Newcastle-upon-Tyne 1939; Fellow and Lecturer in Divinity, King's Coll., Cambridge 1938–48; Asst. Master, Eton Coll. 1940–44; Fellow and Chaplain, Keble Coll., Oxford 1949–71; Ely Prof. of Divinity, Cambridge and Canon Residentiary of Ely Cathedral 1971–80, Canon Emer. 1981–; Fellow, King's Coll., Cambridge 1971–85, Professorial Fellow 1971–80; Emer. Fellow, Keble Coll., Oxford 1981–. *Publications:* Divine Substance 1977, Substance and Illusion in the Christian Fathers 1985, Philosophie und Theologie I, Alte Kirche 1990, Philosophy in Christian Antiquity 1994; contrib. to books, encyclopaedias, journals, etc. *Leisure interests:* walking, sailing, music. *Address:* 13 Station Road, Haddenham, Ely, Cambs., England. *Telephone:* (01353) 740575.

STEADMAN, Alison; British actress; b. 26 Aug. 1946, Liverpool; d. of George Percival Steadman and the late Margorie Evans; m. Mike Leigh (q.v.); two s.; ed. drama school, Loughton, Essex; began career in repertory theatre in Lincoln, Bolton, Liverpool, Worcester and Nottingham; Hon. M.A. (Univ. of E. London); stage appearances include Sandy in The Prime of Miss Jean Brodie, Beverley in Abigail's Party, Mae-Sister Woman in Cat on a Hot Tin Roof, Nat. Theatre (NT) 1988, Mari Hoff in The Rise and Fall of Little Voice, Nat. Theatre, David Edgar's Maydays, RSC, Tartuffe, RSC, Joking Apart, Kafka's Dick, Royal Court, Marvin's Room 1993, The Plotters of Cabbage Patch Corner, The Provok'd Wife, Old Vic 1997; TV appearances in Z Cars, Hard Labour, Abigail's Party, Nuts in May, The Singing Detective, Virtuoso, Newshounds, The Short and Curlies, Gone to Seed, Selling Hitler, Pride and Prejudice, The Wimbledon Poisoner, Karaoke, No Bananas, The Missing Postman. *Films:* Champions, Number One, P'Tang Kipperbang, A Private Function, Wilt, Shirley Valentine, Life is Sweet, Blame It On the Bellboy. *Address:* c/o Peters, Fraser and Dunlop, The Chambers, Chelsea Harbour, London, SW10 0XF, England. *Telephone:* 0171-352 4446. *Fax:* 0171-352 7356.

STEADMAN, Ralph Idris; British cartoonist, writer and illustrator; b. 15 May 1936; s. of Raphael Steadman and Gwendoline Steadman; m. 1st Sheila Thwaite 1959 (divorced 1971); two s. two d.; m. 2nd Anna Deverson 1972; one d.; ed. London School of Printing and Graphic Arts; with de Havilland Aircraft Co. 1952; Cartoonist Kemsley (Thomson) Newspapers 1956–59; freelance for Punch, Private Eye, Daily Telegraph during 1960s; political cartoonist New Statesman 1978–80; retrospective exhbns.: Nat. Theatre 1977, Royal Festival Hall 1984, Wilhelm Busch Museum, Hanover 1988, One on One Gallery, Denver 1997; designed set of stamps Halley's Comet 1986; Hon. D. Litt. (Kent) 1995; Designers and Art Dirs. Asscn. Gold Award 1977, Silver Award 1977. *Publications:* Jelly Book 1968, Still Life with Raspberry: collected drawings 1969, The Little Red Computer 1970, Dogs Bodies 1971, Bumper to Bumper Book 1973, Two Donkeys and the Bridge 1974, Flowers for the Moon 1974, The Watchdog and the Lazy Dog 1974, America: drawings 1975, America: collected drawings 1977 (r.e. Scar Strangled Banger 1987), I, Leonardo 1983, Between the Eyes 1984, Paranoids 1986, The Grapes of Ralph 1992, Teddy Where Are You? 1994; *written and illustrated:* Sigmund Freud 1979, A Leg in the Wind and Other Canine Curses 1982, That's My Dad 1986, The Big I Am 1988, No Room to Swing a Cat 1989, Near the Bone 1990, Tales of Weirrd 1990, Still Life with Bottle, Whisky According to Ralph Steadman; *illustrator:* many books from 1961, including Friendship 1990 (in aid of John McCarthy), Adrian Mitchell, Heart on the Left, Poems 1953–84 1997. *Leisure interests:* gardening, sheep husbandry, fishing, guitar, trumpet.

STEEDS, John Wickham, PH.D., F.R.S., F.INST.P.; British professor of electron microscopy; b. 9 Feb. 1940, London; s. of John Henry William Steeds and Ethel Amelia Steeds, née Tyler; m. Diana Mary Kettlewell 1969; two d.; ed. Haberdashers' Aske's School, Univ. Coll. London, Cambridge Univ.; Mullard Research Fellow, Selwyn Coll. Cambridge 1964–67; Lecturer, Physics Dept., Univ. of Bristol 1967–77, Reader 1977–85, Prof. of Electron Microscopy 1985–; fmr. mem. Council European Pole Univ. of Lille; Chair. Electron Diffraction Comm. of Int. Union of Crystallography, Emersons Innovations Ltd.; Holweck Medal (Soc. Française de Physique and Inst. of Physics) 1996. *Publications:* Introduction to Anistropic Elasticity Theory of Dislocations 1973, Electron Diffraction of Phases in Alloys (with J. F. Mansfield) 1984, Thin Film Diamond (co-ed.) 1994. *Leisure interests:* tennis, cycling. *Address:* Physics Department, University of Bristol, Bristol, BS8 1TL (Office); 21 Canynge Square, Clifton, Bristol, BS8 3LA, England (Home). *Telephone:* (0117) 9288730 (Office); (0117) 9732183 (Home).

STEEL, Danielle (Danielle Fernande Schüelein-Steel); American writer; b. 14 Aug. 1950, New York; d. of John Steel and Norma (Stone) Schüelein-Steel; m. 2nd Bill Toth 1977; m. 3rd John A. Traina Jr.; four s. five d.; ed. Lycée Français, Parsons School of Design, New York, Univ. of New York; worked as public relations and advertising exec., Manhattan, New York; published first novel 1973, then wrote advertising copy, and poems for women's magazines; wrote first bestseller, The Promise 1979. *Publications:* Going Home 1973, Passion's Promise 1977, Now and Forever 1978, Season of Passion 1978, The Promise 1979, Summer's End 1980, To Love Again 1981, Palomino 1981, Loving 1981, Remembrance 1981, A Perfect Stranger 1982, Once in a Lifetime 1982, Crossings 1982, Thurston House 1983, Full Circle 1984, Having a Baby (Contrib., non-fiction) 1984, Family Album 1985, Wanderlust 1986, Fine Things 1987, Kaleidoscope 1987, Zoya 1988, Star 1989, Daddy 1989, Heartbeat 1991, Message from Nam 1991, No Greater Love 1991, Jewels 1992, Mixed Blessings 1992, Vanished 1993, Accident 1994, The Gift 1994, Wings 1995, Lightning 1995, Five Days in Paris 1995, Malice 1995, Silent Honor 1996, The Ranch 1996, The Ghost 1997, Special Delivery 1997, The Ranch 1998, The Long Road Home 1998, The Klone and I 1998, Mirror Image 1998; eight children's books, one book of poetry. *Leisure interest:* my children. *Address:* c/o Dell Publishing, 1540 Broadway, New York, NY 10036 (Office); P.O. Box 1637, New York, NY 10156, U.S.A. (Home).

STEEL, Sir David (Edward Charles), Kt., D.S.O., M.C., T.D.; British company director; b. 29 Nov. 1916; s. of late Gerald Arthur Steel; m. Ann Price 1956 (died 1997); one s. two d.; ed. Rugby School and Univ. Coll., Oxford; Officer, Q.R. Lancers, serving in France, the Middle East, N. Africa and Italy 1940–45; admitted as Solicitor 1948; worked for Linklaters and Paines 1948–50; in Legal Dept., British Petroleum Co. Ltd. 1950–56; Pres. British Petroleum (N. America) Ltd. 1959–61, Regional Co-ordinator, Western Hemisphere, B.P. Co. Ltd. 1961–62; Man. Dir. Kuwait Oil Co. Ltd. 1962–65, Dir. 1965–; a Man. Dir. British Petroleum Co. Ltd. 1965–72, Deputy Chair. 1972–75, Chair. 1975–81; Chair. B.P. Oil 1976–77; Dir. Bank of England 1978–84, Kleinwort, Benson, Lonsdale 1985–92; Trustee, The Economist 1979–95; Chair. Wellcome Trust 1982–89; Deputy Chair. Governing Body, Rugby School 1982, Chair. 1984–88; Pres. London Chamber of Commerce and Industry 1982–85; Hon. Fellow, Univ. Coll., Oxford 1982; Hon. D.C.L. (City) 1983; Hon. D.Univ. (Heriot-Watt Univ.) 1996. *Address:* c/o 22 Hill Street, London, W1X 7FU, England.

STEEL OF AIKWOOD, Baron (Life Peer), cr. 1997, of Ettrick Forest in the Scottish Borders; **David Martin Scott Steel,** K.B.E., P.C., M.A., LL.B.; British (Scottish) politician, journalist and broadcaster; b. 31 March 1938, Kirkcaldy; s. of Very Rev. Dr. David Steel; m. Judith Mary MacGregor 1962; two s. one d.; ed. Prince of Wales School, Nairobi, Kenya, George Watson's Coll. and Edinburgh Univ.; Pres. Edin. Univ. Liberals 1959; mem. Students' Rep. Council 1960; Asst. Sec., Scottish Liberal Party 1962–64; M.P. for Roxburgh, Selkirk and Peebles 1965–83, for Tweeddale, Ettrick and Lauderdale 1983–97; Scottish Liberal Whip 1967–70, Liberal Chief Whip 1970–75; Leader of Liberal Party 1976–88; co-founder Social and Liberal Democrats 1988; Vice-Pres. Liberal Int. 1978–93, Pres. 1994–96; mem. Parl. del. to UN Gen. Ass. 1967; fmr. Liberal spokesman on Commonwealth Affairs; Sponsor, Pvt. Member's Bill to reform law on abortion 1966–67; Pres. Anti-Apartheid Movement of U.K. 1966–69; Chair. Shelter, Scotland 1969–73, Countryside Movt. 1995–97; BBC TV Interviewer in Scotland 1964–65; Presenter of weekly religious programme for Scottish TV 1966–67, for Granada 1969, for BBC 1971–76; Dir. Border T.V. 1991–; Rector Univ. of Edin. 1982–85; Chubb Fellow, Yale Univ., U.S.A. 1987; D.L. Ettrick and Lauderdale and Roxburghshire; Hon. Dr. (Stirling) 1991, Heriot Watt 1996; Hon. D.Litt. (Buckingham) 1994; Hon. LL.D. (Edin.) 1997; Freedom of Tweeddale 1989, of Ettrick and Lauderdale 1990; Bronze Medal London-Cape Town Rally 1998. *Publications:* Boost for the Borders 1964, No Entry 1969, A House Divided 1980, Border Country 1985, Partners in One Nation 1985, The Time Has Come (with David Owen) 1987, Mary Stuart's Scotland (with Judy Steel) 1987, Against Goliath 1989. *Leisure interests:* angling, classic cars. *Address:* House of Lords, London, SW1A 0PW, England; Aikwood Tower, Ettrick Bridge, Selkirkshire, Scotland (Home).

STEELE, John Hyslop, D.SC., F.R.S., F.R.S.E.; British scientist; b. 15 Nov. 1926, Edinburgh, Scotland; s. of Adam Steele and Annie Hyslop Steele; m. Margaret Evelyn Travis 1956; one s.; ed. George Watson's Boys' Coll., Edin., Univ. Coll., Univ. of London; Marine Lab., Aberdeen, Scotland 1951–77, Marine Scientist 1951–66, Sr. Prin. Scientific Officer 1966–73, Dir. Dept. 1973–77; Dir. Woods Hole Oceanographic Inst., Mass. 1977–89, Pres. 1986–91, Pres. Emer. 1991–; Dir. Exxon Corpn. 1989–97; Trustee Robert Wood Johnson Foundation 1990–; mem. Nat. Geographic Soc. Cttee. Research and Exploration 1987–; Fellow American Acad. of Arts and Sciences 1980, A.A.A.S. 1987; Hon. Prof. Univ. of Aberdeen 1993–; Agassiz Medal (N.A.S.) 1973. *Publications:* Structure of Marine Ecosystems 1974, over 100 articles in oceanographic and ecological journals. *Leisure interest:* sailing. *Address:* Woods Hole Oceanographic Institution, Woods Hole, MA 02543, U.S.A. *Telephone:* (508) 548-1400. *Fax:* (508) 457-2184.

STEELE, John Roderic, C.B., M.A., F.C.I.T.; British fmr. civil servant and shipping company executive; b. 22 Feb. 1929, Wakefield; s. of late Harold Graham Steele and Doris (née Hall) Steele; m. Margaret Marie Stevens 1956; two s. two d.; ed. Queen Elizabeth Grammar School, Wakefield, Queen's Coll., Oxford; Asst. Prin., Ministry of Civil Aviation 1951–54, Pvt. Sec. to Parl. Sec. 1954–57; Prin., Rd. Transport Div. 1957–60, Sea Transport 1960–62, Shipping Policy 1962–64; Asst. Sec. (Shipping Policy), Bd. of Trade 1964–67; Counsellor (Shipping), British Embassy, Washington 1967–71; Asst. Sec. (Civil Aviation Div.), Dept. of Trade and Industry 1971–73, Under-Sec., Space Div. 1973–74, Shipping Policy Div. 1974–75, Gen. Div., Dept. of Trade 1975–76, Deputy Sec. 1976–80; Deputy Sec., Dept. of Industry 1980–81; Dir.-Gen. for Transport, Comm. of the European Communities 1981–86; Transport Consultant 1986–; Chair. P & O European Transport Service 1989–95; Dir. P & O Container Line 1987–96, P & O Steam Navigation Co. 1992–; mem. Dover Harbour Bd. 1990–92. *Leisure interests:* cricket, tennis, opera. *Address:* 4 Wickham Court, Stapleton, Bristol, BS16 1DQ, England; 30 Square Ambiorix, Bte 30, 1000 Brussels, Belgium.

STEELE, Tommy, O.B.E.; British actor and singer; b. (as Thomas Hicks) 17 Dec. 1936, Bermondsey, London; s. of Thomas Walter Hicks and Elizabeth Ellen Bennett; m. Ann Donoughue 1960; one d.; ed. Bacon's School for Boys, Bermondsey; entered Merchant Navy 1952; first stage appearance Empire Theatre, Sunderland 1956, London début 1957; roles include Buttons (Cinderella) London 1958/59, Tony Lumpkin (She Stoops to Conquer) 1960, Arthur Kipps (Half A Sixpence) 1963/64, New York 1965/66, Truffaldino (The Servant of Two Masters) 1968, title role in Hans Andersen, London 1974/75, 1977/78, 1981, Don Lockwood (Singin' in the Rain), London 1983–85, 1989 (also dir.), Some Like it Hot 1991 (also dir.), What a Show! 1995; film debut in Kill Me Tomorrow 1956; sculpted tribute to the Beatles' Eleanor Rigby 1982. *Films include:* The Tommy Steele Story, The Duke Wore Jeans 1957, Tommy the Toreador 1959, Light Up the Sky 1963, Its All Happening 1966, The Happiest Millionaire 1967, Half A Sixpence, Finian's Rainbow 1968, Where's Jack 1971; TV début in Off the Record 1956, cabaret début, Caesar's Palace, Las Vegas 1974; composed and recorded musical autobiog. My Life, My Song 1974. *Live performances:* An Evening with Tommy Steele 1979, Tommy Steele in Concert 1998; Quincy's Quest (TV) 1979. *Publications:* Hans Andersen (co-author, stage version), Quincy 1981, The Final Run 1983. *Leisure interests:* squash, painting, sculpture. *Address:* c/o Laurie Mansfield, International Artistes, 235 Regent Street, London, W1R 8AX, England. *Telephone:* 0171-439 8401. *Fax:* 0171-409 2070.

STEELE-PERKINS, Christopher Horace, B.SC.; British photographer; b. 28 July 1947, Burma; s. of Alfred Steele-Perkins and Mary Lloyd; m. Jacqueline de Gier 1984; two s.; ed. Christ's Hospital, Horsham, Sussex, Univ. of Newcastle; mem. Exit Group, London 1974–82; Assoc. Viva Agency, Paris 1976–79; mem. Photography Cttee., Arts Council of G.B. 1977–79; mem. Magnum Photos 1983–, Pres. 1996–98; TV Films: Dying for Publicity 1993, Afghan Taliban 1995; World Press Oskar Barnack 1988, Tom Hopkinson Award for Photo-journalism 1988, Robert Capa Gold Medal 1989, Cooperative Award, One World Award (both for Film Dying for Publicity) 1994, Naçion-Premier Photojournalism Award. *Publications:* The Teds 1979, About 70 Photographs 1980, Survival Programmes 1982, Beirut: Frontline Story 1982, The Pleasure Principle 1989, St. Thomas' Hospital 1992. *Leisure interests:* boxing, chess, photography, film, music, literature. *Address:* 5 St. John's Buildings, Canterbury Crescent, London, SW9 7QB, *Telephone:* 0171-733 9406.

STEENBURGEN, Mary; American film actress; b. 1953, Newport, Ariz.; m. 1st Malcolm McDowell (q.v.) 1980 (divorced); one s. one d.; m. 2nd Ted Danson (q.v.) 1995; ed. Neighborhood Playhouse. *Films include:* Goin' South 1978, Time After Time 1979, Melvin and Howard 1980 (Acad. Award for Best Supporting Actress), Ragtime 1981, A Midsummer Night's Sex Comedy 1982, Romantic Comedy 1983, Cross Creek 1983, Sanford Meisner—The Theatre's Best Kept Secret 1984, One Magic Christmas 1985, Dead of Winter 1987, End of the Line 1987 (also exec. producer), The Whales of August 1987, The Attic: The Hiding of Anne Frank 1988, Parenthood 1989, Back to the Future Part III 1989, Miss Firecracker 1989, The Long Walk Home 1990, The Butcher's Wife 1991, What's Eating Gilbert Grape 1993, Philadelphia 1993, Pontiac Moon 1994, Clifford 1994, It Runs in the Family 1994, Pontiac Moon, My Family, Powder, The Grass Harp, Nixon. *Theatre appearances include:* Holiday (Old Vic, London) 1987, Candida (Broadway) 1993. *Address:* c/o Ames Cushing, William Morris Agency Inc., 151 S. El Camino Drive, Beverly Hills, CA 90212, U.S.A.

STEENSBERG, Axel, DR.PHIL.; Danish academic; b. 1 June 1906, Sinding; s. of Jens Steensberg and Maren Steensberg; m. Frida Sillesen 1934 (died 1964); two s. one d.; working farmer until 1928; Asst. to Gudmund Hatt surveying prehistoric fields and excavating villages of the Iron Age 1934–37; Head, Third Dept. Nat. Museum 1946–59; Chair. Int. Secr. for Research on History of Agricultural Implements 1954–; Prof. of Material Culture, Copenhagen 1959–70; consultant, UNESCO, S. Pacific 1970–71; Ed. Tools and Tillage 1968–; Patron Techniques et Culture 1982–; excavations of deserted Danish villages 1937–82; research in Papua New Guinea, 1968, 1971, 1975, 1983; Hon. mem. Gustav Acad. Uppsala, Asscn. Int. des Musées d'Agriculture, Ethnographic Soc. Budapest; Hon. Vice-Pres. Medieval Settlement Research Group, Cambridge, U.K.; Dr. Agr. h.c.; Culture Prize (Nordic Agrarian Cttee.) 1993. *Publications include:* Ancient Harvesting Implements 1943, Atlas of Borup Fields 1968, Store Valby I-III 1974, Draved, an experiment in Stone Age agriculture, burning, sowing and harvesting 1979, New Guinea Gardens 1980, Borup A.D. 700-1400 I-II 1983, Man the Manipulator 1986, Hard Grains, Irrigation, Numerals and Script in the Rise of Civilizations 1989, Danish Peasant Furniture I–II 1989 (with Grith Lerche), Fire Clearance Husbandry: Traditional Techniques Throughout the World 1993. *Address:* Caeciliavej 30, Copenhagen-Valby, Denmark.

STEENSGAARD, Niels Palle, D.PHIL.; Danish academic; b. 7 March, 1932, Rødovre; s. of Knud Steensgaard and Kirstine (née Knop) Steensgaard; m. Illa Frilis 1954; two d.; ed. Univ. of Copenhagen, S.O.A.S., London; Assoc. Prof. Inst. of History, Univ. of Copenhagen 1962, Dean, Faculty of Humanities 1974–76, Prof. 1977–; mem. Danish Research Council for the Humanities 1980–88, Chair. 1985–87; mem. Nordic Cttee. Humanities Research Councils 1983–88, Chair. 1985–87; Danish Rep., Standing Cttee. for the Humanities, European Science Foundation 1983–88; mem. Swedish Council for Research in the Humanities and Social Sciences 1992–96; Chair. Nat. Cttee. of Danish Historians 1989; mem. Royal Danish Acad. of Sciences and Letters 1982, Acad. Europaea 1989, Royal Historical Soc. 1997. *Publications:* The Asian Trade Revolution of the Seventeenth Century 1973, Verden På Opdagelsernes tid 1984, Verdensmarked og kulturmøter 1985. *Leisure interests:* losing my way in large books or towns. *Address:* Institute of History, University of Copenhagen, Njalsgade 102, Copenhagen 2300 S (Office); Lemnosvej 19, Copenhagen 2300 S, Denmark (Home).

ŞTEFĂNESCU, I. Ştefan, PH.D.; Romanian historian; b. 24 May 1929, Goicea, Dolj Co.; s. of Ion and Dumitra Ştefănescu; m. Teodora Ştefănescu 1958; one s. one d.; ed. Coll. of History, Bucharest Univ. Lomonosov Univ. Moscow; researcher in history 1951–65; Head Romanian Medieval History Dept. of the N. Iorga Inst. of History of the Romanian Acad. 1965–66, Deputy Dir. 1966–70, Dir. 1970–90; Dean of the Coll. of History and Philosophy, Bucharest Univ. 1977–85; mem. Romanian Acad. of Social and Political Sciences 1970–90; corresp. mem. Romanian Academy 1974, mem. 1992; mem. Romanian Soc. for Historical Sciences (on main bd.), Int. Comm. for Hist. of State Ass., Comm. int. des études slaves; Vice-Chair. of the Nat. Cttee. of Historical Sciences; Chair. of the Dept. of History and Archaeology,

Romanian Acad. of Social and Political Sciences 1970–90; mem. European Acad. of History 1981–; Prize of the Romanian Acad. 1967; Order of Scientific Merit 1966, Star of the Repub. 1971; Deputy Nat. Ass. 1975–80, 1985–90. *Works include:* The History of the Romanian People 1970, Medieval Wallachia from Basarab I the Founder until Michael the Brave, 1970, History of Dobrudja, Vol. III (with I. Barnea) 1971, Demography—a Dimension of History 1974, Encyclopedia of Romanian Historiography 1978, The Romanian Nation 1984, The Beginnings of Romanian Principalities 1991, The Romanian Principalities in the 14th–16th Centuries 1992, Romania's Economic History (co-author) 1994, History of the Romanians in the 17th Century 1996, Romania. Historical-Geographic Atlas (co-author) 1996, The Illustrated History of Craiova (co-author) 1996, The Romanian Principalities in the Eighteenth Century 1998, Studies of Economic History and History of Economic Thought (co-author) 1998. *Address:* 214 Calea Victoriei, Apt. 44, 71104 Bucharest, Romania (Home). *Telephone:* 659.39.32.

STEFANIUK, Franciszek Jerzy; Polish politician and farmer; b. 4 June 1944, Drelów, Biała Podlaska Prov.; m.; five c.; ed. Economic Tech. School, Międzyrzec Podlaski; manages his own farm; Chair. Cooperative of Agricultural Circles, Drelów 1978–82; mem. United Peoples' Party (ZSL) 1963–90, Chair. Commune Cttee., Drelów 1982–89; Chair. Voivodship of Polish Peasants' Party, Biała Podlaska 1990–, mem. Supervisory Bd., Vice-Chair. Bd. Supreme Exec. Cttee. 1992–97; Deputy to Sejm (Parl.) 1989–; mem. Polish Peasant Party Parl. Club 1989–97, Deputy Chair. 1993–97; Vice-Marshal Sejm 1997–. *Address:* Kancelaria Sejmu RP, ul. Wiejska 4/6/8, 00-902 Warsaw, Poland. *Telephone:* (22) 628 91 65.

STEFFE, Horst-Otto, D.ECON.; German economist and financial executive; b. 27 Aug. 1919, Berlin; m. Margareta Spangl; three c.; ed. Leipzig and Vienna Univs.; mil. service 1937–45; Economist, Austrian Inst. for Econ. Research 1948; Asst., then Deputy Section Head, Fed. Ministry of Econ. Affairs 1952; Man. Dir. Gemeinschaft zum Schutz der deutschen Sparer 1957; Dir. Nat. Econ. and Econ. Trends, EEC Comm., Brussels 1960, also Chair. EEC Cttee. of Experts for Business Cycle Analysis and of Working Parties on Econ. Budgets, Cyclical Statistics and Econ. Tendency Surveys 1960; mem. Short Term Econ. Policy and Budgetary Policy Cttees.; alt. mem. Monetary Cttee.; Man. Econ. and Research Dept., European Investment Bank (EIB) 1967–72, Vice-Pres., Vice-Chair. Bd. of Dirs. 1972–84, Hon. Vice-Pres. 1984–89; Bundesverdienstkreuz. *Publications:* numerous works on economics, investment and related subjects. *Address:* 76 Grand Rue, 1660 Luxembourg, Luxembourg.

STEGER, Joseph A., PH.D.; American university president; b. 17 Feb. 1937, Philadelphia, Pa.; s. of Joseph A. Steger and Georgianna Kirby; m. Carol R. Steger 1977; one s. one d.; ed. Gettysburg Coll. and Kansas State Univ.; Sr. Research Analyst, Prudential Insurance Co. 1964–66; Asst. Prof., Assoc. Prof. Dept. of Psychology, State Univ. of New York 1966–71; Prof. School of Man. Rensselaer Polytechnic Inst. 1971–74, Dean, School of Man. 1974–79, Dean and Vice-Pres. for Admin. and Budget 1977–78, Dean and Acting Provost 1978–79; Dir. Organizational Devt. and Human Resources, Colt Industries Inc. 1979–82; Sr. Vice-Pres. and Provost, Univ. of Cincinnati 1982–84, Pres. 1984–. *Publication:* Readings in Statistics for the Behavioral Scientist 1971. *Leisure interests:* sailing, golf. *Address:* Office of the President, University of Cincinnati, P.O. Box 210063, Cincinnati, OH 45221-0063, U.S.A. *Telephone:* (513)-556-2201.

STEGER, Norbert; Austrian politician and lawyer; b. 6 March 1944, Vienna; s. of Karl and Anna Steger; m. Margarete Steger 1970; ed. Univ. of Vienna; started private law office, Vienna 1975; mem. FPÖ (Austrian Freedom Party) Fed. Exec. 1974, Deputy Chair. 1978, Chair. 1980; mem. Nationalrat 1979–; Vice-Chancellor and Fed. Minister of Commerce, Trade and Industry 1983–86. *Leisure interests:* music, skiing, basketball.

STEHELIN, Dominique Jean Bernard, PH.D.; French research scientist; b. 4 Sept. 1943, Thoisy; s. of Robert Stehelin and Berthe Zimmermann; m. Liliane Fachan 1969 (divorced 1975); one d.; ed. Lycée Fustel, Strasbourg and Univ. Louis Pasteur, Strasbourg; Perm. Researcher, sponsored by C.N.R.S., at Louis Pasteur Univ. 1969–71; Post-doctoral studies at Institut de la Recherche Scientifique sur le Cancer with Dr. A. Lwoff, Villejuif 1970–71; Visiting Scientist with J. M. Bishop at Univ. of Calif. Medical Center, San Francisco, U.S.A. 1972–75; Head of Molecular Oncology Research Unit, Institut Pasteur, Lille 1979–84, Prof. 1984–; Dir. of Research C.N.R.S. 1985–, C.N.R.S. Inst. of Biology, Lille 1996–; mem. American Soc. of Microbiology, European Molecular Biology Org., Editorial Bd. Oncogene; Grand Prix, Académie des Sciences 1975; Louis Jeantet Award (Medicine), Geneva 1987, and four other awards; Chevalier de l'Ordre Nat. du Mérite, Officier, Légion d'honneur. *Publications:* more than 170 int. publs. on cancer research (cancer genes, retrovirus, angiogenesis). *Leisure interests:* skiing, diving, music. *Address:* C.N.R.S. Institut de Biologie, 1 rue Calmette, 59019 Lille (Office); 7 allée du Trianon, 59650 Villeneuve d'Ascq, France (Home). *Telephone:* (3) 20.87.79.78 (Office); (3) 20.91.38.94 (Home).

STEICHEN, René, D. EN D.; Luxembourg politician; b. 27 Nov. 1942, Luxembourg; m.; three c.; ed. Lycée Classique, Diekirch, Cours Supérieurs, Luxembourg, Faculties of Law, Aix-en-Provence and Paris and Inst. d'Etudes Politiques, Paris; lawyer, Diekirch 1969–84; mem. Diekirch Town Council 1969, Mayor 1974–84; Christian Social Deputy in Parl. 1979; Sec. of State for Agric. and Viticulture 1984, of Agric., Viticulture and Rural Devt. and Minister-Del. for Cultural Research and Scientific Research 1989–93; Commr. for Agric. and Rural Devt., EC 1993–95. *Address:* c/o European Commission, 200 rue de la Loi, 1049 Brussels, Belgium.

STEIGER, Rod; American actor; b. 14 April 1925, W. Hampton, N.Y.; s. of Frederick Steiger and Lorraine Driver; m. 1st Sally Gracie 1952; m. 2nd Claire Bloom (q.v.) 1959 (divorced), one d.; m. 3rd Sherry Nelson 1973 (divorced 1979); m. 4th Paula Ellis 1986; one s.; ed. public schools; Berlin Film Festival Award 1964; British Film Acad. Award; Acad. Award (Oscar) Best Actor 1967. *Stage appearances include:* Night Music 1951, An Enemy of the People 1953, Rashomon 1959. *Numerous film appearances include:* On the Waterfront 1953, Big Knife 1955, Oklahoma 1956, Jubal 1957, Across the Bridge 1958, Al Capone 1959, Seven Thieves 1959, The Mark 1960, The World in my Pocket 1960, The Tiger Among Us 1961, The Longest Day 1961, Convicts 4 1961, The Time of Indifference 1962, Hands on the City 1963, The Pawnbroker 1964, The Loved One 1964, Doctor Zhivago 1966, In the Heat of the Night 1967, No Way to Treat a Lady 1968, The Illustrated Man 1968, The Sergeant 1968, Three into Two Won't Go 1969, Waterloo 1970, The Lolly Madonna War, Lucky Luciano 1973, The Heroes 1974, Les innocents aux mains sales 1975, Hennessy 1975, W.C. Fields and Me 1976, Jesus of Nazareth (TV) 1977, F.I.S.T. 1978, The Amityville Horror 1979, The Chosen 1980, Lion of the Desert 1981, The Magic Mountain 1982, Portrait of a Hitman 1984, The Naked Face 1985, The January Man 1988, American Gothic 1988, The Ballad of the Sad Café 1991, Tennessee Nights, Guilty as Charged 1992, That Summer of White Roses, The Player 1992, The Specialist 1994, Mars Attacks 1996, Incognito 1997, Animals 1997, Legacy 1998, Crazy in Alabama 1998. *Address:* c/o Gold/Marshak & Associates, 3500 W. Olive Avenue, Suite 1400, Burbank, CA 91505; 6342 Zumirez Drive, Malibu, CA 90265, U.S.A.

STEIN, Cyril; British business executive; b. 20 Feb. 1928; m. Betty Young 1949; two s. one d.; Chair. and Jt. Man. Dir. Ladbroke Group PLC 1966–93, Dir. (non-exec.) –1994; Chair. St James's Club Ltd. 1995–.

STEIN, Elias M., M.A., PH.D.; American professor of mathematics; b. 13 Jan. 1931, Antwerp, Belgium; s. of Elkan Stein and Chana Goldman Stein; m. Elly Intrator 1959; one s. one d.; ed. Univ. of Chicago; Instr. M.I.T. 1956–58; Asst. Prof. Univ. of Chicago 1958–61, Assoc. Prof. 1961–63; mem. Inst. for Advanced Study, Princeton 1962–63, 1984–85; Prof. Princeton Univ. 1963–, Chair. of Dept. of Math. 1968–70, 1985–87; Guggenheim Fellow 1976–77, 1984–85; mem. American Acad. of Arts and Sciences, N.A.S., American Mathematical Soc.; A.M.S. Steele Prize 1984, Shock Prize 1993. *Publications:* Singular Integrals and Differentiability Properties of Functions 1970, Topics in Harmonic Analysis Related to the Littlewood-Paley Theory 1970, Introduction to Fourier Analysis on Euclidean Spaces (with G. Weiss) 1971. *Address:* Department of Mathematics, Princeton University, Fine Hall, Washington Road, Princeton, NJ 08544 (Office); 132 Dodds Lane, Princeton, NJ 08544, U.S.A. (Home). *Telephone:* (609) 452-3497 (Office); (609) 924-9335 (Home).

STEIN, Herbert, PH.D.; American economist; b. 27 Aug. 1916, Detroit; s. of David and Jessie Stein; m. Mildred Fishman 1937; one s. one d.; ed. Williams Coll. and Univ. of Chicago; Economist, U.S. Govt. 1938–45; Economist, Cttee. for Econ. Devt. 1945–48, Assoc. Dir. of Research 1948–56, Dir. of Research 1956–66, Vice-Pres. and Chief Economist 1966–67; Sr. Fellow, Brookings Inst. 1967–69; mem. President's Council of Econ. Advisers 1969–72, Chair. 1972–74; A. Willis Robertson Prof. of Econs., Univ. of Va. 1971–84; Sr. Fellow American Enterprise Inst. 1977–87; mem. Bd. of Contributors Wall Street Journal 1974–; Sr. Fellow American Enterprise Inst. 1977–; mem. Econ. Advisory Panel Congressional Budget Office 1976–89; mem. Pres.'s Econ. Policy Advisory Bd. 1981–89, Blue Ribbon Comm. on Defence Man. 1985–86; mem. American Acad. of Arts and Sciences 1983–; Pres. Southern Econ. Assen. 1983–84; Co-Chair. Comm. to Fight Inflation 1982; mem. Exec. Cttee., Cttee. on the Present Danger; fmr. Columnist Scripps-Howard Newspapers; frequent contrib. to Fortune Magazine; Ed. AEI Economist 1977–88; Dir. Reynolds Metals Co.; Hon. LL.D. (Rider Coll.) 1971, (Hartford Univ.) 1973, (Williams Coll.) 1980, (Roanoke Coll.) 1984, (New Haven Univ.) 1987, (Hofstra Univ.) 1994. *Publications:* The Fiscal Revolution in America 1969, On the Brink (with Benjamin Stein) 1977, Moneypower (with Benjamin Stein) 1980, Presidential Economics 1984 (revised edn. 1994), Washington Bedtime Stories 1986, Governing the $5 Trillion Economy 1989, An Illustrated Guide to the American Economy (jtly.) 1992, A New Illustrated Guide to the American Economy 1995, On the Other Hand . . . 1995; ed. Policies to Combat Depression 1956, Tax Policy for the Twenty-First Century 1988. *Address:* American Enterprise Institute, 1150 17th Street, N.W., Washington, DC 20036 (Office); 1704 Yorktown Drive, Charlottesville, VA 22901, U.S.A. (Home).

STEIN, Peter Gonville, F.B.A.; British professor of law; b. 29 May 1926, Liverpool; s. of Walter O. Stein and Effie D. Walker; m. 1st Janet Chamberlain 1953, three d.; m. 2nd Anne Howard 1978; one step-s.; ed. Liverpool Coll., Gonville and Caius Coll. Cambridge and Univ. of Pavia, Italy; served R.N. 1944–47; admitted solicitor 1951; Prof. of Jurisprudence, Univ. of Aberdeen 1956–68; Regius Prof. of Civil Law, Univ. of Cambridge 1968–93, now Prof. Emer., Fellow of Queens' Coll. Cambridge 1968–; mem. Univ. Grants Cttee. 1971–76; J.P., Cambridge 1970–; Fellow, Winchester Coll. 1976–91; Pres. Soc. of Public Teachers of Law 1980–81; mem. U.S.-U.K. Educational Comm. 1985–91; Fellow Acad. Europaea 1989; Foreign Fellow, Accademia Nazionale dei Lincei, Accademia di Scienze Morali e Politiche di Napoli, Accad. degli Intronati di Siena, Kon. Akad. v. Wetenschappen,

Brussels; Dr. Juris h.c. (Göttingen) 1980; Dott. Giur. h.c. (Ferrara) 1990; Hon. Q.C. 1993. *Publications:* Regulae Iuris: from juristic rules to legal maxims 1966, Legal Values in Western Society (with J. Shand) 1974, Legal Evolution 1980, Legal Institutions 1984, The Character and Influence of the Roman Civil Law: essays 1988, The Teaching of Roman Law in England around 1200 (with F. de Zulueta) 1990, Notaries Public in England since the Reformation (ed. and contrib.) 1991, Römisches Recht und Europa 1996, Roman Law in European History 1999. *Leisure interest:* gardening. *Address:* Queens' College, Cambridge, CB3 9ET; Wimpole Cottage, 36 Wimpole Road, Great Eversden, Cambridge, CB3 7HR, England (Home). *Telephone:* (01223) 262349 (Home).

STEINBERG, Saul; American artist and architect; b. 15 June 1914, Romanic-Sarat, Romania; s. of Maurice and Rosa (née Jacobson) Steinberg; m. Hedda Lindenberg Sterne 1944; ed. Milan Polytechnic School; Cartoonist 1936–39; practising architect 1939–41; moved to U.S. 1942; illustrator for the New Yorker 1941–; represented in Museum of Modern Art N.Y.; numerous one-man exhbns. 1953–; Gold Medal, American Acad. of Arts and Sciences 1974. *Publications:* All in Line 1945, The Art of Living 1949, The Passport 1954, The Labyrinth 1960, The Inspector 1973.

STEINBERGER, Jack, PH.D.; American physicist; b. 25 May 1921, Germany; s. of Ludwig Steinberger and Bertha (May) Steinberger; m. 1st Joan Beauregard 1943; m. 2nd Cynthia Eve Alff 1961; three s. one d.; ed. Univ. of Chicago; Visiting mem. Inst. of Advanced Study, Princeton 1948–49; Research Asst., Univ. of Calif. (Berkeley) 1949–50; Prof. Columbia Univ., New York 1950–71, Higgins Prof. 1967–71; Staff mem. Centre Européen pour la Recherche Nucléaire 1968–; mem. N.A.S. 1967–, Heidelberg Acad. of Sciences 1967–, American Acad. of Arts and Sciences 1969–, Acad. Nat. dei Lincei 1997; Hon. Prof., Heidelberg 1968; Pres.'s Science Medal, U.S. 1988, Nobel Prize in Physics (jtly.) 1988, Mateuzzi Medal, Società Italiana delle Scienze 1991; Hon. D. Litt. (Glasgow) 1990; Dr. h.c. (IU. Inst. of Tech.), (Dortmund), (Columbia), (Barcelona), (Univ. Blaise Pascal). *Publications:* Muon Decay 1949, Pi Zero Meson 1950, Spin of Pion 1951, Parity of Pion 1954, 1959, Σ° Hyperon 1957, Properties of "Strange Particles" 1957–64, Two Neutrinos 1962, CP Violating Effects in K° Decay 1966–74, High Energy Neutrino Physics 1975–83, Preparation of Lep Detector 1981, 3 Families of Matter 1989, Electroweak physics experiments 1989–97. *Leisure interests:* mountaineering, flute, cruising. *Address:* CERN, Geneva 23; 25 chemin des Merles, 1213 Onex, Geneva, Switzerland (Home). *Telephone:* 7934612 (Home).

STEINEM, Gloria, B.A.; American writer, journalist and feminist activist; b. 25 March, 1934, Toledo; d. of Leo and Ruth (Nuneviller) Steinem; ed. Smith Coll.; Chester Bowles Asian Fellow, India 1957–58; Co-Dir., Dir. Ind. Research Service, Cambridge, Mass. and New York 1959–60; editorial asst., contributing ed., ed., freelance writer various nat. and New York publs. 1960–; Co-Founder New York Magazine, contrib. 1968–72, Ms Magazine 1972 (Ed. 1971–87, columnist 1980–87, consulting ed. 1987–); feminist lecturer 1969–; active various civil rights and peace campaigns including United Farmworkers, Vietnam War Tax Protest, Cttee. for the Legal Defense of Angela Davis and political campaigns of Adlai Stevenson, Robert Kennedy, Eugene McCarthy, Shirley Chisholm, George McGovern; Co-Founder and Chair Bd. Women's Action Alliance 1970–; Convenor, mem. Nat. Advisory Cttee. Nat. Women's Political Caucus 1971–; Co-Founder, Pres. Bd. Dirs. Ms. Foundation for Women 1972–; founding mem. Coalition of Labor Union Women; Penney-Missouri Journalism Award 1970; Ohio Gov.'s Award for Journalism 1972; named Woman of the Year, McCall's Magazine 1972; Woodrow Wilson Int. Center for Scholars Fellow 1977. *Publications:* The Thousand Indias 1957, The Beach Book 1963, Outrageous Acts and Everyday Rebellions 1983, Marilyn 1986, Revolution From Within: A Book of Self-Esteem 1992, Moving Beyond Words 1994; contribs. to various anthologies. *Address:* c/o Ms Magazine, 135 W. 50th Street, Floor 16, New York, NY 10020, U.S.A.

STEINER, George, D.PHIL., F.B.A., F.R.S.L.; writer and scholar; b. 23 April 1929, Paris, France; s. of Dr. and Mrs. F. G. Steiner; m. Zara Shakow 1955; one s. one d.; ed. Univs. of Paris and Chicago, Harvard Univ. and Balliol Coll., Oxford; Editorial staff The Economist, London 1952–56; Fellow, Inst. for Advanced Study, Princeton 1956–58; Gauss Lecturer, Princeton Univ. 1959–60; Fellow and Dir. of English Studies, Churchill Coll., Cambridge 1961–69, Extraordinary Fellow 1969–, Pensioner Fellow 1996–; Albert Schweitzer Visiting Prof., New York Univ. 1966–67; Visiting Prof. Yale Univ. 1970–71; Prof. of English and Comparative Literature, Univ. of Geneva 1974–94, Prof. Emer. 1994–; Visiting Prof., Collège de France 1992; First Lord Weidenfeld Visiting Prof. of Comparative Literature Oxford Univ. 1994–95; Pres. The English Asscn. 1975–76; Corresp. mem. German Acad.; Hon. mem. American Acad. of Arts and Sciences 1989; Hon. Fellow, Balliol Coll. Oxford; delivered Massey Lectures 1974, Ransom Memorial Lectures 1976, F. D. Maurice Lectures, Univ. of London 1984; Leslie Stephen Lecturer, Cambridge Univ. 1985; W. P. Ker Lecturer, Univ. of Glasgow 1986; Robertson Lecturer, Courtauld Inst., London 1985; Page-Barbour Lectures, Univ. of Va. 1987; Gifford Lectures 1990; Priestley Lectures, Univ. of Toronto 1995; Hon. D.Litt. (East Anglia) 1976, (Louvain) 1979, (Bristol) 1989, Hon. D.Litt. (Glasgow, Liège) 1990, (Ulster) 1993, (Kenyon Coll., U.S.A.) 1995, (Trinity Coll., Dublin) 1995, (Univ. of Rome) 1998, (Sorbonne) 1998; O. Henry Award 1958, Jewish Chronicle Book Award 1968, Zabel Prize of Nat. Inst. of Arts and Letters 1970, Le Prix du Souvenir 1974, King Albert Medal of the Royal Belgian Acad. 1982; Chevalier, Légion d'honneur. *Publications:* Tolstoy or Dostoevsky 1959, The Death of Tragedy 1961, Anno Domini: Three Stories 1964, Language and Silence 1967, Extraterritorial 1971, In Bluebeard's Castle 1971, The Sporting Scene: White Knights in Reykjavík 1973, Fields of Force 1974, A Nostalgia for the Absolute (Massey Lectures) 1974, After Babel 1975, Heidegger 1978, On Difficulty and Other Essays 1978, The Portage of A.H. to San Cristobal 1981; Ed. Penguin Book of Modern Verse Translation 1967, Antigones 1984, George Steiner: A Reader 1984, Real Presences: Is there anything in what we say? 1989, Proofs and Three Parables 1992, No Passion Spent 1996, The Deeps of the Sea 1996, Errata: An Examined Life 1998. *Leisure interests:* chess, music, mountain walking. *Address:* 32 Barrow Road, Cambridge, England; Harvard Club, New York, NY, U.S.A.

STEINHOFF, Janusz Wojciech, PH.D.; Polish politician; b. 24 Sept. 1946, Gliwice; m.; one d.; ed. Silesian Tech. Univ., Gliwice; with Coal Industry Construction and Mechanization Plants, Gliwice 1974–75; Mining Dept. Silesian Tech. Univ., Gliwice 1976–89, 1994–97; Chair. Higher Mining Office 1990–94; advisor State Hard Coal Agency 1994–95; Vice-Chair. Regional Chamber of Commerce, Katowice 1996–97; Minister of the Economy 1997–; co.-founder NSZZ Solidarity, Silesian Tech. Univ. 1980; underground Solidarity activist during martial law; Solidarity expert on mining and protection of the environment during Round Table debates, 1989; deputy to Sejm (Parl.) 1989–93, 1997–; mem. Presidium Citizens Parl. Club (OKP) 1989–91; mem. Solidarity Election Action (AWS) Parl. Club 1997–; author AWS programme for restructuring the mining sector; co.-founder and Vice-Leader Christian Democratic Party. *Address:* Ministerstwo Gospodarki, pl. Trzech Krzyży 5, 00-950 Warsaw, Poland. *Telephone:* (22) 628 73 27. *Fax:* (22) 629 51 01.

STEINKÜHLER, Franz; German trade union executive; b. 20 May 1937, Würzburg; m.; one c.; trained as toolmaker and became Chief of Production Planning 1951–60; joined IG Metall 1951, mem. Youth Group 1952, Chair. Youth Del. 1953, numerous local exec. positions 1953–63, Sec. Regional Exec. Bd., Stuttgart 1963–72, Dir. Stuttgart Region 1972–83, Vice-Pres. IG Metall 1983–86, Pres. 1986–93; Pres. Int. Metalworkers' Fed. June 1987; mem. SPD 1951–, Vice-Pres. in Baden-Württemberg 1975–83, mem. Programme Cttee. of Exec. Bd. 1984; Workers' Rep. VW-AG, Wolfsburg Mannesmann AG, Supervisory Bd., Daimler Benz AG Supervisory Bd. –1993, Thyssen AG; Deputy Chair. Supervisory Bd. Volkswagen AG; mem. State Tribunal of Baden-Württemberg 1983; Hon. Senator Univ. of Konstanz 1983. *Address:* c/o Industriegewerkschaft Metall, Wilhelm-Leuschner Strasse 79-85, 60329 Frankfurt am Main, Germany.

STEINNES, Eiliv, D.PHIL.; Norwegian professor of environmental science; b. 21 Sept. 1938, Elverum; s. of Eirik Steinnes and Aslaug Steinnes; m. Randi Surdal 1962; three d.; ed. Univ. of Oslo; scientist, Norwegian Inst. for Atomic Energy 1964–68, Research leader 1969–79; Prof. in Environmental Science, Univ. of Trondheim Coll. of Arts and Science 1980–, Rector 1984–90; mem. Norwegian Acad. of Tech. Sciences, Norwegian Acad. of Science and Letters (Oslo), Royal Norwegian Soc. of Science and Letters (Trondheim). *Publications:* about 420 scientific papers, two books. *Leisure interests:* outdoor life, in particular cross-country skiing and mountain tours. *Address:* Department of Chemistry, University of Science and Technology, 7034 Trondheim (Office); Trollahaugen 16, 7069 Trolla, Norway (Home). *Telephone:* (47) 73 59 62 35 (Office); (47) 73 52 99 90 (Home). *Fax:* (47) 73 59 69 40.

STELLE, Kellogg Sheffield, PH.D., F.INST.P.; American physicist; b. 11 March 1948, Washington, D.C.; s. of Charles C. Stelle and Jane E. Kellogg; ed. Phillips Acad. Andover, Mass., Harvard Coll. and Brandeis Univ.; field observer, Bartol Research Foundation, South Pole, Antarctica 1970–72; lecturer in Math. King's Coll. London 1977–78; Research Fellow, Imperial Coll. London 1978–80, Advanced Fellow 1982–87, lecturer in Physics 1987–88, Reader 1988–95, Prof. 1995–; mem. Inst. for Advanced Study, Princeton, N.J. 1986; Scientific Assoc. CERN, Geneva 1980–81, 1987; Ed. Classical and Quantum Gravity 1984–93; mem. American Physical Soc., Fed. of American Scientists, Inst. of Physics, A.A.A.S. *Publications:* numerous articles in scientific journals. *Address:* The Blackett Laboratory, Imperial College, Prince Consort Road, London, SW7 2BZ, England.

STELMACHOWSKI, Andrzej, LL.D.; Polish politician and lawyer; b. 28 Jan. 1925, Poznań; s. of Bronisław Stelmachowski and Wisława Stelmachowska; m.; two s.; ed. Poznań Univ.; scientific worker, Poznań Univ. 1947–50; lecturer, Warsaw Univ. 1950–58, Asst. Prof. 1958–62, Prof. 1969–; Prof. Wrocław Univ. 1962–69, Acad. of Catholic Theology, Warsaw 1970–; mem. Solidarity Ind. Self-governing Trade Union 1980–; expert, Social and Labour Study Centre attached to Nat. Comm. of Solidarity Trade Union 1980–81; adviser to Strike Cttee. in Lenin Shipyard, Gdańsk 1980, to Nat. Comm. of Solidarity Trade Union 1980–89, to Solidarity of Private Farmers 1981–, to Temporary Co-ordinating Comm. of Solidarity Trade Union during martial law, then to Nat. Exec. Comm. of Solidarity Trade Union; mem. Civic Cttee. attached to Lech Wałęsa (q.v.), Chair. of Solidarity Trade Union 1988; participant Round Table debates, Co-Chair. team for agric. matters Feb.–April 1989; Senator of the Polish Rep. 1989–91, Marshal (Speaker) of the Senate 1989–91; Minister of Nat. Educ. 1991–92; mem. Catholic Intelligentsia Club, Warsaw 1972– (Pres. 1987–90); Chair. Org. Cttee. of Agric. Foundation 1982–85; Pres. Polish Community Asscn. 1990–; mem. numerous cttees. *Publications:* about 150 works on civil law and agrarian law, including Przysposobienie małoletnich w prawie polskim 1957, Posiadanie w prawie polskim 1958, Kontraktacje produktów rolnych 1960, Wstęp do teorii prawa cywilnego 1969, Prawo rolne (with Jan Selwa) 1967, Zarys prawa gospodarczego (with Marek Madey) 1980, Prawo rolne (with Bohdan Zdziennicki) 1987, (with others) 1994. *Leisure interests:* swimming, agric. problems. *Address:* ul. P. Gojawiczyńskiej 3 m. 6, 01-773, Warsaw, Poland. *Telephone:* 33 96 11. *Fax:* 635 04 40.

STEMPEL, Robert C., M.B.A.; American engineer; b. 15 July 1933, Trenton, N.J.; ed. Worcester Polytechnic Inst., Mass., Mich. State Univ.; joined Oldsmobile 1958, Constructor, undercarriage devt., Driving Track Engineer 1964, Engineer 1969, Deputy Chief Engineer 1972; Asst. to Pres. Gen. Motors 1973–74; Chief Engineer for Engines and Components, Chevrolet 1974; Dir. Construction Dept. 1975; Gen. Dir. Pontiac 1978–80; Vice-Pres. Gen. Motors 1978–87, Pres. and C.O.O. 1987–90, Chair., C.E.O. 1990–92; Chair. Bd. and Gen. Dir. Adam Opel AG, Fed. Repub. of Germany 1980–82; Head of Chevrolet Div., Gen. Motors 1982–, Head of Buick-Oldsmobile-Cadillac Group 1984–; mem. Soc. of Automotive Engineers, American Soc. of Mechanical Engineers. *Address:* c/o General Motors Corporation, 3044 West Grand Boulevard, Detroit, MI 48202, U.S.A. (Office).

STEMPLOWSKI, Ryszard, LL.M., PH.D.; Polish diplomatist, lawyer and historian; b. 25 March 1939, Wygoda; s. of Kazimierz Stemplowski and Eugenia Białecka; m. Irena Zasłona 1975; two d.; ed. Tech. Lycée, Bydgoszcz, Dept. of Ecological Eng., Wrocław Univ. of Tech., Dept. of Law, Wrocław Univ., Inst. of History, Polish Acad. of Sciences, Warsaw; Research Fellow, Inst. of History 1973–90; Chief Clerk of Chamber of Deputies 1990–93; Amb. to U.K. 1994–; Visiting Fellow St. Antony's Coll. Oxford, 1974; A. von Humboldt Research Fellow, Univ. of Cologne 1981–82. *Publications:* Dependence and Defiance: Argentina and the Rivalries among the U.S.A., Germany and the UK 1930–46 1975, Economic Nationalism in East Central Europe and South America 1918–39 (co-author) 1990, The Slavic Settlers in Misiones 1898–1947 (co-author) 1992, State Socialism in Real Capitalism: Chile in the Year 1932 1996. *Leisure interests:* music, astrophysics. *Address:* Polish Embassy, 47 Portland Place, London, W1N 4JH, England. *Telephone:* 0171-580 2969. *Fax:* 0171-323 4018.

STENBÄCK, Pär Olav Mikael, M.A.; Finnish international administrator and fmr. politician; b. 12 Aug. 1941, Porvoo (Borgå); s. of Arne Mikael and Rakel Stenbäck; m. Liv Sissel Lund 1970; two s.; Ed. with Finnish Broadcasting Co. 1964–69; Chair. Svensk Ungdom (youth org. of Swedish People's Party of Finland) 1967–70; M.P. 1970–85; Chair. Swedish People's Party 1977–85; Minister of Educ. 1979–82, of Foreign Affairs 1982–83; Dir. Hanaholmen Swedish-Finnish Culture Centre 1974–85; Sec.-Gen. Finnish Red Cross 1985–88; Sec. Gen. Int. Fed. (fmrly. League) of Red Cross and Red Crescent Socs., Geneva 1988; Sec.-Gen. Nordic Council of Ministers, Copenhagen 1992–96; Pres. Finnish Red Cross 1996–; Chair. Foundation for Swedish Culture in Finland 1996–; Vice-Pres. for Europe, Int. Youth Foundation 1996–; Grand Cross, Royal Order of Northern Star (Sweden), Grand Cross of the Falcon (Iceland), Grand Cross St. Olav (Norway), Grand Cross of Dannebrog (Denmark), Commdr. of the Order of the Lion (Finland), Grand Cross of Santa Miranda (Venezuela). *Leisure interests:* literature, fishing, stamps. *Address:* Hirbölebågen 15, FIN-02160 Esbo, Finland. *Telephone:* 0-428725.

STENFLO, Jan Olof, M.S., PH.D.; Swedish astronomer; b. 10 Nov. 1942; s. of Carl Stenflo and Signe Rödén; m. Joyce E. Tucker 1971; two s.; ed. Univ. of Lund; Assoc. Prof. Univ. of Lund 1969–75; Sr. Research Scientist, Swedish Natural Science Research Council 1975–80; Prof. of Astronomy, Eidgenössische Technische Hochschule (ETH), Zürich and Univ. of Zürich 1980–; Dir. Inst. of Astronomy, ETH 1980–; Pres. LEST Foundation 1983–97; mem. Royal Swedish Acad. of Sciences, Norwegian Acad. of Science and Letters, Royal Physiographic Soc. Lund; Prize of Royal Swedish Acad. 1974. *Publications:* Solar Magnetic Fields 1994; about 160 scientific papers on astronomy in int. journals. *Leisure interests:* classical music, mountain hiking, skiing. *Address:* Institute of Astronomy, ETH-Zentrum, CH-8092 Zürich (Office); Haldeweg 4, CH-5436 Würenlos, Switzerland (Home). *Telephone:* 41-1-632 3804 (Office); 41-56-4242886.

STENLUND, Bengt Gustav Verner, D.TECH.; Finnish professor of polymer technology; b. 17 Aug. 1939, Kristinestad; s. of Gustav Stenlund and Linda Hofman; m. Kerstin Ottosson 1964; one s.; Research Assoc. The Finnish Pulp and Paper Research Inst. 1965–77; Acting Prof. of Polymer Tech., Åbo Akad. 1977–79, Prof. 1979–, Dean. Dept. of Chemical Eng. 1982–85, Vice-Rector 1985–88, Rector 1988–97; Chair. Council of Tech., Finnish Acad. of Sciences 1986–88; Chair. Finnish Rectors' Council 1990–92; Chair. LC Working Group on EC Research Policy 1993–95; Chair. Steering Group, Baltic Univ. Programme 1995–; mem. Scientific Del. of Finnish Chemical Industry 1985–90; mem. Bd. Nordic Foundation of Tech. 1987–90; mem. Steering Cttee. Finnish Centres of Expertise 1996–; mem. Bd. CRE; mem. European Science and Tech. Council; mem. Finnish Acad. of Eng., Finnish Soc. of Science and Letters, Royal Swedish Acad. of Eng. *Publications:* Gel Chromatography of Lignosulfonates 1970; about 50 publs. about natural and synthetic polymers. *Leisure interests:* art, downhill skiing, sailing, university history. *Address:* Åbo Akademi University, Domkyrkotorget 3, 20500 Åbo, Finland. *Telephone:* (2) 2654100. *Fax:* (2) 2517553.

STENT, Gunther Siegmund, PH.D.; American professor of molecular biology; b. 28 March 1924, Berlin, Germany; s. of George and Elizabeth Stensch; m. Inga Loftsdottir 1951; one s.; ed. Hyde Park School, Chicago and Univ. of Illinois; Research Asst. U.S. War Production Bd., Synthetic Rubber Research Programme 1944–48; Document Analyst, Field Intelligence Agency, Occupied Germany 1946–47; Merck Postdoctoral Fellow Calif. Inst. of Tech. 1948–50; American Cancer Soc. Postdoctoral Fellow Univ. of Copenhagen and Inst. Pasteur, Paris 1950–52; Asst. Research Biochemist Univ. of Calif., Berkeley 1952–56, Assoc. Prof. of Bacteriology 1956–59, Prof. of Molecular Biology 1959–94, Prof. Emer 1994–, Chair. Molecular Biology and Dir. Virus Lab. 1980–86, Chair. Molecular and Cell Biology 1987–92; Natural Science Foundation Sr. Fellow Univs. of Kyoto and Cambridge 1960–61; Guggenheim Fellow Harvard Medical School 1969–70; mem. N.A.S., American Acad. of Arts and Sciences, American Philosophical Soc.; External mem. Max Planck Inst. for Molecular Genetics, Berlin 1966–; Fellow, Inst. for Advanced Studies, Berlin 1985–90; Fogarty Scholar, N.I.H. 1990–91; Hon. D.Sc. (York, Toronto Univs.) 1984. *Publications:* Molecular Biology of Bacterial Viruses 1963, Phage and the Origins of Molecular Biology 1966, The Coming of the Golden Age 1969, Molecular Genetics 1970, Function and Formation of Neural Systems 1977, Paradoxes of Progress 1978, Morality as a Biological Phenomenon 1978, Shinri to Satori 1981, Nazis, Women and Molecular Biology 1998. *Leisure interest:* car repairs. *Address:* 145 Purdue Avenue, Kensington, CA 94708, U.S.A. (Home).

STEPANKOV, Valentin Georgievich; Russian lawyer; b. 17 Sept. 1951, Perm; s. of Georgii Vassilyevich and Antonia Andreyevna; m. Luisa Pavlovna 1975; one s.; ed. Perm State Univ.; investigator, Office of Public Prosecutor, Sverdlovsk Dist. 1975–76; Public Prosecutor of Perm 1976–77; Public Prosecutor of town of Gubakh Perm Region 1977–81; instructor Div. of Regional Cttee. of CPSU 1981–83; Public Prosecutor of Perm 1983–87; Deputy-Dir. Investigation Dept. Office of Public Prosecutor of the U.S.S.R. 1987–88; Public Prosecutor of Khabarovsk Region 1986–90; First Deputy Public Prosecutor of R.S.F.S.R. 1990–91; Procurator-Gen. of Russia 1991–93; Deputy Head of Admin., Perm Region 1994–; mem. State Duma 1996–. *Publications:* monograph on Kremlin conspiracy and numerous articles. *Leisure interests:* painting, reading, walks in the forest. *Address:* State Duma, Okhotny Ryad 1, 103265 Russia (Office). *Telephone:* 292 8000.

STEPANOV, Victor Nikolayevich, C.PHIL.SC.; Karelian politician; b. 1947, Vidnitsa, Karelia; ed. Karelia State Pedagogical Inst., Higher CP School in Leningrad, Higher Political School of CP Czechoslovakia; worked as carpenter in lumber factory, then dir. village club 1962–66; mem. CPSU 1969–91; took number of posts in Komsomol and CP orgs. 1966–87; Head of Div. Karelian Regional CPSU Cttee. 1987–88; mem. Cen. CPSU Cttee. 1988–89; mem. Cen. Cttee. and Politburo R.S.F.S.R. CP 1990–91; Chair. Presidium Supreme Soviet Karelian Autonomous S.S.R. 1990–; Chair. Supreme Soviet 1993; mem. Union of Communists of Karelia 1992–; People's Deputy of Russia 1989–91; mem. Russian Council of Fed. (Parl.) 1993–98; Chair. Karelian Govt. 1995–98; Head Exec. Cttee. Union of Russia and Belarus Jan. 1999–. *Address:* Government of Karelia, Lenina prospect 19, 185020, Petrozavodsk, Karelia, Russia (Office). *Telephone:* (81400) 76-41-41. *Fax:* 77-41-48.

STEPASHIN, Lieut.-Gen. Sergey Vladimirovich, LL.D.; Russian security official; b. 2 March 1952, Port Arthur; m.; one s.; ed. Higher Political School, U.S.S.R. Ministry of Internal Affairs, Mil. Acad.; mem. staff U.S.S.R. Ministry of Foreign Affairs 1973–80; Lecturer, Higher Political Coll., Leningrad 1981–90; Deputy to R.S.F.S.R. Supreme Soviet 1989–93; after attempted coup Aug. 1991 Head Cttee. on Investigation of KGB Activities of Supreme Soviet; author Programme of reorg. of state security system; Chief Leningrad KGB Admin. and Deputy Chair. KGB (later Agency of State Security) 1991–92; Dir. Fed. Service of Counter-espionage 1994–95; Head of Admin., Dept. of Govt. 1995–97; Minister of Justice 1997–98, of Internal Affairs 1998–99; Acting Chair. of Govt. (Acting Prime Minister) May 1999–; Acting Chair. Exec. Council of Russia and Belarus Union May 1999–. *Leisure interests:* sports, jogging. *Address:* Government of Russia, Kasnopresnenskaya Embankment 2, 103274 Moscow, Russia. *Telephone:* (095) 205-54-56; (095) 205-81-89.

STEPHANOPOULOS, George Robert, A.B.; American federal official; b. 10 Feb. 1961, Fall River, Mass.; s. of Robert Stephanopoulos and Nikki C. Stephanopoulos; ed. Univs. of Columbia and Oxford; fmrly. admin. asst. to Edward Feighan, Washington; Deputy Communications Dir. Dukakis–Bentsen Campaign 1988; fmrly. Exec. Floor Man., later House Majority leader; Sr. Adviser to Pres. of U.S.A. 1993–96; fmrly. Communications Dir. Clinton Gore Campaign; Communications Dir. The White House 1997–; Visiting Prof. of Political Science Columbia Univ. 1977–; contrib. ABC News, ABC Newsweek 1997–; Medal of Excellence, Columbia Univ. 1993. *Publication:* All Too Human 1999. *Address:* The White House, 1600 Pennsylvania Avenue, N.W. Washington, DC 20502; International Affairs Building, 420 W. 118th Street, Room 1315, New York, NY 10027, U.S.A.

STEPHANOPOULOS, Konstantinos; Greek politician and lawyer; b. 1926, Patras; s. of Demetrius and Vrisiis Stephanopoulos; m. Eugenia El. Stounopoulou 1959; two s. one d.; ed. Univ. of Athens; pvt. law practice 1954–74; M.P. for Achaia (Nat. Radical Union) 1964, (New Democracy) 1974, 1977, 1981, 1985, (Democratic Renewal) 1989; Under-Sec. of Commerce July–Nov. 1974; Minister of the Interior 1974–76, of Social Services 1976–77; in Prime Minister's Office 1977–81; Pres. of Greece 1995–; Parl. Rep., New Democracy Party 1981–85, Pres. Party of Democratic Renewal 1985–94. *Publications:* The National Interest and Security Policy (co-author) 1995,

Nouvelles Etudes d'Histoire, Vol. IX (co-author) 1995. *Address:* Presidential Palace, Herodou Atticou Street, Athens, Greece.

STEPHEN, Rt. Hon. Sir Ninian Martin, K.G., A.K., G.C.M.G., G.C.V.O., K.B.E.; Australian lawyer; b. 15 June 1923, Oxford, England; s. of the late Frederick and Barbara (née Cruickshank) Stephen; m. Valery Mary Sinclair 1949; five d.; ed. George Watson's School, Edinburgh Acad., St. Paul's School, London, Chillon Coll., Switzerland, Scotch Coll., Melbourne, Melbourne Univ.; served World War II, Australian Army; admitted as barrister and solicitor, Victoria 1949; Q.C. 1966; Judge, Supreme Court, Victoria 1970; Justice, High Court, Australia 1972–82; Gov.-Gen. of Australia 1982–89; Chair. Nat. Library of Australia 1989–94; Amb. for the Environment 1989–92; Chair. Strand Two, Northern Ireland Talks 1992, UN Group of Experts on Cambodia, Australian Citizenship Council; Judge, Int. Criminal Tribunals for Yugoslavia 1993–97, for Rwanda 1995–97; Hon. Bencher Gray's Inn 1981; K.St.J. 1982; Commdr. Légion d'honneur 1993. *Address:* Flat 121, 193 Domain Road, South Yarra, Vic., Australia. *Telephone:* (03) 8202787.

STEPHENS, Olin James II; American naval architect and yacht designer; b. 13 April 1908, New York City; s. of Roderick Stephens and Marguerite Dulon; m. Florence Reynolds 1930; two s.; ed. M.I.T.; Partner, Sparkman & Stephens 1928; design agent U.S.N. 1939–; Chief Designer, Vice-Pres. and Dir., Sparkman & Stephens Inc. 1929–64, Chief Designer, Pres. and Dir. 1964–78, Chair and Dir. Jan. 1979–85, Dir. Emer. 1987; Chair. Int. Tech. Cttee. of Offshore Racing Council 1967–74, 1977–79, Councillor of honour 1979; Chair. of Research Cttee. of Offshore Racing Council 1980; mem. Jt. Cttee. of Soc. of Naval Architects and U.S. Yacht Racing Union on Yacht Capsize 1980–85; mem. Royal Designers for Industry, London; Hon. mem. and Fellow, Soc. of Naval Architects and Marine Engineers; Hon. M.S. (Stevens Inst. of Tech.) 1945; Hon. M.A. (Brown Univ.) 1959; Dr. h.c. Istituto Universitario di Architettura di Venezia, Italy 1991; David W. Taylor Medal (Soc. of Naval Architects and Engineers) 1954, Beppe Crole Award, Int. Yacht Racing Union 1992, Gibbs Brothers Medal (N.A.S.) 1993; some yachts designed: Dorade 1930, Stormy Weather 1934, (with W. Starling Burgess) Ranger 1937, Vim, Goose, Bolero 1938, Finisterre 1954, Columbia 1958, Constellation 1964, Intrepid 1967, Morning Cloud 1969, 1971, 1973, 1975, Courageous 1974, Flyer 1977, Freedom 1979. *Leisure interest:* computer studies. *Address:* Sparkman & Stephens Inc., 529 Fifth Avenue, New York, NY 10017 (Office); 80 Lyme Road, Apt. 160, Kendal at Hanover, Hanover, NH 03755, U.S.A. (Home).

STEPHENS, Toby; British actor. *RSC performances include:* Measure for Measure, Coriolanus in Coriolanus (Sir John Gielgud Award for Best Actor 1994, Ian Charlson Award 1995), Young Beamish in Unfinished Business, Wallenstein, Bertram in All's Well That Ends Well, Pompey in Anthony and Cleopatra. *Other stage appearances include:* Ring around the Moon, Lincoln Center Theater, N.Y., Britannicus, Phedre, Almedia & Brooklyn Acad., N.Y., A Streetcar Named Desire, The Haymarket, Damis in Tartuffe, Playhouse Theatre. *Films include:* Eugene Onegin, Sunset Heights, Photographic Fairies, Cousin Bette, Twelfth Night, Orlando. *Television includes:* Tenant of Wildfell Hall (BBC), A View from the Bridge, Oliver in Camomile Lawn. *Address:* c/o ICM, Oxford House, 76 Oxford Street, London, W1N 0AX, England. *Telephone:* 0171-636 6565. *Fax:* 0171-223 0101.

STEPHENSON, Hugh; British journalist and professor; b. 18 July 1938, Simla, India; s. of late Sir Hugh Stephenson and Lady Stephenson; m. 1st Auriol Stevens 1962 (divorced 1987); two s. one d.; m. 2nd Diana Eden 1990; ed. New Coll., Oxford, Univ. of California, Berkeley; served diplomatic service, London and Bonn 1964–68; with The Times, London 1969–81, Ed., The Times Business News 1971–81; Ed. The New Statesman 1982–86; Prof. of Journalism, The City Univ. 1986–; Dir. History Today Ltd. 1981–. *Publications:* The Coming Clash 1972, Mrs. Thatcher's First Year 1980, Claret and Chips 1982, Libel and the Media (with others) 1997. *Address:* Department of Journalism, City University, Northampton Square, London, EC1V 0HB, England.

STEPHENSON, (James) Ian (Love), B.A., R.A.; British painter and professor; b. 11 Jan. 1934, Meadowfield, Co. Durham; s. of James Stephenson and May Stephenson (née Emery); m. Kate Brown 1959; one s. one d.; ed. King Edward VII School of Art, King's Coll., Univ. of Durham; tutorial student, then Studio Demonstrator, King's Coll., Newcastle upon Tyne 1955–58; Boise Scholar in Italy, Univ. of London 1958–59; Visiting Lecturer, Polytechnic School of Art, London 1959–62; Visiting Painter, Chelsea School of Art 1959–66; Dir. Foundation Studies, Dept. of Fine Art, Univ. of Newcastle 1966–70; Dir. M.A. Postgrad. Painting, Chelsea School of Art 1970–89; Fine Art Adviser, Canterbury Art Coll. 1974–79; mem. Visual Arts Panel, Northern Arts Asscn., Newcastle 1967–70, Fine Art Panel, NCDAD 1972–74, Perm. Cttee., New Contemporary Asscn. 1973–75, Fine Art Bd., CNAA 1974–75, Advisory Cttee., Nat. Exhbn. of Children's Art, Manchester 1975–92, Working Party, R.A. Jubilee Exhbn. 1976–77, Selection Cttee., Arts Council Awards 1977–78, Recommending Cttee., Chantrey Bequest 1979–80, R.A. Council 1979–80, 1988–90, 1996–98, R.A. Steward, Artists' Gen. Benevolent Inst. 1979–80, Chief Hanger R.A. Summer Exhbn. 1998; Vice-Pres. Sunderland Arts Centre 1982–86, Boise Scholarship Cttee. 1983; Sr. Examiner London Univ. 1975–83, Heriot-Watt and Edin. Univs. 1989–96 and numerous art schools; juror numerous competitions; Hon. mem. Accademia Italia 1980–, Mark Twain Soc., U.S.A. 1978–; numerous exhbns. London, Amsterdam, Lugano, Paris, Berlin, Antwerp, Milan, Washington, Geneva, Rio de Janeiro, Hong Kong etc.; work in many collections, including: Arts Council of G.B., British Council, Birmingham and Bristol City Art Galleries, BP Chemicals & Co., Contemporary Art Soc., The Economist Newspaper, Granada TV, Gulbenkian Foundation, Hatton Gallery, Leeds City Art Gallery, Madison Art Center, Marzotto Roma, NatWest Bank, Northern Arts Asscn., Nuffield Foundation, Queen Elizabeth II Conf. Centre, Stuyvesant Foundation, Sunderland Art Gallery, Tate Gallery, Unilever Ltd., V&A Museum, Victoria Nat. Gallery, Welsh Nat. Museum, Whitworth Art Gallery; prizes include: Jr. Section, Moores Exhbn., Liverpool 1957; European Selection, Premio Marzotto, Valdagno 1964; First, Northern Painters' Exhbn., Newcastle 1966. *Address:* 49 Elm Park Gardens, London, SW10 9PA, England.

STEPIN, Vyacheslav Semenovich; Russian philosopher; b. 19 Aug. 1934, Bryansk; s. of Semen Nikolaievich Stepin and Antonina Grigorievna (Petrova) Stepina; m. Tatiana Ivanovna Vagranova 1957; ed. Belorussia State Univ.; Prof., Chair.; Dir. Inst. of History of Natural Sciences and Tech. 1987–88; Dir. Inst. of Philosophy 1988–; corresp. mem. U.S.S.R. (now Russian) Acad. of Sciences 1987, mem. 1994; research in theory of cognition, philosophy of science and tech., history of science; Vice-Pres. Philosophy Soc., Pres. Asscn. For Humanitarian Dialogue. *Publications include:* Contemporary Positivism and Science 1963, Practical Nature of Cognition and Methodical Problems of Contemporary Physics 1970, Methods of Scientific Cognition 1974, Scientific Revolutions in Dynamics of Culture 1987, Philosophical Anthropology and Philosophy of Science 1992, Scientific Picture of the World in the Culture of Technogenic Civilization 1994, Philosophy of Science and Technics 1995, Age of Changes and Scenarios of the Future 1996. *Address:* Institute of Philosophy, Russian Academy of Sciences, Volkhonka str. 14, 119842 Moscow (Office); D.M. Ulianov str. 3, Ap. 130, Moscow, Russia (Home). *Telephone:* (095) 203-95-69 (Office). *Fax:* (095) 200-32-50.

STERCKEN, Hans, DR.PHIL.; German politician; b. 2 Sept. 1923, Aachen; s. of Josef Stercken and Johanna Jeuckens; m. Annemarie Wittelsberger 1953; one s. four d.; ed. Kaiser-Karl-Gymnasium, Aachen and Univ. of Bonn; Ed. Bonner Rundschau 1952–54; Head of Div. Press and Information Office of Fed. Govt. 1954–68; Adviser to Govt. of Turkey 1957–58, to Govts. of Cameroon, Guinea, Mauritania and Senegal 1965; Man. Dir. Fed. Centre for Political Educ. 1969–76; mem. Bundestag (for Aachen) 1976–94, Chair. Cttee. on Foreign Affairs 1985–94; Pres. German-Greek Asscn. 1961–, German Africa Foundation 1978–86, German-Turkish Asscn. 1983–, German Atlantic Asscn. 1990–, Swiss-German Asscn. 1990–; Leader German Del. IPU 1982–85, mem. Exec. Cttee. IPU 1983–88, Pres. Inter-Parl. Council of IPU 1985–88, Hon. Pres. 1990–; decorations from Fed. Repub. of Germany, Austria, Belgium, Cameroon, Finland, France, Greece, Guinea, Italy, Portugal, Spain, Order of Malta, German Red Cross; Christian Democrat. *Publications:* De Gaulle hat gesagt 1968, Vive l'Europe 1969, Zurück zum Leben 1980. *Address:* Annastrasse 36, 52062 Aachen, Germany. *Telephone:* (0241) 20880.

STERLING, Michael John Howard, B.ENG., PH.D., F.ENG., F.I.E.E., F.R.S.A.; British professor of engineering; b. 9 Feb. 1946, Paddock Wood, Kent; s. of Richard Howard Sterling and Joan Valeria Sterling, née Skinner; m. Wendy Karla Anstead 1969; two s.; ed. Hampton Grammar School, Middx., Univ. of Sheffield; student apprentice, AEI/GEC 1964–68; GEC Research Engineer 1968–71; Lecturer in Control Eng., Univ. of Sheffield 1971–78, Sr. Lecturer 1978–80; Prof. of Eng., Univ. of Durham 1980–90; Vice-Chancellor and Prin., Brunel Univ. 1990–; mem. Council I.E.E. 1991–93, Vice-Pres. 1997–; mem. Science & Eng. Research Council Eng. Bd. 1989–92, Electricity Research Council 1987–89, Royal Acad. of Eng. Standing Cttee. for Educ., Training and Competence to Practise 1993–97, Cttee. 2 for Int. Co-operation in Higher Educ., British Council 1991–96; Chair. OCEPS Ltd. 1990–, Higher Educ. Statistics Agency 1992–, Higher Educ. Funding Council Steering Cttee. on Performance Indicators 1992–95 (mem. Quality Assessment Cttee. 1992–95), WASMACS Ltd. 1994–; Fellow Inst. of Measurement and Control (Pres. 1988, Council mem. 1983–91); Gov. Burnham Grammar School 1990–, Hampton School 1991– (Chair. of Govs. 1997–); Hon. D.Eng. (Sheffield) 1995; Inst. of Measurement and Control 1980 ICI Prize, I.E.E. Hartree Premium 1985; Liveryman Worshipful Co. of Engineers 1997. *Publications:* Book-Power System Control 1978; over 200 tech. papers and book contribs. *Leisure interests:* gardening, D.I.Y., computers, model railways. *Address:* Brunel University, Uxbridge, Middx., UB8 3PH, England. *Telephone:* (01895) 274000. *Fax:* (01895) 232806.

STERLING OF PLAISTOW, Baron (Life Peer), cr. 1990; **Jeffrey Maurice Sterling,** Kt., C.B.E.; British business executive; b. 27 Dec. 1934; s. of Harry Sterling and Alice Sterling; m. Dorothy Ann Smith 1985; one d.; ed. Reigate Grammar School, Preston Manor County School and Guildhall School of Music, London; Paul Schweder & Co. (Stock Exchange) 1955-57; G. Eberstadt & Co. 1957–62; Financial Dir. General Guarantee Corpn. 1962–64; Man. Dir. Gula Investments Ltd. 1964–69; Chair. Sterling Guarantee Trust PLC 1969–85 (merged with P&O 1985), P & O Steam Navigation Co. 1983–, Chair. P&O Asia 1992–; Special Adviser to Sec. of State for Industry 1982–83, to Sec. of State for Trade and Industry 1983–90; mem. British Airways Bd. 1979–82; mem. Exec., World Org. for Rehabilitation by Training Union 1966–, Chair. Org. Cttee. 1969–73, Chair. ORT Tech. Services 1974–, Vice-Pres. British ORT 1978–; Pres. Gen. Council of British Shipping 1990–91, EC Shipowners' Asscns. 1992–94; Deputy Chair. and Hon. Treasurer London

Celebrations Cttee. Queen's Silver Jubilee 1975–83; Chair. Young Vic Co. 1975–83; Vice-Chair. and Chair. of Exec. Motability 1977–94, Chair. 1994–; Chair. of the Govs. Royal Ballet School 1983–; Hon mem. Royal Inst. of Chartered Surveyors 1993; Fellow, I.S.V.A. 1995; Hon. Fellow Inst. of Marine Engineers 1991, Inst. of Chartered Shipbrokers 1992, Royal Inst. of Chartered Shipbrokers 1992, Royal Inst. of Naval Architects 1997; Gov. Royal Ballet 1986–; Freeman City of London; Hon. Capt. R.N.R. 1991–; Hon. D.B.A. (Nottingham Trent) 1995; Hon. D.C.L. (Durham) 1996; Elder Brother Trinity House 1991. *Leisure interests:* music, swimming, tennis. *Address:* The Peninsular and Oriental Steam Navigation Company, 79 Pall Mall, London, SW1Y 5EJ, England.

STERN, Ernest, M.A., PH.D.; American international official; b. 25 Aug. 1933, Frankfurt, Germany; s. of Henry Stern; m. Zina Gold 1957; ed. Queens Coll., New York, and Fletcher School of Law and Diplomacy; Economist, U.S. Dept. of Commerce 1957–59; Program Economist, U.S. Agency for Int. Devt. (USAID) 1959–63; Instructor, Middle East Tech. Univ. 1960–61; Economist, Office of Pakistan Affairs, USAID 1963–64, Officer in Charge of Pakistan Affairs 1964–64, Asst. Dir. for Devt. Policy USAID India 1965–67, Deputy Dir. USAID Pakistan 1967–68, Deputy Staff Dir. Comm. on Int. Devt. (Pearson Comm.) 1968–69; Lecturer, Woodrow Wilson School of Public and Int. Affairs, Princeton 1971; Sr. Staff mem. Council on Int. Econ. Policy, White House 1971; joined Int. Bank for Reconstruction and Devt. (World Bank) 1972, various posts incl. Deputy Chair. Econ. Cttee., Sr. Adviser on Devt. Policy, Dir. Devt. Policy, then Vice-Pres. S. Asia until 1978; Vice-Pres. Operations, World Bank July 1978–, Sr. Vice-Pres., Operations 1980–87, Sr. Vice-Pres., Finance 1987, Man. Dir. 1991–95; mem. Bd. Advisors Inst. for Int. Econs., Washington D.C.; mem. Bd. of Overseers, Int. Center for Econ. Growth, Calif.; William A. Jump Memorial Foundation Meritorious Award 1964, 1966.

STERN, Fritz, PH.D.; American historian and professor; b. 2 Feb. 1926, Breslau, Germany; s. of Rudolf A. Stern and Catherine B. Stern; m. 1st Margaret J. Bassett 1947 (divorced 1992); one s. one d.; m. 2nd Elisabeth Niebuhr Sifton 1996; ed. Bentley School, New York, Columbia Univ.; Lecturer and Inst. Columbia Univ. 1946–51; Acting Asst. Prof. Cornell Univ. 1951–53; Asst. Prof. Columbia Univ. 1953–57, Assoc. Prof. 1957–63, Full Prof. 1963–67, Seth Low Prof. 1967–92, Univ. Prof. 1992–96, Univ. Prof. Emer. 1997–, Provost 1980–83; Visiting Prof. Free Univ. of Berlin 1954, Yale Univ. 1963, Fondation Nationale des Sciences Politiques, Paris 1979; Perm. Visiting Prof. Konstanz Univ. 1966–; Consultant U.S. State Dept. 1966–67; Guggenheim Fellowship 1969–70; mem. OECD team on German Educ. 1971–72; Netherlands Inst. for Advanced Study 1972–73; Trustee German Marshall Fund 1981–, Aspen Inst. Berlin 1983–; Sr. Adviser, U.S. Embassy, Bonn 1993–94; mem. American Acad. of Arts and Sciences 1969–, Trilateral Comm. 1983–90, American Philosophical Soc. 1988, German-American Academic Council 1993–97; corresp. mem. Deutsche Akad. für Dichtung und Sprache 1988; Senator, Deutsche Nationalstiftung 1993–; Hon. D.Litt. (Oxford) 1985; Hon. LL.D (New School for Social Research, New York) 1997, (Columbia Univ.) 1998; Lucas Prize (Tübingen) 1984, Kulturpreis Schlesien (Wrocław) 1996, Lionel Trilling Book Award 1977; Orden pour le Mérite (Germany) 1994. *Publications:* The Politics of Cultural Despair: A Study in the Rise of the Germanic Ideology 1961, Gold and Iron: Bismarck, Bleichroeder, and the Building of the German Empire 1977, The Failure of Illiberalism: Essays in the Political Culture of Modern Germany 1972, Dreams and Delusions: The Drama of German History 1987, ed. The Varieties of History from Voltaire to the Present 1956, Der Nationalsozialismus als Versuchung, in Reflexionen Finsterer Zeit 1984, Verspielte Grösse. Essays zur deutschen Geschichte 1996. *Leisure interests:* reading, hiking, cross-country skiing. *Address:* 324 Fayerweather Hall, Columbia University, New York, NY 10027 (Office); 15 Claremont Avenue, New York, NY 10027, U.S.A. *Telephone:* (212) 666-2891 (Home). *Fax:* (212) 316 0370 (Home).

STERN, Isaac; American violinist; b. 21 July 1920, Russia; s. of Solomon and Clara Stern; m. 1st Nora Kaye 1948; m. 2nd Vera Lindenblit 1951; two s. one d.; m. 3rd Linda Reynolds 1996; studied San Francisco, notably with Naoum Blinder; début, San Francisco Symphony 1935; New York début 1937; world tours every year 1947–; appearances with major orchestras; extensive recordings; frequent appearances major festivals—Edin., Casals, Tanglewood, etc.; Pres. Carnegie Hall 1960–; Chair. Bd. of Dirs., American Israel Cultural Foundation; fmr. mem. Nat. Arts Council; Chair., Founder Jerusalem Music Centre 1973; Dr. h.c. (Harvard) 1992; awarded first Albert Schweitzer Music Award 1975, Grammy Award 1971, Acad. Award 1981 (for documentary From Mao to Mozart), Kennedy Center Award 1984, Wolf Foundation Prize in Arts 1987, Grammy Lifetime Achievement Award 1987, Emmy Award (Carnegie Hall Re-opening) 1987, Nat. Medal of the Arts 1991, Presidential Medal of Freedom 1992; Commdr., Ordre de la Couronne, Légion d'honneur; Order of the Rising Sun 1997. *Address:* Carnegie Hall Corpn., 881 7th Avenue, New York, NY 10019; ICM, 40 W. 57th Street, New York, NY 10019, U.S.A.

STERN, Jacques, M.SC.; French business executive; b. 21 March 1932, Paris; m. Janine Riemer 1956; three s.; ed. Ecole Polytechnique, Ecole Nationale supérieure de l'Aéronautique, Harvard Univ., U.S.A.; in charge of devt. of air defence computer system, French Air Force 1958–64; f. Société d'Etudes des Systèmes d'Automation (SESA) 1964; apptd. Chair. and C.E.O. Bull 1982, Chair. Honeywell Bull Inc. 1987, Hon. Pres. Bull 1989–; Founder, Pres. Sycomore 1989–; Founder Stern Systèmes d'information 1998; Founder and Pres. Synesys 1998–; mem. Acad. of Sciences Applications Cttee. 1987–; Vice-Pres. Fondation Fyssen 1992–; Officier, Ordre Nat. du Mérite; Chevalier, Légion d'honneur. *Publications:* several tech. books. *Address:* Synesys, Bâtiment Saint Germain, 12 boulevard des Iles, 92130 Issy Les Moulineaux, France. *Telephone:* 41-23-09-40. *Fax:* 41-23-09-49.

STERN, Klaus, DR.IUR.; German professor of law and judge; b. 11 Jan. 1932, Nuremberg; m. Helga Stern 1976; ed. Humanistisches Gymnasium, Nuremberg and Univs. of Erlangen and Munich; Dozent, Univ. of Munich 1961; Prof. Berlin Univ. 1962; Prof. and Dir. Inst. für öffentliches Recht und Verwaltungslehre, Univ. of Cologne 1966–, Rector 1971–73, Pro-Rector 1973–75; Head of Studies Verwaltungs- und Wirtschaftsakademie Düsseldorf 1966–; Judge, Constitutional Court, Nordrhein-Westfalen 1976–; mem. Rheinland- Westfälische Akademie der Wissenschaften 1978; Grosses Bundesverdienstkreuz. *Publications:* Staatsrecht der Bundesrepublik Deutschland (4 vols.); many other books and articles on constitutional and admin. law. *Address:* Universität Köln, Institut für öffentliches Recht und Verwaltungslehre, Albertus-Magnus-Platz, 50931 Cologne, Germany.

STERN, Robert Arthur Morton, B.A., M.ARCH., F.A.I.A.; American architect and educator; b. 23 May 1939, New York; s. of Sidney Stern and Sonya (Cohen) Stern; m. Lynn G. Solinger 1966 (divorced 1977); one s.; ed. Columbia and Yale Univs.; Program Dir. Architectural League New York 1965–66; designer, Richard Meier, architect, New York 1966; consultant Small Parks Program, Dept. of Parks, New York 1966–70; urban designer, Housing and Devt. Admin. New York 1967–70; partner Robert A.M. Stern & John S. Hagmann, Architects, New York 1969–77, Prin. Robert A.M. Stern Architects 1977–89, Prin. Partner 1989–; lecturer to Prof. of Architecture, Columbia Univ. 1970–72, Prof. 1982–; Acting Dir. Historical Preservation Program 1991–; mem. Bd. of Regents American Architecture Foundation 1989–, Bd. of Dirs. Chicago Inst. for Architecture and Urbanism 1990–93, Bd. of Dirs. Preservation League of N.Y., Exec. Cttee., Architectural League of New York 1977– (Pres. 1973–77); numerous awards including A.I.A. Nat. Honour awards 1980, 1985, 1990. *Publications include:* New Directions in American Architecture 1969, The House that Bob Built 1991, The American Houses of Robert A. M. Stern 1991, New York 1960 (with Thomas Mellins and David Fishman) 1995. *Address:* 460 West 34th Street, 18th Floor, New York, NY 10001 (Office); 177 East 77th Street, New York, NY 10021, U.S.A. (Home). *Telephone:* (212) 967-5100 (Office).

STERZINSKY, H.E. Cardinal Georg Maximilian; German ecclesiastic; b. 9 Feb. 1936, Warlack, Warmia; ordained priest 1960; elected Bishop of Berlin 1989, consecrated 1989; cr. Cardinal 1991; Archbishop of Berlin 1994–; mem. Congregation for Catholic Educ., Pontifical Council for the Pastoral Care of Migrants and Itinerant People. *Address:* Erzbischöfl. Ordinariat, Postfach 15 60, 14005 Berlin, Germany.

STETTER, Ib; Danish politician and businessman; b. 1 March 1917, Odense; s. of Egon Madsen; m. Ivy Stetter 1944; one s. two d.; ed. Copenhagen School of Business Admin.; Man. Dir. of large co. in Ålborg, Pres. of North Jutland Econ. Council; M.P. 1964–87; Cttee. Chair. Parl. Group of Conservative Party, Nat. Chair. 1977–81; fmr. Pres. of Nordic Council; Minister for Industry 1982–86; Conservative. *Address:* Provstejorden 62, 9000 Ålborg, Denmark. *Telephone:* 98-184762.

STEVEN, Stewart Gustav; British journalist; b. 30 Oct. 1935, Hamburg, Germany; s. of Rudolph Steven and Trude Steven; m. Inka Sobieniewska 1965; one s.; ed. Mayfield Coll., Sussex; political reporter, Cen. Press Features 1961–63; political corresp., Western Daily Press 1963–64; political reporter, Daily Express 1964–65, Diplomatic Corresp. 1965–67, Foreign Ed. 1967–72; Asst. Ed. Daily Mail 1972–74, Assoc. Ed. 1974–82; Ed. Mail on Sunday 1982–92, columnist 1996–; Dir. Associated Newspapers Holdings Ltd. 1989–95; Ed. Evening Standard 1992–95; Chair. Liberty Publishing & Media Ltd. 1996–97; Chair. Equity Theatre Comm. 1995–96, Nat. Campaign for the Arts 1996–; mem. Bd. Better English Campaign 1995–97, Thames Advisory Group 1995–97, London Film Comm. 1996–; Hon. perpetual student Bart's Hosp. 1993. *Publications:* Operation Splinter Factor 1974, The Spymasters of Israel 1976, The Poles 1982. *Leisure interest:* swimming pool maintenance. *Address:* 29 Priory Avenue, Chiswick, London, W4 1TZ, England. *Telephone:* 0181-995 5212. *Fax:* 0181-994 2560.

STEVENS, Graeme Roy, Q.S.O., M.SC., PH.D., D.SC., F.R.S.N.Z.; New Zealand palaeontologist; b. 17 July 1932, Lower Hutt; m. Diane L. M. Ollivier 1962; two s. one d.; ed. Waterloo School, Hutt Valley High School, Victoria Univ. and Cambridge Univ.; Jr. Lecturer in Geology, Vic. Univ., Wellington 1954–56; Palaeontologist, N.Z. Geological Survey 1956–, Chief Palaeontologist, Hon. Research Assoc.; demonstrator, Cambridge Univ. 1956–59; Hamilton Award (Royal Soc. of N.Z.) 1959 and other awards. *Publications:* eleven books and 175 scientific papers. *Leisure interests:* cross-country running, walking, local history, popularization of science. *Address:* N.Z. Geological Survey, P.O. Box 30368, Lower Hutt (Office); 19A Wairere Road, Belmont, Lower Hutt, New Zealand (Home). *Telephone:* 5699059 (Office); 5697543 (Home).

STEVENS, Sir Jocelyn Edward Greville, Kt., C.V.O., F.R.S.A.; British publisher; b. 14 Feb. 1932, London; s. of Major C.G.B. Stewart-Stevens and Betty Hulton; m. Jane Armyne Sheffield 1956 (dissolved 1979); one s. two d. (one s. deceased); ed. Eton, Cambridge; mil. service Rifle Brigade 1950–52; journalist Hulton Press 1955–56; Chair. and Man. Dir. Stevens Press Ltd.,

Ed. Queen Magazine 1957–68; Personal Asst. to Chair. Beaverbrook Newspapers 1968, Dir. 1971–81, Man. Dir. 1974–77; Man. Dir. Evening Standard Co. Ltd. 1969–72, Daily Express 1972–74; Deputy Chair. and Man. Dir. Express Newspapers 1974–81; Ed. and Publr. The Magazine 1982–84; Dir. Centaur Communications 1982–84; Gov. Imperial Coll. of Science, Tech. and Medicine 1985–92, Winchester School of Art 1986–89; Rector and Vice-Provost R.C.A. 1984–92; Chair. The Silver Trust 1990–93, English Heritage 1992–; Deputy Chair. Independent TV Comm. 1991–96; Dir. (non-exec.) The TV Corpn. 1996; Pres. The Cheyne Walk Trust 1989–93; Trustee Eureka! The Children's Museum 1990–; Hon. D.Litt. (Loughborough) 1989, Hon. F.C.S.D. 1990, Sr. Fellow R.C.A. 1990. *Leisure interests:* skiing. *Address:* 14 Cheyne Walk, London, SW3 5RA, England. *Telephone:* 0171-351 1141. *Fax:* 0171-351 7963.

STEVENS, John Edgar, C.B.E., M.A., PH.D., F.B.A.; British university professor (retd.); b. 8 Oct. 1921, London; s. of William C. J. Stevens and Fanny Stevens; m. Charlotte E. M. Somner 1946; two s. two d.; ed. Christ's Hospital, Horsham and Magdalene Coll., Cambridge; served R.N.; Bye Fellow, 1948, Research Fellow 1950, Fellow, Magdalene Coll., Cambridge 1950, Tutor 1958–74, Pres. Magdalene Coll. 1983–88, now Pres. Emer.; Univ. Lecturer in English 1954–74, Reader in English and Musical History 1974–78, Prof. of Medieval and Renaissance English 1978–88, now Prof. Emer.; Chair. Plainsong and Medieval Music Soc. 1988–94; Hon. D. Mus. (Exeter) 1989; Derek Allen Prize for Musicology 1989. *Publications:* Medieval Carols 1952, Music and Poetry in the Early Tudor Court 1961, Music at the Court of Henry VIII 1962, Medieval French Plays (with R. Axton) 1971, Medieval Romance 1973, Early Tudor Songs & Carols 1975, Words and Music in the Early Middle Ages 1986. *Leisure interest:* viol-playing. *Address:* 4 & 5 Bell's Court, Castle Street, Cambridge, CB3 0AH, England.

STEVENS, John Paul, J.D.; American judge; b. 20 April 1920, Chicago, Ill.; s. of Ernest James Stevens and Elizabeth Street; m. 1st Elizabeth Jane Sheeren 1942; one s. three d.; m. 2nd Maryan Mulholland Simon 1979; ed. Univ. of Chicago, Northwestern Univ. School of Law; served U.S.N. (Bronze Star Medal) 1942–45; Co-Ed. of Law Review at Northwestern Univ. School of Law 1947; Law Clerk to Supreme Court Justice Wiley Rutledge 1947; worked with Poppenhusen, Johnston, Thompson and Raymond law practice 1948–51, 1952; Partner, Rothschild, Stevens, Barry and Myers 1952–70; Circuit Judge, Seventh Circuit Court of Appeals 1970–75; Assoc. Justice, U.S. Supreme Court Dec. 1975–; Assoc. Counsel, Monopoly Power Sub-Cttee. of House of Reps. Judiciary Cttee. 1951; mem. Attorney Gen.'s Nat. Cttee. on Antitrust Laws 1953–55; part-time teacher, Northwestern Univ. School of Law, later Univ. of Chicago Law School 1952–56; admitted to Ill. Bar 1949, to U.S. Supreme Court 1954; mem. American Law Inst. *Publications:* numerous articles on commercial monopoly affairs. *Address:* United States Supreme Court, 1 First Street, N.E., Washington, DC 20543, U.S.A.

STEVENS, Robert Bocking, M.A., D.C.L.; lawyer and academic; b. 8 June 1933; s. of John S. Stevens and Enid Dorothy Bocking Stevens; m. 1st Rosemary Wallace 1961 (divorced 1983); m. 2nd Katherine Booth 1985; one s. two d.; ed. Keble Coll. Oxford and Yale Univ.; mem. Essex Court Chambers, Lincoln's Inn Fields 1965–, Midland Circuit 1962–76; Asst. Prof. of Law, Yale Univ. 1959–61, Assoc. Prof. 1961–65, Prof. 1965–76, Fellow, Jonathan Edwards Coll. 1963–76; Prof. of Law and Adjunct Prof. of History, Tulane Univ. 1976–78, Provost 1976–78; Pres. Haverford Coll. 1978–87; Prof. of History, Univ. of Calif. Santa Cruz 1987–93, Chancellor 1987–91; Counsel, Covington & Burling (Washington, D.C.), London 1991–; mem. Council, Justice (U.K. Br., Int. Comm. of Jurists) 1992–; Master, Pembroke Coll. Oxford 1993–; numerous other academic and legal appts. etc.; four hon. degrees. *Publications include:* Law and Politics: The House of Lords as a Judicial Body 1800–1976 1978, The American Law School: Legal Education in America 1850–1980 1983, The Independence of the Judiciary: The View from the Lord Chancellor's Office 1993; co-author and ed. of other books on law, history and welfare; articles and monographs. *Address:* Master's Lodgings, Pembroke College, Oxford, OX1 1DW; Covington & Burling, Leconfield House, Curzon Street, London, W1Y 8AS; 77 Little Barrington, Glos., OX18 4TE, England. *Telephone:* (01865) 276401 (Oxford); 0171-495 5655 (London); (01451) 844536 (Glos.). *Fax:* (01865) 276446 (Oxford); 0171-495 3101 (London).

STEVENS, Rosemary Anne, PH.D.; American university professor; b. 18 March 1935, U.K.; d. of William E. Wallace and Mary A. Wallace; m. 1st Robert B. Stevens 1961 (divorced 1983); one s. one d.; m. 2nd Jack D. Barchas 1994; ed. Oxford and Manchester Univs., U.K. and Yale Univ., U.S.A.; trained in hosp. admin. and worked as hosp. admin. Nat. Health Service, U.K.; mem. Faculty, Prof. of Public Health, Prof. in Inst. of Policy Studies, Yale Univ., U.S.A. 1962–76; Prof., Dept. of Health Systems Man. (Chair. 1977-78) and Adjunct Prof. of Political Science, Tulane Univ. 1976–79; Prof. of History and Sociology of Science, Univ. of Pa. 1979–, Chair. 1980–83, 1986–91; UPS Foundation Prof. in Social Sciences 1990–91, Dean, Thomas S. Gates Prof. 1991–96; Stanley I. Sheerr Prof. 1997–; mem. Inst. of Medicine of N.A.S.; Fellow American Acad. of Arts and Sciences; Rockefeller Humanities Award 1983–84, Guggenheim Award 1984–85, Baxter Foundation Prize for Health Services Research 1990. *Publications:* Medical Practice in Modern England 1966, American Medicine and the Public Interest 1971, Foreign Trained Physicians and American Medicine 1972, Welfare Medicine in America 1974, The Alien Doctors: Foreign Medical Graduates in American Hospitals 1978, In Sickness and in Wealth: American Hospitals In the Twentieth Century 1989; various articles. *Leisure interests:* painting, reading, flea markets. *Address:* Department of History and Sociology of Science, University of Pennsylvania, 3440 Market Street, Philadelphia, PA 19104; 324 Logan Hall, University of Pennsylvania, 249 South 36th Street, Philadelphia, PA 19104 (Office); 1900 Rittenhouse Square, # 18A, Philadephia, PA 19103, U.S.A. (Home). *Telephone:* (215) 898-8400. *Fax:* (215) 573-2231.

STEVENS, Theodore Fulton, LL.B.; American politician and lawyer; b. 18 Nov. 1923, Indianapolis, Ind.; s. of George A. and Gertrude (née Chancellor) Stevens; m. 1st Ann Cherrington 1952 (died 1978); three s. two d.; m. 2nd Catherine Chandler 1980; one d.; ed. High School, Redondo Beach, Calif., Univ. of Calif. at L.A., and Harvard Law School; U.S. Attorney, Fairbanks, Alaska 1953–56; Legis. Counsel, Dept. of Interior, Washington, D.C. 1956–58; Asst. to Sec. of Interior 1958–60; Solicitor of Interior Dept. 1960; pvt. law practice, Anchorage, Alaska 1961–68; Senator from Alaska 1968–; Asst. Minority Leader U.S. Senate 1977–80, Asst. Majority Leader 1981–85; U.S. Senate del. to Canadian-U.S. Interparl. Conf., to British-U.S. Interparl. Conf.; Admin. Co-Chair., Senate Arms Control Observer Group; Chair. Senate Appropriations Cttee.; Senate Commerce Cttee.; Senate Governmental Affairs Cttee; Senate Rules Cttee.; Republican. *Address:* Room 522, Hart Senate Office Building, Washington, DC 20510 (Office); P.O. Box 100879, Anchorage, AK 99510, U.S.A. (Home). *Telephone:* (202) 224-3004 (Office).

STEVENS OF LUDGATE, Baron (Life Peer), cr. 1987, of Ludgate in the City of London; **David Robert Stevens,** M.A.; British business executive; b. 26 May 1936; s. of (Arthur) Edwin Stevens; m. 1st Patricia Rose (divorced 1971); one s. one d.; m. 2nd Melissa Milicevich 1977 (died 1989); m. 3rd Meriza Giori 1990; ed. Stowe School and Sidney Sussex Coll. Cambridge; man. trainee, Elliott Automation 1959; Dir. Hill Samuel Securities 1959–68, Drayton Group 1968–74; Chair. City & Foreign (now Alexander Proudfoot PLC) 1976–95, Drayton Far East 1976–93, English & Int. 1976–79, Consolidated Venture (fmrly. Montagu Boston) 1979–93, Drayton Consolidated 1980–92, Drayton Japan 1980–93, Econ. Devt. Cttee. for Civil Eng. 1984–86; Dir. United News & Media PLC (fmrly. United Newspapers PLC) 1974–, Chair. 1981–; C.E.O. INVESCO MIM 1980–87, Deputy Chair. 1987–89, Chair. 1989–93; Chair. MIM Britannia Ltd. (fmrly. Montagu Investment Man. Ltd.) 1980–92 (C.E.O. 1980–87), Express Newspapers 1985–. *Leisure interests:* golf, gardening. *Address:* Ludgate House, 245 Blackfriars Road, London, SE1 9UY, England.

STEVENSON, Adlai E., III; American politician and lawyer; b. 10 Oct. 1930, Chicago, Ill.; s. of late Adlai Stevenson II (fmr. Gov. of Illinois, presidential candidate and Amb. to UN); great-grandson of Adlai E. Stevenson (Vice-Pres. of U.S.A. 1893-97); m. Nancy L. Anderson 1955; two s. two d.; ed. Milton Acad., Mass., and Harvard Univ.; law clerk to a justice of Ill. Supreme Court 1957; joined Chicago law firm of Mayer, Brown and Platt 1958–66, partner 1966–67, 1981–83, of Counsel 1983–91; elected to Ill. House of Reps. 1964; State Treas. of Ill. 1966–70; Senator from Illinois 1970–81; Democratic Cand. for Gov. of Ill. 1982, 1986; Chair. SC&M Int. Ltd. 1991–95, Pres. 1995–; numerous awards, hon. degrees and directorships; Democrat. *Address:* SC&M International Ltd., 225 West Wacker Drive, Chicago, IL 60606, U.S.A. (Office). *Telephone:* (773) 281-3578. *Fax:* (773) 281-4812.

STEVENSON, Sir Henry Dennistoun, Kt., C.B.E.; British business consultant; b. 19 July 1945, Edin.; s. of Alexander James Stevenson and Sylvia Florence Stevenson (née Ingleby); m. Charlotte Susan Stevenson (née Vanneck); four s.; ed. Glenalmond School and King's Coll., Cambridge; Dir. Pearson Employee Share Trustees Ltd., Chair. Pearson PLC 1997–; Chair. Trustees of the Tate Gallery 1988–98, Sinfonia 21 1989–, GPA Group PLC 1993–; mem. Bd. of dirs. Manpower Inc. 1988–, J. Rothschild Assurance PLC 1991–97, J. Rothschild Holdings PLC 1991–, English Partnerships 1993–, British Sky Broadcasting Group PLC 1994–, British Council 1996–, Lazard Bros. & Co. Ltd. 1997–, St. James's Place Capital PLC 1997–; Dir. Cloaca Maxima Ltd. 1996–, Saxton Bampfylde Int. PLC 1996–; mem. Take Over Panel 1993; Gov. L.S.E. 1996–. *Publication:* Information and Communications Technology in UK Schools (The Stevenson Report) 1997. *Address:* 68 Pall Mall, London, SW1Y 5ES, England. *Telephone:* 0171-976 2870. *Fax:* 0171-976 2875.

STEVENSON, Juliet; British actress; b. 30 Oct. 1956; d. of Michael Guy Stevens and Virginia Ruth Marshall; one d.; ed. Hurst Lodge School, Berks., St. Catherine's School, Surrey, Royal Acad. of Dramatic Arts; with R.S.C. (now assoc. artist). *Plays include:* Midsummer Night's Dream, Measure for Measure, As You Like It, Troilus and Cressida, Les Liaisons Dangereuses, Caucasian Chalk Circle, Not I, Footfalls (all for R.S.C.), Other Worlds, Yerma, Hedda Gabler, Death and the Maiden (Olivier Award 1992), Duchess of Malfi. *Films include:* Drowning by Numbers, Ladder of Swords, Truly Madly Deeply, The Trial, The Secret Rapture, Emma; several TV roles including The Politician's Wife, Cider with Rosie. *Publications:* Clamorous Voices (jtly.) 1988, Shall I See You Again? (jtly). *Leisure interests:* talking, piano, travelling. *Address:* c/o Markham and Froggatt Ltd., Julian House, 4 Windmill Street, London, W1P 1HF, England.

STEVENSON, Robert Wilfrid, M.A., F.C.C.A.; British public affairs consultant; b. 19 April 1947, Lochalsh; s. of James Stevenson and Elizabeth Macrae; m. 1st Jennifer Grace Antonio 1972 (divorced 1979); m. 2nd Elizabeth Ann

Minogue 1991; one s. two d.; ed. Edinburgh Acad. and Univ. Coll., Oxford; Research Officer Univ. of Edin. Students Asscn. 1970–74; Sec. and Acad. Registrar, Napier Polytechnic, Edin. 1974–87; Deputy Dir. B.F.I. 1987–88, Dir. 1988–97; Dir. The Smith Inst. 1997–. *Leisure interests:* cinema, hill walking, squash, bridge, choral singing. *Address:* Missenden House, Little Missenden, Amersham, Bucks., HP7 0RD, England. *Telephone:* (01494) 890689. *Fax:* (01494) 868127.

STEVER, Horton Guyford, PH.D.; American scientist and company director; b. 24 Oct. 1916, Corning, N.Y.; s. of Ralph Raymond Stever and Alma Matt; m. Louise Risley Floyd 1946; two s. two d.; ed. Colgate Univ. and Calif. Inst. of Tech.; mem. Staff Radiation Lab. and Instructor, Officers' Radar School, M.I.T. 1941–42; Science Liaison Officer, London Mission, Office of Scientific Research and Devt. 1942–45; Asst. Prof. of Aeronautical Eng. Mass. Inst. of Tech. 1946–51, Assoc. Prof. 1951–56, Prof. 1956–65; Chief Scientist, U.S.A.F. 1955–56; Assoc. Dean of Eng., Mass. Inst. of Tech. 1956–59, Head Depts. of Mechanical Eng. Naval Architecture and Marine Eng. 1961–65; Pres. Carnegie-Mellon Univ. 1965–72; Chair. U.S.A.F. Scientific Advisory Bd. 1962–69, Aeronautics and Space Eng. Bd. 1967–69, Foreign Sec. 1984–88; mem. Exec. Cttee. Defense Science Bd., Dept. of Defense 1962–69; mem. Panel on Science and Tech. U.S. House of Reps. Comm. on Science and Tech., 1959–72, Science and Tech. Adviser to Pres. 1976–77; Science Consultant, Corp. Trustee 1977–; Trustee, Colgate Univ. 1962–72, Sarah Mellon Scaife Foundation 1965–72, Shady Side Acad. 1967–72, Univ. Research Asscn. 1977– (Pres. 1982–84); Dir. Fisher Scientific Co. 1965–72, Koppers Co. 1965–72, System Devt. Corpn. 1965–70, United Aircraft Corpn. 1966–72, TRW 1977–88, Saudi Arabian Nat. Center for Science and Tech. 1978–80, Schering Plough 1980–89, Goodyear 1981–86; mem. Nat. Acad. of Eng., Nat. Science Bd. 1970–72; Dir. Nat. Science Foundation 1972–76; Science Adviser to Pres. of U.S.A. and Chair. Fed. Council for Science and Tech., Exec. Cttee. Nat. Science Bd., Energy R & D Advisory Council; U.S. Chair. U.S.-U.S.S.R. Jt. Comm. on Scientific and Tech. Co-operation 1973–77; mem. Carnegie Comm. on Science, Tech. and Govt. 1988–93; mem. N.A.S. 1973–; Foreign mem. Fellowship of Eng. 1989–, Japan Acad. of Eng. 1989–; mem. U.S.-Japan Cttee. on Scientific Co-operation, Fed. Council on the Arts and Humanities, Nat. Council on Educational Research, and many other Govt. bodies; 18 hon. degrees; President's Certificate of Merit 1948, Exceptional Civilian Service Award, U.S.A.F. 1956, Scott Gold Medal of American Ordnance Asscn. 1960, Alumni Distinguished Service Award Calif. Inst. of Technology 1966, Distinguished Public Service Medal, Dept. of Defense 1969, Nat. Medal of Science 1991, Vannevar Bush Award 1997; Commdr., Order of Merit, Poland 1976, Distinguished Public Service Medal, NASA 1988. *Publication:* Flight (with J. J. Haggerty) 1965. *Leisure interests:* skiing, fishing, golf, hiking. *Address:* 588 Russell Avenue, Gaithersburg, MD 20877, U.S.A.

STEWART, Alec James, M.B.E.; British cricketer; b. 8 April 1963, Merton, London; s. of Michael James Stewart and Sheila Stewart; m. Lynn Stewart; one s. one d.; ed. Tiffin Boys' School, Kingston upon Thames; right-hand opening batsman; wicket-keeper; Surrey 1981– (Capt. 1992–97); 86 Tests for England 1989–90 to 1 June 1999, 13 as Capt., scoring 5,968 runs (average 41.15) including 12 hundreds; scored 21,996 first-class runs (44 hundreds) to 1 April 1999; held 11 catches, equalling world first-class record, for Surrey v Leicestershire, Leicester, 19–22 Aug. 1989; toured Australia 1990–91, 1994–95 and 1998–99 (Capt.); 105 limited-overs internationals (10 as Capt.) to 31 Dec. 1998. *Leisure interests:* soccer (Chelsea), spending time with his family. *Address:* c/o Surrey County Cricket Club, Kennington Oval, London, SE11 5SS, England.

STEWART, Brian John, M.SC., C.A.; British brewery executive; b. 9 April 1945, Stirling, Scotland; s. of Ian M. Stewart and Christina McIntyre; m. Seonaid Duncan 1971; two s. one d.; ed. Perth Acad., Edinburgh Univ.; joined Scottish & Newcastle Breweries (now Scottish and Newcastle PLC) 1976, Corp. Devt. Dir. 1985–88, Group Finance Dir. 1988–91, Group Chief Exec. 1991–, Deputy Chair. 1997–; Dir. (non-exec.) Booker 1993–, Standard Life Assurance Co. 1993–. *Leisure interests:* skiing, golf. *Address:* Scottish & Newcastle PLC, Abbey Brewery, 111 Holyrood Road, Edinburgh, EH8 8YS, Scotland. *Telephone:* 0131-556 2591. *Fax:* 0131-556 4665.

STEWART, Dave; British pop musician; b. 1952, Sunderland; m. 1st Pam Stewart (divorced); m. 2nd Siobhan Fahey 1988; two s.; formed band Longdancer and entered recording contract with Elton John's Rocket label 1973; later formed band The Tourists which reached No. 1 in charts with remake of I Only Want To Be With You 1979; The Tourists disbanded 1980; formed group Eurythmics with Annie Lennox in 1980s (disbanded 1989); albums include Sweet Dreams, Touch, Revenge, Savage, We Too Are One; solo album Greetings from the Gutter; now produces records, shoots short films, writes soundtracks for films (including Disney film The Ref), directs films, produces computer-enhanced films and collects art; has produced records and written songs for Mick Jagger, Bob Dylan, Tom Hall, etc.; Hon. D.Mus. (Westminster) 1998.

STEWART, Sir Frederick Henry, K.B., B.SC., PH.D., D.SC., F.R.S., F.R.S.E.; British geologist; b. 16 Jan. 1916, Aberdeen; s. of Frederick R. Stewart and Hester Alexander; m. Mary Florence Elinor Rainbow 1945; ed. Fettes Coll., Edinburgh, Univ. of Aberdeen, Emmanuel Coll., Cambridge; Mineralogist in Research Dept., ICI Ltd. 1941–43; Lecturer in Geology, Durham Univ. 1943–56; Regius Prof. of Geology, Edin. Univ. 1956–82; Chair. Natural Environment Research Council 1971–73, Advisory Bd. for the Research Councils 1973–79; mem. Advisory Council for Applied Research and Devt. 1977–79; Trustee British Museum (Natural History) 1983–88; Hon. D.Sc. (Aberdeen) 1975, (Leicester) 1977, (Heriot-Watt) 1978, (Durham) 1983, (Glasgow) 1988; Lyell Fund Award, J. B. Tyrrell Fund, Lyell Medal, Geological Soc. of London; Mineralogical Soc. of America Award; Clough Medal, Geological Soc. of Edinburgh; Sorby Medal, Yorkshire Geological Soc. 1975. *Publications:* The British Caledonides, Marine Evaporites and papers in Mineralogical Magazine, Journal of Geological Soc. of London and other journals dealing with igneous and metamorphic petrology and salt deposits. *Leisure interests:* fishing and fossil fishing. *Address:* House of Letterawe, Lochawe, Argyll, PA33 1AH, Scotland. *Telephone:* (01838) 200329 (Lochawe).

STEWART, Jane, B.SC.; Canadian politician; b. 1955, St. George, Ont.; m.; two s.; ed. Trent Univ.; worked in area of human resources for many cos. in Canada and U.S.A. including Imperial Oil; M.P. for Brant 1993–; Minister of Nat. Revenue 1996–97, of Indian Affairs and Northern Devt. 1997–; Chair. Nat. Liberal Caucus 1994–; fmr. mem. House of Commons Standing Cttees. on Finance, and on Aboriginal Affairs. *Address:* Indian and Northern Affairs Canada, Les Terrasses de la Chaudière, Bureau 1400, 10 rue Wellington, Hull, PQ K1A 0A4, Canada.

STEWART, John Young (Jackie), O.B.E.; Scottish racing driver; b. 11 June 1939, Milton, Scotland; s. of the late Robert Paul Stewart and Jean Clark Young; m. Helen McGregor 1962; two s.; ed. Dumbarton Acad.; first raced 1961; competed in 4 meetings driving for Barry Filer, Glasgow 1961–62; drove for Ecurie Ecosse and Barry Filer, winning 14 out of 23 starts 1963, 28 wins out of 53 starts 1964; drove Formula 1 for British Racing Motors (BRM) 1965–67, for Ken Tyrrell 1968–73; has won Australian, New Zealand, Swedish, Mediterranean, Japanese and many other non-championship major int. motor races; set new world record by winning his 26th World Championship Grand Prix (Zandvoort) 1973, 27th (Nürburgring) 1973; Third in World Championship 1965, 2nd in 1968 and 1972, World Champion 1969, 1971, 1973; retd. 1973; involved with son, Paul, in operation of Stewart Grand Prix, a Formula One team cr. 1996; Chair. Stewart Grand Prix; Hon. Dr. Aut. Eng. (Lawrence Inst. of Tech., U.S.A.) 1986, Dr. h.c. (Glasgow Caledonian) 1993; Hon. D.Eng. (Heriot-Watt Univ.) 1996; British Automobile Racing Club Gold Medal 1971, 1973, Daily Express Sportsman of the Year 1971, 1973, BBC Sports Personality of the Year 1973, Scottish Sportsman of the Year 1973, U.S. Sportsman of the Year 1973, Segrave Trophy 1973; film: Weekend of a Champion 1972. *Publications:* World Champion (with Eric Dymock) 1970, Faster! (with Peter Manso) 1972, On the Road 1983, Jackie Stewart's Principles of Performance Driving 1986, The Jackie Stewart Book of Shooting 1991. *Leisure interests:* shooting (clay pigeon champion), golf, tennis. *Address:* Stewart Grand Prix, The Stewart Building, Bradbourne Drive, Tilbrooks, Milton Keynes, MK7 8BT, England. *Telephone:* (01908) 216122. *Fax:* (01908) 216892.

STEWART, Martha Kostyra, B.A.; American editor and author; b. Jersey City, N.J.; d. of Edward Kostyra and Martha (née Ruszkowski) Kostyra; m. Andy Stewart 1961 (divorced 1990); one s.; ed. Barnard Univ.; fmr. model, stockbroker, caterer, magazine owner, ed.-in-chief; owner, Ed.-in-Chief Martha Stewart Living magazine 1990–; also appears in cooking feature on Today Show. *Publications include:* (with Elizabeth Hawes) Entertaining 1982, Weddings 1987; (as sole author) Martha Stewart's Hors d'Oeuvres: The Creation and Presentation of Fabulous Finger Food 1984, Martha Stewart's Pies and Tarts 1985, Martha Stewart's Quick Cook Menus 1988, The Wedding Planner 1988, Martha Stewart's Gardening: Month by Month 1991, Martha Stewart's New Old House; Restoration, Renovation, Decoration 1992, Martha Stewart's Christmas 1993, Martha Stewart's Menus for Entertaining 1994, Holidays 1994. *Address:* c/o Susan Magrino Agency, 40 West 57th Street, 31st Floor, New York, NY 10019; 10 Saugatuck Avenue, Westport, CT 06880, U.S.A. (Home).

STEWART, Robert W., O.C., M.SC., PH.D., F.R.S.C., F.R.S.; Canadian oceanographer, b. 21 Aug. 1923, Smoky Lake, Alberta; m. 1st V. Brande 1948 (divorced 1972); three s. one d.; m. 2nd Anne-Marie Robert 1973; one s. one d.; ed. Queen's Univ., Kingston, Ont., Cambridge Univ.; research scientist, Canadian Defence Research Bd., Victoria, B.C. 1950–61; Prof. of Physics and Oceanography, Univ. of British Columbia, Vancouver 1961–70, Hon. Prof. 1971–; Dir.-Gen., Pacific Region, Ocean and Aquatic Sciences, Dept. of the Environment, Victoria, B.C. 1970; Asst. Deputy Minister, Science and Tech., Ministry of Educ., Science and Tech. 1979, Deputy Minister, Ministry of Univs., Science and Communications, Victoria, B.C. 1979–84; Pres. Alberta Research Council 1984–87; Dir. Centre for Earth and Ocean Research, Univ. of Vic. 1987–89, Adjunct Prof. 1989–; Visiting Prof., Dalhousie Univ. 1960–61, Harvard Univ. 1964, Pa. State Univ. 1964, Cambridge Univ. 1967–68; mem. Jt. Organzing Cttee., Global Atmospheric Research Programme 1967–80, Vice-Chair. 1968–72, Chair. 1972–76; mem. Council, American Meteorological Soc. 1977–81; mem. Cttee. on Climate Change and the Ocean 1978–89, Chair. 1983–87; Vice-Chair. Science Cttee. Int. Geosphere-Biosphere Programme 1990–94; Science Officer Int. Council of Scientific Unions, Paris; Hon. D.Sc. (McGill) 1972. LL.D. (Dalhousie) 1974; Patterson Medal, Canadian Meteorological Soc. 1973; IMO Lecturer 1975; Sverdrup Gold Medal, American Meteorological Soc. 1976. *Publications:* approx. 60 publs. on turbulence, oceanography and meteorology. *Address:* School of Earth and Ocean Studies, University of Victoria, P.O. Box 1700, Victoria, B.C., V8W 2Y2, Canada.

STEWART, Rod (Roderick David); British pop singer; b. 10 Jan. 1945, London; m. 1st Alana Collins 1979 (divorced 1984); one s. one d.; d. with Kelly Emberg; m. 2nd Rachel Hunter 1990; one d.; singer with Jeff Beck Group 1968–69, Faces 1969–75. *Solo albums include:* Rod Stewart, Gasoline Alley, Every Picture Tells a Story, Never a Dull Moment, A Night on the Town, Atlantic Crossing, Smiler, Footloose and Fancy Free, Blondes Have More Fun, Foolish Behaviour, Body Wishes, Out of Order, Vagabond Heart, The Best of Rod Stewart (compilation) 1993; Rock Star of the Year, Rolling Stone Magazine 1971; British Rock and Pop Award for Lifetime Achievement 1992. *Address:* c/o Warner Music, 28 Kensington Church Street, London, W8 4EP, England. *Telephone:* 0171-937 8844.

STEWART, S. Jay, B.S., M.B.A.; American business executive; b. 18 Sept. 1938; s. of Virgil Harvey Stewart and Lena Rivers Repair; m. Judith Daniels 1961; one s. two d.; ed. West Virginia Univ. and Univ. of Cincinnati; eng. marketing and mfg., Monsanto Corpn. 1961–73; Dir. of Devt., Dir. of Marketing, Gen. Man. Ventron Div., Thiokol Corpn. 1973–79, Pres. Dynachem Div. 1979–82, Group Vice-Pres. for Chemicals 1982; Pres. Thiokol Chemical Div., Morton Thiokol, Inc. 1982–83, Group Vice-Pres. Chemicals 1983–86, Pres., C.O.O. and Dir. 1986–89; Pres., C.O.O. and Dir. Morton Int. Inc. 1986–94, Chair. C.E.O. 1994–; Advisory Bd. Nat. Foundation for History of Chem. 1991–; mem. American Chemical Soc., American Inst. of Chemical Engs., Commercial Devt. Asscn. *Address:* Morton International Inc., 100 N. Riverside Plaza, Chicago, IL 60606, U.S.A.

STEWART, Thomas, MUS.B.; American opera singer; b. 29 Aug. 1928, San Saba, Tex.; s. of Thomas James Stewart and Gladys Naomi (Reavis) Stewart; m. Evelyn Lear (q.v.) 1955; one s. one d.; ed. Baylor Univ., Juilliard School of Music; joined Berlin Opera 1958; first performance at Bayreuth Festival 1960; has performed at Metropolitan Opera, New York, Royal Opera House, Covent Garden, London, La Scala, Milan, Vienna State Opera, Grand Opera, Paris, Bavarian State Opera, San Francisco Opera, Chicago Opera, Hamburg Opera; appears with all major orchestras of the world; gives recitals internationally with Evelyn Lear; hon. mem. Advisory Bd. George London Foundation for Singers, N.Y. 1994; Artistic Advisor Vocal Arts Soc. 1995; numerous awards and prizes. *Major roles include:* Hans Sachs (The Mastersingers of Nuremberg), Falstaff, Wotan (The Ring cycle), The Flying Dutchman, Scarpia (Tosca), Iago (Otello), Golaud (Pelléas et Mélisande), Amfortas (Parsifal); Fellow, American Univ. 1967; Berlin Kammersänger 1963, Richard Wagner Medal 1963, Grammy Awards 1969, 1971. *Leisure interests:* theatre, tennis, golf. *Address:* c/o Columbia Artists Management Incorporated, 165 West 57th Street, New York, NY 10019, U.S.A.

STEWART, Sir William, Kt., PH.D., D.SC., F.R.S., F.R.S.E.; British university professor; b. 7 June 1935, Glasgow; s. of John Stewart and Margaret Stewart; m. Catherine Macleod 1958; one s.; ed. Univ. of Glasgow; Asst. Lecturer, Univ. of Nottingham 1961–63; Lecturer, Westfield Coll., Univ. of London 1963–68; Visiting Research Worker, Univ. of Wis., U.S.A. 1966, 1968; Boyd Baxter Prof. of Biology, Univ. of Dundee 1968–94, Vice-Prin. 1985–87; Sec. and Deputy Chair. to Agricultural and Food Research Council 1988–90; Chief Scientific Adviser, Cabinet Office 1990–95, Head of Office of Science and Tech. 1992–95; Deputy Chair. Council for Science and Tech. 1993–95; Pres. Bio-industry Asscn. 1995–; Chair. Dundee Teaching Hosps. NHS Trust 1996–; ind. consultant; Dir. (non-exec.) Water Research Centre PLC 1995–; has held numerous other public appointments; Visiting Prof., Univ. of Kuwait 1980, Univ. of Otago, N.Z. 1984; Chair. Royal Soc. Educ. Cttee. 1977–80; Vice-Pres. British Phycological Soc. 1973–75, Pres. 1975–77; Trustee, Estuarine and Brackish-Water Sciences Assoc. 1978–88; Sec. Int. Cttee. on Microbiological Ecology (ICOME) 1980–83, Chair. 1984–86; mem. of Council, Royal Soc. of Edinburgh 1976–79, of Royal Soc. 1984–86; Chair. Council, Scottish Marine Biological Asscn. 1985–87; Chair. Royal Soc. Study Group on the Nitrogen Cycle 1979–83, on Educ. and Training for Biotech. Leeuwenhoek Lecturer, Royal Soc. 1984; Distinguished Lecturer, Phycological Soc. of America 1977; Fellow Queen Mary and Westfield Coll. 1993, Hebrew Univ., Jerusalem 1996; Hon. D.Sc. (East Anglia) 1991, (Glamorgan) 1994, (Napier) 1995, (Dundee) 1995, (Paisley) 1996, numerous other awards. *Publications:* The Blue-Green Algae (co-author) 1973, Algal Physiology and Biochemistry (ed.) 1974, Nitrogen Fixation (ed.) 1976 and 1980, The Nitrogen Cycle of the United Kingdom (ed.) 1984; more than 200 scientific papers. *Leisure interests:* music, house-renovation. *Address:* Dundee Teaching Hospitals NHS Trust, Ninewells Hospital, Dundee, DD1 9SY; 45 Fairfield Road, Broughty Ferry, Dundee, DD5 1PL, Scotland. *Telephone:* (01382) 660111.

STEYN, Baron (Life Peer), cr. 1995, of Swafield in the County of Norfolk; **Johan Steyn,** Kt., P.C., Q.C., M.A.; British judge; b. 15 Aug. 1932; m. Susan Leonore Lewis; two s. two d. by previous m.; one step-s. one step-d.; ed. Jan van Riebeeck School, Cape Town, S. Africa, Univ. of Stellenbosch, S. Africa, Univ. Coll. Oxford; began practising at S. African Bar 1958; Sr. Counsel of Supreme Court of S.A. 1970; settled in U.K.; began practising at English Bar 1973, Bencher, Lincoln's Inn 1985, Q.C. 1979; a Presiding Judge, Northern Circuit 1989–91; Judge of the High Court 1985–91; a Lord Justice of Appeal 1992–95, a Lord of Appeal in Ordinary 1995–; mem. Supreme Court Rule Cttee. 1985–89; Chair. Race Relations Cttee. of the Bar 1987–88; mem. Lord Chancellor's Advisory Cttee. on Legal Educ. and Conduct 1993–96; Pres. British Insurance Law Asscn. 1992–94; Hon. Fellow Univ. Coll. Oxford 1995; Hon. LL.D. (London, E. Anglia) 1997. *Address:* House of Lords, London, SW1A 0PW, England.

STEYN, Hon. Jan Hendrik, B.A., B.LL.; South African lawyer; b. 4 March 1928, Cape Town; s. of H.P.M. Steyn and Zerilda Steyn; ed. Jan van Riebeeck School, Univ. of Stellenbosch; began practising as lawyer, Cape Town 1950, took Silk 1963, apptd. Justice of Supreme Court, Cape Prov. Div. 1964, retd. 1981; apptd. First Exec. Dir. The Urban Foundation 1977 (on leave of absence from Supreme Court), now Hon. Chair.; Chair. Independent Devt. Trust 1990–94, S.A. Media Council 1989–; Judge Court of Appeal, Lesotho 1992–, Botswana 1994–; Acting Judge of Cape Supreme Court; Jt. Ombudsman to Life Assurance Industry 1996; Chair. Bd. of Investigation into Saldanha Steel Project 1995, Comm. of Enquiry into Remuneration of Election Reps.; Dir. First Nat. Bank, Anglo-American Corpn., Barlow Rand Ltd., Metropolitan Life of S.A. Ltd.; Founder The Inst. of Criminology, Univ. of Cape Town; Trustee numerous charitable orgs.; four hon. degrees; Businessman of the Year Award, S.A. Inst. of Housing 1984, Paul Harris Fellowship Award, Rotary Int., Harvard Business School Business Statesman Award 1985. *Publications:* Crime and Punishment in South Africa (jt. Ed.); numerous publs. on crime and its control. *Leisure interest:* golf. *Address:* Court of Appeal, Maseru, Lesotho.

STICH, Michael; German tennis player; b. 18 Oct. 1968, Pinneberg; m. Jessica Stockmann 1992; Nat. Jr. Champion 1986; semi-finalist, French Open 1990; mem. W. German Davis Cup Team 1990; won first professional title, Memphis 1990; winner, Men's Singles Championship, Wimbledon 1991; Men's Doubles (with John McEnroe q.v.)) 1992; won ATP World Championship 1993; retd. 1997. *Address:* Ernst-Barlach-Strasse 44, 2200 Elmshorn, Germany.

STICH, Otto, D.ECON.; Swiss politician; b. 10 Jan. 1927, Dornach, Canton Solothurn; m.; two c.; ed. Basle; teacher –1971; mem. Dornach Accounts Audit Comm. 1953; Communal Councillor and part-time Mayor of Dornach 1953–65; Prefect of Dornach-Thierstein 1961–70; mem. Nat. Council (Fed. Parl.) 1963–83, mem. External Trade Cttee. 1965–71 (Chair. 1969–71), Finance Cttee. 1971–77, 1982–83, Econ. Affairs Cttee. 1978–81, fmr. mem. other cttees.; Fed. Councillor Dec. 1983–, Head Fed. Dept. of Finance 1984–95, Vice-Pres. Fed. Council 1987, Pres. of Swiss Confed. Jan.–Dec. 1988, Jan.–Dec. 1994; Chair. of Ministers, IMF Group of 10; joined Swiss SDP 1947, Chair. Solothurn cantonal party 1968–72, mem. Man. Cttee. of Swiss SDP 1970–75, Vice-Chair. parl. party 1980; Chair. Trade Union Group of Asscn. of Staffs of Pvt. Transport Firms and Swiss Railwaymen's Asscn.; Man. Cen. Personnel Dept., Co-op Switzerland 1971–80, Deputy Dir. and Head of Personnel and Training Dept. 1980.

STICH, Stephen Peter, PH.D.; American professor of philosophy and cognitive science; b. 9 May 1943, New York; s. of Samuel J. Stich and Sylvia L. Stich; m. Judith Ann Gagnon 1971; one s. one d.; ed. Univ. of Pennsylvania, Princeton Univ.; mem. staff Univs. of Mich. 1968–78, Md. 1978–86, Calif. at San Diego 1986–89; Prof. of Philosophy and Cognitive Science, Rutgers Univ., 1989–, Bd. of Govs. Prof. 1998–, Dir. Research Group on Evolution and Higher Cognition; Adjunct Prof., City Univ. of New York Grad. Center 1994–97; Pres. Soc. for Philosophy and Psychology 1982–83; Fulbright Sr. Research Scholar 1978–79; Fellow, Center for Advanced Study in the Behavioral Sciences 1983–84; Visiting Fellow, Research School of Social Sciences, Australian Nat. Univ. 1992; Erskine Fellow, Canterbury Univ., Christchurch, N.Z. 1996. *Publications:* From Folk Psychology to Cognitive Science 1983, The Fragmentation of Reason 1990, Philosophy and Connectionist Theory (Co-author) 1991, Deconstructing The Mind 1996. *Address:* Department of Philosophy, Davison Hall, Douglass Campus, Rutgers University, New Brunswick, NJ 08901, U.S.A. *Telephone:* (732) 932-9091. *Fax:* (732) 932-8617.

STICHT, J. Paul; American business executive (retd.); b. 3 Oct. 1917, Clairton, Pa.; s. of Joseph P. and Adah M. Sticht; m. A. Ferne Cozad 1940; two s.; ed. Grove City Coll. and Univ. of Pittsburgh Graduate School; started as shipping clerk, U.S. Steel Co. 1939, industrial engineer 1941–44; Air Transport Command, TWA airlines div. 1944–48; Vice-Pres. Campbell Soup Co. 1949–57, Int. Pres. 1957–60; Exec. Vice-Pres. Federated Dept. Stores 1960–65, Vice-Chair. 1965–67, Pres. 1967–72; Chair Exec. Cttee. and Dir. R. J. Reynolds Industries Inc. 1972–73, Pres., C.O.O. and Dir. 1973–78, Pres., C.E.O. and Dir. 1978–79, Chair. 1979–84, C.E.O. 1979–83; Acting Chair. R. J. R. Nabisco March–Oct. 1987, Feb. 1989, C.E.O. 1989; Pres. Castle Springs Inc., Winston Salem 1992–; Chair. Caribbean/Latin American Action; fmr. Chair. Nat. Chamber Foundation; fmr. Dir. Textron Inc., Chrysler Corpn.; fmr. Sr. mem. The Conference Bd. Inc.; Visitor, Bowman Gray School of Medicine, Fuqua School of Business of Duke Univ.; Trustee, Grove City Coll. *Leisure interests:* golf, boating, fishing. *Address:* c/o Castle Springs Inc., 119 Brookstown Avenue, Winston Salem, NC 27101 (Office); 11732 Lake House Court, North Palm Beach, FL, U.S.A. (Home).

STICKLER, H.E. Cardinal Alfons, S.D.B.; Austrian ecclesiastic; b. 23 Aug. 1910, Neunkirchen, Vienna; ordained 1937; consecrated Archbishop (Titular See of Volsinium) 1983; cr. Cardinal 1985; fmr. Chief Vatican Librarian and Archivist; Priest of S. Giorgio of Velabro. *Address:* Piazza del S. Uffizio 11, 00193 Rome, Italy.

STIEFLER, Jeffrey E., M.B.A.; American financial services executive; b. 1946; ed. Williams Coll., Harvard Univ.; Gen. Man. Boise Cascade 1971–75; Pres. Mintz & Hoke Inc., Minneapolis 1975–77; Sr. Vice-Pres. Citicorp, Minneapolis 1977–82; Exec. Vice-Pres. J. B. Coleman & Co. 1982–83; with Phila. Saving Fund Soc. 1986–87, IDS Financial Services Inc. 1983–86,

1987–, with IDS Finance Corpn. 1983–86, Exec. Vice-Pres. (Sales & Marketing) 1987–90, Pres. 1990–91, Pres. and C.E.O. 1991–93; Pres. American Express Co., New York 1993–95.

STIGLITZ, Joseph Eugene, PH.D.; American professor of economics; b. 9 Feb. 1943, Gary, Ind.; s. of Nathaniel D. Stiglitz and Charlotte Fishman; m. Jane Hannaway 1978; two s. two d.; ed. Amherst Coll., Mass. Inst. of Tech. and Univ. of Cambridge (Fulbright Scholar); Prof. of Econs. Cowles Foundation, Yale Univ. 1970–74; Visiting Fellow, St. Catherine's Coll. Oxford 1973–74; Prof. of Econs. Stanford Univ. 1974–76, 1988–; Oskar Morgenstern Distinguished Fellow, Inst. of Advanced Studies, Princeton 1978–79; Drummond Prof. of Political Econ. Univ. of Oxford 1976–79; Prof. of Econs. Princeton Univ. 1979–88; mem. Pres.'s Council of Econ. Advisers 1993–95, Chair. 1995–97; consultant to World Bank, Bell Communications Research, numerous consultancies in public and pvt. sector, editorial bd. memberships etc.; Fellow, American Acad. of Arts and Sciences, N.A.S., Econometric Soc., Inst. for Policy Research (Sr. Fellow 1991–93); Guggenheim Fellow 1969–70; John Bates Clark Award, American Econ. Asscn. 1979; Int. Prize, Acad. Lincei, Rome 1988; UAP Scientific Prize, Paris 1989; Hon. D.H.L. (Amherst Coll.) 1974. *Address:* World Bank Group, Room MC 4-315, 1818 H. Street N.W., Washington DC, 20433, U.S.A.

STIGWOOD, Robert Colin; Australian business executive; b. 16 April 1934, Adelaide; s. of Gordon Stigwood and Gwendolyn (née Burrows) Stigwood; ed. Sacred Heart Coll., Adelaide; est. Robert Stigwood Orgn. (RSO) 1967; formed RSO Records 1973; founder, Music for UNICEF; *Producer of films:* Jesus Christ Superstar, Bugsy Malone, Gallipoli, Tommy, Saturday Night Fever, Grease, Sergeant Pepper's Lonely Hearts Club Band, Moment by Moment, Times Square, The Fan, Grease 2, Staying Alive, Evita, Gallipoli; *Producer of stage musicals:* Hair, Oh! Calcutta, The Dirtiest Show in Town, Pippin, Jesus Christ Superstar, Evita, Grease (London) 1993; TV Producer in England and U.S.A. of The Entertainer and The Prime of Miss Jean Brodie; Chair. of Bd. Stigwood group of companies; Key to cities of Los Angeles and Adelaide; Tony Award 1980 for Evita; Int. Producer of the Year, ABC Interstate Theatres Inc. *Leisure interests:* tennis, swimming, sailing, reading. *Address:* c/o Robert Stigwood Organization, Barton Manor, Whippingham, East Cowes, Isle of Wight, PO32 6LB, England.

STIHL, Hans Peter; German business executive; b. 18 April 1932, Stuttgart; s. of Andreas Stihl and Maria Giersch; m.; ed. Technische Hochschule, Stuttgart; Chair. and partner, Andreas Stihl Fabrik; Pres. Deutsche Industrie und Handelstag, Bonn 1988–; Vice-Pres. Inst. of German Economy, Cologne 1983–88, Treas. 1983–88; mem. Man. Bd. Verein Deutscher Maschinen- und Anlagenbau (VDMA) until 1988; numerous other business and professional appts. *Address:* Badstrasse 115, 71336 Waiblingen, Germany.

STILL, Ray; American oboist; b. 12 March 1920, Elwood, Ind.; s. of Roy R. Still and Lillian Taylor; m. Mary Powell Brock 1940; two s. two d.; ed. Juilliard School of Music and privately under Phillip Memoli and Robert Bloom; oboist, Kansas City Philharmonic Orchestra 1939–41; mil. service 1941–46; Buffalo Philharmonic Orchestra 1947–49; Prof. of Oboe and mem. Baltimore Symphony 1949–53; solo oboist, Chicago Symphony Orchestra 1956–; Prof. of Oboe, Northwestern Univ. 1960–; Conductor, Stratford Music Festival, Canada 1964–69; mem. of a Quintet for 100th anniversary of Yamaha Co., recordings, Tour of Japan, judge int. oboe competition, Japan 1988; has undertaken coaching of many symphony orchestra wind and brass sections; numerous recordings, including Oboe Quartettes (with Perlman, Zuckermann, Harrel) and Mozart Oboe Concerto with Chicago Symphony Orchestra, conducted by Claudio Abbado. *Leisure interests:* collecting classical comedy films, listening to great jazz artists of '20s, '30s and '40s, records of great lieder singers. *Address:* c/o Chicago Symphony Orchestra, 220 South Michigan Avenue, Chicago, IL 60604; 585 West Hawthorne Place, Chicago, IL 60657, U.S.A.

STILWELL, Richard Dale, MUS.B.; American baritone; b. 6 May 1942, St. Louis; s. of Otho John Clifton and Tressie (née Parrish) Stilwell; m. 1st Elizabeth Louise Jencks 1967 (divorced); m. 2nd Kerry M. McCarthy 1983; ed. Anderson Coll., Univ. of Indiana; with Metropolitan Opera Co., New York 1970–; appearances in maj. roles Washington Opera Soc., Marseilles Opera Co., Santa Fe Opera, San Francisco Opera Co., Paris Opera Co., La Scala, Covent Garden, Hamburg State Opera, Glyndebourne Opera Festival, Van. Opera Co., Chicago Opera Co., Tanglewood Festival, Israel Philharmonic, Boston Symphony, L.A. Philharmonic, etc.; soloist with Nat. Symphony, Washington, Chicago Symphony, American Symphony, Carnegie Hall, Boston Symphony, Los Angeles Philharmonic, etc.; Nat. Soc. of Arts and Letters award 1963, Fisher Foundation award Metropolitan Opera Auditions 1965; mem. American Guild Musical Artists. *Address:* c/o Columbia Artists Management, Arbib Division, 165 W. 57th Street, New York, NY 10019, U.S.A.

STING (see Sumner, Gordon Matthew).

STIPE, Michael; American rock musician; b. 1960, Decatur, Ga.; ed. Univ. of Georgia; lead singer and song writer R.E.M. band. *Albums include:* (for IRS): Murmur 1982–83, Document; (for Warner): Green 1988, Out of Time 1991, Automatic for the People 1992, Monster 1994, New Adventures in Hi-Fi 1996. *Address:* c/o Warner Bros. Records, 3300 Warner Boulevard, Burbank, CA 91505, U.S.A.

STIRLING, Sir Angus Duncan Aeneas, Kt., C.B.I.M., F.R.S.A.; British arts administrator; b. 10 Dec. 1933, London; s. of late Duncan Alexander Stirling and of Lady Marjorie Stirling; m. Armyne Morar Helen Schofield 1959; one s. two d.; ed. Eton Coll., Trinity Coll. Cambridge, London Univ. (Extra-mural); mem. staff Christie, Manson & Woods Ltd. 1954–57, Lazard Bros. and Co. Ltd. 1957–66; Asst. Dir. Paul Mellon Foundation for British Art 1966–69, Jt. Dir. 1969–70; Deputy Sec.-Gen. Arts Council of G.B. 1971–79; Deputy Dir.-Gen. The Nat. Trust 1979–83, Dir.-Gen. 1983–95; Sr. Policy Adviser Nat. Heritage Memorial Fund 1996–97; Dir. Royal Opera House, Covent Garden 1979–96, Chair. 1991–96, Chair. Friends of Covent Garden 1981–91, Deputy Chair. Royal Ballet Bd. 1988–91; Chair. Greenwich Foundation for the Royal Naval Coll. 1996–, Policy Cttee., Council for Protection of Rural England (CPRE) 1996–, Jt. Nature Conservation Cttee. 1997–; mem. Crafts Council 1980–85, Council of Man. Byam Shaw School of Art 1965–89, Man. Cttee. Courtauld Inst. of Art 1981–83, Advisory Cttee. London Symphony Orchestra 1979–, Bd. of Govs. Live Music Now 1982–89, Council Royal School of Church Music 1996–98; Trustee The Theatres Trust 1983–91, Heritage of London Trust 1983–95, Samuel Courtauld Trust 1984–, Stowe House Preservation Trust 1998–. *Leisure interests:* music, travel, walking. *Address:* 49 Whitehall, London, S.W.1 (Office); 25 Ladbroke Grove, London, W11 3AY, England. *Telephone:* 0171-839 0454 (Office).

STIRLING, Charles James Matthew, PH.D., D.SC., C.CHEM., F.R.S.C., F.R.S.; British professor of organic chemistry; b. 8 Dec. 1930, Croydon; s. of Brig. A. D. Stirling and Isobel M. Matthew; m. Eileen G. Powell 1956; three d.; ed. Edinburgh Acad., Univ. of St. Andrews and King's Coll. London; Civil Service Research Fellow Chemical Defence Experimental Establishment 1955–57; ICI Fellow, Univ. of Edin. 1957–59; Lecturer in Organic Chem. Queen's Univ. Belfast 1959–65; Reader in Organic Chem. King's Coll. London 1965–69; Prof. of Organic Chem. Univ. Coll. of N. Wales, Bangor 1969–90; Prof. of Organic Chem., Univ. of Sheffield 1990–98, Head Dept. of Chem. 1991–94; mem. various int. scientific cttees. etc.; Hon. D.Sc. (St. Andrews) 1994, Hon. D.ès Sc. (Marseille) 1999; Public Orator, Univ. of Sheffield 1995–. *Publications:* 190 scientific articles and papers. *Leisure interests:* Christianity, choral music, travel, furniture restoration. *Address:* Department of Chemistry, University of Sheffield, Sheffield, S3 7HF, England. *Telephone:* (0114) 276 8555; (014) 222 9453. *Fax:* (0114) 273 8673.

STIRN, Olivier, L. EN D.; French civil servant; b. 24 Feb. 1936, Boulogne-Billancourt; s. of Alexandre Stirn and Geneviève Dreyfus; m. Evelyn Toledano 1989; one s. one d. (and two s. from previous m.); ed. Univ. of Paris; Deputy for Calvados 1968–86 (Gen. Councillor 1994–), for Manche 1986–88; Councillor Gen., Mayor of Vire 1971–; Sec. of State for Parl. Relations 1973, for Overseas Territories 1974–78, for Foreign Affairs 1978–81, for Defence 1980–81; Minister Del. for Overseas Territories May–June 1988, Minister Del. attached to Minister of Industry and Territorial Devt. 1988–89, to Minister of Industry, Territorial Devt. and Tourism (with special responsibility for Tourism) 1989–90; Amb. to Council of Europe, Strasbourg 1991–93; Pres. Louis Harris Conseil. *Publications:* Le Piège (with Bernard Stasi and J. P. Soisson) 1973, Une certaine idée du centre 1985, Tourisme: chance pour l'économie, risque pour les sociétés? *Address:* 49 boulevard Lannes, 75116 Paris, France.

STOCKHAUSEN, Karlheinz; German composer; b. 22 Aug. 1928, Mödrath bei Köln; s. of Simon Stockhausen and Gertrud Stupp; m. 1st Doris Andreae 1951; m. 2nd Mary Bauermeister 1967; two s. four d.; ed. Cologne State Music Conservatory, Univs. of Cologne and Bonn; worked with Olivier Messiaen and with the "Musique Concrète" Group in Paris 1952–53; with Westdeutscher Rundfunk Electronic Music Studio, Cologne 1953–, Artistic Dir. 1963–75; first composition of purely electronic music (Studie 1 for sinewaves) 1953; Co-ed. Die Reihe (Universal Edn.) 1954–59; Dozent for composition and analysis at the Int. Summer School for New Music, Darmstadt 1955–74; concert tours throughout the world since 1958; Founder, composition classes in Kölner Kurse für Neue Musik 1963–68; f. ensemble for live electronic music 1964–; Int. World Fair Expo 70, Osaka; Prof. for Composition Staatliche Hochschule für Musik, Cologne 1971–77; mem. Royal Swedish Acad., Akademie der Künste, Berlin, American Acad. and Inst. of Arts and Letters and others; Hon. mem. Royal Acad. of Music, London; many prizes including Preis der deutschen Schallplattenkritik 1964, Grand Prix du Disque 1968, Diapason d'Or 1983, UNESCO Picasso Medal 1992; Bundesverdienstkreuz (1st Class), Commdr., Ordre des Arts et des Lettres (France) 1985. *Compositions:* 252 works including Chöre für Doris 1950, Drei Lieder (alto voice and chamber orchestra) 1950, Choral (chorus) 1950, Sonatine (violin and piano) 1951, Kreuzspiel 1951, Formel (orchestra) 1951, Etude (musique concrète) 1952, Schlagtrio 1952, Spiel (orchestra) 1952, Punkte (orchestra) 1952 (new version 1962), Klavierstücke I-IV 1952–53, Kontra-Punkte (ten instruments) 1952–53, Elektronische Studien 1953–54, Klavierstücke V-X 1954–61, Zeitmasze (five woodwind) 1955–56, Gruppen (three orchestras) 1955–57, Klavierstück XI 1956, Gesang der Jünglinge (electronic) 1955–56, Zyklus (percussionist) 1959, Refrain (three players) 1959, Carré (four orchestras and four choruses) 1959–60, Kontakte (piano, percussion and/or electronic sounds) 1959–60, Originale (musical theatre) 1961, Momente (soprano, four choral groups and 13 instrumentalists) 1962–64, Plus Minus 1963, Mikrophonie 1 (tam-tam, two microphones, two filters and potentiometers) 1964, Mixtur (orchestra, four sine-generators and ring-modulators) 1964, Mikrophonie II (choir, Hammond organ and four ring-modulators) 1965, Stop (orchestra) 1965, Telemusik (electronic music) 1966, Solo (melodic instrument and feed-back) 1966, Adieu (wind quintet) 1966, Hymnen (electronic and concrete music with or without soloists)

1966–67, Prozession (tam-tam, viola, electronium, piano, filters and potentiometers) 1967, Ensemble (process planning) 1967, Kurzwellen (six players) 1968, Stimmung (six vocalists) 1968, Aus den sieben Tagen (fifteen compositions of intuitive music) 1968, Musik für ein Haus (process planning) 1968, Spiral (soloist) 1968, Dr. K-Sextett 1969, Fresco (four orchestral groups) 1969, Hymnen Dritte Region (hymns with orchestra) 1969, Pole (two players/singers) 1970, Expo (three players/singers) 1970, Mantra (two pianists) 1970, Sternklang (park music for 5 groups instrumentalists/singers), Trans (orchestra) 1971, Für kommende Zeiten (17 texts of intuitive music) 1968–70, Alphabet for Liège (13 musical pictures for soloists and duos) 1972, "Am Himmel wandre ich" (12 American Indian songs) 1972, Ylem (19 or more players) 1972, "Atmen gibt das Leben" (choir with orchestra or tape) 1974, Inori (Adorations for soloists and orchestra) 1973–74, Herbstmusik (4 players) 1974, Musik im Bauch (six percussionists and music boxes) 1975, Tierkreis (12 melodies of the star-signs) 1975, Harlekin (clarinet) 1975, The Little Harlequin (clarinet) 1975, Sirius (electronic music and trumpet, bass-clarinet, soprano and bass) 1975–77, Amour (5 pieces for clarinet or flute) 1976, Jubiläum (for orchestra) 1977, In Freundschaft 1977, Licht, die sieben Tage der Woche (for solo voices/instruments, dancers, choir, orchestra, ballet, electronic and concrete music) 1977–, an operatic cycle that includes Donnerstag aus Licht 1981, Samstag aus Licht 1984, Montag aus Licht 1988, Dienstag aus Licht 1991, Freitag aus Licht 1996, and other scenes for a combination of forces; over 100 records. *Publications:* Texte (10 vols.) 1952–62, 1963–70, 1970–77, 1977–84, 1984–91, Stockhausen on Music-Lectures and Interviews 1989, Towards a Cosmic Music 1990. *Address:* Stockhausen-Verlag, 51515 Kürten, Germany.

STOCKMAN, David Allen, B.A.; American politician and administrator; b. 10 Nov. 1946, Fort Hood, Tex.; s. of Allen and Carol (Bartz) Stockman; m. Jennifer Blei 1983; two d.; ed. Michigan State Univ., East Lansing, and Harvard Univ. Divinity School; Special Asst. to Congressman John Anderson 1970–73; Exec. Dir. Republican Conf., House of Reps. 1972–75; mem. House of Reps. from 4th Dist. of Mich. 1977–79, mem. Interstate and Foreign Commerce Cttee., Admin. Cttee.; Chair. Republican Econ. Policy Task Force 1977–81; Dir. U.S. Office of Man. and Budget 1981–85; with Salomon Bros. 1985–88; Sr. Man. Dir. The Blackstone Group 1988–; Man. Partner Stockman and Co. 1988–; mem. Nat. Comm. on Air Quality 1978; Jefferson Award 1981. *Publication:* The Triumph of Politics: Why the Reagan Revolution Failed 1986. *Address:* The Blackstone Group, 345 Park Avenue, New York, NY 10154, U.S.A.

STOCKTON, 2nd Earl of; **Alexander Daniel Alan Macmillan,** F.B.I.M., F.R.S.A.; British publisher; b. 10 Oct. 1943, Oswestry; s. of the late Maurice Victor Macmillan (Viscount Macmillan of Ovenden) and of Dame Katherine Macmillan (Viscountess Macmillan of Ovenden), D.B.E.; grandson of the late 1st Earl of Stockton (fmrly., as Harold Macmillan, Prime Minister of U.K. 1957–63); m. 1st Hélène Birgitte Hamilton 1970 (divorced 1991); one s. two d.; m. 2nd Miranda Elizabeth Louise Nultall 1995; ed. Eton Coll. and Paris and Strathclyde Univs.; Sub.-Ed. Glasgow Herald 1963–65; Reporter, Daily Telegraph 1965–67, Foreign Corresp. 1967–68, Chief European Corresp., Sunday Telegraph 1968–70; Dir. Birch Grove Estates Ltd. 1969–86, Chair. 1983–89; Dir. Macmillan and Co. Ltd. 1970–76, Deputy Chair. 1976–80, Chair. 1984–90, Pres. 1990–; Chair. Macmillan Publrs. Ltd. 1980–90 (Pres. 1990–), St. Martin's Press, New York 1983–88 (Dir. 1974–90), Sidgwick and Jackson 1989–90; Chair. Cen. London Training & Enterprise Council 1990–95; Dir. Book Trade Benevolent Soc. 1976–88, Chair. Bookrest Appeal 1978–86; Dir. United British Artists Ltd. 1984–90 (Chair. 1985–90); mem. Lindemann Fellowship Cttee. 1979– (Chair. 1983–), British Inst. of Man. 1981–, Council of Publrs. Asscn. 1985–88, Carlton Club Political Cttee. 1975–88 (Chair. 1984); Gov. Archbishop Tenison's School 1979–86, Merchant Taylor's School 1980–82, 1990–, English Speaking Union 1980–84, 1986–93; Liveryman Worshipful Co. of Merchant Taylors 1972, Court Asst. 1987, of Stationers 1973, Master 1991–92; Hon. D.Litt. (De Montfort) 1993, (Westminster) 1995, Hon. D.Univ. (Strathclyde) 1993. *Leisure interests:* shooting, fishing, aviation. *Address:* Macmillan Publishers Ltd., 25 Eccleston Place, London, SW1W 9NF, England. *Telephone:* 0171-881 8000. *Fax:* 0171-881 8001.

STOIBER, Edmund, DR.JUR.; German politician and lawyer; b. 1941; m. Karin Stoiber; three c.; ed. Univ. of Munich and Hochschule für Politische Wissenschaft; personal counsellor to Bavarian State Minister for Devt. and Foreign Affairs 1972–74, Dir. of Ministerial Office 1974; admitted solicitor 1978; Gen. Sec. Christian Social Union (C.S.U.) 1978–83; State Sec. and Dir. Bavarian State Chancellery 1982–86, State Minister and Dir. 1986–88; Bavarian State Minister for Internal Affairs 1988–93, Minister Pres. of Bavaria 1993–; Pres. CSU 1999–; Bayerischer Verdienstorden. *Publications:* Politik aus Bayern 1976, Der Hausfriedensbruch im Licht akt. Problemen 1984. *Leisure interests:* skiing, football. *Address:* Christlich-Demokratische Union Deutschlands, Konrad-Adenauer-Haus, Friedrich-Ebert-Allee 73–75, 53113 Bonn, Germany.

STOICHEFF, Boris Peter, O.C., PH.D., F.R.S., F.R.S.C.; Canadian professor of physics; b. 1 June 1924, Bitol, Yugoslavia; s. of Peter Stoicheff and Vasilka (née Tonna) Stoicheff; m. Lillian Joan Ambridge 1954; one s.; ed. Jarvis Collegiate Inst., Toronto, Canada and Univ. of Toronto; Postdoctoral Fellow, Physics, Nat. Research Council, Ottawa 1951–53, Research Officer 1953–64; Visiting Scientist, M.I.T., U.S.A. 1963–64; Prof. of Physics, Univ. of Toronto 1964–89, Univ. Prof. 1977–89, Prof. Emer. 1989–; Chair., Eng. Science 1972–77; I.W. Killam Scholar 1977–79; Visiting Scientist, Stanford Univ., U.S.A. 1978; Exec. Dir., Ont. Laser and Lightwave Research Centre 1988–91; U.K. and Canada Rutherford Lecturer 1989; professional interests include lasers, atomic and molecular spectroscopy and structure, light scattering and two-photon processes, nonlinear optics and generation of ultraviolet radiation; determined structures of many molecules by light scattering, and discovered inverse Raman effect and stimulated Brillouin scattering (or the generation of sound by light); mem. Gov. Council of Nat. Research Council, Ottawa 1977–83; Vice-Pres. Int. Union of Pure and Applied Physics (IUPAP) 1993–96; Co-Foreign Sec., Royal Soc. of Canada 1995–; Hon. Foreign mem. American Acad. of Arts and Sciences 1989; Hon. Fellow, Indian Acad. of Sciences, Macedonian Acad. of Science and Arts, Yugoslavia, Hon. D.Sc. (Skopje) 1982, (York Univ., Canada) 1982, (Univ. of Windsor, Canada) 1989, (Toronto) 1994; Medal of Achievement in Physics, Canadian Asscn. of Physicists 1974 (Pres. 1983), William F. Meggers Medal 1981, Frederic Ives Medal, Optical Soc. of America 1983 (Pres. 1976), Henry Marshall Tory Medal, Royal Soc. of Canada 1989. *Publications:* over 170 scientific publs. in int. journals. *Leisure interests:* travel, art, music. *Address:* Department of Physics, University of Toronto, Toronto, Ont., M5S 1A7 (Office); 66 Collier Street, Apt. 6B, Toronto, Ont., M4W 1L9, Canada (Home). *Telephone:* (416) 978-2948 (Office); (416) 923-9622 (Home). *Fax:* (416) 978-2537.

STOKER, Sir Michael George Parke, Kt., C.B.E., M.A., M.D., F.R.S., F.R.S.E., F.R.C.P.; British medical researcher; b. 4 July 1918, Taunton, Somerset; s. of S. P. Stoker and D. Stoker (née Nazer); m. Veronica Mary English 1942; three s. two d.; ed. Sidney Sussex Coll., Cambridge, and St. Thomas's Hosp., London; Capt. R.A.M.C. 1942–47; lecturer in Pathology, Univ. of Cambridge 1947–58, Fellow of Clare Coll., Cambridge 1948–58; Prof. of Virology, Univ. of Glasgow 1959–68; Dir. Imperial Cancer Research Fund Labs., London 1968–79; Visiting Prof., Univ. Coll., London 1968–79; Fellow Clare Hall, Cambridge 1978, Pres. 1980–87; Foreign Sec., Vice-Pres. Royal Soc. 1976–81; mem. Gen. Cttee. Int. Council of Scientific Unions 1977–82, Scientific Cttee., Ludwig Inst. for Cancer Research 1985–91; Chair. Governing Body Strangeways Research Lab. 1981–93; Foreign mem. Czech. Acad. of Sciences; Hon. Foreign mem. American Acad. of Arts and Sciences; Hon. D.Sc. (Glasgow) 1982; Mendel Gold Medal 1984. *Publications:* over 150 articles and reviews on virology, oncology and cell biology. *Leisure interest:* painting. *Address:* 3 Barrington House, Southacre Drive, Cambridge, CB2 2TY, England.

STOKER, Richard, J.P., F.R.A.M., A.R.C.M.; British composer, author, poet and painter; b. 8 Nov. 1938; s. of late Capt. Bower Morrell Stoker and of Winifred Harling; m. 1st Jacqueline Margaret Trelfer (divorced 1985); m. 2nd Dr. Gillian Patricia Watson 1986; ed. Breadalbane House School, Castleford, Huddersfield School of Music and School of Art, Royal Acad. of Music; studied with Sir Lennox Berkeley at R.A.M. and Nadia Boulanger in Paris (Mendelssohn Scholar 1962); Prof. of Composition R.A.M. 1963–86 (tutor 1970–80); Composition teacher St. Paul's School 1972–74, Magdalen Coll., Cambridge 1974–76; APC Assoc. Prof. of Composition 1984–; Ed. Composer Magazine 1969–80; mem. Composers' Guild 1962– (mem. Exec. Cttee. 1969–80), R.A.M. Guild Cttee. 1994– (Hon. Treas. 1995–); mem. European-Atlantic Group 1993–, Byron Soc. 1993–, Magistrates' Asscn. 1995–, English and Int. PEN 1996–; mem. and Treas. Steering Cttee. Lewisham Arts Festival 1990, 1992; two exhbns. (as artist); Founder-mem. Atlantic Council 1993; Nat. Library of Poetry (U.S.A.) Ed.'s Choice Award 1995, 1996, 1997; American Biographical Inst. Man of the Year Award 1997; numerous awards for music 1950–. *Works include:* Johnson Preserv'd (opera), three string quartets, three piano trios, Organ Symphony, Piano Concerto, Piano Variations, two piano sonatas, A York Suite, Partita for Mandolin and Harp, two overtures, Benedictus, three violin sonatas, Sonatina for Guitar, Organ Partita, Three Improvisations, Kristallnacht Monody, Songs of Love and Loss, Music that Brings Sweet Sleep, Four Shakespeare Songs, Four Yeats Songs, Aspects of Flight, Make Me a Willow Cabin, Canticle of the Rose, A Chinese Canticle (Szuma Chien), Ecce Homo, Proverbs, O Be Joyful, A Landscape of Truth, Zodiac Variations, Regency Suite, A Poet's Notebook; recordings of Sonatina for clavichord and piano, Eric Parkin's Eight Piano Works, Four Piano Duos and Five Song Cycles, etc.; music for film and stage includes: Troilus and Cressida, Portrait of a Town, Garden Party, My Friend–My Enemy; compositions on the Internet. *Publications:* Portrait of a Town 1974, Words Without Music 1974, Strolling Players 1978, Open Window–Open Door 1985, Tanglewood 1990, Between the Lines 1991, Diva 1992, Collected Short Stories 1993, Thomas Armstrong—A Celebration 1998, Turn Back the Clock 1998, poems in numerous anthologies. *Leisure interests:* squash, skiing, tennis, swimming. *Address:* c/o Ricordi & Co. (London) Ltd., 210 New King's Road, London, SW6 4NZ, England.

STOKES, Baron (Life Peer), cr. 1969, of Leyland in the County Palatine of Lancaster; **Donald Gresham Stokes,** Kt., T.D., D.L., F.ENG., F.I.MECH.E., F.I.C.E.; British engineer and business executive; b. 22 March 1914, London; s. of Harry Potts Stokes; m. Laura Lamb 1939 (died 1995); one s.; ed. Blundell's School and Harris Inst. of Tech., Preston; student engineer Leyland Motors 1930–33; Tech. Asst. 1933–39; mil. service 1939–45; Export Man. Leyland Motors 1946–50, Gen. Sales and Service Man. 1950, Dir. 1954; Man. Dir. Leyland Motors Corpn. 1963, Chair. 1967; Man. Dir. British Leyland Motors Corpn. 1968–73, Chair. 1968–75, Chief Exec. 1973–75, Pres. British Leyland Ltd. 1975–80, Consultant 1980–81; fmr. Chair. British Leyland U.K. Ltd., NV Leyland Industries Belgium S.A., NV British Leyland (Belgium) S.A., British Leyland Motors Inc. U.S.A.; Chair. British Arabian

Advisory Co. Ltd 1977–85, Two Counties Radio Ltd. 1979–84 (Pres. 1984–90, Chair. 1990–94); Chair. Jack Barclay Ltd. and Jack Barclay (Service) Ltd. 1980–90; fmr. Dir. British Leyland Motor Corpn. of Australia Ltd., Leyland Motor Corpn. of S. Africa Ltd., N.Z. Motor Corpn., Ashok Leyland Ltd. India, Ennore Foundries Ltd. India, British Leyland Motors Canada Inc., Automóviles de Turismo Hispano Ingleses S.A., Metalúrgica de Santa Ana, British Leyland France S.A., Leyland Motor Corpn. (Malawi) Ltd.; Dir. Nat. Westminster Bank Ltd. 1969–81, OPUS Public Relations Ltd. 1979–85, Scottish and Universal Investments Ltd. 1980–92, The Dutton-Forshaw Motor Group Ltd. 1980–90 (Chair. 1981–90), KBH Communications Ltd. 1985 (Chair. 1987–96), Beherman Auto-Transports N.V. 1982–89, The Dovercourt Motor Co. 1982–90, GWR Group PLC 1990–94; Vice-Pres. Empresa Nacional de Auto-camiones S.A. (Spain) 1969–73; mem. Council of Soc. of Motor Mfrs. and Traders 1953, Vice-Pres. 1961, Pres. 1962, Deputy Pres. 1963; mem. Worshipful Co. of Carmen 1964, North West Econ. Planning Council 1967–70, E.D.C. for the Motor Mfg. Industry 1967, Nat. Advisory Council for the Motor Mfg. Industry 1967; Vice-Pres. Eng. Employers Fed. 1967–75, Inst. of Motor Industry 1967; Vice-Pres. U.M.I.S.T. 1968, Pres. 1972; Deputy Lieut. for the Lancashire County Palatine 1968; Deputy Chair. Ind. Reorganization Corpn. 1968–71; Vice-Pres. I.Mech.E. 1971, Pres. 1972; Cdre. Royal Motor Yacht Club, Poole 1979–81; Hon. Fellow, Keble Coll., Oxford 1968; Fellow, Inst. of Road Transport Engineers 1968, Pres. 1982–84; Fellow Royal Acad. of Eng.; Hon. LL.D. (Lancaster Univ.) Hon. D.Tech. (Loughborough), Hon. D.Sc. (Southampton and Salford); U.K. Marketing Award 1964; Officier, Ordre de La Couronne (Belgium); Commdr., Ordre de Léopold II (Belgium) 1972. *Leisure interest:* yachting. *Address:* 2 Branksome Cliff, Westminster Road, Poole, Dorset, BH13 6JW, England.

STOKES, Kerry Matthew, A.O., F.A.I.M.; Australian business and broadcasting executive; b. 13 Sept. 1940, Vic.; s. of M. P. Stokes; m. Peta Toppano; two s.; ed. St George's Christian Boys Coll., W.A. Tech. Coll.; Dir., mem. Sydney Dance Co. 1980; Chair. Australian Capital Equity Pty. Ltd (Dir. 1981–), Austrim Ltd., Golden West Network (TV), Westrac Equipment Pty. Ltd.; Chair. Canberra Theatre Trust 1981–86, Dir. 1989–91; fmr. Dir. V.A. Holdings Ltd.; Chair. Art Gallery Foundation, W.A. 1989–91; Chair. The Fed. Capital Press Pty. Ltd. (Canberra Times), Seven Network Ltd. 1995–, Nat. Gallery of Australia 1996–; Chair. Corp. Gifts Cttee. SCITECH 1987–89, Dir. 1989–91; Pres. Appeal Campaign for Inst. for Child Health Research; founder, mem. council Nat. Gallery of Australia, Chair. 1996–; Citizen of the Year Award 1994. *Publications:* Boyer Lectures (Advance Australia Where) 1994. *Leisure interests:* photography, sailing, scuba diving. *Address:* Seven Network Ltd., 14th Floor, 1 Pacific Highway, N. Sydney, N.S.W. 2060; c/o Australian Capital Equity Pty. Ltd., Level 3, 30 Kings Park Road, West Perth, WA 6005, Australia.

STOL, Marten; Netherlands university professor; b. 10 Nov. 1940, Oldekerk; m. Rose C. van Wyngaarden 1968; one s. one d.; ed. Gymnasium Middelburg and State Univ. Leiden; Research Assoc. State Univ. Leiden 1968–70, Asst. Prof. 1970–82; Research Assoc. Chicago Assyrian Dictionary, Oriental Inst., Univ. of Chicago 1973–74; Prof. of Akkadian (Assyriology), Ugaritic and History of Ancient Near East, Free Univ. Amsterdam 1983–; Gen. Sec. Soc. Ex Oriente Lux 1973–; mem. Royal Netherlands Acad. *Publications:* Studies in Old Babylonian History 1976, On Trees, Mountains and Millstones in the Ancient Near East 1979, Letters from Yale 1981, Pregnancy and Birth in Babylonia and in the Bible 1983, Letters from Collections in Philadelphia, Chicago and Berkeley 1986, Epilepsy in Babylonia 1993, Langs 's Heeren wegen 1997. *Address:* Heivlinder 27, 2317 JS Leiden, Netherlands.

STOLL, Jean-François; French civil servant; b. 19 Jan. 1950, Isle-Adam; ed. Inst. of Political Studies, Paris, Nat. School of Admin.; joined Ministry of Econ., Commercial Attaché Indonesia 1982–84, Tech. Adviser 1982–86, Commercial Adviser Mexico 1987–90, Tech. Adviser 1990–93, Head Service for Promotion of External Trade 1993–, Dir. External Econ. Relations 1998–. *Address:* c/o Ministry of the Economy, Finance and Industry, 139 rue de Bercy, 75572 Paris Cédex 12, France. *Telephone:* (1) 40-04-04-04. *Fax:* (1) 43-43-75-97.

STOLLEY, Paul David, M.D., M.P.H.; American professor of medicine; b. 17 June 1937, Pawling, New York; s. of Herman Stolley and Rosalie Chertock; m. Jo Ann Goldenberg 1959; one s. two d.; ed. Lafayette Coll., Cornell Univ. Medical School and Johns Hopkins School of Public Health; Medical Officer, U.S. Public Health Service 1964–67; Asst. and Assoc. Prof. of Epidemiology, Johns Hopkins School of Public Health 1968–76; Herbert C. Rorer Prof. of Medical Science, Univ. of Pennsylvania School of Medicine 1976–90; Prof. and Chair. Dept. of Epidemiology, Univ. of Md. 1991–; fmr. mem. Editorial Bd. New England Journal, Milbank Quarterly; fmr. Assoc. Ed. Clinical Pharmacology and Therapeutics; Pres. American Coll. of Epidemiology 1987–88; mem. Inst. of Medicine, N.A.S., Soc. for Epidemiologic Research (Pres. 1984), Int. Epidemiology Asscn. (fmr. Treas.), Johns Hopkins Soc. of Scholars, Science Advisory Cttee. to Fed. Drugs. Admin. Commr. 1993; Hon. M.A. (Pennsylvania) 1976. *Publications:* Case Control Studies (co-author) 1982, Foundations of Epidemiology (co-author) 1994, Epidemiology 1994, Investigating Disease Patterns 1995 (received American Medical Writers Asscn. Award 1996), and numerous articles on epidemiological subjects. *Leisure interests:* classical music, history, literature. *Address:* University of Maryland School of Medicine, 660 W. Redwood Street, Baltimore, MD 21201; 6424 Brass Knob, Columbia, MD 21044, U.S.A. (Home). *Telephone:* (410) 997-9567 (Home). *Fax:* (410) 997-9574 (Home).

STOLOJAN, Theodor, D.ECON., PH.D.; Romanian politician and economist; b. 24 October 1943, Tîrgoviste; s. of Theodor Stolojan and Nadejda Stolojan; m. Elena Stolojan; one s. one d.; ed. Acad. of Econ. Studies, Coll. of Finances, Credit and Accountancy, Bucharest; worked as economist, Ministry of the Food Industry 1966–72; first as economist and then as Chief of Division, State Budget Dept. of Ministry of Finance 1972–82; Deputy Dir., then Dir. of Dept. Foreign Currencies and Int. Financial Relations 1982–87; Gen. Insp. Dept. of State Revenues 1988–89; First Deputy Minister of Finance 1989–90, Minister of Finance 1990–91, Sec. of State, Pres. of Nat. Agency of Privatization; Prime Minister of Romania 1991–92; economist at IBRD 1992–; Assoc. Prof. of Public Finance, Acad. for Econ. Studies 1974–80, 1990–91. *Publications:* numerous studies. *Leisure interests:* skiing, travelling in mountains, jogging. *Address:* c/o World Bank, 1818 H Street, Washington, DC 20433, U.S.A. *Telephone:* (202) 473-7485. *Fax:* (202) 522-3181.

STOLPE, Manfred; German politician; b. 16 May 1936, Stettin, Germany (now Szczecin, Poland); m. Ingrid Ehrhardt; one d.; legal studies in Jena and Berlin; formerly in charge of organizational work of Protestant Church in East Germany; Consistorial Pres. Berlin-Brandenburg Church 1982–90; active in human rights movt.; joined Social Democratic Party (SPD) 1990; Prime Minister of Brandenburg Oct. 1990–. *Address:* Staatskanzlei, Heinrich-Mann-Allee 107, 14473 Potsdam, Postfach 601051, Germany. *Telephone:* (331) 866-1200. *Fax:* (331) 866-1400.

STOLTE, Dieter; German television administrator and professor; b. 18 Sept. 1934, Cologne; ed. Univs. of Tübingen and Mainz; Head of Science Dept., Saarländischer Rundfunk 1961; Personal adviser to Dir.-Gen. of Zweites Deutsches Fernsehen (ZDF) 1962, Controller, Programme Planning Dept. 1967, Programming Dir. 1976–82, Dir.-Gen. ZDF March 1982–; Dir. and Deputy Dir. Gen., Südwestfunk 1973; Prof. Univ. of Music and Presentation Arts, Hamburg 1980–; mem. Admin. Council, German Press Agency (dpa), Hamburg, European Broadcasting Union (EBU); Chair. Admin. Council TransTel, Cologne; Chair. Bd. Dirs. DeutschlandRadio, Cologne; mem. Int. Broadcast Inst., London; mem. Council, Nat. Acad. of TV Arts, New York, Int. Acad. of Arts and Sciences, New York; Int. Emmy Directorate 1997; Bundesverdienstkreuz, Officer's Cross, Golden Order of Merit (Austria), Bavarian Order of Merit, Hon. Citizen of State of Tenn., U.S.A. *Publications:* ed. and co-author of several books on programme concepts and function of television, etc.; several essays on subjects relating to the philosophy of culture and the science of communication. *Address:* ZDF-Strasse, 55100 Mainz (Office); Essenheimerstrasse, P.O. Box 40 40, 6500 Mainz, Germany (Home). *Telephone:* (0 61 31) 70-2000.

STOLTENBERG, Gerhard, DR.PHIL.; German politician and scientist; b. 29 Sept. 1928, Kiel; s. of Gustav Stoltenberg and Christine Stoltenberg; m. Margot Rann 1958; one s. one d.; ed. Grammar School, Bad Oldesloe, and Kiel Univ.; Scientific Asst., Kiel Univ. 1954–60, lecturer 1960–65; Deputy Chair. CDU, Schleswig-Holstein 1955, Chair. 1971; Fed. Chair. "Junge Union" 1955–61; mem. Schleswig-Holstein Parl. 1954–57, 1971–82; mem. Bundestag 1957–71, 1982–; Fed. Minister for Scientific Research 1965–69; Fed. Vice-Chair. CDU 1969–; Minister-Pres. Land Schleswig-Holstein 1971–82; Minister of Finance 1982–89, of Defence 1989–92; mem. Bd. of Man. Fried. Krupp, Essen 1965, 1969–70; Bundesverdienstkreuz. *Publications:* Der Deutsche Reichstag 1871–73, Politische Strömungen im schleswig-holsteiner Landvolk 1919–33, Staat und Wissenschaft: Zukunftsaufgaben der Wissenschafts- und Bildungspolitik 1969, Schleswig-Holstein: heute und morgen 1978, Wendepunkte. Stationen deutscher Politik 1947–1990 1997. *Leisure interests:* reading, oriental art, classical painting. *Address:* Bundeshaus, 53113 Bonn, Germany.

STOLTENBERG, Thorvald; Norwegian diplomatist; b. 8 July 1931, Oslo; s. of Emil Stoltenberg and Ingeborg Stoltenberg; m. Karin Stoltenberg 1957; one s. two d.; joined Foreign Service 1959; served in San Francisco, Belgrade, Lagos and Foreign Ministry; Int. Sec. Norwegian Fed. of Trade Unions 1970–71; Under-Sec. of State, Foreign Ministry 1971–72, 1976–79; Under-Sec. of State, Ministry of Defence 1973–74, Ministry of Commerce 1974–76; Minister of Defence 1979–81, of Foreign Affairs 1987–89, 1990–93; Amb. to UN, New York 1989–90; UN High Commr. for Refugees 1989–90; Special Rep. for UN Sec.-Gen. in fmr. Yugoslavia 1993–94; Co-Chair. Steering Cttee., Int. Conf. on the Fmr. Yugoslavia 1994–96; Amb. to Denmark 1996–. *Address:* Norwegian Embassy, Amaliegade 39, 1256 Copenhagen K, Denmark. *Telephone:* 33140124. *Fax:* 33140624.

STONE, Francis Gordon Albert, C.B.E., SC.D., F.R.S.; British professor of chemistry; b. 19 May 1925, Exeter; s. of Sidney Charles Stone and Florence Stone; m. Judith M. Hislop 1956; three s.; ed. Christ's Coll., Univ. of Cambridge; Fulbright Scholarship, Univ. of Southern Calif. 1952–54; Instructor and Asst. Prof., Harvard Univ. 1954–62; Reader, Queen Mary Coll., Univ. of London 1962–63; Head, Dept. of Inorganic Chem. and Prof., Univ. of Bristol 1963–90, Prof. Emer. 1990–; Robert A. Welch Distinguished Prof. of Chemistry Baylor Univ., Texas 1990–; Visiting Prof., numerous univs.; Pres. Dalton Div., Royal Soc. of Chem. 1981–83; Guggenheim Fellow 1961; Sr. Visiting Fellow, Australian Acad. of Sciences 1966; mem. Council, Royal Soc. of Chem. 1968–70, 1981–83, Chem. Cttee., Science and Eng. Research Council 1971–74, 1982-85; mem. Council of Royal Soc. 1986–88 (Vice-Pres. 1987–88); Hon. D.Sc. (Exeter, Waterloo) 1992, (Durham, Salford)

1993, (Zaragoza) 1994; Royal Soc. of Chem. Medals for Organometallic Chem. 1972, Transition Metal Chem. 1979; Chugaev Medal and Diploma, Kurnakov Inst., U.S.S.R. Acad. of Sciences 1978; American Chemical Soc. Award in Inorganic Chem. 1985; Davy Medal of Royal Soc. 1989. *Publications:* over 600 articles in scientific journals and books; Advances in Organometallic Chemistry, Vols. 1–42 (Ed.); Comprehensive Organometallic Chemistry, Vols. 1–9 (Co-Ed.) 1982, Comprehensive Organometallic Chemistry II, Vols. 1-13 (Co-Ed.) 1995. *Leisure interest:* travel. *Address:* 60 Coombe Lane, Bristol, BS9 2AY, England; 88 Hackberry Avenue, Waco, TX 76706, U.S.A.

STONE, John O., B.A., B.SC.; Australian politician and financial executive; b. 31 Jan. 1929, Perth; s. of Horace Stone and Eva Stone (née Hunt); m. Nancy Hardwick 1954; four s. one d.; ed. Univ. of Western Australia and New Coll., Oxford; Asst. to Australian Treasury Rep. in London 1954–56, Australian Treasury Rep. in London 1958–61; in Research and Information Div., Gen. Financial and Econ. Policy Branch, Dept. of Treasury, Canberra 1956–57, in Home Finance Div. 1961–62, Asst. Sec. Econ. and Financial Surveys Div. 1962–66; Exec. Dir. for Australia, New Zealand and S. Africa, Int. Monetary Fund (IMF) and IBRD—World Bank 1967–70; First Asst. Sec., Revenue, Loans and Investment Div., Treasury 1971; Sec. Australian Loan Council, Sec. Australian Nat. Debt Comm. 1971; Deputy Sec. (Econ.) Treasury 1971–76, Deputy Sec. Treasury 1976–78, Sec. 1979–84; Visiting Prof. Centre of Policy Studies, Monash Univ., Melbourne 1984; Consultant, Potter Partners, Stockbrokers 1985–87; weekly columnist Melbourne Herald, Sydney Morning Herald 1985–87, The Australian 1987–89, Sunday Telegraph 1989, The Australian Financial Review 1990–98; Dir. Sperry (Australia) Ltd. 1985–87, Peko-Wallsend Ltd. 1986–87; Chair. J. T. Campbell & Co. Ltd. 1994–96; Senator for Queensland 1987–90; mem. Defence Efficiency Review 1996–97; Leader of Nat. Party in the Senate, Shadow Minister for Finance; Sr. Fellow, Inst. of Public Affairs, Melbourne 1985–87, 1990–95. *Publication:* Upholding the Australian Constitution, Proceedings of the Samuel Griffith Society, Vols 1–10 1992– (ed. and publr.). *Leisure interests:* reading, wine and food. *Address:* 70 Gipps St, E. Melbourne, Vic. 3002, Australia. *Telephone:* (3) 9416-0253. *Fax:* (3) 9416-0675.

STONE, Lawrence; American professor of history; b. 4 Dec. 1919, Epsom, Surrey, England; s. of Lawrence Frederick Stone and Mabel Annie Julia Stone; m. Jeanne Caecilia Fawtier 1943; one s. one d.; ed. Charterhouse School, Sorbonne, Paris, Christ Church, Oxford; Lieut. R.N.V.R. 1940–45; Bryce Research Student, Univ. of Oxford 1946–47, Jt. Lecturer, Univ. and Corpus Christi Colls., Oxford 1947–50, Fellow of Wadham Coll., Oxford 1950–63; mem. Inst. for Advanced Study, Princeton, N.J. 1960–61, Dodge Prof. of History, Princeton Univ. 1963–90, Chair. of History Dept. 1967–69, Dir. Shelby Cullom Davis Center for Historical Studies 1969–90; mem. American Philosophical Soc. 1970; Fellow of American Acad. of Arts and Sciences 1968; Hon. D.Hum.Litt. (Chicago) 1979, (Pennsylvania) 1986; Hon. D.Litt. (Edin.) 1983, (Glasgow) 1993, (Oxford) 1994, (Princeton) 1995. *Publications:* Sculpture in Britain: The Middle Ages 1955, An Elizabethan: Sir Horatio Palavicino 1956, The Crisis of the Aristocracy, 1558–1641 1965, Social Change and Revolution in England, 1540–1642 1965, The Causes of the English Revolution 1529–1642 1972, Family and Fortune: Studies in Aristocratic Finance in the 16th and 17th Centuries 1973, The Family, Sex and Marriage in England 1500–1800 1977, The Past and Present 1981, An Open Elite? England 1540–1880 1984, The Past and the Present Revisited 1987, Road to Divorce: England 1530–1987 1990, Uncertain Unions: Marriage in England 1660–1753 1992, Broken Lives: Separation and Divorce in England 1660–1857 1993. *Leisure interest:* travel. *Address:* 266 Moore Street, Princeton, NJ 08540, U.S.A.; 231A Woodstock Road, Oxford, OX2 7AD, England. *Telephone:* (609) 921-2717 (U.S.A.); (01865) 59174 (England).

STONE, Norman, M.A.; British historian; b. 8 March 1941, Glasgow; s. of late Norman Stone and Mary Robertson Stone (née Pettigrew); m. 1st Marie-Nicole Aubry 1966 (dissolved 1977); two s.; m. 2nd Christine Booker (née Verity) 1982; one s.; ed. Glasgow Acad. and Gonville & Caius Coll., Cambridge; research student, Christ's Coll., Cambridge attached to Austrian and Hungarian insts. 1962–65; Research Fellow, Gonville & Caius Coll. 1965–67; Asst. Lecturer, Faculty of History, Univ. of Cambridge 1967–72, lecturer in History (Russian) 1973–84; Fellow, Jesus Coll., Cambridge and Dir. of Studies in History 1971–79; Fellow, Trinity Coll., Cambridge 1979–84; Prof. of Modern History, Univ. of Oxford and Fellow, Worcester Coll., Oxford 1984–97; Prof. of Int. Relations, Bilkent Univ., Ankara 1997–; Wolfson Prize 1976; Order of Merit (Poland) 1993. *Publications:* The Eastern Front 1914–17 1976, Hitler 1980, Europe Transformed 1878–1919 1982, Czechoslovakia: Crossroads and Crises (Ed.) 1989, The Other Russia (with Michael Glenny) 1990, articles in the press. *Leisure interests:* music, Eastern Europe, languages. *Address:* Bilkent University, 06533 Bilkent, Ankara, Turkey (Office); 22 St. Margaret's Road, Oxford, OX2 6RX, England (Home). *Telephone:* (01865) 439481 (Oxford). *Fax:* (312) 266-4326 (Ankara).

STONE, Oliver, B.F.A.; American film director and screenwriter; b. 15 Sept. 1946, New York; s. of Louis Stone and Jacqueline Goddet; m. 1st Najwa Sarkis (divorced); m. 2nd Elizabeth Stone (divorced); ed. Yale Univ. and New York Univ. Film School; Teacher, Cholon, Vietnam 1965–66; U.S. Merchant Marine 1966, U.S. Army, Vietnam 1967–68; taxi driver, New York 1971. Wrote screenplay for films Midnight Express (Acad. Award for best screenplay adapted from another medium) 1978, Conan the Barbarian (co-wrote) 1982, Scarface 1983. Directed and wrote films: Seizure 1973, The Hand 1981, Year of the Dragon (with Michael Cimino) 1985, Salvador (co-wrote) 1986, Platoon (Acad. Awards for Best Film, Best Dir.) 1986, Wall Street 1987, Talk Radio (co-wrote) 1988, Born on the Fourth of July 1989 (Acad. Award Best Dir. 1990), No One Here Gets Out Alive 1990, The Doors 1991, JFK 1991, Heaven and Earth 1993, Natural Born Killers 1994, Nixon 1995, Evita, A Child's Night Dream 1997, U-Turn 1998, Saviour 1998; producer Reversal of Fortune, Iron Maze, South Central, Zebrahead, Wild Palms (TV series) 1993, New Age 1994, The People vs. Larry Flynt; exec. producer Killer: A Journal of Murder 1995, Indictment: The McMartin Preschool 1995. *Address:* Ixtlan, 6th Floor, 201 Santa Monica Boulevard, 6th Floor, Santa Monica, CA 90401, U.S.A. (Office).

STONE, Roger, B.S.(ECON.); American business executive; b. 16 Feb. 1935, Chicago, Ill.; s. of Marvin Stone and Anita Masover; m. Susan Kessert 1955; three d.; ed. Wharton School of Finance, Univ. of Pennsylvania; joined Stone Container Corpn. 1957, Vice-Pres. Gen. Man. Container Div. 1970–75, Pres. and C.O.O. 1975–79, Pres., C.E.O. 1979–, Chair. 1983–; Bd. Dirs. Morton Int., McDonalds Corpn., Option Care Inc.; mem. Advisory Council for Econ. Devt. *Leisure interest:* golf. *Address:* Stone Container Corporation, 150 North Michigan Avenue, Chicago, IL 60601-7568, U.S.A. *Telephone:* (312) 346-6600.

STONE, Sharon; American actress; b. 10 March 1958, Meadville, Pa.; m. 1st Michael Greenburg 1984 (divorced 1987); m. 2nd Phil Bronstein 1998; ed. high school in Pennsylvania and Edinboro Coll.; TV appearances in Bay City Blues (series), Tears in the Rain (film), War and Remembrance (mini-series), Calendar Girl Murders (film), The Vegas Strip Wars (film); film debut in Star Dust Memories. *Films include:* Above the Law, Action Jackson, King Solomon's Mines, Allan Quatermain and the Lost City of Gold, Irreconcilable Differences, Deadly Blessing, Personal Choice, Basic Instinct, Diary of a Hit Man, Where Sleeping Dogs Lie, Sliver, Intersection, The Specialist, The Quick and the Dead, Casino, Last Dance, Diabolique 1996, Sphere, The Mighty 1999; Chevalier, Ordre des Arts et des Lettres.

STOPFORD, Michael; British international civil servant; b. 22 June 1953, London; s. of Edward Stopford and Patricia Carrick; ed. Oxford Univ.; fmr. mem. H.M. Diplomatic Service, U.K. Perm. Mission to UN, New York, Second Sec. and Press Attaché, Embassy in Vienna; Assoc. then Second Officer, Exec. Office of Sec.-Gen. of UN 1979–83, Special Projects Officer, Dept. of Public Information 1983–87, Chef de Cabinet to Dir.-Gen., UN Office in Geneva and Under-Sec.-Gen. for Human Rights 1987–91, Chef de Cabinet to Exec. Del. of Sec.-Gen. for Inter-Agency Humanitarian Programme in Iraq, Kuwait and Iraq—Turkey and Iraq—Iran border areas 1991–92, with Dept. for Humanitarian Affairs 1992, Special Asst. to Under Sec.-Gen. for Public Information, Dept. of Public Information, UN, New York 1992, Dir. UN Information Centre, Washington, D.C., Nov. 1992–. *Address:* IFAD, 1775 K Street, N.W., Washington, DC 20006, U.S.A.

STOPPARD, Sir Tom, Kt., C.B.E., F.R.S.L.; British writer; b. (as Thomas Straussler) 3 July 1937, Zlin, Czechoslovakia; s. of the late Dr. Eugene Straussler and Martha Straussler; stepson of Kenneth Stoppard; m. 1st Jose Ingle 1965 (divorced 1972); two s.; m. 2nd Dr. Miriam Moore-Robinson 1972 (divorced 1992); two s.; ed. Pocklington Grammar School, Yorks.; Journalist, Bristol 1954–60; freelance journalist, London 1960–64; mem. Cttee. of the Free World 1981–; mem. Royal Nat. Theatre Bd. 1989–; Hon. M.Litt. (Bristol, Brunel Univs.), Hon. Litt.D. (Leeds Univ.) 1979, (Sussex) 1980, (Warwick) 1981, (London) 1982, Dr. h.c. (Kenyon Coll.) 1984, (York) 1984; John Whiting Award, Arts Council 1967, Italia Prize (radio drama) 1968, New York Drama Critics Best Play Award 1968, Antoinette Perry Award 1968, 1976, Evening Standard Awards 1967, 1972, 1974, 1978, 1982, 1993, 1997. *Publications:* plays: Rosencrantz and Guildenstern are Dead 1967, The Real Inspector Hound 1968, Enter a Free Man 1968, After Magritte 1970, Dogg's Our Pet 1972, Jumpers 1972, Travesties 1975, Dirty Linen 1976, New-Found-Land 1976, Every Good Boy Deserves Favour (with music by André Previn, (q.v.)) 1978, Night and Day 1978, Dogg's Hamlet, Cahoots Macbeth 1979, Undiscovered Country 1980, On the Razzle 1981, The Real Thing 1982, Rough Crossing 1984, Hapgood 1988; Dalliance (adaption of Schmitzler's Liebelei) 1986, Arcadia 1993 (Evening Standard Award for Best Play), Indian Ink 1995, The Invention of Love 1997, The Seagull (trans. 1997); radio plays: The Dissolution of Dominic Boot 1964, M is for Moon among other things 1964, Albert's Bridge 1967, If You're Glad I'll be Frank 1968, Where Are They Now? 1970, Artist Descending a Staircase 1972, The Dog it was that Died 1983, In the Native State 1991; short stories: Introduction 2 1963; novel: Lord Malquist and Mr. Moon 1966; screenplays: The Romantic Englishwoman (co-author) 1975, Despair 1977, film scripts: The Human Factor 1979, Brazil (with Terry Gilliam, q.v. and Charles McKeown) 1984, Empire of the Sun 1987, Rosencrantz and Guildenstern are Dead 1989 (also dir.), Russia House 1989, Billy Bathgate 1990, Shakespeare in Love (jtly.) 1998 (jt. winner Acad. Award Best Original Screenplay 1999); television plays: Professional Foul 1977, Squaring the Circle 1984, The Television Plays 1965–84 1993; radio: The Plays for Radio 1964–91, 1994. *Address:* c/o Peters, Fraser & Dunlop Ltd., The Chambers, Chelsea Harbour, Lots Road, London, SW10 0XF, England.

STORARO, Vittorio; Italian cinematographer; b. 1940, Rome; ed. Centro Sperimentale; started with shorts then moved to feature length films; cinematographer for: Ciovinezza, Ciovinezza 1968, Delitto al Circolo del Tennis, La Strategia del Rango 1969, Il Conformista, L'Eneide 1970, Addio Fratello Crudele 1971, Giornata nera per l'Ariete 1971, Orlando Furioso

1971, Last Tango in Paris 1972, Bleu Gang. . ., Malizia 1972, Giordano Bruno 1973, Le Orme 1974, Novecento 1974, Scandalo 1975, Agatha, La Luna 1978, Apocalypse Now 1979, Reds 1979, Tarzan, the Ape Man 1980, One from the Heart 1981, Wagner 1982, Ladyhawke 1983, The Last Emperor 1984, Tucker: The Man and His Dream, New York Stories (Life Without Zoe), Dick Tracy, The Sheltering Sky, Tosca, Little Buddha, Roma!, Imago Urbis, Flamenco, Taxi.

STORCH, Marcus, M.SC.; Swedish business executive; b. 28 July 1942, Stockholm; s. of Hilel Storch and Anna Storch; m. Gunilla Berglund 1972; one d.; ed. Royal Inst. of Tech., Stockholm; Dept. Head, Welding 1968–72; Pres. Welding Div. AGA AB 1972–75, Pres. Gas Div. 1975–81, Exec. Vice-Pres. AGA AB 1978–81, Pres. and C.E.O. 1981–96; Chair. Connova AB; mem. Bd. A. Johnson AB, Nobel Foundation, Dagens Industrie AB, Acta Oncologica Foundation; Hon. M.D. *Address:* Grevgatan 65, 114 59 Stockholm, Sweden. *Telephone:* 08/6617195.

STOREY, David Malcolm; British author and playwright; b. 13 July 1933, Wakefield, Yorkshire; s. of Frank Richmond and Lily (née Cartwright) Storey; m. Barbara Hamilton 1956; two s. two d.; ed. Wakefield Grammar School, Wakefield Coll. of Art and Slade School of Art; Fellow, Univ. Coll. London 1974. *Publications:* novels: This Sporting Life (MacMillan Award) 1960, Flight into Camden (John Llewellyn Rhys Memorial Prize 1961, Somerset Maugham Award 1963) 1960, Radcliffe 1963, Pasmore (Faber Memorial Prize 1972) 1972, A Temporary Life 1973, Saville (Booker Prize 1976) 1976, A Prodigal Child 1982, Present Times 1984; plays: The Restoration of Arnold Middleton (Evening Standard Award 1967), In Celebration 1969 (also film), The Contractor (New York Critics' Prize 1974) 1969, Home (Evening Standard Award, New York Critics' Prize) 1970, The Changing Room (New York Critics' Prize) 1971, Cromwell 1973, The Farm 1973, Life Class 1974, Night 1976, Mother's Day 1976, Sisters 1978, Dreams of Leaving 1979, Early Days 1980, The March on Russia 1989, Stages 1992; poems: Storey's Lives: Poems 1951–1991 1992, A Serious Man 1998. *Address:* c/o Jonathan Cape Ltd., Random Century House, 20 Vauxhall Bridge Road, London, SW1V 2SA, England.

STORK, Gilbert, PH.D.; American professor of chemistry; b. 31 Dec. 1921, Brussels, Belgium; s. of Jacques Stork and Simone Weil; m. Winifred Elizabeth Stewart 1944 (died 1992); one s. three d.; ed. Univ. of Wisconsin; Instructor, Harvard Univ. 1946–48, Asst. Prof. 1948–53; Assoc. Prof., Columbia Univ. 1953–55, Prof. 1955–67, Eugene Higgins Prof. of Chem. 1967–92, Prof. Emer. 1992–, Chair. of Dept. 1973–76; mem. N.A.S., American Acad. of Arts and Sciences, American Philosophical Soc., Acad. des Sciences (France); Hon. Fellow, Royal Soc. of Chemistry; Hon. Fellow Pharmaceutical Soc. of Japan; Hon. D.Sc. (Lawrence Coll.) 1961, (Paris) 1979, (Rochester) 1982, (Emory) 1988, (Columbia) 1993, (Wis.) 1997; Award in Pure Chemistry of A.C.S. 1957, Baekeland Medal of N. Jersey Section of A.C.S. 1961, Harrison Howe Award 1962, Edward Curtis Franklin Memorial Award of Stanford Univ. 1966, A.C.S. Award in Synthetic Organic Chemistry 1967, Nebraska Award 1973, Roussel Prize 1978, Nichols Medal 1980, Arthur C. Cope Award, A.C.S. 1980, N.A.S. Award in Chemical Sciences 1982, Willard Gibbs Medal 1982, Nat. Medal of Science 1983, Tetrahedron Prize 1985, Roger Adams Award 1991, George Kenner Award 1992, Robert Welch Award 1993, shared Wolf Prize 1995, numerous other awards and medals. *Address:* Department of Chemistry, Columbia University, Chandler Hall, New York, NY 10027 (Office); 459 Next Day Hill Drive, Englewood, NJ 07631, U.S.A. (Home).

STORM, Colin A.; British business executive; b. 26 June 1939, Jersey; s. of Archibald Storm and Dorothy Storm (née Lamy); m. Jennifer Pitcher 1965; one s. two d.; joined Guinness Group as Under-Brewer 1961, various posts in Personnel Dept. 1966–76, Personnel Man. Guinness G.B. 1976–84, Personnel Dir. 1984, later Personnel Dir. Guinness Brewing Worldwide, Man. Dir. Guinness Brewing Int. 1990–92, Man. Dir. Guinness Ireland Group 1992–97, Deputy Man. Dir. Guinness Brewing Worldwide and Man. Dir. Guinness G.B. 1997–98, Chief Exec. Guinness 1998–; mem. Exec. Cttee. and Dir. Diageo PLC; Vice-Pres. Exec. Cttee. Middx. Young People's Clubs; mem. Inst. of Personnel Man. *Leisure interests:* sailing, fishing. *Address:* Guinness Limited, Park Royal Brewery, London, NW10 7RR, England. *Telephone:* 0181-963 5353. *Fax:* 0181-963 5215.

STORMER, Horst Ludwig, PH.D.; German physicist; b. 6 April 1949, Frankfurt-am-Main; s. of Karl-Ludwig Stormer and Marie Ihrig; m. Dominique A. Parchet 1982; ed. Univ. of Stuttgart; with tech. staff AT&T Bell Labs. 1977–83, head of dept. 1983–91, Dir. Physics Research Lab. 1992–; Bell Labs. Fellow 1982; Fellow American Physics Soc., American Acad. of Arts and Sciences; Buckley Prize, American Physics Soc. 1984, Otto Klug Prize, Germany 1985. *Address:* Lucent Technologies, 700 Mountain Avenue, New Providence, NJ 07974, U.S.A.

STORR, (Charles) Anthony, F.R.C.P., F.R.S.L.; British psychiatrist and writer; b. 18 May 1920, Bentley; s. of Vernon Faithfull Storr and Katherine Cecilia Storr; m. 1st Catherine Cole 1942, 2nd Catherine Peters 1970; three d., three step-s.; ed. Winchester Coll., Christ's Coll., Cambridge, Westminster Hosp. Medical School; qualified in medicine 1944; various positions as psychiatrist; Consultant Psychotherapist, Oxford Health Authority 1974–84; Fellow, Green Coll., Oxford 1979, Emer. Fellow 1984–; Hon. Consulting Psychiatrist, Oxford Health Authority 1984–. *Publications:* The Integrity of the Personality 1960, Human Aggression 1968, The Dynamics of Creation 1972, Jung 1973, The Art of Psychotherapy 1979, Solitude 1989, Churchill's Black Dog 1989, Freud 1989, Human Destructiveness 1991, Music and the Mind 1992, Feet of Clay: a study of gurus 1996. *Leisure interests:* music, journalism, broadcasting. *Address:* 45 Chalfont Road, Oxford, OX2 6TJ, England. *Telephone:* (01865) 553348.

STOTHARD, Peter, M.A.; British journalist; b. 28 Feb. 1951; s. of Wilfred Stothard and Patricia Savage; m. Sally Ceris Emerson 1980; one s. one d.; ed. Brentwood School, Essex and Trinity Coll. Oxford; journalist, BBC 1974–77; Shell Petroleum 1977–79; business and political writer, Sunday Times 1979–80; Features Ed. and leader writer, The Times 1980–85; Deputy Ed. The Times 1985–92, U.S. Ed. 1989–92, Ed. 1992–. *Leisure interests:* ancient and modern literature. *Address:* 1 Pennington Street, London, E1 9XN, England. *Telephone:* 0171-782 5000. *Fax:* 0171-782 5436.

STOTT, Kathryn Linda, A.R.C.M.; British pianist; b. 10 Dec. 1958, Nelson, Lancs.; s. of Desmond Stott and Elsie Cheetham; m. 1st Michael Ardron 1979; m. 2nd John Elliot 1983; one d.; ed. Yehudi Menuhin School (under Marcel Ciampi, Vlado Perlemuter, Louis Kentner) and Royal Coll. of Music, London (under Kendall Taylor); fifth prizewinner, Leeds Int. Piano 1978; has since performed extensively in recitals and concertos both in U.K. and in Europe, Far East, Canada and U.S.A.; ten appearances at Henry Wood Promenade concerts; 20 recordings including premieres of concertos by George Lloyd and Michael Nyman; Dir. Fauré and the French Connection Festival, Manchester 1995; Chevalier Ordre des Arts et Lettres 1996. *Leisure interests:* horse-riding, travel, film noir. *Address:* Askonas Holt Ltd., Lonsdale Chambers, 27 Chancery Lane, London, WC2A 1PF, England. *Telephone:* 0171-400 1700. *Fax:* 0171-400 1799.

STOTT, Richard Keith; British journalist; b. 17 Aug. 1943, Oxford; s. of Fred B. Stott and Bertha Stott; m. Penny Scragg 1970; one s. two d.; ed. Clifton Coll., Bristol; Bucks. Herald 1963–65; Ferrari Press Agency 1965–68; reporter Daily Mirror 1968–79, Features Ed. 1979–81, Asst. Ed. 1981; Ed. The People 1984–85, 1990–91; Ed. Daily Mirror 1985–89, 1991–92, Today 1993–95; British Press Awards Reporter of the Year 1977; What the Papers Say Ed. of the Year 1993. *Leisure interests:* theatre, reading. *Address:* 20 Albany Park Road, Kingston-upon-Thames, Surrey, KT2 5SW, England.

STOWE, David Henry, Jr., B.A.(ECONS.); American business executive; b. 11 May 1936, Winston-Salem, N.C.; s. of David Henry Stowe and Mildred (Walker) Stowe; m. Lois Burrows 1959; one s. one d.; ed. Amherst Coll., Massachusetts Inst. of Tech.; Vice-Pres. First Nat. Bank Boston 1961–68; Man. Deere & Co. 1968–71, Dir. 1971–77, Vice-Pres. 1977–82, Sr. Vice-Pres. 1982–87, Exec. Vice-Pres. 1987–90, Pres. and C.O.O. 1990–96. *Address:* 4510 5th Ave, Moline, IL 61265, U.S.A.

STOWE, Madeleine; American actress; b. 18 Aug. 1958, Los Angeles, Calif.; m. Brian Benben; ed. Univ. of Southern Calif.; began acting career at Solari Theatre, Beverly Hills; appeared in TV series The Gangster Chronicles, mini-series Beulah Land and TV films The Nativity, The Deerslayer, Amazons, Blood and Orchids. *Films:* Stakeout 1987, Tropical Snow, Worth Winning 1989, Revenge 1990, The Two Jakes 1990, Closet Land 1991, China Moon, Unlawful Entry 1992, The Last of the Mohicans, Another Stakeout, Short Cuts 1993, Blink, Bad Girls, Twelve Monkeys 1995, The Proposition 1998, Dancing About Architecture 1999. *Address:* c/o David Schiff, UTA, 9560 Wilshire Boulevard, 5th Floor, Beverly Hills, CA 90212, U.S.A.

STOYANOV, Petar; Bulgarian politician and lawyer; b. 1952, Plovdiv; ed. Sofia Univ.; m. Antonina Stoyanova; one s. one d.; fmr. divorce lawyer; became politically active 1989; mem. Union of Democratic Forces (SDS); Deputy Minister of Justice 1992; mem. Parl. 1994–96; Pres. of Bulgaria Jan. 1997–. *Address:* Office of the President, Sofia, Bulgaria.

STRACHAN, Ian Charles, M.A., M.P.A.; British business executive; b. 7 April 1943, Oldham; s. of Dr. Charles Strachan and Margaret Craig; m. 1st Diane Shafer 1967 (divorced 1987); one d.; m. 2nd Margaret Auchincloss 1987; one step-s. one step-d.; ed. Fettes Coll. Edinburgh, Christ's Coll. Cambridge and Princeton and Harvard Univs.; Assoc. Ford Foundation, Malaysia 1967–69; various positions, Exxon Corpn. 1970–86; Sr. Vice-Pres. and Chief Financial Officer, Johnson & Higgins, New York 1986–87; Finance Dir. RTZ Corpn. PLC 1987–91, Deputy Chief Exec. 1991–95; Man. Dir. BTR PLC July–Dec. 1995, Chief. Exec 1996–; Dir. (non-exec.) Commercial Union 1992–95. *Leisure interests:* tennis, golf, reading. *Address:* BTR PLC, BTR House, Carlisle Place, London SW1P 1BX, England.

STRAKHOV, Vladimir Nikolayevich; Russian physicist; b. 3 May 1932; ed. Moscow Inst. of Geological Prospecting; sr. engineer, researcher, Head of Lab. O. Schmidt Inst. of Earth Physics, U.S.S.R. (now Russian) Acad. of Sciences 1959–89, Dir. 1989–; Corresp. mem. U.S.S.R. (now Russian) Acad. of Sciences 1987, mem. 1992; main research in math., geophysics, gravitational and magnetic methods of prospecting mineral deposits, magnetic anomalies of oceans; went on hunger strike in protest at the state of scientific research and its financing 1996. *Address:* Institute of Earth Physics, Bolshaya Gruzinskaya 10, 123 810 Moscow, Russia. *Telephone:* (095) 252 0726 (Office).

STRANG, Rt. Hon. Gavin Steel, P.C., PH.D.; British politician; b. 10 July 1943; s. of James Steel Strang and Marie Finkle; m.; ed. Univs. of Edinburgh and Cambridge; mem. Tayside Econ. Planning Consultative Group 1966–68; scientist with Agric. Research Council 1968–70; mem. Parl. for Edin. East

1970–; Opposition Spokesman on Scottish Affairs 1972–73, on Energy 1973–74; Parl. Under-Sec. of State, Dept. of Energy March–Oct. 1974; Parl. Sec. Ministry of Agric., Fisheries and Food 1974–79; Opposition Spokesman on Agric. 1979–82, on Employment 1987–89, on Agric. and Rural Affairs 1992–97; Minister of Transport 1997–98; Labour. *Leisure interests:* golf, swimming, watching football. *Address:* House of Commons, London, SW1A 0AA, England.

STRANGE, Curtis Northrop; American golfer; b. 30 Jan. 1955, Norfolk, Va.; s. of Thomas Wright Strange Jr. and Nancy Neal; m. Sarah Jones; two s.; ed Wake Forest Univ.; turned professional 1976; won Pensacola Open 1979, Sammy Davis Jr. Greater Hartford Open 1983, LaJel Classic 1984, Honda Classic, Panasonic-Las Vegas Int. 1985, Canadian Open 1985, Houston Open 1986, Canadian Open, Fed. Express-St. Jude Classic, NEC Series of Golf 1987, Sandway Cove Classic, Australia 1988, Ind. Insurance Agent Open, Memorial Tournament, U.S. Open, Nabisco Championships 1988, U.S. Open, Palm Meadows Cup, Australia 1989, Holden Classic, Australia 1993; mem. PGA Tour Charity Team, Michelob Championship, Kingsmill 1996. *Leisure interests:* hunting, fishing. *Address:* c/o IMG, 1 Erieview Plaza, Suite 1300, Cleveland, OH 44114; PGA America, P.O. Box 109601, 100 Avenue of the Champions, Palm Beach Gardens, FL 33410, U.S.A.

STRÁNSKÝ, Jiří; Czech writer; b. 12 Aug. 1931, Prague; m. Jitka Balíková; one s., one d.; ed. High School; manual worker until 1989–; political prisoner 1950–58, 1970–72; after "velvet revolution" 1989–, mem. of Confed. of Political Prisoners, Pres. of Czech Centre of Int. PEN 1992–; Chair. M. Havel Foundation; Egon Hostovský Prize 1991. *Publications include:* Happiness, Tales 1969, The Land that Became Wild (Zdivočelá země) 1991; prose Auction; script for film Bumerang 1996 (Czech Literary Fund Prize 1998). *Leisure interests:* scouting, riding. *Address:* Czech Centre of International PEN, P.O. Box 23, 118 00 Prague 1, Czech Republic.

STRASSER, Valentine E. M.; Sierra Leonean politician and army officer; b. *c.* 1965, Allen Town, Freetown; m. Gloria Strasser; ed. Sierra Leone Grammar School, Gbenguema Mil. School; rank of Capt., retd. from army Sept. 1996; mem. mil. junta who overthrew govt. of Pres. Momoh April 1992; Chair. Nat. Provisional Ruling Council 1992–96, also fmr. Minister of Defence; student, Warwick Univ., U.K. 1996.

STRATAS, Teresa, O.C.; Canadian opera singer; b. 26 May 1938, Toronto, Ont.; d. of Emmanuel Stratas and Argero Stratakis; began singing career in nightclubs in Toronto; début at Toronto Opera Festival 1958; noted opera performances at Metropolitan Opera, New York include Berg's Lulu and Jenny in Brecht and Weill's Mahagonny; appeared as Violetta in Zeffirelli's film of La Traviata 1983; appeared in Broadway musical Rags 1986; created role of Marie Antoinette in Ghosts of Versailles, premièred Metropolitan Opera, N.Y. 1992; LL.D. h.c. (McMaster Univ.) 1986; Drama Desk Award for Leading Actress in a Musical on Broadway 1986–87. *Address:* c/o Vincent & Farrell Associates, 157 W. 57th Street, Suite 502, New York, NY 10019; Metropolitan Opera Company, Lincoln Center Plaza, New York, NY 10023, U.S.A.

STRATHCLYDE, 2nd Baron, cr. 1955; **Thomas Galloway Dunlop du Roy de Blicquy Galbraith,** P.C.; British politician; b. 22 Feb. 1960; s. of the late Sir Thomas Galbraith and Simone Clothilde Fernande Marie Ghislane; m. Jane Skinner 1992; two d.; ed. Sussex House, London, Wellington Coll., Univs. of E. Anglia and Aix-en-Provence; insurance broker Bain Clarkson Ltd. (fmrly. Bain Dawes) 1982–88; Govt. Whip House of Lords 1988–89; fmr. spokesman for Dept. of Trade and Industry, Under-Sec. of State 1993, Minister of State 1994; Parl. Under-Sec. of State Dept. of Employment 1989–90, Dept. of Environment July–Sept. 1990, 1992, Scottish Office 1990–92; Minister for Tourism 1989–90; Minister for Agric., Fisheries, Highlands and Islands 1990–92; Chief Govt. Whip 1994–97; Opposition Chief Whip House of Lords 1997–98, Shadow Leader Dec. 1998–; Conservative cand. European Election, Merseyside E. 1984. *Address:* House of Lords, Westminster, London, SW1A 0PW, England.

STRAUME, Janis; Latvian politician; b. 1962, Sigulda, Latvia; m.; one s. two d.; ed. Riga State Medical Inst.; physician, Riga City clinic, endoscopist, Latvian Diagnostics Centre 1986–90; political activities 1988–; mem. Latvian Human Rights Group Helsinki 86 (Riga Chapter), Latvian Nat. Independence Movt., Citizen's Congress of Latvian Repub., Union of 18th Nov.; mem. Saeima 1990–; Chair., Union for Fatherland and Freedom Faction Nov. 1998–. *Address:* Saeima, Jecaba str. 11, 226811 Riga, Latvia. *Telephone:* (371) 708 7111 (Office).

STRAUS, Robert, PH.D.; American professor of behavioural science, sociology and pharmacy; b. 9 Jan. 1923, New Haven; s. of Samuel H. Straus and Alma Fleischner; m. Ruth E. Dawson 1945; two s. two d.; ed. Yale Univ.; Instructor, Dept. of Applied Physiology, Yale Univ. 1947–48, Asst. Prof. 1948–51, Research Assoc. 1951–53; Asst. Prof., Dept. of Public Health and Preventive Medicine, State Univ. of New York 1953–55, Assoc. Prof. 1955–56; mem. Medical Center Planning Staff, Ky. Univ. 1956–60, Prof. of Sociology 1956, Prof. Dept. of Behavioral Science 1959, Chair. 1959–87, Prof. of Pharmacy 1975, Prof. Emer. 1987–; Dir. for Scientific Devt., Medical Research Inst. of San Francisco 1991–93; Visiting Prof., Calif. Univ. (Berkeley) 1978, Visiting Scholar 1986; Scientific Achievement Award, Ky. Medical Asscn., 1966; mem. Inst. of Medicine, N.A.S. 1975; Lifetime Achievement Award, American Public Health Asscn., Section on Alcohol, Tobacco and other Drugs 1993; Leo G. Reeder Award for Distinguished Career in Medical Sociology, American Sociological Asscn. 1998. *Publications:* Medical Care for Seamen 1950, Drinking in College (co-author) 1953, Medicine and Society (co-ed.) 1963, Alcohol and Society 1973, Escape from Custody 1974, A Medical School is Born 1996. *Leisure interests:* music, theatre, history of transportation. *Address:* 656 Raintree Road, Lexington, KY 40502, U.S.A. *Telephone:* (606) 268-0873 (Home).

STRAUS, Roger W., Jr.; American publisher and editor; b. 3 Jan. 1917, New York; s. of Roger Williams and Gladys (Guggenheim) Straus; m. Dorothea Liebmann 1938; one s.; ed. Hamilton Coll., Univ. of Missouri; reporter, Daily Reporter, White Plains, New York 1936, feature writer 1939–40; Editorial Writer, reporter Columbia Missourian 1937–49; Ed., Publr. Asterisk 1939; Editorial Asst. Current History 1940, Assoc. Ed. 1940–45; Assoc. Ed. Forum 1940–45; Pres. Book Ideas Inc. 1943–46; f. Farrar, Straus & Co. Inc. (now Farrar, Straus & Giroux Inc.) 1945, Pres. 1987–, also C.E.O.; Pres. Hill & Wang 1971–87; Dir. Univ. of Missouri Press; Chair. Publishing Bd. American Judaism magazine 1955–65; Vice-Pres. Fred L. Lavanburg Foundation 1950–80, Daniel and Florence Guggenheim Foundation 1960–76; mem. Bd. of Dirs. Harry Frank Guggenheim Foundation 1970–76, John Simon Guggenheim Foundation, Center for Inter-American Relations; mem. PEN, Emerson Literary Soc., Union of American Hebrew Congregations; Hon. D. Litt. (Missouri) 1976. *Publications:* (Co-Ed.) The Sixth Column 1941, War Letters from Britain 1941, The New Order 1941. *Address:* Farrar, Straus & Giroux Inc., 19 Union Square West, New York, NY 10003, U.S.A. (Office).

STRAUSS, Botho; German playwright and novelist; b. 2 Dec. 1944, Naumburg; moved with family to Remscheid, Ruhr region; on staff of Theater heute, West Berlin; Dramaturg at Schaubühne Theater, West Berlin 1970–75; Literaturpreis, Bayerische Akademie der Schönen Künste 1981; Mülheimer Drama Prize 1982. *Plays include:* Die Hypochonder (first play, 1971, winner Hannover Dramaturgie Award), Trilogie des Wiedersehens, Gross und Klein Kalldeway and Der Park, Das Gleichgewicht 1994. *novels include:* Die Widmung 1979, Rumor 1980, Paare, Passanten 1981, Der Junge Mann 1984, Niemand Anderes 1987. *Address:* Keithstrasse 8, 10787 Berlin, Germany.

STRAUSS, Robert Schwarz, LL.B.; American politician and trade negotiator; b. 19 Oct. 1918, South Central Texas; s. of Charles H. and Edith V. (née Schwarz) Strauss; m. Helen Jacobs 1941; two s. one d.; ed. Univ. of Texas Law School; Special Agent for Fed. Bureau of Investigation (FBI) in Ia., Ohio and Dallas, Tex. 1941–45; admitted to Texas Bar 1941; co-founder of law firm Akin, Gump, Strauss, Hauer and Feld 1945; Pres. Strauss Broadcasting Co. 1965; Dir. Archer Daniels Midland, Lone Star Industries, MCA, Memorex Telex; mem. Texas State Banking Bd. 1963–68; mem. Advisory Cttee. Forstmann Little & Co.; mem. Democratic Nat. Cttee. 1968–70, Treas. 1970–72; Chair. 1972–77; U.S. Prin. Trade Negotiator (rank of Amb.) 1977–79; Special Envoy of Pres. to Middle East April–Nov. 1979; Chair. Pres. Carter's Campaign Cttee. 1979–80; mem. Nat. Bipartisan Comm. of Cen. America 1983–84; Co-Chair. Nat. Econ. Comm. 1988–; Amb. to Russia 1991–93; partner Akin, Gump, Strauss, Hauer and Feld, Dallas 1945–77, 1981–; Presidential Medal of Freedom 1981. *Leisure interests:* golf, horse racing. *Address:* Akin, Gump, Strauss, Hauer & Feld, 4100 First City Center, Dallas, TX 75201; 1333 New Hampshire Ave, Suite 400, N.W., Washington, DC 20036, U.S.A.

STRAUSS-KAHN, Dominique Gaston André; French politician; b. 25 April 1949, Neuilly-sur-Seine; s. of Gilbert Strauss-Kahn and Jacqueline Fellus; m. 3rd Anne Sinclair 1991; one s. three d. from fmr. marriages; lecturer Univ. of Nancy II 1977–80; Scientific Counsellor Nat. Inst. of Statistics and Econ. Studies (INSEE) 1978–80; Dir. Cerepi (CNRS) 1980–; Prof. Univ. of Paris-X Nanterre 1981; Chief of Financial Services Commissariat Gen., Plan, Asst. Commr. Plan 1984–86; elected Socialist Deputy Val-d'Oise 1988–91; Pres. of Comm. on Finances, Assemblée Nationale 1988, Minister Del. of Industry and Foreign Trade to the Minister of State, Minister of the Economy, Finance and Budget 1991–92; Minister of Industry and Foreign Commerce 1992–93, of the Econ., Finance and Industry 1997–; mem. Socialist Party Cttee. of Dirs. 1983–, Nat. Sec. 1984–89; mem. Socialist Party Bureau 1995–; Mayor City of Sorcelles (Val d'Oise) 1995–97, First Deputy Mayor 1997–. *Publications:* La Richessse des Français 1977, Economie de la Famille et Accumulation patrimoniale 1977, l'Epargne et la Retraite 1982. *Leisure interests:* piano, cinema, skiing, rugby. *Address:* Ministry of the Economy, Finance and Industry, 139 rue de Bercy, Télédoc 151, 75572 Paris cedex 12; 5 avenue Georges V, 75008 Paris; Mairie de Sarcelles, 3 rue de la Résistance, 95200 Sarcelles, France.

STRAUSZ-HUPÉ, Robert, A.M., PH.D.; American diplomatist; b. 25 March 1903, Vienna, Austria; s. of Rudolph Strausz-Hupe and Doris (née Hedwig) Strausz-Hupe; m. 1st Eleanor de Graff Cuyler 1938 (died 1976), 2nd Mayrose Ferreira 1979; ed. Univ. of Pennsylvania; engaged in investment banking 1927–37; Assoc. Ed., Current History 1939–41; Assoc. Prof. of Political Science, Univ. of Pa. 1946–52, Prof. 1952; Dir. Foreign Policy Research Inst. 1955–69; Amb. to Ceylon and Repub. of Maldives 1970–72, to Belgium 1972–74, to Sweden 1974–75, to Turkey 1981–89; Perm. Rep. to N. Atlantic Council 1976–77; fmr. Dir. Atlantic Council of U.S.A.; Diplomat-in-Residence Foreign Policy Research Inst., Philadelphia 1977; Guest Prof. Geschwister Scholl Inst. Ludwig-Maximilians Univ., Munich 1978–79; Distinguished Fellow U.S. Inst. of Peace 1992–93; mem. Council on Foreign Relations,

American Political Science Asscn.; Bd. of Visitors Nat. Defense Univ. 1977–78; Distinguished Public Service Medal (U.S. Dept. of Defense), Marilla Ricker Award (U.S. Dept. of State) 1975; Ehrenkreuz für Wissenschaft und Kunst (Austria) 1982, and other honours and awards. *Publications:* The Russian-German Riddle 1940, Axis-America 1941, Geopolitics 1942, The Balance of Tomorrow 1945, International Relations 1950, The Zone of Indifference 1952, Power and Community 1956, Protracted Conflict (co-author) 1959, A Forward Strategy for America 1961 (co-author), Building the Atlantic World (co-author) 1963, In My Time 1967, Dilemmas Facing the Nation 1979, Democracy and American Foreign Policy 1995 (jtly.); over 40 articles on int. affairs. *Address:* White Horse Farm, 864 Grubbs Mill Road, Newtown Square, PA 19073, U.S.A.

STRAW, Rt. Hon. Jack (John Whitaker Straw), P.C., M.P.; British politician and lawyer; b. 3 Aug. 1946, Buckhurst Hill, Essex; s. of Walter A. W. Straw and Joan S. Straw; m. 1st Anthea L. Watson 1968 (divorced 1978); one d. (deceased); m. 2nd Alice E. Perkins 1978; one s. one d.; ed. Brentwood School, Essex and Univ. of Leeds; Pres. Nat. Union of Students 1969–71; mem. Islington Borough Council 1971–78, Inner London Educ. Auth. 1971–74 (Deputy Leader 1973–74); called to Bar, Inner Temple 1972, Bencher 1997, practised as barrister 1972–74; special adviser to Sec. of State for Social Services 1974–76, to Sec. of State for Environment 1976–77; on staff of Granada TV (World in Action) 1977–79; mem. Parl. for Blackburn 1979–; Opposition Treasury Spokesman 1980–83, Local Govt. Spokesman 1983–87; mem. Parl. Cttee. of Labour Party (Shadow Cabinet) 1987–97; Shadow Sec. of State for Educ. 1987–92, for the Environment (Local Govt.) 1992–94; Shadow Home Sec. 1994–97; Home Sec. May 1997–; mem. Council, Inst. for Fiscal Studies 1983–, Lancaster Univ. 1988–92; Vice-Pres. Asscn. of District Councils; Visiting Fellow, Nuffield Coll. Oxford 1990–; Gov. Blackburn Coll. 1990–, Pimlico School 1994– (Chair. 1995–); Fellow Royal Statistical Soc. 1996–; Labour. *Publications:* contribs. to pamphlets, newspaper articles, Policy and Ideology 1993. *Leisure interests:* walking, cooking puddings, music. *Address:* House of Commons, London, SW1A 0AA, England.

STRAWSON, Sir Peter Frederick, Kt., F.B.A., M.A.; British professor of metaphysical philosophy; b. 23 Nov. 1919, London; s. of Cyril Walter Strawson and Nellie Dora Strawson; m. Grace Hall Martin 1945; two s. two d.; ed. Christ's Coll., Finchley, St. John's Coll., Oxford; served in the army with rank of Capt. 1940–46; Asst. Lecturer in Philosophy, Univ. Coll. of N. Wales 1946–47; Lecturer in Philosophy, Univ. Coll., Oxford 1947–48, Fellow and Praelector 1948–68, Univ. Reader in Philosophy 1966–68, Waynflete Prof. of Metaphysical Philosophy and Fellow of Magdalen Coll., Oxford 1968–87; Woodbridge Lecturer, Columbia Univ., U.S.A. 1983; Visiting Prof., Collège de France, Paris 1985; Immanuel Kant Lecturer, Munich Univ. 1985; mem. Acad. Europaea 1990; Foreign hon. mem. American Acad. of Arts and Sciences 1971; Hon. Fellow of St. John's, Univ. and Magdalen Colls.; Dr. h.c. (Munich) 1998; John Locke Prize 1946. *Publications:* Introduction to Logical Theory 1952, Individuals 1959, The Bounds of Sense 1966, Logico-Linguistic Papers 1971, Freedom and Resentment 1974, Subject and Predicate in Logic and Grammar 1974, Naturalism and Skepticism 1985, Analyse et Metaphysique 1985, Analysis and Metaphysics: an Introduction to Philosophy 1992, Entity and Indentity 1997. *Leisure interests:* reading, travel. *Address:* Magdalen College, Oxford; University College, Oxford, OX1 4BH; 25 Farndon Road, Oxford, OX2 6RT, England (Home). *Telephone:* (01865) 276662 (Univ. Coll.); (01865) 515026 (Home).

STREEP, Meryl (Mary Louise), A.B., M.F.A.; American actress; b. 22 June 1949, Summit, N.J.; d. of Harry Streep, Jr. and Mary W. Streep; m. Donald Gummer 1978; one s. two d.; ed. singing studies with Estelle Liebling; studied drama at Vassar, Yale School of Drama; stage début in New York in Trelawny of the Wells; 27 Wagons Full of Cotton, New York; New York Shakespeare Festival 1976 in Henry V, Measure for Measure; also acted in Happy End (musical), The Taming of the Shrew, Wonderland (musical), Taken in Marriage and numerous other plays; Acad. Award for Best Supporting Actress for Kramer vs. Kramer 1980; Best Supporting Actress awards from Nat. Soc. of Film Critics for The Deer Hunter, New York Film Critics Circle for Kramer vs. Kramer, The Seduction of Joe Tynan and Sophie's Choice; Emmy Award for Holocaust, British Acad. Award 1982, Acad. Award for Best Actress, for Sophie's Choice 1982; Hon. Dr. (Yale) 1983, (Dartmouth) 1981, (Lafayette) 1985, Bette Davis Lifetime Achievement Award 1998. *Films acted in include:* Julia 1976, The Deer Hunter 1978, Manhattan 1979, The Seduction of Joe Tynan 1979, The Senator 1979, Kramer vs. Kramer 1979, The French Lieutenant's Woman 1980, Sophie's Choice 1982, Still of the Night 1982, Silkwood 1983, Plenty 1984, Falling in Love 1984, Out of Africa 1985, Heartburn 1985, Ironweed 1987, A Cry in the Dark (Best Actress Award, New York Critics 1988, Cannes 1989) 1988, The Lives and Loves of a She Devil 1989, Hollywood and Me 1989, Postcards from the Edge 1991, Defending Your Life 1991, Death Becomes Her 1992, The House of the Spirits, The River Wild 1994, The Bridges of Madison County 1995, Before and After, Marvin's Room, One True Thing 1998, Dancing at Lughnasa 1999. *TV appearances include:* The Deadliest Season, Uncommon Women, Holocaust, Velveteen Rabbit, First Do No Harm 1997; Special Award Berlin Int. Film Festival 1999. *Leisure interests:* peace and anti-nuclear causes, gardening, skiing, raising family, visiting art galleries and museums. *Address:* c/o Creative Artists Agency, 9830 Wilshire Boulevard, Beverly Hills, CA 90212, U.S.A.

STREET, Anthony Austin; Australian business executive and fmr. politician; b. 8 Feb. 1926, Victoria; s. of Brig. the Hon. G.A. Street, M.C.; m. V.E. Rickard 1951; three s.; ed. Melbourne Grammar; Royal Australian Navy; primary producer; mem. for Corangamite, House of Reps. 1966–84; Sec. Govt. Mems. Defence and Wool Cttees. 1967–71; mem. Joint Parl. Cttee. on Foreign Affairs 1969; Chair. Fed. Rural Cttee. of Liberal Party 1970–74; mem. Fed. Exec. Council 1971–; Asst. Minister for Labour and Nat. Service 1971–72; mem. Liberal Party Shadow Cabinet for Social Security, Health and Welfare 1973, for Primary Industry, Shipping and Transport 1973, for Science and Tech. and A.C.T. 1974, for Labour 1975; Minister for Labour and Immigration Nov.-Dec. 1975; Minister Assisting the Prime Minister in Public Service Matters 1975–77; Minister for Employment and Industrial Relations 1975–78, for Industrial Relations 1979–80, for Foreign Affairs 1980–83; resgnd. from Parl. Jan. 1984; now Man. and Co. Dir. *Leisure interests:* flying, cricket, golf, tennis. *Address:* 153 The Terrace, Ocean Grove, Vic. 3226, Australia (Home).

STREET, Sir Laurence Whistler, A.C., K.C.M.G., LL.B., Q.C.; Australian lawyer; b. 3 July 1926, Sydney, N.S.W.; s. of late Sir Kenneth Street; m. 1st Susan Gai Watt 1952, two s. two d.; m. 2nd Penelope Patricia Ferguson 1989; one d.; ed. Cranbrook School, Sydney, Univ. of Sydney; served in Royal Australian Navy 1943–47; barrister N.S.W. 1951; lecturer Univ. Sydney Law School 1962–65; Q.C. 1963; Commdr. and Sr. Officer R.A.N.R. Legal Branch 1964–65, Pres. Courts Martial Appeal Tribunal 1971–74; Judge Supreme Court N.S.W. 1965–88; Judge Court of Appeal 1972–74; Chief Judge in Equity 1972–74; Chief Justice of N.S.W. 1974–88; Lieut.-Gov. N.S.W. 1974–89; Pres. Cranbrook School Council 1966–74, St. John Ambulance Australia (N.S.W.) 1974–; Chair. Inaugural Planning Cttee., Australian Commercial Disputes Centre 1985–86; Fellow UTS Sydney 1990; Hon. Col. 1st/15th Royal N.S.W. Lancers 1986–96; Hon. Fellow Inst. of Arbitrators Australia (Grade I) 1989; mem. London Court of Int. Arbitration 1988–; Pres. LCIA Asia-Pacific Council 1989–; Chair. Advisory Bd. Dispute Resolution Centre, Bond Univ. 1989–, UTS Centre for Dispute Resolution 1994–; Pres. Australian Branch Int. Law Asscn. 1990–94, World Pres. 1990–92, Life Vice-Pres. 1992–; Pres. Sydney Univ. Law School Foundation 1990–; Chair. Australian Govt. Int. Legal Services Advisory Council 1990–, Legalcare Group 1997–; Fellow Chartered Inst. of Arbitrators (U.K.) 1992; Dir. John Fairfax Holdings Ltd. 1991–94, Chair. 1994–97; mem. WIPO Arbitration Consultative Comm., Geneva 1994–; Chair. Judiciary Appeals Bd. N.S.W. Rugby League 1998–; Australian Govt. Designated Conciliator to ICSID, Washington 1995–; Hon. LL.D. (Sydney), (Macquarie); Hon. D.Econ. (New England Univ.) 1996; K. St. J. 1976; Grand Officer of Merit Order of Malta 1977. *Address:* 1 Wolseley Crescent, Point Piper, N.S.W. 2027, Australia.

STREET, Robert, A.O., PH.D., D.SC., F.A.A.; Australian physicist; b. 16 Dec. 1920, Wakefield, England; s. of Joe Street and Edith Elizabeth Street; m. Joan Marjorie Bere 1943; one s. one d.; ed. Univ. of London; Scientific Officer, Dept. of Supply, U.K. 1942–45; Lecturer Dept. of Physics, Univ. of Nottingham 1945–54; Sr. Lecturer, Dept. of Physics, Univ. of Sheffield 1954–60; Foundation Prof. of Physics, Monash Univ., Melbourne, Victoria 1960–74; Dir. Research School of Physical Sciences, Australian Nat. Univ. 1974–77; Vice-Chancellor Univ. of Western Australia 1978–86; Dir. Magnetics Group, Research Centre for Advanced Materials and Minerals Processing 1991–; fmr. Pres. Australian Inst. of Nuclear Science and Eng.; mem. and Chair. Australian Research Grants Cttee. 1970–76; Chair. Nat. Standards Comm. 1967–78; F.A.A. 1973, Treas. 1976–77; Pres. Int. Inst. of Business and Tech., Perth, W.A. 1987–90; Chair. Child Health Research Foundation of Western Australia 1988–93; Consultant CRA Advanced Tech. Devt. 1992–96. *Publications:* scientific papers on magnetism in learned journals. *Address:* The University of Western Australia, Department of Physics, Nedlands, W.A. 6009, Australia.

STREET-PORTER, Janet, F.R.T.S.; British journalist and television producer and presenter; b. 27 Dec. 1946; m. 1st Tim Street-Porter 1967 (divorced 1975); m. 2nd A. M. M. Elliott 1976 (divorced 1978); m. 3rd Frank Cvitanovich (divorced 1988, died 1995); m. 4th David Sorkin 1996 (divorced); ed. Lady Margaret Grammar School and Architectural Asscn.; columnist and fashion writer, Petticoat Magazine 1968, Daily Mail 1969–71, Evening Standard 1971–73; own show, LBC Radio 1973; presenter, London Weekend Show, London Weekend Television (LWT) 1975, Saturday Night People (with Clive James (q.v.) and Russell Harty), The Six O'Clock Show (with Michael Aspel), Around Midnight 1976–80, co-cr. Network 7 (Channel 4); Head, Youth and Entertainment Features, BBC TV 1988–94; Head, Ind. Production for Entertainment 1994; writer and presenter Coast to Coast with Janet Street-Porter, TV series and book (BBC 2) 1998, The Midnight Hour (BBC 2) 1998, As The Crow Flies, TV series and book (BBC 2) 1999; Pres. Ramblers' Asscn. 1994–97; British Acad. Award for Originality 1988, Prix Italia 1992. *Publication:* Coast to Coast 1998. *Leisure interests:* walking, modern art. Address: c/o Bob Storer, Harbottle & Lewis, 14 Hanover Square, London, W1R 0BE, England. *Telephone:* 0171-629 7633. *Fax:* 0171-667 5100.

STREISAND, Barbra Joan; American actress and singer: b. 24 April 1942, Brooklyn, N.Y.; d. of Emanuel and Diana (née Rosen) Streisand; m. 1st Elliot Gould 1963 (divorced 1971); one s.; m. 2nd James Brolin 1998; ed. Erasmus Hall High School; nightclub debut at Bon Soir 1961; appeared in off-Broadway revue Another Evening with Harry Stoones 1961; appeared at Caucus Club, Detroit and Blue Angel New York 1961; played in musical comedy I Can Get It for You Wholesale 1962; began recording career with

Columbia records 1963; appeared in musical play Funny Girl, New York 1964, London 1966; television programme My Name is Barbra shown in England, Holland, Australia, Sweden, Bermuda and the Philippines, winning five Emmy awards; second programme Color Me Barbra also shown abroad; numerous concert and nightclub appearances; New York, Critics Best Supporting Actress Award 1962; Grammy awards for Best Female Pop Vocalist 1963, 1964, 1965, 1977, 1986; London Critics' Musical Award 1966; Academy Award (Oscar) for film Funny Girl 1968; American Guild of Variety Artists' Entertainer of the Year Award 1970, Commdr. des Arts et Lettres 1984. *Films include:* Funny Girl 1968, Hello Dolly 1969, On a Clear Day you can see Forever 1969, The Owl and the Pussycat 1971, What's up Doc? 1972 Up the Sandbox 1973, The Way We Were 1973, For Pete's Sake 1974, Funny Lady 1975, A Star is Born 1977, Yentl 1983 (also dir. and produced), Nuts 1987, Sing 1989, Prince of Tides 1990 (also dir., co-producer), The Mirror Has Two Faces 1996 (also dir.). *Address:* c/o Jeff Berg, ICM, 8942 Wilshire Boulevard, Beverly Hills, CA 90211, U.S.A.

STREISSLER, Erich W., DR.IUR.; Austrian professor of economics, econometrics and economic history; b. 8 April 1933, Vienna; s. of Albert Streissler and Erna Leithe; m. Monika Ruppe 1961; two s. (one deceased) three d.; ed. Vienna Law School, Univ. of Vienna, Oxford Univ., U.K., Hamilton Coll., New York, U.S.A.; studied also in France and Spain; Prof. of Statistics and Econometrics, Univ. of Freiburg/Br., Germany 1962–68, twice Dean of Law and Social Science Faculty 1965–67; Prof., Univ. of Vienna 1968–, Dean of Law and Social Science Faculty 1973–74; Vice-Pres. Austrian Inst. of Econ. Research 1990–; Distinguished Austrian Visiting Prof., Stanford Univ., U.S.A. 1983; Pres. Austrian Economic Asscn. 1988–94, Pres. Confed. of European Econ. Asscns. 1990–91; mem. Bd. of Control, Vienna Stock Exchange 1990–98; Treas. Int. Econ. Asscn.; Hon. mem. Hungarian Acad. of Sciences; Foreign mem. Bavarian Acad. of Sciences; mem. Austrian Acad. of Sciences. *Publications:* numerous articles in scientific journals on econ. growth, distribution, monetary matters, analysis of econ. systems and especially on the history of thought in econs. *Leisure interests:* hiking, history. *Address:* Faculty of Social Sciences and Economics, Vienna University, Hohenstaufeng 9, Vienna 1010; 18 Khevenhuellerstrasse 15, A-1180 Vienna, Austria. *Telephone:* 44 05 770.

STREITWIESER, Andrew, Jr., M.A., PH.D.; American professor of chemistry; b. 23 June 1927, Buffalo, N.Y.; s. of Andrew Streitwieser and Sophie Streitwieser; m. 1st Mary Ann Good 1950 (died 1965); m. 2nd Suzanne Cope 1967; one s. one d.; ed. Stuyvesant High School and Columbia Univ.; Atomic Energy Comm. Postdoctoral Fellow, M.I.T. 1951–52; Instructor in Chem. Univ. of Calif. at Berkeley 1952–54, Asst. Prof. 1954–59, Assoc. Prof. 1959–63, Prof. of Chem. 1963, Prof. Emer. 1993–, Prof. Grad. School 1995–; Consultant to Industry 1957–; Guggenheim Fellow 1969; mem. N.A.S., American Acad. of Arts and Sciences, Bavarian Acad. of Sciences; A.C.S. awards: Calif. Section 1964, Award in Petroleum Chem. 1967; Humboldt Sr. Scientist Award (Bonn) 1976, Humboldt Award (Bonn) 1979, Norris Award in Physical Organic Chemistry 1982, Cope Scholar Award 1989. *Publications:* Molecular Orbital Theory for Organic Chemists 1961, Solvolytic Displacement Reactions 1962, Supplemental Tables of Molecular Orbital Calculations (with J. I. Brauman) Vols. I and II 1965, Progress in Physical Organic Chemistry (co-ed.) Vols I-XI 1963–74, Dictionary of π-Electron Calculations (with C. A. Coulson) 1965, Orbital and Electron Density Diagrams (with P. H. Owens) 1973, Introduction to Organic Chemistry (with C. H. Heathcock) 1976, 1981, 1985, (also with E.L. Kosower) 1992, Solutions Manual and Study Guide for Introduction to Organic Chemistry (with C. H. Heathcock and P. A. Bartlett) 1985 (3rd edn.), A Lifetime of Synergy with Theory and Experiment 1996. *Leisure interests:* music (especially opera), wine, photography. *Address:* Department of Chemistry, University of California, Berkeley, CA 94720, U.S.A. *Telephone:* (510) 642-2204. *Fax:* (510) 643 6232.

STRENGER, Hermann-Josef; German business executive; b. 26 Sept. 1928, Cologne; m. Gisela Buchholtz 1956; two s. two d.; joined Bayer AG as commercial trainee 1949; Chemical Sales Dept. –1954; assigned to subsidiary, Brazil 1954–57, to Bayer subsidiary, A.B. Anilin Kemi, Sweden 1958–61; Head, Sales Dept. for raw materials for surface coatings, Leverkusen 1961–65; Head, Polyurethanes Dept. 1965–69, Dir. 1969–70; Commercial Head, Polyurethanes Div. 1970–72; mem. Bd. of Man. 1972–; Deputy Chair. Man. Bd. Bayer AG 1978–84, Chair. and Chief Exec. 1984–92, Chair. Supervisory Bd. 1992–; Chair. Supervisory Bd. VEBA AG; Chair. Carl Duisberg Gesellschaft 1987–; Chair. Supervisory Bd. Linde AG 1996; mem. Supervisory Bd. Hapag-Lloyd AG 1983, Karstadt AG 1983. *Address:* VEBA AG, Postfach 30 10 51, 40410 Düsseldorf; Bayer AG, 51368 Leverkusen, Germany.

STRETTON, James, B.A., F.F.A.; British business executive; b. 16 Dec. 1943; m. Isobel Christine Robertson 1968; two d.; ed. Laxton Grammar School, Oundle, Worcester Coll., Oxford; Deputy Man. Dir. Standard Life Assurance Co. 1988–94, Chief Exec. U.K. Operations 1994–. *Address:* Standard Life Assurance Company, 3 George Street, Edinburgh, EH2 2XZ, Scotland. *Telephone:* 0131-225 2552. *Fax:* 0131-245 6010.

STRICK, Joseph; American film director and company executive; b. 6 July 1923, Braddock, Pa.; s. of Frank Strick and Rose Abramovitz; m. 1st Anne Laskin 1945 (divorced 1968); two s. one d.; m. 2nd Martine Rossignol 1970; one s. one d.; studied physics in Los Angeles; aerial photographer during World War II; formed Electrosolids Corpn., Physical Sciences Corpn.; Venice Critics Award for The Savage Eye, Acad. Award for Interviews with My Lai Veterans. *Films directed:* Muscle Beach (also producer, documentary), The Savage Eye, The Balcony, Ulysses (also co-writer and producer), Interviews with My Lai Veterans (documentary), Portrait of the Artist, Tropic of Cancer.

STRICKLAND, John, M.A., J.P.; British banker; b. 23 Oct. 1939; s. of William F. Strickland and Nora N. Strickland; m. Anthea Granville-Lewis 1963; three s.; ed. Univ. of Cambridge; Asst. Gen. Man. TSV, Hongkong and Shanghai Banking Corpn. 1980-82, Gen. Man. TSV 1983–88, Exec. Dir. Services 1989–96, Chair. 1996–; Dir. HSBC Holdings PLC 1988, Marine Midland Bank 1991–96, Midland Bank PLC 1993–96; Chair. Hongkong Bank Malaysia Berhad 1996–98, Hong Kong and Shanghai Banking Corpn. May 1996–; Vice-Chair. Hang Seng Bank Ltd. 1996; mem. Council Outward Bound Trust of Hong Kong. *Leisure interests:* mountaineering, reading. *Address:* c/o The Hongkong and Shanghai Banking Corporation Ltd., Level 34, 1 Queen's Road Central, Hong Kong.

STRINGER, Howard; American broadcasting executive; b. 1942, Cardiff, Wales; m. Jennifer K. Patterson 1978; ed. Merton Coll. Oxford; served with U.S. Army in Vietnam 1965–67; researcher and producer, CBS News 1967–76; Exec. producer, CBS Reports 1976–81, CBS Evening News 1981–84; Exec. Vice-Pres. CBS News 1984–86, Pres. 1986–88; Pres. CBS Broadcast Group 1988–95; Chair., C.E.O. Tele-TV 1995–97; Pres. Sony Corpn. of America 1997, Chair. 1998–; Chair. Sony Canada, Sony Electronics 1997, Sony Pictures Entertainment 1998; Vice-Chair. American Film Inst.; dir. Applied Graphics Techs.; Gov. Nature Conservancy, United Cerebral Palsy, Motion Picture and TV Fund Foundation; Trustee Presbyterian Hosp. *Address:* Sony Corporation of America, 550 Madison Avenue, New York, NY 10022, U.S.A.

STRITCH, Elaine; American singer and actress; b. 2 Feb. 1926, Detroit; d. of George J. Stritch and Mildred (née Tobe) Stritch; m. John Bay 1973 (died 1982); ed. Sacred Heart Convent, Detroit, Drama Workshop, New School for Social Research; Broadway début as Pamela Brewster in Loco 1946; other performances include, Three Indelicate Ladies 1947, Yes M'Lord 1949, Melba Snyder in revival of Pal Joey 1952, Bus Stop 1955, Mimi Paragon in Sail Away, New York 1961, London 1962, Martha in Who's Afraid of Virginia Woolf? 1962 and 1965, Joanne in Company, New York 1970, London 1971, Love Letters, London 1990; *films include,* The Scarlet Hour 1956, Three Violent People 1956, A Farewell to Arms 1957, The Perfect Furlough 1958, Who Killed Teddy Bear 1965, Pigeons 1971, September 1988, Cocoon: The Return, Cadillac Man 1990, Out to Sea; numerous television appearances, including My Sister Eileen 1962, Two's Company (British Series) 1975–76 and 1979, Stranded 1986. *Publication:* Am I Blue?: Living With Diabetes and, Dammit, Having Fun 1984.

STRITTMATTER, Erwin; German writer; b. 14 Aug. 1912, Spremberg; s. of Heinrich Strittmatter and Helene Strittmatter; m. Eva Braun; eight s.; ed. Grammar School; various jobs, Ed. 1945–, full-time writer 1951–; Lessing Prize, Fontane Prize, Nat. Prize. *Publications:* Ochsenkutscher 1952, Tinko 1954, Wundertäter (3 vols.) 1957, 1973, 1980, Ole Bienkopp 1963, Der Laden (2 vols.) 1983, 1987, Nachtigallsgeschichten 1985. *Leisure interests:* horse-breeding, riding. *Address:* Frankfurter Allee 22, Berlin 1035, Germany. *Telephone:* 588 0046.

STROESSNER, Gen. Alfredo; Paraguayan politician and army officer; b. 3 Nov. 1912; ed. Military Coll., Asunción; entered Paraguayan army; commissioned 1932, served through all ranks to Gen; C.-in-C. of Armed Forces 1951; Pres. of Paraguay 1954–89; overthrown in coup Feb. 1989; flown to exile in Brazil 1989; mem. Partido Colorado; Cruz del Chaco, Cruz del Defensor, decorations from Argentina and Brazil. *Address:* Lago Sul, Brasília, Brazil.

STRÖMHOLM, Stig Fredrik, LL.D., D.JUR.; Swedish fmr. university vice-chancellor; b. 16 Sept. 1931, Boden; s. of Major Frederik Strömholm and Gerda Jansson; m. Gunilla M. Forslund 1958; one s. two d.; ed. Univs. of Uppsala, Cambridge and Munich; Clerk, Southern Dist. Court of Uppsala 1958–60; Jr. Judge, Stockholm Court of Appeal 1961; Asst. Prof. of Comparative Law, Uppsala Univ. 1966, Prof. of Jurisprudence 1969, Dean, Faculty of Law 1973–79, Deputy Vice-Chancellor 1978–89, Vice-Chancellor 1989–97; Pres. Royal Swedish Acad. of Letters, History and Antiquities 1985–93, Academia Europaea, London 1997–; mem. several Swedish and foreign acads.; Dr. h.c. at several Swedish and foreign univs.; Orden pour le Mérite (Fed. Repub. of Germany) and other decorations; several prizes. *Publications:* 25 vols. of legal science including Le droit moral de l'auteur, 3 vols. 1967–73, A Short History of Legal Thinking in the West 1985; some 20 vols. of criticism and fiction. *Leisure interests:* reading, travelling. *Address:* Norra Rudbecksgatan 5, 752 36 Uppsala, Sweden. *Telephone:* (018) 515045; (018) 548208.

STROMINGER, Jack L.; American professor of biochemistry; b. 7 Aug. 1925, New York; m.; four c.; ed. Harvard and Yale Univs.; Intern, Barnes Hosp., St. Louis 1948–49; Research Fellow, American Coll. of Physicians, Dept. of Pharmacology, Washington Univ. School of Medicine, St. Louis 1949–50, Research Asst. 1950–51; Sr. Asst. Surgeon, U.S. Public Health Service, Nat. Inst. of Arthritis and Metabolic Diseases, Bethesda 1951–54; leave of absence, Carlsberg Lab., Copenhagen, Denmark and Molteno Inst., Cambridge Univ., England, Commonwealth Fund Fellow 1955; Asst. Prof. of

Pharmacology, Dept. of Pharmacology, Washington Univ. School of Medicine, Markel Scholar in Medical Science 1958–60, Prof., 1960–61, Forsyth Faculty Fellow 1960, Prof. of Pharmacology and Microbiology, Depts. of Pharmacology and Microbiology 1961–64; Prof. of Pharmacology and Chemical Microbiology, Univ. of Wis. Medical School, Madison, Chair. Dept. of Pharmacology, mem. Univ. Cttee. on Molecular Biology 1964–68; Prof. of Biochemistry, Dept. of Biochemistry and Molecular Biology, Harvard Univ., Cambridge, Mass. 1968–83, Chair. Dept. of Biochemistry and Molecular Biology 1970–73, Dir. of Basic Sciences, Sidney Farber Cancer Center 1974–77; Head Tumor Virology Div., Dana-Farber Cancer Inst., Boston 1977–, Higgins Prof. of Biochemistry 1983–; mem. Steering Cttee. Biomedical Sciences Scientific Working Group, WHO; mem. N.A.S., American Acad. of Arts and Sciences, Nat. Inst. of Medicine, A.A.A.S., American Soc. of Biological Chemists, of Microbiologists, of Pharmacology and Experimental Therapeutics, American Asscn. of Immunologists, American Chemical Soc.; Hon. D.Sc. (Trinity Coll., Dublin) 1975; Guggenheim Fellowship1974–75; John J. Abel Award in Pharmacology 1960, Paul-Lewis Labs. Award in Enzyme Chem. 1962, N.A.S. Award in Microbiology in Honour of Selman Waxman 1968, Rose Payne Award, American Soc. for Histocompatibility and Immunogenetics 1986, Pasteur Medal 1990, Albert Lasker Award for Basic Medical Research 1995, other awards. *Address:* Department of Biochemistry, Dana Faber Cancer Institute, 44 Binney Street, Boston, MA 02115, U.S.A.

STRONG, David F., PH.D., F.R.S.C.; Canadian geologist and university president; b. 26 Feb. 1944, Botwood, Newfoundland; m. Lynda Joan Marshall; two d.; ed. Memorial Univ. of Newfoundland, Lehigh Univ., Pa., U.S.A., Univ. of Edinburgh, Scotland; Asst. Prof., Dept. of Geology, Memorial Univ. of Newfoundland 1970–72, Assoc. Prof. 1972–74, Acting Head of Dept. 1974–75, Prof., Dept. of Earth Sciences 1974–90, Univ. Research Prof. 1985–90, Special Adviser to Pres. 1986–87, Vice-Pres. (Academic) 1987–90; Pres., Vice-Chancellor Univ. of Vic. 1990–; Visiting Prof., Université de Montpellier, France 1976–77; W.F. James Prof. of Pure and Applied Sciences, St. Francis Xavier Univ., Nova Scotia 1981–82; mem. Bd. of Dirs. Seabright Corpn. Ltd. 1986–; Assoc. Ed. Canadian Journal of Earth Sciences 1977–83, Transactions of the Royal Soc. of Edin. 1980–; Chair. Natural Sciences and Eng. Research Council of Canada 1983–86, mem. 1982–88; mem. Research Council, Canadian Inst. of Advanced Research 1987–, Newfoundland and Labrador Advisory Council on Science and Tech. 1988–; Fellow Geological Asscn. of Canada, Geological Soc. of America, Soc. of Econ. Geologists; mem. Canadian Inst. of Mining and Metallurgy, Mineralogical Asscn. of Canada; APICS Young Scientist Award (now the Frazer Medal) 1973, Foreign Exchange Fellowships to Japan 1976, to France 1976–77, Canadian Inst. of Mining and Metallurgy Distinguished Service Award 1979, Geological Asscn. of Canada Past Pres.'s Medal 1980, Univ. of Edin. Swiney Lecturer 1981. *Address:* Office of the President and Vice-Chancellor, University of Victoria, P.O. Box 1700, Victoria, B.C. V8W 2Y2, Canada. *Telephone:* (604) 721 7002.

STRONG, Liam (Gerald Porter), B.A.; British business executive; b. 6 Jan. 1945, Enniskillen, Northern Ireland; s. of Gerald James Strong and Geraldine Crozier Strong; m. Jacqueline Gray 1970; one s. one d.; ed. Trinity Coll. Dublin; joined Procter & Gamble, Newcastle upon Tyne 1967–71; Household Man., Reckitt & Colman 1971, moved to Corp. Planning Unit, London 1973, Marketing and Sales Dir., then Gen. Man. Reckitt & Colman 1975–80, Vice-Pres. Sunset Designs, Calif., U.S.A. 1980–82, Head Int. Pharmaceuticals Div., Reckitt & Colman 1982–86, Pres. Durkee French, U.S.A. 1986–89; Dir. of Marketing British Airways 1989–90, Dir. Marketing and Operations 1990–91; Chief Exec. Sears PLC 1991–97; Head of World Comm. 1997–. *Leisure interests:* reading, shooting, opera. *Address:* c/o 40 Duke Street, London, W1A 2HP, England.

STRONG, Maurice F., O.C., F.R.S.A., F.R.S.C.; Canadian environmentalist, international official and business executive; b. 29 April 1929, Oak Lake, Manitoba; s. of Frederick Milton Strong and Mary Fyfe Strong (deceased); m. 1st Pauline Olivette Williams 1950 (divorced 1980), two s. three d.; m. 2nd Hanne Marstrand 1981; one foster d.; served in UN Secr. 1947; Pres. or Dir. of various Canadian and int. corpns. 1954–66; also involved in leadership of various pvt. orgs. in field of devt. and int. affairs; Dir.-Gen. External Aid Office of Canadian Govt. 1966 (now Canadian Int. Devt. Agency); Chair. Canadian Int. Devt. Bd.; Alt. Gov. IBRD, ADB, Caribbean Devt. Bank; UN Under-Sec. Gen. with responsibility for environmental affairs 1970–72, Chief Exec. for 1972 Conf. on Human Environment, Stockholm, June 1972; Exec. Dir. UN Environment Programme 1973–75; Chair. Petro Canada 1976–78; Pres. Stronat Investments Ltd. 1976–80; Chair. Bd. of Govs. Int. Devt. Research Centre 1977–78; Chair. Strouest Holdings Inc., Procor Inc. 1978–79, AZL Resources Inc. 1978–83, Int. Energy Devt. Corpn. 1980–83, N.S. Round Table Soc. for Int. Devt., Canadian Devt. Investment Corpn., 1982–84, and dir. or mem. numerous business and conservation groups in Canada and internationally; Under Sec.-Gen., U.N. 1985–87, 1989; Pres. World Fed. UNA 1987–, The Baca Corpn.; Dir. Better World Soc. 1988–; Chair., Pres. American Water Devt. Inc., Denver 1986–89; Sec.-Gen. UN 1992 Conf. on Environment and Devt.; Chair. Ontario Hydro 1992–95, World Resources Inst.; Sr. Adviser to Pres. of World Bank 1995; Under Sec.-Gen. and Exec. Co-ordinator for UN Reform 1997; Special Adviser to Sec.-Gen. of UN 1998–; mem. Bd. Dirs. UN foundation; several hon. degrees; Onassis Int. Award 1993, Jawaharlal Nehru Award for Int. Understanding 1994, numerous other awards and prizes. *Publications:* various articles in journals. *Address:* Suite #401, 255 Consumers Road, Toronto, Ont., M2J 5B6, Canada.

STRONG, Sir Roy Colin, Kt., PH.D.; British historian, writer on gardening, and fmr. museum director; b. 23 Aug. 1935, London; s. of George Edward Clement Strong and Mabel Ada Smart; m. Julia Trevelyan Oman (q.v.) 1971; ed. Queen Mary Coll., Univ. of London and Warburg Inst.; Asst. Keeper, Nat. Portrait Gallery, London 1959–67, Dir. 1967–73; Dir. Victoria and Albert Museum, London 1974–87; Vice-Chair. South Bank Bd. (now S. Bank Centre) 1985–90; Dir. Oman Productions Ltd., Nordstern Fine Art Insurance 1988–; organizer of exhbns. including The Elizabethan Image (Tate Gallery) 1969, The Destruction of the Country House (Victoria and Albert Museum) 1974, Artists of the Tudor Court (Victoria and Albert Museum) 1983; mem. Arts Council of G.B. 1983–87 (Chair. Arts Panel 1983–87), Council, R.C.A. 1979–87; Patron, Pallant House, Chichester 1986–; Fellow, Royal Soc. of Antiquaries, Queen Mary Coll., Univ. of London; Hon. D.Litt. (Leeds) 1983, (Keele) 1984; Shakespeare Prize 1980 (F.V.S. Foundation, Hamburg). *Publications:* Portraits of Queen Elizabeth I 1963, Leicester's Triumph (with J. A. Van Dorsten) 1964, Holbein and Henry VIII 1967, Tudor and Jacobean Portraits 1969, The English Icon: Tudor and Jacobean Portraiture 1969, Van Dyck: Charles I on Horseback 1972, Inigo Jones: The Theatre of the Stuart Court 1972 (with S. Orgel), Elizabeth R (with Julia Trevelyan Oman (q.v.)) 1971, Mary Queen of Scots (with Julia Trevelyan Oman) 1972, Splendour at Court: Renaissance Spectacle and The Theatre of Power 1973, Nicholas Hilliard 1975, An Early Victorian Album (with Colin Ford) 1974, The Cult of Elizabeth: Elizabethan Portraiture and Pageantry 1977, And When Did You Last See Your Father? The Victorian Painter and British History 1978, The Renaissance Garden in England 1979, Britannia Triumphans, Inigo Jones, Rubens and Whitehall Palace 1980, Holbein 1980, The English Miniature (with J. Murdoch, J. Murrell and P. Noon) 1981, The English Year (with Julia Trevelyan Oman) 1982, The English Renaissance Miniature 1983, Artists of the Tudor Court (with J. Murrell) 1983, Glyndebourne, A Celebration (Contrib.) 1984, Art and Power, Renaissance Festivals 1450–1650 1984, Strong Points 1985, Henry Prince of Wales and England's Lost Renaissance 1986, C. V. Wedgwood Festschrift (Contrib.) 1986, Creating Small Gardens 1986, Gloriana, Portraits of Queen Elizabeth I 1987, The Small Garden Designers Handbook 1987, Cecil Beaton: the Royal Portraits 1988, Creating Small Formal Gardens 1989, Lost Treasures of Britain 1990, A Celebration of Gardens 1991, Small Period Gardens 1992, Royal Gardens 1992, Versace Theatre 1992, William Larkin 1994, A Country Life 1994, Successful Small Gardens 1994, The Tudor and Stuart Monarchy 1995, The Story of Britain 1996, The English Arcadia 1996, Country Life 1897–1997 1997, The Roy Strong Diaries 1967–1987 1997, On Happiness 1997, The Tudor and Stuart Monarchy 1998 and numerous articles in newspapers and periodicals. *Leisure interests:* gardening, cooking, country life. *Address:* The Laskett, Much Birch, Hereford, HR2 8HZ, England.

STROSSEN, Nadine, B.A., J.D.; American human rights lawyer; b. 18 Aug. 1950, Jersey City; d. of Woodrow John Strossen and Sylvia Strossen; m. Eli Michael Noam 1980; ed. Harvard Law School, Radcliffe Coll.; assoc. attorney Sullivan and Cromwell 1978–83; partner Harvis and Zeichner 1983–84; mem. Nat. Bd. Dirs. American Civil Liberties Union 1983–, Pres. 1991–, mem. advisory cttee. on Reproductive Freedom Project 1983–, Nat. Exec. Cttee. 1985–, Nat. Gen. Council 1986–91; Asst. Prof. of Clinical Law Univ. of New York 1989–; Adjunct Prof. Grad. School of Business Univ. of Columbia 1990–; mem. Exec. Cttee. Human Rights Watch 1989–91; mem. Bd. Dirs. Coalition to Free Soviet Jewry 1984–; mem. Asia Watch 1987–, Vice-Chair. 1989–91; mem. Nat. Coalition Against Censorship 1988, Middle East Watch 1989–91, The Fund for Free Expression 1990–; mem. steering cttee. New York Legal Council for Soviet Jewry 1987–. *Publications include:* Regulating Campus Hate Speech; A Modest Proposal? 1990, Recent US and International Judicial Protection of Individuals Rights: A Comparative Legal Process Analysis and Proposed Synthesis 1990, In Defense of Pornography: Free Speech and the Fight for Women's Rights 1995, numerous articles in professional journals. *Address:* New York Law School, 57 Worth Street, New York, NY 10013, U.S.A.

STROYEV, Yegor Semyonovich, D.ECONS.; Russian politician; b. 25 Feb. 1937, Stroyevo, Khotynetsky, Orel Region; m. Nina Semvyovna; one d.; ed. I.V. Michurin Horticultural Inst., Acad. of Social Sciences, Moscow; mem CPSU 1958–91; worked at Progress collective farm, Khotynetsky Region; Orel Regional Sec., First Sec. Regional Cttee. CPSU, Chair. Exec. Cttee. Regional Soviet of People's Deputies, Sec., First Sec. CPSU Cttee. 1985–89; mem. Politburo of CPSU Cen. Cttee. 1986–91, Sec. 1989–91; resgnd. after the Aug. coup d'état; fmr. People's Deputy of U.S.S.R; mem. Council of Fed. of Fed. Ass. of Russian Fed. 1995–, Chair. 1996–; Chair. Council of Interparl. Ass. of C.I.S. 1996–; Head of Admin., Gov. Orel Region 1993–; Dir. All-Russia Scientific Research Inst. of Fruit Crop Breeding 1991–93; Corresp. mem. Russian Acad. of Agricultural Sciences; Hon. mem. Russian Acad. of Literature. *Address:* Council of Federation, Bolshaya Dmitrovka str. 26, 103790 Moscow; Governor's Office, Lenina pl. 1, 30200 Orel, Russia. *Telephone:* (095) 292 06 98 (Moscow); (0362) 41-63-13 (Orel).

STRUBE, Jürgen, DR. JUR.; German business executive; b. 1939, Bochum; m.; one d.; joined BASF 1969, several posts, then with BASF Brasileira S.A., São Paulo 1974–85, Head, Glasurit do Brasil Ltda. 1980–, Head, Brazil Regional Div. 1982–, in charge of Information Systems and Fibres Operating

Divs. and Regional Divs. in N. America 1985–88, of Foams, Polyolefins and PVC, and Information Systems Operating Divs. and Brazil and Latin American Regional Divs. 1988–90, mem. Bd. Exec. Dirs. BASF AG, Ludwigshafen, Germany 1985–, Chair. 1990–; Pres. Asscn. of Chemical Industry (VCI) 1996–97. *Address:* BASF Aktiengesellschaft, 67056 Ludwigshafen, Germany.

STRUCHKOVA, Raisa Stepanovna; Russian ballerina; b. 5 Oct. 1925, Moscow; ed. Bolshoi Theatre Ballet School; Soloist, Bolshoi Theatre Ballet 1944–67; lecturer in classical dancing Lunacharsky State Inst. of Theatrical Art 1968, Prof. 1978–; mem. CPSU 1962–91; People's Artist of U.S.S.R. 1958; Ed.-in.-Chief Sovetskiy Balet (now Balet) 1981–96; Coach, Bolshoi Theatre 1996–. *Principal roles include:* Cinderella (Cinderella, Prokofiev), Juliet (Romeo and Juliet, Prokofiev), Giselle (Giselle, Adan), Princess Aurora (Sleeping Beauty, Tchaikovsky), Odette-Odile (Swan Lake, Tchaikovsky), Kitri (Don Quixote), Parasha (Copper Rider, Glier), Tao Khoa (Red Poppy, Glier), Maria (Fountain of Bakhshisarai, Asafyev), Janne, also Diana de Mirrel (Flames of Paris, Asafyev), Gayane (Gayane, Khachaturyan), Vakchanka (Walpurgisnacht, Gounod); films: Crystal Slipper, Your Name. *Address:* Bolshoi Theatre, Teatralnaya pl. 1, 103009 Moscow, Russia. *Telephone:* (095) 915-40-57.

STRUGATSKY, Boris Natanovich; Russian science-fiction writer and astronomer; b. 15 April 1933, Leningrad; s. of Natan Strugatsky; ed. Leningrad Univ.; astronomer's post in Pulkovo Observatory, Leningrad 1955–65; started publishing science-fiction (with his brother) 1957; Victor Hugo Prize (France). *Publications (with A. N. Strugatsky) include:* The Land of Purple Clouds 1959, The Return 1962, Escape Attempt 1962, The Far-Away Rainbow 1964, Rapacious Things of the Century 1965, The Inhabited Island 1971, The Ugly Swans 1972, Stories 1975, The Forest 1982, The Lame Fortune 1986, One Billion Years Before the End of the World 1988, Collected Works 1991, Burdened by Evil 1988, The Search of Destination 1994. *Address:* Pobeda Str. 4, Apt. 186, 196070 St. Petersburg, Russia. *Telephone:* (812) 291-37-55.

STRUNK, Klaus Albert, D.PHIL.; German professor of linguistics; b. 22 Aug. 1930, Düsseldorf; s. of Albert Strunk and Hedwig Schäfer; m. Marion Kriegeskotte 1957; two s. one d.; Prof., Univ. of Saarland and Dir. Inst. of Indo-European Linguistics and Indo-Iranian Philology 1967–77; Prof., Univ. of Munich and Dir. Inst. of Gen. and Indo-European Linguistics 1977–, Dean Dept. I (Linguistics and Literature) 1985–87; Ed. Kratylos review 1969–83; Co-Ed. Glotta review 1974–, series Studies in Indo-European Language and Culture (Berlin and New York) 1985–, Münchener Studien zur Sprachwissenschaft review 1992–; Pres. Indogermanische Gesellschaft 1983–92; mem. Bayerische Akademie der Wissenschaften 1979–, Sec. Philosophy and History section 1989–; mem. Société de Linguistique de Paris 1978–, Philological Soc., London 1993–. *Publications:* Die sogenannten Aeolismen der homerischen Sprache 1957, Nasalpraesentien und Aoriste. Ein Beitrag zur Morphologie des Verbums im Indo-Iranischen und Griechischen 1967, Probleme der lateinischen Grammatik (Ed.) 1973, Lachmanns Regel für das Lateinische 1976, Generative Versuche zu einigen Problemen in der historischen Grammatik indogermanischer Sprachen 1976, Typische Merkmale von Fragesätzen und die altindische Pluti 1983, Zum Postulat 'vorhersagbaren' Sprachwandels bei unregelmässigen oder komplexen Flexionsparadigmen 1991, numerous articles and reviews on Greek, Latin, Indo-Iranian and Indo-European linguistics. *Leisure interests:* reading books on history, literature, classical music, sport. *Address:* Ringbergstrasse 11, 83707 Bad Wiessee, Germany. *Telephone:* (08022) 82198.

STRUZIK, Adam; Polish politician; b. 1 Jan. 1957, Kutno; m.; one s. one d.; ed. Medical Acad., Łódź; mem. Solidarity Trade Union 1980–; mem. Polish Peasant Party (PSL) 1989–, Exec. Council; Senator 1991–; Marshal of the Senate 1993–97; mem. Programming Bd. TVP S.A. *Leisure interests:* politics, literature, tourism. *Address:* Senat RP, ul. Wiejska 6, 00-902 Warsaw, Poland. *Telephone:* (22) 694 19 29, 625 59 15.

STRZEMBOSZ, Adam Justyn; Polish state official and lawyer; b. 11 Nov. 1930, Warsaw; s. of Adam Strzembosz and Zofia (née Gadomska) Strzembosz; m. Zofia Strzembosz 1957; two s. two d.; ed. Jagiellonian Univ., Cracow, Warsaw Univ.; legal adviser, Ministry of Labour and Social Security 1953–56; judge, County Court 1956–68, Provincial Court 1968–81; researcher Research Inst. of Judicial Law 1974–81; Prof. Catholic Univ. of Lublin 1982–90; Vice-Minister of Justice 1989–90; judge, Supreme Court 1990–; First Pres. Supreme Court 1990–98; Head Solidarity Group, Ministry of Justice 1980–81; mem. Bd. Solidarity Mazowsze Region 1980; Del. to 1st Solidarity Conf., jt. leader Appeal Comm., Gdańsk-Oliwa 1981; mem. Polish Sociological Asscn., Catholic Univ. of Lublin Scientific Asscn., Penal Law Asscn. *Publications:* six books, over 80 treatises and articles. *Leisure interests:* cycling, literature. *Address:* Sąd Najwyższy, ul. Ogrodowa 6, 00-951 Warsaw, Poland. *Telephone:* (22) 620 03 71. *Fax:* (22) 620 37 14.

STUART, Francis; Irish novelist and poet; b. 29 April 1902, Australia; s. of Henry Irwin Stuart and Elizabeth Montgomery; m. 1st Iseult Gonne 1920, one s. one d.; m. 2nd Gertrude Meissner 1954; m. 3rd Finola Graham 1987; ed. Rugby School; born of Northern Irish parents and brought up in Co. Antrim, ed. at English schools; Irish republican 1922–23, interned by Free State Govt.; Lecturer Berlin Univ., Germany during 2nd World War, subsequently imprisoned in French-occupied Germany, lived in Paris 1949–51, London 1951–58, settled in Ireland 1958. *Publications:* two vols. of poetry and 22 novels, including We Have Kept the Faith (poems) 1923, Women and God 1931, Pigeon Irish 1931, The Pillar of Cloud 1948, Redemption 1949, Black List, Section H. 1971, The High Consistory 1981, Faillandia 1985, The Abandoned Snail Shell 1987, Night Pilot (poems) 1988, A Compendium of Lovers 1990, Collected Poems 1992, Arrow of Anguish 1995, King David Dances 1997. *Address:* 2 Highfield Park, Dublin 14, Ireland.

STUART, Sir Kenneth Lamonte, Kt., M.D., F.R.C.P., F.A.C.P., F.F.P.M., F.F.P.H.M.; Barbadian physician; b. 16 June 1920, Barbados; s. of Egbert Stuart and Louise Stuart; m. Barbara Cecille Ashby 1958; one s. two d.; ed. Harrison Coll., Barbados, Queen's Univ., Belfast, Northern Ireland; Rockefeller Foundation Fellow in Cardiology, Mass. Gen. Hosp., Boston, U.S.A. 1956–57; Wellcome Research Fellow, Harvard Univ., U.S.A. 1960–61; Prof. of Medicine, Univ. of W. Indies 1966–76, Dean Medical School 1969–73, Head Dept. of Medicine 1972–76; Commonwealth Medical Adviser 1976–85; Consultant Adviser, Wellcome Tropical Inst. 1985–; Hon. Medical and Scientific Adviser, Barbados High Comm., London 1991–; mem. Bd. of Govs., Liverpool School of Tropical Medicine 1980–, Int. Research Centre of Canada 1985–; Chair. Court of Govs., London School of Hygiene and Tropical Medicine 1983–86; Chair. Commonwealth Caribbean Medical Research Council 1988; Chair. Errol Barrow Memorial Trust 1989–; mem. of Council and Trustee The London Lighthouse 1994–; mem. of Council Royal Over-seas League 1994–, United Medical and Dental Schools of Guy's and St. Thomas's Hosps. 1994–98, Guy's, King's and St. Thomas's Hosp. Medical and Dental School 1998; Freeman of City of London 1992; Trustee Schools Partnership Worldwide 1990–; Gresham Prof. of Physic, Gresham Coll., London 1988; Hon. D.Sc. (Queen's, Belfast) 1986. *Leisure interests:* tennis, music, literature. *Address:* Barbados High Commission, 1 Great Russell Street, London WC1B 3JY (Office); 3 The Garth, Cobham, Surrey, KT11 2DZ, England (Home). *Telephone:* 0171-631 4975 (Office); (01932) 863826 (Home).

STUART, Lyle; American publishing company executive; b. 11 Aug. 1922, New York; s. of Alfred Stuart and Theresa (Cohen) Stuart; m. 1st Mary Louise Strawn 1946; one s. one d.; m. 2nd Carole Livingston 1982; one d.; reporter, Int. News Service 1945, Variety 1945–46; script writer, Dept. of State, Voice of America 1946; Ed. Music Business magazine 1946–48; f. Expose 1951; Publr. The Independent 1951–75; Business Man. MAD magazine 1952–54; Pres. Lyle Stuart Inc. 1954–89, Citadel Press 1970–89, University Books Inc.1983–, Hot News 1983, Barricade Books 1990–; f. N. Bergen, N.J. Public Library; Producer Chinese Festival of Music 1952–62; mem. American Booksellers' Asscn., Nat. Acad. of TV Arts and Sciences, New York Zoological Soc.; Hon. Ph.D. (State of Calif.). *Publications:* God Wears a Bowtie 1949, The Secret Life of Water Winchell 1953, Mary Louise 1970, Casino Gambling for the Winner 1978, Lyle Stuart on Baccarat 1983, Map of Life 1993, Winning at Casino Gambling 1995, Map of Life 1996. *Address:* Barricade Books Inc., 150 5th Avenue, New York, NY 10011 (Office); 1530 Palisade Avenue, Apartment 6-L, Fort Lee, NJ 07024, U.S.A. (Home).

STUART, Robert Douglas, Jr., J.D.; American business executive; b. 26 April 1916, Hubbard Woods, Ill.; s. of Robert Douglas Stuart and Harriet (McClure) Stuart; m. 1st Barbara McMath Edwards 1938 (died 1993), three s. one d.; m. 2nd Ingegjerd Lovenskiold 1995; ed. Princeton Univ. and Yale Law School; with Quaker Oats Co., Chicago 1947–84; Chair. and C.E.O. 1966–82; fmr. Dir. Molson Cos. of Canada, United Airlines, Inc., First Nat. Bank of Chicago, Deere & Co.; mem. Business Council 1972–; Amb. to Norway 1984–89; Pres. North Star Investments Inc., Chicago 1989–; Pres. Council of American Ambs. 1989–92; mem. Bd. Volcker Comm.; Dir. Atlantic Cttee.; Chair. Midwest Advisory Bd. Inst. of Int. Educ.1991–96; mem. Base Closure and Realignment Comm. 1991, 1993. *Address:* 100 Field Drive, Suite 150, Lake Forest, IL 60045 (Office); 1601 Conway Road, Lake Forest, IL 60045, U.S.A. (Home). *Telephone:* (847) 295-7100 (Office); (847) 234-3894 (Home). *Fax:* (847) 295-7167 (Office); (847) 234-8107 (Home).

STUBBS, Imogen Mary, M.A.; British actress; b. 20 Feb. 1961, Rothbury; d. of late Robin Stubbs and Heather McCracken; m. Trevor Nunn (q.v.) 1994; one s. one d.; ed. St. Paul's Girls School, London, Exeter Coll. Oxford and Royal Acad. of Dramatic Art; appeared with RSC in The Rover, Two Noble Kinsmen, Richard II 1987–88, Othello 1991, Heartbreak House 1992, St. Joan 1994, Twelfth Night 1996, Blast from the Past 1998, Betrayal 1998; TV appearances include: The Rainbow, Anna Lee, After the Dance; Gold Medal, Chicago Film Festival. *Films include:* Nanon, A Summer Story, Erik the Viking, True Colours, A Pin for the Butterfly, Fellow Traveller, Sandra c'est la vie, Jack and Sarah, Sense and Sensibility 1995, Twelfth Night 1996. *Leisure interests:* writing, skiing, collecting junk. *Address:* c/o Michael Foster, I.C.M., Oxford House, 76 Oxford Street, London, W1N 0AX, England. *Telephone:* 0171-636 6565.

STÜCKLEN, Richard; German politician and electrical engineer; b. 20 Aug. 1916; s. of Georg S. and Mathilde (née Bach) Stücklen; m. Ruth Geissler 1943; one s. one d.; ed. vocational school, tech. coll.; fmr. Industrial Dept. Man.; Army Service 1940–44; then Man. in family business; mem. Bundestag 1949–; Deputy Chair. Christian Democratic Union/Christian Social Union (CSU) Group and Chair. CSU in Bundestag 1953–57, 1966–76; Fed. Minister of Posts and Telegraphs 1957–66; Vice-Pres. Bundestag 1976–79, 1983–90, Pres. 1979–83; awards include Grosskreuz des Verdienstordens der Bundesrepublik Deutschland, Bayerische Verdienstorden. *Leisure interests:* tennis, football, chess, card games. *Address:* Eichstätter Strasse 27, 91781 Weissenburg, Germany (Home). *Telephone:* 27-20.

STUDENIKIN, Mitrofan Yakovlevich; Russian pediatrician; b. 2 Dec. 1923, Listopadovka, Voronezh Region; s. of Yakov Fedorovich and Praskovia Illarionovna Studenikin; m.; one s. one d.; ed. Moscow Pirogov Medical Inst.; asst., docent, Prof., Chair. of Children's Diseases Pirogov Medical Inst. 1952–70, Head 1970–; Dir. Research Inst. of Pediatrics, Russian Acad. of Medical Sciences 1960–; Corresp. mem. U.S.S.R. (now Russian) Acad. of Medical Sciences 1971, mem. 1975; Chair. Scientific Council on Pediatrics; expert WHO, mem. Exec. Cttee. Int. Asscn. of Pediatrics; Hon. mem. American Acad. of Pediatrics, European Soc. of Pediatrics, Dr. h.c. Univs. of Helsinki, Budapest, Rostok. *Publications:* eight books and more than 250 articles on perinatal pathology, chronic diseases of the intestine, cardiovascular diseases of children. *Address:* Institute of Pediatrics, 117296 Moscow, Lomonosovskii pr. 2/62 (Office); Frunzenskaya emb. 24/1 Apt. 99, Moscow, Russia. *Telephone:* (095) 134-03-61 (Office); 242-24-73 (Home). *Fax:* (095) 134-13-08.

STUDER, Cheryl; American soprano opera singer; b. 24 Oct. 1955, Midland, Mich.; m. 2nd Ewald Schwarz; two d. (one by previous m.); ed. Interlochen Arts Acad., Oberlin Coll. Cleveland, Ohio and Univ. of Tenn.; studied singing with Gwendolyn Pike, at Berks. Music Centre, at Tanglewood with Phyllis Curtin and at Hochschule für Musik, Vienna with Hans Hotter; engaged for concert series with Boston Symphony Orch. by Seiji Ozawa (q.v.) 1979; opera debut as the First Lady in The Magic Flute, Munich 1980–82; with Darmstadt State Theatre, Germany 1982–84, Deutsche Oper, Berlin 1984–86; U.S. debut as Micaela in Carmen, Lyric Opera of Chicago 1984; debut at Bayreuth 1985, Royal Opera House, Covent Garden 1987, Metropolitan Opera, New York 1988; sings wide variety of roles, especially Wagner, Verdi, Mozart and Strauss; Int. Music Award 1993, Vocalist of the Year (U.S.A.) 1994). *Address:* c/o International Performing Artists Inc., 125 Crowfield Drive, Knoxville, TN 37922, U.S.A.

STUHR, Jerzy; Polish actor and film director; b. 18 April 1947, Cracow; s. of Tadeusz Stuhr and Maria Stuhr; m. 1971; one s. one d.; ed. Jagiellonian Univ. and High Theatre School, Cracow; main theatrical roles at Stary Theatre, Cracow with Andrzej Wajda (q.v.), notably Hamlet 1982, Dostoevsky's The Possessed and Crime and Punishment 1984, P. Süskind's Double Bass (actor and dir.) 1985, Le Bourgeois Gentilhomme 1993, Harold Pinter's Ashes to Ashes 1996, Merry Wives of Windsor (dir.) 1998; dir., actor and teacher, Italy 1980–; dir. List of Adultresses 1994, Love Stories 1997; Rector, High Theatre School, Cracow 1990–98, lecturer 1998–; lecturer Faculty of Radio and TV, Silesia Univ. 1998–; mem. European Film Acad. 1998; Best Actor, Chicago Festival 1978, Gdańsk Film Festival 1979, San Remo Film Festival 1988 (for title role in Citizen Piszczyk) 1989, City of Cracow Award 1989, Premio Fipreseii, Venice Film Festival 1997, Grand Prix for Love Stories, Polish Film Festival, Gdynia 1997. *Publication:* Heart Illness, or My Life in Art (autobiog.) 1992. *Address:* Graffiti Ltd., ul. SW Gertrudy 5, 31-107 Cracow, Poland. *Telephone:* 421-42-94. *Fax:* 421-14-02.

STUIVER, Minze, PH.D.; American professor of geological sciences; b. 25 Oct. 1929, Vlagtwedde, Netherlands; s. of Albert Stuiver and Griet Welles; m. Annie Hubbelmeyer 1956; two d.; ed. Univ. of Groningen; Research Assoc. Yale Univ. 1959–62; Sr. Research Assoc. and Dir. Radiocarbon Lab. 1962–69; Prof. of Geological Sciences and Zoology, Univ. of Washington, Seattle 1969–82, Prof. of Geological Sciences and Quaternary Sciences 1982–, Dir. Quaternary Isotope Lab. 1972–; Ed. Radiocarbon 1976–88; mem. Geological Soc. of America, American Quaternary Asscn.; Alexander von Humboldt Sr. Scientist, Fed. Repub. of Germany 1983. *Address:* University of Washington, Box 351360, Seattle, WA 98195, U.S.A.

STUMP, Nicholas Withrington; Australian mining executive; b. 16 Dec. 1941, Adelaide; s. of Stanley Withrington and Dorothy Ellen; m. Alison Goode 1966; one s. two d.; ed. Scotch Coll. Adelaide, Unley High School, Univ. of Adelaide and S. Australian Inst. of Tech.; worked for CRA Group 1970–95; held several tech. and operating man. positions with Zinc Corpn. Broken Hill 1970–77; transferred to Mary Kathleen Uranium Ltd. (CRA subsidiary) 1977; Man. Planning and Evaluation, CRA Group, Melbourne 1980; Gen. Man. CRA's Sulphide Corpn. zinc smelter, Cockle Creek, NSW 1983; Man. Dir. Comalco Rolled Products, Sydney 1985; Pres. Commonwealth Aluminum Corpn. Ltd. U.S.A. 1988; Chief Exec. Comalco Ltd. and Group Exec. CRA Ltd. 1991–95; Chief Exec. M.I.M. Holdings Ltd. 1995–; mem. Senate Univ. of Queensland 1996–; Pres. Minerals Council of Australia 1997– (mem. 1995–); Vice-Pres. Queensland Mining Council Ltd. *Address:* M.I.M. Holdings Ltd., G.P.O. Box 1433, Brisbane, Queensland 4001, Australia. *Telephone:* (07) 3833 8222. *Fax:* (07) 3832 6828.

STUMPF, Paul Karl, PH.D.; American professor of biochemistry; b. 23 February 1919, New York; s. of Karl Stumpf and Annette Shreyer; m. Ruth Rodenbeck 1947; two s. three d.; ed. Harvard and Columbia Univs.; Instructor, School of Public Health, Univ. of Mich. 1946–48; Asst. Prof. of Plant Nutrition, Univ. of Calif., Berkeley 1948–52, Assoc. Prof. of Plant Biochemistry 1952–57, Prof. 1957–58; Prof. of Biochemistry, Univ. of Calif., Davis 1958–84, Emer. Prof. 1984–; Consultant, Palm Oil Research Inst., Malaysia 1982–92; Chief Scientist Competitive Research Grants Office 1988–91, Nat. Research Initiative for Competitive Grants, USDA 1990–91; mem. scientific advisory bd., Calgene Inc., Calif. 1990–93, Md. Biotech. Inst. 1990–92; Guggenheim Fellow 1962, 1969, Alexander von Humboldt Fellow 1976; mem. Royal Danish Acad. of Sciences, N.A.S., American Soc. of Plant Physiologists (Chair., Bd. of Trustees 1986–89, Pres. 1979–80); Fellow A.A.A.S. 1994; Stephens Hales Award 1974, Lipid Chem. Award 1974, Charles Reid Barnes Life Membership Award 1992, Unit Award for Superior Service, USDA 1992, Award of Excellence, Calif. Aggie Alumni Foundation 1996. *Publications:* Outlines of Enzyme Chemistry (with J. B. Nielands), Outlines of Biochemistry (with E. E. Conn); Ed.-in-Chief Biochemistry of Plants (12 vols.), Exec. Ed. Archives of Biochemistry 1965–88; over 250 scientific publs. *Leisure interests:* gardening, golf, travel. *Address:* Department of Molecular and Cellular Biology, University of California, Davis, CA 95616; 764 Elmwood Drive, Davis, CA 95616, U.S.A. (Home). *Telephone:* (916) 752-3523 (Office); (916) 753-5022 (Home). *Fax:* (916) 752-3085.

STURRIDGE, Charles; British television, film and theatre director; b. 24 June 1951, London; s. of Jerome Sturridge and Alyson Sturridge (née Burke); m. Phoebe Nichols; three c.; ed. Oxford Univ.; début in film If . . .; fmr. mem. Nat. Youth Theatre; fmr. Pres. Oxford Univ. Dramatic Soc.; worked as actor and theatre dir.; debut as actor in film If . . . 1995; debut as professional dir., musical version of Hard Times, Belgrade Theatre, Coventry; joined Granada Television 1974. *TV documentaries and drama include:* World in Action, episodes of Coronation Street, Strangers and Crown Court, Brideshead Revisited; (12 awards including BAFTA award for Best Series, two American Golden Globe awards, Grand Award of New York Film and TV Festival, Primetime Emmy for Outstanding Mini Series), Soft Targets (BBC TV) 1982, The Storyteller 1988, Gulliver's Travels 1996, A Foreign Field. *Feature films include:* Runners 1982, A Handful of Dust 1988, Where Angels Fear to Tread 1991, Fairytale—A True Story (co-writer) 1997; Contrib. Dir. to Aria (La Vergine degli angeli from La Forza del Destino). *Theatre includes:* Dir. own trans. of The Seagull, Queens Theatre, London 1985; trans. (with Tania Alexander) Uncle Vanya. *Address:* c/o Peters, Fraser & Dunlop Ltd., 503 The Chambers, Chelsea Harbour, Lots Road, London, SW10 0XF, England.

STURTEVANT, Julian Munson, PH.D.; American professor of chemistry and research scientist; b. 9 Aug. 1908, Edgewater, N.J.; s. of Edgar Howard Sturtevant and Bessie Fitch Sturtevant; m. Elizabeth Caroline Reihl 1929; one s. one d.; ed. Columbia and Yale Univs.; Instructor, Asst. Prof., Assoc. Prof., Prof. of Chemistry Yale Univ. 1931–77, Prof. of Molecular Biophysics and Biochemistry 1965–77, Prof. Emer. and Sr. Research Scientist 1977–; Staff mem., Radiation Lab., M.I.T. 1943–46; Guggenheim Fellow, Fulbright Scholar, Cambridge Univ. 1955–56; Fulbright Scholar, Univ. of Adelaide, Australia 1962–63; Alexander von Humboldt Sr. Scientist Award, Univ. of Regensburg, Fed. Repub. of Germany 1978–79; Fellow American Acad. of Arts and Sciences; mem. N.A.S.; Hon. D.Sc. (Illinois Coll.) 1962, Hon. D.Sc. (Regensburg) 1978; William Clyde DeVane Medal (Yale Univ.) 1978, Huffman Award (U.S. Calorimetry Conf.) 1964, Innovator in Biochemistry Award, Medical Coll. of Va. 1984, Wilbur Cross Medal, Yale Univ. 1986. *Publications:* 295 scientific papers etc. *Leisure interests:* biocalimetry, general science, hiking, chemistry. *Address:* Department of Chemistry, Yale University, P.O. Box 208107, New Haven, CT 06520-8107 (Office); 88 Notch Hill Road No. 347, North Branford, CT 06471, U.S.A. (Home). *Telephone:* (203) 432-3997 (Office); (203) 432-5206 (Laboratory); (203) 488-2894 (Home).

STURUA, Robert Robertovich; Georgian theatrical director; b. 31 July 1938, Tbilisi; m. Dudana Kveselava 1968; two s.; trained at Georgian Theatre Inst. 1956–61; Dir. Rustaveli Theatre, Tbilisi 1961–, Artistic Dir. 1978–; U.S.S.R. State Prize 1979, Georgian State Prize 1981, U.S.S.R. People's Artist 1982; has directed over 50 productions, including The Crucible (Miller), Italian Straw Hat (Labiche), The Good Woman of Szechuan (Brecht), Caucasian Chalk Circle, Medea (Anouilh), King Lear, Tartuffe (in Tel Aviv) 1989, Three Sisters (in London) 1990, Eugene Onegin (in Bologna) 1991, Comedy of Errors (in Helsinki) 1992, Hamlet (in London) 1992, Richard III (toured theatres around world), Antigone, and many Russian and Georgian plays; first guest Dir. at Saarbrücken State Theatre; Opera productions: Music for Alive (G. Kancheli) 1984, Keto and Kote (V. Dolidze) 1986. *Address:* Rustaveli Theatre, Tbilisi, Georgia. *Telephone:* 998587.

STÜTZLE, Walther K. A., DR. RER. POL.; German journalist; b. 29 Nov. 1941, Westerland-Sylt; s. of the late Moritz Stützle and of Annemarie Ruge; m. Dr. H. Kauper 1966; two s. two d.; ed. Westerland High School and Univs. of Berlin, Bordeaux and Hamburg; researcher, Inst. for Strategic Studies, London 1967–68, Foreign Policy Inst. Bonn 1968–69; Desk Officer, Ministry of Defence, Planning Staff, Bonn 1969–72, Pvt. Sec. and Chef de Cabinet, 1973–76, Head, Planning Staff, Under-Sec. of Defence, Plans and Policy 1976–82; editorial staff, Stuttgarter Zeitung 1983–86; Dir. Stockholm Int. Peace Research Inst. (SIPRI) 1986–91; Ed.-in-Chief Der Tagesspiegel. *Publications:* Adenauer und Kennedy in der Berlinkrise 1961–62 1972, Politik und Kräfteverhältnis 1983; co-author: Europe's Future—Europe's Choices 1967, ABM Treaty—To Defend or Not to Defend 1987. *Leisure interests:* history, reading, sailing, mountain walking. *Address:* Der Tagesspiegel, Potsdamer Str. 87, 10785 Berlin (Office); Traunsteiner Str. 2, 10781 Berlin, Germany. *Telephone:* (030) 26009466 (Office); (030) 2137742 (Home).

STYLES, Margretta, ED.D.; American professor of nursing; b. 19 March 1930, Mt. Union, Pa.; d. of Russell B. and Agnes Wilson Madden; m. Douglas F. Styles 1954; two s. one d.; ed. Juniata Coll., Yale Univ., Univ. of Florida; Prof. and Dean, School of Nursing, Univ. of Texas, San Antonio 1969–73, Wayne State Univ., Detroit 1973–77, Univ. of Calif., San Francisco 1977–87, Prof. and Livingston Chair. in Nursing 1987–; Pres. Int. Council of Nurses 1996–, American Nurses Credentialing Center 1996–; mem. Nat. Comm. on

Nursing 1980–; First Distinguished Scholar, American Nurses' Foundation; mem. N.A.S., Inst. of Medicine; American Nurses' Asscn. Hon. Recognition Award (Pres. 1986–88). *Publications:* On Nursing: Toward a New Endowment, Project on the Regulation of Nursing, Int. Council of Nurses 1985. *Leisure interest:* skydiving. *Address:* c/o International Council of Nurses, 3 place Jean-Marteau, 1201 Geneva, Switzerland; School of Nursing, N 531C-D, Box 0608, University of California (San Francisco), San Francisco, CA 94143 (Office); 44 Sabal Palm, Largo, FL 33770; 12 Commons Lane, Foster City, CA 94404, U.S.A. (Home). *Telephone:* (415) 476 6701 (Office), (415) 754 3870 (Home).

STYLES, Richard Geoffrey Pentland, B.COMM.; Canadian banker (retd.); b. 3 Dec. 1930, Regina, Sask.; s. of Alfred G. Styles and C. Ila (Pentland) Styles; m. Jacqueline Joyce Frith 1959; one s. one d.; ed. Univ. of Saskatchewan; joined Royal Bank of Canada, Victoria, B.C. 1951, served in various posts, Canada, U.S.A. and U.K., Vice-Chair. 1987; Chair. and Dir. Grosvenor Int. Holdings Ltd.; Dir. Echo Bay Mines Ltd., Fairwater Capital Corpn., Geon Co., Onex Corpn., The Royal Trust Co., Working Ventures Canadian Fund Inc.; Dir. Toronto Symphony Foundation. *Address:* Suite 3115, Royal Bank Plaza, Toronto, Ont., M5J 2J5, Canada.

STYLIANOU, Petros Savva, PH.D.; Cypriot politician, journalist and writer; b. 8 June 1933, Kythrea; s. of Savvas and Evanthia Stylianou; m. Voula Tzanetatou 1960; two d.; ed. Pancyprian Gymnasium, Univs. of Athens and Salonika; served with Panhellenic Cttee. of the Cyprus Struggle (PEKA) and Nat. Union of Cypriot Univ. Students (EFEK), Pres. EFEK 1953–54; co-founder Dauntless Leaders of the Cypriot Fighters Org. (KARI); joined liberation movement of Cyprus 1955; imprisoned in Kyrenia Castle 1955, escaped; leader, Nat. Striking Group; sentenced to 15 years' imprisonment 1956, transferred to U.K. prison, released 1959; mem. Cen. Cttee. United Democratic Reconstruction Front (EDMA) 1959; Deputy Sec.-Gen. Cyprus Labour Confed. (SEK) 1959, Sec.-Gen. 1960–62; f. Cyprus Democratic Labour Fed. (DEOK) 1962, Sec.-Gen. 1962–73, Hon. Pres. 1974–; mem. House of Reps. 1960–70, 1985–91, Sec. 1960–62; Deputy Minister of Interior 1980–82; Special Adviser to Pres. on Cultural Affairs 1982–85; Mayor of Engomi 1992–; Founder Pancyprian Orgs. for Rehabilitation of Spastics, Rehabilitation from Kidney Disease, from Haemophilia and from Myopathy; Pres. Cyprus Historical Museum and Archives; numerous awards and prizes from Cyprus, Greece and U.S.A. *Publications:* numerous works on poetry, history, etc. *Address:* Erecthiou Street, P.O. Box 7504, Engomi (Office); Kimonos 10, Engomi, Nicosia, Cyprus (Home). *Telephone:* 02-353240 (Office); 02-445972 (Home).

STYRON, William, A.B.; American writer; b. 11 June 1925, Newport News, Va.; s. of William Styron and Pauline Abraham; m. Rose Burgunder 1953; one s. three d.; ed. Davidson Coll., Duke Univ.; Advisory Ed., Paris Review 1953–; Hon. Consultant, Library of Congress; Pres. Cannes Film Festival 1983; mem. Signet Soc. Harvard Univ.; Fellow, Silliman Coll., Yale Univ.; Fellow, American Acad. of Arts and Sciences; mem. American Acad. of Arts and Letters 1966–; Hon. mem. Acad. Goncourt; Duke Univ. Distinguished Alumni Award; Pulitzer Prize for best novel 1968, Howells Medal for Fiction 1970, Conn. Arts Award 1984, Prix Mondial Cino del Duca 1985, Edward MacDowell Medal 1988, Elmer Holmes Bobst Award 1989, Nat. Medal of Arts 1993, Nat. Arts Club Medal for Literature 1995, Common Wealth Award 1995; Commdr., Légion d'honneur, Ordre des Arts et des Lettres. *Publications:* Lie Down in Darkness 1951, The Long March 1955, Set this House on Fire 1960, The Confessions of Nat Turner 1967, In the Clap Shack (play) 1973, Sophie's Choice 1979 (American Book Award 1980), This Quiet Dust (Essays) 1982, Darkness Visible: A Memoir of Madness 1990, A Tidewater Morning 1993. *Leisure interests:* tennis, sailing. *Address:* 12 Rucum Road, Roxbury, CT 06783; Vineyard Haven, MA 02568, U.S.A. (Summer). *Telephone:* (508) 693-2535.

SU, Chi, PH.D.; Chinese government official; b. 1 Oct. 1949, Taichung; s. of Chan-Wu Su and Kuo-Yin Ni; m. Grace Chen; one s. one d.; ed. Nat. Chengchi Univ., Johns Hopkins Univ., Columbia Univ.; Assoc. Prof. Dept. of Diplomacy Nat. Chengchi Univ. 1984–90, Prof. 1990–, Deputy Dir. Inst. of Int. Relations 1990–93; Sec. Gen. Office of the Univ. Pres. 1989–90; mem. Exec. Yuan Research, Devt. and Evaluation Comm. 1990–94; Sec.-Gen. China Political Science Asscn. 1990–91; Deputy Dir. Kuomintang Cen. Cttee. Dept. of Mainland Affairs 1992–93; Vice-Chair Exec. Yuan Mainland Affairs Council 1993–96; Dir.-Gen. Govt. Information Office 1996–97; Exec. Yuan Minister of State 1997; Nat. Policy Adviser to Pres. of Repub. 1997, Deputy Sec.-Gen. to Pres. 1997–. *Publications:* The Normalization of Sino-Soviet Relations, over 20 papers and articles. *Address:* Office of the President, 122 Chung-Ching S. Road, Sec. 1, Taipei, Taiwan. *Telephone:* (02) 23889011. *Fax:* (02) 23141814.

SU BUQING; Chinese mathematician; b. 23 Sept. 1902, Pingyang Co., Zhejiang Prov.; ed. Tokyo Industrial School, Imperial Tohoku Univ.; lecturer, Zhejiang Univ. 1931–, Dir. Dept. of Math. 1946–; Dean, Shanghai Fudan Univ. 1954–57; mem., Dept. of Physics, Math. and Chemistry, Acad. Sinica 1955; in disgrace during Cultural Revolution 1966–77; mem. Standing Cttee. 5th NPC 1978–83; Vice-Pres. Math. Society of China 1978–; Vice-Chair. Cen. Cttee. of China Democratic League 1979–97, Hon. Chair. 1997–; mem., Standing Cttee. 6th NPC 1983–88; Hon. Pres. Shanghai Fudan Univ. 1983–; Chair. Cen. Advisory Cttee. 1987–; mem. Standing Cttee. 7th NPC 1988–93; Vice-Chair. 7th Nat. Cttee. CPPCC 1988–93, 8th Nat. Cttee. 1993–98. *Address:* Room 61, Bldg. 9, Fudan University, Shanghai, People's Republic of China. *Telephone:* 480080.

SU SHAOZHI, M.A.; Chinese research professor; b. 25 Jan. 1923, Peking; s. of Su Xiyi and Jin Yunquan; m. Hu Jianmei; two d.; ed. Chongqing Univ. and Nankai Inst. of Econs.; Assoc. Prof. Fudan Univ. 1949–63; ed. Theoretical Dept. Renmin Ribao (People's Daily) 1963–79; Deputy Dir. Inst. of Marxism-Leninism-Mao Zedong Thought (MLMT) 1979–82, Dir. 1982–87; Research Prof. Chinese Acad. of Social Sciences (CASS) 1982–87, mem. Acad. Cttee. of CASS 1982–85, Prof. Graduate School of CASS 1982–; Ed. Studies of Marxism (quarterly) 1983–. *Publications:* Democracy and Socialism in China 1982, Marxism in China 1983, Democratization and Reform 1988; books and articles on politics and economics. *Leisure interests:* calligraphy and paintings, classical music. *Address:* Institute of Marxism-Leninism-Mao Zedong Thought, The Chinese Academy of Social Sciences, 5 Jianguomen Nei Dajie, Beijing 100732 (Office); 5–3 Building 28, Guang Hua Li, Jianguomen Wai, Beijing 100020, People's Republic of China (Home). *Telephone:* 507744-3149 (Office); 594552 (Home).

SUÁREZ, The Duke of; Adolfo Suárez González; Spanish politician and lawyer; b. 25 Sept. 1932, Cebreros, Avila Province; m. Amparo Illana; five. c.; ed. Univs. of Salamanca and Madrid; Civil Gov. of Segovia 1969, then Dir.-Gen. Radio and TV; Pres. Empresa Nacional de Turismo; Pres. Unión del Pueblo Español; Vice-Sec.-Gen. Falange until 1975, Sec.-Gen. 1975–76; Prime Minister and Pres. of Council of Ministers 1976–81; named Duke of Suárez 1981; Leader Unión Centro Democrático (UCD) 1977–81, Hon. Pres. Jan.–Dec. 1981, resigned July 1982; f. and Leader Centro Democrático y Social (CDS) 1982–91, Pres. 1982–91; M.P. for Madrid 1982–; Pres. Int. Liberals 1988–91; Pres. Inst. of European-Latin American Relations (IRELA). *Address:* c/o Antonio Maura 4, 1°, 28014 Madrid, Spain. *Telephone:* 222.10.06.

SUAREZ PERTIERRA, Gustavo, LL.D.; Spanish politician; b. 1949, Cudillero, Oviedo; m.; two c.; ed. Univs. of Oviedo, Valladolid and Munich; Prof. in Canon Law, Complutense Univ. Madrid 1978, also sometime Vice-Dean of Law and mem. Academic Council of Human Rights Inst.; Dir.-Gen. of Religious Matters, Ministry of Justice and Pres. of Advisory Comm. on Religious Freedom 1982; Deputy Sec. Ministry of Defence 1984; Sec. of State for Mil. Admin. 1990–93; Minister of Educ. and Science 1993–95, of Defence 1995–96; Pres. Parl. Comm. for Public Admin. 1996–. *Address:* Palacio de las Cortes, c/Carrera de San Jerónimo, Madrid 14, Spain.

SUBANDRIO, Dr.; Indonesian politician, diplomatist and surgeon; b. 1914; ed. Medical Univ., Jakarta; active in Nat. Movement as student and gen. practitioner; worked with underground anti-Japanese Forces during Second World War; forced to leave post at Jakarta Cen. Hosp. and then established a pvt. practice at Semarang; following declaration of independence abandoned practice to become Sec.-Gen., Ministry of Information and was later sent by Indonesian Govt. as special envoy to Europe; est. Information Office, London 1947; Chargé d'affaires, London 1949, Amb. to U.K. 1950–54, to U.S.S.R. 1954–56; Foreign Minister 1957–66; Second Deputy First Minister 1960–66, concurrently Minister for Foreign Econ. Relations 1962–66; convicted of complicity in attempted communist coup and sentenced to death Oct. 1966; sentence commuted to life imprisonment 1970; pardoned by Pres. Suharto, released 15 Aug. 1995.

SUBBA ROW, Raman, C.B.E., M.A.; British cricketer (retd.), company director and public relations consultant; b. 29 Jan. 1932, Streatham, London; s. of the late Panguluri Venkata Subba Row and of Doris Pinner; m. Anne Harrison 1960; two s. one d.; ed. Whitgift School and Trinity Hall, Cambridge; Pilot Officer R.A.F. 1956–58; left-hand opening batsman; played for Cambridge Univ. 1951–53, Surrey 1953–54, Northants. 1955–61 (Capt. 1958–61); 13 Tests for England 1958–61; toured Australia 1958–59; scored 14,182 first-class runs with 30 hundreds; Assoc. Dir. W. S. Crawford Ltd. 1963–69; Man. Dir. Man. Public Relations Ltd. 1969–92; Chair. Surrey Co. Cricket Club 1974–79, Test and County Cricket Bd. 1985–90; Int. Cricket Council referee 1992–99; mem. Inst. of Dirs. *Leisure interests:* sports generally. *Address:* Leeward, 13 Manor Way, South Croydon, Surrey, CR2 7BT, England. *Telephone:* 0181-688 2991. *Fax:* 0181-688 2991.

SUBBOTIN, Valery Ivanovich; Russian physicist; b. 12 Dec. 1919, Baku; s. of Ivan Subbotin and Tatiana Subbotin; m. Irina Subbotin 1945; two s. one d.; ed. Baku Industrial Inst.; engineer, then chief of section Kavkazenergomash 1943–48; jr. then sr. researcher Energy Inst. Azerbaijan Acad. of Sciences 1952–53; Head of Lab., of Div., Deputy Dir. Inst. of Physics and Energy Obninsk 1953–75; Dir. Research Production enterprise Energiya 1975–77; Chair. Moscow Inst. of Physics and Eng. 1977–88, also Prof.; Scientific Sec. Research group, Research Construction Inst. of Energy Tech. 1988–; Corresp. mem. U.S.S.R. (now Russian) Acad. of Sciences 1967, mem. 1987; mem. Presidium 1991; main research on thermophysics of nuclear energy plants, methods of modelling of active zones of nuclear reactors, turbulence laws of liquid currents; Lenin Prize and other decorations. *Publications:* Liquid Metals 1967, Physical-Chemical Basis for Application of Liquid Metal Heat Carriers 1978, Structure of Turbulent Flow and Mechanism of Heat Exchange in Channels 1978, On Thermophysics of Focusing Mirrors of Laser Nuclear Reactors 1983, Interchannel Heat Exchange at Transversal Water Flow Around a Bunch of Pipes 1985, Reflections on Atomic Energetics 1995; articles in scientific journals. *Leisure interest:* literature. *Address:* Leninsky prospect 14, Moscow, 117901; Research Construction Institute of Energy Technology, M. Krasnoselskaya str. 2/8, 107112 Moscow, Russia (Office). *Telephone:* 264 7489 (Office); 240 8932 (Home).

SUBBULAKSHMI, Madurai Shanmugavadivu; Indian classical Karnatic musician; b. 16 Sept. 1916, Madurai; m. Sri T. Sadasivam 1940; ed. privately; recitals with her mother, Guru Veena Shanmugavadivu 1928–32; gave solo performances and became a leading musician before age 18; acted title role in Hindi film Meera; numerous benefit performances, donated royalties from many of her records to social and religious causes; rep. Karnatic music at Edinburgh Festival 1963; concerts in London, Frankfurt, Geneva, Cairo; 7-week tour of U.S.A. 1966; performed in Tokyo, Bangkok, Hong Kong, Manila, Singapore, Malaysia, New York, Pittsburgh, Moscow; Pres. Madras Music Acad. Conf. 1968; Nat. Prof. (Music) 1990–; Nat. Research Prof. 1995–; Producer Emer., All India Radio and Doordarshan 1979–; Life mem. Int. Music Council 1981; Trustee Indira Gandhi Nat. Centre for Arts; Hon. D.Litt. (Ravindra Bharati Univ.) 1967, (Shri Venkateswara Univ.) 1971, (Delhi Univ.) 1973, (Madhya Pradesh Univ.) 1979, (Banaras Hindu Univ.) 1980, (Madras Univ.) 1987, (Tirupati) 1989, (Madurai Kamaraj Univ.) 1994; numerous awards including: President's Award for Karnatic Music 1956, Ramon Magsaysay Award for Public Service (Philippines) 1974, Melvin Jones Fellowship Award for outstanding humanitarian services 1986, Indira Gandhi Award 1990, Woman of the Year Award (Int. Women's Assoc.) 1992, Swaralaya Puraskaram–Delhi Award 1997; Sangeet Natak Acad. Fellowship 1974; Padma Bhushan 1954; Padma Vibhushan 1975; hon. title Sangeetha Khalanidhi; hon. title Sapthagiri Sangeetha Vidwanmani 1975, Thanipperum Kalaignyar 1980, Gayaka Ratnam 1990. *Address:* 'Sivam-Subham', 11 First Main Road, Kotturpuram, Madras 600085, India. *Telephone:* 414775.

SUBOTNICK, Morton Leon, M.A.; American composer; b. 14 April 1933, Los Angeles; s. of Jack Jacob Subotnick and Rose Luckerman; m. 1st Linn Pottle 1953 (divorced 1971); one s. one d.; m. 2nd Doreen Nelson 1976 (divorced 1977); m. 3rd Joan La Barbara 1979; one s.; ed. Univ. of Denver, Mills Coll.; Co-Founder, San Francisco Tape Music Center 1961–65; fmr. Music Dir., Ann Halprin's Dance Co. and San Francisco Actors' Workshop, fmr. Music Dir. of Lincoln Center Repertory Theatre; Dir. of electronic music at original Electric Circus, St. Mark's Place, New York 1967–68; Artist-in-Residence at New York Univ. School of the Arts 1966–69; Dir. Center for Experiments in Art, Information and Tech. 1969–, also Co-Chair. Composition Dept.; Visiting Prof. in Composition, Univ. of Maryland 1968, Univ. of Pittsburgh 1969, Yale Univ. 1982, 1983; has toured extensively as a lecturer and composer/performer; Composer-in-Residence DAAD, West Berlin 1981, M.I.T. 1986; Brandeis Award for Music 1983, and numerous other grants and awards. *Compositions include:* Silver Apples of the Moon, The Wild Bull, Trembling, The Double Life of Amphibians, The Key to Songs, Return: The Triumph of Reason (electronic composition in honour of the return of Halley's Comet) 1986, In Two Worlds 1987–88, And The Butterflies Begin to Sing 1988, A Desert Flowers 1989, All my Hummingbirds have Alibis, Jacob's Room (opera) 1993. *Address:* c/o European-American, P.O. Box 850, Valley Forge, PA 19482, U.S.A.

SUBRAMANIAM, Chidambaram, B.A., B.L.; Indian politician; b. 30 Jan. 1910, Pollachi, Coimbatore District of Tamil Nadu; ed. Madras Univ.; joined Satyagraha Movement and imprisoned 1932; started legal practice Coimbatore 1936; political imprisonment 1941, 1942; Pres. Coimbatore Dist. Congress Cttee. and mem. Working Cttee. of All-India Congress Cttee.; mem. Constituent Ass. of India 1946–51, Madras Legis. Ass. 1952–62; Minister of Finance, Educ. and Law, Madras State 1952–62; mem. Lok Sabha 1962–67, 1971–; Minister of Steel 1962–63, of Steel, Mines and Heavy Eng. 1963–64, of Food and Agriculture 1964–66, of Food, Agriculture, Community Devt. and Co-operation 1966–67, of Planning, Science and Tech. 1971–72, of Industrial Devt., Science and Tech. 1972–74, of Finance 1974–77, of Defence 1979–80; Chair. Nat. Comm. on Agric. 1970; Chair. Rajaji Int. Inst. of Public Affairs and Admin. 1980–; Pres. Madras Voluntary Health Services 1987–; Deputy Chair. Nat. Planning Comm. 1971; Hon. Pres. Int. Centre for Public Enterprises in Developing Countries, Ljubljana, Yugoslavia 1985–87; Pres. Bharatiya Vidya Bhavan Feb. 1990–; Gov. of Maharashtra 1990–93; mem. Governing Council of Int. Wheat and Maize Improvement Centre, Mexico; mem. Bd. of Govs. Int. Rice Research Inst., Manila; Pres. All-India Tennis Asscn. *Publications:* Travelogues in Tamil: Countries I Visited, Around the World, India of my Dreams, War on Poverty, New Agricultural Strategy. *Address:* River View, Kotturpuram, Madras 600085, India. *Telephone:* (44) 414208.

SUBRAMANYAN, Kalpathi Ganapathi; Indian artist and professor of art; b. 5 Feb. 1924, Kerala; s. of K. P. Ganapathi and Alamelu Ammal; m. Susheela Jasra 1951; one d.; ed. Univ. of Madras, Kalabhavana, Visvabharati and Slade School of Art, London; Lecturer in Painting, Faculty of Fine Arts, M. G. Univ., Baroda 1951–59, Reader 1961–66, Prof. 1966–80, Dean, Faculty of Fine Arts 1968–74; Prof. of Painting, Kalabhavana, Visva Bharati, Santiniketan 1980–89, Prof. Emer. 1989–; Deputy Dir. (Designs), All India Handloom Bd., Bombay 1959–61, Design Consultant 1961–65; Visiting Lecturer, Canada 1976; Visiting Fellow, Visvabharati, Santiniketan 1977–78; Christensen Fellow, St. Catherine's Coll., Oxford 1987–88; JDR III Fund Fellowship, New York 1967–68; Fellow Lalit Kala Acad. 1984; numerous solo exhbns.; work has been displayed in many countries; Hon. D.Litt. (Rabindra Bharati Univ., Calcutta) 1992, (Banaras Hindu Univ., Varanasi) 1997; Hon. Mention (São Paulo Biennale) 1961, Nat. Award 1965, Gold Medal, 1st Indian Triennale 1968; Padma Shri (India) 1975; Kalidas Samman 1981. *Publications:* Moving Focus (essays on art) 1978, Living Tradition 1985, Creative Circuit (collection of lectures) 1991. *Leisure interests:* reading, handicraft. *Address:* Kalabhavana, Santiniketan, 731235, West Bengal (Office); Kailas, 13 Purvapalli, Santiniketan, 731235, West Bengal, India (Home). *Telephone:* 03463-53106.

SUBROTO, M.A., PH.D.; Indonesian politician; b. 19 Sept. 1928, Surakarta; s. of Sindurejo Subroto and Ibu Subroto; m. Trisnowati Harsono 1958; three s.; ed. Univ. of Indonesia, McGill, Stanford and Harvard Univs.; fmr. Dir.-Gen. of Research and Devt., Ministry of Trade; Prof. in Int. Econs., Univ. of Indonesia; Minister of Resettlement and Co-operatives 1971–73, of Manpower, Transmigration and Co-operatives 1973–78, of Mines and Energy 1978–88; Chair. of Bd. Pertamina 1978–88; Sec.-Gen. OPEC 1988–95. *Leisure interests:* tennis, golf, reading. *Publications:* numerous books on econ. topics. *Address:* c/o Ministry of Foreign Affairs, Jalan Taman Pejambon, 6 Jakarta Pusat, Indonesia.

SUCHET, David; British actor; b. 2 May 1946; s. of Jack Suchet and late Joan Jarché; m. Sheila Ferris 1976; one s. one d.; ed. Wellington School, Somerset, LAMDA, London; fmr. mem. Nat. Youth Theatre, Chester Repertory Co.; joined R.S.C. 1973, Assoc. Artist; *roles for R.S.C. include:* Tybalt in Romeo and Juliet 1973, Orlando in As You Like It 1973, Tranio in Taming of the Shrew 1973, Zamislov in Summerfolk 1974, 1975, Wilmer in Comrades 1974, The Fool in King Lear 1974, 1975, Pisanio in Cymbeline 1974, Hubert in King John, Ferdinand King of Navarre in Love's Labour's Lost 1975, Shylock in The Merchant of Venice 1978, Gruio in Taming of the Shrew 1978, Sir Nathaniel in Love's Labour's Lost 1978, Glougauer in Once in a Lifetime 1978, Caliban in The Tempest 1978, Sextus Pompey in Antony and Cleopatra 1978, Angelo in Measure for Measure 1979, Iago in Othello, Every Good Boy Deserves Favour, Bolingbroke in Richard II 1981, Achilles in Troilus and Cressida, Mercutio in Romeo and Juliet; *other stage roles include:* Lucio in Measure for Measure 1977, Thomas Gilthead in The Devil is an Ass 1977, The Kreutzer Sonata 1978, Tsaravitch and George Wochner in Laughter! 1978, Joe Green in Separation 1987, This Story of Yours, Litvanoy in The Wedding Feast, Estragon in Waiting for Godot, John Aubrey in Brief Lives, Mole in Toad of Toad Hall, Timon in Timon of Athens 1991, John in Oleanna 1993, Sid Field in What a Performance 1994, George in Who's Afraid of Virginia Woolf? 1996, Salieri in Amadeus 1998. *Films:* Tale of Two Cities 1978, Schiele in Prison 1980, The Missionary 1982, Hunchback of Notre Dame 1982, Red Monarch 1983, Trenchcoat 1983, Greystoke: The Legend of Tarzan, Lord of the Apes 1984, Little Drummer Girl 1984, Song for Europe (video title Cry for Justice) 1985, Thirteen to Dinner 1985, Falcon and the Snowman 1985, Gulag 1985, Iron Eagle 1986, Murrow 1986, Big Foot and The Hendersons 1986, Crime of Honor 1987, The Last Innocent Man 1987, A World Apart 1988, To Kill a Priest (also known as Popielusko) 1988, The Lucona Affair, When the Whales Came 1990, Executive Decision 1995, Deadly Voyage 1995, Sunday 1996, A Perfect Murder 1997; *televison includes:* dramatisation of Agatha Christie's Poirot novels (for LWT) Series I 1989, II 1990, III 1991, IV 1992, V 1993, VI 1994, 100th Anniversary Special: The Mysterious Affair at Styles 1990, Oppenheimer 1978, Being Normal, Saigon—the Last Days, Time to Die, The Life of Freud, Blott on the Landscape, Oxbridge Blues 1986, Playing Shakespeare 1983, Master of the Game 1984, Reilly—Ace of Spies 1984, Mussolini: The Untold Story 1985, James Joyce's Ulysses, Cause Célèbre 1988, The Life of Agatha Christie 1990, Once in a Lifetime, Bingo, Long Ago and Far Away 1989, Days of Majesty 1994, Fighting Fund (episode of The Protectors), Separation 1990, Secret Agent, Kings and Castles, Nobody Here but Us Chickens 1989, The Cruel Train, The Curious 1994, Moses 1995, Solomon 1997, See Saw 1997; Visiting Prof. of Theatre, Univ. of Neb., U.S.A.; several radio drama roles and audio recordings; mem. Fight Directors' Asscn.; Brown Belt in Aikido; a First Master of Japanese Samurai; Best Radio Actor of the Year for The Kreutzer Sonata (one-man show) 1979, Best Actor for Beria in Red Monarch, Marseilles Film Festival 1983, Best Actor for Stress, British Industry/Scientific Film Asscn. 1986, Best Actor for Song for Europe, Freud, Blott on the Landscape, Royal TV Soc. Performance Awards 1986, Best Actor, Variety Club Award for John in Oleanna 1994, for Salieri in Amadeus 1998; several BAFTA, SWET, Olivier and other nominations. *Publications:* essays in Players of Shakespeare 1985. *Leisure interests:* photography, clarinet, ornithology, theology, narrow boating. *Address:* c/o Ken McReddie Ltd., 91 Regent Street, London, W1 7TB, England. *Telephone:* 0171-439 1456. *Fax:* 0171-734 6530.

SUCHOCKA, Hanna, LL.M.; Polish politician and lawyer; b. 3 April 1946, Pleszew; ed. Adam Mickiewicz Univ., Poznań; scientific worker, Dept. of Constitutional Law of Adam Mickiewicz Univ., Poznań 1972–89, Catholic Univ. of Lublin 1988–, Polish Acad. of Science 1989–; mem. Democratic Party (SD) 1969–84; Deputy to Sejm (Parl.) 1980–85, 1989–; mem. Civic. Parl. Club 1989–91, mem. Democratic Union Parl. Club (now Freedom Union) 1991–, Deputy Chair. Parl. Legis. Cttee. 1989–92; Chair. Council of Ministers 1992–93; Minister of Justice and Attorney-Gen. 1997–; mem. Pontifical Acad. of Social Sciences 1994–; Dr. h.c. (Oklahoma Univ.). *Publications:* author of reports and articles for professional publs. and int. confs. *Address:* Ministerstwo Sprawiedliwości, Al. Ujazdowskie 11, 00-950 Warsaw, Poland. *Telephone:* (22) 628 44 31.

SUCKLING, Charles W., C.B.E., D.SC., PH.D., F.R.S.C., F.R.S.; British chemist; b. 24 July 1920, Teddington; s. of Edward Ernest Suckling and Barbara

Suckling (née Thomson); m. Eleanor Margaret Watterson 1946; two s. one d.; ed. Oldershaw Grammar School, Wallasey, Univ. of Liverpool; with Imperial Chemical Industries PLC 1942–82, Deputy Chair. Mond Div. 1969–72, Chair. Paints Div. 1972–77, Gen. Man. Research and Tech. 1977–82; Chair. Bradbury, Suckling and Partners Ltd. 1981–92; Dir. (non-exec.) Albright and Wilson 1982–89; Visiting Prof. Stirling Univ. 1969–92; mem. Science Consultative Group, BBC 1979–82; mem. Royal Comm. on Environmental Pollution 1981–92; Treas. Royal Coll. of Art, London 1984–90; mem. Electricity Supply Research Council 1983–90; mem. Nat. Curriculum Working Parties for English and Modern Foreign Languages 1988–91; numerous other appointments; Hon. D.Sc. (Liverpool) 1980, Hon. D. Univ. (Stirling) 1985; John Scott Medal of City of Philadelphia for invention of anaesthetic halothane 1973; Leverhulme Prize Soc. Chem. Industry 1942, Medal of Royal Coll. of Anaesthetists 1992. *Publications:* Research in the Chemical Industry 1969, Chemistry Through Models (with C. J. and K. E. Suckling) 1978. *Leisure interests:* music, writing, horticulture, languages. *Address:* 1 Desborough Drive, Tewin, Welwyn, Herts, AL6 0HQ, England. *Telephone:* (01438) 798250.

SUCKSDORFF, Arne Edvard; Swedish film producer; b. 3 Feb. 1917; ed. Stockholm. *Films include:* documentaries: Shadow over the Snow, Cliff Face, The Open Road, Rhythm of a City, Summer Interlude, Indian Village, and The Divided World; feature films: The Great Adventure, The Flute and the Arrow, The Boy in the Tree.

SUDEARY, Abdelmuhsin M. Al–, M.AGR.; Saudi Arabian diplomatist; b. 7 Feb. 1936, Riyadh; s. of Mohammed and Lululua Al-Sudeary; m. Hissa Al-Sudeary; one s. two d.; ed. Colorado State Univ. and Arizona Univ.; worked at Ministry of Agric. and Waters; Amb. to FAO 1972, Chair. N.E. Group; Chair. OPEC during UN Conf. on the Establishment of Int. Fund for Agric. Devt. (IFAD) June 1975; Chair. World Food Programme Cttee. on Food Aid Policies and Programmes 1976, Preparatory Comm. for IFAD 1976–77; Pres. IFAD 1977–84; Amb. to Sudan 1987–89, to the Netherlands 1990–; Hon. Ph.D. (Mich. State Univ.); Gold Medal Award (Pio Manzu Centre, Italy) 1978, Int. Prize of the Italian Agricultural Press Asscn. 1978; Order Francisco de Miranda (Venezuela) 1979, Chevalier, Ordre Nat. de la Légion d'honneur 1986, and numerous other awards. *Address:* Embassy of Saudi Arabia, Alexanderstraat 19, 2514 JM The Hague, Netherlands. *Telephone:* (070) 3614391.

SUDHARMONO, Gen.; Indonesian politician; b. 12 March 1927, Gresik; ed. Mil. Law Acad., Mil. Law Inst., Army Staff and Command Coll.; Commdr. Reserve Troops, Ronggolawe Div., E. and Cen. Java 1945–49; army officer, Bandung Educ. Centre 1950–52; Staff Officer, Cen. War Authority 1957–61; Alternate Mil. Attorney/Staff Officer, Supreme War Authority Office 1962–63; Asst. to Special Affairs Div. of Consultative Team to Leadership of the Revolution 1963–66; Sec. Econ. Stabilisation Council 1966; Cabinet Sec. 1966; Chair., Co-ordinator, Cttee. for Int. Tech. Co-operation 1966; Sec. Audit Team 1971; became Major-Gen. 1971; State Sec. (and Cabinet Sec.) 1972; Minister, State Sec. 1973–88; Vice-Pres. of Indonesia 1988–93; Head Advisory Bd. for Promotion of Pancasila (state ideology) 1994–. *Address:* Senopati Street 44B, Jakarta Selatan, Indonesia.

SUDOMO; Indonesian politician; b. 20 Sept. 1926, Malang, E. Java; ed. Navigation High School, Cilacap, Cen. Java, Artillerie School Koninklijke Marine Den Helder, Netherlands, Inst. for Nat. Defence (LEMHANAS), School for Marine Commdrs., Surabaya and Naval Staff and Command Coll., Jakarta; Battalion III Base IX 1945–50; Commdr. Flores and First Officer Gajah Madah 1950–56; Head, Directorate of Operations and Training Credits, Naval H.Q., Commdr. Special Fighting Unit, promoted Vice-Adm. 1956–62; Theatre Naval Commdr. for liberation of W. Irian 1962–64; Asst. to Minister of Sea Communications 1964–66; Insp.-Gen. of Navy 1966–68; Commdr. Cen. Maritime Territory 1968–69; Chief of Staff of Indonesian Navy, promoted Admiral 1969–73; Deputy Chief of Command for Restoration of Security and Order 1973–74; Chief of Staff 1974–78; Deputy Commdr. in charge of Armed Forces 1978–83; Minister of Manpower 1983–88, Co-ordinating Minister of Political Affairs and Security 1988–93; Chair. Supreme Advisory Council 1993–98. *Address:* c/o Supreme Advisory Council, Jalan Merdeka Utara 15, Jakarta Pusat 10110, Indonesia.

SUGAÏ, Kumi; Japanese painter; b. 1919; ed. Osaka School of Fine Arts; one-man shows, Galerie Cruen, Paris, Palais des Beaux Arts, Brussels 1954, St. George's Gallery, London 1955, Galerie Legendre, Paris 1957; rep. at Pittsburgh Carnegie Int. Exhbn. 1955, and Salon des Réalités Nouvelles 1956, 1957, Salon de Mai 1957, 1958, Salon Biennale 1957 (all Paris) and Dunn Int. Exhbn., London 1963; Int. Painting Prize, São Paulo Bienal 1965. *Publication:* La quête sans fin.

SUGAR, Alan Michael; British business executive; b. 24 March 1947; s. of Nathan Sugar and Fay Sugar; m. Ann Simons 1968; two s. one d.; ed. Brooke House School, London; Chair. and Man. Dir. Amstrad PLC 1968–97, C.E.O. –1993; Chair., co-owner Tottenham Hotspur PLC 1991–; Exec. Dir. Betacom 1997–; Dir. (non-exec.) Viglen 1997–; Hon. D.Sc. (City Univ.) 1988. *Leisure interest:* tennis. *Address:* 169 King's Road, Brentwood, Essex, CM14 4EF, England. *Telephone:* (01277) 228888.

SUGISAKI, Shigemitsu; Japanese international official and fmr. civil servant; b. 1941; ed. Univ. of Tokyo, Columbia Univ.; positions with Ministry of Finance 1964–76, 1979–94 including mem. Minister's Secr., Deputy Vice-Minister of Finance for Int. Affairs 1990–91, Deputy Dir.-Gen. Int. Finance Bureau 1991–92, Commr. Tokyo Regional Taxation Bureau 1992–93, Sec.-Gen. Exec. Bureau Securities and Exchange Surveillance Comm. 1993–94; Personal Asst. to Pres. Asian Devt. Bank 1976–79; Special Advisor to Man. Dir. IMF 1994–97, Deputy Man. Dir. Feb. 1997–. *Address:* IMF, 700 19th Street, NW, Washington, DC 20431, U.S.A. *Telephone:* (202) 623-7430. *Fax:* (202) 623-6772.

SUGITA, Katsuyuki, B.ECON.; Japanese banker; b. 13 Oct. 1942; ed. Tokyo Univ.; joined Nippon Kangyo Bank 1966 (later merged with Dai-Ichi Bank Ltd. to form Dai-Ichi Kangyo Bank); Man. Dir. and Gen. Man. Planning and Co-ordination Div., Dai-Ichi Kangyo Bank 1995–96, Man. Dir. of Div. V, Nat. Banking Admin. April–May 1996, Man. Dir. 1996–, now Pres. and C.E.O. *Address:* The Dai-Ichi Kangyo Bank, 1-1-5, Uchisaiwai-cho, Chiyoda-ku, Tokyo 100, Japan. *Telephone:* (3) 3596-1111.

SUHARTO, Gen. Mohamed, T.N.I.; Indonesian politician and army officer; b. 8 June 1921, Kemusu, Yogjakarta; m. Siti Hartinah 1947 (died 1996); six c.; ed. mil. schools and Indonesian Army Staff and Command Coll.; Officer in Japanese-sponsored Indonesian Army 1943; Battalion, later Regimental Commdr., Yogjakarta 1945–50; Regimental Commdr., Cen. Java 1953; Brig.-Gen. 1960, Maj.-Gen. 1962; Deputy Chief of Army Staff 1960–65; Chief of Army Staff 1965–68, Supreme Commdr. 1968–73; Minister of Army 1965; assumed emergency exec. powers March 1966; Deputy Prime Minister for Defence and Security 1966; Chair. of Presidium of Cabinet, in charge of Defence and Security, also Minister of Army 1966–67; Full Gen. 1966; Acting Pres. of Indonesia 1967–68; Prime Minister 1967, concurrently Minister for Defence and Security 1967–73; Pres. of Indonesia March 1968–98; UN Population Award 1989. *Publication:* Suharto, My Thoughts, Words and Deeds 1989. *Address:* 8 Jalan Cendana, Jakarta, Indonesia (Home).

SUHL, Harry, PH.D.; American professor of physics; b. 18 Oct. 1922, Leipzig, Germany; s. of Bernhard Suhl and Klara Bergwerk; m. 1949 (deceased); no c.; ed. Univ. Coll., Cardiff and Oriel Coll., Oxford; Temp. Experimental Officer, Admiralty, London 1943–46; Tech. Staff, Bell Labs., N.J. 1948–60; Prof. of Physics, Univ. of Calif. (San Diego) 1961–; Consultant, Aerospace Corpn. 1961–, Exxon Research and Eng., N.J. 1977–; Fellow, American Physics Soc., N.A.S.; Guggenheim Fellow 1968–69; Nat. Science Foundation Fellow 1971; Co-Ed. Magnetism 1961–74; ed. Solid State Communications 1961–; Alexander V. Humboldt Sr. Fellow 1991. *Publication:* Magnetism—a Treatise on Modern Theory and Materials (with G.T. Rado) 1966. *Address:* Physics Department, University of California, 9500 Gilman Drive, La Jolla, CA 92093, U.S.A. *Telephone:* (619) 534-4748.

SUI MINGTAI, Lieut.-Gen.; Chinese army officer; b. 1942, Zhaoyuan Co., Shandong Prov.; joined PLA 1960; joined CCP 1962; Vice-Dir. then Dir. Political Dept. of PLA Second Artillery Force 1990–; mem. 15th CCP Cen. Cttee. 1997–. *Address:* People's Liberation Army Second Artillery Force Headquarters, Beijing, People's Republic of China.

SUI YONGJU, Lieut.-Gen.; Chinese army officer; b. Nov. 1932, Dalian City; engaged in secret communist activities while still at school as mem. New Democratic Youth; joined CCP 1950; joined PLA; Clerk Luda Garrison Command responsible for Communist Youth League work; Sec. Political Office Public Security Militia Luda Border Defence Regt. 1953; Co. Political Guidance Officer Eng. Regt. Second Artillery, Regt. Org. Section Chief, Div. Chief Political Dept. 1969, Political Commissar, Dir. Base Political Dept., Asst. Political Commissar, Base Political Commissar; elected. mil. rep. 7th NPC 1988; selected as activist to study Mao's works 1968; trained Second Artillery Eng. Acad. 1985, Dir. Political Office Second Artillery 1988, promoted to Maj. Gen. 1988; Second Asst. Political Commissar Second Artillery 1990, Political Commissar 1992; mem. Cen. Comm. for Disciplinary Inspection; rank of Gen. 1996. *Address:* People's Liberation Army, c/o Ministry of National Defence, Jingshanqian Jie, Beijing, People's Republic of China.

SUISSA, Eli; Israeli politician; b. 1955, Afula; m.; four c.; mem. Shas (Sephardic Torah Guardians); joined Ministry of Interior, firstly in charge of Jerusalem Dist., then as Deputy Dir.-Gen.; Minister of the Interior and of Religious Affairs 1996–. *Address:* Ministry of the Interior, P.O. Box 6158, 2 Rehov Kaplan, Kiryat Ben-Gurion, Jerusalem 91061, Israel. *Telephone:* (2) 6701411. *Fax:* (2) 6701628.

SUITNER, Otmar; Austrian conductor; b. 16 May 1922, Innsbruck; s. of Karl Suitner and Maria Rizzi; m. Marita Wilckens 1948; ed. Pädagogium Innsbrück, Mozarteum Salzburg; Music Dir. in Remscheid 1952–57; Gen. Dir. of Pfalz-orchester in Ludwigshafen 1957–60; Gen. Dir. of State Opera Dresden 1960–64; Gen. Dir. German State Opera Berlin 1964–89; Hon. Conductor Nippon Hoso Kyokai Orchestra, Tokyo 1973–88; Guest Conductor San Francisco, Tokyo, Vienna, Bayreuth Festival, etc.; many recordings; led course for conductors, Int. Summer Acad. Univ. Mozarteum, Salzburg 1975, 1976; Prof. 1968; Prof. in Conducting, Hochschule für Musik, Vienna 1977–88; Commendatore, Gregorian Order 1973. *Address:* Platanenstr. 13, 13156 Berlin, Germany; Widerhoferplatz 4/48, 1090 Vienna, Austria.

SUK, Josef; Czech violinist; b. 8 Aug. 1929, Prague; great-grandson of Antonin Dvořák; grandson of Josef Suk; s. of Josef Suk and Marie Suková; m. Marie Poláková 1951; ed. Prague Conservatory and studied with Jaroslav Kocian; First violinist, Prague String Quartet 1950; f. Suk Trio 1952; soloist with Czech Philharmonic Orchestra 1961–; Prof., Vienna Conservatoire 1979–86; gives concerts as a soloist or with trio throughout the world; Pres.

Prague Spring Foundation, Antonin Dvořák Foundation; Artistic Dir. Suk Chamber Orchestra 1992–; numerous recordings; Grand Prix du Disque 1960, 1966, 1968, 1974, 1978, Czechoslovak State Prize 1964, Edison Prize 1972, Wiener Flötenuhr 1974, Honoured Artist 1970, National Artist 1977, Golden Disc of Nippon Columbia 1978, Plaque of 100th Anniversary of Béla Bartók's Birth 1981. *Leisure interests:* music, literature. *Address:* Karlovo náměstí 5, 12000 Prague 2, Czech Republic. *Telephone:* (2) 299407. *Fax:* (2) 299407.

SUKSELAINEN, Vieno Johannes; Finnish politician and economist; b. 12 Oct. 1906, Paimio; m. Elma Bonden 1938; three s. one d.; Lecturer School of Social Sciences, Helsinki 1939; Sec. to Prime Minister 1941–45; teacher of political econs., Univ. of Turku 1945–47; Prof. School of Social Sciences, Univ. of Tampere 1947–54, Rector 1953–54, Chancellor 1969–78; Pres. of the Agrarian Union 1945–64; mem. Finnish Parl. 1948–70, 1972–79, Speaker 1956–57, 1958–59, 1968–70, 1972–75; Minister of Finance 1950–51 and 1954; Minister of Interior 1951–53; Gen. Dir. People's Pension Inst. 1954–71; Prime Minister May-Nov. 1957, 1959–61; fmr. mem. Nordic Council, Pres. 1972, 1977. *Leisure interest:* agriculture. *Address:* Päivättärenpolku 2, 02100 Tapiola, Finland.

SULAIM, Suliman Abd al aziz as-; Saudi Arabian politician; b. 1941; ed. Cairo Univ., Univ. of Southern Calif., Johns Hopkins Univ.; Dir. Dept. of Foreign Relations and Confs., Ministry of Labour; Asst. Dir.-Gen. Gen. Org. of Social Insurance; Prof. Political Science, Riyadh Univ. 1972–74; Deputy Minister of Commerce and Industry for Trade and Provisions 1974–75; Minister of Commerce 1975–95; Chair. Bd. Saudi Arabian Specifications and Standardization Org., Wheat Silos and Flour Mills Org. *Address:* c/o Ministry of Commerce, P.O. Box 1774, Airport Road, 11162 Riyadh, Saudi Arabia.

SULEIMENOV, Olzhas Omarovich; Kazakhstan politician and writer; b. 1936; ed. Kazak State Univ., Maxim Gorky Inst. of Literature in Moscow; mem. CPSU 1989–90; debut as writer in 1960; Ed.-in-Chief Studio Kazakhfilm 1962–71; Head of div. Prostor (magazine) 1971–; Sec. Bd. Kazakh Writers' Union 1971–; Chair. Kazakh Cttee. on relations with writers of Asia and Africa 1980–; actively participates in ecological movt., actions of protest against nuclear tests in Semipalatinsk since late 1980s; Deputy to U.S.S.R. Supreme Soviet 1984–89; People's Deputy, mem. U.S.S.R. Supreme Soviet 1989–91; founder and leader of People's Progress Party of Kazakhstan 1992–95; Amb. to Italy 1995–; U.S.S.R. Komsomol Prize, State Abai Prize of Kazakh S.S.R. *Publications:* collections of poetry including Argamaki 1961, Sunny Nights 1962, The Night of Paris 1963, The Kind Time of the Sunrise 1964, The Year of Monkey 1967, Above White Rivers 1970, Each Day—Morning 1973, Repeating in the Noon 1973, A Round Star 1975, Definition of a Bank 1976 and others. *Address:* Via Cassia 185, Rome, Italy (Office); Karla Marksa str. 96, Apt. 6, 480100 Alma-Ata, Kazakhstan (Home). *Telephone:* (6) 30889107 (Office); (3272) 68 20 65 (Home). *Fax:* (6) 30889103 (Office).

SULEIMENOV, Tuleutai Skakovich; Kazakh diplomatist; b. 1941, Semipalatinsk; ed. Karaganda Polytech. Inst., Diplomatic Acad. of U.S.S.R. Ministry of Foreign Affairs; foreman Karaganda Metallurgic factory –1969, Comsomol and CP functionary 1969–80; mem. U.S.S.R. Ministry of Foreign Affairs 1980–; Counsellor U.S.S.R. Embassy to Iran 1988–91; Kazakhstan Minister of Foreign Affairs 1991–94; Amb. to U.S.A. 1994–95; Amb. to Hungary 1995–. *Address:* 1025 Budapest, III ker., Kapi út 59, Hungary (Office); Aiteke-bi 65, Alma-Ata, Kazakhstan. *Telephone:* (1) 275-1300 (Office). *Fax:* (1) 275-2092 (Office); (3272) 507181.

SULIOTIS, Elena; Greek soprano opera singer; b. 28 May 1943, Athens; d. of Constantino Souliotis and Gallia Cavalengo; m. Marcello Guerrini 1970; one d.; ed. Buenos Aires and Milan; grew up in Argentina; went to Milan and was introduced to Gianandrea Gavazzeni 1962; studied singing with Mercedes Llopart; debut in Cavalleria Rusticana, Teatro San Carlo, Naples 1964; sang Amelia in Un Ballo in Maschera, Trieste 1965 and has since sung frequently throughout Italy; debut at La Scala as Abigail in Nabucco 1966; U.S. debut as Helen of Troy in Mefistofele, Chicago 1966; debut at Covent Garden as Lady Macbeth 1969; has also appeared at Teatro Colon, Buenos Aires and in Rio de Janeiro, São Paulo, Mexico City, New York, Dallas, Philadelphia, San Antonio, Montreal, Paris, Kiel, Lübeck, Höchst, Tokyo, Lisbon, Athens and Madrid; *repertoire includes:* Manon Lescaut, La Giaconda, Macbeth, Norma, Otello, Aida, Luisa Miller, Il Trovatore, Tosca, Loreley, La Forza del Destino, etc.; has recorded Norma, Cavalleria Rusticana, Nabucco, Anna Bolena, Macbeth and arias for Decca; recipient of several prizes. *Leisure interests:* country life, looking after plants and animals. *Address:* Villa il Poderino, Via Incontri 38, Florence, Italy.

SULLIVAN, Andrew, PH.D.; journalist; b. 20 Aug. 1963, Godstone, Surrey; ed. Magdalen Coll., Oxford Univ., Dept. of Govt., Harvard Univ., U.S.A.; joined New Republic magazine 1986, Ed. 1991–96; columnist The Sunday Times, London. *Publication:* Virtually Normal: An Argument About Homosexuality 1995. *Address:* c/o New Republic, Suite 600, 1220 19th Street, N.W., Washington, DC 20036, U.S.A.

SULLIVAN, Barry F., M.B.A.; American politician and business executive; b. 21 Dec. 1930, Bronx, N.Y.; m.; four s. one d.; ed. Georgetown and Columbia Univs. and Univ. of Chicago; with Chase Manhattan Bank 1957–80, mem. Man. Cttee. 1974–80; Chair. of Bd. and C.E.O. First Chicago Corpn., First Nat. Bank of Chicago 1980–91; Deputy Mayor, Finance and Econ. Devt., New York 1992–; mem. Econ. Devt. Comm. of Chicago, Asscn. of Reserve City Bankers, Mayor's Airport Study Comm., Chicago Clearing House Cttee., World's Fair Finance Cttee.; Vice-Pres. Exec. Cttee., Chicago Asscn. of Commerce and Industry; Dir. United Way: Crusade of Mercy Chicago, Campaign Dir. 1985; Trustee and mem. Exec. Cttee., Univ. of Chicago, also Chair. of Council of Graduate School of Business; Trustee, Art Inst. of Chicago.

SULLIVAN, Dennis P., PH.D.; American mathematician; b. 12 Feb. 1941, Port Huron, Mich.; three s. two d.; ed. Rice and Princeton Univs.; NATO Fellow, Univ. of Warwick, U.K. 1966; Miller Fellow, Univ. of Berkeley 1967–69; Sloan Fellow of Math. M.I.T. 1969–72, Prof. of Math. 1972–73; Prof. Perm., Institut des Hautes Etudes Scientifiques, Paris, France 1974–; Einstein Prof. of Sciences, Queens Coll. and CUNY Grad. School, CUNY, New York 1981–; mem. N.A.S.; Hon. Dr. (Warwick) 1984; Oswald Veblen Prize in Geometry 1971; Elie Cartan Prix en Géométrie, French Acad. of Sciences 1981. *Publications:* several papers in math. journals. *Leisure interest:* people. *Address:* Department of Mathematics, 33 West 42nd Street, Room 708, New York, NY 10036, U.S.A. *Telephone:* (212) 642-2461. *Fax:* (212) 642-1823.

SULLIVAN, Louis Wade, M.D.; American politician and physician; b. 3 Nov. 1933, Atlanta; s. of Walter Wade Sullivan and Lubirda Elizabeth (née Priester) Sullivan; m. Eve Williamson 1955; three c.; ed. Morehouse Coll., Atlanta, Boston Univ.; Intern New York Hosp.-Cornell Medical Centre, New York 1958–59, resident in internal medicine 1959–60; Fellow in Pathology, Mass. Gen. Hosp., Boston 1960–61; Research Fellow Thorndike Memorial Lab., Harvard Medical School, Boston 1961–63, Instructor of Medicine 1963–64; Asst. Prof. Medicine N.J. Coll. Medicine 1964–66; Co-Dir. Haematology, Boston Univ. Medical Centre 1966, Assoc. Prof. 1968–74, Prof. of Medicine and Physiology 1974–75; Dir. Hematology, Boston City Hosp.; Dean School of Medicine, Morehouse Coll. 1975–89, Pres. –1989, 1993–; Sec. of State for Health and Human Services 1989–93; Dir. (non-exec.) Gen. Motors 1993–; mem. sickle cell anaemia Advisory Cttee., Nat. Insts. of Health 1974–75, Medical Advisory Bd., Nat. Leukemia Asscn. 1968–70, (Chair. 1970); mem. American Soc. of Hematology, American Soc. of Clinical Investigation, Inst. of Medicine. *Publications:* numerous papers on medical matters. *Address:* Office of the President, Morehouse School of Medicine, 720 Westview Drive, S.W., Atlanta, GA 30310 (Office); 223 Chestnut Street, Atlanta, GA 30314, U.S.A.

SULLIVAN, Michael J., J.D.; American politician and lawyer; b. 23 Sept. 1939, Omaha; s. of Joseph B. Sullivan and Margaret Hamilton; m. Jane Metzler 1961; one s. two d.; ed. Univ. of Wyoming; Assoc. Brown, Drew, Apostolos, Barton & Massey, Casper, Wyoming 1964–67; partner, Brown, Drew, Apostolos, Massey & Sullivan, Casper 1967–; Gov. of Wyoming 1987–95; mem. A.B.A.; Democrat.

SULLO, Fiorentino; Italian politician; b. 29 March 1921, Paternopoli, Avellino; s. of Clorindo and Guilia Emilia (née Calienno) Sullo; m. Elvira de Laurentiis 1961; one d.; mem. Constituent Ass. 1946–48, Chamber of Deputies 1948–; fmr. Under-Sec. for Defence, Under-Sec. for Industry and Commerce, Under-Sec. for State Participation; Minister of Transport 1960, of Labour and Social Insurance 1960–62, of Public Works 1962–63, of Educ. 1968–69; Minister without portfolio for scientific and tech. research 1972–73, for Regions 1973; Pres. Interior Comm., Chamber of Deputies 1966–68; Pres. Public Works Comm. 1979–81; now State Councillor; Ed. Le Discussione 1966–69; editorial contrib. Roma di Napoli; Contributor to Il Punto, Politica and Mattino 1977–79, to Roma 1979–; Pres. Christian Democrat group in Parl. 1968; resigned from Christian Democrat Party 1974; mem. Social Democrat Party 1974–82; returned to Christian Democrat Party Aug. 1982, to Chamber of Deputies 1983–87; mem. Majority of Regulation, Constitutional Affairs Comm., Regional Questions Comm., Chamber of Deputies, Admin. Law Council in Sicilian Region 1988, Second Section of State Council 1989, Nat. Revenue Cttee. 1989; Co-Pres. Italy-U.S.S.R. Cultural Asscn.; Grand Officier, Légion d'honneur, Grand Cross Kt. of Italian Repub. *Publication:* Lo Scandalo Ubanistico 1964. *Leisure interest:* tennis. *Address:* Via Venanzio Fortunato 54, 00136 Rome, Italy. *Telephone:* 345 10 31.

SULSTON, John Edward, PH.D., F.R.S.; British scientist; b. 27 March 1942, Fulmer; s. of the late Rev. Canon Arthur Edward Aubrey Sulston and of Josephine Muriel Frearson Blocksidge; m. Daphne Edith Bate 1966; one s. one d.; ed. Merchant Taylor's School and Pembroke Coll., Cambridge; Postdoctoral Fellowship at the Salk Inst., Calif. 1966–69; Staff scientist, MRC Lab. of Molecular Biology, Cambridge 1969–; Dir. The Sanger Centre 1992–; W. Alden Spencer Award (jtly.) 1986, Gairdner Foundation Award (jtly.) 1991, Darwin Medal, Royal Soc. 1996, Rosenstiel Award (jtly.) 1998. *Publications:* papers in scientific journals. *Leisure interests:* gardening, walking, avoiding people. *Address:* The Sanger Centre, Wellcome Trust Genome Campus, Hinxton, Cambridge, CB10 1SA; 39 Mingle Lane, Stapleford, Cambridge, CB2 5BG, England (Home). *Telephone:* (01223) 834244 (Office); (01223) 842248 (Home). *Fax:* (01223) 494919.

SULTAN, Altoon, B.A., M.F.A.; American artist; b. 29 Sept. 1948, Brooklyn, New York; s. of Raymond Sultan and Adele Chalom Sultan; ed. Abraham Lincoln High School, Brooklyn and Brooklyn Coll.; *solo exhbns.:* Marlborough Gallery, New York 1977–98, Middendorf Gallery, Washington, D.C. 1987, Hokin-Kaufman Gallery, Chicago 1990, D.P. Fong & Spratt, San Jose, Calif.

1992, Pinnacle Gallery, Savannah, Ga. 1997; *group exhbns.:* Museum of Fine Arts, Boston 1982, San Francisco Museum of Modern Art 1985, Butler Inst. Youngstown 1987, Metropolitan Museum 1991, Flint Inst. of Arts, Mich., Nat. Museum of Women in the Arts, Washington, D.C., Wichita Art Museum, Kan., Currier Gallery of Art, Manchester, N.H.; work in public collections: Metropolitan Museum of Art, New York, Hunter Museum, Chattanooga, Tenn., Museum of Fine Arts, Boston and Yale Univ. Art Gallery; mem. Nat. Acad. of Design, New York; Nat. Endowment for the Arts Fellowship Grant 1983, 1989, Karolyi Foundation Fellowship 1984 and other awards. *Leisure interests:* horseback riding, gardening. *Address:* P.O. Box 2, Groton, VT 05046, U.S.A. *Telephone:* (802) 584-4052.

SULTAN, Donald Keith, M.F.A.; American painter, printmaker and sculptor; b. 5 May 1951, Asheville, N.C.; s. of Norman Sultan and Phyllis Sultan; m. Susan Reynolds 1978; one s. one d.; ed. Univ. of N. Carolina, Art Inst. of Chicago; represented by: Willard Gallery 1979–82, Blum Helman Gallery 1982–89, M. Knoedler Gallery New York 1989; work in collections: Art Inst. of Chicago, Hirsh Museum and Sculpture Garden, Washington D.C., The Metropolitan Museum of Art, N.Y., The Museum of Fine Arts, Boston, The Museum of Modern Art, N.Y., The Solomon R. Guggenheim Museum, N.Y., Walker Art Center, Minneapolis, Bibliothèque Nationale, Paris 1992; Public Service Grant N.Y. State 1978–79, Nat. Endowments for the Arts 1980–81. *Address:* 19 E. 70th Street, New York, NY 10021, U.S.A.

SULTAN, Fouad, B.SC.; Egyptian politician; b. 26 Jan. 1931; s. of Abdel Latif Sultan and Farida Torky; m. Ferial Fikry 1956, one s. one d.; ed. Univ. of Cairo; worked for 21 years with Cen. Bank of Egypt; seconded to IMF, North Yemen 1971–74; C.E.O. Misr-Iran Bank 1974–85; head of several cttees. in Fed. of Egyptian Banks; Minister of Tourism and Civil Aviation 1985–93; Chair. and C.E.O. AlAhly for Devt. and Investment (ADI) 1995–. *Leisure interests:* rowing, tennis, swimming. *Address:* ADI, 1191 Cornish El Nil, World Trade Center, 10th floor, Cairo, Egypt. *Telephone:* (2) 5780790. *Fax:* (2) 5780793.

SULTAN IBN ABDUL AZIZ AS-SA'UD, H.R.H. Prince; Saudi Arabian government minister; b. 1928; s. of the late King Abdul Aziz ibn Saud and Hassa Bint Sudairi; brother of King Fahd and of the late King Khalid; Gov. of Riyadh 1947; Minister of Agric. 1954, of Transportation 1955; Vice-Pres. Supreme Cttee. of Educ. Policy; Minister of Defence and Aviation and Insp.-Gen. 1963–82; Chair. Bd. Saudia Airlines 1963; Chair. Bd. of Gen. Enterprise of Mil. Industries; Chair. Council of Manpower 1980; Second Deputy Prime Minister and Minister of Defence and Civil Aviation, Insp.-Gen. 1982–; Chair. Supreme Council for Islamic Affairs 1994; various orders and decorations. *Address:* Ministry of Defence and Aviation, P.O. Box 26731, Airport Road, Riyadh 11165, Saudi Arabia. *Telephone:* (1) 476-9000. *Fax:* (1) 405-5500.

SULTANGAZIN, Umirzak Makhmutovich, D.PHYSICS AND MATHS.; Kazakhstan scientist; b. 10 April 1936, Kustanai Region; s. of Sultangazy Makhmutov and Nurila Makhmutova; m. Raikhan Meirmanova 1958, two c.; ed. Kazakh State Univ. and U.S.S.R. (now Russian) Acad. of Sciences, Novosibirsk; Asst. Prof. Kazakh State Univ. 1958–60, Assoc. Prof. 1960–64, Prof. of Math. 1972–78; Dir. Inst. of Math. and Mechanics, Acad. of Sciences of Kazakh S.S.R. 1978–88, Vice-Pres. of Acad. 1986–88, Pres. 1988–94; Dir. Space Research Inst. 1991–95; Visiting Prof. Karlov Univ. Czechoslovakia 1972, Kyoto Univ. Japan 1994–95; Chair. Fed. of Cosmonautics 1985, Peace Fund of Kazakh S.S.R. 1987, Math Cttee. of Rep. of Kazakhstan 1994; Corresp. mem. Acad. of Sciences of Kazakh S.S.R. 1975, mem. 1983; CPSU 1968–91, Cen. Cttee. 1989–91; mem. Parl. Kazakh S.S.R. 1987–89, Parl. of U.S.S.R. 1989–91; Korolev's Medal 1986, State Prize of U.S.S.R. for Science and Tech. 1987, Red Banner Order 1987, Prize of Acad. of Sciences of U.S.S.R. and Czechoslovakia for Nat. Sciences 1988. *Publications:* Concentrated Capacity in the Problems of Heat Physics and Microelectronics 1972, Method of Spherical Harmonics in Kinetic Transport Theory 1979, Mathematical Problems of Kinetic Transport Theory 1986, Discrete Nonlinear Models of Boltzmann Equation 1987, Ecological and Economical Model of Kazakhstan 1995; 150 articles on mathematical physics, numerical mathematics and ecology. *Leisure interests:* history, mountain tourism. *Address:* Institute of Space Research, 480034 Almaty, Akademgorodok (Office); Shevchenko 15, Almaty 480100, Kazakhstan. *Telephone:* (3272) 62-38-96 (Office); (3272) 616853. *Fax:* (3272) 494355.

SULTANOV, Outkir Tukhtamuradovich; Uzbekistan politician; b. 14 July 1939; m.; one d.; ed. Tomsk State Polytech. Inst.; electrician Tomsk plant of cutting metals 1963; master, Head of lab., Head of production automatization, Deputy Chief Engineer, Deputy Dir.-Gen. Tashkent Aviation Production Union 1964–85; Head Scientific Production Unit Vostok 1985–91; Chair. State Cttee. for Foreign Trade and Int. Relations 1991–92; Minister of External Econ. Relations, Deputy Prime Minister 1992–95; Prime Minister of Uzbekistan Dec. 1995–; People's Deputy of Uzbekistan; awarded Mekhnat Shukhradi; Merited Engineer Repub. of Uzbekistan. *Address:* Government House, Mustarilik 5, 700008 Tashkent, Uzbekistan (Office). *Telephone:* (993) 139 82 95; 139 86 19 (Office). *Fax:* (993) 139 86 01 (Office).

SULZBERGER, Arthur Ochs; American newspaper executive; b. 5 Feb. 1926, New York; s. of Arthur Hays and Iphigene (née Ochs) Sulzberger; m. 1st Barbara Grant 1948 (divorced 1956), one s. one d.; m. 2nd Carol Fox 1956 (died 1995), two d.; m. 3rd Allison Stacey Cowles 1996; ed. Columbia Univ.; U.S. Marine Corps, Second World War and Korean War; The New York Times Co., New York 1951–, Asst. Treas. 1958–63, Pres. 1963–79, Publr. 1963–92, Chair., C.E.O. 1992–97, Chair. Emer. 1997–; Co-Chair. Bd. Int. Herald Tribune 1983; Chair. Newspaper Pres. Asscn. 1988; Dir., Times Printing Co., Chattanooga, Gapesia Pulp and Paper Co. Ltd. of Canada; Trustee Columbia Univ., mem. Coll. Council; Trustee Metropolitan Museum of Art, Chair. Bd. of Trustees 1987–99; Hon. L.H.D. (Montclair State Coll.), (Tufts Univ.) 1984; Columbia Journalism Award 1992; Alexander Hamilton Medal 1982, Vermeil Medal (City of Paris) 1992. *Address:* New York Times Co., 229 West 43rd Street, New York, NY 10036, U.S.A. *Telephone:* 556-1234.

SUMAYE, Frederick; Tanzanian politician; fmr. Minister of Agric.; Prime Minister of Tanzania Oct. 1995–; mem. C.C.M. (Party for Democracy and Progress). *Address:* Office of the Prime Minister, P.O. Box 980, Dodoma, Tanzania. *Telephone:* (61) 20511.

SUMITA, Satoshi, LL.B.; Japanese banker; b. 4 Sept. 1916; m. Emiko Sumita; one s. one d.; ed. Univ. of Tokyo; Admin. Vice-Minister of Finance 1969–71; Pres. Export-Import Bank of Japan 1972–78; Deputy Gov. Bank of Japan 1979–84, Gov. 1984–89; Commdr. Légion d'honneur, Grand Officier, Ordre de la Couronne, Grand Cordon, Order of the Rising Sun. *Leisure interest:* art appreciation. *Address:* c/o Bank of Japan, 2-1-1, Hongoku-cho, Nihonbashi, Chuo-ku, Tokyo 100, Japan. *Telephone:* (3) 3279-1111.

SUMMER, Donna; American singer and actress; b. 31 Dec. 1948, Boston; d. of Andrew Gaines and Mary Gaines; m. 1st Helmut Sommer (divorced); one d.; m. 2nd Bruce Sudano; one s. one d.; singer 1967–; appeared in German stage production Hair; in Europe 1967–75, appearing in Vienna Folk productions of Porgy and Bess, and German productions of The Me Nobody Knows; Best Rhythm and Blues Female Vocalist, Nat. Acad. of Recording Arts and Sciences 1978, Best Female Rock Vocalist 1979, Favourite Female Pop Vocalist, American Music Awards 1979, Favourite Female Vocalist of Soul Music 1979, Ampex Golden Reel Award for single and album On the Radio 1979, album Bad Girls, Soul Artist of Year, Rolling Stone Magazine 1979, Best Rock Performance, Best of Las Vegas Jimmy Award 1980, Grammy Award for Best Inspirational Performance 1984; several awards for best-selling records; has sold over 20 million records. *Albums:* The Wanderer, Star Collection, Love to Love You Baby, Love Trilogy, Four Seasons of Love, I Remember Yesterday, The Deep, Shut Out, Once upon a Time, Bad Girls, On the Radio, Walk Away, She Works Hard for the Money, Cats without Claws, All Systems Go 1988, Another Time and Place 1989. *Address:* 2401 Main Street, Santa Monica, CA 90405, U.S.A.

SUMMERFIELD, Arthur, B.SC.TECH., B.SC., C.PSYCHOL., F.B.PS.S.; British psychologist; b. 31 March 1923, Wilmslow; s. of the late Arthur Summerfield and Dora Gertrude (née Perman Smith) Summerfield; m. 1st Aline Whalley 1946, one s. one d.; m. 2nd Angela Barbara Steer 1974; ed. Manchester Grammar School, Victoria Univ. of Manchester, Univ. Coll., London; Electrical Officer, R.N.V.R. (Naval Air Stations 1943–46, Dept. of Sr. Psychologist to Admiralty 1946); lecturer in Psychology, Univ. Coll. London 1949–61, Hon. Research Assoc. 1961–70, Hon. Research Fellow 1970–; Prof. of Psychology, Univ. of London, and Head, Dept. of Psychology, Birkbeck Coll. 1961–88, Prof. Emer. 1988–, Gov. 1982–86; Chair. Cttee. on 'Psychologists in Educ. Services' (Summerfield Report), Dept. of Educ. and Science 1965–68; Chair. LearnIT Ltd. 1991–; Pres. British Psychological Soc. 1963–64 (Hon. Life mem. 1993–), Int. Union of Psychological Science 1976–80, Section J (Psychology), British Asscn. for the Advancement of Science 1976–77, Int. Social Science Council (UNESCO) 1977–81, mem. Exec. Cttee. 1981–83; mem. Cttee. on Int. Relations in Psychology, American Psychological Asscn. 1977–79; mem. Bd. of Dirs., European Co-ordination Centre for Research and Documentation in Social Sciences 1977–81, British Journal of Educ. Psychology Ltd. 1976–93; mem. Social Science Research Council (G.B.) 1979–81; mem. Int. Council of Scientific Unions Study Group on the Biological, Medical and Physical Effects of the Large-scale Use of Nuclear Weapons 1983–87; Asst. Ed. British Journal of Psychology (Statistical Section) 1950–54, Ed. British Journal of Psychology 1964–67; Scientific Ed. British Medical Bulletin (experimental psychology) 1964, (cognitive psychology) 1971, with D. M. Warburton (psychobiology) 1981. *Publications:* Animals and Men (translated and ed. jtly.) 1951, Meeting Points in Dyslexia (ed. jtly.) 1990. *Address:* Rose Bank, Sutton-under-Whitestonecliffe, Thirsk, North Yorkshire, YO7 2PR, England (Home). *Telephone:* (01845) 597097 (Office); (01845) 597395 (Home). *Fax:* (01845) 597005 (Office).

SUMMERS, Lawrence, PH.D.; American economist; b. 1954, New Haven; m. Victoria Summers, one s. two d.; ed. Mass. Inst. of Tech and Harvard Univ.; domestic policy economist, U.S. Council of Econ. Advisers 1982–83; Nathaniel Ropes Prof. of Econs. Harvard Univ. 1983–93; fmr. consultant to U.S. Fed. Reserve system; adviser to governmental agencies in Canada, Jamaica, Japan, Indonesia, Mexico; Chief Economist and Vice-Pres. of Devt. Econs. IBRD 1991–93; Econ. Adviser to Pres. Bill Clinton; Treasury Under-Sec. for Int. Affairs 1993–95; Deputy Treasury Sec. 1995–99; Sec. of Treasury May 1999–; Fellow, American Acad. of Arts and Sciences; Alan T. Waterman Award, Nat. Science Foundation 1987. *Publications:* Understanding Unemployment, Reform in Eastern Europe (co-author), more than 100 articles. *Address:* Department of the Treasury, 1500 Pennsylvania Avenue, N.W., Washington, DC 20220, U.S.A. *Telephone:* (202) 622-1100. *Fax:* (202) 622-0073.

SUMNER, Gordon Matthew ("Sting"); British singer, bass-player, song-writer and actor; b. 2 Oct. 1951, Northumberland; m. 1st Frances Tomelty (divorced 1984); five c.; m. 2nd Trudie Styler 1992; fmr. primary school teacher, Cramlington, Newcastle; singer, bass-player and songwriter for The Police (rock group) 1977–; first solo album The Dream of the Blue Turtles 1985; songs include: Nothing Like the Sun 1987, The Soul Cages 1991; has undertaken major tours in U.K., Europe and U.S.A.; Hon. D.Mus. (Northumbria) 1992; *film appearances include:* Brimstone and Treacle 1984, Quadrophenia, The Bride of Frankenstein, Plenty, Dune 1985, The Adventures of Baron von Munchausen 1989, Stormy Monday 1989, Rosencrantz and Guildenstern are Dead, Resident Alien, The Music Tells You, The Grotesque, Mercury Falling 1996; Ivor Novello Award for Best Song 'They Dance Alone' 1989, four songwriting awards (BMI) 1998; Stage debut in The Threepenny Opera 1989. *Publication:* Jungle Stories: The Fight for the Amazon 1989. *Address:* c/o Publicity Department, Polydor Records, 72 Black Lane, London, W.6, England. *Telephone:* 0181-910 4800.

SUMPTION, Jonathan Philip Chadwick, Q.C., M.A.; British barrister and author; b. 12 Sept. 1948, London; s. of A. J. Sumption and Mrs. H. Sumption; m. Teresa Mary Whelan 1971; one s. two d.; ed. Eton Coll., Magdalen Coll., Oxford; Fellow in History Magdalen Coll., Oxford 1971–75; called to Bar (Inner Temple) 1975; Recorder 1992–; Judge of Courts of Appeal of Guernsey and Jersey 1995–. *Publications:* Pilgrimage: An Image of Medieval Religion 1975, The Albigensian Crusade 1979, The Hundred Years War (Vol. 1) 1989. *Leisure interests:* music, history. *Address:* Brick Court Chambers, 15/19 Devereux Court, London, WC2R 3LD, England. *Telephone:* 0171-379 3550. *Fax:* 0171-379 3558.

SUN CHEN; Chinese politician; fmrly. Minister of Defence; mem. Kuomintang Cen. Standing Cttee. 1994–. *Address:* c/o Ministry of Nat. Defence, P.O. Box 9001, Taipei, Taiwan.

SUN DAO LIN; Chinese actor and film director; b. 18 Dec. 1921; s. of Sun Wen-Yao and Fan Nian-Hua; m. Wang Wenjuan 1962; one d.; ed. Yanjing Univ.; Hon. mem. China Fed. of Literary and Art Circles 1996–; Best Film Actor (Lian-Ho Daily, Singapore) 1987, Outstanding Film Artist Prize (Wen-Hui Daily, Shanghai) 1989, One of Ten Most Popular Film Stars (China Film Weekly) 1990. *Films include:* Reconnaissance Over Yangtze River 1954, The Family 1956, Constant Beam 1958, Early Spring in February 1963, Go Master 1982 (Grand Prix, Montreal Film Festival 1984), Thunderstorm 1983, Special President 1986, Stepmother 1992. *Publication:* Anthology of Sun Daolin's Poems and Prose 1994. *Leisure interests:* literature, music (especially singing). *Address:* Shanghai Film Studio, 595 Tsao Hsi North Road, Shanghai 200030, People's Republic of China. *Telephone:* (021) 4387100. *Fax:* 4391650.

SUN FULING; Chinese party official and business executive; b. 1921, Shaoxing City, Zhejiang Prov.; Vice-Mayor Beijing 1983–93; Vice-Chair. Beijing Mun. Cttee. CPPCC 1988–92; mem. 5th Nat. Cttee. CPPCC 1978–82; Perm. mem. 6th Nat. Cttee. 1983–87, 7th Nat. Cttee. 1988–92; Vice-Chair. 8th Nat. Cttee. CPPCC 1993–98, 9th Nat. Cttee. 1998–. *Address:* National Committee of Chinese People's Political Consultative Conference, 23 Taiping Qiao Street, Beijing, People's Republic of China.

SUN HONGLIE; Chinese agronomist; b. 2 Jan. 1932, Henan; m. Wu Huanning 1956; one s. one d.; ed. Beijing Agric. Univ., Shenyang Inst. of Forestry and Soil Science, Chinese Acad. of Sciences; Research Fellow Comm. for Integrated Survey of Natural Resources (Chinese Acad. of Sciences) 1961–, Dir. 1983; Head Multi-disciplinary Expedition of Qinghai-Tibet Plateau 1973; Visiting Scholar Inst. of Alpine and Arctic Research, Colorado Univ. 1981–82; Vice-Pres. Chinese Acad. of Sciences 1984–; Chair. Academic Cttee. of Antarctic Research of China 1986; Chair. Nat. Cttee. of China for MAB, UNESCO; Vice-Chair. Int. Mountain Soc., State Antarctic Cttee.; a Vice-Pres. Soc. Social Devt. Science Society 1992–; Dir. Cttee. for Comprehensive Survey of Natural Resources; Fellow Third World Acad. of Sciences 1987; mem. Gen. Cttee. of ICSU 1990; mem. Div. of Earth Sciences, Chinese Acad. of Sciences Jan. 1992–; mem. Standing Cttee. of 8th Nat. People's Congress 1993–, mem. Credentials Cttee., Environmental and Resources Protection Cttee.; mem. 21st Century Cttee. for China–Japan Friendship; Special Prize, Chinese Acad. of Sciences 1986; First Prize, State Natural Sciences Awards 1987; Chen Jiagen Prize 1989. *Publications:* The Soil of Heilongjiang River Valley 1960, The Land Resources Assessment of North-East China, Inner Mongolia and West China 1966, The Soils of Tibet 1970, Land Types of Qinghai-Tibet Plateau and the Principles of Agricultural Assessment 1980, Land Resources and Agricultural Utilization in Tibet Autonomous Region, Mountain Research and Development 1983, Integrated Scientific Survey on Tibetan Plateau (series) 1983–89. *Leisure interest:* photography. *Address:* Chinese Academy of Sciences, 52 Sanlihe Road, Beijing 100864, People's Republic of China. *Telephone:* 3297235.

SUN JIAZHENG; Chinese politician; b. 1944, Siyang Co., Jiangsu Prov.; ed. Nanjing Univ.; joined CCP 1966, mem. 14th CCP Cen. Cttee. 1992–97, 15th CCP Cen. Cttee. 1997–; Minister of Radio, Film and TV 1994–98; Minister of Culture 1998–; Hon. Chair. Bd. of Dirs. Beijing Film Coll. *Address:* Ministry of Culture, Jia 83, Donganmen Bei Jie, Dongcheng Qu, Beijing 100701, People's Republic of China.

SUN QI; Chinese politician; b. 1930, Changtu Co., Liaoning; joined CCP 1949; Vice-Gov. Liaoning Prov. 1983–84; mem. Standing Cttee. and Deputy Sec. Liaoning Prov. CCP Cttee. 1985–86, Deputy Sec. CPC 7th Liaoning Prov. Cttee. 1986–; Chair. CPPCC 7th Liaoning Prov. Cttee. 1993–; alt. mem. CCP Cen. Cttee. 1987–; Deputy for Liaoning Prov., 7th NPC 1988; Chair. Cttee. for Comprehensive Man. and Social Security 1991–; Sec. Political Science and Law Cttee. 1991–. *Address:* Central Committee of the Chinese Communist Party, Zhongnanhai, Beijing, People's Republic of China.

SUN QIMENG; Chinese party official; b. 1911, Xiuning Co., Anhui Prov.; ed. Dept. of Political Science, Dongwu Univ.; Pres. Cen. Cttee. China Democratic Nat. Construction Asscn. 1987–96, Hon. Pres. 1997–; Vice-Chair. Standing Cttee. 7th NPC 1988–92, 8th NPC 1993–98. *Address:* c/o Standing Committee, National People's Congress, 19 Xi-Jiaomin Xiang Road, Xicheng District, Beijing 100805, People's Republic of China.

SUN WEIBEN; Chinese politician; b. 1928, Yingkou Co., Liaoning; joined CCP 1947; alt. mem. 12th CCP Cen. Cttee. 1982, mem. 1985, mem. 13th Cen. Cttee. 1987–92, 14th Cen. Cttee. 1992–; Sec. CCP Cttee., Liaoning Prov. 1983–85; Chair. Heilongjiang 7th Provincial People's Congress Standing Cttee. 1988, 8th Cttee. 1993–; 1st Sec. Party Cttee., PLA Heilongjiang Provincial Command 1985–94; Ed.-in-Chief Dictionary of Party Affairs of the CCP June 1989–. *Address:* Heilongjiang Provincial 8th People's Congress, Heilongjiang, People's Republic of China.

SUN WEIYAN; Chinese economist; b. 1937, Cixi, Zhejiang Prov.; ed. Beijing Foreign Trade Inst.; Pres. Univ. of Int. Business ands Econs. 1984–. *Publications:* A Handbook of International Commerce and Trade (Chief Ed.), Multi-National Management Encyclopaedia for Chinese Enterprises (Chief Ed.). *Address:* University of International Business and Economics, Huixin Dong Jie, Beijing 100029, People's Republic of China.

SUN WENSHENG; Chinese government official; b. Feb. 1942, Weihai City, Shandong Prov.; ed. Shandong Metallurgical Inst.; joined CCP 1966; workshop dir. Zhuzhou Smeltery 1963–81, Deputy Dir. 1981–83; Sec. CCP Zhuzhou City Cttee. 1983; Vice-Dir. Org. Dept. CCP Hunan Prov. Cttee., CCP 1984, Dir. 1985, Vice-Sec. 1989; alt. mem. 12th CCP Cen. Cttee. 1985–, 13th CCP Cen. Cttee. 1987, 14th CCP Cen. Cttee. 1992; Vice-Sec. CCP Shanxi Prov. Cttee., Vice-Gov., Acting Gov. of Shanxi Prov. 1993, Gov. 1994–98; mem. 15th CCP Cen. Cttee. 1997–. *Address:* c/o Office of the Governor, Shanxi Provincial Government, 101 Fudong Street, Taiyuan City, Shanxi Province, People's Republic of China.

SUN YING; Chinese politician; b. Nov. 1936, Baodi Co., Tianjin City; joined CCP 1956; ed. Shanxi Teachers College 1958; Sec. CCP Taiyuan City Cttee.; Vice-Sec. CCP Gansu Provincial Cttee. 1992–98, Sec. 1998–; Gov. Gansu Prov. 1997–98; mem. 15th CCP Cen. Cttee. 1997–. *Address:* Gansu Provincial Government, Lanzhou, Gansu Province, People's Republic of China.

SUN YUN-SUAN, B.S.; Chinese politician and engineer; b. 11 Nov. 1913, Penglai, Shantung; m. Yu Hui-hsuan 1947; two s. two d.; ed. Harbin Polytechnic Inst.; engineer with Nat. Resource Comm. 1937–40; Supt. Tienshui Electric Power Plant 1940–43; Training Engineer Tenn. Valley Authority, U.S.A. 1943–45; Head Engineer, Electrical and Mechanical Dept., Taiwan Power Co. 1946–50, Chief Engineer 1950–62, Vice-Pres. 1953–62, Pres. 1962–64; C.E.O. and Gen. Man. Electricity Corpn. of Nigeria 1964–67; Minister of Communications 1967–69, of Econ. Affairs 1969–78; Premier of Taiwan 1978–84; Sr. Adviser to the Pres. 1984–; Fellow Int. Acad. of Man. 1983; Cravat of the Order of Brilliant Star 1952; Eng. Award of the Chinese Inst. of Engineers 1954. *Leisure interests:* reading, classical music, sports. *Address:* 7th Floor, 106 Ho Ping E. Road, Sector 2, Taipei, Taiwan.

SUNADA, Shigetami; Japanese politician; ed. Rikkyo Univ.; mem. House of Reps., Hyogo Pref. 8th term; Chair. Nat. Org. Cttee., Liberal Democratic Party (LDP), Research Comm. on Election System LDP, Cttee. on the Budget; fmr. Minister of Educ.; Dir.-Gen., Hokkaido Devt. Agency and Okinawa Devt. Agency, Minister of State 1990. *Address:* c/o Hokkaido Development Agency, 3-1-1, Kasumigaseki, Chiyoda-ku, Tokyo, Japan.

SUNDERLAND, Eric, LL.D., PH.D., F.I.BIOL.; British anthropologist and fmr. university vice-chancellor; b. 18 March 1930, Ammanford, Carmarthenshire; s. of Leonard Sunderland and Mary Agnes Davies; m. Jean Patricia Watson 1957; two d.; ed. Univ. of Wales, Univ. Coll. London; Prof. of Anthropology, Univ. of Durham 1971–84, Pro-Vice-Chancellor 1979–84; Prin. Univ. Coll. of N. Wales, Bangor 1984–94, Vice-Chancellor 1994–95; Vice-Chancellor Univ. of Wales 1989–91, Emer. Prof. 1995–; Sec.-Gen. Int. Union of Anthropological and Ethnological Sciences (IUAES) 1978–98, Pres. 1998–(2003); Pres. Royal Anthropological Inst., London 1989–91; Chair. of Dirs. Gregynog Press 1991–; Chair. Local Govt. Boundary Comm. for Wales 1994–(2000), Bd. Wales Cttee.; mem. Bd. British Council, Chair. 1996; mem. B.B.C. Broadcasting Council for Wales 1995–(2000); Chair. Environment Agency Advisory Cttee. for Wales 1996–(99); High Sheriff of Gwynedd 1998–(99); D.L.; Pres. Univ. of Wales, Lampeter 1998–(2001); Hon. mem. Gorsedd of Bards, Royal Nat. Eisteddfod of Wales; Hon. Fellow, Univ. of Wales, Lampeter, Univ. of Wales, Bangor; Gold Medal of IUAES, Zagreb XIIth Int. Congress 1988. *Publications:* Elements of Human and Social Geography—Some Anthropological Perspectives 1973, Genetic Variation in Britain (Co-Ed.) 1973, The Exercise of Intelligence; biological pre-conditions for the operation of intelligence (Co-Ed.) 1980, Genetic and Population Studies in Wales (Co-Ed.) 1986. *Leisure interests:* travelling, book collecting, gardening, paintings. *Address:* Faculty of Health Studies, University of Wales-Bangor, Bangor, Gwynedd LL57 2EF (Office); Y Bryn, Ffriddoedd Road, Bangor, Gwynedd, LL57 2EH, Wales (Home). *Telephone:* (01248) 353265. *Fax:* (01248) 355043.

SUNDLUN, Bruce George, LL.B.; American politician; b. 19 Jan. 1920, Providence, R.I.; s. of Walter I. Sundlun and Jane Z. Colitz; m. 2nd Marjorie G. Lee 1985; three s. three d. by previous m.; ed. Williams Coll., Harvard Univ. and Air Command and Staff School; served to Capt. U.S.A.A.F 1942–45; admitted Bars of R.I. and D.C. 1949; Asst. U.S. Attorney, Washington, D.C. 1949–51; special asst. to U.S. Attorney-Gen. 1951–54; partner, Amram, Hahn & Sundlun, Washington, D.C. 1954–72, Sundlun, Tirana & Scher 1972–76; Vice-Pres., Dir. and Gen. Counsel, Outlet Co., Providence 1960–76, Pres. and C.E.O. 1976–84, Chair. Bd. and C.E.O. 1984–91; Pres. Exec. Jet Aviation Inc., Columbus, O. 1970–76, Chair. of Bd. 1976–84; Dir. Questech Inc. 1972–91; Incorporator, Dir. Communications Satellite Corpn. 1962–91; Dir. Hal Roach Studios Inc. 1986–91; numerous other public appts.; del. Democratic Nat. Convention 1964, 1968, 1980, 1990, R.I. Constitutional Convention 1985; Gov. of Rhode Island 1990–95; D.F.C.; Air medal with oak leaf cluster; Purple Heart; Chevalier, Légion d'honneur; Prime Minister's Medal (Israel); Hon. D.S.B.A. (Bryant Coll.) 1980; Hon. D.B.A. (Roger Williams Coll.) 1980. *Address:* 191 Carroll Avenue, Newport, RI 02840, U.S.A. (Home).

SUNDQUIST, Donald Kenneth (Don), B.A.; American politician and business executive; b. 15 March 1936, Moline, Ill.; s. of Kenneth Sundquist and Louise Rohren; m. Martha Swanson 1959; one s. two d.; ed. Augustana Coll. Rock Island, Ill.; Div. Man. Josten's Inc. 1961–72; Exec. Vice-Pres. Graphic Sales of America, Memphis 1973, Pres. 1973–82; mem. 98th–103rd Congresses from 7th Tenn. Dist. 1983–95; Gov. of Tennessee Jan. 1995–; Republican. *Address:* Office of the Governor, State Capitol Building, Nashville TN 37243, U.S.A. *Telephone:* (615) 741-2001. *Fax:* (615) 741-1416.

SUNDQVIST, Ulf Ludvig, M.POL.SC.; Finnish business consultant and fmr. politician; b. 22 Feb. 1945, Sipoo; s. of Karl Eric Sundqvist and Helga Linnea Lönnkvist; m. Eine Kristiina Joki 1969; one s. one d.; ed. Univ. of Helsinki; Asst. Lecturer, Faculty of Political Science, Helsinki Univ. 1968–70; mem. Parl. 1970–83; Minister of Educ. 1972–75, of Trade and Industry 1979–81; Gen. Sec. Finnish Social Democratic Party 1975–81, Chair. 1991–93; mem. Supervisory Bd. Neste Ltd. 1970–, Chair. 1976–94; Deputy Chief Gen. Man. STS-Bank Ltd. 1981, Chief Gen. Man. 1982–91, mem. Bd. 1992–94; pvt. consultant 1993–; Hon. Ph.D. (Kuopio). *Leisure interests:* music, literature. *Address:* Ergo Consult, Mikonkatu 2D, 00100 Helsinki, Finland.

SUNGURLU, Mahmut Oltan; Turkish politician; b. 1936, Gümüşhane; m.; one c.; ed. Bursa Lycée, Istanbul Univ.; practised law in Gümüşhane; f. Motherland Party prov. org. in Gümüşhane; Deputy for Gümüşhane 1983–; Minister of Justice 1986–87, 1987–88, 1989–92, 1997–98; Deputy Chair. Motherland Party June 1988. *Address:* c/o Ministry of Justice, Adalet Bakanlığı, Bakanlıklar, Ankara, Turkey.

SUNTRANGKOON, Gen. Prachuab; Thai army officer and politician; b. 4 April 1920, Sukhothai; m. Khunying Pimpa; one s. one d.; ed. Mil. Acad. (now Chulachomklao Royal Mil. Acad.), Bangkok Metropolis and Cavalry School, Royal Thai Army, Ground Gen. School, Fort Riley and Armour School, Fort Knox, U.S.A., Nat. Defence Coll.; rank of Col. 1957; Dir. Port Authority of Thailand 1959–72; Maj.-Gen., Chief Cavalry Div. 1962–69; Lieut.-Gen., Army Adviser 1969–72; Deputy Dir.-Gen. Police Dept., with rank of Police Lieut.-Gen. 1972, Dir.-Gen., then Police Gen.; Deputy Minister of Communications 1973–74; Deputy Minister of Interior 1974–75; attached to Office of Supreme Commdr. of Armed Forces, with rank of Army Gen.; Deputy Prime Minister 1981–86; Minister of Interior 1986–88. *Address:* c/o Ministry of the Interior, Atasadang Road, Bangkok 10200, Thailand.

SUNUNU, John H., PH.D.; American politician; b. 2 July 1939, Havana, Cuba; m. Nancy Hayes 1958; five s. three d.; founder, Chief Engineer Astro Dynamics 1960–65; Pres. J.H.S. Eng. Co. and Thermal Research Inc., Salem, N.H. 1965–82; Assoc. Prof. Mechanical Eng., Tufts Univ. 1966–82, Assoc. Dean Coll. of Eng. 1968–73; mem. N.H. House of Reps. 1973–74, Govt. Energy Council; Chair. Govt. Council on N.H. Future 1977–78; mem. Govt. Advisory Cttee. on Science and Tech. 1977–78; Gov. State of N.H. Concord 1983–89; Chair. coalition of N.E. Govs. 1985–86; White House Chief of Staff 1989–91, Counsellor to the Pres. 1991–92; Chair. Task force on Tech.; Pres. JHS Assoc. Ltd. 1992; Vice-Chair. Alliance for Acid Rain Control; Chair. Republican Gov.'s Asscn., New England Gov.'s Asscn.; Vice-Chair. Advisory Comm. on Intergovt. Relations. *Address:* 24 Samoset Drive, Salem, NH 03079, U.S.A.

SUNYAYEV, Rashid Aliyevich; Russian astrophysicist; b. 1 March 1943; m.; three s. one d.; ed. Moscow Inst. of Physics and Tech.; jr., sr. researcher Inst. of Applied Math. U.S.S.R. Acad. of Sciences; head of div., head of dept. Inst. of Space Studies U.S.S.R. Acad. of Sciences; Scientific Head Int. Orbital Observatory ROENTGEN on complex space station Mir, Orbital Observatory GRANAT; corresp. mem. U.S.S.R. (now Russian) Acad. of Sciences 1984, mem. 1992; research in high energy astrophysics, cosmology, theoretical astrophysics, X-ray astronomy; Foreign mem. U.S.A. Nat. Acad. of Sciences, mem. European Acad. of Sciences, mem. Int. Acad. of Astronautics, Adjunct Prof. Columbia Univ. (U.S.A.); Bruno Rossi Prize. *Publications:* Black Holes in Double Systems 1973, Observation of Relict Irradiation as Method of Studying the Nature of X-ray Irradiation of Galaxy Clusters 1973, Comptonization of X-ray Irradiation in Plasma Clouds: characteristic spectra 1980, numerous articles. *Address:* Institute of Space Studies, Russian Academy of Sciences, Profsoyuznaya str. 84/32, 117910 Moscow, Russia. *Telephone:* (095) 333 3373 (Office); (095) 331 3805 (Home). *Fax:* (095) 233 5377.

SUOMINEN, Ilkka Olavi, M.POL.SC.; Finnish business executive and fmr. politician; b. 8 April 1939, Nakkila; s. of Leo Suominen and Anna Suominen; m. Riitta Suhonen 1977; one s. two d.; Dept. Head, J. W. Suominen Oy 1960–72, Deputy Man. Dir. 1972–74, Man. Dir. 1975–79, mem. Man. Bd. 1982–; mem. Parl. 1970–75, 1983–94; Leader Nat. Coalition Party 1979–91; Vice-Chair. European Democrat Union 1986–93; Speaker of Parl. 1987, 1991–96; Minister of Trade and Industry 1987–91; Pres. CSCE Parl. Ass. 1992–94; Chair. Admin. Bd. Oy Alko AB 1980–88, 1991–94, Gen. Man. 1994–; Chair. Bd. of Dirs. ICL Data (Finland) 1992–; Vice-Chair. Confed. of Finnish Industries 1978–79. *Leisure interests:* hunting, fishing. *Address:* Oy Alko AB, P.O. Box 350, 001021 Helsinki, Finland.

SUONIO, Kaarina Elisabet; Finnish politician, lawyer and psychologist; b. 7 Feb. 1941, Helsinki; d. of Prof. Karl Otto Brusiin and Ulla Helena Raassina; m. 1st Reino Kalevi 1961; m. 2nd Kÿosti Kullervo Suonio 1967; one s. one d.; psychologist, Inst. of Occupational Health 1963–71; Researcher, Ministry of Justice 1971–75; mem. Helsinki City Council 1973–; M.P. 1975–86; Alt. mem. Exec. Finnish Social Democratic Party 1981–84; Second Minister of Educ. (Minister of Culture and Science) 1982–83, Minister of Educ. 1983–86; Deputy Mayor of Tampere 1986–94; Gov. Province of Häme 1994–; Man. Dir. Tampere Hall Conf. and Concert Centre 1997–. *Address:* Tampere Hall, c/o Box 16, 33101 Tampere, Finland. *Fax:* (03) 2434199.

SUPEK, Ivan, D.SC.; Croatian scientist and author; b. 8 April 1915, Zagreb; ed. Zagreb Univ., studied in Zurich and Leipzig with W. Heisenberg; arrested by Gestapo 1941; Prof. Zagreb Univ. 1946–; founder of R. Boskovic Inst. 1950; mem. Croatian Acad. of Sciences and Arts 1960; f. Inst. of Sciences and Arts 1961–; Ed. Encyclopedia Moderna 1966; Rector Zagreb Univ. 1969; f. Interuniv. Cen. in Dubrovnik 1970; banned from public life due to nationalist activities 1971, ban later lifted. *Publications:* Scientific Theoretical Physics and Structure of Matter, Superbomb and Crisis of Conscience 1962, Cognition 1971, Philosophy of Science and Humanism 1979, History of Physics 1980; novels: Heretic 1969, Rebellion of Janus Pannonius 1990; plays: Mirakul 1965, Heretic 1968. *Address:* Hrvatska Akademija Znanosti i Umetnosti, Zringjski trg 11, 41000 Zagreb, Croatia (Office).

SUPINIT, Vijit; Thai banker; ed. Manchester Univ., U.K. and in U.S.A.; mem. staff Econ. Research Dept., Bank of Thailand, subsequently dept. Dir., then Head of Banking Policy, Deputy Gov. March–Sept. 1990, Gov. Sept. 1990. *Address:* c/o Bank of Thailand, P.O. Box 154, 273 Samsen Road, Bangkunprom, Bangkok 10020, Thailand.

SUPPES, Patrick, B.S., PH.D.; American educationist; b. 17 March 1922, Tulsa, Okla.; m. 1st Joan Farmer 1946 (divorced 1970), one s. two d.; m. 2nd Joan Elizabeth Sieber 1970 (divorced 1973); m. 3rd Christine Johnson 1979, one s. one d.; ed. Univ. of Chicago and Columbia Univ.; mem. faculty Stanford Univ. 1950–, Prof. of Phil., Statistics Educ. and Psychology, Dir. Inst. for Mathematical Studies in the Social Sciences 1959–92; Pres. Computer Curriculum Corpn. 1967–90; Fellow A.A.A.S., American Psychological Asscn.; mem. Nat. Acad. of Educ. (Pres. 1973–77), American Acad. of Arts and Sciences, Finnish Acad. of Science and Letters, N.A.S., European Acad. of Sciences and Arts; Corresp. mem. Yugoslav Acad. of Sciences and Arts 1990; Foreign mem. U.S.S.R. (now Russian) Acad. of Pedagogical Sciences, Norwegian Acad. of Science and Letters; Hon. mem. Chilean Acad. of Sciences; Dr. h.c. (Social Sciences) (Nijmegen) 1979; Dr. h.c., Acad. de Paris, Univ. René Descartes 1982; Palmer O. Johnson Memorial Award, American Educational Research Asscn. 1967; Distinguished Scientific Contribution Award, American Psychological Asscn. 1972; Columbia Univ. Teachers College Medal for Distinguished Service 1978, E. L. Thorndike Award for Distinguished Psychological Contribution to Educ., American Psychological Asscn. 1979; Nat. Medal of Science 1990. *Publications:* Introduction to Logic 1957, Decision Making: An Experimental Approach (with D. Davidson and S. Siegel) 1957, Axiomatic Set Theory 1960, Markov Learning Models for Multiperson Interactions (with R. C. Atkinson) 1960, First Course in Mathematical Logic (with S. Hill) 1964, Experiments in Second-Language Acquisition (with E. Crothers) 1967, Computer Assisted Instruction: Stanford's 1965–66 Arithmetic Program (with M. Jerman and D. Brian) 1968, Studies in the Methodology and Foundations of Science 1970, A Probabilistic Theory of Causality 1970, Foundations of Measurement (with D. Krantz, R. D. Luce, A. Tversky) Vol. I 1971, Vol. II 1989, Vol. III 1990, Computer-assisted Instruction at Stanford, 1966–68 (with M. Morningstar); Probabilistic Metaphysics 1974, The Radio Mathematics Project: Nicaragua 1974–1975 (with B. Searle and J. Friend) 1976, Logique du Probable 1981, Estudios de Filosofía y Metodología de la Ciencia 1988, Language for Humans and Robots 1991, Models and Methods in the Philosophy of Science 1993, Language and Learning for Robots (with C. Crangle) 1994, Foundations of Probability with Applications (with M. Zanotti) 1996, and over 300 articles in professional journals. *Address:* 678 Mirada Avenue, Stanford, CA 94305, U.S.A.

SUPPLE, Barry Emanuel, PH.D., F.R.HIST.S., F.B.A.; British professor of economic history; b. 27 Oct. 1930; s. of Solomon Supple and Rose Supple; m. Sonia Caller 1958; two s. one d.; ed. Hackney Downs Grammar School, L.S.E. and Christ's Coll. Cambridge; Asst. Prof. of Business History, Grad. School of Business Admin., Harvard Univ., U.S.A. 1955–60; Assoc. Prof. of Econ. History, McGill Univ. 1960–62; Lecturer in Econ. and Social History, Univ. of Sussex, Reader, then Prof. 1962–78, Dean, School of Social Sciences 1965–68, Pro-Vice-Chancellor (Arts and Social Studies) 1968–72, Pro-Vice-

Chancellor 1978; Reader in Recent Social and Econ. History, Univ. of Oxford 1978–81, Professorial Fellow, Nuffield Coll. 1978–81; Prof. of Econ. History Univ. of Cambridge 1981–93, Prof. Emer. 1993–, Professorial Fellow, Christ's Coll. 1981–83, Hon. Fellow 1984; Master of St. Catharine's Coll., Cambridge 1984–93, Hon. Fellow 1993; Dir. Leverhulme Trust 1993–; Pres. Econ. History Soc. 1992–95, Foreign Sec. British Acad. 1995–; mem. Social Science Fellowship Cttee., Nuffield Foundation 1974–94; Hon. Fellow Worcester Coll., Oxford 1986; Co-Ed. Econ. History Review 1973–82; Hon. D.Litt. (Sussex) 1998. *Publications:* Commercial Crisis and Change in England, 1600–42, 1959, The Experience of Economic Growth (Ed.) 1963, Boston Capitalists and Western Railroads 1967, The Royal Exchange Assurance: a history of British insurance 1720–1970, 1970, Essays in Business History (Ed.) 1977, History of the British Coal Industry, Vol. IV (1914–46), The Political Economy of Decline 1987, The State and Economic Knowledge: the American and British Experience (ed.) 1990, The Rise of Big Business (ed.) 1992, articles and reviews in learned journals. *Leisure interests:* tennis, photography. *Address:* Leverhulme Trust, 15–19 New Fetter Lane, London, EC4A 1NR, England. *Telephone:* 0171-822 6938.

SUQUÍA GOICOECHEA, H.E. Cardinal Angel; Spanish ecclesiastic; b. 2 Oct. 1916, Zaldivia, San Sebastián; ordained 1940; consecrated Bishop of Almería 1966, of Málaga 1969; Archbishop of Santiago de Compostela 1973, of Madrid 1983, Archbishop Emer. 1994–; cr. Cardinal 1985; mem. Congregation for Catholic Educ., Congregation for the Bishops, and several others. *Address:* c/o Javier de Barcaiztegui No. 7, 3°, 20010 San Sebastián, Spain.

SURÁNYI, György, PH.D, DR. ECON.; Hungarian economist; b. 3 Jan. 1954, Budapest; m.; two c.; ed. Univ. of Econ., Budapest, Hungarian Acad. of Sciences; Research Fellow, Head of Dept. Financial Research Inst. Budapest 1977–86; Consultant World Bank, Washington 1986–87; Counsellor to Deputy Prime Minister, Council of Ministers 1988–89; Sec. of State, Nat. Planning Office 1989–90; Pres. Nat. Bank of Hungary 1990–91; Man. Dir. Cent. European Int. Bank Ltd. 1992–95; Pres. Nat. Bank of Hungary 1995–. *Publications:* author of several articles and books on monetary and financial issues. *Address:* Magyar Nemzeti Bank, H-1850 Budapest, Szabadság tér 8/9, Hungary. *Telephone:* 302-3000. *Fax:* 332-3913.

SUREAU, Claude, M.D.; French obstetrician and gynaecologist; b. 27 Sept. 1927, Paris; s. of Maurice Sureau and Rita Jullian; m. Janine Murset 1956; one s. two d.; ed. Paris Univ.; Visiting Fellow, Columbia Presbyterian Medical Center 1955–56; Asst. Prof., Paris Univ. 1956–61, Assoc. Prof. 1961–74; Prof. and Chair., Dept. of Obstetrics and Gynaecology, St. Vincent de Paul Hosp., Paris 1974–76, Univ. Clinique Baudelocque 1976–89; Pres., Int. Fed. of Obstetricians and Gynaecologists 1982–85, Pres., Standing Cttee. on Ethical Aspects of Human Reproduction 1985–94; Pres. European Asscn. of Gynaecology and Obstetrics 1988–91; Dir. Unit 262, Physiology and Physiopathology of Reproduction, Nat. Inst. of Health and Medical Research 1983–90; Active Staff mem. American Hosp. of Paris 1989–93, Chief of Gynaecological Unit 1990–93, Medical Dir. American Hosp. of Paris 1994–95; Pres. Theramex Inst. 1996–; mem. Nat. Acad. of Medicine of France 1978–, Pres. (elect) 1999; Officier, Légion d'honneur 1989; Commdr. Ordre nat. du Mérite. *Publications:* Le Danger de Naître 1978, Ethical Dilemmas in Assisted Reproduction 1996, Alice au pays des clones 1999; Co-Ed.: Clinical Perinatology 1980, Immunologie de la Réproduction Humaine 1983, Aux Débuts de la Vie 1990, Ethical Aspects of Human Reproduction 1995. *Address:* 147 Avenue de Malakoff, 75116 Paris, France. *Telephone:* (1) 45-02-19-70. *Fax:* (1) 45-02-19-80.

SURJÁN, László, M.D., PH.D.; Hungarian politician and physician; b. 7 Sept. 1941, Kolozsvár (now Cluj, Romania); s. of László Surján and Margit (née Göttinger) Surján; m. Zsófia Stverteczky 1966; one s. two d.; ed. Roman Catholic Theologic Acad. Semmelweis Univ. Medical School, Budapest; specialist in pathology 1973; lecturer Semmelweis Medical Univ. 1969–70, Postgrad. Medical School 1970–90; mem. numerous socs.; joined Hungarian Christian Democratic Party (Pres. 1990–95); mem. Hungarian Parl. 1990–; Minister of Welfare 1990–94; Pres. Employment and Labour Affairs Cttee. of Parl. 1994–98; Head Hungarian Del. to Parl. Ass. of Council of Europe and Vice-Chair. Foreign Affairs Cttee. 1998–; Chair. WHO Regional Cttee. for Europe 1992–93; Vice-Chair. European Union of Christian Democrats. *Publications:* author of 48 scientific publs. *Address:* Parlamenti Hivatal, Széchenyi rkp. 19, 1054 Budapest, Hungary. *Telephone:* (1) 2685886. *Fax:* (1) 2685464.

SURLYK, Finn C., PH.D.; Danish professor of geology; b. 17 March 1943, Copenhagen; s. of C. Surlyk and K. Surlyk; m. Nanna Noe-Nygaard; two s.; Adjunct Prof. Univ. of Copenhagen 1968–69, Assoc. Prof. 1969–80, Prof. 1984–; Head Dept. of Oil Geology, Geological Survey of Greenland, Copenhagen 1981–84; Gen.-Sec. Int. Asscn. of Sedimentologists 1986–94; Gold Medal, Univ. of Copenhagen 1969. *Publications:* over 100 papers, particularly on the geology of Greenland. *Leisure interests:* jazz, bass-playing, outdoor life. *Address:* Geological Institute, Øster Voldgade 10, 1350 Copenhagen K (Office); Islandsvej 11, 2800 Lyngby, Denmark (Home). *Telephone:* 35322453 (Office); 45877209 (Home). *Fax:* 33148322 (Office).

SURTEES, John, M.B.E.; British racing motorcyclist and driver; b. 11 Feb. 1934, Tatsfield, Surrey; s. of Jack Surtees; m. Jane Sparrow 1987; one s. two d.; ed. Ashburton Secondary School, London; began motorcycle road racing 1949, 350 c.c. World Champion 1958, 1959 and 1960, 500 c.c. World Champion 1956, 1958, 1959 and 1960; began car racing 1960, World Champion 1964, runner-up 1966, CanAm Champion 1966. *Grand Prix wins:* 1963 German (Ferrari), 1964 German (Ferrari), 1964 Italian (Ferrari), 1966 Belgian (Ferrari), 1966 Mexican (Cooper-Maserati), 1967 Italian (Honda); retd. 1972; now motor sport and eng. consultant. *Leisure interests:* restoration of period property, Grand Prix motor cycles and cars, antiques, food and wine. *Address:* Team Surtees Ltd., Monza House, Fircroft Way, Edenbridge, Kent, TN8 6EJ, England. *Telephone:* (01732) 865496. *Fax:* (01732) 866945.

SUSCHITZKY, Wolfgang, B.SC.; British cameraman and photographer (retd.); b. 29 Aug. 1912, Vienna, Austria; m. three times; two s. one d.; ed. Graphische Lehr- und Versuchsanstalt Vienna; started in documentary films with Paul Rotha 1937; first feature film No Resting Place 1950; freelance cameraman, mainly on commercials; exhbns. London 1982, 1988, 1989, 1997, Amsterdam 1982; mem. British Soc. of Cinematographers; mem. BAFTA; Hon. mem. Asscn. of Cinematograph, Television and Allied Technicians, Royal Photographic Soc. *Publications:* Photographing Animals 1941, Photographing Children 1942, Kingdom of the Beasts (with Julian Huxley) 1956. *Leisure interests:* photography, film, music, literature. *Address:* Flat 11, Douglas House, 6 Maida Avenue, London, W2 1TG, England. *Telephone:* 0171-723 6269.

SUSHCHENYA, Leonid Mikhailovich, D.BIOL.SC.; Belarus scientist; b. 11 Nov. 1929, Maly Luky, Brest Region; ed. Belarus Univ.; m. Nina Nikolayevna Khmeleva; three c.; Asst. Prof. Byelorussian State Univ., Minsk 1956–59; Sr. researcher, Inst. of Biology of Southern Seas, Ukrainian Acad. of Sciences 1959–67, Head of Div. of Marine Animal Physiology 1967–71; Head of Div., Dir. Inst. of Zoology, Belarus Acad. of Sciences, 1971–95, Academician Sec., Div. of Biological Sciences 1979–92, Head of Div., Hon. Dir. Inst. of Zoology 1995–; Pres. Belarus Acad. of Sciences 1992–; Vice-Pres. Int. Asscn. of Acads. of Sciences of C.I.S. and other cos. 1996–; Ed.-in-Chief Doklady Akademii nauk Belarusi; mem. Belarus and U.S.S.R. (now Russian) Acads. of Sciences; mem. Int. Soc. of Limnology, Hydrobiological Socs. of Belarus and Russia (Hon. Pres. –1989); mem. Peace Cttee. (Chair. Environmental Protection section); mem. All European Acads. Ass.; Foreign mem. Polish and Lithuanian Acads. of Sciences 1994; represents Belarus in ICSU; Hon. Scientist of Repub. of Belarus 1978; Hon. Awards of Supreme Soviet of Repub. of Belarus 1979, 1994; Order of People's Friendship 1986, Order of Red Banner of Labour 1989. *Publications:* more than 190 articles on hydrobiology, gen. ecology, ecology of animals and environment, including monographs Respiration of Crustacea 1972, Quantitative Regularities of Crustacea Feeding 1975, Growth of Water Animals at Changing Temperatures 1978, Fundamentals of Rational Use of Nature 1980, Biology and Products of Ice-age Relic Crayfish 1985, Ecology of Animals in the Radioactive Contaminated Zone 1993. *Leisure interests:* travelling, reading, music. *Address:* Presidium of the Academy of Sciences of Belarus, Prospekt F. Skoriny 66, 220072 Minsk (Office); 15 fl. 41 Kulman Street, 220100 Minsk, Belarus (Home). *Telephone:* (3752) 39-32-54, (3752) 68-46-72 (Office); (02) 34-44-05 (Home). *Fax:* (3752) 39-31-63.

SÜSKIND, Patrick; German author; b. 1949; fmr. writer for TV. *Publications:* Perfume: the Story of a Murderer (novel), The Double Bass, The Pigeon, Three stories and a Reflection. *Address:* c/o Diogenes Verlag AG, Sprecherstr. 8, 8032 Zürich, Switzerland. *Telephone:* (01) 254 8511. *Fax:* (01) 252 8407.

SÜSSENGUTH, Hans, DIPL.ING.; German aviation executive; b. 8 Sept. 1913, Neustadt/Coburg; s. of Franz H. and Rosalie Süssenguth; m. Christa Reischel 1942; one s. one d.; ed. Oberrealschule, Coburg and Tech. Hochschule, Darmstadt; Technician in Research and Devt. and Maintenance and Operations Depts. Deutsche Lufthansa A.G., Berlin 1939–45; Engineer in father-in-law's business 1945–50; Engineer at Gummi-Werke Fulda 1950–52; rejoined Lufthansa in Eng. Div., Hamburg 1952, Tech. Dir. 1954, Head of Traffic Division 1958, Deputy mem. Exec. Bd. 1959, mem. 1963–, responsible for sales, worldwide field org., in-flight services and marketing, retd. June 1978, mem. Bd. Deutsche Lufthansa AG June 1978–; Chair. Advisory Bd., Berlin Penta Hotelgesellschaft, DSG-Deutsche Schlafwagen- und Speisewagen GmbH Frankfurt, AMK-Ausstellungs-Messe-Kongress GmbH, Berlin; mem. Exec. Bd. and Vice-Pres., German Tourist Bd.; mem. Advisory Bd., Hansa Luftbild GmbH, Münster, Deutscher Aerokurier, Cologne; mem. Bd. of Trustees, Hessian Inst. for Aviation; mem. Chartered Inst. of Air Transport, London; Dir. START-Datentechnik für Reise und Touristik GmbH, Frankfurt; Hon. Consul Repub. of Togo; Hon. Prof. Technische Univ., Berlin; Grosses Bundesverdienstkreuz 1978. *Address:* 61476 Kronberg, Taunusstrasse 2, Germany (Home). *Telephone:* (06173) 79538 (Home).

SÜSSMUTH, Rita, D.PHIL; German politician; b. 17 Feb. 1937, Wuppertal; m. Prof. Dr. Hans Sussmüth; one d.; ed. Univs. of Münster, Tübingen and Paris; Asst. Univs. of Stuttgart and Osnabrück 1963–66; lecturer, Coll. of Educ. Pädagogische Hochschule Ruhr 1966–69; Prof. Ruhr Univ. Bochum 1969; Prof. of Educ. Sciences, Pädagogische Hochschule Ruhr 1971, Univ. of Dortmund 1980; Dir. Research Inst. Frau und Gesellschaft (Women and Society), Hanover 1982; mem. Scientific Advisory Cttee. on Family Affairs, Fed. Ministry for Youth, Family Affairs and Health 1971–85 and many other cttees. on youth, marriage and family affairs; Fed. Chair. Christian Democratic Union (CDU) Women's Asscn. 1986; Fed. Minister for Youth, Family Affairs and Health 1985, for Youth, Family Affairs, Women and

Health 1986–88; mem. Bundestag 1987–; Pres. of Bundestag 1988–98; mem. Advisory Council, Bertelsmann Stiftung 1997–. *Publications:* Frauen: Der Resignation keine Chance 1985, Aids: Wege aus der Angst 1987, Kämpfen und Bewegen: Frauenreden 1989. *Leisure interest:* tennis. *Address:* Bundeshaus, 53113 Bonn, Germany.

SUTER, Albert Edward, B.M.E., M.B.A.; American business executive; b. 18 Sept. 1935, New Jersey; s. of Joseph V. Suter and Catherine Clay; m. Michaela S. Suter 1966; two s. one d.; ed. Cornell Univ.; Knight & Assocs., Chicago 1959–79, fmr. Pres. and C.E.O.; Vice-Chair. Emerson Electric Co., St. Louis, Mo. 1979–87; Pres. and C.O.O. Firestone Tire & Rubber Co., Akron, Ohio 1987–88; Pres. and C.O.O. Whirlpool Co. 1988–89; Pres. C.O.O. Emerson Electric Co. 1990–92, Sr. Vice-Chair., C.O.O. 1992–97, Sr. Vice-Chair., C.E.O. 1997–; Bd. Dirs. NationsBank Corpn. *Address:* Emerson Electric Co., P.O. Box 4100, Saint Louis, MO 63136, U.S.A.

SUTHERLAND, Donald McNichol, O.C.; Canadian actor; b. 17 July 1935, St. John, N.B.; s. of Frederick McLae and Dorothy Isabel (McNichol) Sutherland; m. 1st Lois May Hardwick 1959; m. 2nd Shirley Jean Douglas 1966 (divorced); one s. one d.; m. 3rd Francine Racette 1971; three s.; ed. Bridgewater, N.S., High School, Univ. of Toronto; TV Hallmark Hall of Fame; Officier, Ordre des Arts et des Lettres, Order of Canada; appeared on television (BBC and ITV) in Hamlet, Man in the Suitcase, The Saint, Gideon's Way, The Avengers, Flight into Danger, Rose Tattoo, March to the Sea, Lee Harvey Oswald, Court Martial, Death of Bessie Smith, Max Dugan Returns, Crackers, Louis Malle, The Disappearance. *Films include:* The World Ten Times Over 1963, Castle of the Living Dead 1964, Dr. Terror's House of Horrors 1965, Fanatic 1965, The Bedford Incident 1965, Promise Her Anything 1966, The Dirty Dozen 1967, Billion Dollar Brain 1967, Oedipus Rex 1968, Interlude 1968, Joanna 1968, The Split 1968, Start the Revolution Without Me 1969, Act of the Heart 1970, M*A*S*H* 1970, Kelly's Heroes 1970, Little Murders 1970, Alex in Wonderland 1971, Klute 1971, Johnny Got His Gun (as Christ) 1971, Steelyard Blues 1972, Lady Ice 1972, Alien Thunder 1973, Don't Look Now 1973, S*P*Y*S* 1974, The Day of the Locust 1975, 1900 1976, Casanova (Fellini) 1976, The Eagle Has Landed 1977, The Great Train Robbery 1978, Blood Relatives 1978, Bear Island 1979, Ordinary People 1980, Lolita 1981, Eye of the Needle 1981, Threshold 1982, Winter of Our Discontent, Ordeal by Innocence 1984, Revolution 1985, Gauguin 1986, The Wolf at the Door 1987, A Dry White Season 1988, Bethune: The Making of a Hero 1989, Lock Up 1989, Apprentice to Murder 1989, Lost Angels 1989, The Railway Station-man 1991, Scream from Stone 1991, Faithful 1991, JFK 1991, Backdraft, Agaguk, Buffy the Vampire Slayer, Shadow of the Wolf 1993, Benefit of the Doubt, Younger and Younger 1993, Six Degrees of Separation 1993, The Puppet Masters, Disclosure, Outbreak, Hollow Point, The Shadow Conspiracy, A Time to Kill, Virus 1999. *Play:* Lolita (Broadway) 1981; Pres. McNichol Pictures Inc.; Hon. Ph.D. *Leisure interests:* sailing, baseball, Montreal. *Address:* 760 N. La Cienega Boulevard, Los Angeles, CA 90069; PMK, c/o Katherine Olin, 955 Carrillo Drive, Los Angeles, CA 90048, U.S.A. *Telephone:* (213) 306-1633.

SUTHERLAND, Grant Robert, A.C., PH.D., F.R.S., F.A.A.; Australian geneticist; b. 2 June 1945, Bairnsdale, Victoria; s. of John Sutherland and Hazel Wilson Mason McClelland; m. Elizabeth Dougan 1979; one s. one d.; ed. Numurkah High School, Univs. of Melbourne and Edinburgh; Dir. Dept. of Cytogenetics and Molecular Genetics, Women's and Children's Hosp., Adelaide 1975; Affiliate Prof. Dept. of Paediatrics, Univ. of Adelaide 1991–, Dept. of Genetics 1998–; Int. Research Scholar Howard Hughes Medical Inst., Bethesda, Md. 1993–97; Pres. Human Genetics Soc. of Australasia 1989–91, Human Genome Org. 1996–97; Hon. Fellow Royal Coll. of Pathologists of Australasia 1994; co-recipient Australia Prize in Molecular Genetics 1998. *Publications include:* two books and over 400 papers in medical and scientific journals on human genetics. *Leisure interest:* beef cattle farming. *Address:* Department of Cytogenetics and Molecular Genetics, Women's and Children's Hospital, Adelaide, SA 5006; P.O. Box 300, Macclesfield, SA 5153, Australia. *Telephone:* (8) 8204 7284 (Adelaide); (8) 8388 9524 (Macclesfield). *Fax:* (8) 8204 7342 (Adelaide).

SUTHERLAND, James, C.B.E., M.A., LL.B., LL.D.; British lawyer; b. 15 Feb. 1920, Glasgow; s. of James Sutherland and Agnes Walker; m. 1st Elizabeth Kelly Barr 1948, 2nd Grace Williamson Dawson 1984; two s.; ed. Queens Park Secondary School, Glasgow and Glasgow Univ.; war service in Royal Signals 1940–46; partner McClure Naismith, Solicitors, Glasgow, Edin., London 1951–87, Consultant 1987–90; examiner, Glasgow Univ. 1951–55, 1968–69; Dean Royal Faculty of Procurators in Glasgow 1977–80; mem. Bd. of Man., Glasgow Maternity and Women's Hosps. 1964–74, Chair. 1966–74; mem. Council Law Soc. of Scotland 1959–77, Vice-Pres. 1969–70, Pres. 1972–74; mem. Council Int. Bar Asscn. 1972–88, Chair. Gen. Practice Section 1978–80, Sec.-Gen. 1980–84, Pres. 1984–86, Hon. mem. 1988–; mem. Gen. Dental Council 1975–89, Court Univ. of Strathclyde 1977–92, Scottish Dental Estimates Bd. 1982–87. *Leisure interest:* golf. *Address:* Greenacres, Easter Belmont Road, Edinburgh, EH12 6EX, Scotland. *Telephone:* (0131) 337 1888. *Fax:* (0131) 346-0067.

SUTHERLAND, Dame Joan, O.M., A.C., D.B.E.; Australian opera singer (retd.); b. 7 Nov. 1926, Sydney; d. of William McDonald Sutherland and Muriel Beatrice (née Alston) Sutherland; m. Richard Bonynge (q.v.) 1954; one s.; ed. St. Catherine's School, Waverley, Sydney; début as Dido in Purcell's Dido and Aeneas, Sydney 1947; Royal Opera Co., Covent Garden, London 1952–88; retd. from performing 1991. *Has sung leading soprano roles at:* the Vienna State Opera, La Scala, Milan, Teatro Fenice, Venice, the Paris Opera, Glyndebourne, San Francisco and Chicago Operas, The Metropolitan, New York, the Australian Opera, Hamburg, the Canadian Opera, etc.; leading roles in Lucia di Lammermoor, La Traviata, Adriana Lecouvreur, Les Contes D'Hoffmann, Lucrezia Borgia, Semiramide, Don Giovanni, Faust, Die Zauberflöte, Dido and Aeneas, The Merry Widow, Les Huguenots etc.; Hon. life mem. Australia Opera Co. 1974; Hon. D.Mus. (Sydney) 1984; F.R.C.M. 1981. *Publication:* The Joan Sutherland Album (autobiography, with Richard Bonynge) 1986. *Leisure interests:* reading, needlepoint. *Address:* c/o Ingpen and Williams, 14 Kensington Court, London, W8 5DN, England; c/o Wendy Hill, The Australian Opera, P.O. Box 291, Strawberry Hills, N.S.W. 2012, Australia.

SUTHERLAND, John Andrew, PH.D., F.R.S.L.; British professor of English Literature; b. 9 Oct. 1938; s. of Jack Sutherland and Elizabeth (née Salter) Sutherland; m. Guilland Watt 1967; one s.; ed. Colchester Royal Grammar School, Leicester and Edinburgh Univs.; nat. service, 2nd Lieut. Suffolk Regt. 1958–60; lecturer in English Univ. of Edin. 1965–72; lecturer in English U.C.L. 1972–84, Lord Northcliffe Prof. of Modern English Literature 1992–. *Publications include:* Thackeray at Work 1974, Victorian Novelists and Publishers 1976, Fiction and the Fiction Industry 1978, Bestsellers 1980, Offensive Literature 1982, The Longman Companion to Victorian Fiction 1989, Mrs Humphry Ward 1992, The Life of Walter Scott: A Critical Biography 1995, Victorian Fiction: Writers, Publishers, Readers 1995, Is Heathcliffe a Murderer? 1996, Can Jane Eyre be Happy? 1997. *Leisure interest:* walking. *Address:* Department of English, University College London, Gower Streeet, London, WC1E 6BT, England. *Telephone:* 0171-387 7050.

SUTHERLAND, Kiefer; American actor; b. Dec. 1966, Los Angeles; s. of Donald Sutherland (q.v.) and Shirley Douglas; m. Camelia Kath (divorced); two d.; debut with Los Angeles Odyssey Theatre in Throne of Straw aged 9; TV appearances include: Amazing Stories, Trapped in Silence, Brotherhood of Justice, Last Light (also dir.). *Films:* Max Dugan Returns 1983, The Bay Boy 1984, At Close Range 1986, Crazy Moon 1986, Stand By Me 1986, The Lost Boys 1987, The Killing Time 1987, Promised Land 1987, Bright Lights, Big City 1988, Young Guns 1988, Renegades 1989, Chicago Joe and the Showgirl 1990, Flashback 1990, Flatliners 1990, The Nutcracker Prince (voice) 1990, Young Guns II 1990, Article 99 1991, Twin Peaks: Fire Walk With Me 1992, A Few Good Men 1992, The Vanishing 1993, The Three Musketeers, The Cowboy Way, Teresa's Tattoo, Eye for an Eye, A Time to Kill 1996, Truth or Consequences N.M. (also dir.) 1997, Dark City 1997, Ground Control 1998, The Breakup 1998. *Address:* International Creative Management, 8942 Wilshire Boulevard, Beverly Hills, CA 90211, U.S.A.

SUTHERLAND, Peter Denis, S.C., B.C.L.; Irish international civil servant, lawyer and politician; b. 25 April 1946; s. of W. G. Sutherland and Barbara Sutherland; m. Maria del Pilar Cabria Valcarcel 1971; two s. one d.; ed. Gonzaga Coll., Univ. Coll., Dublin and King's Inns; called to Irish Bar (King's Inns), English Bar (Middle Temple) and New York Bar; admitted to Bar of the Supreme Court of the United States; practising mem. of Irish Bar 1968–81; Tutor in Law, Univ. Coll., Dublin 1968–71; apptd. Sr. Counsel 1980; Attorney-Gen. 1981–82, 1982–85; mem. Strategy Cttee. Fine Gael Party 1978–81, Dir. Policy Programme, 1981 General Election; mem. Comm. of the European Communities (responsible for Competition and Relations with the European Parliament) 1985–89; Dir.-Gen. GATT (later World Trade Org.) 1993–95; Chair. Allied Irish Banks 1989–93; Dir. Telefonaktiebolaget, L. M. Ericsson, Delta Airlines, ABB Asea Brown Boveri Ltd.; Dir. British Petroleum Co. PLC (Deputy Chair. 1995–97, Chair. 1997–); Gen. Partner, Goldman Sachs 1995–; Chair and Man. Dir. Goldman Sachs Int. 1995–; Dir. Investor AB 1995–; Visiting Fellow Kennedy School of Govt., Harvard Univ. 1989; Hon. Fellow London Business School 1997; Visiting Prof. Univ. Coll. Dublin; Bencher of the Hon. Soc. of the King's Inns; mem. Bar Council of Ireland Action Cttee. for Europe, Foundation Bd., World Econ. Forum; Hon. LL.D. (St. Louis), (Nat. Univ. of Ireland); several hon. degrees including Hon. D.Phil. (Dublin City Univ.); Gold Medal of European Parl. 1988; First European Law Prize Paris 1988; Grand Cross of Civil Merit, Spain 1989, Grand Cross of King Leopold II, Belgium 1989, N.Z. Centenary Medal 1990, Chevalier Légion d'honneur, Order of Rio Branco, Brazil 1996. *Publications:* 1er janvier 1993—ce qui va changer en Europe 1989; and numerous articles in law journals. *Leisure interests:* reading, sport. *Address:* Goldman Sachs International, Peterborough Court, 133 Fleet Street, London, EC4A 2BB; British Petroleum Company PLC, Britannic House, 1 Finsbury Circus, London, EC2M 7BA, England; 68 Eglinton Road, Dublin 4, Ireland.

SUTHERLAND, Sir Stewart Ross, Kt., M.A.; British university vice-chancellor; b. 25 Feb. 1941, Scotland; s. of George Sutherland and Ethel Masson; m. Sheena Robertson 1964; one s. two d.; ed. Woodside School, Robert Gordon's Coll., Univ. of Aberdeen and Corpus Christi Coll. Cambridge; Asst. Lecturer in Philosophy, Univ. Coll. of N. Wales 1965; lecturer in Philosophy, Univ. of Stirling 1968, Sr. Lecturer 1972, Reader 1976; Prof. of History and Philosophy of Religion, King's Coll. London 1977–85, Vice-Prin. 1981–85, Prin. 1985–90, Fellow 1983; Vice-Chancellor, Univ. of London 1990–94; H.M. Chief Insp. of Schools 1992–94; Vice-Chancellor and Prin. Univ. of Edin. 1994–; mem. Council of Science and Tech. 1993–; Hon. Fellow, Corpus Christi Coll. Cambridge 1989, Univ. Coll. at Bangor 1991; Hon.

L.H.D. (Coll. of Wooster, Ohio) 1975, (Commonwealth Univ. of Va.) 1992, Hon. LL.D. (Aberdeen) 1991, (Nat. Univ. of Ireland) 1992; Hon. D.Univ. (Stirling) 1993; Liveryman, Goldsmiths Co. 1991. *Publications:* Atheism and the Rejection of God 1977, The Philosophical Frontiers of Christian Theology (ed. with B. L. Hebblethwaite) 1983, God, Jesus and Belief 1984, Faith and Ambiguity 1984, The World's Religions (ed.) 1988, Religion, Reason and the Self (jt. ed.) 1989; articles in books and learned journals. *Leisure interests:* Tassie medallions, theatre, jazz. *Address:* University of Edinburgh, Old College, South Bridge, Edinburgh, EH8 9YL, Scotland. *Telephone:* (0131) 650 2149.

SUTHERLAND, Dame Veronica Evelyn, D.M.G., M.A.; British diplomatist; b. 25 April 1939; d. of late Lieut.-Col. Maurice G. Beckett and of Constance M. Cavenagh-Mainwaring; m. Alex J. Sutherland 1981; ed. Royal School, Bath, Univs. of London and Southampton; joined diplomatic service 1965, Second Sec., then First Sec. Copenhagen 1967–70, New Delhi 1975–78; with FCO 1970–75, 1978–80, Counsellor 1981, 1984–87, Asst. Under-Sec. of State (Personnel) 1990–95; Perm Del. to UNESCO 1981–84; Amb. to Côte d'Ivoire 1987–90, to Ireland 1995–99; Deputy Sec. Gen. of the Commonwealth Feb. 1999–; Hon. LL.D (Trinity Coll., Dublin) 1998. *Address:* Commonwealth Secretariat, Marlborough House, Pall Mall, London, SW1Y 5HX, England. *Telephone:* 0171-839 3411.

SÜTŐ, András; Hungarian writer; b. 17 June 1927, Pusztakamarás, Transylvania; s. of András Sütő and Berta Sütő; m. Éva Szabó 1949; two s.; ed. Bethlen Gábor Coll., Nagyenyed, and Reformed Coll., Kolozsvár (now Cluj, Romania); started as journalist with daily newspaper Világosság, Kolozsvár; contrib., later Ed.-in-Chief, Falvak Népe 1949–54; Deputy Chief Ed. literary monthly Igaz Szó, Marosvásárhely (Târgu Mureş) 1955–57; Chief Ed. pictorial Uj Élet, Marosvásárhely 1957–89; Vice-Pres. Writers' Fed. of Socialist Repub. of Romania 1973–81; State Prize for Literature Romania 1953, 1954; Herder Prize, Vienna 1979, Kossuth Prize for Literature 1992. *Publications include:* Emberek indulnak (short stories) 1953, Félrejáró Salamon (short novel) 1956, Anyám könnyü álmot igér (novel) 1970, Rigó és apostol (essays, travelogue) 1970, Engedjétek hozzám jönni a szavakat (novel) 1977, Az Idő Markában (essays) 1984; A lőttlábu madár nyomában 1988, Mese és reménység (short stories) 1991, Vadpávamenyegző (tales) 1994; dramatic works: Tékozló szerelem (play) 1963, Pompás Gedeon (play) 1968, Egy lócsiszár virágvasárnapja 1978, Csillag a máglyán 1978, Cain and Abel 1978, A szuzai menyegző 1979, Advent a Hargitán 1985, Kalandozások Ihajcsuhajdiában (play) 1986, Álomkommandó 1987, Naplójegyzetek 1990, Szemet szóért (diary notes) 1993, Az ugató madár (play) 1993, Herodes napjai (diary notes) 1994; collected works: Színművek (plays) I, II, III, 1989, 1992, 1995, Omló egek alatt (essays) 1990, Sárkány alszik veled (interviews) 1991, Csipkerózsika ébresztése (essays) 1993, Engedjétek hozzám jönni a szavakat (essays, novel) 1994, Kék Álhalál (short stories) 1997, Balkáni gerle (play) 1998; books translated into Romanian, German, Russian, Bulgarian, Slovak and Ukrainian; plays performed in Budapest, Bucharest, Cluj, Novi-Sad, Zagreb, Bratislava, New York and Aachen. *Address:* Târgu Mureş (Marosvásárhely), Str. Mărăşti Nr. 36, Romania. *Telephone:* 65-211179.

SUTRESNA, Nana S., M.A.; Indonesian diplomatist; b. 21 Oct. 1933, Ciamis; m. 1973; two s. one d.; ed. Univ. of Wales, Aberystwyth, Acad. for the Foreign Service; foreign news ed. for the Indonesian News Agency, ANTARA, 1955–57; joined Dept. of Foreign Affairs 1957, Head of Public Relations and Spokesman 1972–76, Dir. for European Affairs 1979–81, Dir.-Gen. for Political Affairs 1984–88; served at Indonesian Embassy in Washington D.C. and in Mexico City, as Minister Counsellor then Minister in Vienna 1976–79; Head of Indonesian Del. to Disarmament Conf., Geneva 1981–83; Deputy Perm. Rep. to the UN, Geneva 1981–84, Perm. Rep. to the UN (also accred to Bahamas, Jamaica and Nicaragua) 1988–92; now Amb.-at-large, Head Exec. to Pres. of Indonesia in his capacity as Chair. Non-Aligned Movt. *Leisure interest:* golf. *Address:* c/o Ministry of Foreign Affairs, Jalan Taman Pejambon 6, Jakarta, Pusat, Indonesia.

SUTRISNO, Gen. Try; Indonesian army officer; mil. engineer; Aide-de-Camp to Pres. 1974–78; Army Chief of Staff 1986–88; Commdr. of the Armed Forces 1988–93; Vice-Pres. of Indonesia March 1993–; left Golkan Party to found Justice and Unity Party 1998–. *Address:* Office of the Vice-President, Jalan Merdeka Selatan 6, Jakarta, Indonesia.

SUTTON, Rt. Rev. Keith Norman; British ecclesiastic; b. 23 June 1934, London; s. of Norman Sutton and Irene Sutton; m. Edith M. J. Geldard 1963; three s. one d.; ed. Woking and Battersea Grammar Schools and Jesus Coll. Cambridge; Curate, St. Andrew's, Plymouth 1959–62; Chaplain, St. John's Coll. Cambridge 1962–67; Tutor and Chaplain, Bishop Tucker Coll. Mukono, Uganda 1968–72; Prin. Ridley Hall, Cambridge 1973–78; Bishop Suffragan of Kingston-upon-Thames 1978–84; Bishop of Lichfield 1984–; Hon. D.Univ. (Keele); Hon. D.Litt. (Wolverhampton) 1994. *Publication:* The People of God 1983. *Leisure interests:* Russian literature, Third World issues, music. *Address:* Bishop's House, 22 The Close, Lichfield, WS13 7LG, England. *Telephone:* (01543) 306000. *Fax:* (01543) 306009.

SUTTON, Philip John, R.A.; British artist; b. 20 Oct. 1928, Poole, Dorset; s. of L. L. Sutton and Anne Sutton; m. Heather Cooke 1954; one s. three d.; ed. Slade School of Fine Art and Univ. Coll., London; Lecturer, Slade School of Fine Art, Univ. Coll. 1954–; artist-in-residence, Fulham Pottery 1987–; one-man exhbns. bi-annually at Roland Browse & Delbanco and Browse & Darby 1956–84; Leeds City Art Gallery retrospective 1960; travelled in Australia and Fiji painting landscapes 1963–64; retrospective exhbn. Diploma Gallery, Royal Acad. 1977; toured Israel with ten British artists 1979; visited Australia 1980; exhbns. Royal Acad. of Arts, London 1992, Agnews, London 1992, Glyn Vivian Art Gallery, Graham Sutherland Gallery 1994, Tenby Museum 1995, Royal Acad. of Arts, London, Armoury Museum, Leeds 1997; touring exhbn., Wales 1993; exhbn. of 'Shell' tapestry at Royal Acad. 1985; ceramic wall, NMB Bank HQ, Amsterdam 1987; ceramic exhbn. Odette Gilbert Gallery, London 1987; painting exhbn., Paris 1988; designed Post Office Greeting Stamps 1989. *Leisure interests:* swimming, running. *Address:* 3 Morfa Terrace, Manorbier, Tenby, Pembrokeshire, SA70 7TH, Wales.

SUVIRANTA, Antti Johannes, LL.M., S.J.D.; Finnish judge, professor of law and legal administrator; b. 30 Nov. 1923, Helsinki; s. of Bruno Suviranta and Aino (née Tarjanne) Suviranta; m. Dr. Annikki Elosuo 1953; three d.; ed. Helsinki Experimental High School, Univ. of Helsinki and Harvard Law School; clerk, Rector's office, Univ. of Helsinki 1949–55; dist. judge's clerk and deputy, dist. of Janakkala 1951; civil servant, Ministry of Finance 1956–59; teaching fellow, Faculty of Law, Univ. of Helsinki 1958–62, Acting Prof. of Labour Law 1962–67, Prof. of Labour Law (on leave of absence 1968, 1971–82) 1967–82; Auxiliary Justice, Supreme Admin. Court of Finland 1968; Pres. The Finnish Labour Court 1970–82; Pres. Supreme Admin. Court of Finland 1982–93; part-time lecturer on Fiscal Law, Univ. of Turku 1963–70; Chair. Finnish Labour Council 1973–79, Finnish Labour Law Soc. 1974–82, Finnish Lawyers' Asscn. 1977–79; mem. Exec. Cttee., Int. Soc. for Labour Law and Social Security 1970–85; mem. ILO Cttee. of Experts for Application of Conventions and Recommendations 1984–93; Chair. Finnish Branch Int. Asscn. of Legal Science 1986–94; Pres. Int. Asscn. of Supreme Admin. Jurisdictions 1986–89; mem. European Comm. for Democracy through Law 1990–98; mem. Finnish Acad. of Sciences; Assoc. mem. Int. Acad. of Comparative Law; Hon. LL.D. (Univ. of Stockholm) 1984; Grand Cross, Order of Finnish White Rose; Grand Cross, Order of Judiciary Merit of Labour (Brazil); Grand Cross, Royal Order of the North Star (Sweden). *Publications:* The Notion of Employment in Tax Law 1961, Joint Taxation of Spouses 1962, The Role of the Member States in the Unification Work of the ILO 1966, Direct taxation in Finland 1972, Labour Law and Industrial Relations in Finland 1997, also learned articles. *Leisure interest:* gardening. *Address:* Vuorimiehenkatu 19A 8, 00140 Helsinki, Finland. *Telephone:* 654661. *Fax:* 1853202.

SUZMAN, Helen, B.COM.; South African politician (retd.); b. 7 Nov. 1917, Germiston, Transvaal; m. Dr. M. M. Suzman 1937 (died 1994); two d.; ed. Parktown Convent, Univ. of Witwatersrand; Asst. statistician, War Supplies Bd. 1941–44; part-time lecturer, Dept. of Econs. and Econ. History, Univ. of Witwatersrand 1944–52; M.P. Houghton 1953–89; (United Party) 1953–61, Progressive Party (now Progressive Fed. Party) 1961–89 (merged with Democratic Party 1989); Pres. S. African Inst. of Race Relations 1991–93; part-time mem. S. African Human Rights Comm. 1996–98; Hon. Fellow St. Hugh's Coll., Oxford 1973, L.S.E. 1975, New Hall, Cambridge 1990; 26 hon. doctorates; recipient Human Rights Award UN 1978; Medallion of Heroism (New York) 1980; American Liberties Medallion (American Jewish Cttee.) 1984; recipient Moses Mendelssohn Award, Berlin Senate 1988; Hon. D.B.E. 1989; Order of Merit (Golá) 1997. *Publication:* In No Uncertain Terms (memoirs) 1993. *Leisure interests:* bridge, fishing. *Address:* 52 Second Avenue, Illovo, Sandton 2196, South Africa (Home). *Telephone:* (11) 788-2833. *Fax:* (11) 788-2833.

SUZMAN, Janet, B.A.; South African actress; b. 9 Feb. 1939, Johannesburg; d. of Saul Suzman and Betty Sonnenberg; m. Trevor Nunn (q.v.) 1969 (divorced 1986); one s.; ed. Kingsmead Coll., Univ. of the Witwatersrand, London Acad. of Music and Dramatic Art; moved to Britain 1960; Best Actress, Evening Standard Drama Award 1973, 1976, Plays and Players Award 1976, Barclays Award for Best Director 1997. *Roles for Royal Shakespeare Co. include:* Lady Anne, La Pucelle, Lady Percy, Luciana, Lulu in The Birthday Party 1963–64, Portia, Rosaline 1965, Carmen in The Balcony, She Stoops to Conquer 1966, Katharina, Celia and Berinthia in The Relapse 1967, Beatrice, Rosalind 1968–69, Cleopatra and Lavinia 1972–73, Hester in Hello and Goodbye (Kings Head) 1973, Masha in Three Sisters (Cambridge Theatre) 1976, The Death of Bessie Smith (Market Theatre, Johannesburg 1976), Shen Te in The Good Woman of Setzuan (Tyneside Theatre Co.) 1976, at Royal Court Theatre 1977; Hedda Gabler (Duke of York's Theatre) 1977, Duchess of Malfi 1978, The Greeks (Aldwych) 1980, Cowardice (Ambassadors Theatre) 1983, Boesman and Lena (Hampstead) 1984, Vassa (Greenwich Theatre) 1985, Andromache (Old Vic) 1987, Another Time (Wyndhams) 1989–90, Hippolytus (Almeida) 1991, The Sisters Rosenweig (Old Vic) 1994. *Directed:* Othello, (Market Theatre, Johannesburg) 1987, A Dream of People (The Pit) 1990, The Cruel Grasp (Edin. Festival) 1991, No Flies on Mr. Hunter (Chelsea Centre) 1992, Death of a Salesman (Theatr Clwyd) 1993, The Deep Blue Sea (Theatr Clwyd) 1996, The Good Woman of Sharkville (Market Theatre, Johannesburg) 1996 and UK tour 1997, The Cherry Orchard (Birmingham Rep.) 1997, The Snow Palace (tour 1998) and Tricycle Theatre 1998. *Film appearances:* A Day in the Death of Joe Egg 1970, Nicholas and Alexandra 1971, Nijinsky 1978, Priest of Love 1981, The Draughtsman's Contract 1981, E la Nave Va 1982, A Dry White Season 1988, Nuns on the Run 1990, Leon the Pig-Farmer 1992. *Television plays since 1966 include:* The Family Reunion 1967, Saint Joan 1968, The Three Sisters 1969, Macbeth 1970, Hedda Gabler 1972, Twelfth Night 1973,

Shakespeare or Bust 1973, Antony and Cleopatra 1974, Miss Nightingale, Clayhanger (serial) 1975–76, Robin Hood (CBS TV) 1983, Mountbatten: The Last Viceroy 1985, The Singing Detective 1986, The Miser 1987, Revolutionary Witness 1989, Hildegard (Omnibus) 1994, Front Seat 1996; directed Othello for television 1988, Cripples 1989, The Amazon 1989; Masterclass: Shakespearian Comedy 1990; The Ruth Rendell Mysteries (TV) 1996; The Tanner Lectures Brasenose Coll., Oxford 1995; Vice-Chair. Council of LAMDA; Hon. Assoc. Artist R.S.C.; Hon. M.A. (Open Univ.) 1984; Hon. D.Lit. (Warwick) 1990, (Leicester) 1992; Hon. D.Lit. London (QMW) 1997. *Publications:* Acting with Shakespeare: Three Comedies 1996, The Applause Shakespeare Library, Antony and Cleopatra 1999. *Address:* William Morris Agency (U.K.) Ltd., 1 Stratton Street, London, W1X 6HB, England. *Telephone:* 0171-355 8500. *Fax:* 0171-355 8600.

SUZUKI, Haruo, LL.B.; Japanese business executive; b. 31 March 1913, Hayama, Kanagawa Pref.; s. of Chuji and Masu Suzuki; m. Itoko Hibiya 1941; two d.; ed. Tokyo Imperial Univ.; with Nomura Securities Co. Ltd. 1936–38; joined Showa Denko K.K. 1939, Exec. Vice-Pres. 1959–71, Pres. 1971–81, Chair. 1981–87, Hon. Chair. 1987–; Pres. Japan Chemical Industry Asscn. 1976–78, New Materials Study Group 1983–, Japan Fine Ceramics Asscn. 1986–91; Perm. Trustee Japan Cttee. for Econ. Devt. 1946–; Dir. Int. Primary Aluminium Inst. 1974–76, 1980–82; Exec. Dir. Fed. of Econ. Orgs. 1972–87; Chair. Japan-Southern U.S. Asscn. 1984–91; Sr. Counsellor Japan Econ. Research Inst. 1997–, Asscn. for Corp. Support for the Arts in Japan 1990–94, Hon. Chair. 1994–; Trustee Emer. The Aspen Inst. 1994–; Consultant Village Shonan Inc. 1996–; Chair. Club Franco-Japonais 1991–; Sr. Adviser Kanagawa Foundation for Academic and Cultural Exchange (K-FACE) 1996–; mem. Industrial Structure Council of Ministry of Int. Trade and Industry (MITI) 1972–92, Legis. Council, Ministry of Justice 1982–92; mem. Industrial Property Council, Patent Office, MITI 1983–92, Japan-China Cttee. for Friendship in the 21st Century, Ministry of Foreign Affairs 1984–, Comité de réflexion sur l'avenir des relations franco-japonaises, Ministry of Foreign Affairs 1982–84. *Publications:* Chemical Industry 1968, What the Classics Have Taught Me 1979, and others. *Leisure interests:* reading, art appreciation, painting, golf, travelling. *Address:* Showa Denko K.K., 13-9, Shiba Daimon 1-chome, Minato-ku, Tokyo 1-810; 7 Mita 2-chome, Minato-ku, Tokyo, Japan (Home). *Telephone:* 432-5111 (Office).

SUZUKI, Kazumi; Japanese politician; fmr. labour union official; Minister of State and Dir.-Gen. Nat. Land Agency 1996–97; mem. House of Councillors, Social Democratic Party of Japan (SDPJ). *Address:* c/o National Land Agency, 1-2-2, Kasumigaseki, Chiyoda-ku, Tokyo 100, Japan.

SUZUKI, Osamu; Japanese business executive; b. 30 Jan. 1930, Gero, Gifu; s. of Shunzo and Toshiko Suzuki; m. Shoko Suzuki 1958; two s. one d.; ed. Chuo Univ.; joined Suzuki Motor Co. Ltd. 1958, Dir. 1963–66, Jr. Man. Dir. 1967–72, Sr. Man. Dir. 1973–77, Pres. 1978–; Award 'Sitara-i-Pakistan' (Pakistan) 1985; Medal of Honour with Blue Ribbon 1987; Mil. Cross of Order of Repub. of Hungary 1993. *Leisure interest:* golf. *Address:* Suzuki Motor Corporation, 300 Takatsuka-cho, Hamamatsu, Shizuoka-ken, Japan. *Telephone:* (053) 440-2027.

SUZUKI, Shunichi, LL.D.; Japanese politician; b. 6 Nov. 1910, Tokyo; s. of Toshio and Kii Suzuki; m. Atsu Suzuki 1935; two s. one d.; ed. Tokyo Imperial Univ.; joined Ministry of Home Affairs; lecturer on public admin. law at Komazawa Univ. 1941–46; lecturer on local autonomy system at Waseda Univ. 1945–57; Vice-Minister, Ministry of Home Affairs 1950–58; Deputy Chief Cabinet Sec. 1958; Vice-Gov. of Tokyo 1959–67, Gov. 1979–; Sec.-Gen., Expo '70 in Osaka 1967–70; Pres., Tokyo Expressway Public Corpn. 1971–77, Finance Corpn. of Local Public Enterprise 1978–79; Conservative. *Leisure interest:* golf. *Address:* 2-8-1 Nishi-shinjyuku, Shinjyuku-ku, Tokyo 163-01, Japan. *Telephone:* (03) 5321-1111.

SUZUKI, Tadashi; Japanese theatre director and producer; b. 20 June 1939, Shimizu City; m. Hiroko Takeuchi 1969; one s.; ed. Kitazono High School and Waseda Univ.; founded Waseda Sho-Gekijo 1966; changed name to Suzuki Co. of Toga (SCOT) 1984; apptd. Artistic Dir. of Iwanami Hall 1974; built Toga Theatre, Toga Village, Toyama Pref. 1976; Guest Prof. at various schools including Juilliard School, Univ. of Wis. (Milwaukee), Univ. of Calif. (San Diego) and Univ. of Del.; founded Japan Performing Arts Center 1982; began annual Toga Int. Arts Festival 1982, Toga Int. Actor Training Programme 1983; apptd. Artistic Dir. of Acting Co. Mito (ACM) Theatre 1989–94, Artistic Dir. Shizuoka Performing Arts Center 1997; mem. Int. Cttee. Theatre Olympics 1994; work has included own texts On the Dramatic Passions I 1969, II 1970, III 1970 and Night and Clock 1975, A Greek trilogy and works by Chekhov and Shakespeare, many of these in theatres around the world; Kinokuniya Theatre Award 1976, Educ. Minister's Art Encouragement Prize of Theatre 1981. *Publications:* The Sum of the Internal Angles 1973, Dramatic Language 1977, On the Dramatic Passions 1977, Horizon of Deception 1980, Force that Crosses the Border 1984, The Way of Acting 1986, What Theatre Is 1988, The Way of Directing 1994. *Leisure interest:* collecting costumes (especially hats). *Address:* Japan Performing Arts Center, 2-14-19-302, Shimo-ochiai, Shinjuku-ku, Tokyo 161, Japan. *Telephone:* 03-3951 4843.

SUZUMURA, Kotaro, PH.D.; Japanese economist; b. 7 Jan. 1944, Aichi; s. of Hidetaro Suzumura and Sumie Suzumura; three d.; ed. Hitotsubashi Univ.; lecturer Dept. of Econs., Hitotsubashi Univ. 1971–73, Prof. of Public Econs., Inst. of Econ. Research 1984–; Assoc. Prof. Inst. of Econ. Research, Kyoto Univ. 1973–82; lecturer L.S.E. 1974–76; Visiting Assoc. Prof. of Econs., Stanford Univ. 1979–80; Visiting Fellow Dept. of Econs., Univ. of Pennsylvania 1987, All Souls Coll., Oxford 1988; Dir.-Gen. Tokyo Centre for Econ. Research 1990–92; Chair. Far Eastern Standing Cttee. Econometric Soc. 1995–, Fellow 1990–, mem. Council 1995–; Ed.-in-Chief Japanese Econ. Review 1995–97; mem. Council Soc. for Social Choice and Welfare; Nikkei Prize 1984, 1988. *Publications:* Rational Choice, Collective Decisions and Social Welfare 1983, Competition, Commitment and Welfare 1995, Social Choice Re-examined (Jt. Ed. 2 vols.) 1996, 1997, Development Strategy and Management of the Market Economy (jtly.) 1997. *Leisure interests:* reading novels. *Address:* Institute of Economic Research, Hitotsubashi University, Naka 2-1, Kunitachi, Tokyo (Office); 1-29-3 Asagaya Minami, Suginami-ku, Tokyo, Japan (Home). *Telephone:* (42) 850-8353 (Office); (3) 3311-5110 (Home). *Fax:* (42) 850-8353 (Office); (3) 3311-5110 (Home).

SVANIDZE, Nikolay Karlovich; Russian journalist; b. 2 April 1955; m.; one s.; ed. Moscow State Univ.; researcher Inst. of U.S.A. and Canada U.S.S.R. Acad. of Sciences 1978–91; on staff Russian TV 1992–; commentator Information programme Vesti 1991–94; author and narrator Information programmes Contrasts, Mirror 1996–; Deputy Dir. Information programmes, Head Studio Information and Analytical programmes 1996–97; Chair. All Russian State TV and Radio Co. 1997–98; Teffi Prize of Russian Acad. of TV for the best information programme. *Address:* Russian TV and Radio Company, Leninsky prosp. 27/2, 125040 Moscow, Russia (Office). *Telephone:* (095) 213 3052 (Office).

ŠVANKMAJER, Jan; Czech stage designer and film director; b. 4 Sept. 1934, Prague; m. Eva Dvořáková 1960; one s. one d.; ed. Theatrical Acad. of Performing Arts, Prague 1954–58; freelance artist 1958–; numerous drawings, graphic sheets, collages, stage sets and (with his wife) art pottery; directed film Dimensions of Dialogue 1990, The End of Stalinism in the Czechlands 1990–, Food 1992, The Faust Lesson 1994, Conspirators of Pleasure 1996; exhbn.: Speaking Painting, Prague 1997; Prix Special ASIFA 1990, Award for Lifetime Work U.K. 1995. *Address:* Černínská 5, 118 00 Prague 1 (Home), Studio Athanor, Knovíz, 274 01 Slaný, Czech Republic (Office). *Telephone:* 02-536 793 (Home).

SVARTVIK, Jan, PH.D.; Swedish professor of English; b. 18 Aug. 1931, Fryksände; s. of Gustaf Svartvik and Sigrid Svartvik; m. Gunilla Berner 1958; two s. one d.; ed. Uppsala Univ.; Research Asst. and Asst. Dir. Survey of English Usage, Univ. Coll. London 1961–65; lecturer, Univ. of Gothenburg 1965–70; Visiting Prof. Brown Univ., R.I., U.S.A. 1969; Prof. of English, Lund Univ. 1970–95; Pres. Asscn. Int. de Linguistique Appliquée 1981–84; Chair. Org. Cttee., Nobel Symposium on Corpus Linguistics 1991; Chair. Steering Cttee. for Evaluation of Linguistics in Sweden 1990–92; mem. Royal Acad. of Letters, History and Antiquities, Royal Swedish Acad. of Sciences, Academia Europaea, Societas Scientarum Fennica, New York Acad. of Sciences. *Publications:* On Voice in the English Verb 1966, The Evans Statements 1969, A Grammar of Contemporary English 1972, A Comprehensive Grammar of the English Language 1985, The London-Lund Corpus of Spoken English: Description and Research 1990; Directions in Corpus Linguistics: Proceedings of Nobel Symposium 82 1992 (Ed.), A Communicative Grammar of English 1994, Words: Proceedings (Ed.). *Leisure interest:* sailing. *Address:* Tumlaregränden 7, 22651 Lund, Sweden. *Telephone:* (46) 248412. *Fax:* (46) 2484436.

SVEDBERG, Bjoern, M.SC.; Swedish business executive; b. 4 July 1937, Stockholm; s. of Inge and Anna-Lisa Svedberg; m. Gunnel Nilsson 1960; four c.; ed. Royal Inst. of Tech., Stockholm and Man. Devt. Inst. (IMEDE), Univ. of Lausanne; Man. Eng. Telephone Exchange Div., L. M. Ericsson Telephone Co. 1972–76, Sr. Vice-Pres. Research and Devt. 1976–77, Pres. 1977–90, Chair. May 1990–; Mo och Domsjo A.B., Chair. 1991–92; Dir. AB Volvo 1994–; mem. Bd. Fed. of Swedish Industry, L. M. Ericsson and several other cos.; mem. Royal Swedish Acad. of Eng. Sciences. *Address:* Telefonaktiebolaget L. M. Ericsson, S 126 11 Stockholm 32, Sweden. *Telephone:* 719 00 00.

SVEJGAARD, Arne, M.D., D.SC.; Danish scientist; b. 13 March 1937, Odense; m. Else Lyngsoe 1960; two s. one d.; ed. Univ. of Aarhus Medical School and Univ. Hosp. of Aarhus; Dir. Tissue Typing Lab., Univ. Hosp. of Copenhagen 1970–87, Dept. of Clinical Immunology 1987–; Prof. of Clinical Immunology, Univ. of Copenhagen 1991–; Councillor Int. Histocompatibility Workshops 1975–; Chair. Danish Cttee. for Immunology 1985–; mem. Royal Danish Acad. of Sciences and Letters 1981–; Gaardon Prize 1980, Novo Prize 1981. *Publications:* Iso-antigenic Systems of Human Blood Platelets 1969, The HLA System (with others) 1975, HLA and Disease (with J. Dausset) 1977, numerous scientific articles. *Address:* University of Copenhagen, Faculty of Medicine, Frue Plads Noerregade 10, P.O. Box 2177, 1017 Copenhagen K; Department of Clinical Immunology, University Hospital, Tagensvej 20, 2200 Copenhagen; Skovvang 67, 3450 Allerod, Denmark. *Telephone:* 35-45-76-30; 42-273211.

SVĚRÁK, Jan; Czech film director; b. 6 Feb. 1965, Žatec; m.; one s. one d.; ed. Film Acad. of Arts; partner of the film production co. Luxor 1996; Co. Biograf Jan Svěrák Pictures 1996–; *Films directed include:* Ropáci 1988, Primary School 1991, Akumulátor I 1994, Ride 1994, Kolya 1996; numerous awards including Acad. Award for best foreign student film 1989, Czech Lion Awards for direction 1996, 1997, Golden Globe Award, Acad. Award and Czech Lion Award for Kolya; Time for Peace Prize 1997. *Leisure interest:* painting. *Address:* P.O. Box 33, 155 00 Prague 515, Czech Republic.

SVERDLOV, Yevgeny Davidovich; Russian biochemist; b. 16 Nov. 1938; ed. Moscow State Univ., sr. lab., jr., sr. researcher Inst. of Bio-organic Chem. 1965–88; Dir. Inst. of Molecular Genetics 1988–; corresp. mem. U.S.S.R. (now Russian) Acad. of Sciences 1984, mem. 1994; research in molecular genetics, structure and functions of nucleic acids; mem. Russian Acad. of Agricultural Sciences 1994; mem. Scientific Council of Biotech. Russian Acad. of Sciences; Lenin Prize; U.S.S.R. State Prize. *Publications include:* Organic Chemistry of Nucleic Acids 1970, over 200 scientific articles. *Address:* Institute of Molecular Genetics, Kurchatov pl. 46, 123182 Moscow, Russia. *Telephone:* (095) 196 0000 (Office). *Fax:* (095) 196 0221 (Office).

SVETLANOV, Yevgeniy Fyodorovich; Russian conductor, composer and pianist; b. 6 Sept. 1928, Moscow; s. of Fyodor Svetlanov and Tatiana Svetlanova; m. Nina Nikolayeva-Svetlanov 1980; ed. Gnesiny Music Educ. Inst. and Moscow Conservatoire; Asst. Conductor, Moscow Radio 1954; Conductor, Bolshoi Theatre, Moscow 1955–63, Chief Conductor 1963–65; Chief Conductor, U.S.S.R. (now Russia) State Symphony Orchestra 1965–; Prin. Guest Conductor, London Symphony Orchestra 1979–; Chief Conductor Royal Residentsije Orchestra, The Hague 1992–; Hon. Academician, Int. Acad. of Sciences, Industry, Educ. and Arts, U.S.A. 1996; People's Artist of R.S.F.S.R., of U.S.S.R. 1968; Lenin Prize 1972, Grand Prix (France); Order of Lenin, State Glinka Prize 1975, State Prize 1983, and other decorations. *Compositions include:* Symphony, Tone-Poems Festival 1950, Daugava 1953, Siberian Fantasy 1953, Rhapsody 1954, Cantata Home Fields 1949, Concerto 1951, five Sonatas 1946–52, five Sonatinas 1946–51, Preludes 1945–51, Symphony 1957, Beautiful Kalina (symphonic poem) 1975; about 50 Romances and Songs. *Leisure interests:* fishing, reading. *Address:* Residentie Orchestra, P.O. Box 11543, 2502 AM The Hague, Netherlands (Office); Leontyevski per. 14, Apt. 41, 103009 Moscow, Russia (Home). *Telephone:* (70) 367925 (Office); (095) 229-68-75 (Home).

SVIDERSKY, Vladimir Leonidovich; Russian physiologist; b. 19 Sept. 1931; m.; one d.; ed. Mil. Navy Acad. of Medicine; mil. doctor 1954–58; lab. asst., researcher, Head of Lab. Sechenov Inst. of Evolutionary Physiology and Biochemistry U.S.S.R. (now Russian) Acad. of Sciences 1958–, Dir. 1988; Corresp. mem. U.S.S.R. (now Russian) Acad. of Sciences 1981, mem. 1987; main research in mechanisms of nervous control of movt. behaviour of higher invertebrates, problems of evolutionary physiology; Ed.-in-Chief Zhurnal Evolutsii Biokhimii i Phisiologii; U.S.S.R. State Prize 1987, L. Orbeli Prize. *Publications include:* Neurophysiology of Flights of Insects 1973, Fundamentals of Neurophysiology of Insects 1980, Locomotion of Insects: Neurophysiological Aspects 1988. *Leisure interests:* poetry, chess, cars, mushroom hunting. *Address:* Institute of Evolutionary Physiology and Biochemistry, M. Toreza prospekt, 194223 St. Petersburg, Moscow. *Telephone:* (812) 552 7901 (Office); (812) 552 1554 (Home). *Fax:* (812) 552 3012 (Office).

SVIRSKY, Grigoriy Tsezarevich; Russian writer; b. 1921; m.; one c.; served in Soviet Army 1941–45 in Arctic; mem. CPSU –1968; began publishing novels 1947; dissident activity 1965–72; expelled from U.S.S.R. Writers' Union 1971; left U.S.S.R. 1972, now lives in Canada; nine awards and medals. *Publications:* Hostages 1967, The Arctic Tragedy 1971, On Lobnoye Mesto 1979, A History of Post-War Soviet Writing: The Literature of Moral Opposition 1981, Parting with Russia (novel) 1986, The Bashkir Honey (stories), The Breakthrough (novel) 1992.

SVOBODA, Jiří; Czech film director; b. 5 May 1945, Kladno; s. of Jiří Svoboda and Božena Svobodová (née Procházková); m. 1973; two d.; studied drama at Acad. of Performing Arts, Prague, expelled for political reasons 1963; worked as warehouseman and driver 1963–66; ed. Film Acad. of Performing Arts, Prague; dir. and script-writer, Film Studios Barrandov 1971–93; freelance film dir. and scriptwriter 1994–; mem. CP of Czechoslovakia 1975–90; Deputy Chair. Union of Czech Dramatic Artists 1987–89; Chair. Film Section of Union of Czech Dramatic Artists 1987–89; Chair. CP of the Czechlands and Moravia 1990–93; Deputy to House of Nations, Fed. Ass. of C.S.F.R. 1990–92; seriously wounded in attempt on his life Dec. 1992; Prof., Acad. of Performing Arts; Merited Artist 1986. *Films include:* (as dir. or scriptwriter): Hostage 1975, A Mirror for Christine 1975, House on the Embankment 1976, The Break Time 1977, The Blue Planet 1979, Girl with a Shell 1980, The Chain 1981, A Meeting with Shadows 1982, The End of the Lonely Berhof Farmstead 1983, The Lancet, Please 1985, Papilio 1986, The World Knows Nothing 1987, A Curse on the Hajnůs' House 1988, Only About Family Orders (about political trials in 1950s) 1989; also directed many TV plays. *Leisure interests:* philosophy, political theory, literature. *Address:* Na Balkáně 120, Prague 3, Czech Republic. *Telephone:* 02/6848395.

SVOBODA, Josef; Czech architect and stage designer; b. 10 May 1920, Čáslav; s. of Růžena Svoboda and Josef Svoboda; m. Libuše Hrubešová 1948; one d.; ed. Special School for Interior Architecture, Prague and School of Fine and Applied Arts, Prague; Stage designer, Nat. Theatre, Prague 1947, Head Designer 1951–; Prof. Acad. of Applied Arts 1968–; mem. Union of Czech Dramatic Artists 1975–, Union of Czech Designers, Union of Czech Architects, Union of United Scenic Artists, U.S.A.; Gen. Sec. Int. Org. of Scenographers and Theatre Technicians 1971–; Artistic Dir. of Laterna Magika 1973–; chief designer, Nat. Theatre, Prague 1990–; created over 500 stage sets in Czechoslovakia and for theatres in Belgium, France, Italy, Germany, U.S.S.R., U.K., U.S.A., etc.; solo exhbn. in Stockholm 1998; Hon. Degree, R.C.A. 1969, Denison Univ., Ohio 1977; Hon. D.F.A. (Univ. of Ohio) 1978, (Univ. of Western Mich.) 1984; State Prize 1954, Order of Labour 1963, Honoured Artist 1966; Best Stage Designer Art Biennale São Paulo 1961, London Theatre Critics' Award for the Best Stage Set (The Insect Comedy, Čapek and Tempest, Ostrovsky) 1966, Nat. Artist 1968, Nederlands Sikkenprijs 1969, L.A. Drama Critics Circle Award for Distinguished Set Design (The Three Sisters) 1970, Kulturpreis, German Photographic Soc. 1971, Int. Theatre Award, American Theatre Asscn. 1976; Premio Internazionale della Scenografia del Costume, Teatro dell'Europa 1984, Royal Industry Designer, RDIHC London 1989; Chevalier, Ordre des Arts et des Lettres 1976, Légion d'honneur 1993. *Leisure interest:* motoring. *Address:* Laterna Magika, Liliová 9, 11000 Prague 1; Filmårská 17, 15200 Prague 5, Czech Republic (Home). *Telephone:* 266-446 (Office); 581 39 24 (Home). *Fax:* 24 22 75 67 (Office).

SWAELEN, Frank, LL.D.; Belgian politician; b. 23 March 1930, Antwerp; m. M. J. Gobin 1958; one s. two d.; ed. Coll. of St.-Lievens, Antwerp, Catholic Univ. of Louvain, Harvard Int. Seminar; Sec.-Gen. Nat. Confed. of Parents' Asscns. 1956–66; Nat. Chair. Young Christelijke Volks Partij (CVP) 1964–66; Gen. Sec. Political CVP-PSC (Christian Democrats) 1966–76; mem. Chamber of Reps. 1968–85, Senator 1985–, Polit. Bureau of European Union of Christian Democrats, Nat. Bureau CVP 1971–; Vice-Chair. CVP group in Chamber of Reps. 1979–80; Chair. CVP group in Council of the Flemish Cultural Community 1979–80; Minister of Defence 1980–81; Nat. Pres. CVP 1981–88; Mayor of Hove 1971–88; Pres. of Belgian Senate 1988–; Pres. Parl. Ass. of CSCE (now OSCE) 1994–96; Grand Cross, Order of Leopold II, Commdr. Order of Leopold. *Leisure interests:* tennis, reading. *Address:* Paleis der Natie, Natieplein, 1009-Brussels (Office); Leliestraat 82, 2540 Hove, Belgium (Home). *Telephone:* 02-515 82 11 (Office); 03-455 26 12 (Home).

SWALES, John Douglas, M.D., F.R.C.P.; British professor of medicine; b. 19 Oct. 1935, Leicester; s. of Frank Swales and Doris Flude; m. Kathleen P. Townsend 1967; one s. one d.; ed. Wyggeston Grammar School, Leicester, Clare Coll. Cambridge and Westminster Hosp. Medical School; House Physician and Sr. House Officer, Westminster Hosp. 1961–63, Registrar 1964–68; Sr. Registrar/Research Fellow, Royal Postgrad. Medical School 1968–70; Sr. lecturer in Medicine, Univ. of Manchester 1970–73; Prof. of Medicine, Univ. of Leicester 1974–; Dir. of Research and Devt., Dept. of Health 1996–98; Hon. Fellow, Australian High Blood Pressure Council 1983; Fellow American High Blood Pressure Research Council. *Publications:* Sodium Metabolism in Disease 1975, Clinical Hypertension 1979, Platt versus Pickering 1985, Classic Papers in Hypertension 1987, Textbook of Hypertension 1994, Manual of Hypertension. *Leisure interest:* bibliophilism. *Address:* Department of Medicine and Therapeutics, Clinical Sciences Building, Royal Infirmary, P.O. Box 65, Leicester, LE2 7LX (Office); 21 Morland Avenue, Leicester, LE2 2PS, England (Home). *Telephone:* (0116) 2523182 (Office); (0116) 270 7161 (Home). *Fax:* (0116) 2523273 (Office).

SWAMINATHAN, Jagdish; Indian painter; b. 21 June 1928, Simla; m. Bhavani 1955; two s.; ed. Delhi Polytechnic and Acad. of Fine Arts, Warsaw; early career of freedom fighter, trade unionist, journalist, and writer of children's books; mem. Delhi State Cttee. of Congress Socialist Party and Ed. of its weekly organ, Mazdoor Awaz; Sr. Art Teacher, Cambridge School, New Delhi; Founder-mem. Group 1890 (avant-garde group of India artists); mem., Nat. Cttee., Int. Asscn. of the Arts 1967, Exec. Cttee. Delhi Slipi Chakra 1967–, also Founder-Ed. monthly journal, Contra 1966 and full-time painter; one-man exhbns. in New Delhi 1962, 1963, 1964, 1965, 1966, in Bombay 1966; in group shows Warsaw 1961, Saigon 1963, Tokyo Biennale 1965, Art Now in India, London, Newcastle and Brussels 1965–66, Seven Indian Painters, London 1967; Dir. Roopankar Museum of Fine Art; Jawaharlal Nehru Research Fellow; represented in various public and pvt. collections in India and abroad. *Address:* c/o Gallery Chemould, Jahangir Art Gallery, Mahatma Gandhi Road, Bombay 1; 6/17 W.E.A., New Delhi 5, India.

SWAN, Sir John William David, K.B.E., B.A.; Bermudian politician; b. 3 July 1935, Bermuda; s. of John Nicholas and Margaret Swan; m. Jacqueline Roberts 1965; one s. two d.; ed. Cen. School and Howard Acad., Bermuda and W. Virginia Wesleyan Coll.; Real-Estate Salesman with Rego Ltd. 1960–62; Founder, C.E.O. and Chair. of John W. Swan Ltd. 1962–; mem. Parl. 1972–, Minister for Marine and Air Services, Labour and Immigration 1977–78, Home Affairs 1978–82, Premier of Bermuda 1982–95; fmr. Parl. Sec. for Finance, Chair. Bermuda Hosp. Bd., Chair. Dept. of Civil Aviation; mem. Chief. Execs. Org. and World Business Council; mem. and Fellow, Senate, Jr. Chamber Int. 1992; Hon. LL.D. (Tampa Univ.) 1986, (W. Va. Wesleyan Coll.) 1987, (Atlantic Union Coll., Mass.) 1991; St. Paul's Anniversary Citation 1969, Outstanding Young Man of the Year 1969, Int. Medal of Excellence (first recipient), Poor Richard Club of Phila. 1987, and other awards; Hon. Freeman City of London 1985; United Bermuda Party. *Leisure interests:* tennis, sailing. *Address:* Swan Building, 26 Victoria Street, Hamilton, HM12; 11 Grape Bay Drive, Paget PG06, Bermuda (Home). *Telephone:* (441) 295-4255 (Office); (441) 236-1303 (Home).

SWANEPOEL, Rev. Frederik, B.A., B.D.; South African ecclesiastic; b. 5 Oct. 1938, Barkley-West Dist.; s. of David Swanepoel and Johanna Swanepoel; m. Marié Kathleen Hobden; two s. two d.; ed. Wonderboom High School and Univ. of Pretoria; Sec. Synod of Eastern Transvaal 1979–87, Moderator 1987–95; Chair. Gen. Cttee. for Youth, Dutch Reformed Church 1977–81; Vice-Chair. Parents' Educ. Soc. Transvaal 1985–89; mem. Transvaal Educ.

Council 1985–89; Chair. Curatorium, Univ. of Pretoria 1991; Moderator, Dutch Reformed Church 1994–. *Publications:* Daniel. Bible Study for the Youth 1980; articles in church periodicals. *Leisure interests:* music, reading, gardening, family. *Address:* P.O. Box 4445, Pretoria 0001, South Africa. *Telephone:* (012) 322-7658 (Office); (012) 803-5703 (Home). *Fax:* (012) 803-5703.

SWANSON, David Heath, M.A.; American business executive; b. 3 Nov. 1942, Illinois; s. of Neil H. Swanson and Helen M. Swanson; m. 1st Elizabeth Farwell 1963 (divorced); two s.; m. 2nd Cynthia Tripp 1990; m. 3rd Carolyn Breitinger; ed. Harvard Coll. and Univ. of Chicago; Account Exec. First Nat. Bank of Chicago 1966–69; Deputy Man. Brown Bros. Harriman 1969–72; Treas. Borden Int. 1972–75; Chief Financial and Admin. Officer, Continental Grain, then Sr. Vice-Pres. and Group Pres., Sr. Vice-Pres. and Gen. Man. World Grain Div. 1975–86; Pres. and C.E.O. Central Soya Co. Inc. 1986–94; Chair. Premier Agricultural Tech. Inst. 1994–; Chair., C.E.O. Explorer Nutrition Group, New York 1994–96; Pres. C.E.O. Countrymark Cooperative Inc., Indianapolis 1996–98; mem. Council on Foreign Relations; mem. Advisory Bd. Export-Import Bank of U.S.; mem. Bd. Int. Policy Council on Trade and Agric. *Publications:* articles on mountaineering and exploration. *Address:* c/o Countrymark Cooperative Inc., 950 N. Meridian Street, Indianapolis, IN 46204, U.S.A.

SWANTON, Ernest William, C.B.E.; British author and journalist, b. 11 Feb. 1907; s. of late William Swanton; m. Ann Swanton 1958; ed. Cranleigh; with Evening Standard 1927–39; played cricket for Middx. 1937–38; served in World War II, captured at Singapore, prisoner of war 1942–45; Acting Maj. Beds. Yeomanry; cricket and rugby corresp. Daily Telegraph 1946–75; Editorial Dir. The Cricketer 1967–68, Pres. 1988–; mem. Marylebone Cricket Club Cttee. 1975–84, Hon. Life Vice-Pres. 1989; mem. Cttee. Kent County Cricket Club 1971–91, Pres. 1981; Pres. Sandwich Town Cricket Club 1976–, Cricket Soc. 1976–83, Forty Club 1983–86. *Publications include:* (with H. S. Altham) A History of Cricket 1938, Denis Compton, A Cricket Sketch 1948, Elusive Victory 1951, Victory in Australia 1954–55, Sort of a Cricket Person (memoirs) 1972, Follow On (memoirs) 1977, As I Said at the Time: a Lifetime of Cricket 1983, Last Over 1996. *Leisure interests:* cricket, golf. *Address:* Delf House, Sandwich, Kent, CT13 9HB, England.

SWAR AL-DAHAB, Gen. (see Dahab, Gen. Swar al-).

SWART, Karel, B.CHEM.ENG.; Netherlands oil company executive; b. 26 May 1921, Singapore; m. Wilhelmina A. Bruinsma 1950; ed. Delft Univ.; with Royal Dutch Shell-Laboratory, Amsterdam 1948; Refinery Start-up Team, Shell Berre 1953; Bombay 1954, Geelong 1955; Cen. Office, The Hague 1956; various tech. and managerial posts at Cardón Refinery, Compañía Shell de Venezuela Ltd. 1958–65; Gen. Man. Curaçao 1965; Dir. Mfg. and Supply, Venezuela 1967; Special Assignment, Cen. Office, The Hague 1968; Man. Dir. N.V. Koninklijke Nederlandsche Petroleum Maatschappij (Royal Dutch) 1979, The Shell Petroleum Co. Ltd. 1979, Prin. Dir. Shell Petroleum N.V. 1970–79; Chair. Supervisory Bd., Royal Boskalis Westminster NV (Papendrecht) 1980–; Kt. Order of Netherlands Lion. *Address:* Brouwerlaan 6, Voorschoten, Netherlands (Home).

SWARTZ, Col. the Hon. Sir Reginald William Colin, K.B.E., M.B.E., E.D., F.B.I.M., F.A.I.M., F.A.I.C.D.; Australian fmr. politician and company director; b. 14 April 1911; ed. Toowoomba and Brisbane Grammar Schools; Parl. Under-Sec. Ministry of Commerce and Agric. 1952–56; Parl. Sec. Ministry of Trade 1956–61; Minister for Repatriation 1961–64; Minister for Health 1964–66; Minister for Social Services 1965–, for Civil Aviation 1966–69, for Nat. Devt. 1969–72; Leader of House of Reps. 1971–72; (retd.); fmr. Dir. eight Australian cos.; fmr. Councillor, Inst. of Dirs.; life mem. Liberal Party. *Address:* 56 Immanuel Gardens, Maroochydore South, Queensland 4558, Australia. *Telephone:* (07) 5443 0656. *Fax:* (07) 5443 0656.

SWAYZE, Patrick; American actor and dancer; b. 18 Aug. 1954, Houston; s. of Patsy Swayze; m. Lisa Niemi 1976; ed. Harkness and Joffrey Ballet Schools; began as dancer in Disney on Parade on tour as Prince Charming; appeared on Broadway as dancer in Goodtime Charley, Grease; television appearances in North and South: Books I and II, The New Season, Pigs vs. Freaks, The Comeback Kid, The Return of the Rebels, The Renegades. *Films:* Skatetown USA 1979, The Outsiders, Uncommon Valor, Red Dawn, Grandview USA (also choreographer), Dirty Dancing (co-wrote song and sings She's Like the Wind), Steel Dawn, Tiger Warsaw, Road House, Next of Kin, Ghost, Point Break, City of Joy, Father Hood, Tall Tales, To Wong Foo—Thanks for Everything—Julie Newmar, Three Wishes, Letters from a Killer 1997, Vanished 1998, Black Dog 1998. *Address:* c/o William Morris Agency, 151 El Camino Drive, Beverly Hills, CA 90212, U.S.A.

SWE, U Ba; Myanma politician; b. 19 April 1915, Tavoy; s. of U Tun Hlaing and Daw Pe Lay Swe; m. Daw Nu Nu Swe 1944; six s. four d.; ed. Rangoon Univ.; Pres. Rangoon Univ. Students' Union 1940–41; one of the founders of People's Revolutionary Party 1939; Chief of Civil Defence in the "Kebotai" 1942–45; one of leaders of Anti-Japanese Resistance Movement, in charge of Rangoon, Hanthawaddy and Insein Dists. 1944–45, arrested and detained by Japanese; Pres. Socialist Party (originally People's Revolutionary Party) 1945, later Sec.-Gen.; Pres. Asia Socialist Conf. 1952–56, 1956–60; Sec.-Gen. Anti-Fascist People's Freedom League 1947–58; Leader of "Stable" Group 1958; fmr. M.P. from Taikkyi; Minister of Defence 1952–58, concurrently Prime Minister 1956; Deputy Prime Minister 1957–59; Leader of Opposition 1958; under political arrest 1963–66; Yugoslav Banner, First Class, Noble Order of the White Elephant (Thailand), Star of Revolution, First Degree, Naing-Ngani Gon Yi, Title Class 1 1980. *Leisure interests:* gardening, billiards, writing. *Address:* 84 Innes Road, Yangon, Myanmar. *Telephone:* 21355.

SWEDEN, King of (see Carl XVI Gustaf).

SWEENEY, John Joseph; American trades union official; b. 5 May 1934, New York; s. of John Sweeney and Patricia Sweeney; m. Maureen Power; one s. one d.; ed. Iona Coll.; with IBM (Int. Business Machines Corpn.); researcher Int. Ladies Garment Workers Union; fmr. Pres. Service Employees Int. Union; Pres. AFL-CIO (American Fed. of Labor and Congress of Industrial Orgs.) 1995–. *Publication:* America Needs a Raise 1996. *Address:* AFL-CIO, 815 16th Street, NW, Washington, DC 20006, U.S.A. *Telephone:* (202) 637-5000. *Fax:* (202) 637-5058.

SWENSEN, Joseph Anton; American conductor and composer; b. 4 Aug. 1960, New Jersey; m. 2nd Kristina Algot-Sörensen; two s. (one from previous marriage); Prin. Guest Conductor Stockholm Chamber Orchestra 1994–, Lahti Symphony Orchestra 1995–; Prin. Conductor Scottish Chamber Orchestra (SCO) 1996–; toured Japan with SCO 1995, U.S.A. 1999; debut at Edin. Int. Festival with SCO 1998; cycle of Beethoven performances to mark 25th anniversary of SCO 1999/2000; regular appearances with Royal Stockholm Philharmonic and Swedish Radio Symphony Orchestras; guest conductor with Los Angeles Philharmonic, Toronto Symphony, London Philharmonic, City of Birmingham Symphony, Oslo Philharmonic, Finnish Radio Symphony, Gothenburg Symphony and Ulster Orchestras, BBC Nat. Orchestra of Wales, Lausanne Chamber Orchestra; own orchestral works have been performed by various orchestras. *Address:* c/o Van Walsum Management Ltd., 4 Addison Bridge Place, London, W14 8XP, England. *Telephone:* 0171-371 4343. *Fax:* 0171-371 4344.

ŚWIĘCICKI, Marcin, D.ECON.SC.; Polish politician and economist; b. 17 April 1947, Warsaw; s. of Andrzej Święcicki and Jadwiga Święcicka; m. Joanna Święcicka 1969; three s., one d.; ed. Warsaw Univ.; Asst., Econ. Sciences Inst., Warsaw Univ. 1971–72; Councillor, then Chief Specialist in Planning Comm. attached to the Council of Ministers 1972–82; Dir. for study and analysis matters 1982–87, Gen. Sec. of Consultative Econ. Council 1987–89; mem. PZPR 1974–90, PZPR Cen. Cttee. 1989–90, Sec. PZPR Cen. Cttee. Aug.–Sept. 1989; participant Round Table debates, mem. group for economy and social policy Feb.–April 1989; Deputy to Sejm (Parl.) 1989–91, 1993–96; Minister for Foreign Econ. Co-operation 1989–91; Deputy Chair. Sejm Cttee. on Foreign Econ. Relations 1993–95; Mayor of Warsaw 1994–; Co-Chair. Govt. and Territorial Self-Govt. Jt. Comm. 1994–; Adviser to Lithuanian Govt. 1993; co-f. Tax Reform Movt. 1993–; Co-founder Cen. European Forum 1995; Pres. Union of Polish Metropolises 1994–; mem. Polish Econ. Soc. 1978–; Co-founder Consensus Dialogue Group 1986–90, mem. Secr. 1986–89; Co-founder and Treas. Polish Asscn. for the Club of Rome 1987–91; scientific worker, Inst. of Econ. Sciences, Polish Acad. of Sciences 1991–93; independent adviser 1991–94; mem. Democratic Union (now Freedom Union) 1991– (mem. Council, Warsaw br. 1991–93, mem. Nat. Council 1993–); Co-founder and Vice-Pres. Polish Fulbright Alumni Asscn. 1993–96; Fellowship, George Washington Univ., Washington, D.C. 1975–76, Harvard Univ., Cambridge, Mass., U.S.A. 1984–85; Hon. mem. Union of Warsaw Uprising Veterans (Związek Powstańców Warszawskich); Labour and Wages Comm. Award 1971, Award of Chair. of Radio and TV Cttee. 1988, Daily Trybuna Ludu Award 1989; Gold and Bronze Cross of Merit; Bronze Medal in long jump, European Junior Athletic Championship, Odessa 1966. *Publications include:* Perspektywiczne programowanie problemowe w Polsce 1978, Revolution in Social Sciences and Future Studies Movement 1978, Rozwój sytuacji i polityki gospodarczej (Ed.) 1985, Reforma własnościowa 1989, The Economy of Ukraine (with Stanisław Wellisz) 1993. *Leisure interests:* mountain hiking, jogging, volley-ball, political books, memoirs, essays. *Address:* Zarząd Miasta Stołecznego Warszawy, pl. Bankowy 3/5, 00-950 Warsaw (Office); Węgrzyna 29, 00-769 Warsaw, Poland (Home). *Telephone:* (22) 6201395 (Office); (22) 6423651 (Home). *Fax:* (22) 695 62 63 (Office); (22) 642 36 51 (Home).

SWIFT, Graham Colin, F.R.S.L.; British writer; b. 4 May 1949, London; s. of Lionel Allan Stanley Swift and Sheila Irene (née Bourne) Swift; ed. Dulwich Coll., Queens' Coll., Cambridge, Univ. of York; Geoffrey Faber Memorial Prize, Guardian Fiction Prize, Royal Society of Literature Winifred Holtby Award 1983, Premio Grinzane Cavour (Italy) 1987, Prix du meilleur livre étranger (France) 1994, Booker Prize, James Tait Black Memorial Prize 1996; Hon. L.H.D. (East Anglia) 1998. *Publications:* (novels) The Sweet Shop Owner 1980, Shuttlecock 1981, Waterland 1983, Out of This World 1988, Ever After 1992, Last Orders 1996; (short stories) Learning to Swim and Other Stories 1982; The Magic Wheel (ed. with David Profumo) 1986. *Leisure interest:* fishing. *Address:* c/o A. P. Watt, 20 John Street, London, WC1N 2DR, England.

SWIFT, Hewson Hoyt, PH.D.; American biologist; b. 8 Nov. 1920, Auburn, New York; s. of Arthur L. Swift Jr. and Hildegarde Hoyt Swift; m. Joan Woodcock 1942; two d.; ed. Swarthmore Coll., State Univ. of Iowa and Columbia Univ.; Curator of Spiders, U.S. Nat. Museum, Washington, D.C. 1945–46; Instr. in Zoology, Univ. of Chicago 1949–51, Asst. Prof. 1951–55, Assoc. Prof. 1955–58, Prof. of Zoology 1958–68, Prof. of Biology 1968–71, Distinguished Service Prof. of Biology and Pathology and Chair. Dept. of Biology 1973–77, George Wells Beadle Distinguished Service Prof. of Biology and Pathology 1977–84, of Molecular Genetics and Cell Biology and of Pathology 1984–90, Prof. Emer. 1990–; Visiting Prof. Harvard Univ. 1970–71; Sr. Visiting Research Fellow, CSIRO, Canberra 1977–78; mem. N.A.S., N.A.S. (India), American Acad. of Arts and Sciences; various awards. *Publications:* about 150 scientific research articles. *Leisure interests:* wildlife study, photography. *Address:* Department of Molecular Genetics and Cell Biology, 1103 East 57th Street, Chicago, IL 60637, U.S.A. *Telephone:* (773) 702-8041. *Fax:* (773) 702-9270.

SWINBURNE, Richard Granville, M.A., B.PHIL., F.B.A.; British professor of philosophy; b. 26 Dec. 1934, Smethwick; s. of William H. Swinburne and Gladys E. Swinburne; m. Monica Holmstrom 1960 (separated 1985); two d.; ed. Univ. of Oxford; Fereday Fellow, St. John's Coll. Oxford 1958–61; Leverhulme Research Fellow in History and Philosophy of Science, Univ. of Leeds 1961–63; lecturer in Philosophy, Univ. of Hull 1963–72; Prof. of Philosophy, Univ. of Keele 1972–84; Nolloth Prof. of the Philosophy of the Christian Religion, Univ. of Oxford 1985–; Visiting Assoc. Prof. Univ. of Md. 1969–70. *Publications:* Space and Time 1968, The Concept of Miracle 1971, An Introduction to Confirmation Theory 1973, The Coherence of Theism 1977, The Existence of God 1979, Faith and Reason 1981, The Evolution of the Soul 1986, Responsibility and Atonement 1989, Revelation 1991, The Christian God 1994, Is There a God? 1996, Providence and the Problem of Evil 1998. *Address:* Oriel College, Oxford, OX1 4EW, England. *Telephone:* (01865) 276589. *Fax:* (01865) 791823.

SWING, William Lacy, M.TH.; American diplomatist; b. 11 Sept. 1934, Lexington, North Carolina; s. of Baxter D. and Mary F. (née Barbee) Swing; m. Yuen Cheong 1993; one s. one d. from previous marriage; ed. Catawba Coll. and Yale Univ.; Vice-Consul, Port Elizabeth, S. Africa 1963–66; int. economist, Bureau of Econ. Affairs, Dept. of State 1966–68; Consul, Hamburg 1968–72; Dept. of State 1972–74; Deputy Chief of Mission, U.S. Embassy, Bangui, Cen. African Repub. 1974–76; Sr. Fellow, Center for Int. Affairs, Harvard Univ. 1976–77; Deputy Dir., Office of Cen. African Affairs, Dept. of State 1977–79; Amb. to People's Repub. of Congo 1979–81, to Liberia 1981–85, to S.A. 1989–93, to Nigeria 1992–93, to Haiti 1993–98, to Democratic Repub. of Congo 1998–; Dir. Office of Foreign Service Assignments and Career Devt. 1985–87; Deputy Asst. Sec. for Personnel 1987–89; Hon. LL.D. (Catawba Coll.), (Hofstra) 1994; Presidential Distinguished Service Award 1985. *Publication:* U.S. Policy Towards South Africa: Dilemmas and Priorities 1977. *Leisure interests:* tennis, squash. *Address:* c/o Department of State, 2201 C Street, NW, Washington, DC 20520, U.S.A.

SWINNERTON-DYER, Sir (Henry) Peter Francis, Bt., K.B.E., M.A., F.R.S.; British mathematician and university professor; b. 2 Aug. 1927, Ponteland; s. of the late Sir Leonard Dyer; m. Dr. Harriet Crawford 1983; ed. Eton and Trinity Coll., Cambridge; Research Fellow, Trinity Coll. 1950–54; Commonwealth Fund Fellow, Univ. of Chicago 1954–55; Coll. Lecturer in Math., Trinity Coll. 1955–71, Dean 1963–70; Lecturer in Math., Cambridge Univ. 1960–71, Prof. of Math. 1971–88, Master of St. Catharine's Coll. 1973–83; Vice-Chancellor, Cambridge Univ. 1979–81; Chair. Univ. Grants Cttee. 1983–89, Chief Exec. Univs. Funding Council 1989–91, European Scientific and Tech. Ass. 1994–; Chair. Sec. of State for Nat. Heritage's Advisory Cttee., Library and Information Services Council 1992–95; mem. Advisory Bd. for Research Councils 1977–90; Vice-Pres. Inst. of Manpower Studies 1983; Visiting Prof. Harvard Univ. 1970–71; Chair. Cttee. on Acad. Org., Univ. of London 1980–81; mem. Advisory Council on Science and Tech. 1987–89; Hon. Fellow, Worcester Coll., Oxford 1980, St. Catharine's Coll., Cambridge 1983, Trinity Coll., Cambridge 1983; Hon. D.Sc. (Bath) 1981, (Wales) 1991; Hon. Sc.D. (Ulster) 1991, (Birmingham) 1992, (Nottingham) 1992; Hon. LL.D. (Aberdeen) 1991. *Publications:* Analytic Theory of Abelian Varieties 1974, and papers in learned journals. *Leisure interest:* gardening. *Address:* The Dower House, Thriplow, Royston, Herts., SG8 7RJ, England. *Telephone:* (01763) 208220.

SWINTON, Tilda; British actress; ed. New Hall, Cambridge; performance art appearance sleeping in a glass case, Serpentine Gallery, London 1996. *Films include:* The Last of England, The Garden 1990, Edward II 1991, Orlando 1993, Wittgenstein 1993, Female Perversions 1996, Love is the Devil 1997, Conceiving Ada 1997, The War Zone 1998; TV: Your Cheating Heart 1989.

SWIRE, Sir Adrian (Christopher), Kt., M.A.; British business executive; b. 15 Feb. 1932; s. of the late John Kidston Swire and Juliet Richenda Barclay; m. Lady Judith Compton 1970; two s. one d.; ed. Eton, Univ. Coll., Oxford; served Coldstream Guards 1950–52; fmrly. with R.A.F.V.R., Royal Hong Kong A.A.F.; joined Butterfield & Swire in Far East 1956, Hon. Pres., Exec. Dir. John Swire and Sons Ltd. 1997–; Pro-Chancellor Southampton Univ. 1995–; Chair. China Navigation Co. Ltd. 1968–88; Dir. Brooke Bond Group 1972–82, Navy, Army and Air Force Insts. 1972–87; Pres. Gen. Council of British Shipping 1980–81, Deputy Chair. 1982–85; Chair. Int. Chamber of Shipping 1982–87; mem. Gen. Cttee. Lloyds Register 1967–, Int. Advisory Council, China Int. Trust and Investment Corpn. 1995–; Chair. R.A.F. Benevolent Fund 1996–; Pres. Spitfire Soc. 1996–; Trustee R.A.F. Museum 1983–91; Hon. Air Commodore No. 1 (Co. Hertford) Maritime HQ Unit, Royal Auxiliary Air Force 1987–; Hon. D.L. (Oxford) 1989; Hon. D.Sc. (Cranfield) 1995. *Address:* Swire House, 59 Buckingham Gate, London, SW1E 6AJ, England.

SWIRE, Sir John (Anthony), Kt., M.A., C.B.E.; British business executive; b. 28 Feb. 1927; s. of the late John Kidston Swire and Juliet Richenda Barclay; m. Moira Cecilia Ducharne 1961; two s. one d.; ed. Eton, Univ. Coll., Oxford; served Irish Guards UK and Palestine 1945–48; joined Butterfield and Swire, Hong Kong 1950, Exec. Dir. John Swire and Sons Ltd. 1955–92, Chair. 1966–87, Hon. Pres., Dir. 1987–, Dir. Swire Pacific Ltd. 1965–92; Dir. Royal Insurance PLC 1975–80, British Bank of Middle East 1975–79, James Finlay PLC 1976–92, Ocean Transport and Trading PLC 1977–83, Shell Transport and Trading Co. 1990–95; Chair. Hong Kong Asscn. 1975–87, Cook Soc. 1984; mem. London Advisory Cttee. Hongkong and Shanghai Banking Corpn. 1969–89, Euro-Asia Centre Advisory Bd. 1980–91, Advisory Council School of Business Stanford Univ. 1981–90, Council Univ. of Kent at Canterbury 1989– (Deputy Pro-Chancellor 1993–); Hon. Fellow St Antony's Coll., Oxford 1987, Univ. Coll., Oxford 1989; Hon. LL.D. (Hong Kong) 1989; Hon. D.C.L. (Kent) 1995; D.L. (Kent) 1996. *Address:* Swire House, 59 Buckingham Gate, London, SW1E 6AJ, England.

SWOBODA, Peter, D.B.A.; Austrian professor of finance; b. 13 April 1937, Bad-Deutsch Altenburg; s. of Gottfried Swoboda and Maria Magdalena Swoboda; m. 1st Eva Swoboda 1959; m. 2nd Birgit Swoboda 1978 (divorced 1988); one s. three d.; ed. Hochschule für Welthandel, Vienna; Asst. Prof. Hochschule für Welthandel, 1959–64; Visiting Assoc. Prof. in Accountancy, Univ. of Ill. (Urbana-Champaign) 1965–66; Full Prof. in Accountancy and Finance, Johann Wolfgang Goethe Univ., Frankfurt 1966–70; Prof. of Industrial Econs., Karl Franzens Univ., Graz 1970–; Pres. European Finance Asscn. 1980–81; Assoc. mem. Austrian Acad. of Sciences 1980, Full mem. 1983. *Publications:* Investition und Finanzierung 1992, Betriebliche Finanzierung 1994. *Address:* c/o Faculty of Business Administration and Economics, Karl Franzens University Graz, Universitätsplatz 3, 8010 Graz, Austria.

SYBERBERG, Hans-Jürgen; German film producer; b. 8 Dec. 1935, Pomerania; m.; ed. studies in literature and history of art at Munich; produced over 80 short TV films 1963–65; Stage adaptation of Die Marquise von O 1990. *Films:* Fritz Kortner Rehearses Schiller's Intrigue and Love 1965, Shylock Monolog 1966, The Count Pocci 1967, How Much Earth Does a Man Need 1968, Sexbusiness Made in Passing 1969, San Domingo 1970, After My Last Removal 1971, Ludwig—Requiem for a Virgin King 1972, Ludwig's Cook 1972, Karl May—In Search of Paradise Lost 1974, The Confessions of Winifred Wagner 1975, Hitler, A Film from Germany 1977, Parsifal (Kritiker Preis, Berlin 1983) 1982, Die Nacht 1984, Edith Clever liest Joyce-Molly 1985, Fräulein Else 1987, Penthesilea 1988, Marquise von O. 1990, Ein Traum, was sonst? 1994. *Publications:* The Film as the Music of the Future 1975, Filmbuch 1976, Die Kunst als Rettung aus der deutschen Misere (essay) 1978, Unglück und Glück der Kunst in Deutschland nach dem letzten Kriege 1991. *Address:* Genter Strasse 15A, 80805 Munich, Germany.

SYCHOU, Alyaksandr; Belarus diplomatist; b. 19 Sept. 1951, Homel, Belarus; m. Natalia Vedmedenko 1976; one s. one d.; ed. Moscow State Inst. of Int. Relations; Third then Second Sec., Ministry of Foreign Affairs 1979–84; Del. Perm. Mission of the Repub. of Belarus to UN office and other int. orgs., Geneva 1984–90; Head Dept. of Foreign Econ. Relations, Ministry of Foreign Affairs 1991–92, Deputy Minister for Foreign Affairs 1992–94; Perm. Rep. Repub. of Belarus to the UN 1994–; Chair. First Cttee. of the 51st session of the UN Gen. Ass., 19th Special Session 1996–97; Vice-Pres. ECOSOC 1998. *Leisure interests:* art, opera, tennis, soccer. *Publications:* numerous articles on Belarus foreign policy and int. affairs. *Address:* Permanent Mission of Belarus to the United Nations, 136 East 67th Street, New York, NY 10021, U.S.A. *Telephone:* (212) 535-3420. *Fax:* (212) 734-4810.

SYDOW, Max von; Swedish actor; b. 10 April 1929, Lund, Sweden; s. of Carl W. von Sydow and Greta Rappe; m. 1st Kerstin Olin 1951 (divorced 1995), two s.; m. 2nd Catherine Brelet 1997; ed. Royal Dramatic Theatre School, Stockholm; Norrköping-Linköping Theatre 1951–53, Hälsingborg Theatre 1953–55, Malmö Theatre 1955–60, Royal Dramatic Theatre, Stockholm 1960–74, 1988–; Best Actor, European Film Award, Berlin 1988. *Plays acted in include:* Peer Gynt, Henry IV (Pirandello), The Tempest, Le misanthrope, Faust, Ett Drömspel, La valse des toréadors, Les sequestrés d'Altona, After the Fall, The Wild Duck, The Night of the Tribades 1977, Duet for One 1981, The Tempest 1988, Swedenhielms 1990, And Give Us the Shadows 1991, The Ghost Sonata 1994. *Films acted in include:* Bara en mor 1949, Miss Julie 1950, Det sjunde inseglet (The Seventh Seal) 1957, Ansiktet (The Face) 1958, The Virgin Spring 1960, Såsom i en spegel (Through a Glass Darkly) 1961, Nattvardsgästerna (Winter Light) 1963, The Greatest Story Ever Told 1963, 4×4 1965, Hawaii 1965, Quiller Memorandum 1966, The Hour of the Wolf 1966, The Shame 1967, A Passion 1968, The Emigrants 1969, The New Land 1969, The Exorcist 1973, Steppenwolf 1973, Heart of a Dog 1975, Three Days of the Condor 1975, The Voyage of the Damned 1976, The Desert of the Tartars 1976, Cadaveri Eccelenti 1976, Deathwatch 1979, Flash Gordon 1979, Victory 1980, The Flight of the Eagle 1981, Hannah and Her Sisters 1985, Duet for One 1986, Pelle the Conqueror 1986, Father 1989, Until the End of the World 1990, The Ox 1991, The Silent Touch 1991, The Bachelor 1991, A Kiss Before Dying, Grandfather's Journey 1992, Time is Money 1993, Needful Things 1994, Judge Dredd, Hamsun 1996, What Dreams May Come 1997; Dir. Katinka 1989. *Television:* The Last Civilian, Christopher Columbus, Samson and Delilah 1983, The Last Place on Earth 1984, The Belarus File 1984, Gosta Berling's Saga 1985, The Wisdom and the Dream 1989, Red King White Knight, Hiroshima Out of the Ashes 1990, Best Intentions 1991, Radetzky March 1994, Citizen X

1995, Confessions 1996, Solomon 1997. *Leisure interest:* nautical history. *Address:* c/o London Management, 2-4 Noel Street, London W1V 3RB, England; c/o Agence Anne Alvares Correa, 18 rue Troyon, 75017 Paris, France.

SYED PUTRA BIN SYED HASSAN JAMALULLAIL (see Perlis).

SYKES, Alfred Geoffrey, PH.D., D.SC., C.CHEM., F.R.S.C.; British professor of inorganic chemistry; b. 12 Jan. 1934, Huddersfield; s. of Alfred H. Sykes and Edith Wortley; m. Elizabeth Blakey; two s. one d.; ed. Huddersfield Coll. and Univ. of Manchester; lecturer, Univ. of Leeds 1961–70, Reader 1970–80; Prof. of Inorganic Chem. Univ. of Newcastle-upon-Tyne 1980–; mem. SERC BBSRC/EPSRC Panels/Cttees.; Ed. Advances in Inorganic Chemistry; mem. editorial bds. various specialist journals; Visiting Prof. Argonne Nat. Labs. 1968, Heidelberg Univ. 1975, Northwestern Univ. 1978, Univ. of Sydney 1984, Univ. of Kuwait 1989, Univs. of Adelaide and Melbourne 1992, Newfoundland 1995, W. Indies 1997, Lausanne 1998 etc.; Tilden Medal and Prize, Royal Soc. of Chem. 1984. *Publications:* Kinetics of Inorganic Reactions 1964; over 420 papers and reviews in chemistry journals. *Leisure interests:* travel, classical music, sport. *Address:* Department of Chemistry, University of Newcastle-upon-Tyne, NE1 7RU (Office); 73 Beech Court, Darras Hall, Newcastle-upon-Tyne, NE20 9NE, England (Home). *Telephone:* (0191) 2226700 (Office); (01661) 825425 (Home).

SYKES, Eric, O.B.E.; British actor, writer and director; b. 4 May 1923; s. of Vernon Sykes and Harriet Sykes; m. Edith Eleanor Milbradt; one s. three d.; ed. Ward Street School, Oldham; left school at 14; long-running TV comedy show Sykes (with Hattie Jacques); many other TV appearances. *Films include:* actor: Orders are Orders, Watch Your Stern, Very Important Person, Heavens Above, Shalako, Those Magnificent Men in Their Flying Machines, Monte Carlo or Bust!, The Boys in Blue, Absolute Beginners. *Plays include:* Big Bad Mouse 1977–78, A Hatful of Sykes 1977–78, Run For Your Wife 1992, The 19th Hole 1992, Two of a Kind 1995, Fools Rush In 1996, The School For Wives 1997, Kafka's Dick 1998–99; Freeman City of London 1988, Lifetime Achievement Award, Writers' Guild 1992. *Leisure interest:* golf. *Publications:* The Great Crime of Grapplewick 1996, UFOs Are Coming Wednesday 1995, Smelling of Roses 1997. *Address:* 9 Orme Court, London, W2 4RL, England. *Telephone:* 0171-727 1544. *Fax:* 0171-792 2110.

SYKES, Lynn R., PH.D.; American professor of geological sciences; b. 16 April 1937, Pittsburgh, Pa.; s. of Lloyd A. Sykes and Margaret Woodburn Sykes; m. 1st (divorced); m. 2nd Katherine Flanz 1986 (divorced); m. 3rd Kathleen Mahoney 1998; ed. Massachusetts Inst. of Tech. and Columbia Univ.; Research Asst., Lamont-Doherty Geological Observatory, Columbia Univ. 1961–64, Research Assoc. 1964–66, Adjunct Asst. Prof. of Geology 1966–68, Head of Seismology Group 1973–83, Higgins Prof. of Geological Sciences 1978–; main areas of interest are seismology, tectonics and arms control, earthquake prediction and the detection and identification of underground atomic tests; Chair. Nat. Earthquake Prediction Evaluation Council; Fellow American Geophysical Union, Geological Soc. of America, Royal Astronomical Soc., A.A.A.S.; mem. N.A.S., American Acad. of Arts and Sciences, Geological Soc. of London, Arms Control Asscn.; Walter H. Bucher Medal of American Geophysical Union for original contribs. to basic knowledge of earth's crust 1975. *Publications:* numerous articles in scientific journals. *Leisure interests:* hiking, canoeing, opera, travel. *Address:* Lamont-Doherty Earth Observatory, Columbia University, Palisades, New York, NY 10964; 100 Washington Spring Road, Palisades, NY 10964, U.S.A. *Telephone:* (914) 365-8880. *Fax:* (914) 359-5215.

SYKES, Peter, B.SC., M.SC., PH.D., F.R.S.C., C.CHEM.; British chemistry teacher; b. 19 Feb. 1923, Manchester; s. of Charles Hyde Sykes and Alice Booth; m. Joyce Tyler 1946; two s. one d.; ed. Rydal School, Colwyn Bay, Univ. Manchester, Clare Coll., Cambridge; Research Fellow, St. John's Coll., Cambridge 1947–50, Univ. Demonstrator in Organic Chem. 1947–55, Lecturer 1955–82, Fellow, Christ's Coll. 1956–, Vice-Master 1984–88; Visiting Research Prof., Coll. of William and Mary, Williamsburg, Va. 1970–71, 1977–78; Visiting Prof., Univ. of Cape Town 1974, 1980, Univs. of São Paulo and Campinas, Brazil 1976, Univ. of Melbourne 1983–84; Mellor Medal, Univ. of N.S.W. 1984. *Publications:* The Search for Organic Reaction Pathways 1972, A Guidebook to Mechanism in Organic Chemistry 1986, A Primer to Mechanism in Organic Chemistry 1995 (all trans. into several languages); numerous papers on organic reaction mechanisms. *Leisure interests:* chamber music, church architecture, talking, wine. *Address:* Christ's College, Cambridge, CB2 3BU, England. *Telephone:* (01223) 334917.

SYLVESTRE, (Joseph Jean) Guy, O.C., M.A.; Canadian librarian and author; b. 17 May 1918, Sorel, Quebec; s. of Maxime A. Sylvestre and Yvonne Lapierre; m. Françoise Poitevin 1943; two s. one d.; ed. Univ. of Ottawa; Private Sec. to Prime Minister 1948–50; Assoc. Parl. Librarian 1953–68; Nat. Librarian of Canada 1968–83; Pres. Canadian Inst. for Historical Microreproductions 1983–86; Fellow (past Pres.), Royal Soc. of Canada, Hon. Librarian 1975–91; numerous hon. degrees; Commdr. Ordre int. du Bien public, Order of Merit of Poland. *Publications:* Louis Francoeur, journaliste 1941, Situation de la poésie canadienne 1942, Anthologie de la poésie canadienne d'expression française 1943, Poètes catholiques de la France contemporaine 1944, Jules Laforgue 1945, Sondages 1945, Impressions de théâtre 1950, Panorama des lettres canadiennes-françaises 1964, Canadian Writers/Ecrivains canadiens 1964, Un siècle de littérature canadienne 1967, Guidelines for National Libraries 1987. *Leisure interests:* golf, reading. *Address:* 2286 Bowman Road, Ottawa, Ont., KIH 6V6, Canada.

SYMON, Lindsay, C.B.E., T.D., M.B.CH.B., F.R.C.S., F.R.C.S.(E.); British professor of neurological surgery; b. 4 Nov. 1929, Aberdeen; s. of William L. Symon and Isabel Symon; m. Pauline Barbara Rowland 1954; one s. two d.; ed. Aberdeen Grammar School and Aberdeen Univ.; house physician/surgeon Aberdeen Royal Infirmary 1952–53; Clinical Officer/Jr. Specialist in Surgery, British troops in Austria 1953–55; Surgical Registrar Aberdeen Royal Infirmary 1956–58; Clinical Research Fellow MRC 1958–61; Rockefeller Travelling Fellow Wayne Univ., U.S.A. 1961–62; Sr. Registrar Neurosurgery Nat. Hosps. 1962–65, Consultant Neurosurgeon 1965–78; mem. External Staff MRC 1965–78; Prof. of Neurological Surgery, Sr. Surgeon, Nat. Hosps. 1978–95; Hon. Consultant Neurosurgeon St. Thomas' Hosp., London 1973–95, Hammersmith Hosp., London 1978–95, Royal Nat. Throat, Nose and Ear Hosp. 1979–95, The Italian Hosp. 1981–89; Adjunct Prof. Dept. of Surgery, Southwestern Medical School, Dallas 1982–95; Civilian Adviser in Neurosurgery, R.N. 1979–95; Pres. World Fed. of Neurosurgical Socs. 1979–93, Hon. Pres. 1993–; Pres. Harveian Soc., London 1997–98; Hon. F.A.C.S.; Jamieson Medal, Australasian Neurosurgical Soc. 1982, John Hunter Medal, Royal Coll. of Surgeons 1985, Joachim Zulch Prize, Max Planck Inst. 1993, Otfrid Förster Medal, German Soc. Neurosurgery 1998. *Publications:* texts on cerebrovascular surgery, physiology of the cerebral circulation, surgery of acoustic neuroma, general neurosurgical topics. *Leisure interests:* golf, prehistory. *Address:* Maple Lodge, Rivar Road, Shalbourne, nr. Marlborough, Wilts., SN8 3QE, England. *Telephone:* (01672) 870501. *Fax:* (01672) 870501.

SYMS, Sylvia; British actress and director; b. 6 Jan. 1934, London; m. Alan Edney 1957 (divorced 1989); one s. one d.; ed. Royal Acad. of Dramatic Art; Founder-mem. and Artistic Dir. Arbela Production Co.; numerous lectures, including Dodo White McLarty Memorial Lecture 1986; mem. The Actors' Centre 1986–91. *Films include:* Ice Cold in Alex 1953, The Birthday Present 1956, The World of Suzie Wong 1961, Run Wild Run Free 1969, The Tamarind Seed 1974, Chorus of Disapproval 1988, Shirley Valentine 1989, Shining Through 1991, Dirty Weekend. *Television includes:* Love Story 1964, The Saint 1967, My Good Woman 1972–73, Nancy Astor 1982, Ruth Rendell Mysteries 1989, Dr. Who 1989–90, May to December 1989–90, The Last Days of Margaret Thatcher 1991, Natural Lies, Mulberry, Peak Practice. *Theatre includes:* Dance of Death, Much Ado About Nothing, An Ideal Husband, Ghosts, Entertaining Mr. Sloane 1985 (Best Actress Award, Manchester Evening News), Who's Afraid of Virgina Woolf? 1989, The Floating Lightbulb 1990, Antony and Cleopatra 1991. *Radio includes:* Little Dorrit, Danger in the Village, Post Mortems. *Plays and television directed:* Better in my Dreams 1988, The Price 1991, Natural Lies 1991–92; Variety Club Best Actress in Films Award 1958, Ondas Award for Most Popular Foreign Actress (Spain) 1966. *Address:* c/o Barry Brown and Partners, 47 West Square, London, SE11 4SP, England. *Telephone:* 0171-582 6622.

SYQUIA, Enrique, LL.D.; Philippine lawyer and professor of law; b. 22 May 1930, Manila; s. of late Vicente A. Syquia and Consolacion P. Syquia; m. Leticia Corpus Syquia 1964; five s.; ed. Univ. of Santo Tomas, Univ. of Madrid and Hague Acad. of Int. Law; Head Syquia Law Offices, Manila 1954–; Prof. of Law 1976–; Publr. The Lawyers Review 1987–, The Diplomats Review 1989–; Dir. Philippine Bar Asscn. 1971–, Pres. 1981–84; mem. Exec. Council, Int. Bar Asscn. 1974–, Vice-Pres. 1982–84; Pres. Int. Law Asscn. 1978–80, Vice-Chair. 1989–; Pres. Philippines Council for Foreign Relations 1987–; Vice-Pres. Union Int. des Avocats 1989–; Pres. Int. Inst. of Humanitarian Law 1991–; Special Adviser Philippine Del. to UN Gen. Ass. 1989–; mem. and/or officer of numerous nat. and int. law orgs. including A.B.A., American Judicature Soc., American Soc. of Int. Law, Inst. Hispano-Luso-Americano de Derecho Internacional; Hon. Consul-Gen. of Kingdom of Jordan in the Philippines 1987; del. to numerous law confs. at home and abroad since 1953; Patron American Soc. of Int. Law 1989–; various hon. trusteeships etc.; Sovereign Mil. Order of Malta. *Publications:* The Tokyo Trial 1955, A Manual on International Law 1957, Twenty Papers on World Affairs 1989; articles in legal journals. *Leisure interests:* reading, heraldry, stamp-collection. *Address:* 6th Floor, Cattleya Condominium, 235 Salcedo Street, Legaspi Village, Makati, Manila (Office); 127 Cambridge Circle, North Forbes, Makati, Manila, Philippines (Home). *Telephone:* 817-1089; 817-1095/1098 (Office); 810-7975; 810-7977 (Home).

SYRADEGHYAN, Vano Sumbatovich; Armenian politician; b. 13 Nov. 1946, Koti, Noyemberyan Region; m.; five c.; ed. Yerevan State Univ.; army service 1966–69; journalist in a number of publs. of the Repub. -1988; mem. Cttee. Karabakh 1988; Chair. of Bd. Armenian Nat. Movt.; Deputy to Armenian Supreme Soviet 1990–92; Minister of Internal Affairs Repub. of Armenia 1992–96; Mayor of Yerevan 1996–98. *Publications include:* articles, essays in numerous publs. of Armenia. *Address:* c/o Office of the Mayor, Yerevan, Armenia.

SYRON, Richard Francis, PH.D.; American bank executive and economist; b. 25 Oct. 1943, Boston; s. of Dominick Syron and Elizabeth (McQuire) Syron; m. Margaret Mary Garatoni 1972; one s. one d.; ed. Boston Coll., Tufts Univ.; Deputy Dir. Commonwealth of Mass. 1973–74; Vice-Pres., Economist Fed. Reserve Bank of Boston 1974–82, Sr. Vice-Pres., Econ. Advisor 1982–85, Pres., C.E.O. 1989–94; Chair. American Stock Exchange 1994–; Exec. Asst. to Sec. U.S. Treasury, Washington 1979–80, Deputy Asst.

to Sec. for Econ. Policy 1980–81; Asst. to Chair. Volcker Fed. Reserve, Washington 1981–82; Pres. Fed. Home Loan Bank of Boston 1986–88; mem. 20th Century Fund Task Force on Financial Speculation, Boston Chamber of Commerce; Chair. Boston Coll. and American Business Conf.; mem. Bd. of Dirs. John Hancock, Thermo Electron, The Dreyfus Corpn. *Address:* American Stock Exchange, 86 Trinity Place, New York, NY 10006, U.S.A. *Telephone:* (212) 306-1000. *Fax:* (212) 306-5464.

SYRYJCZYK, Tadeusz; Polish politician; b. 9 Feb. 1948, Kraków; m.; ed. Acad. of Mining and Metallurgy, Kraków; lecturer Acad. of Mining and Metallurgy, Kraków 1971–89; with ABAKS, Kraków 1987–89; Minister of Industry 1989–90; Chief Prime Minister's team of advisers and Under-Sec. of State in Council of Ministers 1992–93; Minister of Transport and Maritime Economy 1998–; deputy to Sejm (Parl.) 1991–; mem. Democratic Union Parl. Club 1991–94, Freedom Union Parl. Club 1994–, Chair. 1997–98; mem. Parl. Comm. for Privatisation, Econ. System and Industry 1991–92, Parl. Comm. for Econ. Policy, Budget and Finances 1993–97, Parl. Comm. for Public Finances 1997–98, Parl. Comm. for Nat. Defence 1998–; mem. Democratic Union 1991–94; mem. Solidarity Trade Union 1980–; mem. Presidium Małopolska Region 1981; interned during state of martial law 1981–82; mem. regional authorities, Kraków 1982–84; mem. Freedom Union 1994–, Nat. Council and Regional Council, Kraków 1983–; Vice-Pres. Freedom Union 1995–; co-founder Industrial Soc. of Kraków 1987; mem. Polish Tourist Country-Lovers' Asscn., Polish Informatics Soc. *Publications:* papers on automatics and informatics, articles in nat. magazines. *Leisure interest:* tourism. *Address:* Ministry of Transport and Maritime Economy, ul. Chałubińskiego 4/6, 00-928 Warsaw, Poland. *Telephone:* (22) 624 43 00.

SYSUYEV, Oleg Nikolayevich; Russian politician; b. 23 March 1953, Kuybyshev (now Samara); m.; one s. one d.; ed. Kuybyshev Moscow Aviation Inst.; master, head. of tech. div., engineer, Sec. CP Cttee. Kuibyshev aviation team 1976–87; Sec. Krasnoglinsk Dist. CP Cttee. of Kuybyshev 1987–91; del. to 18th CP Congress; Head Samara Admin. 1991–94; Mayor of Samara 1994–97; active participant movt. Russia Our Home; Co-Chair. Union of Mayors of Russian towns 1995–97; Deputy Head Russian Govt., Minister of Labour and Social Devt. 1997–98; Co-ordinator Russian Comm. on Regulation of Trade-Social Relations 1997–98; First Deputy Head Admin. of Pres. Yeltsin 1998–. *Leisure interests:* playing guitar, piano, violin. *Address:* The Kremlin, korp. 14, Moscow, Russia. *Telephone:* (095) 910 10 96.

SZABAD, György, PH.D.; Hungarian politician and historian; b. 4 Aug. 1924, Arad, Romania; s. of Erzsébet Blantz; m. Andrea Suján; one d.; ed. Loránd Eötvös Univ., Budapest; served in forced labour camp 1944; on staff of Nat. Archives 1949, univ. asst. lecturer 1954, lecturer 1956, Prof. 1970; Corresp. mem. Hungarian Acad. of Sciences 1982, mem. 1998–; mem. Revolutionary Cttee. 1956; founding mem. and nat. bd. mem. Hungarian Democratic Forum 1987; founding mem. Hungarian Democratic People's Party; Speaker of Hungarian Parl. 1990–94, mem. Parl. 1994–98. *Publications include:* Kossuth on the Political System of the United States of America 1975, Hungarian Political Trends between the Revolution and the Compromise 1849–1867 1977, Conceptualization of a Danubian Federation 1998. *Address:* Kelenhegyi ut. 40/B.1118, 1054 Budapest, Hungary. *Telephone:* 385-3761.

SZABO, Denis, O.C., D. ÈS SC., F.R.S.C.; Canadian/Belgian professor of criminology; b. 4 June 1929, Budapest, Hungary; s. of Jenö Denes and Catherine Zsiga; m. Sylvie Grotard 1956; two d.; ed. Univs. of Budapest, Louvain and Paris; Asst. Univ. of Louvain 1952–56; lecturer in Sociology, Catholic Univ. of Paris and Lyon 1956–58; Asst. Prof. Univ. of Montreal 1958–59, Assoc. Prof. 1959–66, Prof. of Criminology 1966–95, Prof. Emer. 1995–; founder and Dir. School of Criminology, Univ. of Montreal 1960–70; founder and Dir. Int. Center for Comparative Criminology, Univ. of Montreal 1969–84, now Chair. of Bd.; consultant to Canadian, U.S., French, Hungarian and UN comms. and bodies on crime prevention; Hon. Pres. Int. Soc. of Criminology; mem. Hungarian Acad. of Sciences 1993–; Dr. h.c. (Siena, Budapest, Aix-Marseille, Panteios-Athens); Sutherland Award, American Soc. of Criminology 1968, Golden Medal Beccaria, German Soc. of Criminology 1970; Commdr. Ordre Nat. du Mérite, Côte d'Ivoire, Commdr. Ordre Nat. du Mérite, Hungary, Chevalier des Arts et des Lettres, France. *Publications:* Crimes et Villes 1960, Criminologie et Politique Criminelle 1978, The Canadian Criminal Justice System (with A. Parizeau), Science et Crimes 1986, Criminologie Empirique au Québec (ed. with Marc Le Blanc), De l'anthropologie à la criminologie comparée 1993, Traité de Criminologie Empirique (ed. with Marc Le Blanc). *Leisure interest:* gardening, swimming. *Address:* University of Montreal, C.P. 6128, Montreal, H3C 3J7 (Office); C.P. 26, Georgeville, JOB 1TO, Canada (Home). *Telephone:* (514) 343-7065 (Office); (819) 843-4343 (Home). *Fax:* (514) 343 2269.

SZABÓ, István; Hungarian film director and writer; b. 18 Feb. 1938; s. of Dr. István Szabó and Mária Vita; m. Vera Gyürey; ed. Budapest Acad. of Theatre and Film Arts; started as mem. Balázs B. Studio, Budapest; leading mem. Hungarian Film Studios; Tutor, Coll. of Theatre and Film Arts, Budapest; mem. Acad. of Motion Picture Arts and Sciences, Akademie der Künste, Berlin; Béla Balázs Prize 1967, Kossuth Prize 1975. *Productions: short films:* Concert 1961; Variations upon a Theme 1961, Te (You) 1963 (Grand Prix de Tours), Budapest, amiért szeretem (Budapest, Why I Love It), 1971; a series including: Álom a házról (Dream about the House) 1971 (Main Prize of Oberhausen); *documentaries:* Kegyelet (Piety) 1967, Várostérkép (City Map) 1977 (Grand Prix of Oberhausen), Steadying the Boat 1996; *TV plays:* Osbemutató (Première) 1974, Katzenspiel (Cat Play) 1982, Bali 1983; *TV film:* Offenbach 1995; *full-length films:* Álmodozások kora (The Age of Day-Dreaming) 1964, Apa (Father) 1966, Szerelmesfilm (A Film of Love) 1970, Tüzoltó utca 25 (No. 25 Fireman's Street) 1973 (Grand Prix of Locarno), Budapesti mesék (Budapest Tales) 1976, Bizalom (Confidence) 1979 (Silver Bear of Berlin, Acad. Award Nomination 1981), Der grüne Vogel (The Green Bird) 1979, Mephisto 1981 (Acad. Award 1982, David di Donatello Prize (Italy), Prize of Italian Critics, Prize of Critics, U.K.), Colonel Redl 1985 (Acad. Award Nomination 1986, BAFTA Award 1986, Best W. German Film—Golden Band), Hanussen 1988 (Acad. Award Nomination), Meeting Venus 1990, Sweet Emma, Dear Böbe 1991 (Silver Bear of Berlin, European Acad. Award for Best Screenplay); *operas:* Boris Godunov, Leipzig 1993, Il Trovatore, Vienna 1993. *Address:* I. S. L.-Film, 1149 Budapest, Róna utca 174; 1132 Budapest, Váci-6, Hungary. *Telephone:* (01) 251-9369; (01) 340-55-59. *Fax:* (01) 340-55-59.

SZABÓ, Iván, PH.D.; Hungarian politician, engineer and economist; b. 8 Jan. 1934, Budapest; s. of Ferenc Szabó and Mária Sallai; m. Ildikó Zemenszky; two d.; ed. Budapest Tech. Univ. and Budapest Econ. Univ.; construction engineer with Road and Railway Bldg. Co. 1957–59; tech. dir. Bldg. Mechanization Trust 1959–69; chief engineer Civil Eng. Co. 1969–78; export man. Water Construction Trust 1978–85; Pres. Eng. and Constructing Co-operative 1985–90; arrested for activity in revolutionary students movt. 1956; joined Hungarian Democratic Forum 1988; mem. of Parl. 1990–98; Chair. Econ. Comm. of Parl. 1990–91; Minister of Trade and Industry 1991–93, of Finance 1993–94, Man. Pres., and Leader of Parl. Group of Hungarian Democratic Forum 1994–96; Pres. and Leader of Parl. Group of Hungarian Democratic People's Party 1996–98, Hon. Pres. 1998–. *Leisure interest:* gardening. *Address:* Hungarian Democratic People's Party, 1011 Budapest, Iskola u. 16 (Office); H-1092 Budapest, Ra'day u. 4, Hungary (Home). *Telephone:* (1) 218-74-75. *Fax:* (1) 218-74-75.

SZABÓ, Magda; Hungarian author; b. 5 Oct. 1917, Debrecen; d. of Alex Szabó and Madeleine Jablonczay; m. Tibor Szobotka 1948; graduated as a teacher 1940; worked in secondary schools 1940–44, 1950–59; started literary career as poet and has since written novels, plays, radio dramas, essays and film scripts; works have been translated into 33 languages including English, French, German, Italian, Russian, Polish, Swedish; mem. Acad. of Sciences of Europe, Hungarian Széchenyi Acad. of Art and Literature; Hon. D.Phil.; Baumgarten Prize 1949; József Attila Prize 1959 and 1972, Kossuth Prize 1978, Getz Corpn. Prize (U.S.A.) 1992, Szén Ernő Prize for Dramatic Art. *Publications:* poems: Neszek (Noises); autobiog.: Ókut (Old Well); novels for children: Szigetkék (Island-Blue), Tündér Lala (Lala the Fairy), Abigél (Abigail); novels: Azőz (The Fawn), Fresko (Fresco), Disznótor (Night of Pig-Killing), Pilatus (Pilate), A Danaida (The Danaid), Mózes 1.22 (Genesis 1.22), Katalin utca (Kathleen Street), A szemlélők (The Onlookers), Régimódi történet (Old-Fashioned Story), Az ajtó (The Door), The Moment 1990; plays: Kiálts város (Cry Out, Town!), Az a szép fényes nap (That Bright Beautiful Day), A meráni fiu (The Boy of Meran), A csata (The Battle) 1982, Béla Király (King Béla), A Macskák Szerdája (The Wednesday of the Cats) 1985, Outside the Circle 1980, The Lethargy of the Semigods (essays) 1986, The Logic of the Butterfly (essays) 1997. *Leisure interest:* pets. *Address:* H-1026 Budapest II, Julia-utca 3, Hungary.

SZABÓ, Miklós, PH.D., D.SC.; Hungarian archaeologist; b. 3 July, 1940 Szombathely; s. of Dezső Szabó and Irén Süle; m. Ágnes Molnár; three s.; ed. Eötvös Loránd Univ. of Arts and Sciences (ELTE); with Dept. of Archaeology Hungarian Nat. Museum 1963–66; with Dept. of Antiquities Museum of Fine Arts 1966–85, Deputy Dir. Gen. 1985–87; asst. prof. Dept. of Classical Archaeology of ELTE 1983–89, Prof. and head of Dept. 1989, gen. vice-rector 1991–93, Rector 1993–; research into Ancient Greek and Celtic archaeology, involved in excavations in Greece by the French Inst. of Archaeology in Athens 1970–78; in France 1978, led the Hungarian excavation expedition in Bibracte, France 1988; Visiting Prof. Sorbonne 1980–81, Ecole normale supérieure, Paris 1985, Coll. de France 1989; Pres. Archaeological Cttee. Hungarian Acad. of Sciences 1994; corresp. mem. Hungarian Acad. of Sciences 1995; corresp. mem. of the German Archaeological Inst. 1977, Royal Acad. of Barcelona 1997; mem. Editorial Bd. of Acta Archaeologica and Études Celtiques; Hon. mem. Greek Archaeological Soc. 1998; Dr. h.c. (Univ. of Burgundy, Dijon) 1997; Kuzsinszky Medal 1984, College de France Medal 1989, Rómer Flóris Commemorative Medal 1990, City of Dijon Commemorative Medal 1991, Chevalier de l'Ordre Nat. du Mérite (France) 1995. *Publications:* The Celtic Heritage in Hungary 1971, Hellász fénykora (The Golden Age of Greece) 1972, Világtörténelem képekben I, (World History in Pictures I, co-author) 1972, A keleti kelta művészet (Eastern Celtic Art, co-author) 1974, Les Celtes (co-author) 1978, Les Celtes en Pannonie. Contribution à l'histoire de la civilisation celtique dans la cuvette des Karpates 1988, I Celti (co-author) 1991, Les Celtes de l'Est: Le second âge du Fer dans la cuvette des Karpates 1992, Decorated Weapons of the La Tène Iron Age in the Carpathian Basin (co-author) 1992, Archaic Terracottas of Boeotia 1994, Storia d'Europa II (co-author) 1994, A la frontière entre l'Est et l'Ouest (co-author) 1998. *Address:* ELTE, 1053 Budapest, Egyetem tér 1–3, Hungary. *Telephone:* (1) 266-3119.

SZABOLCSI, Miklós; Hungarian literary critic and historian; b. 3 March 1921, Budapest; s. of Lajos Szabolcsi and Erzsébet Mészáros; m. Hedvig Margulesz 1948; one s.; ed. Budapest Univ.; Gymnasium teacher 1945–48, 1950–53; Prof., Kossuth Lajos Univ., Debrecen 1964–70; Prof., Eötvös Loránd

Univ., Budapest 1979–94; Visiting Prof., Univ. of Paris 1965–66; Corresp. mem. Hungarian Acad. of Sciences 1965, mem. 1976–; Dept. Head, Hungarian Acad. of Sciences Inst. for History of Literature 1957, Man. Dir. 1967–81; Pres. Section I (Language and Literature), Hungarian Acad. of Sciences 1970–85; Gen. Dir. Nat. Inst. of Pedagogy 1981–88; Pres. Féd. Int. des Langues et Littératures Modernes 1981–84; Vice-Pres. Asscn. Int. des Critiques Littéraires 1972–; Ed. literary periodicals: Csillag 1953–56, Élet és Irodalom 1959–61, Neohelicon; State Prize 1980. *Publications:* Költészet és korszerűség 1959, Kis Magyar Irodalomtörténet 1960, Elődök és Kortársak 1962, Biography of Attila József Vols. I–IV 1963–98, A verselemzés kérdéseihez 1969, Jel és kiáltás 1971, Szocialista irodalom—változó világ 1973, A clown mint a művész önarcképe a modern művészetben 1979, A neoavantgarde 1981, A XX. század világirodalmi áramlatai (20th Century World Literature Trends) 1987; about 80 studies on comparative and Hungarian literature and theory of literature in Hungarian and foreign scientific papers. *Address:* XII. Németvölgyi u. 75/a, 1124 Budapest, Hungary. *Telephone:* (1) 175-8921.

SZAJNA, Józef; Polish theatre director, author, scenographer and painter; b. 13 March 1922, Rzeszów; s. of Julian Szajna and Karolina Pieniążek; m. Bożena Sierosławska 1953; one s.; ed. Acad. of Fine Arts, Cracow; mem. Anti-Nazi Resistance, in Auschwitz and Buchenwald 1939–45; Lecturer, Acad. of Arts, Cracow 1954–65; Co-founder and scenographer Teatr Ludowy, Nowa Huta 1955–63, Man. Dir. 1963–66; Dir. and Scenographer, Teatr Stary, Cracow 1966–70; Man. Dir. Teatr Klasyczny, now Art Gallery and experimental theatre called Teatr Studio, Warsaw 1971–82; Prof. Acad. of Arts, Warsaw 1972–, and Dir. School for Stage Designers 1972–78; mem. jury World Council of Culture, Mexico; Dir. Acropolis 1962, Inspector 1963, Puste Pole 1965, Zamek 1965; Dir. and Scenario Faust 1971, Replika I, Göteborg 1971, Replika II, Edin. Festival 1972, Replika III, Nancy Festival 1973, Replika IV, Poland 1973, Replika V, France, Théâtre des Nations 1980, Replika VI, Istanbul Festival 1984, Replika VII, Tel-Aviv 1986, Witkacy 1972, Gulgutiera 1973, Dante, Int. Theatre Festival, Florence 1974, Witkacy II 1975, Cervantes 1976, (Special Prize, XIII Kalisz Theatre Encounters 1977), Majakowski 1978, Śmierć na gruszy 1978, Dante żywy (Dante Alive), Dubrovnik 1981, Dante III, Essen 1985, Dante 1992, Slady, Slady II, Ankara 1993, Workshop, Ziennia, Cairo 1993, Vida y muerte del Poeta Cervantes, Alcalá de Henares 1993, Szczątki, Int. Theatre Festival, Portugal 1995; one-man exhbn. Reminiscence, XXXV Venice Biennale 1970, Gegenwart einer Vergangenheit (Present of the Past), Frankfurt-am-Main 1978, Silhouettes, São Paulo 1979, Pictures of Man, West Berlin 1980, Essen 1984, Tel-Aviv, Jerusalem 1986, Cracow 1986, Warsaw 1987, Moscow 1987, Biennial Sao Paulo 1989, Venice Biennale 1990, Paris 1990, Gdańsk 1991, Warsaw 1992, Poznań 1992, Centrum Scenografii, Katowice 1993, Museum, Ankara 1993, Círculo de Bellas Artes, Madrid 1993; contrib. to many int. exhbns. and theatre festivals, including Quebec Festival 1986 (award winner); works of art in galleries and museums in Poland and abroad; Hon. mem. Int. Asscn. of Art; numerous awards including Gold Centaur Award 1982, Meritorious Award for Nat. Culture 1986, Gold Medal, 40th Anniversary of War Veterans, U.S.S.R. 1987, Int. Hon. Citation from Experimental Theatre, Cairo 1992, Alfred Jurzykowski Foundation Award (U.S.A.) 1995; Kt.'s and Commdr.'s Cross with Star of Order of Polonia Restituta, Great Cross of Polonia Restituta 1997, Order of Banner of Labour (1st Class). *Publications:* Teatr Organiczny (Organic Theatre), On the New Function of Scenography, The Open Theatre, The Matter of Spectacle, Visual Narrative. *Leisure interests:* sport, tourism. *Address:* ul. Smulikowskiego 14 m.8, 00-389 Warsaw, Poland. *Telephone:* 826 47 52.

SZASZ, Thomas Stephen, M.D.; American psychiatrist, psychoanalyst, author and lecturer; b. 15 April 1920, Budapest, Hungary; s. of Julius Szasz and Lily Wellisch; m. Rosine Loshkajian 1951 (divorced 1971); two d.; ed. Cincinnati Univ. and Medical Coll.; staff mem., Chicago Inst. for Psychoanalysis 1951–56; mil. service with U.S. Naval Hosp., Bethesda (attained rank of Commdr.) 1954–56; Prof. of Psychiatry, State Univ. of N.Y., Upstate Medical Center 1956–90, Prof. Emer. 1990–; Co-founder and Chair. Bd. of Dirs., American Asscn. for the Abolition of Involuntary Mental Hospitalization Inc.; mem. Bd. of Dirs., Nat. Council on Crime and Delinquency; Consultant, Cttee. on Mental Hygiene, N.Y. State Bar Asscn. and other advisory positions; mem. A.A.A.S. and other asscns., Int. Editorial Bd. The International Journal of the Addictions, Contemporary Psychoanalysis, Editorial Bd. Journal of Humanistic Psychology, The Humanist, also consulting positions with journals; Hon. Pres. Int. Comm. for Human Rights 1974; D.Sc. h.c. (Allegheny Coll.) 1975, (Univ. Francisco Marroquin, Guatemala) 1979. *Publications:* Pain and Pleasure 1957, The Myth of Mental Illness 1961, 1974, Law, Liberty and Psychiatry 1963, Psychiatric Justice 1965, The Ethics of Psychoanalysis 1965, Ideology and Insanity 1970, The Manufacture of Madness 1970, The Age of Madness 1973, The Second Sin 1973, Ceremonial Chemistry 1974, Heresies 1976, Schizophrenia: The Sacred Symbol of Psychiatry 1976, Karl Kraus and the Soul-Doctors 1976, Psychiatric Slavery 1977, The Theology of Medicine 1977, The Myth of Psychotherapy 1978, Sex By Prescription 1980, Sex: Facts, Frauds and Follies 1981, The Therapeutic State 1984, Insanity: The Idea and its Consequences 1987, The Untamed Tongue: A Dissenting Dictionary 1990, Our Right to Drugs 1992, A Lexicon of Lunacy 1993, Cruel Compassion 1994, The Meaning of Mind 1996, Fatal Freedom: The Ethics and Politics of Suicide 1999. *Address:* Department of Psychiatry, State University of New York, Upstate Medical Center, 750 East Adams Street, Syracuse, NY 13210 (Office); 4739 Limberlost Lane, Manlius, NY 13104, U.S.A. (Home). *Telephone:* (315) 464-3106 (Office); (315) 637-8918 (Home). *Fax:* (315) 464-3163 (Office).

SZCZEPAŃSKI, Jan, PH.D.; Polish sociologist; b. 14 Sept. 1913, Ustroń, Cieszyn Dist.; s. of Paweł Szczepański and Ewa Szczepańska (née Cholewa); m. Eleonora Poczobut 1937; one s. one d.; ed. Univ. of Poznań; Asst. Poznań Univ. 1935–39; during Nazi occupation forced labour in Germany; Asst. Łódź Univ. 1945–52, Extraordinary Prof. 1952–63, Prof. 1963–70, Rector 1952–56; Chief Sociological Dept. Inst. of Philosophy and Sociology, Polish Acad. of Sciences 1957–58, Deputy Dir. 1961–68, Dir. 1968–75; Corresp. mem. Polish Acad. of Sciences 1964, mem. 1969, Vice-Pres. 1971–80; Pres. Int. Sociological Asscn. 1966–70; Vice-Chair. All-Poland Cttee. of Nat. Unity Front 1971–83; Deputy to Sejm (Parl.) 1957–60, 1972–85, Chair. Sejm Socio-Econ. Council 1982–84; Chair. Chief Council of Science, Higher Educ. and Tech., Ministry of Science, Higher Educ., and Tech. 1973–82; Chair. Scientific Council of Intercollegiate Inst. for Research on Higher Educ. 1973–91; mem. Council of State 1977–82; Chair., Sejm Extraordinary Comm. for Control of the Realization of Gdansk, Szczecin and Jastrzębie-Zdrój Agreements 1981; mem. Consultative Council attached to Chair. of State Council 1986–89; mem. Bd. UNRISD, Asscn. Int. de Sociologie (AIS); mem. Nat. Acad. of Educ., U.S.A.; Foreign mem. Finnish Acad. of Science and Literature; Hon. mem. American Acad. of Arts and Sciences 1972; Dr. h.c. (Brno Univ.) 1969, (Łódź Univ., Silesian Univ., Katowice) 1973, (Warsaw Univ.) 1979, (Sorbonne) 1980; Hon. C.B.E. 1978; Commdr.'s Cross with Star, Commdr.'s and Knight's Cross, Order Polonia Restituta 1969, Order of the Builders of People's Poland 1974, State Prize (1st Class) 1974 and others. *Publications:* Structure of Intelligentsia in Poland (in Polish) 1960, History of Sociology (in Polish) 1961, Sociological Problems of Higher Education (in Polish, French, Hungarian) 1963, edited Studies in Polish Class Structure (28 vols.), Introduction to Sociology (in Polish, Czech, Russian, Hungarian and Finnish) 1963, Problems of Contemporary Sociology (in Polish) 1965, Industry and Society in Poland (in Polish) 1969, Sociology and Society (in Bulgarian) 1970, Changes of the Present Time (in Polish) 1970, Co-editor Social Problems of Work Production (in Polish, Russian) 1970, Considerations on the Republic (in Polish) 1971, Reflections on Education (in Polish) 1973, Changes of Polish Community in the Process of Industrialization 1973, Essays on Higher Education 1976, Sprawy ludzkie (Res Humanae) 1979, Konsumpcja a rozwój człowieka (Consumption and Development of Man) 1981, Zapytaj samego siebie 1983, Korzeniami wrosłem w ziemię 1985, O indywidualności 1985, Polska wobec wyzwań przyszłości 1989, Historia mistrzynią życia? 1990. *Address:* Mokotowska 46a m. 23, 00-543 Warsaw, Poland. *Telephone:* 628 21 93.

SZCZYPIORSKI, Andrzej; Polish writer and journalist; b. 3 Feb. 1928, Warsaw; m.; one s.; worked with Polish radio 1951–54, 1959–69; literary head Stanisław Wyspiański Theatre, Katowice 1955–56; diplomatic service 1956–58; worked with numerous magazines, including Kultura, Twórczość, Miesięcznik Literacki, Polityka, Odra; Senator 1989–92; numerous awards including PEN Club Prize 1972, Austrian State Award for European Literature 1988, Nelly Sachs Prize 1989, German Catholics Culture and Art Prize 1990, Herder Prize 1994. *Works include:* novels: Czas przeszły (Time past) 1960, Msza za miasto Arras (A Mass for the Town of Arras) 1971, Początek (Beginning) 1986, Noc, dzień i noc (Night, Day and Night) 1991, Autoportret z kobietą (Self-portrait with Woman) 1994; numerous articles, tales, radio talks, short stories and essays. *Leisure interests:* looking after animals, swimming, walking. *Address:* ul. Idzikowskiego 17, 02-704 Warsaw, Poland.

SZÉKELY, Gábor, M.A.; Hungarian theatre director and university professor of theatre direction; b. 26 May 1944, Jászberény; s. of late Árpád Székely and of Irma Csuka; m. Erika Székely 1967; one s. two d.; ed. Könyves Kalmán Grammar School, Budapest, Budapest Acad. of Dramatic and Cinematic Art; Asst. Dir., Szolnoki Szigligeti Theatre 1968–71, Prin. Dir. 1971–72, Theatre Man. and Prin. Dir. 1972–78; Prin. Dir. Budapest Nat. Theatre 1978–82, apptd. Theatre Man. 1982; Theatre Man. Budapest Katona József Theatre 1982–89; teacher of dramatic art and theatre direction, Acad. of Dramatic and Cinematic Art 1972–, Head Theatre Dirs. Faculty 1990–; has directed in Novi Sad, Stuttgart, Prague Nat. Theatre; invited to direct at Deutscher Theatre, Berlin, Comédie Française, Paris 1991, Helsinki City Theatre 1993; guest teacher Paris Acad. of Dramatic and Cinematic Art 1993; Jászai Mari Prize, Merited Artist, Outstanding Artist, Kossuth Prize, critics' prize for best theatre performance and best theatre direction, several times. *Plays directed include:* As You Like It, Troilus and Cressida, Timon of Athens (Shakespeare), Georges Dandin, L'impromptu de Versailles (Molière), The Death of Tarelkin (Kobilin), The Death of Danton, Woyzeck (Büchner); guest performances abroad with Budapest Nat. and Katona József theatres (among others): Cat's Play (Orkény), Family Toth (Orkény), Moscow, Bucharest, Prague, Helsinki; Catullus (Fust), Vienna, Paris (Odeon), Zürich; Le Misanthrope (Molière), Moscow; Coriolanus (Shakespeare), Berlin; The Escape (Bulgakov), Prague. *Leisure interests:* architecture, fine arts. *Address:* Jókai u. 36. II/12, H-1066 Budapest, Hungary. *Telephone:* (1) 132-4284.

SZILÁGYI, János György, PH.D.; Hungarian art historian; b. 16 July 1918, Budapest; s. of Hugo Szilágyi and Adél Braun; m. Mária Rabinovszky; one d.; ed. Pázmány Péter Univ. of Arts and Sciences; research fellow at the Classical Dept., Museum of Fine Arts of Budapest 1941, Head of Dept. 1952, prof. of Budapest Univ. of Arts and Sciences 1952; mem. Cttee. History of Ancient Civilizations of the Hungarian Acad. of Sciences, Istituto Nazionale di Studi Etruschi, Florence, Deutsches Archäologisches Institut; Ábel Jenő Commemorative Medal, Móra Ferenc Commemorative Medal, Kossuth Award 1991, Eötvös Wreath 1996. *Publications include:* Ceramica etrusco-corinzia figurata I-II 1992–98 and numerous works on Greek and Etruscan art and culture. *Address:* Szépmüvészeti Múzeum, 1396 Budapest, P.O. Box 463, Hungary. *Telephone:* (1) 343-9759.

SZMAJDZIŃSKI, Jerzy Andrzej; Polish politician; b. 9 April 1952, Wrocław; m.; two s.; ed. Acad., Wrocław 1975; with Polish Socialist Youth Union 1975–89; Cen. Cttee. Polish United Workers' Party, (PZPR) 1989–90; mem. Social Democracy of Polish Repub. (SdRP) 1990–, Sec. Gen. 1993–98, Deputy Chair. 1998–; Deputy to Sejm (Parl.) 1985–89, 1991–; Chair. Comm. for Nat. Defence 1993–97, Deputy Chair. 1997–; Chair. Sejm Democratic Left Alliance (SLD) 1996–97, Deputy Chair. 1997–. *Leisure interests:* swimming, tennis, historical books. *Address:* Socjaldemokracja Rzeczypospolitej Polskiej, ul. Rozbrat 44a, 00-419 Warsaw, Poland. *Telephone:* 621 03 41. *Fax:* 621 66 57.

SZOKA, H.E. Cardinal Edmund Casimir; American ecclesiastic; b. 14 Sept. 1927, Grand Rapids; ordained 1954, elected to Gaylord 1971, consecrated bishop of Detroit 1971, prefect 1981, Archbishop Emer. 1990; cr. Cardinal 1988; Pres. of Pref. of Econ. Affairs of Holy See 1990; Pres. Pontifical Comm. for Vatican City State; Second Sec. Council for Relations with States; mem. Congregations for the Causes of Saints, for the Bishops, for the Evangelization of Peoples, for the Clergy, for Insts. of Consecrated Life and for Socs. of Apostolic Life. *Address:* Prefecture for Economic Affairs, 00120 Vatican City.

SZOKOLAY, Sándor; Hungarian composer; b. 30 March 1931, Kunágota; s. of Bálint Szokolay and Erzsébet Holecska; m. 1st Sári Szesztay 1952; m. 2nd Maja Weltler 1970; four s. one d.; ed. Békéstardos Music High School, Budapest Music Acad.; currently musical adviser Hungarian TV; Chair. Hungarian Kodály Soc.; has won prizes in Warsaw, Moscow, Vienna, Merited Artist Distinction 1976, Honoured Artist Distinction 1986, Bartok-Pasztory Prize 1987. *Works include:* Blood Wedding (opera) 1963, Hamlet (opera) 1968, Az iszonyat balladája (The Ballad of Horror), Tetemrehivás (Ordeal of the Bier), Samson (opera) 1973, Csalóka Péter (children's opera, text by Sándor Weöres) 1985, Ecce Homo (passion-opera) 1987; Oratorios: A tüz márciusa (March Fire), Istár pokoljárása (Ishtar's Descent to Hell), Hungarian Psalm; has also written cantatas, songs, chamber music and choral works. *Leisure interests:* car driving, mountaineering.

SZŐLLŐSY, András, D.PH.; Hungarian composer and music historian; b. 27 Feb. 1921, Szászváros, Transylvania; s. of János Szőllősy and Julia Tóth; m. Éva Keményfy 1944; ed. Univ. of Budapest; studied composition, Music Acad., Budapest, under Zoltán Kodály, Accademia di Santa Cecilia, Rome, under Goffredo Petrassi; Prof. of History and Theory of Music, Liszt Ferenc Music Acad., Budapest 1950–; top qualifier, UNESCO Prize, Tribune Int. des Compositeurs, Paris 1970, Merited Artist title 1974, Outstanding Artist 1982, Kossuth Prize 1985, Bartok-Pasztory Prize 1986; Commandeur, Ordre des Arts et Lettres 1987. *Compositions include:* Oly korban éltem (Improvisation of Fear) (ballet) 1963; orchestral works: five Concertos, Musica per Orchestra 1972, Trasfigurazioni 1972, Musica Concertante 1973, Preludio, Adagio e Fuga 1973, Sonorita 1974, Musiche per Ottoni 1975, Concerto for Harpsichord and Strings 1979, Pro Somno Igoris Stravinsky Quieto 1979, Fabula Phaedri for vocal ensemble 1982 (composed for the King's Singers), In Pharisaeos (for choir) 1982, Tristia (for strings) 1983, Planctus Mariae (for female choir) 1983, Suoni di tromba 1984, Miserere (composed for the King's Singers) 1985, Fragments 1985, Quartetto di Tromboni 1986, Canto d'autunno (for orchestra) 1986; Due Paesaggi (for piano) 1987, String Quartet 1988, Elegy (for dixtuor) 1992, Passacaglia Achatio Máthè in memoriam (for string quartet and cello) 1997; songs; incidental music for plays and films. *Publications:* Kodály művészete 1943, Honegger 1960, 1980; Ed. writings of Kodály and Bartók. *Address:* 1118 Budapest, Somlói ut 12, Hungary. *Telephone:* (1) 466-0035.

SZŐNYI, Erzsébet; Hungarian musician; b. 25 April 1924; d. of Jenő Szőnyi and Erzsébet Piszanoff; m. Dr. Lajos Gémes 1948; two s.; ed. Music Acad., Budapest and Paris Conservatoire; teacher of music at a Budapest grammar school 1945–48, Music Acad., Budapest 1948–; leading Prof. of Music Acad. 1960–81; Vice-Pres. Int. Soc. for Music Educ. 1970–74; Co-Chair. Hungarian Kodály Soc. 1978–; Gen. adviser on methodology, Int. Kodály Soc. 1979–; mem. Chopin Soc. of Warsaw, Liszt Soc. of Hungary; Erkel Prize 1959, Hungarian Repub. Medal 1993 Apácai Csere János Prize 1994, Bartók-Pászthory Prize 1995. *Compositions include:* Concerto for Organ and Orchestra; symphonic works: Musica Festiva, Divertimento 1 and 2, Prelude and Fugue, Three Ideas in Four Movements; operas: Tragedy of Firenze, A Gay Lament, Break of Transmission, Elfrida (madrigal opera) 1987–, several children's operas; chamber music, oratorios, vocal compositions, etc. *Publications:* Methods of Musical Reading and Writing, Kodály's Principles in Practice, Travels on Five Continents, Twentieth Century Music Methods. *Leisure interests:* gardening, cooking. *Address:* Ormódi-utca 13, 1124 Budapest XII, Hungary. *Telephone:* (1) 356-7329.

SZUMSKI, Henryk; Polish army officer; b. 6 April 1941, Potulice; m. Wiesława Jawor; three s. one d.; ed. Officer's School, Poznań, Gen. Staff Acad. Polish Armed Forces, Warsaw, Gen. Staff Acad. Armoured Forces of U.S.S.R. Armed Forces, Moscow; career soldier 1964–; Commdr. section and co. of brigade 1964–68, Chief of Staff and Commdr. 1971–76, Chief of Staff and Commdr. of 16th Armoured Div. 1976–78, Commdr., 12th Mechanised Div., Szczecin 1980–84, Chief of Staff of Pomeranian Mil. Dist. 1984–86, deputy chief Gen. Staff for Operational Matters, 1984–87, Commdr Silesian Mil. Dist. 1987–89, First Deputy Chief Gen. Staff, 1989–90, Chief Main Bd. of Combat Training, 1990–92; inspector of Leadership of Gen. Staff 1993–97, Chief of Gen. Staff 1997–, Brig. Gen. 1983, Maj. Gen. 1988, Lieut. Gen. 1997. *Leisure interests:* history, literature, sport. *Address:* Sztab Generalny WP, ul. Rakowiecka 4A, Warsaw, Poland.

SZŰRÖS, Mátyás, PH.D.; Hungarian politician and diplomatist; b. 11 Sept. 1933, Püspökladány; ed. Moscow Univ. Inst. of Int. Relations; on staff of Foreign Ministry 1959–65; staff mem. HSWP 1965–74, Deputy Leader Foreign Dept. HSWP Cen. Cttee. 1974–75, Head 1982–83; Amb. to G.D.R. 1975–78, to U.S.S.R. 1978–82; mem. Cen. Cttee. HSWP 1978, Secr. 1983–89; mem. Parl. 1985–, Chair. Foreign Relations Parl. Cttee. 1985–89 (mem. 1998–), Pres. of Parl. March–Oct. 1989, Acting Pres. 1989–, Vice-Speaker 1990–94; Chair. Hungarian Group of IPU 1989–90, 1994–, mem. Exec. Cttee. IPU 1994–96; Chair. Ópusztaszer Historical Commemorative Cttee. 1989–98, Bd. Trustees Illye's Foundation 1994–98. *Publications:* Hazánk és a nagyvilág (Homeland and World) 1985, Hazánk és Európa (Homeland and Europe) 1987, Magyarságról-Külpolitikáról (Hungary and Foreign Policy) 1989, Cselekvő politikával a magyarságért-Politikai portré (1988–96) (Active policy for Hungary, portrait of a politician) 1996. *Address:* Hungarian National Assembly, 1055 Budapest, Kossuth Lajos tér 1-3, Hungary. *Telephone:* 269-0488.

SZYMBORSKA, Wisława; Polish poet, translator and literary critic; b. 2 July 1923, Kórnik, nr. Poznań; m.; ed. Jagiellonian Univ., Cracow; first work published 1945; mem. Polish Writers' Asscn. 1952–83, mem. Gen. Bd. 1978–83; mem. Editorial Staff Życie Literackie (weekly) 1953–81; Nobel Prize for Literature 1996; Gold Cross of Merit 1955, Kt.'s Cross, Order of Polonia Restituta 1974, Goethe Award (Frankfurt) 1991, Herder Award 1995, Polish PEN Club Award 1996. *Publications:* poetry: Dlatego żyjemy (That's Why We're Alive) 1952, Pyłania Szadawane sobie (Questioning Oneself) 1954, Wołanie do Yeti (Calling Out to Yeti) 1957, Sól (Salt) 1962, Sto pociech (No End of Fun) 1967, Poezje 1970, Wszelki wypadek (Could Have) 1972, Wybór wierszy (Selected Poems) 1973, Wielka liczba (A Large Number) 1976, Ludzie na moście (The People on the Bridge) 1986, Koniec i początek 1993, Widoł 2 ziarmkiem piasku (View With a Grain of Sand) 1996, Poems New and Collected 1957–97 1998. *Address:* Stowarzyszenie Pisarzy Polskich, ul. Kanonicza 7, 31-002 Cracow, Poland.

T

TABAI, Ieremia T., C.M.G.; I-Kiribati politician; b. 1950, Nonouti; m.; two c.; ed. King George V School, Tarawa, St. Andrew's Coll., Christchurch, N.Z., Victoria Univ., Wellington, N.Z.; mem. Gilbert Islands (later Kiribati) House of Ass. 1974–91; fmr. Leader of the Opposition; Chief Minister of the Gilbert Islands 1978–79, also Minister of Local Govt.; Pres. of Kiribati and Minister of Foreign Affairs (fmrly. Gilbert Islands) 1979–91; Sec.-Gen. South Pacific Forum 1991–; Hon. LL.D. (Vic. Univ. of Wellington). *Address:* South Pacific Forum Secretariat, GPO Box 856, Suva, Fiji.

TABAKOV, Oleg Pavlovich; Russian film actor, stage actor and director; b. 17 Aug. 1935, Saratov; s. of Pavel K. Tabakov and Maria A. Beresovskaya; m. 1st Lyudmila Krilova 1959 (divorced), one s. one d.; m. 2nd Marina V. Zudina 1995, one s.; ed. Moscow Arts Theatre Studio-School; co-founder and actor with Sovremennik Theatre 1957–83; with Moscow Arts Theatre 1983–; stage debut 1956; film debut 1957; mem. CPSU 1965–91; master of theatre training 1976–; Assoc. Prof. State Inst. of Theatre Arts (GITIS) 1976–85; Prof. Moscow Arts Theatre Studio School 1985–, Chancellor 1986–; founder and producer, Moscow Theatre Studio 1974–; directed and taught in numerous countries; f. and teacher Stanislavsky Summer School, Cambridge, Mass. 1992–; f. and Pres. Russian-American Performing Arts Center 1992–; State Prize for Acting 1967; People's Artist of the U.S.S.R. 1987. *Film roles include:* Oleg Komelev in The Tight Knot 1956, Nikolay Rostov in War and Peace 1967, Oleg Savin in Noisy Day 1960, Iskremas in Light My Star, Light 1969, Clown in Kashtanka 1975, Shcherbuk in Unfinished Play for Mechanical Piano 1977, Oblomov in A Few Days of I. I. Oblomov's Life 1979 (Oxford Int. Festival Prize for best male actor 1980), Nikolay Pavlovich in Flights of Fancy 1983, Cudechkis in The Art of Living in Odessa 1989, Gen. Vlasik in The Inner Circle 1991, Klaverov in The Shadows 1991, Soukhodritchev in Shirly-Mirly 1995, etc. *Stage roles include:* Misha in Always Alive 1956, Aleksandr in The Same Old Story 1966, Brother Lymon in The Ballad of Sad Cafe 1966, Klava in Always on Sale 1965, Major in Tooth, Others and Major 1971, Balalaykin in Balalaykin and Co. 1974, Anchugin in Provincial Anecdotes 1975, 1996, Malvolio in Twelfth Night 1975, Peter Stockman in Dr. Stockman 1979, Salieri in Amadeus 1983, Hailmayer in Judgers 1985, Sorin in Seagull 1987, Buton in Cabal of Hippocrates 1989, Tacker in I Ought to be in Pictures 1990, Meyer Volf in My Big Land 1991, Famusov in Woe from Wisdom 1992, Uncle in The Same Old Story 1993, Tallyran in Le Souper 1994, Ivan Kolomiytsev in The Last Ones 1995; has directed Champions, Every Wise Man Has a Fool in his Sleeve, The Same Old Story, Goldoni's Revenge. *Leisure interest:* driving a car. *Address:* Moscow Oleg Tabakov Theatre, Chaplygina str. 1A, Moscow 103062 (Office); Chernysherskogo 39, Apt. 3, 103062 Moscow, Russia (Home). *Telephone:* (095) 924-61-37 (Office); 924-76-90 (Home). *Fax:* (095) 200-42-41.

TABONE, Anton; Maltese politician; b. 15 Nov. 1937; s. of Anton Tabone; m. Margerite Stivala; three s.; ed. St. Aloysius Coll.; employee, Nat. Bank of Malta 1955–66; mem. Parl. for Gozo (Nationalist Party) 1966–98; mem. Gozo Civic Council 1966–73; Party spokesman for Agric. and Fisheries, later for Gozo Affairs 1973–87; Minister for Gozo 1987–96; Shadow Minister for Gozo 1996–98; Speaker House of Reps. 1998–. *Address:* House of Representatives, The Palace, Valletta, Malta. *Telephone:* (356) 222294. *Fax:* (356) 242552.

TABONE, Vincent, G.C.B., M.D., D.O.(OXON), D.O.M.S., D.M.J., F.R.C.S.(E), F.E.C.S., K.U.O.M.; Maltese politician and ophthalmic specialist; b. 30 March 1913, Victoria, Gozo; m. Maria Wirth 1941; three s. five d.; ed. St. Aloysius Coll., Univ. of Malta and Univ. of Oxford; served Royal Malta Artillery during World War II; has held sr. ophthalmic posts in various hosps. in Malta; mem. Exec. Cttee. Nationalist Party 1961, Sec.-Gen. 1962–72, First Deputy Leader 1972–77, Pres. 1978–85; mem. Parl. (Nationalist Party) 1966–89; Minister of Labour, Employment and Welfare 1966, of Foreign Affairs 1987–89; Pres. of Repub. of Malta 1989–94; Visiting Prof. Univ. of Malta; Hon. LL.D. (Univ. of Malta) 1989; UN Testimonial for Service to UN Programme on Aging 1989; Grand Cross, Order of Merit (Fed. Repub. of Germany) 1990, Pro Merito Medal (Council of Europe) 1991, Presidential Gold Medal (Royal Coll. of Surgeons of Edin.) 1991, Cavaliere di Gran Croce 1991. *Address:* 33 Carmel Street, Sliema, Malta. *Telephone:* 330994.

TABOR, David, B.SC., PH.D., SC.D., F.R.S., F.INST.P. ; British physicist; b. 23 Oct. 1913, London; s. of Charles Tabor and Rebecca Weinstein; m. Hannalene Stillschweig 1943; two s.; ed. Royal Coll. of Science, London, Cambridge Univ.; Tribophysics, CSIRO, Melbourne, Australia 1940–46; Asst. Dir. of Research, Cambridge Univ. 1946–61, Lecturer in Physics 1961–64, Reader 1964–73, Prof. 1973–81, Emer. Prof. 1981–, Head of Physics and Chem. of Solids, Cavendish Lab. 1969–81; Visiting Prof. Imperial Coll., London 1981–88; Fellow of Gonville and Caius Coll., Cambridge 1957–; Int. Fellow, Stanford Research Inst. 1956; UNESCO Visiting Prof., Israel 1961; Russell Springer Visiting Prof. Univ. of Calif., Berkeley 1970; Foreign Assoc. U.S. Nat. Acad. of Eng. 1995; Hon. D.Sc. (Bath Univ.) 1985; Nat. Award, American Soc. for Lubrication Engineers 1955, Wilson Award, American Soc. of Metals 1969, Inaugural Gold Medal for Tribology, Inst. of Mechanical Engineers 1972, Mayo D. Hersey Award, American Soc. of Mechanical Engineers 1974, Guthrie Medal, Inst. of Physics 1974, Royal Medal, Royal Soc. 1992. *Publications:* Hardness of Metals 1951, Gases, Liquids and Solids 1969 (new edn. Gases, Liquids and Solids and Other States of Matter 1991); (with F. P. Bowden) Friction and Lubrication of Solids, Part I 1950, 1986, Part II 1964, Friction—an Introduction to Tribology 1973; contributions to learned journals on friction and adhesion. *Leisure interest:* Judaica. *Address:* 8 Rutherford Road, Cambridge, CB2 2HH, England. *Telephone:* (01223) 337200 (Office); (01223) 841336 (Home).

TABOR, Hans, DR.RER.POL.; Danish diplomatist; b. 25 April 1922, Copenhagen; s. of Svend Tabor and Dagny Tabor Rasmussen; m. Inger Petersen 1945; two d.; ed. Birkerød Statsskole and Univ. of Copenhagen; Sec., Gen. Secr. OEEC, Paris 1948–50; Sec. Ministry of Foreign Affairs, Copenhagen 1950–52; Asst. Head Danish del. to OEEC 1952–56; Branch Head Ministry of Foreign Affairs 1956, 1957–59; Deputy Sec.-Gen. Suez Canal Users' Asscn., London 1957; Econ. Counsellor, Asst. Head Danish Mission to the European Communities 1959–61, Minister and Head 1961–64, Amb. 1963–64; Perm. Rep. to the UN 1964–67; Minister of Foreign Affairs 1967–68; Rep. of Denmark on the UN Security Council 1967–68; Amb. to Italy (also accred. to Malta) 1968–74; Perm. Rep. to UN 1974; Amb. to Canada 1975–79; Amb. and Perm. Rep. at OECD 1979–86, Chair. OECD Exec. Cttee. 1983; Amb. to Norway 1986–92. *Publications:* Danmark og Marshallplanen (Denmark and the Marshall Plan) 1961, De Seks og det økonomiske samarbejde i Vesten (The Six and Economic Co-operation in the Western World) Krig og Krise—Trods FN (War and Crisis—in spite of the United Nations) 1977, Diplomat blandt politikere (Diplomat Among Politicians) 1995. *Leisure interests:* tennis, swimming, reading, writing. *Address:* Johannes V. Jensens Allé 48, 2000 Frederiksberg, Denmark. *Telephone:* 36-17-38-52.

TABOR, Harry Zvi, PH.D.; British/Israeli research physicist; b. 7 March 1917, London; s. of Charles Tabor and Rebecca Tabor; m. Vivienne Landau 1947; two d.; ed. Quintin Hogg School, London, Univ. of London and Hebrew Univ. of Jerusalem; research physicist in U.K. instrument industry (including defence-related research and devt. 1939–45) 1939–49; Research Council of Israel 1949–74; Dir. Nat. Physical Lab. of Israel 1950–74; Chair. and Scientific Dir. Scientific Research Foundation, Jerusalem 1969–; mem. research cttees. Ministry of Science & Tech., Ministry of Energy and Infrastructure 1975–; Pres. Int. Solar Energy Soc. (ISES) 1981–83; guest lecturer N.A.S. 1961 and at numerous univs.; consultant to UNESCO, etc.; Hon. Ph.D. (Weizmann Inst.) 1992; Royal Soc. Gold Medal Energy Award 1975 for pioneering work on exploitation of solar energy; Diesel Gold Medallist 1977; Farrington Daniels Award (ISES) 1981; Alfred Krupp Energy Prize 1981; Quality of Life Award (Knesset, Israel) 1995, and other honours. *Publications:* book chapters and some 90 papers in scientific journals. *Leisure interests:* music, theatre, study of social problems (non-party). *Address:* P.O. Box 3745, Jerusalem 91036, Israel. *Telephone:* (02) 6435785. *Fax:* (02) 6437470.

TACHI, Ryuichiro; Japanese professor of economics; b. 11 Sept. 1921, Yokohama; m. Yoko Shinmel 1951; two s.; ed. Univ. of Tokyo; Assoc. Prof. of Econs., Univ. of Tokyo 1950–61, Prof. 1961–82, Emer. Prof. 1982–, Dean Faculty of Econs. 1972, Vice-Pres. 1979–81; Prof. of Econs., Aoyama Gakuin Univ. 1984–; Chief Counsellor Inst. for Monetary and Econ. Studies, Bank of Japan 1982–; Dir. Inst. of Public Finance 1982–84; Pres. Japan Soc. of Monetary Econs. 1982–88, Inst. of Fiscal and Monetary Policy, Ministry of Finance 1985–; mem. Japan Acad. 1986–. *Address:* 2-6-20 Kamiosaki, Shinagawa-ku, Tokyo 141, Japan. *Telephone:* (03) 441 0558.

TADLAOUI, Mohammed, B.SC.; Moroccan engineer; b. 1939, Meknes; m.; two s. one d.; ed. Imperial Coll. London and Inst. of Civil Engs. U.K.; research eng. U.K. 1963, project eng. 1966; consulting eng. Morocco 1973; Founder, Pres. and Gen. Dir. SOCOPLAN (consulting engs.) 1975; Co-founder and mem. Moroccan Asscn. of Consulting Engs. (AMCI) 1976; Gen. Sec. Regional Asscn. Grande Ismailia, Rabat Section 1994. *Leisure interests:* swimming, tennis, history, Arabic literature. *Address:* Residence Al Mansour, Zankat Moulay Slimane, Rabat, Morocco.

TADROS, Tharwat Fouad, M.SC., PH.D.; British/Egyptian scientist and academic; b. 29 July 1937, Kena, Egypt; s. of Fouad Tadros Mikhail and Rosa Wasif El-Gouhary; m. Jantina Lodewijka Buter 1969; two s.; ed. Secondary School, Luxor, Egypt, Alexandria Univ.; lecturer in Physical Chem., Faculty of Science, Alexandria Univ. 1962–66; Agric. Univ. Wageningen, Netherlands 1966–68; research worker Lab. for Applied Research, Delft, Netherlands 1968–69; Tech. Officer ICI 1969–74, Sr. Research Officer 1974–78, Research Assoc. 1978–89, Sr. Research Assoc. 1989–; Visiting Prof. Bristol Univ. 1983–84, Imperial Coll., London 1988–; Royal Soc. of Chem. Colloid and Surface Chem. Award and Medal, Silver Medal 1990, Industrial Lecturer. *Publications:* c. 160 scientific articles in learned journals. *Leisure interests:* chess, reading, debates. *Address:* Zeneca Agrochemicals, Jealottis Hill Research Station, Bracknell, Berks., RG12 6EY (Office); 89 Nash Grove Lane, Wokingham, Berks., RG40 4HE, England (Home). *Telephone:* (01344) 424701 (Office); (01734) 732621 (Home).

TAFT, Bob, J.D., M.A.; American politician; b. 8 Jan. 1942; m. Hope Taft; one d.; ed. Yale, Princeton and Cincinnati Univs.; rep. Ohio House of Reps.

1976–80, Commr. Hamilton Co., Ohio 1981–90, Sec. of State of Ohio 1990–99, Gov. of Ohio 1999–; Republican. *Address:* Office of the Governor, 77 South High Street, Columbus, OH 43215, U.S.A.

TAFT, William Howard, IV; American diplomatist, lawyer and government official; b. 13 Sept. 1945, Washington; s. of William Howard and Barbara Hoult Bradfield; m. Julia Vadala 1974; one s. two d.; ed. Yale and Harvard Univs.; Assoc. Winthrop, Stimson, Putnam & Roberts, New York City 1969–70; Adviser to Chair. FTC, Washington 1970; Prin. Asst. to Deputy Dir. of The Office of Man. and The Budget, Washington 1970–72, Exec. Asst. to Dir. 1972–73; Exec. Asst. to Sec. HEW 1973–76, Gen. Counsel 1976–77; Partner Leva, Hawes, Symington, Martin & Oppenheimer 1977–81; Gen. Counsel, The Pentagon 1981–84; Deputy Sec., Dept. of Defense 1984–89; Perm. Rep. to NATO 1989–92; partner Fried, Frank, Harris, Shriver and Jacobson 1992–. *Address:* 1001 Pennsylvania Avenue, N.W., Washington, DC 20004-2505, U.S.A.

TAHER, Abdul Hadi, PH.D.; Saudi Arabian government official; b. 1930, Medina; ed. Ain Shams Univ., Cairo, and Univ. of Calif.; entered Saudi Arabian Govt. service 1955; Dir.-Gen. Ministry of Petroleum and Mineral Resources 1960; Gov., Gen. Petroleum and Mineral Org. (PETROMIN), Riyadh 1962–86; Man. Dir. Saudi Arabian Fertilizers Co. (SAFCO) 1966–76, Jeddah Oil Refinery 1970–; Chair. Arab Maritime Petroleum Transport Co. –1981; Dir. Arabian American Oil Co. (ARAMCO), Saudi Govt. Railways Corpn.; Trustee, Coll. of Petroleum and Minerals; mem. Industrial Research and Devt. Center, Saudi Arabia; Hon. mem. American Soc. of Petroleum Engineers. *Publications:* Income Determination in the International Petroleum Industry 1966, Development and Petroleum Strategies in Saudi Arabia (Arabic) 1970, Energy—A Global Outlook 1981; lectures and papers on economic and petroleum affairs. *Address:* c/o General Petroleum and Mineral Organization (PETROMIN), P.O. Box 757, Riyadh, Saudi Arabia.

TÄHKÄMAA, Taisto Toivo Johannes; Finnish politician and agrologist; b. 11 Dec. 1924, Parainen; s. of Toivo Oskar Rudolf Tähkämaa and Laina Siviä Engblom; m. Riita-Leena Kokolahti 1961; one s, one d.; Consultant, Dist. beet growing 1954–56; State Office, Turku 1956–64; Head, Primary Production Devt. Dept., S.W. Finland Co-operative Abattoir 1964–70; M.P. 1970–91; Minister of Defence 1977–79, of Agric. and Forestry 1979–83; mem. Centre Party. *Leisure interests:* hunting, fishing. *Address:* c/o Keskustapuolue, Pursimiehenkatu 15, Helsinki, Finland.

TAILLANDIER, François, M.A.; French writer; b. 20 June 1955, Chamalières; teacher 1980–83; full-time writer 1984–, also contrib. Le Figaro newspaper and L'Atelier du Roman periodical. *Publications:* (novels) Personnages de la rue du Couteau 1984, Tott 1985, Benoît ou les contemporains obscurs 1986, Les Clandestins (Prix Jean-Freustié) 1990, Les Nuits Racine (Prix Roger-Nimier, Prix Emile Zola), Mémoires de Monte-Cristo 1994, Des hommes qui s'éloignent 1997, Anielka 1999; (essays) Jorge Luis Borges 1993, Aragon (Prix de la critique de l'Acad. française) 1997; Tous les secrets de l'avenir 1996, Journal de Marseille 1999. *Address:* 58 avenue Georges Clemenceau, 94700 Maisons Alfort, France. *Telephone:* (1) 43-76-16-47. *Fax:* (1) 43-76-16-47.

TAILLIBERT, Roger René; French architect; b. 21 Jan. 1926, Châtres-sur-Cher; s. of Gaston Taillibert and Melina Benoit; m. Béatrice Pfister 1965; one d.; ed. schools in Toulouse, Dreux, Argenton-sur-Creuse, Tours, Vaureal and Ecole Nat. des Beaux-Arts, Paris; own practice 1963–; Curator Grand Palais des Champs-Elysées 1977–82, of Palais de Chaillot 1983–86; Pres. Taillibert Gulf Int., U.S.A. *Main works:* Olympic Complex (Parc des Sports, indoor sports hall, swimming pool), Montreal, Canada; Olympic swimming pool, Luxembourg; Nat. Geographic Centre, Amman, Jordan; Officers' Club, Abu Dhabi, U.A.E.; sports complex, Baghdad, Guests' Palace, Bahrain, univ. bldgs., Sousse, Gabès, Tunisia, sports facilities, Cameroon, sports and golf club houses, Yamoussoukro and Abidjan, Côte d'Ivoire; in France: School of Pharmacy, Toulouse, Coca Cola plant, Grigny, pharmaceutical lab. P. Fabre, Castres, DAF plant, Survilliers, skiing and mountaineering nat. school, Chamonix, Parc des Princes stadium, Paris, Nat. Inst. for Sports and Physical Educ., Paris, pre-Olympic centre, Font-Romeu, nuclear plants Penly and Civaux, swimming complex at Nogent-sur-Oise 1995; Lycée Raspail, Paris 1995, Commercial and residential complex, St.-Quentin-en-Yvelines 1995; studies for projects in Iraq and Lebanon; feasibility studies for projects in Argentina and Uruguay (hotels, sports facilities, leisure parks, etc.).; mem. Acad. d'architecture 1974–; mem. Acad. des Beaux-Arts, Inst. de France, Acad. des Sports, Royal Soc. of Arts; Commdr., Légion d'honneur, Commdr., ordre nat. du Mérite, Officier des Palmes Académiques, Commdr. des Arts et des Lettres, Chevalier du Mérite industriel et commercial. *Publications:* Montreal—Jeux Olympiques 1976, Construire l'avenir 1977, Roger Taillibert (autobiog.) 1978. *Leisure interests:* photography, music, painting. *Address:* 163 rue de la Pompe, 75116 Paris, France. *Telephone:* (1) 47-04-29-92. *Fax:* (1) 42-27-37-71.

TAIPALE, Vappu Tuulikki, D.M.; Finnish politician and psychiatrist; b. 1 May 1940, Vaasa; m. 1965; two s. two d.; psychiatrist, Aurora Youth Polyclinic 1970–74; Paediatric Clinic 1975–79; Asst. Prof. of Child Psychiatry, Kuopio Univ. 1980–83, Tampere Univ. 1983–; First Minister of Social Affairs and Health July 1982–May 1983, Second Minister 1983–84; Dir.-Gen. Nat. Bd. of Social Welfare 1984–90; Dir.-Gen. Nat. Agency for Welfare and Health 1991–92, Nat. Research and Devt. Centre for Welfare and Health 1992–; Chair. COST A5 Ageing and Tech.; mem. SDP. *Address:* STAKES National Research and Development Centre for Welfare and Health, Siltasaarenkatu 18, P.O. Box 220, 00531 Helsinki, Finland. *Telephone:* (09) 3967 2011. *Fax:* (09) 3967 2417.

TAIT, Alan A., PH.D.; British international civil servant, academic and consultant; b. 1 July 1934, Edinburgh; s. of Stanley Tait and Margaret Anderson; m. Susan Somers 1963; one s.; ed. Heriots School, Univs. of Edinburgh and Dublin; Lecturer Trinity Coll., Dublin Univ. 1959–70, Fellow 1967, Sen. Tutor 1968; Prof. of Money and Finance Univ. of Strathclyde 1970–76; Visiting Scholar IMF 1971; Consultant to Sec. of State for Scotland 1972–76; Advisor to Pakistan Taxation Comm. 1973, Chief Fiscal Analysis Div., IMF 1975–82, Dep. Dir. Fiscal Affairs Dept. 1982–94, Dir. of Geneva Office 1995–98. *Publications:* Taxation of Personal Wealth 1967, Economic Policy in Ireland (ed. with J. Bristow) 1968, Value-Added Tax 1988; contribs. to numerous acad. journals on public finance and macroeconomics. *Address:* c/o IMF, 58 rue de Moillebeau, 1209 Geneva (Office); Cramond House, Harnet Street, Sandwich, Kent, CT13 9ES.

TAIT, James Francis, PH.D., F.R.S.; British/American scientist; b. 1 Dec. 1925, Stockton-on-Tees; s. of H. Tait and C. L. Brotherton; m. Sylvia A. S. Wardropper 1956; ed. Univ. of Leeds; lecturer in Medical Physics, Middx. Hospital Medical School 1947–57, Joel Prof. of Medical Physics 1970–82, Dir. Biophysical Endocrinology Unit 1970–85; External Scientific Staff, MRC 1955–58; Sr. Scientist, Worcester Foundation, U.S.A. 1958–70; Prof. Emer., Univ. of London 1982–; Hon. D.Sc. (Hull) 1979; Reichstein Award, Int. Soc. of Endocrinology 1976, CIBA Award, American Heart Asscn. for Hypertension Research 1977, Dale Medal, Soc. for Endocrinology 1979, R. Douglas Wright Lecturer, Melbourne 1989. *Publications:* numerous papers on medical physics and endocrinology. *Leisure interests:* gardening, walking, chess, photography. *Address:* Moorlands, Main Road, East Boldre, Nr. Brockenhurst, Hants., SO42 7WT, England. *Telephone:* (01590) 626312. *Fax:* (01590) 626312.

TAIT, Marion, O.B.E.; British ballet mistress; b. 7 Oct. 1950, London; d. of Charles Tait, O.B.E. and Betty Hooper; m. David Morse 1971; ed. Royal Acad. of Dancing and Royal Ballet School; joined Royal Ballet School aged 15, graduating to Royal Ballet's touring co. (later known as Sadler's Wells Royal Ballet, now Birmingham Royal Ballet); Prin. dancer 1974; danced all the classics and other prin. roles including Juliet, Elite Syncopations, Las Hermanas, The Invitation, Hobson's Choice, The Dream, The Burrow, Lizzie Borden in Fall River Legend and Hagar in Pillars of Fire; created many roles for Kenneth MacMillan and David Bintley; guest appearances worldwide; Ballet Mistress, Birmingham Royal Ballet 1995–; Dancer of Year 1994; Evening Standard Ballet Award 1994. *Leisure interests:* needlework. *Address:* Birmingham Royal Ballet, Thorp Street, Birmingham, B5 4AU, England. *Telephone:* 0121-622 2555.

TAITT, Branford Mayhew, LL.B., M.P.A.; Barbadian politician; b. 15 May 1938; m. Marjorie C. Taitt (deceased); one s. two d.; ed. Univ. of West Indies, New York Univ. and Brooklyn Coll., New York; Cable and Wireless 1954–62; Conf. Officer, UN Secr. 1962–65; U.S. Rep. Barbados Industrial Devt. Corpn. 1965–67; mem. Barbados del. to UN 1966–71; Consul-Gen. of Barbados, New York 1967–71; mem. Barbados Senate 1971–76; Minister of Trade, Industry and Commerce, of Tourism and Industry 1986–88, of Health 1988–93, of Foreign Affairs 1993–94; Pres. Democratic Labour Party 1978–84; fmr. part-time Lecturer in Law, Univ. of W. Indies, Cave Hill, Barbados and visiting or guest lecturer and univs. and colls in U.S.A. *Publications:* over 200 articles in newspapers and periodicals. *Address:* 10 Stanmore Crescent, Black Rock, St. Michael, Barbados (Home). *Telephone:* 424 4113. *Fax:* 424 5436.

TAITTINGER, Anne-Claire; French business executive; d. of Jean Taittinger (q.v.) and Corinne Deville; m.; two s.; ed. Inst. de l'Assomption, Paris; fmr. urban planner; fmrly, held positions within several Soc. du Louvre cos., Head Soc. du Louvre 1997–; Dir. Marengo Soc., Deville Soc. *Address:* c/o Taittinger S.A., 9 place Saint-Nicaise, Reims; Société du Louvre, 58 boulevard Gouvion Saint-Cyr, 75858 Paris cedex 17, France.

TAITTINGER, Jean; French politician and vintner; b. 25 Jan. 1923, Paris; s. of Pierre Taittinger; m. Marie Corinne Deville 1948; three s. two d.; ed. Coll. Stanislas, Paris; Dir. Champagne Taittinger 1946, Vice-Chair. 1958–94, Chair. 1994–; Deputy for Marne, Nat. Assembly 1958–73; Mayor of Rheims 1959–77; Nat. Sec. UNR-UDT (Union Démocratique du Travail) 1967; mem. Exec. Office and Nat. Treas. UDR Feb.-Oct. 1968, Deputy Sec.-Gen. 1974–76; Vice-Pres. Finance Comm. of Nat. Assembly 1967–68, Pres. 1968–71; Sec. of State, Ministry of Finance and Econ. Affairs 1971–73; Minister of Justice 1973–74; Minister of State for Justice March–May 1974; Chair Imprimerie Union Républicaine 1960, Soc. du Louvre 1977, Soc. des Hôtels Concorde 1978–90, Cofidev 1979, Société Deville 1979, Société Hôtelière Martinez 1981, Banque Privée de Dépôt et de Crédit 1987; Vice-Chair. Société Taittinger 1947, Société Hôtelière Lutetia Concorde 1980–; Dir. Banque de l'Union Occidentale 1976–85, Banque Worms 1978–82, Etablissements V.Q. Petersen 1979–84; Pres., Dir.-Gen. Banque du Louvre 1987–90 (Hon. Pres. 1990–), Cie. Cristalleries de Baccarat 1992–94, Hon. Pres. 1994–; Dir. Gen. Compagnie Financière Taittinger 1989–94, Chair. 1994–; Pres. Supervisory Council Euro Disneyand S.A. 1989–95; Vice-Chair. Deville SA 1993–95. *Leisure interest:* breeding basset hounds. *Address:* Compagnie financière Taittinger, 58 boulevard Gouvion, Saint-Cyr, 75017 Paris; Cristallerie de

Baccarat, 30 bis rue de Paradis, 75010 Paris, France. *Telephone:* (1) 40-68-04-28.

TAKÁCS-NAGY, Gábor; Hungarian violinist; b. 17 April 1956, Budapest; s. of László Takács-Nagy and Matild Pataki; m. Lesley (née Townson) de Senger 1991, two d.; ed. Béla Bartók Conservatory and Franz Liszt Music Acad. of Budapest; f. Takács String Quartet 1976, Takács Piano Trio 1996; concert tours from 1980 every year throughout Europe, every other year in Australia, U.S.A., Japan, South America; Leader, Festival Orchestra of Budapest 1993–; Prof. Conservatoire de Musique, Geneva 1997–; first prize Evian competition 1977, Menuhin competition (Portsmouth) 1979, Scholarship award, Banff School of Fine Arts, Liszt Prize 1983. *Address:* Case postale 186, 1245 Collonge-Bellerive, Switzerland. *Telephone:* (22) 752 55 68. *Fax:* (22) 752 55 68.

TAKAGAKI, Tasuku; Japanese banker; b. 1928, Tokyo; m.; two d.; ed. Univ. of Tokyo; joined The Bank of Tokyo Ltd. (merged with Mitsubishi Bank Ltd. 1996, now Bank of Tokyo-Mitsubishi Ltd.) 1953, Gen. Man. Int. Investment Div. 1975–76, mem. Bd. 1979–, Dir. and Gen. Man. Planning and Personnel Div. 1979–82, Resident Man. Dir. for Europe 1982–84, Man. Dir. Head Office 1984, Sr. Man. Dir. 1986, Deputy Pres. 1989, Pres. 1990–98, Chair. of Bd. 1998–; Deputy Treasurer Asian Devt. Bank 1966–71; mem. Council of Foreign Econ. Cooperation; mem. Export and Import Transaction Council and Int. Trade and Insurance Council, Ministry of Int. Trade and Industry; Vice-Chair. Keizai Doyukai (Japan Asscn. of Corp. Execs.), Chair. Cttee. on Int. Relations; Co-Chair. Cttee. on Latin America Keidanren (Fed. of Econ. Orgs.); Deputy Chair. Int. Economic Affairs Cttee., Tokyo Chamber of Commerce and Industry; Gran Cruz, Orden Nacional al Mérito (Colombia), Medal of Honour with Blue Ribbon (Japan), Grã-Cruz, Ordem do Mérito Agrícola, Comercial e Industrial (Portugal). *Address:* c/o The Bank of Tokyo Mitsubishi, 7-1, Marunouchi 2-chome, Chiyoda-ku, Tokyo 100, Japan.

TAKAGI, Masaaki; Japanese politician; fmr. Parl. Vice-Minister of Finance; mem. House of Councillors, fmr. Chair. Cttee. on Agric., Forestry and Fisheries and Cttee. on Rules and Admin.; Minister of State, Dir.-Gen. Hokkaido Devt. Agency and Okinawa Devt. Agency 1995–96; mem. LDP. *Address:* c/o Hokkaido Development Agency, 3-1-1, Kasumigaseki, Chiyoda-ku, Tokyo 100; c/o Okinawa Development Agency, 1-6-1, Nagata-cho, Chiyoda-ku, Tokyo 100, Japan. *Telephone:* (3) 3581-9111; (3) 3581-2361.

TAKAMATSU, Shin, PH.D.; Japanese architect; b. 5 Aug. 1948, Shimane Pref.; s. of Toshio Takamatsu and Yuriko Takamatsu; m. Toshiko Hariguchi 1970; two d.; ed. Ohda High School, Kyoto Univ.; Prin. Architect, Shin Takamatsu Architects and Assocs., Kyoto 1980; mem. Nihon Kenchiku Gakai (Japan Architecture Inst.) 1989–, Japan Inst. of Architecture 1993–; Hon. Fellow A.I.A. 1995; work exhibited Venice Biennale 1985, Krin Plaza, Paris 1988, Killing Moon, London 1988, Nimes 1989, Berlin 1991, San Francisco Museum of Modern Art 1992, Kyoto Municipal Museum of Art 1995; several prizes and awards including Japan Architects Asscn. Prize 1984, Venice Biennale Prize 1985, Second Int. Interior Design Award 1987, Architectural Inst. of Japan Prize 1989, Grand Prize, Journal of Japanese Soc. of Commercial Space Designers 1989, Architectural Inst. of Japan Prize 1990, Kyoto Pref. Meritorious Cultural Service Award 1994, Art Encouragement Prize, Ministry of Educ. 1996. *Publications:* Works 1984, Shin Takamatsu & Gabriel E. Lahyani 1994, To the Poetic Space 1998. *Address:* Shin Takamatsu Architects and Associates, 195 Jobodaiin-cho Takeda, Fushimi-ku, Kyoto 612, Japan.

TAKEMI, Taro; Japanese physician; b. 7 March 1904, Kyoto; m. Eiko Akizuki 1941; two s. two d.; ed. Keio Univ. School of Medicine; Pioneer in study of medical application of nuclear physics; mem. team measuring radioactivity of atomic bomb, Hiroshima 1945; built the first portable electrocardiograph 1937; invented the vectorcardiograph 1939; also patented the method of extracting chlorophyll and the mfg. process for pentose nucleotide; Asst., Keio Univ. Hosp. 1930–37; Inst. of Physical and Chemical Research 1938–50; Takemi Clinic 1939; now also Visiting Prof. at Keio, Kitasoto and Tokai Univs.; Vice-Pres. Japan Medical Asscn. 1950, Pres. 1957–82; Pres. World Medical Asscn. 1975–76; also of Japan-Latin America Medical Asscn. and Japan-Italy Medical Asscn.; Vice-Pres. Japan-WHO Asscn.; Adviser, Nat. Cancer Centre; Trustee, Japan Cancer Soc., Princess Takamatsu Cancer Research Fund; Auditor, Nishina Memorial Foundation, Waksman Foundation; Pres. Keio Univ. Medical School Alumni Asscn.; Commdr., Order of Merit (Italy) 1963, Cultural Gold Medal (Italy) 1964, Award for Cultural Merit (Italy) 1964, Silver Medal from Pope Paul VI 1966, Diploma from Lisbon Univ. 1968, Gold Medal from Milan Univ. 1967, from Italian Tuberculosis Soc. 1968, Medal of Grand Distinction from Brazilian Acad. of Mil. Medicine 1972, Grand Cross of Honour of Fed. German Order of Merit 1974, Order of Rising Sun (First Class) 1975, Special Cravat of Order of Brilliant Star (Taiwan) 1976, Nat. Order of Southern Cross (Brazil) 1976, Hon. K.B.E. 1977, Grande Ufficiale nell'Ordine (Italy), Civil Merit Mu Gung Hua Medal (Repub. of Korea), The Golden Heart Presidential Award (Philippines). *Publications:* An Epigram on Medical Affairs, My Memoirs, numerous papers. *Address:* 48-8, Moto-Azabu 3-chome, Minato-ku, Tokyo 104, Japan (Home). *Telephone:* 03-401 2439 (Home).

TAKEMURA, Masayoshi; Japanese politician; b. 26 Aug. 1934, Youkaichi City, Shiga Pref.; ed. Tokyo Univ.; joined Ministry of Home Affairs 1962, at Saitama Pref. offices 1967–70, Research Counsellor to Minister of Home Affairs 1970–71; Mayor of Youkaichi City, Shiga Pref. 1971–74, Gov. of Shiga Pref. 1974–86; Pres. New Party Sakigake (Harbinger) 1993–96; Minister of State, Chief Cabinet Sec. 1993–94; Minister of Finance 1994–96; mem. House of Reps., Shiga Pref. 1986– (Chair. Environment Cttee.). *Address:* New Party Sakigake, Akasaka Annex 1F, 2-17-42 Akasaka, Minato-ku,Tokyo 107, Japan. *Telephone:* (3) 5570-1341. *Fax:* (3) 5570-6941.

TAKESHITA, Noboru; Japanese politician; b. 26 Feb. 1924; m.; three d.; ed. School of Commerce, Waseda Univ.; Jr. High School Teacher; elected to Shimane Prefectural Ass. (two terms) 1951; mem. House of Reps. 1958–, Parl. Vice-Minister for Int. Trade and Industry 1963–64; Deputy Chief Cabinet Sec. 1964–65, Chief Cabinet Sec. 1971–72, Nov.–Dec. 1974; Minister of Construction 1976; Chair. Budget Cttee. of House of Reps. 1978–79; Minister of Finance 1979–80, 1982–86; Chair. Diet Policy Cttee., Nat. Org. Cttee. of Liberal Democratic Party (LDP), Standing Cttee. on Budget, House of Reps. 1978; Sec.-Gen. LDP 1986–87; Pres. 1987–89; Prime Minister of Japan 1987–89; Chair. Bd. of Govs. IMF and World Bank 1984, Group of Ten 1985; Hon. LL.D. (Columbia) 1986. *Publications:* six books including Waga michi o yuku (Seeking after the path) 1979, Magokoro no seiji (Honest Politics) 1983, Subarashi kuni Nihon (Wonderful Japan) 1987. *Leisure interests:* judo (holds 5th dan), golf, reading, fine arts (especially Japanese-style painting), yachting. *Address:* 955 Oaza-Kakeai, Iishi-gun, Shimane 690-27, Japan.

TAKEYAMA, Yutaka; Japanese politician; b. 1934, Shizuoka Pref.; ed. Keio Univ.; worked for a fishery co. for over 25 years; mem. LDP; mem. for Shizuoka House of Councillors; fmr. Parl. Vice-Minister for Science and Tech.; Dir.-Gen. Science and Tech. Agency 1998–; fmr. Chair. House of Councillors panels on Finance, Local Admin. and the Cabinet, Head Fishery Div., LDP Policy Research Council. *Leisure interests:* yachting, golf, singing traditional Japanese songs. *Address:* Science and Technology Agency, 2-2-1, Kasumigaseki, Chiyoda-ku, Tokyo 100, Japan. *Telephone:* (03) 3581-5271.

TAKLA, Laila I., LL.B., PH.D.; Egyptian politician and diplomatist; m.; two c.; ed. Cairo Univ., Egypt, Univ. of Southern Calif., New York Univ.; lecturer in Admin., New York Univ.; lecturer, Higher Inst. of Admin., Cairo Univ.; Public Admin. Expert, Arab League 1969; Chair. Foreign Affairs Cttee., People's Ass.; mem. of the Cen. Cttee. of Arab Socialist Union 1971; mem. of Nat. Specialised Councils 1972; Rep. of Egypt, UN Gen. Ass. 1973; Vice Pres., Int. Parl. Union 1977; Chair. Cttee. on Educ.; Pres. Finnish-Egyptian Soc. 1976; Chair, Nat. Cttee. on Environmental Law; Chair, UN Experts Group on the Advancement of Women 1976. *Publications:* Public Administration Principles and Dynamics (2 vols.) 1968, 1971, 1976; The Six Hour War: An Analysis of the Arab-Israeli October War 1973; The Ombudsman: A Comparative Study 1971. *Leisure interests:* swimming, tennis, sculpture, folk arts. *Address:* People's Assembly, Cairo, Egypt.

TAKLA, Philippe; Lebanese politician and banker; b. 3 Feb. 1915; ed. Univ. Law School, Beirut; Law practice, Beirut 1935–45; M.P. 1945, 1947; Minister of Nat. Economy and Communications 1945–46; Minister of Foreign Affairs 1949, 1961–63, 1964–65, 1966; Gov. Bank of Lebanon 1963–66, 1966–67; Perm. Rep. to UN 1967–68; Amb. to France 1968–71; Minister of Foreign Affairs 1974–76, also of Educ. and Planning 1975–76. *Address:* Rue Maarad, Beirut, Lebanon.

TAKRITI, Saddam Hussein (see Saddam Hussein).

TALAL IBN ABDUL AZIZ, H.R.H. Prince; Saudi Arabian politician and international official; b. 1934; s. of the late King Abdul Aziz ibn Saud; ed. Prince's School, Royal Palace, Riyadh; positions held in his early 20s include responsibility for the Royal Palaces, Minister of Communications; fmr. Minister of Economy and Finance; fmr. Amb. to France; f. Riyadh's first girls' school 1957, first pvt. hosp. 1957 and Mecca's first coll. for boys 1957; passport cancelled 1962; exile in Egypt (for activities promoting human rights and democracy); returned to Saudi Arabia 1964; fmr. Special Envoy, UNICEF; Pres. Arab Gulf Programme for UN Devt. Orgs. "AGFUND"; Pres. Arab Council for Childhood and Devt. *Leisure interests:* history, amateur radio, swimming. *Address:* 7 rue Beaujon, 75008 Paris, France. *Telephone:* (1) 43-80-22-97.

TALBOT, Frank Hamilton, PH.D.; Australian marine scientist and museum director; b. 3 Jan. 1930, Pietermaritzburg, S. Africa; s. of Ralph W. Talbot and Willemina Altmann; m. Mabel S. Logeman 1953; three s. one d.; ed. Univs. of the Witwatersrand and Cape Town; fisheries research scientist, British Colonial Service, Zanzibar 1954–57; marine biologist, S. African Museum, Cape Town 1958–59, Asst. Dir. 1960–63; Curator of Fishes, Australian Museum, Sydney 1964–65, Dir. 1966–74; Prof. of Environmental Studies, Macquarie Univ. Sydney 1975–81; Exec. Dir. Calif. Acad. of Sciences, San Francisco 1982–88; Dir. Nat. Museum of Natural History, Smithsonian Inst. 1989; Pres. Australian Marine Science Asscn. 1971–72, Museums Asscn. of Australia 1973–74; Fellow, Royal Zoological Soc. of N.S.W., Calif. Acad. of Science, American Asscn. for Advancement of Science. *Publications:* The Great Barrier Reef, Readers Digest (scientific ed.) 1983, The Fishes of Tasmania (jt. author) 1984; some 60 scientific papers. *Leisure interests:* yachting, fly fishing, exploring wild places.

TALBOT, Godfrey Walker, L.V.O., O.B.E.; British author and broadcaster; b. 8 Oct. 1908; s. of Frank Talbot and Kate Bertha Talbot; m. Bess Owen 1933; one s.; ed. Leeds Grammar School; with Yorkshire Post 1928; ed. Manchester City News 1932–34; editorial staff Daily Dispatch 1934–37; joined BBC 1937; war correspondent for BBC 1941–45 (despatches); Chief

Reporter, BBC Home Reporting Unit; Sr. News Reporter and Commentator on staff of BBC 1946–69; official BBC observer accred. to Buckingham Palace 1948–69; Pres. Queen's English Soc.; Vice-Chair. Royal Over-Seas League 1985–96, Vice-Pres. 1996–. *Publications:* Speaking from the Desert 1944, Ten Seconds from Now 1973; Queen Elizabeth the Queen Mother 1973, Permission to Speak 1976, Royal Heritage 1977, The Country Life Book of Queen Elizabeth the Queen Mother 1978, The Country Life Book of the Royal Family 1980, Queen Elizabeth, The Queen Mother 1990, Forty Years the Queen 1992, and numerous articles on the British monarchy. *Leisure interest:* keeping quiet. *Address:* Holmwell, Hook Hill, Sanderstead, Surrey, CR2 0LA, England. *Telephone:* 0181-657 3476.

TALBOTT, Strobe; American journalist and politician; b. 25 April 1946, Dayton, Ohio; m. Brooke Lloyd Shearer 1971; two s.; ed. Hotchkiss School, Connecticut, Yale and Oxford Univs.; joined Time magazine; Diplomatic Corresp., White House Corresp., Eastern Europe Corresp., Washington Bureau Chief 1984–89, Ed.-at-large 1989–94; Amb.-at-Large State Dept. Feb.–Dec. 1993; Deputy Sec. of State 1994–; Rhodes Scholar Oxford Univ. 1969; Dir. Carnegie Endowment for Int. Peace; mem. Council on Foreign Relations. *Publications:* several books on the Soviet Union, author and co-author of various books on the Reagan Admin.'s Foreign Policy, translator and ed. Nikita Khrushchev's memoirs. *Address:* Department of State, 2201 C Street, N.W., Washington, DC 20520, U.S.A.

TALBOYS, Rt. Hon. Sir Brian Edward, K.C.B., P.C., C.H.; New Zealand fmr. politician and farmer; b. 7 June 1921, Wanganui; s. of F. P. Talboys; m. P. F. Adamson 1950; two s.; ed. Wanganui Collegiate School, Univ. of Manitoba, Canada, Victoria Univ., Wellington; served R.N.Z.A.F. in Second World War; joined N.Z. Dairy Exporter 1950, later Asst. Ed.; M.P. 1957–81; Parl. Under-Sec. to Minister of Trade and Industry 1960–62; Minister of Agric. 1962–69, of Educ. 1969–72, of Science 1964–72; Minister of Trade and Industry and Minister of Overseas Trade Feb.-Dec. 1972; Deputy Prime Minister, Minister of Foreign Affairs and Minister of Overseas Trade 1975–81, of Nat. Devt. 1975–77; mem. Nat. Party, Deputy Leader 1974–81; Chair. Bd. Indosuez New Zealand Ltd. 1982–87, Genestock N.Z. 1983–, Ericsson Communications 1983–89; Dir. Sedgwick Group N.Z. 1984–96; Hon. D.Sc. (Massey Univ.) 1980, Hon. D.Litt. (Chung-Ang Univ., Seoul) 1981; Hon. A.C. 1982. *Address:* 1 Hamilton Avenue, Winton, New Zealand (Home). *Telephone:* 2368-729 (Home).

TALEB, Gen. Yusef Sabri Abu; Egyptian politician; b. 24 May 1929, Cairo; m.; three s.; ed. Mil. Acad.; Artillery Commdr., Third Field Army and Chief of Staff, Armed Forces Artillery 1969–74; Artillery Dir. Armed Forces 1974–79; Asst. Defence Minister 1979–80; Gov. N. Sinai 1980–82; State Minister for Popular Devt. 1982; Gov. of Cairo 1983; Minister of Defence and Mil. Production, Commdr. Gen. of Armed Forces 1989–91; Order of the Repub. (Second Degree), Order of Science and Arts. *Address:* c/o Ministry of Military Production, 5 Sharia Ismail Abaza, Kasr el-Eini, Cairo, Egypt. *Telephone:* (02) 3553063.

TALEYARKHAN, Homi J. H., B.A.; Indian politician; b. 9 Feb. 1918, Bombay; s. of Jehangir and Tehmina Taleyarkhan; m. Padma Sri Thrity Rustomjee Lichmore 1946; one s. (died 1991); ed. Univ. of Bombay, King's Coll., London, Lincoln's Inn, London; mem. Bombay Municipal Corpn. and Chair. Works Cttee. and Sr. mem. Standing Cttee. 1948–52; mem. Maharashtra State Legis. Ass. 1952–71; Gen. Sec. Congress Legis. Party, Chief Whip and Cabinet Minister, Maharashtra 1952–67 (consecutively Minister of Health, Family Planning, Food, Civil Supplies, Housing, Tourism, Nat. Savings, Fisheries and Printing Presses); Amb. to Libya 1971–77; Chair. Maharashtra State Financial Corpn.; Gov. Sikkim State 1981–84; Amb. to Italy and FAO 1984–85; mem. Nat. Minorities Comm., Govt. of India 1985–92; Chair. Fertilizers Comm. F.A.O. 1985–87; Pres. Int. Tourism Council 1970–; del. to Int. Conf. on Peace and Security in Asia and Pacific Ocean Region Oct. 1988, Chair. Political and Mil. session; del. to Int. Conf. on a non-Nuclear and non-Violent World Nov. 1988; Chair. Steering Cttee. Annual Int. Congress on World Marketing 1986–; Chair. Nat. Conf. of Energy Feb. 1989; Pres., Centre for U.N. Studies, Indo-Yugoslav Friendship Soc., Indo-Libyan Friendship Soc.; del. to UNCTAD II, Delhi; Chair. Nat. Savings Re-organization Cttee., Land Re-organization Cttee., Govt. of India; mem. Small Family Norms Cttee., All India Congress Cttee.; Chair. Project Implementation Comm. for Earthquake Relief and Rehabilitation in Affected Areas; Vice-Pres. Bombay Regional Congress Cttee.; Dir. Shipping Corpn. of India; Vice-Pres. Indian Council of Foreign Trade; mem. Working Cttee., All India Mfrs. Org., Exec. Cttee., Asscn. of Industries, Eng. Asscn., Nat. Productivity Council, Maharashtra State Industries Advisory Cttee., State High-Power Co-ordination Cttee.; Sr. mem. Prime Minister's Bd. of Small Scale Industries; Chair. Maharashtra branch, World Ass. of Small and Medium Enterprises (Delhi), Special Council of Small Scale Industries of AIMO, Urja (Energy) Research Foundation, Consumers' Grievances Cttee. of Council of Fair Business Practices, Advisory Cttee. Nowea Int.; Vice-Pres. Indian Council of Small Industries; mem. Senate, Univ. of Bombay; Adviser to Red Cross, to Fed. of Zoroastrian All India Parsi Anjumans; Padma Shri Presidential Award (India), Rotary Int. Award for Peace and Welfare Work, Inst. of Econ. Studies Awards, Asian Congress of Alternative Medicine Award, Vijay Shree Award, Urja (Energy) Research Foundation Award, Parsi Community Award and many other awards. *Publications include:* I Have It from Gandhiji, They Told Me So, Hyderabad and Her Destiny, United India in Australia, In the Land of the Blue Hills, Three Graces of Kashmir, Roads to Beauty around Bombay, Village Welfare on the Way, Community Projects in India, Escape from the City, Splendour of Sikkim, Environment and Forestry in Economic Development, From Warfare to Welfare—the Ideal of National Integration, The Role of Small Scale Industries, The Importance of Tourism for Goodwill, Foreign Exchange and Employment Opportunities; numerous papers and pamphlets. *Leisure interests:* reading, writing, riding, tennis, dogs, walking, trekking, driving, music. *Address:* Currimbhoy Manor, 41 Warden Road, Bombay 400 026, India. *Telephone:* 2611446 (Office); 4937272 (Home). *Fax:* 2670738.

TALIB, Maj.-Gen. Naji; Iraqi politician and soldier; b. 1917; ed. Iraqi Staff Coll., and Sandhurst, England; Mil. Attaché, London 1954–55; Commdr. Basra Garrison 1957–58; Minister of Social Affairs 1958–59; lived abroad 1959–62; Minister of Industry 1963–64; mem. U.A.R.-Iraq Jt. Presidency Council 1964–65; Minister of Foreign Affairs 1964–65; Prime Minister and Minister of Petroleum Affairs 1966–67.

TALLAWY, Mervat; Egyptian diplomatist and politician; b. 1 Dec. 1937; d. of Mehani Tallawy and Soraya Abdel-Hamid; m. Dr. Ali Abdel-Rahman Rahmy 1964; one d.; ed. American Univ. Cairo, Inst. for Diplomatic Studies, Cairo and Grad. Inst. of Int. Studies, Geneva; joined Ministry of Foreign Affairs 1963; served Geneva, New York and Caribbean countries, Vienna and Tokyo; Deputy Dir. UN Inst. for the Advancement of Women 1982–85; Minister Plenipotentiary, Deputy Dir. Dept. of Int. Orgs. Ministry of Foreign Affairs 1985–88; Amb. to Austria and Resident Rep. to IAEA, UNIDO and UN Centre for Social and Humanitarian Affairs 1988–91; Dir. of Int. Econ. Dept., Ministry of Foreign Affairs 1991; Asst. Minister for Int. Political and Econ. Affairs 1992–93; Amb. to Japan 1993–97; Minister of Insurance and Social Affairs 1997–; Asst. UN Sec. for UNDP, Arab countries 1997; Rapporteur-Gen. UN Conf. on Adoption of Int. Convention on Prevention of Illicit Drug Trafficking, Vienna 1988; mem. UN Cttee. on Elimination of Discrimination against Women (CEDAW) (Chair. 1990–92); Chair. UN Comm. on Status of Women 1991–93; Chair. workshop on Women and Violence leading to adoption of UN Declaration on Elimination of Violence Against Women, Vienna 1992; Chair. Working Group on Health, UN Int. Conf. for the Advancement of Women, Beijing 1995; Head Egyptian Del. to Multilateral Middle East Peace Talks Working Group on Econ. Regional Co-operation, Brussels 1992, Paris 1992, Rome 1993, and to Steering Cttee. of Multilateral Middle East Talks, Tokyo 1994; Head Egyptian Del. to UN World Conf. on Natural Disasters, Yokohama 1994; Del. to UN Environment Conf., Rio de Janeiro 1992, to UN Int. Conf. on Population and Devt., Cairo 1994; initiator of proposal leading to adoption of UN Declaration for the Protection of Women and Children in Time of Armed Conflicts 1974; mem. Club of Rome. *Leisure interests:* theatre, classical music, walking, reading, painting. *Address:* Ministry of Insurance and Social Affairs, Sharia Sheikh Rihan, Cairo (Office); 18 el-Mansour Mohammed St., Apt. 15, Zamalak, 11211, Cairo, Egypt. (Home). *Telephone:* 02-3370039 (Office); 02-3408102 (Home). *Fax:* 02-3375390 (Office); 02-3408102 (Home).

TALLCHIEF, Maria; American ballet dancer; b. 24 Jan. 1925, Fairfax, Okla.; d. of Ruth Porter Tallchief and Alexander Tallchief; m. 1st George Balanchine 1946; m. 2nd Henry D. Paschen 1956, one d.; studied with Bronislava Nijinska; joined Ballet Russe de Monte Carlo 1942; Prima Ballerina, New York City Ballet 1948–66; toured worldwide with the co., cr. numerous roles including Four Temperaments, Stravinsky's Firebird; Guest Prima Ballerina, American Ballet Theatre, touring U.S.S.R., Romania, Bulgaria and Greece 1960; Guest Star, Paris Opéra Ballet 1947; Guest Artist, Royal Danish Ballet, Copenhagen 1961; fmr. teacher, School of American Ballet, New York; gave up performing career 1966; Dir. of Ballet, Lyric Opera of Chicago; guest speaker on dance and dance educ. at several univs.; mem. Nat. Soc. of Arts and Letters; numerous hon. degrees; received Woman of the Year Award from Pres. Eisenhower 1953, Hon. Princess, Osage Indian Tribe 1953, Achievement Award, Women's Nat. Press Club 1953, Dance Educators American Award 1956, Dance Magazine Award 1960, Capezio Award 1965, Distinguished Service Award, Univ. of Okla. 1972, Kennedy Center Honor 1996; inducted into Nat. Women's Hall of Fame 1996, Int. Women's Forum Hall of Fame 1997. *Address:* Lyric Opera Ballet, 20 North Wacker Drive, Suite 860, Chicago, IL 60606 (Office); 502 North Ocean Boulevard, Delray Beach, FL 33483; 48 Prospect, Highland Park, IL 60035, U.S.A.

TALLCHIEF, Marjorie; American ballerina; b. 1927; d. of the Chief of the Osages Indians; m. George Skibine 1947 (died 1981); two s.; ed. Beverly Hills High School, Calif.; studied with Bronislava Nijinska; joined American Ballet Theatre; *created role of:* Medusa in Undertow; Prima Ballerina, Ballet de Monte Carlo 1948, American Ballet Theater 1960; *created leading roles in:* Somnambula, Concerto Barrocco, Les Biches, Boléro, Idylle, Prisoner of the Caucasus and Annabel Lee; Première Danseuse Etoile, Paris Opera 1957–; *leading roles in:* The Firebird, Les Noces Fantastiques, Giselle, Conte Cruel, Concerto and numerous other ballets; Prima Ballerina, Hamburg State Opera 1965–; Chevalier du Nicham-Iftikar.

TALLING, John Francis, PH.D., F.R.S.; British freshwater biologist; b. 23 March 1929, Grange Town; s. of Frank Talling and Miriam Talling; m. Ida Björnsson 1959; one s. one d.; ed. Sir William Turner's School, Coatham, Yorks., Univ. of Leeds and Univ. of London; Lecturer in Botany, Univ. of Khartoum 1953–56; Postdoctoral Fellow, Univ. of Calif. 1957; Biologist, Freshwater Biological Asscn., England 1958–89, Sr. Research Fellow 1991–;

Visiting Prof. Univ. of Lancaster 1992–. *Publications:* Ecological Dynamics of Tropical Inland Waters (with J. Lemoalle) 1998 and about 70 scientific papers. *Leisure interests:* walking, archaeology. *Address:* Freshwater Biological Association, Ambleside, Cumbria, England. *Telephone:* (015394) 42468.

TALMI, Igal, DR.SC.NAT.; Israeli professor of physics; b. 31 Jan. 1925, Kiev, Ukraine (U.S.S.R.); s. of Moshe Talmi and Lea (née Weinstein) Talmi; m. Chana (née Kivelewitz) Talmi 1949; one s. one d.; ed. Herzlia High School, Hebrew Univ. of Jerusalem and Swiss Fed. Inst. of Tech.; served in Israeli Defence Forces 1947–49; Research Fellow Princeton Univ. 1952–54, Visiting Assoc. Prof. 1956–57, Visiting Prof. 1961–62, 1966–67; Prof. of Physics, Weizmann Inst. of Science 1958–, Head Dept. of Nuclear Physics 1967–76, Dean Faculty of Physics 1970–84; mem. Israel Acad. of Sciences and Humanities 1963–, Chair. Div. of Sciences 1974–80; Weizmann Prize of the Tel Aviv Municipality 1962, Israel Prize (with A. de Shalit) 1965, Rothschild Prize 1971. *Publications:* Nuclear Shell Theory (with A. de Shalit) 1963, Simple Models of Complex Nuclei 1993, numerous publs. on theoretical nuclear physics. *Leisure interest:* bird watching. *Address:* Department of Particle Physics, The Weizmann Institute of Science, Rehovot 76100, Israel (Work). *Telephone:* (8) 9342060 (Work); (8) 9468166 (Home).

TALU, Umur E., B.A. ECON.; Turkish journalist; b. 7 Aug. 1957, Istanbul; s. of M. Muvakkar and G. Güzin; m. Şule Talu 1987; two d.; ed. Galatasaray High School and Bosphorus Univ.; Educ. specialist, Railway Workers' Union 1977–78; Int. Econ. Cooperation Sec. Union of Municipalities 1978–80; Econ. Corresp. Günaydin (newspaper) 1980–82; Chief, Econ. Dept. Günes (newspaper) 1982–83; Ed. with Cumhuriyet (newspaper) 1983–85; Chief, Econ. Dept. Milliyet (newspaper) 1985–86, News Ed. 1986–87, 1988–92, Ed.-in-Chief 1992–94, columnist 1994–; News Ed. Hürriyet (newspaper) 1987–88; Freedom of the Press Award (Turkish Journalists' Asscn.) 1996. *Publications:* Social Democracy in Europe (co-author) 1985, Keynes (translation) 1986, Mr Uguran's Post Office 1996. *Leisure interests:* sport, music, films. *Address:* Milliyet, Dogan Medya Centre, Bagcilar 344554, Istanbul, Turkey. *Telephone:* 90-212-5056111. *Fax:* 90-212-5056233.

TAM YIU CHUNG; Chinese trade unionist and government official; b. 15 Dec. 1949, Hong Kong; m. Lai Xiang Ming; two c.; ed. Australian Nat. Univ., L.S.E.; trade union officer; Vice-Chair. Hong Kong Fed. of Trade Unions; Employees' Retraining Bd., fmr. mem. Preparatory Cttee. for Hong Kong Special Admin. Region; mem. Exec. Council Hong Kong Special Admin. Region, Vocational Training Bd., Standing Comm. on Civil Service Salaries and Conditions of Service, Ind. Comm. Against Corruption Complaints Ctte., Services Promotion Strategy Unit, Democratic Alliance for Betterment of Hong Kong; Hon. Life Fellow Inst. of Commercial Man., U.K. *Address:* Executive Council Secretariat, 1st Floor, Main Wing, Central Government Offices, Central, Hong Kong Special Administrative Region, People's Republic of China.

TAMAGNINI, Giulio; Italian diplomatist; b. 24 July 1921, Milan; s. of Egidio Tamagnini and Giulia Giorgetti; m. 1st Maria R. Torrealba 1950 (died 1987), one s. two d.; m. 2nd Sirkku Talja 1989; ed. Beccaria Classical High School, Milan, Coll. Ghislieri, Pavia and Univs. of Pavia and Paris; served in Italian Navy 1940–45; joined Italian foreign service 1948; served in Egypt, U.K., Yugoslavia and Rome 1950–64; Counsellor, Italian Del. to NATO 1964–69; Minister-Counsellor, Moscow 1969–73, Washington, D.C. 1974–77; Amb. to Iran 1978–80, to People's Repub. of China 1980–83; Head, Italian Dels. to CSCE conferences in Ottawa, Budapest, Berne 1984–86; Prof. of Diplomacy, School of Political Science, Univ. of Pavia 1987–91; Croce di guerra (twice); Cavaliere di Gran Croce. *Publications:* La caduta dello Scià 1990, Una visita a Lhasa, Tibet (in Professione: diplomatico) 1990. *Leisure interests:* tennis, bridge. *Address:* Via Minucio Felice 1, 00136 Rome, Italy; 267 rue Saint-Honoré, 75001 Paris, France. *Telephone:* (06) 3724293 (Rome); (01) 42-60-84-38 (Paris).

TAMAMES GÓMEZ, Ramón, LL.D., D.ECON.; Spanish professor of economics; b. 1 Nov. 1933, Madrid; s. of Manuel Tamames, M.D. and Carmen Tamames; m. Carmen Prieto 1960; one s. two d.; ed. French Lycée, Madrid, Univ. of Madrid, London School of Econs.; Services Dir., Ministry of Commerce 1957–59; Full Prof., Univ. of Granada 1968, Univ. Autónoma de Madrid 1975; lectures and courses at Univs. of Mexico, Venezuela, Santo Domingo, Bologna, Rome, Marseilles, Berlin (Free Univ.), Brussels (Free Univ.), Sydney, Harvard; mem. Communist Party of Spain 1956–81; mem. Exec. Comm. July 1976–; M.P. for Madrid prov. 1977–; Deputy Mayor of Madrid 1979–81; founder, Progressive Fed. 1981; imprisoned several times for political opinions; United Left M.P. 1986–. *Publications:* 30 books incl. Introduction to the Economy of Spain, Economic Structure of Spain 1960, International Economic Structure 1971, The Spanish Republic and the Era of Franco 1973, Ecology and Development 1977, The Future and the Nation 1981, The European Common Market: A Guide 1986, The Spanish Economy: An Introduction 1986. *Leisure interests:* painting, swimming.

TAMARÓN, Marqués de; Santiago de Mora-Figueroa, 9th Marqués de Tamarón; Spanish diplomatist; b. 18 Oct. 1941, Jerez de la Frontera; s. of José de Mora-Figueroa, 8th Marqués de Tamarón and Dagmar Williams; m. Isabelle de Yturbe 1966; one s. one d.; ed. Univ. of Madrid and Escuela Diplomática; Lieut. Spanish Marine Corps 1967; Sec. Embassy, Nouakchott 1968–70, Paris 1970–73; Banco del Noroeste 1974; Counsellor, Copenhagen 1975–80; Minister-Counsellor, Ottawa 1980–81; Pvt. Sec. to Minister of Foreign Affairs 1981–82; Head of Studies and Deputy Dir. Escuela Diplomática 1982–88; Dir. Inst. de Cuestiones Internacionales y Política Exterior (INCIPE) 1988–96; Dir. Instituto Cervantes 1996–; mem. Trilateral Comm. 1989–96; Commdr. Order of Carlos III, Officier, Ordre Nat. du Mérite (France), Commdr. Order of Dannebrog, Commdr. Order of Merit (Germany). *Publications:* Pólvora con Aguardiente 1983, El Guirigay Nacional 1988, Trampantojos 1990, El Siglo XX y otras Calamidades 1993, El Peso de la Lengua Española en el Mundo (co-author) 1995. *Leisure interests:* philology, mountain walking, gardening. *Address:* Instituto Cervantes, Francisco Silvela 82, 28028 Madrid, Spain (Office). *Telephone:* (91) 436-76-60. *Fax:* (91) 355-67-36.

TAMEN, Pedro, LL.B.; Portuguese foundation executive and poet; b. 1 Dec. 1934, Lisbon; s. of Mário Tamen and Emília Tamen; m. Maria da Graça Seabra Gomes 1975; two s. two d.; ed. Lisbon Univ.; Dir. Moraes Publishing House 1958–75; Pres. Portuguese PEN Club 1987–90; Trustee Calouste Gulbenkian Foundation, Lisbon; mem. Bd. Portuguese Asscn. of Writers; D. Diniz Prize 1981; Grand Prix for Translation 1990; Critics Award 1993; INAPA Prize for Poetry 1993, Nicola Prize for Poetry 1998. *Publications:* 12 books of poetry since 1958; Tábua das Matérias (Collected Works) 1991, Depois de Ver 1995, Guião de Caronte 1997. *Address:* Calouste Gulbenkian Foundation, Av. de Berna 45–A, P-1067 Lisbon Codex (Office); Rua Luís Pastor de Macedo, lote 25, 5° esq., P-1750 Lisbon, Portugal (Home). *Telephone:* 7935131 (Office). *Fax:* 7937499 (Office).

TAMM, Ditlev, DR.JUR., DR.PHIL.; Danish professor of legal history; b. 7 March 1946, Copenhagen; s. of Henrik Tamm and Lizzie Knutzen; m. Maria Pilar Lorenzo 1973 (separated 1987); two d.; ed. Univ. of Copenhagen and in Germany and France; Prof. of Legal History, Univ. of Copenhagen 1978–; mem. Royal Danish Acad.. and several other Danish and int. scientific bds. and cttees.; A.S. Orsted Award 1974. *Publications:* Fra lovkyndighed til retsvidenskab 1976, Retsopgøret efter besaettelsen 1984, Roman Law 1997; several books and articles on Danish and European legal history. *Address:* 13 Svanemøllevej, 2100 Copenhagen Ø, Denmark. *Telephone:* 39-29-93-92; 35-32-31-67.

TAMM, Peter; German publisher; b. 12 May 1928, Hamburg; s. of Emil Tamm; m. Ursula Weisshun 1958; one s. four d.; ed. Univ. of Hamburg; Shipping Ed., Hamburger Abendblatt 1948–58; Man. Dir. Ullstein GmbH (Publr.) 1960–62, 1984; Man. Dir. Bild-Zeitung 1962–64; Dir., Verlagshaus Axel Springer, Berlin 1964–70, mem. Exec. Bd. 1970–82, Chair. Man. Bd. 1982–91; Vice-Pres. Bundesverband Deutscher Zeitungsverleger 1980–; Bayerischer Verdienstorden, Grosses Bundesverdienstkreuz. *Publication:* Maler der See 1980. *Leisure interests:* model ships, marine books. *Address:* Elbchaussee 277, 22605 Hamburg, Germany.

TAMURA, Hajime; Japanese politician; b. May 1924, Mie Pref.; m.; one d.; mem. House of Reps. 12 times 1955–; Parl. Vice-Minister of Construction 1960, of Labour 1962; Chair., House of Reps. Cttee. on Construction 1966, Cttee. on Finance 1968; Chair. Liberal Democratic Party (LDP) Public Relations Cttee. 1971; Minister of Labour 1972, of Transport 1976; Chair. House of Reps. Cttee. on Budget 1980; Chair. LDP Nat. Org. Cttee. 1980, LDP Diet Policy Cttee. 1981, Research Comm. on Party's Fundamental Policy and Operation 1984, LDP Party Presidential Election Control Cttee. 1986; Minister of Int. Trade and Industry 1986–88. *Leisure interests:* sumo, reading, go, gardening, photography.

TAN, Amy Ruth, M.A., L.H.D.; American writer; b. 19 Feb. 1952, Oakland, Calif.; d. of John Yuehhan and Daisy Ching (Tu) Tan; m. Louis M. DeMattei 1974; ed. San José State Univ., Calif., Dominican Coll., San Rafael; specialist in language devt. Alameda Co. Asscn. for Mentally Retarded 1976–80; Project Dir. M.O.R.E., San Francisco 1980–81; freelance writer 1981–88; Best Fiction Award for The Joy Luck Club 1990 (Commonwealth Club and Bay Area Book Reviewers), Best American Essays Award 1991. *Film:* The Joy Luck Club (screenwriter, producer) 1993. *Publications:* The Joy Luck Club 1989, The Kitchen God's Wife 1991, The Moon Lady 1992, The Chinese Siamese Cat 1994, The Hundred Secret Senses 1995, numerous short stories and essays.

TAN, Melvyn; British concert pianist and early music specialist; b. 13 Oct. 1956, Singapore; s. of Tan Keng Hian and Wong Sou Yuen; ed. Anglo-Chinese School, Yehudi Menuhin School, Royal Coll. of Music; performs on historical keyboard instruments, which he has introduced to audiences round the world; has now extended repertory to include modern piano; performs regularly in music festivals in U.S.A., Japan, Far East, Australia and throughout Europe. *Leisure interests:* swimming, wine, travelling without having to perform. *Address:* c/o Valerie Barber Management, Suite 305, Mappin House, 4 Winsley Street, London, W1N 7AR, England. *Telephone:* 0171-436 1115/1116. *Fax:* 0171-436 5090.

TAN DUN; Chinese composer; b. 8 Aug. 1957, Hunan; s. of Tan Xiang Qiou and Hwang Quin Yin; ed. Cen. Conservatory of Music, Beijing, Columbia Univ., U.S.A.; fmr. violinist, Beijing Opera; Vice-Pres. Cen. Conservatory of Music 1978–; Second place, Weber Int. Chamber Music Composition Competition, Dresden 1983; numerous awards; works performed by maj. orchestras in China and at Aspen Music Festival, U.S.A. 1982, Dresden Music Festival 1983, Contemporary Chinese Composers' Festival, Hong Kong 1986, and by Cen. Philharmonic of China during U.S. tour 1987; four recordings of his maj. orchestral works, oriental instrumental music, chamber music and electronic music issued by China Nat. Recording Co.;

works also include 14 film scores for U.S. and Chinese films, six modern ballet scores, music for several stage plays; Nine Songs (opera) premiered New York 1989; orchestral piece commissioned by Inst. for Devt. of Intercultural Relations Through the Arts, U.S.A. for Beijing Int. Music Festival 1988. *Leisure interests:* painting in ink, calligraphy. *Address:* School of the Arts, Music Division, Dodge Hall, Columbia Univ., New York, NY 10027, U.S.A. *Telephone:* (212) 662 7437.

TAN HAOSHENG, PH.D.; Chinese academic; b. 1 Dec. 1916, Wujin Co., Jiangsu Prov.; m. Deng Tuantz 1969; ed. Jiaotong Univ., California Inst. of Tech., Cornell Univ.; Faculty mem. Cornell Univ. 1950–53, Notre Dame Univ. 1953–56; Dir. Therm Advanced Research 1957–62; Prof. Ill. Inst. of Tech. 1962–65; returned to China from U.S.A. 1965; Prof. Mechanics Inst. 1966–; mem. Acad. Sinica 1980–; mem. Standing Cttee. 6th CPPCC 1984–88, 7th CPPCC 1989–93, 8th CPPCC 1993–. *Address:* Mechanics Institute, Academia Sinica, Zhong Guan Cun, Beijing 100080, People's Republic of China.

TAN JIAZHEN; Chinese biologist; b. 15 Sept. 1909, Ningbo; s. of C. Y. Tan and M. Y. Yang; m. 1st M. Y. Fu 1932 (deceased); m. 2nd Dr. Y. F. Qiu 1973; three s. one d.; ed. Calif. Inst. of Tech., U.S.A.; Research Asst. Calif. Inst. of Tech. 1936–37; Prof. Nat. Chekiang Univ. 1937–52, Dean, Science Coll. 1950–52; Visiting Prof. Colo. Univ. 1945–46; Dir. Genetics Inst., Fudan Univ. 1961–90, Vice-Pres. 1961–82, Provost, School of Life Sciences 1986–90; Sr. Research Fellow, Eleanor Roosevelt Inst. for Cancer Research, Denver, Colo. 1984–; Vice-Chair. Scientific Advisory Cttee., China Center of Biotechnology Devt. 1984–; Pres. Chinese Soc. of Biological Eng. 1994–; Vice-Pres., 16th Int. Congress of Genetics 1988; Editorial Consultant, The Scientist 1986–; mem. Bd. Dirs. Int. Council for Devt. of Underutilized Plants 1983–; mem., NGO Steering Cttee., UN Centre for Science and Tech. for Devt. 1984–, Panel of Scientific Advisers, ICGEB, UNIDO 1984–, Advisory Editorial Bd. of Journal of Genetics 1985–, Int. Advisory Cttee. for Global Science Journal 1987; Vice-Pres. Genetics Soc. of China 1978, Pres. 1983–; a Vice-Chair. China Democratic League 1983–97, Hon. Chair. 1997–; Vice-Chair. Shanghai Municipal 10th People's Congress 1983–; mem. Chinese Acad. of Sciences 1980; Foreign mem. Italian Nat. Acad. of Sciences of 40 1987; Foreign Assoc. N.A.S. 1985; Fellow Third World Acad. of Sciences 1985; Founding mem. World Inst. of Sciences 1991; Hon. Pres. Ningbo Univ. 1986–, Shanghai Agric. Coll. 1988–; mem. Standing Cttee. 8th CPPCC 1993–; Hon. D.Sc. (York Univ.) 1984, (Univ. of Md.) 1985; Distinguished Alumni Award, Calif. Inst. of Tech. 1983; Medal of Merit, Konstanz Universität, Fed. Repub. of Germany 1989; Hon. Citizen of State of Calif. 1990. *Address:* Genetics Institute, Fudan University, 220 Handan Road, Shanghai 200433, People's Republic of China. *Telephone:* 65492222, ext. 2426 (Office); 64739282 (Home); *Fax:* 65491875.

TAN KENG YAM, Tony, PH.D.; Singaporean politician and banker; b. 7 Feb. 1940, Singapore; s. of late Tan Seng Hwee and of Lim Neo Swee; m. Mary Chee Bee Kiang 1964; four c.; ed. St. Patrick's School, St. Joseph's Inst., Univ. of Singapore, Mass. Inst. of Tech. and Univ. of Adelaide; Lecturer in Maths., Univ. of Singapore 1967–69; Sub-Man. Overseas Chinese Banking Corpn. 1969, Gen. Man. 1978; M.P. 1979–; Sr. Minister of State (Educ.) 1979; Minister of Educ. 1980, concurrently Vice-Chancellor, Nat. Univ. of Singapore; Minister for Trade and Industry, concurrently Minister in charge of Nat. Univ. of Singapore and Nanyang Tech. Inst. 1981–83; Minister of Finance 1983–85, of Educ. and Health Jan.–April 1985, for Trade and Industry 1985–86, of Educ. 1985–91; Chair. People's Action Party Cen. Exec. Cttee. 1993; Chair. and C.E.O. Oversea-Chinese Banking Corpn. Ltd. 1992; Deputy Prime Minister and Minister of Defence Aug. 1995–. *Leisure interests:* swimming, golf and walking. *Address:* Ministry of Defence, Gombak Drive, Singapore. *Telephone:* 7608188. *Fax:* 7620112.

TANABE, Makoto; Japanese politician; b. 25 Feb. 1922, Maebashi City, Gunma Pref.; Chair. All Japan Postal Workers Union, Gunma District 1949; Pres. Workers Unions Council, Gunma Dist. 1951–60; mem. Gunma Pref. Ass. 1955–60; mem. House of Reps. 1960–; Vice-Chair. Cen. Exec. Cttee. Socialist Party of Japan (SPJ) 1982–83, Gen. Sec. 1983–86, Vice-Chair. 1990–91; Chair. Cen. Exec. Cttee. Social Democratic Party of Japan (SDPJ) 1991–. *Address:* Social Democratic Party of Japan, 1-8-1, Nagata-cho, Chiyoda-ku, Tokyo, Japan. *Telephone:* (813) 3592-7512, 3580-1171.

TANAKA, Makiko; Japanese politician; fmr. Deputy Dir.-Gen. LDP Int. Bureau; Minister of State, Dir.-Gen. Science and Tech. Agency 1994–95; mem. House of Reps. for Nigata; mem. House Cttee. on Health and Welfare. *Address:* c/o Science and Technology Agency, 2-2-1, Kasumigaseki, Chiyoda-ku, Tokyo, Japan.

TANAKA, Shoji, PH.D.; Japanese research director; b. 19 Sept. 1927, Odawara, Kanagawa; m. Kimiko Tanaka 1956; one s.; ed. Univ. of Tokyo; lecturer, Faculty of Eng. Univ. of Tokyo 1955, Assoc. Prof. 1958, Prof. 1968, Prof. Emer. 1988; Prof. Tokai Univ. 1988–93; Vice-Pres. Int. Superconductivity Tech. Center (ISTEC) 1988–; Dir. Superconductivity Research Lab. (SRL) 1988–; Purple Ribbon Medal; professional awards. *Publications:* Research of Semiconductor Physics 1950–75, Research of Superconductivity 1975. *Leisure interests:* golf, reading. *Address:* Superconductivity Research Laboratory, 1-10-13, Shinonome, Koto-ku, Tokyo 135 (Office); 2-5-3, Ichigaya kaga-cho, Shinjuku-ku, Tokyo 162, Japan (Home). *Telephone:* 81-3-3536-5700 (Office); 81-3-3260-5500 (Home).

TANAKA, Shun-ichi, DR.ENG.; Japanese professor of optics; b. 28 May 1926, Tokyo; m. Yuriko Tanaka 1957; two d.; ed. The First Higher School, Univ. of Tokyo; Assoc., Univ. of Tokyo 1954–58, lecturer 1958–60, Assoc. Prof. 1960–71, Prof. 1971–87; Prof. Faculty of Physics, Scientific Univ. of Tokyo 1987–; Ed.-in-Chief Japanese Journal of Applied Physics 1976–78; Ed. Journal of Modern Optics (Taylor & Francis) 1984–97; Postdoctoral Fellow NRC Canada 1963–64; Fellow Optical Soc. of America 1986–; Optics Paper Award 1960 and Micro-optics Award 1991, Japanese Soc. of Applied Physics, Distinguished Service Award, Minister of Int. Trade and Industry 1990. *Publications:* Dictionary of Optical Terms 1981, Handbook of Optical Engineering 1986, Fundamentals and Applications of Lightwave Sensing 1990, Dictionary of Optoelectronic Terms 1996; more than 70 scientific papers on optics, mostly in English. *Address:* 3-7-7 Zoshigaya, Toshima-ku, Tokyo 171, Japan.

TANAKA, Shusei; Japanese politician; fmr. Parl. Vice-Minister Econ. Planning Agency; Minister of State and Dir.-Gen. Econ. Planning Agency Jan.–Nov. 1996; mem. House of Reps., mem. New Party Sakigake (NPS). *Address:* c/o Economic Planning Agency, 3-1-1, Kasumigaseki, Chiyoda-ku, Tokyo 100, Japan.

TANFORD, Charles, PH.D.; American professor of physiology; b. 29 Dec. 1921, Halle, Germany; s. of Max Tanford and Charlotte Tanford; m. 1st Lucia Brown 1948 (divorced 1969), two s. one d.; m. 2nd Jacqueline Reynolds 1971; ed. New York and Princeton Univs.; Lalor Fellow, Harvard Univ. 1947–49; Asst. Prof., Univ. of Iowa 1949–54, Assoc. Prof. 1954–59, Prof. 1959–60; Prof. Duke Univ. 1960–70, James B. Duke Prof. of Physical Biochem. 1970–80, James B. Duke Prof. of Physiology 1980–88; mem. Whitehead Medical Research Inst. 1977–83; George Eastman Visiting Prof., Oxford Univ. 1977–78; Pres. Biophysical Soc. 1979; Walker-Ames Prof. Univ. of Washington 1979, Reilly Lecturer, Univ. of Notre Dame 1979; Guggenheim Fellow 1956–57; mem. N.A.S., American Acad. of Arts and Sciences; Alexander von Humboldt Prize 1984, Merck Award (American Soc. for Biochem. and Molecular Biology) 1992. *Publications:* Physical Chemistry of Macromolecules 1961, The Hydrophobic Effect 1973, Ben Franklin Stilled the Waves 1989, The Scientific Traveller (with J. A. Reynolds) 1992, Travel Guide to Scientific Sites of the British Isles (with J. A. Reynolds) 1995; 200 scientific articles in various journals. *Leisure interests:* photography, hiking, travel. *Address:* Tarlswood, Back Lane, Easingwold, York, YO61 3BG, England. *Telephone:* (01347) 821029.

TANG, Bishop Dominic; Chinese ecclesiastic; b. 13 May 1908, Hong Kong; ordained May 1941; Apostolic Administrator, Canton 1951–57; imprisoned China 1957; released 1980; apptd. Archbishop of Canton by Pope John Paul II June 1981; appointment rejected by Chinese Catholics. *Address:* Wah Yan College, 56 Waterloo Road, Kowloon, Hong Kong; Catholic Mission, She-Se, Guangzhou, Guangdong, People's Republic of China.

TANG, Pan-Pan, M.A.; Taiwanese broadcasting executive; b. 3 April 1942, Hunan Province; m. Helen Chao; one s. one d.; ed. Political Warfare Coll. Taipei and S. Illinois Univ., Carbondale, Ill.; Chief Ed. Free China Weekly 1968–72; Deputy Dir. English Dept. Central News Agency, Taipei 1973–79; City Ed. China News 1973–75; Chief Ed. Central Daily News (overseas edn., Chinese) Taipei 1976–77; Deputy Ed.-in-Chief, Cen. Daily News (Chinese-language daily), Taipei 1977–79, Ed.-in-Chief –1996; Dir. Dept. of Media Research, Govt. Information Office 1979–80; News and Overseas Programmes Dir. Broadcasting Corpn. of China (BCC) 1980–83; Pres. BCC 1986–92; Pres. Chinese Taipei Baseball Asscn. 1986–; Commr. Chinese Professional Baseball Org. 1990–. *Publications:* more than 500 features, commentaries and analytical articles.

TANG, Pascal Biloa, B.A.; Cameroonian diplomatist; b. 20 Nov. 1937, Ebolowa; m.; six c.; ed. Univs. of Aix-en-Provence and Grenoble, France, Institut Universitaire des Hautes Etudes Internationales, Geneva, Switzerland; Dir. Dept. of Admin., Consular and Cultural Affairs, Ministry of Foreign Affairs 1965, Dept. of African and Asian Affairs 1976–77, Dept. of Legal Affairs and Treaties 1985–86; served in Embassy in Addis Ababa and London, then First Counsellor, Embassy in Bonn 1979–81, Chargé d'Affaires, Algiers 1982, First Counsellor, Brussels 1982–85; Chargé de Mission, Presidency of Repub. 1977–79, Diplomatic Adviser to Pres. and Tech. Adviser to Presidency 1986–90; Perm. Rep. of Cameroon to UN, New York 1990–95. *Address:* c/o Ministry of Foreign Affairs, Yaounde, Cameroon.

TANG, Raili Kaarina; Finnish painter; b. 19 Dec. 1950, Helsinki; d. of Leo Tang and Vilma Tang (née Urb); ed. The Free Art School, Univ. of Industrial Arts, School of Finnish Acad. of Fine Arts; one-person shows Helsinki, Malmö, Norrköping, Stockholm, Turku, Bonn 1980–; group exhbns. 1976–; Dukat Prize for Young Artist 1979. *Leisure interests:* jogging, dogs, art. *Address:* Luotsikatu 11 A 3, 00160 Helsinki, Finland. *Telephone:* 358-0-656 450.

TANG AOQING, PH.D.; Chinese professor of chemistry; b. 18 Nov. 1915, Yixing Co., Jiangsu Prov.; s. of Tang Linking and Chu Yongmei; m. Shi Guangxia 1943; three s. three d.; ed. Beijing and Colombia Univs.; taught at Nat. South-West Associated Univ., Kunming after graduation; Prof. Beijing Univ. 1950–52; Prof. Jilin Univ. 1952–, Vice-Pres. 1956–78, Pres. 1978–86, Hon. Pres. 1986–; Chair. Nat. Natural Science Foundation of China 1986–91, Hon. Chair. 1991–; Chair. Nat. Natural Science Reward Cttee. of China 1991–; Vice-Pres. China Asscn. for Int. Tech. 1986–; Pres. Soc. of

Chem. 1986–; Vice-Pres. China Asscn. for Int. Exchange of Personnel 1986–; a leading researcher in quantum chemistry and in the physical chemistry of macromolecules; announced irreducible tensorial method of Ligand field theory, Beijing symposium on physics symmetry conservation and the statistical theory of polymer reactions; mem., Presidium Chinese Acad. of Sciences 1981–, Acad. Degree Cttee., State Council of China 1981–, Int. Acad. of Quantum and Molecular Science 1982–, Advisory Editorial Bd. 1982–88, Editorial Bd. of Int. Journal of Quantum Chemistry 1989–, Standing Cttee. 8th CPPCC 1993–; Ed.-in-Chief, Chem. Journal of Chinese Univs. 1985–; Fellow Chinese Acad. of Sciences 1955–; Third Class Award, Chinese Acad. of Sciences 1956, Nat. Science Award (First Class) 1982, 1987, (Second Class) 1989, Chen Jiang Chem. Award 1994. *Publications:* Theoretical Method of Ligand and Field Theory 1979, Graph Theoretical Molecular Orbitals 1980, Quantum Chemistry 1982, Statistical Theory on Polymeric Reactions 1985, Applied Quantum Chemistry 1987, Introduction to Irreducible Density Matrix 1989, Dynamics of Molecular Reactions 1989, Supplement to Theoretical Method of Ligand and Field 1989; over 300 articles in various books and journals. *Leisure interests:* quantum chemistry, physical chemistry of macromolecules, literature. *Address:* Institute of Theoretical Chemistry, Jilin University, Changchun 130023 (Office); 35 Huayuan Beilu, Haidian District, Beijing 100083, People's Republic of China. *Telephone:* 8923189-3244 (Changchun), 2016655-313 (Beijing).

TANG JIAXUAN; Chinese diplomatist; b. Jan. 1938, Zhenjiang City, Jiangsu Prov.; ed. Peking Univ.; joined CCP 1973; First Sec., then Minister Embassy, Japan; Vice-Minister of Foreign Affairs 1993–98, Minister 1998–; mem. 15th CCP Cen. Cttee. 1997–. *Address:* Ministry of Foreign Affairs, 225 Chaoyangmennei Dajie, Dongsi, Beijing 100701, People's Republic of China.

TANG SHUBEI; Chinese government official; b. Jan. 1931, Shanghai; m. Liang Wenfeng; one s. one d.; joined CCP 1949; fmrly. official Shanghai Fed. of Trade Unions, Ed., Head of Reporters Centre Fujian Daily; Chief Editorial Dept. New Vietnamese-Chinese News 1955–57; Sec., then Deputy Dir. then Dir. China News Service 1957–69; Deputy Div. Chief Dept. of Consular Affairs 1971–78; First Sec. Tokyo Embassy 1978–82; Div. Chief Dept. of Consular Affairs 1982–83; Consul-Gen. San Francisco 1983–86; envoy of Embassy, U.S.A. 1986–88; Dir. Office for Taiwan Affairs of Foreign Ministry 1988–89, Deputy Dir. for Taiwan Affairs of State Council 1989–; Deputy Dir. CCP Cen. Cttee. Taiwan Affairs Office 1991–; Exec. Vice-Chair. Asscn. for Relations Across the Taiwan Straits 1991–; Deputy Dir. CCP Cen. Cttee. Coordinating Cttee. for Reunification of the Motherland 1993–; mem. Standing Cttee. 8th Nat. Cttee. CCP Cen. Cttee. *Address:* Office for Taiwanese Affairs, c/o State Council, Beijing, China. *Telephone:* 68328307; 68467577. *Fax:* 68328321; 68478780.

TANG TIANBIAO, Lieut.-Gen.; Chinese army officer; b. Oct. 1940, Shimen Co., Hunan Prov.; ed. Harbin Inst. of Mil. Eng., Inst. of PLA Engineer Corps, Propaganda and Theoretical Cadre Training Course of CCP Cen. Cttee. Party School and Univ. of Nat. Defence; mem. CCP 1961–; held various posts in Guangzhou Mil. Region; Deputy Dir. Propaganda Dept. Guangzhou Mil. Region 1983; Deputy Office Head and Deputy Dir. Cadre Dept. of PLA Gen. Political Dept.; Deputy Dir. PLA Navy's Political Dept.; Dir. Cadre Dept. of Gen. Political Dept.; Deputy Dir. Leading Group for the Placement of Demobilized Army Officers 1993–; Asst. Dir. PLA Gen. Political Dept. 1993–95, Deputy Dir. 1995–; rank of Lieut.-Gen. 1994–; Deputy to 8th NPC 1993; mem. 15th CCP Cen. Cttee. 1997–. *Address:* c/o Ministry of National Defence, Jingshanqian Jie, Beijing, People's Republic of China. *Telephone:* (1) 6370000.

TANG TING YEN, Henry, J.P.; Chinese business executive and official; b. 6 Sept. 1952, Hong Kong; m. Lisa Kuo; four c.; ed. Univ. of Michigan; Man. Dir. Peninsula Knitters Ltd.; Chair. Fed. of Hong Kong Industries; Dir. Meadville Ltd.; Hong Kong Affairs Adviser to Chinese Govt.; fmr. mem. Legis. Council; mem. Exec. Council Hong Kong Special Admin. Region July 1997–, Selection Cttee. for First Govt. of the Hong Kong Special Admin. Region, CPPCC Shanghai Cttee., Hong Kong Trade Devt. Council, Liberal Party. *Address:* Executive Council Secretariat, 1st Floor, Main Wing, Central Government Offices, Central, Hong Kong Special Administrative Region, People's Republic of China.

TANG XIAOWEI; Chinese physicist; b. Oct. 1931, Wuxi Co., Jiangsu Prov.; ed. Qinghua Univ.; researcher Physics Inst. 1981–; mem. of Dept. Math. and Physics, Academia Sinica 1985–; Nat. Scientific Prize of China. *Address:* High Energy Physics Institute, Yu Quan Lu, Beijing, People's Republic of China.

TANG ZHISONG; Chinese computer scientist; b. 7 Aug. 1925, Changsha, Hunan; s. of Tang Shousong and Zhu Chunxuan; m. Tong Enjian 1959; two s.; researcher, Computer Tech. Inst., Acad. Sinica, 1956–, Software Inst. 1983–; visited Stanford Univ., U.S.A. 1979–81; mem. Acad. Sinica 1992; Hon. First Nat. Prize of Sciences 1989. *Leisure interest:* Chinese classical poetry. *Address:* Institute of Software, Academia Sinica, P.O. Box 8718, 1000 80 Beijing, People's Republic of China. *Telephone:* (10) 62556910 (Office); (10) 62561363 (Home). *Fax:* (10) 2562533.

TANG ZHONGWEN; Chinese state official; b. 1930, Shanghai; ed. Qinghua Univ., Beijing; joined CCP 1952; cadre of the 5th Ministry of Machine Bldg. 1975–77; Vice-Minister of Ordnance Industry 1977–86, of Machine Bldg. and Electronics Industry 1987–91; Vice-Chair. China Northern Industrial Corpn. 1980–86; Pres. Chamber of Commerce for Importers and Exporters of Machinery and Electronics 1991–; alt. mem. 12th CCP Cen. Cttee. 1982–87; mem. 7th and 8th CPPCC 1988–. *Address:* c/o Chamber of Commerce for Importers and Exporters of Machinery and Electronics, 95 Beiheyan Street, Dongchengqu, Beijing 100006, People's Republic of China.

TANGAROA, Hon. Sir Tangaroa, Kt., M.B.E.; Cook Islands administrator (retd.); b. 6 May 1921; s. of Tangaroa and Mihiau; m. 1941; two s. seven d.; ed. Avarua Primary School, Rarotonga; radio operator 1939–54; shipping clerk, Donald and Ingram Ltd. 1955–63; M.P. for Penrhyn 1958–84; Minister of Educ., Works Survey Printing, and Electric Power Supply, then Minister of Internal Affairs 1978–80; Minister of Educ. 1980–84; Queen's Rep. Cook Islands 1984–90; Pres. Cook Island Crippled Children's Soc. 1966–; Deacon Cook Islands Christian Church; fmr. Pres. Cook Islands Boys Brigade; Del. Islands Sports Asscn. *Leisure interest:* black pearls farming. *Address:* P.O. Box 870, Avarua, Rarotonga, Cook Islands. *Telephone:* 21690.

TANGE, Kenzo, DR.ENG.; Japanese architect; b. 4 Sept. 1913, Osaka; s. of Tokiyo and Tei (Komaki) Tange; m. 1st Toshiko Kato 1949; m. 2nd Takako Iwata 1973; one s. one d.; ed. Tokyo Univ.; Prof. Univ. of Tokyo 1946–74, Emer. 1974–; Pres. Japanese Architects Asscn. 1986–; Hon. mem. American Acad. of Arts and Letters, Akad. der Künste, West Berlin, Colegio de Arquitectos de Venezuela 1978; Hon. Fellow American Inst. of Architects; Royal Gold Medal, R.I.B.A. 1965; Founding mem. Foundation Arquitectura y Urbanismo, Argentina 1978; Assoc. mem. Paris Acad. of Fine Arts 1984; Foreign corresp. l'Acad. d'Architecture pour Japon, France 1979; Academic corresp. in Japan of Nat. Acad. of Fine Arts, Argentina 1978; Hon. Prof. (Univ. Nacional Federico Villarreal, Peru) 1977, (Univ. Buenos Aires) 1978; Hon. Dr. Arts (Harvard); Hon. doctorate (Sheffield Univ.); Hon. Dr. Fine Arts (Univ. of Buffalo); Hon. Dr.-Ing. (Technische Hochschule, Stuttgart); Hon. Dr. Arch. (Politecnico di Milano, Italy); Hon. D.Sc. (Univ. of Hong Kong); AIA Gold Medal, American Inst. of Architects 1966; Medal of Honour, Danish Royal Acad. of Fine Arts, Grand Prix, Architectural Inst. of Japan 1986, Pritzker Architecture Prize 1987, and several other awards; Grande Médaille d'Or, Acad. française 1973, Ordre pour le Mérite (Fed. Repub. of Germany) 1976, Commdr., Ordre nat. du Mérite 1977, Mexican Order of the Aguila Azteca (Grade Encomienda) 1978, Commendatore nell' Ordine al Merito della Repubblica Italiana 1979, Person of Cultural Merit, Japan 1979, Order of Culture, Japan 1980, Commdr., Ordre des Arts et des Lettres 1984, Grande Ufficiale nell'Ordine al Merito, Italy 1984, Pritzker Architecture Prize 1987. *Buildings include:* Peace Memorial Park and Buildings, Hiroshima, Tokyo City Hall, Tokyo, Kurashiki City Hall, Kurashiki, Kagawa Prefectural Govt. Office, Takamatsu, Roman Catholic Cathedral, Tokyo, Nat. Gymnasiums for 1964 Olympic Games, Tokyo, Kuwait Int. Air Terminal Bldg., Skopje City Centre Reconstruction Project, Skopje, Yugoslavia, Yamanashi Press and Broadcasting Centre, Yamahashi, Master Plan for Expo 1970, Osaka, Int. Fairs' Fiera Dist. Centre, Bologna, Italy, Univ. Hospital and Dormitory, Oran, Algeria, Baltimore Inner Harbour Project, residential redevt., Royal State Palace, Jeddah, Saudi Arabia 1977–82, Royal Palace for H.M. the King, Jeddah, Saudi Arabia 1977–82, new capital of Nigeria 'Abuja' Urban Design for Cen. Civic Axis 1979, Overseas Union Bank Centre Bldg., Singapore 1980, Naples Admin. Centre, Italy 1980, Int. Tech. Centre, Singapore 1982, Ekime Culture Centre, Japan 1982, Yokohama City Museum, Japan 1983, Singapore Indoor Stadium 1985–, Ohutsu Prince Hotel, Japan 1985–, The UN Univ., Tokyo 1986–, New Tokyo City Hall Complex, Tokyo 1986–, Mil. Acad. Complex, Singapore 1986–; Imperial Award (Japan) 1993. *Publications:* Katsura, Tradition and Creation in Japanese Architecture 1960, A Plan for Tokyo, 1960 1961, Ise 1962, Japan in the Future 1966, Kenzo Tange, 1946–1958 1966, Kenzo Tange, 1958–1964 1966, Kenzo Tange 1964–1969 1970, Japan in the 21st Century 1971. *Address:* 7-2-21 Akasaka, Minato-ku, Tokyo (Office); 1702, 2-3-34 Mita, Minato-ku, Tokyo 108, Japan (Home). *Telephone:* 408-7121/4 (Office); 455-2787 and 453-7301/3 (Home).

TANIGUCHI, Makoto, M.A.; Japanese diplomatist; b. 1930, Osaka; s. of Yoshio Taniguchi and Tomiko Tamura; m. Hiroko Kanari 1972; one. s.; ed. Hitotsubashi Univ., St. John's Coll. Cambridge, U.K.; joined Ministry of Foreign Affairs 1959; specialized in econ. affairs; Dir. for UN Specialized Agencies 1972, Dir. for UN Econ. Affairs 1973–74, Counsellor of Japanese Mission to Int. Orgs., Geneva, in charge of UNCTAD Affairs 1974–76, Minister and Consul-Gen., Manila 1976–79, Minister, Japanese Mission to UN, in charge of Econ. Matters 1979–83; Amb. Extraordinary and Plenipotentiary to Papua New Guinea 1983–86, to UN, New York 1986–90; Deputy Sec.-Gen. OECD 1990–96, Special Adviser to Sec.-Gen. 1997; Prof. Inst. of Asia-Pacific Studies, Waseda Univ., Tokyo 1998–99, Toyo Eiwa Women's Univ., Tokyo 1998–99; Chair. Preparatory Cttee. for UN Conf. on New and Renewable Sources of Energy 1980–81, Chair. Cttee. I 1981; Chair. Cttee. I, UNCTAD VII; Vice-Pres., Pres. Exec. Bd. UNICEF 1987–88; Visiting Prof. Univ. of Int. Trade and Econs. Beijing 1995; External Auditor Hitachi Metals 1995–; Head Japanese Del. to UN Comm. on Human Rights 1987–89. *Publications:* North-South Issues—A Path to Global Solutions (in Japanese) 1993; many articles. *Address:* Institute of Asia-Pacific Studies, Waseda University, Sodai-Nishiwaseda Bldg. 6F, 1-21-1 Nishiwaseda, Shinjuku-ku, Tokyo 169, Japan. *Telephone:* (03) 5286-3938. *Fax:* (03) 3232-7075.

TANNER, Alain; Swiss film director; b. 1933, Geneva; ed. in London; made numerous documentaries before directing feature films. *Films include:* Charles Dead or Alive 1969; The Salamander, The Middle of the World,

Jonah Who Will be 25 in the Year 2000, Light Years Away (Special Jury Prize, Cannes Film Festival 1985) 1981, No Man's Land 1985, Une Flamme Dans Mon Coeur 1987, The Woman of Rose Hill 1989.

TANNER, Roger Ian, PH.D.; British professor of mechanical engineering; b. 25 July 1933, Wells, Somerset; s. of R. J. Tanner and E. Tanner; m. Elizabeth Bogen 1957; two s. three d.; ed. Univs. of Bristol, Calif. (Berkeley) and Manchester; eng. apprentice, Bristol Aero Engines 1950–53; lecturer in Mechanical Eng. Univ. of Manchester 1958–61; Sr. Lecturer, Reader, Univ. of Sydney 1961–66, P.N. Russell Prof. of Mechanical Eng. 1975–, Pro-Vice-Chancellor (Research) 1994–97; Prof. Brown Univ. Providence, R.I. 1966–75; Edgeworth David Medal 1966, Australian Soc. of Rheology Medallion 1993. *Publication:* Engineering Rheology 1985. *Leisure interests:* tennis, opera. *Address:* Department of Mechanical Engineering, University of Sydney, N.S.W. 2006 (Office); Marlowe, Sixth Mile Lane, Roseville, N.S.W. 2069, Australia (Home). *Telephone:* (02) 9351-7153 (Office). *Fax:* (02) 9351-7060.

TAŃSKI, Adam; Polish politician and economist; b. 5 March 1946, Nieznanowice, Kielce Prov.; s. of Kazimierz Tański and Władysława Tańska; m. Konstancja Szczygieł 1968; two s. one d.; ed. Agricultural Acad., Warsaw; employee land reclamation enterprises 1969–73; Dir. Dept. of Food Econs., Ministry of Finance 1973–90; Under-Sec. of State, Ministry of Agric. 1990; Minister of Agric. and Food Econs. Jan.–Dec. 1991; Pres. Agric. Property Agency of State Treasury 1992–; Episcopal Cttee. of Foundation for Water Supply to Agric. 1983–; mem. Solidarity Trade Union 1980–81. *Leisure interest:* swimming. *Address:* ul. Dolańskiego 2, 00-215 Warsaw, Poland. *Telephone:* 635 5353. *Fax:* 635 0060.

TANZI, Vito, PH.D.; American economist; b. 29 Nov. 1935, Italy; s. of Luigi Tanzi and Maria Tanzi; m. Maria T. Bernabé 1997; three s.; ed. George Washington and Harvard Univs.; Chair. of Econs. Dept., American Univ. 1971–74, Prof. of Econs. 1971–74; Head Tax Policy Div. IMF 1974–81, Dir. Fiscal Affairs Dept. 1981–; Commendatore della Repubblica Italiana. *Publications:* ten books, over 200 articles in professional journals. *Leisure interests:* naive art, African art, photography, music, travel. *Address:* 5912 Walhondine Road, Bethesda, MD 20816, U.S.A. *Telephone:* (202) 6238723 (Office); (301) 2292827 (Home). *Fax:* (202) 623 4259 (Office).

TAO BOJUN, Gen.; Chinese army officer; Chief of Staff Guangzhou Mil. Region 1992; promoted to Lieut.-Gen. 1993; Deputy Commdr. Guangzhou Mil. Region 1993–96; Commdr. Guangdong Mil. Region 1996–; rank of Gen. 1998; mem. 15th CCP Cen. Cttee. 1997–. *Address:* People's Liberation Army, c/o Ministry of National Defence, Jingshanqian Jie, Beijing, China.

TAO DAYONG; Chinese economist; b. 12 March 1918, Shanghai; m. Niu Ping-Qing 1942; one s. one d.; ed. Nat. Cen. Univ.; lecturer Nat. Sun Yat-sen Univ. 1942–43; Assoc. Prof., Nat. Guangxi Univ. 1943–44, Nat. Jiaotong Univ. 1944–45; Prof. Nat. Szechwan Univ. 1945–46; Visiting Prof. (invited by British Council) 1946–48; Prof. Beijing Univ. 1949–51; Prof. Beijing Normal Univ. 1952–; Ed.-in-Chief, New Construction 1951–54, Qunyan 1985–; mem. Standing Cttee. 6th CPPCC 1982–88; mem. Standing Cttee. 6th, 7th, 8th NPC 1993–; Vice Chair. Cen. Cttee. Chinese Democratic League 1985–97, Hon. Vice-Chair. 1997–; Vice-Pres. World Econs. Soc. of China 1980–85, Chinese Soc. of Foreign Econ. Theories 1983–; Adviser, Centre for Hongkong and Macao Studies 1982; Int. Order of Merit 1990, Medal of The First Five Hundred 1991, Int. Register of Profiles 1993, 20th Century Award for Achievement 1993. *Publications:* Economic Reconstruction of Post-War Eastern Europe 1948, Post-war Capitalism 1950, History of Socialism 1949, Introduction to World Economy 1951, Studies in Contemporary Capitalistic Economy 1985, A Critique of Henry George's Economic Thought 1982, A New History of Foreign Economic Thoughts 1990, Selected Works of Tao Dayong 1992. *Leisure interests:* reading, travel, music. *Address:* Economics Department, Beijing Normal University, Beijing, People's Republic of China. *Telephone:* (10) 62200012.

TAO HO; Chinese artist and architect; b. 1936; ed. Williams Coll. Massachusetts and Harvard Univ.; worked with architect Walter Gropius; in practice as architect in Hong Kong; art work includes acrylic paintings, lithographs, pen-and-ink sketches and sculptures in marble, wood and rusty scrap iron; works exhibited at Hong Kong Univ. Museum.

TAO SIJU; Chinese party official; b. 1935, Jingjiang Co., Jiangsu Prov.; joined CCP 1949; Vice-Minister of Public Security 1984–90, Minister 1990–98; Vice-Chair. Internal Affairs and Judicial Cttee. 9th NPC 1998–; mem. 14th CCP Cen. Cttee. 1992–97, 15th CCP Cen. Cttee. 1997–; Chair. Nat. Narcotics Control Comm. 1993–; First Political Commissar Chinese People's Armed Police Force 1991–; mem. Cen. Comm. of Political Science and Law. *Address:* c/o Standing Committee of National People's Congress, Beijing, People's Republic of China. *Telephone:* (10) 65122831.

TAOFINU'U, H.E. Cardinal Pio; Samoan ecclesiastic; b. 8 Dec. 1923, Falealupo, Savaii; s. of Solomona Taofinu'u and Mau Solia; ordained priest 1954; Bishop of Samoa Apia 1968–73, Archbishop 1982–; cr. Cardinal by Pope Paul VI March 1973. *Publication:* The Kava Ceremony is a Prophecy 1973. *Leisure interests:* gardening, music, art. *Address:* Cardinal's Office, P.O. Box 532, Apia, Western Samoa. *Telephone:* 20400. *Fax:* 20402.

TAPE, Gerald Frederick, A.B., M.S., PH.D.; American physicist and scientific administrator; b. 29 May 1915, Ann Arbor, Mich.; s. of Henry A. Tape and Flora Simmons Tape; m. Josephine Waffen 1939; three s.; ed. Eastern Michigan Univ., and Univ. of Michigan; Asst. in Physics, Eastern Mich. Univ. 1933–35, Univ. of Mich. 1936–39; Instructor in Physics, Cornell Univ. 1939–42; Staff mem. Radiation Lab. M.I.T. 1942–46; Asst., later Assoc. Prof. of Physics Univ. of Ill. 1946–50; Asst. to Dir. 1950–51, Deputy Dir., Brookhaven Nat. Lab. 1951–62; Vice-Pres. Associated Univs. Inc. 1962, Pres. 1962–63, 1969–80, Special Asst. to Pres. 1980–82; U.S. Atomic Energy Commr. 1963–69; U.S. Rep. to IAEA with rank of Amb. 1973–77; mem. Pres.'s Science Advisory Cttee. 1969–73; mem. Defense Science Bd. 1970–74, Chair. 1970–73; mem. AEC High Energy Physics Advisory Panel 1969–74, IAEA Scientific Advisory Panel 1972–74, Energy Research and Devt. Admin. Gen. Advisory Cttee. 1975–77, Nat. Science Foundation Advisory Group on Science Programs 1975–76, Dept. of Energy Advisory Cttee. on Nuclear Facility Safety 1988–91; Dir. Atomic Industrial Forum Inc. 1970–73, Science Service Inc. 1971–, Electric Power Research Inst. Advisory Council 1978–85; Univ. Chicago, Bd. of Govs. for Argonne Nat. Lab. 1982–85; Consultant, Defense Nuclear Facilities Safety Bd. 1992–; mem. Nat. Acad. of Eng., American Astronomical Soc.; Fellow, American Physical Soc., American Nuclear Soc., A.A.A.S.; Hon. D.Sc. (E. Mich. Univ. 1964); Army-Navy Certificate of Appreciation 1947; Dept. of State Tribute of Appreciation 1969; Sec. of Defense Meritorious Civilian Service Medal 1969; Dept. of Defense Distinguished Public Service Medal 1973; Henry DeWolf Smyth Nuclear Statesman Award, Atomic Industrial Forum, American Nuclear Soc. 1978; Commdr., Order of Leopold II (Belgium) 1978; Nat. Science Foundation Distinguished Public Service Award 1980; Distinguished Assoc. Award, Dept. of Energy 1980, Enrico Fermi Award 1987. *Publications:* co-author with L. J. Haworth Relay Radar Chapter of M.I.T. Radiation Laboratory Technical Series; co-author with Dr. F. K. Pittman and M. F. Searl Future Energy Needs and the Role of Nuclear Power 1964, Proceedings of Third International Conference on Peaceful Uses of Atomic Energy 1964, Proceedings of the Thermionic Electrical Power Generation Symposium, Stresa 1968, Why We Test 1968, National Policy on Peaceful Uses of Nuclear Explosives 1969, The Next Twenty Years—IAEA's Role 1977. *Address:* 4970 Sentinel Drive 502, Bethesda, MD 20816, U.S.A. *Telephone:* (301) 229-6264.

TÀPIES PUIG, Antoni; Spanish painter; b. 13 Dec. 1923, Barcelona; m. Teresa Barba; three c.; ed. Inst. Menéndez Pelayo and Univ. of Barcelona; first one-man exhbn., Barcelona 1948, later in Paris, New York, London, Zürich, Rome, Milan, Munich, Stockholm, Hanover, Washington, Pasadena, Buenos Aires, Caracas, Düsseldorf, Bilbao, Madrid and Barcelona; cr. Mural for Saint Gallen Theatre, Switzerland 1971; French Govt. Scholarship 1950; Officier des Arts et des Lettres; UNESCO Prize, Venice Biennale and Pittsburgh Int. Prize 1958, Guggenheim Prize 1964, Rubens Prize 1972, City of Barcelona Prize 1979, Rembrandt Prize, Goethe Foundation, Basle 1984, French Nat. Grand Prize for Painting 1985, Prince of Asturias Prize 1990. *Publications:* La pràctica de l'art, L'art contra l'estètica, Memòria personal (autobiog.) 1978, La realitat com a art 1983. *Address:* C. Zaragoza 57, 08006 Barcelona, Spain. *Telephone:* (93) 2173398.

TAPLIN, Guy Christie; British artist; b. 5 March 1939, London; s. of George Frederick Taplin and Gladys Lillian Taplin (née Peters); m. Robina Dunkery Jack 1989; one s. one d.; ed. Norlington Secondary Modern School, Leyton; self-taught artist (sculptor) 1978–; fmrly. worked as window cleaner; Post-Office messenger 1954–58, meat porter 1960, driver 1961, ladies' hairdresser 1961–62, lifeguard 1962–68, cook 1964, birdkeeper Regent's Park 1970–76; also had own fashion business during 1960s. *Leisure interests:* life, art. *Address:* Anglesea Cottage, Anglesea Road, Wivenhoe, Colchester, Essex, CO7 9JR, England. *Telephone:* (01206) 822160.

TAPPER, Colin Frederick Herbert, M.A., B.C.L.; British professor of law; b. 13 Oct. 1934, W. Drayton; s. of H. F. Tapper and F. G. Tapper (née Lambard); m. M. White 1961; one d.; ed. Magdalen Coll., Oxford; teacher L.S.E. 1959–65; barrister Grays Inn 1961; tutor Magdalen Coll. 1965–79, Fellow 1965–, Reader 1979–91, Prof. 1992–; Dir. Butterworth Group 1979–84, Butterworth Telepublishing 1979–89; consultant to Masons (solicitors) 1990–. *Publications:* Computers and the Law 1973, Computer Law 1978, Cross on Evidence (ed.) 1990, Handbook of European Software Law (ed.) 1995, Cross and Tapper on Evidence (ed.) 1995. *Leisure interests:* computing, reading, writing. *Address:* Magdalen College, Oxford, OX1 4AU (Office); Corner Cottage, Woodstock Road, Stonesfield, Witney, Oxon., OX8 8QA, England (Home). *Telephone:* (01865) 276055 (Office); (01993) 891284 (Home). *Fax:* (01865) 276103 (Office); (01993) 891395 (Home).

TAPSELL, Peter, M.B.E., M.B., CH.B., F.R.C.S.(E.), F.R.C.S.; New Zealand politician; b. 21 Jan. 1930, Rotorua; s. of May Sheehan and Peter Tapsell; m. Margaret Bourke 1951; two s. two d.; ed. Otago Univ., Medical School, Dunedin; House Surgeon, Waikato Hosp., Hamilton, demonstrator in Anatomy, School of Medicine, Dunedin; Resident Surgical Officer, Dunedin Public Hosp.; orthopaedic surgeon to Rotorua and Queen Elizabeth Hosps. 1971–84; M.P. for Eastern Maori 1981–96; Minister of Internal Affairs, Civil Defence and the Arts, and Assoc. Minister of Local Govt. and Tourism 1984–87, of Recreation and Sport, of Lands, Survey and Information, of Valuation Dept. 1987–90, of Science (concurrently) 1989–90, of Defence, Lands, Recreation and Sport Jan.–Oct. 1990; Speaker, House of Reps. 1994–96; Deputy Mayor Rotorua City; Chair. N.Z. Maori Arts and Crafts Inst., Ngati Whakaue Lands Corpn.; mem. Cabinet Select Cttee. of Maori Affairs; Vice-Capt. Maori All Blacks Fiji Tour 1954; Labour. *Leisure interests:* rugby, hunting, fishing, skiing. *Address:* 2 Ngahu Street, Rotorua, New Zealand. *Telephone:* (7) 3485432.

TARAND, Andres; Estonian politician; b. 11 Jan. 1940, Tallinn; s. of Helmut Tarand and Leida Tarand; m. Mari (née Viiding) Tarand 1963; two s.; ed. Tartu Univ.; hydrometeorologist 1963; research asst. Tallinn Botanical Gardens 1965–68; researcher Antarctic Expedition 1968–70; engineer, Dir. Tallinn Botanical Gardens 1970–89; Chair. Environment Cttee. Supreme Soviet Estonian S.S.R. 1990; mem. Council of Estonia 1990–92; mem. Constitutional Ass. 1991–92; mem. Riigikogu (Parl.) 1992, 1995–; Minister of Environment 1992–94; Prime Minister of Estonia 1994–95. *Publications:* numerous articles on climatology, urban ecology, politics. *Leisure interests:* chess, ornithology, traditional style gardening. *Address:* Riigikogu, Lossi plats 1a, Tallinn 10130, Estonia (Office). *Telephone:* (3726) 316651 (Office). *Fax:* 316653 (Office).

TARANDA, Gediminas Leonovich; Russian/Lithuanian ballet dancer; b. 26 Feb. 1961, Kaliningrad; ed. Moscow School of Choreography; soloist Bolshoi Theatre 1980–94, dismissed after conflict with admin.; Dir. Imperial Russian Ballet of Vienna; performer of leading roles of classical and contemporary Russian repertoire including Espado (Don Quixote), Correchidor (Carmen), Forest Warden (Giselle), Kuman (Prince Igor), Severyan (Stone Flower), Yashka (Golden Age), Kurbsky (Ivan the Terrible), Abderakhman (Raimonda), Vizir (Legend of Love) and others. *Address:* Imperial Russian Ballet, Vienna, Austria. *Address:* Imperial Ballet, Trekhprudny per. 11/13, bldg. 2b, Office 45, 103001 Moscow, Russia. *Telephone:* 299-13-98.

TARANTINO, Quentin; American film director; b. 27 March 1963, Knoxville, Tenn.; s. of Tony Tarantino and Connie McHugh; worked in Video Archives, Manhattan Beach; brief acting career; producer, Killing Zoe; wrote screenplay for True Romance, Natural Born Killers. *Films directed:* Reservoir Dogs, Pulp Fiction (Golden Palm, Cannes Film Festival) 1994; appearances include Sleep With Me 1994, Destiny Tunes on the Radio 1995, Desperado 1995, Girl 6 1996, From Dusk Till Dawn 1996. *Films produced:* Red Rain 1995, Four Rooms 1995, From Dusk Till Dawn 1996, Curdled 1996. *Publications:* True Romance 1995, Natural Born Killers 1995, Jackie Brown 1998. *Address:* WMA, 151 El Camino Drive, Beverly Hills, CA 90212; 6201 Sunset Boulevard, Suite 35, Los Angeles, CA 90028, U.S.A.

ŢĂRANU, Cornel, D.MUS.; Romanian composer and conductor; b. 20 June 1934, Cluj; s. of Francisc Ţăranu and Elisabeta Ţăranu; m. Daniela Mărgineanu 1960; one d.; ed. Cluj Conservatory; Prof. of Composition, Cluj Conservatory; Conductor of Ars Nova, contemporary music ensemble; Vice-Pres. Romanian Composers' Union 1990–; mem. Romanian Acad. 1993–; Prize of the Romanian Composers' Union 1972, 1978, 1981, 1982, Prize of the Romanian Acad. 1973, The Koussevitsky Prize 1982. *Works include:* sonatas for flute, oboe, clarinet and percussion, sonata for double bass solo, viola sonata, one piano concerto, cantatas, four symphonies, Séquences, Incantations, Symmétries, Raccords for orchestra, two Sinfoniettas for strings, Garlands (for chamber orchestra), Don Giovanni's Secret (chamber opera), Chansons nomades (oratorio), Chansons sans amour, lieder, Sempre Ostinato, Chansons sans réponse, Hommage à Paul Célan, Memento and Dedications (cantatas), Miroirs (for saxophone and orchestra), Garlands, Prolégomènes (for chamber orchestra), Orpheus (cantata), Tombeau de Verlaine (mixed choir), Mosaïques (for saxophone and ensemble), Chansons interrompues (voice and ensemble) 1993, Cadenze Concertante (cello and chamber orchestra) 1993, Trajectoires (for ensemble) 1994, Crisalide (for saxophone, tape and ensemble), Five Tzara Songs (for voice and piano), Remembering Bartók (for oboe and ensemble), Enescu's 'Caprice Roumain' for violin and orchestra (new arrangement) 1995, Responsorial (for clarinet) 1996, Antiphona (for flute and orchestra) 1996, Flaine Quintette (for winds) 1997, Laudatio per Clusium (for voice and instruments) 1997, Saturnali (baritone and ensemble) 1998, three Labiş Poems (bass and piano) 1998, Cadenze per Antiphona (flute and solo) 1998, Siciliana Blues (piano and chamber orchestra) 1998, Concerto (oboe and strings) 1998; also film music. *Leisure interest:* chess. *Address:* Str. Nicolae Iorga 7, Cluj-Napoca 3400, Romania. *Telephone:* (64) 147331. *Fax:* (64) 193879.

TARAR, Muhammad Rafiq; Pakistani politician and lawyer; b. 2 Nov. 1929, Pir Kot, Ghakkar Mandi; ed. Government Islamia High School, Gujranwala, Guru Nanak Khalsa Coll., Gujranwala, Punjab Univ. Law Coll.; legal practice Gujranwala; Additional Sessions Judge, Gujranwala, Bahawalnagar, Sargodha; mem. Lahore High Court 1974, Chief Justice 1989; mem. Electoral Comm. of Pakistan 1980–89; mem. Supreme Court 1991–94; Senator, Pakistan Muslim League March–Dec. 1997; Pres. of Pakistan Jan. 1998–. *Address:* Office of the President, Aiwan-e-Sadr, Islamabad, Pakistan. *Telephone:* (51) 9206060. *Fax:* (51) 9211018.

TARASOV, Gennady Pavlovich; Russian diplomatist; b. 14 Sept. 1947; ed. Moscow State Inst. of Int. Relations; on staff Ministry of Foreign Affairs 1970–; worked in Egypt, U.S.S.R. Mission in U.N.O. and other posts –1986; Deputy Head of Dept. Near E. and S. African Countries U.S.S.R. Ministry of Foreign Affairs 1986–90; Amb. of U.S.S.R., then of Russia to Saudi Arabia 1990–96; Dir. Dept. of Information and Press Ministry of Foreign Affairs 1996–98, to Portugal 1998–. *Address:* Embaixada da Russia, Rua Visconde de Santarém 59, 241000 Lisbon, Portugal. *Telephone:* 846-25-24. *Fax:* 846-30-08.

TARASYUK, Boris Ivanovich; Ukrainian politician; b. 1 Jan. 1949, Zhitomir Region, Ukraine; m.; one s. two d.; ed. Kiev State Univ.; attaché, Third, Second, First Sec. Ukrainian Ministry of Foreign Affairs 1975–81; Second, First Sec. Perm. Mission of Ukrainian S.S.R. to UN 1981–86; First Sec. Div. of Int. Orgs., Ukrainian Ministry of Foreign Affairs 1986–87; instructor Div. of Foreign Relations, Ukrainian CP Cen. Cttee. 1987–90; Head, Dept. of Political Analysis and Planning, Ukrainian Ministry of Foreign Affairs 1991–92; Deputy, First Deputy Minister of Foreign Affairs, Head, Nat. Cttee. on Disarmament Problems 1992–95; Amb. to Belgium (also accred. to Netherlands, Luxembourg) 1995–98; Head, Ukrainian Mission to NATO 1997–; Minister of Foreign Affairs 1998–. *Address:* Ministry of Foreign Affairs, 1st Mikhailovska Square, 252018 Kiev, Ukraine. *Telephone:* (381) 293 2472 (Office).

TARBELL, Dean Stanley, A.M., PH.D.; American professor of chemistry; b. 19 Oct. 1913, Hancock, New Hampshire; s. of Sanford M. Tarbell and Ethel L. Millikan; m. Ann Tracy 1942; two s. one d.; ed. Thayer High School, Winchester, N.H., and Harvard Univ.; Postdoctoral Fellow, Univ. of Ill. 1937–38; Instructor, rising to Houghton Prof. of Chem. and Chair. of Dept., Univ. of Rochester 1938–67; Distinguished Prof. of Chem., Vanderbilt Univ. 1967, Branscom Distinguished Prof. 1975–76, Distinguished Prof. Emer. 1981–; R. C. Fuson Lecturer, Nevada 1972; Consultant, U.S. Public Health Service; mem. N.A.S., American Acad. of Arts and Sciences, American Chemical Soc., Chemical Soc. of London; Herty Medallist 1973, Dexter Award of the Div. of the History of Chemistry 1989. *Publications:* Roger Adams, Scientist and Statesman (with Ann Tarbell) 1981, Essays on the History of Organic Chemistry in the United States, 1875–1955 (with Ann Tarbell) 1986, Autobiography 1996, and about 215 research papers in organic chemistry and history of chemistry 1936–. *Leisure interests:* history, out of doors, music. *Address:* 6033 Sherwood Drive, Nashville, TN 37215, U.S.A. (Home).

TARCHER, Jeremy Phillip, B.A.; American publisher; b. 2 Jan. 1932, New York; s. of Jack D. Tarcher and Mary Bregor Tarcher; m. Shari Lewis 1958; one d.; ed. St. John's Coll., Annapolis, Md.; Founder and Pres. Jeremy P. Tarcher Inc., L.A. 1964–; Vice-Pres. Houghton Mifflin, Boston 1980–83; Chair. Bd. Audio Renaissance Tapes, L. A. 1985–; mem. Bd. Trustees The Esalen Inst., Big Sur, Calif. 1986–; Producer Shari Lewis Show, NBC Network 1959–62; Exec. Producer A Picture of U.S. (Emmy Award for Children's Programming 1976) 1976. *Leisure interests:* entheogenic research, travel, reading, primitive oceanic art. *Address:* Jeremy P. Tarcher Inc., 11150 W. Olympic Blvd., Suite 600, 603 North Alta Drive, Beverly Hills, CA 90210, U.S.A. *Telephone:* (213) 935 9980; (213) 274-7207.

TARJÁN, Imre; Hungarian physicist; b. 26 July 1912, Szabadka; s. of József Tarján and Erzsébet Tomasics; m. 1st Magda Kincsek 1940; m. 2nd Margit Kardos 1955; three d.; ed. Budapest Univ. of Sciences; Prof. Budapest Coll. of Pedagogy 1949; Prof. Budapest Univ. of Medicine and Dir. of Univ. Inst. of Biophysics 1950–82, including Research Group for Crystal Physics of Hungarian Acad. of Science 1961–76, research advisor 1982–; Dean Budapest Medical Univ. Faculty of General Medicine 1959–63, Univ. Vice-Rector 1970–73; Corresp. mem. Hungarian Acad. of Sciences, Section III (Mathematics and Physical Sciences) 1970–76, ordinary mem. 1976–, mem. Presidium 1976–90; mem. Eötvös Loránd Physical Soc., Biophysical Soc., European Physical Soc.; Medal of Merit (Korean People's Repub.) 1953, Golden Order of Labour 1960, 1964, Kossuth Prize 1961, Inventor's Silver Degree 1970, State Prize 1985; Hungarian Order of Merit 1982, Middle Cross, Hungarian Order of Merit 1993; specialized in crystal defects and growth, biological macromolecular structure and function. *Publications:* Fizika orvosok és biológusok számára (Physics for Physicians and Biologists) textbook 1964, 1968, 1971, Laboratory Manual on Crystal Growth (UNESCO) 1972, A biofizika alapjai (An Introduction to Biophysics) 1977–98; 200 contribs. to science magazines and books in Hungarian and other languages. *Leisure interest:* literature. *Address:* Semmelweis University of Medicine, Institute of Biophysics, 1088 Budapest, Puskin utca 9, Hungary. *Telephone:* (1) 267-6261. *Fax:* (1) 266-6656.

TARJANNE, Pekka, D.TECH.; Finnish international telecommunications official; b. 19 Sept. 1937, Stockholm; s. of P.K. Tarjanne and Annu Ritavuori; m. Aino Kairamo 1962; two s. one d.; ed. Helsinki Univ. of Tech.; research and teaching at univs. in Denmark and U.S.A. 1961–66; Prof. of Theoretical Physics, Univ. of Oulu 1965–66, Univ. of Helsinki 1967–77; mem. Parl. 1970–77; Minister for Transport and Communications 1972–75; Dir.-Gen. of Posts and Telecommunications, Finland 1977–89; Sec.-Gen. Int. Telecommunication Union 1989–; Vice-Chair. Project Oxygen 1999–; Commdr. Order of White Rose of Finland. *Publication:* A Group Theoretical Model for Strong Interaction Dynamics 1962. *Address:* International Telecommunication Union, Place des Nations, 1211 Geneva 20, Switzerland. *Telephone:* (022) 7305111. *Fax:* (022) 7337256.

TARSCHYS, Daniel, PH.D.; Swedish international civil servant; b. 21 July 1943, Stockholm; s. of Bernhard Tarschys and Karin Alexanderson; m. Regina Rehbinder 1970; two d.; ed. Univs. of Stockholm, Leningrad and Princeton; Research Assoc. Stockholm Univ. 1972–76, Prof. of Political Science and Public Admin. 1985– (on leave); Adviser with Ministry of Finance 1976–78, 1979–83; Sec. of State, Prime Minister's Office 1978–79; Prof. of Soviet and E. European Studies Uppsala Univ. 1983–85; contrib. to Dagens Nyheter 1983–94; M.P. 1976–82, 1985–94; Chair. Parl. Social Affairs Cttee. 1985–91, Foreign Affairs Cttee. 1991–94; Vice-Pres. Liberal Int. 1992–94; mem. Council of Europe Parl. Ass. 1986–94, alt. mem. 1981–83; Sec.-Gen. Liberal, Democratic and Reformers Group (LDR) 1987–91, Chair. 1991–94; Sec.-Gen. Council of Europe 1994–99; Chair. of several govt. cttees.

Publications: numerous books and articles on political philosophy, budgetary policy, public admin. and comparative politics. *Address:* Council of Europe, Avenue de L'Europe, 67075 Strasbourg Cedex; 1 rue Joseph Massol, 67000 Strasbourg, France. *Telephone:* (3) 88 41 20 50. *Fax:* (3) 88 41 27 99.

TARTAKOVSKY, Vladimir Aleksandrovich; Russian chemist; b. 10 Aug. 1932; m.; one d.; ed. Moscow State Univ.; worked as researcher, teacher; Head of lab., Inst. of Organic Chem., U.S.S.R. (now Russian) Acad. of Sciences 1955–86; Dir. N. D. Zelinsky Inst. of Organic Chem. 1987–; corresp. mem., U.S.S.R. (now Russian) Acad. of Sciences 1987, mem. 1992–; main research in organic synthesis, chem. of nitrocompounds; Lenin Prize 1976, A.M. Butlerov Prize. *Address:* N. D. Zelinsky Institute of Organic Chemistry, Leninsky prosp. 47, 117913 GSP-1 Moscow, Russia. *Telephone:* (095) 137 2944 (Office).

TASCA, Catherine, L. EN D.; French government official; b. 13 Dec. 1941, Lyons; d. of Angelo Tasca and Alice Naturel; one d.; ed. Inst. d'Etudes Politiques, Paris and Ecole Nat. d'Admin.; civil servant, Ministry of Culture 1967; Dir. Maison de la Culture de Grenoble 1973; Gen. Man. Ensemble Intercontemporain 1978; Co-Dir. Théâtre de Nanterre-Amandiers 1982; mem. Comm. Nat. de la Communication et des Libertés (CNCL) 1986; Minister Del. attached to the Minister of Culture and Communications 1988–91; Sec. of State for Francophone Countries and External Cultural Relations 1992–93; Pres. Admin. Bd. Canal+Horizons 1993–97; Deputy to Nat. Ass. from Yvelines 1997–, mem. Socialist Party. *Address:* Canal+Horizons, 101 rue Leblanc, 75015 Paris; Assemblée nationale, 75355 Paris; 21 rue Saint-Amand, 75015 Paris, France.

TASCHEREAU, Pierre, Q.C., LL.L.; Canadian airline administrator; b. 13 Jan. 1920, Quebec; s. of the late Edouard Taschereau and Juliette (Carroll) Taschereau; m. Yseult Beaudry 1945; two s. one d.; ed. Garnier Coll., Que., Laval Univ., Que., Univ. of Western Ontario; called to Bar of Quebec 1941; Sec. Advisory Cttees., Dept. of Justice, Ottawa 1941–42; Attorney, Canadian Nat. Railways, Montreal 1946–63; Sr. mem. Geoffrion & Prud'homme, barristers and solicitors, Montreal 1963–67; Vice-Pres. Canadian Transport Comm., Ottawa 1967–71; Vice-Pres. Law, Canadian Nat. Railways 1971–72, Exec. Vice-Pres., Corporate Affairs 1972–74, Chair. Bd. 1974–77; Chair. Bd. Air Canada 1976–81; Gov. Montreal General Hosp. *Leisure interest:* bridge. *Address:* 4911 Côte-des-Neiges, Apt. 703, Montreal, Que. H3V 1H7, Canada (Home). *Telephone:* (514) 345-0536.

TASHIRO, Kikuo; Japanese newspaper and television executive; b. 22 April 1917; ed. Waseda Univ.; joined Asahi Shimbun 1940; City Ed. 1959; Man. Ed. 1966; Exec. Dir. in charge of Editorial Affairs 1969; Pres. Asahi Nat. Broadcasting Co. Ltd. (TV Asahi) 1983. *Address:* 6-4-10 Roppongi, Minato-ku, Tokyo 106, Japan (Home). *Telephone:* 03-405-3211 (Home).

TATA, Jamshed Rustom, D.SC., F.R.S.; British medical research scientist; b. 13 April 1930, Bombay, India; s. of Dr. Rustom J. Tata and Gool Tata (née Contractor); m. Renée S. Zanetto 1954; two s. one d.; ed. Univ. of Bombay, Indian Inst. of Science, Bangalore, Coll. de France, Paris and Univ. de Paris, Sorbonne; Postdoctoral Fellow, Sloan-Kettering Inst., New York 1954–55; Beit Memorial Fellow, Nat. Inst. for Medical Research, London 1956–60; Visiting Scientist, Wenner-Gren Inst., Univ. of Stockholm 1960–62; mem. Scientific Staff, MRC, Nat. Inst. for Medical Research, London 1962–96, Sr. Scientist 1996–, Head, Lab. of Developmental Biochem. 1973–96; Visiting Prof., Univ. of Calif. (Berkeley) 1969–70; Fogarty Int. Scholar, Nat. Insts. of Health, Bethesda, Md. 1983–89, Visiting Scientist 1997; Chair. Cell and Molecular Panel, Wellcome Trust 1990–92, Int. Relations Group 1997; mem. Indian Nat. Acad. of Sciences; corresp. mem. Soc. de Biologie, France; Fellow Third World Acad. of Sciences; Trustee Oxford Int. Biomedical Centre 1996–; various awards. *Publications:* The Thyroid Hormones 1959, Chemistry of Thyroid Diseases 1960, Metamorphosis 1972, The Action of Growth and Developmental Hormones 1983, Metamorphosis 1986, Hormonal Signalling and Post-embryonic Development 1998. *Leisure interests:* gardening, reading, travel, tennis. *Address:* 15 Bittacy Park Avenue, Mill Hill, London, NW7 2HA, England (Home). *Telephone:* 0181-346 6291 (Home).

TATA, Ratan; Indian business executive; b. 1937; nephew of J. R. D. Tata; fmr. dir. of various cos. in Tata group Pres. Tata Sons Ltd. (holding co. comprising 98 cos.) 1991–; Chair., Man. Dir. Tata Iron and Steel (TISIO) 1993. *Address:* Bombay House, 24 Homi Mody Street, Hutatmu Chowk, Mumbai 400 023, India (Office).

TATARELLA, Giuseppe; Italian politician and lawyer; b. 17 Sept. 1953, Cerignola, Foggia; fmr. mem. Movimento Sociale Italiano (MSI) party, mem. several local councils, mem. party's Secr.; MSI Deputy 1979–94, fmr. Chair. MSI Deputies; Alleanza Nazionale Deputy March 1994–; Minister of Posts and Telecommunications 1994–95. *Address:* Camera dei Deputati, Rome, Italy.

TATARINOV, Leonid Petrovich; palaeontologist and zoologist; b. 12 Nov. 1926, Tula; s. of Petr Lukich Tatarinov and Anna Nikolayevna Tatatrinova; m. Bulat Susanna Gurgenovna 1959; two d.; ed. Moscow Univ.; mem. CPSU 1964–91; served in Soviet Army 1943–44; sr. scientific ed. of Foreign Language Publishing House 1953–54; mem. staff U.S.S.R. Acad. of Sciences Inst. of Palaeontology (jr. research fellow, then head of lab. and sr. research fellow) 1955–73, Dir. 1975–92, Vice-Sec. Dept. of Gen. Biology of U.S.S.R. (now Russian) Acad. of Sciences 1975–; Chair. Council for Study of Palaeobiology and Evolution 1981; mem. Council Russian Acad. of Sciences 1992–; Scientific Chief of Jt. Soviet- (now Russian-) Mongolian Palaeontological Expedition 1975–96; Ed.-in-Chief Palaeontology Journal 1978–88, 1993–, Zoological Journal 1988–93; Corresp. mem. U.S.S.R. (now Russian) Acad. of Sciences 1974, mem. 1981–; Foreign mem. Linnean Soc., London; U.S.S.R. State Prize 1978. *Publications:* Sketches on the Theory of Evolution 1987, Palaeontology and Evolutionary Doctrine 1989, and other works on origins and early evolution of tetrapods. *Leisure interests:* music, history. *Address:* Palaeontological Institute, Academy of Sciences, Profsoyunaya str. 123, 117647 Moscow V-647, Russia. *Telephone:* (095) 339-07-00 (Office); 438-33-21 (Home). *Fax:* (095) 339-12-66.

TATE, Jeffrey Philip, C.B.E., M.A., M.B., B.CHIR.; British conductor; b. 28 April 1943, Salisbury, Wilts.; s. of Cyril H. Tate and Ivy Ellen Naylor (née Evans); ed. Farnham Grammar School, Christ's Coll. Cambridge and St. Thomas' Hosp. London; trained as medical dr. 1961–67; joined London Opera Centre 1969; joined staff of Royal Opera House, Covent Garden 1970; made recordings as harpsichordist 1973–77; Asst. to Pierre Boulez (q.v.) for the Ring, Bayreuth 1976–81; Asst. to Sir John Pritchard, Cologne Opera 1977; conducted Gothenburg Opera, Sweden 1978–80; Metropolitan Opera début 1979; Covent Garden début 1982; Chief Guest Conductor, Geneva Opera 1983–95; Prin. Conductor, English Chamber Orchestra 1985–, Royal Opera House, Covent Garden 1986–91; Prin. Guest Conductor, Royal Opera House, Covent Garden 1991–94, Orchestre Nat. de France 1989–; Chief Conductor and Artistic Dir. Rotterdam Philharmonic Orchestra 1991–94; Chief Conductor Minnesota Orchestra Summer Festival 1997–; appears with maj. orchestras in Europe and America; numerous recordings with English Chamber orchestra; Pres. Asscn. for Spina Bifida and Hydrocephalus 1989–, Music Space; other charitable positions; Hon. Fellow Christ's Coll., Cambridge, St. Thomas' and Guy's Hosp. Medical School; Hon. D.Mus. (Leicester) 1993; Chevalier des Arts et des Lettres 1990. *Leisure interests:* church-crawling, with gastronomic interludes. *Address:* c/o English Chamber Orchestra, 2 Coningsby Road, London, W5 4HR, England. *Telephone:* 0181-840 6565. *Fax:* 0181-567 7198.

TATE, Robert Brian, PH.D., F.B.A., F.R.HIST.S.; British professor of Hispanic studies; b. 27 Dec. 1921, Belfast, Northern Ireland; s. of Robert Tate and Jane Grantie Tate; m. Beth Ida Lewis 1951; one s. one d.; ed. Royal Belfast Academical Inst., The Queen's Univ., Belfast; Asst. Lecturer, Manchester Univ. 1949–52; Lecturer, The Queen's Univ., Belfast 1952–56; Reader in Hispanic Studies, Nottingham Univ. 1956–58, Prof. 1958–83, Emer. Prof. 1983–; Corresp. Fellow of Institut d'Estudis Catalans, of Real Acad. de Buenas Letras, Barcelona, of Real Acad. de Historia, Madrid. *Publications:* numerous publications on Hispanic topics. *Leisure interests:* art, architecture, jazz, walking. *Address:* 11 Hope Street, Beeston, Nottingham, England. *Telephone:* (0115) 925 1243.

TATHAM, David Everard, C.M.G., B.A.; British diplomatist; b. 28 June 1939; s. of Lieut.-Col. Francis Everard Tatham and Eileen Mary Wilson; m. Valerie Ann Mylechreest 1963; three s.; ed. St. Lawrence Coll., Ramsgate, Wadham Coll. Oxford; entered H.M. Diplomatic Service 1960, Third Sec. U.K. Mission to UN, New York 1962–63; Vice-Consul (Commercial), Milan 1963–67; Middle East Centre for Arabic Studies 1967–69; served Jeddah 1969–70, FCO 1971–74, Muscat 1974–77; Asst. Head Middle East Dept. FCO 1977–80; Counsellor, Dublin 1981–84; Amb. to Yemen Arab Repub. (also accred. to Djibouti) 1984–87; Head Falkland Islands Dept., FCO 1987–90; Amb. to Lebanon 1990–92; Gov. Falklands Islands 1992–96, concurrently Commr. S. Georgia and S. Sandwich Islands; High Commr. to Sri Lanka (also accred. to Maldives) 1996–99. *Leisure interests:* walking uphill, historical research. *Address:* British High Commission, 190 Galle Road, Kollupitiya, P.O. Box 1433, Colombo 3, Sri Lanka. *Telephone:* (1) 437336. *Fax:* (1) 430308.

TATISHVILI, Tsisana Bezhanovna; Georgian opera singer (soprano); b. 30 Dec. 1939, Tbilisi, Georgia; ed. Sarandzhishvili Conservatoire, Tbilisi; soloist with Tbilisi (now Georgian) State Opera 1963–; has toured in Germany, Poland, Czechoslovakia and other countries; People's Artist of Georgian S.S.R. 1973, Paliashvili Prize 1979, 1987, People's Artist of U.S.S.R. 1979. *Roles include:* Tatiana in Eugene Onegin, Liza in Queen of Spades, Aida, Leonora in Il Trovatore, Donna Anna in Don Giovanni, Ortrud in Lohengrin, Salome, Desdemona in Otello, Santuzza in Cavalleria Rusticana, Eteri in Paliashvili's Absalom and Eteri. *Address:* c/o Georgian State Opera, Tbilisi, Georgia.

TATON, René André, D. ÈS L.; French historian; b. 4 April 1915, L'Echelle (Ardennes); s. of André and Marie-Thérèse (née Launoy) Taton; m. Juliette Battesti 1945; two d.; ed. Faculté des Sciences, Nancy and Paris, Ecole Normale Supérieure de St. Cloud; Research Asst., Centre Nat. de la Recherche Scientifique 1946, rising to Research Dir. 1952–83; Dir. Ecole pratique des Hautes Etudes en Sciences Sociales 1964–, Dir. Centre Alexandre-Koyré for Research into History of Science 1964–83; mem. Acad. Int. d'Histoire des Sciences; Sec.-Gen. of Int. Union of the History and Philosophy of Sciences 1955–71, Vice-Pres. 1972–74, Pres. 1975–78; Lauréat Acad. des Sciences and George Sarton Medal 1975; Chevalier, Légion d'honneur, Commdr. des Palmes académiques. *Publications:* L'oeuvre scientifique de Gaspard Monge 1951, L'oeuvre mathématique de G. Desargues 1951, Causalités et accidents de la découverte scientifique 1958 (translated into English, Spanish, Japanese), ed. Histoire générale des sciences (4 vols.) (translated into English, Italian, Spanish, Portuguese), numerous articles on the history of mathematics and the history of sciences in general. *Address:* Centre Alexandre Koyné, EHESS-CNRS, 54 rue Cuvier, 75005 Paris; 64 rue Gay-Lussac, 75005 Paris, France (Home).

TÁTRAI, Vilmos; Hungarian violinist; b. 7 Oct. 1912, Kispest; s. of Vilmos Tátrai and Maria Obernauer; m. Zsuzsa Kreismann 1938; one s. one d.; ed. National Conservatoire, Budapest; First Violinist, Budapest Symphony Orchestra 1933; mem. Radio Orchestra 1938; Leading Violinist Metropolitan State Concert Orchestra 1940–; teacher 1946–53; Founder-Leader Tátrai String Quartet 1946, tours throughout Europe 1952–; 64 Hungarian world premieres, 52 foreign premieres; Founder-Leader Hungarian Chamber Orchestra 1957–; Prof. of Music, Budapest Acad. of Music 1965–; Chair. and mem. of juries at 36 int. contests; leader of several int. seminars; mem. Revolutionary Cttee. of Musical Artists 1956 (prohibited from performing abroad); Hon. mem. Hungarian Kodály Soc., Asscn. of Hungarian Musicians, Fészek Artists' Club; 200 recordings including Haydn and Mozart complete works, Bartók string quartet; First prize, Béla Bartók Competition 1948, Liszt Prize 1952, 1972, Kossuth Prize 1958, Pro Urbe Budapest 1979, Bartók-Pasztori Grand Prix 1985, Hungarian Flag Order 1987, Musica Omnium Grand Prix 1993, Eminent Artist of Hungarian People's Republic, Labour Order of Merit (Golden Degree), Cross of Merit of Hungary. *Leisure interests:* walking, photography. *Address:* R. Wallenberg u. 4, 1136 Budapest XIII, Hungary. *Telephone:* 111-0529.

TATSUMI, Sotoo, LL.B.; Japanese banking executive; b. 7 Oct. 1923, Fukui; s. of Kennosuke Nakano and Hisa Nakano; m. Tomoko Araki 1949; one s. one d.; ed. Kyoto Univ.; joined The Sumitomo Bank Ltd. 1947, Dir. 1972, Man. Dir. 1975–79, Sr. Man. Dir. 1979–82, Deputy Pres. 1982–87, Pres. 1987–93, Chair. 1993; Co-Chair. Kansai Community for Econ. Devt. 1987–88; Vice-Chair. Osaka Bankers' Asscn. 1988–89. *Leisure interests:* driving, literature, music. *Address:* c/o Sumitomo Bank, 4-6-5 Kitahama, Chuo-ku, Osaka 541, Japan.

TATTENBACH-YGLESIAS, Christian, LL.B.; Costa Rican diplomatist and politician; b. 1924; ed. Univ. of Costa Rica; mem. Nat. Wage Bd. 1949; Amb. to Guatemala 1951, to Nicaragua 1952; Deputy, Legis. Ass. 1962–66, 1978–82, 1986–90, Pres. Legis. Ass. 1981–82; Minister of Interior, Police and Justice 1966–70; Alt. Sec.-Gen. Cen. American Inst. for Extension of Culture and Dir. Escuela para Todos publs. programme 1970–77; Co-founder and Chair. Union Popular Party 1977; Head Parl. Group of Coalición Unidad 1980–81; Pres. Union Popular 1982–84, now Hon. Pres. Unidad Social Cristiana; Perm. Rep. to UN, New York 1990–94; mem. Bd. Inter-American Inst. of Human Rights 1982. *Address:* c/o Ministry of Foreign Affairs, 1000 San José, Costa Rica.

TAUBE, Henry, B.S., M.S., PH.D.; American professor of chemistry; b. 30 Nov. 1915, Saskatchewan, Canada; s. of Samuel Taube and Albertina Tiledetzki Taube; m. Mary Alice (née Wesche) 1952; two s. two d.; ed. Univs. of Sask. and Calif. (Berkeley); Instructor Univ. of Calif. at Berkeley 1940–41; Instructor-Asst. Prof. Cornell Univ. 1941–46; Asst. Prof., Prof. Univ. of Chicago 1946–61; Prof. of Chem., Stanford Univ., Calif. 1962–90, Prof. Emer. 1990–; Guggenheim Fellow 1949–55; mem. N.A.S., Royal Physiographical Soc. of Lund, American Philosophical Soc.; foreign mem. Royal Soc. 1988; Hon. mem. Hungarian Acad. of Science 1988; Hon. Fellow R.S.C. 1989; Hon. Fellow Indian Chem. Soc. 1989; Hon. Fellow Royal Soc. of Canada 1997; Hon. LL.D. (Univ. of Sask.) 1973, Ph.D. h.c. (Hebrew Univ. of Jerusalem) 1979, Hon. Dr. Sc. (Univ. of Chicago) 1983, (Lajos Kossuth Univ. of Debrecen) 1988, (Seton Hall Univ.) 1988; Baker Lecture, Cornell Univ. 1965, Priestley Lecture, Pa. State 1976; American Chem. Soc. Awards 1955, 1960, Chandler Medal of Columbia Univ., Kirkwood Award, Harrison Howe Award, Rochester Section, ACS, 1960; Nichols Medal, New York Section, ACS 1971; Willard Gibbs Medal, Chicago Section, ACS 1971; F. P. Dwyer Medal, Univ. of N.S.W. 1973; Nat. Medal of Science 1977; Allied Chemical Award for Excellence in Graduate Teaching and Innovative Science 1979; T. W. Richards Medal, Northeastern Sec. ACS 1980, ACS Award in Inorganic Chem. of the Monsanto Co. 1981, Linus Pauling Award, Puget Sound Section ACS 1981, N.A.S. Award in Chemical Sciences 1983, Baillar Medal, Univ. of Ill. 1983, Robert A. Welch Foundation Award in Chem. 1983, Nobel Prize for Chem. 1983, Priestley Medal 1984, Distinguished Achievement Award, Precious Metals Inst. 1986, Oesper Award 1986, G. M. Kospaloff Award 1990, Brazilian Order of Science Merit Award 1994. *Publications:* Approx. 330 scientific articles in chemical journals. *Leisure interests:* record-collecting, gardening. *Address:* Department of Chemistry, Stanford University, Stanford, CA 94305 (Office); 441 Gerona Road, Stanford, CA 94305, U.S.A. (Home). *Telephone:* (415) 723-1736 (Office), (415) 328-2759 (Home).

TAUBMAN, A. Alfred; American entrepreneur; b. 31 Jan. 1925, Pontiac, Mich.; s. of Philip Taubman and Fannie Taubman; m. 1st Reva Kolodney 1949 (divorced 1977), two s. one d.; m. 2nd Judith Mazor 1982; ed. Univ. of Michigan, Lawrence Inst. of Tech.; Chair. and C.E.O. The Taubman Co., Bloomfield Hills, Michigan (specializing in shopping-centre design, planning and devt.) 1950–; Chair. Sothebys Holdings 1983–; owner of Sotheby's (art auctioneers) 1983–; Bd. Dirs. Live Entertainment of Canada Inc. *Address:* The Taubman Co., 200 E. Long Lake Road, Bloomfield Hills, MI 48304, U.S.A.

TAUFA'AHAU Tupou IV, G.C.V.O., G.C.M.G., K.B.E., B.A., LL.B.; H.M. the King of Tonga; b. 4 July 1918; eldest son of the late Queen Salote Tupou III of Tonga and the late Hon. Uiliami Tungi, C.B.E., Premier of Tonga; brother of Prince Fatafehi Tu'ipelahake (q.v.); m. H.R.H. Princess Halaevalu Mata'aho 1947; three s. one d., of whom the eldest, H.R.H. Crown Prince Tupoutoa, is heir to the throne; ed. Newington Coll. and Sydney Univ., N.S.W.; Minister of Educ. 1943, of Health 1944–49, Premier of Tonga, also Minister of Foreign Affairs and Agric. 1949–65; King of Tonga 1965–; est. Teachers' Training Coll. and revised Tonga alphabet 1944; f. Tonga High School 1947, Broadcasting Station 1961, Govt. newspaper 1964; Chancellor Univ. of the S. Pacific 1970–73; Hon. LL.D.; Kt. Commdr., Order of Merit (Fed. Repub. of Germany) 1978; numerous citations and awards. *Address:* The Palace, P.O. Box 6, Nuku'alofa, Tonga. *Telephone:* Nuku'alofa 21-000.

TAUS, Josef, LL.D.; Austrian politician, banker and industrialist; b. 8 Feb. 1933, Vienna; s. of Josef Taus and G. Schinko; m. Martha Loibl 1960; ed. Univ. of Vienna, Hochschule für Welthandel; Journalist; law practice; with Austrian Inst. of Econ. Research; Sec. and Head of Econ. Div., Girozentrale und Bank der Österreichischen Sparkassen AG 1958, mem. Man. Bd. 1967–68, Chair. and Man. Dir. 1968–75; fmr. Man. Sparinvest-Kapitalanlage GmbH; mem. Parl. 1975–91; State Sec. Fed. Ministry of Communications and Nationalized Enterprises 1966–67; Fed. Chair. Austrian People's Party (ÖVP) 1975–79; Man. Partner Constantia IndustrieverwaltungsgesmbH. 1979–86; mem. Bd. Constantia Industrieholding AG 1986–89; mem. Bd. ECO TRUST Holding AG 1989, Man. Trust Holding AG 1989–, Trust Invest AG 1990–; Managing Dir. Fremdenverkehrsbetriebe Gesmbh and Co. OHG. *Leisure interests:* skiing, music, reading, swimming. *Address:* Management Trust Holding AG, Salztorgasse 5, 1010 Vienna (Office); Zahnradbahnstrasse 17, A-1190 Vienna, Austria (Home). *Telephone:* (1) 535 61 03 (Office). *Fax:* (1) 535 61 03-30.

TAVARD, Rev. Georges Henri, S.T.D.; American ecclesiastic; b. 6 Feb. 1922, Nancy, France; s. of Ernest Henri Tavard and Marguerite Wasser; ed. Ecole St. Sigisbert, Nancy, Grand Séminaire, Nancy and Facultés Catholiques, Lyon; mem. Order of Austinians of the Assumption; ordained 1947; lecturer in Theology, Capenor House, Surrey, U.K. 1949–51; Assoc. Ed. Documentation Catholique Paris 1951–52; lecturer in Theol. Assumption Coll., Worcester, Mass. 1953–58; Chair. and Prof. Dept. of Theology, Carlow Coll. Pittsburgh, Pa. 1959–66; Prof. of Religious Studies, Penn. State Univ. 1966–69; Prof. of Theology, Methodist Theological School, Ohio 1970–87, Prof. Emer. 1987–; Medal of St. Augustine of Canterbury; Hon. D.D. (Kenyon Coll.). *Publications:* Holy Writ or Holy Church 1959, The Quest for Catholicity 1963, Woman in Christian Tradition 1973, The Seventeenth Century Tradition 1978, Poetry & Contemplation in St. John of the Cross 1988, Juana Inés de la Cruz and the Theology of Beauty 1991, The Church, Community of Salvation 1992, The Thousand Faces of the Virgin Mary 1996; under pseudonym Henri Wasser: Song for Avalokita, Poems 1979. *Address:* 330 Market Street, Brighton, MA 02135, U.S.A. *Telephone:* (617) 787-3682. *Fax:* (617) 783-8030.

TAVENER, John; British composer; b. 28 Jan. 1944, London; s. of Kenneth Tavener and Muriel Tavener; m. 1st Victoria Marangopoulou 1974 (divorced 1980); m. 2nd Maryanna Schaefer 1991; two d.; ed. Highgate School and R.A.M.; Organist St. John's Church, London 1960; Prof. of Composition, Trinity Coll. of Music, London 1968–; youngest composer ever performed at Promenade Concert, London 1969, at Royal Opera House, Covent Garden (Thérèse) 1979; works performed in U.K., U.S.A., fmr. U.S.S.R., Greece, Poland, Australia, Germany, Scandinavia, S. America and elsewhere; converted to Russian Orthodox Church 1974; works recorded on numerous labels; Hon. F.R.A.M., Hon. Fellow Royal School of Church Music, Hon. Fellow Trinity Coll. of Music, London; Hon. D.Mus. (New Delhi) 1990, (City of London Univ.) 1996; Prince Rainier Int. Prize 1965, First Prize Sacred Music Int. Composition Contest 1972, Gramophone Award (for The Protecting Veil) 1992. *Compositions include:* The Whale, Celtic Requiem, Ultimos Ritos, Palintropos, Antigone, Thérèse, Akhmatova-Rekviem, Liturgy of St. John Chrysostom, 16 Haiku of Seferis, Sappho—Lyrical Fragments, Great Canon of St. Andrew of Crete, Prayer for the World, Kyklike Kinesis, Ikon of Light, A Gentle Spirit, All-Night Vigil Service of the Orthodox Church (commissioned by Orthodox and Anglican Churches, for Christ Church Cathedral, Oxford 1985), Two Hymns to the Mother of God, Trisagion, Mandelion; Eis Thanaton (a ritual), Ikon of St. Cuthbert, God is with Us, Acclamation for Patriarch Demetrios, Akathist of Thanksgiving, Meditation on the Light, Panikhida, Ikon of Saint Seraphim, The Protecting Veil, Resurrection, Magnificat and Nunc Dimittis, The Hidden Treasure, Eonia, Mary of Egypt, The Repentant Thief, We Shall See Him as He Is, The Last Sleep of the Virgin, The Annunciation, Hymns of Paradise, Akhmatova Songs, The Child Lived, The Apocalypse, Let's Begin Again, Wake Up and Die, The Toll Houses, Agraphon, Vlepondas, The Last Discourse, Diodia, Song for Athene (performed at funeral of Diana, Princess of Wales). *Leisure interests:* iconography, love of Greece. *Address:* c/o Chester Music, 8–9 Frith Street, London, W1V 5TZ, England.

TAVERNAS-GUZMÁN, Juan Aristides, B.A., D.JUR.; Dominican Republic diplomatist; b. 24 Nov. 1936, Moca; m.; three c.; ed. Univ. Autónoma de Santo Domingo; practised law 1966–69; Sec. of State for Interior and Police 1969–71; Attorney-Gen. 1971–73; Sec. of State without Portfolio 1973–78, for Labour 1978–87; Perm. Rep. to UN 1987–89; founding mem. and preliminary cand. for Pres. Partido Reformista. *Publications:* La IV República, la de Balaguer, Por los Fueros de Cibao and over 800 newspaper articles. *Address:* c/o Secretariat of State for External Relations, Avda. Independencia, Santo Domingo, DN, Dominican Republic.

TAVERNER, Sonia; Canadian ballerina; b. 18 May 1936, Byfleet, Surrey; d. of H. J. Taverner; ed. Elmhurst Ballet School, and Royal Ballet School, London, and ballet school in New York; joined Royal Ballet 1955, toured U.S.A. and Canada; joined Royal Winnipeg Ballet 1956, leading dancer 1957, ballerina 1962–66; appeared with Royal Winnipeg Ballet, Commonwealth Arts Festival, London 1964; joined "Les Grands Ballets Canadiens" as prin. dancer 1966–74; appeared as guest artist with the Boston Ballet Co., in Swan Lake 1967; Guest teacher Les Grands Ballets Canadiens Summer School 1970; prin. artist with The Pa. Ballet 1971–72; Head of Ballet Div., Grant MacEwan Community Coll. 1975–80; Dir. Professional Program Devt., Alberta Ballet School, Alberta Sept. 1981–; f. School of Classical Ballet, Alberta Sept. 1982; Producer own concert variations 1977; guest artist with Vancouver Opera 1977, Les Grands Ballets Canadiens in Giselle and The Nutcracker 1977, 1978, Alberta Ballet Co. in The Nutcracker and Raymonda 1978, 1979; guest teacher with Alberta Ballet Summer School 1975, 1976, Pacific Ballet Theatre Summer School 1979; guest artist with Toronto, Winnipeg and Vancouver Symphony Orchestras; guest teaching in Penticton, B.C. 1984–85; has toured extensively over North America, Jamaica and U.K.; mem. Royal Acad. of Dancing, Actors Equity Asscn., American Guild of Musical Artists. *Leisure interests:* cooking, books. *Address:* P.O. Box 129, Stony Plain, Alberta, Canada.

TAVERNIER, Bertrand René Maurice; French film director; b. 25 April 1941, Lyon; s. of René Tavernier and Geneviève Dumond; m. Claudine O'Hagan 1965; one s. one d.; ed. Ecole St.-Martin de Pontoise, Lycées Henri-IV, Fénelon, Paris, Univ. de Paris (Sorbonne); press attaché and journalist, then film dir. *Films include:* Le baiser de Judas, Une charge explosive, La chance et l'amour, L'horloger de Saint-Paul (Louis Delluc prize 1973), Que la fête commence (César Best Screenplay, Best Direction) 1975, Le juge et l'assassin (César Best Screenplay 1976) 1976, Des enfants gâtés 1977, La mort en direct (Foreign Press Award 1979) 1979, Une semaine de vacances 1980, Coup de torchon 1981, Mississippi Blues 1983, Un dimanche à la campagne (Best Dir. Award, Cannes Film Festival, N.Y. Critics Award) 1984, Autour de minuit 1986, La passion béatrice 1987, La vie et rien d'autre 1988 (European Film Festival Special Prize 1989), Daddy nostalgie 1990, La guerre sans nom 1991, L.627 1991, La fille d'Artagnan 1994, L'Appât 1995, De l'autre côté du periph (TV documentary) 1997, Ça commence aujourd'hui 1999; jt. screenplay La trace 1983; (Producer) Veillées d'Armes 1994, Capitaine Conan 1996 (Méliès Prize for Best French Film 1996), César for Best Dir. 1997). *Publications:* 30 ans de cinéma américain (jtly.) 1970, 50 ans de cinéma américain (jtly.) 1991, Qu'est-ce qu'on attend? 1993, Amis américains 1994. *Leisure interests:* jazz, food, literature, movies. *Address:* Little Bear, 7–9 rue Arthur Groussier, 75010 Paris, France.

TAVIANI, Paolo; Italian film director; b. 8 Nov. 1931, San Miniato; brother of Vittorio Taviani (q.v.); ed. Univ. of Pisa; co-dir. with Vittorio Taviani of the following films: Un uomo da bruciare 1963, I fuorilegge del metraimonio 1963, Sovversivi 1967, Sotto il segno dello scorpione 1969, San Michele aveva un gallo 1971, Allonsanfan 1974, Padre Padrone 1977, The Meadow 1979, La notte di San Lorenzo (The Night of the Shooting Stars) 1981, Xaos 1984, Good Morning, Babylon 1988, Il Sole anche di Notte 1990, Fiorile 1993.

TAVIANI, Paolo Emilio; Italian politician; b. 6 Nov. 1912; s. of Ferdinando and Elide (née Banchelli) Taviani; m. Vittoria Festa; seven c.; ed. Univ. of Genoa; Prof. History of Econ. Theory at Genoa Univ.; leader Partisan War 1943–45; organizer of Christian Democratic Party (in Genoa area) 1943; mem. Constituent Ass. 1946–48; M.P. 1948–; Deputy Sec. Christian Democratic Party 1946–49, Sec. 1949–50; Ed. and Dir. Civitas, monthly magazine of political studies, 1950–; Italian Rep. to Schuman Plan Conf. 1951 and to later E.D.C. Confs.; Under-Sec. for Foreign Affairs 1951–53; Minister of Defence 1953–58, of Finance 1959–60, of Treasury 1960–62, of Interior 1962–68, for interventions in Southern Italy 1968–73, of the Interior 1973–74; Pres. of F.I.V.L. (Nat. Fed. of Partisans War 1943–45) 1972; Pres. of Foreign Affairs Cttee. of Senate 1979–87; Vice-Pres. of Senate 1987–92, Senator for Life 1992–; 20 hon. degrees. *Publications include:* Social Reformers of the Italian Risorgimento 1940, Social Prospects 1945, Ownership 1946, The Schuman Plan 1952, Atlantic Solidarity and European Community 1957, Defence of Peace 1958, Christian Principles and Democratic Systems 1965, The Concept of Utility in Economic Theory Vol. I 1968, Vol. II 1970, Utility, Economics and Morals 1970, The Problem of Development and the "Cassa del Mezzogiorno" Experience 1972, Christopher Columbus: The Genesis of the Great Discovery 1974, Ligurian Lands 1976, The Voyages of Columbus 1984, Christopher Columbus: The Grand Design 1985, Christopher Columbus, Genius of the Sea 1991. *Address:* Federazione Italiana Volontari della Libertà, Via Nemorense, 81, 00199, Rome; Senato della Repubblica, Piazza Madama, 00186 Rome, Italy. *Telephone:* 86320507.

TAVIANI, Vittorio; Italian film director; b. 20 Sept. 1929, San Miniato; brother of Paolo Taviani (q.v.); ed. Univ. of Pisa; co-dir. with Paolo Taviani of the following films: Un uomo da Bruciare 1963, I fuorilegge del metraimonio 1963, Sovversivi 1967, Sotto il segno dello scorpione 1969, San Michele aveva un gallo 1971, Allonsanfan 1974, Padre Padrone 1977, The Meadow (Italian-French) 1979, La notte di San Lorenzo (The Night of the Shooting Stars) 1981, Xaos 1984, Good Morning, Babylon 1988, Il Sole Anche di Notte 1990, Fiorile 1993.

TAXELL, (Lars Evald) Christoffer, LL.M.; Finnish business executive; b. 14 Feb. 1948, Turku; s. of Lars Erik Taxell and Elna Hillevi Brunberg; m. Rachel Margareta Nygård 1974; Chair. Youth Org., Swedish People's Party 1970–72, Party Chair. 1985–90; Political Sec. 1970–71; Asst., School of Econ., Åbo Akademi, Turku 1973–75; M.P. 1975–91; Minister of Justice 1979–87, of Educ. and Science 1987–90; Pres. and C.E.O. Partek Corpn. 1990–. *Address:* Partek Corporation, 21600 Pargas, Finland. *Telephone:* 21 74261. *Fax:* 21 742 6340.

TAYA, Col. Maawiya Ould Sid'Ahmed; Mauritanian politician and army officer; b. 1943; served in Saharan War 1976–78, Chief of Mil. Operations, then Commdr. garrison at Bir Mogkrein; Minister of Defence 1978–79; Commdr. nat. gendarmerie 1979–80; Minister in charge of Perm. Secr., Mil. Cttee. for Nat. Recovery 1979–81; Army Chief of Staff 1980–81, March–Dec. 1984; Prime Minister and Minister of Defence 1981–84, Dec. 1984–92; Pres. of Mauritania and Chair. Mil. Cttee. for Nat. Salvation 1984–92, elected Pres. of Mauritania 1992–. *Address:* Présidence de la République, B.P. 184, Nouackchott, Mauritania. *Telephone:* 523-17.

TAYLOR, Allan Richard, O.C.; Canadian banker; b. 14 Sept. 1932, Prince Albert, Saskatchewan; s. of Norman Taylor and Anna Lydia Norbeck Taylor; m. Shirley Irene Ruston 1957; one s. one d.; joined Royal Bank of Canada 1949, Dir., Head Int. Div. 1977–83, Pres. and C.O.O. 1983–86, C.E.O. 1986–94, Chair. 1986–95; Dir. Royal Bank of Canada, Canadian Pacific Ltd., Calgary, Alberta, TransCanada PipeLines Ltd., Calgary, Alberta, General Motors of Canada Ltd., Canadian Inst. for Advanced Research, Toronto, Neuroscience Network, Montreal, United Dominion Industries, Charlotte, N.C., Max Bell Foundation, Calgary; Pres. Int. Monetary Conf. 1992–93; Chair. Canadian Bankers Asscn. 1984–86; fmr. Chair. Corporate Program IMAGINE, currently mem. Nat. Advisory Council; Chair. Council of Patrons, Canadian Outward Bound; mem. Advisory Council Canadian Exec. Service Overseas; mem. Advisory Bd. Canadian Journalism Foundation, Bd. of Advisors of Asscn. Int. des étudiants en sciences économiques et commerciales Canada, Advisory Bd., Canadian Foundation for AIDS Research; Founding Dir. Corp.–Higher Educ. Forum, currently hon. mem.; Exec. Advisor, Public Policy Forum; Gov., Olympic Trust of Canada; Hon. D. Jur. (Univ. of Regina) 1987, (Concordia Univ.) 1988, (Queen's Univ.) 1991; Hon. D.B.A. (Laval) 1990; Dr. h.c. (Ottawa) 1992. *Leisure interests:* golf, tennis, fishing. *Address:* Suite 1835, North Tower, Royal Bank Plaza, Toronto, Ont., M5J 2J5, Canada. *Fax:* (416) 974-8713.

TAYLOR, Ann (see Taylor, (Winifred) Ann).

TAYLOR, Arthur Robert, M.A.; American business executive; b. 6 July 1935, Elizabeth, N.J.; s. of Arthur Earl Taylor and Marion Hilda Scott; m. Marion McFarland 1959 (divorced); three d.; m. 2nd Kathryn Pelgrift; ed. Brown Univ.; Asst. Dir. of Admissions, Brown Univ. 1957–60; with The First Boston Corpn. 1961–70, Vice-Pres. Underwriting Dept. 1966–70, Dir. 1970; Vice-Pres. (Finance), Int. Paper Co. 1970–71, Exec. Vice-Pres. 1971–72, Dir. 1971–72; Pres. and Dir. CBS Inc. 1972–76; Dir. Arthur Taylor & Co., New York 1977– (Chair. 1977–), Travelers Corpn., Rockefeller Centre Inc., American Friends of Bilderberg, Pitney Bowes Inc., Louisiana Land and Exploration, Eastern Airlines, Nomura Pacific Basin Fund, etc.; Vice-Chair. Forum Corpn., Boston, Mass 1988–; Dean, Faculty of Business, Fordham Univ. 1985–89; Pres. Muhlenberg Coll., Pa. 1992–; mem. Council on Foreign Relations, Nat. Cttee. on American Foreign Policy, Center for Inter-American Relations, Japan Soc.; Trustee, Brown Univ., Franklin Savings Bank, N.Y. Hospital, William H. Donner Foundation; Commr. Trilateral Comm. *Publications:* article in Harvard Review of Business History 1971, chapter in The Other Side of Profit 1975. *Address:* Office of the President, Muhlenberg College, 2400 W. Chew Street, Allentown, PA 18104; Main Street, Salisbury, CT 06068, U.S.A. (Home).

TAYLOR, Bernard David, C.B.E., B.SC., C.B.I.M.; British business executive; b. 17 Oct. 1935, Coventry; s. of Thomas Taylor and Winifred (Smith) Taylor; m. Nadine B. Taylor 1959; two s. two d.; ed. Univ. of Wales and London Business School; science teacher, Coventry Educ. Authority until 1958; Sales and Marketing, SKF 1960–64; Sales and Marketing Man. Glaxo New Zealand 1964–67; New Products Man. Glaxo U.K. 1967–72; Man. Dir. Glaxo Australia 1972–84; Dir. Glaxo Holdings PLC and Man. Dir. Glaxo Pharmaceuticals U.K. 1984–86; Chief Exec. Glaxo Holdings PLC 1986–89; Exec. Chair. Medeva PLC 1990–96; mem. CBI Europe Cttee. 1987–89, British Overseas Trade Bd. 1987–96; Chair. Cambridge Labs. 1997–; Fellow, London Business School 1988; Trustee, World Wildlife Fund 1990-96. *Address:* c/o Medeva PLC, 10 St. James's Street, London, SW1A 1EF, England.

TAYLOR, Charles; Liberian Head of State and guerrilla leader; leader Nat. Patriotic Front of Liberia (NPFL) which was part of combined rebel force which overthrew fmr. Pres. Samuel Doe; engaged in civil insurrection 1991–96; mem. Transitional Exec. Council of State 1996–97; Pres. of Liberia 1997–. *Address:* c/o Office of the President, Monrovia, Liberia.

TAYLOR, Charles, D.PHIL., F.B.A.; Canadian professor of philosophy; b. 5 Nov. 1931, Montreal; s. of Walter Margrave Taylor and Simone Beaubien; m. Alba Romer 1956 (deceased), five d.; m. 2nd Aube Billard; ed. McGill and Oxford Univs., Fellow of All Souls Coll., Oxford 1956–61; Asst. Prof. of Political Science and Philosophy 1961, Prof. of Political Science and Prof. of Philosophy 1973–; Prof. of Philosophy, Univ. of Montreal 1962–71; Chichele Prof. of Social and Political Theory, Oxford Univ. and Fellow of All Souls Coll. 1976–81; mem. Royal Soc. of Canada, corresp. mem. American Acad. of Arts and Sciences; John Locke Prize, Oxford 1955. *Publications:* The

Explanation of Behaviour 1964, Hegel 1975, Hegel and Modern Society 1979, Human Agency and Language 1985, Philosophy and the Human Sciences 1985, Sources of Self 1989, The Malaise of Modernity 1991, Philosophical Arguments 1995. *Leisure interests:* skiing, swimming, hiking. *Address:* Department of Philosophy, McGill University, Stephen Leacock Bldg., Room 908, 855 Sherbrooke Street W., Montreal, Quebec H3A 2T7; 6603 Jeanne Mance, Montreal, Quebec, H2V 4L1, Canada (Home).

TAYLOR, Elizabeth Rosemond; British film actress; b. 27 Feb. 1932, London; d. of Francis Taylor and Sara Sothern; m. 1st Conrad Nicholas Hilton, Jr. 1950 (divorced); m. 2nd Michael Wilding 1952 (divorced); two s.; m. 3rd Mike Todd 1957 (died 1958); one d.; m. 4th Eddie Fisher 1959 (divorced); m. 5th Richard Burton 1964 (divorced 1974, remarried 1975, divorced 1976); one adopted d.; m. 7th Senator John Warner (q.v.) 1976 (divorced 1982); m. 8th Larry Fortensky 1991 (divorced 1996); ed. Byron House, Hawthorne School, and Metro-Goldwyn-Mayer School; active in philanthropic and relief charitable causes internationally including Israeli War Victims Fund for the Chaim Sheba Hosp. 1976, UNICEF, Variety Children's Hosps., medical clinics in Botswana; inititiated Ben Gurion Univ.-Elizabeth Taylor Fund for Children of the Negev 1982; supporter AIDS Project L.A. 1985; founder, Nat. Chair. Council for AIDS Research (AmFAR) 1985–, int. fund 1985–; founder Elizabeth Taylor AIDS Foundation 1991–; Commdr. Ordre des Arts et des Lettres 1985; Légion d'honneur (for work with AmFAR) 1987; Aristotle S. Onassis Foundation Award 1988, Jean Hersholt Humanitarian Acad. Award (for work as AIDS advocate), Life Achievement Award, American Film Inst. 1993, Lifetime Achievement Award, Screen Actors Guild 1998, BAFTA Fellowship 1999; honoured with dedication of Elizabeth Taylor Clinic, Washington 1993; licensed fragrances: Elizabeth Taylor's Passion, Passion for Men, White Diamonds/Elizabeth Taylor, Elizabeth Taylor's Diamonds and Emeralds, Diamonds and Rubies, Diamonds and Sapphires, jewelry: The Elizabeth Taylor Fashion Jewelry Collection for Avon. *Films include:* Lassie Come Home 1942, There's One Born Every Minute 1943, The White Cliffs of Dover 1943, Jane Eyre 1943, National Velvet 1944, Courage of Lassie 1946, Life with Father 1946, Cynthia 1947, A Date With Judy 1948, Julia Misbehaves 1948, Little Women 1948, Conspirator 1949, The Big Hangover 1949, Father's Little Dividend 1950, Father of the Bride 1950, A Place in the Sun 1950, Love is Better Than Ever 1951, Ivanhoe 1951, Rhapsody 1954, Elephant Walk 1954, Beau Brummel 1954, The Last Time I Saw Paris 1955, Giant 1956, Raintree Country 1957, Cat on a Hot Tin Roof 1958, Suddenly Last Summer 1959, Butterfield 8 1960, Cleopatra 1962, The VIPs 1963, The Sandpiper 1965, Who's Afraid of Virginia Woolf? 1966, The Taming of the Shrew 1967, The Comedians 1967, Reflections in a Golden Eye 1967, Doctor Faustus 1968, Boom 1968, Secret Ceremony 1968, The Only Game in Town 1969, Under Milk Wood 1971, X, Y and Zee 1972, Hammersmith is Out 1972, Night Watch 1973, Ash Wednesday 1974, The Driver's Seat 1975, Blue Bird 1976, A Little Night Music 1977, The Mirror Crack'd 1980, Between Friends 1983, The Young Toscanini 1988, The Flintstones 1994. *Television appearances include:* Divorce His, Divorce Hers 1973, Victory at Entebbe 1977, Return Engagement 1979, Between Friends 1982, Hotel (series) 1984, Malice in Wonderland 1986, North and South (mini-series) 1986, There Must be a Pony 1986, Poker Alice 1987, Sweet Bird of Youth 1989. *Plays include:* The Little Foxes (New York) 1981, (Los Angeles) 1981, (London) 1982, Private Lives (New York) 1983. *Publications:* World Enough and Time (with Richard Burton) 1964, Elizabeth Taylor 1965, Elizabeth Taylor Takes Off—On Weight Gain, Weight Loss, Self-Esteem and Self Image 1988. *Address:* c/o Nat Rubin, 245 Fifth Avenue, New York, NY 10016, U.S.A.

TAYLOR, Gregory Frank, A.O., B.ECONS.; Australian civil servant and diplomatist; b. 1 July 1942, Adelaide; s. of Frank Taylor and Constance Rischbieth; m. Jill Beatrice Bodman 1967; one s. one d.; ed. Univ. of Adelaide; Chair. Industries Assistance Comm., Canberra 1988; C.E.O. Dept. of Employment Educ. and Training 1989–94, Dept. of Primary Industries and Energy 1993–95, Dept. of Industry, Tech. and Commerce 1996; now Exec. Dir. IMF, Washington, D.C. *Leisure interest:* skiing. *Address:* International Monetary Fund, 700 19th Street, N.W., Washington, D.C.; 3915 Ivy Ice Court, N.W., Washington, D.C. 20007, U.S.A. (Office). *Telephone:* (202) 623-7430 (Office). *Fax:* (202) 623-6701 (Office).

TAYLOR, J(ames) Herbert, PH.D.; American university professor; b. 14 Jan. 1916, Texas; s. of Charles Aaron Taylor and Delia May (McCain); m. Shirley C. Hoover 1946; one s. two d.; ed. Southeastern Oklahoma State, Univ. of Oklahoma, Univ. of Virginia; Asst. Prof. of Plant Science, Univ. of Okla. 1946–47; Assoc. Prof. of Botany, Univ. of Tenn. 1947–51; Asst. Prof. of Botany, Columbia Univ. 1951–54, Assoc. Prof. 1954–58, Prof. of Cell Biology 1958–64; Prof. of Biological Science and Assoc. Dir. Inst. of Molecular Biophysics, Florida State Univ. 1964–80, Dir. 1980–85, Robert O. Lawton Distinguished Prof. of Biological Science 1983–90, Prof. Emer. 1990–; mem. N.A.S.; Guggenheim Fellow at Calif. Inst. of Tech. 1958–59; Pres. American Soc. of Cell Biology 1969. *Publications:* Selected Papers on Molecular Genetics 1965, Molecular Genetics (3 vols.) 1963, 1967 and 1979, DNA Methylation and Cellular Differentiation 1984. *Leisure interests:* canoeing and hiking in wilderness areas, travel to wild areas of the world. *Address:* Institute of Molecular Biophysics, Florida State University, Tallahassee, FL 32306, U.S.A.

TAYLOR, Rt. Rev. John Bernard, K.C.V.O., M.A.; British ecclesiastic; b. 6 May 1929, Newcastle-upon-Tyne; s. of George Taylor and Gwendoline Taylor; m. Linda Courtenay Barnes 1956; one s. two d.; ed. Watford Grammar School, Christ's and Jesus Colls. Cambridge, Hebrew Univ. of Jerusalem and Ridley Hall, Cambridge; R.A.F. service 1952–54; ordained deacon 1956, priest 1957; Vicar of Henham and Elsenham, Essex 1959–64; Vice-Prin. Oak Hill Theological Coll. London 1964–72; Vicar of All Saints' Woodford Wells, Essex 1972–75; Archdeacon of West Ham 1975–80; Bishop of St Albans 1980–95; Chair. Council, Wycliffe Hall, Oxford 1985–; Lord High Almoner to H.M. the Queen 1988–97; Pres. The Bible Soc. 1997–; Pres. and Chair. of Council, Haileybury 1980–95; Pres. Hildenborough Evangelistic Trust 1986–, Garden Tomb Asscn. 1987–, Church's Ministry Among Jewish People 1996–; Hon. LL.D. *Publications:* Tyndale Commentary on Ezekiel 1969, Preaching through the Prophets 1983, Preaching on God's Justice 1994. *Leisure interests:* bird-watching, walking. *Address:* 22 Conduit Head Road, Cambridge, CB3 0EY, England. *Telephone:* (01223) 313783.

TAYLOR, John Bryan, PH.D., F.R.S.; British physicist; b. 26 Dec. 1928, Birmingham; s. of Frank H. Taylor and Ada Taylor (née Stinton); m. Joan M. Hargest 1951; one s. one d.; ed. Oldbury Co. High School and Birmingham Univ.; served R.A.F. 1950–52; Physicist, Atomic Weapons Research Establishment, Aldermaston 1955–59, 1961–62; Harkness Fellow, Univ. of Calif. 1959–60; on staff of UKAEA, Culham Lab. 1962–89, Head of Theory Div. 1963–81, Chief Physicist Culham Lab. 1981–89, Consultant 1994–; Fondren Foundation Prof. of Plasma Theory, Univ. of Texas at Austin 1989–94; mem. Inst. for Advanced Study, Princeton, N.J. 1969, 1980 and 1981; Fellow American Physical Soc.; Maxwell Medal (Inst. of Physics) 1971, Max Born Prize and Medal (German Physical Soc.) 1979, Award for Excellence in Plasma Research (American Physical Soc.) 1986. *Publications:* contribs. to scientific learned journals. *Leisure interests:* gliding, model engineering. *Address:* Radwinter, Winterbrook Lane, Wallingford, OX10 9EJ, England. *Telephone:* (01491) 837269.

TAYLOR, John Russell, M.A.; British writer and professor of cinema studies; b. 19 June 1935, Dover, Kent; s. of Arthur Russell Taylor and Kathleen Mary (née Picker) Taylor; ed. Dover Grammar School, Jesus Coll., Cambridge, Courtauld Inst. of Art; Sub Ed., Times Educ. Supplement 1959–60; Editorial Asst., Times Literary Supplement 1960–62; Film Critic, The Times 1962–73; Prof., Div. of Cinema, Univ. of Southern Calif., U.S.A. 1972–78; Art Critic, The Times 1978–; Ed. Films and Filming 1983–90. *Publications:* Anger and After 1962, Anatomy of a Television Play 1962, Cinema Eye, Cinema Ear 1964, Penguin Dictionary of the Theatre 1966, The Art Nouveau Book in Britain 1966, The Rise and Fall of the Well-Made Play 1967, The Art Dealers 1969, The Hollywood Musical 1971, The Second Wave 1971, Directors and Directions 1975, Hitch 1978, Impressionism 1981, Strangers in Paradise 1983, Ingrid Bergman 1983, Alec Guinness 1984, Vivien Leigh 1984, Hollywood 1940s 1985, Portraits of the British Cinema 1986, Orson Welles 1986, Edward Wolfe 1986, Great Movie Moments 1987, Meninsky 1990, Impressionist Dreams 1990, Liz Taylor 1991, Muriel Pemberton 1993, Ricardo Cinalli 1993, Igor Mitoraj 1993, Claude Monet 1995, Bill Jacklin 1997, The World of Michael Parkes 1998, Antonio Smiola 1998, The Sun is God 1999; edited: Look Back in Anger: A Casebook 1968, The Pleasure Dome (Graham Greene on Film) 1972, Masterworks of British Cinema 1974. *Leisure interest:* book collecting. *Address:* c/o The Times, 1 Pennington Street, London, E1 9XN, England. *Telephone:* 0171-782 5000.

TAYLOR, Joseph Hooton, Jr., PH.D.; American radio astronomer and physicist; b. 29 March 1941, Philadelphia; s. of Joseph Taylor and Sylvia Evans; m. Marietta Bisson 1976; one s. two d.; ed. Haverford Coll. and Harvard Univ.; Research Fellow and lecturer, Harvard Univ. 1968–69; Asst. Prof. of Astronomy, Univ. of Mass., Amherst 1969–72, Assoc. Prof. 1973–77, Prof. 1977–81; Prof. of Physics, Princeton Univ. 1980–; James McDonnell Distinguished Prof. of Physics 1986–; Fellow, American Acad. of Arts and Sciences; mem. N.A.S., American Astronomy Soc., Int. Scientific Radio Union, Int. Astronomy Union; Wolf Prize in Physics 1992; shared Nobel Prize for Physics 1993; Hon. D.Sc. (Chicago) 1985, (Mass.) 1994 and other awards and distinctions. *Publication:* Pulsars 1977. *Address:* Department of Physics, Princeton University, Jadwin Hall, P.O. Box 708, Princeton, NJ 08544 (Office); 272 Hartley Avenue, Princeton, NJ 08540, U.S.A. (Home).

TAYLOR, Joyce, B.A.; British television executive; b. 14 March 1948, Glasgow; d. of Lord and Lady Taylor of Gryfe; m. John Lloyd-Richards 1982; one s. one d.; ed. Hutchesons' Girls' Grammar School, Glasgow and Univ. of Strathclyde; worked in production, BBC 1968–70; producer, audio-visual service, Univ. of Glasgow 1977–85; Head of Programming, Clyde Cablevision 1985–89; Chief Exec. Programming, United Artists 1989–95; Man. Dir Discovery Communications Europe Nov. 1995–. *Leisure interests:* theatre, reading, walking. *Address:* Discovery Communications Europe, 160 Great Portland Street, London, W1, England. *Telephone:* 0171-462 3600.

TAYLOR, Ken; British screenwriter; b. 1922, Bolton, Lancs.; m. Gillian Dorothea Black 1953; two s. two d. *Plays for TV include:* One of Us, Special Occasion, The Tin Whistle Man, China Doll, Into the Dark, Parkin's Primitives, The Long Distance Blue, The Slaughtermen, The Devil and John Brown (Writers' Guild Award 1964), The Seekers, The Magicians, The Edwardians: E. Nesbit, Death or Liberty (Churchill's People), The Pankhursts, Christabel Pankhurst, Sylvia Pankhurst (3 plays for BBC's Shoulder to Shoulder), The Poisoning of Charles Bravo, The Devil's Crown (5 plays on Henry II), Cause Célèbre 1988, The Camomile Lawn 1992, The Peacock Spring 1995; many adaptations for TV of works by Somerset Maugham,

D.H. Lawrence, Jane Austen, Muriel Spark, Rebecca West, Mary Wesley etc. also The Jewel in the Crown from Paul Scott's The Raj Quartet (Royal Television Soc.'s Writers' Award 1984). *Stage plays:* The Strange Affair of Charles Bravo 1979, Staying On 1997. *Address:* c/o Peters Fraser and Dunlop, 503/4 The Chambers, Chelsea Harbour, London, SW10 0XF, England. *Telephone:* 0171-344 1000.

TAYLOR, Lance Jerome, B.S., PH.D.; American university professor; b. 25 May 1940, Montpelier, Idaho; s. of W. Jerome Taylor and Ruth R. Taylor; m. Yvonne S.M. Taylor 1963; one s. one d.; ed. Calif. Inst. of Tech., Harvard Univ.; Asst. and Assoc. Prof. Harvard Univ. 1968–74; Prof., M.I.T. 1974–93; Prof., New School for Social Research 1993–; Visiting Prof. Univ. of Brasília 1973–74, Delhi School of Econs. 1987–88, Stockholm School of Econs. 1990; consultant for UN agencies and over 25 govts. and agencies; Marshall lecturer Univ. of Cambridge 1987; V.K. Ramaswamy lecturer Delhi School of Econs. 1988. *Publications:* Structuralist Macroeconomics 1983, Varieties of Stabilization Experience 1988, Income Distribution, Inflation and Growth 1991, The Market Meets its Match: Restructuring the Economies of Eastern Europe 1994. *Leisure interests:* reading, woodchopping. *Address:* Graduate Faculty, New School for Social Research, 65 Fifth Avenue, New York, NY 10003 (Office); Old County Road, P.O. Box 378, Washington, ME 04574, U.S.A. (Home). *Telephone:* (207) 845-2722 (Home). *Fax:* (207) 845-2589 (Home).

TAYLOR, Martin; British banker; b. 1952; ed. Eton Coll. and Balliol Coll. Oxford; joined Reuters news agency, Paris; subsequently ed., Lex comment column, Financial Times; personal asst. to Chair. of Courtaulds, later Dir. Courtaulds Clothing Div.; CEO Courtaulds PLC 1990–93, Chair. 1993; Dir. Barclays Bank PLC Nov. 1993–, Chief Exec. 1994–98; Leader New Whitehall Task Force 1997–; Dir. (non-exec.) WH Smith Group PLC. *Address:* c/o Barclays Bank PLC, 54 Lombard Street, London, EC3P 3AH, England. *Telephone:* 0171-699 5000.

TAYLOR, Mervyn, B.A., LL.B.; Irish politician; b. Dec. 1931, Dublin; m. Marilyn Fisher; two s. one d.; ed. Wesley Coll., Dublin and Trinity Coll. Dublin; solicitor; mem. Dublin Co. Council 1974–; mem. Dáil 1981–; Labour Party Whip 1981–88; Govt. Asst. Chief Whip 1981–82, 1982–87; Chair. The Labour Party 1987–; Minister for Equality and Law Reform 1993–97. *Address:* The Labour Party, 17 Ely Place, Dublin 2, Ireland.

TAYLOR, Rev. Michael Hugh, O.B.E., M.A., B.D., D.LITT., S.T.M.; British minister of religion and charity administrator; b. 8 Sept. 1936, Northampton; s. of Albert Taylor and Gwendolen Taylor; m. Adele May Dixon 1960; two s. one d.; ed. Northampton Grammar School, Manchester Univ., Union Theological Seminary, New York; Baptist Minister, North Shields, Northumberland and Hall Green, Birmingham 1960–69; Prin. Northern Baptist Coll., Manchester 1970–85; lecturer in Theology and Ethics, Univ. of Manchester 1970–85; Examining Chaplain to Bishop of Manchester 1975–85; Dir. Christian Aid 1985–97; Pres. Selly Oak Colls., Birmingham 1998–; Chair. Audenshaw Foundation Trustees 1979–93; mem. Comm. on Theological Educ., WCC 1972–91, Vice-Moderator 1985–91; mem. Council, Overseas Devt. Inst. 1986–; mem. Comm. IV: Sharing and Service; Chair. Asscn. of Protestant Devt. Agencies in Europe 1991–94; Pres. Jubilee 2000 U.K. Coalition 1997–; Trustee Mines Advisory Group 1998–; Fulbright Travel Award 1969. *Publications:* Variations on a Theme 1971, Learning to Care 1983, Good for the Poor 1990, Christianity and the Persistence of Poverty 1991, Not Angels but Agencies 1995, Jesus and the International Financial Institutions 1996, Past their Sell-By Date? The Role of Northern NGOs in the Future of Development 1998. *Leisure interests:* walking, theatre, cooking. *Address:* Central House, Selly Oak Colleges, Birmingham, B29 6LQ, England. *Telephone:* 0121-415 2220.

TAYLOR, Paul B.; American dancer and choreographer; b. 29 July 1930, Allegheny Co., Pa.; s. of Paul B. Taylor and Elizabeth P. Rust; ed. Virginia Episcopal School, Syracuse Univ., Juilliard School, Metropolitan School of Ballet and Martha Graham School of Contemporary Dance; fmr. dancer with the cos. of Martha Graham, George Balanchine, Charles Weidman, Anna Sokolow, Merce Cunningham, Katherine Litz, James Waring and Pearl Lang; Dancer-Choreographer-dir. The Paul Taylor Dance Co. 1955–; co. has performed in 300 U.S. cities, made 42 overseas tours, to 54 countries; choreographed 101 dances, 22 of them taken up by 50 other dance cos. worldwide; Guggenheim Fellowship 1961, 1965, 1983; Hon. Mem. American Acad. and Inst. of Arts and Letters 1989; Hon. Dr. Fine Arts (Connecticut Coll., Duke Univ.) 1983, (Syracuse Univ.) 1986; Centennial Achievement Award (Ohio State Univ.), 1970; Brandeis Univ. Creative Arts Award gold medal 1978, Dance Magazine Award 1980, Samuel H. Scripps/American Dance Festival Award 1983, MacArthur 'Genius' Award 1985, New York State Governor's Award 1987, New York City Mayor's Award of Honor for Art and Culture 1989, Kennedy Center Honour 1992, Nat. Medal of Arts 1993, Award from Chicago Int. Film Festival 1993; Commdr. Ordre des arts et des lettres. *Choreography includes:* Three Epitaphs 1956, Rebus 1958, Tablet 1960, Junction 1961, Fibers 1961, Insects and Heroes 1961, Tracer 1962, Piece Period 1962, Aureole 1962, Party Mix 1963, Scudorama 1963, Duet 1964, From Sea to Shining Sea 1965, Post Meridian 1965, Orbs 1966, Agathes' Tale 1967, Lento 1967, Public Domain 1968, Private Domain 1969, Churchyard 1969, Foreign Exchange 1970, Big Bertha 1970, Fêtes 1971, Book of Beasts 1971, Guests of May 1972, So Long Eden 1972, Noah's Minstrels 1973, American Genesis 1973, Untitled Quartet 1974, Sports and Follies 1974, Esplanade 1975, Runes 1975, Cloven Kingdom 1976, Polaris 1976, Images 1976, Dust 1977, Aphrodisiamania 1977, Airs 1978, Diggity 1978, Nightshade 1979, Profiles 1979, Le Sacre du Printemps (subtitled The Rehearsal) 1980, Arden Court 1981, Lost, Found and Lost 1982, Mercuric Tidings 1982, Sunset 1983, Snow White 1983, Musette 1983, Equinox 1983, Byzantium 1984, Roses 1985, Last Look 1985, A Musical Offering 1986, Ab Ovo Usted Mala 1986, Syzygy 1987, Kith and Kin 1987, Minikin Fair 1989, Speaking in Tongues 1989, The Sorcerer's Sofa 1989, Of Bright and Blue Birds and The Gala Sun 1990, Company B 1991, Fact and Fancy (3 Epitaphs and All) 1991, Oz 1992, A Field of Grass 1993, Spindrift 1993, Moonbine 1994, Funny Papers 1994, Offenbach Overtures 1995, Eventide 1996, Prime Numbers 1996; Algur H. Meadows Award for Excellence in the Arts 1995. *Publication:* Private Domain (autobiog.) 1987. *Leisure interests:* gardening, snorkelling. *Address:* Paul Taylor Dance Co., 552 Broadway, New York, NY 10012, U.S.A.

TAYLOR, Richard Edward, PH.D., F.R.S.C., F.R.S.; Canadian physicist; b. 2 Nov. 1929, Medicine Hat, Alberta; s. of Clarence Richard Taylor and Delia Alena (Brunsdale) Taylor; m. Rita Jean Bonneau 1951; one s.; ed. Univ. of Alberta, Edmonton, Stanford Univ., Calif., U.S.A.; Boursier, Laboratoire de l'Accélérateur Linéaire, Orsay, France 1958–61; physicist, Lawrence Berkeley Lab., Berkeley, Calif. 1961–62; staff mem. Stanford Linear Accelerator Center, Calif. 1962–68, Assoc. Prof. 1968–70, Prof. 1970–, Assoc. Dir. 1982–86; Dr. h.c. (Paris-Sud) 1980, (Blaise-Pascal) 1997; Hon. D.Sc. (Alberta) 1991, (Lethbridge, Alberta) 1993, (Vic., B.C.) 1994; Hon LL.D. (Calgary, Alberta) 1993; Guggenheim Fellow 1971–72, von Humboldt Sr. Scientist Award 1982, W.K.H. Panofsky Prize (with H.W. Kendall and J.I. Friedman) 1989, Nobel Prize in Physics (with H.W. Kendall and J.I. Friedman) 1990. *Publications:* numerous scientific papers. *Address:* Stanford Linear Accelerator Center (SLAC), Mail Stop 96, P.O. Box 4349, Stanford, CA 94309 (Office); 757 Mayfield Avenue, Stanford, CA 94305, U.S.A. (Home). *Telephone:* (650) 926-2417 (Office); (650) 857-1345 (Home). *Fax:* (650) 926-2923 (Office).

TAYLOR, Stuart Ross, M.A., PH.D., D.SC., F.A.A.; Australian geochemist; b. 26 Nov. 1925; s. of late T.S. Taylor; m. Noel White 1958; three d.; ed. Ashburton High School, N.Z., Canterbury Univ. Coll., Univ. of N.Z. and Indiana Univ.; lecturer in Mineralogy, Univ. of Oxford 1954–58; Sr. Lecturer in Geochemistry, Univ. of Cape Town 1958–60; Professorial Fellow, Research School of Earth Science, Australian Nat. Univ. (A.N.U.) 1961–90, Visiting Fellow, Research School of Physical Sciences 1991, 1993–98; mem. Council, A.N.U. 1971–76; mem. Lunar Sample Preliminary Examination Team, Houston, Tex. 1969–70, Prin. Investigator, Lunar Sample Analysis Program 1970–90; Visiting Prof., Univ. of Vienna 1992, 1996; Foreign Assoc. N.A.S. (U.S.A.); Fellow Geochemical Soc., American Geophysical Union; Hon. Fellow, U.K. and Indian Geological Socs., Royal Soc. of N.Z.; Goldschmidt Medal, Geochemical Soc. 1993, Gilbert Award, Geological Soc. of America 1994, Leonard Medal, Meteoritical Soc. 1998, Asteroid 5670 named Ross Taylor. *Publications include:* Spectrochemical Analysis (jtly.) 1961, Moon Rocks and Minerals (jtly.) 1971, Lunar Science: A Post-Apollo View 1975, Planetary Science: A Lunar Perspective 1982, The Continental Crust: Its Composition and Evolution (jtly.) 1985, Solar System Evolution: A New Perspective 1992, Destiny or Chance: Our Solar System and Its Place in the Cosmos 1998, and some 220 papers in scientific journals. *Leisure interests:* reading history, gardening, classical music. *Address:* 18 Sheehan Street, Pearce, A.C.T. 2607, Australia.

TAYLOR, Wendy Ann, C.B.E., L.D.A.D., F.Z.S., F.R.B.S; British sculptor; b. 29 July 1945, Stamford, Lincs.; d. of Edward P. Taylor and Lilian M. Wright; m. Bruce Robertson 1982; one s.; ed. St. Martin's School of Art; 10 one-woman exhbns.; participated in more than 100 group exhbns. 1964–82; work represented in collections in U.K., Europe, U.S.A. etc.; over 40 major comms. in towns and cities throughout U.K.; mem. Fine Art Bd. Council of Acad. Awards 1980–85, Specialist Adviser 1985–93; Specialist Adviser, Cttee. for Art and Design 1988–93; mem. Cttee. for Art and Design, Council of Nat. Acad. Awards; mem. Royal Fine Art Comm. 1981–; mem. Council, Morley Coll. 1984–88; mem. Court R.C.A.; Design consultant, New Towns Comm. (Basildon) 1985–; Design Consultant, London Borough of Barking and Dagenham 1989–93, 1997–; Advisory Bd., London Docklands Devt. Corpn. 1989–98; mem. Advisory Group of the Polytechnics and Colls. Funding Council 1989–90; Fellow Queen Mary and Westfield Coll. (London Univ.); Trustee, Leicestershire's Appeal for Music and the Arts 1993–; Walter Neurath Award 1964, Pratt Award 1965, Sainsbury Award 1966, Arts Council Award 1977, Duais Na Riochta Gold Medal, Eire 1977. *Leisure interest:* gardening. *Address:* 73 Bow Road, London, E3 2AN, England. *Telephone:* 0181-981 2037. *Fax:* 0181-980 3153.

TAYLOR, Sir William, Kt., C.B.E.; British academic; b. 31 May 1930, Crayford, Kent; s. of Herbert Taylor and Maud Taylor; m. Rita Hague 1954; one s. two d.; ed. London School of Econs.; fmr. school teacher and deputy head teacher, Kent; later worked in two colls. of educ. and Dept. of Educ., Oxford Univ.; Prof. of Educ. Univ. of Bristol 1966; Dir. London Inst. of Educ. 1973–83; Prin., Univ. of London 1983–85; Vice-Chancellor, Univ. of Hull 1985–91; Chair. Council for Accreditation of Teacher Educ. (CATE) 1984–93; Chair. Bd. NFER/Nelson publishing co. 1988–99; Chair. of Convocation, Univ. of London 1994–97; Pres. Soc. for Research in Higher Educ. 1996–; Vice-Chancellor, Univ. of Huddersfield 1994–95, Thames Valley Univ. 1998–99; Chair. Northern Ireland Cttee. for Teacher Educ. 1994–; Visiting Prof. Univ. of Oxford 1991–97; Gov. Polytechnic of Wales, Christ Church

Coll. Canterbury; Charter Fellow, Coll. of Preceptors; Hon. Fellow, Green Coll., Westminster Coll., Oxford, Thames Polytechnic, Commonwealth Council for Educ. Admin., Inst. of Educ.; Dr. h.c. (Aston, Leeds, Kent, Loughborough, Open Univ., Huddersfield, Hull, Kingston, Plymouth, Oxford Brookes, Univ. of West of England, Queen's Univ. Belfast, Southampton). *Publications include:* The Secondary Modern School, Society and the Education of Teachers, Planning and Policy in Post-secondary Education, Heading for Change, Research and Reform in Teacher Education, The Metaphors of Education, Universities under Scrutiny. *Leisure interest:* work. *Address:* Yew Trees, 20 Hinton Fields, King's Worthy, Winchester, Hants., England. *Telephone:* (01962) 883485. *Fax:* (01962) 883485.

TAYLOR, Rt. Hon. (Winifred) Ann, P.C., M.P.; British politician; b. 2 July 1947, Motherwell; m. David Taylor 1966; one s. one d.; ed. Bolton School, and Univs. of Bradford and Sheffield; fmr. teacher and part-time tutor, Open Univ.; M.P. for Bolton West 1974–83, for Dewsbury 1987–; Parl. Pvt. Sec. to Sec. of State for Educ. and Science 1975–76, to Sec. of State for Defence 1976–77; an Asst. Govt. Whip 1977–79; Opposition Spokesman on Educ. 1979–81, on Housing 1981–83, on Home Affairs 1987–90, on Environment 1990–92, on Educ. 1992–94; Shadow Leader of House of Commons 1994–97; Lord Pres. of the Council and Leader of the House of Commons 1997–98; Chief Whip July 1998–; Spokesperson on Citizen's Charter 1994–95; mem. Select Cttee. on Standards and Privileges 1995–97; Hon. Fellow, Birkbeck Coll. London; Labour. *Address:* House of Commons, London, SW1A 0AA; Glyn Garth, Stoney Bank Road, Thongsbridge, Huddersfield, Yorks., HD7 2SL, England.

TAZAWA, Tomoharu; Japanese politician; fmr. Parl. Vice-Minister of Int. Trade and Industry; mem. House of Councillors, fmr. Chair. Cttee. on Educ.; Minister of Justice 1995–96; mem. LDP.

TCHAIKOVSKY, Aleksandr Vladimirovich; Russian composer and pianist; b. 19 Feb. 1946, Moscow; ed. Moscow State Conservatory; m. 1st; one s. one d.; m. 3rd; one d.; performs as pianist and chamber musician 1967–, author of compositions in various genres including operas Grandfather Is Laughing 1976, Three Sisters (after A. Chekhov) 1994, ballets Inspector 1960, Battleship Potemkin 1988, symphonies 1985, 1991 (Aquarius), two piano concertos, two viola concertos, Distant Dreams of Childhood for violin and viola 1990, Concerto-Buff for violin and marimba 1990, Triple Concerto for piano, violin and cello 1994, Tsar Nikita for two soloists and folk instruments, Quartet (after A. Pushkin) 1997, chamber music, incidental music to theatre and film productions; teacher Moscow State Conservatory 1976, Prof. 1994–; Artistic Consultant, Mariinski Theatre, St. Petersburg; winner Hollybush Festival Prize (U.S.A.) 1987; People's Artist of Russia 1998. *Leisure interests:* collecting models of cars, table hockey. *Address:* Leningradsky prosp. 14, Apt. 4, 125040 Moscow, Russia (Home). *Telephone:* 151 5418 (Home).

TCHERINA, Ludmila (Tchemerzine, Monika); French actress, dancer, painter, sculptor and writer; b. 10 Oct. 1924, Paris; d. of Prince Avenir Tchemerzine and Stéphane Finette; m. 1st Edmond Audran (deceased), 2nd Raymond Roi 1953; ed. privately and studied under Yvan Clustine; First dancer and choreographer, Grands Ballets de Monte Carlo (youngest-ever prima ballerina) 1940–44, Ballets de Paris 1951–58; f. Compagnie de Ballet Ludmila Tcherina 1958. *Chief appearances include:* Ballets: Romeo and Juliet (with Serge Lifar) Paris 1942, Giselle La Scala, Milan 1954, Bolshoi Theatre, Moscow 1959, Le martyre de Saint Sébastien Paris Opera 1957, Buenos Aires 1967, Les amants de Teruel Théâtre Sarah Bernhardt, Paris 1959, Gala (by Salvador Dali and Maurice Béjart) Venice 1961, Brussels and Paris 1962, La muette de Portici Florence 1968, Anna Karénine Versailles 1975, etc. *Films include:* The Red Shoes, The Tales of Hoffmann, Clara de Montargis, La légende de Parsifal, La nuit s'achève, Oh! Rosalinda, A la mémoire d'un héros, La fille de Mata-Hari, Honeymoon, Les amants de Téruel (Cannes Film Festival, French Entry 1962; New York Critics Award), Jeanne au bûcher, etc. *TV appearances include:* Le Mandarin marveilleux, Bonaparte (title role), Salomé, Bonaparte, La possédée, La dame aux camélias, La passion d'Anna Karénine, La création de la Féminine (based on her career), La Reine de Saba, Portrait de Ludmila Tcherina. *Works:* exhibited Sully Museum and Centre Georges Pompidou, Paris, Universal Exhbn. of Sevilla 1992, the European Parl., Strasbourg, and in many capital cities worldwide; Prize for Best Feminine Performance, Vichy Film Festival for La nuit s'achève 1950, First Prize Dance Film Festival, Buenos Aires for A la mémoire d'un héros 1952, "Oscar" for Best Performance by a Foreign Actress in Tales of Hoffmann 1952, Paris Gold Medal 1959, Oscar Italien de la Popularité 1959, Prix Michel Ange 1973, Prix d'honneur Gemail-1973, Grande Médaille de Vermeil de la Ville de Paris 1978, Prix d'interpretation (Monte Carlo), Europa operanda 1995; Officier, Légion d'honneur 1980, Chevalier des Arts et des Lettres, des Palmes académiques. *Publications:* L'amour au miroir (novel) 1983, La Femme à l'envers (novel) 1986. *Address:* 42 cours Albert 1er, 75008 Paris, France. *Telephone:* 43-59-18-33.

TCHOBANU, Ion; Moldovan writer; b. 6 Nov. 1927, Budai; m.; one s.; ed. Moscow Univ., Higher Literary Courses, U.S.S.R. Writers' Union; mem. CPSU 1947–91; worked as teacher, Prin. of school, Sec. regional Comsomol Cttee.; Sec., First Sec. Writers' Union of Moldova 1961–91; U.S.S.R. People's Deputy 1989–91; People's Writer of Moldova 1984; State Prize of Moldova. *Publications:* novels include Kodry 1957, Bridges (trilogy) 1966, Podgoryane 1971; Responses (collection of essays) 1964; Force of Belle Lettres, numerous short stories and articles. *Address:* Ştefan cel Mare prospekt 6, apt. 135, 277001 Chişinău, Moldova. *Telephone:* (3732) 26-58-71.

TCHUKHONTSEV, Oleg Grigoryevich; Russian poet; b. 8 March 1938, Pavlov Posad, Moscow Region; ed. Moscow Pedagogical Inst.; ed. poetry section, Novy Mir; published in Druzhba Narodov, Yunost, Molodaya Gvardiya, Novy Mir; State Prize of Russia 1993. *Publications:* From Three Notebooks (cycles Posad, Name, Sparrow's Night) 1976, The Dormer Window 1983, Poetry 1989, By Wind and Heat 1989 and other books of poetry. *Address:* Uglovoy per. 2, Apt. 122, 103055 Moscow, Russia (Home). *Telephone:* 258 3989 (Home).

TCHURUK, Serge; French engineer and business executive; b. 13 Nov. 1937, Marseille; s. of Georges Tchurukdichian and Mathilde Dondikian; m. Hélèna Kalfus 1960; one d.; ed. Lycée Thiers à Marseille, Ecole nationale supérieure de l'armament; various refining and research positions Mobil/Oil BV Rotterdam 1964–68, Dir. French research centre 1968–70, Dir. of Information, France 1971–73, attaché int. planning, New York and Dir. plans and programmes France 1973–77, Dir. social and external relations 1977–79, Pres. and Dir.-Gen. 1979–80; Dir.-Gen. fertilizer div. Rhône-Poulenc Inc. 1981, Asst. Dir.-Gen. Rhône-Poulenc Group 1982, Dir.-Gen. special chemicals 1983, Dir.-Gen. Rhône-Poulenc Group 1983; Pres. Bd. Dirs. CdF Chimie 1986, Pres. Dir.-Gen. 1987–90 (became Orkem 1988); Dir. Total 1989, 1995–, Pres. 1990–95; Pres., Dir.-Gen. Alcatel Alsthom 1995–. Chevalier, Légion d'honneur, Officier, Ordre du Mérite. *Leisure interests:* music, skiing, tennis. *Address:* Alcatel-Alsthom, 54 rue La Boétie, 75008 Paris, France (Office).

TE KANAWA, Dame Kiri, D.B.E., O.N.Z.; New Zealand opera singer (soprano); b. 6 March 1944, Gisborne; m. Desmond Park 1967 (divorced 1997); one s. one d.; ed. St. Mary's Coll., Auckland, London Opera Centre; first appearance at Royal Opera, Covent Garden, London, 1970, Santa Fe Opera, U.S.A. 1971, Lyons Opera, France 1972, Metropolitan Opera, New York, U.S.A. 1974; appeared at Australian Opera, Royal Opera House Covent Garden, Paris Opera during 1976–77 season; appeared at Houston Opera, U.S.A., and Munich Opera 1977; début La Scala, Milan 1978, Salzburg Festival 1979; San Francisco Opera Co. 1980; Edin. Festival, Helsinki Festival 1980. *Operas:* Boris Godunov 1970–71, Parsifal 1971, The Marriage of Figaro 1971, 1972, 1973, 1976, 1979, Otello 1972, 1973, 1974, Simon Boccanegra 1973, 1974, 1975, 1976, 1977, 1979, 1980, Carmen 1973, Don Giovanni 1974, 1975, 1976, 1979, 1981, Faust 1974, The Magic Flute 1975, 1980, La Bohème 1975, 1976, 1977, 1979, 1980, Eugene Onegin 1975, 1976, Così fan tutte 1976, 1981, Arabella 1977, 1980, 1981, Die Fledermaus 1978, La Traviata 1978, 1980, Der Rosenkavalier 1981, Manon Lescaut 1983, Don Giovanni (film) 1979; sang at Wedding of H.R.H. the Prince of Wales July 1981; Hon. Fellow Somerville Coll., Oxford 1983, Wolfson Coll., Cambridge 1997; Hon. LL.D. (Dundee) 1982, Hon. D.Mus. (Durham) 1982, (Oxford) 1983, (Nottingham) 1992, (Cambridge) 1997; Hon. D. Litt. (Warwick) 1989. *Recordings include:* Don Giovanni (as Elvira), Così fan tutti (as Fiordiligi), Carmen (as Michela), Mozart Vespers, Mozart C Minor Mass, The Magic Flute (Pamina), The Marriage of Figaro, Hansel and Gretel, Strauss Songs with Orchestra, recital records. *Publication:* Land of the Long White Cloud 1989. *Leisure interests:* golf, swimming, cooking. *Address:* c/o Jules Haefliger, Impresario AG, Postfach 4113, 6002 Lucerne, Switzerland.

TEANNAKI, Teatao; I-Kiribati politician; mem. Parl. for Abiang; fmr. Vice-Pres. of Kiribati; Pres. of Kiribati 1991–94. *Address:* c/o Office of the President, Tarawa, Kiribati.

TEAR, Robert, C.B.E., M.A., F.R.S.A., R.C.M., R.A.M.; British opera and concert singer; b. 8 March 1939, Barry, Wales; s. of Thomas Arthur and Edith Tear; m. Hilary Thomas 1961; two d.; ed. Barry Grammar School, King's Coll., Cambridge; embarked on solo career as tenor after singing as member of King's Coll. Choir 1957–60, and St. Paul's Cathedral Choir; joined English Opera Group 1964; worked with leading conductors (including Karajan, Giulini, Bernstein, Solti), and appeared in numerous operas by Benjamin Britten 1964–68; Artistic Dir. London Royal Schools Vocal Faculty; first Prof. of Int. Singing, Royal Acad. of Music 1985–; first appearance at Covent Garden in The Knot Garden, other appearances: Eugene Onegin 1970, Die Fledermaus 1977, Peter Grimes 1978, The Rake's Progess 1979, Thérèse 1979, Rheingold 1980, Alceste 1981, Die Meistersinger 1982, Billy Budd 1982, Turn of the Screw 1989, Death in Venice 1989; début with Scottish Opera in works including La Traviata, Alceste, Don Giovanni, Peter Grimes 1974; Paris Opera 1976, Lulu 1979; appearances in all major festivals; close asscn. with Sir Michael Tippett 1970–97; numerous recordings including premier recording of Tippett's opera King Priam 1981; Hon. Fellow, King's Coll., Cambridge 1989, Welsh Coll. of Music and Drama 1994. *Publications:* Victorian Songs and Duets, Tear Hear (autobiog.) 1990, Singer Beware 1995. *Leisure interests:* sport, 18th- and 19th-century English watercolours. *Address:* c/o Askonas Holt Ltd., 27 Chancery Lane, London, WC2A 1PF, England. *Telephone:* 0171-400 1700. *Fax:* 0171-400 1799.

TEARE, Andrew; British business executive; b. 8 Sept. 1942; m. Janet Slidmore; three s.; with Turner and Newall 1964–72, CRH 1972–83, Rugby Group 1983–90; Group Chief Exec. English China Clays 1990–96; Chief Exec. Rank Group. 1996–98; Dir. (non-exec.) Prudential Insurance Co. 1992, Nat. Freight Corpn. 1989. *Leisure interests:* skiing, opera. *Address:* Rank Organisation, 6 Connaught Place, London, W2 2EZ, England.

TEBALDI, Renata; Italian soprano; b. 1 Feb. 1922, Pesaro; d. of Teobaldo Tebaldi and Guisseppina (née Barbieri) Tabaldi; ed. Arrigo Boito Conservatory, Parma, Gioacchino Rossini Conservatory, Pesaro, then pupil of Carmen Melis and Giuseppe Pais.; début as Elena in Mefistofele, Rovigo 1944; has sung the principal soprano operatic roles in America and Europe.

TEBBIT, Baron (Life Peer) cr 1992, of Chingford in the London Borough of Waltham Forest; **Norman Beresford Tebbit,** P.C., C.H.; British politician; b. 29 March 1931, Enfield; s. of Leonard Tebbit and Edith Tebbit; m. Margaret Elizabeth Daines 1956; two s. one d.; ed. state primary schools, Edmonton Co. Grammar School; R.A.F. Officer 1949–51; commercial pilot and holder of various posts, British Air Line Pilots' Asscn. 1953–70; M.P. for Epping 1970–74, for Chingford 1974–92; Parl. Pvt. Sec. Dept. of Employment 1972–73; Under-Sec. of State, Dept. of Trade 1979–81; Minister of State, Dept. of Industry Jan.-Sept. 1981; Sec. of State for Employment 1981–83, for Trade and Industry 1983–85; Chancellor of the Duchy of Lancaster 1985–87; Chair. Conservative Party 1985–87; Dir. B.E.T. PLC 1987–96, British Telecom PLC 1987–96, Sears PLC, Spectator Ltd.; Co-Presenter, Target, Sky TV 1989–97; columnist The Sun 1995–97, Mail on Sunday 1997–. *Publications:* Upwardly Mobile 1988, Unfinished Business 1991. *Leisure interests:* peace and quiet. *Address:* House of Lords, Westminster, London, SW1A 0PW, England. *Telephone:* 0171-219 6929.

TEBBIT, Sir Donald Claude, G.C.M.G., M.A.; British diplomatist (retd.); b. 4 May 1920, Cambridge; m. Barbara Margaret Olson Matheson 1947; one s. three d.; ed. Perse School, Cambridge, Trinity Hall, Cambridge Univ.; Royal Naval Volunteer Reserve 1941–46; Foreign Office 1946–48; Second Sec. British Embassy, Washington, D.C. 1948–51; Foreign Office 1951–54; First Sec. (Commercial), Bonn 1954–58; Private Sec. to Minister of State, Foreign Office 1958–61, Counsellor 1962, Sec. Cttee. on Representational Services Overseas 1962–64; Counsellor and Head of Chancery, Copenhagen 1964–67; Head of W. and Cen. Africa Dept., Commonwealth Office 1967; Asst. Under-Sec. of State, FCO 1968; Commercial Minister, Washington, D.C. 1970–71, Minister 1971–72; Deputy Under-Sec. of State, FCO 1973–76; High Commr. in Australia 1976–80; Pres. (U.K.) Australia-British Chamber of Commerce 1980–90; Dir.-Gen. British Property Fed. 1980–85; Dir. Rio Tinto Zinc Corpn. Ltd. 1980–90; Chair. English-Speaking Union of the Commonwealth 1983–87; Gov. (Deputy Chair.) Nuffield Hospitals 1980–90; Chair. Diplomatic Service Appeals Bd. 1980–87, Marshall Aid Commemoration Comm. 1985–95, Jt. Commonwealth Socs.' Council 1987–93; mem. Appeals Bd. Council of Europe 1981–93. *Address:* Priory Cottage, Toft, Cambridge, England.

TEBEKARU, Nikolae; Moldovan politician and diplomatist; b. 20 Aug. 1955, Nadrechnoye, Odessa Region, Ukraine: m.; two c.; ed. Moldovan State Univ., Moscow Diplomatic Acad., diplomatic service 1989–; Head, Protocol Dept., Moldovan Ministry of Foreign Affairs 1990; First Sec. Perm. Mission of Repub. of Moldova to UN 1991–92; Head, Dept. for UN and Disarmament, Moldovan Ministry of Foreign Affairs 1992–93; Head, Protocol Diplomatic Dept. 1993; Counsellor, Minister-Counsellor, Embassy, Belgium (also accred. to Luxembourg, U.K., NATO and EC) 1993–96; Head, Dept. of Europe and N. America, Ministry of Foreign Affairs 1996–97; adviser on Problems of Foreign Policy to Moldovan Pres. 1997–; Minister of Foreign Affairs 1997–. *Address:* Ministry of Foreign Affairs, Piaţa Marii Adunari Nationale 1, 2033 Chişinău, Moldova. *Telephone:* (3732) 23 39 40 (Office).

TÉCHINÉ, André Jean François; French author and film-maker; b. 13 March 1943, Valence, Tarn-et-Garonne. *Films:* Paulina s'en va 1969, Souvenirs d'en France 1975, Barocco 1976, Les Soeurs Bronté 1979, Hôtel des Amériques 1981, Rendez-vous 1985 (Prize for Best Director, Cannes Int. Film Festival 1985), Le Lieu du crime 1986, Les Innocents 1987, J'embrasse pas 1991, Ma saison préférée 1993, Les Roseaux sauvages 1994 (Prix Louis-Delluc 1994, César for Best French Film, Best Dir. and Best Original Screenplay or Adaptation 1995), Les Voleurs 1996; television: La Matiouette. *Address:* Artmédia, 10 avenue George V, 75008 Paris, France.

TEDESCHI, Michele; Italian business executive; b. 28 April 1940, Bari; m.; three s.; ed. Univ. of Rome; joined STET 1960, Deputy Dir., Man. Dir. 1993–94; Dir. EFIM Group 1977; Dir. Personnel and Labour Affairs Dept. IRI 1980, Asst. Gen. Man., Head of Information System Dept., responsible for IRI Cttee. for Strategies 1987–88, Gen. Man. 1989–92, Man. Dir., Gen. Man. 1992–93, Chair., C.E.O. 1994–98. *Leisure interests:* listening to classical music, playing tennis. *Address:* IRI, via Vittorio Veneto 89, 00187 Rome, Italy. *Telephone:* (6) 47271. *Fax:* (6) 47272308.

TEER, Kees, F.I.E.E.E.; Netherlands scientist; b. 6 June 1925, Haarlem; m. Jozina A. Kas 1951; four c.; ed. Tech. Univ. Delft; joined Philips Research Labs., Eindhoven 1950, Sr. Researcher, Deputy Head of Acoustics, 1958, Deputy Dir. 1966, Man. Dir. 1968, Chair. Man. Cttee. 1982–85; Prof. Tech. Univ. Delft 1987–91; mem. Netherlands Scientific Council for Govt. 1985–88; mem. Royal Netherlands Acad. of Sciences; mem. Bd. of Dirs. Royal Dutch PTT, Nedap Industries. *Publications:* several publs. on electro-acoustics, television systems, electronic principles, information tech. and society, R & D management etc. *Address:* Hoge Duinlaan 3, 5582 KD Waalre, Netherlands. *Telephone:* (40) 22 16861. *Fax:* (40) 22 19222.

TEETS, John William; American businessman (retd.); b. 15 Sept. 1933, Elgin, Ill.; s. of John William Teets and Maudie Teets; m. Nancy Teets 1965; four d.; ed. Elgin High School and Univ. of Illinois; Pres. and partner, Winter Garden Restaurant, Carpenterville 1957–63; Vice-Pres. Greyhound Food Man. Co.; Pres. Post Houses and Horne's Enterprises, Chicago 1964–68; Pres. and C.O.O. John R. Thompson Co., Chicago 1968–71; Pres., Corp. Vice-Pres. Public Restaurant Div. Canteen Corpn., Chicago and Div. Pres. Jacques Restaurant Group 1971–75; Exec. Vice-Pres. Bonanza Int. 1975; Group Vice-Pres. Food Services and Pres. Greyhound Food Man. Inc., Phoenix (now Restaura Inc.) 1975; Vice-Chair. Greyhound Corpn. (now The Dial Corpn.) 1980, Chair. C.E.O. 1981, Pres. 1982–95, Chair., Pres., C.E.O. The Dial Corpn. 1996–97; Hon. LL.D. (Trinity Coll., Deerfield, Ill.) 1982; Hon. D.Comm.Sc. (Western Int. Univ., Phoenix, Ariz.) 1992; several awards, including Nat. Human Relations Award, American Jewish Cttee. 1986, Forbes Magazine Award, Top Business Speaker of the Year 1990, Capts. of Achievement Award, American Acad. of Achievement 1992; Order of the Crown, Belgium 1990, other awards and prizes. *Leisure interests:* golf, running, weightlifting. *Address:* J.W. Teets Enterprises LLC, 1850 North Central Avenue, Phoenix, AZ 85077 (Office); 5303 Desert Park Lane, Scottsdale, AZ 85253, U.S.A. (Home).

TEICH, Malvin Carl, PH.D., F.I.E.E.E.; American professor of electrical and biomedical engineering science and of physics; b. 4 May 1939, New York; s. of Sidney R. Teich and Loretta K. Teich; ed. Massachusetts Inst. of Tech., and Stanford and Cornell Univs.; Research Scientist, M.I.T. Lincoln Lab., Lexington, Mass. 1966–67; Prof. of Eng. Science, Columbia Univ. 1967–96, Emer. Prof. 1996–, Chair. Dept. of Electrical Eng. 1978–80, mem. Applied Physics Faculty, Columbia Radiation Lab.; Prof. of Electrical and Computer Eng., Prof. of Biomedical Eng., Physics, Boston Univ. 1995–; Deputy Ed. Journal of European Optical Soc. B: Quantum Optics 1988–92; mem. Bd. of Eds. Optics Letters 1977–79, Journal of Visual Communication and Image Representation 1989–92, Jemná Mechanika a Optika 1994–; mem. Scientific Bd. Czech Acad. of Sciences Inst. of Physics; mem. Photonics Center; Hearing Research Center, Center for Adaptive Systems, Center for BioDynamics; Fellow A.A.A.S., American Physical Soc., Optical Soc. of America, Acoustical Soc. of America; I.E.E.E. Browder Thompson Memorial Prize 1969, John Simon Guggenheim Memorial Foundation Fellow 1973, Citation Classic Award, Inst. for Scientific Information 1981, Memorial Gold Medal (Palacký Univ.) 1992, I.E.E.E. Morris E. Leeds Award 1997. *Publications:* Fundamentals of Photonics (with B.E.A. Saleh) 1991; 250 articles in tech. journals; two U.S. patents. *Address:* Department of Electrical and Computer Engineering, Boston University, 8 Saint Mary's Street, Boston, MA 02215, U.S.A. *Telephone:* (617) 353-1236. *Fax:* (617) 353 1459.

TEITELBAUM, Philip, PH.D.; American professor of psychology; b. 9 Oct. 1928, Brooklyn, New York; s. of Bernard Teitelbaum and Betty Schechter; m. 1st Anita Stawski 1955, m. 2nd Evelyn Satinoff 1963, m. 3rd Osnat Boné 1985; five s.; ed. Johns Hopkins Univ.; Instructor and Asst. Prof. in Psychology, Harvard Univ. 1954–59; Assoc., Full Prof., Univ. of Pa. 1959–73; Prof., Univ. of Ill. 1973–85, Emer. Prof. 1985–; Fellow in Center for Advanced Studies, Univ. of Ill. 1979–85; Grad. Research Prof. in Psychology, Univ. of Fla. 1984–; mem. N.A.S., A.A.A.S.; Guggenheim Fellow; Fulbright Fellow; American Psychology Asscn. Scientific Contrib. Award. *Publications:* Fundamental Principles of Physiological Psychology 1967, Vol. on Motivation, Handbook of Behavioral Neurobiology (with Evelyn Satinoff) 1983. *Address:* Psychology Department, University of Florida, Gainesville, FL 32611, U.S.A. *Telephone:* (904) 392-0615 and (904) 372-5714.

TELIČKA, Pavel; Czech diplomatist and lawyer; b. 24 Aug. 1965, Washington, U.S.A.; m. Eva Telička; one s.; ed. Charles Univ., Prague; with Ministry of Foreign Affairs 1986–, mem. of del. for talks on Czech membership of EU 1991, with Czech Standing Mission to EU 1991–95, Deputy Amb. to Brussels 1993–95; Dir. of Dept. Ministry of Foreign Affairs 1995–98, Dir.-Gen. Dept. for EU and NATO 1998–; Deputy Chair. Comm. for Czech Integration to EU 1998–; Deputy Minister for Foreign Affairs 1998–. *Leisure interests:* sport, music, travel. *Address:* Ministry of Foreign Affairs, Loretánské nám. 5, 110 00 Prague 1, Czech Republic. *Telephone:* (24) 18-11-11.

TELLA, Guido José Mario di, D.ECON.; Argentine politician; b. 12 June 1931, Buenos Aires; ed. Univ. of Buenos Aires and Mass. Inst. of Tech.; Dir. Inst. for Econ. and Social Research, Univ. of Buenos Aires 1965, now Titular Prof. of Econ. Devt.; Titular Prof. of Econ. Devt. Argentine Catholic Univ.; Fellow, St. Antony's Coll. Oxford; Dir. Torcuato Di Tella Inst. 1958; Pres. Nat. Foundation for Arts 1974–75; Sec. of State for Econ. Coordination and Programmation 1975–76; Nat. Deputy for Justicialist Party, Buenos Aires Prov. 1988–89; Minister for Foreign Affairs and Worship 1995–. *Publications include:* Las Etapas del Desarrollo Económico Argentino 1962, Los Ciclos Económicos Argentinos 1973, La Estrategía del Desarrollo Indirecto 1973, Perón-Perón 1973–76 1982; other books in collaboration; articles in economic journals. *Address:* Ministry of Foreign Affairs and Worship, Reconquista 1088, 1003 Buenos Aires, Argentina. *Telephone:* (1) 311-0071. *Fax:* (1) 311-5730.

TELLENBACH, Gerd, PH.D.; German university professor; b. 17 Sept. 1903, Berlin-Lichterfelde; s. of Leo Tellenbach and Margarete Eberty; m. Marie-Elisabeth Gerken 1945; two s. one d.; ed. Univs. of Freiburg and Munich; Asst., Prussian Historical Inst. in Rome 1928–33; Lecturer, Heidelberg, Giessen, and Würzburg Univs. 1933–38; Prof., Giessen 1938–42, Münster 1942–44; Prof. of Medieval and Modern History, Univ. of Freiburg, and Dir. Historical School 1944–62; Dir. German Historical Inst., Rome 1962–72, Prof. Emer. 1972; corresp. mem. Bavarian Acad. of Sciences;

corresp. F.B.A.; Foreign Fellow Nat. Acad. Naz. dei Lincei; D. h.c. Ph. et Litt. (Louvain), Hon. D.Litt. (Glasgow), Hon. D. Hist. (Pisa); Public Service Order Medal, with Star, of Fed. Repub. of Germany; Commdr. Order of Merit of the Italian Repub.; Verdienstmedaille des Landes Baden-Württemberg. *Publications include:* Die bischöflich passauischen Eigenklöster und ihre Vogteien 1928, Römischer und christlicher Reichsgedanke in der Liturgie des früheren Mittelalters 1934, Libertas, Kirche und Weltordnung im Zeitalter des Investiturstreites 1936, Königtum und Stämme in der Werdezeit des deutschen Reiches 1939, Church, State and Christian Society 1940, Die Entstehung des deutschen Reiches 1940, Goethes geschichtlicher Sinn 1949, Europa im Zeitalter der Karolinger, Historia Mundi V 1956, Studien und Vorarbeiten zur Geschichte des grossfränkischen und frühdeutschen Adels 1957, Zur Bedeutung der Personenforschung für die Erkenntnis des früheren Mittelalters 1957, Kaisertum, Papsttum und Europa im hohen Mittelalter, Historia Mundi VI 1958, Neue Forschungen über Cluny und die Cluniacenser 1959, Repertorium Germanicum II 1933–61, Der Sibyllinische Preis, Schriften und Reden zur Hochschulpolitik 1946–1963 1963, Empfehlungen zur Neuordnung des Studiums in den Philosophischen Fakultäten 1966, Saeculum Weltgeschichte III und IV 1967, V 1970, Aus erinnerter Zeitgeschichte 1981, Die westliche Kirche vom 10. bis zum frühen 12. Jahrhundert 1988 (English transl. by T. Reuter, The Church in Western Europe from the Tenth to the Early Twelfth Century 1992), Ausgewählte Abhandlungen und Aufsätze, 5 Bände 1988–96; Ed.: Monumenta Germaniae historica: Liber memorialis Romaricensis (with E. Hlawitschka and K. Schmid) 1970. *Address:* Hintere Steige 4, 79104 Freiburg/Br., Germany (Home). *Telephone:* 56497.

TELLEP, Daniel Michael, M.S.; American business executive (retd.); b. 20 Nov. 1931, Forest City, Pa.; m. Pat Tellep; six c.; ed. Univ. of Calif. (Berkeley) and Harvard Univ. Advanced Man. Program; with Lockheed Missiles & Space Co. 1955–, Chief Eng. Missile Systems Div. 1969–75, Vice-Pres., Asst. Gen. Man. Advanced Systems Div. 1975–83, Exec. Vice-Pres. 1983–84, Pres. 1984–; Pres. Lockheed Missiles and Space Group 1986–; Chair. and C.E.O. Lockheed Corpn. 1989–95 (merged with Martin Marietta to form Lockheed Martin 1994), Chair., C.E.O. Lockheed Martin 1996–97; now consultant; mem. Interstate Bancorp Bd. 1991–, Bd. Govs. Music Center L.A. Co. 1991–95, Calif. Business Round Table 1992–; Fellow, A.I.A.A., American Astronautical Soc.; mem. Nat. Acad. of Eng.; James V. Forrestal Award 1995, Calif. Mfrs. Award 1996, Nat. Eng. Award 1996, and numerous other awards. *Address:* c/o Lockheed Martin Corporation, 6801 Rockledge Drive, Bethesda, MD 20817, U.S.A.

TELLER, Edward, PH.D.; American scientist; b. 15 Jan. 1908, Budapest, Hungary; s. of Ilona and Max Teller; m. Augusta Maria Harkanyi 1934; one s. one d.; ed. Karlsruhe Technical Inst., and Univs. of Munich and Leipzig; Research Assoc., Leipzig 1929–31, Göttingen 1931–33; Rockefeller Fellow, Copenhagen 1934; Lecturer, Univ. of London 1934–35; Prof. of Physics, George Washington Univ. 1935–41, Columbia Univ. 1941–42; Physicist, Manhattan Engineer Dist. 1942–46; Prof. of Physics, Univ. of Chicago 1946–52; Physicist, and Asst. Dir. Los Alamos Scientific Lab. 1949–52; Consultant, Univ. of Calif. Radiation Lab. Livermore 1952–53, Assoc. Dir. Lawrence Livermore Radiation Lab. 1954–75, Dir. 1958–60, Dir. Emer. 1975–; Prof. of Physics Univ. of Calif. 1953–60, Prof. of Physics-at-Large 1960–70, Univ. Prof. 1970–75, Prof. Emer. 1975–; Chair. Dept. of Applied Science, Univ. of Calif. 1963–66; Visiting Prof., Arthur Spitzer Chair of Science, Pepperdine Univ. 1975–77; mem. N.A.S., American Acad. of Arts and Sciences, U.S.A.F. Scientific Advisory Bd., etc.; Fellow, American Nuclear Soc., American Acad of Arts and Sciences etc.; Sr. Research Fellow, Hoover Inst. for War, Revolution and Peace 1975–; Joseph Priestley Memorial Award 1957, Albert Einstein Award 1958, Mid-West Research Inst. Award, Living History Award 1960, Enrico Fermi Award 1962, Robins Award of America 1963, Harvey Prize 1975, Nat. Medal of Science 1983, Sylvanus Thayer Award 1986, Presidential Citizen Medal 1989, Order of Banner with Rubies of Hungary 1990. Hon. D.Sc. (Yale, Alaska, Fordham, George Washington, S. Calif., St. Louis, Clarkson Coll. Clemson Univ., Maryland); Hon. LL.D. (Mount Mary). *Publications:* The Structure of Matter (with F. O. Rice) 1949, Magneto-Hydrodynamic Shocks (with F. de Hoffmann) 1950, Theory of Origin of Cosmic Rays 1954, Our Nuclear Future (with A. Latter) 1958, Legacy of Hiroshima (with Allen Brown) 1962. The Reluctant Revolutionary 1964, Constructive Uses of Nuclear Explosives (with Talley, Higgins & Johnson) 1968, Great Men of Physics (with others) 1969, General Remarks on Electronic Structure 1970, The Hydrogen Molecular Ion 1970, General Theory of Electron Structure 1970, Energy from Heaven and Earth 1979, The Pursuit of Simplicity 1980, Better a Shield than a Sword 1987, Conversations on the Dark Secrets of Physics 1991. *Leisure interests:* chess, swimming, piano. *Address:* Hoover Institution, Stanford University, Stanford, CA 94305 (Office); PO Box 808 Livermore, CA 94551, U.S.A. (Home).

TELLO, Manuel, B.A.; Mexican diplomatist; b. 15 March 1935, Mexico City; s. of Manuel Tello and Guadalupe M. de Tello; m. Rhonda Mosesman 1983; three step-d.; ed. Georgetown Univ., Washington, D.C., U.S.A., Escuela Libre de Derecho, Mexico City; Dir.-Gen. for Int. Orgs., Ministry of Foreign Affairs 1970–72, Head of Div. of Int. Orgs. 1972–74, of Political Affairs 1975–76; Amb. to the U.K. 1977–79; Vice-Minister of Multilateral Affairs 1979–82; Perm. Rep. of Mexico to Geneva-based int. orgs. 1983–88, Rep. to GATT 1986–88; Amb. to France 1989–92; Perm. Rep. of Mexico to UN, New York 1993–94, Feb. 1995–; Minister of Foreign Affairs 1994–95; Alt. Rep. on Council of Agency for Prohibition of Nuclear Weapons in Latin America 1970–73; Rep. to Third UN Conf. on Law of the Sea 1971–82; several foreign decorations. *Publications:* various papers and articles on Mexico's foreign policy, the law of the sea etc. *Leisure interests:* reading, tennis. *Address:* 2 UN Plaza, 28th Floor, New York, NY 10017, U.S.A. *Telephone:* (212) 752-0220. *Fax:* (212) 688-8862.

TELMER, Frederick Harold, M.A.; Canadian business executive; b. 28 Dec. 1937, Edmonton, Alberta; s. of Ingar Telmer and Bernice Telmer; m. Margaret Goddard Hutchings; three s.; ed. Garneau High School, Edmonton, Univ. of Alberta; joined Industrial Relations Dept., Stelco Inc. 1963, various man. positions in Marketing Div., subsequently Gen. Man. Field Sales, apptd. Gen. Man. Corp. Affairs and Strategic Planning 1984, Vice-Pres. 1985, Pres. Stelco Steel 1988, Dir. Stelco Inc. 1989, Chair. and C.E.O. 1991–97, Chair. 1997–; Chair. Spar Aerospace Ltd., Boliden Ltd.; Dir. CT Financial Services Inc.; Founding Dir. Japan Soc. *Leisure interests:* golf, tennis, skiing. *Address:* Stelco Inc., P.O. Box 2030 Hamilton, Ont., L8N 3T1 (Office); 4451 Lakeshore Road, Burlington, Ont., L7L 1B3, Canada (Home). *Telephone:* (905) 528-2511 (Office). *Fax:* (905) 577-4449 (Office).

TELTSCHIK, Horst; German fmr. politician; b. 14 June 1940, Klantendorf; s. of Richard Teltschik and Anja Teltschik; m. Gerhild Ruff 1967; one s. one d.; ed. Gymnasium Tegernsee and Freie Univ. Berlin; formerly held various positions in CDU offices and in Fed. Chancellery; then Ministerial Dir. Dept. 2, Fed. Chancellery; C.E.O. Bertelsmann Foundation; mem. Bd. of Man. BMW AG 1993–; organiser Werkunde Conf.; Hon. Gen. Consul of India for Bavaria and Thuringia; Hon. D.Univ. (Sogang, Seoul) 1997; Bundesverdienstkreuz; Commdr., Légion d'honneur. *Publication:* 329 Tage—Innenansichten der Einigung. *Leisure interests:* literature, tennis. *Address:* Petuelring 130, 80788 Munich, Germany. *Telephone:* (089) 382-26800. *Fax:* (089) 382-26008.

TEMERLIN, Liener, B.F.A.; American advertising executive; b. 27 Nov. 1928, Norman, Okla.; s. of S. Pincus Temerlin and Julie Kahn Temerlin; m. Karla Samuelsohn 1950; four c.; ed. Ardmore, Okla. High School, Univ. of Oklahoma; C.O.O. Glenn Advertising 1970–74; Pres. Glenn, Bozell & Jacobs 1974–79; Chair. of Bd. Bozell & Jacobs 1979–85; Chair. Bozell, Jacobs, Kenyon & Eckhardt 1985–88, Bozell 1989–92, Temerlin McClain 1992–; Algur H. Meadows Distinguished Prof. of Advertising, Meadows School of the Arts, Southern Methodist Univ.; Chair. Dallas Museum of Art Devt. Cttee. 1993–96; Pres. Council Dallas Symphony Asscn. 1989–; Trustee American Film Inst. 1992–; Bill D. Kerss Award, Dallas Advertising League 1983, Nat. Conf. of Christians and Jews Brotherhood Award 1984, Susan G. Komen Foundation for Breast Cancer Research 1989, Community Service Award, Jas. K. Wilson Silver Cup Award, Dallas 1990, Linz Award for civic service 1990. *Address:* 201 E. Carpenter Freeway, Irving, TX 75062, U.S.A.

TEMIRKANOV, Yuriy Khatuyevich; Russian conductor; b. 10 Dec. 1938, Nalchik; s. of Khatu Sagidovich Temirkanov and Polina Petrovna Temirkanova; m. Irina Guseva (deceased); one s.; ed. Leningrad Conservatoire; first violinist with Leningrad Philharmonic Orchestra 1961–66; Conductor for Maly Theatre and Opera Studio, Leningrad 1965–68; Chief Conductor, Leningrad Philharmonic Orchestra 1968–76, Kirov Opera and Ballet Co. 1976–88; Prof. Leningrad Conservatoire 1979–88; Artistic Dir. State Philharmonia 1988–; Prin. Guest Conductor Royal Philharmonic Orchestra and Philadelphia Orchestra; Chief Conductor, London Philharmonic Orchestra 1992–; guest conductor in a number of countries, including Scandinavia (Sweden 1968), U.S.A. and G.B. (Royal Philharmonic Orchestra 1981–); U.S.S.R. People's Artist 1981, Glinka Prize, U.S.S.R. State Prize 1976, 1985; *Opera productions include:* Porgy and Bess (at Maly), Peter the Great (at Kirov), Shchedrin's Dead Souls (at Bolshoi and Kirov), Tchaikovsky's Queen of Spades and Eugene Onegin (Kirov) 1979. *Address:* State Philharmonia, Mikhailovskaya 2, St. Petersburg, Russia. *Telephone:* (812) 110-42-14.

TEMPLE, Joseph George, Jr., B.S. (CHEM. ENG.); American business executive; b. 29 Aug. 1929, Brooklyn, New York; s. of Joseph George Temple and Helen Frances (Beney) Temple; m. Ann Elizabeth McFerran 1952; two s. one d.; ed. Purdue Univ.; joined Dow Chem. U.S.A. 1951, Vice-Pres. 1976–78, Dir. Dow Chemical Co. 1979–94, Group Vice-Pres. for Human Health 1980–83, Exec. Vice-Pres. 1983–87; Pres. Dow Chemical Latin America 1978–80; Pres. Merrell Dow Inc. 1983–88, Chair., C.E.O. Jan. 1988–89; C.E.O., Chair. Marion, Murrell Dow Inc., Kansas 1989–92, Chair. Marion Merrell Dow Pharmaceuticals Inc. 1992–94 (Vice-Chair. 1994–95); mem. Pres.'s Council Purdue Univ. 1978–; Distinguished Alumni Award, Purdue Univ. 1978, Silver Kt. Award, Nat. Man. Asscn. 1976, Gold Kt. Award 1982, Outstanding Chemical Eng. Award 1993.

TEMPLE, Shirley (see Black, Shirley Temple).

TEMPLEMAN, Baron (Life Peer), cr. 1982, of White Lackington in the County of Somerset; **Sydney William Templeman,** P.C., Q.C., M.B.E., M.A.; British judge; b. 3 March 1920, London; s. of Herbert W. and Lilian (née Pheasant) Templeman; m. 1st Margaret Rowles 1946 (died 1988); two s.; m. 2nd Sheila Barton Edworthy 1996; ed. Southall Grammar School and St. John's Coll., Cambridge; served 4/1st Gurkha Rifles 1941–46; mem. Middle Temple 1946–, Treas. 1987–; mem. Bar Council 1961–65, 1970–72; Q.C. 1964; Attorney-Gen., Duchy of Lancaster 1970; Judge, Chancery Div., 1972; Pres. Senate of Inns of Court and Bar 1974; mem. Royal Comm. on Legal Services 1976; Lord Justice of Appeal 1978–82; Lord of Appeal in Ordinary

1982–95; Visitor Essex Univ. 1990; Pres. Bar European Group 1987–; Hon. Fellow, St. John's Coll., Cambridge 1982; Hon. mem. Canadian Bar Asscn. 1976, American Bar Asscn. 1976, Newfoundland Law Soc. 1984; Hon. D.Litt. (Reading) 1980, Hon. L.L.D. (Birmingham) 1986, (Exeter) 1991, Hon. LL.D. CNAA (Huddersfield Polytechnic) 1989, (West of England) 1993, Nat. Law School of India 1994. *Address:* House of Lords, London, SW1A 0PW, England.

TEMPLETON, Sir John M., Kt., M.A.; British investment counsellor; b. 29 Nov. 1912, Winchester, Tenn., U.S.A.; s. of Harvey Maxwell Templeton and Vella Handly Templeton; m. 1st Judith Dudley Folk 1937 (died 1951), two s. one d.; m. 2nd Irene Reynolds Butler 1958 (died 1994); one step-s. one step-d.; ed. Yale Univ., Balliol Coll., Oxford Univ. (Rhodes Scholar); Sec.-Treas., Vice-Pres. and Dir. Nat. Geophysical Co., Dallas and New York 1937–41; Pres. and Dir. Templeton, Dobbrow and Vance, Inc., New York 1941–65, Templeton Growth Fund Canada Ltd., Toronto 1954–85, Templeton Funds, Inc. 1977–86, Templeton Global Funds, Inc. 1981–86; Chair. Templeton Damroth Corpn. 1959–62; Vice-Pres. and Dir. First Trust Bank Ltd. 1963–; Dir. Magic Chef, Inc., Cleveland, Tenn. 1965–86; Chase Manhattan Trust Co. 1972–82, British-American Insurance Co. 1973–82; Chair. Templeton, Galbraith and Hansberger Ltd. 1986–92; Chair. Bd. of Trustees Princeton Theological Seminary 1967–73, 1979–85; Chair. and Trustee Templeton Theological Seminary 1985–94; Pres. World Thanksgiving Alliance 1990–96; Trustee Templeton Foundation Inc. 1952–, Wilson Coll. 1951–73, Englewood Hosp. 1953–56, Center of Theological Inquiry, Princeton 1967–93, Buena Vista Coll. 1981–94, Soc. for Promoting Christian Knowledge (U.S.A.) 1984–88, Balliol Coll. Oxford Endowments Fund 1984–94, Templeton Project Trust (England) 1984–, America European Community Asscn.; mem. Bd. of Visitors Harvard Divinity School 1982–88, Advisory Bd. Harvard Center for Study of World Religions 1975–85, Council on Theological Seminaries, United Presbyterian Church of the U.S.A. 1959–84, Bd. Corporators Presbyterian Ministers' Fund Inc. 1960–93, Comm. on Ecumenical Mission 1961–70, Bd. of Mans. American Bible Soc. 1973–93, Man. Council Templeton Coll. (Oxford) 1982–95, Bd. of Trustees for Restoration of Westminster Abbey 1991–96; Chancellor Fla. Southern Coll. 1992–94; mem. New York Soc. of Security Analysts 1942–; mem. Royal Inst. (U.K.) 1996; Hon. Rector Dubuque Univ. 1988–93; Hon. Fellow Templeton Coll. 1991; Paul Harris Fellow (Rotary Int.) 1992; 20 hon. degrees; Benjamin Franklin Medal of Royal Soc. of Arts 1995, R. E. Lee Distinguished Service Award 1996; K.St.J. *Publications:* The Humble Approach 1981, The Templeton Touch (co-author) 1985, The Templeton Plan 1987, The God Who Would be Known 1989, Riches for the Mind and Spirit 1990, Looking Forward 1993, Is God the Only Reality? (co-author) 1994, Discovering the Laws of Life 1994, Evidence of Purpose (ed.) 1994, World Wide Laws of Life 1996, The Good News 1997; articles in financial and religious journals. *Address:* P.O. Box N-7776, Lyford Cay, Nassau, Bahamas (Home). *Telephone:* 3624904. *Fax:* 3624880.

TEN HOLT, Friso; Netherlands painter and etcher; b. 6 April 1921, Argelès-Gazost, France; m. A. Taselaar 1946; two s. one d.; ed. Rijksakademie van Beeldende Kunsten, Amsterdam; paintings mainly of swimmers, landscapes and nudes, portraits and figures; Prof. of painting, Rijksakademie van Beeldende Kunsten, Amsterdam 1969–83; one-man exhibitions in Netherlands since 1952, London 1959, 1962, 1963, 1965, 1969, 1973; Group exhbns. at Beaverbrook Art Gallery, Canada, and Tate Gallery, London 1963, Biennale Salzburg 1964, Carnegie Inst., Pittsbugh 1964, Netherlands travelling exhbn. 1957–58; works in collections in Netherlands, Sweden, U.K., France and America. *Major works:* stained-glass windows for churches in Amsterdam and The Hague and for Haarlem cathedral. *Leisure interest:* reading. *Address:* Keizersgracht 614, Amsterdam, Netherlands. *Telephone:* 02248-1727 (Studio); 6230736 (Home).

TENET, George J., M.I.A.; American government official; b. New York; m. A. Stephanie Glakas; one s.; ed. Georgetown Univ. School of Foreign Service, School of Int. Affairs, Columbia Univ.; legis. asst., legis. dir., staff of Senator John Heinz 1982–85; fmr. head of supervision of arms control negotiations between U.S.S.R. and U.S.A., subsequently Staff Dir., Senate Select Cttee. on Intelligence; fmr. Special Asst. to Pres. and Sr. Dir. for Intelligence Programs, Nat. Security Council, Deputy Dir. of CIA 1995–96, Acting Dir. 1996–97, Dir. 1997–. *Address:* Central Intelligence Agency, Washington, DC 20505, U.S.A.

TENG JINXIAN; Chinese film director; b. 24 May 1937, Tianjin; s. of Teng Hairu and Lu Shuyun; m. Yan Junxi 1965; one s.; fmrly. in charge of Ermei Film Studio; Dir. Film Industry Admin., Ministry of Radio, Film and TV 1987–96; mem. CPPCC. *Publications:* several articles on film and politics. *Leisure interests:* reading, swimming, travelling. *Address:* Ministry of Radio, Film and Television, 2 Fuxingmenwaidajie, Beijing, People's Republic of China. *Telephone:* (10) 6201-0212.

TENG TENG; Chinese politician; b. 1930, Jiangyin Co., Jiangsu Prov.; ed. Qinghua Univ. and in U.S.S.R.; joined CCP 1948; Vice Minister in charge of State Educ. Comm. 1993; Vice Pres. Chinese Acad. of Social Sciences 1993–; mem. 8th NPC, mem. Educ., Science, Culture and Public Health Cttee. *Address:* State Education Commission, 37 Damucang Hutong Road, Beijing 100816, People's Republic of China.

TENG WENSHENG; Chinese politician; b. 1940, Changning Co., Hunan Prov.; ed. Chinese People's Univ., joined CCP 1965; research fellow Research Office, Secr. of CCP Cen. Cttee.; Vice-Dir. Policy Research Office of CCP Cen. Cttee.; mem. 15th CCP Cen. Cttee. 1997–. *Address:* Policy Research Office of Chinese Communist Party Central Committee, 1 Zhong Nan Hai, Beijing, People's Republic of China.

TENGBOM, Anders, D.ARCH.; Swedish architect; b. 10 Nov. 1911, Stockholm; s. of Ivar Tengbom and Hjördis Tengbom; m. Margareta Brambeck 1937; two s. two d.; ed. Royal Inst. of Tech. and Royal Acad. of Fine Arts, Stockholm, Cranbrook Acad., Mich., U.S.A.; travelled in Europe, U.S.A., Japan, China and the U.S.S.R. 1935–36; architectural practice in Stockholm 1938–, designed bldgs. for many different functions in Sweden, Belgium, Venezuela and Saudi Arabia; Asst. Prof. of Architecture, Royal Inst. of Tech., Stockholm 1947; Pres. Nat. Asscn. of Swedish Architects (SAR) 1963–65; mem. Bd. Swedish Hospitals Fed. 1962–70; Pres. Swedish Asscn. of Consulting Architects (SPA) 1972–75; mem. Royal Acad. of Fine Arts, Stockholm 1973–, Pres. 1980–86; Hon. corresp. mem. R.I.B.A. 1963: Hon. Fellow, American Inst. of Architects 1978. *Leisure interests:* skiing, sailing. *Address:* Kornhamnstorg 6, 111 27 Stockholm (Office); Canton 2, 178 93 Drottningholm, Sweden (Home). *Telephone:* 08-4125200 (Office); 08-759 01 75 (Home).

TENNANT, Sir Anthony John, Kt., B.A.; British business executive; b. 5 Nov. 1930, London; s. of the late Maj. John Tennant and of Hon. Antonia (later Viscountess) Radcliffe; m. Rosemary Violet Stockdale 1954; two s.; ed. Eton Coll., Trinity Coll., Cambridge; Mather and Crowther 1953–66, Dir. 1960–66; Marketing Consultancy 1966–70; Marketing Dir. then Deputy Man. Dir., Truman Ltd. 1970–72; Sales and Marketing Dir. then Deputy Chief Exec., Watney, Mann and Truman Brewers 1972–76; Deputy Man. Dir., later C.E.O., then Chair. Int. Distillers and Vintners Ltd. 1976–87; Dir., later Group Man. Dir., then Deputy Chief Exec., Grand Metropolitan 1977–87; C.E.O. Guinness PLC 1987–89, Chair. 1989–92; Dir. Christie's Int. PLC 1993–, (Chair. 1993–96); Chair. Priorities Bd. 1992–93; Deputy Chair. (non-exec.) Wellcome PLC 1994–95; Deputy Chair. (non-exec.) Arjo Wiggins Appleton PLC 1996–; Dir. Guardian Royal Exchange 1989–, Guardian Royal Exchange Assurance 1989–94, Banque Nat. de Paris 1990–91, BNP UK Holdings Ltd. 1991–, London Stock Exchange 1991–94; Deputy Chair. Forte PLC 1992–96; Sr. Adviser and Dir. Morgan Stanley U.K. Group 1993–; Chair. Bd. of Trustees, Royal Acad. Trust, Univ. of Southampton Devt. Trust; mem. Supervisory Bd. LVMH, Moët Hennessy Louis Vuitton, Paris 1988–92; Hon. D.B.A. (Nottingham Trent Univ.) 1996; Médaille de la ville de Paris; Légion d'honneur. *Leisure interest:* gardening. *Address:* Morgan Stanley Dean Witter, 9 Upper Grosvenor Street, London, W1X 9PA (Office); 18 Hamilton House, Vicarage Gate, London, W8 4HL, England. *Telephone:* 0171-425 5902 (Office); 0171-937 6203. *Fax:* 0171-499 1524 (Office).

TENNANT, Emma Christina, F.R.S.L.; British author; b. 20 Oct. 1937; d. of 2nd Baron Glenconner and Elizabeth Lady Glenconner; one s. two d.; ed. St. Paul's Girls' School; former freelance journalist; founder ed. Bananas 1975–78; gen. ed. In Verse 1982–, Lives of Modern Women 1985–; Hon. D. Litt. (Aberdeen) 1996. *Publications include:* The Colour of Rain (under pseudonym Catherine Aydy) 1963, The Time of the Crack 1973, The Last of the Country House Murders 1975, Hotel de Dream 1976, Bananas Anthology (ed.) 1977, Saturday Night Reader (ed.) 1978, The Bad Sister 1978, Wild Nights 1979, Alice Fell 1980, Queen of Stones 1982, Woman Beware Woman 1983, Black Marina 1985, Adventures of Robina by Herself (ed.) 1986, Cycle of the Sun: The House of Hospitalities 1987, A Wedding of Cousins 1988, The Magic Drum 1989, Two Women of London 1989, Faustine 1992, Tess 1993, Pemberley 1993, An Unequal Marriage 1994, Strangers: A Family Romance 1998. children's books: The Boggart (with M. Rayner), The Search for Treasure Island 1981, The Ghost Child 1984, Emma In Love 1996, Girlitude 1999. *Leisure interest:* walking in Dorset. *Address:* c/o Toby Eady Assocs., 9 Orme Court, London W2 4RL, England.

TENNANT, Stella; British model; b. 1971; d. of Lady Emma Tennant; granddaughter of Duke of Devonshire; one s. by David Lasnet 1998; ed. St Leonard's Girls School, Kingston Polytechnic and Winchester School of Art; first assignment, cover shoot for Italian Vogue; now works in London, New York and Paris and with photographers including Mario Testino, Paolo Roversi and Bruce Weber; selected by Karl Lagerfeld as new face of Chanel 1996; announced retirement from modelling 1998. *Address:* c/o Select Model Management, Thomas Archer House, 43 King Street, London, WC2E 8RJ, England. *Telephone:* 0171-470 5220. *Fax:* 0171-470 5233.

TENNEKES, Hendrik, D.S. (ENG.); Netherlands meteorologist; b. 13 Dec. 1936, Kampen; s. of late Cornelis Tennekes and of Harmpje Noordman; m. Olga Vanderpot 1964 (divorced 1998); one s. one d.; ed. Delft Tech. Univ.; Asst. Prof., Assoc. Prof., Prof. of Aerospace Eng., Pennsylvania State Univ. 1965–77; Dir. of Research, Royal Netherlands Meteorological Inst. 1977–90, Dir. of Strategic Planning 1990–95; Prof. of Meteorology, Free Univ., Amsterdam 1977–; Visiting Prof. Univ. of Washington, Seattle 1976–77; Visiting Sr. Scientist, Nat. Center for Atmospheric Research, Boulder, Colo. 1987; mem. Royal Netherlands Acad. of Sciences. *Publications:* A First Course in Turbulence (with J. L. Lumley) 1972, The Simple Science of Flight 1996; numerous publs. on turbulence, predictability, chaos, boundary-layer meteorology and environmental philosophy. *Leisure interests:* poetry, landscape painting. *Address:* Acacialaan 18-B, 3707 EV Zeist, Netherlands (Home). *Telephone:* (30) 692 3653.

TENORIO, Pedro Pangelinan; American politician; b. 18 April 1934, Saipan, Northern Mariana Islands; s. of the late Blas Pangelinan Tenorio and of Guadalupe Sablan Pangelinan; m. Sophia Pangelinan 1959; four s.

four d.; ed. George Washington High School, Guam; mem. House of Reps., Congress of Micronesia; Senator Marianas Dist. Legislature; Vice-Pres. The Senate, Northern Mariana Commonwealth Legislature 1978–80, Pres. 1980–82; Gov. Commonwealth of the Northern Mariana Islands 1982–91, 1998–; Hon. LL.D. (Univ. of Guam) 1998. *Leisure interest:* golf. *Address:* Office of the Governor, Caller Box 10007, Saipan, MP 96950, Commonwealth of the Northern Mariana Islands. *Telephone:* 670 664 2280. *Fax:* 670 664 2211.

TER BEEK, Relus; Netherlands politician; b. 18 Jan. 1944; ed. Univ. of Amsterdam; mem. Parl. 1971; Int. Sec. Partij van de Arbeid (PvdA); mem. Parl. Assemblies of Council of Europe and WEU; Minister of Defence 1989–94. *Address:* c/o Partij van de Arbeid, Nicolaas Witsenkade 30, 1017 ZT Amsterdam, Netherlands.

TERASAWA, Yoshio, B.A. (ECONS.); Japanese international public servant; b. Tokyo; s. of Tsunesaburo Terasawa and Kura Terasawa; m. 1960; one s. three d.; ed. Waseda Univ., Tokyo, Wharton Business School, Univ. of Pennsylvania, U.S.A.; Pres. Nomura Securities Int. 1970–80, Chair. 1980–85, Exec. Vice-Pres. Nomura Securities, Tokyo 1985–88; Dir.-Gen. Econ. Planning Agency May–June 1994; Exec. Vice-Pres. Multilateral Investment Guarantee Agency (MIGA) 1988–; fmr. Fulbright Scholar; mem. New York Stock Exchange 1971–; Hon. Citizen New York City 1972. *Publications:* Night and Day on Wall Street, Windblown on Wall Street, Think Big!!, From the Window of Washington, D.C. *Address:* 2500 Virginia Avenue, N.W., Washington, DC 20037, U.S.A. *Telephone:* (202) 473-6138 (Office); (202) 342-6453 (Home).

TEREKHOV, Vladislav Petrovich; Russian diplomatist; b. 5 Nov. 1933, Rostov-on-Don; m. Galina Michailovna Terekhova; one s.; ed. Moscow State Inst. for Int. Relations; joined diplomatic service 1957; served in U.S.S.R. Embassies, Austria and Germany 1976–81; Deputy Man. 3rd European Dept. Foreign Ministry 1981–86; Embassy, Germany 1986–88; Admin. Chief, Staff and Teaching Insts., mem. Bd. Foreign Ministry 1988–90; U.S.S.R., then Russian Amb. to Germany 1990–97; Amb.-at-Large; several state prizes and awards. *Address:* Ministry of Foreign Affairs, Smolenskaya-Sennaya pl. 32/34, 121200 Moscow, Russia.

TEREKHOVA, Margarita Borisovna; Russian actress; b. 25 Aug. 1942, Turinsk, the Urals; d. of Galina Stanislavovna Tomashevich and Boris Ivanovich Terekhov; one s. one d.; ed. Tashkent Univ. and Mossoviet Studio School; with Mossoviet Theatre 1964–83; Founder and Dir. of Theatre Studio (Balaganchik) 1987–; film début 1966; R.S.F.S.R. Artist of Merit 1976, K. Stanislavsky Prize 1992. *Films include:* Hi! It's Me! 1966, Byelorussian Station 1971, My Life 1972, Monologue 1973, Mirror 1975, Day Train 1976, Who'll go to Truskovets? 1977, Dog in a Manger 1977, Kids, Kids, Kids 1978, D'Artagnan and the Three Musketeers 1978, Let's get Married 1983, Only for Crazy 1991 (San Remo Int. Film Festival Prize), Forbidden Fruit 1993, The Way 1995. *Theatre:* (dir. and actress) When Five Years Elapse (Lorca), The Tsars Hunt, Mossoviet Theatre. *Leisure interest:* son's upbringing and educ. *Address:* Bolshaya Gruzinskaya Str. 57, Apt. 92, 123056 Moscow, Russia. *Telephone:* (095) 254-96-95. *Fax:* 299-44-37.

TERENIUS, Lars Yngve, PH.D.; Swedish medical research scientist; b. 9 July 1940, Örebro; s. of Yngve Terenius and Margareta Hallenborg; m. 1st Malin Åkerblom 1962 (divorced 1986), 2nd Mona Hagman 1989; two s.; ed. Faculties of Science and Medicine, Uppsala Univ.; Asst. Prof. of Pharmacology, Medical Faculty, Uppsala Univ. 1969–79, Prof. of Pharmacology, Faculty of Pharmacy 1979–89; Prof. of Experimental Drug Dependence Research, Karolinska Inst. 1989–; Visiting Scientist Nat. Inst. for Medical Research, London 1972–73, Univ. of Aberdeen, Scotland 1975, Hebrew Univ., Jerusalem 1983, 1986; Fogarty Scholar, N.I.H., U.S.A. 1988–89; mem. Royal Swedish Soc. of Sciences, Royal Swedish Acad. of Sciences, Academia Europaea; Pacesetter Award 1977, Gairdner Award 1978, Jahre Award 1980, Björkén Award of Uppsala Univ. 1984. *Publications:* 400 papers on experimental endocrinology, cancer research, neurobiology. *Address:* Department of Experimental Drug Dependence Research, Karolinska Institute, 17176 Stockholm (Office); Kyrkogårdsgatan 27/II, 75312 Uppsala, Sweden (Home). *Telephone:* (08) 51774860 (Office).

TERENTYEVA, Nina Nikolayevna; Russian singer (mezzo-soprano); b. 9 Jan. 1946, Kusa, Chelyabinsk Region; d. of Nikolai Fedorovich and Tatyana Vladimirovna Terentyev; one d.; ed. Leningrad State Conservatory (class of Olga Mshanskaya); soloist Kirov (now Mariminsky) Theatre 1971–77, Bolshoi 1979; leading solo mezzo-soprano; Russian repertoire includes Marta (Khovanshchina), Lubasha (Tsar's Bride), Lubava (Sadko), Marina Mnishek (Boris Godunov), also Amneris (Aida), Azucena (Il Trovatore), Delila (Samson and Delila), Eboli (Don Carlos), Santuzza (Cavalleria Rusticana) and others; participated in productions of maj. theatres of the world including Covent Garden (Amneris, 1995), Metropolitan-Opera (Eboli, 1993), La Scala (oratorio Ivan Grozny with R. Muti, 1994), also in Deutsche Opera and Staatsoper Berlin, Munchen, Hamburg, Bordeaux, Los Angeles opera houses; participated in int. festivals; concert repertoire comprises Russian classics; People's Artist of Russia. *Leisure interests:* driving. *Address:* Bolshoi Theatre, Teatralnaya pl. 1, 103009 Moscow, Russia (Office). *Telephone:* (095) 971 6761 (Home).

TERENZIO, Pio-Carlo, LL.D.; Italian international civil servant; b. 4 Sept. 1921, Lausanne, Switzerland; s. of Rodolfo Arnoldo Terenzio and Katherine Agopian; m. Luisa de Notaristefani 1950; two s.; ed. Univs. of Rome and Geneva; joined Int. Labour Office (ILO) 1948; Officer in charge of Relations with Int. Orgs, UNESCO 1948–60, Dir. in charge of Congo Operations 1960–63, Dir. Bureau of Relations with Member States 1963–69, Dir. Bureau of Personnel 1969–70; Sec.-Gen. Inter-Parl. Union (IPU) 1970–86; mem. cttees. on human rights and disarmament, of Italian Nat. Acad. of Sciences 1986–. *Publications:* La rivalité anglo-russe en Perse et en Afghanistan 1947. *Address:* Via della Minerva, 12, 00186 Rome, Italy. *Telephone:* 69920922.

TERESHCHENKO, Sergey Alexandrovich; Kazakhstan politician; b. 30 March 1961, Chimkent Region; ed. Alma-Ata Inst. of Agric.; held offices in state power organs of Chimkent Region 1986–89, Chair. of the Exec. Cttee. of Chimkent Region 1990–91; First Deputy-Chair. Council of Ministers of Kazakh Soviet Repub. 1989–90; Vice-Pres. of Kazakhstan April–May 1991; Prime Minister of Kazakhstan 1991–94; Amb. at large, Ministry of Foreign Affairs 1994–95; works as business consultant. *Address:* Parliament Building, pl. Respubliki, 1480091 Almaty, Kazakhstan.

TERESHKOVA, Maj.-Gen. Valentina Vladimirovna; Russian politician and fmr. cosmonaut; b. 6 March 1937, Maslennikovo, Yaroslavl Region; d. of late Vladimir Aksyonovich Tereshkov and Elena Fyodorovna Tereshkova; m. 1963 (divorced); one d.; ed. Yaroslavl Textile Coll. and Zhukovsky Air Force Engineering Acad.; former textile worker, Krasny Perekop textile mill, Yaroslavl, and textile mill Sec., Young Communist League 1960; joined Yaroslavl Air Sports Club 1959 and started parachute jumping; mem. CPSU 1962–91, Cen. Cttee. CPSU 1971–90; began cosmonaut training March 1962; made 48 orbital flights of the earth in spaceship Vostok VI 16th–19th June 1963; first woman in world to enter space; Deputy to U.S.S.R. Supreme Soviet 1966–90; U.S.S.R. People's Deputy 1989–91; Chair. Soviet Women's Cttee. 1968–87; mem. Supreme Soviet Presidium 1970–90; Head Union of Soviet Socs. for Friendship and Cultural Relations with Foreign Countries 1987–92; Chair. of Presidium, Russian Asscn. of Int. Co-operation 1992–; Pres. Moscow House of Europe 1992–; Head Russian Centre for Int. Scientific and Cultural Co-operation 1994–; Visit to U.K. 1977; Pilot-Cosmonaut of U.S.S.R., Hero of Soviet Union, Order of Lenin (twice), Gold Star Medal, Order of October Revolution, Joliot-Curie Gold Medal, World Peace Council 1966, Order of the Nile (Egypt) 1971, Order of the Red Banner of Labour 1986. *Address:* Russian Association of International Co-operation, Vozdvizhenka Str. 14-18, 103885 Moscow, Russia. *Telephone:* 290-12-45.

TERKEL, Studs Louis, PH.B., J.D.; American author, actor and interviewer; b. 16 May 1912, New York; s. of Samuel and Anna (née Finkel) Terkel; m. Ida Goldberg 1939; one s.; ed. Chicago Univ.; stage appearances include: Detective Story 1950, A View from the Bridge 1958, Light up the Sky 1959, The Cave Dwellers 1960; star TV programme Studs Place 1950–53, radio programme Wax Museum 1945–, Studs Terkel Almanac 1952–, Studs Terkel Show (station WFMT-FM Chicago 1952–97); master of ceremonies, Newport Folk Festival 1959, 1960, Ravinia Musical Festival 1959, Chicago Univ. Folk Festival 1961 and others; lecturer and film narrator; Prix Italia, UNESCO Award for best Radio Programme (East-West Values) 1962; Communicator of the Year Award (Chicago Univ. Alumni Asscn.) 1969. *Publications:* Giants of Jazz 1956, Division Street America 1966, Amazing Grace (play) 1959, Hard Times 1970, Working 1974, Talking to Myself 1977, American Dreams: Lost and Found 1980, The Good War: An Oral History of World War Two 1985, Talking to Myself: A Memoir of My Times 1986, Chicago 1986, The Great Divide: Second Thoughts on the American Dream 1988, Race: How Blacks and Whites Think and Feel About the American Obsession 1992, Coming of Age 1995, My American Century 1997 and short stories. *Address:* WFMT Radio, 5400 N. St. Louis Avenue, Chicago IL 60625, U.S.A. (Office).

TER-PETROSYAN, Levon Akopovich, D.LIT.; Armenian politician and philologist; b. 9 Jan. 1945, Aleppo, Syria; m. Lyudmila Pletnitskaya; one s.; ed. Yerevan State Univ., Leningrad Inst. of Orientology; family moved to Armenia in 1946; jr. researcher Armenian Inst. of Literature 1972–78, sr. researcher, then Scientific Sec. Matenadaran Archive 1978–90; took part in dissident movt., arrested 1966, 1988–89; mem. Chair. Karabakh Cttee. in Matenadaran 1988; Deputy Supreme Soviet of Armenian S.S.R. 1989, Chair. 1990–91; mem. Bd., Chair. Armenian Nat. Movt.; Pres. of Armenia 1991–98. *Publications:* six books and over 70 papers on the history of Armenia. *Leisure interests:* reading, chess. *Address:* Marshal Baghramian Prospect 19, 375016 Yerevan, Armenia. *Telephone:* (02) 52-57-00; 52-54-04.

TERRAGNO, Rodolfo H., D.JUR.; Argentinian politician; b. 16 Nov. 1945, Buenos Aires; m. Sonía Pascual Sánchez; two s.; ed. Univ. de Buenos Aires; Asst. Prof. Univ. de Buenos Aries 1973–80; researcher Inst. of Latin American Studies, London 1980–82, L.S.E. 1980–82; Pres. Terragno S.A. de Industrias Químicas 1970–76; Exec. Vice-Pres. El Diario de Caracas S.A. 1976–80; Vice-Pres. Alas Enterprises Inc., N.Y. 1982–86; Dir. Letters S.A.R., Luxembourg 1982–86, Latin American Newsletters Ltd., London and Paris 1982–86; also columnist on several newspapers; rep. at int. conferences, including dispute with U.K. over Falkland Islands 1983–85; Sec. to Cabinet 1987, Minister of Works and Public Services 1987–89; Pres. Fundación Argentina Siglo 21 1986–87. *Publications:* Los dueños del poder 1972, Los 400 días de Perón 1974–75, Contratapas 1976, Muerte y resurrección de los políticos 1981, La Argentina del Siglo 21 1985–87, also numerous research papers.

TERRAINE, John Alfred, F.R.HIST.S.; British writer; b. 15 Jan. 1921, London; s. of Charles William Terraine and Evelyn Holmes; m. Joyce

Elizabeth Waite 1945; one d.; ed. Stamford School, Keble Coll., Oxford; Recorded Programmes Section, BBC 1943, Radio Newsreel 1945, Russian Section 1947, Pacific and S. African Programme Organizer 1953; free-lance writer 1963–; f. and Pres. Western Front Assn. 1980–; Screenwriters' Guild Documentary Award 1964, Soc. of Film and TV Arts Script Award 1969. *Publications:* Mons 1960, Douglas Haig: The Educated Soldier 1963, The Great War (TV series) 1964, The Western Front 1964, General Jack's Diary (Ed.) 1964, The Life and Times of Lord Mountbatten 1968 (TV series), Impacts of War, 1914 and 1918 1970, The Mighty Continent 1974 (TV series), Trafalgar 1976, The Road to Passchendaele 1977, To Win a War: 1918 The Year of Victory 1978, The Smoke and the Fire 1980, White Heat: the New Warfare 1914–18 1982, The First World War 1914–18 1983, The Right of the Line: The Royal Air Force in the European War 1939–45 1985, Business in Great Waters: The U-Boat Wars 1916–1945 1989, White Heat: The New Warfare 1914–18 1992, The Smoke and the Fire: Myths and anti-myths of war 1992; Chesney Gold Medal, Royal United Service Inst. 1982, Yorkshire Post Book of the Year 1985, C. P. Robertson Memorial Trophy, Air Public Relations Assn. 1985. *Address:* 77 Sirdar Road, London, W11 4EQ, England. *Telephone:* 0171-229 8152.

TERRY, John Quinlan, A.A.DIP., F.R.I.B.A.; British architect; b. 24 July 1937, London; s. of Philip Terry and Phyllis Terry; m. Christina de Ruttié 1961; one s. four d.; ed. Bryanston School, Architectural Assn.; joined late Raymond Erith R.A. 1962–73; work includes Kingswalden Bury, the New Common Room Bldg. at Gray's Inn, the restoration of St. Mary's Church on Paddington Green; Partner Erith and Terry 1967–; in pvt. practice 1973–, work includes large classical pvt. houses in stone erected in England, U.S.A. and Germany including three pvt. villas in Regent's Park for Crown Estate Commrs., offices, shops and flats at Richmond Riverside, new Lecture Theatre, Jr. Common Room, Library and residential bldgs. for Downing Coll. Cambridge, Brentwood Cathedral, restoration of State Room at 10 Downing Street, restoration of St. Helen's Church, Bishopsgate; mem. Royal Fine Art Comm. 1994–97; Rome Scholar 1969, Prix Internationale de la Reconstruction 1983. *Publication:* Architectural Monographs 1993. *Address:* Old Exchange, Dedham, Colchester, Essex, CO7 6HA, England. *Telephone:* (01206) 323186.

TERZIEFF, Laurent Didier Alex; French actor and theatre director; b. 27 June 1935, Toulouse; s. of Jean Terzieff and Marie (née Lapasset) Terzieff; ed. Lycée Buffon, Paris; actor 1952–; *theatre includes:* (as dir. and actor): Fragments 1978, Le Pic du bossu 1979, Le Philanthrope 1979, L'Ambassade 1982, Guérison americaine 1984–85, Témoignage sur Ballybey 1986, A pied 1987, Ce que voit Fox 1988, 1990, Temps contre temps 1993; (as actor): Les Amis 1981, Henri IV 1989, Richard II 1991, Meurtre dans la cathédrale 1994, Le Bonnet du jou 1997; *cinema includes:* Noces de sang 1980, La Flambeuse 1981, Détective 1984, Diésel 1984, Rouge baiser 1985, Hiver 54 1989, Germinal 1993, Fiesta 1994; *television includes:* Bérénice, Le Beau François, Moïse, Hedda Gabler, Rimbaud, Le Martyre de saint Sébastien, La Flèche dans le coeur 1985, La Fille aux lilas 1985; numerous prizes and awards including Prix du disque français 1975, Grand prix nat. du théâtre (Ministry of Culture) 1984, Molière Prizes for best dir. and for best play of the year for Ce que voit Fox 1988, Pirandello Prize (Italy) 1989, Molière Prizes for best dir. and for best play at a pvt. theatre, for Temps contre temps 1993; Officier Ordre Nat. du Mérite, Commdr. des Arts et des Lettres. *Address:* 8 rue du Dragon, 75006 Paris, France.

TESAURO, Giuseppe; Italian professor of international law; b. 15 Nov. 1942, Naples; m. Paola Borrelli 1967; three c.; ed. Liceo Umberto, Naples, Univ. of Naples, Max Planck Inst. Volkerrecht-Heidelberg; Asst. Prof. of Int. Law, Univ. of Naples 1965–71; Prof. of Int. Law and Int. Org., Univs. of Catania, Messina, Naples, Rome 1971–88; Dir. EEC Law School, Univ. of Rome 1982–88; mem. Council Legal Affairs, Ministry of Foreign Affairs 1986–; Judge, First Advocate Gen. European Court of Justice 1988–98; Pres. Italian Competition Authority 1998–. *Publications:* Financing International Institutions 1968, Pollution of the Sea and International Law 1971, Nationalizations and International Law 1976, Movements of Capital in the EEC 1984, Course of EEC Law 1988. *Leisure interests:* tennis, football, sailing. *Address:* c/o European Court of Justice, Palais de la Cour de Justice, 2925 Luxembourg.

TESCH, Emmanuel Camille Georges Victor; Luxembourg iron and steel company executive and engineer; b. 9 Dec. 1920, Hespérange; s. of Georges Tesch and Marie-Laure Weckbecker; m. Thérèse Laval 1949; one s.; ed. Technische Hochschule, Aachen and Eidgenössische Technische Hochschule, Zürich; Engineer, Manufacture de Tabacs Heintz van Landewyck 1948–51; fmr. Man. Dir. Soc. Générale pour le Commerce de Produits Industriels (SOGECO); joined ARBED as auditor 1958, Dir. 1968, Chair. Bd. of Dirs. 1972–91; Chair. Bd. of Dirs. ARBED Finance S.A. –1992, Electro Holding Co., S.A. Luxembourgeoise d'Exploitations Minières; Dir. SIDMAR S.A., Compagnie Maritime Belge, SOGECO S.A., LE FOYER S.A., Banque Générale du Luxembourg S.A.; Adviser Société Générale de Belgique, Companhia Siderurgica Belgo-Mineira; mem. Internationaler Beraterkreis der Allianz-Versicherungs-Gesellschaft, Conseil Economique et Social (Luxembourg); Pres. Chambre de Commerce du Grand-Duché de Luxembourg, Médaille de la Résistance (France); Grand Officer Ordre de la Couronne de Chêne (Luxembourg); Commdr. avec Couronne dans l'Ordre de mérite civil et militaire d'Adolphe de Nassau (Luxembourg); Ordre de la Couronne (Belgium); Commdr. Order of Orange-Nassau (Netherlands); Cavaliere di Gran Croce (Italy); Order of Tudor Vladimirescu (Romania); Hon. K.B.E.; Grosses Goldenes Ehrenzeichen mit Stern des Verdienstordens der Republik Österreich; Grosses Verdienstkreuz mit Stern des Verdienstordens der Bundesrepublik Deutschland; Encomienda de numero, Mérito Civil, Spain. *Leisure interests:* fishing, literature. *Address:* La Cléchère, 45 Route de Bettembourg, L-1899 Kockelscheuer, Luxembourg (Home). *Telephone:* 47921 (Office); 36-81-68 (Home).

TESHABAEV, Fatikh, PH.D.; Uzbekistan diplomatist; b. 18 Oct. 1939, Tashkent; s. of Gulam Ahmad Teshabaev and Hajiniso Teshabaev; m. Mauluda Teshabaev 1966; two s. one d.; ed. Univs. of Tashkent and Delhi; First Deputy Minister for Foreign Affairs 1991–93; Amb. to U.S.A. and Perm. Rep. of Repub. of Uzbekistan at UN 1993–95, Amb. at large 1995–; Nehru Award. *Publications:* articles on political thought in oriental countries. *Leisure interest:* tennis. *Address:* c/o Ministry of Foreign Affairs, ul. Gogolya 87, 700047, Tashkent, Uzbekistan.

TESHIGHARA, Hiroshi; Japanese film director; b. 1927, Tokyo; ed. Tokyo Art Inst.; worked as a film critic, then began directing documentary shorts in the early 1950's. *Films include:* The Pitfall 1961, Woman the Dunes (Jury Prize, Cannes Film Festival 1964), La Fleur de l'Age ou les Adolescentes (The Adolescents/That Tender Age) 1964, The Face of Another 1966, The Man Without a Map 1968, Summer Soldiers 1972, Rikyu 1989.

TESSON, Philippe, D. ÈS L.; French journalist; b. 1 March 1928, Wassigny (Aisne); s. of Albert Tesson and Jeanne Ancely; m. Dr. Marie-Claude Millet 1969; one s. two d.; Sec. of Parl. Debates 1957–60; Ed.-in-Chief, Combat 1960–74; candidate in legis. elections 1968; Diarist and Drama Critic, Canard Enchaîné 1970–83; Co-Man. and Dir. Société d'Editions Scientifiques et Culturelles 1971, Pres. 1980; Dir. and Ed.-in-Chief, Quotidien de Paris 1974; Dir. Nouvelles Littéraires 1975–83; Drama Critic, L'Express Paris 1986; Dir. and Co.-Man. Quotidien du Maire 1988; Animator (TV programme with France 3) A Quel Titre 1994–; ed. Valeurs actuelles 1994–; Drama Critic Revue des deux Mondes 1990–, Figaro Magazine 1995–; Chevalier, Légion d'honneur. *Publication:* De Gaulle 1er 1965. *Address:* Le Quotidien du Médecin, 140 rue Jules Guesde, 92593 Levallois-Perret cedex (Office); France 3, 116 Ave. du Président Kennedy, 75016 Paris, France.

TETLEY, Glen; American ballet director and choreographer; b. 3 Feb. 1926, Cleveland, Ohio; s. of Glenford Andrew Tetley and Mary Eleanor Byrne; ed. Franklin and Marshall Coll., Lancaster, Pa. and New York Univ.; performed with Hanya Holm, José Limon, Pearl Lang, John Butler modern dance cos.; prin. dancer, New York City Opera 1951–54; leading soloist, Robert Joffrey Ballet 1955–56, Martha Graham Dance Co. 1957–59, American Ballet Theater 1959–61, Jerome Robbins' Ballet U.S.A. 1961–62; f. own co. 1962–69; dancer and choreographer, Nederlands Dans Theater, Co-Artistic Dir. 1969; guest choreographer Royal Danish, Swedish, Norwegian Ballets, Hamburg State Opera; choreographer Royal Ballet, Covent Garden, American Ballet Theatre, Ballet Rambert; Dir. Stuttgart Ballet 1974–76; Artistic Assoc. Nat. Ballet of Canada 1987–; German Critics Award (for Die Feder) 1969, Queen Elizabeth II Coronation Award 1981, Prix Italia 1982, RAI Prize 1982, Tennant Caledonian Award 1983, Ohioana Career Medal for 1986, N.Y. Univ. Achievement Award 1988; Kt, Order of Merit, Norway 1997–. *Performances:* Kiss me Kate, Out of this World, Amahl and the Night Visitors; choreography: Pierrot Lunaire, Sargasso, The Anatomy Lesson, Circles, Imaginary Film, Arena, Small Parades, Mutations, Embrace Tiger and Return to Mountain, Ziggurat, Rag Dances, Ricercare, Field Figures, Laborintus, Mythical Hunters, Gemini, Chronocromie, Threshold, Moveable Garden, Voluntaries, Le sacre du printemps, Greening, Nocturne, Sphinx, Praeludium, Contredances, The Tempest, Summer's End, Dances of Albion, Dark Night: Glad Day, Fire Bird, Murderer Hope of Women, Revelation and Fall, Pulcinella, Dream Walk of the Shaman, Alice, Orpheus, La Ronde, Tagore, Dialogues, Oracle, Amores. *Leisure interests:* farming, reading, archaeology. *Address:* 15 West 9th Street, New York, NY 10011, U.S.A. *Telephone:* (212) 475 4604.

TETT, Sir Hugh Charles, Kt., A.R.C.S., B.SC., D.I.C.; British businessman; b. 28 Oct. 1906, Exeter, Devon; s. of late James Charles Tett and of Florence Tett (née Lihou); m. 1st Katie Sargent 1931 (died 1948); m. 2nd Joyce Lilian Mansell 1949 (died 1979); m. 3rd Barbara Mary Riley 1980; two d.; ed. Univ. Coll., Exeter, and Royal Coll. of Science, London; Esso Petroleum Co. 1928–67, Chair. 1959–67; Chair. Addis Ltd. 1973–76; Dir. Esso-Europe 1966–68, Pirelli Gen. Cable Works Ltd. 1970–80, Black and Decker Ltd. 1970–77, Bristol Composite Materials Ltd. 1972, Chair. 1974–79; Pro-Chancellor Univ. of Southampton 1967–79; Fellow Imperial Coll., London 1964; Hon. D.Sc. (Southampton 1965, Exeter 1970). *Leisure interest:* travel. *Address:* Primrose Cottage, Bosham, Chichester, West Sussex, PO18 8HZ, England. *Telephone:* (01243) 572705. *Fax:* (01243) 572765.

TETTAMANZI, H.E. Cardinal Dionigi; Italian ecclesiastic; b. 14 March 1934, Renate; ordained priest 1957; Bishop 1989; Archbishop of Genoa 1995; cr. Cardinal Feb. 1998. *Address:* Arcivescovado, Piazza Matteotti 4, 16123 Genoa, Italy. *Telephone:* (010) 27 001. *Fax:* (010) 29 25 54.

TEUFEL, Erwin; German politician; b. 4 Sept. 1939, Rottweil; m.; four c.; Dist. Admin. Rottweil and Trossingen municipality 1961–64; Mayor of Spaichingen 1964–72; mem. State Parl. of Baden-Württemberg 1972–, Leader CDU Parl. Group 1978–91; Sec. of State for Environmental Affairs, Baden-Württemberg 1976–78; Minister-Pres. of Baden-Württemberg Jan.

1991–; Chair. CDU-Baden-Württemberg 1991–; mem. Fed. Cttee. of CDU. *Address:* Staatsministerium Baden-Württemberg, Büro Ministerpräsident, Richard-Wagner-Strasse 15, 70184 Stuttgart (Office); Dreifaltigkeitsbergstrasse 44, 78549 Spaichingen, Germany (Home). *Telephone:* (0711) 2153438.

TEULADE, René; French politician; b. 17 June 1931, Monceaux-sur-Dordogne; s. of Léon Teulade and Marie Don; m. Bernadette Chassagne 1953; two d.; ed. Ecole Normale d'Instituteurs; schoolteacher 1951–56; Prof. Centre d'Etudes Supérieures, Argentat 1956–66, Deputy Prin. 1966–89, Prin. 1989; Departmental Sec. FEN 1968–72; Pres. Union Nat. des Mutuelles Retraite des Instituteurs et Fonctionnaires de l'Education Nationale 1974–92; Pres. Union Nat. des Caisses autonomes et Service de prévoyance (UNCASP) 1976–79; Pres. Féd. Nat. de la Mutualité française 1979–92; Minister of Social Affairs and Integration 1992–93; Co. Councillor Argentat canton, Corrèze; Vice-Pres. Asscn. Int. de la Mutualité, CASDEN-BP, MATMUT; mem. Econ. and Social Council 1980; Pres. Comm. for Social Affairs and mem. various other comms.; Officier, Légion d'honneur, Officier, Ordre Nat. du Mérite. *Leisure interests:* walking, gardening, hunting. *Address:* 8 bis rue de Solférino, 75007 Paris, France.

TÉVOÉDJRÈ, Albert, D. ÈS SC.ECON. ET SOC., L. ÈS L.; Benin politician and international civil servant; b. 10 Nov. 1929, Porto Novo; s. of Joseph Tévoédjrè and Jeanne Singbo Tévoédjrè; m. Isabelle Ekué 1953; three s.; ed. Toulouse Univ., Fribourg Univ., Institut Universitaire de Hautes Etudes Internationales, Geneva, Sloan School of Management and M.I.T. (Advanced Programme for Sr. Executives); teaching assignments include: Lycée Delafosse, Dakar, Senegal 1952–54, Ecole Normale d'Institutrices, Cahors, France 1957–58, Lycée Victor Ballot, Porto Novo 1959–61, Geneva Africa Inst. 1963–64, Georgetown Univ., Washington D.C. 1964; Sec. of State for Information 1961–62; Sec.-Gen. Union Africaine et Malgache (U.A.M.) 1962–63; Research Assoc. Harvard Univ., Centre for Int. Affairs 1964–65; Int. Labour Office 1965–, Regional Dir. for Africa March 1966, Asst. Dir.-Gen. 1969–75, Deputy Dir.-Gen. 1975; Dir. Int. Inst. for Labour Studies 1975–84; Sec.-Gen. World Social Prospects Asscn. (AMPS) 1980–; fmr. Chief Ed. L'Etudiant d'Afrique Noire; founder mem. Promotion Africaine (society to combat poverty in Africa); founder-mem. Nat. Liberation Movt. and mem. Cttee. 1958–60; Deputy Sec.-Gen. of Nat. Syndicate of Teachers, Dahomey 1959–60; Visiting Prof. Sorbonne 1979–, Univ. des Mutants, Dakar 1979–, Nat. Univ. of Ivory Coast 1979–, Northwestern Univ., Ill. 1980; Int. Humanitarian Medal 1987. *Publications:* L'Afrique revoltée 1958, La formation des cadres africains en vue de la croissance économique 1965, Pan-Africanism in Action 1965, L'Afrique face aux problèmes du socialisme et de l'aide étrangère 1966, Une stratégie du progrès social en Afrique et la contribution de l'OIT 1969, Pour un contrat de solidarité 1976, La pauvreté—richesse des peuples 1978, etc.

THAHANE, Timothy Thahane, B.COMM., M.A.; Lesotho government official and diplomatist; b. 2 Nov. 1940, Leribe; s. of Nicodemus and Beatrice Thahane; m. Dr. Edith Mohapi 1972; one s. one d.; ed. Lesotho High School, Univs. of Newfoundland and Toronto, Canada; Asst. Sec., Prin. Asst. Sec., Cen. Planning Office 1968–70, Dir. of Planning 1968–73; Amb. to EEC for Negotiations of Lomé Convention 1973–74; Alt. Exec. Dir. (Africa Group 1) World Bank 1974–76, Exec. Dir. 1976–78, representing 15 African countries and Trinidad and Tobago; Vice-Chair. and Chair., Jt. Audit Cttee. of World Bank Group 1976–78; Amb. to the U.S.A. 1978–80; Vice-Pres. UN Affairs, IBRD 1990–96; Deputy Gov. Reserve Bank of S.A. April 1996–; Vice-Pres. and Sec., IBRD 1980–96; Dir. Bd. of Global Coalition for Africa, Washington 1992–; mem. Bd. of Lesotho Bank (Vice-Chair. 1972–73), Third World Foundation, Centre for Econ. Devt. and Population Activities, Washington. *Publications:* articles on econ. planning and investment in Lesotho, Southern Africa and Africa in general. *Leisure interests;* reading, music. *Address:* South African Reserve Bank, 370 Church Street, Pretoria 0001, South Africa.

THAILAND, King of (see Bhumibol Adulyadej).

THALÉN, Ingela; Swedish politician; b. 1 Oct. 1943, Gothenburg; m. Lars Thalén; one s. two d.; fmr. shop asst., later clerk at Social Democratic Youth League, Gothenburg, Social Democratic Party, Stockholm County Council and at ARE-Bolagen 1959–74; District Sec. Gothenburg branch, Social Democratic Party 1975–78, Stockholm City branch 1979; engaged in local politics, Järfälla 1979–87, Municipal Commr. and Chair. Municipal Exec. Bd. 1983–87; Minister of Labour 1987–90; Minister of Social Health and Welfare 1990–91, of Health and Social Affairs 1994–96; mem. of Parl. 1991–; Sec. Gen. Social Democratic Party 1996–. *Address:* Partistyrelsen, 10560 Stockholm, Sweden.

THALER, Zoran; Slovenian politician; b. 21 Jan. 1962, Kranj; m.; one c.; ed. Univ. of Ljubljana; with Yugoslavian Foreign Ministry 1987; took part in various int. confs; Deputy Minister of Foreign Affairs Slovenian Repub. 1990–93; mem. of Parl. 1990; mem. Liberal Democracy of Slovenia 1992; Chair. Parl. Cttee. for Foreign Affairs 1993–95; Pres. Slovenian Interparl. Group; Minister of Foreign Affairs 1995–96; in pvt. business 1996–. *Leisure interests:* sailing, skiing, gardening, travelling. *Address:* c/o Ministry of Foreign Affairs, Gregorciceva 25, 61000 Ljubljana, Slovenia.

THAN SHWE, Gen.; Myanma politician and army officer; Prime Minister and Minister of Defence April 1992–; Chair. State Law and Order Restoration Council (SLORC) 1992–97, Chair. State Peace and Devt. Council (SDP) 1997–. *Address:* Office of the Prime Minister, Theinbyu Road, Botahtaung Township, Yangon, Myanmar. *Telephone:* (01) 665480.

THANHAWLA, Lal, B.A.; Indian politician; b. 19 May 1942, Durtlang, Aizawl, Mizoram; s. of H. P. Sailo and Lalsawmliani Thanhawla; m. Lal Riliani 1970; one s. two d.; ed. Gauhati Univ.; joined Indian Nat. Congress 1968, mem. All India Congress Cttee. 1973, Pres. Mizoram Pradesh Congress Cttee. 1973–98; mem. Mizoram Legis. Ass. 1978–, Chief Minister 1984–87, 1989–98, Leader of Opposition 1978–84, 1987–89; mem. Congress Working Cttee.; mem. 9th Finance Comm. of India; Chair. Sports Comm. N.E. Region of India; Founder-Ed. Remna Arsi & Mizo Aw (daily newspaper); Chair. Literary Cttee. of Nat. Devt. Council; Pres. Mizoram Olympic Asscn.; Life mem. YMCA, Evangelical Fellowship of India, Bible Soc. of India; 10 nat. and int. awards for contribs. to peace etc. *Leisure interests:* gardening, reading. *Address:* c/o Chief Minister's Secretariat, Aizawl, Mizoram, India.

THANI, Sheikh Abdul Aziz ibn Khalifa al-, B.S.; Qatari politician; b. 12 Dec. 1948, Doha; one s. three d.; ed. Northern Indiana Univ., U.S.A.; Deputy Minister of Finance and Petroleum June-Dec. 1972, Minister of Finance and Petroleum, State of Qatar 1972; Chair. State of Qatar Investment Bd. 1972–, Qatar Nat. Bank 1972, Qatar Gen. Petroleum Corpn. 1973–; Gov. IMF and IBRD (World Bank) 1972; rep. at numerous int. confs. including OPEC, OAPEC, and Arab, Islamic and Non-Aligned summit confs. *Leisure interest:* scuba diving. *Address:* c/o Qatar General Petroleum Corporation, P.O. Box 3212, Doha, Qatar.

THANI, Sheikh Abdullah bin Khalifa al-; Qatari politician; fmrly. Deputy Prime Minister, Minister of the Interior; Prime Minister of Qatar 1996–. *Address:* Office of the Prime Minister, Doha, Qatar.

THANI, Sheikh Hamad bin Khalifa al-; Emir of Qatar; b. 1950, Doha; ed. Royal Mil. Coll., Sandhurst, U.K.; apptd. Heir-Apparent May 1977; Commdr. First Mobile Bn, (now Hamad Mobile Bn.); Maj., then Maj.-Gen., Commdr.-in-Chief Armed Forces of Qatar; Minister of Defence May 1977–; Emir of Qatar June 1995–; Prime Minister 1995–96; Supreme Pres. Higher Planning Council; Pres. Higher Youth Council 1979–91; f. Mil. Sports Fed.; mem. Int. Mil. Sports Fed.; orders of merit from Egypt, France, Indonesia, Lebanon, Morocco, Oman, Saudi Arabia, U.K., Venezuela. *Address:* The Royal Palace, P.O. Box 923, Doha, Qatar.

THANI, Sheikh Khalifa bin Hamad al-; fmr. Emir of Qatar; b. 1932, Doha; s. of the late Heir Apparent Sheikh Hamad bin Abdullah bin Jassim al-Thani; ed. Royal Mil. Coll., Sandhurst, U.K.; appointed Heir-Apparent 1948; served successively as Chief of Security Forces, Chief of Civil Courts, Minister of Educ., Finance and Petroleum; Deputy Ruler 1960–72, also Minister of Educ. 1960–70; Prime Minister 1970–72, Minister of Finance 1970–72; Chair. Investment Bd. for State Reserves 1972; deposed his cousin Sheikh Ahmad and took office as Emir of Qatar 1972, deposed by his son June 1995.

THANIN KRAIVICHIEN (see Kraivichien, Thanin).

THAPA, Surya Bahadur; Nepalese politician; b. 20 March 1928, Muga, East Nepal; s. of Bahadur Thapa; m. 1953; one s. two d.; ed. Allahabad Univ., India; House Speaker, Advisory Ass. to King of Nepal 1958; mem. Upper House of Parl. 1959; Minister of Forests, Agric., Commerce and Industry 1960; Minister of Finance and Econ. Affairs 1962; Vice-Chair. Council of Ministers, Minister of Finance, Econ. Planning, Law and Justice 1963; Vice-Chair. Council of Ministers, Minister of Finance, Law and Gen. Admin. 1964–65; Chair. Council of Ministers, Minister of Palace Affairs, 1965–69; Prime Minister of Nepal and Minister of Palace Affairs 1979–83; Minister of Finance 1979–80, of Defence 1980–81, 1982–83, of Foreign Affairs 1982; Prime Minister of Nepal 1997–98; mem. Royal Advisory Cttee. 1969–72; arrested 1972, 1975; Tri-Sahkti-Patta 1963, Gorkha Dakshinbahu I 1965, Om Rama Patta 1980; several Nepalese and foreign awards. *Address:* Tangal, Kathmandu, Nepal.

THARP, Twyla; American dancer and choreographer; b. 1 July 1941, Portland, Ind.; m. 1st. Peter Young (divorced), 2nd Robert Huot (divorced); one s.; ed. Pomona Coll., American Ballet Theatre School, Barnard Coll.; studied with Richard Thomas, Merce Cunningham, Igor Schwezoff, Louis Mattox, Paul Taylor, Margaret Craske, Erick Hawkins; with Paul Taylor Dance Co. 1963–65; freelance choreographer with own modern dance troupe and various other cos., including Joffrey Ballet and American Ballet Theatre 1965–87; Artistic Assoc. Choreographer American Ballet Theatre, New York 1988–91; maj. works choreographed include Tank Dive 1965, Re-Moves 1966, Forevermore 1967, Generation 1968, Medley 1969, Fugue 1970, Eight Jelly Rolls 1971, The Raggedy Dances 1972, As Time Goes By 1974, Sue's Leg 1975, Push Comes to Shove 1976, Once More Frank 1976, Mud 1977, Baker's Dozen 1979, When We Were Very Young 1980, Amadeus 1984, White Nights 1985, Rules of the Game 1989, choreographed Cutting Up 1993 for U.S. tour, Demeter and Persephone 1993, 1994, Waterbaby Bagatelles 1994, Red White and Blues 1995, How Near Heaven 1995, Mr. Worldly Wise 1996; films Hair 1979, I'll do Anything 1992; videotape Making Television Dance 1977, CBS Cable Confessions of a Corner Maker 1980; Hon. D. Performing Arts (Brown) 1981 and others; Dance Magazine Annual Award 1981, Laurence Olivier Award 1991. *Publication:* Push Comes to Shove (autobiog.) 1992. *Address:* Tharp Productions, 336 Central Park West, Flat 17B, New York, NY 10025, U.S.A.

THATCHER, Baroness; (Life Peer) cr. 1992, of Kesteven in the County of Lincolnshire, **Rt. Hon. Margaret Hilda Thatcher,** L.G., O.M., P.C., M.A., B.SC., F.R.S.; British politician and barrister; b. 13 Oct. 1925; d. of the late

Alfred Roberts and of Beatrice Ethel Stephenson; m. Denis Thatcher (now Sir Denis Thatcher, Bt.) 1951; one s. one d. (twins); ed. Grantham High School and Somerville Coll., Oxford; Research chemist 1947–51; called to the Bar, Lincoln's Inn 1953; M.P. for Finchley 1959–92; Parl. Sec. Ministry of Pensions and Nat. Insurance 1961–64; Chief Opposition Spokesman on Educ. 1969–70; Sec. of State for Educ. and Science 1970–74; Leader of Conservative Party 1975–90; Leader of H.M. Opposition 1975–79; Prime Minister 1979–90; First Lord of the Treasury and Minister for the Civil Service 1979–90; Pres. No Turning Back Group 1990–; Dir. Tiger Man. 1998–; Vice-Pres. Royal Soc. of St. George 1999–; Hon. Pres. Bruges Group 1991–; Chair. Advisory Bd. Univ. of London's Inst. of U.S. Studies 1994–; Hon. Bencher, Lincoln's Inn 1975; Hon. Master of the Bench of Gray's Inn 1983; Hon. Fellow Royal Inst. of Chem. 1979; Freedom of Royal Borough of Kensington and Chelsea 1979, of London Borough of Barnet 1980, of Falkland Is. 1983, of City of London 1989, of the City of Westminster 1990; Chancellor Univ. of Buckingham 1992–98, William and Mary Coll., Va. 1994–; mem. Worshipful Co. of Glovers 1983–, Int. Advisory Bd. British-American Chamber of Commerce 1993–; Hon. LL.D. (Univ. of Buckingham) 1986, Dr. h.c. (Rand Afrikaans Univ. S.A.) 1991, (Weizmann Inst. of Science) 1992, (Mendeleyev Univ.) 1993, (Brunel) 1996; MacArthur Foundation Fellowship 1992; Presidential Medal of Freedom (U.S.A.) 1991, Order of Good Hope (SA) 1991; Hilal-i-Imitaz 1996; Hon. Citizen of Gorasde 1993; Conservative. *Publications:* In Defence of Freedom 1986, The Downing Street Years 1979–1990 1993, The Path to Power 1995, The Collected Speeches of Margaret Thatcher 1997. *Address:* House of Lords, Westminster, London, SW1A 0PW; P.O. Box 1466, London, SW1X 9HY, England.

THAW, John Edward, C.B.E.; British actor; b. 3 Jan. 1942; s. of John E. Thaw and Dorothy Abblott; m. 1st (divorced); one d.; m. 2nd Sheila Hancock 1973; one d. one step-d.; ed. Ducie Tech. High School, Manchester and Royal Acad. of Dramatic Art; stage appearances include: The Fire Raisers, Royal Court 1961, So What About Love? Criterion Theatre 1969, Random Happenings in the Hebrides, Edin. Festival 1970, Collaborators, Duchess Theatre 1973, Absurd Person Singular (tour) 1976, Sergeant Musgrave's Dance, Nat. Theatre 1982, Pygmalion, Shaftesbury Theatre 1984, All My Sons, Manchester 1988, Absence of War, Nat. Theatre 1993; for RSC: Twelfth Night, The Time of Your Life, Henry VIII 1983. *TV appearances include:* The Sweeney 1974–78, Home to Roost 1985–89, title role in Inspector Morse 1986–93, Stanley and the Women 1991, A Year in Provence 1993, Kavanagh Q.C. 1994–98, Absence of War 1995, Goodnight Mr. Tom 1998, The Waiting Time 1999. *Films include:* The Bofors Gun 1968, The Sweeney 1976, The Sweeney II 1977, The Grass is Singing 1982, Cry Freedom 1987, Charlie 1992. *Address:* c/o John Redway Associates, 5 Denmark Street, London, WC2H 8LP, England.

THÉ, Guy Blaudin de (see de Thé, Guy Blaudin).

THEIS, Adolf; German university president; b. 24 March 1933, Karlsruhe; s. of Ludwig and Maria Theis; m. H. Genzmer; two s.; ed. Univs. of Marburg, Heidelberg, Freiburg and Munich; asst. judge 1960–61; legal adviser in a state ministry 1961–65; Head of Admin. Univ. of Hohenheim 1965–68; Fed. Ministry for Scientific Research, Bonn 1968; mem. Fed. Ministry of Interior's Project Group for Govt. and Admin. Reform for Ministry of Science and Research 1969, Deputy Chair. 1971; Ministerial Adviser, Fed. Chancellery 1970; consultant for planning methods and techniques 1971; Pres. Univ. of Tübingen 1972–95; Bundesverdienstkreuz; Hon. LL.D. (Temple Univ.), (Hanyang) 1987; Hon. Prof. (Heilongjiang) 1987; Hon. D.H.L. (Valparaiso Univ., Ind.) 1988; Hon. Citizen (Tübingen) 1996. *Publications:* articles on political planning and university organization. *Address:* Wilhelmstrasse 5, 72074 Tübingen, Germany. *Telephone:* (07071) 292512.

THEOCHARIS, Reghinos D., PH.D.; Cypriot economist; b. 10 Feb. 1929, Larnaca; s. of Demetrios Theocharis and Florentia Theocharis; m. Madeleine Loumbou 1954; one s. one d.; ed. Graduate School of Economics, Athens, Univ. of Aberdeen, and London School of Economics; Insp. of Commercial Educ., Cyprus 1953–56; at L.S.E. 1956–58; Bank of Greece, Athens 1958–59; Minister of Finance in Cyprus Provisional Govt. 1959–60; Minister of Finance 1960–62; Gov. of Bank of Cyprus 1962–75; Prof. Athens Univ. of Econs. and Business 1975–96; Dir.-Gen. Center of Planning and Econ. Research (KEPE), Athens 1978–81; Hon. Fellow, L.S.E. 1971. *Publications:* On the Stability of the Cournot Solution on the Oligopoly Problem 1960, Early Developments in Mathematical Economics 1983. *Leisure interests:* chess, gardening. *Address:* 2 Raidestou Street, Kessariani, Athens, 16122, Greece. *Telephone:* 7214531.

THEODORAKIS, Mikis; Greek composer; b. 29 July 1925, island of Chios; s. of Georges Michel Theodorakis and Aspasia Poulaki; m. Myrto Altinoglou 1953; one s. one d.; ed. Athens Conservatoire and Paris Conservatoire; joined resistance against German occupation of Greece 1942; arrested and deported during civil war 1947–52; moved to Paris 1953 and studied under Olivier Messiaen; first public concert Sonatina (for pianoforte), Paris 1954; set to bouzouki music the poem Epitaphios by Iannis Ritsos 1958–59 and subsequently wrote numerous other successful songs; Ballet music for Antigone (first performed in London by Dame Margot Fonteyn), Stuttgart Ballet, etc.; returned to Greece 1962; leader Lambrakis youth movement; M.P. 1963; imprisoned for political activities 1967, released April 1970; lived in Paris 1970–74; resgnd. from CP March 1972; M.P. 1981–1986 (resgnd.), 1989–93 (resgnd.), Minister of State 1990–92 (resgnd.); f. Cttee. for Greek-Turkish Friendship 1986; Gold Medal, Moscow Shostakovitch Festival 1957, Copley Prize, U.S.A. 1957, First Prize Athens Popular Song Festival 1961, Sibelius Award, London 1963, Gold Medal for Film Music, London 1970, Socrates Prize, Stockholm 1974, First Literary Prize, Athens 1987; Lenin Int. Peace Prize 1982. *Works include:* Sinfonia (oratorio) 1944, Love and Death (voice, strings) 1945–48, Assi-Gonia (orchestra) 1945–50, Sextet for Flute 1946, Oedipus Tyrannus (strings) 1946, Greek Carnaval (ballet suite) 1947, First Symphony (orchestra) 1948–50, Five Cretan Songs (chorus, orchestra) 1950, Orpheus and Eurydice (ballet) 1952, Barefoot Battalion (film) 1953, Suite No. 1 (four movements, piano and orchestra) 1954, Poèmes d'Eluard (Cycle 1 and Cycle 2) 1955, Suite No. 2 (chorus, orchestra) 1956, Suite No. 3 (five movements, soprano, chorus, orchestra) 1956, Ill Met by Moonlight (film) 1957, Sonatina No. 1 (violin, piano) 1957, Les amants de Teruel (ballet) 1958, Piano Concerto 1958, Sonatina No. 2 (violin, piano) 1958, Antigone (ballet) 1958, Epitaphios (song cycle) 1959, Deserters (song cycle) 1958, Epiphania (song cycle) 1959, Honeymoon (film) 1960, Phoenician Women—Euripides (theatre music) 1960, Axion Esti (pop oratorio) 1960, Electra-Euripides (film), Phaedra (film) 1962, The Hostage (song cycle) 1962, The Ballad of the Dead Brother (musical tragedy) 1962, Zorba the Greek (film), The Ballad of Mathausen (song cycle) 1965, Romiossini (song cycle) 1965, Lusistrata—Aristophanes (theatre music) 1966, Romancero Gitano (Lorca) (song cycle) 1967, Sun and Time (song cycle) 1967, Arcadias Nos. 1-10 (song cycles) 1968–69, Canto General (Pablo Neruda) (pop oratorio) 1972, Z (film), Etat de Siège (film) 1973, Ballads (song cycle) 1975, Symphony No. 2 (orchestra and piano) 1981, Messe Byzantine (Litourgia) 1982, Symphony No. 3 (orchestra, chorus, soprano) 1982, Sadoukeon Passion (cantata for orchestra, chorus, soloists) 1983, Litourgie No. 2 1983, Symphony No. 7 (orchestra, chorus, soloists) 1983, Requiem 1985, Kostas Kariotakis (opera in two acts) 1985, Beatrice (song cycle) 1987, Faces of the Sun (song cycle) 1987, Symphony No. 4 1987, Memory of Stone (song cycle) 1987, Like an Ancient Wind (song cycle) 1987, Canto Olympico (symphony) 1991, Medea (opera) 1990, Electra (opera) 1993. *Publications include:* La Dette, Journals of Resistance 1972, Ballad of the Dead Brother, Culture et dimensions politiques 1973, Star System, Antimanifest, Les chemins de l'Archange (autobiog.), 4 vols. 1986–92. *Address:* Epifanous 1, Akropolis, 117 42 Athens, Greece. *Telephone:* (1) 92 14 863. *Fax:* (1) 92 36 325.

THÉODORE, Jean-François; French public servant; b. 5 Dec. 1946, Paris; s. of Charles Théodore and Aimée Chevallier; m. Claudine Lefèbvre 1976; one s. two d.; ed. Lycées Montaigne and Louis-le-Grand, Faculty of Law, Paris, Institut d'études politiques de Paris; Ecole nationale d'admin. 1971–74; civil servant, Ministry of Econ. and Finance 1974–78, Crédit nat. 1978–80, Head, Bureau des états africains et de la zone franc 1980–82, Head, Bureau des investissements étrangers en France et français à l'étranger 1982–84, Asst. Dir Etablissements de crédit 1984–86, Deputy Dir., Head of Funding and Investment Dept., Treasury 1986–90; Gen. Man. Société des bourses françaises 1990–91, Chair. and C.E.O. 1991–; Pres. Int. Fed. of Stock Exchanges 1993–94; Vice-Pres. Société interprofessionnelle de compensation des valeurs mobilières (Sicovam) 1992, Chair. 1993–; Pres. Matif SA 1998–; Chevalier, Ordre nat. du Mérite, Légion d'honneur. *Address:* Matif, 115 rue Réaumur, Paris; Société des bourses françaises, 39 rue Cambon, 75001 Paris, France.

THEROUX, Paul Edward, B.A., F.R.S.L., F.R.G.S.; writer; b. 10 April 1941, Medford, Mass.; s. of Albert Eugene Theroux and Anne Dittami Theroux; m. 1st Anne Castle 1967 (divorced 1993), two s.; m. 2nd Sheila Donnelly 1995; ed. Univ. of Massachusetts, U.S.A.; lecturer, Univ. of Urbino, Italy 1963, Soche Hill Coll., Malawi 1963–65, Makerere Univ., Kampala, Uganda 1965–68, Univ. of Singapore 1968–71; Writer-in-Residence, Univ. of Va. 1972; Hon. D.Litt. (Tufts Univ., Trinity Univ.) 1983, (Univ. of Mass.) 1988. *Publications:* (*novels*) Waldo 1967, Fong and the Indians 1968, Girls at Play 1969, Murder in Mount Holly 1969, Jungle Lovers 1971, Sinning with Annie 1972, Saint Jack 1973 (filmed 1979), The Black House 1974, The Family Arsenal 1976, The Consul's File 1977, Picture Palace 1978 (Whitbread Award 1978), A Christmas Card 1978, London Snow 1980, World's End 1980, The Mosquito Coast 1981 (James Tait Black Award), The London Embassy 1982, Doctor Slaughter 1984 (filmed as Half Moon Street 1987), O-Zone 1986, My Secret History 1989, Chicago Loop 1990, Dr. DeMarr 1990, Millroy the Magician 1993, My Other Life 1996, Collected Short Novels 1998; (*play*) The White Man's Burden 1987; (*criticism*) V.S. Naipaul 1972; (*travel*) The Great Railway Bazaar 1975, The Old Patagonian Express 1979, The Kingdom by the Sea 1983, Sailing through China 1983, Riding the Iron Rooster: By Train Through China (Thomas Cook Prize for Best Literary Travel Book 1989) 1988, Travelling the World 1990, The Happy Isles of Oceania: Paddling the Pacific 1992, The Pillars of Hercules 1995, Collected Stories 1997, Kowloon Tong 1997, Sir Vidia's Shadow 1998. (*screenplay*) Saint Jack 1979; reviews in New York Times, etc. *Leisure interest:* rowing. *Address:* c/o Hamish Hamilton Ltd., 27 Wrights Lane, London, W8 5TZ, England.

THESIGER, Sir Wilfred, K.B.E., D.S.O., M.A., F.R.S.L.; British traveller; b. 3 June 1910, Addis Ababa, Ethiopia; s. of the Hon. Wilfred Thesiger, D.S.O., and Kathleen Mary Vigors, C.B.E.; ed. Eton Coll. and Magdalen Coll., Oxford; explored Danakil country of Abyssinia 1933–34; Sudan Political Service, Darfur and Upper Nile Provinces 1935–39; served in Ethiopia, Syria and Western Desert with Sudan Defence Force and Special Air Service, Second World War; explored the Empty Quarter of Arabia 1945–50; lived with the

Madan in the Marshes of Southern Iraq 1950–58; Hon. Fellow, British Acad. 1982, Magdalen Coll., Oxford 1982; Hon. D.Litt. (Leicester) 1967, Bath) 1992; awarded Back Grant, Royal Geographical Soc. 1936, Founder's Medal 1948, Lawrence of Arabia Medal, Royal Central Asian Soc. 1955, David Livingstone Medal, Royal Scottish Geographical Soc. 1961, W. H. Heinemann Bequest, Royal Soc. of Literature 1964, Burton Medal, Royal Asiatic Soc. 1966. *Publications:* Arabian Sands 1959, The Marsh Arabs 1964, Desert, Marsh and Mountain: The World of a Nomad 1979, The Life of My Choice (autobiog.) 1987, Visions of a Nomad (photographs) 1987, My Kenya Days 1994, The Danakil Diary 1996, Travels in Asia 1998, Among the Mountains 1998. *Leisure interests:* photography, travel in remote places. *Address:* Woodcote Grove House, Meadow Hill, Coulsdon, Surrey, CR5 2XL, England. *Telephone:* 0181-668 5309.

THEWLIS, David; British actor; b. 20 March 1963; s. of Alec Raymond Wheeler and Maureen Wheeler (née Thewlis); m. Sara Jocelyn Sugarman 1992; ed. Highfield High School, Blackpool, St. Anne's Coll. of Further Educ., Guildhall School of Music and Drama, London. *Theatre includes:* Buddy Holly at the Regal, Ice Cream, Lady and the Clarinet (winner Edin. Fringe First), The Sea. *Television includes:* Dandelion Dead, Valentine Park, Road, The Singing Detective, Bit of a Do, Skulduggery, Journey to Knock (Best Actor, Rheims Film Festival 1992), Filipina Dreamgirls, Frank Stubbs Promotes, Prime Suspect 3. *Films include:* Short and Curlies, Vroom, Resurrected, Afraid of the Dark, Life is Sweet, Damage, The Trial, Naked (Best Actor, Cannes Film Festival 1993), Black Beauty, Divorcing Jack. *Leisure interest:* painting. *Address:* c/o ICM Ltd., Oxford House, 76 Oxford Street, London, W1N 0AX, England. *Telephone:* 0171-636 6565. *Fax:* 0171-323 0101.

THEWS, Gerhard, DR. RER. NAT., DR. MED.; German professor of physiology; b. 22 July 1926, Königsberg; m. Dr. Gisela Bahling 1958; three s. one d.; ed. Univ. of Kiel; Research Fellow Univ. of Kiel 1957–61, Asst. Prof. 1961–62, Assoc. Prof. 1962–63, Prof. 1964–, Dir. Physiological Inst. 1964–, Dean Faculty Medicine 1968–69; Vice-Pres. Acad. Science and Literature 1977–85, Pres. 1985–93; Pres. German Physiological Soc. 1968–69; mem. German Scientific Council 1970–72; Pres. Int. Soc. for Oxygen Transport 1973–75; Wolfgang Heubner Prize (Berlin) 1961, Feldberg Prize (London) 1964, Carl Diem Prize 1964, Adolf Fick Prize (Würzburg) 1969, Ernst von Bergmann Medal (Germany) 1986. *Publications:* Human Anatomy, Physiology and Pathophysiology 1985, Autonomic Functions in Human Physiology 1985, Human Physiology 1989. *Address:* Weidmannstrasse 29, 55131 Mainz, Germany.

THIAM, Habib, L. EN D.; Senegalese politician; b. 21 Jan. 1933, Dakar; ed. Brevet Ecole Nat. de la France d'Outre-mer; Sec. of State for the Devt. Plan 1963; Minister for the Plan and Devt. 1964–67, of Rural Econ. 1968–73; mem. Nat. Ass. 1973–, Pres. 1983–84; Prime Minister 1981–83, 1991–96; Press Sec. Union progressiste sénégalaise (now Parti socialiste sénégalais—PS); Pres. Parl. Group PS 1978; Chair. Bd. Banque Int. pour le Commerce et l'Industrie du Sénégal; Dir. Ethiopique 1976–, L'Unité Africaine 1976–.

THIANDOUM, H.E. Cardinal Hyacinthe; Senegalese ecclesiastic; b. 2 Feb. 1921, Poponguine; s. of François Fari Thiandoum and Anne Ndiémé Sène; ed. Univ. de la Propagande and Gregorian Univ., Rome; ordained Priest at Dakar Cathedral April 1949; Dir. of Works at Dakar 1955–60; Vicar-Gen. at Dakar 1960–62; Archbishop of Dakar 1962–, cr. Cardinal 1976; fmrly. mem. Congregation for the Doctrine of the Faith; fmr. Pres. Episcopal Conf. of Senegal and Mauritania; fmrly. mem. Perm. Cttee. Episcopal Conf. of Francophone West Africa (CERAO); fmrly. Pres. Symposium of Episcopal Confs. of Africa and Madagascar (SECAM); mem. Pontifical Comm. for Social Communications, Congregation for Consecrated Life Inst. and Apostolic Life Socs., Sacred Congregation for the Clergy, Congregation for People Evangelization; fmr. mem. Pontifical Council for Culture, Council of Secr. Gen. of the Rome Synod of Bishops (Deputy Pres. 1977); Gen. Reporter to the Synod 1987, to the African Synod 1994; mem. Post-Synodal Council of African Synod; mem. Episcopal Comm. for Mass Media, CERAO; Hon. Chaplain with Grand Cross, Order of Malta 1972; Grand Cross, Order of Lion 1976; Commdr. Légion d'honneur 1980. *Address:* Archevêché, Avenue Jean XXIII, B.P. 1908, Dakar, Senegal. *Telephone:* 23-69-18.

THIBAUDET, Jean-Yves; French pianist; b. 7 Sept. 1961, Lyon; ed. Paris Conservatoire; now based in New York and Paris; appears with maj. orchestras in U.S.A. and with Royal Concertgebouw, London Philharmonic, Royal Philharmonic, Orchestre Nat. de France etc.; regular visitor to maj. U.S. and European music festivals; in recital has appeared frequently with mezzo soprano Brigitte Fassbaender and cellist Truls Mørk; debut, BBC Promenade Concerts 1992; engaged in recording complete Rachmaninov Piano Concertos with Cleveland Orchestra under Vladimir Ashkenazy; records exclusively for Decca. *Address:* c/o IMG Artists, Media House, 3 Burlington Lane, London, W4 2TH, England. *Telephone:* 0181-233 5800. *Fax:* 0181-233 5801.

THIEBAUD, Wayne; American artist; b. 15 Nov. 1920, Mesa, Ariz.; m. 1st Patricia Patterson 1945 (divorced 1959); two d.; m. 2nd Betty Jean Carr 1959; one s. one step s.; ed. Frank Wiggins Trade School, Long Beach Jr. Coll., San. José State Coll. (now San José State Univ.), Calif. State Coll. (now Calif. State Univ.); worked as commercial artist and freelance cartoonist from 1938; served U.S.A.A.F. 1942–45; started career as painter 1947; Asst. Prof., Dept. of Art, Univ. of Calif. at Davis 1960, Assoc. Prof. 1963–67, Prof. 1967–, Faculty Research Lecturer 1973–; Co-founder Artists Co-operative Gallery (now Artists Contemporary Gallery), Sacramento 1958; numerous one-man exhbns. in U.S.A. since 1950; one-man exhbn. Galleria Schwarz, Milan, Italy 1963; represented U.S.A. at São Paulo Bienal, Brazil 1968; commissioned to do paintings of Wimbledon tennis tournament, England 1968; selected as Nat. Juror for Nat. Endowment for the Arts, Washington, D.C. 1972; commissioned by U.S. Dept. of Interior to paint Yosemite Ridge Line for Bicentennial Exhbn., America 1976; mem. American Acad., Inst. of Arts and Letters, New York City 1985, Nat. Acad. of Design, New York City; Award of Distinction, Nat. Art Schools Asscn. and Special Citation Award, Nat. Asscn. of Schools of Art and Design 1984. *Publication:* Wayne Thiebaud: Private Drawings—The Artist's Sketchbook 1987. *Address:* c/o Department of Art, University of California (Davis), CA 95616, U.S.A.

THIER, Samuel Osiah, M.D.; American physician; b. 23 June 1937, Brooklyn, New York; s. of Sidney Thier and May H. Kanner Thier; m. Paula Dell Finkelstein 1958; three d.; ed. Cornell Univ., State Univ. of New York, Syracuse; Intern, Mass. Gen. Hosp. 1960–61, Asst. Resident 1961–62, 1964–65, Postdoctoral Fellow 1965; Clinical Assoc. Nat. Inst. of Arthritis and Metabolic Diseases 1962–64; Chief Resident in Medicine, Mass. Gen. Hosp. 1966; Instr. to Asst. Prof. Harvard Medical School 1967–69; Assoc. Prof. then Prof. of Medicine, Univ. of Pa. Medical School 1969–74; Prof. and Chair. Dept. of Medicine, Yale Univ. School of Medicine and Chief of Medicine, Yale-New Haven Hosp. 1975–85; Pres. Inst. of Medicine, N.A.S. 1985–91; Prof. Brandeis Univ. 1991–94; Pres. Mass. Gen. Hosp. 1994–97, Partners Healthcare System Inc. 1994–, C.E.O. 1996–; Prof. of Medicine and Health Care Policy Harvard Medical School 1994–. *Publications:* numerous articles and chapters in medical journals and textbooks. *Address:* 99-20 Florence Street, Apartment 4B, Chestnut Hill, MA 02167, U.S.A.

THIESSEN, Gordon, PH.D.; Canadian banker; b. 1938, South Porcupine, Ont.; m. Annette Hillyar 1964; two c.; ed. Univ. of Saskatchewan and London School of Econs. and Political Science; joined Bank of Canada 1963; Visiting Economist, Reserve Bank of Australia 1973–75; Adviser to Gov. Bank of Canada 1979, Deputy Gov. responsible for econ. research and financial analysis 1984, Sr. Deputy Gov. 1987, Chair. Bd. Dirs.; mem. Exec. Cttee. 1987–, Gov. 1994–. *Address:* Bank of Canada, 234 Wellington Street, Ottawa, ON, K1A O99, Canada. *Telephone:* (613) 782-8111. *Fax:* (613) 782-8655.

THIEU, Lt.-Gen. Nguyen Van (see Nguyen Van Thieu).

THIN, U Tun, PH.D.; Myanma economist; ed. Rangoon, Michigan and Harvard Univs.; Chair. Econ. Dept., Univ. of Rangoon; Dir. Cen. Statistics and Econs. Dept., Ministry of Planning, Burma; Alt. Exec. Dir. IMF for Burma, Ceylon, Japan and Thailand; Asst. Dir. IMF Asian Dept. 1959–66, Deputy Dir. 1966–72, Dir. 1972–86; Special Adviser to the Rector, UN Univ. 1986–; Dir. Tun Foundation Bank, Rangoon; Econ. Adviser to Govt. of Burma. *Publication:* Theory of Markets 1970. *Address:* 2212 South Lynn Street, Arlington, VA 22202, U.S.A. *Telephone:* (703) 892-5348.

THINLEY, Lyonpo Jigme Yoser; Bhutanese politician; Chair. Council of Ministers and Foreign Minister of Bhutan July 1998–. *Address:* Council of Ministers, Thinphu, Bhutan.

THIRRING, Walter E., PH.D.; Austrian professor of physics; b. 29 April 1927, Vienna; s. of Hans Thirring and Antonia Thirring; m. Helga Georgiades 1952; two s.; ed. Univ. of Vienna and Dublin Inst. of Advanced Studies; Fellow, Univ. of Glasgow 1950; Asst. Max-Planck-Inst. Göttingen 1950–51; UNESCO Fellow, Fed. Inst. of Tech. Zürich 1951–52; Asst. Univ. of Berne 1952–53; mem. Inst. of Advanced Study, Princeton 1953–54; Docent, Univ. of Berne 1954–56, Prof. 1958; Prof. Univ. of Vienna 1959; mem. CERN Directorate 1968–71; Visiting Prof. M.I.T. 1956–57, Univ. of Washington, Seattle 1957–58; mem. Austrian Acad., Pontifical Acad. of Sciences, Akad. der Naturforscher Leopoldina (G.D.R.); Hon. mem. Hungarian Physical Eötvös Soc., Hungarian Acad. of Sciences; Dr. h.c. (Comenius Univ., Bratislava). *Publications:* A Course in Mathematical Physics, 4 vols.; more than 120 scientific papers. *Leisure interest:* music. *Address:* Nussberggasse 7a/5/7, 1190 Vienna, Austria. *Telephone:* 31 88 250.

THIRSK, (Irene) Joan, C.B.E., PH.D., F.B.A., F.R.HIST.S.; British historian and academic; b. 19 June 1922, London; d. of William Henry Watkins and Daisy Watkins (née Frayer); m. James Wood Thirsk 1945; one s. one d.; ed. Camden School for Girls, London and Westfield Coll., Univ. of London; war service in Auxiliary Territorial Service (ATS) 1942–45; Asst. Lecturer in Sociology, L.S.E. 1950–51; Sr. Research Fellow in Agrarian History, Dept. of English Local History, Leicester Univ. 1951–65; Reader in Econ. History, Oxford Univ. 1965–83, Professorial Fellow of St. Hilda's Coll. 1965–83, Hon. Fellow 1983–; mem. Royal Comm. on Historical Monuments of England 1977–86, Historical Manuscripts 1989–96; Pres. British Agricultural Hist. Soc. 1983–86, 1995–98, British Asscn. for Local History 1986–92, Kent History Fed. 1990–; Gen. Ed. Agrarian History of England and Wales 1975–; Mellon Sr. Fellow, Nat. Humanities Center, N.C., U.S.A. 1986–87; Foreign mem. American Philosophical Soc.; Corresp. mem. Colonial Soc. of Massachusetts; Hon. Fellow Queen Mary and Westfield Coll. London 1997; Hon. D.Litt. (Leicester) 1985, (East Anglia) 1990, (Kent) 1993, (Sussex) 1994; Hon. D. Univ. (Open Univ.) 1991; Hon. D. Agricultural and Environmental Sciences (Wageningen, Netherlands) 1993. *Publications:* Ed. and Contrib., The Agrarian History of England and Wales, IV 1500–1640 1967, V 1640–1750 1985; Seventeenth-Century Economic Documents (with J. P. Cooper) 1972, The Restoration 1976, Economic Policy and Projects: The

Development of a Consumer Society in Early Modern England 1978, The Rural Economy of England: Collected Essays 1984, England's Agricultural Regions and Agrarian History 1500–1750 1987, Alternative Agriculture: a History from the Black Death to the Present Day 1997. *Leisure interests:* gardening, sewing and machine knitting. *Address:* 1 Hadlow Castle, Hadlow, Tonbridge, Kent, TN11 0EG, England.

THOMAS, André Jean, D. EN MED., D. ÈS SC.; French biologist; b. 4 April 1905, Besançon; s. of Albert Thomas and Marie-Louise Sulter; m. Suzanne Anne-Marie Dautremant 1940; one s. two d.; ed. Lycée de Besançon, Faculté de Médecine and Faculté des Sciences, Paris; Prof., Faculté des Sciences, Paris 1943–, Titular Prof. of Cellular Biology 1951–76, Dir. Centre for Cellular Physiology 1955–76, Prof. Emer. 1984–; Deputy Dir. Ecole des Hautes Etudes 1942, Dir. 1946–77; mem. Inst. Pasteur 1929–84, Head of Cellular Biology Science 1951–68; mem. Acad. des Sciences 1972 (Inst. de France), Acad. nat. de Médecine 1960 (Pres. 1988), and many other scientific socs.; Hon. Fellow, Int. Coll. of Surgeons, New York Acad. of Science; Officier, Légion d'honneur, Ordre de Léopold (Belgium); Médaille de la Résistance. *Address:* Université Pierre et Marie Curie, Centre de Physiologie cellulaire, 7 quai Saint-Bernard, 75005 Paris (Office); 8 rue Pierre et Marie Curie, 75005 Paris, France (Home). *Telephone:* 44-27-34-20, Ext. 34-20 (Office); 43-26-59-04 (Home).

THOMAS, Betty; American director and actress; b. 27 July 1949, St. Louis, Mo.; ed. Ohio Univ., Chicago Art Inst., Roosevelt Univ.; fmr. mem. Second City improvisation group, Chicago; performed at the Comedy Store, L.A. *Films:* (Dir.) Only You, The Brady Bunch Movie 1995, Private Parts, Dr. Dolittle 1998; (actress) Tunnelvision, Chesty Anderson—U.S. Navy, Loose Shoes, Used Cars, Homework, Troop Beverly Hills, Jackson County Jail. *TV:* (Dir.) (series) Doogie Howser M.D., Dream On (Emmy Award 1993), Hooperman, Mancusco FBI, Arresting Behavior, Couples; (film) My Breast; (documentary drama) The Late Shift (Dirs' Guild of America Award 1997); (actress) (series) Hill Street Blues (Emmy Award 1985); (films) Outside Chance, Nashville Grab, When Your Lover Leaves, Prison for Children.

THOMAS, Clarence; American judge; b. Pinpoint, Savannah, Ga.; ed. Immaculate Conception Seminary, Conception Junction, Mo., Holy Cross Coll. Worcester and Yale Law School; worked for Mo. Attorney-Gen. for 2½ years; pvt. legal practice 1977–79; legislative asst. U.S. Senate 1979; Asst. Sec. for Civil Rights, Dept. of Educ. Washington, D.C. 1981; Chair. Equal Employment Comm. 1982–90; Judge, U.S. Court of Appeals, D.C. 1990–91; Assoc. Justice, U.S. Supreme Court 1991–. *Address:* United States Supreme Court, 1 First Street, N.E., Washington, DC 20543, U.S.A.

THOMAS, Craig, B.S.; American politician; b. 17 Feb. 1933, Cody, Wyo.; s. of Craig E. Thomas and Marge Lynn; m. Susan Roberts; four s.; ed. Univ. of Wyoming; Exec. Vice-Pres. Wyo. Farm Bureau, Laramie 1960–69; Asst. Legis. Dir. American Farm Bureau, Washington, D.C. 1969–71; Dir. Nat. Resource, American Farm Bureau, Chicago 1971–75; Gen. Man. Wyo. Rural Electrical Assen. 1975–89; mem. Wyo. House of Reps. 1985–89; mem. 101st–103rd U.S. Congresses from Wyo. 1989–94; Senator from Wyoming Jan. 1995–; Republican. *Address:* U.S. Senate, 109 Hart Senate Office Building, Washington, DC 20510, U.S.A.

THOMAS, David; British singer; b. 26 Feb. 1943, Orpington; m. Veronica Joan Dean 1982; three d.; ed. St. Paul's Cathedral Choir School, London, King's School, Canterbury, King's Coll., Cambridge; has performed all over the world in most of the major concert halls with leading conductors, particularly works of the Baroque and Classical period; Chair. Artistic Advisory Cttee.; mem. Bd. Blackheath Concert Halls. *Works include:* more than 50 records, including Handel's Messiah, Athalia, La Resurrectione, Suzanna, Orlando; Bach's B Minor Mass, Cantata "Ich habe genug", St. John Passion; Haydn's Creation; Mozart's Requiem; solo record Aria for Montagnana. *Leisure interest:* woodwork. *Address:* 74 Hyde Vale, Greenwich, London, SE10 8HP, England.

THOMAS, (David) Craig Owen, M.A.; British author; b. 24 Nov. 1942; s. of John Brinley George Thomas and the late Gwendoline Megan Thomas (née Owen); m. Jill Lesley White 1967 (died 1987); ed. Cardiff High School, Univ. Coll. Cardiff; schoolteacher 1966–77; full-time novelist 1977–; mem. Bd. Lichfield Int. Arts Festival; mem. Soc. of Authors. *Publications:* Rat Trap 1976, Firefox 1977, Wolfsbane 1978, Snow Falcon 1979, Sea Leopard 1981, Jade Tiger 1982, Firefox Down 1983, The Bear's Tears 1985, Winter Hawk 1987, All the Grey Cats 1988, The Last Raven 1990, There to Here—Ideas of Political Society 1991, A Hooded Crow 1992, Playing with Cobras 1993, A Wild Justice 1995, A Different War 1997, Slipping into the Shadow 1998; (as David Grant) Moscow 5000 1979, Emerald Decision 1980. *Leisure interests:* history, philosophy, jazz, classical music, gardening, cricket.

THOMAS, Sir Derek Morison David, K.C.M.G., M.A.; British fmr. diplomatist and business consultant; b. 31 Oct. 1929, London; s. of K. P. D. Thomas and Mali Thomas; m. Lineke Van der Mast 1956; one s. one d.; ed. Radley Coll. and Trinity Hall, Cambridge; articled apprentice, Dolphin Industrial Devts. Ltd. 1947; entered H.M. Foreign Service 1953; R.N.V.R. 1953–55; appointments overseas included Moscow, Manila, Sofia, Ottawa, Paris, Washington; Deputy Under-Sec. of State for Europe and Political Dir. FCO 1984–87; Amb. to Italy 1987–89; European Adviser to N.M. Rothschild and Sons Ltd. 1990–, Dir. 1991–; Dir. Rothschild Italia 1990–97, Christow Consultants Ltd. 1990–, Rothschild Europe 1991–97; Dir., Assoc. CDP Nexus 1990–92; Dir. New Court Int. Ltd., Moscow, Consilium Spa, Prague 1994–; mem. Export Guarantees Advisory Council 1991–97; Chair. British Invisibles Lotis Cttee. 1992–96, Council S.O.S. Sahel 1991, Council Royal Inst. of Int. Affairs 1994–97. *Leisure interests:* exploring the past and present, music, theatre, wines, reading when there is time, water. *Address:* Flat 1, 12 Lower Sloane Street, London, SW1W 8BJ, England. *Telephone:* 0171-730 1473. *Fax:* 0171-730 4674.

THOMAS, Deroy C., B.A., LL.B.; American business executive and lawyer; b. 16 Feb. 1926, Utica, N.Y.; ed. Iona Coll. and Fordham Univ.; admitted N.Y. Bar 1952; Asst. Prof. of Law, Fordham Univ. 1953–58; Asst. counsel, Asscn. of Casualty and Surety Cos. New York 1959–64; with firm Watters & Donovan 1964; with Hartford Fire Insurance Co. and subsidiaries, Conn. 1964–, gen. counsel 1966–69, Vice-Pres. 1968–69, Sr. Vice-Pres. 1969–73, Exec. Vice-Pres. 1973–76, Pres. and C.E.O. 1976–83, Chair. and C.E.O. 1979–; Exec. Vice-Pres. ITT Corpn. New York 1983–85, Vice-Chair. 1985–88, Pres. and C.O.O. 1988–; Pres. and C.E.O. ITT Diversified Services Corpn. 1983–. *Address:* ITT Corporation, 1330 Avenue of the Americas, New York, NY 10019; Hartford Life Insurance Co., Hartford Place, Hartford, CT 06115, U.S.A.

THOMAS, Donald Michael, M.A.; British novelist and poet; b. 27 Jan. 1935, Redruth, Cornwall; s. of Harold Redvers Thomas and Amy Thomas (née Moyle); two s. one d.; ed. Redruth Grammar School, Univ. High School, Melbourne, New Coll., Oxford; English teacher, Teignmouth, Devon 1959–63; lecturer, Hereford Coll. of Educ. 1963–78; full-time author 1978–; Gollancz/Pan Fantasy Prize, PEN Fiction Prize, Cheltenham Prize, Los Angeles Times Fiction Prize. *Publications:* Two Voices 1968, Logan Stone 1971, Love and Other Deaths 1975, Honeymoon Voyage 1978, The Flute-Player 1978, Birthstone 1980, The White Hotel 1981, Dreaming in Bronze 1981, Ararat 1983, Selected Poems 1983, Swallow 1984, Sphinx 1986, Summit 1987, Memories and Hallucinations 1988, Lying Together 1989, Flying in to Love 1992, The Puberty Tree (new and selected poems) 1992, Pictures at an Exhibition 1993, Eating Pavlova 1994, Lady with a Laptop 1996, Alexander Solzhenitsyn 1998. *Address:* The Coach House, Rashleigh Vale, Tregolls Road, Truro, Cornwall, TR1 1TJ, England. *Telephone:* (01872) 78885.

THOMAS, Edward Donnall, M.D.; American physician; b. 15 March 1920, Mart, Tex.; s. of Edward E. Thomas and Angie Hill Donnall Thomas; m. Dorothy Martin 1942; two s. one d.; ed. Univ. of Tex., Harvard Univ.; U.S. Army 1948–50; Chief Medical Resident, Sr. Asst. Resident Peter Bent Brigham Hosp. 1951–53; Research Assoc. Cancer Research Foundation Children's Medical Centre, Boston 1953–55; Instructor in Medicine, Harvard Medical School 1953–55; Physician-in-Chief Mary Imogene Bassett Hosp., Cooperstown, N.Y. 1955–63; Assoc. Clinical Prof. of Medicine Coll. of Physicians and Surgeons, Columbia Univ. 1955–63; Prof. of Medicine Univ. of Wash. Medical School, Seattle (Head Div. of Oncology 1963–85), Attending Physician, Univ. of Wash. Hosp., Seattle 1963–90, Prof. Emer. 1990–; mem. Fred Hutchinson Cancer Research Centre, Seattle 1974–, Dir. Medical Oncology 1974–89, Assoc. Dir. Clinical Research Programs 1982–89; mem. Haematology Study Section Nat. Insts. of Health 1965–69; mem. Bd. of Trustees and Medical Science Advisory Cttee. Leukaemia Soc. America, Inc. 1969–73; mem. Clinical Cancer Investigation Review Cttee., Nat. Cancer Inst. 1970–74; mem. numerous editorial bds.; hon. mem. numerous socs.; received McIntyre Award 1975, Levine Award 1979, Kettering Prize 1981, de Villiers Award 1983, Landsteiner Award 1987, Fox Award 1990, Gairdner Foundation Award 1990, Nat. Medal of Science 1990, shared Nobel Prize for Medicine and Physiology 1990 for pioneering bone marrow transplants in leukaemia patients, Kober Medal 1992; numerous guest lectures; Hon. M.D. (Cagliari) 1981, (Verona) 1991, (Parma) 1992, (Barcelona) 1994. *Publications:* numerous articles. *Address:* Fred Hutchinson Cancer Center, 1100 Fairview Avenue North, D5-100, P.O. Box 19024, Seattle, WA 98109, U.S.A.

THOMAS, Gareth, PH.D.; American professor of science; b. 9 Aug. 1932, Maesteg, Wales; s. of David Basset Thomas and Edith May Gregory; m.; one s.; ed. Univ. of Wales, Cambridge Univ.; with Univ. of Calif., Berkeley 1960–, Prof. 1967–; Assoc. Dean, Graduate Div. 1968–69, Asst. to Chancellor 1969–72, Acting Vice-Chancellor, Acad. Affairs 1971–72, Chair. Faculty of Coll. of Eng. 1977–78, Sr. Faculty Scientist, Materials and Molecular Research Div., Scientific Dir., Nat. Center for Electron Microscopy, Prof. Dept. of Materials and Mineral Eng. 1982–93; mem. N.A.S., Nat. Acad. of Eng. and numerous cttees.; Hon. Sc.D. (Cambridge) 1969 and numerous other awards. *Publications:* several books and 600 research papers. *Leisure interests:* squash, skiing, cricket. *Address:* Department of Materials Science and Mineral Engineering, University of California, 561 Evans Hall, Berkeley, CA 94720, U.S.A. *Telephone:* (510) 486 5696. *Fax:* (510) 643 0965.

THOMAS, Iwan, B.SC.; British athlete; b. 5 Jan. 1974, Godmanchester, Hunts.; ed. Stamford School, Brunel Univ.; fourth-ranked BMX rider, Europe 1988; fifth Olympic Games 400m. 1996, Silver Medal 4 x 400m. relay; Gold Medal Amateur Athletics Asscn. Championships 400m. 1997 (British record, 44.36 seconds), 1998; Silver Medal World Championships 4 x 400m. relay 1997; Gold Medal European Championships 400m. 1998; Gold Medal World Cup 400m. 1998; Gold Medal Commonwealth Games 400m. 1998; British Athletics Writers Male Athlete of the Year 1998.

THOMAS, Jean Olwen, C.B.E., SCD., F.R.S., C.CHEM.; British professor of macromolecular biochemistry; b. 1 Oct. 1942; d. of John Robert Thomas and Lorna Prunella (née Harris) Thomas; ed. Llwyn-y-Bryn High School for

Girls, Swansea, Univ. Coll., Swansea, Univ. of Wales; demonstrator in Biochem., Univ. of Cambridge 1969–73, lecturer 1973–87, reader in the Biochem. of Macromolecules 1987–91, Prof. of Macromolecular Biochemistry, Univ. of Cambridge 1991–, Chair. Cambridge Centre for Molecular Recognition 1993–; Coll. lecturer 1969–91; tutor, New Hall, Cambridge 1970–76, Vice-Pres. 1983–87; mem. European Molecular Biology Org.; Royal Soc. Council, SERC, Academia Europaea, Council and Scientific Advisory Cttee. Imperial Cancer Research Fund 1994–, Scientific Advisory Cttee. Lister Inst. 1994–; Trustee British Museum 1994–; Fellow, New Hall, Cambridge 1969–; mem. Royal Soc. of Chemistry; Beit Memorial Fellow; Hon. Fellow, U.C.W., Swansea 1987, Cardiff Univ. 1998; Hon. D.Sc. (Wales) 1992. *Awards include:* Ayling Prize 1964, Hinkel Research Prize 1967, K. M. Stott Research Prize, Newnham Coll., Cambridge 1976. *Publications:* Companion to Biochemistry: Selected Topics for Further Study Vol. 1 1974, Vol. 2 1979 (jt. ed. and contrib.), numerous papers in scientific journals. *Leisure interests:* reading, music, walking. *Address:* Department of Biochemistry, Tennis Court Road, Cambridge, CB2 1QW (Office); 26 Eachard Road, Cambridge, CB3 0HY, England (Home). *Telephone:* (01223) 333670 (Office); (01223) 62620 (Home).

THOMAS, Jeremy; British film producer; b. 26 July 1949, London; s. of Ralph and Joy Thomas; m. 1st Claudia Frolich 1977 (divorced 1981), one d.; m. 2nd Vivien Coughman 1982, two s.; began work in film-processing lab., later worked as asst. and ed. in cutting room; worked with dir. Philippe Mora, editing Brother Can You Spare a Dime; went with Mora to Australia where he produced first film Man Dog Morgan 1974; returned to U.K. 1976; Chair. B.F.I. 1993–97; set up own film distribution co. Recorded Releasing 1985; founded Recorded Cinemas; Grand Prix de Jury, Cannes Film Festival for The Shout, Crash; Vittorio de Sica Prize 1986, Special Award, Evening Standard Film Awards 1991, BAFTA Award 1991. *Films:* Mad Dog Morgan 1976, The Shout 1977, The Great Rock'n'Roll Swindle 1978, Bad Timing 1979, Eureka 1982, Merry Christmas Mr Lawrence 1982, The Hit 1983, Insignificance 1985, The Last Emperor 1987 (winner of 9 Acad. Awards), Everybody Wins, The Sheltering Sky, The Naked Lunch 1991, Let Him Have It 1991, Little Buddha 1992, Stealing Beauty 1995, Blood and Wine 1995, Victory 1995, The Ogre (co-production) 1996, The Brave 1996, Crash 1996, All The Little Animals (dir.) 1997. *Address:* Recorded Picture Company Ltd., 24 Hanway Street, London, W1P 9DD, England. *Telephone:* 0171-636 2251. *Fax:* 0171-636 2261.

THOMAS, John David Ronald, D.SC., F.R.S.C.; British professor of chemistry; b. 2 Jan. 1926, Gwynfe, Wales; s. of John Thomas and Betty (née Watkins); m. Gwyneth Thomas 1950; three d.; ed. Llandovery Grammar School, Univ. Coll. Cardiff, Univ. of Wales; served R.A.M.C. (India) 1944–47; analytical chemist Spillers Ltd., Cardiff 1950–51, Glamorgan County Council 1951–53; Asst. Lecturer, Cardiff Coll. of Tech. 1953–56; Lecturer, S. East Essex Tech. Coll. 1956–58; Sr. Lecturer, Newport and Monmouthshire Coll. of Tech. 1958–61; Sr. Lecturer and Reader, UWIST and Univ. of Wales, Cardiff 1961–90; Prof., Univ. of Wales, Cardiff 1990–93, Prof. Emer. 1994–; Hon. Ed. Newsletter, Analytical Div., Royal Soc. of Chem. 1995–; Hon. Prof. Univ. 'Politehnica', Bucharest, Romania 1996–; Hon. Course Adviser Hong Kong Baptist Univ. 1991–; mem. Court Univ. of Wales 1989–, Council 1997–; mem. Council Univ. of Wales Coll. of Medicine 1993–; Foreign Expert Hunan, North West (Xian) and Shanghai Teachers Univs. 1983, 1985; Visiting Prof. Japan Soc. for the Promotion of Science 1985; Royal Soc. of Chem. Schools lecturer in Analytical Chem. 1986; Distinguished Visiting Fellow La Trobe Univ., Australia 1989; mem. Govt. High-Level Mission on Analytical Instrumentation to Japan 1991; Pres. Analytical Div. Royal Soc. of Chem. 1990–92, mem. Council 1977–80, 1990–; Hon. mem. Romanian Soc. of Analytical Chem. 1994–; mem. Council, Baptist Union of Wales 1994–97; Royal Soc. of Chem. Medal and Award 1981, J. Heyrovsky Centenary Medal of the Czechoslovak Acad. of Sciences 1990. *Publications:* Ed: Selective Electrode Reviews, Vols. 1–14 1979–92; Co-author: Calculations in Advanced Physical Chemistry 1962, Noble Gases and Their Compounds 1964, Selective Ion-Sensitive Electrodes 1971, Dipole Moments in Inorganic Chemistry 1971, Practical Electrophoresis 1976, Chromatographic Separations and Extraction with Foamed Plastics and Rubbers 1982; over 300 articles in scientific journals. *Leisure interests:* travel, reading (current affairs and history) and carpentry. *Address:* 4 Orchard Court, Gresford, Wrexham, LL12 8EB, Wales. *Telephone:* (01978) 856771. *Fax:* (01978) 856771.

THOMAS, (John) Harvey Noake, C.B.E.; British public relations consultant; b. 10 April 1939, London; s. of the late John Humphrey Kenneth Thomas and of Olga Rosina Thomas; m. Marlies Kram 1978; two d.; ed. Westminster School, London, Northwestern Coll., Minn., U.S.A., Univ. of Minnesota, Univ. of Hawaii, Honolulu; articled in law 1957–60; mem. staff Billy Graham Evangelistic Asscn. 1960–75, N. of England Crusade 1960–61, Direct Mail, Minneapolis 1961–63, Press Relations, Southern Calif. Crusade 1963, KAIM Radio, Honolulu 1963–64, Billy Graham London Crusades 1965–67, Press Office, World Congress on Evangelism, Berlin 1966, Co-ordination Australia and N.Z. Crusades 1967–69, Dir. Euro 70 Crusades 1969–70, Dir. European Congress on Evangelism, Amsterdam 1970–71, research in 80 countries for 1974 Int. Congress on World Evangelisation Lausanne 1971–72, Nat. Promotion SPRE-E 73, London 1973, Dir. Billy Graham LAUSTADE Rally, Lausanne 1974, Gen. Sec. Eurofest 75 and Billy Graham Belgian Crusade 1974–75; Public Relations and Project Consultant 1976–; European Co-ordinator Berlin 1981, Co-ordinator Int. Exposition for Tech. Transfer 1984; Public Relations, Luis Palau Mission to London 1984; Dir. of Presentation, Conservative Party 1978; Field Dir. Prime Minister's Election Tour 1987; mem. Bd. London Cremation Co. PLC; mem. Asscn. of Conf. Execs., Inst. of Dirs.; Fellow Inst. of Public Relations; Fellow Inst. of Journalists. *Publications:* In the Face of Fear 1985, Making an Impact 1989, If they haven't heard it—you haven't said it 1995. *Leisure interests:* travel, broadcasting, public speaking, journalism, Europe. *Address:* 23 The Service Road, Potters Bar, Herts., EN6 1QA, England. *Telephone:* (01707) 649910. *Fax:* (01707) 662653.

THOMAS, Sir John Meurig, Kt., M.A., D.SC., LL.D., F.R.S.; British scientist; b. 15 Dec. 1932, Llanelli, Wales; s. of David J. Thomas and Edyth Thomas; m. Margaret Edwards 1959; two d.; ed. Gwendraeth Grammar School, Univ. Coll., Swansea, Queen Mary Coll., London; Scientific Officer, UKAEA 1957–58; Asst. Lecturer, Lecturer, Sr. Lecturer then Reader, Dept. of Chem., Univ. Coll. of N. Wales, Bangor 1958–69; Prof. and Head Dept. of Chem., Univ. Coll. of Wales, Aberystwyth 1969–78; Head of Dept. of Physical Chem., Cambridge Univ., Professorial Fellow of King's Coll. 1978–86, Master of Peterhouse 1993–; Dir. Royal Inst. of G.B. 1986–91, Resident Prof. 1986–88, Fullerian Prof. of Chem. 1988–94, Prof. of Chem. 1994–; Deputy Pro-Chancellor, Univ. of Wales 1991–94; Dir. Davy Faraday Labs. 1986–91; Chair. Chem. Research Applied to World Needs, IUPAC 1987–95; Pres. Chem. Section, B.A.A.S. 1988–89; Hon. Visiting Prof. of Physical Chem., Queen Mary Coll., London 1986–, of Chem., Imperial Coll., London 1986–91, Miller Prof., Univ. of Calif., Berkeley 1998; Linus Pauling Lectureship, Calif. Inst. of Tech. 1999; Trustee British Museum (Natural History) 1986–91, Science Museum 1989–95; Commr., 1851 Royal Exhbn. 1995– (Chair. Scientific Research Cttee. 1996–); Zetelman Fellow, Yale Univ. 1997; Hon. Professorial Fellow Academia Sinica (Shanghai), Imperial Coll. London, Queen Mary Coll. London; Hon. Fellow Indian Acad. (Bangalore), Indian Acad. (Delhi), UMIST, Univ. Coll. Swansea, American Acad. of Arts and Science, American Philosophical Soc., Venezuelan Acad. of Sciences, Russian Acad. of Sciences; Hon. Foreign Fellow Hungarian and Polish Acad. of Sciences 1998; mem. Academia Europaea 1989; Rutherford Memorial Lecturer of Royal Soc. in New Zealand 1997; Hon. Bencher, Gray's Inn 1986; Hon. D.Sc. (Heriot-Watt Univ.) 1989, (Birmingham) 1991, (Claude Bernard Univ., Lyon) 1994, (Complutense Univ., Madrid) 1994, (Western Univ., Ont.) 1995, (Eindhoven Univ., Netherlands, Hull Univ.) 1996, (Aberdeen, Surrey) 1997; numerous awards including Faraday and Longstaff Medals, Royal Soc. of Chem. 1990, Messel Gold Medal, Soc. of Chemical Industry 1992, Davy Medal, Royal Soc. 1994, Willard Gibbs Gold Medal (A.C.S.) 1995, Hon. Medal Polish Acad. of Sciences, Warsaw 1996, Award for Creative Research in Catalysis, American Chemical Soc. 1999. *Publications:* Principles of Heterogeneous Catalysis 1967, Characterization of Catalysts 1980, Heterogeneous Catalysis: Principles and Practice 1997, Michael Faraday and the Royal Institution: the genius of man and place 1991, Perspectives in Catalysis (with K. I. Zamaraev) 1992, Topics in Catalysis 1994; Pan Edrychwyf ar y Nefoedd (Welsh Radio Lecture) 1978; Founding Co-Ed.-in-Chief Catalysis Letters 1988–; over 850 articles on catalysis solid-state and surface science. *Leisure interests:* walking, Welsh literature, ancient civilizations, birdwatching, popularization of science. *Address:* Master's Lodge, Peterhouse, Cambridge, CB2 1RD; The Royal Institution, 21 Albemarle Street, London, W1X 4BS, England. *Telephone:* (01223) 338202 (Cambridge); 0171-409 2992 (London). *Fax:* (01223) 337578 (Cambridge); 0171-495 7395 (London).

THOMAS, Sir Keith Vivian, Kt., M.A., F.B.A.; British historian; b. 2 Jan. 1933, Wick, Glamorgan, Wales; s. of Vivian Thomas and Hilda Thomas; m. Valerie June Little 1961; one s. one d.; ed. Barry County Grammar School and Balliol Coll. Oxford (Brackenbury Scholar); nat. service in Royal Welch Fusiliers 1950–52; Fellow of All Souls Coll. Oxford 1955–57; Fellow of St. John's Coll. Oxford 1957–86, Tutor 1957–85; Reader in Modern History, Univ. of Oxford 1978–85, Prof. 1986, Pres. Corpus Christi Coll. 1986–, Pro-Vice-Chancellor, Univ. of Oxford 1988–; Del., Oxford Univ. Press 1980–; G. M. Trevelyan Lecturer, Univ. of Cambridge 1979; mem. Econ. and Social Research Council 1985–90, Reviewing Cttee. on Export of Works of Art 1990–92, Royal Comm. on Historical Manuscripts 1992–; Trustee, Nat. Gallery 1991–98; Pres. British Acad. 1993–97; Chair. British Library Advisory Cttee. for Arts, Humanities and Social Sciences 1997–; Hon. Fellow Balliol Coll., Oxford 1984, St. John's Coll., Oxford 1986; Foreign hon. mem. American Acad. of Arts and Sciences 1983; mem. Academia Europaea 1993; Hon. D.Litt. (Kent) 1983, (Wales) 1987, (Hull) 1995, (Leicester) 1996, (Sussex) 1996, (Warwick) 1998; Hon. Litt.D. (Sheffield) 1992, (Cambridge) 1995; Hon. LL.D. (Williams) 1988, (Oglethorpe, Atlanta, Ga.) 1996; Wolfson Literary Award for History 1971; Cavaliere Ufficiale, Ordine al Merito della Repubblica Italiana 1991. *Publications:* Religion and the Decline of Magic 1971, Puritans and Revolutionaries (Ed., with Donald Pennington) 1978, Man and the Natural World 1983, The Oxford Book of Work (Ed.) 1999. *Leisure interest:* visiting second-hand bookshops. *Address:* Corpus Christi College, Oxford, OX1 4JF (Office); The President's Lodgings, 3 Merton Street, Oxford, OX1 4JE, England (Home). *Telephone:* (01865) 276739 (Office). *Fax:* (01865) 276769.

THOMAS, René François, L. EN D.; French administrator; b. 13 Jan. 1929, Brest; s. of François Thomas and Jeanne Milbéo; m. 1st Nicole Larrousse 1956 (deceased), one s. one d.; m. 2nd Laurence Carvallo 1994; ed. Voltaire High School and Univ. of Paris; Inspecteur Général des finances 1955; del. in Morocco for Moroccan Ministry of Finance 1959; mem. Comm. of Enquiry into public cos'. accounting 1960; Sec.-Gen. Banque Nat. de Paris 1961–62, Deputy Dir. 1962–65, Dir. 1965–72, Cen. Dir. 1972–79, Deputy Dir.-Gen. 1979–82, Chair. 1982–93, Hon. Chair. 1993–; Vice-Pres. French Asscn. of Banks 1982–86; Dir. BMCI, Casablanca, UBCI, Tunis, BNP UK Holdings, London, BNP España, Madrid, BNP Essilor, Usinor-Sacilor, Pathé, Compagnie Générale des Eaux, Havas, Compagnie d'Investissements de Paris, BNPI, "Censeur" Compagnie Bancaire, Chargeurs Int., Paris; Vice-Chair. Advisory Bd. BANEXI; Commdr. Légion d'honneur, Commdr. Ordre nat. du Mérite. *Address:* BNP, 16 boulevard des Italiens, 75450 Paris Cedex 09 (Office); 59 boulevard d'Inkermann, 92200 Neuilly-sur-Seine, France.

THOMAS, Richard Lee, M.B.A.; American banker (retd.); b. 11 Jan. 1931, Marion, Ohio; s. of Marvin C. and Irene (Harruff) Thomas; m. Helen Moore 1953; two s. one d.; ed. Kenyon Coll., Univ. of Copenhagen, Denmark, Harvard Business School; served army 1954–56; joined First Nat. Bank of Chicago 1958, Vice-Pres. 1963, Sr. Vice-Pres. 1969, Exec. Vice-Pres. 1972, Dir. 1973, Vice-Chair. Bd. 1973, Pres. 1975; Sr. Vice-Pres., Gen. Man. First Chicago Corpn. 1969–72, Exec. Vice-Pres. 1972–73, Vice-Chair. 1973–74, Pres. 1974–94, Chair. and C.E.O. 1992–94; Chair., C.E.O. First Chicago NBD Corpn. 1995–96; Dir. CNA Financial Corpn. 1970, Sara Lee Corpn. 1976, Sabre Group Holdings Inc., Scotsman Industries Inc., IMC Global Inc. etc.; Trustee Northwestern Univ., Rush-Presbyterian-St. Luke's Medical Center 1971, Kenyon Coll. 1971; Chair. Bd. of Trustees Chicago Symphony Orchestra, Orchestral Asscn. 1976; Hon. LL.D. (Kenyon Coll.). *Leisure interests:* golf, tennis, various outdoor sports, travel, reading. *Address:* First Chicago NBD Corporation, 1 First National Plaza, Chicago, IL 60603, U.S.A.

THOMAS, Robert Kemeys, M.A., D.PHIL., F.R.S.; British chemist; b. 25 Sept. 1941, Harpenden; s. of Rev. Herbert Thomas and Agnes Thomas (née McLaren); m. Pamela H. Woods 1968; one s. two d.; ed. St. John's Coll., Oxford; researcher Univ. of Oxford 1968–78, Fellow Merton Coll. 1975–78, lecturer in Physical Chemistry 1978–, also Fellow and tutor Univ. Coll.; Tilden Lecturer, Royal Soc. of Chemistry. *Publications:* papers in scientific journals. *Leisure interests:* music, flora, fungi, Chinese. *Address:* Physical and Theoretical Chemistry Laboratory, South Parks Road, Oxford, OX1 3QZ, England. *Telephone:* (01865) 275422. *Fax:* (01865) 275410.

THOMAS, Ronald Stuart; Welsh poet and clergyman; b. 29 March 1913, Caerdydd; m. Mildred E. Eldridge (died 1991); one s.; ed. Univ. of Wales and St. Michael's Coll., Llandaff; ordained Deacon 1936, Priest 1937; Curate of Chirk 1936–40, of Hammer 1940–42; Rector of Manafon 1942–54; Vicar of St. Michael's Eglwysfach 1954–68, of St. Hywyn, Aberdaron 1968–78; Rector of Rhiw with Llanfaelrhys 1973–78; Heinemann Award of Royal Soc. of Literature 1956 for Song at the Year's Turning; Sovereign's Gold Medal for Poetry 1964, Cholmondeley Award 1978. *Publications:* Stones of the Field (privately published) 1947, Song at the Year's Turning 1955, Poetry for Supper 1958, Tares 1961, The Bread of Truth 1963, Pieta 1966, Not That He Brought Flowers 1968, H'm 1972, Selected Poems 1946–1968 1974, Laboratories of the Spirit 1975, Frequencies 1978, Between Here and Now 1981, Later Poems 1972–1982 1983, Neb (autobiog.) 1985, Experimenting with an Amen 1986, The Echoes Return Slow 1988, Mass for Hard Times 1992, Collected Poems 1945–1990 1993, No Truth with the Furies 1995, Autobiographies 1997. *Address:* Cefn Du Ganol, Llanfairynghornwy, Holyhead, LL65 4LG, Wales. *Telephone:* (01407) 730943.

THOMAS ELLIS, Alice (see Haycraft, Anna Margaret).

THOMAS OF SWYNNERTON, Baron (Life Peer), cr. 1981, of Notting Hill in Greater London; **Hugh Swynnerton Thomas,** M.A.; British historian; b. 21 Oct. 1931, Windsor; s. of Hugh Whitelegge and Margery (née Swynnerton) Thomas; m. Vanessa Jebb 1962; two s. one d.; ed. Sherborne School, Queens' Coll., Cambridge, and Sorbonne, Paris; Foreign Office 1954–57; Sec. U.K. Del. to UN Disarmament Sub-Cttee. 1955–56; worked for UNA 1959–61; Prof. of History, Univ. of Reading 1966–76; Chair. Graduate School of European Studies 1973–76, Centre for Policy Studies 1979–91; King Juan Carlos I Prof. New York Univ. 1995; Visiting Prof. of History Univ. of Boston 1996, Univ. Prof. 1997–; Corresp. mem. Real Academia de la Historia, Madrid; Fellow, Royal Historical Soc.; Somerset Maugham Prize 1962, Arts Council Nat. Book Award for History 1980, Commdr., Order of Isabel la Católica, Spain 1986, Order of the Aztec Eagle 1995. *Publications include:* The Spanish Civil War 1961, The Suez Affair 1966, Cuba or the Pursuit of Freedom 1971, Goya and the Third of May 1808 1973, John Strachey 1973, An Unfinished History of the World 1979, A Case for the Round Reading Room 1983, Havannah! (novel) 1984, Armed Truce: the beginnings of the Cold War 1945–46 1986, Klara (novel) 1988, Madrid: A Traveller's Companion (Ed.) 1988, Ever Closer Union: Britain's Destiny in Europe 1991, The Conquest of Mexico 1993, The Slave Trade 1997. *Address:* 29 Ladbroke Grove, London, W.11; Well House, Sudbourne, Suffolk, England. *Telephone:* 0171-727 2288 (London).

THOMASEN, Ole; Danish central banker; b. 9 Feb. 1934, Randers; m. Charlotte Ingwersen 1965; Asst. Prin. Ministry of Commerce 1961–63; Asst. Head of Div. Jt. Council of Danish Commercial Banks 1963, Head Dept. 1965–68; Asst. Man. Amagerbanken A/S 1969, Deputy Man. 1972, Man. 1975, Man. Dir. 1978–79; mem. Bd. of Govs. Danmarks Nationalbank 1980–96; mem. Bd. Danish Inter-Bank Transfer Centre 1971–79, Regional Banks 1974–79, Housing Mortgage Fund 1979, Finance for Danish Industry A/S 1980–98, Mortgage Fund for Danish Agric. 1981–, Ship Credit Fund of Denmark (Deputy Chair. 1982–), Danish Air Lines 1986–97, Laurits Andersens Foundation 1990–, Bombebøssen Foundation 1990–, Copenhagen Stock Exchange 1992–93, Danish Securities Centre 1992–93, Bank of Greenland A/S 1996–. *Address:* Danmarks Nationalbank, Havnegade 5, 1093 Copenhagen K, Denmark. *Telephone:* 33-63-63-63. *Fax:* 33-14-94-37.

THOMPSON, Alan Eric, PH.D., F.R.S.A., F.S.A. (SCOT.); British professor of economics; b. 16 Sept. 1924; s. of Eric Thompson and Florence Thompson; m. Mary Heather Long 1960; three s. one d.; ed. Univ. of Edinburgh; Lecturer in Econs., Univ. of Edinburgh 1953–59, 1964–71; Labour M.P. for Dunfermline 1959–64; Econ. Consultant, Scotch Whisky Asscn. 1965–70; Visiting Prof., Graduate School of Business, Stanford Univ., Calif. 1966, 1968; A. J. Balfour Prof. of Econs. of Govt., Heriot-Watt Univ., Edin. 1972–87, Prof. of Econs., School of Business and Financial Studies 1987–88, Prof. Emer. 1988–; mem. Scottish Council for Adult Educ. in H.M. Forces 1973–; mem. Local Govt. Boundaries Comm. for Scotland 1975–82; mem. Joint Mil. Educ. Cttee., Edin. and Heriot-Watt Univs. 1975–; mem. Court, Heriot-Watt Univ. 1980; Chair. Northern Offshore Maritime Resources Study 1974–84; BBC Nat. Gov. for Scotland 1976–79; mem. Royal Fine Art Comm. for Scotland 1975–80, Scottish-Soviet Co-ordinating Cttee. for Trade and Industry 1985–; Parl. Adviser to Scottish TV 1966–76, to Pharmaceutical Gen. Council (Scotland) 1985–; Adviser, Robert Burns Memorial Trust 1995–; Chair. Bd. of Govs., Newbattle Abbey Coll. 1980–82; Hon. Vice-Pres. Asscn. of Nazi War Camp Survivors 1960–; Dir. Scottish AIDS Research Appeal 1991–. *Publications:* The Development of Economic Doctrine (with Alexander Gray) 1980; contributions to learned journals. *Leisure interest:* writing children's stories and plays, croquet, bridge. *Address:* 11 Upper Gray Street, Edinburgh, EH9 1SN (Home); Ardtrostan Cottage, St. Fillian's, Perthshire, Scotland, PH6 2NL. *Telephone:* (0131) 667-2140 (Edin.); (01764) 485275 (Perthshire).

THOMPSON, Caroline Warner, B.A.; American screenwriter, film producer and director; b. 23 April 1956, Washington, D.C.; d. of Thomas Carlton Jr. and Bettie Marshall Thompson (née Warner); m. Alfred Henry Bromell 1982 (divorced 1985); ed. Amherst Coll., Harvard Univ.; fmr. freelance journalist. *Screenplays include:* Edward Scissorhands (also assoc. producer) 1990, The Addams Family 1991, Homeward Bound: The Incredible Journey 1993, The Secret Garden (also assoc. producer) 1993, Tim Burton's The Nightmare Before Christmas 1993, Black Beauty (also dir.) 1994, Buddy (also dir.) 1997. *Publication:* First Born 1993. *Address:* c/o William Morris Agency Inc., 151 El Camino Drive, Beverly Hills, CA 90212, U.S.A.

THOMPSON, Sir Clive Malcolm, Kt.; British business executive; b. 4 April 1943, Bristol; s. of H. L. Thompson and P. D. Thompson (née Stansbury); m. Judith Howard 1968; two s.; ed. Clifton Coll., Bristol and Birmingham Univ.; Marketing Exec. Royal Dutch Shell Group 1964–67; Marketing Exec. and Gen. Man. Boots Co. PLC 1967–70; Gen. Man. Jeyes Group Ltd. 1970–78; Man. Dir. Health and Hygiene Div., Cadbury Schweppes 1978–82; Chief Exec. Rentokil Initial PLC 1982–; fmr. Deputy Pres. CBI, Pres. 1998–; fmr. Dir. (non-exec.) Wellcome PLC, Seeboard PLC, Caradon PLC, BAT Industries PLC; now Dir. (non-exec.) Sainsbury PLC, Farepak PLC; mem. Hampel Cttee. On Corp. Governance. *Leisure interests:* the stock market, current affairs, walking, golf. *Address:* Rentokil Initial PLC, Felcourt, East Grinstead, West Sussex, RH19 2JY, England.

THOMPSON, Daley (Francis Morgan), M.B.E.; British athlete; b. 30 July 1958, Notting Hill, London; m. Tisha Quinlan 1987; one c.; Sussex Schools 200m. title 1974; first competitive decathlon, Welsh Open Championship June 1975; European Junior Decathlon Champion 1977; European Decathlon Silver Medallist 1978, Gold Medallist 1982 and 1986; Commonwealth Decathlon Gold Medallist 1978, 1982 and 1986; Olympic Decathlon Gold Medallist 1980 (Moscow) and 1984 (L.A.); World Decathlon Champion 1983; established new world record for decathlon (at Olympic Games, L.A.), retd. July 1992. *Publications:* Going for Gold 1987, The Greatest 1996.

THOMPSON, Emma; British actress; b. 15 April 1959; d. of Eric Thompson and Phyllida Law; m. Kenneth Branagh (q.v.) 1989; ed. Camden Girls' School and Newnham Coll. Cambridge; appeared with Cambridge Footlights; television appearances in Alfresco, Carrott's Lib, Saturday Night Live, Tutti Frutti (Best Television Actress Award), Fortunes of War (Best Television Actress Award), Thompson 1988; stage appearances include Me and My Girl, Look Back in Anger 1989. *Films:* Henry V 1989, Impromptu 1991, Howards End (Acad. Award, BAFTA Award, Evening Standard Award) 1991, Dead Again 1991, Much Ado About Nothing 1993, Remains of the Day 1993 (Evening Standard Award 1994), In the Name of the Father 1993, My Father the Hero 1994, Junior 1994, Carrington 1995, Sense and Sensibility (also wrote screenplay) (Acad Award for Best Screenplay Adaptation) 1996, The Winter Guest 1996, Primary Colors 1998. *Address:* c/o Hamilton Asper Ltd., Ground Floor, 24 Hanway Street, London, W1P 9DD, England. *Telephone:* 0171-636 1221.

THOMPSON, Francis Michael Longstreth, C.B.E., D.PHIL., F.B.A.; British professor of history; b. 13 Aug. 1925, Purley, Surrey; s. of Francis Longstreth-Thompson; m. Anne Challoner 1951; two s. one d.; ed. Bootham School, York and The Queen's Coll., Oxford; Lecturer in History, Univ. Coll. London 1951–63, Reader in Econ. History 1963–68; Prof. of Modern History, Univ. of London and Head of Dept. of History, Bedford Coll. London 1968–77, Prof. of History and Dir. of Inst. of Historical Research 1977–90, Prof. Emer. 1990–; Ford's Lecturer, Univ. of Oxford 1993–94; Pres. Econ. History Soc. 1983–86, Hon. Vice-Pres. 1986–; British mem. Standing Cttee. for Humanities, European Science Foundation 1983–93; Pres. Royal Historical Soc. 1988–92; Pres. British Agric. History Soc. 1989–92. *Publications:* English Landed Society in the 19th century 1963, Chartered Surveyors: the growth of a profession 1968, Victorian England: the horse-drawn society 1970, Hampstead: building a borough, 1650–1964 1974, Countrysides (in The Nineteenth Century, ed. Asa Briggs) 1970, Britain (in European Landed Elites in the Nineteenth Century, ed. David Spring) 1977, Landowners and Farmers (in The Faces of Europe, ed. Alan Bullock) 1980, The Rise of Suburbia (Ed.) 1982, Horses in European Economic History (Ed.) 1983, The Rise of Respectable Society: A Social History of Victorian Britain 1988, The Cambridge Social History of Britain 1750–1950, 3 vols. (Ed.) 1990, The University of London and the World of Learning 1836–1986 (Ed.) 1990, Landowners, Capitalists, and Entrepreneurs (Ed.) 1994. *Leisure interests:* gardening, walking, carpentry, tennis. *Address:* Holly Cottage, Sheepcote Lane, Wheathampstead, Herts., AL4 8NJ, England. *Telephone:* (0158 283) 3129 (Home).

THOMPSON, Fred Dalton, J.D.; American politician, actor and lawyer; b. 19 Aug. 1942, Sheffield, Ala.; m. (divorced); three c.; ed. Vanderbilt Univ.; Minority Staff Counsel to Watergate Cttee.; Senator from Tennessee Jan. 1994–; Chair. Senate Cttee. to Investigate Fund Raising during 1996 Presidential Election 1997; Republican. *Films include:* In the Line of Fire, The Hunt for Red October, No Way Out. *Address:* United States Senate, 523 Dirksen Senate Building, Washington, DC 20510, U.S.A.

THOMPSON, Harold Lindsay, M.B., B.S., F.R.A.C.G.P., A.M.; Australian medical practitioner; b. 23 April 1929, Aberdeen, Scotland; s. of Harold Thompson and Johan D. Thompson; m. Audrey J. Harpur 1957; three s. two d.; ed. Aberdeen, Melbourne and Sydney Grammar Schools and postgrad. training in U.K.; Surgeon-Lieut. Royal Australian Navy 1956–60; now in gen. practice in Lakemba, N.S.W.; Exec. Dir. Canterbury Div. of Gen. Practice 1996–; Assoc-Prof., Faculty of Medicine, Univ. of Sydney 1996–; Fellow Australian Medical Asscn. 1973, Pres. 1982–85; Pres. Confed. of Medical Asscns. of Asia and Oceania 1985–87, Immediate Past Pres. 1987–89; Chair. Australian Urban Divs. of Gen. Practice 1995–; Vice-Chair. Australian Council on Healthcare Standards 1985–89; Vice-Pres. Australian Council of Professions 1985–, Pres. 1989–; mem. Council, World Medical Asscn. 1984–, Pres. 1988–89; mem. Econ. Planning Advisory Cttee. 1989–91, Bd. Southern Sydney Area Health Service 1991–95; Chair. of Council Confed. of Medical Asscns. of Asia and Oceania 1989–95; mem. numerous advisory bds., cttees., etc.; Gold Medal, Australian Medical Asscn. 1986; Medal, Australian Council on Healthcare Standards 1990, Award of Merit, Confed. of Medical Asscns. of Asia and Oceania 1996. *Leisure interests:* golf, skiing, fishing. *Address:* 63 Tudor Street (P.O. Box 495), Belmore, N.S.W. 2192 (Office); 4/100 Milsom Road, Cremorne, N.S.W. 2090, Australia (Home). *Telephone:* (2) 9787 9033 (Office); (2) 9908 2980 (Home). *Fax:* (2) 9787 9200.

THOMPSON, Homer Armstrong, B.A., M.A., PH.D.; American classical archaeologist; b. 7 Sept. 1906, Devlin, Ont.; s. of William J. Thompson and Gertrude Thompson; m. Dorothy Burr 1933; three d.; ed. Univs. of British Columbia and Michigan; Staff mem., American School of Classical Studies excavations of the Athenian Agora 1929–, Field Dir. 1945–67; Prof. of Classical Archaeology, Toronto Univ. 1933–47, Head of Dept. of Art and Archaeology 1946–47; Prof., Princeton Inst. for Advanced Study 1947–77, Emer. 1977–; Asst. Dir., Curator of Classical Collection, Royal Ont. Museum, Toronto 1933–47; George Eastman Visiting Prof., Oxford Univ. 1959–60; Geddes-Harrower Prof. of Greek Archaeology and Art, Aberdeen Univ. 1964–65; Distinguished Visitor Australian-American Educ. Foundation; Corresp. Fellow British Acad.; Hon. mem. German Archaeological Inst., Soc. for Promotion of Hellenic Studies, Greek Archaeological Soc. (Hon. Vice-Pres.), Royal Soc. of Arts and Letters (Gothenburg), Acad. of Sciences (Heidelberg), Royal Swedish Acad., Soc. of Antiquaries (London); mem. American Philosophical Soc., American Acad. of Arts and Sciences; Hon. LL.D. (Toronto and British Columbia); Litt.D. (Michigan); L.H.D. (Dartmouth Coll., Univs. of Athens, Lyons, Freiburg, New York, Wooster Coll., Paris, Queen's); Commdr. Order of the Phoenix (Greece); Gold Medal Archaeological Inst. of America 1972; Drexel Medal, Univ. of Pa. 1978, British Acad. Kenyon Medal for Classical Studies 1991, Onassis Center Award, New York Univ. 1992, Thomas Jefferson Medal, American Philosophical Soc. 1996. *Publications:* studies in topography, architecture, sculpture and ceramics of ancient Athens (chiefly in Hesperia) 1934–; The Agora of Athens (with R. E. Wycherley) 1972. *Leisure interest:* gardening. *Address:* Meadow Lakes, Apt. 30-06 Hightstown, NJ 08520, U.S.A.

THOMPSON, James R., LL.D.; American politician and lawyer; b. 8 May 1936, Chicago, Ill.; s. of Dr. J. Robert Thompson and Agnes Thompson; m. Jayne Carr 1976; one d.; ed. Univ. of Illinois, Washington Univ., St. Louis, Mo., Northwestern Univ. Law School; admitted to Illinois Bar 1959; Prosecutor, State Attorney's Office, Cook County, Ill. 1959–64; Assoc. Prof. North Western Univ. Law School, Ill. 1964–69; Chief, Dept. of Law Enforcement and Public Protection, Office of Ill. Attorney-Gen. 1969–70, First Asst. U.S. Attorney 1970–71, U.S. Attorney for Northern Dist. of Ill. 1971–75; Counsel, Winston and Strawn law firm, Chicago 1975–77, partner, Chair. Exec. Cttee. 1991–; Gov. of Ill. 1977–91; mem. Exec. Cttee. Nat. Govs.' Asscn. (NGA) 1980–82, Chair. 1983–84; Co-Chair. Attorney Gen.'s Task Force on Violent Crime 1981; Chair./President's Intelligence Oversight Bd. 1989–93; mem. Presidential Advisory Cttee. on Federalism 1981, Advisory Bd. of Fed. Emergency Man. Agency 1991–93; Chair. Republican Govs.' Asscn., Mid-western Govs.' Conf., NGA Task Force on Job Creation and Infrastructure 1982; Chair. Council of Great Lakes Govs. 1985; Vice-Chair. Martin Luther King Jr. Nat. Holiday Cttee. 1985; Chair. Ill. Math. and Science Foundation; Hon. LL.D. (Lincoln Coll.) 1975, Hon. D.Hum.Litt. (Roosevelt Univ.) 1979, Hon. D.Jur. (Northwestern Univ. and Illinois Coll.) 1979, Hon. LL.D. (Monmouth Coll.) 1981, (Marshall Law School) 1984, (Elmhurst Coll.) 1985, Dr. h.c. (Pratt Inst.) 1984; Justice in Legislation Award, American Jewish Congress 1984; Distinguished Public Service Award, Anti-Defamation League 1984, Swedish-American of the Year, Vasa Order of America 1985; Republican. *Publications:* Co-author of four textbooks incl. Cases and Comments on Criminal Procedure; numerous articles in professional journals. *Address:* Winston & Strawn, 35 W. Wacker Drive, Chicago, IL 60601, U.S.A.

THOMPSON, J(ay) Lee; British writer, stage actor, film director and producer; b. 1914, Bristol; m. Lucille Steiner 1967; one s. one d.; ed. Dover Coll.; stage actor and playwright 1931–34; film scriptwriter 1934–50; film dir. 1950–; living in U.S.A. 1959–; Cannes Film Festival Special Award for Yield to the Night; Silver Bear for Best Picture, Berlin Film Festival, Int. Critics Award, Golden Globe for Best Picture for Woman in a Dressing-Gown; Int. Critics Award for Tiger Bay; Int. Critics Award for Ice Cold in Alex; Int. Critics Award for I Aim at the Stars; numerous awards for The Guns of Navarone; San Sebastian Film Award for Return from the Ashes; Best Science Thriller Award (Paris) for Eye of the Devil; European Best Thriller Award for Reincarnation of Peter Proud. *Films directed include:* Yield to the Night 1956, Woman in a Dressing-Gown 1957, Ice Cold in Alex (U.S. title Desert Attack) 1958, Tiger Bay 1959, Northwest Frontier 1959, I Aim at the Stars 1960, The Guns of Navarone 1961, Cape Fear 1961, Taras Bulba 1962, Kings of the Sun 1963, What a Way to Go 1964, John Goldfarb, Please Come Home! 1965, Return from the Ashes 1965, Mackenna's Gold 1968, Before Winter Comes 1968, The Chairman 1969, Country Dance (U.S. title Brotherly Love) 1970, Conquest of the Planet of the Apes 1972, The Reincarnation of Peter Proud 1975, St. Ives 1976, The White Buffalo 1976, The Greek Tycoon 1978, The Passage 1978, Cabo Blanco, Happy Birthday to Me, The Ambassador, 10 to Midnight, The Evil That Men Do, King Solomon's Mines, Murphy's Law, Firewalker, Death Wish IV, Messenger of Death, Kinjite. *Publications.* plays: Murder Happens, Double Error, Murder Without Crime, The Human Touch, Getting Away with Murder, The Curious Dr. Robson.

THOMPSON, Very Rev. Prof. John, B.A., B.D., PH.D., D.D.; British ecclesiastic; b. 14 July 1922, nr. Bushmills, N. Ireland; s. of James Thompson and Catherine Mogey; m. 1st Ann M. Norminton 1960 (died 1984); m. 2nd Heather M. Lewis 1988 (died 1995); m. 3rd Ingrid Victoria Barnes 1996; two s. one d.; ed. Ballycastle High School, Magee Coll. Londonderry, Trinity Coll. Dublin, New Coll. Edin., Basle Univ. and Presbyterian Coll. Belfast; Asst. Minister, St. Enoch's, Belfast 1949–52; Minister, Sandymount Presbyterian Church, Dublin and Lecturer in Catechetics, Trinity Coll. Dublin 1952–61; Minister, Fortwilliam Park Presbyterian Church, Belfast 1961–76; Prof. of Systematic Theology and Apologetics, Union Theological Coll. Belfast 1976–94; External Lecturer, Queen's Univ. Belfast 1976–94, mem. Senate 1985–; Moderator, Gen. Ass. of Presbyterian Church in Ireland 1986; various guest and part-time lectureships; Hon. D.D. (Presbyterian Theological Faculty, Ireland) 1986. *Publications:* Commentary on the Shorter Catechism (with J. L. M. Haire) 1966, Christ in Perspective: Christological Perspectives in the Theology of Karl Barth 1976, Theology Beyond Christendom (Ed.) 1986, The Holy Spirit in the Theology of Karl Barth 1991, Modern Trinitarian Perspectives 1994; essays and articles in theological journals. *Leisure interests:* sport, especially hockey, tennis, soccer, English literature, gardening. *Address:* Union Theological College, Botanic Avenue, Belfast, BT7 1LN (Office); 95 Malone Road, Belfast, BT9 6SP, N. Ireland (Home). *Telephone:* (01232) 325374 (Office); (01232) 666662 (Home).

THOMPSON, Mark John, B.A., F.R.T.S.; British broadcasting executive; b. 31 July 1957; s. of Duncan John Thompson and Sydney Columba Corduff Thompson; m. Jane Emilie Blumberg 1987; two s. one d.; ed. Stonyhurst Coll., Merton Coll. Oxford; Research Asst. Trainee, BBC TV 1979–1980, Asst. Producer Nationwide 1980–1982, Producer Breakfast Time 1982–84, Output Ed. London Plus 1984–85, Newsnight 1985–87, Ed. Nine O'Clock News 1988–90, Panorama 1990–92, Head of Features 1992–94, Head of Factual Programmes 1994–96, Controller BBC2 1996–98; Dir. of Nat. and Regional Broadcasting 1998–. *Leisure interests:* walking, cooking. *Address:* c/o BBC Television, Wood Lane, London, W12 8QT, England. *Telephone:* 0181-743-8000.

THOMPSON, Sir Michael Warwick, Kt., D.SC., F.INST.P.; British physicist and university vice-chancellor; b. 1 June 1931; s. of Kelvin W. Thompson and Madeleine Walford; m. Sybil N. Spooner 1956; two s.; ed. Rydal School and Univ. of Liverpool; research scientist, A.E.R.E., Harwell, Reactor Physics and Metallurgy 1953–65; Prof. of Experimental Physics, Univ. of Sussex 1965–80, Pro-Vice-Chancellor 1972–78; Vice-Chancellor, Univ. of E. Anglia 1980–86; Vice-Chancellor and Prin. Univ. of Birmingham 1987–96, Emer. Prof. 1996–; Chair. Council John Innes Research Inst. 1980–86, British Council Cttee. for Academic Research Collaboration with Germany 1988–; mem. S.R.C. Physics Cttee. (also Chair.) 1972–79, E. Sussex Educ. Cttee. 1973–78, E. Sussex Area Health Authority 1973–80, W. Midlands Regional Health Authority 1987–90 (non-exec. Dir. 1990–96), Council for Nat. Academic Awards 1988–91, Council of Asscn. of Commonwealth Univs. 1990–95, Council for Industry and Higher Educ. 1991–; Dir. (non-exec.) Alliance Bldg.

Soc. 1979–85 (Alliance and Leicester Bldg. Soc., now Alliance & Leicester PLC) 1985–, Deputy Chair. 1995–; COBUILD Ltd. 1987–96, TPIC Ltd. 1987–, Council of the Cttee. of Vice-Chancellors and Prins. 1989–96 (Chair. Medical Cttee. 1994–); Trustee Barber Inst. of Fine Art 1987–, St Bartholomew's Medical Coll.; Hon. LL.D. (Birmingham) 1997; Hon. D.Sc. (Sussex) 1998; C.V. Boys Prize, Inst. of Physics; Grosses Bundesverdienstkreuz 1997. *Publications:* Defects and Radiation Damage in Metals 1968; over 100 papers in scientific journals on the interaction of radiation with solids. *Leisure interests:* sailing, the arts. *Address:* The University of Birmingham, Edgbaston, Birmingham, B15 2TT (Office); Stoneacre, The Warren, Polperro, Cornwall, PL13 2RD (Home). *Telephone:* (0121) 414-4536 (Office).

THOMPSON, (Rupert) Julian (de la Mare), M.A.; British business executive; b. 23 July 1941; s. of Rupert Spens and Florence Elizabeth (de la Mare) Thompson; m. Jacqueline Julie Ivimy 1965; three d.; ed. Eton Coll. and King's Coll., Cambridge; joined Sotheby's 1963, Dir. 1969–, Chair. 1982–86, Deputy Chair. 1987–92, Chair. Sotheby's Asia 1992–97, Co-Chair. 1997–. *Address:* 47 Warrington Crescent, London, W9 1EJ, England. *Telephone:* 0171-289 3145.

THOMPSON, Tommy George, J.D.; American state governor; b. 19 Nov. 1941, Elroy, Wis.; s. of Allan Thompson and Julie Dutton; m. Sue Ann Mashak 1969; one s. two d.; ed. Univ. of Wisconsin; political intern, U.S. Rep. Thomson 1963; legis. messenger, Wis. State Senate 1964–66; sole practice, Elroy and Mauston, Wis. 1966–87; self-employed real estate broker, Mauston 1970–; mem. Dist. 87 Wis. State Ass. 1966–87, Asst. Minority Leader 1972–81, Floor Leader 1981–87; Gov. of Wisconsin 1987–; Chair. Republican Govs.' Asscn. 1991–92; mem. Exec. Cttee. Nat. Govs.' Asscn.; mem. American Bar Asscn.; Nature Conservancy Award 1988, Thomas Jefferson Freedom Award (American Legis. Exchange Council) 1991; Leadership in Natural Energy Conservation Award, U.S. Energy Asscn. 1994, and numerous other awards; Republican. *Leisure interests:* hunting, fishing, sports. *Address:* Office of the Governor, State Capitol, P.O. Box 7863, Madison, WI 53707, U.S.A. *Telephone:* (608) 266-1212. *Fax:* (608) 267-8983.

THOMSEN, Niels Jørgen, DR.PHIL.; Danish university professor; b. 21 April 1930; s. of late Sigurd Thomsen and Gudrun Kirkegaard; m. Birgit Nüchel Petersen 1953; two s.; ed. Univ. of Copenhagen; Dir. Danish Press Museum, Aarhus 1958–65; lecturer, School of Journalism, Aarhus 1962–65; Asst. Prof. of Econ. History, Univ. of Copenhagen 1965–71, Asst. Prof. of Political Science 1971–73, Prof. of Modern History 1973–; Danish Ed. Pressens Årbog 1968–82; Chair. Soc. for History and Econs., Copenhagen 1980–83; Chair. Soc. for Contemporary History 1982–; mem. Royal Danish Acad. of Science and Letters. *Publications:* Partipressen 1965, Dagbladskonkurrencen 1870–1970 I–II 1972, Københavns Universitet 1936–66 1986, De danske aviser 1634–1989 (with Jette Søllinge) I–III 1987–91, Industri, stat og samfund 1870–1939 1991, Hovedstrømninger 1870–1914 1998; about 80 articles on political and media history in professional journals. *Address:* Institute of History, University of Copenhagen, Njalsgade 102, 2300 Copenhagen S (Office); Vitus Berings allé 15, 2930 Klampenborg, Denmark (Home). *Telephone:* 35 32 82 85 (Office); 32 64 33 16 (Home). *Fax:* 35 32 82 41.

THOMSON, Sir Adam, Kt., C.B.E.; British businessman; b. 7 July 1926, Glasgow, Scotland; s. of late Frank Thomson and of Jemina Rodgers; m. Dawn Elizabeth Burt 1948; two s.; ed. Rutherglen Acad., Coatbridge Coll., Royal Tech. Coll. Glasgow; pilot Fleet Air Arm 1944–47; Flying Inst. British European Airways (BEA) 1947–50, pilot with BEA and Britavia 1951–59; founded Caledonian Airways 1961, Chair., C.E.O. British Caledonian Airways Ltd. 1970–88; Chair., C.E.O. The Caledonian Aviation Group PLC 1970–88 (fmrly. Airways Interests (Thomson) Ltd., Chair. and Man. Dir. 1964–70); Chair. Asscn. of European Airlines 1977–78, Caledonian Airmotive Ltd. 1978–87; Chair. Gold Stag 1988–94; Deputy Chair. Martin Currie Pacific Trust PLC 1985–92, Inst of Dirs. 1988– (Chair. 1988–90); Dir. Royal Bank of Scotland PLC 1982–91 (mem. 1977–), MEPC PLC 1982–89; Hon. LL.D. (Glasgow) 1979, (Sussex) 1984, (Strathclyde) 1986; Hambro Award Businessman of the Year 1970. *Publication:* High Risk (autobiog.) 1989. *Leisure interests:* golf, sailing. *Address:* 5 Green Ridge, Westdene, Brighton, East Sussex, BN1 5LT, England.

THOMSON, Brian Edward; Australian film, theatre and opera designer; b. 5 Jan. 1946, Sydney; s. of Austin Thomas Thomson and Adoree Gertrude Thomson; ed. Applecross Sr. High School, Perth Tech. Coll., Univ. of New South Wales. *Musicals:* Hair, Jesus Christ Superstar (London and Australia), The Rocky Horror Show (original London production and worldwide), Chicago, The Stripper, Company, Chess, The King and I (Broadway production 1996), How to Succeed in Business Without Really Trying, South Pacific, Hello, Dolly!, Merrily We Roll Along. *Theatre:* Housewife Superstar!!! (London and New York); The Threepenny Opera (opening season, Drama Theatre, Sydney Opera House); Big Toys (the Old Tote); A Cheery Soul, Chinchilla, Macbeth, The Doll Trilogy, The Ham Funeral, A Midsummer Night's Dream, The Crucible, The Homecoming, Uncle Vanya, Death and the Maiden, Coriolanus, Falsettos, King Lear, Arcadia, Medea, Mongrels, Third World Blues (all for Sydney Theatre Co.); Arturo Ui, Rock-Ola (Nimrod); Lulu, Shepherd on the Rocks Crow (State Theatre Co. of S. Australia); Ghosts, The Tempest, The Master Builder, Buzz, Frogs, Aftershocks, Radiance, Up the Road (Belvoir St.); Angels in America (Melbourne Theatre Co.). *Film and television:* Barlow and Chambers, Shadow of the Cobra (both mini-series); The Rocky Horror Picture Show, Starstruck, Rebel, Night of Shadows (also dir.), Ground Zero, Turtle Beach, Frauds. *Dance:* Synergy, Fornicon (Sydney Dance Co.). *Opera:* Death in Venice, The Makropulos Affair (Adelaide Festival); Turandot, Aida, Summer of the Seventeenth Doll (Vic. State Opera); Voss, Death in Venice, Tristan und Isolde, Katya Kabanova, The Eighth Wonder (The Australian Opera); Australian Film Inst. Award for production design, Rebel 1985, Ground Zero 1987, Sydney Theatre Critics' Award for Best Designer 1989, 1992, 1993, 1994, Mo Award 1994, 1995, Tony Award for The King and I 1996. *Leisure interests:* movies, sport (Aussie rules, cricket, tennis). *Address:* 5 Little Dowling Street, Paddington, N.S.W. 2021, Australia. *Telephone:* (02) 9331 1584. *Fax:* (02) 9360 4314.

THOMSON, David Spence, P.C., C.M.G., M.C., E.D., M.P.; New Zealand fmr. politician and dairy farmer; b. 14 Nov. 1915, Stratford; m. June Grace Adams 1942; one s. three d.; ed. Stratford Primary and High School; Territorial Army 1931–59, served Middle East 1939–42, Prisoner of war 1942–45, Brigadier (Reserve of Officers); Chair. Federated Farmers Sub-provincial Exec. 1959–63; M.P. for Stratford 1963–84; Minister of Defence, Minister in charge of Tourism, Minister in charge of Publicity 1966–67; Minister of Defence, Minister Asst. to Prime Minister, Minister in charge of War Pensions, Minister in charge of Rehabilitation Feb.–March 1967; Minister of Defence, Minister of Tourism, Minister Asst. to Prime Minister, Minister in charge of Publicity, Minister in charge of War Pensions, Minister in charge of Rehabilitation 1967–69; Minister of Defence, of Police, in charge of War Pensions, in charge of Rehabilitation 1969–72; Assoc. Minister of Labour and Immigration 1971–72, Minister Feb.–Dec. 1972; Minister of Justice 1975–78; Minister of State, of State Services, Leader of the House Dec. 1978–84; also Minister of Defence and Minister in Charge of War Pensions and Rehabilitation 1980–84; National Party. *Leisure interests:* fishing, golf, music. *Address:* 22 Bird Road, Stratford, New Zealand (Home).

THOMSON, James Alan, M.S., PH.D.; American business executive; b. 21 Jan. 1945, Boston, Mass.; s. of James Thomson and Mary Pluff; m. 1st Linda Eggert 1967–88; m. 2nd Darlene Wilson 1990; one s. one d.; ed. Univ. of New Hampshire and Purdue Univ.; Research Fellow, Univ. of Wis. Madison 1972–74; Systems Analyst, Office of Sec. of Defense, U.S. Dept. of Defense, Washington, D.C. 1974–77; staff mem. Nat. Security Council, Washington, D.C. 1977–81; Vice-Pres. RAND, Santa Monica, Calif. 1981–88, Pres. and C.E.O. 1989–; Dir. L.A. World Affairs Council; mem. Int. Inst. for Strategic Studies Council on Foreign Relations 1985–, Univ. of Calif., L.A. Bd. of Visitors; Hon. D.Sc. (Purdue) 1992. *Publications:* Conventional Arms Control and the Security of Europe 1988; articles on defence issues. *Address:* RAND, 1700 Main Street, Santa Monica, CA 90401, U.S.A. *Telephone:* (310) 393-0411. *Fax:* (310) 393-4818.

THOMSON, Sir John Adam, G.C.M.G., M.A.; British diplomatist (retd.); b. 27 April 1927, Aberdeenshire; s. of the late Sir George Thomson, Kt., F.R.S. and Kathleen Smith; m. 1st Elizabeth Anne McClure 1953 (died 1988); three s. one d.; m. 2nd Judith Ogden Bullitt 1992; ed. Philips Exeter Acad., N.H., U.S.A., Aberdeen Univ., Trinity Coll., Cambridge; Third Secretary, Embassy in Jeddah 1951, in Damascus 1954; Foreign Office 1955; Private Sec. to Perm. Under-Sec. 1958; First Sec., Embassy in Washington, D.C. 1960; Foreign Office 1964; Acting Head of Planning Staff 1966; Counsellor, Head of Planning Staff 1967; seconded to Cabinet Office as Chief of Assessment Staff 1968; Minister, Deputy Perm. Rep. to NATO 1972; Asst. Under-Sec. of State, Foreign and Commonwealth Office 1973; High Commr. in India 1977–82; Perm. Rep. to UN 1982–87; Leader CSCE Humanitarian Mission to Bosnia-Herzegovina 1992; Prin. Dir., 21st Century Trust 1987–90; Chair. Minority Rights Group Int. 1991–, Flemings Emerging Markets Investment Trust 1991–; int. advisor ANZ Grindlays Bank 1996– (Dir. 1987–96); mem. Council Int. Inst. of Strategic Studies, Governing Body Inst. of Devt. Studies, Sussex, Council Overseas Devt. Inst., London, Howie Cttee. for Secondary Educ. in Scotland 1990–92; Trustee Nat. Museums of Scotland 1991– (Dir. 1987–96); Assoc. mem. Nuffield Coll., Oxford 1988–91; Hon. LL.D. (Ursinus Coll., Penn.) 1984, (Aberdeen) 1986. *Publication:* Crusader Castles (with Robin Fedden). *Leisure interests:* castles, oriental carpets. *Address:* Fleming Emerging Markets Investment Trust PLC, 25 Copthall Avenue, London, EC2R 7DR, England.

THOMSON, Peter Alexander Bremner, C.V.O.; British diplomatist (retd.); b. 16 Jan. 1938, Orpington, Kent; s. of Alexander Thomson and Dorothy Scurr; m. Lucinda Sellar 1965; three s.; ed. Canford School, Royal Naval Coll. Dartmouth and S.O.A.S., London; serving officer, R.N. 1958–74; First Sec. H.M. Diplomatic Service, London, Lagos and Hong Kong 1975–84; Counsellor, Peking 1984–87; High Commr. in Belize 1987–90, in Seychelles 1995–97; Counsellor at FCO 1991–95. *Leisure interests:* sailing, walking. *Address:* The Red House, Charlton Horethorne, Sherborne, Dorset, DT9 4NL, England (Home).

THOMSON, Peter William, C.B.E.; Australian golfer; b. 23 Aug. 1929, Melbourne; m. Stella Mary 1960; one s. three d.; turned professional 1949; British Open Champion 1954, 1955, 1956, 1958, 1965 (only player to win three successively since Open became 72-hole event 1892); won British P.G.A. Match-Play Championship four times and 16 major tournaments in Britain; Australian Open Champion 1951, 1967, 1972, N.Z. Open Champion nine times; won open titles of Italy, Spain, Hong Kong, Philippines, India and Germany; played 11 times for Australia in World Cup (won twice); won World Seniors Championship 1984, PGA Seniors Championship of America

1984; Capt. Pres.'s Cup Int. Team 1996, 1998; fmr. Pres. Professional Golfers' Asscn. of Australia; Dir. Thomson, Wolveridge, Perrett; mem. James McGrath Foundation, Vic. *Leisure interests:* classical music, literature. *Address:* Carmel House, 44 Mathoura Road, Toorak, Vic. 3142, Australia.

THOMSON, Richard Murray, B.A.SC.(ENG.), M.B.A.; Canadian banker; b. 14 Aug. 1933, Winnipeg, Man.; s. of H. W. Thomson and Mary Thomson; m. Heather Lorimer 1959; ed. Univ. of Toronto, Harvard Business School, Queen's Univ., Kingston, Ont.; joined Toronto-Dominion Bank, Head Office 1957, Senior Asst. Man., St. James & McGill, Montreal 1961, Asst. to Pres., Head Office 1963, Asst. Gen. Man. 1965, Chief Gen. Man. 1968, Vice-Pres., Chief Gen. Man., Dir. 1971, Pres. 1972–79, Pres. and C.E.O. 1977–79, C.E.O. 1978–97, Chair. 1978–98; Dir. Eaton's of Canada, Canadian Gypsum Co., S. C. Johnson & Co. Ltd., Cadillac Fairview Corpn. Ltd., Union Carbide of Canada, The Prudential Insurance Co. of America, Toronto Dominion Bank, Inco Ltd., Int. Thomson Org. Ltd.; Trustee, Hospital for Sick Children. *Leisure interests:* golf, tennis, skiing. *Address:* c/o Toronto-Dominion Bank, P.O. Box 1, Toronto-Dominion Centre, 55 King Street, P.O. Box 1, Toronto, Ont. M5K 1A2, Canada.

THOMSON, Sir Thomas James, Kt., C.B.E., M.B., CH.B., F.R.C.P.; British gastroenterologist (retd.) and consultant physician; b. 8 April 1923, Airdrie; s. of Thomas Thomson and Annie Jane Grant; m. Jessie Smith Shotbolt 1948; two s. one d.; ed. Airdrie Acad. and Univ. of Glasgow; posts in clinical medicine continuously 1945–87, teacher 1948–87; posts as Lecturer in Dept. Materia Medica, Univ. of Glasgow 1953–87, Hon. Lecturer 1961–87; Consultant Physician and Gastroenterologist Stobhill Gen. Hosp., Glasgow 1961–87; Postgraduate Clinical Tutor to Glasgow Northern Hosps. 1961–80; Chair., Greater Glasgow Health Bd. 1987–93; mem. Court, Univ. of Strathclyde 1992–97, Chair. Staff Cttee. 1993–97; Sec. Specialist Advisory Cttee. for Gen. Internal Medicine for U.K. 1970–74; Chair., Medico-Pharmaceutical Forum 1978–80, ed. Advisory Bd. 1979–84, Conf. of Royal Colls. and Faculties in Scotland 1982–84, Nat. Medical Consultative Cttee. for Scotland 1982–87; Hon. Sec. Royal Coll. of Physicians and Surgeons, Glasgow 1965–73, Pres. 1982–84; Hon. Fellow American Coll. of Physicians; Fellow, Royal Coll. of Physicians of Ireland; Hon. LL.D. (Glasgow) 1988, D.Univ. (Strathclyde) 1997. *Publications:* Dilling's Pharmacology (jt. ed.) 1969, Gastroenterology—an integrated course 1972. *Leisure interests:* swimming and golfing. *Address:* 1 Varna Road, Glasgow, G14 9NE, Scotland. *Telephone:* 0141-959 5930.

THOMSON, William Cran, C.A., C.B.I.M.; British business executive; b. 11 Feb. 1926, Glasgow; s. of William Thomson and Helen Cran; m. Jessie Wallace 1951; four s.; ed. Hutcheons (Boys) Grammar School; joined Royal Dutch/Shell Group 1951, Shell Co. of Egypt 1951–54, of Sudan 1954–56, of Aden 1956–58, Finance Dir. P.T. Shell Indonesia 1961–64, Finance Co-ordinator Shell Int. Chemical Co. 1966–70, Chemical Co-ordinator Shell Int. Chemical Co. 1970–79, Chair. Shell Chemicals U.K. 1974–79, Finance Dir. Shell Petroleum Co. 1979–86, Man. Dir. Royal Dutch/Shell Group 1979–86, Man. Dir. Shell Transport and Trading 1979–86 (Dir. 1986–), Chair. Shell Holdings (U.K.) 1981–86; Chair. Shell Pensions Trust Ltd. 1986–, (Dir. 1976–); Chair. The Nickerson Group 1990– (Dir. 1986–); Dir. Coats Viyella PLC 1986–, Romaga AG 1986–. *Leisure interests:* golf, shooting. *Address:* Royal Dutch/Shell Group, Shell Centre, London, SE1 7NA, England.

THOMSON, William Reid, M.PHIL., M.SC.; American/British international financial adviser; b. 10 Aug. 1939, London, England; s. of the late Wing-Commdr. W. Thomson and of Nellie Hendry Thomson; m. 1st Mary Cormack 1967 (divorced 1986); m. 2nd Jeannette Vinta 1987; two s. one d.; ed. George Washington Univ., Univ. of Washington and Univ. of Manchester (U.K.); operations analyst and economist various cos. 1961–72; investment analyst Legg Mason & Co. 1973–74; mem. staff U.S. Treasury Dept., in posts including financial economist, Office of Debt Analysis and later as sr. economist, Office of Int. Devt. Banks 1974–85; Exec. Dir. African Devt. Bank 1982–83; Alt. Exec. Dir. Asian Devt. Bank (ADB) 1985–90, Vice-Pres. (Operations) ADB 1990–94, Sr. Counsellor to Pres. of ADB 1994–95; Sr. Adviser Fiduciary Trust Int. Asia 1995–; Man. Dir. Economic and Financial Consultants 1995–; Chair. Yamamoto Int. Co (Japan) 1996–, Siam Recovery Fund 1997–, Momentum Asia Ltd. 1997–, PEDCA LLC 1997–. *Leisure interests:* jogging, cricket, reading, writing. *Address:* Suite 6C, Trafalgar Plaza, 105 HV de la Costa Street, Makati, Metro Manila, Philippines (Office); Rumah, Martyr Road, Guildford, GU1 4LF, England (Home). *Telephone:* (632) 814-0131 (Office); (01483) 440825 (Home). *Fax:* (632) 814-0130 (Office); (01483) 440825 (Home).

THOMSON OF FLEET, 2nd Baron (cr. 1964), of Northbridge in the City of Edinburgh; **Kenneth Roy Thomson,** M.A.; Canadian newspaper proprietor; b. 1 Sept. 1923, Toronto; s. of the late Roy Thomson, the 1st Lord Thomson of Fleet, and Edna Anna Irvine; m. Nora Marilyn Lavis 1956; two s. one d.; ed. Upper Canada Coll. and Cambridge Univ.; served with Canadian Air Force during Second World War; in Editorial Dept., Timmins Daily Press, Timmins, Ont. 1947; Advertising Dept. Galt Reporter 1948–50, Gen. Man. 1950–53; directed U.S. and Canadian Operations of Thomson Newspapers in Toronto 1953–68; Deputy Chair. Times Newspapers Ltd. 1966–67, Chair. 1968–70, Co-Pres. 1971–81; Chair. of Bd., Pres., C.E.O. and Dir. Thomson Newspapers Ltd. (owners of 39 newspapers in Canada); Chair. of Bd. and Dir. Int. Thomson Org. PLC, Thomson Corpn. Ltd., Thomson Int. Corpn. Ltd., Thomson Org. PLC, Woodbridge Co. Ltd., Ontario Newspapers Ltd., TECL Holdings Ltd., Thomson Equitable Corpn. Ltd., Thomson Investments Ltd., Thomson US Inc. (owners of 115 newspapers in U.S.A.); The Standard St. Lawrence Co. Ltd.; Pres. and Dir. Dominion-Consolidated Holdings Ltd., Fleet Street Publrs. Ltd., Kenthom Holdings Ltd., Thomfleet Holdings Ltd., Thomson Mississauga Properties Ltd., Thomson Works of Art Ltd.; Vice-Pres. and Dir. Cablevue (Quinte) Ltd., Veribest Products Ltd.; Dir. Abitibi-Price Inc., The Advocate Co. Ltd., Caribbean Trust Ltd., Cen. Canada Insurance Service Ltd., IBM (Canada) Ltd., Hudson's Bay Co., Victoria Insurance Co. of Canada, Scottish and York Insurance Ltd., Load & Go Transport Inc., McCallum Transport Inc., Nipa Lodge Co. Ltd., Orchid Lodge Co. Ltd., Scottish & York Holdings Ltd., Simpsons Ltd., Thomson Scottish Assocs. Ltd., Thomson Television Ltd., The Toronto-Dominion Bank. *Leisure interests:* collecting antiques and paintings, art and golf. *Address:* Thomson Newspapers Ltd., Thomson Building, 65 Queen Street West, Toronto, Ontario M5H 2M8, Canada; The International Thomson Organisation PLC, The Quadrangle, P.O. Box 4YG, 180 Wardour Street, London WIA 4YG, England (Offices); 8 Castle Frank Road, Toronto 5, Ontario M4W 2Z4, Canada; 8 Kensington Palace Gardens, London, W.8, England (Homes). *Telephone:* 864-1710 (Thomson Newspapers); 0171-437 9787 (Thomson Organisation).

THOMSON OF MONIFIETH, Baron (Life Peer), cr. 1977, of Monifieth in the District of the City of Dundee; **George Morgan Thomson,** K.T., P.C., F.R.T.S.; British politician and journalist; b. 16 Jan. 1921, Stirling, Scotland; s. of James Thomson; m. Grace Jenkins 1948; two d.; ed. Grove Acad., Dundee; Royal Air Force 1940–45; Ed. Forward 1946–53; M.P. 1952–72; Chair. Commonwealth Educ. Council 1959–64; Chair. Parl. Group for World Govt. 1962–64; Minister of State, Foreign Office 1964–66, Jan.–Aug. 1967; Chancellor of Duchy of Lancaster 1966–67; Sec. of State for Commonwealth Affairs 1967–68; Minister without Portfolio 1968–69; Chancellor of Duchy of Lancaster and Deputy Foreign Sec. (with special responsibility for European Affairs and Common Market negotiations) 1969–70; Opposition Spokesman on Defence 1970–72; Chair. Standing Conf. of British Refugee Orgs. 1971–72, David Davies Memorial Inst. 1971–77, Labour Cttee. for Europe 1972–73, European Movement 1977–79; mem. Comm. of European Communities, with special responsibility for Regional Policy 1973–76; First Crown Estate Commr. 1977–80; Chair. Advertising Standards Authority 1977–80; Deputy Chair. Ind. Broadcasting Authority 1980–81, Chair. 1981–88; mem. S.L.D. 1989–; Vice-Pres. Royal Television Soc. 1982–89; Chair. Franco-British Council 1979–81, Anglo-Romanian Round Table 1979–81; Chancellor, Heriot-Watt Univ. 1977–92; Chair. Value & Income Investment Trust; Dir. ICI 1977–89, Royal Bank of Scotland 1977–90, Woolwich Equitable Bldg. Soc. (Sr. Vice-Chair. 1988–90); Pres. History of Advertising Trust 1985–, Prix Italia 1989–91; Dir. English Nat. Opera 1987–92; Chair. Suzy Lamplugh Trust 1990–92; Trustee Thomson Foundation; mem. Standing Cttee. Standards in Public Life 1994–97; Chair. Leeds Castle Foundation 1994–; Scottish Peers Asscn. 1996–98; Hon. LL.D. (Dundee) 1967, D.Litt. (Heriot-Watt) 1973, (New Univ. of Ulster) 1984; Hon. D.Sc. (Aston) 1976, (Loughborough) 1980; Hon. D.C.L. (Kent) 1989. *Leisure interests:* swimming, hill walking. *Address:* House of Lords, London, SW1A 0PW, England.

THONEMANN, Peter Clive, M.SC., D.PHIL.; British physicist and emeritus professor; b. 3 June 1917, Melbourne, Australia; s. of Frederick Emil Thonemann and Mabel Jessie Thonemann; one s. one d.; ed. Univs. of Melbourne and Sydney and Trinity Coll., Oxford; Commonwealth Research Scholar Sydney Univ. 1944–46; ICI Fellow, Clarendon Lab., Oxford, proposed principles and initiated research for a fusion reactor, 1946–49; Head of Research on Controlled Thermonuclear Reactions, A.E.R.E., Harwell 1949–60, designed and built prototype fusion reactor Zeta, Deputy Dir., Culham Lab. of the Atomic Energy Authority 1965–66; Prof. of Physics and Head of Dept., Univ. Coll. of Swansea (now Univ. of Wales Swansea) 1968–84. *Leisure interests:* physics, musical composition. *Address:* 130 Bishopston Road, Swansea, SA3 3EU, Wales. *Telephone:* (01792) 232669.

THORBURN, Cliff(ord) Charles Devlin, C.M.; Canadian snooker player; b. 16 Jan. 1948, Victoria, B.C.; s. of James Thorburn and Adel Hanna Thorburn; m. 1981; two s.; World Professional Champion 1980; 27 tournament wins (worldwide); winner 13 Canadian Championships; first player in World Professional Championship to make a 147 break (Crucible Theatre, Sheffield) 1983. *Publications:* Cliff Thorburn's Snooker Skills, Playing for Keeps (autobiography). *Leisure interests:* golf, chess, reading. *Address:* 31 West Side Drive, Markham, Ontario, Canada.

THORENS, Justin Pierre, D. EN D.; Swiss professor of law; b. 15 Sept. 1931, Collonge-Bellerive; s. of Paul L. Thorens and Germaine Falquet; m. Colette F. Vecchio 1963; one s. one d.; ed. Univ. of Geneva, Freie Univ. Berlin and Univ. Coll. London; attorney-at-law, Geneva Bar 1956–; Alt. Pres. Jurisdictional Court, Geneva 1971–78; lecturer, Faculty of Law, Univ. of Geneva 1967, Assoc. Prof. 1970, Prof. 1973–96, Dean 1974–77, Hon. Prof. 1996–; Rector, Univ. of Geneva 1977–83; Visiting Scholar, Stanford and Calif. (Berkeley) Univs. 1983–84; Guest Prof. Univ. of Munich 1984; mem. Cttee. European Center for Higher Educ. (CEPES), Bucharest 1981–95, Pres. 1986–88; mem. Admin. Council Asscn. des Universités Partiellement ou Entièrement de Langue Française (AUPELF), Montreal 1978–87, Vice-Pres. 1981–87, Hon. Vice-Pres. 1987–, mem. Gov. Council 1987–; Pres. Bd. Int. Asscn. of Univs. (AIU), Paris 1985–90, Hon. Pres. 1990–; mem. Council UN Univ. Tokyo 1986–92, Pres. 1988–89; mem. UNESCO Swiss Nat. Comm. 1989–; Pres. Latsis Int. Foundation 1989–; other professional appts.; various prizes, awards and distinctions. *Publications:* publs. on pvt. law, civil procedure, arbitration, Anglo-American property law, univ. politics, cultural questions. *Leisure interests:* history and all its aspects, both European and the rest of the world; interaction of cultures of various times and regions. *Address:* 7 rue de la Fontaine, 1204 Geneva (Office); 18 chemin du Nant d'Aisy, 1246 Corsier, Switzerland (Home). *Telephone:* (022) 3118766 (Office); 7511262 (Home). *Fax:* (022) 7810216.

THORN, Gaston, D. EN D.; Luxembourg politician; b. 3 Sept. 1928, Luxembourg; s. of Edouard Thorn and Suzanne Weber; m. Liliane Petit 1957; one s.; ed. Univs. of Montpellier, Lausanne and Paris; admitted to Luxembourg Bar; Pres. Nat. Union of Students, Luxembourg; mem. Legis. 1959–; mem. European Parl. 1959–69, Vice-Pres. Liberal Group; Pres. Democratic Party, Luxembourg 1961; Minister of Foreign Affairs and Minister of Foreign Trade 1969–80, also Minister of Physical Educ. and Sport 1969–77, Prime Minister and Minister of State 1974–79, Minister of Nat. Econ. and Middle Classes 1977–80, of Justice 1979–80; Deputy Prime Minister 1979–80; Pres. Comm. of the European Communities 1981–84, also responsible for Secr. Gen., Legal Service, Spokesman's Group, Security and Cultural Affairs; Pres. Liberal Int. 1970–82; Pres. of 30th Session of the UN Gen. Ass. 1975–76; Pres. Fed. of Liberal and Democratic Parties of European Community 1976–80; Chair. Banque Int., Luxembourg 1985–; Pres. Mouvement Européen Int. 1985–; Pres., Dir.-Gen. RTL Luxembourg 1985–, Pres. 1987–; Pres. Centre of European Studies, Strasbourg 1995–; numerous decorations. *Leisure interests:* lecturing, tennis, golf. *Address:* 1 rue de la Forge, Luxembourg (Home). *Telephone:* 420-77 (Home).

THORN, George Widmer, M.D.; American physician; b. 15 Jan. 1906, Buffalo, N.Y.; s. of George W. and Fanny R. (Widmer) Thorn; m. 1st Doris Weston 1931 (died 1984); one s.; m. 2nd Claire Steinert 1985 (died 1990); ed. Coll. of Wooster, Ohio; House Officer, Millard Fillmore Hosp., Buffalo (N.Y.) 1929–30; Asst. Univ. of Buffalo 1931–34; Rockefeller Fellow in Medicine, Harvard Medical School and Mass. Gen. Hosp. 1934–35; Asst. Prof. Dept. of Physiology, Ohio State Univ. 1935–36; Assoc. Prof. of Medicine, Johns Hopkins Medical School, Assoc. Physician Johns Hopkins Hosp. 1936–42; Physician-in-Chief, Peter Bent Brigham Hosp., Hersey Prof. of Theory and Practice of Physic, Harvard Univ. 1942–72, Emer. 1972–; Samuel A. Levine Prof. of Medicine, Harvard Medical School 1967–72, Emer. 1972–; Dir. of Research, Howard Hughes Medical Inst. 1956–78, mem. Exec. Cttee. 1978–, Chair. Medical Advisory Bd. 1978–, Pres. 1981–84, Chair. Bd. Dirs. and Trustee 1984–; mem. Corpn. and of Exec. Cttee. of Corpn. of M.I.T. 1965–; First Wingate Johnson Visiting Prof., Bowman Gray School of Medicine, Wake Forest Univ. 1972; Consultant U.S. Public Health Service, etc.; Fellow, Royal College of Physicians, London; mem. Nat. Advisory Cttee. on Radiation; Trustee, Diabetic Fund; Chair. Scientific Review Bd., Whitaker Foundation Biomed. Eng., Bd., Hippocrates Int. Medical Foundation; Hon. mem. Soc. Colombiana de Endocrinología (Bogotá), Royal Soc. of Medicine (Great Britain); mem. Royal Acad. of Medicine (Belgium), Norwegian Medical Soc., Swedish Medical Soc.; First Lilly Lecturer, Royal Coll. of Physicians, London 1966; numerous awards including John Philips Memorial Award (American Coll. of Physicians) 1955, Modern Medicine Award 1961, George Minot Award (American Medical Asscn.) 1963, Robert H. Williams Award (Asscn. of Profs. of Medicine) 1972; Commdr. Order of Hipólito Unanue (Peru), Public Welfare Medal, N.A.S. 1997. *Leisure interests:* tennis, arboretum. *Address:* Howard Hughes Medical Institute, 320 Longwood Avenue, Enders 661, Boston, MA 02115; 16 Gurney Street, Cambridge, MA 02138, U.S.A. *Telephone:* (617) 876-1230.

THORN, Niels Anker, M.D.; Danish professor of physiology; b. 1 Aug. 1924; s. of Niels Johan Thorn and Dagny Thorn; m. Dr. Ingrid Thorn 1954; two s.; ed. Univ. of Copenhagen 1951; Fellow Rockefeller Univ., N.Y. 1953–56; Resident, Assoc. Univ. of Copenhagen 1956, Assoc. Prof. of Physiology 1957, Prof. 1967–95; Chair. Danish Nat. Cttee. for US Public Health Service 1970–85; Ed. Acta Physiologica Scandinavia 1981–; leader Danish Govt. Biotech. Center for Neuropeptide research 1988; f. Danish Nat. Cttee. for Physiology 1989–; mem. Danish Medical Research Council 1973–77, European Medical Research Council 1975–79, Royal Danish Acad. of Sciences 1982; Sec.-Gen. Scandinavian Physiology Soc. 1973–82; Hon. and Visiting Prof. Univ. of Canton and Shanghai 1988; Alfred Benzon Prize 1959; Thorvald Madsen Prize 1967, Gaardon Prize 1989, Ernst Carlsen Prize 1993. *Publications:* Antidiuretic Hormones and Their Analogues (thesis) 1960, The Alkalai Metal Ions in Biology 1960, Neurohypophysical Hormones and Similar Polypeptides 1968, Transport Mechanism in Epithelia 1973, Secretory Mechanism of Exocrine Glands 1974, Calcium Transport in Contraction and Secretion 1975, the Secretory Granule 1982, Molecular Mechanisms in Secretion 1988. *Leisure interests:* travel, sailing, skating. *Address:* Tonysvej 17, 2920 Charlottenhund, Denmark.

THORNBURGH, Dick, B.ENG., LL.B.; American lawyer; b. 16 July 1932, Pittsburgh; s. of Charles G. Thornburgh and Alice Sanborn; m. Virginia W. Judson 1963; four s.; ed. Yale Univ. and Univ. of Pittsburgh; admitted to Pa. Bar 1958, U.S. Supreme Court Bar 1965; attorney, Kirkpatrick & Lockhart LLP, Pittsburgh 1959–79, 1977–79, 1987–88, 1994–; U.S. attorney for Western Pa., Pittsburgh 1969–75; Asst. Attorney-Gen. Criminal Div. U.S. Justice Dept. 1975–77; Gov. of Pennsylvania 1979–87; Dir. Inst. of Politics, J.F. Kennedy School of Govt., Harvard Univ. 1987–88; Attorney-Gen. of U.S.A. 1988–91; Under Sec. Gen. for Admin. and Man. U.N. 1992–93; Chair. State Science and Tech. Inst., Legal Policy Advisory Bd., Washington Legal Foundation; Vice-Chair. World Cttee. on Disability; Fellow, American Bar Foundation; mem. American Judicature Soc., Council on Foreign Relations; Trustee Urban Inst., Nat. Acad. of Public Admin.; 30 hon. degrees; Special Medallion Award, Fed. Drug Enforcement Admin. 1973, Distinguished Service Medal, American Legion 1992; Republican. *Publications:* articles in professional journals. *Address:* 1800 Massachusetts Avenue, N.W., Washington, DC 20036-1800, U.S.A.

THORNE, Kip Stephen, PH.D.; American research physicist, university professor and writer; b. 1 June 1940, Logan, Utah; s. of David Wynne Thorne and Alison Comish; m. 1st Linda Jeanne Peterson 1960 (divorced 1977); m. 2nd Carolee Joyce Winstein 1984; one s. one d.; ed. Calif. Inst. of Tech. and Princeton Univ.; Postdoctoral Fellow, Princeton Univ. 1965–66; Research Fellow in Physics, Calif. Inst. of Tech. 1966–67, Assoc. Prof. of Theoretical Physics 1967–70, Prof. 1970–, William R. Kenan Jr. Prof. 1981–91; Feynman Prof. of Theoretical Physics 1991–; Adjunct Prof. of Physics, Univ. of Utah 1971–98; Fulbright Lecturer, France 1966; Visiting Prof., Moscow Univ. 1969, 1975, 1978, 1981, 1982, 1986, 1988, 1990, 1998; Andrew D. White Prof.-at-Large, Cornell Univ. 1986–92; Chair. Topical Group on Gravity of American Physical Soc. 1997–98; Alfred P. Sloan Research Fellow 1966–68; Guggenheim Fellow 1967; mem. Int. Cttee. on Gen. Relativity and Gravitation 1971–80, 1992–, Cttee. on U.S.-U.S.S.R. Co-operation in Physics 1978–79, Space Science Bd., NASA 1980–83; Hon. D.Sc. (Ill. Coll.) 1979, Dr. h.c. (Moscow State Univ.) 1981; Fellow American Acad. of Arts and Sciences, American Physical Soc., A.A.A.S.; mem. N.A.S.; American Inst. of Physics Science Writing Award in Physics and Astronomy 1967 and 1994, Julius Edgar Lilienfeld Prize, American Physical Soc. 1996, Karl Schwarzschild Medal, German Astronomical Soc. 1996. *Publications:* (co-author) Gravitation Theory and Gravitational Collapse 1965, High Energy Astrophysics, Vol. 3 1967, Gravitation 1973, Black Holes: The Membrane Paradigm 1986; (sole author) Black Holes and Time Warps: Einstein's Outrageous Legacy 1994. *Address:* California Institute of Technology, 130-33 Theoretical Astrophysics, 1200 East California Boulevard, Pasadena, CA 91125, U.S.A. *Telephone:* (626) 395-4598. *Fax:* (626) 796 5675.

THORNHILL, Arthur Horace, Jr., B.A.; American book publisher; b. 1 Jan. 1924, Boston, Mass.; s. of Arthur Horace Thornhill and Mary J. Peterson; m. Dorothy M. Matheis 1944; one s. one d.; ed. Englewood School for Boys and Princeton Univ.; joined Little, Brown & Co. 1948, Vice-Pres. 1955–58, Exec. Vice Pres. 1958–62, Pres. and C.E.O. 1962–86, Chair. of Bd. 1970–87; Pres. Little, Brown & Co. (Canada) 1955–84; Vice-Pres. Time Inc. 1968–87; Dir. Bantam Books Inc. 1965–67, Conrac Corpn. 1972–87; Treas. and Trustee, Princeton Univ. Press. 1971–86; Dir. Asscn. of American Publrs. 1978–81; Trustee Bennington Coll. 1969–76; Fellow Emer. Center for Creative Photography, Univ. of Ariz.; Air Medal (U.S.A.F.); Princeton Univ. Press Medal, Distinguished Alumnus Award, Dwight-Englewood School 1998. *Leisure interests:* American history, tennis. *Address:* 50 S. School Street, Portsmouth, NH 03801, U.S.A. (Home).

THORNING-PETERSEN, Rudolph Anton, LL.M.; Danish diplomatist; b. 17 July 1927, Snekkersten; s. of Erik Thorning-Petersen and Helga Westergaard; m. Britta Leyssac 1949; one s. one d.; ed. Copenhagen Univ.; joined Ministry of Foreign Affairs 1952, Amb. in Beirut, Baghdad, Amman, Damascus, Nicosia 1975–80, Peking 1980–83, Moscow 1983–89, London 1989–96, Amb. at large 1996–97; Kt.-Commdr., Order of the Dannebrog and several foreign decorations. *Leisure interests:* modern history, genealogy, history of art. *Address:* Jaegersborg Alle 23, 2, 2920 Charlottenlund, Denmark.

THORNTON, Billy Bob; American actor, director and writer; b. 4 Aug. 1955, Hot Springs, Ariz. *Films include:* Sling Blade (also dir., screenplay; Acad. Award for Best Adapted Screenplay 1996, Chicago Film Critics Award for Best Actor, Independent Spirit Awards), U-Turn 1997, A Thousand Miles 1997, A Simple Plan 1997, The Apostle 1997, A Gun A Car A Blonde, Primary Colors 1998, Homegrown 1998. *Television:* The 1,000 Chains, Don't Look Back (actor, writer), The Outsiders (series), Hearts Afire. *Address:* c/o Miramax, 7966 Beverly Boulevard, Los Angeles, CA 90048, U.S.A.

THORNTON, Clive Edward Ian, C.B.E., LL.B., B.A., F.C.I.B.; British lawyer and business executive; b. 12 Dec. 1929, Newcastle upon Tyne; s. of Albert Thornton and Margaret Thornton; m. Maureen Crane 1956; one s. one d.; ed. St Anthony's School and Coll. of Commerce, Newcastle upon Tyne and Coll. of Law, London; articled, Kenneth Hudson, Solicitor, London 1959; Solicitor to Cassel Arenz (merchant bankers), London 1964; Chief Solicitor, Abbey Nat. Bldg. Soc. 1967, Deputy Chief Gen. Man. 1978, Chief Gen. Man. 1979–83, Dir. 1980–83; Chair. Commerce and Industry Group, The Law Soc. 1974–75; mem. Council, Bldg. Socs. Asscn. 1979–83, Housing Corpn. 1980–86; Chair. Shelter Housing Aid Centre 1983–86, Mirror Group of Newspapers Jan.-July 1984, Thorndale Farm 1984–, Financial Weekly Ltd. 1984–87, Thamesmead Town Ltd. 1986–90, Gabriel Communications Ltd. 1986–96, Universe Publs. 1986–96, Armstrong Capital Holdings Ltd. 1988–; Dir. Investment Data Services 1986–90, Melton Mowbray Building Soc. 1988–, LHW Futures 1988–96, Burgon Hall Ltd. 1988–96; Council mem., St. Mary's Hosp. Medical School 1986–96; Partner, Stoneham Langton and Passmore (int. lawyers) 1984–88; Solicitor of Supreme Court. *Publications:* Building Society Law: Cases and Materials 1975, 1989, History of Devon Cattle. *Leisure interests:* antique collecting, music, reading, breeding Devon cattle. *Address:* Lansbury House, 3 St. Mary's Place, Stamford, Lincs., PE9 2DN; Keythorpe Grange, East Norton, Leics., LE7 9XL; Belford Hall, Belford,

Northumberland, England. *Telephone:* (01162) 598201 (East Norton); (01668) 213667 (Belford).

THOROGOOD, Kenneth Alfred Charles; British international trade financier; b. 1924, London; s. of Albert Jesse and Alice Lucy Thorogood; m. 1st J. Patricia Smith 1947; two d.; m. 2nd Gaye Lambourne 1979; ed. Highbury County Grammar School; Flight Lieut., R.A.F. 1942–46; Chair. British Export Houses Asscn. 1968–70, Vice-Pres. 1973–76; mem. Cttee. of Invisible Exports 1968–70; Exec. Chair., Tozer Kemsley & Millbourn (Holdings) PLC (int. finance and investment group) 1971–81; Dir. Alexanders Discount Co. Ltd. 1973–83, Royal Insurance Co. Ltd. 1973–83, Liverpool & London & Globe Insurance Co. Ltd. 1973–78, London & Lancashire Insurance Co. Ltd. 1973–78, Welbeck Finance PLC 1984–88; consultant to various cos. *Leisure interests:* aviation, music. *Address:* Flat 1, 18 Lowndes Square, London, SW1X 9HB, England.

THORPE, James, M.A., PH.D., LITT.D., L.H.D., LL.D., H.H.D.; American literary scholar; b. 17 Aug. 1915, Aiken, S.C.; s. of J. Ernest Thorpe and Ruby E. Holloway; m. Elizabeth M. Daniells 1941; one s. one d.; ed. The Citadel, Charleston, S.C., Univ. of N. Carolina and Harvard Univ.; Col., U.S.A.F. 1941–46; Prof. of English, Princeton Univ. 1946–66; Dir. Huntington Library, Art Gallery and Botanical Gardens 1966–83, Sr. Research Assoc. 1966–; Pres. Soc. for Textual Scholarship; Guggenheim Fellow 1949–50, 1965–66; Fellow, American Philosophical Soc., A.A.A.S., American Antiquarian Soc. *Publications:* Rochester's Poems 1950, Etherege's Poems 1963, Literary Scholarship 1964, Principles of Textual Criticism 1972, Use of Manuscripts in Literary Research 1974, Gifts of Genius 1980, A Word to the Wise 1982, John Milton: The Inner Life 1983, The Sense of Style: Reading English Prose 1987, Henry Edwards Huntington: A Biography 1994, Henry Edwards Huntington: A Brief Biography 1996, A Pleasure of Proverbs 1996, Proverbs for Friends 1997, Proverbs for Thinkers 1998. *Leisure interest:* gardening. *Address:* Huntington Library, Art Gallery and Botanical Gardens, San Marino, CA 91108 (Office); 1199 Arden Road, Pasadena, CA 91106, U.S.A. (Home). *Telephone:* (626) 405-2121 (Office); (626) 405-0938 (Home).

THORPE, Rt. Hon. (John) Jeremy, P.C.; British politician; b. 29 April 1929; m. 1st Caroline Allpass 1968 (died 1970); one s.; m. 2nd Maria (Marion) Stein, fmr. Countess of Harewood, 1973; ed. Rectory School, Conn., Eton Coll. and Trinity Coll., Oxford; Barrister, Inner Temple 1954; M.P. for N. Devon 1959–79; Treas. UN Parl. Group 1962–67; Hon. Treas. Liberal Party 1965–67, Leader 1967–76; Pres. N. Devon Liberal Asscn. 1987–; Consultant, Stramit; Chair. Jeremy Thorpe Assocs. Ltd. 1984–; Hon. Fellow, Trinity Coll. Oxford Univ.; Hon. DCL, Exeter Univ. *Publications:* To All Who Are Interested in Democracy 1951, Europe: The Case for Going In 1971, In My Own Time (autobiog.) 1999. *Address:* 2 Orme Square, Bayswater, London, W2 4RS, England.

THORPE, Marjorie, PH.D.; Trinidad and Tobago diplomatist; b. 8 July 1941, Trinidad; d. of Lester Thorpe and Violet Thorpe; ed. McGill Univ. Montreal and Queen's Univ. Ont.; Asst. lecturer, Univ. of the West Indies 1965, Sr. lecturer 1982, Head, Dept. of English 1979–85, Vice-Dean, Faculty of Arts and Gen. Studies 1983–84, Dean 1987–88; Sr. Fellowship Award, Howard Univ. Washington, D.C. 1985; Ford Foundation Fellowship, Inst. of Devt. Studies, Univ. of Sussex, England 1986; frequent engagement in activities, confs. etc. relating to women and devt. issues; Perm. Rep. to UN 1988–92. *Address:* c/o Ministry of Foreign Affairs, Knowsley Building, Queen's Park West, Port of Spain, Trinidad and Tobago.

THOULESS, David James, PH.D., F.R.S.; American (b. British) physicist; b. 21 Sept. 1934, Bearsden, Scotland; s. of Robert Thouless and Priscilla (née Gorton) Thouless; m. Margaret Scrase 1958; two s. one d.; ed. Winchester Coll., Trinity Hall, Cambridge, Cornell Univ.; Physicist, Lawrence Radiation Lab., Berkeley 1958–59; ICI Research Fellow, Birmingham Univ. 1959–61, Prof. of Mathematical Physics 1965–79; Lecturer at Cambridge and Fellow of Churchill Coll. 1961–65, Royal Soc. Research Prof. and Fellow of Clare Hall, Cambridge 1983–86; Prof. of Applied Science, Yale Univ. 1979–80; Prof. of Physics, Univ. of Washington 1980–; mem. N.A.S. 1995; Fellow American Acad. of Arts and Sciences 1980, American Physical Soc. 1987; Maxwell Prize 1973, Holweck Medal 1980, Fritz London Award 1984, Wolf Prize for Physics 1990, Dirac Prize 1993. *Publications:* Quantum Mechanics of Many-Body Systems 1961, Topological Quantum Numbers in Nonrelativistic Physics 1998. *Address:* Department of Physics, Box 351560, University of Washington, Seattle, WA 98195, U.S.A. *Telephone:* (206) 685-2393.

THRANE, Hans Erik, M.ECON.; Danish diplomatist; b. 14 April 1918, Copenhagen; s. of Julius Peter Thrane and Frieda Jensen; m. Gerda Boye 1941; two s.; ed. Copenhagen Univ.; Danish Foreign Service 1945–88; Econ. Attaché, Paris 1948–52; Ministry of Foreign Affairs, Copenhagen 1952–56; Econ. Counsellor, Washington 1956–59; Alt. Exec. Dir., IBRD (World Bank) 1958–59; Ministry of Foreign Affairs, Copenhagen 1959–66, Minister 1962, Asst. Under-Sec. of State for Econ. Affairs 1964; Amb. and Perm. Rep. EFTA, and Perm. Rep. to UN Office and other int. orgs. in Geneva 1966–74; Chair. Council, GATT 1968–71; Amb. to Norway 1974–79, to Switzerland 1980–86, to the Holy See 1982–86; Ministry of Foreign Affairs 1986–88; mem. Bd. of Dirs., Nordic Investment Bank 1986–92, (Chair. 1988–90), Nordic Devt. Fund for the Western North 1987–92. *Leisure interests:* sailing, skiing, mountaineering, modern art. *Address:* Rude Vang 53, 2840 Holte, Denmark.

THRUSH, Brian Arthur, M.A., SC.D., F.R.S.; British professor of physical chemistry; b. 23 July 1928, London; s. of late Arthur Thrush and Dorothy Thrush; m. Rosemary C. Terry 1958; one s. one d.; ed. Haberdashers' Aske's Hampstead School and Emmanuel Coll., Cambridge; Univ. Demonstrator, Asst. Dir. of Research, Lecturer, Reader in Physical Chem. Univ. of Cambridge 1953–78, Prof. of Physical Chem. 1978–95; Head Dept. of Chem., Univ. of Cambridge 1988–93; Fellow, Emmanuel Coll., Cambridge 1960–, Vice-Master 1986–90; mem. Natural Environment Research Council 1985–90; Visiting Prof. Chinese Acad. of Sciences 1980–; mem. Council, Royal Soc. 1989–91, Academia Europaea 1992–; Tilden Lecturer (Royal Soc. of Chem.) 1965; M. Polanyi Medal (Royal Soc. of Chem.) 1980, Rank Prize for Opto-Electronics 1992. *Publications:* papers on spectroscopy, gas reactions and atmospheric chem. in learned journals. *Leisure interests:* wine, walking, gardens. *Address:* Department of Chemistry, University of Cambridge, Lensfield Road, Cambridge, CB2 1EW (Office); Brook Cottage, Pemberton Terrace, Cambridge, CB2 1JA, England (Home). *Telephone:* (01223) 336458 (Office); (01223) 357637 (Home).

THUBRON, Colin Gerald Dryden, F.R.S.L.; British author; b. 14 June 1939, London; s. of Brig. Gerald Ernest Thubron and Evelyn Kate Dryden; ed. Eton Coll.; mem. Editorial Staff, Hutchinson & Co. Publishers Ltd. 1959–62; freelance documentary film maker 1963–64; Production Ed., The Macmillan Co., U.S.A. 1964–65; freelance author 1965–; Silver Pen Award of PEN 1985, Thomas Cook Award 1988, Hawthornden Prize 1988. *Publications:* Mirror to Damascus, The Hills of Adonis, Jerusalem, Journey into Cyprus, The God in the Mountain (novel), Emperor (novel), Among the Russians, A Cruel Madness (novel), Behind the Wall, Falling (novel), Turning Back the Sun (novel), The Lost Heart of Asia, Distance (novel) 1994. *Scenario:* The Prince of the Pagodas (ballet at The Royal Opera House, Covent Garden). *Address:* Garden Cottage, 27 St. Ann's Villas, London, W.11, England. *Telephone:* 0171-602 2522.

THULIN, Ingrid; Swedish actress and director; b. 27 Jan. 1929, Sollefteå; d. of Adam Thulin and Nanna Larsson; m. 1st Claes Sylwander 1951; m. 2nd Harry Schein 1956; ed. Royal Dramatic Theatre School, Stockholm; has appeared in many modern and classical plays for Royal Dramatic Theatre, Stockholm, and for municipal theatres of Malmö and Stockholm until 1962; has also appeared on Broadway, the Italian stage and U.S. T.V.; many nat. and int. awards. *Films include:* When Love Comes to the Village 1950, Wild Strawberries 1957, So Close to Life 1958, The Face 1958, The Judge 1960, The Four Horsemen of the Apocalypse 1961, Winter Light 1962, The Silence 1963, La guerre est finie 1968, The Damned 1970, Cries and Whispers 1973, A Handful of Love 1974, La cage 1975, Cassandra Crossing 1976, Agnes Will Die 1977, One and One 1978, The Rehearsal, Il Corsario 1983, La Casa Sorire 1991, Rabbit Face; wrote and dir. feature film Broken Skies 1983. *Publication:* Någon jag kände (Somebody I Knew) 1993. *Address:* Kevingestrand 7B, 18231 Danderyd, Sweden; 00060 Sacrofano, Rome, Italy. *Telephone:* 08-755-68-98 (Sweden); 06-9084171 (Italy).

THUNBORG, Anders; Swedish diplomatist; b. 9 June 1934, Stockholm; m. Ingalill Thunborg; three s. two d.; Organizing Sec. of Stockholm branch, Social Democratic Party 1958, transferred to party Exec. 1960, later Information Sec. and then Int. Sec.; Asst. Party Sec. 1967–69; Under-Sec. of State, Ministry of Defence 1969–74, Ministry of Foreign Affairs 1974–76; Perm. Rep. to UN 1977–83; Chair. UN Trust Fund S.A. 1977–82; Vice-Chair. UN Comm. on Decolonisation 1978–79; Chair. UN Study Group on Nuclear Weapons 1979–82; Minister of Defence 1983–85; Amb. to U.S.S.R. and Mongolia 1986–89, to U.S.A. 1989–93, to Greece 1993; Consultant, Ministry of Foreign Affairs 1994–95; Amb. to the Holy See 1996–. *Publications:* a number of books, handbooks and essays mainly on int. affairs and defence policy. *Address:* Embassy of Sweden to the Holy See, c/o Ministry of Foreign Affairs, Box 16121, 10323 Stockholm, Sweden; Via Maurizio Bufalini 2, 00161 Rome, Italy. *Telephone:* (6) 6784351 (Italy). *Fax:* (6) 6784355 (Italy).

THUNHOLM, Lars-Erik, K.B.E.; Swedish business executive; b. 2 Nov. 1914, Stockholm; s. of Nils Thunholm and Ebba Olsson; m. May Bruzelli 1939; ed. Stockholm School of Economics, Univ. of Stockholm; joined Svenska Handelsbanken 1938, Econ. Adviser and Man. of Econ. Dept. 1948–55, Dir. 1951–55; Head of Fed. of Swedish Industries 1955–57; Man. Dir. Skandinaviska Banken, Stockholm (now Skandinaviska Enskilda Banken) 1957–65, Chief Man. Dir. 1965–76, Chair. of Bd. 1976–84; Chair. Nobel Industrier Sverige AB 1975–91; Chair. Bd., Banque Scandinave en Suisse, Scandinavian Bank Ltd. –1984, Swedish Match –1985, Billerud, Hon. Chair. 1982–84, AB, Svenska Dagbladet, AB Bofors –1984; Hon. Ph.D.; Kt. Commdr. of the Royal Order of Vasa; Grand Cross, Order of the North Star. *Publications:* Svenskt Kreditvasen 1969, Bankvasendet i utlandet 1969, Bankerna och penningpolitiken 1964, Bankerna och samhället 1974, Oscar Rydbeck och hans tid 1991, Ivar Kreuger 1995. *Address:* Döbelnsgatan 13, 4 tr. S-111 40 Stockholm, Sweden (Home).

THURAU, Klaus Walther Christian, M.D.; German physiologist; b. 14 June 1928, Bautzen; s. of Walther Thurau and Helene Engel; m. Antje Wiese 1957; two s.; ed. High School, Berlin, and Univs. of Erlangen and Kiel; Lecturer in Physiology, Univ. of Göttingen 1955–65; Chair. Dept. of Physiology, Univ. of Munich 1968–; Visiting Prof. American Heart Asscn. 1964; Gilman Prof., Dartmouth Medical School 1968; Visiting Prof., American Kidney Foundation 1980; Pres. Int. Soc. of Nephrology; Treas. and Councillor Int. Union of Physiological Science; mem. Exec. Bd. Int. Council of Scientific Unions; Chair. Verum-Foundation, German UNESCO Comm. on Natural Sciences; mem. German Physiological Soc., Soc. for Clinical Investigation,

American Soc. of Physiology, Int. Soc. for Hypertension, Int. Soc. of Nephrology; Hon. mem. Australian Soc. of Nephrology, S. African Soc. of Nephrology, Heidelberg Acad. of Sciences; Chief Ed. European Journal of Physiology (Pflügers Archiv.). *Publications:* various papers on renal function (in medical journals). *Leisure interest:* music. *Address:* Josef-Vötterstrasse 6, 81545 Munich, Germany. *Telephone:* (89) 5996 528. *Fax:* (89) 5996 532.

THURLOW, 8th Baron, cr. 1792; **Francis Edward Hovell-Thurlow-Cumming-Bruce,** K.C.M.G.; British diplomatist; b. 9 March 1912, London; s. of 6th Baron Thurlow and Grace Catherine Trotter; m. Yvonne Diana Aubyn Wilson 1949 (died 1990); two s. (one deceased) two d.; ed. Shrewsbury School and Trinity Coll., Cambridge; Asst. Prin., Dept. of Agric. for Scotland 1935–37, Dominions Office 1937; Asst. Sec. Office of U.K. High Commr. in New Zealand 1939–44, in Canada 1944–46; Prin. Pvt. Sec. to Sec. of State 1946–48; Asst. Sec. Commonwealth Relations Office (C.R.O.) 1948; Head of Political Div., U.K. High Commr. in India 1949–52; Establishment Officer, C.R.O. 1952–54, Head of Commodities Dept. 1954–55; Adviser on External Affairs to Gov. of Gold Coast 1955–57, Deputy High Commr. for U.K. in Ghana 1957–58; Asst. Under-Sec. of State, C.R.O. 1958; Deputy High Commr. for U.K. in Canada 1958–59, High Commr. in New Zealand 1959–63, High Commr. in Nigeria 1964–66; Gov. and C.-in-C. Bahamas 1968–72; K.St.J. 1969; independent peer. *Address:* 102 Leith Mansions, Grantully Road, London, W9 1LJ; Philham Water, Hartland, Bideford, N. Devon, EX39 6EZ, England. *Telephone:* 0171-289 9664 (London); (01237) 441433 (Bideford).

THURMAN, Uma; American actress; b. 29 April 1970, Boston; d. of Robert Thurman and Nena Schlebrugge; m. Gary Oldman 1991 (divorced); worked as model, dishwasher. *Films:* The Adventures of Baron Munchhausen 1988, Dangerous Liaisons 1988, Even Cowgirls Get the Blues, Final Analysis, Where the Heart Is, Henry and June, Mad Dog and Glory, Pulp Fiction, Robin Hood, Dylan, A Month by the Lake, The Truth About Cats and Dogs, Batman and Robin, Gattaca, The Avengers, Les Miserables. *Address:* c/o CAA, 9830 Wilshire Boulevard, Beverly Hills, CA 90212, U.S.A.

THURMOND, Strom; American politician, farmer and lawyer; b. 5 Dec. 1902, Edgefield, S.C.; s. of J. William Thurmond and Eleanor Gertrude (née Strom) Thurmond; m. 1st Jean Crouch 1947 (died 1960); m. 2nd Nancy Moore 1968 (separated 1991); two s. two d. (one deceased); ed. Clemson Coll.; Teacher, S. Carolina Schools 1923–29, Supt. 1929–33; admitted to the Bar 1930, served as City and County Attorney; State Senator 1933–38; Circuit Judge 1938–46; active service in Europe and Pacific 1942–46; Maj.-Gen. in U.S. Army Reserve (retd.); Gov. of South Carolina 1947–51; U.S. Senator from S. Carolina 1954–; Chair. Senate Judiciary Cttee. 1981–87, Ranking Minority mem. 1987–92; Chair. Senate Armed Services Cttee. 1995–99; Pres. U.S. Senate pro tempore 1981–87, 1995–; Trustee, Bob Jones Univ.; Chair. S.C. Democratic del. and mem. Nat. Exec. Cttee. 1948; mem. American Bar Asscn., Clemson Alumni Asscn.; numerous hon. degrees; decorations include Legion of Merit with Oak Leaf Cluster, Bronze Star with "V", Purple Heart, Croix de guerre, Croix de la Couronne, Army Commendation Ribbon, Congressional Medal, Honor Soc. Nat. Patriot's Award 1974, American Legion Distinguished Public Service Award 1975, American Judges Distinguished Service Award 1981, Presidential Citizens Medal 1989, Presidential Medal of Freedom 1993 and numerous other awards; Republican. *Address:* US Senate, 217 Russell Senate Office Building, Washington, DC 20510; Aiken, SC 29801, U.S.A. (Home). *Telephone:* (202) 224-5972.

THWAITE, Anthony (Simon), O.B.E., M.A., F.R.S.L., D.LITT.; British writer; b. 23 June 1930, Chester; s. of Hartley Thwaite and Alice Thwaite (née Mallinson); m. Ann Harrop 1955; four d.; ed. Kingswood School, Bath, Christ Church, Oxford; Visiting lecturer in English Literature Univ. of Tokyo 1955–57; radio producer BBC 1957–62; Literary Ed. The Listener 1962–65; Asst. Prof. of English, Univ. of Libya, Benghazi 1965–67; Literary Ed. New Statesman 1968–72; Co-Ed. Encounter 1973–85; Editorial Dir., Editorial Consultant André Deutsch 1986–95; Richard Hillary Memorial Prize 1968. *Publications:* Philip Larkin: Collected Poems (ed.) 1988, Poems 1953–88 1989, Selected Letters of Philip Larkin (ed.) 1992, Selected Poems 1956–1996 1997. *Leisure interests:* archaeology, travel. *Address:* The Mill House, Low Tharston, Norfolk, NR15 2YN, England. *Telephone:* (01508) 489 569. *Fax:* (01508) 489 221.

THYSSEN-BORNEMISZA DE KASZON, Baron Hans Heinrich; Swiss industrialist and administrator; b. 13 April 1921, Gröningen; m. 1st Princess Theresa Von Lippe 1939; m. 2nd Nina Ryer; m. 3rd Fiona Campbell-Walker; m. 4th Denise Short; m. 5th Carmen Barker; four s. (one adopted) one d.; ed. Realgymnasium, The Hague, Fribourg Univ.; Chair., Hon. Pres. Supervisory Bd. Thyssen-Bornemisa Group NV (now TBG Holdings N.V.) 1991–, Advisory Bd. BHF-Bank, Frankfurt; Hon. Chair. Bremer Vulkan Schiffbau- und Maschinenfabrik, Bremen, Thyssengas GmbH, Duisburg; Dir. Heineken NV, Heineken Holding NV, Nederlandse Credietbank NV, Amsterdam; mem. Trustee Council Nat. Gallery of Art, Washington, DC, Sotheby's Holdings Advisory Bd.; picture collection housed and exhibited in Villa Favorita; Gran Cruz, Orden Carlo III (Spain) 1988. *Address:* Camino del Golf, 3la Moraleja, 28109 Madrid, Spain; 56 Chester Square, London, SW1W 9AE, England; Villa Favorita, 6976 Castagnola di Lugano, Switzerland.

TIAN CHENGPING; Chinese administrator; b. 1940; alt. mem. 13th Cen. Cttee. CCP 1987–91; a Deputy Sec. CPC 8th Qinghai Prov. Cttee. 1988–; mem. 14th CCP Cen. Cttee. 1992–97, 15th CCP Cen. Cttee. 1997–; Gov. of Qinghai Prov. 1993; Sec. CCP Qinghai Prov. Cttee. 1997–. *Address:* c/o Office of the Governor, Qinghai Provincial Government, Xining City, Qinghai Province, People's Republic of China.

TIAN CONGMING; Chinese politician; b. May 1943, Fugu, Shaanxi Prov.; ed. Beijing Normal Univ.; joined CCP 1965; corresp. Xinhua News Agency Nei Monggol Br., Chief Sec. then Vice-Sec. CCP Nei Monggol Autonomous Region Cttee., Vice-Sec. CCP Tibetan Autonomous Region Cttee. 1970–90; Vice-Minister of Radio, Motion Picture and TV 1990–98; Dir. State Gen. Admin. of Radio, Motion Picture and TV 1998–; mem. CCP Cen. Cttee. for Discipline Inspection 1992–. *Address:* General Administration of Radio, Motion Picture and Television, Beijing, People's Republic of China.

TIAN FENGSHAN; Chinese administrator; b. Oct. 1940; joined CCP 1970; mem. CCP Suihua Prefectural Cttee. Heilongjiang Prov. 1985–88; Deputy Commr., Prov. Admin. Office 1985–88; alt. mem. 13th CCP Cen. Cttee. 1987–91; Sec. CCP Mudanjiang Municipal Cttee. 1988–89; Vice-Gov. Heilongjiang Prov. 1989–94, Acting Gov. 1994–95, Gov. 1995–; Sec. CCP Harbin Municipal Cttee. 1992; alt. mem. 14th CCP Cen. Cttee. 1992–97; mem. 15th CCP Cen. Cttee. 1997–; Deputy to 8th NPC from Heilongjiang Prov. 1996; Deputy Sec. CCP Heilongjiang Prov. Cttee. *Address:* Office of the Governor, Heilongjiang Provincial Government, Harbin City, People's Republic of China.

TIAN JIYUN; Chinese politician; b. June 1929, Feicheng Co., Shandong; joined CCP 1945; Deputy Sec.-Gen. State Council 1981–83, Sec.-Gen. 1983–88; mem. 12th CCP Cen. Cttee. 1982–87, 13th CCP Cen. Cttee. 1987–92, 14th CCP Cen. Cttee. 1992–97, 15th CCP Cen. Cttee. 1997–; mem. Politburo 1985–; Vice-Premier 1983–93; Head, Commodity Prices Group, State Council 1984–93; mem. Secr. CCP Cen. Cttee. 1985–87; Head State Flood Control HQ 1988–93, Cen. Forest Fire Prevention HQ 1987–93; Vice-Chair. Standing Cttee., 8th NPC 1993–98, 9th NPC 1998–. *Address:* Standing Committee of National People's Congress, Beijing, People's Republic of China.

TIAN ZENGPEI; Chinese politican; b. 1930, Raoyang Co., Hebei Prov.; ed.Nankai Univ.; Vice-Minister of Foreign Affairs 1988–96; mem. 14th CCP Cen. Cttee. 1992–97; Chair. Foreign Affairs Cttee., 9th Nat. Cttee. of CPPCC 1998–. *Address:* National Committee of Chinese People's Political Consultative Conference, Taipingqiao Street, Beijing, People's Republic of China. *Telephone:* (01) 553 831.

TIAN ZHAOWU; Chinese scientist and university administrator; b. 1927, Fuzhou City, Fujian Prov.; ed. Xiamen Univ.; mem. Dept. of Chem. Academia Sinica 1985–; Pres. of Xiamen Univ. 1986; mem. Standing Cttee. 8th CCP Nat. Cttee. 1993–; Hon. Nat. Prize of Sciences 1987. *Address:* c/o Xiamen University, Xiamen, Fujian Province, People's Republic of China.

TIBERI, Jean, L. EN D.; French politician; b. 30 Jan. 1935, Paris; s. of Charles Tiberi and Hélène Pallavicini; m. Xavière Casanova; two d.; ed. Coll. Sainte-Barbe, Lycées Montaigne and Louis-le-Grand and Faculté de Droit, Paris; Acting Judge, Colmar 1958; Deputy Public Prosecutor, Metz 1959, Meaux 1959; Judge, Beauvais 1959, Nantes 1960; Chancellery 1960–63; Dir. of Studies, Faculté de Droit, Paris 1961–; Conseiller de Paris 1965–; First Vice-Pres. Conseil de Paris 1983–95; Deputy to Mayor of Paris 1977–83, First Deputy 1983–95; Deputy to Nat. Ass. 1968–; fmr. Sec. of State at Ministries of Agric., Industry and Research; Mayor of 5th arrondissement of Paris 1983–95; Sec. Paris R.P.R. 1985–; Mayor of Paris 1995–. *Address:* Assemblée Nationale, 75355 Paris; Hôtel de Ville, 75196 Paris (Offices); 1 place du Panthéon, 75005 Paris, France (Home).

TICKELL, Sir Crispin (Charles Cervantes), G.C.M.G., K.C.V.O., F.R.G.S., F.Z.S.; British university chancellor and fmr. diplomatist; b. 25 Aug. 1930; s. of late Jerrard Tickell and Renée Haynes; m. 1st Chloë Gunn 1954 (divorced 1976); two s. one d.; m. 2nd Penelope Thorne Thorne 1977; ed. Westminster School and Christ Church, Oxford; entered H.M. Diplomatic Service 1954; served at The Hague 1955–58, Mexico 1958–61, Paris 1964–70; Pvt. Sec. to Chancellor of Duchy of Lancaster 1970–72; Head, Western Orgs. Dept. FCO 1972–75; Fellow, Center for Int. Affairs Harvard Univ. 1975–76; Chef de Cabinet to Pres. of Comm. of European Communities 1977–81; Visiting Fellow, All Souls Coll. Oxford 1981; Amb. to Mexico 1981–83; Deputy Under-Sec. of State FCO 1983–84; Perm. Sec. Overseas Devt. Admin. 1984–87; Perm. Rep. to UN 1987–90; Warden Green Coll. Oxford 1990–97; Dir. Green Coll. Centre for Environmental Policy and Understanding 1992–; Chancellor Univ. of Kent at Canterbury 1996–; Dir. (non-exec.) IBM UK 1990–95 (mem. IBM Advisory Bd. 1995–), Govett Mexican Horizons Investment 1991–96, Govett American Smaller Companies Trust 1996–98; Dir. BOC Foundation 1990–; Pres. Royal Geographical Soc. 1990–93, Earth Centre 1996–, Nat. Soc. for Clean Air 1997–, Gaia Soc. 1998–; Chair. Int. Inst. for Environment and Devt. 1990–94, Earthwatch Europe 1990–97, Climate Inst. of Washington, D.C. 1990–, Marine Biological Asscn. 1990–, Advisory Cttee. on Darwin Initiative 1992–99; Trustee Nat. History Museum 1991–, World Wildlife Fund (U.K.) 1993–99; Convenor Govt. Panel on Sustainable Devt. 1994–; Hon. Fellow Westminster School 1993, St. Edmund's Coll., Cambridge 1995, Green Coll., Oxford 1997; Dr. h.c. (Univs. of Stirling, E. Anglia, Mass., Bristol, Birmingham, Sussex, Westminster,

Cranfield, Loughborough, Sheffield Hallam, East London); Officer, Order of Orange-Nassau (Netherlands), Order of Aztec Eagle with sash (Mexico). *Publication:* Climatic Change and World Affairs 1977, Mary Anning of Lyme Regis 1996, contribs. to many other works. *Leisure interests:* climatology, palaeohistory, art, mountains. *Address:* Ablington Old Barn, Ablington, Cirencester, Glos., GL7 5NU, England. *Telephone:* (01285) 740569. *Fax:* (01285) 740671.

TICKNER, Robert, LL.M., B.ECONS.; Australian politician; b. 24 Dec. 1951, Sydney; m. Jody Tickner; one c.; ed. Univ. of Sydney; lecturer, Faculty of Business Studies, N.S.W. Inst. of Tech. 1974–78, Faculty of Law 1978–79; Prin. Solicitor, Aboriginal Legal Service, Redfern, Sydney 1979–83; Alderman Sydney City Council 1977–84; M.P. for Hughes, N.S.W. 1984–96; Minister for Aboriginal and Torres Strait Islander Affairs 1990–96; Office holder Fed. Electorate Council and other Australian Labor Party bodies; Pres. N.S.W. Soc. of Labor Lawyers; Cttee. mem. N.S.W. Council for Civil Liberties; Founding Cttee. mem. Citizens for Democracy; Convenor Labor Parliamentarians for Nuclear Free Australia; Chair. Parl. Group of Amnesty Int. *Address:* c/o 762 Princes Highway, Sutherland, N.S.W. 2232, Australia.

TIDBURY, Sir Charles Henderson, Kt.; British company director; b. 26 Jan. 1926, Camberley; s. of the late Brig. O. H. Tidbury, M.C. and Beryl (née Pearce) Tidbury; m. Anne Russell 1950; two s. three d.; ed. Eton Coll.; King's Royal Rifle Corps 1944–52; joined Whitbread & Co. Ltd. 1952, a Man. Dir. 1959, Chief Exec. 1974, Deputy Chair. 1977, Chair. 1978–84; Chair. Brickwoods Brewery Ltd. 1966–71; Dir. Whitbread & Co. PLC 1984–88, Whitbread Investment Co. PLC, Barclays PLC 1978–91, Barclays Bank PLC 1985–91, Barclays Bank UK Ltd., Mercantile Group PLC 1988–91, Nabisco Group Ltd. 1985–88, Vaux Group PLC 1985–91, ICL (Europe) 1985–94, Pearl Assurance PLC 1985–94, Gales Brewery 1990–96; Deputy Chair. Int. Speciality Chemicals (Inspec) PLC 1994–98; Pres. Inst. of Brewing 1976–78, Vice-Pres. 1978; Chair. Brewers' Soc. 1982–84, Vice-Pres. 1985–; Pres. Shire Horse Soc. 1986–88, British Inst. of Innkeeping 1985–92 (Vice-Pres. 1992–); Chair. Mary Rose Devt. Trust 1980–86, William and Mary Tercentenary Trust Ltd. 1986–93, Brewing Research Foundation (now Brewing Research Foundation Int.) 1985–93 (Pres. 1993–); mem. Portsmouth and S.E. Hants. Health Comm. 1992–96, Hants. Enterprise Partnership 1992–; Trustee, Nat. Maritime Museum 1984–96; Gov. Nat. Heart and Chest Hosps. 1988–90, Portsmouth Polytechnic (now Univ.) 1988–96; mem. Centre for Policy Studies 1988–93; Hon. LL.D. (Portsmouth) 1997. *Leisure interests:* family, sailing, shooting, countryside. *Address:* Crocker Hill Farm, Forest Lane, Wickham, Hants., PO17 5DW, England (Home). *Telephone:* (01329) 833229. *Fax:* (01329) 833229.

TIE NING; Chinese writer; b. 1957, Beijing; s. of Tie Yang and Xu Zhi-ying; council mem. of Writers' Asscn. 1985–. *Publications:* Path in the Night 1980, Xiangxue (won Nat. Short Story Prize) 1982, Red Shirt With No Buttons (won Nat. Fiction Prize) 1984, Rose Gate 1988, Hay Stack (short stories) 1991, Women's White Night (non-fiction) 1991, Straw Ring (non-fiction) 1992. *Leisure interests:* music, gourmet cooking. *Address:* 40-2-201 Luo Sizhuang, Baoding City, Hebei Prov., People's Republic of China. *Telephone:* (0312) 34341.

TIEMANN, Susanne, D.JUR.; German lawyer; b. 20 April 1947, Schwandorf; d. of Hermann Bamberg and Anna-Maria Bamberg; m. Burkhard Tiemann 1969; one s. two d.; ed. Ludwig-Maximilian Univ. Munich; called to the Bar and established as lawyer in Munich 1975; lawyer, Cologne 1980; mem. Econ. and Social Cttee. of EC 1987–, Chair. 1992–; mem. Bd. German Fed. of Liberal Professions 1988–; mem. Exec. Bd. and Vice-Pres. European Secr. of the Liberal, Intellectual and Social Professions (SEPLIS) 1988, Pres. 1989–95; Chair. German Taxpayers' Asscn. 1992–94; mem. Bundestag 1994–; Frauen für Europa Prize 1993. *Address:* Bonner Str. 324, 50968 Cologne, Germany. *Telephone:* (221) 9347540 (Cologne); (228) 16-81168 (Bonn). *Fax:* (221) 93475420 (Cologne); (228) 16-86226 (Bonn)

TIEN, Chang-Lin, PH.D.; Chinese/American academic; b. 24 July 1935, Wuhan, China; s. of Yun Chien and Yun Di (Lee) Tien; m. Di-Hwa Liu 1959; one s. two d.; ed. Nat. Univ. of Taiwan, Univ. of Louisville, U.S.A., Univ. of Princeton, U.S.A.; acting Asst. Prof. Dept. of Mechanical Eng. Univ. of Calif., Berkeley 1959–60, Asst. Prof. 1960–64, Assoc. Prof. 1964–88, Prof. 1968–88, 1990–, A. Martin Berlin Prof. 1987–88, 1990–, Dept. Chair. 1974–81, Vice-Chancellor for Research 1983–85, Chancellor 1990–97; Exec. Vice-Chancellor Univ. of Calif. at Irvine 1988–90; Chair. Int. Advisory Panel, Univ. of Tokyo Inst. of Ind. Science 1995; Gov. Bd. of Dirs., Cttee. of 100 1991–; mem. Bd. of Dirs. Wells Fargo Bank 1991–, A.A.A.S. 1992– Berkeley Community Foundation 1993–, Raychem Corpn 1996–; mem. Bd. of Trustees, Chiang Industrial Charity Foundation Ltd., Hong Kong 1991–, Princeton Univ. 1991–95, Asia Foundation 1993–, Carnegie Foundation for the Advancement of Teaching 1994–97, U.S. Cttee. on Econ. Devt. 1994–, Council on Foreign Relations 1996; mem. Aspen Inst. Domestic Strategy Group 1992–97; mem. Nat. Advisory Council, American Soc. for Eng. Educ. 1993, Int. Advisory Panel, Nat. Univ. of Singapore 1993; Ed. Int. Journal of Heat and Mass Transfer 1981–, Int. Communications in Heat and Mass Transfer 1981–; Ed.-in-Chief Experimental Heat Transfer 1987–, Microscale Thermophysical Eng. 1997–; consultant for numerous industrial, governmental and educational orgs.; Guggenheim Fellow 1965; Hon. mem. or Fellow of numerous socs. including mem. Nat. Acad. of Eng. 1976, Fellow Academia Sinica (Taiwan) 1988, Fellow A.A.A.S. 1989, Fellow American Acad. of Arts and Sciences 1991; Hon. Prof. at 12 leading Univs. in China since 1981; seven hon. doctor's degrees; Heat Transfer Memorial Award 1974, Gustus L. Larson Memorial Award 1975, Thermophysics Award 1977, Max Jakob Memorial Award 1981. *Publications:* Statistical Thermodynamics (jtly.) 1971, ed. of 12 titles, author of 280 research papers. *Address:* Department of Mechanical Engineering, University of California, 6101 Etcheverry Hall # 1740, Berkeley, CA 94720, U.S.A.

TIEN, PING-KING, M.S., PH.D.; Chinese research engineer; b. 2 Aug. 1919, Checking Prov., China; s. of N. S. Tien and C. S. (Yun) Tien; m. Nancy Chen 1952; two d.; ed. Nat. Cen. Univ., China and Stanford Univ.; Vice-Pres. Tien-Sun Industrial Co. 1942–47; Research Assoc. Stanford Univ. 1948–52; mem. Tech. Staff, AT & T Bell Labs. 1952–61, Head, Electronics Physics Research 1961–80, Head, Microelectronics Research 1980–84, Ed.-in-Chief High Speed Electronics and Systems; Fellow, AT & T Bell Labs. 1984 (Fellow Emer. 1990–), I.E.E.E., Optical Soc. of America; mem. Nat. Acad. of Eng., N.A.S.; Chinese Inst. of Eng. Achievement Award. *Publications:* numerous technical publs. *Address:* AT & T Bell Laboratories, Lucent Technologies, Holmdel, NJ 07733 (Office); 9 Carolyn Court, Holmdel, NJ 07733, U.S.A. (Home). *Telephone:* 201-949-6925 (Office).

TIEN HUNG-MAO, M.A., PH.D.; American professor of political science; b. 7 Nov. 1938, Tainan, Taiwan; m. Amy Tien; one s. one d.; ed. Tunghai Univ. and Univ. of Wisconsin; fmr. Prof. of Political Science, Univ. of Wisconsin; Pres. Inst. for Nat. Policy Research 1991–; mem. Nat. Unification Research Council, Office of Pres. of Taiwan 1994–; Nat. Policy Adviser to Pres. of Taiwan 1996–; Dir. Foundation for Int. Co-operation and Devt. 1996–. *Publications include:* Government and Politics in Kuomintang China 1927–37, The Great Transition, Social and Political Change in the Republic of China, Taiwan's Electoral Politics and Democratic Transition: Riding the Third Wave 1995. *Leisure interests:* golf, tennis, table-tennis. *Address:* 5F, #111, Sung-chiang Road, Taipei (Office); #225, Tung-shih Street, Hsi-chih, Taipei County, Taiwan (Home). *Telephone:* 886-2-509-9181 (Office); 886-2-660-0145 (Home). *Fax:* 886-2-509-2949.

TIETMEYER, Hans, DR.RER.POL.; German banker, economist and civil servant; b. 18 Aug. 1931, Metelen; s. of Bernhard and Helene Tietmeyer; m. 1st Marie-Luise Tietmeyer (died 1978); m. 2nd Maria-Therese Tietmeyer 1980; one s. one d.; ed. Univs. of Münster, Bonn and Cologne; Sec. Bischöfliche Studienforderung Cusanuswerk 1959–62; Fed. Ministry of Econs. 1962–82, Head of Div. of Gen. Econ. Policy 1973–82; mem. Econ. Policy Cttee. of European Community and OECD 1972–82; Sec. of State, Ministry of Finance 1982–89; mem. Bd. of Dirs., Bundesbank 1990, Vice-Pres. 1991–93, Pres. 1993–99. *Publications:* more than 100 articles on economics. *Leisure interests:* sport, rambling. *Address:* c/o Deutsche Bundesbank, Wilhelm-Epstein-Strasse 14, 95661 Frankfurt, Germany.

TIGERMAN, Stanley, M.ARCH., F.A.I.A.; American architect; b. 20 Sept. 1930, Chicago, Ill.; s. of Samuel B. Tigerman and Emma L. Stern; m. Margaret I. McCurry 1979; one s. one d.; ed. Mass. Inst. of Tech. and Yale Univ.; architectural draughtsman, George Fred Keck, Chicago 1949–50; Skidmore Owings & Merrill, Chicago 1957–59; Paul Rudolph, New Haven 1959–61; Harry Weese 1961–62; Partner, Tigerman & Koglin, Chicago 1962–64; Prin. Stanley Tigerman & Assoc. Chicago 1964–82; partner, Tigerman Fugman McCurry, Chicago 1982–88, Tigerman McCurry, Chicago 1988–; co-founder, Archeworks Design Lab. Chicago 1993; Prof. of Architecture, Univ. of Ill. Chicago 1967–71, 1980–93, Dir. School of Architecture 1985–93; Davenport Prof. of Arch. Yale Univ. 1979, Bishop Prof. 1984; Architect-in-residence, American Acad. Rome 1980; Visiting Prof. Harvard 1982; mem. Advisory Cttee. Princeton Univ. 1997; ACSA Citation 1989 and numerous other awards. *Publications:* Chicago's Architectural Heritage: A Romantic Classical Image . . . & Work of the Current Generation of Chicago Architects 1979, VERSUS: An American Architect's Alternatives 1982, Stanley Tigerman Architoons 1988, The Architecture of Exile 1988, Stanley Tigerman, Buildings & Projects 1966–89 1989. *Leisure interests:* tennis, skiing, reading. *Address:* Tigerman McCurry Ltd., 444 North Wells Street, Suite 206, Chicago, IL 60610, U.S.A. (Office). *Telephone:* (312)-644-5880.

TIGRID, Pavel; Czech journalist, publisher, radio presenter and politician; b. 27 Oct. 1917, Prague; m. Ivana Myšková 1947; one s. two d.; radio presenter BBC, London 1939–45; returned to Czechoslovakia 1945; fled Czechoslovakia 1948; set up and worked for Czech Section of Radio Free Europe, Munich 1952–89; returned to Czechoslovakia 1990–; advisor to Pres. Havel 1991–92; Minister of Culture Govt. of Czech Repub. 1994–95; Adviser to Pres.'s Office for Czech-German Relations 1997–; a Co-ordinator, Co-ordination Council of Czech-German Discussion Forum 1998–; European Cultural Prize 1998; Officier, Légion d'honneur 1992, Order of T. G. Masaryk 1995. *Publications:* The Prague Spring 1968, An Intelligent Woman's Guidebook through Her Own Life 1988; articles and radio plays. *Leisure interests:* skiing, tourism. *Address:* U starého hřbitova 248/3, 110 00 Prague 1, Czech Republic (Home).

TIGYI, József; Hungarian biophysicist; b. 19 March 1926, Kaposvár; s. of András Tigyi and Julianna Mátrai; m. Anna Sebes; two s.; ed. Medical Univ. of Pécs; Prof. and Dir. of Biophysical Inst. Medical Univ. Pécs 1971–91, Vice-Rector 1967–73, Rector 1973–79; corresp. mem. Hungarian Acad. of Sciences 1967–76, mem. 1976–, Vice-Pres. 1988, Pres. Regional Cttee., Pécs 1996–; Pres. Acad. Section No. 8 (Biological sciences) 1980–88; Pres. Hungarian Biophysical Soc. 1972–91, Hon. Pres. 1991–; Pres. UNESCO European

Collaboration in Biophysics 1976–86; Chief Ed. Acta Biochimica et Biophysica 1981–91; mem. Royal Soc. of Medicine, New York Acad. of Sciences 1980–, European Acad. of Arts, Sciences and Humanities, Paris 1990–; WHO Exec. Bd. 1972–75; Int. Council of Scientific Unions (ICSU) Gen. Cttee.; Cttee. on the Teaching of Science 1986–93; Gesellschaft für mathematische u. physikalische Biologie (G.D.R.), Biophysical Soc. of Romania, of India; Gen. Sec. Int. Union of Pure and Applied Biophysics (IUPAB) 1984–93, Co-Chair. Special Cttee. on Radiation and Environmental Biophysics 1993–; Labour Order of Merit (Silver) 1966, (Gold) 1970, 1979. *Publications:* Application of Radioactive Isotope in Experimental Medicine 1965; Biophysics—Theory of bioelectric phenomena, Biological semi-conductors; Energetics of cross-striated muscle 1977. *Address:* Biophysical Institute of the Medical University, 7643 Pécs, Szigeti ut 12, Hungary. *Telephone:* (72) 314-017. *Fax:* (72) 314-017.

TIJDEMAN, Robert; Netherlands professor of mathematics; b. 30 July 1943, Oostzaan; ed. Univ. of Amsterdam; scientific worker, Univ. of Amsterdam 1967–70; Reader, Univ. of Leiden 1970–75, Prof. of Math. 1975–; mem. Royal Netherlands Acad. of Sciences 1987. *Publication:* Exponential diophantine equations (with T. N. Shorey) 1986. *Address:* Mathematical Institute, P.O. Box 9512, 2300 RA Leiden, Netherlands. *Telephone:* (71) 5277138. *Fax:* (71) 527 6985.

TIKHVINSKY, Sergej Leonidovich; Russian historian; b. 1 Sept. 1918, Petrograd; s. of Leonid Tikhvinsky and Kira Tikhvinsky; m. Vera Nikitichna 1940; one s. one d.; ed. Oriental Inst., Moscow; mem. CPSU 1941–91; diplomatic service in China, U.K. and Japan 1939–57; Head of Asian Dept. of U.S.S.R. State Cttee. with Council of Ministers for Foreign Cultural Relations 1957–60; Prof. Moscow Univ. 1959; Dir U.S.S.R Acad. of Sciences Inst. of Sinology 1960–61; Deputy Dir. of Acad. of Sciences Inst. of the Peoples of Asia 1961–63; Deputy Dir. of Acad. of Sciences Inst. of World Socialist Economies 1963–65; Corresp. mem. of Acad. of Sciences 1968–81, mem. 1981–; Chief of History of Diplomacy Dept., Head of Asia Section in Foreign Policy Planning Dept. U.S.S.R. Ministry of Foreign Affairs 1965–80; Rector of Diplomatic Acad. of U.S.S.R. Ministry of Foreign Affairs 1980–86; Academician-Sec. of Historical section of U.S.S.R. Acad. of Sciences 1982–88; Pres. Nat. Cttee. of Soviet (now Russian) Historians 1980–; Chair. Scientific Council for The History of Russia's Foreign Policy and Int. Relations 1987–; Hon. Chair. All-Russia Assn. of Sinologues 1988; Adviser to the Presidium of Acad. of Sciences 1988–; Hon. mem. Accademia Fiorentina delle Arti 1984. *Publications include:* The Reform Movement in China and K'ang Youwei 1959, Sun Yatsen Foreign Affairs Theories and Practice 1964, Manchu Rule in China 1966, History of China and Present time 1976, The Reform Movements in China at the end of the 19th Century 1980, China and her Neighbours 1980, China and World History 1988, China: History through Personalities and Events 1991, China in my Life 1992, China's Road to Unity and Independence 1996, Eternal Sleep in China's Earth: Memorial Album 1996, Russia–Japan, Doomed to Good Neighbourhood 1996; numerous articles on Soviet and Russian foreign policy and int. affairs. *Leisure interest:* angling. *Address:* National Committee of Historians, Leninsky prosp. 32A, 117334 Moscow, Russia. *Telephone:* (095) 938-00-08, 123-90-73 (Office); (095) 915-45-20 (Home).

TILEY, John, LL.D., M.A., B.C.L.; British professor of law of taxation; b. 25 Feb. 1941, Leamington Spa; s. of the late William Tiley and Audrey Tiley; m. Jillinda Draper 1964; two s. one d.; ed. Winchester Coll. and Lincoln Coll. Oxford; called to the Bar, Inner Temple 1964, Hon. Bencher 1993; Recorder 1989; lecturer, Lincoln Coll. Oxford 1963–64, Univ. of Birmingham 1964–67; Fellow, Queens' Coll. Cambridge 1967–; Asst. lecturer, Univ. of Cambridge 1967–72, lecturer 1972–87, Reader 1987–90, Prof. of Law of Taxation 1990–, Chair. Faculty Bd. of Law 1992–95; Pres. Soc. of Public Teachers of Law 1995–96; Visiting Prof. Dalhousie Univ., Canada 1972–73, Univ. of Auckland 1973, Univ. of Western Ont. 1978–79, Univ. of Melbourne 1979, Case Western Reserve Univ. 1985–86, 1996–. *Publications:* Revenue Law 1976; ed. of various works on taxation and contrib. to legal journals. *Leisure interests:* walking, visits to art galleries, listening to music. *Address:* Queens' College, Cambridge, CB3 9ET, England. *Telephone:* (01223) 335511. *Fax:* (01223) 335522.

TILLSLEY, Bramwell Harold, B.A.; Canadian Salvation Army officer; b. 18 Aug. 1931, Kitchener, Ont.; s. of Harold Tillsley and Doris Tillsley; m. Maude Pitcher 1953; two s. one d.; ed. Kitchener Waterloo Collegiate, Univ. of Western Ontario, Wycliffe Coll., Toronto; Sec. for Educ. Salvation Army Training Coll., Toronto 1960–70; Prin. Newfoundland Training Coll. 1970–74, School for Officer Training 1974–78, William Booth Int. Coll. 1981–84; Provincial Commdr. Newfoundland 1978–81; Chief Sec. U.S.A. Southern Territory 1984–88; Territorial Commdr. Australia Southern Territory 1988–91; Chief of Staff Salvation Army 1991–93, Gen. 1993–94; Rotary Citizenship Award 1954, Queen's Jubilee Award Medal 1980. *Publications.* Life in the Spirit, Manpower for the Master, Life More Abundant, This Mind in You. *Leisure interests:* music, reading, travel, writing, sports: basketball, golf, hockey. *Address:* 65 Spring Garden Avenue, Unit 604, North York, Ont. M2N 6H9, Canada.

TILSON, Joseph (Joe), A.R.C.A., R.A.; British artist; b. 24 Aug. 1928, London; m. Joslyn Morton 1956; one s. two d.; ed. St. Martin's School of Art, Royal Coll. of Art, British School, Rome; Visiting Lecturer Slade School, Univ. of London, 1962–63, King's Coll., Univ. of Durham 1962–63, exhibited at Venice Biennale 1964; Lecturer School of Visual Arts, New York 1966, Staatliche Hochschule, Hamburg 1971–72; retrospective Exhbn. Boymans van Beuningen Museum, Rotterdam 1978; Rome Prize 1955, Grand Prix Fifth Biennale, Cracow 1974, Henry Moore Prize, Bradford 1984, Grand Prix, 15th Biennale, Ljubljana 1985 and 21st Biennale 1995. *Address:* 2 Brook Street Mansions, 41 Davies Street, London, W1Y 1FJ, England. *Telephone:* 0171-491 0620.

TILSON THOMAS, Michael; American conductor and pianist; b. 21 Dec. 1944; s. of Theodor Thomas and Roberta Thomas; ed. Univ. of S. Calif.; conductor, Young Musicians' Foundation Debut Orchestra, Los Angeles 1963–67; conductor and pianist, Monday Evening Concerts 1963–68; musical asst. Bayreuth 1966–67; Asst. Conductor, Boston Symphony Orchestra 1969, Assoc. Conductor 1970–71, Prin. Guest Conductor 1972–74; New York début 1969; London début with London Symphony Orchestra (LSO) 1970; Music Dir. Buffalo Philharmonic 1971–79; Prin. Guest Conductor, Los Angeles Philharmonic 1981–85; Music Dir. Great Woods Inst. 1985, Music Dir. Great Woods Festival 1987–88; Prin. Conductor, LSO 1988–95, Prin. Guest Conductor 1995–; Artistic Adviser, New World Symphony 1987–; Music Dir. San Francisco Symphony Orchestra 1995–; guest conductor with orchestras and opera houses in U.S.A. and Europe; Koussevitzky Prize, Tanglewood 1968. *Address:* c/o Columbia Artists Management Ltd., 28 Cheverton Road, London, N19 3AY, England; 888 7th Avenue, 37th Floor, New York, NY 10106, U.S.A. *Telephone:* 0171-272 8020 (London). *Fax:* 0171-272 8991 (London).

TIMAKATA, Fred; Ni-Vanuatu politician; b. 1936, Shepard Islands; Speaker of Parl. 1985–88; Minister of Health 1988–89; Pres. of Vanuatu 1989–94. *Address:* c/o Office of the President, Port Vila, Vanuatu.

TIMMER, J.D. (Jan); Netherlands business executive; b. 20 Feb. 1933, Lienden; joined Philips 1952; Man. Ethiopia 1963; Head of Regional Bureau Tropical Africa, Netherlands 1968; Corp. Staff Bureau 1970, Dir. 1973; Head, Philips activities in S. Africa 1977; mem. Group Management, PolyGram 1981; Pres. and C.E.O. PolyGram Int. Ltd. 1983; mem. Group Management Cttee. NV Philips Gloeilampenfabrieken and Chair. Man. Consumer Electronics Div. 1987; Pres., Chair. Bd. of Man. and Group Man. Cttee. Philips 1990–96.

TIMOFEYEVA, Nina Vladimirovna; Russian ballet dancer and teacher; b. 11 June 1935, Leningrad; one d.; ed. Leningrad Ballet School; with Ballet Company of the Leningrad Kirov State Academic Theatre of Opera and Ballet 1953–56; Deputy to Supreme Soviet of the U.S.S.R. 1966–70; mem. Bolshoi Theatre 1956–88, ballet teacher 1989–; in Israel 1991–; has toured with Bolshoi Ballet in U.S.A., Fed. Repub. of Germany and other countries; People's Artist of the R.S.F.S.R. 1963; People's Artist of U.S.S.R. 1969; prizewinner at three int. classic dance competitions; various decorations. *Principal roles:* Odette-Odile (Swan Lake), Marta (Giselle), Laurensia (Laurensia), Yegina (Spartacus), Kitri (Don Quixote), Mistress of the Copper Mountain (Stone Flower), Diane Mireille (Flames of Paris), Gayane (Gayane), Raymonda (Raymonda), Princess Aurora (Sleeping Beauty), Leili (Leili and Medjnun), Mekhmene Banu (Legend of Love), Giselle (Giselle), Asel (Asel), Bacchante (Faust), Masha (Nutcracker), Shopeniana, Beatrice (Much Ado About Nothing), Juliet (Romeo and Juliet) 1976, Lady Macbeth (Macbeth) 1980, Le Tambour Mystérieux, Boviser de la Vée, Adan par de deux. *Films:* White Nights (Dostoevsky), Phaedra (Euripides), The Way the Heart Reveals Itself, Raymonda, Classic Duets, Spartacus, Macbeth, This Wonderful World, Improvisations, The Three Cards, Allegro, Something More About Ballet, Grand Pas, Five Corners 1988. *Leisure interests:* autosports, music.

TIMON, Clay S.; American business executive; m. Barbara Timon; two c.; ed. Univ. of Colorado; fmr. Bd. Dir., Man. Supervisor (Paris) McCann-Erickson, Man. Services Dir. (Tokyo), Sr. Vice-Pres./Man. Supervisor; fmr. Sr. Vice-Pres. Int. Doyle Dane Bernbach; fmr. Vice-Pres./Dir. Worldwide Advertising Colgate-Palmolive; fmr. Regional Vice-Pres. Saatchi & Saatchi, Paris; Chair., Pres., C.E.O. Landor Assocs. 1994–; World Pres. Int. Advertising Assn. 1988–90; fmr. Chair. Int. Cttee. of American Assn. of Advertising Agencies; mem. Business Advisory Council School of Business, Univ. of Colorado. *Leisure interests:* travel, reading, tennis, vintage automobiles. *Address:* Landor Associates, 1001 Front Street, San Francisco, CA 94111, U.S.A. *Telephone:* 415-955-1400.

TINDEMANS, Leo; Belgian politician; b. 16 April 1922, Zwyndrecht; s. of Frans Tindemans and Margaret Vercruyssen; m. Rosa Naesens 1960; two s. two d.; ed. State Univ. of Ghent, Catholic Univ. of Louvain; mem. Chamber of Deputies 1961–89; Mayor of Edegem 1965–76; Minister of Community Affairs 1968–71; Minister of Agric. and Middle Class Affairs 1972–73; Deputy Prime Minister and Minister for the Budget and Institutional Problems 1973–74; Prime Minister 1974–78; Minister of Foreign Affairs 1981–89, Minister of State 1992; Vice-Pres. European Union of Christian Democrats, Leader 1992–; Pres. European People's Party 1976–85; mem. European Parl. 1979–81, 1989–; Pres. Group of European People's Party, European Parl. 1992–; Pres. Belgian Christian People's Party (CVP) 1979–81; Prof., Faculty of Social Sciences, Catholic Univ., Louvain; Hon. D.Litt. (City Univ., London) 1976; Dr. h.c. (Heriot-Watt Univ., Edinburgh) 1978, (Georgetown Univ.) 1984, (Deusto Univ., Bilbao) 1991; Charlemagne Prize 1976; St.-Liborius-Medaille für Einheit und Frieden 1977; Stresemann Medal 1979; Robert Schuman Prize 1980; Christian Democrat. *Publications:* Ontwikkeling van de Benelux 1958, L'autonomie culturelle 1971, Regionalized Belgium, Transition from the Nation State to the Multinational State 1972, Een handvest voor woelig België 1972, Dagboek van de werkgroep Eyskens 1973, European Union 1975, Europe, Ideal of Our Generation 1976, Open Brief aan Gaston Eyskens 1978, Atlantisch Europa 1980, Europa zonder Kompas 1987, L'Europe de l'Est vue de Bruxelles 1989, Duel met de Minister 1991, De toekomst van een idee 1993, Cain in the Balkans 1996. *Leisure interests:* reading, writing, walking. *Address:* Jan Verbertlei 24, B-2650 Edegem, Belgium (Home). *Telephone:* 02/284.59.79 (Office). *Fax:* 03/455.66.58.

TINDLE, David, R.A.; British artist; b. 29 April 1932, Huddersfield, Yorks.; m. 1969 (divorced); one s. two d.; ed. Coventry School of Art; numerous exhbns. in London and provinces since 1952; first one-man exhbn. London 1953, regular one-man shows, Piccadilly Gallery 1954–83, Hamburg Gallerie XX 1974–85, Los Angeles and San Francisco 1964, Bologna and Milan 1968; one-man show, Fischer Fine Art 1985, 1989, 1992, Redfern Gallery, London 1994, 1996, 1998–99, St. Edmund Hall, Oxford 1994, The Shire Hall Gallery, Stafford 1994; has participated in numerous group exhbns. and int. biennales in Europe; works in many public and private collections including the Tate Gallery, Nat. Portrait Gallery; designed and painted set for Iolanta (Tchaikovsky), Aldeburgh Festival 1988; Visiting Tutor, Royal Coll. of Art 1973–83, Fellow 1981, Hon. Fellow 1984; Ruskin Master of Drawing, St. Edmund Hall, Oxford 1985–87, Hon. Fellow 1988–; Hon. mem. Royal Birmingham Soc. of Artists; Hon. M.A. (St. Edmund Hall, Oxford) 1985; R.A. Johnson Wax Award 1983. *Leisure interest:* music. *Address:* c/o The Redfern Gallery, 20 Cork Street, London, W.1., England.

TING, Samuel Chao Chung, B.S.E., PH.D.; American physicist; b. 27 Jan. 1936, Ann Arbor, Mich.; s. of Prof. Kuan Hai Ting and Prof. Tsun-Ying Wang; m. 1st Kay Louise Kuhne 1960; two d.; m. 2nd Susan Carol Marks 1985; one s. two d.; ed. primary and secondary schools in China, Univ. of Michigan; Ford Foundation Fellow, European Org. for Nuclear Research (CERN), Geneva 1963; Instructor, Columbia Univ., N.Y. 1964, Asst. Prof. 1965–67; Group Leader, Deutsches Elektronen Synchrotron (DESY), Hamburg, Fed. Repub. of Germany 1966; Assoc. Prof. of Physics, M.I.T., Cambridge 1967–68, Prof. 1969–, Thomas Dudley Cabot Inst. Prof. 1977–; Programme Consultant, Div. of Particles and Fields, American Physical Soc. 1970; Hon. Prof. Beijing Normal Coll., China 1984, Jiatong Univ., Shanghai, China 1987; Assoc. Ed. Nuclear Physics B 1970; mem. Editorial Bd. Nuclear Instruments and Methods 1977, Mathematical Modelling, Chinese Physics; worked chiefly on physics of electron or muon pairs, investigating quantum electro-dynamics, production and decay of photon-like particles, searching for new particles which decay to electron or muon pairs; Fellow, American Acad. of Arts and Sciences 1975; mem. American, Italian and European Physical Socs.; Foreign mem. Academia Sinica, Taiwan 1975, Pakistani Acad. of Science 1984, U.S.S.R. Acad. of Science 1989, Hungarian Acad. of Science 1993; mem. N.A.S. 1977–; Forum Engelberg Prize 1996; Hon. Sc.D. (Michigan) 1978, (Chinese Univ. of Hong Kong) 1987, (Bologna) 1988, (Columbia) 1990, (Univ. of Science and Tech., China) 1990, (Moscow State Univ.) 1991, (Bucharest) 1993; Ernest Orlando Lawrence Award 1976, Nobel Prize for Physics, jointly with Burton Richter (q.v.), for discovery of the heavy, long-lived 'J' (or 'psi') particle 1976, Eringen Medal, Soc. of Eng. Scientists 1977, De Gasperi Gold Medal for Science, Italy 1988, Gold Medal for Science, City of Brescia, Italy 1988. *Address:* Department of Physics, Massachusetts Institute of Technology, 51 Vassar Street, Cambridge, MA 02139, U.S.A.

TING GUOMA; Chinese business executive; b. 1940; Gen. Man., China State Construction Eng. Corpn. 1993. *Address:* China State Construction Engineering, 7 Beihuan West Road, Beijing 100088, People's Republic of China.

TINKHAM, Michael, M.S., PH.D.; American professor of physics; b. 23 Feb. 1928, near Ripon, Wis.; s. of Clayton H. Tinkham and Laverna Krause Tinkham; m. Mary S. Merin 1961; two s.; ed. Ripon Coll., Ripon, Wis., M.I.T. and Univ. of Oxford; Research Asst., Univ. of Calif. (Berkeley) 1955–57, Asst. Prof. of Physics 1957–59, Assoc. Prof. of Physics 1959–61, Prof. of Physics 1961–66; Gordon McKay Prof. of Applied Physics and Prof. of Physics, Harvard Univ. 1966–80, Rumford Prof. of Physics and Gordon McKay Prof. of Applied Physics 1980–, Chair. Dept. of Physics 1975–78; Richtmyer Lecturer (of American Physical Soc. and American Asscn. of Physics Teachers) 1977; Visiting Miller Research Prof., Univ. of Calif. (Berkeley) 1987; Visiting Prof., Delft Univ. of Tech. 1993; mem. N.A.S.; Fellow, American Acad. of Arts and Sciences; Guggenheim Fellow 1963–64; Hon. Dr. Sc. Nat. (ETH Zürich) 1997; Buckley Prize 1974, Alexander von Humboldt Foundation Award 1978–79. *Publications:* Group Theory and Quantum Mechanics 1964, Superconductivity 1965, Introduction to Superconductivity 1996; numerous articles in journals. *Address:* Department of Physics, Harvard University, Cambridge, MA 02138 (Office); 98 Rutledge Road, Belmont, MA 02178, U.S.A. (Home). *Telephone:* (617) 495-3735 (Office).

TIRIMO, Martino, F.R.A.M., DIP. R.A.M. ; British concert pianist and conductor; b. 19 Dec. 1942, Larnaca, Cyprus; s. of Dimitri Tirimo and Marina Tirimo; m. Mione J. Teakle 1973; one s. one d.; ed. Bedales School, England (Cyprus Govt. Scholarship), Royal Acad. of Music, London, Vienna State Acad.; first public recital, Cyprus 1949; conducted 7 performances of La Traviata with singers and musicians from La Scala, Milan, at Cyprus Opera Festival 1955; prizewinner Int. Beethoven Competition, Vienna 1965; London début Wigmore Hall 1965; Jt. Winner Munich Int. Piano Competition 1971; Winner Geneva Int. Piano Competition 1972; gave first public performance of complete Schubert sonatas (including unfinished ones with own completions), London 1975; first public performance of Beethoven piano concertos cycle directed from keyboard in two consecutive evenings, Dresden 1985, London 1986; first performance Tippett piano concerto in several European countries 1986–87; concerto performances with major orchestras worldwide as well as recitals, radio and TV appearances Europe, U.S.A., Canada, S. Africa and Far East 1965–; recordings include Brahms piano concertos, Chopin concertos, Tippett piano concerto, Rachmaninov concertos, complete Debussy piano works, complete Schubert piano sonatas, several other recordings with mixed repertoire; composed film score "The Odyssey"; Liszt Scholarship, Boise Foundation Scholarship, Gulbenkian Foundation Fellowship 1967–69; Gold Medal, Associated Bd. of Royal Schools of Music 1959, Macfarren Medal, Royal Acad. of Music 1964, Silver Disc 1988 and Gold Disc 1994 for recording of Rachmaninov 2nd Concerto and Paganini Rhapsody, and other prizes and awards. *Publications include:* edn. of complete Schubert piano sonatas. *Leisure interests:* chess, reading, self-knowledge, theatre, badminton. *Address:* 1 Romeyn Road, London, SW16 2NU, England. *Telephone:* 0181-677 4847. *Fax:* 0181-677 6070.

TISCHNER, Józef, PH.D.; Polish ecclesiastic and professor of philosophy; b. 12 March 1931, Stary Sącz; ed. Jagiellonian Univ., Kraków, Acad. of Catholic Theology, Warsaw; ordained Priest 1955; lecturer in philosophy Pontifical Theological Acad., Kraków, 1968–; Dean Philosophy Faculty Pontifical Theological Acad., also head Dept. of Human Philosophy; lecturer Faculty of Arts, Jagiellonian Univ.; lecturer in Philosophy of Drama State Higher Theatrical School, Kraków; Pres. Inst. of Human Science, Vienna 1981–; journalist Tygodnik Powszechny (weekly). *Publications:* World of Human Hope 1975, Solidarity Ethics 1981, Polish Shape of Dialogue 1981, Thinking According to Values 1982, Poland is the Fatherland 1985, Philosophy of Drama 1990, Homo Sovieticus 1992, Unfortunate Gift of Freedom 1993, Between Man and Vicar 1995 (jtly), A Highland History of Philosophy 1997. *Address:* ul. Kanoniczna 20, 31-002 Kraków, Poland.

TISHCHENKO, Boris Ivanovich; Russian composer; b. 23 March 1939, Leningrad; s. of Ivan I. Tishchenko and Zinaida A. Tishchenko; m. Irina A. Donskaya 1977; three s.; ed. Leningrad Conservatory, with post-grad. course under D. D. Shostakovich; Prof. at St. Petersburg Conservatory; 1st Prize, Int. Contest of Young Composers, Prague 1966, R.S.F.S.R. State Prize (Glinka) 1978, People's Artist of R.S.F.S.R. 1987; Prize of Mayor of St. Petersburg 1995. *Compositions include:* The Stolen Sun (opera) 1968, The Twelve (ballet) 1963, Fly-bee (ballet) 1968, Jaroslavna (The Eclipse, ballet) 1974, Beatriche (ballet) 1999, Lenin Lives (cantata) 1959, Requiem (words by A. Akhmatova) 1966, A Cockroach (operetta) 1968; *symphonies:* French Symphony 1958, Sinfonia Robusta 1970, Violin Symphony (2nd Violin Concerto) 1981, The Siege Chronicle 1984, Pushkin's Symphony 1998, 10 symphonies 1961–97, 10 piano sonatas 1957–97; violin and cello solo sonatas; Rondo, Capriccio and Fantasy for violin and piano; also concertos for violin, piano, cello, flute and harp 1962–77, Concerto alla marcia for 16 soloists 1989, The Dog's Heart—Novels for chamber ensemble based on M. Bulgakov 1988, Concerto for clarinet and piano trio 1990, Piano Quintet 1985, String quartets 1957–84, Twelve Inventions and Twelve Portraits for Organ 1964, 1994, orchestral and instrumental suites and pieces, vocal cycles and ensembles, choral works, music for drama productions and films; edns. and instrumentations of some works by Monteverdi, Grieg, Mahler, Prokofiev and Shostakovich. *Address:* Rimsky-Korsakoff Avenue 79, Apt. 10, St. Petersburg 190121, Russia. *Telephone:* 114-75-16.

TISHKOV, Valery Aleksandrovich, D. HIST.; Russian historian; b. 1941; m.; one s.; ed. Moscow State Univ.; teacher, Magadan State Pedagogical Inst. 1964–66; aspirant, Moscow State Pedagogical Inst. 1966–69; docent, Dean, Magadan State Pedagogical Inst. 1969–72; researcher, Inst. of Gen. History U.S.S.R. (now Russian) Acad. of Sciences, Scientific Sec., Dept. of History, U.S.S.R. Acad. of Sciences, also Head of Sector, Inst. of Ethnogeography; Deputy Dir., Dir. N. Miklukho-Maklai Inst. of Ethnology and Anthropology Russian Acad. of Sciences 1972–. *Leisure interest:* fishing. *Address:* N. Miklukho-Maklai Institute of Ethnology and Anthropology, Leninsky prosp. 32A, korp. 8, 117334 Moscow, Russia. *Telephone:* (095) 938 1747 (Office).

TITARENKO, Mikhail Leont'yevich, PH.D.; Russian specialist on international relations with the Far East and Chinese philosophy; b. 27 April 1934, Bryansk region; s. of the late Leonty Titarenko and Maria Titarenko; m. Galina Titarenko 1957 (died 1997); two s.; ed. Moscow State Univ., Beijing Univ., Fudan Univ., Shanghai; diplomatic service 1961–65; researcher and consultant in govt. bodies 1965–85; Dir. Inst. of Far East Studies, Russian Acad. of Sciences 1985–; mem. Editorial Bd. of Far Eastern Affairs 1986–; Chair. of Academic Council on Problems of Modern China, Russian Acad. of Sciences 1987–; Pres. All-Russian Asscn. of Sinologists 1988–; Corresp. mem. Russian Acad. of Sciences 1997–; mem. Russia Acad. of Natural Sciences, Int. Acad. of Informatization. *Publications:* Anthology of Ancient Chinese Philosophy (two vols.), Ancient Chinese Philosopher Mo Di 1985, Development of Productive Forces in China 1989, History of Chinese Philosophy 1989, Economic Reform in China: Theory and Practice 1990, Russia and East Asia: Issues of International and Cross-Civilization Relations 1994, and numerous articles. *Leisure interests:* collecting stamps and matchboxes. *Address:* Institute of Far East Studies, Russian Academy of Sciences, 27 Krasikova Str., 117218 Moscow, Russia. *Telephone:* (095) 124-01-17 (Office); 198-55-38 (Home). *Fax:* 310-7056.

TITHERIDGE, John Edward, PH.D., F.R.S.N.Z.; New Zealand research scientist; b. 12 June 1932, Auckland; s. of Leslie Edward Titheridge and Clarice Muriel Barnes; m. Patricia Joy Brooker 1970; one s. one d.; ed. Avondale Coll., Univ. of Auckland and Univ. of Cambridge; Research Fellow Univ. of Auckland 1960–, Sr. Research Fellow 1961, Assoc. Prof. 1967–; Cheeseman-Pond Memorial Prize 1962, Mechaelis Memorial Prize 1972, N.Z. Geophysics Prize, Wellington Branch Royal Soc. of N.Z. 1977. *Publications:* 100 refereed scientific papers 1959–. *Leisure interests:* music, photography, reading, woodwork, electronics. *Address:* Physics Department, University of Auckland, Auckland (Office); 1500 Dominion Road, Auckland 4, New Zealand (Home). *Telephone:* (09) 373-7999 Ext. 8866 (Office); (09) 620-6231 (Home). *Fax:* (09) 373-7445.

TITO, Teburoro, B.SC.; I-Kiribati politician; b. 25 Aug. 1953, Tabiteuea North; m. Nei Keina; one c.; ed. King George V Secondary School, Univ. of South Pacific, Suva, Papua New Guinea Admin. Coll.; student co-ordinator, Univ. of S. Pacific Students' Asscn. 1977–79; scholarship officer, Ministry of Educ. 1980–82, Sr. Educ. Officer 1983–87; mem. Maneaba ni Maungatabu (Parl.) and Leader of Opposition 1987–94; mem. Parl. Public Accounts Cttee. 1987–90; Pres. of Kiribati 1994–, also Minister of Foreign Affairs and Int. Trade; mem. CPA Exec. Cttee. for Pacific Region 1989–90; Chair. Kiribati Football Asscn. 1980–94. *Leisure interests:* sports, especially soccer. *Address:* Office of the President, P.O. Box 67, Bairiki, Tarawa, Kiribati. *Telephone:* 21183. *Fax:* 21145.

TITOV, Col.-Gen. German Stepanovich, CAND.MIL.SC.; Russian cosmonaut and air force officer (retd.); b. 11 Sept. 1935, Altaiski Krai; s. of Stepan Pavlovich Titov and Alexandra Mikhailovna Titova; m. Tamara Vasilevna; two d.; ed. secondary school, Stalingrad (now Volgograd) Pilots' School and Zhukovsky Air Force Eng. Acad.; training for space flight 1960–61; in space-ship Vostok II circled earth 17 times during a journey of 25 hours 11 minutes 6–7 Aug. 1961; mem. Young Communists' League; mem. CPSU 1961–91; graduate, Zhukovsky Air Force Eng. Acad. 1968; K.E. Voroshilov Acad. of Gen. Staff 1972–; Deputy, Supreme Soviet of U.S.S.R. 1962–70; Major-Gen. of Air Force 1975–79, First Deputy Commdr. of Space Forces of the Ministry of Defence 1979, Lieut.-Gen. 1979–88, Col.-Gen. 1988–92; Pres. of Cosmoflot 1992–; mem. State Duma 1993–; Hon. M.Sc. 1980; Pres. Viet Nam-Soviet Friendship Soc., Fed. of Aerial Views of Sport; Hon. Master of Sport of U.S.S.R.; Hero Soviet Union 1961, Order of Lenin (twice), Gold Star Medal, Order of the Workers' Red Flag, Lenin Award for Science and Tech. 1990; named Honorable Mil. Specialist of U.S.S.R. 1991, Hero of Mongolian People's Repub., Hero of Labour of Viet Nam, Hero of Socialist Labour of Bulgaria and other awards; mem. C.P. of Russian Fed. 1992–. *Publications:* 700,000 km. in Space 1961, Seventeen Cosmic Dawns 1963, Aviation and Cosmonautics 1963, My Sky-blue Planet 1973, On Space and Earth Orbits 1987. *Leisure interests:* hunting, fishing, theatre, playing with grandson. *Address:* Khovanskaya Str. 3, Apt. 8, Moscow 129515, Russia.

TITOV, Konstantin Alekseyevich, CAND. ECON.; Russian politician; b. 30 Oct. 1944, Moscow; m.; one s.; ed. Kuybyshev (now Samara) Aviation Inst., Kuybyshev Inst. of Planning; metalworker aviation factory 1962–63; machine operator aviation factory, Kuybyshev 1968–69; Deputy Sec. Komsomol Cttee. Kuybyshev Aviation Factory 1969–70; Deputy Head Div. of Youth Kuybyshev City Komsomol Cttee. 1970–73; Sec. Komsomol Cttee., jr., sr. researcher, head of group, Head Research Lab. Kuybyshev Inst. of Planning 1973–88; Deputy Dir. Research Cen. Informatika 1988–90; Deputy Chair., Chair. Samara City Soviet 1990–91; Head of Admin. Samara Region 1991–93; Governor Samara Region 1996–; mem. Russian Council of Fed. 1993–, Chair. Cttee. on Budget, Financial, Credit and Currency Regulation; Pres. Interregional Asscn. of Econ. Interaction Bolshaya Volga 1994; Deputy Chair. Our Home Russia movt. 1995–. *Leisure interests:* football, photography, music, hunting. *Address:* Molodogvardeyskaya str. 210, 443006 Samara, Russia (Office). *Telephone:* (095) 32 22 68 (Moscow), (8462) 32-19-44 (Samara).

TITOV, Vladimir Georgievich; Russian cosmonaut; b. 1 Jan. 1947, Sretensk, Chita Region; m. Vera Evdokimovna Titova; one s. one d.; ed. Chernigov Higher Mil. Aviation School, Yuriy Gagarin Air Force Acad.; pilot instructor, commdr. of aviation unit 1970–76; mem. Cosmonauts' team since 1976; Commdr. of space flights on spacecraft Soyuz T-8 1983 and record-breaking flight on Soyuz TM-4 and space station MiR; Deputy Head Dept. of Man. Centre of Cosmonauts' Training 1988–; Hero of Soviet Union; Officier Légion d'honneur and other decorations. *Address:* Yuriy Gagarin Centre for Cosmonauts' Training, Zvezdny Gorodok, Moscow Region, Russia.

TITOV, Yuriy Evlampievich; Russian gymnast; b. 27 Nov. 1935, Omsk; s. of Evlampiy Titov and Marina Titova; m. Valerie Kouzmenko 1960; one s. one d.; ed. Kiev Inst. of Physical Culture; all-round champion of U.S.S.R. 1958, 1961, of Europe 1959 and the world 1962; Honoured Master of Sports 1956; Olympic gymnastics champion 1956; won 13 gold medals at European, world championships and Olympic Games; int. class judge 1968; mem. CPSU 1969–91; Vice-Pres. Int. Gymnastic Fed. 1972–76, Pres. 1976–96, Hon. Life Pres. 1996–; Head Dept. of Gymnastics, U.S.S.R. State Sports Cttee. 1968–87; lecturer Moscow Acad. of Physical Culture 1980–, Leningrad (now St. Petersburg) Acad. of Physical Culture 1988–, Prof. 1993–; Sec. Nat. Olympic Cttee. 1987–88, mem. Int. Olympic Cttee. (IOC) Working Group on Women and Sport 1995–, ex officio mem. IOC 1995–96; inducted into U.S. Hall of Fame 1999. *Publications:* The Sum of Points 1971, The Ascent 1982, The Notes of the President 1984, Rhythmic Gymnastics (jtly.) 1998; works on methodology of gymnastics. *Leisure interests:* history, carpentry, doing nothing with pleasure. *Address:* Kolokolnikov per. 6, Apt. 19, 103045 Moscow, Russia. *Telephone:* (095) 208-46-57. *Fax:* (095) 208-46-57.

TITS, Jacques Léon, DR.SC.; French professor of mathematics (group theory); b. 12 Aug. 1930, Uccle, Belgium; s. of Léon Tits and Louisa (née André) Tits; m. Marie-Jeanne Dieuaide 1956; ed. Univ. of Brussels; Asst. Univ. of Brussels 1956–57, Assoc. Prof. 1957–62, Prof. 1962–64; Prof. Univ. of Bonn 1964–74; Assoc. Prof. Coll. de France, Paris 1973–74, Prof. of Group Theory 1975–; Visiting Teacher and Prof. Eidgenössische Technische Hochschule, Zürich 1950, 1951, 1953, Inst. for Advanced Study, Princeton 1951–52, 1963, 1969, 1971–72, Univ. of Rome 1955, 1956, Univ. of Chicago 1963, Univ. of Calif., Berkeley 1963, Univs. of Tokyo and Kyoto 1971, Yale Univ. 1966–67, 1976, 1980, 1984, 1990; mem. editorial bds. of periodicals and scientific collections; Ed.-in-Chief Math. Publs. of IHES 1980–; guest speaker at Int. Congresses of Mathematicians, Stockholm 1962, Nice 1970, Vancouver 1974; lecture tours in U.S.A., U.K., Israel, etc.; mem. Deutsche Akad. der Naturforscher Leopoldina 1977; Corresp. mem. Acad. des Sciences, Paris 1977, mem. 1979; Foreign mem. Royal Netherlands Acad. of Arts and Sciences 1988; Foreign Assoc. Royal Belgian Acad. 1991; mem. American Acad. of Arts and Sciences 1992, N.A.S. 1992; Hon. mem. London Math. Soc. 1993; Foundation mem. Academia Europaea; Dr. h.c. (Utrecht) 1970, (Ghent) 1979, (Bonn) 1987, (Louvain) 1992; Prix scientifique Interfacultataire L. Empain 1955, Prix Wettrems, Acad. de Belgique 1958, Grand Prix des Sciences mathématiques et physiques, Acad. des Sciences 1976, Wolf Prize 1993; Chevalier, Légion d'honneur, Commdr. des Palmes académiques. *Publications:* over 150 scientific papers. *Leisure interests:* languages, literature, arts. *Address:* Collège de France, 11 place Marcelin-Berthelot, 75231 Paris, Cedex 05 (Office); 12 rue du Moulin des Prés, 75013 Paris, France (Home). *Telephone:* 44.27.17.23 (Office); 45.88.96.03 (Home). *Fax:* 44.27.17.04.

TIWARI, Narayan Datt, M.A.; Indian politician; b. 18 Oct. 1925, Balyuti, Nainital Dist., U.P.; s. of Poorna Nand Tiwari; m. Sushila Tiwari 1954; ed. Allahabad Univ.; joined Indian Freedom Movt. aged 13; joined "Quit India Movt." 1942; imprisoned for 15 months; Pres. Allahabad Univ. Students' Union 1947; Sec. Political Sufferers' Distress Relief Soc.; Ed. Hindi monthly Prabhat; mem. U.P. Ass. 1952–62; Leader of Opposition and Chair. Public Accounts Cttee. 1957; mem. U.P. Vidhan Sabha 1969; Minister for Planning, Labour and Panchayats, also Deputy Chair. State Planning Comm., Govt. of U.P. 1969, Minister for Finance and Parl. Affairs 1970–76, for Heavy Industries and Cane Devt. 1973–76; Chief Minister of U.P. 1976–77, 1984–85, 1988–89; Leader of Opposition (U.P. Congress (I) Legis. Party) 1977–80; mem. Lok Sabha 1980–; Minister of Planning, Govt. of India 1980–81, of Labour 1980–82, of Industry 1981–84, 1985–86, of External Affairs 1986–87, of Finance and Commerce 1987–88, of Steel and Mines 1982–83; expelled from Congress (I) Party 1995. *Leisure interests:* cricket, hockey. *Publication:* European Miscellany. *Address:* Village Padampuri, P.O. Padampuri, Dist. Nainital, U.P., India.

TIZARD, Dame Catherine (Anne), G.C.M.G., G.C.V.O., D.B.E., Q.S.O.; New Zealand public official; b. 4 April 1931, Auckland; d. of Neil Maclean and Helen Montgomery Maclean; m. Hon. Robert James Tizard (q.v.) 1951 (divorced 1983); one s. three d.; ed. Matamata Coll. and Auckland Univ.; tutor in Zoology, Univ. of Auckland 1967–84; Mayor of Auckland 1983–90; Gov.-Gen. of New Zealand 1990–96; Chair. N.Z. Worldwide Fund for Nature 1996–, N.Z. Historic Places Trust 1996–; mem. Auckland City Council 1971–83, Auckland Regional Authority 1980–83. *Leisure interests:* music, reading, drama, scuba diving. *Address:* 12A Wallace Street, Herne Bay, Auckland 1, New Zealand. *Telephone:* (9) 376 2555. *Fax:* (9) 360 0656.

TIZARD, Rt. Hon. Robert James, P.C., M.A.; New Zealand politician (retd.) and teacher; b. 7 June 1924, Auckland; s. of Henry James Tizard and Jessie May Tizard (née Phillips); m. 1st Catherine Anne Maclean (Catherine Anne Tizard, q.v.) 1951 (divorced 1983); one s. three d.; m. 2nd Mary Nacey 1983; one s.; m. 3rd Beryl Vignale 1989; ed. Auckland Grammar School, Auckland Univ.; served in R.N.Z.A.F., Canada, U.K. 1943–46; Jr. Lecturer in History, Auckland Univ. 1949–53, teaching posts 1955–57, 1961–62; M.P. 1957–60, 1963–90; Minister of Health and State Services 1972–74; in charge of State Advances Corpn. 1972–73; Deputy Prime Minister, Minister of Finance 1974–75; Deputy Leader of Opposition 1975–79; Minister of Energy, Statistics, Science and Tech., Minister in Charge of Audit Dept. 1984–87, Minister of Defence, Research, Science and Tech. 1987–90. *Leisure interest:* golf. *Address:* 8 Glendowie Road, Glendowie, Auckland, New Zealand (Home).

TJEKNAVORIAN, Loris-Zare; American/Armenian composer and conductor; b. 13 Oct. 1937; s. of Haikaz and Adriné Tjeknavorian; m. 1st Linda Pierce 1964 (divorced 1979); one s.; m. 2nd Julia Cory Harley-Green 1986; ed. Vienna Acad. of Music, Salzburg Mozarteum; studied with the late Carl Orff 1963–64; worked in U.S.A. until 1970; fmr. Teaching Fellow, Univ. of Michigan; fmr. Composer-in-Residence, Concordia Coll., Minnesota; Composer-in-Residence, Ministry of Culture and Fine Arts; Prin. Conductor, Teheran Opera 1972–79; artist with RCA 1976–; Composer-in-Residence American-Armenian Int. Coll., La Verne Univ., Calif. 1979–; Prin. Conductor and Artistic Dir. Armenian Philharmonic Orchestra, Yerevan, Armenia 1989–; principally associated with London Symphony Orchestra with whom he has recorded; Chair. Bd. of Trustees, Inst. of Armenian Music, London

1976–80; Order of Homayoun; several int. tours as a conductor. *Works include:* Requiem for the Massacred 1975, Simorgh (ballet music), Lake Van Suite, Erebouni for 12 strings 1978, a piano concerto, several operas, several chamber works, Credo Symphony Life of Christ (after medieval Armenian chants) 1976, Liturgical Mass, Violin Concerto, oratorios Lucifer's Fall and Book of Revelation, Mass in Memoriam 1985, Othello (ballet), ballet suites for orchestra, five symphonies. *Address:* c/o Thea Dispeker Artist Representative, 59 East 54th Street, New York, NY 10022 (Agent); 347 West 57th Street, Apt. 37C, New York, NY 10019, U.S.A. (Home); c/o State Philharmonia, Mashtotsi Prospekt 46, Yerevan, Armenia. *Telephone:* (212) 421-7676 (Agent).

TKACHENKO, Aleksander Nikolayevich; Ukrainian politician; b. 1939, Ukraine; worked as First Sec., Tarashansk Comsomol Cttee., then Ukrainian CP functionary in agric. sector; State Minister on Agric. Policy and Food Ukrainian S.S.R. 1991; Head, Agric. Asscn. Zemlya i Lyudi; leader Ukrainian Farmers' Party; mem. Verkhovna Rada (Parl.); First Vice-Chair. Verkhovna Rada 1994–98, Chair. (Speaker) July 1998–. *Address:* Verkhovna Rada. Hrushevskoga str. 5, 252008 Kiev, Ukraine. *Telephone:* (381) 226 2825 (Office).

TLASS, Lieut.-Gen. Mustapha el–; Syrian politician and army officer; b. 11 May 1932, Rastan City, Mouhafazat Homs; m. Lamyaa al-Jabri 1958; two s. two d.; ed. Mil. and Law Colls. and Voroshilov Acad., Moscow; active mem. Baath Arab Socialist Party 1947–, Sec. of Rastan Section 1951; Sports teacher, Al-Kraya School, Mouhafazat al-Soueda 1950–52; attended Mil. Coll. 1952–54; deputed to Egyptian army 1959–61; Insp. Ministry of Supply 1962; mem. Free Officers' Movement 1962–63, detained 1962–63; Commdr. Tank Bn. and Chief of Cen. Region of Nat. Security Court 1963; Chief of Staff, 5th Armoured Brigade 1964–66; mem. Regional Command, Regional Congress of Baath Arab Socialist Party 1965, 1968, 1969, 1975, of Politbureau 1969–, of Nat. Council of Revolution 1965–71; participated in movement of 23 Feb., promoted to Commdr. of Cen. Region and of 5th Armoured Brigade; rank of Major-Gen. 1968, Chief of Staff of Armed Forces 1968–70, First Deputy Minister of Defence 1968–72; participated in coup installing Pres. Hafez Al-Assad Nov. 1970; First Deputy C.-in-C. Armed Forces 1970–72, Deputy C.-in-C. 1972–; mem. People's Council 1971–; Minister of Defence 1972–, now also Deputy Prime Minister; Deputy Chief of Joint Supreme Mil. Council of Syrian and Egyptian Armed Forces 1973; rank of Lieut.-Gen. 1978; 33 orders and medals. *Publications include:* Guerilla War, Military Studies, An Introduction to Zionist Strategy, The Arab Prophet and Technique of War, The Armoured Brigade as an Advanced Guard, Bitter Memories in the Military Prison of Mezzah, The Fourth War between Arabs and Israel, The Second Chapter of the October Liberation War, Selections of Arab Poetry, The Steadfastness Front in confrontation with Camp David, The Algerian Revolution, Art of Soviet War, American Policy under the Carter Regime, The Technological Revolution and Development of the Armed Forces. *Leisure interests:* reading and writing books, military and historical studies, photography. *Address:* Ministry of Defence, Damascus, Syria.

TLOU, Thomas, M.A.T., M.A., PH.D.; Botswana professor of history and diplomatist; b. 1 June 1932, Gwanda, S. Rhodesia (now Zimbabwe); s. of Malapela Tlou and Moloko Nare; m. Sheila Dinotshe 1977; two s. one d.; ed. schools in Rhodesia, Luther Coll., Decorah, Iowa, Johns Hopkins Univ., Baltimore and Univ. of Wisconsin; primary school teacher, Rhodesia 1957–62; lecturer in history, Luther Coll. 1969, Univ. of Wis. 1970–71; lecturer in history, Univ. of Botswana, Lesotho and Vice-Swaziland 1971, later Prof., Dean of Faculty of Humanities and Head of History; mem. Bd. Nat. Museum and Art Gallery of Botswana 1974–76, 1981–, mem. Univ. Senate and Council of UBLS 1974–76; Acting Dir. Nat. Research Inst. 1976; Perm. Rep. to UN 1977–80; Deputy Vice-Chancellor Univ. of Botswana 1980, Vice-Chancellor 1984–98, mem. Senate and Council of Univ. of Botswana and Swaziland (now Univ. of Botswana) 1980–, mem. Nat. Archives Advisory Council, mem. Univ. of Botswana Review Comm.; mem. Pres.'s Comm. on Incomes Policy 1989–90; mem. Namibian Pres. Comm. on Higher Educ. 1991, Univ. of Botswana Review Comm. 1990, UNESCO Bd. 1992–95; Chair. SADCC Consultancy on Human Resources Devt. 1991, Asscn. of Eastern and Southern African Univs. 1992–93; Vice-Chair. Asscn. of Commonwealth Univs. 1993, Chair. 1994; mem. Bd. Botswana Tech. Centre; mem. Nat. Employment, Manpower and Incomes Council; Chair. Asscn. of Eastern and Southern Africa Univs.; mem. Exec. Bd. Asscn. of African Univs. 1993–96; mem. Council, Univ. of Swaziland 1993–95; mem. American-African Studies Asscn., life mem. Botswana Soc.; mem. Bd. Lutheran World Fed. (L.W.F.) 1998–, mem. L.W.F. Study Group on African Religion 1998–; Hon. D.Litt. (Luther Coll.) 1978; Hon. LL.D. (Ohio) 1986; Chevalier, Ordre des Palmes Académiques 1982, Presidential Order of Honour 1994. *Publications:* History of Botswana (co-author), A Political History of North West Botswana 1750–1906, Biography of Seretse Khama 1995, and several articles and book chapters on history of Botswana and Ngamiland. *Leisure interest:* swimming. *Address:* P.O. Box 1004, Gaborone, Botswana. *Telephone:* 3552661 (Office); 351681 (Home). *Fax:* 3552279.

TO HUU; Vietnamese politician and poet; b. 4 Oct. 1920, Hué; m. Vu Thi Thanh 1946; one s. two d.; poet and leading intellectual; in charge of propaganda and ideological training in Lao Dong Party (now CP of Viet Nam); alt. mem. Politburo, CP of Viet Nam 1976; Vice-Premier, Council of Ministers 1980–86; mem. Nat. Defence Council 1981. *Publications:* Tu Ay (Since), Vietbac, Gio Long (Wind Blowing), Ra Tran (To the Front), Vietnam Mau va Hoa (Vietnam Blood and Flower), Theo Chan Ba Ho (Going with Uncle Ho). *Address:* Central Committee of the Communist Party of Viet Nam, No. 1-C, rue Hoang Van Thu, Hanoi, Viet Nam.

TOBBACK, Louis; Belgian politician; b. 3 May 1938, Louvain; teacher, Athenee Royal de Louvain; mem. CPAS Louvain 1965–70; Deputy Mayor, Louvain 1971–76; town councillor, Louvain 1971–; Deputy for Louvain 1974–; Pres. Parti Socialiste Group, Chamber of Reps. 1978–88; Minister of the Interior and the Civil Service 1988–94, 1998. *Address:* c/o Ministry of the Interior and the Civil Service, 60–62 Konings-straat, Rue Royale 94, 1000 Brussels, Belgium (Office).

TOBIA, Maguid, B.SC.; Egyptian author; b. 25 March 1938, Minia; teacher of math. 1960–68; mem. Higher Council of Arts and Literature 1969–78; mem. staff Ministry of Culture 1978–; mem. Writers' Union, Chamber of Cinema Industry, Soc. of Egyptian Film Critics, Fiction Cttee. of Supreme Council of Culture; several literary prizes. *Film scripts include:* Story from Our Country, Sons of Silence, Stars' Maker. *Publications:* (collections of short stories): Vostock Reaches the Moon, Five Unread Papers, The Coming Days, The Companion; (novels): Circles of Impossibility, Sons of Silence, The They, The Room of Floor Chances, The Music Kiosk, Hanan, The Strange Deeds of Kings and the Intrigues of Banks, The Emigration to the North Country of Hathoot's Tribe (3 Vols.), The Story of Beautiful Reem; contribs. to Al Ahram and several Arabic magazines. *Leisure interests:* reading, travel. *Address:* 15 El-Lewaa Abd El Aziz Aly, Heliopolis 11361, Cairo, Egypt.

TOBIAS, Phillip Vallentine, PH.D., D.SC., M.B.B.CH., F.R.C.P.; South African professor of anatomy; b. 14 Oct. 1925, Durban; s. of late Joseph Newman Tobias and Fanny Rosendorff; ed. St. Andrew's School, Bloemfontein, Durban High School, Univ. of the Witwatersrand and Emmanuel Coll., Cambridge; Lecturer in Anatomy, Univ. of Witwatersrand 1951–52, Sr. Lecturer 1953, Dir. Palaeo-anthropology Research Unit 1966–96, Prof. and Head of Anatomy Dept. 1959–90, Dean of Faculty of Medicine 1980–82, Hon. Professorial Research Fellow 1993–; fmr. Visiting Prof. Cambridge Univ., Univ. of Pennsylvania; founder Pres. Inst. for the Study of Man in Africa, Anatomical Soc. of Southern Africa, S. African Soc. for Quaternary Research; Hon. mem. and mem. numerous int. asscns.; Foreign Assoc. N.A.S.; Hon. Fellow, Royal Anthropological Inst. of Great Britain and Ireland, Royal Soc. of S. Africa; Fellow Linnean Soc. of London; sometime Vice-Pres. and acting Exec. Pres. S. African Asscn. for the Advancement of Science; Pres. Royal Soc. of S. Africa 1970–72. Int. Asscn. of Human Biologists 1994–96; Perm. Council mem. Int. Union of Prehistoric and Protohistoric Sciences, Pan-African Congress of Prehistory and Quaternary Studies, Int. Asscn. of Human Biologists; Trustee, Leakey Foundation, Pasadena, Calif.; Hon. Prof. of Palaeo-anthropology, Bernard Price Inst. for Palaeontological Research; Hon. Prof. of Zoology; Overseas Fellow, Austrian Acad. of Sciences 1978; Paul Harris Fellow of Rotary Int. 1981, 1991; Hon. D.Sc. (Natal) 1980, (Cambridge) 1988, (Univ. of Western Ont.) 1986, (Alberta) 1987, (Cape Town) 1988, (Guelph) 1990, (S. Africa) 1990, (Durban-Westville) 1993, (Pennsylvania) 1994, (Witwatersrand) 1994; British Asscn. Medal 1952, Simon Biesheuvel Medal 1966, South Africa Medal 1967, Sr. Captain Scott Medal 1973, Rivers Memorial Medal 1978, Anisfield-Wolf Award for Race Relations 1978, Foundation Award 1983, Phillip Tobias Medal 1983, Certificate of Honour, Univ. of Calif. 1983, Balzan Prize 1987, John F.W. Herschel Medal 1990, Silver Medal-Medical Asscn. of S. Africa 1990, 1st John Grant Distinguished Lecturer Award 1991, 1st L.S.B. Leakey Prize 1991, Carmel Merit Award (Haifa) 1992, Huxley Memorial Medal of Royal Anthropological Inst. 1996; Order for Meritorious Service (Gold Class) of S. Africa 1992. *Publications:* Chromosomes, Sex-cells and Evolution 1956, Olduvai Gorge Vol. II 1967, Man's Anatomy (with M. Arnold) 1968, The Brain in Hominid Evolution 1971, The Meaning of Race 1972, The Bushmen 1978, Dart, Taung and the Missing Link 1984, Hominid Evolution: Past, Present and Future 1985, Olduvai Gorge Vol. IVA and *B* 1991, Paleo-antropologia 1992, Il Bipede Barcollante 1992; about 900 scientific and other publs. *Leisure interests:* people, books, music, philately, art, writing. *Address:* Department of Anatomical Sciences, University of the Witswatersrand Medical School, 7 York Road, Parktown, Johannesburg, 2193, South Africa.

TOBIAS, Randall L., B.S.; American business executive; b. 20 March 1942, Lafayette, Ind.; m. 1st Marilyn Jane Salyer 1966 (died 1994); one s. one d.; m. 2nd Marianne Williams 1995; one step-s. one step-d.; ed. Indiana Univ.; served U.S. Army 1964–66; numerous positions Ind. Bell 1964–81, Ill. Bell 1977–81; Vice-Pres. (residence marketing, sales and service) AT & T 1981–82; Pres. American Bell Consumer Products 1983–84, Sr. Vice-Pres. 1984–85, Chair. and C.E.O. AT & T Communications, New York 1985–91, AT & T Int., Basking Ridge, N.J. 1991–93, Vice-Chair. Bd. AT & T, New York and Chair. Bd. Dirs. 1986–93; Chair., Pres. and C.E.O. Eli Lilly & Co., Indianapolis 1993–; mem. Bd. Dirs. Eli Lilly & Co., Kimberly-Clark, Knight-Ridder, Phillips Petroleum; Chair. Bd. of Trustees Duke Univ.; Vice-Chair. Colonial Williamsburg Foundation; mem. Council on Foreign Relations, numerous other appointments. *Leisure interests:* skiing, shooting. *Address:* Eli Lilly & Co., Lilly Corporation Center, Indianapolis, IN 46285, U.S.A.

TOBIN, James, PH.D.; American economist; b. 5 March 1918, Champaign, Ill.; s. of late Louis Michael and Margaret Edgerton; m. Elizabeth Ringo 1946; three s. one d.; ed. Harvard Univ.; U.S. Navy 1942–46; Teaching Fellow in Econs., Harvard Univ. 1946–47, Junior Fellow 1947–50; Assoc.

Prof. of Econs., Yale Univ. 1950–55, Prof. 1955, Dir. Cowles Foundation for Research in Econs., Yale Univ. 1955–61, Sterling Prof. of Econs., Yale Univ. 1957–88, Chair. Dept. of Econs. 1974–76, Prof. Emer. 1988–; Visiting Prof. Univ. of Nairobi, Kenya 1972–73; Ford Visiting Prof. Univ. of California, Berkeley Jan.–June 1983; mem. Pres.'s Council of Econ. Advisers 1961–62; Fellow American Acad. of Arts and Sciences, Econometric Soc.; mem. N.A.S. 1972–; Foreign Assoc. mem. Acad. das Ciências de Lisboa; Fellow American Statistical Assen.; mem. American Philosophical Soc.; Corresp. mem. British Acad.; Pres. Econometric Soc. 1958; Pres. American Econ. Assen. 1971; Nobel Prize in Econs. 1981; Grand Order of Sacred Treasure, Japan 1988; Centennial Medal, Harvard Grad. School 1989; numerous hon. degrees. *Publications:* National Economic Policy 1966, Essays in Economics Vol. I Macroeconomics 1972, Vol. II Consumption and Econometrics 1975, Vol. III Theory and Policy 1982, Vol. IV National and International 1996, The New Economics One Decade Older 1974, Asset Accumulation and Economic Activity 1980, Policies for Prosperity: Essays in a Keynesian Mode 1987, Two Revolutions in Economic Policy (co-author) 1988, Full Employment and Growth: Further Essays in a Keynesian Mode 1996, Money, Credit and Capital 1997. *Leisure interests:* skiing, sailing, tennis. *Address:* Department of Economics, Yale University, P.O. Box 208281, New Haven, CT 06520 (Office); 117 Alden Avenue, New Haven, CT 06515 (Home). *Telephone:* 203-432-3720 (Office); 203-389-2540 (Home).

TODD, Sir David, Kt., C.B.E., M.D., F.A.M., F.R.C.P., F.R.C.P.E., F.R.C.P.GLAS., F.R.A.C.P., F.R.C.PATH.; British professor of medicine; b. 17 Nov. 1928, China; s. of Paul J. Todd and Margaret S. Todd; ed. Univ. of Hong Kong; Prof. Dept. of Medicine, Univ. of Hong Kong 1972–96, Head, Dept. of Medicine 1974–89, Sub-Dean, Faculty of Medicine 1976–78, Pro-Vice-Chancellor 1978–80; consultant (medicine) to Govt. of Hong Kong 1974–89; Pres. Hong Kong Acad. of Medicine 1992–96, Council for AIDS Trust Fund, Hong Kong 1993–96; Hon. D.Sc. (Chinese Univ. of Hong Kong) 1990, (Hong Kong Univ.) 1992. *Publications:* numerous articles in professional journals. *Leisure interests:* classical music, stamp collecting, swimming. *Address:* c/o Department of Medicine, The University of Hong Kong, Queen Mary Hospital, Pokfulam Road, Hong Kong Special Administrative Region; D12 Breezy Court, 2A Park Road, Mid-levels, Hong Kong Special Administrative Region, People's Republic of China.

TODD, Olivier, M.A.; French writer; b. 19 June 1929, Neuilly; s. of Julius Oblatt and Helen Todd; m. 1st Anne-Marie Nizan 1948; m. 2nd France Huser 1982; two s. two d.; ed. Sorbonne, Corpus Christi Coll., Cambridge; teacher Lycée Int. du Shape 1956–62; Univ. Asst. Saint-Cloud 1962–64; reporter Nouvel Observateur 1964–69; Ed. TV Programme Panorama 1969–70; Asst. Ed. Nouvel Observateur 1970–77; columnist and Man. Ed. L'Express 1977–81; worked for BBC (Europa, 24 Hours) 1964–69; Prix Cazes 1981, Prix France Télévision 1997, Prix du Mémorial 1997. *Publications:* Une demi-campagne 1957, La traversée de la Manche 1960, Des trous dans le Jardin 1969, L'année du Crabe 1972, Les Canards de Ca Mao 1975, La marelle de Giscard 1977, Portraits 1979, Un fils rebelle 1981, Un cannibale très convenable 1982, Une légère gueule de Bois 1983, La balade du chômeur 1986, Cruel Avril 1987, La Négociation 1989, La Sanglière 1992, Albert Camus, une vie 1996. *Leisure interest:* walking. *Address:* 21 rue de l'Odéon, 75006 Paris; 8 rue du Pin, 83310 La Garde Freinet, France. *Telephone:* 43.29.55.26; (94) 43-63-34.

TODD, Hon. Sir (Reginald Stephen) Garfield, Kt., D.D., LL.D.; Zimbabwean politician and rancher; b. 13 July 1908, Invercargill, New Zealand; s. of Thomas and Edith Todd; m. Jean Grace Wilson; three d.; ed. Otago Univ., Glen Leith Theological Coll. and Univ. of Witwatersrand, S.A.; worked with Thomas Todd & Sons Ltd., Invercargill, N.Z.; Supt. Dadaya Mission, Southern Rhodesia 1934–53, Chair. Governing Bd. 1963–85; M.P. for Shabani 1946–58; Pres. United Rhodesia Party 1953–58; Prime Minister 1953–58; Minister of Labour 1954–58, of Native Educ. 1955–57, of Labour and Social Welfare 1958; f. (with Sir John Moffat) Cen. Africa Party 1959, Pres. 1959–60; f. New African Party, July 1961; Dir. Hokonui Ranching Co. Ltd.; restricted to his ranch for 12 months Oct. 1965; imprisoned Jan. 1972, under house arrest 1972–76; Adviser to Joshua Nkomo (q.v.) at Constitutional Conf. on Rhodesia, Geneva 1976; mem. Senate 1980–85; Hon. LL.D.; received medal from Pope Paul for efforts for peace and justice in Southern Rhodesia 1973. *Leisure interest:* ranching. *Address:* Box FM 693, Bulawayo, Zimbabwe. *Telephone:* 64307.

TODD, Richard Andrew Palethorpe, O.B.E.; British actor and producer; b. 11 June 1919, Dublin, Ireland; s. of Major A. W. Palethorpe Todd and Marvilla Palethorpe Todd (née Agar-Daly); m. 1st Catherine Stewart Crawford Grant-Bogle 1949 (divorced 1970); one s. one d.; m. 2nd Virginia Anne Rollo Mailer 1970 (divorced 1992); two s. (one deceased); ed. Shrewsbury, privately; began theatrical career, London 1937; founder-mem. Dundee Repertory Co. 1938–39, rejoined 1947; served in King's Own Yorkshire Light Infantry and Parachute Regt. 1940–46; entered film industry in For Them That Trespass 1948. *Other films include:* The Hasty Heart 1949, Stage Fright 1950, Lightning Strikes Twice (U.S.A.) 1951, Robin Hood 1952, Twenty-Four Hours of a Woman's Life, The Venetian Bird 1953, Rob Roy 1954, The Sword and the Rose 1954, The Dam Busters 1955, A Man Called Peter 1955, The Virgin Queen (U.S.A.) 1955, The Sixth of June, Yangtse Incident 1956, Saint Joan, Chase a Crooked Shadow 1957, The Naked Earth, Danger Within 1958, The Long, the Short and the Tall 1959, Don't Bother to Knock (for own film co. Haileywood Films Ltd.) 1960, The Hellions 1960, Never Let Go 1961, The Longest Day 1962, The Boys 1962, Sanders 1963, Operation Crossbow 1965, Coast of Skeletons 1965, The Last of the Long-Haired Boys 1968, Dorian Gray 1970, Asylum 1972, Secret Agent 008 1976, The House of the Long Shadows 1982, The Olympus Force 1988; returned to London stage as Lord Goring (An Ideal Husband) 1965, Nicholas Randolph (Dear Octopus), Haymarket 1967; formed Triumph Theatre Production 1970, appeared in numerous productions in Britain, as the Comte (The Marquise), U.S.A. 1972, as Andrew Wyke (Sleuth), Australia and New Zealand 1972–73, English tour 1976, R.S.C. productions of The Hollow Crown and Pleasure and Repentance, Canada and U.S.A. 1974, as Martin Dysart (Equus) for Australian Nat. Theatre Co., Perth Festival 1975, toured as John (Miss Adams Will Be Waiting) 1975, toured S.A. in On Approval 1976, in Quadrille 1977, The Heat of the Moment 1977, appeared in Double Edge in U.K. and Canada 1978, in Nightfall, South Africa 1979, in This Happy Breed, U.K. 1980; The Business of Murder (Duchess Theatre 1981, Mayfair Theatre 1981–88), The Woman in Black (Sydney Opera House) 1991; as Lord Caversham (An Ideal Husband), Old Vic 1996, Albery Theatre, Theatre Royal Haymarket 1998. *TV appearances include:* Wuthering Heights, Dr. Who, Virtual Murder, as H.G. Wells in Beautiful Lies; nominated for Best Actor Award, Acad. Awards 1950, won British Nat. Film Award, Picturegoer Award, Hollywood Golden Globe; Past Grand Steward, Grand Lodge of England, Past Master Lodge of Emulation No. 21; Pres. Birmingham Age Concern 1990–. *Publications:* Caught in the Act (Vol. I of autobiog.) 1986, In Camera (Vol. II of autobiog.) 1989. *Leisure interests:* game shooting, fishing, gardening. *Address:* Chinham Farm, Faringdon, Oxon., SN7 8EZ; Little Ponton House, nr. Grantham, Lincs. NG33 5BS, England. *Telephone:* (01367) 710294. *Fax:* (01367) 710294.

TODD, Ronald (Ron); British trade union official (retd.); b. 11 March 1927, Walthamstow; s. of George Todd and Emily Todd; m. Josephine Tarrant 1945; one s. two d.; ed. St. Patrick's School, Walthamstow; served Royal Marine Commandos; joined Transport and Gen. Workers' Union (T&GWU) while employee of Ford Motor Co., Deputy Convenor 1954–62, full-time Union Officer, Metal, Eng. and Chemical Sections 1962–69, Regional Officer 1969–75, Regional Secretary, Region No. 1 1976–78, Nat. Organiser 1978–84, Gen. Sec. 1985–92; mem. TUC Gen. Council, TUC Econ. Cttee., Equal Rights, Health Service Cttees., TUC Gen. Council mem. of NEDC 1985–92, TUC/Labour Party Liaison Cttee.; Chair. TUC Int. Cttee.; Commr. on Manpower Services Comm.; mem. Employment Appeal Tribunal; Pres. Unity Trust 1986–89; Hon. Vice-Pres. Campaign for Nuclear Disarmament, Nat. Cttee. World Disarmament Campaign; mem. Nat. Council Royal Marines Assen.; Trades Union rep. Anti-Apartheid Cttee., T&GWU rep. on Nat. Union of Mineworkers Dispute Co-ordinating Cttee., Past Commr., Manpower Services Comm.; Past Pres. Unity Trust; Vice-Pres. British Deaf Assen. *Publications:* On His Todd (collection of poems, sold in aid of Royal London Hosp. Leukaemia Appeal Fund), Still on His Todd (collection of poems, sold in aid of David Jenkinson Memorial Fund). *Leisure interests:* palaeontology and collecting Victorian music covers. *Address:* 65 Surrey Road, Dagenham, RM10 8ET, England. *Telephone:* 0181-593 8683.

TODEA, H.E. Cardinal Alexandru, S.T.D., D.THEOL.; Romanian ecclesiastic; b. 5 June 1912, Teleac; s. of Gheorghe Todea and Maria Todea; ed. De Propaganda Fide Inst., Rome; ordained priest of Greek Catholic Church 1939; Prof. of Theology, Blaj 1940; Chair. Reghin Deanery 1945; arrested by secret police 1948; consecrated Bishop 1950; imprisoned for his faith 1952, released 1964; elected Archbishop secretly by the Romanian Bishops 1986, recognised and named by Pope, Archbishop and Metropolitan 1990; cr. Cardinal 1991; Archbishop Emer. 1994; mem. Romanian Acad. 1992. *Publications:* Cascada Tinereţii, Pentru tine, tânără învăţătoare, Rugăciunea tineretului. *Address:* Arhidieceza de Alba Iulia şi Făgăraş, Str. P.P. Aron 2, 3175 Blaj, Romania. *Telephone:* 58.71.20.57; 58.71.08.55. *Fax:* 58.88.15.85.

TODOROVSKY, Piotr Yefimovich; Russian film director, cameraman and scriptwriter; b. 26 Aug. 1925; m. Myra Grigoryevna Todorovskaya; one s.; ed. All-Union Inst. of Cinematography; started as cameraman film studios of Kishinev (Moldovafilm) and Odessa in films Moldavian Tunes 1955, Spring in the Zarechnaya Street 1956, Two Fyodors 1958, Thirst 1960; debut as film dir. Never 1962. *Film productions include:* Faithfulness 1965 (Prize of Int. Festival in Venice), Juggler 1968, City Romance 1971, Our Own Land 1973, The Last Victim 1976, On Holiday 1979, The Beloved Woman of Mechanic Gavrilov 1982, Wartime Romance 1984, Intergirl 1988, Encore, Encore 1993, What a Wonderful Game 1995; frequently author of scripts and music for his own films; numerous prizes All-Union and Int. Festivals in Tokyo, Venice, Berlin, San-Remo and others; Nica Prize 1992, State Prize 1995; People's Artist of Russia 1985. *Leisure interests:* composition and performance of guitar music. *Address:* Vernadskogo prospect 70A, Apt. 23, 117454 Moscow, Russia (Home). *Telephone:* 193 5206 (Home).

TOENNIES, Jan Peter, PH.D.; American physicist; b. 3 May 1930, Philadelphia, Pa.; s. of Dr. Gerrit Toennies and Dita Jebens; m. Monika Zelesnick 1966; two d.; ed. Amherst Coll., Brown Univ.; Asst., Bonn Univ., Fed. Repub. of Germany 1962–65, Privat Dozent 1965–67, Dozent 1967–69; Scientific mem. and Dir. Max-Planck-Inst. für Strömungsforschung (Fluid Dynamics) 1969; Assoc. Prof. Göttingen Univ. 1971–; Hon. Prof. Bonn Univ. 1971; Physics Prize, Göttingen Acad. of Sciences 1964, Gold Heyrovsky Medal of the Czechoslovak Acad. of Sciences 1991, 1991 Hewlett-Packard Europhysics Prize (for outstanding achievement in condensed matter research). *Publica-*

tions: Chemical Reactions in Shock Waves (with E.F. Greene) 1964, A Study of Intermolecular Potentials with Molecular Beams at Thermal Energies (with H. Pauly) in Advances in Atomic and Molecular Physics 1965, Molecular Beam Scattering Experiments, contribution in Physical Chemistry, an Advanced Treatise 1974, Rotationally and Vibrationally Inelastic Scattering of Molecules (Chem. Soc. Review) 1974, Scattering Studies of Rotational and Vibrational Excitation of Molecules (with M. Faubel) 1977, Advances in Atomic and Molecular Physics 1977, The Study of the Forces between Atoms of Single Crystal Surfaces 1988. *Leisure interest:* sailing. *Address:* Max-Planck-Institut für Strömungsforschung, Bunsenstrasse 10, 37073 Göttingen (Office); Ewaldstrasse 7, 37085 Göttingen, Germany (Home). *Telephone:* 0551-5176-600 (Office); 0551-57172 (Home).

TOGNOLI, Carlo; Italian politician and journalist; b. 16 June 1938, Milan; ed. Univ. Bocconi, Milan; Dir. Critica Sociale (monthly); joined Italian Socialist Party (PSI) 1957; Town Councillor, Cormano (Milan) 1960–70; City Councillor, Milan 1970–; Pres. Istituto di Tecnologia Urbana, Milan; mem. European Parl. 1984; mem. Nat. Cttee. of PSI 1984; Deputy to Parl. 1987; Minister for Urban Problems in Goria Govt.; Minister of Tourism and the Performing Arts 1990–92.

TOH CHIN CHYE, PH.D.; Singaporean politician and physiologist; b. 10 Dec. 1921, Malaya; s. of Toh Kim Poh and Tan Chuan Bee; m. Yeapp Sui Phek; one d.; ed. Raffles Coll., Singapore, Univ. Coll., London Univ., and National Inst. for Medical Research, London; Founder, People's Action Party, Chair. 1954–; Reader in Physiology, Univ. of Singapore 1958–64; Research Assoc., Univ. of Singapore 1964; Deputy Prime Minister of Singapore 1959–68; Minister for Science and Tech. 1968–75, for Health 1975–81; M.P. Singapore 1959–88; Chair. Bd. of Govs., Singapore Polytechnic 1959–75; Vice-Chancellor, Univ. of Singapore 1968–75; Chair. of Bd. of Govs. Regional Inst. for Higher Educ. and Devt. 1970–75; Chair. Applied Research Corpn. 1973–75; Hon. D.Litt. (Univ. of Singapore) 1976; Nila Utama, First Class 1990. *Publications:* papers in journals of physiology, etc. *Leisure interests:* orchids, reading. *Address:* 23 Greenview Crescent, Singapore 289332.

TOIBIN, Colm; Irish journalist and writer; b. 1955; journalist, columnist Dublin Sunday Independent 1985–; E. M. Forster Award, American Acad. of Arts and Letters 1995. *Publications:* Seeing is Believing: Moving Statues in Ireland 1985, Walking Along the Border 1987, Homage to Barcelona 1990, Dubliners 1990, The South (novel) 1990, The Trial of the Generals: Selected Journalism 1980–90, The Heather Blazing 1993, Soho Square 6: New Writing from Ireland 1993; articles. *Address:* 23 Carnew Street, Dublin 7, Ireland.

TOIVO, Andimba Toivo ya; Namibian politician; b. 22 Aug. 1924, Omangundu, Ovamboland; s. of Andimba Toivo ya Toivo and Nashikoto Elizabeth; m. 2nd Vicki Lynn Erenstein 1990; three s. two d.; ed. St. Mary's Mission School, Odimbo; taught at St. Mary's Mission School, Odimbo; served in S.A. Army 1942–43; worked in S.A. gold mines and on railways; mem. African Nation Congress and Modern Youth Soc.; deported to Ovamboland 1958; f. (with Sam Nujoma) S.W. African People's Org. (SWAPO); arrested 1966; sentenced to 20 years' imprisonment, Robben Island 1968; released in Windhoek, Namibia 1984; mem. Politburo and Sec.-Gen. SWAPO 1984–91; Minister of Mines and Energy 1990–; leader SWAPO del. to UN 1984. *Leisure interests:* volleyball, tennis, jogging, swimming and reading. *Address:* P.O. Box 2038, Windhoek, Namibia. *Telephone:* (61) 2848111. *Fax:* (61) 238643.

TOKAYEV, Kasymzhomart Kemelevich; Kazakhstan diplomatist and politician; b. 17 May 1953, Almaty, Kazakhstan; s. of late Kemel Tokayev and of Turash Shabyrbayeva; m. Nadeyda Poznanskaya 1983; one s.; ed. Moscow Inst. of Int. Relations, Diplomatic Acad., U.S.S.R. Ministry of Foreign Affairs; with U.S.S.R. Ministry of Foreign Affairs 1975; Embassy, Singapore 1975–79; Attaché, Third Sec. Ministry of Foreign Affairs 1979–83; Second Sec. of Dept. 1984–85; Second, First Sec. Embassy, People's Repub. of China 1985–91; rank of Amb. of Kazakhstan 1994; Deputy, First Deputy Minister of Foreign Affairs Repub. of Kazakhstan 1992–94, Minister Oct. 1994–; Parasat (Nat. Award) 1996. *Leisure interests:* reading, playing tennis. *Address:* Ministry of Foreign Affairs, Aiteke-bi str. 65, Almaty; 10 Beibitshilif, Astana, Kazakhstan. *Telephone:* (3172) 32-71-22.

TŐKEI, Ferenc, M.A., D.LITT.SC.; Hungarian philosopher and sinologue; b. 3 Oct. 1930, Budapest; s. of Ferenc Tőkei and Irma Kiss; m. Margit Egry; two s. one d.; ed. Eötvös Loránd Univ. Budapest; on staff Hopp Ferenc Museum of East-Asian Arts, Budapest 1956–57; Ed. Europa Publishing House, Budapest 1957–67; acad. researcher 1967–69; Dir. Inst. of Philosophy, Hungarian Acad. of Sciences 1969–72; corresp. mem. of Acad. 1973–, mem. 1985–; Head of Orientalistic Research Group 1972–; Chair. Hungarian Philosophical Asscn. 1987–90; mem. Bd. Kőrösi Csoma Soc., ed. Acta Orient. Hung. 1977–90; Pres. Cttee. for Orientalistic Studies, Hungarian Acad. of Sciences 1976–86; Prof. of Philosophy Eötvös L. Univ. Budapest 1970–90, Prof. of Chinese 1990–; State Prize Award 1970. *Publications:* A kínai elégia születése 1959, Naissance de l'élégie chinoise 1967, Az ázsiai termelési mód kérdéséhez 1965, Zur Frage der asiatischen Produktionsweise 1969, Műfajelmélet Kínában a III-VI. században 1967, Genre Theory in China in 3rd-6th Centuries 1971, Kínai filozófia, Ókor I-III 1962–67, 1980, 1986, A szépség szíve 1973, Sinológiai műhely 1974, A társadalmi formák marxista elméletének néhány kérdése 1977, 1988, Zur marxistischen Geschichtstheorie I-III 1977, Essays on the Asiatic Mode of Production 1979, Primitive Society and the Asiatic Mode of Production 1989, Kortársunk-e Marx? 1984, Karl Marx—unser Zeitgenosse? 1990, Kínai buddhista filozófia 1993, 1996, Kínai szofisztika és logika 1997, A kínai festészet elmélete 1997, A kínai költészet elméleteiből 1998. *Leisure interests:* travelling, tourism. *Address:* 1022 Budapest, Felvinci út 22, Hungary. *Telephone:* (01) 316 62-44. *Fax:* (01) 316-62-44.

TŐKÉS, Rev. László; Romanian ecclesiastic; b. 1 April 1952, Cluj/Kolozsvár; s. of István Tőkés and Erzsébet Vass; m. Edit Joó 1985; two s. one d.; ed. Protestant Theological Inst. Cluj; asst. minister at Braşov/Brassó, then at Dej/Dés 1975–84; discharged for political reasons and suspended from church service 1984–86; reinstalled as chaplain then pastor, Timişoara/Temesvár 1986–89; banished to small parish of Mineu/Menyő, threatened with eviction, demonstration by supporters was beginning of revolution that overthrew Communist govt. 1989; Bishop of Királyhágómellék Diocese, Oradea/Nagyvárad 1990–; mem. Temporary Nat. Salvation Council; Co-Chair. Hungarian Reformed Synod of Romania; Hon. Pres. Hungarian Democratic Alliance of Hungarians in Romania; Hon. Pres. Hungarian World Fed.; Pres. Reformed Hungarian World Fed.; Dr. h.c. (Theological Acad. of Debrecen) 1990, (Regent Univ., Va. Beach, U.S.A.) 1990, (Hope Coll., Holland, Mich.) 1991; Berzsenyi Prize, Hungary 1989, Roosevelt Prize of The Netherlands 1990, Bethlen Gábor Prize, Hungary 1990, Geuzenpenning Prize, Netherlands 1991, Pro Fide Prize, Finland 1993, Bocskay Prize, Hungary 1995, Hungarian Heritage Prize 1996, Minority Prize of Catalan CIEMEN Centre, Spain 1996, Leopold Kunschak Prize, Austria 1998; Freeman Cities of Sárospatak amd Székelyudvarhely and of 5th and 11th dists. of Budapest; mem. Johannit Order of Knighthood. *Publications:* Where the Lord's Soul, there Freedom (selections of sermons) 1990, The Siege of Timişoara '89 1990, With God for the People 1990, There is a Time to Speak (with David Porter) 1993, A Phrase—and what is Behind 1993, In the Spirit of Timişoara 1997; sermons, articles in ecclesiastical and secular publs. *Address:* Calvin Str. 1, 3700 Oradea, Romania. *Telephone:* (59) 43-28-37. *Fax:* (59) 43-28-37.

TOKODY, Ilona; Hungarian soprano; b. Szeged; d. of András Tokody and Ilona Nagy; ed. Liszt Ferenc Music Acad., Budapest; won Kodály singing competition 1972, Erkel competition of Inter-konzert Agency 1973, Ostend competition operatic category 1976; joined State Opera, Budapest 1976; regular guest performer Staatsoper Wien and Deutsche Oper West-Berlin; appearances in opera houses and concert halls worldwide, including Metropolitan Opera House, Royal Opera House Covent Garden, Vienna State Opera, San Francisco Opera, Teatro Colón, Buenos Aires, Liceo, Barcelona, Bavarian State Opera, San Carlo, Naples, Rome Opera, Bolshoi, Carnegie Hall, New York, Musikverein, Vienna. *Operatic roles include:* leading roles in La Forza del Destino, Don Carlo, Suor Angelica, Madama Butterfly, Il Trovatore, Aida, La Juive, La Bohème; Nedda (I Pagliacci), Micaela (Carmen), Alice (Falstaff), Giselda (I Lombardi). *Recordings:* Suor Angelica, Nerone, La Fiamma, Brahms Requiem, Il Tabarro, Guntram, Iris. *Leisure interests:* cooking, badminton, gymnastics, table tennis, reading. *Address:* c/o Hungarian State Opera, 1062 Budapest, Andrássy ut 22, Hungary. *Telephone:* (1) 312-550.

TOKOMBAYEVA, Aysulu Asanbekovna; Kyrgyzstan ballerina; b. 22 Sept. 1947, Frunze (now Bishkek); ed. Vaganova Dancing School, Leningrad; soloist with Theatre of Kirghizia 1966–; mem. CPSU 1973–91; *major roles include:* Odette-Odile (Swan Lake); Aurore (Sleeping Beauty); Giselle; Bayadère: Frigia (Spartacus); Lady Macbeth (by K. Molchanov); U.S.S.R. State Prize 1976; People's Artist of Kirghizia 1976; U.S.S.R. People's Artist 1981. *Address:* Kyrgyz Opera Theatre, Bishkek, Kyrgystan.

TOLBA, Mostafa Kamal, D.I.C., PH.D.; Egyptian international official, scientist and administrator; b. 8 Dec. 1922, Gharbiah; s. of Kamel Tolba and Shafika Abu Samra; m. Saneya Zaki Labib; ed. Cairo Univ., Imperial Coll., London; Asst. Lecturer, later Lecturer and Prof. of Microbiology, Cairo Univ., Egyptian Nat. Research Centre and Baghdad Univ., Iraq 1943–59; Asst. Sec.-Gen., later Sec.-Gen. Supreme Science Council, Egypt 1959–63; Cultural Counsellor and Dir. Egyptian Educ. Bureau, Washington, D.C., U.S.A. 1963–65; Under-Sec. of State for Higher Educ. 1965–71; Minister of Youth 1971; Pres. Acad. of Scientific Research and Tech. 1971–73; Deputy Exec. Dir. UNEP 1973–75, UN Under-Sec.-Gen., Exec. Dir. UNEP 1976–92; Hon. Prof. Beijing Univ.; Fellow Imperial Coll.; Hon. Dr. (Moscow); Hon. D.Sc. (Seoul), (Gembloux, Belgium) 1985, (Nairobi) 1989; Hon. LL.D. (Williams Coll.) 1990; State Prize in Biology 1959, Environment Prize (UN Environment Programme) 1993; decorations and prizes from 21 countries. *Publications:* Development without Destruction 1982, Earth Matters 1983, Sustainable Development: Constraints and Opportunities 1987, Evolving Environmental Perceptions: from Stockholm to Nairobi 1988; 95 scientific papers in journals of seven countries. *Leisure interest:* reading. *Address:* 46 Mosaddak Street, Dokki, Giza, Egypt.

TOLNAY, Lajos, PH.D.; Hungarian business executive; b. 27 Sept. 1948, Sajószentpéter; m.; four c.; ed. Heavy Industries Tech. Univ. Miskolc and Budapest Univ. of Econs.; various positions DIMAG Co. Ltd. 1971–92, Gen. Dir. 1989–92; Man. Dir. Dunaferr Trading House Ltd. 1992–93; Pres.-Man. Dir. PTW Investment Co. Ltd. 1993–95; Pres.-Man. Dir. Rákóczi Bank 1994, Pres. Aug. 1994–; Chair. Hungarian Chamber of Commerce 1990–93, Hungarian Chamber of Commerce and Industry 1994–; Man. Dir. Inota Aluminium Co. Ltd. 1996–; Chair. Bd. Magyar Aluminium Inc. 1997–; Chair. Controlling Cttee. Életút First Nat. Pension Fund; Chair. NAT Hungarian

Accreditation Bd.; mem. Exec. Bd. ICC, Hon. Chair. ICC Hungary; mem. Supervisory Bd. Hungexpo Co. Ltd., Bankár Investment Co. Ltd.; various awards and decorations. *Address:* Hungarian Chamber of Commerce and Industry, 1055 Budapest, Kossuth Lajos tér 6–8, Hungary. *Telephone:* (1) 353-3333. *Fax:* (1) 269-4628.

TOLSTAYA, Tatyana Nikitichna; Russian writer; b. 3 May 1951, Leningrad (now St Petersburg); d. of Mikhail Lozinsky; m. Andrey V. Lebedev; two s.; ed. Univ of Leningrad; Ed. of Eastern Literature Nauka Publishing, Moscow 1987–89; lecturer, Skidmore Coll., N.J., U.S.A. *Publications:* On the Golden Porch (short story) 1983, Sleepwalkers In A Fog 1992. *Address:* c/o Penguin Books Ltd., Bath Road, Harmondsworth, Middx. UB7 ODA, England. *Telephone:* (095) 238-22-15 (Moscow); (908) 821-3007 (U.S.A.); (01856) 770474 (U.K.).

TOMALIN, Claire, M.A., F.R.S.L.; British writer; b. 20 June 1933, London; d. of Emile Delavenay and Muriel Emily Herbert; m. 1st Nicholas Osborne Tomalin 1955 (died 1973); two s. three d. (one d. and one s. deceased); m. 2nd Michael Frayn 1993; ed. Hitchin Girls' Grammar School, Dartington Hall School, Newnham Coll., Cambridge; publr.'s reader and Ed. 1955–67; asst. Literary Ed. New Statesman 1968–70, Literary Ed. 1974–77; Literary Ed. Sunday Times 1979–86; mem. London Library Cttee. 1997–, Advisory Cttee. for the Arts, Humanities and Social Sciences, British Library 1997–, Council Royal Soc. of Literature 1997; Trustee Nat. Portrait Gallery 1992–; Whitbread Prize 1974, James Tait Black Prize 1990, NCR Book Award 1991, Hawthornden Prize 1991. *Publications:* The Life and Death of Mary Wollstonecraft 1974, Shelley and his World 1980, Katherine Mansfield: A Secret Life 1987, The Invisible Woman 1990, The Winter Wife 1991, Mrs Jordan's Profession 1994, Jane Austen: A Life 1997. *Address:* c/o Peters, Fraser and Dunlop, 503/4 The Chambers, Chelsea Harbour, London, SW10 0XF; 57 Gloucester Crescent, London, NW1 7EG, England.

TÓMASSON, Tómas Ármann, M.A.; Icelandic diplomatist; b. 1 Jan. 1929, Reykjavík; s. of Tómas Tómasson and Gudrun Thorgrimsdottir; m. Heba Jónsdóttir 1957 (divorced); three s. one d.; ed. Reykjavík Grammar School, Univ. of Illinois, Fletcher School of Law and Diplomacy and Columbia Univ.; entered Icelandic foreign service 1954; Sec. Moscow 1954–58; Ministry for Foreign Affairs 1958–60; Deputy Perm. Rep. to NATO and OECD 1960–66; Chief of Div., Ministry for Foreign Affairs 1966–69, Deputy Sec.-Gen. of Ministry 1970–71; Amb. to Belgium and EEC and Perm. Rep. on N. Atlantic Council 1971–77, 1984–86, also accred. to Luxembourg 1976–77, 1984–86; Perm. Rep. to UN 1977–82, 1993–94; Amb. to France (also accred. to Portugal, Spain, Cape Verde) 1982–84; Amb. to U.S.S.R. (also accred. to Bulgaria, G.D.R., Hungary, Mongolia and Romania) 1987–90; Amb., Head of Del. to CSBMs and CFE negotiation, Vienna 1990; Amb. to U.S.A. (also accred. to Canada) 1990–93; Amb., Head of Del. to CSCE Review Conf. and Summit, Budapest Oct.–Dec. 1994; Ministry for Foreign Affairs, Reykjavík 1994–; Order of the Falcon (Iceland), and decorations from France, Belgium, Luxembourg, Portugal and Sweden. *Address:* Ministry for Foreign Affairs, 150 Reykjavík, Iceland. *Telephone:* (1) 5609900. *Fax:* (1) 5622386.

TOMASZEWSKI, Henryk; Polish choreographer, ballet master and mime artist; b. 20 Nov. 1919, Poznań; ed. Ballet School, Ivo Gall's Studio; mem. F. Parnell Ballet Ensemble, then of Wrocław Opera Ballet 1949–56; organized Mime Studio 1956 (now Mime Theatre); now Artistic Man. Wrocław Mime Theatre; won 1st Prize, World Festival of Youth, Moscow with his first programme 1957; Medal of French Critics, Festival of Nations 1962, Gold Medal, Swedish Soc. of Dance 1963, Gold Star, VIII Int. Festival of Dance 1971, Venezuelan Theatre Critics' Prize (for Przyjeżdżam jutro) 1978), Officer's Cross, Order of Polonia Restituta 1976, Commdr.'s Cross 1986, Minister of Culture and Arts Prize, 2nd Class 1962; performances in Europe, America and Africa; *ballets:* for Theatre of Drama: Process (from Kafka) 1966, Klątwa (by Wyspiański) 1969, Peer Gynt 1974, Księżniczka Turandot (by C. Gozzi) 1974, Gra w zabijanego (by Ionesco) 1975, dir. Hammerman and Baker (film for Norwegian TV) 1978, Equus 1978, Historia konia 1981, Pericles (Shakespeare) (in co-operation with Mime Theatre) 1982, for Mime Theatre: Gilgamesh 1968, Odejście Fausta 1970, Menażeria Cesarzowej Filissy (with F. Wedekinda) 1972, Przyjeżdżam jutro 1974, Sceny fantastyczne z legendy o Panu Twardowskim 1976, Spór (by Pierre de Marivaux) 1978, Hamlet, Ironia i Zagłoba 1979, Rycerze Króla Artura 1981, Syn marnotrawny (based on Hogarth's A Rake's Progress) 1983, Action—A Midsummer Night's Dream 1986, Król siedmiodniowy 1988, Cardenio i Celinda 1990, Schluck und Jan (G. Hauptmann) 1995. *Address:* Mime Theatre, al. Dębowa 16, 53-121 Wrocław, Poland. *Telephone:* (71) 367 52 80 (Office). *Fax:* (71) 367 52 80 (Office).

TOMASZEWSKI, Janusz; Polish politician and union activist; b. 13 Sept. 1956, Pabianice; m.; two s.; worked as motor-car mechanic; mem. Solidarity Trade Union 1980–, (Chair. Factory Comm. 1980, Chair. Local Comm. 1981, interned 1982, underground activist Łódź Region 1990–92, Chair. 1992–95, Vice-Chair. Region of Łódź Dist. 1995–97, Vice-Chair. Nat. Comm. 1995–97, Vice-Chair. Solidarity Election Action (AWS); co-founder Social Movt. of Solidarity Election Action (RS AWS) 1998–; Deputy Prime Minister and Minister of Internal Affairs and Admin. 1997–. *Address:* Kancelaria Rady Ministrów, Al. Ujazdowskie 1/3, 00-583 Warsaw, Poland. *Telephone:* (22) 628 44 18. *Fax:* (22) 694 73 93.

TOMBS, Baron (Life Peer), cr. 1990, of Brailes in the County of Warwickshire; **Francis Leonard Tombs,** B.SC., LL.D., D.SC., F.ENG.; British business executive; b. 17 May 1924, Walsall; s. of Joseph Tombs and Jane Tombs; m. Marjorie Evans 1949; three d.; ed. Elmore Green School, Walsall and Birmingham Coll. of Tech.; with British Electricity Authority 1948–57; Gen. Man., Gen. Electric Co. Ltd. 1958–67; Dir. and Gen. Man. James Howden and Co. 1967–68; Dir. of Eng., S. of Scotland Electricity Bd. 1969–73, Deputy Chair. 1973–74, Chair. 1974–77; Chair. Electricity Council for England and Wales 1977–80; Dir. N. M. Rothschild and Sons Ltd. 1981–94; Chair. The Weir Group Ltd. 1981–83; Dir. Rolls-Royce Ltd. 1982–92, Chair. 1985–92; Dir. Old Mutual S.A. Fund 1994–98; Dir. Shell (U.K.) Ltd. 1983–94; Chancellor Univ. of Strathclyde 1991–97; Chair. Eng. Council 1985–88; Hon. F.I.C.E.; Hon. F.I.Mech.E.; Hon. F.I.Chem.E.; Hon. F.I.E.E. (and fmr. Pres.); Hon. F.R.S.E. 1996; Hon. D.Sc. (Aston) 1979, (Lodz, Poland) 1980, (Cranfield Inst. of Tech.) 1985, (The City Univ., London) 1986, (Bradford) 1986, (Queen's Univ., Belfast) 1988, (Surrey) 1988, (Nottingham) 1989, (Warwick) 1990, (Cambridge) 1990, (Warwick) 1990; Hon. D. Univ. (Strathclyde Univ.) 1991; Hon. D. Tech. (Loughborough) 1979; Dr. h.c. (Council for Nat. Acad. Awards) 1988. *Publications:* Nuclear Energy Past, Present and Future—Electronics and Power 1981, Reversing the Decline in Manufacturing Industry (Mountbatten Lecture 1993). *Leisure interests:* music and golf. *Address:* Honington Lodge, Honington, Shipston-upon-Stour, Warwicks., CV36 5AA, England.

TOMIĆ, Dragan; Yugoslav politician and engineer; b. 9 Dec. 1935, G. Bukovica; s. of Boško Tomić and Mitra Tomić; m. Milica Tomić 1964; two d.; ed. Belgrade Univ.; various positions Rekord Rubber Works, Rakovica 1962–86, Gen. Dir. 1986; Pres. Eng. Soc. of Yugoslavia; Gen. Dir. NIS – Jugopetrol Co.; Chair. Man. Bd. RTV Politika Co. 1993–; mem. Nat. Parl. (Skupština) of Serbia 1994–, Chair. 1994–97; Chair. Union of Yugoslav Engineers and Technicians 1993–. *Leisure interests:* chess, walking with his dog. *Address:* Skupština Srbije, Srpskih Vladara 14, 11000 Belgrade, Yugoslavia. *Telephone:* 324-8604. *Fax:* 685-092.

TOMKO, H.E. Cardinal Jozef, D.THEOL., DR.IUR.; Slovak ecclesiastic; b. 11 March 1924, Udavské, Humenné; s. of Andrej Tomko and Anna Tomko; ordained priest 1949; consecrated Bishop (Titular See of Doclea) 1979; cr. Cardinal 1985; Sec.-Gen. of Synod of Bishops; mem. Comm. for Admin. of State of Vatican 1985–; Prefect of the Congregation for the Evangelization of Peoples 1985–; Adviser, Sec. of Vatican State 1996–; numerous missions worldwide; Prize of Grand Duchy of Luxembourg 1988. *Publications include:* Light of Nations 1972, Christianity and the World 1974, Christ Yesterday and Today 1976, Ecumenism 1977. *Address:* Via Urbano VIII 16, 00165 Rome, Italy. *Telephone:* (06) 687.03.31.

TOMKYS, Sir (W.) Roger, K.C.M.G., D.L., M.A.; British diplomatist and academic; b. 15 March 1937, Bradford; s. of Arthur Tomkys and Edith Tomkys; m. Margaret Abbey 1963; one s. one d.; ed. Bradford Grammar School and Balliol Coll. Oxford; entered H.M. Diplomatic Service 1960; served Amman, Benghazi, Athens, Rome; Amb. to Bahrain 1981–84, to Syria 1984–86; Asst. Under-Sec., later Deputy Under-Sec. of State, FCO 1986–90; High Commr. in Kenya 1990–92; Master of Pembroke Coll., Cambridge 1992–; Commendatore dell'Ordine al Merito; Order of Bahrain. *Leisure interests:* travel, books, golf, tennis (real). *Address:* The Master's Lodge, Pembroke College, Cambridge, CB2 1RF, England.

TOMLINSON, John, C.B.E.; British (bass) opera singer; b. 22 Sept. 1946, Accrington, Lancs.; s. of Rowland Tomlinson and Ellen Greenwood; m. Moya Joel 1969; one s. two d.; ed. Accrington Grammar School, Manchester Univ. and Royal Manchester Coll. of Music; debut at Glyndebourne Festival 1972, English Nat. Opera 1974, Royal Opera House, Covent Garden 1976; since then has appeared in many operatic roles throughout Europe and N. America; sang role of Wotan in The Ring cycle, Bayreuth Festival 1988–92, Hans Sachs in Die Meistersinger, Covent Garden 1993, 1997; numerous broadcasts, recordings, opera videos and concert performances; Hon. D.Mus. (Manchester) 1998. *Address:* c/o Music International, 13 Ardilaun Road, Highbury, London, N5 2QR, England. *Telephone:* 0171-359 5183.

TOMLINSON, Lindsay Peter, M.A., F.I.A.; British financial executive; b. 7 Oct. 1951, Derby; s. of P. Tomlinson and J. M. Tomlinson; m. Sarah Caroline Anne Martin 1973; four s. one d.; ed. Clifton Coll., St. John's Coll., Cambridge; actuarial student Commercial Union Assurance Co. 1973–77; sr. pensions consultant Metropolitan Pensions Asscn. 1977–81; Sr. Investment Man. Provident Mutual Managed Pension Funds 1981–87; Chief Exec. (Europe) Barclays Global Investors (fmrly. BZW Investment Man.) 1987–. *Address:* Barclays Global Investors Limited, Murray House, 1 Royal Mint Court, London, EC3N 4HH, England. *Telephone:* 0171-668 8866. Fax: 0171-668 8381.

TOMLINSON, Mel Alexander, B.F.A.; American dancer; b. 3 Jan. 1954, Raleigh, N.C.; s. of Tommy W. A. Tomlinson and Marjorieline Henry Tomlinson; ed. F. J. Carnage Jr. High School, J. W. Ligon High School, N.C. Gov.'s School and N.C. School of the Arts; Prin., Agnes DeMille's Heritage Dance Theater 1973, Dance Theatre of Harlem Inc. 1974–77, Alvin Ailey American Dance Theatre 1977–78, Dance Theatre of Harlem Inc. 1978–81; mem. corps de ballet, New York City Ballet 1981, soloist 1982–; guest appearance, DeMille Tribute, Jofferey Ballet. *Leisure interests:* knitting, swimming, gymnastics, reading, sewing, games. *Address:* New York City Ballet, Lincoln State Theater, New York, NY 10023; 790 Riverside Drive, Apt. 6B, New York, NY 10032; 1216 Bunche Drive, Raleigh, NC 27610, U.S.A. *Telephone:* (212) 234-3320; (919) 834-7010.

TOMOS; Chinese artist; b. 26 Nov. 1932, Tumed Banner, Inner Mongolia (Nei Monggol); s. of Yun Yao and Xing Yu; m. Xiahe-xiou 1967; two s.; ed. Cen. Inst. of Fine Arts, Beijing; Assoc. Prof. of Fine Arts, Inner Mongolia Normal Coll.; Dean of Fine Arts, Inner Mongolia Teachers' Training Coll. 1984–; Adviser on Fine Arts to Children's Palace, Huhehot, Inner Mongolia; Vice-Chair. Inner Mongolian Branch of Chinese Artists' Asscn. 1980–; Dir. Standing Cttee., Chinese Artists' Asscn. May 1985–, mem. Oil Art Cttee. 1985–; mem. Selection Cttee. for Sixth Nat. Art Exhbn. of oil paintings; mem. Art Educ. Cttee. of Nat. Educ. 1986–; Dir. Inner Mongolia branch of China External Culture Exchange Asscn.; Dir. Cheng's Style Tai-Chi Chuan Asscn. 1993–; Chair. Judges' Cttee. for 8th Annual Chinese Art Exhbn., Inner Mongolia 1994, 8th Annual Best Chinese Artwork Exhbn. 1994; Consultant, The Watercolour Asscn., Inner Mongolia 1994; Dir. China Oil Painting Asscn. 1995–; Chair. Inner Mongolian Artists' Asscn. 1996–; First Prize for Art, Inner Mongolia; exhbns. include: oil paintings and sketches, Huhehot 1979, oil paintings Exhbn. Hall of Cen. Inst. of Fine Arts, Cultural Palace of minority nationalities, Beijing 1981, oil paintings and sketches, Changsha, Hunan Prov. 1984, Modern Oil Painting Exhbn., China Art Gallery, China Modern Oil Painting Exhbn., U.S.A. 1987, Far East Art Museum of U.S.S.R. 1991, Modern Gallery, Tai Zhong, Taiwan 1993; Head of del. of Inner Mongolian painters to Hong Kong 1993; Merit of Art Educ. Award, Wu Zuo Ren Int. Art Foundation 1990, Expert and Scholar award of Govt. 1991. *Works include:* Mine, Wind on the Grasslands, Having a Break, Dawn, Milkmaid, A Woman Hay-making (Nat. Silver Medal 1985), At Dusk, Polo (Nat. Copper Medal 1985), Spring Wind, White Horse and Wind, At Dark and many others. *Publications:* Selection of oil-paintings, Tomos's Album of Paintings (sketches and oil paintings) 1993. *Leisure interests:* Chinese Gongfu, Peking opera, Chinese medicine. *Address:* Art Department, Normal College, Nei Monggol Autonomous Region, People's Republic of China.

TOMOWA-SINTOW, Anna; Austrian opera singer; b. 22 Sept. 1943, Stara Zagora, Bulgaria; m. Albert Sintow 1963; one d.; ed. Nat. Conservatory of Sofia; début Leipzig Opera 1967; joined Deutsche Staatsoper, Berlin 1969; guest engagements at most leading European and U.S. opera houses, including La Scala, Milan, Vienna, Covent Garden, London, Paris, Bavarian State Opera and Bolshoi, Moscow; début N. America at Metropolitan Opera, New York 1978; has toured Japan with Scala di Milano and Berlin Philharmonic under von Karajan; regular guest at Salzburg Festival since 1973; major roles include Arabella, Ariadne, Madelaine (in Capriccio), Countess Almaviva, Elsa (in Lohengrin), Elisabeth (in Tannhäuser), Aida, Tosca, Butterfly, Traviata, Manon Lescaut, Maddalena (in Andrea Chenier), Leonora (in La Forza del Destino), Marschallin (Rosenkavalier), Yaroslavna, etc.; has sung in several TV productions; recordings include Lohengrin, Le nozze di Figaro, Don Giovanni, Die Zauberflöte, Mozart Coronation Mass, Mozart Requiem, Brahms German Requiem, Strauss Four Last Songs and Capriccio monologue, Beethoven Missa Solemnis, Ariadne auf Naxos (in preparation), Madame Butterfly, La Traviata, Tosca, Eugen Onegin, recitals of Verdi arias and of Italian and German arias; recording and film of Verdi Requiem with von Karajan; winner Kammersängerin Prize. *Leisure interests:* nature, reading books, singing.

TOMUR DAWAMAT; Chinese party official; b. 1927, Toksun, Xinjiang; s. of Ziweidihan Dawamat; m. Gulzirahan 1944; five s. two d.; ed. Cen. Nationalities Coll., Beijing; village chief 1950; joined CCP 1952; Sec. CCP Cttee., Toksun Cttee., Tunpan Basin 1956, First Sec. 1960; Vice-Chair. Xinjiang Autonomous Region 1964; Deputy for Xinjiang, 3rd NPC; mem. Standing Cttee., Autonomous Regional Revolutionary Cttee., Xinjiang 1968; disappeared until 1976; Deputy for Xinjiang, 5th NPC 1978; mem. Standing Cttee., 5th NPC 1978; Deputy Sec. CCP Cttee. Xinjiang 1978–; Vice-Minister of State Nationalities Affairs Comm., State Council 1979; Chair. Autonomous Regional People's Congress, Xinjiang 1979–85; mem. 12th Cen. Cttee., CCP 1982; Gov. Xinjiang Autonomous Region 1986–93; Vice-Sec. Xinjiang Autonomous Region CCP Cttee. 1985; mem. 13th Cen. Cttee., CCP 1987–92; mem. 14th Cen. Cttee. CCP 1992–; a Vice-Chair. Standing Cttee. 8th NPC 1993–98, 9th NPC 1998–. *Leisure interests:* writing poetry, playing Chinese Checkers. *Address:* Standing Committee of National People's Congress, Beijing, People's Republic of China.

TONČIĆ-SORINJ, Lujo, LL.D.; Austrian politician and landowner; b. 12 April 1915, Vienna; s. of Dušan Tončić-Sorinj and Mabel Plason de la Woesthyne; m. Renate Trenker 1956; one s. four d.; ed. Grammar School, Salzburg, and Univs. of Vienna and Zagreb; Asst. to Chair. S.E. Europe Dept., Berlin Univ. 1940–44; Mil. Service 1941–44; Head of Political Dept., Austrian Research Inst. for Econs. and Politics 1946–49, Ed. Berichte und Informationen 1946–49; M.P. for Land Salzburg 1949–66; Chair. Legal Cttee. of Austrian Parl. 1953–56, Foreign Affairs Cttee. 1956–59; in charge of Foreign Affairs questions, Austrian People's Party 1959–66; Austrian mem. Consultative Ass. of Council of Europe 1953–66, Vice-Chair. Political Cttee.; Vice-Pres. Council of Europe 1961–62; Minister of Foreign Affairs 1966–68; Sec.-Gen. Council of Europe 1969–74; Pres. Austrian Asscn. of UN 1977–92; Perm. Rep. Austrian People's Party to Christian-Democratic Group in European Parl. 1980–92; Perm. Rep. Croatian Democratic Union to EU of Christian Democratic Parties 1991–; Pres. Union Int. de la Propriété Immobilière 1987–; Grosses Goldenes Ehrenzeichen am Bande (Austria) and other decorations. *Publications:* Erfüllte Träume (autobiog.) 1982, Am Abgrund vorbei 1991, Usamljena borba Hrvatske 1998, and about 400 articles and essays on history and int. politics. *Leisure interests:* history, geography, swimming, diving. *Address:* 5020 Salzburg, Schloss Fürberg, Pausingerstrasse 11, Austria. *Telephone:* 0662-642886.

TONEGAWA, Susumu, PH.D.; Japanese immunologist and neuroscientist; b. 5 Sept. 1939, Nagoya; s. of Tsutomu Tonegawa and Miyuko Tonegawa; m. Mayumi Yoshinari 1985; two c.; ed. Kyoto Univ. and Univ. of Calif. San Diego; postgraduate work at Dept. of Biology, Univ. of Calif. San Diego 1968–69, The Salk Inst. San Diego 1969–70; mem. Basle Inst. for Immunology, Basle, Switzerland 1971–81; Prof. of Biology, Center for Cancer Research and Dept. of Biology, M.I.T. 1981–; investigator Howard Hughes Medical Inst. 1988–; mem. American Acad. of Arts and Sciences; Foreign Assoc. mem. N.A.S.; Hon. mem. American Asscn. of Immunologists, Scandinavian Soc. for Immunology; numerous awards and prizes including Avery Landsteiner Prize 1981, Gairdner Foundation Int. Award 1983, Robert Koch Prize 1986, Lasker Prize 1987, Nobel Prize for Medicine 1987; Bunkakunsho Order of Culture 1984. *Address:* Center for Learning and Memory, Department of Biology, Massachusetts Institute of Technology, 77 Massachusetts Avenue, Cambridge, MA 02139, U.S.A.

TONG YIN CHU; Chinese politician; b. 1915, Hefei City, Anhui Prov.; ed. Shanghai Jiaotong Univ.; living in Indonesia 1938–47; joined China Democratic Construction Asscn. 1948; Chair. Cen. Cttee. of China Zhi Gong Dang 1988–97, Hon. Chair. 1997–; Vice-Chair. 8th Nat. Cttee. CPPCC 1993–98; Advisor, China Council for Promotion of Peaceful Nat. Reunification, All China Fed. of Returned Overseas Chinese. *Address:* National Committee of Chinese People's Political Consultative Congress, 23 Taiping Qiao Street, Beijing, People's Republic of China.

TONG ZENGYIN; Chinese banker; b. 1934, Yinxian, Zhejiang Prov.; joined CCP 1954; fmrly. Vice-Gov. Chinese People's Bank; Vice-Chair. China Securities Supervisory Cttee.; Pres. Minsheng Bank (China's first privately owned nat. bank) 1996–. *Address:* Minsheng Bank, Beijing, People's Republic of China.

TONG ZHIGUANG; Chinese government official; mem. Standing Cttee. 8th NPC, mem. NPC Foreign Affairs Cttee., del. of Hebei Prov. to 8th NPC; Deputy Head State Council Leading Group for Right to Intellectual Property 1991–; Vice-Minister of Foreign Trade and Econ. Co-operation 1991–93; Chair. Bd. of Dirs., The Export-Import Bank of China 1994–98. *Address:* c/o The Export-Import Bank of China, 75 Chongnei St., Beijing 100005, People's Republic of China.

TONGA, King of (see Taufa'ahau Tupou IV).

TONKIN, Hon. David Oliver, A.O., M.B., B.S., D.O., F.R.A.C.O.; Australian politician and ophthalmologist; b. 20 July 1929, S. Australia; s. of Oliver Athelstone Prisk Tonkin and Bertha Ida Louise Kennett; m. Prudence Anne Juttner 1954; three s. three d.; ed. St. Peter's Coll., Adelaide, Univ. of Adelaide, Inst of Ophthalmology, London; Private ophthalmic practice and visiting staff Royal Adelaide Hosp. 1958–68; mem. Social Welfare Advisory Council, Govt. of S. Australia 1968–70; Liberal M.P. for Bragg, S. Australia Parl. 1970–83, Leader of the Opposition 1975–79; Premier, Treas., Minister for State Devt., Minister for Ethnic Affairs, Govt. of S. Australia 1979–82; Sec.-Gen. Commonwealth Parl. Asscn. 1986–92; Gov. Commonwealth Trust 1990–94, Royal Commonwealth Soc. for the Blind (now Sightsavers) 1990–94, Queen Elizabeth House, Oxford 1987–94, Vision Aid Overseas 1989–92; Chair. S. Australian Film Corpn. 1994–; Freeman City of London 1981; mem. Worshipful Co. of Spectacle Makers 1992. *Publication:* Patient Care Review—Quality Assurance in Health Care 1986. *Leisure interests:* family, music and theatre. *Address:* 5A Glenferrie Avenue, Myrtle Bank SA 5064, Australia.

TONOMURA, Hitoshi; Japanese banker; fmr. Pres. and Chair. Nomura Int., Head of Overseas Operations 1995–. *Address:* Nomura International, 1 St Martins-le-Grand, London E.C.1, England. *Telephone:* 0171-236-8811.

TOOLEY, Sir John, Kt., M.A.; British administrator and arts consultant; b. 1 June 1924, Rochester, Kent; s. of late H. R. Tooley; m. 1st Judith Craig Morris 1951 (dissolved 1965); three d.; m. 2nd Patricia J. N. Bagshawe 1968 (divorced 1990); one s.; m. 3rd Jennifer-Anne Shannon 1995; ed. Repton School and Magdalene Coll., Cambridge; Sec. Guildhall School of Music and Drama 1952–55; Asst. to Gen. Admin., Royal Opera House, Covent Garden 1955–60, Asst. Gen. Admin. 1960–70, Gen. Admin. 1970–80, Gen. Dir. 1980–88; Chair. Almeida Theatre 1990–97, Fabric Advisory Cttee. Salisbury Cathedral 1992–, Nureyev Foundation 1995–97; Chair. Monument Insurance Brokers Ltd. 1997–; Pres. Salisbury Festival 1988–; Consultant Int. Man. Group 1988–97, Ballet Opera House, Toronto 1989–90, Istanbul Int. Festival 1992–, Antelope Films 1993–; Dir. Britten Estate 1989–96, South Bank Bd. 1991–97, Compton Verney Opera Project 1991–97, Welsh Nat. Opera 1992–, David Gyngell Holdings Ltd. 1996–97; Trustee Britten Pears Foundation 1988–, Walton Trust 1988–, Wigmore Hall 1989–, Performing Arts Labs. 1992–, Cardiff Bay Opera House 1995–96; Gov. Royal Ballet 1994–97; Hon. F.R.A.M., Hon. G.S.M.; Hon. mem. Royal Northern Coll. of Music, ISM; Hon. D. Univ. (Univ. of Central England) 1996; Commendatore of Italian Repub. *Leisure interests:* walking, theatre. *Address:* 163A High Street, Aldeburgh, Suffolk, IP15 5AN, England. *Telephone:* (01728) 454864. *Fax:* (01728) 454870.

TOON, Malcolm, M.A.; American diplomatist; b. 4 July 1916, Troy, N.Y.; s. of George Toon and Margaret Broadfoot; m. Elizabeth J. Taylor 1943; one

s. two d.; ed. Tufts Univ., Fletcher School of Law and Diplomacy, and Harvard Univ.; Research Technician, Nat. Resources Planning Bd. 1939–41; Ensign, Lt.-Commdr., U.S. Naval Reserve 1942–46; in U.S. Foreign Service 1946–79; Amb. to Czechoslovakia 1969–71, to Yugoslavia 1971–75, to Israel 1975–76, to U.S.S.R. 1976–79; Dir. McKesson Corpn., San Francisco; mem. Bd. of Trustees Tufts Univ., Bd. of Visitors, Fletcher School of Law and Diplomacy 1992; Hon. LL.D. (Tufts Univ.) 1977, (Middlebury Coll.) 1978, (Drexel Univ.) 1980, (American Coll. of Switzerland) 1985; Superior Honor Award, Dept. of State 1965; Distinguished Honor Award, Dept. of State 1979; Freedom Leadership Award Hillsdale Coll., Mich. 1980, Freedom Award 1981, Wallace Award 1984, Gold Medal, Nat. Inst. of Social Sciences 1987, degree of Prof. Acad. of Natural Sciences of the Russian Fed. 1996. *Leisure interests:* golf, tennis, hunting, fishing. *Address:* 375 Pee Dee Road, Southern Pines, NC 28387, U.S.A. (Home).

TOPCHEYEV, Yuriy Ivanovich, DR. TECH. SC.; Russian cyberneticist; b. 26 Sept. 1920, Yaroslavl; s. of Ivan Yakovlevich Topcheyev and Vera Aleksandrovna Topcheyeva; m. Inna Ivanovna Smirnova 1965; one s.; ed. Moscow Aviation Inst.; mem. CPSU 1948–91; Chief Dept. of Scientific Research Inst. of Automatic Systems 1943–72; mem. staff and Prof., Inst. of Physical Eng., Moscow 1968–89, Chief of Faculty 1972–88; Prof. Int. G. Soros Science Educ. Programme 1996–97, Emer. Prof. 1997–; mem. Comm. of Co-ordination Cttee. on Computers of U.S.S.R. (now Russian) Acad. of Sciences 1978–85, Co-ordination Cttee. on Robotics 1980–87; Chair. Council on Systems of Automated Design, Ministry of Higher Educ. 1977–87; mem. Council Specialized Scientific and Technological Activities of U.S.S.R. (now Russian) Acad. of Sciences 1989–; Order of Labour Banner 1950, State Prize 1972, Korolev Medal 1977, Gagarin Medal 1981. *Publications include:* Encyclopaedia for Automatic Regulation Systems Design 1989; (co-author) Basics of Automatic Regulation 1954, Technical Cybernetics (4 vols.) 1967–89, Philosophy of Nonlinear Control Systems 1990, Nonlinear Systems of Automatic Control (vols. 1–9) 1970–92, People and Robotics (Vol. 1) 1995, (Vol. 2) 1998; about 270 articles. *Leisure interests:* nonlinear systems design, the history of the development of automatic systems and robotics. *Address:* Leningradskoye sch. 31, Apt. 147, 125212 Moscow, Russia. *Telephone:* (095) 156-63-06.

TÖPFER, Klaus, PH.D.; German politician; b. 29 July 1938, Waldenburg, Silesia; m.; three c.; ed. Univs. of Mainz, Frankfurt-am-Main and Munster; family expelled from Silesia, settled in Höxter/Weser 1945; Head, Political Economy Dept., Inst. of Devt. Planning, Munster 1970–71; Head, Planning and Information Section, Saarland State Chancellery, Saarbrucken; lecturer, Coll. of Admin., Speyer 1971–78; Prof. Ordinarius, Hanover Univ., Dir. Inst. of Environmental Research and Regional Planning 1978–79; Hon. Prof. Mainz Univ. 1985–; joined Christian Democratic Union (CDU) 1972, CDU Dist. Chair., Saarbrucken, mem. CDU State Exec., Saar 1977–79; State Sec., Rhineland Palatinate Ministry of Social Affairs, Health and Environment, Mainz 1978–85; Deputy Chair. CDU Fed. Cttee. of Experts on the Environment 1983; Minister of Environment and Health, Rhineland Palatinate 1985–87; CDU Dist. Chair., Rhein-Hunsrück 1987–; Fed. Minister for the Environment, Nature Conservation and Nuclear Safety 1987–94, of Regional Planning, Housing and Urban Devt. 1994–98; Head of UN Environment Secretariat, Nairobi 1998–.

TOPOL, Chaim; Israeli actor, producer and director; b. 9 Sept. 1935, Tel Aviv; s. of Yaakov Topol and Rela Goldman; m. Galia Finkelstein 1956; one s. two d.; joined entertainment unit during army service 1953; f. The Green Onion satirical theatre 1956, Municipal Theatre of Haifa 1959; starred in stage productions of Fiddler on the Roof in London 1967, 1983, 1994, on Broadway NY, 1990 and in Melbourne 1998, Ziegfield 1988, in The Caucasian Chalk Circle, Romanov and Juliet, Othello, View From The Bridge, Chichester Festival Theatre; Actor, Producer, Director for the Genesis Project, filming the Bible, New York, N.Y.; Golden Globe Award, San Francisco Film Festival Winner. *Films include:* Cast A Giant Shadow 1965, Sallah 1966, Before Winter Comes 1969, A Time for Loving, Fiddler on the Roof 1971, The Public Eye, Galileo 1974, Flash Gordon, For Your Eyes Only 1980, The Winds of War 1981, A Dime Novel, Ervinka, Left Luggage 1997; several TV films. *Publication:* Topol by Topol (autobiog.) 1981, To Life! (A Treasury of Jewish Wisdom, Wit and Humour) 1995. *Address:* 22 Vale Court, 28 Maida Vale, London, W9 1RT, England. *Telephone:* 0171-286 5361. *Fax:* 0171-266 2155.

TOPORNIN, Boris Nikolayevich; Russian legal specialist; b. 29 Dec. 1929; m.; two s.; ed. Moscow Inst. of Int. Relations; jr., sr. researcher, Scientific Sec. Inst. of Law U.S.S.R. (now Russian) Acad. of Sciences 1955–62; Deputy Chief Scientific Sec. Presidium of U.S.S.R. Acad. of Sciences 1962–67; head of div., First Deputy Dir. Inst. of Law and State U.S.S.R. Acad. of Sciences 1967–89; Dir. 1989–; corresp. mem. U.S.S.R. (now Russian) Acad. of Sciences 1987, mem. 1991, Sec. Dept. of Phil. and Law; research in constitutional law and state law 1991–; Deputy Pres. Int. Asscn. of Constitutional Law; Mem. Int. Acad. of Law. *Publications include:* Political Foundation of Socialism 1972, New Constitution of U.S.S.R. 1980, Development of Socialist Democracy 1985, Foreign Policy and Science 1990. *Address:* Institute of State and Law, Russian Academy of Sciences, Znamenka str. 10, 119841 Moscow, Russia. *Telephone:* (095) 291 8756, 203 9212.

TOPOROV, Col.-Gen. Vladimir Mikhailovich; Russian army officer; b. 7 Feb. 1946, Baranovichi; ed. Odessa Artillery School, Frunze Mil. Acad., Gen. Staff Acad.; commdr. of platoon, battery 1968–75, Deputy Commdr. of regt., Commdr. 1976–79, Deputy Commdr. of Div., Commdr. 1979–84, First Deputy Commdr., Commdr. of army 1987–89; Head of Staff, First Deputy Commdr. of troops of Far East Mil. Dist. 1989–92; Commdr. of troops of Moscow Mil. Dist. 1991–92; Deputy Minister of Defence 1992–; C.-in-C. of airborne (expeditionary) forces 1995–. *Address:* Ministry of Defence, Znamenka 19, Moscow, Russia. *Telephone:* (095) 296-33-66 (Office).

TOPOROV, Vladimir Nikolayevich; Russian writer, literary historian and linguist; b. 5 July 1928, Moscow; ed. Moscow Univ.; first articles published 1958; Sr. Research Fellow at Inst. of Slavic and Balkan Studies, U.S.S.R. (now Russian) Acad. of Sciences 1954–86, Chief Scientific Researcher 1986–; specialist in Indo-European languages and semiotics; mem. U.S.S.R. (now Russian) Acad. of Sciences 1990–; U.S.S.R. State Prize 1990. *Publications:* Dictionary of Prussian Language (5 vols.) 1975–90, Akhmatova and Blok 1981, Gospodin Prokharchin 1982, Pushkin and Goldsmith 1992, Aeneas—the Man of Fate 1993; articles in Soviet and int. professional journals, some in collaboration with Vjacheslav Ivanov (q.v.), some works published abroad. *Address:* Institute of Slavic and Balkan Studies, Leninski prosp. 32A, 117334 Moscow, Russia. *Telephone:* 938-19-43.

TÖRMÄLÄ, Pertti, DR.PHIL.; Finnish professor of biomaterials technology; b. 26 Nov. 1945, Tampere; s. of Matti Törmälä and Elma Virtanen; m. 1st Kirsti Miettinen 1967 (dissolved); two d.; m. 2nd Mirja Talasosa 1995; Assoc. Prof. of Non-Metallic Materials, Tampere Univ. of Tech. 1975, Prof. of Fibre Raw Materials, Prof. of Plastics Tech. and Head Inst. of Plastics Tech. 1985–; fmr. Research Prof. Acad. of Finland, Acad. Prof. 1995–; Nat. Inventor Prize 1986; Nordic Tech. Prize 1988. *Publications:* eight textbooks, 100 patents, over 700 scientific papers. *Leisure interests:* exercise, music. *Address:* Tampere University of Technology, Institute of Biomaterials, P.O. Box 527, 33101 Tampere, Finland. *Telephone:* (3) 3652111.

TORNATORE, Giuseppe; Italian film director; b. 1956, Bagheria, Palermo, Sicily; debut as dir. at age 16, with short film Il Carretto. *Television films include:* Ritratto di un Rapinatore, Incontro con Francesco Rosi, Scrittori Siciliani e Cinema: Verga, Pirandello, Brancati and Sciascia, and Il Diario di Guttuso; *feature films include:* Il Camorrista 1987, Cinema Paradiso 1988 (Special Jury Prize, Cannes Festival 1989), Stanno Tutti Bene 1991, A Pure Formality 1994, Uomo delle Stelle 1995; *documentaries include:* Ethnic Minorities in Sicily (Best Documentary, Salerno Film Festival 1982).

TÖRNUDD, Klaus, PH.D.; Finnish diplomatist; b. 26 Dec. 1931, Helsinki; s. of Allan Törnudd and Margit Niininen; m. Mirja Siirala 1960; one s. one d.; ed. Univ. of Helsinki, Univ. of Paris and School of Advanced Int. Studies, Johns Hopkins Univ., Washington D.C.; entered Finnish Foreign Service 1958, served at Finnish Mission to UN 1961–64, Cairo Embassy 1964–66, Moscow Embassy 1971–73, CSCE 1973–74; Deputy Dir. of Political Affairs in the Ministry for Foreign Affairs 1974–77, Dir. 1977–81, Under-Sec. of State for Political Affairs 1983–88; Perm. Rep. to the UN 1988–91; Fellow Harvard Univ., U.S.A. 1991–92; Sr. Adviser, Ministry for Foreign Affairs 1992–; Amb. to France and to UNESCO 1993–96; Prof. of Int. Politics, Univ. of Tampere, Finland 1967–71; Ed. Co-operation and Conflict (Nordic Journal of Int. Politics) 1968–70, mem. Editorial Bd. 1976–79; mem. Editorial Bd. of Ulkopolitiikka-Utrikespolitik 1983–87; Chair. of Bd. Tampere Peace Research Inst. 1978–82; Chair. UN Study Group on Nuclear-Weapon-Free-Zones 1983–85; mem. Bd. of Trustees UNITAR 1984–88; mem. of Bd. of Govs. IAEA 1985–87; mem. UN Sec.-Gen.'s Advisory Bd. on Disarmament Matters 1991–. *Publications:* several books on Finnish politics and int. affairs. *Address:* c/o Embassy of Finland, 2 rue Fabert, 75007 Paris, France.

ToROBERT, Sir Henry Thomas, K.B.E., B.ECON.; Papua New Guinea banker; b. 1942, Kokopo; ed. Univ. of Sydney; Asst. Research Officer, Reserve Bank of Australia, Port Moresby 1965, Deputy Man. 1971, Man. 1972; Gov. and Chair. of Bd. Bank of Papua New Guinea 1973–93; Chair. Papua New Guinea Inst. of Applied Social and Econ. Research 1975–82; Chair. Man. Bd. Bankers' Coll. 1973–; partner Deloitte Touche Tohmatsu 1993–; Chair. Credit Corpn. (PNG) Ltd. 1993–, Govt. Super Task Force on Project Implementation 1994–; Pres. Amateur Sports Fed. and PNG Olympic and Commonwealth Games Cttee. 1980–. *Address:* P.O. Box 898, Port Moresby, Papua New Guinea.

TÖRÖK, László, PH.D.; Hungarian archaeologist; b. 13 May, 1941, Budapest; s. of László Török and Mária Giesz; m. Erzsébet Sződy 1984; ed. Budapest Univ. of Tech. Sciences, Eötvös Loránd Univ.; research fellow Archaeological Inst. Hungarian Acad. of Sciences 1964, sr. research fellow 1985, adviser 1991; lecturer, Eötvös Loránd Univ. of Arts and Sciences, Dept. of Egyptology 1972, Hon. Prof. 1992–; Visiting Prof. Dept. of Classics, Univ. of Bergen, Norway 1980, 1989–92, 1994–96; Overseas Visiting Scholar, St. John's Coll. Cambridge 1998; Vice-Pres. of the Int. Soc. for Nubian Studies 1990; Gen. Ed. of Antaeus (periodical) 1984; mem. Norwegian Acad. of Science 1994; Albert Reckitt Archaeological Lecture, British Acad. 1995; research into ancient history and archaeology of Middle Nile Region, and Hellenistic and late antique art of Egypt. *Publications:* Economic Offices and Officials in Meroitic Nubia 1978, Der meroitische Staat 1986, The Royal Crowns of Kush 1987, Late Antique Nubia 1988, Coptic Antiquities I–II 1993, Fontes Historiae Nubiorum I 1994, II 1996, III 1998 (with co-authors), Hellenistic and Roman Terracottas from Egypt 1995, The Birth of an Ancient African State 1995, Meroe City: An Ancient African Capital 1997, The Kingdom of Kush: Handbook of the Napatàn-Meroitic Civilization 1997, The

Hunting Centaur 1998; over 100 articles. *Leisure interest:* reading (belles-lettres). *Address:* MTA Régészeti Intézete, 1014 Budapest, Úri utca 49, Hungary. *Telephone:* (1) 175-9011.

TORP, Niels A., DIP.ARCH.; Norwegian architect; b. 8 March 1940, Oslo; s. of Ernst Torp and Nini Torp (née Butenschøn); m. Bente Poulsson; one s. three d.; ed. Norges Tekniske Høgskole, Trondheim, The Norwegian Inst. Rome; joined Torp & Torp Arkitekter MNAL 1965, partner 1970, Man. 1974, Man. Niels Torp Arkitekter MNAL 1984; visiting lecturer at architectural schools in Norway and other European countries. *Major Works:* Giskehagen residential homes 1986, Scandinavian Airlines System (SAS) HQ, Stockholm 1987, Aker Brygge (dockland devt. Oslo) 1988, HQ Den Norske Bank 1988, Hamar Olympiahall 1991, Alna Shopping Centre, Oslo 1996, Railway station/Bus terminal, Gothenburg 1996, Christiania Qvartalet 1996, B.A. HQ, London 1997, Colosseum Park, Oslo 1997, Oslo Airport Gardermoen (with Aviaplan) 1998, Airport control tower and airport hotel, Oslo 1998, development plans for towns of Larvik, Sandefjord and Drammen; awards include: A. C. Houens Legacy, Sundts Prize for Architectural Merits, Awards from the Stone Asscn., Fine Art Award (Oslo City Council), Carl M. Egers Legacy, Europa Nostra Awarda, Prize for Built Environment (Norwegian Dept. of Environment), Kasper Salin Prize (Sweden), European Award for Steel Structures, Swedish Stone Asscn. Award, Concrete Award (Norway), British Construction Industry Award 1998, Brunel Award 1998. *Leisure interests:* music, playing piano, sailing. *Address:* Industrigaten 59, P.O. Box 5387, 0304 Oslo, Norway (Office). *Telephone:* 23 36 68 00 (Office). *Fax:* 23 36 68 01.

TORRANCE, Sam, M.B.E.; British golfer; b. 24 Aug. 1953; s. of Bob Torrance and June Torrance; m. Suzanne Torrance; one s. two d.; professional golfer 1970–; has played in eight Ryder Cups and represented Scotland on numerous occasions; winner Scottish PGA Championship 1978, 1980, 1985, 1991, 1993; mem. Dunhill Cup team (eight times), World Cup team (11 times), Hennessy Cognac Cup team (five times), Double Diamond team (three times); Capt. winning European team in Asahi Glass Four Tours Championship, Adelaide 1991; winner of 28 tournaments worldwide since 1972 including Italian Open 1987, Germany Masters 1990, Jersey Open 1991, Kronenbourg Open 1993, Catalan Open 1993, Honda Open 1993, Hamburg Open 1993, British Masters. *Leisure interests:* snooker, tennis. *Address:* c/o Katrina Johnston, Carnegie Sports International, The Glassmill, 1 Battersea Bridge Road, London, SW11 3BZ, England. *Telephone:* 0171-924 4882. *Fax:* 0171-924 4883.

TORRANCE, Very Rev. Prof. Thomas Forsyth, M.B.E., M.A., DR.THEOL., D.D., D.LITT., D.SC., F.B.A., F.R.S.E.; British minister of religion and university professor; b. 30 Aug. 1913, Chengtu, China; s. of Rev. Thomas and Annie Elizabeth (Sharp) Torrance; m. Margaret Edith Spear 1946; two s. one d.; ed. Bellshill Acad., Univs. of Edinburgh, Basel and Oxford; war service with Church of Scotland Huts and Canteens, Middle East and Italy 1943–45; Prof. of Systematic Theol., Auburn Theol. Seminary, U.S.A. 1938–39; Minister, Alyth Barony Parish, Church of Scotland 1940–47, Beechgrove Parish Aberdeen 1947–50; Prof. of Church History, Univ. of Edinburgh 1950–52, of Christian Dogmatics, also Head of Dept. 1952–79; Cross of St. Mark, Cross of Aksum, Protopresbyter of Greek Orthodox Church; Collins Prize, Templeton Prize; Hon. D.D. (Montreal, St. Andrews, Edin.); Hon. D.Theol. (Geneva, Faculté Libre Paris); Hon. Dr.Teol. (Oslo); Hon. D.Sc. (Heriot Watt Univ.) 1983; Hon. D.Theol. (Debrecen). *Publications:* The Doctrine of Grace in the Apostolic Fathers 1948, Calvin's Doctrine of Man 1949, Royal Priesthood 1955, Kingdom and Church 1956, Conflict and Agreement in the Church (two vols.) 1959, 1960, Karl Barth: Introduction to his Early Theology 1962, Theology in Reconstruction 1965, Theological Science 1969, Space, Time and Incarnation 1969, God and Rationality 1971, Theology in Reconciliation 1975, Space, Time and Resurrection 1976, The Ground and Grammar of Theology 1980, The Incarnation (ed.) 1980, Belief in Science and in Christian Life (ed.) 1980, Christian Theology and Scientific Culture 1980, Divine and Contingent Order 1981, Reality and Evangelical Theology 1981, Juridical Law and Physical Law 1982, Transformation and Convergence in the Frame of Knowledge 1984, James Clerk Maxwell. A Dynamical Theory of the Electromagnetic Field (ed.) 1982, Reality and Scientific Theology 1985, The Mediation of Christ 1983, The Christian Frame of Mind 1985, The Trinitarian Faith 1988, The Hermeneutics of John Calvin 1988, Karl Barth, Biblical and Evangelical Theologian 1990, Trinitarian Perspectives 1994, Preaching Christ Today, The Gospel and Scientific Thinking 1994, Divine Meaning, Studies in Patristic Hermeneutics 1995, The Christian Doctrine of God, One Being, Three Persons 1996, Scottish Theology from John Knox to John McLeod Campbell 1996. *Leisure interests:* walking, travel. *Address:* 37 Braid Farm Road, Edinburgh, EH10 6LE, and Sea Spray, Canty Bay, North Berwick, East Lothian, Scotland (Homes). *Telephone:* (0131) 447 3224 (Home); (01620) 2508 (Home). *Fax:* (0131) 447 3224; (01620) 2508.

TORRELIO VILLA, Gen. Celso; Bolivian politician and army officer; b. 3 June 1933, Sucre; m. Teresa Toledo; ed. School of Arms Application, School of Motors, Panama, School of Command; Head, 6th EMGE Dept.; Commandant, Mil. Coll.; Chief Div. Commdr., 5th Army Div.; Head, 4th Logistical Dept., EMGE; Commdt., Mil. and Army Coll.; Minister of the Interior Feb.–June 1981; C.-in-C. of Army 1981–82; mem. ruling mil. junta June–Sept. 1981; Pres. of Bolivia 1981–82; Guerrilleros Lanza; Constancia Militar (second class). *Address:* c/o Oficina del Presidente, La Paz, Bolivia.

TORRES, Angel, M.A.; Spanish economist and international public servant; ed. Universidad Autónoma de Barcelona, Grad. Inst. of Int. Studies, Geneva, Switzerland; Head Balance of Payments Div., Ministry of Econ. and Finance 1983–85, Head Research Dept. 1985–89; Deputy Gen. Man. Instituto de Crédito Oficial 1989–90; mem. IMF Exec. Bd. 1990–91, of IBRD 1992–93.

TORRES Y TORRES LARA, Carlos; Peruvian politician; fmr. Minister of Labour; Prime Minister and Minister of Foreign Affairs 1991–92. *Address:* c/o Office of the Prime Minister, Ucayali 363, Lima, Peru.

TORRICELLI, Robert G., J.D., M.P.A.; American politician; b 26 Aug. 1951, Paterson, N.J.; ed. Rutgers and Harvard Univs.; called to bar, N.J. 1978; Deputy legis. counsel, Office of Gov. of N.J. 1975–77; counsel to Vice-Pres. Mondale, Washington, D.C. 1978–81; pvt. practice, Washington, D.C. 1981–82; mem. 98th-104th Congresses 1983–97; Senator from New Jersey Jan. 1996–; Democrat. *Address:* United States Senate, 113 Dirksen Senate Office Building, Washington, DC 20510, U.S.A.

TORROJA MENENDEZ, José María, DR.SC.; Spanish professor of astronomy and geodesy; b. 29 Aug. 1916, Madrid; s. of José María Torroja Menendez and Isabel Menendez; m. Aurora Cifuentes 1962; two s.; ed. Univ. of Madrid; Geographical Engineer, Instituto Geográfico, Madrid 1942–52; Astronomer, Observatory of Madrid 1952–67; Prof. of Astronomy and Geodesy, Univ. of Madrid 1945–83; Vice-Rector, Univ. of Madrid 1971–76; Sec.-Gen. Real Academia de Ciencias Exactas, Físicas y Naturales 1977–92, Pres. Real Sociadad Geográfica. *Publications:* several publications on astronomy and geodesy. *Address:* Avda Filipinas 50, 28003 Madrid, Spain. *Telephone:* 15544721.

TORSTENDAHL, Rolf, PH.D.; Swedish professor of history; b. 9 Jan. 1936, Jönköping; s. of Torsten Torstendahl and Ragnhild (née Abrahamsson) Torstendahl; m. 1st Anna-Maria Ljung 1960 (died 1987); two s.; m. 2nd Tamara A. Salycheva 1996; ed. Uppsala Univ.; lecturer, Dept. of History, Uppsala Univ. 1964–67, Assoc. Prof. 1968–78, Sven Warburg Prof. of History 1978–80, Prof. 1981–; Dir. Swedish Collegium for Advanced Study in the Social Sciences 1985–90, Dean of Faculty 1994–; mem. Royal Swedish Acad. of Letters, History and Antiquities 1982, Norwegian Acad. of Science and Letters 1989, Acad. Europaea 1989, Russia Acad. of Sciences, Urals Div. 1995; Björnstiernas pris (Royal Swedish Acad. of Letters, History and Antiquities) 1976. *Publications include:* Teknologins nytta 1975, Dispersion of Engineers in a Transitional Society 1975, Bureaucratization in Northwestern Europe 1880–1985 1991, State Theory and State History (Ed.) 1992, History-making (Ed.) 1996. *Address:* Uppsala University, St Larsgatan 2, 75310 Uppsala (Office); St Olofsgatan 4, 75312 Uppsala, Sweden (Home). *Telephone:* (018) 471 1534 (Office); (018) 125298 (Home).

TORTELIER, Yan Pascal; French conductor and violinist; b. 19 April 1947, Paris; s. of the late Paul Tortelier and of Maud Tortelier; m. Sylvie Brunet-Moret 1970; two s.; ed. Paris Conservatoire and Berks. Music Centre; début as concert violinist, Royal Albert Hall 1962; has since toured extensively all over the world; Konzertmeister, Assoc. Conductor of Orchestre du Capitole de Toulouse 1974–82; Prin. Conductor and Artistic Dir., Ulster Orchestra 1989–92; Prin. Conductor BBC Philharmonic 1992–; Hon. D.Litt. (Ulster) 1992. *Publication:* première orchestration of Ravel's Piano Trio (world première concert 1992). *Leisure interests:* skiing, windsurfing, scuba diving, nature. *Address:* c/o IMG Artists Europe, Media House, 3 Burlington Lane, Chiswick, London, W4 2TH, England.

TORUMTAY, Gen. Necip; Turkish army officer; b. 1926, Vakfikebir, Trabzon; s. of Nihat Torumtay and Edibe Torumtay; m. Mrs. Türkân 1949; one s. one d.; ed. Army War Coll., Artillery School, War Acads. Unit Commdr. at platoon, battery and bn. levels; Deputy Attaché Turkish Embassy, Tokyo; Turkish Mil. Rep. Planning Officer NATO Mil. Cttee., Washington; Regt. Commdr. and Br. Chief Turkish Gen. Staff H.Q.; promoted Brig.-Gen. 1970; Deputy Div. Commdr., Brigade Commdr., Br. Chief at SHAPE and T.G.S. H.Q., Army Corps. C.-in-C. Operations, then Plan and Policy; promoted to Gen. 1982; Deputy Sec.-Gen. to the Presidency, Sec.-Gen. to the Presidency and Nat. Security Council; Deputy Chief of T.G.S. and First Army Commdr.; Commdr. Turkish Land Forces; Chief of Gen. Staff 1987–90. *Leisure interest:* aviation. *Address:* c/o Ministry of Defence, Savunma Bakantig 1, Ankara, Turkey. *Telephone:* 118 77 94.

TORVILL, Jayne, M.B.E.; British ice skater; b. 7 Oct. 1957; d. of George Torvill and Betty (née Smart) Torvill; m. Philip Christensen 1990; insurance clerk 1974–80; British Pair Skating Champion (with Michael Hutchinson) 1971; British Ice Dance Champion (with Christopher Dean, q.v.) 1978–83, 1993; European Ice Dance Champion (with Christopher Dean) 1981–82, 1984, 1994; World Ice Dance Champion (with Christopher Dean) 1981–84; World Professional Ice Dance Champion (with Christopher Dean) 1984, 1985, 1990, 1995; Olympic Ice Dance Champion (with Christopher Dean) 1984; Hon. M.A. (Nottingham Trent) 1994; BBC Sportsview Personality of the Year (with Christopher Dean) 1983–84. *Publications:* (with Christopher Dean) Torvill and Dean: An Autobiography 1984, Torvill and Dean: Face the Music and Dance 1995, Facing the Music (with Christopher Dean) 1995. *Leisure interests:* theatre, ballet, dogs. *Address:* c/o Mrs. Sue Young, P.O. Box 32, Heathfield, East Sussex, TN21 0BW, England. *Telephone:* (01435) 867825.

TOSAR, Héctor A.; Uruguayan composer and pianist; b. 1923; ed. Montevideo, and Conservatoire Nationale de Musique, Paris, and Ecole Normale de Musique, Paris (under D. Milhaud, J. Rivier and A. Honegger); Prof. of History of Music and Musical Analysis, Conservatorio de Música, Montevideo

1951–60; Prof. of Harmony, Composition and Analysis, and Head of Theory Dept., Conservatorio de Música de Puerto Rico 1961; Guggenheim Fellowships, U.S.A. 1946–47, 1960–61. *Principal works:* Symphony for Strings 1959, Te Deum for bass, chorus and orchestra 1959, Sinfonia Concertante for piano and orchestra 1961.

TOSCAN du PLANTIER, Daniel; French business executive; b. 7 April 1941, Chambéry, Savoie; s. of Jacques Toscan du Plantier and Françoise de Ganay; m. 1st Marie-Christine Barrault (divorced); one s. one d.; m. 2nd Francesca Comencini (divorced); one s.; m. 3rd Sophie Bouniol 1991 (died 1996); ed. Lycée de Chambéry, Lycées Claude-Bernard and Janson-de-Sailly, Faculté de droit and Faculté des lettres, Paris, Institut d'Etudes Politiques de Paris; Advertising Man., France-Soir 1969; Gen. Man. Régie-Presse 1974; Deputy Gen. Man. Gaumont 1975, Man. Dir. 1985; Chair. Editions Ramsay 1981; Chairman and Man. Dir. Editions Costallat-Erato 1981, Erato Disques et Films 1986; mem. Bd. Opéra de Paris 1985–91, 1991; Founder-mem. Académie des Arts de la Télévision 1985; Programme Adviser on films, broadcaster, Canal + 1985; Vice-Pres. Union des Producteurs de Films 1987; Pres. Unifrance Film Int. 1988, Groupement d'Intérêt Economique France Cinéma Diffusion 1990; Vice-Pres. Supervisory Cttee. of SEPT 1991–; Pres. Acad. of Arts and Cinematic Technique 1992–, Acad. of Césars for cinema 1992, Cinémathèque de Toulouse 1996–; produced Don Giovanni, Opéra de Monte-Carlo 1983; Officier, Ordre Nat. du Mérite, Commdr. des Arts et Lettres 1985, Chevalier, Légion d'honneur 1989. *Publications:* Donnez-nous notre quotidien 1974, Les enfants d'Al Capone et de Rossellini 1981, Bouleversifiant 1992, L'Emotion Culturelle 1995. *Address:* Euripide Productions, 10 rue Affre, 75018 Paris, France. *Telephone:* 49.25.89.00. *Fax:* 49.25.89.09.

TOŠOVSKÝ, Josef, B.COM.; Czech banker; b. 28 Sept. 1950, Náchod; m. Bohunka Světlíková; two d.; ed. School of Econs. Prague; banker with Czechoslovak State Bank 1973–, Deputy Dir. 1978–, consultant to Bank Chair. 1982; Chief Economist, Živnobanka, London 1984–85, Deputy Dir. June–Dec. 1989; Consultant to Bank Chair., Prague 1986–89; Chair. Czechoslovak State Bank 1989–92, Gov. 1992, for Czech Nat. Bank 1993–97, 1998–; Gov. IMF 1990–97; Prime Minister of Czech Repub. 1997–98; named Cen. Bank Gov. of 1993 by U.K. magazine Euromoney, European Man. of the Year 1994, Karel Engliš Prize 1994, named Banker of the Year 1995. *Publications:* numerous articles in professional press. *Leisure interests:* sports. *Address:* Czech National Bank, Na Příkopě 28, 110 00 Prague 1, Czech Republic. *Telephone:* (2) 441 11 11. *Fax:* (2) 441 85 22, 24 21 78 65.

TÓTH, Július, C.SC.; Slovak politician and engineer; b. 6 May 1935, Zvolen; m. Mária Tóthová; held numerous positions in various iron-processing plants, participated in the privatization of these plants 1990; Minister of Finance 1992–94; Chair. Econ. Council of Slovak Repub. 1992–98, Council for Regional Devt. July 1992–; Vice-Premier, Govt. of Slovakia –March 1994; Alt. Gov. IMF July 1992–; mem. Movt. for Democratic Slovakia; Chair. Bd. of Supervisors, E. Slovak Iron Works, Košice 1994–; Deputy Chair. Bd. of Dirs. Industrial Bank, Košice 1994–. *Address:* Movement for Democratic Slovakia, Tomášikova 32/a, Bratislava, Slovakia. *Telephone:* (7) 23 01 44, 23 47 42.

TO'THOVÁ, Katarína, J.U.DR., DR.SC.; Slovak politician and lawyer; b. 6 Feb. 1940, Bratislava; legal counsellor; Minister of Justice 1992–94; Chair. Legis. Council of Slovak Repub. 1992–98; Vice-Premier, Govt. of Slovakia 1994–98; Chair. Govt. Council for Mass Media 1995–96; mem. Movt. for Democratic Slovakia. *Address:* Movement for Democratic Slovakia, Tomášikova 32/a, Bratislava, Slovak Republic. *Telephone:* (7) 23 01 44, 23 47 42.

TOTSKY, Col.-Gen. Konstantin Vasilyevich; Russian army officer; b. 23 Feb. 1950, Kagan, Uzbekistan; m.; two d.; ed. Higher Frontier Mil. School, Frunze Mil. Acad., Gen. Staff Mil. Acad.; army service in Pacific, Cen. Asian, Transcaucasian, N.W. Border Dist. 1977–89; participated in mil. operations in Afghanistan; Head, Acad. of Fed. Border Service of Russian Fed. 1996–; Dir. Fed. Border Service Sept. 1998–; Chair. Council of Border Forces of C.I.S. Countries 1998–. *Address:* Federal Border Service, Myasnitskaya str. 1, 101000 Moscow, Russia. *Telephone:* (095) 224 1973 (Office).

TÖTTERMAN, Richard Evert Björnson, JUR.LIC., D.PHIL.; Finnish diplomatist; b. 10 Oct 1926, Helsinki; s. of B. Björn Tötterman and Katharine Clare Wimpenny; m. Camilla S. Veronica Huber 1953; one s. one d.; ed. Univ. of Helsinki and Brasenose Coll., Oxford; entered Ministry for Foreign Affairs 1952; diplomatic posts in Stockholm 1954–56, Moscow 1956–58, at Ministry of Foreign Affairs 1958–62, Berne 1962–63, Paris 1963–66; Deputy Dir. Ministry of Foreign Affairs 1966; Sec.-Gen. Office of Pres. of Finland 1966–70; Sec. of State Ministry of Foreign Affairs 1970–75; Amb. to U.K. 1975–83, to Switzerland 1983–90, concurrently to the Holy See 1988–90; Chair. Multilateral Consultations preparing Conf. on Security and Co-operation in Europe 1972–73; Hon. Fellow, Brasenose Coll. 1982; Hon. G.C.V.O., Hon. O.B.E; Kt. Commdr. Order of the White Rose (Finland); Grand Cross, Order of Dannebrog (Denmark), Order of Merit (Austria), Order of Orange-Nassau (Netherlands), Order of the Pole Star (Sweden), Order of the Falcon (Iceland); Grand Officier Ordre de la Couronne (Belgium), Order of St. Olav (Norway), Order of Merit (Poland), Order of Lion (Senegal), Order of the Banner (Hungary), Commandeur, Ordre Nat. du Mérite (France). *Address:* Parkgatan 9A, 00140 Helsinki, Finland. *Telephone:* 62-77-21.

TOTTIE, Thomas, FIL.LIC.; Swedish librarian; b. 3 July 1930, Waxholm; s. of the late John Tottie and Gerda (née Willers) Tottie; m. 1st; two d.; m. 2nd Marianne Sandels 1972; two s.; ed. Stockholm Univ.; Asst. Librarian, Royal Library, Stockholm 1961; Sec. Swedish Council of Research Libraries 1966–73; Deputy Dir. Stockholm Univ. Library 1975–76; Dir. Library of Royal Carolingian Medico-Chirurgical Inst., Stockholm 1977; Chief Librarian, Uppsala Univ. 1978–96; mem. and official of various professional orgs.; Dr. h.c. (Uppsala) 1994. *Publications:* 2 books and numerous articles and reports on librarianship. *Leisure interests:* biography, sailing. *Address:* Kyrkogardsgatan 5A, 753 10 Uppsala, Sweden. *Telephone:* 018-51 46 83 (Office); 018-12 32 00 (Home).

TOUBERT, Pierre Marcel Paul, PH.D.; French professor of medieval history; b. 29 Nov. 1932, Algiers; s. of André Toubert and Paola Garcia y Planes; m. Hélène Poggioli 1954; one s.; ed. Ecole Normale Supérieure, Paris, Ecole des Hautes-Etudes, Paris, Univ. of Paris and Ecole Française d'Archéologie, Rome; mem. Ecole Française, Rome 1958–61; Dir. of Studies, Ecole des Hautes-Etudes 1964–92; Prof. Dept. of History, Univ. of Paris (Sorbonne) 1969–92; mem. Nat. Council for Scientific Research, CNRS 1992–, Prof. Coll. de France 1992–; mem. Acad. Française, Acad. Europaea 1989–, Nat. Cttee. of Evaluation of Univs. 1996–; Chevalier, Légion d'honneur, Ordre Nat. du Mérite, Ordre des Arts et des Lettres, Commdr. des Palmes académiques. *Publications include:* Les structures du Latium médiéval, 2 vols. 1973, Etudes sur l'Italie médiévale 1976, Histoire du haut Moyen Age et de l'Italie médiévale 1987, Dalla terra aì castelli nell'Italia medioevale 1994; many other books and publs. on medieval Italy, econ. and social history of the Middle Ages. *Address:* Collège de France, 11 place Marcelin Berthelot, 75231 Paris Cedex 05; 34 rue Guynemer, 75006 Paris, France. *Telephone:* (1) 44.27.10.32. *Fax:* (1) 44.27.11.09.

TOUBON, Jacques, L. EN D.; French politician; b. 29 June 1941, Nice; s. of Pierre-Constant and Yolande (Molinas) Toubon; m. 1st Béatrice Bernascon; m. 2nd Lise Weiler 1982; ed. Lycée Masséna, Nice, Lycée Jean Perrin, Lyon, Faculté de Droit, Lyon, Inst. d'Etudes Politiques, Lyon, and Ecole Nat. d'Admin.; civil servant 1965–76, Chef de Cabinet, to Minister of Agric. 1972–74, to Minister of Interior 1974, Tech. Adviser, Office of Prime Minister 1974–76; Minister of Culture and the French Language 1993–95, of Justice May 1995–; Dir. Fondation Claude Pompidou 1970–77; Asst. Sec.-Gen. Rassemblement pour la République (RPR) 1977–81, Sec.-Gen. 1984–88; Deputy to Nat. Ass. 1981–93; Mayor 13th Arrondissement, Paris 1983–, Deputy Mayor of Paris 1983–; Pres. Club 89 1993–; Minister of Justice 1995–97; adviser to Pres. Jacques Chirac 1997–98; Chevalier du Mérite Agricole. *Publication:* Pour en finir avec la peur 1984. *Address:* Présidence de la République, 55–57 rue du Faubourg-Saint-Honoré, 75008 Paris (Office); 86 rue Notre-Dame des Champs, 75006 Paris, France (Home).

TOULOUSE, Gérard, D.SC.; French research scientist; b. 4 Sept. 1939, Vattetot-sur-mer; s. of Robert Toulouse and Thérèse Toulouse (née Tiret); m. Nicole Schnitzer 1970; one s. one d.; ed. Ecole Normale Supérieure, Ulm, Orsay; research scientist CNRS 1965–, Laboratoire de Physique de l'Ecole Normale Supérieure 1976–; post-doctoral Fellow UCSD, La Jolla, CA 1969–71; Vice-Pres. Cttee. of Exact and Natural Sciences (French nat. comm. for UNESCO) 1997; Visitor Ecole Supérieure de Physique et Chimie, Paris 1985–86; Fellow Inst. for Advanced Studies, Jerusalem 1987–88; Corresp. Acad. of Sciences, Paris 1990; Foreign hon. mem. American Acad. of Arts and Sciences 1996; Langevin Prize 1976, Triossi Prize 1979, Holweck Prize 1983, CEA Prize 1989; Chevalier Ordre Nat. du Mérite. *Publications:* Introduction au groupe de renormalisation 1975, Biology and Computation: a Physicist's Choice 1994, Regards sur l'éthique des sciences 1998. *Address:* Laboratoire de physique de l'ENS, 24 rue Lhomond, 75231 Paris, France. *Telephone:* (1) 44.32.34.87. *Fax:* (1) 43 36 76 66.

TOURAINE, Alain Louis Jules François, D. ÈS L.; French sociologist; b. 3 Aug. 1925, Hermanville; s. of Albert Touraine and Odette Cleret; m. Adriana Arenas 1957 (deceased); one s. one d.; ed. Lycées Montaigne and Louis-le-Grand, Paris and Ecole Normale Supérieure; Dir. of Studies, Ecole Pratique des Hautes Etudes (now Ecole des Hautes Etudes en Sciences Sociales) 1960–; Prof. Faculté des Lettres de Paris-Nanterre 1966–69; f. Lab. de Sociologie Industrielle (now Centre d'Etude des Mouvements Sociaux) 1958–80; f. and Dir. Centre d'Analyse et d'Intervention Sociologiques 1980; mem. Haut Conseil à l'Intégration 1994–96; mem. Acad. Europea, American Acad. of Arts and Sciences; Officier, Légion d'honneur, Officier des Arts et Lettres. *Publications:* Sociologie de l'Action 1965, La Société post-industrielle 1969, Production de la société 1973, Pour la sociologie 1974, La voix et le regard 1978, Mort d'une gauche 1979, L'après-socialisme 1980, Solidarité 1982, Le mouvement ouvrier (with Dubet and Wieviorka) 1984, Le retour de l'acteur 1984, La parole et le sang? Politique et société en Amérique Latine 1988, Critique de la modernité 1992, Qu'est-ce que la démocratie 1994, Lettre à Lionel, Michel, Jacques, Martine, Bernard, Dominique . . . et vous 1995, le Grand refus, réflexion sur la grève de décembre 1995 1996 (jtly.), Pourrons-nous vivre ensemble? 1997. *Leisure interest:* Latin America. *Address:* CADIS, 54, blvd Raspail, 75006 Paris (Office); 32, blvd de Vaugirard, 75015 Paris, France (Home). *Telephone:* 45 44 39 79 (Office); 43 20 61 06 (Home).

TOURE, Lieut.-Col. Amadou Toumani; Malian army officer; paratroop commdr.; leader Nat. Reconciliation Council 1991–92. *Address:* National Reconciliation Council, Bamako, Mali.

TOURE, Sidia; Guinean politician; fmr. Dir. Office of the Prime Minister of Côte d'Ivoire; Prime Minister of Guinea 1996–, Minister of Economy,

Finance and Planning 1996–97. *Address:* Office of the Prime Minister, Conakry, Guinea.

TOURÉ, Younoussi; Malian politician; b. 27 Dec. 1941, Niodougou, Timbuktu Region; s. of Singoro Touré and Santadji Tamoura; m. Alimata Traore 1970; two s. three d.; studied in Dakar, Senegal and Abidjan, Côte d'Ivoire; joined Cen. Bank of Mali 1969, Dir. Gen. 1983; rep. at Banque Centrale des états de l'Afrique de l'ouest (BCEAO); Prime Minister 1992–93; Special Adviser to Gov. of BCEAO 1993–94; Commissaire, Union Economique et Monétaire Ouest Africaine (UEMOA) 1994–. *Leisure interests:* reading, sport. *Address:* c/o Union Economique et Monétaire Ouest Africaine (UEMOA), 01 BP 543, Ouagadougou 01, Burkina Fasso. *Telephone:* (226) 306015.

TOURET, Jacques Léon Robert; French geologist; b. 2 Jan. 1936, Fumay; s. of late Martial Touret and Suzanne Gouilly; m. 1st Christiane Poinsignon 1960 (divorced 1972); one s. two d.; m. 2nd Lydie Mohammed 1974; one d.; ed. Lycée Chanzy, Charleville, Ecole Nat. Supérieure de Géologie Appliquée, Nancy and Univ. of Nancy; Asst., Ecole Nat. Supérieure de Géologie, Nancy 1958–64, Asst. lecturer in Geology 1964–69; Lecturer in Geology, Univ. of Nancy 1969–74; Prof. Univ. of Paris 7 1974–80; Prof. Earth Science Inst., Free Univ., Amsterdam, Netherlands 1980–; Invited Prof., Ecole Normale Supérieure, Paris 1994–97; chargé de mission, C.N.R.S., Paris 1978–80; mem. Royal Netherlands Acad. of Sciences, Norwegian Acad. of Science and Letters, Academia Europaea; Prix Carrière, Acad. des Sciences, Paris 1970; Dumont Medal (Belgian Geological Soc.) 1992, Van Waterschoot van der Gracht Medal (Netherlands) 1996; Chevalier, Ordre nat. du mérite. *Publications include:* Le Socle précambrien de Norvège méridionale 1969, The deep Proterozoic Crust in the North Atlantic province (with A. C. Tobi) 1985, Collisional Ologens: Zones of Active Transfer between Crust and Mantle (with H. Austrheim) 1997. *Leisure interests:* classical music, French literature. *Address:* Department of Petrology, Vrije Universiteit, 1081 HV Amsterdam, De Boelelaan 1085 (Office); Regentesselaan 1, 2015 BW Haarlem, Netherlands (Home). *Telephone:* (020) 4447270 (Office); (023) 5314549 (Home). *Fax:* (020) 646-2457.

TOURNIER, Michel, L. ÈS L., L. EN D., D.PHIL.; French author; b. 19 Dec. 1924, Paris; s. of Alphonse Tournier and Marie-Madeleine (née Fournier) Tournier; ed. Saint-Germain-en-Laye, and Univs. of Paris (Sorbonne) and Tübingen; radio and television production 1949–54; press attaché, Europe No. 1 1955–58; head of literary services, Editions Plon 1958–68; contrib. to le Monde, Figaro; mem. Acad. Goncourt 1972–; Officier, Légion d'honneur; Commdr., Ordre nat. du Mérite; Grand Prix du Roman, Acad. Française 1967, Prix Goncourt 1970. *Publications:* Vendredi ou les limbes du Pacifique 1967, Le Roi des Aulnes 1970, Les météores 1975, Le vent paraclet 1977, Le coq de bruyère 1978, Des clefs et des serrures 1979, Gaspard, Melchior et Balthazar 1980, Le vol du Vampire 1981, Gilles et Jeanne 1983, La Goutte d'Or 1986, Le Tabor et le Sinaï 1989, Le Médianoche amoureux 1989, le Crépuscule des masques 1992, le Miroir des Idées 1994, Le Pied de la lettre 1994, La Couleuvrine 1994, Les Pieds de la lettre 1996. *Leisure interest:* photography. *Address:* Le presbytère, Choisel, 78460 Chevreuse, France. *Telephone:* (1) 30.52.05.29.

TOUSIGNANT, Claude, O.C.; Canadian artist; b. 23 Dec. 1932, Montreal; s. of Alberic Tousignant and Gilberte Hardy-Lacasse; m. Judith Terry 1968; two d.; ed. School of Art and Design, The Montreal Museum of Fine Arts; many solo and group nat. and int. exhbns. 1956–; works included in major N. American public and pvt. collections; 1st Prize, Salon de la jeune peinture 1962, 1st Prize, Painting, Art Gallery of Ont. 1967, Canadian Inst. in Rome Award 1973, Prix Paul-Emile Borduas 1989. *Address:* 181 Bourget Street, Montreal, Quebec, H4C 2M1 (Studio); 460 Avenue Bloomfield, Outremont, Quebec, H2V 3R8, Canada (Home). *Telephone:* (514) 934-3012 (Studio); (514) 948-1463 (Home).

TOWNE, Robert; American scriptwriter; b. 1936; m. Luisa Towne; two c.; screenplays include: The Tomb of Ligeia 1964, Villa Rides 1967, The Last Detail 1967, Chinatown 1974, Shampoo (with Warren Beatty) 1974, The Yazuka (jtly.) 1975, Personal Best (also producer-dir. 1984), Greystoke 1984, Tequila Sunrise 1988, Days of Thunder, The Two Jakes, The Firm (co-screenwriter) 1993, Love Affair (co-screenwriter), Mission: Impossible (co-screenwriter), Without Limits (also dir.) 1998. *Address:* c/o CAA, 9830 Wilshire Boulevard, Beverly Hills, CA 90212, U.S.A.

TOWNES, Charles Hard, PH.D.; American physicist; b. 28 July 1915, Greenville, S. Carolina; s. of Henry Keith Townes and Ellen Sumter Hard; m. Frances H. Brown 1941; four d.; ed. Furman and Duke Univs., California Inst. of Technology; Asst. Calif. Inst. of Tech. 1937–39; mem. Tech. staff, Bell Telephone Labs. 1939–47; Assoc. Prof. of Physics, Columbia Univ. 1948–50, Prof. 1950–61; Exec. Dir. Radiation Lab. 1950–52, Chair. Dept. of Physics 1952–55; Vice-Pres. and Dir. of Research, Inst. for Defense Analyses 1959–61; Provost and Prof. of Physics, M.I.T. 1961–66, Inst. Prof. 1966–67; Univ. Prof., Univ. of Calif. 1967–86, Prof. Emer. 1986–94, Prof. in the Grad. School 1994–; Trustee Carnegie Inst. of Washington 1965–, Bd. of Dirs. Perkin-Elmer Corpn. 1966–85, Gen. Motors 1973–86, Bulletin of the Atomic Scientists 1964–69; Chair. Science and Tech. Advisory Comm. for Manned Space Flight, Nat. Aeronautics and Space Admin. 1964–69; Chair. Space Science Bd., N.A.S. 1970–73; Guggenheim Fellow 1955–56; Fulbright Lecturer, Paris 1955–56, Tokyo 1956; Richtmeyer Lecturer, American Physical Soc. 1959; Scott Lecturer, Cambridge 1963; Centennial Lecturer, Univ. of Toronto 1967; Jansky Lecturer, Nat. Radio Astronomy Observatory 1971; Lincoln Lecturer 1972–73; Halley Lecturer, Oxford 1976; Schiff Memorial Lecturer, Stanford 1982, Michelson Memorial Lecturer, U.S. Naval Acad. 1982; Faculty Research Lecturer, Univ. of Calif. at Berkeley 1986; Beckman Lecturer, Univ. of Ill. 1986; Schultz Lecturer, Yale Univ. 1987; Fulbright Fellow Lecturer, Collège de France 1987; Darwin Lecturer, Cambridge Univ. 1988; Houston Memorial Lecturer, Rice Univ., Houston 1990; VanVleck Lecturer, Univ. of Minn. 1990; Henry Norris Russell Lectureship, American Astronomical Soc. 1998; mem. Bd. of Trustees Rand Corpn. 1965–70; Trustee, Calif. Inst. of Tech. 1979–; mem. Pres.'s Science Advisory Cttee. 1966–70, Vice-Chair. 1967–69; Trustee Pacific School of Relations 1983–; mem. Bd. of Dirs. Grad. Theological Union 1993–, Center for Theology and the Natural Sciences 1987–94; mem. Bd. of Advisors, Templeton Foundation Humility Theology Center 1993–; mem. Astronomical Soc. of the Pacific 1989–; mem. Editorial Bd. Review of Scientific Instruments 1950–52, Physical Review 1951–53, Journal of Molecular Spectroscopy 1957–60, etc.; Fellow, American Physical Soc. (Council mem. 1959–62, 1965–71, Pres. 1967), Inst. of Electrical and Electronics Engineers; mem. American Acad. of Arts and Sciences, American Philosophical Soc., American Astronomical Soc., Space Program Advisory Council, NASA, N.A.S. (council mem. 1967–72, 1978–81); Hon. mem. Optical Soc. of America; Foreign mem. Royal Soc. 1976, Nat. Acad. of Sciences, India, Indian Nat. Science Acad.; Hon. Fellow Rozhdestvensky Optical Soc. of Russia 1995; mem. Pontifical Acad. of Science 1983, Russian Acad. of Sciences 1993; Fellow of Calif. Acad. of Sciences; hon. degrees include D.Litt., Sc.D., Dott.Ing., LL.D., L.H.D., D. Med Sc.; awards include Comstock Award (N.A.S.) 1959, Stuart Ballantine Medal (Franklin Inst.) 1959, 1962, Rumford Premium (American Acad. of Arts and Sciences) 1961, David Sarnoff Award in Electronics (American Inst. of Electrical Engineers) 1961, John A. Carty Medal (N.A.S.) 1962, Thomas Young Medal and Prize (Inst. of Physics and Physical Soc., England) 1963, Nobel Prize for Physics 1964, Distinguished Public Service Medal (NASA) 1969, Medal of Honor, Inst. of Electrical and Electronics Engineers 1967, Wilmer Exner Award 1970, Plyler Prize American Physical Soc. 1977, Niels Bohr Int. Gold Medal 1979, LeConte Medal 1980, Nat. Medal of Science 1982, L. W. Frolich Award 1986, Berkely Citation 1986, Nat. Inventors' Hall of Fame 1976, Eng. and Science Hall of Fame 1983, Common Wealth Award 1993, ADION Medal, Observatory of Nice 1995, Frederick Ives Medal, Optical Soc. of America 1996; Officier, Légion d'honneur; holder of patents in electronics, including fundamental patents on masers and lasers, etc. *Publications:* Microwave Spectroscopy 1955, Quantum Electronics 1960, Quantum Electronics and Coherent Light 1964; other scientific papers on microwave spectroscopy, molecular and nuclear structures, radio and infra-red astronomy, masers and lasers, etc. *Leisure interest:* natural history. *Address:* University of California, Department of Physics, 366 LeConte, # 7200, Berkeley, CA 94720, U.S.A. *Telephone:* (510) 642-1128. *Fax:* (510) 643-8497.

TOWNSEND, Sue; British author; b. 2 April 1946, Leicester; m. (divorced); three c.; started writing professionally early 1980s; stage plays include Ten Tiny Fingers, Nine Tiny Toes, Groping for Words 1984, Womberang 1984, The Great Celestial Cow 1985; wrote, narrated and presented Think of England (TV) 1991; Hon. M.A. (Leicester) 1991. *Publications:* The Secret Diary of Adrian Mole Aged 13¾ (trans. in 20 languages), The Growing Pains of Adrian Mole, True Confessions of Adrian Albert Mole, Margaret Hilda Roberts and Susan Lilian Townsend, Rebuilding Coventry, Ten Tiny Fingers, Nine Tiny Toes 1990, Adrian Mole: From Minor to Major 1991, The Queen and I (adapted for stage 1994) 1992, Adrian Mole: The Wilderness Years 1993, Plays 1996, Ghost Children 1997. *Address:* c/o Tessa Sayle Agency, 11 Jubilee Place, London, SW3 3TE; c/o Curtis Brown Group Ltd., 28–29 Haymarket, London, SW1Y 4SP, England.

TOWNSHEND, Peter Dennis Blandford; British composer, performer of rock music, publisher and author; b. 19 May 1945, Isleworth, London; s. of Clifford and Betty Townshend; m. Karen Astley 1968; one s. two d.; ed. Acton County Grammar School and Ealing Art Coll.; contracted as mem. of The Who to Fontana Records 1964, M.C.A. Records 1965, W.E.A. Records 1979; retd. from The Who 1984; contracted as solo artist to Atco Records (U.S.A.) 1979–, to Virgin Records 1986–; owner, Eel Pie Recording Ltd. 1972–83; est. Eel Pie (bookshops and publishing co.) 1976–83; est. Meher Baba Oceanic (U.K. archival library) 1976–81; Ed., Faber & Faber (publrs.) 1983–; final tour with The Who 1989; Ivor Novello Award 1981, British Phonographic Industry Award 1983; Rock and Roll Hall of Fame 1990, Olivier Award 1997. *Recordings include:* with The Who: I Can't Explain 1965, My Generation, Tommy (rock opera), Quadrophenia (rock opera), The Iron Man 1989; solo: Empty Glass 1980, Chinese Eyes 1982, White City 1985, Iron Man 1989. *Publications:* The Story of Tommy (with Richard Barnes), Horse's Neck: 1985, Tommy: The Musical 1995, London 1996. *Leisure interest:* sailing. *Address:* c/o Trinifold Management, 12 Oval Road, London, NW1 7DH; Box 305, Twickenham, TW1 1TT, England. *Telephone:* 0171-419 4300. *Fax:* 0171-419 4325 (London).

TOY, Sam, M.A.; British business executive; b. 21 Aug. 1923, Mabe, Cornwall; s. of Edward and Lilian Toy; m. 1st Jean Balls 1944, one s.; m. 2nd Joan Franklin Rook 1950, two s. one d.; m. 3rd Janetta McMorrow 1984; ed. Falmouth Grammar School and Univ. of Cambridge; R.A.F. pilot 1942–48; joined Ford Motor Co. Ltd. 1948, Chair. and Man. Dir. 1980–86; Vice-Pres. Soc. Motor Mfrs. and Traders Ltd. 1982–86, Pres. 1986–87, Deputy Pres. 1987–88; Chair. Norman Cordiner Ltd. 1991–96. *Leisure interests:* trout and salmon fishing, golf. *Address:* 1 Primrose Bay, Invermoriston, Inverness,

IV3 6YD, Scotland; 35 Stanhope Terrace, Lancaster Gate, London, W2 2UA, England.

TOYE, Wendy, C.B.E.; British theatrical producer, film director, choreographer, actress and dancer; b. 1 May 1917; d. of Ernest W. Toye and Jessie Crichton (Ramsay) Toye; ed. privately, trained with Euphen MacLaren, Tamara Karsavina, Anton Dolin, Morosoff, Legat, Marie Rambert; first performance aged 3 years, Albert Hall; first professional appearance as Cobweb (Midsummer Night's Dream), Old Vic 1929; prin. dancer Hiawatha, Albert Hall 1931; played Marigold and Phoebe, and produced dances, Toad of Toad Hall, Royalty 1931–32; masked dancer Ballerina, Gaiety 1933; danced and choreographed for Carmargo Soc. of Ballet; mem. Ninette de Valois' original Vic Wells Ballet, danced in C. B. Cochran's The Miracle, Lyceum 1932, prin. dancer The Golden Toy, Coliseum 1934; toured with Anton Dolin's Ballet (choreographer for divertissements and short ballets) 1934–35; Tulip Time, Alhambra, then prin. dancer and choreographer, Markova-Dolin Ballet 1935; arranged dances and ballets for many shows and films 1935–42, including most of George Black's productions notably Black Velvet (also prin. dancer) 1939; Shakespearean season, Open Air Theatre 1939; *Theatre productions:* Big Ben, Bless the Bride, Tough at the Top (for C. B. Cochran), Adelphi, The Shepherd Show, Prince's, Peter Pan (co-dir. and choreographer), New York, And So To Bed, New Theatre, Feu d'Artifice (co-dir. and choreographer), Paris, Night of Masquerade, Queen, Second Threshold, Vaudeville, Three's Company (choreographer) in Joyce Grenfell Requests the Pleasure, Fortune, Wild Thyme, Duke of York's, Lady at the Wheel and Robert and Elizabeth, Lyric, Hammersmith, Majority of One, Phoenix, Magic Lantern and On the Level, Saville, As You Like It, Old Vic, Virtue in Danger, Mermaid and Strand, A Midsummer Night's Dream, Shakespeare quatercentenary, Latin American tour 1964, Soldier's Tale, Edinburgh Festival 1967, Boots and Strawberry Jam, Nottingham Playhouse 1968, The Great Waltz, Drury Lane 1970, Showboat, Adelphi 1971, She Stoops to Conquer, Young Vic 1972, Cowardy Custard, Mermaid 1972, Stand and Deliver, Roundhouse 1972; at Chichester R. Loves J 1973, The Confederacy 1974, Follow The Star 1974, Made in Heaven 1975, Make Me a World 1976, Once More with Music 1976, Oh Mr. Porter, Mermaid 1977, Gingerbread Man, Watermill Theatre 1981, This Thing Called Love, Watermill Theatre 1982, Ambassadors Theatre 1983, Singing in the Rain (Assoc. Producer), Palladium 1983, Noel and Gertie, Monte Carlo 1983, Birds of A Feather 1984, Barnum (Assoc. Producer) 1985, Madwoman of Chaillot, Torville and Dean World Tour (Assoc. Producer) 1985, Once Upon A Mattress, Watermill Theatre 1985, Kiss Me Kate, Copenhagen 1986, Laburnham Grove, Palace Theatre, Watford 1987, Miranda, Chichester Festival Theatre 1987, Get the Message, Molecule 1987, Songbook, Watermill 1988, Mrs Dot, Watford 1981, When that I was, Manitoba 1988–89, Cinderella, Watford 1989, Penny Black, Wavendon 1990, Moll Flanders, Watermill 1990, Heaven's Up., Playhouse 1990, Bernard Shaw and Mrs Patrick Campbell (musical), Wavendon 1990, Mrs Pat's Profession, Wavendon 1991, The Drummer, Watermill 1991, Sound of Music 1992, See How They Run, Watermill 1992, Vienna 1992, The Kingfisher, Vienna 1993, Under Their Hats, King's Head 1994, Vienna 1995, The Anastasia File, Watermill 1994, Der Apotheker, Menton, France 1995, Warts and All, Watermill 1996, Sadler's Wells Finale Gala 1996, Rogues to Riches, Watermill 1996. *opera productions:* Bluebeard's Castle (Bartók), Sadler's Wells and Brussels, The Telephone (Menotti), Rusalka (Dvořák), and La Vie Parisienne, Sadler's Wells, Die Fledermaus, Coliseum and Sadler's Wells, Orpheus in the Underworld, Sadler's Wells and Australia, The Abduction from the Seraglio, Bath Festival 1967, The Impresario, Don Pasquale (for Phoenix Opera Group) 1968, The Italian Girl in Algiers, Coliseum 1968, Orpheus 1978, Merry Widow 1979–80, Orpheus 1981, Mikado (Turkey) 1982, The Italian Girl in Algiers 1982, Serva Padrona and the Apothecary Operas for Aix-en-Provence Festival 1991; *films directed:* The Stranger Left No Card 1952, The Teckman Mystery, Raising a Riot, The Twelfth Day of Christmas, Three Cases of Murder 1954, All for Mary 1955, True as a Turtle 1956, We Joined the Navy 1962, The King's Breakfast, Cliff in Scotland, A Goodly Manor for a Song, Girls Wanted—Istanbul; productions for TV, Follow the Star 1979, Tales of the Unexpected 1981, Trial By Jury 1982, Di Ballo 1982; retrospective of films, Paris Film Festival 1990, Nat. Film Theatre 1995; musicals, variety, cabaret; Guest Artist with Sadler's Wells Ballet and Mme. Rambert's Ballet Club; prin. dancer with British Ballet organized by Adeline Genée, Denmark 1932, lectured in Australia 1977; Adviser, Arts Council Training Scheme 1978–; mem. Grand Council, Royal Acad. of Dancing, Council LAMDA, Wavendon All Music scheme, Richard Stilgoe Award scheme, original Accreditation Bd., Nat. Council of Drama Training for Acting Courses; The Queen's Silver Jubilee Medal, Hon. D.Litt. (City) 1997. *Leisure interests:* embroidery, gardening. *Address:* c/o Jean Diamond, London Management, 2 Noel Street, London W.1, England. *Telephone:* 0171-287 9000.

TOYODA, Shoichiro, D.ENG.; Japanese business executive; b. 27 Feb. 1925, Nagoya; s. of Kiichiro Toyoda and Hatako Toyoda; m. Hiroko Mitsui 1952; one s. one d.; ed. Nagoya and Tohoku Univs.; joined Toyota Motor Corpn. 1952, Man. Dir. 1961, Sr. Man. Dir. 1967, Exec. Vice-Pres 1972, Pres. Marketing Org. 1981, Pres. Toyota Motor Corpn. 1982, Chair. 1992, Sr. Adviser, mem. Bd. June 1996–; fmr. Chair. Japanese Automobile Mfrs. Asscn.; Vice-Chair. Keidanren (Fed. of Industrial Orgs.) 1990–94, Chair. 1994–98; Deming Prize 1980; Medal with Blue Ribbon for Outstanding Public Service. *Leisure interests:* go, gardening, golf. *Address:* c/o Keidanren, 1-9-4 Ohtemachi, Chiyoda-ku, Tokyo 100, Japan.

TOYODA, Tatsuro, B.MECH.ENG., M.B.A.; Japanese motor manufacturing executive; b. 1 June 1929, Nagoya; s. of Kiichiro Toyoda and Hatako Mitsui; m. Shimizu Ayako; one s. one d.; ed. Univ. of Tokyo, New York Univ.; joined Toyota Motor Corpn. 1953, apptd. Dir. 1974, supervised creation of New United Motor Mfg. Inc. (NUMMI), jt. venture with General Motors in Calif., U.S.A. 1984, Pres. NUMMI 1984–88, Exec. Vice-Pres. Toyota 1988–92, Pres. 1992–95, Vice-Chair 1995–96, Sr. Adviser 1996–; fmr. Chair. Japan Automobile Mfrs.' Asscn.; Vice-Chair. Japan Asscn. of Corp. Execs. (Keizai Doyukai); Order of the Blue Ribbon. *Leisure interest:* listening to music. *Address:* c/o Toyota Motor Corporation, 1 Toyota-cho, Toyota-cho, Toyota 471-71, Japan.

TRABOULSY, Antoun; Syrian lawyer; b. 1919, Homs; s. of Badih Traboulsy; m. 1944; one s. three d.; fmr. Rep. Ordre des avocats, Homs 1946, fmr. Leader, mem. Council, Damascus 1973–. *Address:* Boustan Diwane, Homs, Syria. *Telephone:* 224406 (Office); 224655, 225286 (Home).

TRACHTENBERG, Stephen Joel, J.D., M.P.A.; American university president; b. 14 Dec. 1937, Brooklyn; s. of Oscar Trachtenberg and Shoshana Weinstock; m. Francine Zorn 1971; two s.; ed. Columbia, Yale and Harvard Univs.; admitted New York Bar 1964, U.S. Supreme Court Bar 1967; attorney, Atomic Energy Comm. 1962–65; Special Asst. to U.S. Educ. Comm., Health, Educ. and Welfare, Washington, D.C. 1966–68; Assoc. Prof. of Political Science, Boston Univ. 1969–77, Assoc. Dean 1969–70, Dean 1970–74, Assoc. Vice-Pres., co-Counsel 1974–76, Vice-Pres. Academic Services 1976–77; Pres., Prof. of Law, Univ. of Hartford, Conn. 1977–88; Pres., Prof. of Man. George Washington Univ., Washington 1988–; Dir. NationsBank, Greater Washington Bd. of Trade, Nat. Educ. Telecommunications Org., Washington Research Library Consortium, DC Tax Revision Comm., Newcomen Soc.; Adviser to Presidency; numerous awards and several hon. degrees. *Address:* Office of the President, George Washington University, Washington, DC 20052; 843 Bruce Avenue, Flossmoor, IL 60422, U.S.A.

TRAILL, Sir Alan, G.B.E., Q.S.O., M.A., D.MUS.; British insurance broker; b. 7 May 1935, London; s. of George and Margaret (Matthews) Traill; m. Sarah Jane Hutt 1964; one s.; ed. Charterhouse and Jesus Coll., Cambridge; Dir. Morice Tozer Beck (insurance brokers) 1960; Underwriting mem. Lloyd's 1963–89; Founder Dir. Traill Attenborough (Lloyd's brokers) 1973, Chair. 1980; Man. Dir. Colburn Traill Ltd. 1989–96; Div. Dir. First City Insurance Brokers Ltd. 1996–; Dir. City Arts Trust Ltd., Grandactual Ltd. 1993–97; mem. Pathfinder Team Consulting 1992–; Assoc. Chartered Inst. of Arbitrators; mem. Royal Shakespeare Theatre Trust 1982–, Advisory Council and Educ. Cttee., London Symphony Orchestra 1997–; Chair. UK/NZ 1990 Cttee. 1989–90; Chair. Trustees, Waitangi Foundation 1991–; Trustee, St. Paul's Cathedral Choir School Foundation 1985–; Gov./Almoner Christ's Hosp. 1980–; Gov. Lord Mayor Treloar School 1985–; Trustee Morden Coll. 1995–; mem. Court of Common Council (of City of London) 1970, Alderman 1975, Sheriff 1982–83, Lord Mayor of London 1984–85; K. St. J. 1985. *Leisure interests:* shooting, skiing, DIY, travel, opera, music, assisting education. *Address:* 13/15 Folgate Street, London, E1 6BX, England. *Telephone:* 0171-410 4832. *Fax:* 0171-410 5631.

TRÂN DUC LUONG; Vietnamese politician and fmr. mining engineer; b. 1937; apptd. a Vice-Prime Minister 1992; mem. Dang Cong san Viet Nam (Communist Party of Viet Nam) Politburo 1996–97. *Address:* c/o Dang Cong san Viet Nam, 1 Hoang Van Thu, Hanoi, Viet Nam.

TRAN TAM TINH, Rev., PH.D., F.R.S.C.; Vietnamese/Canadian professor of classical archaeology; b. 16 April 1929, Nam Dinh; ed. Séminaire Pontifical, Università Laterano, Université de Fribourg, Ecole Pratique des Hautes Etudes, Paris, C.N.R.S.; ordained Priest 1956; excavations at Soli, Cyprus 1965–74, Pompeii and Herculaneum 1969–76; Co-f. Fraternité Vietnam 1976; Prof. of Classical Archaeology, Laval Univ. 1964–, Sr. Prof. 1971–94; Tatiana Warscher Award for Archaeology (American Acad. at Rome) 1973, Prix G. Mendel (Académie des Inscriptions et Belles-Lettres, France) 1978. *Publications:* Le culte d'Isis à Pompéi 1964, Le culte des divinités orientales à Herculanum 1971, Le culte des divinités orientales en Campanie 1972, Isis lactans 1973, Catalogue des peintures romaines au musée du Louvre 1974, I cattolici nella storia del Vietnam 1975, Dieu et César 1978, Sérapis debout 1983, Soloi I, La Basilique 1985, La casa dei Cervi à Herculanum 1988, Tôi vê Hanoi 1974, Tro vê nguôn 1974, Corpus des lampes antiques conservées au Québec I 1991, Corpus des lampes à sujets isiaques du musée gnéco-romain d'Alexandrie 1993, and numerous articles on classical iconography and religion. *Address:* 2995 Maricourt, Suite 300, Ste.-Foy, Québec, G2W 4T8, Canada. *Telephone:* (418) 653-3513.

TRÂN THIEN KHIEM, Gen.; Vietnamese politician and army officer; b. 15 Dec. 1925; Army service 1947–75; held off attempted coup against Pres. Diem 1960, took part in coup against him 1963; with Gen. Nguyen Khan led coup removing Gen. Duong Van Minh 1964; Defence Minister and C.-in-C. 1964; Amb. to U.S.A. 1964–65, to Repub. of China 1965–68; Minister of the Interior 1968–73, Deputy Prime Minister March-Aug. 1969, Prime Minister 1969–75, Minister of Defence 1972–75; fled to Taiwan April 1975.

TRAN VAN HUONG; Vietnamese politician; b. 1 Dec. 1903; fmr. schoolteacher; participated in Viet-Minh resistance against French; Prefect of Saigon 1954 and 1964; Prime Minister Repub. of Viet Nam 1964–65, 1968–69; Vice-Pres. of Repub. of Viet Nam 1971–75, Pres. 21-28 April 1975.

TRAORÉ, Gen. Amadou Toumani; Malian politician and army officer; leader coup which overthrew Gen. Moussa Traoré (q.v.) March 1991; Chair. Transition Cttee. for the Salvation of the People (CTSP) 1991–92. *Address:* Bamako, Mali.

TRAORÉ, Col. Diara; Guinean politician and army officer; Prime Minister of Guinea April–Dec. 1984, Minister of Nat. Educ. 1984–85; mem. Comité militaire de redressement nat. (CMRN) 1984–85; staged abortive coup d'état July 1985; arrested and sentenced to death; sentence commuted to life imprisonment; released Dec. 1988.

TRAORÉ, Gen. Moussa; Malian politician and army officer; b. 25 Sept. 1936, Kayes; ed. Training Coll., Fréjus, Cadets Coll., Kati; became N.C.O. in French Army; returned to Mali 1960; promoted Lieut. 1964, Col. 1971, Brig.-Gen. 1978; at Armed Forces Coll., Kati until 1968; led coup to depose Pres. Modibo Keita Nov. 1968; Pres. Mil. Cttee. for Nat. Liberation (Head of State) and C.-in-C. of the Armed Forces 1968–91, also Prime Minister 1969–80; Pres. of Mali 1979–91; Minister of Defence and Security 1978–86, of the Interior 1978–79, of Nat. Defence 1988–90 (overthrown in coup, under arrest); Chair. OAU 1988–89; Sec.-Gen. Nat. Council Union Démocratique du Peuple Malien 1979–80, fmr. mem. Cen. Exec. Bureau; Pres. Conf. of Heads of State, Union Douanière des Etats de l'Afrique de l'Ouest 1970; overthrown March 1991; stood trial Nov. 1992; sentenced to death for mass murder Feb. 1993; sentence commuted to life imprisonment 1997; charged with embezzlement Oct. 1998.

TRAPP, Joseph Burney, C.B.E., M.A., F.B.A., F.S.A.; British/New Zealand administrator and scholar; b. 16 July 1925, Carterton, N.Z.; s. of H. M. B. Trapp and Frances M. Trapp (née Wolters); m. Elayne Margaret Falla 1953; two s.; ed. Dannevirke High School and Victoria Univ. Coll., Wellington, N.Z.; Asst. Librarian, Alexander Turnbull Library, Wellington 1946–50; Jr. Lecturer, Victoria Univ. Coll. 1950–51; Asst. Lecturer, Univ. of Reading, England 1951–53; Asst. Librarian, then Librarian, Warburg Inst., London 1953–76, Dir. and Prof. of the History of the Classical Tradition 1976–90; Vice-Pres. British Acad. 1983–85, Foreign Sec. 1988–95; Chair. Advisory Cttee., and Trustee, Lambeth Palace Library 1987–98; Gray Lecturer (Cambridge) 1990, Panizzi Lecturer (British Library) 1990, Lyell Reader (Oxford) 1994; Foreign mem. Royal Swedish Acad. of Letters, History and Archaeology 1995–. *Publications:* Ed. Apology of Sir Thomas More 1979, Essays in the Renaissance and the Classical Tradition 1990, Erasmus, Colet and More: The Early Tudor Humanists and their Books 1991, Cambridge History of The Book in Britain, III: 1400–1557 (co-ed.) 1999; articles in learned journals. *Address:* Warburg Institute, Woburn Square, London, WC1H 0AB, England. *Telephone:* 0171-580 9663. *Fax:* 0171-436 2852.

TRAUNER, Sergio; Italian business executive and lawyer; b. 9 March 1934, Athens, Greece; s. of Livio Trauner and Nada Mandich; m. (divorced); ed. Univ. of Trieste; lawyer in pvt. practice; counsellor to Trieste Municipality 1962–75, 1982–, to Friuli Venezia Giulia Region 1964–78; Dir. Finmare Co. (IRI Group) 1981–84, EFIM 1984–87; mem. Presidential Cttee. and Bd. of Dirs. IRI 1986–91; Pres. ILVA S.p.A. 1991–; Commendatore of Italian Repub., Officer, Order of Merit of Italian Repub. *Publications:* books on art and history. *Leisure interests:* reading, travel. *Address:* ILVA S.p.A., Viale Castro Pretorio 122, 00185 Rome, Italy. *Telephone:* 06/44596200; 06/44596459.

TRAUTMAN, Andrzej; Polish theoretical physicist; b. 4 Jan. 1933, Warsaw; s. of Mieczysław and Eliza Trautman; m. Róża Michalska 1962; two s.; ed. Warsaw Univ. of Tech., Warsaw Univ.; Asst. Inst. of Radiolocation, Warsaw Univ. of Tech. 1952–53, Inst. of Applied Math. 1953–55; postgraduate studies, Inst. of Physics, Polish Acad. of Sciences (PAN) 1955–58, Doctorate 1959; Lecturer 1959; scientific training, Imperial Coll., King's Coll., London, Univ. of Syracuse, U.S.A. 1959–61; Scientist, Inst. of Theoretical Physics, Warsaw Univ. 1961–, Asst. Prof. and Head of Dept. Electrodynamics and Theory of Relativity 1962–68, Extraordinary Prof. 1964–71, Ordinary Prof. 1971–; Deputy Dir. Inst. of Theoretical Physics 1968–74, Dir. 1975–85; Corresp. mem. Polish Acad. of Sciences 1969–76, mem. 1977–, mem. Presidium 1972–83, Vice-Pres. 1978–80, Chair. Cttee. of Physics, Polish Acad. of Sciences; Deputy Chair. Gen. Bd. of Polish Physics Asscn. 1970–73, Foreign mem. Czechoslovak Acad. of Sciences 1980–90; mem. Int. Cttee. of Theory of Relativity and Gravitation 1965–80, Editorial Staff Annales de l'Inst. H. Poincaré, Reports on Mathematical Physics, Int. Journal of Theoretical Physics, Lett. Math. Phys., Journal of Geometric Physics; Visiting Prof., American Math. Soc., Santa Barbara 1962, Coll. de France, Paris 1963 and 1981, Brandeis Univ., U.S.A. 1964, Univ. of Chicago 1971, Univ. of Pisa, Italy 1972, The Schrödinger Professorship, Univ. of Vienna 1972, State Univ. of N.Y. at Stony Brook 1976–77, Univ. of Montreal 1982, 1990, Univ. of Tex. at Dallas 1985, 1986; State Prize 1st Class 1976, Alfred Jurzykowski Foundation Award in Physics 1984, Gold Cross of Merit, Cross of Order of Polonia Restituta. *Publications:* Differential Geometry for Physicists 1984, The Spinorial Chessboard (with P. Budinich) 1988, Space Time and Gravitation (with W. Kopczyński) 1992, and numerous works on theory of gravitation waves, energy of gravitation field, modern methods of differential geometry and their application in physics, Einstein-Cartan's Theory. *Leisure interest:* chess. *Address:* Instytut Fizyki Teoretycznej UW, ul. Hoża 69, 00-681 Warsaw, Poland. *Telephone:* (22) 621 40 97 (Office).

TRAVKIN, Nikolai Ilyich; Russian politician; b. 19 March 1946, Novo-Nikolskoe, Moscow region; m.; two s.; ed. Kolomna Pedagogical Inst., Higher Party School; mem. CPSU 1970–90; worker, brigade-leader, Head of the Dept. of "Glavmosstroi"; initiator self-financing and self-man. into construction industry 1969–; Deputy Head of construction union 1967–89; mem. of the Movt. "Democratic Russia" 1988–; People's Deputy of the U.S.S.R. 1989–91; People's Deputy of Russia 1990–93; a founder and Chair. Democratic Party of Russia 1990–94; Chair. of the Subcttee., Supreme Soviet of the U.S.S.R. (supervising local soviets and devt. of self-man.) 1989–90; Chair. Cttee. Supreme Soviet of Russia; supervising local soviets and devt. of self-man. May–Dec. 1990; head of local admin. Shakhovskoy Dist. 1991–96; co-leader Civic Union coalition 1992–93; mem. State Duma (Parl.) Dec. 1993–; Minister without Portfolio 1994–96; mem. Cttee. on Problems of Fed. and Regional Politics 1996–; Hero of Socialist Labour 1986. *Leisure interests:* theatre, literature. *Address:* Okhotny Ryad 1, 103265 Moscow, Russia. *Telephone:* 292-33-47 (Duma).

TRAVOLTA, John; American actor; b. 18 Feb. 1954, Englewood, N.J.; s. of Salvatore Travolta and late Helen (née Burke) Travolta; m. Kelly Preston 1991; one s. *Films:* Carrie 1976, The Boy in the Plastic Bubble (for TV) 1976, Saturday Night Fever 1977, Grease 1978, Moment by Moment 1978, Urban Cowboy 1980, Blow-Out 1981, Staying Alive 1983, Two of a Kind 1983, Perfect 1985, The Experts 1988, Chains of Gold 1989, Look Who's Talking 1989, Look Who's Talking Now 1990, The Tender 1991, All Shook Up 1991, Look Who's Talking 3 1994, Pulp Fiction 1994, White Man's Burden 1995, Get Shorty 1995, Broken Arrow 1996, Phenomenon 1996, Michael 1997, Face Off 1997, She's So Lovely 1997, Primary Colors 1998, A Civil Action 1998; TV series Welcome Back Kotter 1975–77; l.p. records 1976, 1977; Billboard Magazine Best New Male Vocalist Award 1976; Best Actor Award, Nat. Bd. of Review 1978; Male Star of the Year, Nat. Asscn. of Theatre Owners 1983, Alan J. Pakula Prize 1998. *Publication:* Staying Fit 1984. *Leisure interest:* flying.

TRAXLER, Vieri; Italian diplomatist; b. 23 May 1928, Pisa; s. of Augusto Traxler and Adele Camerana; m.; five c.; ed. Univ. of Florence; fmr. Deputy Dir.-Gen. for Political Affairs, Ministry of Foreign Affairs; Amb. to Zaïre 1976, to Brazil 1983–86; Head Italian del. to Vienna meetings of Conf. on Security and Co-operation in Europe (CSCE) 1986–89; Perm. Rep. to UN, New York 1989–93; Under-Sec.-Gen. of UN as Special Envoy of Dept. of Humanitarian Affairs 1993. *Leisue interests:* history (particularly military history), biographies. *Address:* c/o Department of Humanitarian Affairs, Room 3600, United Nations, New York, NY 10017, U.S.A.

TREACY, Philip, M.A., R.C.A.; Irish milliner; b. 26 May 1967, Ballinsoe, Co. Galway; s. of the late James Vincent Treacy and Katie Agnes Treacy; ed. Nat. Coll. of Art and Design, Dublin, Royal Coll. of Art, London; while still a student, worked for designers including Rifat Ozbek, John Galliano and Victor Edelstein; f. Philip Treacy Millinery, London 1991; house milliner for Marc Bohan at Hartnell and for Victor Edelstein; has collaborated with Karl Lagerfeld, Chanel's couture and ready-to-wear shows 1991–; his own ready-to-wear range sold in New York and London 1991–; designed head dresses for Pola John's production of My Fair Lady 1992; presented own show, London 1993; launched accessory range 1997; first show in New York 1997; British Accessory Designer of the Year award 1991, 1992, 1993, 1996, 1997, Irish Fashion Oscar 1992. *Address:* Philip Treacy Ltd., 69 Elizabeth Street, London, SW1W 9PJ, England. *Telephone:* 0171-259 9605. *Fax:* 0171-824 8559.

TRECHSEL, Stefan, D.IUR.; Swiss lawyer; b. 25 June 1937, Berne; s. of Manfred F. Trechsel and Steffi Friedlaender; m. Franca Julia Kinsbergen 1967; two d.; ed. Univ. of Berne and Georgetown Univ., Washington; Asst. and Main Asst. for Criminal Law, Univ. of Berne 1964–71; Swiss Fed. Dept. for Tech. Cooperation 1966–67; Public Prosecutor, Dist. of Bern-Mittelland 1971–75; Guest Prof. of Criminal Law and Procedure, Univ. of Fribourg 1975–77; Prof., Hochschule St. Gallen 1979–99; Prof. Univ. of Zurich 1999–; mem. European Comm. of Human Rights 1975–, 2nd Vice-Pres. 1987, Chamber Pres. 1993–94, Pres. 1995–; Hon. Dr. New York Law School 1975. *Publications:* Der Strafgrund der Teilnahme 1967, Die Europäische Menschenrechtskonvention, ihr Schutz der persönlichen Freiheit und die Schweizerischen Strafprozessrechte 1974, Strafrecht Allgemeiner Teil I (4th edn. of textbook by Peter Noll) 1994, Schweizerisches Strafgesetzbuch, Kurzkommentar 1997. *Leisure interests:* skiing, music, literature, psychology, chamber music ('cello). *Address:* Tigerbergstrasse 21, CH 9000, St. Gallen, Switzerland. *Telephone:* (071) 224 21 60.

TREDE, Michael, M.B., B.CHIR., M.D.; German surgeon; b. 10 Oct. 1928, Hamburg; s. of Hilmar Trede and Gertrud (Daus) Trede; m. Ursula Boettcher 1956; one s. four d.; ed. The Leys School, Cambridge and Univ. of Cambridge; Surgeon-in-training, Freie Universität Berlin 1957–62, Heidelberg Univ. 1962–72; now Prof. and Chair. Dept. of Surgery, Klinikum Mannheim, Univ. of Heidelberg; Pres. Deutsche Gesellschaft für Chirurgie, Int. Surgical Soc. 1993–95; Hon. mem. Greek and Yugoslav Surgical Asscns.; Hon. F.R.C.S. (England, Ireland, Glasgow); Hon. F.A.C.S. *Publications:* Surgery of the Pancreas (with D. C. Carter); 200 articles on surgery in scientific journals. *Leisure interests:* painting, violin-playing, mountaineering, skiing. *Address:* Nadlerstrasse 1A, 68259 Mannheim, Germany. *Telephone:* (0621) 796301.

TREEN, David Conner, B.A., LL.B.; American politician and lawyer; b. 16 July 1928, Baton Rouge, La.; s. of Joseph Paul Treen and Elizabeth Speir Treen; m. Dolores Brisbi 1951; one s. two d.; ed. Fortier High School, New Orleans, La., Tulane Univ., Tulane Univ. Law School; U.S.A.F. legal corps

1951–52; Vice.-Pres. and legal counsel, Simplex Manufacturing Corpn. 1952–57; Assoc. Attorney with law firm Beard, Blue and Schmitt, then partner Beard, Blue, Schmitt and Treen 1957–72; mem. House of Reps. for 3rd Dist. of La. 1973–80; Gov. of Louisiana 1980–84. *Publication:* Can You Afford This House? *Address:* c/o Deutsch, Kerrigan & Stiles, 755 Magazine Street, New Orleans, LA 70130, U.S.A. *Telephone:* (504) 581-5141.

TREGLOWN, Jeremy Dickinson, M.A., B.LITT., PH.D., F.R.S.L.; British university professor, writer and journalist; b. 24 May 1946, Anglesey, N. Wales; s. of Rev. G. L. Treglown; m. 1st Rona Bower 1970 (divorced 1982); one s. two d.; m. 2nd Holly Eley (née Urquhart) 1984; ed. Bristol Grammar School, St. Peter's Coll., Oxford; Lecturer in English Literature, Lincoln Coll., Oxford 1973–76, Univ. Coll., London 1976–79; Asst. Ed. The Times Literary Supplement 1979–81, Ed. 1982–90; Prof. of English, Univ. of Warwick 1993–; contrib. The Guardian, Plays and Players, New Statesman, The Times, The Sunday Times, Independent on Sunday, New Yorker etc.; Chair. of Judges, Booker Prize 1991, Whitbread Book of the Year Award 1998; Co-ed. Liber, a European Review of Books 1989; Contributing Ed., Grand Street magazine, New York 1991–98; Visiting Fellow, All Souls Coll., Oxford 1986; Fellow Huntington Library 1988, R.S.L. 1989– (mem. Council 1989–94); Hon. Research Fellow, Univ. Coll. London 1991–; Mellon Visiting Assoc., Calif. Inst. of Tech.; Ferris Visiting Prof., Princeton Univ. 1992; Jackson Brothers Fellow, Beinecke Library, Yale Univ. 1999. *Publications:* The Letters of John Wilmot, Earl of Rochester 1980, Spirit of Wit 1982, The Lantern-Bearers and Other Essays by R. L. Stevenson 1988, Roald Dahl: A biography 1994, Grub Street and the Ivory Tower: Literary Journalism and Literary Scholarship from Fielding to the Internet (co-ed.) 1998; various articles and introductions on poetry, drama and literary history. *Address:* Gardens Cottage, Ditchley Park, Enstone, Oxfordshire, OX7 4EP, England.

TREICHL, Heinrich; Austrian banker; b. 31 July 1913, Vienna; s. of Dr. Alfred and Dorothea (née Baroness Ferstel) Treichl; m. Helga Ross 1946; two s.; ed. Univs. of Frankfurt, Germany and Vienna; Dir. Banque des Pays de l'Europe Centrale, Paris, Mercur Bank AG and Länderbank Wien AG, Vienna 1936–39; Partner, Ullstein and Co., Vienna 1946–55; Dir. Österreichische Industrie- und Bergbauverwaltungs GmbH, Vienna 1956–58; Dir. Creditanstalt-Bankverein, Vienna 1958–, Chair. of Man. Bd. 1970–81; Hon. Chair. Supervisory Bd. Bank für Kärnten und Steiermark AG, Bank für Oberösterreich und Salzburg, Bank für Tirol und Vorarlberg AG; mem. Int. Advisory bd. Verwaltungs-und Privatbank AG, Vaduz; Pres. Austrian Red Cross Soc.; Grande Ufficiale Ordine del Merito (Italy); Commdr., Order Homayoun; Commdr., Légion d'honneur; Kt. Commdr., Order of St. Gregory, Grand Decoration of Honour in Gold for Services to Repub. of Austria, Grand Decoration in Silver with Star for Services to Repub. of Austria. *Leisure interests:* literature, hunting, skiing. *Address:* 1030 Vienna, Salmgasse 2, Austria. *Telephone:* 713 31 50.

TREIKI, Ali A., PH.D.; Libyan diplomatist and politician; b. 10 Oct. 1938, Misurata; s. of Abdussalem Treiki and Amna Treiki; m. Aisha Dihoum 1969; one s. three d.; ed. Univ. of Benghazi, Libya, and Toulouse Univ., France; joined Foreign Ministry 1970; Minister Plenipotentiary 1970, Dir. of Political Admin. 1970–73, Dir. of African Admin. 1973–74, Asst. Deputy for Political Affairs 1974–76; Sec. of State for Foreign Affairs 1971–77, Foreign Sec. 1977–81, Sec. of Liaison for Foreign Affairs 1981–86; Foreign Minister 1984–86; Head of Libyan del. to UN Gen. Ass. 1977–80; Perm. Rep. of Libya to the UN 1982–84, 1986–91, to League of Arab States, Cairo 1991–93; Amb. to France 1995–. *Address:* Libyan People's Bureau, 2 rue Charles Lamoureux, 75116 Paris, France. *Telephone:* (1) 47 04 71 60. *Fax:* (1) 47 55 96 25.

TREIMAN, Sam Bard, PH.D.; American professor of physics; b. 27 May 1925, Chicago, Ill.; s. of Abraham Treiman and Sarah (Bard) Treiman; m. Joan Little 1952; one s. two d.; ed. Northwestern Univ. and Univ. of Chicago; joined Princeton Univ. 1952, Prof. of Physics 1963–, Eugene Higgins Prof. 1976–, Chair. of Dept. 1981–87; Chair. Univ. Research Bd. 1988–; Sloan Fellow; Guggenheim Fellow; mem. N.A.S., American Acad. of Arts and Sciences. *Publications:* Formal Scattering Theory (with M. Grossjean), Lectures on Current Algebra (with R. Jackiw and D. Gross) 1972; and numerous papers in professional journals. *Leisure interests:* tennis, reading. *Address:* Joseph Henry Laboratories, Jaduin Hall, P.O. Box 708, Princeton University, Princeton, NJ 08540 (Office); 60 McCosh Circle, Princeton, NJ 08540, U.S.A. (Home). *Telephone:* 452-4350 (Office); 924-0592 (Home).

TREITEL, Sir Guenter Heinz, Kt., Q.C., M.A., D.C.L., F.B.A.; British fmr. professor of law; b. 26 Oct. 1928, Berlin, Germany; s. of Dr. Theodor Treitel and Hanna (née Levy) Treitel; m. Phyllis M. Cook 1957; two s.; ed. Kilburn Grammar School and Magdalen Coll., Oxford; came to U.K. 1939; Fellow of Magdalen Coll., Oxford 1954–79, Emer. Fellow 1979–; All Souls Reader in English Law 1964–79; Vinerian Prof. of English Law, Univ. of Oxford, and Fellow of All Souls Coll. 1979–96, Emer. Prof. and Emer. Fellow 1996–; Visiting Lecturer, Univ. of Chicago 1963–64, Visiting Prof. 1968–69, 1971–72; Visiting Prof., Univ. of W. Australia 1976, Univ. of Houston 1977, Southern Methodist Univ. 1978, 1988–89, 1994, Univ. of Va. 1978–79, 1983–84, Univ. of Santa Clara 1981; Visiting Scholar, Ernst von Caemmerer Gedächtnisstiftung 1990; Consultant to Law Comm. on law of contract 1972–84; Trustee, British Museum 1983–98; mem. Council Nat. Trust 1984–93; Hon. Bencher, Gray's Inn. *Publications:* The Law of Contract 1962, An Outline of the Law of Contract 1975, Remedies for Breach of Contract: a comparative account 1988, Unmöglichkeit, "Impracticability" und "Frustration" im anglo-amerikanischen Recht 1991, Frustration and Force Majeure 1994; (co-author) Benjamin's Sale of Goods 1974; ed. of other law books. *Leisure interests:* reading, music. *Address:* All Souls College, Oxford, OX1 4AL, England. *Telephone:* (01865) 279379. *Fax:* (01865) 279299.

TREJOS FERNÁNDEZ, José Joaquín; Costa Rican politician and university professor; b. 18 April 1916, San José; s. of Juan Trejos and Emilia F. de Trejos; m. Clara F. de Trejos 1936; five s.; ed. Univ. of Chicago; Prof. of Statistical Theory and Dean, Faculty of Econ., Univ. de Costa Rica 1952–56, Dean, Faculty of Sciences and Letters 1957–62, Prof. Emer. School of Statistics 1979–; Pres. of Costa Rica 1966–70; Partido Unidad Social Cristiana. *Publications:* Reflexiones sobre la Educación, 2nd edn. 1968, Ocho Años en la Política Nacional—Ideales Políticos y Realidad Nacional, Vol. I 1973, Vol. III 1973, Vol. IV 1973, Vol. II 1974, Ideas Políticas Elementales 1985. *Leisure interests:* music, history. *Address:* Apartado 10.096, San José, Costa Rica. *Telephone:* 224-2411.

TRELFORD, Donald Gilchrist, M.A., F.R.S.A.; British journalist; b. 9 Nov. 1937, Coventry; s. of T. S. Trelford; m. 1st Janice Ingram 1963; two s. one d.; m. 2nd Katherine Louise Mark 1978; one d.; ed. Bablake School, Coventry, Selwyn Coll., Cambridge; Pilot Officer, R.A.F. 1956–58; worked on newspapers in Coventry and Sheffield 1961–63; Ed. Times of Malawi and Corresp. in Africa, The Times, Observer, BBC 1963–66; joined Observer as Deputy News Ed. 1966, Asst. Man. Ed. 1968, Deputy Ed. 1969–75, Dir. and Ed. 1975–93, C.E.O. 1992–93; Dir. Optomen Television 1988–97, Observer Films 1989–93, Cen. Observer TV 1990–93; Dir., Prof. Dept. of Journalism Studies, Sheffield Univ. 1994–; Chair. Soc. of Gentlemen, Lovers of Musick 1996–; mem. British Exec. Cttee., Int. Press Inst. 1976–, Asscn. of British Eds. 1984–, Guild of British Newspaper Eds. 1985– (mem. Parl. and Legal Cttee. 1987–91); Vice Pres. British Sports Trust 1988–; Ind. Assessor BBC TV Regional News 1997; mem. Council, Media Soc. 1981–98, Judging Panel, British Press Awards 1981–, Scottish Press Awards 1985, Olivier Awards Cttee., SWET 1984–93, Defence, Press and Broadcasting Cttee. 1986–93, Cttee., MCC 1988–; Vice-Pres. Newspaper Press Fund (Chair. Appeals Cttee. 1991), Vice-Pres. 1992–; Acting Ed. The Oldie 1994; Judge, Whitbread Literary Awards 1992; Sports columnist Daily Telegraph 1993–; Dir. St. Cecilia Int. Festival of Music 1995–; Hon. D.Litt. (Sheffield), Granada Newspaper of the Year Award 1983, 1993; commended, Int. Ed. of the Year (World Press Review) 1984, Freeman City of London 1988; George Orwell Prize 1998. *Publications:* Siege 1980, Snookered 1986, Child of Change (with Garry Kasparov q.v.) 1987, Saturday's Boys 1990, Fine Glances 1990; (Contrib.) County Champions 1982, The Queen Observed 1986, Len Hutton Remembered 1992, World Chess Championships (with Daniel King) 1993, W. G. Grace 1998; (Ed.) Sunday Best 1981, 1982, 1983, The Observer at 200 1992; contrib. Animal Passions 1994. *Leisure interests:* golf, snooker. *Address:* 15 Fowler Road, London, N1 2EA, England. *Telephone:* 0171-226 9356.

TRELLES MONTES, Oscar; Peruvian politician and physician; b. 23 Aug. 1904, Lima; s. of Juan Antonio Trelles Cáceres and María Antonia Montes Cano; m. Estela Orihuela 1964; three s.; Dir. Hosp. Neurológico Santo Toribio de Mogrovejo 1944–74; Head Dept. of Neurology Univ. Cayetano Heredia 1961–74; Minister of Public Health 1945–46; Prime Minister and Minister of Interior 1963–64; Amb. to France 1964–65; Sec.-Gen. Partido Acción Popular 1965–67; Pres. of Senate 1980–81; Dir. Revista de Neuro-Psiquiatría; mem. Editorial Bd. Review of Neurological Sciences, La Revue de Neuro-Psychologie, Handbook of Clinical Neurology; Senator-Pres. Comm. Defensa Nacional y Orden Interno; Hon. Prof. Santiago (Chile) 1959; Hon. Prof. John F. Kennedy Univ. (Argentina) 1976; Hon. Prof. Sorbonne (Paris) 1977; mem. American Acad. of Neurology 1956, Acad. de Médecine (Paris) 1963; Dr. h.c. (Aix-en-Provence); numerous prizes and awards. *Publications:* about 350 books, including Les Ramollissements Protubérantiels 1935, Précis d'Anatomo-Phisiologie Normale et Pathologique du Système Nerveux Central (with F. Masquin) 1937, La Cisticercosis Cerebral (with J. Lazarte) 1941, Traumatismos craneo-encefálicos (with M. Davila) 1942, Oliva Bulbar, Estructura, Función, Patología 1944, Jean Lhermitte, Vida y Obra 1959, and articles on medicine and the Neurological Sciences. *Address:* Av. Salaverry 1971, Lince, Lima 14 and Quilca 499, Lima 1, Peru. *Telephone:* 711881 and 238564.

TREMAIN, Edwin Garrick; New Zealand landscape artist and cartoonist; b. 4 Feb. 1941, Wellington; s. of Edwin Rex Tremain and Linda Joyce Tremain; m. Jillian Mary Butland; two d.; ed. Palmerston North Boys' High School; fmrly. worked as shepherd; fmr. artist and art dir. for advertising cos. in N.Z., U.K. and elsewhere; full-time artist 1973–; syndicated cartoonist 1988–; N.Z. Commemoration Medal 1990; Cartoonist of the Year 1996. *Leisure interests:* golf, piano, Harley Davidson motorbike. *Address:* Beggars Roost, Malaghan Road, R.D.I., Otago, New Zealand. *Telephone:* (03) 4429530. *Fax:* (03) 4429459.

TREMAIN, Rose, B.A., F.R.S.L.; British writer; b. 2 Aug. 1943, London; d. of Keith Thomson and Viola Mabel Thomson; m. 1st Jon Tremain 1971; one d.; m. 2nd Jonathan Dudley 1982 (dissolved 1990); ed. Sorbonne, Paris and Univ. of East Anglia; full-time novelist/playwright 1971–; part-time lecturer Univ. of East Anglia 1984–94; Dylan Thomas Short Story Prize 1984, Giles Cooper Award 1985, Angel Literary Award 1986, Sunday Express Book of the Year Award 1989, James Tait Black Memorial Prize 1993, Prix Femina Etranger 1994. *Publications:* (novels) Sadler's Birthday 1976, Letter to Sister Benedicta 1978, The Cupboard 1981, The Swimming Pool Season 1984,

Restoration 1989, Sacred Country 1992; (short stories) The Colonel's Daughter 1982, The Garden of the Villa Mollini 1988, Evangelista's Fan 1994, The Way I Found Her 1997. *Leisure interests:* yoga, gardening. *Address:* 2 High House, South Avenue, Thorpe St. Andrew, Norwich, NR7 0EZ, England. *Telephone:* (01603) 439682. *Fax:* (01603) 434234.

TREMBLAY, Marc-Adélard, O.C., M.A., L.S.A., PH.D.; Canadian professor of social anthropology; b. 24 April 1922, Les Eboulements; s. of Wellie Tremblay and Lauretta Tremblay; m. Jacqueline Cyr 1949; one s. five d.; ed. Montreal, Laval and Cornell Univs.; research assoc., Cornell Univ. 1953–56; Asst. Prof., Dept. of Sociology and Anthropology, Laval Univ. 1956, Prof. of Social Anthropology 1963–; Founding Pres., Canadian Sociology and Anthropology Asscn. 1965–67; Pres. Canadian Ethnology Soc. 1976–77, Royal Soc. of Canada 1981–84, Asscn. of Canadian Univs. for Northern Studies 1985–87, Quebec Council for Social Research 1987–91; Dir. Groupe d'études Inuit et Circumpolaires 1990–94; mem. many other professional and scientific orgs.; Dr. h.c. (Ottawa) 1982, (Guelph) 1984, (Univ. of N. British Columbia) 1994, (Carleton) 1995, (Ste.-Anne) 1997, (McGill) 1998; Prix de la Province de Québec 1964, Innis-Gérin Medal, Royal Soc. of Canada 1979; Molson Prize, The Canada Council 1987, Marcel Vincent Prize, French Canadian Asscn. for the Advancement of Science 1988; Grand Officier Ordre Nat. du Québec 1995. *Publications:* People of Cove and Woodlot: communities from the viewpoint of social psychiatry 1960, Les comportements économiques de la famille salariée 1964, Initiation à la recherche dans les sciences humaines 1968, Famille et Parenté en Acadie 1971, Communities and culture in French Canada 1973, Patterns of Amerindian Identity 1976, L'identité québécoise en péril 1983, Conscience et Enquête 1983, L'Anthropologie à l'Université Laval: Fondements historiques, pratiques, académiques, dynamismes d'évolution 1989, Les Fondements historiques et pratiques de l'anthropologie appliquée 1990; 25 books and monographs and 200 articles. *Leisure interests:* gardening, cross-country skiing, classical music, skating. *Address:* Département d'Anthropologie, Université Laval, Cité Universitaire, Sainte Foy, Quebec (Office); 835 rue Nouvelle Orléans, Sainte-Foy, Quebec, Canada (Home). *Telephone:* (418) 653-5411 (Home). *Fax:* (418) 653-9865.

TREMBLAY, Michel; Canadian writer; b. 25 June 1942, Montreal; ed. Graphic Arts Inst. of Quebec; worked as linotypist 1963–66; won first prize for young writers sponsored by CBC for play Le Train (written 1959) 1964; plays include: Les Belles Soeurs 1968, En pièces detachées 1969, La Duchesse de Langeais 1969, Les Paons 1971, Hosanna 1973, Bonjour Là, Bonjour 1974, Ste. Carmen de la Main 1976, Damnée Manon, Sacrée Sandra 1977, l'Impromptu d'Outremont 1980, Les grandes vacances 1981, Les Anciennes Odeurs 1981, Albertine en cinq temps 1984, Le vrai monde? 1987, La Maison suspendue 1990, Marcel poursuivi par les chiens 1992; opera libretto: Nelligan, Opera de Montréal 1990; film scripts: Françoise Durocher, Waitress 1972, Il était une fois dans l'Est 1973, Parlez-nous d'amour 1976, Le Soleil se lève en retard 1977; radio plays: Le Coeur découvert 1986, Le Grand Jour 1988, Six Heures au plus tard 1988; Dr. h.c. (Concordia, McGill, Stirling, Windsor); several hon. degrees, numerous prizes and awards; Officier Ordre des Arts et des Lettres (France). *Publications:* Contes pour buveurs attardés 1966 (English trans. 1977), La Cité dans l'oeuf 1969, C't'à ton tour, Laura Cadieux 1973, La Grosse Femme d'à côté est enceinte 1973 (English trans. 1981), Thérèse et Pierrette à l'école des Saints-Anges 1980 (English trans. 1984), La Duchesse et le roturier 1982, Des Nouvelles d'Edouard 1984, Le Coeur découvert 1986 (English trans. 1988), Le Premier Quartier de la lune 1989, Les vues animées 1991, Douze coups de théâtre 1992. *Address:* c/o Agence Goodwin, 839 Sherbrooke est, Suite 2, Montreal, Quebec, H2L 1K6, Canada. *Telephone:* (514) 598-5252. *Fax:* (514) 598-1878.

TREMLETT, David Rex; British artist; b. 13 Feb. 1945, Cornwall; s. of Rex Tremlett and Dinah Tremlett; m. Laure Florence 1987; one s. two d.; ed. St. Austell Grammar School, Falmouth Art Coll. and Royal Coll. of Art; exhibited widely in U.K., U.S.A., Europe, Africa, Australia, Mexico, Japan etc.; recent projects include: walls of Law Courts, Amsterdam, Benesse Guesthouse, Naoshima Island, Japan, façade of St. Denis Univ., Paris, main hall of B.B.L. Bank Kortrijk, Belgium, walls at Eaton Hall, Chester, U.K., walls of castle of Marchese di Barolo, Barolo, Italy, lobby of Central Landesbank, Dresden, Germany, ceiling at Eaton Hall, Chester. *Publications:* Some Places to Visit 1974, On the Waterfront 1978, Scrub 1978, On the Border 1979, Restless 1983, Rough Ride 1985, Ruin 1987, Dates/Differents 1987, Sometimes We All Do 1988, Tremlett-West Bengal 1990, Written Form 1990, Internal 1991, From Wall to Wall 1991, Mjimwema Drawings 1991, A Quiet Madness 1992, P.A.C. Catalogue 1993, Abandoned Drawings 1993, Casa de Dibujos 1993, Nouveaux Plans 1994, Rooms in Vienne 1994, Walls at the Palais Jacques Coeur, Bourges 1994, Wall Drawings 1969–1995, Columns 1995, How Far in that Direction 1996, Walls and their Drawings 1997, Pages (Eritrea) 1998. *Leisure interests:* pole vaulting, African music, Saharan architecture. *Address:* Broadlawns, Chipperfield Road, Bovingdon, Herts., England. *Telephone:* (0442) 832214.

TRENGGANU, H.R.H. The Sultan of; Mahmud Al Muktafi Billah Shah, D.K.T., D.K., D.M.N., S.S.M.T., S.P.M.T.; Malaysian ruler of Trengganu State; b. 29 April 1930; s. of the late Sultan Ismail Nasiruddin Shah; m. Tengku Bariah 1951; ed. Grammar Crown English School; mil. training 1955, officer Territorial Army; Yang di-Pertuan Muda 1951, Regent of Trengganu 1954, 1965, Sultan 1979–98; numerous hon. degrees. *Leisure interest:* golf. *Address:* Istana Badariah, 20500 Kuala Trengganu, Malaysia.

TRENTHAM, David R., F.R.S., PH.D.; British medical research scientist; b. 22 Sept. 1938, Solihull; s. of John A. Trentham and Julia A. M. Trentham; m. Kamalini Bhargava 1966; two s.; ed. Uppingham School and Cambridge Univ.; Faculty mem., Biochemistry Dept., Bristol Univ. 1972–77; Chair. and Edwin M. Chance Prof., Dept. of Biochemistry and Biophysics, School of Medicine, Univ. of Pa., Philadelphia, U.S.A. 1977–83; Head, Physical Biochemistry Div., Nat. Inst. for Medical Research, London 1984–; Colworth Medal, Biochemistry Soc. 1974, Wilhelm Feldberg Prize 1990. *Publications:* numerous articles in biochemical and academic journals. *Address:* National Institute for Medical Research, The Ridgeway, Mill Hill, London, NW7 1AA, England (Office). *Telephone:* 081-959 3666.

TRETYAKOV, Viktor Viktorovich; Russian violinist; b. 17 Oct. 1946, Krasnoyarsk; ed. Moscow Conservatory (pupil of Yury Yankelevich); First Prizes, All-Union Competition of violinists 1965, Int. Tchaikovsky Competition 1966; concert career since mid-1960s, soloist of Moscow Philharmonic 1969; tours Europe, America, Japan; participant of numerous European music festivals; Artistic Dir. and Conductor Moscow (now Russian) Chamber Orchestra 1983–90; Prof., Head of Chair of Violin, Moscow Conservatory 1983–90; Prof., Hochschule für Musik, Cologne 1996–; U.S.S.R. People's Artist 1979; State Prize of Russia 1981. *Address:* Concerto Winderstein GmbH, Leopoldstr. 25, D-80802 Munich, Germany; Columbia Artists Management, 165 West 57th Street, New York, N.Y. 10019, U.S.A. *Telephone:* (89) 349050 (Munich); (095) 291-45-51 (Moscow). *Fax:* (89) 337938.

TREVINO, Lee Buck; American golfer; b. 1 Dec. 1939, Dallas, Tex.; s. of Joe Trevino and Juanita Barrett; m. Claudia Bove 1983; three s. three d.; professional 1961–; U.S. Open Champion 1968, 1971; British Open Champion 1971, 1972; Canadian Open Champion 1971 and numerous other championships 1965–80; U.S. P.G.A. Champion 1974, 1984; has won over $3m. in prize money in U.S.A.; Champion U.S. Sr. Open 1990, P.G.A. Sr. Championship 1994; Chair. Bd. Lee Trevino Enterprises, Inc. 1967–; U.S. P.G.A. Player of the Year 1971, sr. Tour Player of the Year 1990, 1992, 1994. *Publication:* Super Mex (autobiog.) 1983. *Address:* Lee Trevino Enterprises, 5757 Alpha Road, Suite 620, Dallas, TX 75240, U.S.A.

TREVOR, William, C.B.E., C.LIT.; Irish author; b. 24 May 1928, Co. Cork; s. of James William Cox and Gertrude Cox; m. Jane Ryan 1952; two s.; ed. St. Columba's, Dublin, Trinity Coll., Dublin; Hawthornden Prize 1965, Royal Soc. of Literature Prize 1978, Whitbread Prize for Fiction 1978, Allied Irish Banks Award for Services to Literature 1978, Whitbread Prize 1983, 1994; Sunday Express Book of the Year Award 1994; Hon. D.Litt. (Exeter) 1984, (Dublin) 1986, (Queen's Univ., Belfast) 1989, (Nat. Univ. Cork) 1990. *Publications:* The Old Boys 1964, The Boarding House 1965, The Love Department 1966, The Day We Got Drunk on Cake 1967, Mrs Eckdorf in O'Neill's Hotel 1968, Miss Gomez and the Brethren 1969, The Ballroom of Romance 1970, Elizabeth Alone 1972, Angels at the Ritz 1973, The Children of Dynmouth 1977, Lovers of Their Time 1979, Other People's Worlds 1980, Beyond the Pale 1981, Fools of Fortune 1983, A Writer's Ireland: Landscape in Literature 1984, The News from Ireland 1986, Nights at the Alexandra 1987, The Silence in the Garden 1988, Family Sins and Other Stories 1989, The Oxford Book of Irish Short Stories (ed.) 1989, Two Lives 1991, William Trevor: The Collected Stories 1992, Juliet's Story 1992, Excursions in the Real World (essays) 1993, Felicia's Journey 1994, Ireland: Selected Stones 1995, After Rain 1996, Cocktails at Doney's and Other Stories 1996, Death in Summer 1998. *Address:* c/o A. D. Peters, 5th Floor, The Chambers, Chelsea Harbour, London, SW10 0XF, England.

TREVOR-ROPER, Hugh Redwald (see Dacre of Glanton).

TRIANTAFYLLIDES, Michalakis Antoniou; Cypriot judge; b. 12 May 1927, Nicosia; m.; two c.; ed. Gray's Inn, London; practised as a lawyer in Cyprus 1948–60, serving for three years as Sec. of Human Rights Cttee. of Bar; mem. Greek Cypriot del. to Joint Constitutional Comm. which drafted Cyprus Constitution 1959–60; Greek Cypriot Judge, Supreme Constitutional Court 1960–64, Judge 1964–71, Pres. Supreme Court 1971–88; Attorney Gen. 1988–94. *Address:* c/o Office of the Attorney General, Supreme Court, Char. Mouskos Street, Nicosia, Cyprus.

TRIBE, Laurence Henry, J.D.; American professor of law; b. 10 Oct. 1941, Shanghai, China; s. of George I. Tribe and Paulina Diatlovitsky; m. Carolyn R. Kreye 1965; one s. one d.; ed. Harvard Univ.; admitted Calif. Bar 1966, U.S. Supreme Court Bar 1966; law clerk, Calif. Supreme Court 1966–67, U.S. Supreme Court 1967–68; Exec. Dir. Tech. Assessment Panel, N.A.S. 1968–69; Asst. Prof. of Law, Harvard Univ. 1969–72, Prof. 1972–82, Ralph S. Tyler Jr. Prof. of Constitutional Law 1982; Adviser to Hoylake Investments Ltd. Aug. 1989–; Chair. Marshall Islands Judicial Service Comm. 1979–80; Chief Appellate Counsel, Calif. Nuclear Litigation 1978–83; Special Deputy Attorney-Gen. Hawaii 1983–84; various consultancies; Fellow, American Acad. of Arts and Sciences; mem. A.B.A.; Triennial Coif Award 1978–80, Scribe Award 1980, etc.; Hon. LL.D. (Gonzaga) 1980, (Pacific) 1987. *Publications:* American Constitutional law 1978, Constitutional Choice 1985, God Save this Honorable Court 1985, Abortion: The Clash of Absolutes 1990; articles in professional journals. *Address:* c/o Harvard Law School, Cambridge, MA 02138, U.S.A.

TRIBOULET, Raymond, L. EN DR., L. ÈS L.; French politician; b. 3 Oct. 1906, Paris; s. of Maurice Triboulet and Josèphe Wagner; m. Luce Chauveau 1928 (died 1995); three s. (one deceased) three d.; ed. Univ. of Paris; active in French Resistance 1941–44; Sous-Préfet for Bayeux region 1944–46; Regional Insp. for Rhine-Palatinate 1946; M.P. 1946–; founder of European Federalist group in French Parl.; Pres. of Gaullist Parl. Group (Social Republicans) 1954–58; Minister of War Veterans Jan.-Oct. 1955; mem. ECSC Common Ass. 1957; Pres. Union of New Republic (UNR) Parl. Group 1958; Minister of War Veterans 1959–63, of Co-operation 1963–66; re-elected Deputy 1958, 1962, 1967 and 1968; mem. European Parl. 1967–73; Pres. UDE group 1968–73; Pres. and founder D-Day Commemoration Cttee.; mem. Inst. (Acad. des Sciences morales et politiques) 1979; Grand Officier Légion d'honneur, Croix de guerre; Médaille de la Résistance; Hon. C.B.E., and other decorations. *Publications:* Les Billets du Négus 1939, Sens dessus dessous 1951, Des Vessies pour des Lanternes 1958, Halte au Massacre 1966, Correspondance de Gaston de Renty (1611–1649) 1978, A tous ceux qui sont mal dans leur peau 1980, Un gaulliste de la IVe 1985, Un Ministre du général 1986, Vie de Gaston de Renty, homme de ce monde et homme de Dieu 1992, Tous comptes faits 1998. *Address:* 119 rue Brancas, 92310 Sèvres, France. *Fax:* (1) 45 07 11 39.

TRICART, Jean Léon François; French university professor; b. 16 Sept. 1920, Montmorency; s. of François Tricart and Lea Cordonnier; m. Denise Casimir 1944; four s.; ed. Lycée Rollin, Paris, and Univ. de Paris à la Sorbonne; Asst. Lecturer, Univ. de Paris 1945–48; Lecturer Univ. of Strasbourg 1948–49, Asst. Prof. 1949–55, Prof. 1955–88, Emer. Prof. 1988–; Vice-Dean, mem. of Univ. Senate 1967–70; Prin. Asst., Geological Map of France 1960; Founder-Dir. Centre of Applied Geography, Strasbourg 1956–; Pres. Applied Geomorphology Comm. of Int. Geographical Union 1960–68; Head of numerous tech. co-operation missions in Senegal, Mauritania, Ivory Coast, Guinea, Togo, Mali, Argentina, Brazil, Chile, Venezuela, Peru, Panama, El Salvador, Colombia, Uruguay, Mexico; FAO, UNDP, WMO and UNESCO Sr. Consultant 1968; scientific assessor of Inst. de Recherche Agronomique Tropicale; Expert, Int. Hydrological Programme, UNESCO; Chair. French Nat. Cttee. of INQUA 1976–79; Chair. Comm. of Arid and Subarid Regions, CNFG 1989–94; Corresp. mem. Colombian Acad. of Science 1986–, GAEA 1991–; Dr. h.c. (Łódź, Poland, Bahia, Brazil, Los Andes, Venezuela); Busk Medal (Royal Geographical Soc.) 1985; medals and prizes in Argentina, Belgium, France, Germany, Hungary, Italy, Netherlands; Chevalier, Légion d'honneur 1992. *Publications include:* numerous scientific articles and Principes et méthodes de la Géomorphologie 1965, Traité de Géomorphologie (with A. Cailleux), 5 vols., La terre, Planète vivante, Ecogeography and Rural Management (with Kiewiet de Jonge), Ecogéographie des espaces ruraux. *Leisure interest:* philately. *Address:* Centre de Géographie Appliquée, Université Louis-Pasteur, Strasbourg, 3 rue de l'Argonne, 67083 Strasbourg-CEDEX; 85 route de la Meinau, 67100 Strasbourg-Meinau, France. *Telephone:* (3) 88.35.82.59 (Office); (3) 8839-09-86 (Home).

TRICHET, Jean-Claude, L. ÈS SC. ECON.; French banker; b. 20 Dec. 1942, Lyon; s. of Jean Trichet and Georgette Vincent-Carrefour; m. Aline Rybalka 1965; two s.; ed. Ecole des Mines, Nancy, Inst. d'Etudes Politiques, Paris and Ecole Nat. d'Admin.; Insp. of Finances 1971–76; Sec.-Gen. Business Restructuring Interministerial Cttee. 1976–78; Adviser, Ministry of Economy 1978; Counsellor to Pres. of Repub. 1978–81; Deputy Asst. Sec. and Asst. Sec. of Treasury 1981–86; Chief of Staff to Minister of Finance 1986–87; Under-Sec. of Treas. 1987–93; Gov. Bank of France 1993–; Pres. Paris Club 1985–93; mem. Bd. of Dirs. BIS 1993–, EMI 1994–98; a Gov. IBRD 1993–95; Vice-Gov. IMF 1995; Chair. Monetary Cttee. of EC 1992–93; Dir. Cen. European Bank 1998–; mem. Bd. Dirs. BNP; Censor, Banque de France; Chevalier, Légion d'honneur; decorations from Austria, Argentina, Brazil, Ecuador, Yugoslavia. *Publications:* various articles on finance and economy. *Leisure interest:* poetry. *Address:* Banque de France, 39 rue Croix des Petits Champs, 75001 Paris (Office); 5 rue de Beaujolais, 75001 Paris, France.

TRIER, Peter Eugene, C.B.E., M.A., M.SC., F.ENG., F.I.E.E., F.INST.P., F.I.M.A.; British research director and consultant; b. 12 Sept. 1919, Darmstadt, Germany; s. of Ernst J. Trier and Nellie M. (née Bender) Trier; m. Margaret N. Holloway 1946 (died 1998); three s.; ed. Mill Hill School, London and Trinity Hall, Cambridge; Royal Naval Scientific Service 1941–50; Mullard Research Labs. (now Philips Research Labs.), Redhill 1950–69, Dir. 1953–69; Dir. of Research and Devt. Philips Electronics 1969–81, mem. Bd. 1969–85; Chair. of Council, Brunel Univ. 1973–79, Pro-Chancellor 1980–; Chair. Electronics Research Council 1976–80, Defence Scientific Advisory Council 1981–85; Pres. Inst. of Math. and its Applications (IMA) 1982, 1983; mem. Man. Cttee. The Wine Soc. 1977–92; Hon.D.Tech. (Brunel) 1975; Glazebrook Prize and Medal, Inst. of Physics 1984. *Publications:* Strategic Implications of Micro-Electronics 1982, Mathematics & Information 1983; papers in scientific and technical journals. *Leisure interests:* travel, mathematics, railway history, Trier family history. *Address:* Yew Tree House, Bredon, Tewkesbury, Glos., GL20 7HF, England. *Telephone:* (01684) 772200.

TRIGANO, Gilbert; French business executive; b. 28 July 1920, St. Maurice, Val-de-Marne; s. of Raymond Trigano and Félicie Bensaïd; m. Simone Sabah 1945; one s. three d.; Man. Dir. Soc. des villages de vacances 1959, en Guadeloupe 1973; Man. Dir. Club Méditerranée 1963, Pres. Minerve (affiliated to Club Méditerranée) 1991; Man. Dir. Bureau Suisse S.A., Culip S.A., Spain; mem. supervisory Bd. holding co. 1969; Admin. Tourisme France Int. 1973; Pres. Soc. Island-Properties, Man. Dir. Soc. nouvelle Victoria, Switzerland; Dir. Cie. int. des wagons-lits 1984, mem. Conseil économique et social 1983–; Deputy to Prime Minister, in charge of training 1985–86; Dir. Banque Verne et Commerciales de Paris 1988, Crédit Lyonnais 1989; Pres. Minerve (affil. to Club Médi-terranée) 1991, Maison de la France 1992–; Officier, Légion d'honneur, Officier, ordre nat. du Mérite. *Address:* Club Méditerranée, 25 rue Vilvienne, 75002 Paris, France.

TRIGONA, Alex Sceberras, LL.D., M.A., M.P.; Maltese politician; b. 3 March 1950; s. of Alexander and Connie Trigona; m. Joanna Borg 1985; ed. St. Joseph's High School, the Lyceum, Univs. of Malta and Oxford; Pres. Univ. Students' Rep. Council 1971–72; Lecturer in Int. Politics and Econ., Univ. of Malta; Int. Sec. of Ghaqda Zghazagh Socjalisti (Young Socialists Org.) 1976–79, Malta Labour Party 1977–82; Counsellor American Univ. Cairo 1978–79; Dir. Bank of Valletta 1978–81; Ed. magazine Il-Hsieb 1978, Dir. Mediterranean Conf. Centre 1980–81, Minister of Foreign Affairs and Culture 1981–87; Labour; founder and Hon. Pres. Tigne' Sports Asscn. *Address:* c/o Ministry of Foreign Affairs, Palazzo Parisio, Valletta; 43 Paola Road, Tarxien, Malta.

TRIMBLE, Rt. Hon. David, P.C., LL.B.; British politician, barrister and university lecturer; b. 15 Oct. 1944, Belfast; s. of the late William Trimble and of Ivy Jack; m. Daphne Orr 1978; two s. two d.; ed. Bangor Grammar School and Queen's Univ. Belfast; mem. N. Ireland Constitutional Convention 1975–76; mem. Parl. for Upper Bann 1990–; Leader Ulster Unionist Party 1995–; First Minister, Northern Ireland Ass. 1998–; shared Nobel Peace Prize 1998. *Address:* 2 Queen Street, Lurgan, Co. Armagh, BT66 8BQ, Northern Ireland. *Telephone:* (01762) 328088. *Fax:* (01762) 322343.

TRINH, Xuan Lang, B.A.; Vietnamese diplomatist; b. 4 Sept. 1927, Hanoi; m.; three c.; took part in Viet Nam's independence movt. 1945–54; joined Ministry of Foreign Affairs 1955, Consul-Gen., Rangoon 1960–64, Counsellor of Embassy in New Delhi 1969–73; Amb. to Indonesia 1981–84; Dir. Press and Information Dept. and spokesman for Ministry of Foreign Affairs 1984–88; Perm. Rep. to the UN 1988–93. *Address:* c/o Ministry of Foreign Affairs, Hanoi, Viet Nam.

TRINTIGNANT, Jean-Louis (Xavier); French actor; b. 11 Dec. 1930, Piolenc (Vaucluse); s. of Raoul Trintignant and Claire Tourtin; m. 1st Colette Dacheville (the actress Stéphane Audran, q.v.) 1954 (divorced); m. 2nd Nadine Marquand 1961; one s. two d. (one deceased); ed. Faculté de Droit, Aix-en-Provence; theatre début 1951; film roles 1955–; Prix d'interprétation de l'Acad. du Cinéma (for Mata Hari, Agent H21) 1965; Prize, Cannes Festival (for Z) 1969; Prix David de Donatello, Taormina Festival 1972; Officier des Arts et des Lettres. *Plays include:* Macbeth, Jacques ou la Soumission (Ionesco), Hamlet, Bonheur, impaire et passe (Sagan), Deux sur la balançoire, etc. *Films include:* Et Dieu créa la femme 1956, Club de femmes 1956, Les liaisons dangereuses 1959, L'été violent 1959, Austerlitz 1959, La millième fenêtre 1959, Pleins feux sur l'assassin 1960, Coeur battant 1960, Le jeu de la vérité 1961, Horace 62 1961, Les sept péchés capitaux 1961, Il sorpasso 1962, Il successo 1962, Chateau en Suède 1963, La bonne occase 1964, Mata Hari, Agent H21 1964, Angélique marquise des anges 1964, Meurtre à l'italienne 1965, La longue marche 1965, Le 17e ciel 1965, Paris brûle-t-il? 1965, Un homme et une femme 1966, Safari diamants 1966, Trans-Europ-Express 1966, Mon amour, mon amour 1967, L'homme qui ment 1967, Les biches 1968, Le voleur de crimes 1968, Z 1969, Ma nuit chez Maud 1969, Disons un soir à diner 1969, L'Américain 1969, La mort a pondu un oeuf 1969, Le conformiste 1970, Si douces, si perverses 1970, Le grand silence 1971, Une journée bien remplie (author and dir.) 1973, Le train 1973, Les violins du bal 1973, Le mouton enragé 1974, Le secret 1974, Le jeu avec le feu 1975, Shattering 1977, Le désert des Tartares 1977, The French Way 1978, L'argent des autres 1978, Le maitre nageur 1979 (also Dir.), La terrasse 1980, Je vous aime 1980, La femme d'à côté 1981, Un assassin qui passe 1981, Malevil 1981, Passion d'amour 1981, Une affaire d'hommes 1981, Eaux profondes 1981, Le grand-pardon 1982, Boulevard des assassins 1982, Le bon plaisir 1983, Vivement dimanche! 1983, La crime 1983, Le bon plaisir, Femmes de personne 1984, Under Fire, Viva la vie 1984, L'été prochain, Partir, revenir 1985, Rendez-vous, David, Thomas et les autres 1985, L'homme aux yeux d'argent 1985, Un homme et une femme: vingt ans déja 1986, La femme de ma vie 1986, La vallée fantôme 1987, Le Moustachu 1987, Bunker Palace Hotel 1989, Merci la vie 1991, L'Instinct de l'ange 1993, Rouge 1994, Regarde les hommes tomber 1994, Fiesta 1995, C'est jamais loin 1996, Ceux qui m'aiment prendrout le train 1998. *Address:* c/o Artmédia, 10 avenue George V, 75008 Paris; 30 rue des Francs-Bourgeois, 75003 Paris, France (Home).

TRITTIN, Jürgen; German politician; b. 25 June 1954, Bremen; one d.; worked as journalist 1973; business man. Alternative-Greens-Initiative List (AGIL) group Göttingen City Council 1982–84; press spokesman for Green Party group Lower Saxony Landtag 1984–85, Chair. 1985–86, 1988–90, Deputy Chair. Alliance '90/Greens group 1994–95, spokesman Fed. Exec. 1994–98; mem. Lower Saxony Landtag 1985–90, 1994–95, Lower Saxony Minister for Fed. and European Affairs 1990–94, also head state mission to fed. insts. in Bonn; mem. Bundestag 1998–; Fed. Minister for the Environment, Nature Conservation and Reactor Safety 1998–. *Address:* Ministry of the Environment, Kennedyallee 5, 53175 Bonn (Office); Baunscheidstrasse 1A, 53113 Bonn, Germany (Home). *Telephone:* (228) 6150 (Office); (228) 916-61-36 (Home). *Fax:* (228) 615-44-36 (Office); (228) 916-62-35 (Home).

TRIVEDI, Ram Krishna, M.A.; Indian state governor (retd.); b. 1 Jan. 1921, Myingyan, Burma (now Myanmar); s. of Pandit Mahavir Trivedi and Rama Trivedi; m. Krishna Trivedi 1944 (deceased); four s. one d.; joined civil service 1943; Dist. Magistrate, Tehri Garhwal, Faizabad, Allahabad and Kanpur; Vice-Prin., IAS Training School, Delhi 1957–58, Acting Prin. 1958–59, Deputy Dir. Nat. Acad. of Admin. 1959–62; Sec. Medical and Health Dept. Govt. of Uttar Pradesh 1968–70; Commr. and Sec. Dept. of Finance 1968–71; Commr. Allahabad 1970–71; Chair. U.P. State Electricity Bd. 1972–73; Sec. Dept. of Civil Supplies and Cooperation 1974–75; Dept. of Personnel & Admin. Reforms, Govt. of India 1975–77; Chair. and Man. Dir. STC 1978; Vice-Chancellor, Bundelkhand Univ. 1979; Adviser to Gov. of Madhya Pradesh; Chair. British India Corpn. Kanpur 1980; Central Vigilance Commr. Govt. of India 1980–82; Chief Election Commr. of India 1982–85; Gov. of Gujarat 1986–90; Vice-Pres. Exec. Council, Indian Inst. of Public Admin.; mem. Gov. Body, Asian Centre for Devt. Admin. Kuala Lumpur; Pres. Ramkrishna Mission, Lucknow; Hon. D.Litt. (Lucknow); Hon. LL.D. (Bundelkhand); Padma Bhushan. *Publication:* The Greening of Gujarat. *Leisure interests:* yoga, serious reading, philately, photography. *Address:* Anand Niwas, B-7, Niralanagar, Lucknow, U.P., 226020, India. *Telephone:* 370515.

TROCCOLI, Antonio Américo, DR.; Argentinian politician and lawyer; b. 21 Feb. 1925, Tres Arroyos; m. Dolores Cecilia Bustos; ed. Nat. Univ. of La Plata; mem. Chamber of Deputies 1963–66, and in 1972; Minister of the Interior 1983–87. *Address:* c/o Ministerio del Interior, Balcarce 24 C.P. 1004, Buenos Aires, Argentina.

TROFIMUK, Andrey Alekseyevich; Russian petroleum geologist; b. 16 Aug. 1911, Khvetkovichi, Byelorussia; s. of Aleksey Ustinovich Trofimuk and Yelizaveta Onisimovna; m. Amina Taufikovna 1931; three s. one d.; ed. State Univ. of Kazan; Head Geologist and Scientific Leader of Central Research Lab. of the "Vostokneft" Trust 1934–40; Chief Geologist "Ishimbaineft" Trust 1940–42, "Bashneft" Soc. 1942–50; Chief Geologist, Main Oil and Gas Exploration Dept., Ministry of Oil Industry of U.S.S.R. 1950–53; Deputy Dir. All-Union Oil and Gas Scientific Research Inst. 1953–55, Dir. 1955–58; Dir. Inst. of Geology and Geophysics, Siberian Branch, U.S.S.R. (now Russian) Acad. of Sciences 1958–88, Hon. Dir. 1988–; Deputy to U.S.S.R. Supreme Soviet 1962–74, Deputy to R.S.F.S.R. Supreme Soviet 1980–85; mem. U.S.S.R. (now Russian) Acad. of Sciences 1958–; mem. Presidium U.S.S.R. (now Russian) Acad. of Sciences 1963–88, Adviser to Presidium 1988–; First Vice-Chair. Siberian Branch; Ed. Geology and Geophysics; Hero of Socialist Labour 1944, State Prizes 1946, 1950. *Publications:* On the Nature of Ishimbaevo Oil-Bearing Limestone Massifs 1936, An Outline of Tectonics and Oil Content of Volga-Ural Region 1939, Oil Content of Paleozoic Beds of Bashkiria 1950, Conditions of Formation of Oil Deposits of Ural-Volga Oil-Bearing Region 1955, Gas Resources of the U.S.S.R. 1959, Oil and Gas Content of Siberian Platform 1960, Gas-Bearing Prospects of the U.S.S.R. 1963, Geology and Oil and Gas Content of West Siberian Lowland, a New Oil-Bearing Province of the U.S.S.R. 1960, Oil- and Gas-Bearing Basins of the U.S.S.R. 1964, Tectonics and Oil and Gas-Bearing prospects of Platform Regions of Siberia (with Yu. A. Kosygin) 1965, Some Questions on the Theory of Organic Origin of Oil and the problem of Diagnostics of Oil-Source Beds (with A. E. Kontorovich) 1965, On the Methods of Calculation of Prognostic Reserves of Oil 1966, Geology of Oil and Gas of Western Siberia (co-author) 1975, Oil and Gas Geology of Siberian Platform 1981, The Ways of Gas Hydrate Deposits Exploration 1982 (co-author), Nature Factor of Fossil Organic Matter Transformation (co-author) 1982, Nepsko-Botubinskaya arch, 1986. *Leisure interests:* fishing, hunting. *Address:* c/o Institute of Geology and Geophysics, Universitetski prosp. 3, 630090 Novosibirsk 90, Russia. *Telephone:* (3832) 35-46-50 (Office); 35-06-21 (Home).

TROISGROS, Pierre Emile René; French hotelier and restaurateur; b. 3 Sept. 1928, Châlon-sur-Saône; s. of Jean-Baptiste Troisgros and Marie Badaut; m. Olympe Forte 1955; two s. one d.; ed. Lycée Bourgneuf, Roanne; worked Roanne-Etretat 1944–45, Armenonville, Paris 1946, St Jean de Luz 1947; mil. service, Tunisia 1948; at Lucas Carton, Paris 1950–52, Point, Vienne 1954, then Maxim's and Retour à Roanne; now Man. Dir. Restaurant Troisgros, Roanne; Ordre du Mérite Nat. 1969; Officier des Arts et des Lettres 1985; Chevalier, Légion d'honneur 1987. *Publications:* Cuisiniers à Roanne (with Jean Troisgros) 1977, Toc et Toque 1983, Les Petits Plats des Troisgros (with Michel Troisgros) 1985, Cuisine de famille chez les Troisgros (jtly.) 1998. *Leisure interests:* tennis, basketball. *Address:* Place Jean Troisgros, 42300 Roanne; 20 route de Commelle, 42120 Le Coteau, France. *Telephone:* 77.71.66.97.

TROITSKAYA, Natalia Leonidovna; Russian soprano singer; b. 18 May 1956, Moscow; ed. Gnesins Music Inst.; left U.S.S.R. 1980, winner of int. competitions in Toulouse, Vercelli, Barcelona; debut as opera singer in Theatro Liseo, Barcelona with José Carreras 1981; performs as guest singer La Scala, Covent Garden, Deutsche Oper Berlin, Wiener Staatsoper, Colón Buenos Aires, Rome Opera; participated in numerous music festivals including Arena di Verona; debut in Moscow as Adrienna Lecouvrer with La Scala 1989; roles include Lisa (Queen of Spades), Violetta (La Traviata), Aida, Maddalena (Andre Chenier), Leonora (Il Trovatore), Elisabeth (Don Carlos), Desdemona (Othello), Amelia (Un Ballo in Maschera), Mavra (Mavra), Yaroslavna (Prince Igor); f. fund for promotion of young singers, Moscow 1994; Gold Rose Prize of Critics (Germany).

TROLLOPE, Joanna, O.B.E., M.A.; British author; b. 9 Dec. 1943; d. of Arthur Trollope and Rosemary Hodson; m. 1st David Potter 1966; two d.; m. 2nd Ian Curteis 1985; two step-s.; ed. Reigate Co. School and St. Hugh's Coll. Oxford; Information and Research Dept. Foreign Office 1965–67; various teaching posts 1967–79; Chair. Advisory Cttee. on Nat. Reading Initiative, Dept. of Nat. Heritage 1996; mem. Advisory Cttee. on Nat. Year of Reading, Dept. of Educ. 1998; Vice-Pres. Trollope Soc.; Trustee Joanna Trollope Charitable Trust 1995–; Patron County of Glos. Community Foundation 1994–. *Publications:* Eliza Stanhope 1978, Parson Harding's Daughter 1979, Leaves from the Valley 1980, The City of Gems 1981, The Steps of the Sun 1983, Britannia's Daughters: A Study of Women in the British Empire 1983, The Taverners' Place 1986, The Choir 1988, A Village Affair 1989, A Passionate Man 1990, The Rector's Wife 1991, The Men and the Girls 1992, A Spanish Lover 1993, The Country Habit 1993, The Best of Friends 1995, Next of Kin 1996, Faith 1996, Other People's Children 1998; as Caroline Harvey: Legacy of Love 1992, A Second Legacy 1993, A Castle in Italy 1993, The Brass Dolphin 1997; contribs. to newspapers and magazines. *Leisure interests:* reading, conversation, very long baths. *Address:* c/o Peters Fraser and Dunlop, 503/4 The Chambers, Chelsea Harbour, London SW10 0XF, England.

TRONCHETTI PROVERA, Marco; Italian business executive; b. 1948, Milan; three c.; ed. Bocconi Univ., Milan; worked in family maritime transport business 1973–86; joined Pirelli Group as Partner, Pirelli & C. 1986, Man. Dir. and Gen. Man. Soc. Int. Pirelli S.A., Basle 1988–92, Man. Dir. and Gen. Man. (Finance and Admin. and Gen. Affairs) Pirelli S.p.A. 1991–92, Exec. Deputy Chair. and Man. Dir. Pirelli S.p.A. 1992–96, Deputy Chair. Pirelli & Co. 1995–, Chair. and C.E.O. Pirelli S.p.A. 1996–; Chair. Bd. and Exec. Cttee. CAMFIN S.p.A., Milan; Chair. Bd. Editrice Il Sole 24 Ore; mem. Exec. Council and Bd. Confindustria (nat. employers' org.); mem. Bd. Mediobanca, HPI, RAS, Università Commerciale Luigi Bocconi; mem. European Round Table of Industrialists; Italian Chair. Council for U.S. and Italy; mem. Italian Group of Trilateral Comm. *Address:* Pirelli S.p.A., Viale Sarca 222, 20126, Milan, Italy. *Telephone:* (02) 6442.2650. *Fax:* (02) 6442.3733.

TROST, Barry Martin, PH.D.; American professor of chemistry; b. 13 June 1941, Philadelphia, Pa.; s. of Joseph and Esther Trost; m. Susan Paula Shapiro 1967; two s.; ed. Univ. of Pennsylvania and M.I.T.; Asst. Prof. of Chem., Dept. of Chem., Univ. of Wis. 1965–68, Assoc. Prof. 1968–69, Prof. 1969–76, Helfaer Prof. 1976–82, Vilas Prof. 1982–87; Prof. of Chemistry, Stanford Univ. 1987–, Tamaki Prof. of Humanities and Sciences 1990–; Consultant E.I. du Pont de Nemours and Merck, Sharp & Dohme; mem. ARCO Science Bd.; mem. Cttee. on Chemical Sciences, N.A.S. 1980–83; mem. and Chair. NIH Medicinal Chem. Study Section 1982–; Commr., Nat. Research Council Comm. on Eng. and Tech. Systems; Ed.-in-Chief Comprehensive Organic Synthesis (Vols. 1–9) 1991, Chair. 1996–; Ed. Chemical Tracts/Organic Chem.; mem. N.A.S., American Chemical Soc., A.A.A.S.; Dr. h.c. (Univ. Claude Bernard, Lyon); A.C.S. Award in Pure Chem. 1977, for Creative Work in Synthetic Organic Chem. 1981, Backland Award 1981, Chemical Pioneer Award of A.I.C. 1983, Alexander von Humboldt Award (Fed. Repub. of Germany) 1984, Cope Scholar Award of A.C.S. 1989, Guenther Award of A.C.S. 1990, Dr. Paul Janssen Prize for Creativity in Organic Synthesis 1990, Merit Award (N.I.H.) 1988, Roger Adams Award 1995. *Publications:* Problems in Spectroscopy 1967, Sulfur Ylides 1974, Organic Synthesis Today and Tomorrow (Ed.) 1981, Selectivity: a Goal for Synthetic Efficiency (Ed.) 1984; more than 510 scientific articles in leading chemical journals. *Address:* Department of Chemistry, Stanford University, Stanford, CA 94305, U.S.A. *Telephone:* (415) 723-3385.

TROTMAN, Baron (Life Peer) cr. 1999, of Osmotherley in the County of North Yorkshire; **Alexander Trotman,** Kt., M.B.A.; American business executive; b. 22 July 1933, Middx.; m.; ed. Mich. State Univ.; joined Ford Motor Co. 1955, car planner, Chief Product Analyst 1960s, Dir. Sales and Marketing Planning 1971–72, Exec. Dir. Product Planning Research 1972–75, Corp. Vice-Pres. 1979, Pres. Ford Asia-Pacific 1983–84, Pres. Chair. Ford Europe 1984, Head World-Wide Auto Operations 1992–93, Pres., Chair., C.E.O. 1993–99; Dir. ICI 1997–; Dr. h.c. (Edin.) 1998. *Address:* c/o Ford Motor Co., The American Road, Dearborn, MI 48121, U.S.A.

TROTMAN-DICKENSON, Sir Aubrey Fiennes, Kt., D.SC.; British university vice-chancellor and principal (retd.); b. 12 Feb. 1926, Wilmslow, Cheshire; s. of late Edward Trotman-Dickenson and Violet Murray (née Nicoll); m. Danusia Hewell 1953; two s. one d.; ed. Winchester Coll., Balliol Coll. Oxford and Univs. of Manchester and Edinburgh; Fellow, Nat. Research Council, Ottawa, Ont. 1948–50; Asst. lecturer, ICI Fellow, Univ. of Manchester 1950–53; E.I. Du Pont de Nemours, Wilmington, U.S.A. 1953–54; lecturer, Univ. of Edin. 1954–60; Prof. of Chem. Univ. Coll. of Wales, Aberystwyth 1960–68; Prin. Univ. of Wales Inst. of Science and Tech. 1968–88, Univ. Coll. Cardiff 1987–88, Univ. of Wales Coll. of Cardiff 1988–93; Vice-Chancellor, Univ. of Wales 1975–77, 1983–85, 1991–93; Tilden Lecturer 1963; Hon. LL.D. (Wales). *Publications:* Gas Kinetics 1955, Free Radicals 1959, Tables of Biomolecular Gas Reactions 1967, Comprehensive Inorganic Chemistry (ed. 1973); 150 contribs. to learned journals. *Address:* Siston Court, Bristol, BS16 9LU, England. *Telephone:* (0117) 937 2109.

TROVOADA, Miguel dos Anjos da Cunha Lisboa; São Tomé e Príncipe politician; fmrly. in charge of foreign relations for the São Tomé and Príncipe Liberation Movement (MLSTP), fmr. mem. Political Bureau; Prime Minister of São Tomé and Príncipe 1975–78, also Minister of Defence and Foreign

Affairs July-Dec. 1975, of Econ. Co-ordination, Co-operation and Tourism 1975–78, of Trade, Industry and Fisheries 1978–79; arrested and imprisoned 1979, released 1981, then in exile in Lisbon; Pres. and C.-in-C. of the Armed Forces of São Tomé and Príncipe 1991–95 (deposed in coup 15 Aug. 1995), reinstalled Aug. 1995–. *Address:* Office of the President, São Tomé, São Tomé and Príncipe.

TROWBRIDGE, Alexander Buel Jr.; American business executive; b. 12 Dec. 1929, Englewood, N.J.; s. of Alexander Buel Trowbridge and Julie Chamberlain; m. 1st Nancey Horst 1955; two s. one d.; m. 2nd Eleanor Hutzler 1981; ed. Phillips Acad., Andover, Mass., and Princeton Univ.; U.S. Marine Corps during Korean War; with overseas operations of several petroleum cos. in Cuba, El Salvador, Panama and Philippines; Pres. and Div. Man. Esso Standard Oil Co. of Puerto Rico 1963–65; Asst. Sec. of Commerce for Domestic and Int. Business 1965–67; Acting Sec. of Commerce Feb.-May 1967, Sec. of Commerce 1967–68; Pres. American Man. Asscn. 1968–70, Conf. Bd. Inc. 1970–76; Dir. Allied Chemical Corpn., then Vice-Chair. of Bd. 1976–79; mem. Bd. Dirs. Nat. Asscn. of Mfrs. 1978–, Pres. 1980–89; Dir. New England Life Insurance Co., The Rouse Co., Waste Management Inc., The Sun Co., The Gillette Co., Harris Corpn., ICOS Corpn., Warburg Pincus Counsellors Funds, Sun Resorts Int., S.A.; I.R.I. Int. Corpn.; Charter Trustee Phillips Acad., Andover, Mass.; mem. Competitiveness Policy Council, Washington, D.C., Council on Foreign Relations. *Leisure interests:* tennis, skiing. *Address:* 1317 F Street, NW, Suite 500, Washington DC 20004; 1823 23rd Street, NW, Washington DC 20008 (Office); 1823 23rd Street, N.W., Washington, DC 20008, U.S.A. (Home).

TROYANOVSKY, Oleg Aleksandrovich; Russian diplomatist (retd.); b. 24 Nov. 1919, Moscow; s. of Aleksandr Troyanovsky and Nina Troyanovskaya; m. Tatyana Troyanovskaya 1953; one d.; ed. Moscow Foreign Languages Inst., Moscow Inst. of Philosophy, Literature and History; Diplomatic service 1944; mem. CPSU 1947–91; took part in many important confs.; Amb. to Japan 1968–76, to People's Repub. of China 1986–90; Perm. Rep. to UN 1977–86; Counsellor, Ministry of Foreign Relations 1990–92; mem. CPSU Cen. Auditing Comm. 1981–86; cand. mem. CPSU Cen. Cttee. 1986–90; Lenin Prize 1960. *Publications:* Across the Years and Distances (memoirs) 1997; numerous articles. *Leisure interests:* tennis, chess. *Address:* 3d Frunsenskaya str. 7, Apt. 183, 119270 Moscow, Russia.

TROYAT, Henri (pseudonym of Tarasoff); French writer; b. 1 Nov. 1911, Moscow, Russia; s. of Aslan Tarasoff and Lydie Abessolomoff; m. Marguerite Saintagne 1948; one s. one step-d.; ed. Lycée Pasteur, and Law Faculty, Univ. of Paris; mem. Acad. Française 1959–; Grand Officier Légion d'honneur, Commdr. Ordre nat. du Mérite, Ordre des Arts et des Lettres. *Publications:* Faux-jour (Prix Populiste) 1935, L'araigne (Prix Goncourt) 1938, La neige en deuil (Grand prix littéraire de Monaco) 1952, Tant que la terre durera (three vols.) 1947–50, Les semailles et les moissons (five vols.) 1953–58, La lumière des justes (five vols.) 1960–, Les Eygletière (three vols.) 1965–67, Les héritiers de l'avenir 1968, Anne Predaille 1973, Le Moscovite 1974, La dérision 1983, Le bruit solitaire du coeur 1985, Aliocha, A Demain Sylvie 1986, Le Troisième bonheur 1987, Toute ma vie sera mensonge 1988, Le Défi d'Olga 1995; biographies: Dostoïevsky, Pouchkine, Tolstoi, Gogol, Catherine la Grande, Pierre le Grand, Alexandre Ier, Ivan le Terrible, Tchekhov, Turgenev, Gorki, Flaubert, Maupassant, Alexandre II, Nicolas II, Zola, Verlaine, Baudelaire, Raspoutine, l'Affaire Crémonnière 1997, Le fils du satrape 1998. *Address:* Académie Française, 23 quai de Conti, 75006 Paris, France.

TRUBETSKOI, Kliment Nikolayevich; Russian geochemist; b. 3 July 1933; m.; two c.; ed. Moscow Inst. of Nonferrous Metals and Gold; jr., sr. researcher Moscow Inst. for Problems of Complex Utilisation of Mineral Resources 1961–81; Head of Lab. 1981–87, Deputy Dir. 1987–92, Dir. 1992–; Corresp. mem. U.S.S.R. (now Russian) Acad. of Sciences 1987, mem. 1991; Vice-Pres. Acad. of Mining Sciences; took part in devt. of tech. to save resources in quarries, developed theoretical fundamentals of projecting, prognosis and tech. of complex utilisation of mineral deposits; U.S.S.R. State Prize 1990, N. Melnikov Gold Medal and Prize. *Publications:* author of books and scientific articles in periodicals. *Leisure interests:* chess, swimming, photography, travelling. *Address:* Institute of Problems of Complex Utilisation of Mineral Resources, Krukovsky tupik 4, 111020 Moscow, Russia. *Telephone:* (095) 360 8960 (Office); 331 5255 (Home).

TRUBETSKOV, Dmitry Ivanovich, PH.D.; Russian physicist; b. 14 June 1938, Saratov; s. of Ivan Trubetskov and Varvara Trubetskova; m. Sofya Vasilyeva 1962; one s.; ed. Saratov State Univ.; aspirant 1960–64; teacher 1961–68; Docent 1968; Prof. Saratov State Univ. 1981–, Head Chair of Electronics and Wave Processes 1981–, Rector 1994; mem. I.E.E.E. Electron Devices Soc. 1995; corresp. mem. U.S.S.R. (now Russian) Acad. of Sciences 1991; research in theoretical radiophysics and electronics, microwave electronics, applied nonlinear dynamics. *Publications include:* Analytical Methods of Calculation in Microwave Electronics (with V.N. Shevchik) 1970, Electronics of Backward-Wave Tubes 1975, Introduction into the Theory of Oscillations and Waves 1984, Nonlinear Dynamics in Action (with A.A. Koronovsky) 1995, Lectures on Microwave Vacuum Microelectronics (with A.Y. Rozgenev and D.V. Sokolov) 1996. *Leisure interest:* reading. *Address:* Saratov State University, Astrakhanskaya str. 83, 410071 Saratov, Russia. *Telephone:* (8452) 241-696 (Office). *Fax:* (8452) 240-446.

TRUBNIKOV, Gen. Vyacheslav Ivanovich; Russian security officer; b. 25 April 1944, Irkutsk; m.; one d.; ed. Moscow State Inst. of Int. Relations; served in U.S.S.R. KGB (First Main Directorate, intelligence) 1967–91; staff mem. HQ of First Main Dept. (intelligence) 1977–84; KGB station officer in India (as corresp. Press Agency Novosti) 1971–77; mem. Union of Journalists 1973; resident in Bangladesh and India 1984–90; Head Div. of S. Asia KGB 1990–92; First Deputy Dir. Russian Intelligence Service 1992–96, Dir. 1996–; mem. Security Council, Defence Council and Foreign Policy Council of Russia 1996. *Address:* Russian Foreign Intelligence Service, 51/10 Ostozhenka Street, 119034 Moscow, Russia. *Telephone:* (095) 247-1938, 245-3368. *Fax:* (095) 247-0529.

TRUDEAU, Garry B.; American cartoonist; b. 1948, New York; m. Jane Pauley 1980; one s. one d.; ed. Yale Univ. School of Art and Architecture; created comic strip Doonesbury syndicated nationwide, Pinhead: selected cartoons from You Ask for Many; conceived (with Robert Altman, q.v.) Tanner '88 (TV) 1988, *Publications include:* Any Grooming Hints for Your Fans, Rollie, But the Pension Fund was Just Sitting There, The Doonesbury Chronicles, Guilty, Guilty, Guilty, We Who are about to Fry, Salute You: selected cartoons in In Search of Reagan's Brain, Vol. 2, Is This Your First Purge, Miss ?, Vol. 2, It's Supposed to be Yellow, Pinhead: selected cartoons from You Ask for Many, Seetle for June, Vol. 1, The Wreck of the Rusty Nail, Dressed for Failure 1983, Confirmed Bachelors are Just So Fascinating 1984, Sir I'm Worried About Your Mood Swings 1984, Doonesbury Dossier: The Reagan Years 1984, Check Your Egos at the Door 1986, Talking 'Bout My G-G-Generation 1988, We're Eating More Beets 1988, Read My Lips, Make My Day, Eat Quiche and Die 1989, Recycled Doonesbury 1990, You're Smoking Now Mr Butt! 1990, In Search of a Cigarette Holder Man: A Doonesbury Book 1994, Doonesbury Nation 1995; The Portable Doonesbury 1993; contribs. to The People's Doonesbury and many others; *plays include:* Doonesbury 1983, Rapmaster Ronnie, A Partisan Review (with Elizabeth Swados) 1984.

TRUDEAU, Rt. Hon. Pierre Elliott, C.H., C.C., P.C.; Canadian politician and lawyer; b. 18 Oct. 1919, Montreal, Quebec; s. of Charles-Emile Trudeau and Grace Elliott; m. Margaret Sinclair 1971 (divorced 1984); three s. (one deceased); one d. by Deborah Coyne; ed. Collège Jean-de-Brébeuf, Montreal, Univ. of Montreal, Harvard Univ., Univ. of Paris, and L.S.E.; called to Bar, Prov. of Quebec 1944, then studied at Harvard, Paris and London; subsequently employed with Cabinet Secr., Ottawa; later practised law, Prov. of Que.; one of founders of Cité Libre (Quebec review); Assoc. Prof. of Law, Univ. of Montreal 1961; mem. House of Commons 1965–84; Parl. Sec. to Prime Minister 1966–67; Minister of Justice and Attorney-Gen. 1967–68; Leader of Liberal Party 1968–84; Prime Minister of Canada 1968–79, 1980–84; Sr. Consultant Heenan, Blaikie 1984–; mem. InterAction Council 1985; numerous hon. degrees; Freedom of City of London 1975; Albert Einstein Int. Peace Prize 1984. *Publications:* La grève de l'amiante 1956, Canadian Dualism/La dualité Canadienne 1960, Deux innocents en Chine rouge 1961, Federalism and the French Canadians 1968, Réponses 1968, Memoirs 1993, The Canadian Way: Shaping Canada's Foreign Policy 1968–84 (with Ivan Head) 1995, Against the Current 1996; and numerous articles in Canadian and foreign journals. *Address:* c/o Heenan, Blaikie, 1250 boulevard René-Lévesque Ouest, Bureau 2500, Montreal, Quebec H3B 4Y1, Canada.

TRUJILLO MOLINA, General Héctor Bienvenido; Dominican Republic army officer and politician; b. 1908; ed. Univ. Autónoma de Santo Domingo; entered Army 1926; Chief of Staff of Army 1936; Supervisor-Gen. of Nat. Police 1938–43; Secretary of War, C.-in-C. of Army and Navy 1944; succeeded his brother as Pres. of the Dominican Republic 1952–60; Prof. American Int. Acad., Washington; corresp. mem. Nat. Athenaeum Arts and Sciences, Mexico; holds numerous military and other decorations of his own and foreign countries; living abroad.

TRUKHANOVSKY, Vladimir Grigoryevich; Russian historian; b. 15 July 1914, Botvinovka, Byelorussia; s. of Grigory Trukhanovsky and Anna Trukhanovskaya; m. Natalya (née Dumovna) Trukhanovskaya 1969; two c.; ed. Leningrad Pedagogical Inst., High Diplomatic School; Head Chair History of Int. Relations, Inst. of Int. Relations (MGIMO) 1947–75; Dir. Inst. of History U.S.S.R. Acad. of Sciences 1953–60; Ed.-in-Chief Problems of Hist 1960–87; leading scientific consultant Inst. of Comprehensive History U.S.S.R. Acad. of Sciences; corresp. mem. U.S.S.R. (now Russian) Acad. of Sciences 1964, mem. 1992; research in comprehensive history, history of England, int. relations and foreign policy; mem. Int. Council of Pugwash Movt. of Scientists for Peace. *Publications include:* Foreign Policy of England: 1917–1957 (3 vols.) 1957–65, Winston Churchill 1968, Anthony Eden 1974, Admiral Nelson 1980, History of British Nuclear Armaments 1985, Benjamin Disraeli 1993. *Address:* Institute of Comprehensive History, Russian Academy of Sciences, Leninsky pr. 32A, 117334 Moscow, Russia. *Telephone:* (095) 938-1009 (Office).

TRUMAN, James; British journalist; b. Nottingham; news and arts reporter Hampstead and Highgate Express; American Ed., columnist The Face; joined Condé Nast Publs. 1988, Features Ed. Vogue, Ed.-in-Chief Details 1990–93, Editorial Dir. Condé Nast Publs. April 1993–. *Address:* Condé Nast Publications Inc., 350 Madison Avenue, New York, NY 10017, U.S.A.

TRUMKA, Richard Louis, J.D.; American lawyer and industrialist; b. 24 July 1949, Waynesburg, Pa.; s. of Frank Richard Trumka and Eola Elizabeth

Bertugli; m. Barbara Vidovich 1982; one s.; ed. Philadelphia State Univ., Villanova Univ.; served at bar U.S. Dist. Court 1974, U.S. Court of Appeals 1975, U.S. Supreme Court 1979; Attorney United Mine Workers of America, Washington 1974–77, 1978–79, mem. Int. Exec. Bd. Dist. 4, Masontown, Pa. 1981–83, Int. Pres., Washington 1982–95; Sec. Treasurer AFL-CIO, Washington 1995–; Miner-Operator Jone and Loughlin Steel, Nemacolin, Pa. 1977–78, 1979–81; Pres. Emer. United Mine Workers Asscn. 1995–; Dir. Nat. Bank, Washington 1983–85, Dinamo Corpn. 1983–; mem. Bd. Dirs. American Coal Fund 1983–; Trustee Philadelphia State Univ. *Address:* AFL-CIO, 815 16th Street, NW, Washington, DC 20006, U.S.A.

TRUMP, Donald John, B.A.; American property developer; b. 14 June 1946, New York; s. of Fred C. Trump and Mary Trump; m. 1st Ivana Zelnicek 1977 (divorced 1991); two s. one d.; m. 2nd Marla Maples 1993; one d.; ed. Fordham Univ., Univ. of Pennsylvania; Pres. Trump Org.; holdings include: (New York) Trump Tower on Fifth Avenue; (Fla.) Mar-A-Lago at Palm Beach, Trump Plaza; (Atlantic City) Trump Plaza Hotel Casino, Trump Castle Casino, Trump Taj Mahal Casino Resort; acquired 50 per cent stake in Empire State Bldg. 1994; mem. Bd. of Dirs. Police Athletic League; Advisory Bd. mem., Lenox Hill Hosp. and United Cerebral Palsy; dir. Fred C. Trump Foundation; Founder-mem. Cttee. to complete construction of Cathedral of St. John the Divine, and Wharton Real Estate Center; fmr. Co-Chair. New York Vietnam Veterans Memorial Fund. *Publications:* Trump: The Art of the Deal 1987, Trump: Surviving at the Top 1990, The Art of the Comeback 1997. *Address:* Trump Organization, 725 Fifth Avenue, New York, NY 10022, U.S.A. *Telephone:* (212) 832-2000.

TRUONG NHU TANG; Vietnamese lawyer and politician; b. 1923, Cholon; ed. Univ. of Paris; Controller-General, Viet Nam Bank for Industry and Commerce; Dir.-Gen. Viet Nam Sugar Co., Saigon; Sec.-Gen. People's Movement for Self-Determination 1964–65; mem. Saigon Cttee. for Restoration of Peace; Pres. Viet Nam Youth Union 1966–67; imprisoned 1967–68; joined Nat. Liberation Front 1968; Minister of Justice, Provisional Revolutionary Govt. of S. Viet Nam 1969–76 (in Saigon 1975–76). *Address:* c/o Council of Ministers, Hanoi, Viet Nam.

TRZECIAKOWSKI, Witold Mieczysław, D.ECON.SC.; Polish economist and politician; b. 6 Feb. 1926, Warsaw; s. of Witold Trzeciakowski and Zofia Trzeciakowska; m. Anna Przedpelska 1951; three s.; ed. Cen. School of Planning and Statistics, Warsaw, Harvard Univ., Cambridge, Mass. and Columbia Univ., New York, N.Y.; mem. underground Home Army 1942–44, took part in Warsaw uprising 1944; Asst. Prof. 1966, Extraordinary Prof. 1972, Ordinary Prof. 1979; Dir. Podkowiak Metal Wares Factory, Szydłowiec 1946–49; Vice-Pres. Asscn. of Pvt. Producers of Metal Wares 1946–49; designer, Transport Design Office, Warsaw 1949–57; consultant, Inst. of Foreign Trade Conjuncture and Prices, Warsaw 1959–60, Deputy Dir. 1960–76, Dir. 1976–78, Prof. 1972–81; Prof., Econ. Sciences Inst., Polish Acad. of Sciences (PAN), Warsaw 1981–91; mem. Solidarity Trade Union 1980–, Civic Cttee. attached to Chair. of Solidarity Trade Union, Lech Wałęsa 1988–; participant Round Table plenary debates, co-Chair. group for econ. and social policy Feb.–April 1989; Senator 1989–91, Chair. Senate Comm. of Nat. Econ. 1989–91; Minister, mem. Council of Ministers 1989–90, Chair. Econ. Council 1989–91; mem. Primatial Social Council 1983–85; Chair. Church Agric. Cttee. 1987–89, mem. 1987–; Kt.'s Cross of Polonia Restituta Order, Gold Cross of Merit, Cross of Valour, Prime Minister's Prize for achievements in economics of transformation 1995. *Publications include:* Modele pośredniego kierowania gospodarką planową w sterowaniu handlem zagranicznym 1975, Structural Adjustments in Trade Dependent Small Centrally Planned Economies 1984, Reforma–restrukturyzacja–zadłużenie 1987, Transition in Poland 1993. *Leisure interests:* skiing, horse-riding. *Address:* ul. Langiewicza 2 m. 2, 02-071 Warsaw, Poland. *Telephone:* (22) 625 66 15. *Fax:* (22) 629 58 97.

TSABAN, Yair; Israeli journalist and politician; b. 1930, Tel Aviv; Chair. political bureau of Maki (Israeli CP) 1972–73; co-founder of Sheli Coalition 1977; Political Sec. Mapam (United Workers' Party), Chair. Mapam's faction in the Histadrut; Minister of Immigrant Absorption 1992–96; mem. Knesset 1981– (Meretz), served on numerous cttees. 1981–92. *Publications:* various articles on political, social and economic topics. *Address:* c/o Ministry of Immigrant Absorption, P.O. Box 883, 2 Rehov Kaplan, Kiryat Ben-Gurion, Jerusalem 91006, Israel.

TSANG, Sir Donald Yam-kuen, K.B.E.; Chinese government official; b. 7 Oct. 1944, Hong Kong; m.; two s.; ed. in Hong Kong and U.S.A.; joined Govt. of Hong Kong 1967; served in various govt. depts. and brs. of Govt. Secr.; Dist. Officer, Shatin; Deputy Dir. of Trade responsible for trade relations with N. America; Deputy Sec. of Gen. Duties Br. responsible for Sino-British Jt. Declaration 1985; Dir. of Admin. Office of Chief Sec. 1989; Dir.-Gen. of Trade 1991–93; Sec. for Treasury 1993–95; Financial Sec. 1995–. *Leisure interests:* golf, music. *Address:* Government Secretariat, Central Government Offices, Lower Albert Road, Hong Kong Special Administrative Region, People's Republic of China.

TSANG YOK-SING; Chinese politician; Chair. Democratic Alliance for the Betterment of Hong Kong (DAB); mem. political section, Preparatory Cttee. for Hong Kong Special Admin. Region (SAR). *Address:* Democratic Alliance for the Betterment of Hong Kong, 12/F., SUP Tower, 83 King's Road, North Point, Hong Kong Special Administrative Region, People's Republic of China. *Telephone:* 25280136. *Fax:* 25284339.

TSAO, Robert H.C., M.S.; Taiwanese electronics industry executive; b. 24 Feb. 1947, Shantung; ed. Nat. Univ. of Taiwan, Nat. Chiao Tung Univ.; Deputy Dir. Electrical Research Service Org. 1979–81; Vice-Pres. United Microelectronics Corpn. (UMC) 1980, Pres. 1981–91, Chair. 1991–; Chair. Unipac Microelectronics Corpn. 1989–, World Wiser Electrical Inc. 1989–; Vice-Chair. TECO Information System Co. Ltd. 1995–; mem. Standing Bd. Chinese Nat. Fed. of Industry (CNFI), Chair. Intellectual Property Protection Cttee. 1991–94; Chair. Asscn. of Allied Industries in Science-Based Industry Park 1987–93. *Address:* 13 Chuang Hsin 1st Road, Science-Based Industry Park, Hsinchu, Taiwan.

TSAPOGAS, Makis Joakim, M.D., D.SC., M.CH., M.R.C.S., L.R.C.P., F.A.C.S.; professor of vascular diseases; b. Greece; m. Lily Philossopoulou; lecturer in Surgery, King's Coll. Hosp. Medical School, London 1961–63, Sr. lecturer 1963–67; Assoc. Prof. of Surgery, Albany Medical Coll. Union Univ. New York 1967–70, Prof. 1970–75; Adjunct Prof. Rensselear Polytechnic Inst. New York 1970–75; Prof. of Surgery, Rutgers Medical School, N.J. 1976; Prof. of Vascular Diseases, State Univ. of New York 1977–; Prof. Univ. of London 1993–; adviser, WHO 1986–; consultant, UN, New York 1993–; Visiting Prof. in many univs. in Europe and N. America; Hunterian Prof. Royal Coll. of Surgeons; corresp. mem. Acad. of Athens; hon. mem. many scientific socs.; Red Cross Gold Medal; Hon. Ph.D.; Hon. D.M. *Publications include:* Atherosclerosis in the Lower Limb 1959, Treatment of Thrombosis 1965, Management of Vascular Diseases 1985, Medical Education 1992; numerous articles in scientific medical journals. *Leisure interests:* classical music, reading, travelling. *Address:* P.O. Box 457, Northport, NY 11768, U.S.A. *Telephone:* (516) 261-4114. *Fax:* (516) 261-4114.

TSATSOS-SYMEONIDIS, Dora; Greek dancer, teacher and choreographer; b. 23 Aug. 1932, Athens; d. of Constantine Tsatsos and Joanna Seferiades; m. Alexander Symeonidis 1960 (died 1972); two s.; ed. Athens Univ., Martha Graham School of Contemporary Dance; dancer, teacher, choreographer with Hellenikom Chorodrama Dance Co. 1952–59; Dir. (ancient drama chorus) Northern Greece Nat. Theatre 1962–74, State School of Dance 1980–88; choreographer Nat. Theatre of Greece 1975–82, Dir. 1992–93; choreographer, Greece, (in collaboration with Laban Centre for Movt. and Dance, London) 1990–96; mem. bd. of dirs. Cancer Inst., Thessaloniki 1973–86. *Address:* 9 Kydathimeon Street, Athens 105 58, Greece. *Telephone:* 32-27-330. *Fax:* 32-20-513.

TSCHUDI, Hans-Peter, LL.D.; Swiss politician; b. 22 Oct. 1913; ed. Basle Univ.; Prof. of Labour Law, Basle Univ. 1952–59; Head of Home Dept. Govt. of Basle 1953–59; mem. Council of States, Fed. Ass. 1956–59; mem. Fed. Council 1960–73, Vice-Pres. Jan.-Dec. 1964, Jan.-Dec. 1969, Pres. Jan.-Dec. 1965, Jan.-Dec. 1970; Head of Dept. of the Interior 1960–73; mem. Ass., Int. Red Cross; Socialist. *Publications:* Die Ferien im schweizerischen Arbeitsrecht 1948, Koalitionsfreiheit und Koalitionszwang 1948, Die Sicherung des Arbeitsfriedens durch das schweizerische Recht 1952, Gesamtarbeitsvertrag und Aussenseiter 1953. *Address:* c/o Comité International de la Croix-Rouge, avenue de la Paix 17, 1211 Geneva, Switzerland.

TSCHUDI-MADSEN, Stephan, PH.D.; Norwegian art historian; b. 25 Aug. 1923, Bergen; s. of Dr. Stephan Tschudi-Madsen and Aagot (née Stoltz) Tschudi-Madsen; m. Elizabeth Kverndal 1954; two s. one d.; ed. Univ. of Oslo; Keeper, Nat. Gallery, Oslo 1950–51, Vigelands Museum, Oslo 1951–52; Asst. Prof. Univ. of Oslo 1953–58; Chief Antiquarian, Cen. Office of Historic Monuments, Oslo 1959–78, Dir.-Gen. 1978–91, Special Counsellor 1991–93; Keeper, Akershus Castle 1961–79; Prof. Univ. of Calif. 1966–67, 1973; Sec. Gen. The Architectural Heritage Year 1974–76; Pres. Advisory Cttee. of Int. Council on Monuments and Sites 1981–88, Vice-Pres. 1988–90; Pres. Norwegian Nat. Comm. 1978–92; Chair. Akershus Slotts Venner 1992–; Vice-Pres. World Heritage Comm. 1984–87; Chair. State Council of Cultural Heritage 1992–96, Council of Norsk Folkemuseum 1992–; mem. Norwegian Nat. Comm. of UNESCO 1988–92; mem. Norwegian Acad.; Hon. mem. Norwegian Soc. of Preservation, Icomos (int. and nat.); Cultural Prize of Science and Letters of Oslo City; Commdr. of the Order of St. Olav, Commdr. of Order of Oranje-Nassau, Kt. of Order of King Leopold. *Publications:* To kongeslott 1952, Vigelands Fontenerelieffer 1953, Sources of Art Nouveau 1957, Rosendal 1965, Art Nouveau 1967, Chateauneuf's Works in London and Oslo 1968, Restoration and Anti-Restoration 1976, Henrik Bull 1983, (Ed.) Norges Kulturhistorie, 8 vols. 1979–81, (Ed.) Norges Kunsthistorie, 7 vols. 1981–83, (Ed.) Norsk Kunstnerleksikon, 4 vols. 1981–86, (Ed.) Norway: A Cultural Heritage 1987, Vakrest i Norge 1991, På Nordmanns vis 1993, Norske antikviteter 1994, Quantum Satis (Ed.) 1995, Our Nordic Heritage (Ed.), The Norwegian Supreme Court (Ed.) 1998, Akershus Castle 1999. *Leisure interest:* skiing. *Address:* Bjørn Farmannsgt. 8, Oslo 2, Norway. *Telephone:* (22) 430373.

TSELKOV, Oleg; Russian artist; b. 1934, Moscow; ed. Moscow secondary school, Minsk Inst. of Theatre Art and Leningrad Acad. of Art; expelled from both for 'formalism'; later graduated from Leningrad Theatre Inst. as stage-designer 1958; designed numerous productions; mem. of Artists' Union; left U.S.S.R. 1977, now lives in Paris. *Exhibitions:* Moscow 1965, 1970, 1975, Austria 1975, Fed. Germany, France 1976, in Russia after 1991.

TSENG, Kwang-shun, LL.B.; Taiwanese politician; b. 24 Dec. 1924, Haifeng Co., Guangdong Prov.; m. Wan Yee-mui; one s. two d.; ed. Prov. Coll. of Law and Commerce, Kwangtung; teacher Wan-kiu Coll. and Chuhai Univ., Hong Kong 1952–57; Deputy Dir. China Youth Corps 1958–70; Deputy Dir. 3rd

Section, Cen. Cttee. of Kuomintang (KMT) 1969–72, Deputy Dir., Acting Dir. Dept. of Overseas Affairs, KMT 1969–77, Dir. Dept. of Overseas Affairs, Cen. Cttee. of KMT 1978–84, mem. Cen. Standing Cttee., KMT 1988–93, mem. Cen. Advisory Council, KMT 1993–; Minister Overseas Chinese Affairs Comm. 1984–93; Pres. Overseas Chinese Culture and Educ. Foundation 1993–; Hon. Ph.D. (Yeungnam Univ., Korea) 1985. *Address:* Overseas Chinese Culture and Education Foundation, 7F, 30 Kungyuan Road, Taipei, Taiwan. *Fax:* (2) 2371-1815.

TSENG CHENG KUI, M.SC.; Chinese scientist; b. 18 June 1909, Xiamen (Amoy), Fujian Prov., China; s. of Tseng Pi-chang and Lin Sui-qing; m. 1st Ye Nu-ying 1931; m. 2nd Zhang Yi-fan 1954; two s. two d.; ed. Amoy, Lingnan and Mich. Univs.; Asst., Botany Dept. Amoy Univ. 1930–32; instructor, Biology Dept. 1934–35; lecturer in Biology Nat. Shandong Univ. 1935–37, Assoc. Prof. 1937–38; Assoc. Prof. in Biology, Lingnan Univ. 1938–40; Rackham Postdoctoral Fellow, Univ. of Mich. 1942–43; Research Assoc. in charge of Seaweed Research, Scripps Inst. of Oceanography, U.C.L.A., La Jolla, Calif., U.S.A. 1943–46; Prof. and Chair. Dept. of Botany and Deputy Dir., Inst. of Oceanography Nat. Shandong Univ., Qingdao 1946–52, Chair., Dept. of Fisheries, 1946–47; Research Prof., Deputy Dir., Marine Biological Lab. 1950–56, with Inst. of Marine Biology 1957–58; Deputy Dir., Inst. of Oceanography 1959–77, Dir. 1978–84, Dir. Emer. 1984–; Dir., Experimental Marine Biology (Open) Lab., CAS 1987–91, Dir. Emer. 1991–; mem. Chinese Acad. of Sciences 1980; Fellow, Third World Acad. of Sciences 1985; mem. Chinese Society of Oceanology and Limnology 1951–63 (Pres., 1979–88, Pres. Emer. 1988–), Chinese Fisheries Soc. 1964–77 (Vice-Pres. 1981–90, Hon. mem. 1991–), Chinese Phycological Soc. (Pres. 1979–84, Pres. Emer. 1985–), Pres., Chinese Scientific Cttee. of Oceanic Research 1985–89, Pres. Emer., Chinese Oceanographic Soc. 1989–; Hon. Life mem. World Aquaculture Soc. 1991; Dr. h.c. (Ohio State Univ.) 1987; Nat. Natural Science Award, 1956, 1987, Nat. Science Congress Award 1978, Nat. Educational Comm. Textbook Award 1987; CAS Natural Science Award 1990, Shintoshi Hatai Medal, Pacific Science Asscn. 1995, Quishi Natural Science Prize, Quishi Science and Tech. Foundation 1996, Science and Tech. Progress Prize, HLHL Science and Tech. Foundation 1997. *Publications:* over 250 scientific articles. *Leisure interest:* music. *Address:* Institute of Oceanology, Chinese Academy of Sciences, 7 Nanhai Road, Qingdao 266071, People's Republic of China. *Telephone:* 0532-8670220 (Office); 0532-2869117 (Home). *Fax:* 0532-8670882; 0532-8679235.

TSEPOV, Boris Anatolyevich, C.JUR.; Russian diplomatist; b. 13 June 1948; ed. Moscow Inst. of Int. Relations, Diplomatic Acad.; diplomatic service 1971–; different posts in U.S.S.R. Embassy, Kuwait 1971–76; in Third African Div., U.S.S.R. Ministry of Foreign Affairs 1976–78; Secr. of Deputy Minister 1978–86, with Dept. for Int. Humanitarian Cooperation and Human Rights 1986–90; counsellor Perm. U.S.S.R. (now Russian) Mission to UN (New York) 1991–94; Dir. of Dept., concurrently Exec. Sec. Russian Ministry of Foreign Affairs 1994–98; Amb. to Kenya (also accred. Perm. Rep. to int. orgs., Nairobi). *Address:* Embassy of Russian Federation, P.O. Box 30049, Lenana Road, Nairobi, Kenya. *Telephone:* (2) 72-87-00, 72-02-33. *Fax:* (2) 72-18-88.

TSERETELI, Zurab Konstantinovich; Georgian sculptor and artist; b. 4 Jan. 1934, Tbilisi; m. Inessa Andronikashvili; one d.; ed. Tbilisi Acad. of Arts; mem. Russian Acad. of Fine Arts, Pres. 1997–, Head Dept. of Design; Pres. Int. UNESCO Foundation in Moscow; Vice-Pres. Russian Acad. of Creativity; author of numerous sculptures, mosaics, monumental murals, stained-glass windows, revived old technique of traditional Georgian enamel; author of numerous monuments including Friendship in Moscow (with poet A. Voznesensky), Kindness Wins over Evil (New York, UN Bldg.), Happiness for Children of the World (Univ. of Fine Arts, Brockport), Columbus (Miami), Birth of a New Man (London), Moment of Victory (Moscow), Peter the Great (Moscow), and others in Tbilisi, Tokyo, Seville, Osaka, Brasília; U.S.S.R. People's Deputy 1989–90; Hero of Labour 1990, U.S.S.R. People's Artist 1980, People's Artist of Russia; Lenin and State Prizes. *Address:* Bolshaya Gruzinskaya str. 17, Moscow, Russia. *Telephone:* 254-7767.

TSHERING, Lyonpo Dago; Bhutanese diplomatist and politician; b. 17 July 1941, Paro; ed. Univ. of Bombay, Indian Admin. Service Training, Mussoorie and Indian Audit and Accounts Service Training, Simla, India, Univ. of Manchester, England; Asst., Ministry of Devt. 1961–62; Asst., Office of the Chief Sec., Royal Secretariat 1962–63; returned to Ministry of Devt. 1963, Sec. 1965–70; mem. Nat. Ass., mem. Royal Advisory Council 1968–70; First Sec. Bhutan Embassy in India 1971–73; Deputy Perm. Rep. to UN 1973–74, Perm. Rep. 1974–80, 1984–85; Amb. to Bangladesh 1980–84; Minister of Home Affairs 1985–98; Orange Scarf. *Address:* c/o Ministry of Home Affairs, Tashichho Dzong, Thimphu, Bhutan.

TSHERING, Ugyen, B.A.; Bhutanese public servant; b. 8 Aug. 1954, Thimphu; m.; ed. Univ. of Calif., Berkeley, U.S.A.; joined Govt. Planning Comm. 1978, Co-ordinator bilateral and multilateral assistance to govt. 1983–, Project Co-ordinator, Computer Support Centre 1984, Sec. Computerization Cttee. 1983–, Dir. Planning Comm. 1986–89; Perm Rep. of Bhutan to UN 1989–98; Editorial Adviser to Nat. Ass. 1980–; fmr. Chair. Asian Devt. Bank; Chair. World Bank Projects Implementation Cttee. 1984–; Chair. Tech. Cttee. on Rural Devt., S.-E. Asian Asscn. of Regional Co-operation 1988–89. *Address:* c/o Ministry of Foreign Affairs, Convention Centre, P.O. Box 103, Thimphu, Bhutan.

TSHISEKEDI, Etienne; Democratic Republic of the Congo politician; leader Union for Democracy and Social Progress (UDSP); Prime Minister of Zaire and C.-in-C. of Armed Forces Sept.–Oct. 1991; Prime Minister 1992–94 (dismissed by Pres. Mobutu March 1993); Prime Minister of Zaire (now Democratic Repub. of the Congo) April 1997.

TSHWETE, Steve Vukile; South African civil servant; b. 1938, Springs, Transvaal; m. Pamela Zondki; two c.; teacher; arrested 1964, charged with furthering the aims of ANC, sentenced to 15 years imprisonment, released 1979; lawyer's clerk 1983; Border Pres. United Democratic Front (UDF) 1983–85, mem. UDF Nat. Exec. Cttee. 1983–85; in exile 1985; addressed UN Comm. Against Apartheid 1985; mem. ANC del. to Bonn, Fed. Repub. of Germany 1986; Co-ordinator ANC's Internal Political Cttee., ANC 75th Anniversary Commemoration 1987; Political Commissar Umkhonto weSizwe–1988; mem. ANC Nat. Exec. Cttee. 1988–; Head ANC Sports Desk 1991–94; Minister of Sport and Recreation, Govt. of Nat. Unity 1994–. *Address:* Private Bag X869, Pretoria 0001, South Africa.

TSOHATZOPOULOS, Apostolos Athanasios; Greek politician; b. 1939, Athens; m. Gudrun Moldenhauer; one s. one d.; ed. Tech. Univ. of Munich, Fed. Repub. of Germany; deprived of citizenship by mil. dictatorship 1969; active in Panhellenic Liberation Movt., mem. Nat. Council during dictatorship; returned to Greece 1974; mem. Cen. Cttee. and Exec. Office PASOK 1974–90, Gen. Sec. 1990–95, mem. Exec. Office 1995–; M.P. 1981–; Minister of Public Works 1981–84, to the Prime Minister 1986–87, of the Interior 1987–89, of Transport and Communications 1989, of Interior 1993–94, 1995–96, of Defence 1996–. *Address:* Komna Traka 3, 11257 Athens; Omirou 8, 10564 Athens, Greece. *Telephone:* (1) 3233478, 3231975.

TSOVOLAS, Dimitris; Greek politician; b. 1942, Melissourgi, Arta; m. Ekaterini Yoti; one s. one d.; ed. Salonika Univ.; practised law at Arta until 1977; PASOK M.P. 1977–92; mem. Parl. Working Cttees. on Labour, Public Order and Premiership 1977–81; elected Sec. of Presidium of Parl.; Minister of Finance 1985–89; f. and Pres. Democratic Social Movement (DHKKI) Dec. 1995–. *Address:* 48 Serifou Street, 112 54, Athens, Greece. *Telephone:* 01-2020 469.

TSUI, Daniel C., PH.D.; American (b. Chinese) professor of physics; b. 1939, Henan, China; ed. Univ. of Chicago; Prof. Dept. of Electrical Eng., Princeton Univ.; Nobel Prize in Physics for discovery of fractional quantum Hall effect (jtly. with Robert B. Laughlin and Horst L. Störmer) 1998. *Address:* Department of Electrical Engineering, Princeton University, P. O. Box 5263, Princeton, NJ 08544, U.S.A. *Telephone:* 609-258-4621. *Fax:* 609-258-6279.

TSUI, Lap-Chee, O.C., PH.D., F.R.S.C., F.R.S.; Canadian geneticist; b. 21 Dec. 1950, Shanghai, China; s. of Jing Lue Hsue and Hui Ching Wang; m. (Ellen) Lan Fong 1977; two s.; ed. The Chinese Univ. of Hong Kong, Univ. of Pittsburgh, U.S.A.; staff geneticist, Dept. of Genetics, and scientist, The Research Inst., Hosp. for Sick Children, Toronto, Canada 1983–, Sr. Research Scientist 1988–, Sellers Chair in Cystic Fibrosis Research 1989–, Geneticist-in-Chief 1996–; Asst. Prof. Depts. of Medical Genetics and Medical Biophysics, Univ. of Toronto 1983–88, Assoc. Prof. 1988–90, Prof., Dept. of Molecular and Medical Genetics 1990–, Univ. Prof. 1994–; Howard Hughes Int. Scholar 1991–96; Assoc. Ed. Clinical Genetics 1991–; Ed. Int. Journal of Genome Research 1990, Assoc. Ed. Genomics 1994–; mem. Editorial Bd. several scientific journals; Adviser, European Journal of Human Genetics 1992–; Dir. American Soc. of Human Genetics, Mon Sheong Foundation, Educ. Foundation, Fed. of Chinese Canadian Professionals; mem. or fmr. mem. numerous scientific cttees.; mem. The Human Genome Org. and other professional bodies; Hon. D.Sc. (Univ. New Brunswick) 1991, (Chinese Univ. of Hong Kong) 1992, Hon. D.C.L. (Univ. King's Coll.) 1991; numerous prizes and awards including Scientist Award, Medical Research Council (Canada) 1989–93, Gold Medal of Honor, Pharmaceutical Mfgs. Asscn. of Canada 1989, Royal Soc. of Canada Centennial Award 1989, Award of Excellence, Genetic Soc. of Canada 1990, Gairdner Int. Award 1990, Canadian Achiever Award 1991, Sarstedt Research Prize 1993, XII San Remo Int. Award for Genetic Research 1993, J.P. Lecocq Prize 1994, Henry Friesen Award, Canadian Soc. of Clinical Investigation and Royal Coll. of Physicians and Surgeons of Canada 1995, Medal of Honour, Canadian Medical Asscn. 1996. *Publications:* numerous scientific papers and reviews. *Leisure interests:* travel, good food. *Address:* Department of Genetics, The Hospital for Sick Children, 555 University Avenue, Toronto, Ont., M5G 1X8, Canada. *Telephone:* (416) 813-6015. *Fax:* (416) 813-4931.

TSUJI, Yoshifumi; Japanese business executive; b. 6 Feb. 1928, Kagawa Pref.; ed. Univ. of Tokyo; joined Nissan Motor Co., Ltd. 1954, Gen. Man. Tochigi Plant 1984, Dir., mem. Bd. and Gen. Man. Tochigi Plant 1985, Man. Dir. in charge of Product Planning 1987, Exec. Man. Dir. in charge of Plant Operations, Eng. Depts. 1989, Exec. Vice-Pres. in charge of Product Operation Group, Purchasing Group, Non-Automotive Operations Group, etc. 1990, Exec. Vice-Pres. in charge of Production Operation Group, Non-automotive Operations Group 1991, Pres. 1992–96, Chair. 1996–. *Leisure interests:* golf, reading. *Address:* Nissan Motor Co., 17-1 Ginza 6-chome, Chuo-ku, Tokyo 104-23, Japan.

TSUKA, Kohei (Bong Woong Kim); Korean author and theatre director; b. 24 April 1948, Iizuka City, Fukuoka Pref., Japan; m. Naoko Ikoma; one d.; ed. Keio Univ. Tokyo; wrote first play, Red Beret for You 1969; writer and dir. for Waseda Univ. Theatre Club 1972; publ. first plays The Murder of Atami 1975; est. Thukakoahei office for plays 1975–82; est. Kitaku Thukakoahei Gekidan 1994, Ôita City Thukakoahei Gekidan 1996; dir. Ginchan Ga Yuku, New Nat. Theatre 1997; Japan Acad. Award for film Kamata March Song 1983; 42nd Yomiuri Literature Prize for play of The Tale of Hiryu '90 1990, and other awards. *Publications:* novels: The Murder of Atami 1975, For the Father Who Couldn't Die in the War 1976, Introduction to Revolution, The Tale of Hiryu 1977, Sun is in Your Mind 1978, Kamata March Song 1981, Town with Well 1985, The Day that they Bombed Hiroshima 1986, A Stripper's Story 1984, Birth of a Star 1986, My Country, Tell it to my Daughter 1990, The Story of Ryoma 1992; many other plays and essays. *Address:* Room 401, Villa Kamimura, Tabata, 6-3-18 Tabata, Kita-ku, Tokyo 114-0014, Japan. *Telephone:* (3) 5814-5177. *Fax:* (3) 5814-5178.

TSUKAHARA, Shunpei; Japanese politician; fmr. Minister of Labour, of Int. Trade and Industry Jan.–Nov. 1996; mem. House of Reps.; mem. LDP. *Address:* c/o Ministry of International Trade and Industry, 1-3-1, Kasumigaseki, Chiyoda-ku, Tokyo 100, Japan.

TSUMBA, Leonard Ladislas, PH.D.; Zimbabwean banker; b. 27 June 1943, Harare; s. of Ladislus Million Tsumba and Regina Tsumba; m. Nola Arne Yasinski 1969; two d.; Instructor in Econs. Hampton Inst. U.S.A. 1970–72; Asst. Prof. of Econs. Trinity Coll. U.S.A. 1975–77; consultant, Money and Finance Div. UNCTAD 1979; CitiBank NA, U.S.A. 1977–81; Exec. Asst. to Gov. Reserve Bank of Zimbabwe 1981–82, Gen. Man. 1982–86, Deputy Gov. 1986–87, Group Chief Exec. 1987–83, Gov. 1993–; Man. Dir. Finhold/ Zimbabwe Banking Corpn. 1987–93. *Leisure interest:* golf. *Address:* Reserve Bank of Zimbabwe, P.O. Box 1283, 80 Samora Machel Avenue, Harare, Zimbabwe. *Telephone:* (4) 703000. *Fax:* (4) 705978.

TSUR, Yaakov; Israeli diplomatist and politician; b. 18 Oct. 1906, Vilno; s. of Samuel and Bella Tsur; m. Vera Gotlib 1928; one s. one d.; ed. Hebrew Coll., Jerusalem, Univs. of Florence and Sorbonne; mem. staff daily newspaper Haaretz, Tel-Aviv 1929; Dir. French Dept. and later Co-Dir. Propaganda Dept. Jewish Nat. Fund, Jerusalem 1930; special Zionist missions, Belgium, Greece, France 1934–35, Bulgaria and Greece 1940; Liaison officer with G.H.Q. British Troops in Egypt 1943–45; Head del. to Greece 1945; Pres. Israeli Army Recruiting Cttee. Jerusalem 1948; Minister, Argentina 1949–53, Uruguay 1949–53, Chile 1950–53, and Paraguay 1950–53, Amb. to France 1953–59; mem. Jewish Agency Exec. Cttee. 1960–61; Chair. Zionist Gen. Council (Action Cttee.); Grand Officier, Légion d'honneur. *Publications:* Juifs en guerre 1947, The Birth of Israel 1949, Shacharit Shel Etmol (Autobiography) 1965, Ambassador's Diary 1967, La révolte juive 1970, Portrait of the Diaspora 1975, The Saga of Zionism 1976, The Day is Near 1979, Credentials No. 4 1981. *Address:* 5 Mero Yoram, Jerusalem, Israel.

TSURUMI, Kazuko, PH.D.; Japanese professor of sociology; b. 10 June 1919, Tokyo; s. of Yusuke Tsurumi and Aiko Tsurumi; ed. Peeresses' School, Tsuda Coll., Vassar Coll. and Princeton Univ.; Asst. Prof. Univ. of British Columbia 1964–65, Seikei Univ. 1966–69; Prof. of Sociology and mem. Inst. of Int. Relations, Sophia Univ. 1969–89, Prof. Emer. 1989–; Visiting Prof. Univ. of Toronto 1973–74, Princeton Univ. 1976–77; Bobbs-Merrill Award 1964; Mainichi Publication-Culture Prize 1979; Tohata Prize (Nat. Inst. for Research and Achievement) 1990. *Publications:* Social Change and the Individual: Japan Before and After Defeat in World War II 1970, Itinerants and the Settled: Yanagita Kunio's Theory of Social Change 1977, Minakata Kumagusu: A Globe-oriented Comparativist 1979, A Theory of Endogenous Development (co-ed.) 1989, Prospect and Retrospect 1997. *Leisure interests:* Japanese Tanka poetry, Japanese theatrical dancing. *Address:* 3-20-52, Sekimachi-kita, Nerima-ku, Tokyo 177, Japan. *Telephone:* 03-3920-2519. *Fax:* 03-3920-2519.

TSURUMI, Shunsuke, B.S.; Japanese author; b. 25 June 1922, Tokyo; s. of Yusuke Tsurumi and Aiko Tsurumi; m. Sadako Yokoyama 1960; one s.; ed. Harvard Coll.; founded The Science of Thought (philosophical journal) 1946; Asst. Prof. Univ. of Kyoto 1949, Tokyo Inst. of Tech. 1954; Prof. Doshisha Univ. 1960; freelance author 1970–; Visiting Prof. El Colegio de Mexico 1972–73, McGill Univ. 1979–80; Takano Chóei Prize 1976; Osaragi Jiro Prize 1982; Mystery Writers' Soc. Prize 1989, Asahi Prize 1994. *Publications:* Collected Works (5 vols.) 1974, An Intellectual History of Wartime Japan 1986, A History of Mass Culture in Postwar Japan 1987, Collected Works (12 vols.) 1992, Conversation (10 vols.) 1996. *Leisure interest:* reading. *Address:* 230-99 Nagatanicho, Iwakura, Sakyōku, Kyoto, Japan.

TSVETKOV, Aleksey, PH.D.; Russian poet and critic; b. 2 Feb. 1947, Stanislaw (now Ivano-Frankivsk), Ukraine; s. of Petr Tsvetkov and Bella Tsvetkov (née Tsyganov); m. Olga Samilenko 1978; ed. Odessa and Moscow Univs., Univ. of Mich., U.S.A.; journalist in Siberia and Kazakhstan; poetry recitals and participant in Volgin's Moscow Univ. literary soc. Luch 1970–75; emigrated to U.S.A. 1974; co-ed. of Russkaya zhizn', San Francisco 1976–77; Prof. of Russian Language and Literature, Dickinson Coll., Pa. 1981–85; broadcaster, Voice of America; poetry has appeared in Kontinent, Ekho, Vremya i my, Apollon, Glagol and elsewhere; Dr. h.c. (Univ. of Mich.) 1977. *Publications include:* A Collection of Pieces for Life Solo 1978, Three Poets: Kuzminsky, Tsvetkov, Limonov, 1981, Dream State 1981, Eden 1985, Simply Voice 1991. *Leisure interest:* collecting baroque opera records.

TU GUANGCHI, PH.D.; Chinese scientist; b. 14 Feb. 1920; ed. Univ. of Minnesota; Deputy, 5th NPC 1978–83, 6th NPC 1983–87, 7th NPC 1988–; Pres. Soc. of Mineral-Rocks Geochem. 1980–; Dir. Dept. of Earth Sciences, Acad. Sinica 1981–; Dir. Guiyang Inst. of Geochem. 1985–; Vice-Chair. People's Congress of Guizhou Prov. 1987–; mem. Nat. Acad. Degrees Cttee. 1988–. *Address:* Institute of Geochemistry, Guiyang City, Guizhou Province, People's Republic of China.

TUCKER, Jim Guy, B.A., J.D.; American politician and lawyer; b. 13 June 1943, Oklahoma City; s. of James Tucker and Willie White; m. Betty Allen; one s. three d.; ed. Harvard Univ. and Univ. of Arkansas; assoc. attorney, Rose, Barron, Nash, Williamson, Carroll and Clay, Little Rock 1968–70; partner, Tucker & Stafford (Attorneys) 1979–82, Mitchell, Williams, Selig & Tucker 1982–; Prosecuting Attorney, Sixth Judicial Dist., Pulaski and Perry Counties, Ark. 1971–72; Attorney-Gen. Ark. 1973–74, 1975–76; Rep. Second Dist., Ark. 1977–78; mem. U.S. House of Reps. and Lieut.-Gov. Ark. 1991–92; Gov. of Arkansas 1992–96; convicted of two charges of fraud May 1996; Democrat. *Publication:* Arkansas Men at War 1968.

TUCKWELL, Barry Emmanuel, A.C., O.B.E., F.R.C.M., F.R.S.A.; Australian musician; b. 5 March 1931, Melbourne, Australia; s. of Charles Tuckwell and Elizabeth Hill; m. 1st Sally E. Newton 1958; one s. one d.; m. 2nd Hilary J. Warburton 1971; one s.; m. 3rd Susan T. Levitan 1992; ed. Sydney Conservatorium; French Horn player with Melbourne Symphony Orchestra 1947, Sydney Symphony Orchestra 1947–50, Hallé Orchestra 1951–53, Scottish Nat. Orchestra 1954–55, Bournemouth Symphony Orchestra, London Symphony Orchestra 1955–68; Horn Prof., R.A.M. 1963–74; f. Tuckwell Wind Quintet 1968; int. soloist and recording artist; Conductor of Tasmanian Symphony Orchestra 1980–83; Music Dir. and Conductor Md. Symphony Orchestra 1982–98; Pres. Int. Horn Soc. 1969–76, 1993–95; Guest Conductor Northern Sinfonia 1993–; mem. Bd. of Dirs., London Symphony Orchestra 1957–68, Chair. 1961–68; mem. Chamber Music Soc. of Lincoln Center 1974–81; Hon. degrees from R.A.M., Guildhall School of Music and Drama, Sydney Univ.; Harriet Cohen Int. Award for Solo Instruments 1968, George Peabody Medal for outstanding contributions to music in America. *Publications:* Playing the Horn, 50 1st Exercises 1978, The Horn (Yehudi Menuhin Music Guides) 1981, entire horn repertoire of G. Schirmer Inc. (Ed). *Address:* 13140 Fountain Head Road, Hagerstown, MD 21742, U.S.A.

TUDJMAN, Franjo, D.HIST.SC.; Croatian head of state, historian and author; b. 14 May 1922, Veliko Tgrovišće; m. Ankica Zumbar; two s. one d.; ed. Higher Military Acad., Belgrade, Univ. of Zagreb; mem. Partisan movt. in Croatia in World War II; with Ministry of Nat. Defence; Gen. Staff of Yugoslav Nat. Army 1991; Dir. Inst. of Workers Movt. of Croatia 1961–67; Prof. of Contemporary History, School of Political Science, Univ. of Zagreb 1963; resgnd. from all posts 1967 because of his support for Declaration on Croatian Literary Language 1967; imprisoned twice for nationalist activities 1972, 1982; Founder and Chair. Croatian Democratic Union (HDZ) 1989–; elected Pres. of Croatia 1990, re-elected 1992; mem. PEN Club Int., Asscn. of Croatian Writers; guest lecturer at several univs. N. America and Europe; co-ed. several scientific publs. *Publications include:* War against War 1957, Great Ideas and Small Nations 1969, National Questions and Contemporary Europe 1981, Waste lands of Historical Reality 1989–90; numerous articles on historical problems, mil. theory, philosophy of history, int. relations. *Address:* Office of the President, Presidential Palace, Pantovcak 241, Zagreb 10000, Croatia.

TUENI, Ghassan, M.A.; Lebanese newspaper editor; b. 5 Jan. 1926, Beirut; s. of Gebran Tueni and Adile (née Salem) Tueni; m. Nadia Hamadeh (deceased); one s.; ed. American Univ. of Beirut and Harvard Univ.; lecturer in Political Science, American Univ. of Beirut 1947–48; Ed.-in-Chief, An-Nahar (daily newspaper) 1948, Pres.; Man.-Dir. An-Nahar Publishing Co. (now Dar an-Nahar SAL) 1963–; Co-founder Lebanese Acad. of Law and Political Science 1951, lecturer 1951–54; M.P. for Beirut 1953–57; mem. Lebanese del. to UN Gen. Assembly 1957; founded Middle East Business Services and Research Corpn. 1958, Chair. 1958–70; founder, Chair. and Man.-Dir. of Press Cooperative, S.A.L. 1960–; Deputy Prime Minister and Minister of Information and Nat. Educ. 1970–71; arrested Dec. 1973, appeared before mil. tribunal and then released in accordance with press laws; Minister for Social Affairs and Labour, Tourism, Industry and Oil 1975–76; Perm. Rep. to UN 1977–82; mem. Nat. Dialogue Cttee. 1975. *Address:* Dar an-Nahar SAL, P.O. Box 55-454, rue Zahret el-Ihsan, Achrafiyé, Beirut (Office); Ras Kafra, Beit Mery, Lebanon (Home).

TUGENDHAT, Baron (Life Peer), cr. 1993, of Widdington in the County of Essex; **Christopher Samuel Tugendhat,** Kt., M.A.; British fmr. international official and politician; b. 23 Feb. 1937, London; s. of late Dr. Georg Tugendhat; m. Julia Lissant Dobson 1967; two s.; ed. Ampleforth Coll., Gonville and Caius Coll., Cambridge; Pres. Cambridge Union; Mil. Service, Commissioned in The Essex Regt. 1955–57; Leader and Feature Writer, The Financial Times 1960–70; Consultant to Wood Mackenzie & Co. Ltd., stockbrokers 1968–77; Conservative M.P. for Cities of London and Westminster 1970–74, for City of London and Westminster South 1974–76; Dir. Sunningdale Oils 1971–77, Phillips Petroleum Int. (U.K.) Ltd. 1972–77, Nat. Westminster Bank PLC 1985–91 (Deputy Chair. 1990–91), BOC Group PLC 1985–96, Commercial Union PLC 1988–91, LWT (Holdings) PLC 1991–94; Dir. (non-exec.), Eurotunnel PLC 1991–, Rio Tinto PLC; Chair. Civil Aviation Authority 1986–91; Chair. Abbey Nat. PLC 1991–, Blue Circle Industries PLC; mem. Comm. of EEC with responsibility for Budget and Financial Control, Financial Institutions, Personnel and Admin. 1977–81,

Vice-Pres. with responsibility for Budget and Financial Control, Financial Institutions and Taxation 1981–85; Chancellor Univ. of Bath 1998–; Chair. Royal Inst. of Int. Affairs (Chatham House) 1986–95; Gov. and mem. Council of Man., Ditchley Foundation; mem. Devt. Cttee. Nat. Portrait Gallery; Chair. European Policy Forum, Cambridge Univ. Library Devt. Cttee.; Pres. The Construction Industry Trust for Youth; Vice-Pres. British Lung Foundation; Freeman City of London; Hon. Fellow Gonville and Caius Coll., Cambridge; Hon. LL.D. (Bath Univ.); McKinsey Foundation Book Award 1971. *Publications:* Oil: the Biggest Business 1968, The Multinationals 1971, Making Sense of Europe 1986, Options for British Foreign Policy in the 1990s (with William Wallace) 1988; numerous articles. *Leisure interests:* reading, family, conversation. *Address:* 35 Westbourne Park Road, London, W2 5QD, England.

TUGWELL, Very Rev. Simon Charles ffoster, O.P., S.T.M., D.D., S.T.D.; British ecclesiastic; b. 4 May 1943, Brighton; s. of Major Herbert Tugwell and Mary Brigit Tugwell (née Hutchinson); ed. Lancing Coll. and Corpus Christi Coll. Oxford; received into Roman Catholic Church 1964; joined Dominican Order 1965; ordained priest 1971; lecturer and tutor, Blackfriars, Oxford 1972–92, Regent of Studies 1976–90; mem. Faculty of Theology, Oxford Univ. 1982–92; Fellow Istituto Storico Domenicano 1987– (Pres. 1992–97); Ed. Monumenta Ordinis Praedicatorum Historica 1992–; Visiting Lecturer, Pontifical Univ. of St. Thomas, Rome 1977–93; Flannery Prof. of Theology, Gonzaga Univ. Spokane 1982–83; Read-Tuckwell Lecturer on Human Immortality, Bristol Univ. 1988; Consultor to Congregation for Causes of Saints 1994–97; has lectured in many countries around the world. *Publications:* The Way of the Preacher 1979, Early Dominicans 1982, Ways of Imperfection 1984, Albert and Thomas 1988, The Apostolic Fathers 1989, Letters of Bede Jarrett (ed.) 1989, Human Immortality and the Redemption of Death 1990, Saint Dominic 1995, Miracula S. Dominici . . . Petri Calo legendae S. Dominici (ed.) 1997, Bernardi Guidonis: Scripta de Sancto Dominico (ed.) 1998; articles on aspects of theology and Dominican history, especially sources for the life of St. Dominic. *Leisure interests:* music, science fiction, teddy bears, avoiding sightseeing. *Address:* Istituto Storico Domenicano, Largo Angelicum 1, 00184 Rome, Italy.

TU'IPELAHAKE, H.R.H. Prince Fatafehi, K.B.E.; Tongan politician; b. 7 Jan. 1922; second son of the late Queen Salote Tupou III and the late Prince Uiliami Tungi, C.B.E., Prime Minister of Tonga; brother of King Taufa'ahau Tupou IV (q.v.); m. H.R.H. Princess Melenaite Topou Moheofo 1947; two s. four d.; ed. Newington Coll., Sydney, N.S.W., and Gatton Agricultural Coll., Queensland; Gov. of Vava'u 1952–65; Prime Minister of Tonga 1965–91, also fmr. Minister for Agric. and Marine Affairs, Forestry and Fisheries; Chair. Commodities Bd.; 'Uluafi Medal 1982. *Address:* c/o Office of the Prime Minister, Nuku'alofa, Tonga.

TUITA, Baron Siosaia Aleamotu'a Laufilitonga Tuita, C.B.E.; Tongan government official and civil servant; b. 29 Aug. 1920, Lapaha, Tongatapu; s. of 'Isileli Tupou Tuita and Luseane Halaevalu Fotofili; m. Fatafehi Lapaha Tupou 1949; two s. two d.; ed. Tupou Coll., Wesley Coll., Auckland, New Zealand, Oxford Univ.; Lieut. Officer, Tonga Defence Service 1942–43; Court Interpreter and Registrar, Supreme Court 1945; Asst. Sec. Prime Minister's Office 1954; Acting Gov. of Vava'u 1956, Gov. 1957; Acting Minister of Lands 1962, of Police 1964–65; Chair. Niuafo'ou evacuation 1965; Minister of Lands and Survey and Minister of Health 1965; assumed title of Tuita 1972, conferred with title of Baron Tuita of 'Utungake 1980; Deputy Prime Minister and Minister of Lands, Survey and Natural Resources 1972–89; mem. Privy Council; Chair. Town Planning Cttee., Energy Standing Cttee., Royal Land Comm., Tonga Broadcasting Comm.; mem. numerous socs. *Leisure interests:* rugby, cricket, driving, fishing. *Address:* Mahinafekite, Nuku'alofa, Tonga (Home). *Telephone:* 22451 (Home).

TUIVAGA, Hon. Sir Timoci (Uluiburotu), Kt., B.A.; Fijian judge; b. 21 Oct. 1931; s. of Isimeili Siga Tuivaga and Jessie Hill; m. Vilimaina Leba Parrott Tuivaga 1958; three s. one d.; ed. Univ. of Auckland; native magistrate 1958–61, called to the Bar, Gray's Inn 1964, N.S.W. 1968; Crown Counsel 1965–68, Prin. Legal Officer 1968–70, Puisne Judge 1972, Acting Chief Justice 1974, Chief Justice of Fiji 1980–87, 1988–; sometime Acting Gov.-Gen. 1983–87. *Leisure interests:* golf, gardening. *Address:* 228 Ratu Sukuna Road, Suva, Fiji. *Telephone:* 303-782.

TUKE, Sir Anthony Favill, Kt.; British banker; b. 22 Aug. 1920, Berkhamsted, Herts.; s. of late Anthony William Tuke and Agnes Edna Tuke (née Gannaway); m. Emilia Mila Antic 1946; one s. one d.; ed. Winchester Coll., Magdalene Coll., Cambridge; Scots Guards 1940–46; joined Barclays Bank Ltd. 1946; various appts. in Barclays Bank Ltd. including Chair. Birmingham Bd. 1964–68; Dir. Barclays Bank Ltd. 1965–90, Barclays Bank U.K. 1971–81, Barclays Bank Int. 1966–87; Vice-Chair. Barclays Bank Int. Ltd. (fmrly. Barclays Bank D.C.O.) 1968–72, Chair. 1972–79; Vice-Chair. Barclays Bank Ltd. 1972–73, Chair. 1973–81; Dir. Rio Tinto-Zinc Corpn. Ltd. 1980–91, Chair. 1981–85; Dir. Royal Insurance PLC 1978–92, Deputy Chair. 1985–92; Dir. Merchants Trust PLC 1969–94, Whitbread Investment Co. PLC 1984–93; mem. Bd. various subsidiary cos. in Barclays Group; Deputy Chair. Cttee. of London Clearing Bankers 1974–76, Chair. 1976–78; fmr. Vice-Pres. Inst. of Bankers; Pres. MCC 1982–83; Dir. Savoy Hotel 1982–94, Chair. 1984–94. *Leisure interests:* lawn tennis, gardening. *Address:* Freelands, Wherwell, nr. Andover, Hants., SP11 7JS, England.

TUKEY, John W(ilder), PH.D., SC.D.; American statistician; b. 16 June 1915, New Bedford, Mass.; s. of Ralph H. Tukey and Adah M. Tasker; m. Elizabeth Louise Rapp 1950; ed. Brown Univ. and Princeton Univ.; Fine Instructor, Mathematics, Princeton Univ. 1939–41, Asst. Prof. 1941–48, Assoc. Prof. 1948–50, Prof. 1950–66, Prof. of Statistics 1965–, Donner Prof. of Science 1976–; mem. Tech. Staff, Bell Telephone Labs. 1945–58, Asst. Dir. of Research 1958–61, Assoc. Exec. Dir. Research 1961–; mem. Pres.'s Science Advisory Cttee. 1960–63, Nat. Advisory Cttee. for Oceans and Atmosphere 1975–; mem. N.A.S. 1967, American Acad. of Arts and Sciences, American Philosophical Soc.; Hon. mem. Royal Statistical Soc.; Guggenheim Fellow 1949–50; Fellow, Inst. of Mathematical Statistics (Pres. 60), American Statistical Asscn. (Vice-Pres. 1955–57), American Soc. of Quality Control, American Asscn. for the Advancement of Science (Chair. 1972, 1974); Samuel Wilks Medal, American Statistical Asscn. 1965; Nat. Medal of Science 1973; Hon. Sc.D. (Brown Univ., Yale Univ., Case Inst. of Technology, Univ. of Chicago). *Publications:* Convergence and Uniformity in Topology, Statistical Problems of the Kinsey Report (with W. G. Cochran and F. Mosteller), The Measurement of Power Spectra from the Point of View of Communications Engineering (with R. B. Blackman) 1959, Exploratory Data Analysis, Vols. I-III 1970–71, Robust Estimates of Location: Survey and Advances (with others) 1972, The Statistics Cum Index, Vol. I (with T. L. Dolby) 1973, Index to Statistics and Probability, Vols. II-V (with others) 1973–75; more than 150 technical papers. *Leisure interest:* table tennis. *Address:* c/o Statistics Department, Princeton University, Princeton, NJ 08540 (Offices); 115 Arreton Road, Princeton, NJ 08540; Summer: P.O. Box 304, Westport Point, MA 02791, U.S.A. (Home). *Telephone:* (609) 924-5095 (Home); (617) 636-2612 (Summer).

TULEYEV, Aman Gumirovich (Aman-geldy Moldagazyevich); Russian politician; b. 13 May 1944, Krasnovodsk, Turkmenistan; m.; two s.; ed. Tikhoretsk Railway Tech. School, Novosibirsk Inst. of Railway Eng., Acad. of Social Sciences at Cen. Cttee. CPSU; worked on railway station Kemerovo Region, head Mezhdurechensk Railway Station, Head Novokuznetsk Dept. Kemerovo Railway 1978–88; Head Div. of Transport and Communications Regional Cttee. CPSU 1988–90; Chair, Kemerovo Regional Soviet 1991; Peoples' Deputy of Russian Fed. 1990–93; Cand. for Presidency 1991; supported coup d'etat attempt 1991; Chair. Legis. Ass. Kemerovo Region 1994–96; Minister of Co-operation with C.I.S. 1996–97; Gov. Kemerovo Region 1997–; mem. Council of Fed. 1993–95, 1997–. *Address:* Office of the Governor, Sovetsky prosp. 62, 650099 Kemerovo, Russia (Office). *Telephone:* (3842) 36 34 09 (Office). *Fax:* (3842) 36 48 33.

TULIN, Dmitri Vladislavovich, M.B.A., PH.D.; Russian economist; b. 26 March 1956; s. of late Vladislav Tulin and of Emma S. Tulin; m. Vera Nerod 1977; two s.; ed. Moscow Financial Inst. and U.S.S.R. Inst. of Econs. and Finance; economist, Int. Monetary and Econ. Dept. U.S.S.R. State Bank (Gosbank) 1978, Sr. Economist 1980, Chief Economist 1985, Man. 1989, Man. Dir., mem. Bd. Securities Dept. 1990; Deputy Chair. Cen. Bank of Russian Fed. 1991–94; Exec. Dir. for Russian Fed. IMF 1994–96; Chair. Bd. Vneshtorgbank (Bank for Foreign Trade) 1996–. *Publications:* articles on monetary econs. and banking in Russian professional journals. *Leisure interests:* gardening, chess. *Address:* Vneshtorgbank, 16 Kuznetsky Most, 103031 Moscow, Russia. *Telephone:* (095) 258-4709. *Fax:* (095) 234-0475.

TULLY, Daniel Patrick, (retd.); American finance executive; b. 2 Jan. 1932, New York; m. Grace Tully; four c.; ed. St. John's Univ. New York and Harvard Business School; army service 1953–55; joined Merrill Lynch & Co., Inc. 1955; Account Exec. Stamford Office 1959, Man. 1970, Vice-Pres. 1971; Individual Sales Dir. New York HQ 1976; mem. Bd. Dirs. Merrill Lynch, Pierce, Fenner & Smith 1977, Chair. and C.E.O. 1985; Exec. Vice-Pres. Marketing 1979; Pres. Individual Services Group 1982 and Exec. Vice-Pres. Merrill Lynch & Co. Inc. 1982, Pres. and C.O.O. 1985–92, Chair. Bd. and C.E.O. 1992–, Chair., C.E.O., Pres. 1993–97, now Chair. Emer.; Vice-Chair. American Stock Exchange 1984–86, Securities Industry Asscn. 1985–86; Dir. New York Stock Exchange. *Address:* Merrill Lynch & Co. Inc., World Headquarters, North Tower, World Financial Center, 250 Vesey Street, New York, NY 10281, U.S.A. *Telephone:* (212) 449-1000.

TULLY, (William) Mark, O.B.E., M.A.; British journalist; b. 24 Oct. 1935, Calcutta, India; s. of William S.C. Tully and Patience T. Tully; m. Frances M. Butler 1960; two s. two d.; ed. Marlborough Coll., Trinity Hall, Cambridge; Regional Dir. Abbeyfield Soc. 1960–64; Personnel Officer BBC 1964–65, Asst. Rep. then Rep. (a.i.), BBC, Delhi 1965–69, Hindi Programme Organizer BBC External Services, London 1969–70, Chief Talks Writer 1970–71, Chief of Bureau BBC, Delhi 1971–93, BBC South Asia Corresp. 1993–94; now freelance writer, broadcaster, journalist 1994–; Hon. Fellow Trinity Hall, Cambridge 1994; Hon. D.Litt. (Strathclyde) 1997; Dimbleby Award (BAFTA) 1984, Padma Shri (India) 1992 etc. *Leisure interests:* bird watching, reading, railways, theology. *Publications:* Amritsar Mrs Gandhi's Last Battle (jtly.) 1985, Raj to Rajiv (jtly.) 1988, No Full Stops in India 1991, The Heart of India 1995, The Lives of Jesus 1996. *Address:* 1 Nizamuddin East, Delhi 110013, India. *Telephone:* 462-9687. *Fax:* 460-2878.

TUMANOV, Vladimir Aleksandrovich, D.JUR.; Russian lawyer and university professor; b. 20 Oct. 1926, Kropotkin, Krasnodar Dist.; s. of Aleksandr Tumanov and Serafima Tumanov; m. 1948; one s.; ed. Inst. of Foreign Trade, U.S.S.R. Ministry of Foreign Trade, All-Union Inst. of Law; scientific researcher All-Union Inst. of Law 1952–59; chief scientific researcher, Head of Comparative Law Dept., Inst. of State and Law U.S.S.R. (now Russian) Acad. of Sciences; Pres. Int. Asscn. of Legal Science at UNESCO (resgnd.); mem. State Duma (Russian Parl.) 1993–94; mem. Constitutional Court of Russian Fed. Oct. 1994–, Chair. 1995–97; mem. European Court of Human Rights 1997–. *Publications include:* Force-majeure in Civil Law 1958, Constitutional Law of Foreign Countries (Vols. 1, 2) 1987–88, Legal Nihilism and Prospects of the Rule of Law 1991, Constitution of the Russian Federation of 1993 (an encyclopaedic guide) 1994. *Leisure interests:* canoeing, travel. *Address:* 13th Parkovaya str. 25-1-40, 105215 Moscow, Russia. *Telephone:* 206-18-39.

TUMI, H.E. Cardinal Christian Wiyghan; Cameroonian ecclesiastic; b. 15 Oct. 1930, Kikaikelaki; ordained 1966, elected to Yagoua 1979, consecrated bishop 1980, coadjutor bishop 1982, diocesan bishop 1984; Archbishop of Douala; cr. Cardinal 1988. *Address:* Archevêché, B.P. 179, Douala, Cameroon. *Telephone:* 423714. *Fax:* 421837.

TUMIM, Sir Stephen, Kt., M.A.; British judge and university official; b. 15 Aug. 1930, London; s. of Joseph Tumim and Renee Tumim; m. Winifred Borthwick 1962; three d.; ed. St. Edward's School, Oxford, Worcester Coll., Oxford; called to the Bar 1955; Co. Court Judge 1978; H.M. Chief Insp. of Prisons in England and Wales 1987–95; Prin. St. Edmund's Hall, Oxford 1996–98; Bencher Middle Temple 1990. *Leisure interests:* books and pictures. *Address:* 18 Stafford Place, London, SW1E 6NP, England.

TUNCER, Cengiz; Turkish politician; b. 1942, Manavgat, Antalya; m.; two c.; ed. Univ. of Ankara; has worked as sr. exec. in various pvt. firms; Parl. Deputy 1983; Minister of Transport 1989–91; fmr. Chair. Planning and Budget Comm.; fmr. Deputy Chair. Motherland Party. *Address:* c/o Anavatan Partisi, 13 Cad. 3, Balgat, Ankara, Turkey.

TUNE, Tommy (Thomas James); American theatrical performer, director and choreographer; b. 28 Feb. 1939, Witchita Falls, Tex.; s. of Jim Tune and Eva Tune; ed. Lamar High School, Houston, Lon Morris Junior Coll., Univ. of Tex. at Austin and Univ. of Houston; began professional career as chorus dancer on Broadway; appeared in films Hello, Dolly! and The Boyfriend; appeared on Broadway in Seesaw (Tony Award, Best Supporting Actor); Off-Broadway Dir. The Club, Cloud 9 (Obie and Drama Desk Awards), Stepping Out 1987; Choreographer, A Day in Hollywood/A Night in the Ukraine (Tony Award); Dir. The Best Little Whorehouse in Texas, Nine (Tony Award 1982); actor and choreographer, My One and Only (Tony Award 1983), Grand Hotel 1989 (London 1992), The Will Rogers Follies, Bye, Bye Birdie 1991–92; recipient of many other awards. *Leisure interests:* cooking, yoga, reading, drawing. *Address:* c/o International Creative Management, 40 W. 57th Street, New York, NY 10019; 1501 Broadway, 1312, New York, NY 10036, U.S.A. *Telephone:* (212) 719-2166.

TUNG CHEE-HWA, B.SC.; Chinese business executive; b. 29 May 1937, China; m. Betty H.P. Tung; two s. one d.; ed. Univ. of Liverpool; Chair. Island Navigation Corpn. Ltd., fmr. Chair. Orient Overseas (Holdings) Ltd.; Dir. Sing Tao Newspapers Ltd., Sun Hung Kai Bank Ltd., Hsin Chong Properties Ltd., Mass Transit Railway Corpn.; Vice-Chair. Preparatory Cttee. for Hong Kong Special Admin. Region; mem. Exec. Council, Hong Kong Govt. 1992–96; Chief Exec. of Hong Kong Special Admin. Region 1997–; mem. 8th NPC 1993–; numerous civic appts. etc.; Hon. Consul of Monaco in Hong Kong. *Address:* Suite 705–708 Asia Pacific Finance Tower, Citibank Plaza, 3 Garden Road, Hong Kong Special Administrative Region, People's Republic of China.

TUNLEY, David Evatt, A.M., D.LITT., B.MUS., F.A.H.A.; Australian professor of music; b. 3 May 1930, Sydney; s. of Dr. Leslie Tunley and Dr. Marjorie Tunley; m. Paula Patricia Laurantus 1959; one s. two d.; ed. The Scots Coll., Sydney, State Conservatorium of Music, Sydney; music master, Fort Street Boys' High School, Sydney 1952–57; joined staff of Dept. of Music, Univ. of Western Australia 1958, Personal Chair. of Music 1980–, now Emer., Head Dept. of Music 1985–90, Hon. Sr. Research Fellow in Music 1994–; studied under Nadia Boulanger with French Govt. Scholarship 1964–65; Scholar-in-residence, Rockefeller Foundation, Bellagio, Italy 1987; Fowler Hamilton Visiting Research Fellow, Christ Church, Oxford 1993; Visiting Scholar, Wolfson Coll. Oxford 1996; Founder/Conductor Univ. Collegium Musicum, 1976–83; Founder/Chair. York Winter Music Festival, 1982–; Nat. Pres. Musicological Soc. of Australia 1980–81; Chair. Music Bd., Australia Council 1984–85; Chevalier dans l'ordre des Palmes Académiques. *Publications:* Couperin 1982, Harmony in Action 1984, The French Cantata in Facsimile, 17 vols. 1990, Romantic French Song in Facsimile (6 vols.) 1994, The 18th Century French Cantata 1997, contribs. to the New Grove Dictionary of Music and Musicians, The New Oxford History of Music. *Leisure interests:* reading, travel, theatre. *Address:* Department of Music, University of Western Australia, Nedlands 6009, Western Australia (Office); 100 Dalkeith Road, Nedlands 6009, Western Australia, Australia (Home). *Telephone:* (08) 9386 1934 (Home).

TUNNEY, John V., B.A., LL.B.; American politician; b. 26 June 1934, New York City; s. of Gene Tunney and Mary Lauder Tunney; m. 2nd Kathinka Osborne 1977; two s. two d.; ed. Westminster School, Simsbury, Conn., Yale Univ., Univ. of Virginia School of Law and Acad. of Int. Law, The Hague; practised law, New York City 1959–60, Riverside 1963–; Judge Advocate, U.S. Air Force 1960–63; taught Business Law at Univ. of Calif., Riverside; mem. U.S. House of Representatives 1964–70; Senator from California 1971–77; mem. Manatt, Phelps, Rothenberg and Tunney, Los Angeles 1977–86; Chair., Bd. of Dirs. Cloverleaf Group Inc., Los Angeles 1986–, Enterprise Plan Inc., Trusted Brands Inc.; Gen. Partner Sun Valley Ventures 1994–. Democrat. *Leisure interests:* tennis, sailing, skiing, handball. *Address:* 1819 Ocean Ave, Santa Monica, CA 90401, U.S.A.

TUPOLEV, Aleksey Andreyevich, D. TECH. SC.; Russian aircraft designer; b. 20 May 1925, Moscow; s. of A. N. Tupolev; m.; two c.; ed. Moscow Aviation Inst.; mem. CPSU 1959–91; engineer, Leading Constructor, Head of Dept., Deputy Constructor, Chief Constructor, Deputy Gen. Constructor, Gen. Constructor, Moscow Machine Bldg. Plant, Opyt (later A. N. Tupolev Aviation Scientific Constructing Bureau) 1949–; Prof. 1964–; mem. U.S.S.R. (now Russian) Acad. of Sciences 1987–; Deputy to U.S.S.R. Supreme Soviet 1974–89; People's Deputy 1989–; developed with father various supersonic jets (among which TU-144, in 1968); State Prize 1967, Lenin Prize 1980; Hero of Socialist Labour 1972, other orders and medals. *Address:* A. Tupolev ANTK, Acad. Tupolev Nab. 15, 111250 Moscow, Russia. *Telephone:* (095) 263-7067 (Office); (095) 244-7765 (Home).

TURABI, Dr Hassan Al-; Sudanese politician; Pres. Nat. Ass. April 1996–; Leader Nat. Islamic Front (NIF). *Address:* National Islamic Front, Khartoum, Sudan.

TURANDJONZODA, Khodji Akbar; Tajikistan ecclesiastic and politician; b. 16 Feb. 1954; ed. Tashkent Islam Inst., Amman Univ., Jordan; teacher Tashkent Islam Inst. 1980–82; Chief Kasikolon of Tajikistan 1988–; elected mem. Supreme Soviet Tajik S.S.R., active participant of democratic movt. against Islamic fundamentalists; denounced as Enemy of the People 1992, forced to emigrate, in hiding 1993; Deputy Chair. Islamic Resurrection Party of Tajikistan 1994; took active part in negotiations between Govt. and Opposition 1995–97; Deputy Prime Minister of Coalition Govt. 1998–. *Address:* House of Government, Ruduki prospect 42, 734051 Dushanbe, Tajikistan. *Telephone:* (3772) 232758.

TURBAY AYALA, Julio César; Colombian diplomatist and politician; b. 18 June 1916, Bogotá; m.; one s. three d.; mem. House of Reps. 1943–53; Minister of Mines and Energy 1957–58, of Foreign Affairs 1958–61; Senator 1962–70; twice elected Vice-Pres. of Colombia, Pres. of Colombia 1978–82; Perm. Rep. to UN 1967; Amb. to U.K. 1970, to U.S.A. 1974–76, now Amb. to Holy See; Hon. LL.D. (Univ. of Cauca) 1957. *Address:* Colombian Embassy, Via Cola di Rienzo 285/12B, 00192 Rome, Italy. *Telephone:* (6) 3211681. *Fax:* (6) 3211703.

TURECK, Rosalyn; American concert artist, conductor and professor; b. 14 Dec. 1914, Chicago; d. of Samuel Tureck and Monya Lipson; m. George Wallingford Downs 1964; ed. Juilliard School of Music, New York; debut in Chicago 1924; first New York appearance 1932; concert tours U.S.A.and Canada 1937–, Europe 1947–, South Africa 1959, South America 1963, Israel 1963, World Tour (Far East and India) 1971, Europe, Israel, S. America, N. American Bach Festivals 1985/86; repeated appearances at major int. festivals; specializes in the keyboard works of J. S. Bach, played on the piano, harpsichord, clavichord, organ, antique and electronic instruments; conductor 1956–; Conductor-soloist, London Philharmonic 1958, New York Philharmonic 1958, Israel Philharmonic 1963, Kol Israel Orchestra 1963, Int. Bach Soc. Orchestra 1967, 1968, 1970, Madrid Chamber Orchestra 1972, Washington Nat. Symphony 1972, Tureck Bach Players (Carnegie Hall) 1981, Bach Triennial Celebration Series (solo recitals and orchestral concerts conducting Tureck Bach Players), Carnegie Hall 1984/85, soloist, Casals Festival 1991; Visiting Prof. of Music, Washington Univ., St. Louis 1963–64; Prof. of Music, Univ. of Calif., San Diego 1966–72, Regents Lecturer 1966; Visiting Prof., Univ. of Md. 1982–84, Yale Univ. 1992; Regents Prof. U.C.L.A. 1995–; lecturer numerous univs. and colls. of music, including Univ. of Winnipeg, Canada, Southern Methodist Univ., Dallas, Tex. 1989, Brandeis and Yale Univs., Menendez Pelayo Inst., Univ. of Santander, Spain 1990; Visiting Fellow, St. Hilda's Coll., Oxford 1974, Hon. Life Fellow 1974–; Visiting Fellow, Wolfson Coll., Oxford 1975–; Founder-dir. of Composers of Today 1951–55, Tureck Bach Players 1957, Int. Bach Soc. 1966 (now Tureck Bach Inst.), Int. Bach Soc. Orchestra 1967, Inst. for Bach Studies 1968, Tureck Bach Research Foundation 1994; mem. many musical socs.; Hon. D.Mus., (Colby Coll. 1964, Roosevelt Univ. 1968, Wilson Coll. 1968, Oxford Univ. 1977, etc.); First Prize, Greater Chicago Piano Playing Tournament 1928, Winner Schubert Memorial Contest, Nat. Fed. of Music Clubs 1935; Officer's Cross of Order of Merit, Fed. Repub. of Germany 1979. *Recordings:* The Well-tempered Clavier (Books I and II), Goldberg Variations, Six Partitas, Italian Concerto, French Overture, Introduction to Bach, A Bach Recital, A Harpsichord Recital, Goldberg Variations and Aria and Ten Variations in the Italian Style (harpsichord), Italian Concerto, Chromatic Fantasia and Fugue, Four Duets (piano), Rosalyn Tureck Plays Bach (Live at the Teatro Colón, Buenos Aires) 1992, Live in St. Petersburg (5 vols.) 1995. *Publications:* An Introduction to the Performance of Bach (3 vols.) 1959–60 (trans. into Japanese 1966, Spanish 1972), A Critical and Performance Edition of J. S. Bach's Chromatic Fantasia and Fugue; numerous articles in various periodicals; Editor: Paganini, Niccolo—Perpetuum Mobile 1950, J. S. Bach—Sarabande, C Minor 1960, Scarlatti, Alessandro—Sarabande and Gavotte; Ed. Tureck Bach Urtext Series, Publr. Italian Concerto 1983, Lute Suite, E Minor 1984, Lute Suite C Minor 1985, Authenticity 1994. *Films:* Fantasy and Fugue: Rosalyn Tureck plays Bach 1972, Rosalyn Tureck plays Bach on Harpsichord and Organ 1977, Joy of Bach (Rosalyn Tureck Soloist and

Consultant) 1979, Bach on the Frontier of The Future 1980, Rosalyn Tureck Plays Bach in Ephesus, Turkey 1985, Rosalyn Tureck plays Bach, Live at the Teatro Colón, Buenos Aires 1992, Live in St. Petersburg 1995. *Address:* c/o Lies Askonas, 6 Henrietta Street, London W.C.2, England; Tureck Bach Research Foundation, Windrush House, Davenant Road, Oxford, OX2 8BX, England; Tureck Bach Institute, 215 E. 68th Street, New York, NY 10021, U.S.A. *Telephone:* (01865) 515760 (Oxford). *Fax:* (01865) 512620 (Oxford).

TURKEVICH, Anthony Leonid, PH.D.; American professor of chemistry; b. 23 July 1916, New York; s. of Rev. L. J. Turkevich and Anna (Chervinsky) Turkevich; m. Ireene T. Podlesak 1948; one s. one d.; ed. Columbia Grammar School, Curtis High School, Dartmouth Coll., Hanover N.H., Princeton Univ.; Research Assoc. Physics Dept. Univ. of Chicago 1940–41; Research Assoc. Manhattan Project, Columbia Univ., Univ. of Chicago, Los Alamos Scientific Lab. 1942–46; participant in test of first nuclear bomb, Almagordo, N.M. 1945, in theoretical work on and test of thermonuclear reactions 1945–, calculations on the production of helium during the first minutes of the Big Bang Universe 1949, chemical analysis of the moon 1967–; Asst. Prof. Enrico Fermi Inst. and Chemistry Dept. Univ. of Chicago 1946–48, Assoc. Prof. 1948–53, Prof. 1953–86, James Franck Prof. of Chemistry 1965–70, Distinguished Service Prof. 1970–86, Prof. Emer. 1986; Consultant to U.S. Atomic Energy Comm. Labs. 1946–; Del. to Geneva Conf. on Nuclear Test Suspension 1958, 1959; Fellow Los Alamos Science Lab. 1972–; mem. of N.A.S., American Chem. Soc., American Physical Soc., A.A.A.S., American Acad. of Arts and Sciences; Hon. D.Sc. (Dartmouth Coll.) 1971; E. O. Lawrence Award of U.S. Atomic Energy Comm. 1962, Atoms for Peace Prize 1969, Nuclear Applications Award (American Chemical Soc.) 1972, New York Acad. Pregel Award 1986. *Publications:* Global atmospheric diffusion; Double beta decay of U-238; articles on intra-nuclear cascades, on chemical analysis of the moon and on high energy nuclear reactions. *Leisure interests:* hiking, reading. *Address:* Department of Chemistry, University of Chicago, 5640 South Ellis Avenue, Chicago, IL 60637 (Office); 175 Briarwood Loop, Oak Brook, IL 60521, U.S.A. (Home).

TURKI, Abdul Aziz Al-Abdullah Al-, B.A.; Saudi Arabian oil official; b. 12 Aug. 1936, Jeddah; m.; two d.; ed. Univ. of Cairo; U.S. Embassy, Jeddah 1953–54; ARAMCO 1954–66; Dir. Office of Minister of Petroleum and Mineral Resources 1966–68; Dir. of Gen. Affairs, Directorate of Mineral Resources 1968–70; Asst. Sec.-Gen. OAPEC 1970–75; Sec.-Gen. Supreme Advisory Council for Petroleum and Mineral Affairs, Saudi Arabia 1975–90; Saudi Gov. for OPEC 1975–90; Deputy Minister, Ministry of Petroleum and Mineral Resources 1975–; Chair. Arab Maritime Petroleum Transport Co., Kuwait 1981–87, Pemref 1982–89; mem. Bd. of Dirs. Petromin 1975–89, ARAMCO 1980–89; Sec.-Gen. OAPEC 1990–. *Leisure interests:* tennis, swimming. *Address:* Organization of Arab Petroleum Exporting Countries, P.O. Box 20501, Safat 13066, Kuwait. *Telephone:* 4844500. *Fax:* 4815747.

TÜRKMEN, Ilter; Turkish politician and diplomatist; b. 1927, Istanbul; s. of Behçet Türkmen and Nuriye Türkmen; m. Mina Türkmen 1953; one s. one d.; ed. Galatasaray Lycée, Istanbul, Faculty of Political Sciences, Ankara; Dir.-Gen. of Policy Planning Dept., Ministry of Foreign Affairs 1964, Asst. Sec.-Gen. for Political Affairs 1967; Amb. to Greece 1968, to U.S.S.R. 1972, to France 1988–90; Perm. Rep. to UN in New York 1975–78, 1985–88, in Geneva 1983–85; Special Rep. to UN Sec.-Gen. for Human Affairs in South East Asia 1979–80; Minister of Foreign Affairs 1980–83; fmr. Commr.-Gen. UNRWA. *Address:* c/o Ministry of Foreign Affairs, Dişişleri Bakanligi, Yeni Hizmet Binasi, 06520 Balgat, Ankara.

TURLINGTON, Christy; American fashion model; b. 2 Jan. 1969, Walnut Creek, Calif.; discovered at age 14; with Ford Models Inc. 1985; model for Revlon, Maybelline 1993; face of Calvin Klein's Eternity Fragrance; promotes advertisement campaigns for Michael Kors, Camay Soap, Special K Cereal. *Film:* Catwalk 1996; appeared in George Michael's video Freedom. *Address:* c/o Ford Models Inc., 344 E 59th Street, New York, NY 10022, U.S.A.

TURNAGE, Mark-Anthony; British composer; b. 10 June 1960, Corringham, Essex; s. of Roy Turnage and Patricia Knowles; m. 1st Susan Shaw 1989 (divorced 1990); m. 2nd Helen Reed 1992; two s.; ed. Hassenbrook Comprehensive School, Palmers Sixth Form, Grays and Royal Coll. of Music (RCM); studied composition at RCM with Oliver Knussen and John Lambert; Mendelssohn scholarship to study with Gunther Schuller and Hans Werner Henze in Tanglewood, U.S.A. 1983; first opera, Greek, premiered at first Munich Biennale 1988; Composer in asscn. with City of Birmingham Symphony Orchestra (CBSO), composing three maj. works 1989–93; Composer in asscn. with E.N.O. 1995–99; works include: Night Dances 1980–81, On All Fours 1985, Greek 1986–88, Three Screaming Popes 1988–89, Some Days 1989, Drowned Out 1992–93, Your Rockaby 1992–93, Blood on the Floor 1994–95, Dispelling the Fears 1995, Twice Through the Heart 1997, Country of the Blind 1997, Four-Horned Fandango 1997, The Silver Tassie 1997–99, Silent Cities 1998. *Leisure interests:* football, films, theatre. *Address:* c/o Schott & Co. Ltd., 48 Great Marlborough Street, London, W1V 2BN, England. *Telephone:* 0171-494 1487. *Fax:* 0171-287 1529.

TURNBERG, Sir Leslie Arnold, Kt., M.B., CH.B., M.D.; British professor of medicine; b. 22 March 1934, Manchester; s. of Hyman Turnberg and Dora Bloomfield; m. Edna Barme 1968; one s. one d.; ed. Stand Grammar School, Whitefield and Univ. of Manchester; lecturer, then Sr. lecturer in Gastroenterology, Univ. of Manchester, Manchester Royal Infirmary 1968–73; Prof. of Medicine Univ. of Manchester 1973–97; hon. consultant physician, Hope Hosp. 1973–97; Pres. Royal Coll. of Physicians 1992–97, Asscn. of Physicians of G.B. and Ireland 1996–97; Chair. Conf. of Medical Royal Colls. 1993–95, Strategic Review of London's Health Services 1997; Pres. Medical Protection Soc. 1997–, Medical Council on Alcoholism 1997–; Chair. Bd. of Public Health Lab. Service 1997–; Scientific Adviser Asscn. of Medical Research Charities 1997–; Pres. (elect) British Soc. of Gastroenterology; Hon. F.R.C.P. (Edin.), F.R.C.P. (Glasgow), F.R.C.P.I., F.R.C.O.G.; Hon. Fellow Royal Colls. of Ophthalmologists, Psychiatrists, Surgeons of England; Hon. Fellow Royal Australian Coll. of Physicians, S. African Coll. of Medicine, Pakistan Coll. of Physicians, Acad. of Medicine of Hong Kong and of Singapore and several others; Hon. D.Sc. (Salford) 1996, (Manchester) 1998. *Publications:* Intestinal Secretion 1982, Mechanisms of Mucosial Protection in the Upper Gastro-Intestinal Tract 1983, Clinical Gastroenterology 1989. *Leisure interests:* reading, antiquarian books, walking, talking, Chinese ceramics. *Address:* c/o Public Health Laboratory Service, 61 Colindale Avenue, London, NW9 5DF, England. *Telephone:* 0181-200 6868.

TURNBULL, Andrew, C.B., C.V.O.; British civil servant; b. 21 Jan. 1945; s. of Anthony Turnbull and Maria Turnbull; m. Diane Clarke 1967; two s.; ed. Enfield Grammar School, Christ's Coll., Cambridge; Overseas Devt. Inst. Fellow working as economist to Govt. of Zambia 1968–70; Asst. Principal H.M. Treasury 1970, Prin. 1972, Asst. Sec. 1978, Head of Gen. Expenditure Policy Group 1985–88, Deputy Sec. (Public Finance) 1992, Second Perm. Sec. 1993–94; Pvt. Sec. to Prime Minister 1983–85, Under Sec. 1985, Prin. Pvt. Sec. 1988–92; Perm. Sec. Dept. of Environment 1994–. *Leisure interests:* walking, running, opera. *Address:* Department of the Environment, 6th Floor, Eland House, Bressenden Place, London, SW1E 5DU, England.

TURNBULL, Lyle E. J., A.O.; Australian company director; b. 13 April 1928, Geelong; s. of H. W. Turnbull and Hilda Turnbull; m. 1st Jeanette Mashado 1953 (died 1982); one s. one d.; m. 2nd Jennifer Malone 1984; ed. Geelong Coll.; joined The Herald and Weekly Times Ltd. 1946; journalist The Sun News-Pictorial 1946–67, in Asia, Middle East and Europe 1950, New York Bureau 1950–51, London 1956–58, Asst. Ed. 1958–62, Ed. 1965–67; Deputy Ed.-in-Chief Herald and Weekly Times Ltd. 1962–65, 1967–70, Ed.-in-Chief 1970–75, Man. Ed. 1975–84, Dir. 1972–89, Exec. Dir. 1984–89; Chair. Australian Associated Press 1985–95, Consultant 1995–; Chair. Australian Section Commonwealth Press Union 1974–86, London Council of the Commonwealth Press Union 1986–; Dir. Reuters Ltd., London 1974–89, Reuters Holdings U.K. 1984–89, Trustee Reuters 1993–; mem. Exec. Bd. Int. Press Inst., Vienna 1995–; Astor Award (U.K.) 1984. *Leisure interest:* sailing. *Address:* Australian Associated Press, Level 5, 530 Collins Street, Melbourne, Vic. 3000, Australia. *Telephone:* (61-3) 499-3725. *Fax:* (61-3) 499-3170.

TURNBULL, Malcolm Bligh, B.A., LL.B., B.C.L.; Australian banker and lawyer; b. 24 Oct. 1954, Sydney; s. of Bruce B. Turnbull and Coral Lansbury; m. Lucinda M. F. Hughes 1980; one s. one d.; ed. Sydney Grammar School, Univ. of Sydney and Univ. of Oxford (Rhodes Scholar); State Parl. Corresp. for Nation Review 1976; journalist, The Bulletin 1977–78; Exec. Asst. to Chair. Consolidated Press Holdings Ltd. 1978; journalist, The Sunday Times, London 1978–79; barrister, Sydney 1980–82; Gen. Counsel and Sec. Consolidated Press Holdings Ltd. 1983–85; solicitor in pvt. practice, Turnbull McWilliam, Sydney 1986–87; Prin. Turnbull and Co. (Solicitors) 1987; Man. Dir. Turnbull & Partners Ltd. (Investment Bankers), Sydney 1987–97; Chair. Axiom Forest Resources Ltd. (HK) 1991–92; Dir. Perseverance Corpn. Ltd. 1993–94, Star Mining Corpn. NL 1993–95; Dir. Australian Republican Movt. 1991–, Chair. 1993–; Chair. Cttee. to advise on changing Australia to Republic; Chair., Man. Dir. Australian and N.Z. Operations, Goldman Sachs Australia 1997–; Henry Lawson Prize for Poetry 1975. *Publication:* The Spycatcher Trial 1988, The Reluctant Republic 1993. *Leisure interests:* reading, walking, riding, gardening. *Address:* Goldman Sachs Australia, Level 48, Governor Phillip Tower, 1 Farrer Place, Sydney, N.S.W. 2000; Level 8, 1 Chifley Square, Sydney, N.S.W. 2000, Australia. *Telephone:* (02) 2235899.

TURNBULL, Rt. Rev. Michael, M.A.; British ecclesiastic; b. 27 Dec. 1935, Yorks; s. of George Turnbull and Adeline Awty; m. Brenda Merchant 1963; one s. two d.; ed. Ilkley Grammar School, Keble Coll. Oxford and St. John's Coll. Durham; ordained deacon 1960, priest 1961; curate, Middleton 1960–61, Luton 1961–65; Domestic Chaplain to Archbishop of York 1965–69; Rector of Heslington and Chaplain, York Univ. 1969–76; Chief Sec. Church Army 1976–84; Archdeacon of Rochester 1984–88; Bishop of Rochester 1988–94, of Durham 1994–; mem. Gen. Synod of Church of England 1970–75, 1987–; mem. Archbishops' Council 1999–, Chair. Ministry Div. 1999–; Chair. Archbishops' Comm. on Org. of Church of England; Hon. D.Litt. *Publications:* Unity: the Next Step? (contrib.) 1972, God's Front Line 1979, Parish Evangelism 1980, Learning to Pray 1981. *Leisure interests:* cricket, family life. *Address:* Auckland Castle, Bishop Auckland, Co. Durham, DL14 7NR, England. *Telephone:* (01388) 602576. *Fax:* (01388) 605264.

TURNBULL, William; British sculptor, painter and print-maker; b. 11 Jan. 1922, Dundee, Scotland; m. Cheng Kim Lim 1960; two s.; ed. Slade School of Fine Art, London; one-man exhbns. in London, New York, San Francisco, Berlin, Stuttgart, Latin America, Toronto, Luxembourg, Singapore etc. since 1950 including IX Bienal, São Paulo and tour of S. American countries (sculpture and painting) 1967, Hayward Gallery, London (painting) 1968, Tate Gallery Retrospective (sculpture and painting) 1973 and exhbns.

at Waddington Galleries, London 1967, 1969, 1970, 1976, 1978, 1981, 1985, 1987, 1991, 1998, Serpentine Gallery 1995; has participated in numerous group exhbns. around the world since 1950; works in public collections in U.K., U.S.A., Australia and Germany. *Leisure interests:* reading, music, chess, swimming. *Address:* c/o Waddington Galleries, 11 Cork Street, London, W1X 1PD, England. *Telephone:* 0171-437 8611. *Fax:* 0171-734 4146.

TURNER, George, DR.IUR.; German academic; b. 28 May 1935, Insterburg; s. of Albert Turner and Martha Turner; m. Edda Horstmann 1963; three s.; law clerk 1959–63; Legal Asst. 1963–66; Docent 1966–68; legal counsel and Prof. 1968–70; Pres. Univ. of Hohenheim 1970–86; Senator for Science and Research in W. Berlin 1986–89; Pres. West German Rectors' Conf. 1979–83. *Publications:* ten books and numerous essays and articles on legal topics, and university management. *Leisure interests:* sport, literature. *Address:* Hohenheim University, 70593 Stuttgart, Germany. *Telephone:* 0711/ 4592786.

TURNER, George William, M.A., F.A.H.A.; Australian reader in English (retd.); b. 26 Oct. 1921, Dannevirke, N.Z.; s. of Albert George Turner and Elinor Jessie Turner; m. Beryl Constance Barbara Horrobin 1949; two s.; ed. Univ. of N.Z., Univ. Coll. London, and N.Z. Library School; secondary school teacher, N.Z. 1944–46; librarian, Christchurch 1949–54; English Dept., Univ. of Canterbury 1955–64; Reader in English, Univ. of Adelaide, Australia 1965–86; Festschrift: Lexicographical and Linguistic Studies: Essays in honour of G. W. Turner (Ed. T. L. and Jill Burton) 1988. *Publications:* The English Language in Australia and New Zealand 1966, Stylistics 1973, The Australian Pocket Oxford Dictionary (Ed.) 1984, The Australian Concise Oxford Dictionary (Ed.) 1987, The Australian Oxford Paperback Dictionary (Ed. with Beryl C. B. Turner) 1989, The Annotated Such Is Life (with others) 1991. *Address:* 3 Marola Avenue, Rostrevor, South Australia 5073, Australia. *Telephone:* (8) 83372257.

TURNER, Grenville, D.PHIL., F.INST.P., F.R.S.; British professor of isotope geochemistry; b. 1 Nov. 1936, Todmorden; s. of Arnold Turner and Florence Turner; m. Kathleen Morris 1961; one s. one d.; ed. St. John's Coll., Cambridge and Balliol Coll., Oxford; Asst. Prof., Univ. of Calif., Berkeley 1962–64; Lecturer, Sheffield Univ. 1964–74, Sr. Lecturer 1974–79, Reader 1979–80, Prof. of Physics 1980–88; Prof. of Isotope Geochem., Manchester Univ. 1988–; Visiting Assoc. in Nuclear Geophysics, Calif. Inst. of Tech. 1970–71; Council mem. Royal Soc. 1990–92; Fellow Meteoritical Soc. 1980, Geochemical Soc. and European Soc. of Geochem. 1996, American Geophysical Union 1998; Rumford Medal, Royal Soc. 1996, Leonard Medal, Meteoritical Soc. 1999. *Publications:* numerous scientific papers. *Leisure interests:* photography, walking, theatre. *Address:* Department of Earth Sciences, University of Manchester, Manchester, M13 9PL (Office); 42 Edgehill Road, Sheffield, S7 1SP, England (Home). *Telephone:* (0161) 275-3800 (Office). *Fax:* (0161) 275-3947.

TURNER, Rt. Hon. John Napier, P.C., C.C., Q.C., M.P., M.A., B.C.L.; Canadian politician and lawyer; b. 7 June 1929, Richmond, Surrey, England; s. of Leonard and Phyllis (née Gregory) Turner; m. Geills McCrae Kilgour 1963; three s. one d.; ed. schools in Ottawa, and Univs. of British Columbia, Oxford and Paris; M.P. 1962–76, 1984–93; Minister without Portfolio 1965; Registrar-Gen. 1967–68; Minister of Consumer and Corp. Affairs Jan.-July 1968; Solicitor-Gen. April-July 1968; Minister of Justice and Attorney-Gen. 1968–72; Minister of Finance 1972–75; Leader Liberal Party of Canada 1984–90; Prime Minister of Canada June–Sept. 1984, Leader of Opposition 1984–90; Partner, McMillan, Binch (law firm), Toronto 1976–84; Partner, Miller Thomson (law firm), Toronto 1990–; mem. Bd. Dirs. The Dominion of Canada General Insurance Co., The Empire Life Insurance Co., The Loewen Group, McDermott Int., Noranda Forest, Purolator Courier Ltd. *Publications:* The Senate of Canada 1961, Politics of Purpose 1968. *Leisure interests:* tennis, canoeing, skiing. *Address:* Miller Thomson, 20 Queen Street West, Box 27, Suite 2500, Toronto, Ont., M5H 3S1 (Office); 27 Dunloe Road, Toronto, Ont., M4V 2W4, Canada (Home).

TURNER, (Jonathan) Adair, M.A.; British business executive; b. 5 Oct. 1955; s. of Geoffrey Vincent Turner and Kathleen Margaret Turner; m. Orna Ni Chionna 1985; two d.; ed. Hutcheson's Grammar School, Glasgow, Glenalmond School, and Gonville & Caius Coll. Cambridge; Pres. Cambridge Union; began career with British Petroleum PLC 1979; Chase Manhattan Bank 1979–82; McKinsey & Co. 1982–95, Dir. 1994–95; Dir.-Gen. CBI 1995–; mem. British Overseas Trade Bd., Nat. Advisory Cttee. for Educ. and Training Targets; Sr. Scholar Cambridge Univ. *Leisure interests:* skiing, opera, theatre, gardening. *Address:* Confederation of British Industry, Centre Point, 103 New Oxford Street, London, WC1A 1DU, England. *Telephone:* 0171–379 7400. *Fax:* 0171–497 2596.

TURNER, Kathleen, M.F.A.; American actress; b. 19 June 1954, Springfield, Mo.; m. Jay Weiss 1984; one d.; ed. Cen. School of Speech and Drama, London, S.W. Mo. State Univ., Univ. of Md.; various theatre roles including Broadway debut, Gemini 1978; *TV Series include:* The Doctors 1977. *Films include:* Body Heat 1981, The Man With Two Brains 1983, Crimes of Passion 1984, Romancing the Stone 1984, Prizzi's Honour 1985, The Jewel of the Nile 1985, Peggy Sue Got Married 1986, Julia and Julia 1988, Switching Channels 1988, The Accidental Tourist 1989, The War of the Roses 1990, V.I. Warzhawski 1991, House of Cards, Undercover Blues 1993, Serial Mom 1994, Naked in New York 1994, Moonlight and Valentino, A Simple Wish, The Real Blonde; producer Hard Boiled 1990. *Address:* c/o ICM, 8942 Wilshire Boulevard, Beverly Hills, CA 90211, U.S.A.

TURNER, Admiral Stansfield, M.A.; American naval officer (retd.), lecturer and author; b. 1 Dec. 1923, Chicago, Ill.; s. of Oliver Stansfield Turner and Wilhelmina Josephine (née Wagner) Turner; m. Eli Karin Gilbert 1985; ed. Amherst Coll., U.S. Naval Acad., Annapolis, Oxford Univ., U.K.; Rhodes Scholar, Oxford Univ. 1947; active duty, U.S. Navy, serving minesweeper, destroyers, U.S.S. Horne (guided missile cruiser in action in Vietnamese conflict); served in Office of Chief of Naval Operations, then in Office of Asst. Sec. of Defence for Systems Analysis; Advanced Man. Program, Harvard Business School; Exec. Asst. and Naval Aide to Sec. of the Navy 1968–70; Rear Admiral 1970; C.O. Carrier Task Group in U.S.S. Independence, U.S. Sixth Fleet 1970; Dir. Systems Analysis Div. of Office of Chief of Naval Operations, Dept. of the Navy 1971–72; Vice-Admiral 1972; Pres. U.S. Naval War Coll., Newport, R.I. 1972–74; Commdr. U.S. Second Fleet and NATO Striking Fleet Atlantic 1974–75; Admiral 1975; C.-in-C. Allied Forces Southern Europe, NATO 1975–77; Dir. Cen. Intelligence (CIA) 1977–81; Prof. Graduate School of Public Affairs, Univ. of Md. 1991–; Hon. Fellow, Exeter Coll., Oxford 1981–; Nat. Security Medal, Legion of Merit, Bronze Star. *Publications:* Secrecy and Democracy: The CIA in Transition 1985, Terrorism and Democracy 1991, Caging the Nuclear Genie: An American Challenge for Global Security 1997. *Leisure interests:* tennis, reading. *Address:* 1320 Skipwith Road, McLean, VA 22101, U.S.A. *Telephone:* (703) 528-2023.

TURNER, Ted (Robert Edward, III); American broadcasting executive and yachtsman; b. 19 Nov. 1938; s. of Robert Turner and Frances Rooney; m. 1st Judy Nye (divorced); one s. one d.; m. 2nd Jane S. Smith 1965 (divorced 1988); one s. two d.; m. 3rd Jane Fonda (q.v.) 1991; ed. Brown Univ.; Gen. Man. Turner Advertising, Macon, Ga. 1960–63; Pres. and C.E.O. various Turner cos., Atlanta 1963–70; Chair. Bd. and Pres. Turner Broadcasting System, Inc. (merged with Time Warner to form Time Warner Inc.) 1970–96; Vice-Chair. Time Warner Inc. 1996–; Pres. Atlanta Braves 1976–, and now owner; Chair. Bd. Atlanta Hawks 1977–, Better World Soc., Wash. 1985–90; f. and Chair. UN Foundation; Dir. Martin Luther King Center, Atlanta; acquired New Line Cinema Corpn. 1993; sponsor, creator, The Goodwill Games, Moscow 1986; winner 1977 America's Cup in yacht Courageous; named Yachtsman of Year four times; numerous awards. *Address:* Turner Broadcasting System Inc., One CNN Center, Box 105366, Atlanta, GA 30348, U.S.A.

TURNER, Tina (Annie Mae Bullock); American singer; b. 26 Nov. 1939, Brownsville, Tenn.; m. Ike Turner 1956 (divorced 1978); four s.; singer with Ike Turner Kings of Rhythm, Ike and Tina Turner Revue; concert tours of Europe 1966, 1983–84, Japan and Africa 1971; Grammy Award 1972, 1985 (three), 1986; Chevalier des Arts et des Lettres. *Films:* Gimme Shelter 1970, Soul to Soul 1971, Tommy 1975, Mad Max Beyond Thunderdome 1985, What's Love Got to Do with It (vocals) 1993, Last Action Hero 1993. *Recordings include:* River Deep, Mountain High 1966, Proud Mary 1970, Blues Roots 1972, Nutbush City Limits 1973, The Gospel According to Ike and Tina 1974; solo albums: Let Me Touch Your Mind 1972, Tina Turns the Country On 1974, Acid Queen 1975, Rough 1978, Private Dancer 1984, Break Every Rule 1986, Foreign Affair 1989, Simply the Best 1991, The Collected Recordings: Sixties to Nineties (with others) 1994, Wildest Dreams 1996. *Address:* c/o CAA, 9830 Wilshire Boulevard, Beverly Hills, CA 90212, U.S.A.

TURNER, Wilfred, B.SC., C.M.G., C.V.O.; British former diplomatist and civil servant; b. 10 Oct. 1921, Littleborough, Lancs.; s. of Allen Turner and Eliza (née Leach) Turner; m. June Gladys Tite 1947; two s. one d.; ed. Heywood Grammar School and London Univ.; Ministry of Labour and Nat. Service 1938–42, 1947–55; served in British army 1942–47; Asst. Labour Adviser, British High Comm. in India 1955–59; Sr. Wages Insp., Ministry of Labour 1959–60; Prin. at Ministry of Health 1960–66, Sec. Cttee. of Safety of Drugs 1963–66; joined Foreign and Commonwealth Office 1966; First Sec. Kaduna, N. Nigeria 1966–69, Kuala Lumpur, Malaysia 1969–73; Deputy High Commr. in Ghana 1973–77; High Commr. in Botswana 1977–81; Dir. Southern Africa Assen. 1983–88, Transportation Systems and Market Research Ltd., British Rail 1987–90; mem. Royal Inst. of Int. Affairs, Royal African Soc. *Leisure interest:* hill-walking. *Address:* 44 Tower Road, Twickenham, Middx., TW1 4PE, England. *Telephone:* 0181-892 1593.

TURNER, William Cochrane, B.S.; American diplomatist and business executive; b. 27 May 1929, Red Oak, Iowa; s. of James Lyman Turner and Josephine Cochrane Turner; m. Cynthia Dunbar 1955; two s.; ed. Northwestern Univ.; Vice-Pres. and Dir., Western Man. Consultants Inc. 1955–60, Pres., C.E.O. and Dir. 1960–74, Chair. and Dir. Western Man. Consultants Europe S.A. 1969–74; Dir. Ryan-Evans Drug Stores Inc. 1964–68, First Nat. Bank of Arizona 1970–74; Trustee American Graduate School of Int. Man. 1972–, Vice-Chair. 1972–86, Chair. 1986–88; mem. Advisory Cttee. for Trade Negotiations 1982–84; Amb. and U.S. Rep. to OECD 1974–77; mem. U.S. Advisory Comm. on Int. Educ. and Cultural Affairs 1969–74, Nat. Review Bd., Center for Cultural and Tech. Interchange between East and West 1970–74, Western Int. Trade Group, U.S. Dept. of Commerce 1972–74; Pres. and Dir. Phoenix Symphony Asscn. 1957–72; Gov. Atlantic Inst. for Int. Affairs, Paris 1977–88, Joseph H. Lauder Inst. of Man. and Int. Studies, Univ. of Pa. 1983–; Chair. and C.E.O. Argyle Atlantic Corpn. 1977–, Avon Int. Advisory Council, Avon Products Inc. 1985–98, Int.

Advisory Council, Plasma Tech. Inc. 1992–97; Chair Bd. GO Wireless Int. Ltd. 1995–97; Chair. European Advisory Council, Asia Pacific Advisory Council, AT&T Int. 1981–88; Dir. Pullman Inc. 1977–80, Nabisco Brands Inc. 1977–85, Goodyear Tire and Rubber Co. 1978–, Salomon Inc. 1980–93, Energy Transition Corpn. (also Vice-Chair.) 1979–86, The Atlantic Council of the U.S. 1977–92, AT&T Int. 1980–84, Swensen's Inc. 1981–84, Atlantic Inst. Foundation Inc. 1984–90, Rural/Metro Corpn. 1993–, Microtest Inc. 1995–; mem. Caterpillar Tractor Co. Asia Pacific Advisory Council 1984–90, Spencer Stuart Advisory Council 1984–90; mem. European Community-U.S. Business Council, Washington, D.C. 1978–79, Advisory Bd. Center for Strategic and Int. Studies, Georgetown Univ. 1978–81, Nat. Councils, The Salk Inst. 1978–82, Council of American Ambs. 1984–, Council on Foreign Relations 1980–, US-Japan Business Council 1987–93, Nat. Advisory Council on Business Educ., Council on Int. Educ. Exchange, New York City 1987–, Trade and Environment Cttee. Nat. Advisory Council for Environmental Policy and Tech., U.S. Environmental Protection Agency, Washington, D.C. 1991–95, Gov.'s Strategic Partnership for Econ. Devt., Phoenix 1992–95; Chair. and mem. ASM Int. Advisory Council, Advanced Semi-conductor Materials Int. NV, Bilthoven 1985-88; Trustee and mem. Exec. Cttee., U.S. Council for Int. Business 1977–, Heard Museum, Phoenix 1983–85 (mem. Nat. Advisory Bd. 1985–93); Nat. Trustee, Nat. Symphony Orchestra Asscn. 1973–84; mem. Bd. of Govs. American Hosp. of Paris 1974–77, Bd. of Trustees, American School of Paris, Saint-Cloud 1975–77, Greater Phoenix Leadership 1979–97; Chair. Bd. of Dirs. Mercy Ships Int., A Ministry of Youth with a Mission, Lindale, Tex. 1986–; Dir. Ariz. Econ. Council, Phoenix 1989–93, mem. Nat. Council, World Wildlife Fund and The Conservation Foundation, Washington, D.C. 1989–95; f. mem. Pacific Council on Int. Policy 1995; Hon. LL.D. (American Grad. School of Int. Man.) 1993. *Leisure interests:* tennis, symphony, opera, international political and economic relations. *Address:* 5434 East Lincoln Drive, No. 74, Paradise Valley, AZ 85253, U.S.A. *Telephone:* (602) 840-1530. *Fax:* (602) 840-1657.

TURNER-WARWICK, Dame Margaret, D.B.E., M.A., D.M., PH.D., F.R.C.P., F.R.C.P.E., F.R.A.C.P., F.F.P.H.M.; British physician; b. 19 Nov. 1924, London; d. of William Harvey Moore, Q.C. and Maude Baden-Powell; m. Richard Turner-Warwick 1950; two d.; ed. Maynard School, Exeter, St. Paul's School for Girls, Univ. of Oxford and Univ. Coll. Hosp.; consultant physician, Royal Brompton Hosp., London Chest Hosp 1965–72; Prof. of Medicine, Cardiothoracic Inst. 1972–87, Dean 1984–87; Pres. Royal Coll. of Physicians 1989–92; Chair. Royal Devon & Exeter Health Care NHS Trust; Fellow Univ. Coll. London 1991; Hon. Bencher, Middle Temple; Fellow Royal Coll. of General Practitioners, Faculty of Occupational Medicine, Royal Coll. of Physicians Canada, Royal Coll. of Pathologists, Royal Coll. of Physicians Ireland and others; Hon. F.A.C.P.; Hon. Fellow Lady Margaret Hall, Oxford, Green Coll., Oxford, Girton Coll., Cambridge, Univ. Coll., London, Imperial Coll., London; Hon. F.R.C.P. & S. (Canada); Hon. D.Sc. (New York, Sussex, Hull, Exeter, London, Oxford, Cambridge) and numerous other honours. *Publications:* Immunology of the Lung 1978, Occupational Lung Disease (jtly.) 1981; chapters in textbooks and articles in medical journals. *Leisure interests:* gardening, water-colour painting, violin playing, country life and family. *Address:* Pynes House, Thorverton, Exeter, EX5 5LT, Devon, England. *Telephone:* (01392) 861173. *Fax:* (01392) 860940.

TURNQUEST, Sir Orville (Alton), G.C.M.G., Q.C., LL.B.; Bahamian politician and lawyer; b. 19 July 1929, Grants Town, New Providence; s. of late Robert Turnquest and Gwendolyn Turnquest; m. Edith Louise Thompson 1955; one s. two d.; ed. Govt. High School, Univ. of London; articled in chambers of Hon. A.F. Adderley 1947–53; called to The Bahamas Bar 1953, to English Bar (Lincoln's Inn) 1960; Counsel and Attorney of Supreme Court of Bahamas; Notary Public; in pvt. practice 1953–92; stipendiary and circuit magistrate and coroner 1959; law tutor and mem. Examining Bd., The Bahamas Bar 1965–92; Pres-Bahamas Bar Asscn.; Chair. Bahamas Bar Council 1970–72; Sec.-Gen. Progressive Liberal Party 1960–62; M.P. for S. Cen. Nassau 1962–67, for Montagu 1982–94; Opposition Leader in Senate 1972–79; Deputy Leader Free Nat. Movt. 1987–94; Attorney-Gen. 1992–94, Minister of Justice 1992–93, of Foreign Affairs 1992–94, Deputy Prime Minister 1993–94; Gov.-Gen. The Bahamas Jan. 1995–; mem. Del. to first Bahamas Constitutional Conf., London 1963, Bahamas Independence Conf., London 1972; Pres. Commonwealth Parl. Asscn. 1992–93; Patron The Bahamas Games; Chancellor of Diocese of Nassau and The Bahamas; mem. Anglican Cen. Educational Authority, Nat. Cttee. of United World Colls., Bd. of Govs. St. John's Coll., St. Anne's High School; fmr. mem. Prov. Synod, Anglican Church of W.I. *Leisure interests:* tennis, swimming, music, reading. *Address:* Government House, P.O. Box N-8301, Nassau, Bahamas.

TUROW, Scott F., J.D.; American author and lawyer; b. 12 April 1949; s. of David Turow and Rita Pastron; m. Annette Weisberg 1971; three c.; ed. Amherst Coll. and Stanford and Harvard Univs.; mem. Bar, Ill. 1978, U.S. Dist. Court. Ill. 1978, U.S. Court of Appeals (7th Circuit) 1979; Assoc. Suffolk Co. Dist. Attorney, Boston 1977–78; Asst. U.S. Attorney, U.S. Dist. Court, Ill., Chicago 1978–86; partner Sonnenschein, Nath & Rosenthal, Chicago 1986–; mem. Chicago Council of Lawyers. *Publications:* One L.: An Inside Account of Life in the First Year at Harvard Law School 1977, Presumed Innocent 1987, The Burden of Proof 1990, Pleading Guilty 1993, The Laws of our Fathers 1996; contribs. to professional journals. *Address:* Sonnenschein, Carlin, Nath & Rosenthal, Sears Tower, Suite 8000, 233 S. Wacker Drive, Chicago, IL 60606, U.S.A.

TURRO, Nicholas John, PH.D.; American professor of chemistry; b. 18 May 1938, Middletown, Conn.; s. of Nicholas J. Turro and Philomena Russo; m. Sandra J. Misenti 1960; two d.; ed. Wesleyan Univ. and Calif. Inst. of Tech.; Instr. Columbia Univ. 1964–65, Asst. Prof. 1965–67, Assoc. Prof. 1967–69, Prof. of Chem. 1969–82, William P. Schweitzer Prof. of Chem. 1982–, Chair. Dept. of Chem. 1981–84, Co-Chair. Dept. of Chemical Eng. and Applied Chem. 1997–; Sloan Fellowship 1966–70; Guggenheim Fellowship, Univ. of Oxford 1984; mem. N.A.S., American Acad. of Arts and Sciences; Fellow, New York Acad. of Science; several awards and distinctions; Hon. D.Sc. (Wesleyan Univ.) 1984. *Publications:* Molecular Photochemistry 1965, Modern Molecular Photochemistry 1978. *Leisure interests:* racquet ball, music, reading. *Address:* Department of Chemistry, Columbia University, 3030 Broadway, New York, NY 10027 (Office); 125 Downey Drive, Tenafly, NJ 07670, U.S.A. (Home).

TURTURRO, John; American actor; b. 28 Feb. 1957; s. of Nicholas Turturro and Katherine Turturro; m. Katherine Borowitz; one s.; ed. State Univ. of New York at New Paltz and Yale Drama School; fmr. labourer; Best Actor Award, Cannes Film Festival, for role in Barton Fink 1991; Obie Award for stage appearance in Danny and the Deep Blue Sea. *Films include:* Raging Bull, Desperately Seeking Susan, Exterminator III, The Flamingo Kid, To Live and Die in L.A., Hannah and Her Sisters, Gung Ho, Offbeat, The Color of Money, The Italian Five Corners, Do the Right Thing, Miller's Crossing, Men of Respect, Mo' Better Blues, Jungle Fever, Barton Fink, Brain Doctors, Mac (co-author, dir. and actor), Being Human, Quiz Show, Fearless, Clockers, Search and Destroy, Unstrung Heroes, Sugartime (dir.), Grace of My Heart (dir.), Box of Moonlight (dir.), The Truce (dir.), The Big Lebowski 1997, Animals 1997, Lesser Prophets 1998, Rounders 1998, Illuminata (dir.) 1998. *Address:* c/o ICM, 8942 Wilshire Boulevard, Beverly Hills, CA 90211, U.S.A.

TUSA, John, M.A.; British broadcaster and administrator; b. 2 March 1936, Zlín, Czechoslovakia (now Czech Repub.); s. of Jan Tusa and Lydie Sklenarova; m. Ann Hilary Dowson 1960; two s.; ed. Gresham's School, Holt, Trinity Coll., Cambridge; joined BBC as general trainee 1960; Producer, Talks and Features, BBC World Service 1964–66; Ed., Forum World Features 1966–67; Presenter, The World Tonight, Radio 4 1970–78, 24 Hours, BBC World Service 1972–78, Newsweek, BBC2 1978–79, Newsnight, BBC2 1979–86, Timewatch, BBC2 1982–84, One O'Clock News BBC 1993–95; Chair. London News Radio 1993–94; Pres. Wolfson Coll., Cambridge Feb.–Oct. 1993; Man. Dir. BBC World Service 1986–92; Man. Dir. Barbican Centre July 1995–; Chair. Advisory Cttee., Govt. Art Collection 1993, BBC Marshall Plan of the Mind Trust 1992–; mem. Bd. English Nat. Opera 1994–; Freeman City of London 1997; Trustee Nat. Portrait Gallery 1988–, Wigmore Hall Trust, Thomson Foundation 1993–95; Dr. h.c. (Heriot Watt) 1993; Hon. LL.D. (London) 1993; Hon. D.Litt. (City Univ.) 1997; Royal TV Soc. TV Journalist of the Year 1984, BAFTA Richard Dimbleby Award 1984, Broadcasting Press Guild Award 1991, RTS Presenter of the Year 1995, Broadcasting Press Guild Radio Programme of the Year (for "20/20—A View of the Century") 1995, Order of the White Rose (Finland) 1998. *Publications:* The Nuremberg Trial 1983 (with Ann Tusa), The Berlin Blockade (with Ann Tusa) 1988, Conversations with the World 1990, A World in Your Ear 1992. *Leisure interests:* tennis, string quartets, listening. *Address:* 21 Christchurch Hill, London, NW3 1JY, England. *Telephone:* 0171-435 9495. *Fax:* 0171-435 9495.

TUSK, Donald Franciszek; Polish politician; b. 22 April 1957, Gdańsk; m.; one s. one d.; ed. Gdańsk Univ.; journalist Maritime Publishing House, with magazines Pomerania and Samorządność; with Gdańsk Height Services Work Co-operative; ed. Gazeta Gdańska 1990; mem. Liquidation Cttee. RSW Press-Books-Ruch; assoc. Free Trade Unions by the Coast; co.-f. Independent Students Union (NZS); mem. Solidarity Trade Union 1980–; founder and ed. underground publ. Przegląd Polityczny; leader Programme Council for Liberals Foundation; leader Congress of Liberals 1989, later the Liberal-Democratic Congress (KLD); Vice-Chair. Freedom Union (UW) 1994 following the merger with Democratic Union (UD); deputy to Sejm (Parl.) 1991–93; leader Parl. Liberal-Democratic Club and Special Cttee. for Consideration of Constitutional Acts; Senator and Vice-Marshal of Senate 1997–. *Leisure interest:* football. *Address:* Kancelaria Senatu RP, ul. Wiejska 6, 00-902 Warsaw, Poland. *Telephone:* (22) 694 14 43, 694 10 44.

TUSQUETS BLANCA, Oscar; Spanish architect and designer; b. 14 June 1941, Barcelona; m. Victoria Roqué; one c.; ed. Arts & Crafts School, Barcelona, School of Architecture, Barcelona; with Luis Clotet, Studio Per 1964–84; co-founder B.D. Ediciones de Diseño 1972; Prof., School of Architecture, Barcelona 1975–76, 1979–80; f. Tusquets, Diaz & Assoc. Architects' Office, with Carlos Diaz 1987. *Work includes:* Casa Fullá, Barcelona, Belvedere Regas, Girona, Casa Vittoria, Sala Mae West, Dali Museum, Figueras, re-modelling of Music Palace, Barcelona, Pavilion, Parc de la Villette, Paris, Chandon Vinery, Barcelona, dwellings in Kashii, Fukuoka, and in Olympic Village, Barcelona, La Coupole, Montpellier, music auditorium, Canary Islands, public square, shopping mall and dwellings, Den Bosch, Netherlands; design of furniture and objects for various producers, bus stop for Hanover, Germany; FAD Architecture Prize (five times), FAD Design prize (six times), Sant Jordi Cross 1987, Ciutat de Barcelona Prize 1988, 1989, Nat. Prize for Design 1988, Fukuoka Beautification Award 1994, Medalla de Oro 1998; Chevalier des Arts et des Lettres. *Leisure interest:* painting. *Address:* Tusquets, Diaz & Assoc., Cavallers 50, 08034 Barcelona, Spain. *Telephone:* 280.55.99. *Fax:* 280.40.71.

TUTIN, Dorothy, C.B.E.; British actress; b. 8 April 1930, London; d. of late Dr. John Tutin and of A. E. Fryers; m. Derek Waring 1963; one s. one d.; ed. St. Catherine's Bramley, Surrey, and Royal Acad. of Dramatic Art, London; appeared at Stratford Festival 1958, 1960; took part in Shakespeare Memorial Theatre tour of Russia 1958; Shakespeare recital before Pope, Vatican 1964; Evening Standard Award as Best Actress 1960, Variety Club of Great Britain Award for Best Film Actress 1972; Soc. of the West End Theatre Award for Actress of the Year in a Revival 1976. *Principal roles:* Rose (The Living Room), Katherine (Henry V), Sally Bowles (I am a Camera), St. Joan (The Lark), Catherine (The Gates of Summer), Hedwig (The Wild Duck), Viola (Twelfth Night), Ophelia (Hamlet), Dolly (Once More, With Feeling), Portia (The Merchant of Venice), Cressida (Troilus and Cressida), Sister Jeanne (The Devils) 1961, 1962, Juliet (Romeo and Juliet) and Desdemona (Othello), Stratford-on-Avon 1961, Varya (The Cherry Orchard) 1961, Prioress (The Devils), Edinburgh 1962, Polly Peachum (The Beggar's Opera) 1963, Queen Victoria (Portrait of a Queen) 1965 and in New York 1968, Rosalind (As You Like It), Stratford-on-Avon 1967, Los Angeles 1968; Cleopatra (Antony and Cleopatra) 1977, Madame Ravanskaya (The Cherry Orchard); has also played in The Hollow Crown, New York 1963, Old Times 1971, Peter Pan 1971, 1972, What Every Woman Knows 1973, 1975, A Month in the Country 1974, 1976, Macbeth 1976, The Cherry Orchard 1978, The Double Dealer 1978, Undiscovered Country 1979, Reflections 1980, The Provok'd Wife 1980, The Deep Blue Sea 1981, After The Lions 1982, Ballerina 1984, Other Places, London 1985, Are You Sitting Comfortably 1986, Brighton Beach Memoirs 1986, Chalk Garden 1986, Thursdays Ladies 1987, Harlequinade and The Browning Version 1988, Desirée in A Little Night Music 1989, Party Time 1991, Henry VIII (Chichester) 1991, The Seagull 1992, Getting Married 1993, After October 1997. *Films include:* The Beggar's Opera, The Importance of Being Earnest, A Tale of Two Cities, Cromwell, Savage Messiah, South Riding 1978, The Shooting Party 1984. *Television appearances include:* The Double Dealer 1980, The Eavesdropper 1981, The Combination 1981, Life After Death 1981, La Ronde 1982, King Lear 1982, Landscape 1982, A Kind of Alaska, Murder with Mirrors, The Demon Lover, The Father 1985, Evensong 1986, Young Indy 1992, Body and Soul 1992, Jake's Progress, The Great Kandinsky 1994, Great Moments in Aviation, Alive and Kicking, Maybe It's the Last Time 1997. *Leisure interest:* music. *Address:* c/o Michael Whitehall, 125 Gloucester Road, London, SW7 4TE, England.

TUTT, Leo Edward, F.C.A., F.A.I.M., F.C.P.A.; Australian business executive; b. 6 April 1938, Sydney; s. of Leo Edward Tutt and Dorothy Tutt; m. Heather Coombe 1961; two s. one d.; ed. Knox Grammar School, Univ. of Sydney and Inst. of Chartered Accountants, Australia; C.A. 1966–71; Man. Dir. Tutt Bryant Ltd. 1971–74; C.E.O. Bowater Industries Australia Ltd. 1974–96; Chair. Royal and Sun Alliance Insurance Australia Ltd. 1994–, MIM Holdings Ltd. (Australia) 1998– (Dir. 1991–); Dir. Rexam PLC (fmrly. Bowater PLC) 1978–96, Friends Provident 1984–94, Grad. School of Man., Univ. of Sydney 1989–, State Rail Authority of N.S.W. (Australia) 1989–94, Metway Bank Ltd. (Australia) 1992–96; Hon. Fellow Univ. of Sydney 1996. *Leisure interests:* sailing, golf, reading. *Address:* 58 Prince Albert Parade, Newport, N.S.W. 2106, Australia 2106. *Telephone:* (2) 92211966 (Office); (2) 99795744 (Home). *Fax:* (2) 92352585 (Office); (2) 99973119 (Home).

TUTU, Most Rev. Desmond Mpilo, L.TH., M.TH.; South African ecclesiastic; b. 7 Oct. 1931, Klerksdorp; s. of Zachariah Tutu and Aletta Tutu; m. Leah Nomalizo Tutu 1955; one s. three d.; ed. Bantu High School, Bantu Normal Coll., Univ. of South Africa, St. Peter's Theological Coll., Rosettenville, King's Coll., Univ. of London; Schoolmaster 1954–57; Parish Priest 1960–; Theological Seminary Lecturer 1967–69; Univ. Lecturer 1970–71; Assoc. Dir. Theological Educ. Fund, World Council of Churches 1972–75; Dean of Johannesburg 1975–76; Bishop of Lesotho 1977–78, of Johannesburg 1984–86; Archbishop of Cape Town, Metropolitan of the Church of the Prov. of Southern Africa 1986–95, Archbishop Emer. 1995–; Chancellor Univ. of Western Cape 1988–; Chairperson Truth and Reconciliation Comm. 1995–99; Pres. All Africa Conf. of Churches 1987–97; Sec.-Gen. South African Council of Churches 1979–84; Visiting Prof. of Anglican Studies New York Gen. Theological Seminary 1984; elected to Harvard Univ. Bd. of Overseers 1989; Dir. Coca-Cola 1986–; Visiting Prof. Emory Univ., Atlanta 1998–; mem. Third Order of the Soc. of St. Francis; Hon. D.D., D.C.L., LL.D., Th.D. (Gen. Theol. Sem. New York, Kent Univ., Harvard Univ., Ruhr Bochum Univ.); Hon. D.Div. (Aberdeen) 1981; S.T.D. (Columbia) 1982; Dr. h.c. (Mount Allison Univ., Sackville, N.B., Strasbourg) 1988, Dr. h.c. (Oxford) 1990; Hon. LL.D. (South Bank Univ.) 1994; Hon. D.D. (Exeter) 1997; F.K.C. (Fellow of King's Coll. London); numerous awards including Onassis Award, Family of Man Gold Medal 1983, Nobel Peace Prize 1984, Carter—Menil Human Rights Prize 1986, Martin Luther King Jr. Humanitarian Award 1986, Third World Prize (jt. recipient) 1989, Grand Cross of Merit, Germany 1996, Bill of Rights Award, American Civil Liberation Union Fund 1997, Henry W. Edgerton Civil Liberties Award, American Civil Liberties Union 1997, One Hundred Black Men Award, U.S.A. 1997, Peace Prize, Int. Community of UNESCO, Athens 1997; Order of Jamaica; Freedom of Borough of Merthyr Tydfil (Wales), Durham, Hull, Borough of Lewisham (U.K.), Florence, Lecco (Italy), Kinshasa (Democratic Repub. of Congo), Krugersdorp, Cape Town (S.A.). *Publications:* Crying in the Wilderness 1982, Hope and Suffering 1983 (both collections of sermons and addresses), The Rainbow People of God 1994, An African Prayer Book 1996. *Address:* c/o Truth and Reconciliation Commission, P.O. Box 3162, Cape Town 8000, South Africa. *Telephone:* 021 24 51 61. *Fax:* 021 24 52 25.

TUWAIJRI, Abdulrahman Al-, PH.D.; Saudi Arabian economist; b. 23 Feb. 1955, Almajmaah; s. of Abdulaziz Al-Tuwaijri and Hussah Al-Tuwaijri; m. Norah Alabdulatif 1982; three s. two d.; ed. King Saud Univ. and Iowa State Univ., U.S.A.; grad. asst. Dept. of Econs., King Saud Univ. 1978–84, Asst. Prof. 1985–88; Econ. Adviser Gen. Secr. Cooperation Council for the Arab States of the Gulf 1988–90; Alt. Exec. Dir. IMF 1991–95, Exec. Dir. 1995–. *Leisure interests:* reading, swimming. *Address:* International Monetary Fund, 700 19th Street, N.W., Room 11-306, Washington, DC 20431, U.S.A. *Telephone:* (202) 623 7284. *Fax:* (202) 623 4760.

TUYA, Nyam-Osoryn, M.A.; Mongolian politician; b. 1958, Ulan Bator; m.; two s. one d.; ed. Moscow State Inst. of Int. Relations, Univ. of Sorbonne, Univ. of Leeds; Ed., later Ed.-in-Chief Foreign Service Broadcasting Dept. State Cttee. for Radio, TV and Information 1980–90; researcher Strategic Studies Centre 1990–95; Sec. Elections Cttee. Mongolian Nat. Democratic Party 1995–96; Head Policy Planning Dept., Ministry of External Relations 1996–98; Minister for External Relations Dec. 1998–. *Address:* Ministry of External Relations, Ulan Bator, Mongolia.

TWIGGY (see Lawson, Lesley).

TWIN, Peter John, O.B.E., PH.D., F.R.S.; British professor of experimental physics; b. 26 July 1939, London; s. of Arthur James Twin and Hilda Ethel Twin; m. Jean Leatherland 1963; one s. one d.; ed. Sir George Monoux Grammar School, Walthamstow, London and Univ. of Liverpool; lecturer, Univ. of Liverpool 1964, Sr. lecturer, Prof. of Experimental Physics 1987–; Head, Nuclear Structure Facility, Daresbury Lab. Cheshire 1983–88; Weatherill Medal, Franklin Inst. U.S.A. 1991; Bonner Prize, Americal Physical Soc. 1991. *Publications:* articles in professional journals. *Address:* Oliver Lodge Laboratory, University of Liverpool, Liverpool, L69 3BX, England. *Telephone:* 0151-794 3378.

TWITCHETT, Denis Crispin, F.B.A.; British professor of Chinese studies (retd.); b. 23 Sept. 1925, London; m. Umeko Ichikawa 1956; two s.; ed. St. Catharine's Coll., Cambridge and Inst. of Far Eastern Culture, Tokyo Univ.; Lecturer in Far Eastern History, S.O.A.S., London Univ. 1954–56; Lecturer in Classical Chinese, Cambridge Univ. 1956–60; Prof. of Chinese and Head of Dept. of Far East, S.O.A.S. 1960–68; Prof. of Chinese, Cambridge Univ. 1968–80, Professorial Fellow of St. Catharine's Coll. 1968–80; Visiting Fellow, Inst. for Advanced Study, Princeton, U.S.A. 1973–74; Visiting Prof., Princeton Univ. 1978–79, Gordon Wu Prof. of Chinese Studies 1980–94. *Publications:* Financial Administration of the T'ang Dynasty 1963, Confucian Personalities (with A. F. Wright) 1963, Perspectives on the T'ang (with A. F. Wright) 1973, Times Atlas of China 1974, Printing and Publishing in Medieval China 1984, Reader T'ang History 1986, The Writing of Official History under the T'ang 1992, The Historian, His Readers, and the Passage of Time 1997; Gen. Ed. of Cambridge History of China 1977–. *Leisure interests:* music, fine arts. *Address:* 24 Arbury Road, Cambridge, CB4 2JE, England.

TWOMBLY, Cy; American artist; b. 25 April 1929, Lexington, Va.; ed. Boston Museum School of Fine Arts, Washington & Lee Univ., Art Students League, and Black Mountain Coll. with Frank Kline and Robert Motherwell; Head, Art Dept. Southern Seminary and Jr. Coll. Buena Vista, Va. 1955–56; one-man shows include: Milwaukee 1968, Nicholas Wilder Gallery 1969, Heron Inst. of Art, Indianapolis 1969, Guggenheim Museum, New York 1976, Museum of Modern Art, New York 1976, Vancouver Art Gallery 1982, Museum Hans Lange, Krefeld, Germany 1982, Santa Barbara Contemporary Arts Forum 1984; retrospective exhbn. Whitney Museum of Art, New York 1979; has participated in numerous group exhbns. including New York Univ. 1967, Whitney Museum American Art Annual 1967, Royal Acad. London 1981, Larry Gagosian Gallery, L.A. 1982, Young Hoffman Gallery, Chicago 1982, Blum Gallery, New York 1982; works in numerous public and pvt. collections in U.S.A. and Europe; Fellow American Acad. of Arts and Letters; Imperial Praemium Prize 1996. *Address:* c/o Gagosian Gallery, 980 Madison Avenue, New York, NY 10021, U.S.A.

TYAZHLOV, Anatoly Stepanovich; Russian politician; b. 11 Oct. 1942, Kopeisk, Chelyabinsk Region; m.; two c.; ed. Chelyabinsk Polytech. Inst.; metalworker, master, head of workshop, head of div., chief engineer Orenburg factory of prefabricated ferro-concrete structures 1959–69; chief engineer Orekhovo-Zuyevo house construction factory, Egoryevsk agric. construction factory 1969–73; chief engineer, man. of div., Head Moscow Region Dept. of Construction, Chair. State Production Asscn. Mosoblstroimatelialy 1973–82; Head Elektrostal Construction Trust 1982–90; Chair. Exec. Cttee. Moscow Region Soviet 1990–91; Head Moscow Region Admin. 1991–; Gov. of Moscow Region. 1995–; mem. Russian Council of Fed. 1993–; Pres. Int. Asscn. of Fraternised Towns; Pres. Asscn. of Admin. Heads of Regions and Territories—Chair. Union of Govs. of Russia 1992–; mem. Co-ordination Council on Introduction of Privatisation Cheques by Russian Govt. 1992–; mem. Fed. State Comm. on Problems of Reforms 1993–; mem. Int. Acad. of Ecological Sciences. *Address:* Office of the Governor, Staraya pl. 6, 103070 Moscow, Russia (Office). *Telephone:* (095) 206-60-93, 206-62-78.

TYCZKA, Mieczysław; Polish lawyer; b. 13 April 1925, Witków; s. of Szczepan Tyczka and Maria Tyczka; m. 1956; two d.; ed. Adam Mickiewicz Univ., Poznań; with Investment Bank 1950–53, Dist. Arbitration Comm.,

Poznań 1953–61, Adam Mickiewicz Univ., Poznań 1961–; Head Civil Procedure of Law and Admin. Faculty; Inst. for Environmental Foundations of Tourism and Recreation of Physical Educ. Acad., Poznań; Pres. of Constitutional Tribunal 1989–; mem. Cttee. for Legal Sciences of Polish Acad. of Sciences; mem. Poznań Friends of Learning Soc. (Chair. Comm. for Legal Sciences), Democratic Party (SD) 1963–. *Publications:* Organization of the Polish Judicature, Law-making Procedure in the Polish National Economy Governmental Agencies, Arbitration Proceedings, Proceedings in Law on Inventions and Industrial Designs. *Leisure interest:* tourism.

TYLER, Anne, B.A.; American author; b. 25 Oct. 1941, Minneapolis; d. of Lloyd Parry Tyler and Phyllis (Mahon) Tyler; m. Taghi M. Modarressi 1963; two c.; ed. Duke Univ., Columbia Univ.; Pulitzer Prize for Fiction for Breathing Lessons 1989. *Publications:* If Morning Ever Comes 1964, The Tin Can Tree 1965, A Slipping-Down Life 1970, The Clock Winder 1972, Celestian Navigation 1974, Searching for Caleb 1976, Earthly Possessions 1977, Morgan's Passing 1980, Dinner at the Homesick Restaurant 1982, The Accidental Tourist 1985, Breathing Lessons 1988, Saint Maybe 1991, Ladder of Years 1995, A Patchwork Planet 1998; short stories in magazines. *Address:* 222 Tunbridge Road, Baltimore, MD 21212, U.S.A.

TYLER, Liv; American actress; b. 1977; d. of Steve Tyler and Bebe Buell; fmrly. model Eileen Ford Agency. *Film appearances include:* Silent Fall, Empire Records, Heavy, Stealing Beauty, That Thing You Do!, Inventing the Abbotts, Plunkett and Macleane 1999, Armageddon 1998, Cookie's Fortune 1999.

TYMIŃSKI, Stanisław; Canadian/Peruvian politician and business executive; b. 1948, Pruszkow, Warsaw; m.; four c. (one by 1st marriage); trained as radio technician; went to Sweden, then Canada 1970; studied computer science; became Canadian citizen 1975; f. Transduction Ltd., Mississauga, Toronto, Ont. 1979; lived in Peruvian Amazonia, f. TV co. TVS Iquitos 1981–85; became Peruvian citizen 1990; Pres. Party X 1990; unsuccessful cand. presidential elections, Poland Dec. 1990. *Publication:* Sacred Dogs (in Polish).

TYNDALE-BISCOE, Cecil Hugh, PH.D.; Australian research scientist and university teacher; b. 16 Oct. 1929, Kashmir, India; s. of Eric Dallas Tyndale-Biscoe and Phyllis Mary (née Long) Tyndale-Biscoe; m. Marina Szokoloczi 1960; two s. one d.; ed. Wycliffe Coll., England, Canterbury Univ., N.Z., Univ. of Western Australia and Washington Univ., St. Louis, U.S.A.; Animal Ecology, Dept. of Scientific and Industrial Research, N.Z. 1951–55; lecturer Edwardes Coll., Peshawar, Pakistan 1955–58, Univ. of W.A., Perth 1961; Deputy Leader, Biologist, N.Z. Alpine Club Antarctic Expedition 1959–60; lecturer, Sr. Lecturer, Reader in Zoology, Australian Nat. Univ., Canberra 1962–75, Adjunct Prof. 1996–(99); Sr. Prin. Research Scientist Div. of Wildlife Research, CSIRO, Canberra 1976–78, Chief Research Scientist Div. of Wildlife and Ecology 1978–91; Dir. Co-operative Research Centre for Biological Control of Vertebrate Pest Populations 1992–95; Hayward Fellow, Manaaki Whenua Landcare Research, N.Z. 1996–97; mountaineering in N.Z., including first north-south traverse of Mt. Cook, first ascent of Torres from the Balfour; in the Karakorum, including first ascents of Falak Sar, Barteen and Buni Zom; Fellow Australian Acad. of Science, Australian Inst. of Biologists; Hon. mem. R.S.N.Z.; Clarke Medal, Royal Soc. of N.S.W., Troughton Medal, Aitken Medal, CSIRO Medal. *Publications:* Life of Marsupials 1973, Reproduction and Evolution (Ed.) 1977, Reproductive Physiology of Marsupials (with M. B. Renfree) 1987, Developing Marsupials (Ed. with P. A. Janssens) 1988; about 80 papers in scientific journals of reproduction, ecology and endocrinology. *Leisure interests:* mountaineering, agroforestry, earth houses, woodwork, history of N. India. *Address:* Research School of Biological Science, Australian National University, GPO Box 475, Canberra, A.C.T. 2601 (Office); 114 Grayson Street, Hackett, A.C.T. 2602, Australia (Home). *Telephone:* (2) 6249 5093 (Office); (2) 6249 8612 (Home). *Fax:* (2) 6249 3808.

TYRA (b. Tyra Banks); American model; b. 4 Dec. 1973; d. of Carolyn London; ed. Immaculate Heart High School; has modelled since 1991 for Karl Lagerfeld (q.v.), Yves St Laurent (q.v.), Oscar De La Renta (q.v.), Chanel, etc.; featured on covers of Elle, GQ, Sports Illustrated, German Cosmopolitan, Spanish Vogue, Scene, Arena. *Video appearances include:* Too Funky by George Michael (q.v.), Black or White by Michael Jackson (q.v.), Love Thing by Tina Turner (q.v.). *Film appearances include:* Higher Learning, Love Changes. *TV appearances include:* Fresh Prince of Bel Aire, NY Undercover.

TYSON, Alan Walker, C.B.E., M.A., M.B., B.S., F.B.A.; British musicologist and former psychoanalyst; b. 27 Oct. 1926, Glasgow; s. of Henry Alan Maurice Tyson and Dorothy (Walker) Tyson; ed. Rugby School, Magdalen Coll. Oxford, Inst. of Psychoanalysis, London and Univ. Coll. Hospital, London; Fellow, All Souls Coll. Oxford 1952–94, Sr. Research Fellow 1971–94; Lecturer in Psychopathology and Developmental Psychology, Oxford Univ. 1968–70, James P. R. Lyell Reader in Bibliography 1973–74; Visiting Lecturer in Psychiatry, Montefiore Hospital, New York 1967–68; Visiting Prof. of Music, Columbia Univ., New York 1969; Ernest Bloch Prof. of Music, Univ. of Calif. (Berkeley) 1977–78; mem. Inst. for Advanced Study, Princeton 1983–84; Visiting Prof. of Music, Graduate Center, City Univ., New York 1985. *Publications:* The Authentic English Editions of Beethoven 1963, English Music Publishers' Plate Numbers (with O. W. Neighbour) 1965, Thematic Catalogue of the Works of Muzio Clementi 1967, The Beethoven Sketchbooks: History, Reconstruction, Inventory (with Douglas Johnson and Robert Winter) 1985, Mozart: Studies of the Autograph Scores 1987, Mozart's Thematic Catalogue; a facsimile (with Albi Rosenthal) 1990, Mozart's Watermarks, two vols. in Neue Mozart-Ausgabe 1992; ed. Beethoven Studies 1 1973, 2 1977, 3 1982. *Address:* c/o Stanecroft, Jarvis Lane, Steyning, Sussex, BN44 3GL, England (Home). *Telephone:* (01903) 879031.

TYSON, Harvey Wood; South African journalist; b. 27 Sept. 1928, Johannesburg; two s. one d.; ed. Kingswood Coll., Rhodes Univ., Grahamstown; Ed.-in-Chief The Star and the Sunday Star, Johannesburg 1974–90; Dir. Argus Holdings 1991–94, Argus Newspapers 1991–94, Sussens Mann Tyson Ogilvie & Mather, Omni Media Holdings 1994–. *Publication:* Editors Under Fire 1993. *Leisure interests:* writing, golf. *Address:* c/o The Star, 47 Sauer Street, P.O. Box 1014, Johannesburg 2000, South Africa. *Telephone:* (011) 886-7153. *Fax:* (011) 886-7676.

TYSON, Laura D'Andrea, PH.D.; American professor of economics; b. New Jersey; m. Erik Tarloff; one s.; ed. Smith Coll., Northampton, Mass and M.I.T.; Asst. Prof. Princeton Univ. 1974–77; Nat. Fellows Program Fellowship, Hoover Inst. 1978–79; consultant, IBRD 1980–86, Pres.'s Comm. on Industrial Competitiveness 1983–84, Hambrecht & Quist 1984–86, PlanEcon 1984–86, Western Govs. Asscn. 1986, Council on Competitiveness 1986–89, Electronics Industry Asscn. 1989, Motorola 1989–90; Visiting Prof. Harvard Business School 1989–90; Prof. Dept. of Econs. and Business Admin. and Dir. Inst. of Int. Studies, Univ. of Calif. Berkeley; Chair. Council of Econ. Advisers to Pres. Clinton 1993–95, Nat. Econ. Adviser to Pres. U.S. Nat. Econ. Council 1995–97; Visiting Scholar, Inst. of Int. Econs.; mem. Bd. of Economists, Los Angeles Times; mem. Council on Foreign Relations, numerous other professional and public appts. *Publications:* The Yugoslav Economic System and its Performance in the 1970s 1980, Economic Adjustment in Eastern Europe 1984, Who's Bashing Whom?, Trade Conflict in High Technology Industries 1992; articles in professional journals. *Address:* Haas School of Business, S-545 Haas, Berkeley, CA 94720, U.S.A.

TYSON, Mike G.; American boxer; b. 30 June 1966, New York City; s. of the late John Kilpatrick Tyson and Lorna Tyson; m. Robin Givens 1988 (divorced 1989); defeated Trevor Berbick to win WBC Heavyweight Title 1986; winner WBA Heavyweight Title March 1987, IBF Heavyweight Title Aug. 1987; fmr. undefeated World Champion, winner all 32 bouts, lost to James Buster Douglas 1990, defeated Donovan Ruddock 1991; Hon. Chair. Cystic Fibrosis Asscn. 1987, Young Adult Inst. 1987; sentenced to six years' imprisonment for rape and two counts of deviant sexual practice March 1992; appealed against March sentence; appeal rejected by U.S. Supreme Court March 1994; released March 1995; regained title of Heavyweight World Champion after defeating Frank Bruno March 1996; lost to Evander Holyfield Dec. 1996; licence revoked by Nevada State Athletics Comm. after disqualification from rematch against Holyfield 1996, reinstated on appeal Oct. 1998; sentenced to a year's imprisonment for assault Feb. 1999.

TYSZKIEWICZ, Zygmunt Jan Ansgary, B.A.; British administrative official; b. 4 Feb. 1934, Warsaw; m. Kerstin Barbro Ekman 1958; two s. two d.; ed. Downside School, Somerset and Univ. of Cambridge; service with Royal Lancers 1955–57; with Shell Int. Petroleum Co., Ltd. 1957–85; served in U.K., Venezuela, Côte d'Ivoire, Benin, Tanzania, France, Netherlands and Greece; Man. Dir. Shell and BP Tanzania Ltd. 1970–73; Gen. Man. Shell Cos. in Greece; Sec.-Gen. Union of Industrial and Employers' Confederations of Europe (UNICE) 1985–98; mem. Advisory Council, Involvement and Participation Asscn., London 1998–; Gov. European Policy Forum 1998–; Hon. C.M.G.; Order of Leopold (Belgium) 1998. *Publications:* articles, interviews, speeches. *Leisure interest:* European affairs. *Address:* c/o UNICE, rue Joseph II 40 (Bte. 4), B-1000 Brussels, Belgium.

TZANNETAKIS, Tzannis; Greek politician; b. 13 Sept. 1927, Gytheion; s. of Petros Tzannetakis and Maria Tzannetakis; m. Maria Ragoussi 1954; one s. one d.; ed. Naval Acad., War Acad.; served Greek Navy 1945–67; business exec. 1967–74; Sec.-Gen. Nat. Tourist Org. 1975; mem. Parl. 1977, 1981, 1985, 1993–; Minister of Public Works 1980–81; Prime Minister 1989; Minister of Defence 1990; Vice-Premier 1990–91; Deputy Prime Minister 1992–93; Minister of Culture 1990–93; Grand Cross (Greece, Luxembourg). *Publications:* The Greek Agora: Public Political Space 1994, India: Another Way of Life 1994; translations into Greek. *Leisure interests:* reading, sailing, travelling. *Address:* Omirou 54, Athens (Office); Odos Pefkon 25, Kifissia, Athens, Greece (Home). *Telephone:* 36.08.573. *Fax:* 36.45.028.

U

UCHIDA, Mitsuko; Japanese pianist; b. 20 Dec. 1948, Tokyo; d. of Fujio Uchida and Yasuko Uchida; ed. Vienna Acad. of Music; recitals and concerto performances with all maj. London orchestras, Chicago Symphony, Boston Symphony, Cleveland Orchestra, Berlin Philharmonic, New York Philharmonic, Los Angeles Philharmonic, and others; played and directed the cycle of 21 Mozart piano concertos with the English Chamber Orchestra in London 1985–86; recordings include Mozart Complete Piano Sonatas and 21 Piano Concertos (English Chamber Orchestra and Jeffrey Tate), Chopin Piano Sonatas, Schubert Piano Sonatas, Beethoven Piano Concertos; First Prize Beethoven Competition Vienna 1969, Second Prize Chopin Competition Warsaw 1970, Second Prize Leeds Competition 1975. *Leisure interest:* bicycling (preferably on the flat). *Address:* c/o Van Walsum Management Ltd., 4 Addison Bridge Place, London, W14 8XP, England. *Telephone:* 0171-371 4343. *Fax:* 0171-371 4344.

UDALL, Stewart Lee; American politician; b. 31 Jan. 1920, St. Johns, Ariz.; s. of Levi S. and Louise (née Lee) Udall; brother of Morris Udall (q.v.); m. Ermalee Webb 1947; four s. two d.; ed. Univ. of Arizona; served U.S. Air Force, Second World War; admitted to Arizona Bar 1948, practised law, Tucson 1948–54, Washington 1969–; of Counsel, Hill, Christopher and Phillips, Washington; mem. House of Reps. 1955–61, mem. Interior and Insular Affairs Cttee., Labor and Education Cttee.; Sec. of the Interior 1961–69; Chair. of Bd., Overview Group (int. consulting firm working to create a better environment for mankind) 1969–; writer syndicated column Udall on the Environment 1970–; Writer Visiting Prof. in Environmental Humanism, Yale School of Forestry; Democrat. *Publications:* The Quiet Crisis 1963, Agenda For Tomorrow 1968, America's Natural Treasures 1971, The National Parks of America (with others) 1972, The Energy Balloon (co-author) 1974.

UDAY HUSSEIN; Iraqi militia leader and business executive; b. 1964; s. of Saddam Hussein (Pres. of Iraq, q.v.) and Sajida Saddam; ed. Baghdad Univ.; Ed. Babil (pro-government newspaper); Ed. and owner Al-Baath ar-Riyadhi; owner, TV and radio station; Head, Fedaycen of Saddam (militia). *Address:* c/o Presidential Palace, Kawadaf Mariam, Baghdad, Iraq.

UDENFRIEND, Sidney, PH.D.; American biologist; b. 5 April 1918, New York; s. of Max Udenfriend and Esther Tabak; m. Shirley Frances Reidel 1943; one s. one d.; ed. Coll. of the City of New York and New York Univ.; Lab. Asst., New York City Dept. of Health 1940–42; Jr. Chemist, New York Univ. Research Service 1942–43, Asst. Chemist 1943–44, Research Chemist 1944–46; Research Asst., New York Univ. Medical School 1946–47, Instructor 1947–48; Instructor, Washington Univ. Medical School 1948–50; Biochemist, Lab. of Chemical Pharmacology, Nat. Heart Inst., Nat. Inst. of Health 1950–53, Head, Section on Cellular Pharmacology 1953–56, Chief, Lab. of Clinical Biochemistry 1956–68; Dir. Roche Inst. of Molecular Biology 1968–83, Dir. Emer. and Head, Lab. of Molecular Neurobiology 1983–96; Dir. Dana Inst., Drew Univ. 1996–; Adjunct Prof., Columbia Univ. 1969–75, City Univ. New York 1968–95, Cornell Univ. Medical School 1982–95; mem. N.A.S., American Acad. of Arts and Sciences and numerous scientific socs.; Fellow New York Acad. of Sciences; Gairdner Foundation Award 1967, Rudolph Virchow Gold Medal 1979, and others. *Publications:* Fluorescence Assay in Biology and Medicine, Vol. I 1962, Vol. II 1969, The Peptides, Analysis, Synthesis, Biology: Opioid Peptides (ed., with Johannes Meienhofer) 1984; 486 publs. on peptide chem. and neurochemistry. *Leisure interests:* reading, music. *Address:* Dana Institute, Drew University, Madison, NJ 07940, U.S.A.

UDOVENKO, Gennady Yosipovich, PH.D.; Ukrainian diplomatist; b. 22 June 1931, Kryvy Rih; s. of Yosyp Udovenko and Maria Kharenko; m. Dina Boutenko 1953; one d.; ed. Kiev State Univ.; joined Diplomatic Service, First Sec., Counsellor 1959–64; Sr. Recruitment Officer, UN Tech. Assistance Recruitment Service 1965–71; Chief of Depts., Ministry of Foreign Affairs 1972–76; Dir. Interpretation and Meetings Div., Dept. of Conf. Services, UN Secr., New York 1977–80; Deputy Minister for Foreign Affairs of Ukrainian S.S.R. 1980–85; Rep. of Ukrainian S.S.R. on Governing Body of ILO 1981–85; Rep. to UN Security Council 1985; Perm. Rep. of Ukrainian S.S.R. to UN 1985–91; Ukrainian Amb. to UN 1992; Amb. to Poland 1992–94; Minister of Foreign Affairs 1994–98; Hon. D.Hum.Litt. (Bridgeport Univ., U.S.A.) 1997. *Leisure interest:* jogging. *Address:* Ministry of Foreign Affairs, 1 Mykhaylivska Square, 252018 Kiev, Ukraine. *Telephone:* (44) 226-3379. *Fax:* (44) 226-3169.

UDUGOV, Brig.-Gen. Movladi; Russian/Chechen politician; b. 9 Feb. 1962, Grozny; m. 1st; m. 2nd; four c.; ed. Chechen-Ingush State Univ. as economist; political activities 1986–; one of founders Soc. Kavkaz, political group Bart and newspaper Bart 1987; f. and ed. Orientir (newspaper) banned by Soviet regime 1988; organiser Mil. Patriotic Union Mansur 1990; participant Congress of Chechen People 1990; Sec. all sessions of Chechen Nat. Congress, leader formation Cttee. Nat. Congress of Chechen People, one of orgs. anti-Russian resistance Nov. 1991; participant overthrowing of Communist leadership of Chechen-Ingushetia 1991; Minister of Information and Press, Dudayev Govt. 1991; Head propaganda service of separatists 1994–96; took part in negotiations on peaceful resolution of conflict; First Vice-Minister Coalition Govt. Chechen Repub. Ichkeria 1996–97; First Deputy Prime Minister 1997–98; Foreign Minister Jan. 1998–.

UEBERROTH, Peter; American sports administrator; b. 2 Sept. 1937, Evanston, Ill.; s. of Victor Ueberroth and Laura Larson; m. Ginny Nicolaus 1959; one s. three d.; ed. San Jose Univ.; Operations Man., Trans Int. Airlines 1959, later part owner; f. Transportation Consultants (later First Travel); Head, Los Angeles Olympic Games Organizing Cttee. 1984; Major League Baseball Commr. 1984–89; named Head "Rebuild L.A." 1992–93; Co-Chair. Doubletree Hotels Corpn. 1993–; mem. Young Presidents' Org.; Scopus Award 1985. *Publication:* Made in America (autobiog.) 1986. *Leisure interests:* reading (especially historical non-fiction), golf. *Address:* Doubletree Hotels Corporation, 410 N. 44th Street, Suite 700, Phoenix, AZ 85008, U.S.A.

UEHARA, Kosuke; Japanese politician; mem. House of Reps., fmr. Chair. Cttee. on Disasters; Dir.-Gen. Nat. Land Agency, Hokkaido Devt. Agency, Okinawa Devt. Agency 1993–94; mem. Social Democratic Party of Japan (SDPJ). *Address:* c/o National Land Agency, 1-2-2 Kasumigaseki, Chiyoda-ku, Tokyo 100, Japan.

UEMATSU, Kunihiko, D.ENG.; Japanese engineer; b. 1931, Kochi; m.; three c.; ed. Kyoto Univ. and M.I.T.; Head, Fuel and Materials Devt. for Fast Breeder Reactor Project, Japanese Power Reactor and Nuclear Fuel Devt. Corpn. (PNC) 1968, Dir. Fuel Devt. Div. 1982, Exec. Dir. 1983–88, Exec. Vice-Pres. 1995–98, Special Tech. Advisor 1998–; Dir.-Gen. OECD Nuclear Energy Agency (NEA) 1988–95. *Publications:* numerous papers on tech. and policy issues in field of nuclear energy. *Address:* c/o PNC, 1-9-13 Akasaka, Minato-ku, Tokyo, Japan.

UFFEN, Kenneth James, C.M.G., M.A.; British diplomatist (retd.); b. 29 Sept. 1925, Chiswick; s. of late Percival J. Uffen and late Gladys E. James; m. Nancy E. Winbolt 1954; one s. two d.; ed. Latymer Upper School and St. Catharine's Coll., Cambridge; served R.A.F.V.R. 1943–48; Third Sec. Foreign Office 1950–52, Paris 1952–55; Second Sec. Buenos Aires 1955–58; First Sec. Foreign Office 1958–61, Moscow 1961–63; seconded to H.M. Treasury 1963–65; F.C.O. 1965–68; Counsellor, Mexico City 1968–70; Econ. Counsellor, Washington 1970–72; Commercial Counsellor, Moscow 1972–76; Resident Assoc. Inst. of Strategic Studies 1976–77; Amb. to Colombia 1977–82; Amb. and U.K. Perm. Rep. to OECD, Paris 1982–85. *Leisure interests:* music, photography. *Address:* 40 Winchester Road, Walton-on-Thames, Surrey, KT12 2RH, England. *Telephone:* (01932) 225049.

UFFEN, Robert James, O.C., PH.D., D.SC., P.ENG., F.R.S.C., F.G.S.A., F.C.A.E.; Canadian geophysicist; b. 21 Sept. 1923, Toronto, Ont.; s. of James Frederick Uffen and Elsie May (Harris) Uffen; m. Mary Ruth Paterson 1949; one s. one d.; ed. Univ. of Toronto, Western Ontario; war service 1942–45; Lecturer, Univ. of Western Ont. 1951–53, Asst. Prof. of Physics and Geology 1953–57, Assoc. Prof. of Geophysics 1957–58, Prof. and Head of Dept. of Geophysics 1958–61, Acting Head Dept. Physics 1960–61; Prin. Univ. Coll. of Arts and Science, London, Ont. 1961–65; Dean, Coll. of Science, Univ. of Western Ont. 1965–66; Vice-Chair. Defence Research Bd., Ottawa 1966–67, Chair. 1967–69; Chief Science Adviser to the Cabinet 1969–71; Dean, Faculty of Applied Science, Queen's Univ., Kingston, Ont. 1971–80, Prof. of Geophysics 1971–89, Prof. Emer. 1989–; Commr. Ont. Royal Comm. on Asbestos 1980–84, on Truck Safety 1981–83; Research Fellowship, Inst. of Geophysics, Univ. of Calif., Los Angeles 1953; mem. Council of Regents Colls. of Applied Arts and Tech. 1966–69, 1973–76, Nat. Research Council of Canada 1963–66, Science Council of Canada 1967–71; Dir. Canadian Patents and Devt. Ltd. 1965–70; mem. Club of Rome 1969–83; Chair. Canadian Eng. Manpower Council 1973–74; Dir. Centre for Resource Studies 1973–76, 1980–83, Ont. Hydro 1974–, (Vice-Chair. 1975–79); Councillor, Asscn. of Professional Engineers of Ont. 1975–78; Chair. Ont. Exploration Tech. Devt. Fund 1981–84; Consultant to E.E.C. on energy research 1987–88; Tech. Advisor to A.E.C.L. on nuclear wastes 1988–91; mem. Fisheries Research Bd. of Canada 1974–78; Visiting Fellow, Univ. of Sussex 1976–77; Fellow American Asscn. for the Advancement of Science 1986, Canadian Acad. of Eng. 1988–; Hon. D.Sc. (Queen's Univ.) 1967, (Univ. of Western Ontario) 1970, (Royal Mil. Coll. of Canada) 1978, Hon. D.Sc. (McMaster Univ.) 1983; Centennial Medal, Canada 1967, A.P.E.O. Public Service Award 1985, Distinguished Service Award, Queen's Univ. 1990, Eng. Hall of Distinction, Univ. of Toronto 1990, 1867–1992 Commemorative Medal 1992, John Orr Award (Queen's Univ.) 1993. *Publications:* papers on geophysics, operations research, evolution, science policy and radioactive waste management. *Leisure interests:* painting, boating, old bottles. *Address:* 185 Ontario Street, No. 1504, Kingston, Ont., K7L 2Y7, Canada. *Telephone:* (613) 546-4981.

UGEUX, Georges; Belgian financier; b. 20 April 1945, Brussels; m. Francine Godet 1970; two s. two d.; ed. Catholic Univ. of Louvain; lecturer in Economics, Faculty of Law, Univ. of Louvain 1970–72; fmr. Gen. Man. Investment Banking & Trust Div., Générale Bank; Man. Dir. Morgan Stanley 1985–88; Group Finance Dir. Société Générale de Belgique 1988–92; Pres. Kidder Peabody-Europe 1992–95; Chair. Belgian Privatisation Comm. 1995–96; Pres. European Investment Fund 1995–96; Group Exec. Vice-Pres., Int. and

Research, New York Stock Exchange 1996–. *Publication:* Floating Rate Notes 1985. *Leisure interests:* music, arts, philosophy. *Address:* New York Stock Exchange, 11 Wall Street, New York, NY 10005, U.S.A. (Office). *Telephone:* 212-656-2077 (Office). *Fax:* 212-656-2016 (Office).

UGGLAS, Baroness Margaretha af, B.A.; Swedish politician; b. 1939; ed. Harvard-Radcliffe Program in Business Admin., Stockholm School of Econs.; leader-writer Svenska Dagbladet 1968–74; Chair. Save the Children Fed., Stockholm 1970–76; mem. Stockholm County Council 1971–73; M.P. 1974–; fmr. Moderate Party Spokesman on Foreign Affairs; Chair. Swedish Section European Union of Women 1981–; mem. Parl. Standing Cttee. on Foreign Affairs 1982–, Advisory Council on Foreign Affairs, Swedish Del. to Council of Europe; observer European Parl.; Minister for Foreign Affairs 1991–94. *Leisure interests:* art, walking, sailing. *Address:* c/o Moderata Samlingspartiet, P.O. Box 1243, 111 82 Stockholm, Sweden.

UGLOW, Euan; British artist and lecturer; b. 10 March 1932, London; s. of Ernest R. Uglow and Elizabeth J. Williams; ed. Strand Grammar School for Boys, Camberwell School of Arts and Crafts and Slade School of Fine Art, Univ. Coll., London; Spanish State Scholarship, Spain 1952; Abbey Minor (Prix de Rome) Scholar 1953; Teacher St. Albans School of Art, Herts. 1958–62, Camberwell School 1959–77, Slade School of Fine Art, Univ. Coll. London 1961–; Fellow Univ. Coll. London; Trustee, Nat. Gallery 1990–; work exhibited at John Moores, Liverpool, Beaux Arts Gallery, Arts Council, Camden Arts Centre, Marlborough Fine Art, London, Univ. of Stirling, Whitechapel Art Gallery, Browse & Darby, London, Hayward Annual, Tate Gallery, Corner House, Manchester, British Council. *Address:* c/o Browse and Darby, 19 Cork Street, London, W1X 2LP, England. *Telephone:* 0171-734 7984.

UHDE, Milan, PH.D.; Czech politician, journalist and playwright; b. 28 July 1936, Brno; m.; two c.; ed. Masaryk Univ., Brno; Ed. of literary monthly A Guest Is Coming 1958–70; signed Charter 77; published essays in unofficial periodicals and abroad; Reader, Faculty of Philosophy, Masaryk Univ., Brno Dec. 1989–; Ed.-in-chief, Atlantis Publishing House, Brno March–June 1990; Minister of Culture, Czech Repub. 1990–92; Pres. of Foundation for Preservation of Cultural Monuments 1991–; mem. Civic Democratic Party (ODS) 1991–98, Unie Svobody 1998; Deputy to Czech Nat. Council June 1992–; mem. Presidium; Pres. of Parl., Czech Repub. 1992–96; Chair. Civic Democratic Party in Parl. 1996–97; Czechoslovak Radio Prize 1966. *Publications:* plays including King Vávra 1964, The Tax-Collector 1965, Witnesses 1966, The Tart from the Town of Thebes 1967, The Gang 1969, A Dentist's Temptation 1976, Lord of the Flames 1977, The Hour of Defence 1978, The Blue Angel 1979; novels: Like Water off a Duck's Back 1961, A Mysterious Tower in B. 1967. *Address:* Barvířova 59, 602 00 Brno, Czech Republic.

UHL, Petr; Czech human rights activist; b. 8 Oct. 1941, Prague; s. of Bedřich Uhl and Marie Kohoutová; m. Anna Šabatová 1974; three s. one d.; ed. Czech. Univ. of Tech., Prague; designer and patent clerk 1964–66; teacher, Coll. of Tech. Prague 1966–69; imprisoned for political activities 1969–73; designer 1974–78; co-founder of Charter 77; co-founder of Cttee. for Protection of the Unjustly Prosecuted 1978; imprisoned for political activities 1979–84; stoker 1984–89; ed. of East European Information Agency 1988–90; leading rep. of Civic Forum, Prague 1989–90; Dir.-Gen., Czechoslovak News Agency 1990–92, Ed. 1992–94; Ed.-in-Chief Listy (magazine) 1994–96; Ed. Právo (daily) 1996–98; Commr. of Govt. of Czech Repub. for Human Rights 1998–; Deputy to House of the Nations, Fed. Ass. 1990–92; Chair., Control and Auditing Comm. of Prison Staff Corps, Czech Repub. 1990; mem. Working Group on Arbitrary Detention of UN Comm. on Human Rights 1991–. *Publications:* The Programme of Social Self-government 1982, On Czechoslovak Prison System (co-author) 1988, Right and Unjustness in Petr Uhl's Eyes 1998, and numerous articles in Czechoslovak and foreign press. *Address:* Anglická No 8, 120 00 Prague 2, Czech Republic (Home).

UHRIG, John Allan, A.O.; Australian business executive; b. 24 Oct. 1928; s. of L. J. Uhrig; m. Shirley Attwood 1956; two s. two d.; ed. Newcastle Tech. High School, Univ. of New South Wales; Man. Dir. Simpson Ltd. 1975–85; Dir. CRA Ltd. (now Rio Tinto Ltd.) 1983–, Chair. (non-exec.) 1987–; Chair. Codan Pty. Ltd. 1986–, Australian Mineral Devt. Laboratories Ltd. (Amdel) 1989–, Australian Minerals and Energy Environment Foundation 1991–; fmr. Chair. Australian Mfg. Council; Dir. Westpac Banking Corpn. 1989–, Chair. Oct. 1992–; Deputy Chair. Santos Ltd. 1992–94, Chair. 1994– (Dir. 1991–); Deputy Chair. RTZ 1995–; mem. Remuneration Tribunal of South Australia 1985–89. *Address:* c/o Rio Tinto Ltd., G.P.O. Box 384D, Melbourne, Vic. 3001, Australia.

UJFALUSSY, József, PH.D.; Hungarian musicologist; b. 13 Feb. 1920, Debrecen; s. of Dr. Géza Ujfalussy and Margit Mándy; ed. Debrecen Univ., Music Academy, Budapest; Secondary school teacher 1943–46; education organizer, Budapest 1946–48; Section Head, then Chief Dept. Leader Ministry of Culture 1949–55; Prof. of Aesthetics of Music and Theory of Music, Budapest Acad. of Music 1955–, Rector 1980–88; Fellow Inst. of Musicology 1969, Dir. 1973–80; Fellow Hungarian Acad. of Sciences Bartók Archives 1961, Dir. 1973–80; Corresp. mem. Hungarian Acad. of Sciences 1973–85, ordinary mem. and Vice-Pres. 1985–93; mem. Acad. Europaea 1991; Erkel Prize 1961, Kossuth Prize 1966, Herder Prize 1987. *Publications:* Bartók breviárium 1958, 2nd edn. (with Vera Lamperth) 1974, Debussy 1959, A valóság zenei képe (The Musical Image of Reality) 1962, Béla Bartók Vols. I-II 1965 (3rd edn. 1976), On Music, on Aesthetics 1981, Tamino a válaszuton (Tamino at the cross-way) 1986. *Address:* Hungarian Academy of Sciences (Magyar Tudományos Akadémia), Roosevelt-ter 9, 1051 Budapest; Csévi-utca 13b, H-1025 Budapest II, Hungary. *Telephone:* 1328-344; 176-2159.

ULIKI (WU LIJI); Chinese politician; b. 1940, Inner Mongolia; Chair. Govt. of the Inner Mongolia Autonomous Region 1993–97. *Address:* c/o Office of Government for Inner Mongolia, Hohhot City, Inner Mongolia Autonomous Region, People's Republic of China.

ULLENDORFF, Edward, M.A., D.PHIL., F.B.A.; British university professor; b. 25 Jan. 1920; s. of Frederic and Cilli Ullendorff; m. Dina Noack 1943; ed. Univs. of Jerusalem and Oxford; war service in Eritrea and Ethiopia 1941–46; Asst. Sec., Govt. of Palestine 1946–47; Research Officer, Oxford Univ. Inst. of Colonial Studies 1948–49; Lecturer, later Reader, in Semitic Languages, St. Andrews Univ. 1950–59; Prof. of Semitic Languages, Manchester Univ. 1959–64; Prof. of Ethiopian Studies, London Univ. 1964–79, of Semitic Languages 1979–82, Prof. Emer. 1982–; Head of Africa Dept., School of Oriental and African Studies (SOAS) 1972–77; Chair. Asscn. of British Orientalists 1963–64, Anglo-Ethiopian Soc. 1965–68, Editorial Bd. of Bulletin of SOAS 1968–78; Schweich Lecturer, British Acad. 1967; Pres. Soc. for Old Testament Study 1971; Vice-Pres. Royal Asiatic Soc. 1975–79, 1981–85; Fellow, British Acad. 1965–, Vice-Pres. 1980–82; Foreign Fellow, Accad. Nazionale dei Lincei, Rome 1998; Haile Selassie Prize for Ethiopian Studies 1972; Hon. D.Litt. (St. Andrews Univ.), Hon. Dr. Phil. (Hamburg Univ.) 1990. *Publications:* Exploration and Study of Abyssinia 1945, Catalogues of Ethiopic MSS in the Bodleian Library 1951, The Royal Library, Windsor Castle 1953, Cambridge Univ. Library 1961; The Semitic Languages of Ethiopia 1955, The Ethiopians 1960, 3rd edn. 1973, Comparative Grammar of the Semitic Languages 1964, An Amharic Chrestomathy 1965, Ethiopia and the Bible 1968, Solomon and Sheba 1974, translated and annotated Emperor Haile Sellassie's autobiography 1976, Studies in Semitic Languages and Civilizations 1977, The Ethiopic Enoch (with M. A. Knibb, 2 vols.) 1978, The Amharic Letters of Emperor Theodore to Queen Victoria 1979, The Bawdy Bible, The Hebrew Letters of Prester John 1982, A Tigrinya Chrestomathy 1985, Studia Aethiopica et Semitica 1987, The Two Zions 1988, From the Bible to Enrico Cerulli 1990, H.J. Polotsky's Selected Letters 1992, From Emperor Haile Sellassie to H.J. Polotsky 1995, and others; articles and reviews in journals of learned socs. *Leisure interests:* music, motoring in Scotland. *Address:* 4 Bladon Close, Oxford, OX2 8AD, England.

ULLMAN, Tracey; British actress and singer; b. 30 Dec. 1959, Slough; d. of the late Anthony John Ullman and of Dorin Cleaver; m. Allan McKeown 1984; one s. one d.; ed. Italia Conti Stage School, London; stage appearances include roles in Gigi, Elvis, Grease, Four in a Million (London Theatre Critics' Award 1981); TV appearances include series The Tracey Ullman Show 1987–90, The Best of the Tracey Ullman Show 1990; Tracey Takes On 1996; record album: You Broke My Heart in Seventeen Places; British Acad. Award 1983, Rudolph Valentino Cinema Lifetime Achievement Award 1992. *Films include:* The Rocky Horror Picture Show, Give My Regards to Broad Street, Plenty 1985, Jumpin' Jack Flash 1986, I Love You To Death 1990, Robin Hood: Men in Tights 1993, Household Saints, Bullets over Broadway 1995, Pret-a-Porter 1995, Everybody Says I Love You 1996. *Address:* c/o ICM, Oxford House, 76 Oxford Street, London, W1N 0AX, England; c/o CAA, 9830 Wilshire Boulevard, Beverly Hills, CA 90212, U.S.A. *Telephone:* 0171-636 6565 (London). *Fax:* 0171-323 0101 (London).

ULLMANN, Liv Johanne; Norwegian actress; b. 16 Dec. 1938, Tokyo, Japan; d. of late Viggo Ullmann and of Janna (Lund) Ullmann; m. 1st Dr. Gappe Stang 1960 (dissolved 1965); one d.; m. 2nd Donald Saunders 1985; worked in repertory company, Stavanger 1956–59; has appeared at Nat. Theatre and Norwegian State Theatre, Oslo; work for UNICEF as Goodwill Amb. 1980–; Vice-Chair. Int. Rescue Cttee.; 12 hon. doctorates; Best Actress of the Year, Nat. Soc. of Critics in America 1969, 1970, 1974; N.Y. Film Critics Award 1973, 1974; Hollywood Foreign Press Asscn.'s Golden Globe 1973; Best Actress of the Year, Swedish T.V. 1973, 1974; Donatello Award (Italy) 1975; Bambi Award (Fed. Repub. of Germany) 1975; nominated for Tony Award as Best Stage Actress, debut on Broadway in The Doll's House 1975; Los Angeles Film Critics' Award (Face to Face) 1976; New York Film Critics' Award (Face to Face) 1977; Nat. Bd. of Review of Motion Pictures Award (Face to Face) 1977; Peer Gynt Award (Norway), Eleanor Roosevelt Award 1982, Roosevelt Freedom Medal 1984, Dag Hammarskjold Award 1986; Commdr. of Olav 1994. *Films include:* Pan 1965, Persona 1966, The Hour of the Wolf 1968, Shame 1968, The Passion of Anna 1969, The Night Visitor 1971, The Emigrants 1972, Cries and Whispers 1972, Pope Joan 1972, Lost Horizon 1973, 40 Carats 1973, The New Land 1973, Zandy's Bride 1973, Scenes from a Marriage 1974, The Abdication 1974, Face to Face 1975, The Serpent's Egg 1978, Sonate d'automne 1978, Richard's Things 1980, The Wild Duck 1983, Love Streams 1983, Let's Hope It's a Girl 1985, Baby Boy 1984, Dangerous Moves 1985, Gaby Brimmer 1986, Moscow Adieu 1986, Time of Indifference 1987, La Amiga 1987, Mindwalk, The Ox, The Long Shadow; Dir. Sophie 1993, Kristin Lavrandsdatter (wrote screenplay also). *Plays include:* Brand 1973, The Doll's House 1975, Anna Christie 1977, I Remember Mama 1979, Ghosts 1982, Old Times 1985, The Six Faces of Women (TV), Mother Courage. *Publication:* Changing (autobiog.) 1976, Choices (autobiog.) 1984. *Leisure interest:* reading. *Address:* 2 Commonwealth Avenue, Boston, MA 02116, U.S.A. *Fax:* (617) 267-9632.

ULLSTEN, Ola; Swedish politician and diplomatist; b. 23 June 1931, Umeå; s. of C. A. and Stina Ullsten; graduated in social sciences 1956; Sec. Parl.

Group Liberal Party 1957–61; journalist Dagens Nyheter 1962–64; mem. Riksdag (Parl.) 1965–84; Chair. Liberal Party Stockholm County 1972–76; Minister of Int. Devt. Co-operation 1976–78; Deputy Prime Minister March-Oct. 1978, Prime Minister 1978–79; Minister for Foreign Affairs 1979–82, Deputy Prime Minister 1980–82; Chair. Liberal Party 1978–83; Amb. to Canada 1983–89, to Italy 1989; mem. Interaction Council of Former Heads of Govt. *Address:* c/o Ministry for Foreign Affairs, Gustav Adolfstorg 1, P.O. Box 16121, 103 23 Stockholm, Sweden.

ULMANIS, Guntis; Latvian politician; b. 13 Sept. 1939, Riga; m. Aina Ulmane; one s. one d.; as a child was exiled to Russia together with his parents, returned to Latvia in 1946; ed. Univ. of Latvia; mem. CPSU 1965–89; economist, municipal employee in Riga 1963–92; mem. Bd. of Cen. Bank of Latvia 1992–, Deputy to Parl. (Saeima) June–July 1993; elected Pres. of Latvia July 1993–; Hon. Chair. Union of Farmers 1993–. *Publication:* Autobiography 1995. *Address:* Office of the State President, Pils Laukums 3, Riga, Latvia. *Telephone:* (2) 379519. *Fax:* (2) 7325800.

ULUFA'ALU, Bartholomew; Solomon Islands politician; Leader Solomon Islands Liberal Party; Prime Minister of Solomon Islands Aug. 1997–; Acting Minister of Finance 1998–. *Address:* Office of the Prime Minister, P.O. Box G1, Honiara, Solomon Islands. *Telephone:* 21863.

ULUSU, Adm. Bülent; Turkish politician and naval officer; b. 7 May 1923, Istanbul; s. of M. Salih Ulusu and Seniye Ulusu; m. Mizat Erensoy 1951; one d.; ed. Naval Acad.; various command posts in navy; rank of Rear-Adm. 1967, Vice-Adm. 1970, Adm. 1974; fmr. Commdr. of War Fleet; Commdr. of Turkish Naval Forces until 1980; fmr. Under-Sec., Ministry of Defence; Prime Minister of Turkey 1980–83; M.P. 1983–87. *Address:* Ciftehavuzlar Yesilbahar 50K. 8/27, Kadikoy/Istanbul, Turkey. *Telephone:* 90-(1)-350 1311.

ULYANOV, Mikhail Aleksandrovich; Russian actor and director; b. 20 Nov. 1927, Tara, Omsk Dist.; s. of Aleksandr Andreevich Ulyanov and Elizaveta Mikhailovna Ulyanova; m. Alla Petrovna Parfanyak 1958; one d.; ed. Shchukin Theatre School; worked with Vakhtangov Theatre 1950–, Chief Theatre Dir. 1987–; mem. CPSU 1951–91; with Soviet TV; début as dir. 1973; Chair. Russian Union of Theatre Workers 1986–96; U.S.S.R. People's Deputy 1989–91; U.S.S.R. People's Artist 1969, R.S.F.S.R. State Prize 1975 for work in theatre; Hero of Socialist Labour 1986. *Roles in films include:* They Were The First 1956, The Volunteers 1958, A Simple Story 1960, The Battle on the Way 1961, The Chairman 1964 (Lenin Prize 1966), Brothers Karamazov 1969, Escape 1971, Egor Bulychev and Co. 1973, Liberation 1970–72, The Blockade 1975–78, Soldiers of Freedom 1977, Call me to the Bright Distant Horizon 1978, The Last Escape 1981, Private Life 1982 (U.S.S.R. State Prize 1988), Unless the Enemy Surrenders 1983, No Witnesses 1983, Tevie the Milkman 1985, Choice 1987, Our Armoured Train 1989, The Home under Starry Skies 1991, The Co-operative Store called 'Political Bureau' 1992, Me I'm the Native of Viatka 1992, The Master and Margarita 1992. *Films directed include:* The Very Last Day 1973, Brothers Karamazov (part 3). *Leisure interest:* reading. *Address:* Theatre Vakhtangov, 26 Arbat, 121002 Moscow, Russia (Office). *Telephone:* 241-10-77, 241-07-44 (Theatre); 299-96-76 (Home). *Fax:* (095) 241-26-25.

UMBA DI LUTETE, L. EN D.; Democratic Republic of the Congo diplomatist and former government official; b. (as Jean-Théodore Umba-di-Lutete) 30 June 1939, Kangu; s. of late Umba Julien and Mdbuilu Matsumba; m. Diomi Kiese 1967; three s. three d.; ed. Univ. of Lovanium, Univ. Libre de Bruxelles, Belgium; training with U.S. Agency for Int. Devt. and with Belgian Parl. and Foreign Ministry; taught at Univ. of Lovanium; at Nat. Univ. of Zaire; Minister at the Presidency 1969–70, of Energy 1970–71, of Mining 1971–74, for Foreign Affairs 1974–75, for Politics 1975–76, for State Affairs, Foreign Affairs and Int. Co-operation 1977–79, for Nat. Guidance, Culture and the Arts 1979–80; mem. Political Bureau of Mouvement populaire de la révolution (MPR), also MPR Perm. Cttee.; Perm. Rep. to UN 1976–77, 1982–84; State Commr. for Foreign and Int. Affairs 1984–85; fmr. leader of dels. to UN Gen. Ass. and Security Council, to OAU, OCAM, UNCTAD. *Address:* c/o Ministry of Foreign Affairs, Kinshasa, Democratic Republic of the Congo.

UMRI, Gen. Hassan; Yemeni politician; took part in revolution against Imamate 1962; Minister of Transport Sept.-Oct. 1962, of Communications 1962–63; mem. Council of Revolutionary Command 1962–63; Vice-Pres. of Yemen 1963–66; mem. Political Bureau 1963–66; Prime Minister Jan.-April 1965, 1965–66, 1967–68; Mil. Gov.-Gen. of Yemen 1968–69; also C.-in-C. of Army; Prime Minister Aug.-Sept. 1971; in exile in Lebanon until Jan. 1975; returned to Yemen Arab Repub. Jan. 1975.

UNCKEL, Per; Swedish politician; b. 24 Feb. 1948, Finspång, Östergötland; m. Christina Lagenquist 1977; two s.; ed. Uppsala Univ.; Chair. Swedish Young Moderates 1971–76, M.P. (Östergötland) 1976, Moderate Party Spokesman on Energy Questions 1978–82, Nat. Campaign Leader 1980 Referendum on Nuclear Power, Party Spokesman on Educ. and Science 1982–86, Sec. Moderate Party 1986–91; Minister of Educ. and Science 1991–94. *Leisure interest:* music. *Address:* c/o Riksdag, 10012 Stockholm, Sweden.

UNDERWOOD, Cecil H., LL.D.; American politician and businessman; b. 5 Nov. 1922, Joseph's Mills, West Va.; s. of Silas H. Underwood and Della N. Underwood; m. Hovah Hall 1948; one s. two d.; ed. Salem Coll., West Virginia Univ.; U.S. Army Reserve Corps 1942–43; high-school teacher 1943–46; mem. staff Marietta Coll. 1946–50; Vice-Pres. Salem Coll. 1950–56; mem. West Virginia House of Delegates 1944–56 and Minority Floor Leader 1949–54; Gov. of West Virginia 1957–61, 1997–; Temporary Chair. Republican Nat. Convention 1960; Vice-Pres. Island Creek Coal Co. 1961–64; Dir. Civic Affairs, Northeastern Region, Monsanto Co. 1965–66; Vice-Pres. Govt. and Civic Affairs, Monsanto Co., Washington, D.C. 1967; Pres. Franswood Inc., Huntington 1968–75; Pres. Cecil H. Underwood Asscns. 1965–80; field underwriter New York Life Insurance Co. 1976–78; Pres. Bethany Coll. 1972–75, Princess Coals Inc. 1978–81, Chair. Bd. 1981–83; Pres. Morgantown Industrial Park Inc. 1983–86, Chair. Bd. 1986–96; Pres. Software Valley Corpn. 1989–92, Mon View Heights of WV 1993–96; Bd. of Dirs. Huntington Fed. Savings and Loan Asscn. 1961–96, American Cancer Soc. 1973–; mem. Bd. of Trustees Salem-Teikyo Univ. 1990–; Chair. W. Va. State Council on Vocational Educ. 1982–96; Pres. Nat. Asscn. of State Councils on Vocational Educ. (NASCOVE) 1994–96; mem. Bd. WV State Coll. System (Chair. 1991–93); Vice-Chair. Huntington Foundation 1986–94, Chair. 1994–; 12 hon. degrees. *Address:* Governor's Office, 1900 Kanawha Blvd. East, Charleston, WV 25305 (Office); Governor's Mansion, 1716 Kanawha Blvd. East, Charleston, WV 25305, U.S.A. (Home). *Telephone:* (304) 558-2000 (Office); (304) 558-3588 (Home).

UNGARO, Emanuel Mattéotti; French fashion designer; b. 13 Feb. 1933, Aix-en-Provence; s. of Cosimo Ungaro and Concetta Casalino; m. Laura Bernabei; one d.; ed. Lycée d'Aix-en-Provence; worked as tailor at Aix-en-Provence then with Camps, Paris, Balenciaga Paris and Madrid 1958–64, Courrèges, Paris 1964; Couturier, Paris 1965–. *Leisure interests:* music, reading. *Address:* 2 avenue Montaigne, 75008 Paris, France.

UNGER, Felix, DR.MED.; Austrian surgeon; b. 2 March 1946, Klagenfurt; s. of Carl Unger and Maria Unger; m. Monika von Fioreschy 1971; two s.; lecturer Univ. of Vienna 1978–83, Prof. Univ. of Innsbruck 1983; Head of Heart Surgery Salzburg State Hospital; Founder and Pres. European Acad. of Sciences and Arts; Hon. Dr. Med.; Bundesverdienstkreuz 1992; Dr. Karl Renner Prize 1975, Sandoz Prize 1980, Plannsee Prize 1982. *Publications:* numerous articles in specialist journals. *Leisure interest:* arts. *Address:* Schwimmschulstrasse 31, A-5020 Salzburg, Austria. *Telephone:* 43-662-82 47 41. *Fax:* 433 840.

UNGER, Michael Ronald; British newspaper editor and executive; b. 8 Dec. 1943, Surrey; s. of Ronald Unger and Joan Stanbridge; m. 1st Eunice Dickens 1966 (divorced 1992); one s. one d. (deceased); m. 2nd Noorah Ahmed 1993; ed. Wirral Grammar School, Liverpool Polytechnic; trainee journalist, Stockport 1963–65; Production Ed., Reading Evening Post 1965–67; News Ed., Perth, Australia 1967–71; Deputy Ed. Daily Post, Liverpool 1971–79, Ed. 1979–82; Ed. Liverpool Echo 1982–83; Ed. Manchester Evening News 1983–97; Dir. Guardian Media Group 1983–97, Manchester Evening News PLC 1983–; Chair. The Lowry Centre 1996–, Youth Charter for Sport 1996–; Trustee Scott Trust 1986–97; various newspaper awards including Newspaper Design 1980, 1981, 1982, 1994; Ed. of the Year 1988. *Publication:* The Memoirs of Bridget Hitler 1979. *Leisure interests:* books, theatre. *Address:* c/o Manchester Evening News, 164 Deansgate, Manchester, M60 2RD, England (Office). *Telephone:* 0161-832 7200.

UNGERER, Werner, DR. RER. POL.; German diplomatist; b. 22 April 1927, Stuttgart; s. of Max Ungerer and Elisabeth (Mezger) Ungerer; m. Irmgard Drenckhahn 1959; one s. two d.; ed. Dillman Gymnasium, Stuttgart, Technical Univ. Stuttgart, Univ. of Tübingen and Coll. of Europe, Bruges; Attaché, diplomatic service 1952–54; Vice-Consul, Boston 1954–56; Consul, Bombay 1956–58; Head of Div. Euratom Comm. Brussels 1958–64; Ministry of Foreign Affairs 1964–70; Resident Lecturer on Diplomacy and European Integration, Univ. of Bonn 1965–66; rep. to int. orgs. in Vienna 1970–75; Consul-Gen. New York 1975–79; Ministry of Foreign Affairs 1979–85; Dir.-Gen. Dept. of Econ. Affairs 1984–85; Perm. Rep. to EEC Brussels 1985–89; Rector Coll. of Europe 1990–93; lecturer, Univ. of Bonn 1994–98; Pres. European Cooperation Fund 1994–98; Bundesverdienstkreuz, Order Leopold II of Belgium, Medal of Merit, Europa-Union Germany. *Publications:* numerous articles on European integration, energy problems and int. orgs. in reviews. *Leisure interests:* history, religions, playing piano and composing. *Address:* Nachtigallenweg 19, 53343 Wachtberg, Germany. *Telephone:* (49) 228-325572. *Fax:* (49) 228-328755.

UNGERS, Oswald Mathias, DIPL.ENG.; German architect and university professor; b. 12 July 1926, Kaisersesch; s. of Anton and Maria (née Mitchels) Ungers; m. Liselotte Gabler 1956; one s. two d.; ed. Technical Univ., Karlsruhe; architectural practice, Cologne 1950–62, Berlin 1962–69, Ithaca, N.Y. 1969–; Prof. of Architecture, Technische Universität, Berlin 1963–73, Dean, Faculty of Architecture 1965–67; Prof. of Architecture, Cornell Univ. 1968–, Chair. of Dept. 1968–74; Visiting Prof., Harvard Univ. 1972, 1977, Univ. of Calif. (Los Angeles) 1973; mem. Accademia Nazionale di San Luca, Rome, Akademie der Wissenschaft, Berlin. *Publications:* Optimization Models for Housing, New York State Pattern Development, Settlements of the 20th Century, The Urban Block, The Urban Villa, The Urban Garden, O. M. Ungers 1951–84: Bauten und Projekte, O.M. Ungers-Architetture 1951–90. *Address:* Belvederestrasse 60, 50933 Cologne, Germany. *Telephone:* (0221) 49 23 43.

UNO, Osamu, B.L.; Japanese business executive; b. 29 May 1917, Kyoto; s. of Kenichiro and Tami Uno; m. Yoshie Uno 1945; one s. two d.; ed. Tokyo Univ.; Dir. Toyobo Co. Ltd. 1971, Man. Dir. 1974–76, Sr. Man. Dir. 1976–77, Deputy Pres. 1977–78, Pres. 1978–83, Chair. 1983–92, Hon. Chair. and Dir.

1992–94, Sr. Adviser 1994–97, Hon. Sr. Adviser 1997–; Vice-Pres. Japan Chemical Fibres Asscn. 1980–81, Pres. 1981–82; Vice-Pres. Japanese Spinners' Asscn. 1982–83, Pres. 1983–84; Vice-Chair. Kansai Econs. Fed. 1983–87, Chair. 1987–94, Exec. Adviser 1994–; Blue Ribbon Medal Japan 1982, Kt. Commdr.'s Cross (Badge and Star) of Order of Merit of Fed. Repub. of Germany 1990, Officier, Légion d'honneur 1990, Grand Cordon, Order of the Sacred Treasure 1991, Order of Diplomatic Service Merit, Heung-In Medal 1992. *Leisure interest:* golf. *Address:* 2-8 Dojima Hama 2-chome Kitaku, Osaka 530-8230 (Office); 1-46 Showa-cho, Hamadera Sakai, Osaka 592-8345, Japan (Home). *Telephone:* (06) 348-3252 (Office).

UNSELD, Siegfried, DR.PHIL.; German publisher and editor; b. 28 Sept. 1924, Ulm; s. of Ludwig and Lina (née Kögel) Unseld; one s.; ed. Univ. of Tübingen; joined Suhrkamp Verlag 1952, Pres. 1959–; Pres. Insel Verlag 1963–; Guest Prof., Univ. of Texas, Austin 1976; Hon. Prof. Univ. of Heidelberg 1992; Regents-Lecturer, Univ. of Southern Calif., San Diego-La Jolla 1978; Dr. h.c. (Washington Univ., St. Louis, Mo., Goethe Univ., Frankfurt); Hermann Hesse Medal 1967, Heinrich Merck Award 1975, Goethe Medal (City of Frankfurt) 1977, Wilhelm Leuschner Medal of Hessen 1981, Ricarda Huch Prize 1984; Grosses Bundesverdienstkreuz; Order of Merit of Poland. *Publications:* Encounters with Hermann Hesse 1974, Hermann Hesse: A History of his Works 1973, Peter Suhrkamp—A Biography 1975, Goethe's 'The Diary' and Rilke's 'Seven Poems' 1978, The Author and his Publisher 1978, Goethe and his Publishers 1991; ed. of numerous works. *Address:* Suhrkamp Verlag–Insel Verlag, Suhrkamp Haus, Lindenstrasse 29, 60325 Frankfurt, Germany. *Telephone:* (069) 756010.

UNSWORTH, Barry; British writer; b. 10 Aug. 1930, Wingate, Co. Durham; s. of the late Michael Unsworth and Elsie Unsworth; m. 1st Valerie Irene Moore 1959 (divorced 1991); three d.; m. 2nd Aira Pohjanvaara-Buffa 1992; ed. Manchester Univ.; nat. service; taught English in France and at Univs. of Athens and Istanbul; Writer-in-Residence Ambleside, Cumbria 1979, Univ. of Liverpool 1985; Visiting Literary Fellow Univs. of Durham and Newcastle 1982; moved to Helsinki 1987, now lives in Italy. *Publications:* The Partnership 1966, The Greeks Have A Word For It 1967, The Hide 1970, Mooncranker's Gift (winner Heinemann Fiction Prize) 1973, The Big Day 1976, Pascali's Island 1980, The Rage of the Vulture 1982, Stone Virgin 1985, Sugar and Rum 1988, Sacred Hunger 1992 (joint winner, Booker Prize 1992), Morality Play 1995, After Hannibal 1996. *Leisure interests:* gardening, bird-watching. *Address:* c/o Giles Gordon, Curtis Brown, Haymarket House, 28–29 Haymarket, London, SW1Y 4SP, England; Casella Postale 24, 06060 Agello (PG), Italy (Home). *Telephone:* 0171-396 6600 (London); (75) 5050084 (Italy). *Fax:* 0171-396 0110 (London); (75) 5050084 (Italy).

UNTERMANN, Jürgen, DR.PHIL.; German professor of linguistics; b. 24 Oct. 1928, Rheinfelden; ed. Univs. of Frankfurt and Tübingen; Asst. Prof. Univ. of Tübingen 1953–58, Pvt. Tutor 1962–65; project on Pre-Roman inscriptions in the Iberic Peninsula 1958–62; Full Prof. Comparative Linguistics, Univ. of Cologne 1965–94, Dean, Faculty of Letters 1971–72, Emer. Prof. 1994–; Dr. h.c. (Salamanca). *Publications:* Die Venetischen Personennamen 1961, Monumenta Linguarum Hispanicarum, Vol. I 1975, Vol. II 1980, Vol. III 1990, Vol. IV 1997, Einführung in die Sprache Homers 1987. *Address:* Institut für Sprachwissenschaft, Universität Köln, 50923 Cologne (Office); Pfalzgrafenstrasse 11, 50259 Pulheim, Germany (Home). *Telephone:* 02234-82274 (Home).

UNWIN, Sir (James) Brian, K.C.B., M.A.; British banker and fmr. government official; b. 21 Sept. 1935; s. of Reginald Unwin and Winifred Walthall; m. Diana Scott 1964; three s.; ed. Chesterfield School, New Coll. Oxford and Yale Univ.; Asst. Prin. Commonwealth Relations Office 1960; Pvt. Sec. to British High Commr. Salisbury, Rhodesia 1961–64; First Sec. British High Comm. Accra 1964–65; FCO 1965–68; transferred to H.M. Treasury 1968; Pvt. Sec. to Chief Sec. Treasury 1970–72, Asst. Sec. 1972, Under-Sec. 1976, Deputy Sec. 1983–85; seconded to Cabinet Office 1981–83; Dir. European Investment Bank (EIB) 1983–85, Pres. 1993–; Deputy Sec. Cabinet Office 1985–87; Chair. Bd. H.M. Customs & Excise 1987–93; Gov. EBRD 1993–; Chair. Supervisory Bd. European Investment Fund 1994–; mem. Advisory Bd. IMPACT 1990–93; mem. Bd. of Dirs. E.N.O. 1993–94, Fondation Pierre Werner; mem. Bd. Centre d'Etudes Prospectives (CEPROS) 1996–; Hon. Fellow New Coll. Oxford 1997; Gold Medal, Fondation du Mérite Européen. *Leisure interests:* opera, bird-watching, Wellingtoniana, cricket. *Address:* European Investment Bank, 100 blvd. Konrad Adenauer, 2950 Luxembourg.

UNWIN, Peter William, C.M.G., M.A.; British diplomatist and international official (retd.); b. 20 May 1932, Middlesbrough; s. of the late Arnold and Norah Unwin; m. Monica Steven 1955; two s. two d.; ed. Ampleforth Coll., York, Christ Church, Oxford; joined H.M. Foreign Service 1956, British Legation, Budapest 1958, British Embassy, Tokyo 1961, FCO 1963, British Information Services, New York, 1967, FCO 1970, British Embassy, Bonn 1973, Head of Personnel Policy Dept., FCO 1976, Harvard Univ., U.S.A. 1979, Minister (Econ.), British Embassy, Bonn 1980, Amb. to Hungary 1983–86, to Denmark 1986–88; Commonwealth Deputy Sec.-Gen. 1989–93; Chair. British-Hungarian Soc. 1993–, Abbeyfield Int. 1996–; Vice-Chair. Anglo-Danish Soc. 1997–, U.K. Cttee. UNICEF 1997–; Dir. David Davies Memorial Inst. of Int. Studies 1995–. *Publications:* Voice in the Wilderness, Imre Nagy and the Hungarian Revolution 1991, Baltic Approaches 1996, Hearts, Minds and Interests 1998. *Address:* 30 Kew Green, Richmond, Surrey, TW9 3BH, England. *Telephone:* 0181-940 8037.

UPDIKE, John Hoyer, A.B.; American writer; b. 18 March 1932, Shillington, Penn.; s. of Wesley R. and Linda Grace Hoyer Updike; m. 1st Mary Pennington 1953; two s. two d.; m. 2nd Martha Bernhard 1977; ed. Shillington High School, Pennsylvania, and Harvard Coll.; Reporter on the magazine New Yorker 1955–57; mem. Nat. Inst. of Arts and Letters, American Acad. of Arts and Sciences; Dr. h.c. (Harvard) 1992; Rosenthal Award, Nat. Inst. of Arts and Letters 1960; O'Henry Story Award 1967, 1991, U.S. Nat. Book Critics Circle Award 1982, Pulitzer Prize 1982, 1991, Nat. Medal of Arts 1989, Scanno Prize 1991. *Publications:* The Carpentered Hen (poems) 1958, The Poorhouse Fair (novel) 1959, The Same Door (short stories) 1959, Rabbit, Run (novel) 1960, Pigeon Feathers and Other Stories 1962, The Centaur (novel) 1963, Telephone Poles and Other Poems 1963, Assorted Prose 1965, Of the Farm (novel) 1965, The Music School (short stories) 1966, Couples (novel), Midpoint and other poems 1969, Bech: A Book 1970, Rabbit Redux (novel) 1972, Museums and Women and Other Stories 1972, Buchanan Dying (play) 1974, A Month of Sundays (novel) 1975, Picked-up Pieces 1976, Marry Me (novel) 1976, The Coup (novel) 1978, Tossing and Turning (poems) 1978, Problems (short stories) 1979, Your Lover Just Called 1980, Rabbit is Rich (novel) 1981, Bech is Back 1982, Hugging the Shore (essays and criticism) 1984, The Witches of Eastwick (novel) 1984, Facing Nature 1984, The Year's Best American Short Stories (ed.) 1985, Roger's Version (novel) 1986, Trust Me (short stories) 1987, S (novel) 1988, Self-Consciousness (autobiog.) 1989, Just Looking (essays) 1989, Rabbit at Rest 1990, Odd Jobs (essays and criticism) 1991, Memories of the Ford Administration (novel) 1992, Collected Poems 1953–1993 1993, Brazil (novel) 1993, The Afterlife and Other Stories 1994, In the Beauty of the Lilies 1996, Golf Dreams (writings on golf) 1996, Toward the End of Time 1997, Bech at Bay: A quasi-novel 1999. *Leisure interest:* golf. *Address:* Beverly Farms, MA 01915, U.S.A.

UPTON, Arthur Canfield, M.D.; American professor of environmental medicine; b. 27 Feb. 1923, Ann Arbor, Mich.; s. of Herbert Hawkes Upton and Ellen Canfield Upton; m. Elizabeth Bache Perry 1946; one s. two d.; ed. Phillips Acad., Andover, Univ. of Michigan, Ann Arbor; Chief, Pathology-Physiology Section, Oak Ridge Nat. Lab. 1954–69; Prof. of Pathology, State Univ. of New York at Stony Brook 1969–77, Chair. Dept. of Pathology 1969–70, Dean, School of Basic Health Sciences 1970–75; Dir. Nat. Cancer Inst., Bethesda, Md. 1977–79; Prof. and Chair. Dept. of Environmental Medicine and Dir. Inst. of Environmental Medicine, New York Univ. School of Medicine, New York 1980–92, Prof. Emer. 1993–; Prof. of Pathology, School of Medicine, New Mexico Univ., Albuquerque 1991–95, Prof. of Radiology 1993–; Clinical Prof. of Environmental and Community Medicine, UMDNJ-Robert Wood Johnson Medical School 1995–; mem. Editorial Bd. Cancer, Risk Analysis, Environmental Research, Experimental Gerontology, Gerontology and Geriatrics Educ., Health and Environmental Digest; Corresp. mem. Int. Comm. for Protection Against Environmental Mutagens and Carcinogens; fmr. Chair. Biology Div. Advisory Cttee., Oak Ridge Nat. Lab.; mem. Inst. of Medicine of N.A.S., A.A.A.S., American Asscn. for Cancer Research (fmr. Pres.), American Asscn. of Pathologists and Bacteriologists, American Coll. of Toxicology, American Soc. for Experimental Pathology (fmr. Pres.), Int. Acad. of Pathology, Int. Asscn. for Radiation Research (fmr. Pres.), Radiation Research Soc. (fmr. Pres.) and many other professional and scientific orgs.; E. O. Lawrence Award 1965, Comfort Crookshank Award for Cancer Research 1978, Claude M. Fuess Award 1980, Sarah L. Poilley Award 1983, CHUMS Physician of the Year Award 1985, Basic Cell Research in Cytology Lectureship Award 1985, Lovelace Insts. Award 1993, Distinguished Achievement Award, Soc. for Risk Analysis 1997. *Leisure interests:* theatre, museums, music, art, literature. *Address:* 401 East 86th Street, Apt. 12B, New York, NY 10028, U.S.A. *Telephone:* (212) 348-4361. *Fax:* (212) 410-9847.

URANO, Yasuoki; Japanese politician; fmr. Parl. Vice-Minister of Foreign Affairs, of Int. Trade and Industry; mem. House of Reps., Chair. Cttee. on Commerce and Industry; Minister of State, Dir.-Gen. Science and Tech. Agency 1995–96. *Address:* c/o Science and Technology Agency, 2-2-1, Kasumigaseki, Chiyoda-ku, Tokyo 100, Japan. *Telephone:* (3) 3581-5271.

URBAIN, Robert; Belgian politician; b. 24 Nov. 1930, Hornu; ed. Ecole Normale, Mons; fmr. teacher; Deputy for Mons 1971–; Sec. of State for Planning and Housing 1973, for Econ. Affairs (French region) 1977–79; Minister of Posts and Telephones 1979–80, of Foreign Trade 1980–81, of Health and Educ. (French sector) 1981–85, of Social Affairs and Health Feb.–May 1988, of Foreign Trade 1988–92, of European Affairs 1992–95; mem. Senate 1995–. *Address:* Palais de la Nation, 1000 Brussels; Hôtel de Ville, 7300 Boussu, Belgium. *Telephone:* (65) 770511 (Boussu).

URBAN, Horst W.; German business executive; b. 1 June 1936, Lauban, Silesia; m. Dorothea Kiffer 1963; trained as tax inspector, Stuttgart 1953–56; IBM Deutschland GmbH, Stuttgart 1957–61; Ford-Werke AG, Cologne 1962–70; Vice-Pres. Bayerische Motoren Werke AG (BMW), Munich 1971–74; mem. Exec. Bd. Continental AG, Hannover 1974–87, Chair. Exec. Bd. 1987–91; Chair. H.W. Urban GmbH u. Co. Man. KG, Berlin 1992–96. *Leisure interests:* golf, skiing. *Address:* Wietzendiek 20, 30657 Hannover, Germany. *Telephone:* (511) 651281. *Fax:* (511) 651196.

URBAN, Jerzy; Polish journalist; b. 3 Aug. 1933, Łódź; s. of Jan and Maria Urban; m. 1st 1957; one d.; m. 3rd Małgorzata Daniszewska 1986; ed. Warsaw Univ.; staff writer, weekly Po Prostu, Warsaw 1955–57; Head of home section, weekly Polityka, Warsaw 1960–63, 1968–81; columnist of satirical weekly Szpilki, articles written under pen-names including Jan Rem and Jerzy Kibic; Govt. Press Spokesman 1981–89; Minister without portfolio Head Cttee. for Radio and Television April–Sept. 1989; Dir. and Ed.-in-Chief, Nat. Workers' Agency Nov. 1989–90; Dir. and Ed.-in-Chief Unia-Press Feb.–May 1990; Pres. Kier Co. Ltd. 1990–; Pres. URMA Co. Ltd., Warsaw 1991–; Ed.-in-Chief, political weekly Nie Oct. 1990–; participant Round Table debates, mem. group for mass media Feb.–April 1990; mem. Journalists' Asscn. of Polish People's Repub. 1982–; mem. Polish Writers' Union; Victor Prize (TV) 1987. *Publications:* Kolekcja Jerzego Kibica 1972, Impertynencje: Felietony z lat 1969–72 1974, Wszystkie nasze ciemne sprawy 1974, Grzechy chodzą po ludziach 1975, Gorączka 1981, Romanse 1981, Robak w jabłku 1982, Na odlew 1983, Samosądy 1 1984, Felietony dla cudzych zon 1984, Samosądy 2 1984, Z pieprzem i solą 1986, Jakim prawem 1988, Rozkosze podglądania 1988, Cały Urban 1989, Alfabet Urbana 1990, Jajakobyły 1991, Prima aprilis towarzysze 1992, Klątwa Urbana 1995. *Leisure interest:* social life. *Address:* URMA Co. Ltd., ul. Słoneczna 25, 00 789 Warsaw, Poland. *Telephone:* 48 84 48. *Fax:* 49 72 58.

URBANOVÁ, Eva; Czech opera and concert singer (soprano); b. 20 April 1961, Slaný; ed. Acad. of Musical Arts; opera début Plzeň Josef Kajetan Tyl Theatre 1987; soloist Plzeň Opera 1988–90; Chief of opera singer section Conservatory Plzeň 1989; soloist Nat. Theatre Prague 1990–, Metropolitan Opera New York 1996–; charity concert tours with Karel Gott, Czech Repub. 1998; *recordings:* Duets (with Karel Gott) 1998, Czech Opera Airs 1998. *Leisure interests:* cooking, piano. *Address:* Národní divadlo, National Theatre, Prague 1 – Ostrovní 1 110 00, Czech Republic. *Telephone:* 24 91 03 12. *Fax:* 24 91 15 24.

URE, Sir John Burns, K.C.M.G., L.V.O., M.A.; British diplomatist, author and company director; b. 5 July 1931, London; s. of the late Tam Ure; m. Caroline Allan 1972; one s. one d.; ed. Uppingham School, Magdalene Coll., Cambridge, Harvard Business School, U.S.A.; served in Scottish Rifles, Malaya 1950–51; appointments in British Embassies Moscow, Léopoldville, Santiago and Lisbon, and at Foreign Office, London 1956–79, Asst. Under-Sec. of State (Americas) in FCO 1981–83; Amb. to Cuba 1979–81, to Brazil 1984–87, to Sweden 1987–91; UK Commr.-Gen. for Expo '92, Seville; Dir. Thomas Cook Group, Sotheby's Scandinavia AB, CSE Aviation Ltd. 1992–94; consultant, Robert Fleming (merchant bankers) 1995–98, Ecosse Films 1996–99; Chair. Anglo-Swedish Soc. 1992–96, Brazilian Chamber of Commerce 1994–96, Panel of judges for Travel Book of the Year Award; Trustee Leeds Castle Foundation. *Publications:* Cucumber Sandwiches in the Andes 1973, Prince Henry the Navigator 1977, The Trail of Tamerlane 1980, The Quest for Captain Morgan 1983, Trespassers on the Amazon 1986, Royal Geographical Soc. History of World Exploration (section on Cen. and S. America) 1991, A Bird on the Wing 1992, Diplomatic Bag 1994; regular book reviews in Times Literary Supplement. *Leisure interests:* travel, writing. *Address:* Netters Hall, Hawkhurst, Kent, TN18 5AT, England. *Telephone:* (01580) 752191. *Fax:* (01580) 754532.

UREN, Thomas, A.O.; Australian politician; b. 28 May 1921, Balmain, N.S.W.; s. of Thomas Uren and Agnes Uren; m. 1st Patricia Uren 1947 (died 1981); one s. one d.; m. 2nd Christine Anne Logan 1992; one d.; served with Royal Australian Artillery 1939, 2nd Australian Imperial Force 1941, in Japanese prisoner-of-war camp 1942–45 (Burma–Siam Railway); Labor M.P. for Reid 1958–90; mem. Opposition cabinet 1969–72; mem. Fed. Parl. Labor Party Exec. 1969–72, Deputy Leader 1976–77; First Minister of Urban and Regional Devt. 1972–75; Fed. Labor Spokesman, Urban and Regional Devt. 1976–77, on Urban and Regional Affairs, Decentralization, Local Govt., Housing and Construction 1977–80, on Urban and Regional Affairs 1980–83; Minister for the Territories and Local Govt. and Minister assisting Prime Minister for Community Devt. and Regional Affairs 1983–84, Minister for Local Govt. and Admin Services 1984–87; del. to Australasian Area Conf. of Commonwealth Parl. Asscn., Darwin 1968, to Australian Parl. Mission to Europe 1968, to Commonwealth Parl. Asscn. Conf., Canberra 1970; Leader Australian del. to IPU 1987–90, Chair. Asian-Pacific Group 1989–90; brought back Australian hostages from Baghdad 1990; Chair. Australia-Vietnam Soc., Parramatta Park Trust; Pres. H. V. Evatt Foundation; Hon. D.Univ. (Charles Sturt Univ.) 1997; Patron Defenders of Sydney Harbour Foreshores; Life Mem. Australian Labor Party 1993. *Publication:* Tom Uren Stright Left 1994. *Leisure interests:* gardening, theatre, opera, music, art, environmental issues, photography. *Address:* 8 Gilchrist Place, Balmain, N.S.W. 2041, Australia.

URINSON, Yakov Moiseyevich, DR. ECON.; Russian politician; b. 12 Sept. 1944; m.; one s. one d.; ed. Moscow Plekhanov Inst. of Nat. Econs.; researcher Centre Inst. of Econ. and Math. U.S.S.R. Acad. of Sciences 1968–72; Deputy Head of Div., Deputy Dir. Computation Centre U.S.S.R. State Planning Cttee. 1972–91; Dir. Centre of Econ. Conjuncture and Prognosis, Russian Govt. 1992–94; mem. Exec. Bd. Russian Ministry of Science and Tech. 1993–97; First Deputy Chair. Russian Govt., Minister of Econs. 1997–98; mem. Defence Council 1997–98. *Publications:* over 50 papers and articles in specialised periodicals. *Address:* Ministry of Economics, Novy Arbat 19, 103025 Moscow, Russia (Office). *Telephone:* (095) 205 51 22, 205 45 95 (Office).

URIS, Leon Marcus; American writer; b. 3 Aug. 1924, Baltimore; s. of Wolf William and Anna (Blumberg) Uris; m. 1st Betty Beck 1945 (divorced 1968); two s. one d.; m. 2nd Margery Edwards 1968 (died 1969); m. 3rd Jill Peabody 1971; one d.; ed. High School, Baltimore City Coll; served with the U.S. Marine Corps 1942–45. *Publications:* Battle Cry 1953 (novel and screenplay), The Angry Hills 1955, Exodus 1957, Mila 18 1960, Gunfight at the OK Corral (screenplay), Armageddon 1964, Topaz 1967, QB VII 1970, Trinity 1976, Ireland: A Terrible Beauty (with Jill Uris) 1976, The Haj 1984, Mitla Pass 1988, Redemption 1995; with others Exodus Revisited (Photo essay) 1959. *Address:* c/o Doubleday & Co. Inc., 1540 Broadway, New York, NY 10036, U.S.A.

URNOV, Mark Yuryevich, CAND. ECON.; Russian politician; b. 12 May 1947, Moscow; m.; one d.; ed. Moscow State Inst. of Int. Relations; on staff Inst. of Conjuncture U.S.S.R. Ministry of Foreign Trade 1970–76; researcher Inst. of World Econs. and Int. Relations U.S.S.R. Acad. of Sciences 1976–79; sr. researcher Inst. of Culture Ministry of Culture R.S.F.S.R. 1979–82; sr. researcher Leningrad Inst. of Information and Automatisation 1982–86; sr. researcher Inst. of Int. Workers' Movt. U.S.S.R. Acad. of Sciences 1986–89; leading researcher U.S.S.R. Acad. of Nat. Econ. 1989–90; Dir. of political programmes and studies Research Cen. Ekspertiza, concurrently worked in All-Union Cen. on study of public opinion Int. Foundation of Social Econ. and Political Studies Gorbachev Foundation 1990–94; Head of div. Politika Analytical Centre, Russian Presidency April 1994–; Deputy Head, Dir. Analytical Centre, Russian Presidency 1994–98; mem. Political Council, Russian Presidency 1994–, Dir. 1995–98. *Address:* Office of the President, Kremlin, korpus 1, Moscow, Russia (Office). *Telephone:* (095) 206 0766 (Office).

URQUHART, Sir Brian, K.C.M.G., M.B.E.; British international official (retd.); b. 28 Feb. 1919, Bridport, Dorset; s. of Murray Urquhart and Bertha (née Rendall); m. 1st Alfreda Huntington 1944 (dissolved 1963); two s. one d.; m. 2nd Sidney Howard 1963; one s. one d.; ed. Westminster School and Christ Church, Oxford; Army service 1939–45; Personal Asst. to Exec. Sec. of Preparatory Comm. of UN. London 1945–46; Personal Asst. to Trygve Lie, First Sec.-Gen. of UN 1946–49; served in various capacities relating to peace-keeping operations in Office of UN Under-Sec.-Gen for Special Political Affairs 1954–71; Exec. Sec. 1st and 2nd UN Int. Confs. on Peaceful Uses of Atomic Energy 1955, 1958; Deputy Exec. Sec. Preparatory Comm. of IAEA 1957; Asst. to Sec.-Gen.'s Special Rep. in the Congo July-Oct. 1960; UN Rep. in Katanga, Congo, 1961–62; Asst. Sec.-Gen. UN 1972–74; Under-Sec.-Gen. for Special Political Affairs UN 1974–86; Scholar in residence, Ford Foundation 1986–95; Hon. LL.D. (Yale Univ.) 1981, (Tufts Univ.) 1985; Dr. h.c. (Essex Univ.) 1981, (Westminster) 1993; Hon. D.C.L. (Oxford Univ.) 1986, Hon. degrees (City Univ. of New York, Grinnell Coll., State Univ. of New York—Binghamton) 1986, (Univ. of Colorado, Keele) 1987, (Hobart Coll., William Smith Coll.) 1988, (Warwick Univ.) 1989, (Williams Coll.) 1992, (Lafayette Coll.) 1993; Roosevelt Freedom Medal 1984, Int. Peace Acad. Prize 1985. *Publications:* Hammarskjöld 1973, A Life in Peace and War 1987, Decolonization and World Peace 1989, A World in Need of Leadership: Tomorrow's United Nations (with Erskine Childers) 1990, Ralph Bunche: An American Life 1993, Renewing the United Nations System (with Erskine Childers) 1994, A World in Need of Leadership: A Fresh Appraisal (with Erskine Childers) 1996. *Address:* 50 West 29th Street, New York, NY 10001; Jerusalem Road, Tyringham, MA 01264, U.S.A.

URQUHART, Lawrence McAllister, LL.B., C.A.; British business executive; b. 24 Sept. 1935, Liverpool; s. of the late Robert Urquhart and Josephine McEwan Urquhart, née Bissell; m. Elizabeth Catherine Burns 1961; three s. one d.; ed. Strathallan School, Perthshire, King's Coll., London Univ., Inst. of Chartered Accountants of Scotland; Price Waterhouse 1957–62; Shell Int. Petroleum 1962–64; PA Man. Consultants 1964–68; Sr. Group Exec. Charterhouse Group Ltd. 1968–74; Group Finance Dir. Tozer Kemsley & Millbourn Holdings 1974–77, Burmah Oil Co. Ltd. 1977–82; Chief Exec. Castrol Ltd. 1982–85; Group Man. Dir. The Burmah Oil PLC 1985–88, Group Chief Exec. 1988–90; C.E.O. Burmah Castrol PLC 1988–93, Chair. 1990–98; Dir. (non-exec.) Premier Consolidated Oilfields PLC 1986, English China Clays PLC 1991– (Chair. 1995–), BAA PLC 1993– (Deputy Chair. 1997–98, Chair. 1998–), Scottish Widows' Fund and Life Assurance Soc. 1992– (Deputy Chair. 1993–95, Chair. 1995–), Kleinwort Benson PLC 1994–98. *Leisure interests:* golf, music. *Address:* English China Clays PLC, 1015 Arlington Business Park, Theale, Reading, RG7 4SA, England. *Telephone:* (0118) 930 9601.

URRUTIA MONTOYA, Miguel, PH.D.; Colombian banker; b. 20 April 1939, Bogotá; s. of Francisco Urrutia and Genoveva Montoya; m. Elsa Pombo 1963; three c.; ed. Univ. de los Andes, Bogotá; Gen. Sec. Ministry of Finance 1967–68, Advisor to Monetary Bd. 1969; Deputy Tech. Man. Banco de la República 1970–74; Dir. Nat. Planning Dept. 1974–76; Minister of Mines and Energy 1977; Vice-Rector Univ. of the UN, Tokyo 1981–85; Man. Econ. and Social Devt. Dept., Interamerican Devt. Bank 1985–89; Exec. Dir. Fedesarrollo 1978–81, 1989–91; mem. Bd. of dirs. Banco de la República 1991–93; Gov. Cen. Bank of Colombia (Banco de la República) 1993–; has taught various courses at Univ. de los Andes at various times; fmr. weekly columnist for El Tiempo newspaper. *Publications:* Empleo y Desempleo en Colombia 1968, The Development of the Colombia Labor Movement 1969, Income Distribution in Colombia 1975, Winners and Losers in Colombia's Economic Growth of the 1970s 1985, Development Planning in Mixed Economies (with Setsuko Yukawa) 1988, Financial Liberalization and the Internal Structure of Capital Markets in Asia and Latin America 1988, Economic

Development Policies in Resource Rich Countries (with Setsuko Yukawa) 1988, The Political Economy of Fiscal Policy (with Shinichi Ichimura and Setsuko Yukawa) 1989. *Leisure interests:* golf, reading. *Address:* Banco de la República, Cra. 7a. No. 14–78, piso 5o., Santafé de Bogotá, D.C., Colombia. *Telephone:* (57-1) 283 2492. *Fax:* (57-1) 281 7445.

URSI, H.E. Cardinal Corrado; Italian ecclesiastic; b. 26 July 1908, Andria, Bari; s. of Riccardo Ursi and Apollonia Sterlicchio; ordained Priest 1931; Bishop of Nardo 1951, Archbishop of Acorensa 1961, Archbishop of Naples 1966–87, Archbiship Emer. 1987–; created Cardinal by Pope Paul VI 1967; mem. Congregation for Catholic Educ. *Address:* Via Capodimonte 13, 80136 Naples, Italy. *Telephone:* (081) 741.39.85.

URSU, Ioan, PH.D.; Romanian physicist; b. 5 April 1928, Mânăstireni Commune, Cluj Co.; s. of Ioan Ursu and Ana Abrudan; m. Lucia Flămându 1930; two s. one d.; ed. Univ. of Cluj and Univ. of Princeton, U.S.A.; Asst. Prof., Univ. of Cluj 1949, Prof. and Head of Dept. 1960–68; Prof. and Head of Dept., Univ. of Bucharest 1968–89, Sr. Scientist 1990–; Visiting Prof., ICTP (Italy) 1991; Dir.-Gen., Inst. for Atomic Physics 1968–76; Pres. State Cttee. for Nuclear Energy 1969–76; Pres. Nat. Council for Science and Tech. 1976–79, Vice-Chair. 1979–86, First Vice-Chair. Nat. Cttee. for Science and Tech. 1986–89; Corresp. mem. Romanian Acad. 1963, mem. 1974, Pres. Physics Section 1988–; mem. Scientific Council of the Jt. Inst. for Nuclear Research, Dubna 1969; mem. Bd. of Govs. IAEA 1971, Vice-Pres. 1972; mem. Scientific Advisory Cttee., IAEA 1979–90; mem. Exec. Council, European Physical Soc. 1968, Vice-Pres. 1975, Pres. 1976–79; Pres. Balkan Physical Union 1987; Ed. two Romanian journals of physics, and int. journals of magnetic resonance, lasers, materials and energy; mem. Romanian Soc. of Physics and Chem., Physical Socs. of U.S.A., Belgium, France; mem. Bd. of Int. Soc. of Magnetic Resonance; mem. Cttee. Atomes et Molécules par Etudes Radioélectriques (AMPERE); mem. American Nuclear Asscn. 1976, Canadian Nuclear Asscn. 1976; Corresp. mem. Ecuadorian Inst. of Natural Sciences 1976, Centre for Scientific Culture "Ettore Majorana" (Erice, Italy) 1977; mem. European Acad. of Sciences, Arts and Humanities 1980. *Publications:* Rezonanța Electronică de Spin 1965, La résonance paramagnétique electronique 1968, Magnetic Resonance and Related Phenomena (Ed.) 1971, Energia atomică 1973, Magnetic Resonance in Uranium Compounds 1979, Magnitny Rezonans v Soedynenyah Urana 1982, Fizica și Tehnologia Materialelor Nucleare 1982, Physics and Technology of Nuclear Materials 1985, Interactiunea Radiației Laser cu Metalele (with others) 1986, Fizika i technologyia iadernyh materialov, Vzaimodeistwie lazernovo izluchenyia s metallami 1988, Laser Heating of Metals 1990, and about 300 papers on atomic and nuclear physics, nuclear materials, nuclear technologies, solid state physics, interaction of radiation with matter. *Address:* Str. Iuliu Tetrat 26, Bucharest 1, Romania (Home).

URWICK, Sir Alan (Bedford), K.C.V.O., C.M.G., M.A.; British fmr. parliamentary official and retd. diplomatist; b. 2 May 1930, London; s. of the late Lyndall Fownes Urwick and Joan Saunders; m. Marta Yolanda (née Montagne) 1960; three s.; ed. Dragon School, Rugby, New Coll. Oxford; joined Foreign Service 1952; served in Embassies in Belgium 1954–56, U.S.S.R. 1958–59, Iraq 1960–61, Jordan 1965–67, U.S.A. 1967–70, Egypt 1971–73; seconded to Cabinet Office as Asst. Sec., Cen. Policy Review Staff 1973–75; Head of Near East and North Africa Dept., Foreign and Commonwealth Office 1975–76; Minister, British Embassy in Madrid 1977–79; Amb. to Jordan 1979–84, to Egypt 1984–87; High Commr. in Canada 1987–89; Serjeant at Arms, House of Commons 1989–95; Chair. Anglo-Jordanian Soc. 1997. *Leisure interests:* reading, gardening. *Address:* The Moat House, Slaugham Place, Nr. Hayward's Heath, Sussex, RH17 6AL, England. *Telephone:* (01444) 400458.

USAMI, Tadanobu; Japanese trade unionist; b. 31 Oct. 1925, Tokyo; m. 1948; two d.; ed. Takachiho Coll. of Econs.; joined Fuji Cotton Spinning Co. 1946; joined staff of Japanese Fed. of Textile, Garment, Chemical, Distributive and Allied Industry Workers' Unions (ZENSEN) 1946, successively held posts of Treas., Sec., Dir. of Gen. Affairs, mem. Cen. Exec. Cttee. ZENSEN 1947–55, Asst. Gen. Sec. 1955–61, Gen. Sec. 1961–71, Pres. 1971–88, Adviser 1988–; mem. Exec. Bd. ICFTU Asian Regional Org. 1960–65, Pres. 1981–89; Vice-Pres. Japanese Confed. of Labour (DOMEI) 1972–80, Pres. 1980–87; Pres. Japan Int. Labour Foundation (JILAF) 1989–95, Fuji Social Educ. Centre 1995–. *Leisure interest:* golf. *Address:* 1F, Sixth Central Building, 1-19-10 Toranomon, Minato-ku, Tokyo (Office); 4-16-19, Wakabayashi, Setagaya-ku, Tokyo, Japan (Home).

USHAKOV, Nikolay Aleksandrovich, D.SC.; Russian international lawyer; b. 19 Nov. 1918, Moscow; Research Prof., Chief Scientific Researcher, Inst. of State and Law, U.S.S.R. (now Russian) Acad. of Sciences 1948–; Chief of Editorial Board, International Law (annual); mem. Perm. Court of Arbitration, The Hague; mem. UN Int. Law Comm. 1967–; Exec. Sec. UN Asscn. in U.S.S.R.; mem. Int. Law Asscn.; Vice-Pres. Soviet Int. Law Asscn.; lectures in int. public law at Moscow, Kiev and Leningrad Univs.; has participated in various confs. on questions of int. law. *Publications:* over 40 learned publications in the field of int. law. *Address:* Institute of State and Law, Znamenka Str. 10, 119841 GSP, Moscow, Russia. *Telephone:* (095) 264-82-42.

USHAKOV, Yuri Viktorovich, CAND. HIS. SC.; Russian diplomatist; b. 13 March 1947, Moscow; m.; one d.; ed. Moscow State Inst. of Int. Relations, Diplomatic Acad., diplomatic service 1970–; trans., expert, attaché U.S.S.R. Embassy to Denmark 1970, Second then First Sec. 1975–82; counsellor-envoy 1986–92; adviser Gen. Secr. U.S.S.R. Ministry of Foreign Affairs 1982–86; Head Dept. of Security and Co-operation Dept. of Europe, Ministry of Foreign Affairs 1992–96; Rep. of Russia to Conf. on Security and Co-operation in Europe (CSCE) 1996–98; Deputy Minister of Foreign Affairs 1998; Amb. to U.S.A. 1999–. *Address:* Embassy of the Russian Federation, 1125 16th Street, N.W., Washington, DC 20036, U.S.A. *Telephone:* (202) 298-5770, 298-5700, 298-5701. *Fax:* (202) 298-5722.

USHER ARSÉNE, Assouan, M.A.; Côte d'Ivoirian politician and lawyer; b. 24 Oct. 1930; ed. Dakar, Bordeaux and Poitiers Univ.; Lawyer, Court of Appeals, Poitiers 1955–56; Cabinet attaché of M. Houphouet-Boigny 1956; Asst. Dir. Caisse des Allocations Familiales 1957–59; Conseiller Général 1957–59; Deputy Vice-Pres. Nat. Assembly 1959–60; Lawyer, Court of Appeals, Abidjan 1959; Head, Ivory Coast (now Côte d'Ivoire) Perm. Mission to UN 1961–67; Minister of Foreign Affairs 1967–77; mem. UN Security Council 1964–67, Political Bureau Parti Démocratique de Côte d'Ivoire responsible for Mass Educ. 1970; Pres. Société des Ananas de la Côte d'Ivoire 1987; Nat. Order of Côte d'Ivoire.

USHERWOOD, Nicholas John, B.A.; British curator and art critic; b. 4 June 1943, Bucks.; s. of Stephen Usherwood and Hazel Usherwood (née Weston); m. 1st Henrietta Mahuffy (dissolved 1990); one s.; m. 2nd Jilly Szaybo 1991; ed. Westminster School, Courtauld Inst. of Art, Univ. of London; lecturer in art history, Portsmouth and Wimbledon Colls. of Art 1965–68; researcher, Pelican History of Art 1966–68; Admin., Press Officer R.A. 1969–74, Exhbns. Sec. 1974–77; Deputy Keeper in charge of exhbns. and public relations, British Museum 1977–78; freelance exhbn. curator and organizer, art-critic, lecturer, writer 1978–; Features Ed. Galleries Magazine 1998–; Chevalier Order of Léopold II of Belgium. *Publications include:* exhbn. catalogues for Algernon Newton 1980, Tristram Hillier 1983, Alfred Munnings 1986, Richard Eurich 1991, 1994, Nolanis Nolanis 1997, Julian Trevelyan 1998. *Leisure interests:* new maps, reading poetry, talking to artists, contemporary music. *Address:* 17A Abinger Road, Bedford Park, London, W4 1EU, England. *Telephone:* 0181-994 2604. *Fax:* 0181-747 3865.

USLAR-PIETRI, Arturo; Venezuelan writer and politician; b. 16 May 1906, Caracas; s. of Arturo Uslar and Helena Pietri de Uslar; m. Isabel Braun 1939; two s.; ed. Univ. Central de Venezuela; Prof. of Political Economy, Univ. Cen. de Venezuela 1937–41; Sec. to Pres. of Venezuela 1941–43; Minister of Nat. Educ. 1939–41, of Finance 1943, Home Office Sec. 1945; Prof. of Latin American Literature, Columbia Univ., New York 1947, of Venezuelan Literature, Univ. Central de Venezuela; mem. Acad. Venezolana de la Lengua, Acad. of Social and Political Sciences, Acad. of History, Venezuela; Senator, Nat. Congress 1958; Ind. Candidate for Pres. Dec. 1963; Perm. Del. and mem. Exec. Bd. UNESCO; holds numerous int. awards, including Príncipe de Asturias award for literature in Spanish 1990, Rómulo Gallegos 7th Int. Novel Award for La visita en el tiempo 1991. *Publications:* novels: Las lanzas coloradas 1931, El camino de El Dorado 1947, El laberinto de fortuna 2 vols., Oficio de Difuntos 1976, La Isla de Robinson 1981, La visita en el tiempo 1990; stories: Barrabás y otros relatos 1926, Red 1936, Treinta hombres y sus sombras 1949, Pasos y Pasajeros 1965, Los Ganadores 1980; essays: Las Nubes 1951, Del hacer y deshacer de Venezuela 1963, La ciudad de nadie 1960, Oraciones para despertar, La Otra América 1974, Fantasmas de dos mundos 1979, Godos, Insurgentes y Visionarios 1986; poems: Manoa 1972, El hombre que voy siendo 1986; plays: Teatro 1958, Chúo Gil y las tejedoras 1960, and several monographs. *Address:* Avenida Los Pinos 49, La Florida, Caracas, Venezuela. *Telephone:* 74-40-61. *Fax:* (58-2) 71-73-87.

USPENSKY, Boris Andreyevich; Russian linguist, philologist, critic and semiotician; b. 1 March 1937, Moscow; s. of Andrej Uspensky and Gustava Mekler; m. 1st Galina Korshunova 1963 (died 1978); m. 2nd Tatiana Vladyshevskaya 1985; two s.; ed. Moscow Univ.; dissertation on structural typology of languages published 1965 and partly translated into English 1968; studied under Hjelmslev at Univ. of Copenhagen 1961; expedition to Siberia to study Ket language 1962; research at U.S.S.R. Acad. of Sciences Inst. of African Languages 1963–65; research mem. of Lab. of Computational Linguistics, Moscow Univ. 1965–77, Prof., Moscow Univ. 1977–92; Fellow Inst. for Advanced Studies, Russian State Univ. for the Humanities 1992–93; Visiting Prof. Vienna Univ. 1988, Harvard Univ. 1990–91, Graz Univ. 1992, Cornell Univ. 1994; Fellow Wissenschaftskolleg (Berlin) 1992–93; Prof., Oriental Univ. of Naples 1993–; major structuralist publications 1962–; Foreign Corresp. mem. Austrian Acad. of Science 1987; mem. Int. Asscn. for Semiotic Studies 1976, Academia Europaea 1990, Russian Acad. of Natural Science 1992, Russian PEN Centre 1994, Acad. of Humanities Research 1995, Soc. Royale des Lettres de Lund 1996; Hon. mem. Slavonic and E. European Medieval Studies Group 1987, Asscn. Int. de sémiologie de l'image 1990, Hon. Cttee., American Friends of the Warburg Inst. 1993. *Publications include:* Principles of Structural Typology 1962, Structural Typology of Languages 1965, The Archaic System of Church Slavonic Pronunciation 1968, A Poetics of Composition 1970 The First Russian Grammar in the Native Language 1975, The Semiotics of the Russian Icon 1976, Tipologia della cultura (with Yu. M. Lotman) 1976, Philological Investigations in the Field of Slavic Antiquities 1982, The History of the Russerary Language of XVIII to early XIX centuries 1985, The History of the Russian Literary Language XI–XVII centuries 1987, Sémiotique de la culture russe (with Yu. M. Lotman) 1990, Semiotik der Geschichte 1991, Storia della lingua letteraria russa: Dall'antica Rus' a Puškin 1993, Semiotics of Art 1995, Linguistica, semiotica, storia della cultura 1996, Selected Works (3 vols.) 1996–97, Tsar and Patriarch 1998; numerous articles. *Leisure interest:* travelling. *Address:* Via Principe Eugenio 15, Rome 00185, Italy; Chasovaja ul. 19/8 Apt. 20, Moscow 125315, Russia. *Telephone:* (6) 4468157 (Italy); (095) 152-52-39 (Russia).

USPENSKY, Nikolay Nikolayevich; Russian diplomatist (retd.); b. 10 Oct. 1938; ed. Higher Diplomatic School; fmr. mem. CPSU; Official, Ministry of Foreign Affairs 1973–75, Third Sec., Second European Countries Dept., 1975–77, Head, Second European Dept. 1986–87; Second Sec., U.S.S.R. Embassy, U.K. 1977–82, First Sec. 1982–83, Amb. to Sweden 1987–91; Counsellor, European Dept., Ministry of Foreign Affairs 1992–97. *Address:* Ministry of Foreign Affairs, 32/34 Smolenskaya-Sennaya, Moscow, Russia.

USPENSKY, Vladislav Aleksandrovich; Russian composer; b. 7 Sept. 1937, Omsk; s. of Alexander Grigoryevich Kolodkin and Vera Pavlovna Uspenskaya; m. Irina Yevgenyevna Taimanova 1963; ed. Moscow State Conservatory, postgrad. studies Leningrad State Conservatory (pupil of Dmitri Shostakovich); teacher of music theory Leningrad State Conservatory 1965–67, Dean of Musicology 1967–72, Prof. of Composition 1982–; Guest Composer-in-Residence Seoul Univ., Korea 1995, Lima Univ., Peru 1997; Chair. Music Council of Cultural Cttee., St. Petersburg Govt. 1996–; Vice-Pres. Union of Composers of St. Petersburg 1972–; Gen. Dir. Int. Musical Children's Festival 1995–; People's Artist of Russia. *Compositions:* operas – The War Against Salamanders 1967, Intervention 1970; 8 ballets including A Road to the Day 1974, For You to the Sea 1978, Cranes Flying 1984, The Mushroom's Alarm 1990; works for orchestra, choir, instrumental ensembles, songs (over 100), music for films and theatre productions. *Leisure interest:* love. *Address:* Admiralteysky canal 5 Apt. 26, St. Petersburg, Russia (Home). *Telephone:* (812) 311 3548 (Office), (812) 311 7435 (Home). *Fax:* (812) 311 3548 (Office).

USTINOV, Sir Peter Alexander, Kt., C.B.E., F.R.S.A.; British actor and dramatist; b. 16 April 1921; s. of late Iona Ustinov and Nadia Benois; m. 1st Isolde Denham 1940 (divorced 1950); one d.; m. 2nd Suzanne Cloutier 1954 (divorced 1971); one s. two d.; m. 3rd Hélène du Lau d'Allemans 1972; ed. Westminster School and London Theatre Studio; entered theatre as actor 1939; first appearance in revue writing own material Ambassador's Theatre, London 1940; served in army 1942–46; UNICEF Amb. of Goodwill; Pres. World Federalist Movt. 1992–96; appeared in plays: Crime and Punishment 1946, Frenzy 1948, Love in Albania 1949, The Love of Four Colonels 1951, Romanoff and Juliet 1956 (British Critics' Best Play Award), Photo Finish 1962, The Unknown Soldier and his Wife 1973, King Lear 1979–80, Beethoven's Tenth 1983, (in Berlin) 1987–88, An Evening with Peter Ustinov 1990–94, 1995–97; appeared in films: The Way Ahead (collaborated on screenplay) 1944, Odette 1950, Hotel Sahara 1951, Quo Vadis 1951, Beau Brummel 1954, The Egyptian 1954, We're no Angels 1955, Lola Montes 1955, Spartacus 1961 (Acad. Award for Best Supporting Actor, Golden Globe Award), Billy Budd 1962, Topkapi 1963 (Acad. Award for Best Supporting Actor), John Goldfarb 1964, Lady L 1965, Blackbeard's Ghost 1966, The Comedians 1967, Viva Max! 1970, Hot Millions (part-author and star) 1968, Hammersmith is Out (also dir.) 1971, One of Our Dinosaurs is Missing 1975, Treasure of Matcumbe 1977, The Last Remake of Beau Geste 1977, The Thief of Baghdad 1978, Death on the Nile 1978, Ashanti 1978, Charlie Chan and the Curse of the Dragon Queen 1981, Evil Under the Sun 1981, Memed My Hawk (wrote and dir.) 1984, Appointment with Death 1988, The French Revolution 1989, The Man Who Loved Hitchcock 1989, Lorenzo's Oil 1992, The Old Curiosity Shop 1994, The Phoenix and the Magic Carpet 1994; has appeared in numerous TV productions; dir. operas Magic Flute, Hamburg 1968, Don Quichotte, Paris 1973 (also designed and produced), Don Giovanni, Edinburgh 1973 (also designed), Les Brigands, Berlin 1978, Mavra, Milan 1982, Katja Kabanowa, Hamburg 1985, The Marriage of Figaro (Salzburg and Hamburg) 1987, The Love of the Three Oranges (Moscow) 1997; recorded Peter and the Wolf (Grammy Award); Rector Univ. of Dundee 1968, 1971–73; Chancellor Durham Univ. 1992–; Pres. World Federalist Movt. 1992; Foreign mem. Acad. of Fine Arts, Paris 1988; Hon. D.Mus. (Cleveland Inst. of Music) 1967, Hon. LL.D. (Univ. of Dundee) 1969, (La Salle Coll., Philadelphia) 1971, (Ottawa Univ.) 1991; Hon. D.Litt. (Univ. of Lancaster) 1972; Hon. Dr. (Univ. of Toronto) 1984, (Pontifical Inst. of Medieval Studies, Univ. of Toronto) 1995; Hon. D.H.L. (Georgetown Univ.) 1988, Dr. h.c. (Free Univ. of Brussels) 1995; UNICEF Award 1978, 1995, Variety Club Award 1979; Benjamin Franklin Medal, R.S.A.; Gold Medal (City of Athens) 1990; Greek Red Cross Medal 1990; Medal of Honour (Prague Univ.) 1991; Britannia Award (B.A.F.T.A.) 1992; Critics' Circle Award 1993; Commdr. Ordre des Arts et des Lettres 1985; Ordem Nacional do Cruzeiro de Sul (Brazil) 1994; German Cultural Award 1994, German Bambi Award 1994; Int. Child Survival Award, UNICEF 1995; German Video Prize (for life-time achievement) 1997; Order of Istiqlal (Jordan); Order of the Yugoslav Flag; Bundesverdienstkreuz 1998; Bayerischer Fernsehpreis 1998. *Publications:* plays: House of Regrets 1942, Blow Your Own Trumpet 1943, The Banbury Nose 1944, The Tragedy of Good Intentions 1945, The Indifferent Shepherd 1948, The Man in the Raincoat 1949, The Love of Four Colonels 1951, The Moment of Truth 1951, No Sign of the Dove 1953, Romanoff and Juliet 1956, Photo Finish 1962, The Life in My Hands 1963, Half Way up the Tree 1967, The Unknown Soldier and his Wife 1967, Who's Who in Hell 1974, Overheard 1981, Beethoven's Tenth 1983; short stories: Add a Dash of Pity 1959, The Frontiers of the Sea 1966; novels: The Loser 1960, Krumnagel 1971, The Old Man and Mr. Smith 1990; autobiogs.: Dear Me 1977, My Russia 1983; Ustinov at Large 1991, Ustinov Still at Large 1993, Quotable Ustinov 1995; The Disinformer (novellas) 1989; articles, etc. *Leisure interests:* sailing, travel. *Address:* c/o William Morris Agency (UK) Ltd., 1 Stratton Street, London, W1X 6HB, England; 11 rue de Silly, 92100 Boulogne, France. *Telephone:* 0171-355 8500 (London). *Fax:* 0171-355 8600.

USTVOLSKAYA, Galina Ivanovna; Russian composer; b. 17 June 1919, Petrograd; ed. Leningrad Conservatory (pupil of D. Shostakovich); author of maj. orchestral compositions rarely performed in U.S.S.R. up to late 1980s due to ban of contemporary sacred music including 5 symphonies: 1 1955, 2 (Genuine Eternal Beauty) 1979, 3 (Jesus, Messiah, Rescue Us) 1983, 4 (Pray) 1987, 5 (Amen) 1989/90; also numerous compositions for different instruments and piano pieces, including Dona nobis pacem, for piccolo, tuba and piano 1970/71, Dies irae, for 8 double basses, percussion and piano 1972/73, Benedictus qui Venit, for 4 flutes, 4 bassoons and piano 1974/75; teacher, then Prof. of Composition N. Rimsky-Korsakov School of Music in St. Petersburg 1947–. *Address:* Prospect Gagarina 27, Apt. 72, 196135 St. Petersburg, Russia (Home). *Telephone:* (812) 293 1512 (Home).

USUI, Hideo; Japanese politician; fmr. Parl. Vice-Minister Econ. Planning Agency; Minister of State and Dir.-Gen. Defence Agency Jan.–Nov. 1996; mem. House of Reps., mem. LDP. *Address:* c/o Defence Agency, 9-7-45, Akasaka, Minato-ku, Tokyo 107, Japan.

UTEEM, Cassam, G.C.S.K., L. ÈS L.; Mauritian politician; b. 22 March 1941, Plaine Verte; m. 1967; two s. one d.; ed. Univs. of Mauritius and Paris VII; fmr. supervisor, Cable & Wireless Ltd.; personnel man. Currimjee Jeewanjee & Co., Ltd.; Sec.-Gen. Mauritius Nat. Youth Council 1971–72; Treas. Mauritius Council of Social Service 1971–73; Rep. of World Ass. of Youth (WAY) to UNESCO 1974–76; municipal councillor, Port Louis 1969, 1977–79, 1986–88; Lord Mayor of City of Port Louis 1986; mem. Legis. Ass. 1976–92; Minister of Employment, Social Security and National Solidarity 1982–83; Opposition Whip 1983–87; Chair. Public Accounts Cttee. 1988–90; Deputy Leader, Mouvement Militant Mauricien (MMM) 1988; Deputy Prime Minister and Minister of Industry and Industrial Tech. 1990–92; Pres. Republic of Mauritius 1992–; mem. h.c. Acad. Nationale Malgache 1995; Hon. D.C.L. (Univ. of Mauritius) 1994; Dr. h.c. (Univ. of Marseille III) 1994. *Address:* State House, Le Réduit, Mauritius. *Telephone:* 4543021. *Fax:* 4645370.

UTKIN, Vladimir Fedorovich, D.TECH.SC.; Russian scientist; b. 17 Oct. 1923, Shostye Kasimov; m. Valentina Pavlovna Pronkina 1949 (died 1994); one s. one d.; ed. Kasimov, Ryazan and Leningrad Mechanical Inst.; design engineer, later Dept. Head, Deputy Chief Designer, Design Office 1952–71, Chief Designer and Man. 1971–79, Gen. Designer and Man. 1979–86; Gen. Designer and Gen. Dir. Scientific Unit South (Dnepropetrovsk) 1986–90; Dir. Cen. Research Inst. of Machine Construction 1990–; mem. Ukrainian Acad. of Sciences 1976, U.S.S.R. (now Russian) Acad. of Sciences 1984; Pres. K. Tsiolkovski Acad. of Cosmonautics, Int. Acad. of Astronautics; Hero of Socialist Labour 1969, 1976, Lenin Prize 1972, State Prize of the U.S.S.R. 1980, six Orders of Lenin, Order of the Red Banner, other medals. *Publications:* scientific works on applied mechanics, investigation of tech. and econ. effectiveness of mechanical systems, design of space rocket systems and spacecraft. *Address:* Central Research Institute of Machine Construction 141070 Korolev, Moscow Region (Office); Alexandr Nevsky St. 1, Apt. 91, 125047 Moscow, Russia (Home). *Telephone:* 513-50-00, 187-49-44 (Office); 973-15-65 (Home). *Fax:* (095) 274-00-25, 516-61-29.

UTTLEY-MOORE, William James, C.B.E., B.SC., F.ENG.; British electronic engineer; b. 19 July 1944, Crayford, Kent; s. of late William Uttley-Moore and of Louisa Clara Dixon; m. Jennifer Bencer 1966; one s.; ed. Erith Tech. School, London Univ.; student apprentice and devt. engineer, Cintel Ltd. 1960–68; project leader, Molins Machine Co. Ltd. 1968–69; Chief Engineer, Computing Devices Co. Ltd. 1969–75, Tech. Dir. 1979–85, Chair. and Man. Dir. 1985–; Founder Dir. Southern F.M. 1989–92, Conqueror F.M. 1996–; Chair. E. Sussex Econ. Partnership 1998–; mem. Bd., Defence Scientific Advisory Council 1994–. *Publications:* numerous tech. papers on reconnaissance, avionics and digital battlefield. *Leisure interests:* practical eng., farming, running, classical music. *Address:* Computing Devices Company Ltd., St. Leonards-on-Sea, East Sussex, TN35 5EL; Tilekiln Farm, Fairlight Road, Ore, Hastings, East Sussex, TN35 5EL, England. *Telephone:* (01424) 426322.

UTZERATH, Hansjörg; German theatre director; b. 20 March 1926; m. Renate Ziegfeld 1957; one s. two d.; ed. Kepler Oberschule, Tübingen; began as actor, later in theatre man. in Düsseldorf, and then in production; Chief Stage Man., Düsseldorfer Kammerspiele 1955–59; Dir. 1959–66; Intendant, Freie Volksbühne, Berlin 1967–73; Dir. Städtische Bühnen, Nuremberg 1977–; Guest Producer at Staatstheater Stuttgart, Münchener Kammerspiele and Schiller-Theater, Berlin 1959–. *Productions include:* Tango 1971, Der Vater 1972, Viele heissen Kain (TV). *Address:* Städtische Bühnen Schauspiel, Richard-Wagner-Platz 2-10, 90443 Nuremberg, Germany.

UTZON, Jørn, O.A.; Danish architect; b. 9 April 1918, Copenhagen; ed. Royal Acad. of Fine Arts, Copenhagen; joined Helsinki Office of Alvar Aalto after Second World War; won travelling scholarships to Morocco and U.S.A.; designer of furniture and glassware; won competition for design of Sydney Opera House 1957, worked on project in Denmark 1957–63, in Sydney

1963–66 (resgnd. as architect); won competition for design of Zürich Schauspielhaus 1966; architect of a housing scheme near Fredensborg, his own house, Bank Melli Iran, Teheran, etc.; Fellow, Royal Australian Inst. of Architects 1965, R.I.B.A. 1978–; Ehrenpreis, Bund Deutscher Architekten 1966, Gold Medal, Royal Australian Inst. of Architects 1973, R.I.B.A. 1978, Wolf Prize (jtly.) 1992, and other awards. *Address:* 3150 Hellebaek, Denmark.

UYEDA, Seiya, D.SC.; Japanese geophysicist; b. 28 Nov. 1929, Tokyo; s. of the late Seiichi and Hatsuo Uyeda; m. Mutsuko Kosaka 1952; one s. two d.; ed. Univ. of Tokyo; Research Fellow Earthquake Research Inst., Univ. of Tokyo 1955–63, Assoc. Prof. Geophysical Inst. 1963–69, Prof. Earthquake Research Inst. 1969–89; Prof., School of Marine Science and Tech., Tokai Univ. 1990–95; Harris Prof. of Geophysics, Texas A & M Univ. 1990–95; RIKEN Int. Frontier Program on Earthquake Research 1996–; Tanakadate Prize, Soc. of Terrestrial Electricity and Magnetism 1955; Okada Prize, Oceanographical Soc. of Japan 1968; Alexander Agassiz Medal, Nat. Acad. of Sciences 1972, Japan Acad. Prize 1987, George P. Woollard Award, Geological Soc. of America 1989, Walter H. Bucher Medal, American Geophysical Union 1991. *Publications:* Debate about the Earth 1967, Island Arcs 1973, The New View of the Earth 1977; 300 scientific papers. *Leisure interest:* skiing. *Address:* Earthquake Prediction Research Centre, Tokai University, 3-20-1 Orido, Shimizu City, Shizuoka (Office); 2-39-6 Daizawa, Setagaya-ku, Tokyo 113, Japan (Home). *Telephone:* 81-543-36-2862 (Office); 81-3-3412-0237 (Home). *Fax:* 81-543-36-0920 (Office).

UYS, Pieter-Dirk, B.A.; South African playwright, performer and producer; b. 28 Sept. 1945, Cape Town; s. of Helga Bassel and Hannes Uys; ed. Univ. of Cape Town, London Film School, U.K.; joined Space Theatre, Cape Town 1973; f. Syrkel Theatre Co.; Dir. P. D Uys Productions, Bapetikosweti Marketing Enterprises; produced and performed 30 plays in revues throughout S.A. and in U.K., U.S.A., Australia, Canada, Netherlands; several videos and TV films and documentaries. *Publications:* Die van Aardes van Grootoor 1979, Paradise is Closing Down 1980, God's Forgotten 1981, Karnaval 1982, Selle ou storie 1983, Farce about Uys 1984, Appassionata 1985, Skote! 1986, Paradise is Closing Down and Other Plays 1989, No one's Died Laughing 1986, P.W. Botha: In His Own Words 1987, A Part Hate, A Part Love 1990, Funigalore 1995. *Leisure interests:* films, music, people, S. African politics. *Address:* 17 Station Road, Darling 7345, South Africa. *Telephone:* (2241) 3208. *Fax:* (2241) 3208.

UZAWA, Hirofumi, PH.D.; Japanese professor of economics; b. 21 July 1928, Tottori Province; s. of Tokio and Toshiko Uzawa; m. Hiroko Aoyoshi 1957; two s. one d.; ed. Univ. of Tokyo; Research Assoc., Lecturer, Asst. Prof., Dept. of Econs., Stanford Univ., Calif. 1956–60, Assoc. Prof. of Econs. and Statistics 1961–64; Asst. Prof. of Econs. and Math., Univ. of Calif., Berkeley 1960–61; Prof. of Econs. Univ. of Chicago 1964–68, Univ. of Tokyo 1969–89, Prof. Emer. 1989–; Prof. of Econs., Niigata Univ. 1989–; mem. The Japan Acad. 1989–; Matsunaga Memorial Prize 1969, Yoshino Prize 1971, Mainichi Prize 1974, desig. as Person of Cultural Merits 1983. *Publications:* in English: Studies in Linear and Nonlinear Programming (co-author) 1958; in Japanese: Economic Development and Fluctuations (co-author) 1972, Social Costs of the Automobile 1974, A Re-examination of Modern Economic Theory 1977, Transformation of Modern Economics 1986, A Critique of Japanese Economy 1987, Towards a Theory of Public Economics 1987, Preference, Production, and Capital 1988, Optimality, Equilibrium and Growth 1988, A History of Economic Thought (in Japanese) 1989, Poverty amid Economic Prosperity (in Japanese) 1989, Economic Analysis (in Japanese) 1990. *Leisure interest:* walking. *Address:* University of Tokyo, Hongo, Bunkyo-ku, Tokyo; Higashi 1-3-6, Hoya, Tokyo, Japan.

V

VĂCĂROIU, Nicolae; Romanian politician and economist; b. 5 Dec. 1943, Bolgrad, Bessarabia; m. Marinela Văcăroiu; one s.; ed. Bucharest Acad. of Econ. Studies; Economist, Ilfov Co. Inst. of Design and Systemization; then with State Planning Cttee., promoted to Dir. Econ.-Financial Synthesis Dept.; apptd. Deputy Minister of Nat. Economy 1990; subsequently Head of Price Dept., Ministry of Finance, Sec. of State and Head of Tax Dept., Chair. Interministerial Cttee. of Foreign Trade Guarantees and Credits; Prime Minister 1992–96; Senator 1996–; Pres. Privatisation Cttee. 1997–. *Publications:* numerous articles on econ. and financial matters. *Address:* Romanian Senate, Piaţa Revoluţiei, 71243 Bucharest, Romania.

VACEK, Miroslav; Czech politician and army officer (retd.); b. 29 Aug. 1935, Kolín; m. Helena Vacek 1958; one s.; ed. A. Zápotocký Mil. Acad. Brno and Mil. Acad. of U.S.S.R.; Commdr. Western Mil. Dist. 1985; Chief of Gen. Staff of Czechoslovak Army and First Deputy of Minister of Nat. Defence 1987; Minister of Nat. Defence 1989–90; Advisor to Ministry of Defence 1990–91; Pres. Victoria (business) 1992–; mem. Parl. of Czech Repub. 1996–98; mem. Comm. for Defence and Security in Parl. 1996–98; Communist Party of Bohemia and Moravia (KSČM). *Publications:* Why Should I Keep Silent? 1991, In Fairness 1994; articles on mil. problems published in mil. press. *Address:* Communist Party of Bohemia and Moravia, Politických vězňů 9, 110 00 Prague 1, Czech Republic. *Telephone:* 242 101 72. *Fax:* 24 22 77 21.

VACHON, H.E. Cardinal Louis-Albert, C.C., D.PH., D.TH.; Canadian ecclesiastic; b. 4 Feb. 1912, St. Frédéric, Beauce Co., Quebec; s. of Napoléon Vachon and Alexandrine Gilbert; ed. Laval Univ. and St. Thomas Aquinas Univ., Rome; ordained priest 1938; Prof. of Philosophy, Laval Univ. 1941–47, of Theology 1949–55; Superior, Grand Seminaire de Quebec 1955–59, Gen. Superior 1960–77; Domestic Prelate 1958; Vice-Rector Laval Univ. 1960–72; Vicar-Gen., Diocese of Quebec 1960–81; Protonotary Apostolic 1963–77; Auxiliary Bishop of Quebec 1977–81; Archbishop of Quebec and Primate of Canada 1981–90, Archbishop Emer. 1990; cr. Cardinal 1985; mem. Sacred Congregation for the Clergy 1986–, Canadian Soc. of Theology, Canadian Soc. of Authors, Admin. Bd. of English Speaking Union of Commonwealth in Canada, Royal Soc. of Canada, Admin. Bd. of Canadian Conf. Catholic Bishops, and many other bodies; Fellow Royal Soc. of Canada; Kt. Great Cross, Equestre du Saint-Sépulchre de Jérusalem 1985, Officier, Légion d'honneur (France) 1988; Hon. degrees from several univs. *Publications:* Espérance et présomption 1958, Vérité et liberté 1962, Unité de l'université 1962, Apostolat de l'universitaire catholique 1963, Mémorial 1963, Communauté universitaire 1963, Progrès de l'université et consentement populaire 1964, Responsabilité collective des universitaires 1964, Les humanités d'aujourd'hui 1966, Excellence et loyauté des universitaires 1969. *Leisure interests:* reading, fine art. *Address:* Séminaire de Québec, 1 rue des Remparts, Québec, Qué. G1R 5LY, Canada. *Telephone:* (418) 692-3981. *Fax:* (418) 692-4345.

VADIM, Roger (Plemiannikov); French film director; b. 26 Jan. 1928, Paris; s. of Igor Plemiannikov and Marie-Antoinette Ardilouze; m. 1st Brigitte Bardot (q.v.) 1952 (divorced); m. 2nd Annette Stroyberg 1958 (divorced); one d.; m. 3rd Jane Fonda (q.v.) 1967 (divorced); one d.; m. 4th Catherine Schneider 1975 (divorced); one s.; m. 5th Marie-Christine Barrault 1990; one s. by Catherine Deneuve (q.v.); actor; script-writer and Asst. Dir. with Marc Allegret; reporter Paris-Match 1952–54; ind. film dir. 1955–; scriptwriter Futures vedettes, Cette sacrée gamine, En effeuillant la marguerite; dir. and scriptwriter Et Dieu créa la femme, Sait-on jamais, Les bijoutiers du Clair de Lune, Les liaisons dangereuses, Et mourir de plaisir, Le repos du guerrier, Le vice et la vertu, La ronde, La curée, Histoires extraordinaires, Barbarella, Metzengerstein 1969, Pretty Maids in a Row, Hellé, Don Juan 1973, La jeune fille assassinée 1974, La femme fidèle 1976, Night Games 1979, Surprise Party 1983. *Publications:* Memoirs of the Devil 1976, The Hungry Angel 1984, Bardot, Deneuve and Fonda 1986, Le Fou amoureux 1988. *Address:* c/o Editions Fixot, 24 avenue Marceau, 75381 Paris, France (Office); 24-29 Beverly Avenue, Santa Monica, CA, U.S.A. (Home).

VĂDUVA, Leontina; French soprano; b. Romania, 1962; d. of Maria Ciobanu; m. Gheorghe Codre; ed. Bucharest Conservatoire; came to West in 1988, subsequently gaining political asylum in France; début in Massenet's Manon, Toulouse 1987; Covent Garden début as Manon 1988; appeared at Covent Garden as Gilda in Rigoletto 1989 and as Juliet in Romeo and Juliet 1995; has also sung in Paris, Munich, Hamburg, Zurich, Brussels, Barcelona, Florence, Buenos Aires, San Francisco and Tokyo; Olivier Award for Outstanding Achievement in Opera 1988, Chevalier Ordre des Arts et des Lettres 1998. *Address:* c/o Theateragentur Luisa Petrov, Glauburgstr. 95, 60318 Frankfurt, Germany.

VAEA, Baron (Baron Vaea of Houma); Tongan politician; b. 15 May 1921, Nuku'alofa; s. of Vilai Tupou and Tupou Seini Vaea; m. Hon. Tuputupu-'o-Pulotu Ma'afu 1952; three s. three d.; ed. Tupou Coll., Wesley Coll., N.Z., St. Edmund's Hall, Oxford Univ., Kidlington Air Training School; inherited title 'Vaea' 1942; military service with R.N. Z.A.F. 1942–44; joined Tonga Civil Service 1945; Aide-de-Camp to H.M. Queen Salote Tupou III 1954–59; Gov. of Ha'apai 1960–68; Commr. and Consul for Tonga in London 1969–70, High Commr. and Consul 1970–72; given title of Baron by H.M. King Taufa'ahau Tupou IV 1970; Minister for Labour, Commerce and Industries 1973–91; Acting Deputy Prime Minister 1989; Prime Minister, Minister for Agric. and Forestry, for Fisheries 1991–, for Telecommunications 1991–, for Women's Affairs 1991–, of Marines and Ports 1994–; mem. Tonga Defence Bd. 1973; Chair. Shipping Corpn. of Polynesia 1978, Nat. Reserve Bank 1989, Tonga Telecommunications Comm., Tonga Broadcasting Comm. 1991, Tonga Investment Ltd. 1992. *Leisure interests:* tennis, rugby, farming. *Address:* P.O. Box 62, Nuku'alofa, Tonga. *Telephone:* 24-644. *Fax:* 23-888.

VAES, Baron Robert, cr. 1985, LL.D.; Belgian diplomatist; b. 9 Jan. 1919, Antwerp; s. of Louis Vaes; m. Anne Albers 1947; one d.; Parl. Pvt. Sec. to Minister of Foreign Trade 1958–60; Dir.-Gen of Political Affairs 1964–66; Perm. Under-Sec. of State, Ministry of Foreign Affairs, Foreign Trade and Devt. Co-operation 1966–72; fmr. Chair. Council of Benelux Union; postings to Washington, Paris, Hong Kong, London, Rome, Madrid 1972–76; Amb. to U.K. 1976–84; Dir. Sotheby's 1984–; decorations include Grand Officer of the Order of Léopold, Grand Officier Légion d'honneur, Grand Officer of the Order of the Crown, Hon. K.C.M.G. *Address:* Sotheby's, 34/35 New Bond Street, London, W1A 2AA (Office); The Orangery, Langley Park, Bucks., SL3 6DW, England. *Telephone:* (01753) 528815 (Office).

VAGELOS, Pindaros Roy, M.D.; American pharmaceutical industry executive; b. 8 Oct. 1929, Westfield, N.J.; s. of Roy John Vagelos and Marianthi Lambrinides; m. Diana Touliatos 1955; two s. two d.; ed. Univ. of Pennsylvania and Columbia Univ. Coll. of Physicians and Surgeons; Intern in Medicine, Mass. Gen. Hosp. 1954–55, Asst. Res. in Medicine 1955–56; Surgeon, Lab. of Cellular Physiology, Nat. Insts. of Health 1956–59, Surgeon, Lab. of Biochemistry 1959–64, Head, Section on Comparative Biochemistry 1964–66; Prof. of Biochemistry, Chair. Dept. of Biological Chem., Washington Univ. School of Medicine, St. Louis, Mo. 1966–75, Dir. Div. of Biology and Biomedical Sciences 1973–75; Sr. Vice-Pres. Research, Merck Sharp & Dohme Research Labs., Rahway, N.J. 1975–76, Pres. 1976–84, Corporate Sr. Vice-Pres. Merck & Co., Inc. 1982–84, Exec. Vice-Pres. 1984–85, C.E.O. 1985–86, Chair. and C.E.O. 1986–95; Chair Regeneron Pharmaceuticals Inc. 1995–; Trustee Rockefeller Univ. 1976–94, Univ. of Pa. 1988– (Chair. Bd. 1994–), Danforth Foundation 1978–; Dir. TRW Inc. 1987–, Prudential Insurance Co. of America 1989–, PepsiCo Inc. 1992–, numerous other appointments; mem. N.A.S., American Acad. of Arts and Sciences; Enzyme Chem. Award, American Chemical Soc. 1967, N.J. Science/Tech. Medal 1983, Pupin Medal 1995; discoverer of acyl-carrier protein. *Leisure interests:* jogging, tennis. *Address:* Regeneron Pharmaceuticals Inc., 777 Old Saw Mill River Road, Tarrytown, NY 10591 (Office); 82 Mosle Road, Far Hills, NJ 07931, U.S.A. (Home).

VAGNORIUS, Gediminas, DR.ECON.SC.; Lithuanian politician; b. 10 June 1957, Plunge district; m. Niele Vagnorenė; one s. one d.; ed. Inst. of Eng. and Construction, Vilnius; engineer-economist, jr. researcher, then researcher, Inst. of Econs., Lithuanian Acad. of Sciences 1980–90; Deputy to Lithuanian Supreme Soviet, mem. Presidium 1990–91; Chair. Council of Ministers of Lithuania 1991–92, 1996–; mem. Seimas 1992–; Chair. Bd. Homeland Union/Lithuanian Conservative Party 1993–. *Leisure interest:* jogging. *Address:* Government of Lithuania, Gedimino Prospekt 11, 2039 Vilnius, Lithuania. *Telephone:* (2) 622101. *Fax:* (2) 221088.

VAGO, Constant, PH.D., D.SC.; French pathologist and university professor; b. 2 May 1921, Debrecen, Hungary; s. of Vincent Vago and Françoise Schibl; m. Catherine Sary 1944; one s. one d.; ed. Lycée of Debrecen, Univ. of Marseilles; Dir. Lab. of Cytopathology, Nat. Inst. for Agron. Research, Saint-Christol 1958–; Prof. of Pathology and Microbiology, Univ. of Science, Montpellier 1964–; Dir. Centre of Comparative Pathology, Univ. of Montpellier and WHO Research Centre 1964–; mem. Acad. of Sciences of France, Acad. of Agric. of France, New York Acad. of Sciences, Hungarian Acad. of Sciences, Nat. Acad. of Sciences of India, European Acad. of Sciences, Int. Acad. of Sciences; Past Pres. Int. Soc. for Invertebrate Pathology; Pres. Nat. Cttee. of Biological Sciences of France; mem. numerous scientific socs.; Dr. h.c. (Medical Univ., Debrecen, Hungary); Prof. h.c. (Univ. of Cen. China); Int. Ishida Prize of Cytology, Int. El Fasi Great Prize for Science, Institut Pasteur Prize; Légion d'honneur, Ordre nat. du Mérite, and other decorations. *Publications:* Invertebrate Tissue Culture 1972, and about 400 publications on comparative pathology, tissue culture, molecular virology, chlamydial diseases, comparative oncology. *Leisure interests:* sculpture, swimming. *Address:* University of Sciences, Place Eugène Bataillon, 34095 Montpellier, France. *Telephone:* (4) 67143220. *Fax:* (4) 66524699.

VAGO, Pierre; French architect and town planner; b. 30 Aug. 1910, Budapest, Hungary; s. of Joseph and Ghita (Lenart) Vago; m. 1st Monique Lesourd (deceased); two s. two d.; m. 2nd Nicole Cormier 1968; ed. Ecole spéciale d'Architecture, Paris; Ed.-in-Chief Architecture d'Aujourd'hui 1932–48, Pres. of Cttee. 1948–75; Founder and Sec.-Gen. Int. Reunions of Architects 1932–48 and Int. Union of Architects 1948–69, Hon. Pres. 1969–; Head Architect for Reconstruction 1948–56; Pres. Int. Council, Soc. of Industrial

Design 1963–65; fmr. Vice-Pres. Confed. of French Architects; Council mem., Comité Int. Critiques d'Architecture 1979–; Chair. Co-ordinating Group NGO's in Man-Made Environment 1981–90; Vice-Pres. Int. Acad. of Architecture 1987–98; mem. jury of many int. competitions; architect and town planner in Belgium, Austria, France, Germany, Tunisia, Mexico, Luxembourg, Israel and Italy; Prof. and Dir. of Studies Ecole Supérieure d'Architecture St. Luc de Belgique; Prof. Int. Sommerakadamie, Salzburg 1972–78; honours include Hon. mem. of R.I.B.A., American Inst. of Architects, Bund Deutscher Architekten, Acad. d'Architecture (Paris), Akad. der Künste, Berlin and mem. of numerous architectural socs.; Dr. h.c. (Univ. of Stuttgart), Prof. h.c. (Tech. Univ., Budapest); Chevalier, Légion d'honneur, Commdr. Grégoire le Grand, Commdr. Ordre des Arts et des Lettres, Medal Résistance. *Major works include:* Basilica St. Pius X, Lourdes and other churches, Cen. Bank of Tunis, Library of Univ. of Bonn, Univ. of Lille, several buildings in France, Germany, N. Africa, Mexico and Israel. *Leisure interest:* history. *Address:* Le Valparon, 77123 Noisy-sur-Ecole, France (Home). *Telephone:* (1) 64 24 56 00.

VÄHI, Tiit; Estonian politician; b. 10 Jan. 1947, Valgamaa; m.; two c.; ed. Tallinn Polytechnic Inst.; fmr. Production Man. Valga Motor Depot, later Deputy Dir., Chief Engineer, Dir., Chair. Transport Cttee.; fmr. Minister of Transport and Communications; Prime Minister of Estonia Jan.–Oct. 1992, April 1995–; mem. of Bd., Coalition Party, Chair. 1995–; attended refresher courses in Germany 1993; Chair. Tallinn City Council 1993–95. *Address:* Coalition Party Eesti Koonderakond, Kuhlbarsi 1, Tallinn 0104, Estonia. *Telephone:* (3726) 431-551. *Fax:* (3726) 433-122.

VAILLANT, Daniel; French politician; b. 19 July 1949, Lormes (Nièvre); s. of Raymond Vaillant and Germaine Andre; three c.; ed. Ecole supérieure de biologie et biochimie; joined Convention des Institutions Républicaines 1966; Parti Socialiste (PS) official, 18th arrondissement Paris 1971–95; Special Asst. to François Mitterrand, presidential election campaign 1981; Asst. Nat. Sec. for PS Feds. 1986, Nat. Sec. for PS Feds. 1988–94, Nat. Sec. without specific assignment 1994–95; campaign dir., Lionel Jospin's parl. and regional election campaigns 1986, Organizer and Co-ordinator Jospin's gen. election campaign 1997; city councillor 18th arrondissement Paris 1977–95, Mayor of 18th arrondissement 1995; Ile-de-France regional councillor 1986–89; Nat. Ass. Deputy for 19th Paris constituency 1988–93; Minister for Relations with Parl. 1997–. *Address:* Ministère des Relations avec le Parlement, 69 rue de Varenne, 75700 Paris; Mairie, 1 place Jules Joffrin, 75877 Paris, France.

VAILLAUD, Pierre; French oil executive; b. 15 Feb. 1935, Paris; s. of Marcel Vaillaud and Rose Larrat; m. Geneviève Dreyfus 1960; two s.; ed. Lycée Janson-de-Sailly, Paris, Ecole Polytechnique, Ecole des Mines, Ecole Nat. Supérieure du Pétrole et des Moteurs; engineer, Ministry of Industry 1959–63; project man. Technip 1964–68, Dir., Vice-Pres. Eng. and Construction Atochem (affiliate of Total) 1968–72; Vice-Pres. Natural Gas Div., Total 1972–74, Vice-Pres. Devt. and Construction Div., Vice-Pres. Exploration and Production Operations then Pres., Total Exploration Production 1974–89, Exec. Vice-Pres. Total, Pres. and C.E.O. Total Chimie 1989–92, Chair. and C.E.O. Technip 1992–; Pres. Asscn. des techniciens du pétrole 1985–87; Commdr., Ordre nat. du Mérite, Chevalier, Légion d'honneur. *Leisure interests:* tennis, sailing, golf. *Address:* Technip, La Défense 6, 92973 Paris-la-Défense Cédex (Office); 5 villa Madrid, 92200 Neuilly-sur-Seine, France (Home). *Telephone:* (1) 47 78 20 04. *Fax:* (1) 47 78 35 02.

VAINBERG, Lev Iosifovich, C.TECH.SC.; Russian business executive; b. 6 May 1944, Kuibyshev; m.; one d.; ed. Moscow Aviation Inst., Moscow Univ.; worked Computer Centre of Moscow Aviation Inst. –1987; founder and Dir.-Gen. French-Italian-Soviet Co. Interquadro 1987–90; Chair. of Bd. Asscn. of jt. ventures, trusts and int. orgs., U.S.S.R. 1988–90; Vice Pres. U.S.S.R. Scientific-Industrial Union 1990–92; Deputy Chair. Council on Enterprise of Pres. of U.S.S.R. 1991; Vice-Pres. Int. Foundation for Promotion of Privatization and Foreign Investments 1991; Deputy Chair. Russian Union of Businessmen and Entrepreneurs 1992–; Chair. Bd. Centrinvest, Technobank; Pres. SOLEV Int. Corpn.; mem. Council on Enterprise of Pres. of Russia 1992–. *Address:* SOLEV, Svetlyi Proyezd 4, Korp. 4, 125080 Moscow, Russia (Office). *Telephone:* (095) 943-0014 (Office).

VAINIO, Vesa Veikko; Finnish business executive; b. 2 Dec. 1942, Helsinki; s. of Veikko Vainio and Aune Vainio; m. Marja-Liisa Harjunen 1968; two s.; Circuit Court Notary, Rovaniemi Circuit Court 1966–67; Counsellor, Union of Finnish Lawyers 1968; Sec. Finnish Employers' Confed. 1969, Counsellor and Asst. Head of Dept. 1969–72; Admin. Dir. Aaltonen Footwear Factory 1972, Deputy Man. Dir. 1974–76; Man. Dir. Aaltonen Factories Oy 1976–77; Dir. Confed. of Finnish Industries 1977–83, Deputy Man. Dir. 1983–85; Exec. Vice-Pres. Kymmene Corpn. 1985–91, Pres. 1991–92; Pres. and C.E.O. Unitas Ltd. 1992–94; Chair. and C.E.O. Union Bank of Finland 1992–94, (after merger with Kansallis-Osake-Pankki into Merita Bank Ltd.) Merita Bank Ltd. 1994–97, Pres. and C.E.O. of Merita Ltd. 1994–97, Pres. Merita PLC 1998–, Chair. Bd. MeritaNordbanken PLC 1998, Vice-Chair. Nordbanken Holding PLC 1998–, Vice-Chair. Bd. MeritaNordbanken PLC 1999; Kt., Order of Finnish Lion, Commdr. of Finnish Lion. *Leisure interests:* hunting, fishing. *Address:* MeritaNordbanken PLC, Aleksanterinkatu 30, 00100 Helsinki, Finland. *Telephone:* (9) 1651. *Fax:* (9) 16542211.

VAISEY, David George, C.B.E., M.A., F.S.A., F.R.HIST.S.; British librarian; b. 15 March 1935; s. of William Thomas Vaisey and Minnie Vaisey (née Payne); m. Maureen Anne Mansell 1965; two d.; ed. Rendcomb Coll., Glos., Exeter Coll. Oxford; archivist, Staffordshire Co. Council 1960–63; Asst., then Sr. Librarian, Bodleian Library 1963–75, Keeper of Western Manuscripts 1975–86, Bodley's Librarian 1986–96, Bodley's Librarian Emer. 1997–; Deputy Keeper, Oxford Univ. Archives 1966–75, Keeper 1995–; Professorial Fellow, Exeter Coll., Oxford 1975–96, Fellow by Special Election 1997–; Hon. Fellow, Kellogg Coll., Oxford 1996–; Visiting Prof. Library Studies, Univ. of Calif., L.A. 1985; Hon. Research Fellow, Dept. of Library, Archive and Information Studies, Univ. Coll., London 1987–; Chair. Nat. Council on Archives 1988–91; mem. Royal Comm. on Historical Manuscripts 1986–98, Advisory Council on Public Records 1989–94. *Publications:* Staffordshire and the Great Rebellion (jtly.) 1964, Probate Inventories of Lichfield and District 1568–1680 1969, Victorian and Edwardian Oxford from old photographs (jtly.) 1971, Oxford Shops and Shopping 1972, Art for Commerce (jtly.) 1973, Oxfordshire: a handbook for students of local history 1973, The Diary of Thomas Turner 1754–65 1984. *Address:* 12 Hernes Road, Oxford, OX2 7PU, England.

VAJDA, György; Hungarian engineer; b. 18 June 1927, Budapest; s. of László Vajda and Mária Daróczi; m. 1st Magdolna Krasznai 1969 (died 1987); one s. one d.; m. 2nd Dr. Klára Berei 1988; ed. Tech. Univ., Budapest; Asst. Lecturer 1949–50; on staff of Hungarian Acad. of Sciences 1950–52; Deputy Dir. Inst. of Measurements 1952–57, Research Inst. of Electric Energetics 1957–63; Deputy Section Leader, Ministry of Heavy Industry 1963–70; Dir. Inst. for Electrical Power Research 1970–93, Prof. 1993–97; Dir. Gen. Nat. Atomic Energy Authority 1997– (Vice-Pres. 1979–97); Pres. European Atomic Energy Soc.; Hon. Pres. Hungarian Electrotech. Soc.; mem. Hungarian Nat. Comm. for Tech. Devt., Hungarian Acad. of Eng.; Corresp. mem. Hungarian Acad. of Sciences 1976–81, mem. and Section Pres. 1982–92; mem. Admin. Comm. Conference Int. des Grands Reseaux Électriques, Paris; Chair. ECE Electric Power Comm. 1972–76; mem. New York Acad. of Sciences; State Prize 1975. *Publications:* A szigetelések romlása (Deterioration of Insulations) 1964, Szigetelések villamos erőterei (Electric Power Fields of Insulation) 1970, Energia és Társadalom (Energy and Society) 1975, Energetika (Energetics), Vol. I–II, Risk and Safety; 150 papers in int. trade journals. *Leisure interest:* gardening. *Address:* National Atomic Energy Authority, Margit bld. 85, 1024 Budapest, Hungary. *Telephone:* (1) 355-0419. *Fax:* (1) 355-3372.

VAJPAYEE, Atal Bihari, M.A.; Indian politician; b. 25 Dec. 1926, Gwalior, Madhya Pradesh; s. of Krishna Bihari Vajpayee; ed. Victoria (now Laxmibai) Coll., Gwalior, D.A.V. Coll., Kanpur; mem. Rashtriya Swayamsewak Sangh 1941, Indian Nat. Congress 1942–46; mem. Lok Sabha 1957–62, 1967–84 (for New Delhi March 1977–84), 1991–, Rajya Sabha 1962–67; founder mem. Bharatiya Jana Sangh 1951, Parl. Leader 1957–77; Chair. Public Accounts Cttee. Lok Sabha 1969–70, 1991–93; detained during Emergency 1975–77; founder mem. Janata Party 1977, Pres. Bharatiya Janata Party 1980–86, Parl. Leader 1980–84, 1986; Minister of External Affairs 1977–79; Leader Opposition, Lok Sabha 1993–98, Chair. Standing Cttee. on External Affairs 1993–95; Minister of External Affairs 1998; Prime Minister of India 15–28 May 1996, March 1998–, also Minister of Health and Family Welfare, Atomic Energy and Agric. March 1998–; Chair. Nat. Security Council 1998–; mem. Nat. Integration Council 1961–; Hon. Ph.D. (Kanpur Univ.) 1993; Bharat Ratna Pt. Govind Ballabh Pant Award 1994; Padma Vibhushan; Lokmanya Tilak Puruskar. *Publications:* New Dimensions of India's Foreign Policy, Jan Sangh Aur Musalmans, Three Decades in Parliament; collections of poems and numerous articles. *Leisure interests:* reading, writing, travelling, cooking. *Address:* Office of the Prime Minister, S. Block, New Delhi 110001, India. *Telephone:* (11) 3013040. *Fax:* (11) 3016857.

VAKHROMEYEV, Kyril Varfolomeyevich (see Philaret).

VALCOURT, Bernard, P.C., D.H.C., B.A., LL.B.; Canadian politician and lawyer; b. 18 Feb. 1952, St. Quentin de Restigouche, N.B.; s. of Bertin Valcourt and Geraldine Allain; m.; two d.; ed. Académie St. Joseph, Collège St. Louis—Maillet, Univ. of New Brunswick; practised law, mem. Canadian Bar Asscn. and N.B. Lawyers Asscn.; M.P. 1984–93, Parl. Sec. to Minister of State for Science and Tech., Parl. Sec. to Minister of Revenue 1985–86; Minister of State for Small Business and Tourism 1986–89, Minister of State for Indian Affairs and Northern Devt. 1987–89; Minister for Consumer and Corp. Affairs Jan.–Aug. 1989, of Fisheries and Oceans 1990–91, of Employment and Immigration 1991–93; Leader Progressive Conservative Party of N.B. 1995; mem. N.B. Legis. Ass. 1995–, Leader of Opposition 1995. *Address:* 90–48th Avenue, Edmundston, N.B. E3V 3C9, Canada.

VALDEZ ALBIZU, Hector, B.ECON.SC.; Dominican Republic central bank governor; b. 10 Nov. 1947, Dominican Repub.; s. of Hector Manuel Valdez Albizu and Ana Rita Valdez Albizu; m. Fior d'Aliza Martinez 1971; one s.; Tech. Asst. (Publs.), Cen. Bank of Dominican Repub. 1970–75, Head of Banking and Monetary Div., Tech. Co-ordinator of Econ. Studies 1975–82, Econ. Asst. to Gov. 1982–84, Dir. Econ. Studies Dept. 1984–86, Asst. Man., Monetary and Exchange Policy 1986–90, Adviser to Monetary Bd. 1987–89, Rep. of Cen. Bank at Banco de Reservas (State commercial bank) 1991–92, Asst. Gen. Man. and Gen. Admin. Banco de Reservas 1992–94, Gov. Cen. Bank and Pres. Monetary Bd. 1994–; mem. Bd. of Dirs. Consejo Estatal del Azucar (State Sugar Council) 1993–94; Prof., Universidad Cen. del Este and Instituto de Estudios Superiores 1975–89. *Publications:* Financial Programs for the Dominican Republic 1976–1990, Dimensions of the National Banking

System and its Enhancement 1976, Exchange Emergency Regime 1985. *Address:* Banco Central de la Republica Dominicana, Calle Pedro Henriquez Ureña, Esq. Leopoldo Navarro, Apdo. 1347, Santo Domingo, DN, Dominican Republic. *Telephone:* 221-9111. *Fax:* 687-7488.

VÁLEK, Vladimír; Czech conductor; b. 2 Sept. 1935, Nový Jičín; m. 1st Jana Adamová; m. 2nd Hana Patočková 1986; two s. one d.; ed. Acad. of Musical Arts, Bratislava, Acad. of Musical Arts, Prague; conductor 1962–85; Chief Conductor Symphonic Orchestra of Czechoslovak Radio, Prague 1985–; Guest Conductor Czech Philharmonic 1996–. *Works:* many classical music recordings; concert tours include Japan, France, Spain, U.S.A. *Leisure interest:* aviation. *Address:* Na Vápenném 6, 140 00 Prague 4 (Home), Český rozhlas, Vinohradská 12, 120 00 Prague 2, Czech Republic (Office). *Telephone:* 02-24218085 (Office); 02-434341 (Home).

VALENCIA-RODRÍGUEZ, Luis, LL.D.; Ecuadorean diplomatist and professor of law; b. 5 March 1926, Quito; s. of Pedro Valencia and María Rodríguez; m. Cleopatra Moreno 1952; two s. three d.; ed. Cen. Univ., Quito; entered Ecuadorean Foreign Service 1944; Counsellor, Buenos Aires 1957–59; Minister-Counsellor, UN, New York 1959–64; Minister of Foreign Affairs 1965-66, 1981–84; legal adviser on foreign affairs 1964–65, 1966–69, 1980–81, 1990–; Amb. to Bolivia 1969–71, to Brazil 1971–74, to Peru 1974–78, to Venezuela 1978–79, to Argentina 1988–91; Perm. Rep. to UN 1994–; Prof. Cen. Univ., Quito 1984–; mem. Cttee. on the Elimination of Racial Discrimination 1974–86, 1992–; special citation of Ecuadorean Nat. Ass. 1966 and decorations from Ecuador, Italy, Nicaragua, Bolivia, Brazil, Peru, Venezuela, Colombia, Argentina, El Salvador, Dominican Republic and Korea. *Publications:* books on legal matters, foreign affairs etc. *Leisure interests:* swimming, reading. *Address:* Permanent Mission of Ecuador to the United Nations, 866 United Nations Plaza, Room 516, New York, NY 10017, U.S.A. *Telephone:* (212) 935-1680. *Fax:* (212) 935-1835.

VALENTI, Jack; American film executive and fmr. government official; b. 5 Sept. 1921, Houston, Tex.; s. of late Mr. and Mrs. Joseph Valenti; m. Mary Margaret Wiley 1962; one s. two d.; ed. High School, Houston, Univ. of Houston and Harvard Business School; fmr. office boy, oil company; U.S.A.F., Second World War; co-f. Weekly & Valenti Advertising 1951; Special Asst. to Pres. Johnson 1963–66; Pres. and C.E.O. Motion Picture Asscn. of America 1966–; Chair. Alliance of Motion Picture and Television Producers Inc. 1966–; Chair., C.E.O. Motion Picture Export Asscn. of America; Dir. American Film Inst. 1967–; mem. Bd. Riggs Nat. Corp.; mem. Bd. of Trustees, J.F.K. Center for the Performing Arts, American Film Inst.; Chevalier, Légion d'honneur. *Publications:* The Bitter Taste of Glory 1971, A Very Human President 1976, Speak Up with Confidence 1982, Protect and Defend 1992. *Address:* Motion Picture Association, 1600 I Street, N.W., Washington, DC 20006, U.S.A.

VALENTIČ, Nikica; Croatian politician and business executive; b. 24 Nov. 1950, Gospić; m. Antoneta Valentič; one s. one d.; ed. Zagreb Univ.;. journalist for Radio Zagreb 1969–71; Ed. Pravnik (magazine) 1972–74; legal adviser in Zeljko Jurkovič office; f. and Gen. Man. S2 Stanograd and Stanogradinvest consultancy co. 1978–83; own legal firm 1984–90; Gen. Man. INA Industria Nafte 1990–93; Prime Minister of Croatia 1993–95; Pres. Niva co. 1995–. *Leisure interests:* painting, music. *Address:* c/o Office of the Prime Minister, 41000 Zagreb, Jordanovac 71, Croatia.

VALENTINO (Valentino Garavani); Italian fashion designer; b. 11 May 1932, Voghera, nr. Milan; ed. Ecole des Beaux-Arts, Paris, Ecole de la Chambre Syndicale de la Couture, Paris; asst. designer at Paris fashion houses of Jean Dessès 1950–55, Guy Laroche 1956–58; est. Valentino fashion house with Giancarlo Giammetti in Rome 1959; owner boutiques Rome, Milan and other cities; other Valentino boutiques opened and licensing agreements signed Europe, U.S.A. and Far East since 1970s; f. Valentino Acad. for AIDS research and assistance to victims of the disease; f. L.I.F.E. 1990; retrospective exhbn. of creations at Columbus Festivities, New York 1991; numerous int. awards; Ufficiale di Gran Croce. *Address:* Palazzo Mignanelli, Piazza Mignanelli 22, 00187 Rome, Italy (Office); 823–825 Madison Avenue, New York, NY 10021, U.S.A. (Office).

VALENZUELA, Luisa; Argentinian writer and journalist; b. 26 Nov. 1938, Buenos Aires; d. of Luisa Mercedes Levinson and Pablo F. Valenzuela; m. Théodore Marjak 1958 (divorced); one d.; ed. Belgrano Girls' School, Colegio Nacional Vicente Lopez, Buenos Aires; lived in Paris, writing for Argentinian newspapers and for the RTF 1958–61; Asst. Ed. La Nación Sunday Supplement, Buenos Aires 1964–69; writer, lecturer, freelance journalist in U.S.A., Mexico, France, Spain 1970–73, Buenos Aires 1973–79; taught in Writing Div., Columbia Univ., New York 1980–83; conducted writers' workshops, English Dept., New York Univ. and seminars, Writing Div. 1984–89; returned to Buenos Aires 1989; Fulbright Grant 1969–70; Guggenheim Fellow 1983; Fellow New York Inst. for the Humanities; mem. Acad. of Arts and Sciences, Puerto Rico; Dr. h.c. (Knox Coll., Ill., U.S.A.) 1991; Machado de Assis Medal, Brazilian Acad. of Letters 1997. *Publications:* novels: Hay que sonreír 1966, El Gato Eficaz 1972, Como en la guerra 1977, Cambio de armas 1982, Cola de largartija 1983, Novela negra con argentinos 1990, Realidad Nacional desde la cama 1990, Antología personal 1998; short stories: Los heréticos 1967, Aquí pasan cosas raras 1976, Libro que no muerde 1980, Donde viven las águilas 1983, Simetrías (Cuentos de Hades) 1993; most books in English trans. *Leisure interests:* masks, anthropology, ceremonies. *Address:* Artilleros 2130, 1428 Buenos Aires, Argentina. *Telephone:* (114) 781-3593.

VALLANCE, Sir Iain David Thomas, Kt., B.A., M.SC.; British business executive; b. 20 May 1943; s. of Edmund Thomas Vallance and Janet Wright Bell Ross Davidson; m. Elizabeth Mary McGonnigill 1967; one s. one d.; ed. Edinburgh Acad., Dulwich Coll., Glasgow Acad., Brasenose Coll., Oxford, London Grad. School of Business Studies; Asst. Postal Controller, Post Office 1966, Personal Asst. to Chair. 1973–75, Head of Finance Planning Div. 1975–76, Dir. Cen. Finance 1976–78, Telecommunications Finance 1978–79, Materials Dept. 1979–81; mem. Bd. for Org. and Business Systems, British Telecommunications 1981–83, Man. Dir., Local Communications Services Div. 1983–85, Chief of Operations 1985–86, Chief Exec. 1986–95, Chair. 1987–; Vice-Chair. Royal Bank of Scotland 1994–; founding mem. Pres.'s Cttee. of European Foundation for Quality Man. 1988–, CBI Pres.'s Cttee., Advisory Council of Business in the Community, Gov. Body London Business School, Advisory Council of Prince's Youth Business Trust 1988–, Advisory Bd. British-American Chamber of Commerce 1991–; Trustee Monteverdi Trust; Fellow London Business School 1989; Hon. Gov. Glasgow Acad. 1993–; Hon. D.Sc. (Ulster) 1992, (Napier) 1994, Hon. D. Tech. (Loughborough) 1992, (Robert Gordon) 1994, Hon. D.B.A. (Kingston) 1993, Hon. D.Eng. (Heriot-Watt) 1995, Hon. D.C.L. (City Univ.) 1996; Liveryman of Worshipful Co. of Wheelwrights; Freeman of the City of London. *Address:* c/o 81 Newgate Street, London, EC1A 7AJ, England.

VALLANCE-OWEN, John, M.A., M.D., F.R.C.P., F.R.C.P.I., F.R.C.PATH., F.H.K.C.P.; British professor of medicine and physician; b. 31 Oct. 1920, London; s. of Edwin Augustine Vallance-Owen and Julia May; m. Renee Thornton 1950; two s. two d.; ed. Epsom Coll., Surrey, Cambridge Univ., The London Hospital; various appts. including Pathology Asst. and Medical First Asst., London Hosp. 1946–51; Medical Tutor, Royal Postgraduate Medical School, Hammersmith Hosp., London 1952–55, 1956–58; Consultant Physician and Lecturer in Medicine, Univ. of Durham 1958–64; Consultant Physician and Reader in Medicine, Univ. of Newcastle upon Tyne 1964–66; Prof. and Chair., Dept. of Medicine, Queen's Univ. of Belfast, and Consultant Physician to Royal Victoria Hosp., Belfast City Hosp. and Forster Green Hosp., Belfast 1966–82; Dir. of Medical Services, The Maltese Islands 1981–82; Foundation Prof. and Chair. Dept. of Medicine, The Chinese Univ. of Hong Kong 1983–88, Assoc. Dean 1984–88; Consultant in Medicine to Hong Kong Govt. 1984–88, to British Army in Hong Kong 1985–88; Medical Adviser on Clinical Complaints, N.E. Thames Regional Health Authority 1989–96; Visiting Prof. Imperial Coll. of Science, Tech. and Medicine, Hammersmith Hosp.; Consultant Physician London Ind. Hosp.; Rockefeller Travelling Fellowship, held at Univ. of Pa., U.S.A. 1955–56; Oliver-Sharpey Prize, Royal Coll. of Physicians 1976. *Publications:* Essentials of Cardiology 1961, Diabetes: Its Physiological and Biochemical Basis 1974; numerous papers in scientific journals on carbohydrates and fat metabolism and the aetiology of diabetes mellitus, with special reference to insulin antagonism. *Leisure interests:* music, tennis, golf, trees. *Address:* 17 St Matthews Lodge, Oakley Square, London, NW1 1NB; 10 Spinney Drive, Great Shelford, Cambridge, England; Cuildochart, Killin, Perthshire, Scotland. *Telephone:* 0171-388 3644; (01223) 842767; (01567) 820337.

VALLEE, Bert Lester, M.D.; American biochemist, physician and university professor; b. 1 June 1919, Hemer, Westphalia, Germany; s. of Joseph Vallee and Rosa (Kronenberger) Vallee; m. Natalie Kugris 1947; ed. Univ. of Berne, Switzerland and New York Univ. Coll. of Medicine; went to U.S.A. 1938, naturalized 1948; Research Fellow, Harvard Medical School, Boston 1946–49, Research Assoc. 1949–51, Assoc. 1951–56, Asst. Prof. of Medicine 1956–60, Assoc. Prof. 1960–64, Prof. of Biological Chem. 1964–65, Paul C. Cabot Prof. of Biological Chem. 1965–80, Paul C. Cabot Prof. of Biochemical Sciences 1980–89, Prof. Emer. 1989–, Distinguished Sr. Prof. Biochemical Sciences 1989–90, Edgar M. Bronfman Distinguished Sr. Prof. 1990–; Research Assoc., Dept. of Biology, M.I.T. 1948–; Physician Peter Bent Brigham Hosp., Boston 1961–80; Biochemist-in-Chief, Brigham and Women's Hosp., Boston 1980–89, Emer. 1989–; Scientific Dir. Biophysics Research Lab., Harvard Medical School, Peter Bent Brigham Hosp. 1954–80; Head, Center for Biochemical and Biophysical Sciences and Medicine, Harvard Medical School 1980–; Hon. Prof. Shanghai Inst. of Biochemistry 1997; Founder and Trustee Boston Biophysics Foundation 1957–; Founder, Pres. Endowment for Research in Human Biology, Inc. 1980–; Fellow A.A.A.S., N.A.S., American Acad. of Arts and Sciences, N.Y. Acad. of Sciences; mem. American Chemical Soc., Hon. Foreign mem. Royal Danish Acad. of Sciences and Letters; Hon. mem. Japan Soc. for Analytical Chemistry; Hon. Prof., Tsinghua Univ. 1987; Messenger Lecturer, Cornell Univ. 1988; Hon. A.M. (Harvard) 1960, Hon. M.D. (Karolinska Inst.) 1987; Hon. D.Sc. (Naples Univ.) 1991, (Ludwig Maximillian Univ., Munich) 1995; Linderstrøm-Lang Award and Gold Medal 1980, Willard Gibbs' Gold Medal 1981, William C. Rose Award in Biochemistry 1982; Order Andres Bello (1st Class) (Venezuela). *Publications:* over 500 publs. on zinc and other metalloenzymes; their structure, function and mechanism of action; emission, absorption, CD and MCD spectroscopy; organic chemical modification of proteins; organogenesis. *Leisure interest:* riding. *Address:* 300 Boylston Street, Apartment 712, Boston, MA 02116, U.S.A.

VALTICOS, Nicholas, D. EN D.; Greek judge; b. 8 April 1918, Cairo, Egypt; s. of Michael Valticos and Helen Valticos; m. Nelly Valticos 1951; one s. one d.; ed. Univ. of Paris; barrister at law in Athens 1941–42; Chief of section Comm. administering Relief in Greece 1942–45; joined ILO 1949, Chief of Application of Conf. Decisions Div. 1955–64, Chief Int. Labour Standards

Dept. 1964–76, Asst. Dir.-Gen. and Adviser for Int. Labour Standards 1976–81; Assoc. Prof. at Faculty of Law, Univ. of Geneva 1972–81; Sec.-Gen. Inst. de droit int. 1981–91; ad hoc Judge at Int. Court of Justice 1984–94 (case concerning Continental Shelf, Libya/Malta), (case-frontier dispute, El Salvador/Honduras), (Qatar-Bahrain); Judge at the European Court of Human Rights 1986–98, First Vice-Pres. Inst. of Int. Law 1991–93; Henri Rolin Professor of Int. Law, Belgium 1979–80; Pres. Curatorium, Acad. of Int. Law, The Hague 1996–; mem. Perm. Court of Arbitration; mem. and Chair. of various int. arbitral tribunals and comms. of inquiry; mem. Council of Int. Inst. of Human Rights, Société francaise de droit int., Int. Law Asscn., Greek Soc. of Int. Law, Acad. of Athens; hon. mem. American Soc. of Int. Law, Hellenic Inst. of Int. and Foreign Law; Dr. h.c. Univs. of Athens, Leuven, Utrecht, Neuchâtel; Prix de la Faculté and Prix Dupin Aîné, Paris; Grand Cross of San Raimundo de Peñafort, Spain 1989; Officier, Légion d'honneur, of Isabella la Catolica (Spain) 1986, of the Order of Merit (Poland) 1992, Great Commdr. of the Order of Honour (Greece) 1998. *Leisure interest:* writing. *Address:* 22 avenue William Favre, 1207 Geneva, Switzerland. *Telephone:* (22) 736.07.72.

VALTINOS, Thanassis; Greek author; b. 16 Dec. 1932, Karatoula Kynourias; m.; one d.; ed. Athens Univ.; Visiting Prof. War Research Inst., Frankfurt 1993–; Pres. Greek Soc. of Authors; mem. European Acad. of Sciences and Arts, Int. Inst. of Theatre, Greek Society of Playwriters; Scenario Award Cannes Festival 1984; Nat. Literary Award 1990. *Address:* 66 Astidamantos Street, 116 34 Athens, Greece. *Telephone:* 7218.793.

VÁMOS, Tibor, PH.D., D.SC.; Hungarian electrical engineer; b. 1 June 1926, Budapest; s. of Miklós Vámos and Ilona Rausnitz; m. Mária Fekete; one s.; ed. Tech. Univ. Budapest; started in process control automation of power plants and systems, worked later in computer control of processes, robot vision, artificial intelligence; Chief Eng. Research Inst. of Power System Eng. Co. 1950–54, Automation Dept. Head 1954–64; Dir. Computer and Automation Inst. of the Hungarian Acad. of Sciences 1964–85, Chairman 1986–; Prof. Budapest Tech. Univ. 1969–; Distinguished Visiting Prof., George Mason Univ. 1992–93, Distinguished Affiliate Prof. 1993–94; Corresp. mem. Hungarian Acad. of Sciences 1973, mem. 1979, mem. Governing Bd. 1980–; Pres. Int. Fed. of Automatic Control 1981–84, IFAC Lifetime Adviser 1987–; Hon. mem. Austrian Computer Soc. 1992, Austrian Soc. for Cybernetic Studies 1994; mem. editorial bd. 6 int. scientific journals; Fellow IEEE Inc. 1986–; Hon. Pres. John Neumann Soc. of Computer Science; Dr. h.c. (Tallinn Univ.); State Prize 1983; Chorafas Prize (Swiss Acads.) 1994; Order of Hungarian Repub. 1996. *Publications:* Nagy ipari folyamatok irányitása (Control of Large-Scale Processes) 1970, Computer Epistemology 1991; Co-author: Applications of Syntactic Pattern Recognition 1977, Progress in Pattern Recognition 1981; Co-ed.: The Neumann Compendium 1995; 270 contribs. to scientific journals. *Leisure interests:* fine arts, mountaineering. *Address:* Lágymányosi u. 11, 1111 Budapest, Hungary. *Telephone:* (36-1) 2095274. *Fax:* (36-1) 2095275.

VAN AGT, Andries A. M. (see Agt, Andries A. M. van).

VAN ALLAN, Richard; British opera singer; b. 28 May 1935, Clipstone, Notts.; s. of Joseph Arthur and Irene Hannah Jones; m. 1st Elizabeth Mary Peabody 1963 (divorced 1974); m. 2nd Rosemary Pickering 1976 (divorced 1987); two s. one d.; ed. Brunt's Grammar School, Mansfield, Worcester Teaching Training Coll., Birmingham School of Music; studied singing under David Franklin and Jani Strasser; first appearance with Glyndebourne Festival Opera 1964; with Welsh Nat. Opera 1967, with Sadler's Wells Opera (now English Nat. Opera) 1968, as prin. bass, Royal Opera House, Covent Garden 1971–, with Paris Opera 1975, with Boston Opera, Mass., and San Diego Opera, Calif. 1976; debut Colón Theatre, Buenos Aires 1978, Le Monnaie, Brussels 1982, Miami 1985, Seattle 1987, Metropolitan, New York 1987, Madrid 1991, Barcelona 1992, Vic. State Opera, Melbourne 1995; Dir. Nat. Opera Studio, London 1986–; mem. Bd. of Dirs. English Nat. Opera 1995–98; John Christie award, Glyndebourne 1967, Grammy Award (The Nat. Acad. of Performing Arts and Sciences) for Don Alfonso (Così fan tutte), Sir Charles Santley Memorial Prize, Worshipful Co. of Musicians 1995; Hon. mem. R.A.M. 1987; Fellow Birmingham Schools of Music 1991. *Leisure interests:* cricket, tennis, shooting. *Address:* 18 Octavia Street, London, SW11 3DN, England. *Telephone:* 0171-228 8462. *Fax:* 0171-228 4367.

VAN ALLEN, James Alfred, PH.D.; American physicist; b. 7 Sept. 1914, Mount Pleasant, Iowa; s. of Alfred Morris and Alma (Olney) Van Allen; m. Abigail Fithian Halsey 1945; two s. three d.; ed. Iowa Wesleyan Coll. and State Univ. of Iowa; Research Fellow, Carnegie Inst., Washington 1939–41, Physicist (Dept. of Terrestrial Magnetism) 1941–42; Applied Physics Lab., Johns Hopkins Univ. 1942, 1946–50; Lieut.-Commdr. in U.S. Navy 1942–46; Prof. of Physics, Univ. of Iowa, Head of Dept. 1951–85, Carver Prof. of Physics 1985–92, Regent Distinguished Prof. 1992–; Prin. Investigator, Pioneers 10 and 11, and Interdisciplinary Scientist, Galileo project; Guggenheim Research Fellow at Brookhaven Nat. Lab. 1951; Research Assoc. Princeton Univ. Project Matterhorn 1953–54; Dir. expeditions to study cosmic radiation, Cen. Pacific 1949, Alaska 1950, Arctic 1952, 1957, Antarctic 1957; mem. Rocket and Satellite Research Panel 1946, Chair. 1947–58, Exec. Cttee. 1958; mem. Advisory Cttee. on Nuclear Physics, Office of Naval Research 1957–60; mem. Space Science Bd., N.A.S. 1958–70, Foreign mem. The Royal Swedish Acad. of Sciences 1981; Consultant, Pres.'s Science Advisory Cttee.; mem. Cosmic Radiation, Rocket Research and Earth Satellite Panel, Int. Geophysical Year; Fellow, American Physical Soc., American Geophysical Union, American Rocket Soc., Inst. of Electrical and Electronics Engineers, American Astronautical Soc., American Acad. of Arts and Sciences, A.A.A.S., Regents' Fellow, Smithsonian Inst. 1981; Pres.-elect American Geophysical Union 1980–82, Pres. 1982–84; mem. N.A.S., Royal Astronomical Soc. (U.K.) (Gold Medal 1978); founder mem. Int. Acad. of Astronautics; Assoc. Ed. Physics of Fluids 1958–62, Journal of Geophysical Research 1959–67; mem. Editorial Bd. Space Science Reviews 1962–; Distinguished Civilian Service Medal (U.S. Army) 1959, NASA Medal for Exceptional Scientific Achievement 1974, Distinguished Public Service Award (U.S. Navy) 1976, Award of Merit, American Consulting Engineers Council 1978, Space Science Award, American Inst. of Aeronautics and Astronautics 1982, Crawford Prize, Swedish Royal Acad. of Sciences 1989; numerous Hon. D.Scs.; discoverer of the "Van Allen Belt" of radiation around the earth and a pioneer of high-altitude rocket research. *Publications:* Physics and Medicine of the Upper Atmosphere, Rocket Exploration of the Upper Atmosphere, Origins of Magnetospheric Physics 1983, and 225 scientific papers; Ed. Scientific Use of Earth Satellites. *Address:* Department of Physics and Astronomy, 701 Van Allen Hall, University of Iowa, Iowa City, IA 52242 (Office); 5 Woodland Mounds Road, R.F.D. 6, Iowa City, IA 52240, U.S.A. (Home).

VAN BENTHEM, Johannes F.A.K., M.A., PH.D.; Netherlands professor of mathematical logic; b. 12 June 1949, Rijswijk; s. of A.K. van Benthem and J.M. Eggermont; m. Lida Blom 1977; two s.; ed. 's Gravenhaags Christelijk Gymnasium and Univ. of Amsterdam; Asst. Prof. of Philosophical Logic, Univ. of Amsterdam 1972–77, Chair. Dept. of Philosophy 1974–75; Assoc. Prof. of Philosophical Logic, Univ. of Groningen 1977–86, Chair. Dept. of Philosophy 1979–81; Prof. of Mathematical Logic, Univ. of Amsterdam 1986–, Chair. Dept. of Math. and Computer Science 1987–89, Scientific Dir. Research Inst. for Logic, Language and Computation 1991–98; Sr. Researcher, Center for Study of Language and Information, Stanford Univ. 1992–; Bonsall Visiting Chair. in the Humanities, Stanford Univ. 1994–; other professional appts.; mem. Acad. Europaea, Royal Dutch Acad. of Sciences; Dr. h.c. (Liège Univ.) 1998; Spinoza Prize, Netherlands Org. for Scientific Research 1996. *Publications:* The Logic of Time 1983, Modal Logic and Classical Logic 1985, Essays in Logical Semantics 1986, A Manual of Intensional Logic 1988, Language in Action, Categories, Lambdas and Dynamic Logic 1991, Exploring Logical Dynamics 1996; co-author of various textbooks in logic; (ed.) Handbook of Logic and Language 1997; articles in scientific journals. *Address:* Department of Mathematics and Computer Science, University of Amsterdam, Plantage Muidergracht 24, 1018 TV Amsterdam, The Netherlands. *Telephone:* (20) 525 6051. *Fax:* (20) 525 5206.

VAN CAENEGEM, Raoul C.; Belgian academic; b. 14 July 1927, Ghent; s. of Jozef Van Caenegem and Irma Barbaix; m. Patricia Carson 1954; two s. one d.; ed. Univs. of Ghent, Paris and London; Ordinary Prof. 1964, Prof. Emer. Univ. of Ghent 1992–; Visiting Fellow, Univ. Coll. Cambridge 1968; Goodhart Prof. of Legal Science, Cambridge 1984–85; Visiting Fellow, Peterhouse, Cambridge 1984–85; Sir Henry Savile Fellow, Merton Coll. Oxford 1989; Erasmus Lecturer on History and Civilization of the Netherlands, Harvard Univ. 1991; Francqui Prize 1974; Solvay Prize, Nat. Fund for Scientific Research, Brussels 1990; Dr. h.c. (Tübingen) 1977, (Louvain) 1984, (Paris) 1988. *Publications:* Royal Writs in England from the Conquest to Glanvill. Studies in the Early History of the Common Law 1959, The Birth of the English Common Law 1973, Guide to the Sources of Medieval History 1978, English Lawsuits from William I to Richard I (two vols.) 1990–91, An Historical Introduction to Private Law 1992, An Historical Introduction to Western Constitutional Law 1995. *Leisure interests:* bridge, swimming, wine. *Address:* Veurestraat 47, 9051 Afsnee, Belgium. *Telephone:* 9/222.62.11. *Fax:* 9/222.62.11.

VAN CITTERS, Robert L., M.D.; American professor of medicine, physiology and biophysics; b. 20 Jan. 1926, Alton, Ia.; s. of Charles J. Van Citters and Wilhelmina T. Van Citters; m. Mary E. Barker 1949; two s. two d.; ed. Univ. of Kansas; Intern, Univ. of Kansas Medical Center 1953–54; Medical Officer, Air Research and Devt. Command, Kirtland AFB, N.M. 1954–55; Resident, Internal Medicine, Univ. of Kansas Medical Center 1957–58; Research Fellow Cardiovascular Physiology, Univ. of Washington 1958–62; Research Assoc. Cardiopulmonary Inst., Scripps Clinic and Research Foundation, La Jolla, Calif. 1962; Exchange Scientist, Jt. U.S.-U.S.S.R. Scientific Exchange Agreement 1962; Robert L. King Chair. of Cardiovascular Research 1963–; Asst. Prof. of Physiology and Biophysics School of Medicine, Univ. of Washington 1963–65, Assoc. Prof. 1965–68, Assoc. Dean for Research and Grad. Programs 1968–70, Chair. Bd. of Health Sciences 1970, Dean, School of Medicine 1970–81, Dean Emer. 1981-, Prof. of Medicine (Cardiology), Prof. of Physiology and Biophysics 1981–; mem. Inst. of Medicine, N.A.S.; Hon. D.Sc. (Northwestern Coll.) 1978. *Publications:* 150 publications in scientific journals. *Leisure interests:* fishing, gardening. *Address:* Division of Cardiology, Box 356422, Department of Medicine, School of Medicine, University of Washington, Seattle, WA 98195, U.S.A. *Telephone:* (206) 543-9952. *Fax:* (206) 543-3639.

VAN CREVELD, Martin L.; Israeli academic; b. 5 March 1946, Rotterdam; s. of L. van Creveld and M. van Creveld (née Wyler); two step c.; ed. Hebrew Univ., L.S.E.; lecturer in History, Hebrew Univ. 1971–; Fellow War Studies Dept. King's Coll. Univ. of London 1975–76; Fellow von Humboldt Inst., Freiburg 1980–81; Faculty mem. Nat. Defense Univ., Washington D.C.

1986–87; Prof. Marine Corps. Univ., Quantico, Va. 1991–92; now Prof. of History, Hebrew Univ.; Best Book Award, Mil. History Inst. U.S.A. 1990. *Publications:* Supplying War 1977, Fighting Power 1987, Command in War 1985, Technology and War 1988, The Transformation of War, 1991. *Leisure interests:* reading, walking. *Address:* Hebrew University of Jerusalem, Mount Scopus, 91 905 Jerusalem, Israel (Office). *Telephone:* 2-588-3769 (Office); 2-534-4923 (Home). Fax: 2-532-2545.

VAN CUYLENBURG, Peter; British business executive; b. 5 March 1948; s. of Flight Lieut. Brian van Cuylenburg and Margaret Budd; m. Mary-Rose Sabberton 1972; one s. one d.; ed. Sir William Borlase School, Marlow St. John's, Singapore and Bristol Polytechnic; Man. Dir. Texas Instruments Ltd. 1984–87; Vice-Pres. Data Systems Group, Texas Instruments 1987–89; Chief. Exec. Mercury Communications Ltd. 1989; Group Dir. Cable & Wireless PLC 1991–. *Leisure interest:* sailing. *Address:* c/o Cable and Wireless PLC, Mercury House, Theobald's Road, London, W.C.1, England.

VAN DAM, José; Luxembourg opera singer; b. 25 Aug. 1940, Brussels, Belgium; m.; ed. Académie de Musique, Brussels, Conservatoire Royal, Brussels; début in Paris in Carmen (Escamillo) 1961, with Grand Théâtre, Geneva 1965–67, Deutsche Oper, Berlin 1967–, Salzburg Festival, opera and concerts 1966–, Festival d'Aix en Provence 1966–, title role in St-François d'Assise (Messiaen) Paris 1983–84, Wozzeck at Royal Opera House, Covent Garden 1983–84, début in Meistersinger (Hans Sachs), Brussels 1985; awards include Grand Prix de l'Académie Française du Disque 1979, Orphée d'Or, Académie Lyrique Française 1980, Prix Européen des Critiques 1985. *Address:* c/o Artist's Management Zürich, Frau Rita Schütz, Rütistrasse 52, CH-8044 Zürich-Gockhausen, Switzerland.

VAN DAMME, Jean-Claude; Belgian actor; b. 1 Apr. 1961, Brussels; m. 1st Gladys Portugues; m. 2nd Darcy LaPier 1994; one s. one d.; fmr. European Professional Karate Asscn. Middleweight Champion. *Films include:* Predator, Bloodsport, Death Warrant, Kickboxer, Cyborg, AWOL, Universal Soldier, No Retreat, No Surrender, Nowhere to Run, Monaco Forever, Hard Target, Streetfighter, Time Cop, Sudden Death, The Quest (also dir.), Maximum Risk, Double Team. *Address:* United Talent Agency, 9560 Wilshire Boulevard, Beverly Hills, CA 90212, U.S.A.

VAN DE KAA, Dirk Jan, PH.D.; Netherlands professor of demography; b. 5 Jan. 1933, Scherpenzeel; m. Anna Jacomina van Teunenbroek 1961; one s. one d.; ed. Univ. of Utrecht, A.N.U., Canberra; Dept. Dir., Demographic Research Project, Western New Guinea 1961–66; Research Fellow, Dept. of Demography, Research School of Social Sciences, Inst. for Advanced Studies, A.N.U., Canberra 1966–71; Dir. Netherlands Interuniversity Demographic Inst. (NIDI), The Hague 1971–87; Project Dir. World Fertility Survey, London 1981–82; Dir. Int. Statistical Research Centre, The Hague 1982–84; Prof. of Demography, Univ. of Amsterdam 1977–; Dir. Netherlands Inst. for Advanced Study (NIAS), Wassenaar 1987–95; Vice-Chair. Nat. Science Foundation, The Hague 1988–; mem. Royal Netherlands Acad. of Arts and Sciences (Vice-Pres. 1984–87); Pres. European Asscn. for Population Studies 1983–87, Hon. Pres. 1987–. *Publications:* (author, co-author or ed.) Results of the Demographic Research Project Western New Guinea 1964–67, The Demography of Papua and New Guinea's Indigenous Population 1971, Science for Better and for Worse 1984, Population: Growth and Decline 1986, Europe's Second Demographic Transition 1987. *Address:* Van Hogenhoucklaan 63, 2596 TB The Hague, Netherlands.

VAN DEN BERGH, Sidney, O.C., M.SC., DR.RER.NAT., F.R.S., F.R.S.C.; Canadian astronomer; b. 20 May 1929, Wassenaar, Netherlands; s. of Sidney J. van den Bergh and S. M. van den Berg; m. 2nd (wife deceased); one s. two d.; m. 3rd Paulette Brown; ed. Princeton Univ. and Ohio State Univ., U.S.A., Univ. of Göttingen, Fed. Repub. of Germany; Asst. Prof., Ohio State Univ. 1956–58; Prof., Univ. of Toronto, Canada 1958–77; Dir. Dominion Astrophysical Observatory, Victoria 1977–86, Astronomer 1986–98; Adjunct Prof., Univ. of Vic. 1978–; Pres. Canadian Astronomy Soc. 1990–92; Assoc. Royal Astronomical Soc.; Killam Laureate 1990; NRC Pres.'s Medal. *Publications:* about 600 scientific publs. *Leisure interests:* archaeology, photography. *Address:* Dominion Astrophysical Observatory, 5071 West Saanich Road, Vic., B.C. V8X 4M6; 418 Lands End Road, Sidney, B.C. V8L 5R9, Canada (Home). *Telephone:* (250) 363 0006 (Office); (250) 656-6020 (Home). *Fax:* (250) 363-0045.

VAN DEN BOOGAARD, Hans Albert Dirk; Netherlands business executive; b. 5 Nov. 1939, Hengelo; m. Ina Mulder 1967; one s. one d.; ed. Rotterdam School of Econs.; joined Stork N.V. 1968, mem. Man. Bd. 1986–, Chief Financial Officer, Bd. of Man. 1991–; Chair. Stichting Pensioenfonds Stork; Chair. Supervisory Bd. NethCorp III, IV and V, Venture; mem. Supervisory Bd. Wärtsilä NSD Nederland, ICT Automatisering, Delaval-Stork, Van der Hoop Effektenbank, VSB Bank, Koninklijke IBC; Chair. Foundation Certifying Friesland Coberco Dairy Foods; mem. Supervisory Bd. Energieonderzoek Centrum Nederland 1996–; Treas. Exec. Cttee. FME (Employers' Asscn.); mem. Bd. Coöperatie Achmea, Foundation Univ. Fund Twente; mem. Advisory Bd. Univ. of Twente. *Leisure interests:* hockey, skiing, reading. *Address:* Stork N.V., 7 Amersfoortsestraatweg, 1412 KA Naarden, The Netherlands. *Telephone:* (0) 35-6957403. *Fax:* (0) 35-6957471.

VAN DEN BROEK, Hans; Netherlands politician; b. 11 Dec. 1936, Paris, France; m.; two c.; ed. Alberdingk Thym Grammar School, Hilversum, Univ. of Utrecht; attended Sr. Man. training, De Baak, Noordwijk; solicitor in Rotterdam 1965–68; Sec. Man. Bd. ENKA B.V., Arnhem 1969–73, Commercial Man., 1973–76; City Councillor, Rheden 1970–74; mem. Second Chamber, States-Gen. (Parl.) 1976–81; served on Standing Cttees. on Foreign Affairs, Devt. Co-operation and Justice; Sec. of State for Foreign Affairs 1981–82, Minister 1982–93; Commr. for External Relations, Foreign and Security Policy Enlargement Negotiations, Comm. of EC (now European Comm.) 1993–95, for External Relations with Cen. and Eastern Europe, fmr. Soviet Union and others for Common Foreign and Security Policy and External Service 1995–. *Address:* European Commission, 200 rue de la Loi, 1049 Brussels, Belgium. *Telephone:* (02) 295 3892. *Fax:* (02) 295 3609.

VAN DEN HOVEN, Helmert Frans; Netherlands business executive; b. 25 April 1923, IJsselmonde; m. 1st Dorothy Ida Bevan 1950 (dissolved 1981); one s.; m. 2nd Cornelia Maria van As 1981; joined Unilever NV, Rotterdam 1938, at London Office 1948–50, at Unilever Office, Turkey 1951–62, Chair. 1958–62; Chair. Van den Bergh en Jurgens BV 1962; Dir. Unilever 1970; Vice-Chair. Unilever Ltd. (now PLC), Chair. Unilever NV 1975–83; Vice-Pres. ICC 1982–84, Pres. 1985–86, Immediate Past Pres. 1987–; Chair. Save the Children Netherlands 1984–94; Chair. Supervisory Bd. ABN/AMRO Bank 1992–94; mem. Supervisory Bd. Shell 1985–94; mem. Council Kellogg (North Western) Grad. School of Man.; Kt. of Order of Netherlands Lion 1978, Hon. K.B.E. 1980. *Address:* Marevista 35, 2202 BX, Noordwijk, Netherlands.

VAN DER AVOIRD, Ad, PH.D.; Netherlands professor of theoretical chemistry; b. 19 April 1943, Eindhoven; s. of H. J. van der Avoird and M. A. (née Kerkhofs) van der Avoird; m. T. G. M. Lange 1964; two s.; ed. Tech. Univ., Eindhoven; Research Fellow, Inst. Battelle, Geneva, Switzerland 1965–67; Section Man. Unilever Research Lab., Vlaardingen 1967–71; Assoc. Prof., Univ. of Nijmegen, Nijmegen 1968–71, Prof. 1971–; mem. Netherlands Acad. of Sciences 1979–. *Publications:* Interacties tussen moleculen 1989; articles in scientific journals. *Leisure interests:* sailing, windsurfing, tennis. *Address:* Institute of Theoretical Chemistry, University of Nijmegen, Toernooiveld, 6525 ED Nijmegen, The Netherlands. *Telephone:* (024) 3653037.

VAN DER BYL, Hon. Pieter Kenyon Fleming-Voltelyn, B.A.; Zimbabwean politician; b. 11 Nov. 1923, Cape Town, S. Africa; s. of the late Major the Hon. P. V. G. and Mrs. Joy Clare Fleming van der Byl; m. Princess Charlotte of Liechtenstein 1979; two s.; ed. Cape Town, Cambridge and Harvard Univs.; Officer 7th Queen's Hussars (served in Middle East, Italy and Austria) 1943–46; tobacco farmer in Zimbabwe 1946–; M.P. 1962; Jr. Govt. Whip 1963; Deputy Minister of Information 1964–68; Minister of Information, Immigration and Tourism 1968–74, of Foreign Affairs 1974–79, of Defence 1974–76, of Public Service 1976–77, of Information, Immigration and Tourism 1977–79, Co-Minister 1978–79; Minister of Transport, Power and Posts in Bishop Muzorewa's Govt. 1979–80; mem. Senate 1985–87; Deputy Leader of Rhodesian Govt. Del. at Geneva Conf. on future of Rhodesia 1976; mem. Rhodesia Tobacco Asscn. Council 1956–62; Deputy Chair. Selous Farmers' Asscn. 1957. *Leisure interests:* big game hunting, shooting and fishing. *Address:* 4 Bath Road, Harare, Zimbabwe 22320; Fairfield, Napier, Cape, South Africa. *Telephone:* 722320 (Harare); (02841) 3615 (Napier).

VAN DER EB, Alex Jan, PH.D.; Netherlands professor of molecular carcinogenesis; b. 16 Jan. 1936, Bandung, Java; s. of Wijnand Jan van der Eb and Gertrude Leonie van der Eb-Blekkink; m. Titia Brongersma 1961; two s. one d.; ed. Univ. of Leiden; mil. service 1962–63; Assoc. Prof. of Tumor Virology, Univ. of Leiden 1974–80, Prof. of Molecular Carcinogenesis 1980–; mem. Royal Acad. of Sciences and Letters 1987–, European Molecular Biology Org. 1981–, Acad. Europaea, Human Genome Org., Holland Science Asscn. of 1752 1987–; Postdoctoral Fellow, Calif. Inst. Tech., Pasadena, Calif., U.S.A. 1968–69; AKZO Prize 1975, Korteweg Overwater Fund Award 1977, Beijerinck Virology Medal 1978, Robert Koch Prize 1989. *Publications:* numerous publs. on virology. *Address:* Sylvius Laboratory, Wassenaarseweg 72, 2333 AL Leiden (Office); Prinses Beatrixlaan 53, 2341 TW Oegstgeest, The Netherlands (Home). *Telephone:* (31) 71-5276115 (Office); (31) 71-5172178 (Home). *Fax:* (31) 71-5276284.

VANDER ESPT, Georges J.H.; Belgian diplomatist; b. 16 Jan. 1931, Ostend; m. Marie-Jeanne Schaeverbeke; two s. two d.; ed. Univ. of Ghent; public prosecutor 1957; joined diplomatic service 1961; served in the Netherlands 1963, U.K. 1969, Portugal 1975, Italy 1979; Dir. Cabinet of Minister of Foreign Affairs 1980–88; Amb. to Germany 1988–96; many Belgian and foreign distinctions. *Leisure interests:* reading, swimming, modern painting. *Address:* c/o Ministry of Foreign Affairs, 2 rues des Quatre Bras, 1000 Brussels, Belgium.

VAN DER KEMP, Gerald, M.V.O.; French museum curator (retd.); b. 5 May 1912, Charenton-le-Pont; m. Florence Harris-Downs; one step s. two step d.; one s. from previous marriage; ed. Institut d'Art et d'Archéologie, Sorbonne; with Musée du Louvre 1936–41; Asst. Musée Nat. d'Art Moderne 1941–45; Curator of the Museums of Versailles, Trianons and Jeu de Paume 1945–53, Chief Curator 1953–80, Insp.-Gen. Nat. Museums 1972–80; Curator, Claude Monet Foundation at Giverny 1977–80; Hon. Pres. Christie's Europe 1980–84; mem. Inst. de France (Acad. des Beaux-Arts) 1968–; Commdr., Légion d'honneur, Ordre des Arts et des Lettres, Grand Officier du Mérite de l'Ordre Souverain de Malte. *Address:* c/o Fondation Claude Monet, Giverny, 27620 Gasny, France.

VAN DER KLAAUW, Christoph Albert; Netherlands politician and diplomatist; b. 13 Aug. 1924, Leyden; m. 1st Henriette van Everdingen (deceased);

five c.; m. 2nd Leontine van Noort 1989; ed. Leyden Municipal Gymnasium, State Univ. of Leyden; entered Ministry of Foreign Affairs as trainee 1952; Legation Attaché, Budapest 1952–53; Staff mem., Western Co-operation Dept. (NATO and European Defence Affairs Section), Ministry of Foreign Affairs; Second Sec., Oslo 1956–59; First Sec., Combined Perm. Netherlands Del. to N. Atlantic Council and OEEC, Paris 1959–63; Head of NATO and WEU Political Affairs Section, Ministry of Foreign Affairs, and Sec. of dels. to ministerial NATO and WEU Council sessions 1963–66; Counsellor, Rio de Janeiro 1966–70; Deputy Perm. Rep. to UN, New York 1970–74; Amb. serving as Perm. Rep. at UN and other int. orgs., Geneva 1975–77; Dir.-Gen. for European Co-operation 1977; Minister for Foreign Affairs 1977–81; Amb. to Belgium 1981–86, to Portugal 1986–89; mem. People's Party for Freedom and Democracy (VVD), Advisory Cttee. on Foreign Policy 1964–66; mem. Telders Foundation 1964–66; fmr. Corresp. mem. Univ. Alumni Fund and advisory mem. Student Asscn., State Univ. of Leyden; Vice-Chair. Dutch Protestant League, Paris 1961–63; Chair. Asscn. of Liberal Reformed Protestants of The Hague and Scheveningen 1964–66; Chair. Supervisory Bd. Netherlands Inst. for Int. Relations 1989–98; Commdr. of Order of Orange-Nassau, Kt. of the Order of the Netherlands Lion, Grand Cross of the Order of Leopold (Belgium), Grand Cross of the Order of the Crown (Belgium) and other foreign decorations. *Publications:* Political Relations between the Netherlands and Belgium 1919–1939 1953, Integration at the Ministry of Foreign Affairs (article in Internationale Spectator) March 1977, Een Diplomatenleven (memoirs) 1995. *Leisure interests:* family, water sports, reading, contemporary and 19th century history. *Address:* Ary Schefferstraat 151, 2597 VS The Hague, The Netherlands. *Telephone:* (070) 3282427.

VAN DER MEER, Jan, M.D.; Netherlands physician; b. 30 Aug. 1935, Leeuwarden; s. of L. van der Meer and G. Bakker; m. Joan Alkema 1962; one d.; ed. Univ. of Amsterdam; intern 1968; Sr. Registrar in Internal Medicine, Binnengasthuis, Amsterdam 1970–76; Head of Coagulation Lab., Cen. Lab. of Bloodtransfusion Service of Dutch Red Cross 1969–76; Prof. of Internal Medicine, Chair. of Dept., Acad. Hosp. of Free Univ. Amsterdam 1976–; Chair. Govs., Cen. Lab. of Blood Transfusion Service, Netherlands Red Cross 1994–. *Publications:* Meting van de plasma renine-activiteit met behulp van een radioimmunologische bepaling van angiotensine I 1969. *Leisure interests:* music, skating, sailing. *Address:* Academic Hospital Free University, Department of Internal Medicine, P.O. Box 7057, 1007 MB Amsterdam, Netherlands. *Telephone:* (020) 4444307. *Fax:* 4444313.

VAN DER MEER, Simon; Netherlands engineer and physicist; b. 24 Nov. 1925, The Hague; m. Catharina M. Koopman 1966; one s. one d.; ed. gymnasium, The Hague and Univ. of Tech., Delft; Philips Physical Lab., Eindhoven 1952–56; Sr. Engineer European Org. for Nuclear Research (CERN) 1956–90; Foreign Hon. mem. American Acad. of Arts and Sciences; corresp. Royal Netherlands Acad. of Sciences; Nobel Prize for Physics 1984; Hon. Dr. (Amsterdam, Geneva, Genoa). *Publications:* scientific papers. *Leisure interest:* reading. *Address:* 4 Chemin des Corbillettes, 1218 GD-Saconnex, Switzerland. *Telephone:* 7984305.

van der MEULEN, Robert Paul; Netherlands diplomatist; b. 25 May 1950, Eindhoven; m. Christine Bayle 1982; two d.; ed. Univ. of Leyden; Asst., European Inst., Univ. of Leyden 1974–76; Dir. European Integration, Foreign Econ. Relations Dept., Ministry of Econ. Affairs 1976, Head of Bureau, Accession of Greece, Spain and Portugal, Co-operation with Mediterranean cos. and EFTA cos. 1979; with Perm. Representation of Netherlands to EC, Brussels 1981–82; First Sec. Embassy in Washington, D.C. 1982–84, Counsellor 1984–85; Deputy Head Office of Vice-Pres. of EC 1985–88; Head Del. of European Comm. to Brunei, Indonesia and Singapore 1989–94, to Tunisia 1994–98; Head Maghreb Div. (DGIB-A3), European Comm. 1998–. *Leisure interest:* collecting Chinese porcelain. *Address:* c/o European Commission, Charlemagne 4/207, rue de la Loi 170, 1040 Brussels (Office); 12 avenue de la Sapinière, 1180 Uccle, Belgium (Home). *Telephone:* (02) 296.14.99 (Office). *Fax:* (02) 296.66.10.

VAN DER STOEL, Max, LL.M., M.A.; Netherlands politician; b. 3 Aug. 1924, Voorschoten; one s. four d.; ed. Univ. of Leiden; Int. Sec. Labour Party (Partij van de Arbeid) 1958–65; mem. Exec. Bd. Socialist Int. 1958–65; mem. First Chamber of States-Gen. (Parl.) 1960–63, Second Chamber 1963–65, 1967–73, 1978–; State Sec. of Foreign Affairs 1965–66; mem. Ass. Council of Europe 1967–72; N. Atlantic Ass., European Parl. 1972–73; Minister of Foreign Affairs 1973–77, 1981–82; Perm. Rep. to the UN 1983–86; mem. Council of State 1986–92; CSCE High Commr. on Nat. Minorities 1993–; Minister of State of the Netherlands 1991; appt. a Special Rapporteur of UN Comm. on Human Rights on the situation of human rights in Iraq June 1991; Grand Cross, Order of Merit (Italy), Order of Repub. (Tunisia), Order of the White Rose (Finland) and other decorations. *Address:* P.O. Box 20062, Prinsessegracht 22, 2514 AP The Hague, Netherlands. *Telephone:* (070) 3125500.

VAN DER WEE, Baron Herman Frans Anna, LL.D., PH.D.; Belgian historian (retd.); b. 10 July 1928, Lier; s. of Jos van der Wee and Martha Planckaert; m. Monique Verbreyt 1954; one s. one d.; ed. Leuven Univ., Sorbonne, Paris, London School of Econs., U.K.; Fellow Nat. Foundation for Scientific Research of Belgium 1953–55; lecturer, Leuven Univ. 1955, Assoc. Prof. 1966, Prof. of Econ. History 1969–93, Prof. Emer. 1993–, Sec. Dept. of Econs. 1970–72, Chair. 1972–74, Chair. Bd. of Trustees Leuven Univ. Press 1971–93; Visiting Prof. St. Aloysius Univ., Brussels 1972–76, Dean Faculty of Econ., Political and Social Sciences 1972–75; Visiting Prof. Université Catholique de Louvain, Louvain-la-Neuve 1972–80, 1991–92; Research Fellow, Woodrow Wilson Int. Center for Scholars, Washington, D.C. 1975–76; Visiting Fellow, Inst. for Advanced Study, School of Historical Studies, Princeton, N.J., U.S.A. 1981–82, 1991, All Souls Coll. Oxford 1985; Ellen MacArthur Chair., Cambridge Univ. 1989; P.P. Rubens Chair., Univ. of Calif. at Berkeley 1994; Visiting Fellow Inst. for Advanced Study (RSSC), Canberra, Australia 1994; Erasmus Chair, Harvard Univ. (1997); Visiting Prof. or Fellow at various univs. U.S.A., U.K., Australia, Netherlands, France and Switzerland 1968–94; Pres. Int. Econ. History Asscn. 1986–90, Hon. Pres. 1990–; Chair. Royal Acad. of Belgium (Class of Letters) 1987, Leuven Inst. of Cen. and E. European Studies 1990–93, Advisory Council of W. European Program at Wilson Int. Center for Scholars, Washington, D.C. 1986–91, Academic Advisory Council of European Asscn. for Banking History 1991–; mem. Royal Acad. of Belgium; Corresp. Foreign mem. Royal Acad. of Netherlands; Corresp. Fellow British Acad. 1987; Foundation mem. Acad. Europaea; Foreign Hon. mem. American Acad. of Arts and Sciences; Dr. h.c. (Brussels) 1994, (Leicester) 1995; De Stassart Prize for Nat. History 1961–67 (Royal Acad. of Belgium) 1968, Fulbright-Hayes Award 1975, 1981, Quinquennial Solvay Prize for the Social Sciences 1976–80 (Nat. Foundation of Scientific Research of Belgium) 1981, Amsterdam Prize for Historical Sciences 1992, Golden Medal for Special Merits, Flemish Parl. 1995. *Publications:* Prix et salaires: Manuel Méthodologique 1956, The Growth of the Antwerp Market and the European Economy (14th–16th centuries), 3 vols. 1963, The Great Depression Revisited 1972, The Rise of Managerial Capitalism 1974, La Banque Nationale de Belgique et la politique monétaire entre les deux guerres 1975, Monetary, Credit and Banking Systems in Western Europe, 1400–1750, in The Cambridge Economic History of Europe (part V) 1977, Prosperity and Upheaval, the World Economy, 1945–1980 1983 (trans. in several languages), The Rise and Decline of Urban Industries in Italy and in the Low Countries (Late Middle Ages—Early Modern Times) 1988, Histoire économique mondiale 1945–1990 1990, History of European Banking 1991, Winkler Prins. History of the Low Countries, 1500–1800 (Ed.) 1992, The Economic Development of Europe, 950–1950 1992, Constructing the World Economy 1750–1990 1992, The Low Countries in the Early Modern World 1993, The General Bank 1822–1997: A Continuing Challenge 1997, Economic Development in Belgium Since 1870 1997. *Leisure interests:* literature, music, tennis, skiing. *Address:* Katholieke Universiteit Leuven, Centrum voor Economische Studiën, Naamsestraat 69, 3000 Leuven (Office); Ettingestraat 10, 9170 Sint-Pauwels, Belgium (Home). *Telephone:* (16) 32 67 25 (Office); (3) 776 03 33 (Home). *Fax:* (16) 32 67 96 (Office); (3) 765 90 28 (Home).

Van DEURSEN, Arie Theodorus; Netherlands professor of modern history (retd.); b. 23 June 1931, Groningen; s. of Arie van Deursen and Trijntje Smilde; m. Else Ruth Junkers 1962; two s. two d.; ed. Groningen Grammar School and Groningen State Univ.; research asst. Univ. of Groningen 1957; staff mem. Bureau, Royal Comm. of Dutch History 1958–67; Prof. of Modern History, Free Univ. Amsterdam 1967–96; mem. Royal Acad. of Science 1978, Wijnaends Francken Award 1983. *Publications:* Professions et métiers interdits 1960, Honni soit qui mal y pense 1965, Jacobus de Rhoer 1970, Bavianen en slijkgeuzen 1974, Het kopergeld van de gouden eeuw (4 vols.) 1978–80, Willem van Oranje (with H. C. de Schepper) 1984, Plain Lives in a Golden Age 1991, Een Dorp in de Polder 1994, Graft. Ein Dorf im 17. Jahrhundert 1997. *Address:* Bispinck Park 35, 2061 SH Bloemendaal, Netherlands. *Telephone:* (23) 5265592.

Van DIJK, Petrus, LL.M., S.J.D.; Netherlands public servant and fmr. professor of international law; b. 21 Feb. 1943, De Lier; s. of A. A. M. van Dijk and J. H. van Straelen; m. Francisca G. M. Lammerts 1969; one s. one d.; ed. Utrecht and Leyden Univs.; lecturer in Int. Law, Utrecht Univ. 1967–76, Prof. 1976–90; judge European Court of Human Rights 1996–98; Fullbright-Hays Scholar, Univ. of Mich. Law School 1970–71; Visiting Prof. Wayne State Univ. Law School 1978; Chair. Netherlands Inst. of Human Rights 1982–97, Netherlands Inst. of Social and Econ. Law 1986–90; mem. Court of Appeal of The Hague 1986, mem. Court of Appeal for Business and Industry 1992, Netherlands Council of State; mem. Bd. of Trustees Inst. of Social Sciences 1992–98, Anne Frank Foundation 1994–; State Councillor 1990–; mem. various advisory cttees.; mem. Royal Netherlands Acad. of Arts and Sciences; mem. Netherlands Del. to UN Gen. Ass. 1981, 1983, 1986. *Publications include:* Theory and Practice of the European Convention on Human Rights (with G. J. H. van Hoof) 1979, The Final Act of Helsinki: Basis for a Pan-European System? 1980, Contents and Function of the Principle of Equity in International Economic Law 1987, Normative Force and Effectiveness of International Economic Law 1988, Access to Court 1993, Universality of Human Rights 1994; book chapters and ed. of numerous legal publs. *Address:* Council of State, P.O. Box 20019, 2500 EA The Hague, Netherlands.

VAN DÚNEM, Fernando José França; Angolan politician; fmr. Minister of External Affairs; Prime Minister of Angola 1991–; mem. Marxist-Leninist Popular Movement for the Liberation of Angola-Worker's Party (MPLA). *Address:* Office of the Prime Minister, Luanda, Angola.

VAN DUYN, Mona, M.A.; American poet; b. 9 May 1921, Waterloo, Iowa; d. of George Van Duyn and Lora Kramer; m. Jarvis Thurston 1943; instr. in English, Univ. of Iowa 1943–46, Univ. of Louisville, Ky. 1946–50; lecturer in English, Washington Univ., St. Louis 1950–67; Ed. Perspective: A Quarterly of Literature, St. Louis 1947–67; named U.S. Poet Laureate 1992–93; mem. Nat. Acad. of Arts and Letters, N.A.A.S.; Fellow Acad. of American Poets; numerous awards and hon. degrees; Pulitzer Prize for Poetry 1991. *Publications:* Valentines to the Wide World 1959, A Time of Bees 1964, To See, To Take 1970, Bedtime Stories 1972, Merciful Disguises 1973, Letters from a Father and Other Poems 1982, Near Changes 1990, Firefall 1993, If It Be Not I 1993. *Address:* 7505 Teasdale Avenue, St. Louis, MO 63130, U.S.A.

VAN EEKELEN, Willem Frederik, D.LL.; Netherlands politician and diplomatist; b. 5 Feb. 1931, Utrecht; m. Johanna Wentink; two c.; ed. Utrecht and Princeton Univs.; diplomatic service 1957–77; mem. Consultative Ass. Council of Europe and WEU 1981–82; Sec. Gen. WEU 1989–94; Sec. of State for Defence 1978–81, for Foreign Affairs 1982–86; Minister of Defence 1986–88; Senator 1995–. *Leisure interests:* old maps, trekking, sailing. *Address:* Else Manhslaan 187, 2595 HE The Hague, Netherlands. *Telephone:* (70) 3241103. *Fax:* (70) 3241103.

VAN FRAASSEN, Bastiaan Cornelis, PH.D.; Canadian professor of philosophy; b. 5 April 1941, Goes, The Netherlands; s. of Jan Bastiaan van Fraassen and Dina Landman; m. Judith Ann Brown 1962; two s.; ed.Univ. of Alberta, Canada, Univ. of Pittsburgh, U.S.A.; Asst. Prof., Yale Univ. 1966–68, Assoc. Prof. 1969, Assoc. Prof., Univ. of Toronto 1969–73, Prof. 1973–82; Prof., Univ. of Southern Calif. 1976–81; Prof. of Philosophy, Princeton Univ. 1982–; John Simon Guggenheim Fellowship 1970–71; co-winner Franklin Matchette Award 1982, co-winner Imre Lakatos Award 1986. *Publications:* Introduction to the Philosophy of Time and Space 1970, Formal Semantics and Logic 1971, The Scientific Image 1980, Laws and Symmetry 1989, Quantum Mechanics: An Empiricist View 1991. *Leisure interest:* rock climbing. *Address:* 308 Western Way, Princeton, NJ 08544, U.S.A. *Telephone:* (609) 258-4304. *Fax:* (609) 258-1502.

VAN GERVEN, Walter M., DR.JUR.; Belgian lawyer; b. 11 May 1935, St. Niklaas; s. of Willy van Gerven and Germaine van Bel; m. Frieda Sintobin 1959; four s.; ed. Catholic Univ. of Louvain; Teaching Fellow, Univ. of Chicago Law School 1959–60; Assoc. Prof. of Law, Catholic Univ. of Louvain 1962–67, Prof. of Law 1967–82, Extraordinary Prof. 1982–, Vice-Rector 1970–76; Extraordinary Prof. Univ. of Amsterdam 1981–86; mem. Brussels Bar. 1970–80; Pres. Banking Comm. of Belgium 1982–88; mem. Bd. of Dirs. of several commercial cos.; Advocate-Gen. Court of Justice of European Communities 1988–95; Visiting Prof. Univ. of Chicago 1968–69; mem. Royal Belgian Acad., Royal Netherlands Acad., Acad. Europaea *Publications:* Principles of Belgian Private Law 1968, Commercial and Economic Law (3 vols.) 1973–86, The Policy of the Judge 1973, In Law and Equity 1987. *Leisure interests:* modern art, music, golf. *Address:* Demarsinstraat 42, 3010 Wilsele, Belgium (Home). *Telephone:* 016/22.91.54 (Home).

VAN HAMEL, Martine; American ballerina; b. 16 Nov. 1945, Brussels, Belgium; d. of D. A. van Hamel and Manette van Hamel-Cramer; ed. Nat. Ballet School of Canada; started ballet training at age four; début aged 11 with Nat. Ballet of Venezuela; joined Nat. Ballet of Canada as soloist 1963; moved to New York and danced with Joffrey Ballet 1969–70; joined American Ballet Theatre 1970, as Prin. Ballerina danced classic roles including Swan Lake, Sleeping Beauty, Raimonda as well as contemporary works choreographed by Petipa, Balanchine, Glen Tetley, Anthony Tudor, Kenneth MacMillan, Mark Morris, Twyla Tharp, Alvin Ailey; danced with Nederlands Dans Theater III 1993–98; Artistic Dir. New Amsterdam Ballet (f. 1986); mem. Founding Bd. Kaatsbaan Int. Dance Center; Gold Medal, Varna Competition 1996, Prix de Varna 1996, Dance Magazine Award, Cue Magazine Award, Award for Excellence, Washington Coll., Dance Educators of America Award. *Choreography:* Amnon V'Tamar for American Ballet Theatre 1984 and creator of works for Milwaukee Ballet, Washington Ballet, Royal Winnipeg Ballet and New Amsterdam Ballet. *Leisure interests:* singing. *Address:* c/o American Ballet Theatre, 890 Broadway, New York, NY 10003, U.S.A. *Telephone:* (212) 749-1942. *Fax:* (212) 678-0320.

VAN HEERDEN, Neil Peter, B.A.; South African diplomatist; b. 30 July 1939, East London; s. of J. van Heerden and C. Nel; m. Evelin Nowack 1961; one s. one d.; ed. Wonderbom High School, Pretoria and Univ. of S. Africa, Pretoria; joined Dept. of Foreign Affairs 1959; Vice-Consul, Tokyo 1963; opened S. Africa's first mission in Taipei 1967–68; opened first S. African mission in Tehran 1970–71; First Sec. Washington, D.C. 1971–75; Amb. to Fed. Repub. of Germany 1980; Deputy Dir. Gen., Dept. of Foreign Affairs, Pretoria 1985–87, Dir.-Gen. of Foreign Affairs 1987–92, Amb. to EC (now EU) 1992–96; Exec. Dir. S. Africa Foundation 1996–; *Publications:* articles in journals dealing with foreign affairs. *Leisure interests:* music, hiking, sailing, golf. *Address:* P.O. Box 7006, Johannesburg 2000, South Africa.

Van HOOFF, Jan A. R. A. M.; Netherlands professor of comparative physiology and ethology; b. 15 May 1936, Arnhem; s. of R. A. Th. van Hooff and L. E. Burgers; m. Anna C. M. Bluemink 1964; two s. one d.; ed. Canisius Coll., Nijmegen; scientific collaborator, Faculty of Biology, Utrecht Univ. 1963–73, lecturer in Comparative Physiology 1973–80, Prof. of Comparative Physiology 1980–96, Dean Faculty of Biology 1993–96; Dir. Science Bd., Burgers Zoo, Arnhem 1969–; Pres. Research Council of Ethology, Netherlands Foundation for Biological Research 1972–78, Dir. 1978–83; Pres. Soc. pour l'Etude et la Protection des Mammifères 1985–89; mem. numerous scientific foundations and socs.; Fellow, Royal Netherlands Acad. of Arts and Sciences. *Publications include:* Facial expressions in higher primates 1962, The comparison of facial expressions in man and higher primates 1976, Categories and sequences of behavior: methods of description and analysis 1982, Oorlog 1990. *Address:* c/o Utrecht University, P.O. Box 80.086, 3508 TB Utrecht (Office); Vermeerlaan 24, 3723 EN Bilthoven, The Netherlands (Home). *Telephone:* (030) 535404 (Office); (030) 287639 (Home). *Fax:* (030) 521105.

VAN HOOVEN, Eckart, DR.JUR.; German company executive; b. 11 Dec. 1925; Chair. Supervisory Bd. Giesecke & Devrient GmbH, Munich, Mobil Oil AG, Hamburg; Deputy Chair. Supervisory Bd. Hapag-Lloyd AG, Hamburg; mem. Supervisory Bd. Kaufhof AG, Cologne, Reemtsma Cigarettenfabriken GmbH, Hamburg. *Address:* Deutsche Bank AG, Taunusanlage 12, 60325 Frankfurt am Main, Germany. *Telephone:* (069) 7150-3075.

van INWAGEN, Peter Jan, PH.D.; American professor of philosophy and scholar; b. 21 Sept. 1942, Rochester, New York; s. of George Butler van Inwagen and Mildred Gloria Knudsen; m. 1st Margery Naylor 1967 (divorced 1988); one d.; m. 2nd Elisabeth Bolduc 1989; ed. Rensselaer Polytechnic Inst., Univ. of Rochester; served U.S. Army 1969–70; Visiting Asst. Prof. of Philosophy Univ. of Rochester 1970–71; Asst. Prof., Assoc. Prof., then Prof. of Philosophy, Syracuse Univ. 1971–95; John Cardinal O'Hara Prof. of Philosophy, Univ. of Notre Dame, S. Bend, Ind. 1995–; Visiting Prof. Univ. of Ariz. 1981, Rutgers Univ. 1987; Research grants, Nat. Endowment for the Humanities 1983–84, 1990–91. *Publications:* An Essay on Free Will 1983, Material Beings 1990, Metaphysics 1993, God, Knowledge and Mystery (essays) 1995, The Possibility of Resurrection and Other Essays in Christian Apologetics 1997. *Address:* Department of Philosophy; University of Notre Dame, IN 46556, U.S.A. *Telephone:* (219) 631-5910. *Fax:* (219) 631-8209.

VAN ITTERSUM, Baron Boudewijn F.; Netherlands financial official; b. 1939; ed. Univ. of Amsterdam; joined Ministry of Finance; seconded to IMF, IBRD, Washington, D.C. 1970–72; subsequently Dir. of Int. Affairs, Ministry of Finance; Chair. Amsterdam Stock Exchange 1981–96, Dir. 1996–. *Address:* Amsterdam AEX, Beursplein 5, 1012 JW, Amsterdam, Netherlands.

VAN LIEROP, Robert F.; Ni-Vanuatu diplomatist, television journalist, university lecturer and lawyer; b. 17 March 1939; m.; one s.; ed. New York Univ. U.S.A.; practised law; subsequently worked as journalist, writer and univ. lecturer, New York; mem. Vanuatu dels. to meetings of Non-Aligned Movt. including summits New Delhi 1983, Harare 1986, Belgrade 1989, and to several UN Gen. Ass. sessions, Vice-Pres. 43rd session; Vanuatu's Rep. to Preparatory Comm. for the Int. Sea-Bed Authority and Int. Tribunal for Law of the Sea; Perm. Rep. of Vanuatu to UN 1988–93; elected Chair. Gen. Ass. Fourth Cttee. (Decolonization) 1989. *Address:* c/o Department of Foreign Affairs, PMB 51, Port Vila, Vanuatu.

VAN LINT, Jacobus Hendricus, PH.D.; Netherlands professor of mathematics; b. 1 Sept. 1932, Bandung, Indonesia; s. of J. H. van Lint and P. C. E. Minkman; m. Elisabeth Barbara Janna Teunissen 1961; one s. one d.; ed. Univs. of Utrecht, Göttingen and Munster; Prof. of Math., Eindhoven Univ. of Tech. 1959–, Rector Magnificus 1991–96; Dir. Stan Ackermans Inst. 1997–; mem. Tech. Staff, Bell Labs. 1966, 1971, 1977; Visiting Prof. Calif. Inst. of Tech. 1970–71, 1988–89; Pres. Wiskundig Genootschap 1968–70; mem. Royal Netherlands Acad. of Arts and Sciences. *Publications:* Coding Theory 1971, Algebra en Analyse (with S. T. M. Ackermans) 1974, Combinatorial Theory Seminar 1973, Graphs, Codes and Designs (with P. J. Cameron) 1980, Introduction to Coding Theory 1983, A Course in Combinatorics (with R. M. Wilson) 1991. *Leisure interests:* philately, swimming, bridge. *Address:* Department of Mathematics and Computing Science, Eindhoven University of Technology, Den Dolech, P.O. Box 513, 5600 MB Eindhoven; Beukenlaan 15, Nuenen 5671 AH, Netherlands. *Telephone:* (40) 2831466; (40) 2474763. *Fax:* (40) 2435810.

VAN MIERLO, Henricus Antonius Franciscus Maria Oliva (Hans), D.JUR.; Netherlands politician; b. 18 Aug. 1931, Breda; ed. Canisius Coll. Nijmegen and Univ. of Nijmegen; journalist, Het Algemeen Handelsblad, Amsterdam 1960–67; first Chair. newly formed political party Democrats '66 (D66) 1966; mem. Lower House of States Gen. 1967–77, 1986–94; Leader D66 Parl. Party 1967–74, 1986–94; mem. Upper House of States Gen. 1983–86; Deputy Prime Minister and Minister of Foreign Affairs 1994–; fmr. mem. Netherlands-Suriname Devt. Comm., Advisory Council on Defence; co-producer of TV programmes; various positions in literary and other cultural orgs. *Address:* Ministry of Foreign Affairs, Bezuidenhoutseweg 67, P.O. Box 20061, 2500 EB The Hague, Netherlands. *Telephone:* (70) 3486486. *Fax:* (70) 3484848.

VAN MIERT, Karel; Belgian international official and politician; b. 17 Jan. 1942, Oud-Turnhout; m.; one c.; ed. State University of Ghent; Researcher, Fonds National de la Recherche Scientifique 1968–70; Asst. in Int. Law, Free Univ. of Brussels 1971–73; Head. Admin. attached to Pvt. Office of Vice-Pres. of European Comm. 1973–75; part-time lecturer, Free Univ. of Brussels 1978–; Int. Sec. Belgian Socialist Party 1976, Co-Chair. 1977; subsequently Chair. Flemish Socialists; Vice-Chair. Confed. of Socialist Parties of European Community 1978–80; mem. European Parl. 1979–85; mem. House of Reps. 1985–88; Vice-Chair. Socialist Int. 1986–92; EEC (now European Commission) Commr. for Transport, Credit, Investment and Consumer Affairs 1989–94, for Environment (acting) 1992–93, for Competition Policy, Personnel and Admin. 1993–95, for Competition 1992–, a Vice-Pres. 1993–95. *Address:* The European Commission, 200 rue de la Loi, 1049 Brussels, Belgium. *Telephone:* (02) 295-25-30. *Fax:* (02) 295-95-83.

VAN MONTAGU, Baron, Marc Charles Ernest, PH.D.; Belgian plant geneticist; b. 11 Nov. 1933, Ghent; s. of Jean Van Montagu and Irene Van Beveren; m. Nora Podgaetchi 1957; ed. State Univ. Ghent; Asst., State Univ. Ghent 1962–64, Lab. Dir. and Lector, Dept. of Histology 1964–78, Assoc. Prof. and Co-Dir. Lab. of Genetics 1979–87, Full Prof. and Dir. Lab. of Genetics 1987–; Scientific Dir. Plant Genetic Systems N.V. 1983–95; mem. Royal Belgium Acad. of Sciences; Foreign Assoc. N.A.S. (U.S.A.); Foreign mem. Russian Agric. Acad., Royal Swedish Acad. of Eng. Sciences, Acad. d'Agriculture de France; Hon. D.Phil. (Helsinki) 1990; Rank Prize for Nutrition, U.K. 1987, IBM-Europe Prize 1988, Prize of the Flemish Community 1989, Dr. A. De Leeuw-Damry-Bourlart Prize 1990, Charles Leopold Mayer Prize, Acad. of Sciences, Paris 1990, Japan Prize 1997; title of Baron granted by King Baudoin I. *Publications:* about 600 articles in specialized journals and books. *Leisure interest:* travel. *Address:* University of Ghent, Laboratory of Genetics, Ledeganckstraat 35, 9000 Ghent (Office); De Stassartstraat 120, 1050 Brussels, Belgium (Home). *Telephone:* (32) 9-264 5170 (Office); (32) 2-511 2557 (Home). *Fax:* (32) 9-264 5349.

van MUNSTER, Hans, DR.PHIL.; Netherlands ecclesiastic; b. 17 Nov. 1925, Gouda; s. of J. M. van Munster and A. C. B. Faay; ed. Univ. of Louvain; entered Order of St. Francis of Assisi 1944; ordained priest 1951; lecturer in Logic and Methodology, Philosophical Inst., Venray 1955–67; Regent, R.C. Lycee, Venray 1963–67; Prof. of Philosophy, Catholic Theological Faculty of Utrecht 1967–71, Rector 1968–71; Vicar-Gen. of Archdiocese of Utrecht 1970–81; Sec.-Gen. Dutch Bishops' Conf. 1981–91; Pres. Cttee. on Justice and Peace 1991–; Pres. Catholic Bible Soc. 1992–98, Franciscan Asscn. 1992–98; Officer Order of Oranje-Nassau, Kt. of Netherlands Lion. *Publications include:* Kierkegaard een keuze uit zijn dagboeken 1957, De filosofische gedachten van de jonge Kierkegaard 1958, Kierkegaards redevoeringen 1959, Over de vertwijfeling 1963, Sören Aabye Kierkegaard 1963, Naar woorden moet je luisteren 1981, Vanwaar? Waarheen? 1982, Drie prioriteiten voor de kerk van Europa 1983, Kantelt de Koets wel? 1989, Een steen in de vijver, vrede en gerechtigheid na de dood van Marx 1993, Te Doen gerechtigheid 1993, De ware vrede 1993, 't is een vreemdeling zeker 1994. *Leisure interests:* cycling, literature. *Address:* Jan van Scorelstraat 75, 3583 CL Utrecht, Netherlands. *Telephone:* (30) 2510153. *Fax:* (30) 2523326.

VAN NIEKERK, André Isak (Kraai), PH.D.; South African politician and agricultural scientist; b. 7 Oct. 1938, Eshowe, Natal; m. Theresa Claassens 1964; three s.; ed. Univ. of Stellenbosch; taught Science and Agric. Eshowe Bantu Training Coll. 1962; specialist officer, Dept. of Agric. Tech. Services, Univ. of Stellenbosch 1964–67; Research at Rowett Inst., Aberdeen, Scotland 1968, Wageningen Agricultural Univ., The Netherlands 1969; farmer, Kenhardt Dist. 1971–81; elected M.P. for Prieska 1981; Deputy Minister of Agric. 1986, of Agric. and Water Supply in Ministers' Council 1989, of Agricultural Devt. 1989; Minister of Agric. in Cabinet, of Agricultural Devt. in Ministers' Council 1991–94, of Agric., Govt. of Nat. Unity 1994–96; Leader Nat. Party for the Northern Cape 1994–; mem. Senate (for Northern Cape) 1994–, Deputy Leader 1994–. *Address:* Private Bag X5066, Kimberley 8300, South Africa.

VAN PEEBLES, Mario, B.ECONS.; American actor and film director; b. 15 Jan. 1957, Mexico; s. of Melvin Van Peebles and Maria Marx; ed. Columbia Univ.; film début aged 11, A Thousand Clowns, then appeared in Dirty Harry, Sweet Sweetback's Badass Song; worked as budget analyst in New York mayor's office; studied acting and script interpretation with Stella Adler. *Theatre:* Champion, Jungle Fever, Midnight, Friday The 13th, Deadwood Dick, Bodybags (also co-dir.). *Television:* The American Masters Series, Children of the Night, L.A. Law, One Life to Live, Gang in Blue, Riot. *Films include:* Cotton Club, Exterminator II, Rappin (also as singer), Hot Shots, The Last Resort, Heartbreak Ridge, New Jack City (also dir.), Posse (also dir.), Gunmen (also dir.), Panther (also dir., producer), Jaws IV: The Revenge, Solo, Los Locos (also dir., wrote screenplay), Stag 1997, Love Kills (also dir., producer) 1998.

Van ROIJEN, Jan Herman Robert Dudley, LL.M.; Netherlands diplomatist; b. 17 Dec. 1936, Tokyo, Japan; s. of late Dr Jan Herman van Roijen and Anne née Jonkvrouwe Snouck Hurgronje; m. Jonkvrouw Caroline H.W. Reuchlin 1963; one s. two d.; ed. Groton School, Mass., U.S.A. and Univ. of Utrecht; entered foreign service 1963; Third Sec. Jakarta 1965–67; Second Sec. Perm. Mission at NATO, Paris and Brussels 1967–70; Head, Recruitment and Training Section, Foreign Office 1970–73; Chargé d'Affaires, Saigon 1973–75; Counsellor, Athens 1975–78, Ottawa 1978–81; Minister Plenipotentiary, Jakarta 1981–83; Deputy Dir.-Gen. Int. Cooperation, Ministry of Foreign Affairs 1983–86; Amb. to Israel 1986–89; Prin. Dir. Personnel, Diplomatic Budget and Bldgs., Ministry of Foreign Affairs 1989–91; Amb. to Indonesia 1992–94, to U.K. 1995–98 (also accred. to Iceland). *Leisure interests:* tennis, skiing. *Address:* c/o Ministry of Foreign Affairs, Bezuidenhoutseweg 30, P.O. Box 20061, 2500 EB The Hague, The Netherlands.

VAN SANT, Gus, Jr., B.A.; American film director and screenwriter; b. 1952, Louisville, Ky.; ed. Rhode Island School of Design; fmr. production asst. to Ken Shapiro. *Films include:* Mala Noche, Drugstore Cowboy 1989 (with Daniel Yost); Nat. Soc. of Film Critics Awards for Best Dir. and Screenplay 1990, New York Film Critics and L.A. Film Critics Award for Best Screenplay 1989, PEN Literary Award for Best Screenplay Adaptation (jtly. 1989), My Own Private Idaho 1991, Even Cowgirls Get the Blues 1993, To Die For 1995, Kids 1995, Ballad of the Skeletons 1996, Good Will Hunting 1997, Psycho 1998. *Address:* c/o William Morris Agency Inc., 151 South El Camino Drive, Beverly Hills, CA 90212, U.S.A.

Van SCHAIK, Ben; Netherlands business executive; b. 1945; worked in sales for Mercedes Benz in U.K., Netherlands, Germany; Chair. Fokker (aircraft maker) 1994–. *Address:* Fokker, P.O. Box 1222, 1100 AE Amsterdam-Juidoost, Netherlands.

VAN SCHAIK, Gerard, F.C.I.S.; Netherlands businessman; b. 29 March 1930, Haarlem; s. of the late Gerard Van Schaik and Maria Mulder; m. Moyra Colijn 1963; two s. one d.; ed. Free Univ. of Amsterdam, IMEDE, Switzerland; officer Royal Netherlands Air Force 1956–58; joined Heineken's Bierbrouwerij Maatschappij N.V. 1959, mem. Exec. Bd. Heineken N.V. 1974, Deputy Chair. 1983, Chair. 1989–93; Pres. Supervisory Bd. Aegon NV 1993–; Dir. of numerous cos.; Pres. European Foundation of Man. Devt., Brussels; Dr. h.c. (State Acad. for Man., Moscow) 1997; Kt. Order of Dutch Lion; Hon. Fellow London Business School. *Leisure interests:* golf, music. *Address:* Duinvoetlaan 7, 2243 GK Wassenaar, The Netherlands. *Telephone:* (31) 70.5179008. *Fax:* (31) 70.5179008.

VAN SWAAIJ, Willibrordus Petrus Maria, PH.D.; Netherlands professor of chemical engineering; b. 18 Jan. 1942, Nijmegen; s. of Christian van Swaaij and C. Bosman; m. J. J. T. van den Berk 1966; one s. four d.; ed. Tech. Univ. of Eindhoven, Univ. of Nancy, France; joined Shell Research 1965, worked in lab. Shell Research B.V. (KSLA), Amsterdam 1966–72, Section Chief, Gasification 1971–72; Prof. of Chemical Eng. Science, Twente Univ.; Consultant to DSM, AKZO, Unilever, Netherlands Govt., EEC; mem. Royal Netherlands Acad. of Sciences 1986; Australian European Fellowship Award 1984; Dr. h.c. (Inst. Nat. Polytechnique de Lorraine, France) 1996; Dow Energy Prize 1985, Grand Prix du Génie des Procédés, Inst. de France 1996. *Publications:* Chemical Reactor Design and Operation (with Westerterp and Beenackers); about 340 scientific papers, contribs. to books etc. *Leisure interests:* sailing, surfing, photography, gardening. *Address:* University of Twente, Department of Chemical Technology, P.O. Box 217, 7500 AE Enschede; Sportlaan 60, 7581 BZ Losser, Netherlands (Home). *Telephone:* (53) 489 2880 (Office); (53) 538 2677 (Home). *Fax:* (53) 489 4774 (Office); (53) 538 4368 (Home).

VAN VUUREN, Jacobus Lukas Jansen, B.COM.; South African banker; b. 6 June 1931, De Aar; s. of Stephanus van Vuuren; m. Anna van der Merwe 1953; three d.; ed. De Aar High School and UNISA; Chief Accountant, Volkskas Bank Ltd. 1978, Asst. Gen. Man. 1980, Gen. Man. 1981, Sr. Gen. Man. 1984, now Man. Dir. and C.E.O.; Exec. Dir. Volkskas Group Ltd.; Chair. MLS Bank Ltd., Volkskas Motor Bank Ltd.; Exec. Dir. Amalgamated Banks of S.A. Ltd.; Dir. Bank of Transkei Ltd., United Bank Ltd., Priceforbes Federale Volkskas Holdings (Pty) Ltd. *Leisure interests:* gardening, golf.

VAN WACHEM, Lodewijk Christiaan; Netherlands business executive and mechanical engineer; b. 31 July 1931, Pangkalan Brandan, Netherlands E. Indies (now Indonesia); m. Elisabeth G. Cristofoli 1958; two s. one d.; ed. Technological Univ., Delft; joined Bataafsche Petroleum Maatschappij, The Hague 1953; Mech. Engineer, Cía Shell de Venezuela 1954–63; Chief Engineer, Shell-BP Petroleum Devt. Co. of Nigeria 1963–66, Eng. Man. 1966–67, Chair. and Man. Dir. 1972–76; Head Tech. Admin. Brunei Shell Petroleum Co. Ltd. 1967–69, Tech. Dir. 1969–71; Head of Production Div. Shell Int. Petroleum Maatschappij, The Hague 1971–72, Co-ordinator Exploration and Production 1976–79; Man. Dir. Royal Dutch Petroleum Co. until 1982, Pres. 1982–92; mem. Presidium of Bd. of Dirs., Shell Petroleum N.V.; Man. Dir. Shell Petroleum Co. Ltd. 1977–92, Chair. Shell Oil Co. U.S.A. 1982–92, Dir. Shell Canada Ltd. 1982–92; Chair. Jt. Cttee. of Man. Dirs. of the Royal Dutch/Shell Group 1985–92, Chair. Supervisory Bd. Royal Dutch Petroleum Co. 1992–; mem. Bd. of Dirs. Crédit Suisse Holding 1992–96, Zürich Insurance Group (now Zürich Financial Services) 1993–, Supervisory Bd. Akzo-Nobel NV 1992–, Philips Electronics NV 1993–, BMW (Munich) 1994–, Bayer AG 1997–; Dir. (non-exec.) IBM Corpn. 1992–, ATCO Ltd. 1993–, AAB Brown Boveri Ltd. 1996–; Hon. K.B.E. 1989, Kt. Order of Netherlands Lion 1981, Commdr., Order of Oranje Nassau 1990, Public Service Star, Singapore 1998. *Address:* Royal Dutch Petroleum Co., Carel van Bylandtlaan 30, 2596 HR The Hague, Netherlands. *Telephone:* (070) 3772118 (Office). *Fax:* (070) 3772616.

VAN WIJNGAARDEN, Leendert, PH.D.; Netherlands professor of fluid mechanics; b. 16 March 1932, Delft; s. of Cornelis M. van Wijngaarden and Jeanne Severijn; m. Willy F. de Goede 1962; two s.; ed. Gymnasium B, Delft and Technological Univ. of Delft; Netherlands Ship Model Basin, Wageningen 1962–66, latterly Head of Hydrodynamics Dept.; Prof. of Fluid Mechanics, Twente Univ. 1966–; mem. of Bureau and Treasurer Int. Union of Theoretical and Applied Mechanics 1984–88, Pres. 1992–; mem. Royal Netherlands Acad. of Science. *Publications:* about 60 publs. in professional journals. *Leisure interests:* tennis, chess, literature, music. *Address:* University Twente, P.O. Box 217, 7500 AE Enschede (Office); Von Weberlaan 7, 7522 KB Enschede, The Netherlands (Home). *Telephone:* 31-53 893086 (Office); 31-53-352078 (Home).

VAN WINDEN, Jacobus Cornelis Maria; Netherlands ecclesiastic and professor of Greek; b. 10 Oct. 1922, Schipluiden; ed. in Franciscan convents and Leiden Univ.; mem. Franciscan Order (OFM) 1941; ordained priest 1948; Asst. to J. H. Waszink, Prof. of Latin, Leiden 1954–56; teacher of

Greek and Latin, Rotterdam 1956–66; Reader, Leiden Univ. 1966–80, Prof. of Greek of Late Antiquity 1980–87, Prof. Emer. 1987–; Ed.-in-Chief Vigiliae Christianae (review of Early Christian Life and Language) 1977–; mem. Royal Netherlands Acad. *Publications:* Calcidius on Matter: His Doctrine and Sources 1959, An Early Christian Philosopher: Justin Martyr's Dialogue with Trypho 1971, Tertullianus, De idolatria (critical text, trans. and commentary with J. H. Waszink) 1987, De ware wijsheid: Wegen van vroegchristelijk denken 1992, Bonaventura, Itinerarium. De Weg die de geest naar God voert (Dutch transl. with commentary) 1996, Arche. A Collection of Patristic Studies 1997. *Address:* Haarlemmerstraat 106, 2312 GD Leiden, Netherlands. *Telephone:* 071-5120401.

VAN WYK, Andreas Herculas, B.A., LL.D.; South African professor of law and university rector; b. 17 Sept. 1941, Pretoria; s. of Andries Hercules du Preez van Wyk and Hendrina Louise van Wyk (née Kruger); m. Magdalena Krüger 1967; two d.; ed. Helpmekaar Boys' High School, Johannesburg, Univs. of Stellenbosch and Leiden; lecturer, then Prof., then Dean, Faculty of Law, Univ. of Stellenbosch 1966–84, Dir. Gen. Dept. of Constitutional Devt. 1984–87, Prof. Faculty of Law 1987–91, Vice-Rector Operations 1991–93, Rector and Vice-Chancellor 1993–; Dir. Distillers Corpn., Stellenbosch 1988–; mem. Bd. and Exec. Comm. of Old Mutual 1992–; guest U.S.A./S.A. Leadership Exchange Programme 1978; Alexander von Humboldt Foundation Fellowship 1981; Hon. LL.D. (Leuven); William of Orange Medal (Leiden) 1995. *Publications:* The Power to Dispose of the Assets of the Universal Matrimonial Community of Property 1976, Die Suid-Afrikaanse Kontraktereg en Handelsreg (jtly.) 1992, Family, Property and Succession 1983 and numerous articles in academic journals; has drafted various pieces of legislation. *Address:* Rector's Office, University of Stellenbosch, Private Bag XI, Matieland 7602, South Africa. *Telephone:* 27-21-808-4490. *Fax:* 27-21-808-3714.

VAN ZYL SLABBERT, Dr. F. (see Slabbert, F. Van Zyl).

VAN-CULIN, Rev. Canon Samuel, A.B., B.D.; American ecclesiastic; b. 20 Sept. 1930, Honolulu; s. of Samuel Van-Culin and Susie Mossman; ed. Princeton Univ. and Virginia Theological Seminary; Curate St. Andrew's Cathedral, Honolulu 1955–56; Canon Precentor and Rector Hawaiian Congregation, Honolulu 1956–58; Asst. Rector St. John's, Washington D.C. 1958–60; Gen. Sec. Lyman Int., Washington D.C. 1960–61; Asst. Sec. Overseas Dept., Exec. Council of the Episcopal Church U.S.A. 1962–68, Sec. for Africa and Middle E. 1968–76, Exec. for World Mission 1976–83; Sec. Gen. Anglican Consultative Council 1983–94; Sec. to Lambeth Conf. 1988; Hon. D.D. (Virginia Theological Seminary); Hon. Canon Canterbury, Jerusalem, Honolulu, Ibadan and Cape Town. *Leisure interests:* music and travel. *Address:* 16a Burgate, Canterbury, Kent, CT1 2EA, England. *Telephone:* (01227) 458018.

VANCE, Cyrus Roberts, B.A., LL.B.; American former government official and lawyer; b. 27 March 1917, Clarksburg, W. Va.; s. of John Carl and Amy (Roberts) Vance; m. Grace Elsie Sloane 1947; one s. four d.; ed. Kent School, Yale Law School and Yale Univ.; Lieut., U.S. Navy 1942–46; Asst. to Pres. The Mead Corpn. 1946–47; Simpson Thacher and Bartlett, New York (law firm) 1947–98, Partner 1956–61, 1967–76, 1980–98; Chair. Bd. of Govs., Fed. Reserve Bank, New York 1989–92; Special Counsel, Preparedness Investigating Subcttee., Cttee. on Armed Services of the U.S. Senate 1957–60; Consulting Counsel to Special Cttee. on Space and Astronautics, U.S. Senate 1958; Gen. Counsel, Dept. of Defense 1961–62; Chair. Cttee. Adjudication of Claims of the Admin. Conf. of the U.S. 1961–62; Sec. of the Army 1962–64; Deputy Sec. of Defense 1964–67; Pres. Johnson's Special Envoy on Cyprus Situation 1967, on Korean Situation 1968; negotiator at Paris talks on Viet Nam 1968–69; Sec. of State 1977–80; Co-Chair. UN-EC Jt. Peace Conf. on Yugoslavia, London 1992–93; UN Peace Negotiator to fmr. Yugoslavia 1991–93; mem. Cttee. investigating Alleged Police Corruption, New York 1970–72, Ind. Comm. on Disarmament and Security 1980–; Pres. Bar Assen. of City of New York 1974–76; Chair. UN Devt. Corpn. 1976; Dir. New York Times Co.; Chair. Bd. of Rockefeller Foundation 1975–77; UN Special Rep. in S.A. 1992; in Nagorno-Karabakh 1992; Court apptd. mediator in Olympia & York and Macy bankruptcy negotiations 1994; mem. U.S. Supreme Court, American Bar Assen., N.Y. State Bar Assen., Council of Foreign Relations; Fellow, American Coll. Trial Lawyers; Hon. D.C.L. (New York Univ.) 1993 and numerous other hon. degrees; Medal of Freedom 1969, Hon. K.B.E.; Légion d'honneur; Grand Cordon, Order of Rising Sun (Japan). *Publication:* Hard Choices (autobiog.) 1983. *Address:* Simpson, Thacher and Bartlett, 425 Lexington Avenue, New York, NY 10017-3954, U.S.A. *Telephone:* (212) 455-7190.

VANDEPUTTE, Robert M. A. C., D. EN D., D. EN SC., POL. ET SOC.; Belgian banker and university professor; b. 26 Feb. 1908, Antwerp; m. Marie-Louise Cauwe 1938; three c.; ed. Univs. of Louvain, Nijmegen, Paris, Berlin and Berne; called to Antwerp Bar 1930–40; Prof. Univ. of Louvain 1936–78; Chef de Cabinet, Ministry of Econ. Affairs 1939–40; Sec.-Gen. Assoc. Belge des Banques 1940–42; Dir. Banque Nat. de Belgique 1943–44, Regent 1954–71, Gov. 1971–75; Man. Dir. Soc. Nat. de Crédit à l'Industrie 1944–48, Pres. 1948–71; mem. Caisse Gén. d'Epargne et de Retraite 1958–75; Dir. and mem. Directing Cttee. Société Nat. d'Investissement 1962–71; Pres. Inst. de Réescompte et de Garantie 1973–78; Minister of Finance April–Dec. 1981; Administrateur, Palais des Beaux-Arts de Belgique 1966–84; mem. Conseil Supérieur des Finances 1969–71; Pres. Administratieve en Economische Hogeschool 1959–91; Pres. Faculty Univ. Saint-Louis 1982–93; Commdr., Order of the Crown and Knight, Order of Léopold (Belgium); Officer, Order of Merit (Italian Repub.); Commdr., Order of St. Gregory the Great (Holy See); Grand Officer, Order of Léopold II (Belgium), and other awards. *Publications:* Beginselen van Nijverheidsrecht, Handboek voor Verzekeringen en Verzekeringsrecht, Wat ik rondom mij zag, De Overeenkomst, Een Machteloos Minister, De harde strijd—Beknopte geschiedenis van het A.C.V., Economische geschiedenis van Belgie 1944–84, Het Aquilaans foutbegrip, Verbintenissen en Overeenkomsten in Kort bestek, Sociale geschiedenis van België 1944–85, Economie in België in Kort Bestek, De Schoolkwestie en de Guimardstraat; in French: Quelques aspects de l'activité de la Société Nationale de Crédit à l'industrie, Le statut de l'entreprise, Ministre sans pouvoir, Les institutions financières belges. *Address:* Institut de Réescompte et de Garantie, rue du Commerce 78, 1040 Brussels (Office); rue au Bois 376 Bte. 21, 1150 Brussels, Belgium (Home). *Telephone:* 511-73-30 (Office).

VANDER ZALM, William N.; Canadian politician; b. 29 May 1934, Noordwykerhout, Holland; s. of Wilhelmus Nicholaas van der Zalm and Agatha C. Warmerdam; m. Lillian B. Mihalick 1956; two s. two d.; ed. Phillip Sheffield High School, Abbotsford, B.C., Canada; emigrated to Canada 1947, became Canadian citizen; purchased Art Knapp Nurseries Ltd., became Co. Pres. 1956; elected to Surrey Municipal Council as Alderman 1965, as Mayor 1969–; elected to Prov. Legis. for Social Credit Party, Minister of Human Resources 1975; Minister of Municipal Affairs and Minister responsible for Urban Transit Authority (now B.C. Transit) 1978; Minister of Educ. and Minister responsible for B.C. Transit 1982; est. Fantasy Garden World, major tourist attraction in Richmond 1983; Leader B.C. Social Credit Party July 1986–; Premier of B.C. 1986–91. *Leisure interests:* fishing, swimming. *Address:* 3553 Arthur Drive, Ladner B.C., V4K 3N2, Canada. *Telephone:* (604) 946-1774. *Fax:* (604) 946-1981.

VANDERPOORTEN, Herman, LL.D.; Belgian politician; b. 25 Aug. 1922; ed. Atheneum Berchem-Antwerp and Rijksuniversiteit te Gent; Attorney 1945; Co. Councillor, Antwerp 1949–58; Town Councillor and Deputy Justice of the Peace, Lier 1959; mem. Chamber of Reps. 1961–65; Senator 1965; Minister of Interior 1966–68, of Justice 1973–77; Deputy Prime Minister and Minister of Justice and Institutional Reforms May–Oct. 1980; Pres. Liberal Flemish Assen. 1957–66; mem. European Parl. 1979–80; Govt. Councillor to the King 1981–. *Address:* Antwerpsesteenweg 2, Lier, Belgium.

VANDROSS, Luther; American singer, songwriter and producer; b. New York; s. of Mary Ida Vandross; started career by singing advertising jingles and with backing groups; featured on David Bowie's record Young Americans 1975; signed contract with Epic Records 1981; has produced albums by Aretha Franklin and Cheryl Lynn. *Albums include:* Never Too Much, Forever, for Always, for Love, Busy Body, Give Me The Reason, The Night I Fell In Love, Any Love, Never Let Me Go, The Best of Luther Vandross, The Power of Love, One Night With You, The Best of Love. *Address:* Epic Records, 550 Madison Avenue, New York, NY 10022, U.S.A.

VANE, Sir John Robert, D.SC., D.PHIL., F.R.S.; British pharmacologist; b. 29 March 1927, Tardebigg, Worcs.; s. of Maurice Vane and Frances Florence Vane; m. Elizabeth Daphne Page 1948; two d.; ed. King Edward VI High School, Birmingham, and Univs. of Birmingham and Oxford; Therapeutic Research Council Fellow, Oxford 1946–48; research worker, Sheffield and Nuffield Inst. for Medical Research, Oxford 1948–51; Stothert Research Fellow, Royal Soc. 1951–53; Instructor in Pharmacology, Yale Univ. 1953–54, Asst. Prof. 1954–55; Sr. Lecturer in Pharmacology, Inst. of Basic Medical Sciences of Univ. of London at Royal Coll. of Surgeons of England 1955–61, Reader 1961–65, Prof. of Experimental Pharmacology 1966–73; Group Research and Devt. Dir., The Wellcome Foundation Ltd. 1973–85; Dir. The William Harvey Research Inst., St. Bartholomew's Hosp. Medical Coll. 1986–90, Dir.-Gen. 1990–97, Hon. Pres. 1997–; Prof. of Pharmacology and Medicine New York Medical Coll. 1986–; mem. British Pharmacological Soc. (Foreign Sec. 1979–85), Physiological Soc., Soc. for Drug Research, Royal Acad. of Medicine of Belgium; Fellow, Inst. of Biology; Hon. Fellow, Royal Coll. of Physicians, American Coll. of Physicians, Swedish Soc. of Medical Sciences, St. Catherine's Coll., Oxford, American Physiological Soc., Council on Clinical Cardiology, American Heart Assen., British Pharmacological Soc., Physiological Soc., Royal Coll. of Surgeons, Royal Nat. Acad. of Medicine, Spain; Foreign mem. N.A.S., Polish Acad. of Sciences, A.A.A.S., Royal Netherlands Acad. of Arts and Sciences, Nat. Acad. of Medicine, Buenos Aires; numerous memorial lectures in U.K. and abroad, especially U.S.A.; hon. doctorates from Copernicus Acad. of Medicine, Cracow, René Descartes Univ., Paris, Aberdeen Univ., London Univ., Mount Sinai Medical School, New York, New York Medical Coll. and Birmingham, Surrey, Camerino, Louvain and Buenos Aires Univs.; shared Nobel Prize for Physiology or Medicine for discoveries concerning prostaglandins and related substances 1982, Royal Medal, Royal Soc. 1989; numerous other awards, prizes and distinctions. *Publications:* numerous review articles and over 700 papers on pharmacology and related topics; jt. ed. of five books. *Leisure interests:* photography, travel, underwater swimming. *Address:* The William Harvey Research Institute, St. Bartholomew's and The Royal London School of Medicine and Dentistry, Charterhouse Square, London, EC1M 6BQ, England. *Telephone:* 0171-982-6119. *Fax:* 0171-251 1685.

VANGELIS (pseudonym of **Vangelis Papathanassiou**); Greek composer and conductor; b. Greece; began performing own compositions at age of six;

moved to Paris in late 1960s; composed and recorded symphonic poem Faire que ton rêve soit plus long que la nuit and album, Terra; composed La Cantique des Créatures for film-maker Frederic Rossif; returned to Greece, after period in London, 1989; formed band Formynx in Greece. *Film scores:* Chariots of Fire (Acad. Award), Antarctica, Missing, Blade Runner, The Bounty, Wonders of Life, Wild and Beautiful, Francesco, 1492: Conquest of Paradise, Bitter Moon.

VANNECK, Air Commodore The Hon. Sir Peter Beckford Rutgers, G.B.E., C.B., A.F.C., A.E., M.A., D.SC., J.P., D.L.; British air force officer and fmr. Lord Mayor of London; b. 7 Jan. 1922; s. of Baron Huntingfield and Margaret Eleanor Crosby; m. 1st Cordelia Errington 1943 (divorced 1984); one d. (one d. deceased); m. 2nd Elizabeth Forbes 1984; one step-s. one step-d.; ed. Geelong Grammar School, Stowe School, Trinity Coll., Cambridge and Harvard; Cadet, R.N. 1939; served in Nelson, King George V, Eskimo, 55th LCA Flot., Wren, MTB 696; in command 771 Sqdn., 807 Sqdn. FAA, resigned 1949; Cambridge Univ. Air Sqdn. 1949; 601 (Co. of London) Sqdn. R.Aux.A.F. 1950–57; 3619 (Co. of Suffolk) Fighter Control Unit 1958–59, in command 1959–61; No. 1 Maritime HQ Unit 1961–63; Group Capt. 1963; Insp. R.Aux.A.F. 1963–73, Hon. Insp.-Gen. 1974–83; Hon. Air Cdre. No. 1 (Co. Hertford) Maritime HQ Unit, 1973–87; ADC to the Queen 1963–73, Gentleman Usher 1967–79; Conservative mem. European Parl. for Cleveland 1979–84, for Cleveland and Yorkshire North 1984–89; Alderman of Cordwainer Ward, City of London 1969–79; DL Greater London 1970; Sheriff, City of London 1974–75; Lord Mayor of London 1977–78; Warden, Fishmongers' Co., Prime Warden 1981; Master, Gunmakers' Co. 1977; Past Master, Guild of Air Pilots and Air Navigators; mem. Bd., Ipswich Group Hosps. 1956–62, Gov. Body British Post Graduate Medical Fed., Univ. of London 1963–71, St. Bartholomew's Hosp. Bd. of Govs. 1971–73, City and E. London Area Health Authority 1973–77; Pres. Anglo-Netherlands Soc. 1989–; Hon. Trustee, St. Bartholomew's Hosp. 1974–82; Trustee, R.A.F. Museum 1976–87, Royal Acad. Trust 1981–87; Gov. Royal Shakespeare Theatre 1974–87; Churchwarden of St. Mary-le-Bow; K.St.J. (mem. Chapter Gen.). *Leisure interests:* sailing, shooting, skiing, bad bridge. *Address:* 10 Brompton Square, London, SW3 2AA; Red House, Sudbourne, Woodbridge, Suffolk, IP12 2AT, England. *Telephone:* 0171-606 1066 (London).

VANNI, Carla, LL.D.; Italian journalist; b. 18 Feb. 1936, Leghorn; m. Vincenzo Nisivoccia; two c.; ed. Univ. of Milan; joined Mondadori publrs., working on fashion desk of Grazia magazine 1959, Head fashion desk 1964, Jt. Ed.-in-Chief 1974, Ed.-in-Chief 1978–, responsible for launch of Marie Claire magazine in Italy 1987, Publishing Dir. Marie Claire and Cento Cose-Energy 1987–, Donna Moderna 1995–; has created several new supplements of Grazia: Grazia Bricolage, Grazia Blu and Grazia Int. and introduced coverage of social problems; also Ed.-in-Chief Grazia Casa; mem. juries of several nat. and int. literary awards and many beauty competitions; Montenapoleone d'Oro (Best Journalist) 1970, The Oner (Journalist of the Year) 1987, Gullace (for coverage of women's interest issues) 1995. *Address:* c/o Grazia, Via Arnoldo Mondadori, 20090 Segrate, Milan, Italy. *Telephone:* (02) 75421. *Fax:* (02) 75422515.

VANNI D'ARCHIRAFI, Raniero; Italian diplomatist; entered diplomatic service 1956; attached to office of Italy's Perm. Rep. to EC, Brussels 1961–66; with Ministry of Foreign Affairs 1966–73; First Counsellor, Madrid 1973; Minister Plenipotentiary 1980; Prin. Pvt. Sec. to Minister of Foreign Affairs 1980; Amb. to Spain 1984–87, 1995–, to Germany 1987–90; Dir.-Gen. for Econ. Affairs 1990, for Political Affairs 1991; mem. Comm. for Institutional Questions, The Internal Market, Financial Services, Enterprise Policy, Small and Medium-sized Enterprises, Trade Services, Crafts and Tourism, EC 1993–95. *Address:* Italian Embassy, Lagasca 98, 28006 Madrid, Spain. *Telephone:* (1) 5776529. *Fax:* (1) 5757776.

VANRIET, Jan; Belgian artist; b. 21 Feb. 1948, Antwerp; m. Simone Lenaerts 1971; two s. one d.; ed. Royal Acad. of Fine Arts, Antwerp; Dir. Antwerp Acad. of Fine Arts, Hoboken 1980–; participated in São Paulo Biennale 1979, Venice Biennale 1984, Art at Olympics, Seoul 1988; works in several museums in Europe, U.S.A. and Asia; Special Prize, Art Festival, Seoul 1990. *Publications:* poetry: Staat van Beleg 1982, Geen Hond de Brood Lust 1984. *Address:* Louizastraat 22, 2000 Antwerp 1, Belgium. *Telephone:* 03 2324776; 03 2480703. *Fax:* 03 2261350.

VANSITTART, Peter, F.R.S.L.; British novelist and historian; b. 27 Aug. 1920, Bedford; s. of Edwin Vansittart and Mignon Vansittart; ed. Haileybury Coll. and Worcester Coll., Oxford; school teacher 1940–60; writer 1942–; Hon. Fellow Worcester Coll., Oxford. *Publications:* The Overseer 1948, The Game and the Ground 1955, The Friends of God 1963, The Story Teller 1968, Dictators 1973, The Death of Robin Hood 1983, Paths from a White Horse 1985, London 1994, A Safe Conduct 1995, In the Fifties 1995, In Memory of England 1998, Survival Tactics 1998. *Address:* Little Manor, Church Hill, Kersey, Ipswich, Suffolk, IP7 6DZ, England. *Telephone:* (01753) 823163.

VARDA, Agnès; French film writer and director; b. 30 May 1928, Ixelles, Belgium; d. of Eugène Jean Varda and Christiane Pasquet; m. Jacques Demy 1962 (died 1990); one s. one d.; ed. Sète, Hérault, and Univ. de Paris à la Sorbonne and Ecole du Louvre; Official Photographer, Théâtre Nat. Populaire 1951–61; reporter and photographer, film-maker 1954–; Prix Méliès 1962 (Cleo de 5 à 7), Prix Louis Delluc 1965 (Le Bonheur), David Selznick Award 1965 (Le Bonheur), Bronze Lion, Venice Festival 1964 (Salut les Cubains), Silver Bear, Berlin Festival 1965 (Le Bonheur); 1st Prize, Oberhausen (Black Panthers), Popular Univs. jury (Lions Love) 1970, Grand Prix, Taormina, Sicily 1977 (L'une chante, l'autre pas), Firenze 1981 (Mur Murs); César Award 1984 (Ulysse); Golden Lion, Best Film Venice Film Festival (Sans toit ni loi) 1985; Prix Méliès (Sans toit ni loi) 1985; L.A. Critics Best Foreign Film (Sans toït ni loi) 1985; Commdr. des Arts et des Lettres, Chevalier Légion d'honneur. *Full-length films:* La pointe-courte 1954, Cleo de 5 à 7 1961, Le bonheur 1964, Les créatures 1965, Loin du Vietnam 1967, Lions Love 1969, Nausicaa 1970, Daguerreotypes 1975, L'une chante, l'autre pas 1976, Mur Murs 1980, Documenteur (An Emotion Picture) 1981, Sans toit ni loi (Vagabond) 1985, Jane B par Agnés V 1987, Kung Fu Master 1987, Jacquot de Nantes 1990, Les demoiselles ont eu 25 ans 1992, L'univers de Jacques Demy 1993, Les Cent et Une nuits 1994. *Short-length films:* O saisons, O châteaux 1957, L'opéra-Mouffe 1958, Du côté de la côte 1958, Salut les cubains 1963, Uncle Yanco 1967, Black Panthers 1968, Réponse de femmes 1975, Plaisir d'amour en Iran 1975, Ulysse 1982, Les dites Cariatides 1984, T'as de beaux escaliers . . . tu sais 1986. *Publication:* Varda par Agnès 1994. *Address:* c/o Ciné-Tamaris, 88 rue Daguerre, 75014 Paris, France. *Telephone:* (1) 43.22.66.00. *Fax:* (1) 43.21.75.00.

VARENNIKOV, Gen. Valentin Ivanovich; Russian army officer (retd.); b. 1923, R.S.F.S.R.; ed. Frunze Mil. Acad.; mem. CPSU 1944–91; joined army 1941; active service 1941–45; Commdr. of a corps 1967–69, of a unit 1969–71; First Deputy Supreme Commdr. Soviet Forces in Germany 1971–73; Commdr. Carpathian Mil. Dist. 1973–82; First Deputy Chief of Gen. Staff 1982–91; First Deputy Head of HQ of U.S.S.R. Armed Forces 1984–91; People's Deputy of the U.S.S.R. 1989; Army Gen. 1978; arrested Aug. 1991 as an alleged accomplice in attempted coup d'état; charged with conspiracy; released 1992; on trial 1993–94, released 1994; cleared of high treason by Supreme Court after rejecting amnesty Aug. 1994; active in Communist movt.; mem. State Duma (Parl.) 1995–, Chair. Cttee. on War Veterans 1996–; mem. CP of Russian Fed. 1994–. *Address:* State Duma, Okhotny Ryad 1, Moscow, Russia. *Telephone:* (095) 292-93-60, 292-92-10.

VARFIS, Grigorios; Greek politician; b. 1927, Athens; ed. Univs. of Athens and Paris; journalist in Paris, 1952–58; on staff of OECD 1953–62; Econ. Adviser to perm. Greek del. to the EEC, Brussels 1963–74; apptd. Gen. Dir., Co-ordination Ministry, with jurisdiction over Directorate of Relations with the European Communities 1974, resgnd. Jan. 1977; contributed to econ. programme of Panhellenic Socialist Movt. (PASOK) 1979–; Co-ordination Under-Sec. and Under-Sec. at Foreign Affairs Ministry, responsible for EEC Affairs 1981–83; mem. European Parl. 1984; mem. Comm. of the European Communities (responsible for Regional Policy and Relations with European Parl.) 1985–86, for Structural Funds and Consumer Protection 1986–89. *Address:* Spefsipou 35, 10676 Athens, Greece.

VARGA, Imre; Hungarian sculptor; b. 1 Nov. 1923, Budapest; s. of Mátyás Varga and Margit Csepeli; m. Ildikó Szabó 1944; two s.; ed. Budapest Coll. of Visual Arts; Pres. FÉSZEK Artists Club; mem. American Acad. of Arts and Sciences, Académie Européenne des Arts et des Sciences, Paris; Munkácsy Prize 1969, Kossuth Prize 1973, Merited Artist 1975, Eminent Artist 1980, Herder Prize 1981; Order of the Flag 1983, Commdr., Ordre des Arts et des Lettres (France), Cavaliere dell'Ordine al Merito (Italy). *Works:* Prometheus 1965 and The Professor 1969 in Middelheim, Belgium, Madách Memorial 1968, Radnóti Memorial 1970, Partisans Memorial 1971, Lenin Memorial, Heroes Monument, Oslo 1974, plurifigural St. Stephen composition, St. Peter's Basilica, Vatican 1980, Bartók Memorial, Paris 1983, Béla Kun memorial, Budapest 1986, Raoul Wallenberg memorial 1987; perm. collection of work in Budapest; smaller sculptures: Erölltetett menet (Forced March), A la Recherche, Baudelaire kedvese (Baudelaire's Sweetheart), Páholy (Theatre box), statue of St. Stephen in Aachen Cathedral, Germany 1993, Bartók Memorial, Carrefour de l'Europe Square, Brussels 1995, Ferenc Rákóczi II, commemorative statue, Bad Kissingen, Germany 1992. *Address:* 1126 Budapest XII, Bartha-utca 1, Hungary. *Telephone:* (1) 560-278.

VARGAS LLOSA, Mario, PH.D.; Spanish/Peruvian writer; b. 28 March 1936, Arequipa, Peru; s. of Ernesto Vargas Llosa and Dora Vargas Llosa; m. 1st Julia Urquidi 1955 (divorced 1964); m. 2nd Patricia Llosa Urquidi 1965; two s. one d.; ed. Colegio Nacional San Miguel, Piura, Peru, Univ. Nacional Mayor de San Marcos, Lima, and Universidad Complutense de Madrid, Spain; journalist on local newspapers, Piura, Peru 1952, for magazines Turismo and Cultura Peruana, and for Sunday supplement of El Comercio 1955; news ed. Radio Panamericana, Lima 1955; journalist Agence-France Presse 1959; broadcaster Latin American services of Radiodiffusion Télévision Française 1959; lecturer in Latin American Literature, Queen Mary Coll., London Univ. 1967, Prof. King's Coll. 1969; trans. UNESCO 1967; Visiting Prof. Washington State Univ., U.S.A. 1968, Univ. de Puerto Rico 1969, Columbia Univ., U.S.A. 1975; Prof. Univ. of Cambridge 1977; writer-in-residence Woodrow Wilson Int. Center for Scholars, Smithsonian Inst., U.S.A. 1980; f. Movimiento Libertad political party and co-f. Frente Democrático (FREDEMO) coalition 1988; cand. for Pres. of Peru 1990; Visiting Prof. Harvard Univ., U.S.A. 1992, Princton Univ., U.S.A. 1993, Georgetown Univ., U.S.A. 1994; Pres. PEN Club Int. 1976–79; mem. Acad. Peruana de la Lengua 1977, Real Acad. Española 1994, Int. Acad. of Humanism 1996; Neil Gunn Int. Fellow, Scottish Arts Council 1986; Fellow Wissenschaftskolleg, Berlin 1991–92, Deutscher Akademischer Austauschdienst, Berlin 1997–98; Hon. Fellow Hebrew Univ., Israel 1976, Modern

Language Asscn. of America 1986, American Acad. and Inst. of Arts and Letters 1986; Hon. D.Hum.Litt (Conn. Coll., U.S.A.) 1991; Dr. h.c. of 13 universities; numerous prizes including Premio de la Crítica, Argentina 1981, Príncipe de Asturias Prize, Spain 1986, Castiglione de Sicilia Prize, Italy 1990, Miguel de Cervantes Prize, Spain 1994, Jerusalem Prize, Israel 1995; Congressional Medal of Honour, Peru 1982, Golden Palm Award, INTAR Hispanic American Arts Center, New York 1992, Pluma de Oro Award, Spain 1997, Medal and Diploma of Honour, Univ. Católica de Santa María, Arequipa, Peru 1997; Légion d'honneur, Commdr. Ordre des Arts et Lettres. *Publications include: plays:* La huída del Inca 1952, La señorita de Tacna (The Lady of Tacna) 1981, Kathie y el hipopótamo (Kathie and the Hippopotamus) 1983, La Chunga 1986, El loco de los balcones (The Madman of the Balconies) 1993; *short stories:* El desafío (The Challenge) 1957 (Revue Française Prize), Los jefes 1959 (Leopoldo Alas Prize, Spain), Los cachorros (The Cubs) 1967; *novels:* La cuidad y los perros (The Time of the Hero) 1963 (Biblioteca Breve Prize, Spain), La casa verde (The Green House) 1966 (Crítica Española Prize, Spain 1966, Premio Nacional de Novela, Peru 1967), Conversación en La Catedral (Conversation in the Cathedral) 1969, Pantaleón y las visitadoras (Captain Pantoja and the Special Service) 1973 (co-dir. of film version 1975), La tía Julia y el escribidor (Aunt Julia and the Scriptwriter) 1977 (ILLA Prize, Italy 1982), La guerra del fin del mundo (The War of The End of the World) 1981 (Pablo Iglesias Literature Prize, Spain 1982, Ritz Paris Hemingway Prize, France 1985), Historia de Mayta (The Real Life of Alejandro Mayta) 1984, ¿ Quién mató a Palomino Molero? (Who Killed Palomino Molero?) 1986, El hablador (The Storyteller) 1987 (Scanno Prize, Italy 1989), Elogio de la madrastra (In Praise of the Stepmother) 1988, Lituma en los Andes (Death in the Andes) 1993 (Planeta Prize, Spain 1993, Arzobispo Juan de San Clemente Literary Prize, Spain 1994, Antico Fattore Int. Literary Prize, Italy 1995), Los cuadernos de Don Rigoberto 1997; *anthology:* Contra viento y marea, vol. I (1962–72) 1986, vol. II (1972–83) 1986, vol. III (1983–90) 1990; *autobiography:* El pez en el agua (A Fish in the Water) 1993. *Address:* Las Magnolias 295, 6° Piso, Barranco, Lima 4, Peru. *Fax:* (14) 477 3518.

VARLEY, Baron (Life Peer), cr. 1990, of Chesterfield in the County of Derbyshire; **Eric Graham Varley;** British politician; b. 11 Aug. 1932, Poolsbrook, Derbys.; s. of Frank and Eva Varley; m. Marjorie Turner 1955; one s.; ed. Secondary Modern and Tech. Schools, and Ruskin Coll., Oxford; apprentice engineer's turner 1947–52; engineer's turner 1952–55; mining industry craftsman 1955–64; Nat. Union of Miners' Branch Sec. 1955–64; mem. Area Exec. Cttee., Derbys. 1956–64; M.P. for Chesterfield 1964–84; Asst. Govt. Whip 1967–68; Parl. Pvt. Sec. to Prime Minister 1968–69; Minister of State, Ministry of Tech. 1969–70; Chair. Trade Union Group of Labour M.P.'s 1971–74; Sec. of State for Energy 1974–75, for Industry 1975–79; Opposition Spokesman for Employment 1979–83; Treas. Labour Party 1981–83; mem. Nat. Exec. Cttee. Labour Party 1981–83; Exec. Deputy Chair. Coalite Group Jan.–Nov. 1984, Chair. and C.E.O. 1984–89; North and East Midlands Regional Dir. Lloyds Bank Group 1987–89, Midlands and N. Wales Regional Dir. 1989–91; mem. House of Lords European Communities Select Cttee. 1992–96; Dir. Ashgate Hospice Ltd. 1987–96, Cathelco Ltd. 1991–92, Laxgate Ltd. 1991–92. *Leisure interests:* gardening, reading, music, sport. *Address:* c/o House of Lords, London, SW1A 0AA, England.

VARLOOT, Denis; French engineer; b. 25 Oct. 1937, Lille; s. of Jean and Madeleine (née Boutron) Varloot; m. Marie J. Kennel 1963; two s.; ed. Lycées in Paris, Ecole Polytechnique and Ecole Nat. Supérieure des Télécommunications; Centre Nat. d'Etudes des Télécommunications 1962–68; with Direction Gén. des Télécommunications, Service des Programmes et des Etudes Economiques 1968–73, deputized for head of service 1973–75; Dir. of Telecommunications, Orléans 1975–76; Head of Telecommunications Personnel 1976–81; Dir. of Scientific and Tech. Information, Ministry of Educ. 1981–82; Dir. Libraries, Museums and Scientific and Tech. Information, Ministry of Educ. 1982–87; Special Adviser to Pres. of France-Télécom 1987, Adviser 1992–; Chair. and C.E.O. Télésystemes 1988–92; Chair. Admin. Bd. Palais de la découverte 1996–; Chevalier, Arts et Lettres, Ordre des Palmes Académiques, Officier, Légion d'honneur, Ordre nat. du Mérite. *Leisure interest:* sailing. *Address:* France Télécom, 6 Place d'Alleray, 75505 Paris Cedex 15 (Office); 14 rue Campagne Première, 75014 Paris, France (Home). *Telephone:* (01) 44.44.46.52 (Office); (01) 43 22 31 31 (Home).

VARMUS, Harold Eliot, M.A., M.D.; American microbiologist and university professor; b. 18 Dec. 1939, Oceanside, N.Y.; s. of Frank Varmus and Beatrice (Barasch) Varmus; m. Constance Louise Casey 1969; two s.; ed. Amherst Coll., Harvard Univ., Columbia Univ.; physician, Presbyterian Hosp., New York 1966–68; Clinical Assoc., N.I.H., Bethesda, Md. 1968–70; lecturer, Dept. of Microbiology, Univ. of Calif. at San Francisco 1970–72, Asst. Prof. 1972–74, Assoc. Prof. 1974–79, Prof. 1979–83, American Cancer Soc. Research Prof. 1984–93; Dir. Nat. Insts. of Health 1993–; Consultant, Chiron Corp., Emoryville, Calif.; Assoc. Ed. Cell Journal; mem. Editorial Bd. Cancer Surveys; Calif. Acad. of Sciences Scientist of the Year 1982, Lasker Foundation Award 1982 (Co-recipient), Passano Foundation Award 1983, Armand Hammer Cancer Prize 1984, Gen. Motors Alfred Sloan Award, Shubitz Cancer Prize (N.A.S.) 1984, Nobel Prize 1989; mem. American Soc. of Virology, American Soc. of Microbiology, A.A.A.S. *Publications:* (Ed.) Molecular Biology of Tumor Viruses 1982, 1985, Readings in Tumor Virology 1983. *Address:* National Institutes of Health, 1 Center Drive, Bethesda, MD 20892 (Office); 2841 29 Street, N.W., Washington, DC 20008, U.S.A. (Home).

VARSZEGI, Gabor; Hungarian/American business executive and musician; bass guitarist with Gemini 1970s; emigrated to USA 1980; diamond trader, N.Y.; owner photograph developing business 1985; buyer of numerous cos. which were privatized by the state (in Hungary); C.E.O. Fotex (retailing group). *Address:* Fotex, Nagy Jeno Utch 12, 1126 Budapest, Hungary.

VARTY, Keith, M.A.; British couturier and business executive; b. 9 Jan. 1952, Darlington; s. of Thomas Varty and Dorothy Craggs; ed. Hurworth Co. School, Queen Elizabeth Grammar School, Middlesbrough School of Art, St. Martins Coll. of Art and R.C.A.; Asst. Designer Dorothy Bis, Paris 1975–79, Design Consultant Geoffrey Beene, New York 1975–79; Designer 'Complice' Collection 1979–80, Byblos, Ancona, Italy and U.S.A. 1980–; Chair. and Founder United S.R.L., Milan 1986–; Visiting Lecturer R.C.A. 1986–. *Leisure interests:* travel, bull terrier breeding, Italian opera, collecting antiques. *Address:* Piazza Plebiscito 55, Ancona; Bosco di San Francesco N°6, Sirolo; Via Vallone, Monte Conero, Sirolo, Italy. *Telephone:* (071) 203790; (071) 936 225; (071) 936 203.

VÁSÁRY, Tamás; Hungarian concert pianist and conductor; b. 11 Aug. 1933; s. of Jozsef and Elizabeth (Baltazàr) Vasary; m. Ildiko Kovacs 1967; ed. Franz Liszt Univ. of Music, Budapest under Lajos Hernadi, Jozsef Gat and Zoltan Kodály; first solo performance at eight years; studied at Franz Liszt Acad. until 1954; remained at Liszt Ferenc Music Acad. to teach theory; recitals in Leningrad, Moscow and Warsaw; settled in Switzerland 1958; London début 1961, New York 1962; début as conductor in Menton Festival of Music 1971; has since appeared in Europe, S. Africa, S. America, U.S.A., Canada, India, Thailand, Hong Kong, Australia, Japan and Mexico; Jt. Music Dir. Northern Sinfonia, Newcastle 1979–; Musical Dir. Bournemouth Sinfonietta 1988–, Hungarian Radio Orchestra 1993–; records for Deutsche Grammophon; Liszt Prizes: Queen Elizabeth (Belgium), Marguerite Longue (Paris); Chopin Prizes: Int. Competition, Warsaw, Int. Competition, Brazil; Bach and Paderewski Medals (London), Kossuth Prize, Presidential Gold Medal 1998. *Principal recordings:* three records of works of F. Liszt; eight of works of Chopin, three of works of Rachmaninoff, one each of works of Debussy and Mozart; all symphonies and overtures of Beethoven, Schubert and Schumann 1997–98. *Leisure interest:* writing fiction. *Address:* 9 Village Road, London, N.3, England; 1181 Budapest, Kossuth Lajos u. 106, Hungary. *Telephone:* 0181-346 2381 (London); (1) 328-8326 (Budapest). *Fax:* (1) 328-8910 (Budapest)..

VASILE, Radu, PH.D.; Romanian politician and academic; b. 10 Oct. 1942, Sibiu; m. Mariuca Vasile; two s. one d; ed. Univ. of Bucharest; historian The Village Museum, Bucharest 1967–69; scientific researcher History Inst. Nicolae Iorga, Romanian Acad. 1969–72; asst. lecturer Acad. of Econ. Studies, Bucharest 1972; Asst. Prof., Vice-Dean, Faculty of Trade, Acad. of Econ. Studies, Bucharest 1990, Prof. 1993; Vice-Pres. Romanian Senate 1996–98, Head Romanian Del. to Parl. Ass. of Council of Europe 1996–98; Vice-Pres. Parl. Ass. of Council of Europe 1997–98; Dir. Dreptatea (daily newspaper) 1992–94; mem. Christian Democratic Nat. Peasant Party CDNPP 1990–, Sec. Gen. 1996–98, Pres. Senate Parl. Group 1996–98; Prime Minister of Romania April 1998–. *Publications:* World Economy; Avenues and Stages of Modernization 1987, Currency and Economy 1994, Currency and Fiscal Policy 1995, From the Iron Century to the Second World War 1998. *Leisure interests:* poetry, satirical literature, chess, football. *Address:* Office of the Prime Minister, 71201 Bucharest, Piaţa Victoriei 1, Romania. *Telephone:* (1) 143400. *Fax:* (1) 592018.

VASILIU, Emanuel, PH.D.; Romanian linguist; b. 7 Sept. 1929, Chişinău; s. of Nicolae and Gabriela Vasiliu; m. Maria-Laura Vasiliu 1952; ed. Univ. of Bucharest; Assoc. Prof. Univ. of Bucharest 1968, Prof. 1970; Visiting Prof. Univ. of Chicago 1964–65, 1970–71, of Boston 1971; Dean Faculty of Letters, Univ. of Bucharest 1990–92; Dir. "Al. Rosetti" Inst. of Phonetics and Dialectology 1990–; mem. Romanian Acad. 1992; mem. Soc. Linguistica Europaea, Soc. Européenne de Culture, Romanian Linguistic Soc. (SRL), Romanian Soc. of Romance Linguistics (SRLR), Int. Cttee. of Linguists 1977–87; mem. editorial bd. Studii şi cercetări lingvistice (Linguistic Studies and Researches), Revue roumaine de linguistique, Fonetică şi dialectologie (Phonetics and Dialectology), Cahiers de linguistique théorique et appliquée. *Publications:* Fonologia limbii române (Romanian Phonology) 1965, Fonologia istorică a dialectelor dacoromâne (Historical Phonology of Daco-Romanian Dialects) 1968, Elemente de teorie semantică a limbilor naturale (Some Principles of a Semantic Theory of Natural Languages) 1970, Outline of a Semantic Theory of Kernel Sentences 1972, Preliminarii logice la semantica frazei (Logic Preliminaries to Compound Sentence Semantics) 1978, Scrierea limbii române în raport cu fonetica şi fonologia (Romanian Writing in relation to Phonetics and Phonology) 1979, Sens, adevăr analitic, cunoaştere (Meaning, Analytic Truth and Knowledge) 1984, Introducere în teoria textului (Introduction to Textual Theory) 1990, Introducere în teoria limbii (Introduction to the Theory of Language) 1992, Elemente de filosofie a limbajului (Elements of Language Philosophy) 1995, The Transformational Syntax of Romanian (with Sanda Golopentia-Eretescu) 1972, Limba Română în Secolele al XII-lea- al XV-lea. Fonetică—Fonologie—Gramatică (Romanian in the XII–XV Centuries. Phonetics—Phonology—Grammar) (with Liliana Ionescu-Ruxăndoiu) 1986; contrib. to several works on Romanian language. *Address:* Institutul de Fonetică şi Dialectologie "Al. Rosetti",

Str. 13 Septembrie 13, 76117 Bucharest (Office); Intrarea Lucaci 3, 74111 Bucharest, Romania (Home). *Telephone:* 320-63-37 (Home).

VASILYEV, Anatoli Aleksandrovich; Russian theatre director; b. 4 May 1942, Danilovka, Penza Region; m. Nadezhda Kalinina; one d.; ed. Rostov State Univ., State Inst. of Dramatic Art, Moscow; Founder and Dir. Theatre Co. School of Dramatic Art, Moscow 1987; staged all works by Pirandello; numerous tours in Europe 1985–; Nuova Realita Europea Prize, Taormina, Italy 1990, Pirandello Prize, Agrigento, Italy 1992, Stanislavsky Fund Prize 1995, Stanislavsky Prize of Russian Fed. 1998; Chevalier Ordre des Arts et des Lettres 1989, Honoured Art Worker of Russia 1993. *Productions include:* Vassa Zheleznova 1978, Grown-up Daughter of a Young Man (V. Slavkin) 1979, Cerceau (V. Slavkin) 1985, Six Characters in Search of an Author (Pirandello) 1987, Masquerade (Lermontov) at Comédie Française 1992, Uncle's Dream (Dostoyevsky), Budapest 1994, The Lamentation of Jeremiah (Martynov) 1996 (Golden Mask Prize of Russian Fed. 1997), The Queen of Spades (Tchaikovsky), German Nat. Theatre, Weimar 1996, Don Juan (Pushkin) 1998. *Address:* School of Dramatic Art, Povarskaya 20, Moscow, Russia. *Telephone:* (095) 291-50-39 (Office); 299-91-09 (Home). *Fax:* (095) 291-86-42.

VASILYEV, Boris Lvovich; Russian writer, dramatist and essayist; b. 21 May 1924, Smolensk; m. Zorya Albertovna Vasilyeva; two adopted s.; served in Red Army in World War II, seriously wounded; ed., then engineer with Acad. of Armoured Troops 1943–54; U.S.S.R. People's Deputy 1989–91; mem. U.S.S.R. Supreme Soviet 1991; U.S.S.R. State Prize 1975; K. Simonov Prize; Dovzhenko Gold Medal. *Publications include:* Dawns are Quiet Here 1969, Do Not Shoot the White Swans 1975, My Horses are Flying 1983, And Tomorrow was War (novel) 1984, The Burning Bush 1987, Regards from Baba Vera 1988, Absent from the Casulty List (novel) 1988, There was Evening, There was Morning 1989, The Short Castling 1989, The Carnival (novel) 1990, The House Built by the Old Man 1991, Kahunk and Prince Prophetic Oleg (novel) 1996, Two Bananas in one Peel (novel) 1996; many screenplays. *Leisure interests:* gardening, history, English literature. *Address:* Chasovaya Str. 58, Apt. 40, 125319 Moscow, Russia. *Telephone:* (095) 152-99-01.

VASILYEV, Sergey Aleksandrovich, DR. ECON.; Russian politician; b. 8 June 1957, Leningrad; m.; one c.; ed. Leningrad State Univ.; Head Research Lab. Leningrad Inst. of Finance and Econs.; took part in activities of Moscow-Leningrad group of young economists 1983–; mem. Leningrad Political Club Perestroika 1986; deputy Leningrad City Soviet 1990; Head Working Cttee. of Econ. Reforms, Russian Govt. 1991–; Deputy Minister of Econs. Russian Fed.; First Deputy Head Office of Russian Govt. 1997–98. *Address:* House of Government, Krasnopresnenskaya nab. 2, 103274 Moscow, Russia (Office). *Telephone:* (095) 205 44 14 (Office).

VASILYEV, Vladimir Viktorovich; Russian ballet dancer; b. 18 April 1940, Moscow; m. Yekaterina Maksimova; ed. Bolshoi Theatre Ballet School; with Bolshoi Theatre Ballet 1958–88; guest appearances with Kirov ballet, Paris 1988; f. Kremlin Ballet 1990; Man. and Artistic Dir. Bolshoi Theatre 1995–; People's Artist of the R.S.F.S.R. 1969; Lenin Prize 1970, Leninist Komsomol Prize 1968, Nijinsky Prize 1964, Grand Prix at Varna Int. Competition 1964, People's Artist of U.S.S.R. 1973. *Principal roles:* The Prince (Nutcracker), Pan (Valpurgis Night), The Poet (Chopiniana), Danila (Stone Flower), Prince Charming (Cinderella), Batyr (Shurale), Andrei (A Page of Life), Basil (Don Quixote), Albert (Giselle), Frondoso (Laurencia), Medjnun (Leili and Medjnun); also appeared in The Humpbacked Horse, Spartacus, Petrushka and Icarus 1978; dir. (ballets) Anyuta, Macbeth, Icarus, These Charming Sounds, Romeo and Juliet, Don Quixote, Cinderella, new version of Swan Lake and Giselle, Bolshoi Theatre 1996–97; (opera) Così fan tutte (with N. Kasatkina) 1978. *Address:* State Academic Bolshoi Theatre, Teatralnaya pl. 1, Moscow, Russia. *Telephone:* (095) 292-05-93 (Office); 224-02-27 (Home).

VASILYEVA, Larisa Nikolayevna; Russian poet and writer; b. 23 Nov. 1935, Kharkov, Ukraine; d. of Nikolai Alekseyevich and Yekaterina Vasilievna Kucherenko; m. Oleg Vasiliyev 1957; one s.; ed. Moscow Univ.; started publishing 1957; first collection of verse 1966; Sec. of Moscow Br. of Russian Union of Writers; Pres. Fed. of Russian Women Writers 1989–, Int. Publishing League Atlantida 1992–; Moscow Komsomol Prize 1971. *Publications include: Poetry:* Fire-fly 1969, The Swan 1970, Blue Twilight 1970, Encounter 1974, A Rainbow of Snow 1974, Meadows 1975, Fire in the Window 1978, Russian Names 1980, Foliage 1980, Fireflower 1981, Selected Poetry 1981, Grove 1984, Mirror 1985, Moskoverechie 1985, Lantern 1985, Waiting For You In The Sky 1986, A Strange Virtue 1991. *Stories, prose works:* Albion and the Secret of Time 1978, Novel About My Father 1983, Cloud of Fire 1988, Selected Works (2 vols.) 1989, The Kremlin Wives 1992, The Kremlin Children 1996. *Address:* Usievicha str. 8, Apt. 86, 125319 Moscow, Russia. *Telephone:* (095) 155-7486.

VASNETSOV, Andrei Vladimirovich; Russian painter; b. 24 Feb. 1924, Moscow; ed. Moscow Inst. of Applied Arts; Sec. U.S.S.R. Union of Artists 1983–88, Chair. 1988–92; First Sec. of Bd. R.S.F.S.R. Union of Artists 1987–88; mem. Presidium, Russian Acad. of Fine Arts; author of monumental panels for Soviet pavilions at exhbns. in Leipzig 1953, New York 1957, Brussels 1958, participated in decorating maj. architectural edifices in Moscow; one-man exhbns. 1962–; Hon. Pres. Vasnetsovs' Foundation; R.S.F.S.R. People's Deputy 1989–91; People's Artist of Russia, U.S.S.R. State Prize 1979, Pres.'s Prize, Russian Fed. *Address:* Russian Academy of Fine Arts, Prechistenka str. 21, 119034 Moscow, Russia (Office). *Telephone:* (095) 201-40-31.

VASSANJI, Moyez G., PH.D.; Canadian fiction writer; b. 30 May 1950, Nairobi, Kenya; s. of Gulamhussein V. Nanji and Daulatkhanu V. Nanji; m. Nurjehan Vassanji (née Aziz); two s.; ed. Mass. Inst. of Tech. and Univ. of Pennsylvania; grew up in Dar-es-Salaam, Tanzania; Post-doctoral Fellow Atomic Energy of Canada Ltd. 1978–80; Research Assoc. Univ. of Toronto 1980–89; first novel published 1989, full-time writer 1989–; Writer-in-Residence Int. Writing Program, Univ. of Ia. 1989; Commonwealth (Regional) Prize 1990, Giller Prize for Best Novel (Canada) 1994, Harbour Front Literary Award 1994, Bressani Award 1994. *Publications:* The Gunny Sack (novel), No New Land (novel) 1991, Uhuru Street (short stories) 1992, The Book of Secrets (novel) 1994. *Address:* 39 Woburn Avenue, Toronto, M5M 1K5, Canada.

VASSILIKOS, Vassilis; Greek author; b. 18 Nov. 1934, Kavala; m. Vasso Papantoniou 1985; one d.; ed. Univ. of Salonika Law School and School of Radio and Television, New York; Dir.-Gen. of Greek TV (public) 1981–85; presenter of weekly TV show on books; Amb. to UNESCO 1996–; Officier, Ordre des Arts et des Lettres. *Publications* (in English trans.): The Plant, The Well, The Angel 1963, Z– 1968, The Harpoon Gun 1972, Outside the Walls 1973, The Photographs 1974, The Monarch 1976, . . . And Dreams Are Dreams 1996; some 80 titles in Greek; translations into many languages (15 French titles). *Address:* 27 rue Galilée, 75116 Paris, France. *Telephone:* (1) 45-68-30-64.

VASSILIOU, George Vassos, D.ECON.; Cypriot politician and consulting company executive; b. 20 May 1931, Famagusta; s. of Vasos Vassiliou and Sophia Othonos (Yiavopoulou) Vassiliou; m. Androulla Georgiadou 1966; one s. two d.; ed. Univs. of Geneva, Vienna, Budapest; Market Researcher Reed Paper Group, London 1960–62; f., Chair., Man. Dir. Middle E. Marketing Research Bureau 1962–; f. Middle E. Marketing Research and Consulting Group, Cyprus 1962, Chair. and C.E.O. 1962–; Founder and Prin. Middle E. Centre for Man. Studies 1984–; Pres. of Cyprus 1988–93; Leader, United Democrats Movt. 1993–; mem. Parl.; fmr. Vice-Pres. Nicosia Chamber of Commerce; Dir. Bank of Cyprus, Synek Fashionwear, Bellfoods, Village Hotel; mem. Bd. Dirs. Cyprus State Fair Authority 1970–78; Visiting Prof., Cranfield School of Man.; Chair. World Inst. For Devt. Econ. Research, UN Univ.; Chair. Foundation for Information, Amsterdam; mem. InterAction Council, Int. Advisory Cttee., Centre for European Policy Research, Brussels; Fellow Royal Econ. Soc., Royal Statistical Soc.; mem. European Soc. of Opinion and Marketing Research, Market Research Soc., Industrial Market Research, Market Research Asscn.; Grand Cross, Légion d'honneur, Grand Cross of Order of the Saviour, Greece, Grand Cross of the Holy Sepulchre, Greek Orthodox Patriarchate of Jerusalem, Standard (Flag) Order, Hungary, and other distinctions, awards and decorations. *Publications:* Marketing in the Middle East 1980, Marketing Handbook 1986; articles in various publs. *Leisure interests:* listening to music, reading, swimming, body-exercise. *Address:* P.O. Box 874, 21 Academiou Avenue, Aglandjia, Nicosia, Cyprus.

VASTAGH, Pál, PH.D.; Hungarian politician and jurist; b. 23 September 1946; m. Erzsébet Fenyvesi; one s. two d.; ed. József Attila Univ. of Arts and Sciences, Szeged; asst. lecturer, later lecturer, then sr. lecturer Dept. of Theory of State and Law, József Attila Univ. of Arts and Sciences 1988–89, Dean 1989; mem. of Presidium of Hungarian Socialist Party (HSP) 1989; mem. Parl. 1990–; mem. Parl.'s Cttee. on Constitutional Affairs, Codification and Justice Cttee. on European Integration Affairs; Minister of Justice 1994–98; Deputy Leader of Socialist faction. *Publications:* articles in nat. newspapers and professional periodicals. *Leisure interests:* reading, hiking, travelling, soccer. *Address:* Képviselői Irodaház, 1358 Budapest, Széchenyi Rep. 19, Hungary. *Telephone:* (1) 268-5512.

VATOLIN, Nikolay Anatolevich; Russian metallurgist; b. 13 Nov. 1926; m.; one s.; ed. Urals Polytech. Inst.; scientific researcher, scientific sec., Head of Lab., Dir. U.S.S.R. (now Russian) Acad. of Sciences Inst. of Metallurgy (Urals Branch) 1950–98, Adviser Russian Acad. of Sciences 1998–; mem. CPSU 1952–91; Prof. at Urals Mining-Geological Acad. 1973–; Corresp. mem. of U.S.S.R. (now Russian) Acad. of Sciences 1970–81, mem. 1981; U.S.S.R. State Prize 1982, 1991, Kurnakow Gold Medal, Russian Acad. of Sciences 1995, Govt. Prize, Russian Fed. 1997, Dernidov's Prize 1997. *Publications:* (co-author): Physico-chemical Foundations of Steel Hot Leading 1977, Oxidation of Vanadium Slags 1978, Interparticle Interaction in Molten Metals 1979, Diffraction Studies of High Temperature Melts 1980, Computerization of Thermodynamic Calculations of Metallurgical Processes 1982, Electrical Properties of Oxide Melts 1984, Hydrometallurgy of Ferropowders 1984, Computer Simulation of Amorphous Metals 1985, Vanadium Slags 1988, Thermodynamic Modelling in High Temperature Inorganic Systems 1994. *Address:* Institute of Metallurgy, Russian Academy of Sciences, 101 Amundsen Street, 620016 Yekaterinburg, Russia. *Telephone:* (3432) 28-53-12 (Office); 59-49-25 (Home).

VAUGHAN, David Arthur John, Q.C., F.R.S.A.; British lawyer; b. 24 Aug. 1938; s. of late Capt. F.H.M. Vaughan and J.M. Vaughan; m. 1st 1967 (divorced); m. 2nd Leslie A.F. Irwin 1985; one s. one d.; ed. Eton Coll. and Trinity Coll. Cambridge; called to Bar, Inner Temple 1962, Bencher 1988; mem. Bar Council 1968–72, 1984–86, Bar Cttee. 1987–88; mem. Int. Relations Cttee. of Bar Council 1968–86, Bar/Law Soc. Working Party on EEC (now EC) Competition Law 1977– (Chair. 1978–88), U.K. Del. to Consultative Cttee. of Bars and Law Socs. of the EC 1978–81, and other cttees. etc.; Chair. EC Section, Union Int. des Advocats 1987–91; Chair. Editorial Bd. European Law Reports; Visiting Prof. of Law Durham Univ. 1989–; mem. Advisory Bd., Centre for European Legal Studies, Cambridge Univ. 1991–; mem. Council of Man., British Inst. of Int. and Comparative Law 1992–; mem. Editorial Advisory Bd. European Business Law Review 1998–; Fellow Soc. for Advanced Legal Studies 1998; Bronze Medal, Bar of Bordeaux 1985. *Publications:* co-ordinating ed. vols. on EC Law, Halsbury's Laws of England 1986; Vaughan on the Law of the European Communities (ed.) 1986–97, consultant ed. European Court Practice 1993, Current EC Legal Development series. *Leisure interests:* fishing, tennis. *Address:* 7–8 Essex Street, London, WC2R 3LD, England (Home). *Telephone:* 0171-379 3550. *Fax:* 0171-379 3558.

VAUTRIN, Jean (Jean Herman); French novelist and film director; b. 17 May 1933, Pagny sur-Moselle, Meurthe-et-Moselle; s. of Raymond Herman and Maria Schneider; m. 2nd Anne Doat; two s. one d. (and one s. from first m.); ed. Lycée Jacques-Amyot, Auxerre, Institut des hautes études cinématographiques; Lecturer in French Literature, Univ. of Bombay 1955; Asst. to Roberto Rossellini 1955–57, to Jacques Rivette 1958, to Vincente Minelli 1958; Asst. at ORTF, Dir., Armed Forces film div. 1959–61; Asst. to Jean Cayrol, then made advertising films and shorts 1958–63, full-length films 1963–; Dir. Julliard 1990–; began writing career 1973; films (made under name Jean Herman) include: Voyage en Boscavie 1958 (Prix Emile Cohl), Actua-Tilt 1960 (Grand Prix, Festival Int. de Tours, Critics' Prize, Oberhausen), La Quille 1961 (Jury's Special Prize, Venice Festival), Le Dimanche de la Vie 1965 (Marilyn Monroe Prize), Garde à vue 1981 (Prix de l'Académie française); several films for television; Ed. Atelier Julliard series; Conseiller Régional d'Aquitaine; Chevalier Légion d'honneur, Officier du Mérite, Officier des Arts et des Lettres. *Publications:* (under name of Jean Vautrin) include: A bulletins rouges 1973, Billy-Ze-Kick 1974, Bloody Mary 1979 (Prix Mystère de la Critique), Canicule 1982, Patchwork 1984 (Prix des Deux-Magots), Baby Boom 1985 (Prix Goncourt de la Nouvelle), La Vie Ripolin 1986 (Grand Prix du Roman de la Société des gens de lettres), Un grand pas vers le Bon Dieu 1989 (Prix Goncourt), 18 Tentatives pour devenir un saint 1989; (with Dan Franck): La Dame de Berlin 1988, Le Temps des cerises 1991, Romans Noirs 1991, Courage, chacun 1992, Les Noces de Guernica (jtly.) 1994, Symphonie-Grabuge 1994 (Prix Populiste); Mademoiselle Chat (jtly.) 1996, Jamais comme avant (co-author) 1996, Le Roi des ordures 1997, Un Monsieur bien mis 1997, Le cri du peuple. *Leisure interest:* drawing cartoons. *Address:* c/o Editions Grasset, 61 rue des Saints-Pères, 75007 Paris; 33730 Uzeste, France. *Telephone:* (5) 56.25.88.40 (Uzeste). *Fax:* (5) 56.25.87.67 (Uzeste).

VAUZELLE, Michel Marie; French politician and lawyer; b. 15 August 1944, Montelimar, Drome; s. of Fernand Vauzelle and Marine Faure; m. Sylvie Fauvet 1980; two s. one d.; ed. Collège St-Joseph, Lyon, Faculty of Law, Paris; barrister 1968; Chargé de mission Prime Minister's Office 1969–72; mem. Finance Section Econ. and Social Council 1972–73; town councillor, Arles 1983–95; Nat. Del. of Socialist Party Council of Civil Liberties 1978–81; Spokesman for the President of the Republic 1981–86; Préfet hors cadre 1985, Socialist Deputy for Bouches-du-Rhône 1986–92, 1997–; Pres. Comm. for Foreign Affairs Nat. Assembly 1989–92; Minister of Justice and Keeper of the Seals 1992–93; Pres. Nat. School of Photography 1982–86; Vice-Pres. Gen. Council Bouches du Rhône 1992–97; Mayor of Arles 1995–98; Pres. Regional Council Provence-Alpes-Côte d'Azur 1998–. *Publication:* Éloge de Daniel Manin, avocat veritien 1978. *Leisure interest:* riding. *Address:* Assemblée nationale, 75355 Paris; Mairie, 13200 Arles; Hôtel de la Région, 27 place Jules Guesde, 13481 Marseille cedex 20, France.

VÁVRA, Otakar; Czech scriptwriter and film director (retd.); b. 28 Feb. 1911, Hradec Králové; s. of Alois Vávra and Marie Vávrová; m. 1st Helena Vávrová 1946 (deceased); m. 2nd Jitka Němcová 1997; one s.; ed. Czech Tech. Coll.; scriptwriter, dir. Moldavia-film, Elektafilm, Lucernafilm companies 1931–45; scriptwriter, dir. Barrandov Film Studios, Prague 1945–; art team man. Barrandov Film Studios, Prague 1947–51; teacher, Film Faculty, Acad. of Music and Dramatic Arts, Prague 1949–51, Head, Film and Television direction dept. 1956–70, Prof. 1963–; mem. collective man. bd., Barrandov Film Studios, Prague 1951–54; art team man. Barrandov Film Studios, Prague 1954–56; Chair. feature film section, Union of Czechoslovak Film and Television Artists 1965; mem. Cen. Cttee., Union of Czechoslovak Film and Television Artists 1966–70; Pro-Rector Acad. of Music and Dramatic Arts, Prague 1967–70; scriptwriter and dir. of short films Light Penetrates Darkness 1931, We Live in Prague 1934, November 1935; *author and co-author of films:* The Eleventh Commandment, Maryša 1935, The Lane in Paradise, A Camel through a Needle's Eye 1936, Guard No. 47, Morality above All 1937; Dir.: Gaudeamus igitur, Virginity 1937, The Guild of the Maids of Kutná Hora 1938, Humoresque 1939, The House of Magic 1939, The Enchanted Masqued Lover, The Girl in Blue, The Mistress in Disguise, Dr. Hegl's Patient, The May Tale 1940, The Turbine 1941, Come Right Back 1942, Happy Journey 1942, Rozina the Bastard 1945, The Mischievous Bachelor 1946, Presentiment 1947, Krakatit 1948, The Silent Barricade 1949, Deployment 1952, Jan Hus 1955, A Hussite Warrior 1956, Against All 1957, Citizen Brych 1958, The First Rescue Party 1959, The Curfew 1960, August Sunday 1960, The Night Guest 1961, The Burning Heart 1962, The Golden Queening 1965, Romance for a Bugle 1966, 13 Chamber 1968, Witch-Hunt 1969, The Days of Betrayal 1973, Sokolovo 1974, The Liberation of Prague 1977, A Story of Love and Honour 1977, The Dark Sun 1980, Jan Amos Commenius 1982, Comedian 1983, Oldřich a Božena 1984, Veronika 1985, Temptation Catherine, Chief Witness 1985–87, Till 1987, Europe was Waltzing 1989; directed Genus 1996; written 89 film scripts and dir. 46 films; Czechoslovak Film Prize 1937, 1938, Nat. Prize 1941, Czech Land Prize 1948, State Prize 1949, Artist of Merit 1955, Order of Labour 1961, State Prize of Klement Gottwald 1968, Nat. Artist 1968, Prize of Antonín Zápotocký 1973, State Prize of Klement Gottwald 1977, Order of Repub. 1981 and various other awards. *Publication:* Strange Life of the Film Director 1996. *Address:* Academy of Music and Dramatic Arts, Faculty of Film and TV, Smetanovo nábřezí 2, 11000 Prague 1, Czech Republic.

VÄYRYNEN, Paavo Matti, D.POL.SC.; Finnish politician; b. 2 Sept. 1946, Keminmaa; s. of Juho Eemeli and Anna Liisa (Kaijankoski) Väyrynen; m. Vuokko Kaarina Tervonen 1968; one s. two d.; M.P. 1970–; Political Sec. to Prime Minister 1970–71; Vice-Chair. Centre Party 1972–80, Chair. 1980; mem. Nordic Council 1972–75; Minister of Educ. 1975–76, of Labour 1976–77; Minister for Foreign Affairs 1977–82, 1991–93; Chair. Supervisory Bd. Rautaruukki Oy 1994–. *Publications:* Köyhän asialla (Speaking for the Poor) 1971, On muutoksen aika (This is a Time of Change) 1974, Kansallisia kysymyksiä 1981. *Address:* Keskustapuolue (KP), Pursimiehenkatu 15, 00150 Helsinki, Finland.

VEALE, Sir Alan John Ralph, Kt., F.ENG.; British engineer; b. 2 Feb. 1920, Exeter; s. of Leslie Henry Veale and Eleanor Veale; m. Muriel Edwards 1946; two s.; ed. Exeter School, Manchester Coll. of Tech. (now UMIST), London Business School; Dir. and Gen. Man. A.E.I. Motor and Control Group 1966–68; Man. Dir. G.E.C. Diesels Ltd. 1968–70, G.E.C. Power Eng. Ltd. 1970–85, Dir. G.E.C. PLC 1973–85; Chair. Rossmore Warwick Ltd. 1987–89, R.F.S. Industries Ltd. 1987–92, Exeter Enterprise Ltd. 1989–97; Dir. Lloyds Register Quality Assurance Ltd. 1986–, The Throgmorton Trust 1986–91; Hon. D.Sc. (Salford) 1984. *Leisure interests:* sailing, walking. *Address:* 41 Northumberland Road, Leamington Spa, Warwicks., CV32 6HF, England. *Telephone:* (01926) 424349.

VEASEY, Josephine, C.B.E.; British (mezzo-soprano) opera singer (retd.) and teacher; b. 10 July 1930, London; m. Ande Anderson 1951 (divorced 1969); one s. one d.; mem. chorus Covent Garden Opera Company 1948–50, returned as soloist 1955; prin. mezzo-soprano, Royal Opera House, Covent Garden; has sung every major mezzo-soprano role in repertory; many foreign engagements have included Salzburg Festival, La Scala, Milan, Metropolitan Opera House, New York, and Paris Opera; has made recordings with Karajan, Solti, Bernstein and Colin Davis; Prof. Royal Acad. of Music 1982–83; Vocal consultant, English Nat. Opera 1985–94; Hon. R.A.M. *Address:* 5 Meadow View, Whitchurch, Hants., RG28 7BL, England. *Telephone:* (01256) 896813.

VEBER, Francis Paul; French film screenplay writer and director; b. 28 July 1937, Neuilly; s. of Pierre Gilles Veber and Catherine Veber (née Agadjaniantz); m. Françoise Marie Ehrenpreis 1964; two s.; ed. Paris Univ. of Science, Paris Medical School; began career as journalist, also wrote short stories, stand-up comedy material and theatre plays; wrote first film screenplay 1969; directed first film, Le Jouet, 1976; first American film, Three Fugitives 1989; stage play Le Dîner des Cons 1993 (film The Dinner Game 1997); Pres. EFVE Films 1976, Escape Film Production Co. 1988; mem. Bd. dirs. EuroDisney 1988; Chevalier, Légion d'honneur, Officier des Arts et des Lettres. *Publications:* Tall Blond Man with One Black Shoe 1972, L'Emmerdeur 1973, Le Magnifique 1973, Le Jouet 1976, La Cage aux Folles (adaptation) 1978, La Chèvre 1981, Les Compères 1983, Les Fugitifs 1986, Le Jaguar 1996, Le Dîner des Cons 1998. *Leisure interests:* tennis, swimming. *Address:* Creative Artists Agency, 9830 Wilshire Boulevard, Beverly Hills, CA 90210, U.S.A. *Telephone:* (310) 288 4545.

VECSEI, Eva Hollo, B.ARCH., F.R.A.I.C.; Canadian/Hungarian architect; b. 21 Aug. 1930, Vienna, Austria; m. André Vecsei 1952; one s. one d.; ed. School of Architecture, Univ. of Tech. Sciences, Budapest; Assoc. Prof., School of Architecture, Univ. of Budapest, designer of various public bldgs. and winner of housing competition, Budapest 1952–56; Assoc., ARCOP Architects, Montreal, Canada 1958–71; Assoc. of D. Dimakopoulos, architect, Montreal 1971–73; in pvt. practice, Eva Vecsei, architect 1973–84, in partnership with husband, Vecsei Architectes 1984–; *major projects include:* design and execution La Cité 7-acre redevelopment project, Montreal 1973–76, commercial and financial centre, Karachi, Pakistan, drama faculty and experimental theatre, Sainte-Thérèse, Canada, Inter-Municipal Library and Recreational Centre, Dollard-des-Ormeaux, Canada, new elementary school and gymnasium, Montreal, Residence Montefiore, Montreal; mem. Nat. Capital Comm. Advisory Cttee. on Design 1982–87; juror for several architectural competitions; Hon. Fellow American Inst. of Architects; lecture tour in China 1984; exhbn. Int. Union of Women Architects, Paris 1978; Award of Excellence, The Canadian Architect, for office bldg. McGill Coll. Ave., Montreal, Prix Orange for renovation of Passage du Musée, Montreal. *Publications:* numerous articles. *Address:* Vecsei Architectes, 1425 rue du Fort, Montreal, Quebec, H3H 2C2, Canada (Office).

VEGA DE SEOANE AZPILICUETA, Javier; Spanish mining engineer; b. 13 Sept. 1947, San Sebastián; s. of Joaquín Vega de Seoane and Rosa Azpilicueta; m. Mercedes Pérez de Villaamil Lapiedra 1970; two s. one d.; ed. Escuela Técnica Superior de Ingenieros de Minas, Madrid and Glasgow

Business School, Scotland; Asst. Production Dir., Fundiciones del Estanda S.A. 1972–75; Asst. to C.E.O., Leyland Ibérica S.A. 1975–77; Gen. Man. SKF Española S.A. 1977–83, Pres. and C.E.O. 1983–84; Gen. Man. Instituto Nacional de Industria 1984–. *Leisure interests:* golf, squash, scuba diving.

VÉGH VILLEGAS, Alejandro; Uruguayan politician and industrial engineer; b. 22 Sept. 1928; ed. Escuela de Ingeniería de Montevideo, Univ. of Harvard; Prof. Escuela de Ingeniería, Montevideo; Prof. Univ. Nacional de Buenos Aires; consultant in power economy in Venezuela; Planning Adviser, Hidronor S.A., Argentina; Adviser, Planning Ministry of Brazil; Consultant of IDB, OAS, ECLA and IBRD; Under-Sec. of State, Ministry of Industry and Trade 1967; Dir. Planning and Budget Office 1968; Minister of Finance 1974–76, of Econ. and Finance 1983–85; mem. Council of State 1976–83; Amb. to U.S.A. 1982–83; Exec. Dir. IMF 1990–93. *Address:* c/o Ministry of Finance, Colonia 1089, 3° Montevideo, Uruguay.

VEIGA, Carlos Alberto Wahnon de Carvalho, PH.D.; Cape Verde politician and lawyer; Prime Minister of Interim Govt. Jan. 1991, officially inaugurated April 1991–, also with responsibility for Defence; Chair. Movimento para Democracia (MPD). *Address:* Office of the Prime Minister, Palácio do Governo, Várzea CP 16, Praia, Santiago, Cape Verde. *Telephone:* 61-04-05. *Fax:* 61-30-99.

VEIL, Simone, L. EN D.; French politician and fmr. lawyer; b. 13 July 1927, Nice; d. of André Jacob and Yvonne Steinmetz; m. Antoine Veil 1946; three s.; ed. Inst. d'Etudes Politiques de Paris; Attaché Ministry of Justice 1957–59; Tech. Adviser to Office of René Pleven, Keeper of the Seals 1969; Sec.-Gen. Conseil Supérieur de la Magistrature 1970–74; mem. ORTF Admin. Council 1972–74; Minister of Health 1974–76, of Health and Social Security 1976–79, of Social Affairs, Health and Urban Devt. 1993–95; mem. European Parl. 1979–93, (Pres. 1979–82, Chair. of Legal Affairs Cttee. 1982–84), Chair. Liberal and Democratic Group 1984–89; mem. Conseil Constitutionnel 1998–; Leader Centre-Right List for European elections 1989; Dr. h.c. (Princeton) 1975, (Weizmann Inst.) 1976, (Bar Ilan) 1980, (Yale) 1980, (Cambridge) 1980, (Edin.) 1980, (Georgetown) 1981, (Urbino) 1981, (Sussex) 1984, (Yeshiva) 1982, (Free Univ., Brussels) 1984, (Brandeis) 1989, (Pennsylvania) 1997; Hon. LL.D. (Glasgow) 1995; Onassis Foundation Prize 1980, Charlemagne Prize 1981, Louise Weiss Foundation Prize 1981, Louise Michel Prize 1983, European Merit Prize 1983, Jabotinsky Prize (U.S.A.) 1983, Prize for Everyday Courage 1984, Special Freedom Prize 1984, Fiera di Messina 1984, Thomas Dehler Prize 1988, Klein Foundation Prize, Phila. 1991, Truman Prize for Peace, Jerusalem 1991, Giulietta Prize, Verona 1991, Atlantide Prize, Barcelona 1991, and other prizes; Chevalier Ordre nat. du Mérite, Médaille pénitentiaire, Médaille de l'Education surveillée; numerous foreign decorations including Grand Officer, National Order of the Lion (Senegal), Order of Merit of the Repub. (Ivory Coast), Isabel la Católica (Spain), Grand Cross Order of Merit (Fed. Repub. of Germany), Order of Rio Branco (Brazil), Order of Merit (Luxembourg), Order of the Phoenix (Greece); Hon. D.B.E. (U.K.) 1998. *Publication:* Les données psycho-sociologiques de l'adoption (with Prof. Launay and Dr. Soule) 1969. *Address:* 1 rue Bixio, 75007 Paris; Conseil constitutionnel, 2 rue Montpensier, 75001 Paris; 11 Place Vauban, 75007 Paris, France (Home). *Telephone:* (1) 40-56-48-75 (Home).

VELASQUEZ-GÁZTELU RUIZ, Cándido; Spanish business executive; b. 1937, Jerez de la Frontera; ed. Univ. of Granada; Dir. Coca-Cola and other cos.; Head of sales and Commercial Dir. Tabalcera S.A. 1973, Gen. Dir. 1981, Chair. 1982–89; Pres. Compañía Telefónica Nacional de España 1989–.

VELAYATI, Ali Akbar; Iranian politician; b. 1945, Teheran; s. of Ali Asghar and Zobeideh Asgah; m. Skina Khosshnevissan; three c.; ed. Teheran Univ.; joined Nat. Front (of Mossadegh) 1961; a founder of the Islamic Asscn. of Faculty of Medicine, Teheran Univ. 1963; underground political activities in support of Ayatollah Khomeini 1979; Vice-Minister, Ministry of Health 1979–80; proposed for Prime Minister by Ayatollah Khomeini Oct. 1981 (candidature rejected by the Majlis); Minister of Foreign Affairs 1981–97. *Publications:* Infectious Diseases (3 vols.) 1979, numerous articles. *Address:* c/o Ministry of Foreign Affairs, Teheran, Iran.

VELDHUIS, Johannes (Jan) G.F.; Netherlands university president; b. 4 Oct. 1938, Hengelo; m. Monica M. H. Thier 1969; three s.; ed. Univs. of Utrecht and Minnesota; Ministry of Foreign Affairs 1968–70; Sec. Univ. Bd. Univ. of Leiden 1970–74; Deputy Sec.-Gen. Ministry of Educ. and Science 1974–79, Dir.-Gen. and Insp.-Gen. of Educ. and Science 1979–86; Pres. Utrecht Univ. 1986–; Sec. Bd. Medical Inst. Paramaribo, Suriname 1972–74; Chair. Netherlands del. OECD Educ. Cttee. 1984–86; Chair. Bd. Netherlands-America Comm. for Educational Exchange (Fulbright Comm.) 1984–, Netherlands Inst. for Art History, Florence; mem. Bd. Netherlands History Inst., Rome, Netherlands Archaeological Inst., Cairo, Japan-Netherlands Inst., Tokyo; mem. bds. of several hosps. in The Hague area; Fulbright Grant; Fellow, Int. Visitor Pogram. *Publications:* various publs. in the field of educ. and public admin. *Leisure interests:* comparative educ., literature, botany, tennis, skiing, bridge. *Address:* Heidelberglaan 8, P.O. Box 80125, 3508 TC Utrecht (Office); Roucooppark 12, 2251 AV Voorschoten, Netherlands (Home). *Telephone:* (30) 2539111 (Office); 071-617696 (Home). *Fax:* 030-521818.

VELICHKO, Vladimir Makarovich; Russian fmr. politician and business executive; b. 23 April 1937, Mozhaisk, Voronezh Region; s. of Makar Petrovich Velichko and Maria Ivanovna Velichko; m. Eleanora Dmitrievna Bestouzheva 1961, one d.; ed. Leningrad Inst. of Mechanics, Leningrad Inst. of Eng. and Econs.; joined CPSU 1962; started career as foreman, later dir. of machine bldg. plant; First Deputy Minister, Ministry of Power Eng. of U.S.S.R. 1975–83, Minister 1983–87; Minister of Heavy Power and Transport Eng. 1987–89; Minister of Heavy Machine-Building Industry 1989–91; U.S.S.R. First Deputy Prime Minister Jan.–Dec. 1991; Deputy to U.S.S.R. Supreme Soviet 1984–89; Deputy of the U.S.S.R. 1989; mem. Political Consultative Council, Sept.–Dec. 1991; Chair. Bd. Tyazhenergomash (now jt. stock co. TENMA) 1992; Pres. Financial and Industrial Group 1996; Academician, mem. Presidium Russian Acad. of Eng.; U.S.S.R. State Prize 1974. *Leisure interests:* literature, art. *Address:* TENMA, Nizhni Kislovsky per. 5, GSP, 103906 Moscow K-9, Russia. *Telephone:* 203 1500. *Fax:* 291 6826.

VELIKHOV, Yevgeniy Pavlovich; Russian physicist; b. 2 Feb. 1935, Moscow; s. of Pavel Pavlovich Velikhov and Natalia Vsevolodoma Velikhova; m. Natalia Alekseevna Arseniyeva 1959; two s. one d.; mem. of staff, Kurchatov Inst. of Atomic Energy 1958–, Head of Lab. 1962–70, Deputy Dir., then Dir. of branch of Inst. 1971–89; Dir. Russian Scientific Centre, Kurchatov Inst. 1989–; f. and Dir. Inst. for Security Problems of Nuclear Energy Devt. 1988–91; Prof., Moscow Univ. 1973–; mem. CPSU Cen. Cttee. 1989–90; mem. U.S.S.R. (now Russian) Acad. of Sciences 1974, Vice-Pres. 1978–96, Academician-Sec. Dept. of Information Technology, Cybernetics and Automatic Systems 1985–92; mem. Supreme Soviet of U.S.S.R.; People's Deputy of the U.S.S.R. 1989–91; mem. Pres. Council 1992–93; Chair. Cttee. of Soviet Scientists for Peace against Nuclear Threat; Co-founder Int. Foundation for Survival and Devt. of Humanity; del. to numerous scientific and peace confs.; Chair. Soviet Nuclear Soc. 1989–; Co-Chair. Jr. Achievement of Russia 1991–; Chair. Council, Int. Thermonuclear Experimental Reactor 1992–; mem. Presidential Council of Science and Tech. 1995–; Pres. Shelf-Developing Co. Rosshelf 1992–; mem. American Geophysical Soc. 1981; Foreign mem. Swedish Royal Acad. of Eng. Sciences 1989; Dr. h.c. (Notre Dame, Susquachana, Tafts, London); U.S.S.R. State Prize 1977, Lenin Prize 1984, Hero of Socialist Labour 1985, Science for Peace Prize, Italy, Szillard Award, American Physical Soc.; Order of Lenin (three times). *Publications:* numerous, related both to science and the problems of prevention of nuclear war. *Leisure interests:* mountain skiing, underwater swimming, windsurfing. *Address:* RNTs Kurchatovskiy Institute, Kurchatova pl. 1, 123182 Moscow, Russia. *Telephone:* (095) 196-92-41.

VELLIDIS, Katerina; Greek publisher; b. 1947, Thessaloniki; d. of Ioannis Vellidis and Anna Vellidis; m. (divorced); one d.; ed. Univ. of Geneva and Sorbonne, Paris; Pres. Bd. and Man. Dir. I. K. Vellidis Press Org. of Northern Greece (publrs. of newspapers and magazines) 1980–; Pres. Ioannis and Anna Vellidis Foundation; numerous awards including Silver Medal of Acad. of Athens. *Address:* Tsimiski 77, 54622 Thessaloniki, Greece. *Telephone:* 031.521.621.

VENABLES, Terry Frederick; British football manager and coach; b. 6 Jan. 1943; m. Yvette Venables; two d.; ed. Dagenham High School; professional footballer, Chelsea 1958–66 (Capt. 1962), Tottenham Hotspur 1966–68 (FA Cup winners 1967), Queens Park Rangers 1968–73; coach, Crystal Palace 1973–76, Man. 1976–80; Man. Queens Park Rangers 1980–84; Man. Barcelona 1984–87 (winners Spanish Championship 1984, European Cup finalists 1985); Man. Tottenham Hotspur 1987–91 (FA Cup winners 1991); Chief Exec. Tottenham Hotspur PLC 1991–93; coach, England Nat. Team 1994–96; Dir. of Football, Portsmouth Football Club 1996–98; coach, Australian Nat. Team 1996–98; Head Coach Crystal Palace 1998; only player to have rep. England at all levels; co-author, Hazell (TV detective series); Hon. Fellow Univ. of Wolverhampton. *Publications:* They Used to Play on Grass, The Best Game in the World 1996, Venables' England—The Making of the Team 1996. *Address:* Terry Venables Holdings Ltd., 213 Putney Bridge Road, London, SW15 2NY, England. *Telephone:* 0181-874 5001. *Fax:* 0181-874 0064.

VENDLER, Helen Hennessy, PH.D.; American professor and literary critic; b. 30 April 1933, Boston, Mass.; d. of George Hennessy and Helen Conway; one s.; ed. Emmanuel Coll. and Harvard Univ.; Instructor Cornell Univ. 1960–63; lecturer, Swarthmore Coll., Pa. and Haverford Coll., Pa. 1963–64; Asst. Prof. Smith Coll. Northampton, Mass. 1964–66; Assoc. Prof. Boston Univ. 1966–68, Prof. 1968–85; Visiting Prof. Harvard Univ. 1981–85, Kenan Prof. 1985–, Assoc. Acad. Dean 1987–92, Porter Univ. Prof. 1990–; Sr. Fellow, Harvard Soc. of Fellows 1981–92; poetry critic, New Yorker 1978–; mem. American Acad. of Arts and Sciences, Norwegian Acad., American Philosophical Soc., Educ. Advisory Bd. Guggenheim Foundation, Pulitzer Prize Bd.; Fulbright Fellow 1954; A.A.U.W. Fellow 1959; Guggenheim Fellow 1971–72; American Council of Learned Socs. Fellow 1971–72; N.E.H. Fellow 1980, 1985, 1994; Wilson Fellow 1994; Fulbright Lecturer, Univ. of Bordeaux 1968–69; Overseas Fellow, Churchill Coll. Cambridge 1980; Parnell Fellow, Magdalene Coll. Cambridge 1996, Hon. Fellow 1996–; several hon. degrees; Lowell Prize 1969, Explicator Prize 1969, Nat. Inst. of Arts and Letters Award 1975, Nat. Book Critics Award 1980. *Publications include:* Yeats's Vision and the Later Plays 1963, On Extended Wings: Wallace Stevens' Longer Poems 1969, The Poetry of George Herbert 1975, Part of Nature, Part of Us 1980, The Odes of John Keats 1983, Wallace Stevens: Words Chosen Out of Desire 1985, Harvard Book of Contemporary American Poetry 1985, The Music of What Happens 1988, The Given and the Made 1995, The Breaking of Style 1995, Soul Says 1995, Poems, Poets, Poetry 1996,

The Art of Shakespeare's Sonnets 1997, Seamus Heaney 1998. *Address:* Harvard University, Department of English, Barker Center, Cambridge, MA 02138; 54 Trowbridge Street, Apt. B, Cambridge, MA 02138, U.S.A. *Fax:* (617) 496-8737.

VENETIAAN, Runaldo; Suriname politician; mem. New Front for Democracy and Development (NF); elected Pres. of Suriname 1991–96. *Address:* c/o Office of the President, Paramaribo, Suriname.

VENGEROV, Anatoly Borisovich, LL.D.; Russian lawyer; b. 10 Feb. 1928, Kremenchug, Ukraine; ed. Moscow Inst. of Law; worked in judicial investigation bodies in Lithuania, Lvov Region of W. Ukraine; lecturer, Drogobych Pedagogical Inst., Saratov Inst. of Law; researcher, All-Union Research Inst. of Soviet Law, Acad. of Nat. Econs., U.S.S.R. Council of Ministers; Head of Dept., All-Union Inst. of Law by correspondence 1989, Head of Dept., U.S.S.R. State Cttee. on Science and Tech. 1989–91; Head of Chair, Moscow State Acad. of Law 1991–94; Head of Arbitration, Chamber on Information Disputes of Russian Presidency 1994–. *Publications:* over 200 scientific works. *Address:* Court Chamber, Ilyinka str. 10, etr. 9, Moscow, Russia. *Telephone:* (095) 206 5680, 206 8844 (Office).

VENIAMIN, Christodoulos; Cypriot government official; b. Sept. 1922; ed. in Nicosia and Middle Temple, London; junior officer in govt. service 1942, admin. officer 1949; served as Asst. Sec. in Depts. of Local Govt. and Admin., Personnel, Finance, Commerce and Industry, Social Services, Communications and Works, Agric. and Natural Resources; Asst. Dist. Commr., Larnaca; Asst. Sec. Ministry of Interior during transitional period; Dist. Officer, Limassol Dist. 1960–68; Dir.-Gen. Ministry of Foreign Affairs 1968; Minister of Interior and Defence 1975–84, of Interior 1988–93; mem. House of Reps. 1997–. *Address:* Kleanthi Ierodiaconou No. 5, 2433 Engomi, Nicosia, Cyprus. *Telephone:* (02) 360339 (Office); (02) 352400. *Fax:* (02) 361821.

VENKATARAMAN, Ramaswamy, M.A., B.L.; Indian politician; b. 4 Dec. 1910; s. of Ramaswami Iyer; m. Janaki Venkataraman; three d.; ed. Madras Univ.; Advocate, Madras High Court and Supreme Court; detained during Quit India Movt. 1942–44; mem. Provisional Parl. 1950–52; mem. Lok Sabha 1952–57, 1977–84; Sec. Congress Party 1952–54; mem. Standing Finance Cttee., Estimates Cttee., Public Accounts Cttee., Privileges Cttee.; Minister for Industry and Labour and leader of the House, Govt. of Madras 1957–67, mem. Planning Comm. 1967–71; Chair. Nat. Research and Devt. Corpn.; Man. Ed. Labour Law Journal 1971; Minister of Finance and Industry 1980–82, of Defence 1982–84; Vice-Pres. of India 1984–87, Pres. of India 1987–92; del. to ILO 1958, UN Gen. Ass. 1953–61. *Publications:* My Presidential Years (in Tamil) 1994, Travelogue in Socialist Countries 1996. *Leisure interests:* arts, music, tennis. *Address:* c/o Rashtrapati Bhavan, New Delhi 110004; Pothigai, Greenways Road, Madras 600028, India.

VENNAMO, Pekka Veikko; Finnish politician; b. 1944, Helsinki; ed. Helsinki Univ. of Tech.; Asst. Helsinki Inst. of Tech. 1964–65; mem. Parl. 1972–75, 1979–; Chair. Finnish Rural Party 1979–89; reporter Suomen Uutiset (party newspaper) 1970–71, Man. Dir. 1976–; Minister, Ministry of Finance 1983–87; Minister of Transport and Communications 1987–90; Chair., C.E.O. Posts and Telecommunication Authority 1989. *Address:* c/o Ministry of Transport and Communications, Eteläesplanadi 16, 00130 Helsinki, Finland.

VENTURI, Franco; Italian professor of modern history; b. 16 May 1914, Rome; s. of Lionello Venturi; m. Gigliola Spinelli 1945; one s.; ed. Univ. of Paris; Partisan in the Alps 1943–45; Cultural Attaché, Moscow 1947–50; Prof. of Modern History in Cagliari and Genoa from 1952, now in Turin; Visiting Prof. in Cambridge (Mass.), Oxford, Chicago; Corresp. Fellow of British Acad.; Hon. Degree of Univs. of London, Geneva, Chicago and Cambridge. *Publications:* Il Populismo Russo 1952, Settecento Riformatore, Vol. I Da Muratori a Beccaria 1969, Vol. II. La Chiesa e la Repubblica entro i loro Limiti 1976, Vol. III. La Prima Crisi dell'Antico Regime (1768–1776) 1979, Vol. IV, La Caduta dell'Antico Regime 1984, Vol. V.1, L'Italia dei lumi 1987, Vol. V. 2, Venezia, Utopia and Reform in the Enlightenment 1971, The End of the Old Regime in Europe: The First Crisis 1768–1776 1990. *Leisure interests:* skiing, mountaineering. *Address:* Piazza Amedeo Peyron 7, Turin, Italy. *Telephone:* 771 0380.

VENTURI, Robert, A.B., M.F.A.; American architect; b. 25 June 1925, Philadelphia, Pa.; s. of Robert C. Venturi and Vanna Lanzetta; m. Denise (Lakofski) Scott Brown 1967; one s.; ed. Princeton Univ.; Designer, Oskar Stonorov 1950, Eero Saarinen & Assoc. 1950–53; Rome Prize Fellow, American Acad. in Rome 1954–56; Designer, Louis I. Kahn 1957; Assoc. Prof., School of Fine Arts, Univ. of Pennsylvania 1957–65; Charlotte Shepherd Davenport Prof., Yale Univ. 1966–70; Prin., Venturi, Cope & Lippincott 1958–61, Venturi and Short 1961–64, Venturi and Rauch 1964–80, Venturi, Rauch and Scott Brown (architects and planners) 1980–89; Venturi, Scott Brown and Assocs. June 1989–; *works include:* Vanna Venturi House, Phila., Pa. 1961, Guild House, Phila. 1961, Franklin Court, Phila. 1972, Allen Memorial Art Museum Addition, Oberlin, Ohio 1973, Inst. for Scientific Information Corpn. HQ, Phila. 1978, Gordon Wu Hall, Princeton Univ., N.J. 1980, Seattle Art Museum, Seattle, Wash. 1984, Clinical Research Bldg., Univ. of Pa. 1985 (with Payette Assocs.), Nat. Gallery, Sainsbury Wing, London, U.K. 1986, Fisher-Bendheim Hall, Princeton Univ. 1986, Charles P. Stevenson Library, Bard Coll. 1989, Regional Govt. Bldg., Toulouse, France 1992, Kirifuri Resort facilities, Nikko, Japan 1992, Univ. of Del. Student Center, Newark, Del. 1992, Memorial Hall Restoration and Addition, Harvard Univ. 1992, The Barnes Foundation Restoration and Renovation, Merion, Pa. 1993, Disney Celebration Bank, Celebration, Fla. 1993, Princeton Campus Center, Princeton Univ. 1996; Fellow American Inst. of Architects, American Acad. in Rome, Accademia Nazionale di San Luca, American Acad. of Arts and Sciences; Hon. Fellow Royal Incorporation of Architects in Scotland, American Acad. and Inst. of Arts and Letters, R.I.B.A.; Hon. D.F.A. (Oberlin, Yale, Penn., Princeton, Phila. Coll of Art), Hon. L.H.D. (N.J. Inst. of Tech.), Laurea h.c. (Univ. of Rome La Sapienza) 1994; Nat. Medal of Arts 1992, and numerous other awards. *Publications:* Complexity and Contradiction in Architecture 1966, Learning from Las Vegas (with Denise Scott Brown and Steven Izenour) 1972, A View from the Campidoglio: Selected Essays, 1953–1984 (with Denise Scott Brown) 1984, Iconography and Electronics upon a Generic Architecture 1996; numerous articles in professional journals. *Leisure interest:* travel. *Address:* Venturi, Scott Brown and Associates, 4236 Main Street, Philadelphia, PA 19127, U.S.A. *Telephone:* (215) 487-0400 (Office).

VERBA, Sidney, PH.D.; American academic; b. 26 May 1932, Brooklyn, New York; s. of Morris Verba and Recci Salman; m. E. Cynthia Winston 1955; three d.; ed. Harvard Coll. and Princeton Univ.; Asst., then Assoc. Prof. of Politics Princeton Univ. 1960–64; Prof. of Political Science Stanford Univ. 1964–68; Sr. Study Dir. Nat. Opinion Research Center 1968–72; Prof. of Political Science Univ. of Chicago 1968–72; Prof. of Govt. Harvard Univ. 1972–, Clarence Dillon Prof. of Int. Affairs 1983–84, Carl H. Pforzheimer Univ. Prof. 1984–, Assoc. Dean for Undergraduate Educ., Faculty of Arts and Sciences 1981–84, Dir. Harvard Univ. Library 1984–; Chair. Bd. of Dirs. Harvard Univ. Press 1991–; Pres. American Political Science Asscn. 1994–95; mem. N.A.S., American Acad. of Arts and Sciences; Guggenheim Fellow; Woodrow Wilson and Kammerer Book Awards, James Madison Award (American Political Science Asscn.). *Publications:* Small Groups and Political Behavior 1961, The Civic Culture 1963, Participation in America 1972, Participation and Political Equality 1978, The Changing American Voter 1979, Injury to Insult 1979, Equality in America 1985, Elites and the Idea of Equality 1987, Designing Social Inquiry 1994, Voice and Equality 1995. *Address:* Wadsworth House, Harvard University, Cambridge, MA 02138 (Office); 142 Summit Avenue, Brookline, MA 02146, U.S.A. (Home). *Telephone:* (617) 495-3650 (Office); (617) 232-4987 (Home).

VERBURGT, Paul Adriaan; Netherlands banker; b. 23 Jan. 1935, Bussum; s. of Dr. G. Verburgt and A. C. (née Koole) Verburgt; m. 1958; one s. one d.; ed. Econ. High School and Private Banking School; Dutch Banking Group, South Africa 1955–57, Belgium 1957–65; joined Bank of America, Antwerp Branch 1965, Man. Rotterdam br. until 1972, Regional Vice-Pres. for Scandinavia and Benelux countries 1972–73; Sr. Vice-Pres., Head of Int. Financial Centre, London 1973–82, Head of Middle East Area 1979–82, Exec. Vice-Pres. Europe, Middle East and Africa Div. 1982–86; Dir. of banks, and financial consultant 1986–. *Leisure interests:* photography, vintage cars. *Address:* Hillside, St. George's Hill, Weybridge, Surrey, England. *Telephone:* (01932) 851669.

VERDAN, Claude Edouard; Swiss hand surgeon (retd.); b. 21 Sept. 1909, Yverdon; s. of Edouard and Adeline (née Henrioud) Verdan; m. Sylva Malan 1934; one s. (deceased) one d.; ed. Faculty of Medicine, Univ. of Lausanne, Univ. of Zürich; specialist in surgery, Foederatio Medicorum Helveticorum (FMH); Chief surgeon and founder of Clinique chirurgicale et Permanence de Longeraie, Lausanne; Prof. Univ. of Lausanne; Sr. Dean Faculty of Medicine 1972–74; Pres. Soc. suisse de médecine des accidents et des maladies professionnelles 1961–66; Pres. Soc. française de chirurgie plastique et reconstructive 1964; Sec.-Gen. and Founder, Groupe suisse d'étude de chirurgie de la main 1966–72; Pres. Comm. for war surgery, Fed. Mil. (Defence) Dept. (médecin-Col.) 1965–69; Pres. Soc. française de chirurgie de la main 1975–76; retd. from medical practice 1980; f. Museum of the Human Hand (Foundation Claude Verdan), Lausanne 1981, first exhbn. "Man's Hand" 1983, several other exhbns. in Switzerland and France; Hon. Pres. Claude Verdan Foundation 1990; Hon. mem. British Soc. for Surgery of the Hand 1959; Corresp. mem. Belgian Soc. for Forensic Traumatology 1963, Italian Soc. for Hand Surgery 1970; Assoc. mem. Acad. of Surgery, Paris 1974; Hon. mem. American Soc. for Surgery of the Hand 1960, Swiss Soc. for Medicine in Casualty 1966, Swiss Soc. for Orthopedics 1967, German-speaking Asscn. for Hand Surgery 1971, Soc. vaudoise de médecine 1975, Spanish Soc. for Hand Surgery, French Soc. for Orthopedics and Traumatology 1979, French Soc. of Hand Surgery 1979; Hon. mem. de l'Association française de chirurgie 1981; Specialist FMH in plastic and reconstructive surgery 1977; Ed. Annales de chirurgie de la main 1982–, Ed.-in-Chief Emer. 1985; Hon. Prof., Univ. of Lausanne 1979; Gold Medal and Prix César Roux (Faculty of Medicine, Lausanne) 1933; nominated Pioneer of Hand Surgery, 3rd Congress JFSSH, Tokyo 1986; Chevalier Légion d'honneur. *Publications:* The Hand—A Whole Universe, with catalogue of Museum of the Human Hand 1994, and numerous other books and articles on the hand. *Leisure interests:* sculpting, painting, collecting articles concerning the hand, objets d'art, writing memoirs. *Address:* The Museum of the Human Hand (Foundation Claude Verdan), 21 rue du Bugnon, 1005 Lausanne; 9 avenue de la Gare, 1003 Lausanne; 63 route de Lausanne, 1096 Cully, Switzerland. *Telephone:* (021) 314 4955; (021) 3122210; (021) 7991330. *Fax:* (021) 314 4963.

VERDEŢ, Ilie; Romanian politician; b. 10 May 1925, Comăneşti, Bacău County; m. Regina Manescu (sister of Nicolae Ceauşescu); ed. Acad. of Econ. Studies, Bucharest; mem. Romanian CP (RCP) 1945; worked in the Party local organs of Banat Region 1948–54; Head of Section in Central Cttee. RCP 1954; First Sec. Hunedoara Regional Party Cttee. 1954–65; mem. Cen. Cttee. RCP 1960–89; mem. Grand Nat. Ass. 1961–89; Alt. mem. Exec. Cttee. of Cen. Cttee. of RCP 1965–66, mem. 1966–86; Deputy Chair. Council of Ministers 1965–66, First Deputy Chair. 1966–74, First Vice Prime Minister 1978–79, Prime Minister 1979–82; Minister of Mines 1985–86; mem. Perm. Presidium of Cen. Cttee. 1966–74, 1984–86; mem. Standing Bureau Exec. Political Cttee. 1977–86, Chair. Cen. Auditing Cttee. 1986–89; Sec. Cen. Cttee. 1974–78, 1982–85; Chair. Cen. Council of Workers' Control over Econ. and Social Activity 1974–78, 1982–89; Vice Chair. Supreme Council on Social and Econ. Devt. 1973–86; Chair. State Planning Cttee. 1978–79; Pres. Labour Socialist Party 1991–; mem. Nat. Council Front of Socialist Democracy and Unity 1980–89; Hero of Socialist Labour 1971. *Leisure interests:* sport, travelling, hunting, fishing.

VERE-JONES, David, M.SC., D.PHIL., F.R.S.N.Z.; British professor of mathematics; b. 17 April 1936, London; s. of Noel W. Vere-Jones and Isabel M. I. Wyllie; m. Mary To Kei Chung 1965; two s. one d.; ed. Cheadle Hulme School, Cheshire, Hutt Valley High School, N.Z., Vic. Univ. of Wellington and Univ. of Oxford; emigrated to New Zealand 1949; Rhodes Scholar 1958–61; sr. scientist, Applied Math. Div. Dept. of Scientific & Industrial Research, N.Z. 1961–65; Fellow, Sr. Fellow, Dept. of Statistics, A.N.U. 1965–69; Prof. of Statistics Vic. Univ. of Wellington 1970–; Founding Pres. N.Z. Math Soc. 1975; Chair. Int. Statistical Inst. (ISI) Educ. Comm. 1987–91; Pres. Interim Exec., Int. Asscn. for Statistical Educ. 1991–93; other professional affiliations; ISI Henri Willem Methorst Medal 1995. *Publications:* An Introduction to the Theory of Point Processes (with D. J. Daley) 1988; about 100 papers on probability theory, seismology, mathematical educ. *Leisure interests:* tennis, walking, languages. *Address:* Institute of Statistics and O.R., Victoria University of Wellington, P.O. Box 600, Wellington (Office); 15 Farm Road, Northland, Wellington 5, New Zealand (Home). *Telephone:* (04) 471-5391 (Office); (04) 475-7249 (Home). *Fax:* (04) 495-5118.

VERESHCHETIN, Vladlen Stepanovich; Russian professor of law; b. 8 Jan. 1932, Briansk; m.; one d.; mem. staff, Presidium of U.S.S.R. Acad. of Sciences 1958–67; First Vice-Chair. and Legal Counsel, Intercosmos, U.S.S.R. Acad. of Sciences 1967–81; Prof. of Int. Law, Univ. of Friendship of Peoples 1979–82; Deputy Dir. and Head, Dept. of Int. Law, Inst. of State and Law, Russian Acad. of Sciences 1981–95, Chair. Scientific Council on Int. and Comparative Law 1981–; mem. Perm. Court of Arbitration, The Hague 1984–; Vice-Pres. Russian (fmrly. Soviet) UN Asscn. 1984–; Vice-Pres. Russian (fmrly. Soviet) Asscn. of Int. Law 1985–; Distinguished Visiting Prof. Univ. of Akron, U.S.A. 1991; mem. UN Int. Law Comm. 1992–, Chair. 1994–. *Publications:* numerous books and 150 articles on int. law, law of the sea, space law, state responsibility, int. criminal law and constitutional law. *Address:* Institute of State and Law, Russian Academy of Sciences, Leninskii Prospekt 14, 117901 Moscow, Russia. *Telephone:* (095) 291-33-81.

VEREY, Michael John, T.D., M.A.; British merchant banker; b. 12 Oct. 1912, London; s. of late Henry Edward Verey and Lucy Alice Verey; m. Sylvia Mary Wilson 1947; two s. one d.; ed. Eton Coll., Trinity Coll., Cambridge; joined Helbert Wagg and Co. Ltd. 1934; served in Warwickshire Yeomanry 1939–45 (Iraq, Syria, Persia, Western Desert and Italy), rank of Lieut.-Col. Commdg. 1945; Chair. Brixton Estate Ltd. 1971-83, Schroders Ltd. 1973–77, Accepting Houses Cttee. 1974–77, Broadstone Investment Trust Ltd. 1963–83, Charities Official Investment Fund 1974–83, London American Energy Investments Ltd. 1981–84; Vice-Chair. Commercial Union Assurance Co. Ltd. 1975–78, Deputy Chair. 1978–82; Dir. Boots Co. Ltd. (Vice-Chair. 1978–83), Invest. SpA (Italy) 1970–85, British Petroleum Co. 1974–82, Invest International Holdings; mem. Covent Garden Market Authority 1961–66; High Sheriff of Berks. 1968; Pres. Royal Worcs. and Warwicks. Yeomanry Regimental Asscn. 1971–86; Gov. Pangbourne Coll. 1972–82. *Leisure interests:* gardening and travel. *Address:* The Lodge, Little Bowden, Pangbourne, Berks., England. *Telephone:* (0118) 984 2210.

VERGE, Pierre, M.A., LL.L., LL.M., LL.D., F.R.S.C.; Canadian professor of law; b. 9 Jan. 1936, Quebec City; m. Colette Habel 1963; two s. one d.; ed. Univ. Laval, McGill Univ. and Univ. of Toronto; mem. Quebec Bar 1961; Q.C. 1976; Prof. of Law, Univ. Laval 1967–, Dean, Faculty of Law 1973–77; Commonwealth Fellowship, St. John's Coll. Cambridge 1977; mem. Canadian Asscn. of Law Teachers (Pres. 1972–73), Royal Soc. of Canada. *Publications:* Le droit de grève, fondement et limites, Droit du travail (co-author), Le droit et les syndicats (co-author) 1991, Un droit du travail? (co-author) 1997. *Address:* Faculté de droit, Université Laval, Québec, G1K 7P4, Canada. *Telephone:* (418) 656-559.

VERGÈS, Jacques; French lawyer; b. 5 March 1925, Thailand; of Vietnamese-French parentage; m. Djamila Bouhired; two c.; ed. legal studies in Paris; served with Free French in World War II in N. Africa, Italy, France and Germany; joined French CP 1945; Sec. Int. Union of Students, Prague 1951–55; joined Paris Bar 1955; defended many Algerian FLN militants; pvt. legal practice in Algeria 1965–70; activities unknown 1970–78; returned to Paris Bar 1978; appeared for defence, at trial in Lyons of Nazi war criminal Klaus Barbie who was gaoled for atrocities committed during World War II, 1987. *Publications:* De la stratégie judiciare 1968, Beauté du Crime 1988, La justice est un jeu 1992. *Address:* 20 rue de Vintimille, 75009 Paris, France. *Telephone:* 42.81.51.61. *Fax:* 42.82.90.30.

VERGHESE, Rev. Thadikkal Paul (see Gregorios, Bishop Paul).

VERHAEGEN, Georges, PH.D.; Belgian university professor; b. 26 March 1937, Brussels; s. of Col. J. Verhaegen and L. Nefcoeur; m. M. van de Keere 1965; two s.; ed. Ashbury Coll., Ottawa, Canada, Univ. Libre, Brussels, C.N.R.S., France; Pres. Dept. of Chemistry, Univ. Libre de Bruxelles 1973–75, Dean Faculty of Sciences 1978–81, Prof. 1979–, mem. Governing Body 1975–84, 1986–, Rector 1986–90, Pro-Rector 1990; Pres. Belgian Conf. of Rectors (French speaking) 1986–90, Belgian Nat. Science Foundation 1990, Network of Univs. of Capital Cities of Europe (UNICA) 1989–; winner of three Belgian scientific prizes. *Publications:* around sixty scientific publs. *Leisure interests:* reading, tennis, handicrafts, travelling. *Address:* C.P. 160, Université Libre de Bruxelles, 50 ave. F.D. Roosevelt, B 1050 Brussels, Belgium. *Telephone:* 6502424. *Fax:* 6504232.

VERHOEVEN, Paul; Netherlands film director; b. 18 July 1938, Amsterdam; ed. Leiden Univ.; worked as a documentary film-maker for the Dutch navy and then for TV; directed: (shorts) A Lizard too Much 1960, Let's have a Party 1963, The Wrestler 1971; (feature length) Wat zien ik (Business is Business/Any Special Way) 1971, Turks fruit (Turkish Delight) 1973, Keetje Tippel 1975, Soldaat van Oranje 1940–45 (Soldier of Orange/ Survival Run) 1978, Spetters 1980, De vierde man (The Fourth Man) 1984, Flesh and Blood 1985, RoboCop 1987, Total Recall 1989, Basic Instinct, Showgirls, Starship Troopers.

VERHOFSTADT, Guy; Belgian politician; b. 11 April 1953, Dendermonde; s. of Marcel Verhofstadt and Gaby Stockmans; m. Dominique Verkinderen 1981; one s. one d.; fmr. Pres. Young Liberals; Pres. Partij voor Vrijheid en Vooruitgang (PVV) –1982; Vice-Premier and Minister for the Budget 1985–88; Pres. Flemish Liberals and Democrats (V.L.D.) 1992–95, 1997–. *Leisure interests:* cycling, literature, Italy. *Address:* Rondonkstraat 44, 9030 Mariakerke, Belgium. *Telephone:* (9) 227.90.92.

VERLINDEN, (Jean) Charles (Alphonse), M.A., PH.D.; Belgian historian; b. 3 Feb. 1907, St. Gilles, Brussels; s. of Emile Verlinden; m. Nelly Noulard 1931; ed. Univ. of Ghent, Sorbonne, Ecole des Hautes Etudes, Paris, Ecole des Chartes, Paris and Centro de Estudios Historicos, Madrid; Studies and research Paris 1933, Madrid 1934, Italy 1938; Asst. Prof. of Econ. History, Business Univ., Antwerp 1940; Asst. Prof. of History, Univ. of Ghent 1944, Prof. 1944–74, Emer. 1974–; Dir. Belgian Acad., Rome 1959–77; Dir. Belgian Historical Inst., Rome 1955–86; Pres. Int. Comm. of Maritime History (Int. Comm. of Historical Sciences) 1980–85; mem. Royal Belgian Acad. (Flemish Section), Acad. de la Historia, Madrid, Royal Historical Soc., Medieval Acad. of America, Accademia dei Lincei, Rome, Società Nazionale di Scienze, Lettere ed Arti, Naples, Acad. da Historia, Lisbon, Acad. das Ciencias, Lisbon, Inst. Coimbra, Soc. de Historia, Lima, Comisión Panamericana de Historia, Caracas, Assoc. Siciliana Lettere ed Arti, Palermo; has taught and lectured in 46 univs. in Europe and America; Dr. h.c. (Seville) 1968, (Coimbra) 1988; Int. Prize Galileo Galilei 1970. *Publications:* L'esclavage dans l'Europe médiévale, Vol. I Péninsule Ibérique, France 1955, Vol. II Italie, Colonies italiennes du Levant. Levant latin, Empire byzantin 1977, Documents sur l'histoire des prix et salaires en Flandre et en Brabant (XIII–XIXe siecle), 5 vols. 1959–73, Les origines de la civilisation atlantique, De la renaissance à l'âge des lumières 1966, Cristóbal Colón 1967, The beginnings of modern colonization 1970, De Koloniale expansie in de XVe en XVIe eeuw 1975, Die mittelalterlichen Ursprünge der europäischen Expansion 1986. *Leisure interests:* classical music, travel.

VERNEUIL, Henri; French film director; b. 15 Oct. 1920, Rodosto, Turkey; s. of Agop Malakian and Araxi Kirazian; m. 1st Françoise Bonnot (divorced); m. 2nd Véronique Sedro 1984; two s. two d.; journalist and critic 1944–48; made 30 short films 1948–50, 29 full-length films 1950–78; Best Foreign Language Film (U.S.A.) 1963, Victoire du Cinéma Français 1963, Mystery Writers' Award (U.S.A.) 1964, Prix Saint-Simon for Mayrig 1986; Commdr. Légion d'honneur, des Arts et des Lettres. *Films include:* La vache et le prisonnier 1959, Le Président 1960, Un singe en hiver 1962, Melodie en sous-sol (Any Number Can Win) 1963, Weekend à Zuydcoote 1964, La 25ème heure 1966, Le clan des siciliens 1969, Le casse 1970, Le serpent 1972, Peur sur la ville 1975, Le corps de mon ennemi 1976, I comme Icare 1979, Mille milliards de dollars 1981, Les Morfalous 1983, Mayrig, 588 rue Paradis. *Publication:* Mayrig 1985, Le Cheval Vartan 1997. *Leisure interest:* magic. *Address:* Artmédia, 10 avenue George V, 75008 Paris, France.

VERNIER, Jacques; French politician and environmentalist; b. 3 July 1944, Paris; s. of Charles Vernier and Georgette Mangin; m. Bertille Janssen 1968; two s. two d.; ed. Ecole Polytechnique and Ecole des Mines, Paris; engineer Service des Mines, Strasbourg 1968–72; Sec.-Gen. Agence de Bassin Seine-Normandie 1972–74; Dir. Agence de Bassin Artois-Picardie 1974–83; Mayor of Douai 1983–; Conseiller Régional 1983–90; mem. European Parl. 1984–93; Deputy (R.P.R.) to Nat. Ass. 1993–97; Pres. Agence de l'Environnement 1994–97; Chevalier Ordre nat. du Mérite, Ordre du Palmes académiques. *Publications:* several publs. on environmental matters. *Leisure interest:* tennis. *Address:* Mairie de Douai, 59500 Douai; 162 quai du Petit Bail, 59500 Douai, France (Home). *Telephone:* (3) 27.93.58.00. *Fax:* (3) 27.96.58.22.

VERNIER-PALLIEZ, Bernard Maurice Alexandre, L. EN D.; French business executive and diplomatist; b. 2 March 1918; m. Denise Silet-Pathe

1952; one s. three d.; ed. Ecole Libre des Sciences Politiques, Ecole des Hautes Etudes Commerciales; Head of Welfare, Régie Nat. des Usines Renault 1945–47, Sec. to Sec.-Gen. 1947–48, Sec.-Gen. 1948–67, Deputy Man. Dir. 1967–71, Chair. and Man. Dir. 1975–81; Chair. and Man. Dir. SAVIEM 1967–74; Del.-Gen. for commercial vehicles, coaches and buses, Régie Renault; Pres. Berliet 1975–76; Vice-Pres. Supervisory Bd. SAVIEM 1975; Amb. to U.S.A. 1982–84; mem. Int. Advisory Bd. A.I.G.; Ambassadeur de France 1984; Commdr., Légion d'honneur, Croix de guerre, Médaille de la Résistance. *Address:* 25 Grande Rue, 78170 La Celle St.-Cloud, France. *Telephone:* (01) 39.69.30.11.

VERNON, Sir James, A.C., C.B.E., PH.D., F.R.A.C.I., F.A.I.M., F.T.S.; Australian business executive; b. 13 June 1910, Tamworth; s. of Donald Vernon; m. Mavis Lonsdale-Smith (deceased); two d.; ed. Sydney Univ., Univ. Coll. London; Chief Chemist, Colonial Sugar Refining Co. Ltd. (C.S.R.) 1938–51, Sr. Exec. Officer 1951–56, Asst. G. Man. 1956–57, Gen. Man. 1958–72; Dir. C.S.R. Ltd. 1958–82, Chair. 1978–80; Chair. CIBC Australia Ltd. 1974–89, Volvo Australia Pty. Ltd. 1980–89; Chair. Commonwealth Cttee. of Econ. Inquiry 1963–65, Australian Post Office Comm. of Inquiry 1973–74; Int. Pres. Pacific Basin Econ. Council 1980–82; Fellow, Australian Inst. of Man., Australian Acad. of Tech. Sciences; Royal Australian Chemical Inst.; Hon. D.Sc. (Univs. of Sydney and Newcastle); Order of the Sacred Treasure, 1st class (Japan); Leighton Memorial Medal, Royal Australian Chemical Inst. 1965; John Storey Medal, Australian Inst. of Management 1971. *Leisure interests:* fishing, music. *Address:* 27 Manning Road, Double Bay, N.S.W. 2028, Australia.

VERNON, Raymond, PH.D.; American professor of international affairs; b. 1 Sept. 1913, New York; s. of Hyman Wisotsky and Lillian Sonenberg; m. Josephine Stone 1935; two d.; ed. City Coll. of New York and Columbia Univ.; Securities and Exchange Comm. 1935–46; Dept. of State 1946–54; Sr. Economist, Comm. on Foreign Policy 1953–54; Planning and Control Dir. Hawley and Hoops Inc. 1954–56; Dir. New York Metropolitan Region Study 1956–59; Prof. of Int. Trade and Investment, Harvard Business School 1959–69, Herbert F. Johnson Prof. of Int. Business Man. 1969–80; Dir. Center for Int. Affairs, Harvard Univ. 1973–78; Clarence Dillon Prof. of Int. Relations, Govt. Dept. Harvard Univ. 1978–84, Prof. Emer. 1983–; consultant to Under-Sec. for Monetary Affairs, Treasury Dept. 1978–79; Visiting Scholar, IBRD 1986; Eminent Scholar in Int. Political Economy (Int. Studies Assen.); Dept. of State Meritorious Service Award; Order of Rising Sun (Japan). *Publications:* Anatomy of a Metropolis 1963, Dilemma of Mexico's Development 1963, Sovereignty at Bay 1971, Storm over the Multinationals 1977, Two Hungry Giants 1983, Beyond Globalism 1989, In the Hurricane's Eye 1998; Ed.: Iron Triangles and Revolving Doors (jtly.) 1991, Defense and Dependence in a Global Economy (jtly.) 1992. *Leisure interests:* sculling, cross-country skiing. *Address:* Kennedy School of Government, 79 Kennedy Street, Cambridge, MA 02138 (Office); 1 Dunstable Road, Cambridge, MA 02138, U.S.A. (Home). *Telephone:* (617)-495-1145 (Office); (617) 547-3494 (Home). *Fax:* (617) 496-0063.

VERNON, Sir (William) Michael, Kt., M.A.; British business executive (retd.); b. 17 April 1926, Cheshire; s. of late Sir Wilfred Vernon; m. 1st Rosheen O'Meara 1952 (dissolved 1977); one s.; m. 2nd Jane Kilham-Roberts 1977 (died 1998); ed. Marlborough Coll. and Trinity Coll., Cambridge; joined Spillers (millers and animal food mfrs.) as trainee 1948, Dir. 1960–80, Joint Man. Dir. 1962–67, Deputy Chair. 1967–68, Chair. 1968–80; Chair. Famous Names Ltd. 1981–85, Granville Meat Co. Ltd. 1981–94; Dir. Electrical and Musical Industries (later EMI) Ltd. 1973–80, Strong and Fisher (Holdings) PLC 1980–91; Pres. British Food Export Council 1977–79; Vice-Pres. Royal Nat. Lifeboat Inst. 1975–96, Deputy Chair. 1980–89, Chair. 1989–96. *Leisure interests:* sailing, shooting, skiing. *Address:* Fyfield Manor, Andover, Hants., SP11 8EN, England (Home).

VEROSTA, Stephan Eduard, LL.D.; Austrian lawyer and diplomatist; b. 16 Oct. 1909, Vienna; s. of Rudolf Verosta and Elisabeth (née Szalay) Verosta; m. Maria Stuehler, M.D. 1942; two s. one d.; ed. Gymnasium, Vienna, Univ. of Vienna and studied in Paris, Geneva and Acad. of Int. Law, The Hague; legal practice 1932–35, Judge 1936; Legal Dept., Austrian Foreign Office 1935–38, Deputy Legal Adviser 1945–48, 1949–51; Counsellor, Austrian Legation, Rome, Minister, Budapest 1951–52; Head of Legal Dept., Foreign Office 1953–56; Amb. to Poland 1956–61; Austrian Del. to various int. confs. and UN; mem. Perm. Court of Arbitration, The Hague 1957–; Consultant to Foreign Office 1962; Dozent in Int. Law, Univ. of Vienna 1946, Prof. of Int. Law, Jurisprudence and Int. Relations 1962–80; Chair. U.S.-Finnish Comm. of Conciliation 1964; mem. Dutch-Fed. German Comm. of Conciliation, Inst. de Droit Int. 1961; mem. Founding Cttee. UN Univ. 1972; mem. Appeals Board, Council of Europe 1974; mem. Int. Law Comm. of UN 1977–82, Council, UN Univ. 1977–83; mem. Austrian Acad. of Science 1964; numerous decorations. *Publications:* Les avis consultatifs de la Cour Permanente de Justice Internationale, etc. 1932, Jean Dumont und seine Bedeutung für das Völkerrecht 1934, Liberale und planwirtschaftliche Handelspolitik (with Gottfried Haberler) 1934, Richterliches Gewohnheitsrecht in Österreich 1942, Die Satzung der Vereinten Nationen 1946, Die internationale Stellung Österreichs von 1938–1947 1947, Die geschichtliche Kontinuität des österreichischen Staates und seine europäische Funktion 1954, Johannes Chrysostomus, Staatsphilosoph 1960, Geschichte des Völkerrechts 1964, International Law in Europe and Western Asia between 100-650 A.D. 1966, Dauernde Neutralität 1967, Theorie und Realität von Bündnissen Heinrich Lammasch, Karl Renner und der Zweibund 1897-1914 1971, L'histoire de l'Académie de Droit International de la Haye 1973, History of the Law of Nations 1648 to 1815 1984, Kollektivaktionen der Mächte des Europäischen Konzerts bis 1914 1988, Die völkerrechtliche Praxis der Donaumonarchie von 1859 bis 1918, 2 vols. (Co-ed. with Ignaz Seidl-Hohenveldern) 1996. *Leisure interest:* collecting old books. *Address:* 1180 Vienna, Hockegasse 15, Austria. *Telephone:* 479-13-48.

VERPLAETSE, Alfons Remi Emiel; Belgian central banker; b. 19 Feb. 1930, Zulte; m. Odette Vanhee 1954; three s. two d.; ed. Katholieke Universiteit Leuven; Nat. Bank of Belgium 1953–81; Office of the Prime Minister 1981–88; Dir. Nat. Bank of Belgium 1988–, Deputy Gov. 1988–89, Gov. 1989–. *Address:* National Bank of Belgium, Boulevard de Berlaimont 14, 1000 Brussels (Office); Schaveyslaan 25, 1650 Beersel, Belgium (Home).

VERRETT, Shirley; American soprano singer; b. 31 May 1931, New Orleans; d. of Leon Verrett and Elvira Verrett; m. Louis Lomonaco 1963; one d.; ed. Juilliard School of Music, New York; Prof. of Voice, School of Music, Univ. of Mich. 1996–; operatic début as mezzo-soprano taking title role of Carmen, Spoleto Festival 1962; same role for début at Bolshoi Opera, Moscow 1963, New York City Opera 1966, Florence 1968, Metropolitan Opera, New York 1968; sang at Covent Garden, London in roles of Ulrica (Un Ballo in Maschera) 1966, Amneris (Aida) 1967, Eboli (Don Carlos) 1968, Azucena (Il Trovatore) 1970; début at San Carlo, Naples as Elisabetta (Maria Stuarda) 1969, at La Scala, Milan as Delilah (Samson et Dalila) 1970, at Vienna Staatsoper as Eboli 1970, at Teatro Liceo, Barcelona as Eboli 1971, at Paris Opera as Azucena 1972; other mezzo-soprano roles in Orfeo (Gluck), as Dido (Les Troyens), Judith (Bluebeard's Castle), Neocle (Siege of Corinth), Adalgisa (Norma, first performance at Metropolitan, New York 1976); made début as soprano in title role of La Favorita, Dallas Civic Opera 1971; début at San Francisco Opera in title role of L'Africaine 1972; first artist to sing roles of both Dido and Cassandra in one single full-length production of Les Troyens, Metropolitan 1973; other soprano roles: Lady Macbeth, La Scala 1975, and with La Scala at Kennedy Center, Washington, D.C. 1976, also with Opera Co. of Boston 1976; title role of Norma, Metropolitan Opera 1976 (in the same season took mezzo-soprano role of Adalgisa, being the first singer since Grisi to sing both roles); New Prioress in Dialogues of the Carmelites, Metropolitan 1977; now sings only soprano roles; Amellia, La Scala 1978, title role in Favorita, Metropolitan 1978; in Tosca at Metropolitan, New York 1978; début appearance at Opera Bastille, Paris 1990; appeared in film Maggio Musicale 1990, as Nettie Fowler in Broadway production of Carousel 1994–95; frequent appearances with U.S. and European opera houses, with U.S. symphony orchestras; has appeared as soloist on Milan's RAI; was subject of BBC TV feature Profiles in Music 1971, of documentary Black Diva 1985; Dr. h.c. (Holy Cross Coll., Worcester, Mass., Northeastern Univ.); Commdr. des Arts et des Lettres 1984. *Address:* School of Music, University of Michigan, Ann Arbor, MI 48109, U.S.A.

VERSACE, Donatella; Italian designer; b. 1955, Reggio Calabria; d. of Antonio Versace and Francesca Versace; sister of the late Gianni Versace; m.; one s. one d.; joined Versace 1978, fmrly. overseer of advertising and public relations, accessories designer, children's collection designer, sole designer Versus and Isante lines; Creative Dir. Gianni Versace Group 1997–. *Address:* c/o Keeble Cavaco and Duka Inc., 450 West 15th Street, Suite 604, New York, NY 10011, U.S.A.

VERSHBOW, Alexander R., B.A., M.A.; American diplomatist; b. 3 July 1952, Boston; s. of Arthur E. Vershbow and Charlotte Z. Vershbow; m. Lisa K. Vershbow 1976; two s.; ed. Yale Coll. and Russian Inst., Columbia Univ.; joined Foreign Service 1977, Bureau of Politico-Military Affairs 1977–79, U.S. Embassy, Moscow 1979–81, Office of Soviet Union Affairs 1981–85, U.S. Embassy, London 1985–88; advisor U.S. Del. to S.A.L.T. II and S.T.A.R.T. negotiations; Dir. State Dept.'s Office of Soviet Union Affairs 1988–91; U.S. Deputy Perm Rep. to NATO and Chargé d'affaires U.S. Mission 1991–93; Prin. Deputy Asst. Sec. of State for European and Canadian Affairs (responsibilities covered the Balkan conflict) 1993–94; Special Asst. to the Pres. and Sr. Dir. for European Affairs at Nat. Security Council 1995–97 (worked on U.S. policy which laid foundations of the Dayton Peace Agreement, adaptation and enlargement of NATO and its new relationship with Russia); Perm. Rep. to NATO Jan. 1998–; Anatoly Sharansky Freedom Award, Union of Councils of Soviet Jews 1990, first Joseph J. Kruzel Award for contribs. to the cause of peace 1997. *Publications:* articles on arms control, speeches on NATO issues. *Leisure interests:* music, theatre. *Address:* U.S. Mission to NATO, 1110 Brussels, Belgium.

VERSTRAETE, Baron Marc, M.D., PH.D., F.R.C.P., F.A.C.P.; Belgian professor of medicine; b. 1 April 1925, Bruges; s. of Louis Verstraete and Jeanne Coppin; m. Bernadette Moyersoen 1955; one s. four d.; ed. Leuven and Oxford Univs. and Cornell Univ. Medical Coll., New York; Lecturer, Univ. of Leuven 1957, Asst. Prof. 1961, Assoc. Prof. 1963, Prof. 1968–, Dir. Centre for Thrombosis and Vascular Research; Visiting Prof., Harvard Medical School, Boston, U.S.A.; Past-Pres. Royal Acad. of Medicine of Belgium; mem. Acad. of Medicine of South Africa and of Argentina; Dr. h.c. (Edin., Córdoba, Argentina, Bologna, Bordeaux, London). *Publications:* Arterial Hypertension 1966, 1972, Haemostatic Drugs 1977, Methods in Angiology 1980, Haemostasis 1980, Thrombosis 1982, Thrombolysis 1985, Thrombosis in Cardiovascular Disorders 1992; numerous articles in scientific journals. *Leisure interests:* reading, skiing, swimming, tennis. *Address:* Minderbroedersstraat

29, 3000 Leuven (Home); Centre for Molecular and Vascular Biology, Campus Gasthuisberg, University of Leuven, Herestraat 29, 3000 Leuven, Belgium. *Telephone:* (016) 34 57 75 (Office); (016) 22 66 74. (Home). *Fax:* (016) 34 59 90.

VERTINSKAYA, Anastasiya Aleksandrovna; Russian actress; b. 19 Dec. 1944, Moscow; d. of Aleksander Vertinsky; ed. Schukin Theatre School; actress Theatre Sovremennik 1969–80, Moscow Art Theatre 1980–90; works as theatre teacher in Oxford, Switzerland (European Film School), France (Comédie Française); f. Russian Drama troupe in Paris; dir. production Mirage or The Route of The Russian Pierrot, Chekhov, Act III (with A. Kalyagin); cinema début 1961. *Films include:* Red Sails 1961, A Man-Amphibia 1962, Hamlet 1964, War and Peace 1967, Anna Karenina 1968, Do Not Grieve! 1969, A Man Before His Time 1973, Master and Margarita 1994. *Address:* Malaya Dmitrovka str. 31/22, Apt. 38, 103006 Moscow, Russia (Home).

VESSEY, Gen. John W., Jr., D.SC., D.S.M.; American army officer; b. 22 June 1922, Minneapolis, Minn.; s. of John William and Emily (née Roche) Vessey; m. Avis C. Funk; two s. one d.; enlisted in Minn. Nat. Guard 1939; commissioned 2nd Lieut., Field Artillery, Anzio May 1944; served successively with 34th Infantry Div., N. Africa and Italy, 4th Infantry and 3rd Armoured Div., Germany, 25th Infantry Div., S. Viet Nam; promoted Gen. 1976; Commdr. U.S. Forces, S. Korea 1976–79; Army Vice-Chief of Staff 1979–82; Chair. Joint Chiefs of Staff 1982–85; Presidential Emissary to Hanoi 1987–93; Chair. Bd. Center for Preventive Action (Council on Foreign Relations) 1995–; mem. Defense Science Bd. 1987–90, 1992–, Defense Policy Bd. 1990–93, Bd. of Dirs. Martin Marietta, Illinois Tool Works, Nat. Computer Syst., United Services Life Insurance, Nat. Flag Day Foundation, Youth Services U.S.A., Advisory Bd. Gen. Atomics; Trustee AAL Mutual Funds; Legion of Merit, Bronze Star, Air Medal, Jt. Services Commendation Medal, Purple Heart, Presidential Medal of Freedom 1992, and other decorations. *Address:* HCR-1, Box 136A, Garrison, MN 56450, U.S.A. *Telephone:* (320) 692-4488. *Fax:* (320) 692-4939.

VEST, Charles Marstiller, M.S.E., PH.D.; American university president; b. 9 Sept. 1941, Morgantown, W. Va.; s. of Marvin Vest and Winifred Buzzard; m. Rebecca McCue 1963; one s. one d.; ed. W. Va. Univ. and Univ. of Mich.; Asst. Prof., Assoc. Prof. Univ. of Mich. Ann Arbor 1968–77, Prof. of Mechanical Eng. 1977–90, Assoc. Dean of Academic Affairs, Coll. of Eng. 1981–86, Dean, Coll. of Eng. 1986–89, Provost, Vice-Pres. for Academic Affairs 1989–90; Pres. M.I.T., Cambridge, Mass. 1990–; Visiting Assoc. Prof. Stanford Univ. 1974–75; Fellow, Optical Soc. of America, American Acad. of Arts and Sciences, A.A.A.S. *Publications:* Holographic Interferometry 1979; articles in professional journals. *Address:* Office of the President, Massachusetts Institute of Technology, 77 Massachusetts Avenue, Cambridge, MA 02139, U.S.A.

VESTEY, Edmund Hoyle, D.L., F.R.S.A., F.C.I.T.; British business executive; b. 19 June 1932; s. of Ronald Arthur Vestey; m. Anne Moubray Scoones 1960; four s.; ed. Eton Coll.; 2nd Lieut. Queens Bays 1951; Lieut. City of London Yeomanry; Dir. Vestey Group Ltd.; Chair. Albion Insurance Co. 1970–91, Blue Star Line 1971–95, Union Int. PLC and assoc. cos. 1988–91; Pres. Essex County Scout Council 1979–87, Gen. Council of British Shipping 1981–82; Pres. Chamber of Shipping 1992–94; Chair., Masters of Foxhounds Asscn. 1992–96; High Sheriff, Essex 1977; D.L. Essex 1978–91, Suffolk 1991–. *Leisure interest:* fox-hunting. *Address:* Little Thurlow Hall, Haverhill, Suffolk, England.

VETCHÝ, Vladimír, DR.RER.NAT., C.SC.; Czech politician; b. 8 May 1949, Třebíč; m. Alena Vetcha; one s. one d.; ed. Masaryk Univ., Brno, Pedagogue Mil. Acad., Brno; mem. Czech Social Democratic Party 1991–; various functions 1989–98 including mem. Council, Brno, mem. Czecho-Moravian Chamber of Labour Unions; Minister of Defence 1998–. *Leisure interests:* sport, especially basketball, volleyball. *Address:* Ministry of Defence, Tychonova 1, 160 00 Prague 6, Czech Republic. *Telephone:* (20) 20-11-11.

VETLESEN, Vesla; Norwegian politician; b. 19 Oct. 1939, Farsund; m.; worked in Uganda 1968–70; fmr. leader Norwegian Save the Children Fund, Norwegian People's Relief Asscn; fmr. Sec. Devt. Co-operation for LO's (Norwegian TU Fed.); Minister of Devt. Co-operation 1986–88.

VÉZINA, Monique; Canadian politician; b. Rimouski; m.; four c.; Dir. and Chair. Fédération des caisses populaires Desjardins du Bas Saint-Laurent; Chair. Gérardin-Vaillancourt Foundation; Sec. and Dir. Confédération des caisses populaires Desjardins du Québec; Minister for External Relations 1984–86, of Supply and Services 1986–87, of State (Transport) 1987–88, of State for Employment and Immigration 1988–93, for Sr. Citizens 1988–93, for External Affairs Jan.–Nov. 1993; mem. Bd. of Dirs., Rimouski Chamber of Commerce, Soc. immobilière du Québec; fmr. Chair. Comm. on Secondary Educ.; fmr. Vice-Pres. Régie de l'assurance automobile du Québec; fmr. mem. Superior Council of Educ.; Progressive Conservative. *Address:* c/o Progressive Conservative Party of Canada, 275 Slater Street, Suite 501, Ottawa, ON K1P 5H9, Canada.

VIAL, Martin Marie-Charles François; French civil servant and economist; b. 8 Feb. 1954, Lyon; s. of René Vial and Thérèse Giuliani; m. Nelly Waldmann 1978; two s. two d.; ed. Lycée Ampère, Inst. of Political Studies Paris; Prof. of Econ. and Reform Inst. of Tech. of Commerce Algiers 1977–78, Prof. of Finance Higher School of Applied Commercial Sciences 1978–82; with Office of Gen. Compatibility and Budget for External Services 1982–84, also Head; Head of Office of the Treasury and Financial Man. 1984–86; with Office of Banks and Nat. Financial Cos. 1986–88, tech. adviser Postal sector 1988–89, charged with reform of Post, Telecommunications and Broadcasting (PTT) 1989–91, Jt. Dir. office of Minister for Post, Telecommunications and Space 1991, Dir. Ministry of Post and Telecommunications 1992–93, Jt. Dir. for Space Equipment, Accommodation and Transport 1991, Dir. 1991–92; Pres. Aéropostale 1993–97; Dir. La Poste 1997–; mem. Cen. Cttee. Union of Air Transport and Nat. Fed. of Aviation Trade 1994–96, Pres. 1996–. *Leisure interests:* tennis, skiing. *Address:* 2 rue Alençon, 75015 Paris, France (Home).

VIARDO, Vladimir Vladimirovich; Russian pianist; b. 14 Nov. 1949; m. Natalia Viardo; two s.; ed. Moscow State Conservatory; Asst. Prof., Prof., Moscow State Conservatory 1975–; Grand Prix Marguerite Long Int. Competition; Gold Medal and 1st Prize, Van Clibern Int. Competition, U.S.A. 1973; resident in U.S.A. 1988–; Prof. Univ. of N. Texas 1988–; Visiting Prof. Moscow State Conservatory 1998–; played with conductors Mehta, Kitayenko, Maazel, Spivakov, Comissiona, Penderecki; toured in major European, N. American and Canadian cities, Asia and S. Africa, Israel, Central and S. America. *Address:* 457 Piermont Road, Cresskill, N.J. 07626, U.S.A. *Telephone:* (201) 816 1339 (Home). *Fax:* (201) 894 5352 (Home).

VIBE, Kjeld, LL.D.; Norwegian diplomatist; b. 5 Oct 1927, Stavanger; s. of Christopher Andreas Vibe and Thordis Amundsen; m. Beate Meyer 1953; one s. three d.; ed. Univ. of Oslo; entered foreign service 1954; Sec., Del. to NATO and OEEC, Paris 1956–59; First Sec. Ministry of Foreign Affairs 1959–62; Temp. Head, Norwegian Mil. Mission, Berlin 1961; Personal Sec. to Minister of Foreign Affairs 1962–65; Counsellor, Norwegian Embassy, Wash. 1965–69; Deputy Dir.-Gen. for Political Affairs, Ministry of Foreign Affairs 1969–72, Dir.-Gen. 1972–77; Amb., Perm. Rep. to NATO 1977–84; Sec.-Gen. Ministry of Foreign Affairs 1984–89; Amb. to U.S.A. 1989–97. *Leisure interests:* skiing, history, music.

VICKERS, John Stuart, F.B.A., M.A., D.PHIL.; British economist; b. 7 July 1958, Eastbourne; s. of Aubrey Vickers and Kay Vickers; m. Maureen Freed 1991; one s. two d.; ed. Eastbourne Grammar School and Oriel Coll. Oxford; Fellow, All Souls Coll. Oxford 1979–84, 1991–; Shell U.K. Oil 1979–81; Roy Harrod Fellow, Nuffield Coll. Oxford 1984–90; Drummond Prof. of Political Econ. Univ. of Oxford 1991–98; Chief Economist, Bank of England 1998–; Visiting Lecturer, Princeton Univ. 1988, Harvard Univ. 1989, 1990; Visiting Prof. London Business School 1996. *Publications:* Privatization: An Economic Analysis (jtly.) 1988, Regulatory Reform (jtly.) 1994; articles on innovation, competition, regulation, industrial org. etc. *Address:* Bank of England, Threadneedle Street, London, EC2R 8AH, England. *Telephone:* 0171-601 4999. *Fax:* 0171-601 4112.

VICKERS, Jon, C.C.; Canadian tenor; 29 Oct. 1926, Prince Albert, Saskatchewan; s. of William Vickers and Myrle Mossip; m. Henrietta Outerbridge 1953; three s. two d.; began career as concert and opera singer in Canada; joined Royal Opera House, Covent Garden (London) 1957; sang at Bayreuth Festival, Vienna State Opera, San Francisco, Chicago Lyric Opera, Metropolitan Opera, La Scala, Milan, Paris Opera, Boston, Buenos Aires, Athens, Ottawa, Houston, Dallas, Hamburg, Berlin, Munich, Athens Festival, Salzburg Festival, Festival of Orange, Tanglewood Festival, Rio de Janeiro; mem. Royal Acad. Music, London; Hon. LL.D. (Sask.); Hon. C.L.D. (Bishop's Univ.); Mus.D. (Brandon Univ., Univ. of Western Ont.), LL.D. (Univ. of Guelph), Civ. L.D. (Univ. of Laval), D.Mus. (Univ. of Ill.); Critics Award, London 1978, Grammy Award 1979. *Films include:* Carmen, Pagliacci, Norma, Otello. *Recordings:* Messiah, Otello, Aida, Die Walküre, Samson and Delilah, Fidelio, Italian Arias, Verdi Requiem, Peter Grimes, Das Lied von der Erde, Les Troyens, Tristan und Isolde. *Address:* Collingtree, 18 Riddells Bay Road, Warwick, WK-04 Bermuda.

VID, Leonard Bernhardovich, CAND. ECON.; Russian banker; b. 9 Nov. 1931, Zaporozhye, Ukraine; m.; two d.; ed. Moscow Inst. of Non-ferrous Metals and Gold; with Norilsk Ore Mining and Processing enterprise, master then Deputy Dir. 1955–77; First Deputy Chair. U.S.S.R. State Planning Cttee. 1977–91; Deputy Minister of Econs. of U.S.S.R. 1991–92; Dir. Cen. of Econ. State of Affairs at Russian Govt. 1992–95, Chair. Bd. of Dirs. Alfa-Bank 1996–; Exec. Dir. Our Home Russia Movt. 1995–96; mem. Comm. on Co-ordinating State Programme of Transition to the Int. System of Statistics and Accountancy. *Address:* Alfa-Bank, Mashi Poryvayevoy str. 11, Moscow, Russia (Office). *Telephone:* (095) 208 8142 (Office).

VIDAL, Gore; American writer; b. 3 Oct. 1925, West Point, NY; s. of Eugene L. and Nina (Gore) Vidal; ed. Phillips Acad., Exeter, N.H.; served in U.S. Army 1943–46; Edgar Allen Poe award for Television 1955; Drama Critic Reporter (magazine) 1959, Democratic-Liberal Cand. for U.S. Congress from New York 1960; Pres. Kennedy's Advisory Council on the Arts 1961–63; Co-Chair. People's Party 1970–72; Hon. Citizen, Ravello, Italy 1983; Chevalier Ordre nat. des Arts et des Lettres. *Publications: Novels:* Williwaw 1946, In a Yellow Wood 1947, The City and the Pillar 1948, The Season of Comfort 1949, A Search for the King 1950, Dark Green, Bright Red 1950, The Judgment of Paris 1952, Messiah 1954, Julian 1964, Washington, D.C. 1967, Myra Breckinridge 1968, Two Sisters 1970, Burr 1972, Myron 1974, 1876 1976, Kalki 1978, Creation 1980 (Prix Deauville), Duluth 1983, Lincoln 1984, Empire 1987, Hollywood 1990, Live from Golgotha 1992, With Honors 1994, Dark Green, Dark Red 1995, The Season of Conflict 1996, The Essential Vidal 1998, The Smithsonian Institution: a novel 1998. *Short stories:* A Thirsty Evil 1956; *Plays:* Visit to a Small Planet 1956, The Best Man 1960,

Romulus 1962, Weekend 1968, An Evening with Richard Nixon 1972, Gore Vidal's Lincoln 1988; *Travel:* Vidal in Venice 1986. *Film scripts and adaptations:* Wedding Breakfast, I Accuse, Ben Hur, Suddenly Last Summer, The Best Man (Cannes Critics' Prize 1964), Caligula, Dress Gray 1986, Billy the Kid 1989; *Essays:* Rocking the Boat 1963, Reflections upon a Sinking Ship 1969, Homage to Daniel Shays 1972, Matters of Fact and Fiction: Essays 1973–76, 1977, The Second American Revolution 1982, Armageddon? 1987, At Home: Essays 1982–88 1988, A View from the Diners Club: Essays 1987–1991 1991, United States: Essays 1952–1992 1993 (Nat. Book Award), Virgin Islands: A Dependency of United States Essays 1992–97 1997; acted in film Bob Roberts 1992; writes thrillers under pseudonym Edgar Box; *Memoirs:* Screening History 1992, Palimpsest 1995; criticism in Partisan Review, The Nation, New York Review of Books, Esquire, etc. *Address:* c/o Random House, 201 East 50th Street, New York, NY 10022, U.S.A.

VIDAL, H.E. Cardinal Ricardo; Philippine ecclesiastic; b. 6 Feb. 1931, Mogpog, Marinduque; s. of Fructuoso Vidal and Natividad Jamin; ordained 1956; consecrated Bishop (Titular Church of Claterna) 1971; Archbishop of Lipa 1973–82, of Cebu 1982–; cr. Cardinal 1985; Chair. Episcopal Comm. on Clergy; mem. Congregation for the Evangelization of Peoples, Congregation for Catholic Educ., Pontifical Council for Pastoral Assistance to Health Care Workers. *Leisure interests:* walking, classical music, gardening. *Address:* D. Jakosalem Str., P.O. Box 52, Cebu City 6000, Philippines. *Telephone:* (032) 253-3382. *Fax:* 54-458.

VIDAL-NAQUET, Pierre Emmanuel; French historian; b. 23 July 1930, Paris; s. of Lucien Vidal-Naquet and Marguerite Valabrègue; m. Geneviève Railhac 1952; three s.; ed. Lycées Périer, Carnot, Henri-IV and Thiers, Faculté des lettres, Paris; teacher Lycée d'Orléans 1955–56; asst. Faculté des lettres Univ. of Caen 1955–60, Univ. of Lille 1961–62; research asst. Nat. Centre for Scientific Research 1962–64; lecturer Faculté des lettres Univ. of Lyon 1964–66; Deputy Dir. of Studies School of Higher Studies in Social Sciences 1966–69, Dir. of Studies 1969–; now Dir. Centre Gernet Paris; Chevalier Légion d'honneur, Commdr. Order of Phoenix, Greece; Eschilo Oro, Syracuse 1986; Dr. h.c. (Free Univ. of Brussels) 1987, (Dublin) 1989; Grand Prix des sciences humaines de la Ville de Paris 1996. *Publications include:* L'Affaire Audin 1958, La Raison d'Etat 1962, Flavius Josèphe ou du bon usage de la trahison 1977, Le Chasseur noir 1981, Les Assassins de la mémoire 1987, Atlas historique 1987, Face à la raison de l'Etat: Un histoire dans la guerre d'Algérie 1989, La Démocratie grecque vue d'ailleurs 1990, Les Juifs, la mémoire et le présent (2 Vols.) 1981, 1991, Le Trait empoisonné, Réflexions sur l'affaire de Jean Moulin 1993, Réflexions sur le génocide 1995, Mémoires: la Brisure et l'attente (Vol. 1) 1995. *Address:* Centre Louis Gernet, 10 rue Monsieur le Prince, 75006 Paris (Office); 11 rue du Cherche-Midi, 75006 Paris, France (Home).

VIDELA, Lt.-Gen. Jorge Rafael; Argentinian fmr. Head of State and army officer; b. 2 Aug. 1925, Mercedes, Prov. of Buenos Aires; m. Alicia Hartridge; six c.; ed. Nat. Mil. Coll. and War School; commissioned in Infantry 1944; Lieut. in Vigilance Co., Ministry of War 1946; with Motorized Army Regt. 1947–48; Nat. Mil. Coll. 1948; Student, War School, with rank of Army Capt. 1951–54; Staff Officer, Nat. Mil. Coll. 1954–56; Adviser to Office of Mil. Attaché, Washington, D.C. 1956–58; Staff Officer, Army Gen. Command 1962–65, 1966–68; Col. 1965; engaged on course in Strategy, Army Centre of Higher Studies 1965–66; Lieut.-Col., Chief of Cadet Corps 1968; Second in Command and Chief of Staff, Fifth Infantry Brigade 1968–70; Chief of Operations, Third Army Corps 1970–71; Brig., Head of Nat. Mil. Coll. 1971–73; Chief of Army Gen. Staff 1973–75, of Joint High Command 1975; C.-in-C. of Army 1975–78; led coup to depose Pres. María Perón March 1976; Pres. of Argentina 1976–81; fmr. mem. Inter-American Defence Bd., Washington, D.C.; arrested Aug. 1984, on trial for human rights offences 1985, sentenced to life imprisonment Dec. 1985, granted pardon Dec. 1990.

VIDENOV, Jan Vassilev; Bulgarian politician; b. 22 March 1959, Plovdiv; m.; one c.; ed. Moscow State Inst. for Int. Relations; specialist with Biotech Corpn. and Autoelectronics; mem. Supreme Council of Presidency, Bulgarian Socialist Party (BSP) 1990, Chair. 1994; mem. Parl.; Prime Minister of Bulgaria 1995–97. *Address:* c/o Council of Ministers, Blvd. Knjaz Dondukov 1, 1000 Sofia, Bulgaria.

VIEIRA, Brig.-Gen. João Bernardo; Guinea-Bissau politician; b. 1939, Bissau; joined Partido Africano da Indepêndencia da Guiné e Cabo Verde (PAIGC) 1960; Political and Mil. Chief of Catió 1961–64; Mil. Chief of the Southern Front and mem. Political Bureau 1964–65; Vice-Pres. Council of War 1965–67; Rep. of the Political Bureau for the Southern Front 1967–70; mem. Council of War, responsible for mil. operations 1970–71; mem. Exec. Cttee. and Council of War 1971–73; mem. Perm. Secr. of PAIGC 1973–; Pres. of People's Nat. Ass. 1973–78; State Commr. for the Armed Forces Sept. 1973–78; Chief State Commr. 1978–84; Pres. of Guinea-Bissau Nov. 1980–; C.-in-C. of Armed Forces 1982, Minister of Defence and of Interior 1982–92; led coup to depose Pres. Luiz Cabral (q.v.); Sec. Gen. Revolutionary Council Nov. 1980–. *Address:* Conselho de Estado, Bissau, Guinea-Bissau.

VIENOT, Marc, L. ÈS L.; French banker; b. 1 Nov. 1928, Paris; s. of the late Jacques Vienot and of Henriette Brunet; m. Christiane Regnault 1953; two s. two d.; ed. Nat. Inst. of Politicial Studies and Ecole Nat. d'Admin.; Inspector of Finance 1955; special envoy to Cabinet of Minister of Econ. and Finance April–June 1957, to Cabinet of Minister of Finance, Econ. and Planning June–Nov. 1957; special envoy to cabinet of Pres. of French Parl. 1957–58; special envoy to Treasury Div. July 1958; Chair. Study Cttee. OECD 1961–65; Sec. to Bd. of Econ. and Social Devt. Fund 1963–65; Under-Sec. Treasury Div. 1965; Head, Financial Activities Service, Treasury Div. 1967; Minister (Financial Counsellor), French embassies in U.S.A. and Canada and Dir. IBRD and IMF 1970–73; Deputy Gen. Man. Société Générale 1973, Gen. Man. 1977–86, Chair. and C.E.O. 1986–97, now Hon. Chair; Interim Pres. Alcatel Alsthom April-July 1995; Dir. Alcatel Alsthom, Havas, Schneider, Compagnie générale des eaux, Rhône Poulenc; mem. Supervisory Bd. Compagnie bancaire, Carnaud Metalbox; mem., fmr. Vice-Pres. French Banks Asscn.; Officier, Légion d'honneur; Commdr., Ordre Nat. du Mérite. *Address:* 29 boulévard Haussmann, 75009 Paris (Office); 4 avenue Raymond Poincaré, 75016 Paris, France.

VIERECK, Peter, B.S., M.A., PH.D.; American poet, historian and dramatist; b. 5 Aug. 1916, New York; s. of George S. and Margaret (Hein) Viereck; m. 1st Anya de Markov 1945 (divorced 1970); one s. one d.; m. 2nd Betty Martin Falkenberg 1972; ed. Harvard Univ. and Christ Church, Oxford; Teaching Asst., Harvard Univ. 1941–42, Instructor in German Literature and tutor 1946–47; History Instructor, U.S. Army, Univ. of Florence, Italy 1945; Asst. Prof. History, Smith Coll. 1947–48; Assoc. Prof. Mount Holyoke Coll. 1948–55, Prof. of European and Russian History 1955–, Distinguished William R. Kenan Prof. 1979–; U.S. State Dept. mission of cultural exchange to U.S.S.R. 1961; awarded Tietjens Prize for Poetry 1948, Pulitzer Prize for Poetry 1949, Sadin Poetry Prize New York Quarterly 1977, Varouja Prize 1983; Guggenheim Fellow, Rome 1949–50; Visiting Lecturer Univ. of Paris, American Univ., Beirut, and American Univ. Cairo 1966; L.H.D. (Olivet Coll.) 1959. *Publications:* Metapolitics—From the Romantics to Hitler 1941, Terror and Decorum (poems) 1948, Who Killed the Universe? 1948, Conservation Revisited—The Revolt Against Revolt—1815-1849 1949, Strike Through the Mask: New Lyrical Poems 1950, The First Morning: New Poems 1952, Shame and Glory of the Intellectuals 1953, Dream and Responsibility: The Tension Between Poetry and Society 1953, The Unadjusted Man: a New Hero for Americans 1956, Conservatism: From John Adams to Churchill 1956, The Persimmon Tree (poems) 1956, The Tree Witch: A Poem and Play 1961, Metapolitics: The Roots of the Nazi Mind 1961, Conservatism Revisited and the New Conservatism: What Went Wrong? 1962, New and Selected Poems 1967, Soviet Policy Making 1967, Outside Looking In 1972, A Question of Quality 1976, Archer in the Marrow (poems) 1987, Tide and Continuities: Last & First Poems 1995; numerous articles and poems. *Address:* Mount Holyoke College, South Hadley, MA 01075 (Office); 12 Silver Street, South Hadley, MA 01075, U.S.A. (Home). *Telephone:* (413) 534-5504 (Home).

VIGNAL, Renaud; French diplomatist; b. 18 April 1943, Valence; s. of Jean Vignal and Reine Mouet; m. 1st Monique Tuffelli 1966 (deceased); two d.; m. 2nd Anne de Villiers de la Noue 1983 (deceased); one s.; ed. Lycées Montaigne and Louis-le-Grand, Paris, Facultés de Droit et des Lettres, Paris, Inst. d'Etudes Politiques and Ecole Nat. d'Admin.; Second Sec. Embassy Cairo 1971–74; mem. policy planning staff, Ministry of Foreign Affairs 1974–75; Press Officer, Washington 1975–77; Deputy Spokesman, Ministry of Foreign Affairs 1980–81; Prin. Sec. to Minister for Co-operation and Devt. 1981–82; Consul-Gen. Quebec 1983–87; Amb. to Seychelles 1987–89, to Romania 1990–93, to Argentina 1993–97; Conseiller gen. de la Drôme 1988–94, Chevalier Légion d'honneur, Ordre nat. du Mérite, Grande croix du Mérite (Argentina); Commdr. du Mérite (Egypt). *Leisure interest:* horses. *Address:* Ministère des Affaires étrangères, 37 quai d'Orsay, 75007 Paris; 15 rue Moncey, 75009 Paris, France.

VIKSTRÖM, John Edvin, D.THEOL.; Finnish ecclesiastic (retd.); b. 1 Oct. 1931, Kronoby; s. of Edvin and Hilma (née Lindström) Vikström; m. Birgitta Hellberg 1957 (died 1994); two s. one d.; ordained 1956; Pastor for Porvoo (Borgå) Diocese 1957–61; Asst. in Theological Faculty of Åbo Akademi, Turku 1962–65, Instructor 1966–70, Assoc. Prof. 1970; Bishop of Porvoo (Borgå) Diocese 1970–82; Archbishop of the Evangelical-Lutheran Church of Finland 1982–98; mem. Cen. Cttee. World Council of Churches 1983–91; Dr. h.c. (Theological Acad. of Leningrad) 1985, (Theological Acad. of Budapest) 1987; Great Award of the Swedish Culture Foundation 1981, Grosses Bundesverdienstkreuz (Fed. Germany) 1989, Great Cross Order of the White Rose (Finland) 1986, Cross of Apostle and Evangelist Mark (First Class) 1989, Commdr. Order of the Holy Lamb (1st Class) 1991, Independence Medal of the First Order (Jordan) 1993, Lambeth Cross 1994. *Publications:* Religion och kultur 1966, Effekten av religiös fostran 1970, Tro i kris 1972, Fråga biskopen om tro 1980, Herdestaven 1982, Ihmisen usko 1982, Kuitenkin 1983, Uusi rohkeus elää 1985, Kirjeen Kääntöpiiri 1987, Suuntaviittoja 1988, Myös maan päällä 1992. *Leisure interests:* history of ideas and culture, sports. *Address:* c/o Satamakatu 11, P.O. Box 185, 00161 Helsinki, Finland.

VIKTYUK, Roman Grigoryevich; Russian/Ukrainian theatre director; b. 28 Oct. 1936, Lvov; ed. A. Lunacharcky State Inst. of Theatre Art; Chief Dir. Kalinin Theatre of Lenin Komsomol 1968–71; Dir. Russian Drama Theatre in Vilnius 1971–77; Artistic Dir. Students' Theatre of Moscow Univ. 1977–91; concurrently theatre productions in maj. theatres of Moscow and Leningrad; f. and Artistic Dir. Viktyuk Theatre 1991–; directed productions in Swedish Theatre Helsinki, theatres of Brescia, Rome, San Diego; U.S.A. tour 1998; several TV productions. *Address:* Tverskaya 4, Apt. 87, 103009 Moscow, Russia. *Telephone:* (095) 292 6895 (Home).

VIKULOV, Vladimir Ivanovich; Russian ice-hockey player; b. 27 July 1946, Moscow; ed. Moscow Inst. of Physical Culture; Honoured Master of

Sport 1967; joined CPSU 1971; champion of World, Europe and U.S.S.R. 1966–79; champion of Winter Olympic Games 1968 and holder of Cup of European Champions for ice-hockey 1969–70, 1972. *Address:* Russian Ice Hockey Federation, Luzhnetskaya nab. 8, Moscow, Russia. *Telephone:* 201-09-74.

VILADECANS, Joan-Pere; Spanish artist; b. 1948, Barcelona; s. of Joan-Pere Viladecans and Carme Viladecans; one-man shows include: Sala Gaspar, Barcelona 1967, Galerie Dresdnere, Toronto 1967, Galerie Dreiseitel, Cologne 1971, 1990, Galeria Pecanins, Mexico 1974, Galleri Uddenberg, Gothenburg 1975, M.L. Museum Gallery, New York 1977, Aaron Gallery, Washington, D.C. 1978, Guild Gallery, New York 1981, Museo Español Arte Contemporáneo, Madrid 1983, Duszka Patÿn-Karolczak Galerie d'Art, Brussels 1983, Galeria Art-Inter, Luxembourg 1985, Brompton Gallery, London 1985, Baukunst Galerie, Cologne 1988, Galerie Dreiseitel, Cologne 1990, Museo Rufino Tamayo, Mexico 1991, Casa de Goya, Bordeaux 1991, Espace Sphonisbe, Tunis 1991, Expo '92, Seville 1992, Sala Gaspar, Barcelona 1992, Galeria Quadrado Azul, Oporto 1993, Galerie Joan Gaspar, Barcelona 1994, Galeria Benedet, Oviedo 1995; Chevalier, Ordre des Arts et des Lettres. *Address:* Córcega 589, 08025 Barcelona, Spain. *Telephone:* (3) 455.93.85; 2076388.

VILARDELL, Francisco, M.D., D.SC.(MED.); Spanish physician; b. 1 April 1926, Barcelona; s. of Jacinto Vilardell and Mercedes Viñas; m. Leonor Vilardell 1958; one s. two d.; ed. Univs. of Barcelona and Pennsylvania; Dir. Gastroenterology Service, Hosp. Santa Cruz y San Pablo, Barcelona 1963–; Dir. Postgrad. School of Gastroenterology, Autonomous Univ. of Barcelona 1969–; Pres. European Soc. for Digestive Endoscopy 1970–74, European Asscn. for Study of the Liver 1975–76, World Org. of Gastroenterology 1982– (Sec.-Gen. 1974–82), Council of Int. Orgs. in Medical Science 1987–93, Perm. Adviser 1994–; Dir.-Gen. Health Planning, Ministry of Health 1981–82, mem. Advisory Council 1997–; Gold Medal, Barcelona Acad. of Medicine; Gold Medal, Spanish Soc. of Gastroenterology; Chevalier, Légion d'honneur. *Publications:* ed. of six books; 170 papers in medical journals. *Leisure interests:* music, philology. *Address:* Escuela de Patología Digestiva, Hospital de la Santa Cruz y San Pablo, 08025 Barcelona (Office); CIOMS, c/o World Health Organization, 1211 Geneva 27, Switzerland; Juan Sebastian Bach 11, 08021 Barcelona, Spain (Home). *Telephone:* (93) 219.73.43 (Office); (22) 91.34.06 (CIOMS); (93) 201.45.11 (Home). *Fax:* (93) 201.01.91 (Home).

VILARIÑO PINTOS, Daría; Spanish librarian (retd.); b. 26 Jan. 1928, Santiago de Compostela; d. of José Vilariño de Andrés and Daría Pintos Castro; mem. staff, state library, museum and archives depts. 1957–70; Deputy Dir. Library of Univ. of Santiago 1970–73, Dir. 1973–93. *Publications:* O Libro Galego onte e hoxe (with Virtudes Pardo) 1981, Hechos de D. Berenguel de Landoria (Co-author) 1983, Vasco de Aponte. Recuento de las Casas Antiguas del Reino de Galicìa. Edición crítica (co-author) 1986, Ordoño de Celanova: Vida y Milagros de San Rosendo. Edición crítica (co-author) 1990; articles in professional journals, bibliographical catalogues. *Leisure interest:* reading. *Address:* Calle San Miguel No. 5, 2°, 15704 Santiago de Compostela, La Coruña, Spain. *Telephone:* 58 36 58.

VILHJALMSSON, Thor; Icelandic lawyer; b. 9 June 1930, Reykjavík; s. of Vilhjalmur Th. Gislason and Inga Arnadóttir Gislason; m. Ragnhildur Helgadóttir Vilhjalmsson 1950; one s. three d.; ed. Reykjavík Grammar School, St. Andrews Univ., Scotland, Univ. of Iceland, New York Univ. and Univ. of Copenhagen; Asst. Lecturer, Univ. of Iceland 1959–62, part-time Lecturer 1962–67, Prof. 1967–76, and Dean, Faculty of Law 1968–70, Dir. Inst. of Law 1974–76; Deputy Judge Reykjavík Civil Court 1960–62, Judge 1962–67; Judge European Court of Human Rights 1971–98; Assoc. Justice of the Supreme Court of Iceland 1976–93, Pres. 1983–84, 1993; Judge, EFTA Court, Geneva 1994–96, Luxembourg 1996–; mem. Icelandic Del. to UN Gen. Ass. 1963, UN Sea-Bed Cttee. 1972, 1973 to Law of the Sea Conf. 1974, 1975, and other int. confs.; Pres. Asscn. of Icelandic Lawyers 1971–74; Ed. Icelandic Law Review 1973–83. *Publications:* Civil Procedure I-IV and studies on human rights and legal history. *Address:* EFTA Court, 1 rue du Fort Thüngen, 1499 Luxembourg. *Telephone:* 42 108 1. *Fax:* 43 43 89.

VILJOEN, Gerrit van Niekerk, D.LITT. ET PHIL., M.A.; South African fmr. politician and academic; b. 11 Sept. 1926, Cape Town; s. of late Hendrik Geldenhuys Viljoen; m. Magdalena Maria van der Merwe 1951; two s. five d.; ed. Afrikaanse Hoër Seunskool, Pretoria, Univ. of Pretoria, King's Coll., Cambridge, Ryksuniversiteit, Leiden, Sorbonne; Sr. Lecturer in Classics, Univ. of S.A. 1955–57, Prof. 1957–67; Admin.-Gen. Namibia (S.W. Africa) 1979–80; Minister of Nat. Educ. 1980–84, of Co-operation and Devt. and (Black) Educ. (renamed Devt. Aid and Educ.) 1984–86, of Devt. Aid and Educ. 1986–89, of Nat. Educ. 1989–90, of Constitutional Devt., Planning 1989–92, of State Affairs May–Nov. 1992; Rector, Rand Afrikaans Univ. 1967–79; Chancellor Rand Afrikaans Univ. 1985–; Corresp. mem. Royal Netherlands Acad. of Sciences; mem. Suid-Afrikaanse Akad.; Hon. Pres. Classical Asscn. of S.A.; Hon. LL.D. (Rand Afrikaans) 1980, Hon. D.Ed. (Orange Free State Univ.). *Address:* P.O. Box 95173, Waterkloof 0145, Pretoria, South Africa.

VILJOEN, Hendrik Christo, PH.D.; South African broadcasting executive and electronics engineer; b. 31 Aug. 1937, Graaff-Reniet; s. of Hendrik Christoffel Viljoen and Anna Pienaar; m. Hana Stehlik 1965; one s. two d.; ed. Univ. of Stellenbosch; engineer, Dept. of Posts and Telecommunications, Pretoria 1961–65; Sr. Lecturer, Univ. of Stellenbosch 1966–70, Prof. 1970–, Dean of Eng. 1979–93, Vice-Rector of Operations 1993–; Chair. Bd. of Control SABC 1989–91, Chair. SABC 1989–93; Visiting Prof. Ga. Inst. of Tech., Atlanta, U.S.A. 1975–76, Nat. Chiao Tung Univ., Hsinchu, Taiwan 1981; mem. Bd. S.A. Bureau of Standards, Pretoria, Electricity Council, Johannesburg; mem. Electricity Control Bd., Pretoria; Chair. Task Group on Broadcasting in S.A. 1987–91; Sr. mem. Inst. of Electrical and Electronic Engineers, U.S.A. 1978–; Fellow S.A. Akademie vir Wetenskap en Kuns. *Leisure interests:* philately, genealogy, perlemoen diving at Betty's Bay, squash. *Address:* 6 Hof Avenue, Stellenbosch 7600, South Africa. *Telephone:* 883-3754. *Fax:* 808-3743.

VILKAS, Eduardas, D.PHYS.-MATH.SC.; Lithuanian mathematician and economist; b. 3 Oct. 1935, Girgzday; m. Stefa Vilkienė; two s. one d.; ed. Lithuanian State Univ.; mem. CPSU 1959–90; researcher Inst. of Physics and Math., Lithuanian Acad. of Sciences 1958–77; researcher Inst. of Math. and Cybernetics 1977–79, Deputy Dir. 1979–85; Dir. Inst. of Econs. 1985–; teacher Vilnius State Univ. 1958–, Prof. 1976; Chair. Govt. Comm. for Privatization 1996; mem. Chief Learned Sec., Lithuanian Acad. of Sciences; main research on probability theory, theory of games, math. economy and its application in nat. econ. *Publications:* What is the Theory of Games? 1976, Mathematical Methods in the Economy 1980, Solutions, Theory, Information, Modelling (together with E. Maiminas) 1981, articles in scientific periodicals. *Address:* Ekonomikos Institutas, A. Goštanto 12, 2600 Vilnius; Lietuvos M.A. Prezidiumas, Gedimino pr. 3, 2600 Vilnius (Offices); Žirgo 20, 2040 Vilnius, Lithuania. *Telephone:* (2) 623502 (Office); (2) 700404 (Home).

VILLA, José García, A.B.; Philippine poet and critic; b. 5 Aug. 1914, Manila; s. of Dr. Simeon Villa and Maria García; two s.; ed. Univs. of the Philippines, of New Mexico and Columbia Univ.; Assoc. Ed. New Directions Books 1949; Cultural Attaché Philippine Mission to UN 1953–63; Dir. N.Y. City Coll. Poetry Workshop 1952–63, Prof. of Poetry, New School for Social Research 1964–73; Philippines Presidential Adviser on Cultural Affairs 1968–; Guggenheim Fellowship 1943, Bollingen Fellowship 1951, Rockefeller Grant 1964; American Acad. of Arts and Letters Award 1942, Shelley Memorial Award 1959, Pro Patria Award 1961, Philippines Cultural Heritage Award 1962, Nat. Artist in Literature 1973; Hon. D.Litt. (Far Eastern Univ.) 1959, Hon. L.H.D. (Philippines) 1973. *Publications:* Footnote to Youth (stories) 1933, Many Voices 1939, Poems by Doveglion 1941, Have Come, Am Here 1942, Volume Two 1949, Selected Poems and New 1958, Poems Fifty-five 1962, Poems in Praise of Love 1962, Selected Stories 1962, The Portable Villa 1963, The Essential Villa 1965, Appassionata 1979; Ed.: A Celebration for Edith Sitwell 1948, Doveglion Book of Philippine Poetry 1975, Bravo: the Poet's Magazine 1981, New Doveglion Book of Philippine Poetry 1993. *Leisure interests:* dogs, plants, cooking.

VILLA-VICENCIO, Rev. Charles, S.T.M., PH.D.; South African professor of religion and society; b. 7 Nov. 1942, Johannesburg; s. of Charles Villa-Vicencio and Paula Villa-Vicencio; m. Eileen van Sittert 1968; two d.; ed. Rhodes Univ. Grahamstown, and Natal, Yale and Drew Univs.; with Standard Bank of S.A. 1961–64; Probationer Minister, Methodist Church of Southern Africa 1965–70; ordained Minister 1970; Minister of various congregations in S. Africa and U.S.A.; Teaching Fellow, Drew Univ. 1974–75; part-time lecturer, Univ. of Cape Town 1976–77; Sr. Lecturer, Univ. of S. Africa 1978–81, Assoc. Prof. 1981–82; Sr. Lecturer, Univ. of Cape Town 1982–, Assoc Prof. 1984–88, Head, Dept of Religious Studies 1986–97, Prof. of Religion and Society 1988–97; mem. S.A. Theological Soc.; del. to numerous confs. etc. *Publications include:* Between Christ and Caesar: Classical and Contemporary Texts 1986, Trapped in Apartheid 1988, Civil Disobedience and Beyond 1990, A Theology of Reconstruction 1992, A Spirit of Hope: Conversations on Politics, Religion and Values 1993; ed. or co-ed. of and contrib. to several vols. of essays; numerous articles including many on the church and politics in South Africa. *Address:* 14 Annerley Road, Rosebank, Cape Town 7700, South Africa (Home). *Telephone:* 021-6868643 (Home). *Fax:* 021-6503761.

VILLAGRAN DE LEON, Francisco, M.A.; Guatemalan diplomatist; b. 29 March 1954, Guatemala City; m.; one c.; ed. Georgetown Univ., Washington, D.C. and Universidad Rafael Landivar, Guatemala; Deputy Dir. Guatemalan Foreign Service 1979; Political Counsellor, Washington, D.C. 1983; Alt. Rep. Guatemalan Mission to OAS 1984; Deputy Chief of Washington Embassy 1985; Deputy Minister of Foreign Affairs 1986; Amb. to OAS 1987, to Canada 1995–; Perm. Rep. to UN 1988–92. *Address:* Guatemalan Embassy, 130 Albert Street, Suite 1010, Ottawa, Ont. K1P 5G4, Canada; c/o Ministry of Foreign Affairs, Palacio Nacional, Guatemala City, Guatemala. *Telephone:* (613) 233-7237 (Ottawa). *Fax:* (613) 233 0135 (Ottawa).

VILLAIN, Claude Edouard Louis Etienne, L. EN D.; French international civil servant; b. 4 Jan. 1935, Paris; s. of Etienne and Marie Louise (Caudron) Villain; m. Bernadette Olivier 1962; two s.; ed. Lycée Voltaire, Lycée Louis-le-Grand, Univ. of Paris; Trainee in French Overseas Admin. 1956–59, Officer in Dept. of Algerian Affairs 1959–61; Officer for Econ. Studies in Agricultural Devt. Bureau 1962–64; Officer in Ministry of Econ. and Finance 1964, Head of Dept. 1969, Deputy Dir. of Ministry 1973; Tech. Adviser in Office of Valéry Giscard d'Estaing (then Minister of Econ. and Finance) 1973–74; Dir.-Gen. of Competition and Prices in Ministry of Econ. and Finance 1974–78; Administrateur Soc. Nat. des Chemins de fer Français (SNCF) 1974–78; Administrateur Soc. Nat. Elf Aquitaine 1974–79; Dir.-

Gen. of Agric., Comm. of EEC 1979–85; Dir.-Gen. Socopa Int., Vice-Pres. Socopa France 1985; Special Adviser to Minister of Econ. and Finance 1986–88; Inspector-Gen. of Finances 1987–92; Del. Interministerial Mission for Cen. and Eastern Europe (MICECO) 1992–93, for Euro-Disneyland 1993; Chair. Admin. Bd. Etablissement public de réalisation de défaisance 1996–, Comilog SA 1996–; mem. Intergovernmental Comm. of the Channel Tunnel; Officier, Légion d'honneur; Chevalier, Ordre nat. du Mérite; Croix de Valeur Mil.; Commandeur du Mérite Agricole. *Address:* Inspection générale des finances, 139 rue de Bercy, 75572 Paris, cedex 12, France.

VILLAPALOS-SALAS, Gustavo; Spanish university rector; b. 15 Oct. 1949, Madrid; s. of Gustavo Villapalos-Salas and Juana Villapalos-Salas; Prof., Faculty of Law, Universidad Complutense de Madrid 1970–75, Prof. of Law 1976, Dir. Dept. of History of Law 1980–84, Dean Faculty of Law 1984–87, Rector of Univ. 1987–; Research Fellow Instituto de Estudios Juridícos 1972–74, Centro de Investigaciones Juridícas, Económicas y Sociales 1975; Visiting Prof., Univ. of Calif. at Berkeley, U.S.A. 1976, Univ. of Freiburg 1976–77; Dr. h.c. (Paris-Sud, St. Louis, U.S.A., Guanajuato, Mexico, La Plata, Argentina); Gran Cruz de la Orden de Alfonso X el Sabio, Gran Cruz del Mérito Civil, Hon. C.B.E. *Publications:* Colección Diplomática del Archivo Municipal de Santander: Documentos Reales II (1525–1599) 1982, Los Regímenes Económicos Matrimoniales en la Historia del Derecho Español: Prelección 1983, El Fuero de León: Comentarios 1984, Cortes de Castilla en el siglo XV 1986, La Baja Edad Media, Vol. IV, Historia General de Cantabria 1986, La Alta Edad Media, Vol. III 1987. *Leisure interests:* astronomy, cinema, classical music, reading. *Address:* Calle Alberto Aguilera 11, 28015 Madrid, Spain (Home). *Telephone:* 91-445.29.29 (Home).

VILLAR Y ORTIZ DE URDÍA, Francisco, B.L.; Spanish diplomatist; b. 8 Jan. 1945, Salamanca; m.; two c.; ed. Univ. of Salamanca; entered diplomatic service 1971; Sec. of Embassy, Perm. Mission of Spain at UN 1973–78; lecturer and Dir. of Studies, Escuela Diplomatica, Madrid 1978–81; Ministry of Foreign Affairs 1981–83; with Perm. Mission at UN, New York and mem. Spanish Del. to UN Security Council 1982–83; Dir.-Gen. of Int. Orgs. and Confs. Ministry of Foreign Affairs 1983–87; Perm. Rep. to UN 1987–91; del. to numerous int. confs. *Publications:* El Processo de Autodeterminacion del Sahara Occidental 1982, numerous articles on politics and int. relations. *Address:* c/o Ministry of Foreign Affairs, Plaza de la Provincia 1, Madrid 12, Spain.

VILLARROEL-LANDER, Mario Enrique; Venezuelan Red Cross official, lawyer and professor; b. 20 Sept. 1947, Caracas; m. Norka Sierraalta 1969; three s. one d.; ed. Cen. Univ. of Venezuela, Santa María Univ., Caracas; joined Red Cross as a volunteer 1967, Nat. Pres. 1978–, Pres. Int. Fed. of Red Cross and Red Crescent Socs. 1987–; Pres. Mirandino Historical Studies Inst., Henry Dunant Inst. 1992–93; Prof. of Penal Law, Chair. of Criminal Law Santa María Univ.; lawyer pvt. legal practice; fmr. dir. La Voz del Derecho (legal review); numerous memberships of int. orgs.; numerous distinctions from Red Cross orgs. *Publications:* El Cuerpo Técnico de Policía Judicial en el Proceso Penal Venezolano, Habeas Corpus y antejuicio de Mérito, legal articles in Venezuelan and foreign periodicals. *Leisure interest:* journalism. *Address:* International Federation of Red Cross and Red Crescent Societies, 17 Chemin des Crêts, Petit-Saconnex, Case Postale 372, 1211 Geneva 19, Switzerland. *Telephone:* (22) 7304222. *Fax:* (22) 7330395.

VILLAS BÔAS, Orlando; Brazilian anthropologist and explorer; b. 1914, Botucatu, São Paulo; s. of Agnelo and Arlinda Villas Bôas; m. Marina Lopes de Lima Villas Bôas; one s.; brother of late Claudio Villas Bôas; has lived in the Brazilian jungle around the River Xingú and worked among the Indians since 1945; co-founder (with his brother) of the Parque Nacional do Xingú, Dir. 1961–; Gold Medal, Royal Geographical Soc. *Leisure interests:* theatre, reading, travel.

VILLAS-BOAS, José Manuel P. de; Portuguese diplomatist; b. 23 Feb. 1931, Oporto; s. of João and Maria Margarida de Villas-Boas; m. Maria do Patrocinio de Almeida Braga 1956; ed. Lisbon Univ.; Attaché, Ministry of Foreign Affairs 1954; Embassies, Pretoria 1959, London 1963; Counsellor 1969; Head of African Dept., Ministry of Foreign Affairs 1970–72; Consul-Gen., Milan 1972–74; Minister Plenipotentiary, Asst. Dir.-Gen. of Political Affairs, Ministry of Foreign Affairs 1974–77, Dir.-Gen. of Political Affairs 1977–79; Amb. and Perm. Rep. to NATO 1979–84, Amb. to South Africa 1984–89, to People's Repub. of China 1989–93, to Russia 1993–97; Grand Cross Order of Merit (Portugal), Hon. K.C.M.G. (U.K.), Grand Cross of St. Olav (Norway), of Merit (Spain), Cruzeiro do Sul (Brazil), of Rio Branco (Brazil), of Good Hope (S. Africa), Grand Officer of the Order of Merit (Fed. Repub. of Germany), of the Lion (Senegal), Commdr., Légion d'honneur (France), Order of Merit (Italy), etc. *Leisure interests:* music, travelling. *Address:* c/o Ministry of Foreign Affairs, Largo do Rilvas, 1354 Lisbon Codex, Portugal.

VILLEGAS DE CLERCAMP, Eric Auguste Marc Ghislain de, D.IUR., CAND. IN PHIL. AND LETTERS; Belgian business executive and lawyer; b. 19 June 1924, Brussels; s. of late Count de Villegas de Clercamp and of Elisabeth de Lantsheere; m. Béatrice Met den Ancxt 1981; three s.; joined Soc. Gen. de Banque (now Gen. Bank) 1947, Head of Service, Turnhout 1953, Sub-Man. Louvain 1956, Asst. Man. 1958, Man. Ghent 1959, Gen. Man. and mem. Local Man. Cttee., Ghent 1959, Exec. Mem. Local Cttee., Brussels 1963, Dir. 1967, Man. Dir. 1968, Chair. Bd. of Man. Dirs. 1980; Officier de l'Ordre de la Couronne. *Leisure interests:* riding, gardening, antiques. *Address:* Kasteel von Bever, Hof te Beverlaan, 150, 1820 Grimbergen (Strombeer-Bever), Belgium. *Telephone:* 02/269.27.90.

VILLELLA, Edward, B.S.; American ballet dancer; b. 1 Oct. 1936, New York; s. of Joseph and Mildred (De Giovanni) Villella; m. 1st Janet Greschler 1962 (divorced 1980); one s.; m. 2nd Linda Carbonetta 1981; two d.; ed. N.Y. State Maritime Coll.; joined N.Y. City Ballet 1957, becoming soloist within a year, now Premier Dancer; originated leading roles in George Balanchine's Bugaku, Tarantella, Stars and Stripes, Harlequinade, Jewels, Glinkaiana, A Midsummer Night's Dream; first danced his famous role of Prodigal Son 1960; has also danced leading roles in Allegro Brillante, Jeux, Pas de Deux, Raymonda Variations, Scotch Symphony, Swan Lake; choreographed Narkissos; has appeared at Bolshoi Theatre, with Royal Danish Ballet and in London, and made numerous guest appearances; choreographed and starred in revivals of Brigadoon, Carousel; Dance magazine award 1965; Chair. N.Y. City Comm. of Cultural Affairs 1978; Artistic Co-ordinator Eglersky Ballet Co. (now André Eglersky State Ballet of New York) 1979–84, Choreographer 1980–84; Choreographer N.J. Ballet 1980; Artistic Dir. Ballet Okla. 1983–86, Miami City Ballet 1985–; Heritage Chair in Arts and Cultural Criticism George Mason Univ. 1992–93, 1993–94; mem. Nat. Council on the Arts 1968–74; Hon. D.F.A. (S.U.N.Y. Maritime Coll.) 1998; Golden Plate Award (American Acad. of Achievement) 1971, Emmy Award 1975, Gold Medal Award Nat. Soc. of Arts and Letters 1990, Nat. Medal of Arts Award 1997, other awards. *Publication:* Prodigal Son (jtly.) 1992.

VILLEMÉJANE, Bernard de; French business executive; b. 10 March 1930, Marseille; s. of Pierre and Marie-Thérèse (née Getten) de Villeméjane; m. Françoise Boucheronde 1965; two s.; ed. Ecole Polytechnique and Ecole des Mines, Paris; with Direction des Mines et de la Géologie, French W. Africa 1955–60; Ministry of Industry 1960–61; Eng. Adviser, Banque Rothschild 1961–62; Deputy Man. Dir. Société Penarroya 1963, Man Dir. 1967, Chair. of Bd. and Man. Dir. 1971–86, Dir. 1986–88, Vice-Pres. Supervisory Bd. 1988–91; Man Dir. Société Le Nickel 1971–74; Chair. of Bd. and Man. Dir. S.M. le Nickel S.L.N. 1974–83, Dir. 1984; Dir. Imetal 1974, Man. dir. 1974, Chair. 1979–93, Hon. Pres. 1993–; Vice-Chair. Supervisory Bd. Metaleurop 1986–91; Dir. Copperweld Corpn., U.S.A. 1976, Cookson PLC (UK) 1977–86; Dir. Financère d'Angers 1989–, Chair. 1989–91; Chair., Man. Dir. Gravograph 1994–95; Vice-Pres. Moulinex; Dir. of various other European and American cos., including Origny-Desvroise, C-E Minerals Inc., DBK Minerals Inc., Minemet S.A.; Officier, Légion d'honneur, Officier, Ordre Nat. du Mérite, Grand Cross, Orden del Mérito (Spain), Commdr. Ordre de l'Etoile Equatoriale (Gabon). *Address:* Imetal, Tour Maine-Montparnasse, 33 avenue du Maine, 75755 Paris Cedex 15 (Office); 102 rue d'Assas, 75006 Paris, France (Home). *Telephone:* 45-38-48-48 (Office).

VILLENEUVE, Jacques; Canadian racing car driver; b. 9 April 1971; started racing in Italian touring car championship Italian Formula 3 1989, 1990, with Reynaud and Alfa Romeo 1992, Japanese Formula 3 1993, Formula Atlantic 1993, IndyCar driver 1994–95; IndyCar racing champion 1995; now drives Formula One cars with Williams Renault team; Grand Prix winner: Britain 1996, 1997, Brazil 1997, Argentina 1997, Spain 1997, Hungary 1997, Austria 1997, Luxembourg 1997; Formula One Champion 1997.

VILLENEUVE, Jeanne Madeleine; French journalist; b. 29 Jan. 1949, Paris; d. of Henry Villeneuve and Jacqueline Picq; ed. Inst. d'Etudes Politiques; Financial Analyst, Banque Nat. de. Paris 1974–78; Chef de Service, Soc. Générale de Presse 1978–82, daily newspaper Libération 1982–86, weekly l'Express Feb.–Sept. 1986; Chief Reporter, l'Evènement du Jeudi 1986–91; Asst. Ed. Parisien 1991–95; Ed. Libération 1996–97. *Publication:* Le mythe Tapie 1988. *Address:* c/o Journal Libération, 11 rue Béranger,75003 Paris, France.

VILLEPIN, Dominique Marie François René Galouzeau de, L. EN D.; French diplomatist and civil servant; b. 14 Nov. 1953, Rabat; s. of Xavier Galouzeau de Villepin and Yvonne Hétier; m. Marie-Laure Le Guay 1985; two s. one d.; ed. Collège Français, Caracas, Ecole de Caousou, Toulouse, Lycée Français, New York, Paris Univ.; responsible for Horn of Africa, Office of African Affairs 1980–81, Head of Mission attached to Dir.'s Office 1981–84, Asst. Dir. 1992–93; with Centre d'Analyse et de Prévision 1981–84; Adviser, Middle East 1984–87; Embassy Press and Information Dir., New York 1987–89, Ministerial Councillor, India 1989–92; Dir. de Cabinet to Alain Juppe (q.v.), Minister of Foreign Affairs 1993–95; Sec. Gen. to Presidency May 1995–; Chair. Admin. Council Nat. Forests Office (ONF) 1996–. *Publications:* Parole d'Exil 1986 (poetry), le Droit d'Aînesse 1988 (poetry), Elégies barbares 1996. *Address:* Présidence de la République, 55–57 rue du Faubourg Saint-Honoré, 75008 Paris; ONF, 2 Avenue de Saint-Mondé, 75012 Paris, France.

VILLIERS de SAINTIGNON, Philippe le Jolis de; French politician; b. 25 March 1949, Boulogne; s. of Jacques le Jolis de Villiers de Saintignon and Hedwige d'Arexy; m. Dominique de Buor de Villeneuve 1973; four s. three d.; ed. Saint-Joseph Inst., Ecole Nationale d'Admin.; civil servant Ministry of Interior 1978; Prin. Pvt. Sec. to Prefect of La Rochelle 1978; Deputy Prefect Vendôme 1979; f. Alouette FM (regional radio station) 1981, Fondation pour les Arts et les Sciences de la Communication, Nantes 1984; Jr. Minister of Culture and Communications 1986–87; mem. Conseil Gen. de la Vendée 1987–, Pres. 1988–; Deputy to Nat. Ass. from Vendée 1988–94 (U.D.F.), 1997– (ind.); M.E.P. 1994–97, majorité pour l'autre Europe; Nat.

Del. UDF (in charge of youth and liaising with cultural groups) 1988; f. and Pres. Mouvement pour la France 1994. *Publications:* Lettre Ouverte aux Coupeurs de Têtes et aux Menteurs du Bicentenaire 1989, La Chienne qui Miaule 1990, Notre Europe sans Maastricht 1992, Avant qu'il ne soit trop tard 1993, la Société de connivence 1994, Dictionnaire du politiquement correct à la française 1996, La machination d'Amsterdam 1998. *Address:* Assemblée nationale, 75355 Paris; Conseil Général de la Vendée, BP 823, 85021 La Roche-sur-Yon cedex, France. *Telephone:* (1) 40 63 82 05 (Paris). *Fax:* (1) 40 63 82 80 (Paris).

VILLIGER, Kaspar; Swiss politician; b. 5 Feb. 1941, Pfeffikon, Lucerne; m.; two d.; ed. Swiss Fed. Inst. of Tech., Zürich; man. of cigar factory Villiger Söhne AG, Pfeffikon 1966; subsequently bought bicycle factory in Buttisholz; fmr. Vice-Pres. Chamber of Commerce of Cen. Switzerland and mem. cttee. Swiss Employers' Cen. Asscn.; mem. Lucerne Cantonal Parl. 1972–82; mem. Nat. Council, Liberal Party of Switzerland (FDP) 1982; mem. Council of States 1987; Swiss Fed. Councillor 1989–; Head, Fed. Mil. (Defence) Dept. 1989–95; Pres. Swiss Confed. Jan.-Dec. 1995. *Address:* c/o Federal Chancellery Bundeshaus-West, 3003 Berne, Switzerland.

VIMOND, Paul Marcel; French architect; b. 20 June 1922, La Meurdraquière; s. of Ernest Vimond and Marie Lehuby; m. Jacqueline Lefèvre 1945; two s. two d.; ed. Lycée de Coutances, Ecole préparatoire des beaux-arts de Rennes and Ecole nat. supérieure des beaux-arts, Paris; Acad. de France at Rome 1950–52; Chief architect, public buildings & national monuments 1954; mem. Jury of Nat. School of Fine Arts; mem. Diocesan Comm. on Sacred Art, Paris; Nat. Expert for Cour de Cassation, Cours d'Appel, Tribuneaux Administratifs and all French courts; Pres. Architecture section, Salon des Artistes Français; Officier Ordre nat. du mérite; Chevalier, Légion d'honneur, des Palmes académiques, des Arts et des Lettres and of Pontifical Order of Merit; Premier Grand Prix de Rome 1949, Officier, Ordre nat. du Mérite. *Major architectural works include:* Architect in charge of Int. Exhbn. of Sacred Art, Rome 1953; responsible for films and architectural reconstructions of tomb of Saint Peter, Rome; Buildings in Paris for: Assemblée de l'Union française, Conseil économique et social, Union de l'Europe occidentale, Org. de co-opération et de développement économiques; planner and architect for Palais d'Iéna, Paris; town planner for Cherbourg; Atomic Power Station, The Hague; two theatres, three churches in Paris, hotels, restaurants, hospitals, and numerous lycées in France; 800 pvt. houses; 15,000 flats in six new towns; technical insts. at Besançon, Montpellier, Paris, Orsay, Nice, Toulon, Troyes; Faculty of medicine, Nice; a hosp. and a coll. in Lebanon; French Lycée, Brussels; numerous telephone exchanges and 14 large postal sorting offices in Paris region and provinces; sorting offices in Riyadh, Jeddah and Dammam and project for television centre in Saudi Arabia, project for town in Zaire. *Leisure interests:* painting, golf.

VIMONT, Jacques Pierre, L. EN D.; French diplomatist; b. 17 July 1911, Paris; s. of Marcel and Alice (née Durantet) Vimont; m. Anne Brun 1942; one s. two d.; ed. Lycée de Nice, Faculté de Droit, Paris and Ecole Libre des Sciences Politiques; Attaché, Belgrade 1938; Asst. Dir. Office of Resident-Gen., Tunis 1939–42; Ministry of Foreign Affairs 1944–46; Counsellor to Sherifian Govt. 1946–49; Counsellor, Berne 1949–50; Sec.-Gen. Tunisian Govt. 1950–51; Counsellor, Rio de Janeiro 1951–53; Asst. Dir. Office of Minister of Foreign Affairs 1953–54; Minister-Counsellor, Washington 1954–57; Dir. of Personnel, Ministry of Foreign Affairs 1958–65; Amb. to Mexico 1965–69, to Czechoslovakia 1969–73, to U.S.S.R. 1973–76; mem. Admin. Council Air France 1976–80; mem. Council Légion d'honneur 1977–81; Ambassadeur de France 1975; Grand Officier, Ordre nat. du Mérite, Commdr. Légion d'honneur, des Arts et des Lettres, des Palmes académiques. *Address:* 42 avenue Bosquet, 75007 Paris, France.

VINCENT, Francis Thomas, Jr.; American sports executive; b. 29 May 1938, Waterbury, Conn.; s. of Francis Vincent and Alice Lynch; m. Valerie McMahon 1965; two s. one d.; ed. Williams Coll. and Yale Univ.; admitted Conn. Bar 1963, N.Y. Bar 1964, D.C. Bar 1969; Assoc. Whitman & Ransom, New York 1963–68; partner, Caplin & Drysdale, Washington, D.C. 1968–78; Assoc. Dir. Div. of Corporate Finance, SEC, Washington, D.C. 1978; Pres. and C.E.O. Columbia Pictures Industries, Inc, New York 1978–83, Chair. and C.E.O. 1983–87; Pres. and C.E.O. Entertainment Business Section, The Coca Cola Co. New York 1987; Deputy Commr. and C.O.O. Major League Baseball, New York 1989, Commr. 1989–92; Dir. Time Warner Inc. 1993–.

VINCENT, Jean-Pierre, L. ÈS L.; French theatre director; b. 26 Aug. 1942, Juvisy-sur-Orge, Essonne; s. of André Vincent and Paulette Loyot; one s.; ed. Lycées Montaigne, Louis-le-Grand, Paris, Univ. de Paris (Sorbonne); amateur actor Univ. theatre Lycée Louis-le-Grand 1958–64; mem. Patrice Chéreau theatre co. 1965–68, Dir. 1968–72; Dir., Admin. Dir. Espérance Theatre 1972–74; Dir. at Théâtre Nat. and École Supérieure d'art dramatique, Strasbourg 1975–83; Gen. Admin. Comédie-Française 1983–86; Dir. Théâtre de Nanterre-Amandiers July 1990–; Lecturer Inst. d'études théâtrales de Paris 1969–70; Studio Dir. Conservatoire Nat. Supérieur d'art dramatique 1969–70, Prof. 1986–89; Pres. Syndicat Nat. de Dirs. d'entreprises artistiques et culturelles (Syndeac) 1978–82, Vice-Pres. 1992; numerous critics' prizes, including Molière Prize for Best Dir. 1987, Prix de la Critique 1988. *Address:* Nanterre-Amandiers, 6 avenue Pablo Picasso, 92000 Nanterre, France.

VINCENT, Rev. Dr. John James, DR.THEOL.; British minister of religion; b. 29 Dec. 1929, Sunderland; s. of David Vincent and Beatrice Ethel Vincent (née Gadd); m. Grace Johnston Stafford 1958; two s. one d.; ed. Manchester Grammar School, Richmond Coll., London Univ., Drew Univ., Madison, N.J., U.S.A., Basel Univ., Switzerland; ordained in Methodist Church 1956; Minister, Manchester and Salford Mission 1956–62; Supt. Minister, Rochdale Mission 1962–69, Sheffield Inner City Ecumenical Mission 1970–77; Dir. Urban Theology Unit, Sheffield 1969–97, Dir. Emer. and Doctoral Supervisor 1997–; Pres. Methodist Conf. 1989–90; Visiting Prof. of Theology, Boston School of Theology, U.S.A. 1969, New York Theological Seminary 1970, Theological School, Drew Univ. 1977; elected mem. Studiorum Novi Testamenti Societas 1961; Sec. Regional Working Party, WCC Faith and Order 1958–63; mem. British Council of Churches Comm. on Defence and Disarmament 1963–65, 1969–72; N.W. Vice-Pres. Campaign for Nuclear Disarmament 1957–69; Founding mem. Methodist Renewal Group 1961–70; Founding mem. and Leader Ashram Community 1967–; Chair. Alliance of Radical Methodists 1971–74, Urban Mission Training Asscn. of G.B. 1976–77, 1985–90; Co-ordinator, British Liberation Theology Project 1990–; Hon. Lecturer Biblical Studies Dept., Sheffield Univ. 1990–; mem. Bd. Int. Urban Ministry Network 1991–; presented Petition of Distress from the Cities to H.M. the Queen 1993; mem. Independent Del. to Colombia 1994; Chair. Methodist Report on the Cities 1997. *Publications:* Christ in a Nuclear World 1962, Christ and Methodism 1965, Secular Christ 1968, The Race Race 1970, The Jesus Thing 1973, Stirrings 1975, Starting All Over Again 1981, Into the City 1982, O.K. Let's Be Methodists 1984, Radical Jesus 1986, Mark at Work 1986, Britain in the 90s 1989, Discipleship in the 90s 1991, Liberation Theology UK (ed.) 1995, Gospel from the City (ed.) 1997, Hope from the City 1999. *Leisure interests:* jogging, writing. *Address:* 178 Abbeyfield Road, Sheffield, S4 7AY, England. *Telephone:* (0114) 243 6688. *Fax:* (0114) 243 5342.

VINCENT, John Russell, PH.D., F.R.HIST.S.; British historian; b. 20 Dec. 1937, Cheshire; s. of J. J. Vincent; m. Nicolette Kenworthy 1972; two s. (one deceased); ed. Bedales School, Christ's Coll. Cambridge; Fellow of Peterhouse, Cambridge 1962–70, Lecturer in History Univ. of Cambridge 1967–70; Prof. of Modern History, Univ. of Bristol 1970–84, Prof. of History 1984–. *Publications:* The Formation of the Liberal Party 1966, The Governing Passion 1974, The Crawford Papers 1984, Disraeli 1990, An Intelligent Person's Guide to History 1995, Derby Diaries, 1869–1878 1995; various works on political history. *Leisure interest:* journalism. *Address:* 7 Woodland Road, Bristol, BS8 1TB, England. *Telephone:* (0117) 928 8892 (Office); (0117) 929 2700 (Home).

VINCENT, Olatunde Olabode, C.F.R.; Nigerian banker; b. 16 May 1925, Lagos; s. of Josiah O. and Comfort A. Vincent; m. Edith Adenike Gooding 1958; three s. one d.; ed. C.M.S. Grammar School, Lagos, Chartered Inst. of Secs., London, Univ. of Manchester, and Admin. Staff Coll., Henley, England; Nigerian Army 1942–46; Financial Sec.'s Office 1947–56; Fed. Ministry of Finance 1956–61; Asst. Gen. Man. Central Bank of Nigeria 1961–62, Deputy Gen. Man. 1962, Gen. Man. 1963–66, Adviser 1973–75, Deputy Gov. 1975–77, Gov. 1977–82; co-f., then Vice-Pres. African Devt. Bank, Abidjan, Ivory Coast 1966–73; Part-time Lecturer in Econs., Extra-Mural Dept., Univ. Coll. of Ibadan 1957–60; mem. Lagos Exec. Devt. Bd. 1960–61; Dir. Nigerian Industrial Devt. Bank 1964–66, Nigerian Security Printing and Minting Co. Ltd., Lagos, 1975–77; Chair. Sona Dairies Ltd. 1985–90, City Business Computers Ltd. 1985–, Equity and Trust Ltd. 1986–; Chair. Capital Issues Comm., Lagos, 1975–77, Southern Africa Relief Fund 1977–82, Cttee. on Motor Vehicle Advances and Basic Allowance 1978; Fellow Nigerian Inst. of Bankers, Inst. of Dirs.; mem. Nat. Econ. Council 1979–82, Soc. for Int. Devt., Nigerian Econ. Soc., Nigerian Inst. of Man., Nigerian Stock Exchange, Nigeria-Britain Asscn., Nigerian Conservation Foundation, Int. Airline Passengers Asscn., London, Trustee, African Church Cathedral (Bethel); African Church Primatial Honours Award 1981, Distinguished Nigerian Community Leader Award 1983; Commdr. Order of Fed. Repub. 1982. *Leisure interests:* reading, listening to African and light classical music, gardening. *Address:* 8 Balarabe Musa Crescent, Victoria Island, P.O. Box 8780, Lagos, Nigeria. *Telephone:* 615687; 619291.

VINCENT OF COLESHILL, Baron (Life Peer), cr. 1996, of Shrivenham in the County of Oxfordshire; **Field Marshal Sir Richard (Frederick) Vincent,** G.B.E., K.C.B., D.S.O., F.I.MECH.E., F.R.AE.S.; British army officer; b. 23 Aug. 1931, London; s. of the late Frederick Vincent and the late Frances Elizabeth (née Coleshill) Vincent; m. Jean Paterson (née Stewart) 1955; two s. (one deceased) one d.; ed. Aldenham School, Royal Mil. Coll. of Science; nat. service 1950; Germany 1951–55, Gunnery Staff 1959, Radar Research Establishment Malvern 1960–61, B.A.O.R. 1962, Tech. Staff Training, Royal Mil. Coll. of Science 1963–64; Staff Coll. 1965, Commonwealth Brigade, Malaysia 1966–68, Ministry of Defence 1968–70; Commdr. 12th Light Air Defence Regt., Germany, England and N.I. 1970–72; Instructor Staff Coll. 1972–73; Mil. Dir. of Studies, RMCS 1974–75; Commdr. 19 Airportable Brigade 1975–77; RCDS 1978; Deputy Mil. Sec. 1979–80; Commandant Royal Mil. Coll. of Science 1980–83; Master Gen. of Ordnance, Ministry of Defence 1983–87; Vice-Chief Defence Staff 1987–91; Chief of Defence Staff 1991–92; Chair. Mil. Cttee. of NATO 1993–96; Chair. MoDeM Consortium 1997–; Chancellor Cranfield Univ. 1998–; Col. Commandant, REME 1981–87, RA 1983; Hon. Col. 100 (Yeomanry) Field Regt. RA, TA 1982–91, 12th Air Defence Regt. 1987–91; Chair (Non-exec.) Hunting Defence Ltd. 1996–; Dir. (Non-exec.) Hunting Eng. Ltd. 1996– (Chair. 1998–), Vickers Defence Systems 1996–, R. A. Museums Ltd 1996–; Vice-Pres. The Defence

Mfrs. Asscn. 1996–, Officers' Pension Soc. 1997–; Dir. Hunting-BRAE 1997– (Chair. 1998–); Kermit Roosevelt Lecturer 1988; mem. Court, Cranfield Inst. of Tech. 1981–83, Greenwich Univ. 1997–; mem. Guild of Freemen of the City of London 1992–, Comm. on Britain and Europe (Royal Inst. for Internal Affairs) 1996–97; Advisory Council, RMCS 1983–91; Freeman City of London 1992, Freeman of Worshipful Co. of Wheelwrights 1997; Fellow Imperial Coll., London 1996; Gov. Aldenham School 1987–, Ditchley Foundation 1992–, Imperial Coll. of Science, Tech. and Medicine 1995– (Chair. Bd. of Govs. 1996–); Hon. D.Sc. (Cranfield) 1985; Master Gunner St. James's Park 1996; Jordanian Order of Merit (First Class), U.S.A. Legion of Merit (Degree of Cdre.). *Publications:* contrib. to journals and publs. *Leisure interests:* seven grandchildren, pursuing a second career. *Address:* House of Lords, London, SW1A 0PW, England.

VINDE, Pierre L. V., JUR.CAND., PHIL.CAND.; Swedish fmr. civil servant and international civil servant; b. 15 Aug. 1931, Paris, France; s. of Victor Vinde and Rita Wilson; ed. schools in France, Sweden and U.K., Univs. of Uppsala and Stockholm; in Prime Minister's Office 1957–58; Ministry of Trade 1958–60; Ministry of Finance 1961–76, Budget Dir. 1970–74, Under-Sec. 1974–76; mem. Bd. Devt. Assistance Agency 1962–65, Inst. of Defence Org. and Man. 1968–70, Nat. Audit Office 1969–74, Agency for Admin. Devt. 1974–76; Deputy Group of Ten 1974–76; Chair. Bd. of Dirs. Bank of Sweden 1974–76; mem. Police Comm. 1962–64, Defence Comm. 1965–68; Chair. Relocation of Gov. Admin. Comm. 1970–72; Sr. Vice-Pres. PKbanken 1977–80; Asst. Admin. (Finance and Admin.), UN Devt. Program 1980–85, Deputy Sec.-Gen. OECD 1985–96; Adviser, Ministry of Finance 1996–97. *Publications:* Frankr av i dag o i morgon 1960, Hur Sverige styres (The Government of Sweden) 1968, Den sv. statsförvaltningen 1969, Swedish Government Administration 1971. *Address:* 15 rue Méchain, 75014 Paris, France.

VINE, Barbara, (see Rendell, Ruth).

VINES, David Anthony, PH.D.; British/Australian economist; b. 8 May 1949, Oxford; s. of Robert Vines and Vera Vines; m. 1st Susannah Lucy Robinson 1979 (divorced 1992); three s.; m. 2nd Jane E. Bingham 1995; two step-s.; ed. Scotch Coll. Melbourne and Univs. of Melbourne and Cambridge; Fellow, Pembroke Coll. Cambridge 1976–85; Research Officer, Sr. Research Officer, Dept. of Applied Econs., Univ. of Cambridge 1979–85; Adam Smith Prof. of Political Econ. Univ of Glasgow 1985–92; Fellow and Tutor in Econs. Balliol Coll. Oxford 1992–; Adjunct Prof. of Econs., Research School of Pacific Studies, A.N.U. 1991–; Dir. ESRC Research Programme on Global Econ. Insts. 1993–; mem. Bd. Channel 4 TV 1986–92, Glasgow Devt. Agency 1990–92, Analysys, Scottish Early Music Asscn.; econ. consultant to Sec. of State for Scotland 1988–92; consultant to IMF 1988, 1989; mem. Acad. Panel, H.M. Treasury 1986–; mem. Research Programmes Bd., ESRC 1990–92; Reader in Econs., Univ. of Oxford 1997–; other professional appts. *Publications:* Stagflation, Vol. II: Demand Management (with J. E. Meade and J. M. Maciejowski) 1983, Macroeconomic Interactions Between North and South (with D. A. Currie) 1988, Macroeconomic Policy: inflation, wealth and the exchange rate (jtly.) 1989, Deregulation and the Future of Commercial Television (with G. Hughes) 1989, Information, Strategy and Public Policy (with A. Stevenson) 1991, North South Macroeconomic Interactions and Global Macroeconomic Policy (Ed. with D. A. Currie) 1995, papers in professional journals. *Leisure interests:* hillwalking, music. *Address:* Balliol College, Oxford, OX1 3BJ; Institute of Economics and Statistics, Manor Road, Oxford, OX1 3UL, England. *Telephone:* (01865) 277719 (Coll.); (01865) 271067 (Inst.). *Fax:* (01865) 277803 (Coll.); (01865) 271094 (Inst.).

VINES, Sir William Joshua, Kt., A.C., C.M.G.; Australian business executive and farmer (retd.); b. 27 May 1916, Terang; s. of Percy V. and Isabella Vines; m. 1st Thelma J. Ogden 1939 (died 1988); one s. two d.; m. 2nd Judith Anne Ploeg 1990; ed. Haileybury Coll., Victoria; army service, Middle East, New Guinea and Borneo 1939–45; Sec. Alexander Fergusson Pty. Ltd. 1938–40, 1945–47; Dir. Goodlass Wall and Co. Pty. Ltd. 1947–49, Lewis Berger and Sons (Australia) Pty. Ltd. and Sherwin Williams Co. (Aust.) Pty. Ltd. 1952–55; Man. Dir. Lewis Berger and Sons (Victoria) Pty. Ltd. 1949–55, Lewis Berger & Sons Ltd. 1955–60, Berger, Jensen & Nicholson Ltd. 1960–61, Int. Wool Secr. 1961–69, mem. Bd. 1969–79; Chair. Dalgety Australia Ltd. 1969–80, Carbonless Papers (Wiggins Teape) Pty. Ltd. 1970–78, Assoc. Pulp & Paper Mills Ltd. 1978–82; Deputy Chair. and Dir. Tubemakers of Australia Ltd. 1970–86; Dir. Commercial Union Assurance Co. of Australia Ltd. 1969–78, Port Phillip Mills Pty. Ltd., Conzinc Riotinto of Australia Ltd. 1976–84, Dalgety Australia Holdings Ltd. 1980–92, A.N.Z. Banking Group Ltd. (Deputy Chair. 1980–82, Chair. 1982–89), Grindlays Holdings (now A.N.Z. U.K. Holdings PLC) 1985–89, Grindlays Bank 1987–89; Chair. Sir Robert Menzies Memorial Trust 1978–92; Chair. Council, Hawkesbury Agricultural Coll. 1975–85; Hon. D.Sc.(Econs.) (Sydney Univ.). *Address:* 1/10 West Street, Balgowlah, N.S.W., 2093, Australia (Home). *Telephone:* (02) 9948 1147.

VINKEN, Pierre; Netherlands publishing executive; b. 25 Nov. 1927, Heerlen; ed. Univs. of Utrecht and Amsterdam; consultant neurosurgeon, Univ. of Amsterdam 1964–71; Man. Dir. Excerpta Medica Publishing Co. Amsterdam 1963–71, Elsevier Science Publrs., Amsterdam 1971–73; Exec. Dir. Elsevier NV, Amsterdam (now Reed/Elsevier Group) 1972–79, Chair. 1979–99; Co-Chair. Reed Elsevier PLC, London 1993–95; mem. Exec. Cttee. 1993–; leader Republikeins Genootskap 1997–; hon. mem. various scientific asscns.; Dr. h.c. (Paris). *Publications:* Handbook of Clinical Neurology; articles in journals. *Address:* c/o Reed Elsevier PLC, P.O. Box 470, 1000 AL Amsterdam, Netherlands.

VINOGRADOV, Oleg Mikhailovich; Russian ballet master; b. 1 Aug. 1937; ed. Vaganov Choreographic School, Leningrad; danced with Novosibirsk Acad. Theatre and dir. Cinderella 1964, Romeo and Juliet 1965; ballet master at Kirov Ballet, Leningrad 1968–72; R.S.F.S.R. State Prize 1970 for Kazhlaev's Goryanka; Chief Ballet Master of Maly Dance Co. 1973–77; People's Artist of U.S.S.R. 1983; Chief Ballet Master of Kirov (now Mariinsky) Theatre 1977–; Marius Petipa Prize, Paris 1978. *Productions include:* Useless Precaution (Hérold) 1971, Coppélia 1973, Yaroslavna (by Tishchenko) 1974, The Hussar's Ballad (Khrennikov), The Government Inspector, The Battleship Potemkin (A. Chaikovsky), Behests of the Past 1983, and numerous others. *Address:* Mariinsky Theatre, Theatre Square, St. Petersburg, Russia. *Telephone:* 317-57-24.

VINOGRADOV, Vasily Valentinovich; Russian diplomatist; b. 19 Sept. 1948, Port Arthur; m.; one s.; ed. Moscow Inst. of Int. Relations; with U.S.S.R. Ministry of Foreign Affairs 1971–; Consulate Dept. 1971–79; Third Sec. U.S.S.R. Gen. Consulate in New York 1979–88; Third, Second Sec. U.S.S.R. Embassy, U.S.A. 1980–84; First Sec., Head of Div., Deputy Head, Head Consulate Dept. Ministry of Foreign Affairs 1984–92; Dir. Dept. of Consulate Service Russian Ministry of Foreign Affairs 1992–96; Amb. to Australia 1997–98. *Address:* Ministry of Foreign Affairs, Smolenskaya-Sennaya 32/34, Moscow, Russia.

VINOGRADOV, Vladimir Alekseyevich; Russian information specialist and economist; b. 2 July 1921, Kazan; s. of Aleksei Alexandrovich and Maria Alexandrovna; m. Marianna B. Antsuta 1943; one s.; ed. Inst. of Int. Relations, Moscow; served in Soviet Army 1939–41; mem. staff Presidium of U.S.S.R. (now Russian) Acad. of Sciences 1948–60, Deputy Chief Scientific Sec. 1961–71, Dir. Inst. of Scientific Information on Social Sciences 1972–98, mem. Acad. 1984–, Counsellor 1998–; lecturer, Dept. of Political Economy, Moscow Univ. 1954–60; mem. Soviet Cttee. of UNESCO 1965–91; Vice-Pres. Int. Asscn. for Econ. History 1968–78, Int. Social Sciences Council 1978–81; Hon. Vice-Pres. Vienna Centre 1981–93; mem. New York Acad. of Sciences; U.S.S.R. State Prize 1982, Chernishevski Prize (Presidium of Acad. of Sciences) and other awards and prizes. *Publications:* numerous books and articles on the genesis of property in Russian and West European countries and on problems of information in the social sciences and the humanities, including Social Sciences and Information 1978, Workers' Control over Production: Theory, History and Contemporaneity 1983, What Type of Privatization do we Need? 1991, State Property and Privatization in France 1998, Privatization in the Global Context 1998. *Leisure interest:* poetry. *Address:* Institute of Scientific Information in Social Sciences, Nakhimovski prosp. 51/21, 117418 Moscow, Russia. *Telephone:* 128-89-30 (Office); 331-32-16 (Home). *Fax:* 420-2261.

VINOGRADOV, Vladimir Viktorovich; Russian banker; b. 19 Sept. 1955, Ufa, Bashkiria; m.; one s. two d.; ed. Moscow Aviation Inst., Moscow Inst. of Nat. Econ.; master, deputy chief workshop, engineer-constructor Atommash Co. (Volgodonsk) 1979–85, Sec. Comsomol Cttee. Atommash Co. 1983–85; economist, chief economist Promstroybank U.S.S.R. 1985–88; f. and Chair. Exec. Bd. Moscow Innovation Bank Incombank 1988–98 (resgnd.); mem. Enterprise Council of Pres. Gorbachev Sept.-Dec. 1991; mem. Bd. Russian Union of Entrepreneurs and Businessmen 1992–; Chair. Moscow Banking Union. *Leisure interests:* hunting, motoring.

VIOT, Jacques Edmond, L. ÈS L.; French diplomatist; b. 25 Aug. 1921, Bordeaux; m. Jeanne de Martimprey de Romecourt 1950; ed. Bordeaux and Paris lycées and Ecole Normale Supérieure and Ecole nat. d'Admin.; Lecturer in French, Univ. of Dublin 1945–47, Ecole Nat. d'Admin. 1948–50; Foreign Office 1951–53, Second Sec., London 1953–57; First Sec., Rabat 1957–61; held various posts in cen. admin. 1961–72; Amb. to Canada 1972–77; Gen. Insp. for Foreign Affairs 1977–78; Dir. de Cabinet, Ministry of Foreign Affairs 1978–81; Gen. Insp. for Foreign Affairs 1981–84; Amb. to U.K. 1984–86; Chair. Review Cttee. on Foreign Affairs, Paris 1986–87; Chair. France-Grande Bretagne 1987; mem. Admin. Council Alliance-Française 1987–94, Ecole Normale supérieure 1988–94, Conseil supérieur Agence France-Presse 1988–94; Chair. Franco-British Council (French Section) 1992, Alliance Française 1994–; Ambassadeur de France; Commdr., Légion d'honneur, Commdr., Ordre Nat. du Mérite. *Address:* 19 rue de Civry, 75016 Paris, France. *Telephone:* (1) 42-22-63-68.

VIOT, Pierre, L. ÈS L.; French barrister; b. 9 April 1925, Bordeaux; s. of Edmund Viot and Irma Viot; m. Monique Fruchier 1952 (deceased); two s. two d.; ed. Faculté de droit de Bordeaux, Inst. d'études politiques de Paris, Ecole nat. d'admin.; Jr. Official Cour des Comptes 1953, Chief Counsel; Asst. Bureau des Commrs. aux Comptes, NATO 1957–61; Regional and Urban Dept. Head, Gen. Planning Office 1961; Spokesman Nat. and Regional Devt. Cttee. 1961; Sec.-Gen. Conseil des Impôts 1971; Dir.-Gen. Centre nat. de la Cinématographie 1973–84; Pres. Cannes Film Festival 1984–; Pres. Bd. of Dirs., Etablissement public de l'Opéra de la Bastille 1985–89; Officier, Légion d'honneur, Croix de guerre, Grand Officier, Ordre nat. du Mérite, Commdr. Arts et Lettres. *Leisure interests:* tennis, gardening. *Address:* 38 avenue Emile Zola, 75015 Paris, France (Home).

VIRATA, Cesar Enrique, B.S.BUS.ADM., B.S.MECH.ENG., M.B.A.; Philippine politician and banker; b. 12 Dec. 1930, Manila; s. of Enrique Virata and

Leonor Aguinaldo; m. Joy Gamboa 1956; two s. one d.; ed. Univ. of Pennsylvania, U.S.A. and Univ. of the Philippines; Dean, Coll. of Business Admin., Univ. of the Philippines 1961–69; Chair. and Dir. Philippine Nat. Bank 1967–69; Deputy Dir.-Gen. Presidential Econ. Staff 1967–68; Under-Sec. of Industry 1967–69; Chair. Bd. of Investments 1968–70; Minister of Finance 1970–86; Prime Minister of the Philippines 1981–86; Chair. Land Bank of the Philippines 1973–86; mem. Nat. Ass. 1978–86, Monetary Bd., Nat. Econ. and Devt. Authority 1972–86, Comm. on the Future of the Bretton Woods Insts. 1992–; Adviser to the Co-ordinating Council for the Philippines Aid Plan 1989–90; Chair. IMF and IBRD Devt. Cttee. 1976–80; Prin. C. Virata & Assocs. (Man. Consultants) 1986–; Chair. Bd. of Govs., Asian Devt. Bank 1979–80; Dir. Philippine Stock Exchange, Inc. 1992; Chair. Rizal Commercial Banking Corpn. 1996–; L.H.D. h.c., D.P.A. h.c., Dr. h.c. (Philippines). *Leisure interests:* tennis, reading. *Address:* Rizal Commercial Banking Corporation, 333 Sen. Gil. J. Puyat Avenue, Ext., Makati, Metro Manila (Office); 63 East Maya Drive, Quezon City, Philippines (Home). *Telephone:* (2) 8910813 (Office); 99-74-19 (Home). *Fax:* (2) 8190458.

VIREN, Lasse; Finnish athlete; b. 22 July 1949, Myrskylä; m. Päivi Kajander 1976; two s.; competed Olympic Games, Munich 1972, won gold medal at 5,000 m. and 10,000 m.; Montréal 1976, won gold medal at 5,000 m. and 10,000 m., 5th in marathon; Moscow 1980, 5th in 10,000 m.; only athlete to retain 5,000 m. and 10,000 m. titles at successive Olympics; has held World records at 2 miles, 5,000 m. and 10,000 m.; recreation officer. *Address:* Suomen Urheiluliitto ry, Box 25202, 00250, Helsinki 25, Finland.

VIROLAINEN, Johannes, PH.D.; Finnish politician and farmer; b. 31 Jan. 1914, Viipuri; s. of Paavo Virolainen and Anna-Lydia Skyttä; m. Eeva Kyllikki Salojärvi 1981; ed. Helsinki Univ. (Agric. and Forestry); M.P. 1945–; Vice-Chair. Agrarian Party 1946–64, Chair. 1965–80 (name of party changed to Centre Party 1965); Second Minister of Interior 1950–51; Second Minister of Prime Minister's Office 1951; Minister of Educ. 1953–54, 1968–70, of Foreign Affairs 1954–56, 1957, 1958, of Agric. 1961–63, of Agric. and Forestry 1976–78; Deputy Prime Minister 1958, 1962–63, 1968–70, 1977–79; Prime Minister 1964–66; Speaker of Parl. 1966–69, 1979–83; First Minister of Finance 1972–75; Chair. Nat. Planning Council 1956–66; Centre Party Cand. for Pres. of Finland 1982; Councillor of State; Pres. IPU 1982–83; Grand Crosses Orders of Merit (Argentina), Leopold (Belgium), Dannebrog (Denmark), Hawk (Iceland), North Star (Sweden), Sankt Olav (Norway), White Rose (Finland), Hungary, Colombia; Grand Officer Order of Polonia Restituta (Poland). *Publications:* Pöytäkirjat puhuvat 1948, Maaseutuhekinen elämänkatsomus 1949, Maatalousmaan arvioimisesta ja arvosta Suomessa vuosina 1934–38 1950, Karjalainen kotikylä 1955, Maalaisliiton johtavat aatfeet 1961, Pääministerinä Suomessa 1969, Ainoa vaihtoehto, poliittinen kestusta 1971, Kuka ottaa vastuun? 1978, Onko valta kansalla? 1981, Yöpakkasista juhannuspommiin 1982, Sanoi Paasikivi 1983, Muistiinpanoja ja myllykirjeitä 1984, Yhden äänen presidentti 1985, Vallankäyttö Kekkosen aikana 1986, Karjalaiset Suomen Kohtaloissa 1988, Siirtokarjalaiset 1941–44 1989, Viimeinen vaalikausi 1991. *Address:* Kirkniemi, Lohja, Finland.

VIROS, Christian; French business consultant and executive; b. Le Mans; m. Esther Viros; two s.; ed. mil. school, Columbia Univ., New York; joined Booz Allen & Hamilton 1977, with Paris and New York brs., partner 1988; Chief Exec. TAG Heuer 1988–. *Leisure interests:* French cuisine, jazz, modern painting.

VIRSALADZE, Eliso Konstantinovna; Georgian pianist; b. 14 Sept. 1942, Tbilisi; studied under grandmother, Prof. Anastasia Virsaladze; then at Tbilisi Conservatory; won first prize at All-Union Competition of Performing Musicians, Moscow 1961; Bronze Medal at Tchaikovsky Competition 1962, Prize at Schumann Competition; teacher Moscow Conservatory 1962, Prof.; played as a soloist all over the world and on tour in Europe and U.S.A. with Leningrad Philharmonic; soloist with U.S.S.R. Symphony Orchestra in U.K. 1983–84, Germany 1984–85; f. Tkvarcheli Music Festival and Summer School; many other tours as soloist in Europe and Japan; master classes in Munich 1996; U.S.S.R. People's Artist 1989, Georgian State Prize 1983. *Address:* Moscow Conservatory, Bolshaya Nikitskaya str. 13, Moscow, Russia. *Telephone:* (095) 268-69-12 (Home).

VISHNEVSKAYA, Galina Pavlovna; Russian soprano; b. 25 Oct. 1926, Leningrad (now St. Petersburg); m. Mstislav Rostropovich (q.v.); two d.; studied with Vera Garina 1942–52; Leningrad Musical Theatres 1944–52; leading soloist, Bolshoi Theatre 1952–74; left Soviet Union 1974; stripped of citizenship 1978 (citizenship restored 1990); retd. from operatic stage as Tatiana (Eugene Onegin) Paris 1982; numerous parts in operas, notably Leonora in Fidelio, and Tatiana in Eugene Onegin (also in the film), Aida (Aida), Kupava (Snow Maiden), Liza (Queen of Spades), Cio-Cio-San (Madame Butterfly), Margaret (Faust), Natasha (War and Peace), Cherubino (Marriage of Figaro), Marfa (Tsar's Bridge), Violetta (Traviata), Liu (Turandot), Katerina (Lady Macbeth of Mtsensk); acted in A. Chekhov Moscow Arts Theatre 1993–94. *Publication:* Galina (autobiog.) 1985. *Address:* Gazetny per. 13, Apt. 79, 103009 Moscow, Russia. *Telephone:* 229-04-96 (Moscow); (01) 42.27.85.06 (Paris).

VISHNYOVA, Diana Viktorovna; Russian ballerina; b. 13 July 1976, Leningrad; ed. Vaganova Acad. of Russian Ballet; first Russian ballerina to have won Prix de Lausanne 1994; soloist Mariinsky Theatre 1995–; Prizes Divine Isadora, Benoit de la Dance. *Address:* Mariinsky Theatre, Teatralnaya pl. 1. St. Petersburg, Russia (Office). *Telephone:* (812) 315 5724 (Office).

VISSEUR, Pierre, LL.D.; Swiss international administrator; b. 10 June 1920, Bré; s. of Pierre L. Visseur and Charlotte van Aken; m. Suzy Butikoffer 1947; one s. two d.; ed. Univs. of Basel, Geneva and Berne, and Inst. of Int. Studies, Geneva; Sec.-Gen., European Div., World Brotherhood 1950–62; Dir. World Fed. for Mental Health 1963–68; Dir. Pharmaceutical Proprietary Asscn. of Europe (AESGP) 1969–80; fmr. Pres. Fed. of Pvt. and Semi-Official Int. Orgs. in Geneva. *Publication:* Evolution of Control of International Labour Legislation 1946. *Leisure interests:* mountaineering, gardening, history. *Address:* Casa Angelina, 6925 Gentilino, Switzerland. *Telephone:* (091) 9944492.

VISTBACKA, Raimo Viljam, LL.M., M.P.; Finnish politician; b. 19 Oct. 1945, Kauhava; Jr. Constable 1966–68, Sr. Constable 1968–78, Asst. Chief Constable of Hyvinkää and Espoo 1978–81, Chief Constable of Evijärvi, Töysä and Alajärvi 1981–; mem. Alajärvi Town Exec. Bd. 1987–88, of Alajärvi Town Council 1988–; Rural Party of Finland mem. of Parl. 1987–; Minister of Transport and Communications 1989–90; auditor of Postipankki Ltd. 1988; mem. of Bd. Oy Pohjolan Liikenna Ab 1987–89. *Address:* c/o Ministry of Transport and Communications, Eteläesplanadi 16, 00130 Helsinki, Finland.

VITA, Giuseppe, DR. MED.; Italian business executive; b. 28 April 1935, Sicily; ed. in Catania and Rome; qualified as specialist in radiology; Asst. Röntgeninstitut, Univ. of Mainz 1962; joined Schering AG as asst. in clinical research 1964; Gen. Dir. Schering S.p.A. Milan 1965; Deputy mem. Man. Bd. Schering AG 1987, mem. 1988, Chair. 1989–; Cavaliere del Lavoro; Verdienstorden des Landes Berlin. *Address:* Schering AG, Postfach 65 03 11, 13303 Berlin, Germany.

VITALE, Alberto; American publishing executive; b. 1933, Vercelli, Piedmont, Italy; s. of Sergio Vitale and Elena Segre; m. Gemma G. Calori 1961; two s.; ed. Turin Univ., IPSOA Business School and Wharton School, Univ. of Pa. (Fulbright Scholar); joined Olivetti 1958; moved to U.S.A. to assist in Olivetti's acquisition of Underwood 1959; Exec. IFI (Agnelli family holding co.) 1971; Exec. Vice-Pres. for Admin. Bantam Books, New York 1975, Co-C.E.O. 1985, Sole C.E.O. 1986; Pres. and C.E.O. Bantam-Doubleday-Dell 1987; Chair., Pres. and C.E.O. Random House 1990–96, Chair., C.E.O. 1996–; Bd. Dirs. Transworld Publrs. *Address:* Random House Inc., 201 East 50th Street, New York, NY 10022; 505 Alda Road, Mamaroneck, NY 10543, U.S.A.

VITALI, Felice Antonio; Swiss radio and television official; b. 24 March 1907, Bellano, Italy; s. of Battista and Leoni Vitali; m. Hilda Schlatter 1930; ed. St. Gall Gymnasium and Commercial Coll.; Ed. Die Presse 1928; Radio Berne 1929; Ed. Schweizer Radio Zeitung 1930; Dir. Radio Svizzera Italiana 1931–47; corresp. Swiss Radio in Berlin 1948–57; Project-leader UNESCO Radio advisory mission to Libya 1957–58; Head of Information Services, Swiss Television (Zürich) 1958–67; Programme Liaison of Swiss Television, Lugano 1967–85; Prix Pisa of the Prix Italia 1962 (for TV documentary). *Radio plays:* I tre amici, La capanna del Bertuli, Idol und Masse, Kraftwerk Mittelmeer, Flut ohne Ebbe, Kampf um die öffentliche Meinung 1955, Atome für die Politik 1956, Die sieben Kiesel 1961. *Television documentaries:* Der alte Mensch, Was war der Generalstreik? Kranke Menschen, halbe Hilfe, Urteil ohne Richter, Testfall Celerina, Die Polizei des Bürgers, Frau Grossrätin, Hauptmann Grüninger, Die Barriere, Das Wagnis, Partner im Rollstuhl, Betrifft Friedrich Glauser. *Publications:* Reporter erleben England, Confidenze del Microfono, Radiohörer das geht dich an, Der alte Mensch und das Fernsehen, Altersprogramme—Ghetto oder Treffpunkt?, Zwischen den Grenzen, Lebensbericht eines Medienmachers: 1907–83, Die Matusa: Tessiner Dorfgeschichten (1983–90), Radio Monte Ceneri, Quello Scomodo Microfono 1990. *Leisure interests:* walking, gardening. *Address:* Via Ronco Nuovo 11, 6949 Comano, Lugano, Switzerland. *Telephone:* 941.12.50.

VITORINO, António; Portuguese politician and lawyer; b. 1958; mem. Parl. 1981; Sec. of State for Parl. Affairs 1985; has served in Govt. of Macau; Judge, Constitutional Court; Minister for Defence and the Presidency 1995. *Address:* c/o Ministry of Defence, Avenida Ilha de Madeira, 1400 Lisbon, Portugal.

VITRUK, Nikolai Vasilievich, LL.D.; Russian lawyer; b. 4 Nov. 1937, Zharovka, Tomsk Region; m. (divorced 1988); one d.; ed. Tomsk State Univ.; Man. Legal Advice Bureau, Tomsk Regional Lawyers' Bd. 1959; Asst. Chair. of Theory and History of State and Law, Tomsk Univ. 1960–63; Asst., Sr. Teacher, Asst. Prof. Chair. of Theory of State and Law, T. G. Shevchenko Kiev State Univ. 1966–71; Sr. Scientific Researcher, Inst. of State and Law, U.S.S.R. Acad. of Sciences 1971–81; Prof. Chair. of Theory of State and Law and Constitutional Law, Acad. of Ministry of Internal Affairs of U.S.S.R. 1981–84; Chief, Chair of State and Law Discipline, High Correspondence Law Coll. Ministry of Internal Affairs of U.S.S.R. 1984–91; Justice, Deputy Chair. Constitutional Court of Russian Fed. 1991–, Acting Chair. 1993–95; Labour Veteran Medal; Medal for Irreproachable Service. *Publications:* about 300 legal works including three monographs. *Leisure interests:* theatre, modern realistic painting, poetry, art, culture of the Russia of the 'Silver Age'. *Address:* 1st Truzhennikov Lane 17, Apt. 54, 119121 Moscow, Russia. *Telephone:* 248-17-64.

VITTI, Monica (Monica Luisa Ceciarelli); Italian actress; b. 3 Nov. 1931, Rome; ed. Nat. Acad., Rome; films include L'Avventura 1959, La Notte 1960,

L'Eclisse 1962, Dragées au Poivre 1963, The Red Desert 1964, Modesty Blaise 1966, The Chastity Belt 1967, Girl With a Pistol 1969, Le Coppie 1971, La Pacifiste 1971, La Tosca 1971, Teresa la larda 1973, A mezzanotte va la ronda di piacere 1975, Duck in Orange Sauce 1975, An Almost Perfect Affair 1979, Teresa the Thief 1979, The Oberwald Mystery 1981, Tigers in Lipstick, The Flirt, When Veronica Call's, Broadway Danny Rose 1984, Secret Scandal (also wrote and dir.) 1990. *Publication:* A Bed is Like a Rose 1997.

VITUKHNOVSKAYA, Alina Aleksandrovna; Russian poet; b. 27 March 1973, Moscow; first verses published late 1980s in periodicals; arrested on charge of drugs trafficking, freed Oct. 1995, arrested Nov. 1997; mem. Russian PEN Centre, Writers' Union; Pushkin Scholarship, Hamburg, Germany 1998. *Publications include:* Anomaly 1993, Children's Book of the Dead 1994, Pavlov's Dog (with K. Kedrov) 1996, The Last Old Woman Money-lender of Russian Literature (stories) 1996, Land of Zero 1996, Romance with Phenamine (novel). *Address:* Leningradskoye shosse 80, Apt. 89, 125565 Moscow, Russia. *Telephone:* (095) 452-15-31.

VIVARELLI, Roberto; Italian professor of history; b. 8 Dec. 1929, Siena; s. of Lavinio Vivarelli and Margherita Cosci; m. Ann Sheldon West 1960; two s. one d.; ed. Univs. of Siena, Florence and Pennsylvania, U.S.A. and Istituto Italiano di Studi Storici; Research Fellow, St. Antony's Coll. Oxford, U.K. 1961–62; Asst. Prof., Univ. of Siena 1962–70, Full Prof. 1972–75; Assoc. Prof., Univ. of Florence 1970–72, Full Prof. 1975–86; Prof. of History, Scuola Normale Superiore, Pisa 1986–; Visiting Prof., Inst. for Advanced Study, Princeton, U.S.A. 1969–70, 1980–81, Harvard Univ. 1976; Visiting Fellow, All Souls Coll. Oxford 1993–94. *Publications:* Gaetano Salvemini's Scritti sul Fascismo (Ed.) 1961, 1974, Georges Sorel's Scritti politici (Ed.) 1963, Il dopoguerra in Italia e l'avvento del fascismo 1967, Il fallimento del liberalismo 1981, Storia delle origini del fascismo (2 vols.) 1991, Profilo di storia (3 vols.) 1996. *Address:* Scuola Normale Superiore, Piazza dei Cavalieri, 56100 Pisa (Office); Via Dante da Castiglione 1, 50125 Florence, Italy (Home). *Telephone:* 050-509221 (Office); 055-223190 (Home).

VIZZINI, Carlo; Italian politician and university teacher; b. 28 April 1947, Palermo; elected Social Democrat M.P. for Palermo-Trapani-Agrigento-Caltanisetta 1976–; Nat. Deputy Sec. Italian Social Democrat Party and head of Econ. Dept. 1980–88; Under-Sec. of State in Ministry of Budget and Econ. Planning; Minister for Regional Affairs 1986–87, of Cultural Heritage 1987–88, of the Merchant Navy 1989–91, of Posts and Telecommunications 1991–92; Sec. Partido Socialista Democratica Italiano (PSDI); Prof. of History of Econs., Univ. of Palermo. *Address:* c/o PSDI, Piazza di Spagna 35, 00187 Rome; Camera dei Deputati, Rome, Italy.

VLAAR, Nicolaas Jacob; Netherlands professor of geophysics; b. 17 March 1933, Mijnsheerenland; m. 1st Joanna Lambermont 1956 (died 1976); m. 2nd Everdina den Hartog 1980; three s. (one s. deceased) one d.; ed. Bisschoppelijk Coll., Tech. Univ., Delft and Utrecht Univ.; Asst. Calif. Inst. of Tech. 1965–66, St. Louis Univ. 1966–67, Utrecht Univ. 1963–, Prof. of Theoretical Geophysics 1973; Prof. of Theoretical Geophysics, Free Univ. 1983–, Dean of Faculty 1989–92; mem. Royal Netherlands Acad. of Science 1984–; mem. Hollandsche Maatschappij der Wetenschappen 1983–, Bd. Netherlands Science Org. (Biology, Oceanography and Earth Science) 1988–; Royal Dutch/Shell Prize 1982; Kt. Royal Order of the Netherlands Lion 1994. *Publications:* numerous works on seismology and geodynamics. *Leisure interests:* nature, esoterics. *Address:* Mauritslaan 5, 3818 GJ Amersfoort, Netherlands. *Telephone:* (33) 4613516.

VLÁČIL, František; Czech film director; b. 19 Feb. 1924, Český Těšín; s. of František Vláčil and Anna Vláčilová-Vacková; m. 1st Alena Texlová 1949; m. 2nd Věra Peštuková 1955; m. 3rd Olga Stuchlíková 1983; two s.; ed. Masaryk Univ., Brno; asst. Cartoon Film, Brno 1951–52, Armádní film, Prague 1952–58; film dir. Film Studios Barrandov, Prague 1958–88; Pres. Czech Film and TV Acad. 1995–; films include: The Dove 1960, The Devil's Trap 1961, Markéta Lazarová 1967, The Valley of Bees 1968, Adelheid 1968, Smoke of the Potato-Tops 1976, Shadows of the Hot Summer 1978, A Concert at the End of Summer 1979, Snake's Venom 1981, The Shepherd from the Valley 1983, Shadow of the Fern 1984, Magician 1987; dir. numerous TV films; Film Festival Prize in Venice 1960, Cannes 1961, Paris 1961, Rencontres a Prades 1961, Mar del Plata 1968, London 1976, London 1978, Karlovy Vary 1978, 1998, Santander 1982, San Sebastián 1986, Tokyo 1989, V. Vančura Prize, Prague 1997. *Leisure interests:* contemporary painting, folk architecture. *Address:* Čínská 5, 160 00 Prague 6, Czech Republic.

VLADIMIR, Metropolitan (Victor Markianovich Sabodan), B.THEOL.; Ukrainian ecclesiastic; b. 23 Nov. 1935, Khmelnitsky Region; ed. Leningrad and Moscow Theological Acad.; ordained as deacon, then priest 1962–66; Bishop, Archbishop 1966–82; Metropolitan 1982; taught in Odessa Seminary, then Rector; Deputy Chief Russian Orthodox Mission in Jerusalem 1966–68; Bishop of Pereslavl-Zalessky; Archbishop of Dmitrov, Rector Moscow Theological Acad., Prof. 1973–82; Metropolitan of Rostov and Novocherkassk 1982–86; Patriarch Rep. in West Europe 1986–87; man. Moscow Patriarchy, permanent mem. Holy Synod 1987–; Metropolitan of Kiev and All Ukraine 1992–. *Address:* Ukrainian Orthodox Church, Perchevsk Monastery, Sichnevoho Povstannia 25, Kiev, Ukraine. *Telephone:* (044) 290-15-08.

VLADIMIROV, Igor Petrovich; Russian actor and director; b. 1 Jan. 1919; m.; one d.; ed. Leningrad Theatre Inst.; worked with both Lenin Komsomol Theatre, Leningrad and Gorky Theatre 1948–60; artistic dir. of Lensoviet Theatre, Leningrad (now State Acad. Open Theatre, St. Petersburg) 1960–; Prof. Leningrad (now St. Petersburg) Inst. of Theatre and Cinematography; worked in films 1957–; U.S.S.R. People's Artist 1978. *Films include:* Your Contemporary 1968, People on the Nile 1972, Taming of Fire 1972, The Hottest Month 1974, An Ordinary Month 1976, Tales of Old Arbat 1982, An Extra Ticket 1983 etc. *Stage productions:* Mothr (Chapek), Gamblers (Gogol), A Black Man or I'm the Poor So-and-So Yugastivili (V. Korkia), A Group (Galin), Romeo and Juliet, The Taming of the Shrew etc. *Address:* Tavricheskaya Str. 27, Apt. 38, 193015 St. Petersburg, Russia. *Telephone:* (812) 271-70-66.

VLADIMIROV, Vasiliy Sergeyevich, D.SC.; Russian mathematician; b. 9 Jan. 1923, Djaglevo, Petrograd Region; s. of Sergey Ivanovich Vladimirov and Maria Semyonovna Vladimirova; m. Nina Yakovlevna Ovsyannikova 1948; two s.; ed. Leningrad State Univ.; served in Soviet Army 1941–45; Jr. Research Worker, Leningrad Dept., V. A. Steklov Inst. of Math., U.S.S.R. Acad. of Sciences 1948–50; Head Dept. Computer Math., All Russian Research Inst. of Experimental Physics, Arsamas-16, 1950–56; Sr. Research Worker, Steklov Inst. of Maths., Moscow 1956–69, Head, Dept. of Math. Physics 1969–; Prof. Physico-tech. Inst. 1964–86; Vice-Dir. Steklov Inst. 1986–88, Dir. 1988–93, Counsellor 1993–; mem. CPSU 1944–91; corresp. mem. U.S.S.R. (now Russian) Acad. of Sciences 1968–70, mem. 1970–; mem. Saxony Akademie der Wissenschaften 1985, Int. Asscn. of Math. Physics 1980, Acad. of Sciences and Arts Voievodina (Yugoslavia) 1987, Serbian Acad. of Science and Arts 1991; State Prize 1953, 1987 (twice), Bogolyubov Prize, Nat. Acad. of Sciences of Ukraine 1997; Gold Medal of A. N. Liapounov 1971, Gold Medal Bernarda Bolzana CSR Acad. of Science 1982, Hero of Socialist Labour 1983, and numerous other awards. *Publications:* Mathematical Problems of the one-velocity particles transfer 1961, Methods of the Theory of Functions of Several Complex Variables 1964, Equations of Mathematical Physics 1967, Distributions in Mathematical Physics 1976, Many Dimensional Tauberian Theorems for Distributions (with others) 1986, p-Adic Analysis and Mathematical Physics (with others) 1994, and works in the field of numerical methods; analysis of transfer equation; theory of holomorphic functions of several complex variables and distribution theory, and their applications in mathematical physics; about 250 papers and articles. *Leisure interests:* skiing, fishing. *Address:* Steklov Institute of Mathematics, Gubkin Street 8, 117966 GSP-1 Moscow, Russia. *Telephone:* (095) 135-14-49 (Office); 124-78-64 (Home). *Fax:* (095) 135-05-55.

VLADIMOV, Georgiy Nikolayevich (pseudonym of G. N. Volosevich); Russian writer and literary critic; b. 19 Feb. 1931, Kharkov; ed. Law Faculty, Leningrad State Univ.; started literary activity as critic 1954, and as prose-writer 1960; expelled from U.S.S.R. Writers' Union 1982, and refused visa to emigrate; subsequently emigrated and worked for some time as ed. of Grani 1983–86. *Publications include:* Bolshaya Ruda (short story) 1961, Letter to the Presidium of U.S.S.R. Writers' Union (samizdat) 1967, Faithful Ruslan 1975, Three Minutes of Silence 1969, The Sixth Soldier (play) 1981, Do Not Pay Attention, Maestro (short story) 1982, The General and his Army (novel) 1990, (Russian Booker Prize 1995), Bolshaya ruda (novel) 1994, Collected Works (4 vols.) 1998. *Address:* Lenzhahner Weg 38, Niedernhausen/TS, Germany. *Telephone:* (6127) 5896.

VLADISLAVLEV, Alexander Pavlovich, D.TECH.SC.; Russian politician; b. 21 May 1936, Moscow; m. Karina Lisitsian; one s.; ed. Gubkin Petroleum Inst., Moscow, Oil and Gas Inst., Bucharest; mem. CPSU 1959–91; researcher, sr. teacher, docent, Pro-Rector Gubkin Moscow Inst. 1959–74; Vice-Pres. All-Union Soc. Znanie 1974–86; First Vice-Chair. U.S.S.R. Council of Scientific and Eng. Socs. 1988–90; Chair. Exec. Cttee., First Vice-Pres. U.S.S.R. (now Russian) Scientific-Industrial Union 1990–92; Chair. Council of Business of U.S.S.R., Pres. 1991; First Deputy Minister of Foreign Relations of U.S.S.R. Nov.–Dec. 1991; First Vice-Pres. Russian Union of Industrialists and Entrepreneurs 1992–; U.S.S.R. People's Deputy 1989–91; f. and Co-Chair. Democratic Reform Movt. 1991–92; a leader of Civic Union 1992–93; Chair. Bd., ZIL motor co. 1994–95; Pres. Ind. Fund for Realism in Politics 1994–; mem. Presidium of Eng. Acad., founder and mem. of admin. of non-govt. foundations and socs., mem. Advisory Council of UNO on Science and Tech. *Publications:* 6 books; over 200 articles and papers; 15 patents. *Address:* Novy Arbat prosp. 15, Suite 2424, Moscow, Russia (Office). *Telephone:* (095) 202-26-25 (Office); 203-55-15 (Home).

VLASOV, Aleksey Feliksovich; Russian business executive; b. 20 Oct. 1954, Kalinin (Tver'); m.; two s.; ed. Moscow Inst. of Steel and Alloys; mem. research insts. connected with econs. of construction 1977–1991; Chief Man. Russian Commodity and Raw Materials Exchange (now Russian Exchange) 1990–94, Pres. 1994–. *Address:* Russian Exchange, Myasnitskaya str. 26, 101000 Moscow, Russia (Office). *Telephone:* 262-23-52 (Office). *Fax:* 262-57-57 (Office).

VLK, H. E. Cardinal Miloslav, B.SC.; Czech ecclesiastic; b. 17 May 1932, Líšnice; ed. Faculty of Philosophy, Charles Univ. Prague, Faculty of Theology, Litoměřice; archivist Třeboň and Jindřichův Hradec 1960–61, České Budějovice 1961–64; ordained priest 1968; sec. to Roman Catholic Bishop of České Budějovice 1968–71; parish priest Lažiště and Rožmitál pod Třemšínem 1971–78; denied permission to work as priest 1978; window cleaner, Prague 1978–1986; archivist, Czechoslovak State Bank, Prague 1986–88; parish priest, parishes in Šumava Mountains 1989–90; cr. Bishop of České Budějovice 1990, Archbishop of Prague 1991–, cr. Cardinal 1994; mem. Consilium Conferentiarum Episcopalium Europae 1990 (Pres. 1993–), Pontificium Consilium pro Dialogo cum non credentibus 1991–93, Pontificum Consilium de Communicationibus Socialibus 1994–, Congregatio pro Ecclesiis Orientalibus 1994–; Hon. L.H.D. (Ill. Benedictine Coll., U.S.A., Univ. of St. Thomas, Minn., U.S.A.) 1992; Hon. D.Theol. (Univ. Passau, Germany) 1993; Hon. Citizen, Rožmitál pod Třemšínem 1992, Cedar Rapids, U.S.A. 1992, Baltimore, U.S.A. 1992, Kłodzko, Poland 1996, Třeboň 1996, Roudnice nad Labem 1997. *Publications:* numerous ecclesiastical articles. *Leisure interests:* translation from foreign languages, classical and oriental languages, classical music, mountain tourism. *Address:* Arcibiskupství pražské, Hradčanské nám. 16/56, 119 02 Prague 1, Czech Republic. *Telephone:* (2) 20392111; (2) 20392201. *Fax:* (2) 20514647; (2) 20515396.

VLOK, Adriaan; South African politician; b. 11 Dec. 1937, Sutherland; m. Cornelia Burger; two s. one d.; joined Dept. of Justice 1957; became prosecutor and sr. magistrate; Asst. Pvt. Sec. to Prime Minister John Vorster 1967; subsequently entered pvt. business; later Deputy Sheriff, E. Pretoria; M.P. 1974–94; fmr. Deputy Speaker of House of Ass.; Deputy Minister of Defence and Deputy Minister of Law and Order 1985–86; Minister of Law and Order 1986–91, of Correctional Services and the Budget 1991–92, of Correctional Services and of Housing and Works 1992, of Correctional Services 1992–94; Leader House of Ass. 1992–94; mem. Truth and Reconciliation Comm. for amnesty for criminal acts 1998. *Leisure interests:* rugby (referee in Northern Transvaal), military history, chewing biltong.

VO CHI CONG: Vietnamese politician; b. 1913, Central Viet Nam; fmr. mem. Vietcong force; fmr. Sec. Southern People's Party, a main element in Nat. Liberation Front (NLF); mem. Cen. Cttee. of Lao Dong party for many years; Minister for Fisheries, Socialist Repub. of Viet Nam 1976–77; Vice-Premier, Council of Ministers 1976–82, now mem.; Minister for Agric. 1977–78; mem. Politburo of CP of Viet Nam 1976; Pres. of Viet Nam 1987–92. *Address:* c/o Council of Ministers, Bac Thao, Hanoi, Viet Nam.

VO NGUYEN GIAP, Gen.; Vietnamese army officer; b. 1912, Quangbinh Prov.; ed. French Lycée in Hué, and law studies at Univ. of Hanoi; History teacher, Thang Long School, Hanoi; joined Viet Nam CP in early 1930s; fled to China 1939, helped organize Vietminh Front, Viet Nam 1941; Minister of Interior 1945, became C.-in-C. of Vietminh Army 1946; defeated French at Dien Bien Phu 1954; Vice-Chair. Council of Ministers 1976–91, Minister of Defence, C.-in-C., Democratic Repub. of Viet Nam to 1976, Socialist Repub. of Viet Nam 1976–80; mem. Politburo Lao-Dong Party until 1976, CP of Viet Nam 1976–82. *Publications:* People's War, People's Army, Big Victory, Great Task 1968. *Address:* Dang Cong san Viet Nam, 1C boulevard Hoang Van Thu, Hanoi, Viet Nam.

VO VAN KIET; Vietnamese politician; b. 1922, S. Viet Nam; joined CP of Indo-China in 1930s; mem. Lao Dong Party (renamed Communist Party of Viet Nam Dec. 1976), mem. Cen. Cttee. 1958–; mem. Cen. Office for S. Viet Nam during war; alt. mem. Politburo, CP of Viet Nam 1976, now mem.; Vice-Chair. Council of Ministers 1982–91, Chair. 1991; Chair. State Planning Cttee. 1982–88; Chair. party Cttee. in Ho Chi Minh City; Prime Minister of Viet Nam 1992–97. *Address:* c/o Council of Ministers, Hanoi, Viet Nam.

VODIČKA, Jindřich; Czech politician; b. 22 July 1952, Prague; m.; two s.; ed. Univ. of Maritime Studies, Odessa; sailed as deck engineer, later First Officer in merchant navy 1977–90; First Deputy Dir., Office for Protection of Constitutional Officials –1990; Dir. Job Centre, Prague-West Dist. 1990–92; mem. Civic Democratic Party (CDP) 1991–97, 1998–, Unie Svobody Jan.–March 1998; Deputy to House of Nations (Fed. Ass. of Č.S.F.R.) June–Dec. 1992; Minister of Labour and Social Affairs of Czech Repub. 1992–97; Minister of Interior 1997–98. *Address:* Civic Democratic Party, Sněmovní 3, 110 00 Prague 1, Czech Republic. *Telephone:* (2) 311 48 00/01/09.

VOGEL, Bernhard, D.PHIL.; German politician; b. 19 Dec. 1932, Göttingen; s. of Prof. Dr. Hermann Vogel and Caroline (née Brinz) Vogel; ed. Univs. of Heidelberg and Munich; Lecturer, Inst. für Politische Wissenschaft, Heidelberg 1961; mem. Bundestag 1965–67; Minister of Educ. and Culture, Rhineland-Palatinate 1967–76; mem. Rhineland-Palatinate State Parl. 1971; Chair. CDU Rhineland-Palatinate 1974–; Minister-President, Rhineland-Palatinate 1976–88, Thuringia 1992–94; Pres. Bundesrat 1976–77; Chair. Advisory Bd., Zweites Deutsches Fernsehen 1979–; Pres. Bundesverband "Schutzgemeinschaft Deutscher Wald" 1980–84, Stiftung Wald in Not 1984–; Pres. Maximilian-Kolbe Works 1984–; Senator Max-Planck Asscn. 1984–; Pres. Adenauer-Stiftung 1989–; mem. Fed. Bd. of CDU, Head CDU, Thuringia 1992–; Grosses Bundesverdienstkreuz mit Stern und Schulterband; decorations from France, Luxembourg, U.K., Senegal and Vatican; Grosskreuz St. Gregorius; Gold Medal of Strasbourg; Christian Democrat. *Publications:* Wahlen und Wahlsysteme 1961, Kontrolliert der Bundestag die Regierung? 1964, Wahlkampf und Wählertradition 1965; numerous essays and speeches. *Leisure interests:* mountaineering, literature, swimming. *Address:* Regierungsstrasse 73, 99084 Erfurt, Germany.

VOGEL, Dieter H., DR.ING.; German industrialist; b. 14 Nov. 1941; m. Ursula Gross 1970; two c.; ed. Tech. Univ. of Darmstadt, Tech. Univ. of Munich; Asst. Prof., Thermic Turbo Engines, Tech. Univ. of Munich 1967–69; Vice-Pres., Printing Div., Bertelsmann AG 1970–74, Pegulan AG 1975–85 (Chair. 1978); Vice-Chair. Man. Bd. Batig (BAT Industries) 1978-85; joined Thyssen Group 1986, Chair. Thyssen Handelsunion AG 1986–96, mem. Exec. Bd. 1986–91, Deputy Chair. Thyssen AG 1991–96, Chair. 1996–. *Leisure interest:* skiing. *Address:* Thyssen AG, August-Thyssen-Str. 1, 40211 Düsseldorf, Germany. *Telephone:* 0211 8240.

VOGEL, Hans-Jochen, DR.JUR.; German politician; b. 3 Feb. 1926, Göttingen; m. 1st Ilse Leisnering 1951 (divorced 1972), one s. two d.; m. 2nd Liselotte Sonnenholzer (née Biersack) 1972; ed. Univs. of Munich and Marburg; Asst., Bavarian Justice Ministry 1952–54; lawyer, Traunstein Dist. Court 1954–55; Bavarian State Chancellery 1955–58; mem. Munich City Council 1958–60; Chief Burgomaster of Munich 1960–72; mem. Bundestag 1972–81, 1983–94; Minister for Regional Planning, Building and Urban Devt. 1972–81, of Justice 1974; Mayor, West Berlin Jan.–June 1981; Chair. SPD Parl. Party 1984–91; Deputy Chair. SPD 1984–87, Chair. 1987–90; Vice-Pres. Org. Cttee. for Munich Olympic Games 1972; Chair. Gegen Vergessen Project 1993–; numerous decorations including Grosses Bundesverdienstkreuz, Bayerischer Verdienstorden, Hon. C.B.E. and honours from France, Italy, etc. *Leisure interests:* mountain walking, history. *Address:* Bundeshaus, 53113 Bonn, Germany.

VOGT, Marthe Louise, DR.MED., DR. PHIL., PH.D., F.R.S.; British scientist; b. 1903; d. of Oskar Vogt and Cécile Mugnier; ed. Univ. of Berlin; Research Asst., Dept. of Pharmacology, Univ. of Berlin 1930; Research Asst. and Head, Chemical Div., Kaiser Wilhelm Inst. für Hirnforschung, Berlin 1931–35; Rockefeller Travelling Fellow 1935–36; Research Worker, Dept. of Pharmacology, Univ. of Cambridge 1935–40; Alfred Yarrow Research Fellow, Girton Coll., Cambridge 1937–40; mem. Staff, Coll. of Pharmaceutical Soc., London 1941–46; Lecturer, later Reader in Pharmacology, Univ. of Edin. 1947–60; Head, Pharmacology Unit, Agricultural Research Council, Inst. of Animal Physiology 1960–68; Visiting Assoc. Prof. in Pharmacology, Columbia Univ., New York 1949; Visiting Prof., Sydney Univ. 1965, Montreal 1968; Hon. mem. Physiological Soc. 1974, British Pharmacological Soc. 1974, Hungarian Acad. of Sciences 1981, British Asscn. for Psychopharmacology 1983; Foreign Hon. mem. American Acad. of Arts and Sciences 1977; Life Fellow, Girton Coll., Cambridge 1970; Hon. F.R.S.M.; Hon. D.Sc. (Edin.) 1974, (Cambridge) 1983; Schmiedeberg Plakette 1974; Royal Medal, Royal Soc. 1981. *Publications:* papers in neurological, physiological and pharmacological journals. *Leisure interests:* gardening, travel. *Address:* Chateau La Jolla Terrace, 7544 La Jolla Boulevard, La Jolla, CA 92037, U.S.A.

VOGT, Peter K., PH.D.; American professor of microbiology; b. 3 Oct. 1932; s. of Josef Vogt and Else (née Thiemann) Vogt; ed. Univ. of Tubingen; Asst. Prof. of Pathology, Univ. of Colorado 1962–66, Assoc. Prof. 1966–67; Assoc. Prof. of Microbiology, Univ. of Washington 1967–69, Prof. 1969–71; Hastings Prof. of Microbiology, Univ. of Southern Calif. 1971–78, Hastings Distinguished Prof. of Microbiology 1978–80, Chair. Dept. of Microbiology 1980–; Calif. Scientist of the Year 1975, Award of Nat. Acad. of Sciences 1980, Alexander von Humboldt Prize 1983, Ernst Jung Prize for Medicine 1985. *Publications:* Genetics of RNA Tumor Viruses 1977, The Genetic Structure of RNA Tumor Viruses 1977, Class II Defective Avian Sarcoma Viruses: Comparative Analysis of Genome Structure 1982. *Leisure interest:* painting. *Address:* Department of Microbiology, University of Southern California School of Medicine, 2011 Zonal Avenue, HMR-401, Los Angeles, CA 90033, U.S.A. *Telephone:* (213) 224-7139.

VOGT LORENTZEN, Fredrik; Norwegian metal industry executive; b. 4 June 1946, Oslo; s. of Fredrik Vogt Lorentzen and Kirsten (née Meyer) Vogt Lorenzen; m. Elen Wulfsberg; one s. one d.; ed. Norges Nandelshøyskole, Oslo Univ.; trainee, Norema A/S 1966; in Accounting Dept., Spar Espänola A.A., Madrid, Compania de Maderas S.A., Madrid 1967; Consultant, Finance and Control Dept., Norema A/S 1972; Head, Stores and Bathroom Fittings Divs. 1973; Head of Dept., Ministry of Industry 1976; Consultant 1981; Plant Man., Lista Aluminium Factory 1987; Pres. and C.E.O. Elkem A/S 1988–92; Partner Isco Group 1992–; mem. Plyteknisk Forening, Council for Supporting Norwegian Athletic Foundations, Council for Promoting Norwegian Understanding of the European Community. *Leisure interests:* literature, classical music, cross-country and alpine skiing, sailing, farming, family.

VOHOR, Serge; Ni-Vanuatu politician; fmr. Minister of Econ. Affairs; Pres. Union of Moderate Parties (UMP); Prime Minister of Vanuatu 1995–98. *Address:* c/o Office of the Prime Minister, P.O. Box 110, Port Vila, Vanuatu.

VOHS, James Arthur, B.A.; American business executive; b. 26 Sept. 1928, Idaho Falls, Ida.; s. of John D. Vohs and Lucille Packer; m. Janice Hughes 1953; four d.; ed. Univ. of Calif., Berkeley and Harvard School of Business; joined Kaiser org. 1952; Exec. Vice-Pres. Kaiser Foundation Health Plan, Inc. and Kaiser Foundation Hosps. 1969, mem. Bd. of Dirs. 1970, Pres. 1975–92, C.E.O. 1977–92, Chair. 1980–92; mem. Bd. of Dirs. Holy Names Coll. 1981–92; Chair. Marcus Foster Inst. 1981–, Oakland-Alameda County Coliseum Complex 1991–92, Fed. Reserve Bank, San Francisco 1991–94. *Address:* Kaiser Center, Ordway Bldg., Oakland, CA 94612 (Office); 17 Westminster Drive, Oakland, CA 94618, U.S.A. (Home). *Telephone:* (415) 653-5858 (Home).

VOIGHT, Jon, American actor; b. 29 Dec. 1938, Yonkers, New York; s. of Elmer Voight and Barbara (née Camp) Voight; m. 1st Lauri Peters 1962 (divorced 1967); m. 2nd Marcheline Bertrand 1971 (divorced); one s. one d.; ed. Catholic Univ.; Acad. Award (Best Actor) for Coming Home 1979, Best Actor Awards for Midnight Cowboy 1969, Coming Home 1979, Cannes Int.

Film Festival, Golden Globe Award for Best Actor for Coming Home. *Theatre includes:* A View From the Bridge (New York); That Summer That Fall (New York) 1966; played Romeo at the San Diego Shakespeare Festival; Stanley Kowalski in A Streetcar Named Desire, Los Angeles 1973, Hamlet; *Films include:* Hour of the Gun 1967, Fearless Frank 1968, Out of It 1969, Midnight Cowboy 1969, The Revolutionary 1970, The All-American Boy 1970, Catch 22 1970, Deliverance 1972, Conrack 1974, The Odessa File 1974, Coming Home 1978, The Champ 1979, Lookin' to get out (also wrote screenplay) 1982, Table for Five 1983, Runaway Train 1985, Desert Bloom 1986, Eternity, Heat, Rosewood, Mission Impossible 1996, U-Turn, The Rainmaker 1997, Varsity Blues 1998, I Once Had A Life 1998, Enemy of the State 1998. *Television includes:* End of the Game 1976, Gunsmoke and Cimarron Strip, Chernobyl: The Final Warning 1991, The Last of His Tribe 1992, The Tin Soldier (also Dir.), Convict Cowboy. *Address:* c/o Martin Baum, CAA, 9830 Wilshire Boulevard, Beverly Hills, CA 90212, U.S.A.

VOIGT, Hans-Heinrich, DR.RER.NAT.; German professor of astronomy and astrophysics; b. 18 April 1921, Eitzendorf; s. of Pastor Wilhelm and Thea (née Zietz) Voigt; m. Margaret Moericke 1949 (died 1979); two d.; ed. Univs. of Göttingen and Kiel; Research Assoc., Lick Observatory, Mt. Hamilton, Calif. 1951–52; Asst., Univ. Observatory, Göttingen 1952–58; Chief Observer, Hamburger Sternwarte 1958–63; Prof. of Astronomy and Astrophysics, Univ. of Göttingen 1963–86, Rector 1969–70, Dir. of Observatory 1963–86, now Prof. Emer.; Chair. Astronomische Gesellschaft 1972–77; Pres. Acad. of Science of Göttingen 1978–80; mem. Deutsche Akademie der Naturforscher Leopoldina, Braunschweigische Wiss. Gesellschaft. *Publications:* Astronomy and Astrophysics (ed.). Abriss der Astronomie (5th edn.) 1991, Das Universum 1994; several articles in scientific journals. *Address:* Universitäts-Sternwarte, Geismarlandstr. 11, 37083 Göttingen; Charlottenburgerstrasse 19, 37070 Göttingen, Germany (Home). *Telephone:* 0551-395042 (Office); 0551-7992627 (Home).

VOINEA, Radu, PH.D.; Romanian civil engineer and scientist; b. 24 May 1923, Craiova; s. of Policarp Voinea and Gabriela Voinea; m. 1st Maria Marta Gorgos 1951 (divorced 1957); one s. one d.; m. 2nd Aurica Daghie 1959; ed. Polytech. School, Bucharest; Asst. Prof. 1947; Sr. lecturer, Inst. of Civil Eng., Bucharest 1951; Prof., Polytech. Inst., Bucharest 1962, Pro-Rector 1964–67, Rector 1972–81; Corresp. mem. Romanian Acad. 1962, mem. 1974–, Gen. Sec. 1967–74, Pres. 1984–90; mem. European Acad. of Arts, Sciences and Humanities 1985. *Publications:* Curs de rezistența materialelor (Lectures on the Strength of Materials), with A. Beles 1958, Mecanica teoretică (Theoretical Mechanics), with V. Vâlcovici and Ş. Bălan 1959, Metode analitice în teoria mecanismelor (Analytical Methods in the Theory of Mechanisms), with M. C. Atanasiu 1964, Mecanica (Mechanics), with D. Voiculescu and V. Ceausu 1975, 1983, Elasticitate şi Plasticitate (Elasticity and Plasticity), with D. Voiculescu and V. Ceauşu 1976, Vibratii mecanice (Mechanical Vibrations) with D. Voiculescu 1979, Introducere în Mecanica Solidului pentru ingineri (Introduction to mechanics of solids for engineers) with D. Voiculescu and F. Simion 1989, Technical Mechanics (co-author) 1996, Introduction to Mechanics of Elastic Continuous Bodies (co-author) 1997, Mechanics and Mechanical Vibrations 1998.

VOINOVICH, George, V., B.A., J.D.; American lawyer and politician; b. 15 July 1936, Cleveland; m. Janet Voinovich; three c.; ed. Ohio and Ohio State Univs.; called to the Bar, Ohio 1961; mem. U.S. Supreme Court 1968; Asst. Attorney Gen., Ohio 1963–64; mem. Ohio House of Reps. 1967–71; auditor Cuyahoga Co., Ohio 1971–76, commr. 1976–78; Acting Gov. of Ohio 1979; Mayor of Cleveland 1979–90; Gov. of Ohio 1991–98; Senator from Ohio 1998–; mem. Nat. Govs. Asscn. (Chair. Educ. Action Team on School Readiness 1991, Child Support Enforcement Work Group 1991–92, Co-Chair. Task Force on Educ. 1992–93, mem. Exec. Cttee. 1993–; Co-Lead Gov. on Fed. Mandates 1993–); Certificate of Merit Award, Dist. Urban Mayor Award Nat. Urban Coalition, 1987 Ohio Univ., Humanitarian Award N.C.C.J. 1986. Republican. *Address:* U.S. Senate, Washington, DC 20510, U.S.A.

VOLCHEK, Galina Borisovna; Russian stage director and actress; b. 19 Dec. 1933, Moscow; d. of cameraman Boris Volchek and Vera Maimyna; m. 1st Yevgeniy Yevstigneyev 1957 (divorced 1964); m. 2nd Mark Abelev 1966 (divorced 1976); one s.; ed. Studio-School of Moscow Art Theatre; one of founders, actress and stage dir. Theatre Sovremennik 1956–72, Chief Dir. 1972–; Deputy to State Duma (Parl.) 1995–; over 40 productions including Common Story by Goncharov, On the Bottom by Gorky, Cherry Orchard, Three Sisters by Chekhov, Ascent over Fujiyama by Aitmatov, Echelone by Roshchin, Anfissa by Andreyev, Steep Route by Ginzburg; among roles Martha (Who's Afraid of Virginia Woolf?), Miss Amelia (The Ballad of the Sad Café by Albee), Wife of Governor (Inspector by Gogol), roles in films by dirs. Kozintsev (King Lear), Yutkevich, Danelia and others; stage productions in many countries including U.S.A. (first Soviet stage dir. to work in U.S.A.) Alley Theatre, Houston (Echelone by M. Roshchin), Ireland (Abbey Theatre), Hungary, Finland, Bulgaria, Germany, Czechoslovakia; master classes in Tisch School N.Y. Univ.; U.S.S.R People's Artist, State Prize, State Orders of U.S.S.R., Hungary, Bulgaria and Russia. *Leisure interest:* designing clothes. *Address:* Chistoprudny blvd. 19A, 101000 Moscow (Theatre); Povarskaya str. 26, Apt. 43, Moscow, Russia (Home). *Telephone:* (095) 921 2543 (Theatre); 290 1606, 418 4773 (Home). *Fax:* (095) 921 6629 (Office).

VOLCKER, Paul A., M.A.; American government official and banker; b. 5 Sept. 1927, Cape May, N.J.; s. of Paul A. and Alma Klippel Volcker; m. Barbara Marie Bahnson 1954; one s. one d.; ed. Princeton Univ., Harvard Univ. Graduate School of Public Admin., and L.S.E.; Special Asst. Securities Dept., Fed. Reserve Bank of N.Y. 1953–57; Financial Economist, Chase Manhattan Bank, N.Y. 1957–62, Dir. of Forward Planning 1965–69; Dir. Office of Financial Analysis, U.S. Treasury Dept. 1962–63, Deputy Under-Sec. for Monetary Affairs 1963–65, Under-Sec. Monetary Affairs 1969–74; Sr. Fellow, Woodrow Wilson School of Public and Int. Affairs, Princeton Univ. 1974–75; Pres. N.Y. Fed. Reserve Bank 1975–79; Chair. Bd. of Govs., Fed. Reserve System 1979–87; Chair. James D. Wolfensohn Inc. 1988–, C.E.O. 1995–; Frederick H. Schultz Prof. of Inst. Econ. Policy, Princeton Univ. 1988; Henry Kaufman Visiting Prof., Stern School of Business, N.Y. Univ. 1998; Consultant IBRD on Debts; Dir. (non-exec.) ICI 1988–93, Exec. Dir. 1993–; Hon. LL.D. (Adelphi Univ., Notre Dame Univ.) 1980, (Farleigh Dickinson Univ.) 1981, (Princeton Univ., Univ. of N.H.) 1982, (New York Univ., Lamar Univ., Dartmouth Coll.) 1983; Admin. Fellowship (Harvard), Rotary Foundation Fellow (L.S.E.), Arthur S. Flemming Award (Fed. Govt.), U.S. Treasury Dept. Exceptional Service Award, Alexander Hamilton Award, Fred Hirsch Memorial Lecture 1978, Public Service Award (Tax Foundation) 1981, Courage Award 1989.

VOLENÍK, Lubomír, JU.DR.; Czech politician; b. 1 March 1950, Prague; ed. Charles Univ. Prague (corresp. student); electromechanic, EZ Bystřany 1970–75, tech. controller 1975–78; disability pension from 1978; co. lawyer, SČVK Teplice 1983–90; mem. People's Chamber of Fed. Ass. (Civil Forum) 1990–92; mem. Civil Democratic Party 1991–; mem. Cttee. of Conciliation 1991–92; mem. People's Chamber of Fed. Ass. (Civil Democratic Party) 1992; mem. Constitution-Legal Cttee. 1992; Pres. N. Bohemia Regional Asscn. until June 1992; mem. Czech Broadcast Liquidation Group 1993; Pres. Supreme Audit Office 1993–; Vice-Pres. EUROSAI Governing Bd. 1993–96, Pres. 1996–(99). *Publications:* Luxembourg Conception of the Czech State (legal-historical study); numerous articles. *Address:* Nejvyšší kontrolni úřad, Jankovcova 63, 170 04, Prague 7, Czech Republic.

VOLK, Patricia, B.F.A.; American writer; b. 16 July 1943, New York; d. of Cecil Sussman Volk and Audrey Elayne Morgen Volk; m. Andrew Blitzer 1969; one s. one d.; ed. Syracuse Univ., Acad. de la Grande Chaumière, Paris, School of Visual Arts, The New School, Columbia Univ.; Art Dir. Appelbaum and Curtis 1964–65, Seventeen Magazine 1967–68, Harper's Bazaar 1969; copy-writer, Assoc. Creative Dir., Sr. Vice-Pres. Doyle Dane Bernbach Inc. (DDB Needham Worldwide Inc.) 1969–88; Adjunct Instructor of fiction Yeshiva coll. 1991; columnist Newsday, N.Y. 1995–96; mem. PEN Authors Guild; Yaddo Fellow; MacDowell Fellow; Word Beat Fiction Book Award 1984, and numerous other awards. *Publications include:* The Yellow Banana 1985, White Light 1987, All It Takes 1990; contribs. to The New York Times Magazine, The Atlantic, Quarterly, Cosmopolitan, Family Circle, Mirabella, Playboy, 7 Days, Manhattan Inc., The New Yorker, New York Magazine, Red Book; to Anthologies, Good Housekeeping, Allure; Stories About How Things Fall Apart and What's Left When They Do 1985, A Reader for Developing Writers 1990, Exploring Language 1992, Magazine and Feature Writing 1992, Hers 1993, Her Face in the Mirror 1994. *Leisure interests:* fly-fishing, gardening, travel. *Address:* c/o Gloria Loomis, 133 East 35th Street, New York, N.Y. 10016, U.S.A.

VOLKOV, Vladimir Konstantinovich, DR. HIST.; Russian historian; b. 15 Dec. 1930, Voronezh; m.; two d.; ed. Moscow State Univ.; started career as journalist, ed. broadcasting for Bulgaria and Albania 1954–56; researcher, head of div., Deputy Dir. Inst. of Slavonic Studies U.S.S.R. (now Russian) Acad. of Sciences 1956–87, Dir. 1987–; mem. Council Pres. Boris Yeltsin 1993–; Vice Pres. Nat. Cttee. of Historians, mem. several scientific socs. *Publications:* numerous works on problems of culture and history of Slavic peoples. *Address:* Institute of Slavonic Studies, Leningradsky pr. 7, 125040 Moscow, Russia. *Telephone:* (095) 250-77-08 (Office).

VOLLEBAEK, Knut, M.SC.; Norwegian politician; b. 11 Feb. 1946; m.; one c.; ed. Inst. Catholique de Paris, Univs. of Oslo, Madrid and Calif., Norwegian School of Econs. and Business Admin., Bergen; teacher Gjøvik School 1964–65; joined Foreign Service 1973; Second Sec. Embassy of Norway, Delhi 1975–78, First Sec. Embassy of Norway, Madrid 1978–81, Exec. Officer and Sr. Exec. Officer, Ministry of Foreign Affairs 1981–84, Counsellor Embassy of Norway, Harare 1984–86; Head First Political Affairs Div., Ministry of Foreign Affairs 1986–89, State Sec. 1989–90; Amb. to Costa Rica 1991–93; Dir. Gen. Dept. of Bilateral Devt. Cooperation, Ministry of Foreign Affairs 1993; Deputy Co-Chair. Int. Conf. on the fmr. Yugoslavia, Geneva 1993; Asst. Sec. Gen. for Devt. Cooperation 1994–97; Minister of Foreign Affairs 1997. *Address:* c/o Ministry of Foreign Affairs, 7 Juni pl. 1, P.O. Box 8114 Dep., 0032 Oslo, Norway.

VOLODIN, Aleksander Moiseyevich; Russian playwright; b. 10 Feb. 1919, Minsk (now in Belarus); s. of Moses Lifshitz and Haya Lifshitz; m. Frida Lifshitz 1946; two s.; ed. Moscow Aviation Inst., State Inst. of Theatre Art, All-Union Inst. of Cinematography; teacher secondary school Veshki, Moscow Region; army service World War II; freelance 1946–; mem. Editorial Bd. Dramaturg (magazine) 1992–; plays Factory Girl, Five Evenings, Elder Sister, Appointment; Prize All-Union Cinema Festival (films Portrait with Rain and Confusion of Feelings); Brothers Vasilyevs State Prize of R.S.F.S.R. (for Autumn Marathon). *Publications include:* Short Stories 1954, Portrait with Rain 1980, Autumn Marathon (collected plays) 1985, Notes of a Not Sober Man 1998. *Leisure interest:* beautiful women. *Address:* Pushkarskaya str. 44, Apt. 28, 197101 St. Petersburg, Russia (Home). *Telephone:* (812) 238 5928 (Home).

VOLONTIR, Mikhai; Moldovan actor; b. 9 March 1934; s. of Ermolae Volontir and Feodosia Volontir; m. Eufrosinia Volontir 1961; one d.; ed. Actors' Training School; actor and producer with Alecsandri Moldavian Music and Drama Theatre in Beltsy 1957–; work in TV and films 1968–; U.S.S.R. People's Artist 1984. *Theatre includes:* Misfortune (producer), The Twilight (actor, producer), Alecsandri's Agaki Flutur, Bayescu's Preshul (actor, producer), Drutsa's Beautiful and Saint (producer), Tanev's The Last Night of Socrates (actor, producer). *Films:* leading and title roles in numerous films including: A Movement of Answer, The Only Man, The Hunting of Deer, Am I Guilty?, Traces of a Wolf, We Shall Remain Faithful, One-Sided Love. *Leisure interest:* protection of animals. *Address:* Str. Independentsei 34, Apt. 4, 3100 Beltsy, Moldova. *Telephone:* (31) 2-80-52.

VOLSKY, Arkadiy Ivanovich; Russian politician; b. 15 May 1932, Dobrush, Byelorussian S.S.R.; s. of Ivan Pavlovich Volsky and Anna Semyonovna Volsky; m. Ludmila Aleksandrovna Semyonova 1953; one s. one d.; ed. Moscow Steel Inst.; foreman, shop supt., Sec. of Party Cttee. of Likhachev Automobile Plant, Moscow 1955–69; Deputy Head, First Deputy Head of Dept. of Machine Bldg., Cen. Cttee. CPSU 1969–83; Aide to Gen. Sec. Cen. Cttee. 1983–84; Head of Dept. of Machine Bldg., Cen. Cttee. CPSU 1985–91; Rep. of Cen. Cttee. CPSU and Presidium of U.S.S.R. Supreme Soviet in Nagorny-Karabakh autonomous region (Azerbaijan S.S.R.) 1988–89; Chair. Emergency Powers Cttee. in Nagorny-Karabakh 1989–90; Deputy Head Russian Govt.'s del. to negotiations on crisis in Chechen Repub. June 1995; Pres. U.S.S.R. League of Scientific and Industrial Asscns. 1990–92, Russian Industrialists and Entrepreneurs' Union 1992–; Deputy to R.S.F.S.R. Supreme Soviet 1984–86; Deputy to U.S.S.R. Supreme Soviet 1986–89; U.S.S.R. People's Deputy 1989–91; mem. Cen. Cttee. CPSU 1986–91; Deputy Head Governing Cttee. on Nat. Econ. of U.S.S.R. Aug.–Dec. 1991; mem. Constitutional Comm. of Russian Fed. 1993–; Chair, Pres.'s Comm. on Political Stability of Public Chamber 1994–; U.S.S.R. State Prize 1971. *Leisure interest:* football. *Address:* RSSP, Staraya Pl. 10/4, 103070 Moscow, Russia. *Telephone:* 206-54-92. *Fax:* 973-20-13.

VOLSKY, Viktor Vatslavovich, DR.ECON.SC.; Russian specialist on Latin America; b. 10 Aug. 1921; widower; one d.; ed. Moscow Inst. of Int. Relations; army service 1940–45; mem. CPSU 1943–91; lecturer, Inst. of Int. Relations 1953–59; Prof., Head of Chair., Moscow Univ. 1959–; Chief Ed. of encyclopaedia Latin America; Dir. Latin America Inst. (ILA) 1966–93; Corresp. mem. Acad. of Sciences 1984–; Hero of Soviet Union 1945; U.S.S.R. State Prize 1987; Andrés Bello Order of Venezuela 1975, Distinguished Merit Order of Peru 1980, Aztec Eagle Order of Mexico 1984. *Publications:* books and articles on U.S.S.R./Russian relations with Latin American countries; Ivan A. Vitver (biog.) 1991, Socioeconomic Geography of the World 1998. *Address:* Moscow State University, Vorobyovy Gori, 119899 Moscow, Russia. *Telephone:* (095) 939-36-21.

VON BÜLOW, Andreas, DR.JUR.; German politician and lawyer; b. 17 July 1937, Dresden; s. of Georg-Ulrich and Susanne (née Haym) von Bülow; m. Anna Barbara Duden 1961; two s. two d.; law studies in Heidelberg, Berlin and Munich, studied in France and U.S.A.; entered higher admin. service of State of Baden-Württemberg 1966, on staff of Rural Dist. Offices of Heidelberg and Balingen, Pres. Admin. Dist. of Süd-Württemberg Hohenzollern at Tübingen; mem. Bundestag (Parl.) 1969–94; Parl. State Sec. Fed. Ministry of Defence 1976–80; Fed. Minister for Research and Tech. 1980–82; mem. Social Democratic Party 1960–, Public Services and Transport Workers' Union. *Publications:* Die Überwachung der Erdgasindustrie durch die Federal Power Commission als Beispiel der Funktionen der unabhängigen Wirtschaftsüberwachungskommissionen der amerikanischen Bundesverwaltung 1967 (dissertation), Gedanken zur Weiterentwicklung der Verteidigungsstrategien in West und Ost 1984, Alpträume West gegen Alpträume Ost—ein Beitrag zur Bedrohungsanalyse 1984, Skizzen einer Bundeswehrstruktur der 90er Jahre 1985, Die eingebildete Unterlegenheit—das Kräfteverhältnis West-Ost, wie es wirklich ist 1985, The Conventional Defense of Europe, New Technologies and New Strategies 1986. *Leisure interests:* music, geology, history, swimming, hiking, skiing. *Address:* Hesselbergstrasse 15, Balingen 14, Germany. *Telephone:* (0228) 238854.

VON DER DUNK, Hermann Walther; Netherlands professor of history; b. 9 Oct. 1928, Bonn, Germany; s. of Heinrich M. von der Dunk and Ilse Löb; m. Goverdina Schuurmans Stekhoven 1958; two s. one d.; ed. Univ. of Utrecht and Inst. für Europäische Geschichte, Mainz; school teacher, Bilthoven 1961–63; Asst. Prof. Dept. of History, Univ. of Utrecht 1963–67, Prof. of Contemporary History and Head of Dept. 1967–88, Prof. and Head, Dept. of Cultural History 1988–90; mem. Royal Netherlands Acad., Acad. Europaea, Dutch Soc. of Science. *Publications:* Der deutsche Vormärz u. Belgien (thesis) 1966, Kleio heeft 1000 ogen (essays) 1974, Conservatisme 1976, De organisatie van het verleden 1982, Voorbij de verboden drempel: de Shoah 1990, Cultuur & Geschiedenis (articles) 1990, Sprekend over identiteit en geschiedenis 1992, Twee buren, twee culturen 1994, Elke tijd is overgangstijd 1996; articles and contribs. to textbooks, journals and newspapers. *Leisure interests:* music (playing piano), drawing and painting, literature. *Address:* Nicolailaan 20, 3723 HS Bilthoven, Netherlands. *Telephone:* 302285401.

VON DOHNÁNYI, Christoph; German conductor; b. 8 Sept. 1929, Berlin; s. of Hans von Dohnányi and Christine (née Bonhoeffer) von Dohnányi; brother of Klaus von Dohnányi (q.v.); m. 1st Renate Zillessen; one s. one d.; m. 2nd Anja Silja (q.v.) 1979; one s. two d.; abandoned legal training to study music 1948; studied in U.S.A. under grandfather, Ernst von Dohnányi 1951; répétiteur and conductor under Georg Solti, Frankfurt Oper 1952; Gen. Music Dir. Lübeck 1957–63, Kassel 1963–66, chief conductor of Cologne Radio Symphony Orchestra 1964–69, Gen. Music Dir. and Opera Dir., Frankfurt 1968–77, Chief Conductor and Intendant, Hamburg State Opera 1977–84; Music Dir. Desig. Cleveland Orchestra 1982–84, Music Dir. 1984–; Prin. Guest Conductor Philharmonia Orchestra 1994, Prin. Conductor 1997–; numerous guest appearances; numerous recordings of symphonies with Cleveland Orchestra and opera; Commdr. Ordre des arts et des lettres; Commdr.'s Cross, Order of Merit (Germany); Commdr.'s Cross (Austria); recipient Richard Strauss Prize, Bartok Prize, and other awards. *Address:* The Cleveland Orchestra, Severance Hall, Cleveland, OH 44106, U.S.A. *Telephone:* (216) 231-7300.

VON DOHNÁNYI, Klaus, DR.JUR.; German politician; b. 23 June 1928, Hamburg; s. of Johann-Georg and Christine (née Bonhoeffer) von Dohnányi; brother of Christoph von Dohnányi (q.v.); m. 2nd Christa Gross 1966; two s. one d.; ed. Munich, Columbia, Stanford and Yale Univs.; frmly. with Ford Motor Co., Detroit, Mich. and Cologne; Dir. Planning Div. Ford-Werke, Cologne 1956-60; Dir. Inst. für Marktforschung und Unternehmensberatung, Munich 1960–67; Sec. of State, Fed. Ministry of Economy 1968–69; mem. Bundestag 1969–81; Parl. Sec. of State, Ministry of Educ. and Science 1969–72; Minister of Educ. and Science 1972–74; Minister of State and Parl. Sec. of State, Fed. Foreign Office 1976–81, First Burgomaster and Pres. Senate, Hamburg 1981–88; Chair. Bd. TAKRAF A.G., Leipzig 1990–94; mem. Club of Rome 1996–; Social Democrat. *Publications:* Brief an den Deutschen Demokratischen Revolutionäre 1990, Das Deutsche Wagnis 1990, Im Joch des Profits (The German Model) 1997. *Address:* Heilwig Str. 5, 20249 Hamburg, Germany.

VON KLITZING, Klaus; German physicist; b. 28 June 1943, Schroda; s. of Bogislav von Klitzing and Anny (née Ulbrich) von Klitzing; m. Renate Falkenberg 1971; two s. one d.; ed. Tech. Univ. Brunswick, Univ. Würzburg; Prof., Tech. Univ., Munich 1980–84; Dir. Max-Planck Inst. for Solid State Research, Stuttgart 1985–; Schottky Prize, Hewlett-Packard Prize, Nobel Prize for Physics 1985. *Address:* Max-Planck Institut für Festkörperforschung, Heisenbergstr. 1, Postfach 800665, 70506 Stuttgart, Germany. *Telephone:* (0711) 6891571.

VON KYAW, Dietrich, DR.JUR.; German diplomatist; b. 9 June 1934, Stettin; s. of Jobst von Kyaw and Helga von Kyaw; m. Elisabeth von Kyaw 1965; two d.; ed. Univs. of Bonn, Chicago and Liège; joined diplomatic service 1964; Vice-Consul, L.A. 1964–65; Sec. German embassies, Brazzaville and Bangui 1966–69; Econ. Dept. Foreign Office, Bonn 1970–73, 1977–83, 1989–93; Perm. Mission to UN, New York 1973–77; Minister (Econs.), Washington, D.C. 1984–88; Amb. and Perm. Rep. to EU, Brussels 1993–. *Leisure interests:* sports, reading. *Address:* Permanent Mission of Germany to the European Union, 19-21 rue J. de Lalaing, 1040 Brussels, Belgium. *Telephone:* (2) 238.19.42. *Fax:* (2) 238.19.46.

VON MEHREN, Arthur Taylor, S.B., LL.B., PH.D.; American professor of law; b. 10 Aug. 1922, Minn.; s. of Sigurd Anders von Mehren and Eulalia M. Anderson; m. Joan E. Moore 1947; three s; ed. Harvard Univ., Univ. of Zürich and Faculté de Droit, Paris; law clerk, U.S. Court of Appeals 1945–46; Asst. Prof. Harvard Univ. 1946–53, Prof. of Law 1953–76, Story Prof. of Law 1976–93, Prof. Emer. 1993–; Fulbright Research Prof. Univ. of Tokyo 1956–57, Rome 1968–69; Guggenheim Fellow 1968–69; Goodhart Prof. of Legal Science Univ. of Cambridge 1983–84, Fellow, Downing Coll. 1983–84, Hon. Fellow, Univ. of Cambridge 1984–; gave Gen. Course on pvt. int. law, Hague Acad. of Int. Law 1996; other visiting professorships etc.; mem. U.S. del. Hague Conf. on Pvt. Int. Law 1966, 1968, 1978, 1980, 1985, 1993, 1996; mem. American Bar Asscn., American Acad. of Arts and Sciences, Int. Acad. of Comparative Law, Inst. de Droit Int., American Soc. of Comparative Law; Hon. Dr. iur. (Katholeke Univ. Leuven) 1985; Order of the Rising Sun; Theberge Award, American Bar Asscn. 1997. *Publications include:* The Civil Law System 1957, The Law of Multistate Problems 1965, Law in the United States: A General and Comparative View 1988. *Leisure interests:* travel, gardening. *Address:* Harvard Law School, Cambridge, MA 02138 (Office); 68 Sparks Street, Cambridge, MA 02138, U.S.A. (Home). *Telephone:* (617) 495-3193 (Office); (617) 547-8977 (Home). *Fax:* (617) 495-1110.

VON OTTER, Anne Sofie; Swedish singer; b. 9 May 1955, Stockholm; ed. Conservatorium, Stockholm, studied interpretation with Erik Werba (Vienna) and Geoffrey Parsons (London) and vocal studies since 1981 with Vera Rozsa; mem. Basel Opera, Switzerland 1982–85; début France at Opéra de Marseille (Nozze di Figaro—Cherubino) and Aix-en-Provence Festival (La Finta Giardiniera) 1984, Rome, Accad. di Santa Cecilia 1984, Geneva (Così fan tutte—Dorabella) 1985, Berlin (Così fan tutte) 1985, U.S.A. in Chicago (Mozart's C minor Mass) and Philadelphia (Bach's B minor Mass) 1985, London at Royal Opera, Covent Garden (Nozze di Figaro) 1985, Lyon (La Finta Giardiniera) 1986, La Scala, Milan (Alceste) 1987, Munich (Le Nozze di Figaro) 1987, Stockholm (Der Rosenkavalier) 1988, The Metropolitan Opera, New York (Le Nozze di Figaro) 1988, The Royal Albert Hall, London (Faust) 1989, numerous recordings for Philips, EMI, Deutsche

Grammophon and Decca; has given recitals in New York, Paris, Brussels, Geneva, Stockholm and London; Hon. D.Sc. (Bath) 1992. *Address:* c/o IMG, 3 Burlington Lane, London W4 2TH, England.

VON RINGELHEIM, Paul Helmut, B.S., M.A.; American sculptor; b. Vienna, Austria; s. of Henry von Ringelheim and Rosita von Ringelheim (née Altschuler); ed. Brooklyn Coll., Fairleigh Dickinson Univ., Art Students League, New York, Acad. of Fine Arts, Munich; teacher of printmaking Brooklyn 1957–58; Prof. of Sculpture School of Visual Arts, New York 1967–71; one-man shows include Niveau Art Gallery, New York 1958, Am Haus, Berlin, Munich and Hamburg 1960–61, Rose Fried Gallery, New York 1964, 1967, Fairleigh Dickinson Univ. 1964, New Vision Galleries, London 1964, New York Cultural Center 1975, O.K. Harris Gallery, New York 1971–73, 1976, 1978, 1980, 1982, Mitzi Landau Gallery, L.A. 1974, Amarillo Museum of Art 1987, Amarillo Art Center 1987, Robert Berman Gallery, L.A. 1988, Obelisk Gallery 1992, 1994; has participated in numerous group exhbns. internationally; Fulbright scholar 1974–75; mem. Architectural League, New York; Outstanding Young Man of the Year Award, New York World's Fair 1964. *Address:* 9 Great Jones Street, New York, NY 10012, U.S.A. *Telephone:* (212) 777-8757.

VON ROHR, Hans Christoph (see Rohr, Hans Christoph von).

VON SCHLABRENDORFF, Fabian Gotthard Herbert, M.A., DR.IUR.; German lawyer; b. 23 Dec. 1944, Berlin; s. of Fabian von Schlabrendorff and Luitgarde von Schlabrendorff (née von Bismarck); m. Maria de la Cruz Caballero Palomero 1977; one s. one d.; ed. Univs. of Tübingen, Berlin, Geneva, Frankfurt and Chicago; service in Bundeswehr 1964–68; Research co-ordinator, Inst. of Int. and Foreign Trade and Business Law, Frankfurt 1975–82; lawyer with Pünder, Volhard, Weber & Axster, Frankfurt 1982, partner 1984; CEPES award 1987. *Publications:* (co-author) Mining Ventures in Developing Countries, (parts 1 and 2) 1979/81, The Legal Structure of Transnational Forest-Based Investments in Developing Countries 1987; various articles on business law. *Leisure interest:* classical music. *Address:* Pünder, Volhard, Weber & Axster, Mainzer Landstrasse 46, 60325 Frankfurt am Main, Germany. *Telephone:* 069-719901. *Fax:* 069-7199-4000.

VON STADE, Frederica; American mezzo-soprano; b. 1 June 1945, Somerville, N.J.; m. 1st Peter Elkus 1973 (divorced); two d.; m. 2nd Michael G. Gorman 1991; ed. Mannes Coll. of Music, New York; opera début with Metropolitan Opera, New York (in Le nozze di Figaro) 1970; has also sung Paris Opera, San Francisco Opera, Salzburg Festival, Covent Garden, London, Spoleto Festival, Boston Opera Co., Santa Fe Opera, Houston Grand Opera, La Scala, Milan; recital and concert artist; over 60 recordings include Frederica von Stade Sings Mozart and Rossini Opera Arias, French Opera Arias, Songs of the Cat with Garrison Keillor. *Address:* c/o Columbia Artists Management Inc., Jeffrey D. Vanderveen, 165 W. 57th Street, New York, NY 10019, U.S.A.

von SYDOW, Björn, M.S., PH.D.; Swedish politician; b. 26 Nov. 1945, Stockholm; s. of Bengt Sköldenberg and Tallra von Sydow; m. Madeleine von Sydow; three s. one d.; ed. Stockholm and Linköping Univs.; worked as librarian 1970–74; lecturer in Political Science Linköping Univ. 1974–78; Assoc. Prof. of Political Science Stockholm Univ. 1978–83, 1992–96; Prin. School of Social Work and Public Admin. 1983–88; work on study of gen. election of Bd. of Dirs. of Nat. Pension Insurance Fund 1984–86; Visiting Research Scientist Case Western Reserve Univ., Ohio 1986, Pomona and Scripps Colls. Clairmont, Calif. 1992; active in municipal politics in Solna 1979–, Chair. Swedish Social Democratic Party (SAP), Solna 1983–; mem. editorial cttee. Tiden (political journal) 1983–89; mem. SAP programme comm; M.P. 1994–; mem. Parl Cttee. on Constitutional Affairs 1994–96, mem. SI Cttee. on Econ. Policy, Devt. And Environment 1995–96, Chair. SAP Cttee. on EU Affairs, mem. IGC and EU Enlargement Cttee. of Party of European Socialists, Chair. EU Cttee. of Nordic Labour Movt. (SAMAK) 1996–98; Head of Political Planning responsible for Research and Devt., Econ. Growth and Environment, Office of Prime Minister 1988–91; mem. Cttee. on Civil Rights, Ministry of Justice 1993–94; Chair. Cttee. on Environmental Protection, Ministry of Environment 1994–96, Parl. Cttee. preparing EU Treaty revision, Ministry for Foreign Affairs 1995–96; Minister of Trade at Ministry for Industry and Commerce 1996–97; Minister of Defence 1997–; Chair. Univ. Centre for Physics and Astronomy, Stockholm 1992–95. *Leisure interests:* horse riding. *Address:* Ministry of Defence, Jakobsgatan 9, 103 33 Stockholm, Sweden. *Telephone:* 8-405 1000. *Fax:* 8-411 9864.

VON TRIER, Lars; Danish film director; dir. The Element of Crime, Zentropa, Epidemic, The Kingdom, Breaking the Waves.

VON TROTTA, Margarethe; German film director and actress; b. 21 Feb. 1942, Berlin; has written scripts for The Sudden Wealth of the Poor People of Kombach 1971, Summer Lightning 1972, Fangschuss 1974, Unerreichbare Nahe 1984. *Films include:* Die Verlorene Ehre der Katharina Blum (The Lost Honour of Katharina Blum) 1975, Das zweite Erwachen der Christa Klages (The Second Awakening of Christa Klages) 1978, Schwestern, oder die Balance des Glücks (Sisters, or the Balance of Happiness) 1979, Die Bleierne Zeit (The German Sisters) 1981, Heller Wahn (Friends and Husbands) 1983, Rosa Luxemburg 1985, Felix 1987, Paura e amore (Love and Fear) 1988, L'Africana 1990, Il lungo silenzio 1992, Das Versprechen (The Promise) 1994, Winterkind (TV film) 1996, Dunkle Tage (TV film) 1998. *Address:* Bioskop-Film, Turkenstrasse 91, 80799 Munich, Germany.

VON WILPERT, Gero, PH.D., F.A.H.A.; Australian professor of German; b. 13 March 1933, Dorpat, Estonia; s. of Arno von Wilpert and Gerda Baumann; m. Margrit Laskowski 1953; three s.; ed. Univs. of Heidelberg and N.S.W.; publrs. reader and literary dir. Stuttgart 1957–72; Sr. Lecturer in German, Univ. of N.S.W. 1973–78, Assoc. Prof. 1978–81; McCaughey Prof. of German, Univ. of Sydney 1982–94. *Publications include:* Sachwörterbuch der Literatur 1955, Deutsche Literatur in Bildern 1957, Schiller-Chronik 1958, Deutsches Dichterlexikon 1963, Der verlorene Schatten 1978, Die deutsche Gespenstergeschichte 1994, Goethe-Lexikon 1998. *Leisure interests:* 18th century French art and antiques. *Address:* Werrington House, Werrington, N.S.W. 2747, Australia. *Telephone:* (02) 9623 1026 (Home).

VONDRA, Vladimir; Czech writer; b. 6 June 1930, Martinice, nr. Proseč; ed. Charles Univ. Prague; Ed. and publisher; work for Czech. TV 1967–70; on staff of State Library and Nat. Gallery; night watchman, technician 1970–89. *Publications include:* Ballad of Bandits 1956, The Double Face 1960, Veraikon 1974, Icons Marching In 1975.

VONDRAN, Ruprecht, DR.IUR.; German business executive and politician; b. 31 Dec. 1935, Göttingen; s. of Rudolf Vondran and Anneliese Unterberg ; m. Jutta Paul 1970; two s. two d.; ed. Univs. of Göttingen, Bonn and Würzburg; Pres. Wirtschaftsvereinigung Stahl 1987–98, mem. Bundestag 1987–94; Hon. D.Eng. *Leisure interests:* modern graphics, Japanese porcelain. *Address:* Wirtschaftsvereinigung Stahl, Sekretariat der Hauptgeschäftsführung, Breite Strasse 69, 40213 Düsseldorf (Office); Urdenbader Allee 63, 40593 Düsseldorf, Germany (Home).

VONGSAY, Kithong, DR.RER.POL.; Laotian diplomatist; b. 17 May 1937, Vientiane; m.; three c.; ed. Toulouse Univ.; Counsellor, Paris 1970–73; Deputy Minister for Foreign Affairs of Prov. Govt. 1975; Head Press and Information Dept., Ministry of Foreign Affairs 1975–78; Amb. to India, Burma, Sri Lanka and Nepal 1978–83; Perm. Rep. to UN, New York 1983–88. *Address:* c/o Ministry of Foreign Affairs, Vientiane, Laos.

VONNEGUT, Kurt, Jr., M.A.; American author; b. 11 Nov. 1922, Indianapolis; s. of Kurt Vonnegut and Edith Lieber; m. 1st Jane Marie Cox 1945 (divorced 1979); one s. two d. and three adopted s.; m. 2nd Jill Krementz 1979; one d.; ed. Cornell Univ., Univ. of Chicago; served with U.S. Army as Infantry Combat Scout, World War II; P.O.W., Dresden 1945; police reporter, Chicago City News Bureau 1946; in public relations, Gen. Electric Co., Schenectady, N.Y. 1947–50; freelance writer, New York 1950–65, 1974–; lecturer, Writers' Workshop, Univ. of Iowa 1965–67; Lecturer in English, Harvard Univ. 1970; Distinguished Prof., City Coll. of N.Y. 1973–74; Hon. Pres. American Humanist Asscn. 1992–; Guggenheim Fellow 1967–68; mem. Nat. Inst. Arts and Letters (Literary Award 1970). *Publications:* novels: Player Piano 1951, The Sirens of Titan 1959, Mother Night 1961, Cat's Cradle 1963, God Bless you, Mr. Rosewater 1965, Slaughterhouse-Five 1969, Breakfast of Champions 1973, Slapstick 1976, Jailbird 1979, Deadeye Dick 1982, Galápagos 1985, Bluebeard 1987, Hocus Pocus 1990, Timequake 1997; play: Happy Birthday, Wanda June 1971; short stories: Welcome to the Monkey House 1968; essays: Wampeters, Foma and Granfalloons 1974, Sun Moon Star 1980, Palm Sunday (autobiographical collage) 1981; TV script; Between Time and Timbuktu or Prometheus-5 1972, Fates Worse Than Death: An Autobiographical Collage of the 1980s. *Address:* c/o Donald C. Farber, Hartman and Craven, 460 Park Avenue, 11th Floor, New York, NY 10022, U.S.A. *Telephone:* (212) 836-4938. *Fax:* (212) 223-0467.

VORA, Motilal; Indian politician; b. 29 Dec. 1928, Nagor, Rajasthan; s. of Mohanlal Vora; m. Shanti Vora; two s. four d.; fmr. journalist; elected Councillor, Durg Municipality 1968, Congress Party mem. Madhya Pradesh Vidhan Sabha 1972; Minister of State for Educ. and Minister for Local Govt. 1981–82; Minister of Transport, Science and Tech. 1982–83, of Higher Educ. 1983–84, of Health and Family Welfare and Civil Aviation 1988–89; Pres. Madhya Pradesh Congress (I) Cttee. 1984–85; elected Leader Congress (I) Legis. Party 1985; Chief Minister, Madhya Pradesh 1985–88, Jan.–Dec. 1989; Gov. of U.P. 1995–96. *Address:* c/o Raj Bhavan, Lucknow, Uttar Pradesh, India.

VOROBYEV, Andrei Ivanovich, DR. MED.; Russian haematologist; b. 1 Oct. 1928; m.; two s.; ed. First Inst. of Medicine; worked as house-painter 1941–44; practitioner, Head of Polyclinics Volokolamsk Moscow Region 1953–54; docent Cen. Inst. of Advanced Medical Studies 1956–66; Head of div. Inst. of Biophysics 1966–84; mem. Acad. of Medical Sciences 1986; Dir. All-Union (now All-Russian) Scientific Cen. of Haematology 1987–91; Minister of Health of Russia 1991–92; Dir. Haematological Scientific Centre Russian Acad. of Medical Sciences 1993–; U.S.S.R. State Prize. *Leisure interest:* history. *Address:* Haematological Scientific Centre, Novy Zhukovsky pr. 4a, 125167 Moscow, Russia (Office). *Telephone:* (095) 212 2123 (Office).

VORONENKOVA, Galina, PH.D.; Russian professor of journalism; b. 30 Jan. 1947, Kostroma Region; d. of late Fjodor Smirnov and Alexandra Smirnova; m. Mikhail Voronenkov; one d.; ed. Moscow State Univ., Leipzig Univ., G.D.R.; literary contrib. to local newspaper, Kostroma Region 1965–67; mem. staff Journalism Dept., Moscow State Univ. 1974–87; teacher of Russian language, House of Soviet Science and Culture, Berlin, G.D.R. and Business Man. Journalists' Club, Berlin 1987–90; reporter for Soviet Women, Germany 1990–92; Prof. Faculty of Journalism, Moscow State Univ. 1992–; Dir. Free Russian-German Inst. for Publishing 1994–; Corresp. mem. Acad. of Information and Communication; award from Fed. Council of

Russian Fed. 1996. *Publications include:* Bürger in der Demokratie (Russian ed.) 1997, Sredstva massovoj Informatii Germanii v 90-e gody 1998, Neue Technolgien und die Entwicklung der Medien in Russland und Deutschland (Russian ed.) 1998, Nemezkaja journalistika: s momenta osnowanija do segodnjashnego dnja 1999. *Leisure interests:* classical music, world history, science fiction. *Address:* Mochovaja ul. 9, Apt. 235, 103914 Moscow, Russia. *Telephone:* (095) 203-26-43. *Fax:* (095) 251-97-76.

VORONKOV, Mikhail Grigorevich; DR. CHEM. SC.; Russian chemist; b. 6 Dec 1921, Orel; s. of Grigorii Vasilievich and Raisa Mikhailovna Voronkova; m. Lilia Iliinichna Makhnina 1943; one s. one d.; ed. Sverdlovsk Univ.; Sr. Scientist, Chemical Dept., Leningrad Univ. 1944–54; Head of Lab., Inst. of Chem. of Silicates, U.S.S.R. Acad. of Sciences 1954–61; Head of Lab. of Inst. of Organic Synthesis, Latvian Acad. of Sciences 1961–70; Dir. Inst. of Organic Chem., Siberian branch of U.S.S.R. (now Russian) Acad. of Sciences, Irkutsk 1970–94; Scientific Adviser 1994–; Corresp. mem. U.S.S.R. (now Russian) Acad. of Sciences 1970, mem. 1990; mem. Latvian Acad. of Sciences 1966–91, Foreign mem. 1991–; mem. Braunschweig Scientific Soc., Fed. Repub. of Germany 1976, Chem. Soc. of Japan 1991–, Asia-Pacific Acad. of Advanced Materials 1992; Emer. mem. Fla. Center of Heterocyclic Chem., U.S.A. 1998; Dr. h.c. (Gdansk Tech. Univ., Poland); Laureate, State Prize of Ukrainian S.S.R. 1981, Hon. Chemist of the U.S.S.R. 1983, Prize of the U.S.S.R. Council of Ministers 1991, Laureate, State Prize of Russia 1997. *Leisure interests:* numismatics, humour in chemistry. *Address:* Institute of Chemistry, 1 Favorsky Street, 664033 Irkutsk, Russia. *Telephone:* (3952) 46-24-00 (Office); 46-45-81 (Home).

VORONTSOV, Nikolai Nikolayevich, D.BIOL.SC.; Russian geneticist, zoologist and politician; b. 1 Jan. 1934, Moscow; m. Elena Lyapunova 1955; two d.; ed. Moscow Univ.; worked as jr. researcher Leningrad Inst. of Zoology, docent Pirogov Second Medical Inst., Moscow; scientific sec. Presidium of the Siberian br. of U.S.S.R. Acad. of Sciences on problems of biology, head of lab. Inst. of Cytology and Genetics; mem. Presidium of the Far East Scientific Centre of Acad. of Sciences, Dir. Inst. of Biology and Soil 1972–77; sr. researcher Koltsov Inst. of Biology of Devt., Moscow 1977–88, leading researcher 1988–; Chair. U.S.S.R. State Cttee. on nature preservation, then Minister of Use of Nature (the first minister not mem. of CPSU) 1989–91; U.S.S.R. People's Deputy 1989–91; People's Deputy of Russia 1990–93; Visiting Scholar, Prof. Harvard Univ. 1992–93; mem., Vice-Pres. Russian Acad. of Natural Sciences 1991–; active participant in democratic reforms movt.; elected to State Duma (Parl.) Dec. 1993; participant in more than 40 scientific expeditions; mem. Swedish Royal Acad. of Sciences, American Acad. of Art and Science; A. N. Severtsov Prize 1982, First Prize, Moscow Soc. for Nature 1984, U.S.S.R. State Prize 1990, Bruno Schubert Prize (Germany) 1990, Znamya Literature Prize 1996. *Publications:* more than 500 works on evolutionary biology, mammalian taxonomy, genetics, biodiversity, politology, ecology and preservation of environment. *Address:* N. K. Koltsov Institute of Biology of Development, ul. Vavilova 26, 117334 Moscow, Russia. *Telephone:* (095) 135-75-83.

VORONTSOV, Yuliy Mikhailovich; Russian diplomatist (retd.); b. 7 Oct. 1929, Leningrad; ed. Moscow Inst. of Int. Relations; various posts in Ministry of Foreign Affairs 1952–54; mem. CPSU 1956–91; U.S.S.R. rep. at UN 1954–58, 1963–65; Counsellor, U.S.S.R. Embassy to U.S.A. 1966–70, Counsellor-Envoy 1970–77; Amb. to India 1977–83, to France 1983–86, to Afghanistan 1988–90; First Deputy Minister of Foreign Affairs 1986–89; U.S.S.R. (then Russian) Amb. to UN 1990–92; Adviser to Pres. Yeltsin 1992–94; Amb. to U.S.A. 1994–98; Under-Sec. Gen. with responsibility for conflict resolution 1998–. *Address:* United Nations, United Nations Plaza, New York, NY 10017, U.S.A.; Ministry of Foreign Affairs, Smolenskaya-Sennaya 32/34, Moscow, Russia.

VOROTNIKOV, Vitaliy Ivanovich; Russian official (retd.); b. 20 Jan. 1926, Voronezh; ed. Kuibyshev Aviation Inst.; technologist, later sec. party cttee. and chief controller of a plant 1942–44, 1947–60; Sec. Kuibyshev Dist. Cttee. 1961–67; Chair. Kuibyshev Exec. Cttee. of Dist. Soviet of Workers' Deputies 1967–71; Deputy to U.S.S.R. Supreme Soviet 1970–89; First Sec. Voronezh Dist. Cttee. of CPSU 1971–75; mem. Cen. Cttee. of CPSU 1971–90; First Deputy Chair. Council of Ministers of R.S.F.S.R. 1975–79; Chair. U.S.S.R.-Angola Friendship Soc. 1976–79; Amb. to Cuba 1980–82; Cand. mem. Politburo June 1983, mem. 1983–90; Chair. Council of Ministers of R.S.F.S.R. 1983–88; Chair. Supreme Soviet of R.S.F.S.R. 1988–90; a Deputy Chair. Presidium of the Supreme Soviet of the U.S.S.R. 1988–90; U.S.S.R. People's Deputy 1989–91, People's Deputy of Russia, mem. Supreme Soviet 1990–93; mem. R.S.F.S.R. Supreme Soviet 1990–91; Hero of Socialist Labour 1986.

VORRES, Ian, M.A.; Canadian/Greek civil servant; b. 19 Sept. 1924, Athens; s. of Andrew Vorres and Stephanie Vorres; two adopted c.; ed. Queen's Univ. and Toronto Univ.; Founder and Dir. Vorres Museum 1983–; Mayor of Paiania 1991–; decorations from Portugal, Austria and Finland. *Publication:* The Last Grand Duchess (biography of Duchess Olga of Russia) 1964. *Leisure interests:* skiing, swimming, collection of antiques. *Address:* Vorres Museum of Greek Art, Paiania, Attica; Par. Diad. Kon/Noy 1, 190 02 Paiania, Attica, Greece. *Telephone:* 6642520. *Fax:* 6645775.

VOSCHERAU, Henning, LL.D.; German politician; b. 13 Aug. 1941, Hamburg; m.; three c.; qualified as notary public; joined SPD (Social Democratic Party) 1966; mem. Borough of Wandsbek Dist. Ass. 1970–74, Chief Whip SPD Parl. Group 1971–74; mem. Hamburg City Parl., mem. SPD Parl. Exec. Cttee. 1974–, Deputy Chair. 1976–82, Chair. 1982–87, Chair. City Parl. Cttee. on Home Affairs 1974–82, Deputy Party Chair. SPD, Hamburg 1981–89, First Mayor and Pres. of Senate, City of Hamburg 1988–97; Pres. Bundesrat 1990–91; Chair. Jt. Comm. for Reform of the Fed. Constitution 1992–93; SPD Speaker on Financial Policy 1995–97; Chair. Mediation Cttee. 1996–97. *Address:* Alstertor 14, 20095 Hamburg, Germany.

VOUTILAINEN, Pertti Juhani, M.SC.; Finnish banker; b. 22 June 1940, Kuusjärvi; s. of Otto Voutilainen and Martta Voutilainen; m. Raili Juvonen 1963; two s.; ed. Helsinki Univ. of Tech., Helsinki School of Econs., Pennsylvania State Univ., U.S.A.; joined Outokumpu Oy 1964, Man. Corp. Planning 1973–76, Dir. Corp. Planning 1976–78, mem. Bd. 1978–91, Pres. 1980–91, Chair. Exec. Bd. 1983–91; Chair. and C.E.O. Kansallis-Osake-Pankki (to merge with Unitas Ltd.) 1992–; Pres. Merita Bank PLC; Commdr. Order of Lion of Finland. *Leisure interests:* hunting, fishing. *Address:* Kansallis-Osake-Pankki, Aleksanterinkatu 42, 00100 Helsinki, Finland. *Telephone:* 358 0 1631. *Fax:* 358 0 1633077.

VOYNET, Dominique; French politician and doctor; b. 4 Nov. 1958, Montbéliard; two d.; ed. Faculty of Medicine, Besançon; anaesthetist and intensive care specialist, Dole (Jura) public hosp. 1985–89; activist in several ecological and other orgs., Belfort and Besançon 1976–; Co-founder Les Verts ('Green' movt.) 1984, Gen. Sec. Green Group in European Parl. 1989–91, Nat. Spokesperson 1991–; Municipal Councillor, Dole 1989–, Co. Councillor 1998–; mem. Franche-Comté regional council 1992–94 (resgnd.); cand. presidential election 1995; elected Nat. Ass. Deputy (for Les Verts and Parti Socialiste) in Dole-Arbois 1997; Minister for Town and Country Planning and the Environment 1997–. *Address:* Ministry of the Environment, 20 avenue de Segur, 75302 Paris cédex 07, France. *Telephone:* (1) 42.19.20.21.

VOYNOVICH, Vladimir Nikolayevich; author, playwright and film script-writer; b. 26 Sept. 1932, Stalinabad (now Dushanbe), Tajikistan; s. of Nikolai Pavlovich Voinovich and Rosa (née Goikhman) Voinovich; m. 1st Valentina Voinovich; one s. one d.; m. 2nd Irina Braude 1970; one d.; served in Soviet Army 1951–55; worked as carpenter 1956–57; studied Moscow Pedagogical Inst. 1958–59; started literary activity (and song-writing for Moscow Radio) 1960; various dissident activities 1966–80; expelled from U.S.S.R. Writers' Union 1974; elected mem. French PEN Centre 1974; emigrated from U.S.S.R. 1980; U.S.S.R. citizenship restored 1990; mem. Bavarian Acad. of Fine Arts. *Publications include:* The Life and Unusual Adventures of Private Ivan Chonkin (samizdat 1967) 1975 (English trans. 1977), Ivankiada 1976, By Way of Mutual Correspondence 1979, Pretender to the Throne 1981, Moscow-2042 1987, The Fur Hut 1989, The Zero Decision 1990, Case N3484 1992, The Conception 1994, Tales for Adults 1996.

VOYTSEKHOVSKY, Bogdan Vyacheslavovich, D.TECH.SC.; Russian physicist; b. 25 Jan. 1922, Soroka, Vinnitsa Region, Ukraine; m.; four d.; ed. Moscow Inst. of Physics and Eng.; mem CPSU 1948–91; worked on secret mil. plants 1953–56; Head of Lab. Moscow Inst. of Physics and Tech. 1956–58; Head of Div. Inst. of Hydrodynamics Siberian br. of U.S.S.R. (now Russian) Acad. of Sciences 1958–65, Deputy Dir. 1965–90, Head of Lab. 1991–; Corresp. mem. U.S.S.R. (now Russian) Acad. of Sciences 1964, mem. 1991; main research on gas detonation, high-pressure pulse and continuous jets, pulse hydrocurrents, including Spin Detonation 1957, Perspective Energy Sources and Their Technical and Economic Characteristics 1980; Unstable Detonation of Waves in Gases; Lenin Prize and other distinctions. *Leisure interests:* economy. *Address:* Institute of Hydrodynamics, Prospekt akademika Lavrentyeva 15, 630090 Novosibirsk, Russia (Office). *Telephone:* (3832) 35 40 63 (Office); 35 06 28 (Home). *Fax:* (3832) 35 40 50 (Office).

VOZNESENSKY, Andrey Andreyevich; Russian poet; b. 12 May 1933, Moscow; s. of Andrey N. and Antonina S. Voznesensky; m. Zoya Boguslavskaya 1965; one s.; ed. Moscow Architectural Inst.; mem. Union of Soviet Writers, mem. Bd. 1967–; Vice-Pres. Soviet (now Russian) PEN Centre 1989–; Hon. mem. American Acad. of Arts and Letters 1972, Bayerischen Kunst Akad., French Acad. Merime; Int. Award for Distinguished Achievement in Poetry 1978, State Prize 1978. *Publications:* poems: The Masters 1959, Forty Lyrical Digressions from a Triangular Pear 1962, Longjumeau 1963, Oza 1964, Story Under Full Sail 1970, Ice-69 1970, Queen of Clubs 1974, The Eternal Flesh 1978, Andrey Polisadov 1980, Unaccountable 1981, The Ditch 1981; collections: Parabola 1960, Mosaic 1960, Anti-Worlds 1964, Heart of Achilles 1966, Verses 1967, The Shadow of a Sound 1970, The Glance 1972, Let The Bird Free 1974, Violoncello Oak Leaf 1975, The Master of Stained Glass 1976, Temptation 1978, Metropol (poetry and prose, co-author with 22 others) 1979, Selected Poems 1979, Collected Works (vols. 1–3) 1984, Aksioma Samoiska 1990, Videomes 1992, Rossia-Casino 1997; *in English:* Selected Poems 1964, Anti-worlds 1966, Anti-worlds and the Fifth Ace 1967, Dogalypse 1972, Story under Full Sail 1974, Nostalgia for the Present 1978. *Address:* Kotelnicheskaya nab. 1/15, korp. B., Apt. 62, Moscow 109240, Russia. *Telephone:* (095) 915-49-90.

VRAALSEN, Tom Eric, M.ECON.; Norwegian diplomatist; b. 26 Jan. 1936, Oslo; m.; five c.; ed. Århus School of Econs. and Business Admin., Denmark; joined Norwegian Foreign Service 1960; various diplomatic positions, Beijing 1962–64, 1969–70, Cairo 1964–67, Manila 1970–71, Jakarta 1971; in charge of Norwegian relations with Africa, Asia and Latin America, Political Dept., Ministry of Foreign Affairs 1971–73, in charge of UN and int. org. affairs 1973–75; Deputy Perm. Rep. to UN 1975–79, Perm. Rep. 1982–89; Dir.-Gen.

Political Dept., Ministry of Foreign Affairs 1981–82; Minister for Devt. Co-operation, for Nordic Co-operation 1989–90; Sr. Vice-Pres. Saga Petroleum 1991–92; Asst. Sec.-Gen. Ministry of Foreign Affairs 1992–94; Amb. to U.K. 1994–96, to U.S.A. 1996–. *Address:* 3401 Massachusetts Avenue N.W., Washington, D.C. 20007, U.S.A.

VRANITZKY, Franz, D.COMM.; Austrian politician and banker; b. 4 Oct. 1937, Vienna; s. of Franz Vranitsky and Rosa Vernitsky; m. Christine Kristen; one s. one d.; ed. Vienna XVII High School, Coll. (now Univ.) of Commerce, Vienna; joined Siemens-Schuckert Gesellschaft m.b.H., Vienna 1961; Dept. of Nat. Econs., Austrian Nat. Bank 1961–69, seconded to the Office of the First Vice-Pres. 1969–70; Advisor on Econ. and Financial Policy to Minister of Finance 1970–76; Deputy-Chair. Bd. of Dirs. Creditanstalt-Bankverein 1976–81, Österreichische Länderbank 1981, Chair. Bd. of Dirs. 1981–84; Fed. Minister of Finance 1984–86; Fed. Chancellor 1986–96; fmr. Chair. Austrian Socialist Party (now Social Democratic Party of Austria); Pres. Vienna Inst. for Devt. and Co-operation 1990–; Hon. K.C.M.G. 1995. *Address:* c/o Office of the Federal Chancellor, Ballhausplatz 2, 1014 Vienna, Austria.

VREDELING, Henk; Netherlands politician; b. 20 Nov. 1924, Amersfoort; m. Jola Schouten 1948; three s. one d.; ed. Agricultural Univ., Wageningen; mem. Second Chamber of States-Gen. (Parl.) 1956–73; mem. European Parl. 1958–73; Socio-econ. Adviser to Agricultural Workers' Union 1950–73; Minister of Defence 1973–76; Commr. for Employment and Social Affairs and for Tripartite Conf., Comm. of European Communities 1977–81; mem. Equal Opportunities Council 1981–85, Advisory Council on Peace and Security 1987–94, Supervisory Bd. Weekbladpers 1983–96. *Address:* Rembrandtlaan 13A, 3712 A J Huis ter Heide, Netherlands. *Telephone:* 030-6931633.

VUILLEMIN, Jules Marie Etienne, DR.PHIL.; French professor of philosophy; b. 15 Feb. 1920, Pierrefontaine; s. of Etienne Vuillemin and Marie Cuenot; m. 1st Suzanne Pannier 1946 (divorced 1967); m. 2nd Gudrun Diem 1967; one s. one d.; ed. Coll. des Jesuits de Metz, Lycée Louis le Grand, Ecole Normale Supérieure, Paris and Sorbonne, Paris; Prof. Lycée de Besançon 1943–44; CNRS 1944–48; Prof. Univ. of Clermont-Ferrand 1948–61; Prof. of Philosophy of Cognition, Coll. de France 1962–90, now Prof. Emer.; Dr. h.c. (Liège, Fribourg, Montreal); Prix Paul Pelliot; Chevalier Légion d'honneur. *Publications:* Physique et métaphysique kantiennes 1955, Mathématiques et métaphysique chez Descartes 1960, Introduction à la philosophie de l'algèbre 1962, Le miroir de Venise 1965, De la logique à la théologie, cinque études sur Aristote 1967, Leçons sur la première philosophie de Russell 1968, Le dieu d'Anselm et les apparances de la raison 1971, La logique et le monde sensible, étude sur les théories contemporaines de l'abstraction 1971, Nécessité ou contingence, l'aporie de Diodore et les systèmes philosophiques 1984, What are Philosophical Systems? 1986, Eléments de Poétique 1991, Trois histoires de guerre 1991, L'Intuitionnisme Kantien 1994, Necessity or Contingency, the Master Argument 1996. *Address:* 11 Place Marcelin-Berthelot, 75005 Paris; 18 Les Granges Berrard, 25300 Les Fourgs, France.

VUNIBOBO, Berenado, C.B.E., B.AGR.SC.; Fijian government official and agronomist; b. 24 Sept. 1932, Nukutubu, Rewa; s. of Mateo Vunibobo and Maria Kelekeletabua; m. Luisa Marama Tabumoce 1953; two s. three d.; ed. St. Joseph's Catholic Mission School, Rewa, Marist Brothers High School, Suva, Queensland State Agric. Coll., Queensland Univ. Imperial Coll. of Tropical Agric., Trinidad; Govt. Service 1951–, Dist. Agric. Officer 1962–67, Sr. Agric. Officer and later Chief Agric. Officer 1968–69; Deputy Dir. of Agric. 1969–70, Dir. of Agric. 1970–71; Perm. Sec. for Agric., Fisheries and Forests 1971–72, for Works 1973–76; Perm. Rep. to UN, Amb. to U.S.A., High Commr. in Canada 1976–80; Perm. Sec. for Tourism, Transport and Civil Aviation 1980–81; Resident Rep. UNDP, Repub. of Korea 1981–86; Resident Rep. UNDP, Pakistan 1986–87; Minister of Trade and Commerce 1987–92, for Home Affairs, Immigration, Employment, Youth and Sports 1994, of Finance and Econ. Devt. 1994–97, for Foreign Affairs and External Trade 1997–; Chair. UN Visiting Mission to Cayman Islands and U.S. Virgin Islands 1978; Vice-Pres. UN Gen. Ass.; Pres. UN Pledging Conf., Governing Council, UNDP; Chair. UN Observer Mission to New Hebrides (Vanuatu); Chair. Coconut Pests and Diseases Bd., Banana Marketing Bd., Nat. Marketing Authority 1970–72; Chair. Civil Aviation Authority, Fiji, Air Terminal Services, Fiji; mem. Bd., Fiji Devt. Bank 1970–72; mem. Native Lands Trust Bd. 1968–75, Fijian Affairs Bd. 1968–76, Great Council of Chiefs 1968–76, Cen. Whitley Council 1970–76, Jt. Industrial Council 1970–76, Fiji Electricity Authority 1975–76. Gold Medal (Queensland Agric. Coll.) 1986. *Leisure interests:* reading, debating, walking, gardening, swimming, golf. *Address:* Ministry of Foreign Affairs, Government Buildings, P.O. Box 2220, Suva, Fiji. *Telephone:* (679) 211458. *Fax:* (679) 301741.

VUONG VAN BAC; Vietnamese diplomatist; b. 1927, Bac Ninh, N. Viet Nam; ed. Hanoi Univ., Michigan State Univ., Vanderbilt Univ., U.S.A.; admitted to Hanoi Bar Asscn. 1952, Saigon Bar Asscn. 1954; Prof. of Constitutional and Political Science, Nat. Inst. of Admin. 1955; Chair. Dalat Univ. 1965; Sec.-Gen. Viet Nam Lawyers' Fed. 1961; mem. Council of Lawyers, Saigon High Court 1962–68, Bd. of Dirs. Viet Nam Council on Foreign Relations 1968; Legal Adviser to Repub. of Viet Nam Liaison and Observation Del. at Paris talks 1968; Amb. to U.K. 1972–73; Minister of Foreign Affairs 1973–75; has attended numerous int. confs. on legal and econ. affairs.

VUONO, Gen. Carl E., B.S.ENG., M.S.; American army officer; b. 18 Oct. 1934, Monongahela, Pa.; ed. U.S. Mil. Acad.; commissioned 2nd Lieut. U.S. Army 1957, advanced through ranks to Gen.; Chief of Staff Dept. of Army, Washington, D.C. *Address:* Chief of Staff, The Pentagon, Washington, DC 20310; 5796 West Chester, Alexandria, VA 22310, U.S.A.

VUURSTEEN, Karel; Netherlands business executive; b. 25 July 1941, Arnhem; s. of Cornelis Vuursteen and Hendrika Weddepohl; m. Juliette Pronk 1964; one s. two d.; ed. Agricultural Univ. Wageningen; several marketing functions, Philips, Netherlands 1968; Man. Dir. Consumer Goods, Philips, Sweden 1979; C.E.O. Philips Norway 1982; Man. Dir. Consumer Goods, Philips Germany 1984; C.E.O. Philips Austria 1987, Philips Lighting Co. U.S.A. 1990; mem. Exec. Bd. Heineken N.V. 1991, Deputy Chair. Exec. Bd. 1992, C.E.O. 1993–. *Leisure interest:* golf. *Address:* Heineken N.V., Tweede Weteringplantsoen 21, Postbus 28, 1000 AA Amsterdam (Office); Kortrijk 19, 3621 LZ Breukelen, Netherlands (Home). *Telephone:* 31.20.5239 600 (Office). *Fax:* 31.20.6265 962.

VYACHIREV, Rem Ivanovich; Russian business executive; b. 23 Aug. 1934, Bolshaya Chernigovka, Kuibyshev Dist; m.; two c.; ed. Kuibyshev Inst. of Oil and Gas; worked in Oil Producers' Union, Ozenburg (Ordobycha) 1976–78; Chief Engineer Orenburggazprom 1978–82; Deputy Minister of Gas Industry of U.S.S.R. 1983–85, 1986–89; Gen. Man. Tyumengazprom 1985–86; Deputy Chair. Bd., State (later Jt. Stock) Gazprom Co. 1989–92, Chair. 1992–; Chair Bd. of Dirs. Siberian Oil Co. 1996–. *Address:* RAO Gazprom, Nametkina str. 16, 117884 Moscow, Russia. *Telephone:* (095) 719-30-01; 719-21-09. *Fax:* 719-83-33/34/35.

VÝBORNÝ, Miloslav, D.IUR.; Czech politician and lawyer; b. 19 Feb. 1952, Chrudim; m. Vaclava Výborný; three s.; ed. Charles Univ., Prague; M.P. 1990–, Chair. Parl. Constitutional Juridical Cttee. 1992–96; Vice-Chair. Christian and Democratic Union–Czech People's Party (KDU–CSL) 1993–; Chair. KDU–ČSL Parl. Club 1995–96; Minister of Defence 1996–97, of Legislative Affairs Jan.–July 1998; Vice-Pres. Govt. Cttee. for Integration of Czech Repub. into NATO 1997–98. *Address:* Parliament of the Czech Republic, Sněmovní 4, 118 26 Prague 1, Czech Republic. *Telephone:* (2) 571 111, 24 59 2111 (Office).

W

WAALER, Bjarne Arentz, DR.MED.; Norwegian professor of medicine; b. 18 April 1925, Bergen; s. of Prof. Rolf and Gudrun Waaler; m. Gudrun Arentz 1950; two s. one d.; ed. Univ. of Oslo; various positions in Norwegian hospitals 1950–56; research fellow in haematology and physiology, Univ. of Oslo 1956–58; research fellow in physiology, Univ. of Oxford 1958–61; Prof. of Medicine (Physiology), Univ. of Oslo 1962–92, Dean, Faculty of Medicine 1974–77; Rector, Univ. of Oslo 1977–84; mem. Norwegian Acad. of Science and Letters (Pres. 1990–96), mem. U.K. Physiological Soc.; Commdr. Order of St. Olav. *Publications:* about 120 publications in the fields of blood coagulation, blood circulation, and university matters. *Leisure interests:* fly fishing, literature. *Address:* University of Oslo, Department of Physiology, P.B. 1103, Blindern, 317 Oslo 3; Kaptein Oppegaards vei 36B, 1152 Oslo, Norway (Home). *Telephone:* (22) 85 12 32 (Office); (22) 28 23 65 (Home).

WACHTMEISTER, Count Wilhelm Hans Frederik; Swedish diplomatist; b. 29 April 1923, Wanås; s. of Count Gustaf Wachtmeister and Countess Margaretha Wachtmeister (née Trolle); m. Countess Ulla Wachtmeister (née Leuhusen) 1947; one s. two d.; ed. Stockholm Univ.; Attaché, Foreign Office 1946–47, Embassy in Vienna 1947–49, in Madrid Feb.-May 1949, in Lisbon 1949–50, Foreign Office 1950–52; Second Sec. Foreign Office 1952–55; Second Sec. Embassy in Moscow 1955–56, First Sec. 1956–58; Special Asst. to Sec.-Gen. of UN 1958–62; Head of Div. for UN Affairs, Foreign Office 1962–63, Head of Div. 1963–65, Head of Dept. July–Oct. 1965, Asst. Under-Sec. of State 1965–66; Amb. to Algeria 1966–68; Deputy Under-Sec. of State and Head of Political Div. 1968–74; Amb. to U.S.A. 1974–89; Dean of the Diplomatic Corps 1986–89; Sr. Adviser to Chair. of AB Volvo 1989–93; Int. Adviser Coudert Bros. (law firm) 1989–93; Chair. Swedish-American Chamber of Commerce (US) 1993–; Hon. LL.D. *Leisure interest:* tennis. *Address:* c/o Ministry of Foreign Affairs, P.O. Box 16121, 10323 Stockholm, Sweden.

WADA, Akiyoshi, PH.D.; Japanese research director; b. 28 June 1929, Tokyo; s. of Koroku Wada and Haruko Kikkawa; m. Sachiko Naito 1958; two s.; ed. Gakushūin High School and Univ. of Tokyo; Prof. of Physics, Univ. of Tokyo 1971–90, Prof. Emer. 1990–, Dean, Faculty of Science 1989–90; Dir. Sagami Chemical Research Center 1991–; Vice-Pres. Advanced Tech. Inst. 1988–; Dir. Kazusa DNA Research Inst. 1991–; mem. Science Council of Japan 1991–; Pres. Nestlé Science Foundation (Japan) 1992–; Dir. Genomic Sciences Centre, Inst. of Physical and Chemical Research 1998–; Matsunaga Prize 1971, Shimadu Prize 1983, Polymer Soc. Prize 1995, Purple Ribbon Medal 1995, 10th Anniversary Award, Human Frontier Science Program 1998. *Publications:* Macrodipole of α-helix 1976, Molten Globule State of Proteins 1980, Automated DNA Sequencing 1987, Stability Distribution of DNA Double Helix 1987. *Leisure interests:* orchid cultivation, stamp collection. *Address:* 11-1-311, Akasaka 8, Minato-ku, Tokyo 107, Japan. *Telephone:* 03-3408-2932.

WADA, Emi; Japanese costume designer; b. 18 March 1937, Kyoto; d. of Nobu Wada and Sumiko Noguchi; m. Ben Wada 1957; one s.; ed. Kyoto City Coll. of Arts (now Kyoto Univ. of Arts). *Costumes designed:* (theatre) Aoi Hi (Blue Fire) 1957, Image Mandala 1987, King Lear 1993; (films) Marco 1972, Ran 1985, Rokumeikan 1986, Princess from the Moon 1987, Momotaro Forever 1988, Rikyu 1989, Dreams 1990, Prospero's Books 1991; (dance) Carmen 1991; (TV) Silk Art by Emi Wada 1991; (opera) Oedipus Rex 1992; (exhbn.) Emi Wada Recreates the Momoyama Period, Kyoto 1989; mem. Acad. of Motion Picture Art and Sciences, U.S.A., Costume Designers' Guild, U.S.A.; Acad. Award, Best Costume Design for Ran 1986, Gold Medal, Cannes Film Festival 1987, Grand Prix, Montreux Int. HDTV Festival, for Silk Art by Emi Wada 1991. *Publication:* My Costume—Emi Wada 1989. *Leisure interest:* reading. *Address:* 3-31-3-105 Kinuta, Setagaya-ku, Tokyo 157, Japan. *Telephone:* (3) 3417-0425. *Fax:* (3) 3417-1773.

WADDINGTON, Baron (Life Peer), cr. 1990, of Read in the County of Lancashire, **David Waddington,** G.C.V.O., P.C., Q.C., D.L.; British politician; b. 2 Aug 1929, Burnley; s. of Charles Waddington and Minnie Hughan Waddington; m. Gillian Rosemary Green 1958; three s. two d.; ed. Sedbergh and Hertford Coll., Oxford; Pres. Oxford Union Conservative Asscn. 1950; called to the Bar Gray's Inn 1951, Recorder of the Crown Court 1972; M.P. for Nelson and Colne 1968–74, for Clitheroe (Ribble Valley constituency from 1983) March 1979–91; Parl. Pvt. Sec. to Attorney-Gen. 1970–72; Lord Commr. of the Treasury 1979–81, Parl. Under-Sec. of State for Employment 1981–83; Minister of State at the Home Office 1983–87, Parl. Sec. to H.M. Treasury and Govt. Chief Whip 1987–89, Home Sec. 1989–90, Lord Privy Seal and Leader of the House of Lords 1990–92; Gov. and C.-in-C. of Bermuda 1992–97. *Leisure interests:* golf, sailing. *Address:* House of Lords, Westminster, London, SW1A 0PW; Stable House, Sabden, Clitheroe, Lancs., BB7 9HP, England.

WADDINGTON, Leslie; British art dealer; b. 9 Feb. 1934, Dublin; s. of Victor Waddington and Zelda Waddington; m. 2nd Clodagh F. Waddington 1985; two d. by first marriage; ed. Portora Royal School, Enniskillen and Ecole du Louvre, Paris; Dir. Waddington Galleries 1957, Man. Dir. 1966–; Chair. Modern Painting Section Maastricht Art Fair 1994–95, Pictura Section 1996; Sr. Fellow R.C.A. 1993; Dr. h.c. (Royal Coll. of Art) 1993. *Leisure interests:* chess, reading. *Address:* Waddington Galleries, 11 Cork Street, London, W1X 1PD, England. *Telephone:* 0171-437 8611.

WADE, Sir (Henry) William (Rawson), Kt., Q.C., LL.D., D.C.L., F.B.A.; British professor of law (retd.); b. 16 Jan. 1918, London; s. of Col. H. O. Wade and E. L. Wade; m. 1st Marie Osland-Hill 1943 (died 1980); m. 2nd Marjorie Grace Hope Browne 1982; two s.; ed. Shrewsbury School, Gonville and Caius Coll. Cambridge and Harvard Law School, U.S.A.; Temporary Officer, H.M. Treasury 1940–45; Barrister, Lincoln's Inn 1946; Fellow, Trinity Coll. Cambridge and Univ. Lecturer/Reader 1946–61; Prof. of English Law, Oxford Univ., and Fellow of St. John's Coll. 1961–76; Master of Gonville and Caius Coll. Cambridge 1976–88; Prof. of English Law, Cambridge Univ. 1978–82; Guest Lecturer in many countries; mem. Council on Tribunals 1958–71, Relationships Comm., Uganda 1961, Royal Comm. on Tribunals of Inquiry 1966; Vice-Pres. British Acad. 1981–83; Hon. Bencher, Lincoln's Inn 1964; Hon. Fellow, St. John's Coll., Oxford 1976, Trinity Coll., Cambridge 1991. *Publications:* The Law of Real Property (with Sir Robert Megarry), 5th edn. 1984, Administrative Law (with C. F. Forsyth), 7th edn. 1994, Towards Administrative Justice 1963, Legal Control of Government (with B. Schwartz) 1972, Constitutional Fundamentals (Hamlyn Lectures) 1980; articles in legal journals. *Leisure interests:* climbing, gardening and music. *Address:* Gonville and Caius College, Cambridge, CB2 1TA (Office); The Green, 1A Ludlow Lane, Fulbourn, Cambridge, CB1 5BL, England (Home). *Telephone:* (01223) 332400 (Office); (01223) 881745 (Home).

WADE, Kenneth, D.SC., F.R.S.; British university professor; b. 13 Oct. 1932, Sleaford, Lincs.; s. of the late Harry K. Wade and Anna E. Wade (née Cartwright); m. Gertrud Rosmarie Hetzel 1962; one s. two d.; ed. Carre's Grammar School, Sleaford, Lincs., Nottingham Univ.; postdoctoral research asst. Cambridge Univ. 1957–59, Cornell Univ., Ithaca, N.Y. 1959–60; Lecturer in Chem. Derby Coll. of Tech. 1960–61; lecturer in Chem. Durham Univ. 1961–71, Sr. Lecturer 1971–77, Reader 1977–83, Head of Inorganic Chem. 1980–98, Prof. 1983–, Chair. Dept. of Chem. 1986–89; Visiting Prof. Warsaw 1974, Amsterdam 1977, USCLA 1979, Notre Dame 1983, McMaster 1984, London, Ont. 1990; Pres. Royal Soc. of Chem. Dalton Div. 1995–97; Main Group Award Royal Soc. of Chem. 1982, Tilden Lecturer 1987, Mond Lecturer 1998, E. Merck Lecturer, Darmstadt 1994. *Publications:* Organometallic Compounds: The Main Group Elements (jtly.) 1967, Principles of Organometallic Chemistry (jtly.) 1968, Electron Deficient Compounds 1971, Hypercarbon Chemistry (jtly.) 1987, Electron Deficient Boron and Carbon Clusters (jtly.) 1990. *Leisure interest:* walking. *Address:* Chemistry Department, Durham University Science Laboratories, South Road, Durham, DH1 3LE (Office); 7 Hill Meadows, High Shincliffe, Durham, DH1 2PE, England (Home). *Telephone:* (0191) 374 3122 (Office); (0191) 386 5139 (Home). *Fax:* (0191) 386-1127.

WADE, (Sarah) Virginia, O.B.E., B.SC.; British tennis player; b. 10 July 1945, Bournemouth, Hants. (now Dorset); d. of Canon Eustace Wade (fmr. Archdeacon of Durban, S.A.); ed. Univ. of Sussex; amateur player 1962–68, professional 1968–; British Hard Court Champion 1967, 1968, 1973, 1974; U.S.A. Champion 1968 (singles), 1973, 1975 (doubles); Italian Champion 1971; Australian Champion 1972; Wimbledon Ladies Champion 1977; played Wightman Cup for G.B. 1965–81, Capt. 1973–80; played Fed. Cup for G.B. 1967–81, Capt. 1973–81; commentator BBC 1980–; mem. Cttee. All England Lawn Tennis Club 1983–91; Hon. LL.D. (Sussex) 1985; Int. Tennis Hall of Fame 1989. *Publications:* Courting Triumph (with Mary Lou Mellace) 1978, Ladies of the Court 1984. *Leisure interest:* reading. *Address:* c/o International Management Group, Pier House, Strand on the Green, London, W4 3NN, England.

WADE-GERY, Sir Robert (Lucian), K.C.M.G., K.C.V.O., M.A.; British fmr. diplomatist and banker; b. 22 April 1929, Oxford; s. of Prof. H. T. and V. Wade-Gery; m. Sarah Marris 1962; one s. one d.; ed. Winchester Coll. and New Coll., Oxford; Fellow, All Souls Coll., Oxford 1951–73, 1987–89, 1997–; joined Foreign (now Diplomatic) Service 1951; in Foreign Office (FO) Econ. Relations Dept. 1951–54; at Embassy in Bonn 1954–57, Tel-Aviv 1961–64, Saigon (now Ho Chi Min City) 1967–68; FO 1957–60, 1964–67; Cabinet Office 1968–69; Counsellor 1969; on loan to Bank of England 1969; Head of Financial Policy and Aid Dept., FCO 1970; Under-Sec., Cen. Policy Review Staff, Cabinet Office 1971–73; Minister at Embassy, Madrid 1973–77, Moscow 1977–79; Deputy Sec. of Cabinet 1979–82; High Commr. in India 1982–87; Vice-Chair. Barclays de Zoete Wedd 1994–98 (Exec. Dir. 1987–93), Vice-Chair. Barclays Capital 1998–; Chair. SOAS 1990–98; Chair. Anglo-Spanish Soc. 1995–98. *Leisure interests:* walking, sailing, travel, history. *Address:* 14 Hill View, 2 Primrose Hill Road, London, NW3 3AX; The Old Vicarage, Cold Aston, Cheltenham, Glos., GL54 3BW, England. *Telephone:* 0171-773 3813 (Office); 0171-722 4754, (01451) 821115 (Homes). *Fax:* 0171-586 5966, (01451) 822496.

WADIA, Jim, F.C.A., F.R.S.A.; British chartered accountant; b. 12 April 1948; m. Joelle Garnier 1972; one s. one d.; ed. Le Rosey, Rolle, Switzerland, Inns of Court School of Law; called to Bar, Inner Temple 1969; partner, Arthur

Andersen 1982–, Managing Partner, U.K. 1993–97, Worldwide Managing Partner 1997–. *Leisure interests:* tennis, theatre. *Address:* Arthur Anderson, 1 Surrey Street, London, WC2R 2RS; 28 Eldon Road, London, W8 5PT, England. *Telephone:* 0171-438 3501.

WAELBROECK, Jean Louis, PH.D.; Belgian professor of economics (retd.); b. 2 May 1927, Petit Saconnet (Sw.); s. of Pierre G. Waelbroeck and Elisabeth M. Varlez; m. Isabelle Gogneaux 1954; two s. three d.; ed. Strathcona High School, McGill Univ. and Free Univ. of Brussels; Research Dept., Nat. Bank of Belgium 1952–55; Econ. Office, NATO 1955–59, Head, Soviet Section 1958; Chargé de cours, Free Univ. of Brussels 1959–63, Prof. 1963–92, Prof. Emer. 1992–; Ed. European Econ. Review 1969–90; Fellow, Econometric Soc. *Publication:* Activity Analysis and General Equilibrium Modelling (with V. Ginsburgh). *Leisure interests:* fruit growing, music. *Address:* 29 rue d'Heuval, 1490 Court-St.-Etienne, Belgium. *Telephone:* 010/612326.

WAELSCH, Salome G., PH.D.; American geneticist; b. 6 Oct. 1907, Danzig, Germany (now Gdańsk, Poland); d. of Ilyia and Nadia Gluecksohn; m. Heinrich B. Waelsch 1943; one s. one d.; ed. Univs. of Königsberg, Berlin, Freiburg; Research Assoc. in Genetics, Columbia Univ., New York 1936–55; Assoc. Prof. of Anatomy (Genetics), Albert Einstein Coll. of Medicine, Bronx, N.Y. 1955–58, Prof. of Anatomy (Genetics) 1958–63, Chair. of Dept. of Genetics 1963–76, Prof. of Genetics 1963–; mem. N.A.S.; Fellow, American Acad. of Arts and Sciences. *Publications:* more than 100 articles in the field of developmental genetics in various scientific journals. *Address:* Department of Molecular Genetics, Albert Einstein College of Medicine, 1300 Morris Park Avenue, Bronx, NY 10461 (Office); 90 Morningside Drive, New York, NY 10027, U.S.A. (Home). *Telephone:* (718) 430-3185 (Office). *Fax:* (718) 822-0845 (Office).

WAGGONER, Paul Edward, PH.D.; American scientist; b. 29 March 1923, Appanoose County, Ia.; s. of Walter Loyal Waggoner and Kathryn Maring Waggoner; m. Barbara Ann Lockerbie 1945; two s.; ed. Univ. of Chicago and Iowa State Coll., Ames; Asst., then Assoc., then Chief Scientist, Connecticut Agricultural Experiment Station, New Haven 1951–71, Vice-Dir. 1969–71, Dir. 1972–87, Distinguished Scientist 1987–; lecturer, Yale Forestry School, New Haven 1962–; Guggenheim Fellow 1963; mem. N.A.S.; Fellow A.A.A.S., American Soc. of Agronomy, American Phytopathological Soc.; received Anton-de Bary Medal 1996. *Publications:* Agricultural Meteorology (Ed.) 1965 and articles on phytopathology. *Leisure interest:* gardening. *Address:* The Connecticut Agricultural Experiment Station, Box 1106, New Haven, CT 06504 (Office); 314 Vineyard Point Road, Guilford, CT 06437, U.S.A. (Home). *Telephone:* (203) 789-7214 (Office); (203) 453-2816 (Home).

WAGNER, Falk (Oskar Paul Alfred), DR.THEOL.; German professor of theology; b. 25 Feb. 1939, Vienna, Austria; s. of Robert Wagner and Friedel Wagner; m. Inamaria Winnefeld 1968; two d.; ed. Gymnasium Wiesbaden and Univs. of Frankfurt and Mainz; Research Fellow for Economic Ethics and Adult Educ., Karlsruhe 1968–69; Research Fellow, Deutsches Inst. für Int. Pädagogische Forschung, Frankfurt-am-Main 1969–72; Asst. Univ. of Munich 1970–72, Lecturer in Systematic Theology 1972, Prof. 1978–; Prof. Vienna Univ. *Publications include:* Über die Legitimität der Mission 1968, Der Gedanke der Persönlichkeit Gottes bei Fichte und Hegel 1971, Schleiermachers Dialektik 1974, Geld oder Gott? 1985, Was ist Religion? 1986, Die vergessene spekulative Theologie 1987, Was ist Theologie? 1989, Zur gegenwärtigen Lage des Protestantismus 1995, Ende der Religion—Religion ohne Ende? (with M. Murrmann-Kahl) 1996, Religion und Gottesgedanke 1996, Zeitenwechsel und Beständigkeit (co-Ed.) 1997; numerous articles on theological, philosophical and ethical questions. *Address:* Universität Wien, Evangelisch-Theologische Fakultät, Institut für Systematische Theologie, Rooseveltplatz 10, 1090 Vienna (Office); Kaiserstrasse 32, 1070 Vienna, Austria (Home). *Telephone:* (1) 406 5981-16 (Office).

WAGNER, Heinz Georg, DR.RER.NAT.; German professor of physical chemistry; b. 20 Sept. 1928, Hof, Bavaria; s. of Georg Wagner and Frida Spiess; m. Renate C. Heuer 1974; ed. Tech. Hochschule, Darmstadt and Univ. of Göttingen; lecturer, Univ. of Göttingen 1960–65, Prof. of Physical Chem. 1971–97; Prof. Ruhr Univ. Bochum 1965–70; Dir. Max-Planck-Inst. für Strömungsforschung, Göttingen 1971–97; Vice-Pres. Deutsche Forschungsgemeinschaft 1983–89; mem. Exec. Council ESF; scientific mem. Max-Planck-Gesellschaft; mem. Göttingen Acad., Acad. Leopoldina, Int. Acad. of Astronautics, Heidelberg Acad., Acad. of Natural Sciences of Russia, Academia Europaea, American Physical Soc., Royal Soc. of Chem. etc.; Dr. h.c.; Bundesverdienstkreuz; Fritz-Haber Prize, Bernard Lewis Gold Medal, Achema Medal, Numa Manson Medal, Dionizy Smoleński Medal, Walther-Nernst-Denkmünze, Dechema Medal. *Publications:* articles on combustion, reaction kinetics, thermodynamics of liquid mixtures. *Address:* Institut für Physikalische Chemie, Universität Göttingen, Tammannstr. 6, 37077 Göttingen, Germany. *Telephone:* (49-551) 393112. *Fax:* (49-551) 393117.

WAGNER, Robert; American actor; b. 10 Feb. 1930, Detroit; m. 1st Natalie Wood 1957 (divorced 1962, re-married 1972, died 1981); one d.; m. 2nd Marion Marshall Donen; one d. *Films include:* Halls of Montezuma, The Frogmen, Let's Make It Legal, With a Song in My Heart, What Price Glory?, Stars and Stripes Forever, The Silver Whip, Titanic, Star of Tomorrow, Beneath the 12-Mile Reef, Prince Valiant, Broken Lance, White Feather, A Kiss Before Dying, The Mountain, The True Story of Jesse James, Stopover Tokyo, In Love and War, Say One For Me, Between Heaven and Hell, The Hunters, All the Fine Young Cannibals, Sail a Crooked Ship, The Longest Day, The War Lover, The Condemned of Altona, Harper, Banning, The Biggest Bundle of Them All, The Pink Panther, The Curse of the Pink Panther, Winning, The Affair, The Towering Inferno, Critical List, Pearl, Dragon, Austin Powers, Crazy in Alabama, Wild Things. *Television series include:* Hart to Hart 1979–84, It Takes a Thief 1967–70, Madame Sin (producer and actor); numerous other television appearances. *Address:* c/o William Morris Agency, 151 S. El Camino Drive, Beverly Hills, CA 90212, U.S.A.

WAGNER, Wolfgang; German opera director; b. 30 Aug. 1919, Bayreuth; s. of Siegfried and Winifred (née Williams) Wagner; m. 1st Ellen Drexel 1943; one s. one d.; m. 2nd Gudrun Mack (née Armann) 1976; one d.; mil. service 1938–40; stage man. at Bayreuth Festival 1940; Asst. with Preussische Staatsoper, Berlin 1940–44; returned to Bayreuth after war, worked with brother (the late Wieland Wagner) as dir. annual Wagner operatic festival 1951–66, on his own 1967–; directed more than 400 performances 1953–; numerous guest appearances and int. tours; mem. Bayerische Akademie der Schönen Künste 1986; Dr. h.c. 1994; Bayerischer Maximiliansorden 1984; Ehrensenator Graz 1987, Munich 1988, Tübingen 1988. *Productions include:* Andreasnacht (Berlin 1944), The Rhinegold (Naples 1952), The Valkyrie (Naples 1952, 1953, Barcelona 1955, Venice 1957, Palermo 1962, Osaka 1967), Lohengrin (Bayreuth 1953, 1967, Taormina 1991, Tokyo 1997), Siegfried (Naples 1953, Brussels 1954, Venice 1957, Bologna 1957), The Flying Dutchman (Bayreuth 1955, Dresden 1988), Tristan and Isolde (Barcelona 1955, Bayreuth 1957, Venice 1958, Palermo 1960, Osaka 1967, Milan 1978), Parsifal (Barcelona 1955, Bayreuth 1975, 1989), Don Giovanni (Brunswick 1955), The Mastersingers of Nuremberg (Rome 1956, Bayreuth 1968, 1981, 1996, Dresden 1985), The Nibelung's Ring (Venice 1957, Bayreuth 1960, 1970), Götterdämmerung (Venice 1957), Tannhäuser (Bayreuth 1985). *Publication:* Acts (autobiog.). *Address:* Festspielhügel Nr. 3, 95445 Bayreuth, Germany. *Telephone:* 921-78780.

WAGNER TIZON, Allan; Peruvian politician and diplomatist; b. 7 Feb. 1942, Lima; ed. Universidad Católica and Universidad de San Marcos; joined Ministry of Foreign Affairs 1963; joined Diplomatic Service 1968; Minister of Foreign Affairs 1985–89. *Address:* c/o Ministry of Foreign Affairs, Ucayali 363, Lima, Peru.

WAGONER, Dan; American dancer, choreographer and dance company director; b. 1932, West Va.; studied pharmacy; joined Martha Graham co. 1957; danced with Merce Cunningham's and Paul Taylor's cos.; f. own dance co. 1969; has choreographed about 40 works; Artistic Dir. London Contemporary Dance Theatre (LCDT), London 1989–90. *Address:* c/o Contemporary Dance Theatre, The Place, 17 Duke's Road, London, WC1H 9AB, England.

WAGONER, David Russell, M.A.; American writer and university professor; b. 5 June 1926, Massillon, Ohio; m. 1st Patricia Parrott 1961 (divorced 1982); m. 2nd Robin H. Seyfried 1982; two d.; ed. Pennsylvania State Univ., Indiana Univ.; served U.S.N. 1944–46; Instructor DePauw Univ., Greencastle, Ind. 1949–50, Pennsylvania State Univ. 1950–54; Assoc. Prof. Univ. of Washington, Seattle 1954–66, Prof. of English 1966–; Elliston lecturer Univ. of Cincinnati 1968; Ed. Poetry Northwest, Seattle 1966–, Ed. Princeton Univ. Press Contemporary Poetry Series 1977–81; Poetry Ed. Mo. Press 1983–; Guggenheim Fellowship 1956, Ford Fellowship 1964, American Acad. Grant 1967, Morton Dauwen Zabel Prize (Poetry, Chicago) 1967, Nat. Endowment for the Arts Grant 1969; Ruth Lilly Prize 1991, Levinson Prize (Poetry, Chicago) 1994, Union League Prize (Poetry, Chicago) 1997. *Publications: Novels* The Man in the Middle 1955, Money, Money, Money 1955, Rock 1958, The Escape Artist 1965, Baby, Come On Inside 1968, Where is My Wandering Boy Tonight? 1970, The Road to Many a Wonder 1974, Tracker 1975, Whole Hog 1976, The Hanging Garden 1980; *Short Stories:* Afternoon on the Ground 1978, Wild Goose Chase 1978, Mr. Wallender's Romance 1979, Cornet Solo 1979, The Water Strider 1979, Fly Boy 1980, The Bird Watcher 1980, Snake Hunt 1980; *Play:* An Eye for an Eye for an Eye 1973; *Verse:* Dry Sun, Dry Wind 1953, A Place to Stand 1958, Poems 1959, The Nesting Ground 1963, Five Poets of the Pacific Northwest (with others) 1964, Staying Alive 1966, New and Selected Poems 1969, Working Against Time 1970, Riverbed 1972, Sleeping in the Woods 1974, A Guide to Dungeness Spit 1975, Travelling Light 1976, Who Shall Be the Sun? Poems Based on the Lore, Legends and Myths of Northwest Coast and Plateau Indians 1978, In Broken Country 1979, Landfall 1981, First Light 1983, Through the Forest 1987, Walt Whitman Bathing 1996. *Address:* University of Washington, 4045 Brooklyn Avenue N.E., Seattle, WA 98105; 5416 154th Place, S.W., Edmonds, WA 98026, U.S.A. *Telephone:* (425) 745-6964.

WAHL, Jacques Henri; French administrator; b. 18 Jan. 1932, Lille; s. of Abraham Wahl and Simone Kornbluth; m. Inna Cytrin 1969; two s. one d.; ed. Inst. d'Etudes Politiques, Paris, Univs. of Lille and Paris, Ecole Nat. d'Admin.; Insp. des Finances 1961–; Treasury Dept. 1965–68; Special Asst. to Ministers of Econ. and Finance, François Ortoli 1968–69, Valéry Giscard d'Estaing 1969–71; Asst. Dir. of the Treasury for Int. Affairs 1971–73; Chair. Invisible Transactions Cttee., OECD 1971–73; lecturer, Inst. d'Etudes Politiques and Ecole Nat. d'Admin., Paris 1969–73; Financial Minister, French Embassies, U.S.A. and Canada 1973–78; Exec. Dir. IMF, IBRD 1973–78; Sec.-Gen. to the Presidency of the French Repub. 1978–81; Insp.-Gen. des Finances 1981; Dir.-Gen. Banque Nat. de Paris 1982 (Vice-Chair.

1993–97, Adviser to Chair. 1994); Chair. Banque Nat. de Paris Intercontinentale 1993–97; Officier, Légion d'honneur, Officier Ordre Nat. du Mérite, Commdr. Ordre Nat. de Côte d'Ivoire, Officier Ordre du Mérite de la République Centrafricaine, Chevalier Ordre du Mérite de Haute Volta. *Address:* 15 avenue de la Bourdonnais, 75007 Paris, France (Home).

WAHLSTRÖM, Jarl Holger; Finnish Salvation Army officer (retd.); b. 9 July 1918, Helsinki; s. of Rafael Alexander and Aina Maria (née Dahlberg) Wahlström; m. Maire Helfrid Nyberg 1944; two s. one d.; ed. Salvation Army Int. Training Coll., Denmark Hill, London; Salvation Army Field Officer, Finland 1939–45, Youth Officer 1945–52, 1954–60, Pvt. Sec. to Territorial Commdr. 1952–54, Div. Commdr. 1960–63, Training Coll. Prin. 1963–68; Chief Sec., Finland 1968–72, Canada and Bermuda 1972–76; Territorial Commdr., Finland 1976–80, Sweden 1981; Int. Leader of the Salvation Army 1981–86; Hon. D.Hum.Litt. (Western Illinois Univ.); Kt., Order of Lion of Finland, Finnish Liberty Cross (Fourth Class), Order of Civil Merit, Mugunghwa Medal (Repub. of Korea), Commdr., Order of White Rose of Finland 1989. *Publication:* autobiography: Matkalaulu (Finnish), En Vallfartssång (Swedish) 1989. *Leisure interest:* music. *Address:* Borgströminkuja 1A10, 00840 Helsinki 84, Finland. *Telephone:* 698-2413.

WAIGEL, Theodor, DR.JUR.; German politician; b. 22 April 1939, Oberrohr; s. of August Waigel and Genoveva Konrad; m. 1st Karin Hönig 1966 (divorced 1994); m. 2nd Irene Epple 1994; two s. one d.; ed. Univs. of Munich and Würzburg; Bavarian Ministries of Finance and of Econ. and Transport 1969–72; mem. Bundestag 1972–; Chair. CSU Land (Bavarian) Group in Bundestag 1982–89; Chair. of CSU 1988–98; Minister of Finance 1989–98; Bayerischer Verdienstorden. *Leisure interests:* climbing, theatre. *Address:* c/o Ministry of Finance, Graurheindorfer Strasse 108, 53117 Bonn, Germany.

WAIHEE, John David, III, B.A., J.D.; American state governor; b. 19 May 1946, Honokaa, Hawaii; m. Lynne Kobashigawa; one s. one d.; ed. Andrews Univ., Central Mich. Univ. and Univ. of Hawaii; admitted to Hawaii Bar 1976; Community Educ. Co-ordinator, Benton Harbor (Mich.) area schools 1968–70; Asst. Dir. Community Educ. 1970–71; Program Evaluator, Admin. Asst. to Dirs., Planner, Honolulu Model Cities Program 1971–73; Sr. Planner, Office of Human Resources, City and Co. of Honolulu 1973–74, Program Man. 1974–75; Assoc. Shim, Sigal, Tam & Naito, Honolulu 1975–79; partner, Waihee, Manuia, Yap, Pablo & Hoe, Honolulu 1979–82; mem. Hawaiian House of Reps. 1980–82; Lieut. Gov. of Hawaii 1982–86, Gov. 1986–95; Democrat. *Address:* 745 Fort Street Mall, # 600, Honolulu, HI 96813, U.S.A.

WAINWRIGHT, Rev. Geoffrey, M.A., D.D., DR. THÉOL.; British ecclesiastic and university professor; b. 16 July 1939, Yorkshire; s. of Willie Wainwright and Martha Burgess; m. Margaret H. Wiles 1965; one s. two d.; ed. Gonville & Caius Coll. Cambridge and Univ. of Geneva; Prof. of Dogmatics, Protestant Faculty of Theology, Yaoundé, Cameroon 1967–73; lecturer in Bible and Systematic Theology, Queen's Coll. Birmingham 1973–79; Roosevelt Prof. of Systematic Theology, Union Theological Seminary, New York 1979–83; Cushman Prof. of Christian Theology, Duke Univ. 1983–; mem. Faith and Order Comm. WCC 1977–91; Co-Chair. Jt. Comm. between World Methodist Council and Roman Catholic Church 1986–; Sec. American Theological Soc. 1988–95, Pres. 1996–97; Leverhulme European Fellow 1966–67; Pew Evangelical Fellow 1996–97; Berakah Award, N. American Acad. of Liturgy 1999. *Publications include:* Christian Initiation 1969, Eucharist and Eschatology 1971, Doxology 1980, The Ecumenical Moment 1983, On Wesley and Calvin 1987, Methodists in Dialogue 1995, Worship With One Accord 1997, For Our Salvation: Two Approaches to the Work of Christ 1997. *Leisure interests:* music, art, cricket, tennis. *Address:* The Divinity School, Duke University, Durham, NC 27708 (Office); 4011 W. Cornwallis Road, Durham, NC 27705, U.S.A. (Home). *Telephone:* (919) 660-3460 (Office); (919) 489-2795 (Home). *Fax:* (919) 660-3473 (Office).

WAITE, Terence Hardy, C.B.E.; British religious adviser; b. 31 May 1939, Bollington; s. of Thomas William Waite and Lena (née Hardy) Waite; m. Helen Frances Watters 1964; one s. three d.; ed. Wilmslow School, Stockton Heath, Cheshire, Church Army Coll., London; Lay Training Adviser to Bishop and Diocese of Bristol 1964–68; Adviser to Archbishop of Uganda, Rwanda and Burundi 1968–71; int. consultant working with Roman Catholic Church 1972–79; Adviser to Archbishop of Canterbury on Anglican Communion Affairs 1980–92, Iranian hostages mission 1981, Libyan hostages mission 1985; kidnapped in Beirut Jan. 1987; released Nov. 1991; mem. Church of England Nat. Ass. 1966–68; Co-ordinator Southern Sudan Relief Project 1969–71; mem. Royal Inst. of Int. Affairs 1980–, Butler Trust (Prison Officers Award Programme); Pres. Y-Care Int. (YMCA Int. Devt. Cttee.) 1998, Emmaus U.K. 1998; Founder Chair. Friends of Victim Support 1992–; Patron Strode Park Foundation for the Disabled, Hearne, Kent, Rainbow Trust, Warrington Male Voice Choir; Consultant Freeplay Co.; Fellow Commoner Trinity Hall, Cambridge 1992–; Hon. Chancellor Florida Southern Univ. 1992; Trustee Freeplay Foundation; Hon. D.C.L. (Kent) 1986, (City of London), (Durham) 1992; Hon. D.LL. (Liverpool); Hon. LL.D. (Sussex) 1992; Hon. L.H.D. (Wittenberg Univ.) 1992; Hon. Dr. Int. Law (Florida Southern Univ.) 1992; Dr. h.c. (Yale Univ. Divinity School) 1992; Roosevelt Freedom Medal 1992; U.K. 'Man of the Year' 1985 (Radar Award), Freeman City of Canterbury 1992, Borough of Lewisham 1992. *Publications:* Taken on Trust 1993, Footfalls in Memory 1995. *Leisure interests:* music, walking, travel, Jungian studies, international affairs and politics. *Address:* Trinity Hall, Cambridge, England. *Telephone:* (01284) 830005.

WAITT, Theodore (Ted) W.; American computer executive; f. Gateway (with Mike Hammond) 1985, C.E.O. Gateway 2000, Inc. 1992–, also Chair., Pres.; Hon. D.Sc. (Univ. of S. Dakota); U.S. Small Business Asscn. Young Entrepreneur of the Year, U.S. Jr. Chamber of Commerce Ten Outstanding Young Americans award, Nat. Alliance of Business Henry Ford II Award. *Address:* Gateway 2000, Inc., 610 Gateway Drive, North Sioux City, SD 57049, U.S.A.

WAJDA, Andrzej; Polish film and theatrical director; b. 6 March 1926, Suwałki; s. of Jakub Wajda and Aniela Wajda; m. 1st Beata Tyszkiewicz 1967 (divorced); one d.; m. 2nd Krystyna Zachwatowicz 1975; ed. Acad. of Fine Arts, Cracow and Higher Film School, Łódź; Film Dir. 1954–; Theatre Dir. Teatr Stary, Cracow 1962–98; Man. Dir. Teatr Powszechny, Warsaw 1989–90; Senator of Repub. of Poland 1989–91; Pres. Polish Film Asscn. 1978–83, 'Solidarity' Lech Wałęsa Council 1981–89, Presidential Council for Culture 1992–94; mem. Inst. de France 1997–, Acad. des Beaux Arts, France 1997–; Hon. mem. Union of Polish Artists and Designers (ZPAP) 1977; Dr. h.c. (American Univ. Washington) 1981, (Bologna) 1988, (Jagiellonian Univ., Cracow) 1989, (Lyon Univ.) 1995, (Univ. Libre, Brussels) 1995; numerous prizes including State First Class Prize 1974, Konrad Swinarski Prize 1976, Premio David di Donatello 'Luchino Visconti' 1978, Prize of Cttee. for Polish Radio and TV 1980, Onassis Prize, Greece 1982, Kyoto Prize, Japan 1987, Praemium Imperiale, Japan 1997; BAFTA Fellowship 1982, César Award, France 1983, Pirandello Artistic Award, Italy 1986, 'Felix' European Film Awards—Lifetime Achievement Award 1990, Golden Lion, Venice 1998; Order of the Banner of Labour (Second Class) 1975, Officer's Cross of Order of Polonia Restituta, Order of Kirill and Methodius (First Class), Bulgaria 1978, Officier, Légion d'honneur 1982, Order of Rising Sun, Japan 1995. *Films:* Pokolenie (A Generation) 1954 (Polish State Prize), Idę do słońca (I'm Going to the Sun) 1955, Kanal 1957 (Jury Special Silver Palm Award, Cannes 1957), Popiół i diament (Ashes and Diamonds) 1957 (Fipresci Prize, Venice 1959, David O'Selznick's 'Silver Laurel' Award 1962), Lotna 1959, Niewinni czarodzieje (Innocent Sorcerers) 1960, Samson 1961, Sibirska Ledi Makbet (Serbian Lady Macbeth) 1962, L'Amour à Vingt Ans (Love at Twenty) 1962, Popioły (Ashes) 1965, Gates to Paradise 1968, Wszystko na sprzedaż (Everything for Sale) 1969, Polowanie na muchy (Hunting Flies) 1969, Krajobraz po bitwie (Landscape After Battle) 1970 (Golden Globe, Milan 1971), Brzezina (The Birch Wood) 1970 (Fipresci Prize, Milan 1970, Golden Medal, Moscow 1971), Wesele (The Wedding) 1973 (Silver Shell, San Sebastián 1973), Ziemia obiecana (The Promised Land) 1975 (Gdańsk Golden Lions 1975, Golden Medal, Moscow 1975), Człowiek z marmuru (Man of Marble) 1977 (Fipresci Prize, Cannes 1978, Jury Special Prize, Cartagena 1980), Bez znieczulenia (Without Anaesthetic) 1978 (OCIC Prize, Cannes 1979), Panny z Wilka (The Maids of Wilko) 1979 Dyrygent (The Orchestral Conductor) 1980, Czlowiek z żelaza (Man of Iron) 1981 (Palme d'Or, Cannes 1981), Danton 1982 (Prix Luis Delluc 1982), Eine Liebe in Deutschland (A Love in Germany) 1983, Kronika wypadków miłosnych (Chronicle of Love Affairs) 1986, Les Possédés (The Possessed) 1987, Korczak 1990, Pierścionek z orłem w koronie (The Crowned-Eagle Ring) 1992, Nastasya 1994, Wielki Tydzień (The Holy Week) 1995 (Silver Bear, Berlin 1996), Panna Nikt (Miss Nobody) 1996. *TV:* Przekładaniec (Roly-Poly) 1968, Macbeth 1969, Pilatus und Andere (for German TV ZDF) 1971 (Bambi Award 1972), Noc listopadowa (November Night) 1975, The Shadow Line (for Thames TV, London) 1976, Z biegiem lat z beiegiem dui (Gone with the Years, Gone with the Days) 1978–79, Zbroduia i kara (Schuld und Suhne) 1985, Wieczernik (The Last Supper) 1985, Hamlet IV 1989, Silniejsza (The Stronger One) 1990, Mishima 1995. *Plays:* Kapelusz pełen deszczu (Hatful of Rain) 1959, Hamlet 1960, 1980, 1989, Dwoje na huśtawce (Two on the Seesaw) 1960, 1990, Demons 1963, Wesele (The Wedding) 1962, 1991, Play Strindberg 1970, Sticks and Bones (Moscow) 1972, Noc listopadowa (November Night) 1974, Sprawa Dantona (The Danton Case) 1975, 1980, Kiedy rozum śpi (When Reason is Asleep) 1976, Emigranci (Emigrés) 1976, Nastasya Filipowna (improvisation based on Dostoyevsky's The Idiot) 1977, Rozmowy z Katem (Conversation with the Executioner) 1977, White Marriage (Yale Repertory) 1977, Z biegiem lat z biegiem dui (Gone with the Years, Gone with the Days) 1978, Antygone 1984, Zbrodnia i kara (Crime and Punishment) 1984, Wieczernik (The Last Supper) 1985, Zemsta (Revenge) 1986, Panna Julia (Miss Julia) 1988, Dybuk 1988, Lekcja polskiego (Lesson of Polish Language) 1988, Romeo and Juliet 1990, The Ghost Sonata (Stockholm) 1994, Mishima 1994, Klątwa (The Curse) 1997, Słomkowy Kapelusz (The Straw Hat) 1998. *Publication:* My Life in Film 1989. *Address:* Centre for Japanese and Technology, ul. Konopnickiej 26, 30-302 Cracow, Poland.

WAKEFIELD, Sir Peter George Arthur, K.B.E., C.M.G.; British diplomatist; b. 13 May 1922; s. of John Bunting and Dorothy Ina (née Stace) Wakefield; m. Felicity Maurice-Jones 1951; four s. one d.; ed. Cranleigh School and Corpus Christi Coll., Oxford; served in Army 1942–47; Mil. Govt., Eritrea 1946–47; Hulton Press 1947–49; entered Diplomatic Service 1949; Middle East Centre for Arab Studies 1950; Second Sec., British Embassy, Jordan 1950–52; Foreign Office 1953–55, 1964–66; First Sec., British Middle East Office, Nicosia 1955–56; First Sec. (Commercial), Egypt 1956, Austria 1957–60, Japan 1960–63; Admin. Staff Coll., Henley 1957; Consul-Gen. and Counsellor, Benghazi 1966–69; Econ. and Commercial Counsellor, Tokyo 1970–72, Econ. and Commercial Minister 1973; seconded as Special Adviser on the Japanese Market, British Overseas Trade Bd. 1973–75; Amb. to Lebanon 1975–78, to Belgium 1979–81; Dir. Nat. Art Collections Fund London 1982–92; U.K. Dir., Trust for Museum Exhbns.; Gov. European

Cultural Foundation 1988–92; Chair. Heritage Co-ordination Group 1993–97, Asia House, London, Richmond Theatre; Chair. of Judges, Jerwood Painting Prize 1994/95; Hon. LL.D. (St. Andrews) 1991. *Leisure interests:* modern British painting, ceramics, restoring ruins. *Address:* Lincoln House, Montpelier Row, Twickenham, Middx., England; La Molineta, Frigiliana, nr. Málaga, Spain. *Telephone:* 0181-892 6390 (England). *Fax:* 0181-744 0961.

WAKEHAM, Baron (Life Peer), cr. 1992, of Maldon in the County of Essex, **John Wakeham,** J.P., F.C.A.; British politician; b. 22 June 1932, Godalming, Surrey; s. of late Major W. J. Wakeham and Mrs. E. R. Wakeham; m. 1st Anne Roberta Bailey 1965 (died 1984); two s.; m. 2nd Alison Bridget Ward 1985; one s.; ed. Charterhouse; J.P. Inner London 1972–; M.P. for Maldon 1974–83, for Colchester S. and Maldon 1983–92; Asst. Govt. Whip 1979–81, Govt. Whip 1981, Govt. Chief Whip 1983–87; Lord Commr. of H.M. Treasury 1981, Minister of State 1982–83, Parl. Sec. 1983–87; Parl. Under-Sec. of State, Dept. of Industry 1981–82; Lord Privy Seal 1987–88; Leader of House of Commons 1987–89, Sec. of State for Energy 1989–92; Lord Privy Seal and Leader of the House of Lords 1992–94; Lord Pres. of Council 1988–89; Chair. Carlton Club 1992–, Press Complaints Comm. 1995–, British Horse-racing Bd. 1996–98 (mem. 1995–98); Chair. Michael Page Group PLC 1995–97 (Pres. 1997–), Vosper Thorneycroft PLC 1995–, Kalon Group PLC 1995–, Genner Holdings Ltd. 1994–, Alexander Rose Day 1998–; Chair. Royal Comm. on Lords Reform 1999–; Dir. (non-exec.) Bristol & West Bldg. Soc. 1995–, N.M. Rothschild & Sons Ltd. 1995–, Ehron Corpn. 1994–; Chancellor Brunel Univ. 1998–; Trustee, mem. Cttee. of Man. Royal Nat. Lifeboat Inst. 1995–; Trustee H.M.S. Warrior 1860 1997–. *Leisure interests:* farming, sailing, racing and reading. *Address:* House of Lords, London, SW1A 0PW, England.

WAKELEY, Amanda; British fashion designer; b. 15 Sept. 1962; d. of Sir John Wakeley; m. Neil David Gillon 1992; ed. Cheltenham Ladies' Coll.; worked in fashion industry, N.Y. 1983–85; began designing for pvt. clients in U.K. 1986; launched own label 1990; operation includes retail, wholesale worldwide, bridal, high street brand Amanda Wakeley for Principles and corporatewear consultancy; Glamour Award, British Fashion Awards 1992, 1993, 1996. *Address:* First Floor, 79-91 New Kings Road, London, SW6 4SQ, England. *Telephone:* 0171-471 8807. *Fax:* 0171-471 8833.

WAKIL, Abdul; Afghanistan politician; b. 1945, Kabul province; ed. Kabul Univ.; fmr. Sec. Gen. of Afghan Foreign Ministry, Minister of Finance, Amb. to U.K. and to Viet Nam; mem. People's Democratic Party of Afghanistan (PDPA) 1964, mem. Cen. Cttee. 1977; mem. of Revolutionary Council of Afghanistan; Minister of Foreign Affairs 1986–89. *Address:* c/o Ministry of Foreign Affairs, Kabul, Afghanistan.

WAKOSKI, Diane, B.A.; American poet; b. 3 Aug. 1937, Whittier, Calif; ed. Univ. of Calif. at Berkeley; began writing poetry, New York 1960–73; worked as a book shop clerk, a junior high school teacher and by giving poetry readings on coll. campuses; Poet-in-Residence Michigan State Univ. 1975–; Prof. of English, Michigan State Univ. 1975–. *Publications:* Coins and Coffins 1962, Discrepancies and Apparitions 1966, The George Washington Poems 1967, Inside the Blood Factory 1968, The Magellanic Clouds 1970, The Motorcycle Betrayal Poems 1971, Smudging 1972, Dancing on the Grave of a Son of a Bitch 1973, Trilogy (reprint of first three collections) 1974, Virtuoso Literature for Two and Four Hands 1975, Waiting for the King of Spain 1976, The Man Who Shook Hands 1978, Cap of Darkness 1980, The Magician's Feastletters 1982, Norii Magellanici (collection of poems from various vols. trans. into Romanian) 1982, The Collected Greed 1984, The Rings of Saturn 1986, Emerald Ice (selected poems 1962–87) 1988 (William Carlos Williams Prize 1989), The Archaeology of Movies and Books: Vol. I Medea The Sorceress 1991, Vol. II Jason The Sailor 1993, Vol. III The Emerald City of Las Vegas 1995, Vol. IV Argonaut Rose 1998; (criticism) Towards A New Poetry 1980. *Address:* 607 Division Street, East Lansing, MI 48823, U.S.A. (Home). *Telephone:* 517 355 0308 (University); 517 332 3385 (Home).

WALCOTT, Derek; Saint Lucia poet and playwright; b. 23 Jan. 1930, Castries; s. of Warwick Walcott and Alix Walcott; m. 1st Fay Moston 1954 (divorced 1959); one s.; m. 2nd Margaret R. Maillard 1962 (divorced); two d.; m. 3rd Norline Metivier (divorced); ed. Univ. of Wisconsin; Prof. of English, Univ. of Boston, U.S.A.; fmr. Visiting Prof. Harvard Univ.; Queen's Gold Medal for Poetry 1988, W. H. Smith Literary Award 1991 for epic poem Omeros; awarded Nobel Prize for Literature 1992. *Publications:* numerous vols. of poetry, Collected Poems 1948–1984; plays include Odyssey, The Last Carnival, Dream on Monkey Mountain, The Joker of Seville, O Babylon!, Steel, The Bounty 1997, The Capeman 1997 (musical, jtly.), What the Twilight Says 1998, Homage to Robert Frost (jtly.) 1998. *Address:* c/o Faber & Faber, 3 Queen Square, London, WC1N 3AU; 71 St. Mary's Street, Brookline, MA 02215, U.S.A.

WALD, Patricia McGowan, LL.B.; American judge; b. 16 Sept. 1928, Torrington, Conn.; d. of Joseph and Margaret (née O'Keefe) McGowan; m. Robert L. Wald 1952; two s. three d.; ed. Connecticut Coll. for Women, Yale Law School; Law Clerk, U.S. Court of Appeals for the Second Circuit 1951–52; Assoc. Arnold, Fortas and Porter, Washington, D.C. 1952–53; mem. Nat. Conf. on Bail and Criminal Justice 1963–64; Consultant, Nat. Conf. on Law and Poverty 1965; mem. President's Comm. on Crime in the Dist. of Columbia 1965–66, on Law Enforcement and Admin. of Criminal Justice 1966–67; Attorney, Office of Criminal Justice, Dept. of Justice 1967–68, Neighborhood Legal Services Program 1968–70; Co-Dir., Ford Foundation Drug Abuse Research Project 1970; Attorney, Center for Law and Social Policy 1971–72, Mental Health Law Project 1972–77; Asst. Attorney for Legis. Affairs, Dept. of Justice 1977–79; Circuit Judge, U.S. Court of Appeals for the Dist. of Columbia Circuit 1979–, Chief Judge 1986–91; First Vice-Pres. American Law Inst.; mem. Exec. Bd. CEELI (ABA) 1994–97; 16 hon. degrees; August Voelmer Award, American Soc. of Criminology 1976, Woman Lawyer of the Year, Women's Bar Assen. 1984; Sandra Day O'Connor Medal of Honor (Seton Hall Law School) 1993; Margaret Brent Award for Distinguished Women in the Legal Profession 1994; numerous hon. degrees. *Publications:* Bail in the United States (with Daniel J. Freed) 1964, Bail Reform: A Decade of Promise Without Fulfillment, Vol. 1 1972, Juvenile Detention in 'Pursuing Justice for the Child' 1977, The Rights of Children and the Rites of Passage in 'Child Psychiatry and the Law' 1980, Dealing with Drug Abuse: A Report to the Ford Foundation (with Peter Barton Hutt) 1972, Law and Poverty: Report to the Nat. Conf. on Law and Poverty 1965, and numerous learned articles. *Address:* US Courthouse, 3rd & Constitution Avenues N.W., Washington, DC 20001 (Office); 2101 Connecticut Avenue, N.W., Apartment 38, Washington, DC 20008, U.S.A. (Home). *Telephone:* (202) 232 1158 (Home).

WALD, Richard C., M.A.; American journalist; b. New York; s. of Joseph S. Wald and Lily (Forstate) Wald; m. Edith May Leslie; two s. one d.; ed. Columbia Univ. and Clare Coll., Cambridge; reporter, later Man. Ed. Herald Tribune 1955–66; Asst. Man. Ed. Washington Post 1967; Exec. Vice-Pres. Whitney Communications Corpn. New York 1968; Vice-Pres. NBC News, Pres. 1968–77; Sr. Vice-Pres. ABC News 1978–; Chair. of Bd. Columbia Spectator; Chair. Worldwide TV News. *Address:* ABC News, 47 West 66th Street, New York, NY 10023, U.S.A. (Office).

WÄLDE, Thomas, DR.IUR., LL.M.; German lawyer; b. 9 Jan. 1949, Pluderhausen; s. of Dr Ernst Wälde; m. Gabriele Wälde-Sinigoj 1981; one s.; ed. Univs. of Heidelberg, Lausanne, Berlin and Frankfurt and Harvard Law School; Research Fellow, Inst. for Foreign and Int. Econ. Law, Frankfurt 1973–77; Legal Officer, UN Centre on Transnational Corpns. New York 1976–77; Resident Investment Adviser, UNIDO, Vienna 1978–79; Interregional Adviser on Mineral Devt. Legislation, Dept. of Tech. Co-operation for Devt., UN, New York 1980–85, Interregional Adviser on Petroleum and Mineral Legislation 1986–; Maier Leibnitz Award 1978; American Inst. of Mining Engineers Award 1985. *Publications:* Decision Analysis and Economic Legislation 1976, Transnational Investment Agreements 1978, Renegotiation of Transnational Agreements 1978, Methods and Mechanisms of International Industrial Enterprise Cooperation 1979, International Economic Development Law 1982, Permanent Sovereignty over Natural Resources 1985, Petroleum Investment in Developing Countries 1988. *Leisure interests:* history, anthropology. *Address:* DC1-846, NRED/DTCD, United Nations, One UN Plaza, New York, NY 10017, U.S.A. *Telephone:* (212) 963-8783.

WALDEGRAVE, Rt. Hon. William, P.C., J.P.; British politician; b. 15 Aug. 1946; m. Caroline Burrows 1977; one s. three d.; ed. Eton Coll., Corpus Christi Coll. Oxford, Harvard Univ., U.S.A.; fmr. Pres. Oxford Union; Fellow All Souls Coll. Oxford 1971–86; attached to Cabinet Office as mem. Cen. Policy Review Staff 1971–73; mem. staff political office of Rt. Hon. Edward Heath (q.v.) 1973–76; M.P. for Bristol W. 1979–97; Parl. Under-Sec. of State, Dept. of Educ. and Science 1981–83, Dept. of Environment and Spokesman for the Arts 1983–85; Minister of State, Dept. of the Environment (Minister for the Environment, Countryside and Local Govt., subsequently Minister for Housing and Planning) 1985–88; Minister of State, FCO 1988–90; Sec. of State for Health 1990–92, Chancellor of the Duchy of Lancaster 1992–94; Sec. of State for Agric., Fisheries and Food 1994–95; Chief Sec. to Treasury 1995–97; Dir. Bristol and West Bldg. Soc. 1997–, Corp. Finance, Dresdner Kleinwort Benson 1998–, several other directorships; worked for GEC PLC 1975–85. *Publication:* The Binding of Leviathan—Conservatism and the Future 1977. *Address:* 66 Palace Gardens Terrace, London, W8 4RR, England.

WALDEN, (Alastair) Brian; British broadcaster and journalist; b. 8 July 1932; s. of W. F. Walden; m. Hazel Downes; one s., and three s. from fmr. marriages; ed. West Bromwich Grammar School, Queen's Coll. and Nuffield Coll., Oxford; univ. lecturer; M.P. for Birmingham All Saints 1964–74, Birmingham Ladywood 1974–77, Labour; TV presenter, Weekend World (London Weekend TV) 1977–86; mem. W. Midland Bd., Cen. Ind. TV 1982–84; Columnist London Standard 1983–86, Thomson Regional Newspapers 1983–86; columnist, The Sunday Times; presenter, The Walden Interview (L.W.T. for ITV network) 1988, 1989, 1990–94, Walden on Labour Leaders (BBC) 1997, Walden on Heroes (BBC) 1998, Walden on Villains 1999; Shell Int. Award 1982, BAFTA Richard Dimbleby Award 1985; Aims of Industry Special Free Enterprise Award 1990; ITV Personality of the Year 1991. *Publication:* The Walden Interviews 1990. *Leisure interests:* chess, gardening. *Address:* Landfall, Fort Road, St. Peter Port, Guernsey.

WALDENSTRÖM, Jan Gosta, M.D.; Swedish professor of medicine; b. 17 April 1906, Stockholm; s. of Prof. Henning Waldenström and Elsa Laurin; m. 1st Elisabet Waldenström 1932; m. 2nd Karin Nordsjö 1957; five s. two d.; ed. Univs. of Uppsala and Cambridge, Tech. Hochschule, Munich; various positions at Academic Hosp., Uppsala; Prof. of Theoretical Medicine, Uppsala 1947; Prof. of Practical Medicine, Univ. of Lund 1950–72; Physician-in-Chief, Dept. of Gen. Medicine, Gen. Hospital, Malmö 1950–72; foreign mem.

N.A.S., U.S.A., French Acad. of Sciences; Hon. mem. Royal Soc. of Medicine, London and other foreign acads.; mem. Academia Europaea; Jahre Scandinavian Prize in Medicine 1962, Gairdner Award 1966, Paul Ehrlich Prize 1972; hon. degrees from Univs. of Oslo, Dublin, Mainz, Oxford, Paris, London, Innsbruck and Poitiers, Freiburg im Breisgau. *Publications:* Studien über Porphyrie, 1937, Monoclonal and polyclonal hypergammaglobulinemia 1968, Diagnosis and Treatment of Multiple Myeloma 1970, Paraneoplasia 1978, Reflections and Recollections from a Long Life with Medicine 1994; numerous publs. on metabolic, hematologic and other subjects of internal medicine; chapters in many textbooks. *Leisure interests:* history, botany, travelling, art. *Address:* Roskildevägen 11A, 217 46 Malmö, Sweden *Telephone:* 46-40-91-62-02.

WALDHEIM, Kurt, LL.D.; Austrian fmr. Head of State, fmr. United Nations official and diplomatist; b. 21 Dec. 1918; m. Elisabeth Ritschel Waldheim 1944; one s. two d.; ed. Consular Acad. of Vienna, Univ. of Vienna; entered foreign service 1945; served Ministry of Foreign Affairs; mem. Austrian Del. to Paris, London and Moscow for negotiation on Austrian State Treaty; First Sec. 1945–47; served Paris 1948–51; Counsellor and Head of Personnel Div., Ministry of Foreign Affairs 1951–55; Perm. Austrian Observer to UN 1955–56; Minister to Canada 1956–58, Amb. to Canada 1958–60; Dir.-Gen. for Political Affairs, Ministry for Foreign Affairs 1960–64; Perm. Rep. to UN 1964–68; Chair. Outer Space Cttee. of UN 1965–68, 1970–71; Fed. Minister for Foreign Affairs 1968–70; Perm. Rep. to UN 1970–71; Cand. for Pres. of Austria 1971, Pres. of Austria 1986–92; Sec.-Gen. of UN 1972–82; Guest Prof. of Diplomacy, Georgetown Univ., Washington, D.C. 1982–84; Chair. InterAction Council of Fmr. Heads of State and Govt. 1982–85; numerous hon. degrees; several decorations include Order of Pius IX (Vatican) 1994. *Publications:* Der österreichische Weg (The Austrian Example), Un métier unique au monde, Der schwierigste Job der Welt, The Challenge of Peace 1980, Building The Future Order 1980, In the Eye of the Storm 1985. *Address:* 1 Lobkowitz platz, 1010 Vienna, Austria.

WALES, H.R.H. The Prince of, and Earl of Chester (cr. 1958); **Prince Charles Philip Arthur George,** K.G., K.T., G.C.B., P.C., M.A., Duke of Cornwall and Rothesay, Earl of Carrick, Baron of Renfrew, Lord of the Isles and Great Steward of Scotland (cr. 1952); b. 14 Nov. 1948, London; eldest son of Princess Elizabeth (now H.M. Queen Elizabeth II, q.v.) and Prince Philip, Duke of Edinburgh (q.v.); m. Lady Diana Spencer (subsequently Diana, Princess of Wales) 29 July 1981 (divorced 28 Aug. 1996, died 31 Aug. 1997); two s., H.R.H. Prince William Arthur Philip Louis, b. 21 June 1982, H.R.H. Prince Henry Charles Albert David, b. 15 Sept. 1984; ed. Cheam School, Gordonstoun School, Geelong Grammar School, Trinity Coll., Cambridge, and Univ. Coll. of Wales, Aberystwyth; mem. Gray's Inn 1974, Hon. Bencher 1975; Personal A.D.C. to H.M. the Queen 1973–; Capt. R.N. 1988–; Group Capt. R.A.F. 1988–; Col.-in-Chief The Royal Regt. of Wales (24th/41st Foot) 1969–; Col. Welsh Guards 1974–; Col.-in-Chief The Cheshire Regt. 1977–, Lord Strathcona's Horse (Royal Canadian) Regt. 1977–, The Parachute Regt. 1977–, The Royal Australian Armoured Corps 1977–, The Royal Regt. of Canada 1977–, The Royal Winnipeg Rifles 1977–, Royal Pacific Islands Regt., Papua New Guinea 1984–, Royal Canadian Dragoons 1985–, Army Air Corps 1992–, Royal Dragoon Guards 1992–, Royal Gurkha Rifles 1994–; Deputy Col.-in-Chief The Highlanders (Seaforth, Gordons, Camerons) 1994–; Group Capt. 1988–; Hon. Air Cdre. R.A.F. Valley 1994–; Air Cdre.-in-Chief R.N.Z.A.F. 1977–; Col.-in-Chief Air Reserves Group of Air Command in Canada 1977–; Pres. Soc. of St. George's and Descendants of Knights of the Garter 1975–; Dr. h.c. (Royal Coll. of Music) 1981; Adm. Royal Thames Yacht Club 1974–; High Steward, Royal Borough of Windsor and Maidenhead 1974–; Chair. The Mountbatten Memorial Trust 1979–; King Edward VII Fund for London Hosps. 1987; Chair. The Prince of Wales's Cttee. 1971–; Pres. The Prince's Trusts 1977–, Royal Forestry Soc. 1982–, Royal Acad. of Music 1985–, Prince's Youth Business Trust 1986–, The Prince's Scottish Youth Business Trust, Business in the Community 1985, Prince of Wales's Inst. of Architecture 1992–, Prince of Wales's Business Leaders Forum 1990–; Hon. Pres. Royal Acad. Trust 1993–; Chancellor, Univ. of Wales 1976–; mem. Bd. Commonwealth Devt. Corpn. 1979–89; Trustee, Royal Opera House, Gurkha Welfare Fund 1989; Patron Oxford Centre for Islamic Studies 1993–, British Orthopaedic Asscn. 1993–, Royal Coll. of Music 1993–, Prague Heritage Fund 1993–, Nat. Gallery 1993–, Nat. Trust Centenary Appeal 1994–, ActionAid 1995–, Help the Aged 1997–, Welsh Nat. Opera 1997–, Guinness Trust 1997–; represented H.M. the Queen at Independence Celebrations in Fiji 1970, at Requiem Mass for Gen. Charles de Gaulle 1970, at Bahamas Independence Celebrations 1973, at Papua New Guinea Independence Celebrations 1975, at Coronation of King of Nepal 1975, at funeral of Sir Robert Menzies 1978, at funeral of Jomo Kenyatta 1978, at funeral of Rajiv Gandhi 1990, at funeral of King Olav of Norway 1991; Spoleto Prize 1989; Author of the Year 1989; Premio Fregene 1990; Coronation Medal 1953, The Queen's Silver Jubilee Medal 1977, Grand Cross of The Southern Cross of Brazil 1978, Grand Cross of The White Rose of Finland 1969, Grand Cordon of the Supreme of the Chrysanthemum of Japan 1971, Grand Cross of The House of Orange of the Netherlands 1972, Grand Cross Order of Oak Crown of Luxembourg 1972, Kt. of The Order of Elephant of Denmark 1974, Grand Cross of The Order of Ojasvi Rajanya of Nepal 1975, Order of the Repub. of Egypt (First Class) 1981; Grand Croix, Légion d'honneur 1984; Order of Mubarak the Great of Kuwait 1993; cr. Prince of Wales and Earl of Chester (invested July 1969); K.G. 1958 (invested and installed 1968), K.T. 1977, P.C. 1977, G.C.B. and Great Master of Order of the Bath 1975; Royal Fellowship of the Australian Acad. of Science 1979; Hon. Fellowship of Royal Coll. of Surgeons 1978, Royal Aeronautical Soc. 1978, Inst. of Mechanical Engineers 1979, Inst. of Architecture 1992; received Freedom of City of Cardiff 1969, of Royal Borough of New Windsor 1970, of City of London 1971, of Chester 1973, of City of Canterbury 1978, City of Portsmouth 1979, City of Lancaster 1993, City of Swansea 1994; Hon. Fellow, Trinity Coll., Cambridge 1988; Liveryman of Fishmongers' Co. 1971; Freeman of Drapers' Co. 1971; Freeman of Shipwrights' Co. 1978; Hon. Freeman and Liveryman of Goldsmiths Co. 1979, Liveryman of Farmers' Co. 1980, of Pewterers' Co. 1982, of Fruiterers' Co. 1989; Hon. Liveryman of Worshipful Co. of Carpenters 1992; Hon. mem. of Hon. Co. of Master Mariners 1977 (Master 1988), of Merchants of City of Edinburgh 1979; Hon. Life mem. Incorporation of Gardeners of Glasgow 1989; Hon. D.C.L. (Durham) 1998. *Publications:* The Old Man of Lochnagar 1980, A Vision of Britain 1989, H.R.H. The Prince of Wales Watercolours 1990, Urban Villages 1992, Highgrove: Portrait of An Estate 1993, Prince's Choice: A Selection from Shakespeare by the Prince of Wales 1995. *Address:* St. James's Palace, London, SW1A 1BS; Highgrove House, Doughton, Nr. Tetbury, Gloucs., GL8 8TN, England.

WALES, H.R.H. Prince William of, William Arthur Philip Louis; elder s. of H.R.H. The Prince of Wales (q.v.) and the late Diana, Princess of Wales; b. 21 June 1982; ed. Mrs. Mynors' Nursery School, Wetherby School, Ludgrove School, Eton Coll. *Address:* St. James's Palace, London, SW1A 1BS, England.

WAŁĘSA, Lech; Polish politician and trade union activist; b. 29 Sept. 1943, Popowo; s. of Bolesław and Feliksa Wałęsa; m. Danuta Wałęsa 1969; four s. four d.; ed. primary and tech. schools; electrician, Lenin Shipyard, Gdańsk 1966–76, 1983–; Chair. Strike Cttee. in Lenin Shipyard 1970; employed Zremb and Elektromontaż 1976–80; Chair. Inter-institutional Strike Cttee., Gdańsk Aug.–Sept. 1980; co-founder and Chair. Solidarity independent trade union 1980–90, Chair. Nat. Exec. Comm. of Solidarity 1987–90; interned 1981–82; founder of Civic Cttee. attached to Chair. of Solidarity 1988–90; participant and co-Chair. Round Table debates 1989; Chair. Country Defence Cttee. 1990–95; Supreme Commdr. of Armed Forces of Polish Republic for Wartime 1990–95; Pres. of Polish Republic 1990–95; founder of Lech Wałęsa Inst. Foundation 1995, Christian Democratic Labour Party (ChDSP) 1997, Pres. 1998–; 60 hon. doctorates; Hon. citizen of Buffalo, N.Y. 1981, Osaka 1981; Man of the Year, Financial Times 1980, The Observer 1980, Die Welt 1980, Die Zeit 1981, L'Express 1981, Le Soir 1981, Time 1981, Le Point 1981; Awarded "Let us Live" peace prize of Swedish journal Arbetet 1981, Love International Award (Athens) 1981, Freedom Medal (Philadelphia) 1981, Medal of Merit, (Congress of Polish Community in U.S.A.) 1981, Free World Prize (Norway) 1982, Social Justice Award 1983, Nobel Peace Prize 1983, Human Rights Prize, Council of Europe 1989, White Eagle Order 1989, Meeting-90 Award (Rimini) 1990, and other awards and prizes. *Publications:* autobiographies: Droga nackiei (The Way of Hope) 1987, Droga dowolności (The Way to Freedom) 1991, Wszystko co robię, robię dla Polski (Everything I Do, I Do for Poland) 1995. *Leisure interests:* crossword puzzles, fishing. *Address:* ul. Polanki 54, 80-308 Gdańsk-Oliwa, Poland.

WALIGÓRSKI, Ewaryst, M.SC.MECH.ENG.; Polish government official and union leader; b. 19 Aug. 1937, Pobiedziska; m. 1962; two s. one d.; ed. Szczecin Tech. Univ.; employee of Polish State Railways 1961–, exec. positions in Szczecin; arrested under martial law, acquitted by Dist. Mil. Tribunal, Bydogoszcz, then interned; Under-Sec. of State in Ministry of Transport and Maritime Econ. 1989–90; Minister of Transport and Maritime Econ. 1990–92; mem. Solidarity Trade Union 1980–. *Address:* ul. Boryny 48 m. 7, 70-017 Szczecin, Poland. *Telephone:* (91) 82 29 24.

WALKEN, Christopher; American actor; b. 31 March 1943, Astoria, N.Y.; s. of Paul Walken; ed. Hofstra Univ.; numerous stage appearances including: West Side Story, Macbeth, The Lion in Winter (Clarence Derwent Award 1966), The Night Thoreau Spent in Jail (Joseph Jefferson Award 1970–71), Cinders 1984, A Bill of Divorcement 1985. *Films include:* The Anderson Tapes, Next Stop Greenwich Village, Roseland, Annie Hall, The Deer Hunter (New York Film Critics and Acad. Awards for Best Supporting Actor), Dogs of War, Heaven's Gate, Pennies from Heaven, The Dead Zone 1983, Brainstorm 1983, A View to a Kill 1984, At Close Range 1986, The Milagro Beanfield War 1988, Biloxi Blues 1988, Communion 1989, The Comfort of Strangers 1989, King of New York 1990, True Romance 1993, A Business Affair 1994, Scam 1994, Wayne's World II 1994, Pulp Fiction 1994, Things To Do In Denver When You're Dead, Nick of Time, The Funeral, Last Man Standing, Touch, Excess Baggage, Suicide Kings, Blast from the Past 1999. *Address:* William Morris Agency, 151 South El Camino Drive, Beverly Hills, CA 90212, U.S.A.

WALKER, Rev. Sir Alan, Kt., O.B.E., M.A., D.D.; Australian ecclesiastic; b. 4 June 1911, Sydney; s. of Rev. Alfred E. and Violet L. Walker; m. Winifred G. Channon 1938; three s. one d.; ed. Fort Street Boys' High School, Sydney, Leigh Theological Coll., Enfield, Sydney and Univ. of Sydney; ordained Minister of Methodist Church of Australia 1934; Assoc. Dir. Methodist Young People's Dept., N.S.W. Conf. 1936–38; Minister, Cessnock, N.S.W. 1939–44; Supt. Waverley Methodist Mission, Sydney 1944–54; Dir. Mission to the Nation, Methodist Church of Australia 1953–56; Mission to America, Mission to Canada 1956–57; Visiting Prof. of Evangelism, Boston School of Theology, U.S.A. 1957–58; Supt. Cen. Methodist Mission, Sydney 1958–78; Dir. of

World Evangelism, World Methodist Council 1978–88; Prin. Pacific Coll. for Evangelism 1988–95, Prin. Emer. 1995–; Chair. Australian Nat. Goals and Directions Inc.; has undertaken many lecturing and preaching engagements in U.S.A. and elsewhere; received (jtly. with Lady Walker) World Methodist Peace Award 1986. *Publications:* more than 20 books including: Life Begins at Christ 1980, Standing up to Preach 1983, Life in the Holy Spirit 1986, Try God 1990, Herald of Hope 1994. *Leisure interests:* swimming, gardening, reading. *Address:* 14 Owen Stanley Avenue, Beacon Hill, N.S.W. 2100, Australia. *Telephone:* (02) 4513923.

WALKER, Alice Malsenior; American author; b. 9 Feb. 1944, Eatonton, Ga.; d. of Willie L. Walker and Minnie (Grant) Walker; m. Melvyn R. Leventhal 1967 (divorced 1977); one d.; ed. Sarah Lawrence Coll.; Lillian Smith Award 1974, Rosenthal Award, Nat. Inst. of Arts and Letters 1973, Guggenheim Foundation Award 1979, American Book Award 1983, Pulitzer Prize 1983; Hon. Ph.D. (Russell Sage Univ.) 1972 Hon. D.H.L. (Univ. of Mass.) 1983. *Publications:* Once 1968, The Third Life of George Copeland 1970, In Love and Trouble 1973, Langston Hughes, American Poet 1973, Revolutionary Petunias 1974, Meridian 1976, I Love Myself When I am Laughing 1979, You Can't Keep a Good Woman Down 1981, Good Night Willi Lee, I'll See You in the Morning 1979, The Colour Purple 1982, In Search of Our Mothers' Gardens 1983, Horses Make a Landscape Look More Beautiful 1984, To Hell with Dying 1988, Living By the Word 1988, The Temple of My Familiar 1989, Her Blue Body Everything We Know: Earthling Poems (1965–90) 1991, Possessing the Secret of Joy 1992, Warrior Marks (with Pratibha Parmar) 1993, Double Stitch; Black Women Write About Mothers and Daughters (jtly.) 1993, Everyday Use 1994, Alice Walker Banned 1996, Everything We Love Can Be Saved 1997. *Address:* c/o Random House, 201 E. 50th Street, New York, NY 10022, U.S.A.

WALKER, Catherine, M. ÈS L.; French couturier; b. 27 June 1945, Pas de Calais; d. of Remy Baheux and Agnes Lefebvre; m. John Walker (deceased); two d.; ed. Univs. of Lille and Aix-en-Provence; Dir. Film Dept., French Inst., London 1970, Lecture Dept., French Embassy, London 1971, The Chelsea Design Co. Ltd. 1978–; Founder sponsor Gilda's Club and Hon. mem. of Bd.; Founder sponsor Haven Trust; Designer of the Year for British Couture 1990–91, Designer of the Year for Glamour Award 1991–92. *Publication:* Catherine Walker, an Autobiography by the Private Couturier to Diana, Princess of Wales 1998. *Address:* 65 Sydney Street, Chelsea, London, SW3 6PX, England. *Telephone:* 0171-352 4626.

WALKER, Charls Edward, M.B.A., PH.D.; American economist; b. 24 Dec. 1923, Graham, Tex.; s. of Pinkney Clay Walker and Sammye McCombs Walker; m. Harmolyn Hart 1949; one s. one d.; ed. Univs. of Texas and Philadelphia; Pilot, U.S.A.F. World War II; Instructor in Finance and later Asst. and Assoc. Prof., Univ. of Tex. 1947–54; Instructor in Finance, Wharton School 1948–50; Assoc. Economist, Fed. Reserve Bank of Philadelphia 1953–54; Economist and Special Asst. to Pres. of the Repub. Nat. Bank of Dallas 1955–56; Vice-Pres. and Financial Economist, Fed. Reserve Bank of Dallas 1958–61; Asst. to the Sec. of the Treasury 1959–61; Exec. Vice-Pres., American Bankers' Asscn. 1961–69; Under-Sec. of the Treasury 1969–72; Deputy Sec. of the Treasury 1972–73; Adjunct Prof. for Finance and Public Affairs Univ. of Texas at Austin 1986–; Chair. American Council for Capital Formation; Co-Chair. Presidential Debates 1976; Chair., Pres. Reagan's Task Force on Tax Policy 1980; Co-founder Cttee. on the Present Danger; Founder Chair. Bretton Woods Cttee., Advisory Cttee. on Nat. Issues Convention; Hon. LL.D. (Ashland Coll.) 1970. *Publications:* The Banker's Handbook 1978 (co-Ed.), New Directions in Federal Tax Policy 1983 (co-Ed.), The Consumption Tax: A Better Alternative (co-Ed.) 1987, Intellectual Property Rights and Capital Formation in the Next Decade 1988, Saving: The Challenge for the U.S. Economy 1990; numerous articles in economic and other journals. *Leisure interests:* golf, music. *Address:* 10120 Chapel Road, Potomac, MD 20854, U.S.A. *Telephone:* (301) 299-5414 (Home).

WALKER, David Alan, PH.D., D.SC., F.R.S.; British professor of photosynthesis; b. 18 Aug. 1928, Hull; s. of Cyril and Dorothy Walker; m. Shirley Wynne Mason 1956; one s. one d.; ed. Univ. of Newcastle; Royal Naval Air Service 1946–48; at Univ. of Newcastle 1948–58, Purdue Univ., Indiana 1953–54; Reader in Botany, Queen Mary Coll., Univ. of London 1963; Reader in Enzymology, Imperial Coll., Univ. of London 1964–70; Prof. of Biology, Univ. of Sheffield 1970–84, Dir. Research Inst. for Photosynthesis 1984–88, Prof. of Photosynthesis 1988–93, Emer. Prof. 1993–; Visiting Fellow, Connecticut Agricultural Experimental Station 1965; Corresp. mem. American Soc. of Plant Physiology 1979, Academia Europaea 1994; von Humboldt Prize 1991. *Publications:* Energy, Plants and Man 1979, 1992, C_3C_4 (with Gerry Edwards) 1983, A Leaf in Time 1999; over 200 publications on photosynthetic carbon assimilation. *Leisure interest:* singing the Sheffield carols and changing the Biddlestone landscape. *Address:* 6 Biddlestone Village, Morpeth, Northumberland, NE65 7DT, England. *Telephone:* (0114) 2305904. *Fax:* (0870) 0554915.

WALKER, Sir David Alan, Kt., M.A.; British financial executive; b. 31 Dec. 1939; m. Isobel Cooper 1963; one s. two d.; ed. Chesterfield School and Queens' Coll., Cambridge; joined H.M. Treasury 1961, Pvt. Sec. to Jt. Perm. Sec. 1964–66, Asst. Sec. 1973–77; seconded to staff IMF, Washington, D.C. 1970–73; joined Bank of England as Chief Adviser, then Chief Econ. Intelligence Dept. 1977, Asst. Dir. 1980, Dir. 1982–88 (non-Exec. 1988–93); Chair. Johnson Matthey Bankers Ltd. (later Minories Finance Ltd.) 1985–88, Financial Markets Group, L.S.E. 1987–, Securities and Investments Bd. 1988–92, Agric. Mortgage Corpn. PLC 1993–94, Morgan Stanley (Europe) 1994–, Morgan Stanley Int. 1995–; Deputy Chair. Lloyds Bank Ltd. 1992–94; Dir. (non-exec.), British Invisibles 1993–, Nat. Power 1990–93, Morgan Stanley Inc. 1994–; part-time Bd. mem. Cen. Electricity Generating Bd. 1987–89; mem. Council, Lloyd's of London 1988–92; Gov. Henley Man. Coll. 1993–, L.S.E. 1993–; Chair. Exec. Cttee. of Int. Org. of Securities Comms. 1990–92, Cttee. of Inquiry into Lloyd's Syndicate Participations and the LMX Spiral; mem. Group of Thirty 1993–; Hon. Fellow Queens' Coll., Cambridge 1990. *Leisure interests:* music, architecture, long-distance walking. *Address:* c/o Morgan Stanley, 25 Cabot Square, Canary Wharf, London, E14 4QA, England. *Telephone:* 0171-425 5400. *Fax:* 0171-425 8975.

WALKER, David Maxwell, C.B.E., Q.C., PH.D., LL.D., F.B.A., F.R.S.E., F.S.A.-SCOT., F.R.S.A.; British university professor and barrister; b. 9 April 1920, Glasgow, Scotland; s. of James Mitchell Walker and Mary Paton Colquhoun Irvine; m. Margaret Knox, O.B.E. 1954; ed. High School of Glasgow, Univs. of Glasgow, Edinburgh and London; army service in India, N. Africa and Italy, Capt., Indian Army 1939–46; practised at Scottish Bar 1948–53; Prof. of Jurisprudence, Glasgow Univ. 1954–58, Regius Prof. of Law 1958–90, Dean of Faculty of Law 1956–59, Convener of School of Law 1984–88, Sr. Research Fellow 1990–; Chair. Hamlyn Trust 1988–93; Hon. LL.D. (Edin.) 1974. *Publications:* Law of Damages in Scotland 1955, Law of Civil Remedies in Scotland 1974, The Oxford Companion to Law 1980, Law of Delict in Scotland (2nd edn.) 1981, Stair's Institutions (Ed.; 6th edn.) 1981, The Scottish Jurists 1985, Principles of Scottish Private Law (4th edn.) 1988, Legal History of Scotland, Vol. I 1988, Vol. II 1990, Vol. III 1995, Vol. IV 1996, Vol. V 1997, Law of Contracts in Scotland (3rd edn.) 1994, Law of Prescription in Scotland (5th edn.) 1996, The Scottish Legal System (7th edn.) 1997. *Leisure interest:* book collecting. *Address:* School of Law, University of Glasgow, Glasgow, G12 8QQ (Office); 1 Beaumont Gate, Glasgow, G12 9EE, Scotland (Home). *Telephone:* (0141) 339 8855 (Office); (0141) 339 2802 (Home).

WALKER, Derek, M.ARCH., R.I.B.A., F.R.C.A., F.R.S.A.; British architect, town planner, university professor and designer; b. 15 June 1931, Ribchester, Lancs.; s. of late William Walker and Ann Nicholson; m. 1st Honora Jill Messenger 1957; two s.; m. 2nd Jan Larrance 1983; one d.; f. Derek Walker Assocs., Architects & Urban Planners 1960, Walker, Wright, Schofield, Interior Design/Furniture Design 1966; Chief Architect and Planner, New City of Milton Keynes 1969–76; re-formed practices, Sr. Partner Derek Walker Assocs., Walker Wright 1976–; Prof. of Architecture & Design, R.C.A. 1984–90, Chair. Design Faculty; Prin. projects: New City of Milton Keynes 1969–82, Sculpture Park, Milton Keynes 1972, Master Planning New City of Jubail, Saudi Arabia 1979–82, WonderWorld Themepark 1982–, StarSite Birmingham Urban Plan 1984, Commodores Point, Jacksonville, Fla. Urban Plan, U.S.A. 1985, Ski Resort, Telluride, Colo., U.S.A. 1986–88, Lijnbaan Shopping Centre, Rotterdam 1987–89, Gyosei Japanese School 1985–87, Kowloon Park, Hong Kong 1985–87, Energy World, Corby 1986, Olympic Pool and Sports Hall, Kowloon 1986–88, Happy Valley Racecourse Redevt., Hong Kong 1990–96, Ushiku New Town Plan, Japan 1991–95, Clarence Dock Master Plan, Leeds 1991, Royal Armouries Museum, Leeds 1992–96, Museum of British History, London 1996–, Newmarket Racing Museum and Stables 1996–; Architectural Design Awards, pvt. houses, urban devts., village plans 1965 (two), 1966 (two), 1967, 1968, Civic Trust Awards 1965, 1967, 1968, Financial Times Architectural Awards 1969, first prize numerous nat. and int. competitions for theatres, new towns, shopping bldgs., waterside devts. and parks, R.I.B.A. Awards 1979, 1980. *Publications:* British Architects 1981, Los Angeles 1982, Architecture and Planning of Milton Keynes 1982, Animated Architecture 1995, The Royal Armouries: The Making of a Museum (with Guy Wilson) 1996; numerous articles. *Leisure interests:* fine art, classical music, jazz, literature and most sports. *Address:* 80 Warwick Gardens, London, W14 8PR, England; 12 North Drive, Marion, MA 02738, U.S.A. *Telephone:* 0171-371 1749 (England); (508) 748–0203 (U.S.A.). *Fax:* (508) 748–0203 (U.S.A.)

WALKER, George Alfred; British business executive; b. 14 April 1929, London; s. of William James Walker and Ellen Walker (née Page); m. Jean Maureen Hatton 1957; one s. two d.; ed. Jubilee School, Bedford, Essex; Chief Exec. Walkers Int. 1992; declared bankrupt April 1993; Chair. Premier Telesports Ltd. 1995–; Freeman City of London 1978. *Leisure interests:* skiing, ocean racing, climbing. *Address:* Pell House, High Road, Fobbing, Essex, SS17 9JJ, England. *Telephone:* (01375) 672082. *Fax:* (01375) 643315.

WALKER, George P. L., PH.D., F.R.S.; British geologist and volcanologist; b. 2 March 1926, London; s. of L. R. T. Walker and E. F. Walker (née McConkey); m. Hazel R. Smith 1958; one s. one d.; ed. Wallace High School, Lisburn, Northern Ireland, Queen's Univ. of Belfast and Univ. of Leeds; Asst. Lecturer, Imperial Coll. of Science and Tech., Univ. of London 1951–54, Lecturer 1954–64, Reader in Geology 1964–80; Capt. James Cook Research Fellow of Royal Soc. of N.Z., based at Univ. of Auckland 1978–80; Gordon A. Macdonald Prof. of Volcanology, Univ. of Hawaii, Manoa 1981–96; Visiting Prof. Univ. of Bristol; Fellow Geological Soc. of America 1987, American Geophysical Union 1988; Hon. mem. Visindafelag Islendinga (Iceland), Royal Soc. of N.Z.; Hon. D.Sc. (Univ. of Iceland) 1988; Moiety of Lyell Fund, Lyell Medal and Wollaston Medal, Geological Soc. of London 1963, 1982, 1995, McKay Hammer Award, Geological Soc. of N.Z. 1982, Excellence in Research Award, Univ. of Hawaii 1985, Thorarinsson Medal, Int. Asscn. of Volcanology and Geochem. of Earth's Interior 1989; Icelandic Order of the Falcon, Kt.'s

Class 1980. *Publications:* scientific papers on the geology and mineralogy of Iceland, and processes in volcanology. *Leisure interest:* visiting volcanoes. *Address:* Department of Geology, University of Bristol, Bristol BS8 1RJ; Geology Department, Cheltenham and Gloucester College of Higher Education, Glos., GL50 4AZ, England.

WALKER, Sir John Ernest, Kt. M.A., D.PHIL., F.R.S.; British scientist; b. 7 Jan. 1941; s. of Thomas Ernest Walker and Elsie Walker (née Lawton); m. Christina Jane Westcott 1963; two d.; ed. Rastrick Grammar School, W. Yorks., St. Catherine's Coll. Oxford; Visiting Research Fellow Univ. of Wis., U.S.A. 1969–71; NATO Research Fellow, C.N.R.S., Gif-sur-Yvette, France 1971–72; EMBO Research Fellow, Pasteur Inst., Paris 1972–74; Staff Scientist, MRC Lab. of Molecular Biology, Cambridge 1974–; Head, Dunn Nutrition Unit, Cambridge 1998–; mem. EMBO 1983; Fellow Sidney Sussex Coll., Cambridge; Hon. Fellow St. Catherine's Coll., Oxford; Dr. h.c. (Univs. of Bradford, Huddersfield, Buenos Aires); Johnson Foundation Prize, Univ. of Pa. 1994, Ciba Medal and Prize, Biochemistry Soc. 1996, Nobel Prize for Chem. (jtly, with Paul Boyer, q.v.) 1997. *Publications:* research papers and reviews in scientific journals. *Leisure interests:* cricket, opera music, walking. *Address:* Medical Research Council Laboratory of Molecular Biology, Hills Road, Cambridge, CB2 2QH, England. *Telephone:* (01223) 402239.

WALKER, Gen. Sir Michael John Dawson, K.C.B., C.M.G., C.B.E.; British army officer; b. 7 July 1944; s. of William Hampden Dawson Walker and Dorothy Helena (née Shiach) Walker; m. Victoria Margaret Holme 1973; two s. one d.; ed. Royal Mil. Acad. Sandhurst; joined Royal Anglian Regt. 1966, Regimental and Staff Duties 1966–82, with Staff Coll. 1976–77, Mil. Asst. to Chief of Gen. Staff 1982–85, C.O. 1985–87, Col. 1996–; Commdr. 20th Armoured Brig. 1987–89; Chief of Staff 1 (Br.) Corps 1989–91; G.O.C. N.E. Dist. and Commdr. 2nd Infantry Div. 1991–92; Col. Commdt. Queen's Div. 1991–, Army Air Corps 1994–; G.O.C. Eastern Dist. 1992; Asst. Chief of the Gen. Staff Ministry of Defence 1992–94; Commdr. Ace Rapid Reaction Corps 1994–95; Head NATO Ground Forces, Bosnia 1995–96; C.-in-C. Land Command 1997–; Aide de Camp Gen. to the Queen 1997–. *Address:* HQ Land Command, Wilton, Salisbury, Wilts., SP2 0AG, England.

WALKER, Sir Miles Rawstron, Kt., C.B.E.; British politician; b. 13 Nov. 1940, Isle of Man; s. of George D. Walker and Alice Rawstron; m. Mary L. Cowell 1966; one s. one d.; ed. Castle Rushen High School and Shropshire Agricultural Coll.; co. dir. farming and retail trade; mem. and fmr. Chair. Arbory Parish Commrs. 1970–76; mem. House of Keys (Ind.) 1976–; mem. Bd. of Agric., Local Govt. Bd., Manx Museum 1976–81; Chair. Broadcasting Comm. 1979, Local Govt. Bd. 1981–86; mem. Exec. Council 1981–; mem. Assessment Bd. 1983–86; Vice-Chair. Post Office Authority 1984–86; Chief Minister, Isle of Man Govt. 1986–96. *Address:* Office of the Clerk of Tynwald, Legislative Buildings, Douglas; Magher Feailley, Main Road, Colby, IM9 4AD, Isle of Man (Home). *Telephone:* (01624) 685505 (Office); (01624) 833728 (Home). *Fax:* (01624) 685710 (Office).

WALKER, Robert Mowbray, PH.D.; American physicist; b. 6 Feb. 1929, Philadelphia; s. of Robert Walker and Margaret Seivwright; m. 1st Alice J. Agedal 1951 (divorced 1973); two s.; m. 2nd Ghislaine Crozaz 1973; ed. Union Coll., Schenectady, New York, Yale Univ.; Research Physicist, Gen. Electric Lab., Schenectady, N.Y. 1954–66; Adjunct Prof. Metallurgy Dept. Rensselaer Polytechnic Inst., Troy, N.Y. 1958, Physics Dept. 1965–66; Nat. Science Foundation Sr. post-doctoral Fellow and Visiting Prof. Univ. of Paris 1962–63; McDonnell Prof. of Physics and Dir. Lab. for Space Physics, Washington Univ. 1966–75; Visiting Prof. of Physics and Geology, Calif. Inst. of Tech. Jan.–June 1972; Visiting Scientist, Laboratoire René Bernas, Univ. of Paris, France May–Aug. 1975; McDonnell Prof. of Physics and Dir. McDonnell Center for the Space Sciences, Washington Univ. 1975–; Chair. Antarctic Meteorite Working Group 1990–92; mem. N.A.S. Polar Research Bd. 1995–, Cosmic Dust Allocation Cttee., NASA 1998; Visiting Scientist Physical Research Lab., Ahmedabad, India 1981; Visiting Scientist, Inst. d'Astrophysique, Paris, and Laboratoire René Bernas, France March–Aug. 1981; Founder Vols. in Tech. Assistance (VITA) 1960, Pres. 1960–62, 1965–66, mem. Bd. of Dirs. 1961–; Fellow American Physical Soc., A.A.A.S.; numerous honours and awards. *Publications:* 198 scientific papers and book: Nuclear Tracks in Solids. *Address:* McDonnell Center for the Space Sciences, Box 1105, Washington University, 1 Brookings Drive, St. Louis, MO 63130 (Office); 3 Romany Park Lane, Saint Louis, MO 63132, U.S.A. (Home). *Telephone:* (314) 935-6257.

WALKER, Roger Neville, B.ARCH., F.N.Z.I.A.; New Zealand architect; b. 21 Dec. 1942, Hamilton; s. of Andrew Frank Walker and Margaret Clothier; m. 1985; three s. one d.; ed. Hamilton Boys' High School, Univ. of Auckland School of Architecture; with corp. architectural practice, Wellington 1968–70; own practice 1970–; designs include Rainbow Springs, Rotorua, Waitomo Visitor Centre, Whakatane Airport, Gardens Park Royal Hotel, Queenstown, City Centre Shopping Devt., New Plymouth, Marist Provincial Bldg., Ropata Medical Centre, Thorndon New World Shopping Devt., Willis Street Village, Wellington, over 100 houses and apartment devts. in New Zealand, Australia and U.K.; lecturer Auckland School of Architecture, Wellington School of Architecture; received New Zealand Steel Award 1984; 13 N.Z. Inst. of Architecture Awards; 5 N.Z. Tourism Awards. *Leisure interests:* photography, travel, motor sport, basketball. *Address:* 8 Brougham Street, Mount Victoria, Wellington, New Zealand. *Telephone:* (04) 3859307. *Fax:* (04) 3859348.

WALKER, Sarah Elizabeth Royle, C.B.E., L.R.A.M., F.R.C.M.; British mezzo-soprano; b. Cheltenham; d. of Elizabeth Brownrigg and Alan Royle Walker; m. Graham Allum 1972; ed. Pate's Grammar School for Girls, Cheltenham, and R.C.M.; studied violin and cello and then voice (with Ruth Packer and Cuthbert Smith) at R.C.M.; Martin Musical Trust Scholarship to begin vocal studies with Vera Rozsa 1967; operatic débuts: Kent Opera, Ottavia in Coronation of Poppea 1969, Glyndebourne Festival, Diana/Giove in La Calisto 1970, Scottish Opera, Didon in Les Troyens 1971, English Nat. Opera, Wellgunde in The Ring 1971; Prin. singer with English Nat. Opera 1972–76; début Royal Opera House, Covent Garden as Charlotte in Werther 1979; début Metropolitan Opera, New York, as Micha in Handel's Samson 1986; has sung opera in Chicago, San Francisco, Göttingen, Geneva, Vienna and Brussels; concert repertoire includes, in addition to standard works, contemporary and avant-garde works by Berio, Boulez, Cage, Ligeti, Xenakis and others; sang Rule Britannia at last night of 1985 and 1989 BBC Promenade concerts, London; recital début, Wigmore Hall, London 1979; recital tours Australia, N. America, Europe; numerous recordings including Handel's Hercules and Julius Caesar and Stravinsky's Rake's Progress; video recordings of Gloriana (title role), Julius Caesar (Cornelia) and King Priam (Andromache); Pres. Cheltenham Bach Choir 1986–; Hon. G.S.M.; Liveryman Worshipful Co. of Musicians. *Leisure interests:* interior design, gardening, battling against incipient laziness. *Address:* c/o Askonas Holt Ltd., Lonsdale Chambers, 27 Chancery Lane, London, WC2A 1PF; 152 Inchmery Road, London, SE6 1DF, England. *Fax:* 0181-461 5659.

WALKER OF WORCESTER, Baron (Life Peer), cr. 1992, of Abbots Morton in the County of Hereford and Worcester; **Peter Edward Walker,** P.C., M.B.E., M.P.; British politician and businessman; b. 25 March 1932; s. of Sydney and Rose Walker; m. Tessa Joan Pout 1969; three s. two d.; ed. Latymer Upper School; Chair. Rose, Thomson, Young and Co. Ltd. (Lloyd's Brokers) 1956–70; Deputy Chair. Slater Walker Securities Ltd. 1964–70; Dir. Adwest Ltd. 1963–70; mem. Lloyd's 1969–75; Parl. cand. for Dartford 1955 and 1959, M.P. for Worcester 1961–92; mem. Nat. Exec. of Conservative Party 1956–; Nat. Chair. Young Conservatives 1958–60; mem. Conservative Commonwealth Council Gen. Cttee. 1960; Parl. Pvt. Sec. to Leader of House of Commons 1963–64; Opposition Spokesman Finance and Econs. 1964–66, Transport 1966–68, Housing and Local Govt. 1968–70; Minister of Housing and Local Govt. 1970; Sec. of State for the Environment 1970–72, for Trade and Industry 1972–74; Opposition Spokesman on Trade and Industry 1974, Defence 1974–75; Sec. of State for Agric., Fisheries and Food 1979–83, for Energy 1983–87, for Wales 1987–90; Head Urban Regeneration Agency 1992–; Dir. N.M. Rothschild (Wales) 1990–, D.C. Gardner 1990–, Tate and Lyle 1990–, British Gas 1990–96, Worcester Group 1990–, Dalgety 1990–96, Smith New Court 1990–, Liffe 1995–, Kleinwort Benson 1996– (non-exec. Chair. 1997–); Dept. Co-ordinator on Coal Industry 1992–; Chair. Thornton and Co. 1991–97, Cornhill Insurance 1992–, English Partnerships' (urban regeneration agency) 1993–, London Int. Financial Futures and Options Exchange 1995–, Kleinwort Benson Group 1996–; Dir. Viet Nam Fund; Hon. LL.D. (Wales) 1991; Commdr.'s Cross of Order of Merit (Germany) 1994; Conservative. *Publications:* The Ascent of Britain 1977, Trust the People 1987, Staying Power (autobiog.) 1991. *Address:* Abbots Morton Manor, Grooms Hill, Abbots Morton, Worcester, WR7 4LT, England (Home).

WALL, Brian; American sculptor; b. 5 Sept. 1931, London, England; s. of Arthur F. Wall and Dorothy Seymour; m. Sylvia Brown 1973; two s.; ed. Luton Coll. of Art, England; numerous one-man exhbns. since 1957 including, recently: Lowinsky Gallery, New York City 1987, 1998, Francis-Graham-Dixon Gallery, London 1992, Sheldon Memorial Art Gallery, Univ. of Nebraska 1995, Jernigan Wicker Fine Arts, San Francisco 1995; has participated in numerous group exhbns. in U.K., Europe, N. America, Australia and N.Z.; retrospective exhbns. in Seattle Art Museum 1982, San Francisco Museum of Modern Art 1983,; works in many public collections including Tate Gallery, London, Art Gallery of N.S.W., Sydney, Museum of Art, Dublin, Seattle Art Museum, Univ. Art Museum, Berkeley, Oakland Museum, Calif., Sheldon Memorial Art Gallery, Univ. of Neb.; Asst. Prof. of Art, Univ. of Calif., Berkeley 1975–77, Assoc. Prof. 1977–81, Prof. 1981–94, Emer. Prof. 1994–. *Address:* 306 Lombard Street, San Francisco, CA 94133, U.S.A. *Telephone:* (510) 652-6042.

WALL, Charles Terence Clegg, PH.D., F.R.S.; British professor of mathematics; b. 14 Dec. 1936, Bristol; s. of Charles Wall and Ruth Wall (née Clegg); m. Alexandra Joy Hearnshaw 1959; two s. two d.; ed. Marlborough Coll. and Trinity Coll. Cambridge; Fellow of Trinity Coll. 1959–64; Harkness Fellow, Inst. for Advanced Study, Princeton, U.S.A. 1960–61; Reader in Math. and Fellow of St. Catherine's Coll. Oxford 1964–65; Prof. of Pure Math. Univ. of Liverpool 1965–; Royal Soc. Leverhulme Visiting Prof., CIEA, Mexico 1967; Science and Eng. Research Council (SERC) Sr. Research Fellow 1983–88; mem. Council of Royal Soc. 1974–76, Council of London Math. Soc. 1972–80, 1992–96, Pres. 1978–80; Foreign mem. Royal Danish Acad.; Treas. Wirral Area SDP 1985–88, Wirral West Liberal Democrat Party 1988–; Jr. Berwick Prize, Whitehead Prize, Polya Prize (London Math. Soc.), Sylvester Medal (Royal Soc.). *Publications:* Surgery on Compact Manifolds 1971, A Geometric Introduction to Topology 1971, The Geometry of Topological Stability 1995; over 140 research publs. in math. journals. *Leisure interests:* reading, walking, gardening, home winemaking. *Address:* Department of Mathematical Sciences, The University of Liverpool, Liverpool, L69 3BX

(Office); 5 Kirby Park, West Kirby, Wirral, Merseyside, L48 2HA, England (Home). *Telephone:* (0151) 794 4060 (Office); (0151) 625 5063 (Home).

WALL, Frank A., B.C.L., LL.B.; Irish public official and solicitor; b. 10 Oct. 1949, Limerick; s. of Frank M. Wall and Eileen Pierse; m. Margot Hourigan 1977; three s. one d.; ed. Mungret Coll., Limerick, Univ. Coll., Cork, Inc. Law Soc., Dublin and Free Univ. of Brussels; Adviser Group of European Progressive Democrats, European Parl. 1974–79; Adviser to Minister for Agric., Dublin 1980; Nat. Dir. of Elections 1982; Senator 1982–83; mem. Exec. Cttee., Irish Council of the European Movt. 1980–91; Gen. Sec. Fianna Fáil 1981–91; mem. Bd., Friends of Fianna Fáil Inc., U.S.A. 1986–91; Chair. Irish Council of European Movt. 1987–91; Co-founder Inst. of European Affairs 1990; Dir. Parl. and Institutional Affairs, Council of the European Union. *Publications:* European Regional Policy (with Sean Brosnan) 1978. *Leisure interests:* politics, gaelic football, golf, rugby, gardening. *Address:* Council of the European Union, Rue de la Loi 175, 1048 Brussels, Belgium. *Telephone:* (2) 285 8055. *Fax:* (2) 285 7393.

WALL, Frederick Theodore, B.CHEM., PH.D.; American physical chemist; b. 14 Dec. 1912, Chisholm, Minn.; s. of Peter Wall and Fanny Rauhala Wall; m. Clara Vivian 1940; two d.; ed. Univ. of Minnesota; Instructor to Prof. of Chem., Univ. of Ill. 1937–64, Dean of Grad. Coll. 1955–63; Prof. of Chem., Univ. of Calif. at Santa Barbara 1964–66, Vice-Chancellor Research 1965–66; Vice-Chancellor Grad. Studies and Research, and Prof. of Chem., Univ. of Calif. at San Diego 1966–69; Ed. Journal of Physical Chemistry 1965–69; Exec. Dir. of American Chem. Soc. 1969–72; Prof. of Chem., Rice Univ. 1972–78, San Diego State Univ. 1979–81; Adjunct Prof. Univ. of Calif., San Diego 1982–90; Fellow American Acad. of Arts and Sciences; mem. N.A.S.; Corresp. mem. Finnish Chemical Soc.; American Chemical Soc. Award in Pure Chem. 1945, Univ. of Minn. Outstanding Achievement Award 1959. *Publications:* Chemical Thermodynamics 1958; numerous scientific articles on statistics of macromolecular configurations and discrete quantum mechanics. *Address:* 2468 Via Viesta, La Jolla, CA 92037-3935, U.S.A. *Telephone:* (619) 459-8570.

WALL, Sir (John) Stephen, K.C.M.G., L.V.O.; British diplomatist; b. 10 Jan. 1947, Croydon; s. of John Wall and Maria Whitmarsh; m. Catharine Reddaway 1975; one s.; ed. Douai School and Selwyn Coll. Cambridge; entered FCO 1968; served Addis Ababa 1969-72, Paris 1972–74; First Sec. FCO 1974–76; Press Officer, No. 10 Downing St. 1976–77; Asst. Pvt. Sec. to Sec. of State for Foreign and Commonwealth Affairs 1977–79; First Sec. Washington, D.C. 1979–83; Asst. Head, later Head, European Community Dept. FCO 1983–88; Pvt. Sec. to Sec. of State for Foreign and Commonwealth Affairs 1988–90, to Prime Minister 1991–93; Amb. to Portugal 1993–95; Perm. Rep. of U.K. to the European Union 1995–. *Leisure interests:* walking, photography. *Address:* United Kingdom Permanent Mission to the EU, 10 avenue D'Anderghem, 1040 Brussels, Belgium. *Telephone:* (2) 287-82-11. *Fax:* (2) 287-83-98.

WALL, Patrick David, M.A., B.M., B.CH., D.M., F.R.C.P., F.R.S.; British professor of anatomy; b. 5 April 1925, Nottingham; s. of T. Wall and R. Cresswell; ed. St. Paul's School and Christchurch, Oxford; Instructor of Physiology, Yale Univ. 1948–50; Asst. Prof. of Anatomy, Chicago Univ. 1950–53; Instructor of Physiology, Harvard Univ. 1953–55; Assoc. Prof. of Biology, M.I.T. 1957–59, Prof. 1959–67; Prof. of Anatomy, Univ. Coll., London 1967, now Prof. Emer.; Visiting Prof., Hebrew Univ., Jerusalem 1972–; Ed. Pain 1975–; Hon. Fellow Royal Coll. of Anaesthetists; Dr. h.c. (Siena, Debrecen); Sherrington Medal (Royal Soc. of Medicine), Bonica Medal. *Address:* 1 Lake House, South Hill Park, London, NW3 2SH, England. *Telephone:* 0171-439 9139. *Fax:* 0171-439 9139.

WALLACE, Bruce, PH.D.; American professor of genetics; b. 18 May 1920, McKean, Pa.; s. of George E. and Rose Paterson Wallace; m. Miriam Covalla 1945; one s. one d.; ed. Columbia Coll. and Columbia Univ.; Research Assoc., Dept. of Genetics, Carnegie Inst. of Washington 1947–49; Geneticist, later Asst. Dir., Biological Lab., Cold Spring Harbour, N.Y. 1949–58; Assoc. Prof., Cornell Univ. 1958–61, Prof. of Genetics 1961–81; Univ. Distinguished Prof. of Biology, Virginia Polytech. Inst. and State Univ. 1981–94; Prof. Emer. 1994–; mem. N.A.S., American Acad. of Arts and Sciences. *Publications:* Radiation, Genes, and Man (with Th. Dobzhansky) 1959, Adaptation (with A. M. Srb) 1961, Chromosomes, Giant Molecules and Evolution 1966, Topics in Population Genetics 1968, Genetic Load 1970, Essays in Social Biology (3 vols.) 1972, Basic Population Genetics 1981, Dobzhansky's Genetics of Natural Populations I–XLIII (with others) 1982, Human Culture: A Moment in Evolution (with others) 1983, Biology for Living (with G. M. Simmons, Jr.) 1987, Fifty Years of Genetic Load: An Odyssey 1991, The Search for the Gene 1992, The Study of Gene Action (with J. O. Falkinham) 1997, Environmental Literacy: As I See It, Science Is Not Enough 1998. *Leisure interest:* promotion of environmental literacy. *Address:* 940 McBryde Drive, Blacksburg, VA 24060, U.S.A. *Telephone:* (540) 951-2464.

WALLACE, David James, PH.D., F.R.S., F.R.S.E., F.INST.P., F.R.S.A., C.ENG.; British university vice-chancellor; b. 7 Oct. 1945, Hawick, Scotland; s. of Robert Elder Wallace and Jane McConnell Wallace (née Elliot); m. Elizabeth Anne Yeats 1970; one d.; ed. Hawick High School and Edinburgh Univ.; Harkness Fellow, Princeton Univ., U.S.A. 1970–72; Lecturer in Physics, Univ. of Southampton 1972–78, Reader 1978–79; Tait Prof. of Math. Physics, Univ. of Edin. 1979–93, Head of Physics 1984–87; Vice-Chancellor Loughborough Univ. 1994–; Assoc. Dir. Research Initiative on Pattern Recognition, RSRE, Malvern 1986–90; Dir Edin. Concurrent Supercomputer 1987–89, Edin. Parallel Computing Centre 1990–93; Chair. Physics Cttee., Science and Eng. Research Council 1987–90, Science Bd. 1990–94, mem. Council 1990–94; mem. Council and Chair. Tech. Opportunities Panel, Eng. and Physical Sciences Research Council 1994–98; mem. LINK Bd. Office of Science and Tech. 1995–, scientific and industrial award cttees. of Royal Soc. 1990–95, High Performance Computing and Networking Advisory Cttee., European Comm. 1991–92, Physics Panel of Human Capital and Mobility Programme 1991–94, Large Scale Facilities Evaluation Panel 1995–97; mem. Scottish Higher Educ. Funding Council 1993–97; Pres. Physics Section, British Assen. for Advancement of Science 1994; Maxwell Medal, Inst. of Physics 1980. *Leisure interests:* eating at la Potinière, running. *Address:* Loughborough University of Technology, Loughborough, Leics., LE11 3TU, England. *Telephone:* (01509) 222001. *Fax:* (01509) 223900.

WALLACE, Helen, PH.D.; British professor of European studies; b. 25 June 1946, Manchester; d. of late Edward Rushworth and of Joyce Rushworth (née Robinson); m. William Wallace (now Lord Wallace of Saltaire) 1968; one s. one d.; ed. Univs. of Oxford, Bruges, Belgium and Manchester; Lecturer in European Studies, UMIST 1974–78, in Public Admin., Civil Service Coll 1978–85; Head W. European Programme, Royal Inst. of Int. Affairs 1985–92; Prof. of Contemporary European Studies and Dir. of Sussex European Inst., Univ. of Sussex 1992–; Visiting Prof., Coll. of Europe, Bruges 1976–; mem. Planning Staff, FCO 1979–80. *Publications:* Policy-Making in the European Community (jtly.) 1983, French and British Foreign Policies in Transition (jtly.) 1990, The Wider Western Europe (Ed.) 1991, The European Community: the Challenge of Enlargement (jtly.) 1992, Policy-Making in the European Union (Ed.) 1996, The Council of Ministers (jtly.) 1997. *Leisure interests:* gardening, walking. *Address:* Sussex European Institute, University of Sussex, Falmer, Brighton, BN1 9QN, England. *Telephone:* (01273) 606 755; (01273) 678 560. *Fax:* (01273) 678 571.

WALLACE, Ian, O.B.E., M.A.; British singer, actor and broadcaster; b. 10 July 1919, London; s. of the late Sir John Wallace and Mary Temple; m. Patricia G. Black 1948; one s. one d.; ed. Charterhouse and Trinity Hall, Cambridge; appeared in buffo roles at Glyndebourne 1948–60 and continued to appear in opera in Britain and briefly in Italy until 1970s; later appeared on concert platforms and also in straight plays, reviews, musicals and pantomimes as well as in many television and radio shows notably My Music; Pres. Inc. Soc. of Musicians 1979–80, Council for Music in Hosps. 1987–99; Hon. mem. Royal Acad. of Music, Royal Coll. of Music.; Hon. Mus.D. (St. Andrews Univ.) 1991. *Film appearances include;* Plenty, Porterhouse Blue. *Publications:* autobiog.: Vol. I Promise Me You'll Sing Mud 1975, Vol. II Nothing Quite Like It 1982, Reflections on Scotland 1988. *Leisure interests:* walking, photography, birdwatching, sport, reading. *Address:* c/o Fraser & Dunlop Ltd., 5th Floor, The Chambers, Chelsea Harbour, Lots Road, London, SW10 0XF, England. *Telephone:* 0171-344 1010.

WALLACE-CRABBE, Christopher Keith, M.A., F.A.H.A.; Australian poet and critic; b. 6 May 1934, Melbourne; s. of Kenneth Eyre Inverell Wallace-Crabbe and Phyllis Vera May Wallace-Crabbe (née Cock); m. 1st Helen Margaret Wiltshire 1957; one s. one d.; m. 2nd Marianne Sophie Feil 1979; two s.; ed. Melbourne Univ., Yale Univ., U.S.A.; cadet metallurgist 1951–52; then journalist, clerk, schoolteacher; Lockie Fellow in Australian Literature, Univ. of Melbourne 1962; Harkness Fellow, Yale Univ. 1965–67; Sr. Lecturer in English, Univ. of Melbourne 1967, Reader 1976, Prof. 1987–, Personal Chair. 1987–97; Visiting Chair. in Australian Studies, Harvard Univ., U.S.A. 1987–88; Masefield Prize for Poetry 1957, Farmer's Poetry Prize 1964, Grace Leven Prize 1986, Dublin Prize 1987, Christopher Brennan Award 1990, Age Book of the Year Prize 1995. *Publications:* The Music of Division 1959, Selected Poems 1974, Melbourne or the Bush 1974, The Emotions are not Skilled Workers 1980, Toil and Spin: Two Directions in Modern Poetry 1980, Splinters (novel) 1981, The Amorous Cannibal 1985, I'm Deadly Serious 1988, Sangue è l'Acqua 1989, For Crying out Loud 1990, Falling into Language 1990, Poetry and Belief 1990, From the Republic of Conscience 1992, Rungs of Time 1993, Selected Poems 1956–94 1995. *Leisure interests:* drawing, tennis, surfing. *Address:* Department of English, University of Melbourne, Parkville, Vic. 3052; 910 Drummond Street, North Carlton, Vic. 3054, Australia. *Telephone:* (03) 344-6864.

WALLACH, Eli, M.S. IN ED.; American actor; b. 7 Dec. 1915, Brooklyn, N.Y.; s. of Abraham Wallach and Bertha Schorr; m. Anne Jackson 1948; one s. two d.; ed. Univ. of Texas, City Coll. of New York, Neighborhood Playhouse School of Theatre; started theatre career 1946, film career 1955; Donaldson Award, Tony Award, British Film Acad. Award 1956; acted in plays: The Rose Tattoo, The Teahouse of the August Moon 1954–55, Camino Real, Luv, Typists and Tiger 1964, Promenade All 1973, Waltz of the Toreadors 1974, The Diary of Anne Frank 1978, Opera Comique 1987, The Flowering Peach in Florida 1987, Visiting Mr. Green 1997. *Films include:* Baby Doll 1956, The Line-Up 1958, Seven Thieves 1959, The Magnificent Seven 1960, The Misfits 1961, How the West Was Won 1962, The Victors 1963, The Moonspinners 1964, Lord Jim 1965, Genghis Khan 1965, How to Steal a Million 1966, The Good, the Bad and the Ugly 1967, The Tiger Makes Out 1967, Mackenna's Gold 1968, Cinderella Liberty 1973, Domino Principle 1975, The Sentinel 1975, The Deep 1975, Winter Kills 1975, The Silent Flute 1978, Movie Movie 1978, The Hunter 1979, The Wall 1980, The Executioner's Song 1982, Sam's Son 1985, Tough Guys 1986, Rocket to the Moon 1986, Nuts 1987, The Rose Garden 1989, The Godfather III 1990, The Two Jakes

1990, Article 99, Mistress 1991, Night and the City 1991, Honey Sweet Love 1993, Two Much Film 1995, The Associate 1996. *Leisure interest:* photography.

WALLENBERG, Peter, LL.M.; Swedish business executive; b. 29 May 1926, Stockholm; s. of Dr. Marcus Wallenberg and Dorothy Mackay; m. (divorced); two s. one d.; ed. Univ. of Stockholm; various positions with Atlas Copco Group; fmr. Chair. Atlas Copco AB, STORA, ASEA; fmr. Co-Chair. ASEA Brown Boveri (AAB); First Vice-Chair. Skandinaviska Enskilda Banken 1984–96; Chair. Investor AB 1982–97, Wallenberg Foundation 1982–; mem. Swiss Bank Corpn. Council of Int. Advisers, Gen. Motors European Advisory Council; mem. Bd. Stockholm School of Econs. 1976–, Per Jacobson Foundation, U.S.A. 1983–, Joseph H. Lauder Inst., U.S.A. 1983–, Nobel Foundation 1986; Dr. h.c. (Stockholm School of Econs., Augustana Coll., and Uppsala Coll., U.S.A.); Hon. Kt. 1989. *Leisure interests:* hunting, tennis, sailing. *Address:* Investor AB, 10332 Stockholm, Sweden. *Telephone:* 8221900. *Fax:* 86142815.

WALLER, Robert James; American writer and musician; b. 1 Aug. 1939; s. of Robert Waller Sr. and Ruth Waller; m. Georgia A. Wiedemeier; one d.; ed. Northern Iowa and Indiana Univs.; Prof. of Man. Univ. of N. Iowa 1968–91, Dean Business School 1979–85; singer; guitarist; flautist; album: The Ballads of Madison County 1993. *Publications:* Just Beyond the Firelight 1988, One Good Road is Enough 1990, Iowa: Perspectives on Today and Tomorrow 1991, The Bridges of Madison County 1992, Slow Waltz at Cedar Bend 1994, Old Songs in a New Café 1994, Selected Essays 1994, Border Music 1995, Puerto-Vallarta Squeeze 1995. *Leisure interests:* photography, basketball. *Address:* c/o Aaron Priest Literary Agency, 708 3rd Avenue, 23rd Floor, New York, NY 10017, U.S.A.

WALLERSTEIN, Ralph O., M.D.; American professor of medicine; b. 7 March 1922, Düsseldorf, Germany; s. of O. R. Wallerstein and Ilse Hollander; m. Betty A. Christensen 1952; two s. one d.; ed. Univ. of California Medical School, San Francisco; Chief of Clinical Hematology, San Francisco Gen. Hosp. 1953–81, Clinical Dir. of Blood Bank 1955–80; Chief of Staff, Children's Hosp. 1968–72; Clinical Prof., Univ. of Calif. 1969–; mem. Exec. Cttee. American Soc. of Hematology 1971–78, Pres. 1978; Chair. Bd. of Govs. American Bd. of Internal Medicine 1982–83, Chair. Cttee. on Hematology 1974–77; Gov., N. Calif., American Coll. of Physicians 1977–81, Chair. Bd. of Govs. 1980–81, Regent 1981–87, Pres. 1987–88; mem. Residency Review Cttee. for Internal Medicine 1985–; Fellow A.A.A.S., A.C.P.; mem. American Medical Assn., American Fed. for Clinical Research, American Assn. of Blood Banks, American Soc. of Hematology, Inst. of Medicine, American Soc. of Clinical Oncology. *Publications:* Iron in Clinical Medicine (with S. R. Mettier) 1958, 27 articles in specialized journals. *Leisure interest:* photography. *Address:* 3838 California Street, Room 707, San Francisco, CA 94118 (Office); 3447 Clay Street, San Francisco, CA 94118, U.S.A. (Home). *Telephone:* (415) 668-0160 (Office).

WALLOP, Malcolm, B.A.; American politician; b. 27 Feb. 1933, New York; s. of Oliver M. Wallop and Jean Moore; m. French Carter 1984; three s. one d.; ed. Yale Univ.; owner, operator, Canyon Ranch, Big Horn, Wyo.; service U.S. army 1955–57; mem. Wyo. House of Reps. 1969–73, Wyo. Senate 1973–77; Senator from Wyoming 1976–95; official observer from Senate on arms control negotiations; mem. Comm. on Security and Co-operation in Europe; Republican.

WALLOT, Jean-Pierre, O.C., L. ÈS L., PH.D.; Canadian historian and archivist; b. 22 May 1935, Valleyfield, Quebec; s. of late Albert Wallot and of Adrienne Thibodeau; m. 1st Rita Girard 1957; m. 2nd Denyse Caron 1990; two s. one d.; ed. Univ. de Montréal; Prof. and Dir. History Dept. Univ. de Montréal 1961–66, 1973–85, Vice-Pres. (Academic) 1982–85; Historian Museum of Man of Canada 1966–69; Prof. Univ. of Toronto 1969–71, Concordia Univ. 1971–73; Nat. Archivist of Canada 1985–97; Dir. d'études associé, Ecole des Hautes Etudes en Sciences Sociales, Paris 1975, 1979, 1981, 1983, 1985, 1987, 1989, 1994; Guest Lecturer Univ. of Ottawa 1986–(2000); mem. Bd. of Govs. Univ. of Ottawa 1988–90; Pres. Int. Council of Archives 1992–96; Pres. Royal Soc. of Canada 1997–(99); Pres. Int. Advisory Cttee. on Memory of the World, UNESCO 1993–(99); Dr. h.c. (Rennes) 1987, (Ottawa) 1996; Jacques Ducharme Prize, Assn. Archiv. du Québec 1997; Marie Tremaine Medal (Canadian Bibliographic Soc.) 1973, Tyrrell Medal (Royal Soc. of Canada) 1983, Centenary Medal of Royal Soc. of Canada 1994; Officier Ordre des Arts et Lettres (France) 1987. *Publications:* Intrigues françaises et américaines au Canada 1965, Les Imprimés dans le Bas-Canada (with John Hare) 1967, Un Québec qui bougeait 1973, Patronage et Pouvoir dans le Bas-Canada (with G. Paquet) 1973. *Leisure interests:* reading, hiking, drums. *Address:* 26-635 Richmond Road, Ottawa, Ont., K2A 0G6, Canada. *Telephone:* (250) 761-7472. *Fax:* (250) 761-9405.

WALLS, Daniel Frank, PH.D., F.R.S., F.R.S.N.Z.; New Zealand professor of physics; b. 13 Sept. 1942, Napier; s. of James R. Walls and Barbara G. Walls; m. Fari Khoy 1968; one s.; ed. Auckland Grammar School and Auckland and Harvard Univs.; Asst. Prof. Univ. of Stuttgart 1970; Postdoctoral Fellow, Univ. of Auckland 1971; Sr. Lecturer, Univ. of Waikato 1972–76, Reader 1976–80, Prof. 1980–87; Prof. Univ. of Auckland 1987–; Adjunct Prof. Univ. of Arizona 1986–; Fellow, American Physical Soc., Optical Soc. of America; Frank Knox Memorial Fellow; Fulbright Fellow. *Publications:* 200 publs. in scientific journals; ed. of 6 books. *Leisure interests:* tennis, swimming, skiing. *Address:* Department of Physics, University of Auckland, Private Bag 92019, Auckland 1; 75A Selwyn Avenue, Mission Bay, Auckland, New Zealand. *Telephone:* 64 9 585 212.

WALLS, Gen. (George) Peter, M.B.E.; Zimbabwean fmr. army officer; b. 28 July 1926, Salisbury; ed. Plumtree School, Royal Mil. Acad., Sandhurst, and Camberley Staff Coll., U.K.; enlisted in Southern Rhodesian Army 1944; commissioned into the Black Watch (Royal Highland Regt.), British Army 1946; attested back to Southern Rhodesian Perm. Staff Corps 1948, commissioned 1949; Commdr. C. Squadron, 22nd Special Air Service in Malaya 1951–53; Officer Commdg. Tactical Wing, later Chief Instructor, School of Infantry 1954–56; Co. Commdr. Northern Rhodesian Regt. 1956–59; Brigade Maj. Copperbelt Area and later N. Rhodesia District 1961–62; Adjutant-Gen. Rhodesian Army 1962–64; C.O. 1st Bn. Rhodesian Light Infantry 1964–67; Commdr. 2nd Brigade 1967–68; Chief of Staff, Rhodesian Army 1968–72, Commdr. 1972–77; Commdr. Combined Operations 1977–80, of Jt. Operations 1980; Grand Officer of the Legion of Merit, Defence Cross for Distinguished Service.

WALLSTRÖM, Margot; Swedish politician; b. 28 Sept. 1954, Kåge, Västerbotten Co.; m. Håkan Olsson; one s.; Organizing Sec. Värmland br., Social Democratic Youth League; bank clerk, Sparbanken Alfa, Värmland 1977–79; Chief Accountant 1986–88; M.P. 1979–85; fmr. mem. Värmland Co. Council, Directorate of Bd. of Civil Aviation, Directorate of Nat. Environment Protection Bd. etc.; Minister with responsibility for Ecclesiastical, Consumers, Equality and Youth Affairs, Ministry of Public Admin. 1988–92; Minister of Cultural Affairs 1994–96, of Health and Social Affairs 1996–98. *Address:* c/o Ministry of Health and Social Affairs, Jakobsgt. 26, 103 33 Stockholm; Riksdagen, 10012 Stockholm, Sweden.

WALMSLEY, David George, PH.D., M.R.I.A.; British professor of physics; b. 3 Feb. 1938, Newtownstewart, N. Ireland; s. of Robert Walmsley and Elizabeth Johnston; m. Margaret H. Edmonstone 1965; two s.; ed. Royal School, Armagh, Queen's Univ. Belfast and McMaster Univ., Hamilton, Ont.; NRC Canada Post-doctoral Fellow, MacMaster Univ. 1965; Scientific Officer, Sr. Scientific Officer, A.E.R.E. Harwell 1966–70; Lecturer, Sr. Lecturer, Reader in Physics, New Univ. of Ulster 1970–84; Prof. of Physics, Univ. of Ulster 1984–88; Prof. of Physics, Queen's Univ. Belfast 1988–, Dir. School of Math. and Physics 1993–98, Dean Faculty of Science and Agric. 1998–; mem. Royal Irish Acad. *Publications:* articles in professional journals. *Address:* 5 Newforge Grange, Belfast, BT9 5QB; 25 Swilly Road, Portstewart, BT55 7DJ, Northern Ireland. *Telephone:* (01232) 664141; (01265) 833257.

WALSER, Martin, DR. PHIL.; German writer; b. 24 March 1927, Wasserburg/Bodensee; s. of Martin Walser and Augusta Schmid; m. Käthe Jehle 1950; four d.; ed. Theologisch-Philosophische Hochschule, Regensburg, and Univ. of Tübingen; writer 1951–; Group 47 Prize 1955, Hermann-Hesse Prize 1957, Gerhart-Hauptmann Prize 1962, Schiller Prize 1980, Büchner Prize 1981. *Publications:* short stories: Ein Flugzeug über dem Haus 1955, Lügengeschichten 1964; novels: Ehen in Philippsburg 1957, Halbzeit 1960, Das Einhorn 1966, Fiction 1970, Die Gallistlische Krankheit 1972, Der Sturz 1973, Jenseits der Liebe 1976, Ein fliehendes Pferd 1978, Seelenarbeit 1979, Das Schwanenhaus 1980, Brief an Lord Liszt 1982, Brandung 1985, Dorle und Wolf 1987, Jagd 1988, Die Verteidigung der Kindheit 1991, Ohne einander 1993, Finks Krieg 1996, Ein springender Brunnen 1998; plays: Der Abstecher 1961, Eiche und Angora 1962, Überlebensgross Herr Krott 1963, Der schwarze Schwan 1964, Die Zimmerschlacht 1967, Ein Kinderspiel 1970, Das Sauspiel 1975, In Goethe's Hand 1982, Die Ohrfeige 1986, Das Sofa 1992, Kaschmir in Parching 1995; essays: Beschreibung einer Form, Versuch über Franz Kafka 1961, Erfahrungen und Leseerfahrungen 1965, Heimatkunde 1968, Wie und wovon handelt Literatur 1973 Wer ist ein Schriftsteller 1978, Selbstbewusstsein und Ironie 1981, Messmers Gedanken 1985, Über Deutschland reden 1988, Vormittag eines Schriftstellers 1994; poems: Der Grund zur Freude 1978. *Address:* 88662 Überlingen-Nussdorf, Zum Hecht 36, Germany. *Telephone:* (7551) 4131. *Fax:* (7551) 68494.

WALSH, Sir Alan, Kt., M.SC.TECH., D.SC., F.INST.P., F.A.I.P., F.A.A., F.R.S., F.T.S.; British research physicist; b. 19 Dec. 1916, Darwen, Lancs.; s. of late Thomas Haworth Walsh and Betsy Alice Robinson; m. Audrey Dale Hutchinson 1949; two s.; ed. Darwen Grammar School and Manchester Univ.; at British Non-Ferrous Metals Research Assn. 1939–46; seconded to Ministry of Aircraft Production 1943; joined Commonwealth Scientific and Industrial Research Org. (CSIRO), Australia 1946, Asst. Chief of Div. of Chemical Physics, CSIRO 1961–76; Consultant, Perkin-Elmer Corpn., Norwalk, U.S.A. 1977; Hon. mem. Soc. for Analytical Chem., Royal Soc. of N.Z., Japan Soc. for Analytical Chem.; Foreign mem. Royal Acad. of Sciences, Stockholm; Pres. Australian Inst. of Physics 1968–69; Hon. Research Fellow, Monash Univ.; Hon. Fellow, Chemical Soc., London 1972, Australian Inst. of Physics 1979; Torbern Bergman Memorial Lecturer, Swedish Chem. Soc. 1976; Hon. D.Sc. (Manchester) 1984, (Monash); Britannica Australia Science Award 1966; Royal Soc. of Victoria Medal 1969, Talanta Gold Medal 1969, Kronland Medal, Czechoslovak Spectroscopic Soc. 1975, Matthew Flinders Medal, Australian Acad. of Science 1980, Robert Boyle Medal (Royal Soc. of Chem.) 1982; Maurice Hasler Award, Soc. for Applied Spectroscopy (U.S.A.) 1972; James Cook Medal, Royal Soc. of N.S.W. 1976; Royal Medal of Royal Soc. 1976; John Scott Award (City of Philadelphia) 1978; K. L. Sutherland Medal, Australian Acad. of Technological Sciences 1982; Inaugural Colloquium Spectroscopicum Int. Award 1991. *Publications:* numerous papers in scientific journals. *Leisure interests:* gardening, golf. *Address:* 43A Carpenter Street, Brighton, Vic. 3186, Australia (Home). *Telephone:* 03-9592 4897.

WALSH, Arthur Stephen, C.B.E., M.A., F.ENG., F.I.E.E.; British business executive; b. 16 Aug. 1926, Wigan; s. of Wilfrid Walsh and Doris Walsh; m. 1st. Gwendoline Mary Walsh (divorced 1983); m. 2nd Judith Martha Westenborg 1985; one s. one d.; ed. Selwyn Coll., Cambridge; joined G.E.C. 1952, various sr. appointments, including Tech. Dir. of G.E.C./A.E.L. 1952–79; Man. Dir. Marconi Space and Defence Systems 1979–82; Man. Dir. The Marconi Co. 1982–85; Chief Exec., STC PLC (now Northern Telecom Europe Ltd) 1985–91; Chair. Telemetrix PLC 1991–97, Simoco Int. Ltd. Jan. 1998–; Dir. FKI PLC 1991–, Deputy Chair. 1993–; Hon. D.Sc. (Ulster) 1988, (Southampton) 1993. *Leisure interests:* sailing, skiing. *Address:* Simoco International Ltd., P.O. Box 24, St Andrews Road, Cambridge, CB4 1DP (Office); Aiglemont, Trout Rise, Loudwater, Rickmansworth, Herts., WD3 4JS, England. *Telephone:* (01223) 877830 (Office); (0923) 770883. *Fax:* (01223) 8793000.

WALSH, Don, PH.D., M.S., M.A., B.S.; American business executive, fmr. university administrator and fmr. naval officer; b. 1931; Berkeley, Calif.; s. of J. Don and Marta G. Walsh; m. Joan A. Betzmer 1962; one s. one d.; ed. San Diego State Coll., Texas A. & M. Univ. and U.S. Naval Acad.; entered navy 1950, submarine service 1956; became Officer-in-Charge Submersible Test Group and Bathyscaph Trieste 1959, made record dive to 35,780 ft., Jan. 1960; Submarine service 1962–64; at Dept. of Oceanography, Texas A. & M. Univ. 1965–68; commanded submarine Bashaw 1968–69; Scientific Liaison Officer Submarine Devt. Group One 1969–70; Special Asst. to Asst. Sec. of the Navy for Research and Devt., Washington, D.C. 1970–73; Resident Fellow, Woodrow Wilson Int. Center for Scholars 1973–74; Deputy Dir. Naval Labs. 1974–75; retd. from navy with rank of Capt. 1975; Dir. Inst. for Marine and Coastal Studies and Prof. of Ocean Eng., Univ. of Southern Calif. 1975–83; Pres., C.E.O. Int. Maritime Inc. 1976–; Vice-Pres. Parker Diving Service 1985–94; mem. Marine Bd., Nat. Research Council 1990–93; Exec. Dir. Deep Ocean Eng. 1990–; mem. Bd. of Dirs. Explorers Club 1994–; mem. American Geophysical Union, A.A.A.S., U.S. Naval Inst., Nat. Advisory Cttee. on Oceans and Atmosphere 1979–86, Law of the Sea Advisory Cttee. (U.S. State Dept.) 1979–83, Soc. of Naval Architects and Marine Engineers, American Soc. for Naval Engineers, Bd. of Govs., Calif. Maritime Acad. 1985–94, etc.; Ed. Marine Tech. Soc. Journal 1976–80; Hon. Life mem. Explorers Club, Adventurers Club, Marine Tech. Soc. 1980; Legion of Merit (two awards); Gold Medals from City of Trieste and Chicago Geographic Socs., U.S. Coast Guard Meritorious Public Service Medal 1980, Meritorious Service Medal (two awards), Lowell Thomas Award from Explorers' Club 1987 and other awards. *Publications:* author of about 200 papers, articles, etc. on marine subjects; ed. and contrib. Law of the Sea: Issues in Ocean Resources Management; Energy and Resource Development of the Continental Margins (co-ed.) 1980, Energy from the Sea: Challenge for the Decade (ed.) 1982, Waste Disposal in the Oceans: Minimum Impact, Maximize Benefits (co-Ed.) 1983. *Leisure interests:* writing, travel, sailing, flying. *Address:* International Maritime Inc., HC-86, Box 101, Myrtle Point, OR 97458, U.S.A. *Telephone:* (541) 572-2313. *Fax:* (541) 572-4041.

WALSH, Edward M., PH.D., F.I.E.E.; Irish university president; b. 3 Dec. 1939, Cork; s. of Michael Walsh and Margaret Walsh (née Leonard); m. Stephanie Barrett 1965; three s. one d.; ed. Nat. Univ. of Ireland, Iowa State Univ., U.S.A.; Assoc., U.S. Atomic Energy Comm. Lab., Ames, Iowa 1963–65; Founding Dir. Energy Research Group Programme and Assoc. Prof., Va. Polytechnic Inst. and State Univ., U.S.A. 1966–69; Chair. Planning Bd. and Pres. Univ. of Limerick 1970; Founding Chair. and Vice-Chair. Nat. Technological Park Limerick 1983–; Founding Chair. Nat. Council for Curriculum and Assessment 1984–90, Nat. Self-Portrait Collection of Ireland, Univ. of Limerick 1982–; Founding Dir. Nat. Microelectronics Applications Centre Ltd. 1981–84; Vice-Pres. (Europe) and Rep. to UN, Geneva, Int. Asscn. of Univ. Pres.'s 1987–; Trustee Int. Asscn. of Science Parks 1987–; mem. Cttee. of Heads of Irish Univs. 1986–; Dir. Shannon Free Airport Devt. Co. Ltd. 1985–; Fellow Inst. of Engineers of Ireland; Rotary Paul Harris Fellowship; Hon. LL.D. (Dublin). *Publications:* Energy Conversion: electromechanical-direct-nuclear 1967, Fluid Dynamic Energy Conversion 1967 and publs. on science parks, and the role of univs. *Leisure interests:* sailing, riding, skiing, tennis, gardening, silversmithing, painting, violin. *Address:* University of Limerick, Limerick (Office); Oakhampton House, Newport, Co. Tipperary, Ireland (Home). *Telephone:* (61) 333644 (Office). *Fax:* (61) 330316.

WALSH, Joe; Irish politician; b. May 1943, Ballineen, Co. Cork; m. Marie Donegan; three s. two d.; ed. Univ. Coll. Cork; fmr. dairy man.; mem. Irish Creamery Mans. Asscn., Soc. of Dairy Tech., mem. Cork Co. Council 1974–91; mem. Dáil 1977–81, 1982–; Senator 1981–82; Minister of State, Dept. of Agric. and Food 1987, 1989–93; Minister for Agric., Food and Forestry 1993–94, 1997–; Fianna Fáil. *Address:* Dáil Eireann, Dublin 2; 5 Emmet Square, Clonakilty, Co. Cork, Ireland. *Telephone:* (023) 33575 (Home).

WALSH, Lawrence Edward, LL.D.; American lawyer; b. 8 Jan. 1912, Port Maitland, N.S., Canada; s. of Dr. Cornelius E. Walsh and Lila M. Sanders; m. Mary A. Porter; one s. four d.; ed. Columbia Univ.; mem. Bar, New York State 1936, Dist. of Columbia 1981, Oklahoma 1981, U.S. Supreme Court 1951; Special Asst. Attorney-Gen. Drukman Investigation 1936–38; Deputy Asst. Dist. Attorney, N.Y. Co. 1938–41; Assoc. Davis Polk, Wardwell, Sunderland, and Kiendl 1941–43; Asst. Counsel to Gov. of New York 1943–49, Counsel to Gov. 1950–51; Counsel, Public Service Comm. 1951–53; Gen. Counsel, Exec. Dir. Waterfront Comm. of N.Y. Harbor 1953–54; U.S. Judge, S. Dist. N.Y. 1954–57; U.S. Deputy Attorney-Gen. 1957–60; Partner, Davis, Polk & Wardwell 1961–81; Counsel, Crowe & Dunlevy, Oklahoma City 1981–; Independent Counsel, "Iran-Contra" investigation 1986–93; Pres. American Bar Asscn. 1975–76; Trustee Emer., Columbia Univ.; many other public appts. and mem. numerous bar and lawyers' asscns. *Address:* 1800 Mid-America Towers, Oklahoma City, OK 73102 (Office); 1902 Bedford Drive, Oklahoma City, OK 73116, U.S.A. (Home).

WALTER, Bernhard; German banker; joined Dresdner Bank on leaving school; fmr. responsibilities include operations in the fmr. G.D.R., corp. finance, Eastern European operations; mem. Bd. 1987–, Chair. Jan. 1998–. *Leisure interests:* golf, jogging, music. *Address:* Dresdner Bank AG, Jurgen-Ponto-Platz 1, 60301 Frankfurt am Main, Germany. *Telephone:* 69-2-63-111-11. *Fax:* 69-2-63-101-11.

WALTER, Norbert, DR.RER.POL.; German economist; b. 23 Sept. 1944, Weckbach/Unterfranken; s. of Heinrich Walter and Erna Walter; m. Christa Bayer 1967; two d.; ed. Johann Wolfgang Goethe Univ., Frankfurt; affiliated Inst. for Capital Market Research, Frankfurt 1968–71; mem. staff Kiel Inst. of World Econs., Kiel 1971–86, Asst. to Pres. and head various research groups 1971–77, Head Dept. on Business Cycle in the World Economy, subsequently Resource Econs. Dept. 1977–85; fmr. Professorial Lecturer, Christian Albrechts Univ., Kiel; John McCloy Distinguished Research Fellow and Resident Scholar, Johns Hopkins Univ., Washington, D.C. 1986–87; Sr. Economist, Deutsche Bank, Frankfurt 1987–90, Chief Economist Deutsche Bank Group 1990–, Man. Dir. Deutsche Bank Research 1992–. *Publications include:* Was würde Erhard heute tun?, Wohin treibt die Wirtschaft?—Die Wende zu mehr Markt (co-author) 1984, Strengths, Weaknesses and Prospects of the German Economy, in The Future of Germany (Ed. Gary Geipel) 1990, Weniger Staat—Mehr Markt 1993, Der neue Wohlstand der Nation 1993, Der Euro—Kurs auf die Zukunft 1997. *Leisure interest:* jogging. *Address:* Deutsche Bank Research, Postfach, 60272 Frankfurt-am-Main (Office); Bismarckstr. 28, 65812 Bad Soden, Germany (Home). *Telephone:* (69) 910-31810 (Office). *Fax:* (69) 910-31826.

WALTERS, Sir Alan Arthur, Kt., B.SC.; British economist; b. 17 June 1926, Leicester; s. of James Arthur and Clarabel Walters; m. 2nd Margaret Patricia Wilson 1975; one d. by previous marriage; ed. Alderman Newton's Secondary School, Leicester, Univ. Coll., Leicester, and Nuffield Coll., Oxford; Prof. of Econometrics and Social Statistics, Univ. of Birmingham 1961–68; Sir Ernest Cassel Prof. of Econs., L.S.E. 1968–75; Prof. of Econs., Johns Hopkins Univ., Baltimore, Md. 1976–91; Visiting Fellow, Nuffield Coll., Oxford 1982–83; Econ. Adviser to World Bank, Washington, D.C. 1976–80; Econ. Adviser to Margaret Thatcher (now Baroness Thatcher, q.v.) 1981–89 (part-time 1983–89); Deputy Chair. and Dir. AIG Trading Co. 1991–; mem. Referendum Party 1995–; Hon. D.Litt. (Leicester) 1981; Hon. D.Soc.Sci. (Birmingham) 1984; Hon. Ph.D. (Francisco Marroquin Univ.) 1994. *Publications:* Economics of Road User Charges 1968, Money in Boom and Slump 1968, Noise and Prices 1975, Port Pricing and Investment for Developing Countries 1979, Microeconomic Theory (with Richard Layard) 1978, Britain's Economic Renaissance: Margaret Thatcher's reforms 1979–1984 1986, Sterling in Danger 1990, The Economics and Politics of Money 1998. *Leisure interests:* theatre, opera, music. *Address:* AIG Trading Group Inc., 1200 19th Street N.W., Suite 605, Washington, DC 20036, U.S.A.; 3 Chesterfield Hill, London, W1X 7RP, England. *Telephone:* 0171-491 7345 (London). *Fax:* 0171-499 3982 (London).

WALTERS, Barbara, B.A.; American television broadcaster; b. 25 Sept. 1931, Brookline, Mass.; d. of Lou Walters and Dena (Selett) Walters; m. 1st Lee Guber 1963 (divorced 1976); one adopted d.; m. 2nd Merv Adelson 1986 (divorced 1993); ed. Sarah Lawrence Coll., Bronxville, N.Y.; fmr. writer and producer with WNBC TV, then with Station WPIX and CBS TV morning broadcasts; Producer, NBC TV; joined Today programme, NBC TV 1961 as a writer, then gen. reporter, regular panel mem. 1963–74, Co-Host 1974–76; Moderator, Not for Women Only (syndicated TV programme) for five years; Corresp., ABC News, Co-Anchor of evening news programme 1976–78, Co-Host 20/20 1979–; Host Barbara Walters Specials 1976–, Ten Most Fascinating People 1994–; Co.-exec. producer The View (ABC), N.Y. 1997–; contrib. Issues and Answers; retrospective of career at Museum of Broadcasting, N.Y. 1988; Hon. L.H.D. (Ohio State Univ., Marymount Coll., New York Temple Univ., Wheaton Coll., Hofstra Univ.); Broadcaster of the Year, Int. Radio and TV Soc. 1975, Emmy Award of Nat. Acad. of TV Arts and Sciences 1975, 1983, Silver Satellite Award, American Women in Radio and TV 1985, named one of the 100 Most Important Women of the Century, Good Housekeeping 1985, Pres.'s Award, Overseas Press Club 1988, Lowell Thomas Award for Journalism 1990, 1994, Lifetime Achievement Award, Int. Women's Media Foundation 1992, and several other awards. *Publications:* How to Talk with Practically Anybody about Practically Anything 1970; contribs. to Good Housekeeping, Family Weekly, Reader's Digest. *Address:* 20/20, 147 Columbus Avenue, 10th Floor, New York, NY 10023; Barwall Productions, The Barbara Walters Specials, 825 7th Avenue, Third Floor, New York, NY 10019, U.S.A.

WALTERS, Julie; British actress; b. 22 Feb. 1950, Birmingham; d. of late Thomas Walters and Mary Bridget O'Brien; m. Grant Roffey 1998; one d.;

ed. St Pauls Prep. School, Edgbaston, Holly Lodge Grammar School for Girls, Smethwick, Manchester Poly; School Gov., Open Univ. 1990; Variety Club Best Newcomer Award 1980, Best Actress Award 1984, British Acad. Award for Best Actress 1984, Golden Globe Award 1984, Variety Club Award for Best Actress (for Stepping Out) 1991. *Stage appearances include:* Educating Rita 1980, Fool for Love 1984/85, When I was a Girl I used to Scream and Shout 1986/87, Frankie and Johnny in the Clair de Lune 1989, The Rose Tattoo 1991. *Films include:* Educating Rita 1983, She'll be Wearing Pink Pyjamas 1984, Personal Services 1986, Prick Up Your Ears 1986, Buster 1987, Mack the Knife 1988, Killing Dad 1989, Stepping Out 1991, Just Like a Woman 1992, Sister My Sister 1994, Intimate Relations 1996, Titanic Town 1997, Girls Night 1997. *TV includes:* Talent 1980, Wood and Walters 1981, Boys from the Blackstuff 1982, Say Something Happened 1982, Victoria Wood as seen on TV 1984, 1986, 1987, The Birthday Party 1986, Her Big Chance 1987, GBH 1991, Stepping Out 1991, Julie Walters and Friends 1991, Clothes in the Wardrobe 1992, Wide Eyed and Legless 1993, Bambino Mio 1993, Pat and Margaret 1994, Jake's Progress 1995, Little Red Riding Hood 1995, Intimate Relations 1996, Julie Walters is an Alien 1997, Dinner Ladies 1998, Jack and the Beanstalk 1998. *Publication:* Baby Talk 1990. *Leisure interests:* reading, travel. *Address:* c/o ICM, 76 Oxford Street, London, W1R 1RB, England.

WALTERS, Sir Peter Ingram, Kt., B.COM.; British oil executive; b. 11 March 1931, Birmingham; s. of late Stephen and of Edna F. (née Redgate) Walters; m. 1st Patricia Anne Tulloch 1960 (divorced 1991); two s. one. d.; m. 2nd Meryl Marshall 1992; ed. King Edward's School, Birmingham and Univ. of Birmingham; served R.A.S.C. 1952–54; joined BP 1954, Vice-Pres. BP North America 1965–67, Gen. Man. Supply and Devt. 1969–70, Regional Dir. Western Hemisphere 1971–72; Dir. BP Trading Ltd. 1971–73, BP Chemicals Int. 1972, Chair. 1978–90; Deputy Chair. The British Petroleum Co. Ltd. 1980–81, Chair. 1981–90; Vice-Pres. Gen. Council of British Shipping 1974–76, Pres. 1977–78; Pres. Soc. of Chemical Industry 1978–79, Inst. of Manpower Studies 1980–86; Dir. Post Office 1978–79, Nat. Westminster Bank 1981– (Deputy Chair. 1988–89); Dir. Thorn EMI (now EMI) 1989–, Deputy Chair. 1990–; Dir. SmithKline Beecham PLC 1989–, Deputy Chair. 1990–94, Chair. 1994–; Chair. Blue Circle Industries Ltd. 1990–96, Midland Bank PLC 1992; Vice-Chair. AIG Trading 1991–; Deputy Chair. HSBC Holdings 1992–; Adviser Union Bank of Switzerland 1990–; Dir. (non-exec.) Saatchi and Saatchi 1993; mem. of Council, Industrial Soc.; Gov. London Business School 1981–91; Pres. Inst. of Dirs. 1986–92; Trustee, mem. Foundation Bd. Nat. Maritime Museum 1982–83; Chair. Int. Man. Inst., Geneva 1984–86; Hon. D. Univ. (Stirling) 1987. *Leisure interests:* golf, gardening, sailing. *Address:* SmithKline Beecham PLC, New Horizons Court, Brentford, TW8 9EP; 22 Hill Street, London, W1X 7FU, England. *Telephone:* 0181-975 2000. *Fax:* 0181-975-2040.

WALTERS, Sir Roger Talbot, K.B.E., F.R.I.B.A., F.I.STRUCT.E.; British architect; b. 31 March 1917, Chorley Wood, Herts.; s. of Alfred Bernard Walters; m. Claire Myfanwy Chappell 1976; ed. Oundle School, Architectural Asscn. School of Architecture, Liverpool Univ. and Birkbeck Coll.; entered office of Sir. E. Owen Williams 1936; Directorate of Constructional Design, Ministry of Works 1941–43; served in Royal Engineers 1943–46; Architect, Timber Devt. Asscn. 1946–49; Prin. Asst. Architect, E. Region, British Railways 1949–59; Chief Architect (Devt.), Directorate of Works, War Office 1959–62; Deputy Dir.-Gen. Research and Devt., Ministry of Public Bldgs. and Works 1962–67, Dir.-Gen. for Production 1967–69, Controller Gen. 1969–71; Architect and Controller of Construction Services, Greater London Council 1971–78; Prin. The Self-Employed Agency 1981–83; pvt. practice 1984–87; Hon. F.A.I.A. *Address:* 46 Princess Road, London, NW1 8JL, England (Home). *Telephone:* 0171-722 3740.

WALTERS, Lieut.-Gen. Vernon Anthony; American army officer and diplomatist; b. 3 Jan. 1917, New York City; s. of Frederick J. and Laura (O'Connor) Walters; ed. St. Louis Gonzaga School, Paris, Stonyhurst Coll., England; Second Lieut. U.S. Army 1941, rising to rank of Lieut.-Gen., served N. Africa, Italy; Mil. Attaché, Brazil 1945–48; Mil. Attaché at large, Paris 1948–50; Asst. to Deputy Chief of Staff, SHAPE, Paris 1951–56; staff asst. to Pres. Eisenhower 1956–60; mem. NATO Standing group 1956–60; Army Attaché, Rome 1960–62; Defence Attaché, Rio de Janeiro 1962–67; served Viet Nam 1967; Defence Attaché, Paris 1967–72; Deputy Dir. CIA 1972–76; Roving U.S. Amb. for Special Missions 1981–85; Perm. Rep. to UN 1985–89; Amb. to Germany 1989–91; interpreter to Pres. Truman, Eisenhower, Nixon; Distinguished Service Medal with oak leaf cluster, Distinguished Intelligence Medal, Legion of Merit with oak leaf cluster, Bronze Star, Air Medal (U.S.), Army Commendation, Nat. Security Medal 1976, Commdr., Légion d'honneur, Croix de guerre with palms, War Cross (Brazil), Bronze Medal Valor (Italy), Presidential Medal of Freedom 1991. *Publication:* Silent Missions 1978.

WALTHER, Herbert, DR.RER.NAT.; German professor of physics; b. 19 Jan. 1935, Ludwigshafen; s. of Philipp Walther and Anna Lorenz; m. Margot Gröschel 1962; one s. one d.; ed. Univ. of Heidelberg and Tech. Univ. of Hannover; Asst. Univ. of Hannover 1963–68, Lecturer in Physics 1968–69; Prof. of Physics, Univ. of Bonn 1971, Univ. of Cologne 1971–75, Univ. of Munich 1975–; Dir. Max-Planck-Inst. für Quantenoptik 1981–; Vice-Pres. Max-Planck Soc. 1991–96; mem. Bavarian Acad. of Sciences, Acad. Leopoldina, Academia Europaea; Hon. mem. Loránd Eötvös Physical Soc., Hungary, Romanian Acad.; Corresp. mem.. Acad. of Sciences, Heidelberg, Nordrhein-Westfälische Akademie der Wissenschaften; Foreign Hon. mem. Acad. of Arts and Sciences; Hon. Prof. Academia Sinica, China; Dr. h.c. (Hanover Univ., Lomonosov Univ., Moscow); Max Born Prize, Inst. of Physics 1978, Einstein Prize 1988, Carl-Friedrich-Gauss Medal 1989, Townes Medal (American Optical Soc.) 1990, Michelson Medal (Franklin Inst.) 1993, King Faisal Prize for Physics 1993, Humboldt Medal, Alexander von Humboldt-Stiftung 1997, Stern Gerlach Medal, German Physical Soc. 1998, Ernst Hellmut-Vits Prize 1998. *Publications:* 8 books on laser spectroscopy and high power lasers and applications; 420 articles in professional journals. *Address:* Sektion Physik, Universität München, Am Coulombwall 1, 85748 Garching; Max-Planck-Institut für Quantenoptik, 85748 Garching (Office); Egenhoferstrasse 7a, 81243 Munich, Germany (Home). *Telephone:* (89) 2891-4142; (89) 32905-704 (Office); (89) 8349859 (Home). *Fax:* (89) 32905-200.

WALTON, Henry John, M.D., PH.D., F.R.C.P.(E), F.R.C.PSYCH., D.P.M.; British psychiatrist, physician and medical educator; b. 15 Feb. 1924, Kuruman, South Africa; m. Dr. Sula Wolff 1959; ed. Univs. of Cape Town, London and Edinburgh and Columbia Univ., New York; Registrar in Neurology and Psychiatry, Univ. of Cape Town 1946–54, Head, Dept. of Psychiatry 1957–60; Sr. Registrar, Maudsley Hosp. London 1955–57; Sr. Lecturer in Psychiatry, Univ. of Edin. 1962–70, Prof. of Psychiatry 1970–85, Prof. of Int. Medical Educ. 1986–; Ed. Medical Educ. 1976–; Pres. Asscn. for Medical Educ. in Europe 1972–86, Hon. Life Pres. 1986–; Pres. World Fed. for Medical Educ. 1983–97, mem. Exec. Bd. 1997–; frequent consultant to WHO and mem. Advisory Panel on Health Manpower; led worldwide inquiry into training of doctors since 1983; presided at World Summit on Medical Educ., Edin. 1988, 1993, organized six Regional Confs. 1994–95; Dir. Edin. Printmakers; mem. Soc. of Medical Studies of Greece; Academician, Acad. of Medical Sciences of Buenos Aires, Polish Acad. of Medicine, Royal Acad. of Medicine of Belgium; Foundation mem. Nat. Asscn. for Medical Educ. of Czechoslovakia; Hon. M.D. (Uppsala, New Univ. of Lisbon, Tucuman); Hermann Salhi Medal, Univ. of Berne 1976, Thureus Prize, Swedish Acad. of Medical Sciences 1982, De Lancey Prize, Royal Soc. of Medicine 1984, Jofre Medal, Spanish Soc. for Advancement of Psychiatry 1985, WHO Medal 1988, Medicus Magnus Medal, Polish Acad. of Medicine. *Publications:* Alcoholism (with N. Kessel) 1966, 1988, Small Group Psychotherapy (Ed.) 1974, Dictionary of Psychiatry (Ed.) 1985, Newer Developments in Assessing Clinical Competence (Ed. with others), Problem-based Learning (Ed. with M. B. Matthews) 1988, Proc. of World Summit on Medical Educ. (Ed.) 1994. *Leisure interests:* literature, visual arts, particularly Western painting, Chinese and Japanese art. *Address:* 38 Blacket Place, Edinburgh, EH9 1RL, Scotland. *Telephone:* (0131) 667 7811. *Fax:* (0131) 662 0337.

WALTON OF DETCHANT, Baron (Life Peer), cr. 1989, of Detchant in the County of Northumberland; **John Nicholas Walton,** Kt., T.D., M.A., M.D., D.SC., F.R.C.P.; British neurologist; b. 16 Sept. 1922, Rowlands Gill, Co. Durham; s. of Herbert and Eleanor Watson (née Ward) Walton; m. Mary Elizabeth Harrison 1946; one s. two d.; ed. Alderman Wraith Grammar School, Spennymoor, Co. Durham, King's Coll., Medical School, Univ. of Durham; served R.A.M.C. 1947–49; Medical Registrar, Royal Victoria Infirmary, Newcastle upon Tyne 1949–51; Nuffield Foundation Travelling Fellow, Mass. Gen. Hosp., Harvard Medical School, Boston, U.S.A., King's Coll. Travelling Fellow, MRC Neurology Unit, Nat. Hosp., Queen Sq., London 1954–55; First Asst. in Neurology, Univ. of Durham (Newcastle upon Tyne) 1955–58; Consultant Neurologist, Newcastle Hosps. 1958–83; Prof. of Neurology, Univ. of Newcastle upon Tyne 1968–83, Dean of Medicine 1971–81; Warden, Green Coll., Oxford 1983–89; mem. MRC 1974–78, Gen. Medical Council (Chair. Educ. Cttee.) 1971–89, Pres. 1982–89; Chair. Muscular Dystrophy Group of G.B. 1971–95; Pres. British Medical Asscn. 1980–82; Pres. Royal Soc. of Medicine 1984–86; First Vice-Pres. World Fed. of Neurology 1981–89, Pres. 1989–97; Hon. F.A.C.P.; Hon. F.R.C.P. (Edin.); Hon. F.R.C.P. (Canada); Hon. F.R.C. Path.; Hon. F.R.C. Psych.; Hon. F.R.C.P.C.H.; Hon. Dr. de l'Univ. (Aix-Marseille) 1975; Hon. D.Sc. (Leeds) 1979, (Leicester) 1980, (Hull) 1988, (Oxford Brookes) 1994; Hon. M.D. (Sheffield) 1987, (Mahidol Univ., Thailand) 1998; Hon. D.C.L. (Newcastle) 1988; Laurea h.c. (Genoa) 1992. *Publications:* Subarachnoid Haemorrhage 1956, Polymyositis (with R. D. Adams) 1958, Oxford Companion to Medicine (Ed.) 1986, Essentials of Neurology (6th edn.) 1989, Skeletal Muscle Pathology (with F. L. Mastaglia, 2nd edn.) 1992, Brain's Diseases of the Nervous System (Ed., 10th edn.) 1993, The Spice of Life (autobiog.) 1993, Disorders of Voluntary Muscle (Ed., 6th edn.) 1994, Oxford Medical Companion (Ed.) 1994, and numerous articles in scientific journals. *Leisure interests:* music, golf, reading, cricket. *Address:* 13 Norham Gardens, Oxford, OX2 6PS, England. *Telephone:* (01865) 512492. *Fax:* (01865) 512495.

WALY, Youssef, PH.D.; Egyptian politician; b. 1930; ed. Faculty of Agric., Cairo Univ. and in U.S.A.; Reader, later Prof. Faculty of Agric., Cairo Univ.; Consultant, Ministry of Scientific Research and Ministry of Agric. and Land Reform; fmr. Agric. Planning Consultant in Libya; Deputy Prime Minister Sept. 1985–; Minister of State for Agric. and Food Security 1982–87, Minister of Agric. and Land Reclamation 1987–. *Address:* Ministry of Agriculture and Land Reclamation, Sharia Wizaret az-Ziraa, Dokki, Giza, Egypt. *Telephone:* (2) 702677.

WAMBAUGH, Joseph, M.A.; American author; b. 22 Jan. 1937, East Pittsburgh, Pa.; s. of Joseph A. Wambaugh and Anne Malloy; m. Dee Allsup 1955; two s. (one deceased), one d.; ed. Calif. State Coll. Los Angeles; served U.S. Marine Corps 1954–57; police officer, Los Angeles 1960–74; creator, TV series, Police Story 1973. *Publications:* The New Centurions 1971, The Blue Knight 1972, The Onion Field 1973, The Choirboys 1975, The Black Marble 1978, The Glitter Dome 1981, The Delta Star 1983, Lines and Shadows 1984, The Secrets of Harry Bright 1985, Echoes in the Darkness 1987, The Blooding 1989, The Golden Orange 1990, Fugitive Nights 1992, Finnegan's Week 1993, Floaters 1996.

WAMYTAN, Rock, M.A.; New Caledonian politician; b. 13 Dec. 1950, Nouméa; s. of late Benjamin Wamytan and Philomène Pidjot; three s. one d.; ed. Grand Séminaire St. Paul, Nouméa, Univ. of Lyon II and Centre d'Etudes Financières Economiques et Bancaires, Paris; fmr. Head, Office for the Devt. of the Interior and Islands; Attaché to Econ. Devt. Sec. 1988; mem. Caledonian Union; Chief, St. Louis tribal village; mem. Mt. Dore town council; mem. Southern Provincial Govt.; Deputy Speaker, Congress of New Caledonia, responsible for external relations 1989–; Vice-Pres. Kanak Socialist National Liberation Front (FLNKS) 1990, Pres. 1995; Pres. New Caledonian Diocese Pastoral Council 1996. *Address:* B.P. 288, Mont-Dore, 98810 New Caledonia. *Telephone:* 26 58 83; 27 31 29. *Fax:* 26 58 88; 27 32 04.

WAN GUOQUAN; Chinese politician; b. March 1919, Nong' an Co., Jilin Prov.; ed. Zhonghua Univ.; Perm. mem. Exec. Cttee., All-China Fed. of Industry and Commerce 1978–83; Vice-Pres. China Democratic Nat. Construction Asscn. 1983–97, Hon. Vice-Pres. 1997–; mem. 5th Nat. Cttee. CPPCC 1978–82, Perm. mem. 6th Nat. Cttee. 1983–87, 7th Nat. Cttee. 1988–92, 8th Nat. Cttee. 1993–98 (Vice-Chair. 1994–98), Vice-Chair. 9th Nat. Cttee. 1998–; Jt. Pres. China Council for Promoting Peaceful Reunification 1993–; Vice-Pres. Asscn. for Int. Understanding of China 1993–. *Address:* National Committee of Chinese People's Political Consultative Conference, 23 Taipingqiao Street, Beijing, People's Republic of China.

WAN LI; Chinese government official; (retd.); b. Dec. 1916, Dongping Co., Shandong Prov.; m. Bian Tao; four s. one d.; joined CCP 1936; trained as teacher; various posts in Dongping Co. CCP Cttee.; served on Hebei-Shangdong CCP Cttee., Deputy Dir. Financial and Econ. Cttee., Nanjing Mil. Control Comm.; Head Econ. Dept. and Dir. Construction Bureau 1947–49; Deputy Head, then Head Industrial Dept., Southwest China Mil. and Admin. Cttee.; Vice-Minister of Bldg., Minister of Urban Construction 1949–58; subsequently Sec. Beijing Municipal CCP Cttee., Deputy Mayor of Beijing, Asst. to Premier Zhou Enlai in planning and organizing work of Ten Major Projects of the Capital (including Great Hall of the People) and other important construction projects; persecuted during Cultural Revolution 1966–73; Vice-Chair. Municipal Revolutionary Cttee.; fmr. Minister of Railways, Head Provisional Leading Party mems.' group in Ministry; closely allied with Deng Xiaoping's policies; dismissed as Minister when latter fell from favour 1976; First Vice-Minister of Light Industry 1977; First Sec. Anhui Prov. CCP Cttee., Chair. Anhui Prov. Revolutionary Cttee., First Political Commissar, Anhui Mil. Area 1977–80; Vice-Premier, State Council and Chair. State Agricultural Comm., Sec. Leading Party Group, Chair. Cen. Afforestation Comm. 1982–89, State People's Air Defence Comm. 1980; Deputy to 2nd, 3rd, 4th, 5th and 7th NPC, Chair. Standing Cttee. 7th NPC 1988–93; elected mem. CCP 11th Cen. Cttee., mem. Secr. CCP 11th Cen. Cttee.; elected mem. Politburo CCP Cen. Cttee. and mem. Secr. 1982, 1987; mem. Presidium 14th Nat. Congress CCP 1992; Hon. Chair. Chinese Tennis Asscn. 1982–; Hon. Pres. Bridge Asscn. 1980–, Literature Foundation 1986–, Hon. Pres. Chinese Youth Devt. Foundation 1993–, Greening Foundation 1989–, China Environmental Protection Foundation 1993–; visited Canada and U.S.A. 1989. *Leisure interests:* tennis, bridge. *Address:* Standing Committee, National People's Congress, Tian An Men Square, Beijing, People's Republic of China.

WAN SHAOFEN; Chinese party official, economist and lawyer; b. 1930, Nanchang; ed. Zhongzheng Univ.; joined CCP 1952; Leading Sec. CCP Cttee., Jiangxi 1985–87; mem. 13th CCP Cen. Cttee. 1985–92; Chair. Prov. Women's Fed., Jiangxi 1983–85; Deputy Head United Front Work Dept. of CCP Cen. Cttee. 1988–; Vice-Chair. Overseas Chinese Affairs Cttee.; mem. CCP Cen. Discipline Inspection Comm. 1992–97, 8th NPC Standing Cttee. 1993–98, Preliminary Working Cttee. of the Preparatory Cttee. of the Hong Kong Special Admin. Region 1993–96; Vice-Chair. Internal Affairs and Judicial Cttee. of the 9th NPC 1998. *Address:* c/o Standing Committee of National People's Congress, Beijing, People's Republic of China.

WAN XUEYUAN; Chinese administrator; b. 1941, joined CCP 1964; alt. mem. 13th CCP Cen. Cttee. 1987–91; mem. 14th CCP Cen. Cttee. 1992; Gov. of Zhejiang Prov. 1994–97; Deputy Sec. CCP 9th Zhejiang Prov. Cttee. 1994–97; Vice-Minister of Personnel 1997, Head of Bureau of Foreign Experts 1997. *Address:* c/o Ministry of Personnel, 12 Hepinglizhong Jie, Dongcheng Qu, Beijing 100716, People's Republic of China.

WAN ZHEXIAN; Chinese mathematician; b. Nov. 1927; ed. Qinghua Univ.; mem. Chinese Sciences Acad. 1992. *Address:* Institute of System Science, Zhong Guan Cun, Beijing 100080, People's Republic of China.

WANAMAKER, Zoë; British actress; b. New York, U.S.A.; d. of late Sam Wanamaker and Charlotte Wanamaker; m. Gawn Grainger 1994; one step-s. one step-d.; ed. Cen. School of Speech and Drama; professional debut as Hermia in A Midsummer Night's Dream, Manchester 1970; repertory at Royal Lyceum 1971–72, Oxford Playhouse 1974–75, Nottingham 1975–76; work with R.S.C. and Nat. Theatre includes Toine in Piaf, London and New York 1980, Viola in Twelfth Night 1983, Adriana in A Comedy of Errors 1983, Kitty Duval in Time of Your Life 1983, Kattrin in Mother Courage 1984, Othello 1989, The Crucible 1990, The Last Yankee 1993; appeared as Fay in Loot, Broadway 1986, as Ellie in Terry Johnson's new play Dead Funny, London 1994, as Amanda in The Glass Menagerie, London 1995/96, Sylvia 1996, Electra, Chichester and London 1997, Princeton and Broadway 1998 (Laurence Olivier Award 1998), The Old Neighbourhood, Royal Court 1998; TV appearances include Enemies of the State, Edge of Darkness (BBC), Paradise Postponed, Poor Little Rich Girl (NBC mini-series), Love Hurts, Prime Suspect, The Widowing of Mrs. Holroyd (BBC) 1995; *films include:* The Last Ten Days of Hitler, Inside the Third Reich, The Hunger 1982, The Raggedy Rawney 1987, Wilde, Swept by the Sea 1997; Hon. Vice-Pres. Voluntary Euthanasia Soc.; Hon. D.Litt. (South Bank Univ.) 1993. *Address:* c/o Conway van Gelder Ltd, 18-21 Jermyn Street, London SW1Y 6HP, England. *Telephone:* 0171-287 0077. *Fax:* 0171-287 1940.

WANG, Charles B., B.S.; Chinese computer executive; b. 19 Aug. 1944, Shanghai; ed. Queen's Coll.; Chair., C.E.O. Computer Assocs. 1976–. *Address:* Computer Associates International Inc., 1 Computer Associates Plaza, Islandia, NY 11788, U.S.A.

WANG, Wayne; Chinese/American film director; b. 1949, Hong Kong; m. Cora Miao; ed. Coll. of Arts and Crafts, Oakland, Calif. *Films directed:* Chan is Mission, Dim Sum, Slamdance, Eat a Bowl of Tea, Life is Cheap . . . But Toilet Paper is Expensive, The Joy Luck Club, Smoke, Blue in the Face.

WANG BINGQIAN; Chinese politician; b. 1925, Li Co., Hebei Prov.; Deputy Section Chief, Auditing Div., Dept. of Finance 1948–49; Section Chief, later Dir., Vice-Minister, Minister of Finance, Cen. Govt.; Dir. Budget Dept. 1963; Deputy Minister of Finance 1973–80, Minister of Finance 1980–92; mem. 12th Cen. Cttee. CCP 1982, 13th Cen. Cttee. 1987; Pres. Accounting Soc. 1980–; Chinese Gov., World Bank 1986; Hon. Chair. Bd. of Dirs., China Investment Bank 1981–; State Councillor 1983–93; Chair. Cen. Treasury Bond Sales Promotion Cttee. 1984–; Vice-Chair. Standing Cttee. of 8th NPC 1993–98; mem. State Planning Comm. 1988–92; Hon. Pres. Auditing Soc. 1984–, China Scientific Research Soc. for Policy Study; NPC Deputy Hebei Prov. *Address:* c/o Standing Committee of National People's Congress, Beijing, People's Republic of China.

WANG CHANG-CHING, M.SC.; Taiwanese politician; b. 22 Sept. 1920, Chingshan Co., Hupeh; s. of C. S. Wang and Si Teng (deceased); m. Hsueh Chen L. Wang; one s. one d.; ed. Nat. Chiaotung Univ. and Johns Hopkins Univ.; Sr. Eng. and concurrently Div. Chief, Dept. of Communications, Taiwan Provincial Govt. 1949–58; Dir. Public Works Bureau, Taiwan Provincial Govt. 1958–69; Dir. Dept. of Public Works, Taipei City Govt. 1967–69; Vice-Minister, Ministry of Communications 1969–77; Vice-Chair. Council for Econ. Planning and Devt. 1977–84; Sec.-Gen. Exec. Yuan 1984–88; Chair. China External Trade Devt. Council 1988–; Vice-Chair. Straits Exchange Foundation 1993–. *Leisure interest:* golf. *Address:* 7th Floor, 333 Keelung Road, Sec. 1, Taipei 10548, Taiwan. *Telephone:* (02) 757-6293. *Fax:* (02) 757-6653.

WANG CHAOWEN; Chinese politician; b. 1930, Huangping, Guizhou; joined CCP 1951; Sec. Guizhou Communist Youth League 1973; Vice-Chair. Prov. Revolutionary Cttee., Guizhou 1977–79; Sec. CCP Cttee., Guizhou 1980–81, Deputy Sec. 1981–; Vice-Gov. of Guizhou 1980–83, Gov. 1983–93; Chair. Guizhou Prov. 8th People's Congress 1994–98; Chair. Nationalities Cttee. of 9th NPC 1998–; mem. 12th Cen. Cttee. CCP 1982–87, 13th Cen. Cttee. 1987–92, 14th Cen. Cttee. 1992–97; Deputy Sec. CPC 6th Guizhou Prov. Cttee. 1980–93. *Address:* The Standing Committee of the National People's Congress, 19 Xi-Jiaoming Xiang Road, Xicheng District, Beijing 100805, People's Republic of China.

WANG CHIEN-SHIEN; Taiwanese politician; b. 7 Aug. 1938, Anhwei; m. Fa-jau Su; ed. Harvard Univ., U.S.A.; Sr. Specialist Taxation & Tariff. Comm. Ministry of Finance 1971–73; Dir. 1st Div. Dept. of Taxation 1973–76, 4th Dept. Exec. Yuan 1976–80; Dir.–Gen. Dept. of Customs Admin. Ministry of Finance 1980–82, Public Finance Training Inst. 1982–84; Admin. Vice-Minister of Econ. Affairs 1984–89, Political Vice-Minister 1989–90, Minister of Finance 1990–92; mem. Legis. Yuan 1993–, Sec.-Gen. New Party 1994; Asian Finance Minister of the Year 1992. *Publications:* several works on income tax and business. *Address:* c/o New Party, 4th Floor, 65 Guang Fuh S. Road, Taipei, Taiwan. *Telephone:* (2) 7562222.

WANG DAN; Chinese dissident; imprisoned for four years for role in Tiananmen Square pro-democracy demonstrations 1989; sentenced to eleven years' imprisonment for conspiring to subvert govt. 1996.

WANG DESHUN; Chinese mime artist; b. 1938; m. Zhao Aijun; one s. one d.; fmr. street performer; with army drama co. 1960–70; joined state-run Changchun Theatre Troupe, N.E. China 1970; since 1984 has been appearing in 'modelling pantomime' show in which he adopts series of sculpture-like poses to develop a theme; has taken his show to France, Germany and Macao and China's first int. mime festival, Shanghai 1994.

WANG DEYAN; Chinese banker; b. 1931; ed. Qinhua Univ., Cen. Inst. of Finance and Econ., Beijing Foreign Languages Inst.; joined Bank of China 1953, served as Sec., Asst. Man., Deputy Gen. Man. 1953–84, Vice-Pres. 1984–85, Pres. 1985–93, Chair., Bd. Dirs. 1986–93; Dir., Council's Office of People's Bank of China, Welfare Fund for Chinese Disabled Persons; Guest Adviser, China Council for Promotion of Int. Trade; Adviser to Coordination

Group for Sino-Japanese Econ. and Trade Affairs; Vice-Chair. China Int. Finance Soc.; Hon. Dir. Research Fund for Prevention of AIDS in China; mem. Leading Group for Introduction of Foreign Capital under State Council; mem. Nat. Geographic Soc., U.S.A.; Asian Banker of 1987, Asian Finance. *Address:* Bank of China, 410 Fuchengmennei Dajie, Beijing, People's Republic of China.

WANG DEZHAO; Chinese academic; b. Aug. 1940, Wujin Co., Jiangsu Prov.; Dir. Electronics Inst., Academia Sinica 1983–; Dir. Acoustics Inst., Academia Sinica 1990–; mem. Presidium CPPCC 1989–.

WANG FOSONG; Chinese administrator and chemist; b. 1933, Xingning Co., Guangdong Prov.; ed. Wuhan Univ.; Vice-Pres. Chinese Sciences Acad. 1988; mem. 8th Nat. People's Congress 1993–, mem. Foreign Affairs Cttee. *Address:* Chinese Academy of Sciences, 52 San Li He Road, Beijing 100864, People's Republic of China.

WANG FUZHOU; Chinese mountaineer and sports administrator; b. 1931, Xihua, Henan Province; s. of Wang Daikuang and Shen Xiozhen; m. Lia Aihua; one d.; mem. of Chinese mountaineering team which conquered Mt. Everest for first time from North 1960; Sec.-Gen. Chinese Mountaineering Asscn. 1980–93, Pres. 1993–; Gen. Man. of China Int. Sports Travel Co. 1983–. *Address:* State Physical Culture and Sports Commission, 9 Tiyuguang Road, Beijing; Chinese Mountaineering Association, 10 Zuoanmen Nei Street, Beijing, People's Republic of China. *Telephone:* 7017810. *Fax:* 5114859.

WANG GANCHANG; Chinese nuclear physicist; b. 28 May 1907, Changshu, Jiangsu Prov.; m.; two s. three d.; ed. Qinhua Univ. and Berlin Univ.; Research Prof. of Nuclear Physics, Shandong and Zhejiang Univs. 1934–50, and suggested first detecting the neutrino by 7Be in 1942; Vice-Dir. Inst. of Modern Physics, Acad. of Sciences of China 1950–56; Vice-Dir. Jt. Inst. of Nuclear Research, Dubna, U.S.S.R. 1959–60, led research team and discovered anti-sigma negative hyperon 1960; working in nuclear bases in north-western deserts in 1960s, was one of group of leading scientists guiding devt. of China's first atomic bomb in 1964 and first hydrogen bomb in 1967; independently suggested the concept on inertia confine fusion by strong laser 1964; Dir. Inst. of Atomic Energy, Beijing 1978–; Vice-Chair. China Asscn. for Science and Tech. 1980–86; Hon. Pres. Soc. of Nuclear Physics 1980–, Soc. of Advanced Science and Industrial Admin.; Pres. Chinese Nuclear Soc. 1980–83, Hon. Pres. 1985–; Vice-Pres. Comm. of Science and Tech., Minister of Nuclear Industry 1983; mem. Standing Cttee. 6th NPC 1983; mem. Educ., Science, Culture and Public Health Cttee., NPC 1983; Deputy Head China-Turkey Friendship Group 1985; Hon. Pres. Research Inst. of Atomic Energy 1986–; Vice-Pres. China Asscn. for Int. Exchange of Personnel 1986–; Head China Nuclear Instruments Asscn. 1987–; Chair. Cen. Advisory Cttee., Jiusan (Sept. 3) Soc. 1989–97, Hon. Chair. 1997–; Hon. Ph.D. (Moscow) 1990; Natural Science Award (First Class) 1982. *Address:* Chinese Nuclear Society, P.O. Box 2125, Beijing, People's Republic of China.

WANG GUANGYING; Chinese business executive; b. 1919, Beijing; m. 1943; ed. Catholic Fudan Univ.; set up own business in Tianjin 1943; Vice-Chair. China Democratic Nat. Construction Asscn. 1954; gaoled for eight years during cultural revolution 1967–75; Vice-Chair. All China Fed. of Industry and Commerce 1982, Hon. Chair. 1993–; f., Chair. and Pres. China Everbright Co. (China's first trans-nat. corpn.), Hong Kong 1983–90; Exec. Chair. Presidium CPPCC 1983–; Vice-Chair. 6th CPPCC 1983–87, 7th CPPCC 1988–, Standing Cttee. of 8th NPC 1993–98, 9th NPC 1998–; NPC Deputy Tianjin Municipality; a Pres. China Council for Promoting Peaceful Reunification 1990–; Hon. Vice-Chair. Red Cross Soc. of China 1994–. *Address:* All China Federation of Industry and Commerce, 93 Beiheyan Dajie, Beijing, People's Republic of China.

WANG GUNGWU, C.B.E., PH.D., F.A.H.A.; historian and university vice-chancellor; b. 9 Oct. 1930, Indonesia; s. of Wang Fo Wen and Ting Yien; m. Margaret Lim Ping-Ting 1955; one s. two d.; ed. Nat. Central Univ., Nanjing, Univ. of Malaya and Univ. of London; Asst. Lecturer Univ. of Malaya, Singapore 1957–59, lecturer 1959; lecturer, Univ. of Malaya, Kuala Lumpur 1959–61, Sr. Lecturer 1961–63, Dean of Arts 1962–63, Prof. of History 1963–68; Rockefeller Fellow, Univ. of London 1961–62, Sr. Visiting Fellow 1972; Prof. of Far Eastern History, A.N.U. 1968–86, Emer. Prof. 1986–, Dir. Research School of Pacific Studies 1975–80; Visiting Fellow, All Souls Coll. Oxford 1974–75; John A. Burns Distinguished Visiting Prof. of History, Univ. of Hawaii 1979; Rose Morgan Visiting Prof. of History, Univ. of Kansas 1983; Vice-Chancellor, Univ. of Hong Kong 1986–95; Chair. Inst. of E. Asian Political Economy, Nat. Univ. of Singapore 1996–97, Dir. East Asian Inst. 1997–; Distinguished Sr. Fellow Inst. of Southeast Asian Studies, Singapore 1996–; Fellow and Hon. Corresp. mem. for Hong Kong of Royal Soc. of Arts 1987–95; Pres. Australian Acad. of the Humanities 1980–83, Asian Studies Asscn. of Australia 1978–80; Chair. Australia-China Council 1984–86, Environmental Pollution Advisory Cttee. 1988–95, Council for the Performing Arts 1989–94, Asia-Pacific Council, Griffith Univ. 1997–; mem. Exec. Council, Hong Kong 1990–92; Adviser Chinese Heritage Centre, Nanyang Tech. Univ. 1995–, Southeast Asian Studies, Academia Sinica, Taipei 1994–; mem. Council Int. Inst. for Strategic Studies, London 1992–; mem. Nat. Arts Council, Singapore 1996–, Nat. Heritage Bd. 1997–, Nat. Library Bd. 1997–; mem. Academia Sinica; Foreign Hon. mem. American Acad. of Arts and Science; Hon. Fellow S.O.A.S., London; Hon. Sr. Fellow Chinese Acad. of Social Sciences, Beijing; Hon. Prof. Beijing Univ., Fudan Univ.; Hon. D.Litt. (Sydney), Hon. LL.D. (Monash, A.N.U., Melbourne), D. Univ. (Griffith, Soka). *Publications:* 17 books, including The Chineseness of China 1991, China and the Chinese Overseas 1991, Community and Nation: China, South-East Asia and Australia 1992, Zhongguo yu Haiwai Huaren 1994, The Chinese Way: China's Position in International Relations 1995; Hong Kong's Transition: A Decade after the Deal (Ed.) 1995, Global History and Migrations 1997, The Nanhai Trade 1998; also numerous articles on Chinese and South-East Asian history; Gen. Ed. East Asian Historical Monographs series. *Leisure interests:* music, reading, walking. *Address:* East Asian Institute, Block AS5, National University of Singapore, Kent Ridge Crescent, Singapore 119260. *Telephone:* 7752033. *Fax:* 7793409.

WANG HAI, Gen; Chinese army officer; b. 1925, Weihai City, Shandong Prov.; ed. China's North-East Aviation Acad.; joined PLA 1945; Group Commdr., air force brigade and sent to Korean battlefield 1950; promoted Col. PLA 1964; Commdr., Air Force of Guangzhou Mil. Region 1975–83; Deputy Commdr., PLA Air Force 1983–85; Commdr., PLA Air Force 1985; mem., CCP 12th Cen. Cttee. 1985–87, 13th Cen. Cttee. 1987–92, 14th Cen. Cttee. 1992–; promoted Gen. PLA 1988. *Address:* Ministry of Defence, Beijing, People's Republic of China.

WANG HANBIN; Chinese state and party official; b. 28 Aug. 1925, Fujian Prov.; m. Peng Peiyun; two s. two d.; joined CCP in Burma 1941; Deputy Sec.-Gen. NPC Legal Comm. 1979–80; Vice-Chair. and Sec.-Gen. NPC Legal Comm. 1980–83; Deputy Sec.-Gen., Political and Legal Comm. of CCP Cen. Cttee. 1980–82, Constitution Revision Cttee. of P.R.C. 1980–82; Vice-Pres. Chinese Law Soc. 1982–91, Hon. Pres. 1991–; mem. 12th CCP Cen. Cttee. 1982–86, 13th Cen. Cttee. 1987–92, 14th Cen. Cttee. 1992–97; Sec.-Gen. NPC Standing Cttee. 1983–87, Vice-Chair. NPC 7th Standing Cttee. 1988–93; Chair. Legis. Affairs Comm. 1983–87; Vice-Chair. Cttee. for Drafting Basic Law of Hong Kong Special Admin. Zone of People's Repub. of China 1985–90, for Drafting Basic Law of Macau Special Admin. Region of People's Republic of China 1988–, Preparatory Cttee., Hong Kong Special Admin. Region 1995–97; alt. mem. Politburo CCP 1992–97; Vice-Chair. Standing Cttee. 8th NPC 1993–98. *Leisure interest:* bridge. *Address:* c/o National People's Congress Standing Committee, Beijing, People's Republic of China.

WANG JIDA; Chinese sculptor; b. 27 Oct. 1935, Beijing; s. of Wang Sho Yi and Chiu Chen Shin; m. Jin Gao 1971; one s. one d.; ed. Cen. Inst. of Fine Arts, Beijing; worked in Nei Monggol 1966, 1976–84; moved to U.S.A. 1984; exhbn. in Grand Cen. Art Gallery 1986, 1987. *Works include:* The Struggle 1987, (commissioned by Exec. Council on Foreign Diplomats), Natural Beauty 1987 (a collection of 18 pieces portraying women and animals), Statue of Liberty (commissioned by Statue of Liberty/Ellis Island Foundation), several monumental sculptures in Chairman Mao's image, in China; Asst. Dir. Standing Council, Nei Monggol Sculptors' Asscn.; mem., Chinese Artist's Asscn., American Nat. Sculpture Soc. 1988–; Honour Prize, China 1977. *Leisure interests:* athletics, music, literature. *Address:* Inner Mongolia Artist's Association, 33 W Street, Hohhot, Inner Mongolia, People's Republic of China; 76-12 35th Avenue, Apartment 3E, Jackson Heights, NY 11372, U.S.A. *Telephone:* 25775 (China); (718) 651 3944 (U.S.A.).

WANG JIYING, Vice-Adm.; Chinese naval officer; b. 1933, Jiyuan City, Henan Prov.; ed. Navy Submarine School and Naval Acad; joined CCP and PLA 1950; served as naval boat mechanic leader 1956; served as capt., deputy chief of staff of naval boat detachment and naval boat detachment leader; grad. from Naval Acad. 1983; Deputy Commdr. PLA Navy's E. China Sea Fleet 1983–93; Commdr. N. China Sea Fleet 1993–; Deputy Commdr. Jinan Mil Region; rank of Rear Adm. 1988; PLA del. to 8th NPC. *Address:* Ministry of National Defence, Jingshanqian Jie, Beijing, People's Republic of China.

WANG JUN; Chinese business executive; s. of late Wang Zhen; joined China Int. Trust and Investment Corpn. (CITIC) 1979, served as Deputy Gen. Man. then Gen. Man. Business Dept., Vice-Pres., Vice-Chair. and Pres. CITIC Hong Kong (Holdings), Vice-Pres. CITIC 1986–93, Pres. 1993–95, Chair. of Bd. 1995–; Chair. Bd. of Dirs. Poly Group 1991–, Planning Comm. Gansu Prov. People's Govt.; Chief Procurator Guangdong Prov. People's Procuratorate. *Address:* China International Trust and Investment Corporation (CITIC), Capital Mansion, 6 Xianyuan Nan Ju, Chaoyang Qu, Beijing 100004, People's Republic of China. *Telephone:* (1) 4660088. *Fax:* (1) 4661186.

WANG JUNXIA; Chinese athlete; b. Jan. 1973, Dalian, Liaoning Prov.; set new world record for women's 10,000 m race and 1,500 m race in 1993, won Gold Medal in women's 5,000 m race in the 26th Olympics in Atlanta. *Address:* c/o State General Bureau for Physical Culture and Sports, 9 Tiyuguan Road, Chongwen District, Beijing, People's Republic of China.

WANG KE, Gen.; Chinese army officer; b. Aug. 1931, Xiaoxian Co., Jiangsu Prov.; joined CCP-led armed work team 1944; joined CCP 1947; ed PLA Military Acad.; took part in the Korean War 1953; Div. Commdr., Army Group Commdr. 1980–86; Vice-Commdr. Xinjiang Mil. Area Command 1986–90; Vice-Commdr. Lanzhou Mil. Area Command, Commdr. Xinjiang Mil. Area Command 1990–92; rank of Lieut.-Gen. 1988, Gen. 1994; mem. 14th CCP Cen. Cttee. 1992, mem. 15th CCP Cen. Cttee. 1997–; Commdr. Shenyang Mil. Area Command 1992–95; mem. Cen. Mil. Comm. 1995–; Dir. PLA Gen. Logistics Dept. 1995–. *Address:* People's Liberation Army General Logistics Department, Beijing, People's Republic of China.

WANG KEFEN; Chinese dance historian; b. 1 April 1927, Yunyang, Sichuan; d. of Wang Baifan and Liao Huiqing; m. Zhang Wengang 1949; one s. one d.; Research Fellow, Inst. of Dance, China Nat. Arts Acad. (CNAA) 1977–. *Publications:* The History of Chinese Dance 1980, The Stories of Ancient Chinese Dancers 1983, The History of Chinese Dance: Ming Dynasty, Qing Dynasty 1984, Sui Dynasty and Tang Dynasty 1987 (CNAA Research Excellence Award 1989), The History of Chinese Dance Development (CNAA Research Excellence Award 1994); Dictionary of Chinese Dance (Chief Ed.) (Nat. Award for Best Dictionary 1995); Chief Ed. on subject of dance in 10 vol. History of Chinese Civilization (Nat. Award for Best Book 1994); Sui and Tang Culture (Co-Ed. and contrib.) 1990 (Social Science Book Award 1992), Chinese Dance of the 20th Century 1991 (Nat. Best Book Award 1993), Buddhism and Chinese Dance 1991, Chinese Ancient Dance History (Co-author), The Past and Future of Chinese Dance, The Chinese Contemporary History of Dance 1840–1996 (Ed. in chief) and other works on Chinese Dance. *Leisure interests:* choreography and dance. *Address:* 1601-4 Building, Changyungong, Xi Sahuan Bei Lu, Beijing 100044, People's Republic of China. *Telephone:* (10) 68411250.

WANG LEQUAN; Chinese politician; b. Dec. 1944, Shouguang Co., Shandong Prov.; joined CCP 1966; Vice-Sec. Communist Youth League Shandong Provincial Cttee.; Vice-Sec. then Sec. CCP Liaocheng Prefectural Cttee.; Vice-Gov. Shandong Prov.; alt. mem. 14th CCP Cen. Cttee. 1992; Vice-Sec. CCP Xinjiang Uygur Autonomous Regional Cttee., Vice-Chair. Xinjiang Uygur Autonomous Region 1993, then Sec. CCP Xinjiang Uygur Autonomous Regional Cttee.; mem. 15th CCP Cen. Cttee. 1997–. *Address:* Chinese Communist Party Xinjiang Uygur Autonomous Regional Committee, Urumqi City, Xinjiang Uygur Autonomous Region, People's Republic of China.

WANG LIANZHENG; Chinese agronomist and administrator; b. 15 Oct. 1930, Haicheng, Liaoning Prov.; s. of Wang Dianche and Wang Youzhen; m. Li Shuzhen 1959; two d.; ed. Northeast Agricultural Coll., Harbin and Moscow Timiryazeev Agricultural Acad.; Asst. Prof. Heilonjiang Acad. of Agricultural Sciences (HAAS) 1964–78, Assoc. Prof. 1979–82, Prof. 1983–; Dir. Soybean and Crop Breeding Inst. HAAS 1970–78; Vice-Pres. HAAS 1978–82, Pres. 1983–86, Pres. and Prof. Grad. School CAAS 1988–95; Vice-Gov. Heilonjiang Prov. (in charge of Agricultural Production, Science and Tech.) 1983–87; Vice-Minister of Agric. 1988–91; mem. Agricultural Devt. Group at State Council 1988–93; mem. and Convenor Plant Genetics, Breeding, Cultivation Academic Degree Cttee. at State Council 1991–96; Pres. Chinese Acad. of Agricultural Sciences (CAAS) 1987–94, Hon. Chair. Acad. Cttee. of CAAS 1995–; Vice-Chair. Chinese Crop Science Soc. 1988–94, Chair. 1994–; Vice-Chair. Scientific Tech. Cttee. (Ministry of Agric.) 1988–96, Chinese Cttee. for Release of New Crop Varieties 1989–96, China Asscn. for Science and Tech. 1991–, Heilonjiang Asscn. of Science and Tech., Chinese Asscn. of Agricultural Science Socs.; Chair. China Int. Exchange Asscn. of Agricultural Science and Tech. 1992–96; mem. Bd. IFAD, CABI 1994–; Co-Chair. Advisory Cttee. China-EC Centre for Agricultural Tech. 1992–97; mem. Chinese dels. to numerous int. confs.; has developed 10 soyabean cultivars; Foreign mem. Russian Acad. of Agricultural Sciences; Foreign Fellow Indian Nat. Acad. of Agricultural Sciences; Second Class Chinese State Prize for Invention, for new soyabean cultivar "Heinong 26", Second Class Chinese State Prize for Invention, for new potato cultivar "Kexin No. 1", First Class Prize for Scientific Progress, Ministry of Agric.; Second Class Heilongjiang Prov. Prize for Tech. Progress, for high-yielding high-protein soyabean cultivar "Heinong 35" 1994. *Publications:* Feeding a Billion (co-author) 1987, Soyabean Breeding and Genetics (Ed.-in-chief) 1992, Agriculture in Modern China (Co-ed.) 1992, Soyabean Cultivation for High Yielding (Ed.-in-chief) 1994, and more than 124 papers. *Leisure interest:* classical music. *Address:* Chinese Academy of Agricultural Sciences, 30 Baishiqiao Road, Haidian District, Beijing 100081, People's Republic of China. *Telephone:* (010) 62173585; (010) 62172991. *Fax:* (010) 62174142.

WANG LINXIANG; Chinese business executive; b. 1951, Baotou, Nei Monggol Autonomous Region; joined CCP 1974; Dir. Erdos Cashmere Sweater Mill 1983–89; Pres. Erdos Group 1989–. *Address:* Erdos Group, Baotou, Nei Monggol, People's Republic of China.

WANG LUOLIN; Chinese economist; b. June 1938, Wuchang City., Hunan Prov.; ed. Beijing Univ.; joined CCP 1978; Asst. Lecturer, Lecturer, Assoc. Prof. Amoy Univ. 1961–84; Vice-Pres. Amoy Univ. 1984 then Vice-Pres. Chinese Acad. of Social Sciences; alt. mem. 13th CCP Cen. Cttee. 1987, mem. 14th CCP Cen. Cttee. 1992; 15th CCP Cen. Cttee. 1997–. *Address:* Chinese Academy of Social Sciences, Jianguomennei Dajie 5 Hao, Beijing 100732, People's Republic of China.

WANG MAOLIN; Chinese party and government official; b. 1935, Qidong, Jiangsu; ed. Shanghai Financial and Econ. Coll.; Vice-Chair. Shanxi Prov. Revolutionary Cttee. 1977–78; Vice-Gov. Shanxi Prov. 1979–88; Vice-Chair. Shanxi Prov. People's Congress 1981–88; Deputy Sec. Shanxi Prov. Cttee. 1988–91, Sec. 1991; Chair. CPPCC 7th Shanxi Prov. Cttee. 1993; Sec. CPC 7th Hunan Prov. Cttee. 1993–98; mem. CCP 13th Cen. Cttee. 1987–92, 14th Cen. Cttee. 1992–97; mem. 15th CCP Cen. Cttee. 1997–. *Address:* c/o Central Committee of the Chinese Communist Party, Zhongnanhai, Beijing, People's Republic of China.

WANG MAORUN, Gen.; Chinese army officer; b. May 1936, Rongcheng, Shandong Prov.; joined PLA 1951; mem. CCP 1956–; ed. PLA Mil. Acad.; staff officer, Qingdao Garrison 1962; various posts in a corps political dept. 1969–73; Deputy Sec.-Gen. Political Dept. Jinan Mil. Region 1973–76; dir. of a corps political dept. 1976–83; corps deputy political commissar 1983–85; Dir. Political Dept. PLA Lanzhou Mil. Region 1985–90; Deputy Political Commissar and Sec. CCP Comm. for Inspecting Discipline, Lanzhou Mil. Region 1990; Political Commissar, Nat. Defence Univ. 1995–; rank of Gen. 1998; mem. 15th CCP Cen. Cttee. 1997–. *Address:* National Defence University, Beijing, People's Republic of China.

WANG MENG; Chinese politician and writer; b. 15 Oct. 1934, Beijing; s. of Wang Jindi and Tong Min; m. Cui Ruifang 1957; two s. one d.; criticized 1957–76; rehabilitated 1979; Alt. mem. 12th Cen. Cttee. CCP 1982, mem. 12th Cen. Cttee. CCP 1985, mem. 13th Cen. Cttee. 1987–92; Minister of Culture 1986–89; mem. Secr. Chinese Writers' Asscn. 1981–86, Vice-Chair. 1985–; Vice-Pres. China PEN Centre 1982–; Vice-Pres. Asscn. for Int. Understanding 1985–; Chief Ed. People's Literature 1983–86; mem CPPCC 8th Nat. Cttee. March 1994–. *Publications include:* The Young Newcomer in the Organization Department 1956, Long Live the Youth 1957, Bolshevik State: A Modernist Chinese Novel 1979, The Barber's Tale 1979, A Night in the City 1979, A Spate of Visitors 1980, The Butterfly 1980, The Metamorphosis of Human Nature 1986, Selected Works (Vols. I–IV) 1986, Adventures of a Soccer Star 1990, You Can Come into My Dream Again 1991, Revelation from The Dream of Red Mansion 1991, Notes on Styles (collection of literary criticisms) 1991, The Seasons for Love 1992, Hard Gruel (short stories) 1992. *Leisure interests:* swimming, drinking. *Address:* China PEN, Shatan Beijie 2, Beijing, People's Republic of China.

WANG MENGKUI; Chinese academic; b. April 1938, Wenxian Co., Henan Prov.; joined CCP 1956; ed. Beijing Univ.; Assoc. Research Fellow then Research Fellow Research Office of Secr. CCP Cen. Cttee. 1981–87; Exec. Vice-Dir. Econs. Research Centre of State Planning Comm. 1987; Vice-Dir. Research Office of State Council 1990, Dir. 1995–; alt. mem. 14th CCP Cen. Cttee. 1992; mem. 15th CCP Cen. Cttee. 1997–. *Address:* Research Office of the State Council, Beijing, People's Republic of China.

WANG QIMIN; Chinese business executive; b. 1937; ed. Beijing Petroleum Inst.; joined CCP 1978; technician, Vice-Chief Geologist, Sr. Engineer and then Vice-Pres. Oilfield Devt. Research Inst. of Daqing Oilfield 1961–96, Pres. 1996–. *Address:* Oilfield Development Research Institute, Daqing, Heilongjiang Province, People's Republic of China.

WANG RUILIN, Gen.; Chinese army officer and party official; b. Dec. 1929, Zhaoyuan Co., Shandong Prov.; joined PLA 1946, CCP 1947; decoder and staff officer, Confidential Div., PLA Northeast Mil. Dist. 1947–49; Deputy Section Chief, Confidential Div., Govt. Admin. Council 1949–52; Sec. Office of Vice-Premier Deng Xiaoping 1973–76; Dir. Vice-Chairmen's Office of CCP Cen. Cttee. Mil. Comm., Chair.'s Office; Deputy Dir. of Gen. Office, CCP Cen. Cttee. 1983–97, Vice-Dir. PLA Gen. Political Dept. 1992– (concurrently Dir. Office of Deng Xiaoping –1997); rank of Lieut.-Gen. 1988; mem. 13th CCP Cen. Cttee. 1987–92; Sec. Comm. for Discipline Inspection CCP Cen. Cttee. Mil. Comm. 1990–93; mem. 14th CCP Cen. Cttee. 1992–97, mem. Cen. Mil. Comm. 1995–; mem. 15th CCP Cen. Cttee. 1997–. *Address:* Central Office, Chinese Communist Party Central Committee, Beijing, People's Republic of China.

WANG SENHAO; Chinese government official; b. 1932, Cixi, Zhejiang; two s.; Deputy Sec. CCP Cttee., Shaanxi 1983–93; Gov. of Shaanxi Prov. 1983–93; Minister of Coal Industry 1993–98; mem. CCP 12th Cen. Cttee. 1985–87, 13th Cen. Cttee. 1987–92, 14th Cen. Cttee. 1992–97; Chair. Soc. and the Rule of Law Cttee., 9th Nat. Cttee. of CPPCC 1998–. *Address:* National Committee of Chinese People's Political Consultative Conference, 23 Taipingqiao Street, Beijing, People's Republic of China.

WANG SHOUGUAN; Chinese astronomer and university professor; b. 15 Jan. 1923, Fuzhou; s. of B. L. Wang and S. Y. Gao; m. Lin Zhihuan 1955; one s. one d.; Deputy Head, Div. of Math. and Physics, Chinese Acad. of Sciences 1981–; Prof., Beijing Normal Univ. 1987–, Univ. of Science and Tech. of China 1991–; Hon. Dir. Beijing Astronomical Observatory 1987–; Hon. Pres. Chinese Astronomical Soc. 1988–; Chief Ed. Vol. Astronomy, Chinese Encyclopaedia 1980; Chief Ed. Astrophysics Sinica; mem. Chinese Acad. of Sciences 1981; Nat. Science Congress Award 1978, Nat. Science and Tech. Progress Award 1985. *Leisure interest:* poetry. *Address:* No. 404, Block 808, Zhong-Guan-Cun, Beijing 100080, People's Republic of China. *Telephone:* 28-5228.

WANG TAIHUA; Chinese politician; b. Oct. 1945, Xingguo, Jiangxi Prov.; ed. Jiangxi Teachers Coll.; joined CCP 1973; Vice-Sec. CCP Anhui Prov. Cttee. and Sec. CCP Hefei City Cttee. 1992–98; Deputy Gov. Anhui Prov. 1998–; alt. mem. CCP 14th and 15th Cen. Cttee. 1992–. *Address:* Anhui Provincial People's Government, 1 Changjiang Road, Hefei, Anhui Province, People's Republic of China.

WANG TAO; Chinese politician and geologist; b. 1931, Leting, Hebei; Chief Geologist, Dagang Oil Field; Chief Geologist, Liaohe Petroleum Prospecting Bureau; Gen. Man., South China Sea Eastern Br. of China Nat. Offshore Oil Corpn.; Minister of Petroleum Industry 1985–88; Pres. China Nat. Petroleum Corpn. 1988–97; mem. CCP 12th Cen. Cttee 1985–87, 13th Cen. Cttee. 1987–92, 14th Cen. Cttee. 1992–97, Vice-Chair. Environment and Resources Protection Cttee., 9th NPC 1998–. *Address:* c/o Standing Committee of the National People's Congress, Beijing, People's Republic of China.

WANG TIAN-REN; Chinese sculptor, artist and calligrapher; b. 26 July 1939, Henan; s. of Zheng-gang Wang and Shu-zheng Ren; m. Zhang Pei 1969; one s.; ed. Xi'an Acad. of Fine Arts; worked as art designer and sculptor at Shaanxi Exhbn. Hall 1963–79, worked on construction 1964–65; cr. sculptures for Yanan Revolution Memorial Hall 1968–71; dir. group sculptures for Shaanxi Exhbn. Hall 1972–75; participated in group sculptures for Chairman Mao Memorial Hall 1976–78; *works include:* Hou Ji 1980–81, Flower, The Morning Rooster, Qin Ox, Zebra, Tang Dynasty Musicians in Nishang and Yuyi (Copper Medal, Nat. City Sculptures Designing Exhbn. 1983), Letter Carrier Goose (Copper Medal, Nat. City Sculptures Designing Exhbn. 1983), Biaoqi General of Han Dynasty Huo Qu-bing' (Excellent Prize, 6th Nat. Art Works Exhbn. 1984, First Prize, Shaanxi Art Works Exhbn. 1984), Rising to the Sky (for Urumuqi, Xinjing; Prize for Excellence, Nat. Ministry of Urban Construction, Nat. Asscn. of Artists 1987) 1985, Qin Unification 1992, Unification of Qin Dynasty (selected for 2nd Nat. City Sculpture, Nat. Prize from Nat. Construction Ministry, Ministry of Culture and Asscn. of Nat Artists) 1994, Yu Youren (selected for 8th Nat. Arts Exhbn.) 1994, sign sculpture for Xijiang Chemical Fertilizer Factory 1995, civic scenery sculpture for Hejin, Shaanxi Prov. 1995, Soar Aloft (sign sculpture for Xi'an Yanliang city) 1996, Zhao Hongzhang (granite-sculpture) 1996, Hou Ji (stone sculpture for Shaanxi) 1996, large city sign sculpture for Shanxi 1996; calligraphy works exhibited in Chinese and Japanese cities; Pres. Shaanxi Sculpture Inst. 1995–; Vice-Dir. of Sculpture Art Cttee., Shaanxi Br. Nat. Asscn. of Artists; Art Dir., Dir. of Creation Office, Shaanxi Sculpture Inst.; mem., Nat. Calligraphers Asscn., Shaanxi Folk Art Inst., Shaanxi Industrial Artists Asscn. *Leisure interests:* Chinese classical literature, poetry, music. *Address:* Shaanxi Sculpture Institute, Longshoucun, Xi'an, Shaanxi 710016, People's Republic of China. *Telephone:* (29) 6261002 (Office); (29) 6253551 (Home). *Fax:* (29) 3237768.

WANG TINGDONG; Chinese politician; b. 1925, Pingding Co., Shanxi Prov.; Chair. Standing Cttee. of Shanxi Prov. People's Congress 1993. *Address:* Standing Committee of Shanxi Provincial People's Congress, Taiyuan City, People's Republic of China.

WANG WEICHENG; Chinese party official; b. 1929, Tonglu Co., Zhejiang Prov.; joined CCP 1948; Deputy head of Propaganda Dept. CCP Cen. Cttee. 1987; Dir. Cen. Policy Research Center 1989–; mem. 14th CCP Cen. Cttee. 1992–97; Vice-Pres. China Asscn. for Int. Exchange of Personnel, Soc. for study of Workers' Political and Ideological Work; Chair. Legal Affairs Cttee. of 9th NPC 1998–. *Address:* c/o Standing Committee of National People's Congress, Beijing, People's Republic of China.

WANG WENSHI; Chinese writer; b. 21 Nov. 1921, Shanxi Prov.; s. of Wang Zhitong and Cui Jinxiu; m. Gao Bin 1949; two s. one d. *Publications:* Comrade-in-Arms (opera libretto), The Night of Wind and Snow, Hei Feng (novel), The Dunes, New Acquaintance, Yiyun Ji (Echo the Views of Others: essay), Wang Wenshi's Prose, Selected Short Stories. *Leisure interests:* playing marjang pieces, calligraphy. *Address:* Union of Chinese Writers, Shaanxi Branch Xi'an, Shaanxi Province, People's Republic of China.

WANG WENYUAN; Chinese politician and economist; b. Feb. 1931, Huangpi, Hubei Prov.; ed. Northeast Finance and Econs. Inst.; teaching asst., lecturer, Assoc. Prof., Prof. and Head, Econs. Dept. of Liaoning Univ. 1958–88; Vice-Gov. of Liaoning Prov. 1988–92; Vice-Chair. Cen. Cttee. of Jiu San Soc. 1988–; Vice-Chair. Supreme People's Procuratorate 1992–98; Vice-Chair. Nat. Cttee. of CPPCC 1998–. *Address:* National Committee of Chinese People's Political Consultative Conference, 23 Taipingqiao Street, Beijing, People's Republic of China.

WANG XIANJIN; Chinese politician; b. 1930, Haiyang, Shandong; fmr. Vice-Sec. Jilin, concurrently Dir. State Bureau of Land Admin.; Pres. Asscn. of Land Valuers of China 1994–. *Address:* Association of Land Valuers of China, Beijing, People's Republic of China.

WANG XIAOFENG; Chinese politician; b. Oct. 1944, Cili Co., Hunan Prov.; ed. Beijing Mining Inst.; joined CCP 1973; Vice-Sec. CCP Changde Prefectural Cttee., Commdr. Changde Prefectural Admin. Comm. 1983; Dir. Hunan Provincial Planning Comm. 1986; Vice-Gov. Hunan 1990; Vice-Sec. CCP Hunan Prov. Cttee. 1992; alt. mem. 14th CCP Cen. Cttee. 1992–97; Vice-Sec. CCP Hainan Provincial Cttee.; Vice-Gov. Hainan Prov. 1993–98, Gov. 1998–; mem. 15th CCP Cen. Cttee. 1997–. *Address:* Office of the Governor, Haikou City, Hainan Province, People's Republic of China.

WANG XIAOGUANG; Chinese jurist; b. 1924, Anguo, Hebei; Deputy Procurator-Gen. 1983; mem. CCP Discipline Inspection Comm. 1982; Sec. Party Cttee. Beijing Univ. 1985; Deputy Procurator Gen., Supreme People's Procuratorate, Pres. Soc. of Procuratorial Work; NPC Deputy Hebei Prov.; mem. 8th NPC 1993–, Internal and Judicial Affairs Cttee. *Address:* Supreme People's Procuratorate, Beijing, People's Republic of China.

WANG XUAN; Chinese computer scientist; b. 5 Feb. 1937, Shanghai; s. of Wang Shou-Qi and Zhou Miao-Qin; m. Chen Kun-Qiu 1967; Prof. and Dir. Research Inst. of Computer Tech., Peking Univ.; mem. Chinese Acad. of Sciences 1992–, Third World Acad. of Sciences 1993–, Chinese Acad. of Eng. 1994–; Science and Tech. Progress Award, UNESCO Science Prize 1995; Vice-Chair. Cttee. of Educ., Science and Public Health of 9th NPC 1998–. *Leisure interests:* Peking Opera, sightseeing. *Address:* Research Institute of Computer Technology, Peking University, Beijing 100871, People's Republic of China. *Telephone:* 10-62981435. *Fax:* 10-62981501.

WANG XUEBING; Chinese banker; with Peoples' Bank of China, mainly in overseas brs. (Dir. New York Br. for 5 years) 1976–93, Chair. Bd. of Dirs. Bank of China Dec. 1993–; Vice-Gen. Man. Everbright Group April–Dec. 1993. *Address:* Bank of China, 410 Fu Cheng Men Nei Dajie, Beijing 100818, People's Republic of China. *Telephone:* (10) 6601-6688. *Fax:* (10) 6601-6869.

WANG YONGGUO; Chinese naval officer; fmr. Commdr. PLA Navy East China Sea Fleet, Zhoushan Base; Deputy Commdr. PLA Navy East China Sea Fleet 1993–95; Commdr. South China Sea Fleet 1995–; Deputy Commdr. Guangzhou Mil. Region. *Address:* c/o Ministry of National Defence, Jingshanqian Jie, Beijing, People's Republic of China.

WANG YOU-TSAO, M.SC., PH.D.; Taiwanese politician; b. 2 July 1925, Chinchiang Co., Fukien; s. of Wang Hsiao-kwei and Wang-Huang Pei-feng; m. Jean Eng-ling 1954; two s. one d.; ed. Nat. Taiwan Univ., Iowa State Univ., U.S.A.; Asst., Instructor, Assoc. Prof. Dept. of Agric. Econs. Nat. Taiwan Univ. 1954–60, Prof. 1960–73; Specialist, Rural Econs. Div., Jt. Comm. on Rural Reconstruction (JCRR) 1960–63, Sr. Specialist 1965–66, Chief, Rural Econs. Div. 1966–71, Chief, Office of Planning and Programming 1971–72, Deputy Sec.-Gen. JCRR 1972–73, Sec.-Gen. 1973–79; Sec.-Gen. Council for Agric. Planning and Devt., Exec. Yuan 1979, Vice-Chair. 1979–84, Chair. 1984, Chair. and Chief Operating Admin. 1984–88, Adviser 1990–; Minister without Portfolio, Exec. Yuan 1988–90; Nat. Policy Adviser to Pres. 1990–96; Dir Asian Agric. Tech. Service Center 1993–95; Pres. Rural Devt. Foundation 1995–98 (Chair. 1998–); Chair. Bd. of Dirs. Harvest (farm magazine); mem. Agric. Asscn. of China, Rural Econs. Asscn. of China. *Publications:* Statistical Analysis of Resources Productivity in Shihmen Reservoir Area of Taiwan 1963, Technological Changes and Agricultural Development of Taiwan 1946–65 1966. *Address:* Council of Agriculture, Executive Yuan, 37 Nanhai Road, Taipei 100 (Office); 14-6 Alley 1, Lane 194, Sect. 4, Chung Hsiao East Road, Taipei, Taiwan (Home).

WANG YUAN; Chinese mathematician; b. 30 April 1930; Dir. Inst. of Math., Acad. Sinica March–Oct. 1985; mem. Dept. of Math. and Physics, Acad. Sinica 1985–; mem. Nat. Cttee. 6th CPPCC 1986; Pres. Mathematics Soc. 1989–; Deputy Dir. State Pharmaceutical Admin. 1991–; mem. Presidium Chinese Acad. of Sciences 1996–. *Address:* Institute of Mathematics, Academia Sinica, Zhong Guan Cun, Beijing 100080, People's Republic of China.

WANG YUEFENG; Chinese politician; b. 1930, Qiangzhong Co., Hainandao; joined CCP 1951; Deputy for Guangdong Prov. to 5th NPC 1978; mem. State Nationalities Comm. 1982–83; alt. mem. 12th CCP Cen. Cttee. 1982, 13th Cen. Cttee. 1987; Vice-Gov. Hainan Prov. 1988–, a Vice-Chair. 1st Hainan Prov. Cttee. 1991, 2nd Cttee. 1991–; mem. 8th NPC Standing Cttee. 1993–; NPC Deputy Hainan Prov. *Address:* c/o Chinese Communist Party Central Committee, Beijing, People's Republic of China.

WANG YUNG-CHING; Taiwanese business executive; b. 18 Jan. 1917, Taiwan; m. Yueh-Lan Wang; two s. eight d.; founder/owner Formosa Plastics Group, a multinational petrochemical conglomerate consisting of over 20 cos. including Nan Ya Plastics Corpn., Formosa Plastics Corpn., Formosa Chemicals & Fibre Corpn., Cyma Plywood & Lumber Co. and three cos. in U.S.A.; Chair. Ming-chi Inst. of Tech. *Address:* Formosa Chemicals and Fibre Corporation., 201 Tun Hua North Road, Taipei, Taiwan.

WANG YUNKUN; Chinese politician; b. Dec. 1942, Liyang Co., Jiangsu Prov.; ed. Tianjin Univ.; joined CCP 1966; Mayor of Jilin City and Vice-Sec. CCP Jilin City Cttee.; Vice-Gov. Jilin Prov.; Sec. CCP Changchun City Cttee.; Acting Gov. Jilin Prov. 1995, Gov. 1996–; Sec. Jilin Prov. Cttee. 1998–; mem. 15th CCP Cen. Cttee. 1997–. *Address:* Jilin Provincial Government, Changchun City, Jilin Province, People's Republic of China.

WANG ZHAOGUO; Chinese party official; b. 1941, Fengrun, Hebei; First Sec. China Youth League 1982–84; mem. 12th Cen. Cttee. CCP 1982–87, 13th Cen. Cttee. 1987–92, 14th Cen. Cttee. 1992–97, 15th Cen. Cttee. 1997–; Deputy for Hubei to 6th NPC 1983; Dir.-Gen. Office Cen. Cttee. CCP 1984–86; Chief Rep. 21st Century Cttee. for Chinese-Japanese Friendship 1984–89; Vice-Gov. and Acting Gov. of Fujian 1987–88, Gov. 1988–90; Dir. Taiwan Affairs Office, State Council 1990–96; mem. Secr., CCP Cen. Cttee. 1985–87; mem. Presidium 6th NPC 1986–88, Standing Cttee. 6th NPC 1986–88; Head United Front Work Dept. 1992–; Vice-Chair. 8th Nat. Cttee. CPPCC 1993–98, 9th Nat. Cttee. 1998–. *Address:* National Committee of the Chinese People's Political Consultative Conference, 23 Taipingqiao Street, Beijing, People's Republic of China.

WANG ZHIBAO; Chinese administrator; b. July 1938, Zhaoyuan, Shandong Prov.; ed. Northeast Electric Power Inst.; joined CCP 1965; Vice-Minister of Forestry 1992–98; Dir. State Forestry Bureau 1998–. *Address:* State Forestry Bureau, Beijing, People's Republic of China.

WANG ZHONGFANG; Chinese lawyer and administrator; b. 1921; Dir. Law Research Inst. 1979; Chair. Legal Consultancy Center 1984–; Pres. of Law Soc. 1985–; Hon. Chair. Shuang Cheng attorneys-at-law 1996–. *Address:* Shuang Cheng attorneys-at-law, Suite 331, Main Building, Jingxin Mansion, 2A Dongsanhuan Road, Beijing 100027, People's Republic of China. *Telephone:* (10) 64641790. *Fax:* (10) 64662652.

WANG ZHONGFU; Chinese politician; b. 1942; ed. Changsha Inst. of Railway Industry; fmr. Dir. Changsha Bureau of Urban Construction, Dir. Changsha Co., Deputy Sec. CCP Changsha Municipal Cttee., then Sec.; Dir. State Admin. Bureau for Industry and Commerce 1994–. *Address:* State

Administration Bureau for Industry and Commerce, Beijing, People's Republic of China.

WANG ZHONGSHU; Chinese archaeologist; b. 15 Oct. 1925, Ningbo; s. of Wang Xuanbing and Ling Sujuan; m. Chen Kai 1960; one s.; Sr. Fellow Inst. of Archaeology, Chinese Acad. of Social Sciences 1979–, Dir. 1982–88; Prof. and Tutor for Doctoral Studies, Chinese Acad. of Social Sciences 1982–; mem. Nat. Council of Cultural Relics 1983–. *Leisure interests:* Chinese and Japanese classical literature. *Address:* Institute of Archaeology, Chinese Academy of Social Sciences, 27 Wangfujing Dajie, Beijing 100710, People's Republic of China. *Telephone:* (10) 65135532. *Fax:* (10) 65135532.

WANG ZHONGYU; Chinese politician; b. 1933, Changchun, Jilin; two s. one d.; joined CCP 1956; Sec. Gen. Jilin Prov. CCP Cttee. 1984, Deputy Sec. 1985–89; Gov. 1989–93; alt. mem. 13th Cen. Cttee. CCP 1987–92, 14th Cen. Cttee. 1992; Deputy, Jilin Prov., 7th NPC 1988–93; Vice-Gov. Jilin Prov. 1988–89, Gov. 1989–93; Minister in charge of State Econ. and Trade Comm. 1993–98; State Councillor and Sec. Gen. State Council 1998–; mem. 15th Cen. Cttee. CCP 1997–. *Address:* State Council, Xi Chang'an Jie, Beijing, People's Republic of China.

WANG ZIKUN; D.SC.; Chinese professor and university administrator; b. 30 April 1929, Jiangxi Prov.; s. of Wang Zhao-ji and Guo Xiang-e; m. Tian Der-Lin 1958; two s.; ed. Wuhan Univ. and Moscow Univ.; Asst. Prof., then Prof. Nankai Univ. 1952–84; Pres. and Prof. Beijing Normal Univ. 1984–; Prof. Shantou Univ. 1993–; Dir. of China Math. Soc.; mem. of Standing Bd. China Probilistical-Statistics Soc., China Higher Educational Soc.; mem. of editorial bd. Society, Scientia Sinica, Science Bulletin of China; mem. Chinese Acad. of Sciences 1991–; D.Sc. h.c. (Macquarie Univ., Australia) 1988; China Science Conference Award 1978, China Natural Science Prize 1982, China Excellent Popular Science Works Award 1981, and numerous other awards. *Publications:* Foundations of Probability Theory and Their Applications 1976, Theory of Stochastic Processes 1965, Brownian Motion and Potentials 1982, Probability Theory and Statistical Prediction 1978, Talks on Scientific Discovery 1978, Birth-Death Processes and Markov Chains 1992, and many other math. articles and popular scientific publs. *Leisure interest:* literature. *Address:* President's Office, Beijing Normal University, Beijing, People's Republic of China. *Telephone:* (10) 62208985.

WANGCHUCK, Jigme Singye; King (Druk Gyalpo) of Bhutan; b. 11 Nov. 1955; s. of late Druk Gyalpo Jigme Dorji Wangchuk and of Queen Ashi Kesang; ed. North Point, Darjeeling, Ugyuen Wangchuk Acad., Paro, also in England; Crown Prince March 1972; succeeded to throne 24 July 1972, crowned 2 June 1974; Chair. Planning Comm. of Bhutan March 1972–; C.-in-C. of Armed Forces; Chair. Council of Ministers 1972–98. *Address:* Royal Palace, Thimphu, Bhutan.

WANIEK, Danuta, D.JUR.; Polish politician; b. 26 Oct. 1946, Włocławek; widowed; two s.; ed. Warsaw Univ.; Institut für Höhere Studien und Wissenschaftliche, Vienna; Inst. of Political Studies, Polish Acad. of Sciences (PAN); mem. Polish United Workers' Party (PZPR) 1967–90; mem. Social Democracy of Polish Repub. (SdRP) 1990–; Deputy to Sejm (Parl.) 1991–, mem. Cttee. of Nat. Defence; Chair. Women's Democratic Union; Deputy Minister of Nat. Defence 1994–95; Minister of State and Head of Chancellery of Pres. of Poland 1995–97. *Leisure interests:* opera, reading newspapers, embroidering. *Address:* Biuro Poselskie, ul. Rozbrat 44A, 00-419 Warsaw, Poland (Office). *Telephone:* (22) 621 58 30.

WANKE, Maj. Daouda Mallam; Niger army officer; Head Nat. Reconciliation Council April 1999–. fmr. Head Presidential Guard. *Address:* National Reconciliation Council, Niamey, Niger.

WANLESS, Derek, M.A., M.I.S., F.C.I.B.; British banker; b. 29 Sept. 1947, Newcastle; s. of late Norman Hall Wanless and of Edna Charlton; m. Vera West 1971; one s. four d.; ed. Royal Grammar School, Newcastle upon Tyne, King's Coll. Cambridge and Harvard Univ.; joined Nat. Westminster Bank PLC 1970, Marketing Man. Domestic Banking Div. 1980–82, Area Dir. North-East Area 1982–85, W. Yorks Area 1985–86, Dir. of Personal Banking Services 1986–88, Gen. Man. U.K. Br. Business 1989–90, Chief Exec. U.K. Financial Services 1990–92, Deputy Group Chief Exec. and Group Head of NatWest Markets (now Hawkpoint Partners Ltd.) 1992, Dir. 1991–, Group Chief Exec. 1992–; Chair. Advisory Cttee. on Business and the Environment 1993–95, Nat. Forum for Man. Educ. and Devt. (NFMED) 1996–; mem. Investors in People U.K. Bd.; Hon. D.Sc. (City) 1995. *Leisure interests:* all sports, chess, music, walking, gardening. *Address:* National Westminster Bank PLC, 41 Lothbury, London, EC2P 2BP, England (Office). *Telephone:* 0171-726 1212. *Fax:* 0171-726 1174.

WAPNEWSKI, Peter, DR.PHIL.; German professor of medieval literature; b. 7 Sept. 1922, Kiel; s. of Harald and Gertrud (née Hennings) Wapnewski; m. 1st Caroline Gräfin Finckenstein 1950 (divorced 1959); m. 2nd Monica Plange 1971; ed. Univs. of Berlin, Freiburg, Jena and Hamburg; Prof. of Medieval German Literature, Heidelberg 1959, Free Univ. of Berlin 1966, Univ. of Karlsruhe 1969, Tech. Univ. of Berlin 1982–; Rector, Wissenschaftskolleg, Berlin 1980–86, Perm. mem. 1986–; Vice-Pres. Goethe Inst. 1977–; mem. Deutsche Akademie für Sprache und Dichtung, PEN Club, American Medieval Acad.; Grosses Bundesverdienstkreuz 1986, (with star) 1992. *Publications:* Wolframs Parzival 1955, Deutsche Literatur des Mittelalters 1960, Walther von der Vogelweide (ed.), Hartmann von Aue 1962, Die Lyrik Wolframs von Eschenbach 1972, Richard Wagner—Die Szene und ihr Meister 1978, Der Traurige Gott 1978, Zumutungen 1979, Tristan der Held Richard Wagners 1981, Minnesang des Codex Manesse 1982, Eduard Hanslick, Aus meinem Leben (Ed.) 1987, Götternot und Göttertrauer 1988, Die unerhörten Künste (Ed.) 1989, Eduard Hanslick: Aus dem Tagebuch eines Rezensenten (Ed.) 1989, Peter Huchel, Gedichte (Ed.) 1989, Betrifft Literatur. Über Marcel Reich-Ranicki (Ed.) 1990, Zuscreibungen. Gesammelte Aufsätze von P.W. Hildesheim 1994; about 200 articles on medieval and modern German literature. *Address:* Wallotstrasse 19, 14193 Berlin, Germany. *Telephone:* (030) 89001-0.

WAQAR YOUNIS; Pakistani cricketer; b. 16 Nov. 1971, Vehari; ed. Pakistani Coll. Sharjah and Govt. Coll. Vehari; right-hand lower-order batsman, right-arm fast bowler; played for Multan 1987–88 to 1990–91, United Bank 1988–89 to date, Surrey 1990–91 and 1993, Glamorgan 1997–98; played in 55 Tests for Pakistan 1989–90 to 31 Dec. 1998, 1 as Capt. taking 275 wickets (average 21.5); has taken 752 wickets in first-class cricket to 31 Oct. 1998; toured England 1992 and 1996; 172 limited-overs internationals to 31 Dec. 1998 (1 as Capt.). *Leisure interests:* football, badminton, squash.

WARBURTON, Dame Anne Marion, D.C.V.O., C.M.G., M.A., F.R.S.A.; British diplomatist; b. 8 June 1927; d. of Capt. Eliot and Mary Louise (née Thompson) Warburton; ed. Barnard Coll., Columbia Univ., Somerville Coll., Oxford; with Econ. Co-operation Admin., London 1949–52; NATO Secr., Paris 1952–54; Lazard Bros., London 1955–57; entered Diplomatic Service 1957; Second Sec., Foreign Office 1957–59; Second, then First Sec., U.K. Mission to UN, New York 1959–62; First Sec., Bonn 1962–65, Diplomatic Service Admin. Office, London 1965–67, Foreign Office, then FCO 1967–70; Counsellor, U.K. Mission to UN, Geneva 1970–75; Head of Guidance and Information Policy Dept., FCO 1975–76; Amb. to Denmark 1976–83, to UN at Geneva 1983–85; Pres. Lucy Cavendish Coll., Cambridge 1985–94, Hon. Fellow 1994–; Equal Opportunities Commr. 1986–87; mem. British Library Bd. 1989–95, Council of Univ. of E. Anglia 1991–97, Cttee. on Standards in Public Life (Nolan Cttee.) 1994–97; Hon. Fellow Somerville Coll. Oxford 1977–; Hon. Dr. (Arkansas) 1994; Verdienstkreuz (First Class), Fed. Repub. of Germany 1965; Grand Cross, Order of Dannebrog, Denmark 1979; Order of Isabel la Católica (Spain) 1988. *Leisure interests:* performing arts, walking, travel. *Address:* Ansted, Thornham Magna, Eye, Suffolk, IP23 8HB, England.

WARD, Ian Macmillan, M.A., D.PHIL., F.R.S.; British professor of physics; b. 9 April 1928, Stockton-on-Tees; s. of Harry Ward and Joan Moodie (née Burt); m. Margaret Linley 1960; two s. one d.; ed. Royal Grammar School, Newcastle upon Tyne and Magdalen Coll., Oxford; Tech. Officer, ICI Fibres 1954–61; seconded to Div. of Applied Math. Brown Univ., U.S.A. 1961–62; Head, Basic Physics Section, ICI Fibres 1962–65; Sr. Lecturer in Physics of Materials, Univ. of Bristol 1965–69; Prof. of Physics, Univ. of Leeds 1970–93, Cavendish Prof. 1987–94 (Chair. of Dept. 1975–78, 1987–89; Dir., IRC in Polymer Science and Tech. 1989–94); Pres., British Soc. of Rheology 1984–86; A. A. Griffith Medal 1982, S. G. Smith Memorial Medal 1984, Swinburne Award 1988, Charles Vernon Boys Medal 1993. *Publications:* Mechanical Properties of Solid Polymers 1971, Structure and Properties of Oriented Polymers (Ed.) 1975, Ultra High Modulus Polymers 1979. *Leisure interests:* music, walking. *Address:* Kirskill, 2 Creskeld Drive, Bramhope, Leeds, West Yorks., LS16 9EL, England. *Telephone:* (0113) 267 3637 (Home).

WARD, Most Rev. John Aloysius; British ecclesiastic; b. 24 Jan. 1929, Leeds; s. of Eugene Ward and Hannah Cheetham; ed. Prior Park Coll., Bath and Theological Seminaries of Franciscan Order, Olton, Crawley; entered Capuchin Franciscan Order 1945, First Vows 1946, Profession 1950, Priest 1953–; Travelling Missioner of Diocese of Menevia, Wales 1954–60; Superior (Guardian) and Parish Priest of Franciscan Friary, Peckham, London 1960–66; Provincial Definitor (Councillor) of British Prov. of Order 1963–69, Minister Provincial 1969–70; Gen. Definitor (Councillor) of Order in Rome 1970–80; Coadjutor Bishop of Menevia July 1980, Bishop Oct. 1980, succeeded to See 1981; Archbishop of Cardiff and Metropolitan of Welsh Prov. 1983–; Order of Friars Minor Capuchin. *Address:* Archbishop's House, 41–43 Cathedral Road, Cardiff, CF1 9HD, Wales. *Telephone:* (01222) 220411. *Fax:* (01222) 345950.

WARD, John Stanton, C.B.E., R.P.; British artist; b. 10 Oct. 1917; s. of the late Russell S. Ward and Jessie E. Ward; m. Alison C.M. Williams 1950; four s. twin d.; ed. St. Owen's School, Hereford and Royal Coll. of Art; served Royal Engineers 1939–46; with Vogue Magazine 1948–52; exhbns. at Thomas Agnew Gallery and Maas Gallery; fmr. Vice-Pres. Royal Soc. of Portrait Painters; mem. Exec. Nat. Art-Collections Fund 1976–87; Trustee, Royal Acad.; resgnd. from R.A. 1997; Hon. D.Litt. *Leisure interest:* book illustration. *Address:* Bilting Court, Bilting, Ashford, Kent, TN25 4HF, England. *Telephone:* (01233) 812478.

WARD, Michael Phelps, C.B.E., M.D., F.R.C.S.; British consultant surgeon; b. 26 March 1925, London; m. Felicity Jane Ewbank 1957; one s.; ed. Marlborough Coll., Peterhouse, Cambridge, London Hosp.; House Surgeon, Registrar, Sr. Registrar, London Hosp. 1950–64; lecturer in Clinical Surgery, London Hosp. Medical Coll. 1975–93; Consultant Surgeon, City and East London Area Hosp. Authority (Teaching) 1964–93, St. Andrew's Hosp., Bow 1964–93, Newham Hosp. 1983–93; took part in Everest Reconnaissance 1951, First Ascent 1953, Himalayan Scientific Expedition 1960–61; Leader scientific expeditions N. Bhutan 1964, 1965, Southern Xinjiang (First Ascent Mt. Kongur) 1980, 1981; Royal Soc./Chinese Acad. of Sciences Tibet Geotraverse 1985–86; Chair. Mt. Everest Foundation 1978–80; mem. Court of

Assistants, Soc. of Apothecaries 1985; Hunterian Prof., Royal Coll. of Surgeons 1954; Cuthbert Peek Award, Royal Geographical Soc. 1973, Founders (Royal) Medal, Royal Geographical Soc. 1982, Cullum Medal, American Geographical Soc. 1954. *Publications:* Mountaineer's Companion 1966, In This Short Span 1972, Mountain Medicine 1975, High Altitude Medicine and Physiology (Co-Author) 1989; articles and medical papers on the effects of great altitude, exposure to cold and on exercise; also on exploratory journeys in Nepal, Bhutan, Chinese Cen. Asia and Tibet. *Leisure interests:* mountaineering, skiing. *Address:* c/o St. Andrew's Hospital, Bow, London, E3 3NT, England.

WARD, Simon; British actor; b. 19 Oct. 1941, Beckenham; s. of Leonard Fox Ward and Winifred Ward; m. Alexandra Malcolm; three d.; ed. Alleyn's School, Dulwich, and Royal Acad. of Dramatic Art; mem. Nat. Youth Theatre from its foundation (as Youth Theatre) 1956; first professional stage appearance in Hobson's Choice, Northampton Repertory Theatre 1963; London début in The Fourth of June, St. Martin's Theatre 1964; film début in Frankenstein Must Be Destroyed 1969. *Stage roles include:* Konstantin in The Seagull, Birmingham Repertory 1964; Abel Drugger in The Alchemist and Hippolytus in Phèdre, Playhouse, Oxford 1965–66; Dennis in Loot, Jeannetta Cochrane and Criterion 1966; the Unknown Soldier in The Unknown Soldier and His Wife, Ferdinand in The Tempest and Henry in The Skin of Our Teeth, Chichester Festival 1968; Donald in Spoiled, Haymarket 1971; Romeo in Romeo and Juliet, Shaw 1972; Troilus in Troilus and Cressida, Young Vic 1976; *other stage performances include:* House Guest 1982, Whose Life is it Anyway?, Birmingham 1982, Heartbreak House 1983, Dial M for Murder 1983, Ross 1986, Paris Match 1988, Henceforward 1990, Rumours 1990, Don't Dress for Dinner 1992, Cell Mates 1995, An Ideal Husband 1997. *Films include:* I Start Counting 1970, Young Winston 1971, Hitler—The Last Ten Days 1972, The Three Musketeers 1973, The Four Musketeers, Deadly Strangers, All Creatures Great and Small 1974–75, Aces High 1975, Battle Flag 1976, The Four Feathers 1978, Zulu Dawn 1979, Supergirl, Around The World in 80 Days, Double X 1992, Wuthering Heights, Ghost Writers. *TV includes:* The Black Tulip, The Roads to Freedom, Holocaust (serials). *Leisure interests:* music, gardening, reading, badminton. *Address:* c/o Shepherd & Ford Associates Ltd, 13 Radner Walk, London, SW3 4BP, England. *Telephone:* 0171-352 2200. *Fax:* 0171-352 2277.

WARD, Vincent; New Zealand film director; b. 1956, Greytown; ed. Elam School of Fine Art, Christchurch (graduated in film). *Films include:* A State of Siege 1977, In Spring one Plants Alone 1979 (Grand Prix co-winner in 1982 Cinéma du Réel, Silver Hugo at Chicago Film Festival), Vigil 1984 (Grand Prix at Madrid and Prades Film Festivals), The Navigator 1988, Map of the Human Heart. *Address:* P.O. Box 423, Kings Cross, Sydney, N.S.W. 2011, Australia. *Telephone:* (02) 360-2769.

WARDHANA, Ali, M.A., PH.D.; Indonesian politician and economist; b. 6 May 1928, Surakarta, Central Java; m. Renny Wardhana 1953; one s. three d.; ed. Univ. of Indonesia, Jakarta and Univ. of California (Berkeley) U.S.A.; Dir., Research Inst. of Econ. and Social Studies 1962–67; Prof. of Econs., Univ. of Indonesia 1967–, Dean Faculty of Econs. 1967–78; Adviser to Gov. of Cen. Bank 1964–68; mem. team of experts of Presidential Staff 1966–68; Minister of Finance 1968–83; Co-ordinating Minister for Econ., Finance, Industry and Devt. Control 1983–88; Chair. Cttee. of Bd. of Governors of the IMF on Reform of the Int. Monetary System and Related Issues 1972–74; Grand Cross Order of Léopold II (Belgium) 1970, Grand Cross Order of Orange Nassau (Netherlands) 1971, Mahaputra Adipradhna II Award (Indonesia) 1973. *Leisure interests:* reading, tennis, bowling, swimming. *Address:* 5, Jalan Brawijaya III, Kebayoran Baru, Jakarta, Indonesia.

WARLOW, Charles Picton, M.D., F.R.C.P.; British professor of medical neurology; b. 29 Sept. 1943, Nottingham; s. of Charles Warlow and Nancy Hine; m. Ilona McDowell 1976; three c.; ed. Univ. of Cambridge and St. George's Hosp. Medical School, London; Lecturer in Medicine, Aberdeen 1971; specialist training in neurology, London and Oxford 1974–77; Clinical Reader in Neurology and Hon. Consultant Neurologist, Oxford 1977–87; Prof. of Medical Neurology, Univ. of Edin. 1987–; Tenovus-Scotland Margaret MacLellan Award 1989–90, Osler Oration, Royal Coll. of Physicians 1998. *Publications include:* Handbook of Clinical Neurology 1991, Transient Ischaemic Attacks of the Brain and Eye (with G. J. Hankey) 1994, Stroke: A Practical Guide to Management (co-author) 1996. *Leisure interests:* sailing, photography, mountains. *Address:* Department of Clinical Neurosciences, Western General Hospitals NHS Trust, Crewe Road, Edinburgh, EH4 2XU, Scotland. *Telephone:* 0131-537 2082. *Fax:* 0131-332 7886.

WARNE, Shane Keith; Australian cricketer; b. 13 Sept. 1969, Ferntree Gully, Melbourne; m. Simone Warne; one d.; ed. Hampton High School, Mentone Grammar School; leg-break and googly bowler; right-hand lower-order batsman; 68 Tests for Australia 1991–92 to 1 Feb. 1999, taking 315 wickets (average 24.9) and scoring 1,240 runs (average 14.7), took hat-trick v England, Melbourne, 1994; took 530 wickets and scored 2,141 runs in first-class cricket to 31 Oct. 1998; toured England 1993, 1997; 96 limited-overs internationals (1 as Capt.) to 31 Dec. 1998. *Address:* c/o Victorian Cricket Association, 86 Jolimont Street, Vic. 3002, Australia.

WARNER, Bishop Bennie D., M.SC., TH.M., D.D.; Liberian ecclesiastic; b. 30 April 1935, Caresburg District; ed. Monrovia Gbargna United Methodist Mission School, Booker Washington Inst., Kakata, Cuttington Univ. Coll., Suakoto, Syracuse Univ. and Boston Univ. School of Theology (U.S.A.); ordained Deacon 1961; Acting Dir. Pastors' Inst. of the United Methodist Church 1961; educ. counsellor and maths. and social studies teacher, W.V.S. Tubman Elementary School 1962–68; fmr. Chair. Nat. Student Christian Council of Liberia; later ordained Elder; fmr. Pastor, St. John's United Methodist Church, Gbarnga, and Reeves Memorial United Methodist Church, Crozierville; fmr. Chair. Interim Cttee. for the Admin. of the Coll. of W. Africa, Bd. of Ministry, Liberia Annual Conf. of United Methodist Church; ordained Bishop 1973; later Chair. Bd. of Trustees of the Coll. of W. Africa; Vice-Pres. of Liberia 1977–80; mem. Bd. of Trustees, Cuttington Coll. and Divinity School, Bd. of the Booker Washington Inst., Nat. Disaster Comm., Council of Bishops, World Methodist Council; Grand Band, Order of the Star of Africa; in exile in U.S.A.

WARNER, Brian, PH.D., M.A., D.SC., F.R.A.S., F.R.S. (S.A.); British astronomer; b. 25 May 1939, Sussex; s. of Leslie Warner and Edith M. (née Bashford) Warner; m. 1st Carole Christian 1965 (divorced 1973); one s. one d.; m. 2nd Nancy Russell 1976 (divorced 1987); ed. Univs. of London and Oxford; Research Asst., Univ. of London Observatory 1964–65; Radcliffe-Henry Skynner Sr. Research Fellow, Balliol Coll., Oxford 1965–67; Asst. Prof., Univ. of Texas at Austin 1967–69, Assoc. Prof. 1969–72; Prof. and Head, Dept. of Astronomy, Univ. of Cape Town 1972–, Fellow 1978; Alfred P. Sloan Fellow 1969–71; Visiting Fellow, Univ. of Colo. 1977; Visiting Sr. Fellow, Dept. of Astrophysics Univ. of Oxford 1985; Visiting Prof. Dartmouth Coll. and Univ. of Texas 1986–87, Univ. of Sussex 1997; Visiting Fellow, Univ. of Calif. Santa Cruz 1990, A.N.U. 1989, 1993, 1996, 1998; Visiting Scientist, European Southern Observatory 1996; Assoc. Royal Astronomical Soc. 1994; Pres. Royal Soc. of South Africa 1981–83, Foreign Sec. 1996–; Founder mem. Acad. of Sciences of S.A. 1994–; Pres. Comm. 42 of Int. Astronomical Union 1978–82; Pres. Astronomical Soc. of Southern Africa 1977–78, The Owl Club 1985–86; mem. Bd. of Trustees, South African Museum 1981–, Deputy Chair. 1988–91, Chair. 1991–; mem. Council S.A. Library 1991–; Hon. mem. Royal Astronomical Soc. of N.Z. 1995; Boyden Premium, Franklin Inst. 1980; McIntyre Award, Astronomical Soc. of Southern Africa 1983, John F. W. Herschel Medal, Royal Soc. of S.A. 1988, South African Medal, S.A. Asscn. for the Advancement of Science 1989, Ernest Oppenheimer Travelling Fellowship 1990, Gill Medal, Astronomical Soc. of Southern Africa 1992, Univ. of Cape Town Book Award 1997. *Publications:* Astronomers at the Royal Observatory, Cape of Good Hope 1979, Charles Piazzi Smyth 1983, Maclear and Herschel 1984, The Journal of Lady Jane Franklin 1985, High Speed Astronomical Photometry 1988, William Mann 1989, Lady Herschel 1991, Cataclysmic Variable Stars 1995, Dinosaurs' End 1996, Flora Herscheliana 1998; over 200 scientific research papers. *Leisure interests:* 19th-century science and exploration, baroque music. *Address:* Department of Astronomy, University of Cape Town, Rondebosch, 7700 Cape; 401 Blenheim, Marlborough Park, Claremont, 7700 Cape, South Africa (Home). *Telephone:* (2721) 6502391 (Office). *Fax:* 6503352.

WARNER, David; British actor; b. 29 July 1941, Manchester; s. of Herbert Simon Warner; ed. Feldon School, Leamington Spa, and Royal Acad. of Dramatic Art; worked as bookseller; stage début as Snout in A Midsummer Night's Dream, Royal Court 1962; film début in Tom Jones 1963; joined Royal Shakespeare Co. (RSC) 1963 and appeared as Trinculo in The Tempest, Cinna in Julius Caesar, title role in Henry VI, Edward IV in adaptation of Henry VI (Parts I, II and III) comprising first two parts of trilogy The Wars of the Roses (Stratford). *Other roles include:* Henry VI in The Wars of the Roses, Aldwych 1964; Richard II, Mouldy in Henry IV (Part II) and Henry VI in The Wars of the Roses, RSC, Stratford 1964; Valentine Brose in Eh?, Aldwych 1964, Hamlet, Stratford and Aldwych 1965; the Postmaster in The Government Inspector, Aldwych 1965; Hamlet, Sir Andrew Aguecheek in Twelfth Night, Stratford 1966; Claudius in I, Claudius, Hampstead 1972. *Films include:* Morgan—A Suitable Case for Treatment 1966, Work is a Four Letter Word 1967, The Bofors Gun, The Fixer, The Seagull 1968–69, The Ballad of Cable Hogue 1970, Straw Dogs 1971, A Doll's House 1972, The Omen 1975, Cross of Iron, Providence, Silver Bears 1976, The Disappearance 1977, The Thirty Nine Steps 1978, Nightwing, Time After Time 1979, The Island 1980, Hanna's War 1988, The Secret Life of Ian Fleming 1990, Dark at Noon, Mortal Passions, In the Mouth of Madness, Titanic 1997. *TV includes:* Clouds of Glory 1977, Holocaust 1977, Charlie 1984, The Choir 1995.

WARNER, Deborah; British theatre and opera director; b. 12 May 1959, Oxford; d. of Ruth Warner and Roger Warner; ed. Sidcot School, Avon, St. Clare's Coll. Oxford, Cen. School of Speech and Drama, London; Artistic Dir. Kick Theatre Co. 1980–86; Resident Dir. R.S.C. 1987–89; Assoc. Dir. Royal Nat. Theatre; freelance dir. Abbey Theatre, Dublin 1991, BBC TV 1992, 1995, Opera North, Leeds 1993, 1996, Salzburg Festival, Austria 1993, 1994, Garrick Theatre, London 1994, Glyndebourne Festival Opera 1994, 1995, Royal Nat. Theatre 1995, Brussels 1995; Evening Standard Award 1988, 1998, Laurence Olivier Award 1989, 1992, S. Bank Arts Award 1998; Chevalier, Ordre des Arts et des Lettres. *Address:* c/o Conway van Gelder Ltd., 18–21 Jermyn Street, London, SW1Y 6HP, England. *Telephone:* 0171-287 0077. *Fax:* 0171-287 1940.

WARNER, Denis Ashton, C.M.G., O.B.E.; Australian journalist and author; b. 12 December 1917, Tasmania; s. of Hugh Ashton Warner and Nelly Callan; m. Peggy Strafford Hick 1945; one s. two d.; ed. Hutchins School, Hobart, Harvard Univ.; war corresp. Australian Publications 1944–45; Reuter-AAP Editorial Man., Tokyo 1947–49; Roving Far Eastern Corresp.

Melbourne Herald and Daily Telegraph (London) 1949–55; Far Eastern Corresp. Reporter Magazine 1957–68; Asian Corresp. Look Magazine 1968–72; Author of syndicated column on Far Eastern Affairs 1957–89; Ed. Pacific Defence Reporter 1981–95; Australian Corresp. London Daily Telegraph 1958–86; mem. Editorial Bd., Conflict, Int. Advisory Bd., Political Communication and Persuasion; Pres. Australian Defence Correspondents' Asscn. 1985–87; Citations Overseas Press Club of New York for Best Magazine Reporting 1966, 1968. *Publications:* Out of the Gun 1956, The Last Confucian 1963, Not with Guns Alone 1977; with Peggy Warner: The Tide at Sunrise: A History of the Russo-Japanese War 1904–05 1974, The Great Road, Japan's Highway to the 20th Century 1980, The Sacred Warriors 1982, Disaster in the Pacific: New Light on the Battle of Savo Island 1992, Wake Me if there's Trouble 1995, Not Always on Horseback 1997. *Leisure interest:* dry fly fishing. *Address:* Ramslade, Nepean Highway, Mt. Eliza, Vic. 3930, Australia. *Telephone:* (359) 752706. *Fax:* (359) 759632.

WARNER, Douglas Alexander III, B.A.; American banker; b. 9 June 1946, Cincinnati; s. of Douglas Alexander Warner Jr. and Eleanor (Wright) Warner; m. Patricia Grant 1977; two s. one d.; ed. Yale Univ.; Officer's Asst. Morgan Guaranty Trust Co., New York 1968–70, Asst. Treas. 1970–72, Asst. Vice-Pres. 1972–75, Vice-Pres. 1975–85, Sr. Vice-Pres. Morgan Guaranty Trust Co., London 1983–87, Exec. Vice-Pres. Morgan Guaranty Trust Co., New York 1987–89, Man. Dir. 1989–90, Pres. 1990–95, Chair. and C.E.O. 1995–; mem. Bd. Dirs. General Electric Co., Anheuser-Busch Cos. Inc.; Chair. Bd. of Man. Overseers Memorial Sloan-Kettering Cancer Center, New York; Trustee Pierpoint Morgan Library, Cold Spring Harbor Lab. *Leisure interests:* golf, tennis, shooting. *Address:* J.P. Morgan & Co. Inc., 60 Wall Street, New York, NY 10005, U.S.A. (Office).

WARNER, Sir Frederick Edward, Kt., F.ENG., F.R.S.; British engineer and university professor; b. 31 March 1910, London; s. of Frederick Warner; m. 1st Margaret Anderson McCrea; two s. two d.; m. 2nd Barbara Ivy Reynolds; ed. Bancrofts School, Univ. Coll., London; chemical engineer with various cos. 1934–56; partner in firm of consulting chemical engineers working in U.K., Ireland, U.S.S.R., India, Iran, Jordan, Africa 1956–80; Sr. Partner, Cremer and Warner 1963–80; Visiting Prof. Bartlett School of Arch., Univ. Coll., London 1970; Visiting Prof. Imperial Coll., London 1970–78, 1993–; Visiting Prof. Univ. of Essex 1983–; Pro-Chancellor, Open Univ. 1974–79; mem. Advisory Council on Energy Conservation, Dept. of Energy 1974–80; Pres. British Standards Inst. 1980–83, Vice-Pres. 1976–80, 1983–89; Pres. British Asscn. for Commercial and Industrial Educ. 1977–90, Inst. of Quality Assurance 1987–90; Chair. British Nat. Cttee. on Problems of Environment, Royal Soc. 1973–80, Council of Science and Tech. Insts. 1987–90; Treas. SCOPE 1982; Pres. Fédération Européenne d'Associations Nationales d'Ingénieurs 1968–71; Hon. mem. Royal Inst. of Engineers, Netherlands 1972; Fellow, Univ. Coll., London 1967; Hon. Fellow, School of Pharmacy, London 1979, UMIST 1986; Académico Correspondiente la Academia de Ingeniería, Mexico; Hon. D.Tech. (Bradford) 1969, Hon. D.Sc. (Aston) 1970, (Cranfield) 1978, (Heriot-Watt) 1978, (Newcastle) 1979, Hon. D.Univ. (Open) 1980, (Essex) 1992; Gold Medal, Czechoslovak Soc. for Int. Relations 1969; Medal, Insinöö riliitto, Finland 1969, Bronze Medal, Associazione Nazionale Ingegneri e Architetti d'Italia 1971, Leverhulme Medal (Royal Soc.) 1978, Buchanan Medal 1982, Gold Medal World Fed. of Eng. Orgs.; Tuev Rheinland Prize 1984. *Publications:* Problem in Chemical Engineering Design (with J. M. Coulson) 1949, Risk (ed.) 1983, Quality 2000 1992 (ed.), Radioecology after Chernobyl (ed. with J. M. Harrison) 1993, Nuclear Test Explosions (ed. with R. J. Kirchmann) 1999; papers on nitric acid, heat transfer, underground gasification of coal, air and water pollution, contracts, planning, safety, risk, technology transfer, professional and continuous educ., nuclear winter, Chernobyl, nuclear weapons tests. *Leisure interests:* monumental brasses, ceramics, gardens. *Address:* 1 Ropewalk, Southwell, Notts., NG25 0AL, England. *Telephone:* (01636) 816483. *Fax:* (01636) 816399.

WARNER, John W., B.S., LL.B.; American politician; b. 18 Feb. 1927, Washington, D.C.; s. of late Dr. John W. Warner and of Martha (Budd) Warner; m. 1st Catherine Conover Mellon (divorced 1973); one s. two d.; m. 2nd Elizabeth Taylor (q.v.) 1976 (divorced 1982); ed. public schools in Washington, D.C., school of Naval Research Laboratory, Washington, D.C., Washington and Lee Univ. and Univ. of Virginia Law School; in U.S.N., attained rank of Electronic Technician 3rd Class 1944–46; subsequently enlisted in U.S. Marine Corps Reserve, active duty as Communications Officer 1950–52, Capt. in Marine Corps Reserve 1952–61; admitted to the Bar 1954; pvt. practice 1954–56; in U.S. Attorney's office as Special Asst. 1956, Asst. 1957, fmr. trial lawyer; joined campaign staff of then Vice-Pres. Richard Nixon 1960; associated with law firm Hogan & Hartson 1960, gen. partner 1964; Dir. of Ocean Affairs as rep. of Dept. of Defense 1971; Under-Sec. of U.S. Navy 1969–72, Sec. 1972–74; Dir. American Revolution Bicentennial Admin. 1974–76; Senator from Virginia 1979–; head of U.S. Del. to Moscow on Naval Affairs; Republican. *Address:* 225 Russell Senate Office Building, The Senate, Washington, DC 20510 (Office); Atoka Farm, P.O. Box 1320, Middleburg, VA 22117; 700 New Hampshire Avenue, N.W., Washington, DC 20037, U.S.A. (Homes).

WARNER, Marina Sarah, M.A.; British author; b. 9 Nov. 1946, London; d. of Esmond Warner and Emilia Terzulli; m. 1st William Shawcross 1971; one s.; m. 2nd John Dewe Mathews 1981; ed. St. Mary's Convent, Ascot and Lady Margaret Hall, Univ. of Oxford; Getty Scholar, Getty Centre for the History of Art and the Humanities 1987–88; Tinbergen Prof. Erasmus Univ. Rotterdam 1990–91; Visiting Prof., Queen Mary and Westfield Coll., Univ. of London 1994, Univ. of Ulster 1994, Univ. of York 1996–; Tanner Lecturer, Yale Univ. 1999; Fellow Commonership, Trinity Coll., Cambridge 1998; mem. Exec. Cttee. Charter 88 –1997, Literature Panel Arts Council of England –1997, Advisory Council British Library –1997, Man. Cttee. Nat. Council for One-Parent Families, Bd. Artangel, Cttee. London Library; Hon. D.Litt. (Exeter) 1998; Dr. h.c. (Sheffield Hallam, York, N. London, St. Andrews) 1998; Fawcett Prize 1986, Harvey Darton Award 1996, Mythopoeic Fantasy Award 1996. *Publications:* Alone of All Her Sex: the myth and the cult of the Virgin Mary 1976, Monuments and Maidens: the allegory of the female form 1985, The Lost Father 1988, Indigo 1992, Mermaids in the Basement (short stories) 1993, Six Myths of Our Time—The 1994 Reith Lectures, From the Beast to the Blonde: On Fairy Tales and Their Tellers 1994, No Go the Bogeyman: On Scaring, Lulling and Making Mock 1998; Wonder Tales (ed.) 1994. *Leisure interests:* travel, photography, friendship. *Address:* c/o Rogers, Coleridge & White, 20 Powis Mews, London, W11 1JN, England. *Telephone:* 0171-221 3717. *Fax:* 0171-229 9084.

WARNKE, Jürgen, LL.D.; German politician; b. 20 March 1932, Berlin; s. of Dr Franz Warnke and Marianne (née Gensel) Warnke; m.; six c.; registered for legal practice 1961; Sec. Chemical Industry Asscn. in Bavaria 1962–64; Gen. Sec. Ceramics Industry Assn., Selb, Bavaria; joined Christian Social Union (CSU) 1958, Academic Asst. to CSU Group in Deutscher Bundestag 1959–62; mem. Bavarian State Parl. 1962–70; mem. Deutscher Bundestag 1969–; apptd. Chair. Bundestag Cttee. on Trade Policy 1971, Vice-Pres. Cttee. for European and Int. Co-operation 1978; Fed. Minister of Econ. Co-operation 1982–87, 1989–91, of Transport 1987–89; Chair. Supervisory Bd. Königliche Porzellan Manufaktur GmbH, Berlin 1995–; mem. Synod, Protestant Church of Germany (EKD) 1985–; Grosses Bundesverdienstkreuz 1986, (with star) 1994. *Address:* Bundeshaus, 53113 Bonn, Germany.

WARNKE, Paul Culliton, B.A., LL.B.; American government official and lawyer; b. 31 Jan. 1920, Webster, Mass.; s. of Paul Martin and Lillian (née Culliton) Warnke; m. Jean Farjeon Rowe 1948; three s. two d.; ed. Yale Univ., Columbia Univ., New York; served U.S. Coast Guard, to Lieut. (sr. grade) 1942–46; admitted to D.C. Bar 1948; Assoc., Covington and Burling, Washington, D.C. 1948–57, Partner 1957–66; Gen. Counsel, Dept. of Defense 1966–67; Asst. Sec. of Defense for Int. Security Affairs 1967–69; Partner, Clifford, Warnke, Glass, McIlwain and Finney 1969–77; Dir. U.S. Arms Control and Disarmament Agency (ACDA) 1977–78; Chief Negotiator for Strategic Arms Limitation Talks (SALT) 1977–78; part-time Consultant to State Dept. 1978–80; mem. Scientific and Policy Advisory Cttee., ACDA 1995–, Presidential Advisory Bd. on Arms Proliferation Policy 1995–; Chair. Cttee. for Nat. Security; Partner Clifford and Warnke 1978–91, Howrey & Simon 1991–; Adjunct Prof. Georgetown Univ. School of Foreign Service 1996–; mem. Md. and D.C. Advisory Comms. to U.S. Comm. on Civil Rights 1962–66; Dir. Exec. Cttee. of Int. Voluntary Services 1972; mem. Exec. Cttee. of Trilateral Comm.; mem. Bd. of Govs., D.C. Bar 1976; Trustee, Potomac School 1958–66, Chair. Bd. 1965–66; mem. Bd. of Dirs., Health and Welfare Council of Nat. Capital Area 1966–67; Trustee, Northland Coll. 1970–76; Chair. Bd. of Visitors, Georgetown Univ. School of Foreign Service 1971–76; mem. Bd. of Visitors, Columbia Univ. School of Law 1971–; mem. Bd. of Dirs. Georgetown Univ. 1979–91; mem. American Soc. of Int. Law, Council on Foreign Relations, Council of American Ambs., American Acad. of Diplomacy, American Bar Asscn. Standing Cttee. on World Order under Law 1986– (Chair 1989–91); Fellow, American Bar Foundation; Alumni Trustee, Columbia Univ. 1984–90; Democrat. *Address:* Howrey and Simon, 1299 Pennsylvania Avenue, N.W., Washington, DC 20004; 5037 Garfield Street, N.W., Washington, DC 20016, U.S.A. (Home). *Telephone:* (202) 383-6509 (Office); (202) 966-0397 (Home).

WARNOCK, Baroness (Life Peer), cr. 1985, of Weeke in the City of Westminster; **(Helen) Mary Warnock,** D.B.E., F.C.P., F.R.S.M.; British philosopher and university administrator; b. 14 April 1924; d. of the late Archibald Edward Wilson; m. Geoffrey J. Warnock 1949 (died 1995); two s. three d.; ed. St. Swithun's, Winchester and Lady Margaret Hall, Oxford; Tutor in Philosophy, St. Hugh's Coll., Oxford 1949–66; Headmistress, Oxford High School 1966–72; Talbot Research Fellow, Lady Margaret Hall 1972–76; Sr. Research Fellow, St. Hugh's Coll. 1976–84; Mistress of Girton Coll., Cambridge 1985–91; Chair. Cttee. of Inquiry into Special Educ. 1974–78, Advisory Cttee. on Animal Experiments 1979–86, Cttee. of Inquiry into Human Fertilization 1982–84, Educ. Cttee. Girls' Day School Trust 1994–; mem. Independent Broadcasting Authority (IBA) 1973–81, Royal Comm. on Environmental Pollution 1979–84, Social Science Research Council 1981–85, U.K. Nat. Comm. for UNESCO 1981–85, Archbishop of Canterbury's Advisory Group on Medical Ethics 1992–; Hon. Master of the Bench, Gray's Inn 1986; Hon. F.I.C. 1986; Hon. Fellow, Hertford Coll., Oxford 1997; Hon. D.Univ. (Open Univ.) 1980, (St Andrews) 1992, Hon. LL.D. (Manchester) 1987, (Liverpool) 1991, (London) 1991, Hon. D.Litt. (Glasgow) 1988; Dr h.c. (Univ. of York) 1989; R.S.A. Albert Medal 1998. *Publications:* Ethics since 1900 1960, J.-P. Sartre 1963, Existentialist Ethics 1966, Existentialism 1970, Imagination 1976, Schools of Thought 1977, What Must We Teach? (with T. Devlin) 1977, Education: A Way Forward 1979, A Question of Life 1985, Teacher Teach Thyself (Dimbleby Lecture) 1985, Memory 1987, A Common Policy for Education 1989, Universities: knowing our minds 1989, The Uses of Philosophy 1992, Imagination and Time 1994, An Intelligent

Person's Guide to Ethics 1998; Women Philosophers (Ed.) 1996, An Intelligent Person's Guide to Ethics 1998. *Leisure interests:* music, gardening. *Address:* 3 Church Street, Great Bedwyn, Wilts., SN8 3PE, England. *Telephone:* (01672) 870214.

WARRELL, David Alan, M.A., D.M., D.SC., F.R.C.P., F.R.C.P. (E.), F.MED.SCI.; British specialist in tropical medicine and venoms; b. 6 Oct. 1939, Singapore; s. of Mr and Mrs A. T. Warrell; m. Dr. Mary J. Prentice 1975; two d.; ed. Portsmouth Grammar School, Christ Church, Oxford and St. Thomas's Hosp. Medical School, London; Oxford Univ. Radcliffe Travelling Fellow, Univ. of Calif. San Diego 1969; Sr. Lecturer, Ahmadu Bello Univ., Nigeria and Lecturer and Consultant Physician, Royal Postgrad. Medical School, London and Hammersmith Hosp. 1970–75; Founding Dir. Wellcome-Mahidol Univ., Oxford Tropical Medicine Research Programme, Bangkok and Wellcome Reader in Tropical Medicine, Univ. of Oxford 1979–86; Prof. of Tropical Medicine and Infectious Diseases and Dir. Centre for Tropical Medicine, Univ. of Oxford 1987–; Hon. Consultant in Malariology to British Army 1989–; Hon. Medical Advisor, Royal Geographical Soc. 1993–; WHO Consultant 1979–; mem. WHO Expert Advisory Panel on Malaria 1989–; Fellow St. Cross Coll. 1975–; Chair. AIDS Therapeutic Trials Cttee., MRC; Trustee, Tropical Health and Education Trust; Patron, Cambodia Trust; Pres. British Venom Gp. 1992–, Int. Fed. for Tropical Medicine 1996–, Royal Soc. of Tropical Medicine and Hygiene 1997–; Marc Daniels, Bradshaw and Croonian Lecturer (Ambuj Nath Bose Prize), Royal Coll. of Physicians; Runme Shaw Lecturer, Acad. of Medicine, Singapore 1997; Chalmer's Medal, Royal Soc. of Tropical Medicine and Hygiene 1981. *Publications:* scientific papers and book chapters; Ed. Oxford Textbook of Medicine, Bruce-Chwatt's Essential Malariology, Expedition Medicine. *Leisure interests:* book-collecting, music, bird-watching, mountain-walking. *Address:* Centre for Tropical Medicine, University of Oxford, John Radcliffe Hospital, Headington, Oxford, OX3 9DU, England. *Telephone:* (01865) 220968. *Fax:* (01865) 220984.

WARREN, Sir Frederick Miles, K.B.E., F.N.Z.I.A., A.R.I.B.A., DIP.ARCH.; New Zealand architect; b. 10 May 1929, Christchurch; s. of M. B. and J. Warren (née Hay); ed. Christ's Coll., Auckland Univ. School of Architecture; worked for late C. W. Wood, 1946–47, for late R. C. Munroe, A.N.Z.I.A. 1948; joined partnership with late G. T. Lucas 1956; started firm Warren and Mahoney 1958, Sr. Partner 1958–; Fellow, New Zealand Inst. of Architects 1965; Pres. Canterbury Soc. of Arts 1972–76; Warren and Mahoney awarded N.Z.I.A. Gold Medal for Dental Nurses' Training School 1960, for Christchurch Memorial Garden Crematorium 1964, for Christchurch Coll. Halls of Residence 1969, for Christchurch Town Hall and Civic Centre 1973; won Architectural Competition for design of Condominium Offices, New Hebrides 1966; Gold Medal N.Z.I.A. 1980, 1981, 1983, 1984, 1985, 1986, 1988–91. *Publication:* Warren & Mahoney Architects 1990. *Leisure interests:* yachting, watercolouring, sketching. *Address:* 65 Cambridge Terrace, Christchurch 1, New Zealand. *Telephone:* 799.640.

WARREN, Jack Hamilton, O.C.; Canadian diplomatist and business executive (retd.); b. 10 April 1921; m. Hilary J. Titterington; four c.; ed. Queen's Univ., Kingston, Ont.; Royal Canadian Navy 1941–45; joined Dept. of External Affairs 1945; served in London 1948–51; transferred to Dept. of Finance and served as Financial Counsellor, Washington, D.C. and as Alt. Dir. for Canada, IMF and IBRD 1954–57; Canadian Del. to OECD and NATO 1957–58; Asst. Deputy Minister of Trade and Commerce 1958–64; Chair. GATT Contracting Parties 1962–65; Deputy Minister of Trade and Commerce 1964–68, of Industry, Trade and Commerce 1968–71; High Commr. in U.K. 1971–74; Amb. to U.S.A. 1975–77; Canadian Coordinator for the Multilateral Trade Negotiations 1977–79; Vice-Chair. Bank of Montréal 1979–86; Chair. Bank of Montréal Int. Ltd. 1983–86; Prin. Adviser on trade policy, Govt. of Quebec 1986–94; Deputy N. American Chair. Trilateral Comm. 1986–90; Hon. LL.D. (Queen's Univ.) 1974; Outstanding Achievement Award, Public Service of Canada 1975. *Address:* Box 282, R.R.1, Chelsea, Que. J0X 1N0, Canada (Home).

WARRINGTON, Elizabeth Kerr, PH.D., D.SC., F.R.S.; British professor of clinical neuropsychology; d. of the late Prof. John A. V. Butler, F.R.S. and Margaret L. Butler; m.; one d.; ed. Univ. Coll. London; Research Fellow, Inst. of Neurology 1956; Sr. Clinical Psychologist, Nat. Hosp. 1960, Prin. Psychologist 1962, Top Grade Clinical Psychologist 1972–82, Prof. of Clinical Neuropsychology 1982–96, Consultant Neuropsychologist to Dementia Research Group 1996–; Emer. Prof. of Clinical Neuropsychology, London Univ. 1996–; Fellow Univ. Coll. London; Dr. h.c. Psiccologia (Bologna) 1998. *Publications:* Cognitive Neuropsychology (co-author) 1990; numerous papers in professional journals. *Address:* Dementia Research Group, National Hospital for Neurology and Neurosurgery, Queen Square, London, WC1N 3BG, England. *Telephone:* 0171-837 3611.

WARWICK, Dionne; American singer; b. 12 Dec. 1941, East Orange, N.J.; m. Bill Elliott (divorced 1975); two s.; ed. Hartt Coll. of Music, Hartford, Conn.; as teenager formed Gospelaires; later sang background for recording studio 1966; début, Philharmonic Hall, Lincoln Center, New York 1966; appearances at London Palladium, Olympia, Paris, Lincoln Center; co-host, Solid Gold (TV show); host, A Gift of Music (TV show) 1981; star, Dionne Warwick Special (TV show); appeared in Sisters in the Name of Love on TV 1986; records include: I'll Never Love this Way Again, That's What Friends are For; albums include: Valley of the Dolls and Others 1968, Promises, Promises 1975, Dionne 1979, Then Came You, Friends 1986, Reservations for Two 1987, Greatest Hits 1990, Dionne Warwick Sings Cole Porter 1990, Hidden Gems: The Best of Dionne Warwick (Vol. 2) 1992, Friends Can Be Lovers (with Whitney Houston) 1993, Dionne Warwick and Placido Domingo 1994, Aquarela do Brasil 1994, From the Vaults 1995; Grammy Awards 1969, 1970, 1980. *Films:* The Slaves 1969, No Night, So Long, Hot! Live and Otherwise. *Address:* c/o Arista Records Inc., 6 West 57th Street, New York, NY 10019, U.S.A.

WĄSACZ, Emil; Polish economist; b. 1 Aug. 1945, Zabratówka, Rzeszów Prov.; m.; three c.; ed. Łódź Tech. Univ., Main School of Commerce (SGH), Warsaw; employee Katowice Steelworks 1976–94, Supreme Dir. and then Chair. Katowice Steelworks S.A. 1991–94; advisor Chair. Bank Śląski S.A., Bank PeKaO S.A., and enterprise Stalexport S.A.; Chair. Szczecin Steelworks S.A. 1995–97; Vice-Leader Supervisory Bd., later Chair. Progress Nat. Investment Fund 1995–97; Minister of the Treasury 1997–; mem. Solidarity Trade Union, leader Plant Cttee. in the Katowice Steelworks 1989–90; voluntary worker Catholic Family Clinic, Sosnowiec 1983–90. *Leisure interests:* tourism, history, astronomy, literature and romantic poetry. *Address:* Ministerstwo Skarbu Państwa, ul. Krucza 36, 00-522 Warsaw, Poland. *Telephone:* (22) 695 85 90, 695 87 90. *Fax:* (22) 628 19 14.

WASER, Peter Gaudenz, M.D., D.PHIL.; Swiss professor of pharmacology; b. 21 July 1918, Zürich; s. of Ernst Waser and Margrit Ruttiman; m. Marion Edmée Bodmer 1946; one s. two d.; ed. Univ. of Zürich, Basle Univ. Hosp., California Inst. of Tech.; Prof. of Medicine, Univ. of Zürich 1959, Dir. Inst. of Pharmacology 1963–87, Prof. of Pharmacy 1965–87, Dean of Faculty of Medicine 1970–72, Rector 1978–80; research in psychopharmacology, Univ. Clinic, Zürich 1987–95; Pres. Engadine Collegium in Philosophy 1967–, Int. Union of Pharmacology 1978–81, Int. Council of Scientific Unions 1981–84. *Publications:* Mechanisms of Synaptic Transmission 1969 (with Akert), Cholinergic Mechanisms 1975, Praktische Pharmakotherapie 1987 (with C. Steinbach), The Cholinergic Receptor 1987, Psychiatrie, Psychopharmaka und Drogen in Zurich 1990. *Leisure interests:* mountaineering, skiing, gardening, painting. *Address:* Institute of Pharmacology, Winterthurerstr. 190, 8057 Zürich; Research Department of Psychiatry, University Clinic, Lenggstrasse 31, 8029 Zürich; Ob. Heuelsteig 12, 8032 Zürich, Switzerland (Home). *Telephone:* 01-257-5911 (Pharmacology); 01-384 2111 (Psychiatry); 01-251-2814 (Home).

WASHINGTON, Denzel, B.A.; American film actor; b. 28 Dec. 1954, Mt. Vernon, N.Y.; m. Pauletta Pearson 1983; two s. two d.; ed. Fordham Univ. and American Conservatory Theater, San Francisco; worked at New York Shakespeare Festival and American Place Theater; off-Broadway appearances include: Ceremonies in Dark Old Men, When the Chickens Come Home to Roost and A Soldier's Play (Negro Ensemble Co.); played young doctor in TV series St. Elsewhere. *Films include:* A Soldier's Story 1984, The Mighty Quinn, Cry Freedom 1987, Heart Condition 1989, Glory (Acad. Award for Best Supporting Actor) 1990, Love Supreme 1990, Mo' Better Blues 1990, Ricochet 1991, Mississippi Masala 1991, Much Ado About Nothing, Malcolm X 1992, The Pelican Brief 1993, Philadelphia 1993, Devil in a Blue Dress 1995, Courage Under Fire 1996, The Preacher's Wife 1996, Fallen 1997, He Got Game 1998, The Siege 1998. *Address:* c/o ICM, 8942 Wilshire Boulevard, Beverly Hills, CA 90211, U.S.A.

WASIM AKRAM; Pakistani cricketer; b. 3 June 1966, Lahore; ed. Islamia Coll.; left-hand middle-order batsman, left-arm fast bowler; played for PACO 1984–85, Lahore 1985–86, Lancashire 1988–98 (Capt. 1998); played in 83 Tests for Pakistan 1984–85 to 31 Dec. 1998, 17 as Capt., scoring 2,111 runs (average 21.1) including 2 hundreds and taking 354 wickets (average 22.8); has scored 6,044 runs (6 hundreds) and taken 912 wickets in first-class cricket to 31 Oct. 1998; toured England 1987, 1992 and 1996 (Capt.); 254 limited-overs internationals (72 as Capt.) taking record 363 wickets to 31 Dec. 1998.

WASMOSY, Juan Carlos, D.C.E.; Paraguayan politician and civil engineer; b. 15 Dec. 1938; s. of Juan Bautista Wasmosy and María Monti Paoli; m. Maria Teresa Carrasco Dos Santos; five s. (one deceased) one d.; ed. San José School, Asunción and Nat. Univ. of Asunción; fmr. Asst. Prof. Univ. of Asunción; sometime Pres. ECOMIPA, CONEMPA, COCEP, GOYA (pvt. construction and industrial cos.); other business affiliations; mem. construction holding which built Itaipú Hydroelectric Power Station; currently engaged in construction of Yacyretá power station; Pres. Int. Fed. of Zebu Cattle Breeders; mem. Colorado Party 1973–; Minister of Integration 1993; Pres. of Paraguay 1993–98, Senator for Life 1998–; Orden de Solidaridad de Brasil; other medals and awards. *Address:* The Senate, Asunción, Paraguay.

WASS, Sir Douglas William Gretton, G.C.B., M.A.; British fmr. civil servant and business executive; b. 15 April 1923, Wallasey, Cheshire; s. of late Arthur W. Wass and Elsie W. Wass; m. Dr. Milica Pavičić 1954; one s. one d.; ed. Nottingham High School, St. John's Coll., Cambridge; Scientific Research with Admiralty 1943–46; Asst. Prin., Treasury 1946, Prin. 1951; Commonwealth Fund Fellow, U.S.A. 1958–59; Fellow, Brookings Inst., Washington 1959; Pvt. Sec. to Chancellor 1959–61; Pvt. Sec. to Chief Sec. 1961–62; Alt. Exec. Dir. to IMF and Financial Counsellor, British Embassy, Washington, D.C. 1965–67; Under-Sec. of Treasury 1968, Deputy Sec. 1970, Second Perm. Sec. 1973, Perm. Sec. 1974–83; Jt. Head, Home Civil Service 1981–83; Chair. Econ. Policy Cttee., OECD 1982; Reith Lecturer, BBC 1983; Chair. British Selection Cttee., Harkness Fellowships 1981–84, Governing Body of the Ditchley Foundation, Council of the Policy Studies Inst.; Chair.

Nomura Int. PLC 1986–98 (Sr. Adviser 1998–), Axa Equity and Law Life Assurance Soc. PLC 1986–95, N.C.M. (Credit Insurance) Ltd. 1991–95; Gov. Centre for Econ. Policy Research 1983–90; Adviser to Campaign for Freedom of Information; Dir. De La Rue Co. PLC 1983–93, Coopers and Lybrand 1984–86, Barclays Bank PLC 1984–87, African Capacity Bldg. Foundation, Harare 1991–98, Equitable Cos. Inc. New York 1992–95; Administrateur, Cie. du Midi S.A. (now Axa S.A.) 1987–95; Vice-Pres. Constitutional Reform Centre 1984–92; mem. Council of Univ. of Bath 1985–91; Pres. Market Research Soc. 1987–91; mem. Overseas Devt. Council 1990–96; mem. Council British Heart Foundation 1990–96; Dir. Soho Theatre Co. 1996–; Hon. D.Litt. (Bath); Hon. Fellow, St. John's Coll., Cambridge. *Publications:* The Changing Problems of Economic Management 1978, The Public Service in Modern Society 1982, Government and the Governed 1984, The Civil Service at the Crossroads 1985, What Sort of Industrial Policy? 1986, Checks and Balances in Public Policy Making 1987. *Leisure interest:* swimming. *Address:* 6 Dora Road, Wimbledon, London, SW19 7HH, England. *Telephone:* 0181-946 5556.

WASSERBURG, Gerald Joseph, M.SC., PH.D.; American professor of geology and geophysics; b. 25 March 1927, New Brunswick, N.J.; s. of Charles Wasserburg and Sarah Levine Wasserburg; m. Naomi Z. Orlick 1951; two s.; ed. Univ. of Chicago; Rifleman, U.S. Army Second Infantry Div. 1943–46; with Resurrection Mining Co. 1947; Juneau Ice Field Research Project, Alaska 1950; Consultant Argonne Nat. Laboratory, Lamont, Ill. 1952–55; Research Assoc., Inst. for Nuclear Studies, Chicago 1954–55; Asst. Prof. of Geology, Calif. Inst. of Tech. 1955–59, Assoc. Prof. of Geology 1959–62, Prof. of Geology and Geophysics 1962–82; Adviser to NASA 1968–88; Vice-Chair. Lunar Sample Analysis Planning Team, MSC, NASA 1970; mem. Lunar Sample Review Bd. 1970–72, Science Working Panel 1971–73, Physical Sciences Cttee. 1971–75; Ed. Earth and Planetary Science Letters 1967–74; Chair. Comm. for Planetary and Lunar Exploration, Space Science Bd. 1975–78; Vinton Hayes Sr. Fellow, Harvard 1980; Jaeger-Hales Lecture, Australian Nat. Univ. 1980; Harold Jeffreys Lecture, Royal Astronomical Soc. 1981; John D. MacArthur Prof. of Geology and Geophysics, Calif. Inst. of Tech. 1982–, Chair. Div. of Geological and Planetary Sciences 1987–89; Pres. Meteoritical Soc. 1987–88; mem. N.A.S.; Fellow, American Acad. of Arts and Sciences, American Geophysical Union, Geological Soc. of America; Regents Fellow, Smithsonian Inst. 1982; Hon. Fellow Geological Soc. London; Geochemistry Fellow Geochemical Soc. and European Asscn. for Geochemistry 1996; mem. American Philosophical Soc.; Foreign mem. Norwegian Acad. of Science and Letters 1988; Hon. Foreign Fellow European Union of Geosciences (EUG) 1983; Dr. h.c. (Brussels) 1985, (Chicago) 1992, (Pennes) 1998, (Torino) 1999; Hon. D.Sc. (Ariz.) 1987; Combat Infantryman's Badge; Exceptional Scientific Achievement Medal, NASA 1970; Arthur L. Day Medal, Geological Soc. of America 1970; Distinguished Public Service Medal, NASA 1972, and with cluster 1978; James Furman Kemp Medal, Columbia Univ. 1973, Leonard Medal, Meteoritical Soc. 1975; V. M. Goldschmidt Medal, Geochemical Soc. 1978, Univ. of Chicago Alumni Asscn. Professional Achievement Award 1978; Arthur L. Day Prize, N.A.S. 1981, J. Lawrence Smith Medal, N.A.S. 1985, Wollaston Medal, Geological Soc. of London 1985, Sr. U.S. Scientist Award, Alexander von Humboldt-Stiftung 1985, Harry H. Hess Medal, American Geophysical Union, Crafoord Prize, Swedish Royal Acad. 1986, Holmes Medal, EUG 1987, Gold Medal (Royal Astronomical Soc.) 1991. *Publications:* research papers in several scientific journals, in the fields of geochemistry, geophysics and astrophysics, and the application of the methods of chemical physics to problems in the earth and planetary sciences; major researches: determination of the time scale of the solar system, chronology of the moon, establishment of dating methods using long-lived natural radioactivities, study of geological processes using nuclear and isotopic effects as a tracer in nature and the application of thermodynamic methods to geological systems. *Leisure interests:* hiking, music, art. *Address:* California Institute of Technology, Division of Geological and Planetary Sciences, Pasadena, CA 91125; 1207 Arden Road, Pasadena, CA 91106, U.S.A. (Home). *Telephone:* (426) 395-6139 (Office); (426) 449-7852 (Home).

WASSERMAN, Lew R.; American film and record company executive; b. 15 March 1913, Cleveland, Ohio; m. Edith T. Beckerman 1936; one d.; Nat. Dir. Advertising and Publicity, Music Corpn. of America (MCA) 1936–38, Vice-Pres. 1938–39, apptd. Vice-Pres. Motion Picture Div. 1940, then Chair. Bd. of Dirs., C.E.O. and mem. Exec. Cttee. MCA Inc., Chair. Emer. 1995; also Chair. Bd., C.E.O. and Dir. subsidiary corpns.; Dir. American Airlines; Chair. Emer. Asscn. of Motion Picture and TV Producers; Trustee John F. Kennedy Library, John F. Kennedy Center for the Performing Arts, Calif. Inst. of Tech., Jules Stein Eye Inst., Carter Presidential Center, Lyndon Baines Johnson Foundation; Pres. Hollywood Canteen Foundation; Chair. Research to Prevent Blindness Foundation; Hon. Chair. Bd. Center Theatre Group L.A. Music Center; mem. Bd. of Dirs. Amateur Athletic Foundation of L.A., L.A. Music Center Foundation; Dir. Seagram Co. 1995–; mem. Bd. of Govs. Ronald Reagan Presidential Foundation; Dr. h.c. (Brandeis Univ., New York Univ.); Jean Hersholt Humanitarian Award, Acad. of Motion Picture Arts and Sciences 1973. *Address:* Universal City Studios Inc., 100 Universal City Plaza, Universal City, CA 91608, U.S.A.

WASSERMAN, Robert Harold, PH.D.; American professor of sciences; b. 11 Feb. 1926, Schenectady, New York; s. of Joseph Wasserman and Sylvia Rosenburg; m. Marilyn Mintz 1950; three d.; ed. Mount Pleasant High School, N.Y., Cornell Univ., Michigan State Univ.; Research Assoc. and Assoc. Prof. of Biochem. Univ. of Tenn. Atomic Energy Comm. Agricultural Research Program, Oak Ridge 1953–55; Sr. Scientist Medical Div., Oak Ridge Inst. of Nuclear Studies 1955–57; Research Assoc. in Radiation Biology N.Y. State Veterinary Coll., Cornell Univ. 1957–59; Assoc. Prof. of Radiation Biology, Dept. of Physical Biology 1959–63, Prof. of Radiation Biology 1963–80, Prof. of Physiology, Coll. of Veterinary Medicine 1980–89, Prof. and Chair. of Dept. and Section 1983–87, James Law Prof. of Physiology 1989–, Prof. Emer. 1998–; Chair. Cttee. Meat and Poultry Inspection, Nat. Research Council 1983–85, mem. Food and Nutrition Bd. 1984–87; Visiting Scientist Inst. of Biological Chem., Copenhagen, Denmark 1964–65; Guggenheim Fellowship 1964, 1972; mem. N.A.S. 1980–; Fellow American Inst. of Nutrition 1992; Mead-Johnson Award in Nutrition 1969; Wise and Helen Burroughs Lectureship 1974, 1987; A. Lichtwitz Prize (INSERM) 1982, Merit Status, NIH 1989, Newman Award (American Soc. Bone and Mineral Research) 1990, Career Recognition Award, Vitamin D Workshop 1994. *Publications:* numerous articles in specialist journals. *Leisure interests:* sailing, reading, sports, computers, cards. *Address:* Department and Section of Physiology—T8-020B VRT, College of Veterinary Medicine, Cornell University, Ithaca, NY 14853; 207 Texas Lane, Ithaca, NY 14850, U.S.A. (Home). *Telephone:* (607) 253-3437.

WASSERSTEIN, Bruce, M.B.A.; American investment banker; b. 25 Dec. 1947, New York; s. of Morris Wasserstein and Lola Wasserstein; m. Christine Parrott; two s. one d.; ed. Univ. of Mich., Harvard Univ. and Univ. of Cambridge; Assoc. Cravath, Swaine & Moore, New York 1972–77; Man. Dir. First Boston Corpn. 1977–88; Pres. Wasserstein, Perella & Co. 1988–; mem. Council on Foreign Relations. *Address:* Wasserstein, Perella & Co., 31 West 52nd Street, 27th Floor, New York, NY 10019, U.S.A.

WASSERSTEIN, Wendy, M.F.A.; American playwright and author; b. 18 Oct. 1950, Brooklyn; ed. Mount Holyoake Coll. and Yale School of Drama; mem. Council, Dramatists' Guild; mem. Bd. British American Arts Asscn.; mem. Artistic Bd. Playwrights Horizons; taught fmrly. at Columbia and New York Univs.; contrib. ed. New York Woman; recipient of Pulitzer Prize, N.W. Drama Critics Circle Prize, Drama Desk Award, Outer Critics Circle Award, Susan Smith Blackburn Prize and Tony Award, all for play The Heidi Chronicles; other plays include: Isn't It Romantic, Any Woman Can't, Montpelier, Pa-Zazz, Miami, Uncommon Women and Others, The Sisters Rosenzweig 1993; dir. Channel Thirteen, MacDowell Colony, British American Arts Asscn.; Dr. h.c. (Mt. Holyoake Coll.). *Publications:* Bachelor Girls, The Heidi Chronicles and Other Plays; collection of essays, Pamela's First Musical (for children) 1995. *Address:* c/o Royce Carlton Inc., 866 United Nations Plaza, Suite 4030, New York, NY 10017, U.S.A. *Telephone:* (212) 355-7700.

WASTBERG, Olle, B.A.; Swedish politician, writer and banker; b. 6 May 1945, Stockholm; s. of Erik Wastberg and Greta Hirsch; m. Inger Claesson 1968; two s.; ed. Univ. of Stockholm; Vice-Pres. Liberal Youth Sweden 1968–71; mem. Bd. Liberal Party 1972–93, 1997–, Pres. Exec. Cttee. 1982–83, teacher of political science, Univ. of Stockholm 1967–68; journalist, political dept. Expressen 1968–71; Research Fellow, Business and Social Research Centre 1971–76; Pres. Akieframjandet 1976–82; mem. Parl. 1976–82; Pres. Swedish Newspaper Promotion Asscn. 1983–91; Under-Sec. of State, Ministry of Finance 1991–93; Ed. Expressen 1994–95; Dir. Stockholm Stock Exchange 1977–82, 1988–94; Pres. Nordic Investment Bank 1992–94; Chair. Bd. Swedish Broadcasting Corpn. 1996–, Stockholm City Theatre 1998–; mem. govt. comms. on S. African consumer politics, stock market and media; Gold Medal, Swedish Marketing Group 1982. *Publications:* books on African problems, immigration policies and economic topics; articles in professional journals. *Address:* Bellmangatan 6, 11820 Stockholm, Sweden. *Telephone:* (8) 6436879. *Fax:* (8) 7021388.

WATANABE, Youji; Japanese architect; b. 14 June 1923, Naoetsu City; ed. Waseda Univ.; Asst. to Prof. Takamasa Yosizaka (q.v.), Architectural Inst., Waseda Univ. 1955–58; lecturer in Architecture, Waseda Univ. 1959, Special Postgraduate Student of City Planning 1968–73; Visiting Lecturer, Montana State Univ. 1983; Oceanic Architectural Students' Congress, Auckland Univ. 1983; prizes in architectural competitions; exhbns. at VIII Salone Internazionale della Industrializzazione Edilizia, Bologna 1972, Georges Pompidou Centre, Paris 1977, Centro Edile, Milan 1977, Museum of Modern Art, New York 1978, The Peak Competition, Hong Kong 1982, Paris Opera Bastille Competition 1982. *Publication:* Approach to Architecture 1974.

WATERHOUSE, Douglas Frew, A.O., C.M.G., D.SC., F.A.A., F.R.S.; Australian entomologist; b. 3 June 1916, Sydney; s. of Prof. E. G. Waterhouse and J. F. (née Kellie) Waterhouse; m. Allison D. Calthorpe 1944; three s. one d.; ed. Univs. of Sydney and Cambridge; Research Officer, CSIR Div. of Econ. Entomology 1938; Asst. Chief., CSIRO Div. of Entomology until 1960, Chief 1960–81, Hon. Research Fellow 1981–; Consultant, Australian Centre for Int. Agricultural Research 1983–; Pres. Nat. Trust of Australia (ACT) 1983–88; many other professional appts.; Foreign Assoc. N.A.S.; Foreign mem. U.S.S.R. Acad. of Sciences, etc.; Hon. D.Sc. (Australian Nat. Univ.). *Publications:* Butterflies of Australia (jtly.), Biological Control: Pacific Prospects (jtly.) 1987 and supplements 1989, 1993, Major Pests and Weeds of South-East Asia 1993, Biological Control of Weeds: South-East Asian Prospects 1994, Biological Control of Insect Pests: Southeast Asian Prospects 1998; over 100 articles in scientific journals. *Leisure interests:* gardening, fishing, Gyotaku (ancient Japanese art of fish painting). *Address:* Division of Entomology, CSIRO Box 1700 City, Canberra 2601 (Office); 60 National Circuit, Canberra, A.C.T. 2600, Australia (Home). *Telephone:* (02) 6246-4049 (Office); (02) 6273-1772 (Home). *Fax:* (02) 6246-4133.

WATERHOUSE, Keith Spencer, C.B.E., F.R.S.L.; British writer; b. 6 Feb. 1929, Leeds; s. of Ernest Waterhouse and Elsie Edith Waterhouse; m. 2nd Stella Bingham 1984 (divorced 1989); one s. two d. by previous marriage; journalist 1950–, columnist, Daily Mirror 1970–86, Daily Mail 1986–, contrib. to various periodicals; mem. Kingman Cttee. on Teaching of the English Language 1987–88; Granada Columnist of the Year Award 1970; IPC Descriptive Writer of the Year Award 1970; IPC Columnist of the Year Award 1973; British Press Awards Columnist of the Year 1978, 1989; Granada Special Quarter Century Award 1982; Evening Standard Comedy of the Year 1990 (Jeffrey Bernard is Unwell). *Films (with Willis Hall) include:* Billy Liar, Whistle Down the Wind, A Kind of Loving, Lock Up Your Daughters. *Plays:* Mr. and Mrs. Nobody 1986, Jeffrey Bernard is Unwell 1989, Bookends 1990, Our Song 1992, Good Grief 1998, Bing-Bong 1999. *Plays (with Willis Hall) include:* Billy Liar 1960, Celebration 1961, All Things Bright and Beautiful 1963, Say Who You Are 1965, Whoops-a-Daisy 1968, Children's Day 1969, Who's Who 1972, The Card (musical) 1973, Saturday, Sunday, Monday (adapted from play by de Filippo) 1973, Filumena (adapted from de Filippo) 1977, Worzel Gummidge 1981, Budgie (musical) 1988. *TV series:* Budgie, Queenie's Castle, The Upper Crusts, Billy Liar, The Upchat Line, The Upchat Connection, Worzel Gummidge, West End Tales, The Happy Apple, Charters and Caldicott. *TV films:* Charlie Muffin 1983, This Office Life 1985, The Great Paperchase 1986. *Publications:* (novels) There is a Happy Land 1957, Billy Liar 1959, Jubb 1963, The Bucket Shop 1968, Billy Liar on the Moon 1975, Office Life 1978, Maggie Muggins 1981, In the Mood 1983, Thinks 1984, Our Song 1984, Bimbo 1990, Unsweet Charity 1992, Good Grief 1997; *Others:* Café Royal (with Guy Deghy) 1956, Writers' Theatre (Ed.) 1967, The Passing of the Third-floor Buck 1974, Mondays, Thursdays 1976, Rhubarb, Rhubarb 1979, Fanny Peculiar 1983, Mrs Pooter's Diary 1983, Waterhouse At Large 1985, Collected Letters of a Nobody 1986, The Theory and Practice of Lunch 1986, The Theory and Practice of Travel 1988, Waterhouse on Newspaper Style 1989, English Our English 1991, Jeffrey Bernard is Unwell and Other Plays 1992, Sharon & Tracy and the Rest 1992, City Lights 1994, Streets Ahead 1995. *Address:* c/o Alexandra Cann Representation, 12 Abingdon Road, London, W8 6AF; 29 Kenway Road, London, SW5 0RP, England.

WATERLOW, John Conrad, C.M.G., M.D., SC.D., F.R.S.; British professor of human nutrition; b. 13 June 1916, London; s. of Sir Sydney Waterlow and Margery H. Eckhard; m. Angela P. Gray 1939; two s. one d.; ed. Eton Coll., Trinity Coll., Cambridge and London Hosp. Medical Coll.; Persia/Iraq force 1943; mem. scientific staff, MRC 1942–70; Dir. Tropical Metabolism Research Unit, Univ. of the West Indies 1954–70; Prof. of Human Nutrition, London School of Hygiene and Tropical Medicine 1970–82, Prof. Emer. 1982–; Foreign Assoc. mem. N.A.S. (U.S.A.); Murgatroyd Prize for Tropical Medicine; Bristol-Myers Prize for Nutrition. *Publications:* Protein Turnover in the Whole Body and in Mammalian Tissues 1978, Protein Energy Malnutrition 1992; many papers and reviews on malnutrition and protein metabolism. *Leisure interest:* mountain walking. *Address:* 15 Hillgate Street, London, W8 7SP; Oare, Marlborough, Wilts, SN8 4JA, England. *Telephone:* 0171-727 7456 (London).

WATERMAN, Ewen Leith, B.ECONS.; Australian civil servant; b. 2 Dec. 1943, Adelaide, S. Australia; s. of Gordon Waterman and Elsie Waterman (née Batty); m. Barbara Prideaux 1966; two s. one d.; ed. Pulteney Grammar School, Adelaide, Univ. of Adelaide; Gen. Financial and Econ. Policy Div., Australian Treasury 1967–72, Overseas Econ. Relations Div., 1973–75, Asst. Sec. State and Local Govt. Finances Br. 1982–84, Prin. Adviser, Gen. Financial and Econ. Policy Div., 1984–85, First Asst. Sec., Revenue Loans and Investment Div. 1985–87, Capital Markets Div. 1987–89, Deputy Sec. (Financial) 1989–93; Prime Minister's Dept. 1972; Counsellor (Financial), Australian Embassy, Washington, D.C. 1976–79; Sec. Australian Loan Council 1986–87, Australian Nat. Debt Comm. 1986–87; Exec. Dir. IMF, Washington, D.C. 1993–97; Exec. Dir. Access Economica June 1997–. *Leisure interests:* tennis, golf. *Address:* 39 Brisbane Avenue, Barton, ACT 2600, Australia. *Telephone:* (2) 6273 1222. *Fax:* (2) 6273 1223.

WATERSTONE, Timothy John Stewart, M.A.; British business executive; b. 30 May 1939; s. of Malcolm Waterstone and Sylvia Sawday; m. 1st Patricia Harcourt-Poole (divorced); two s. one d.; m. 2nd Clare Perkins (divorced); one s. two d.; m. 3rd Mary Rose Alison; two d.; ed. Tonbridge School and St. Catharine's Coll. Cambridge; Carritt Moran, Calcutta 1962–64; Allied Breweries 1964–73; W. H. Smith 1973–81; Founder and Chair. Waterstone & Co. (booksellers) 1982–93; Chair. Daisy & Tom's Children's Stores 1996–; Chair. The Principals Ltd. 1987–, Metronome Radio Ltd. 1989–, Priory Investments Ltd. 1990–95, Golden Rose Radio (London Jazz FM) 1992–93; Chair. HMV Media Group (merger between Waterstones and Dillons) 1998–; Deputy Chair. Sinclair-Stevenson Ltd. 1989–92; mem. Bd. of Trustees, English Int. (Int. House) 1987–92; mem. Bd. London Philharmonic Orchestra 1992–97, Acad. of Ancient Music, Yale Univ. Press. 1992–, Virago Press 1995–96. *Publications:* Lilley and Chase 1994, An Imperfect Marriage 1995, A Token for Good 1996, A Passage of Lives 1996. *Leisure interest:* books. *Address:* c/o Ed Victor Ltd., 6 Bayley Street, London, WC1B 3HB, England.

WATHELET, Melchior, L. EN D., LL.M.; Belgian politician; b. 6 March 1949, Petit-Rechain; m.; one c.; ed. Univ. of Liège, Harvard Univ., U.S.A.; researcher, Univ. of Liège 1973–77; Sec. of State for Regional Economy (French Sector) and for Housing 1980–81, Minister of New Tech., Planning and Foresty (French sector) 1981–85; Minister and Chair. French Regional Exec. responsible for New Tech., Foreign Affairs, Gen. Afffairs and Personnel 1985–88; Deputy Prime Minister and Minister of Justice and of the Middle Classes 1988–92, Vice-Prime Minister 1992–95, Minister of Justice and of Economic Affairs 1992–95, of Nat. Defence June–Sept. 1995; Pres. Parti Social Chrétien (PSC) 1992–94. *Address:* c/o Office of Vice-Prime Minister, Rue Lambermont 8, 1000 Brussels, Belgium.

WATKINS, Alan Keith, PH.D.; British business executive; b. 9 Oct. 1938, Birmingham; s. of late Wilfred Watkins and of Dorothy Watkins; m. Diana E. Wynne 1963; two s.; ed. Moseley Grammar School and Univ. of Birmingham; Mfg. Process Research, Lucas Group Research 1962–69; Mfg. and Production Eng. Lucas Batteries Ltd. 1969–75; Div. Dir. Electrical Div. Lucas Aerospace Ltd. 1975–82; Man. Dir. Lucas Aerospace Ltd. 1982–87; Man. Dir. Aerospace, Lucas Industries PLC 1987–89; Man. Dir. and Chief Exec. Hawker Siddeley Group PLC 1989–91; C.E.O. London Transport 1992–94, Vice-Chair. 1992–93, Deputy Chair. 1993–94, Dir. Senior Eng. Group 1994–, Deputy Chair. 1995–96, Chair. 1996–; Dir. (non-exec.) Dobson Park Industries PLC 1992–95, Hepworth PLC 1995–98; mem. Review Bd. for Govt. Contracts 1993–. *Leisure interests:* tennis, photography, golf, hot-air ballooning, vintage cars. *Address:* Senior Engineering Group PLC, 59/61 High Street, Rickmansworth, Herts, WD3 1RH, England.

WATKINS, Winifred May, D.SC., F.R.C.PATH., F.R.S.; British scientist; b. 6 Aug. 1924, London; d. of Albert E. Watkins and Annie B. Watkins; ed. Godolphin and Latymer School, London, Univ. of London; Research Student, St. Bartholomew's Hosp. Medical School, London 1948–50; MRC Grantee, Lister Inst. Preventive Medicine, London 1950–52, Beit Memorial Research Fellow 1952–55, mem. scientific staff 1955–75, Prof. of Biochem. and Head, Dept. of Biochem. 1968–75; Wellcome Travelling Fellow, Univ. of Calif., Berkeley 1960–61; Reader in Biochem., Univ. of London 1965–68; Head of Div. of Immunochemical Genetics, MRC Clinical Research Centre 1976–89; Visiting Prof. and Sr. Research Fellow, Royal Postgrad. Medical School 1990–; Hon. mem. Int. Soc. of Blood Transfusion 1984, British Blood Transfusion Soc. 1996; Hon. F.R.C.P. 1990; Hon. mem. Japanese Biochemical Soc. 1990; Foreign mem. Polish Acad. of Sciences 1988, Royal Swedish Acad. of Sciences 1998; Hon. D.Sc. Chem. (Utrecht) 1990; Award of Oliver Memorial Fund for outstanding contribs. in blood transfusion 1965, Karl Landsteiner Award, American Asscn. of Blood Banks (jtly.) 1967, Paul Erhlich-Ludwig Darmstädter Medal and Prize (jtly.) 1969, William Julius Mickle Fellowship Award, Univ. of London 1970, Kenneth Goldsmith Award of British Blood Transfusion Soc. 1986, Royal Medal of Royal Soc. 1988, Franz-Oehleckler Medal of the German Soc. of Transfusion Medicine and Immunohaematology 1989, Philip Levine Award (jtly.) (American Soc. of Chemical Pathologists 1990). *Publications:* numerous papers in scientific journals. *Leisure interests:* reading. *Address:* Department of Haematology, Imperial College School of Medicine, Hammersmith Hospital, Du Cane Road, London, W12 0NN, England (Office). *Telephone:* 0181-383 2171. *Fax:* 0181-742 9335.

WATSON, Emily; British actress; b. 1966, London; *films:* Breaking the Waves (New York Soc. of Film Critics Award, Nat. Soc. of Film Critics Award), Mill on the Floss, Metroland, The Boxer, Hilary and Jackie. *Address:* c/o ICM Ltd., Oxford House, 76 Oxford Street, London, W1N 0AX, England.

WATSON, James Dewey, B.S., PH.D.; American biologist; b. 6 April 1928, Chicago, Ill.; s. of James D. Watson and Jean Mitchell Watson; m. Elizabeth Lewis 1968; two s.; ed. Univ. of Chicago, and Univ. of Indiana; Research Fellow, U.S. Nat. Research Council, Univ. of Copenhagen 1950–51; Fellow U.S. Nat. Foundation, Cavendish Lab., Univ. of Cambridge, England 1951–53, 1955–56; Sr. Research Fellow in Biology, Calif. Inst. of Tech. 1953–55; Asst. Prof. of Biology, Harvard Univ. 1956–58, Assoc. Prof. 1958–61, Prof. 1961–76; Dir. Cold Spring Harbor Lab. 1968–93, Pres. 1994–; Assoc. Dir. NIH (USA) 1988–89, Dir. Nat. Center for Human Genome Research, NIH 1989–92; Newton-Abraham Visiting Prof., Oxford Univ., U.K. 1994; discovered structure of DNA (with F. W. Crick) 1953; mem. N.A.S., Danish Acad. of Arts and Sciences, American Acad. of Arts and Sciences, American Soc. of Biological Chemists; Sr. Fellow, Soc. of Fellows, Harvard Univ. 1964–70; Hon. Fellow of Clare Coll., Univ. of Cambridge 1967; mem. American Philosophical Soc. 1978; Foreign mem. Royal Soc. 1981, U.S.S.R. (now Russian) Acad. of Sciences 1989; Hon. D.Sc. (Chicago, Indiana, Long Island, Adelphi, Brandeis, Hofstra, Harvard, Rockefeller, State Univ. of New York, Albert Einstein Coll. of Medicine, Clarkson Coll., Stellenbosch, Fairfield, Cambridge, Oxford); Hon. LL.D. (Notre Dame) 1965; Hon. M.D. (Buenos Aires) 1986; Hon. D.Sc. (Rutgers Univ.) 1988, (Bard Coll.) 1991, (Melbourne) 1997; Eli Lilly Award in Biochem. 1959, Lasker Prize (American Public Health Asscn.) 1960, Nobel Prize for Medicine (with F. H. C. Crick and M. F. H. Wilkins) 1962, John J. Carty Gold Medal (Nat. Acad. of Sciences) 1971, Medal of Freedom 1977, Gold Medal Award, Nat. Inst. of Social Sciences 1984, Kaul Foundation Award for Excellence 1992, Capley Medal of Royal Soc. 1993, Nat. Biotech. Venture Award 1993; Lomosonov Medal 1994, Nat. Medal of Science 1997. *Publications:* Molecular Biology of the Gene 1965 (2nd edn. 1970, 3rd edn. 1976), The Double Helix 1968, The DNA Story 1981 (with John Tooze), Recombinant DNA: A Short Course 1983 (with others), The Molecular Biology of the Cell (with others) 1986, Recombinant

DNA, 2nd edn. 1992 (with others); papers on structure of deoxyribonucleic acid (DNA), on protein synthesis and on the induction of cancer by viruses. *Address:* Cold Spring Harbor Laboratory, P.O. Box 100, Cold Spring Harbor, Long Island, New York, NY 11724 (Office); Bungtown Road, Cold Spring Harbor, New York, NY 11724, U.S.A. (Home). *Telephone:* (516) 367-8310.

WATSON, James Kay Graham, PH.D., F.R.S., F.R.S.C.; British research scientist; b. 20 April 1936, Denny, Scotland; s. of Thomas Watson and Mary C. Miller; m. Carolyn M. L. Kerr 1981; ed. Denny High School, High School of Stirling and Univ. of Glasgow; Carnegie Sr. Scholar, Dept. of Chem., Univ. Coll. London 1961–63; Postdoctoral Fellow, Nat. Research Council, Ottawa 1963–65; ICI Research Fellow, Univ. of Reading 1965–66, lecturer in Chemical Physics 1966–71; Visiting Assoc. Prof. in Physics, Ohio State Univ. 1971–75; S.R.C. Sr. Research Fellow in Chem. Univ. of Southampton 1975–79, 1980–82; Visiting Scientist, Nat. Research Council, Ottawa 1979–80, Sr. Research Officer 1982–87, Prin. 1987–; Fellow American Physical Soc. 1990; Chem. Soc. Award 1974; Plyler Prize, American Physical Soc. 1986. *Publications:* 130 articles on molecular physics in learned journals. *Leisure interests:* music, golf, tree-watching. *Address:* 183 Stanley Avenue, Ottawa, Ont., K1M 1P2, Canada. *Telephone:* (613) 990-0739 (Office); (613) 745-7928 (Home).

WATSON, Lyall, PH.D., F.Z.S., F.L.S.; British author and biologist; b. 12 April 1939, South Africa; m. Vivienne Mawson 1961 (divorced 1966); ed. Rondebosch Boys High School, Witwatersrand Univ. and Univs. of Natal and London; Dir. Johannesburg Zoo 1964–65; Producer and Reporter, BBC Television 1966–67; Founder and Dir. Biologic of London (Consultancy) 1968–; organizer and leader of numerous expeditions 1970–; Commr. for Seychelles on Int. Whaling Comm. 1978–82; lives on ocean-going trawler "Amazon" and in a cottage in West Cork, Ireland; Kt. Order of Golden Ark, Netherlands 1983. *Publications:* Omnivore 1970, Supernature 1972, The Romeo Error 1974, Gifts of Unknown Things 1976, Lifetide 1978, Lightning Bird 1980, Whales of the World 1982, Heavens Breath 1984, Earthworks 1986, Beyond Supernature 1986, Supernature II 1986, The Water Planet 1987, Sumo 1988, Neophilia 1988, The Nature of Things 1990, Turtle Islands 1995, Dark Nature 1996, Monsoon 1996, Warriors, Warthogs and Wisdom 1997, Perfect Speed 1998, Jacobson's Organ 1999, Natural Mystery 1999. *Leisure interests:* bird-watching, ethnobotany, archaeology, tribal art, conchology. *Address:* c/o BCM-Biologic, London, WC1N 3XX, England.

WATSON, Thomas Sturges (Tom); American golfer; b. 4 Sept. 1949, Kansas City, Mo.; s. of Raymond Etheridge Watson and Sarah Elizabeth Ridge; m. Linda Tova Rubin 1973; one s. one d.; ed. Stanford Univ.; professional 1971–; British Open Champion 1975, 1977, 1980, 1982, 1983; record low aggregate for British Open of 268, record two single round scores of 65, lowest final 36-hole score of 130, Turnberry 1977; won U.S. Masters title 1977, 1981; won U.S Open 1982; won World Series 1975, 1977, 1980; winner numerous other open championships 1974–; top money winner on U.S. P.G.A. circuit 1977, 1978, 1979, 1980; U.S. P.G.A. Player of the Year 1977, 1978, 1979, 1980, 1982; first player ever to win in excess of $500,000 in prize money in one season 1980; Ryder Cup Player 1977, 1981, 1983, 1989 (Capt. 1992–); mem. PGA World Golf Hall of Fame 1988–. *Publication:* Getting Back into Basics (jtly.) 1992. *Address:* PGA America, P.O. Box 109801, 100 Avenue of the Champions, Palm Beach Gardens, FL 33410; 1901 West 47th Place, Suite 200, Shawnee Mission, KS 66205, U.S.A..

WATSON, William, C.B.E., F.B.A.; British professor of Chinese and Japanese Art History; b. 9 Dec. 1917, Darley Abbey; s. of Robert Scoular Watson and Lily Waterfield; m. Katherine Sylvia Mary Armfield 1940; four s.; ed. Glasgow High School, Herbert Strutt School and Gonville and Caius Coll., Cambridge; Asst. Keeper, British Museum, first in Dept. of British and Medieval Antiquities, then in Dept. of Oriental Antiquities 1947–66; Slade Prof. of Fine Art, Cambridge Univ. 1975–76; Prof. of Chinese Art and Archaeology, Univ. of London (S.O.A.S.) 1966–83, Prof. Emer. 1983–; Pres. of Oriental Ceramic Soc. 1981–84; Hon. D. Litt. (Chinese Univ. of Hong Kong) 1973; Trustee British Museum 1980–90. *Publications:* The Sculpture of Japan 1959, Archaeology in China 1960, China before the Han Dynasty 1961, Ancient Chinese Bronzes 1961, Jade Books in the Chester Beatty Library 1963, Cultural Frontiers in Ancient East Asia 1971, The Genius of China 1973, Style in the Arts of China 1974, L'Art de l'Ancienne Chine 1980; Ed. Catalogue of the Great Japan Exhibition 1981–82, Tang and Liao Ceramics 1984, Pre-Tang Ceramics of China 1991, The Arts of China to AD 900 1995. *Leisure interests:* Iberia, claret, Welsh literature. *Address:* Cefn y Maes, Parc, Bala, Gwynedd, LL23 7YS, Wales. *Telephone:* (01678) 540 302.

WATT, James Gaius, B.S., J.D.; American politician and lawyer; b. 31 Jan. 1938, Lusk, Wyo.; s. of William G. and Lois M. (Williams) Watt; m. Leilani Bomgardner 1957; one s. one d.; ed. Univ. of Wyoming; Instructor, Coll. of Commerce and Industry, Univ. of Wyo. 1960–62; admitted to Wyo. bar 1962, U.S. Supreme Court bar 1966; Legis. Asst., Counsel to Senator Simpson of Wyo. 1962–66; Sec. Natural Resources Comm. and Environmental Pollution Advisory Panel, U.S. Chamber of Commerce 1966–69; Deputy Asst. Sec. for Water and Power, Dept. of the Interior 1969–72; Dir. Bureau of Outdoor Recreation, U.S. Dept. of the Interior 1972–75; Vice-Chair. Fed. Power Comm. 1975–77; Pres., Chief Legal Officer, Mountain States Legal Foundation, Denver 1977–80; U.S. Sec. of the Interior 1981–83; practising law, Washington 1983–86, Jackson Hole, Wyo. 1986–; Chair. of Bd. Environmental Diagnostics Inc. 1984–87, Disease Detection Int. 1987–90. *Publication:* The Courage of a Conservative (with Doug Wead) 1985. *Address:* P.O. Box 3705, 755 East Paintbrush Drive, Box 3705, Jackson, WY 83001, U.S.A.

WATT, James Park, M.B.E.; Scottish boxer (retd.); b. 18 July 1948, Glasgow; s. of James and Ina Watt; m. Margaret Black; two s. one d.; ed. Glasgow Grammar School; rep. Scotland, amateur boxing; Amateur Boxing Asscn. (ABA) lightweight champion 1968; declined invitation to join British Olympic team 1968; turned professional Oct. 1968; beaten in British lightweight championship fight v. Willie Reilly Feb. 1972; won title, beating Tony Riley after Willie Reilly relinquished it May 1972; lost title to Ken Buchanan Jan. 1973; won vacant title v. Johnny Cheshire Jan. 1975; won Lonsdale Belt outright by retaining British title v. Johnny Claydon Feb. 1977; beaten by Jonathan Dele for vacant Commonwealth lightweight title May 1975; won vacant European title, beating André Holyk in first round Aug. 1977; relinquished British title July 1977; retained European title twice in 1978; won vacant World Boxing Council (WBC) version of world lightweight championship April 1979, beating Alfredo Pitalua; defended it v. Roberto Vasquez Nov. 1979, Charlie Nash March 1980, Howard Davis June 1980 and Sean O'Grady Nov. 1980; 45 fights, 38 wins; now works as TV commentator. *Leisure interests:* football and music.

WATTS, Sir Arthur Desmond, K.C.M.G., Q.C., LL.M.; British international lawyer; b. 14 Nov. 1931, Wimbledon; s. of the late Col. A. E. Watts and Eileen May (née Challons) Watts; m. Iris Ann Collier 1957; one s. one d.; ed. Haileybury, Royal Mil. Acad. and Downing Coll., Cambridge; called to Bar, Gray's Inn 1957, Bencher 1996; Legal Asst. Foreign Office 1957–59, Asst. Legal Adviser 1962–67; Legal Adviser British Property Comm. (later British Embassy), Cairo 1959–62; Embassy, Bonn 1967–69; Asst. Solicitor Law Officer's Dept. 1969–70; Legal Counsellor FCO 1970–73, 1977–82; Legal Counsellor, Perm. Rep. to EEC, Brussels 1973–77; Deputy Legal Adviser 1982–87, Legal Adviser 1987–91; Special Negotiator for Succession Issues (fmr. Yugoslavia) 1996–. *Publications:* Legal Effects of War (with Lord McNair) 1966, Encyclopaedic Dictionary of International Law (with Parry, Grant) 1986, Oppenheim's International Law, Vol. I (with Sir Robert Jennings) 1992, International Law and the Antarctic Treaty System 1992, Self-Determination and Self-Administration (with Danspeckgruber) 1997, International Law Commission 1949–1998 (3 vols.) 1999. *Address:* 20 Essex Street, London, WC2R 3AL, England. *Telephone:* 0171-583 9294.

WATTS, Charlie (Charles Robert); British musician; b. 2 June 1941; m. Shirley Anne Shepherd 1964; one d.; drummer with Rolling Stones 1963–; albums with The Rolling Stones include: The Rolling Stones 1964, The Rolling Stones No. 2 1965, Out of Our Heads 1965, Aftermath 1966, Big Hits 1966, got LIVE if you want it! 1967, Between the Buttons 1967, Their Satanic Majesties Request 1967, Beggars Banquet 1968, Let it Bleed 1969, Get Yer Ya-Ya's Out! 1970, Stone Age 1971, Sticky Fingers 1971, Goats Head Soup 1973, It's Only Rock'N'Roll 1974, Black and Blue 1976, Love You Live 1977, Some Girls 1978, Emotional Rescue 1980, Tattoo You 1981, Still Life 1981, Dirty Work 1986, Steel Wheels 1989, Flashpoint 1991, Voodoo Lounge 1994; solo albums include: Charlie Watts Orchestra—Live at Fulham Town Hall 1986, From One Charlie 1992, Warm and Tender 1993, From One Charlie 1995, Long Ago and Far Away 1996; toured with Charlie Watts Orchestra 1985–86; films include: Sympathy For The Devil 1969, Gimme Shelter 1970, Ladies and Gentlemen, The Rolling Stones 1977, Let's Spend the Night Together 1983, Flashpoint 1991. *Publication:* Ode to a High Flying Bird 1965. *Leisure interest:* jazz music. *Address:* c/o Munro Sounds, 5 Church Row, Wandsworth Plain, London SW18 1ES, England.

WATTS, Donald Walter, A.M., PH.D., F.T.S.E., F.R.A.C.I., F.A.C.E., F.A.I.M.; Australian business executive; b. 1 April 1934, Western Australia; s. of Horace Frederick Watts and Esme Anne White; m. Michelle Rose Yeomans 1960; two s.; ed. Hale School, Perth, Univ. of Western Australia, University Coll. London, U.K.; Personal Chair. in Physical and Inorganic Chem., Univ. of Western Australia 1977–79; Dir. Western Australian Inst. of Tech. 1980–86; Vice-Chancellor Curtin Univ. of Tech. 1987; Pres. and Vice-Chancellor Bond Univ. 1987–90, Emer. Prof. 1990; C.E.O. Trade Devt. Zone Authority, Darwin 1990–91; Chair. N.T. Employment & Training Authority 1991–93; Dean Coll. of Arts and Sciences, Univ. of Notre Dame, Western Australia 1995–97, Dean of Research 1998–, Prof. of Science and Educ. 1995–; Dir. Advanced Energy Systems 1995–96 (Chair. 1997–); Fellow Royal Australian Chemical Inst., Australian Acad. of Tech. Sciences and Eng.; mem. American Chemical Soc., Chemical Educ. Sub.-Cttee., Australian Acad. of Science; Hon. Fellow Marketing Inst. of Singapore; Hackett Scholar 1953, Gledden Fellow 1957, CSIRO Postdoctoral Fellow 1959, DSIR Postdoctoral Fellow 1961, Fulbright Scholar 1967; Japan Foundation Visiting Fellow 1984; Hon. D. Tech. (Curtin Univ. of Tech.) 1987; Rennie Medal 1967, Leighton Medal Royal Australian Chemical Inst. 1987. *Publications:* The School Chemistry Project—A Secondary School Chemistry Syllabus for Comment (with N. S. Bayliss) 1978, Chemical Properties and Reactions (with A. R. H. Cole and R. B. Bucat) 1978, Chemistry for Australian Secondary School Students (with N. S. Bayliss) 1979, Elements of Chemistry: Earth, Air, Fire and Water 1984, Higher Education in Australia: A Way Forward, Policy Paper No. 8 1986, The Private Potential of Australian Higher Education 1987, A Private Approach to Higher Education 1987; numerous articles. *Leisure interests:* golf, tennis, reading. *Address:* 87 Evans Street, Shenton Park, WA 6008, Australia. *Telephone:* (8) 9239-5533 (Office); (8) 9381-1667 (Home).

WATTS, Helen Josephine, C.B.E.; British contralto (retd.); b. 7 Dec. 1927, Milford Haven, Wales; d. of Thomas Watts and Winifred Morgan; m. Michael

Mitchell 1980; ed. St. Mary and St. Anne's School, Abbot Bromley; singer in Glyndebourne and BBC choruses; toured Russia with English Opera Group 1964; Concert tours in U.S.A. 1967–85 (retd.); has appeared with all major European and American orchestras; numerous recordings; has sung at the Salzburg Festival, Covent Garden and the Hong Kong Festival; major appearances include: The Ring at Covent Garden; Mozart Opera at Salzburg Festival; four Promenade concerts 1974; Hon. F.R.A.M. *Recordings include:* Handel Arias, Orfeo, B Minor Mass, Beethoven's Mass in C Minor, The Dream of Gerontius, The Apostles, Götterdämmerung. *Leisure interest:* gardening.

WATTS, Philip Beverley, M.SC.; British oil company executive; b. 25 June 1945, Leicester; s. of Samuel Watts and Philippa Watts (née Wale); m. Janet Edna Watts (née Lockwood) 1966; one s. one d.; ed. Wyggeston Grammar School, Leicester and Leeds Univ.; science teacher, Methodist Boys High School, Freetown, Sierra Leone 1966–68; joined Shell Int. 1969; held various posts: seismologist, Indonesia 1970–74, geophysicist UK/Europe 1974–77, Exploration Man., Norway 1978–81, Div. Head, Malaysia, Brunei, Singapore, London 1981–83, Exploration Dir., U.K. 1983–85; Head EP Liaison—Europe, The Hague 1986–88, Head EP Econs. and Planning, The Hague 1989–91, Man. Dir., Nigeria 1991–94, Regional Co-ordinator, Europe, The Hague 1994–95; Dir. Planning, Environment and External Affairs, London 1996–97; Group Man. Dir. Royal Dutch/Shell Group, Man. Dir. Shell Transport and Trading 1997–; mem. Exec. Cttee. World Business Council for Sustainable Devt. 1998–; Chair. Governing Body ICC-UK 1998– (mem. 1997), Worldwide ICC, Exec. Bd. 1997–. *Leisure interests:* travel, gardening, reading. *Address:* Shell Centre, London, SE1 7NA, England. *Telephone:* 0171-934 5554. *Fax:* 0171-934 5557.

WATTS, William Arthur, M.A., SC.D.; Irish university provost; b. 26 May 1930; s. of William Watts and Bessie Dickinson; m. Geraldine Magrath 1954; two s. one d.; ed. St. Andrew's Coll. Dublin and Trinity Coll. Dublin; Lecturer in Botany, Univ. of Hull 1953–55; Lecturer in Botany, Trinity Coll. Dublin 1955–65, Prof. of Botany 1965–80, Prof. of Quaternary Ecology 1980–81, Provost 1981–91; Adjunct Prof. of Geology, Univ. of Minnesota 1975–; mem. Dublin Inst. for Advanced Studies 1981–; Chair. Federated Dublin Voluntary Hospitals 1983–, Mercer's Hosp. 1973–83, Mercer's Hosp. Found. 1983–, Health Research Bd. 1987–89; Fellow, Irish Man. Inst.; Pres. Royal Irish Acad. 1982–85; Gov. Nat. Gallery of Ireland 1982–85, Marsh's Library 1981–; Hon. L.L.D. (Queen's Univ., Belfast) 1990, Hon. D.Sc. (Nat. Univ. of Ireland) 1991. *Publications:* numerous articles on aspects of quaternary ecology. *Leisure interests:* walking, conservation studies, music. *Address:* c/o Trinity College, Room 24.02, Dublin 2, Ireland. *Telephone:* (1) 772941.

WAUGH, Auberon Alexander; British writer; b. 17 Nov. 1939, Dulverton, Somerset; s. of late Evelyn Waugh and Laura Waugh; m. Teresa Onslow 1961; two s. two d.; ed. Downside School, Christ Church, Oxford; editorial staff, Daily Telegraph 1960–63; special writer, IPC Publications 1964–67; political corresp., Spectator 1967–70, Chief Fiction Reviewer 1970–73, weekly columnist 1976–90; political corresp. and columnist, Private Eye 1970–86; Chief Book Reviewer, The Independent 1986–89; columnist The Times 1970–71, The Sunday Telegraph 1981–90, 1996–, The Daily Telegraph 1990–; weekly columnist, New Statesman 1973–76; Chief Fiction Reviewer, Evening Standard 1973–80; monthly columnist, Books and Bookmen 1973–80; Chief Fiction Reviewer, Daily Mail 1980–86; Ed. The Literary Review Jan. 1986–; British Press Award, "Critic of the Year" commendations 1977 and 1978, Granada TV "What the Papers Say", Columnist of the Year 1979, 1988. *Publications:* The Foxglove Saga 1960, Consider the Lilies 1968, Biafra: Britain's Shame (with S. Cronje) 1969, Country Topics 1974, Four Crowded Years 1976, In the Lion's Den 1979, The Last Word: The Trial of Jeremy Thorpe 1980, Auberon Waugh's Yearbook 1981, The Diaries of Auberon Waugh, A Turbulent Decade 1976–85 1985, Waugh on Wine 1986, Another Voice (essays) 1986, The Literary Review, Anthology of Real Poetry 1991 (ed.), Will This Do? The First Fifty Years of Auberon Waugh: An Autobiography 1991, Way of the World 1995, The Forgotten Years 1997. *Leisure interest:* gossip. *Address:* Combe Florey House, Combe Florey, Taunton, Somerset, TA4 3JD; 7 Phoenix Lodge Mansions, Brook Green, London, W6 7BG, England; La Pesegado, 11320 Montmaur, Labastide d'Anjou, France. *Telephone:* (01823) 432297 (Somerset). *Fax:* (01823) 432502.

WAUGH, John Stewart, PH.D.; American professor of chemistry; b. 25 April 1929, Willimantic, Conn.; s. of Albert E. Waugh and Edith S. Waugh; m. Susan M. Walsh 1983; one s. one d.; ed. Windham High School, Dartmouth Coll. and Calif. Inst. of Tech.; mem. Faculty, M.I.T. 1953–, A. A. Noyes Prof. of Chem. 1973–88, Inst. Prof. 1989–; Visiting Scientist, U.S.S.R. Acad. of Sciences 1962, Univ. of Calif. 1963, Harvard Univ. 1975; Visiting Prof. Max Planck Inst. for Medical Research 1971, East China Normal Univ., Shanghai 1984, Texas A & M Univ. 1986; Joliot-Curie Prof. Ecole Supérieure de Physique et Chimie, Paris 1985, 1997; Fairchild Scholar, Calif. Inst. of Tech. 1989; Chair. Div. of Chem. Physics, American Physical Soc. 1984–85; Vice-Pres. Int. Soc. of Magnetic Resonance 1996–98, Pres. 1998–; mem. N.A.S., American Acad. of Arts and Sciences 1962–96, Slovenian Acad. of Sciences and Arts; von Humboldt Award 1971, Langmuir Award 1974, Pittsburgh Spectroscopy Award 1978, Wolf Laureate 1984, Pauling Medal 1985, Richards Medal 1992. *Publications:* many scientific research papers. *Leisure interest:* sailing. *Address:* Department of Chemistry, Massachusetts Institute of Technology, 77 Massachusetts Avenue, Cambridge, MA 02139, U.S.A. *Telephone:* (617) 253 1901. *Fax:* (617) 253-7030.

WAUGH, Stephen Rodger; Australian cricketer; b. 2 June 1965, Canterbury, Sydney; elder twin of Mark Edward; s. of Rodger Waugh and Beverley Waugh; ed. East Hills High School; right-hand batsman and right-arm medium-fast bowler; teams—New South Wales 1984–85 to date, Somerset 1987–88; 111 Tests for Australia 1985–86 to 6 Jan. 1999, scoring 7,213 runs (average 50.4) including 17 hundreds and a record 9 nineties, and taking 89 wickets (average 34.8); has scored 16,623 first-class runs (average 51.9) with 49 hundreds to 1 Oct. 1998; shared world record 5th wicket stand of 464 (unbroken) with M. E. Waugh for N.S.W. v W. Australia, Perth, 1990–91; toured England 1989, 1993, 1997; 249 limited-overs internationals to 31 Dec. 1998 (30 as Capt.). *Publications:* South African Tour Diary 1995, Steve Waugh's West Indies Tour Diary 1996, Steve Waugh's World Cup Diary 1997.

WAX, Ruby; American comedienne and actress; b. 19 April 1953, Ill.; d. of Edward Wax and Berta Wax (née Goldmann); m. Edward Richard Morison Bye 1988; one s. two d.; ed. Evanston High School, Berkeley Univ., Royal Scottish Acad. of Music and Drama; with Crucible Theatre 1976; with RSC 1978–82. *Television includes:* Not the Nine O'Clock News 1982–83, Girls on Top 1983–85, Don't Miss Wax 1985–87, Hit and Run 1988, Full Wax 1987–92, Ruby Wax Meets . . . 1996, 1997, 1998, Ruby 1997, 1998. *Films include:* Miami Memoirs 1987, East Meets Wax 1988, Class of '69, Ruby Takes a Trip 1992. *Address:* c/o Peters & Dunlop, 503 The Chambers, Chelsea Harbour, Lots Road, London, SW10 0XF, England. *Telephone:* 0171-344 1010. *Fax:* 0171-352 8135.

WAZZAN, Chafiq al-, LL.B.; Lebanese politician and lawyer; b. 1925, Beirut; m.; two s.; ed. al-Makassed Coll., St. Joseph's Univ., Beirut; law practice 1947–; Deputy for Beirut, Nat. Ass. 1968; Minister of Justice Jan.–Oct. 1969; Pres. Higher Islamic Council 1963, Lebanese Muslim Congress; fmr. mem. Presidium al-Hayat al-Wataniya party; Prime Minister 1980–84. *Address:* Rue Haroun el-Rashid, Immeuble Wazzan, Beirut, Lebanon (Home).

WEAIRE, Denis Lawrence; British/Irish physicist; b. 17 Oct. 1942; s. of Allen M. Weaire and Janet E. Rea; m. Colette O'Regan 1969; one s.; ed. Belfast Royal Acad. and Cambridge Univ.; Harkness Fellowship 1964–66; Fellow, Clare Coll. Cambridge 1967–69; Instructor, Assoc. Prof. Yale Univ. 1970–74; Sr. Lecturer, Prof. Heriot-Watt Univ. 1974–79; Chair. of Experimental Physics, Univ. Coll. Dublin 1980–84; Erasmus Smith's Prof. of Natural and Experimental Philosophy, Trinity Coll. Dublin 1984–, Dean of Science 1989; mem. Royal Irish Acad.; Hon. Sec. European Asscn. of Deans of Science 1991–93; Vice-Pres. European Physical Soc. 1995–96, Pres. 1997–. *Publications:* Introduction to Physical Mathematics (co-author) 1985; co-ed. of several other vols. *Leisure interests:* sport, sea-fishing, theatre. *Address:* University of Dublin, Trinity College, Faculty of Science, Dublin 2; 26 Greenmount Road, Terenure, Dublin, Ireland.

WEARING, Gillian, B.A.; British artist and photographer; b. 1963, Birmingham; ed. Chelsea School of Art, Goldsmith's Coll., London; first solo exhbn. City Racing, London 1993, numerous exhbns. around the world; concentrates on photography. *Works include:* Signs that say what you want them to say and not signs that say what someone else wants you to say, 10-16, Sixty Minutes' Silence (winner of Turner Prize 1997); Phaidon Press Award 1999. *Address:* c/o Maureen Paley Interim Art, 21 Beck Road, London, E8 4RE, England. *Telephone:* 0171-254 9607. *Fax:* 0171-254 6445.

WEATHERALL, Sir David John, Kt., M.D., F.R.S., F.R.C.P.; British professor of medicine; b. 9 March 1933, Liverpool; s. of the late Harry Weatherall and Gwendoline Weatherall; m. Stella Nestler 1962; one s.; ed. Calday Grammar School and Univ. of Liverpool; various resident posts in medicine 1956–58; jr. medical specialist, Royal Army Medical Corps, Singapore 1959–60; Research Fellow, Johns Hopkins Hosp. 1961–65; Reader in Haematology, Univ. of Liverpool 1969–71, Prof. 1971–74; consultant to WHO 1967–82; Nuffield Prof. of Clinical Medicine, Univ. of Oxford 1974–92, Regius Prof. of Medicine 1992–, Fellow, Magdalen Coll. 1974–92, Emer. Fellow 1992, Student, Christ Church 1992–; Hon. Dir. MRC Molecular Haematology Unit 1979–, Inst. of Molecular Medicine 1988–; Trustee Wellcome Trust 1990–; Pres. British Asscn. for the Advancement of Science 1993, Int-Soc. of Haematology 1993; mem. American Acad. of Arts and Sciences; Watson-Smith Lecture 1974, Croonian Lecture 1984, Foundation Lecture (F.R.C. Path.) 1979, Darwin Lecture (Eugenics Soc.) 1979; Sims Visiting Prof. 1982; Fellow Imperial Coll.; Foreign Assoc. N.A.S., Inst. of Medicine; Hon. F.R.C.O.G.; Hon. F.A.C.P.; Hon. F.R.C.P.C.H.; Hon. M.D. (Leeds) 1988, (Sheffield) 1989, (Nottingham) 1993; Hon. D.Sc. (Manchester) 1989, (Edin.) 1989, (Aberdeen) 1991, (Leicester) 1991, (London) 1992, (Keele) 1993, (Mahidol Univ., Thailand) 1997; Hon. D.Hum.Litt. (Johns Hopkins Univ.) 1990; Hon. D.Sc. (Oxford Brookes) 1995, (South Bank) 1995, (Exeter) 1998; Hon. LL.D. (Liverpool) 1992, (Bristol) 1994; Stratton Award and Medal (Int. Haematology Soc.) 1982, Ballantyne Prize (R.C.P. Edin.) 1983, Feldberg Foundation Award 1984, Royal Medal (Royal Soc.) 1989, Conway Evans Prize (Royal Soc. and Royal Coll. Physicians) 1991, Gold Medal, Royal Soc. of Medicine 1992, Buchanan Medal (Royal Soc.) 1994, Helmut Horten Int. Prize in Biomedical Science 1995. *Publications:* The New Genetics and Clinical Practice 1982, The Thalassaemia Syndromes (with J. B. Clegg) 1982, Oxford Textbook of Medicine (with others) 1983. *Leisure interest:* music. *Address:* Institute of Molecular Medicine, John Radcliffe Hospital, Headington, Oxford, OX3 9DU (Office); 8 Cumnor Rise Road, Cumnor Hill, Oxford, OX2 9HD, England (Home). *Telephone:* (01865) 222359 (Office). *Fax:* (01865) 222501.

WEATHERALL, Vice-Adm. Sir James (Lamb), K.B.E.; British naval officer and Marshal of the Diplomatic Corps; b. 28 Feb. 1936, Newton Mearns, Renfrewshire; s. of the late Lieut. Commdr. Alwynne Weatherall and Joan Cuthbert; m. Hon. Jean Stewart Macpherson 1962; two s. three d.; ed. Glasgow Acad., Gordonstoun School; commanded H.M. Ships Soberton 1966–67, Ulster 1970–72, Tartar 1975–76, Andromeda 1982–84 (in Falklands Conflict), Ark Royal 1985–87; on staff of SACEUR as Rear Adm. 1987–89; Deputy Supreme Allied Commdr. Atlantic 1989–91; H.M. Marshal of the Diplomatic Corps 1992–; Chair. Sea Cadet Asscn. 1992–; Liveryman Worshipful Co. of Shipwrights 1985, Asst. to Court 1989, 4th Warden 1998; Younger Brother Trinity House 1986; Trustee Marwell Zoological Preservation Trust 1992; Gov. Box Hill School 1992– (Chair. 1994), Gordonstoun School 1994– (Chair. 1996); Pres. Int. Social Service 1996–. *Leisure interests:* fishing, stamp collecting. *Address:* Clock Tower House, St. James's Palace, London, SW1A 1BN; Craig House, Ashton Lane, Bishop's Waltham, Hants., SO32 1FS, England. *Telephone:* 0171-930 4749 (Clock Tower); (01489) 892483 (Home).

WEATHERHEAD, Rt. Rev. James Leslie, C.B.E., M.A., LL.B.; British ecclesiastic in Church of Scotland; b. 29 March 1931, Dundee; s. of Leslie Binnie Weatherhead and Janet Hood Arnot Smith; m. Anne Elizabeth Shepherd 1962; two s.; ed. High School, Dundee and Univ. of Edinburgh; nat. service in R.N. 1955–56; ordained 1960; Parish Minister Trinity Church, Rothesay 1962–69; The Old Church, Montrose 1969–85; Prin. Clerk of Gen. Ass. of Church of Scotland 1985–93, 1994–96 Moderator 1993–94; a Chaplain to H.M. The Queen in Scotland 1991–. *Publication:* The Constitution and Laws of the Church of Scotland (Ed.) 1997. *Leisure interests:* music and sailing. *Address:* Church of Scotland Offices, 121 George Street, Edinburgh, EH2 4YN (Office); Newton Park, 59 Brechin Road, Kirriemuir, DD8 4DE, Scotland (Home). *Telephone:* 0131-225 5722 (Office); (01575) 572237 (Home).

WEATHERILL, Baron (Life Peer), cr. 1992, of North East Croydon in the London Borough of Croydon; **(Bruce) Bernard Weatherill;** British politician and master tailor; b. 25 Nov. 1920, Sunningdale, Surrey; s. of the late Bernard Weatherill and of Gertrude Creak; m. Lyn Eatwell 1949; two s. one d; ed. Malvern Coll.; served Royal Dragoon Guards, Indian Army, 19th King George V's Own Lancers 1939–45; Man. Dir. Bernard Weatherill Ltd. 1957–70, Pres. 1992–; M.P. for Croydon North East 1964–92; Opposition Whip 1967–70; Lord Commr. of H.M. Treasury 1970–71; Vice-Chamberlain of the Royal Household 1971–72, Comptroller 1972–73; Treasurer of the Household and Deputy Chief Whip 1974–79; Chair. Ways and Means and Deputy Speaker 1979–83; Speaker of the House of Commons 1983–92; Convenor of Cross-bench Peers, House of Lords 1995–; Chair. Commonwealth Speakers and Presiding Officers 1986–88; High Bailiff of Westminster Abbey 1989–; Chair. The Parl. Channel, Industry and Parliament Trust; Vice-Chancellor The Order of St. John of Jerusalem 1992–; Hon. D.C.L. (Kent) 1990, (Univ. of William and Mary, Williamsburg), (Denver, Colo.); Hon. D.Univ. (Open Univ.). *Publication:* Acorns to Oaks. *Leisure interests:* golf, tennis. *Address:* House of Lords, London, SW1A 0PW; Emmetts House, Ide Hill, Kent, TN14 6BA, England. *Telephone:* 0171-219 5353.

WEATHERSTONE, Sir Dennis, K.B.E., F.I.B.; British banker; b. 29 Nov. 1930, London; s. of Henry Philip Weatherstone and Gladys Hart; m. Marion Blunsum 1959; one s. three d.; ed. Acland High School, Northwestern Polytechnic, London; Vice-Pres. Morgan Guaranty Trust Co. 1965–72, Sr. Vice-Pres. 1972–77. Exec. Vice-Pres. and Treas. 1977–79; Vice-Chair. Morgan Guaranty Trust Co. (now J. P. Morgan & Co. Inc.) 1979–80, Chair. Exec. Cttee. 1980–86, Pres. 1987–89, Chair. 1989–94, C.E.O. 1990–94; mem. Bd. of Banking Supervision of Bank of England 1994–. *Leisure interest:* tennis. *Address:* J.P. Morgan & Co., 60 Wall Street, New York, NY 10260, U.S.A.

WEAVER, A. Vernon; American diplomatist; b. 16 April 1922, Miami, Fla.; s. of A. Vernon Weaver, Sr. and Genevieve Weaver; m. Joyce McCoy 1947; three d.; ed. U.S. Naval Acad.; with U.S. Navy 1946–49, 1951–53; with Southern Venetian Blind Co., Miami 1949–51 (Vice-Pres.), 1953–59; Pres. Lanotan Inc., Miami 1952–62; Man. Hollis & Co., Little Rock 1962–64; Pres. Union Life Insurance, Little Rock 1954–77; Admin. U.S. Small Business Admin., Washington D.C 1977–81; Asst. to Chair., Stephens, Inc., Washington D.C. 1981–96; Amb. to EU July 1996–. *Leisure interests:* reading, tennis. *Address:* Permanent Mission of the United States to the European Union, 40 Boulevard du Régent, Brussels 1000, Belgium. *Telephone:* (2) 508-2750. *Fax:* (2) 514-4339.

WEAVER, Michael; American boxer; b. 7 July 1952, Gatesville, Tex.; m.; three d.; ed. High School; joined U.S. Marines 1969; began amateur boxing 1971; served in Viet Nam; American Services heavyweight champion; professional Sept. 1972–; sparring partner for leading heavyweights Ken Norton and Bernardo Mercado; knocked out Mercado Oct. 1978; won U.S. heavyweight title Jan. 1979; lost in 12 rounds to Larry Holmes for World Boxing Council (WBC) version of world heavyweight title June 1979; won World Boxing Asscn. version of title by knocking out John Tate in 15th round, Knoxville, U.S.A. March 1980; retained title, knocking out Gerrie Coetzee, Bophuthatswana, S.A. Oct. 1980; 31 fights, 22 wins.

WEAVER, Sigourney; American actress; b. 8 Oct. 1949, New York; d. of Pat Weaver and Elizabeth Inglis; m. James Simpson 1984; one d. *Films include:* Annie Hall 1977, Tribute to a Madman 1977, Camp 708 1978, Alien 1979, Eyewitness 1981, The Year of Living Dangerously 1982, Deal of the Century 1983, Ghostbusters 1984, Une Femme ou Deux 1985, Half Moon Street 1986, Aliens 1986, Gorillas in the Mist (Golden Globe Best Actress Award) 1988, Working Girl (Best Supporting Actress Award Golden Globe) 1988, Ghostbusters II 1989, Aliens 3 1992, 1492: Conquest of Paradise 1993, Dave 1993, Death and the Maiden 1994, Jeffrey 1995, Copycat 1996, Snow White in the Black Forest 1996, Ice Storm 1996, Alien Resurrection 1997. *Address:* c/o ICM, 8942 Wilshire Boulevard, Beverly Hills, CA 90211, U.S.A.

WEBB, James H., Jr., J.D.; American government official; b. 9 Feb. 1946, Arlington, Va.; m.; three c.; ed. U.S. Naval Acad. and Georgetown Univ.; Asst. Minority Counsel, House Cttee. on Veterans Affairs, Washington 1977–78, Chief Minority Counsel 1979–81; Visiting Writer, U.S. Naval Acad. 1979; Asst. Sec. for Reserve Affairs, Dept. of Defense 1984–87; Sec. of the Navy 1987–88. *Publications include:* A Country Such As This, Something to Die For 1991.

WEBB, Leslie Roy, B.COM., PH.D.; Australian university vice-chancellor; b. 18 July 1935, Melbourne; s. of Leslie Hugh Charles Webb and Alice Myra Webb; m. Heather Brown 1966; one s. one d.; ed. Wesley Coll., Melbourne, Univ. of Melbourne, London School of Economics; Sr. Lecturer in Econs., Univ. of Melbourne 1962–68, Truby Williams Prof. of Econs. 1973–84, Prof. Emer. 1985–, Pro-Vice-Chancellor 1982–84, Chair. Academic Bd. 1983–84; Reader in Econs., La Trobe Univ. 1969–72; Vice-Chancellor Griffith Univ. 1985–; Visiting Prof. Cornell Univ., U.S.A. 1967–68; Consultant, UNCTAD 1974–75; Jt. Ed. The Economic Record 1973–77; Chair. Cttee. of Inquiry into S. Australian Dairy Industry 1977; Assoc. mem. Prices Justification Tribunal 1978–79, 1980–81; mem. Council of Advice, Bureau of Industry Econs. 1982–84; Chair. Bd. of Dirs. Australian-American Educational Foundation (Fulbright Program) 1986–90; mem. Bd. of Govs., Foundation for Devt. Co-operation 1990; Dir. and mem. Australian Vice-Chancellors' Cttee. Bd. of Dirs. 1991; Pres. Victorian Br., Econ. Soc. of Australia and N.Z. 1976; Award for Outstanding Achievement, U.S. Information Agency 1987; Cavaliere, Ordine al Merito (Italy). *Publications:* Industrial Economics: Australian Studies (Jt. Ed.) 1982; articles in learned journals. *Leisure interests:* music, art. *Address:* Griffith University, Kessels Road, Nathan, Queensland 4111 (Office); 3 Davrod Street, Robertson, Queensland 4109, Australia (Home). *Telephone:* (07) 3875-7340 (Office); (07) 3345-7141 (Home). *Fax:* (07) 3875-7507.

WEBBER, Tristan, M.A.; British fashion designer; ed. S.E. Essex Coll. of Arts and Tech., Cordwainers Coll., London and St. Martin's School of Art and Design; work exhibited at Colette, Paris and Powerhouse Exhbn., London 1998; third collection shown at London Fashion Week (Sept. 1998) and MTV Fashionably Loud event, Miami (Dec. 1998). *Address:* c/o Brower Lewis PR, 74 Gloucester Place, London, W1H 3HN, England. *Telephone:* 0171-935 2735. *Fax:* 0171-935 2739.

WEBER, Bruce; American photographer, film director and producer; b. 29 March 1946, Greensburg, Pa.; ed. Hun School at Princeton, Denison Univ., Ohio, New York Art and Film School, New School for Social Research, New York; numerous exhbns. New York, Los Angeles, Chicago, Dallas, San Francisco, Atlanta, New Orleans, St. Louis, Paris, London, Dortmund, Basel, Lausanne, Tokyo, Frankfurt etc. 1973–; Dir. and Producer films: Broken Noses 1987, Let's Get Lost 1988, Beauty Brothers 1988; numerous awards including: Council of Fashion Designers of America for Achievement in Photography 1984, 1985, American Soc. of Magazine Photographers Fashion Photographer of the Year 1984, Int. Film and TV Festival of New York Silver Medal 1985, Int. Advertising Film Festival Silver Lion for Beauty Brothers 1988, The Critics' Award, Venice Film Festival, for Let's Get Lost 1988, Int. Documentary Asscn. Award for Broken Noses 1988, for Let's Get Lost 1989. *Publication:* Gentle Giants: A Book of Newfoundland 1995, Branded Youth and other stories 1997. *Address:* c/o Robert Miller Gallery, 41 East 57th Street, New York, NY 10022, U.S.A.

WEBER, George Brian, M.A.; Canadian Red Cross official; b. 18 April 1946, Montreal; s. of Harry Weber and Johanna Alexopoulos; m. Mary Morris 1976; ed. McGill Univ., Harvard Univ.; voluntary instructor/examiner Canadian Red Cross 1963–73; Field Del. Vietnam, Int. Red Cross 1973–74; Disaster Relief Officer, Chief Del. League of Red Cross Socs. 1974–76; Nat. Dir. Int. Affairs, Canadian Red Cross 1976–81, Nat. Dir. of Programmes 1981–83, Sec. Gen. Canadian Red Cross 1983–93, Hon. Vice Pres. 1993–, Sec. Gen. and C.E.O. Int. Fed. of Red Cross and Red Crescent Socs. 1993–. mem., dir. numerous bodies, including Canadian Inst. of Int. Affairs, Amundsen Foundation, Earth Foundation, American Coll. of Sports Medicine, Canadian Soc. Assoc. Execs. Awards include Vanier Award 1984. *Leisure interests:* diving, tennis, squash, skiing. *Address:* P.O. Box 372, 1211 Geneva 19 (Office); Chemin Moise-Duboule 29, 1209 Geneva, Switzerland (Home).

WEBER, John William, B.A.; American art dealer; b. 10 Dec. 1932, Los Angeles, Calif; s. of John William Weber and Helen M. Curran; m. Joyce Nereaux 1981; four c.; ed. Admiral Farragut Acad., Fla., Antioch Coll. Yellow Springs, Ohio and Inst. of Fine Arts, New York Univ.; Assoc. Curator, Dayton Art Inst. Dayton, Ohio 1958; Dir. Martha Jackson Gallery, New York 1960–62, Dwan Gallery, L.A. and New York 1962–71; founder and Pres. John Weber Gallery, New York 1971–; Chevalier, Ordre des Arts et des Lettres. *Publications:* de Europa 1972, Papunya Tula 1989, Political Arm 1991. *Leisure interests:* amateur radio, boating, mountaineering.

Address: John Weber Gallery, 529 W. 20th Street, New York, NY 10011, U.S.A. *Telephone:* (212) 966-6115. *Fax:* (212) 941-8727.

WEBER, Jurgen; German business executive; b. 17 Oct. 1941; m. Sabine Rossberg 1965; one s. one d.; ed. Stuttgart Tech. Univ., M.I.T.; with Lufthansa Eng. Div. 1967–74, Dir. Line Maintenance Dept. 1974–78, with Aircraft Eng. Sub-div. 1978–87, C.O.O. (Tech.) 1987–89, Deputy mem. Exec. Bd. 1989–90, C.E.O. (Tech.) 1990–91, Chair. Exec. Bd. Lufthansa German Airlines 1991–, C.E.O. 1998–. *Leisure interests:* jogging, skiing. *Address:* Deutsche Lufthansa AG, Lufthansa Basis, 60546 Frankfurt, Germany. *Telephone:* (69) 6962200.

WEBER, Manfred, DR.RER.POL.; German banking official; b. 18 Dec. 1950; ed. Johann Wolfgang Goethe Univ. Frankfurt am Main; Research Asst. Research Dept. Deutsche Bundesbank 1980, Head, Office of Deputy Gov. 1986–91; Monetary and Econ. Dept. B.I.S., Basle 1991–92; Sec.-Gen. and mem. Bd. of Dirs. Bundesverband Deutscher Banken, Cologne 1992–. *Address:* 50667 Cologne, Kattenbug 1, Germany. *Telephone:* 1663 215. *Fax:* 1663 206.

WEBSTER, Peter; business executive; joined Jefferson Smurfit Group 1978, fmr. Regional Operations Dir., Chair. and Chief Exec. 1996–. *Address:* Jefferson Smurfit Group PLC, Beech Hill, Clonskeagh, Dublin 14, Ireland. *Telephone:* 01 269 6622. *Fax:* 01 269 4481.

WEBSTER, William Hedgcock, LL.B.; American government official and judge; b. 6 March 1924, St. Louis, Mo.; s. of Thomas M. and Katherine (Hedgcock) Webster; m. 1st Drusilla Lane 1950 (died 1984); one s. two d.; m. 2nd Lynda Clugston 1990; ed. Amherst Coll., Washington Univ. Law School; admitted to Mo. Bar 1949; attorney with Armstrong, Teasdale, Kramer and Vaughan, and predecessors, St. Louis 1949–50, 1952–59, partner 1956–59, 1961–70; U.S. Attorney, Eastern Dist., Mo. 1960–61; Judge U.S. Dist. Court, Eastern Mo. 1971–73, U.S. Court of Appeals 1973–78; Dir. FBI 1978–87; Dir. of Cen. Intelligence Agency (CIA) 1987–91; Sr. Partner Millbank, Tweed, Hadley & McCloy 1991–; Trustee, Washington Univ. 1974–; Head investigation into police response to L.A. Riots 1992; served as Lieut. U.S.N.R. 1943–46, 1951–52; mem. American, Fed., Mo., and St. Louis Bar asscns., American Law Inst., Council 1978–, Inst. of Judicial Admin. Inc. (Pres.-elect 1982); Fellow, American Bar Foundation; Hon. LL.D. (Amherst Coll. 1975, DePauw Univ. 1978, Washington Univ. 1978, William Woods Coll. 1979 and numerous others); Wash. Univ. Distinguished Alumnus Award 1977; American Legion Distinguished Service Award 1979; Order of the Coif; St. Louis Globe-Democrat Man of the Year 1980; Washington Univ. William Greenleaf Elliot Award 1981; Riot Relief Fund of N.Y. Award 1981, Young Lawyers of the American Bar Asscn. Award 1982, Fordham-Stein Award 1982, William Moss Inst.-American Univ. Award 1983, Freedoms Foundation Medal 1985. *Leisure interest:* tennis. *Address:* 1825 I Street, N.W., Suite 1100, Washington, DC 20006, U.S.A.

WECHMAR, Rüdiger Baron Von; German diplomatist and journalist; b. 15 Nov. 1923, Berlin; s. of Irnfried Baron von Wechmar and Ilse Baroness von Wechmar (née von Binzer); m. 1st Rosemarie Warlimont 1947 (divorced); one s. one d.; m. 2nd Susanne Woldenga 1961; one d.; with German News Service (DPD); joined United Press 1948, Head of Bonn Bureau 1954–58; Press Attaché, German Consulate-Gen., N.Y. 1958; Head of E. European Bureau, Zweites Deutsches Fernsehen, Vienna 1963; Dir. German Information Center, New York 1968; Deputy Head of Govt. Press and Information Office 1969, State Sec., Head of Govt. Press and Information Office, Chief Govt. Spokesman 1972–74; Perm. Rep. to UN 1974–81, Pres. UN Gen. Ass. 1980–81; Amb. to Italy 1981–83, Amb. to U.K. 1984–88; mem. European Parl. 1989–94; mem. Deutsche Gesellschaft für Auswärtige Politik; Paul Klinger Prize 1973, Dag Hammarskjöld Gold Medal 1981, UN Gold Medal 1981 and other decorations. *Publications:* numerous works and articles on foreign and UN affairs. *Address:* Hiltensperger Strasse 15, 80798 Munich, Germany. *Telephone:* (089) 271-1224. *Fax:* (089) 271-1224.

WECKMANN-MUÑOZ, Luis, PH.D., LL.D., M.A.; Mexican diplomatist and historian; b. 7 April 1923, Ciudad Lerdo, Durango; s. of José Bernardo Weckmann and Ana Muñoz; ed. Univ. Nacional Autónoma de México, Univs. of Paris and Calif., Inst. des Hautes Etudes Int. and Ecole des Chartes, Paris; successively Sec. of Legation and Chargé d'affaires, Czechoslovakia, Sec. of Embassy and Chargé d'affaires, France 1952–59; Dir.-Gen. for Int. Educ. Affairs and Exec. Sec.-Gen. Mexican Nat. Council for UNESCO 1959–64; Minister Plenipotentiary and Chargé d'affaires, France 1965–66; Amb. to Israel 1967–69, to Austria 1969–72, to Fed. Repub. of Germany 1973–74; Special Rep. of UN Sec.-Gen. to Iran and Iraq 1974; Special Rep. of UN Sec.-Gen. in Cyprus 1974–75; Amb. to Iran 1976–79, to UN 1979–80, to Italy 1981–86, to Belgium and the EEC 1986–88; Consul-Gen. in Rio de Janeiro 1988–90; Vice-Pres. 1st Interamerican Meeting on Science and Tech., Washington; UNESCO's expert for Latin America on Cultural Exchanges. *Publications:* La Sociedad Feudal 1944, Las Bulas Alejandrinas de 1943 y la Teoría Política del Papado Medieval 1949, El Pensamiento Político Medieval y una nueva base para el Derecho Internacional 1950, Les origines des Missions Diplomatiques Permanentes 1953, Panorama de la Cultura Medieval 1962, Las Relaciones Franco-Mexicanas (1823-1885) vol. I 1961, vol. II 1963, vol. III 1972, La Herencia Medieval de México, vols. I and II 1984, new edn. in one vol. 1994, Carlota de Bélgica: Correspondencia y Escritos sobre México en los archivos Europeos, 1861–1868 1989, Constantino el Grande y Cristóbal Colón 1992, The Medieval Heritage of Brazil 1993. *Leisure interest:* reading. *Address:* Villa del Cardo, Calzado del Cardo 4, 37700 San Miguel Allende, Gto., Mexico.

WEDDERBURN OF CHARLTON, Baron (Life Peer), cr. 1977; **Kenneth William Wedderburn,** Q.C., M.A., LL.B., F.B.A.; British professor of law; b. 13 April 1927, London; s. of Herbert John Wedderburn and Mabel Ethel Wedderburn; m. 1st Nina Salaman 1951 (divorced 1961); one s. two d.; m. 2nd Dorothy Cole 1962 (divorced 1969); m. 3rd Frances Ann Knight 1969; one s.; ed. Aske's (Hatcham) Grammar School, Whitgift School, Queens' Coll., Cambridge; Lecturer in Law, Cambridge Univ. 1952–64; Fellow, Clare Coll., Cambridge; Cassel Prof. of Commercial Law, L.S.E. 1964–92, Emer. Prof. 1992–; Visiting Prof., Harvard Law School 1969–70, Univ. of Calif., Los Angeles 1969; Barrister at Law (Middle Temple) 1953–, Q.C. 1990; Gen. Ed. Modern Law Review 1970–88; mem. Civil Service Arbitration Tribunal 1973–; Chair. Trades Union Congress Ind. Review Cttee. 1975–; Hon. Pres. Industrial Law Soc. 1996–; Fellow, British Acad. 1981; Hon. D. Giur. (Pavia); Hon. D. Econ. (Siena); Hon. LL.D. (Stockholm); Chancellor's Medal for English Law (Cambridge) 1949. *Publications:* Employment Grievances and Disputes Procedures in Britain (with P. L. Davies) 1969, Cases and Materials on Labour Law 1967, The Worker and the Law 1971, 1986, Industrial Conflict—A Comparative Legal Survey (co-ed. with B. Aaron) 1972, Democrazia Politica e Democrazia Industriale 1978, Discrimination in Employment (co-ed.) 1978, Labour Law and the Community (with W. T. Murphy) 1983, Labour Law and Industrial Relations (with R. Lewis and J. Clark) 1983, Diritto del Lavoro in Europa (with B. Veneziani and S. Ghimpu) 1987, The Social Charter, European Company and Employment Rights 1990, Employment Rights in Britain and Europe 1991, Labour Law and Freedom 1995, I Diritti del Lavoro 1998; numerous articles on legal subjects. *Leisure interest:* Charlton Athletic Football Club. *Address:* London School of Economics, Aldwych, London, WC2A 2AE (Office); 29 Woodside Avenue, Highgate, London, N6 4SP, England (Home). *Telephone:* 0171-405 7686 (Office); 0181-444 8472 (Home). *Fax:* 0171-955 7366 (Office); 0181-444 8472 (Home).

WEDEMEIER, Klaus; German politician; b. 12 Jan. 1944, Hof, Bavaria; m.; one c.; apprentice with wholesale export/import firm 1969; co. clerk until 1979; mem. Social Democratic Party (SDP) 1964–; Chair. Young Socialists, Bremen 1970–76; mem. Bremen Parl. 1971–85, Chair. SDP Parl. Group 1979–85; Mayor and Pres. of Senate of Free Hanseatic City of Bremen 1985–95; President of Federal Council 1993. *Address:* c/o Rathaus, D-28309 Bremen 1, Germany. *Telephone:* 0421/361-1. *Fax:* 361-6363.

WEE CHONG JIN, M.A.; Singaporean judge; b. 28 Sept. 1917, Penang, Malaya; s. of late Wee Gim Puay and Lim Paik Yew; m. Cecilia Mary Henderson 1955; three s. one d.; ed. Penang Free School, St. John's Coll., Cambridge; called to Bar, Middle Temple, London 1938, admitted Advocate and Solicitor of Straits Settlements 1940; practised in Penang and Singapore 1940–57; Puisne Judge, Singapore 1957; Chief Justice 1963–90; Acting Pres. of Singapore March–Aug. 1985; Head Presidential Council for Religious Harmony 1992–; Hon. D.C.L. (Oxford) 1987. *Leisure interest:* golf. *Address:* 1 Colombo Court, # 09-05, Singapore 0617.

WEE KIM WEE; Singaporean politician and diplomatist; b. 4 Nov. 1915; s. of Wee Choong Lay and Chua Hay Luan; m. Koh Sok Hiong 1936; one s. six d.; ed. Raffles Inst.; clerk Circulation Dept. Straits Times, then Advertising Dept. then reporter, rejoined as Deputy Ed. (Singapore) 1959, covered civil war in Belgian Congo (now Democratic Repub. of Congo) and was first Singapore journalist to enter Jakarta during Confrontation 1966; joined United Press Asscn. 1941, rejoined 1945–59; served in Air Raid Precautions during attack on Malaya and Singapore; worked as clerk in Japanese mil. establishments during occupation; High Commr. to Malaysia 1973–80; Dean Diplomatic Corps, Kuala Lumpur 1978–80; mem. Singapore Del. to UN Gen. Ass. 1977; Amb. to Japan 1980–84, to Repub. of Korea 1981–84; Chair. Singapore Broadcasting Corpn. 1984–85; Pres. Repub. of Singapore 1985–93; fmr. Pres. Singapore Badminton Asscn., Chair. Singapore Anti-Tuberculosis Asscn.; fmr. mem. Rent Control Bd., Film Appeal Cttee., Land Acquisition Bd., Bd. of Visiting Justices, Nat. Theatre Trust; J.P. 1966; Hon. D. Litt. (Nat. Univ. of Singapore) 1994; Public Service Star 1963, Meritorious Service Medal 1979; Hon. G.C.B. 1989, Laila Utama (Brunei) 1990; Order of Temasek (First Class) 1993; Jr. Singles Badminton Champion of Singapore 1937. *Leisure interests:* golf, walking and writing. *Address:* 25 Siglap Plain, Singapore 456014, Singapore.

WEEDON, Basil Charles Leicester, C.B.E., F.R.S., D.SC., F.R.S.C.; British chemist and university administrator; b. 18 July 1923, London; s. of the late Charles William Weedon and Florence May Weedon; m. Barbara Mary Dawe 1959; one s. one d.; ed. Wandsworth School, Imperial Coll. of Science and Tech., Univ. of London; Research Chemist, ICI Ltd. (Dyestuffs Div.) 1945–47; Lecturer in Organic Chem., Imperial Coll. of Science and Tech. 1947–55, Reader 1955–60; Prof. of Organic Chem., Queen Mary Coll., Univ. of London 1960–75; Vice-Chancellor, Univ. of Nottingham 1976–88; Chair. Food Additives and Contaminants Cttee. 1968–83, Nat. Stone Centre 1985–91, East Midlands Electricity Consumers' Cttee. 1990–95; Hon. Prof. (Nottingham) 1988–; Scientific Ed., Pure and Applied Chemistry 1960–75; mem. EEC Scientific Cttee. for Food 1974–81; Fellow Queen Mary Coll. 1984; Hon. D.Tech. (Brunel) 1975; Hon. LL.D. (Nottingham) 1988; Meldola Medal, Royal Inst. of Chem.; Tilden Lecturer of Chem. Soc. *Publications:* numerous papers in scientific journals, mainly in Journal of the Chemical Society. *Leisure interests:* music, gardening. *Address:* Sheepwash Grange, Heighington Road, Canwick, Lincoln, LN4 2RJ, England. *Telephone:* (01522) 522488.

WEEKS, John Reginald, C.B.E., F.R.I.B.A.; British architect; b. 5 March 1921, London; s. of Victor J. Weeks and Beatrice Beasley; m. Barbara L. Nunn 1955; one s. one d.; ed. Dulwich Coll. London and Architectural Asscn. School of Architecture, London; Deputy Dir. Nuffield Foundation Div. of Architectural Studies 1956–60; architectural partnership with Richard Llewelyn-Davies 1960–81; Chair. Llewelyn-Davies Weeks 1981–86, Consultant 1986–91; Sr. lecturer, Bartlett School of Architecture, Univ. of London 1961–72; mem. Council, Architectural Asscn. 1975–83 (Vice-Pres. 1976–78); Chair. British Hosps. Export Council 1982–84; Hon. mem. China Soc. of Architects, Beijing; maj. works include: student housing, Imperial Coll. of Tropical Architecture, Trinidad 1960; Northwick Park Hosp. and Clinical Research Centre, London 1961–71; Tel Hashomer Teaching Hosp. Israel 1967; devt. plan for Health Sciences Centre, Memorial Univ. Newfoundland 1968; Univ. Children's Hosp. Leuven, Belgium 1970; Flinders Medical Centre, Adelaide 1971–74; Gen. Hosp. Singapore 1972; redevt. St. Mary's Hosp. Paddington 1978–86; exhbn.: This is Tomorrow 1956. *Publications include:* Studies in the Function and Design of Hospitals (jtly.) 1955; many articles on medical architecture. *Address:* 39 Jackson's Lane, Highgate, London, N6 5SR, England.

WEERAMANTRY, Christopher Gregory, B.A., LL.D.; Sri Lankan judge; b. 17 Nov. 1926, Colombo; ed. Univ. of London; advocate Supreme Court of Sri Lanka 1948–65, Commr. of Assize 1965–67, Justice of Supreme Court 1967–72; Sir Hayden Starke Prof. of Law, Monash Univ., Melbourne, Australia 1972–91, Emer. Prof. of Law 1991–; mem. Int. Court of Justice 1991–, Vice-Pres. 1997–; lecturer and Examiner, Council of Legal Educ. 1951–56; mem. Council of Legal Educ. 1967–72; Visiting Prof. Univs. of Tokyo 1978, Stellenbosch 1979, Papua New Guinea 1981, Fla. 1984, Lafayette Coll., Pa. 1985, Hong Kong 1989; Hon. Visiting Prof. Univ. of Colombo 1984; Chair Comm. of Inquiry into Int. Responsibility for Phosphate Mining on Nauru 1987–88; mem. Editorial Bd. Sri Lankian Journal of Int. Law, Human Rights Quarterly (Johns Hopkins Univ.), Interdisciplinary Peace Research (La Trobe Univ.), Journal of Ceylon Law; mem. Advisory Bd. China Law Reports; Vice Chair. UN Centre against Apartheid/Govt. of Nigeria Conf. on Legal Status of Apartheid Regime, Lagos 1984; Co.-ordinator UN Univ./Netherlands Inst. of Human Rights Workshop on Science, Tech., and Human Rights, Utrecht 1989; Assoc. Academician, Int. Acad. of Comparative Law, Paris; Vice-Pres. Int. Comm. of Jurists, Vic.; Past Pres. World Fed. of Overseas Sri Lankan Orgs.; Vice-Patron UN Asscn. of Sri Lanka; mem. Club of Rome (Australia); mem. Commonwealth Lawyers' Asscn. and other professional bodies; Hon. Life mem. Bar Asscn. of Sri Lanka; LL.D. Hon. (Colombo); Mohamed Sahabdeen Award for Int. Understanding in the SAARC Region 1993; Order of Deshamanya. *Publications:* numerous books on law, human rights and other topics; numerous articles in law journals worldwide and published lectures. *Address:* International Court of Justice, Peace Palace, 2517 KJ The Hague, The Netherlands. *Telephone:* (070) 302 23 23. *Fax:* (070) 364 99 28.

WEESE, Harry M.; American architect; b. 30 June 1915, Evanston, Ill.; s. of Harry Ernest Weese and Marjorie Mohr Weese; m. Kate Baldwin 1945; three d.; ed. Yale Univ. School of Architecture, M.I.T., Cranbrook Acad. of Art; Research Asst. Bemis Housing Foundation, M.I.T. (prefabricated and low-cost housing) 1939; Principal, Baldwin & Weese (architects) 1940–42; U.S. Navy 1942–46; Sr. Designer, Chicago office Skidmore, Owings & Merrill 1946–47; ind. practice as Harry Weese and Assocs., Chicago 1947–; Fellow, A.I.A. and Pres. Chicago Chapter 1975; Publr. Inland Architect Magazine 1977–; Co-Chair. Mayor Byrne's Architects' Advisory Cttee., Chicago 1979–83; mem. Nat. Acad. of Design, Nat. Council on the Arts, Advisory Bd., Nat. Asscn. of Housing and Redevt. Officials 1985–90, Urban Design Review Bd., San José Redevt. Agency 1984–90, Design Arts Cttee., Nat. Council on Arts 1984–90; Publr. Inland Architect Magazine; fmr. mem. Pres.'s Citizens' Advisory Cttee. on Environmental Quality; Total Design Award, Ill. Chapter, A.I.A. 1975, Firm of the Year Award, A.I.A. 1978, Distinguished Chapter Award, Chicago Chapter, A.I.A. 1981, Diplôme de Lauréat, Biennale Mondiale de l'Architecture, Union of Architects, Bulgaria 1983, Chicago Architecture Award, Architectural Magazine and Ill. Council A.I.A. 1987, Distinguished Ill. Preservationist 1991. *Principal projects:* U.S. Embassy, Accra, Ghana, Hyde Park Redevelopment Project, Chicago, Arena Stage, Washington D.C., Elvehjem Art Center, Univ. of Wis., Milwaukee Center for the Performing Arts, Wis., Metro Rapid Rail Transit System, Washington D.C., IBM Building, Milwaukee, Time & Life Building, Chicago, Technical Center, Cummins Engine Co., Columbus, Ind., Staff Housing Air India, Bombay, First Baptist Church, Columbus, Ind., Crown Center Hotel, Kansas City, Physical Education Building, Educ. and Communications Building, Univ. of Ill. Chicago Circle Campus, U.S. Courthouse Annex, Chicago, Fine Arts Center, Carleton Coll., Social Sciences Campus, New York State Univ., Buffalo-Amherst Campus, Student and Fine Arts Centers, Drake Univ., Terman Eng. Center, Stanford Univ., Calif.; Loop Subway System Study, CTA Determination of System and Design Elements (with American Bechtel) for Chicago Central Transportation District; Dade County Transit System, Miami, Fla. (with Kaiser Eng); Performing Arts Center; Grand Rapids, Mich.; New Town, Riyadh Int. Airport, Saudi Arabia; restoration of Adler-Sullivan Auditorium Theater, Chicago; U.S. Embassy Staff Housing, Tokyo, Wolf Point Landings, Chicago; 200 Wacker Drive, Chicago; Buffalo, N.Y. Rapid Transit System, Metro Rail Project, Los Angeles; Master Plan and Architectural Design, Chinatown, Chicago; Renovation and Master Plan, Field Museum of Natural History, Chicago; Master Plan, Fed. Triangle, Washington, D.C.; Dallas Area Rapid Transit Project, Tex.; Renovation and Master Plan, Henry Ives Cobb Bldg., Newberry Library, Chicago; Printing House Row, Chicago; Oak Park Village Hall, Ill.; First Nat. Bank in Albuquerque, N.M.; Corp. HQ, Union Underwear Co., Bowling Green, Ky.; Navy Pier Marina, Chicago; St. Louis Customs House and Post Office Renovation, Mo.; Harwick Bldg., Mayo Clinic, Rochester, Minn.; Chicago and Northwestern Railroad Station Trainshed, Chicago; 411 E. Wis. Office Bldg., Milwaukee; S. Cove Marina and Condominiums, New Buffalo, Mich.; Swiss Grand Hotel, Chicago *Leisure interests:* sailing, skiing, tennis. *Address:* 10 West Hubbard Street, Chicago, IL 60610 (Office); 314 West Willow Street, Chicago, IL 60610, U.S.A. (Home). *Telephone:* 467-7030 (Office).

WEI CHUNSU; Chinese administrator; b. 1929; joined CCP 1941; del. 12th Nat. Conf. CCP 1982–85, 13th 1986–91, 14th 1992–; del. 6th NPC 1983–87, 7th NPC 1988–92, 8th NPC 1993; Admin. Head, Self- Govt. of Guangxi Zhuang Autonomous Region 1992–. *Address:* Office of the Governor, Guangxi Dangwei, 1 Minlelu Road, Nanning City, People's Republic of China.

WEI JIANXING; Chinese state official; b. Jan. 1931, Xinchang Co., Zhejiang Prov.; ed. Dalian Eng. Inst. and in U.S.S.R.; joined CCP 1949; section chief, Northeast China Light Alloy Processing Factory 1961–64, Dir. 1977–81; Deputy Sec. Harbin Municipality CCP Cttee. 1981–83; Mayor of Harbin City 1981–83; Sec. and mem. Exec. Cttee. All-China Fed. of Trade Unions 1983, Vice-Pres. 1983–84, Pres. 1993–; Deputy Dir. CCP Cen. Cttee. Org. Dept. 1984–85, Dir. 1985–87; Minister of Supervision 1987–93; Sec. Beijing Municipal CCP Cttee. 1995–97; mem. CCP Cen. Cttee. Politburo, Cttee. and Secr. for Inspecting Discipline 1992–; Head Cen. Leading Group for Party Bldg. Work; Sec. Secr. CCP Cen. Cttee.; mem. 15th Cen. Cttee. CCP 1997–; mem. CCP Politburo Standing Cttee. 1997–. *Address:* All-China Federation of Trade Unions, 10 Fu Xing Men Wai Jie, Beijing 100865, People's Republic of China. *Telephone:* (10) 8012200. *Fax:* (10) 8012922.

WEI JINGSHENG; Chinese dissident; fmr. mem. Red Guards and PLA; active in pro-democracy movt., contrib. to underground magazine Exploration 1978; sentenced to 15 years' imprisonment for allegedly leaking mil. secrets to a foreign journalist and for counter-revolutionary activities Spring 1979, released Sept. 1993; held incommunicado and without charge April 1994; sentenced to 14 years' imprisonment for alleged subversive activities 1995; deported March 1998; Sakharov Prize 1996. *Publication:* The Courage to Stand Alone.

WEI WEI; Chinese singer; m. Michael Smith; one s.; singer at 11th Asian Games, Beijing 1990, performed a duet with Julio Iglesias (q.v.) at East Asian Games, Shanghai 1993; tour of China 1995. *Albums include:* Twilight.

WEI YUMING; Chinese business executive and administrator; b. March 1924, Yushe Co., Shanxi Prov.; Vice-Minister of Econ. Relations and Trade 1982–86; Chair. of Bd. of Dirs., Centre of Int. Trade 1987–; mem. 7th CPPCC 1988–92, 8th CPPCC 1993–. *Address:* Centre of International Trade, 2 Dong Chang' an Street, Beijing 100731, People's Republic of China.

WEI YUNG, PH.D.; Taiwanese politician, university professor and consultant; b. 5 May 1937, Hupei; s. of Shao-cheng Wei and Pei-chih Shing; m. Serena Ning Sun Wei 1964; two d.; ed. Nat. Chengchi Univ., Taipei, Univ. of Oregon U.S.A.; Instructor to Asst. Prof., Dept. of Political Science, Univ. of Nevada 1966–68; Asst. Prof., Dept of Political Science, Memphis State Univ. 1968–69, Assoc. Prof. of Political Science 1969–74, Prof. and Chair. of Grad. Program in Political Science 1974; Visiting Scholar, Survey Research Centre, Univ. of Mich. 1969; Visiting Assoc. Prof., Nat. Chengchi Univ. 1970–71; Nat. Fellow, Hoover Inst., Stanford Univ. 1974–75; Deputy Dir. Inst. of Int. Relations 1975–76; Eisenhower Exchange Fellow 1977; Chair. Research, Devt. and Evaluation Comm., Exec. Yuan, Taiwan 1976–88; Chancellor, Sun Yat-sen Inst. on Policy Research and Devt. 1988–90; Prof. of Political Science, Nat. Chiao-tung Univ. 1990–; mem. Legis. Yuan (Parl.) and Chair. Foreign Relations Cttee. 1992–96; Adjunct Prof., Dept. of Political Science, Nat. Taiwan Univ. and Nat. Chengchi Univ.; Pres. Chinese Asscn. of Political Science 1988–92; Chair. Bd., Dir. Policy Research Inst. Vanguard Inst. for Policy Studies 1991–; Pres. Sino-American Cultural and Econ. Asscn. 1997–; mem. Cen. Cttee., Kuomintang. *Publications:* The Nature and Methods of the Social Sciences, Taiwan: A Modernizing Chinese Society, Communist China: A System-Functional Reader, Political Development in the Republic of China on Taiwan: Analysis and Projections, A Methodological Critique of Current Studies on Chinese Political Culture, The Republic of China in the 1970s, Striving for A Future of Growth, Equity, and Security, Policy Planning of the Republic of China in the 1980s, Science, Elite and Modernization, From Multi-System Nations to Linkage Communities. *Leisure interests:* Chinese calligraphy, painting, boating, golf. *Address:* Vanguard Foundation, 4th Floor, 15 Chi-Nan Road, Sec. 1, Taipei (Office); No 1-2, Lane 8, Chin-tien Street, Taipei 106, Taiwan (Home). *Telephone:* (2) 2395-2045 (Office). *Fax:* (2) 2395-2052 (Office).

WEICKER, Lowell Palmer, Jr., LL.B.; American senator; b. 16 May 1931, Paris, France; s. of Lowell Palmer Weicker and Mary (Bickford) Paulsen; m. 1st Camille Di Lorenzo Butler; eight c.; m. 2nd Claudia Testa Ingram 1984; ed. Lawrenceville School, Yale Univ. and Univ. of Virginia; State Rep. in Conn. Gen. Assembly 1963–69; U.S. Rep., Fourth Congressional District, Conn. 1969–71; Senator from Conn. 1971–89; Gov. of Connecticut 1991–95; 1st Selectman of Greenwich 1964–68; mem. Select Cttee. for Investigation of the Watergate Case 1973; fmr. mem. Senate Appropriations Cttee., Senate

Labor and Human Resources Cttee., fmr. Chair. Senate Small Business Cttee., Sub-cttee. on State, Justice, Commerce, the Judiciary and related agencies, Senate Energy and Natural Resources Cttee.; fmr. Republican, then Independent. *Publication:* Maverick: My Life in Politics 1995. *Leisure interests:* tennis, scuba, history. *Address:* c/o Office of the Governor, 210 Capitol Avenue, Room 202, Hartford, CT 06106, U.S.A.

WEIDENBAUM, Murray Lew, M.A., PH.D.; American government official and economist; b. 10 Feb. 1927, Bronx, New York; s. of David Weidenbaum and Rose (Warshaw) Weidenbaum; m. Phyllis Green 1954; one s. two d.; ed. City Coll. New York, Columbia Univ., New York, and Princeton Univ.; Fiscal Economist, Budget Bureau, Washington 1949–57; Corpn. Economist, Boeing Co., Seattle 1958–62; Sr. Economist, Stanford Research Inst., Palo Alto, Calif. 1962–63; mem. Faculty, Washington Univ., St. Louis, Mo. 1964–, Dir. of Center for Study of American Business at Washington Univ. 1975–81, 1982–95, Chair. 1995–, Prof. and Chair. Dept. of Econs. 1966–69, Mallinckrodt Distinguished Univ. Prof. 1971–; Asst. Sec. for Econ. Policy, Treasury Dept., Washington 1969–71; Head, Council of Econ. Advisers, U.S. Govt. 1981–82; Chair. Research Advisory Cttee., St. Louis Regional Industrial Devt. Corpn. 1965–69; Exec. Sec. Pres.'s Cttee. on Econ. Impact of Defense and Disarmament 1964; mem. U.S. Financial Investment Advisory Panel 1970–72; mem. Pres.'s Econ. Policy Advisory Bd. 1982–89, Bd. of Dirs. Harbour Group Ltd., May Dept. Stores Co. 1982–, Tesoro Petroleum Corpn. 1992–, Macroeconomic Advisers 1996–; consultant to various firms and insts.; Fellow, Nat. Asscn. of Business Economists; Treasury Dept. Alexander Hamilton Medal 1971; Distinguished Writer Award, Georgetown Univ. 1975, Free Market Hall of Fame 1983. *Publications:* Federal Budgeting 1964, Economic Impact of the Vietnam War 1967, Modern Public Sector 1969, Economics of Peacetime Defense 1974, Government-Mandated Price Increases 1975, The Future of Business Regulation 1979, Business, Government, and the Public 1990, Rendezvous with Reality; The American Economy After Reagan 1990, Small Wars, Big Defense 1992, Bamboo Network 1996, Business and Government in the Global Marketplace 1999; articles in econ. journals. *Address:* Center for the Study of American Business, Washington University, 1 Brookings Drive, St. Louis, MO 63130; 303 N. Meramec No. 103, St. Louis, MO 63105, U.S.A. (Home). *Telephone:* (314) 935-5662. *Fax:* (314) 935-5688.

WEIDENFELD, Baron (Life Peer), cr. 1976, of Chelsea in Greater London; **Arthur George Weidenfeld,** Kt; British publisher; b. 13 Sept. 1919, Vienna, Austria; s. of the late Max Weidenfeld and Rosa (née Eisenstein-ish Horowitz) Weidenfeld; m. 1st Jane Sieff 1952; one d.; m. 2nd Barbara Skelton Connolly 1956 (divorced 1961); m. 3rd Sandra Payson Meyer 1966 (divorced 1976); m. 4th Annabelle Whitestone 1992; ed. Piaristen Gymnasium, Vienna, Univ. of Vienna and Konsular Akademie; came to England 1938; BBC Monitoring Service 1939–42; BBC News Commentator on European Affairs on BBC Empire and N. American service 1942–46; Foreign Affairs columnist, News Chronicle 1943–44; Political Adviser and Chief of Cabinet of Pres. Weizmann of Israel 1949–50; founder of Contact Magazine 1945, George Weidenfeld & Nicolson Ltd 1948–; Chair. George Weidenfeld & Nicolson Ltd. 1948–, Wheatland Corpn., N.Y. 1985–90, Grove Press, N.Y. 1985–90, Wheatland Foundation, San Francisco and New York 1985–92; Dir. (non-exec.) Orion 1991–; Chair. Bd. of Govs., Ben Gurion Univ. of the Negev 1996–; Gov. of Tel-Aviv Univ. 1980–, Weizmann Inst. of Science 1964–; mem., South Bank Bd. 1986–; mem. Bd. English Nat. Opera 1988–; Trustee Nat. Portrait Gallery 1988–94; mem. Governing Council, Inst. of Human Science, Vienna, Einstein Forum, Potsdam; Vice-Chair. Oxford Univ. Devt. Programme; Hon. Fellow St. Peter's Coll., Oxford, St. Anne's Coll., Oxford; Hon. Senator Bonn Univ.; Hon. M.A. (Oxon.); Hon. Ph.D. (Ben Gurion Univ.); Kt. Commdr.'s Cross (Badge and Star) of Order of Merit (Germany), Golden Kt.'s Cross of Order of Merit (Austria), Chevalier, Légion d'honneur. *Publications:* The Goebbels Experiment 1943, Remembering My Good Friends 1994. *Leisure interests:* opera, travel. *Address:* 9 Chelsea Embankment, London, SW3 4LE, England. *Telephone:* 0171-351 0042.

WEIDENFELD, Werner, DR.PHIL.; German professor of political science; b. 2 July 1947, Cochem; s. of Dr. Josef Weidenfeld and Maria (née Walther) Weidenfeld; m. Gabriele Kokott-Weidenfeld 1976; ed. Univ. of Bonn; Prof. of Political Science, Univ. of Mainz 1976–95; Assoc. Prof., Sorbonne, Paris 1986–88; Co-ordinator for German-American Co-operation 1987–; Prof. of Political Science, Univ. of Munich 1995–, Dir. Centre for Applied Policy Research. *Publications:* Die Englandpolitik Gustav Stresemanns 1972, Konrad Adenauer und Europa 1976, Europa 2000 1980, Die Frage nach der Einheit der deutschen Nation 1981, Die Identität der Deutschen 1983, Die Bilanz der Europäischen Integration 1984, Nachdenken über Deutschland 1985, 30 Jahre EG 1987, Geschichtsbewusstsein der Deutschen 1987, Der deutsche Weg 1990, Jahrbuch der Europäischen Integration (Ed.), Die Deutschen—Profil einer Nation 1991, Handwörterbuch zur deutschen Einheit 1992, Osteuropa: Herausforderungen-Probleme-Strategien 1992, Technopoly, Europa im globalen Wettbewerb 1993, Maastricht in der Analyse, Materialien zur Europäischen Union (ed.) 1994, Europa '96. Reformprogramm für die Europäische Union (ed.) 1994, Reform der Europäischen Union 1995, Kulturbruch mit Amerika? 1996, Handbuch zur deutschen Einheit 1996, Demokratie am Wendepunkt? (ed.) 1996, Europa öffnen—Anforderungen an die Erweiterung (ed.) 1997, Aussenpolitik für die deutsche Einheit. Die Entscheidigungsjahre 1989/90 1998, Amsterdam in der Analyse. Strategien für Europa (ed.) 1998, Handbuch zur deutschen Einheit 1949–1989–1999 (ed.) 1999. *Address:* Oettingenstr. 67, 80538 Munich, Germany. *Telephone:* 089-21783040. *Fax:* 089-21783042.

WEIDINGER, Christine; American soprano; fmrly. with Stuttgart Opera; joined Bielefeld opera 1979; appearances at Bielefeld include Malvina in Heinrich Marschner's Der Vampyr, title role in Thea Musgrave's Mary, Queen of Scots, Donizetti's Lucia di Lammermoor, Anina in Bellini's La Sonnambula, Berthe in Meyerbeer's Le Prophète, Elizabeth I in Donizetti's Roberto Devereux and title role in Bellini's Norma 1989; appearances abroad include: Inez in L'Africaine (Barcelona), Lucia and Juliet in I Capuleti e i Montecchi, Pamira in Rossini's Siege of Corinth (Marseilles), title role in Bellini's Beatrice di Tenda (Catania), Eupaforice in Heinrich Graun's Spanish Conquest (Spoleto/Charleston Festival of Two Worlds) and in Tancredi (Los Angeles Music Center Opera) 1989.

WEIDLINGER, Paul, M.S.; American engineer; b. 22 Dec. 1914, Budapest, Hungary; s. of Andrew Weidlinger and Juliette Weidlinger; m. Solveig Højberg 1964; two s. one d.; ed. Tech. Inst., Brno, Czechoslovakia, Swiss Polytechnic Inst., Zürich; Chief Engineer, Bureau of Reclamation, La Paz, Bolivia 1939–42; Prof. of Eng., San Andrés Univ. La Paz 1939–42; went to U.S.A. 1944, naturalized 1949; Chief Engineer, Atlas Aircraft, New York 1944–46; Dir. of Div., Nat. Housing Agency, Washington, D.C. 1946–47; engineer, pvt. practice 1947–; Sr. partner Weidlinger Assocs., New York 1948–; Visiting Lecturer, Harvard Univ., M.I.T.; mem. Scientific Advisory Bd., U.S.A.F.; Consultant to Rand Corpn.; Fellow of Hudson Inst., American Soc. of Civil Engineers (A.S.C.E.), American Concrete Inst., Int. Asscn. of Bridge and Structural Engineers, New York Acad. of Sciences, A.I.A.A., Nat. Acad. of Eng.; J. R. Croes Medal 1963, Moisseiff Award 1975 (both A.S.C.E.), Ernest E. Howard Award (A.S.C.E.) 1985. *Publications:* articles in journals. *Address:* Weidlinger Associates, 375 Hudson Street, New York, NY 10014, U.S.A.

WEIKL, Bernd; Austrian baritone; b. 29 July 1942, Vienna; ed. Mainz Conservatoire and Hochschule für Musik, Hanover; mem. Hamburg State Opera 1973–; guest artist, Bayreuth Festivals 1973–75. *Address:* c/o Lies Askonas Ltd., 6 Henrietta Place, London, WC2E 8LA, England. *Telephone:* 0171-405 1808.

WEILL, Sanford I., B.A.; American banker; b. 16 March 1933, New York; s. of Max and Etta (née Kalika) Weill; m. Joan Mosher 1955; one s., one d.; ed. Peekskill Mil. Acad., Cornell Univ., School Business and Public Admin.; C.E.O. Carter, Berlind and Weill (now Shearson/American Express Inc.) New York 1960–, Pres. and C.E.O. 1978–85; Chair., Pres., C.E.O. Commercial Credit Co., Baltimore 1986–; Chair., C.E.O. Primerica Corpn. 1989–, Pres. 1989–92; now Chair., C.E.O. Travelers Group 1996–; f. Acad. of Finance; dir. Terra Nova Insurance Co. 1984–; Chair. Carnegie Hall 1991–; mem. Midwest Stock Exchange Bd.; Assoc. mem. New York Stock Exchange, Bd. of Overseers Cornell Medical Coll., Business Cttee. Museum of Modern Art, N.Y. *Address:* Travelers Group, 388 Greenwich Street, New York, NY 10013, U.S.A.

WEINBACH, Lawrence, B.S.; American business executive; b. 1 Jan. 1940, Brooklyn, New York; s. of Max Weinbach and Winnefred Weinbach; m. Patricia Lieter 1961; two s. one d.; ed. Univ. of Pennsylvania Wharton; joined Arthur Andersen 1961, Man. Partner and Chief Exec. 1989–97; as Chair., Pres. and C.E.O. Unisys Corpn. Sept. 1997–; *Leisure interests:* reading, golf. *Address:* Unisys Corporation, Unisys Way, Blue Bell, PA 19424, U.S.A. *Telephone:* (215) 986 4011. *Fax:* (215) 986 2886.

WEINBERG, Alvin M., S.M., PH.D.; American physicist and scientific administrator; b. 20 April 1915, Chicago, Ill.; s. of Jacob and Emma Levinson Weinberg; m. 1st Margaret Despres 1940 (died 1969); two s.; m. 2nd Gene K. de Persio 1974; ed. Univ. of Chicago; Biophysics research Univ. of Chicago 1939–42; Hanford reactor design Univ. of Chicago Metallurgical Laboratory 1942–45; Section Chief Physics Div., Oak Ridge Nat. Laboratory 1945–47, Dir. Physics Div. 1947–48, Research Dir. 1948–55; Dir. Oak Ridge Nat. Lab. 1955–73; Dir. Office of Energy Research and Devt., Fed. Energy Office 1974, Inst. for Energy Analysis 1975–85 (Distinguished Fellow 1985–); mem. Scientific Advisory Bd. to the Air Force 1955–59; mem. President's Science Advisory Cttee. 1960–63; Chair. Advisory Cttee. on Carbon Dioxide, Dept. of Energy 1978–80; Fellow, American Nuclear Soc., American Physical Soc.; mem. American Acad. of Arts and Sciences, Nat. Acad. of Eng., N.A.S., Cttee. on Science and Public Policy of Nat. Acad. of Sciences 1963–66, Council of N.A.S. 1967–70, American Philosophical Soc.; Foreign mem. Royal Netherlands Acad. of Sciences; mem. Pres. Nixon's Task Force on Science Policy 1969, Nat. Cancer Plan Evaluation Cttee. 1972; Regents' Lecturer Univ. of Calif., San Diego 1980; co-recipient Atoms for Peace Award 1960, Ernest O. Lawrence Memorial Award of Atomic Energy Comm. 1960, Univ. of Chicago Alumni Medal 1966, Heinrich Hertz Energy Prize 1975, New York Acad. of Sciences Award 1976, Enrico Fermi Award 1980, Harvey Prize 1982, Alvin M. Weinberg Medal of American Nuclear Soc. 1997; contributions to nuclear tech. in reactor theory, reactor design, breeder reactor systems, implications of nuclear energy; formulation of science policy; energy supply and demand. *Publications:* The Physical Theory of Neutron Chain Reactors (with Eugene P. Wigner) 1958, Reflections on Big Science 1967, Continuing the Nuclear Dialogue 1985, The Nuclear Connection (Co-Ed.) 1985, Strategic Defenses and Arms Control (Co-Ed.) 1987, Stability and Strategic Defenses (Co-Ed.) 1991, Nuclear Reactions: Science and Trans-Science 1992, The First Nuclear Era: The Life and Times of a Technological Fixer 1994. *Leisure* *interests:* piano, tennis, swimming. *Address:* Oak Ridge Associated Universities, P.O. Box 117, Oak Ridge, TN 37831 (Office); 111 Moylan Lane, Oak Ridge, TN 37830, U.S.A. (Home). *Telephone:* (423) 576-3249 (Office); (423) 483-6045 (Home).

WEINBERG, Felix Jiri, D.SC., PH.D., F.R.S., M.R.I., C.ENG., F.INST.P., F.C.G.I.; British physicist; b. 2 April 1928; s. of Victor Weinberg and Nelly Marie Weinberg (née Altschul); m. Jill Nesta Piggott 1954; three s.; ed. Univ. of London; Lecturer, Dept. of Chemical Eng. and Chemical Tech., Imperial Coll., London 1956–60, Sr. Lecturer 1960–64, Reader in Combustion 1964–67, Prof. of Combustion Physics 1967–93, Emer. Prof. and Sr. Research Fellow 1993–, Leverhulme Emer. Research Fellow 1993–95; Dir. Combustion Inst. 1978–88, Chair. British Section 1975–80; Founder and First Chair. Combustion Physics Group, Inst. of Physics 1974–77, Rep. on Watt Cttee. on Energy 1979–84; mem. Council, Inst. of Energy 1976–79; Hon. D.Sc. (Technion) 1989; Combustion Inst. Silver Combustion Medal 1972, Bernard Lewis Gold Medal 1980, Royal Soc. Rumford Medal 1988, Italgas Prize in Energy Sciences (Turin Acad.) 1991. *Publications:* Optics of Flames 1963, Electrical Aspects of Combustion 1969, Combustion Inst. European Symposium (ed.) 1973, Advanced Combustion Methods 1986; over 195 scientific papers. *Leisure interests:* eastern philosophies, travel, archery. *Address:* Imperial College, London, SW7 2BY (Office); 59 Vicarage Road, London, SW14 8RY, England (Home). *Telephone:* 0171-594 5580 (Office); 0181-876 1540 (Home). *Fax:* 0171-594 5604.

WEINBERG, Robert A., PH.D.; American biochemist; b. 11 Nov. 1942, Pittsburgh, Pa.; s. of Dr. Fritz E. and Lore W. (née Reichhardt) Weinberg; m. Amy Shulman 1976; one s. one d.; ed. M.I.T.; Instructor in Biology, Stillman Coll., Ala. 1965–66; Fellow Weizmann Inst., Israel 1969–70; Fellow Salk Inst., Calif. 1970–72; Research Assoc. Fellow M.I.T. 1972–73, Asst. Prof., Dept. of Biology and Center for Cancer Research 1973–76, Assoc. Prof. 1976–82, Prof. Whitehead Inst. for Biomedical Research 1982–, mem. 1984–; mem. N.A.S.; numerous awards including Hon. Sc.D. (Northwestern Univ., Ill.) 1984. *Leisure interests:* house building, gardening, genealogy. *Address:* Whitehead Institute, 9 Cambridge Center, Cambridge, MA 02142; Department of Biology, Massachusetts Institute of Technology, Cambridge, MA 02139, U.S.A.

WEINBERG, Steven, PH.D.; American physicist; b. 3 May 1933, New York; s. of Fred Weinberg and Eva Weinberg; m. Louise Goldwasser 1954; one d.; ed. Cornell Univ., Univ. of Copenhagen and Princeton Univ.; Columbia Univ. 1957–59; Lawrence Radiation Lab. 1959–60; Univ. of Calif. (Berkeley) 1960–69; Prof. of Physics, M.I.T. 1969–73; Higgins Prof. of Physics, Harvard Univ. 1973–83; Sr. Scientist, Smithsonian Astrophysical Observatory 1973–83, Sr. Consultant 1983–; Josey Regental Prof. of Science, Univ. of Texas, Austin 1982–; Co-Ed. Cambridge Univ. Press Monographs on Mathematical Physics 1978; Dir. Jerusalem Winter School of Theoretical Physics 1983–, Headliners Foundation 1993–; mem. A.P. Sloan Foundation Science Book Cttee. 1985–90, Einstein Archives Int. Advisory Bd. 1988–, Scientific Policy Cttee., Supercollider Lab. 1989–93, American Acad. of Arts and Sciences 1968–, N.A.S. 1972–, Council for Foreign Relations, President's Cttee. on the Nat. Medal of Science 1979–80, Royal Soc. 1982–, American Philosophical Soc. 1983–; fmr. mem. Council, American Physical Soc., Int. Astronomical Union, Philosophical Soc. of Tex. (Pres. 1994); Loeb Lecturer, Harvard Univ. and Visiting Prof. M.I.T. 1966–69, Richtmeyer Lecturer of American Asscn. of Physics Teachers 1974, Scott Lecturer, Cavendish Lab. 1975, Silliman Lecturer, Yale 1977, Lauritsen Lecturer, Calif. Inst. of Tech. 1979, Bethe Lecturer, Cornell Univ. 1979, Harris Lecturer, Northwestern Univ. 1982, Cherwell-Simon Lecturer, Oxford Univ. 1983, Bampton Lecturer, Columbia Univ. 1983, Hilldale Lecturer, Univ. of Wisconsin 1985, Brickweede Lecturer, Johns Hopkins Univ. 1986, Dirac Lecturer, Univ. of Cambridge 1986, Klein Lecturer, Univ. of Stockholm 1989, Sackler Lecturer, Univ. of Copenhagen 1994, Brittin Lecturer, Univ. of Colorado 1994, Gibbs Lecturer, American Math. Soc. 1996, Bochner Lecturer, Rice Univ. 1997, Sanchez Lecturer, Tex. A & M Int. Univ. 1998; Hon. D.Sc. (Knox Coll.) 1978, (Chicago, Yale, Rochester) 1979, (City Univ., New York) 1980, (Clark Univ.) 1982, (Dartmouth) 1984, (Weizmann Inst.) 1985, (Columbia) 1990, (Salamanca) 1992, (Padua) 1992, (Barcelona) 1996; Hon. D.Litt. (Washington Coll.) 1985; J. R. Oppenheimer Prize 1973, Dannie Heinemann Mathematical Physics Prize 1977, American Inst. of Physics-U.S. Steel Foundation Science Writing Award 1977, Elliott Cresson Medal, Franklin Inst. 1979, Joint Winner, Nobel Prize for Physics 1979, James Madison Medal (Princeton) 1991, Nat. Medal of Science 1991, Piazzi Prize 1998. *Publications:* Gravitation and Cosmology 1972, The First Three Minutes 1977, The Discovery of Subatomic Particles 1982, Elementary Particles and the Laws of Physics (with R. P. Feynman) 1987, Dreams of a Final Theory 1993, The Quantum Theory of Fields (Vol. I) 1995, (Vol. II) 1996, and over 200 articles. *Leisure interest:* medieval history. *Address:* Department of Physics, University of Texas, Austin, TX 78712, U.S.A. *Telephone:* (512) 471-4394.

WEINBERGER, Caspar Willard, A.B., M.C.L.; American government official; b. 18 Aug. 1917, San Francisco; s. of Herman Weinberger and Cerise Carpenter (Hampson) Weinberger; m. Jane Dalton 1942; one s. one d.; ed. Harvard Coll. and Law School; served with AUS 1941–45; with Heller, Ehrman, White and McAuliffe 1947–69, partner 1959–69; mem. Calif. State Legislature 1952–58; Vice-Chair. Calif. Republican Central Cttee. 1960–62, Chair. 1962–64; Chair. Calif. Govt. Cttee. on Org. and Econ. 1967–68; Dir. of Finance, Calif. 1968–69; Chair. Fed. Trade Comm. 1970; Deputy Dir. Office of Man. and Budget 1970–72, Dir. 1972–73; Counsellor to Pres. 1973; Sec. of Health, Educ. and Welfare 1973–75; Sec. of Defense 1981–87; specialist in int. law and finance, Rogers & Wells, Washington 1988–94; Publr. Forbes Magazine 1988–92, Chair. 1989–; Distinguished Visiting Prof. Inst. for Advanced Studies in the Humanities, Edin. Univ. 1988; Gen. Counsel for the Bechtel Group of Cos. including Bechtel Power Corpn. and Bechtel Inc. 1975–80; Chair. Pres.'s Cttee. on Mental Retardation 1973–75; mem. Pres.'s Foreign Intelligence Advisory Bd. 1987–88; Chair. Bd. USA-ROC Econ. Council 1990–94; Bd. Dirs. Chatham House Foundation Inc. 1996–; Earl Mountbatten Memorial Lecture 1991; fmr. Dir. Pepsico Corpn., Quaker Oats Corpn., American Ditchley Foundation, Yosemite Inst.; fmr. Treas. Episcopal Diocese; fmr. Pres. Nat. Trustees of the Nat. Symphony, Washington, D.C.; fmr. mem. American Assembly Bd. of Trustees, Trilateral Comm.; American Bar Asscn., State Bar Calif.; admitted to Dist. of Columbia Bar 1990; Dr. h.c. (Leeds) 1989; Hon. D. Litt. (Buckingham) 1995; Harvard Univ. John F. Kennedy School of Govt. Medal 1982, 1986; Hon. G.B.E. (U.K.) 1988; Grand Cordon of the Order of the Rising Sun (Japan) 1988; Presidential Medal of Freedom (with Distinction) 1987. *Publications:* Fighting for Peace 1990, The Next War (with Peter Schweizer) 1996. *Address:* Forbes Inc., 1901 L Street, N.W., Suite 711, Washington, DC 20036, U.S.A.

WEINER, Gerry, B.A., B.SC.; Canadian politician; b. 26 June 1933, Montreal; m. Judith Weiner 1959; one s. one d.; ed. Univ. of Montreal and McGill Univ.; pharmacist; fmr. Mayor Dollard-des-Ormeaux; fmr. Pres. North Shore Youth Services; exec. mem. B'nai B'rith Univ. Lodge, Lakeshore Gen. Hosps. Foundation and Beechwood Home and Scholastic Asscn.; M.P. 1984–93; Parl. Sec. to Sec. of State for External Affairs, then Parl. Sec. to Minister of Employment 1985–86; Minister of State for Immigration 1986–88, for Multiculturalism and Citizenship 1988–91, Minister 1991–93; Sec. of State for Canada 1989–91; Progressive Conservative. *Address:* 40 Fredmir Street, Dollard-des-Ormeaux, Quebec H9A 2R3, Canada.

WEINER, Mervyn Lester, B.COM., M.PHIL.; Canadian economist; b. 30 Oct. 1922, Montreal; s. of Louis Weiner and Beatrice Feinstein; m. Shirley R. Hurwitz 1951; one s. one d.; ed. McGill Univ., Balliol Coll., Oxford, Univ. of Pennsylvania and Johns Hopkins Univ.; Canadian Army 1943–46; Instructor, Wharton School of Commerce and Finance, Univ. of Pennsylvania 1948–49; Instructor Johns Hopkins Univ. 1949–51; Econ. Affairs Officer UN 1950; IBRD officer 1951–84, Research Economist 1951–55, Country Economist 1955–61, Loan Officer 1961–63, Div. Chief 1963–65, Econ. Adviser, later Chief Economist, Western Hemisphere Dept. 1965–69, Dir. Public Utilities Projects Dept. 1969–72, Dir. Asia Region Projects Dept. 1972–74, Regional Vice-Pres. S. Asia 1974–75, Dir.-Gen. Operations Evaluation 1975–84; Int. Consultant 1984–. *Address:* 3206 Cummings Lane, Chevy Chase, MD 20815, U.S.A. *Telephone:* (301) 656-5675.

WEINGARTEN, David Michael, B.A., M.ARCH.; American architect; b. 22 Jan. 1952, Fort Ord, Calif.; s. of Saul M. Weingarten and Miriam E. Moore; one s.; ed. Monterey High School, Yale Univ. and Univ. of Calif. Berkeley; partner, Ace Architects 1979–; lecturer, Univ. of Calif. Berkeley 1980–81; exhbns. of work, Oakland Museum 1985, San Francisco Fine Arts Comm. 1987, St. Louis Design Center 1988, Avery Library, Columbia Univ. 1991, Smithsonian Inst. 1992, Limn Gallery 1993, San Francisco Museum of Modern Art 1996, Art Inst. of Chicago 1997, Octagon Museum, Washington DC 1997, Smith Coll. Museum of Art, Northampton Mass. 1998–99, Museum of the City of New York 1998–99; various awards and prizes. *Address:* Ace Architects, 330 2nd Street, Oakland, CA 94607, U.S.A. *Telephone:* (510) 452-0775. *Fax:* (510) 452-1175.

WEINGARTNER, Paul Andreas, D.PHIL.; Austrian professor of philosophy; b. 8 June 1931, Innsbruck; s. of Karl Weingartner and Maria Weingartner; five s. one d.; ed. Univ. of Innsbruck; Research Fellow, Univ. of London 1961–62; Research Asst. Inst. für Wissenschaftstheorie, Int. Research Centre, Salzburg 1962–67, Chair. Dept. I (Philosophy of Natural Science) 1967–72; Assoc. Prof. of Philosophy, Univ. of Salzburg 1970, Prof. of Philosophy 1971–, Chair. Inst. für Philosophie 1971–79, 1988–90, 1994–, Chair. Inst. für Wissenschaftstheorie 1972–; Dr. h.c. (M. Curie Univ., Poland) 1995; mem. New York Acad. of Sciences 1997–. *Publications:* Wissenschaftstheorie (2 vols.) 1976, 1978, Logisch-philosophische Untersuchungen zu Werten und Normen 1996, Zu philosophie-historischen Themen 1996, Basic Questions on Truth 1999; ed. of 28 vols.; about 130 research articles. *Leisure interests:* sport (climbing, skiing), photography. *Address:* Institut für Philosophie, Universität Salzburg, Franziskanergasse 1, 5020 Salzburg, Austria. *Telephone:* (662) 8044-4071, (662) 842521-130. *Fax:* (662) 8044-629.

WEINSTEIN, Harvey; American film company executive; Co-Chair. Miramax Films Corpn., New York. *Films produced (jtly.) include:* Playing for Keeps 1986, Scandal 1989, Strike it Rich 1990, Hardware 1990, A Rage in Harlem 1991, The Crying Game 1992, The Night We Never Met 1993, Benefit of the Doubt 1993, True Romance 1993, Mother's Boys 1994, Like Water for Chocolate 1994, Pulp Fiction 1994, Pret-A-Porter 1994, Smoke 1995, A Month by the Lake 1995, The Crossing Guard 1995, The Journey of August King 1995, Things To Do In Denver When You're Dead 1995, The Englishman Who Went Up A Hill But Came Down A Mountain 1995, Blue in the Face 1995, Restoration 1995, Scream 1996, The Pallbearer 1996, The Last of the High Kings 1996, Jane Eyre 1996, Flirting with Disaster 1996, The English Patient 1996, Emma 1996, The Crow: City of Angels 1996, Beautiful Girls 1996, Addicted to Love 1997, Shakespeare in Love 1998.

Address: Miramax Films Corporation, 375 Greenwich Street, New York, NY 10013, U.S.A.

WEINSTEIN, Robert; American film producer and executive; now Co-Chair. Miramax Films Corpn. *Films produced include:* (all with Harvey Weinstein (q.v.)) Playing for Keeps (with Alan Brewer) 1986, Scandal (with Joe Boyd and Nik Powell) 1989, Strike it Rich 1990, Hardware (with Nik Powell, Stephen Woolley and Trix Worrell) 1990, A Rage in Harlem (with Terry Glinwood, William Horberg and Nik Powell) 1991, The Night We Never Met (with Sidney Kimmel) 1993, Benefit of the Doubt 1993, True Romance (with Gary Barber, Stanley Margolis and James G. Robinson) 1993, Mother's Boys (with Randall Poster) 1994, Pulp Fiction (with Richard N. Gladstein) 1994, Pret-A-Porter (with Ian Jessel) 1994, Smoke (with Satoru Iseki) 1995, A Month By the Lake (with Donna Gigliotti) 1995, The Crossing Guard (with Richard N. Gladstein) 1995, The Journey of August King 1995, Things To Do In Denver When You're Dead (with Marie Cantin) 1995, The Englishman Who Went Up a Hill But Came Down a Mountain (with Sally Hibbin and Robert Jones) 1995, Blue in the Face (with Harvey Keitel) 1995, Restoration (with Donna Gigliotti) 1995. *Address:* Miramax Films Corporation, 375 Greenwich Street, New York, NY 10013, U.S.A.

WEINSTOCK, Baron (Life Peer), cr. 1980, of Bowden in the County of Wiltshire; **Arnold Weinstock,** Kt., B.SC.(ECON.), F.S.S.; British business executive; b. 29 July 1924, London; s. of Simon Weinstock and Golda Weinstock; m. Netta Sobell 1949; one s. (died 1996), one d.; ed. Univ. of London; Jr. Admin. Officer, Admiralty 1944–47; with pvt. group of cos. engaged in finance and property devt. 1947–54; joined Radio and Allied Industries Ltd. (now Radio and Allied Holdings Ltd.) 1954, Man. Dir. 1955–61; Dir. General Electric Co. Ltd. 1961–96, Man. Dir. 1963–96; Dir. Rolls-Royce (1971) Ltd. 1971–73; mem. Advisory Council Merrill Lynch 1985–89; Dir. Friends of the Ravenna Festival 1993–; Trustee, British Museum 1985–95; Fellow Royal Statistical Soc.; Hon. Fellow, Peterhouse, Cambridge, L.S.E.; Hon. Master of the Bench, Gray's Inn 1982; Hon. F.R.C.R.; Hon. D.Sc. (Salford) 1975, (Aston) 1976, (Bath) 1978, (Reading) 1978, (Ulster) 1987; Hon. LL.D. (Leeds) 1978, (Wales) 1985, (Keele) 1997; Hon. D.Tech. (Loughborough) 1981, Hon. D.Econ.Sc. (London) 1997; Officier, Légion d'honneur 1992, Commendatore, Order of Merit (Italy) 1991. *Leisure interests:* racing and bloodstock, music. *Address:* 7 Grosvenor Square, London, W1X 9LA, England.

WEIR, Viscount; William Kenneth James Weir, B.A.; British business executive; b. 9 Nov. 1933, Glasgow, Scotland; s. of Lord Weir and Lady Weir (née Crowdy); m. Marina Sevastopoulo 1988; two s. one d.; ed. Eton Coll., Trinity Coll. Cambridge; served Royal Navy 1955–56; Chair. Weir Group PLC 1972–99, BICC PLC 1996–; Dir. Bank of England 1972–84, British Steel Corpn. 1972–76, British Bank of Middle East 1977–79, Canadian Pacific Ltd. 1989–, St. James Place Capital 1990–; Pres. British Electrotechnical Mfrs. Asscn. 1988-89, 1993–95; mem. London Advisory Cttee., Hong Kong Shanghai Bank 1980–92, Export Credit Advisory Cttee. 1991–98; Hon. Fellow, Hon. D. Eng. (Glasgow). *Leisure interests:* shooting, golf. *Address:* BICC PLC, Devonshire House, Mayfair Place, London, W1X 5FH, England (Office); Rodinghead, Mauchline, Ayrshire, KA5 5TR, Scotland (Home). *Telephone:* 0171-629 6622 (Office); (01563) 884233 (Home).

WEIR, Dame Gillian Constance, D.B.E.; British/New Zealand concert organist and harpsichordist; b. 17 Jan. 1941, Martinborough, New Zealand; d. of Cecil Alexander Weir and Clarice Mildred Foy Weir (née Bignell); m. 1st Clive Rowland Webster 1967 (divorced 1971); m. 2nd Lawrence Irving Phelps 1972; ed. Wanganui Girls' Coll., N.Z. and Royal Coll. of Music, London; winner St. Albans Int. Organ Festival Competition 1964; débuts Royal Festival Hall and Royal Albert Hall, London 1965; worldwide career since 1965 as organist and latterly as harpsichordist also; has appeared with all leading British orchestras and with many abroad, under leading conductors; many radio and TV appearances; adjudicator in int. competitions and artist-in-residence at major univs.; gives lectures and master classes in many countries; organ consultant, Birmingham Symphony Hall; Visiting Prof. of Organ, Royal Acad. of Music, London 1996–; many premières including first British performance of Messiaen's Méditations of 1972; many works written for her including concertos by William Mathias and Peter Racine Fricker; many recordings including 7-CD set complete organ works of Olivier Messiaen 1995 and complete works of César Franck 1997; presenter and performer 6-part BBC TV series 1989; Pres. Inc. Asscn. of Organists (first woman Pres.) 1981–83, Inc. Soc. of Musicians 1992–93; mem. Exec. Council, Royal Coll. of Organists (first woman mem.) 1981–85, Council (first woman mem.) 1977–, Pres. (first woman Pres.) 1994-96; mem. Council Royal Philharmonic Soc. 1996–; Hon. F.R.C.O.; Hon. F.R.C.C.O.; Hon. mem. Royal Acad. of Music; Hon. D.Mus. (Victoria Univ. of Wellington, N.Z.) 1983; Hon. D.Litt. (Univ. of Huddersfield) 1997; Int. Performer of Year Award, American Guild of Organists 1983; Turnovsky Prize for Outstanding Achievement in the Arts 1985. *Publication:* contrib. to The Messiaen Companion 1995; articles in professional journals. *Leisure interests:* theatre, reading. *Address:* c/o D. Lyster Artists Management, 25 Courthope Road, London, NW3 2LE, England. *Telephone:* 0171-485 5932. *Fax:* 0171-267 0179.

WEIR, Judith, C.B.E., M.A.; British composer; b. 11 May 1954, Cambridge; ed. North London Collegiate School, King's Coll., Cambridge; composer-in-residence, Southern Arts Asscn. 1976–79; Fellow in Composition Univ. of Glasgow 1979–82, Creative Arts Fellowship, Trinity Coll., Cambridge 1983–85, composer-in-residence Royal Scottish Acad. of Music and Drama 1988–91; Fairbairn Composer in asscn. with City of Birmingham Symphony Orchestra 1995–98; Artistic Dir. Spitalfields Festival 1995–; Hon. Dr. (Aberdeen) 1995; Critics' Circle Award for most outstanding contrib. to British Musical Life 1994. *Works include:* King Harald's Saga 1979, Consolations of Scholarship 1985, A Night At The Chinese Opera 1987, Missa Del Cid 1988, Heaven Ablaze In His Breast 1989, The Vanishing Bridegroom 1990, Music Untangled 1991–92, Heroic strokes of the Bow 1992, Blond Eckbert 1993, Musicians Wrestle Everywhere 1994, Moon and Star 1995, Forest 1995, Storm 1997. *Address:* c/o Chester Music, 8/9 Frith Street, London, W1V 5TZ, England. *Telephone:* 0171-434 0066. *Fax:* 0171-287 6329.

WEIR, Peter Lindsay; Australian film director; b. 21 Aug. 1944, Sydney; s. of Lindsay Weir and Peggy Barnsley; m. Wendy Stites 1966; one s. one d.; ed. Scots Coll., Sydney, Vaucluse Boys' High School, Sydney Univ.; worked in real estate until 1965; worked as stagehand in television, Sydney 1967; dir. film sequences in variety show 1968; dir. amateur univ. reviews 1967–69; dir. for Film Australia 1969–73; made own short films 1969–73, independent feature-film dir. and writer 1973–; various film awards. *Films:* Cars that Ate Paris 1973, Picnic at Hanging Rock 1975, The Last Wave 1977, The Plumber (television) 1978, Gallipoli 1980, The Year of Living Dangerously 1982, Witness 1985, The Mosquito Coast 1986, The Dead Poets Society 1989, Green Card 1991, Fearless 1994, The Truman Show (BAFTA Award for Best Dir.) 1997. *Address:* Salt Pan Films Pty. Ltd., c/o P.O. Box 29, Palm Beach, N.S.W. 2108, Australia.

WEIR, Stuart Peter, B.A.; British journalist and academic; b. 13 Oct. 1938, Frimley, Surrey; s. of Robert H. Weir and Edna F. Lewis; m. 1st Doffy Burnham 1963; two s.; m. 2nd Elizabeth E. Bisset 1987; one s. two d.; ed. Peter Symonds School, Winchester and Brasenose Coll. Oxford; Feature Writer, Oxford Mail 1964–67; Diarist, the Times 1967–71; Dir. Citizens Rights Office 1971–75; Founding Ed. Roof Magazine (Shelter) 1975–77; Deputy Ed. New Society 1977–84; Ed. New Socialist 1984–87; Political Columnist, London Daily News 1987; Ed. New Statesman 1987–88, New Statesman and Society 1988–90; Man. Ed. World Democracy Survey; Founder Charter 88 1988; now Dir.; Jt. Ed. Democratic Audit of the U.K. and Sr. Research Fellow Human Rights Centre, Univ. of Essex 1991–; Series Consultant The People's Parl. (Channel 4 TV) 1994–97; Sr. Int. Facilitator Namibian Govt. and Democracy Project 1994–95; U.K. Facilitator Zimbabwe Parl. Democracy Project; Lecturer on Politics and the Media, L.S.E. 1994. *Publications:* Manifesto 1981, Political Power and Democratic Control in Britain; contributor to: The Other Britain 1982, Consuming Secrets 1982, Defining and Measuring Democracy 1995, Ego Trip (ed.) 1995, Behind Closed Doors 1995, The Three Pillars of Liberty 1996, Making Votes Count 1997. *Leisure interests:* children, cooking, gardening. *Address:* Butts Orchard, Butts Batch, Wrington, Bristol, BS40 5LN, England. *Telephone:* (01934) 863668.

WEIS, Eberhard, DR.PHIL.; German professor of history; b. 31 Oct. 1925, Schmalkalden; m. Ingeborg Koeniger 1953; two s.; ed. Univs. of Munich, Dijon and Paris; Archivist, Bavarian State Archives 1953–69; Prof. of Modern History, Freie Univ. Berlin 1969–70, Univ. of Münster 1970–74, Univ. of Munich 1974–91; Pres. Historical Comm., Bavarian Acad. of Sciences 1987–97; mem. several scientific socs. and insts. *Publications:* Geschichtsschreibung und Staatsauffassung in der französischen Enzyklopädie 1956, Montgelas 1759–1799 1971, Propyläen Geschichte Europas, Vol. IV (1776-1847) 1978, Deutschland und Frankreich um 1800 1990, and more than 100 other publs. *Address:* Ammerseestrasse 102, 82131 Gauting, Germany. *Telephone:* 089/850 54 08.

WEISKRANTZ, Lawrence, PH.D., F.R.S.; American professor of psychology; b. 28 March 1926, Philadelphia; s. of Benjamin Weiskrantz and Rose Weiskrantz (née Rifkin); m. Barbara Collins 1954; one s. one d.; ed. Girard Coll. of Philadelphia, Swarthmore and Univs. of Oxford and Harvard; part-time Lecturer, Tufts Univ. 1952; Research Assoc., Inst. of Living 1952–55; Sr. Postdoctoral Fellow, N.A.S. 1955–56; Research Assoc., Cambridge Univ., England 1956–61, Asst. Dir. of Research 1961–66, Fellow, Churchill Coll. 1964–67, Reader in Physiological Psychology 1966–67; Prof. of Psychology and Head of Dept. of Experimental Psychology, Oxford Univ. 1967–93; Fellow of Magdalen Coll. Oxford; Kenneth Craik Research Award, St. John's Coll. Cambridge 1975–76; Sir Frederick Bartlett Memorial Lecturer 1980; Ferrier Lecturer, Royal Soc. 1989; Hughlings Jackson Lecturer/Medallist (Royal Soc. of Medicine) 1990; Deputy Ed. Brain 1981–91; mem. N.A.S. *Publications:* Analysis of Behavioral Change (Ed.) 1967, Animal Intelligence (Ed.) 1985, Neuropsychology of Cognitive Function (Ed.) 1986, Blindsight 1986, Thought Without Language (Ed.) 1988, Consciousness Lost and Found 1997, and articles in Science, Nature, Quarterly Journal of Experimental Psychology, Journal of Comparative Physiological Psychology, Animal Behaviour and Brain. *Leisure interests:* music, walking. *Address:* Department of Experimental Psychology, University of Oxford, South Parks Road, Oxford, OX1 3UD, England. *Telephone:* (01865) 271444.

WEISS, Ulrich; German banker; b. 3 June 1936; fmr. mem. Bd. of Man. Dirs., Deutsche Bank AG, Frankfurt; Chair. Supervisory Bd. Continental AG, Hanover; Chair. Admin. Council, Deutsche Bank S.A.E., Barcelona/Madrid, Deutsche Bank de Investimento S.A., Lisbon, Deutsche Bank Luxembourg S.A.; Chair. Admin. Council, Deutsche Bank S.p.A., Milan; mem. Supervisory Bd. Asea Brown Boveri AG, Mannheim, BASF AG, Ludwigshafen, Heidelberger Zement AG, Klein, Schanzlin & Becker AG, Frankenthal, Rheinelektra AG, Mannheim, Südzucker AG, Mannheim; mem. Admin. Council Fiat S.p.A., Turin. *Address:* c/o Deutsche Bank AG, 60262 Frankfurt am Main, Germany.

WEISSENBERG, Alexis; Bulgarian pianist; b. 26 July 1929, Sofia; studied piano and composition with Pancho Vladigerov, also with Olga Samaroff at Juilliard School, New York; début at age 14; numerous appearances in Europe, South America, U.S.A., Japan; American début with New York Philharmonic; soloist with Berlin, Vienna, Japan, Czechoslovak Philharmonics, Philadelphia, Cleveland, Minnesota, Royal Danish, and Salzburg Festival orchestras, Boston, Chicago, Pittsburgh Symphony orchestras, Orchestre de Paris and others; recording artist with RCA, Angel; first prize Int. Leventritt competition and Philadelphia Youth competition 1946.

WEISZ, Rachel; British actress; b. 1972. *Film roles:* Seventeen, Chain Reaction, Stealing Beauty, Going All the Way, Amy Foster, Bent, I Want You, Land Girls, The Mummy. *Play:* Suddenly Last Summer 1999.

WEITZ, Raanan; Israeli rural development planner; b. 27 July 1913, Rehovot, Israel; s. of Joseph and Ruchama Weitz; m. Rivka Schechtman; one s. one d.; ed. Hebrew Gymnasia, Jerusalem, Hebrew Univ., and Univ. of Florence; Agricultural Settlement Dept., Jewish Agency 1937–, Village Instructor Head of Dept. 1963–84; service with Intelligence Corps., British 8th Army, Second World War; Chair. Nat. and Univ. Inst. of Agric. 1960–66; Head Devt. Study Centre 1963–; Prof. Rural Devt. Planning, Univ. of Haifa 1973–78, of Rural Devt. Theory Bar-Ilan Univ. 1978–82; fmr. mem. Hagana; mem. Exec., Zionist Org. 1963–84; Israel Prize 1990. *Publications:* Agriculture and Rural Development in Israel: Projection and Planning 1963, Rural Planning in Development Countries (ed.) 1965, Agricultural Development—Planning and Implementation 1968, Rural Development in a Changing World (ed.) 1971, From Peasant to Farmer: a Revolutionary Strategy for Development 1971, Urbanization and the Developing Countries: Report on the Sixth Rehovot Conference (ed.) 1973, Employment and Income Generation in New Settlement Projects 1978, Integrated Rural Development: The Rehovot Approach 1979, Growth and Values in Development: An Alternative Direction, New Roads to Development, a Twentieth Century Fund essay 1986; and papers on problems of comprehensive planning. *Address:* Development Study Centre, P.O. Box 2355, 76 122 Rehovot (Office); 15 Diskin Street, Kiriyat Wolfson, Israel (Home). *Telephone:* 08-9474111 (Office); 02-618764 (Home). *Fax:* 08-9475884.

WEIZMAN, Maj.-Gen. Ezer; Israeli politician and air force officer; b. 15 June 1924, Tel-Aviv; nephew of Chaim Weizmann (1st Pres. of Israel); m.; two c.; ed. R.A.F. Staff Coll.; Officer, Israel Air Force 1948–66 and fmr. C.O., I.A.F.; Chief General Staff Branch 1966–69; Minister of Transport 1969–70, of Defence 1977–80, of Communications 1984–88, of Science 1988–92; Chair. Exec. Cttee. Herut Party 1971–73; mem. Likud front 1973–80; in pvt. business 1980–84; Minister without Portfolio in Cabinet, Head of Yahad Party in Nat. Unity Govt. 1984–89; Pres. of Israel May 1993–. *Publications:* On Eagles Wings 1978, The Battle for Peace 1981. *Address:* Beit Hanassi, Jerusalem; 2 Hadekel Street, Caesarea, Israel.

WEIZSÄCKER, Carl Friedrich, Freiherr von, PH.D.; German professor of philosophy and director of research; b. 28 June 1912, Kiel; s. of Ernst von Weizsäcker and Marianne Graevenitz; m. Gundalena Wille 1937; four c.; ed. Univs. of Berlin, Göttingen and Leipzig; lecturer Kaiser-Wilhelm-Institut, Berlin 1936–42; Assoc. Prof. Univ. of Strasbourg 1942–44; Head Dept. Max-Planck-Inst. for Physics, Göttingen 1946–57; Hon. Prof. Univ. of Göttingen 1946–57; Prof. of Philosophy Univ. of Hamburg 1957–69; Dir. Max-Planck-Inst. for Research on Preconditions of Human Life in the Modern World, Starnberg 1970–80; Emer. Scientific mem. Max-Planck-Gesellschaft, Munich 1980–; Hon. Prof. Univ. of Munich; mem. Deutsche Akademie der Naturforscher, Leopoldina, Göttinger Akademie der Wissenschaften, Sächsische Akademie der Wissenschaften, Leipzig, Österreichische Akademie der Wissenschaften, Bayerische Akademie der Wissenschaften, Bayerische Akademie der Schönen Künste, Deutsche Physikalische Gesellschaft, American Physical Soc., Ordre Pour le Mérite, Académie des Sciences Morales et Politiques, Institut de France; Hon. Dr. Iur. (Vrije Universiteit, Amsterdam) 1975, (Alberta) 1981; Hon. Dr. Theol. (Catholic Theol. Faculty, Tubingen) 1977; Hon. Dr. rer. nat. (Karl-Marx-Universität, Leipzig) 1987; Hon. Dr. Phil. (Freie Universität, Berlin) 1987; numerous prizes and medals including John M. Templeton Prize for Progress in Religion (jtly.) 1989; Bundesverdienstkreuz. *Publications:* Die Atomkerne 1937, Zum Weltbild der Physik 1943, Die Geschichte der Natur 1948, Bedingungen des Friedens 1963, Die Tragweite der Wissenschaft 1964, Gedanken über unsere Zukunft 1966, Der ungesicherte Friede 1969, Die Einheit der Natur 1971, Fragen zur Weltpolitik 1975, Wege in die Gefahr 1977, Der Garten des Menschlichen 1978, Deutlichkeit 1978, Der bedrohte Friede 1981, Wahrnehmung der Neuzeit 1983, Aufbau der Physik 1985, Die Zeit drängt 1986, Bewusstseinswandel 1988, Bedingungen der Freiheit 1990, Der Mensch in seiner Geschichte 1991, Zeit und Wissen 1992, Der bedrohte Friede-heute 1994, Wohin gehen wir? 1997. *Address:* Alpenstrasse 15, 82319 Starnberg, Germany. *Telephone:* 08151 7091.

WEIZSÄCKER, Richard von, DR.JUR.; German politician and lawyer; b. 15 April 1920, Stuttgart; s. of late Baron Ernst von Weizsäcker; m. Marianne von Kretschmann 1953; three s. one d.; ed. Berlin, law studies at Oxford, Grenoble, Göttingen; army service 1938–45; prof. lawyer 1955–; fmr. mem. Bd. Allianz Lebensversicherung-AG, Stuttgart, Robeco-Gruppe, Amsterdam; mem. Robert Bosch Foundation, Stuttgart; mem. Synod and Council of German Protestant Church 1969–84, Pres. Protestant Church Congress 1964–70; mem. Fed. Bd. CDU, Deputy Chair. CDU/CSU Party 1972–79; mem. Bundestag 1969–81, Vice-Pres. 1979–81; Governing Mayor of West Berlin 1981–84; Pres. Fed. Repub. of Germany 1984–94; Hon. Pres. Int. Council of Christians and Jews 1994–; Hon. Senator Max Planck Soc.; Theodor Heuss Prize 1983; Hon. D.C.L. (Oxford) 1988; Dr. h.c. (Cambridge) 1994. *Publications:* Die deutsche Geschichte geht weiter 1983, Von Deutschland aus 1985, Die politische Kraft der Kultur 1987, Von Deutschland nach Europa 1991. *Address:* 14195 Berlin, Germany.

WELCH, John Francis, Jr., PH.D.; American business executive; b. 19 Nov. 1935, Peabody, Mass.; s. of John Francis and Grace (née Andrews) Welch; m. 1st Carolyn B. Osburn 1959 (divorced 1987); two s. two d.; m. 2nd Jane Beasely 1989; ed. Univs. of Massachusetts and Illinois; joined Gen. Electric Co., Fairfield, Conn. 1960–, Vice-Pres. 1972, Vice-Pres. Exec. Components and Materials Group 1973–77, Sr. Vice-Pres. Sector Exec., Consumer Products and Services Sector 1977–79, Vice-Chair, C.E.O. 1979–81, Chair., C.E.O. 1981–; Pres. and C.E.O. Nat. Broadcasting Co. Aug. 1986–, Dir.-Gen. Electric Credit Corpn. *Address:* General Electric Co., 3135 Easton Turnpike, Fairfield, CT 06431, U.S.A.

WELCH, Raquel; American actress; b. 5 Sept. 1940, Chicago, Ill.; d. of Armand and Josepha (née Hall) Tejada; m. 1st James Westley Welch 1959 (divorced); one s. one d.; m. 2nd Patrick Curtis (divorced); m. 3rd Andre Weinfeld 1980 (divorced); fmr. model for Neiman-Marcus stores. *Films include:* Fantastic Voyage 1966, One Million Years B.C. 1967, Fathom 1967, The Biggest Bundle of Them All 1968, Magic Christian 1970, Myra Breckinridge 1970, Fuzz 1972, Bluebeard 1972, Hannie Caulder 1972, Kansas City Bomber 1972, The Last of Sheila 1973, The Three Musketeers 1974, The Wild Party 1975, The Four Musketeers 1975, Mother, Jugs and Speed 1976, Crossed Swords 1978, L'Animal 1979, Chair. of the Board 1998; Right to Die 1987, Scandal in a Small Town 1988, Trouble in Paradise 1989, Naked Gun 33$^1/_3$ 1993; acted in play: Woman of the Year (Broadway) 1982, Torch Song 1993. *Videos:* Raquel: Total Beauty and Fitness 1984, A Week with Raquel 1987, Raquel: Lose 10lbs in 3 Weeks 1989. *Publication:* The Raquel Welch Total Beauty and Fitness Program 1984. *Address:* c/o Innovative Artists, 1999 Avenue of the Stars, 2850 Los Angeles, CA 90067, U.S.A.

WELD, Tuesday Ker (Susan Ker Weld); American actress; b. 27 Aug. 1943, New York; d. of Lathrop M. Weld and Aileen Ker; m. 1st Claude Harz 1965 (divorced 1971); one d.; m. 2nd Dudley Moore (q.v.) 1975 (divorced); one s.; m. 3rd Pinchas Zukerman (q.v.) 1985; ed. Hollywood Professional School; fashion and catalogue model aged three; regular appearances as magazine cover-girl and in child roles on TV by age twelve; appears in numerous TV programmes and TV films inc. Cimarron Strip, Playhouse 90, Climax, Ozzie and Harriet, 77 Sunset Strip, The Millionaire, Tab Hunter Show, Dick Powell Theatre, Adventures in Paradise, Naked City, The Greatest Show on Earth, Mr Broadway, Fugitive. *Films include:* Rock Rock (debut) 1956, Serial, Rally Round the Flag Boys, The Five Pennies, The Private Lives of Adam and Eve, Return to Peyton Place, Wild in the Country, Bachelor Flat, Lord Love a Duck, Pretty Poison, I Walk the Line, A Safe Place, Play it as it Lays, Because They're Young, High Time, Sex Kittens Go to College, The Cincinnati Kid, Soldier in the Rain, Looking for Mr Goodbar, Thief, Author!, Once Upon a Time In America, Heartbreak Hotel, Falling Down, Feeling Minnesota 1996.

WELD, William Floyd, J.D.; American politician; b. 31 July 1945, New York; s. of David Weld and Mary Nichols; m. Susan Roosevelt 1975; two s. three d.; ed. Harvard and Oxford Univs.; admitted Mass. Bar 1970; law clerk, Supreme Judicial Court, Mass. 1970–71; partner, Hill & Barlow, Boston 1971–81; Assoc. Minority Counsel, U.S. House of Reps. Judiciary Comm. Impeachment Inquiry 1973–74; U.S. Attorney for Dist. of Mass. 1981–86; Asst. Attorney-Gen. Criminal Div. U.S. Justice Dept., Washington, D.C. 1986–88; Gov. of Massachusetts 1990–97; mem. American Law Inst., Boston Bar Asscn., American Bar Asscn.; Republican. *Address:* c/o Office of the Governor, State House, Boston, MA 02133, U.S.A.

WELDON, Fay, M.A.; British author; b. 22 Sept. 1931, Alvechurch, Worcs.; d. of Frank T. Birkinshaw and Margaret J. Birkinshaw; m. Ronald Weldon 1960 (divorced 1994); four s.; ed. Girls' High School, Christchurch, New Zealand, and Univ. of St. Andrews; Chair. of Judges, Booker McConnell Prize 1983; fmr. mem. Arts Council Literary Panel; mem. Video Censorship Appeals Cttee.; Hon. D. Litt. (St Andrews) 1992; Women in Publishing Pandora Award 1997. *Publications:* novels: The Fat Woman's Joke 1967 (published in U.S.A. as And the Wife Ran Away 1968), Down Among the Women 1972, Female Friends 1975, Remember Me 1976, Little Sisters 1977 (U.S.A. Words of Advice), Praxis 1978, Puffball 1980, The President's Child 1982, The Life and Loves of a She-Devil 1984, The Shrapnel Academy 1986, The Heart of the Country 1987, The Hearts and Lives of Men 1987, The Rules of Life (novella) 1987, Leader of the Band 1988, The Cloning of Joanna May 1989, Darcy's Utopia 1990, Growing Rich 1992, Life Force 1992, Affliction 1994 (U.S.A. Trouble), (U.S.A. Trouble) Splitting 1995, Worst Fears 1996, Big Women 1997; children's books: Wolf the Mechanical Dog 1988, Party Puddle 1989, Nobody Likes Me! 1997; short story collections: Watching Me Watching You 1981, Polaris 1985, Moon Over Minneapolis 1991, Wicked Women 1995, Angel All Innocence and Other Stories, A Hard

Time to be a Father 1998; plays for theatre: Words of Advice 1974, Friends 1975, Moving House 1976, Mr Director 1977, Action Replay 1979, I Love My Love 1981, Woodworm 1981, Jane Eyre 1986, The Hole in the Top of the World 1987; more than 30 television plays, dramatizations and radio plays. *Address:* Casarotto Co. Ltd., National House, 62/66 Wardour Street, London W1V 3HP, England.

WELDON, Virginia Verral, A.B., M.D.; American university administrator and physician; b. 8 Sept. 1935, Toronto, Canada; d. of John Edward Verral and Carolyn Edith Swift; m. (divorced); two d.; ed. Smith Coll., State Univ. of New York at Buffalo, Johns Hopkins Univ. School of Medicine, U.S.A.; Instructor in Paediatrics, Johns Hopkins Hosp. 1967–68; Washington Univ. School of Medicine 1968–69, Asst. Prof. of Paediatrics 1973–79, Prof. 1979–89, Asst. Vice-Chancellor for Medical Affairs 1975–81, Assoc. Vice-Chancellor 1981–83, Deputy Vice-Chancellor 1983–89, Vice-Pres. Washington Univ. Medical Center 1980–89; Vice-Pres. Scientific Affairs, Monsanto Co. 1989, Vice-Pres. Public Policy 1989–93, Sr. Vice-Pres. Public Policy 1993–98; Dir. Center for Study of American Business, Washington Univ., St Louis 1998–; Adviser, Dir. Monsanto Co. 1989–98; Trustee Calif. Inst. of Tech. 1996–, Whitaker Foundation 1997–, Whitfield School 1997–; mem. Environmental Protection Agency Risk Assessment Man. Comm. 1992–97, Pres's Cttee. of Advisors on Science and Tech. 1994–; Fellow A.A.A.S.; Smith Coll. Medal 1984. *Publications:* numerous articles in scientific journals. *Leisure interest:* civic affairs. *Address:* Monsanto Co., DIA, 800 N. Lindbergh Boulevard, Saint Louis, MO 63141 (Office); 242 Carlyle Lake Drive, Saint Louis, MO 63141, U.S.A. (Home).

WELLAND, Colin (b. Williams); British playwright and actor; b. 4 July 1934, Liverpool; s. of John Arthur Williams and Norah Williams; m. Patricia Sweeney 1962; one s. three d.; ed. Newton-le-Willows Grammar School, Goldsmiths' Coll., London; art teacher 1958–62; entered theatre 1962–, Library Theatre, Manchester 1962–64; Dir. Radio Aire 1981–. *Film roles:* Kes, Villain, Straw Dogs, Sweeney, The Secret Life of Ian Fleming, Dancing through the Dark. *Wrote screenplay for:* Yanks 1978, Chariots of Fire 1980 (Acad. Award), Twice in a Lifetime 1986, A Dry White Season, War of the Buttons 1994. *Stage roles:* Waiting for Godot 1987, The Churchill Play. *Wrote plays:* Say Goodnight to Grandma 1973, Roll on Four O'Clock 1981; *TV plays include* Kisses at 50, Leeds United, Your Man from Six Counties, Bambino Mio. *Publications:* plays Roomful of Holes 1972, Say Goodnight to Grandma 1973. *Leisure interests:* cricket, watching rugby (League and Union) and soccer, films, dining out, politics. *Address:* c/o Peters, Fraser & Dunlop, 5th Floor, The Chambers, Lots Road, Chelsea Harbour, London, SW10 0XF, England.

WELLER, Malcolm Philip Isadore, M.A., M.B., B.S.; British medical practitioner; b. 29 May 1935, Manchester; s. of Solomon George Weller and Esther Weller; m. Davina Reisler 1966; two s.; ed. Perse School, Cambridge, Cambridge and Newcastle Univs.; consultant, Friern, St. Ann's Hosps., London; Hon. Sr. Lecturer, London Univ., Royal Free Hosp. School of Medicine –1997; Hon. Research Prof. Middx. Univ. 1997–; Chair. N. Thames Regional Psychiatric Cttee. 1997–; Vice-Chair. N.E. Thames Regional Cttee. for Hosp. Medical Services 1984–96; Hon. Medical Adviser, Nat. Alliance of Relatives of the Mentally Ill, Jewish Asscn. of the Mentally Ill, Nat. Schizophrenia Fellowship and Founder-mem. Parl. Cttee.; Chair. CONCERN; co-opted mem. Bd. of Studies in Psychology, London Univ., and Higher Degrees Sub-Cttee. 1976–; Founder, Ed.-in-Chief Baillière's Clinical Psychiatry series; External Examiner for Master in Medicine (Psychiatry) Degree, Nat. Univ. of Singapore 1988, 1989; External Examiner Manchester Univ. M.Sc. 1990; mem. Standing Cttee. Bd. of Studies in Medicine, London Univ. 1981–84; mem. Gen. Psychiatry Exec. Cttee. Royal Coll. of Psychiatry, also of Pharmacology, and Social, Community and Rehabilitation Cttees.; Concert organizer, Newcastle Festival 1970–71; co-opted mem. Laing Art Gallery Cttee. 1972–73; Chair. CONCERN 1992–94; Chair. Govs. Gosforth Middle School 1971–74; Fellow British Psychological Soc., Royal Coll. of Psychiatrists, Collegium Internationale Neuro-Psycho-Pharmacologicum (CINP); Ver Heyden de Lancey Prize, Cambridge Univ., Wilfred Kingdom Prize, Newcastle Univ., Mental Health Foundation Undergraduate Scholarship, British Council Travel Award. *Publications:* Scientific Basis of Psychology (Ed.) 1983, International Perspectives in Schizophrenia (Ed.) 1989, Dimensions of Community Care 1993, Progress in Clinical Psychiatry 1997, about 100 editorials and papers in learned journals, mainly on schizophrenia, depression, psychological medicine, and medico-legal matters; about 100 publs. on music in various music journals. *Leisure interests:* fine art, music. *Address:* 30 Arkwright Road, Hampstead, London, NW3 6BH, England (Home). *Telephone:* 0171-794 5804 (Home). *Fax:* 0171-431 1589.

WELLER, Paul; British musician; b. 1958; m.; two c.; founded The Jam 1972, The Style Council 1982; solo 1989–. *Songs include:* Eton Rifles 1979, Going Underground/Dreams of Children 1980, Start 1980, Town Called Malice/Precious 1982, Bitterest Pill (I ever had to swallow) 1982, Beat Surrender 1982, Long Hot Summer 1982. *Albums:* In the City 1977, This is the Modern World 1977, All Mod Cons 1978, Setting Sons 1979, Sound Affects 1980, The Gift 1982, Dig the New Breed 1982, In the City (re-issue), Snap 1983, Greatest Hits 1991, Extras 1992, Live Jam 1993, (The Jam) Cafe Bleu 1984, Our Favourite Shop 1985, Home and Abroad 1986, The Cost of Loving 1987, Confessions of a Pop Group 1988, Singular Adventures of the Style Council 1989, Here's Some That Got Away 1993, (The Style Council) Paul Weller 1992, Wild Wood 1993, Live Wood 1994, Stanley Road 1995. *Address:* c/o Go'Discs Ltd., 72 Black Lion Lane, Hammersmith, London, W6 9BE, England. *Telephone:* 0181-910 4600. *Fax:* 0181-741 2184.

WELLER, Thomas Huckle, A.B., M.S., M.D.; American scientist and university professor; b. 1915, Ann Arbor, Mich.; s. of Carl V. Weller and Elsie H. Weller; m. Kathleen R. Fahey 1945; two s. two d.; ed. Harvard Univ. and Univ. of Michigan; Teaching Fellow, Harvard Medical School 1940–42; served Medical Corps, U.S. Army 1942–45; Asst. Resident, Children's Hospital, Boston 1946–47; Research Fellow, Harvard Medical School 1947–48, Instructor 1948–49; Asst. Prof. Tropical Public Health, Harvard School of Public Health 1949, Assoc. Prof. 1950–54, Richard Pearson Strong Prof. 1954–85, Emer. 1985, and Head of Dept. 1954–81; Asst. Dir. Research Div. of Infectious Diseases, Children's Medical Center, Boston 1949–55; Dir. Comm. on Parasitic Diseases, Armed Forces Epidemiological Bd. 1953–59; Consultant on Tropical Diseases, U.S. Public Health Service; Dir. Center for Prevention of Infectious Diseases, Harvard School of Public Health 1966–81; Consultant practice: viral and parasitic diseases, int. health 1985–; mem. N.A.S.; Hon. Fellow Royal Soc. of Tropical Medicine and Hygiene 1987, Faculty of Public Health Medicine of Royal Coll. of Physicians 1990; Hon. LL.D. (Mich.), Sc.D. (Gustavus Adolphus), L.H.D. (Lowell); winner (jtly.) of E. Mead Johnson Award 1953, Kimble Methodology Award 1954, Nobel Prize in Medicine and Physiology 1954, Weinstein Cerebral Palsy Award 1973, Ledlie Prize 1963, Bristol Award, Infectious Diseases Soc. of America 1980, Gold Medal and Diploma of Honor, Univ. Costa Rica, 1984, VZV Foundation Award for Scientific Achievement 1993, Walter Reed Medal, American Soc. of Tropical Medicine and Hygiene 1996. *Publications:* papers on infectious diseases, tropical medicine, virus cultivation (especially poliomyelitis and mumps), the etiology of varicella, cytomegalic inclusion disease and rubella, herpes zoster, laboratory diagnosis of schistosomiasis. *Leisure interests:* gardening, ornithology, photography. *Address:* 56 Winding River Road, Needham, MA 02492, U.S.A. (Home). *Telephone:* (781) 235-3905. *Fax:* (781) 235-9059.

WELLER, Walter; Austrian conductor; b. 30 Nov. 1939; s. of Walter and Anna Weller; m. Elisabeth Samohyl; 1966; one s.; ed. Realgymnasium, Vienna, Akademie für Musik, Vienna; f. Weller Quartet 1958–69; mem. Vienna Philharmonic 1958–60, First Leader 1960–69; Conductor, Vienna State Opera 1969–75; Guest Conductor with all main European, American and Japan Broadcasting Corpn. orchestras 1973–; Chief Conductor, Tonkünstler Orchestra, Vienna 1974–77; Principal Conductor and Artistic Adviser, Royal Liverpool Philharmonic Orchestra 1977–80, Guest Conductor Laureate 1980; Prin. Conductor, Royal Philharmonic Orchestra 1980–85, Chief Guest Conductor 1985–; Chief Guest Conductor, Nat. Orchestra of Spain 1987–; Prin. Conductor, Music Dir. Royal Scottish Nat. Orchestra 1992–97; Chief Conductor and Artistic Adviser, Opera Basel and Allgemeine Musikgesellschaft Basel 1994–95; Conductor Emer. Royal Scottish Nat. Orchestra; Medal of Arts and Sciences (Austria) 1968, Grand Prix du Disque, Charles Cross for Duke's symphony in C, Great Silver Cross of Honour (Austria) 1998. *Leisure interests:* magic, model railways, sailing, swimming, stamp-collecting, skiing. *Address:* c/o Harrison-Parrott Ltd., 12 Penzance Place, London, W11 4PA, England.

WELLERSHOFF, Dieter, D.PHIL.; German writer; b. 3 Nov. 1925, Neuss/Rhein; s. of Walter Wellershoff and Kläre Weber; m. Dr. Maria von Thadden 1952; one s. two d.; ed. Gymnasium in Grevenbroich and Univ. Bonn; Ed. 1952–55; freelance writer 1956–59, 1981–; Reader Kiepenheuer and Witsch Publishing House, Cologne 1959–81; Hörspielpreis der Kriegsblinden 1961; Literaturpreis Verband der deutschen Kritiker 1970, Heinrich Böll Prize, Cologne 1988. *Publications:* Gottfried Benn, Phänotyp dieser Stunde 1958, Der Gleichgültige 1963, Ein schöner Tag 1966, Literatur und Veränderung 1969, Einladung an alle 1972, Die Schönheit des Schimpansen 1977, Die Sirene 1980, Der Sieger nimmt alles 1983, Die Arbeit des Lebens 1985, Die Körper und die Träume 1986, Der Roman und die Erfahrbarkeit der Welt 1988, Pan und die Engel. Ansichten von Köln 1990, Blick auf einen fernen Berg 1991, Das geordnete Chaos 1992, Angesichts der Gegenwart 1993, Der Ernstfall. Innenansichten des Krieges 1995, Zikadengeschrei 1995, Werke in 6 Bänden 1996–97; (ed.) Gottfried Benn, Gesammelte Werke 1958; works translated into 15 languages. *Address:* Mainzer Strasse 45, 50678 Cologne, Germany. *Telephone:* (0221) 388565.

WELLS, Herman B, B.S., A.M., LL.D.; American educationist; b. 7 June 1902, Jamestown, Indiana; s. of Joseph Granville and Anna Bernice (née Harting) Wells; ed. Univs. of Illinois and Wisconsin, and Indiana Univ.; Asst. Cashier, First Nat. Bank, Lebanon, Ind. 1924–26; Asst., Dept. of Econs., Univ. of Wisconsin 1927–28; Field Sec. Indiana Bankers' Asscn. 1928–31; Sec. and Research Dir. Study Comm. for Indiana Financial Insts. 1931–33; Instructor in Econs. Indiana Univ. 1930–33, Asst. Prof. 1933–35; Supervisor Div. of Banks and Trust Cos. and Div. of Research and Statistics, Dept. of Financial Insts. State of Indiana 1933–35, Sec. Comm. for Financial Insts. 1933–36; Dean and Prof. School of Business Admin. Indiana Univ. 1935–37, Acting Pres. of Univ. 1937–38, Pres. of Univ. 1938–62, Chancellor 1962–; Pres. Indiana Univ. Foundation 1962–69, Chair. of Bd. 1937–62, 1969–72, Chair. Exec. Cttee. 1969–, Vice-Chair. 1975–; Chair. American Council on Educ. 1944–45; Trustee, Carnegie Foundation for Advancement of Teaching 1941–62; Special Advisor Liberated Areas, U.S. Dept. of State 1944; Consultant, American Council on Educ. to U.S. Del. at San Francisco Conf. 1945; mem. Allied Missions for Observation of Greek Elections 1946; adviser cultural affairs Mil. Govt., U.S. Zone, Germany 1947–48; mem. UNESCO

Comm. of Experts on German Questions 1949–50; U.S. mem. Governing Bd. UNESCO Inst. for Educ., Hamburg 1951–57; U.S. Nat. Comm. for UNESCO 1951–55, Vice-Chair. 1953–54; mem. U.S. Del. to UN 1957; adviser to Pakistan Ministry of Educ. 1959; Vice-Pres. Int. Asscn. of Univs. 1955–60; Head U.S. Del. SEATO Preparatory Comm. on Univ. Problems 1960; mem. U.S. Cttee. reviewing activities and org. of UN Secr. 1960–61; Chair. Bd. American Research Inst. for the Arts 1975–78; Chair. Bd. of Trustees, Educ. and World Affairs 1963–70; mem. President's Cttee. on U.S.-Soviet Trade Relations 1965, on Overseas Voluntary Activities 1967; mem. Review Cttee. on Haile Sellassie I Univ. 1966–74; mem. Nat. Cttee. on U.S.-China Relations 1969, numerous Cttees.; mem. Bd. Lilly Endowment; mem. Bd. Chemed Corpn. 1970–85, Hon. mem. 1985–, Lilly Endowment Inc. 1973–; mem. Visiting Cttee., Tulane Univ.; hon. degrees from 25 univs. and colls.; Commdr's Cross of Order of Merit, Fed. Repub. of Germany and numerous other orders. *Leisure interest:* travelling. *Address:* Office of the Chancellor, Owen Hall, Indiana University, Bloomington, IN 47405; 1321 East 10th Street, Bloomington, IN 47408, U.S.A. (Home). *Telephone:* (812) 855-6647 (Office); (812) 336-6275 (Home).

WELLS, Rufus Michael Grant, PH.D., D.SC., F.R.S.N.Z.; New Zealand professor of zoology; b. 3 July 1947, Cardiff, Wales; s. of Peter F. Wells and Jean Chiles; m. Jane Nelson 1969; one s. one d.; ed. Hamilton Boys' High School, Univ. of Auckland, Bedford Coll., Univ. of London, U.K.; researcher in molecular physiology of haemoglobin and respiration (medical, animal, and fisheries science), Antarctic biology; Asst. Lecturer in Statistics, Univ. of Auckland 1970–71; Research Asst. and Ph.D. student Bedford Coll., London 1971–74; Biochemist and MRC Fellow, Univ. Coll. Hosp., London 1974–75; lecturer, then Sr. Lecturer in Zoology, then Prof., Univ. of Auckland 1975–; biological and editorial consultant, specializing in Antarctic Science and Science Educ.; fmr. mem. Nat. Comm. for Antarctic Research; Physiological Soc. of N.Z. Medal 1983, Royal Soc. of N.Z. Hutton Medal 1989. *Publications:* 220 scientific papers. *Address:* School of Biological Sciences, University of Auckland, Private Bag 92019, Auckland 1, New Zealand. *Telephone:* (9) 373 7599.

WELSER-MÖST, Franz (pseudonym of Franz von Bennigsen); Austrian conductor; b. 16 Aug. 1960, Linz; ed. Musikgymnasium, Linz and Staatliche Musikhochschule, Munich; Chief Conductor, Jeunesse Orchestra, Linz 1982–85, Norrköping Symphony Orchestra 1985, Musikkollegium Winterthur, Switzerland 1986; Music Dir. London Philharmonic Orchestra (LPO) 1990–96, Zürich Opera 1995–; *recordings include:* Mendelssohn Symphonies 3 and 4, Schumann Symphonies 2 and 3, Bruckner Symphony 7, Strauss Waltzes, Carl Orff's Carmina Burana, Stravinsky's Oedipus Rex, Bartok's Miraculous Mandarin, Kodaly's Peacock Variations, Kancheli's Symphony 3, Pärt's Symphony 3, Fratres, Schmidt's Symphony 4 (Gramophone Award 1996) (all with LPO); Outstanding Achievement Award from Western Law Centre, L.A., for work for people with disabilities. *Leisure interests:* literature, mountain hiking, marathon. *Address:* c/o IMG Artists Europe, Media House, 3 Burlington Lane, London, W4 2TH, England.

WELSH, Irvine; British writer; lives in Amsterdam and Scotland. *Publications:* Trainspotting (made into film), The Acid House (short stories), Marabou Stork Nightmares 1995, Ecstasy–Three Chemical Romances, Filth 1998. *Address:* c/o Jonathan Cape, 20 Vauxhall Bridge Road, London, SW1V 2SA, England. *Telephone:* 0171-973 9000. *Fax:* 0171-233 6117.

WELSH, Moray Meston, B.A., L.R.A.M., A.R.C.M.; British 'cellist; b. 1 March 1947, Haddington; s. of D. A. Welsh and C. (née Meston) Welsh; ed. York Univ. and Moscow Conservatoire; 'cello solo appearances in U.K., U.S.A., U.S.S.R., Europe and Scandinavia; appeared in concertos and chamber music with major U.K. orchestras, radio, TV; also festivals at Bath, Edin., Aldeburgh, Bergen and Helsinki; records include concertos by Boccherini, Vivaldi, Goehr, Hoddinott, Hugh Wood (record of the year); recorded with James Galway, Kyung-Wha Chung, Allegri Quartet, Alberni Quartet; Prin. 'cello, London Symphony Orchestra 1992–; British Council Award, Gulbenkian Fellowship. *Address:* 28 Summerfield Avenue, Queens Park, London, NW6 6JY, England. *Telephone:* 0181-960 9122.

WELTEKE, Ernst; German banker; b. 21 Aug. 1942, Korbach; ed. Marburg and Frankfurt am Main; Town Councillor, Oberursel 1977–85; Chair. SPD Landtag Party 1984–87, 1988–91; Minister for the Economy, Transport and Tech. in Hessen 1991–94, for Finance 1994–95; Pres. Regional Cen. Bank, Hessen 1995–99; Pres. (desig.) Bundesbank Sept. 1999–; mem. dist. ass., Hochtaunus 1968–89; mem. Landtag, Hessen 1974–95. *Address:* Deutsche Bundesbank, Wilhelm-Epstein-Str. 14, 60006 Frankfurt am Main, Postfach 100602, Germany. *Telephone:* (69) 95661 (Bundesbank). *Fax:* (69) 5601071 (Bundesbank).

WELTING, Ruth Lynn; American opera singer (coloratura soprano); b. 5 Nov. 1948, Memphis, Tenn.; d. of W. E. Welting; ed. Memphis State Univ., Juilliard School of Music and under Jani Strasser (Glyndebourne), Daniel Ferro and Luigi Ricci (Rome Opera); début, New York City Opera in Die Entführung 1971, Metropolitan Opera as Zerbinetta in Ariadne auf Naxos 1975, Chicago Lyric Opera as Olympia in Tales of Hoffmann 1975, Royal Opera House, Covent Garden as Rosina in Il Barbiere di Siviglia 1976, Paris Opera 1983; has appeared at many int. music festivals. *Leisure interests:* Christian ministries, sport, cooking. *Address:* c/o Bob Lombardo Associates, One Harkness Plaza, 61 West 62nd Street, New York, NY 10023, U.S.A. *Telephone:* (212) 586-4453.

WELTY, Eudora, B.A.; American writer; b. 1909, Jackson, Miss.; d. of Christian Webb and Chestina (Andrews) Welty; ed. Mississippi State Coll. for Women, Univ. of Wisconsin and Columbia Univ.; contrib. The New Yorker; mem. American Acad. of Arts and Letters 1969; Chevalier, Ordre des Arts et des Lettres 1987; Gold Medal, Nat. Inst. Arts and Letters 1972; Pulitzer Prize for Fiction for The Optimist's Daughter 1973; Nat. Medal for Literature 1980; Presidential Medal of Freedom 1980. Commonwealth Award for Distinguished Service in Literature (Modern Language Asscn. of America) 1984, Nat. Endowment for the Arts Award 1989, Nat. Book Foundation Medal 1991, Charles Frankel Prize 1992. *Publications:* A Curtain of Green 1941, Robber Bridegroom 1942, The Wide Net 1943, Delta Wedding 1946, The Golden Apples 1949, The Ponder Heart 1954, The Bride of Innisfallen 1955, The Shoe Bird 1964, Losing Battles 1970, One Time, One Place 1971, The Optimist's Daughter 1972, The Eye of the Story 1978, The Collected Stories of Eudora Welty 1980, One Writer's Beginnings 1984, Eudora Welty Photographs 1989, A Writer's Eye: Collected Book Reviews 1994, Monuments to Interruption: Collected Book Reviews 1994. *Address:* 1119 Pinehurst Place, Jackson, MI 39202, U.S.A.

WELTY, John D., M.A., ED.D.; American university president; b. 24 Aug. 1944, Amboy, Ill.; s. of John D. Welty and Doris E. Donnelly; m. Sharon Brown 1996; three d. two s.; ed. Western Illinois, Michigan State and Indiana Univs.; Admissions Counsellor, Mich. State Univ. 1966–67; Asst. Vice-Pres. for Student Affairs, Southwest Minn. State Univ. 1967–74; Dir. of Residences and Asst. Prof. SUNY, Albany 1974–77, Assoc. Dean of Students and Dir. of Residences 1977–80; Vice-Pres. for Student and Univ. Affairs, Ind. Univ. of Pa. 1980–84, Pres. 1984–91; Pres. Calif. State Univ., Fresno 1991–; several distinguished service awards. *Leisure interests:* golf, jogging, reading, racquetball. *Address:* Office of the President, California State University, 5241 N. Maple Ave, Thomas Administration Building, Fresno, CA 93725; 4411 N. Van Ness Boulevard, Fresno, CA 93704, U.S.A. *Telephone:* (209) 222 2920.

WEN, Carson, M.A.; Chinese lawyer; b. 16 April 1953, Hong Kong; s. of Sir Yung Wen and Tsi Fung Chu; m. Julia Fung Yuet Shan 1983; one c.; ed. Diocesan Boys' School, Hong Kong, Nat. Jr. Coll. Singapore, Columbia Univ. New York and Univ. of Oxford; Singapore Govt. Scholar 1971–72; partner, Siao, Wen and Leung (Solicitors), Hong Kong 1982–; Dir. and Sec.-Gen. Hong Kong Kwun Tong Industries and Commerce Asscn. 1982–, Pres. Emer. 1989–; Hon. Life Pres. Hong Kong Sze Yap Industry and Commerce Asscn. 1983–; mem. Kwun Tong Dist. Bd. 1983–85; Dir. Banco Delta Asia SARL, Macau 1992–; Hon. Pres. Hong Kong Industrial Dists., Industry and Commerce Asscn. Ltd. 1993–; Attesting Officer apptd. by Ministry of Justice of China 1992–; mem. Standing Cttee. Fed. of Youth of Shenzhen, China 1992–; Special Adviser to China Sr. Prosecutors Educ. Foundation under the auspices of the Supreme People's Procurate of People's Repub. of China 1993–; Del. People's Congress of Guangdong Prov., China 1993–; Hong Kong Affairs Adviser to Govt. of China 1993–; mem. Selection Cttee. for First Govt. of Hong Kong Special Admin. Region 1996; Vice-Chair. The Hong Kong Progressive Alliance 1994–. *Publications:* contribs. to 13 lectures on Hong Kong Law; articles in journals magazines and newspapers. *Leisure interests:* reading, golf. *Address:* 15th Floor, Hang Seng Building, 77 Des Voeux Road, Central, Hong Kong Special Administrative Region, People's Republic of China (Office); 6B, Wealthy Heights, 35 Macdonnell Road, Hong Kong Special Administrative Region, People's Republic of China (Home). *Telephone:* (852) 28104113 (Office); (852) 28401118 (Home). *Fax:* (852) 28697060 (Office).

WEN JIABAO; Chinese party and state official; b. Sept. 1942, Tianjin; ed. Beijing Geological Coll.; joined CCP 1965; geological research worker in Gansu Prov. 1968–1982; Dir. Reform Research Office of the Geological and Mining Bureau of the State Council 1982–83; Deputy Minister of Geology and Mining 1983–85; Dir. Cen. Gen. Office of CCP Cen. Cttee. 1986–97; Alt. mem. Secr. of Cen. Cttee. 1987; Sec. CCP Cen. Organs Working Cttee. 1988; mem. 14th CCP Cen. Cttee. 1992–97, alt. mem. CCP Politburo 1992–97, mem. 1997–; Sec. Secr. of Cen. Cttee. 1992; mem. 15th CCP Cen. Cttee. 1997–; Vice-Premier State Council 1998–. *Address:* State Council, Beijing, People's Republic of China.

WEN SHIZHEN; Chinese administrator; b. 1940, Haicheng Co., Liaoning Prov.; ed. Faculty of Mechanical Eng., Dalian Inst. of Tech.; joined CCP 1979; with Dalian Oil Pump Nozzle Plant 1980–82; Deputy Dir. Dalian City Machinery Bureau 1983–85; alt. mem. 13th Cen. Cttee. CCP 1987–91, mem. 14th Cen. Cttee. CCP 1992; del. 8th NPC; Vice-Gov. Liaoning Prov. 1986–94, Acting Gov. 1994–95, Gov. 1995, Deputy Sec. CCP 7th Liaoning Prov. Cttee. 1995, Sec. 1997–; mem. 15th Cen. Cttee. CCP 1997–. *Address:* c/o Office of the Governor, Liaoning Provincial Government, Shengyang City, People's Republic of China.

WEN ZONGREN; Chinese army officer; b. Nov. 1940, Chaoxian Co., Anhui Prov.; joined PLA 1959; joined CCP 1961; ed. PLA Tank School 1963, PLA Political Acad. 1979, PLA Mil. Acad. 1984; Regimental Political Commissar 1976; Dir. Divisional Political Dept. 1980; Divisional Political Commissar 1982; Dir. Group Army Political Dept. 1983; Group Army Political Commissar; Dir. Political Dept. of Nanjing Mil. Area Command, Political Commissar Lanzhou Mil. Area Command 1985–; alt. mem. 14th CCP Cen. Cttee. 1992; mem. 15th CCP Cen. Cttee. 1997–. *Address:* People's Liberation Army Lanzhou Military Area Command, Lanzhou City, Gansu Province, People's Republic of China.

WENDERS, Wim; German film director; b. 14 Aug. 1945, Düsseldorf; m. Donata Schmidt 1993; Chair. European Film Acad. 1991–96, Pres. 1996–; mem. Akademie der Künste; Dr. h.c. (Sorbonne, Paris). *Films include:* Summer in the City 1970, The Goalies Anxiety at the Penalty Kick 1972, The Scarlet Letter 1973, Alice in the Cities 1974, The Wrong Move 1975, Kings of the Road 1976, The American Friend 1977, Lightning Over Water 1980, The State of Things 1982, Hammett 1982, Paris, Texas 1984, Wings of Desire 1987 (Cannes Film Festival Award), Aufzeichnungen zu Kleidern und Städten 1989, Until the End of the World 1991, Faraway, So Close! 1993, Lisbon Story, The Million Dollar Hotel 1999. *Publications:* Emotion Pictures 1986, Written in the West 1987, Die Logik der Bilder 1988, The Act of Seeing 1992. *Address:* Road Movies Filmprod. GmbH, Potsdamer Strasse 199, 10783 Berlin, Germany. *Telephone:* (030) 216-80-11.

WENDT, Albert; Samoan author; b. 1939, Apia; three c.; Prof. Head of English Dept., Auckland Univ.; Hon. Ph.D. (Univ. de Bourgogne, France) 1993; Order of Merit (Western Samoa). *Publications include:* Pouliuli (novel), Leaves of the Banyan Tree (novel), Flying Fox in a Freedom Tree (short stories), Sons for the Return Home (novel), Ola (novel), Black Rainbow (novel). *Address:* Department of English, University of Auckland, Private Bag 92019, Auckland 1, New Zealand. *Telephone:* 3737999.

WENDT, Henry, III, A.B.; American business executive; b. 19 July 1933, Neptune City, N.J.; s. of Henry Wendt and Rachel Lindsey Wendt; m. Holly Ann Peterson 1956; one s. one d.; ed. Hackley School, Tarrytown, N.Y., and Princeton, N.J.; joined SmithKline and French Labs. 1955; Pres. SmithKline Corpn. 1976–89, C.E.O. 1982–89; Chair. SmithKline Beckman Corpn. Feb.–July 1989; Chair. SmithKline Beecham PLC 1989–94. *Publications:* Global Embrace, various articles. *Leisure interests:* viniculture, oenology, 16th and 17th century cartography, fly fishing, sailing. *Address:* c/o SmithKline Beecham, One Franklin Plaza, P.O. Box 7929, Philadelphia, PA 19101, U.S.A. *Telephone:* (215) 751-4211.

WENGER, Antoine, Rév. Père; French ecclesiastic and theologian; b. 2 Sept. 1919, Rohrwiller (Bas-Rhin); s. of Charles Wenger and Philomène Gambel; ed. Sorbonne, Strasbourg Univ.; ordained Priest 1943; Dir. of Oriental Theology, Univ. Catholique de Lyon 1948–56, Prof. 1956; Chief Ed. La Croix 1957–69; Pres. Fédération Internationale des Directeurs de Journaux Catholiques 1957–65; mem. Pontifical Marian Acad., Rome 1959; Prof. of Ancient Christian Literature, Strasbourg Univ. 1969–73; Ecclesiastical Counsellor to the French Amb. to the Holy See 1973–83; Adviser to Council for Church (Vatican) and Public Affairs 1983–92, to Pontifical Council for non-believers 1987–92, Counsellor for Religious Affairs, French Embassy in Russia 1992–96; Officier, Légion d'honneur; Commdr. Ordre nat. du Mérite. *Publications:* L'Assomption dans la tradition orientale 1955, Homélies Baptismales inédites de St. Jean Chrysostome 1957, La Russie de Khrouchtchev 1959, Vatican II, Première Session 1963, Vatican II, Deuxième Session 1964, Vatican II, Troisième Session 1965, Quatrième Session 1966, Upsal, le Défi du Siècle aux Eglises 1968, Rome et Moscou, 1900–1950 1987, Le cardinal Jean Villot, Secrétaire d'Etat de trois Papes 1989, Les Trois Romes 1991, Martyrs et confesseurs de l'Eglise catholique en Russie communiste 1917–1980 1997. *Leisure interests:* old books, stamps. *Address:* Via San Pio V, 55, 00165 Rome, Italy. *Telephone:* (6) 66.23.998.

WENT, David, B.A., LL.B., B.L.; Irish business executive; b. 25 March 1947, Dublin; s. of Arthur Went and Phyllis Went (née Howell); m. Mary Christine Milligan 1972; one s. one d.; ed. Trinity Coll. Dublin; Barrister-at-Law, King's Inns, Dublin; grad. trainee, Citibank, Dublin 1970, Gen. Man. 1975, Gen. Man., Jeddah 1975–76; Dir. Ulster Investment Bank 1976, Chief Exec. 1982, Deputy Chief Exec. Ulster Bank Belfast 1987, Chief Exec. 1988–94; C.E.O. Coutts & Co. Group 1994–97; C.E.O. Irish Life Assurance PLC 1998–; Brook Scholar, King's Inns; Paul Prize, Trinity Coll. *Leisure interests:* tennis, reading, theatre. *Address:* Irish Life Assurance PLC, Lower Abbey Street, Dublin, Ireland. *Telephone:* (1) 704 1240.

WERGER, Marinus Johannes Antonius, PH.D.; Netherlands professor of plant ecology and vegetation science; b. 3 May 1944, Enschede; s. of Johannes G. Werger and Gezina M. Zwerink; m. Karin E. Klein 1968; one d.; ed. Jacobus Coll. Enschede and Utrecht, Groningen and Nijmegen Univs.; professional research officer, Botanical Research Inst. Pretoria, S. Africa 1968–73; Asst. Prof., Assoc. Prof. Nijmegen Univ. 1974–79; Prof. of Plant Ecology and Vegetation Science, Utrecht Univ. 1979–, Dean, Faculty of Biology 1990–93; Consultant Prof. S.W. China Univ. Beibei 1984–; Visiting Prof. Univ. of Tokyo 1985; mem. Royal Netherlands Acad.; Mid-America State Univs. Asscn. Award 1986. *Publications:* Biogeography and Ecology of Southern Africa (2 vols.) 1978, The Study of Vegetation 1979, Man's Impact on Vegetation 1983, Plant Form and Vegetation Structure 1988, Tropical Rain Forest Ecosystems. *Leisure interests:* history, travel, cooking. *Address:* Department of Ecology & Evolutionary Biology, Heidelberglaan 8, P.O. Box 80125, 3508 TC Utrecht (Office); Nieuwe Gracht 145, 3512 LL Utrecht, Netherlands (Home). *Telephone:* 030-536700 (Office); 030-311969 (Home).

WERLEIGH, Claudette; Haitian politician and social worker; worked for Caritas (Catholic aid org.) 1976–86; Minister of Social Affairs March–Aug. 1990, of Foreign Affairs 1993–95; Prime Minister of Haiti 1995–96. *Address:* c/o Office of the Prime Minister, Port au Prince, Haiti.

WERNER, Helmut; German business executive; b. 2 Sept. 1936, Cologne; m. Erika Werner; one s. one d.; ed. business studies in Cologne; various man. posts with Englebert & Co. GmbH, Aachen 1961–78, Man. Dir. for marketing, mfg. and devt., Europe 1978; mem. Exec. Bd. Continental Gummi-Werke AG 1979, Chair. 1983–87; mem. Exec. Bd. Daimler-Benz AG 1987–; Chair. Bd. of Man. Mercedes-Benz AG 1993–97; Chair Supervisory Bd. EXPO 2000 Hannover GmbH 1994–, Metallgesellschaft AG 1998–. *Address:* c/o Mercedes-Benz AG, 70322 Stuttgart, Germany.

WERNER, Karl Ferdinand, DR.PHIL.; German historian; b. 21 Feb. 1924, Neunkirchen; s. of Karl Werner and Johanna Kloepfer; m. Brigitte Hermann 1950; one d.; ed. schools in Saarbrücken and Dresden and Univs. of Heidelberg and Paris; Asst. Prof. of Medieval History, Univ. of Heidelberg 1961–65; Prof. of Medieval History, Univ. of Mannheim 1965–68, Hon. Prof. 1968–; Dir. Inst. Historique Allemand, Paris 1968–89; mem. Inst. de France 1992–; Corresp. mem. Munich and Dijon acads.; Dr. h.c. (Sorbonne, Orléans); Commdr. Ordre des Arts et des Lettres; Grosses Bundesverdienstkreuz. *Publications:* Untersuchungen zur Frühzeit des französischen Fürstentums 9–10 Jh. 1960, NS-Geschichtsbild 1967, Kingdom and Principality in Twelfth Century France 1978, Structures Politiques du Monde Franc 1979, L'Histoire médiévale et les ordinateurs 1981, Vom Frankenreich zur Entfaltung Deutschlands und Frankreichs 1984, Les Origines 1984, (German version Ursprünge Frankreichs 1989), Hof, Kultur und Politik im 19. Jahrhundert 1985, Volk, Nation (in Gesch. Grundbegriffe Vol. 7) 1992, Karl d. Gr. oder Charlemagne? 1995, Marc Bloch 1995, Naissance de la Noblesse en Europe 1998. *Leisure interests:* music, chess. *Address:* Karl Theodor Strasse 30, 83700 Rottach-Egern, Germany. *Telephone:* (08022) 65840.

WERNER, Pierre; Luxembourg politician and lawyer; b. 29 Dec. 1913, Saint André, Lille, France; s. of Henri Werner and Marie Schmit; m. Henriette Pescatore 1939; three s. two d.; ed. Univ. of Paris and Luxembourg; practising lawyer 1938–39 and 1944–45; with Banque Générale du Luxembourg 1939–44; with Ministry of Finance 1945; Commr. of Bank Control 1946–53 and of Nat. Savings 1948–53; Sec. to the Council of Govt. 1949–53; Minister of Finance and of the Armed Forces 1953–58; Prime Minister and Minister of Finance 1959–64; Prime Minister, Min. of Foreign Affairs, of Treasury, and of Justice 1964–66; Prime Minister, Minister of Treasury and of Civil Service 1967–69; Prime Minister, Minister of Finance and Minister of Cultural Affairs 1969–74, Prime Minister and Minister of Cultural Affairs 1979–84; Gov. EIB 1958–74, 1979–84; Chair. EEC Cttee. on Monetary Union 1970–71; Chair. Parl. Christian Social group 1974–79; mem. European Parl. 1979; Chair. Compagnie Luxembourg de Télédiffusion 1985–87; Chair. Soc. Européenne des Satellites 1989–96; Christian Social Party; numerous Luxembourg and foreign decorations. *Publications:* Itinéraires Luxembourgeois et Européens 1945–1985 (memoirs) 1993, and various publs. on European and monetary matters. *Leisure interests:* music, walking, swimming, literature, history. *Address:* 2 Rond-Point Robert Schuman, Luxembourg (Home). *Telephone:* 222574 (Home).

WERTENBAKER, Timberlake; British playwright; Resident Playwright, Royal Court Theatre 1984–85. *Plays include:* (for the Soho-Poly): Case to Answer 1980; (for the Women's Theatre Group): New Anatomies 1982; (for the Royal Court): Abel's Sister 1984, The Grace of Mary Traverse 1985, Our Country's Good 1988, Three Birds Alighting on a Field 1991; (for Out of Joint): The Break of Day 1995; (for R.S.C.): The Love of the Nightingale 1988; (for Hampstead Theatre): After Darwin 1998; (for R.S.C.): trans. Arianne Mnouchkine's Mephisto, trans. Sophocles' Thebans; (for San Francisco ACT): trans. Euripides' Hecuba; (for Peter Hall Co): trans. Eduardo de Filippo's Filumena 1998; other trans. include Successful Strategies, False Admissions, La Dispute (Marivaux), Leocadia (Anouilh). *Films:* The Children, Do Not Disturb (BBC TV). Plays and Players Most Promising Playwright (for The Grace of Mary Traverse) 1985, Evening Standard Most Promising Playwright, Olivier Play of the Year (for Our Country's Good) 1988, Eileen Anderson Cen. Drama Award (for The Love of the Nightingale) 1989, Critics' Circle Best West End Play 1991, Writers' Guild Best West End Play, Susan Smith Blackburn Award (for Three Birds Alighting on a Field) 1992, Mrs Giles Whiting Award (for gen. body of work) 1989. *Publications:* Timberlake Wertenbaker: Plays 1996, The Break of Day 1996, After Darwin, Filumena. *Address:* c/o Casarotto Ramsay, National House, 60-66 Wardour Street, London, W1V 4ND, England.

WERTMULLER, Lina; Italian film director; b. (as Arcangela Felice Assunta Wertmuller von Elgg) 14 Aug. 1928, Rome; m. Enrico Job; ed. Rome Theatre Acad.; toured Europe with a puppet show after graduating; worked in theatre for ten years as actress, director and playwright. *Films as director and screenwriter:* I Basilischi (The Lizards) 1963, Questa Volta parliamo di Uomini (Let's Talk About Men) 1965, Rita la zanzara (Rita the Mosquito) 1966, Non stuzzicate la zanzara (Don't Sting the Mosquito) 1967, Mimi Metallurgio Ferito nell'Onore (The Seduction of Mimi) 1972, Film d'amore e d'anarchia (Love and Anarchy) 1973, Tutto a Posto e Niente in Ordine (All Screwed Up), Travolti da un Insolito Destino nell'Azzurro Mare d'Agosto (Swept Away) 1974, Pasqualino Settebellezze (Seven Beauties) 1976, The End of the World in our Usual Bed in a Night Full of Rain, Shimmy Lagano Tarantelle e Vino 1978, Revenge 1979, Summer Night, On a Moonlit Night, Saturday, Sunday, Monday, Ciao, Professore! *Address:* Piazza Clotilde 5, 00196 Rome, Italy.

WESKER, Arnold, F.R.S.L.; British playwright; b. 24 May 1932, Stepney, London; s. of Joseph Wesker and Leah Wesker (née Perlmutter); m. Doreen (Dusty) Cecile Bicker 1958; two s. two d.; ed. mixed elementary schools and

Upton House Central School, Hackney, London; left school 1948, worked as furniture maker's apprentice, carpenter's mate, bookseller's asst.; R.A.F. 1950–52 (ran drama group); plumber's mate, road labourer, farm labourer, seed sorter, kitchen porter and pastry-cook; studied 9 months, London School of Film Technique; Dir. Centre 42, 1961–70; Chair. British Cen. of Int. Theatre Inst. 1978–82; Pres. Int. Cttee. of Playwrights 1979–83; Arts Council Bursary 1959, 1996; Hon. Fellow Queen Mary Coll. London; Hon. D.Litt. (Univ. of E. Anglia) 1989, (Denison Univ., Ohio) 1997; Encyclopaedia Britannica Competition, 1st Prize (for Chicken Soup with Barley), 3rd Prize 1961 (for The Kitchen), Premio Marzotto Drama Prize (for Their Very Own and Golden City) 1964, Gold Medal, Premios el Espectador y la Critica (for The Kitchen) 1973, (for Chicken Soup with Barley) 1979, The Goldie Award (for Roots) 1986. *Directed own plays:* The Four Seasons, Cuba 1968, world première of The Friends at Stadsteatern, Stockholm 1970, London 1970, The Old Ones, Munich, Their Very Own and Golden City, Aarhus 1974, Love Letters on Blue Paper, Nat. Theatre 1978, Oslo 1980, Annie Wobbler, Birmingham 1983, London 1984, Yardsale and Whatever Happened to Betty Lemon, London 1987; also dir. Osborne's The Entertainer, Theatre Clwyd 1983, The Merry Wives of Windsor, Oslo 1989. *Publications:* plays: The Kitchen 1957, Chicken Soup with Barley 1958, Roots 1959, I'm Talking About Jerusalem 1960, Chips with Everything 1962, The Four Seasons 1965, Their Very Own and Golden City 1966, The Old Ones 1970, The Friends 1970, The Journalists 1972, The Wedding Feast 1974, Shylock (previously The Merchant) 1976, Love Letters on Blue Paper (TV play) 1976, (stage play) 1977, One More Ride on the Merry-Go-Round 1978, Fatlips 1980 (revised version Build My Darlings Build 1992), Caritas 1980, Sullied Hand 1981, Breakfast 1981, Annie Wobbler 1982, Four Portraits—of Mothers 1982, Yardsale 1983, Cinders 1983, Bluey 1984, Whatever Happened to Betty Lemon 1986, When God Wanted a Son 1986, Badenheim 1939 1987, Shoeshine & Little Old Lady 1987, Lady Othello 1987, Beorhtel's Hill 1988, The Mistress 1988, Three Women Talking 1990, Letter to a Daughter 1990, Blood Libel 1991, Wild Spring 1992, Vol. 7 of Collected Plays 1994, Circles of Perception 1996, Break My Heart 1997; essays, stories, etc.: Fears of Fragmentation 1971, Six Sundays in January 1971, Love Letters on Blue Paper 1974, Journey into Journalism 1977, Said the Old Man to the Young Man 1978, Distinctions 1985, As Much As I Dare (autobiog.) 1994, The Birth of Shylock and the Death of Zero Mostel (non-fiction) 1997, The King's Daughters 1998; film scripts: The Wesker Trilogy 1979, Lady Othello 1980, Homage to Catalonia 1991, Maudie 1995; opera libretto: Caritas 1988; adaptations for TV: Thieves in the Night (Arthur Koestler) 1984–85, Diary of a Good Neighbour (Doris Lessing) 1989, Phoenix Phoenix Burning Bright (from own story The Visit) 1992, The Birth of Shylock and the Death of Zero Mortel. *Leisure interest:* listening to music. *Address:* 37 Ashley Road, London, N19 3AG, England.

WESLEY, Mary (see Siepmann, Mary Aline).

WESSELMANN, Tom, B.A.; American artist; b. 23 Feb. 1931, Cincinnati, Ohio; s. of Edwin W. and Grace D. Wesselmann; m. 2nd Claire Selley 1963; one s. two d.; ed. Hiram Coll., Ohio, Univ. of Cincinnati, Art Acad. of Cincinnati and Cooper Union, N.Y; taught art New York City Junior and Senior High Schools 1959–62; more than 60 one-man exhbns. 1961–, including Sidney Janis Gallery, New York (19 exhbns.) and many other galleries in the U.S.A., Düsseldorf, Paris, Montreal, Bogotá, London, Tokyo, etc.; touring graphics and multiples retrospective in U.S. galleries and Tokyo 1989–91; retrospective exhbn. painting and sculpture touring Japan, Germany, Belgium, Netherlands, France and Spain 1993–96. *Leisure interest:* writing country music. *Address:* 7A 115 East 9th Street, New York, NY 10003, U.S.A. *Telephone:* (212) 228-3930.

WESSELS, Wolfgang, DR.RER.POL.; German academic; b. 19 Jan. 1948, Cologne; s. of Theodor Wessels and Emma Wessels; m. Aysin Wessels 1973; two d.; Dir. Institut für Europäische Politik, Bonn 1973–94; Dir. Admin. Studies and Prof., Coll. of Europe, Bruges, Belgium 1980–96; Jean Monnet Prof., Univ. of Cologne 1994–. *Publications include:* The European Council, Decision-Making in European Politics (with Simon Bulmer) 1987; (Co-Ed.) Die Europäische Politische Zusammenarbeit in den achtziger Jahren-Eine gemeinsame Aussenpolitik für Westeuropa? 1989, Jahrbuch der Europäischen Integration 1980–, Europa vom A-Z. Taschenbuch der Europäischen Integration 1994, 1995, Foreign Policy of the European Union. From EPC to CFSP and Beyond (jtly.) 1997; papers and articles on European integration. *Address:* Forschungsinstitut für Politische Wissenschaft und Europäische Fragen, Universität zu Köln, Gottfried-Keller-Strasse 6, 50931 Cologne, Germany. *Telephone:* (221) 470 41 31. *Fax:* (221) 470 50 17.

WEST, Edward Mark, C.M.G., M.A.; British administrator; b. 11 March 1923, London; Head of Chancery, U.K. Comm., Singapore 1958–61; Pvt. Sec. to Sec. of State for Commonwealth and Colonial Affairs 1962–64; Head of Natural Resources Dept., Ministry of Overseas Devt. 1964–70; Dir. Programme Formulation, FAO of the UN 1970, Asst. Dir.-Gen. for Admin. and Finance 1974–76, Asst. Dir.-Gen. for Programme Budget and Evaluation 1976–81, Deputy Dir.-Gen. 1982–85, Special Rep. of Dir.-Gen., FAO 1990–92. *Address:* 10 Warwick Mansions, Cromwell Crescent, London, SW5 9QR, England.

WEST, Francis James, PH.D., F.B.A., F.R.HIST.S., F.A.H.A.; British/Australian professor of history; b. 26 June 1927, E. Yorks.; s. of George H. West and Florence C. Selby; m. Katharine White 1963 (divorced 1976); one d.; ed. Hymers Coll. E. Yorks, Univ. of Leeds and Trinity Coll. Cambridge; Fellow, A.N.U. 1952–55; Sr. Lecturer, Victoria Univ. of Wellington 1955–59; Professorial Fellow, Inst. of Advanced Studies, A.N.U. 1960–73; Dean of Arts and Social Studies, Univ. of Buckingham 1973–75; Prof. of History and Govt. and Dean of Social Sciences, Deakin Univ. Geelong 1976–90, Pro Vice-Chancellor (Research) 1986–90, Prof. Emer. 1990–; Overseas Fellow, Churchill Coll. Cambridge 1981–82, 1984–85; mem. Australian Humanities Research Council 1966. *Publications:* Political Advancement in the South Pacific 1961, The Justiciarship in England 1966, Hubert Murray: Australian Pro Consul 1968, Biography as History 1973, University House 1979, Gilbert Murray: A Life 1984, From Alamein to Scarlet Beach 1989. *Leisure interests:* music, occasional journalism and broadcasting. *Address:* c/o Churchill College, Cambridge, CB3 0DS, England; Deputy Vice-Chancellor's Office, Deakin University, Geelong, Vic. 3217; 6 Sylvan Court, Newtown, Vic. 3220, Australia (Home). *Telephone:* 052-212375 (Home).

WEST, John C., LL.B.; American fmr. state governor, lawyer and diplomatist; b. 27 Aug. 1922, Camden, S.C.; s. of late Shelton J. West and of Mattie (Ratterree) West; m. Lois Rhame 1942; two s. one d.; ed. Univ. of S. Carolina; U.S. Army 1942–46; elected to S. Carolina Senate 1954, re-elected 1958, 1962; Lieut.-Gov. of S. Carolina 1966–70; Gov. of S. Carolina 1971–75; Amb. to Saudi Arabia 1977–81; with law firm John C. West, P.A., Hilton Head Is. and Camden 1981–; of Counsel, Bethea, Jordan and Griffin 1993; Distinguished Prof. of Middle East Studies, Univ. of South Carolina 1981–; of Counsel McNair Law Firm 1988–92, Bethea, Jordan & Griffin 1993–; Chair. Bd. Dirs. Seibels Bruce Group Inc., Donaldson, Lufkin & Jenrette Inc.; mem. Bd. Trustees Southern Centre for Int. Studies; Army Commendation Medal, Kt. Commdr. Order of Merit, Fed. Repub. of Germany; Democrat. *Address:* P.O. Box 13, Hilton Head Island, SC 29938, U.S.A.

WEST, Martin Litchfield, D.PHIL, D.LITT., F.B.A.; British scholar; b. 23 Sept. 1937, London; s. of the late Maurice Charles West and Catherine Baker West (née Stainthorpe); m. Stephanie Roberta Pickard 1960; one s. one d; ed. St. Paul's School, London and Balliol Coll., Oxford; Woodhouse Jr. Research Fellow, St. John's Coll., Oxford 1960–63; Fellow and Praelector in Classics, Univ. Coll., Oxford 1963–74; Prof. of Greek, Univ. of London (Bedford Coll., now Royal Holloway and Bedford New Coll.) 1974–91; Sr. Research Fellow, All Souls Coll., Oxford; corresp. mem. Akad. der Wissenschaften, Göttingen; mem. Acad. Europaea, London. *Publications:* Hesiod, Theogony (ed.) 1966, Fragmenta Hesiodea (ed. with R. Merkelbach) 1967, Early Greek Philosophy and the Orient 1971, Sing Me, Goddess 1971, Iambi et Elegi Graeci (ed.) 1971–72 (revised edn. 1989–92), Textual Criticism and Editorial Technique 1973, Studies in Greek Elegy and Iambus 1974, Hesiod, Works and Days (ed.) 1978, Theognidis et Phocylidis fragmenta 1978, Delectus ex Iambis et Elegis Graecis 1980, Greek Metre 1982, The Orphic Poems 1983, Carmina Anacreontea 1984, The Hesiodic Catalogue of Women 1985, Introduction to Greek Metre 1987, Euripides Orestes (ed.) 1987, Hesiod (trans.) 1988, Aeschyli Tragoediae 1990, Studies in Aeschylus 1990, Ancient Greek Music 1992, Greek Lyric Poetry (trans.) 1993, The East Face of Helicon 1997, Homeri Ilias (ed.) Vol. I 1998. *Leisure interest:* music. *Address:* All Souls College, Oxford, OX1 4AL; 42 Portland Road, Oxford, OX2 7EY, England (Home). *Telephone:* (01865) 279289 (College).

WEST, Morris (Langlo), A.O., B.A.; Australian author; b. 26 April 1916, Melbourne; s. of Charles Langlo West and Florence Guilfoyle Hanlon; m. Joyce Lawford 1953; three s. one d.; ed. Univ. of Melbourne; teacher of Modern Languages and Mathematics, New South Wales and Tasmania 1933–39; Army service 1939–43; Sec. to William Morris Hughes, fmr. Prime Minister of Australia 1943; Fellow, Royal Soc. of Literature, World Acad. of Arts and Science; Hon. D.Litt. (Santa Clara Univ., Calif.) 1969, (Mercy Coll., New York) 1982, (Univ. of Western Sydney) 1993, (A.N.U., Canberra) 1995; Nat. Brotherhood Award, Nat. Council of Christians and Jews 1960, James Tait Black Memorial Prize 1960, Royal Soc. of Literature Heinemann Award 1960 (all prizes for The Devil's Advocate), Int. Dag Hammarskjold Prize (Grand Collar of Merit) 1978, Lloyd O'Neil Award 1997. *Publications:* Gallows on the Sand 1955, Kundu 1956, Children of the Sun 1957, The Crooked Road (English title The Big Story) 1957, The Concubine 1958, Backlash (English title Second Victory) 1958, The Devil's Advocate 1959 (filmed 1977), The Naked Country 1960, Daughter of Silence (novel and play) 1961, The Shoes of the Fisherman 1963, The Ambassador 1965, The Tower of Babel 1968, The Heretic, a Play in Three Acts 1970, Scandal in the Assembly (with Robert Francis) 1970, Summer of the Red Wolf 1971, The Salamander 1973, Harlequin 1974, The Navigator 1976, Proteus 1979, The Clowns of God 1981, The World is Made of Glass 1983 (play 1984), Cassidy 1986, Masterclass 1989, Lazarus 1990, The Ringmaster 1991, The Lovers 1993, Vanishing Point 1996, A View From the Ridge 1996, Images and Inscriptions 1997, Eminence 1998. *Address:* P.O. Box 102, Avalon, N.S.W. 2107, Australia.

WEST, Paul, M.A.; American author; b. 23 Feb. 1930, Eckington, Derbyshire, England; s. of Alfred West and Mildred Noden; ed. Oxford and Columbia Univs.; arrived U.S.A. 1961, became naturalized 1971; served with R.A.F. 1954–57; Asst. Prof. of English Memorial Univ., Newfoundland 1957–58, Assoc. Prof. 1958–60; contrib. Washington Post, New York Times 1962–, also contributes to Harper's and GQ magazines, Paris Review; mem. of staff Pa. State Univ. 1962–, Prof. of English and Comparative Literature 1968–; Crawshaw Prof. Colgate Univ. 1972; Melvin Hill Distinguished Visiting Prof. Hobart and William Smith Colls. 1973; Distinguished Writer-in-Residence Wichita State Univ. 1982; Writer-in-Residence Univ. of Arizona 1984; Visiting Prof. of English Cornell Univ. 1986, Brown Univ. 1992; Guggenheim Fellow 1962–63; Nat. Endowment for Arts Creative Writing Fellow 1979, 1984; mem. Author's Guild; Aga Khan Fiction Prize 1973, Hazlett Memorial Award for Excellence in Arts (Literature) 1981, Literature Award, American Acad. and Inst. of Arts and Letters 1985, Pushcart Prize 1987, 1991, Best American Essays Award 1990, Grand Prix Halpérine Kaminsky Award 1992. Lannan Fiction Award 1993, Teaching Award N.E. Asscn. of Grad. Schools 1994; Outstanding Achievement Medal, Pa. State Univ. 1991, Chevalier Ordre Arts et Lettres. *Publications include:* Byron and the Spoiler's Art 1960, I, Said the Sparrow 1963, The Snow Leopard 1965, Tenement of Clay 1965, The Wine of Absurdity 1966, I'm Expecting to Live Quite Soon 1970, Words for a Deaf Daughter 1970, Caliban's Filibuster 1971, Bela Lugosi's White Christmas 1972, Colonel Mint 1973, Gala 1976, The Very Rich Hours of Count von Stauffenberg 1980, Out of My Depths: A Swimmer in the Universe and Other Fictions 1988, The Place in Flowers Where Pollen Rests 1988, Lord Byron's Doctor 1989, Portable People, The Women of Whitechapel and Jack the Ripper 1991, James Ensor 1991, Love's Mansion 1992. *Leisure interests:* swimming, astronomy, classical music, cricket, films. *Address:* c/o Elaine Markson Agency, 44 Greenwich Avenue, New York, NY 10011, U.S.A. *Telephone:* (212) 243 8480. *Fax:* (607) 257 0631.

WEST, Richard G., M.A., SC.D., F.R.S.; British professor of botany; b. 31 May 1926, Hendon, Middx.; m. 1st Janet Abram 1958; one s.; m. 2nd Hazel Gristwood 1973; two d.; ed. King's School, Canterbury and Univ. of Cambridge; Fellow, Clare Coll., Cambridge 1954–; Lecturer in Botany, Univ. of Cambridge 1960–68, Reader in Quaternary Research 1968–74, Prof. of Palaeoecology 1974–77, Prof. of Botany and Head, Dept. of Botany 1977–91, Dir. Sub-dept. of Quaternary Research 1966–87; Hon. mem. Royal Belgian Acad.; Hon. M.R.I.A.; Bigsby Medal, Geological Soc. 1968, Lyell Medal, Geological Soc. 1988. *Publications:* Pleistocene Geology and Biology 1968, The Ice Age in Britain (jtly.) 1972, The Pre-glacial Pleistocene of the Norfolk and Suffolk Coasts 1980, Pleistocene Palaeoecology of Central Norfolk 1991. *Leisure interest:* sailing. *Address:* Clare College, Cambridge; 3A Woollards Lane, Great Shelford, Cambridge, CB2 5LZ, England (Home). *Telephone:* (01223) 842578 (Home).

WEST, Stephen Craig, PH.D., F.R.S.; British scientist; b. 11 April 1952, Hull; s. of Joseph West and Louisa West; m. Phyllis Fraenza 1985; ed. Univs. of Newcastle and Yale; research scientist Yale Univ. 1983–85; Sr. Scientist Imperial Cancer Research Fund 1985–89, Prin. Scientist 1989–; Hon. Prof. Univ. Coll. London 1997–; mem. European Molecular Biology Org. 1994–. *Publications:* over 150 research articles. *Leisure interests:* sport, music. *Address:* Imperial Cancer Research Fund, Clare Hall Laboratories, South Mimms, Herts., EN6 3LD (Office); Meadowbank, Riverside Avenue, Broxbourne, Herts., EN10 6RA, England (Home). *Telephone:* 0171-269 3868 (Office); (01992) 470147 (Home). *Fax:* 0171-269 3811 (Office).

WEST, Timothy Lancaster, C.B.E., F.R.S.A.; British actor and director; b. 20 Oct. 1934, Bradford, Yorks.; s. of the late H. Lockwood West and Olive Carleton-Crowe; m. 1st Jacqueline Boyer 1956 (dissolved); one d.; m. 2nd Prunella Scales (q.v.) 1963; two s.; ed. John Lyon School, Harrow and Regent Street Polytechnic; repertory seasons, Wimbledon, Hull, Salisbury, Northampton 1956–60; Artistic Dir., Old Vic 1980–81; Dir.-in-Residence Univ. of W.A. 1982; Assoc. Dir. Bristol Old Vic. –1991; Chair. London Acad. of Music and Dramatic Art; Hon.D.Litt (E. Anglia, W. of England); Hon. D.Univ. (Bradford). *Stage appearances:* (in London) Caught Napping 1959, Galileo 1960, Gentle Jack 1963, The Trigon 1963, The Italian Girl 1968, Abelard and Heloise 1970, Exiles 1970, The Critic as Artist 1971, The Houseboy 1973, A Month in the Country 1974, A Room with a View 1975, Laughter 1978, The Homecoming 1978, Beecham 1980, Master Class 1984, The War at Home 1984, When We are Married 1986, The Sneeze 1988, A Long Day's Journey into Night 1991, It's Ralph 1991, Twelve Angry Men 1996, Henry IV Parts 1 and 2 1996, King Lear 1997; numerous appearances with Prospect Theatre Co., Royal Shakespeare Co. and regional theatres. *TV appearances include:* The Monocled Mutineer, The Good Doctor Bodkin Adams, Harry's Kingdom, When We Are Married, Breakthrough at Reykjavik, Strife, A Shadow on the Sun, The Contractor, Blore M.P., Survival of the Fittest, Why Lockerbie?, Framed, Smokescreen, Reith to the Nation, Eleven Men Against Eleven, Cuts, Place of the Dead. *Film appearances include:* The Looking Glass War, Nicholas and Alexandra, The Day of the Jackal, The Devil's Advocate, The Thirty-Nine Steps, Oliver Twist, Cry Freedom, Ever After, Joan of Arc. *Publication:* I'm Here I Think, Where Are You? 1997. *Leisure interests:* music, travel, inland waterways, old railways. *Address:* c/o Gavin Barker Associates, 45 South Molton Street, London, W1Y 1HD, England.

WESTBROOK, Roger, C.M.G., M.A.; British diplomatist; b. 26 May 1941, Surrey; s. of Edward George Westbrook and Beatrice Minnie Marshall; ed. Dulwich Coll. and Hertford Coll., Oxford; Foreign Office 1964; Asst. Pvt. Sec. to the Chancellor of the Duchy of Lancaster 1965; held posts in Yaoundé 1967, Rio de Janeiro 1971, Brasilia 1972; Private Sec. to Minister of State, FCO 1975; Head of Chancery, Lisbon 1977; Deputy Head, News Dept., FCO 1980, Deputy Head, Falkland Islands Dept. 1982, Overseas Inspectorate 1984; High Commr., Brunei Darussalam 1986–91; Amb. to Zaire 1991–92; High Commr. in Tanzania 1992–95; Amb. to Portugal 1995–; British Commr.-Gen. EXPO 98. *Leisure interests:* doodling, sightseeing, theatre. *Address:* British Embassy, Rua São Bernardo 33, 1200 Lisbon, Portugal; BFPO 6, London, England.

WESTERBERG, Bengt, MED.KAND., FIL.KAND.; Swedish politician; b. 23 Aug. 1943; s. of late Carl-Eric and of Barbro Westerberg; m. 2nd Marie Ehrling; one s., two d. from a previous marriage; ed. Karolinska Inst., Univ. of Stockholm; joined Liberal Youth League 1965, held elected office at all levels, Chair. Exec. Cttee. 1970–71; joined Liberal Party 1965, held municipal office in Södertälje, elected to Nat. Bd. 1983, mem. Party Exec. 1983, Chair. 1984–95; Pres. Liberal Party 1993–95; Deputy Sec. to Commr. for Greater Stockholm 1969, Sec. to Commr. for Municipal Services 1970, Sec. to Stockholm County Council Traffic Commr. 1971, Research Dir. Traffic Cttee. 1972, Adviser Govt. Comm. on Traffic Policy 1975, Adviser Ministry of Labour 1976, Liberal Party's Coordination Office 1978; Under-Sec. Ministry of Industry 1978, Ministry of the Budget 1979–82; f. Foundation for a Market-Economy Alternative for Sweden (MAS) 1983; M.P. 1984–94; Minister of Social Affairs and Deputy Prime Minister 1991–94; Research and Devt. Leader, Centre of Gender Studies, Univ. of Karlstad 1995–; Chair. Bd. Telia AB 1995–, BTJ 1995–, Media Technology MT AB 1996–; Vice-Chair. Bd. Riksbank (Cen. Bank of Sweden) 1994–; mem. Bd. Morgondagen AB 1995–; Pres. Swedish Athletics Asscn. 1995–, Swedish Foundation of Dyslexia 1995–.

WESTERFIELD, Putney, B.A.; American business executive; b. 9 Feb. 1930, New Haven, Conn.; s. of Ray Bert Westerfield and Beatrice Putney; m. Anne Montgomery 1954; two s. one d.; ed. Choate School and Yale Univ.; Vice-Pres. and Co-founder, Careers Inc. 1950–52; Man. S.E. Asia Operations, Swen Publs.; service with Dept. of State in Korea, Washington, Saigon 1953–59; Asst. to Publr. of Time 1957–59, Asst. to Circulation Dir. 1959–61, Circulation Dir. 1961–66, Asst. Publr. 1966–68; Asst. Publr. of Life 1968–69; Publr. of Fortune 1969–73; Pres. Chase World Information Corpn. 1973–75; Vice-Pres. Boyden Assocs. Int. 1976–80, Sr. Vice-Pres., Western Man. 1980–84, Pres. and C.E.O. 1984–90, Man. Dir. 1990–; Dir. East Meets West Foundation 1991–; Chair. Bd. Dirs. Upside Media Inc. *Leisure interests:* reading, music, tennis, swimming. *Address:* Boyden International, 275 Battery Street, Suite 420, San Francisco, CA 94111 (Office); 10 Green View Lane, Hillsborough, CA 94010, U.S.A. (Home). *Telephone:* (415) 981-7900. *Fax:* (415) 981-0644.

WESTHEIMER, Frank Henry, M.A., PH.D.; American professor of chemistry; b. 15 Jan. 1912, Baltimore, Md.; s. of Henry F. Westheimer and Carrie (Burgunder) Westheimer; m. Jeanne Friedman 1937; two d.; ed. Dartmouth Coll. and Harvard Univ.; Nat. Research Fellow, Columbia Univ. 1935–36; Research Assoc., Instr., Asst. Prof. of Chem., Univ. of Chicago 1936–44; Research Supervisor, NDRC Explosives Research Lab. 1944–45; Assoc. Prof. Dept. of Chem., Univ. of Chicago 1946–48, Prof. 1948–54; Visiting Prof. of Chem. Harvard Univ. 1953–54, Prof. 1954–83, Morris Loeb Prof. of Chem. Emer. 1983–; Visiting Prof., Univ. of Calif. (Berkeley) 1958, Boston Univ. 1984, Ohio State Univ. 1985, Univ. of Calif. (San Diego) 1986, 1988; mem. Pres.'s Science Advisory Cttee. 1967–70; mem. American Acad. of Arts and Sciences, (Sec. 1985-90), N.A.S., American Philosophical Soc.; Foreign mem. Royal Soc.; seven hon. degrees; numerous awards and prizes including Willard Gibbs Medal, Ingold Medal, N.A.S. Award in the Chemical Sciences, Nichols Medal, James Flack Norris Award, Richards Medal, Welch Award, Nat. Medal of Science, Paracelsus Medal (Swiss Chemical Soc.), Priestley Award (American Chemical Soc.), Repligen Award 1992, Nakanishi Prize 1997. *Publications:* Chemistry, Opportunities and Needs 1965; about 200 articles in scientific journals. *Address:* Department of Chemistry, Harvard University, 12 Oxford Street, Cambridge, MA 02138 (Office); 3 Berkeley Street, Cambridge, MA 02138, U.S.A. (Home).

WESTLING, Håkan, M.D., PH.D.; Swedish university administrator and physiologist; b. 9 Aug. 1928, Göteborg; m. Britt Westling 1957; one s. three d.; ed. Lund Univ.; physiologist, Lund 1949–57, clinical physiologist Göteborg 1958–61; physician-in-charge and Prof. of Clinical Physiology Lund Univ. 1962–83, Dean Medical Faculty 1977–82, Vice-Chancellor 1983–92; mem. Swedish Medical Research Council 1967–73, Chair. Govt. Comm. on Higher Educ. 1989–92. *Publications:* around 250 papers in physiology, clinical physiology and nuclear medicine. *Leisure interest:* sailing. *Address:* Department of Clinical Physiology, University Hospital, 22185 Lund, Sweden. *Telephone:* (046) 173335. *Fax:* (046) 151769.

WESTMINSTER, 6th Duke, cr. 1874; **Gerald Cavendish Grosvenor,** O.B.E., T.D., D.L., F.R.S.A.; British landowner and company director; b. 22 Dec. 1951, Northern Ireland; s. of late 5th Duke of Westminister and Hon. Viola Lyttelton; m. Natalia Phillips 1978; one s. three d.; succeeded to title 1979; ed. Harrow School; served Queen's Own Yeomanry 1970–85, promoted to Col. 1995, Deputy Commdr. 143 W. Midlands Brigade 1996–; Dir. Claridges Hotel Ltd. 1981–92, Grosvenor Estate Holdings, Grosvenor Int. Holdings, Marcher Sound Ltd. 1982–97, Sun Alliance Group, Sutton Ridge Pty. Ltd., N.W. Business Leadership Team Ltd., Business in the Community 1988–92, Pres. Abbeyfield Soc. 1989–96, Patron 1996–; Pres. Arthritis Care 1987–, Chester Zoo, Game Conservancy, London Fed. of Boys' Clubs, Royal Nat. Inst. for the Blind, Scope (fmrly. The Spastics Soc.), Youth Clubs UK, British Limbless Ex-Servicemen's Asscn., British Asscn. for Shooting and Conservation, Drug and Alcohol Foundation 1987–97, Holstein Friesian Soc. and many other orgs.; Vice-Pres. Country Landowners Asscn., NSPCC, Chancellor Manchester Metropolitan Univ. (fmrly. Manchester Polytechnic) 1993–; Patron Dyslexia Inst., British Holstein Soc., British Kidney Patients' Asscn., Royal Fine Art Comm., Worcs. Co. Cricket Club; Gov. Royal Agricultural Soc. of England; mem. Cttee. N. American Advisory Group of British

Overseas Trade Bd., Nat. Army Museum, Prince's Youth Business Trust; Trustee The Grosvenor Estate, TSB Foundation for England and Wales, Westminster Abbey Trust, Westminster Foundation, Westminster Housing Trust; Cubitt Memorial Trust, Falcon Trust, Habitat Research Trust, Royal Agricultural Soc. of the Commonwealth; Freeman of Chester, of London, of England; Fellow The Royal Agricultural Socs., Chartered Inst. of Marketing, Chartered Inst. of Bldg., Liverpool John Moores Univ.; mem. Royal Inst. of Chartered Surveyors; Hon. LL.D. (Keele, Westminster Coll., Foulton, Mo.); Hon. D.Litt. (Manchester Metropolitan Univ.); K. St. J.; Deputy Lieut. Co. of Cheshire. *Leisure interests:* shooting, fishing, scuba diving. *Address:* Eaton Hall, Eaton, Chester, Cheshire CH4 9EJ, England. *Telephone:* (01244) 680333.

WESTMORELAND, Gen. William Childs; American retd. army officer; b. 26 March 1914, Spartanburg County, S. Carolina; s. of James R. and Eugenia Childs Westmoreland; m. Katherine S. Van Deusen 1947; one s. two d.; ed. U.S. Mil. Acad.; U.S. Army 1936–72; Maj.Gen. 1956, Lieut.-Gen. 1963, Gen. 1964; Battery Officer, Oklahoma and Hawaii 1936–41; Commdg. Officer, 34th Field Artillery Battalion 1942–44; Exec. Officer 9th Infantry Div. Artillery 1944, Chief of Staff 1944–45, Commdr. 60th Infantry Regt., Germany 1945, 504th Parachute Infantry Regt., Fort Bragg 1946–47; Chief of Staff, 82nd Airborne Div. 1947–50; Instructor, Command and Gen. Staff Coll., and Army War Coll. 1950–52; Commdr. 187th Airborne Regimental Combat Team, Korea and Japan 1952–53; Deputy Asst. Chief of Staff G1, for Manpower Control, Dept. of Army 1953–54, Sec. Gen. Staff 1955–58; Commdg. Gen. 101st Airborne Div. and Fort Campbell, Kentucky 1958–60; Supt. U.S. Mil. Acad., West Point 1960–63; Commdr. 18th Airborne Corps, Fort Bragg 1963–64; Deputy Commdr. U.S. Mil. Assistance Command Viet Nam 1964, Commdr. 1964–68; Chief of Staff, U.S. Army, The Pentagon 1968–72; retd. from army 1972; Man of the Year, Time Magazine 1966, S. Carolina Hall of Fame 1986; numerous awards from veteran and patriotic orgs.; numerous mil. decorations from foreign govts. *Publications:* Report on the War in Vietnam, A Soldier Reports and numerous articles in mil. publs. and the press. *Address:* P.O. Box 1059, Charleston, SC 29402, U.S.A.

WESTON, Garfield Howard; Canadian business executive; b. 28 April 1927; s. of Willard Garfield Weston and Reta Lila Weston (née Howard); m. Mary Ruth Kippenberger 1959; three s. three d.; ed. Sir William Borlase School, New Coll. Oxford, U.K., Harvard Univ., U.S.A.; Man. Dir. Ryvita Co. Ltd. 1951–54, Weston Biscuit Co., Australia 1954–67; Vice-Chair. Assoc. British Foods Ltd. (now PLC), U.K. 1960–, Chair. 1967–; Chair. Fortnum & Mason 1979–, Wittington Investments Ltd. U.K. 1979–, British Sugar PLC 1991–. *Leisure interests:* walking, gardening, tennis. *Address:* Weston Centre, Bowater House, 68 Knightsbridge, London, SW1X 7LQ, England. *Telephone:* 0171-589 6363.

WESTON, Sir John (see Weston, Sir (Philip) John).

WESTON, Sir Michael Charles Swift, K.C.M.G., C.V.O., M.A.; British diplomatist; b. 4 Aug. 1937, Crowborough, Sussex; s. of late Edward C. S. Weston and Kathleen M. Mockett; m. 1st Veronica A. Tickner 1959 (divorced 1990); two s. one d.; m. 2nd Christine J. Ferguson 1990; one s. one d.; ed. Dover Coll. and St. Catharine's Coll. Cambridge; joined H.M. Diplomatic Service 1961; Third Sec. Kuwait 1962; First Sec. Teheran 1968; U.K. mission, New York 1970; Counsellor, Jeddah 1977; Royal Coll. of Defence Studies 1980; Counsellor, Paris 1981, Cairo 1984; Head, S. European Dept. FCO 1987–90; Amb. to Kuwait 1990–92; Leader U.K. del. to Conf. on Disarmament, Geneva 1992–97. *Leisure interests:* squash, tennis, walking. *Address:* c/o Foreign and Commonwealth Office, King Charles Street, London, SW1A 2AH, England.

WESTON, Sir (Philip) John, K.C.M.G.; British diplomatist; b. 13 April 1938; s. of late Philip G. Weston and Edith Ansell; m. Sally Ehlers 1967; two s. one d.; ed. Sherborne School and Worcester Coll. Oxford; served Royal Marines 1956–58; entered H.M. Diplomatic Service 1962; Treasury Centre for Admin. Studies 1964; Chinese language student, Hong Kong 1964–66; Beijing 1967–68; Office of U.K. Perm. Rep. to EEC 1972–74; Asst. Pvt. Sec. to Sec. of State for Foreign and Commonwealth Affairs 1974–76; Counsellor, Head of EEC Presidency Section, FCO 1976–77; Visiting Fellow, All Souls Coll. Oxford 1977–78; Counsellor, Washington, D.C. 1978–81; Head, Defence Dept. FCO 1981–84, Asst. Under-Sec. of State 1984–85; Minister, Paris 1985–88; Deputy Sec. to Cabinet, Cabinet Office 1988–89; Deputy Under-Sec. of State, FCO 1989–90, Political Dir. 1990–91; Amb. and Perm. Rep. to N. Atlantic Council (also accred. to WEU) 1991–95; Perm. Rep. to UN 1995–98; Dir. (non-exec.) British Telecommunications 1998–, Rolls Royce 1998–. *Leisure interests:* fly-fishing, poetry, running, birds. *Address:* 13 Denbigh Gardens, Richmond, Surrey, TW10 6EN, England.

WESTPHAL, Heinz; German politician; b. 4 June 1924, Berlin; s. of Max and Alice (née Dusedau) Westphal; m. Ingeborg Riemann 1950; one d.; trainee aircraft mechanic, Daimler-Benz 1939–42, instructor 1942–43; war service 1943–45; mem. SPD 1945–; mem. staff, Int. Union of Socialist Youth 1948–57; Chair. Die Falken (Socialist youth movt.) 1953–57, German Youth Council 1955–56, Chief Exec. 1958–65; mem. Advisory Council, Zweites Deutsches Fernsehen 1965–74; Chair. Admin. Council, German Volunteer Service 1974-82; mem. Bundestag 1965–90, Vice-Pres. 1983–90; Parl. Sec. of State, Ministry of Youth and Family 1969–74; Minister of Labour and Social Affairs April–Oct. 1982; German rep. Int. Council of Memorial Museum Auschwitz-Birkenau 1993–; mem. Chairs.' Cttee., Internationaler Bund für Sozialarbeit/Jugendserialarbeit 1992–97; Vice-Chair. Archiv der Arbeiterjugendbewegung 1990–. *Publications:* Ungefährdet ist Demokratie nie 1994, Jugend braucht Demokratie—Demokratie braucht Jugend 1994. *Leisure interests:* reading, walking, swimming. *Address:* Droste-Hülshoffstrasse 2, 53129 Bonn, Germany. *Telephone:* 0228/231694.

WESTWOOD, Vivienne, O.B.E.; British fashion designer; b. 8 April 1941, Tintwhistle, Derbys.; d. of Gordon Swire and Dora Swire; m. 1st Derek Westwood; one s.; m. 2nd Andreas Kronthaler 1993; one s. with Malcolm Mclaren; during 1970s worked with Malcolm McLaren, developing 'punk' look; designed for the Sex Pistols, Boy George and Bananarama; created Pirate collection (adopted by Adam Ant and Bow Wow Wow) 1980; ended partnership with Malcolm McLaren 1983; moved to Italy for deal with Sergio Galeotti (partner of Giorgio Armani (q.v.)), 1984; launched 'Mini Crini' 1985; produced collection featuring Harris tweed suits and princess coats; Pagan 5 (latest of England Goes Pagan Collections) 1989; regular fashion shows, Paris, N.Y., London; launch of signature fragrance Boudoir 1998; Prof. of Fashion Acad. of Applied Arts 1989–91, Hochschule der Künste, Berlin 1993–; Dr. h.c. (Royal Coll. of Art) 1992, (Heriot-Watt) 1995; Designer of the Year 1990, 1991; Queen's Award for Export 1998. *Address:* Westwood Studios, 9–15 Elcho Street, London, SW11 4AU, England. *Telephone:* 0171-924 4747.

WETHERILL, George West, PH.D.; American geophysicist; b. 12 Aug. 1925, Philadelphia, Pa.; s. of George W. Wetherill and Leah Hardwick Wetherill; m. Phyllis May Steiss 1950 (died 1995); one s. two d.; ed. Univ. of Chicago; served U.S. Navy 1943-46; mem. Science Staff, Dept. of Terrestrial Magnetism, Carnegie Inst. of Washington 1953–60, Dir. Dept. 1975–91, mem. Science Staff 1991–; Prof. of Geophysics and Geology, Univ. of Calif., Los Angeles 1960–75, Chair. Dept. of Planetary and Space Science 1968–72; Ed. Annual Review of Earth and Planetary Science 1981–96; Pres. Geochemical Soc. 1975–76, Int. Asscn. of Geochemistry and Cosmochemistry 1977–80, Meteoritical Soc. 1983–85; Consultant to NASA, N.S.F., Nat. Acad. of Sciences; Fellow American Acad. of Arts and Sciences; mem. N.A.S.; Leonard Medal (Meteoritical Soc.) 1981, G. K. Gilbert Award (Geological Soc. of America), 1984, G. P. Kuiper Prize (American Astronomical Soc.) 1986, Hess Medal (American Geophysical Union) 1991. *Publications:* about 200 papers in scientific journals. *Address:* Carnegie Institution of Washington, 5241 Broad Branch Road, N.W., Washington, DC 20015, U.S.A. *Telephone:* (202) 686-4370, Ext. 4375. *Fax:* (202) 364-8726.

WETHINGTON, Charles T., Jr., PH.D.; American university president; b. 2 Jan. 1936, Merrimac, Ky.; m. Judy Woodrow 1962; two c.; Instr. Univ. of Ky. 1965–66; Dir. Maysville Community Coll. 1967–71; Asst. Vice-Pres. for the Community Coll. System, Univ. of Ky. 1971–81, Vice-Pres. 1981–82, Chancellor 1982–88, Chancellor for the Community Coll. System and Univ. Relations 1988–89, Interim Pres. Univ. of Ky. 1989–90, Pres. 1990–. *Address:* University of Kentucky, 104 Administration Building, Lexington, KY 40506 (Office); Maxwell Place, 471 Rose Street, Lexington, KY 40508, U.S.A. (Home). *Telephone:* (606) 257-1704 (Office). *Fax:* (606) 257-1760 (Office).

WETTER, H.E. Cardinal Friedrich; German ecclesiastic; b. 20 Feb. 1928, Landau, Speyer; s. of Peter Wetter and Hedwig Böttinger; ordained 1953; consecrated Bishop of Speyer 1968; Archbishop of Munich and Freising 1982–; cr. Cardinal 1985. *Publications:* Zeit-Worte 1993, Er allein trägt 1996. *Address:* Postfach 10 05 51, 80079 Munich, Germany. *Telephone:* (089) 296955. *Fax:* (089) 229871.

WETTSTEIN, Diter von, DR.RER.NAT.; Danish geneticist b. 20 Sept. 1929, Göttingen, Germany; s. of Fritz von Wettstein and Elsa Jesser; m. Penny von Wettstein-Knowles 1967; two d.; ed. school in Innsbruck, Austria, Univ. of Tübingen, Germany, Univ. of Stockholm, Sweden; Research Asst., Genetics Dept., Forest Research Inst., Stockholm 1951–54; Asst. and Assoc. Prof. in Genetics, Univ. of Stockholm 1954–62; Prof. of Genetics and Head, Inst. of Genetics, Univ. of Copenhagen, Denmark 1962–75; Acting Head, Dept. of Physiology, Carlsberg Lab., Copenhagen 1972–75, Prof. of Physiology and Head of Dept. 1975–96; Distinguished Prof. Washington State Univ., Pullman, Wash., U.S.A. 1994–; Rockefeller Fellow 1958; Visiting Prof., Univ. of Calif., Davis 1966, 1972, 1973, 1974, Washington State Univ. 1969; Dr. Agr. h.c. *Publications:* 295 scientific papers on mutation research, developmental physiology and cell research. *Address:* Department of Crop and Soil Sciences, Washington State University, Pullman, WA 99164, U.S.A. (Office); Aasevej 13, 3500 Vaerløse, Denmark (Home). *Telephone:* (509) 335-3635 (Office); (42) 48 19 98 (Home). *Fax:* (509) 335-8674.

WEYMANN, Gert; German theatre director and playwright; b. 31 March 1919, Berlin; s. of Hans Weymann and Gertrud Israel; ed. Grammar School, Berlin, and Berlin Univ.; Asst. Dir., later Dir. Berlin theatre 1947–; worked as Dir. in several W. German cities and New York; lecturer in Drama Dept., American univs. 1963, 1966; lecturer at Goethe Inst., Berlin 1970–; perm. ind. mem. SFB (radio and television plays); Gerhart Hauptmann Prize for Generationen 1954. *Plays:* Generationen, Eh' die Brücken verbrennen, Der Ehrentag; TV Plays: Das Liebesmahl eines Wucherers, Familie; Radio Plays: Der Anhalter, Die Übergabe.

WHALLEY-KILMER, Joanne; British actress; b. 25 Aug. 1964, Salford; m. Val Kilmer 1988; stage career began during teens and has included season of Edward Bond plays at Royal Court Theatre, London and appearances in The Three Sisters, What the Butler Saw (N.W. Manhattan Theatre Club); Lulu (Almeida, London); television appearances include: The Singing Detective, A Kind of Loving, A Quiet Life, The Gentle Touch, Bergerac, Reilly, Edge of Darkness, A Christmas Carol, Save Your Kisses, Will You Love Me Tomorrow?, Scarlett. *Films:* Pink Floyd—The Wall, Dance With a Stranger, No Surrender, The Good Father, To Kill a Priest, Willow, Scandal, Kill Me Again, The Big Man, Navy Seals, Miss Helen, Shattered, Crossing the Line, Storyville, Mother's Boys, A Good Man in Africa, Trial By Jury, The Man Who Knew Too Little. *Address:* Creative Artists Agency, 9830 Wilshire Boulevard, Beverly Hills, CA, 90212, U.S.A.

WHARTON, Clifton R., Jr., PH.D.; American educator, insurance executive and government official; b. 13 Sept. 1926, Boston, Mass.; s. of Hon. Clifton R. Wharton Sr. and Harriette B. Wharton; m. Dolores Duncan 1950; two s.; ed. Boston Latin School, Harvard Univ., Johns Hopkins Univ. School of Advanced Int. Studies and Univ. of Chicago; Head of Reports and Analysis Dept., American Int. Asscn. for Econ. and Social Devt. 1948–53; Research Assoc., Univ. of Chicago 1953–57; Assoc., Agricultural Devt. Council 1957–58, stationed in S.E. Asia 1958–64, Dir. of the Council's American Univs. Research Program 1964–66, Vice-Pres. 1967–69, mem. Bd. of Dirs. 1973–80; Pres. Mich. State Univ. and Prof. of Econs. 1970–78; Chancellor, State Univ. of N.Y. System 1978–87; Chair. and C.E.O. TIAA-CREF 1987–93; Deputy Sec. of State, U.S. Dept. of State 1993; Visiting Prof., Univ. of Malaya 1958–64, Stanford Univ. 1964–65; fmr. Chair. Bd. for Int. Food and Agric. Devt. (AID), U.S. Dept. of State; mem. Presidential Comm. on World Hunger, Presidential Mission to Latin America; Chair. Bd. Rockefeller Foundation 1982–87; Dir. or Trustee of numerous cos. and orgs. including Ford Motor Co. 1973–93, 1994–, Tenneco Inc. 1994, Harcourt Gen. 1994–, Equitable Life 1969–82, Overseas Devt. Council 1969–79, 1994–, Aspen Inst. 1980–93, Time Inc. 1982–89, Federated Dept. Stores 1985–88, Rockefeller Foundation 1970–87; Comm. for Econ. Devt. 1980–93, 1994–; Deputy Chair. Fed. Reserve Bank, New York 1985–86; mem. Knight Foundation Comm. on Inter-collegiate Athletics 1990–93, Council on Foreign Relations 1983–93, Advisory Comm. on Trade Policy and Negotiations 1990–93, N.Y. Stock Exchange 1991–; numerous hon. degrees. *Publications:* Subsistence Agriculture and Economic Development (ed.) 1969, Patterns for Lifelong Learning (co-author) 1973. *Address:* TIAA-CREF, 730 Third Avenue, New York, NY 10017, U.S.A.

WHEATLEY, Glenn Dawson; Australian media executive; b. 23 Jan. 1948, Nambour, Queensland; s. of William Dawson Wheatley and Freda Aileen Evans; m. Gaynor Cherie Martin 1982; one s. two d.; bass guitarist Purple Hearts 1966, Bay City Union 1966–67, The Master's Apprentices 1967–72; Founder, Man. Dir. The Wheatley Org. (TWO Australia Ltd.) 1975–92, Hoyts Media (fmrly. Wheatley Communications Pty. Ltd.) 1987–89, Emerald City Records 1991–, TalentWORKS Pty. Ltd. 1996–; Dir. Int. Media Man. (Holdings) Ltd. 1997–, Int. Media Man. 1997–, Exec. Dir. 1998–; a founding Dir. 92.3 EON FM radio station 1980; Man. Dir. Radio 2BE Bega NSW 1987–89, Radio 3CV Vic. 1987–89; Co-owner and Dir. Sydney Swans Football Club 1988–90; Dir. Advantage Int. (fmrly. Wheatley Sport Pty. Ltd.) 1985–88, Sydney Hard Rock Cafe 1988–89; Bd. mem. Ausmusic 1993; mem. Tourism Task Force 1990–92; Cttee. mem. Austrade (Music) 1986; Trustee AIDS Trust Australia 1990–93; Outstanding Contrib. in Entertainment Industry award, Advance Australia 1987, Marketing Award, Business Review Weekly 1988, Queensland Apprentice of the Year 1965. *Address:* TalentWORKS Pty. Ltd., Suite 1A, 663 Victoria Street, Abbotsford, Vic. 3067, Australia. *Telephone:* (03) 9429 6933. *Fax:* (03) 9428 7433.

WHEELER, Sir (Harry) Anthony, Kt., O.B.E., B.ARCH., P.P.R.S.A., P.P.R.I.A.S., F.R.S.A., F.R.I.B.A.; British architect and town planner (retd.); b. 7 Nov. 1919, Stranraer; s. of Herbert G. Wheeler and Laura E. Groom; m. Dorothy J. Campbell 1944; one d.; ed. Stranraer High School, Royal Tech. Coll. Glasgow, Glasgow School of Art and Glasgow School of Architecture, Univ. of Strathclyde; Asst. City Architect, Oxford 1949; Asst. Sir Herbert Baker & Scott, London 1949; Sr. Architect, Glenrothes New Town 1949–51; Sr. lecturer, Dundee School of Architecture 1952–58; commenced pvt. practice, Fife 1952; Sr. partner, Wheeler & Sproson, Edin. and Kirkcaldy 1954–86, consultant 1986–89; various public appts.; Pres. Royal Scottish Acad. 1983–90; prin. works include St. Columba's Parish Church, Glenrothes, reconstruction The Giles, Pittenweem, redevt. Dysart and Old Buckhaven, Students' Union, Univ. of St. Andrews, Leonard Horner Hall and Students' Union, Heriot-Watt Univ., Hunter Bldg. Edin. Coll. of Art, St. Peter's Episcopal Church, Kirkcaldy, Museum of Childhood, Edin. and town centre renewal, Grangemouth; 22 Saltire Soc. Housing Awards; 12 Civic Trust Awards and commendations; Hon. Pres. Saltire Soc. 1995; Hon. R.A.; Hon. mem. Royal Hibernian Acad., Royal Soc. of British Sculptors; Hon. Royal Glasgow Inst.; Hon. D.Des. *Leisure interests:* sketching and water-colour painting, fishing, gardens, music, drama. *Address:* South Inverleith Manor, 31/6 Kinnear Road, Edinburgh, EH3 5PG, Scotland. *Telephone:* 0131-552 3854.

WHEELER, John Archibald, D.SC., PH.D.; American physicist; b. 9 July 1911, Jacksonville, Fla.; s. of Dr. Joseph Lewis Wheeler and Mabel Archibald; m. Janette Latourette Zabriskie Hegner 1935; one s. two d.; ed. Johns Hopkins Univ.; Nat. Research Council Fellow, New York and Copenhagen 1933–35; Asst. Prof. of Physics, Univ. of N.C. 1935–38; Asst. Prof. of Physics, Princeton Univ. 1938–42, Assoc. Prof. 1945–47, Prof. 1947–66, Joseph Henry Prof. of Physics 1966–76, Emer. 1976–; Prof. of Physics, Univ. of Texas at Austin 1976–86; Ashbel Smith Prof. of Physics 1979–86; Blumberg Prof. of Physics 1981–86, Prof. Emer. 1986–; Physicist, Manhattan project of U.S. Govt., Chicago, Wilmington, Hanford 1942–45; Dir. Project Matterhorn, Princeton 1951–53; Lorentz Prof., Univ. of Leiden 1956; Fulbright Prof., Univ. of Kyoto 1962; Guggenheim Fellow, Paris and Copenhagen 1949–50; Visiting Fellow, Clare Coll., Cambridge 1964; Chair. Jt. Cttee. of American Physical Soc. and American Philosophical Soc. on History of Theoretical Physics; mem. U.S. Gen. Advisory Cttee. on Arms Control and Disarmament 1969–76; Fellow, American Physical Soc. (Pres. 1966, mem. Council), American Philosophical Soc., Tex. Philosophical Soc., A.A.A.S. (mem. Bd. of Dirs. 1963–68); mem. American Acad. of Arts and Sciences, N.A.S., Accad. Naz. dei Lincei, Royal Acad. of Science Uppsala, Sweden, Royal Acad. of Sciences of Denmark, The Royal Soc., London; Trustee Battelle Memorial Inst. 1959–89, Southwest Research Inst. 1977–93; Hon. Sc.D. (Western Reserve, Yeshiva, Rutgers and Yale Univs., Univs. of N.C. and Pa., Middlebury Coll., Catholic Univ. of America, Univ. of Conn., Gustavus Adolphus Univ., and Princeton Univ.); Hon. D.Sc. (Newcastle Univ., England) 1983; Hon. D.Hum. Litt. (Johns Hopkins) 1976; Hon. Ph.D. (Uppsala, Maryland) 1976; Hon. D. Litt. (Drexel) 1987; A. Cressy Morrison Prize, N.Y. Acad. of Sciences 1947, Albert Einstein Prize, Strauss Foundation 1965, Enrico Fermi Award, U.S. Atomic Energy Comm. 1968, Franklin Medal of Franklin Inst. 1969, Nat. Medal of Science 1971, Herzfeld Award 1975, Outstanding Graduate Teaching Award (Univ. of Texas at Austin) 1981, Niels Bohr Int. Gold Medal 1982, Oersted Medal 1983, J. Robert Oppenheimer Memorial Prize 1984, Franklin Medal, American Philosophical Soc. 1989, Wolf Foundation Prize in Physics 1997. *Publications:* Geometrodynamics 1962, Gravitation Theory and Gravitational Collapse 1965, Einstein's Vision 1968, Black Holes, Gravitational Waves and Cosmology (with M. Rees and R.Ruffini) 1974, Gravitation (with Thorne and Misner) 1973, Frontiers of Time 1979, Quantum Theory and Measurement (with Zurek) 1983, Journey into Gravity and Spacetime 1990, At Home in the Universe 1993, Spacetime Physics (with E. Taylor) 1994, Gravitation and Inertia (with Ciufolini) 1995. *Leisure interests:* swimming, sculpture in nature. *Address:* Department of Physics, Princeton University, Princeton, NJ 08544; 1904 Meadow Lakes, Hightstown, NJ 08520, U.S.A. (Home). *Telephone:* (609) 258-5824 (Princeton Univ.); (609) 426-6239 (Home).

WHEELER, Gen. Sir Roger Neil, K.C.B., C.B.E., M.A.; British army officer; b. 16 Dec. 1941, Fulmer, Bucks.; s. of Maj.-Gen. T.N.S. Wheeler, C.B., C.B.E.; m. Felicity Hares 1980; three s. one d. from a previous marriage; ed. All Hallows School, Devon and Hertford Coll. Oxford; commissioned Royal Ulster Rifles 1964; early service in Borneo, the Middle East and Cyprus; Chief of Staff, Falkland Islands June–Dec. 1982; Command, 11th Armoured Brig. 1985–87; Dir. Army Plans 1987–89; Command, 1st Armoured Div. 1989–90; Asst. Chief of Gen. Staff, Ministry of Defence 1990–92; G.O.C. Northern Ireland 1993–96; C.-in-C. Land Command 1996–97; Chief of Gen. Staff. 1997–; ADC Gen. to Queen 1996–; Pres. Army Rugby Football Union 1995, Army Rifle Assoc. 1995; Col. The Royal Irish Regt. 1996–; Col. Commdt. Intelligence Corps 1996; Hon. Fellow, Hertford Coll. Oxford. *Leisure interests:* fly fishing, ornithology, cricket, shooting. *Address:* c/o Ministry of Defence, Whitehall, London, S.W.1., England.

WHELAN, Michael John, PH.D., F.R.S., F.INST.P.; British university professor; b. 2 Nov. 1931, Leeds; s. of William Whelan and Ellen Whelan (née Pound); ed. Gonville and Caius Coll., Cambridge; Royal Soc. Mr. and Mrs. John Jaffé Donation Research Fellow 1959–61; Demonstrator in Physics, Univ. of Cambridge 1961–65, Asst. Dir. of Research 1965–66, Fellow of Gonville and Caius Coll. 1958–66; Reader, Dept. of Materials, Univ. of Oxford 1966–92, Prof. 1992–97, Emer. Prof. 1997–; Fellow, Linacre Coll., Univ. of Oxford 1968–; Hon. Prof. of Univ. of Science and Tech., Beijing 1995; C. V. Boys Prize, Inst. of Physics 1965, Hughes Medal, Royal Soc. 1988. *Publications:* Electron Microscopy of Thin Crystals (co-author) 1965, Worked Examples in Dislocations, numerous papers and articles in scientific journals. *Leisure interests:* gardening, tinkering, Japanese language. *Address:* Department of Materials, Parks Road, Oxford, OX1 3PH; 18 Salford Road, Old Marston, Oxford, OX3 0RX, England (Home). *Telephone:* (01865) 273700 (Office); (01865) 244556 (Home). *Fax:* (01865) 283333.

WHELAN, Noel, B.COMM., M.ECON.SC., PH.D., D.P.A., F.I.MGT.I.; Irish civil servant, international public servant, academic and banker; b. 28 Dec. 1940, Cork; s. of Richard Whelan and Ann Whelan (née Crowley); m. Joan Gaughan 1970; two s. two d.; ed. Nat. School, Buttevant, Co. Cork, Sacred Heart Coll., Buttevant, Univ. Coll., Dublin; Nat. Univ. of Ireland; Exec. Officer, Irish Civil Service 1960–62; Sr. Admin. Officer and Head of Research Evaluation, an Foras Taluntais (Agricultural Research Inst. of Ireland) 1962–69; Asst. Gen. Man. Córas Iompair Éireann (Irish Transport Authority) 1969–74; Deputy Sec. Dept. of Public Service and Dept. of Finance 1974–77; Special Consultant, OECD (part-time) 1975–80, UN 1989–; Sec. Dept. of Econ. Planning and Devt. 1977–80; Second Sec. Dept. of the Taoiseach (Prime Minister) 1980, Sec. 1980–82; Chair. Sectoral Devt. Cttee., Irish Govt. 1980–82; Vice-Pres. and Vice-Chair., Bd. of Dirs. European Investment Bank, Luxembourg 1982–88, Hon. Vice-Pres. 1988–; Sec., Dept. of the Taoiseach 1988–; Vice-Pres. Univ. of Limerick, Dean Coll. of Business 1989–; Chair. Sectoral Devt. Cttee. 1989–97; Special Consultant UN and World Bank 1989–; Chair./Dir. corp. Bds. 1989–; Chair. Nat. Econ. and Social Council of Ireland 1978–84; Chair. Telephone Users' Advisory Council 1993–98; Chair. Caritas Consultative Forum (Health Sector) 1998–; Pres. and Chair. Inst. of Public Admin. (part-time); Council mem. and mem. Exec. Cttee., Econ. and Social Research Inst.; Council mem. Statistical and Social Enquiry Soc.; Council mem. and Fellow Irish Man. Inst. *Publications:* miscellaneous papers and reports in various academic and research journals.

Leisure interests: reading, photography, music. *Address:* Office of the Vice-President, University of Limerick, Limerick; 74 Northbrook Avenue, Ranelagh, Dublin 6, Ireland (Home). *Telephone:* (01) 960646. *Fax:* (01) 4977562.

WHENT, Sir Gerald Arthur, Kt., C.B.E.; British business executive; b. 1 March 1927, India; s. of Major A. Whent and G. A. Whent; m. 1st Coris D. Bellman-Thomas 1956; one s. one d.; m. 2nd Sarah Donaldson; two step-s. one step-d.; ed. St. Mary's School, Southampton; man. trainee, Dent Allcroft & Co. 1952–57, Div. Man. 1957–60; Man. Plessey Co. 1960–63; Man. Controls & Communications 1963–68; Subsidiary Dir. Racal Electronics PLC 1968–82, Main Bd. Dir. 1980; Chief Exec. Vodaphone Group PLC 1991–96, Deputy Chair. 1997–98; Non-Exec. Dir. Racal Electronics PLC 1982–94. *Leisure interests:* golf, horse racing, bridge, chess. *Address:* The Bothy, Horris Hill, Newton Common, Newbury, Berks, England.

WHERRETT, Richard Bruce, O.A., B.A.; Australian theatre director; b. 10 Dec. 1940, Sydney; s. of Arthur Eric Wherrett and Lila Muriel Wherrett; ed. Trinity Grammar School, Sydney, Sydney Univ., Acting School, U.K.; Assoc. Artistic Dir. Old Tate Theatre, Sydney 1971–72, Jt. Artistic Dir. Nimrod Theatre, Sydney 1974–79; Artistic Dir. Sydney Theatre Co. 1979–90, Melbourne Int. Festival 1990–93; OBIE Best Dir. for The Elocution of Benjamin Franklin 1978. *Leisure interests:* performing arts, film, beach. *Address:* c/o Hilar Linstead & Assocs. Pty. Ltd, Suite 302, East Tower, 9-13 Bronte Road, Bonds Junction, N.S.W. 2022, Australia.

WHICKER, Alan Donald, F.R.S.A.; British television broadcaster and journalist; b. 2 Aug. 1925; s. of late Charles Henry Whicker and Anne Jane Cross; ed. Haberdashers' Aske's School; Dir. Army Film and Photo Section, with 8th Army and U.S. 5th Army; war corresp., Korea; joined BBC TV 1957; regular appearances on "Tonight" programme, then series Whicker's World 1959–60, Whicker Down Under 1961, Whicker in Sweden 1963, Whicker's World 1965–67; Founder-mem. Yorkshire TV 1968, made 122 documentaries including Whicker's New World Series, Whicker in Europe, World of Whicker; returned to BBC TV 1982; programmes include: Whicker's World—The First Million Miles! 1982, Whicker's World, A Fast Boat to China (4 programmes) 1983, Whicker! (series talk shows) 1984, Whicker's World—Living with Uncle Sam (10 programmes) 1985, Whicker's World—Living with Waltzing Matilda (10 programmes) 1988, Whicker's World—Hong Kong (eight programmes) 1990, Whicker's World—A Taste of Spain (eight programmes) 1992, Around Whicker's World (four programmes, for ITV) 1992, Whicker's World—The Sultan of Brunei 1992, South Africa: Whicker's Miss World, and Whicker's World—The Sun King 1993, South-East Asia: Whicker's World Aboard the Real Orient Express, Whicker's World — Pavarotti in Paradise 1994, Travel Channel (26 programmes) 1996; Whicker's Wireless World (BBC Radio series) 1983; Around Whicker's World (six programmes for Radio 2) 1998; various awards, including Guild of TV Producers and Dirs., Personality of the Year 1964, Silver Medal, Royal TV Soc., Dimbleby Award, BAFTA 1978, TV Times Special Award 1978, first to be named in Royal Television Soc.'s new Hall of Fame, for outstanding creative contrib. to British TV 1993. *Publications:* Some Rise by Sin 1949, Away—With Alan Whicker 1963, Best of Everything 1980, Within Whicker's World (autobiog.) 1982, Whicker's Business Travellers Guide 1983, Whicker's New World 1985, Whicker's World Down Under 1988. *Address:* Le Gallais Chambers, St. Helier, Jersey.

WHINNERY, John Roy, PH.D.; American professor of electrical engineering; b. 26 July 1916; s. of Ralph Vincent Whinnery and Edith Bent Whinnery; m. Patricia Barry 1944; three d.; ed. Modesto Junior Coll. Calif., Univ. of Calif., Berkeley; Student Engineer to Research Engineer, Gen. Electric Co. 1937–46; Lecturer, Union Coll., Schenectady, N.Y., 1945–46; Lecturer, Univ. of Calif., Berkeley, Assoc. Prof., Prof., Chair. of Dept., Dean of Coll. 1959–63, Univ. Prof. 1980–; Guggenheim Fellow E.T.H., Zurich, Switzerland 1959; Head of Microwave Tube Research at Hughes Aircraft Co., Culver City, Calif. 1952–53; visiting mem. of Tech. Staff, Bell Telephone Labs. 1963–64; Visiting Prof. Stanford Univ. 1969–70; Research Professorship in Miller Inst. for Basic Research in Science 1973–74; mem. Visiting Review Bd., Dept. of Electrical Eng., M.I.T. 1968, Div. of Applied Science, Harvard Univ. 1974, 1979, 1980, 1981, 1982, 1983, Dept. of Eng. and Applied Science, Calif. Inst. of Tech. 1977, 1979, 1980; Hon. Prof. of Chengdu Inst. of Tech., Sichuan, Chengdu, People's Repub. of China 1986; Fellow, Univ. of Calif., Berkeley 1990; IEEE Microwave Theory and Techniques Soc. Distinguished Lecturer for U.S. 1990; mem. Nat. Acad. of Eng. 1965, Pres.'s Cttee. Nat. Medal of Science 1970–72, 1979–81, N.A.S. 1973, Optical Soc. of America, American Acad. of Arts and Sciences; life mem. Inst. of Electronics and Electrical Eng., American Soc. for Eng. Educ.; Fellow A.A.A.S.; Okawa Prize in Information and Telecommunications 1997; Educ. Medal Inst. Electronics and Electrical Engineers, Outstanding Educators of America Award (Univ. of Calif., Berkeley) 1974, Lamme Award of American Soc. on Eng. Educ. 1975, Microwave Career Award of Inst. Electronics and Electrical Eng. 1976, Distinguished Eng. Alumnus Award, Univ. of Calif., Berkeley 1980, Inst. of Electronics and Electrical Eng. Centennial Medallist 1984, Medal of Honor Award from Inst. Electronics and Electrical Eng. 1985, Founder's Award, Nat. Acad. of Eng. 1986, Berkeley Citation, Univ. of Calif., Berkeley 1987, Nat. Medal of Science 1992, American Soc. for Eng. Educ. Hall of Fame and Centennial Medal awards 1993, John R. Whinnery Chair in Electrical Eng. est. at Univ. of Calif., Berkeley 1994. *Publications:* Fields and Waves in Modern Radio (with Simon Ramo) 1944, 1952, World of Engineering 1965, Fields and Waves in Communication Electronics (with Simon Ramo and T. Van Duzer) 1965, Introduction to Electronic Systems Circuits and Devices (with D. O. Pederson and J. J. Studer) 1966, 140 tech. articles and patents on microwaves and lasers. *Leisure interests:* hiking, skiing, golf, writing poetry and children's stories. *Address:* Department of Electrical Engineering and Computer Sciences, Univ. of California., Berkeley, CA 94720 (Office); 1804 Wales Drive, Walnut Creek, CA 94595, U.S.A. (Home). *Telephone:* (510) 642-1030 (Office); (925) 256-9136 (Home). *Fax:* (510) 642-6330.

WHIPPLE, Fred Lawrence, PH.D.; American astronomer; b. 5 Nov. 1906, Red Oak, Iowa; s. of Harry Lawrence Whipple and Celestia (MacFarland) Whipple; m. 1st Dorothy Woods 1928 (divorced 1935); one s.; m. 2nd Babette Samelson 1946; two d.; ed. Univ. of Calif.; mem. Staff Harvard Coll. Observatory 1931–77; in charge of Oak Ridge Station 1932–37; Instructor Harvard Univ. 1932–38, Lecturer 1938–45, Assoc. Prof. 1945–50, Prof. of Astronomy 1950–77, Chair. Dept. of Astronomy 1949–56, Phillips Prof. of Astronomy 1968–77; Chair. Cttee. on Concentration in the Physical Sciences 1947–49; Research Associate Radio Research Lab. 1942–45, in charge of Confusion Reflectors "Window" (radar countermeasure); Dir. Smithsonian Inst. Astrophysical Observatory 1955–73, Sr. Scientist 1973–; mem. Rocket and Satellite Research Panel 1946–58, U.S. Nat. Advisory Cttee. on Aeronautics Sub-Cttee. 1946–52, U.S. Research and Devt. Bd. Panel 1947–52, U.S. Nat. Cttee. I.G.Y. 1955–59, Advisory Panel on Astronomy to the Nat. Science Foundation 1952–55 and Chair. 1954–55, mem. Div. Cttee. for Mathematical and Physical Sciences 1964–70, many other scientific cttees., etc.; Project Leader, Harvard Radio Meteor Project 1958–65; mem. NASA Optical Astronomy Panel, Astronomy Missions Bd. 1968; mem. NASA Science and Tech. Advisory Cttee. 1969; mem. NASA Comet and Asteroid Working Group 1971–72, Chair. 1972; Voting Rep. of U.S.A. in Int. Astronomical Union 1952 and 1955; Assoc. Ed. Astrophysical Journal 1952–54, Astronomical Journal 1954–56, 1964–71; Ed. Planetary and Space Science 1958–83, Hon. Ed. 1983–, Harvard's Announcement Cards 1952–60, Smithsonian Contributions to Astrophysics 1956–73; Lowell Lecturer, Lowell Inst. Boston 1947; Vice-Pres. American Astronomical Soc. 1948–50, 1960–67, Cttee. on Space Research (COSPAR) 1960; Editorial Bd. Space Science Reviews 1961–70; Editorial Cttee. Annual Review of Astronomy and Astrophysics 1965–69; mem. R.S.A., Benjamin Franklin Fellow 1968–; Assoc. Royal Astronomical Soc. 1970; depicted on postage stamp of Mauritania 1986, of St. Vincent and the Grenadines 1994; numerous hon. degrees; Donohue Medals, Pres. Certificate of Merit, J. Lawrence Smith Medal of Nat. Acad. of Sciences, Exceptional Service Award (U.S.A.F.), Liège Univ. Medal, Space Flight Award, Commr. of Order of Merit for Research and Invention; Distinguished Federal Civilian Service Award from President Kennedy, Alumnus of the Year Achievement Award (Univ. of Calif.), Leonard Medal, Meteoritical Soc. 1970, Nat. Civil Service League's Career Service Award for Sustained Excellence 1972, Kepler Medal, A.A.A.S., Gold Medal, Royal Astronomical Soc., London and Astronomical Soc. of the Pacific, Kuiper Award, American Astronomical Soc., Univ. of Calif. at Los Angeles Medal 1997. *Publications:* Earth, Moon and Planets 1942, Orbiting the Sun 1981, The Mystery of Comets 1985 and many scientific papers. *Leisure interests:* scuba diving, stochastic painting, cycling. *Address:* Smithsonian Astrophysical Observatory, 60 Garden Street, Cambridge, MA 02138; 35 Elizabeth Road, Belmont, MA 02178, U.S.A. (Home). *Telephone:* (617) 864-7383 (Office); (617) 484-0988 (Home). *Fax:* (617) 495-7356.

WHISHAW, Anthony, R.A., R.W.A., A.R.C.A.; British artist; b. 22 May 1930, London; s. of Robert Whishaw and Joyce Wheeler; m. Jean Gibson 1957; two d.; ed. Chelsea School of Art, Royal Coll. of Art; numerous one-man exhbns. U.K., including ICA, London 1971, 1992, 1993, Royal Acad. of Arts 1986, 1987; Hamburg 1989; Shanghai 1989, Barbican Centre (London); touring exhbn., UK and Dublin 1994–95; numerous group exhbns. 1957–; work in collections including Arts Council of G.B., Bolton Art Gallery, Chantrey Bequest, City Art Galleries, Sheffield, Coventry Art Gallery, Dept. of the Environment, European Parl., Strasbourg, Leicester City Art Gallery, Museu de Baha, Brazil, Museo de Murcia, Spain, Nat. Gallery of Vic., Melbourne, Australia, Museum of Contemporary Art, Helsinki, Nat. Gallery of Wales, R.C.A., London, Royal Acad., London, Seattle Museum of Art, U.S.A., Tate Gallery, London, Western Australia Gallery, and several pvt. collections. *Address:* 7A Albert Place, Victoria Road, London, W8 5PD, England. *Telephone:* 0181-981 2139 (Studio); 0171-937 5197 (Home).

WHISTLER, Laurence, C.B.E., M.A.; British writer and glass engraver; b. 21 Jan. 1912, Eltham, Kent; s. of Henry Whistler and Helen Ward; brother of the late Rex Whistler; m. 1st Jill Furse 1939 (died 1944); one s. one d.; m. 2nd Theresa Furse (younger sister of Jill Furse) 1950 (divorced 1985); one s. one d.; m. 3rd Carol Dawson (née Groves) 1987 (divorced 1992); ed. Stowe School, Balliol Coll., Oxford; served World War II, commissioned in Rifle Brigade 1941; Hon. Fellow, Balliol Coll.; First Pres. Guild of Glass Engravers 1975–80; exhbns.: Agnews, Bond Street 1969, Marble Hill, Twickenham 1972, Corning Museum, U.S.A. 1974, Ashmolean, Oxford 1976, 1985, Kenwood, Hampstead 1985, Sotheby 1992, S. Wilts. Museum, Salisbury 1993; Hon. D.Lit. (Oxford) 1993; King's Gold Medal for poetry 1935, Atlantic Award for Literature 1945. *Work on glass includes:* goblets in point-engraving and drill, engraved church windows and panels at Sherborne Abbey, Moreton, Dorset, Checkendon, Oxon., Ilton, Somerset, Eastbury, Berks., Guards' Chapel, London, Ashmansworth, Berks., Steep, Hants., Yalding, Kent, Hannington, Hants, Dacre, Cumbria, Abbots Ripton, Hunts., St. Hugh's Coll.

and St. Hilda's Coll., Oxford. *Publications:* Sir John Vanbrugh (biog.) 1938, The English Festivals 1947, Rex Whistler, His Life and His Drawings 1948, The World's Room (Collected Poems) 1949, The Engraved Glass of Laurence Whistler 1952, Rex Whistler: the Königsmark Drawings 1952, The Imagination of Vanbrugh and His Fellow Artists 1954, The View From This Window (poems) 1956, Engraved Glass 1952–58, The Work of Rex Whistler (co-author) 1960, Audible Silence (poems) 1961, The Initials in the Heart: the story of a marriage 1964, To Celebrate Her Living (poems) 1967, Pictures on Glass 1972, The Image on the Glass 1975, Scenes and Signs of Glass 1985, The Laughter and the Urn: The Life of Rex Whistler 1985, Enter (poems) 1987, Point Engraving on Glass 1992. *Address:* Scriber's Cottage, Watlington, Oxford, OX9 5PY, England.

WHITACRE, Edward E., Jr., B.ENG.; American business executive; b. 4 Nov. 1941, Ennis, Tex.; ed. Texas Tech. Univ.; joined Southwestern Bell Telephone Co., Dallas, Tex. 1963, subsequently facility engineer, Lubbock, and various posts in operational depts., Texas, Arkansas and Kansas; Pres. Kansas Div. 1982–85; Group Pres., subsequently Vice-Pres. (Revenues and Public Affairs), Vice-Chair. and Chief Financial Officer, Southwestern Bell Corpn. 1986–88, Pres. and C.O.O. 1988–90, Chair. of Bd. and C.E.O. (now SBC Communications Inc.) 1990–; Dir. Anheuser-Busch Cos. Inc., May Department Stores Co., Emerson Electric Co., Burlington Northern Inc.; mem. Bd. of Regents, Texas Tech. Univ. and Texas Tech. Univ. Health Sciences Center, Bd. of Govs., Southwest Foundation for Biomedical Research; Trustee Southwest Research Inst.; Int. Citizen of the Year Award, World Affairs Council, San Antonio 1997, Spirit of Achievement Award, Nat. Jewish Medical and Research Center 1998, Freeman Award, San Antonio Chamber of Commerce 1998. *Address:* Southwestern Bell Corporation, Room 40, 175 E. Houston Street, San Antonio, TX 78205, U.S.A.

WHITAKER, Thomas Kenneth, M.SC.(ECON.); Irish financial administrator; b. 8 Dec. 1916, Rostrevor, Co. Down; s. of Edward Whitaker and Jane O'Connor; m. Nora Fogarty 1941; five s. one d.; ed. Christian Brothers' School, Drogheda; entered Irish Civil Service 1934; Sec. Dept. of Finance 1956–69; Dir. Cen. Bank of Ireland 1958–69, Gov. 1969–76; Dir. Bank of Ireland 1976–85; mem. Senate 1977–82, Council of State 1991–97; Jt. Chair. Anglo-Irish Encounter 1983–89; fmr. Pres. Econ. and Social Research Inst.; Dir. Arthur Guinness and Sons 1976–84; Chancellor, Nat. Univ. of Ireland 1976–96; Chair. Dublin Inst. for Advanced Studies 1980–95; Pres. Royal Irish Acad. 1985–87; Hon. D.Econ.Sc. (Nat. Univ. of Ireland), Hon. LL.D. (Univ. of Dublin, Queen's Univ. of Belfast, Univ. of Ulster); Hon.Ph.D. (Dublin City Univ.); Commdr., Légion d'honneur. *Publications:* Financing by Credit Creation, Economic Development 1958, Interests 1983. *Leisure interests:* angling, golf, music. *Address:* 148 Stillorgan Road, Donnybrook, Dublin 4, Ireland. *Telephone:* (1) 2693474.

WHITBREAD, Fatima, M.B.E.; fmr. British athlete; b. 3 March 1961, Stoke Newington; adopted d. of Margaret Whitbread; m. Andrew Norman 1997; one s.; UK int. debut as javelin thrower 1977; European Jr. Champion 1979; European Cup Champion 1983; European Cup Silver Medallist 1985; European Champion 1986; Commonwealth Games Bronze Medallist 1982, Silver Medallist 1986; Olympic Games Bronze Medallist 1984, Silver Medallist 1988; World Championships Silver Medallist 1983; World Record Holder 1986; World Champion 1987; founder-mem. and Pres. Chafford Hundred A.C.; marketing consultant; mem. Bd. Eastern Region Sports Council 1992–96; Dir. (non-exec.) Thameside Community Health Care NHS Trust 1993–; Voluntary Service Overseas Amb. 1992–93; Pres. Thurrock Harriers Athletic Club 1993–; BBC Sports Personality of the Year 1987; British Sports Writers Sportswoman of the Year 1986, 1987; British Athletic Writers Woman Athlete of the Year, 1986, 1987. *Leisure interests:* interior design, theatre. *Address:* Chafford Hundred Information Centre, Elizabeth Road, Chafford Hundred, Grays, Essex, RM16 6QZ, England. *Telephone:* (01375) 391099. *Fax:* (01375) 391374.

WHITBREAD, Samuel Charles, J.P.; British business executive; b. 22 Feb. 1937, London; s. of Major Simon Whitbread and H. B. M. Trefusis; m. Jane M. Hayter 1961; three s. one d.; ed. Eton Coll.; served Beds. and Herts. Regt. 1955–57; Dir. Whitbread & Co. 1972, Deputy Chair. 1984, Chair. Whitbread & Co. (Whitbread PLC from 1991) 1984–92, Dir. 1972–; Vice-Pres. East Anglia TA and VRA 1991–; Lord-Lieut. of Bedfordshire 1991–. *Leisure interests:* shooting, travel, photography, music. *Address:* Southill Park, Biggleswade, Beds., SG18 9LL, England (Home). *Telephone:* (01462) 816226 (Home).

WHITE, Baroness (Life Peer), cr. 1970, of Rhymney in the County of Monmouth; **Eirene Lloyd White;** British politician; b. 7 Nov. 1909, Belfast; d. of late Dr. Thomas Jones and Eirene Theodora Lloyd; m. John Cameron White 1948 (died 1968); ed. St. Paul's Girls' School and Somerville Coll., Oxford; Ministry of Labour 1941–45; Political Corresp. Manchester Evening News 1945–49; Labour M.P. for E. Flintshire 1950–70; Parl. Under-Sec. of State, Colonial Office 1964–66; Minister of State, Foreign Office 1966–67; Minister of State for Wales 1967–70; mem. Nat. Exec. Cttee., Labour Party 1947–53, 1958–72, Chair. 1968–69; Deputy Chair. Metrication Bd. 1972–76; Chair. Land Authority for Wales 1975–80; mem. Royal Comm. on Environmental Pollution 1974–81, British Waterways Bd. 1974–80, Univ. Grants Cttee. 1977–79; Deputy Speaker House of Lords 1979–89; Prin. Deputy Chair. of Cttees., House of Lords 1980–82, Chair. Select Cttee. on European Communities 1980–82; Gov. Nat. Library of Wales, British Film Inst. and Nat. Film Theatre 1959–64; Chair. Advisory Cttee. on Pollution at Sea 1974–78; Pres. Council for the Protection of Rural Wales 1976–89; Vice-Pres. Commonwealth Countries' League, Council for Nat. Parks 1985–; Hon. Fellow, Somerville Coll., Oxford 1966; Chair. Univ. of Wales Inst. of Science and Tech. 1983–88, Vice-Pres. Univ. of Wales, Cardiff 1988–93; Hon. LL.D. (Wales) 1979, (Queen's Univ., Belfast) 1981, (Bath Univ.) 1983. *Publication:* The Ladies of Gregynog 1985. *Address:* House of Lords, London, SW1A 0PW, England; 22 Bailey Court, Hereford Road, Abergavenny, Gwent, NP7 5PQ, Wales. *Telephone:* 0171-219 5435 (London); (01873) 859032 (Gwent).

WHITE, Christopher John, PH.D., F.B.A.; British arts administrator (retd.); b. 19 Sept. 1930; s. of Gabriel Ernest E. F. White; m. Rosemary Katharine Desages 1957; one s. two d.; ed. Downside School, Courtauld Inst. of Art, London Univ.; army service 1949–50; Asst. Keeper, Dept. of Prints and Drawings, British Museum 1954–65; Dir. P. and D. Colnaghi 1965–71; Curator of Graphic Arts, Nat. Gallery of Art, Washington 1971–73; Dir. of Studies, Paul Mellon Centre for Studies in British Art 1973–85; Assoc. Dir. Yale Centre for British Art, New Haven 1976–85; Adjunct Prof. of History of Art, Yale Univ. 1977–85; Dir. Ashmolean Museum, Oxford 1985–97; Fellow, Worcester Coll., Oxford 1985–97; Prof. of the Art of the Netherlands, Oxford 1992–97; Hermione Lecturer, Alexandra Coll., Dublin 1959; Adjunct Prof., Inst. of Fine Arts, New York Univ. 1973, 1976; Visiting Prof., Yale Univ. 1976; Conf. Dir., European-American Ass. on Art Museums 1975; Reviews Ed., Master Drawings 1967–80; Trustee Victoria and Albert Museum 1997. *Publications:* Rembrandt and His World 1964, The Flower Drawings of Jan van Huysum 1965, Rubens and His World 1968, Rembrandt as an Etcher 1969, Rembrandt's Etchings: a catalogue raisonné (jtly.) 1970, Dürer: the Artist and His Drawings 1972, English Landscape 1630–1850 1977, The Dutch Paintings in the Collection of H.M. The Queen 1982, Rembrandt in Eighteenth Century England (Ed.) 1983, Peter Paul Rubens: Man and Artist 1987, Drawing in England from Hilliard to Hogarth (jtly.) 1987, Rubens in Oxford (jtly.) 1988, One Hundred Old Master Drawings from the Ashmolean Museum (jtly.) 1991, Dutch and Flemish Drawings at Windsor Castle (jtly.) 1994, Anthony van Dyck: Thomas Howard, the Earl of Arundel 1995. *Address:* 34 Kelly Street, London, NW1 8PH, England.

WHITE, Sir David Harry, Kt.; British business executive; b. 12 Oct. 1929, Nottingham; s. of Harry White and Doris White; m. Valerie White 1971; one s. four d.; ed. Nottingham High School; Master Mariner's Certificate, H.M.S. Conway; apprentice, Shell Co. 1946–56; Terminal Man., Texaco (UK) Ltd. 1956–64; Operations Man., Gulf Oil (GB) 1964–68; Asst. Man. Dir. Samuel Williams, Dagenham 1968–70; Man. Dir. Eastern British Road Services 1970–76; Group Man. Dir. British Road Services 1976–82, Pickfords 1982–84; Deputy Chair. Nat. Freight Corpn. 1984–89; Group Man. Dir. Nat. Freight Consortium Property Group 1984–87; Chair. Pension fund, Nat. Freight Co. 1985–; Chair. Nottingham Devt. Enterprise 1987–93; Dir. (non-exec.) British Coal 1993–94; Chair. Nottingham Health Authority 1986–98, Bd. of Govs. Nottingham Trent Univ. 1988–, Mansfield Brewery PLC 1993–, The Coal Authority 1994–, EPS Ltd. 1997–; D.L. 1989. *Leisure interests:* football, walking. *Address:* Whitehaven, 6 Croft Road, Edwalton, Notts., NG12 4BW, England.

WHITE, Edmund; American author; b. 13 Jan. 1940; s. of E.V. White and Delilah Teddlie; ed. Univ. of Mich.; Prof. of English, Brown Univ., Providence, R.I.; Prof. Brown Univ. 1990–92; Guggenheim Fellowship; Literature Award, American Acad. of Arts and Letters. *Publications include:* novels: Forgetting Elena 1973, Nocturnes for the King of Naples 1978, A Boy's Own Story 1982, Caracole 1985, The Darker Proof 1987, The Beautiful Room is Empty 1988; non-fiction: States of Desire: Travels in Gay America 1980, Gay Short Fiction 1991, The Burning Library 1994, Sketches from Memory 1994; biography: Jean Genet 1992. *Address:* c/o Maxine Groffsky, 2 Fifth Avenue, New York, NY 10011, U.S.A.

WHITE, Gilbert F(owler), PH.D.; American geographer; b. 26 Nov. 1911, Chicago; s. of Arthur E. White and Mary (Guthrie) White; m. Anne E. Underwood 1944; one s. two d.; ed. Univ. of Chicago; Geographer, Miss. Valley Comm. of P.W.A. 1934, Nat. Resources Bd. 1934–35; Sec. Land and Water Comm., Nat. Resources Comm. and Nat. Resources Planning Bd. 1935–40; Bureau of Budget, Exec. Office of Pres. 1941–42; Relief Admin. in France 1942–43; interned Baden-Baden 1943–44; Sec. American Relief for India 1945–46; Pres. Haverford Coll. 1946–55; Prof. of Geography Univ. of Chicago 1956–69; Prof. of Geography and Dir. Inst. of Behavioral Sciences, Univ. of Colorado 1970–78, Gustavson Distinguished Prof. Emer. 1979–; Dir. Natural Hazards Research Information Center 1976–84, 1992–94, American Soc. of Flood Plain Man.'s Foundation 1996–; mem. numerous nat. and int. advisory comms. etc.; Exec. Ed. Environment 1983–93; Visiting Prof. Univ. of Oxford 1962–63; mem. N.A.S., Asscn. of American Geographers; Hon. mem. Royal Geographical Soc., Russian Geographical Soc.; Foreign mem. U.S.S.R. (now Russian) Acad. of Sciences; recipient of numerous awards and hon. degrees. *Publications:* author, co-author and ed. of books on flood management and other environmental issues. *Address:* Campus Box 482, University of Colorado, Boulder, CO 80309 (Office); 624 Pearl Street, Boulder, CO 80302, U.S.A. (Home). *Fax:* (303) 492-2151.

WHITE, Guy Kendall, M.SC., D.PHIL., F.A.A.; Australian physicist; b. 31 May 1925, Sydney; s. of Perceval George White and Eugenie White (née Kendall); m. Judith Kelly McAuliffe 1955; one s. two d.; ed. The Scots Coll., Sydney, Univ. of Sydney, Magdalen Coll., Oxford, U.K.; Research Officer CSIRO Div.

of Physics 1950–54; Assoc. Research Officer, Nat. Research Council of Canada 1955–58; Prin. Research Scientist, CSIRO 1958–62, Sr. Prin. Research Scientist 1962–69, Chief Research Scientist 1969–90, Hon. Fellow 1990–; Hon. D.Sc. (Wollongong) 1994; Syme Medal (Melbourne Univ.) 1966, Armco Iron Award, U.S.A. 1983, Touloukian Award, U.S.A. 1994. *Publication:* Experimental Techniques in Low Temperature Physics 1958. *Leisure interests:* golf, bush-walking, swimming. *Address:* CSIRO Division of Applied Physics, National Measurement Laboratory, P.O. Box 218, Lindfield, N.S.W. 2070, Australia. *Telephone:* (02) 9413-7318. *Fax:* (02) 9413-7202.

WHITE, Adm. Sir Hugo (Moresby), G.C.B., C.B.E.; British naval officer (retd.); b. 22 Oct. 1939, Torquay; s. of late Hugh F.M. White, C.M.G. and Betty White; m. Josephine Pedler 1966; two s.; ed. Dragon School, Nautical Coll. Pangbourne and Britannia Royal Naval Coll. (BRNC) Dartmouth; H.M.S. Blackpool 1960; submarine training 1961; H.M.S. Submarines Tabard, Tiptoe, Odin 1961–65; navigation course 1966; Navigator, H.M.S. Warspite 1967; First Lieut. H.M.S. Osiris 1968–69; C.O. H.M.S. Oracle 1969–70; staff, BRNC Dartmouth 1971–72; submarine sea training 1973–74; C.O. H.M.S. Salisbury (cod war) 1975–76; Naval Sec.'s Dept. 1976–78; Asst. Dir. Naval Plans 1978–80; C.O. H.M.S. Avenger (Falklands) and 4th Frigate Squadron 1980–82; Prin. Staff Officer to Chief of Defence Staff 1982–85; C.O. H.M.S. Bristol and Flag Capt. 1985–87; Flag Officer, Third Flotilla and Commdr. Anti-Submarine Warfare Striking Force Atlantic 1987–88; Asst. Chief of Naval Staff 1988–89; Flag Officer, Scotland and N. Ireland 1991–92; C.-in-C. Fleet, Allied C.-in-C. Channel and E. Atlantic 1992–94; C.-in-C. Fleet, Allied C.-in-C. Atlantic and Naval Commdr. N.W. Europe 1994–95; Gov. and C.-in-C. Gibraltar 1995–97. *Leisure interests:* sailing, travelling, gardening, reading.

WHITE, James Boyd, A.M., LL.B.; American university professor; b. 28 July 1938, Boston, Mass.; s. of Benjamin White and Charlotte Green White; m. 1st Constance Southworth 1959; m. 2nd Mary Fitch 1978; two s. two d.; ed. Groton School, Amherst Coll. and Harvard Univ.; pvt. practice of law, Foley Hoag & Eliot 1964–67; Prof. of Law, Univ. of Colorado 1967–75, Univ. of Chicago 1975–82; Hart Wright Prof. of Law, Prof. of English Language and Literature and Adjunct Prof. of Classics, Univ. of Mich. 1982–. *Publications:* The Legal Imagination 1973, When Words Lose Their Meaning 1984, Heracles' Bow: Essays on the Rhetoric and Poetics of the Law 1986, Justice as Translation: An Essay in Cultural and Legal Criticism 1990, This Book of Starres: Learning to Read George Herbert 1994, Acts of Hope: Creating Authority in Literature, Law and Politics 1994. *Leisure interests:* reading, walking, swimming. *Address:* The University of Michigan Law School, Ann Arbor, MI 48109 (Office); 1606 Morton, Ann Arbor, MI 48104, U.S.A. (Home). *Telephone:* (734) 936-2989 (Office); (734) 662-6464 (Home). *Fax:* (734) 763-9375.

WHITE, Marco Pierre; British chef and restaurateur; b. 11 Dec. 1961, Leeds; s. of Frank White and Maria Rosa Gallina; m. 1st Alexandra McArthur 1988 (divorced 1990); one d.; m. 2nd Lisa Butcher 1992 (divorced 1994); two s. by M. Conejero; ed. Fir Tree School, Leeds, Allerton High School, Leeds; Commis Chef The Box Tree, Ilkley 1978; Commis Chef de Partie Le Gavroche 1981, Tante Claire 1983; Sous Chef Le Manoir aux Quat' Saisons 1984; Chef, Propr. Harveys 1987–, The Restaurant 1993–; The Canteen co-owned with Michael Caine (q.v.) 1992; opened Criterion Restaurant with Sir Rocco Forte (q.v.) 1995; re-opened Quo Vadis (which holds the art collection of Damien Hirst) 1996; Catey Award for Newcomer of the Year 1987, Chef of the Year, Egon Ronay 1992, first British-born chef to win 3rd Michelin Star, and youngest-ever 1995, Restaurant of the Year, Egon Ronay (for The Restaurant) 1997. *Publications:* White Heat 1990, White Heat II 1994, Wild Food from Land and Sea 1994, Canteen Cuisine 1995. *Leisure interests:* fishing, shooting. *Address:* The Restaurant, 66 Knightsbridge, London, SW1X 7LA, England. *Telephone:* 0171-259 5380.

WHITE, Michael Simon; British theatrical and film producer and impresario; b. 16 Jan. 1936; s. of Victor White and Doris White; m. 1st Sarah Hillsdon 1965 (divorced 1973); two s. one d.; m. 2nd Louise Moores 1985; one s.; ed. Lyceum Alpinum, Zuoz, Switzerland, Pisa Univ. and Sorbonne, Paris; began career by bringing Cambridge Footlights to London's West End; Asst. to Sir Peter Daubeny 1956–61; *stage productions include:* Rocky Horror Show, Jabberwocky, Sleuth, America Hurrah, Oh, Calcutta!, The Connection, Joseph and the Amazing Technicolour Dreamcoat, Loot, The Blood Knot, A Chorus Line, Deathtrap, Annie, Pirates of Penzance, On Your Toes, The Mystery of Edwin Drood, Metropolis, Bus Stop, Crazy for You, Looking Through a Glass Onion, Me and Mamie O'Rourke, She Loves Me, Fame, Voyeurz 1996; *films include:* Monty Python and the Holy Grail, Rocky Horror Picture Show, My Dinner with André, Ploughman's Lunch, Moonlighting, Strangers' Kiss, The Comic Strip Presents, The Supergrass, High Season, Eat the Rich, White Mischief, The Deceivers, Nuns on the Run 1989, Robert's Movie, The Pope Must Die, Widow's Peak. *Publication:* Empty Seats 1984. *Leisure interests:* art, skiing, racing. *Address:* 48 Dean Street, London, W1V 5HL, England. *Telephone:* 0171-734 7707.

WHITE, Norman A., PH.D., F.I.MECH.E., F.R.S.A.,; British business executive, academic and international consultant; b. 11 April 1922, Hetton-le-Hole, Durham; s. of Charles Brewster White and Lilian Sarah White (née Finch); m. 1st Joyce Marjorie Rogers 1944 (died 1982); one s. one d.; m. 2nd Marjorie Iris Rushton 1983; ed. Manchester Inst. of Science and Technology, Univ. of London, Univ. of Philippines, London Polytechnic (now Univ. of Westminster), Harvard Business School, London School of Econs.; apprenticeship with George Kent Ltd. and D. Napier and Sons Ltd. 1936–43; Flight Test Engineer, Mil. Aircraft Devt. 1943–45; with Royal Dutch Shell Group 1945–72, numerous posts, including Chair. and Dir. of Royal Dutch/Shell Oil and int. mining cos. 1963–72; f. Norman White Assocs. 1972, Prin. Exec. 1972–92, Chair. 1992–95; tech. consultant to numerous cos. 1972–96; Chair. and Dir. numerous eng. and oil cos. 1972–97; Chair. Millennium Satellite Centre 1995; mem. Council and Chair. Eng.-Man. Div., Inst. Mechanical Engineers 1980–85, 1987–91; mem. Council and Vice-Pres. Inst. of Petroleum 1975–81; Founder, Chair. Jt. Bd. for Engineering Man. of Inst. Mech. E., I.C.E., I.E.E., I. Chem. E. 1990–94, Chair. Academic Bd. 1994–97; Visiting Prof. Univ. of Manchester, Henley Man. Coll., City Univ. 1971–96; mem. numerous academic and educational cttees. including Senate and Advisory Bd. in Eng., Univ. of London; Chair. Transnational Satellite Educ. Centre, Univ. of Surrey 1991–94; mem. House of Commons Parl. and Scientific Cttee. 1977–83, 1987–92; Chair. British Nat. Cttee. of World Petroleum Congresses (WPC) 1987–95 (Deputy Chair. 1977–87), U.K. Rep. WPC Int. Exec. Bd. and Perm. Council 1979–97, Treas. 1983–91, 1994–97, Vice-Pres. 1991–94; mem. Conservation Comm. for World Energy 1979–87; Chair. Int. Task Force on Oil Substitution 1979–84; mem. int. energy/petroleum dels. to U.S.S.R, People's Repub. of China, Romania, G.D.R., Japan, Korea, India, Mexico, Argentina, Brazil, Venezuela, Nepal, Indonesia, Southern Africa, Iran 1979–; mem. numerous professional eng. insts.; f. mem. British Inst. of Energy Econs.; Fellow, Inst. of Man.; mem. American Soc. of Petroleum Engineers, Canadian Inst. of Mining and Metallurgy; Freeman of the City of London; Liveryman, Worshipful Co. of Engineers, Worshipful Co. of Spectacle Makers, Co. of World Traders, Hon. Calgarian, Alberta, Canada; numerous honours. *Publications:* Financing the International Petroleum Industry 1978, The International Outlook for Oil Substitution to 2020 1983, Handbook of Engineering Management 1989, articles in professional journals in U.K. and Canada. *Leisure interests:* family, walking, international affairs, comparative religions, odd-jobbing. *Address:* Green Ridges, Downside Road, Guildford, Surrey, GU4 8PH, England. *Telephone:* (01483) 567523. *Fax:* (01483) 504314.

WHITE, Raymond P., D.D.S., PH.D.; American oral and maxillofacial surgeon; b. 13 Feb. 1937, New York; s. of Raymond P. White and Mabel S. White; m. Betty P. White 1961; one s. one d.; ed. Medical Coll. of Virginia and Washington & Lee Univ.; Asst. Prof. of Oral Surgery, Univ. of Kentucky 1967–70, Assoc. Prof. 1970–71, Chair. Oral Surgery Dept. 1969–71; Prof. of Oral Surgery, Virginia Commonwealth Univ. 1971–74; Dalton L. McMichael Prof. of Oral and Maxillofacial Surgery, Univ. of N.C. School of Dentistry 1974–, Dean 1974–81; Assoc. Dean. Univ. of N.C. School of Medicine 1981–93; Research Assoc. Univ. of N.C. Health Services Research Center 1982–; mem. Inst. of Medicine, N.A.S. *Publications:* co-author, Fundamentals of Oral Surgery 1971, Surgical Correction of Dentofacial Deformities 1980, Surgical Orthodontic Treatment 1990, Rigid Fixation for Maxillofacial Surgery 1991. *Leisure interests:* tennis, sailing. *Address:* 188 Dental Office Building 209H, CB 7450, University of North Carolina, Chapel Hill, NC 27599-7450 (Office); 1506 Velma Road, Chapel Hill, NC 27514, U.S.A. (Home). *Telephone:* (919) 966-1126 (Office); (919) 967-4064 (Home). *Fax:* (919) 966-6019.

WHITE, Robert James, A.O., F.A.I.B., F.A.I.M.; Australian banker; b. 18 Oct. 1923, Deniliquin, N.S.W.; s. of late A. W. White and S. J. White; m. 1st Molly McKinnon 1950 (died 1994); m. 2nd Janice Anne White 1996; ed. War Memorial High School, Hay, N.S.W.; joined Bank of N.S.W. 1940, Asst. Chief Man., New Zealand 1965–66, Deputy Chief Accountant 1967–69, Man., Sydney 1970–71, Chief Man., U.K. and Europe 1972–74, Gen. Man. 1974–77, Dir. and C.E.O. Bank of N.S.W. 1977–82, Man. Dir. Westpac Banking Corpn. (merger of Bank of N.S.W. with Commercial Bank of Australia) 1982–87, Dir. 1977–90; Dir. ICI Australia Ltd. 1987–93, IBM Australia Ltd. 1988–95, Atlas Copco Australia Pty. Ltd. 1989–94; Commr. Electricity Comm. of N.S.W. 1989–95; Pres. Australian Inst. of Bankers 1980–86; Chair. Australian Bankers' Asscn. 1978–79, 1983–84, 1987; Dir. Int. Monetary Conf. 1982–85; Pres. Asian Pacific Bankers' Club 1983–84, Business Council of Australia 1984–86, Australian Coalition of Service Industries 1988–94, Australian Inst. for Int. Affairs 1988–91, German-Australian Chamber of Industry and Commerce 1988–91, Council for Int. Business Affairs 1992–95; mem. Trade Devt. Council 1981–84, Australian Pacific Econ. Co-operation Cttee. 1984–91; mem. Exec. Bd. ICC 1987–90; Storey Medal, Australian Inst. of Man. 1987; Commdr.'s Cross, Order of Merit (Germany). *Publication:* Cheques and Balances (memoir) 1995. *Address:* G.P.O. Box 4046, Sydney, N.S.W. 2001, Australia. *Telephone:* (02) 9233-6539.

WHITE, Robert M., II; American journalist; b. 6 April 1915, Mexico, Mo.; s. of L. Mitchell White and Maude (née See) White; m. 1st Barbara Spurgeon 1948 (died 1983); one s. three d.; m. 3rd Linda Hess Grimsley 1992; ed. Missouri Military Acad., and Washington and Lee Univ.; with United Press 1939; Army service 1940–45; Pres., Ed. and Publr. Mexico (Missouri) Ledger 1945–87, Ed. Emer. 1987–; Ed. and Pres. New York Herald Tribune 1959–61: Dir. American Newspaper Publishers' Asscn. 1955–63, Treas. 1962–63; Dir. New York World's Fair 1964-65; fmr. Chair. Associated Press Nominating Cttee.; fmr. Chair. and Pres., Inland Daily Press Asscn.; Pres. See TV Co. 1965–81; Vice-Chair. American Cttee. Int. Pres. Inst. 1968–71, 1981–91, Chair. 1982–86; Dir. American Soc. of Newspaper Eds. 1968–70; Pres. Soc. of Professional Journalists 1967; Dir. Stephen's Coll., Missouri Mil. Acad.; Visiting Prof., Univ. of Missouri 1968–69; mem. Pulitzer Prize Jury for

Journalism 1964–66; Chair. American Soc. of Newspaper Eds. Freedom of Information Cttee. 1970–72; Chair. Missouri Free Press-Fair Trial Cttee.1970–74; Pres. Missouri Press Assen.; Vice-Pres. Mo. Inst. for Justice 1978–82, Bd. of Dirs. 1982–87; Vice-Pres. Gen. Douglas MacArthur Foundation 1979–81, Pres. 1981–; mem. Bd. of Dirs. Associated Press 1971–80, Bd. of Dirs. Washington Journalism Center 1972–84, State Historical Soc. of Missouri, Missouri Public Expenditure Survey 1980–85 (Pres. 1981–83), Bd. of Dirs. Washington and Lee Univ. Alumni Inc. 1976–80, World Press Freedom Comm. 1984–; Dir. Commerce Bank of Mexico 1971–85, Commerce Bancshares Inc. 1971–85; Dir. Thomson Newspapers (Toronto) 1986–92; mem. Bd. of Dirs. Int. Eye Foundation 1987–89; Distinguished Service to Journalism Award, Univ. of Missouri 1967, Nat. Newspapers Assen. Pres. Award of Merit 1967. *Publications:* A study of the Printing and Publishing Business in the Soviet Union (co-author), China Journey 1972, Second Journey To China 1977. *Leisure interests:* hunting, fishing. *Address:* 4871 Glenbrook Road, NW, Washington DC 20016, U.S.A.

WHITE, Robert Mayer, SC.D.; American meteorologist; b. 13 Feb. 1923, Boston, Mass.; s. of David and Mary (Winkeller) White; m. Mavis Seagle 1948; one s. one d.; ed. Harvard Univ. and M.I.T.; war service with U.S.A.F., exec. at Atmospheric Analysis Lab., Geophysics Research Directorate, Air Force Cambridge Research Center 1952–58, Chief of Meteorological Devt. Lab. 1958; Research Assoc. M.I.T. 1959; Travelers Insurance Cos. 1959–60, Pres. Travelers Research Center, Hartford 1960–63; Chief of Weather Bureau, U.S. Dept. of Commerce 1963–65; Admin. Environmental Science Services Admin., U.S. Dept. of Commerce 1965–70; Perm. Rep. and mem. Exec. Cttee. of World Meteorological Org. 1963–77; Administrator Nat. Oceanic and Atmospheric Admin. 1971–77; Chair. Joint Oceanographic Inst., Inc., 1977–79; Chair. Climate Research Bd. of N.A.S. 1977–79; Admin. Nat. Research Council, Exec. Officer 1979–80; Pres. Univ. Corpn. for Atmospheric Research 1979–83, Sr. Fellow 1995–; Karl T. Compton Lecturer, M.I.T., Cambridge 1995–96; Pres. Washington Advisory Group 1996–; mem. Exec. Cttee. American Geophysical Union, Council Nat. Acad. of Eng., (Pres. 1983–), Marine Tech. Soc., Royal Meteorological Soc., Nat. Advisory Cttee. on Oceans and Atmosphere 1979–84, Nat. Advisory Cttee. on Govt. and Public Affairs, Univ. of Ill. 1987–; Bd. of Overseers Harvard Univ. 1977–79; mem. of numerous weather research cttees., Commr. Int. Whaling Comm. 1973–77; Cleveland Abbe award, American Meteorological Soc. 1969, Rockefeller Public Service award 1974, David B. Stone award, New England Aquarium 1975, Matthew Fontaine Maury award Smithsonian Inst., Int. Conservation award Nat. Wildlife Fed. 1976, Neptune Award American Oceanic Org. 1977, Charles Franklin Brooks award 1978, Int. Meteorological Assen. Prize 1980, Tyler Prize, Univ. of Calif 1992, Vannevar Bush Award 1998. *Leisure interests:* gardening, reading. *Address:* 1200 New York Avenue N.W., Suite 410, Washington, DC 20005, U.S.A. (Office); Somerset House II, 5610 Wisconsin Avenue, Apt. 1506, Bethesda, MD 20815, U.S.A. (Home).

WHITE, Terrence Harold, PH.D.; Canadian university president; b. 31 March 1943, Ottawa; s. of William H. White and Shirley M. Ballantine; m. Susan E. Hornaday 1968; two d.; ed. Univ. of Toronto; Head, Dept. of Sociology and Anthropology, Univ. of Windsor 1973–75; Chair. Dept. of Sociology, Univ. of Alberta 1975–80, Dean, Faculty of Arts 1980–88; Pres. and Vice-Chancellor Brock Univ. 1988–96, Univ. of Calgary 1996–. *Publications:* Power or Pawns: Boards of Directors in Canadian Corporations 1978, Quality of Working Life 1984. *Leisure interests:* hockey, skiing, squash, tennis, painting. *Address:* The University of Calgary, 2500 University Drive N.W., Calgary, Alberta, T2N IN4, Canada. *Telephone:* (403) 220-5460.

WHITE, Willard Wentworth, C.B.E., B.A.; Jamaican/British opera singer; b. 10 Oct. 1946, Ewarton, St. Catherine, Jamaica; s. of Egbert White and Gertrude White; m. Gillian Jackson 1972; three s. one d.; ed. Excelsior School, Kingston and Juilliard School of Music, N.Y.; with New York City Opera 1974–75; European début as Osmin with Welsh Nat. Opera 1976; has performed in most int. opera houses, including Royal Opera House, Covent Garden, England, La Scala, Italy, Glyndebourne, England, Scotland; roles include: Porgy, Orestes, Banquo, King Henry (Lohengrin), Pizarro, Wotan, Golau, Leporello, Prince Kovansky; extensive concert appearances; appeared as Othello, R.S.C., Stratford-upon-Avon; Prime Minister of Jamaica's Medal of Appreciation 1987. *Recordings include:* Porgy and Bess, Mozart Requiem and Orfeo. *Address:* c/o I.M.G. Artists Europe, Media House, 3 Burlington Lane, London, W4 2TH, England.

WHITE, William James, B.S., M.B.A.; American business executive; b. 30 May 1938, Kenosha, Wis.; s. of William H. White and Dorothy Caroline White; m. Jane Schulte 1960; two s. two d.; ed. Northwestern and Harvard Univs.; Mechanical Planning Engineer, Procter & Gamble Corpn. 1961–62; Corp. Vice-Pres. Hartmarx Corpn., Chicago 1963–74; Group Vice-Pres. Mead Corpn., Dayton, Ohio 1974–81; Pres., C.O.O. and Dir. Masonite Corpn., Chicago 1981–85; Exec. Vice-Pres. and Dir. USG Corpn. 1985–88; Pres., C.E.O. Whitestar Enterprises Inc. 1989–90; Chair., Pres., C.E.O. Bell & Howell Co. 1990–95; Chair. C.E.O. Bell and Howell Holdings Co. 1995–; Dir. Midwest Stock Exchange, Chicago, Evanston Hosp., Evanston, Ill., Ill. Math. and Science Foundation, Business Advisory Council, Univ. of Ill.; mem. The Chicago Cttee., Advisory Council Tech. Inst., Northwestern Univ.; Trustee Northwestern Univ., Evanston. *Publication:* Creative Collective Bargaining (Co-author) 1965. *Address:* Bell & Howell Co., 5215 Old Orchard Road, Skokie, IL 60077, U.S.A.

WHITEHEAD, George William, PH.D.; American mathematician; b. 2 Aug. 1918, Bloomington, Ill.; s. of George William Whitehead and Mary Gutschlag Whitehead; m. Kathleen Ethelwyn Butcher 1947; ed. Univ. of Chicago; Instructor in Math. Purdue Univ. 1941–45, Princeton Univ. 1945–47; Asst. Prof. of Math. Brown Univ. 1947–48, Assoc. Prof. 1948–49; Asst. Prof. of Math. M.I.T. 1949–51, Assoc. Prof. 1951–57, Prof. 1957–85, Prof. Emer. 1985–; Fellow, American Acad. of Arts and Sciences 1954; mem. N.A.S. 1972–. *Publications:* Homotopy Theory 1966, Recent Advances in Homotopy Theory 1970, Elements of Homotopy Theory 1978, and articles in scientific journals. *Leisure interests:* bridge, archaeology, genealogy. *Address:* Room 2-235, Department of Mathematics, Massachusetts Institute of Technology, Cambridge, MA 02139; 25 Bellevue Road, Arlington, MA 02476, U.S.A. (Home). *Telephone:* (617) 253-4984 (Office); (781) 643-0911 (Home).

WHITEHEAD, Sir John Stainton, G.C.M.G., C.V.O., M.A. British diplomatist (retd.); b. 20 Sept. 1932; s. of John William Whitehead and Kathleen Whitehead; m. Mary Carolyn Hilton 1964; two s. two d.; ed. Christ's Hosp. and Hertford Coll., Oxford; served H.M. Forces 1950–52; Foreign Office 1955–56, Third Sec., later Second Sec., Tokyo 1956–61, Foreign Office 1961–64, First Sec. Washington 1964–67, First Sec. Econ., Tokyo 1968–71, FCO 1971–76, Head of Personnel Services Dept. 1973–76, Counsellor and Head of Chancery, Bonn 1976–80, Minister, Tokyo 1980–84, FCO, Deputy Under-Sec. of State (Chief Clerk) 1984–86; Amb. to Japan 1986–92; adviser to Pres. of Bd. of Trade 1992–96; sr. adviser, Morgan Grenfell Group PLC 1992–; Chair. Deutsche Morgan Grenfell Trust Bank, Tokyo 1996–; Dir. (non-exec.) Cadbury Schweppes 1993–, Serco PLC 1994–96, BPB Industries PLC 1995–; adviser or consultant to various cos.; Hon. Fellow Hertford Coll. Oxford 1992. *Leisure interests:* new challenges, music, travel, tree-felling, walking, golf. *Address:* Bracken Edge, High Pitfold, Hindhead, Surrey, England (Home). *Telephone:* (01428) 604162. *Fax:* (01428) 607950.

WHITELAW, Billie, C.B.E.; British actress; b. 6 June 1932, Coventry; d. of Perceval Whitelaw and Frances Whitelaw; m. 1st Peter Vaughan (divorced); m. 2nd Robert Muller; one s.; ed. Thornton Grammar School, Bradford; Annenberg-Beckett Fellow, Univ. of Reading 1993; Hon. D.Litt. (Bradford) 1981, (Birmingham, St. Andrews) 1997; Variety Club Silver Heart Award 1961, TV Actress of Year 1961, 1972, British Acad. Award 1968, U.S. Film Critics' Award 1977, Evening News Film Award as Best Actress 1977, Sony Best Radio Actress Award 1987, Evening Standard Best Film Actress Award 1988; Hon. D.Litt. (Birmingham) 1997. *Plays include:* Hotel Paradiso, Winter Garden 1954 and Oxford Playhouse 1956, Progress to the Park, Theatre Workshop and Saville 1961, England our England, Prince's 1962, Touch of the Poet, Venice and Dublin 1962; with Nat. Theatre 1963–65, Othello, London and Moscow, Hobson's Choice, Play (Beckett), Trelawny of the Wells, The Dutch Courtesan, After Haggerty, Criterion 1971, Not I, Royal Court 1973 and 1975, Alphabetical Order, Mayfair 1975, Footfalls, Royal Court 1976, Molly, Comedy 1978, Happy Days, Royal Court 1979, The Greeks, Aldwych 1980, Passion Play, Aldwych 1981, Rockaby, Nat. Theatre 1982, New York 1982, 1984, Riverside Studios 1986, world tour 1985/86, Tales from Hollywood, Nat. Theatre 1983, Who's Afraid of Virginia Woolf?, Young Vic 1987. *Films include:* No Love For Johnnie 1961, Charlie Bubbles 1968, Twisted Nerve 1968, The Adding Machine 1968, Start the Revolution Without Me, Leo the Last, Eagle in a Cage 1969, Gumshoe 1971, Frenzy 1972, Night Watch 1973, The Omen 1976, Leopard in the Snow, The Water Babies 1977, An Unsuitable Job for a Woman 1981, Slayground 1983, The Chain 1984, Shadey 1985, Maurice 1986, The Dressmaker 1988, Joyriders 1989, The Krays 1990, Deadly Advice 1993, Jane Eyre 1994, Canterbury Tales (animated film). *Television includes:* No Trams to Lime Street, Lena Oh My Lena, Resurrection, The Skin Game, Beyond the Horizon, Anna Christie, Lady of the Camelias, The Pity of it all, Love on the Dole, A World of Time, You and I, Poet Game, Sextet (8 plays), Napoleon and Love (9 plays, as Josephine), The Fifty Pound Note (Ten From the Twenties), The Withered Arm (Wessex Tales), The Werewolf Reunion (2 plays), Shades by Samuel Beckett, Not I, Eustace and Hilda (2 plays), The Serpent Son, Happy Days (dir. by Beckett), A Tale of Two Cities, Jamaica Inn, Private Schultz, Camille, Old Girlfriends, The Picnic, The Secret Garden, Imaginary Friends, The Entertainer, The 15 Streets, Footfalls, Rockaby, Eh Joe, Duel of Love, Lorna Doone, Murder of Quality, The Cloning of Joanna May, Firm Friends, Born to Run. *Plays for radio:* The Master Builder, Hindle Wakes, Jane Eyre, The Female Messiah, Alpha Beta, Marching Song, The Cherry Orchard, Vassa, Beckett's All that Fall, Embers, Becket Evening (one-woman) 1997. *Publication:* Billie Whitelaw—Who he! (memoirs) 1995. *Leisure interest:* pottering about the house. *Address:* c/o I.C.M., Oxford House, 76 Oxford Street, London, W.1, England. *Telephone:* 0171-636 6565. *Fax:* 0171-323 0101.

WHITELAW OF PENRITH, 1st Viscount (cr. 1983) of Penrith in the County of Cumbria; **William (Stephen Ian) Whitelaw,** K.T., C.H., M.C., D.L.; British politician; b. 28 June 1918, Edinburgh; s. of Mr. and Mrs. W. A. Whitelaw; m. Cecilia Doriel Sprot 1943; four d.; ed. Winchester Coll. and Trinity Coll., Cambridge; M.P. for Penrith and Border Div. of Cumberland 1955–83; Parl. Pvt. Sec. to Chancellor of Exchequer 1957–58; Asst. Govt. Whip 1959–61; a Lord Commr. of the Treasury 1961–62; Parl. Sec. Ministry of Labour 1962–64; Opposition Chief Whip 1964–70; Lord Pres. of Council and Leader of House of Commons 1970–72; Sec. of State for N. Ireland 1972–73, for Employment 1973–74; Chair. Conservative Party 1974–75; Deputy Leader of the Opposition 1975–79; Deputy Leader of the Conservative

Party 1975–91; Opposition Spokesman on Home Affairs 1975–79; Home Sec. 1979–83; Lord Pres. of the Council and Leader of the House of Lords 1983–87; Chair. Carlton Club 1986–92; Hon. D.Iur. (Durham) 1989. *Publication:* The Whitelaw Memoirs (autobiog.) 1989. *Leisure interest:* golf. *Address:* House of Lords, London, S.W.1, England.

WHITEREAD, Rachel; British sculptor; b. 20 April 1963, London; d. of Thomas Whiteread and Patricia Whiteread; ed. Brighton Polytechnic and Slade School of Art, Univ. Coll. London; one-woman exhbns. London 1988, 1990, 1991, 1994, Bristol 1991, New York, Barcelona 1992, Eindhoven 1992, 1993, Paris, Chicago, Berlin 1993, Basle 1994, Philadelphia 1995, Madrid 1997, The British Pavilion Venice Biennale 1997; participant in numerous group exhbns. in U.K. and abroad 1987–; some works use casts of sinks, baths, beds, mattresses, floors and mortuary slabs; work includes 'Ghost', a white plaster cast of an entire room shown at Chisenhale Gallery, London 1990 and 'House', a cast of an entire London terraced house on show in Bow, East London 1993–94; recipient of Turner Prize 1993, Venice Biennale Award for Best Young Artist 1997. *Address:* c/o Anthony d'Offay, 22 Dering Street, London, W1R 9AA, England *Telephone:* 0171-499 4100.

WHITHAM, Gerald Beresford, PH.D., F.A.A.A.S., F.R.S.; British professor of applied mathematics; b. 13 Dec. 1927, Halifax; s. of Harry Whitham and Elizabeth E. Whitham; m. Nancy Lord 1951; one s. two d.; ed. Elland Grammar School and Univ. of Manchester; Research Assoc. New York Univ. 1951–53; Lecturer in Applied Math. Manchester Univ. 1953–56; Assoc. Prof. of Applied Math., Inst. of Mathematical Sciences, New York 1956–59; Prof. of Math. M.I.T. 1959–62; Prof. of Aeronautics and Math. Calif. Inst. of Tech. 1962–67, of Applied Math. 1967–83, Charles Lee Powell Prof. of Applied Math. 1983–; Wiener Prize 1980. *Publications:* Linear and Nonlinear Waves 1974, Lectures on Wave Propagation 1980. *Address:* Applied Mathematics 217-50, California Institute of Technology, Pasadena, CA 91125, U.S.A. *Telephone:* (818) 395-4561.

WHITLAM, (Edward) Gough, A.C., Q.C., B.A., LL.B.; Australian politician and diplomatist; b. 11 July 1916, Melbourne; s. of late H. F. E. Whitlam and Martha (Maddocks) Whitlam; m. Margaret Dovey 1942; three s. one d.; ed. Knox Grammar School, Sydney, Canberra High School, Canberra Grammar School and Univ. of Sydney; R.A.A.F. 1941–45; admitted to N.S.W. Bar 1947; mem. House of Reps. 1952–78; mem. Parl. Cttee. on Constitutional Review 1956–59; mem. Federal Parl. Exec. of Australian Labor Party 1959–77; Deputy Leader of Australian Labor Party in Fed. Parl. 1960–67, Leader 1967–77; Leader of the Opposition 1967–72, 1975–77; Prime Minister 1972–75, concurrently Minister of Foreign Affairs 1972–73; Rep. to UNESCO, Paris 1983–86, mem. Exec. Bd. 1985–89; mem. Australian Constitutional Convention 1973–76, Independent Comm. on Int. Humanitarian Issues 1983–86, Constitutional Comm. 1986–88; Chair. Australia-China Council 1986–91, Australian Nat. Gallery 1987–90; Visiting Fellow (lecturing in Political Science and Int. Relations) Australian Nat. Univ. 1978–80, Nat. Fellow 1980–81; Fellow Univ. of Sydney Senate 1981–83, 1986–89; Pres. Int. Comm. of Jurists (Australian Section) 1982–83; Visiting Prof. Harvard Univ. 1979; Hon. Pres. Australian Nat. Council for the Celebration of the Bicentenary of the French Revolution 1989; f. Hanoi Architectural Heritage Foundation 1993; mem. Sydney Olympics 2000 del. to Africa 1993; mem. Acad. of Athens 1992; Fellow Australian Acad. of the Humanities; Hon. LL.D. (The Philippines) 1974; Hon. D.Litt. (Sydney) 1981, (Wollongong) 1989, (La Trobe, Wodonga) 1992, (Univ. of Tech., Sydney) 1995; Socialist Int. Silver Plate of Honour 1976, Vice-Pres. 1976–77, Hon. Pres. 1983–; Mem. of Honour Int. Union for Nature Conservation (now World Conservation Union) 1988; Grand Cross, Order of Makarios III (Cyprus) 1983, Australian Library and Information Asscn. Redmond Barry Award 1994, Grand Commdr. Order of Hellenic Repub. 1996, Commendatore dell' Ordine al Merito (Italy) 1997, Grand Cross of the Order of the Phoenix (Greece) 1998. *Publications:* Australian Foreign Policy 1963, Australia—Base or Bridge (Evatt Memorial Lecture) 1966, Beyond Vietnam—Australia's Regional Responsibilities 1968, An Urban Nation 1969, The New Federalism 1971, Towards a New Australia—Australia and Her Region 1972, Labor in Power 1972, Australian Public Administration and the Labor Government (Sir Robert Garran Oration) 1973, Australia's Foreign Policy: New Directions, New Definitions (Roy Milne Memorial Lecture) 1973, Road to Reform: Labor in Government 1975, Government of the People, for the People by the People's House 1975, The Labor Government and the Constitution 1976, On Australia's Constitution (articles and lectures 1957–77) 1977, Reform During Recession 1978, The Truth of the Matter 1979, Labor Essays 1980, The Italian Inspiration in English Literature 1980, A Pacific Community (Harvard lectures) 1981, The Cost of Federalism 1983, The Whitlam Government 1985, International Law-Making 1989, Australia's Administrative Amnesia 1990, National Collecting Institutions 1990, Living with the United States: British Dominions and New Pacific States 1990, National and International Maturity 1991, Coordination of Transport 1992, Hellenism in the Antipodes 1993, Abiding Interests 1997. *Address:* 100 William Street, Sydney, N.S.W. 2011, Australia. *Telephone:* (02) 9358-2022. *Fax:* (02) 9358-2753.

WHITMAN, Christine Todd; American politician; b. 26 Sept. 1946; d. of Webster Bray Todd and Eleanor Schley Todd; m. John Whitman 1974; two c.; ed. Wheaton Coll.; fmr. freeholder, Somerset Co., N.J.; fmr. Pres. State Bd. of Public Utilities; fmr. host, radio talk show, Station WKXW, Trenton, N.J.; fmr. newspaper columnist; Chair. Comm. for an Affordable N.J.; Gov. of New Jersey 1994–; Republican. *Address:* Office of the Governor, State House, Trenton, NJ 08625, U.S.A. *Telephone:* (609) 292-6000. *Fax:* (609) 984-6886.

WHITMAN, Marina von Neumann, PH.D.; American economist; b. 6 March 1935, New York; d. of John von Neumann and Mariette Kovesi (Mrs. J. B. H. Kuper); m. Robert F. Whitman 1956; one s. one d.; ed. Radcliffe Coll. and Columbia Univ.; Lecturer in Econs., Univ. of Pittsburgh 1962–64, Asst. Prof. 1964–66, Assoc. Prof. 1966–71, Prof. of Econs. 1971–73, Distinguished Public Service Prof. 1973–79; Sr. Staff Economist, Council of Econ. Advisers 1970–71; mem. President's Price Comm. 1971–72; mem. President's Council of Econ. Advisers (with special responsibility for int. monetary and trade problems) 1972–73; Vice-Pres., Chief Econ. Gen. Motors Corpn., New York 1979–85, Group Exec. Vice-Pres. for Public Affairs 1985–92; Distinguished Visiting Prof. Business Admin. and Public Policy Univ. of Mich. 1992–94, Prof. 1994–; mem. Trilateral Comm. 1973, Bd. of Dirs. Council on Foreign Relations 1977–87; Mfrs. Hanover Trust Co. 1973, Proctor and Gamble Co. 1976–; Bd. of Trustees, Princeton Univ. 1980–90; mem. Consultative Group on Int. Econ. and Monetary Affairs 1979–. *Publications:* various books and articles on economic topics. *Address:* School of Public Policy, University of Michigan, 411 Lorch Hall, Ann Arbor, MI 48109, U.S.A.

WHITNEY, John Norton Braithwaite, F.R.S.A.; British broadcasting official; b. 20 Dec. 1930, Burnham, Bucks.; s. of Willis Bevan Whitney and Dorothy Anne Whitney; m. Roma Elizabeth Hodgson 1956; one s. one d.; ed. Leighton Park Friends' School, Reading; radio producer 1951–64; set up Ross Radio Productions Ltd. 1951, Autocue Ltd. 1955; f. Radio Antilles 1963; Man. Dir. Capital Radio 1973–82; Dir.-Gen. Ind. Broadcasting Authority 1982–89; Man. Dir. The Really Useful Group 1989–90, Chair. 1990–95, Dir. 1990–97; Dir. VCI PLC 1995–98; Chair. The Radio Partnership Ltd. 1996–; Chair. Caspian Publishing Ltd. 1996–; Dir. Galaxy Media Corp PLC 1997–; wrote, edited and devised numerous TV series 1956–82; mem. Bd. Royal Nat. Theatre 1977–94, City of London Sinfonia 1994–; Founder-Dir. Sagitta Productions 1968–82; Dir. Duke of York's Theatre 1979–82, Consolidated Productions (UK) Ltd. 1980–82, Friends' Provident Life Office 1982– (Chair. Friends' Provident Stewardship Cttee. of Reference 1985–); Chair. Theatre Investment Fund 1990–, Trans-World Communications PLC 1992–94, Sony Music Pace Partnership (Nat. Bowl) 1992–95, Rajar Ltd. 1992–, Friends' Provident Ethical Investment Trust plc 1992–; Trustee Pension and Life Assurance Plan RNT 1994–; Chair. and co-f. Local Radio Asscn. 1964; Chair. Asscn. of Ind. Local Radio Contractors 1973–75, 1980; f. Recidivists Anonymous Fellowship Trust 1962; mem. Films, TV & Video Advisory Cttee., British Council 1983–89, Royal Coll. of Music Centenary Devt. Fund 1982– (Chair. Media & Events Cttee. 1982–94), Royal Jubilee Trusts Industry & Commerce Liaison Cttee. 1986– (mem. Admin. Council of Trusts 1981–85); mem. Council Royal London Aid Soc. 1966–90, Fairbridge Drake Soc. 1981–, Intermediate Tech. Group 1982–85; mem. Council for Charitable Support 1989–92; Pres. TV & Radio Industries Club 1985–86, London Marriage Guidance Council 1983–90; Vice-Pres. Commonwealth Youth Exchange Council 1982–85, RNID 1988–; Chair. Trustees, Soundaround 1981–, Artsline 1983–; Chair. Festival Media Cttee. 1991–92; Trustee Japan Festival Educ. Trust 1992–; Trustee Venture Trust 1982–86; mem. Bd. Open Coll. 1987–89; Gov. English Nat. Ballet 1989–91, Performing Arts and Tech. School; Patron Music Space Trust 1990–; Chair. British American Arts Asscn. 1992–95, Sony Radio Awards 1992–98; Fellow, Vice-Pres. RTS 1986–89; Hon. F.R.C.M.; Hon. mem. B.A.F.T.A. *Leisure interests:* chess, photography, sculpture. *Address:* Heathcoat House, 20 Savile Row, London, W1X 1AE, England.

WHITTAM, Ronald, F.R.S.; British physiologist and university professor; b. 21 March 1925, Oldham, Lancs.; s. of Edward Whittam and May Whittam; m. Christine Patricia Margaret Lamb 1957; one s. one d.; ed. Council and Tech. School, Oldham, Univs. of Manchester, Sheffield, King's Coll., Univ. of Cambridge; served R.A.F. 1943–47; Beit Memorial Research Fellow, Physiological Lab., Univ. of Cambridge 1955–58; Lecturer in Biochem., Univ. of Oxford 1960–66; Prof. of Physiology, Univ. of Leicester 1966–83, Prof. Emer. 1983–, Research Worker 1983–86; Dean of Science Faculty 1979–82; Hon. Sec. Physiological Soc. 1969–74, Hon. mem. 1986; mem. cttees. Univ. Grants Council and MRC 1970–83; mem. Royal Soc. Educ. Cttee. 1974–83. *Publications:* numerous articles and reviews in scientific journals. *Leisure interests:* walking, theology. *Address:* 9 Guilford Road, Stoneygate, Leicester, LE2 2RD, England (Home). *Telephone:* (0116) 2707132 (Home).

WHITTAM SMITH, Andreas; British journalist; b. 13 June 1937; s. of Canon J. S. Smith; m. Valerie Catherine Sherry 1964; two s.; ed. Keble Coll., Oxford; with N. M. Rothschild 1960–62, Stock Exchange Gazette 1962–63, Financial Times 1963–64, The Times 1964–66; Deputy City Ed. The Telegraph 1966–69; City Ed. The Guardian 1969–70; Ed. Investors Chronicle, Stock Exchange Gazette and Dir. Throgmorton Publs. 1970–77; City Ed. Daily Telegraph 1977–85; Ed. The Independent 1986–94, Ed.-in-Chief Independent on Sunday 1991–94, Dir. Newspaper Publishing PLC 1986–, C.E.O. 1987–93, Chair. 1994–95; Chair., Publr. Notting Hill 1995–, Sir Winston Churchill Archive Trust 1995–; Pres. British Bd. of Film Classification 1998–; Vice-Pres. Nat. Council for One Parent Families 1982–86, 1991–; Wincott Award 1975; Journalist of the Year 1987; Hon. Fellow Keble Coll., Oxford, UMIST 1989; Hon. D.Litt. (St. Andrews, Salford) 1989. *Leisure interests:* music, history. *Address:* 31 Brunswick Gardens, London, W8 4AW, England.

WHITTLE, Peter, PH.D., F.R.S.; New Zealand academic; b. 27 Feb. 1927, Wellington; s. of Percy Whittle and Elsie (née Tregurtha) Whittle; m. Kathe Hildegard Blomquist 1951; three s. three d.; ed. Wellington Boys' Coll., Victoria Univ. Coll., N.Z., Uppsala Univ., Sweden; N.Z. Sr. Prin. Scientific Officer 1953–59; Lecturer in Math. Univ. of Cambridge 1959–61, Churchill Prof. of the Math. of Operational Research 1967–94, Prof. Emer. 1994–; Prof. of Math. Statistics, Univ. of Manchester 1961–67; Sr. Fellow Eng. and Science Research Council 1988–91; mem. Royal Soc. of N.Z. 1981; Hon. D. Sc. (Victoria Univ. of Wellington) 1987; Sylvester Medal (Royal Soc.) 1994. *Publications:* Hypothesis Testing in Time Series Analysis 1951, Prediction and Regulation 1963, Probability 1970, Optimisation under Constraints 1971, Optimisation over Time 1982, Systems in Stochastic Equilibrium 1986, Risk-sensitive Optimal Control 1990, Probability via Expectation 1992, Optimal control; basics and beyond 1995, Neural Nets and Chaotic Carriers 1998. *Address:* Statistical Laboratory, 16 Mill Lane, Cambridge, CB2 1SB (Office); 268 Queen Edith's Way, Cambridge, CB1 4NL, England (Home). *Telephone:* (01223) 245422 (Home). *Fax:* (01223) 337956.

WHITTLE, Stephen Charles, LL.B.; British broadcasting executive; b. 26 July 1945; s. of Charles William Whittle and Vera Lillian Whittle (née Moss); m. Claire Walmsley 1988; ed. St. Ignatius Coll., Stamford Hill, Univ. Coll. London; Asst. Ed. New Christian 1968–70; Communications Officer World Council of Churches, Geneva 1970–73; Ed. One World 1973–77, Asst. Head Communications Dept. 1975–77; Sr. Producer BBC Religious Programmes, Manchester 1977–82, Producer Newsnight 1982, Ed. Songs of Praise and Worship 1983–89, Head of Religious Programmes 1989–93, Chief Adviser Editorial Policy 1993–96; Dir. Broadcasting Standards Council 1996–97, Broadcasting Standards Comm. 1997–; Gov. European Inst. for the Media, Düsseldorf 1998; Freeman, City of London 1990. *Publications:* Tickling Mrs. Smith 1970. *Leisure interests:* cinema, theatre, music, reading, exercise. *Address:* Broadcasting Standards Commission, 5/8 The Sanctuary, London, SW1P 3JS, England. *Telephone:* 0171-233 0544. *Fax:* 0171-233 0397.

WHITWORTH-JONES, Anthony, C.A.; British arts administrator; b. 1 Sept. 1945, Bucks; s. of Henry Whitworth-Jones and Patience Martin; m. Camilla Barlow 1974; one d.; ed. Wellington Coll.; Admin. Dir. London Sinfonietta 1972–81; Admin. Glyndebourne Touring Opera 1981–89, Opera Man. Glyndebourne Festival Opera 1981–89, Gen. Dir. Glyndebourne 1989–98; Chair. Michael Tippett Musical Foundation 1998–. *Leisure interests:* contemporary art, jazz, golf, Greece. *Address:* 81 St. Augustine's Road, London, NW1 9RR, England. *Fax:* 0171-482 7017.

WIATR, Jerzy Józef, M.PH; Polish politician and scientist; b. 17 Sept 1931, Warsaw; m.; one s.; ed. Warsaw Univ.; scientific worker Warsaw Univ. 1951–59; Mil. Political Acad. 1959–65; Polish Acad. of Sciences (PAN) 1965–69; Warsaw Univ. 1969–, Dean of Social Sciences 1977–80; participant Round Table debates 1989; Deputy to Sejm (Parl.) 1991–97; mem. Cttee. for Nat. Defence and Cttee. for Constitutional Responsibility 1991–97; mem. Polish United Workers Party (PZPR) 1949–90; mem. Social Democracy of Polish Repub. (SdRP) 1990–; Vice Pres. Int. Political Science Asscn. 1979–82; Vice Pres. Int. Studies Asscn. 1986–; Minister of Educ. 1996–97. *Publications:* over 20 books and numerous articles on sociology. *Leisure interests:* tourism, books, chess. *Address:* ul. K. Sosnkowskiego 2 m. 1, 02-784 Warsaw, Poland.

WIBBLE, Anne, PH.D.; Swedish politician; b. 13 Oct. 1943, Stockholm; m. Jan Wibble; two d.; ed. Stockholm School of Econs., Univ. of Stanford, Calif., U.S.A.; teacher of Econs. Stockholm School of Econs. 1967–77; mem. Täby Municipal Council 1973–85, fmr. mem. Exec. Bd., Chair. Local Educ. Authority 1979–82; mem. State Industrial Subsidies Cttee., Exchange-Control Cttee. 1979–85, Income Tax Cttee. 1987–89; mem. Stockholm County Council 1977–, fmr. Head of Projects Regional Planning Office; Political Adviser Liberal Party, Co-ordination and Planning Secr., Cabinet Office 1980, Admin. Dir. Parl. Exec. 1983–86; M.P. for Stockholm 1985–; Minister of Finance 1991–94; Chair. Bd. Govs. EBRD 1993–94; Vice-Chair. Parl. Standing Cttee. on Finance; mem. Liberal Party Exec. 1986–, Nat. Bd. 1987.

WIBERG, Kenneth Berle, PH.D.; American professor of chemistry; b. 22 Sept. 1927, New York; s. of Halfdan Wiberg and Solveig Berle; m. Marguerite Louise Koch 1951; two s. one d.; ed. Mass. Inst. of Technology and Columbia Univ.; Instructor, Univ. of Washington 1950–52, Asst. Prof. 1952–55, Assoc. Prof. 1955–57, Prof. 1958–62; Prof., Yale Univ. 1962–68, Chair. Dept. of Chem. 1968–71, Whitehead Prof. of Chem. 1968–90, Eugene Higgins Prof. 1990–; Visiting Prof., Harvard Univ. 1957–58; A. P. Sloan Foundation Fellow 1958–62, J. S. Guggenheim Fellow 1961–62; mem. N.A.S., A.A.A.S.; California Section Award of American Chemical Soc. 1962, J. F. Norris Award of American Chemical Soc. 1973, Linus Pauling Award 1992. *Publications:* Laboratory Technique in Organic Chemistry 1960, Interpretation of NMR Spectra 1964, Physical Organic Chemistry 1964, Oxidation in Organic Chemistry (Ed.) 1965, Computer Programming for Chemists 1966, Sigma Molecular Orbital Theory (with Sinanoglu) 1970; approx. 150 articles in scientific journals. *Address:* Department of Chemistry, Yale University, 225 Prospect Street, New Haven, CT 06520 (Office); 160 Carmalt Road, Hamden, CT 06517, U.S.A. (Home). *Telephone:* (203) 436-2443 (Office).

WICKBOM, Sten, LL.B.; Swedish politician; b. 14 March 1931, Stockholm; s. of Börje Wickbom and Elsa Wickbom (née Quiding); m. Gunnel Persson 1991; one s. two d.; trainee legal asst. 1955–57; reporting clerk, Svea Court of Appeal 1958–62, asst. judge 1962–64, Assoc. Judge of Appeal 1964, Judge of Appeal 1969; legal adviser, Ministry of Labour and Housing 1964–67; Deputy Asst. Under-Sec., Ministry of Transport and Communications 1967–69, Under-Sec. for Legal Affairs, Ministry of Physical Planning and Local Govt. 1969–73, Ministry of Housing 1974; Dir.-Gen. and Head of Nat. Land Survey 1974–83; Minister of Justice 1983–87; Gov. Prov. of Kronoberg 1988–95; chair. of various govt. cttees. *Leisure interests:* music, literature. *Address:* Stojby, Västragård 2, 35592 Växjö, Sweden.

WICKER, Thomas Grey, A.B.; American journalist (retd.) and author; b. 18 June 1926, Hamlet, N.C.; s. of Delancey D. Wicker and Esta Cameron; m. 1st Neva J. McLean 1949 (divorced 1973); one s. one d.; m. 2nd Pamela A. Hill 1974; ed. Univ. of North Carolina; Exec. Dir. Southern Pines (N.C.) Chamber of Commerce 1948–49; Ed. Sandhill Citizen, Aberdeen, N.C. 1949; Man. Ed. The Robesonian, Lumberton, N.C. 1949–50; public information dir. N.C. Bd. of Public Welfare 1950–51; copy-ed. Winston-Salem (N.C.) Journal 1951–52, sports ed. 1954–55, Sunday feature ed. 1955–56, Washington corresp. 1957, editorial writer 1958–59; Nieman Fellow, Harvard Univ. 1957–58; assoc. ed. Nashville Tennessean 1959–60; mem. staff, Washington Bureau, New York Times 1960–71, chief of bureau 1964–68; Assoc. Ed. New York Times 1968–85; columnist 1966–91. *Publications:* novels (under pseudonym Paul Connolly): Get Out of Town 1951, Tears are for Angels 1952, So Fair, So Evil 1955; novels (under own name): The Kingpin 1953, The Devil Must 1957, The Judgment 1961, Facing the Lions 1963, Unto this Hour 1984, Donovan's Wife 1992, Easter Lilly 1998; non-fiction: Kennedy without Tears 1964, JFK and LBJ: The Influence of Personality Upon Politics 1968, A Time to Die 1975, On Press 1978, One of Us: Richard Nixon and the American Dream 1991, Tragic Failure: Racial Integration in America 1996; book chapters, contributions to nat. magazines. *Address:* 169 E. 80th Street, New York, NY 10021, U.S.A.

WICKERT, Erwin, PH.D.; German diplomatist (retd.) and author; b. 7 Jan. 1915, Bralitz; s. of Erwin Wickert and Hanna (née Dornbusch) Wickert; m. Ingeborg Weides 1939; two s. one d.; ed. Friedrich-Wilhelm Univ., Berlin, Dickinson Coll., Carlisle, Pa., and Heidelberg Univ.; attaché, German Foreign Office 1939; attaché, Shanghai 1940–41, Tokyo 1941–45; repatriated to Germany 1947 and lived as writer in Heidelberg; re-entered foreign service, Fed. Repub. of Germany 1955; Counsellor, German Embassy NATO, Paris 1955–60; Ministry of Foreign Affairs, Bonn 1960–68; Minister Plenipotentiary, London 1968–71; Amb. to Romania 1971–76, to People's Repub. of China 1976–80; mem. Mainz Acad. of Sciences and Literature; German Radio Play Award of War Blind 1952, Rheinland-Pfalz State Prize for Literature 1992; Grosses Bundesverdienstkreuz. *Publications:* Fata Morgana über den Strassen 1938, Du musst dein Leben ändern, 1949, Dramatische Tage in Hitlers Reich 1952, Der Auftrag des Himmels (novel) 1961, Der Purpur (novel) 1966, China von innen gesehen 1982, The Middle Kingdom 1983, Der verlassene Tempel (novel) 1985, Der Kaiser und der Grosshistoriker (seven radio plays) 1987, Der fremde Osten 1988, Die Frage des Tigers 1990, Mut und Uebermut (autobiog.) 1991, Sonate mit dem Paukenschlag 1993, Zappas oder die Wiederkehr des Herrn (novel) 1995, John Rabe—Der gute Deutsche von Nanking 1997. *Address:* Rheinhöhenweg 22, D-53424 Remagen-Oberwinter, Germany. *Telephone:* (02228) 1726. *Fax:* (02228) 7006.

WICKI-FINK, Agnes; Swiss actress; b. 14 Dec. 1919, Frankfurt-am-Main, Germany; d. of Ludwig Fink and Anna Agnes Klotz; m. Bernhard Wicki 1945; ed. Dr. Hoch's Konservatorium für Schauspielstudium, Frankfurt-am-Main; has appeared in Heidelberg, Leipzig, Munich, Zürich, Stuttgart, Hamburg, Vienna and Berlin; Maria Theater, Hamburg 1989–90; TV Kritikerpreis 1957; Goldene Bildschirm (twice), Grosses Bundesverdienstkreuz. *Address:* 8000 Munich 40, Weisgerberstrasse 2, Germany. *Telephone:* (89) 3612684 (Munich).

WICKRAMASINGHE, Nalin Chandra, M.A., PH.D., SC.D.; British professor of astronomy; b. 20 Jan. 1939, Colombo, Sri Lanka; s. of Percival H. Wickramasinghe and Theresa E. Wickramasinghe; m. Nelum Priyadarshini Pereira 1966; one s. two d.; ed. Royal Coll., Colombo, and Univs. of Colombo and Cambridge; Research Fellow, Jesus Coll., Cambridge 1963–66, Fellow 1967–73, Tutor 1970–73; Staff mem. Inst. of Theoretical Astronomy, Univ. of Cambridge 1968–73; Prof. and Head of Dept. of Applied Math. and Astronomy, Univ. Coll., Cardiff 1973–88; Prof. of Applied Math. and Astronomy, Univ. of Wales Coll. of Cardiff 1988–; Dir. Inst. of Fundamental Studies, Sri Lanka 1982–83; UNDP Consultant and Scientific Adviser to Pres. of Sri Lanka 1970–81; Visiting Prof., Univs. of Ceylon, Maryland, Arizona and Kyoto 1966–70, Univ. of W. Ontario 1974–76, Inst. of Space and Astronomical Science, Japan 1993, Univ. of W. Indies, Mona, Kingston, Jamaica 1994; Visiting Research Prof., Inst. of Fundamental Studies, Sri Lanka 1997–; Hon. Dr. (Soka Univ., Tokyo) 1996; Dag Hammarskjöld laureate in science 1986, Scholarly Achievement Award of Inst. of Oriental Philosophy, Japan 1989, Sahabdeen Award for Science 1996; Vidya Jyothi (Sri Lanka Nat. Honour) 1992. *Publications:* Interstellar Grains 1967, Light Scattering Functions for Small Particles with Applications in Astronomy 1973, The Cosmic Laboratory 1975; with Sir Fred Hoyle (q.v.): Life Cloud: The Origin of Life in the Universe 1978, Diseases from Space 1979, The Origin of Life 1980, Evolution from Space 1981, Space Travellers, The Bringers of Life, Is Life an Astronomical Phenomenon? 1982, Why Neo-Darwinism doesn't work 1982, Proofs that Life is Cosmic 1982, Fundamental Studies and the Future of Science 1984, From Grains to Bacteria 1984, Living Comets 1985, Archaeopteryx, the Primordial Bird: a case of fossil forgery 1986, Cosmic Life Force 1987, The Theory of Cosmic Grains 1991,

Our Place in the Cosmos: the Unfinished Revolution 1993; with F. D. Kahn and P. G. Mezger: Interstellar Matter 1972; with D. J. Morgan: Solid State Astrophysics 1976; with Daisaku Ikeda: 2000 A.D.—Emergent Perspectives 1992, Glimpses of Life, Time and Space 1994, Space and Eternal Life 1997. *Leisure interests:* photography, poetry. *Address:* School of Mathematics, University of Wales College of Cardiff, Senghenydd Road, Cardiff, CF2 4AG, Wales. *Telephone:* (01222) 752146. *Fax:* (01222) 753173.

WICKREMESINGHE, Ranil, LL.B.; Sri Lankan politician and lawyer; b. 24 March 1949, Colombo; s. of Esmond Wickremesinghe; m. Maithree Wickremesinghe 1995; ed. Royal Coll. Colombo, Univ. of Colombo and Sri Lanka Law Coll.; attorney-at-law, Supreme Court; elected mem. Parl. 1977, 1989; Leader of House 1989–93; Deputy Minister of Foreign Affairs 1977–79; Minister of Youth Affairs and Employment 1978–89, of Educ. 1980–89, of Industries 1989–90, of Industries, Science and Tech. 1990–94; Prime Minister 1993–94; Leader Opposition, Leader United Nat. Party 1994–. *Address:* Parliament Building, Sri Jayewardanapura, Kotte, Sri Lanka. *Telephone:* 864253. *Fax:* 864257.

WICKS, Sir Nigel Leonard, G.C.B., C.V.O., C.B.E., M.A.; British civil servant; b. 16 June 1940; s. of late Leonard Charles Wicks and Beatrice Irene Wicks; m. Jennifer Mary Coveney 1969; three s.; ed. Beckenham and Penge Grammar School, Portsmouth Coll. of Tech., Univ. of Cambridge, Univ. of London; British Petroleum 1958–68; served H.M. Treasury 1968–75, 1978–83, Second Perm Sec. (Finance) 1989–; Pvt. Sec. to Prime Minister 1975–78; mem. BNOC Bd. 1980–82; Econ. Minister Embassy, Washington and U.K.; Exec. Dir. IMF and IBRD 1983–85; Prin. Pvt. Sec. to Prime Minister 1985–88; Pres. Monetary Cttee. of EC 1993; fmr. Chair. EU Econ. and Finance Cttee. –1999. *Address:* H.M. Treasury, Parliament Street, London, SW1P 3AG, England. *Telephone:* 0171-270 3000.

WIDDECOMBE, Rt. Hon. Ann (Noreen), P.C., M.A.; British politician; b. 4 Oct. 1947; d. of James Murray Widdecombe; ed. La Sainte Union Convent, Bath, Univ. of Birmingham, Lady Margaret Hall Oxford; with Marketing Dept. Unilever 1973–75; Sr. Admin. Univ. of London 1975–87; contested Burnley 1979, Plymouth Devonport 1983; M.P. for Maidstone 1987–97, Maidstone and The Weald 1997–; Parl. Pvt. Sec. to Tristan Garel-Jones, M.P. 1990; Parl. Under-Sec. State Dept. of Social Security 1990–93, Dept. of Employment 1993–94; Minister for Employment 1994–95, Home Office 1995–97; Shadow Health Minister 1997–; Conservative. *Publication:* Layman's Guide to Defence 1984. *Leisure interests:* reading, researching Charles II's escape. *Address:* 9 Tamar House, Kennington Lane, London, SE11 4X4; Kloof Cottage, Sutton Valence, Maidstone, Kent, England. *Telephone:* 0171-735 5192; (01622) 843868.

WIDDRINGTON, Peter Nigel Tinling, B.A., LL.D., M.B.A.; Canadian business executive; b. 2 June 1930, Toronto; s. of Gerard Widdrington and Margery (MacDonald) Widdrington; m. Betty Ann Lawrence 1956; two d.; ed. Pickering Coll., Newmarket, Ont., Queen's Univ. and Harvard Business School; Asst. Regional Man. Labatt's Ontario Breweries Ltd. 1957, Regional Man. 1958; Gen. Man. Kiewel and Pelissiers, Winnipeg 1961; Gen. Man. Labatt's Manitoba Breweries Ltd. 1962, Labatt's B.C. Breweries Ltd. 1965; Pres. Lucky Breweries Inc., San Francisco 1968; Vice-Pres. Corporate Devt., John Labatt Ltd. 1971, Sr. Vice-Pres. 1973, Pres. 1973–87, Chair. and C.E.O. 1987–89, Chair. 1989–91; Chair. and Dir. Laidlaw Inc., Talisman Energy Inc.; Pres., C.E.O. and Dir. Cuddy Int. Corpn. 1996–; Chair. Talisman Energy Inc. 1996–; Dir. Canadian Imperial Bank of Commerce, CEC Resources Ltd., Dialysis Centers of America Inc., SNC-Lavalin Group Inc.; mem. Advisory Bd. Dana Canada, St. Edmund Hall, Oxford Univ., Olympic Trust of Canada, Richard Ivey School of Business, Univ. of Western Ont.; Hon. LL.D. (Western Ont.). *Address:* 252 Pall Mall Street, Suite 303, London, Ont., N6A 5P6; 1 Doncaster Ave, London, Ont. N6G 2A1, Canada.

WIDMARK, Richard, B.A.; American actor; b. 26 Dec. 1914, Sunrise, Minn.; s. of Carl H. Widmark and Ethel Barr; m. Ora Jean Hazlewood 1942; one d.; ed. Lake Forest Coll.; Drama instructor at Lake Forest Coll. 1936–38; radio actor for New York networks 1938–47; Pres. Heath Productions 1955–; Vice-Pres. Widmark Cattle Enterprises 1957–; Broadway appearances include Kiss and Tell 1943, Get Away Old Man 1943, Trio 1944, Kiss Them For Me 1944, Dunnigan's Daughter 1945, Dream Girl 1946. *Films include:* Kiss of Death 1947, Road House 1948, Yellow Sky 1949, Slattery's Hurricane 1949, Night and the City 1950, No Way Out 1950, Halls of Montezuma 1950, Red Skies of Montana 1950, Full House 1952, Destination Gobi 1953, Hell and High Water 1954, Garden of Evil 1954, Broken Lance 1954, Backlash 1956, St. Joan 1957, Tunnel of Love 1958, The Alamo 1960, Secret Ways 1961, Judgement at Nuremberg 1961, How the West Was Won 1963, Madigan 1969, The Moonshine War 1970, When Legends Die 1972, Murder on the Orient Express 1974, To the Devil a Daughter 1975, The Sellout 1976, The Domino Principle 1976, Roller Coaster 1976, The Swarm 1977, Coma 1978, Bear Island 1979, All God's Children 1980, Who Dares Wins 1982, The Final Option 1983, Against All Odds 1984, True Colours 1990; television includes Vanished 1970, and the series Madigan 1972.

WIDNALL, Sheila Evans, PH.D.; American professor of aeronautics and astronautics; b. 13 July 1938; d. of Rolland Evans and Genevieve Krause; m. William Widnall 1960; one s. one d.; ed. Mass. Inst. of Tech.; Asst. Prof. M.I.T. 1964–70, Assoc. Prof. 1970–74, Prof. of Aeronautics and Astronautics 1974–93, 1997–, Assoc. Provost 1992–93; Dir. Univ. Research, U.S. Dept. of Transport, Washington, D.C. 1974–75; mem. Bd. Dirs. Chemfab Inc., Bennington, Vt., Aerospace Corpn., L.A. and Draper Labs. Cambridge; Trustee, Carnegie Corpn. 1984–92; Sec. of U.S. Air Force 1993–98; Fellow, A.A.A.S., American Inst. of Aeronautics and Astronautics, American Physics Soc.; mem. American Acad. of Arts and Sciences; numerous hon. degrees. *Publications:* articles in professional journals. *Address:* Massachusetts Institute of Technology, 77 Massachusetts Avenue, Building 4-104, Cambridge, MA 02139, U.S.A.

WIDOM, Benjamin, PH.D.; American professor of chemistry; b. 13 Oct. 1927, Newark, N.J.; s. of Morris Widom and Rebecca Hertz Widom; m. Joanne McCurdy 1953; two s. one d.; ed. Stuyvesant High School, New York and Columbia and Cornell Univs.; Research Assoc., Univ. of N.C. 1952–54; Instructor in Chem., Cornell Univ. 1954–55, Asst. Prof. 1955–59, Assoc. Prof. 1959–63, Prof. 1963–, Goldwin Smith Prof. 1983–; van der Waals Prof., Univ. of Amsterdam 1972; Visiting Prof. of Chem., Harvard Univ. 1975; IBM Visiting Prof. of Theoretical Chem., Oxford Univ. 1978; Lorentz Prof., Leiden Univ. 1985; Visiting Prof., Katholieke Univ., Leuven 1988, Université d'Aix Marseille III 1995; Fellow American Acad. of Arts and Sciences, New York Acad. of Sciences; mem. N.A.S., American Philosophical Soc.; Boris Pregel Award (New York Acad. of Sciences), Langmuir Award (American Chemical Soc.), Dickson Prize for Science (Carnegie-Mellon Univ.), Hildebrand Award (American Chemical Soc.), Hirschfelder Prize in Theoretical Chem. (Univ. of Wis.), Bakhuis Roozeboom Medal (Royal Netherlands Acad. of Arts and Sciences), Onsager Medal (Univ. of Trondheim), Boltzmann Medal (IUPAP Comm. on Statistical Physics), Award in Theoretical Chem. (American Chemical Soc.). *Publication:* Molecular Theory of Capillarity (with J. S. Rowlinson) 1982. *Address:* Department of Chemistry, Baker Laboratory, Cornell University, Ithaca, NY 14853, U.S.A. *Telephone:* (607) 255-3363. *Fax:* (607) 255-4137.

WIECK, Hans-Georg, D.PHIL.; German diplomatist; b. 28 March 1928, Hamburg; s. of late John Wieck and Elisabeth Wieck (née Hall); m. Anneliese Dietz 1958 (died 1977); three s. one d.; ed. Univ. of Hamburg; entered Foreign Service, Fed. Repub. of Germany 1954, assignments in Bonn (Soviet Affairs), New York (Fed. German Observer Mission to UN), Washington, D.C. (Fed. German Embassy), Bonn (Berlin Affairs); Chef de Cabinet to Foreign Minister Schroeder 1966, to Defence Minister Schroeder 1966–69; Dir. Policy Planning Staff, Fed. Ministry of Defence, Bonn 1970–74; Amb. to Iran 1974–77, to U.S.S.R. 1977–80, to India 1990–93; Amb. and Perm. Rep. to NATO 1980–85; Pres. Fed. German Intelligence System 1985–90; Head O.S.C.E. Advisory and Monitoring Group in Belarus 1998–99; Chair. Judaeo-German Assen.. *Publications:* The Establishment of the Christian Democratic Union in Germany 1953, The Christian Democrats and the Liberals in Southern Germany 1958. *Leisure interests:* sports, hunting, history, architecture. *Address:* Koenigsallee 5, D 14193, Berlin, Germany. *Telephone:* (30) 8909 6748. *Fax:* (30) 8909 6675.

WIEDEKING, Wendelin; German business executive; b. 28 Aug. 1952, Ahlen; m.; fmrly. engineer Porsche; left Porsche 1988; mem. Bd. Porsche 1991–; Chair. 1994–. *Address:* Porsche AG, Porschestrasse 42, 70435 Stuttgart-Zuffenhausen, Germany. *Telephone:* 7-11-9115805. *Fax:* 7-11-9116375.

WIEDEMANN, Josef; German architect; b. 15 Oct. 1910, Munich; s. of Thomas Wiedemann and Maria (née Anwald) Wiedemann; m. Hilma Bittorf 1939; one d.; ed. Tech. Univ., Munich; worked with Prof. Roderich Fick 1935–42; freelance architect 1946–; Prof. of Design, Conservation and Sacred Bldg., Dept. of Architecture, Tech. Univ., Munich 1955–76, now Prof. Emer.; has lectured on conservation, ornament, architecture, etc. in Munich, Hamburg, Vienna, New York and elsewhere; mem. Bayerische Akad. der Schönen Künste; corresp. mem. Acad. d'Architecture, Paris; Komturkreuz, St.-Sylvester Orden; BDA Prize 1975; work includes reconstruction work and new shops, offices, homes, churches in Munich and other towns and cities, including Glyptothek, Munich, Karmel Hlg. Blut, Dachau, Allianz Head Office, Munich, Verbandsschule and Maria am Wege church, Windach, St. Ignatius, Munich, St. Stephan, Diessen/A. *Publications:* Der Friedhof m.O. Valentien 1963, Ornament heute? 1974, Antoni Gaudi 1974, Sakralbau in "München und seine Bauten" 1983, Musik und Architektur 1986, Neuer Kirchenbau in 'Wörterbuch der Kunst'. *Leisure interests:* theory and philosophy of architecture. *Address:* Im Eichgehölz 11, 80997 Munich, Germany. *Telephone:* 089/811 41 53.

WIEHAHN, Nicholas E., LL.D.; South African university professor and consultant; b. 29 April 1929, Mafeking (now Mafikeng); s. of Johannes Wiehahn and Anna C. Wiehahn; m. Huiberdina J. Verhage 1956; two s.; ed. Univ. of O.F.S., Univ. of S. Africa; research work in Univs. of Hamburg, Cologne, Heidelberg, Munich and London; research visits to labour insts. and univs. in Europe, Israel, Canada, U.S.A. and Japan; Advocate, Supreme Court of S.A. and High Court of Lesotho; Prof. in Labour and Industrial Law at various univs.; Chair. Transkei Nat. Manpower Comm.; Prof. Extra-Ordinarius, Univ. of S.A. 1980–, Dir. Inst. of Labour Relations 1976–77; Prof. Siemens Chair of Industrial Relations, School of Business Leadership, Univ. of S.A., Pretoria, Dir. Oct. 1984–; mem. Council, Univ. of Port Elizabeth 1973–75, Free State Univ. 1980–; Chair. Council, Univ. of Zululand 1981–90; Dir. Bureau for Int. Labour Affairs, Dept. of Manpower 1977–78, Ed.-in-Chief EMPACT 1977–78, Labour Adviser to Minister of Manpower 1977–79; mem. Prime Minister's Econ. Advisory Council 1977; Pres. Industrial Court of S.A. 1979–80, Industrial Court of KwaNdebele; Chair. Comm. of Inquiry into Labour Legis. (Wiehahn Comm.) 1977–80, into Labour Matters (Namibia) 1987–88; Chair. Labour Council, S.A. Transport Services 1988; Chair. Wiehahn Comm., Transkei 1989, KwaNdebele 1990, Royal Comm. of Inquiry, Swaziland; Chair. Lotteries and Gambling Bd.; mem. various govt. comms., advisory cttees., etc.; other public and educational appointments; Chair. and dir. of several public and pvt. cos. 1981–; three hon. doctorates; recipient of several awards and bursaries; Order for Meritorious Service (Gold Class) 1993. *Publications:* articles on labour law and industrial relations in periodicals, commentaries and other publs.; Change in South Africa 1983. *Leisure interests:* reading, gardening. *Address:* P.O. Box 5862, Pretoria 0001, South Africa. *Telephone:* (012) 342-4601/4 (Office); 474438 (Home). *Fax:* (012) 342-4609 (Office).

WIELAND, Joyce, O.C.; Canadian artist and film maker; b. 30 June 1931, Toronto; ed. Cen. Tech. School; solo exhbns. at Isaacs Gallery Toronto 1960, 1963, 1967, 1972, 1974, 1981, 1983, 1987, Vancouver Art Gallery 1968, Museum of Modern Art, New York 1971, Cannes Film Festival 1976, Canadian Film Arts Centre, Hong Kong 1981, Nat. Gallery of Canada 1978, Yajima Gallery, Montreal 1982; has participated in several group exhbns. including Canadian Pavilion at Expo 67, Montreal 1967; maj. travelling retrospective, Art Gallery of Ont., Toronto 1981–82, 1987–88, Canada House, London 1988–89; film The Far Shore received three Canadian awards 1977; Retrospective Films of Joyce Wieland, Whitney Museum, New York 1973, San Francisco Art Inst. 1985, Art Gallery of Ontario (touring) 1987–88, Nat. Film Theatre, London 1988, Georges Pompidou Centre 1989; selection of films screened at Ciné-Club de Saint-Charles, Univ. of Paris, Sorbonne 1986; Artists on Fire film documentary 1987; Artist in Residence, Univ. of Toronto 1988–89; two awards for Rat Life and Diet in N. America, Third Ind. Filmmakers Festival, New York 1969, Award for A and B in Ontario, Ann Arbor Film Festival 1986, YWCA Woman of Distinction Award 1987. *Publications:* True Patriot Love 1971, Joyce Wieland 1987, Joyce Wieland: Quilts, Paintings and Works of Paper 1988. *Address:* 497 Queen Street East, Toronto, Ont. M5A 1V1; 179 John Street, Toronto, Ont. M5T 1X4, Canada. *Telephone:* (416) 366-2986.

WIELGUS, Stanisław; Polish ecclesiastic and professor of history of philosophy; b. 23 April 1939, Wierzchowiska; ed. Catholic Univ. of Lublin, Univ. of Munich; ordained Priest 1962; curate and parish catechist 1962–69; professor, Catholic Univ. of Lublin 1969–, Pro-rector 1988–92, Rector 1989–98; head Dept. of the History of Philosophy in Poland, head Interdisciplinary Centre of the History of Medieval Culture; Head Catholic Univ. of Lublin (KUL) Catholic Encyclopaedia Editing Offices; Vice-Pres. Conf. of Polish Univ. of Rectors 1990–93; del. Extraordinary Synod of European Bishops, Rome 1991; canon Lublin Cathedral Chapter; leader Coll. of Rectors, Lublin Region 1992–93; Chair. Friends of KUL Society; mem. KUL Science Soc. (Gen. Sec. 1985–88), Acad. Council of the John Paul Second Inst., mem. numerous socs.; Award of the Minister of Nat. Educ. *Publications:* Quaestiones Nicolai Peripatetici 1973, Benedykta Hessego Quaestiones super octo libros Physicorum Aristotelis 1983, Bible Research in Ancient Times and in the Middle Ages 1990, Foreign Biblical Literature in Medieval Poland 1990, Mediaeval Biblical Literature in the Polish Language 1991, Mediaeval Polish Bible Studies in the Latin Language 1992, From Research into the Middle Ages 1995. *Leisure interests:* factual literature, memoirs, film. *Address:* Al. Racławickie 14, skr. poczt. 129, 20-950 Lublin, Poland.

WIELICKI, Krzysztof; Polish mountaineer and businessman; b. 5 Jan. 1950, Szklarka Przygodzka; m.; one s. two d.; ed. Tech. Univ. of Wrocław; owner of four commercial cos. (distribution of alpine and outdoor equipment and garments) and mountain agencies; began climbing 1970; joined 27 high mountain expeditions including Dolomites, Alps, Caucasus, Pamir, Hindukush, Karakoram and Himalayas; leader of 11 expeditions; the fifth man in the world to climb all 8,000 m. peaks; first person to climb in winter: Mount Everest (with partner Leszek Cichy) 1980, Kanchenjunga 1986, Lhotse (solo) 1988. *Publications:* Talks about Everest (co-author) 1980, The Crown of Himalayas 1997. *Leisure interest:* travelling. *Address:* ul. A. Frycza Modrzewskiego 21, 43-100 Tychy, Poland. *Telephone:* (32) 227 15 00.

WIELOWIEYSKI, Andrzej, LL.M.; Polish politician, economist and publicist; b. 16 Dec. 1927, Warsaw; m.; one s. six d.; ed. Jagellonian Univ., Cracow; trainee, Radomsko Forest Inspectorate 1942–44; Head Foreign Dept. Bratnia Pomoc students' org. Jagellonian Univ., Cracow 1945–48; mem. Wici Rural Youth Union (ZMW Wici) 1945–48; subsequently councillor and inspector in Ministry of Finance 1948–52; Ed., Słowo Powszechne, Warsaw 1948; inspector, Head Office of Workers' Housing Estates Enterprise Warsaw-South, subsequently Warsaw-Śródmieście 1952–55; inspector, Head Urban Devt. Dept., Municipal Comm. of Econ. Planning, Warsaw 1956–62; Head of Section Więź, Warsaw 1961–80; lecturer, Doświadczenie i Przyszłość (Experience and the Future) Conversatorium, Warsaw 1978–82; Ed. Królowa Apostołów, Warsaw 1982–84, Gość Niedzielny, Katowice 1982–90; mem. Solidarity Ind. Self-governing Trade Union 1980–, adviser to Nat. Comm. of Solidarity 1980–81; Head of Social and Labour Study Centre attached to Nat. Comm. of Solidarity, Warsaw 1981; adviser to Nat. Executive Comm. of Solidarity 1987–89; mem. Civic Cttee. attached to Lech Wałęsa, Chair. of Solidarity 1987–90; participant Round Table plenary debates, Co-Chair. group for economy and social policy Feb.–April 1989; Senator 1989–91, Vice-Marshal of the Senate 1989–91; Chair. Civic Parl. Club of Senate 1989–90; Deputy to Sejm (Parl.) 1991–, mem. Parl. Comm. Foreign Affairs 1991–; Polish del. and Vice-Pres. Council of Europe Parl. Ass. 1992–; mem. Freedom Union 1994–; mem. Pax Romana Catholic Intelligentsia Int. Fed., mem. of Council 1979–83; mem. of European Council 1987–89; co-f. Int. Fed. of Family Life Promotion 1979–; Silver Cross of Merit with Swords, Cross of Valour, Partisan Cross, Cross of Home Army (AK), Victory and Freedom Medal. *Publications:* Przed trzecim przyspieszeniem 1969, Przed nami małżeństwo 1972, over 300 articles on politics, religion, educ. and history. *Leisure interests:* gardening, skiing, yachting, historical and detective stories. *Address:* Sejm RP, ul. Wiejska 4/6/8, 00-902 Warsaw (Office); ul. Kłodzka 59, 04-913 Warsaw-Falenica, Poland (Home). *Telephone:* (22) 694 21 35 (Office); (22) 812 91 95 (Home).

WIESCHAUS, Eric F., PH.D.; American molecular biologist; b. 8 June 1947, South Bend, Ind.; s. of Leroy Joseph Wieschaus and Marcella Carner Wieschaus; m. Trudi Schupbach 1982; three d.; ed. Univ. of Notre Dame, Yale Univ.; Research Fellow Zoological Inst., Univ. of Zurich 1975–78; Group Leader European Molecular Biology Lab., Germany 1978–81; Asst. Prof. then Assoc. Prof., Princeton Univ. 1981–87, Prof. of Biology 1987–; Visiting Researcher Center for Pathobiology, Univ. of Calif., Irvine 1977; Fellow Laboratoire de Génétique Moléculaire, France, A.A.A.S.; mem. Damon Runyon-Walter Winchell Cancer Fund 1987–92, N.A.S.; shared Nobel Prize for Medicine and Physiology 1995. *Publications:* numerous articles. *Address:* Department of Molecular Biology, Princeton University, Princeton, N.J. 08544, U.S.A.

WIESEL, Elie; American author; b. 30 Sept. 1928, Sighet, Romania; s. of Shlomo Wiesel and Sarah (Feig) Wiesel; m. Marion E. Wiesel 1969; one s.; ed. Sorbonne, Paris; naturalized U.S. citizen 1963; Distinguished Prof. Coll. of City of New York 1972–76; Andrew Mellon Prof. in Humanities, Boston Univ. 1976–, Prof. of Philosophy 1988–; Founder The Elie Wiesel Foundation for Humanity 1986; mem. Bd. for Fund for the Holocaust 1997–; Founding Pres. Universal Acad. of Cultures, Paris 1993; mem. numerous bds. of dirs., trustees, govs. and advisers including Int. Rescue Cttee., American Jewish World Service, Yad Vashem, Mutual of America, AmeriCares, U.S. Cttee. for Refugees; mem. PEN, The Authors' Guild, Foreign Press Asscn., Writers and Artists for Peace in the Middle East, Council of Foreign Relations, American Acad. of Arts and Sciences, American Acad. of Arts and Letters (Dept. of Literature), Jewish Acad. of Arts and Sciences, European Acad. of Arts, Sciences and Humanities, Royal Norwegian Soc. of Sciences and Letters; recipient of numerous hon. degrees; Prix Rivarol 1964, Jewish Heritage Award 1965, Remembrance Award 1965, Prix Médicis 1968, Prix Bordin (Acad. Française) 1972, Eleanor Roosevelt Memorial Award 1972, American Liberties Medallion, American Jewish Comm. 1972, Martin Luther King Jr. Award (Coll. of City of New York) 1973, Faculty Distinguished Scholar Award, Hofstra Univ. 1973–74, Congressional Gold Medal of Achievement 1985, Nobel Peace Prize 1986, Medal of Liberty Award 1986, Ellis Island Medal of Honor 1992, Presidential Medal of Freedom 1993, and numerous other awards; Grand Officer, Légion d'honneur. *Publications:* Night 1960, Dawn 1961, The Accident 1962, The Town Beyond the Wall 1964, The Gates of the Forest 1966, The Jews of Silence 1966, Legends of Our Time 1968, A Beggar in Jerusalem 1970, One Generation After 1971, Souls on Fire 1972, The Oath 1973, Ani Maamin, Cantata 1973, Zalmen or the Madness of God (play) 1975, Messengers of God 1966, A Jew Today 1978, Four Hasidic Masters 1978, The Trial of God 1979, Le Testament d'un Poète Juif Assassiné 1980 (Prix Livre-Inter 1980, Prix des Bibliothéquaires 1981), The Testament 1980, Images from the Bible 1980, Five Biblical Portraits 1981, Somewhere a Master: Further Tales of the Hasidic Master 1982, Paroles d'étranger 1982, The Golem 1983, The Fifth Son (Grand Prix de la Littérature, Paris) 1985, Signes d'exode 1985, Against Silence 1985, A Song for Hope 1987, Job ou Dieu dans la tempête (with Josy Eisenberg) 1987, The Nobel Address 1987, Twilight (novel) 1988, The Six Days of Destruction (with Albert Friedlander) 1988, L'Oublie 1989, Silences et mémoire d'hommes 1989, From the Kingdom of Memory, Reminiscences (essays) 1990, Evil and Exile 1990, A Journey of Faith 1990, Sages and Dreamers 1991, Célébration Talmudique 1991, The Forgotten 1992, A Passover Haggadah 1993, All Rivers Run to the Sea (Memoirs, Vol.I) 1995, Et la mer n'est pas remplie (Memoirs, Vol.II) 1996, Célébration prophétique 1998. *Address:* Boston University, 745 Commonwealth Avenue, Boston, MA 02215, U.S.A. *Telephone:* (617) 353-4566.

WIESEL, Torsten N., M.D.; Swedish university president and professor of neurobiology; b. 3 June 1924, Uppsala, Sweden; ed. Karolinska Inst. Stockholm; Instr. Karolinska Inst. 1954–55; Asst. Karolinska Hosp. 1954–55; Fellow in Ophthalmology, Johns Hopkins Univ. Medical School, Baltimore, Md. 1955–58, Asst. Prof. of Ophthalmic Physiology 1958–59; Assoc. in Neurophysiology/Neuropharmacology, Harvard Medical School, Boston 1959–60, Asst. Prof. 1960–64, Asst. Prof. Dept. of Psychiatry 1964–67, Prof. of Physiology 1967–68, Prof. of Neurobiology 1968–74, Chair. Dept. of Neurobiology 1973–82, Robert Winthrop Prof. of Neurobiology 1974–83; Vincent & Brooke Astor Prof. and Head, Lab. of Neurobiology, The Rockefeller Univ. New York 1983–; Pres. The Rockefeller Univ. 1992–; mem. American Physiology Soc., American Acad. of Arts and Sciences, A.A.A.S., N.A.S., etc.; Foreign mem. Royal Soc.; Nobel Prize for Medicine 1981; numerous honours and awards. *Publications:* over 80 articles in medical journals. *Address:* The Rockefeller University, 1230 York Avenue, New York, NY 10021, U.S.A.

WIESENTHAL, Simon; Austrian investigator of Nazi crimes and fmr. architect; b. 31 Dec. 1908, Buczacz, Poland (now Buchach); s. of Hans

Wiesenthal; m. Cyla Müller 1936; one d.; ed. architectural studies in Prague and Lvov (Lemberg); practised architecture until World War II; prisoner in Nazi concentration camps 1941–43, 1944–45; active since the war in searching for Nazi criminals, assisting Jewish victims of Nazi regime and in Jewish civic affairs; Head of Jewish Historical Documentation Centre, Linz, Austria 1947–54; Dir. Jewish Documentation Centre, Vienna 1961–; Chair. Asscn. of Jews Persecuted by the Nazi Regime; Diploma of Honour, Int. Fed. of Resistance Movements, Vienna; Vice-Pres. Int. Union of Resistance and Deportation; Hon. mem. Dutch Resistance, Hon. mem. Danish Asscn. of Freedom Fighters; 16 hon. degrees; many awards and honours, including Medal of Freedom (Netherlands), Congressional Gold Medal (U.S.A.) 1980, Dutch Medal for Freedom, Medal for Freedom of Luxembourg, Jean-Moulin-Médaille of the French Resistance, Kaj-Munk-Medal, Denmark, Justice Louis Brandeis Award of Zionist Org. in U.S.A., Jerusalem Medal, F.D. Roosevelt Freedom from Fear Medal 1991, Nat. Hero Award (New York) 1991, Erasmus Prize 1992; Great Medal of Merit, Fed. Repub. of Germany, Chevalier, Légion d'honneur, Commdr. of Oranje-Nassau (Netherlands), Commendatore della Repubblica Italiana, Austrian Cross of Honour of the Sciences and Arts, Vienna. *Publications:* KZ Mauthausen 1946, Head Mufti, Agent of the Axis 1947, I Hunted Eichmann 1961, Limitation 1964, The Murderers Among Us 1967, Sails of Hope 1973, The Case of Krystyna Jaworska 1975, Max and Helen 1982, Every Day Remembrance Day—A Chronicle of Jewish Martyrdom 1986, Justice not Vengeance 1989, Sunflower 1997. *Leisure interest:* philately. *Address:* Jewish Documentation Centre, Salztorgasse 6, 1010 Vienna, Austria. *Telephone:* (01) 533-91-31. *Fax:* (01) 535-03-97.

WIGGINS, David, M.A., F.B.A.; British university teacher; b. 8 March 1933, London; s. of Norman Wiggins and Diana Wiggins (née Priestley); m. Jennifer Hornsby 1980 (separated 1987); one s.; ed. St. Paul's School and Brasenose Coll., Oxford; Asst. Prin. Colonial Office 1957–58; Jane Eliza Procter Visiting Fellow, Princeton Univ. 1958–59; Lecturer, New Coll., Oxford 1959, Fellow and Lecturer 1960–67; Prof. of Philosophy, Bedford Coll., London 1967–78; Fellow and Praelector in Philosophy, Univ. Coll., Oxford 1981–89; Prof. of Philosophy, Birkbeck Coll., London 1989–94; Wykeham Prof. of Logic, New Coll., Oxford Univ. 1994–; visiting appts. Stanford Univ. 1964, 1965, Harvard Univ. 1968, 1972, All Souls Coll., Oxford 1973, Princeton Univ. 1980, Univ. Coll., Oxford 1989–; Fellow, Center for Advanced Study in Behavioral Sciences, Stanford 1985–86; mem. Independent Comm. on Transport 1973–74, Cen. Transport Consultative Cttee.; Chair. Transport Users' Consultative Cttee. for South-East 1977–79; Foreign Hon. mem. American Acad. of Arts and Sciences 1992. *Publications:* Identity and Spatio Temporal Continuity 1967, Truth, Invention and the Meaning of Life 1978, Sameness and Substance 1980, Needs, Values, Truth 1987; articles in learned journals. *Address:* New College, Oxford, England.

WIGGINS, James Russell; American newspaperman; b. 4 Dec. 1903, Luverne, Minn.; s. of James Wiggins and Edith Binford; m. Mabel E. Preston 1923 (died 1990); two s. (two deceased) two d. (one deceased); ed. Luverne High School, and USAF Air Intelligence School; with Rock County Star 1922–30; Editorial Writer St. Paul Dispatch and St. Paul Pioneer Press 1930–33, Washington Corresp. 1933–38, Man. Ed. 1938–42, 1945–46; U.S. Army Air Force 1942–45; Asst. Publr. New York Times 1946–47; Man. Ed. The Washington Post 1947–55, Vice-Pres. 1953–60, Exec. Ed. 1955–60, Ed. and Exec. Vice-Pres. 1960–68; Perm. Rep. to UN 1968–69; Ed., Publr. Ellsworth American 1969–91, Ed. 1989–; Elijah Lovejoy Award 1954, John Zenger Award 1957, Golden Key Award 1960, Eugene Cervi Award 1987. *Publication:* Freedom or Secrecy 1956. *Address:* Box 509, 30 Water Street, Ellsworth, ME 04605 (Office); HCR 64 Box 506, Carlton Cove, Brooklin, ME 04616-9709, U.S.A. (Home).

WIGHTMAN, Arthur Strong, PH.D.; American professor of mathematics and physics; b. 30 March 1922, Rochester, N.Y.; s. of Eugene Pinckney Wightman and Edith Stephenson Wightman; m. 1st Anna-Greta Larsson 1945 (died 1976); one d.; m. 2nd Ludmila Popova 1977; ed. Yale Coll. and Princeton Univ.; Instructor in Physics, Yale Univ. 1943–44; U.S. Navy 1944–46; Instructor in Physics, Princeton Univ. 1949, Asst. Prof., Assoc. Prof., Prof. of Math. Physics, 1960–, Thomas D. Jones Prof. of Math. Physics 1971–92, Prof. Emer. 1992–; Visiting Prof. Sorbonne, Paris 1957, Ecole Polytechnique, Palaiseau 1977–78; Fellow American Acad. of Arts and Sciences, Royal Society of Arts; mem. N.A.S., American Math. Soc., American Physical Soc.; Dannie Heinemann Prize in Mathematical Physics 1969; D.Sc. h.c. (ETH, Zürich) 1969, (Göttingen) 1987. *Publication:* PCT, Spin and Statistics and All That (with R. F. Streater) 1964. *Leisure interests:* art, music, tennis. *Address:* Joseph Henry Laboratories of Physics, Princeton University, Box 708, Princeton, NJ 08544; 16 Balsam Lane, Princeton, NJ 08540, U.S.A. (Home). *Telephone:* (609) 258-5835 (Office).

WIGLEY, Dafydd, P.C., B.SC.; Welsh politician; b. 1 April 1943, Derby; s. of Elfyn Edward Wigley and Myfanwy (née Batterbee) Wigley; m. Elinor Bennett Owen 1967; three s. (two deceased) one d.; ed. Sir Hugh Owen School, Caernarfon, Rydal School, Colwyn Bay, Victoria Univ. of Manchester; Econ. Analyst, Ford Motor Co. 1964–67; Chief Cost Accountant, Mars Ltd. 1967–71; Financial Controller, Hoover Ltd. 1971–74; Co. Borough Councillor, Merthyr Tydfil 1972–74; Vice-Chair. Plaid Cymru 1972–74, Pres. 1981–84, 1991–; M.P. for Caernarfon 1974–; Chair. All Party House of Commons Reform Group 1983, Vice-Chair. All-Party Disablement Group 1992–; Vice-Chair. Parl. Social Services Group 1985–88; mem. Nat. Ass. for Wales 1999–; Pres. Spastic Soc. of Wales 1985–90; Vice-Pres. Welsh Asscn. of Community Councils 1978–, Nat. Fed. of Industrial Devt. Authorities 1981–; Sponsor, Disabled Persons Act 1981; Hon. mem. Gorsedd of Welsh Bards; Hon. Fellow Univ. of N. Wales Bangor 1995; Grimshaw Memorial Award, Nat. Fed. of the Blind 1982. *Publications:* An Economic Plan for Wales 1970, O Ddifri 1992, Dal Ati 1993, A Democratic Wales in a United Europe 1995, A Real Choice for Wales 1996. *Leisure interests:* football, tennis, swimming, chess. *Address:* House of Commons, London, SW1A 0AA, England; National Assembly for Wales, Cardiff Bay, Cardiff, CF99 1NA; 8 Stryd y Castell, Caernarfon, Gwynedd, LL55 1SE, Wales (Constituency Office). *Telephone:* 0171-219 4182 (London); (01286) 672076 (Caernarfon).

WIGZELL, Hans, M.D., PH.D.; Swedish professor of immunology; b. 28 Oct. 1938; m. Kerstin Largell 1964; one s. three d.; ed. Karolinska Inst., Stockholm; Prof. of Immunology, Uppsala Univ. 1972–82, Karolinska Inst. 1982–; Dir. Nat. Bacteriological Lab., Stockholm 1988–; Chair. Nobel Cttee., Karolinska Inst. 1990; Hon. mem. American Asscn. of Immunologists; Anders Jahres Prize, Oslo 1975, Erik Pernstrom Prize, Uppsala 1981. *Publications:* about 400 scientific articles, textbooks and popular science books. *Leisure interests:* music, nature, tropical plants. *Address:* Karolinska Institute, Department of Immunology, 171 77 Stockholm, Sweden.

WIIN-NIELSEN, Aksel Christopher, DR.SC.; Danish professor of physics; b. 17 Dec. 1929, Klakring; s. of Aage Nielsen and Marie Petre (née Kristoffersen) Nielsen; m. Bente Havsteen Zimsen 1953; three d.; ed. Univs. of Copenhagen and Stockholm; staff mem. Danish Meteorological Inst. 1952–55, Int. Meteorological Inst. 1955–58, Jt. Numerical Weather Prediction 1959–61, Nat. Centre for Atmospheric Research 1961–63; Prof. (Chair.), Univ. of Mich., U.S.A. 1963–73; Dir. European Centre for Medium-Range Weather Forecasts 1974–80; Sec.-Gen. WMO 1980–84; Dir. Danish Meteorological Inst. 1984–87; Prof. of Physics, Univ. of Copenhagen 1988–94; mem. Danish Acad. of Tech. Sciences 1980 (Vice-Pres. 1989–92), Finnish Acad. of Sciences and Letters 1980, Royal Swedish Acad. of Sciences 1981, Royal Danish Acad. of Sciences 1982; Hon. D.Sc. (Reading, Copenhagen); Ohridsky Medal, Univ. of Sofia, Bulgaria, Buys-Ballot Medal, Royal Netherlands Acad. of Science, Wihuri Int. Science Prize, Wihuri Foundation, Helsinki, Finland, Rossby Prize, Swedish Geophysical Soc., Silver Medal, Univ. of Helsinki, Palmen Medal, Finnish Geophysical Soc. *Publications:* Problems in Dynamic Meteorology 1970, Dynamic Meteorology 1973, Predictability 1987, Chaos and Causality 1992, Fundamentals of Atmospheric Energetics (with C.-T. Chen) 1993, and about 100 articles on dynamic meteorology, numerical weather prediction and atmospheric energetics. *Address:* Solbakken 6, 3230 Graested, Denmark. *Telephone:* 48 39 23 84.

WIJDENBOSCH, Jules Albert, CERT.ED., PH.D.; Suriname politician; b. 2 May 1941, Paramaribo; one d.; customs officer 1962–66; civil servant Municipality of Amsterdam 1966–81; mem. State Cttee. on Remigration of Surinamese est. by Dutch govt. 1978–81; sr. civil servant Ministry of Dist. Admin. and Decentralization 1981, Under-Dir. in charge of Bureau for Decentralization of Admin. 1983, Dir. of Dist. Admin., Ministry of Dist. Admin., and Decentralization and Nat. Mobilization 1985; Minister of Home Affairs, Dist. Admin. and Nat. Mobilization and Minister of Justice and Police 1986–87; Prime Minister, Minister of Gen. Affairs and Minister of Foreign Affairs 1987–88; sr. civil servant Ministry of Regional Devt. 1988–91; Vice-Pres. Repub. of Suriname and Minister of Finance Jan.-Sept. 1991; sr. civil servant Ministry of Regional Devt. 1991–; co-ordinator Jongerengroep (Youth Section) of Suriname Nat. Party 1962–63; co-ordinator Verenigung van Bestuurskundigen 1982–; mem. and Acting Chair. Political Advisory Group 25th Feb. Movt. 1983; mem. Higher Political Council on the political and admin. future of Suriname 1985–87; first Chair. Nationale Democratische Partij (NDP) 1987–91, Deputy Chair. 1992–96; mem. Nat. Ass. and floor leader NDP 1991–; Deputy Chair. Foundation for the promotion of remigration of Surinamese; Chair. Amsterdam Welfare Foundation; Chair. Union of Customs Officers 1962–66; co-f. Algemene Jongeren Organisatie (Youth Org.) 1962, Dir. 1963; Chair. Surinamese Basketball Fed., Deputy Chair. Surinamese Football Fed.; mem. editorial bd. Lanti; Grand Master, Order of the Yellow Star, Order of the Palm. *Publications:* Schets voor de Republiek Suriname eigen stijl (A Personal View of the Repub. of Suriname) 1974, Bestuurlijke organisatie in een leefgemeenschap (Administrative Organisation in Surinamese Society) 1980, Politieke orde en legitimiteit (Political Order and Legitimacy) 1981, Statuut van het Koninkrijk der Nederlanden (Charter for the Kingdom of the Netherlands) 1979, Participatie in een waarachtige democratie (Participating in a Modern Democracy) 1983. *Address:* Office of the Prime Minister, Paramaribo, Suriname.

WIJESEKERA, Nandadeva, M.A., D.LITT., PH.D.; Sri Lankan anthropologist, archaeologist and government official (retd.); b. 11 Dec. 1908, Moonamalwatta, Sri Lanka; s. of Muhandiram N. G. de S. Wijesekera and Dona Emaliya de Alwis Gunatilaka; m. Leila Jayatilaka 1941; one d.; ed. Ananda Coll., Colombo, Univ. Coll. Colombo, Trinity Coll. Cambridge, England, Univ. Coll. London, Vienna Univ. and Calcutta Univ.; Asst. in Ethnology, Colombo Museum 1937–44; war service in civilian duties 1940–44; Deputy Supt. of Census 1945–50; Dir. Census and Statistics 1950–55; mem. UNESCO Nat. Comm. 1950; Asst. Sec., Ministry of Finance 1951; Sec. Royal Comm. on Languages 1951; Sec. Gal-Oya Devt. Bd. 1952; Liaison Officer, World Bank Comm. 1952–53; Dir. Official Language Dept. 1956; Deputy Commr. Official Language Affairs 1959–60, Commr. 1960–67; Amb. 1967–70; Leader Science Del. to China 1964, Ceylon Del. to Colombo Plan Conf. 1967; Adviser to

Dept. of Archaeology 1983–; mem. Bd. of Man. Inst. of Indigenous Medicine 1983–; has been mem. of numerous govt. dels. and has held many official appointments; Ed.-in-Chief Mahavamsa (in Pali and Sinhala); represented All-Ceylon cricket team 1932; Pres. Nondescripts Cricket Club 1982; Pundit, Oriental Studies Soc. 1959; Fellow Acad. of Arts, Nat. Acad. of Sciences; mem. Sri Lanka Asscn. for the Advancement of Science 1964; Pres. All-Ceylon Football Asscn. 1963, Royal Asiatic Soc. 1966–67, 1971, 1973–75; Founder Pres. Archaeological Soc. 1966; Hon. D. Litt. (Sri Jayawardenepura; Gold Medal, Royal Asiatic Soc. 1973, Purā vidyā Chakravarti 1986, Desamanya Sri Lanka 1990. *Publications:* many books, including (Sinhala) Lanka Janatawa 1955, Perani Bitusituvam 1964, Perani Murti Kalawa 1970, Proper Names in Sinhala Literature 1988; (English) People of Ceylon 1949, Early Sinhalese Painting 1959, Veddas in Transition 1964, Biography of Sir D. B. Jayatilaka 1973, Selected Writings 1983, Heritage of Sri Lanka 1984, Anthropological Gleanings from Sinhala Literature 1985, Contacts and Conflicts with Sri Lanka 1986, The Sinhalese 1990, Sri Lankave Urumaya 1991, Archaeology Department's Centenary 1890–1990, 5 vols. (Ed.-in-chief); also (autobiog.) 1995, 25 children's books and 200 articles. *Leisure interests:* reading and writing. *Address:* No. 34 Dudley Senanayake Mawata, Borella, Colombo 8, Sri Lanka. *Telephone:* Colombo 694089.

WIJETUNGA, Dingiri Banda; Sri Lankan politician; b. 15 Feb. 1922, Polgahanga, Kandy; m.; one d.; official in Co-operative Dept. 1942–47; joined United Nat. Party 1946; M.P. for Udunuwara 1965–; apptd. Minister of Information and Broadcasting 1977, of Power and Highways 1978, of Power and Energy 1979, of Agricultural Devt. and Research and Minister of Food 1987, Gov. Northwestern Prov. 1988; Prime Minister of Sri Lanka and Minister of Finance 1989–93; elected Exec. Pres. of Sri Lanka 1993–94. *Address:* c/o Office of the President, Republic Square, Colombo 1, Sri Lanka.

WIJNHOLDS, Johannes de Beaufort, PH.D.; Netherlands international civil servant and economist; b. 24 Oct. 1943, Amsterdam; m. Jolanthe de Graaf 1968; one s. one d.; ed. Univ. of Amsterdam; economist, De Nederlandsche Bank, Amsterdam 1968, various positions in bank 1974–84, Deputy Exec. Dir. 1987–94; Asst. to Exec. Dir. IBRD and IMF, Washington, D.C. 1972–74, Alt. Exec. Dir. IMF 1985–87, Exec. Dir. 1994–; Alt. mem. Social Econ. Council of the Netherlands 1987–94; Prof. of Money and Banking, Univ. of Groningen 1992–95. *Publications:* The Need for International Reserves and Credit Facilities 1977, The International Banking System (in Dutch) 1985, A Framework for Monetary Stability (ed. and co-author) 1994; numerous articles on int. financial subjects. *Address:* International Monetary Fund, 700 19th Street, N.W., Washington, DC 20431, U.S.A. *Telephone:* (202) 623-4640. *Fax:* (202) 623-4924.

WIKSTRÖM, Jan-Erik, B.A.; Swedish politician and publisher; b. 11 Sept. 1932, St. Skedvi, Dalarna; s. of Börje Wikström and Essy (Lilja) Wikström; m. Rev. Cecilia Wikström 1995; three s. one d.; ed. Gothenberg Univ.; Man. Dir. Gummessons Bokförlag Publishing House 1961–76; mem. Municipal Council, Stockholm 1962–70; mem. Riksdag (Parl.) 1970–73, 1976–92; Minister of Educ. and Cultural Affairs 1976–82; Gov. of Uppsala 1992–97; mem. Folkpartiet (Liberal Party). *Publications:* Röd och gul och vit och svart 1950, Skall kyrkan skiljas från staten 1958, Storm över Kongo 1961, Indien vid korsvägen 1962, Inför Herrens ansikte 1962, Politik och kristen tro 1964, Skall samhället utbilda präster? 1966, Liberala positioner 1969, Med frisinnat förtecken 1970, En bättre skola 1973, Möten med Mästaren 1975, I väntan på befrielsen 1977, Friket Mångfald Kvalitet 1978, Liberalism med frisinnat förtecken 1981. *Leisure interests:* literary history, biographies, political literature, tennis. *Address:* Doppingvägen 10, 756 51 Uppsala, Sweden. *Telephone:* 018-320918.

WIKTORIN, Gen. Owe Erik Axel, Swedish army officer; b. 7 May 1940, Motala; s. of Erik Wiktorin and Ester Wiktorin (née Johnsson); m. Cajs Gårding 1965; two s.; ed. A.F. Flying Training School, A.F. Acad., Armed Forces Staff and War Coll., U.S.A.F. Air Command and Staff Coll.; figher pilot Skaraborg Wing 1964–69, C.O. squadron 1969–71; staff officer Swedish Defence Staff 1973–79, Head of Planning Section 1980–83, Dir. of Plans and Policy and Deputy Chief 1986–91, Chief 1991–92; Deputy C.O. Jämtland (Sector) Wing 1983–84; Head of Planning Section A.F. Staff 1984–86; C.O. Southern Jt. Command Swedish Armed Forces 1992–94, Supreme Commdr. 1994–; Kt. Commdr. of White Rose of Finland, Chevalier, Légion d'honneur; Gold Medal for Merit, Southern Skåne Regt., Swedish Home Guard; Gold Medal for Merit, Nat. Fed. of A.F. Asscns. *Leisure interests:* sailing, skiing, cooking, sky-diving, hunting. *Address:* Swedish Armed Forces HQ, SE-107 85 Stockholm, Sweden. *Telephone:* (8) 788-8001. *Fax:* (8) 788-8425.

WILANDER, Mats; Swedish tennis player; b. 22 Aug. 1964; m. Sonja Mulholland 1987; Australian Open Champion 1983, 1984, 1988, French Open Champion 1982, 1985, 1988 (finalist 1983, 1987), U.S. Open Champion 1988; winner Wimbledon Men's Doubles Championship (with Joakim Nystrom) 1986; mem. victorious Swedish Davis Cup Team 1984, 1987, 1988; ranked World Number 1 1988; voted official World Champion 1988; won 33 singles and 7 doubles titles (end of 1996). Leisure interests: music, art.

WILBERFORCE, Baron (Life Peer), cr. 1964; **Richard Orme Wilberforce,** C.M.G., O.B.E., F.R.C.M., Q.C., M.A.; British judge; b. 11 March 1907, Jullundur; s. of Samuel Wilberforce and Katherine Sheepshanks; m. Yvette Lenoan 1947; one s. one d.; ed. Winchester Coll. and Oxford Univ.; called to Bar 1932; Fellow, All Souls Coll., Oxford 1932–; Chief, Legal Div., Control Comm., Germany 1945; U.K. Rep. Legal Cttee. ICAO 1949–61; Judge, High Court 1961–64; Lord of Appeal in Ordinary 1964–82; mem. Perm. Court of Arbitration 1964–87; Chair. Exec. Council, Int. Law Asscn. 1965–87; Pres. Appeals Tribunal of Lloyds of London 1983–87; Pres. U.K. Asscn. of European Law; Pres. Int. Fed. for European Law 1978–80; High Steward, Oxford Univ. 1967–90; Chancellor, Hull Univ. 1978–94; Chair. Court of Inquiry into Electricity Workers' Dispute 1970–71, Mineworkers' Dispute 1972; Hon. mem. Faculty of Advocates, Scotland, Canadian Bar Asscn., American Soc. of Int. Law; Hon. D.C.L. (Oxford) 1968, LL.D. (London) 1972, (Hull) 1973, (Bristol) 1983. *Publication:* The Law of Restrictive Practices and Monopolies (joint author) 1957. *Leisure interests:* music, golf, philately, the turf. *Address:* House of Lords, London, SW1A 0PW, England.

WILBUR, Richard (Purdy), M.A.; American poet and fmr. university professor; b. 1 March 1921, New York City; s. of Lawrence L. Wilbur and Helen Purdy Wilbur; m. Charlotte Ward 1942; three s. one d.; ed. Amherst Coll., and Harvard Univ.; Asst. Prof. of English, Harvard Univ. 1950–54; Assoc. Prof. Wellesley Coll. 1954–57; Prof. Wesleyan Univ. 1957–77; Writer in Residence, Smith Coll., Northampton, Mass. 1977–86; mem. American Acad. of Arts and Sciences, Soc. of Fellows of Harvard Univ. 1947–50; Guggenheim Fellow 1952–53, 1963, Ford Fellow 1961; Chancellor, Acad. of American Poets 1961; Poet Laureate of U.S.A. 1987–88; mem. PEN; Pres. American Acad. of Arts and Letters 1974–76, Chancellor 1977–78; mem. Dramatists Guild; Hon. Fellow, Modern Language Asscn. 1986; Harriet Monroe Prize 1948, Oscar Blumenthal Prize 1950, Prix de Rome from American Acad. of Arts and Letters 1954–55, Edna St. Vincent Millay Memorial Award 1956, Nat. Book Award, Pulitzer Prize 1957, co-recipient Bollingen Translation Prize 1963, co-recipient Bollingen Prize in Poetry 1971, Prix Henri Desfeuilles 1971, Brandeis Creative Arts Award 1971, Shelley Memorial Prize 1973, Harriet Monroe Poetry Award 1978, Drama Desk Award 1983, PEN Translation Prize 1983, St. Botolph's Foundation Award 1983, Aiken Taylor Award 1988, L. A. Times Book Award 1988, Pulitzer Prize 1989, Gold Medal for Poetry, American Acad. of Arts and Letters 1991, MacDowell Medal 1992, Nat. Arts Club Medal of Honour for Literature 1994, PEN/Manheim Medal for Translation 1994, Nat. Medal of Arts 1994, Milton Center Prize 1995; Robert Frost Medal, Poetry Soc. of America 1996, T. S. Eliot Award 1996; Chevalier, Ordre des Palmes Académiques 1984. *Publications:* The Beautiful Changes and other poems 1947, Ceremony and other poems 1950, A Bestiary (anthology, with Alexander Calder) 1955, The Misanthrope (trans. from Molière) 1955, Things of this World (poems) 1956, Poems 1943–1956 1957, Candide (comic opera, with Lillian Hellman and others) 1957, Poe (edition of his poems with introduction and notes) 1959, Advice to a Prophet (poems) 1961, Tartuffe (trans. from Molière) 1963, The Poems of Richard Wilbur 1963, Loudmouse (for children) 1963, Poems of Shakespeare (with Alfred Harbage) 1966, Walking to Sleep (new poems and translations) 1969, School for Wives (trans. from Molière) 1971, Opposites (children's verse, illustrated by the author) 1973, The Mind-Reader 1976, Responses: Prose Pieces 1953–1976 1976, The Learned Ladies (trans. from Molière) 1978, Selected Poems of Witter Bynner (editor) 1978, Seven Poems 1981, Andromache (trans. from Racine) 1982, The Whale (translations) 1982, Molière: Four Comedies (contains 4 plays translated previously listed) 1982, Phaedra (trans. from Racine) 1986, Lying and Other Poems 1987, New and Collected Poems 1988, More Opposites 1991, School for Husbands (trans. from Molière) 1992, The Imaginary Cuckold (trans. from Molière) 1993, A Game of Catch 1994, Amphitryon (trans. from Molière) 1995, The Catbird's Song (prose pieces) 1997, The Disappearing Alphabet (for children and others) 1998, Bone Key and other poems 1998. *Leisure interests:* tennis, walking, herb gardening. *Address:* 87 Dodwells Road, Cummington, MA 01026; 715R Windsor Lane, Key West, FL 33040, U.S.A. (Winter). *Telephone:* (413) 634-2275; (305) 296-7499.

WILBUR, Richard Sloan, M.D., J.D.; American association executive and physician; b. 8 April 1924, Boston; s. of Blake Colburn Wilbur and Mary Caldwell Sloan; m. Betty Lou Fannin 1951; three s.; ed. John Marshall Law School, Stanford Univ.; Intern, San Francisco County Hosp. 1946–47; Resident, Stanford Hosp. 1949–51, Univ. of Pa. Hosp. 1951–52; mem. of Staff, Palo Alto Medical Clinic, Calif. 1952–69; Deputy Exec. Vice-Pres., American Medical Asscn., Chicago 1969–71, 1973–74; Asst. Sec., Health and Environment Dept. 1971–73; Sr. Vice-Pres., Baxter Labs Inc., Deerfield, Ill. 1974–76; Exec. Vice-Pres. Council Medical Speciality Socs. 1976–91, Emer. 1992–; Sec., Accreditation Council for Continuing Medical Educ. 1979–91; Assoc. Prof. of Medicine, Georgetown Univ. Medical School 1971–77, Stanford Medical School 1952–69; Vice-Pres. Nat. Resident Matching Plan 1980–91, Pres. 1991–92; Chair. Bd. Calif. Medical Asscn. 1968–69; Chair. Calif. Blue Shield 1966–68; Chair. American Medico-Legal Foundation 1987–, Professional Advisory Bd., Royal Soc. of Medicine Foundation 1995–; Pres. American Coll. of Physician Executives 1988–89; Pres. American Bd. Medical Man. 1992–93; Pres. MedicAlert Foundation Int. 1992–94, MedicAlert Foundation, U.S.A. 1992–94, Dir. MedicAlert Germany 1992–94, Iberica 1992–94, Europe (U.K.) 1992–95; Chair. Bd. and C.E.O. Inst. for Clinical Information 1994–; Sr. Vice-Pres. Healthcare, Buckeye Corpn. Pte. Ltd. 1997–; Chair. Medical Advisory Bd, Medical City, Bangalore 1997–; Pres. Royal Soc. Medicine Foundation 1998–; mem. numerous other medical asscns. *Publications:* contribs. to medical journals. *Address:* Institute for Clinical Information, 207 Westminster Road, Suite 201, Lake Forest, IL 60045-1840, (Office); 985 North Hawthorne Place, Lake Forest, IL 60045, U.S.A. (Home). *Telephone:* (847) 234-6337 (Office). *Fax:* (847) 234-6511.

WILBY, James; British actor; b. 20 Feb. 1958, Rangoon, Burma; s. of Geoffrey Wilby and Shirley Wilby; m. Shana Louise Magraw 1988; two s. one d.; ed. Sedbergh School, Durham Univ., Royal Acad. of Dramatic Art, London. *Stage appearances:* Another Country (West End début), Who's Afraid of Virginia Woolf (Belgrade Theatre, Coventry), Chips With Everything (Leeds Playhouse), As You Like It (Royal Exchange Theatre, Manchester, and tour), Jane Eyre (Chichester), A Patriot for Me (Barbican). *Films:* Dreamchild, Maurice, A Handful of Dust, A Summer Story, The Apple Tree, Howards End 1991, Immaculate Conception 1992, The Chess Game, Une Partie d'Echec, Regeneration, An Ideal Husband, Tom's Midnight Garden, Cotton Mary. *Television:* Sherlock Holmes, The Crooked Man, Dutch Girls, The Siege of Venice, A Tale of Two Cities, Mother Love, Tell Me That You Love Me, Adam Bede, You, Me And It, Lady Chatterley, Crocodile Shoes, Woman in White 1997, The Dark Room. *Leisure interests:* playing piano, tennis, sailing. *Address:* c/o ICM Ltd., Oxford House, 76 Oxford Street, London, W1R 1RB, England. *Telephone:* 0171-636 6565. *Fax:* 0171-636 3524.

WILD, Earl; American pianist and composer; b. 26 Nov. 1915, Pittsburgh, Pa.; s. of Royland and Lillian G. Wild; ed. Carnegie Technical Coll., Pittsburgh; studied with Selmar Jansen, Egon Petri, Helene Barrere, Volya Cossack and Paul Doguereau; first American soloist to perform with NBC Orchestra conducted by Toscanini 1942, has performed with symphony orchestras and given recitals in many cos.; has appeared with Sir Malcolm Sargent, Jascha Horenstein, Sir Georg Solti, Arthur Fiedler; played first TV piano recital 1939; has played for 7 Presidents of U.S., incl. inauguration of Pres. J. F. Kennedy; numerous recordings for RCA, EMI, Columbia, Nonesuch, Readers Digest and Vanguard Records. *Compositions include:* Piano Concerto, The Turquoise Horse (choral work) and ballet music, oratorios, solo piano music, choral work and popular songs. *Leisure interests:* writing poetry, playing piano.

WILD, John Paul, A.C., C.B.E., F.R.S., F.A.A., F.T.S., M.A., SC.D.; Australian radio astronomer; b. 17 May 1923, Sheffield, England; s. of late Alwyn H. Wild and Bessie Wild (née Arnold); m. 1st Elaine Poole Hull 1948 (died 1991); two s. one d.; m. 2nd Margaret Lyndon 1991; ed. Whitgift School, Croydon, England and Peterhouse, Cambridge; Radar Officer, Royal Navy 1943–47; Research Scientist, Div. of Radiophysics, Commonwealth Scientific and Industrial Research Org. (CSIRO), Australia 1947–71, Chief of Div. 1971–77, Assoc. mem. 1977–78, full-time mem. of CSIRO Exec. 1978–85, Chair. and Chief Exec. 1978–85; Chair. Very Fast Train (VFT) Jt. Venture 1986–91; Pres. Radio Astronomy Comm. of Int. Astronomical Union 1967–70; mem. Anglo-Australian Telescope Bd. 1973–82, Chair. 1975–80; Foreign mem. American Philosophical Soc.; Foreign Hon. mem. American Acad. of Arts and Sciences; Corresp. mem. Royal Soc. of Sciences, Liège; Hon. Fellow Peterhouse, Cambridge, Royal Soc. of N.S.W., Royal Soc. of Arts, Inst. of Engineers, Australia; Hon. D.Sc. (Aust. Nat. Univ.) 1979, (Newcastle Univ.) 1982; Hale Prize for Solar Astronomy, American Astronomical Soc. 1980; Edgeworth David Medal, Hendryk Arctowski Gold Medal of N.A.S., Balthasar van der Pol Gold Medal of Int. Union of Radio Science, Herschel Medal of Royal Astronomical Soc., Thomas Rankin Lyle Medal of Australian Acad. of Science, Royal Medal, Royal Soc. of London 1980, ANZAAS Medal 1984, Hartnett Medal, Royal Soc. of Arts 1988. *Publications:* various papers on radio astronomy in scientific journals. *Address:* Unit 4, 1 Grant Crescent, Griffith, A.C.T. 2603, Australia; 800 Avon Road, Ann Arbor, MI 48104, U.S.A. *Telephone:* (06) 295 3473 (Australia); (313) 663-8333 (U.S.A.). *Fax:* (313) 761-1586.

WILDENSTEIN, Daniel Leopold, L. ÈS L.; French art historian; b. 11 Sept. 1917, Verrières-le-Buisson; s. of Georges and Jane (Lévi) Wildenstein; m. 1st Martine Kapferer 1939 (divorced 1968); two s.; m. 2nd Sylvia Roth 1978; ed. Cours Hattemer, Sorbonne; joined Wildenstein and Co. Inc., New York 1940, Vice-Pres. 1943–59, Pres. 1959–68, Chair. 1968–; Pres. Wildenstein Foundation Inc., New York 1964–; Dir. Wildenstein and Co. Ltd., London, and Wildenstein Arte, Buenos Aires 1963–; Founder and mem. American Inst. of France, New York 1947; Dir. of Activities, Musée Jacquemart-André, and of Musée Chaalis (Institut de France), Paris, 1956–62; Dir. Gazette des Beaux-Arts 1963–; mem. French Chamber of Commerce in U.S. (Counsellor) 1942–, Haut Comité du Musée de Monaco 1973–; organizer of art competitions (Hallmark art award); mem. Inst. de France (Académie des Beaux-Arts), Commdr. des Arts et des Lettres, Commdr. de l'ordre de Léopold II (Belgium). *Publications:* Claude Monet (Vol. I) 1975, (Vol. II, III) 1979, (Vol. IV) 1985, (Vol. V) 1991, Edouard Manet (Vol. I) 1976, (Vol. II) 1977, Gustave Courbet (Vol. I) 1977, (Vol. II) 1978. *Leisure interest:* horse racing. *Address:* 57 rue la Boétie, 75008 Paris, France; Seidenstrasse 6, 8853 Lachen SZ, Switzerland (Home).

WILDER, Billy; American film writer, producer and director; b. 22 June 1906, Austria; m. Audrey Young; fmr. reporter, Berlin; film scriptwriter 1930–; wrote People on Sunday, Emil and the Detectives, Germany; writer and dir. Mauvaise Graine, Paris 1933; went to U.S. 1934; writer in collaboration Bluebeard's Eighth Wife 1938, Midnight 1939, Ninotchka 1939, What A Life 1939, Arise, My Love 1940, Hold Back the Dawn 1941, Ball of Fire 1941. *Films directed* (also co-scripted): The Major and the Minor 1942, Five Graves to Cairo 1943, Double Indemnity 1944, The Lost Weekend (Acad. Award) 1945, The Emperor Waltz 1947, A Foreign Affair 1948, Sunset Boulevard (Acad. Award) 1950; Producer, dir. and writer (in collaboration): The Big Carnival (or Ace in the Hole) 1951, Stalag 17 1953, Sabrina 1954, The Spirit of St. Louis 1957, Love in the Afternoon 1957, Witness for the Prosecution 1958, Some Like It Hot 1959, The Apartment (Acad. Award) 1960, One, Two, Three 1961, Irma La Douce 1963, Kiss Me, Stupid 1964, The Fortune Cookie (British title Meet Whiplash Willie) 1966, The Private Life of Sherlock Holmes 1970, Avanti 1972, Fedora 1979; co-producer, dir. and writer (in collaboration) The Seven Year Itch 1955; dir. and writer Buddy Buddy 1981; six Academy Awards (for Lost Weekend, Sunset Boulevard and The Apartment), American Film Inst. Life Achievement Award 1985, Irving G. Thalberg Award 1988, Kennedy Center Award 1990, Nat. Medal of Arts 1993. *Address:* c/o Paul Kohner, 9300 Wilshire Boulevard, Suite 555, Beverly Hills, CA 90212, U.S.A.

WILDER, Gene; pseudonym of Jerry Silberman; American film actor, director and producer; b. 11 June 1935, Milwaukee, Wis.; s. of William J. Silberman and Jeanne Silberman (née Baer); m. 1st Mary Joan Schutz 1967 (divorced 1974); one d.; m. 2nd Gilda Radner 1984 (deceased); m. 3rd Karen Boyer 1991; ed. Univ. of Iowa, Bristol Old Vic. Theatre School; served with U.S. Army 1956–58; Broadway play: The Complaisant Lover 1962, West End play Laughter on the 23rd Floor 1996. *Films include:* Bonnie and Clyde 1966, The Producers 1967, Start the Revolution Without Me 1968, Quackser Fortune Has a Cousin in the Bronx 1969, Willy Wonka and the Chocolate Factory 1970, The Scarecrow 1972, Everything You Always Wanted to Know About Sex, But Were Afraid to Ask 1971, Young Frankenstein 1974, The Little Prince 1974, Rhinoceros 1972, Blazing Saddles 1973, Thursday's Game 1974, The Adventure of Sherlock Holmes's Smarter Brother 1975, Silver Streak 1976, The World's Greatest Lover 1977, The Frisco Kid 1979, Stir Crazy 1980, Sunday Lovers 1980, Hanky Panky 1982, The Woman in Red 1984, Haunted Honeymoon 1986, See No Evil, Hear No Evil 1989, Funny About Love 1990, Another You 1991. *TV appearances include:* The Scarecrow 1972, The Trouble With People 1973, Marlo Thomas Special 1973, Thursday's Games 1973, Something Wilder 1994–. *Address:* William Morris Agency, 151 S. El Camino Drive, Beverly Hills, CA 90212, U.S.A.

WILDER, Lawrence Douglas, B.S., J.D.; American politician and lawyer; b. 17 Jan. 1931, Richmond, Va.; one s. two d.; ed. Virginia Union Univ., Howard Univ.; mem. Va. Bar; served U.S. Army 1952–53 (decorated Bronze Star); mem. Va. Senate 1969–85; Lieut.-Gov. State of Va. 1986–89, Gov. of Virginia 1989–93; Pres. Va. Union Univ., Richmond 1998–; del. Democratic Nat. Convention 1980; mem. Bd. Dirs., United Givers Fund; Chair. Bd. Red Shield Boys' Club; mem. Va. Bar Asscn., Nat. Bar Asscn., American Judicature Soc. *Address:* Wilder and Gregory, P.O. Box 518, Richmond, VA 23218; Office of the President, Virginia Union University, 1500 N. Lombardy Street, Richmond, VA 23220, U.S.A.

WILDHABER, Luzius, DR.IUR., LL.M., J.S.D.; Swiss judge and professor of law; b. 18 Jan. 1937, Basle; m. Simone Wildhaber-Creux 1963 (died 1994); two d.; ed. Basle, Paris, Heidelberg, London and Yale Univs.; Int. Law Div. Fed. Dept. of External Affairs 1968–71; Prof. of Int. Constitutional and Admin. Law, Univ. of Fribourg 1971–77; Prof. of Int. and Constitutional Law, Univ. of Basle 1977–, Rector (desig.) 1990–92, Rector 1992–94, Pro-Rector 1994–96; Judge, Supreme Court of Liechtenstein 1975–88, Admin. Tribunal, IDB 1989–94, European Court of Human Rights 1991–; Pres. European Court of Human Rights 1998–. *Publications:* Advisory Opinions—Rechtsgutachten höchster Gerichte 1962, Treaty-making Power and Constitution 1971, Praxis des Völkerrechts (with J. P. Müller) 1977, Erfahrungen mit der Europäischen Menschenrechtskonvention 1979, Wechselspiel zwischen Innen und Aussen 1996; more than 100 articles. *Leisure interests:* travel, skiing, hiking, mountaineering. *Address:* European Court of Human Rights, Council of Europe, F-67075 Strasbourg, France. *Telephone:* 388-41.31.53. *Fax:* 388-41.27.91.

WILES, Andrew John, PH.D., F.R.S.; British mathematician; b. 11 April 1953; s. of Rev. M. F. Wiles; m.; two d.; ed. Merton Coll. Oxford, Clare Coll. Cambridge; fmr. Fellow Clare Coll.; Prof. of Math., Princeton Univ., U.S.A. 1982–88, 1990–; Royal Soc. Research Prof. in Math. and Professorial Fellow Merton Coll. Oxford 1988–90; Jr. Whitehead Prize (jtly.), London Math. Soc. 1988, Wolfskehl Prize (for proving Fermat's Last Theorem), Göttingen 1997, Special Award, Berlin Int. Congress of Mathematicians 1998. *Address:* Department of Mathematics, Princeton University, Fine Hall, Washington Hall, Princeton, NJ 08544, U.S.A.

WILES, Rev. Maurice Frank, M.A., D.D., F.B.A.; British ecclesiastic and fmr. university professor; b. 17 Oct. 1923, London; s. of Sir Harold Wiles and Lady Wiles; m. Patricia M. Mowll 1950; two s. one d.; ed. Tonbridge School, Christ's Coll. Cambridge and Ridley Hall, Cambridge; curate, St. George's Church, Stockport 1950–52; chaplain, Ridley Hall, Cambridge 1952–55; lecturer, Univ. Coll. Ibadan, Nigeria 1955–59; Dean, Clare Coll. Cambridge and Univ. lecturer, Faculty of Divinity 1959–67; Prof. of Christian Doctrine, King's Coll. London 1967–70; Regius Prof. of Divinity, Univ. of Oxford and Canon of Christ Church Cathedral 1970–91. *Publications:* The Spiritual Gospel 1960, The Christian Fathers 1966, The Divine Apostle 1967, The Making of Christian Doctrine 1967, The Remaking of Christian Doctrine 1974, What Is Theology? 1976, Working Papers in Doctrine 1976, Explorations in Theology 4 1979, Faith and the Mystery of God 1982, God's Action in the World 1986, Christian Theology and Interreligious Dialogue 1992, A Shared Search 1994, Archetypal Heresy 1996. *Address:* 11 Baytree Close, Iffley, Oxford, OX4 4DT, England. *Telephone:* (01865) 777091.

WILHELMSSON, Hans K. B., D.TECH.; Swedish professor of physics; b. 4 Oct. 1929, Göteborg; s. of Wilhelm Petterson and Clara M. Johansson; m.

1st Birgitta Frederikson 1960 (divorced 1995); one s. one d.; m. 2nd Julie Baudin; ed. Chalmers Univ. of Tech.; Prof. and Dir. Inst. for Electromagnetic Field Theory, Chalmers Univ. of Tech. Göteborg 1971; Prof. of Plasma Physics, Fondation de France, Ecole Polytechnique, Palaiseau 1987–93, Prof. Emer. 1993–; mem. Royal Swedish Acad., Royal Swedish Acad. of Eng. Science, Acad. Nationale des Sciences, Belles-Lettres et Arts de Bordeaux; John Ericson Medal (Chalmers Univ.) 1952. *Publications:* 200 scientific articles in theoretical and plasma physics. *Leisure interests:* art, travel. *Address:* 45 rue Condillac, 33000 Bordeaux, France. *Telephone:* (5) 56.01.13.40 (Home, France).

WILKES, Maurice Vincent, PH.D., F.R.S., F.ENG., F.I.E.E., F.B.C.S.; British computer engineer; b. 26 June 1913, Dudley; s. of Vincent J. Wilkes, O.B.E.; m. Nina Twyman 1947; one s. two d.; ed. King Edward VI School, Stourbridge, and St. John's Coll., Cambridge; Univ. Demonstrator 1937; Radar and Operational Research, Second World War; Univ. Lecturer and Acting Dir. of Mathematical Lab., Cambridge 1945, Dir 1946–70; Head of Computer Lab. 1970; Prof. of Computer Technology, Univ. of Cambridge 1965–80; Staff Consultant, Digital Equipment Corpn. 1980–86; Adjunct Prof. M.I.T. 1981–85; mem. for Research Strategy, Olivetti Research Bd. 1986–89, Consultant 1989–; mem. Measurement and Control Section Cttee., Inst. of Electrical Engineers 1956–59; First Pres. British Computer Soc. 1957–60; mem. Council, Int. Fed. for Information Processing 1960–63, Council, Inst. of Electrical Engineers 1973–76, Council, Asscn. for Computing Machinery 1991–94; Turing Lecturer Asscn. for Computing Machinery 1967; Distinguished Fellow, British Computer Soc. 1973; Foreign Hon. mem. American Acad. Arts and Sciences 1974; Foreign Assoc. U.S. Nat. Acad. of Engineering 1977, N.A.S. 1980; 9 hon. degrees including Hon. Sc.D. (Cambridge) 1993; Dr. h.c. (Amsterdam) 1978, (Newcastle-on-Tyne, Hull, Kent, City Univ. London, Linköping, Munich, Bath); Harry Goode Memorial Award, American Fed. of Information Processing Socs. 1968, Eckert-Mauchly Award, American Fed. of Information Processing Socs. 1980, McDowell Award, I.E.E.E. 1981, Faraday Medal, I.E.E. 1981, Pender Award, Univ. of Pa. 1982, C and C Prize, Tokyo 1988, Italgas Prize, Turin 1991, Kyoto Prize 1992, John von Neumann Medal, I.E.E.E. 1997, Mountbatton Medal, Nat. Electronics Council 1997. *Publications:* Oscillations of the Earth's Atmosphere 1949, Preparation of Programs for an Electronic Digital Computer 1951, 1957, Automatic Digital Computers 1956, A Short Introduction to Numerical Analysis 1966, Time-Sharing Computer Systems 1968, The Cambridge CAP Computer and its Operating System 1979, Memoirs of a Computer Pioneer 1985, Computing Perspectives 1995. *Address:* Olivetti and Oracle Research Laboratory, 24A Trumpington Street, Cambridge, CB2 1QA, England. *Telephone:* (01223) 343 213. *Fax:* (01223) 313 524.

WILKINS, Sir Graham John, Kt.; British business executive; b. 22 Jan. 1924, Mudford, Somerset; s. of George W. and Ann May Wilkins (née Clarke); m. 1st Daphne Mildred Haynes 1945; m. 2nd Helen C. McGregor 1990; ed. Yeovil School, Univ. Coll. of South West, Exeter; Man. Dir. Beecham Research Laboratories 1961; Chair. Beecham Pharmaceutical Div., Dir. Beecham Group PLC 1964, Man. Dir. (Pharmaceuticals) 1973; Exec. Vice-Chair. Beecham Group PLC 1974–75, Chair. 1975–84, Pres. 1984–89; Chair. Thorn EMI PLC 1978–89; Dir. Courtaulds PLC 1976–86, Hill Samuel Group 1977–87, Rowntree 1985–88, Eastern Electricity 1989–95; Vice-Chair. Proprietary Asscn. of Great Britain 1966–68, ICC (U.K.); Pres. Asscn. of British Pharmaceutical Industry 1969–71, European Fed. of Pharmaceutical Industries Asscns. 1978–82, Advertising Asscn.; Chair. Medico-Pharmaceutical Forum 1972, 1973, ICC United Kingdom 1985–89; mem. Review Body for Doctors' and Dentists' Remuneration 1986–90, Chair. 1987–90; mem. Council, School of Pharmacy, London Univ. 1984–, Chair. 1987–. *Leisure interests:* golf, travel. *Address:* 'Alceda', Walton Lane, Shepperton-on-Thames, Middlesex, TW17 8LQ, England.

WILKINS, Maurice Hugh Frederick, C.B.E., PH.D., F.R.S.; British molecular biologist; b. 15 Dec. 1916, Pongaroa, New Zealand; s. of late E. H. Wilkins and of Eveline Whittaker; m. Patricia Chidgey 1959; two s. two d.; ed. St. John's Coll., Cambridge; Research on luminescence of solids, Physics Dept. Birmingham Univ.; Ministry of Home Security and Aircraft Production 1938; Manhattan Project (Ministry of Supply), Univ. of Calif. 1944; Lecturer in Physics, St. Andrews Univ. 1945; Medical Research Council, Biophysics Unit, King's Coll., London 1946, Deputy Dir. 1955–70, Dir. 1970–72, Dir. Neurobiology Unit (Cell Biophysics Unit 1974–80), MRC 1972; Prof. of Biophysics and Head of Dept., King's Coll. 1970–82, Emer. Prof. 1981–, Fellow 1973–; mem. Russell Cttee. against Chemical Weapons 1981; Pres. British Soc. for Social Responsibility in Science 1969–91, Food and Disarmament Int. 1984–; Hon. mem. American Soc. of Biological Chemists 1964; Foreign Hon. mem. American Acad. of Arts and Sciences 1970; Hon. LL.D.; Albert Lasker Award, American Public Health Asscn. 1960; Joint Nobel Prize for Physiology or Medicine 1962. *Publications:* Papers on luminescence and topics in biophysics, e.g. molecular structure of nucleic acids and structure of nerve membranes. *Address:* 30 St. John's Park, London, SE3 7JH, England. *Telephone:* 0171-836 5454; 0181-858 1817.

WILKINSON, Sir Denys Haigh, Kt., D.SC., PH.D., SC.D., F.R.S.; British physicist and university professor; b. 5 Sept. 1922, Leeds; s. of Charles Wilkinson and Hilda Wilkinson; m. 1st Christiane Clavier 1947; three d.; m. 2nd Helen Sellschop 1967; ed. Jesus Coll., Cambridge; worked on British Atomic Energy Project 1943–46, on Canadian Atomic Energy Project 1945–46; Demonstrator Cavendish Lab., Univ. of Cambridge 1947–51, Lecturer 1951–56 and Reader 1950–57, Fellow, Jesus Coll., Cambridge 1944–59, Hon. Fellow 1961–; Student of Christ Church, Oxford 1957–76, Emer. 1976–79, Hon. 1979–; Prof. of Nuclear Physics Clarendon Laboratory of Univ. of Oxford 1957–59, Prof. of Experimental Physics 1959–76, Head of Dept. of Nuclear Physics 1962–76; Vice-Chancellor Sussex Univ. 1976–87, Emer. Prof. 1987–; Pres. Inst. of Physics 1980–82; Rutherford Memorial Lecturer of British Physical Soc. 1962; mem. Governing Bd. Nat. Inst. for Research in Nuclear Science 1958–64; Queen's Lecturer, Berlin 1966; Cherwell-Simon Memorial Lecturer, Oxford 1970, Tizard Memorial Lecturer 1975, Lauritsen Memorial Lecturer, Calif. Inst. of Tech. 1976, Schiff Memorial Lecturer, Stanford Univ. 1977, Racah Memorial Lecturer, Univ. of Jerusalem 1977, Solly Cohen Memorial Lecturer, Hebrew Univ. of Jerusalem 1985, Axel Memorial Lecturer, Univ. of Ill. 1985, Breit Memorial Lecturer, Yale Univ. 1987, W.B. Lewis Memorial Lecturer, Chalk River 1989, Humphry Davy Lecturer, Acad. of Science (Paris) 1990, Rutherford Memorial Lecturer, N.Z. 1991, W.V. Houston Memorial Lecturer, Rice Univ., Houston, Tex. 1994, Hudspeth Lecturer, Univ. of Tex. Austin 1994, McPherson Memorial Lecturer, McGill Univ., Montreal 1995; Pickavance Memorial Lecturer, Rutherford Lab., Oxford 1997; Sargent Memorial Lecturer, Queen's Univ., Kingston, Ont. 1998; mem. Science Research Council 1967–70; Chair. S.R.C. Nuclear Physics Bd. 1968–70, Physics III Cttee. CERN, Geneva 1971–75, Radioactive Waste Man. Advisory Cttee. 1978–83; Vice-Pres. IUPAP 1985–93; mem. Council of the Asscn. of Commonwealth Univs. 1981–87; mem. Academia Europaea; Foreign mem. Royal Swedish Acad. of Sciences; Hon. D.Sc. (Univ. of Saskatchewan, Utah State Univ., Univ. of Guelph, Queen's Univ., Ont.); Hon. Fil.Dr. (Univ. of Uppsala); Hon. LL.D. (Sussex); Hon. D.Sc. (Coll. of William and Mary, Williamsburg); Holweck Medallist of French and British Physical Socs. 1957, Hughes Medal of the Royal Soc. 1965, Bruce-Preller Prize of Royal Soc. of Edin. 1969, Battelle Distinguished Prof., Univ. of Washington 1970, Tom W. Bonner Prize of American Physical Soc. 1974, Royal Medal, Royal Soc. 1980, Guthrie Medal of Inst. of Physics 1986, CCSEM Gold Medal 1988. *Publications:* Ionization Chambers and Counters 1950, Our Universes 1991; Editor: Isospin in Nuclear Physics 1969, Progress in Particle and Nuclear Physics 1977–84; Mesons in Nuclei (jt. ed.) 1979; many articles in learned journals. *Leisure interests:* early music and art, ornithology. *Address:* Gayles Orchard, Friston, Eastbourne, BN20 0BA, England. *Telephone:* (01323) 423333. *Fax:* (01323) 423329.

WILKINSON, Paul, M.A., F.R.S.A.; British professor of international relations; b. 9 May 1937, Harrow, Middx.; s. of Walter Ross Wilkinson and Joan Rosemary Paul; m. Susan Wilkinson 1960; two s. one d.; ed. Lower School of John Lyon, Harrow, Univ. Coll., Swansea and Univ. of Wales; regular officer R.A.F. 1959–65; Asst. Lecturer in Politics, Univ. Coll., Cardiff 1966–68, Lecturer 1968–75, Sr. Lecturer 1975–78; Reader in Politics, Univ. of Wales 1978–79; Chair. in Int. Relations, Aberdeen Univ. 1979–89; Head Dept. of Int. Relations, Univ. of St. Andrews 1990–94, Head School of History and Int. Relations 1994–96; Dir. Research Inst. for the Study of Conflict and Terrorism 1989–94; Hon. Fellow Univ. Coll., Swansea 1986; Visiting Fellow, Trinity Hall, Cambridge 1997–98. *Publications:* Social Movement 1971, Political Terrorism 1974, Terrorism versus Liberal Democracy 1976, Terrorism and the Liberal State (revised edn.) 1986, British Perspectives on Terrorism 1981, Terrorism: Theory and Practice (jtly.) 1978, The New Fascists (revised edn.) 1983, Contemporary Research on Terrorism 1987, Lessons of Lockerbie 1989, Terrorism and Political Violence (ed., with David Rapoport) 1990, Technology and Terrorism (ed.) 1993, Terrorism: British Perspectives (ed.) 1993, Research Report (Vol. Two) Lord Lloyd's Inquiry into Legislation Against Terrorism 1996, Aviation Terrorism and Security (ed., with Brian Jenkins) 1998, and numerous articles in specialist journals. *Leisure interests:* modern art, poetry, walking. *Address:* Department of International Relations, University of St. Andrews, North Street, St. Andrews, Fife, KY16 9AL, Scotland. *Telephone:* (01334) 462936.

WILKINSON, Sir Philip William, Kt., F.C.I.B.; British business executive; b. 8 May 1927; m. Eileen Patricia Malkin 1951 (died 1991); one s. two d.; ed. Leyton County High School; joined Westminster Bank (later Nat. Westminster Bank) 1943, Dir. 1979–90, Deputy Chair. 1987–90; Chief Exec. Lombard North Cen. Ltd. 1975; Gen. Man. Related Banking Services Div. 1978, Deputy Group Chief Exec. 1980, Group Chief Exec. 1983–87; Dir. HandelsBank 1983–90 (Deputy Chair. 1987–90); Dir. British Aerospace 1987–91, English Nat. Opera 1988–93, National Power 1990–92; Chair Wishbone Trust 1994–; Vice-Pres. Chartered Inst. of Bankers 1989–; Trustee Baptist Bldg. Fund 1987–; Council mem. Imperial Cancer Research Fund 1990–; mem. U.I.C.C. Finance Cttee. 1993–; Chair. The Wishbone Trust 1994–. *Leisure interests:* opera, theatre, golf, watching sport. *Address:* Pine Court, Whichert Close, Knotty Green, Beaconsfield, Bucks., HP9 2TP, England.

WIŁKOMIRSKA, Wanda; Polish violinist; b. 11 Jan. 1929, Warsaw; d. of Alfred Wiłkomirski and Dorota Temkin; m.; two s.; ed. Łódź Conservatory and in Budapest and France; public debut at age of 7 years; first appearance with orchestra aged 15, in Cracow; studied under Irena Dubiska (Łódź), Ede Zathureczky (Budapest) and Henryk Szeryng (Paris); Polish State Prize 1952, 1964; several foreign prizes, including Bach Competition award of Dem. German radio; Officer's Cross of Polonia Restituta 1953; Order of Banner of Labour 2nd Class 1959, 1st Class 1964; Culture and Arts Prize, 1st Class 1975, Orpheus Prize, Polish Musicians' Asscn. 1979; numerous recordings; now appears frequently with most of the major orchestras throughout the world; defected whilst on tour of Fed. Repub. of Germany March 1982. *Leisure interests:* theatre, literature, sports.

WILLATS, Stephan; British artist; b. 17 Aug. 1943, London; m. Stephanie Craven 1983; three s.; ed. Drayton School and Ealing School of Art; Lecturer, Ipswich School of Art 1965–67; Lecturer, Nottingham Coll. of Art 1968–72; Organiser, Centre for Behavioural Art, Gallery House, London 1972–73; numerous one-person exhbns. including Concerning Our Present Way of Living, Whitechapel Art Gallery, London 1979, Four Islands in Berlin, National Gallery, Berlin 1980, Meta Filter and Related Works, Tate Gallery, London 1982, Another City, Riverside Studios, London 1984, Doppelgänger, Lisson Gallery, Double Crossing, Ralph Wernicke Gallery, Stuttgart 1985, City of Concrete, Ikon Gallery, Birmingham, Fragments of Modern Living, in Regensburg and Cologne, Fed. Repub. of Germany, and Utrecht, Netherlands, Concepts and Models, ICA Gallery, London, Vier Huizen in Den Haag, Netherlands, Striking Back, Mappin Art Gallery, Sheffield 1986, Between Objects and People, Leeds City Art Gallery 1987, Transformers, People's Lives in the Modern World, Laing Art Gallery, Newcastle 1988, Gallery Torch, Amsterdam 1988, Secret Language, Cornerhouse Gallery, Manchester 1989, Mosaics, Kaj Fovsblom Gallery, Helsinki, Barbara Farber Gallery, Amsterdam 1990, Multiple Clothing Inst. of Contemporary Art (ICA) 1993, Tate Gallery, London 1994, Victoria Miro Gallery London 1994, Tramway Glasgow 1995; Galerie Kaj Forsblom, Helsinki 1995; numerous group exhbns. in the U.K., Netherlands, Italy, Fed. Repub. of Germany, Switzerland, Belgium, Australia; numerous project works, including Inside an Ocean, Mile End, London 1979, Two Worlds Apart, Hayes 1981 and Blocks, Avondale Estate, London 1982, Brentford Towers, W. London 1985, White Towers, Helsinki 1989, Private Network, Oxford 1990; D.A.A.D. Fellowship, Berlin 1979–81. *Publications:* several books, including The Artist as an Instigator of Changes in Social Cognition and Behaviour 1973, Art and Social Function 1976, The Lurky Place 1978, Doppelgänger 1985, Intervention and Audience 1986, Concepts and Projects, Bookworks by Stephen Willats; numerous articles in art magazines, including Control Magazine which he f. 1965. *Address:* c/o Lisson Gallery, 67 Bell Street, London, NW1 5DA, England.

WILLCOCKS, Sir David (Valentine), Kt., C.B.E., M.C., M.A., MUS.B., F.R.C.O., F.R.C.M.; British musician; b. 30 Dec. 1919, Newquay, Cornwall; s. of T. H. Willcocks; m. Rachel Blyth 1947; two s. (one deceased) two d.; ed. Clifton Coll. and King's Coll., Cambridge; Fellow, King's Coll., Cambridge 1947–51, Fellow and Dir. of Music 1957–73, Lecturer in Music, Cambridge Univ. and Cambridge Univ. Organist 1957–74; Conductor Cambridge Univ. Music Soc. 1958–73; Organist Salisbury Cathedral 1947–50, Worcester Cathedral 1950–57; Conductor, Worcester Three Choirs Festival and City of Birmingham Choir 1950–57; Musical Dir. Bach Choir, London 1960–98; Pres. Royal Coll. of Organists 1966–68, Incorporated Soc. of Musicians 1978–79, Nat. Fed. of Music Socs. 1980–89, Asscn. of British Choral Dirs. 1993–; Dir. Royal Coll. of Music, London 1974–84; Freeman, City of London 1981; Hon. D.Mus. (Exeter, Bristol and Leicester Univs., Westminster Choir Coll., Princeton, St. Olaf Coll., Luther Coll., Ia., Royal Coll. of Music, Univ. of Victoria, B.C.), Hon. D.Litt. (Sussex Univ.), Hon. D.S.L. (Trinity Coll., Toronto), Hon. M.A. (Bradford Univ.), Hon. R.A.M., Hon. G.S.M., Hon. Fellow, Royal Canadian Coll. of Organists, King's Coll., Cambridge; Harvard Glee Club Medal; F.R.N.C.M., F.R.S.A.M.D., F.R.S.C.M., F.T.C.L. *Address:* 13 Grange Road, Cambridge, CB3 9AS, England. *Telephone:* (01223) 359559. *Fax:* (01223) 355947.

WILLEBRANDS, H.E. Cardinal Johannes Gerardus Maria, DR. PHIL.; Netherlands ecclesiastic; b. 4 Sept. 1909, Bovenkarspel; s. of Herman Willebrands and Afra Kok; ed. Warmond Seminary, Holland, Angelicum, Rome; ordained 1934; Chaplain, Begijnhof Church, Amsterdam 1937–40; Prof. of Philosophy, Warmond 1940, Dir. 1945; Pres. St. Willibrord Asscn. 1946: organized Catholic Conf. on Ecumenical Questions 1951; Sec. Vatican Secretariat for Promoting Christian Unity 1960, Pres. 1969–89; Pres. Emer. Pontifical Council for Promoting Christian Unity 1989–; created Bishop 1964; created Cardinal 1969; now Chamberlain of the Coll. of Cardinals; appointed Archbishop of Utrecht 1975 (retd. 1983); Hon. D.D. (Oxford) 1987, and numerous other hon. degrees. *Publications:* La liberté religieuse et l'oecuménisme; Ecumenismo e problemi attuali, Oecuménisme et problèmes actuels; Bibel, ekumenik och sekularisering; Christus, Zeichen und Ursprung der Einheit in einer geteilten Welt, Mandatum Unitatis: Beiträge zur Oekumene 1989, Church and Jewish People: New Considerations 1992, Una sfida ecumenica, La nuova Europa 1995. *Address:* Piazza della Città Leonina 1, 00193 Rome, Italy.

WILLES, Mark Hinckley, PH.D.; American media executive and economist; b. 16 July 1941, Salt Lake City; s. of Joseph Simmons Willes and Ruth (née Hinckley) Willes; m. Laura Fayone 1961; three s. two d.; ed. Columbia Univ.; with Banking and Currency Cttee. House of Reps. 1966–67; Asst. Prof. of Finance Univ. of Pennsylvania, Phila. 1967–69; economist Fed. Reserve Bank 1967, sr. economist 1969–70, Dir. Research 1970–71, Vice-Pres. 1971, First Vice-Pres. 1971–77; Pres. Fed. Reserve Bank of Minneapolis 1977–80; Exec. Vice-Pres., Chief Finance Officer Gen. Mills Inc. 1980–85, Pres., C.O.O. 1985–92, Vice-Chair. 1992–95; Chair., Pres., C.E.O. Times Mirror Co. 1995–. *Address:* Times Mirror Company, Times Mirror Square, Los Angeles, CA 90053, U.S.A.

WILLEY, Gordon Randolph, PH.D.; American archaeologist; b. 7 March 1913, Chariton, Ia.; s. of Frank Willey and Agnes Caroline Wilson; m. Katharine Winston Whaley 1938; two c.; ed. Univ. of Arizona and Columbia Univ.; Instructor in Anthropology, Columbia Univ. 1942–43; Anthropologist, Bureau of American Ethnology, Smithsonian Inst. 1943–50; Bowditch Prof. of Mexican and Cen. American Archaeology, Harvard Univ. 1950–83, Sr. Prof. of Anthropology 1983–87, Bowditch Prof. Emer. 1987–, Chair. Dept. Anthropology 1954–57; mem. N.A.S.; Hon. D.Litt. (Cambridge) 1977, (Univ. of Arizona) 1981, (Univ. of New Mexico) 1984; Wenner-Gren Medal for Archaeology 1953, Order of Quetzal, Republic of Guatemala 1968, Archaeological Inst. of America Gold Medal 1973, A. V. Kidder Medal for Archaeology (American Anthropological Asscn.) 1974; Huxley Medal, Royal Anthropological Inst. of Great Britain 1979; Walker Prize, Boston Museum of Science 1981, Drexel Medal (Univ. Museum, Philadelphia) 1982, Golden Plate Award, American Acad. of Achievement 1987. *Publications:* Archaeology of the Florida Gulf Coast 1949, Prehistoric Settlement Patterns of the Viru Valley, Peru 1953, Method and Theory in American Archaeology 1958, Prehistoric Maya Settlements in the Belize Valley 1965, An Introduction to American Archaeology Vol. I 1966, Vol. II 1971, Excavations at Altar de Sacrificios, Guatemala 1973, A History of American Archaeology (co-author) 1974, Excavations at Seibal, Guatemala 1975, The Origins of Maya Civilization 1977, Lowland Maya Settlement Patterns: A Summary View 1981, Essays in Maya Archaeology 1987, Portraits in American Archaeology 1988, New World Archaeology and Culture History 1990, Excavations at Seibal: Summary and Conclusions 1990, Excavations in the Copán Residential Zone: Ceramics and Artifacts 1994. *Leisure interests:* tennis, swimming, English literature and literary criticism. *Address:* 25 Gray Gardens E., Cambridge, MA, U.S.A. (Home). *Telephone:* EL4-1287 (Home).

WILLIAM, David, B.A.; British/Canadian director, actor and lecturer; b. 24 June 1926, London, England; s. of Eric Hugh Williams and Olwen Roose; ed. Bryanston School, Blandford, Dorset, Univ. Coll. Oxford; Artistic Dir. New Shakespeare Co., London, England 1962–66, Nat. Theatre of Israel 1968–70; Assoc. Dir. Mermaid Theatre, London 1964–66; f. and first Artistic Dir. Ludlow Festival; Artistic Dir. Stratford Festival, Stratford, Ont., Canada 1989–93. *Productions include:* (at Stratford, Ont.): Bacchae, The Importance of Being Earnest, The Winter's Tale, Murder in the Cathedral, Troilus and Cressida; (elsewhere): Richard II (Nat. Theatre of G.B.), Dear Daddy (Ambassadors Theatre, London), Thérèse (Royal Opera House, Covent Garden), The Lighthouse (Edin. Festival), world première of opera Red Emma (Canadian Opera Co.) 1995, Così fan Tutte, Opera St. Louis, Tosca (Canadian Opera Co.) 1998 and many others in London, New York, San Francisco, Washington, D.C., Gulbenkian Festival, Lisbon. *Recent performances include:* Malvolio, Serebryakov and Jacques. *Publications:* The Tempest on the Stage 1960, Hamlet in the Theatre 1963. *Leisure interests:* walking, dogs. *Address:* 194 Langarth Street, London, Ont., N6C 1Z5, Canada. *Fax:* 519 673 3755.

WILLIAMS, Abraham (Abe), B.A.; South African politician; b. 12 Dec. 1940, Saldanha; m. Esmé Williams; one s. one d.; ed. Univ. of W. Cape; teacher St Andrew's Primary School, Saldanha; Prin. Belhar Primary School, Cape Town 1977–83; M.P. for Mamre 1984; mem. Labour Party, Nat. Organizer 1986, Nat. Sec. 1989–91; joined Nat. Party 1991; Deputy Minister of Educ. and Culture, House of Reps. 1989–91; Deputy Minister of Nat. Educ. and Local Govt. and Nat. Housing 1991–92; mem. Govt. Del. to CODESA 1992; Minister of Sport in Cabinet 1993; Minister of Welfare and Population Devt., Govt. of Nat. Unity 1994–96. *Address:* c/o Private Bag X9153, Cape Town 8000, South Africa.

WILLIAMS, Sir Alwyn, Kt., PH.D., F.R.S., F.R.S.E., M.R.I.A.; British geologist and academic; b. 8 June 1921, Aberdare; s. of D. Daniel Williams and E. May Williams (née Rogers); m. Edith Joan Bevan 1949; one s. one d.; ed. Aberdare Boys' Grammar School and Univ. Coll. of Wales, Aberystwyth; Fellow of Univ. of Wales, Sedgwick Museum, Cambridge 1947–48; Commonwealth Fund (Harkness) Fellow, U.S. Nat. Museum 1948–50; Lecturer in Geology, Univ. of Glasgow 1950–54; Prof. of Geology, Queen's Univ., Belfast 1954–74; Lapworth Prof. of Geology, Univ. of Birmingham 1974–76; Prin. and Vice-Chancellor, Univ. of Glasgow 1976–88; Hon. Sr. Research Fellow, Univ. of Glasgow 1988–; Pres. Royal Soc., Edin. 1985–88; Hon. F.R.C.P.S., F.D.S., R.C.P.S.; Hon. Fellow, Geological Soc. of America; Foreign mem. Polish Acad. of Sciences; Hon. D.Sc. (Wales) 1973, (Queen's Univ. Belfast) 1975, (Edin.) 1979, (Strathclyde) 1982; Hon. D.C.L. (Oxford) 1987, Hon. LL.D. (Glasgow) 1988; Hon. D.Univ. (Paisley). *Publications:* monographs in professional journals. *Leisure interests:* music, art. *Address:* Palaeobiology Unit, University of Glasgow, Glasgow, G12 8QQ (Office); 25 Sutherland Avenue, Pollokshields, Glasgow, GI4 4HG, Scotland (Home).

WILLIAMS, Anthony A., J.D.; American government official; m. Diana Lynn Simmons; one c.; ed. Yale and Harvard Univs.; law clerk U.S. Dist. Court Boston 1987–88; Asst. Dir. Boston Redevt. Authority 1988–89; Exec. Dir. Community Devt. Agency St. Louis 1989–91; Deputy Comptroller State of Conn. 1991–93; Chief Finance Officer Dept. of Agric. 1993–; Adjunct Prof. of Public Affairs Columbia Univ. 1992–93; Nat. Fellow Kellogg Foundation 1991; Democrat. *Address:* Department of Agriculture, 441 4th Street North West, Suite 350N, Washington, DC 20001, U.S.A.

WILLIAMS, Arthur Ronald, O.B.E.; British business executive; b. 29 Oct. 1942, Rawalpindi, India; s. of Alfred Arthur Williams and Marjory Williams (née Heenan); m. 1st Lynne Diana Merrin 1967; m. 2nd Antoinette Catherine Naldrett 1993; two d.; ed. Rossall School, Fleetwood, Lancs. and Selwyn

Coll., Cambridge 1961–64; joined diplomatic service 1964, served in Jakarta 1966–67, Singapore 1967–69, Budapest 1971–74, Nairobi 1976–78; Chief Exec. Timber Growers U.K. 1980–87; Exec. Dir. Forestry Industry Council of G.B. 1987–97; Chief Exec. The Publrs. Assen. 1998–. *Publications:* Montrose, Cavalier in Mourning 1975, The Lords of the Isles 1985, The Heather and the Gale 1997, Sons of the Wolf 1998. *Leisure interests:* fly fishing, Scottish history, walking, real tennis. *Address:* Cobblers, The Old Hill, Wherwell, Hampshire, SP11 7JB, England. *Telephone:* (01264) 860879. *Fax:* (01264) 860003.

WILLIAMS, Bernard Arthur Owen, M.A., F.B.A.; British philosopher; b. 21 Sept. 1929, Westcliff; s. of Owen Williams and Hilda Williams; m. 1st Shirley Catlin (now Baroness Williams of Crosby q.v.) 1955 (divorced 1974); one d.; m. 2nd Patricia Skinner 1974; two s.; ed. Chigwell School, Essex, Balliol Coll., Oxford; Fellow, All Souls Coll., Oxford 1951–54, 1997–, New Coll., Oxford 1954–59; Lecturer, Univ. Coll., London 1959–64; Prof. Bedford Coll., London 1964–67; Knightbridge Prof. of Philosophy, Cambridge 1967–79; Provost, King's Coll., Cambridge 1979–87; Monroe Deutsch Prof. of Philosophy, Univ. of Calif., Berkeley 1988–; White's Prof. of Moral Philosophy and Fellow Corpus Christi Coll., Univ. of Oxford 1990–96; visiting appointments, Univ. Coll. of Ghana 1958–59, Princeton 1963, A.N.U. 1969, Harvard 1973, Univ. of California, Berkeley 1986; Dir. English Nat. Opera 1968–86; author and presenter What Is Truth? series, Channel 4 1988; Hon. Litt.D. (Dublin) 1981, Hon. Litt. (Aberdeen) 1987, (Keele) 1995, Hon. Fellow Balliol Coll., Oxford 1984, Corpus Christi Coll., Oxford 1996. *Publications:* Morality 1972, Problems of The Self 1973, A Critique of Utilitarianism 1973, Descartes: The Project of Pure Enquiry 1978, Moral Luck 1981, Ethics and the Limits of Philosophy 1985, Shame and Necessity 1993, Making Sense of Humanity 1995, Plato 1998, Der Wert der Wahrheit 1998. *Leisure interest:* music. *Address:* All Souls College, Oxford, OX1 4AL, England.

WILLIAMS, Betty; British peace campaigner; b. 22 May 1943, Belfast; m. 1st Ralph Williams 1961 (divorced); one s. one d.; m. 2nd James T. Perkins 1982; ed. St. Teresa's Primary School, Belfast; worked as office receptionist; jt. winner of Nobel Peace Prize for launching the Northern Ireland Peace Movement (later renamed Community of the Peace People) 1976, Jt. Leader 1976–78; Carl von Ossietzky Medal for Courage (Berlin Section, Int. League of Human Rights); Hon. LL.D. (Yale Univ.); Hon. D.Hum.Litt. (Coll. of Sienna Heights, Mich.) 1977. *Leisure interest:* gardening. *Address:* P.O. Box 725, Valparaiso, FL 32580, U.S.A.

WILLIAMS, Brian; American television journalist; b. 1959; m. Jane Stoddart Williams; two c.; ed. Catholic and George Washington Univs.; fmrly. intern The White House, TV reporter KOAM-TV, with WTTG-TV, WCAU-TV; joined WCBS-TV 1993; Chief White House Corresp. 1994–96; anchor, Man. Ed. The News With Brian Williams MSNBC 1996–; Emmy Awards for reporting 1987, 1989, 1993. *Address:* c/o NBC News, 30 Rockefeller Plaza, New York, NY 10112, U.S.A.

WILLIAMS, Sir Bruce (Rodda), K.B.E., M.A.; economist; b. 10 Jan. 1919, Warragul, Vic.; s. of the late Rev. W. J. Williams and of Helen Baud; m. Roma Olive Hotten 1942; five d.; ed. Wesley Coll., Melbourne, Queen's Coll., Univ. of Melbourne; Prof. of Econs., Univ. Coll., North Staffordshire 1950–59; Robert Otley Prof., Stanley Jevons Prof., Univ. of Manchester 1959–67; Sec. and Jt. Dir. of Research, Science and Industry Cttee. 1952–59; mem. U.K. Nat. Bd. for Prices and Incomes 1966–67; Econ. Adviser to U.K. Ministry of Tech. 1966–67; mem. U.K. Cen. Advisory Council on Science and Tech. 1967; Vice-Chancellor and Principal, Univ. of Sydney 1967–81, Prof. 1967–; Dir. Tech. Change Centre 1981–86; Chair. Australian Inquiry into the Eng. Disciplines 1987–88; Chair. N.S.W. State Cancer Council 1967–81; mem. Bd. of Reserve Bank of Australia 1969–81; Chair. Australian Vice-Chancellors' Cttee. 1972–74, Nat. Cttee. of Inquiry into Educ. and Training 1976–79; Dir. Parramatta Hospitals Bd. 1978–81; mem. Commonwealth Working Group on the Man. of Technological Change 1984–85, on Distance Teaching and Open Learning 1986–87; Visiting Fellow, Australian Nat. Univ. 1989–90, 1993–94, Univ. of London Inst. of Educ. 1991–92; Fellow Univ. of Sydney Senate 1994–98; Pres. Sydney Conservatorium of Music Foundation 1994–98; Chair. Exec. Sydney Int. Piano Competition 1986–; Hon. F.I.E. Australia 1989; Hon. D.Litt. (Univ. of Keele) 1973, (Univ. of Sydney) 1982, Hon. D.Econ. (Univ. of Queensland) 1980, Hon. LL.D. (Univ. of Melbourne) 1981, (Univ. of Manchester) 1982, Hon. D.Sc. (Univ. of Aston) 1982. *Publications:* The Socialist Order and Freedom 1942, Industry and Technical Progress (with C. F. Carter) 1957, Investment in Innovation (with C. F. Carter) 1958, Science in Industry (with C. F. Carter) 1959, Technology, Investment and Growth 1967, Science and Technology in Economic Growth 1973, Systems of Higher Education: Australia 1978, Education Training and Employment 1979, Disappointed Expectations 1981, Living with Technology 1982, Knowns and Unknowns in Technical Change 1985, The Influence of Attitudes to New Technology on National Growth Rates 1986, Review of the Discipline of Engineering 1988, Academic Status and Leadership (with D. Wood) 1990, University Responses to Research Selectivity 1991, Higher Education and Employment 1994. *Leisure interests:* music, theatre. *Address:* 106 Grange Road, Ealing Common, London, W5 3PJ, England; 24 Mansfield Street, Glebe, N.S.W. 2037, Australia.

WILLIAMS, David; British international finance official; b. 1934; ed. London School of Econs.; mem. Basle Centre for Econ. and Financial Research; Asst. lecturer, Univ. of Leeds; lecturer, Univ. of Hull; economist, European Dept. IMF 1963; economist and sr. economist, IMF Research Dept.; joined Treasurer's Dept. 1969; Deputy Treasurer IMF 1978, Treasurer 1991–. *Address:* International Monetary Fund, 700 19th Street, N.W., Washington, DC 20431, U.S.A.

WILLIAMS, Sir David Glyndwr Tudor, Kt., M.A., LL.M.; British professor of law; b. 22 Oct. 1930, Carmarthen; s. of Tudor Williams and Anne Williams; m. Sally G. M. Cole 1959; one s. two d.; ed. Queen Elizabeth Grammar School, Carmarthen and Emmanuel Coll. Cambridge; called to Bar, Lincoln's Inn 1956; Commonwealth Fund (Harkness) Fellow, Univ. of Calif., Berkeley and Harvard Univ. 1956–58; lecturer in Law, Univ. of Nottingham 1958–63; Fellow, Keble Coll., Oxford 1963–67; Fellow, Emmanuel Coll., Cambridge 1967–80, Sr. Tutor 1970–76; Pres. Wolfson Coll., Cambridge 1980–92; Rouse Ball Prof. of English Law, Univ. of Cambridge 1983–92, Emer. Prof. 1992–; Vice-Chancellor, Univ. of Cambridge 1989–96, Vice-Chancellor Emer. 1996–, Prof. of Law, Professorial Fellow Emmanuel Coll. 1996–; mem. Royal Comm. on Environmental Pollution 1976–83, Council on Tribunals 1972–83; Chair. Animal Procedures Cttee. 1987–89; mem. Int. Jury for the Indira Gandhi Prize for Peace, Disarmament and Devt. 1992–; Trustee Rajiv Gandhi (U.K.) Foundation; mem. American Law Inst.; Foreign Hon. mem. American Acad. of Arts and Sciences; Hon. Fellow, Emmanuel Coll., Cambridge 1984, Keble Coll., Oxford 1991, Pembroke Coll., Cambridge 1993, Wolfson Coll., Cambridge; Hon. Bencher, Lincoln's Inn 1985; Hon. Q.C. 1994; Hon. D. Litt. (Loughborough, William Jewell Coll., Mo.); Hon. LL.D. (Hull, Nottingham, Sydney, Davidson Coll., N.C., Liverpool, McGill, De Montfort, Duke, Cambridge). *Publications:* Not in the Public Interest 1965, Keeping the Peace 1967; articles in legal periodicals. *Address:* Emmanuel College, Cambridge, CB2 3AP, England. *Telephone:* (01223) 334200. *Fax:* (01223) 334426.

WILLIAMS, Sir Denys Ambrose, K.C.M.G., G.C.M., M.A., B.C.L.; Barbadian attorney-at-law; b. 12 Oct. 1929; s. of George Cuthbert Williams and Violet Irene Gilkes; m. Carmel Mary Coleman 1954; two s. four d.; ed. Combermere School, Harrison Coll., Worcester Coll., Oxford and Middle Temple, London; Asst. Legal Draftsman, Asst. to Attorney Gen., Barbados; Asst. Legal Draftsman, Fed. of West Indies; Sr. Parl. Counsel, Barbados 1963–67, Supreme Court Judge 1967–86, Chief Justice 1987–; Gold Crown of Merit. *Leisure interests:* horse-racing, tennis, gardening, walking. *Address:* 9 Garrison, St. Michael, Barbados, West Indies. *Telephone:* 42 7 11 64.

WILLIAMS, Dudley Howard, PH.D., SC.D., F.R.S.; British professor of biological chemistry; b. 25 May 1937, Leeds; s. of Lawrence Williams and Evelyn Williams; m. Lorna Patricia Phyllis Bedford 1963; two s.; ed. Univ. of Leeds, Stanford Univ., Calif.; Asst. Dir. Research, Univ. Chem. Lab., Univ. of Cambridge 1966–74, Fellow Churchill Coll. 1964–, Reader in Organic Chem. 1974–96, Prof. of Biological Chem. 1996–; Visiting Prof. and Lecturer, Univs. of Calif. 1967, 1986, 1989, 1997, Cape Town 1972, Sydney 1972, Fla. 1973, Wis. 1975, Copenhagen 1976, Australian Nat. Univ., Canberra 1980, Queensland 1994; co-discoverer of metabolism of vitamin D 1971, and of mechanism of action of glycopeptide antibiotics which inhibit resistant bacteria; mem. Acad. Europaea; Tilden Lecturer (Royal Soc. of Chem.) 1983, Arun Guthikonda Memorial Award Lectureship (Columbia Univ.) 1985, Distinguished Visiting Lecturer, Texas A & M Univ. 1986, Rorer Lecturer, Ohio State Univ. 1989, Univ. of Auckland Foundation Lecturer 1991, Pacific Coast Lecturer 1991, Steel Lecturer, Univ. of Queensland 1994; Meldola Medal, Royal Inst. of Chem. 1966; Corday-Morgan Medal, Chemical Soc. 1968, Award for Structural Chem. (R.S.C.) 1984, Bader Award in Organic Chem. (R.S.C.) 1990, Leo Friend Award, American Chem. Soc. 1996. *Publications:* 10 books, including Spectroscopic Methods in Organic Chemistry (with I. Fleming), about 400 scientific publications dealing with the devt. of mass spectrometry and nuclear magnetic resonance, the structure elucidation of complex molecules, the modes of action of antibiotics, and molecular recognition phenomena. *Leisure interests:* music, skiing, squash. *Address:* University Chemical Laboratory, Lensfield Road, Cambridge, CB2 1EW (Office); 7 Balsham Road, Fulbourn, Cambridge, CB1 5BZ, England (Home). *Telephone:* (01223) 336368 (Office); (01223) 502341 (Home).

WILLIAMS, Elizabeth (see Williams, Betty).

WILLIAMS, Sir Glanmor, Kt, C.B.E., M.A., D.LITT., LL.D., F.B.A., F.S.A., F.R.HIST.S.; British professor of history (retd.); b. 5 May 1920, Dowlais, Glam.; s. of Daniel Williams and Ceinwen Williams; m. Margaret F. Davies 1946; one s. one d.; ed. Cyfarthfa Secondary School, Merthyr Tydfil and Univ. Coll. of Wales, Aberystwyth; Lecturer and Sr. Lecturer in History, Univ. Coll. of Swansea 1945–57, Prof. of History 1957–82, Vice-Prin. 1975–78; Vice-Pres. Univ. of Wales, Aberystwyth 1986–96; mem. Bd. of Govs. BBC 1965–71, British Library Bd. 1973–80; Chair. Ancient Monuments Bd. (Wales) 1983–95, Royal Comm. on Ancient and Historical Monuments (Wales) 1986–90; Chair. British Library, Advisory Council 1981–86. *Publications:* The Welsh Church 1962, Welsh Reformation Essays 1966, Religion, Language and Nationality in Wales 1979, Henry Tudor 1985, Recovery, Reorientation and Reformation: Wales, 1415–1642 1987; Glamorgan County History, Vols. I–VI 1971–88 (Ed.), The Welsh and their Religion 1991, Owain Glyndŵr 1993, Wales and the Reformation 1997. *Leisure interests:* music, cine-photography. *Address:* 11 Grosvenor Road, Sketty, Swansea, SA2 0SP, Wales. *Telephone:* (01792) 204113.

WILLIAMS, (John) Gwynn, C.B.E., M.A.; British historian; b. 19 June 1924; s. of the late John Ellis Williams and Annie Maude Rowlands; m. Beryl Thomas 1954; three s.; ed. Holywell Grammar School, Univ. Coll. of North

Wales; with R.N. 1943–46; staff tutor Dept. of Extra Mural Studies Univ. of Liverpool 1951–54; asst. lecturer Univ. of North Wales 1955, Prof. of Welsh History 1963–83, Dean Faculty of Arts 1972–74, Vice-Prin. 1974–79, Vice-Pres. 1993–; Chair. Press Bd. Univ. of Wales 1979–91; Dir. Gregynog Press 1979–; Vice-Pres. Nat. Library of Wales 1984–86, Pres. 1986–96; Pres. Cambrian Archaeological Asscn. 1987–88; Vice-Pres. Hon. Soc. of Cymmrodorion 1988–; Hon. mem. Gorsedd of Bards; mem. Royal Comm. on Ancient and Historical Monuments in Wales 1967–91. *Publications include:* The Founding of the University College of North Wales, Bangor 1985, The University College of North Wales: Foundations 1985, University and Nation 1893–1939 (The Thomas Jones Pierce Memorial Lecture) 1992, The Report on the Proposed University of Wales (ed.) 1993, The University Movement in Wales 1993, numerous articles on 17th century Wales for learned journals. *Leisure interests:* travelling, walking. *Address:* Llywenan, Siliwen, Bangor, Gwynedd, LL57 2BS, Wales. *Telephone:* (01248) 353065.

WILLIAMS, John, A.O., O.B.E.; guitarist; b. 24 April 1941, Melbourne, Australia; s. of Len Williams and Melaan Ket; m. 1st Linda Susan Kendall 1964 (divorced); one d.; m. 2nd Sue Cook 1981 (divorced); one s.; ed. Friern Barnet Grammar School, and Royal Coll. of Music, London; studied guitar with father, Segovia and at Accad. Chigiana, Siena; has toured widely and appears frequently on TV and radio; numerous transcriptions and gramophone recordings as solo guitarist and with leading orchestras; founded The Height Below (ensemble) with Brian Gascoigne 1974, John Williams and Friends (ensemble) and founder mem. groups Sky 1979–84 and John Williams' Attacca 1991–; Artistic Dir. South Bank Summer Music Festival 1984–85, Melbourne Arts Festival 1987; Hon. F.R.C.M., Hon. Fellow Royal Northern Coll. of Music. *Leisure interests:* people, living, chess, table tennis, music. *Address:* c/o Askonas Holt Ltd., 27 Chancery Lane, London, WC2A 1PF, England. *Telephone:* 0171-400 1700. *Fax:* 0171-400 1799.

WILLIAMS, John Ellis Caerwyn, M.A., B.D., D.LITT., D.LITT./CELT., F.B.A., M.R.I.A.; British university professor (retd.); b. 17 Jan. 1912, Glam. Wales; s. of John Williams and Maria Williams; m. Gwenifred Watkins 1946; no c.; ed. Univ. Coll. of N. Wales, Bangor, Nat. Univ. of Ireland, Dublin, Trinity Coll., Dublin, United Theological Coll., Aberystwyth and Bala Theological Coll.; Research Lecturer, Univ. Coll. of N. Wales 1937–39; Fellow, Univ. of Wales 1939–41; Lecturer, Univ. Coll. of N. Wales 1945–51, Sr. Lecturer 1951–53, Prof. of Welsh 1953–65; Prof. of Irish, Univ. Coll. of Wales, Aberystwyth 1965–79, Prof. Emer. 1979–; Hon. Dir. Centre for Advanced Welsh and Celtic Studies 1979–85, Hon. Consultant Ed. 1985–; Leverhulme Fellow 1963–64; Visiting Prof. U.C.L.A. 1968, Harvard Summer School 1968; Chair. Welsh Acad. 1965–75, Pres. 1989–; Hon. D.Litt. Celt. (Ireland) 1967, D.Litt. (Wales) 1983; Derek Allen Prize (British Acad.) 1983. *Publications:* several books. *Leisure interest:* walking. *Address:* 6 Pant-y-Rhos, Waunfawr, Aberystwyth, Dyfed, Wales. *Telephone:* (01970) 612959.

WILLIAMS, Sir (John) Kyffin, Kt., O.B.E., R.A.; Welsh artist; b. 1918, Llangefni; s. of Henry Inglis Wynne Williams and Essyllt Mary Williams (née Williams); ed. Shrewsbury School, Slade School of Art; Sr. Art Master, Highgate School 1944–73; one-man shows Leicester Galleries 1951, 1953, 1956, 1960, 1966, 1970; Colnaghi Galleries 1948, 1949, 1965, 1970; Thackeray Galleries 1975, 1977, 1979, 1981, 1983, 1985, 1987, 1989, 1991; retrospective Nat. Museum of Wales 1987; Pres. Royal Cambrian Acad. 1969–76, 1992–; Winston Churchill Fellow 1968; D.L. Gwynedd 1985; Hon. Fellow, Univ. Coll., Swansea 1989, Univ. Coll. N. Wales, Bangor 1991, Univ. Coll. Wales, Aberystwyth 1992; Hon. M.A. (Wales) 1973; Hon. D.Litt. (Wales) 1993; Medal of Hon. Soc. of Cymmrodorion. *Publications:* Across The Straits (autobiog.) 1973, A Wider Sky (autobiog. Vol. II) 1991, Boyo Ballads 1995, Portraits 1996, Land and Sea 1998. *Leisure interests:* the countryside, sport. *Address:* Pwllfanogl, Llanfairpwll, Gwynedd, LL61 6PD, Wales. *Telephone:* (01248) 714693.

WILLIAMS, John Peter Rhys, M.B.E., M.R.C.S., L.R.C.P., M.B., B.S., F.R.C.S.(E.); Welsh rugby player and orthopaedic surgeon; b. 2 March 1949, Cardiff; s. of Peter and Margaret Williams; m. Priscilla Parkin 1973; one s. three d.; ed. Bridgend Grammar School, Millfield, St. Mary's Hosp. Medical School; British Junior Tennis Champion, Wimbledon 1966; Welsh int. rugby player 1969–79, 1980–81; 55 caps for Wales; on tour with British Lions to New Zealand 1971, South Africa 1974; 8 test matches for British Lions, winning both series; qualified as medical doctor 1973; surgical Registrar, Cardiff Hosp. 1977–80, Orthopaedic Registrar 1980–82; Orthopaedic Sr. Registrar, St. Mary's Hosp., London 1982–85; Consultant Orthopaedic Surgeon, Princess of Wales Hosp., Bridgend Jan. 1986–; Captain of Welsh rugby team 1978–79; Primary F.R.C.S. 1976. *Publications:* Irish Conference on Sporting Injuries, Dublin (ed.) 1975, JPR (autobiography) 1979, Cervical neck injuries in Rugby Football, British Medical Journal 1978, Trans-Oral Fusion of the Cervical Spine, Journal of Bone and Joint Surgery 1985. *Leisure interests:* sport, music. *Address:* Llansannor Lodge, Llansannor, Nr. Cowbridge, Vale of Glamorgan, CF71 7RX, Wales.

WILLIAMS, John T.; American composer of film music; b. 8 Feb. 1932, Flushing, N.Y.; ed. Juilliard School; Conductor Boston Pops Orchestra 1980–84; numerous hon. degrees; Acad. Awards for Fiddler on the Roof, Jaws, Star Wars, E.T., Schindler's List. 14 Grammys; two Emmys; Golden Globe Award 1978. *Filmscores:* The Secret Ways 1961, Diamond Head 1962, None But the Brave 1965, How to Steal a Million 1966, Valley of the Dolls 1967, The Cowboys 1972, The Poseidon Adventure 1972, Tom Sawyer 1973, Earthquake 1974, The Towering Inferno 1974, Jaws 1975, The Eiger Sanction 1975, Family Plot 1976, Midway 1976, The Missouri Breaks 1976, Raggedy Ann and Andy 1977, Black Sunday 1977, Star Wars 1977, Close Encounters of the Third Kind 1977, The Fury 1978, Jaws II 1976, Superman 1978, Dracula 1979, The Empire Strikes Back 1980, Raiders of the Lost Ark 1981, E.T.: The Extra Terrestrial 1982, Return of the Jedi 1983, Indiana Jones and the Temple of Doom 1984, The River 1985, Space Camp 1986, The Witches of Eastwick 1987, Empire of the Sun (BAFTA Best Score Award) 1988, Always 1989, Born on the Fourth of July 1989, Stanley and Iris 1990, Presumed Innocent 1990, Home Alone 1990, Hook 1991, JFK, Far and Away, Home Alone 2: Lost in New York, Jurassic Park 1993, Schindler's List 1993, Sabrina 1995, Nixon 1995, Sleepers 1996, Rosewood 1996, Seven Years in Tibet 1997, The Lost World, Amistad 1997, Saving Private Ryan 1998, The Phantom Menace 1999. *Address:* c/o Michael Gorfaine, Gorfaine & Schwartz, 13245 Riverside Drive, Suite 450, Sherman Oaks, CA 91423, U.S.A.

WILLIAMS, Joseph Dalton, B.SC.; American business executive; b. 15 Aug. 1926, Washington, Pa.; s. of Joseph Dalton Williams and Jane Day; m. Millie E. Bellaire 1973; one s. one d.; ed. Univ. of Nebraska; Sales Rep., Parke-Davis, Kan. City 1950, Field Man. 1956, Asst. Man. Market Research 1958, Asst. to Dir. Sales Research and Devt. 1962, Dir. Medical-Surgical Market Devt. 1967, Dir. U.S. Marketing 1968, Group Vice-Pres., Marketing and Sales 1970; following merger of cos., Vice-Pres., Warner-Lambert, mem. Bd., Parke-Davis; Exec. Vice-Pres. and C.O.O., Parke-Davis 1971, Pres. and C.E.O. 1973; mem. Bd of Dirs. Warner-Lambert 1973–, Sr Vice-Pres. 1973, Exec. Vice-Pres. and Pres. Pharmaceutical Group 1976, Sr. Exec. Vice-Pres., mem. Office of Chair. and Pres. Int. Group 1977, Pres., Dir. Warner-Lambert Corpn. 1979–80, Pres. and C.O.O. 1980–84, Chair., C.E.O. 1985–91, Chair. Exec. Cttee. 1991–; Bd. Dirs. AT&T, Exxon Corpn., Rockefeller Financial Services Inc.; numerous hon. degrees; Remington Honor Medal, American Pharmaceutical Asscn., Rutgers Univ. Award 1982. *Leisure interests:* golf, antique cars. *Address:* Warner-Lambert Company, 55 Madison Avenue, Morristown, NJ 07960 (Office); P.O. Box 836, Bernardsville, NJ 07924, U.S.A. (Home). *Telephone:* (973) 285-3277 (Office). *Fax:* (973) 285-3276 (Office).

WILLIAMS, Lynn Russell; American union official; b. 21 July 1924, Springfield, Ont., Canada; s. of Waldemar Williams and Emma Elizabeth (née Fisher) Williams; m. Audrey Hansuld 1946; two s. two d.; ed. McMaster Univ.; organizer Canadian Labour Congress 1947–55; joined United Steelworkers of America, Toronto, Ont. 1947, Staff Rep. 1956–57, Asst. Dir. Dist. 6 1963–73, Dir. Dist. 6 1973–77; Int. Sec. United Steelworkers of America, Pittsburgh 1977–83, Int. Pres. 1983; Visiting Fellow, Inst. of Politics; mem. Exec. Cttee. AFL-CIO, Washington 1983; Dir. American Arbitration Asscn. 1983; mem. Bd. of Dirs., African-American Labor Center, Cttee. for Nat. Health Insurance, Work in America Inst., American Open Univ. 1983–; American Productivity Centre, Citizen/Labor Energy Coalition, Pittsburgh Symphony Soc., other orgs.; mem. Panel, Econ. Policy Council; Vice-Pres. Americans for Democratic Action; mem.UN Econ. Policy Council, Canada-America Comm. *Leisure interests:* running, jogging, reading, skiing. *Address:* Institute of Politics, 79 JFK Street, Cambridge, MA 02138, U.S.A.

WILLIAMS, Mack Geoffrey Denis, B.A.; Australian diplomatist; b. 16 July 1939, Sydney; s. of Bernard George Williams and Thelma A. McMillan; m. Carla Lothringer 1966; one s. three d.; ed. Fort Street Boys High School, Sydney and Univ. of Sydney; joined Dept. of Foreign Affairs 1961; Third Sec. Brussels 1962–65; Second Sec. Saigon 1965–67; First Sec. Phnom Penh 1969–71; Counsellor, Washington, D.C. 1971–74; Office of Minister of Foreign Affairs, Canberra 1975–76; Deputy High Commr. in Papua New Guinea 1977–78; Royal Coll. of Defence Studies, London 1979; High Commr. in Bangladesh 1980–82; Dept. of Prime Minister, Canberra 1986–87; First Asst. Sec. Dept. of Foreign Affairs and Trade 1987–89; Amb. to the Philippines 1989–94, to Repub. of Korea 1994–. *Leisure interest:* golf. *Address:* Embassy of Australia, KPO Box 562, Seoul, Republic of Korea. *Telephone:* (2) 7306490. *Fax:* (2) 7356601.

WILLIAMS, Martin John, C.V.O., O.B.E., B.A.; British diplomatist; b. 3 Nov. 1941; s. of John Henry Stroud Williams and Barbara Williams (née Benington); m. Susan Dent 1964; two s.; ed. Manchester Grammar School, Corpus Christi Coll. Oxford; joined Commonwealth Relations Office 1963; various posts including Embassy, Manila 1966–69, Consulate-Gen., Milan 1970–72, Embassy, Teheran 1977–80, High Comm., New Delhi 1982–86, Embassy, Rome 1986–90; Head S. Asian Dept., FCO 1990–92; seconded to Northern Ireland Office, Belfast as Asst. Under-Sec. (Political Affairs) 1993–95; High Commr. in Zimbabwe 1995–98, in N.Z. (also accred to Samoa and Gov. Pitcairn Island) 1998–. *Leisure interests:* music, gardening, woodwork. *Address:* British High Commission, 44 Hill Street, P.O. Box 1812, Wellington 1, New Zealand. *Telephone:* (04) 495 0874. *Fax:* (04) 495 0831.

WILLIAMS, Maurice Jacoutot, M.A.; American international civil servant; b. 13 Nov. 1920, Moncton, N.B., Canada; s. of Alfred Jacoutot Williams and Yvonne Theberge; m. Betty Jane Bath 1943; three s.; ed. Northwestern Univ., Evanston, Ill., Victoria Univ. of Manchester, England, Univ. of Chicago, Ill., London School of Econs.; Capt. Mil. Intelligence, U.S. Army 1942–46; Dir. Reynolds Club, Univ. of Chicago 1946–48; Prin. Examiner, Chicago Civil Service Comm. 1948–49; Economist, Int. Trade Policy, Dept. of State, Washingon 1950–53; Foreign Service Officer, London Embassy, 1953–55; Chief of Econ. Defense Co-ordination, Washington 1955–58; Deputy Dir. U.S. Agency for Int. Devt. (AID), Pakistan 1963–66; Asst. Admin. Near East-South Asia Bureau, AID, Washington 1967–69, Deputy Admin. AID 1970–74; U.S. Pres. Co-ordinator, Foreign Disaster Relief, Bangladesh, Peru, African Sahel 1971–74; Co-Chair. U.S.-N. Viet Nam Jt. Econ. Comm. 1974; Chair. Devt. Assistance Cttee., OECD 1975–78; Exec. Dir. UN World Food Council, Rome 1978–86; Sec.-Gen., Pres. Emer. Soc. of Int. Devt. 1986–94; Sr. Assoc. Overseas Devt. Council, Washington 1987–; mem. Acad. of Sr. Professionals, Fla 1993–; U.S. Civil Service Award 1971, AID Distinguished Honor Award 1974, Rockefeller Public Service Award 1974. *Publications:* Development Cooperation in Reviews 1974–78, The UN System and Sustainable Development 1995, Sustaining the Earth 1996, and over 20 articles on econ. devt. and food policy. *Address:* Overseas Development Council, 1875 Connecticut Ave, N.W., Washington, DC 20009; 4515 Willard Avenue, 1704 S., Chevy Chase, Maryland; Suite 402, 4850 Osprey Drive South, St. Petersburg, FL, U.S.A.

WILLIAMS, Michael Leonard; British actor; b. 9 July 1935, Manchester; s. of Michael Leonard Williams and Elizabeth Mulligan; m. Judith Olivia Dench (q.v.) 1971; one d.; ed. St. Edward's Coll. Liverpool and Royal Acad. of Dramatic Art; début, Nottingham Playhouse 1959; London début in Celebration, Duchess Theatre 1961; joined RSC 1963, Assoc. Artist 1966–; roles include: Puck in A Midsummer Night's Dream, Filch in The Beggar's Opera 1963; Oswald in King Lear, Pinch in The Comedy of Errors 1964, Dromio in The Comedy of Errors 1965 (also in musical version 1976), Petruchio in The Taming of the Shrew, Orlando in As You Like It 1967, Fool in King Lear 1968, 1976, Troilus in Troilus and Cressida 1968, Charles Courtly in London Assurance 1970, Bassanio in The Merchant of Venice, Ferdinand in The Duchess of Malfi, title role in Henry V 1971, Autolycus in The Winter's Tale 1976, title role in Quartermaine's Terms (nat. tour) 1982, George in Two Into One (Shaftesbury) 1984, Charles Pooter in Mr and Mrs Nobody (Garrick) 1986, George in Out of Order 1990, Brief Lives 1998; numerous TV appearances. *Films include:* The Marat/Sade 1966, Eagle in a Cage 1969, Dead Cert 1974, In Search of Alexander the Great 1980, Enigma 1981, Educating Rita 1982, Henry V 1990, Tea with Mussolini 1999. *Leisure interests:* family, tennis, pottering, gardening. *Address:* c/o Julian Belfrage Associates, 46 Albemarle Street, London, W1X 4PP, England. *Telephone:* 0171-491 4400.

WILLIAMS, Nigel; British writer and television producer; b. 20 Jan. 1948, Cheshire; s. of the late David Ffrancon Williams; m. Suzani Harrison; three s.; ed. Highgate School, Oriel Coll. Oxford; Sr. Producer, BBC TV; *television plays include:* Double Talk, Talking Blues, Real Live Audience 1977, Baby Love 1981, Breaking Up 1986; *television film:* The Last Romantics 1992; *stage plays include:* Class Enemy 1978 (Plays and Players Award for most promising playwright 1978), Trial Run 1980, Line 'Em 1980, Sugar & Spice 1980, My Brother's Keeper 1985, Country Dancing 1986, Nativity 1989, Harry & Me 1995, The Last Romantics 1997. *Publications:* (novels) My Life Closed Twice 1977 (jt. winner Somerset Maugham Award), Jack Be Nimble 1980, Star Turn 1985, Witchcraft 1987, The Wimbledon Poisoner 1990, They Came from SW19 1992, East of Wimbledon 1994, Scenes from a Poisoner's Life 1994, Stalking Fiona 1997; (travel) Wimbledon to Waco 1995. *Address:* c/o Judy Daish Associates, 2 St. Charles Place, London, W10 6EG, England. *Telephone:* 0181-964 8811. *Fax:* 0181-964 8966.

WILLIAMS, Peter Orchard, C.B.E., F.R.C.P.; British medical director and doctor; b. 23 Sept. 1925, Trinidad; s. of Robert O. Williams and Agnes A. Birkinshaw; m. Billie I. Brown 1949; two d.; ed. Caterham School, Queen's Royal Coll., Trinidad, St. John's Coll., Cambridge and St. Mary's Hosp. Medical School; House Physician, St. Mary's Hosp., London 1950–51; Registrar, Royal Free Hosp. 1951–52; Medical Specialist, R.A.M.C. 1954; Medical Officer, Medical Research Council H.Q. 1955–60; Asst. and Deputy Scientific Sec. Wellcome Trust 1960–64, Scientific Sec. 1964–65, Dir. 1965–91; Pres. Royal Soc. of Tropical Medicine and Hygiene 1991–93; Visiting Fellow, Green Coll. Oxford; Hon. Fellow, London School of Hygiene and Tropical Medicine; Hon. D.Sc. (Birmingham) 1989, (Univ. of the West Indies) 1991, (Glasgow) 1992, Hon. D.M. (Nottingham) 1990, (Oxford) 1993. *Publication:* Careers in Medicine 1952. *Leisure interests:* gardening, travel, golf. *Address:* Courtyard House, Bletchingdon, Kidlington, Oxon., OX5 3DL.

WILLIAMS, Richard Edmund; Canadian animated film producer, director and writer; b. 19 March 1933, Toronto, Ont.; s. of Kenneth D. C. Williams and Kathleen (née Bell) Williams; m. 2nd Margaret French 1976; four c. (including two from a previous marriage); ed. Royal Ontario Coll. of Art; f. Richard Williams Animation Ltd. 1956; produced and directed: The Little Island 1958 (British Acad. Award), Love Me, Love Me, Love Me 1962, A Christmas Carol 1973 (Oscar for Best Animated Short Subject); designed film sequences and titles for: What's New Pussycat 1965, A Funny Thing Happened on the Way to the Forum 1966, Casino Royale 1975, The Charge of the Light Brigade 1967, The Return of the Pink Panther 1975, The Pink Panther Strikes Again 1976; animation for Who Framed Roger Rabbit 1988 (Special Achievement Oscar), Arabian Knight (dir., produced); mem. Acad. of Motion Picture Arts and Sciences; mem. Asscn. of Cinematographers and TV Technicians.

WILLIAMS, Robbie; British popular singer; b. 13 Feb. 1974, Stoke-on-Trent; s. of Pete Williams and Theresa Janette Williams; played the Artful Dodger in Oliver 1982; mem. group Take That 1991–95 (eight 'No. 1' singles); with Chrysalis Records 1996, three Brit Awards 1999. *Albums:* Life Thru a Lens (1.5 million copies sold), I've Been Expecting You 1998. *Singles include:* Freedom 1996, Old Before I Die 1997, Lazy Days 1997, South of the Border 1997, Let Me Entertain You 1998, Millennium 1998, No Regrets/Antmusic 1998, Angels 1999; Levi's Nordoff-Robbins Music Therapy Original Talent Award 1998, three Brit Awards (Best Male Artist, Best Single, Best Video) 1998. *Address:* c/o Chrysalis Records Ltd., EMI House, 43 Brook Green, London, W6 7EF, England. *Telephone:* 0171-605 5256. *Fax:* 0171-605 5130.

WILLIAMS, Robert Joseph Paton, D.PHIL., F.R.S., F.R.C.S.; British professor of chemistry; b. 25 Feb. 1926, Wallasey; s. of Ernest Ivor Williams and Alice Roberts; m. Jelly Klara Buchli 1952; two s.; ed. Oxford Univ.; Rotary Int. Fellow 1951–52; Research Fellow, Merton Coll., Oxford Univ. 1952–55; Fellow, Wadham Coll., Oxford Univ. 1955–, Sr. Research Fellow 1991–; Lecturer, Oxford Univ. 1955–70, Reader 1970–72, Royal Soc., Napier Research Prof. 1974–91; Pres. Dalton Div. Royal Soc. of Chemistry 1991–93; Hon. Fellow, Merton Coll., Oxford; Foreign mem. Royal Swedish Acad. of Science, Lisbon Acad. of Science, Czechoslovak Acad. of Science, Royal Soc. of Science, Liège; Lord Goodman Lecturer 1992; J. D. Bernal Lecturer 1993; Canada Lecturer, Royal Soc. 1996; Hon. D.Sc. (Louvain, Leicester, East Anglia, Keele, Lisbon); Tilden Medal (Chem. Soc. of England), Liversidge Medal (Chem. Soc. of England), Keilen Medal (Biochem. Soc.), Hughes Medal (Royal Soc.), Sir Hans Krebs Medal (European Biochem. Soc.), Linderstrøm-Lang Medal (Denmark), Sigillum Magna (Univ. of Bologna), Heyrovsky Medal (Int. Union of Biochem.), Sir Frederick Gowland Hopkins Medal (Biochem. Soc.), Royal Medal (Royal Soc.). *Publications:* Inorganic Chemistry (with C. S. G. Phillips), NMR in Biology, Recent Trends in Bioinorganic Chemistry, The Biological Chemistry of the Elements (with J.J.R. Frausto da Silva), The Natural Selection of the Chemical Elements (with J.J.R. Frausto da Silva) 1996. *Leisure interest:* walking in the country. *Address:* Wadham College, Oxford, OX1 3QR (Office); 115 Victoria Road, Oxford, OX2 7QG, England (Home). *Telephone:* (01865) 272600 (Office); (01865) 58926 (Home). *Fax:* (01865) 272690 (Office).

WILLIAMS, Robert Martin, C.B., C.B.E., PH.D.; New Zealand mathematician; b. 30 March 1919, Christchurch; s. of the late Canon Henry Williams; m. Mary Constance Thorpe 1944; one s. two d.; ed. Christ's Coll., Canterbury Univ., N.Z., St. John's Coll., Cambridge; Mathematician, Radar Devt. Laboratory, D.S.I.R., N.Z. 1941–44; mem. U.K. Atomic Group in U.S.A. 1944–45; mem. Applied Math. Laboratory, D.S.I.R. 1949–53, Dir. 1953–62; Commr. State Services Comm. N.Z. 1963–66; Vice-Chancellor Univ. of Otago 1967–73, A.N.U. 1973–75; Chair. State Services Comm. 1975–81; mem. Int. Statistical Inst. 1961–; Pres. N.Z. Book Council 1989–92, Nat. Library Soc. of N.Z. 1992–95; Hon. LL.D. (Otago). *Publications:* papers on mathematical statistics. *Address:* 21 Wadestown Road, Wellington, New Zealand (Home). *Telephone:* 726698 (Home).

WILLIAMS, Robin; American actor and comedian; b. 21 July 1951, Chicago; s. of Robert Williams; m. 1st Valerie Velardi 1978 (divorced); one s.; 2nd Marsha Garces 1989; one s. one d.; ed. Claremont Men's Coll., Marin Coll., Kentfield, Calif., Juillard School, New York; started as stand-up comedian. *TV appearances include:* Laugh-In, The Richard Pryor Show, America 2-Night, Happy Days, Mork and Mindy 1978–82, Carol and Carl and Whoopi and Robin (Emmy Award), Royal Gala: Prince's Trust (Emmy Award). *Stage appearances include:* Waiting for Godot. *Films include:* Popeye 1980, The World According to Garp 1982, The Survivors 1983, Moscow on the Hudson 1984, Club Paradise 1986, Good Morning Vietnam 1987 (Golden Globe Award 1988), Dead Poets' Society 1989, Awakenings 1990 (Best Actor, Nat. Bd. of Review), The Fisher King 1991 (Golden Globe Award), Hook 1991, Dead Again 1991, Toys 1992, Being Human 1993, Aladdin (voice) 1993, Mrs Doubtfire 1993, Jumanji 1996, The Birdcage 1996, Jack, Hamlet, Joseph Conrad's The Secret Agent 1996, Good Will Hunting 1997 (Acad. Award), Flubber 1997, What Dreams May Come 1998, Patch Adams 1998. *Recordings:* Reality, What a Concept 1979 (Grammy Award), Throbbing Python of Love, A Night at the Met. *Address:* CAA Creative Artists Agency, 9830 Wilshire Boulevard, Beverly Hills, CA 90212; P.O. Box 480909, Los Angeles, CA 90048, U.S.A.

WILLIAMS, Robin Murphy, Jr., PH.D., D.SC.; American professor of social sciences; b. 11 Oct. 1914, Hillsborough, N.C.; s. of Robin Murphy Williams, Sr. and Mabel Strayhorn Williams; m. Marguerite York 1939; one s. (deceased) two d.; ed. North Carolina State Coll. and Harvard Univ.; Instructor and Research Asst., Univ. of Ky. 1939–42; Statistical Analyst, U.S. War Dept. 1942–46; Assoc. Prof., Cornell Univ. 1946–48, Prof. 1948–67, Dir. Social Science Research Center 1949–54, Chair. Dept. of Sociology and Anthropology 1956–61, Henry Scarborough Prof. of Social Science 1967–85, Prof. Emer. 1985–; Visiting Prof. Univ. of Calif., Irvine 1990–99; Ed. Sociological Forum 1984–91; Chair. Cttee. on Status of Black Americans, Nat. Research Council; mem. American Philosophical Soc., American Acad. of Arts and Sciences, N.A.S. *Publications:* Strangers Next Door 1964, American Society 1970, Mutual Accommodation 1977 (ed. with Gerald David Jaynes), A Common Destiny: Blacks and American Society 1989. *Leisure interest:* work. *Address:* 342 Uris Hall, Cornell University, Ithaca, NY 14853; 414 Oak Avenue, Ithaca, NY 14850, U.S.A. (Home). *Telephone:* (607) 255-1416 (Univ.); (607) 273-9119 (Home).

WILLIAMS, Roger Stanley, C.B.E., M.D., F.R.C.P., F.R.C.S., F.R.C.P.E., F.R.A.C.P.; British consultant physician; b. 28 Aug. 1931; s. of Stanley George Williams and Doris Dagmar Clatworthy; m. 1st Lindsay Mary Elliott 1954 (divorced 1977); two s. three d.; m. 2nd Stephanie Gay de Laszlo 1978; one s. two d.; ed. St Mary's Coll., Southampton, London Hosp. Medical School, Univ. of London; House Doctor London Hosp. 1953–56; Jr. Medical Specialist, Queen Alexandra Hosp. 1956–58; Medical Registrar and Tutor, Royal Postgraduate Medical School 1958–59; Lecturer in Medicine Royal Free Hosp. 1959–65; Consultant Physician Royal S. Hants. and Southampton Gen. Hosp. 1965–66; Consultant Physician and Dir., Inst. of Liver Studies, King's Coll. Hosp. (now King's Coll. School of Medicine and Dentistry), London 1966–96, Prof. of Hepatology; Dir. Inst. of Hepatology and Consultant Physician, Univ. Coll. London Hosps. and Medical School 1996–; mem. WHO Scientific Group on Viral Hepatitis, Geneva 1972, Transplant Advisory Panel DHSS 1974–83, Advisory Group on Hepatitis DHSS 1980–, European Asscn. for the Study of the Liver (Pres. 1983) 1966–, Harveian Soc. of London (Pres. 1974–75), British Asscn. for the Study of the Liver (Pres. 1984), Royal Soc. of Medicine, British Soc. of Gastroenterology (Pres. 1989); Vice-Pres. Royal Coll. of Physicians 1991; Hon. Consultant in Medicine to the Army 1988–98; Hon. F.A.C.P.; Rep. to Select Cttee. of Experts on Organisational Aspects of Co-operation in Organ Transplantation, Congress of Europe; Sir Ernest Finch Visiting Prof. Univ. of Sheffield 1974. *Publications:* Fifth Symposium on Advanced Medicine (Ed.) 1969, Immunology of the Liver 1971, Artificial Liver Support 1975, Immune Reactions in Liver Disease 1978, Drug Reactions and the Liver 1981, Clinics in Critical Care Medicine—Liver Failure 1986, Liver Tumours (Baillière's Clinical Gastroenterology) 1987, The Practice of Liver Transplantation 1995, International Developments in Health Care. A review of Health Systems in the 1990s 1995, Acute Liver Failure 1997; author of over 1,500 papers, reviews and book chapters. *Leisure interests:* tennis, sailing, opera. *Address:* Institute of Hepatology, University College London, 69-75 Chenies Mews, London, WC1E 6HX; 8 Eldon Road, London, W8 5PU, England. *Telephone:* 0171-380 0401 (Office); 0171-937 5301 (Home). *Fax:* 0171-380 0405 (Office).

WILLIAMS, Stephen, PH.D.; American professor of anthropology and archaeologist; b. 28 Aug. 1926, Minneapolis, Minn.; s. of Clyde G. Williams and Lois M. (Simmons) Williams; m. Eunice Ford 1962; two s.; ed. Univ. of Michigan and Yale Univ.; Historical and Archaeological Research on Caddo Indians for U.S. Dept. of Justice 1954–55; Research Fellow in N. American Archaeology, Peabody Museum of Archaeology and Ethnology, Harvard Univ. 1955–58; Lecturer in Anthropology, Harvard Univ. 1956–58, Asst. Prof. of Anthropology 1958–62, Assoc. Prof. 1962–67, Prof. of Anthropology 1967–72, Peabody Prof. 1972–93, Chair. Dept. of Anthropology 1967–69, mem. of Bd. of Freshmen Advisers, Harvard Univ. 1959–60, 1961–65; Asst. Curator of N. American Archaeology, Peabody Museum 1957–58, Curator of N. American Archaeology 1962–93; Dir. Peabody Museum, Harvard Univ. 1967–77, Dir. Lower Mississippi Survey 1958–93, Peabody Prof. Emer. and Hon. Curator N. American Archaeology, 1993–; mem. Bd. of Dirs. Archaeological Conservancy 1984–88; Distinguished Fellow School of American Research, Santa Fe 1977–78; Hon. M.A. (Harvard Univ.). *Publications:* Six monographs incl. Excavations at the Lake George Site, Yazoo County, Miss. 1958–60 (with Jeffrey P. Brain), Fantastic Archaeology: The Wild Side of North American Prehistory 1990, Yazoo Chronicles—The Mississippi Delta from Paleo-Indians to Plantations; numerous articles in journals and magazines. *Address:* P.O. Box 22354, Santa Fe, NM 87502 (Office); 1017 Foothills Trail, Santa Fe, NM 87505, U.S.A. (Home).

WILLIAMS, H.E. Cardinal Thomas Stafford, S.T.L., B.SOC.SC.; New Zealand ecclesiastic; b. 20 March 1930, Wellington; s. of Thomas S. Williams and Lillian M. (née Kelly) Williams; ed. St. Patrick's Coll., Wellington, Victoria Univ., Wellington, St. Kevin's Coll., Oamaru, Holy Cross Coll., Mosgiel, Pontifical Urban Coll. de Propaganda Fide, Rome and Univ. Coll., Dublin; ordained priest, Rome 1959; Asst. St. Patrick's Parish, Palmerston North 1963; Dir. of Studies, Catholic Enquiry Centre, Wellington 1965; parish priest, St. Anne's, Leulumoega, Western Samoa 1971, Holy Family Parish, Porirua East, Wellington 1976; Archbishop of Wellington and Metropolitan of N.Z. 1979–; cr. Cardinal 1983. *Address:* P.O. Box 1937, Wellington 6015; Viard, 21 Eccleston Hill, Wellington 1, New Zealand. *Telephone:* 4961-795. *Fax:* (04) 496-1719.

WILLIAMS-JONES, Michael Robert; British/South African film executive; b. 3 June 1947, Sussex; s. of Hugh E. Williams-Jones and Valerie Lyons; m. 1st. Lynne Williams-Jones 1969 (deceased); m. 2nd Eve Foreman 1994; two s. one step.-s. one step-d; ed. Selborne Coll. East London, S. Africa; trainee, United Artists, Southern Africa region 1967, Man. Dir. 1969, Brazil 1971, U.K. 1975; Sr. Vice-Pres. United Artists Int. 1978; Pres. United Int. Pictures Film Group 1981; Pres. and C.E.O. United Int. Pictures Corpn. 1984–96; owner/co-founder, Merlin Anglesey UK, Ltd. 1996–; Int. Distributor of Year 1995; Lifetime Achievement Award, Locarno, Taiwan. *Leisure interests:* movies, theatre, reading, opera, walking, snorkelling. *Address:* Merlin Anglesey UK, Ltd., 49C Princes Gate, London, SW7 2PG (Office); 11 Kingston House South, Ennismore Gardens, London, SW7 1NF, England (Home). *Telephone:* 0171-584 6065 (Office). *Fax:* 0171-584 7057 (Office).

WILLIAMS OF CROSBY, Baroness (Life Peer), cr. 1993, of Stevenage in the County of Hertfordshire, **Rt. Hon. Shirley Williams,** P.C., M.A.; British politician; b. 27 July 1930, London; d. of the late Sir George Catlin and Vera Brittain; m. 1st Bernard Williams (q.v.) 1955 (divorced 1974); one d.; m. 2nd Richard Neustadt (q.v.) 1987; ed. Summit School, Minn., U.S.A., St. Paul's Girls' School, Somerville Coll., Oxford, and Columbia Univ.; Gen. Sec. Fabian Soc. 1960–64; Labour M.P. for Hitchin 1964–74, for Hertford and Stevenage 1974–79; Social Democratic Party M.P. for Crosby 1981–83; Parl. Pvt. Sec., Minister of Health 1964–66; Parl. Sec. Minister of Labour 1966–67; Minister of State, Dept. of Education and Science 1967–69; Minister of State, Home Office 1969–70; Opposition Spokesman on Health and Social Security 1970–71, on Home Affairs 1971–73, on Prices and Consumer Affairs 1973–74; Sec. of State for Prices and Consumer Protection 1974–76, for Educ. and Science 1976–79; Paymaster-Gen. 1976–79; Sr. Research Fellow (part-time) Policy Research Inst. 1979–85; mem. Labour Party Nat. Exec. Cttee. 1970–81; mem. Council for Social Democracy Jan.–March 1981; left Labour Party March 1981; co-founder Social Democratic Party March 1981, Pres. 1982–88; Prof. of Elective Politics, John F. Kennedy School of Govt., Harvard Univ. 1988–; mem. Social and Liberal Democratic Party 1988–; Fellow Inst. of Politics, Harvard 1979–80 (mem. Sr. Advisory Council 1986–); Dir. Turing Inst., Glasgow 1985–90, Learning by Experience Trust 1986–94, Project Liberty 1990–; TV series: Shirley Williams in Conversation 1979; BBC Radio series: Women in Parliament 1997; Visiting Fellow, Nuffield Coll., Oxford 1967–75; Hon. Fellow Somerville Coll., Oxford, Newnham Coll., Cambridge; Trustee Twentieth Century Fund, U.S.A.; mem. European Comm. Comité des Sages 1995–96; Chair. European Job Creation Competition 1997; Hon. D.Ed., C.N.A.A.; Hon. Dr.Pol.Econ., Univ. of Leuven, Belgium, Radcliffe Coll., U.S.A.; Hon. LL.D. (Leeds Univ.) 1979, (Southampton) 1981, (Ulster) 1997. *Publications:* Politics is for People 1981, A Job to Live 1985, Snakes and Ladders: a diary of a political life 1996, pamphlets on European Community, and economics of Central Africa; articles and broadcasts. *Leisure interests:* riding, rough walking, music. *Address:* House of Lords, Westminster, London, SW1A 0PW, England.

WILLIAMS OF ELVEL, Baron (Life Peer), cr. 1985, of Llansantffraed in Elvel in the County of Powys; **Charles Cuthbert Powell Williams,** C.B.E., M.A.; British business executive and politician; b. 9 Feb. 1933; s. of late Dr. Norman P. Williams and Muriel Cazenove; m. Jane G. Portal 1975; one step-s.; ed. Westminster School, Christ Church, Oxford and London School of Econs.; British Petroleum Co. Ltd. 1958–64; Bank of London and Montreal 1964–66; Eurofinance SA, Paris 1966–70; Baring Brothers & Co. Ltd. 1970–77, Man. Dir. 1971–77; Chair. Price Comm. 1977–79; Man. Dir. Henry Ansbacher & Co. Ltd. 1980–82, Chair. 1982–85; Chief Exec. Henry Ansbacher Holdings PLC 1982–85; Chair. Acoustiguide UK Ltd 1989–95; Pres. Campaign for the Protection of Rural Wales 1989–95, Vice-Pres. and Pres. Radnor Br. 1995–; Pres. Fed. of Econ. Devt. Authorities 1990–96, Vice-Pres. 1996–; parl. cand. (Labour) 1964; Opposition Spokesman for Trade and Industry, House of Lords 1986–92, for Defence 1990–, for Environment 1992–; Deputy Leader of Opposition in House of Lords 1989–92. *Publications:* The Last Great Frenchman: A Life of General de Gaulle 1993, Bradman 1996. *Leisure interests:* cricket, music, real tennis. *Address:* 48 Thurloe Square, London, SW7 2SX, England; Pant-y-Rhiw, Llansantffraed in Elvel, Powys, LD1 5RH, Wales. *Telephone:* 0171-581 1783 (London).

WILLIAMSON, David Keith, A.O., B.E.; Australian playwright and screenwriter; b. 24 Feb. 1942, Melbourne; s. of Edwin Keith David Williamson and Elvie May (née Armstrong) Williamson; m. Kristin Ingrid Lofven 1974; two s. one d.; ed. Monash Univ.; Design Engineer Gen. Motors-Holden's 1965; lecturer Swinbourne Tech. Coll. 1966–72; freelance writer 1972–. *Plays:* The Removalists 1972, Don's Party 1973, Three Plays 1974, The Department 1975, A Handful of Friends 1976, The Club 1977, Travelling North 1979, The Perfectionist 1981, Sons of Cain 1985, Emerald City 1987, Top Silk 1989, Siren 1990, Money and Friends 1992, Brilliant Lies 1993, Sanctuary 1994, Dead White Males 1995. *Screenplays:* Gallipoli 1981, Phar Lap 1983, The Year of Living Dangerously 1983, Travelling North 1986, Emerald City 1988, The Four Minute Mile (2-part TV series) 1988, A Dangerous Life (6-hour TV series) 1988, Top Silk 1989, Siren 1990, Money and Friends 1992, Dead White Males 1995, Heretic 1996, Third World Blues 1997, After the Ball 1997. *Address:* c/o Anthony Williams Management Pty Ltd., 1st Floor, 50 Oxford Street, Paddington, N.S.W. 2021, Australia.

WILLIAMSON, G. Malcolm, F.I.B., F.B.I.M.; British banker; b. 29 Feb. 1939, Oldham; m. Hang Thi Ngo; one s. one d.; one s. one d. by previous marriage; local Dir. Barclays Bank PLC, N. London 1980–81; Asst. Gen. Man. Barclays Bank PLC 1981–83, Regional Man. 1983–85; Dir. Barclays Unit Trust & Insurance Ltd. 1983–85; Man. Dir. Girobank PLC and mem. Bd. The Post Office 1985–89; Group Exec. Dir. Banking (Eastern Hemisphere), Standard Chartered Bank 1989–90, Group Exec. Dir. Banking 1990–91, Group Man. Dir. 1991–93, Group Chief Exec. 1993–98; Dir. Nat. Grid Group 1995–; Chair. Thai-British Group 1997–; Pres. and Chief Exec. Visa Int. 1998–; Fellow, Inst. of Dirs. *Leisure interests:* mountaineering, walking, chess, bridge. *Address:* Visa International, 99 Kensington High Street, London W.8., England. *Telephone:* 0171-937 8111.

WILLIAMSON, John, PH.D.; British economist; b. 7 June 1937, Hereford; s. of A.H. Williamson and Eileen Williamson; m. Denise R. de Souza 1974; two s. one d.; ed. London School of Econs. and Princeton Univ.; Lecturer, Reader, Univ. of York 1963–68; H.M. Treasury 1968–70; Prof. Univ. of Warwick 1970–77; adviser, IMF 1972–74; Prof. Catholic Univ. of Rio de Janeiro 1978–81; Sr. Fellow, Inst. for Int. Econs. 1981–96; Chief Economist South Asia, World Bank 1996–. *Publications:* The Crawling Peg 1965, The Failure of World Monetary Reform 1977, The Exchange Rate System 1983, Targets and Indicators (with M.H. Miller) 1987, Latin American Adjustment: How Much Has Happened? 1990, The Political Economy of Policy Reform 1993, The Crawling Band as an Exchange Rate Regime 1996. *Leisure* *interests:* birding. *Address:* 3919 Oliver Street, Chevy Chase, MD 20815, U.S.A. *Telephone:* (202) 458-9008 (Office); (301)-654-5312 (Home). *Fax:* (202) 477-6050.

WILLIAMSON, Marshal of the Royal Air Force Sir Keith (Alec), G.C.B., A.F.C.; British air force officer; b. 25 Feb. 1928; s. of Percy Williamson and Gertrude Williamson; m. Patricia Ann Watts 1953; two s. two d.; ed. Bancrofts' School, Woodford Green, Market Harborough Grammar School, R.A.F. Coll. Cranwell; commissioned 1950; with R.A.A.F. in Korea 1953; C.O. 23 Squadron 1966–68; C.O., R.A.F. Gütersloh 1968–70; Royal Coll. Defence Studies 1971; Dir., Air Staff Plans 1972–75; Commdt. R.A.F. Staff Coll. 1975–77; Asst. Chief of Staff (Plans and Policy) S.H.A.P.E. 1977–78; Air Officer Commdr. in Chief, R.A.F. Support Command 1978–80; R.A.F. Strike Command and C.-in-C. U.K. Air Forces 1980–82; Chief of Air Staff 1982–85; Air A.D.C. to the Queen 1982–85. *Leisure interest:* golf. *Address:* c/o National Westminster Bank, Fakenham, Norfolk, England.

WILLIAMSON, Malcolm Benjamin Graham, C.B.E., A.O.; British composer, pianist and organist; b. 21 Nov. 1931, Sydney, N.S.W., Australia; s. of George and Bessie (née Wrigley) Williamson; m. Dolores Daniel 1960; one s. two d.; ed. Barker Coll., Hornsby, N.S.W., and Sydney Conservatorium of Music; Asst. organist, Farm Street, London 1955–58; Organist, St. Peter's, Limehouse 1958–60; lecturer in Music, Cen. School of Speech and Drama, London 1961–62; Exec. Cttee., Composers' Guild of Great Britain 1964; Composer-in-Residence Westminster Choir Coll., Princeton, N.J. 1970–71, Fla. State Univ. 1975; Pres. Beauchamp Sinfonietta 1972–, Birmingham Chamber Music Soc. 1975–, Univ. of London Choir 1976–, Purbeck Festival of Music 1976–, Royal Philharmonic Orchestra 1977–82, Sing for Pleasure 1977–, British Soc. for Music Therapy 1977–, Stevenage Music Soc. 1987–, Ditchling Choral Soc. 1989–, Finchley Children's Music Group 1991–; Vice-Pres. Elgar Foundation, St. Michael's Singers, Nat. Music Council of G.B., Nat. Youth Orchestra of G.B.; Creative Arts Fellow, Australian Nat. Univ. 1974–81; Ramasciotti Medical Research Fellow, Univ. of N.S.W. 1982; Visiting Prof., Univ. of Strathclyde 1983–86; Master of the Queen's Music 1975–; Hon. Dr.Mus. (Westminster Choir Coll.) 1970, (Univ. of Melbourne) 1982, (Univ. of Sydney) 1982, (The Open Univ.) 1983; Sir Arnold Bax Memorial Prize 1963; Hon. A.O. 1987. *Compositions include:* Operas: Our Man in Havana 1963, English Eccentrics 1964, The Happy Prince 1964, Julius Caesar Jones 1965, The Violins of St. Jacques 1966, Dunstan and the Devil 1967, The Growing Castle 1968, Lucky-Peter's Journey 1969, The Red Sea 1972; Choral Operas or Cassations: The Moonrakers 1967, The Snow Wolf, Knights in Shining Armour 1968, Genesis, The Stone Wall 1971, The Winter Star 1973, The Glitter Gang 1974, The Terrain of the Kings 1975, The Valley and the Hill 1977, Le Pont du Diable 1982; Ballets: The Display 1964, Sun into Darkness 1966, Perisynthion, Heritage 1985, Have Steps Will Travel 1988; Orchestral: Piano Concertos 1958, 1960, 1961, Organ Concerto 1961, Violin Concerto 1965, Elevamini (Symphony) 1956, Santiago de Espada (Overture) 1956, Sinfonia Concertante 1961, Sinfonietta 1965, Symphonic Variations 1965, Concerto Grosso 1965, Symphony No. 2 1969, Symphony No. 3 (The Icy Mirror) 1972, Symphony No. 4 1977, Symphony No. 5 1980, Symphony No. 6 1982, Symphony No. 7 1984, Bicentennial Anthem 1988; Chorus and Orchestra: Mass of Christ the King 1977, A Pilgrim Liturgy 1984, The True Endeavour 1988, The Dawn is at Hand 1989; Chamber: Variations for Cello and Piano 1964, Concerto for Wind Quintet and Two Pianos, Eight Hands 1965, Pas de Quatre (Piano and woodwind) 1967; Organ: Fons Amoris 1957, Symphony 1960, Vision of Christ Phoenix 1961, Elegy JFK 1964, Peace Pieces 1971, The Lion of Suffolk; works for brass ensemble; numerous songs, carols and other works for chorus, unison voices and solo voices; scores for films, TV and radio. *Leisure interest:* literature. *Address:* c/o Campion Press, Sandon, Buntingford, Herts. SG9 0QW, England. *Telephone:* (01763) 247287. *Fax:* (01763) 249984.

WILLIAMSON, Matthew, B.A.; British fashion designer; ed. St. Martin's School of Art and Design; worked as freelance designer for two years; travelled frequently to India for Marni, Georgina von Ertzdorf and Monsoon fashion retailers; f. Matthew Williamson (with Joseph Velosa) 1996; collections shown in British Fashion Week 1997, 1998, 1999; trademark details are embroidery, beading and sequins. *Address:* c/o Beverly Cable PR, 11 St. Christopher's Place, London, W1M 5HB, England. *Telephone:* 0171-935 1314. *Fax:* 0171-935 8314.

WILLIAMSON, Nicol; British actor; b. 14 Sept. 1938, Hamilton, Scotland; m. Jill Townsend 1971 (divorced 1977); one s.; began career with Dundee Repertory Theatre 1960–61; London début at Royal Court, That's Us 1961; joined R.S.C. 1962; *theatre appearances include:* Satin in The Lower Depths 1962, Leantio in Women Beware Women 1962, Kelly's Eye 1963, The Ginger Man 1963, Vladimir in Waiting for Godot 1964, Bill Maitland in Inadmissible Evidence 1964, 1965, 1978, Diary of A Madman 1968, Hamlet 1969, Uncle Vanya 1973, Coriolanus 1973, Malvolio in Twelfth Night 1974, Macbeth 1974, Rex 1975, Inadmissible Evidence 1981, Macbeth 1982, The Entertainer 1983, The Lark 1983, The Real Thing 1985, Jack—A Night on the Town with John Barrymore 1994; *films include:* Inadmissible Evidence 1967, Laughter in the Dark 1968, Bofors Gun 1968, The Reckoning 1969, Hamlet 1969, The Jerusalem File 1972, The Wilby Conspiracy 1974, Robin and Marian 1976, The Seven Per Cent Solution 1976, The Human Factor 1980, Knights 1980, Excalibur 1980, Venom 1980, I'm Dancing as Fast as I Can 1981, Return to Oz 1984, Black Widow 1986, The Hour of the Pig 1994. *television includes:* Terrible Jim Fitch, Arturo Ui, I Know What I Meant, The Word 1977, Macbeth 1982, Mountbatten—the Last Viceroy 1985, Passion Flower 1985; New York Drama Critics Award for Inadmissible Evidence 1965–66; Evening Standard Award for Best Actor, for Inadmissible Evidence 1964, for Hamlet 1969. *Publication:* Ming's Kingdom (novel) 1996. *Address:* c/o Jonathan Altaras Associates, 13 Shorts Gardens, London, WC2H 9AT, England.

WILLIAMSON OF HORTON, Baron (Life Peer), cr. 1999, of Horton in the County of Somerset, **David Francis Williamson,** G.C.M.G., C.B., M.A., D.C.L., D.ECON.SC.; British government official (retd.); b. 8 May 1934; m. Patricia M. Smith 1961; two s.; ed. Tonbridge School and Exeter Coll. Oxford; Army service 1956–58; entered Ministry of Agric., Fisheries and Food 1958; seconded to H.M. Diplomatic Service as First Sec. (Agric. and Food), Geneva, for Kennedy Round Trade Negotiation 1965–67; Prin. Pvt. Sec. to successive Ministers, Ministry of Agric., Fisheries and Food 1967–70; Head of Milk and Milk Products Div. 1970–74; Under-Sec. 1974; Deputy Dir.-Gen. (Agric.), Comm. of European Communities 1977–83; Deputy Sec. and Head of European Secr. Cabinet Office 1983–87; Sec.-Gen. Comm. of European Communities (now European Comm.) 1987–97; Visiting Prof., Univ. of Bath; Dir. (non-exec.) Whitbread PLC; Knight Commdr.'s Cross of the Order of Merit (Germany); Commdr., Légion d'honneur, Commdr., Grand Cross of the Royal Order of the Polar Star (Sweden). *Address:* Thatchcroft, Broadway, Ilminster, Somerset, TA19 9QZ, England.

WILLIS, Bruce Walter; American actor and singer; b. 19 March 1955, Fed. Repub. of Germany; s. of David Willis and Marlene Willis; m. Demi Moore (q.v.); three d.; ed. Montclair State Coll.; moved to U.S.A. 1957; studied with Stella Adler; mem. First Amendment Comedy Theatre. *Stage appearances:* (off-Broadway): Heaven and Earth 1977, Fool for Love 1984, The Bullpen, The Bayside Boys, The Ballad of Railroad William. *Films:* Prince of the City 1981, The Verdict 1982, Blind Date 1987, Sunset 1988, Die Hard 1988, In Country 1989, Die Hard 2, Die Harder 1990, Bonfire of the Vanities 1990, Hudson Hawk 1991, The Last Boy Scout 1991, Death Becomes Her, Striking Distance, Color of Night 1994, North 1994, Nobody's Fool 1994, Pulp Fiction 1994, Die Hard with a Vengeance 1995, 12 Monkeys 1995, Four Rooms, Last Man Standing 1996, The Jackal 1997, The Fifth Element 1997, Mercury Rising 1998, Armageddon 1998, Breakfast of Champions 1998, The Story of US 1999. *Television:* Trackdown (film), Miami Vice (series), The Twilight Zone (series), Moonlighting 1985–89 (series; People's Choice award 1986, Emmy award 1987, Golden Globe award 1987). *Recordings:* The Return of Bruno 1987, If It Don't Kill You, It Just Makes You Stronger 1989.

WILLIS, Sir Eric Archibald, K.B.E., C.M.G., B.A., F.R.G.S.; Australian fmr. politician; b. 15 Jan. 1922, Murwillumbah, N.S.W.; s. of the late Archibald Clarence Willis and Vida Mabel Willis (née Buttenshaw); m. 1st Norma Dorothy (Knight) Thompson 1951 (divorced); two s. one d.; m. 2nd Lynn Anitra (Roberts) Ward 1982 (divorced); ed. Murwillumbah High School, Univ. of Sydney; mem. N.S.W. Legis. Ass. 1950–78, Deputy Leader of Opposition 1959–65; Minister for Labour and Industry 1965–71, Chief Sec. 1965–72, Minister for Tourism 1965–72, for Sport 1971–72, for Educ. 1972–76, Premier and Treas. Jan.–May 1976; Leader of Opposition 1976–77; Exec. Sec. Royal Australian Coll. of Ophthalmologists 1978–83; Chair. Citizens in Support of Reserve Forces Trust Fund 1978–97; N.S.W. Vice-Pres., Scout Assen. of Australia (N.S.W. Br.) 1979–; Exec. Dir. Arthritis Foundation of N.S.W. 1984–91; mem. exec. Australian Red Cross Soc. (N.S.W. Div.) 1991–, Deputy Chair. 1995–. *Leisure interests:* reading, swimming. *Address:* 5/94 Kurraba Road, Neutral Bay, N.S.W. 2089, Australia. *Telephone:* (02) 99093432.

WILLIS, Norman David; British trade union official; b. 21 Jan. 1933; s. of Victor J. M. Willis and Kate E. Willis; m. Maureen Kenning 1963; one s. one d.; ed. Ashford County Grammar School, Ruskin and Oriel Colls., Oxford; Personal Research Asst. to Gen. Sec. Transport & General Workers' Union (TGWU) 1959–70; Nat. Sec. Research and Educ. TGWU 1970–74; Asst. Gen. Sec. Trades Union Congress 1974–77, Deputy Gen. Sec. 1977–84, Gen. Sec. 1984–93; Councillor (Labour), Staines Urban Dist. Council 1971–74; Chair. Nat. Pensioners Convention Steering Cttee. 1979–93; Vice-Pres. European TUC 1984–91 (Pres. 1991–93), ICFTU 1984–93, Inst. of Manpower Studies 1985–93; Trustee Anglo-German Foundation for Study of Industrial Soc. 1986–95, Duke of Edin.'s Commonwealth Study Conf. 1986–93; Patron West Indian Welfare (U.K.) Trust 1986; mem. NEDC 1984, Council, Overseas Devt. Inst. 1985–93, Council, Motability 1985–93, Exec. Bd. UNICEF 1986–90, Trade Union Advisory Cttee. to OECD 1986–93, Council of Prince of Wales Youth Business Trust 1986–93, Employment Appeal Tribunal 1995–; Vice-Pres. Poetry Soc., West Indian Welfare Trust (U.K.) 1986–93; Patron Docklands Sinfonietta 1986–; Hon. Fellow Oriel Coll., Oxford. *Leisure interests:* embroidery, The Arthur Ransome Society, poetry, natural history, architecture, canals. *Address:* c/o Trades Union Congress, Congress House, Great Russell Street, London, WC1B 3LS, England.

WILLIS, Ralph; Australian politician; b. 14 April 1938, Melbourne; s. of Stanley Willis and Doris Willis; m. Carol Joyce Dawson 1970; one s. two d.; ed. Univ. High School and Melbourne Univ.; research officer, Australian Council of Trade Unions (ACTU) 1960, industrial advocate 1970; mem. House of Reps. 1972; Minister for Employment and Industrial Relations and Minister assisting Prime Minister in Public Service Industrial Matters 1983–87, Minister for Industrial Relations and Minister assisting Prime Minister in Public Service Matters 1987–88, for Transport and Communications 1988–90, for Finance 1990–91, Treasurer 1991, Minister for Finance 1991–93, Treas. 1993–96; Vice-Pres. Exec. Council 1992; Australian Labor Party. *Leisure interests:* tennis, reading, watching football. *Address:* 4 Treasury Place, Melbourne, Vic. 3000, Australia.

WILLOCH, Kåre Isaachsen, CAND. OECON.; Norwegian politician; b. 3 Oct. 1928, Oslo; s. of Haakon Willoch and Agnes Saure; m. Anne Marie Jørgensen 1954; one s. two d.; ed. Ullern Gymnasium and Univ. of Oslo; Sec. Fed. of Norwegian Shipowners 1951–53, Counsellor Fed. of Norwegian Industries 1954–63; mem. Storting 1958–89; mem. Nat. Cttee. Conservative Party 1961–89, Sec.-Gen. Conservative Party 1963–65, Chair. 1970–74, Chair. Conservative Party Parl. Group 1970–81; Minister of Trade and Shipping 1963, 1965–70; Chair. World Bank Group 1967; mem. Nordic Council 1970–86, Pres. 1973; Prime Minister 1981–86; Chair. Int. Democratic Union 1987–89; Chair. Foreign Affairs Cttee. of Parl. 1986–89; Co-Gov. of Oslo and Akershus 1989–98; Chair. Norwegian Defence Comm. 1990–92; Chair. Supervisory Bd., Norwegian Bank 1990–96; Chair. Bd. of Norwegian Broadcasting Corpn. 1998–; Dir. Fridtjof Nansen Inst. 1999–. *Publications:* Personal Savings 1955, Price Policy in Norway (with L. B. Bachke) 1958, Memoirs (Vol. I) 1988, (Vol. II) 1990, Krisetid 1992, A New Policy for the Environment 1996. *Leisure interests:* skiing, touring. *Address:* Fr. Nansens v. 17, 1324 Lysaker, Norway. *Telephone:* 67 11 1900. *Fax:* 67 11 1910.

WILLOTT, (William) Brian, C.B., PH.D.; British government official; b. 14 May 1940; s. of William Harford and Beryl P. M. Willott; m. Alison Leyland Pyke-Lees 1970; two s. two d.; ed. Trinity Coll., Cambridge; Research Assoc., Univ. of Md. 1965–67; Asst. Prin. Bd. of Trade 1967–69, Prin. 1969–73; H.M. Treasury 1973–75; Asst. Sec. Dept. of Industry 1975–78, Sec. Ind. Devt. Unit 1978–80; Sec. Nat. Enterprise Bd. 1980–81; C.E.O. British Tech. Group (Nat. Enterprise Bd. and Nat. Research and Devt. Corpn.) 1981–84; Head, Information Tech. Div., Dept. of Trade and Industry 1984–87, Head, Financial Services Div. 1987–91; Chief Exec. Export Credit Guarantee Dept. 1992–97; C.E.O. Welsh Devt. Agency 1997–. *Leisure interests:* music, reading, ancient history, gardening. *Address:* Welsh Development Agency, Principality House, The Friary, Cardiff, CE1 4AE, Wales. *Telephone:* (01222) 828669.

WILLOUGHBY, Christopher R., M.A.; British economist; b. 24 Feb. 1938, Guildford; s. of Ronald James Edward Willoughby and Constance Louisa (née Sherbrooke) Willoughby; m. Marie-Anne Isabelle Normand 1972; ed. Lambroke School, Marlborough Coll., Univ. of Grenoble, Jt. Services School for Linguists, Balliol Coll., Oxford, Univ. of California, Berkeley; R.N. 1956–58, Lieut., R.N. Reserve 1958; New York Times Wash. Bureau 1962–63; economist World Bank 1963–, Dir. Operations Evaluation Dept. 1973–76, Transport, Water and Telecommunications Dept. 1976–83, Econ. Devt. Inst. 1983–90, Chief, World Bank Mission in Bangladesh 1990–94, in Belarus 1994–97, Infrastructure Lead Adviser Europe and Cen. Asia Region 1997–. *Leisure interests:* running, swimming, house re-modelling. *Address:* World Bank, 1818 H Street, N.W., Washington, DC 20433 (Office); 5340 Falmouth Road, Bethesda, MD 20816, U.S.A. (Home). *Telephone:* 202-473-3407 (Office); 301-263-9116 (Home). *Fax:* 202-522-1165.

WILLS, Dean Robert, A.O.; Australian business executive; b. 10 July 1933, Australia; s. of Walter W. Wills (deceased); m. Margaret F. Williams 1955; one s. two d.; ed. Sacred Heart Coll., S. Australia and S. Australian Inst. of Tech.; Dir. W. D. & H. O. Wills (Australia) 1974–, Man. Dir. 1977–83, Chair. 1983–86; Dir. AMATIL Ltd. 1975–, Deputy Chair. 1983–84, Man. Dir. Coca-Cola AMATIL Ltd. 1984–94, Chair. 1984–; mem. Business Council of Australia 1984–94, Vice-Pres. 1987–88, Pres. 1988–90; mem. Bd. Australian Grad. School of Man. (Univ. of N.S.W.) 1985–92; Gov. Medical Foundation (Univ. of Sydney) 1990–94; mem. Corps. and Securities Panel 1991–94; Vice-Chair. Nat. Mutual Life 1992–97, Chair. 1997–; Deputy Chair. Nat. Mutual Holdings 1995–97, Chair. 1997–; Dir. Microsurgery Foundation, Melbourne 1992–, John Fairfax Holdings Ltd 1994–, Westfield Holdings Ltd 1994–; Trustee Museum of Applied Arts and Sciences 1986–90; Gov. Australian Naval Aviation Museum; Deputy Chair. Australian Grand Prix Corpn. *Leisure interests:* tennis, performance cars. *Address:* Coca-Cola AMATIL Ltd., G.P.O. Box 145, Sydney, N.S.W. 2001, Australia.

WILLSON, Francis Michael Glenn, M.A., D.PHIL.; British university administrator and professor; b. 29 Sept. 1924, Carlisle; s. of the late Christopher Glenn Willson and Elsie Katrine Mattick; m. Jean Carlyle 1945; two d.; ed. Carlisle Grammar School, Univ. of Manchester, Balliol and Nuffield Colls., Oxford; war service in Merchant Navy 1941–42 and R.A.F. 1943–47; seconded to BOAC 1946–47; Research Officer, Royal Inst. of Public Admin. 1953–60; Research Fellow, Nuffield Coll., Oxford 1955–60; Lecturer in Politics, St. Edmund Hall, Oxford 1958–60; Prof. of Govt., Univ. Coll. of Rhodesia and Nyasaland 1961–64, Dean of Social Studies 1962–64; Prof. of Govt. and Politics, Univ. of Calif., Santa Cruz 1965–74, Provost of Stevenson Coll. 1967–74, Vice-Chancellor Coll. and Student Affairs 1973–74, Visiting Prof. 1985–92; Warden of Goldsmith's Coll., London 1974–75; Prin. of London Univ. 1975–78; Vice-Chancellor Murdoch Univ., W. Australia 1978–84, Prof. Emer. 1985–. *Publications:* Organization of British Central Government 1914–1956 (with D. N. Chester) 1957, 2nd edn. 1914–1964 1968, Administrators in Action 1961, A Strong Supporting Cast—The Shaw Lefevres 1789–1936 1993, Our Minerva—The Men and Politics of the University of London 1836–1858 1995, In Just Order Move—The Progress of the Laban Centre for Movement and Dance 1946–96 1997. *Leisure interests:* listening to music, reading. *Address:* 32 Digby Mansions, Hammersmith Bridge Road, London, W6 9DF, England. *Telephone:* 0181-741 1247.

WILMOTT, Peter Graham, C.M.G., M.A.; British consultant and fmr. civil servant; b. 6 Jan. 1947, Cuckfield; s. of John Wilmott and Violet Wilmott; m. Jennifer Plummer 1969; two d.; ed. Hove Grammar School and Trinity Coll. Cambridge; Asst. Prin., H.M. Customs & Excise 1968, Prin. 1973, Asst. Sec. 1983, Commr. 1988; seconded to U.K. Perm. Rep. to EC 1971–73, 1977–79, to EC Court of Auditors 1980–82; Dir.-Gen. Customs and Indirect Taxation, EC Comm. 1990–96; partner with Prisma Consulting Group 1996–; Chair. Int. Value Added Tax Asscn. 1998–; Admin. Office du Développement par l'Automisation et la Simplification du Commerce Extérieur, Paris 1998–. *Address:* 31 Wilbury Avenue, Hove, East Sussex, BN3 6HS, England.

WILSEY, Gen. Sir John, G.C.B., C.B.E., D.L.; British former army officer and business executive; b. 18 Feb. 1939, Frimley, Hants.; s. of late Maj.-Gen. J.H.O. Wilsey and B.S.F. Wilsey; m. Elizabeth P. Nottingham 1975; one s. one d.; ed. Sherborne School and Royal Mil. Acad. Sandhurst; served Cyprus, North Africa, Guyana, U.S.A., Malta, Germany, U.K. (mem. Blue Nile Expedition 1968), Staff Coll. 1973; Commdg. 1st Bn., The Devonshire & Dorset Regt. 1979–82, Col. 1990– (commissioned 1959); Chief of Staff, H.Q. N. Ireland 1982–84; Commdg. 1st Infantry Brigade and U.K. Mobile Force 1985–86; Royal Coll. of Defence Studies 1987; Chief of Staff, H.Q. U.K. Land Forces 1988–90; G.O.C. and Dir. Mil. Operations, Northern Ireland 1990–93; C.-in-C. Land Command 1993–96; ADC Gen. to the Queen 1994–96; Chair. Western Provident Asscn. 1996–; Hon. Col. Royal Jersey Militia, Royal Engineers 1993–; Col. Devonshire and Dorset Regt. 1990–97; Vice-Chair. Sherborne School 1996–; mem. Council Royal Bath & West 1996–, Commonwealth War Graves Comm. 1998–; Commr. Royal Hosp., Chelsea 1996–; Gov. Suttons Hosp. in Charterhouse 1996–, Sherborne School for Girls 1996–. *Publication:* Service for the Nation 1987. *Leisure interests:* skiing, fishing, sailing, breeding alpacas. *Address:* Western Provident Association, Rivergate House, Blackbrook Park, Taunton, Somerset, TA1 2PE, England. *Telephone:* (01823) 623502.

WILSON, Alan Geoffrey, M.A., F.B.A., F.C.G.I.; British professor of geography and mathematician; b. 8 Jan. 1939, Bradford, Yorks.; s. of Harry Wilson and Gladys Naylor; m. Sarah Fildes 1987; ed. Queen Elizabeth Grammar School, Darlington, Corpus Christi Coll., Cambridge; Scientific Officer, Rutherford High Energy Lab. 1961–64; Research Officer, Inst. of Econs. and Statistics, Univ. of Oxford 1964–66; Math. Adviser to Ministry of Transport 1966–68; Asst. Dir. Centre for Environmental Studies, London 1968–70; Prof. of Urban and Regional Geography, Univ. of Leeds 1970–91, Pro-Vice-Chancellor 1989–91, Vice-Chancellor 1991–; Ed. Environment and Planning 1969–91; mem. Academia Europaea 1991–; Gill Memorial Award, Royal Geographical Soc. 1978; Hons. Award, Asscn. of American Geographers 1987, Founder's Medal, Royal Geographical Soc. 1992. *Publications:* Entropy in Urban and Regional Modelling 1970, Urban and Regional Models in Geography and Planning 1974, Spatial Population Analysis (with P. H. Rees) 1977, Mathematics for Geographers and Planners (with M. J. Kirkby) 1980, Models of Cities and Regions (Jt. Ed.) 1977, Catastrophe Theory and Bifurcation: applications to urban and regional systems 1981, Geography and the Environment: Systems Analytical Methods 1981, Mathematical Methods in Geography and Planning (with R. J. Bennett) 1985, Urban Systems (Jt. Ed.) 1987, Urban Dynamics (Jt. Ed.) 1990, Modelling the City: Performance, Policy and Planning (with Bertuglia, Clarke and others) 1994, Intelligent Geographical Information Systems (with Birkin, Clarke and Clarke) 1996. *Leisure interests:* writing, fell running, miscellaneous fads. *Address:* University of Leeds, Leeds, LS2 9JT, England. *Telephone:* (0113) 233 3000. *Fax:* (0113) 233 4122.

WILSON, Alexander, C.B.E., F.L.A.; British librarian; b. 12 Feb. 1921, Greenock, Scotland; s. of late William Wilson and Amelia Wilson; m. Mary Catherin Traynor 1949; two s.; ed. Bolton Co. Grammar School; Dir. Libraries, Museums and Arts with Dudley Co. Borough 1952–68, with Coventry City Council 1968–72, with Cheshire Co. Council 1972–80; Consultant to Nat. Library of Malaysia 1978, Nat. Library of Pakistan 1983; Dir.-Gen. British Library Reference Div. 1980–86; Pres. Library Asscn. 1986; freelance library and information consultant 1986–93; Fellow, Birmingham Polytechnic; Hon. D.Lit. (Sheffield). *Leisure interests:* music, walking. *Address:* 1 Brockway West, Tattenhall, Chester, CH3 9EZ, England (Home). *Telephone:* (01829) 770179 (Home).

WILSON, Alexander (Sandy) Galbraith; British writer and composer; b. 19 May 1924, Sale, Cheshire; s. of George Wilson and Caroline Humphrey; ed. Harrow School, Oxford Univ. and Old Vic Theatre School; contributed to revues Slings and Arrows, Oranges and Lemons 1948; wrote revues for Watergate Theatre, London, See You Later, See You Again 1951–52; wrote musical The Boy Friend for Players Club Theatre 1953, transferred to Wyndhams Theatre and on Broadway 1954 (London revival 1984), The Buccaneer 1955, Valmouth London 1958, U.S.A. 1960, Chichester 1982, Divorce me Darling! 1965 (revival Chichester 1997); Dir. London revival of The Boy Friend 1967; Composed music for As Dorothy Parker Once Said London 1969; songs for BBC television Charley's Aunt 1969; wrote and performed Sandy Wilson Thanks the Ladies (one man show) London 1971; wrote His Monkey Wife London 1971, The Clapham Wonder 1978, Aladdin (London) 1979. *Publications:* This is Sylvia 1954, The Poodle from Rome

1962, I Could be Happy (autobiog.) 1975, Ivor 1975, The Roaring Twenties 1977. *Leisure interests:* cinema, cookery, travel. *Address:* Flat 4, 2 Southwell Gardens, London, SW7 4SB, England. *Telephone:* 0171-373 6172.

WILSON, Andrew N., M.A., F.R.S.L.; British author; b. 27 Oct. 1950; s. of late N. Wilson and of Jean Dorothy (née Crowder) Wilson; m. 1st Katherine Dorothea Duncan-Jones 1971 (divorced 1989); two d.; m. 2nd Ruth Guilding 1991; one d.; ed. Rugby School and New Coll., Oxford; Asst. Master Merchant Taylors' School 1975–76; Lecturer St. Hugh's Coll. and New Coll., Oxford 1976–81; Literary Ed. Spectator 1981–83, Evening Standard 1990–97; Chancellor's Essay Prize 1975, Ellerton Theological Prize 1975. *Publications:* fiction: The Sweets of Pimlico 1977, Unguarded Hours 1978, Kindly Light 1979, The Healing Art (Somerset Maugham Award) 1980, Who Was Oswald Fish? 1981, Wise Virgin (W. H. Smith Award) 1982, Scandal 1983, Gentleman in England 1985, Love Unknown 1986, Stray 1987, Incline Our Hearts 1988, A Bottle in the Smoke 1990, Daughters of Albion 1991, The Vicar of Sorrows 1993, A Watch in the Night 1996, Hazel the Guinea-pig (for children) 1997; non-fiction: The Laird of Abbotsford 1980, A Life of John Milton 1983, Hilaire Belloc 1984, How Can We Know? An Essay on the Christian Religion 1985, The Church in Crisis (jtly.) 1986, The Lion and the Honeycomb 1987, Penfriends from Porlock 1988, Tolstoy (Whitbread Award for Biography and Autobiography) 1988, Eminent Victorians 1989, John Henry Newman: prayers, poems, meditations (ed.) 1989, C. S. Lewis: A Biography 1989, Jesus 1992, The Faber Book of Church and Clergy (ed.) 1992, The Rise and Fall of the House of Windsor 1993, The Faber Book of London (ed.) 1993, Hearing Voices 1995, A Life of Walter Scott: The Laird of Abbotsford 1996, A Life of John Milton 1996, Paul: The Mind of the Apostle 1997, Dream Children 1998. *Address:* 5 Regent's Park Terrace, London, NW1 7EE, England.

WILSON, Sir Anthony, Kt., F.C.A., F.R.S.A.; British accountant; b. 17 Feb. 1928, Leeds; s. of late Charles E. Wilson and Martha C. (née Mee) Wilson; m. Margaret J. Hudson 1955; two s. one d.; ed. Giggleswick School, Yorks.; service in R.N. 1946–49; joined John Gordon Walton & Co. 1945–46, 1949–52; mem. staff, Price Waterhouse 1952–61, Partner 1961–84; mem. Govt. Production Statistics Advisory Cttee. 1972–84; Head, Govt. Accountancy Service and Chief Accountancy Adviser to Treasury 1984–88; mem. Council, Inst. of Chartered Accountants in England and Wales 1985–88, Accounting Standards Cttee. 1985–88, Auditing Practices Cttee. 1987–88, S.W. Regional Arts Asscn. Man. Cttee. 1983–91, Chair. 1988–91, Sr. Salaries Review Body 1989–98; Non-Exec. Dir. Capita Group PLC 1989–92; Chair. Chartered Accountants Compensation Scheme Ltd. 1989–90; Chair. Jt. Disciplinary Scheme of U.K. Accountancy Profession 1990–93; Pres. Chandos Chamber Choir 1986–88; Dir. Opera 80 1989–91; mem. Dorset Opera Cttee. 1981–96, Treas. 1981–88, Chair. 1988–93; Chair. Dorset Musical Instruments Trust 1994–; Chair. Sherborne Soc. Br., Council for the Protection of Rural England; Vice-Chair. Sherborne House Trust; Sr. Warden, Needlemakers' Co., Liveryman, Chartered Accountants' Co. *Leisure interests:* fishing, gardening, collecting pottery, opera, golf. *Address:* The Barn House, 89 Newland, Sherborne, Dorset, DT9 3AG, England (Home). *Telephone:* (01935) 815674 (Home).

WILSON, August; American playwright; b. 1945, Pittsburgh, Pa.; s. of David Bedford Wilson and Daisy Wilson; one d.; f. Black Horizons Theatre Co.; worked in Science Museum of Minn., St. Paul, writing short plays to accompany exhbns.; plays: The Homecoming 1976, The Coldest Day of the Year 1977, Black Bart and the Sacred Hills 1977, Jitney 1979, Ma Rainey's Black Bottom 1982 (N.Y. Drama Critics' Circle Award for Best Play), Fences (N.Y. Drama Critics' Circle Award for Best Play, Tony Award, Pulitzer Prize for Drama), 1983 Joe Turner's Come and Gone 1984 (N.Y. Drama Critics' Circle Award for Best Play), The Piano Lesson 1986 (Pulitzer Prize for Drama, New York Drama Critics' Circle Award, Drama Desk Award), Two Trains Running 1990, Seven Guitars 1995 (N.Y. Drama Critics' Circle Award for Best Play). *Address:* c/o John Breglio, Paul, Weiss, Rifkind, Wharton & Garrison, 1285 Avenue of the Americas, New York, NY 10019, U.S.A.

WILSON, Brian G., A.O., PH.D., F.T.S.; Australian academic (retd.); b. 9 April 1930, Belfast, N. Ireland; s. of Charles W. Wilson and Isobel C. (née Ferguson) Wilson; m. 1st Barbara Wilkie 1959 (divorced 1975); two s. one d.; m. 2nd Jeanne Henry 1978 (divorced 1988); m. 3rd Joan Opdebeeck 1988; three s.; ed. Methodist Coll., Belfast, Queens Univ. Belfast and Nat. Univ. of Ireland; Postdoctoral Fellow, Nat. Research Council of Canada 1955–57; Officer-in-charge, Sulphur Mount Lab., Banff, Alberta 1957–60; Assoc. Prof. of Physics, Univ. of Calgary 1960–65, Prof. 1965–70, Dean of Arts and Science 1967–70; Vice-Pres. Simon Fraser Univ., Burnaby, B.C. 1970–78; Vice-Chancellor Univ. of Queensland 1979–95; Deputy Chair. Australian Vice-Chancellors' Cttee. 1987–88, Chair. 1989–90; mem. Council, Northern Territory Univ. 1988–93, Univ. of the South Pacific 1991–95; Pres. Int. Devt. Program of Australian Univs. and Colls. 1991–92; Chair. Australian Cttee. for Quality Assurance in Higher Educ. 1993–95; Hon. LL.D. (Calgary) 1984; Hon. D.Univ. (Queensland Univ. of Tech.) 1995; Hon. D.Sc. (Queensland) 1995. *Publications:* one book and over 50 scientific articles in int. journals. *Leisure interests:* golf, viniculture. *Address:* Domaine des Tisseyres, 11270 Fanjeaux, France. *Telephone:* (4) 68.24.61.75. *Fax:* (4) 68.24.61.75.

WILSON, Charles; British journalist; b. 18 Aug. 1935, Glasgow, Scotland; s. of Adam Wilson and Ruth Wilson; m. 1st Anne Robinson 1968 (divorced 1973); one d.; m. 2nd Sally O'Sullivan 1980; one s. one d.; ed. Eastbank Acad., Glasgow; copy boy, The People 1951; later reporter with Bristol Evening World, News Chronicle and Daily Mail; Deputy Ed. Daily Mail (Manchester) 1971–74; Asst. Ed. London Evening News 1974–76; Ed., Evening Times, Glasgow 1976; later Ed., Glasgow Herald; Ed. Sunday Standard, Glasgow 1981–82; Exec. Ed., The Times 1982, Jt. Deputy Ed. 1984–85, Ed. 1985–90; Int. Devt. Dir. News Int. 1990–91; Ed.-in-Chief, Man. Dir The Sporting Life 1990–98; Editorial Dir. Mirror Group Newspapers 1991–92, Group Man. Dir. Mirror Group 1992–98; Acting Ed. The Independent 1995–96; mem. Jockey Club. *Leisure interest:* National Hunt racing. *Address:* c/o Mirror Group PLC, 1 Canada Square, Canary Wharf, London, E14 5AP, England.

WILSON, Sir Charles Haynes, Kt., M.A., LL.D., D.C.L., D.LITT.; British university administrator; b. 16 May 1909, Glasgow, Scotland; s. of George Wilson and Florence Hannay; m. Jessie Wilson 1935; one s. two d.; ed. Glasgow Univ. and Oxford Univ.; Fellow and Tutor in Modern History, Corpus Christi Coll., Oxford 1939–52, Jr. Proctor 1945; Prin. Univ. Coll. of Leicester 1952–57; Vice-Chancellor, Univ. of Leicester 1957–61; Prin. and Vice-Chancellor, Univ. of Glasgow 1961–76; Hon. Fellow, Corpus Christi Coll., Oxford 1963. *Address:* Whinnymuir Dalry, Castle Douglas, DG7 3TT, Scotland. *Telephone:* (01644) 430218.

WILSON, Sir Colin Alexander St John, Kt., R.A., F.R.I.B.A.; British architect; b. 14 March 1922; s. of late Rt. Rev. Henry A. Wilson; m. 1st Muriel Lavender 1955 (divorced 1971); m. 2nd Mary J. Long 1972; one s. one d.; ed. Felsted School, Corpus Christi Coll. Cambridge and London Univ. School of Architecture; served R.N.V.R. 1942–46; Asst. Housing Div. Architects Dept. London County Council 1950–55; lecturer, School of Architecture, Univ. of Cambridge 1955–69, Prof. of Architecture 1975–89, now Prof. Emer.; Fellow, Churchill Coll. Cambridge 1962–71, Pembroke Coll. 1977–; Visiting Critic, Yale School of Architecture 1960, 1964, 1983; Bemis Prof. of Architecture, M.I.T. 1970–72; practised in assoc. with Sir Leslie Martin 1955–64; works included bldgs. at Univs. of Oxford, Cambridge, London and Leicester; in own pvt. practice works include extension to British Museum, The British Library, St. Pancras (under construction since 1982), public bldgs. in Leicester, housing etc.; Hon. Fellow Corpus Christi Coll. Cambridge; Dr. h.c. (Essex) 1998; Commdr., Order of the Lion (Finland) 1992. *Publications:* Architectural Reflections 1993, The Other Tradition of Modern Architecture 1995, articles in The Observer, professional journals etc. *Address:* Colin St John Wilson & Associates, Clarendon Buildings, 27 Horsell Road, London, N5 1XL; 31A Grove End Road, London, N.W.8, England. *Telephone:* 0171-607 3084. *Fax:* 0171-607 5621.

WILSON, Colin Henry; British writer; b. 26 June 1931, Leicester; s. of Arthur Wilson and Annetta Jones; m. 1st Dorothy Troop 1951; one s.; m. 2nd Joy Stewart 1960; two s. one d.; ed. Gateway Secondary Technical School, Leicester; laboratory asst. 1948–49, civil servant (taxes) 1949–50; R.A.F. 1950, discharged on medical grounds 1950; then navvy, boot and shoe operative, dish washer, plastic moulder; lived Strasbourg 1950, Paris 1953; later factory hand and dish washer; writer 1956–; Writer in Residence, Hollins Coll., Virginia, U.S.A. 1966–67; Visiting Prof., Univ. of Washington 1967–68, Dowling Coll., Majorca 1969, Rutgers Univ., N.J. 1974. *Publications include:* philosophy: The Outsider 1956, Religion and the Rebel 1957, The Age of Defeat 1958, The Strength to Dream 1961, Origins of the Sexual Impulse 1963, Beyond the Outsider 1965, Introduction to the New Existentialism 1966; other non-fiction: Encyclopaedia of Murder 1960, Rasputin and the Fall of of the Romanovs 1964, Brandy of the Damned (music essays) 1965, Eagle and Earwig (literary essays) 1965, Sex and the Intelligent Teenager 1966, Voyage to a Beginning (autobiog.) 1968, Shaw: A Reassessment 1969, A Casebook of Murder 1969, Poetry and Mysticism 1970, The Strange Genius of David Lindsay (with E. H. Visiak) 1970, The Occult 1971, New Pathways in Psychology 1972, Strange Powers 1973, A Book of Booze 1974, The Craft of the Novel 1975, The Geller Phenomenon 1977, Mysteries 1978, Beyond The Occult 1988; novels: Ritual in the Dark 1960, Adrift in Soho 1961, The World of Violence 1963, Man Without a Shadow 1963, Necessary Doubt 1964, The Glass Cage 1966, The Mind Parasites 1967, The Philosopher's Stone 1969, The Killer 1970, The God of the Labyrinth 1970, The Black Room 1970, The Schoolgirl Murder Case 1974, The Space Vampires 1976, Men of Strange Powers 1976, Enigmas and Mysteries 1977; *other works include:* The Quest for Wilhelm Reich 1979, The War Against Sleep: the Philosophy of Gurdjieff 1980, Starseekers 1980, Frankenstein's Castle 1980, The Directory of Possibilities (ed. with John Grant) 1981, Poltergeist! 1981, Access to Inner Worlds 1983, Encyclopaedia of Modern Murder (with Donald Seaman) 1983, The Psychic Detectives 1984, The Janus Murder Case 1984, The Personality Surgeon 1984, A Criminal History of Mankind 1984, Encyclopaedia of Scandal (with Donald Seaman) 1985, Afterlife 1985, Rudolf Steiner 1985, Strindberg (play) 1970, Spiderworld—the tower 1987, Encyclopaedia of Unsolved Mysteries (with Damon Wilson) 1987, Aleister Crowley: the nature of the beast 1987, The Misfits 1988, Spiderworld—The Delta 1988, Written in Blood 1989, The Serial Killers 1990, Mozart's Journey to Prague (play) 1991, Spider World: the Magician 1992, The Strange Life of P. D. Ouspensky 1993, From Atlantis to the Sphinx 1996, Atlas of Sacred Sites and Holy Places 1996, Alien Dawn 1998, The Books in My Life 1998. *Leisure interests:* music, mathematics, wine. *Address:* Tetherdown, Trewallock Lane, Gorran Haven, Cornwall, PL26 6NT, England.

WILSON, Sir David Mackenzie, Kt., LITT.D., F.B.A., F.S.A.; British fmr. museum director; b. 30 Oct. 1931, Dacre Banks; s. of Rev. J. Wilson; m. Eva Sjögren 1955; one s. one d.; ed. Kingswood School, St. John's Coll., Cambridge, Lund Univ., Sweden; Asst. Keeper, The British Museum 1955–64; Reader in Archaeology, Univ. of London 1964–71, Prof. of Medieval Archaeology 1971–76; Dir. British Museum 1977–92; Commr. English Heritage 1990–97; Hon. Fellow Univ. Coll., London; mem. Royal Swedish Acad. of Science, Norwegian Acad. of Science and Letters, numerous other honours and awards. *Publications:* The Anglo-Saxons 1960, Catalogue of Anglo-Saxon Metalwork 700–1100 in the British Museum 1964, Anglo-Saxon Art 1964, The Bayeux Tapestry 1965, Viking Art (with O. Klindt-Jensen) 1966, Three Viking Graves in the Isle of Man (with G. Bersu) 1966, The Vikings and their Origins 1970, The Viking Achievement (with P. Foote) 1970, St. Ninian's Isle and its Treasure (with A. Small and A. C. Thomas) 1973, The Viking Age in the Isle of Man 1974; Editor: The Archaeology of the Anglo-Saxons 1976, The Northern World 1980, The Art of the Anglo-Saxons 1984, The Bayeux Tapestry 1985, The British Museum: Purpose and Politics 1989, Awful Ends 1992, Showing the Flag 1992, Vikingetidens Konst 1995, Vikings and Gods in European Art 1997; many articles and pamphlets. *Address:* The Lifeboat House, Castletown, IM9 1LD, Isle of Man. *Telephone:* (01624) 822800.

WILSON, Donald M.; American journalist and publishing executive; b. 27 June 1925; m. Susan M. Neuberger 1957; one s. two d.; ed. Yale Univ.; Air Corps Navigator, Second World War; magazine assignments in 35 countries 1951–61; fmr. Far Eastern Corresp., Life magazine, Chief Washington Correspondent 1957–61; Deputy Dir. U.S. Information Agency 1961–65; Gen. Man. Time-Life Int. 1965–68; Assoc. Publisher Life magazine 1968–69; Vice-Pres. Corp. and Public Affairs, Time Inc. 1969–81, Corp. Vice-Pres. Public Affairs Time Inc. 1981–89; Publr. Business News New Jersey 1989–. *Address:* Business News New Jersey, 104 Church Street, New Brunswick, NJ 08901 (Office); 4574 Province Line Road, Princeton, NJ 08540, U.S.A. (Home).

WILSON, Edward Osborne, PH.D.; American university professor and author; b. 10 June 1929, Birmingham, Ala.; s. of the late Edward Osborne Wilson Sr. and of Inez Freeman Huddleston; m. Irene Kelley 1955; one d.; ed. Univ. of Alabama and Harvard Univ.; Jr. Fellow, Soc. of Fellows, Harvard Univ. 1953–56, Prof. of Zoology 1964–76, F. B. Baird Prof. of Science 1976–94, Pellegrino Univ. Prof. 1994–97, Research Prof. 1997–, Curator of Entomology, Museum of Comparative Zoology, 1972–; Fellow, Guggenheim Foundation 1977–78, Advisory Bd. 1979–90, mem. Selection Cttee. 1982–90; mem. Bd. of Dirs., World Wildlife Fund 1983–94; Org. for Tropical Studies 1984–91; American Museum of Natural History 1992–, American Acad. of Liberal Educ. 1993–, Nature Conservancy 1994–; Foreign mem. Royal Soc. 1990; Nat. Medal of Science 1976, Pulitzer Prize for Gen. Non-Fiction 1978, 1981, Tyler Prize for Environmental Achievement 1983, Crafoord Prize, Royal Swedish Acad. of Sciences 1990, Int. Prize for Biology, Govt. of Japan 1993, Schubert Prize, Germany 1996, and some 50 other awards and prizes. *Publications:* The Theory of Island Biogeography (with R. H. MacArthur) 1967, The Insect Societies 1971, Sociobiology: The New Synthesis 1975, On Human Nature 1978, Caste and Ecology in the Social Insects (with G. F. Oster) 1978, Genes, Mind and Culture (with C. J. Lumsden) 1981, Promethean Fire (with C. J. Lumsden) 1983, Biophilia 1984, Biodiversity (Ed.) 1988, The Ants (with B. Hölldobler) 1990, Success and Dominance in Ecosystems 1990, The Diversity of Life 1992, Naturalist 1994, Journey to the Ants (with Bert Hölldobler) 1994, Consilience: The Unity of Knowledge 1998; numerous articles on evolutionary biology, entomology and conservation. *Address:* Museum of Comparative Zoology, Harvard University, Cambridge, MA 02138 (Office); 9 Foster Road, Lexington, MA 02173, U.S.A. (Home).

WILSON, Hon. Geoffrey Hazlitt, C.V.O., B.A., F.C.A., F.C.M.A.; British accountant and business executive; b. 28 Dec. 1929, London; s. of Lord Moran and Dorothy Dufton; m. Barbara Jane Hebblethwaite 1955; two s. two d.; ed. Eton Coll. and King's Coll., Cambridge; with English Electric Co. Ltd. 1956–68, Deputy Comptroller 1967–68; Financial Controller (Overseas), General Electric Co. Ltd. 1968–69; Financial Dir., Cables Div., Delta PLC 1969, Group Financial Dir. 1972, Jt. Man. Dir. 1977, Dir. 1977, Deputy Chief Exec. 1980, Chief Exec. 1981–88, Chair. 1982–94; Dir. Blue Circle Industries PLC 1981–87, Drayton English & Int. Trust PLC 1978–95, Nat. Westminster Bank PLC (W. Midlands and Wales Regional Bd.) 1985–92 (Chair. 1990–92), Southern Electric PLC 1989–96 (Chair. 1993–96), Johnson Matthey PLC 1990– (Deputy Chair. 1994–97); Hon. Treasurer, mem. Admin. Council The Prince's and the Royal Jubilee Trusts 1979–89; Vice-Pres. Eng. Employers' Fed. 1983–86, 1990–94, Deputy Pres. 1986–90; Vice-Chair. King's Coll., Cambridge Campaign Appeal 1994–97; Pres. British Fed. of Electrotechnical and Allied Mfrs'. Asscns. 1987–88; Hon. mem. The Hundred Group of Chartered Accountants (Chair. 1979–81); mem. Court, Worshipful Co. of Chartered Accountants in England and Wales 1982–, Master 1988–89, Financial Repertoire Council 1990–93; mem. O. St. J. 1997. *Leisure interests:* family, reading, vintage cars, skiing.

WILSON, Georges; French theatre and film director; b. 16 Oct. 1921, Champigny-sur-Marne; m. Nicole Mulon 1956; two s.; ed. Centre dramatique de la rue Blanche, Paris; acted in two plays in Grenier-Hussenot Company 1947; entered Comédie de l'Ouest 1950; entered Théâtre Nat. Populaire (T.N.P.) 1952, played important roles in almost all the plays; Dir. L'école des femmes, Le client du matin (Théâtre de l'Oeuvre), Un otage (Théâtre de France), La vie de Galilée, Lumières de Bohème, La folle de Chaillot, Le diable et le bon Dieu, Chêne et lapins angora, Les prodiges 1971, Turandot 1971, Long voyage vers la nuit 1973, Othello 1975, Un habit pour l'hiver 1979, Huis clos, K2 1983, l'Escalier 1985, Je ne suis Rappaport 1987, Meteore (Dir., Actor) 1991, les Dimanches de Monsieur Riley 1992, Show Bis 1994, Henry IV 1994; Dir. T.N.P. 1963–72; Chair. Interim Action Cttee. British Film Authority 1979; Chevalier, Légion d'honneur, Officier, Ordre nat. du Mérite, Commdr., Ordre des Arts et Lettres. *Films directed include:* Une aussi longue absence, La jument verte, Le Caïd, Terrain vague, Lucky Joe, Dragées au poivre, Chair de poule, Max et les ferrailleurs 1970, Blanche 1971, Nous sommes tous en liberté provisoire 1973, Asphalte 1981, L'honneur d'un capitaine 1982, Itinéaires bis 1983, Tango, l'exil de Gardel 1985, La Vouivre 1989, le Château de ma mère 1990, la Tribu 1991; several TV appearances. *Address:* Moulin de Vilgris, 78120 Rambouillet, France (Home).

WILSON, Gordon (see Wilson, (Robert) Gordon).

WILSON, Jean Donald, M.D.; American professor of internal medicine; b. 26 Aug. 1932, Wellington, Tex.; s. of J. D. Wilson and Maggie E. (Hill) Wilson; ed. Hillsboro Coll., Univ. of Texas at Austin and Univ. of Texas Southwestern Medical School, Dallas; Medical Intern and Asst. Resident in Internal Medicine, Parkland Memorial Hosp. Dallas 1955–58; Clinical Assoc. Nat. Heart Inst. Bethesda, Md. 1958–60; Instr. Univ. of Texas Health Science Center 1960–, Prof. of Internal Medicine 1968–; Established Investigator, American Heart Asscn. 1960–65; Travelling Fellow, Royal Soc. of Medicine, Strangeways Research Lab. Cambridge 1970; mem. N.A.S., American Acad. of Arts and Sciences etc.; several honours and awards. *Publications:* 200 scientific articles in various medical journals. *Leisure interests:* gardening, opera. *Address:* Division of Endocrinology and Metabolism, Department of Internal Medicine, University of Texas Southwestern Medical Center at Dallas, 5323 Harry Hines Boulevard, Dallas, TX 75235–8857, U.S.A. *Telephone:* (214) 648-3494. *Fax:* (214) 648-8917.

WILSON, Sir John Foster, Kt., C.B.E., D.C.L.; British international health administrator; b. 20 Jan. 1919, Nottingham; s. of Rev. George Wilson and Leonore Carrick Wilson; m. Chloe J. McDermid 1944; two d.; ed. Worcester Coll. for the Blind and St. Catherine's Coll., Oxford; founded Royal Commonwealth Soc. for the Blind 1950, Dir. 1950–84, Vice-Pres. 1983; First Pres. Int. Agency for Prevention of Blindness 1974–83, Hon. Life Pres. 1982; initiated IMPACT (Int. Initiative against Avoidable Disablement) 1983, Chair. Int. Council 1991–; Sr. Consultant to UNDP 1983–, Helen Keller Int. Award 1970, World Humanity Award 1979, Lasker Special Public Service Award 1979, Albert Schweitzer Int. Prize 1993, other awards; Hon. D.C.L. (Oxford) 1995. *Publications:* Travelling Blind 1964, Preventable Disablement: The Global Challenge 1983, World Blindness and its Prevention (Vol. I) 1979, (Vol. II) 1984. *Leisure interests:* music, radio, gardening, wine making. *Address:* 22 The Cliff, Roedean, Brighton, East Sussex, BN2 5RE, England. *Telephone:* (01273) 607667. *Fax:* (01273) 679624.

WILSON, John P., M.A., T.D.; Irish politician and university lecturer; b. 8 July 1923, Co. Cavan; s. of John Wilson and Brigid Wilson; m. Ita M. Ward 1953; one s. four d.; ed. St. Mel's Coll., Longford, Nat. Univ. of Ireland, Univ. of London and Zaragoza Univ.; taught in England and Ireland 1947–73; mem. of the Dáil 1973–; Opposition Spokesman on Educ. and the Arts 1973–77, Jan.–Dec. 1982; Minister for Educ. 1977–81, for Transport and for Posts and Telegraphs 1982; Opposition Spokesman on Transport 1983–87; Minister for Tourism and Transport 1987–89, for the Marine 1989–93, for Defence 1992–93; Minister for the Gaeltacht, Tánaiste (Deputy Prime Minister) 1990–93; Chair. Irish Govt. del., Northern Ireland talks 1992; Apptd. Victims' Commr. by Irish Govt. 1998; Pres. European Council of Fisheries Ministers; Pres. Perm. Comm., Eurocontrol 1989–; mem. Arts Council; Dir. Tyrone Guthrie Centre, Annaghmakerrig. *Leisure interests:* politics, Irish language and literature, theatre, reading, fishing, Gaelic football and hurling, cruising, arts. *Address:* Kilgolagh, Co. Cavan, via Finea, Mullingar; 13 Braemor Avenue, Churchtown, Dublin 14, Ireland. *Telephone:* (043) 81130; 2981861. *Fax:* 2981861.

WILSON, Kenneth Geddes, PH.D.; American physicist; b. 8 June 1936, Waltham, Mass.; s. of Edgar Bright Wilson, Jr. and Emily Fisher Buckingham Wilson; m. Alison Brown 1982; ed. Harvard Univ., Calif. Inst. of Tech.; Fellow Harvard Univ. 1959–62, Ford Foundation Fellow 1962–63; joined Cornell Univ. N.Y. 1963, Prof. 1970–88, James A. Weeks Chair. in Physical Sciences 1974–88, Dir. Center for Theory and Stimulation in Science and Eng. (Cornell Theory Center) 1985–88; Hazel C. Youngberg Distinguished Prof. Ohio State Univ. 1988–; Co-Prin. Investigator Ohio's Project Discovery; mem. N.A.S., American Acad. of Arts and Sciences, American Philosophical Soc.; Heinemann Prize 1973, Boltzmann Medal 1975, Wolf Prize 1980, Nobel Physics Prize 1982. *Publications:* Redesigning Education 1994; articles in journals. *Address:* Department of Physics, The Ohio State University, 174 W. 18th Avenue, Columbus, OH 43210, U.S.A. *Telephone:* (614) 292-8686. *Fax:* (614) 292-3221.

WILSON, Linda S., PH.D.; American university administrator and chemist; b. 10 Nov. 1936, Washington D.C.; m. 1st Malcolm C. Whatley 1957 (divorced); one d.; m. 2nd Paul A. Wilson 1970; one step-d.; ed. Tulane Univ. and Univ. of Wisconsin (Madison); Asst. Vice-Chancellor for Research, Washington, Univ., St Louis, Mo. 1968–74, Assoc. Vice-Chancellor 1974–75; Assoc. Vice-Chancellor for Research, Univ. of Ill., Urbana, Ill. 1975–85, Assoc. Dean, Graduate Coll. 1978–85; Vice-Pres. for Research, Univ. of

Mich., Ann Arbor, Mich. 1985–89; Pres. Radcliffe Coll., Cambridge, Mass. 1989–; Chair. Advisory Cttee. Office of Science and Eng. Personnel, Nat. Research Council 1990–96; mem., Council on Govt. Relations 1971–77, Nat. Inst. of Health Advisory Council on Research Resources 1978–82, Nat. Comm. on Research 1978–80, NSF Dirs. Advisory Council 1980–89, Govt.-Univ.-Industry Research Roundtable (N.A.S.) 1984–88, Inst. of Medicine Council 1986–89, Inst. of Medicine Cttee. on Govt.-Industry Collaboration in Research and Educ. 1988–89, Bd. of Dirs. A.A.A.S. 1984–88, Mich. Materials Processing Inst. 1986–89, Mich. Biotech. Inst 1986–89, Inst. of Medicine (N.A.S.) American Chemical Soc.; Overseer Museum of Science, Boston 1992–; Trustee Mass. Gen. Hosp. 1992–, Cttee. on Econ. Devt. 1995–; Dir. Citizens Financial Group 1997–, Inacom Corpn. 1997–; Fellow A.A.A.S.; hon. degrees from Tulane Univ., Univ. of Md.; Distinguished Contribution to Research Admin. Award, Soc. of Research Admins., Distinguished Service Award, Univ. of Ill., Centennial Award for Outstanding Accomplishments, Newcomb Coll, Distinguished Alumni Award, Univ. of Wis. 1997. *Publications:* 7 book chapters, 10 journal articles, 6 maj. reports, 4 commissioned studies, 12 papers on chem., science policy and research policy. *Leisure interests:* sailing, reading, music. *Address:* Radcliffe College, Fay House, 10 Garden Street, Cambridge, MA 02138; 76 Brattle Street, Cambridge, MA 02138, U.S.A. (Home). *Telephone:* 617-495-8602. *Fax:* 617-496-3179.

WILSON, Very Rev. Lois Miriam, O.C., D.MIN.; Canadian ecclesiastic; b. 8 April 1927, Winnipeg, Man.; d. of Rev. Dr. E. G. D. Freeman and Ada M. Davis; m. Rev. Dr. Roy F. Wilson 1950; two s. two d.; ordained United Church of Canada 1965; Minister, First Church United, Thunder Bay, Ont. 1965–69, Hamilton, Ont. 1969–78, Chalmers United Church, Kingston, Ont. 1978–80; Pres. Canadian Council of Churches 1976–79; Moderator, United Church of Canada 1980–82; Dir. Ecumenical Forum of Canada 1983–89; Pres. World Council of Churches 1983–91, World Federalists (Canada) 1996–; The United Church of Canada McGeachy Sr. Scholar 1989–91; mem. Bd. Amnesty Int. 1978–90, Canadian Inst. for Int. Peace and Security 1984–89, Refugee Status Advisory Bd. 1985–89, Canadian Assen. of Adult Educ. 1987–90, Civil Liberties Asscn. of Canada 1987–, Co-op Program in Int. Devt., Univ. of Toronto 1987–93, Public Review Bd., Canada 1989–, Bd. of Regents, Victoria Univ. 1990–; Govt. appointee to Environmental Assessment Panel reviewing nuclear waste disposal 1989–97; Chair. Urban Rural Mission (Canada) 1990–95; Chancellor Lakehead Univ. 1990–, Nat. Pres. UNIFEM 1993–95, Int. Centre for Human Rights and Democratic Devt. 1997–; mem. Advisory Bd., Canadian Women's Studies Journal, York Univ., Toronto 1993–, Centre for Studies in Religion and Society, Victoria, B.C. 1992–; Monitor, El Salvador elections 1994; Keynote speaker Christian/Jewish Conf., Jerusalem 1994; 11 hon. degrees; Pearson Peace Prize 1985, World Federalist Peace Prize 1985, Queen's Jubilee Medal, Order of Ont. 1991, commemorative medal for 125th anniversary of Canadian Confed. 1992. *Publications:* Like a Mighty River 1981, Turning the World Upside Down (memoir) 1989, Telling Her Story 1992, Miriam, Mary and Me 1992, Stories Seldom Told 1997. *Leisure interests:* skiing, sailing, canoeing, reading. *Address:* 40 Glen Road, Apt. 310, Toronto, Ont., M4W 2V1, Canada (Home). *Telephone:* (416) 975-0395 (Home and Office). *Fax:* (416) 975-0848.

WILSON, Gen. Louis Hugh, B.A.; American marine corps officer; b. 11 Feb. 1920, Brandon, Miss.; s. of Louis Wilson and Bertha (née Buchann) Wilson; m. Jane Clark 1944; one d.; ed. Millsaps Coll.; enlisted in Marine Corps Reserve 1941, Second Lieut. 1941, 9th Marine Regt., San Diego, Guadalcanal, Efate, Bougainville; Capt. 1943; participated in assault on Guam 1944; Company C.O., Camp Pendleton 1944; Detachment Commdr., Washington, D.C. 1944–46; Dean, later Asst. Dir. Marine Corps Inst., later ADC to Commdg. Gen. of Fleet Marine Force, Pacific; Recruiting Officer, N.Y.; Lieut.-Col. 1951; exec. posts at Basic School, Quantico, Va.; C.O., Camp Barrett 1951–54; with 1st Marine Div. as Asst. G-3 in Korea 1954–55; Head of Operations, HQ Marine Corps 1956–68; C.O., Test and Training Regt., then of Basic School, Quantico 1958–61; Deputy Chief of Staff, HQ Marine Corps 1962–65; Asst. Chief of Staff, G-3 1st Marine Div., Repub. of Viet Nam 1965; Command, 6th Marine Corps District, Atlanta, Ga. 1966; Brig.-Gen. 1966; Legis. Asst. to Commdt. of Marine Corps 1967–68; Chief of Staff, HQ Fleet Marine Force, Pacific 1968–70; Maj.-Gen. 1970; Command, 1st Marine Amphibious Force, 3rd Marine Div., Okinawa 1970; Dir. of Educ., Quantico 1971–72; Lieut.-Gen. 1972; Command, Fleet Marine Force, Pacific 1972–75; 26th Commdt. Marine Corps 1975–79; designated mem. Jt. Chiefs of Staff Oct. 1978–; mem. Bd. Dirs. Merrill Lynch and Co., Fluor Corpn., La. Lands Exploration Co.; Hon. LL.D. 1976; Hon. D.Hum. 1978; Medal of Honor 1944, Legion of Merit with Combat V and 2 Gold Stars, Purple Heart with 2 Stars, Cross of Gallantry with Gold Star (Repub. of Viet Nam) 1965, Order of Nat. Security Merit (Repub. of Korea), GUK-SEON Medal, Commdr., Legion of Honour (Philippines), Outstanding American Award 1975, Int. Order of Merit 1976, Spanish Grand Cross of Naval Merit 1977, Order of Nat. Security Merit, Tong-Il Medal (Korea) 1977, Distinguished American Award 1977, D.S.M. *Leisure interests:* hunting, golf. *Address:* 1338 Wembley Road, San Marino, CA 91108, U.S.A.

WILSON, Lynton Ronald, O.C., M.A.; Canadian business executive; b. 3 April 1940, Port Colborne, Ont.; s. of Ronald Alfred Wilson and Blanche Evelyn Matthews; m. Brenda Jean Black; one s. two d.; ed. Port Colborne High School, McMaster Univ., Cornell Univ., U.S.A.; Deputy Minister, Ministry of Industry and Tourism, Govt. of Ont. 1978–81; Pres. and C.E.O. Redpath Industries Ltd., Toronto 1981–88, Chair. Bd. 1988–89; Man. Dir. N. America, Tate & Lyle PLC 1986–89; Vice-Chair. Bank of Nova Scotia, Toronto 1989–90; Pres. and C.O.O. BCE Inc., Montreal 1990–, C.O.O. 1990–92, C.E.O. 1992–98, Chair. 1993–, Chair. Bd. Dirs. 1998–; Chair. Bell Canada; Dir. BCE Mobile Communications Inc., Bell Canada Int. Inc., Northern Telecom Ltd., Bell-Northern Research Ltd., Teleglobe Inc., Chrysler Canada Ltd., Chrysler Corpn., Tate & Lyle PLC, U.K., Stelco Inc., C.D. Howe Inst., Canadian Inst. for Advanced Research; mem. Business Council on Nat. Issues (Policy Cttee.), Trilateral Comm., Int. Council J.P. Morgan & Co., New York, Bd. of Trustees Montreal Museum of Fine Arts Foundation; Gov. Olympic Trust of Canada, McGill Univ.; Dr. h.c. (Montreal) 1995; Hon. LL.D. (McMaster) 1995. *Address:* BCE Inc., 1000 rue de La Gauchetière Ouest, Bureau 3700, Montreal, Quebec, H3B 4Y7, Canada. *Telephone:* (514) 397-7244.

WILSON, Nigel Guy, M.A., F.B.A.; British academic; b. 23 July 1935, London; s. of Noel Wilson and Joan L. Wilson; m. Hanneke Marion Wirtjes 1996; ed. Univ. Coll. School and Corpus Christi Coll., Oxford; Lecturer, Merton Coll., Oxford 1957–62; Fellow and Tutor in Classics, Lincoln Coll., Oxford 1962–; Gordon Duff Prize 1968. *Publications:* Scribes and Scholars (with L. D. Reynolds) (3rd edn.) 1991, An Anthology of Byzantine Prose 1971, Medieval Greek Bookhands 1973, St. Basil on the Value of Greek Literature 1975, Scholia in Aristophanis Acharnenses 1975, Menander Rhetor (with D. A. Russell) 1981, Scholars of Byzantium 1983, Oxford Classical Text of Sophocles (with Sir Hugh Lloyd-Jones) 1990, From Byzantium to Italy 1992, Photius: the Bibliotheca 1994, Aelian: Historical Miscellany 1997. *Leisure interests:* bridge, real tennis. *Address:* Lincoln College, Oxford, OX1 3DR, England. *Telephone:* (01865) 279794. *Fax:* (01865) 279802.

WILSON, Pete, LL.B.; American politician and lawyer; b. 23 Aug. 1933, Lake Forest, Ill.; s. of James Boone and Margaret (Callahan) Wilson; m. 1st Betty Robertson (divorced); m. 2nd Gayle Edlund Graham 1983; admitted to Calif. Bar; Asst. Exec. Dir. Republican Asscn., San Diego Co. 1963–64; Exec. Dir. San Diego Co. Republican Cen. Comm. 1964–65; legal service officer, Calif. State Republican Cen. Comm. 1965; mem. Calif. Ass. 1967–71; Mayor of San Diego 1971–83; Senator from Calif. 1983–91; Gov. of Calif. 1991–99; mem. Presidential Advisory Cttee. on Environmental Quality, Task Force Land Use and Urban Growth Policy. *Address:* c/o Governor's Office, State Capitol, Sacramento, CA 95814, U.S.A.

WILSON, Richard Thomas James, C.B., LL.B; British civil servant; b. 11 Oct. 1942; s. of the late Richard Ridley Wilson and Frieda Bell Finlay; m. Caroline Margaret Lee 1972; one s. one d.; ed. Radley Coll. and Cambridge Univ.; called to the Bar 1965; asst. Prin. Board of Trade 1966, Pvt. Sec. to Minister of State, Board of Trade 1969–71, Prin. Cabinet Office 1971–73, Dept. of Energy 1974, Asst. Sec. Dept. of Energy 1977–82, Under Sec. 1982, Prin. Establishment and Finance Officer 1982–86; on loan to Cabinet Office Man. and Personnel Office 1986–87, Deputy Sec. Cabinet Office 1987–90; Deputy Sec. (Industry) H.M. Treasury 1990–92; Perm. Sec. Dept. of Employment 1992–94; Perm. Under Sec. of State, Home Office 1994–97; Cabinet Sec. 1997–. *Address:* Cabinet Office, 70 Whitehall, London, SW1A 2AS, England. *Telephone:* 0171-270 1234.

WILSON, Sir Robert, C.B.E., PH.D., F.INST.P., F.R.S.; British astrophysicist; b. 16 April 1927; s. of Robert G. Wilson and Anne Riddle; m. Fiona Nicholson; ed. South Shields High School and Univs. of Durham and Edinburgh; astronomer, Royal Observatory, Edinburgh 1952–57; NRC Research Fellow, Dominion Astrophysical Observatory, B.C., Canada 1957–58; Leader, Plasma Spectroscopy Group, Atomic Energy Research Establishment, Harwell 1958–62; Head, Spectroscopy Div. Culham Lab., Oxon. 1962–68; Dir. SRC Astrophysics Research Unit, Culham 1968–72; Perren Prof. of Astronomy, Univ. Coll. London 1972–94, Dean of Science 1982–85, Head, Dept. of Physics and Astronomy 1987–93; Chair. Anglo-Australian Telescope Bd. 1986–89, James Clerk Maxwell Telescope Bd. 1987–91; mem. Cospar Bureau 1986–90; mem. Council, Royal Inst. 1990–93; Foreign mem. American Philosophical Soc. 1996; Hon. D.Sc. (Queen's Univ., Belfast) 1995; Science Award, Int. Acad. of Astronautics; Herschel Medal, Royal Astronomical Soc, U.S. Design Award for Int. Ultraviolet Explorer Satellite 1988, Pres. Award for Design Excellence (U.S.A.) 1988, Royal Soc./Cospar Massey Award 1994. *Publications:* nearly 200 papers in optical astronomy, plasma spectroscopy, solar physics and ultraviolet astronomy. *Address:* Department of Physics and Astronomy, University College, Gower Street, London, WC1E 6BT, England.

WILSON, (Robert) Gordon, B.L., LL.D.; Scottish politician and solicitor; b. 16 April 1938, Glasgow, Scotland; s. of Robert George Wilson and Robina Wilson; m. Edith Hassall 1965; two d.; ed. Douglas High School and Edinburgh Univ.; Asst. Nat. Sec. Scottish Nat. Party 1963–64, Nat. Sec. 1964–71, Exec. Vice-Chair. 1972–73, Sr. Vice-Chair. 1973–74, Chair. 1979–90, Vice-Pres. 1992–; M.P. for Dundee E. 1974–87; Party Spokesman on Oil and Energy 1974–87, on Energy 1992–93, on Treasury 1993–94; Jt. Spokesman on Devolution 1976–79; Rector, Univ. of Dundee 1983–86; Chair. Marriage Counselling (Tayside) 1989–92; Gov. Dundee Inst. of Tech.; Court mem. Univ. of Abertay Dundee 1991–96. *Leisure interests:* photography, reading, sailing. *Address:* 48 Monifieth Road, Dundee, DD5 2RX, Scotland (Home). *Fax:* (01382) 226745.

WILSON, Robert M.; American actor and artist; b. 4 Oct. 1941, Waco, Tex.; s. of D.M. Wilson and Loree Velma Wilson (née Hamilton); ed. Univ. of Tex., Pratt Inst. *Stage appearances include:* Deafman Glance 1970, The Life and

Times of Joseph Stalin (dir.) 1974, A Letter for Queen Victoria 1974, Einstein on the Beach 1976, 1984, Death, Destruction and Detroit 1979, The Golden Windows 1982, 1985, The Civil Wars 1983–85, Hamletmachine 1986, Doktor Faustus 1989, The Black Rider 1990, King Lear 1990, The Magic Flute 1991, Alice 1993, Der Mond in Gras 1994, The Death of Molière 1994, Hamlet: A Monologue 1995, Prometeo 1997, Saints and Singing 1997. *Films include:* Overture for a Deafman, Murder; videos include: Spaceman 1976, 1984, Video 50 1978, La Femme à la Cafétière 1989, Mr. Bojangles' Memory 1991, La Mort de Molière 1993; one-man exhbns. of drawings and sculpture: Iolas Gallery, N.Y., Palazzi Gallery, Milan, Galerie Fred Lanzenberg Brussels, Musée Galliera, Paris 1972, 1974, Contemporary Art Center, Cincinatti 1980, Galerie der Stadt, Stuttgart, Galerie Herald Behm, Hamburg 1988, Anne Marie Verna Galerie, Zurich 1989, Museum of Fine Arts, Boston 1991, Centre Georges Pompidou, Paris 1991, Galerie Fred Jahn, Munich 1991, IVAM, Valencia 1992, Museum Boymans-Van Beuningen Rotterdam 1993, Galeria Luis Serpa, Lisbon 1995, Thaddeus Ropac Gallery Salzburg and Paris 1996, Cink Street Vaults, London 1996, Art Cologne, Cologne 1996, Villa Stuck Museum , Munich 1997; Le Syndicat de la Critique Dramatique Best Foreign Play Award for Deafman Glance 1970; Lumen Award for Einstein on the Beach 1977, German Critics Award 1979 and German Press Award 1979 for Death Destruction and Detroit 1979, Der Rosenstrauss award for The Golden Windows 1982, Village Voice Obie Award for Direction for Hamletmachine 1986, Italian Theatre Critics Best Production of the Year Award for Doktor Faustus 1989; German Theatre Critics Production of the Year for The Black Rider 1990; Grand Prix Biennale Barcelona Festival of Cinema Art 1989; Inst. Skowhegan Medal for drawing 1987; Brandeis Univ. Poses Creative Arts Award 1991; Venice Biennale Golden Lion Award for Sculpture 1993, Tadeusz Kantor Prize 1997, Harvard Excellence in Design Award 1998; Most Outstanding Theater Designer of the Seventies, U.S. Inst. of Theater Tech. 1977; Guggenheim Fellow 1971, 1980; Trustee Nat. Inst. of Music Theatre; mem. Dramatists Guild, Soc. des Auteurs et Compositeurs Dramatiques, Soc. of Stage Dirs. and Choreographers; PEN American Center; hon. dir. American Repertory Theatre; has given lectures and workshops at numerous insts. *Address:* RW Work Ltd., 131 Varick Street, Room 908, New York, NY 10013, U.S.A. *Telephone:* (212) 620-0220.

WILSON, Robert McLachlan, B.D., PH.D., D.D., F.B.A.; British professor of biblical criticism; b. 13 Feb. 1916, Gourock, Scotland; s. of Hugh McLachlan Wilson and Janet N. Struthers; m. Enid Mary Bomford 1945; two s.; ed. Greenock Acad., Royal High School, Edin., Edin. and Cambridge Univs.; Minister of Rankin Church, Strathaven 1946–54; Lecturer in New Testament Language and Literature, St Mary's Coll., Univ. of St. Andrews 1954–64, Sr. Lecturer 1964–69, Prof. (personal chair) 1969–78, Prof. of Biblical Criticism 1978–83; Assoc. Ed. New Testament Studies 1967–77, Ed. 1977–83; Pres. Studiorum Novi Testamenti Societas 1981; Hon. D.D. (Aberdeen) 1982; Hon. mem. Soc. of Biblical Literature; Burkitt Medal for Biblical Studies (British Acad.) 1990. *Publications:* The Gnostic Problem 1958, Studies in the Gospel of Thomas 1960, The Gospel of Philip 1962, Gnosis and the New Testament 1968, Commentary on Hebrews 1987, Nag Hammadi and Gnosis (Ed.) 1978, The Future of Coptic Studies (ed.) 1978; Transl. Ed. of: Haenchen, Acts 1971, Foerster, Gnosis Vol. 1 1972, Vol. 2 1974, Rudolph, Gnosis 1983, Hennecke-Schneemelcher, New Testament Apocrypha (revised edn.) Vol. I 1991, Vol. II 1992. *Leisure interest:* golf. *Address:* 10 Murrayfield Road, St. Andrews, Fife, KY16 9NB, Scotland. *Telephone:* (01334) 474331.

WILSON, Robert Peter; British businessman; b. 2 Sept. 1943, Carshalton; s. of late Alfred Wilson and Dorothy Wilson (née Mathews); m. Shirley Elisabeth Robson 1975; one s. one d.; ed. Epsom Coll., Sussex Univ., Harvard Business School; Asst. Economist Dunlop Ltd. 1966–67; Economist Mobil Oil Co. Ltd. 1967–70; with Rio Tinto PLC (fmrly. RTZ Corpn. PLC) 1970–, Man. Dir. AM & S Europe 1979–82, Project Dir. RTZ Devt. Enterprise 1982–83, Head of Planning and Devt. RTZ Corpn. PLC 1984–86, Dir. 1987–, Chief Exec. 1991–97, Chair. 1997–; Dir. (non-exec.) Rio Tinto Ltd. (fmrly. CRA Ltd.) (Australia) 1990– (Deputy Chair. 1995–), The Boots Co. PLC 1991–98; Trustee Camborne School of Mines 1993–; Hon. D.Sc. (Exeter) 1993. *Leisure interests:* theatre, opera, tennis. *Address:* Rio Tinto PLC, 6 St. James's Square, London, SW1Y 4LD, England. *Telephone:* 0171-930 2399. *Fax:* 0171-930 3249.

WILSON, Robert Woodrow, PH.D.; American radio astronomer; b. 10 Jan. 1936, Houston; s. of Ralph Woodrow Wilson, and Fannie May (née Willis) Wilson; m. Elizabeth Rhoads Sawin 1958; two s. one d.; ed. Rice Univ., Calif. Inst. of Tech.; mem. of Technical Staff, AT & T Bell Labs., Holmdel, N.J. 1963–76, Head of Radio Physics Research Dept. 1976–94; Sr. Scientist, Harvard-Smithsonian Center for Astrophysics 1994–; mem. N.A.S., American Astronomical Soc., American Physical Soc., Int. Astronomical Union; Henry Draper Award 1977, Herschel Award 1977, Nobel Prize For Physics 1978. *Publications:* numerous articles in scientific journals. *Leisure interests:* running, skiing, playing piano. *Address:* Harvard-Smithsonian Center for Astrophysics, 60 Garden Street, # 42, Cambridge, MA 02138 (Office); 9 Valley Point Drive, Holmdel, NJ 07733, U.S.A. (Home). *Telephone:* (617) 496-7744 (Office); (201) 671-7807 (Home). *Fax:* (617) 496-7554.

WILSON, Rt. Rev. Roger Plumpton, K.C.V.O., M.A., D.D.; British ecclesiastic; b. 3 Aug. 1905, Manchester; s. of Canon Clifford Plumpton and Hester Marion (Wansey) Wilson; m. Mabel Joyce Avery 1935 (died 1995); two s. one d.; ed. Winchester Coll., and Keble Coll., Oxford; Classical Master Shrewsbury School 1928–30 and 1932–34, St. Andrew's, Grahamstown, S. Africa 1930–32; ordained Deacon 1935; Curate St. Paul's Liverpool 1935–38; Curate St. John's, Westminster 1938–39; Vicar of South Shore, Blackpool 1939–45, Radcliffe-on-Trent, Notts. 1945–49; Archdeacon of Nottingham 1945–49; Bishop of Wakefield 1949–58; Bishop of Chichester 1958–74; Clerk of the Closet to the Queen 1963–75; mem. of Presidium of the Conf. of European Churches 1967–74; Hon. Asst. Bishop, Diocese of Bath and Wells 1974–. *Address:* Kingsett, Wrington, Bristol, BS40 5NH, England. *Telephone:* (01934) 862464.

WILSON, Sandy (see Wilson, Alexander Galbraith).

WILSON, Thomas, O.B.E., PH.D., F.B.A., F.R.S.E., F.R.S.A.; British university professor; b. 23 June 1916, Belfast; s. of John B. Wilson and Margaret E. Wilson; m. Dorothy Joan Parry 1945; one s. two d.; ed. Queen's Univ., Belfast and London School of Econs.; Mynors Fellowship in Econ., Univ. Coll., Oxford 1946–58; Ed. Oxford Econ. Papers 1948–58; Adam Smith Prof. of Political Econ., Glasgow Univ. 1958–82; various visiting professorships and govt. consultancies; Prof. Emer. with hon. appointments at Glasgow and Bristol Univs. *Publications:* Fluctuations in Income and Employment 1942, Oxford Studies in the Price of Mechanism 1952, Inflation 1961, Planning and Growth 1964, The Political Economy of the Welfare State 1982, Inflation, Unemployment and the Market 1984, Unemployment and the Labour Market 1987, Ulster: Conflict or Consent 1989, The State and Social Welfare 1991, Churchill and the Prof 1995. *Leisure interests:* walking, photography. *Address:* 1 Chatford House, The Promenade, Clifton, Bristol, BS8 3NG, England. *Telephone:* (0117) 973 0741.

WILSON, Trevor Gordon, M.A., D.PHIL., F.R.HIST.S., F.A.H.A.; New Zealand professor of history; b. 24 Dec. 1928, Auckland; s. of late Gordon Wilson and of Winifred Wilson; m. Jane Verney 1957; two d.; ed. Mount Albert Grammar School, Univs. of Auckland and Oxford; Asst. Lecturer in History Canterbury Univ. 1952, Auckland Univ. 1953–55; Research Asst. in Govt. Univ. of Manchester 1956–59; lecturer then Sr. Lecturer in History Univ. of Adelaide 1960–67, Prof. 1968–; Commonwealth Fellow St. John's Coll., Cambridge 1972; Visiting Fellow Magdalen Coll., Oxford 1987; Drinko Distinguished Visiting Prof., Marshall Univ., W. Va. Fall 1989; Nuffield Dominion Travelling Fellowship 1964–65; Univ. of N.Z. Overseas Travelling Scholarship 1953; Gilbert Campion Prize (jt. winner) 1960, Higby Prize 1965, Adelaide Festival of Arts Literature Award 1988. *Publications:* The Downfall of the Liberal Party (1914–35) 1966, The Political Diaries of C. P. Scott 1911–28 1970, The Myriad Faces of War: Britain and the Great War 1914–18 1986, Command on the Western Front: The Military Career of Sir Henry Rawlinson 1914–1918 (with Robin Prior) 1992, Passchendaele: the Untold Story (with Robin Prior) 1996. *Leisure interests:* listening to jazz, watching musical movies, table tennis. *Address:* Department of History, University of Adelaide, North Terrace, S. Australia 5001.

WILSON OF TILLYORN, Baron (Life Peer), cr. 1992, of Finzean in the District of Kincardine and Deeside and of Fanling in Hong Kong; **David Clive Wilson,** G.C.M.G., PH.D.; British diplomatist; b. 14 Feb. 1935; s. of Rev. William Skinner Wilson and Enid Wilson; m. Natasha Helen Mary Alexander 1967; two s.; ed. Glenalmond School and Keble Coll., Oxford; nat. service, The Black Watch 1953–55; entered Foreign Service 1958, Third Sec., Vientiane 1959–60, Second then First Sec., Peking 1963–65, FCO 1965–68, Cabinet Office 1974–77, Political Adviser, Hong Kong 1977–81, Head S. European Dept., FCO 1981–84, Asst. Under-Sec. of State 1984–87; Gov. and Commdr.-in-Chief of Hong Kong 1987–92; Chancellor, Univ. of Aberdeen 1997–; Vice-Pres. Royal Scottish Geographical Soc. 1996–; Language Student, Hong Kong 1960–62; Ed. China Quarterly 1968–74; Visiting Scholar, Columbia Univ., New York 1972; Chair. Scottish Hydro-Electric PLC 1993– (Scottish and Southern Energy PLC 1998–); mem. Bd. of Govs. S.O.A.S. 1992–97; mem. Bd. British Council 1993– (Chair. Scottish Cttee. 1993–); Chancellor's Assessor, Univ. of Aberdeen 1993–96; mem. Council, Glenalmond Coll. 1994–; Pres. Bhutan Soc. of the U.K. 1993–; Hon. Fellow, Keble Coll. Oxford; Hon. LL.D. (Aberdeen) 1990, (Chinese Univ., Hong Kong) 1996, Hon. D.Litt. (Sydney) 1991, (Abertay Dundee) 1994. *Leisure interests:* mountaineering, reading. *Address:* House of Lords, London, SW1A 0PW, England.

WILSON-JOHNSON, David Robert, B.A., F.R.A.M.; British baritone; b. 16 Nov. 1950, Northampton; s. of Harry K. Johnson and Sylvia C. Wilson; ed. Wellingborough School, Northants., British Inst. of Florence, St. Catharine's Coll., Cambridge and Royal Acad. of Music; début at Royal Opera House, Covent Garden in We Come to the River 1976; has since appeared in Billy Budd, L'Enfant et les Sortilèges, Le Rossignol, Les Noces, Boris Godunov, Die Zauberflöte, Turandot, Werther, Madam Butterfly; Wigmore Hall recital début 1977; BBC Promenade Concert début 1981; appeared at Edin. Festival 1976, Glyndebourne Festival 1980 and at festivals in Bath, Bergen, Berlin, Geneva, Graz, Netherlands, Hong Kong, Jerusalem, Orange, Paris and Vienna; Paris Opéra début in Die Meistersinger 1989; played St. Francis of Assisi (title role) in Olivier Messiaen's 80th birthday celebrations 1988; American début in Paulus (title role) 1990; English Nat. Opera début (in Billy Budd) 1991, Netherlands Opera début in Birtwistle's Punch and Judy 1993; Gulbenkian Fellowship 1978–81; Nat. Fed. of Music Soc. Award 1977; Evening Standard Award for Opera 1989. *Films include:* A Midsummer Marriage 1988. *Recordings include:* Schubert's Winterreise, Mozart Masses from King's College, Cambridge, Haydn's Nelson Mass, Schoenberg's Ode to Napoleon, King Priam, Punch and Judy, La Traviata, Lucrezia Borgia and

Michael Berkeley's Or Shall We Die?, Belshazzar's Feast, L'Enfance du Christ, The Kingdom (Elgar), The Ice Break (Tippett), Odes (Purcell), Caractacus (Elgar), Black Pentecost (Maxwell Davies), Mass in B Minor (Bach) Peter Grimes, Damnation of Faust. *Leisure interests:* swimming, slimming, gardening and growing walnuts in the Dordogne. *Address:* 28 Englefield Road, London, N1 4ET, England. *Telephone:* 0171-254 0941 (London); 65.10.94.11 (France).

WINBERG, (Sven) Håkan, LL.B.; Swedish politician and lawyer; b. 30 July 1931, Ånge; s. of Sven Winberg and Sally Angman; m. Ulla Greta Petersson; Justice, Court of Appeal; M.P. 1971–82; mem. Exec. Swedish Moderate Party 1972–, mem. Steering Cttee. 1975–; mem. Press Assistance Bd. 1971–79, Bd. of Council for Prevention of Crime 1974–79, Co. Boundaries Cttee. 1970–74, Cttee. of Inquiry into the Press 1972–75, New Labour Laws Cttee. 1976–78, Nat. Police Bd. 1977–79, Nordic Council 1977–82; County Councillor 1974–79; Minister of Justice 1979–81; Pres. Court of Appeal, Sundsvall 1982–; mem. Election Review Cttee. of the Riksdag 1983–; mem. Parl. Comm. for Investigation into the murder of Prime Minister Olof Palme 1987–88, new Comm. for same investigation 1994; mem. Security Police Cttee. 1989–, Court of Law Cttee. 1990–. *Leisure interest:* skiing. *Address:* P.O. Box 170, 851 03 Sundsvall, Sweden.

WINBLAD, Ann, B.A.; American finance executive; ed. St. Thomas Coll.; co-f. Open Systems Inc. 1976–83; fmrly. strategic planning consultant; now partner Hummer Winblad Venture Partners. *Publication:* (as co-author) Object-Oriented Software 1990. *Address:* Hummer Winblad Venture Partners, 2nd Floor, 2 South Park, San Francisco, CA 94107, U.S.A.

WINCH, Donald Norman, PH.D., F.B.A., F.R.HIST.S.; British professor of economics; b. 15 April 1935, London; s. of Sidney Winch and Iris Winch; m. Doreen Lidster 1983; ed. Sutton Grammar School, London School of Econs., Princeton Univ.; Visiting Lecturer Univ. of Calif. 1959–60; Lecturer in Econs. Univ. of Edinburgh 1960–63; Univ. of Sussex 1963–66, Reader 1966–69, Prof. History of Econs. 1969–, Dean School of Social Sciences 1968–74, Pro-Vice-Chancellor (Arts and Social Studies) 1986–89; Vice-Pres. British Acad. 1993–94; Visiting Fellow, School of Social Science, Inst. of Advanced Study, Princeton 1974–75, King's Coll., Cambridge 1983, History of Ideas Unit, Australian Nat. Univ. 1983, St. Catharine's Coll., Cambridge 1989, All Souls Coll., Oxford 1994; Visiting Prof. Tulane Univ. 1984; Carlyle Lecturer, Oxford Univ. 1995; Publr. Sec., Royal Econ. Soc. 1971–; Review Ed. The Economic Journal 1976–83. *Publications:* Classical Political Economy & Colonies 1965, James Mill, Selected Economic Writings 1966, Economics and Policy 1969, The Economic Advisory Council 1930–39 (with S. K. Howson) 1976, Adam Smith's Politics 1978, That Noble Science of Politics (with S. Collini and J. W. Burrow) 1983, Malthus 1987, Riches and Poverty 1996. *Leisure interest:* gardening. *Address:* Arts B, The University of Sussex, Brighton, BN1 9QN, England. *Telephone:* (01273) 678634.

WINDLE, Alan Hardwick, PH.D., A.R.S.M., F.I.M., F.INST.P., F.R.S.; British academic; b. 20 June 1942, Croydon, Surrey; s. of Stuart George Windle and Myrtle Lillian Windle (née Povey); m. Janet Susan Carr 1968; one s. three d.; ed. Whitgift School, Imperial Coll. London, Trinity Coll. Cambridge; ICI Research Fellow, Imperial Coll. London 1966–67, lecturer in Metallurgy 1967–75; lecturer in Metallurgy and Materials Science, Cambridge Univ. 1975–92, Fellow Trinity Coll. 1978–, lecturer and Dir. of Studies in Natural Sciences, Trinity Coll. 1978–92, tutor 1983–91, Prof. of Materials Science 1992–, Head of Dept. of Materials Science, Cambridge Univ. 1996–; Visiting Prof. N.C. State Univ., U.S.A. 1980; Bessemer Medal, Imperial Coll. 1963, Silver Medal, R.S.A. 1963, Rosenhain Medal & Prize, Isle of Man 1987, Swinburne Medal & Prize, Plastics and Rubber Inst. 1992. *Publications:* A First Course in Crystallography 1978, Liquid Crystalline Polymers (with A. M. Donald) 1992. *Leisure interest:* flying light aircraft. *Address:* Department of Materials Science and Metallurgy, Pembroke Street, Cambridge, CB2 3Q2, England. *Telephone:* (01223) 334321. *Fax:* (01223) 335637.

WINDLESHAM, 3rd Baron; **David James George Hennessy,** P.C., C.V.O., M.A., D.LITT.; British politician and college principal; b. 28 Jan. 1932; s. of 2nd Baron Windlesham and Angela Mary Duggan; m. Prudence Glynn 1965 (died 1986); one s. one d.; ed. Ampleforth, Trinity Coll., Oxford; Chair. of Bow Group 1959–60, 1962–63; mem. Westminister City Council 1958–62; Dir. Rediffusion Television 1965–67; Man. Dir. Grampian Television 1967–70; Minister of State Home Office 1970–72; Minister of State Northern Ireland 1972–73; Lord Privy Seal, Leader House of Lords 1973–74; Opposition Leader, House of Lords March–Oct. 1974; Jt. Man. Dir. ATV Network 1974–75, Man. Dir. 1975–81, Chair. 1981; Chair. Independent Television Cos. Asscn. 1976–78; Deputy Chair. Queen's Silver Jubilee Appeal 1976–77, and Trust 1977–80; Prin. Brasenose Coll., Oxford 1989–; Pres. Victim Support 1992–; Chair. Oxford Preservation Trust 1979–89, Parole Bd. 1982–88, Oxford Soc. 1985–88; Vice-Chair. Ditchley Foundation 1987–; Dir. W. H. Smith 1986–95, The Observer 1981–89; Trustee, Charities Aid Foundation 1977–81, Int. Inst. of Communications 1981–83, Community Service Volunteers 1981–, Royal Collection Trust 1993–; Trustee British Museum 1981–96, Chair. 1986–96; mem. Museums and Galleries Comm. 1984–86; Hon. Fellow Trinity Coll., Oxford 1982; Visiting Fellow All Souls Coll., Oxford 1986; John L. Weinberg/Goldman Sachs Visiting Prof. Princeton Univ. 1997. *Publications:* Communication and Political Power 1966, Politics in Practice 1975, Broadcasting in a Free Society 1980, Responses to Crime (Vol. 1) 1987, (Vol. 2) 1993, (Vol 3.) 1996, Windlesham/Rampton Report on Death on the Rock 1989, Politics, Punishment and Populism 1998. *Address:* Brasenose College, Oxford, OX1 4AJ, England. *Telephone:* (01865) 277821. *Fax:* (01865) 277514.

WINDSOR, Colin, D.PHIL., F.R.S., F.INST.P.; British physicist; b. 28 June 1938, Beckenham, Kent; s. of George Thomas and Mabel Rayment; m. Margaret Lee 1963; one s. two d.; ed. Magdalene Coll., Oxford, Clarendon Lab., Oxford; Research Assoc. Yale Univ. 1963–64; scientist UKAEA 1964–96, Programme Area Man. UKAEA Fusion 1996–; Visiting Fellow Japanese Asscn. for Advancement of Science, Sendai 1980; Hon. Prof. of Physics Univ. of Birmingham 1990–; Sr. Consultant PenOp U.K. 1998–; Duddell Medal, Inst. of Physics 1986. *Publications include:* Pulsed Neutron Scattering 1981, Four Computer Models 1983, Solid State Science, Past, Present and Predicted (ed.) 1987. *Address:* 521 Harwell Laboratory, Oxon., OX11 0RA (Office); 21 Blackwater Way, Didcot, Oxon., OX11 7RL, England (Home). *Telephone:* (01235) 512036 (Home).

WINFREY, Oprah, B.A.; American broadcaster, actress and producer; b. 29 Jan. 1954, Kosciusko, Miss.; d. of Vernon Winfrey and Vernita Lee; ed. Tennessee State Univ.; worked for WVOL radio, Nashville, Tenn. while still at school, subsequently as reporter/anchor, WTVF-TV, Nashville; joined WJZ-TV news, Baltimore, as co-anchor 1976, became co-host, People Are Talking 1978; joined WLS-TV, Chicago as host, A.M. Chicago, subsequently renamed The Oprah Winfrey Show 1985–(99); numerous awards, including Int. Radio and Television Soc.'s Broadcaster of the Year Award 1988; acting roles: Sofia in The Color Purple 1985, Mrs. Thomas in Native Son 1986, Mattie Michael in The Women of Brewster Place (TV) 1989, Throw Momma From The Train 1988, Listen Up: The Lives of Quincy Jones 1990, Beloved 1998; f. Harpo Productions Inc. 1986, owner and producer 1986–; producer of several TV films; numerous awards. *Publications:* Oprah (autobiog.) 1993, In the Kitchen with Rosie 1996, Make the Connection (with Bob Greene) 1996. *Address:* Harpo Productions, 110 N. Carpenter Street, Chicago, IL 60607, U.S.A.

WINGER, Debra; American actress; b. 16 May 1955, Cleveland; d. of Robert Winger and Ruth Winger; m. Timothy Hutton (q.v.) 1986 (divorced); one s.; ed. Calif. State Univ., Northridge; served with Israeli army 1972; first professional appearance in Wonder Woman TV series 1976–77. *Films include:* Thank God Its Friday 1978, French Postcards 1979, Urban Cowboy 1980, Cannery Row 1982, An Officer and a Gentleman 1982, Terms of Endearment 1983, Mike's Murder 1984, Legal Eagles 1986, Black Widow 1987, Made in Heaven 1987, Betrayed 1988, The Sheltering Sky, Everybody Wins 1990, Leap of Faith 1992, Shadowlands 1993, A Dangerous Woman 1993, Forget Paris 1995. *Address:* c/o CAA, 9830 Wilshire Boulevard, Beverly Hills, CA 90212, U.S.A.

WINGTI, Rt. Hon. Paias, C.M.G., P.C.; Papua New Guinea politician; b. 2 Feb. 1951, Moika Village; five s.; ed. Univ. of Papua New Guinea; M.P. 1977–97; apptd. Asst. Speaker and mem. Public Accounts Cttee; elected Govt. Whip; Minister for Transport and Civil Aviation 1978–80; Deputy Prime Minister and Minister for Nat. Planning and Devt. 1982–84, for Educ. 1984–85; resgnd. from Govt., co-f. People's Democratic Movt. 1985; Leader of Opposition March–Nov. 1985, 1988–92, 1994; Prime Minister 1985–88, 1992–94. *Leisure interests:* playing golf and watching Rugby League. *Address:* People's Democratic Movement, P.O. Box 972, Boroko, Papua New Guinea. *Telephone:* 277631. *Fax:* 277611.

WINKLER, Hans Günter; German showjumper and company executive; b. 24 July 1926, Barmen; s. of Paul Winkler; m. 1st Inge Fellgiebel 1957 (divorced); m. 2nd Comtesse Marianne Moltke 1962; two c.; m. 3rd Astrid Nunez 1976; mem. Exec., German Riding and Motoring Asscn. 1958–, German Olympic Riding Cttee. 1981–; winner of about 1,000 events, incl. over 500 int. events, up to 1964; took part in six Olympiads 1956–76, winning 106 nat. prizes, five Gold Medals, one Bronze Medal (Mexico City) 1968, one Silver Medal (Montreal) 1976; World Riding Champion 1954, 1955; European Champion 1957; Winner, King George V Cup 1965, 1968; Needle of Honour, Senate of West Berlin 1954; Sportsman of the Year 1955, 1956; Gold Band, German Sports Press Asscn. 1956; Best Sportsman of the Decade 1960; Needle of Honour, Int. Riding Asscn. 1964; Grand Cross of Honour of Fed. Repub. of Germany 1974; FN Award in Gold with Olympic Rings, Laurel Wreath and Diamonds 1976; Hon. mem. Riding and Motoring Asscns. of Warendorf, Ludwigsburg, Herborn, Darmstadt, Bayreuth, Salzburg, Frankfurt am Main, Mitterfels, Kassel, Hünfeld; Hon. Citizen of Warendorf; world's most successful Olympic showjumping rider. *Publications:* Meine Pferde und ich (My Horses and I), Pferde und Reiter in aller Welt (Horses and Riders of the World) 1956, Halla D., Geschichte ihrer Laufbahn (Halla D., A History of her Career) 1961, Springreiten (Jumping) 1979, Halla die Olympiadiva: Olympiareiter in Warendorf 1981. *Leisure interests:* skiing, hunting, tennis. *Address:* Dr. Rau Allee 48, 48231 Warendorf, Germany. *Telephone:* 2361.

WINNER, Michael Robert, M.A.; British film producer and director; b. 30 Oct. 1935, London; s. of late George Joseph Winner and Helen Winner; ed. Cambridge Univ.; Ed. and film critic of Cambridge Univ. paper; entered film industry as film critic and columnist for nat. newspapers and magazines 1951; wrote, produced and directed many documentary, TV and feature films for the Film Producers Guild, Anglo Amalgamated, United Artists 1955–61; Chair. Scimitar Films Ltd., Michael Winner Ltd., Motion Picture and Theatrical Investments Ltd. 1957–; Chief Censorship Officer, Dirs. Guild of G.B. 1983, mem. Council 1983–, Sr. mem. 1991–; f. Police Memorial

Trust, Chair. 1984–. *Films:* Play It Cool (Dir.) 1962, The Cool Mikado (Dir., writer) 1962, West 11 (Dir.) 1963, The System (Co-producer and Dir.) 1963–64, You Must Be Joking (original story, Dir.) 1964–65, The Jokers (Writer, Dir.) 1966, I'll Never Forget What's 'is Name (Producer, Dir.) 1967, Hannibal Brooks (Producer, Dir., original story) 1968, The Games (Dir.) 1969, Lawman (Producer, Dir.) 1970, The Nightcomers (Producer, Dir.) 1971, Chato's Land (Producer, Dir.) 1971, The Mechanic (Dir.) 1972, Scorpio (Dir.) 1972, The Stone Killer (Producer, Dir.) 1973, Death Wish (Dir.) 1974, Won Ton Ton—The Dog Who Saved Hollywood (Producer, Dir.) 1975, The Sentinel (Producer, Dir., Screenplay) 1976, The Big Sleep (Producer, Dir., Writer) 1977, Firepower (Producer, Dir., Writer) 1978, Death Wish II (Producer, Dir., Writer) 1981, The Wicked Lady (Dir., Writer) 1982, Scream For Help (Producer, Dir.) 1983, Death Wish III 1985, Appointment with Death (Producer, Dir., Writer) 1987, A Chorus of Disapproval (Dir., co-writer) 1989, Bullseye! (Producer, Dir., Co-Writer) 1990, Dirty Weekend (producer, dir. jt. screenplay writer) 1993, Parting Shots 1997. *Theatre:* A Day in Hollywood, A Night in the Ukraine (Producer) (Evening Standard Award for Best Comedy of the Year 1979). *Leisure interest:* art. *Address:* Scimitar Films Ltd., 6-8 Sackville Street, London, W1X 1DD, England. *Telephone:* 0171-734 8385. *Fax:* 0171-602 9217.

WINNING, H.E. Cardinal Thomas Joseph, S.T.L., D.C.L., D.D.; British ecclesiastic; b. 3 June 1925, Wishaw, Lanarkshire; s. of Thomas Winning and Agnes (née Canning) Winning; ed. St. Mary's Coll., Blairs, Aberdeen, St. Peter's Coll., Bearsden, Pontifical Scots Coll. and Pontifical Gregorian Univ.; ordained priest, Rome 1948; asst. priest, Chapelhall 1949-50, St. Mary, Hamilton 1953–57; Cathedral, Motherwell 1957–58; Chaplain, Franciscans of the Immaculate Conception, Bothwell 1958-61; Diocesan Sec., Motherwell 1956–61; Spiritual Dir. Pontifical Scots Coll., Rome 1961–66; parish priest, St. Luke's, Motherwell 1966–70; Officialis and Vicar Episcopal, Motherwell 1966–70; Pres. Scottish Catholic Marriage Tribunal 1970; Auxiliary Bishop and Vicar Gen., Glasgow 1971–74; parish priest, Our Holy Redeemer's, Clydebank 1972–74; Archbishop of Glasgow 1974–; cr. Cardinal with title of S. Andrea delle Fratte 1994; Pres. Scottish Bishops' Conf. 1985–; mem. Sacred Congregation for the Doctrine of the Faith, Rome 1978–85, Pres.'s Cttee. Pontifical Council for the Family 1994–, Pontifical Council for Promoting Christian Unity 1994–; Hon. D.D. (Glasgow Univ.); Hon. D.Univ. (Strathclyde Univ.) 1992; Hon. LL.D. (Aberdeen) 1996; Hon. F.E.I.S. 1986; Grand Prior of Scottish Lieutenancy of Equestrian Order of Holy Sepulchre of Jerusalem 1989. *Leisure interests:* golf, watching Glasgow Celtic, listening to good music (not necessarily classical). *Address:* 196 Clyde Street, Glasgow, G1 4JY (Office); 40 Newlands Road, Glasgow, G43 2JD, Scotland (Home). *Telephone:* (0141) 226 5898 (Office). *Fax:* (0141) 225 2600.

WINOCK, Michel, D.LITT.; French historian and publisher; b. 19 March 1937, Paris; s. of Gaston Winock and Jeanne Winock (née Dussaule); m. Françoise Werner 1961; two s.; ed. Sorbonne; teacher Lycée Joffre, Montpellier 1961–63, Lycée Hoche, Versailles 1963–66, Lycée Lakanal, Sceaux 1966–68; lecturer, Sr. lecturer Univ. of Paris VIII-Vincennes à St.-Denis 1968–78; Sr. lecturer Institut d'Etudes politiques, Paris 1978–, Prof. 1990–; Publr. Editions du Seuil, Paris 1969–; radio producer France-Inter 1983–85; Ed.-in-Chief l'Histoire magazine 1978–81, Editorial Adviser 1981–. *Publications:* La république se meurt 1978, La Fière hexagonale 1986, Nationalisme, antisemitisme et fascisme en France 1995, Le siècle des intellectuels (essays on the Medicis) 1997. *Address:* Institut d'Etudes politiques, 27 rue Saint-Guillaume, 75337 Paris Cedex 07, France. *Telephone:* (1) 40-46-51-08. *Fax:* (1) 40-46-51-75.

WINOGRAD, Shmuel, PH.D.; American mathematician and computer scientist; b. 4 Jan. 1936, Tel Aviv, Israel; s. of Pinchas Mordecai Winograd and Rachel Winograd; m. Elaine R. Tates 1958; one s. one d.; ed. Massachusetts Inst. of Technology and New York Univ.; IBM Fellow, Thomas J. Watson Research Center 1961–70; MacKay Lecturer, Univ. of Calif., Berkeley 1967–68; Adjunct Prof. New York Univ. Courant Inst. of Math. Sciences 1968; Dir. Mathematical Sciences Dept. IBM Research Center 1970–74, 1981–94, Computing Tech. Dept. 1984–86; Perm. Visiting Prof. Technion, Israel 1972–; Hitchcock Prof. Univ. of Calif. 1970; mem. N.A.S., American Acad. of Arts and Sciences. *Publications:* Reliable Computations in the Presence of Noise (with J. D. Cowan) 1963; articles in professional journals. *Address:* IBM Research, P.O. Box 218, Yorktown Heights, NY 10598 (Office); 235 Glendale Road, Scarsdale, NY 10583, U.S.A. (Home). *Telephone:* (914) 945-2443 (Office).

WINSLET, Kate; British actress; b. Oct. 1975, Reading; d. of Roger Winslet and Sally Winslet; m. Jim Threapleton 1998; ed. Theatre School, Maidenhead; TV appearances in Get Back, Casualty, Anglo-Saxon Attitudes; recipient of BAFTA Award for Best Supporting Actress for role of Marianne in Sense and Sensibility. *Films:* A Kid in King Arthur's Court, Heavenly Creatures 1994, Sense and Sensibility 1996, Jude 1996, Hamlet 1996, Titanic 1997 (Best European Actress, European Film Acad. 1998, Film Actress of the Year, Variety Club of G.B. 1998), Hideous Kinky 1997, Holy Smoke 1998. *Address:* c/o Dallas Smith, Peters Fraser & Dunlop Ltd., 503 The Chambers, Chelsea Harbour, Lots Road, London, SW10 0XF, England. *Telephone:* 0171-344 1010.

WINSTON, Baron (Life Peer) cr. 1995, of Hammersmith in the London Borough of Hammersmith and Fulham, **Robert Maurice Lipson Winston,** M.B., B.S., F.R.C.O.G.; British obstetrician and gynaecologist; b. 15 July 1940; s. of late Laurence Winston and of Ruth Winston-Fox; m. Lira Feigenbaum 1973; two s. one d.; ed. St. Paul's School, London and London Hosp. Medical Coll. Univ. of London; Registrar and Sr. Registrar, Hammersmith Hosp. 1970–74; Wellcome Research Sr. lecturer, Inst. of Obstetrics and Gynaecology 1974–78; Sr. lecturer, Hammersmith Hosp. 1978–81, Consultant Obstetrician and Gynaecologist 1978–; Reader in Fertility Studies, Royal Postgrad. Medical School (RPMS) 1982–86; Prof. of Fertility Studies, Imperial Coll. London 1997–; Chair. Select Cttee. of Science and Tech., House of Lords 1999–; Visiting Prof. Univ. of Leuven 1976–77, Mt. Sinai Hosp. New York 1985; Prof. of Gynaecology, Univ. of Texas at San Antonio 1980–81; founder mem. British Fertility Soc.; many other professional appts.; presenter, Your Life In Their Hands, BBC TV 1979–87, The Human Body 1998; Victor Bonney Prize, Royal Coll. of Surgeons 1991–93; Chief Rabbinate Award for Contribution to Soc. 1992–93; Cedric Carter Medal, Clinical Genetics Soc. 1993; Gold Medal, Royal Soc. of Health 1998. *Publications:* Reversibility of Sterilization 1978, Tubal Infertility (jtly.) 1981, Infertility: A Sympathetic Approach 1987; articles on human and experimental reproduction. *Leisure interests:* theatre, broadcasting, music, wine. *Address:* 11 Denman Drive, London, NW11 6RE, England. *Telephone:* 0181-455 7475. *Fax:* 0181-458 4980.

WINTER, Frederick Thomas, C.B.E.; British racehorse trainer (retd.); b. 20 Sept. 1926, Andover, Hants.; s. of late Frederick N. Winter and of Anne Winter; m. Diana Ruth Pearson 1956; three d.; ed. Ewell Castle School; served with 6 Bn. Parachute Regt. 1944–47; Nat. Hunt Jockey (four times Champion) 1947–64, Trainer (seven times Champion) 1964–87. *Leisure interests:* golf, gardening. *Address:* Montague House, Eastbury, Newbury, Berks., RG17 7JN, England. *Telephone:* (01488) 71438.

WINTER, William Forrest, B.A., LL.B.; American lawyer; b. 21 Feb. 1923, Grenada, Miss.; s. of William A. Winter and Inez P. Winter; m. Elise Varner 1950; three d.; ed. Univ. of Mississippi; Miss. House of Reps. 1948–56; Miss. state tax collector 1956–64; State Treas. 1964–68; Lieut.-Gov. of Miss. 1972–76, Gov. 1980–84; Sr. Partner, Watkins, Ludlam & Stennis, Jackson, Miss. 1985–; Eudora Welty Prof. of Southern Studies, Millsaps Coll. 1989; Jamie Whitten Prof. of Law, Univ. of Miss. 1989; Chair. Advisory Comm. on Intergovernmental Relations 1993–97; mem. Pres.'s Advisory Bd. on Race 1997–. *Address:* 633 North State Street, P.O. Box 427, Jackson, MS 39202, U.S.A. *Telephone:* (601) 949-4800. *Fax:* (601) 949-4804.

WINTERBOTTOM, Michael, D.PHIL., F.B.A.; British classicist; b. 22 Sept. 1934, Sale, Cheshire; s. of Allan Winterbottom and Kathleen Mary Winterbottom (née Wallis); m. 1st Helen Spencer 1963 (divorced 1983); two s.; m. 2nd Nicolette Janet Streatfeild Bergel 1986; ed. Dulwich Coll., London and Pembroke Coll. Oxford; Domus Sr. Scholar, Merton Coll. Oxford 1958–59; Research Lecturer, Christ Church Oxford 1959–62; Lecturer in Latin and Greek, Univ. Coll. London 1962–67; Fellow and Tutor in Classics, Worcester Coll. Oxford 1967–92, Reader in Classical Languages 1990–92; Corpus Christi Prof. of Latin, Fellow of Corpus Christi Coll., Oxford 1993–; Craven Scholar 1954; Derby Scholar 1956; Dr. h.c. (Besançon) 1985. *Publications:* Quintilian (Ed.) 1970, Ancient Literary Criticism (with D. A. Russell) 1972, Three Lives of English Saints 1972, The Elder Seneca (Ed. and Trans.) 1974, Tacitus, Opera Minora (with R. M. Ogilvie) 1975, Gildas (Ed. and Trans.) 1978, Roman Declamation 1980, The Minor Declamations Ascribed to Quintilian (Ed., with commentary) 1984, Sopatros the Rhetor (with D. C. Innes) 1988, Cicero, De Officiis (Ed.) 1994, William of Malmesbury, 'Gesta Regum Anglorum' Vol. I (with R. A. B. Mynors and R. M. Thomson) 1998. *Leisure interests:* travel and hill walking. *Address:* 53 Thorncliffe Road, Oxford, England. *Telephone:* (01865) 513066.

WINTERFELDT, Ekkehard, DR.RER.NAT.; German professor of organic chemistry; b. 13 May 1932, Danzig; s. of Herbert and Herta Winterfeldt; m. Marianne Heinemann 1958; one s. one d.; ed. Tech. Hochschule Braunschweig, Tech. Univ. of Berlin; Asst. Prof., Tech. Univ. of Berlin 1959, Assoc. Prof. 1967; Prof. and Head of Dept. of Organic Chem., Hannover Univ. 1970–; mem. Braunschweigische Wissenschaftliche Gesellschaft, Akad. der Wissenschaften zu Göttingen; Dr. h.c. (Liège) 1991; Dozentenstipendium des Fonds der Chemischen Industrie 1969, Emil Fischer Medal (German Chem. Soc.) 1990, Adolf Windaus-Medaille, Univ. of Göttingen, Richard Kuhn-Medaille (Gesellschaft Deutscher Chem.). *Publications:* 175 publs. in scientific journals. *Address:* Sieversdamm 34, 30916 Isernhagen, Germany. *Telephone:* 0511/77 84 99.

WINTERS, L. Alan, M.A., PH.D.; British professor of economics; b. 8 April 1950, London; s. of Geoffrey Walter Horace Winters and Christine Agnes Ive; m. 1st Margaret Elizabeth Griffin 1971; m. 2nd Zhen Kun Wang 1997; one s. two d.; ed. Chingford Co. High School, Univs. of Bristol and Cambridge; Jr., Research Office, Dept. of Applied Econs., Univ. of Cambridge 1971–80; lecturer in Econs., Univ. of Bristol 1980–86; economist, World Bank 1983–85, Div. Chief/Research Man. 1994–99; Prof. of Econs., Univ. of Wales at Bangor 1986–90, Univ. of Birmingham 1990–94, Univ. of Sussex 1999–. *Publications:* Econometric Model of the British Export Sector 1981, International Economics 1984, Europe's Domestic Market 1987, Eastern Europe's International Trade 1994, Sustainable Development 1995, The Uruguay Round and the Developing Countries 1996. *Leisure interests:* walking, music, cricket. *Address:* School of Social Sciences, University of Sussex, Falmer, Brighton, BN1 9QN, England. *Telephone:* (01273) 877273. *Fax:* (01273) 673563.

WINTERS, Robert Cushing, B.A., M.B.A.; American insurance company executive; b. 8 Dec. 1931, Hartford, Conn.; s. of George Warren and Hazel Keith (Cushing) Winters; m. Patricia Ann Martini 1962; two d.; ed. Yale and Boston Univs.; with Prudential Insurance Co. of America 1953–, Vice-Pres., Actuary 1969–75, Sr. Vice-Pres. Cen. Atlantic Home Office 1975–78, Exec. Vice-Pres., Newark 1978–84, Vice-Chair. 1984–86, Chair. and C.E.O. 1987–94, Chair. Emer. 1995–; Fellow Soc. of Actuaries; mem. and fmr. Pres. American Acad. of Actuaries; mem. Business Council, Business Roundtable. *Address:* c/o Prudential Insurance Company, 751 Broad Street, Newark, NJ 07102, U.S.A.

WINTERS, Shelley; American actress; b. 18 Aug. 1922, St. Louis, Mo.; m. 1st Vittorio Gassmann (divorced); one d.; m. 2nd Anthony Franciosa 1957 (divorced 1960); ed. Wayne Univ; *films include:* A Thousand and One Nights, A Place in the Sun, Playgirl, Executive Suite, The Diary of Anne Frank 1958, Odds Against Tomorrow, Let No Man Write My Epitaph, Lolita 1962, Wives and Lovers 1963, The Balcony 1964, A House is not a Home 1964, A Patch of Blue, Time of Indifference 1965, Alfie 1965, The Moving Target 1965, The Poseidon Adventure 1972, Cleopatra Jones 1973, Blume in Love 1974, Whoever Slew Auntie Roo 1974, Heaven Save Us from Our Friends 1975, Diamonds 1975, That Lucky Touch 1975, Next Stop Greenwich Village 1976, The Tenant 1976, Pete's Dragon 1977, The Magician 1979, The Visitor 1980, Over the Brooklyn Bridge 1983, The Delta Force 1985, Awakenings 1990, Stepping Out 1991, The Pickle, Portrait of a Lady 1996, Gideon's Webb 1998; *stage appearances include:* A Hatful of Rain 1955, Girls of Summer 1957, The Night of the Iguana, Cages, Who's Afraid of Virginia Woolf?; *TV appearances include:* The Vamp 1972–73, Roseanne (TV series); Acad. Awards for best supporting actress in The Diary of Anne Frank 1959, A Patch of Blue 1964, Emmy Award for Best Actress 1964, Monte Carlo Golden Nymph Award 1964, Int. Television Award, Cannes Festival 1965. *Publications:* Shelley also Known as Shirley (autobiog.), One Night Stands of a Noisy Passenger (play) 1971, Shelley II: The Middle of My Century 1989. *Address:* c/o Jack Gilliardi, ICM, 8942 Wilshire Boulevard, Beverly Hills, CA 90211, U.S.A.

WINTERSON, Jeanette; British author; b. 27 Aug. 1959; partner M. Reynolds; ed. Univ. of Oxford. *Publications:* fiction: Oranges Are Not The Only Fruit (Whitbread Prize 1985), The Passion (Llewellyn Rhys Prize 1987), Sexing the Cherry 1989 (E. M. Forster Award), Written on the Body 1992, Art and Lies 1994, Gut Symmetries 1997, The World and Other Places 1998; essays: Art Objects 1995; screenplay: Great Moments in Aviation; Golden Gate Award (San Francisco Int. Film Festival) 1990, and FIPA d'Argent Award (Cannes Film Festival) 1991, for TV adaptation of Oranges Are Not the Only Fruit; Int. Fiction Award, Festival Letteratura Mantova 1998. *Address:* c/o Jonathan Cape Ltd., 20 Vauxhall Bridge Road, London, SW1V 2SA, England.

WINTERTON, George Graham, LL.M., J.S.D.; Australian professor of law; b. 15 Dec. 1946, Hong Kong; s. of Walter Winterton and Rita Winterton; m. Rosalind Julian 1979; two s. two d.; ed. Hale School, Perth, Univ. of W. Australia and Columbia Univ.; Assoc. in Law, Col. Univ. 1973–75; staff mem. Univ. of N.S.W. 1975–, Prof. of Law 1992–; mem. Exec. Govt. Advisory Cttee., Australian Constitutional Comm. 1985–87, Repub. Advisory Cttee. 1993; del. Australian Constitutional Convention 1998; barrister, N.S.W.; barrister and solicitor, Vic. and W. Australia; Fulbright Scholarship 1973. *Publications:* Parliament, The Executive and the Governor-General 1983, Australian Constitutional Perspectives (co-ed.) 1992, Monarchy to Republic: Australian Republican Government 1994, We, the People: Australian Republican Government (ed.) 1994, Judicial Remuneration in Australia 1995, Australian Federal Constitutional Law: Commentary and Material (co-author) 1999. *Leisure interests:* music, reading. *Address:* Faculty of Law, University of New South Wales, Sydney, N.S.W. 2052, Australia. *Telephone:* (02) 9385 2245. *Fax:* (02) 9385 1175.

WINTHER, Eva; Swedish politician; b. 3 Aug. 1921, Stockholm; m. Arne Winther 1946; three c.; qualified as children's nurse 1945; mem. of Exec. of Liberal Party 1971–81; mem. Kiruna Municipal Council and mem. Kiruna Cen. Social Welfare Cttee. 1967–76; mem. Norrbotten Co. Council 1976–78, Chair. Norrbotten Constituency Asscn. until 1978; mem. Riksdag 1976–82; Chair. Standing Cttee. on Labour Market affairs 1978; Minister in Labour Ministry responsible for Immigrant Affairs and Questions concerning Equality between Men and Women 1978–79; mem. Standing Cttee. on Labour Market Affairs 1979–82; mem. Halland County Council 1985–91. *Leisure interests:* art, fiction, poetry, outdoor life. *Address:* Box 101, 42923 Kullavik, Sweden.

WINTOUR, Anna; British journalist; b. 3 Nov. 1949; d. of Charles Wintour (q.v.); m. David Shaffer 1984; one s. one d.; ed. Queen's Coll. School, London and N. London Collegiate School; deputy fashion ed. Harpers & Queen 1970–76, Harpers Bazaar, New York 1976–77; fashion and beauty ed. Viva 1977–78; contributing ed. for fashion and style, Savvy Magazine 1980–81; sr. ed. New York Magazine 1981–83; Creative Dir. U.S. Vogue 1983–86; Ed.-in-Chief, Vogue 1986–87; Ed. House & Garden, New York 1987–88; Ed. U.S. Vogue 1988–. *Address:* Condé Nast Publications Inc., 350 Madison Avenue, New York, NY 10017, U.S.A.

WINTOUR, Charles Vere, M.A., C.B.E.; British journalist; b. 18 May 1917, Wimborne, Dorset; s. of F. Wintour and Blanche Foster; m. 1st Eleanor Baker 1940 (divorced 1979, died 1996); two s. (and one s. deceased) two d.; m. 2nd Audrey Slaughter 1979; ed. Oundle School and Peterhouse, Cambridge Univ.; Royal Norfolk Regiment 1940, G.S.O. Headquarters, Chief of Staff to Supreme Allied Commdr. (desig.) and SHAEF (despatches); Evening Standard 1946, Political Ed. 1952, Deputy Ed. 1954–57, Ed. 1959–76, 1978–80; Asst. Ed. Sunday Express 1952–54, Ed. Sunday Express Magazine 1981–82; Man. Ed. Daily Express 1957–59, Man. Dir. 1977–78; Dir. Beaverbrook Newspapers 1964–82; Chair. Evening Standard Co. 1968–80; Dir. (non-exec.) TV-am News 1982–84; Dir. Wintour Publs. 1984–86; Ed. U.K. Press Gazette 1985–86; Editorial Consultant to Robert Maxwell 1986–87; Ombudsman, Sunday Times 1990–95; Pres. Media Soc. 1989–90; Wilts. Rep. Nat. Art Collections Fund 1995–; Gov. L.S.E.; Croix de guerre 1945; Bronze Star (U.S.) 1945, S.W.E.T. Special Award 1982. *Publications:* Pressures on the Press 1972, The Rise and Fall of Fleet Street 1989. *Leisure interests:* theatre, travel. *Address:* 60 East Hatch, Tisbury, Wilts., SP3 6PH, England. *Telephone:* (01747) 870880. *Fax:* (01747) 870880.

WINWOOD, Stephen Lawrence; British musician and composer; b. Birmingham; s. of Lawrence Samuel Winwood and Lillian Mary Winwood (née Saunders); m. Eugenia Crafton 1987; one s. three d.; singer and musician Spencer Davis Group 1964–67, Traffic 1967–74, Blind Faith 1970; solo artist 1974–; Dir. F.S. Ltd.; 14 Gold Record Awards, 4 Platinum Record Awards, 2 Grammy Awards. *Albums include:* Arc of a Diver 1980, Talking Back to the Night 1982, Back in the Highlife 1986, Roll With It 1988 (Grammy Award 1989), Chronicles, Refugees of the Heart 1991, Traffic, Far from Home 1994, Junction 7 1997. *Address:* c/o Trinley Cottage, Tirley, Gloucs., GL19 4EU, England. *Telephone:* (01452) 780706. *Fax:* (01452) 780196.

WIRAHADIKUSUMAH, Gen. Umar; Indonesian politician and retd. army officer; b. 10 Oct. 1924, Sumedang, West Java; m. Karlinah Djajaatmadja 1957; two d.; platoon commdr. Tasikmalaya 1942; mem. PETA (Self-Defence Forces) 1944; Commdr. TKR (People's Security Army), Cicalengka, West Java 1945; Chief of Staff of Gen. Div., Siliwangi 1949; Commdr. of Mil. Command of Greater City of Djakarta 1959; Commdr. of Mil. Command of Territory V/Jaya and played key role in crushing abortive communist coup 1965; Commdr. of Kostrad 1966; Army Chief of Staff 1969; Chair. Audit Bd. (BPK) 1973–83; Vice-Pres. of Indonesia 1983–88; twelve Indonesian mil. decorations and decorations from U.S.A., Fed. Repub. of Germany, Netherlands, Yugoslavia, Repub. of Korea, Belgium and Malaysia. *Leisure interests:* reading, golf, swimming. *Address:* Jalan Teuku Umar 61, Jakarta 10310, Indonesia. *Telephone:* 3104303.

WIRTH, Timothy Endicott, PH.D.; American politician; b. 22 Sept. 1939, Santa Fé; s. of Cecil Wirth and Virginia Maude Davis; m. Wren Winslow 1965; one s. one d.; ed. Harvard and Stanford Univs.; Special Asst. to Sec. Dept. of Health, Educ. and Welfare 1967, Deputy Asst. Sec. for Educ. 1969; Asst. to Chair., Nat. Urban Coalition 1968; Vice-Pres. Great Western United Corpn., Denver 1970; Man. Arthur D. Little Inc. 1971–73; mem. 94th-99th Congresses from 2nd Dist. Colo.; Senator from Colorado 1987–92; Counsellor Dept. of State 1993–97; Pres. UN Foundation Jan. 1997–; Ford Foundation Fellow 1964–66; Pres. White House Fellows Asscn. 1968–69; mem. Exec. Cttee. Denver Council Foreign Relations 1974–75; mem. Bd. of Visitors, U.S.A.F. Acad. 1978–; Advisor, Pres. Comm. on the 80s 1979–80; Democrat. *Address:* UN Foundation, 1301 Connecticut Avenue, N.W., Washington, DC 20036, U.S.A.

WISE, Michael John, C.B.E., M.C., PH.D., F.R.G.S., F.R.S.A.; British geographer; b. 17 Aug. 1918, Stafford; s. of Harry Cuthbert Wise and Sarah Evelyn Wise; m. Barbara Mary Hodgetts 1942; one s. one d.; ed. Saltley Grammar School, Birmingham and Birmingham Univ.; served with R.A. and Northamptonshire Regt. in Middle East and Italy 1941–46; Lecturer in Geography, Univ. of Birmingham 1946–51, L.S.E. 1951–54; Cassel Reader in Econ. Geography, L.S.E. 1954–58, Prof. of Geography 1958–83; Pro-Dir. L.S.E. 1983–85, (Hon. Fellow 1988); Erskine Fellow, Univ. of Canterbury, N.Z. 1970; Chair. Ministry of Agric. Cttee. of Inquiry into Statutory Smallholdings 1963–67; Chair. Dept. of Transport Landscape Advisory Cttee. 1981–90; Chair. Court of Govs., Birkbeck Coll. 1983–89, Fellow 1990–; Pres. Inst. of British Geographers 1974, Int. Geographical Union 1976–80, Geographical Asscn. 1976–77; Pres. Royal Geographical Soc. 1980–82; Chair. Dudley Stamp Memorial Trust 1986–; mem. Univ. Grants Cttee., Hong Kong 1966–73, Social Science Research Council 1976–82; Hon. mem. Geographical Soc., U.S.S.R. 1975, Paris 1984, Mexico 1984, Poland 1986, Asscn. Japanese Geographers 1980, Inst. of British Geographers 1989, Geographical Asscn. 1990; Hon. Fellow Landscape Inst. 1991; Hon. D.Univ. (Open Univ.) 1978, Hon. D.Sc. (Birmingham) 1982; Gill Memorial Award of Royal Geographical Soc. 1958, Founder's Medal 1977; Alexander Csoma Körös Medal of Hungarian Geographical Soc. 1980, Tokyo Geographical Soc.'s Medal 1981, Lauréat d'honneur, Int. Geographical Union 1984. *Publications:* Hon. Ed., Birmingham and its Regional Setting 1950, A Pictorial Geography of the West Midlands 1958, Ed. (with E. M. Rawstron), R. O. Buchanan and Economic Geography 1973, General Consultant, An Atlas of Earth Resources 1979, The Ordnance Survey Atlas of Great Britain 1982, numerous papers on economic and urban geography. *Leisure interests:* music, gardening. *Address:* London School of Economics, Houghton Street, Aldwych, London, W.C.2; 45 Oakleigh Avenue, Whetstone, London, N20 9JE, England. *Telephone:* 0181-445 6057.

WISE, Robert Earl; American film producer and director; b. 10 Sept. 1914, Winchester, Ind.; s. of Earl W. Wise and Olive Longenecker; m. 1st Patricia

Doyle 1942; one s.; m. 2nd Millicent Franklin 1977; ed. Franklin Coll., Ind.; joined RKO 1933, apprentice sound effects cutter, then Asst. Ed. and later Film Ed.; films edited include Citizen Kane and The Magnificent Ambersons; Film Dir. 1943–, partner in independent film co. 1970–; Vice-Pres. The Filmakers Group; mem. Bd. of Govs., Acad. of Motion Picture Arts and Sciences, Pres. 1985–87; mem. Dirs. Guild of America; mem. Nat. Council on the Arts; four Acad. Awards (Best Film and Best Dir. West Side Story and The Sound of Music), Irving Thalberg Award, Acad. of Motion Picture Arts and Sciences, D. W. Griffith Award 1988. *Films include:* Curse of the Cat People 1944, The Body Snatcher 1945, The Set Up 1949, The Day the Earth Stood Still 1951, The Desert Rats 1953, Executive Suite 1954, Helen of Troy 1955, Tribute to a Bad Man 1956, Somebody Up There Likes Me 1956, Until They Sail 1957, Run Silent, Run Deep 1958, I Want to Live 1958, Odds Against Tomorrow 1959, West Side Story 1961, Two for the Seesaw 1962, The Haunting 1963, The Sound of Music 1965. The Sand Pebbles 1966, Star! 1968, The Andromeda Strain 1971, Two People 1973, The Hindenburg 1975, Audrey Rose 1977, Star Trek 1979, Rooftops 1989. *Address:* Robert Wise Productions, 315 South Beverly Drive, Suite 214, Beverly Hills, CA 90212, U.S.A.

WISNER, Frank George, B.A.; American diplomatist; b. 2 July 1938, New York; s. of Frank G. Wisner and Mary E. Knowles; m. 1st Genevieve de Virel 1969 (deceased 1974); one d.; m. 2nd Christine de Ganay 1976; one s. and one step-s. one step-d.; ed. Woodberry Forest School, Rugby School and Princeton Univ.; joined U.S. Foreign Service 1961; various posts 1961–75; Special Asst. to Under-Sec. for Political Affairs 1975–76; Dir. Office of Southern African Affairs 1976–77; Deputy Exec. Sec. 1977–79; Amb. to Zambia 1979–82; Deputy Asst. Sec. for African Affairs 1982–86; Amb. to Egypt 1986–91, to Philippines 1991–92, to India 1994–97; Under-Sec. of Defense 1993–94; Bd. Dirs. Exxon Oil and Gas; Presidential Meritorious Service Award, Dept. of State Meritorious Honor, Vietnam Service Award, Repub. of Vietnam Mil. Medal of Honour. *Leisure interests:* hunting, squash, horseback riding, golf. *Address:* American International Group Inc., 18th Floor, 70 Pine Street, New York, NY 10270, U.S.A.

WISSMANN, Matthias; German politician; b. 15 April 1949, Ludwigsburg; s. of Paul Wissmann and Margarete Kalcker; unmarried; ed. Univs. of Tübingen and Bonn; lawyer; mem. Fed. Exec. of CDU 1975–; mem. Bundestag 1976–; Pres. European Union of Young Christian Democrats 1976–82; Minister of Research and Technology Jan.–May 1993, of Transport 1993–98; CDU. *Publications include:* Zukunftschancen der Jugend 1979, Einsteigen statt Aussteigen 1983, Marktwirtschaft 2000 1983. *Leisure interests:* piano, literature, hockey, tennis, skiing. *Address:* Am Zuckerberg 79, 71640 Ludwigsburg, Germany (Home).

WISZNIEWSKI, Andrzej; Polish linguist and politician; b. 15 Feb. 1935, Warsaw; m. Ewa Lutosławska; one d.; researcher Wrocław Univ. of Tech. 1957–, Extraordinary Prof. 1972, Ordinary Prof. 1990–, Rector 1990–96; Univ. of Garyounis Benghazi, Libya 1976–79, Head of Scientific Research Cttee. and mem. Council of Ministers 1997–; mem. Speech Communication Asscn. (USA); mem. Solidarity Trade Union 1980–; mem. Social Movt. of Solidarity Election Action 1998–; Kt.'s Cross Order of Polonia Restituta 1997, Grand Cross Order of Saint Stanisław with Star 1998, Commander Order of Saint Sylvester 1998; Dr. h.c. (Cen. Conn. State Univ.) 1993; City of Wrocław Award 1996. *Publications:* over 130 on electrotechnics and electroenergetics include Algorithms of Numeral Measurements in Electroenergetic Automatics 1990, Przekładniki w elektroenergetyce 1992, Schutztechnik in Elektroenergiesystemen (co-author) 1994, Protective Automatics in Electroenergetics Systems 1998, How to Speak and Make Speeches Convincingly 1994, Aphorisms and Quotations: for Orators, Disputants and Banqueters 1997. *Leisure interests:* contemporary literature, dog-walking, skiing, mountaineering, rhetorics. *Address:* Komitet Badań Naukowych, ul. Wspólna 1/3, 00-921 Warsaw, Poland. *Telephone:* (22) 628 19 44. *Fax:* (22) 628 19 44.

WITHEROW, John; journalist; b. 20 Jan. 1952, Johannesburg, S. Africa; s. of Cecil Witherow and Millicent Witherow; m. Sarah Linton 1985, two s. one d.; ed. Bedford School and Univ. of York; two years' voluntary service in Namibia (then S.W. Africa) after school; posted to Madrid for Reuters; covered Falklands War for The Times 1982; joined The Sunday Times 1984, successively Defence and Diplomatic Corresp., Focus Ed., Foreign Ed., Man. Ed. (news), Acting Ed., The Sunday Times 1994, Ed. Jan. 1995–. *Leisure interests:* sailing, skiing, snoozing. *Address:* The Sunday Times, 1 Pennington Street, London, E1 9XW, England. *Telephone:* 0171-782 5640. *Fax:* 0171-782 5420.

WITKOP, Bernhard, PH.D., SC.D.; American chemist; b. 9 May 1917, Freiburg (Baden), Germany; s. of Prof. Philipp W. Witkop and Hedwig M. Hirschhorn; m. Marlene Prinz 1945; one s. two d.; ed. Univ. of Munich; Dozent Univ. of Munich 1946; Matthew T. Mellon Fellow Harvard Univ., U.S.A. 1947; Instructor and Lecturer 1948–50; Special Fellow U.S. Public Health Service 1950–53; Research Fellow Nat. Heart Inst. 1950; Special Fellow, Nat. Inst. of Arthritis and Metabolic Diseases, N.I.H. 1952, Chief of Section on Metabolites 1956–87, Chief of Lab. of Chem., Nat. Inst. of Arthritis, Metabolic and Digestive Diseases 1957–87; N.I.H. Inst. Scholar 1987–92, Hon. Emer. Scholar 1993–; Visiting Prof., Kyoto Univ. 1961, Univ. of Freiburg 1962; Lecturer, Univ. of Zürich 1972; Ed. (U.S.A.) FEBS Letters 1979–; mem. N.A.S., Acad. Leopoldina-Carolina 1972, N.A.S. Comm. on Int. Relations 1978, American Acad. of Arts and Sciences 1978, Paul Ehrlich Foundation, Frankfurt 1979–; Hon. mem. Pharmaceutical Soc. of Japan 1978, Chemical Soc. 1982–, Japanese Biochemical Soc. 1983–, Academia Scientiarum et Artium Europaea, Salzburg 1993–; mem. Bd. of Dirs., Leo Baeck Inst., New York 1992–; Hillebrand Award of American Chemical Soc. 1959, Paul Karrer Medallist, U.S. Sr. A. von Humboldt Award (Univ. of Hamburg) 1979; Order of the Sacred Treasure, Japan. *Publications:* Mushroom Poisons 1940, Curare Arrow Poisons 1942, Yohimbine 1943, Kynurenine 1944, Indole Alkaloids 1947–50, Oxidation Mechanisms, Ozonization, Peroxides 1952, Hydroxyaminoacids, Metabolites, Building Stones and Biosynthesis of Collagen 1955, Mescalin and LSD Metabolism 1958, Pharmacodynamic Amines 1960, Nonenzymatic Cleavage and Modification of Enzymes 1961, Gramicidin A 1964, Rufomycin 1964, Photo-Reductions, -Additions, -Cyclizations 1966, Microsomal Hydroxylations, Arenoxide Metabolites, "NIH-Shift" 1967, Amphibian Venoms, Batrachotoxin, Pumiliotoxin 1968, Norepinephrine Release, Inactivation, False transmitters 1968, Histrionicotoxin, a selective inhibitor of cholinergic receptors 1970–72, Interaction of Polynucleotides Stimulators of Interferon 1973–74, Gephyrotoxin, a Muscarinic Antagonist 1978, Anatoxin-a: The most potent Agonist at the nicotinic receptor 1980–82, Paul Ehrlich: His Ideas and his Legacy, Nobel Symposium 1981, Amphibian Alkaloids 1983, Forty Years of "Trypto-Fun" 1984, Mind over Matter (lecture at Israel Acad. of Sciences, Jerusalem) 1987. *Leisure interests:* languages, etymology, literature, piano, chamber music, hiking, skating, mountaineering. *Address:* National Institute of Health–Department of Health, Education & Welfare, Room B1A-11, Bethesda, MD 20892, U.S.A.

WITTEN, Edward, PH.D.; American physicist; b. 26 Aug. 1951, Baltimore, Md.; s. of Louis Witten and Lorraine Wollach Witten; m. Chiara R. Nappi 1979; one s. two d.; ed. Brandeis and Princeton Univs.; Prof. of Physics, Princeton Univ., N.J. 1980–87, Inst. for Advanced Study, Princeton 1987–; Fellow American Acad. of Arts and Sciences, American Physical Soc., N.A.S.; McArthur Fellowship 1982, Einstein Medal, Einstein Soc. of Berne, Switzerland 1985, Award for Physical and Math. Sciences, New York Acad. of Sciences 1985, Dirac Medal, Int. Center for Theoretical Physics 1985, Alan T. Waterman Award, Nat. Science Foundation 1986, Fields Medal, Int. Union of Mathematicians 1990. *Publication:* Superstring Theory, 2 vols. (with M.B. Green and J.H. Schwarz) 1987. *Address:* Institute for Advanced Study, Olden Lane, Princeton, NJ 08540, U.S.A. *Telephone:* (609) 734-8021.

WOESSNER, Mark Matthias, DR.ING.; German business executive; b. 14 Oct. 1938, Berlin; m.; two c.; ed. Studium TH, Karlsruhe, then apprenticeship; Asst. to Man. Bertelsmann AG 1968–72; Tech. Man. Mohndruck Printing Co. 1972–74, C.E.O. 1974–76; mem. Exec. Bd. Bertelsmann AG, Pres. Printing and Mfg. Div. 1976–83, Pres. and C.E.O. 1983–98, Chair. Supervisory Bd. 1997–, also Chair. Bertelsmann Foundation. *Publications:* several technical publs. at the Univ. of Stuttgart. *Leisure interest:* sport. *Address:* c/o Bertelsmann AG, Carl-Bertelsmann-Strasse 270, 33311 Gütersloh, Germany.

WOFFORD, Harris Llewellyn, LL.B.; American politician; b. 9 April 1926, New York; s. of Harris L. Wofford and Estelle Gardner; m. Emmy Lou Clare Lindgren 1948 (died 1996); two s. one d.; ed. Univ. of Chicago and Yale and Harvard Univs.; admitted D.C. Bar 1954, U.S. Supreme Court Bar 1958, Pa. Bar 1978; Asst. to Chester Bowles 1953–54; law assoc. Covington & Burling, Washington, D.C. 1954–58; legal asst. to Rev. T. Hesburgh, Comm. on Civil Rights 1958–59; Assoc. Prof. Notre Dame Law School 1959–60, on leave 1961–66; Special Asst. to Pres. John F. Kennedy 1961–62; Special Rep. for Africa, Dir. Ethiopian Program, U.S. Peace Corps. 1962–64; Assoc. Dir. Peace Corps, Washington, D.C. 1964–66; Pres. Coll. at Old Westbury, Southern Univ. of N.Y. 1966–70, Bryn Mawr (Pa.) Coll. 1970–78; Counsel, Schnader, Harrison, Segal and Lewis, Philadelphia and Washington 1979–86; Sec. Labor and Industry, Commonwealth of Pa. 1987–92; Senator from Pennsylvania 1991–95; C.E.O. Corpn. for Nat. Service 1995–; mem. Council on Foreign Relations; mem. Bd. Dirs. Int. League for Human Rights; other public appts.; Democrat. *Publications include:* It's Up to Us 1946, India Afire (with Clare Wofford) 1951, Of Kennedys and Kings 1980. *Address:* Corporation for National Service, 1201 New York Avenue, N.W., Washington, D.C. 20525, U.S.A.

WOGAN, Gerald Norman, PH.D.; American educator; b. 11 Jan. 1930, Altoona, Pa.; s. of Thomas B. Wogan and Florence E. (Corl) Wogan; m. Henrietta E. Hoenicke 1957; one s. one d.; ed. Juniata Coll. and Univ. of Illinois; Asst. Prof. of Physiology, Rutgers Univ., New Brunswick, N.J. 1957–61; Asst. Prof. of Toxicology, M.I.T., Cambridge, Mass. 1962–65, Assoc. Prof. 1965–69, Prof. 1969–, Head of Dept. of Applied Biological Sciences 1979–88, Dir. Division of Toxicology 1988–, Prof. of Chemistry 1989–; Consultant to nat. and int. govt. agencies and industries; Fellow American Acad. of Microbiology; mem. N.A.S., Inst. of Medicine. *Publications:* articles and reviews in professional journals. *Address:* Division of Toxicology, Massachusetts Institute of Technology, 77 Massachusetts Avenue, Room 26-9, Cambridge, MA 02139, U.S.A. *Telephone:* (617) 253-3188.

WOGAN, Michael Terence (Terry); O.B.E.; Irish broadcaster; b. 3 Aug. 1938; s. of late Michael Thomas and Rose Wogan; m. Helen Joyce 1965; two s. one d.; ed. Crescent Coll., Limerick, Belvedere Coll., Dublin; announcer RTE 1963, Sr. Announcer 1964–66; various progs. for BBC Radio 1965–67; Late Night Extra BBC Radio 1967–69; The Terry Wogan Show, BBC Radio

One 1969–72, BBC Radio Two 1972–84, 1993, Wake Up to Wogan, BBC Radio Two 1995–; TV shows include: Lunchtime with Wogan, ATV; BBC: Come Dancing, Song for Europe, The Eurovision Song Contest, Children in Need, Wogan's Guide to the BBC, Blankety-Blank, Wogan, Terry Wogan's Friday Night Auntie's Bloomers, Wogan's Web; Pye Radio Award 1980, Radio Industries Award (Radio Personality 3 times; TV Personality 1982, 1984, 1985, 1987); TV Times TV Personality of the Year (10 times); Daily Express Award (twice); Carl Alan Award (3 times); Variety Club of GB: Special Award 1982; Showbusiness Personality 1984; Radio Personality of last 21 Years, Daily Mail Nat. Radio Awards 1988; Sony Radio Award, Barcelona Olympics 1993, Best Breakfast Show 1994. *Publications:* Banjaxed 1979, The Day Job 1981, To Horse, To Horse 1982, Wogan on Wogan 1987, Wogan's Ireland 1988, Bumper Book of Togs 1995. *Leisure interests:* tennis, golf, swimming, reading, writing. *Address:* c/o Jo Gurnett, 2 New Kings Road, London, SW6 4SA, England.

WOJTYŁA, Andrzej Franciszek; Polish politician and paediatrician; b. 1 May 1955, Kalisz; s. Franciszek and Stanisława Wojtyła; m. Ewa Wojtyła; one s. one d.; ed. Medical Acad., Poznań, George Washington, Georgetown and La Salle Univs., U.S.A.; paediatrician, Children's Ward Mun. Hospital, Pleszew 1980–89; Head, Village Health Service Centre, Jastrzębniki 1985–92; Visiting Researcher, George Washington Univ. 1995, Visiting Prof., Center for Health Policy and Research 1995–96; mem. Solidarity Trade Union 1980–89, Solidarity of Individual Farmers Trade Union 1989–; Councillor of Commune of Blizanów 1990; mem. Polish Peasant Party Solidarity (PSL Solidarność) 1990, subsequently Peasant Christian Party (SLCh), Pres. SLCh Voivodship Bd., Kalisz, mem. SLCh Nat. Political Council; mem. Conservative Peasant Party (SKL) 1997–; Deputy to Sejm (Parl.) 1991–93, 1997–, Vice-Chair. Parl. Health Cttee.; mem. Parl. Constitutional Responsibility Cttee. 1991–93; Minister of Health and Social Welfare 1992–93. *Publication:* Third International Conference: Health Education for Children. *Leisure interests:* fitness, walking, history, health care reforms in the world. *Address:* ul. Pawłówek 8A, 62-800 Kalisz, Poland. *Telephone:* (062) 76-72-604. *Fax:* (062) 76-72-604.

WOJTYŁA, H.E. Cardinal Karol (see John Paul II, His Holiness Pope).

WOLF, Christa; German writer; b. 18 March 1929, Landsberg/Warthe, fmr. G.D.R.; ed. Jena and Leipzig; fmr. mem. G.D.R. CP, resgnd. 1989; Heinrich-Mann Prize 1963, Nationalpreis für Kunst und Literatur (G.D.R.) 1964, Georg-Büchner Prize, Deutsche Akad. der Sprache und Dichtung 1980. *Publications include:* Der geteilte Himmel, Unter den Linden, Moskauer Novelle 1961, Nachdenken über Christa T. 1968, Kein Ort. Nirgends 1979, Kassandra 1983, Störfall 1987, What Remains (short story) 1990, Medea: Stimmen 1996, several collections of short stories.

WOLF, Markus Johannes (Mischa); German fmr. state security official; b. Hechingen, Nr. Stuttgart; s. of Friedrich Wolf; m. 3rd Andrea Wolf; ed. Karl-Liebknecht School, Moscow, Comintern School Kuschnarenkovo; emigrated to Switzerland and France 1933, to U.S.S.R. 1934–45; adopted Soviet citizenship 1939; joined CP 1942; reporter Berlin Radio; 1st Councillor G.D.R. Mission Moscow 1949–51 (changed citizenship to E. German); joined Inst. of Econ. Research (secret service) at Ministry for State Security early 1950s, Deputy Minister for State Security; Chief Main Admin. of Foreign Intelligence 1958–87; sentenced to six years imprisonment for treason and bribery Dec. 1993; sentence under appeal; Constitutional Court ruled he should not be held criminally accountable; convicted of three kidnappings and given a two-year suspended sentence May 1997; imprisoned for refusing to identify a Cold War agent Jan. 1998; Maj.-Gen. 1955, Lieut.-Gen. 1966, Col.-Gen. (State Security Service) 1980; fmr. mem. Young Pioneers (radical Stalinist group) 1935, Socialist Unity Party of Germany; Fatherland's Merit Order (Gold) 1969, Order of the Fatherland's War (U.S.S.R., 2nd class) 1970. *Leisure interest:* culinary skills. *Publication:* Troika (autobiographical novel) 1989, Memoirs of a Spymaster 1998.

WOLF, Stephen M.; American airline executive; b. 7 Aug. 1941, Oakland, Calif.; ed. San Francisco State Univ.; American Airlines 1966–81; Pres. and C.O.O. Continental Airlines 1982–83; Pres. and C.E.O. Repub. Airlines 1984–86; Chair., Pres. and C.E.O. Tiger Int. Inc. 1986–88; Chair., C.E.O. UAL Corpn. 1987–94, also fmr. Pres.; Chair. C.E.O. United Airlines 1992–94; Chair. U.S. Air Group Inc. 1996– (Pres. 1987–92); Sr. Adviser Lazard Freres 1994–; Adviser to Chair. of Air France 1994–96; Dir. Air Transport Assn. of America and numerous cos. and orgs. *Address:* U.S. Air Inc., 2345 Crystal Drive, Arlington, VA 22227, U.S.A.

WOLFBEIN, Seymour Louis, PH.D.; American government official and educator; b. 8 Nov. 1915, New York; s. of Samuel Wolfbein and Fannie Katz; m. Mae Lachterman 1941; two d.; ed. Brooklyn Coll., and Columbia Univ.; Research Assoc. U.S. Senate Comm. on Unemployment and Relief 1938; Economist, Research Div., Works Project Admin. 1939–42; Economist, Bureau of Labor Statistics, Dept. of Labor 1942–45, Head, Occupational Outlook Div. 1946–49, Head, Manpower and Productivity Div. 1949–50, Manpower and Employment Div. 1950–59, Deputy Asst. Sec. of Labor 1959–62, Dir. Office of Manpower, Automation and Training 1962–65, Econ. Adviser to Sec. of Labor 1965–67; Visiting Prof. Univ. of Mich. 1950–; Adjunct Prof. American Univ. 1951–; Dean School of Business Admin., Temple Univ. 1967–78, J.A. Boettner Prof. of Business Admin 1978–85; Dean Temple Univ., Japan 1983–85; Pres. T.W.O. Man. Consultants 1986–; Comm. on Human Resources, N.A.S. 1976–; Vice-Pres. World Trade Council 1980–; Fellow, American Statistical Assn., A.A.A.S.; Distinguished Service Award, Dept. of Labor 1955 and 1961; Eminent Man of Guidance Award 1970. *Publications:* Decline of a Cotton Textile City 1942, The World of Work 1951, Employment and Unemployment in the U.S. 1964, Employment, Unemployment and Public Policy 1965, Education and Training for Full Employment 1967, Occupational Information 1968, Emerging Sectors of Collective Bargaining 1970, Work in the American Society 1971, Manpower Policy: Perspectives and Prospects 1973, Labor Market Information for Youths 1975, The Pre-Retirement Years 1977, Establishment Reporting in the U.S.A. 1978, The Demography of the Disabled 1988, The Temporary Help Supply Industry 1989, Working and Not Working in the USA, Working Part Time In the USA 1990, To the Year 2000 1991, Our Industrial Future 1991, Our Occupational Future 1992, The World of Work: To the Year 2000 and Beyond 1993, Occupational Futures in the USA 1994, Guidance and Counseling for the Labor Force: Moving Into the Next Millennium 1995, Schooling in the USA: What a Difference a Year Makes 1996, An Election Lesson in Education 1996, The Philadelphia Story 1996, Employment in the U.S.A. 1997, Making a Living in the U.S.A. 1997, Moving Across the Millennium 1997, The Emerging Geography of the American Economy 1998. *Leisure interest:* painting. *Address:* East 706 Parktowne, 2200 Benjamin Franklin Parkway, PA 19130; 4903 Edgemoor, Bethesda, MD 20814, U.S.A. *Telephone:* (215) 563 6740. *Fax:* (215) 854 1892.

WOLFE, Thomas Kennerly, Jr., A.B., PH.D.; American author and journalist; b. 2 March 1931, Richmond, Va.; s. of Thomas Kennerly and Helen Hughes; m. Sheila Berger; one s. one d.; ed. Washington and Lee Univ., and Yale; reporter Springfield (Mass.) Union 1956–59; reporter, Latin American Corresp. Washington Post 1959–62; reporter, magazine writer New York Herald Tribune 1962–66; magazine writer New York World Journal Tribune 1966–67; Contributing Ed. New York magazine 1968–76, Esquire Magazine 1977–; Contributing Artist Harper's magazine 1978–81; exhibited one-man show of drawings, Maynard Walker Gallery, New York 1965, Tunnel Gallery, New York 1974; mem. American Acad. of Arts and Letters 1999; Hon. D.F.A. (Minneapolis Coll. of Art) 1971, Hon. Litt. D. (Washington and Lee) 1974, Hon. L.H.D. (Va. Commonwealth Univ.) 1983, (Southampton Coll., N.Y.) 1984; Front Page Awards for Humour and Foreign News Reporting, Washington Newspaper Guild 1961, Award of Excellence, Soc. of Magazine Writers 1970, Frank Luther Mott Research Award 1973, Va. Laureate for Literature 1977, Harold D. Vursell Memorial Award, American Acad. and Inst. of Arts and Letters 1980, American Book Award for Gen. Non-Fiction 1980, Columbia Journalism Award 1980, Citation for Art History, Nat. Sculpture Soc. 1980, John Dos Passos Award 1984, Gari Melchers Medal 1986, Benjamin Pierce Cheney Medal (E. Washington Univ.) 1986, Washington Irving Medal (St. Nicholas Soc.) 1986. *Publications:* The Kandy-Kolored Tangerine-Flake Streamline Baby 1965, The Electric Kool-Aid Acid Test 1968, The Pump House Gang 1968, Radical Chic and Mau-mauing the Flak Catchers 1970, The New Journalism 1973, The Painted Word 1975, Mauve Gloves and Madmen, Clutter and Vine 1976, The Right Stuff 1979, In Our Time 1980, From Bauhaus to Our House 1981, Bonfire of the Vanities 1987, Ambush at Fort Bragg 1998, A Man in Full 1998. *Address:* c/o Farrar, Straus and Giroux Inc., 19 Union Square W., New York, NY 10003, U.S.A.

WOLFENDALE, Sir Arnold (Whittaker), Kt., PH.D., F.R.A.S., F.INST.P., F.R.S.; British professor of physics; b. 25 June 1927; s. of Arnold Wolfendale and Doris Wolfendale; m. Audrey Darby 1951; twin s.; ed. Manchester Univ.; Asst. Lecturer, Manchester Univ. 1951–54, Lecturer 1954–56; Lecturer, Univ. of Durham 1956–59, Sr. Lecturer 1959–63, Reader in Physics 1963–65, Prof. 1965–92, Emer. Prof. 1992–, Head of Dept. 1973–77, 1980–83, 1986–89; Chair., Northern Region Action Cttee., Manpower Services Comm. Job Creation Programme 1975–78; Pres. Royal Astronomical Soc. 1981–83, Durham Univ. Soc. of Fellows 1988–, Inst. of Physics 1994–96, European Physical Soc. 1999–; Prof. of Experimental Physics, Royal Inst. of G.B. 1996–; mem. Science and Eng. Research Council 1988–94; Astronomer Royal 1991–95; Fellow Tata Inst. Fund 1996; mem. Academia Europaea 1998; Foreign Fellow, Nat. Acad. of Sciences of India 1990, Indian Nat. Science Acad.; Foreign Assoc. Royal Soc. of S.A. 1996; Hon. Fellow, Lancs. Polytechnic 1991; Pres. Antiquarian Horological Soc.; Dr. h.c. (Potchefstroom, Łódź, Teesside, Newcastle, Open Univ., Paisley, Lancaster); Silver Jubilee Medal 1977, Univ. of Turku Medal 1987, Armagh Observatory Medal 1992, Marian Smoluchowski Medal (Polish Physics Soc.) 1992, Powell Memorial Medal, European Physical Soc. 1996, Freeman Worshipful Co. of Clockmakers, Worshipful Co. of Scientific Instrument Makers, Lancaster. *Publications:* Cosmic Rays 1963; Ed. Cosmic Rays at Ground Level 1973, Origin of Cosmic Rays 1974, Gamma Ray Astronomy 1981, Progress in Cosmology 1982, Gamma Ray Astronomy (with P. V. Ramana Murthy) 1986, Secular, Solar and Geomagnetic Variations in the last 1,000 years 1988; Origin of Cosmic Rays (Co-Ed.) 1981, Obs. Tests of Cosmological Inflation (Co-Ed.) 1991; numerous papers on cosmic radiation. *Leisure interests:* walking, gardening, foreign travel. *Address:* Ansford, Potters Bank, Durham, England. *Telephone:* (0191) 384-5642.

WOLFENSOHN, James D. (Jim); American international official, business executive and arts administrator; b. 1 Dec. 1933, Sydney, Australia; s. of Hyman Wolfensohn and Dora Weinbaum; m. Elaine Botwinick 1961; one s. two d.; ed. Harvard Business School; Pres. J. Henry Schroder Banking Corpn. 1970–76; Chair. Salomon Bros. Int. 1977–81; owner, Pres. James D. Wolfensohn Inc. 1981–; fmr. Chair., also C.E.O.; Bd. Carnegie Hall; Chair.

Kennedy Center for the Performing Arts 1990–95; Chair. Emer. 1995–; Pres. IBRD June 1995–, Int. Devt. Asscn., Int. Finance Corpn., Multilateral Guarantee Agency; Trustee Rockefeller Univ. 1985–94, Howard Hughes Medical Inst. 1987–96; Montblanc de la Culture Award 1992. *Leisure interest:* playing the cello. *Address:* IBRD, 1818 H Street, N.W., Washington, DC 20433, U.S.A.

WOLFENSTEIN, Lincoln, PH.D.; American physics professor; b. 10 Feb. 1923, Cleveland, Ohio; s. of Leo Wolfenstein and Anna Koppel; m. Wilma C. Miller 1957; one s. two d.; ed. Univ. of Chicago; Physicist, Nat. Advisory Comm. for Aeronautics 1944–46; Asst. Prof., Carnegie-Mellon Univ. 1948–57, Assoc. Prof. 1957–60, Prof. 1960–78, Univ. Prof. 1978–; Guggenheim Fellow 1973–74, 1983–84; mem. N.A.S. *Publications:* over 100 papers on theoretical particle and nuclear physics, weak interactions, c.p. violation, neutrino physics. *Address:* Physics Department, Carnegie-Mellon University, 5000 Forbes Avenue, Pittsburgh, PA 15213, U.S.A. *Telephone:* (412) 578-2740.

WOLFF, Otto Herbert, C.B.E., M.D.; British professor of child health; b. 10 Jan. 1920, Hamburg, Germany; s. of the late Dr. and Mrs. H. A. Wolff; m. Jill Freeborough 1952; one s. one d.; ed. Peterhouse, Cambridge, Univ. Coll. Hosp., London; Lieut. and Capt. R.A.M.C. 1944–47; Resident Medical Officer, Registrar and Sr. Medical Registrar, Birmingham Children's Hosp. 1948–51; Lecturer, Sr. Lecturer, Reader Dept. of Pediatrics and Child Health, Univ. of Birmingham 1951–64; Nuffield Prof. of Child Health, Univ. of London 1964–85; Dean Inst. of Child Health until 1985; Consulting Physician Hosp. for Sick Children, London until 1985; Chair. Child-to-Child Trust 1989–93; fmr. Senator London Univ.; fmr. Pres. of British Pediatric Asscn.; fmr. mem. Gen. Medical Council; mem. Royal Soc. of Medicine and British Medical Asscn.; corresp. mem. Société Française de Pédiatrie, Société Suisse de Pédiatrie, and numerous others; Dawson Williams Memorial Prize, Medal of Asscn. Française pour le Dépistage et la Prévention des Maladies Métaboliques et des Handicaps de l'Enfant 1986, Harding Award of Action for the Crippled Child 1987, James Spence Medal of the British Pediatric Asscn. 1988. *Publications:* articles in the Lancet and British Medical Journal. *Leisure interest:* music. *Address:* 53 Danbury Street, London, N1 8LE, England. *Telephone:* 0171-226 0748.

WOLFF, Philippe, D. ÈS L.; French professor of history; b. 2 Sept. 1913, Montmorency; s. of Lucien Wolff and Gabrielle Dubois; m. Odette Desgrées 1944 (deceased); two s. two d.; ed. Lycée de Rennes, Univs. of Rennes and Paris; Liaison Officer, 51st Div. (Highland Div.) 1940; Lecturer, Univ. of Paris (Sorbonne) 1943–45; Prof., Univ. of Toulouse 1945–74, Emer. Prof. 1974–; Hon. Pres. Fed. of Learned Socs. Languedoc-Pyrénées Gascogne 1964–; Visiting Prof., Univs. of São Paulo, Houston, Cambridge (Mass.), Calif. at Berkeley, Mich. at Ann Arbour, Washington at Seattle, Bonn, St. Paul's (Tokyo); mem. Institut de France; Silver Medal (C.N.R.S.); Chevalier, Légion d'honneur, Commdr. Ordre des Arts et des Lettres. *Publications:* Commerces et marchands de Toulouse c. 1350–c. 1450 1954, Histoire de Toulouse 1958, The Awakening of Europe 1968, Les origines linguistiques de l'Europe 1971, Ongles bleus, Jacques et Ciompi, Les révolutions populaires en Europe aux XIVe et XVe siècles (with Michel Mollat) 1970, Automne du Moyen Age ou printemps des Temps Nouveaux? 1986, gen. edition of historical works (with Privat and Éché), Les Toulousains dans l'histoire 1984, L'Economie européenne aux XIVe et XVe siècles 1986. *Leisure interest:* music. *Address:* Residència Clara Rabassa, Avda. Princep Benlloch, 26–30 Andorra-la-Vella, Andorra; 3 rue Espinasse, 31000 Toulouse, France. *Telephone:* 28858.

WOLFF, Tobias J. A., M.A.; American writer; b. 19 June 1945; Birmingham, Ala.; s. of Arthur S. Wolff and Rosemary Loftus; m. Catherine Dolores Spohn 1975; two s. one d.; ed. The Hill School, Univ. of Oxford and Univ. of Stanford; U.S. Army 1964–68; Reporter, Washington Post 1972; Writing Fellow, Stanford Univ. 1975–78; Writer-in-Residence, Ariz. State Univ. 1978–80, Syracuse Univ. 1980–97, Stanford Univ. 1997–; Guggenheim Fellow 1983; Nat. Endowment Fellow 1978, 1984; PEN/Faulkner Award for Fiction 1985, Rea Award for Short Story 1989, Whiting Foundation Award 1989, L.A. Times Book Prize 1989, Ambassador Book Award 1990, Lila Wallace/Reader's Digest Award 1993, Esquire-Volvo-Waterstone Award for Non-Fiction 1994. *Publications:* Hunters in the Snow 1981, The Barracks Thief 1984, Back in the World 1985, This Boy's Life 1989, In Pharaoh's Army: Memories of a Lost War 1994, The Vintage Book of Contemporary American Short Stories 1994, The Best American Short Stories 1994, The Night in Question 1996. *Address:* English Department, Stanford University, CA 94305, U.S.A.

WOLFF, Torben, D.SC.; Danish deep-sea biologist; b. 21 July 1919, Copenhagen; s. of Jørgen Frederik de Lichtenberg Wolff and Karen Margrethe Lunn; m. Lisbeth Christensen; two d.; ed. Copenhagen Univ.; Curator Zoological Museum, Univ. of Copenhagen 1953–66, Chief Curator 1966–80, 1983–89; Dir. Denmark's Aquarium 1980–83, 1990–93; Deputy Leader Danish Galathea Deep-Sea Expedition Round the World 1950–52; mem. Danish Atlantide Expedition to West Africa 1945–46; numerous other expeditions; Hon. mem. R.S.N.Z., 1977, Danish Natural History Soc. 1990; Royal Galathea Medal 1955, G.E.C. Gad's Grant of Honour 1964, Popular Science Prize, Danish Asscn. of Authors 1983. *Publications:* A Year in Nature 1944, The Systematics and Biology of Isopoda Asellota 1962, Danish Expeditions on the Seven Seas 1967, The History of Danish Zoology 1979, The History of the Danish Natural History Society 1933–83, 1983. *Leisure interest:* guiding tours abroad to places off the beaten track. *Address:* Zoological Museum, 2100 Copenhagen Ø (Office); Hesseltoften 12, 2900 Hellerup, Denmark (Home). *Telephone:* 39 62 89 71 (Home). *Fax:* 35 32 10 10.

WOLFF VON AMERONGEN, Otto; German industrialist; b. 6 Aug. 1918; s. of Otto Wolff and Else von Amerongen; m. Winnie Greger; three d.; Chair. and C.E.O. Otto Wolff AG 1966–86, Chair. Supervisory Bd. 1986–90; Chair. and C.E.O. Otto Wolff Industrieberatung und Beteiligungen GmbH 1990–; Chair. and C.E.O. Otto Wolff von Amerongen-Stiftung 1991–; Chair., Deputy Chair. and mem. Supervisory Bds. various nat. and int. corpns.; Chair. Cologne Chamber of Commerce and Industry 1966–90, Hon. Chair. 1990–; Chair. German East-West Trade Cttee. 1955–; Pres. Deutsche Gesellschaft für Osteuropakunde 1971–; Hon. Chair. Asscn. of German Chambers of Commerce and Industry; Officier, Légion d'honneur, Grosses Bundesverdienstkreuz. *Address:* Marienburger Strasse 19, 50968 Cologne, Germany. *Telephone:* (0221) 934770-0. *Fax:* (0221) 934770-50.

WOLFRAM, Herwig, D.PHIL.; Austrian historian; b. 14 Feb. 1934, Vienna; s. of Dr Fritz Wolfram and Rosa Wolfram; m. Adelheid Schorghofer 1958; three s. one d.; ed. Univ. of Vienna; Lecturer 1959–68; Docent, Univ. of Vienna 1967; Assoc. Prof., Los Angeles 1968; Assoc. Prof. of Medieval History 1969, Prof. of Medieval History and Auxiliary Sciences 1971–, Dean Faculty of Arts 1981–83; Dir. Inst. für osterr. Geschichtsforschung, Vienna 1983–; Fellow Austrian Acad. of Sciences 1985–, Medieval Acad. of America 1990. *Publications include:* Splendor Imperii 1963, Intitulatio I 1967, II 1973, III 1988, History of the Goths 1988, Die Geburt Mitteleuropas 1987, Die Goten (3rd ed.) 1990, Das Reich und die Germanen 1990; over 120 articles. *Leisure interests:* sport, music, theatre. *Address:* Universität Wien, Dr. Karl Lueger-Ring 1, 1010 Vienna, Austria. *Telephone:* 40103/2180.

WOLFSON, Baron (Life Peer), cr. 1985, of Marylebone in the City of Westminster; **Leonard Gordon Wolfson,** Kt.; British retail executive; b. 11 Nov. 1927; s. of the late Sir Isaac Wolfson and Lady Edith Wolfson; m. 1st Ruth Sterling 1949 (divorced 1991); four d.; m. 2nd Estelle (née Feldman) 1991; ed. King's School, Worcester; Chair. Great Universal Stores 1981–96, Hon. Pres. 1996– (Dir. 1952, Man. Dir. 1962–81); Chair. Burberrys Ltd. 1978–96, Hon. Pres. 1996–; Founder Trustee Wolfson Foundation 1955–, Chair. 1972–; Patron Royal Coll. of Surgeons 1976; Trustee Imperial War Museum 1988–94; Hon. Fellow Wolfson Coll., Cambridge, Wolfson Coll., St. Catherine's Coll. and Worcester Coll., Oxford, Univ. Coll. London, London School of Hygiene and Tropical Medicine 1985, Queen Mary Coll., London Univ. 1985, Imperial Coll. 1991; Hon. F.R.C.P.; Hon. F.R.C.S.; Hon. F.B.A.; Hon. D.C.L. (Oxon, E. Anglia), Hon. Ph.D. (Tel Aviv and Hebrew Univ., Weizmann Inst.), Hon. LL.D. (Strathclyde, Dundee, Cambridge, London), Hon. D.Sc. (Hull, Univ. of Wales), Hon. D.H.L. (Bar Ilan, Israel), Hon. D. Univ. (Surrey) 1990, (Glasgow) 1997; Hon. Dr. Med. (Birmingham) 1992; Dr. h.c. (Edin.) 1996; Winston Churchill Award (British Technion Soc.) 1989. *Leisure interests:* history, economics, golf. *Address:* 8 Queen Anne Street, London, W1M 9LD; 18–22 Haymarket, London, SW1Y 4DQ, England.

WOLFSON, Dirk Jacob, PH.D.; Netherlands economist; b. 22 June 1933, Voorburg; s. of Dirk Wolfson and Gerdina Akkerhuys; m. Anna Maaike Hoekstra 1960; three c.; ed. Univ. of Amsterdam; Teaching Asst. Univ. of Amsterdam 1961–63; Economist, IMF, Washington, D.C. 1964–70; Dir. (Chief Economist), Econ. Policy Div. Netherlands Treasury Dept. 1970–75; Prof. of Public Finance, Erasmus Univ. Rotterdam 1975–86, Prof. of Econs. 1992–; Rector, Inst. of Social Studies, The Hague 1986–90; mem. Social and Econ. Council 1982–96, Scientific Council for Govt. Policy 1990–98; Royal Supervisor, Netherlands Cen. Bank, and Chair. Banking Council 1990–; mem. Royal Netherlands Acad. of Arts and Sciences 1989. *Publications:* Public Finance and Development Strategy 1979; numerous books and articles on econ. theory and policy. *Leisure interests:* theatre, hiking. *Address:* Aelbrechtskolk 41a, 3025 HB Rotterdam, Netherlands (Home). *Telephone:* 070-479497 (Office); 010-4764667 (Home). *Fax:* 070-3562695.

WOLLHEIM, Richard Arthur, M.A., F.B.A.; British philosopher; b. 5 May 1923, London; s. of Eric Wollheim and Constance Wollheim; m. 1st Anne Toynbee (née Powell) 1950 (divorced 1967); two s.; m. 2nd Mary Day Lanier 1969; one d.; ed. Westminster School, Balliol Coll. Oxford; army service 1942–45; taught at Univ. Coll. London 1949–82, Grote Prof. 1963–82; Emer. Grote Prof. 1982–; Prof. of Philosophy, Columbia Univ., U.S.A. 1982–84; Prof. of Philosophy, Univ. of Calif., Berkeley 1985–; Prof. of Philosophy and the Humanities, Univ. of Calif., Davis 1989–95; Fellow American Acad. of Arts and Sciences. *Publications:* F. H. Bradley 1959, Art and its Objects 1968, A Family Romance 1969, Freud 1971, On Art and the Mind 1973, The Thread of Life (William James Lectures, Harvard) 1984, Painting as an Art (Mellon Lectures, Nat. Gallery of Art) 1987, The Mind and Its Depths (essays and lectures) 1993. *Address:* 20 Ashchurch Park Villas, London, W12 9SP, England; 1814 Marin Avenue, Berkeley, CA 94707, U.S.A. *Telephone:* 0181-743 7708 (London); (510) 525-2599 (Calif.).

WOLPER, David Lloyd; American film and television producer; b. 11 Jan. 1928, New York; s. of Irving S. Wolper and Anna (née Fass) Wolper; m. 1st Margaret Dawn Richard 1958 (divorced); two s. one d.; m. 2nd Gloria Diane Hill 1974; ed. Drake Univ. and Univ. of Southern California; Vice-Pres. and Treasurer Flamingo Films TV Sales Co. 1948–50; Vice-Pres. W. Coast Operations 1954–58; Chair. Bd. and Pres. Wolper Productions 1958–, Wolper Pictures Ltd. 1968–, The Wolper Org. Inc. 1971–; Pres. Fountainhead Int. 1960–, Wolper TV Sales Co. 1964–, Wolper Productions Inc. 1970–; Vice-

Pres. Metromedia Inc. 1965–68; Consultant and Exec. Producer Warner Brothers Inc. 1976–; Dir., fmr. Chair. Amateur Athletic Foundation of Los Angeles; Dir. Acad. of TV Arts and Sciences Foundation, S. Calif. Cttee. for Olympic Games, Univ. of S. Calif. Cinema/TV Dept.; mem. Acad. of Motion Picture Arts and Sciences, Acad. of TV Arts and Sciences, Producers' Guild of America, Caucus for Producers, Writers and Dirs.; mem. Bd. of Govs. Cedars Sinai Medical Center; mem. Bd. of Trustees, American Film Inst., Museum of Broadcasting, Los Angeles Country Museum of Art and numerous other appointments seven Golden Globe Awards, five George Foster Peabody Awards, Distinguished Service Award, U.S. Jr. Chamber of Commerce, 46 Emmy Awards, Acad. of TV Arts and Sciences, Monte Carlo Int. Film Festival Award 1964, Cannes Film Festival Grand Prix for TV Programmes 1964, two Acad. Awards: Best Documentary Film 1972, Jean Hersholt Humanitarian Award 1985; Chevalier, Légion d'honneur 1990. *TV productions include:* The Race for Space, The Making of the President, Hollywood and the Stars, March of Time Specials, The Rise and Fall of the Third Reich, The Undersea World of Jacques Cousteau, China: Roots of Madness, Primal Man, Welcome Back, Kotter, Roots, Victory at Entebbe, Roots: The Next Generations, The Thorn Birds, North and South—Books I and II, The Morning After, Napoleon and Josephine, and numerous TV films including Men of the Dragon, Unwed Father; has produced numerous feature films and several live special events, including Opening and Closing Ceremonies of 1984 Olympic Games, L.A., 100th Anniversary of Unveiling of the Statue of Liberty 1986. *Address:* c/o Warner Brothers Inc., 4000 Warner Boulevard, Burbank, CA 91522, U.S.A.

WOLPERT, Lewis, C.B.E., D.I.C., PH.D., F.R.S.; British professor of biology as applied to medicine; b. 19 Oct. 1929, South Africa; s. of William Wolpert and Sarah Wolpert; m. Elizabeth Brownstein; two s. two d.; civil engineer S. African Council for Scientific and Industrial Research and Israel Water Planning Dept. 1951–54; Reader in Zoology, King's Coll. London 1964–66; Prof. of Biology as Applied to Medicine, Dept. of Anatomy and Developmental Biology Univ. Coll. & Middlesex School of Medicine (fmrly. at Middx. Medical School) 1966–; presenter Antenna (BBC2) 1988–89, TV documentaries and radio interviews with scientists; Chair. MRC Cell Bd. 1984–88; Chair. Comm. on the Public Understanding of Science 1994–; mem. various cttees., scientific panels etc.; Hon. D.Sc. (Westminster) 1997, Hon. D.Univ. (Open Univ.) 1998. *Publications:* A Passion for Science 1988, The Triumph of the Embryo 1991, The Unnatural Nature of Science 1992, Principles of Development 1998, Malignant Sadness. The Anatomy of Depression 1999. *Leisure interests:* cycling, tennis. *Address:* Department of Anatomy and Developmental Biology, University College London, Gower Street, London, WC1E 6BT, England.

WOLSZCZAN, Aleksander; Polish astronomer; b. 29 April 1946, Szczecinek; m.; one d.; ed. Nicolaus Copernicus Univ., Toruń; Dir. Astronomy Centre, Nicolaus Copernicus Univ. 1996–. *Publications include:* Interstellar Interferometry of the Pulsar PSR 1237+25 1987 (co-author), Experimental Constrains on Strong-Field Relativistic Gravity 1992 (co-author), A Planetary System Around the Millisecond Pulsar PSR 1257+12 1992 (co-author), Confirmation of Earth-Mass Planets Orbiting the Millisecond Pulsar PSR B1257+12 1994, Binary Pulsars and Relativistic Gravitation 1994. Young Astronomer Prize, Polish Astronomical Soceity 1977; Annual Award, Foundation of Polish Science 1992; Annual Award, Alfred Jurzykowski Foundation 1993; Faculty Scholar Medal, Pa. State Univ. 1994; Beatrice M. Tinsley Prize, American Astronomical Society 1996; Cosimir Funk Natural Sciences Award, Polish Inst. of Arts and Sciences of America 1996; Kt.'s Cross, Order of Polonia Restituta 1997. *Leisure interests:* climbing, hiking, windsurfing. *Address:* The Pennsylvania State University, Department of Astronomy and Astrophysics, 525 Davey Laboratory, University Park, PA 16802, U.S.A. *Telephone:* (814) 865 2918.

WOLTER, Frank, DR.; German international civil servant; b. 22 Nov. 1943, Seehausen, Bavaria; s. of Dr. Hans Wolter and Ilse Wolter (née Henrici); m. Birgit Rein 1975; one s. one d.; ed. Univs. of Freiburg, Saarbrücken, and Kiel; Research Fellow Kiel Inst. of World Econs. 1969–74, Head Research Groups 1974–83; Dir. Research Project, German Research Foundation 1977–79; Sr. Economist, Econ. Research and Analysis Unit, GATT Secr., Geneva 1983–89, Dir. Trade Policies Review Div. 1989–91, Dir. Agric. and Commodities 1991–. *Publications:* numerous studies and articles on structural change in industry, int. trade and econ. growth. *Leisure interests:* tennis, skiing, classical music, historical literature, golf. *Address:* 154 rue de Lausanne, 1211 Geneva 21, Switzerland; 38 La Clé des Champs, 01280 Moens, France.

WONDER, Stevie; American singer, musician and composer; b. (as Steveland Judkins Morris) 13 May 1950, Saginaw, Mich.; step-s. of Paul Hardaway; m. 1st Syreeta Wright 1971 (divorced 1972); m. 2nd Yolanda Simmons, three c.; ed. Michigan School for the Blind; first appeared as solo singer at Whitestone Baptist Church, Detroit 1959; recording artist with Motown, Detroit 1963–70; f. and Pres. Black Bull Music Inc. 1970–, Wondirection Records 1982–; owner KJLH, Los Angeles; named Best Selling Male Soul Artist of Year (Nat. Asscn. of Record Merchandisers) 1974; Grammy Awards (You Are the Sunshine of My Life, Innervisions, Superstition) 1974, (Fulfillingness' First Finale, Boogie on Reggae Woman, Living for the City) 1975, (Songs in the Key of Life, I Wish) 1977, Acad. and Golden Globe Awards for song I Just Called to Say I Love You 1985. *Numerous recordings include:* singles include Fingertips 1963, Uptight/Purple Raindrops 1965, Someday At Christmas/The Miracles of Christmas, I'm Wondering/Everytime I See You I Go Wild 1966, I Was Made to Love Her/Hold Me 1967, Shoo-Be-Doo-Be-Doo-Da-Day/Why Don't You Lead Me To Love, You Met Your Match/My Girl 1968, For Once in My Life, I Don't Know Why, My Cherie Amour, Yester-Me, Yester-You, Yesterday, Never Had a Dream Come True, Signed, Sealed, Delivered, I'm Yours, Heaven Help Us All, Superstition, You are the Sunshine of My Life, Higher Ground, Living For the City, Boogie on Reggae Women, Don't You Worry About a Thing, I Wish, Sir Duke, Another Star, Lately, Jammin', We Are the World (with others), I Just Called to Say I Love You; albums include: Little Stevie Wonder: The Twelve-Year-Old Genius, Tribute To Uncle Ray, Jazz Soul, With A Song In My Heart, At The Beach, Uptight 1966, Down To Earth 1966, I Was Made To Love Her 1967, Someday At Christmas 1967, Stevie Wonder: Greatest Hits 1968, Music Of My Mind 1972, Innervisions 1973, Fulfillingness' First Finale 1975, Songs in the Key of Life 1976, Journey Through the Secret Life of Plants 1979, Hotter than July 1980, Original Musiquarium 1981, Woman in Red 1984, In Square Circle 1986, Characters 1987, Jungle Fever 1991, Inner Peace 1995, Motown Legends 1995; Polar Music Prize, Swedish Acad. of Music. *Address:* c/o Steveland Morris Music, 4616 W. Magnolia Boulevard, Burbank, CA 91505, U.S.A.

WONG, Kar-Wai, B.A.; Chinese film director; b. 1959, Shanghai. Films: As Tears Go By, Days of Being Wild, Days of Being Wild II, Fallen Angels, Ashes in Time, Chungking Express. *Address:* c/o Jet Tone Films Ltd., Flat E, Third Floor, Kalam Court, 9 Grampian Road, Kowloon, Hong Kong Special Administrative Region, People's Republic of China.

WONG YICK MING, Rosanna; Chinese administrator and official; b. 15 Aug. 1952, Hong Kong; ed. St. Stephen's Girls' School, Univ. of Hong Kong, Univ. of Toronto, L.S.E., Chinese Univ. of Hong Kong, Univ. of California, Davis; Exec. Dir. Hong Kong Fed. of Youth Groups; Chair. Hong Kong Housing Authority, Complaints Cttee. of Hong Kong Ind. Comm. Against Corruption, Children's Thalassaemia Foundation, Social Welfare Advisory Cttee. 1988–91, Comm. on Youth 1990–91, Police Complaints Cttee. 1993; mem. Legis. Council 1985–91, Exec. Council 1988–91, 1992–97, Exec. Council of Hong Kong Special Admin. Region July 1997–; Patron Mother's Choice, Children's Kidney Trust Fund; mem. Co-ordinating Cttee. for Children and Youth at Risk, Exec. Cttee. Hong Kong Council of Social Service, Bd. World Vision Hong Kong; Hon. Fellow Hong Kong Inst. of Housing 1994; Hon. Mem. Chartered Inst. of Housing 1994. *Address:* Executive Council Secretariat, First Floor, Main Wing, Central Government Offices, Central, Hong Kong Special Administrative Region, People's Republic of China.

WOO, John; Chinese film director; b. 1948, Guangzhou; ed. Matteo Ricci Coll., Hong Kong; started making experimental 16mm. films in 1967; entered film industry 1969 as Production Asst. Cathay Film Co., Asst. Dir. 1971; later joined Shaw Bros. as Asst. Dir. to Zhang Che. *Films:* The Young Dragons (debut) 1973, The Dragon Tamers, Countdown in Kung Fu, Princess Chang Ping, From Riches to Rags, Money Crazy, Follow the Star, Last Hurrah for Chivalry, To Hell with the Devil, Laughing Times, Plain Jane to the Rescue, Sunset Warriors (Heroes Shed No Tears), The Time You Need a Friend, Run Tiger, Run, A Better Tomorrow, A Better Tomorrow II, Just Heroes, The Killer, Bullet in the Head, Once a Thief, Hard Boiled, Hard Target, Broken Arrow, Face/Off.

WOO, Peter K. C., J.P., M.B.A., D.LITT., D.SC.; Chinese business executive; b. 1946, Shanghai; ed. Univ. of Cincinnati, Columbia Business School, U.S.A.; Chair. Wheelock & Co. Ltd. 1986–96, Hon. Chair. 1996–; Chair. Wharf (Holdings) Ltd. 1986–94, Hon. Chair 1994–; Founding Chair. Wheelock NatWest Ltd. 1995–, The Wharf (Holdings) Ltd. 1992–; Hong Kong (now Hong Kong Special Admin. Region) Affairs Adviser to People's Repub. of China 1993–; mem. Int. Advisory Bd. Chemical Banking Corpn. 1981–, Nat. Westminster Bank PLC 1992–, Gen. Electric 1994–, Elf Aquitaine 1994–; Dir. Standard Chartered Bank PLC 1986–89; mem. Hong Kong (now Hong Kong Special Admin. Region)/United States Econ. Co-operation Cttee. 1989–95, Hong Kong Gov.'s Business Council 1993–97, Chair. Hong Kong (now Hong Kong Special Admin. Region) Environment and Conservation Fund Cttee. 1994–, Hosp. Authority 1995–; Deputy Chair. Prince of Wales Business Leaders' Forum 1991–; Leader of the Year (Hong Kong Standard) 1995; Cross of Officer, Order of Leopold (Belgium). *Publication:* The Challenge of Hong Kong Plus 1991. *Leisure interests:* golf, tennis. *Address:* Penthouse, Wheelock House, 20 Pedder Street, Central, Hong Kong Special Administrative Region, People's Republic of China.

WOO, Sir PO-SHING, Kt., F.C.I.ARB., F.I.MGT., F.INST.D.; British solicitor; b. 19 April 1929, Hong Kong; s. of late Seaward Woo and of Ng Chiu Man; m. Helen Fong Shuet Fun 1956; four s. one d.; ed. La Salle Coll. Hong Kong and King's Coll. London; admitted to practice as solicitor in England and Hong Kong 1960; Notary Public 1966; admitted to practice as barrister and solicitor, Supreme Court of Victoria, Australia 1983; founder and Sr. Partner, Woo & Kwan Lee Solicitors 1963 (merged to form Woo Kwan Lee & Lo, Solicitors and Notaries 1973); Chair. Kailey Enterprises Ltd., Kailey Devt. Ltd.; Dir. Sun Hung Kai Properties Ltd., Henderson Devt. Co. Ltd. and over 40 other cos.; mem. Inst. of Admin. Man., Inst. of Trade Mark Agents; f. Woo P Shing Medal in Law (Hong Kong Univ.) 1982, Woo Po Shing Overseas Summer School Travelling Scholarship (Hong Kong Univ.) 1983, The Po-Shing Woo Charitable Foundation 1994, Woo Po Shing Chair of Chinese and Comparative Law (City Univ.) 1995; mem. Council Univ. of Hong Kong;

voting mem. Hong Kong Jockey Club, Po Leung Kuk Advisory Bd., Tung Wah Group of Hosps.; Legal Adviser Chinese Gold and Silver Exchange Soc.; Hon. Pres. and Legal Adviser S. China Athletic Asscn.; Patron Woo Po Shing Gallery of Chinese Bronze, Shanghai Museum, The Auckland Observatory (renamed Dr. Po-Shing Woo Auckland Observatory Bldg.); Hon. Prof. Nankai Univ. of Tianjin, China; Fellow Inst. of Man., Inst. of Dirs., King's Coll., London Univ.; Hon. LL.D. (City Univ. Hong Kong); Hon. LL.B. (King's Coll. London); World Fellowship of Duke of Edin.'s Award. *Leisure interests:* travelling, viewing and collecting antiques including Chinese paintings, bronzes and ceramics. *Address:* 21/F Kailey Tower, 16 Stanley Street, Central, Hong Kong Special Administrative Region, People's Republic of China. *Telephone:* 2522 4825. *Fax:* 2537 9747.

WOOD, Adrian John Bickersteth, M.A., M.P.A., PH.D.; British economist; b. 25 Jan. 1946, Woking; s. of late John H.F. Wood and of Mary E. B. (née Ottley) Brain; m. Joyce M. Teitz 1971; two d.; ed. Bryanston School, King's Coll. Cambridge and Harvard Univ.; Fellow, King's Coll. Cambridge 1969–77; Asst. Lecturer, Lecturer, Univ. of Cambridge 1973–77; Economist, Sr. Economist, IBRD 1977–85; Professorial Fellow, Inst. of Devt. Studies, Univ. of Sussex 1985–; Harkness Fellowship 1967–69. *Publications:* A Theory of Profits 1975, A Theory of Pay 1978, Poverty and Human Development (with others) 1981, China: Long-Term Development Issues and Options (with others) 1985, North-South Trade, Employment and Inequality 1994. *Leisure interests:* music, art, walking. *Address:* Institute of Development Studies, University of Sussex, Brighton, Sussex, BN1 9RE, England. *Telephone:* (01273) 678280. *Fax:* (01273) 621202.

WOOD, Sir Andrew Marley, K.C.M.G., M.A.; British diplomatist; b. 2 Jan. 1940; s. of Robert George Wood; m. 1st Melanie LeRoy Masset 1972 (died 1977); one s.; m. 2nd Stephanie Lee Masset 1978; one s. one d.; ed. Ardingly Coll., King's Coll. Cambridge; Foreign Office 1961, served in Moscow 1964, Washington 1967, FCO 1970, Cabinet Office 1971, First Sec., FCO 1973, First Sec. and Head of Chancery, Belgrade 1976, Counsellor 1978, Head of Chancery, Moscow 1979, Head of Western European Dept., FCO 1982, Head of Personnel Operations Dept., FCO 1983, Amb. to Yugoslavia 1985–89, Minister, Washington 1989–92, (Chief Clerk) FCO 1992, Amb. to Russia (also accred. to Moldova) 1995–. *Address:* British Embassy, Sofiiskaya nab. 14, Moscow, Russia. *Telephone:* (095) 956-72-00. *Fax:* (095) 956-74-20.

WOOD, Charles Gerald, F.R.S.L.; British scriptwriter and playwright; b. 6 Aug. 1932; s. of John Edward Wood and Catherine Mae (née Harris) Wood; m. Valerie Elizabeth Newman 1954; one s. one d.; ed. King Charles I School, Kidderminster and Birmingham Coll. of Art; corporal 17/21st Lancers 1950–55; factory worker 1955–57; Stage Man., scenic artist, cartoonist, advertising artist 1957–59; Bristol Evening Post 1959–62; mem. Drama Advisory Panel, South Western Arts 1972–73; consultant to Nat. Film Devt. Fund 1980–82; mem. Council BAFTA 1991–93. *Plays include:* Prisoner and Escort, Spare, John Thomas 1963, Meals on Wheels 1965, Don't Make Me Laugh 1966, Fill the Stage with Happy Hours 1967, Dingo 1967, H 1969, Welfare 1971, Veterans 1972, Jingo 1975, Has 'Washington' Legs? 1978, Red Star 1984, Across from the Garden of Allah 1986; adapted Pirandello's Man, Beast and Virtue 1989, The Mountain Giants 1993, Alexandre Dumas's The Tower 1995. *TV Plays include:* Prisoner and Escort, Drill Pig, A Bit of a Holiday, A Bit of an Adventure, Love Lies Bleeding, Dust to Dust. *Screenplays include:* The Knack 1965, Help! 1965, How I Won the War 1967, The Charge of the Light Brigade 1968, The Long Day's Dying 1969, Cuba 1980, Wagner 1983, Red Monarch 1983, Puccini 1984, Tumbledown 1988, Shooting the Hero 1991, An Awfully Big Adventure 1993, England my England (with John Osborne) 1995, The Ghost Road 1996. *TV Series:* Company of Adventurers 1986, My Family and Other Animals 1987, The Settling of the Sun 1987, Sharpe's Company 1994, Sharpe's Regiment 1996, Mute of Malice (Kavanagh QC) 1997, Sharpe's Waterloo 1997. *Publications:* (Plays) Cockade 1965, Fill the Stage with Happy Hours 1967, Dingo 1967, H 1970, Veterans 1972, Has 'Washington' Legs? 1978, Tumbledown 1987, Man, Beast and Virtue 1990, The Giants of the Mountain 1994, The Tower 1995. *Leisure interests:* military and theatrical studies, gardening. *Address:* c/o Jane Annakin, London Management, 2–4 Noel Street, London, W1V 3RB, England. *Telephone:* 0171-287 9000.

WOOD, Graham Charles, M.A., PH.D., F.R.S., F.ENG.; British professor of engineering; b. 6 Feb. 1934, Farnborough; s. of Cyril Wood and Doris Hilda Wood (née Strange); m. Freda Nancy Waithman 1959; one s. one d.; ed. Bromley Grammar School, Kent, Christ's Coll., Cambridge; lecturer, then sr. lecturer, Reader in Corrosion Science UMIST 1961–72, Prof. of Corrosion Science and Eng. 1972–97, now Emer. Prof. UMIST and Univ. of Manchester; Vice-Prin. for Academic Devt. UMIST 1982–84, Deputy Prin. 1983, Dean of Faculty of Tech. 1987–89, Pro-Vice-Chancellor 1992–97; Chair. Int. Corrosion Council 1993–96; Pres. Inst. of Corrosion Science and Tech. 1978–80; U. R. Evans Award, Inst. of Corrosion, C. Wagner Award of Electrochemical Soc.; Beilby Medal, Griffith Medal, Inst. of Materials, Cavallaro Medal, European Fed. of Corrosion. *Publications:* over 400 papers in various learned journals. *Leisure interests:* travel, cricket, walking, history of art, science and politics. *Address:* University of Manchester Institute of Science and Technology, Corrosion and Protection Centre, P.O. Box 88, Manchester, M60 1QD, England. *Telephone:* (0161) 200-4850; (0161) 200-4851. *Fax:* (0161) 200-4865.

WOOD, John; British actor; ed. Bedford School, Jesus Coll. Oxford; with Old Vic Co. 1954–56, R.S.C. 1971–. *Stage appearances include:* Enemies, The Man of Mode, Exiles, The Balcony 1971, The Comedy of Errors 1972, Julius Caesar, Titus Andronicus 1972, 1973, Collaborators, A Lesson in Blood and Roses 1973, Sherlock Holmes, Travesties 1974 (Evening Standard Best Actor Award 1974, Tony Award 1976), The Devil's Disciple, Ivanov 1976, Death Trap 1978, Undiscovered Country, Richard III 1979, Piaf, The Provok'd Wife 1980, The Tempest 1988, The Man Who Came to Dinner, The Master Builder 1989, King Lear (Evening Standard Best Actor Award 1991), Love's Labours Lost 1990, The Invention of Love 1997. *Television:* A Tale of Two Cities, Barnaby Rudge 1964–65, The Victorians 1965, The Duel 1966. *Films:* Nicholas and Alexandra 1971, Slaughterhouse Five 1972, War Games 1983, The Madness of King George 1994, Sabrina 1996, Richard III 1996, Jane Eyre 1996, The Gambler 1997. *Address:* c/o Royal Shakespeare Company, Barbican Centre, Silk Street, London, EC2Y 8DS, England.

WOOD, L. John, M.A.; New Zealand diplomatist; b. 31 March 1944, Kaikoura; s. of Lionel Wood and Margaret Wood; m. Rosemary Taunt 1969 (died 1995); one s.; ed. Lincoln County Dist. High School, Christchurch Boys' High School, Univ. of Canterbury and Balliol Coll. Oxford; joined Ministry of Foreign Affairs 1969; seconded to Treasury 1971–72; Second Sec., later First Sec. Tokyo 1973–76; seconded to Prime Minister's Dept. 1976–78; First Sec., later Counsellor and Consul-Gen. Bonn 1978–82; Ministry of Foreign Affairs 1982–83; Minister, Deputy Chief of Mission, Washington, D.C. 1984–87; Amb. to Iran (also accred. to Pakistan and Turkey) 1987–90; Dir. N. Asia Div. Ministry of External Relations and Trade 1990–91, Deputy Sec. Econ. and Trade Relations 1991–94; Amb. to U.S.A. 1994–98. *Leisure interests:* rare books and bindings, New Zealand literature, sport. *Address:* c/o Ministry of Foreign Affairs, Private Bag 18901, Wellington, New Zealand.

WOOD, Sir Martin (Francis), Kt., O.B.E., M.A., F.R.S., D.L.; British engineer and business executive; b. 19 April 1927; s. of Arthur Henry Wood and Katharine Mary Altham (née Cumberlege) Wood; m. Audrey Buxton (née Stanfield) Wood 1955; one s. one d. one step-s. one step-d.; ed. Gresham's, Trinity Coll. Cambridge, Imperial Coll. London, Christ Church Oxford; with Nat. Coal Bd. 1953–55; Sr. Research Officer, Clarendon Lab., Oxford Univ. 1956–69; f. Oxford Instruments PLC 1959, Chair. 1959–83, Deputy Chair. 1983–; Chair. Nat. Comm. for Superconductivity 1987–91; mem. Advisory Bd. for Research Councils 1983–89, ACOST 1990–93, Central Lab. of Research Councils 1995–98; Dir. Orbit Precision Machining Ltd. 1965–, Oxford Seedcorn Capital Ltd. 1986–, Oxford Ventures Group Ltd. 1988–, ISIS Innovation Ltd. 1989–, Oxford Innovation Ltd. 1989–, Newport Tech. Group Ltd. 1989–, FARM Africa Ltd. 1985–; Tech. Consultant African Medical and Research Foundation; f. Northmoor Trust (for nature conservation), Oxford Trust (for encouragement of study and application of science and tech.); Trustee Oxon Council for Voluntary Action 1994–; Fellow Wolfson Coll., Oxford 1967–94, Hon. Fellow 1994; Hon. Fellow UMIST 1989; Hon. D.Sc. (Cranfield Inst. of Tech.) 1983; Hon. D.Tech. (Loughborough Univ. of Tech.) 1985, Hon. D.Eng. (Birmingham) 1997; Mullard Medal, Royal Soc. 1982. *Address:* c/o Oxford Instruments Group PLC, Old Station Way, Eynsham, Witney, Oxon., OX8 1TL, England. *Telephone:* (01865) 881437.

WOOD, Maurice, M.B., B.S., F.R.C.G.P., F.A.A.F.P.; American physician; b. 28 June 1922, Pelton, Co. Durham, England; s. of Joseph Wood and Eugenie (Lumley) Wood; m. Erica J. Noble 1948; two s. one d.; ed. Chester-le-Street Grammar School and Univ. of Durham; various hosp. appts. 1945–46, 1949–50; Maj, R.A.M.C. 1946–49; Sr. Partner, Medical Practice, South Shields 1950–71; Gen. Practice Teaching Group, Univ. of Newcastle-upon-Tyne 1969–71; Clinical Asst. Dept. of Psychological Medicine, South Shields Gen. Hosp. 1966–71; Assoc. Prof., Dir. of Research, Dept. of Family Practice, Medical Coll. of Va., Va. Commonwealth Univ., Richmond, Va. 1971–73, Prof. and Dir. of Research 1973–87, Prof. Emer. 1987–; Exec. Dir. N. American Primary Care Research Group 1983–92; Consultant Adviser, WHO 1979–90; other professional appts. and memberships; Sr. mem. Inst. of Medicine, N.A.S. and other awards and distinctions. *Publications:* International Class of Primary Care 1987, The International Classification of Primary Care in the European Community—with a multilanguage layer (Co-ed.) 1993; numerous articles in professional journals and book chapters. *Leisure interests:* sailing, gliding, skiing. *Address:* Department of Family Practice, Medical College of Virginia, Medical College of Virginia Station, Box 251, Richmond, VA 23298-001; Route 1, Box 672, Roseland, VA 22967, U.S.A. *Telephone:* (804) 786-9625; (804) 325-1383. *Fax:* (804) 325-1383.

WOOD, Rt. Rev. Maurice Arthur Ponsonby, D.S.C., M.A.; British ecclesiastic; b. 26 Aug. 1916, London; s. of the late Arthur S. Wood and of Jane Elspeth (née Piper) Wood; m. 1st Marjorie Pennell 1947 (died 1954); two s. one d.; m. 2nd M. Margaret Sandford 1955; two s. one d.; ed. Monkton Combe School, Queens' Coll., Cambridge and Ridley Hall, Cambridge; ordained 1940; Curate, St. Paul's Portman Square, London 1940–43; Royal Naval Chaplain 1943–47; Rector, St. Ebbe's Oxford 1947–52; Vicar and Rural Dean of Islington 1952–61; Prin., Oak Hill Theological Coll., Southgate, London 1961–71; Bishop of Norwich 1971–85; Hon. Chaplain, R.N.R. 1971–, an Hon. Asst. Bishop, Diocese of London 1985–, Diocese of Oxford 1989–94; Resident Priest of Englefield 1987–94; entered House of Lords 1975; Chaplain, Commando Asscn., Worshipful Co. of Weavers –1995, Freeman 1995–; Chair. Order of Christian Unity 1986–96, Pres. 1996–; Gov. Monkton Combe School, Bath, St. Helen's School, Abingdon 1989–; Visitor Luckley-Oakfield School 1990–. *Publications:* Like a Mighty Army 1956, Your Suffering 1959, Christian Stability 1968, To Everyman's Door 1968, Into the Way of Peace 1982, This is our Faith 1985, Comfort in Sorrow 1992.

Leisure interests: painting, supporting Dr Billy Graham (q.v.) and Norwich City Football Club. *Address:* Abbot's Cottage, Horning, Norfolk, NR12 8NE; 41 Fir Tree Walk, Enfield, EN1 3TZ, England. *Telephone:* 0181-363 4491 (Enfield).

WOOD, Peter, C.B.E.; British business executive; m.; five d.; Head European Data Processing Operations, Levi Strauss; fmrly. with Alexander Howden (insurance brokers); Founder, C.E.O. Direct Line Insurance 1985–96, Chair. 1996–97; Chair. Privilege Insurance 1993–; Vice-Chair. Direct Response Corpn. and Homeowners Direct Corpn., U.S.A. *Address:* c/o Privilege Insurance, Wrencote, 123 High Street, Croydon, Surrey, CR0 1QG; Minet House, 66 Prescot Street, London, E1 8HG, England. *Telephone:* 0171-464 2702.

WOOD, Peter (Lawrence); British theatre and television director; b. 8 Oct. 1928; s. of Frank Wood and Lucy E. Meeson; ed. Taunton School and Downing Coll. Cambridge; Resident Dir. Arts Theatre 1956–57; Assoc. Dir. Nat. Theatre 1978–89; Nat. Theatre productions include: The Master Builder 1964, Love for Love 1965, 1985, Jumpers 1972, The Guardsman, The Double Dealer 1978, Undiscovered Country 1979, The Provok'd Wife 1980, On the Razzle 1981, The Rivals 1983, Rough Crossing 1984, Dalliance 1986, The Threepenny Opera 1986, The American Clock 1986, The Beaux Stratagem 1989, The School for Scandal 1990; RSC productions include: Winter's Tale 1960, The Devils 1961, Hamlet 1961, The Beggar's Opera 1963, Travesties 1974, The Strange Case of Dr. Jekyll and Mr. Hyde 1991, Indian Ink 1995; numerous other productions at theatres in London, Edinburgh, New York, Stratford (Ont.), Vienna etc.; dir. of plays for television in U.S.A. and U.K. since 1970; opera productions include: The Mother of Us All, Santa Fe 1976, Il Seraglio, Glyndebourne 1980, 1988, Don Giovanni, Covent Garden 1981, Macbeth, Staatsoper, Vienna 1982, Orione, Santa Fe 1983, Otello, Staatsoper, Vienna 1987. *Leisure interests:* swimming, sailing, travelling. *Address:* The Old Barn, Batcombe, Somerset, BA4 6HD, England.

WOOD, Rt. Hon. Richard Frederick (see Holderness, Baron).

WOOD, Ronald Karslake Starr, F.R.S.; British professor of plant pathology; b. 8 April 1919, Ferndale; s. of Percival T. E. Wood and Florence Dix Starr; m. Marjorie Schofield 1947; one s. one d.; ed. Ferndale Grammar School and Imperial Coll., London; Ministry of Aircraft Production 1942; Lecturer Imperial Coll. 1947, Reader in Plant Pathology 1955, Prof. of Plant Pathology 1964–, mem. Governing Body, Head Dept. of Pure and Applied Biology 1981–84; Dean Royal Coll. of Science 1975; Dir. NATO Advanced Study Insts. 1970, 1975, 1980; Sir C. V. Raman Prof. Univ. of Madras 1980; Regent's Lecturer Univ. of Calif. 1981; Otto-Appel Denkmünster 1978; Sec.-Gen. 1st Int. Congress of Plant Pathology 1968, Hon. Pres. 7th Int. Congress (Edin.) 1998; Founder Pres. Int. Soc. for Plant Pathology 1968, British Soc. for Plant Pathology, now Hon. mem.; Commonwealth Fund Fellow 1950, Research Fellow Conn. Agricultural Experimental Station 1957, Fellow American Phytopathological Soc. 1976, Thurburn Fellow Univ. of Sydney 1979; Vice-Chair. Governing Body E. Malling Research Station; Gov. Inst. of Horticultural Research; Corresp. mem. Deutsche Phytomedizinische Gesellschaft 1973. *Publications:* Physiological Plant Pathology 1967, Phytotoxins in Plant Diseases (Ed. with A. Ballio and A. Graniti) 1972, Specificity in Plant Diseases (Ed. with A. Graniti) 1976, Active Defence Mechanisms in Plants (Ed.) 1981, Plant Diseases: infection, damage and loss (Ed.) 1984; numerous papers in scientific journals. *Leisure interest:* gardening. *Address:* Imperial College, London, SW7 2AZ (Office); Pyrford Woods, Pyrford, Nr. Woking, Surrey, England (Home). *Telephone:* 0171-589 5111 (Office); (0193 23) 43827 (Home). *Fax:* 0171-584 2056.

WOOD, Ronnie (Ronald); British musician; b. 1 June 1947; m. 1st; one s.; m. 2nd Jo Howard 1985; one s. one d.; guitarist with Jeff Beck Group 1968–69, The Faces 1969–75, The Rolling Stones 1975–; albums with Jeff Beck Group: Truth 1968, Beck-Ola 1969, with The Faces: First Step 1970, Long Player 1971, A Nod's As Good As A Wink . . . To A Blind Horse 1971, Ooh La La 1973, Coast To Coast Overtures and Beginners 1974, with The Rolling Stones: Black and Blue 1976, Love You Live 1977, Some Girls 1978, Emotional Rescue 1980, Tattoo You 1981, Still Life 1981, Undercover 1983, Rewind 1971–1984 1984, Dirty Work 1986, Steel Wheels 1989, Flashpoint 1991, Voodoo Lounge 1994, solo albums include: Slide on This 1992; films include: Let's Spend the Night Together 1983, Flashpoint 1991; has also played with Bo Diddley, Rod Stewart, Jerry Lee Lewis. *Address:* c/o Monroe Sounds, 5 Church Row, Wandsworth Plain, London, SW18 1ES, England.

WOOD, William B., III, PH.D.; American professor of biology; b. 19 Feb. 1938, Baltimore, Md.; s. of Dr. W. Barry Wood, Jr. and Mary L. Hutchins; m. Renate Marie-Elisabeth Hartisch 1961; two s.; ed. Harvard Coll., Stanford Univ. and Univ. of Geneva; Nat. Acad. of Sciences—Nat. Research Council Postdoctoral Fellow, Univ. of Geneva 1964; Asst. Prof. of Biology, Calif. Inst. of Tech. 1965–68, Assoc. Prof. 1968–70, Prof. 1970–77; Prof. of Molecular Biology, Univ. of Colo., Boulder 1977–, Chair. of Dept. 1978–83; mem. N.A.S., American Acad. of Arts and Sciences, A.A.A.S., American Soc. of Biological Chemists, Soc. for Developmental Biology. *Publications:* Biochemistry, A Problems Approach (with J. H. Wilson, R. M. Benbow and L. E. Hood) 1974, 1981, Molecular Design in Living Systems 1974, The Molecular Basis of Metabolism 1974, Molecular Biology of Eucaryotic Cells (with L. E. Hood and J. H. Wilson) 1975, Immunology (with L. E. Hood and I. Weissman) 1978, 1984, The Nematode Caenorhaboitis Elegans (Ed.) 1988, articles in professional journals. *Leisure interests:* music, tennis, camping. *Address:* Department of Molecular, Cellular and Developmental Biology, Box 347, University of Colorado, Boulder, CO 80309, U.S.A.

WOODCOCK, Leonard; American labour leader and diplomatist; b. 15 Feb. 1911, Providence, R.I.; s. of Ernest Woodcock and Margaret (née Freel) Woodcock; m. 1st Loula Martin 1941; one s. two d.; m. 2nd Sharon Lee Tuohy 1978; ed. St. Wilfred's Coll. Oakmore, Northampton Town and Country School (England) and intermittent courses at Wayne State Univ.; Regional Dir., United Automobile, Aerospace and Agricultural Implement Workers of America (UAW) 1947–55, Vice-Pres. 1955–70, Pres. Int. Union 1970–77, Pres. Emer. 1977–; Chief U.S. Liaison Office, Peking 1977–78; Amb. to People's Repub. of China 1979–81; Adjunct Prof., Univ. of Mich. 1981–; Bd. mem. America-China Soc., New York 1987–, Nat. Comm. on U.S.-China Relations, New York 1991–; Dir. ATC Int. Inc., Houston, Tex. 1987–. *Leisure interests:* music and literature. *Address:* 2404 Vinewood Boulevard, Ann Arbor, MI 48104, U.S.A. *Telephone:* (734) 662-8963.

WOODHEAD, Christopher Anthony, M.A.; British civil servant; b. 20 Oct. 1946, Middx.; s. of Anthony Woodhead and Doris Woodhead; m. 1970 (divorced 1995); one d.; ed. Wallington Co. Grammar School, Univs. of Bristol and Keele; English teacher Priory School, Shrewsbury 1969–72; Deputy Head of English Newent School, Gloucester 1972–74; Head of English Gordano School, Avon 1974–76; lecturer in English Oxford Univ. 1976–82; English Adviser Shropshire Local Educ. Authority 1982–84, Chief Adviser 1984–86; Deputy Chief Educ. Officer Devon Local Educ. Authority 1988–90, Cornwall Local Educ. Authority 1990–91; Deputy Chief Exec. Nat. Curriculum Council 1990, Chief Exec. 1991–93; Chief Exec. School Curriculum and Assessment Authority 1993–94; H.M. Chief Inspector of Schools 1994–. *Leisure interest:* rock climbing. *Address:* Office for Standards in Education, Alexandra House, 29–33 Kingsway, London, WC2B 6SE, England. *Telephone:* 0171-421 6800. *Fax:* 0171-421 6546.

WOODHOUSE, Rt. Hon. Sir (Arthur) Owen, K.B.E., D.S.C., P.C., LL.B.; New Zealand judge; b. 18 July 1916, Napier; s. of late Arthur James Woodhouse and Wilhemina Catherine (née Allen) Woodhouse; m. Margaret Leah Thorp 1940; four s. two d.; ed. Napier Boys' High School and Auckland Univ.; military and naval service 1939–45; joined Lusk, Willis & Sproule, barristers and solicitors 1946; Crown Solicitor, Napier 1953; Judge of Supreme Court 1961–86; a Judge of Court of Appeal 1974–86; Pres. Court of Appeal 1981–86; Founding Pres. Law Comm. 1986–91; Chair. Royal Comm. on Compensation and Rehabilitation in respect of Personal Injury in New Zealand 1966–67, Chair. inquiry into similar questions in Australia 1973–74; Hon. LL.D. (Victoria Univ. of Wellington) 1978, (Univ. of York, Toronto, Canada) 1981. *Leisure interests:* music, golf. *Address:* 244 Remuera Road, Auckland 1005, New Zealand.

WOODHOUSE, Hon. (Christopher) Montague, D.S.O., O.B.E., M.A., F.R.S.L.; British politician; b. 11 May 1917, London; s. of Lord and Lady Terrington; m. Lady Davina Lytton (Countess of Erne) 1945 (died 1995); two s. one d; ed. Winchester Coll., and New Coll., Oxford; commissioned R.A. 1940; commanded Allied Mil. Mission in German occupied Greece 1943–44; Asst. Sec. Nuffield Foundation 1947; served Foreign Office in Athens 1945 and Teheran 1951; Fellow Trinity Hall, Cambridge 1949; Dir.-Gen. Royal Inst. of Int. Affairs 1955–59; M.P. for Oxford 1959–66, 1970–74; Parl. Sec. Ministry of Aviation 1961–62, Jt. Under-Sec. of State Home Office 1962–64; Chief Ed. Penguin Books 1960; Dir. of Educ. and Training, CBI 1966–70; Chair. Council Royal Soc. of Literature 1977–86; Visiting Prof., King's Coll. London; Special mem. Acad. of Athens 1980; Visiting Fellow Nuffield Coll. 1956; Fellow New Coll., Oxford 1982; Legion of Merit (U.S.A.); Order of Phoenix with Swords (Greece); Conservative. *Publications:* Apple of Discord 1948, One Omen 1950, Dostoievsky 1951, The Greek War of Independence 1952, Britain and the Middle East 1959, British Foreign Policy since the Second World War 1961, Rhodes (with J. G. Lockhart) 1963, The New Concert of Nations 1964, The Battle of Navarino 1965, Postwar Britain 1966, The Story of Modern Greece 1968, The Philhellenes 1969, Capodistria 1973, The Struggle for Greece (1941–1949) 1976, Something Ventured 1982, Karamanlis: The Restorer of Greek Democracy 1982, The Rise and Fall of the Greek Colonels 1985, Gemistos Plethon: the last of the Hellenes 1986, Rhigas Velestinlis 1995. *Leisure interests:* fishing, music. *Address:* 59 Pegasus Grange, Whitehouse Road, Oxford, OX1 4QQ, England. *Telephone:* (01865) 724642.

WOODLAND, Alan Donald, PH.D., F.A.S.S.A.; Australian professor of econometrics; b. 4 Oct. 1943, Dorrigo, N.S.W.; s. of C. J. Woodland and E. Shephard; m. Narelle Todd 1966; one s. two d.; ed. Univ. of New England; lecturer, Univ. of New England 1967–69; Asst. Prof. Univ. of British Col. 1969–74, Assoc. Prof. 1974–78, Prof. of Econs. 1978–81; Prof. of Econometrics, Univ. of Sydney 1982–; Jt. Ed. The Economic Record 1987–92; Fellow, Reserve Bank 1981; Fellow, Econometric Soc. *Publication:* International Trade and Resource Allocation 1982. *Leisure interests:* bridge, tennis. *Address:* 5 Rosebery Road, Killara, N.S.W. 2071, Australia. *Telephone:* (02) 9416-3100; (02) 9351-6825. *Fax:* (02) 9351-6409.

WOODROOFE, Sir Ernest George, Kt., PH.D., F.INST.P., F.I.CHEM.E.; British business executive; b. 6 Jan. 1912, Liverpool; s. of Ernest George Woodroofe and Ada (Dickinson) Woodroofe; m. 1st Margaret Downes 1938 (died 1961); one d.; m. 2nd Enid Grace Hutchinson Arnold 1962; ed. Leeds Univ.; Dir. British Oil and Cake Mills Ltd. 1951–56; Dir. Unilever Ltd. and Unilever N.V., in charge of Research 1956–61, Vice-Chair. Unilever Ltd.

1961–70, Chair. 1970–74; Vice-Chair. Unilever N.V. 1970–74; Dir. Commonwealth Devt. Finance Co. Ltd. 1970–75, Schroders Ltd. 1974–89, British Gas Corpn. 1972–81, Burton Group 1974–83, Guthrie Corpn. 1975–82; Chair. Review Body on Doctors' and Dentists' Remuneration 1975–79, Leverhulme Trust 1975–82; Vice-Chair. Atlantic Salmon Trust 1984–91; Visiting Fellow, Nuffield Coll., Oxford 1972–80; Hon. LL.D., Hon. D.Sc. (from two univs.), Hon. D. Univ.; Commdr. Order of Orange-Nassau 1972. *Leisure interest:* fishing. *Address:* 44 The Street, Puttenham, Guildford, Surrey, GU3 1AR, England. *Telephone:* (01483) 810977.

WOODROW, Bill (William Robert), D.F.A.; British artist and sculptor; b. 1 Nov. 1948, Henley-on-Thames, Oxon.; s. of Geoffrey W. Woodrow and Doreen M. Fasken; m. Pauline Rowley 1970; one s. one d.; ed. Barton Peveril Grammar School, and Winchester, St. Martin's and Chelsea Schools of Art; 67 solo exhbns. in U.K., Fed. Repub. of Germany, France, Australia, Netherlands, Belgium, Italy, U.S.A., Canada, Switzerland, Sweden, Ireland and Yugoslavia since 1979; solo exhbn. Duveen Galleries, Tate Gallery, London 1996; has participated in many group exhbns. around the world including British Sculpture in the 20th Century (Whitechapel Gallery), An Int. Survey of Recent Painting and Sculpture (Museum of Modern Art, N.Y.), Skulptur im 20. Jahrhundert (Basle), Carnegie Int. (Pittsburgh) 1985, British Sculpture since 1965 (toured U.S.A.) 1987, Great Britain to U.S.S.R. (Kiev, Moscow) 1990, Metropolis (Berlin) 1991, Ripples across the Water, Tsurugi and Tokyo 1994–95, Un Siècle de sculpture anglaise, Jeu de Paume, Paris 1996, Sexta Bienal de la Habana (Cuba) 1997, Forjar el Espacio (C.A.A.M., Gran Canaria) 1998; represented Britain at Biennales of Sydney 1982, Paris 1982, São Paulo 1983, 1991, Paris 1985; works in many public collections in U.K. and abroad; finalist in Turner Prize 1986, winner Anne Gerber Award, Seattle Museum of Art, U.S.A. 1988. *Publications include:* Bill Woodrow, Sculpture 1980–86, A Quiet Revolution—Recent British Sculpture, Bill Woodrow, Eye of the Needle, Sculptures 1987–1989, Bill Woodrow, XXI Bienal de São Paulo 1991, In Awe of the Pawnbroker 1994, Fools' Gold 1996. *Address:* 14 Cormont Road, London, SE5 9RA, England. *Telephone:* 0171-733 2435. *Fax:* 0171-733 9585.

WOODRUFF, Judy Carline, B.A.; American broadcast journalist; b. 20 Nov. 1946, Tulsa, Okla.; d. of William Henry and Anna Lee (Payne) Woodruff; m. Albert R. Hunt, Jr. 1980; two s. one d.; ed. Meredith Coll., Duke Univ.; News Announcer, Reporter WAGA-TV, Atlanta 1970–75; News Corresp. NBC News, Atlanta 1975–76; White House Corresp., NBC News, Washington 1977–83; Corresp. MacNeil-Lehrer News Hour, PBS, Washington 1983–93; Anchor, Sr. Corresp. CNN 1993–; Anchor for Frontline (PBS documentary series) 1983–90; mem. Bd. of Advisers Henry Grady School of Journalism, Univ. of Ga. 1979–82, Bd. of Visitors Wake Forest Univ. 1982–88; mem. Bd. of Advisers, Benton Fellowship in Broadcast Journalism, Univ. of Chicago 1984–90, Families and Work Inst. 1989–, Freedom Forum First Amendment Center 1992–, Comm. on Women's Health 1993–, Radio and TV News Dirs.' Foundation 1994–; Trustee Duke Univ. 1985–; Co-Chair. Int. Women's Media Foundation 1991– (f., dir. 1989–); Knight Fellowship in Journalism, Stanford Univ. 1985–; Knight Fellowship in broadcast journalism Stanford Univ. 1985–; mem. Nat. Acad. of TV Arts and Sciences, White House Corresps. Assn.; numerous awards. *Publication:* This is Judy Woodruff at the White House 1982. *Address:* Cable News Network, 820 1st Street, N.E., Washington, DC 20002, U.S.A.

WOODS, James; American actor; b. 18 April 1947, Vernal, Utah; s. of Gail Woods and Martha Woods; m. 1st Kathryn Greko 1980 (divorced 1983), 2nd Sarah Owen 1989; ed. Univ. of Calif. Los Angeles and Mass. Inst. of Tech.; first Broadway appearance in Brendan Behan's Borstal Boy; Obie Award for appearance in Brooklyn Acad. of Music Production of Edward Bond's Saved, New York 1971; other stage appearances in 1970s include Moonchildren 1972, The Trial of the Catonsville Nine, Finishing Touches, Conduct Unbecoming; many appearances in TV films including Holocaust 1978, Promise 1986 (Emmy Award), My Name Is Bill W. 1989 (Emmy Award). *Films include:* The Visitors 1971, The Way We Were 1972, The Gambler 1974, Distance 1975, Alex and the Gipsy 1976, The Choirboys 1977, The Onion Field 1979, Black Marble 1980, Fast Walking 1982, Split Image 1982, Videodrome 1983, Once Upon a Time in America 1984, Against All Odds 1984, Joshua Then and Now 1985, Best Seller 1987, Cop 1987, The Boost 1989, True Believer 1989, Immediate Family 1989, Straight Talk 1992, Diggstown, Chaplin 1992, The Gateway 1994, Curse of the Starving Class 1994, Casino 1995, Nixon 1996, Killer: A Journal of Murder, Ghosts of Mississippi 1996, Hercules (voice) 1997, Contact 1997. *Address:* c/o Guttman Assocs., 118 S. Beverly Drive, Beverly Hills, CA 90212, U.S.A.

WOODS, Michael, PH.D.; Irish politician; b. 8 Dec. 1935, Bray, Co. Wicklow; m. Margaret Maher; three s. two d.; ed. Univ. Coll. Dublin and Harvard Business School, U.S.A.; Lecturer, Franciscan Coll. of Agric., Multyfarnham, Co. Westmeath 1958–59; Head of Dept. and Prin. Officer, Agric. Research Inst. 1960–70; Man. Dir. F11 Produce Ltd. 1970–73, Associated Producer Groups Ltd. 1974–79; mem Dáil 1977–; Minister of State, Depts. of Taoiseach and Defence 1979; Minister for Health and Social Welfare 1979–81, March–Dec. 1982, for Social Welfare 1987–91, for Agric. 1991–92, for the Marine 1992, for Social Welfare 1993–94, Health 1994, for Marine and Natural Resources 1997–; Spokesperson on Equality and Law Reform 1994–97; Fianna Fáil. *Publications:* Research in Ireland—Key to Economic and Social Development; numerous tech. and scientific papers. *Address:* Department of the Marine & Natural Rersources, Leeson Lane, Dublin 2; 13 Kilbarrack Grove, Raheny, Dublin 5, Ireland. *Telephone:* (01) 678 9807. *Fax:* (01) 676 3616.

WOODS, Philip Wells (Phil), B.MUS.; American jazz musician (alto saxophonist), composer and teacher; b. 2 Nov. 1931, Springfield, Mass.; s. of Stanley J. Woods and Clara Markley; m. 1st Beverly Berg 1957 (divorced 1973); one s. one d.; m. 2nd Jill Goodwin 1985; two step-d.; ed. pvtly. with Harvey LaRose in Springfield, Lenny Tristano in New York, Manhattan School of Music and Juilliard Conservatory; numerous appearances and recordings with bands, as featured performer and with own groups Clark Terry Big Bad Band (co-founder), The European Rhythm Machine (his European group 1968–73), The Phil Woods Quartet 1974–83, The Phil Woods Quintet (leader) 1984–, Phil Woods' Little Big Band (leader); featured on soundtrack scores of films The Hustler, Blow-Up, Twelve Angry Men, Boy in a Tree, It's My Turn; recipient of 4 Grammy Awards; Hon. LL.D. (East Stroudsberg Univ.) 1994; Officier, Ordre des Arts et des Lettres (France); elected to American Jazz Hall of Fame 1994. *Compositions include:* Three Improvisations (saxophone quartet), Sonata for Alto and Piano (Four Moods), Rights of Swing, The Sun Suite, I Remember, The Deer Head Suite. *Leisure interests:* computer games, reading, public television, movies. *Address:* P.O. Box 278, Delaware Water Gap, PA 18327, U.S.A. *Telephone:* (717)-421-3145.

WOODS, Tiger (Eldrick); American golfer; b. 30 Dec. 1975, Cypress, Calif.; s. of Lieut.-Col. Earl Woods and Kultida Woods; ed. Stanford Univ.; winner Int. Jr. World Championship 1984–91, Nat. Youth Classic 1990, U.S. Jr. Amateur Championship 1991 (youngest winner), 1992, 1993, U.S. Amateur Championships 1994 (youngest winner), 1995, 1996, Las Vegas Invitational competition 1996, Walt Disney Classic 1996, Honda Asian Classic 1997, Mercedes Championships 1997, U.S. Masters 1997 (youngest winner, broke records for lowest score and greatest margin of victory), Bell South Classic 1998; winner of numerous other titles; mem. U.S. team World Amateur Team Championship 1994, U.S. Walker Cup team 1995 awards include Golf World Player of the Year 1992, Man of the Year 1994, Sports Illustrated Sportsman of the Year 1996. *Address:* PGA, P.O. Box 109601, 100 Avenue of the Champions, Palm Beach Gardens, FL 33418, U.S.A.

WOODWARD, C(omer) Vann, PH.D.; American historian; b. 13 Nov. 1908, Vanndale, Ark.; s. of Hugh Allison Woodward and Bess Vann Woodward; m. Glenn MacLeod 1937 (deceased); one s. (deceased); ed. Emory Univ., Columbia Univ. and Univ. of N. Carolina; Asst. Prof. Univ. of Fla. 1937–39, Univ. of Va. 1939–40; Assoc. Prof. Scripps Coll., Claremont Colls. 1940–43; Lieut. U.S.N.R. 1943–46; Prof. Johns Hopkins Univ. 1947–61; Sterling Prof. of History, Yale Univ. 1962–77, Prof. Emer. 1977–; Pres. American Historical Assn. 1968–69, Org. of American Historians 1968–69, Southern Historical Assn. 1952–53; mem. American Philosophical Soc., American Acad. of Arts and Letters, American Acad. of Arts and Sciences (Vice-Pres. 1987–88); Hon. LL.D. (Mich.) 1971, Hon. L.H.D. (Columbia) 1972, (Northwestern) 1977, (Brandeis) 1983, Hon. D.Litt. (Princeton) 1971, Hon. Litt.D. (Cambridge) 1975; Bancroft Prize for History 1952, Writing Award, American Acad. of Arts and Letters 1953, Pulitzer Prize for History 1982, Talcott Parsons Prize, American Acad. of Arts and Sciences, Gold Medal for History, American Acad. of Arts and Letters. *Publications:* Tom Watson: Agrarian Rebel 1938, The Battle for Leyte Gulf 1947, Reunion and Reaction 1951, Origins of the New South 1951, The Strange Career of Jim Crow 1955, The Burden of Southern History 1960, American Counterpoint 1971, Thinking Back: The Perils of Writing History 1986, The Future of the Past 1989, The Old World's New World 1991; Ed.: The Comparative Approach to American History 1968, Responses of the President to Charges of Misconduct 1973, Mary Chesnut's Civil War 1981, The Private Mary Chesnut (co-ed.) 1984, Oxford History of the United States. *Address:* 83 Rogers Road, Hamden, CT 06517, U.S.A. *Telephone:* (203) 624-4534.

WOODWARD, Edward, O.B.E.; British actor and singer; b. 1 June 1930, Croydon, Surrey; s. of Edward Oliver Woodward and Violet Edith Woodward; m. 1st Venetia Mary Collett 1952; two s. one d.; m. 2nd Michele Dotrice 1987; one d.; ed. Kingston Coll. and Royal Acad. of Dramatic Art; stage debut Castle Theatre, Farnham 1946; in repertory cos. in England and Scotland; London debut, Where There's a Will, Garrick Theatre 1955. *Other stage appearances include:* Mercutio in Romeo and Juliet, Laertes in Hamlet, Stratford 1958, Rattle of a Simple Man, Garrick 1962, Two Cities (musical) 1968, Cyrano in Cyrano de Bergerac, Flamineo in The White Devil, Nat. Theatre Co. 1971, The Wolf, Apollo 1973, Male of the Species, Piccadilly 1975, On Approval, Theatre Royal Haymarket 1976, The Dark Horse, Comedy 1978, Beggar's Opera (also dir.) 1980, The Assassin 1982, Richard III 1982, The Dead Secret 1992; three productions, New York. *Films include:* Becket 1966, The File on the Golden Goose 1968, Hunted 1973, Sitting Target, Young Winston, The Wicker Man 1974, Stand Up Virgin Soldiers 1977, Breaker Morant 1980, The Appointment 1981, Comeback, Merlin and the Sword 1982, Champions 1983, A Christmas Carol, King David 1984, Uncle Tom's Cabin 1989, Mister Johnson 1990, Deadly Advice 1993, A Christmas Reunion 1994, Gulliver's Travels 1995; over 2000 TV productions; title role in TV serials Callan 1966–71, The Equalizer 1985–89, Over My Dead Body 1990, In Suspicious Circumstances (series) 1991–94, In My Defence 1991, America At Risk (series) 1991–92, Harrison (series, U.S.A.) 1993–95, Common as Muck (BBC TV series) 1994, The Woodward File (series) 1995–96, Gulliver's Travels (mini-series) 1995–96; 12 LP records as singer and three of poetry and 14 talking book recordings; numerous int. and nat. acting awards, including Golden Globe Award, Emmy Award,

Variety Award (Best Musical Performance). *Leisure interests:* boating, geology. *Address:* c/o ICM Ltd., Oxford House, 76 Oxford Street, London, W1N 0AX, England. *Telephone:* 0171-636 6565. *Fax:* 0171-636 0101.

WOODWARD, Joanne Gignilliat; American actress; b. 27 Feb. 1930, Thomasville, Ga.; d. of Wade Woodward and Elinor Trimmier; m. Paul Newman (q.v.) 1958; three d.; ed. Louisiana State Univ.; numerous awards including Foreign Press Award for Best Actress 1957, Acad. Award 1957, Nat. Bd. Review Award 1957, Best Actress Award, Soc. of Film and TV Arts 1974; Franklin D. Roosevelt Four Freedoms Medal 1991, Kennedy Center Honor 1992. *Films include:* Count Three and Pray 1955, A Kiss Before Dying 1956, The Three Faces of Eve 1957, The Long Hot Summer 1958, Rally Round the Flag Boys 1958, The Sound and the Fury 1959, The Fugitive Kind 1959, From the Terrace 1960, Paris Blues 1961, The Stripper 1963, A New Kind of Love 1963, Signpost to Murder 1964, A Big Hand for the Little Lady 1966, A Fine Madness 1966, Rachel Rachel 1968, Winning 1969, W.U.S.A. 1970, They Might Be Giants 1971, The Effects of Gamma Rays on Man-in-the-Moon Marigolds 1972, The Death of a Snow Queen 1973, Summer Wishes, Winter Dreams 1973, The Drowning Pool 1975, The End 1978, The Shadow Box 1980, Candida (Play) 1981, Harry and Son 1984, The Glass Menagerie 1987, Mr and Mrs Bridge 1990, Philadelphia 1993. *TV includes:* All the Way Home, See How She Runs 1978, Streets of L.A. 1979, Crisis at Central High 1981, Do You Remember Love? 1985, Blind Spot 1993, Breathing Lessons 1994. *Address:* ICM, 40 W. 57th Street, New York, NY 10019, U.S.A.

WOODWARD, Adm. Sir John Forster, G.B.E., K.C.B.; British naval officer (retd.); b. 1 May 1932, Marazion, Cornwall; s. of late Tom Woodward and Mabel B. M. Woodward; m. Charlotte M. McMurtrie 1960; one s. one d.; ed. Britannia Royal Naval Coll., Dartmouth; Commanding Officer, H.M.S. Tireless 1961–62, H.M.S. Grampus 1964–65; Exec. Officer, H.M.S. Valiant 1965–67; Commdg. Officer, H.M.S. Warspite 1969–71; at Royal Coll. of Defence Studies, then in Directorate of Naval Plans, Ministry of Defence; Commdg. Officer, H.M.S. Sheffield 1976–78; Dir. of Naval Plans, Ministry of Defence 1978–81; Flag Officer, First Flotilla 1981–83; commanded British naval task force during Falkland Islands campaign 1982; Flag Officer, Submarines, and Commdr. Submarines, Eastern Atlantic, NATO May 1983–84; Deputy Chief of Defence Staff (Commitments) 1985–87; C.-in-C. Naval Home Command 1987–89, rank of Adm.; Flag Aide-de-Camp to H.M. the Queen 1987–89; Man. consultant; Yachtmaster Ocean (Royal Yachting Asscn.). *Publications:* Strategy by Matrix 1980, One Hundred Days (autobiog.) 1992. *Leisure interests:* sailing, philately, skiing, desktop computers. *Address:* c/o The Naval Secretary, Victory Building, H.M. Naval Base, Portsmouth, Hants, PO1 3LS, England.

WOODWARD, Kirsten; British couturier; b. 15 Nov. 1959, London; d. of Prof. Woodward and J. B. Woodward; ed. London Coll. of Fashion; stall at Hyper Hyper while still a student 1983; Designer Karl Lagerfeld 1984–; f. Kirsten Woodward Hats 1985–; also designed for Lanvin, Victor Edelstein, Betty Jackson, Alistair Blair, The Emanuels, Belleville Sassoon, Katharine Hammnet. *Leisure interests:* boats, horses, geography and ancient history, anthropology, writing.

WOODWARD, Robert Upshur, B.A.; American journalist; b. 26 March 1943, Geneva, Ill.; s. of Alfred Woodward and Jane Upshur; m. Elsa Walsh 1989; two c.; ed. Yale Univ.; reporter, Montgomery Co. (Md.) Sentinel 1970–71; reporter, Washington Post 1971–78, Metropolitan Ed. 1979–81, Asst. Man. Ed. 1981–. *Publications:* All the President's Men (with Carl Bernstein) 1974, The Final Days 1976, The Brethren (with Scott Armstrong) 1979, Wired 1984, Veil: The Secret Wars of the CIA 1987, The Commanders 1991, The Man Who Would Be President (with D.S. Broder) 1992, The Agenda: Inside the Clinton White House 1994, The Choice 1996. *Address:* Washington Post Co., 1150 15th Street, N.W., Washington, DC 20071, U.S.A.

WOODWARD, Roger Robert, O.B.E., A.C.; Australian pianist, conductor and composer; b. 20 Dec. 1942, Sydney; s. of Francis W. and Gladys A. Woodward; one s. one d.; ed. Conservatorium of Music, Sydney and PWSH, Warsaw; début at Royal Festival Hall, London 1970; subsequently appeared with the five London orchestras; has performed throughout Eastern and Western Europe, Japan and the U.S.A.; has appeared at int. festivals and with the major orchestras throughout world; extensive repertoire and is noted for interpretation of Chopin, Beethoven, Bach and Twentieth Century Music; Artistic Dir. Nat. Chamber Orchestra for Contemporary Music in Australia 'Alpha Centaure' 1989 and festivals in London; performs each season at leading int. festivals works by contemporary composers; Fellow Chopin Inst., Warsaw; Kt. (Breffini). *Leisure interests:* cooking, chess, swimming, gardening, painting, design. *Address:* LH Productions, 2/37 Hendy Avenue, Coogee, N.S.W. 2034, Australia.

WOOLARD, Edgar Smith, Jr., B.SC.; American business executive; b. 15 April 1934, Washington, N.C.; s. of Edgar Smith and Mamie (née Boone) Woolard; m. Peggy Harrell 1956; two d.; ed. North Carolina State Univ.; fmr. Lieut., U.S. Army; industrial engineer, Du Pont at Kinston, N.C. 1957–59, various supervisory and managerial posts 1959–75, Man. Dir. textile marketing div. 1975–76, Man. corp. plans dept. 1976–77, Gen. Dir. products and planning div. 1977–78, Gen. Man. textile fibers, Wilmington, Del. 1978–81, Vice-Pres. textile fibers 1981–83, Exec. Vice-Pres. 1983–85, Vice-Chair. 1985–87, Pres. and C.O.O. 1987–89, Chair., C.E.O. 1989–96, Chair. 1996–98; mem. Bd. of Dirs. Citicorp, New York, Council for Aid to Educ., New York, IBM, New York, Apple Computer Inc., Cupertino, Calif., Jt. Council on Econ. Educ., New York, N.C. Textile Foundation, Raleigh, Seagram Co., Canada; Int. Palladium Medal Soc. Chimie Industrielle (American Section) 1995. *Address:* c/o Du Pont, 1007 Market Street, Wilmington, DE 19801, U.S.A.

WOOLCOTT, Richard, A.C., A.O., B.A.; Australian fmr. diplomatist, consultant and company director; b. 11 June 1927, Sydney; s. of Dr. and Mrs. A. R. Woolcott; m. Birgit Christensen 1952; two s. one d.; ed. Frankston High School, Geelong Grammar School, Univ. of Melbourne and London Univ. School of Slavonic and E. European Studies; joined Australian Foreign Service 1951; served in Australian missions in London, Moscow (twice), S. Africa, Malaya, Singapore and Ghana; attended UN Gen. Ass. 1962; Acting Commr. to Singapore 1963–64; High Commr. to Ghana 1967–70; accompanied Prime Ministers Menzies 1965, Holt 1966, McMahon 1971, 1972, Whitlam 1973, 1974 and Hawke 1988–91 on visits to Asia, Europe, the Americas and the Pacific; Adviser at Commonwealth Heads of Govt. Confs. London 1965, Ottawa 1973, Kuala Lumpur 1989; Pacific Forum 1972, 1973, 1988; Australia-Japan Ministerial Cttee. 1972, 1973, 1988, 1989; Head, S. Asia Div., Dept. of Foreign Affairs 1973; Deputy Sec. Dept. of Foreign Affairs 1974; Amb. to Indonesia 1975–78, to Philippines 1978–82; Perm. Rep. to UN 1982–88; Sec. of Dept. of Foreign Affairs and Trade 1988–92; Prime Minister's Special Envoy to develop Asia Pacific Econ. Co-operation 1989; Australian Rep. on UN Security Council 1985–86; rep. of Australia at Non-aligned Summit meeting, Harare 1986; ASEAN Post-Minsterial Conf. 1989, 1990, 1991; Alt. Australian Gov., inaugural EBRD meeting 1991; Chair. Australia Indonesia Inst. 1992–98, Official Establishments Trust 1992–, Nat. Cttee. on Population and Devt. 1993–95; mem. Int. council of The Asia Soc.; Vice-Pres. Multiple Sclerosis Soc. of Australia 1995–; Dir. Australasia Centre, Asia Soc. 1997–; Dir. or consultant several firms; Life Fellow Trinity Coll., Melbourne Univ. 1995. *Publications:* Australian Foreign Policy 1973; numerous articles, including special features for The Australian, articles for Int. Herald Tribune, Time. *Address:* 19 Talbot Street, Forrest, Canberra, A.C.T. 2603, Australia. *Telephone:* (2) 6295-3206.

WOOLDRIDGE, Dean E., M.S., PH.D.; American engineer; b. May 1913, Chickasha, Okla.; s. of Auttie Noonan Wooldridge and Irene Amanda (née Kerr) Wooldridge; m. M. Helene Detweiler 1936; two s. one d.; ed. Univ. of Okla. and Calif. Inst. of Tech.; mem. tech. staff, Bell Telephone Labs. 1936–46; Dir. of Electronic Research and Devt., Hughes Aircraft Co. 1946, subsequently Vice-Pres. for Research and Devt.; Co-founder & Pres. Ramo-Wooldridge Corpn. 1953–58, Pres. Thompson Ramo Wooldridge Inc. (TRW Inc.) 1958–62, Dir. until 1969; Research Assoc. in Eng., Calif. Inst. of Tech. 1962–79; Chair. Nat. Inst. of Health Study Cttee. 1964, 1965; Fellow, American Acad. of Arts and Sciences, American Physical Soc., A.A.A.S., Inst. of Electrical and Electronic Engineers, A.I.A.A.; mem. N.A.S., Nat. Acad. of Eng.; Citation of Honor, Air Force Asscn.; E. E. Hackett Award 1955; Distinguished Service Citation, Univ. of Okla. 1960, A.A.A.S.—Westinghouse Award for Science Writing, Distinguished Alumni Award, Calif. Inst. of Tech. 1983. *Publications:* The Machinery of the Brain 1963, The Machinery of Life 1966, Mechanical Man: The Physical Basis of Intelligent Life 1968, Sensory Processing in the Brain 1979; several articles in journals and magazines. *Address:* 4545 Via Esperanza, Santa Barbara, CA 93110, U.S.A.

WOOLDRIDGE, Michael Richard Lewis, M.B., B.SC., M.B.A.; Australian politician; b. 7 Nov. 1956; m. Michele Marion Colman 1988; two s.; ed. Scotch Coll., Melbourne, Univ. of Melbourne, Monash Univ.; Resident Medical Staff (Surgical), Alfred Hosp. 1982–85; M.P. (Liberal Party) for Chisholm, Vic. 1987–; pvt. practice 1985–87; Shadow Minister Assisting Leader on Youth Affairs and Shadow Minister for Aboriginal Affairs 1990–92; Shadow Minister for Aboriginal and Torres Strait Islander Affairs 1992–93; Deputy Leader of the Opposition, Shadow Minister for Educ., Employment and Training, Chair. Family and Human Resources Man. Group 1993–94, Shadow Minister for Community Services, Sr. Citizens and Aged Care 1994–95, for Health and Human Services 1995–96; Minister for Health and Family Services March 1996–. *Leisure interests:* royal tennis, skiing, reading. *Address:* Parliament House, Canberra, A.C.T. 2600; 523-525 Station Street, Box Hill, Vic. 3128, Australia.

WOOLF, Baron (Life Peer) cr. 1992, of Barnes in the London Borough of Richmond; **Rt. Hon. Harry Kenneth Woolf,** LL.B.; British judge; b. 2 May 1933, Newcastle upon Tyne; s. of Alexander Woolf and Leah Woolf; m. Marguerite Sassoon 1961; three s.; ed. Fettes Coll., Univ. Coll. London; called to Bar, Inner Temple 1954; Counsel for Inland Revenue 1973–74; First Treasury Jr. Counsel, Common Law 1974–79; Judge, High Court, Queen's Bench Div. 1979–86; Presiding Judge, S.E. Circuit 1981–84; Lord Justice of Appeal 1986–92; Lord of Appeal in Ordinary 1992–96; Master of the Rolls 1996–; Chair. Bd. of Man. Inst. of Advanced Legal Studies 1986–94; Chair. Magna Carta Trust 1996, Advisory Council on Public Records 1996–, Council of Civil Justice, Rules Cttee.; Pro Chancellor London Univ. 1994–; Pres. Cen. Council Jewish Social Services 1987–; Fellow Univ. Coll. London; Hon. Fellow Leeds Metropolitan Univ.; Visitor Nuffield Coll., Oxford 1996, Univ. Coll., London 1996–; Hon. LL.D. (Buckingham, Bristol, London, Manchester Metropolitan). *Publications:* Protection of the Public—A New Challenge 1990, The Declaratory Judgment (Zamir & Woolf) 1992, Judicial Review of Administrative Action (De Smith, Woolf & Jowell) (5th edn.) 1995; reports: Prisons in England and Wales 1991, Access to Justice (Interim)

1995, (Final) 1996. *Address:* Royal Courts of Justice, Strand, London, WC2A 2LL, England. *Telephone:* 0171-936 6002. *Fax:* 0171-936 7475.

WOOLFORD, Harry Russell Halkerston, O.B.E.; British art gallery director; b. 23 May 1905; s. of H. Woolford; m. Nancy Philip 1932; one d.; ed. Edinburgh Coll. of Art; studied art in London, Paris and Italy; Chief, now Consultant Restorer, Nat. Gallery of Scotland; Fellow Museums Asscn., Inst. of Conservation, Int. Inst. for Conservation of Historic and Artistic works; Hon. mem. Asscn. of British Picture Restorers; Hon. M.A. (Dundee Univ.) 1976. *Address:* 7A Barntongate Avenue, Barnton, Edinburgh, EH4 8BD, Scotland. *Telephone:* (0131) 339 6861.

WOOLFSON, Michael Mark, M.A., PH.D. D.SC., F.R.A.S., C.PHYS., F.INST.P., F.R.S.; British professor of physics; b. 9 Jan. 1927, London; s. of Maurice Woolfson and Rose (née Solomons) Woolfson; m. Margaret Frohlich 1951; two s. one d.; ed. Jesus Coll., Oxford, UMIST; Nat. Service, Royal Engineers 1947–49; Research Asst., Cavendish Lab., Cambridge 1952–54; ICI Fellow Univ. of Cambridge 1954–55; lecturer, Faculty of Tech. Univ. of Manchester 1955–61, Reader 1961–65; Prof. of Theoretical Physics, Univ. of York 1965–94, Prof. Emer. 1994–; Chair. Royal Soc. Planetary Sciences Subcttee. 1979–83, British Crystallographic Asscn. 1985–90, British Nat. Cttee. for Crystallography 1985–90; Pres. Yorks. Philosophical Soc. 1985–; Hughes Medal, Royal Soc. 1986, Patterson Award, American Crystallographic Asscn. 1990, Gregori Aminoff Medal and Prize, Royal Swedish Acad. of Sciences 1992, Dorothy Hodgkin Prize, British Crystallographic Asscn. 1997. *Publications:* Direct Methods in Crystallography 1960, The Origin of the Solar System, The Capture Theory 1989, Physical and Non-physical Methods of Solving Crystal Structures 1995, An Introduction to X-ray Crystallography 1997, An Introduction to Computer Simulation 1999. *Leisure interest:* wine-making. *Address:* Department of Physics, University of York, York, YO1 5DD (Office); 24 Sandmoor Green, Leeds, LS17 7SB, England (Home). *Telephone:* (01904) 432230 (Office); (0113) 266 2166 (Home). *Fax:* (01904) 432214.

WOOLLCOMBE, Rt. Rev. Kenneth John, M.A., S.T.D.; British ecclesiastic; b. 2 Jan. 1924, Sutton, Surrey; s. of Rev. Edward P. Woollcombe O.B.E., and Elsie O. Wood; m. 1st Gwendoline R. V. Hodges 1950 (died 1976); m. 2nd Juliet Dearmer 1980; four d.; ed. Haileybury Coll., Technical Coll., Wednesbury, St. John's Coll., Oxford and Westcott House, Cambridge; Sub-Lieut., R.N.V.R. 1945–46; Curate, Grimsby Parish Church 1951–53; Fellow, Chaplain and Tutor, St. John's Coll., Oxford 1953–60; Prof. of Dogmatic Theology, Gen. Theological Seminary, New York 1960–63, Prin. of Episcopal Theological Coll., Edin. and Canon of St. Mary's Cathedral, Edin. 1963–71; Bishop of Oxford 1971–78; Asst. Bishop of London 1978–81, Diocese of Worcester 1989–; Canon Residentiary, St. Paul's Cathedral 1981–89, Precentor 1982–89; Chair. Soc. for Promotion of Christian Knowledge (S.P.C.K.) 1973–79; Chair. Churches' Council for Covenanting 1978–82; Chair. Cttee. for Roman Catholic Relations 1985–88; mem. Court of Ecclesiastical Causes Reserved 1984–89; Hon. Fellow St. John's Coll., Oxford 1971; Hon. S.T.D. (Univ. of the South, Sewanee, Tennessee) 1963; Hon. D.D. (Hartford, Conn.) 1975. *Publications:* Essays on Typology (joint author) 1957, and contributions to other theological publications. *Leisure interests:* reading, music. *Address:* 19 Ashdale Avenue, Pershore, Worcs., WR10 1PL, England.

WOOLLEY, Kenneth Frank, A.M., B.ARCH., L.F.R.A.I.A.; Australian architect; b. 29 May 1933, Sydney; s. of Frank and Doris May (Mudear) Woolley; m. 1st Cynthia Stuart (divorced 1979); m. 2nd Virginia Braden 1980; two s. one d.; ed. Sydney Boys' High School, Univ. of Sydney; Design Architect, Govt. Architect's Office, Sydney 1955–56, 1957–63; Asst. Architect, Chamberlin, Powell and Bon, London 1956–57; Partner, Ancher, Mortlock, Murray & Woolley, Sydney 1964–69, Dir. 1969–75; Dir. Ancher, Mortlock & Woolley Pty. Ltd., Sydney 1975–; mem. Quality Review Cttee. Darling Harbour Redevt. Authority 1985; Visiting Prof., Univ. of N.S.W. School of Architecture 1983; Visiting Tutor and Critic, Visiting Prof., Univ. of Sydney, Univ. of N.S.W., N.S.W. Inst. of Tech., Sydney; mem. N.S.W. Bd. of Architects 1960–72, N.S.W. Bldg. Regulations Advisory Cttee. 1960–74, N.S.W. Bd. of Architectural Educ. 1969–72, Royal Australian Inst. of Architects Aboriginal Housing Panel 1972–76; Life F.R.A.I.A. 1976; Sulman Award 1962, Bronze Medal 1962, Wilkinson Award 1962, 1968, 1982, 1987, Blacket Award 1964, 1967, 1969, 1987, Civic Design Award 1983, Gold Medal, Royal Australian Inst. of Architects 1993, numerous other architectural awards. *Major works include:* Australian Embassy, Bangkok, ABC Radio Bldg., Sydney, Hyatt Hotel, Campbell's Cove, Sydney, Control Tower, Sydney Airport, Sydney Town Hall renovations, The Olympics and RAS Exhbn. Halls and Hockey Stadium, new offices and city sq., three student union bldgs., Univs. in N.S.W., numerous urban housing devts., radio stations, Vanuatu, Solomon Islands, over 4,000 production houses, State Govt. offices, Sydney, Fisher Library, Sydney Univ. *Publications:* numerous papers and articles in architectural journals. *Leisure interests:* golf, sailing, music, drawing. *Address:* LV. 5, 790 George Street, Sydney, N.S.W. 2000, Australia. *Telephone:* 9211 4466 (Office).

WOOLSEY, R. James, LL.D.; American public servant; b. 1941, Tulsa, Okla.; m. Suzanne Haley; three s.; ed. Stanford and Yale Univs.; staff mem. Nat. Security Council 1968–70; Counsel to Senate Armed Services Cttee. 1970–73; Under-Sec. of the Navy 1977–79; negotiator, Conventional Armed Forces in Europe Treaty; del.-at-large to U.S.-Soviet Strategic Arms Reduction Talks and space talks 1983–86; Amb. and U.S. Rep. to negotiations on CFE Treaty 1989–91; Chair. CIA task force on future of satellite spying 1991; Dir. of CIA 1993–95; Partner Shea & Gardner 1991–93, 1995–; Dir. USF&G 1995–, Sun Healthcare Group Inc. 1995–, Yurie Systems Corp. 1996–; Rhodes Scholar 1965. *Address:* Shea & Gardner, 1800 Massachusetts Avenue, N.W., Washington, D.C. 20036, U.S.A.

WOOSNAM, Ian Harold, M.B.E.; British golfer; b. 2 March 1958; s. of Harold Woosnam and Joan Woosnam; m. Glendryth Pugh 1983; two d. one s.; ed. St. Martin's Modern School; professional golfer 1976–; tournament victories: News of the World under-23 Matchplay 1979, Cacharel under-25 Championship 1982, Swiss Open 1982, Silk Cut Masters 1983, Scandinavian Enterprise Open 1984, Zambian Open 1985, Lawrence Batley TPC 1986, 555 Kenya Open 1986, Hong Kong Open 1987, Jersey Open 1987, Cepsa Madrid Open 1987, Bell's Scottish Open 1987, 1990, Lancome Trophy 1987, Suntory World Match-Play Championship 1987, 1990, Volvo PGA Championship 1988, 1997, Carrolls Irish Open 1988, 1989, Panasonic Euro Open 1988, Am Express Mediterranean Open 1990, Torras Monte Carlo Open 1990, Epson Grand Prix 1990, U.S. Masters 1991, USF+G Classic 1991, Fujitsu Mediterranean Open, Torras Monte Carlo Open 1991, European Monte Carlo Open 1992, Lancôme Trophy 1993, Murphy's English Open 1993, British Masters 1994, Cannes Open 1994, Heineken Classic 1996, Scottish Open 1996, Volvo German Open 1996, Johnnie Walker Classic 1996; team events: Ryder Cup 1983–97, Dunhill Cup 1985, 1986, 1988, 1989, 1990, 1991, 1993, 1995, World Cup 1980, 1982, 1983, 1984, 1985, 1987, 1990, 1991, 1992, 1993, 1994, 1996, 1997; finished top Order of Merit 1987, 1990; ranked 1, Sony world rankings 1991; World Cup Individual, PGA Grand Slam 1991. *Publication:* Ian Woosnam's Golf Masterpieces (with Peter Grosvenor) 1991. *Leisure interests:* snooker, water skiing, sports. *Address:* c/o IMG, Pier House, Strand on the Green, London, W4 3NN, England.

WORCESTER, Robert Milton, B.SC., F.R.S.A.; American opinion researcher; b. 21 Dec. 1933, Kansas City; s. of late C. M. and Violet Worcester; m. 1st Joann Ransdell 1958; m. 2nd Margaret Noel Smallbone 1982; two s.; ed. Univ. of Kansas; Consultant with McKinsey & Co. 1962–65; Controller and Asst. to Chair. Opinion Research Corpn. 1965–68; Man. Dir. Market & Opinion Research Int. Ltd. (MORI) 1969–94, Chair. 1973–; Visiting Prof. of Journalism, City Univ., London; Visiting Prof. of Govt., L.S.E.; Visiting Prof. of Marketing, Univ. of Strathclyde 1996–; Consultant to The Times, The Economist; Vice-Pres. Int. Soc. Science Council UNESCO 1989–94; Trustee WorldWide Fund for Nature (WWF-U.K.) 1988–94, Natural History Museum Devt. Trust 1989–94; Chair. Pilgrims Soc.; Vice-Pres. European Atlantic Group, UNA (London), Fulbright Comm.; Adviser, Prince of Wales's Business Leaders Forum; Trustee Magna Carta; Fellow Market Research Soc. 1997; mem. Court of Govs., L.S.E.; Vice-Pres. Royal Soc. for Nature Conservation; Co-Ed. Int. Journal of Public Opinion Research; Hon. D.Sc. (Buckingham) 1998. *Publications:* Political Communications (with Martin Harrop) 1982, Political Opinion Polling: An International Review 1983, Consumer Market Research Handbook (3rd. edn., Ed. with John Downham) 1986, Private Opinions, Public Polls (with Lesley Watkins) 1986, We British (with Eric Jacobs) 1990, British Public Opinion: History and Methodology of Political Opinion Polling in Great Britain 1991, Dynamics of Societal Learning about Global Environmental Change (with Samuel H. Barnes) 1991, Typically British (with Eric Jacobs) 1992. *Leisure interest:* choral music. *Address:* 32 Old Queen Street, London, SW1H 9HP, England. *Telephone:* 0171-222 0232. *Fax:* 0171-222 1653.

WORMS, Gérard Etienne; French company director; b. 1 Aug. 1936, Paris; s. of André Worms and Thérèse Dreyfus; m. Michèle Rousseau 1960; one s. one d.; ed. Lycées Carnot, Saint-Louis, and Ecole Nat. Supérieure des Mines, Paris; Engineer, Org. commune des régions sahariennes 1960–62; Head of Dept., Délégation à l'Aménagement du Territoire et à l'Action Régionale 1963–67; Tech. Adviser, Office of Olivier Guichard (Minister of Industry, later of Planning) 1967–69, Office of Jacques Chaban-Delmas (Prime Minister) 1969–71; Asst. Man. Dir., Librairie Hachette 1972–75, Man. Dir. 1975–81, Dir. 1978–81; Prof., Ecole des Hautes Etudes Commerciales 1962–69, Supervisor of complementary courses, Faculty of Letters and Human Sciences, Paris 1963–69; Prof. Ecole Polytechnique 1974–; Vice-Pres. Syndicat nat. de l'édition 1974–81; Exec. Vice-Pres. Rhône-Poulenc S.A. 1981–83; Chair. and C.E.O. Compagnie de Suez 1990–95; Pres. Banque Indosuez 1994–95; Pres. Bd. of Sleeping Partners Rothschild, Compagnie Banque Paris 1995–, Centre for research into economic expansion and business devt. 1996–, Supervisory Council for health information systems 1997–, History channel 1997–; mem. Bd. Olivetti 1996–; Chevalier, Ordre nat. du Mérite, Chevalier, Ordre du Mérite maritime, Chevalier, Légion d'honneur. *Publications:* Les méthodes modernes de l'économie appliquée 1965; various articles on economic methods in specialized journals. *Address:* Rothschild et Cie, 17 avenue Matignon, 75008 Paris (Office); 61 bis avenue de la Motte Picquet, 75015 Paris, France (Home). *Telephone:* 47-83-99-43 (Home).

WORNER, Howard Knox, C.B.E., D.SC., F.A.A., F.T.S., F.R.A.C.I., F.I.M., F.I.M.M., F.A.I.E., M.A.I.M.E.; Australian metallurgist and scientific consultant; b. 3 Aug. 1913; s. of late John Worner and Ida Worner; m. Rilda B. Muller 1937; two s. (one deceased) one d.; ed. Bendigo School of Mines and Univ. of Melbourne; Lecturer in Metallography, Univ. of Melbourne 1935–38; Research Fellow, Nat. Health and Medical Research Council of Australia 1939–46; Consultant, Defence Forces, on Dental and Surgical Materials 1940–46; tropical scientific service, Australian army 1944–45; Prof. of Metallurgy, Univ. of Melbourne

1947–55, Dean, Faculty of Eng. 1953–55; Dir. of Research, The Broken Hill Pty. Co. Ltd. 1956–62; int. consultant 1963; Dir. of New Process Devt., CRA Ltd. 1964–75; Chair. Nat. Energy Advisory Cttee. 1976–77; Chair. Victoria Brown Coal Cttee. (later Council) and mem. Nat. Energy Research and Devt. Cttee. 1976–81; scientific consultant 1981–; Hon. Sec. Australian Acad. of Tech. Sciences 1975–86; Hon. Prof., Univ. of Wollongong 1987–, Dir. Microwave Applications Research Centre 1987–88, Dir. Microwave and Materials Inst. 1989–, Research Dir. Resources Div., ITC Ltd. (within Univ.) 1991–; Hon. Fellow Inst. Engineers Australia 1988, Australasian Inst. of Mining and Metallurgy 1989, Australian Acad. of Tech. Sciences and Eng. 1993, Australian Inst. of Eng. 1993, Australian Inst. of Energy 1994; Hon. D.Sc. (Newcastle, Wollongong, La Trobe); Hon. D.Eng. (Melbourne); nine medals from professional socs. and univs. and numerous other awards. *Publications:* 200 scientific papers and monographs. *Leisure interests:* mineral collecting, oil painting. *Address:* North Bay, 16/10 Smith Street, Wollongong, N.S.W. 2500, Australia. *Telephone:* (02) 42268805 (Office); (02) 42273578 (Home).

WORRALL, Denis John, PH.D.; South African business executive, politician and lawyer; b. 29 May 1935, Benoni; s. of Cecil John Worrall and Hazel Worrall; m. Anita Denise Ianco 1965; three s.; ed. Univ. of Cape Town, Univ. of S.A. and Cornell Univ., U.S.A.; taught political science, Cornell Univ., Univ. of Calif. at Los Angeles, Univ. of Natal, Univ. of S.A. and Univ. of Witwatersrand; Cornell Research Fellow, Univ. of Ibadan, Nigeria 1962–63; f. and Ed. New Nation 1967–74; Research Prof. and Dir. Inst. for Social and Econ. Research, Rhodes Univ. –1974; Senator for Cape 1974–77; Amb. to Australia 1983–84, to U.K. 1984–87; Advocate, Supreme Court of S.A.; M.P. for Cape Town-Gardens 1977–83; independent cand. for Helderberg in 1987 Election; mem. Pres's. Council 1980–83; f. Ind. Movt. 1988; Leader Ind. Party 1988–89; co-founder Democratic Party 1989; M.P. for Berea, Durban 1989–94; Chair. Omega Investment Research Ltd., Dir. and Vice-Chair. Int. Bank of S. Africa; Exec.-Chair. Tridelta Magnet Technique Holdings Ltd. *Publications:* South Africa: Government and Politics; numerous articles. *Leisure interests:* reading, tennis. *Address:* P.O. Box 5455, Cape Town 8000; 23 Bonair Road, Rondebosch, Cape, South Africa. *Telephone:* 021-689 7881 (Office); 021-685 7502 (Home).

WORSTHORNE, Sir Peregrine Gerard, Kt., M.A.; British journalist; b. 22 Dec. 1923, London; s. of Col. A. Koch de Gooreynd and the late Baroness Norman; m. 1st Claudia Bertrand de Colasse 1950 (died 1990); one d. one step-s.; m. 2nd Lady Lucinda Lambton 1991; ed. Stowe School, Peterhouse, Cambridge and Magdalen Coll., Oxford; editorial staff, Glasgow Herald 1946–48; editorial staff, The Times 1948–50, Washington corresp. 1950–52, Leader writer 1952–55; Leader writer, Daily Telegraph 1955–61; Assoc. Ed. Sunday Telegraph 1961–86, Ed. 1986–89, Ed. Comment Section 1989–91; Granada Television Journalist of the Year 1981, columnist The Spectator 1997–. *Publications:* The Socialist Myth 1972, Peregrinations 1980, By The Right 1987, Tricks of Memory (memoirs) 1993. *Leisure interests:* walking, tennis. *Address:* The Old Rectory, Hedgerley, Bucks., SL2 3UY, England. *Telephone:* (01753) 646167. *Fax:* (01753) 646914.

WORTH, Irene; American actress; b. 23 June 1916; ed. Univ. of Calif. at Los Angeles; Daily Mail Nat. Television Award 1953–54; British Film Acad. Award for Orders to Kill 1958; Page One Award, Newspaper Guild of New York, for Toys in the Attic 1960; American Theatre Wing "Tony" Award for Tiny Alice 1965; Evening Standard Award for Noel Coward Trilogy 1966; Whitbread Anglo-American Theatre Award 1967; Variety Club of Great Britain Award 1967; Tony Award and Jefferson Award for Sweet Bird of Youth 1975; Drama Desk Award for The Cherry Orchard 1977; Whitbread Anglo-American Award 1967; Hon. C.B.E. 1975; first appeared as Fenella in Escape Me Never, New York 1942; debut on Broadway as Cecily Hardern in The Two Mrs. Carrolls 1948; London appearances in Love Goes to Press 1946, The Play's the Thing 1947, Edward My Son 1948, Home is Tomorrow 1948, Champagne for Delilah 1949, The Cocktail Party 1950, Othello 1951, A Midsummer Night's Dream 1952, The Other Heart 1952, The Merchant of Venice 1953, A Day by the Sea 1953–54, The Queen and the Rebels 1955, Hotel Paradiso 1956, Maria Stuart 1958, The Potting Shed 1958, King Lear 1962, The Physicists 1963, The Ides of March 1963, A Song at Twilight 1966, Shadows of the Evening 1966, Come into the Garden Maud 1966, Heartbreak House 1967, Oedipus 1968, Notes on a Love Affair, Lyric Theatre, other appearances include: The Cocktail Party, New York 1950, Old Vic tour of S. Africa 1952, Shakespeare Festival, Stratford, Ont. 1953, 1959, A Life in the Sun, Edinburgh Festival 1955, Maria Stuart, New York 1957, Toys in the Attic, New York 1960, Royal Shakespeare Theatre, Stratford 1962, World tour of King Lear 1964, Tiny Alice, New York 1965, worked with Peter Brook's Int. Theatre Research Centre, Paris and Iran 1970, 1971, Hedda in Hedda Gabler, Stratford, Ont. 1970, The Seagull, Chichester Festival Theatre 1973, Ghosts, The Seagull, Hamlet, Greenwich Theatre 1974, Sweet Bird of Youth, Kennedy Center, Washington D.C., Brooklyn Acad. of Music, and Harkness Theatre, New York, Drake Theatre, Ill. 1975, Misalliance, Drake Theatre, Lake Forest, Ill. 1976, The Cherry Orchard, Lincoln Center 1977, Old Times, Ill. 1977, After the Season 1978, Happy Days, New York 1979, The Lady from Dubuque, New York 1980, L'Olimpiade, Edin. Festival 1982, The Chalk Garden, New York 1982, The Physicists, Washington 1983, The Golden Age, New York 1984, Coriolanus, Nat. Theatre 1984, The Bay at Nice, London 1986, The Mask of the Red Death, New York 1987, You Never Can Tell, London 1987–88, Coriolanus, New York 1988, Lost in Yonkers 1991, The Bay 1986, Edith Wharton 1994, A Week's Worth, 1996, The Gypsy and the Yellow Canary 1997; films include: Orders to Kill 1957, The Scapegoat 1958, King Lear, Nicholas and Alexandra 1971, Eye Witness 1980, Lost in Yonkers 1993, Piece of Cake 1997, Onegin 1998; television: Coriolanus 1984. *Address:* c/o ICM, Sam Cohn, 40 West 57th Street, 6th Floor, New York, NY 10019, U.S.A.

WORTHINGTON, Edgar Barton, C.B.E., F.L.S., F.R.G.S., PH.D.; British biologist; b. 13 Jan. 1905, London; s. of Edgar Worthington and Amy Beale; m. 1st Stella Johnson 1930 (died 1978); three d.; m. 2nd Harriett Stockton 1980; ed. Rugby School, and Gonville and Caius Coll., Cambridge; Frank Smart Student Gonville and Caius Coll. during fishing surveys of African lakes 1927–30; Balfour Student Cambridge Univ. 1930–33, Leader expedition to E. African lakes; Demonstrator in Zoology Cambridge Univ. 1933–37; Scientist for African Research Survey 1934–37; Dir. Freshwater Biological Asscn. of British Empire 1937–46; Scientific Adviser Middle East Supply Council 1943–45; Devt. Adviser, Uganda 1946; Scientific Sec. Colonial Research Council 1946–49; Seconded as Scientific Sec. E. Africa High Comm. 1947–51; Sec.-Gen. Scientific Council for Africa South of the Sahara 1951–55; Deputy Dir.-Gen. (Scientific) Nature Conservancy, London 1956–65; Scientific Dir. of Int. Biological Programme 1965–75; Hon. mem. Int. Union for Conservation of Nature 1978; Hon. mem. Linnean Soc. 1992; Gill Memorial, Royal Geographical Soc. 1931; Mungo Park Medal, Royal Scottish Geographical Soc. 1938, Avicenna Medal, UNESCO 1994; Kt. of the Golden Ark (Netherlands) 1976. *Publications:* Fishing Survey of Lakes Albert and Kioga 1929, Fisheries of Uganda 1932, Inland Waters of Africa (with Stella Worthington) 1933, Science in Africa 1938, Middle East Science 1946, Development Plan for Uganda 1947, Life in Lakes and Rivers (with T. T. Macan) 1951, Survey of Research and Scientific Services in East Africa 1952, Science in the Development of Africa 1958, Man-made Lakes: Problems and Environmental Effects (Ed.) 1973, The Evolution of IBP 1975, Arid-land Irrigation: Environmental Problems (Ed.) 1977, The Nile 1978, The Ecological Century 1983, and over 100 scientific papers and articles in journals. *Leisure interests:* nature conservation, country sports, farming. *Address:* Colin Godmans, Furner's Green, Nr. Uckfield, Sussex TN22 3RR, England. *Telephone:* (01825) 740322.

WOUK, Herman, A.B.; American writer; b. 27 May 1915, New York; s. of Abraham Isaac Wouk and Esther Levine; m. Betty Sarah Brown 1945; three s. (one deceased); ed. Columbia Univ.; radio script-writer for leading comedians, New York 1935–41; presidential consultant to U.S. Treasury 1941; served U.S.N.R. 1942–46; Visiting Prof. of English, Yeshiva Univ., N.Y. 1952–57; Trustee, Coll. of the Virgin Islands 1961–69; mem. Authors' Guild, U.S.A., Authors' League, Center for Book Nat. Advisory Bd., Library of Congress, Advisory Council, Center for U.S.–China Arts Exchange; Hon. L.H.D. (Yeshiva Univ.); Hon. D.Litt. (Clark Univ.); Hon. D.Lit. (American Int. Coll.) 1979; Hon. Ph.D. (Bar Ilan) 1990, (Hebrew Univ.) 1997; Hon. D.S.T. (Trinity Coll.) 1998; Pulitzer Prize for Fiction 1952, Columbia Univ. Medal for Excellence, Alexander Hamilton Medal, Columbia Univ. 1980, Ralph Waldo Emerson Award, Int. Platform Asscn. 1981, Univ. of Calif., Berkeley Medal 1984, Yad Vashem Kazetnik Award 1990, U.S. Navy Memorial Foundation Lone Sailor Award 1987, Washingtonian Book Award (for Inside, Outside) 1986, American Acad. of Achievement Golden Plate Award 1986, Bar Ilan Univ. Guardian of Zion Award 1998, Univ. of Calif. at San Diego UCSD Medal 1998. *Publications:* Aurora Dawn 1947, The City Boy 1948, Slattery's Hurricane 1949, The Traitor (play) 1949, The Caine Mutiny (novel) 1951, The Caine Mutiny Court-Martial (play) 1953, Marjorie Morningstar 1955, Nature's Way (play) 1957, This Is My God 1959, Youngblood Hawke (novel) 1962, Don't Stop the Carnival (novel) 1965, The Winds of War (novel) 1971, War and Remembrance 1978 (screenplay for TV serial 1986), The Winds of War (TV screenplay) 1983, Inside, Outside 1985, The Hope (novel) 1993, The Glory 1994. *Leisure interests:* Hebraic studies, travel. *Address:* c/o BSW Literary Agency, 3255 N Street, N.W., Washington, DC 20007, U.S.A.

WOUTS, Bernard François Emile; French business executive; b. 22 March 1940, Roubaix; s. of Emile Wouts and Marie Vanderbauwede; m. Annick Memet 1965; two s. one d.; ed. Lycée Saint Louis, Paris; engineer, then Deputy Dir.-Gen. and Man. Bayard Presse and Pres. subsidiaries of Bayard Presse group 1966–81; Dir.-Gen. Soc. de Publications et d'Editions Réunies 1980–85; Gen. Man. Le Monde 1985–90; Pres. Coopérative des quotidiens de Paris 1988–90; Pres.-Dir.-Gen. Le Point 1990–; Pres. SPMI (Syndicat de la Presse Magazine et d'Information) 1995–. *Publication:* La presse entre les lignes 1990. *Leisure interest:* sailing. *Address:* Le Point, 74 avenue du Maine, 75014 Paris (Office); 49 rue Alphonse Manceau, 77360 Vaires sur Marne, France (Home).

WOYTOWICZ-RUDNICKA, Stefania; Polish soprano concert singer; b. 8 Oct. 1922, Oryń; d. of Michał and Domicela Zwolakowska Woytowicz; m. 1952; ed. State Higher School of Music; concerts in Europe, U.S.A., Canada, China, Japan; tour of Singapore, Hong Kong, New Zealand, India with Australian Broadcasting Comm.; concert for Pope John Paul II 1995; contract with Deutsche Grammophon; also recorded with RCA Victor, Supraphon, Polskie Nagrania and others; participates in Vienna Festival, Edinburgh Festival, Warsaw Autumn and others; Pres. Gen. Bd., Warsaw Music Asscn.; First Prize in Prague Spring Int. Singing Competition 1954, State Prize (2nd Class) 1964, Officer's Cross, Order of Polonia Restituta 1968, Orpheus Prize, Polish Musicians' Asscn. 1967, Medal of 30th Anniversary of People's

Poland 1974, Prize of Minister of Culture and Arts (1st Class) 1975, Prize of Union of Polish Composers 1978, Polskie Nagrania Gold Record for recording of Górecki's Symphony No. 3 1997, Karol Szymanowski Foundation Award 1998. *Address:* al. Przyjaciół 3 m. 13, 00-565 Warsaw, Poland.

WRAGG, John, A.R.C.A., R.A.; British sculptor; b. 20 Oct. 1937, York; s. of Arthur Wragg and Ethel Wragg; ed. York School of Art and Royal Coll. of Art; one-man exhbns. Hanover Gallery 1963, 1966, 1970, Galerie Alexandre Iolas, Paris 1968, York Festival 1969, Bridge St. Gallery, Bath 1982, Katherine House Gallery, Marlborough 1984, Quinton Green Fine Art, London 1985, Devizes Museum Gallery 1994, 1996, England & Co. London 1994, L'Art Abstrait, London 1995, 1996, Monumental '96, Belgium 1996; participant in numerous group exhbns. in U.K., Europe and U.S.A. 1959–; work represented in several public collections including Tate Gallery, London, Contemporary Art Society, Nat. Gallery of Modern Art, Edin., Israel Museum, Wellington Art Gallery, N.Z.; Sainsbury Award 1960; winner, Sainsbury Sculpture Competition, Chelsea 1966; Arts Council of G.B. Major Award 1977; Chantrey Bequest 1981. *Leisure interests:* walking, listening to music, reading. *Address:* 6 Castle Lane, Devizes, Wilts., SN10 1HJ, England. *Telephone:* (01380) 727087.

WRAN, Neville Kenneth, A.C., Q.C.; Australian business executive and fmr. politician; b. Sydney; m. 2nd Jill Hickson 1976; one s. one d., and one s. one d. by previous marriage; ed. Fort Street Boys' High School, Sydney Univ.; solicitor, then admitted to Bar 1957; apptd. Q.C. 1968; mem. N.S.W. Legis. Council 1970–73; Deputy Leader of Opposition 1971–72; Leader of Opposition in Legis. Council 1972–73; mem. N.S.W. Legis. Assembly for Bass Hill 1973–86; Leader of Opposition 1973–76; Premier of N.S.W. and Minister for Arts (and various other ministerial portfolios) 1976–86; Nat. Pres. Australian Labor Party 1980–86; Chair. CSIRO 1986–91, Lionel Murphy Foundation 1986–, Ghana Gold Mines Ltd.; Exec. Chair. Turnbull and Partners Ltd. 1987, Wran Partners Pty. Ltd.; Sr. Adviser Goldman Sachs Australia LLC 1997–; Dir. British Aerospace Australia Pty. Ltd., Hopetown School, Abigroup Ltd. 1997–; Gov. Australia-Israel Chamber of Commerce; Pres. Soccer Australia; Foundation mem. Australian Republican Movt.; Fellow Powerhouse Museum; Life Gov. Art Gallery of N.S.W. *Leisure interests:* reading, tennis, walking, cycling. *Address:* GPO Box 4545, Sydney, N.S.W. 2001, Australia.

WRAY, Gordon Richard, EUR.ING., PH.D., D.SC., F.R.S., F.ENG., F.I.MECH.E., F.T.I., F.R.S.A.; British professor of engineering design; b. 30 Jan. 1928, Farnworth, Lancs.; s. of Joseph Wray and Letitia Wray (née Jones); m. Kathleen Senior 1954; one s. one d.; ed. Bolton Tech. Coll. and Univ. of Manchester; Eng. Apprentice, Bennis Combustion, Bolton 1943; Design Draughtsman, Dobson and Barlow, Bolton 1946; Sir Walter Preston Scholar, Univ. of Manchester 1949; Devt. Eng., Platts (Barton) 1952; Lecturer in Mechanical Eng., Bolton Tech. Coll. 1953; Lecturer in Textile Eng., UMIST 1955; Reader in Mechanical Eng., Loughborough Univ. 1966–70, Prof. and Head of Dept. 1970–88; Springer Visiting Prof., Univ. of Calif., Berkeley, U.S.A. 1977; Royal Acad. of Eng. Prof. in the Principles of Eng. Design, Loughborough Univ. of Tech. 1988–93, Dir. of Eng. Design Inst. 1988–91, Emer. Prof. 1993–; mem. Council, I.Mech.E. 1964–67, Dept. of Industry Chief Scientist's Requirements Bd. 1974–75, SEFI Cttee. on Innovation, Brussels 1980–82, Royal Soc. Working Group on Agricultural Eng. 1981–82, Royal Soc. Sectional Cttee. 4(1) 1985–89, Cttee. of the Eng. Profs. Conf. 1985–86, Royal Soc./SERC Industrial Fellowships Panel 1986–89, Royal Soc. Mullard Award Cttee. 1987–92, Royal Soc. Tech. Activities Cttee. 1989–93; mem. Editorial Advisory Bd., Int. Journal of Clothing Science and Tech. 1994–; Chair. Judging Panel for William Lee Quater Centenary Tech. Prize 1989, Eng. Council/Design Council Working Party on Attaining Competence in Eng. Design (The ACED Report) 1989–91; Royal Soc./Royal Acad. of Eng. Visiting Lecturer, Australia and N.Z. 1992; Brunel Lecturer to British Asscn. Annual Meeting 1980; Thomas Hawksley Lecturer, Inst. of Mech. Eng. 1989; Bill Aldridge Memorial Lecturer, Textile Inst. (N.Z.) 1994; Hon. mem. Inst. of Eng. Designers 1990; Viscount Weir Prize 1959, Water Arbitration Prize 1972, James Clayton Prize 1975; Warner Medal, Textile Inst. 1976, S. G. Brown Award and Medal, Royal Soc. 1978; First recipient of title 'European Engineer' (Eur. Ing.), Paris 1987. *Publications:* Textile Engineering Processes (contrib.) 1959, Modern Yarn Production from Man-made Fibres 1960, Modern Developments in Weaving Machinery 1961, An Introduction to the Study of Spinning 1962, Contemporary Textile Engineering (contrib.) 1982, State/Industry Linkages 1993, Mechatronic Design in Textile Engineering (contrib.) 1993; numerous papers in learned journals. *Leisure interests:* fell-walking, photography, steam traction engines, theatre, music, gardening, DIY. *Address:* Stonestack, Rempstone, Loughborough, Leics., LE12 6RH, England.

WRIGHT, Alexander (Alastair) Finlay, M.B.E., M.D.; British medical practitioner; b. 19 March 1933, Blantyre, Scotland; s. of Alexander Finlay Wright and Mary Paterson; m. Barbara Lattimer 1957; three s. one d.; ed. Hamilton Acad., Univ. of Glasgow; Gen. Medical Practitioner, medical researcher, teacher 1961–92; Council of Europe Fellowship, France 1976; Chair. Clinical and Research Div. Royal Coll. of Gen. Practitioners 1990–91; mem. Scientific Cttee., Jt. Royal Coll. "Defeat Depression" Campaign 1991–98; Ed. British Journal of Gen. Practice 1991–; Fellow Royal Coll. of Gen. Practitioners; Hon. Fellow Royal Coll. of Psychiatrists 1998; Sima/Jansson Prize for Research in Gen. Practice 1981. *Publications include:* Medicine and the New Towns of France 1976, Female Sterilisation: The View From General Practice 1981, Depression: Recognition and Management in General Practice 1993, Psychiatry and General Practice (jt. ed.) 1994. *Leisure interests:* walking, spoken French, grandchildren. *Address:* 5 Alburne Crescent, Glenrothes, Fife, KY7 5RE, Scotland. *Telephone:* (01592) 753139. *Fax:* (01592) 753139.

WRIGHT, Barbara, M.A., LL.B., PH.D., LITT.D., S.F.T.C.D., M.R.I.A.; Irish professor of French literature; b. 8 March 1935, Dublin; d. of W. Edward Robinson and Rosaleen H. Robinson; m. William Wright 1961 (died 1985); one s.; ed. Alexandra Coll. Dublin, Trinity Coll. Dublin and Newnham Coll. Cambridge; teaching posts at Univs. of Manchester 1960–61, Exeter 1963–65; mem. staff Trinity Coll. Dublin 1965–, Prof. of French Literature 1978–, Dean, Faculty of Arts (Letters) 1983–86, 1990–96; mem. Royal Irish Acad., Academia Europaea; Chevalier, Ordre Nat. du Mérite. *Publications:* Eugène Fromentin's Dominique (critical edn.) 1966; studies on Gustave Drouineau 1969, Edgar Quinet 1982, Charles Baudelaire (with D. Scott) 1987; Correspondence of Eugène Fromentin and Gustave Moreau (with P. Moisy) 1972; La Vie et l'oeuvre d'Eugène Fromentin (with J. Thompson) 1987, Correspondance d'Eugène Fromentin (2 vols.) 1995. *Leisure interest:* music. *Address:* Department of French, Arts Building, Trinity College, Dublin 2 (Office); 1 Lynton Court, Merrion Road, Dublin 4, Ireland (Home). *Telephone:* 6081575 (Office); 6601276 (Home). *Fax:* 6717118.

WRIGHT, Sir David John, K.C.M.G., L.V.O., M.A.; British diplomatist; b. 16 June 1944; s. of J. F. Wright; m. Sally Ann Dodkin 1968; one s. one d.; ed. Wolverhampton Grammar School, Peterhouse, Cambridge; Third Sec., Foreign Office 1966, Third Sec., later Second Sec., Tokyo 1966–72, FCO 1972–75, Ecole Nat. d'Admin., Paris 1975–76, First Sec., Paris 1976–80, Pvt. Sec. to Sec. of Cabinet 1980–82, Counsellor (Econ.), Tokyo 1982–85, Head Personnel Services Dept. FCO 1985–88, Deputy Pvt. Sec. to H.R.H. the Prince of Wales 1988–90 (on secondment), Amb. to Repub. of Korea 1990–94, to Japan 1996–, Deputy Under-Sec. of State, FCO 1994–96. *Leisure interests:* running, golf, cooking, military history. *Address:* c/o Foreign and Commonwealth Office, King Charles Street, London, SW1A 2AH, England.

WRIGHT, Georg Henrik von, M.A., DR. PHIL.; Finnish philosopher; b. 14 June 1916, Helsinki; s. of Tor von Wright and Ragni Elisabeth Alfthan; m. Baroness Maria Elisabeth von Troil 1941; one s. one d.; ed. Helsinki and Cambridge Univs.; Lecturer in Philosophy, Univ. of Helsinki 1943–46; Prof. of Philosophy, Univ. of Helsinki 1946–61; Prof. of Philosophy, Univ. of Cambridge 1948–51; Visiting Prof., Cornell Univ. 1954, 1958, Univ. of Calif. 1963, Univ. of Pittsburgh 1966, Univ. of Karlsruhe 1975; Research Fellow, Acad. of Finland 1961–86; Andrew D. White Prof.-at-Large, Cornell Univ. 1965–77; Leibniz Prof., Univ. of Leipzig 1994–95; Chancellor of Åbo Acad. 1968–77; Gifford Lecturer Univ. of St. Andrews 1959–60; Tarner Lecturer, Trinity Coll., Cambridge 1969; Woodbridge Lecturer, Columbia Univ. 1972; Nellie Wallace Lecturer, Univ. of Oxford 1978; Tanner Lecturer, Univ. of Helsinki 1984; Pres. Philosophical Soc. of Finland 1962–73, Int. Union of History and Philosophy of Science 1963–65, Inst. Int. de Philosophie, Paris 1975–78; sometime Fellow, Trinity Coll., Cambridge, Hon. Fellow 1983; Fellow, Finnish Soc. of Sciences, Royal Swedish Acad. of Sciences, British Acad., Royal Danish Acad. of Sciences, Norwegian Acad. of Sciences and Letters, European Acad. of Arts, Sciences and Humanities, World Acad. of Arts and Sciences, Academia Europaea; Hon. Foreign mem. American Acad. of Arts and Sciences; Dr. h.c. (Helsinki, Liverpool, Lund, Turku, Tampere, St. Olaf Coll., U.S.A., Buenos Aires, Salta, Bologna, Abo Acad., Tromsø, Stockholm, Leipzig, Innsbruck); Wihuri Foundation Int. Prize 1976, Alexander von Humboldt Foundation Research Award 1986, Tage Danielsson Humanist Award 1998. *Publications:* The Logical Problem of Induction 1941, A Treatise on Induction and Probability 1951, An Essay in Modal Logic 1951, Logical Studies 1957, The Varieties of Goodness 1963, Norm and Action 1963, The Logic of Preference 1963, An Essay in Deontic Logic 1968, Explanation and Understanding 1971, Causality and Determinism 1974, Freedom and Determination 1980, Wittgenstein 1982, Philosophical Papers I–III 1983–84, Intellectual Autobiography 1989, Minervan Pöllö (The Owl of Minerva) 1992, Myten om framsteget (The Myth of Progress) 1993, The Tree of Knowledge 1993, Normen, Werte und Handlungen 1994, Six Essays in Philosophical Logic 1996, In the Shadow of Descartes 1998. *Address:* 4 Skepparegatan, Helsinki, Finland. *Telephone:* 655-192.

WRIGHT, James Claude, Jr.; American politician; b. 22 Dec. 1922, Fort Worth, Tex.; s. of James C. Wright and Marie (née Lyster) Wright; m. Betty Hay 1972; one s. three d. (by previous m.); ed. Weatherford Coll. and Univ. of Texas; army service 1942–45, D.F.C., Legion of Merit; Partner, advertising and trade extension firm; mem. Texas Legislature 1947–49; Mayor of Weatherford, Tex. 1950–54; mem. League of Texas Municipalities, Pres. 1953; fmr. Lay Minister in Presbyterian Church; mem. for Fort Worth (12th District of Tex.), U.S. House of Reps. 1954–89, Deputy Democratic Whip until 1976, Majority Leader in House of Reps. 1976–87; Chair. Democratic Steering and Policy Cttee. in House, Vice-Chair. 1976–87, Speaker, House of Reps. 1987–89; mem. Budget Cttee. 1974–87; Sr. Political Consultant, American Income Life Insurance Co. 1989–; Political Consultant, Arch Petroleum 1989–; fmr. ranking mem. Public Works and Transportation Cttee.; fmr. mem. Govt. Operations Cttee.; fmr. Chair. Comm. on Highway Beautification; Cand. for U.S. Senate 1961. *Publications:* You and Your Congressman 1965, The Coming Water Famine 1966, Of Swords and Plowshares 1968, Worth It All 1993, Balance of Power 1996; co-author: Congress and Conscience 1970, Reflections of a Public Man 1984. *Address:* Federal

Building, 819 Taylor Street, Fort Worth, TX 76102, U.S.A. *Telephone:* (817) 978-3450. *Fax:* (817) 978-3714.

WRIGHT, James Robertson Graeme, D.L., M.A.; British university administrator; b. 14 June 1939, Castle Douglas, Scotland; s. of John Wright and Elizabeth Calder Coghill; m. Jennifer Susan Greenberg 1966; two d.; ed. Inverness Royal Acad., Dundee High School, Univ. of Edinburgh, St. John's Coll., Cambridge; asst. lecturer in Humanity (Latin) Univ. of Edin. 1965–66, lecturer in Humanity (Latin) 1966–78, Sr. Warden, Pollock Halls of Residence 1973–78, mem. Univ. Court 1975–78; Fellow, Domestic Bursar and Dir. of Studies in Classics St. Catharine's Coll., Cambridge 1978–87, Bursar 1979–87, Professorial Fellow 1987–91; Sec.-Gen. of the Faculties Univ. of Cambridge 1987–91; mem. Cambridge Dist. Health Authority 1990–91; Vice-Chancellor Univ. of Newcastle upon Tyne 1992–; mem. Council Cttee. of Vice-Chancellors and Prins. 1996–, Sector Strategy Group, HEFCE 1998–; Chair. Higher Educ. Man. Statistics Group 1995–; mem. Gov. Body Shrewsbury School 1986–; mem. Scottish Higher Educ. Funding Council 1992–99; Assoc. Commr. Nat. Comm. on Educ. 1992–93; mem. CICHE 2 (British Council) 1992–94, mem. CICHE 1993–, UKCOSA 1998–; Chair. Exec. Cttee. Council for Int. Educ. 1998–; Dir. The Newcastle Initiative 1993–; non-exec. mem. Northern and Yorkshire Regional Health Authority 1994–96; D.L., Tyne and Wear 1995. *Publications:* various articles and reviews in classical journals. *Address:* 6 Kensington Terrace, Newcastle upon Tyne, NE1 7RU, England. *Telephone:* (0191) 222-6064.

WRIGHT, Sir (John) Oliver, G.C.M.G., G.C.V.O., D.S.C.; British diplomatist; b. 6 March 1921, London; s. of Arthur Wright and Ethel Wright; m. Marjory Osborne 1942; three s.; ed. Solihull School, and Christ's Coll., Cambridge; Royal Navy 1941–45; joined Foreign Office Nov. 1945; served New York 1946–47, Bucharest 1948–50, Singapore 1950–54, Berlin 1954–56, Pretoria 1957–58; Imperial Defence Coll. 1959; Asst. Pvt. Sec. to Foreign Sec. 1960–63, Pvt. Sec. Jan.–Nov. 1963; Pvt. Sec. to Prime Minister 1963–66; Amb. to Denmark 1966–69; U.K. Rep. to Northern Ireland Govt. 1969–70; Deputy Under-Sec. of State and Chief Clerk, FCO 1970–72; Deputy Under-Sec. for EEC and Econ. Affairs 1972–75; Amb. to Fed. Repub. of Germany 1975–81, to U.S.A. 1982–86; King of Arms, Most Distinguished Order of St. Michael and St. George 1987–97; Dir. Gen. Tech. Systems Inc. 1990–95, Enviromed plc 1993–97, Berkeley Hotel 1994–96; Clark Fellow, Cornell Univ. 1987; Lewin Prof., Wash. Univ., St. Louis, Mo. 1988; Trustee British Museum, 1986–91, Bd., British Council, Int. Shakespeare Globe Centre; Co-Chair. Anglo-Irish Encounter 1986–91; Chair. British Königswinter Steering Cttee. 1987–97; Pres. German Chamber of Commerce and Industry in London 1988–92; Chair. of Govs. Reigate Grammar School 1990–97; Hon. Fellow, Christ's Coll., Cambridge 1981. *Leisure interests:* theatre, opera. *Address:* Burstow Hall, Horley, Surrey, RH6 9SR, England. *Telephone:* (01293) 783494.

WRIGHT, Judith Arundell; Australian writer; b. 31 May 1915; Armidale, N.S.W.; d. of late Phillip Arundell Wright and Ethel Mabel Bigg; m. J. P. McKinney; one d.; ed. New England Girls' School, Armidale, N.S.W., and Sydney Univ.; Commonwealth Literary Fund Scholarship 1949, 1962; Lecturer in Australian literature at various Australian univs.; Fellow, Australian Acad. of Humanities; Hon. D.Litt. (New England) 1963, (Sydney) 1976, (Monash) 1977, (Australian Nat. Univ.) 1981, (Griffith Univ.) 1988, (Melbourne) 1988; Emer. Fellowship, Australia Council 1981–93, Emer. Award 1994; Sr. Writers' Fellowship, Australia Council 1977–79; Encyclopaedia Britannica Writers' Award 1964, Robert Frost Memorial Medal 1976, The Alice Award 1980, Asan World Prize 1984, Special Premier's Prize for Poetry 1991, The Queen's Medal for Poetry 1992. *Publications:* Poetry: The Moving Image 1946, Woman to Man 1949, The Gateway 1953, The Two Fires 1955, A Book of Birds 1962, Five Senses 1963, The Other Half 1966, Collected Poems 1971, Alive 1972, Fourth Quarter 1976, The Double Tree 1978, Phantom Dwelling 1985, A Human Pattern 1990, Collected Poems 1942–1985 1994; criticism: Charles Harpur 1963, Preoccupations in Australian Poetry 1964, Because I Was Invited 1975; anthologies: A Book of Australian Verse 1956, New Land, New Language 1957, The Oxford Book of Australian Verse 1968; biography: The Generations of Men 1958, The Cry for the Dead 1981; short stories: The Nature of Love 1966; The Coral Battleground (documentary) 1977, We Call for a Treaty (documentary) 1985, Born of the Conquerors 1991, Going on Talking 1992; also books for children including Tales of a Great Aunt 1998, Half a Lifetime 1999. *Leisure interests:* gardening, walking. *Address:* Flat 1/17 Devonport Street, Lyons, A.C.T. 2060, Australia. *Fax:* 02 62820498.

WRIGHT, Karen Jocelyn, M.A., M.B.A.; American editor and journalist; b. 15 Nov. 1950, New York; d. of Louis David Wile and Grace Carlin Wile; m. 1981; two d.; ed. Brandeis and Cambridge Univs., London Grad. School of Business Studies; founder, owner Hobson Gallery, Cambridge 1981–87; co-f. (with Peter Fuller) Modern Painters magazine 1987–, Ed. 1990–; co-f. (with David Bowie (q.v.), Sir Timothy Sainsbury and Bernard Jacobson) 21 Publishing 1997–; mem. Assen. Int. des Critiques d'Art. *Publication:* (as co-ed.) The Penguin Book of Art Writing 1998. *Leisure interests:* looking at art, children, reading, theatre. *Address:* 31 Storeys Way, Cambridge, CB3 0DP, England. *Telephone:* (01223) 313235. *Fax:* (01223) 461726.

WRIGHT, Sir Oliver (see Wright, Sir John Oliver).

WRIGHT, Paddy; Irish business executive; joined Jefferson Smurfit 1976, fmrly. Chief Exec. U.K. and Ireland, Pres. and C.O.O. 1996–; fmr. Pres. Confed. of Irish Industry. *Address:* Jefferson Smurfit Group PLC, Beech Hill, Clonskeagh, Dublin 14, Ireland (Office).

WRIGHT, Sir Peter Robert, Kt., C.B.E.; British ballet director; b. 25 Nov. 1926, London; s. of Bernard Wright and Hilda Foster; m. Sonya Hana 1954; one s. one d.; ed. Bedales School and Leighton Park School, Reading; debut as professional dancer with Ballets Jooss; during 1950s worked with several dance cos. including Sadler's Wells Theatre Ballet; created first ballet, A Blue Rose, for Sadler's Wells 1957; Ballet Master, Sadler's Wells Opera and teacher, Royal Ballet School 1959; teacher and ballet master to ballet co. formed by John Cranko in Stuttgart 1961; choreographed several ballets in Stuttgart including The Mirror Walkers, Namouna, Design for Dancers, Quintet and mounted his first production of Giselle; producer of TV ballets and choreographer of various London West End musicals and revues during 1960s; Asst. Dir. The Royal Ballet 1969, later Assoc. Dir.; Dir. Sadler's Wells Royal Ballet (now The Birmingham Royal Ballet) 1977–95; Dir. Laureate, Birmingham Royal Ballet 1995–; Gov. Royal Ballet School 1976–, Sadler's Wells Theatre 1987–; Special Prof. of Performance Studies, Univ. of Birmingham 1990; Fellow, Birmingham Conservatoire of Music 1991; Pres. Council of Dance Educ. and Training 1994–, Friends of Sadler's Wells Theatre 1995–, Benesh Inst. of Choreology; Hon. D.Mus. (London) 1990; Hon. D. Litt. (Birmingham) 1994; Evening Standard Award for Ballet 1981; Elizabeth II Coronation Award, Royal Acad. of Dancing 1990; Digital Premier Award 1991; Critics Award for Services to the Arts 1995. *Leisure interests:* ceramics, gardens, travel. *Address:* 10 Chiswick Wharf, London, W4 2SR, England. *Telephone:* 0181-747 1658.

WRIGHT, Robert C., LL.B.; American broadcasting executive; b. Hempstead, N.Y.; m. Suzanne Wright; one s. two d.; ed. Chaminade High School, Holy Cross Coll. and Univ. of Virginia Law School; career in gen. man. marketing, broadcasting, strategic planning and law; fmr. Pres. Cox Cable Communications; later Pres. Gen. Electric Financial Services; Pres. and C.E.O. Nat. Broadcasting Co. (NBC) 1986–. *Address:* National Broadcasting Company, Inc., 30 Rockefeller Plaza, 52nd Floor, New York, NY 10112, U.S.A. *Telephone:* (212) 664-4444.

WRIGHT OF RICHMOND, Baron (Life Peer), cr. 1994, of Richmond-upon-Thames in the London Borough of Richmond-upon-Thames; **Patrick Richard Henry Wright,** G.C.M.G., F.R.C.M.; British diplomatist (retd.); b. 28 June 1931, Reading; s. of the late Herbert H. S. Wright and of Rachel Wright (née Green); m. Virginia Anne Gaffney 1958; two s. one d.; ed. Marlborough Coll., Merton Coll., Univ. of Oxford; served R.A. 1950–51; joined Diplomatic Service 1955, Middle East Centre for Arabic Studies 1956–57, Third Sec., British Embassy, Beirut 1958–60, Pvt. Sec. to Amb., later First Sec., British Embassy, Washington 1960–65, Pvt. Sec. to Perm. Under-Sec., FCO 1965–67, First Sec. and Head of Chancery, Cairo 1967–70, Deputy Political Resident, Bahrain 1971–72, Head of Middle East Dept., FCO 1972–74; Pvt. Sec. (Overseas Affairs) to Prime Minister 1974–77; Amb. to Luxembourg 1977–79, to Syria 1979–81, to Saudi Arabia 1984–86; Deputy Under-Sec., FCO 1982–84; Perm. Under-Sec. of State, FCO and Head Diplomatic Service 1986–91; Dir. Barclays Bank PLC 1991–96, British Petroleum 1991–, De La Rue 1991–, Unilever 1991–99, British Airports Authority 1992–98; mem. Council, Royal Coll. of Music; Chair. Royal Inst. for Int. Affairs 1995–; Vice-Pres. Home-Start; Gov. Wellington Coll. *Leisure interests:* music, philately, travel. *Address:* c/o House of Lords, London, SW1A 0PW, England.

WRIGLEY, Sir Edward Anthony, Kt., M.A., PH.D., F.B.A.; British academic; b. 17 Aug. 1931, Manchester; s. of Edward Wrigley and Jessie Wrigley; m. Maria Laura Spelberg 1960; one s. three d.; ed. King's School, Macclesfield and Peterhouse, Cambridge; William Volker Research Fellow, Univ. of Chicago 1953–54; Fellow, Peterhouse 1958–79, Sr. Bursar 1964–74, Hon. Fellow 1996–; Lecturer in Geography, Cambridge 1958–74; Assoc. Dir. Cambridge Group for the History of Population and Social Structure 1964–95; mem. Inst. of Advanced Study, Princeton 1970–71; Hinkley Visiting Prof., Johns Hopkins Univ. 1975; Tinbergen Visiting Prof., Erasmus Univ., Rotterdam 1979; Prof. of Population Studies, L.S.E. 1979–88; Pres. Manchester Coll., Oxford 1987–96; Sr. Research Fellow All Souls Coll., Oxford 1988–94, Acad. Sec. 1992–94; Prof. of Econ. History, Univ. of Cambridge 1994–97; Master, Corpus Christi Coll. Cambridge 1994–; Ed. Econ. History Review 1985–92; Treas. British Acad. 1989–95, Pres. 1997–; James Ford Special Lecturer, Oxford 1986; Ellen Macarthur Lecturer, Cambridge 1987; Linacre Lecturer, Oxford 1998; Pres. British Soc. for Population Studies 1977–79; Chair. Population Investigation Cttee. 1984–90; I.U.S.S.P. Laureate 1993; Hon. Fellow L.S.E. 1997; Hon. D.Litt. (Manchester) 1997, (Sheffield) 1997, (Bristol) 1998; Hon. D.Soc.Sc. (Edin.) 1998; Founder's Medal, Royal Geographical Soc. 1997. *Publications:* Continuity, Chance and Change 1989, several works on econ. and demographic history. *Leisure interest:* gardening. *Address:* 13 Sedley Taylor Road, Cambridge, CB2 2PW, England. *Telephone:* (01223) 247 614.

WU, Sir Gordon, K.C.M.G.; Chinese businessman; b. 3 Dec. 1935, Hong Kong; s. of Chung Wu and Sum (née Kang) Wu; m. Kwok San-Ping Wu 1970; two s. two d.; Man. Dir. Hopewell Holdings, Hong Kong; responsible for bldg. of colony's tallest bldg., Hopewell Holdings H.Q.; built China Hotel, Canton, China; built new coal-fired power station for Prov. of Guangdong, China; new motorway linking Hong Kong to Shenzen and Canton now under construction; is responsible for design of many of his own bldgs. *Leisure interest:* classical music. *Address:* 641st Floor, Hopewell Centre, 183 Queen's

Road East, Hong Kong Special Administrative Region, People's Republic of China. *Telephone:* 2528-4975. *Fax:* 2861-2068; 286562.

WU BANGGUO; Chinese party official and engineer; b. July 1941, Feidong, Anhui Prov.; ed. Radio Electronics Dept., Qinghua Univ., Beijing; joined CCP 1964; worked at Shanghai No. 3 Electronic Tube Factory, progressing from freight worker to Factory Dir. –1978; Deputy Man. Shanghai Municipal Electronics Components Industry Co., Shanghai Municipal Electrical Vacuum Device Co. 1979–81; Deputy Sec. Parl. Cttee. Shanghai Municipal Instruments Bureau 1981–83; mem. Standing Cttee. Shanghai Municipal CCP Cttee. 1983–85, Deputy Sec. 1986–89, Sec. 1991–94; alt. mem. CCP Cen. Cttee. 1985–92; mem. 14th Cen. Cttee. 1992–97; mem. Politburo CCP 1992–; a Shanghai del. to 8th NPC 1993; mem. CCP Secr. 1994–; Vice-Premier of State Council 1995–; mem. 15th CCP Cen. Cttee. 1997–. *Address:* State Council, Beijing, People's Republic of China.

WU BOSHAN; Chinese banker; b. 1940; ed. Cen. Coll. of Finance and Monetary; joined CCP 1965; Pres. Investment Bank of China 1993. *Address:* c/o Investment Bank of China, Beijing, People's Republic of China.

WU CHENG-CHUNG, H.E. Cardinal John Baptist, D.C.L.; Chinese ecclesiastic; b. 26 March 1925, Kwangtung; s. of Wu Shing Sing and Mary Chow; ed. Ka-Ying Seminary, South China Regional Seminary, Hong Kong, and Pontifical Univ. Urbaniani, Rome; ordained priest 1952; pastoral ministry, Refugee Centre, Tung-tao-tsuen, Kowloon 1952–53; worked at Chancery of Archdiocese of New York, Boston and Chicago 1956–57; pastoral ministry, Taiwan 1957–75 Bishop of Hong Kong 1975–98; cr. Cardinal 1988; mem. Congregation for the Evangelization of Peoples, Pontifical Councils for Inter-Religious Dialogue, for Culture, for Social Communication. *Address:* Caritas House, 2 Caine Road, Hong Kong Special Administrative Region, People's Republic of China. *Telephone:* 2524-2071. *Fax:* 2810-4619.

WU DECHANG; Chinese academic; b. 22 Oct. 1927, Beijing; m. Lin Rhizhu 1951; one s. two d.; ed. Peking Univ. and in U.S.S.R.; Commdt. Mil. Medical Science Acad. of PLA 1991–; del. to 14th Nat. Conf. CCP 1991–; mem. 8th Nat. Cttee. CPPCC 1993–96. *Leisure interest:* classical music. *Address:* Military Medical Science Academy of People's Liberation Army, 27 Tai-Ping Road, Beijing 100850, People's Republic of China. *Telephone:* (10) 68 186211. *Fax:* (10) 682 14653.

WU GUANGYU, Lieut.-Gen.; Chinese air force officer; b. Dec. 1940, Hongze Co., Jiangsu Prov.; ed. middle school and Air Force Aviation School; joined PLA 1958; mem. CCP 1964–; air force pilot and squadron leader 1962–70; various posts in Air Force Aviation 1970–85; Commdr. Air Force units, PLA Shanghai Base 1985; Commdr. PLA Air Force Command Post 1985–90; Deputy Commdr. Nanjing Mil. Regional Air Force 1990–93; Deputy Commdr. and Air Force Commdr. Jinan Mil. Region 1993; Deputy Commdr. PLA Air Force 1995–; Deputy to 6th NPC 1983; alt. mem. 14th CCP Cen. Cttee. 1992–. *Address:* c/o Ministry of National Defence, Jingshanqian Jie, Beijing, People's Republic of China. *Telephone:* (1) 6370000.

WU GUANZHENG; Chinese government official; b. 25 Aug. 1938, Yugan Co., Jiangxi Prov.; s. of Wu Enshui and Dong Gelao; m. Zhang Jinshang 1959; three s.; ed. Power Dept., Qinghua Univ., Beijing; joined CCP 1962; mem. CCP Cttee. of Wuhan Gedian Chemical Plant, Deputy Dir. Revolutionary Cttee. of Wuhan Gedian Chemical Plant 1968–75; Deputy Dir. Wuhan Science and Tech. Cttee., Vice-Chair. Wuhan City Asscn. of Science and Tech., Deputy Commdr. and Dir. of Gen. Office, Wuhan City Technical Innovation Headquarters; Dir., Sec. CCP Cttee. of Wuhan City Eng. Science and Tech. Research Centre 1975–82; standing mem. CCP Cttee. of Wuhan City 1982–83; Sec. CCP Cttee. and Mayor of Wuhan City 1983–86; Deputy Sec. Jiangxi Prov. CCP Cttee., Acting Gov., Gov. Jiangxi Prov. 1986–95; Sec. CCP Cttee. Jiangxi Prov., First Sec. CCP Cttee. Jiangxi Prov. Mil. Command 1995–97, Sec. CCP Cttee. Shandong Prov. and Prin. of School for CCP Shandong Cttee. 1997–; alt. mem. 12th CCP Cen. Cttee. 1982–87; mem. 13th CCP Cen. Cttee. 1987–92; mem. 14th CCP Cen. Cttee. 1992–97; mem. Political Bureau of 15th CCP Cen. Cttee., mem. 15th CCP Cen. Cttee. 1997–. *Leisure interests:* reading, sports. *Address:* 482 Weiyi Road, Jinan City, Shandong, People's Republic of China. *Telephone:* 86 531 2033333.

WU GUANZHONG; Chinese painter and university professor; b. Yixing Co., Jiangsu Prov.; ed. Nat. Inst. of Fine Arts, Hangzhou; Ecole Nat. Supérieure des Beaux Arts, Paris; Prof. Cen. Inst. of Applied Arts 1980–; exhbns. in Japan, France, Singapore and Hong Kong; mem. 6th CPPCC 1983–87, 7th 1988–92, mem. 8th Nat. Cttee. 1993–; Hon. mem. China Fed. of Literary and Art Circles 1996. *Address:* Central Institute of Applied Arts, 34 Dong Sanhuan North Road, Beijing 100020, People's Republic of China.

WU HUALUN; Chinese artist; b. June 1942, Tianjin; s. of Wu Bing-Zheng and Wang Yaxin; m. Zeng Wan 1985; one d.; ed. Cen. Acad. of Arts and Crafts; mem. China Artists' Asscn. 1982–, China Calligraphists' Asscn. 1986–; Sr. Art Ed., China People's Fine Art Publishing House; works have been exhibited many times in Japan, Hong Kong and U.S.A.; one man exhbn. of paintings Oct. 1988, Gallery Triform, Taiwan; First Prize, Chinese Paintings Competition 1988; Gold Medal, Japan-China Art Exchange Centre 1988. *Publication:* Chinese Paintings by Wu Hualun 1989. *Leisure interests:* travelling, playing badminton. *Address:* People's Fine Arts Publishing House, 32 Bei Zong Bu Hutong, Beijing 100735, People's Republic of China. *Telephone:* (10) 65244901.

WU JIANCHANG; Chinese business executive; son-in-law of Deng Xiaoping; fmr. Deputy Gen. Man. China Nat. Nonferrous Metals Import and Export Corpn.; Vice-Pres. China Nat. Nonferrous Metals Industry Corpn. 1984–94, Pres. 1994–. *Address:* China National Nonferrous Metals Industry Corporation, 12B Fuxing Lu, Beijing 100814, People's Republic of China. *Telephone:* (10) 685 14423. *Fax:* (10) 685 15368.

WU JICHUAN; Chinese party and government official; b. 1937, Changning Co., Hunan Prov.; joined CCP 1960; Vice-Minister of Posts and Telecommunications 1984–90, Minister 1993–98; Minister of Information Industry 1998–; Deputy Sec. Henan Prov. CCP Cttee. 1990–93; alt. mem., 14th Cen. Cttee. 1992–97; Vice-Chair. State Radio Regulatory Cttee.; mem. 15th CCP Cen. Cttee. 1997–. *Address:* c/o Ministry of Information Industry, Beijing, People's Republic of China.

WU JIEPING; Chinese urologist; b. 22 Jan. 1917, Jiangsu; s. of Wu Jingyi and Cheng Xia; m. 1st Zhao Junkai 1933; m. 2nd Gao Rui 1984; one s. two d.; Prof. Beijing Medical Coll. 1957–; Pres. 2nd Medical Coll. Beijing 1960–70; Vice-Pres. Chinese Medical Asscn. 1978–84, Pres. 1984–89, Hon. Pres. 1989–; Vice-Pres. Acad. of Medical Sciences 1970–83, Pres. 1983–85, Hon. Pres. 1985–; Vice-Chair. Cen. Council Int. Planned Parenthood Fed. (IPPF) 1986–, Chair. Regional Council 1991–; Vice-Chair. Standing Cttee. 8th NPC 1993–98, 9th NPC 1998–; Chair. Jiusan (Sept. 3) Soc. 1997–; Fellow, Chinese Acad. of Science 1981–98, Sr. Fellow 1998–; Fellow Chinese Acad. of Eng. 1995–98, Sr. Fellow 1998–; Hon. Fellow American Coll. of Physicians 1989, American Urological Asscn. 1995–, Royal Coll. of Surgeons, Edin. 1996–. *Leisure interest:* reading. *Address:* Academy of Medical Sciences, Beijing 100730, People's Republic of China. *Telephone:* 5135844.

WU JINGHUA; Chinese state official; b. 1931, Mianning Co., Sichuan Prov.; Deputy to 4th NPC 1975; Vice-Minister, State Nationalities' Affairs Comm. 1979; Vice-Chair. Sichuan Prov. People's Congress 1979–83; Pres. Sichuan Prov. Soc. for Agricultural Modernization in Areas Inhabited by Minorities 1981–83; mem. 12th CCP Cen. Cttee. 1982–87, 13th Cen. Cttee. 1987–93; Sec. CCP Cttee., Tibet 1985–88; Political Commissar, PLA Tibet Mil. Dist. 1985–88; Vice-Minister State Nationalities Affairs Comm. 1985–88, Deputy Sec. Party Group, State Nationalities Affairs Comm. 1988; Vice-Chair. Agric. and Rural Affairs Cttee. 9th NPC 1998–. *Address:* c/o Standing Committee of National People's Congress, Beijing, People's Republic of China.

WU JINGLIAN; Chinese economist; b. Jan. 1930, Nanjing, Jiangsu Prov.; ed. Fudan Univ.; Asst. Research Fellow, Econs. Research Inst. of Chinese Acad. of Sciences 1954–79; Assoc. Research Fellow, Econs. Inst. of Chinese Acad. of Social Sciences 1979–83, Research Fellow and Prof. 1983–; Vice-Dir. Office for Econ. Reform Programmes of State Council, Vice-Chair. Econ. Cttee. of CPPCC 1984–. *Publications:* Explorations into Problems of Economic Reform, Planned Economy or Market Economy. *Address:* c/o Chinese Academy of Social Sciences, Beijing, People's Republic of China.

WU KUNG-CHAO (known as K. C. Wu), O.B.E.; Chinese banker; b. 20 Nov. 1922, Amoy; s. of Wu Kung Hua and Wu Fu Kan; m. Daisy Chan 1951; one s. one d.; accountant, Bank of China, Rangoon 1939; transferred to Calcutta 1942; joined London br. of Bank of China 1944, Asst. Gen. Man. 1973, Sr. Deputy Gen. Man. 1986, Adviser 1989–; set up New York br. of Bank of China 1981–83; mem. Nat. Cttee. of CPPCC 1988–; Hon. Pres. Foreign Banks and Securities Houses Asscn. 1990–; Hon. D.Sc. (City Univ.) 1993; Hon. Ph.D. (Guildhall Univ) 1996; Courvoisier Leadership Award 1993; Hon. O.B.E.; *Leisure interests:* tennis, travel, reading. *Address:* Bank of China, 90 Cannon Street, London, EC4N 6HA, England. *Telephone:* 0171-282 8888. *Fax:* 0171-282 8873.

WU LENGXI; Chinese party official and journalist; b. 1919, Xinhui, Guangdong; ed. Wuhan Univ., Lu Xun Acad. of Arts; worked for Mass Daily, Henan 1937; Man. Ed. 7 July Daily, Cen. Plain Mil. Region 1937; Deputy Dir. Propaganda Dept., Cen. Plain Mil. Region 1948; Prin. Cadre New China News Agency (NCNA), trained in Pingshanxian, Hebei 1949; Man. Ed. NCNA 1949–50, Deputy Dir. 1950–52, Dir. 1952–Cultural Revolution; Deputy for Tianjin, 1st NPC 1954–59; mem. Comm. for Cultural Relations with Foreign Countries 1954; Man. Ed. Renmin Ribao (People's Daily) 1958–Cultural Revolution; Deputy for Guangdong, 2nd NPC 1958, 3rd NPC 1964; Deputy Dir. Propaganda Dept., CCP Cen. Cttee. 1964–Cultural Revolution; mem. Standing Cttee., 3rd NPC 1965-Cultural Revolution; disappeared 1966–72; leading mem. People's Daily 1972; mem. Standing Cttee., 4th NPC 1975; Alt. mem. 11th Cen. Cttee., CCP 1977, 12th Cen. Cttee. 1982; Deputy for Shanghai, 5th NPC 1978; mem. Standing Cttee., 5th NPC 1978; Deputy Dir. Propaganda Dept., Cen. Cttee. 1978; mem. Standing Cttee., Nat. Cttee., 5th CPPCC 1978, 7th 1988–; fmr. Sec. CCP Cttee., Guangdong; Adviser Beijing Journalism Studies Soc. 1980; Alt. mem. 12th Cen. Cttee. CCP 1982–87; Minister of Radio and TV 1982–86; Chair. All Journalists' Asscn. 1983–; Vice-Pres. China Int. Cultural Exchange Centre 1984–; Pres. Soc. of Radio and TV Oct. 1986–, Soc. for Studies of Radio and TV Oct. 1986–, Chinese Friends Research Foundation 1989–; mem. Standing Cttee. 7th CPPCC 1988–; Vice-Pres. China Int. Cultural Exchange Centre; mem. Educ. and Cultural Cttee. 1988–. *Address:* State Council, Beijing, People's Republic of China.

WU LIANGYONG; Chinese architect; b. 1922, Nanjing, Jiangsu Prov.; ed. Cen. Univ., Cornish Coll. of the Arts 1949; Prof. Tsinghua Univ. 1950–; Fellow Chinese Acad. of Sciences 1981–; Fellow Chinese Acad. of Eng. 1995–;

Vice-Chair. Int. Asscn. of Architects 1987–93, Chair. 1993–. *Publications:* Essays on City Planning and Design, An Outline History of Ancient Chinese Cities. *Address:* Architecture and City Planning Research Institute, Tsinghua University, Beijing, People's Republic of China.

WU POH-HSIUNG, B.SC.; Chinese politician; b. 19 June 1939, Taoyuan County; m. Dai Mei-yu; two s. one d.; ed. Nat. Cheng Kung Univ., Sun Yat-sen Inst. of Policy and Research and Devt.; school-teacher 1963–65; mem. Taiwan Prov. Ass. 1968–72; Assoc. Prof. Nan Ya Jr. Coll. of Tech. 1972–73; Magistrate, Taoyuan County 1973–76; Dir. Inst. of Industry for Workmen and Friends of Labour Asscn., Dir-Gen. Taiwan Tobacco and Wine Monopoly Bureau 1976–80; Dir. Inst. of Industrial and Vocational Training for Workmen 1976–80; Chair. Repub. of China Amateur Boxing Asscn. 1981–82; Dir. Secr., Cen. Cttee., Kuomintang 1982–84, Chair. Cen. Exec. Cttee.; Minister of Interior 1984–88, 1991–94; Mayor of Taipei 1988–90; Minister of State 1990–91; Sec.-Gen. Office of the Pres. 1994–; Chair. Cen. Election Comm. 1991–94, Political Party Review Cttee. 1991–94. *Address:* Office of the President, 122 Chungking South Road, Sec. 1, Taipei, Taiwan. *Telephone:* 02-311371. *Fax:* 02-3140746.

WU SHAOZU, Maj.-Gen.; Chinese politician; b. 1939, Laiyang Co., Hunan Prov.; two s.; ed. Qinghua Univ. Beijing; Chair. Student Fed. 1965–82; Deputy, 3rd NPC 1964–66; Vice-Minister State Comm. of Science, Tech. and Industry for Nat. Defence 1982–88; promoted to Maj.-Gen. PLA 1988; Minister State Physical Culture and Sports Comm. 1988–98; Dir. State Gen. Bureau for Physical Culture and Sports 1998–; mem. 14th and 15th Cen. Cttee. CCP 1992–; Pres. Chinese Olympic Cttee. *Address:* c/o State General Bureau for Physical Culture and Sports, 9 Tiyuguan Road, Chongwen Dist., Beijing 100763, People's Republic of China.

WU TIANMING; Chinese film director; b. Oct. 1939, Shaanxi Prov.; m. Mu Shulan; ed. Xi'an Drama School; Head of Xian Film Studio 1983–89; Visiting Scholar Univ. of Calif. 1990–91. *Films:* Kith and Kin 1981, River Without Buoys 1983, Life 1984, The Old Well 1987.

WU WEIRAN; Chinese surgeon; b. 14 Oct. 1920, Changzhou, Jiangsu Prov.; s. of Wu Jingyi and Zheng Zhixia; m. Huang Wuchiung 1951; three d.; Deputy Dir. Surgery Soc., attached to the Medical Soc. 1972; Deputy Dir. Surgery Dept., Beijing Union Medical Coll. Hosp., Chinese Acad. of Medical Sciences 1972; now Prof. of Surgery, Surgical Dept., Beijing Union Medical Coll. Hosp., Chinese Acad. of Medical Sciences; Hon. Dir. Beijing Hosp.; alt. mem. 12th CCP Cen. Cttee. 1982, mem. 1985, mem. 13th Cen. Cttee. 1987–92; mem. Presidium of 14th CCP Nat. Congress 1992. *Leisure interest:* gardening. *Address:* Surgery Department, Beijing Hospital, 1 Dahalu, Dondan, Beijing 100730, People's Republic of China. *Telephone:* 6513-2266. *Fax:* 6513-2969.

WU WENJUN; Chinese mathematician; b. 12 May 1919, Jiansu Prov.; ed. in U.S.A.; returned to China in 1950; Deputy Dir., Math. Inst. Acad. Sinica 1964; mem. Standing Cttee. of 5th CPPCC 1978; Deputy Dir., Inst. of Systems Science, Acad. Sinica 1980; mem., Standing Cttee. of 6th CPPCC 1983; Pres., Math. Soc. of China 1984; Dir. Mathematics and Physics Div. 1992–; mem., Dept. of Math. and Physics, Chinese Acad. of Sciences 1985, now Dir.; mem. Standing Cttee. of 7th CPPCC 1988; mem. 8th CPPCC Nat. Cttee. 1993–.

WU WENYING; Chinese politician and cotton spinner; b. 1932, Changzhou City, Jiangsu Prov.; ed. E. China Textile Eng. Inst., Shanghai; joined CCP 1949; began work as cotton spinner in a textile mill, Changzhou 1947; held various leading posts in textile mills, Changzhou Municipal Party Cttee. and City Govt.; Chair. Chinese Gen. Asscn. of Textile Industry 1993–; Alt. mem. 12th Cen. Cttee. CCP 1982–85, mem. 1985–87; mem. 13th Cen. Cttee. 1987–92; mem. 14th Cen. Cttee. 1992–97; Minister of Textile Industry 1983–93; Vice-Chair. Motions Cttee., 9th Nat. Cttee. of CPPCC 1998. *Address:* c/o National Committee of Chinese People's Political Consultative Conference, 23 Taipingqiao Street, Beijing, People's Republic of China.

WU XU, Maj.-Gen.; Chinese army officer; b. March 1939, Changsu City, Jiangsu Prov.; ed. 5th Artillery School and PLA Mil. Acad.; joined PLA 1954; mem. CCP 1959–; various posts in artillery, reconnaissance and training 1956–85; army corps political commissar and army corps commdr. 1985–92; Asst. Chief of Gen. Staff 1992; Deputy Chief, PLA Gen. Staff 1995–; mem. 15th CCP Cen. Cttee. 1997–. *Address:* Ministry of National Defence, Jingshanqian Jie, Beijing, People's Republic of China. *Telephone:* (1) 6370000.

WU XUEQIAN; Chinese politician; b. 1921, Shanghai; joined CCP 1939; Council mem. Asscn. for Cultural Relations with Foreign Countries 1954–67; disappeared during Cultural Revolution 1967–77; mem. 5th CPPCC 1978–82; Vice-Minister of Foreign Affairs May–Nov. 1982; Minister of Foreign Affairs 1982–88; State Councillor 1983–88, Vice-Premier State Council 1988–93; mem. 12th Cen. Cttee. CCP 1982, 13th Cen. Cttee. 1987; mem. Political Bureau of Cen. Cttee. 1985–92; Dir. Comm. for Commemorating 40th Anniversary of UN 1985; Chair. State Tourism Cttee. 1988; mem. Presidium of 14th CCP Nat. Congress 1992; Vice-Chair. 8th Nat. Cttee. CPPCC 1993–98; mem. and head numerous dels. abroad; other public appointments. *Address:* State Council, Beijing, People's Republic of China.

WU YI; Chinese politician, engineer and administrator; b. Nov. 1938, Wuhan City, Hubei Prov.; ed. Dept. of Petroleum Refining, Beijing Petroleum Inst.; joined CCP 1962; Vice-Mayor of Beijing 1988–91; Vice-Minister of Foreign Trade 1991–93; Minister of Foreign Trade and Econ. Co-operation 1993–98; alt. mem. 13th CCP Cen. Cttee. 1987–92; mem. 14th 1992–97; Chair. Bd. of Dirs. Foreign Trade Univ. 1995–98; alt. mem. CCP Politburo 1997–; mem. 15th CCP Cen. Cttee. 1997–; State Councillor 1998–. *Address:* c/o State Council, Beijing, People's Republic of China.

WU YIGONG; Chinese film director; b. 1 Dec. 1938, Chongqing, Sichuan Prov.; s. of Wu Tiesan and Yu Minhua; m. Zhang Wen Rong 1967; one s.; Dir. Shanghai Film Bureau, Gen. Man. Shanghai Film Corpn., Vice-Pres. China Film Artists' Asscn. 1985–; alt. mem. 14th CCP Cen. Cttee. 1992–97, mem. 15th CCP Cen. Cttee. 1997–; Vice-Chair. China Fed. of Literary and Art Circles 1996; Golden Rooster Award 1984 for best Dir. of film My Memories of Old Beijing, Magnolia Prize for A Man Aged 18 1988; other films include University in Exile, The Tribulations of a Chinese Gentleman, Bitter Sea. *Leisure interests:* music, sports. *Address:* 52 Yong Fu Road, Shanghai, People's Republic of China. *Telephone:* 4332558. *Fax:* 4370528.

WU ZUGUANG; Chinese author and dramatist; b. 21 April 1917, Beijing; s. of Wu Ying and Zhou Qin Qi; m. Xin Fengxia 1950; two s. one d; ed. China-France Univ.; *plays:* Wind Snow Night, Itinerant Entertainer, Xin Fengxia I–XII (TV plays), and others; mem. 6th CPPCC 1983–87, 7th 1988–92, 8th 1993–; Advisor Chinese Writers' Asscn. 1996. *Address:* 9-5-7 Gongren Tiyuchang Donglu, Beijing 100020, People's Republic of China. *Telephone:* 65524404

WU ZUQIANG; Chinese musician and composer; b. 24 July 1927, Beijing; s. of Jing-zhou Wu and Qin-qi (née Zhou) Wu; m. Li-qin Zheng 1953; one s. one d.; Vice-Pres. Cen. Conservatory of Music 1978–82, Pres. 1982–88, now Prof., Hon. Pres.; Vice-Pres. Chinese Musicians' Asscn. 1985–; Vice-Exec. Chair. China Fed. of Literary and Art Circles 1988–95, Vice-Chair. 1995; Adviser to China Nat. Symphony Orchestra 1996; alt. mem. 12th CCP Cen. Cttee. 1982; Perm. mem. Nat. Cttee. 7th, 8th and 9th CPPCC 1988–. *Leisure interests:* literature, fine arts, tourism. *Address:* Central Conservatory of Music, 43 Baojiajie West District, Beijing 100031, People's Republic of China. *Telephone:* (10) 66414887. *Fax:* (10) 66417211.

WULF-MATHIES, Monika, DR.PHIL.; German fmr. trade union leader; b. 17 March 1942, Wernigerode; d. of Carl-Hermann Baier and Margott Baier (née Meisser); m. Carsten Wulf-Mathies 1968; ed. Univs. of Hamburg and Freiburg; Br. Asst. Fed. Ministry of Econs. 1968–71; Head of Dept. for Social Policy, Fed. Chancellery 1971–76; joined ÖTV (Public Services and Transport Workers' Union) 1971, mem. Man. Exec. Cttee. 1976–95, Chair. of ÖTV 1982–95; Commr. for Regional Policies of EU Jan. 1995–; Pres. Public Services Int. 1989–94; mem. Exec. Bd. Deutsche Lufthansa AG 1978–95 (Deputy Chair. 1988–95), VEBA 1989–95. *Leisure interests:* gardening, cross-country skiing. *Address:* Commission of the European Communities, 200 rue de la Loi, 1049 Brussels, Belgium. *Telephone:* (2) 299 3870.

WUNDERLICH, Paul; German painter, sculptor and lithographer; b. 10 March 1927, Eberswalde; s. of Horst Wunderlich and Gertud Wunderlich (née Arendt); m. 1st Isabella von Bethmann-Hollweg 1957 (divorced 1959), 2nd Karin Székessy 1971; two d.; ed. Academie Hamburg; Prof. of Drawing and Painting, Hamburg Acad. 1963–68; freelance artist 1969–; Premio Marzotto 1967, Kama Kura Prize, Tokyo 1968, Kunstpreis, Schleswig-Holstein 1986. *Publications:* Monographie Paul Wunderlich Vol. I 1978, Vol. II 1980, Werkverseichnis der Grafik 1982, Skulpturen und Objekte 1988. *Address:* Haynstrasse 2, 20249 Hamburg, Germany. *Telephone:* 487387. *Fax:* 476312.

WUNSCH, Carl Isaac, PH.D.; American physical oceanographer and university professor; b. 5 May 1941, Brooklyn, New York; s. of Harry Wunsch and Helen (Gellis) Wunsch; m. Marjory Markel 1980; one s. one d.; ed. Massachusetts Inst. of Technology; Lecturer in Oceanography, M.I.T. 1966–67, Asst. Prof. 1967–70, Assoc. Prof. 1970–75, Prof. of Physical Oceanography 1975–76, Cecil and Ida Green Prof. 1976–, Sec. of Navy Research Prof. 1985–89; Sr. Visiting Fellow, Dept. of Applied Math. and Theoretical Physics, Cambridge Univ., England 1969, 1974–75, 1981–82; Fulbright Scholar 1981–82; John Simon Guggenheim Foundation Fellow 1981–82; Visiting Sr. Scientist, GFDL, Princeton Univ. 1993–94; Visiting Scientist, CNES/CNRS, Toulouse, France 1994; Distinguished Visiting Scientist, Jet Propulsion Lab. 1994–; Chair. Ocean Studies Bd., N.R.C.; Consultant to N.A.S., N.S.F.; Fellow American Acad. of Arts and Sciences, American Geophysical Union, American Meteorological Soc.; mem. N.A.S., Royal Astronomical Soc., Soc. for Industrial and Applied Mathematics; James R. Macelwane Award 1971, Maurice Ewing Medal 1990, American Geophysical Union, Founders Prize, Texas Instrument Foundation 1975, A.G. Huntsman Prize 1988, Public Service Medal, NASA 1993. *Publications:* Evolution of Physical Oceanography (co-ed.), Ocean Acoustic Tomography (co-author), The Ocean Circulation Inverse Problem; many tech. papers. *Leisure interest:* sailing. *Address:* Room 54-1524, Department of Earth, Atmospheric and Planetary Science, Massachusetts Institute of Technology, Cambridge, MA 02139 (Office); 78 Washington Avenue, Cambridge, MA 02140, U.S.A. (Home). *Telephone:* (617) 253-5937 (Office). *Fax:* (617) 253-4464.

WYATT, (Alan) Will, F.R.T.S.; British television executive; b. 7 Jan. 1942; s. of Basil Wyatt and Hettie Evelyn Wyatt (née Hooper); m. Jane Bridgit Bagenal 1966; two d.; ed. Magdalen Coll. School, Oxford, Emmanuel Coll. Cambridge; trainee reporter, Sheffield Telegraph 1964; Sub-Ed. BBC Radio News 1965; joined BBC TV 1968, Producer Late Night Line-Up, In Vision,

The Book Programme, B. Traven—a mystery solved, etc. 1970–77, Asst. Head of Presentation (Programmes) 1977, Head Documentary Features 1981, Features and Documentaries Group 1987, Asst. Man. Dir BBC Network Television 1988–91; Man. Dir. BBC Network TV 1991–96; Chief Exec. BBC Broadcast 1996–; Chair. BBC Guidelines on Violence 1983, 1987; Dir. Broadcasters' Audience Research Bd. 1989–91, BBC Subscription TV 1990–93, BBC Enterprises 1991–93, UKTV 1997–; Vice-Pres. Royal TV Soc. 1997, Euro Broadcasting Union 1998–; Gov. London Inst. 1990–; Huw Weldon Memorial Lecture 1996. *Publication:* The Man Who Was B. Traven 1980. *Leisure interests:* fell walking, horse racing, opera. *Address:* BBC Broadcasting House, Portland Place, London, W1A 1AA, England. *Telephone:* 0171-580 4468.

WYATT, Christopher Terrel, F.ENG., F.I.C.E.; British business executive; b. 17 July 1927, Ewell, Surrey; s. of Lional H. Wyatt and Audrey Vere Wyatt; m. 1st Doreen Mary Emmerson; three s.; m. 2nd Geertruida Willer 1970; one s.; m. 3rd Patricia Perkins 1990; ed. Kingston Grammar School, Battersea Polytechnic and Imperial Coll., London; Charles Brand & Son, Ltd., 1948–54; joined Richard Costain Ltd., 1955, Dir. 1970–87, Group Chief Exec. 1975–80, Deputy Chair. 1979–80, Chair. Costain Group PLC 1980–87; Chair., W. S. Atkins Ltd. 1987–97. *Leisure interest:* sailing. *Address:* The White House, St Martin's Avenue, Epsom, Surrey, KT18 5HS, England. *Telephone:* (01428) 54538.

WYDEN, Ronald Lee, J.D.; American politician; b 3 May 1949, Wichita, Kan.; s. of Peter Wyden and Edith Wyden; m. Laurie Oseran 1978; one s.; ed. Univ. of Santa Barbara, Stanford Univ. and Univ. of Oregon; campaign aide, Senator Wayne Morse 1972, 1974; Co-founder, Co-dir. Oregon Gray Panthers 1974–80; Dir. Oregon Legal Services for Elderly 1977–79; Instructor in Gerontology, Univ. of Oregon 1976, Portland State Univ. 1979, Univ. of Portland 1980; mem. 97th-103rd Congresses from 3rd Oregon Dist. 1981–95; Senator from Oregon 1996–; mem. American Bar Asscn.; Democrat. *Address:* United States Senate, 717 Hart Senate Office Building, Washington, DC 20510, U.S.A.

WYETH, Andrew N.; American artist; b. 12 July 1917, Chadds Ford, Pa.; s. of Newell Converse Wyeth and Carolyn (née Bockius) Wyeth; m. Betsy Merle James 1940; two s.; ed. privately; artist, landscape painter 1936–; first one-man exhbn. William Macbeth Gallery, New York 1937; one-man gallery exhbns. at Doll and Richard, Boston 1938, 1940, 1942, 1944, 1946, 1950; Macbeth Gallery 1937, 1939, 1941, 1943, 1945, 1948, 1950, 1952; M. Knoedler and Co., New York 1953, 1958, Lefevre Gallery, London 1974, Art Emporium, Vancouver 1977, Mitsukoshi Galleries, Japan 1984; Group and other one-man exhbns. in U.S.A., Japan, France, Italy, U.K. and U.S.S.R. 1980–1993; mem. Nat. Inst. of Arts and Letters, American Acad. of Arts and Sciences, Acad. des Beaux Arts, France; Hon. mem. Soviet Acad. of the Arts 1978; Hon. D.F.A. (Maine, Harvard, Dickinson, Swarthmore, Temple Univ., Delaware, Northeastern Univ., Md.); Hon. L.H.D. (Tufts Univ.) 1963; U.S. Presidential Medal of Freedom 1963, Einstein Award 1967, Congressional Gold Medal (first to living American Artist) 1988. *Publication:* Andrew Wyeth: Autobiography (with Thomas Hoving). *Address:* c/o Frank E. Fowler, P.O. Box 247, Lookout Mountain, TN 37350, U.S.A. *Telephone:* (615) 821-3081.

WYLLER, Egil A., D.PHIL.; Norwegian professor emeritus of philosophy; b. 24 April 1925, Stavanger; s. of Trygve Wyller and Anne-Kathrine Wyller; m. Eva Middelthon 1949; three s.; ed. Univs. of Oslo, Tübingen and Freiburg i. Br.; fmr. Prof. of History of the Ideas of Antiquity, Dept. of Philosophy, Univ. of Oslo 1969–95 (now Prof. Emer.); Gold Medal of H.M. King of Norway 1958; Cultural Prize of City of Oslo 1987; Commdr. Order of Phoenix (Greece). *Publications include:* Platons 'Parmenides' 1960, Der späte Platon 1965–70, Enhet og Annethet I-III 1981, Johannes' Apenbaring 1985, Prinsesse Europa 1989, Platonismus/Henologie in der Antike und im Mittelalter I–II (textbook) 1993, Henologisk Skriftserie I–XX 1994–, Henologische Perspektiven I: Platon–Johannes–Cusanus 1995, Platon und Platonismus 1996. *Leisure interests:* music, poetry, natural life. *Address:* Institute of Philosophy, University of Oslo, Blindern, Oslo 3 (Office); Tyslevvn. 46, 1163 Oslo 11, Norway (Home).

WYLLIE, Peter John, PH.D., F.R.S.; British geologist; b. 8 Feb. 1930, London; s. of George W. Wyllie and Beatrice G. Weaver; m. F. Rosemary Blair 1956; two s. one d. (and one d. deceased); glaciologist, British West Greenland Expedition 1950; British North Greenland Expedition 1952–54; Asst. Lecturer in Geology, Univ. of St. Andrews 1955–56; Research Asst. to O. F. Tuttle (q.v.), Pa. State Univ. 1956–58, Asst. Prof. of Geochem. 1959–60; Research Fellow in Chem., Univ. Leeds 1959–60, lecturer in Experimental Petrology 1960–61; Assoc. Prof. of Petrology, Pa. State Univ. 1961–65; Prof. of Petrology and Geochem., Univ. of Chicago 1965–83, Homer J. Livingston Prof. 1978–83; Chair. Dept. of Geophysical Sciences 1979–82; Chair. Div. of Geological and Planetary Sciences, Calif. Inst. of Tech. 1983–87, Prof. of Geology 1983–; Pres. Int. Union of Geodesy and Geophysics 1995–99; Foreign Assoc. N.A.S.; Fellow, American Acad. of Arts and Sciences 1982, Royal Soc., London 1984; Corresp. Fellow, Edin. Geological Soc. 1985–; Hon. mem. Mineralogical Soc. of G.B. and Ireland 1986; Hon. mem. Russian Mineralogical Soc. 1986; Foreign Fellow (Corresp. mem.) Indian Geophysical Union 1987; Foreign mem. U.S.S.R. (now Russian) Acad. of Sciences 1988, Academia Europaea 1996; Foreign Fellow Indian Nat. Science Acad. 1991, Nat. Acad.of Science of India 1992; Louis Murray Visiting Fellow, Univ. of Cape Town March 1987; Pres. Int. Mineralogical Asscn. 1986–90; Vice-Pres. Int. Union of Geodesy and Geophysics 1991–95, Pres. 1995–(99); Hon. D.Sc. (St. Andrews) 1974; Polar Medal 1954, Mineralogical Soc. of America Award 1965, Quantrell Award 1979, Wollaston Medal (Geological Soc., London) 1982, Abraham-Gottlob-Werner-Medaille, German Mineralogical Soc. 1987. *Publications:* Ultramafic and Related Rocks (ed.) 1967, The Dynamic Earth 1971, The Way the Earth Works 1976, Solid-Earth Sciences and Society (Chair. N.A.S. Cttee.) 1993; numerous articles in scientific journals. *Leisure interests:* concerts, theatre. *Address:* Division of Geological and Planetary Sciences, California Institute of Technology, Pasadena, CA 91125, U.S.A. (Office). *Telephone:* (818) 395-6461 (Office). *Fax:* (818) 568-2840.

WYMAN, Bill (William George); British musician; b. 24 Oct. 1941, London; m. 1st (divorced 1969); m. 2nd Mandy Smith 1989 (divorced 1991); m. 3rd Suzanne Accosta 1993; two d.; one s. from first marriage; bass-player with The Rolling Stones 1962–93; owner Ripple Records, Ripple Music, Ripple Publs., Ripple Productions; *albums include:* 12 x 5 1964, New 1965, Big Hits 1966, Got Live If You Want It 1967, Flowers 1967, Sucking in the 70's 1981, Still Life 1981, Rewind, Dirty Work 1986, Emotional Rescue 1988, Steel Wheels 1989, Flashpoint 1991, Voodoo Lounge 1994; solo recordings include: Stone Alone, Monkey Grip, Bill Wyman; *films:* Sympathy for the Devil 1970, Gimme Shelter 1970, Ladies and Gentlemen the Rolling Stones 1974, Let's Spend the Night Together 1982, Digital Dreams 1983. *Publication:* Stone Alone: The Story of a Rock and Roll Band 1990 (with Ray Coleman). *Address:* c/o Ripple Productions Ltd., 344 Kings Road, London, SW3 5UR, England.

WYMAN, Jane (Sarah Jane Fulks); American actress; b. 4 Jan. 1914, St. Joseph, Mo.; d. of R. D. Fulks and Emme Reise; m. 1st Myron Futterman 1937; m. 2nd Ronald Reagan (q.v.) 1940 (divorced 1948); one s. one d.; m. 3rd Fred Karger (divorced); ed. Univ. of Missouri; fmr. radio singer and chorus girl; TV appearances. *Films include:* My Man Godfrey 1936, Brother Rat 1938, The Lost Weekend 1945, The Yearling 1946, Johnny Belinda 1948 (Acad. Award), State Fright 1950, The Glass Menagerie 1950, The Blue Veil 1951, Magnificent Obsession 1954, All That Heaven Allows 1956, Miracle in the Rain 1956, Holiday for Lovers 1959, Pollyanna 1960, Bon Voyage 1962, How to Commit Marriage 1969.

WYNDHAM, Henry Mark; British art expert and company director; b. 19 Aug. 1953, London; s. of Hon. Mark Wyndham and Anne Wyndham; m. Rachel Pritchard 1978; three s.; ed. Wellesley House, Broadstairs, Eton Coll., Sorbonne, Paris and Sotheby's Fine Art Course; joined Christie's 1974; Head, 19th Century European Picture Dept. Christie's, New York 1978–82, Vice-Pres. 1979; Dir. Christie's, London 1983–87; set up Henry Wyndham Fine Art of St. James's Art Group 1987–93; set up Portrait Commissions 1992; Chair. Sotheby's U.K. 1994–, Sotheby's Europe 1997–. *Leisure interests:* cricket, golf, fishing, shooting, travelling, soccer (Brighton & Hove Albion supporter), visiting museums, galleries and houses. *Address:* Sotheby's, 34 New Bond Street, London, W.1 (Office); The Old Rectory, Southease, Nr. Lewes, Sussex, BN7 3HX, England (Home). *Telephone:* 0171-493 8080 (Office); (01273) 513800 (Home).

WYNNE-MORGAN, David; British public relations executive; b. 22 Feb. 1931; s. of John Wynne-Morgan and late Marjorie Wynne-Morgan; m. 1st Romaine Ferguson; two s.; m. 2nd Sandra Douglas-Home (divorced); m. 3rd Karin E. Stines; two s.; ed. Bryanston School; reporter, Daily Mail 1952–55; foreign corresp., later William Hickey, Daily Express 1955–58; contracted to Sunday Times to write biographical features including ghosting autobiog. of late Pres. Nasser of Egypt; founder, Chair. and Man. Dir. Partnerplan 1964–80; Man. Dir. Extel Public Relations 1980–83; Chair. 1983–84; Chair. and Chief Exec. Hill & Knowlton (U.K.) Ltd. 1984–90, Pres. Hill & Knowlton Europe, Middle East and Africa 1990–94, Chair. Worldwide Exec. Cttee., consultant 1994–96; Chair. W.M.C. Communications 1995–; Chair. Marketing Group of G.B. 1989–90; Dir. Horsham Corpn. 1995–97; mem. Inst. of Public Relations. *Publications:* biographies of Pietro Annigoni, Margot Fonteyn, Sir Malcolm Sargent. *Leisure interests:* squash (fmr. Welsh Int.), cricket, tennis, riding, golf. *Address:* W.M.C. Communications, Elsinore House, 77 Fulham Palace Road, London, W6 8JA; 8 Leighton Mansions, Queens Club Gardens, London, W.14, England. *Telephone:* 0181-741 7444 (W.M.C. Communications). *Fax:* 0181-741 7333 (W.M.C. Communications).

WYPLOSZ, Charles, PH.D., DIPL. ENG.; French professor of economics; b. 5 Sept. 1947, Vichy; s. of Jacob Wyplosz and Félicia Zanger; m. Claire-Lise Monod 1967; one s. three d.; ed. Univ. of Paris, Harvard Univ.; Asst., Assoc., then Full Prof. of Econs. INSEAD, Fontainebleau 1978–, Assoc. Dean (Research and Devt.) 1986–89; Directeur d'études, EHESS, Paris 1988–95; Prof. of Econs., Grad. Inst. of Int. Studies, Geneva 1995–; Man. Ed. Economic Policy 1984–; Econ. Adviser EC 1994, 1997, IBRD 1995–97; mem. Scientific Council, Banque de France 1990–; mem. Council of European Econ. Asscn. 1990–; Foreign Corresp. FNRS, Belgium 1989–. *Publications:* numerous publications in professional journals; occasional contribs. to press. *Leisure interests:* skiing, music, family. *Address:* Graduate Institute of International Studies, 11 avenue de la Paix, 1202 Geneva (Office); 3 rue du Valais, 1202 Geneva; les Estras, 26770 Taulignan, Switzerland (Homes). *Telephone:* 22-734-8950 (Office). *Fax:* 22-733-3049 (Office).

WYZNER, Eugeniusz, M.A.; Polish diplomatist; b. 31 Oct. 1931, Chełmno; s. of Henryk Wyzner and Janina (Czaplicka) Wyzner; m. Elżbieta Laudańska 1961; one s.; ed. Jagellonian Univ., Cracow, Warsaw Univ. and Acad. of Int. Law, The Hague; official, Ministry of Foreign Affairs 1952–; Sec. Neutral

States Supervisory Comm. in Korea 1954–55; Deputy Perm. Rep. to UN 1961–68; Deputy Dir. of Dept. at Ministry of Foreign Affairs 1968–71, Dir. of Dept. 1971–73, Amb., Perm. Rep. to UN, Geneva 1973–78; Dir. of Dept., Ministry of Foreign Affairs 1978–81; Perm. Rep. to UN 1981–82, 1998–; UN Under-Sec.-Gen. 1982–94, for Public Information 1992–94; UN Commr.-Gen., Expo 1993–94; Deputy Minister for Foreign Affairs and Parl. Sec., Ministry of Foreign Affairs 1994–95, Acting Minister for Foreign Affairs Dec. 1995, Sec. of State, First Deputy Minister for Foreign Affairs 1996–97; mem. Bd. of Dirs. Int. Inst. of Space Law, Paris, Int. Peace Acad., New York, Int. Congress Inst. 1987–; Chair. UN Steering Cttee. on Status of Women 1989–91, UN Appointments and Promotion Bd. 1991–94, UN Exhibits Cttee. 1992–94; mem. UN Sr. Bd. on Services to the Public 1989–94; Amb. ad personam; Gold Cross of Merit 1964, Commdr.'s Cross of Order of Polonia Restituta, Commdr.'s Cross, Légion d'honneur, and other decorations. *Publications:* Wybrane zagadnienia z działalności ONZ w dziedzinie kodyfikacji i postępowego rozwoju prawa międzynarodowego 1962, Niektóre aspekty prawne finansowania operacji ONZ w Kongo i na Bliskim Wschodzie 1963. *Leisure interests:* cross-country skiing, mountain walking, theatre. *Address:* Permanent Mission of Poland, 9 East 66th Street, New York, NY 10021, U.S.A. *Telephone:* (212) 744-2506. *Fax:* (212) 517-6771.

X

XENAKIS, Yannis; French composer, architect and engineer; b. 1 May 1922, Braïla, Romania; s. of Clearchos Xenakis and Fotini Pavlou; m. Françoise Gargouïl 1953; one d.; ed. Athens Polytechnic Inst., Ecole Normale de Musique, Paris (with Milhaud), Gravesano (with Scherchen) and Paris Conservatoire (under Messiaen); studied eng. in Athens; fought in Greek Resistance, World War II, condemned to death; went into exile in France 1947; collaborated as engineer and architect with Le Corbusier 1947–60; innovator of mass concept of music, Stochastic Music and Symbolic Music through probability calculus and set theory into instrumental, electro-acoustic and computerized musical composition; designer, Philips Pavilion, Brussels World Fair 1958, sonic, sculptural and light composition Polytope for French Pavilion, Expo 1967 Montreal, music and light spectacle Persepolis on ruins and mountain, Persepolis, Iran 1970, Polytope de Cluny, Paris 1972; founder and Dir. Equipe de Mathématique et Automatique Musicales, Paris, 1966–, Center for Math. and Automated Music, Indiana Univ.; Assoc. Prof. Indiana Univ. 1967–72; Emer. Prof. Univ. of Paris I; Gresham Prof. in Music, City Univ., London; mem. C.N.R.S., France; Hon. mem. American Acad. of Arts and Letters, (mem. Council) Acad. des Arts et des Lettres, Acad. des Beaux Arts, France; Hon. D.Mus. (Edin.) 1989, (Glasgow) 1990; Maurice Ravel Gold Medal 1974; Beethoven Prize (Fed. Repub. of Germany) 1977, Kyoto Prize (Japan) 1997, Polar Music Prize (Sweden) 1999; Commdr. de l'Ordre des Arts et des Lettres, Officier Ordre nat. du Mérite, Officier, Légion d'honneur. *Works include:* Metastasis (for orchestra) 1954, Pithoprakta (for string orchestra) 1956, Achorripsis (for 21 instruments) 1957, Symos (for 18 string instruments) 1959, Analogiques (for 9 string instruments and magnetic tape) 1959, ST/10-1,080262 (for 10 instruments) 1957–62, Atrées (for 10 instruments) 1962, Amorsima-Morsima (for 4 instruments) 1962, Stratégie (for 84 instruments and 2 conductors) 1963, ST/4-2 (for string quartet) 1962, Eonta (for piano and brass) 1963, Akrat 1965, Terretektorh 1966, Nuits 1968, Nomos Gamma 1968, Persephassa 1969, Antikhthon 1971, Aroura 1971, Linaia-Agon 1972, Eridanos 1973, Cendrées 1974, Erikhthon 1974, Gmeeoorh 1974, Noomena 1974, Empreintes 1975, Phlegra 1975, Psappha 1975, N'Shima 1975, Khoaï 1976, Retours—Windungen 1976, Epeï 1976, Dmaathen 1976, Akanthos 1977, Kottos 1977, Jonchaies 1977, Le Diatope (Actions of Laser Beams, Electron, Flashes, 7-Track Tape music, computer controlled show in portable structure) 1978, Polytope at Mycenae 1978, Pleiades 1978, Aïs 1980, Nekuïa 1981, Komboï 1981, For the Whales 1982, Shaar 1983, Tetras 1983, Lichens 1984, Naama 1984, Thalein 1984, Alax 1985, Idmen A, B 1985, Keqrops 1986, Horos 1986, A l'île de Gorée 1986, Akea 1986, Keren 1986, Ata 1987, Kassandra 1987, Xas 1987, Tauriphanie 1987, Jalons 1988, Waarg 1988, Echange 1989, Epicycle 1989, Okho 1989, Oo Phaa 1989, Voyage absolu des Unari vers Andromède 1989, Knephas 1990, Kyania 1990, Tetora 1990, Krinoïdi 1991, Roaï 1991, Troorkh 1991, Dox-Orkh 1991, Gendy 3 1991, The Bacchae 1993. *Publications:* Musiques formelles 1963, Formalized Music 1970, Musique Architecture 1970, Xenakis—les Polytopes 1975, Arts/Sciences: Alloys 1979, and many articles. *Leisure interests:* camping and kayaks. *Address:* Institut de France, 23 Quai Conti, 75006 Paris (Office); 9 rue Chaptal, 75009 Paris, France (Home).

XI JINPING; Chinese politician; b. June 1953, Fuping, Shaanxi Prov.; ed. Tsinghua Univ., joined CCP 1974; Sec. CCP Fuzhou City Cttee. 1990–; alt. mem. CCP 15th Cen. Cttee. 1997–. *Address:* Chinese Communist Party Fuzhou City Committee, Fuzhou, Fujian Province, People's Republic of China.

XI ZEZONG; Chinese scientist; b. 9 June 1927, Shanxi Prov.; s. of Xi Renyin and Li Mudan; m. Shi Liuyun 1956; one s. one d.; ed. Zhongshan Univ.; mem. Chinese Acad. of Sciences 1991; mem. Int. Acad. of History of Science 1993–, Int. Eurasian Acad. of Sciences 1995–; Pres. Chinese Soc. of History of Science and Tech. 1994–. *Address:* Institute for History of Natural Science, 137 Chao-Nei Street, Beijing 100010, People's Republic of China. *Telephone:* 4043989. *Fax:* 4017637.

XI ZHONGXUN; Chinese party official; b. 1912, Fuping Co., Shaanxi Prov.; joined CCP 1927; Alt. mem. 7th Cen. Cttee., CCP 1945, Dir. Org. Dept., Cen. Cttee. 1945; Deputy Sec. N.W. Bureau, Cen. Cttee. 1945–48, Sec. 1948; Political Commissar 1st Field Army 1949; Vice-Chair. N.W. Mil. and Admin. Council 1949; Political Commissar N.W. Mil. Region 1949–54; Vice-Chair. Cultural and Educational Cttee., Govt. Admin. Council 1952–54; mem. State Planning Comm. 1952; Vice-Chair. N.W. Admin. Council 1953; Dir. Propaganda Dept., CCP Cen. Cttee. 1953–54; Sec.-Gen. Govt. Admin. Council 1953–54; Deputy for Xi'an, 1st NPC 1954; Sec.-Gen. State Council 1954; mem. 8th Cen. Cttee., CCP 1956; Vice-Chair. Cen. Relief Comm. 1957; Deputy for Shaanxi, 2nd NPC 1958; Vice-Premier State Council 1959; disappeared 1962–66; purged 1967; mem. Standing Cttee., 5th CPPCC 1978; Second Sec. CCP Cttee., Guangdong 1978, First Sec. 1979; Vice-Chair. Prov. Revolutionary Cttee., Guangdong 1978–79, Chair. 1979; mem. 11th Cen. Cttee., CCP 1979; First Political Commissar, Guangdong Mil. Region 1979–80; Vice-Chair. Standing Cttee., 5th NPC 1980–83, Vice-Chair. 7th NPC 1988; Chair. Comm. on Legis. Affairs, NPC 1981–, Bills Cttee. 5th NPC 1981–83; mem. Secr., Cen. Cttee. 1981–85; mem. Politburo, 12th Cen. Cttee. 1982–87; Deputy Sec.-Gen. CCP 12th Nat. Congress 1982; Gov. of Guangdong 1982–83; Adviser, Cen. Party Consolidation Guidance Comm. 1983–; Hon. Pres. Beijing Social Welfare Foundation 1984–, Badminton Asscn. 1985–; Vice-Chair. Standing Cttee. NPC 1988–93; mem. Presidium of 14th CCP Nat. Congress 1992; several hon. and advisory positions. *Address:* Standing Committee of National People's Congress, 19 Xijiaominxiang, Xicheng Qu, Beijing 100805, People's Republic of China.

XIA PEISU; Chinese computer engineer; b. July 1923; Ed.-in-Chief Journal of Computer Science and Tech.; mem. Chinese Acad. of Sciences 1992–; research fellow Computer Tech. Inst. *Address:* Computer Technology Institute, Zhong Guan Cun, Beijing 100080, People's Republic of China.

XIAN DINGCHANG; Chinese nuclear physicist; b. 15 Aug. 1935, Guangzhou; s. of Xian Jiaqi and Li Zuoming; m. Ren Mengmei 1966; two s.; ed. Beijing Univ.; Research Prof. Inst. of High Energy Physics, Academia Sinica; Chair. Chinese Synchrotron Radiation Soc. 1996–; mem. Chinese Acad. of Sciences 1992. *Publication:* Synchrotron Radiation Applications 1997. *Leisure interests:* literature, music. *Address:* Institute of High Energy Physics, 19 Yuquan Road, Beijing 100039, People's Republic of China. *Fax:* (10) 68213374.

XIANG HUAICHENG; Chinese politician; b. 1939, Wujiang Co., Jiangsu Prov.; ed. Shandong Univ.; Joined CCP 1983; Vice-Minister of Finance 1994–98, Minister 1998–; Vice-Minister State Admin. of Taxation 1994–; mem. 15th CCP Cen. Cttee. 1997–. *Address:* Ministry of Finance, 3 Nansanxiang, Sanlihe Road, Xicheng District, Beijing 100820, People's Republic of China.

XIAO YOUNG (XIAOYANG); Chinese party and government official; b. August 1938, Heyuan Co., Guangdong Prov.; ed. People's Univ. of China; joined CCP 1966; imprisoned during "Cultural Revolution" 1968–71; Deputy Dir. Qujiang Co. CCP Cttee. Office, then various party posts 1971–81; Sec. CCP Cttee. of Wujiang Region, Shaoguan City, Guangdong Prov. 1981–83; Deputy Sec. Qingyuang Prefectural CCP Cttee., Guangdong 1983; Deputy Chief Guangdong Prov. Procurator's Office, Deputy Sec. CCP Leadership Group 1983–86; Procurator-Gen. Guangdong Prov. Procurator's Office 1986–90; Deputy Procurator-Gen. Supreme Procurator's Office, Deputy Sec. CCP Leadership Group 1990–92; Minister of Justice 1993–98; alt. mem. 14th CCP Cen. Cttee. 1992–97; mem. 15th CCP Cen. Cttee. 1997–; Pres. Supreme People's Court 1998–. *Address:* Supreme People's Court, 27 Dongjiaominxiang, Beijing, People's Republic of China.

XIE BINGXIN; Chinese writer; b. 5 Oct. 1900, Fuzhou City, Fujian Prov. (as Xie Wanying); d. of Xie Baozhang and Yang Fuci; m. Wu Wenzao 1929; one s. two d.; ed. Bridgeman Acad. for Girls, Women's Union Coll., Yanjing Univ, Wellesley Coll., U.S.A.; participated in May 4th Movt.; Lecturer, Yanjing Univ., Qinghua Univ. and Women's Coll. of Science and Arts 1926–37; taught Tokyo Univ., Japan 1949–50; mem. NPC 1954–59, 1959–64, 1964–69, 1973–78; May 7th Cadres' School, Hubei 1970–72; Cen. Inst. of Nationalities, Beijing 1972–76; Vice-Chair. Asscn. for Promoting Democracy 1979–88, (Hon. Chair. 1988–), China Fed. of Literature and Art 1979–88; mem. Standing Cttee. CPPCC 1978; Hon. Pres. Prose Soc. 1984; Adviser China Literary Foundation 1983–, China Writers' Asscn. 1984–96, Hon. Chair. 1997; Hon. Chair. China Asscn. for Promoting Democracy 1988–. *Publications:* poetry: Spring Water 1922, A Maze of Stars 1922; prose: Letters to Young Readers 1923–26, Things Past 1930, Returning South 1931, A Little Orange Lantern 1957, We Have Awoken Spring 1959, More Letters to Young Readers 1958–60, Ode to Cherry Blossoms 1961, Gleanings 1964; stories: Two Families 1923, Superman 1923, Parting of the Ways 1931, About Women 1943, Empty Nest 1980, About Men 1988; novella: Tao Qi's Diary 1952; translations: Gibran's The Prophet 1931, Sand and Foam 1963, Tagore's Gitanjali, The Gardener 1955, Selected Stories by Tagore 1981, Selected Poems by Tagore 1958, Mahendra's Selected Poems 1965, The Lamplighter by Anton Buttigieg 1981. *Address:* Flat 4, Unit 34, Residential Quarters, Central Institute of Nationalities, Beijing 100081, People's Republic of China. *Telephone:* 831-7601.

XIE FEI; Chinese party official; b. Nov. 1932, Lufeng, Guangdong Prov.; m. Peng Yuzhen 1957; two s.; joined CCP 1949; alt. mem. 12th CCP Cen. Cttee. 1982–87, mem. 13th Cen. Cttee. 1987–92; mem. 14th CCP Cen. Cttee. 1992–97, 15th CCP Cen. Cttee. 1997–; mem. Politburo CCP 1992–; Deputy Sec. CCP Cttee., Guangdong 1983–87; Sec. CCP Cttee., Guangzhou City 1986–88; Deputy Sec. Guangdong Cttee. CCP 1988–91; Sec. Guangdong Prov. Cttee. CCP 1991–98; Vice-Chair. Standing Cttee. 9th NPC 1998–. *Address:* Standing Committee of National People's Congress, Beijing, People's Republic of China.

XIE JIN; Chinese film director; b. 1923, Shangyu Co., Zhejiang Prov.; ed. Sichuan Nat. Drama School; Film Dir., Datong Film Studio, Shanghai 1948–50; Film Dir., Shanghai Film Studio 1953–88; Exec. Vice-Chair. 5th Nat. Cttee. Chinese Fed. of Literary and Art Circles 1988–96, Vice-Chair. 1996–; mem. 8th Nat. Standing Cttee. CPPCC 1994–; a Vice-Pres. Chinese Fed. for the Disabled 1988–; May 1 Labour Medal 1987. *Films include:* Red

Girl's Army (Hundred Flavers Award) 1960, Legend of Tian Yun (1st Golden Rooster Best Film Award) 1981, Lotus Town (Golden Rooster Best Film Dir. Award) 1987. *Address:* c/o Shanghai Film Studio, 595 Caoxi Beilu, Shanghai, People's Republic of China. *Telephone:* 388100 (Shanghai).

XIE SHIJIE; Chinese administrator; b. 1934, Liangping Co., Sichuan Prov.; ed. South-West Agricultural Coll.; joined CCP 1954; Vice-Gov. of Sichuan Prov. 1986–; Sec. CCP Sichuan Prov. Cttee. 1993–; mem. 14th CCP Cen. Cttee. 1992–97, 15th CCP Cen. Cttee. 1997–. *Address:* Sichuan Provincial Government, Chengdu City, Sichuan Province, People's Republic of China.

XIE TIELI; Chinese film director; b. 1925, Huaiyin Co., Jiangsu Prov.; joined CCP 1942; Film Dir. Beijing Film Studio; mem. 5th Nat. Cttee. Chinese Fed. of Literary and Art Circles 1988–, CPCC 8th NPC 1993–; mem. Educ., Science, Culture and Health Cttee.; Vice-Chair. Chinese Film Artists Asscn. 1985. *Films include:* February, Violent Storm. *Address:* Beijing Film Studio, 19 Beihuan Xilu Road, Beijing 100088, People's Republic of China.

XIE XIDE, PH.D.; Chinese physicist; b. 19 March 1921, Jinjiang, Fujian Prov.; d. of late Xie Yuming (Yu Ming Hsieh); m. Cao Tianqin (q.v.) (Tian Chin Tsao) 1952; one s.; ed. Smith Coll. and Massachusetts Inst. of Tech., U.S.A.; joined CCP 1956; taught in Physics Dept., Fudan Univ. 1952–77, Vice-Pres. Physics Soc. 1978, Vice-Pres. Fudan Univ. 1978–83, Pres. 1983–88, Adviser 1988–; mem. Presidium, mem. Scientific Council and Vice-Chair., Vice-Pres. Chinese Physical Soc.; Pres. Shanghai Asscn. of Science and Tech., Science Fund Cttee., Acad. of Sciences 1981; mem. 12th CCP Cen. Cttee. 1982, mem. 13th Cen. Cttee. 1987; mem. CPPCC 8th Nat. Cttee. 1993–; Party Group Sec. Shanghai Municipal Cttee. 1989, CPPCC Shanghai Cttee. 1988; Fellow American Inst. of Physics 1986, The Third World Acad. of Sciences 1988; Hon. D.S. (Smith Coll., Mass.) 1981, (CCNY of Columbia Univ., New York) 1981, (Leeds Univ., U.K.) 1985, (Mount Holyoke Coll., U.S.A.) 1986, (Kansai Univ., Japan) 1986, (Beloit Coll., Wis., U.S.A.) 1987, (State Univ. of N.Y., Albany, U.S.A.) 1987, (Tokyo Univ., Japan) 1987; Hon. D.Eng. (Tokyo) 1987. *Publications:* Semiconductor Physics (with Huang Kun) 1958, Solid Physics (with Fang Junxin) 1962, chapter on Non-crystalline Material, Solid State Physics, Vol. II (by Fang Junxin and Lu Dong) 1982, Group Theory and its Applications (maj. author) 1986; many papers in int. scientific journals. *Leisure interests:* reading, music appreciation, stamp collecting. *Address:* Fudan University, Shanghai, People's Republic of China. *Telephone:* 484906-2644.

XIE ZHENHUA; Chinese civil servant; b. Oct. 1949, Tianjin; ed. Tsinghua Univ., Wuhan Univ.; joined CCP 1977; teaching asst. Tsinghua Univ.; clerk State Construction Comm.; Dir. Radiation Office then Personnel Office of State Environment Protection Bureau (SEPB), Dir. Personnel Dept., Vice-Dir. 1977–93, Dir. 1993–; mem. CCP 15th Cen. Cttee. for Discipline Inspection 1997–. *Address:* State Environment Protection Bureau, Beijing, People's Republic of China.

XIMENES BELO, Mgr. Carlos Filipe, S.D.B.; Indonesian ecclesiastic; b. 3 Feb. 1948, Baucau, Dili; ordained priest 1980; consecrated Titular Bishop of Lorium 1988; Papal Admin. Dili; active in campaign for human rights in E. Timor; jt. winner Nobel Peace Prize (with José Ramos-Horta, q.v.), 1996. *Address:* Bishop's Residence, Dili, East Timor, Indonesia.

XIN DIANFENG; Chinese air force officer; b. Dec. 1933, Shuangliao Co., Jilin Prov.; ed. Air Force Aviation school; joined CCP 1951; joined North-east Democratic United Army 1947, took part in Liaoxi-Shenyang and Marching Southwest campaigns; served as team leader of cultural troop of Political Dept. of Chinese People's Volunteers in Korean War; served as pilot, squadron leader, deputy group commdr., commdr. of ind. group, regt. commdr. and deputy div. commdr. of Air Force Aviation 1957–78; Deputy Dir., then Dir. Mil. Training Dept. PLA Air Force 1978–83, Dir. of a mil. regional Air Force command post 1983–84, Deputy Chief of Staff PLA Air Force 1984–90, Deputy Commdr. of Air Force of Ji'nan Mil. Region 1990–93, Deputy Commdr. and Air Force Commdr. of Shenyang Mil. Region 1993, Chief of Staff PLA Air Force 1993, rank of Air Force Lieut. Gen. 1993, Deputy Commdr. PLA Air Force 1995–. *Address:* Ministry of National Defence, Beijing, People's Republic of China.

XING BENSI; Chinese philosopher and university professor; b. 7 Oct. 1929, Sheng Co., Zhejiang Prov.; s. of Xing Tinxu and Guei Yuyin; m. Zhou Bangyuan 1953; two d.; ed. Special School of Russian Language of CCP Cen. Cttee.; joined CCP 1950; teacher, Beijing Inst. of Russian Language 1952–56; Asst. Researcher and Academic Sec. Inst. of Philosophy under Chinese Acad. of Sciences 1957–66, Deputy Dir., Dir., Vice-Chair. Academic Cttee., under Chinese Acad. of Social Sciences 1978–82, Academician 1983–85; Guest Prof. Qinghua Univ. 1984–; mem. Council for Int. Cultural Exchange 1984; Deputy Gen. Ed. Philosophy Vol. of Chinese Encyclopaedia 1983–; Vice-Pres. CCP Cen. Cttee. Party School 1988–; Ed.-in-Chief Party journal Qiushi 1994–; NPC Deputy, Zhejiang Prov.; mem. NPC Law Cttee.; Visiting Scholar Columbia Univ. 1981. *Publications:* The Dualism of Ludwig Feurbach's Anthropology 1963, The Social Theory and Historical Viewpoint of Saint-Simon 1964, Humanism in the History of European Philosophy 1978, Philosophy and Enlightenment 1979, The Anthropology of Ludwig Feurbach 1981, Philosophy and Time 1984, Philosophy (Introduction to Philosophy Vol. of Chinese Encyclopaedia) 1987, The Past, Present and Future of Philosophy (Introduction, Little Encyclopaedia of Philosophy) 1987, and many other essays. *Leisure interests:* music, literature, Peking Opera, Chinese calligraphy. *Address:* Institute of Philosophy, Chinese Academy of Social Sciences, Beijing, People's Republic of China. *Telephone:* 500.7744-2219.

XING CHONGZHI; Chinese party official; b. 1927, Shexian, Hebei Prov.; joined CCP 1943; mem. Cen. Cttee., Communist Youth League 1964; Vice-Chair. Preparatory Cttee., 10th Congress of Communist Youth League 1978; Vice-Minister of Agric. 1979–82; alt. mem. 12th CCP Cen. Cttee. 1982, mem. 1985, mem. 13th CCP Cen. Cttee. 1987–92; Sec. CCP Cttee., Hebei 1985–92; mem. Presidium 14th CCP Nat Congress 1992; mem. 8th CPPCC Nat. Cttee. 1993–. *Address:* Hebei Provincial Chinese Communist Party, Shijiazhung, Hebei, People's Republic of China.

XING SHIZHONG, Gen.; Chinese army officer; b. Sept. 1938, Licheng Co., Shandong Prov.; ed. Nanjing Eng. Army School; joined CCP 1957; staff officer in a div. engineer section 1959, a div. operational training section 1965, commdr. of corps-affiliated eng. bn. 1969, regt. commdr. 1975, chief of corps operational training div. 1978, div. chief of staff 1978, div. commdr. 1979, corps commdr. 1983, chief of staff Lanzhou Mil. Region 1985; rank of Maj.-Gen. 1988, Lieut.-Gen. 1993; Deputy Commdr. Ji'nan Mil. Region 1995–96; Commandant Nat. Defence Univ. 1995–; rank of Gen. 1998; mem. 15th CCP Cen. Cttee. 1997–. *Address:* National Defence University, Beijing, People's Republic of China.

XIONG GUANGKAI, Lieut.-Gen.; Chinese diplomatist and army officer; b. March 1939, Nanchang City, Jiangxi Prov.; ed. August 1st Middle School, Beijing, PLA Training School for Foreign Langs.; joined PLA 1956; joined CCP 1959; translator, secretarial asst. Office of Mil. Attaché, Chinese Embassy, German Democratic Repub. 1960–72; Asst. Mil. Attaché, Chinese Embassy, Fed. Repub. of Germany 1972–80; student PLA Military Acad. 1981–83; Asst. Div. Chief, Intelligence Dept., Gen. Staff HQ 1983–85, Deputy Dir. 1985–87, Dir. 1987–88, Asst. to Chief of Gen. Staff 1988, Deputy Chief of Gen. Staff 1996–; rank of Maj.-Gen. 1988; alt. mem. 14th CCP Cen. Cttee. 1992–97, mem. 15th CCP Cen. Cttee. 1997–; mem. Central Cttee. Leading Group on Taiwan 1993–; rank of Lieut.-Gen. 1993; Head of mil. delegation to U.S.A. 1995.

XIONG QINGQUAN; Chinese party and state official; b. 1927, Shuangfeng, Hunan Prov.; Mayor of Changsha 1982; alt. mem. 12th CCP Cen. Cttee. 1982, mem. 1985–87; mem. 13th Cen. Cttee. CCP 1987–92; mem. Presidium 14th CCP Nat. Congress 1992; Sec. CCP Cttee., Hunan Prov. 1983–85, Deputy Sec. 1985–88, Sec. 1988–93; Gov. of Hunan 1985–89; fmr. Party Cttee. First Sec. PLA Hunan Prov. Command; mem. 8th NPC 1993–; NPC Deputy, Hunan Prov. *Address:* Hunan Provincial People's Government, Changsha, Hunan, People's Republic of China.

XIONG SHEN; Chinese mechanical engineer and academic; b. 13 Sept. 1935, Jiangsu Prov.; s. of Shen Baozhang and Xu Shifeng; m. Xia Xuejian 1965; one d.; ed.; Tsinghua Univ.; teacher, Dept. of Eng. Mechanics, Tsinghua Univ. 1959–, now Prof., Dir. Fluid Mechanics Lab. 1988–; mem. Evaluation Cttee. of Academic Degree of Mechanics 1989–; mem. Advisory Cttee. of Int. Symposium on Applications of Laser Techniques to Fluid Mechanics 1988–; Nat. Rep., Int. Congress on Laser Anemometry! Advances and Applications 1989–; Ed. Journal of Experimental Mechanics (China) 1991–, Journal of Aerodynamic Experiments and Measurement and Control (China) 1988–; several prizes including State Prize of Science Congress 1978, Prize of Science and Tech. of State Bureau of Instrumentation Industry 1981, State Prize of Invention 1992, Prize of Zhou Peiyuan Foundation 1992. *Publications include:* Modern Techniques and Measurements in Fluid Flows 1989, Turbulent Correlation Measurement with 2-point LDV System 1996. *Leisure interests:* music, playing piano and accordion. *Address:* Department of Engineering Mechanics, Tsinghua University, Beijing 100084, People's Republic of China. *Telephone:* (10) 62784476, 62788649. *Fax:* (10) 62785569.

XONGERIN BADAI; Chinese Inner Mongolia administrator, writer and poet; b. 5 June 1930, Bayinguoltng Prefecture, Hejin Co., Xinjiang; s. of Honger Xongerin and Bayinchahan Xongerin; m. 1952; two s. two d.; Pres. Xinjiang Broadcasting and TV Univ. 1982–; Chair. Cttee. of Xinjiang Uygur Autonomous Region of CPPCC 1989; mem. Standing Cttee. CPPCC 1991. *Publications:* several books of prose and poetry and history in Mongol language and Chinese. *Leisure interests:* history of poetry, writing plays, Mongol history. *Address:* 15 South Beijing Road, Urumqi, Xinjiang, People's Republic of China. *Telephone:* (991) 2825701 (Office); (991) 3839303 (Home). *Fax:* (991) 2823443.

XU BING, M.F.A.; Taiwanese artist; b. 8 Feb. 1955, Chongqing; s. of Hua-min Xu and Shi-ying Yang; ed. Cen. Acad. of Fine Arts, Beijing; Asst. Prof. Printmaking Dept., Cen. Acad. of Fine Arts 1987–, Assoc. Dir. 1988–; Hon. Adviser, Dept. of Art, Beijing Univ. 1989–; Hon. Fellow, Art Dept., Univ. of Wisconsin-Madison 1990; exhbns. in China, France, U.S.A., Switzerland, U.K., Italy, Japan, Germany, Turkey 1979–; one man exhbns. Beijing Art Gallery 1988, Taipei 1988, Taiwan 1990; mem. Chinese Engraving Artists' Asscn. 1981–, Chinese Artists' Asscn. 1982–, Dir. 1985–; Dir. Chinese Engraving Artists' Asscn. 1986–; mem. Acad. Affairs Cttee., of Cen. Acad. of Fine Arts 1988–; mem. Printmaking Artists' Cttee. Chinese Fine Arts Asscn. 1989–; mem. Appraisal Cttee. 7th Chinese Nat. Exhbn. of Fine Arts 1989; prizes from Art Exhbns. of Chinese Young Artists' Works 1980, 1985, 8th Exhbn. of China's Wooden Paintings 1983, Medal, 9th Chinese Engraving Exhbn. 1986, Award for Excellent Prints, Taiwan 1988, Henry E. T. Kok

Educ. Foundation Prize for Young Instructors at Insts. of Higher Learning 1989. *Publications:* Wooden Painting Sketches of Xu Bing 1986, Engravings of Xu Bing; numerous articles in magazines and newspapers. *Leisure interest:* hiking.

XU CAIDONG; Chinese administrator and engineer; b. 1919, Fengxin Co., Jiangxi Prov.; ed. Tangshan Inst., Jiaotong Univ., Hebei, and Grenoble Inst., France; returned to China 1955; Prof., Guizhou Eng. Inst. 1958–; Pres., Science Acad. of Guizhou Prov. 1978; Vice-Gov. Guizhou Prov. 1983; mem. Dept. of Tech. Sciences, Academia Sinica 1985–; Vice-Chair. Jiu San Soc. 1983–; mem. 7th Nat. People's Congress, 8th NPC 1993–, mem. Educ., Science, Culture and Public Health Cttee.; NPC Deputy, Guizhou Prov. *Publication:* The Physical Chemistry of Zinc. *Address:* Guizhou Provincial People's Government, Guiyang, Guizhou Province, People's Republic of China.

XU CAIHOU, Lieut.-Gen.; Chinese army officer; b. 1943, Wafangdian City, Liaoning Prov.; ed. PLA Mil. Eng. Acad.; joined CCP 1971; Dir. Army Group Political Dept. 1985 then Army Group Political Commissar; rank of Maj.-Gen. 1990; Asst. Dir. PLA Gen. Political Dept. 1992 Dir. Jiefangjun Bao (Liberation Army Daily) 1992, Vice-Dir. 1993–; Lieut.-Gen. 1993; mem. 15th CCP Cen. Cttee. 1997–. *Address:* People's Liberation Army General Political Department, Beijing, People's Republic of China.

XU CHENGSHI; Chinese journalist; fmrly. with English service Xinhua official news agency. *Address:* c/o Xinhua News Agency, 57 Xuanwumen Xidajie, Beijing 100803, China.

XU HOUZE; Chinese geodesist and geophysicist; b. 4 May 1934, Anhui; s. of Xu Zuoren and Jiang Xinghua; m. Yang Huiji 1967; one s. one d.; ed. Tongji Univ., Shanghai, Dept. of Geodesy; Asst. Researcher Inst. of Geodesy and Geophysics, Chinese Acad. of Sciences 1963, Assoc. Prof. 1978, Prof. 1982–, Dir. 1983–; Dir. Survey and Geophysics Inst. 1992–; mem. Chinese Geophysics Soc. 1978–; Vice-Pres. Int. Gravimetry Cttee. and Pres. Perm. Cttee. of Earth Tides, Int. Asscn. of Geodesy (IAG) 1983–; Vice-Pres. Science-Tech. Soc. of Hubei Prov. 1984–, Chinese Survey and Mapping Soc. 1985–; Prof. Tongji Univ. 1985–, Wuhan Tech. Univ. of Survey and Mapping 1986–; NPC Deputy, Hubei Prov. *Publications:* The Approximation of Stokes' Function and the Estimation of Trunction Error 1981, The Effect of Oceanic Tides on Gravity Tide Observations 1982, The Tidal Correction in Astrometry 1982, Accuracy Estimation of Loading Correction in Gravity Observation 1984, The Effect of Different Earth Models on Load Tide Correction 1985, Representation of Gravity Field outside the Earth using Fictitious Single Layer Density 1984, Collected Papers on Earth Tides 1988, Model of Oceanic Load Tide Correction in Chinese Continent 1988. *Address:* 54 Xu Dong Road, Wuchang, Hubei 430077, People's Republic of China. *Telephone:* 813405.

XU HUAIZHONG, Maj.-Gen.; Chinese writer; b. 1929, Hebei Prov.; s. of Xu Hongchang and Xin Zhuoliang; m. Yu Zengxiang; one s. two d.; mem. Presidium and Dir. Bd. of Dirs., Chinese Writers' Asscn. 1983–; Deputy Cultural Dir., Gen. Political Dept. of PLA 1985–88, Dir. 1988–; rank of Major Gen. 1988; mem. Nat. Cttee. CPPCC 1993–; Vice-Chair. Chinese Writers' Asscn. 1996–; a Deputy Head Propaganda Dept., CPC 5th Fujian Prov. Cttee. 1989–96. *Publications:* Rainbow over the Earth, On the Tibetan Highlands, Anecdotes from the Western Front, The Wingless Angel (collection of medium-length novels and short stories), The Selected Works of Xu Huaizhong 1989. *Leisure interests:* playing table tennis and traditional Chinese shadow boxing. *Address:* 21 North Street Andeli, East District, Beijing, People's Republic of China.

XU HUIZI, Gen.; Chinese army officer and party official; b. 9 Dec. 1932, Penglai Co., Shandong Prov.; joined PLA 1948, CCP 1950; Deputy Chief of Gen. Staff 1985–95, rank of Lieut.-Gen. 1988, rank of Gen. 1994; Pres. Acad. of Mil. Sciences 1995–97; mem. 14th CCP Cen. Cttee. 1992–97; mem. Preliminary Working Cttee. of the Preparatory Cttee. of the Hong Kong Special Admin. Region 1993–97; Vice-Chair. People's Air Defence Cttee. 1988–; Deputy Sec. for Discipline Inspection 1994–; Vice-Chair. Cttee. of Overseas Chinese Affairs, 9th NPC 1998–. *Address:* c/o Standing Committee of National People's Congress, Beijing, People's Republic of China.

XU JIALU; Chinese linguist; b. June 1937, Huai'an Co., Jiangsu Prov.; ed. Beijing Normal Univ.; Prof., Vice-Pres. Beijing Normal Univ.; joined China Asscn. for Promoting Democracy 1987; Dir. State Language Work Cttee. 1994–; Vice-Chair. 9th Cen. Cttee. of China Asscn. for Promoting Democracy, Chair. 10th Cen. Cttee. 1997–; mem. Standing Cttee. of 7th and 8th NPC; Vice-Chair. Standing Cttee. of 9th NPC 1998. *Address:* Beijing Normal University, Xinjiekouwai Street 19, Beijing 100875, People's Republic of China.

XU JIATUN; Chinese politician; b. 1916, Jiangsu; mem. of CCP, Deputy Sec., Sec., Fuzhou Municipal Cttee. in Fujian 1950; Sec. Nanjing Municipal Cttee. CCP in Jiangsu 1954; Sec. Secr. and mem. Standing Cttee. Jiangsu Provincial Cttee. CCP; Deputy Gov. of Jiangsu 1956; Vice-Chair. Jiangsu Prov. Revolutionary Cttee. 1970, 1974, Chair. 1977–79; Sec., then First Sec. Jiangsu Prov. Cttee. CCP; Chair. Standing Cttee. of Fifth People's Congress of Jiangsu; First Political Commissar of PLA of Jiangsu Prov. Mil. Dist. 1977–90; Chair. Jiangsu Prov. People's Congress 1979–83; First Sec. of Party Cttee. 1977–83, mem. 11th Cen. Cttee. of CCP 1977–82, 12th Cen. Cttee. CCP 1982–85; mem. Cen. Advisory Cttee. 1985–90; mem. Presidium 6th NPC 1986–90; Vice-Chair. Cttee. for Drafting Basic Law of Hong Kong Special Admin. Region 1985–91; Dir. Xinhua News Agency, Hong Kong 1983–90; mem. Standing Cttee., CCP 1988; stripped of all CCP posts 1991, living in Buddhist retreat 1991. *Publication:* Hong Kong Memoirs 1994.

XU KUANGDI; Chinese politician and educationist; b. 1937, Tongxiang Co., Zhejiang Prov.; ed. Beijing Metallurgy Inst.; joined CCP 1983; Prof., Vice-Pres. Shanghai Industrial Univ.; Dir. Shanghai Higher Educ. Bureau; Dir. Shanghai Planning Comm.; Vice-Mayor Shanghai Municipality 1992; Vice-Sec. CCP Shanghai Municipal Cttee. 1994; Mayor Shanghai Municipality 1995–; alt. mem. 14th CCP Cen. Cttee. 1992; mem. 15th CCP Cen. Cttee. 1997–. *Address:* Shanghai Municipal Government, Shanghai, People's Republic of China.

XU QIN; Chinese politician; b. 1928, Suizhong Co., Fengtian (now Liaoning) Prov., joined CCP 1949; Deputy for Jiangxi to 5th NPC 1978; Vice-Gov. Jiangxi 1979–83; Deputy Sec. CCP Cttee., Jiangxi 1981; Vice-Chair. Jiangxi People's Congress 1981, Chair. Feb. 1988; alt. mem. 12th CCP Cen. Cttee. 1982–87; mem. 8th NPC 1993–; NPC Deputy, Jiangxi Prov. *Address:* Jiangxi Provincial Chinese Communist Party, Nanchang, Jiangxi, People's Republic of China.

XU RONGCHU; Chinese government official; Dir. Dept. of Fixed Assets Investment, State Planning Comm. 1988–93; Pres. State Communications Investment Corpn. 1993–.

XU XIN, Gen.; Chinese army officer and party official; b. 1921, Ningshou, Hebei Prov.; joined Red Army and CCP 1937; rank of Maj.-Gen. PLA 1964; Chief of Staff, Beijing Units 1970–80; Political Commissar, Tianjin Garrison 1974; Sec. CCP Cttee., Tianjin 1975; Deputy for PLA, 5th NPC 1978; Deputy Dir. China Inst. for Int. Strategic Studies 1981–87, Dir. Dec. 1987–; Asst. to Chief of Gen. Staff, PLA 1980–82; alt. mem. 12th Cen. Cttee. CCP 1982–87; Deputy Chief of Gen. Staff, PLA 1982–, promoted to Gen. PLA 1988; Chair. Nat. Advertising Asscn. for Foreign Econ. Relations and Trade 1985, China-Romania Friendship Group; Dir. China Inst. for Int. Strategic Studies 1987–; mem. Cen. Advisory Comm. 1987, NPC Foreign Affairs Cttee. *Address:* c/o Beijing Institute for International Strategic Studies, Beijing, People's Republic of China.

XU YINSHENG; Chinese government official; b. 12 June 1938; m. Chen Liwen; one s.; World table tennis champion three times; Vice-Minister State Physical Culture and Sport Comm. 1977–98; Vice-Dir. State Gen. Admin. of Physical Culture; Pres. Chinese Table Tennis Asscn. 1979–, Chinese Boxing Asscn. 1987–; Exec. Vice-Chair. Preparatory Cttee. for 6th Nat. games 1985; Vice-Pres. Chinese Olympic Cttee. 1986–89, 1994–, All-China Sports Fed. 1989–; Exec. Vice-Pres. XIth Asian Games Organizing Cttee. 1990–; Pres. Int. Table Tennis Fed. 1997–. *Publication:* How to Play Table Tennis by Dialectics. *Leisure interests:* tennis, fishing. *Address:* 9 Tiyuguan Road, Beijing, People's Republic of China. *Telephone:* 7012233.

XU YONGQING, Lieut.-Gen.; Chinese army officer; b. 1938, Jiande Co., Zhejiang Prov.; joined PLA 1956; joined CCP 1956; Deputy Army Political Commissar; Army Group Political Commissar; Political Commissar Zhejiang Mil. Provincial Command; Deputy Political Commissar Lanzhou Mil. Area Command 1994; Political Commissar Armed Police; mem. 15th CCP Cen. Cttee. 1997–. *Address:* Armed Police Headquarters, Beijing, People's Republic of China.

XU YOUFANG; Chinese politician; b. 1939, Guangde Co., Anhui Prov.; ed. Anhui Agricultural Coll.; joined CCP 1973; Dir. Forestry Industry Bureau, Ministry of Forestry 1985; Vice-Minister for Forestry 1986–93, Minister 1993–; Deputy Dir. State Council Environment Protection Comm.; Dir. China Forestry Science and Tech. Comm.; Vice-Chair. Nat. Afforestation Comm. 1993–; Chair. Beijing Univ. of Forestry 1994–; Pres. China Wildlife Conservation Asscn. 1993–; Sec. CCP Heilongjiang Prov. Cttee. 1997–; mem. 15th CCP Cen. Cttee. 1997–. *Address:* Office of the Governor, Heilongjiang Provincial Government, Harbin City, People's Republic of China.

XU YUANHE; Chinese philosopher; b. 1942, Rugao, Jiangsu Prov.; ed. Peking Univ.; Asst. Research Fellow, Assoc. Research Fellow then Research Fellow Inst. of Philosophy, Chinese Acad. of Social Sciences 1980–; Dir. Oriental Philosophy Research Centre, Chinese Acad. of Social Sciences. *Publications:* Origin and Development of Luo Studies, The School of Reason and the Yuan Society, Confucianism and Oriental Culture. *Address:* Institute of Philosophy, Chinese Academy of Social Sciences, Beijing, People's Republic of China.

XU ZHENSHI; Chinese photographer, artist and publisher; b. 18 Aug. 1937, Songjiang Co., Shanghai; s. of Xu Weiqing and Jiang Wanying, step-s. of Cheng Shi-fa; m. Zhang Fuhe 1967; one d.; ed. No. 1 High School, Songjiang Co., Zhejiang Acad. of Fine Arts; moved to Beijing 1965; Ed., People's Fine Arts Publishing House 1965–86, Dir. Picture Editorial Dept. 1986–, Ed.-in-Chief 1992–; mem. China Artists' Asscn.; Deputy Sec.-Gen. Spring Festival Pictures Research Centre, Publrs.' Asscn. of China, Deputy Sec.-Gen. and Assoc. Dir. Photography Research Centre; mem. Selection Cttee. 3rd, 4th and 5th Nat. Exhbns. of Spring Festival Pictures and other exhbns.; Assoc. Dir. Standing Cttee. Spring Festival Pictures; Sr. Adviser, Office of East China–UN TIPS Nat. Exploit Bureau 1994–; exhbns. in China, Japan, Korea, Hong Kong, Thailand; Vice-Ed.-in-Chief Gouache Vol. of Anthology of Contemporary Chinese Fine Arts 1996; Vice-Pres. Chinese Fan Art Soc. 1997; organized 1st Nat. Exhbn. of Calligraphy and Paintings to Help the

Poor 1998; Dir. Foundation for Underdeveloped Regions in China 1998–; prepared 6th Nat. Exhbn. of Spring Festival Pictures 1998; numerous awards including Bronze Medal for albums of photographs, Leipzig Int. Book Exhbn. 1987, Nat. Award 1993, Model Ed. Nat. Press and Publs. System 1997, 1998. *Publications:* China's Cultural Relics Unearthed during the Great Cultural Revolution 1973, Travel in China (4 vols.) 1979–80, Tibet 1981, Travel in Tibet 1981, Costumes of China's Minority Nationalities 1981, Travel in Guilin 1981, Travel Leisurely in China 1981, Travel in Yunnan 1982, China's Flowers in Four Seasons 1982, Poet Li Bai 1983, Native Places of Tang Dynasty Poems 1984, Travel along the Yangtse River 1985, Through the Moongate: a guide to China's famous historical sites 1986, Waters and Mountains in China 1986, Travel in Guangzhou 1986, China 1987, The Chinese Nation 1989, Poet Du Fu 1989, Selected Works of Xu Zhenshi 1990, 1993, Selected Paintings of Xu Zhenshi 1993, 1994, Boat on the Plateau 1998, Album of Xu Zhenshi's Sketches 1999. *Leisure interest:* sports. *Address:* People's Fine Arts Publishing House, No. 32 Beizongbu Hutong, Beijing, People's Republic of China. *Telephone:* 65244901 (Office); 65246353 (Home).

XUE JU; Chinese politician; b. 1922, Yuncheng, Shanxi; ed. Datong Univ., Shanghai; joined CCP 1938; Deputy Sec. CCP Cttee., Zhejiang 1978–79; Vice-Chair. Prov. CPPCC Cttee., Zhejiang 1979–83; mem. 12th Cen. Cttee. 1982–87; mem. Presidium 6th NPC 1986; Gov. of Zhejiang 1983–87; Sec. Zhejiang CCP Cttee. 1987–88; Chair. CCP Zhejiang Provincial Advisory Cttee. 1988–92; Exec. Vice-Pres. Cen. Party School 1989; mem. Presidium 14th CCP Nat. Congress 1992, 8th NPC 1993–, NPC Deputy, Zhejiang Prov.; Chair. Law Cttee; mem. Cen. Leading Group for Party Bldg. Work. *Address:* Zhejiang Provincial People's Government, Hangzhou, Zhejiang Province, People's Republic of China.

XUE MUQIAO; Chinese politician and economist; b. 25 Oct. 1904, Wuxi Co., Jiangsu Prov.; m. Luo Qiong 1935; three d.; largely self-taught, ed. later high school; worked in Inst. of Social Sciences attached to Cen. Research Acad. conducting surveys of rural economy 1920s; Prof. of Rural Econs., normal school, Guangxi Prov. 1933; with other organized Soc. for Research in China's Rural Economy and Ed. Rural China monthly, Shanghai; First Dir. of Dept. of Training, Anti-Japanese Mil. and Political Acad. of Cen. China, Sec.-Gen. Anti-Japanese Democratic Govt. of Shandong Prov., war with Japan 1937–45; successively Sec.-Gen. of Financial and Econ. Comm. of Govt. Admin. Council, Vice-Minister in Charge of State Planning Comm., Dir. of State Statistical Bureau, Dir. Nat. Price Comm., mem. Council of Social Sciences, Academia Sinica; del. to First, Second and Third Nat. People's Congresses; mem. Nat. Cttee. Fifth CPPCC; adviser to State Planning Comm. 1979–, Dir. of its Econ. Inst., Prof., Peking Univ., Pres. Statistical Soc. 1979, Nat. Statistical Soc.; Hon. Pres. Soc. of Systems Eng. 1980; Pres. Planning Soc. 1984–; Adviser, Fed. of Econs. Socs. 1981, Office of Restructuring of Econ. System 1984–85; Hon. Dir.-Gen. Devt. Research Centre 1985–; Hon. Chair. Industrial Co-operative Asscn. 1983–; Sr. Adviser All-China Fed. of Industry and Commerce 1988–; mem. Academic Cttees. of the Econ. Inst. and Inst. of the World Economy, Chinese Acad. of Social Sciences. *Publications:* The Elementary Knowledge of China's Rural Economy, The ABC of Rural Economy, The Socialist Transformation of China's National Economy, Some Theoretical Problems Concerning the Socialist Economy, Research on Problems Concerning China's Socialist Economy, Research on Price and Currency Problems, Management of the Economy on the Basis of Objective Economic Law, Selected Works of Xue Muqiao, Reforms and the Theoretical Breakthrough, Selected Papers on the Economy. *Address:* Development Research Centre of the State Council, Beijing, People's Republic of China.

XUE WEI; Chinese violinist; b. 21 Dec. 1963, Henan; s. of Xue-Ming and Shang Yi-qing; ed. Shanghai Conservatory, Beijing Conservatory of Music and Guildhall School of Music, London; now resides in London appearing regularly with the maj. London orchestras; performs in solo recitals and as concert soloist at int. music festivals; guest soloist with Shanghai Symphony on tour in Japan; Prof. Royal Acad. of Music, London 1989–; numerous prizes including Silver Medal, Tchaikovsky Int. Competition (violin), Moscow 1986; Gold Medal, Carl Flesch Int. Competition 1986; London Philharmonic Soloist of the Year 1986. *Leisure interests:* reading, chess, poker. *Address:* 134 Sheaveshill Avenue, London, N.W.9, England.

Y

YAACOBI, Gad, M.A.; Israeli politician, diplomat and author; b. 18 Jan. 1935, Moshav Kfar Vitkin; s. of Alexander and Sara Yaacobi; m. Nela Yaacobi; three s. one d.; ed. Tel Aviv Univ.; mem. Moshavim Movt. 1960–67; Asst. to Minister of Agric., Head of Agric. and Settlement Planning and Devt. Centre 1960–66; mem. Cen. Cttee. Histadrut, Labour Union, Rafi Faction 1966–69; mem. Cen. Cttee., Secr. Labour Party; Deputy to Sec. Labour Party 1966–70; M.P. (Knesset) 1969–, Parl. Finance Cttee. 1969–70, Parl. Defence and Foreign Affairs Cttee. 1974; Deputy Minister of Transport 1971–74, Minister 1974–77, of Econs. and Planning 1984–88, of Communications 1987–90; mem. Inner Cabinet 1990; Chair. Parl. Econ. Cttee. 1977–89; Amb. to UN 1992–97; Chair. Labour Party Econ. Council; Chair. Israel Electric Corpn. 1996–. *Publications:* The Power of Quality 1971, The Freedom to Choose 1975, The Government 1980, A Call for Change 1983, On the Razor's Edge 1990; children's books 1988, 1990; Grace of Time (poems) 1991, A Breakthrough: Israel and the UN 1996, New York Diaries: A Place Nearby (poetry) 1997; many articles on economics and politics. *Leisure interests:* theatre, reading, writing poetry. *Address:* 6 Hadassa Street, Tel Aviv (Home). *Telephone:* (3) 527 0662. *Fax:* (3) 527 3510.

YABLOKOV, Alexey Vladimirovich, D.BIOL.SC.; Russian biologist; b. 3 Oct. 1933, Moscow; s. of Vladimir Yablokov and Tatiana Sarycheva; m. 1st Eleonora Bakulina 1955 (died 1987), one s.; m. 2nd Dil'bar Klado 1989; ed. Moscow Univ.; researcher, head of lab., Prof. N. Koltsov Inst. of Developmental Biology 1959–; political activities since late 1980s; Chair. Ichthyological Comm. of U.S.S.R. Ministry of Fishery 1989–92; U.S.S.R. People's Deputy 1989–91; Deputy Chair. Comm. on Ecology of U.S.S.R. Supreme Soviet 1989–91; State Counsellor on Ecology and Public Health to Pres. of Russia 1991–93; Chair. Interagency Comm. on Environmental Security, Russian Security Council 1993–97, Chair. Center of Russian Environmental Policy 1993–; Corresp. mem. U.S.S.R. (now Russian) Acad. of Sciences 1984; Pres. Moscow Soc. for Protection of Animals 1988–; mem. Exec. Cttee. Stockholm Environmental Inst. 1994–; Pew Fellowship 1994–97; Severtsev Prize, Karpinsky Prize, WASA Prize. *Publications:* 21 books and numerous articles on population, evolution and conservation biology, zoology, ecology, including Nuclear Mythology 1997. *Leisure interests:* writing, fishing, carpentry. *Address:* N. Koltsov Institue of Biology, Vavilova str. 26, 117808 Moscow, Russia. *Telephone:* (095) 952-30-07 (Office); (095) 134-44-21 (Home). *Fax:* (095) 952-30-07 (Office).

YACOUB, Sir Magdi Habib, Kt., F.R.C.S.; Egyptian cardiac surgeon; b. 16 Nov. 1935, Cairo; m.; one s. two d.; ed. Univ. of Cairo; British Heart Foundation Prof. of Cardiothoracic Surgery, Royal Brompton and Nat. Heart Lung Inst. 1986–; Consultant Cardiothoracic Surgeon, Harefield Hosp., Middx. 1969–; pioneered techniques of repair of complex congenital heart disease, homograft valve surgery and heart, heart-lung and lung transplantation; Hon. M.Ch. (Wales) 1986; Hon. D.Sc. (Loughborough Univ. of Tech.), (Keele) 1995. *Publications:* numerous medical papers. *Leisure interest:* orchid growing. *Address:* National Heart and Lung Institute, Dovehouse Street, London, SW3 6LY, England. *Telephone:* 0171-351 8534/3. *Fax:* 0171-351 8229.

YADLIN, Aharon; Israeli politician; b. 17 April 1926, Tel Aviv; s. of Haim Yadlin and Zipora Yadlin; m. Ada Hacohen 1950; three s.; ed. Hebrew Univ.; Co-founder Kibbutz Hatzerim; fmr. mem. Presidium, Israel Scouts Movement; mem. Exec. Council Histadrut (Israel Fed. of Labour) 1950–52; Prin. Beit Berl (Labour Party's centre for Educ.) 1956–58; mem. Knesset (Parl.) 1959–79; Deputy Minister of Educ. and Culture 1964–72; Gen. Sec. Israel Labour Party 1972–74; Minister of Educ. and Culture 1974–77; Chair. Educational and Cultural Cttee., Knesset 1977–79; Chair. Beit Berl Coll. of Educ. 1977–85; Chair. Bialik Inst., Books Publishing House and Acad. for Philosophy, Jewish Studies and World Literature 1990–; Sec.-Gen. United Kibbutz Movt. (TAKAM) 1985–89; Chair. Beer-Sheva Theatre, Janush Korczak Asscn. in Israel, Scientific Cttee. Ben Gurion Research Inst. and Archives 1979–85, Yad Tabenkin (Research Centre of Kibbutz Movt.), Beith Yatziv Educational Centre, Beer-Sheva, World Labour Zionist Movt. 1992–; Chair. Exec. Cttee., Ben Gurion Univ. of the Negev; lecturer and researcher in EFAL (educ. centre of United Kibbutzim movt.). *Publications:* Introduction to Sociology 1957, The Aim and The Movement 1969 and articles on sociology, education and youth. *Leisure interests:* stamps, gardening. *Address:* Kibbutz Hatzerim, Mobile Post Hanegev 85420, Israel. *Telephone:* 07-6473436. *Fax:* 07-6473600.

YADOV, Vladimir Aleksandrovich, DR. PHIL. SC.; Russian sociologist; b. 25 April 1929, Leningrad; m.; one s.; ed. Leningrad State Univ., Univ. of Manchester, London School of Econs.; with Inst. of Sociological Studies U.S.S.R. (now Russian) Acad. of Sciences, Inst. of Social and Econ. Problems U.S.S.R. (now Russian) Acad. of Sciences, Leningrad br. of Inst. of History of Nat. Sciences and Tech.; Dir. Inst. of Sociology Russian Acad. of Sciences 1986–; Dean, Inst. of Sociological Educ. at Repub. Centre of Humanitarian Educ. in St. Petersburg 1995–; Dr. h.c. Univs. of Tartu and Helsinki; Pres. Russian Sociological Soc. 1991–; mem. Int. Sociological Asscn. 1990– (Vice-Pres. 1990–94); mem. European Asscn. of Experimental Social Psychology 1989–, Int. Inst. of Sociology 1990–. *Publications:* numerous papers on theory and methods of sociology, sociology of labour, social psychology of personality and of science. *Address:* Institute of Sociology, Krzhizhanovskogo str. 24/35, korp 5, 117218 Moscow, Russia. *Telephone:* (095) 128 9109 (Office).

YAFI, Abdullah Aref al–; Lebanese politician and lawyer; b. 1901; ed. Collège des Pères Jésuites, Beirut, and Univ. de Paris à la Sorbonne; admitted to Beirut Bar 1926; Prime Minister and Minister of Justice 1938–39; Lebanese del. to preparatory conf. for founding League of Arab States 1944, to San Francisco Conf. 1945; Minister of Justice Dec. 1946–April 1947; Prime Minister 1951–52, 1953–54, March-Nov. 1956, April-Dec. 1966, 1968–69, concurrently Minister of the Interior 1951–52, 1953–54, March-Nov. 1956, July-Oct. 1968, of Defence 1953–54, Feb.-Oct. 1968, of Information 1953–54, April-Dec. 1966, 1968–69, of Finance March-Sept. 1954, of Planning June-Nov. 1956, April-Dec. 1966, Feb.-July 1968, 1968–69, of Social Affairs 1968–69, of Educ. 1968–69.

YAGI, Yasuhiro; Japanese engineer; b. 15 Feb. 1920; m.; one s. two d.; ed. Imperial Univ., Tokyo; joined Kawasaki Heavy Industries Ltd. 1943; Dir. and Asst. Gen. Supt. Mizushima Works 1971–74, Man. Dir. 1974–77, Sr. Man. Dir. Corporate Tech., Engineering and Tubarao Project 1977–79, Exec. Vice-Pres. Corporate Tech. and Tubarao Project 1979–82; Pres. Kawasaki Steel Corpn. June 1982–. *Leisure interests:* golf, "Go". *Address:* Kawasaki Steel Corporation, Hibiya Kokusai Building, 2-3, Uchisaiwaicho 2-chome, Chiyoda-ku, Tokyo 100, Japan.

YAGODIN, Gennadiy Alekseyevich; Russian physical chemist; b. 3 June 1927, Vyass, Penza region; s. of Alexei Yagodin and Alexandra Yagodina; m. 1949; one s. one d.; ed. Mendeleyev Chemical Tech. Inst., Moscow; mem. CPSU 1948–91; Deputy Dean, Mendeleyev Chemical Tech. Inst., Moscow 1956–59, Dean, Dept. of Physical Chemistry 1959–63, Prof. of Chemical Tech. 1959–63, 1966–73, Rector 1973–85; Deputy Dir.-Gen. (Head of Dept. of Training and Technical Information 1963–64, Head of Dept. of Technical Operations 1964–66), IAEA, Vienna 1963–66; U.S.S.R. Minister of Higher and Secondary Specialized Educ. 1985–89; Chair. State Cttee. for Nat. Educ. 1988–91; Rector Int. Univ. in Moscow 1992–; Deputy, U.S.S.R. Supreme Soviet 1986–89; mem. Cen. Cttee. CPSU 1986–89; Corresp. mem. U.S.S.R. (now Russian) Acad. of Sciences 1976–; mem. Russian Acad. of Educ.; Order of Lenin; D.Y. Mendeleyev Prize 1981, State Prize 1985. *Leisure interest:* collecting butterflies. *Address:* International University, Leningradsky prosp. 17, 125040 Moscow, Russia. *Telephone:* (095) 250-03-42. *Fax:* (502) 221-10-60; (095) 250-40-49 (Office); (095) 332-13-15 (Home).

YAKER, Layashi; Algerian civil servant; b. 1930, Algiers; m.; three c.; ed. Ecole de Commerce, Algiers, Ecole des Hautes Etudes at Sorbonne, Inst. d'Etude du Développement Economique et Social, Univ. of Paris and Conservatoire Nat. des Arts et Métiers, Paris; fmr. Prof. Nat. School of Admin. Algiers and Inst. of Political, Diplomatic and Int. Studies, Paris; fmr. Assoc. Dir. Inst. of Strategic Studies, Algiers; Political Sec. Ministry of Foreign Affairs of Provisional Govt. of Algeria in Cairo 1960–61; Head of Mission, Provisional Govt. of Algeria to India for S. Asia 1961–62; Minister Plenipotentiary, Ministry of Foreign Affairs and Dir.–Gen. for Econ. Social and Cultural Affairs and Int. Cooperation 1962–69; mem. Algerian/French Exec. Bd. Org. for Exploitation of Saharan Resources 1963–65; mem. Org. for Industrial Cooperation 1965–70; Gov. African Devt. Bank and Alt. Gov. IBRD 1966–68; Minister of Commerce 1969–77; Pres. Council of Ministers, Econ. Comm. for Africa (UNECA) 1973–76; Pres. Council of African Ministers of Commerce 1974–77; mem. Council IPU 1977–79; head of del. to numerous int. confs. 1961–87; M.P. 1977–79; Amb. to U.S.S.R. 1979–82, to U.S.A. 1982–84; Amb.-at-large 1985–87; int. consultant 1988–92; UN Under-Sec.-Gen. and Exec. Sec. Econ. Comm. for Africa (UNECA) 1992–95. *Address:* c/o Executive Secretary of the Economic Commission for Africa, P.O. Box 3001, Addis Ababa, Ethiopia.

YAKOVLEV, Aleksandr Maksimovich, D.JUR.; Russian lawyer; b. 30 Aug. 1927, Leningrad; s. of Maxim Yakovlev and Maria Yakovleva; m. Eugenia Yakovleva 1950; ed. Moscow Inst. of Law; sr. research fellow Inst. of Law, U.S.S.R. Ministry of Internal Affairs, then U.S.S.R. Ministry of Justice 1957–75; Head Dept. of Criminal Law and Criminology U.S.S.R. (now Russian) Inst. of State and Law, Prof. 1975–94, Sr. researcher 1996–; in democratic movt. since late 1980s; U.S.S.R. People's Deputy 1989–91; mem. Perm. Cttee. on Legis. U.S.S.R. Supreme Soviet 1989–91; Plenipotentiary Rep. of Pres. of Russia at Federal Ass. 1994–96, Expert to Council of Fed. 1997–; Visiting Prof. Univ. of Manitoba 1990, Rutgers Univ. 1991, Alberta Univ., N. York and Toronto Univ. 1992, Emory Univ. Atlanta 1993, 1997; Hon. LL.D. (Alberta Univ., Canada) 1991; mem. Int. Soc. of Social Defense, Paris, mem. Bd. of Dirs.; mem. Inst. of Sociology of Law for Europe. *Publications:* The Bear That Wouldn't Dance; Failed Attempts to Reform the Former Constitution of the Soviet Union (with Dale Gibson) 1992, Striving for Law in a Lawless Land 1995; several other books and more than 100 articles on various aspects of constitutional law, pubs. in journals. *Leisure interest:* travelling. *Address:* Dolgorukovskaya str. 40, Apt. 153, 103030 Moscow, Russia (Home). *Telephone:* (095) 978-84-97. *Fax:* (095) 291-85-74.

YAKOVLEV, Aleksandr Nikolayevich, D.HIST.; Russian politician; b. 2 Dec. 1923; m.; one s. one d.; ed. Yaroslavl Pedagogical Inst.; served in Soviet Army 1941–43; mem. CPSU 1944–91 (expelled); party work, Yaroslavl Dist. Cttee. CPSU 1946–48; chief lecturer at Yaroslavl Party School and corresp. of dist. newspaper 1948–50; Deputy Head of Dept. of Science and Culture, Cen. Cttee. of CPSU 1953–56; Instructor with Dept. of Propaganda and Agitation of Cen. Cttee. CPSU 1962–64; Head of Radio and TV Broadcasting Propaganda Dept. of Cen. Cttee. CPSU 1964–65; mem. of editorial staff of journal Kommunist; First Deputy Head, Acting Head of Cen. Cttee., Propaganda Dept. 1965–73; mem. of Cen. Auditing Comm. of Cen. Cttee. CPSU 1971–76; Amb. to Canada 1973–83; Dir. Inst. of World Econs. and Int. Relations, U.S.S.R. Acad. Sciences 1983–85; mem. of Council of Nationalities, U.S.S.R. Supreme Soviet, mem. of U.S.S.R. Parl. Group Cttee. 1984–89; Head of Cen. Cttee. CPSU Propaganda Dept. 1985–91; mem. Cen. Cttee. CPSU 1986–90; Sec. responsible for Propaganda of Cen. Cttee. CPSU 1986–87; mem. Political Bureau 1987–90; Head. Int. Policy Comm. 1988–90; People's Deputy 1989–91; mem. Presidential Council 1990–91; Sr. Presidential Adviser 1991; Chair. Moscow Public Ass. 1991–; mem. Political Consultative Council Sept.–Dec. 1991; Chair. Presidential Comm. on Rehabilitation of Political Prisoners 1992–; Pres. Democracy Foundation 1993–; Founder and Chair. Russian Party of Social Democracy 1995–; Head, State Radio-TV Co. Ostankino 1993–95; Chair. Bd. of Dirs., Russian Public TV 1995–96; Corresp. mem. Acad. of Sciences (Econs. Dept.) 1984, mem. 1990; Dr. h.c. (Exeter) 1991, (Soka, Japan) 1996. *Publications:* books and articles on Russian 20th century history, critical analyses of Marxist theory and Communist practice. *Leisure interest:* playing chess. *Address:* Presidential Commission on Rehabilitation of Political Prisoners, Ul. Iljinka 8/4, Entr. 20, 103132 Moscow, Russia. *Telephone:* 206-24-94. *Fax:* 206-55-62.

YAKOVLEV, Veniamin Fedorovich, D.JUR.; Russian politician and lawyer; b. 12 Feb. 1932, Petukhovo, Kurgan Region; s. of Fedor Kuzmich Yakovlev and Domna Pavlovna Yakovleva; m. Galina Ivanovna 1956; two d.; ed. Sverdlovsk Inst. of Law; mem. CPSU 1956–91; teacher, then Dir. Yakut School of Law 1953–56; Asst. Procurator/Attorney-Gen. of Yakut Autonomous Repub. 1956–60; aspirant, teacher, docent, Dean, Pro-rector Sverdlovsk Inst. of Law 1960–87; Dir. All-Union Research Inst. of Soviet Legis. 1987–89; Deputy Chair. Public Comm. of Int. Co-operation on Humanitarian Problems and Human Rights 1988; U.S.S.R. Minister of Justice 1989–90; Chair. U.S.S.R. Supreme Arbitration Court 1991, Supreme Arbitration Court of Russian Fed. 1992–. *Publications:* Civil Law Method of Regulation for Social Relations, and more than 150 other publs. *Leisure interests:* skiing and other sports. *Address:* Arbitration Court, Maly Kharitonyevski 12, 101000 Moscow, Russia. *Telephone:* (095) 208-11-19. *Fax:* (095) 208-44-00.

YAKOVLEV, Vladimir Anatolyevich, CAND. ECON. SC.; Russian politician; b. 25 Nov. 1944, Olekminsk, Yakutia; m. Irina Ivanovna Yakovleva; one s.; ed. N.W. Polytech. Inst.; master on construction sites, Head Repair-Construction Trust 1965–80, Deputy Man. Housing Dept., Leningrad 1980–93; First Deputy Mayor of St. Petersburg, Russia. Head Cttee. on Man. of Municipal Econ. 1993–96; elected Mayor of St. Petersburg 1996; mem. Council of Fed. of Russia 1996–; Pres. Ass. of Heads of Regions and Repubs. of N.W. Russia 1997; Pres. Basketball Club Spartacus; Pres. Fed. of Bicycle Sports of St. Petersburg; Merited Constructor of Russia. *Address:* Governor of St. Petersburg, Smolny, 193060 St. Petersburg, Russia. *Telephone:* (812) 278-16-84 (Office). *Fax:* (812) 278 1827 (Office).

YAKOVLEV, Yegor Vladimirovich; Russian journalist and newspaper editor; b. 18 March 1930; ed. Moscow State Historical Archival Inst.; mem. CPSU 1953–91; worked on a number of newspapers: Pravda, Izvestiya, Sovetskaya Rossiya, Moscow Pravda; founding Ed. Zhurnalist monthly; worked in Prague on staff of World Marxist Review 1972–75; worked on Izvestiya, Moscow 1975–85; Ed. Moscow News weekly 1985–91; Pres. All-Russia Radio and TV Co. Ostankino 1991–92; Founder and Ed. Obshchaya Gazeta weekly 1992–; mem. Presidential Political Consultative Council 1991. *Address:* Goncharnaya 1, 109240 Moscow, Russia. *Telephone:* 915-22-88.

YAKUNIN, Gleb Pavlovich; Russian politician and ecclesiastic; b. 4 March 1934; ed. Irkutsk Inst. of Agriculture, Moscow Theological Seminary, expelled for criticism of church admin.; sexton, minister in Zaraisk, Dmitrov; deprived of the right to be a minister for public protest against collaboration of church admin. with CP, f. and leader Christian Cttee. for Protection of Believers, sentenced to five-year imprisonment and five-year term of exile for anti-Soviet propaganda 1979; then Minister in St. Nicholas Church, Shchelykovo Village, Moscow Region; exonerated 1991; active participant of Movt. for Democratic Russia, Co-Chair. Coordination Council; People's Deputy of Russia 1990–93; fmr. mem. Supreme Soviet of Russia; Chair. Cttee. for Protection of Freedom of Conscience 1996; excommunicated by Holy Synod for political activities Dec. 1993; mem. State Duma 1993–95. *Address:* Bolshoy Golovin per. 22, 103045 Moscow, Russia. *Telephone:* (095) 207-60-69. *Fax:* (095) 207-60-69.

YALOW, Rosalyn Sussman, PH.D.; American medical physicist; b. 19 July 1921, New York; d. of Simon and Clara (Zipper) Sussman; m. Aaron Yalow 1943; one s. one d.; ed. Hunter Coll., New York, Univ. of Illinois; Asst. in Physics, Univ. of Ill. 1941–43, Instructor 1944–45; Lecturer and temp. Asst. Prof. in Physics, Hunter Coll., New York 1946–50; Physicist and Asst. Chief, Radioisotope Service, Veterans Admin. Hosp., Bronx 1950–70, Acting Chief 1968–70, Chief Radioimmunoassay Reference Lab. 1969, Chief Nuclear Medicine Service 1970–80, Sr. Medical Investigator 1972–92, Sr. Medical Investigator Emer. 1992–, Dir. Solomon A. Berson Research Lab. Veterans Admin. Medical Center 1973–92; Research Prof., Dept. of Medicine, Mount Sinai School of Medicine, New York 1968–74, Distinguished Service Prof. 1974–79; Distinguished Prof.-at-Large, Albert Einstein Coll. of Medicine, Yeshiva Univ. 1979–85, Prof. Emer. 1985–; Chair. Dept. of Clinical Sciences, Montefiore Hosp., Bronx, N.Y. 1980–85; Solomon A. Berson Distinguished Prof.-at-Large, Mt. Sinai School of Medicine, New York 1986–; Harvey Lecturer 1966, American Gastroenterology Asscn. Memorial Lecturer 1972, Joslyn Lecturer, New England Diabetes Asscn. 1972, Franklin I. Harris Memorial Lecturer 1973, 1st Hagedorn Memorial Lecturer, Acta Endocrinologica Congress 1973; Pres. Endocrine Soc. 1978–79; mem. N.A.S. 1975–, American Physics Soc., Radiation Research Soc., American Asscn. Physicists in Medicine, Biophysics Soc., American Acad. of Arts and Sciences, American Physiology Soc.; Foreign Assoc. French Acad. of Medicine 1981; Fellow New York Acad. of Science, Radiation Research Soc., American Asscn. of Physicists in Medicine; Assoc. Fellow in Physics, American Coll. of Radiology, American Diabetes Asscn., Endocrine Soc., Soc. of Nuclear Medicine; more than 60 hon. doctorates; jt. winner of Nobel Prize for Physiology or Medicine for discoveries concerning peptide hormones 1977, and more than 30 other awards. *Address:* Veterans Administration Medical Centre, 130 West Kingsbridge Road, Bronx, New York, NY 10468, U.S.A.

YAM, Joseph C. K., C.B.E., B.SC.; British banker; b. 9 Sept. 1948, Canton, China; s. of Shun Yam and Hok-chun Shum; m. Grace Fong 1972; one s. one d.; ed. Univ. of Hong Kong, Inst. of Social Studies, The Hague, Netherlands; demonstrator in Econs., Econs. Dept., Univ. of Hong Kong 1970–71; Statistician Census and Statistics Dept., Hong Kong Govt. 1971–76, Economist, Econ. Services Br. 1976–77, Sr. Economist 1977–79, Prin. Asst. Sec. (Econ. Services) 1979–82, (Monetary Affairs) 1982–85, Deputy Sec. for Monetary Affairs 1985–91; Dir. Office of the Exchange Fund 1991–93; Chief Exec. Hong Kong Monetary Authority 1993–; Banker of the Year in Hong Kong 1995. *Leisure interests:* golf, horse racing, swimming, hiking. *Address:* 30/F, 3 Garden Road, Central, Hong Kong. *Telephone:* 2878 8196. *Fax:* 2878 8197.

YAMAGUCHI, Kenji, M.A. (ECON.); Japanese government official; b. 19 July 1933, Yamagata; s. of Futao and Yoshi Yamaguchi; m. Momoe Matsumoto 1962; one s. one d.; ed. Univ. of Tokyo; entered Budget Bureau, Ministry of Finance 1956; Nat. Tax Admin. Agency 1963; Ministry of Interior 1966; Econ. Planning Agency 1968; First Sec. Okinawa Reversion Preparatory Cttee., Foreign Minister's Office and Counsellor, Okinawa Bureau, Prime Minister's Office 1969; Int. Finance Bureau, Ministry of Finance 1971; Consul for Japan, Sydney 1972; Counsellor, Personnel Bureau, Prime Minister's Office 1975; Finance Bureau, Ministry of Finance 1977; Dir.-Gen. North East Japan Finance Bureau, Ministry of Finance 1981; Special Asst. to Minister of Foreign Affairs 1982–87; Exec. Dir. for Japan, IBRD and affiliates 1982–88, Dean IBRD Bd. 1985–87; Sr. Exec. Dir. Water Resources Devt. Public Corpn. 1988–; Co-ordination Leader, Org. for Industry, Science and Cultural Advancement (OISCA) 1987–; Exec. Adviser Mitsui Trust Bank, Tokyo 1993–; Chair. Mitsui Trust Int. Ltd., London 1993–, Mitsui Trust Bank Ltd., Zürich 1993–; Exec. Adviser Chiyoda Mutual Life Insurance Co., Tokyo 1997–; Pres. Honest Club 1995–. *Publications:* The World Bank and its Role in the World Economy 1988, How can Japan contribute to the World?, Land Policy for Prosperity—Land as Public Property, and several books on financial matters, foreign affairs, etc. *Leisure interests:* reading, swimming, golf. *Address:* 3-16-43 Utsukushiga-Oka, Aoba-ku, Yokohama City, 225-0002, Japan. *Telephone:* 045 901 7309.

YAMAGUCHI, Tsuruo; Japanese politician; Chair. Social Democratic Party of Japan (SDPJ) Diet Affairs Cttee., Gen.-Sec. SDPJ; Minister of State, Dir.-Gen. Man. and Co-ordination Agency 1994–95; mem. House of Reps. for Guma, Chair. Budget Cttee. *Address:* c/o Management and Co-ordination Agency, 3-1-1, Kasumigaseki, Chiyoda-ku, Tokyo, Japan.

YAMAHANA, Sadao; Japanese politician and barrister; b. 26 Feb. 1936, Tokyo; s. of Hideo Yamahana and Terumi Yamahana; m. 1964; three s. one d.; fmr. Sec. Gen. Social Democratic Party of Japan (SDPJ) (fmrly. Japan Socialist Party), Chair. 1993–95; Minister of State (in charge of Political Reform) 1993–94. *Leisure interests:* reading books, cooking. *Address:* Social Democratic Party of Japan, 2-2-1-301 Nagata-cho, Chiyoda-ku, Tokyo 100 Japan. *Telephone:* 03-3508-9301. *Fax:* 03-3592-1654.

YAMAMOTO, Takuma, B.ENG.; Japanese businessman; b. 11 Sept. 1925, Kumamoto; joined Fujitsu Ltd. 1949, Bd. Dir. 1975–, Man. Dir. 1976–79, Exec. Dir. 1979–81, Pres. and Rep. Dir. 1981–90, Chair. and Rep. Dir. 1990–98; Vice-Chair. Communication Industries Asscn. of Japan 1986; Chair. Japan Electronic Industry Devt. Asscn. 1987–89, Vice-Chair. 1989–; Chair. Cttee. on Int. Coordination of Econ. Policies (KEIDANREN) 1988–; Blue Ribbon with Medal of Honour 1984; Hon. Dr. Hum. Litt. (Chaminade Univ. of Honolulu). *Leisure interests:* river-fishing, golf, gardening. *Address:* c/o Fujitsu Ltd., 1-6-1 Marunouchi, Chiyoda-ku, Tokyo 100, Japan.

YAMAMOTO, Yohji; Japanese fashion designer; b. 1943, Tokyo; ed. Keio Univ. and Bunkafukuso Gakuin school of fashion, Tokyo; launched first collection Tokyo 1977, Paris 1981, New York 1982, first menswear collection, Paris 1984; costume designer for Opéra de Lyon's production of Madame Butterfly 1990, Wagner Opera's production of Tristan and Isolde, Bayreuth 1993, Kanagawa Art Festival Opera Susanoo 1994; launched first perfume

Yohji 1996, second perfume Yohji Essential 1998; participant in 25th Anniversary of Pina Bausch Co. Wuppertal 1998; subject of Wim Wenders' film Notebook on Cities and Clothes 1989; So-en Award, Endo Award 1969, Fashion Eds. Club Award, Tokyo 1982, 1991, 1997, Mainichi Fashion Award, Tokyo 1986, 1994, Chevalier, Ordre des Arts et des Lettres 1994, Night of Stars Award Fashion Group, New York 1997, Arte e Moda Award, Pitti Imagine, Florence 1998. *Address:* Yohji Yamamoto Inc., 14–15 Conduit Street, London, W1R 9TG, England. *Telephone:* 0171-491 4129. *Fax:* 0171-491 0667.

YAMANI, Sheikh Ahmed Zaki; Saudi Arabian politician; b. 1930, Mecca; ed. Cairo Univ., New York Univ. and Harvard Univ.; Saudi Arabian Govt. Service; private law practice; Legal Adviser to Council of Ministers 1958–60; mem. Council of Ministers 1960–86; Minister of State 1960–62; Minister of Petroleum and Mineral Resources 1962–86; Dir. Arabian American Oil Company 1962–86; Chair. of Bd. of Dirs. General Petroleum and Mineral Org., (PETROMIN) 1963–86, Coll. of Petroleum and Minerals, Dhahran 1963–86, Saudi Arabian Fertilizer Co. (SAFCO) 1966–86; f. Center for Global Energy Studies; Sec.-Gen. Org. of Arab Petroleum Exporting Countries (OAPEC) 1968–69, Chair. 1974–75; mem. several Int. Law Asscns. *Publication:* Islamic Law and Contemporary Issues. *Address:* P.O. Box 14850, Jeddah 21434, Saudi Arabia.

YAMANI, Hashim bin Abdullah bin Hashim al, PH.D.; Saudi Arabian politician; ed. Harvard Univ., Prof. and later Chair., Physics Dept., King Fahd Univ. of Petroleum and Minerals; Vice-Pres., King Abdul Aziz City for Science and Tech. Dir., Dept. of Energy Resources, Research Inst., King Fahd Univ. of Petroleum and Minerals; Minister of Industry and Electricity 1995–. *Address:* Ministry of Industry and Electricity, P. O. Box 5729, Omar bin al-Khatab Street, Riyadh 11432, Saudi Arabia. *Telephone:* (1) 477-6666. *Fax:* (1) 477-5441.

YAMASAKI, Taku; Japanese politician; mem. House of Reps.; fmr. Parl. Vice-Minister of Health and Welfare; Deputy Chief Cabinet Sec., Dir. Gen. Liberal Democratic Party (LDP) Election Bureau; Dir. Gen. Defence Agency; Minister for Construction 1991–92; Chair. LDP Diet Affairs Cttee., LDP Policy Research Council 1995. *Address:* c/o House of Representatives, 1-7-1 Nagata-cho, Chiyoda-ku, Tokyo 100, Japan.

YAMASHITA, Yasuhiro, M.A.; Japanese judo player and coach; b. 1 June 1957, Kumamoto; m. Midori Ono 1986; two s. one d.; ed. Kyushu Gakuin High School, Tokai Univ. Sagami High School and Tokai Univ.; winner nine consecutive times, All Japan Judo Tournament; World Judo Champion 1979, 1981, 1983; achieved unbroken record of 203 consecutive wins since 1977 before retirement; Prof. Dept. of Sports, Tokai Univ. 1986–, fmr. Team Man. Univ. Judo Team; Man. Japanese Nat. Judo Team 1992–; several awards. *Publications include:* Young Days with Black Belt, Enjoyable Judo, The Moment of Fight, Osoto-Gari, Judo with Fighting Spirits. *Leisure interests:* reading, playing with my kids, karaoke (with family), dining out. *Address:* 1117 Kitakaname, Hitatsuka Kanagawa, 259–1207 (Office); 661-104 Higashi Koiso, Oiso-machi, Naka-gun, Kanagawa-ken, Japan (Home). *Telephone:* (81) 463-61-1100. *Fax:* (81) 463-61-2120.

YAMEY, Basil Selig, C.B.E., B.COMM., F.B.A.; British economist; b. 4 May 1919, Cape Town, South Africa; s. of Solomon Yamey and Leah Yamey; m. 1st Helen Bloch 1948 (died 1980); one s. one d.; m. 2nd Demetra Georgakopoulou 1991; ed. Tulbagh High School and Univ. of Cape Town; Prof. of Econs. London School of Econs. 1960–84, Prof. Emer. 1984–; mem. Monopolies and Mergers Comm. 1966–78; Trustee Nat. Gallery, London 1974–81, Tate Gallery, London 1977–81, Inst. of Econ. Affairs 1987–91; Hon. Fellow L.S.E. 1988. *Publications:* Economics of Resale Price Maintenance 1951, Economics of Underdeveloped Countries (with P. T. Bauer) 1956, Economics of Futures Trading (with B. A. Goss) 1976, Essays on the History of Accounting 1978, Arte e Contabilità 1986, Art and Accounting 1989. *Address:* 27B Elsworthy Road, London, NW3 3BT, England. *Telephone:* 0171-586 9344; 0171-405 7686.

YAN DONGSHENG, PH.D.; Chinese academic; b. 10 Feb. 1918, Shanghai; s. of Chi Yan and Yuhan (née Chu) Yan; m. Bi-Rou Sun 1943; one s. one d.; ed. Yanjing and Tsinghua Univ., Beijing, Univ. of Illinois, U.S.A.; Deputy Dir. Inst. of Chem. Eng., Kailan Mining Admin. 1950–54; Research Prof., Inst. of Metallurgy and Ceramics, Acad. of Sciences 1954–60; Deputy Dir. Shanghai Ceramic Inst., Acad. of Sciences 1960, Dir. 1977; mem. ed. Bd., Chinese Science Bulletin 1961; Vice-Pres. Shanghai Univ. of Science and Tech. 1980, Hon. Pres. 1985–, mem. Acad. Degrees Cttee. 1981, Vice-Chair. Fund Cttee. 1981; mem. 12th CCP Cen. Cttee. 1982; mem. Standing Cttee. CPPCC 1987–93, Vice-Chair. Shanghai Municipal CPPCC 1987–93; Pres. Chinese Chemical Soc. 1982–86; Ed.-in-Chief Science in China, Science Bulletin 1987–96, Ceramics Int.; Ed. Material Letters (Int.), Int. Solid State Chem., European Solid State and Inorganic Chem., High Tech Ceramics (Intel); mem. Leading Group for Scientific Work, State Council 1983–88; mem. Chinese Acad. of Sciences (Vice-Pres. 1980–87), Dir. Dept. of Chem. 1981–93; Party Sec. Chinese Acad. of Sciences 1984–87, Special Adviser 1987–, Sr. Fellow 1998–; Sr. Fellow Chinese Acad. of Eng. 1998–; Pres. Chinese Ceramic Soc. 1983–93, Hon. Pres. 1993–; Pres. Chinese Chemical Soc. 1995–98; Vice-Pres. China-U.S. People's Friendship Asscn. 1986–; Hon. mem. Materials Research Socs., India, Japan, U.S.A., Europe; Titular mem. IUPAC 1987–95; Pres. Fed. of Asian Scientific Acads. and Socs. 1990–(95); Hon. D.Sc. (Ill., Bordeaux) 1986, (Hong Kong Polytechnic) 1993. *Leisure interest:* tennis, classical music, bridge. *Address:* Chinese Academy of Sciences, 52 San Li He Road, Beijing, People's Republic of China. *Telephone:* (10) 68597289 (Office); (10) 62554019 (Home). *Fax:* (10) 68512458.

YAN HAIWANG; Chinese politician; b. Sept. 1939, Zhengzhou City, Henan Prov.; ed. Harbin Architectural Eng. Inst.; joined CCP 1966; Vice-Gov. Gansu Prov. 1987, Gov. 1993–97; Vice-Sec. CCP Gansu Provincial Cttee. 1988; alt. mem. 14th CCP Cen. Cttee. 1992; Sec. CCP Gansu Provincial Cttee. 1993–98; mem. 15th CCP Cen. Cttee. 1997–.

YAN LIANGKUN; Chinese orchestral conductor; b. Oct. 1923, Wuchang City, Hubei Prov.; Art Dir. and Conductor, Symphony Orchestra of China Cen. Philharmonic Soc.; Vice-Pres. China Musicians' Asscn. 1992–; mem. 6th Nat. Cttee. CPPCC 1983–87, 7th 1988–92, 8th 1993. *Address:* Central Philharmonic Society, 11-1 Hepingjie (Peace Street), Beijing 100013, People's Republic of China.

YAN WENJING; Chinese writer; b. 15 Oct. 1915, Wuchang, Hubei; m. 1st Li Shuhua 1939 (died 1976); m. 2nd Kang Zhichiang 1976; one s. five d.; joined CCP 1938; worked in literature dept. of Lu Xun Art Acad., Yan'an; Asst. Ed.-in-Chief North East Daily 1945; worked in Propaganda Dept., Cen. Cttee., CCP after 1949; Chief Ed. People's Literature; Dir. People's Literature Publishing House, Head 1973–83; mem. Presidium Chinese Writers' Asscn. 1985–96, Advisor 1996–; Vice-Pres. China Pen Centre 1982–; writes children's stories. *Publications include:* A Man's Troubles (novel), Nannan and Uncle Whiskers, The Echo, The Little Stream Sings, Next Time Port, Fables of Yan Wenjing, Selected Prose Poems of Yan Wenjing. *Address:* People's Literature Publishing House, Beijing, People's Republic of China. *Telephone:* 500 3312.

YANAGISAWA, Hakuo; Japanese politician; mem. LDP; mem. for Shizuoka, House of Reps.; fmr. official in Ministry of Finance; Sec. to Chief Cabinet Sec. 1978–80; mem. House of Reps. 1980–; fmr. Parl. Vice-Minister; Dir.-Gen. Nat. Land Agency 1998–99; Minister of Financial Reconstruction 1999–. *Leisure interest:* karaoke. *Address:* c/o Ministry of Finance, 3-1-1, Kasumigaseki, Chiyoda-ku, Tokyo 100-0013, Japan.

YANAYEV, Gennadiy Ivanovich, CAND.HIST.SC.; Russian politician; b. 1937, Perevoz, Perevozovsky region, Gorky Dist.; ed. Gorky Agric. Inst. and All-Union Law Inst.; mem. CPSU 1962–91; began work as foreman of mechanisation unit 1959–63; komsomol work; Second Sec. Gorky village komsomol Dist. Cttee. (obkom), Second, First Sec. Gorky komsomol Dist. Cttee. (obkom) 1963–68; Chair. Cttee. of U.S.S.R. Youth Orgs., then Vice-Chair. of Presidium of Union of Soviet Asscns. for Friendship and Cultural Relations with Foreign Countries 1968–86; trade-union work, Sec., Vice-Chair. All-Union Trades Union Fed. 1986–90; mem. Cen. Cttee. CPSU, Sec. 1990–91; fmr. People's Deputy; mem. CPSU Politburo 1990–91; Vice-Pres. U.S.S.R. 1990–91; arrested for participation in attempted coup d'état, charged with conspiracy Jan. 1992; on trial 1993–94, released after amnesty 1994.

YANDARBIYEV, Zelimkhan; Chechen politician and writer; b. 12 Sept. 1952, Vydrika, Kazakhstan; ed. Chechen-Ingush State Univ.; worked as bricklayer, gas well driller 1969–76; proof-reader, engineer-technician, head Production Div. Chechen-Ingush Publ. House 1976–85; mem. U.S.S.R. Union of Writers 1985; published a few collections of verses and short stories under pen name Abdul Muslim; Chair. Cttee. of Literature Promotion 1985–86; Ed.-in-Chief Raduga (magazine) 1986–89; participant opposition movt. for ind. of Chechnya since 1980s; Vice-Chair. Ass. of highland peoples of Caucasus 1989; mem. Parl. of Chechnya 1991, Vice-Pres. Chechen Repub. Ichkeriya 1993, Pres. (after decease of D. Dudayev) 1996; Cand. in Pres. elections Jan. 1997.

YAÑEZ-BARNUEVO, Juan Antonio, LL.B.; Spanish diplomatist; b. 15 Feb. 1942, Coria del Río, Seville; s. of late Luis Yañez-Barnuevo and Angeles Yañez-Barnuevo; m. Isabel Sampedro 1969; one s.; ed. Univs. of Seville, Madrid and Cambridge, School for Int. Civil Servants, Madrid, Hague Acad. of Int. Law and Diplomatic School, Madrid; Sec. of Embassy, Perm. Mission of Spain to UN, New York 1970–73; Deputy Head, Office of Int. Legal Affairs, Ministry of Foreign Affairs 1975–78; Deputy Perm. Rep. to Council of Europe, Strasbourg 1978–82; Dir. of Int. Dept. of Presidency of Govt. (Foreign Policy Adviser to Prime Minister) 1982–91; Amb. and Perm. Rep. of Spain at UN, New York 1991–96. *Leisure interests:* reading, music, nature. *Address:* c/o Ministry of Foreign Affairs, Plaza de la Provincia 1, 28071 Madrid, Spain.

YANG, Jerry, M.S.E.E., B.S.; American computer executive; ed. Stanford Univ.; co-creator Yahoo! (on-line guide), co-founder, C.E.O. Yahoo! Inc. 1994–. *Address:* Yahoo! Incorporated, 3420 Central Expressway, 2nd Floor, Santa Clara, CA 95051, U.S.A.

YANG, Hon. Sir Ti Liang, Kt., Hon. Mr Justice Yang, LL.B., F.C.I.A.; British judge; b. 30 June 1929, Shanghai, China; s. of Shao-nan Yang and Elsie Chun; m. Eileen Barbara Tam 1954; two s.; ed. The Comparative Law School of China, Soochow Univ., Shanghai, Univ. Coll. London, U.K.; called to Bar (with hons.), Gray's Inn 1954; Magistrate, Hong Kong 1956, Sr. Magistrate 1963, Dist. Judge, Dist. Court 1968, Judge of High Court 1975, Justice of Appeal 1980, Vice-Pres. Court of Appeal 1987, Chief Justice of Hong Kong 1988–96; mem. Exec. Council, Hong Kong Special Admin. Region 1997–; Pres. of Ct. of Appeal of Negara Brunei Darussalam 1988–92; Rockefeller Fellow, London Univ. 1963–64; Chair. Kowloon Disturbances Claims

Assessment Bd. 1966, Compensation Bd. 1967, Comm. of Inquiry into the Rainstorm Disasters 1972, into Lelung Wing-sang Case 1976, into McLennan Case 1980; mem. Law Reform Comm. (Chair. Sub-Cttee. on law relating to homosexuality 1980) 1980–96; Chair. Chief Justice Working Party on Voir Dire Procs. and Judges' Rules 1979, Univ. and Polytechnic Grants Cttee. 1981–84, Hong Kong Univ. Council 1987–; Pro-Chancellor Hong Kong Univ. 1994–; Patron The Soc. for the Rehabilitation of Offenders, Hong Kong; Hon. Pres. Hong Kong Scouts Asscn., Against Child Abuse; Hon. LL.D. (Chinese Univ. of Hong Kong) 1984, (Hong Kong Polytechnic) 1992; Hon. D.Litt. (Hong Kong Univ.) 1991; Order of Chivalry (First Class), SPMB, Negara Brunei Darus-salam 1990. *Leisure interests:* philately, reading, walking, oriental ceramics, travelling, music. *Address:* Executive Council, Hong Kong Special Administrative Region, People's Republic of China; Flat 8, Duchess of Bedford House, Duchess of Bedford's Walk, London, W8 7QL, England. *Telephone:* 2849-8811 (Hong Kong).

YANG, Yuyu; Taiwanese artist; b. Taiwan; ed. China, Japan, Italy; founder Lifescape Museum, Taipei; Int. F.R.B.S. 1996. *Works include:* Mountain Grandeur, Solar Permanence, Lunar Brilliance, Dragon's Song, Universe and Life.

YANG BAIBING, Gen.; Chinese army officer; b. Sept. 1920, Tongnan Co., Sichuan Prov.; Deputy Political Commissar, Beijing Mil. Region, PLA 1983–85, Political Commissar 1985; Deputy Dir., Bureau under Int. Liaison Dept., State Council 1985–87; Dir. Gen. Political Dept. 1987; mem. Cen. Mil. Comm., PRC April 1988, Sec.-Gen. 1989; rank of Gen. 1988; mem. 13th CCP Cen. Cttee. 1987–92; mem. 14th CCP Cen. Cttee. 1992–97; PLA Deputy to 8th NPC; mem. Politburo 1992–97. *Address:* c/o Politburo, Chinese Communist Party, Beijing, People's Republic of China.

YANG BO; Chinese politician; b. 1920, Shandong; concurrently Dir. Research Office and Comprehensive Dept., State Statistics Bureau, State Council; Deputy Dir. then Dir. Shandong Prov. Statistics Comm.; Vice-Chair. Prov. Revolutionary Cttee., Shandong 1977; Vice-Minister State Planning Comm., State Council 1979; Deputy Man. 7th Dept., China Nat. Tech. Import Corpn. (TECHIMPORT) 1980; Vice-Minister State Energy Comm., State Council 1981; Minister of Light Industry 1982–87; Sec. Party Group 1983; mem. 12th Cen. Cttee., CCP 1982–87; Adviser, China-Japan Personnel Exchange Cttee. 1985–, NPC Finance and Econ. Cttee.; fmr. Adviser Internal and Judicial Affairs Cttee.; Deputy 7th NPC, mem. Standing Cttee. 1988; Chair. Int. Cttee. for Promotion of Chinese Industrial Co-operatives (ICCIC) 1992–.

YANG CHENG-ZHI, B.SC.; Chinese petroleum engineer; b. 8 Aug. 1938, Henan; s. of Yang Xian-zun and Hou Yang; m. Li Yan-qin 1969; one s. one d.; ed. Beijing Univ. of Petroleum; Asst. Prof. Beijing Univ. of Petroleum 1961–75; Asst. Prof., Vice-Dir. Dept. of Petroleum Eng. Sheng-li Coll. of Petroleum 1976–78; Prof., Sr. Research Engineer and Dir. of Research for interface chem., Research Inst. of Petroleum Exploration and Devt. of Beijing 1979–; Dir. Jr. Lab. for colloid and interface science, Acad. Sinica and China Nat. Petroleum Co. 1990–; Hon. Prof. Da-qing Univ. of Petroleum 1988–; Visiting Sr. Research Engineer Inst. Français du Pétrole 1979–80, 1985–87, 1989–90; mem. China Petroleum Soc., Soc. of Petroleum Engineers of U.S.A.; research into enhanced oil recovery, the physical chem. of oil reservoirs, surfactant solution properties, adsorption of surfactants and polymers, colloid and interface chem. etc.; Science-Tech. Award in Petroleum Eng. 1991, 1996, World Lifetime Achievement Award, ABI, U.S.A. 1992 and other awards. *Publications:* Petroleum Reservoir Physics 1975, World Fine Chemical Engineering Handbook (jtly.), Enhanced Oil Recovery Theory and Practice 1995; more than 60 articles in professional journals. *Leisure interests:* collecting stamps and badges. *Address:* Research Institute of Petroleum Exploration and Development, P.O. Box 910, 100083 Beijing (Office); No. 1101, 29 Lodging House, 20 Xue Yuan Road, 100083 Beijing, People's Republic of China (Home). *Telephone:* 62098371 (Office); 62098450 (Home). *Fax:* 62097181.

YANG DEQING; Chinese army officer and politician; b. Sept. 1942, Yingcheng, Hubei Prov.; fmr. Divisional Political Commissar and Army Political Dir. of PLA Armoured Force, Political Commissar of Acad. of Mil. Economy; Deputy Political Commissar PLA Gen. Logistics Dept. 1995–; mem. Cen. Comm. for Discipline Inspection; Mayor Zhangjiakou City, Hebei Prov. *Address:* PLA General Logistics Department, Ministry of National Defence, Beijing, People's Republic of China.

YANG DEZHONG, Gen.; Chinese army officer and politician; b. 1923, Weinan Co., Shanxi Prov.; joined CCP 1938, First Deputy Dir. of Gen. Office 1983–, CCP Cen. Cttee., Dir. of Garrison Bureau 1982–; mem. 12th CCP Cen. Cttee. 1982–87, 13th 1987–92, 14th 1992–96. *Address:* General Office, Chinese Communist Party Central Committee, Zhong Nan Hai, Beijing, People's Republic of China.

YANG DI; Chinese politician; b. 1924, Qingpu Co., Shanghai; joined New 4th Army 1938; joined CCP 1939; Deputy Dir., Shanghai Bureau of Foreign Trade 1960–76; Dir. Shanghai Post and Telecommunications Bureau, Dir. Shanghai Public Security Bureau; Vice-Mayor, Shanghai 1977–83; mem. 12th CCP Cen. Cttee. 1982–87; Del. 12th and 13th CCP Congresses; Sec. CCP Cttee., Shanghai 1983, Deputy Sec. 1983–89; mem. Standing Cttee. 7th CPPCC 1989, 8th 1993–98. *Address:* Shanghai Municipal Chinese Communist Party, Shanghai, People's Republic of China.

YANG GUOLIANG, Gen.; Chinese army officer; b. March 1938, Zunhua City, Hebei Prov.; joined CCP 1961; ed. Beijing Aeronautics Inst.; Vice-Commdr. PLA Second Artillery Force 1985; alt. mem. 12th CCP Cen. Cttee. 1985, 13th CCP Cen. Cttee. 1987; rank of Maj. Gen. 1988, Lieut.-Gen. 1990; Commdr. PLA Second Artillery Force 1992–; rank of Gen. 1998; mem. 14th CCP Cen. Cttee. 1992, 15th CCP Cen. Cttee. 1997–. *Address:* People's Liberation Army Second Artillery Force Headquarters, Beijing, People's Republic of China.

YANG GUOPING, Gen.; Chinese army officer; b. Oct. 1934, Zhongxiang Co., Hubei Prov.; ed. PLA Mil. Acad.; joined PLA 1950, fought in Korean War 1951; joined CCP 1956; Staff Officer of Combat Troops, Deputy Section Chief, Section Chief, Deputy Dept. Chief, Dept. Chief of Combat Troops for Shenyang Mil. Region, Deputy Chief of Staff 1987; Chief of Staff, 14th Army 1983–87; rank of Maj.-Gen. 1988; Chief of Staff, Jinan Mil. Region 1990–94, Deputy Commdr. 1994–96; mil. rep. to 14th Cen Cttee. CCP 1992; rank of Lieut.-Gen. 1993; Commdr. of People's Armed Police Feb. 1996–; rank of Gen. 1998; mem. 15th CCP Cen. Cttee. 1997–. *Address:* People's Liberation Army Headquarters of Armed Police; Beijing, People's Republic of China.

YANG GUOQING, M.D.; Chinese politician and surgeon; b. 1936, Taibei City, Taiwan Prov.; ed. Beijing Medical Univ., Kobe Medical Univ., Japan; Dir. Beijing Overseas Chinese Office 1990; Vice-Chair. China Asscn. of Taiwan Compatriots 1993, Chair. 1997–; Vice-Chair. Cttee. of Overseas Chinese Affairs, 9th NPC 1998–. *Address:* China Association of Taiwan Compatriots, Beijing, People's Republic of China.

YANG HUAIQING; Chinese naval officer; b. Feb. 1939, Shouguang Co., Shandong Prov.; joined PLA 1958, CCP 1960; served as asst. of Org. Section under political dept. of frigate detachment, asst., section chief, deputy dir. and dir. of Cadre Dept. of Navy Fleet, dir. political dept. of a naval base, political commissar of a naval base, Deputy Dir. Political Dept. of PLA Navy, Dir. 1992–95; Political Commissar PLA Navy 1995–; rank of Rear Adm. 1990, Vice Adm. 1994; Deputy to 8th NPC 1993; mem. 15th CCP Cen. Cttee. 1997–. *Address:* Ministry of National Defence, Beijing, People's Republic of China.

YANG HUICHUAN, Maj.-Gen.; Chinese army officer; Political Commissar Tianjin Garrison, PLA –1995, Beijing Garrison March 1995–. *Address:* c/o Ministry of National Defence, Jingshanqian Jie, Beijing, People's Republic of China. *Telephone:* 10-6370000.

YANG JIKE; Chinese scientist and administrator; b. 6 Nov. 1921, Shanghai; m. Wang Anqi; one s. two d.; Prof. Chinese Univ. of Science and Tech. 1966–; Vice-Gov. of Anhui Prov. 1979–88; Vice-Pres. Energy Research Asscn. 1982–90, Pres. 1990–; Vice-Chair. China Zhi Gong Dang (Party for Public Interests) 1988–; Pres. Cen. Coll. of Socialism of China (now Cen. Socialist Acad.) 1991–; Vice-Chair. Environmental and Resources Protection Cttee., 8th NPC 1993–98; Vice-Chair. Population Resources and Environment Cttee., 9th NPC of CPPCC 1998–. *Address:* c/o Zhi Gong Dang, Taiping Qiao Street, Xi Cheng District, Beijing, People's Republic of China.

YANG JINGREN; Chinese politician; b. 1918, Lanzhou City, Gansu Prov.; former High Iman of Islam; First Sec. Ningxia Hui, CCP 1961–67; criticized and removed from office during Cultural Revolution 1967; mem. 11th Cen. Cttee. 1977; Minister in charge of the Comm. for Minority Nationalities 1978–86; Vice-Premier, State Council 1980–82; Dir. United Front Work Dept., Cen. Cttee. CCP 1982–85; mem. 12th Cen. Cttee. CCP 1982–87; Vice-Chair. Credentials Cttee. 5th NPC 1979–83; Vice-Chair. NPC 6th Standing Cttee. 1983–87, 7th NPC 1988–93; Chair. Nationalities Cttee. 1988–93; Vice-Chair. 8th Nat. Cttee. CPPCC 1993–98; Pres. China-Syria Friendship Asscn. 1991–. *Address:* c/o National Committee of Chinese People's Political Consultative Conference, 23 Taipingqiao Street, Beijing, People's Republic of China.

YANG JINGYU; Chinese politician; b. Sept. 1936, Xingyang, He'nan Prov.; ed. Beijing Foreign Trade Inst.; Dir. Legal Affairs Bureau of State Council; Head of Legal Affairs Office of State Council 1991–. *Address:* c/o State Council, Zhongnanhai, Beijing, People's Republic of China.

YANG LE; Chinese mathematician; b. Nov. 1939, Nantong, Jiangsu Prov.; ed. Peking Univ. and Inst. of Mathematics, Chinese Acad. of Sciences; Research Fellow and Dir. Inst. of Mathematics, Chinese Acad. of Sciences. *Address:* Institute of Mathematics, Chinese Academy of Sciences, Zhongguancun, Haidian District, Beijing, People's Republic of China.

YANG RUDAI; Chinese party official; b. 1924; cadre in Sichuan 1977–79; Vice-Gov. of Sichuan 1979–84; mem. 12th Cen. Cttee. CCP 1982–87; mem. 13th Cen. Cttee. CCP 1987–92; mem. Politburo 1987–92; Political Commissar Sichuan Mil. Dist. 1983–86; First Sec. Party Cttee. 1985; Sec. CCP Sichuan 1983–93; mem. Presidium 14th CCP Nat. Congress 1992; Vice-Chair. 8th Nat. Cttee. CPPCC 1993–98, 9th Nat. Cttee. 1998–. *Address:* National Committee of Chinese People's Political Consultative Conference, 23 Taipingqiao Street, Beijing, People's Republic of China.

YANG TAIFANG; Chinese politician and expert in telecommunications technology; b. 30 April 1927, Mei Co., Guangdong Prov.; s. of Yang Shukum and Wen Xinyun; m. Wu Youhong 1957; one s. two d.; ed. Zhongshan Univ.; Vice-Minister of Posts and Telecommunications 1982–84, Minister 1984–92; mem. 12th Cen. Cttee. CCP 1982–87, 13th Cen. Cttee. 1987–92; Chair. Overseas Chinese Cttee. 8th NPC 1993–; mem. Presidium 14th CCP Nat.

Congress 1992; NPC Deputy, Guangdong Prov.; mem. Standing Cttee. 8th NPC 1993–. Chair. All-China Fed. of Returned Overseas Chinese 1994–. *Leisure interests:* music, bridge, Taiji boxing. *Address:* Overseas Chinese Committee of the National People's Congress, 23 Xijiao Minxiang Road, West District, Beijing 100805, People's Republic of China.

YANG XIZONG; Chinese government official; b. 27 Sept. 1928, Dayi Co., Sichuan Prov.; s. of Yang Qunling and Yang Chunbing; m. Zhou Feng; one s. two d.; alt. mem. CPC Cen. Cttee. 1983; Deputy to 6th NPC 1983, NPC Deputy, Sichuan Prov.; Deputy Sec. CPC 4th Prov. Cttee., Sichuan 1983–85; Gov. of Sichuan 1983–85; Chair. Sichuan Prov. 8th People's Congress, Standing Cttee. 1993–; Sec. CCP Prov. Cttee. Henan 1985–89; mem. 12th CCP Cen. Cttee. 1985–87, 13th CCP Cen. Cttee. 1987–92. *Leisure interest:* reading. *Address:* Sichuan Provincial 8th People's Congress, Chengdu, Sichuan Province, People's Republic of China.

YANG YUSHU; Chinese naval officer; fmr. Vice-Commdr. Yulin Base, PLA Navy South China Sea Fleet; fmr. Vice-Commdr. PLA Navy South China Sea Fleet; Commdr. PLA Navy East China Sea Fleet 1994–; Deputy Commdr., Nanjing Mil. Region. *Address:* c/o Ministry of National Defence, Jingshanqian Jie, Beijing, China.

YANG ZHENGWU; Chinese politician; b. Jan. 1941, Longshan Co., Hunan; joined CCP 1969; Deputy Sec. CCP Hunan Prov. Cttee. 1990–98, Sec. 1998–; Chair. Comm. for Comprehensive Man. of Social Security 1993–; Gov. of Hunan Prov. 1995–; mem. 13th CCP Cen. Cttee. 1987–92, 14th CCP Cen. Cttee., 15th CCP Cen. Cttee. 1997–. *Address:* Office of the Governor, Changsha, Hunan Province, People's Republic of China.

YANG ZHENHUAI; Chinese government official; b. Jan. 1928, Anhui; s. of Yang Licuo and Wu Dingshu; m. Yang Duanyi 1960; one s. one d.; Vice-Minister for Water Resources and Electric Power 1983–88, Minister for Water Resources 1988–93; Sec.-Gen. State Flood Control H.Q. 1986–88, Deputy Head 1988; Deputy Head State Leading Group for Comprehensive Agric. Devt. 1990–; Vice-Chair. Environmental and Resources Protection Cttee.; alt. mem. 14th CCP Cen. Cttee. 1992; Vice-Chair. Agric. and Rural Affairs Cttee., 9th NPC 1998–. *Leisure interests:* reading history, geology, humane studies. *Address:* c/o Standing Committee of National People's Congress, Beijing, People's Republic of China.

YANG ZHENYU; Chinese air force officer; b. 1931, Chifeng City, Rehe (Jehol) (now Liaoning Prov.); ed. Air Force Aviation School, Red Flag Air Force Acad., U.S.S.R.; joined PLA 1947, CCP 1948; regt. literacy teacher of N. China Mil. Command 1948–49; joined Chinese People's Volunteers (CPV) in Korea 1951; served in PLA Air Force as regt. commdr. 1962–64, deputy commdr. of div. and chief of staff, PLA Air Force Shanghai Base 1980–81, chief of staff of corps 1983–85, deputy commdr. of command post of PLA Air Force 1985–86; Vice-Pres. Air Force Command Acad. 1986–90, Pres. 1990–; Deputy Commdr. PLA Air Force 1994–96; Vice-Pres. China Soc. of Mil. Future Studies 1988–; rank of Maj.-Gen. 1988; a PLA del. to 8th NPC. *Address:* c/o Ministry of National Defence, Beijing, People's Republic of China.

YANG ZHIGUANG; Chinese artist; b. 11 Oct. 1930, Shanghai; s. of Yang Miaocheng and Shi Qinxian; m. Ou Yang 1958; two d.; ed. Cen. Acad. of Fine Art; Vice-Pres. and Prof., Guangzhou Acad. of Fine Arts; mem. Council, Chinese Artists' Asscn.; mem. Acad. of Traditional Chinese Painting; does traditional Chinese figure painting, calligraphy and seal-making; Artist-in-Residence, Griffis Art Center, Conn., U.S.A. Sept. 1990–; one-man show, Center for Int. Art and Culture, New York (Special Award for Outstanding Contribs. to Chinese painting); Gold Medal winner, 7th Vienna World Youth Festival, for picture Sending Food in Heavy Snow 1959. *Publications:* Skill of Chinese Traditional Figure Painting, Selections of Portraits, Chinese Water Colours, Yang Zhiguang's Sketches in China's North-west, Portraits of Modern Chinese Artists, Painting Selections of Mr. and Mrs. Yang Zhiguang. *Leisure interests:* calligraphy, seal-making, poetry. *Address:* Guangzhou Institute of Fine Art, No. 257, Chang Gang Dong Lu Street, Haizhu District, Guangzhou, People's Republic of China; 1816 Well Springs Drive, Diamond Bar, CA 91765, U.S.A. *Telephone:* 8620-84417598 (Home, China); (909) 861-6283 (U.S.A.). *Fax:* 8620-84432417; (909) 861-0883 (U.S.A.).

YANG-KANG LIN (alias Chih-Hung), B.A.; Taiwanese politician; b. 10 June 1927, Nantou Co., Taiwan Prov.; s. of Chih-Chang Lin and Chen Ruan; m. Chen Ho 1945; one s. three d.; ed. Dept. of Political Science, Nat. Taiwan Univ.; Chief Admin. Civil Affairs Section, Nantou Co. Govt. 1952–61, Sec. 1962–64; Sec. Taiwan Prov. Govt. 1964; Chair. Yunlin Co. HQ, Kuomintang 1964–67; Magistrate, Nantou Co. 1967–72; Commr., Dept. of Reconstruction 1972–76; Mayor, Taipei Special Municipality 1976–78; Gov. of Taiwan Prov. Govt. 1978–81; Minister of Interior 1981–84; Vice-Premier of Exec. Yuan 1984–87; Premier of Judicial Yuan 1987–94; Vice-Chair. Kuomintang 1993–; Sr. Advisor to Pres. 1994–; Order of Diplomatic Service Merit, Korea 1977. *Leisure interests:* hiking, reading and studying, music. *Address:* 5 Chao-Chou Street, Taipei, Taiwan. *Telephone:* (02) 3415668. *Fax:* (886-2) 3923311.

YANGLING DUOJI; Chinese politician and academic; b. 24 April 1931, Batang Co., Sichuan Prov.; s. of Yang Yong-an and Basang-wengmo; m. Qumu-a Ying 1954; two s. one d.; Vice-Gov. Sichuan Prov. 1979–81; Perm. Sec. CCP Cttee., Tibet Autonomous Region 1981–86; Vice-Chair. Tibetan People's Govt. 1982–83; alt. mem. 12th CCP Cen. Cttee. 1982–87; Chair. Tibet Branch, CPPCC 1983–86; Vice-Chair. and Vice-Sec. of Party, Sichuan CPPCC 1986–; del. to 7th People's Congress of China 1988–92; del. to 11th Congress of CCP 1980–82, 12th 1982–86, 13th 1987–91; Chair. Tibetan Studies Asscn., Sichuan Prov.; Dean Acad. of Tibetan Studies, Sichuan Prov. 1990–; Ed. Tibetology Research, History of Kong Tibetan 1996–. *Leisure interest:* reading. *Address:* Office of the Vice-Chairman of the Chinese People's Consultative Council, No. 25 Hong Zhao Bi Street, Chengdu, Sichuan, People's Republic of China. *Telephone:* (028) 6753780 (Home). *Fax:* (028) 663393.

YANIN, Valentin Lavrentyevich; Russian archaeologist; b. 6 Feb. 1929; m.; ed. Moscow State Univ.; jr. then sr. researcher Moscow Univ. 1954–, Prof. 1963, Head Chair of Archaeology Moscow Univ.; researcher of history and archaeology of Middle Age Russia and of old manuscripts; Chair. Russian Humanitarian Scientific Fund (RGNF) 1996–; Corresp. mem. U.S.S.R. (now Russian) Acad. of Sciences 1966, mem. 1990, mem. Presidium 1991; Lenin Prize, U.S.S.R. State Prize, Hon. Citizen of Novgorod. *Publications include:* Money and Weight Systems of Middle Age Russia 1956, Novgorod Posadniki 1962, I Have Sent You a Birch Bark 1965, Act Stamps of Old Russia X–XV Centuries 1970, Novgorod Feudal Ancestral Lands 1982, Novgorod Acts XII–XV Centuries 1991. *Leisure interest:* collecting old vocal recordings. *Address:* RGNF, Yaroslavskaya str. 13, 129366 Moscow, Russia. *Telephone:* 283-55-40 (Office); 335-54-28 (Home).

YANKILEVSKY, Vladimir Borissovich; Russian artist; b. 15 Feb. 1938, Moscow; s. of Boris Yankilevsky and Rosa Yankilevskaya; m. Rimma Solod 1959; one d.; ed. Moscow Secondary Art School and Moscow Polygraphic Inst.; took part in Manège Exhbn. of 1962; *personal exhbns.* in Moscow, Prague, New York, San Francisco, Cologne, Chicago, Paris, Bochum, Düsseldorf, Brussels, Leverkusen; *group exhibitions* in Moscow, Italy, Germany, Switzerland, U.S.A., U.K., Belgium, Japan, Hungary, Korea, Czechoslovakia, Sweden, Poland, Austria. *Leisure interest:* photography. *Address:* 3 square de Port Royal, 75013 Paris, France. *Telephone:* (1) 45.35.91.74. *Fax:* (1) 45.35.91.74.

YANKOVSKY, Oleg Ivanovich; Russian actor; b. 23 Feb. 1944, Jezrazgan; m. Lyudmila Zorina; one s.; ed. Saratov Drama School; actor Saratov Drama Theatre 1967–73, Moscow Theatre of Lenin Komsomol (now Lenkom) 1973–; debut in film I am Francisc Skorina 1968; State Prize of Russia 1989. *Films include:* Ordinary Wonder, Flights in Dreams and Reality, We, the Undersigned . . ., Two Hussars, That Munchhausen, Keep Me, My Talisman and others; Pres. Russian Nat. Festival Kentaurus 1992; People's Artist of Russia 1984, winner of many int. and Russian prizes at maj. film festivals. *Address:* Komsomolsky prospekt 41, Apt. 10, 119270 Moscow, Russia. *Telephone:* 242 32 85 (Home).

YANNARAS, Christos, DR.PHIL., DR. THEOL.; Greek professor of philosophy; b. 10 April 1935, Athens; Univ. of Athens 1953–57; Univ. of Bonn 1964–67; Univ. of Paris (Sorbonne) 1968–72; Visiting Prof. Univ. of Geneva 1977–79, Univ. of Crete (Rethymnon) 1979–82; Prof. of Philosophy, Panteios Univ. of Political and Social Studies, Athens 1982–; mem. Acad. Int. des Sciences Humaines, Brussels. *Publications:* The Freedom of Morality 1981, Philosophie sans Rupture 1982, Person and Eros 1984, Critical Ontology 1985, Heidegger and Areopagita 1988, Europe against Hellenism 1990, Metamodern Meta-physics 1993, The Inhuman Nature of Human Rights 1997, Culture: The Central Problem of Politics 1997, etc. *Address:* 84 Plastira Street, 171 21 Nea Smyrni, Athens, Greece (Home). *Telephone:* 01-92 98 065 (Office). *Fax:* 01-93 53 697.

YANOFSKY, Charles, PH.D.; American professor of biology; b. 17 April 1925, New York, N.Y.; s. of Frank Yanofsky and Jennie Kopatz Yanofsky; m. 1st Carol Cohen 1949 (died 1990); three s.; m. 2nd Edna Crawford 1992; ed. City Coll. of New York and Yale Univ.; Research Asst. in Microbiology, Yale Univ. 1951–53; Asst. Prof. of Microbiology, Western Reserve Univ. 1954–58; Assoc. Prof., Dept. of Biological Sciences, Stanford Univ., Prof., Dept. of Biological Sciences 1961–; Herzstein Prof. of Biology 1967; Pres. Genetics Soc. of America 1969, American Soc. of Biological Chemists 1984; Career Investigator American Heart Asscn. 1969–95; mem. N.A.S., American Acad. of Arts and Sciences; Foreign mem. Royal Soc. 1985–; Hon. mem. Japanese Biochemical Soc. 1985–; Hon. D.Sc. (Univ. of Chicago) 1980, (Yale Univ.) 1981; Eli Lilly Award in Bacteriology 1959, U.S. Steel Award in Molecular Biology 1964, Howard Taylor Ricketts Award 1966, Albert Lasker Award for Basic Medical Research 1971, Selman A. Waksman Award 1972, Louisa Gross Horwitz Prize 1976, Townsend Harris Medal, City Coll. of New York, Mattia Award, Roche Inst. 1982, Genetics Soc. of America Medal 1983, Gairdner Foundation Award 1985, Thomas Hunt Morgan Medal, Genetics Soc. of America 1990, Passano Award 1992, William C. Rose Award of the ASBMB 1997, Abbott-ASM Lifetime Achievement Award 1998. *Publications:* scientific articles in proceedings of Nat. Acad. of Sciences, etc. *Leisure interests:* tennis, growing orchids. *Address:* 725 Mayfield Avenue, Stanford, CA 94305, U.S.A. *Telephone:* (650) 725-1835 (Office); (650) 857-9057.

YAO WENYUAN; Chinese politician and journalist; b. 1924; journalist and youth activist before Cultural Revolution; leading pro-Maoist journalist during Cultural Revolution 1965–68; Ed. Wen Hui Bao 1966, Liberation Daily 1966; mem. Cen. Cultural Revolution Group, CCP 1966; Vice-Chair. Shanghai Revolutionary Cttee. 1967–76; Ed. People's Daily 1967–76; mem. Politburo, CCP Cen. Cttee. 1969–76; Second Sec. CCP Shanghai 1971;

arrested as mem. of "Gang of Four" Oct. 1976; expelled from CCP July 1977; in detention; on trial Nov. 1980–Jan. 1981; sentenced to 20 years' imprisonment; freed Oct. 1996.

YAO XIN, PH.D.; Chinese scientist; b. 1925; ed. Univ. of Edinburgh; Deputy Dir. of Shanghai Cytobiology Inst., Academia Sinica 1981–; Pres. Soc. of Cytobiology 1985. *Address:* Shanghai Cytobiology Institute, 320 Yueyang Road, Shanghai, People's Republic of China.

YAO ZHENYAN; Chinese banker; Vice-Minister of Water Conservancy and Electric Power 1985–88; Gen. Man. State Energy Investment Corpn. 1988–94; Pres. State Devt. Bank 1994–98; Vice-Minister State Planning Comm. *Address:* c/o State Development Bank, 40 Fucheng Lu, Haidian Qu, Beijing, People's Republic of China.

YAO ZHONGHUA; Chinese artist; b. 17 July 1939, Kunming, Yunnan; s. of late Yao Penxien and late Wang Huiyuan; m. Ma Huixian 1969; two s.; ed. Cen. Acad. of Fine Arts; one-man show, Beijing 1980, Cité Int. Arts, Paris 1985 and exhbns. in Paris and E. Europe; numerous group exhbns. China, also China Oil Paintings of Present Age exhbn., New York, U.S.A. 1987, Melbourne, Sydney, Australia 1987, Wan Yu Tang Art Gallery, Hong Kong 1989; group exhbn. Beijing Art Gallery 1992; one-man exhbn. Taiwan 1992, Calif., U.S.A. 1995; mural for Parl. Hall, Yunnan People's Congress; mem. Council China Artists' Asscn.; Vice-Pres. Yunnan Painting Inst. *Works include:* Oh, the Land!, Sani Minority's Festival, The Yellow River, Zhenghe's Voyage, The Jinsha River Flowing beside the Jade Dragon Mountain, Chinese Ink and Water. *Leisure interests:* music, literature. *Publication:* paper on painter Dong Xi Wen, in Chinese Oil Painting and Art Research 1990, Selected Works of Yao Zhonghua 1993.

YAR'ADUA, Major-Gen. Shehu; Nigerian army officer; b. 5 March 1943, Katsina, Kaduna State; m.; three d.; ed. Govt. Secondary School, Katsina, Nigerian Mil. Training Coll., Zaria, Royal Mil. Coll., Sandhurst, U.K., Command and Staff Coll., U.K.; Platoon Commdr. 1964–65, Battalion Adjutant 1965–67, Co. Commdr. 1967, Asst. Adjutant Gen., 2nd Div. 1967; Commanded 6th Infantry Brigade in Second Infantry Div. with service in Onitsha Sector 1968; Commanded 9th Infantry Brigade (based at Warri during civil war) 1969–72; Commr. for Transport 1975–76; Chief of Staff, Supreme HQ (Chief of Army Staff) 1976–79; Vice-Pres. Supreme Mil. Council 1976–79; arrested March 1995; farmer; mem. Social Democratic Party; Chair. Nation House Press, Hamada Carpets, Kaduna; fmr. Chair. Habib Nigeria Bank Ltd. *Address:* Office of the Chairman, Habib Nigeria Bank Ltd., 1 Keffi Street, P.O. Box 54648, Falomo, Ikoyi, Lagos, Nigeria. *Telephone:* (1) 2663121.

YARMOLINSKY, Adam, LL.B., A.B.; American university professor, lawyer, and fmr. government official; b. 17 Nov. 1922, New York; s. of Avrahm Yarmolinsky and Babette Deutsch Yarmolinsky; m. 1st Harriet Rypins 1945 (divorced 1981); m. 2nd Jane C. Vonnegut 1984 (died 1986); m. 3rd Sarah Ames Ellis 1990; three s. one d.; ed. Harvard Univ. and Yale Law School; practised as lawyer 1949–55; Law Clerk, Supreme Court 1950–51; Sec. Fund for the Repub. 1955–57; Special Corresp. The Economist, London 1956–60; consultant to philanthropic foundations 1959–60; Kennedy Presidential Campaign and talent hunt 1960; Special Asst. to Sec. of Defense 1961–64; Deputy Dir. Pres.'s Anti-Poverty Task Force 1964; Prin. Deputy Asst. Sec. of Defense (Int. Security Affairs) 1965–66; Prof. of Law, Harvard Law School, mem. Inst. of Politics, John Fitzgerald Kennedy School of Govt. 1966–72, C.E.O. Welfare Island Devt. Corpn., New York City 1971–72; Ralph Waldo Emerson Univ. Prof., Univ. of Mass. 1972–79; Counsellor, U.S. Arms Control and Disarmament Agency 1977–79; pvt. law practice, Kominers, Fort Schlefer & Boyer (now Fort & Schlefer) 1979–85, counsel 1985–; Prof. of Policy Sciences, Graduate Program in Policy Sciences, Univ. of Md., Baltimore County 1985–93, Provost 1986–93, Regent's Prof. of Public Policy in the Univ. of Md. System 1993–; Trustee Vera Inst. of Justice 1966–, Robert F. Kennedy Memorial 1968–, Bennington Coll. 1984– (Chair. 1986–88), Ind. Sector 1980–89, 1989–95 (Chair. Govt. Relations Comm. 1989–93), New Directions Educ. Fund (Chair. 1981–83), Nat. Acad. of Social Insurance 1996–; mem. Council for Econ. Priorities 1990–93, Center for Nat. Policy 1981–, Cttee. on Nat. Security 1983– (Chair. 1986–92), Coalition for Nat. Service 1986–, New Directions 1976–77, 1979–81; Chair. Hospice Care of D.C. 1991–97, 1998– (Vice-Chair. 1996–97); Bd. Chair. Lawyers' Alliance for World Security 1994–97, Vice-Chair. 1997–; Chair. PACT 1995–; Charter mem. Inst. of Medicine of N.A.S. 1970–; Fellow American Acad. of Arts and Sciences; mem. American Law Inst. (life), Asscn. of Bar of City of New York, Council on Foreign Relations, Int. Inst. for Strategic Studies, Hudson Inst.; mem. Governing Council, Wye Faculty seminar; Moderator Troutbeck Educational Leadership Program 1984–, Aspen Inst. exec. seminars 1976–, Oxford Aspen Seminars 1986–89. *Publications:* Recognition of Excellence 1960, The Military Establishment 1971, Paradoxes of Power 1983; (Ed.) Case Studies in Personnel Security 1955, Race and Schooling in the City 1981, Rethinking Liberal Education 1996. *Leisure interests:* reading, walking. *Address:* University of Maryland Baltimore County, 1000 Hilltop Circle, Baltimore, MD 21250; 3700 33rd Place, N.W., Washington, DC 20008, U.S.A. (Home). *Telephone:* (410) 455-2300 (Office); (202) 363-7642 (Home). *Fax:* 202 363 3077.

YAROSHINSKAYA, Alla Aleksandrovna; Ukrainian/Russian journalist and writer; b. 1953, Zhitomir, Ukraine; m. Aleksander Kirko; two s.; ed. Kiev State Univ., professional courses in journalism (U.S.A., Japan); journalist Radyanska Zhitomirshchina (Ukrainian newspaper) 1976–89; was subjected to admin. sanction for exposing Party corruption and cover-up of Chernobyl disaster; mem. Helsinki Int. Cttee. on Human Rights 1989–; U.S.S.R. People's Deputy, mem. U.S.S.R. Supreme Soviet; mem. Cttee. on Freedom of Press, Human Rights and Ecology 1989–91; Chair. All-Union Cttee. on Rights of Journalists and Freedom of Press 1989–91; Head Mass Media Dept. Ministry of Press and Information of Russian Fed. 1991–92; Head Int. Liaison of Mass Media Dept. Fed. Information Centre of Pres. Boris Yeltsin 1992–93; Adviser to Pres. 1993–; Head Chief Dept. of Mass Media, State Cttee. of Press 1995–98; Sec. Journalists' Union of Russian Fed. 1992–; Pres. Alla Yaroshinskaya Charity Fund to assist victims of nuclear disasters 1993–; mem. Russian branch Int. Green Cross Foundation 1992–. *Publications include:* Earth is Alarmed (with co-authors) 1990, Chernobyl is with Us 1991, Chernobyl: Top Secret 1992, Hunt in the City (novel), numerous short stories and articles in newspapers and magazines; guest lecturer European Parl., Int. A. Sakharov Univ. (Germany), and others; All-Union Golden PEN Award 1980; Int. Journalists' Prize 1985, shared The Right Livelihood Award, Stockholm 1992. *Leisure interests:* chess, poetry, art, travelling. *Address:* Office of the President, The Kremlin, Moscow, Russia (Office). *Telephone:* (095) 203 7590 (Office). *Fax:* (095) 203 9304 (Office).

YAROV, Yuri Fedorovich; Russian politician; b. 2 April 1942, Mariinsk, Kemerovo Region; m.; one s. one d.; ed. Leningrad Tech. Inst., Leningrad Eng. Econ. Inst.; worked in factories in Latvia 1964–68, Leningrad Region 1968–76; Dir. factory Burevestnik 1978–85; First Sec. Gatchina City CPSU Cttee. 1985–87; Deputy Chair. Exec. Cttee. Leningrad Regional Soviet of Deputies 1987–89, Chair. 1989–90; Chair. Leningrad Regional Soviet of People's Deputies 1990–91; People's Deputy of Russian Fed. 1990–92; Deputy Chair. Supreme Soviet of Russia 1991–92; Deputy Prime Minister 1992–96; Deputy Head of Pres. Yeltsin's Admin. 1996–, First Deputy 1997–98; Plenipotentiary Rep. of Pres. of the Russian Fed. in Council of Fed. 1998–. *Address:* Office of the President, Kremlin, korp. 14v, Moscow, Russia. *Telephone:* (095) 206-52-47.

YARROW, Sir Eric Grant, 3rd Bt. (cr. 1916), M.B.E., D.L., F.R.S.E.; British business executive (retd.); b. 23 April 1920, Glasgow; s. of late Sir Harold Yarrow, 2nd Bt., and late Eleanor Etheldreda; m. 1st Rosemary Ann Young 1951 (died 1957); one s. (deceased); m. 2nd Annette Elizabeth Françoise Steven 1959 (divorced 1975); three s.; m. 3rd Joan Botting 1982; ed. Marlborough Coll., Glasgow Univ.; served apprenticeship with G. and J. Weir Ltd.; army service in Burma 1939–45, Major Royal Engineers 1945; trained with English Electric Co. 1945–46; Asst. Man., Yarrow and Co. Ltd. 1946, Dir. 1948, Man. Dir. 1958–67, Chair. 1962–85, Pres. 1985–86; Chair. Yarrow (Shipbuilders) Ltd. 1962–79; Dir. Clydesdale Bank 1962–91, Deputy Chair. 1975–85, Chair. 1985–91; Dir. Standard Life Assurance 1958–90, Nat. Australia Bank Ltd. 1987–91; mem. Council, Royal Inst. Naval Architects 1957–, Vice-Pres. 1965, Hon. Vice-Pres. 1972; mem. Gen. Cttee. Lloyd's Register of Shipping 1960–87; Prime Warden, Worshipful Co. of Shipwrights 1970–71; Deacon, Incorpn. of Hammermen of Glasgow 1961–62; fmr. mem. Council of Inst. Engineers and Shipbuilders in Scotland; Chair. Exec. Cttee. Princess Louise Scottish Hosp., Erskine 1980–86, Hon. Pres. 1986–; Pres. Scottish Convalescent Home for Children 1958–70, Burma Star Asscn. in Scotland 1989–; Officer of Order of St. John. *Leisure interest:* golf. *Address:* Cloak, Kilmacolm, Renfrewshire, PA13 4SD, Scotland. *Telephone:* (0150587) 2067.

YASHIRO, Most Rev. James Takashi, A.B., B.D., TH.L., D.D.; Japanese ecclesiastic; b. 16 July 1931, Kobe; s. of Michael Hinsuke and Ruth Tamiyo; m. Yoko Kuyama 1957; two s. two d.; ed. Kenyon Coll. Ohio, Virginia Theol. Seminary, Univ. of Kyoto Grad. School and St. Augustine's Coll. Canterbury, England; Asst. Prof. of Christian Studies, Momoyama Gakuin Univ. 1968; Asst. Prof. of Church History, Rikkyo Univ. 1971, Prof. 1972, Chancellor 1987–; Visiting Prof. of Religion, Washington and Lee Univ. Lexington, Va. 1980–81; Bishop of Kitakanto, Nippon Seikokai (Anglican Church in Japan) 1985–94, Primate 1994–97; Japan. Soc. of Historical Studies of Christianity Prize 1977; Hon. D.D. (Va. Theol. Seminary) 1982, (Kenyon Coll.) 1991. *Publications:* Christianity and World History, Studies in English Reformation History 1978, New Canterbury Tales: A Short History of the Anglican Communion 1987, Studies in English Reformation History: Second Series 1993. *Leisure interests:* photography, painting. *Address:* Office of the Chancellor, Rikkyo University, Nishi-Ikebukuro, Toshima-ku, Tokyo 171, Japan.

YASIN, Yevgeny Grigoryevich, D.ECON.SC.; Russian politician and economist; b. 7 May 1934, Odessa; s. of Grigory Yasin and Yevgenia Yasina; m. Lydia Yasina (née Fedoulova); one d.; ed. Odessa Inst. of Construction Eng., Moscow State Univ.; worked U.S.S.R. Cen. Dept. of Statistics 1963–73, researcher Cen. Inst. of Econs. and Math., U.S.S.R. Acad. Sciences 1973–89; Head of Div. State Comm. on Econ. Reform, U.S.S.R. Council of Ministers (Abalkin Comm.) 1990–91; one of authors of econ. programme 500 Days; Dir.-Gen. Direction on Econ. Policy of Russian Union of Industrialists and Entrepreneurs 1991; f. and Dir. Expert Inst. of Russian Union of Industrialists and Entrepreneurs 1992–93; mem. Council of Enterprise of Pres. of Russia 1992; Plenipotentiary Rep. of Govt. in Parl. 1992–93; Head Analytical Centre of Pres. 1994–; Minister of Econs. of Russia 1994–97, Minister Without Portfolio 1997–98; co-f., Head of Science and Prof., Higher School of Econs. 1992–; Head of govt. legislation drafting teams 1992–97. *Address:* c/o Office of the Government, Moscow, Krasnopresnenskaya 2, Russia. *Telephone:* 205-42-24; 205-50-96.

YASSIN, Ahmed; Palestinian religious leader; b. 1938, S. Israel; fled Israel to Gaza Strip 1948; fmrly. teacher; fmrly. involved in Muslim Brotherhood, jailed for 45 days because of involvement with Muslim Brotherhood; f. Islamic Centre 1973; arrested and sentenced to 13 years' imprisonment for sedition 1984, released 1985; f. Hamas (Islamic Resistance Movt.) 1987; arrested and sentenced to life imprisonment for manslaughter 1989, released 1997.

YASSIN, Salim, PH.D.; Syrian politician and professor of economics; b. 10 Oct. 1937, Lattakia; m. Najwa Ismail 1962; five c.; Dean of Faculty, Aleppo Univ. 1966–68, Vice-Pres. of Univ. 1969–71; Pres. Lattakia Univ. 1971–78; govt. minister 1978–85, Deputy Prime Minister in charge of Econ. Affairs 1985–. *Publications:* Theory of Corellation, International Trade, Aggregate Economic Analyses. *Leisure interests:* reading, football, swimming. *Address:* Board of Ministers Building, Damascus, Syria. *Telephone:* (11) 331 77 27. *Fax:* (11) 222 53 31; (11) 331 93 02.

YASSUKOVICH, Stanislas Michael, C.B.E.; British banker; b. 5 Feb. 1935, Paris, France; s. of Dimitri Yassukovich and Denise Yassukovich; m. Diana Townsend 1961; two s. one d.; ed. Deerfield Acad., Mass. and Harvard Univ.; U.S. Marine Corps. 1957–61; joined White, Weld and Co. 1961, London Office 1962, Branch Man. 1967–69, Gen. Partner, New York 1969–73, Man. Dir., London 1969–73; Man. Dir. European Banking Co. S.A. Brussels 1983–85, Chief Exec. European Banking Group 1983–85; Chair. Merrill Lynch Europe Ltd. 1985–89, Hemingway Properties 1993–, Vice-Chair. Jt. Deputy Chair. London Stock Exchange 1986–89, Bristol and West Bldg. Soc. (now Bristol & West PLC) 1991–, ABC Int. Bank 1993–; Chair. Securities Asscn. 1988–91; Chair. Cragnotti & Partners Capital Investment (U.K.) 1991–96, Park Place Capital 1994–, Easdaq SA 1996–, Manek Investment Man. Ltd. 1997–; Deputy Chair. Flextech PLC 1989–, South West Water (now Pennon Group PLC) 1993–; Dir. Royal Nat. Theatre 1991–96, Chair. City Disputes Panel 1993–; Non-exec. Dir. Henderson Group PLC 1990–98. *Leisure interests:* hunting, shooting and polo. *Address:* S. M. Yassukovich & Co. Ltd., 42 Berkeley Square, London, W1X 5DB, England.

YASTRZHEMBSKY, Sergey Vladimirovich, CAND. HIS. SC.; Russian politician, journalist and diplomatist; b. 4 Dec. 1953, Moscow; m.; two c.; ed. Moscow State Inst. of Int. Relations, Inst. of Int. Workers' Movt.; jr. researcher Acad. of Social Sciences Cen. Cttee. CPSU 1979–81; on staff journal Problems of the World and Socialism (Prague) 1981–89; sr. staff-mem. Int. Div. Cen. Cttee. CPSU 1989–90; Deputy Ed.-in-Chief Megapolis (journal) 1990–91, Ed.-in-Chief VIP journal 1991–92; Dir. Dept. of Information and Press, Russian Ministry of Foreign Affairs 1992–93; Amb. to Slovakia 1993–96; Press Sec. Pres. B. Yeltsin (q.v.) 1996–; Deputy Head Pres. Yeltsin's Admin. 1997–98; Vice-Chair. Moscow Govt. 1998–. *Publications:* Social Democracy in the Contemporary World 1991, essays and articles on current events, contemporary devt. of Portugal. *Address:* Moscow Government, Tverskaya str. 13, 103032 Moscow, Russia. *Telephone:* (095) 299-49-60.

YASUI, Kaoru, LL.D.; Japanese jurist and poet; b. 25 April 1907, Osaka; s. of Harumoto and Harue Yasuri; m. Tazuko Kuki 1936; one s. one d.; ed. Tokyo Univ.; Asst. Prof. Tokyo Univ. 1932–42, Prof. 1942–48; Prof. Hosei Univ. 1952, Dean Faculty of Jurisprudence 1957–63, Dir. 1963–66, Prof. Emer. 1978–; Leader (Chair. etc.) Japan Council Against Atomic and Hydrogen Bombs 1954–65; Pres. Japanese Inst. for World Peace 1965–; Dir. Maruki Gallery for Hiroshima Panels 1968–; Chair. Japan-Korea (Democratic People's Repub.) Solidarity Cttee. of Social Scientists 1972–; Dir-Gen. Int. Inst. of the Juche Idea 1978–; Hon. mem. Japanese Asscn. of Int. Law 1976–; Hon. D.Jur. (San Gabriel Coll., U.S.A.); mem. Lenin Peace Prize Cttee.; Lenin Peace Prize 1958; Gold Medal (Czechoslovakia) 1965. *Publications:* Outline of International Law 1939, Banning Weapons of Mass Destruction 1955, People and Peace 1955, Collection of Treaties 1960, My Way 1967, The Dialectical Method and the Science of International Law 1970, A Piece of Eternity (Poems) 1977. *Address:* Minami-Ogikubo 3-13-11, Suginami-ku, Tokyo, Japan.

YATES, Peter; British film and theatre producer and director; b. 24 July 1929; s. of Col. Robert Yates and Constance Yates; m. Virginia Pope 1960; two s. two d. (one deceased); ed. Charterhouse, R.A.D.A.; entered film industry as studio man. and dubbing asst. with De Lane Lea; Asst. Dir. The Entertainer, The Guns of Navarone, A Taste of Honey, etc.; *Films directed include:* Summer Holiday 1962, Danger Man, Saint (TV series) 1963–65, Bullitt 1968, John and Mary 1969, Murphy's War, Mother, Jugs and Speed 1975, The Deep 1976, Breaking Away (also produced) 1979, The Janitor (Eyewitness in U.S.A.; also produced) 1980, Krull 1982, The Dresser (also produced) 1983, Eleni 1984, The House on Carroll Street (also produced) 1986, Suspect 1987, An Innocent Man 1989, The Year of the Comet 1992 (also produced), Roommates 1995, The Run of the Country 1996 (also produced), It all Came True 1997. *Plays directed:* The American Dream 1961, The Death of Bessie Smith 1961, Passing Game 1977, Interpreters 1985. *Leisure interests:* tennis, sailing, skiing. *Address:* c/o William Morris Agency, 151 El Camino Drive, Beverly Hills, CA 90212, U.S.A.

YATIM, Dato Rais, M.A., LL.B.; Malaysian politician; b. 1942, Jelebu, Negeri Sembilan; m. Datin Masnah Mohamat; three s. one d.; ed. Univ. of Northern Illinois and Univ. of Singapore; lecturer at ITM, School of Law and also managed own law firm in Kuala Lumpur 1973; mem. Bar Council 1973; mem. Parl. 1974; Parl. Sec. Ministry of Youth, Sport and Culture 1974; Deputy Minister of Law 1976, of Home Affairs 1978; elected to State Ass., Negeri Sembilan 1978; Menteri Besar, Negeri Sembilan 1978; Minister of Land and Regional Devt. 1982, of Information 1984–86, of Foreign Affairs 1986–87; Advocate and Solicitor, High Court of Malaysia 1988–; returned to Law practice, Kuala Lumpur 1988–; mem. United Malays' Nat. Org. (UMNO) Supreme Council of Malaysia 1982–; Deputy Pres. Semangat 1989–; mem. Civil Liberty Cttee. Bar Council, Kuala Lumpur 1996–. *Address:* 41 Road 12, Taman Grandview, Ampang Jaya, 68000 Ampang, Selangor Darul Ehsan, Malaysia (Home). *Telephone:* (03) 456 9621.

YAVLINSKY, Grigory Alekseevich, PH.D., C.ECON.SC.; Russian politician and economist; b. 10 April 1952, Lvov; m.; two s.; ed. Plekhanov Inst. of Nat. Econ.; electrician Lvov Co., Raduga 1968–69; sr. researcher, Research Inst. of Man., Ministry of Coal Industry, Moscow 1976–80; Head of Div. Research Inst. of Labour 1980–84; Deputy Chief, Chief of Div., Chief of Dept. of Man. U.S.S.R. State Labour Cttee. 1984–89; Chief of Div. State Cttee. on Econ. Reform U.S.S.R. Council of Ministers 1988–90; mem. Pres.'s Political Advisory Council 1990–; Deputy Chair. Council of Ministers of Russian Fed., Chair. State Cttee. on Econ. Reform 1990, author of econ. programme 500 days July–Nov. 1990; Econ. Counsellor of Prime Minister of Russia 1991, Chair. of Council of Scientific Soc. EPI-CENTRE (Cen. for Political and Econ. Studies) 1991–; mem. Econ. Council of Pres. of Kazakhstan 1991–, Deputy Chair. U.S.S.R. Cttee. on Operational Man. of Nat. Econ. Aug.–Dec. 1991; mem. Political Advisory Council of Pres. Gorbachev Oct.–Dec. 1991; leader (with Y. Boldyrev and V. Lukin) of pre-election bloc (later political movt.) Yabloko 1993, Chair. 1995–; mem. State Duma (Parl.) 1993–. *Publications:* Russia—the Search for Landmarks 1993; several books on Econ. of U.S.S.R., numerous articles. *Address:* State Duma, Okhotny Ryad 1, 103265 Moscow, Russia. *Telephone:* (095) 292-8944. *Fax:* (095) 292-89-42.

YAZDI, Ibrahim, PH.D.; Iranian politician; b. c. 1933; m.; two s. four d.; studied and worked as physician in U.S.A. for sixteen years; close assoc. of Ayatollah Khomeini during exile in Neauphlé-le-Château, France Oct. 1978–Feb. 1979; mem. Revolutionary Council during Feb. 1979 revolution; Deputy Prime Minister with responsibility for Revolutionary Affairs Feb.–April 1979; Minister of Foreign Affairs April-Nov. 1979; Special Emissary of Ayatollah Khomeini on Provincial Problems 1979; Supervisor Keyhan Org. 1980–81; Deputy in Parl. for Tehran 1980–84; mem. Foreign Affairs, Health and Welfare Parl. Comms.; WHO Adviser 1991; Sec.-Gen. Liberation Movt. of Iran 1995–; arrested Dec. 1997. *Publications:* Final Efforts in Terminal Days: Some Untold Stories of the Islamic Revolution of Iran 1984, Principles of Molecular Genetics 1985, Mutational Changes in Genetic Materials and Repair Systems 1989, The Ills of the Human Heart 1994; papers on herbal and traditional medicine, carcinogenics, the nucleic acid of cancer cells, and Islamic and social topics. *Address:* 21 Touraj Lane, Valiasr Avenue, Teheran, 19666 Iran. *Telephone:* 021/2042558. *Fax:* 021/2042558.

YAZGHI, Mohamed el-, L.EN D.; Moroccan politician, lawyer and newspaper executive; b. 28 Sept. 1935, Fez; m. Balafrej Souada 1972; two s.; ed. Univ. of Rabat and Ecole Nat. d'Admin. Paris; Dir. of Budget, Ministry of Finance 1957–60; Dir. Al-Moharir (daily paper) 1975–81, Liberation (daily paper) 1989–; First Sec. Moroccan Press Union 1977–93; Deputy to Parl. 1977–; mem. Political Bureau, Union Socialiste des Forces Populaires (USFP) 1975–91, First Vice-Sec. 1991–. *Publications:* articles in magazines and journals. *Leisure interests:* reading, travel. *Address:* 5 rue Ibn Tofai, Les Orangers, Rabat, Morocco. *Telephone:* (2127) 77-39-05 (Office); (2127) 72-28-02 (Home). *Fax:* (2127) 72-77-06.

YAZOV, Marshal Dmitri Timofeevich; Russian military official (retd.); b. 1923; ed. Frunze Mil. Acad. and Mil. Acad. of Gen. Staff; entered Soviet army 1941–; active service 1941–45; command posts 1945–76; Deputy Commdr. of Far Eastern Mil. Dist. 1976–79; Commdr. of Cen. Group Forces in Czechoslovakia 1979–80; Deputy to U.S.S.R. Supreme Soviet 1979–89; Commdr. of Cen. Asian Mil. Dist. 1980; Deputy Minister of Defence Feb.–June 1987, Minister of Defence and Head of Armed Forces 1987–91; mem. of Cen. Cttee. of Kazakh CP 1981–87; mem. Presidential Council 1990–91; Cand. mem. of Cen. Cttee. of CPSU 1981–91; fmr. mem. Politburo; rank of Marshal 1990; arrested Aug. 1991, for participation in attempted coup d'état, charged with conspiracy Jan. 1992; on trial 1993; released 1994; Chief Adviser, Ministry of Defence 1998–. *Address:* Ministry of Defence, Znamenka str. 19, 103160 Moscow, Russia. *Telephone:* (095) 296-39-66.

YBARRA Y CHURRUCA, Emilio de; Spanish banker; b. 1936, San Sebastián; m.; four c.; ed. Jesuit Deusto Univ., Bilbao; joined Banco de Bilbao 1964, mem. Bd. of Dirs. 1971, Chief Exec. 1976, Vice-Pres. and Chief Exec. 1986; Sole Vice-Pres. Banco Bilbao-Vizcaya (BBV) (following merger of Banco de Bilbao with Banco de Vizcaya) 1988, Pres. 1990–. *Address:* Banco Bilbao-Vizcaya, Plaza de San Nicolás 4, 48005 Bilbao, Spain. *Telephone:* (94) 4202000. *Fax:* (94) 4202030.

YE GONGQI; Chinese administrator; b. 1930; joined CCP 1948; Deputy Dir. of Shanghai Light Industry Bureau 1976–; Vice-Mayor Shanghai 1985; Chair. Shanghai Municipal 10th People's Congress 1986–. *Address:* Shanghai People's Government, Shanghai, People's Republic of China.

YE LIANSONG; Chinese politician and engineer; b. 1935, Shanghai; ed. Jiaotong Univ., Shanghai; engineer, Shijiazhuang Municipal Diesel Plant 1960–80; Vice-Mayor Shijiazhuang 1982–85; mem. Standing Cttee. Hebei Prov. CCP Cttee. 1983–, Deputy Sec. 1998–; Vice-Gov. Hebei Prov. 1985–93,

Gov. 1993–; alt. mem. 13th Cen. Cttee. CCP 1987–92, mem. 14th Cen. Cttee. 1992–97, 15th CCP Cen. Cttee. 1997–; Deputy to 8th NPC. *Address:* Office of the Governor, Hebei Provincial Government, 1 Weiming Jie Street, Shijiazhuang City, People's Republic of China.

YE RUTANG; Chinese politician; b. 20 March 1940, Zhejiang; s. of Ye Mei and Chen Jiaoru; m. Liu Wenbin 1968; one s. two d.; Minister of Urban and Rural Construction and Environmental Protection 1985–88; Vice-Chair. Environmental Protection Cttee. of State Council 1985–88; Vice-Minister of Construction 1988–; Vice-Chair. Chinese Soc. of Science and Tech. for Social Devt. 1991–; Pres. Architectural Soc. of China 1992–. *Leisure interests:* calligraphy, swimming. *Address:* Architectural Society of China, Bai Wanzhuang, W District, Beijing; Ministry of Construction, 9 Sanlihe Road, Beijing 100835, People's Republic of China.

YE WEILIN; Chinese writer; b. 1935, Huiyang Co., Guangdong Prov.; s. of Ye Wei; m. Chen Jieni; two c.; joined PLA 1950; Chair. Hainan Writer's Asscn. 1990–. *Publications:* The Blue Mulan Rivulet, On the River without Navigation Marks, The First Farewell. *Address:* Hunan Branch of the Writers' Association, Changsha City, Hunan Province, People's Republic of China.

YE XIAOGANG; Chinese musical composer; b. 23 Sept. 1955, Shanghai, China; s. of Ye Chunzi and Ho Ying; m. Xu Jing 1987; ed. Eastman School of Music, U.S.A. (post-graduate); lecturer Cen. Conservatory of Music, Beijing. *Compositions:* Xi Jiang Yue Symphony 1984, Horizon Symphony 1985, Piano Ballade 1987, Dance Drama: The Love Story of Da Lai VI 1988. *Address:* 115 Summit Drive, Rochester, New York 14620, U.S.A. *Telephone:* (716) 244 3835.

YE XUANPING; Chinese state official; b. Nov. 1924, Meixian Co., Guangdong Prov.; s. of late Marshal Ye Jianying and Zeng Xianzhi; ed. Yan'an Coll. of Natural Sciences, Qinghua Univ., studies in U.S.S.R. 1950–54; Dir. Beijing No. 1 Machine-tool Factory 1963; Vice-Gov. Guangdong Prov. 1980–85; Chair. Guangdong Prov. Scientific and Tech. Cttee. 1980–85; alt. mem. 12th CCP Cen. Cttee. 1982, mem. 1985; mem. 13th CCP Cen. Cttee. 1987–92, 14th Cen. Cttee. 1992–97; Deputy Sec. CCP Cttee., Guangzhou Municipality 1983–85; Acting Mayor Guangzhou 1983, Mayor 1983–85; Deputy for Guangdong Prov. to 6th NPC 1983; Exec. Chair. Preparatory Cttee. for 6th NPC Games 1985–89; Gov. of Guangdong 1985–91; Chair. Zhongkai Inst. of Agricultural Tech. 1987–; Vice-Chair. 7th CPPCC Nat. Cttee. 1991–93, 8th Nat. Cttee. 1993–98, 9th Nat. Cttee. 1998–; Hon. Chair. Beijing Science and Eng. Univ. 1995–. *Address:* National Committee of Chinese People's Political Consultative Conference, 23 Taipingqiao Street, Beijing, People's Republic of China.

YE YONGLIE; Chinese writer; b. 1940, Wenzhou, Zhejiang Prov.; ed. Peking Univ. *Publications:* The Biography of Jiang Qing, The Biography of Zhang Chunqiao, The Biography of Yao Wenyuan, The Biography of Wang Hongwen. *Address:* Shanghai Science Education Film Studio, Shanghai, People's Republic of China.

YEFIMOV, Air Marshal Aleksandr Nikolayevich, M.SC.; Russian air force officer (retd.); b. 6 Feb. 1923, Kantemirovka, Voronezh Oblast; ed. Voroshilovograd Mil. Air Acad., Mil. Acad. of Gen. Staff; joined CPSU 1943; served in Soviet army 1941; fought on the Western and on 2nd Byelorussian Fronts at Vyazma, Smolensk, in Byelorussia, Poland and Germany 1942–45; by July 1944 had flown about 100 missions and was made Hero of the Soviet Union; completed his 222nd mission on 8 May 1945; awarded second Gold Star; held various command posts 1945–69; First Deputy C.-in-C., Soviet Air Defence Forces 1969–91; Deputy to Supreme Soviet 1946–50, 1974–89; rank of Air Marshal 1975; Commdr. of Soviet Air Force and Deputy Minister of Defence 1984–91, Mil. Insp.-Adviser, Ministry of Defence 1991; Chair. C.I.S. Interstate Comm. on use of space and control of air services 1992–96, Council for co-operation with war veterans' unions 1995–; mem. CPSU Cen. Cttee. 1986–90; U.S.S.R. People's Deputy 1989; Hero of the Soviet Union 1944, 1945, Order of Lenin (twice), Order of the Red Banner (five times), Aleksandr Nevsky Order, Merited Mil. Pilot of U.S.S.R. 1970 and other decorations. *Publication:* Over the Field of Battle 1976. *Address:* c/o Ministry of Defence, Myasnitskaya str. 37, 101000 Moscow, Russia. *Telephone:* (095) 293-31-76.

YEFREMOV, Oleg Nikolayevich; Russian actor and director; b. 1 Oct. 1927, Moscow; s. of Nicolay Ivanovich Yefremov and Anna Dmitriyevna Yefremova; one s. one d.; ed. Studio School of Moscow Art Theatres 1945–49; Actor and producer at Cen. Children's Theatre 1949–56; Chief Producer Sovremennik Theatre 1956–70; Chief Stage Man. Moscow Art Theatre 1970–87; Artistic Dir. Moscow Chekov Art Theatre 1987–; over 30 stage productions; film work 1955–; U.S.S.R. People's Deputy 1989–91; Merited Art Worker of R.S.F.S.R. 1957, R.S.F.S.R. People's Artist 1969, U.S.S.R. State Prize 1969, 1974, 1983, U.S.S.R. People's Artist 1976, Hero of Socialist Labor 1987. *Films include:* Alive and Dead, Three Poplars on Plushchikha, Aibolit—66, Shine, Shine My Star!, The Old New Year, Rudin, The Driver for One Trip, Look for the Cars. *Address:* Moscow Chekov Art Theatre, Kamergersky pereulok 3, Moscow; Tverskaya str. 9, Apt. 42, 103009 Moscow, Russia (Home). *Telephone:* 229-33-12 (Office); 229-74-66 (Home). *Fax:* 975-21-96.

YEFUNI, Sergey Naumovich; Russian anaesthesiologist and physiologist; b. 24 Jan. 1930; m.; two s.; ed. Second Moscow Inst. of Medicine; Head of surgery div. municipal hosp. 1954–56; researcher First Moscow Inst. of Medicine 1959–63; sr. researcher, Head of lab. All-Union Research Cen. of Surgery, U.S.S.R. Acad. of Medical Sciences 1963–78, Head of Dept. 1978–93; Corresp. mem. U.S.S.R. (now Russian) Acad. of Sciences 1979, mem. 1992; research in physiology of breathing, practical problems of anaesthesia, effect of anaesthesia on cardio-vascular system; mem. United Scientific Council on complex problem Physiology of Man and Animals; Chair. Comm. Acad. of Sciences (now Inst. of) Problems of Hyperbaric Oxygenation; U.S.S.R. State Prize; lives in U.S.A. *Address:* c/o Institute of Hyperbaric Oxygenation, 119435 Moscow, Russia. *Telephone:* (095) 246-49-87 (Office); 201-43-68 (Home).

YEGOROV, Sergey Yefimovich; Russian banker; b. 4 October 1927, Orenburg Region; m.; one s. one d.; ed. Saratov Inst. of Econ., Acad. of Finance; economist Altai territory branch U.S.S.R. Gosbank 1950–60; instructor, Head of Sector Dept. of Planning and Finance Bodies Cen. CPSU Cttee. 1960–74; Chair. of Bd. Russian Repub. Bank 1973–; Deputy to R.S.F.S.R. Supreme Soviet 1973–88; consultant Exec. Bd. U.S.S.R. Gosbank 1988–91; Pres. Asscn. of Russian Banks 1991–; mem. Int. Acad. of Information Processes and Tech.; Corresp. mem. Acad. of Man. and Market. *Leisure interests:* theatre, painting. *Address:* Association of Russian Banks, Skatertny per. 20, st. 1, Moscow, Russia. *Telephone:* (095) 291 66 30 (Office). *Fax:* (095) 291 6666 (Office).

YEGOROV, Vladimir Konstantinovich; Russian politician, philosopher and journalist; b. 30 Oct. 1947, Kanash, Chuvash A.S.S.R.; m.; one s.; ed. Kazan State Univ.; Deputy Ed. Molodoi Komsomolets, also Head, Dept. of Propaganda, Cen. Comsomol Cttee. 1974–85; Rector, Gorky. Inst. of Literature in Moscow 1985–87; Deputy Head, Div. of Culture, Ideological Dept., CPSU Cen. Cttee. 1987–90; asst. to Pres. Gorbachev on Problems of Culture and Religion 1990–91; Chief Scientific Researcher, Analytical Centre at Ministry of Science 1992–96; Prof. Russian Acad. of State Service 1993–; mem. Co-ordination Council, My Motherland; Dir. Russian State Library 1996–98; Minister of Culture Russian Fed. 1998–. *Publications:* books including History in our Lives, Intelligentsia and Power, The Star Turns Pale: Reflections on Russian History, From Deadlock to Uncertainty, Many Faces of Russia, numerous articles. *Address:* Ministry of Culture, Kitaigorodsky proyezd 7, 103693 Moscow, Russia. *Telephone:* (095) 220 4500; (095) 925 2881 (Office).

YEHOSHUA, Abraham B., M.A.; Israeli writer and university professor; b. 9 Dec. 1936, Jerusalem; s. of Yakov Yehoshua and Malka Rosilio; m. Rivka Kirsninski 1960; two s. one d.; served in paratroopers unit 1954–57; Dir. Israeli School in Paris 1964; Gen. Sec. World Union of Jewish Studies, Paris 1964–67; Dean of Students, Haifa Univ. 1967–72, Prof. of Comparative Literature 1972–; Visiting Prof., Harvard Univ., U.S.A. 1977, Univ. of Chicago 1988, 1997, Princeton Univ. 1992–; Co-Ed. Keshet 1965–72, Siman Kria 1973–, Tel Aviv Review 1987–; Brener Prize, Alterman Prize, Bialik Prize, Nat. Jewish Book Award 1990, 1993 (for Five Seasons, Mister Mani), Israeli Booker Prize (for Mister Mani) 1992, European B'nai B'rith Award 1993, Cavour Prize (Italy) (for Five Seasons) 1994, Wingate Prize (U.K.) (for Mr Mani) 1994, Israel Prize 1995, Fliano Prize (Italy) (for A Late Divorce) 1996. *Publications:* Death of the Old Man (short stories) 1963, Three Days and a Child (short stories) 1970, Early in the Summer of 1970 (novella) 1973, Two Plays 1975, The Lover (novel) 1978, Between Right and Right (essays) 1980, A Late Divorce (novel) 1982, Possessions (play) 1986, Five Seasons (novel) 1988, The Wall and the Mountain (essays) 1988, Mister Mani (novel) 1990, The Night's Babies (play) 1991, Open Heart 1994, A Voyage to the End of the Millennium (novel) 1997, The Moral Context of the Literary Text (essays) 1998. *Address:* 33 Shoshanat Ha-Carme, Haifa, 34322, Israel. *Telephone:* 04-8370001. *Fax:* 04-8375569.

YELLAND, David Ian, B.A.(HONS.); British journalist; b. 14 May 1963, Harrogate; s. of John Michael Yelland and Patricia Ann McIntosh; m. Tania Farrell 1996; one s.; ed. Brigg Grammar School, Lincs., Coventry Univ.; grad. trainee Westminster Press 1985; trainee reporter Buckinghamshire Advertiser 1985–87; industrial reporter Northern Echo 1987–88; gen. news and business reporter North West Times and Sunday Times 1988–89; city reporter Thomson Regional Newspapers 1989–90; joined News Corpn. 1990; city reporter, city ed., New York corresp. The Sun 1993–98, Ed. 1998–; Deputy Business Ed., Business Ed., then Deputy Ed. New York Post 1993–98. *Address:* The Sun, 1 Virginia Street, London, E1 9XP, England. *Telephone:* 0171-782 4000.

YELLEN, Janet Louise, PH.D.; American economist and government official; b. 13 Aug. 1946, Brooklyn; d. of Julius Yellen and Anna Ruth Yellen (née Blumenthal); m. George Arthur Akerlof 1978; one s.; ed. Brown Univ., Yale Univ.; Asst. Prof. of Econs. Harvard Univ. 1971–76; lecturer L.S.E. 1978–80; Asst. Prof. of Econs. School of Business Admin. Univ. of Calif., Berkeley 1980–82, Assoc. Prof. 1982–85, Prof. Haas School of Business 1985–; Bernard T. Rocca Jr. Prof. of Int. Business and Trade 1992–; consultant Div. of Int. Finance, Bd. Govs. of Fed. Reserve System 1974–75, economist Trade and Financial Studies section 1977–78, mem. 1994–97; Research Fellow M.I.T. 1974; consultant Congressional Budget Office 1975–76, mem. Panel of Econ. Advisers 1993–; Chair. Council of Econ. Advisers Jan. 1997–; research affiliate, Yale Univ. 1976; mem. Advisory Panel on Econs. Nat. Science Foundation 1977–78, 1991–92; mem. Brookings Panel on Econ. Activity 1987–88, 1990–91, Sr. Adviser 1989–; lecturer on macroeconomic theory, Yrjö Jahnsson Found., Helsinki 1977–78; mem. Council on Foreign Relations 1976–81, American Econ. Assn.; Hon. Woodrow Wilson Fellow 1967; grad. fellow Nat. Science Foundation 1967–71; Guggenheim Fellow 1986–87. *Publications:* The Limits of the Market in Resource Allocation (jtly.) 1977, assoc. ed. Journal of Econ. Perspectives 1987–91, contrib. articles to professional journals. *Address:* Council of Economic Advisers, Old Executive Office Building, 17th Street and Pennsylvania Avenue, N.W., Washington, DC 20500, U.S.A.

YELTSIN, Boris Nikolayevich; Russian politician; b. 1 Feb. 1931, Sverdlovsk; s. of Nikolai Yeltsin and Klavdia Yeltsina; m. Naina Yeltsina (née Girina) 1956; two d.; ed. Urals Polytech. Inst.; construction-worker with various orgs. in Sverdlovsk Dist. 1955–68; mem. CPSU 1961–90 (resgnd.); First Sec. Sverdlovsk Dist. Cen. Cttee. CPSU 1976–85; fmr. Deputy to Supreme Soviet of U.S.S.R.; Sec. of Cen. Cttee. CPSU 1985–86; First Sec. of Moscow City Party Cttee. 1985–87; First Deputy Chair. State Cttee. for Construction 1987–89; Head Cttee. on Construction Architecture 1989–90; Chair. Inter-Regional Group July 1989; elected to Congress of People's Deputies of the U.S.S.R. 1989; mem. U.S.S.R. Supreme Soviet 1989–91; mem. and Chair. R.S.F.S.R. Supreme Soviet 1990–91; President of R.S.F.S.R. 1991, of Russia Dec. 1991–; Acting Head Russian Fed. Defence Ministry 1992; Supreme Commdr. of Russian Army May 1992–; Olympic Gold Order 1992, German Press Award 1996. *Publications:* Against the Grain (autobiog.) 1990, Three Days 1992, Memoirs: The View From the Kremlin 1990, 1994. *Leisure interests:* tennis, hunting, film. *Address:* Office of the President, 103073 The Kremlin, korp. 1, Moscow, Russia. *Telephone:* 910-07-66; 206-85-10.

YELYAKOV, Georgy Borisovich, D.CHEM.SC.; Russian chemist; b. 13 Sept. 1929, Kostroma; m. Lyudmila Elyakova 1960; two d.; ed. Moscow Univ.; mem. CPSU 1965–91; worked in Cen. Mil. Tech. Inst., U.S.S.R. Ministry of Defence 1952–55; sr. researcher Far East br. of U.S.S.R. Acad. of Sciences 1955–69; f. and Head of lab. of Chem. of natural physiologically active compounds, Inst. of Biologically Active Compounds, Far East br. of U.S.S.R. Acad. of Sciences 1959–64; Dir. Pacific Inst. of Bioorganic Chem. 1964–; Corresp. mem. U.S.S.R. (now Russian) Acad. of Sciences 1970, mem. 1987; Vice-Pres. Russian Acad. of Sciences, Chair. Far East Div. 1991–; mem. Int. Soc. of Toxinologists. *Publications:* over 200 works on biologically active compounds (biosynthesis, structure and elucidation of biological functions); synthesis of principally new antibiotics and antioxidants. *Leisure interests:* driving, hunting, computers. *Address:* Pacific Institute of Bioorganic Chemistry, Far East Division of Russian Academy of Sciences, 690022 Vladivostok, Russia. *Telephone:* (4232) 22-25-28 (Vladivostok); (095) 938-17-55 (Moscow). *Fax:* (4232) 31-40-50.

YEMELYANOV, Aleksei Mikhailovich, D.ECON.; Russian politician and economist; b. 1935; ed. Moscow Univ.; mem. CPSU 1959–90; lecturer, Prof., Head of Chair Moscow Univ.; mem. Russian Agric. Acad.; U.S.S.R. People's Deputy 1989–91; Deputy Chair. Cttee. on Agric. Problems, U.S.S.R. Supreme Soviet 1989–91; mem. Pres. Council 1992–; Pres.-Rector Russian State Acad. of State Service 1994–; active participant of democratic movt.; elected to State Duma (Parl.) Dec. 1993–. *Publications:* scientific works and articles on agricultural reforms in Russia. *Address:* Russian Agricultural Academy, Bolshoy Kharitonyevsky per. 21, 107814 Moscow; Academy of State Service, Vernadskogo prosp. 84, 117606 Moscow, Russia. *Telephone:* 923-40-90 (Agricultural Acad.); 434-90-10 (Acad. of State Service).

YEMELYANOV, Stanislav Vasilevich, DR.TECH.SC.; Russian management specialist; b. 18 May 1929, Voronezh; s. of Vasilii Yemelyanov and Ludmila (née Chepkova) Yemelyanova; m. Olga Yemelyanova 1952; one s. one d.; ed. Moscow Univ.; with Inst. of Control Problems, U.S.S.R. (now Russian) Acad. of Sciences 1952–76, with Inst. for Systems Analysis 1976– (Dir. 1991–), mem. Acad. 1984, mem. Presidium 1988, Acad.-Sec., Dept. of Informatics, Computer Science and Automation 1990–; Gen. Dir. Int. Inst. for Man. Science 1976–; Head of Chair of Nonlinear Dynamics and Control Processes, Moscow State Univ.; Chair of Engineering Cybernetics, Moscow Steel and Alloys Inst.; mem. editorial bd. Differential Equations, Automatic and Remote Control, Problems of Theory and Practice of Management, Dynamics and Control; research into variable structure control theory; holder of about 100 patents; Lenin Prize 1972, U.S.S.R. State Prize 1980, Council of U.S.S.R. Ministers Prize 1981, Russian Fed. State Prize 1994. *Publications:* 7 books; 250 journal articles. *Address:* International Institute for Management Science, Shchepkina Street 8, 129090 Moscow (Office); ac. Zelinskii str. 38/8, Apt. 69, Moscow, Russia (Home). *Telephone:* 208-91-06 (Office); 135-54-69 (Home). *Fax:* 938-16-74.

YEMEN, former King of (see Saif al-Islam, Mohammed al-Badr).

YEN CHEN-HSING, PH.D.; Taiwanese government official; b. 10 July 1912, Junan Co., Honan; m. Sou-lien Yen; two s. one d.; ed. Nat. Tsinghua Univ. and Univ. of Iowa; Prof. Nat. Tsinghua Univ. 1941–46; Dean, Coll. of Eng., Nat. Honan Univ. 1947–48; Chief Eng. Kaohsiung Habor Bureau 1949–57; Dean, Coll. of Eng. Nat. Taiwan Univ. 1953–55; Commr. Dept. of Educ. Taiwan Provincial Govt. 1962–63; Pres. Nat. Chengkung Univ. 1957–65; Minister of Educ. 1965–69; Chair. Nat. Youth Comm., Exec. Yuan 1966–70; Pres. Chungshan Inst. 1969–75, Nat. Tsinghua Univ. 1969–70, Nat. Taiwan Univ. 1970–81, Hon. Prof. 1981–; Chair. Atomic Energy Council, Exec. Yuan 1981–; mem. Acad. Sinica 1982–. *Publications:* numerous publs. on construction. *Address:* Atomic Energy Council, 67 Lane 144, Keelung Road, Sec. 4, Taipei; 3, Lane 11, Chingtien Street, Taipei, Taiwan.

YENTOB, Alan, LL.B.; British television administrator; b. 11 March 1947; s. of Isaac Yentob and Flora Yentob (née Khazam); one s. one d. by Philippa Walker; ed. King's School, Ely, Univ. of Grenoble, France, Univ. of Leeds; BBC gen. trainee 1968, Producer/Dir. 1970–, Head of Music and Arts, BBC-TV 1985–88, Controller, BBC 2 1988–93, BBC 1 1993–96, BBC Dir. of Programmes 1996–97; BBC Dir. of TV May 1997–; mem. Bd. of Dirs. Riverside Studios 1984–88, British Film Inst. Production Bd. 1985–93, British Screen Advisory Council, Advisory Cttee., Inst. of Contemporary Arts, Council Royal Court Theatre; Gov. Nat. Film School; Hon. Fellow, R.C.A., R.I.B.A. *Leisure interests:* swimming, books. *Address:* BBC Television, Television Centre, Wood Lane, London, W.12, England.

YEO CHEOW TONG, B.ENG.; Singaporean politician; b. 1947; m.; two d.; ed. Anglo-Chinese School, Univ. of Western Australia; worked in Econ. Devt. Bd. 1972–75; joined LeBlond Makino Asia Pte. Ltd. (LMA) as Staff Engineer 1975, subsequently promoted to Eng. Man., then Operations Dir.; Man. Dir. LMA and subsidiary co., Pacific Precision Castings (Pte.) Ltd. (PPC) 1981–85; elected M.P. for Hong Kah 1984; Minister of State for Health and Foreign Affairs 1985–87; Acting Minister for Health, Sr. Minister of State for Foreign Affairs 1987–90, of Health 1990–94, for Community Devt. 1993–94, for Trade and Industry 1994–97, of Health and Environment 1997–. *Address:* Ministry of Health, 16 College Road, College of Medicine Bldg., Singapore 169854. *Telephone:* 3259220. *Fax:* 2241677.

YEREMIN, Yuri Ivanovich; Russian theatre director; b. 9 March 1944, Kolomna, Moscow Region; s. of Evdokiya Fillippovna Yeremina; m. Nina Petrovna Yeremina 1974; one s. one d.; with Youth Theatre, Rostov-on-Don 1973–77; Gorky Drama Theatre, Rostov-on-Don 1978–80; Cen. Army Theatre, Moscow 1981–87; Dir. Pushkin Theatre, Moscow 1987–; U.S. debut with production of The Paper Gramophone, Hartford Stage Co. 1989; Ward No. 6, dramatic adaptation of Chekhov story, performed at int. drama festivals in U.S.A., France, Italy, Switzerland, Belgium, U.K. and Canada 1989–91; Vice-Pres. Int. Assn. of Theatre Producers 1991–; People's Artist of Russia 1986, Order for Literature and Art (France) 1989. *Recent productions include:* The Possessed (Dostoevsky adaptation) 1989, Black Monk (Chekhov adaptation) 1990, At Kingdom Gate (Hamsun) 1991, Erick XIV (Strindberg) 1992, The Ghosts (De Filippo) 1992, The History of one Staircase (Buero Valejo) 1993, To Moscow! To Moscow! (adaptation of Chekhov's Three Sisters) 1994, Madame Bovary (Flaubert adaptation) 1994, The Inspector (Gogol) 1994, King Oedipus (Sophocles) 1995. *Leisure interests:* painting, writing. *Address:* Pushkin Theatre, Tverskoy bul. 23, Moscow, Russia. *Telephone:* 203-85-82.

YERIN, Army Gen. Victor Fedorovich; Russian politician; b. 17 Jan. 1944, Kazan; ed. Higher School, U.S.S.R. Ministry of Internal Affairs; regional militiaman; mem. Criminal Investigation Dept. Ministry of Internal Affairs, Tatar Autonomous Repub., Chief of Dept. 1980–83; Chief of Div. Admin. of struggle against embezzlement of social property 1983–88; First Deputy Minister of Internal Affairs of Armenian S.S.R. 1988–90; Deputy Minister of Internal Affairs of R.S.F.S.R., Chief Service of Criminal Militia 1990–91; First Deputy Minister of Internal Affairs of U.S.S.R. Sept.–Dec. 1991; First Deputy Minister of Security and Internal Affairs of Russian Fed. 1991–92; Minister of Internal Affairs of Russian Fed. 1992–95; Deputy Dir. of Foreign Intelligence July 1995–. *Address:* Kolpachni per. 11, 101000 Moscow, Russia (Office). *Telephone:* (095) 429-38-50.

YEROFEYEV, Victor Vladimirovich; Russian writer and critic; b. 19 Sept. 1947, Moscow; m. Veslava (née Skura) Yerofeyeva; one s.; ed. Moscow Univ.; expelled from U.S.S.R. Writers' Union for participation in almanac Metropol, membership restored in 1986; lecturer Maxim Gorky Literature Inst.; seminars on Modern Russian Literature at Univ. of South Calif.; contribs. to Moscow News, Moscow Magazine, New York Review of Books; mem. Bd. Russian PEN Centre; named Man of the Year by Moscow Magazine 1990. *Publications:* Anna's Body and End of the Russian Avant-garde (collection of short stories) 1980, Life with an Idiot (novel) 1980, Russian Beauty (novel) 1981, In the Maze of Cursed Questions (collection of essays) 1990, The Pocket Apocalypse 1993, Collected Works (3 vols.) 1994–95, Men 1997, Five Rivers of Life 1998. *Leisure interest:* travelling. *Address:* 1st Smolensky per. 9, Apt. 1, Moscow, Russia. *Telephone:* 241-02-08.

YESIN, Sergey Nikolayevich; Russian writer: b. 18 Dec. 1935, Moscow; s. of Nikolai Yesin and Zinaida (née Afonina) Saprykina; m. Valentina Ivanova; ed. Moscow State Univ.; debut as journalist, corresp. Moskovsky Komsomolets, Ed.-in-Chief Krugozor 1972–74; ed. Drama Broadcasting Div. State TV and Broadcasting Cttee. 1974–81; Rector Literature Inst. 1992–, Prof. 1993; a founder Club of Ind. Writers 1992; founder and Vice-Pres. Acad. of Russian Literature 1996. *Publications include:* Recollections of August, Memoirs of a Forty-Year-Old, The Imitator, The Spy, Standing in the Doorway, Gladiator 1987, Characters 1990, Selected Stories 1994, In the Season of Salting Pickles 1994, The Current Day 1994, The Mars Eclipse 1994, Tutor 1996. *Leisure interests:* building dachas, home maintenance. *Address:* Stroiteley str. 4, korp. 6, Apt. 43, 117311 Moscow, Russia (Home). *Telephone:* 930-35-45 (Home).

YESSENIN VOLPIN, Alexander Sergeyevich; Russian mathematician, philosopher, poet and mentor of Human Rights Movt.; b. 5 Dec. 1924,

Leningrad (now St. Petersburg); s. of poet Sergey Esenin and Nadiezhda Volpina; m. 1st V. B. Volpina; m. 2nd I. G. Kristi; m. 3rd 1994; one c.; studied at Faculty of Math., Moscow Univ. 1941–46; arrested for poetry and committed to mental asylum 1949; in exile Karaganda, Kazakh S.S.R. 1950; amnestied 1953; wrote numerous articles on logic and math. and translated extensively; at U.S.S.R. Acad. of Sciences Inst. of Scientific and Tech. Information 1961–72; dissident activity 1959–; emigrated 1972. *Publications include:* A Free Philosophical Treatise 1959, A Leaf of Spring 1959, 1961, Open Letter to Solzhenitsyn 1970, Report on Committee on Rights of Man 1971, On the Logic of Moral Sciences (in English) 1988; numerous articles in Western and Russian scientific journals (after 1990s). *Leisure interests:* logic, philosophy. *Address:* 1513 North Shore Road, 2nd Floor, Revere, MA 02151, U.S.A. *Telephone:* (781) 289-1072.

YEUTTER, Clayton K.; American government official; b. 10 Dec. 1930, Eustis, Neb.; m. Lillian Jeanne Vierk; two s. two d.; ed. Univ. of Nebraska; served U.S.A.F. 1952–57; ran family farm from 1957; law degree, Univ. of Neb. 1963, agricultural econs. degree 1966, subsequently Prof., Dir. Agricultural and Tech. Assistance Programme in Bogotá, Colombia 1968–70; Asst. Sec. of Agric. in charge of Int. Affairs and Commodity Programs, U.S. Govt. 1970–75; Deputy Special Trade Rep. 1975–77, U.S. Trade Rep. 1985–88; Sec. of State for Agric. 1989–91; Chair. Republican Nat. Cttee. 1991–92; Counsellor to the Pres. for domestic policy 1992; Pres. Chicago Mercantile Exchange 1978–85; Dir. (non-exec.) BAT Industries. *Address:* c/o Republican National Committee, 310 First Street, S.E., Washington, DC 20003, U.S.A.

YEVTUSHENKO, Yevgeniy Aleksandrovich; Russian poet; b. 18 July 1933, Zima, Irkutsk Region; m. 1st Bella Akhmadulina 1954; m. 2nd Galina Sokol 1962; one s.; m. 3rd Jan Butler 1978; two s.; m. 4th Maria Novikova 1986; two s.; ed. Moscow Literary Inst.; geological expeditions with father to Kazakhstan 1948, the Altai 1949–50; literary work 1949–; mem. Editorial Bd. of Yunost magazine 1962–69; People's Deputy of the U.S.S.R. 1989–91; Sec. U.S.S.R. Writers' Union 1986–91; Vice-Pres. Soviet PEN Cttee.; U.S.S.R. Cttee. for Defence of Peace Award 1965, Order of Red Banner of Labour, Badge of Honour, U.S.S.R. State Prize 1984. *Publications include:* verse: Scouts of the Future (collected verse) 1952, The Third Snow (lyric verse) 1955, The Highway of Enthusiasts 1956, Zima Junction 1956, The Promise (collected verse) 1960, Moscow Goods Station, The Nihilist, The Apple 1960–61, Do the Russians Want War?, Babi Yar 1961, The Heirs of Stalin, Fears 1962, A Sweep of the Arm 1962, Tenderness 1962, A Precocious Autobiography 1963, The City of Yes and the City of No, Do the Russians Want War?, Bratskaya Hydro-Electric Power Station 1964, Letter to Yesenin 1965, Italian Tears, A Boat of Communication, Poems Chosen by the Author 1966, Collection of Verses Yelabuga Nail, Cemetery of Whales 1967, That's What Is Happening to Me 1968, It's Snowing White 1969, Kazan University 1971, I am of Siberian Stock 1971, The Singing Domba 1972, Stolen Apples 1972, Under the Skin of the Statue of Liberty (play) 1972, Intimate Lyrics 1973, A Father's Hearing 1975, 1978, From Desire to Desire 1976, Love Poems 1977, People of the Morning 1978, Winter Station 1978, A Dove in Santiago: A Novella in Verse 1978, Heavy Soils 1979, The Face Behind the Face 1979, Ivan the Terrible and Ivan the Fool 1979, Berries (novel) 1981, Ardabiola (short story) 1981, Almost At the End (prose and verse) 1985, A Wind of Tomorrow (essays) 1987, Fatal Half Measures 1989, The Collected Poems 1952–90 1991, Farewell to Red Banner 1992, compiler Twentieth Century Russian Poetry 1994, Don't Die Before You're Dead (novel) 1996, My Very, Very ..... (poetry) 1996; acted in Ascent (film on Tsiolkovsky) 1979; dir. Kindergarten 1983, Stalin's Funeral 1987; photography: Divided Twins: Alaska and Siberia, Invisible Threads, Shadows and Faces. *Address:* Kutuzovski Prospekt 2/1, Apt. 101, 121248 Moscow, Russia. *Telephone:* (095) 243-37-69.

YEZHOV, Valentin Ivanovich; Russian screenplay writer; b. 21 Jan. 1921, Samara; s. of Ivan Yezhov and Anna Yezhov; m. 1st Olga Sherbova 1951, 2nd Natalya Gotovtseva 1976; one s.; ed. All-Union State Inst. of Cinematography; Prof. of Cinematography 1989–; mem. CPSU 1951–91; Lenin Prize 1961 for script of Ballad of a Soldier 1959; co-author scripts for Our Champions 1954, World Champion 1955, Liana 1956, A Man from the Planet Earth 1958, The House of Gold 1959, The Volga Flows 1962, Wings 1966, Thirty Three 1967, White Sun of the Desert 1969, A Nest of Gentry 1969, The Legend 1971, This Sweet Word Liberty 1973, Eleven Hopefuls 1974, Siberiade 1977, Meadow Flowers 1981, The Girl and the Grand 1982, Alexander the Small 1982, Moon Rainbow 1983, The First Cavalry 1984, The Rivals 1985, Bow to the Ground 1985, Strawberry Wine 1985, Last Will and Testament 1986, Your Special Correspondent 1986, Igor Savovich 1987, Fellow Townsmen 1988, The Watchmaker and the Hen 1989, Happiness Never Strikes Twice 1990, Esperanza (Mexican co-production) 1990, Maria and Mirabella II 1990, Adjouba (Indian co-production) 1990, Under Aurora (Japanese co-production) 1990, Lord Silver 1991, Sin 1992, My Best Friend General Vasiliy, Son of Joseph 1992, Siberiada (collected works) 1993, The White Sun of the Desert (collected works) 1994. *Plays:* Nightingale Night 1969, Gunfire Beyond the Dunes 1982, Alyosha 1985. *Leisure interest:* fishing. *Address:* Kutuzovski Prospekt 41, Apt. 20, 121170 Moscow, Russia. *Telephone:* (095) 249-38-74.

YHAP, Laetitia, D.F.A.; British artist; b. 1 May 1941, St. Albans; d. of Leslie Neville Yhap and Elizabeth (née Kogler) Yhap; one s.; ed. Camberwell School of Arts and Crafts, Slade School of Fine Art, Univ. Coll. London; Artist-in-Residence Chatham House Grammar School, Ramsgate 1981; numerous one-woman exhbns. 1965–; most recent maj. solo shows: The Business of the Beach, on tour 1988–89, Life at the Edge, Charleston Farmhouse 1993, Bound By the Sea (retrospective), Berwick Gymnasium 1994, Maritime Counterpoint, Boundary Gallery 1996; works in public collections in U.K.; John Moores Prize 1973. *Leisure interests:* music, attending concerts, playing badminton. *Address:* 12 The Croft, Hastings, Sussex, TN34 3HH, England. *Telephone:* (01424) 426222.

YHOMBI-OPANGO, Brig.-Gen. Jacques-Joachim; Congolese army officer and fmr. Head of State; b. 1939; trained in French army; fmr. military attaché at Congolese Embassy, Moscow; Chief of Staff, People's National Army 1968–73, Insp.-Gen. 1973–74; Sec.-Gen. of Council of State with rank of Minister 1974–75, Council of State Delegate responsible for Defence and Security 1974–75; Pres. of Republic, Pres. Council of Ministers, Pres. Mil. Council of Congolese Labour Party 1977–79; arrested 1979, detained 1979–84, released from detention Nov. 1984, rearrested Sept. 1987; Prime Minister of Congo 1993–96; Leader Rassemblement pour la défense et le developpement (RDP); fmr. Leader Rassemblement pour la Démocratie et le Développement (RDD); Order of Nat. Flag (North Korea) 1978. *Address:* c/o Office of the Prime Minister, Brazzaville, Congo.

YIANNOPOULOS, Evangelos; Greek politician; b. 1918, Gortynia, Peloponnese; m. Konstantina Yiannopoulou 1954; one s. one d.; ed. Athens Univ.; served as officer in Albanian war (wounded) and later in Greek resistance movement in World War II as bn. commdr. in Greek Popular Liberation Army; mem. Nat. Progressive Centre Union; joined Centre Union youth org., Centre Union Party 1960; arrested and deported to remote area 1969, rearrested and imprisoned for political activities 1970; founding mem. Panhellenic Socialist Movement (PASOK); also mem. Cen. Cttee.; Pres. Athens Lawyer's Asscn. 1976–81; mem. Gov. Council, Inst. of Int. and Alien Law; M.P. 1981–; Minister of Labour 1981–85, 1985–86, of Merchant Marine 1987–89, of the Aegean March–July 1989, of Labour 1993–94, of Justice Sept. 1996–. *Address:* Ministry of Justice, Odos Mesogeion 96, 115 27 Athens, Greece. *Telephone:* (1) 775 1303. *Fax:* (1) 775 9879.

YILMAZ, A. Mesut; Turkish politician; b. 6 Nov. 1947, Istanbul; s. of Hasan Yilmaz and Güzide Yilmaz; m. Berna Müren; two s.; ed. Istanbul High School for Boys, Faculty of Political Studies, Ankara and in London and Cologne; fmr. company dir. in pvt. business sector; Deputy for Rize 1983–; fmr. Minister of State; Minister of Culture and Tourism 1986–87, of Foreign Affairs 1987–90, Prime Minister of Turkey June–Nov. 1991, 1996, 1997–98; Leader Motherland Party; Vice-Chair. EDU. *Address:* c/o Başbakanlık, Bakanlıklar, Ankara, Turkey. *Telephone:* (312) 4189056. *Fax:* (312) 4180476.

YIN CHANGMIN; Chinese scientist and party and state official; b. 4 Oct. 1923, Nanchang, Jiangxi Prov.; d. of Yin Renqing and Wu Yahui; m. Bei Xiaoliang 1948; two s.; alt. mem. 12th CCP Cen. Cttee. 1982, mem. 1986; alt. mem. 13th CCP Cen. Cttee. 1987–92; Prof. Hunan Normal Univ. 1979–, Vice-Pres. 1973–81, Pres. 1981–83, Consultant 1985–; Vice-Chair. CPPCC Prov. Cttee., Hunan 1985–92; mem. CCP Cttee., Hunan 1983–85; Vice-Chair. Hunan Branch Asscn. for Science and Tech. 1980–85, Hon. Chair. 1985–; mem. Bd. of Dirs., Chinese Zoological Soc. 1984; Chair. Bd. of Dirs. Hunan Biology Soc. and Zoological Soc. 1981–92, Hunan Zoological Soc. 1992–; Deputy, Nat. Cultural and Educational Conf. 1960; Nat. Red Banner Women's Pacesetter 1959, Model Worker of Hunan Prov. 1960, First Prize for Improvement of Science and Tech., Dept. of Agric. and Forestry 1980, First Prize, Nat. Cttee. of Educ., and other prizes. *Publications:* Field Spiders 1980, Textbook of Zoology 1983, Spiders in China: One Hundred New and Newly Recorded Species of the Araneidae and Agelenidae Family 1990, Fauna Sinica; 70 research papers. *Leisure interests:* literature, collecting postage stamps. *Address:* Department of Biology, Hunan Normal University, Changsha, Hunan Province, People's Republic of China. *Telephone:* (731) 8883310. *Fax:* (731) 8851226.

YIN JUN; Chinese politician; b. Sept. 1932; alt. mem. 12th CCP Cen. Cttee. 1982; Chair. and Gov., Dali Bai Autonomous Pref., Yunnan Prov. 1982–84; Sec. Discipline Inspection Cttee., Yunnan CCP Prov. Cttee. 1985; alt. mem. 13th CCP Cen. Cttee. 1987; Deputy Sec. Yunnan Prov. Cttee. 1989; Chair. Yunnan Prov. 8th People's Congress 1993–. *Address:* Dali Bai Autonomous Prefectural People's Government, Yunnan, People's Republic of China.

YIN KESHENG; Chinese politician; b. 1932; ed. Beijing Petroleum Inst.; Vice-Gov., Qinghai 1983; Sec. CCP Cttee., Qinghai 1985–97; mem. 12th CCP Cen. Cttee. 1985–87; mem. 13th CCP Cen. Cttee. 1987–92, 14th Cen. Cttee. 1992–97; Vice-Chair. Nationalities Cttee. of 9th NPC 1998–. *Address:* c/o Standing Committee of National People's Congress, Beijing, People's Republic of China.

YIN WENYING; Chinese entomologist; b. Oct. 1923, Pingxiang Co., Hebei Prov.; ed. Zhongyang Univ.; mem. Chinese Acad. of Sciences 1992–; Science and Tech. Progress Award. *Address:* Shanghai Institute of Entomology, 225 Chongqing Nan Road, Shanghai Municipality, People's Republic of China.

YING, Diane; Taiwanese journalist and publisher; b. Xian, China; ed. Univ. of Iowa, U.S.A.; emigrated with family from mainland China to Taiwan 1949; fmr. reporter, The Philadelphia Inquirer, U.S.A., Taiwan corresp. at various times for Asian Wall Street Journal, New York Times and United Press Int.; Co-founder, Chief Ed. and Publr. Commonwealth financial monthly 1981–; teaches journalism at Nat. Chengchi Univ.; Commr. Nat. Unification Council. *Address:* 4th Floor, 87 Sungkiang Road, Taipei, Taiwan.

YISHAI, Eliyahu; Israeli politician; b. 1963, Jerusalem; m.; four c.; fmr. head of Interior Minister's bureau; acting Sec.-Gen. Shas (Sephardic Torah Guardians) 1991–, Dir.-Gen. Shas-affiliated El ha-Ma'ayan movt.; Minister of Labour and Social Welfare 1996–. *Address:* Ministry of Labour and Social Welfare, P.O. Box 915, 2 Rehov Kaplan, Kiryat Ben-Gurion, Jerusalem 91008, Israel. *Telephone:* 2-6752311. *Fax:* 2-6752803.

YODER, Hatten Schuyler, Jr., PH.D.; American petrologist; b. 20 March 1921, Cleveland, Ohio; s. of Hatten Schuyler Yoder and Elizabeth Katherine Yoder (née Knieling); m. Elizabeth Marie Bruffey 1959; one s. one d.; ed. Univs. of Chicago and Minnesota and Massachusetts Inst. of Tech.; active duty, U.S. Naval Reserve 1942–46, MOKO expedition to Siberia 1945–46, Lieut.-Commdr., retd.; Petrologist, Geophysical Lab., Carnegie Inst. of Washington 1948–71, Dir. 1971–86, Dir. Emer. 1986–; public mem. Foreign Service Selection Bds., Dept. of State 1990; mem. Editorial Bd. Geochimica et Cosmochimica Acta 1958–68; N. American Ed., Journal of Petrology 1959–68, Hon. mem. Advisory Bd. 1968–79; Assoc. Ed. American Journal of Science 1972–90; Editorial Bd. Earth Sciences History 1993–; Consultant Los Alamos Nat. Lab. 1971–; Visiting Prof. of Geochemistry, Calif. Inst. of Tech. 1958; Visiting Prof. of Petrology, Univ. of Tex. 1964, Univ. of Colo. 1966, Univ. of Cape Town 1967; new mineral, Yoderite named in his honour; Participant, Nobel Symposium, Royal Swedish Acad. of Sciences 1979; mem. N.A.S. 1958– (Geology Section Chair. 1973–76); mem. U.S. Nat. Cttee. for Geology 1973–76, for Geochemistry 1973–76, on the history of Geology 1982–90, American Philosophical Soc. 1979, (Council 1983–85), Exec. Cttee. 1994–99, Geochemical Soc. (Organizing and Founding mem., Council 1956–58); Hon. mem. All-Union Mineralogical Soc. of U.S.S.R. (now Russia) 1977–, Mineralogical Soc. of Great Britain 1983–, Soc. Française de Minéralogie et de Cristallographie 1986–; Fellow, Mineralogical Soc. of America (mem. Council 1962–64, Vice-Pres. 1970–71, Pres. 1971–72), Geological Soc. of America (mem. Council 1966–68), American Geophysical Union (Pres. Volcanology, Geochemistry and Petrology Section 1961–64, mem. Council 1965–68), American Acad. of Arts and Sciences 1979, Geological Soc. of S.A. 1988–, Public Mems. Asscn. of the Foreign Service (Vice-Pres. 1994–95, 1998–99); Pres. History of Earth Sciences Soc. 1995–99; Independent Trustee The Cutler Trust 1992–; Sec.-Treas. Bd. of Advisors, The Coll. of Democracy 1985–; Corresp. Fellow, Edinburgh Geological Soc.; Hon. Fellow Geological Soc. of London 1988, Geological Soc. of Finland, Mineralogical Asscn. of Canada; Hon. D.Eng. (Colorado School of Mines) 1995; Dr. h.c. (Univ. of Paris VI) 1981; Mineralogical Soc. of America Award 1954, Columbia Univ. Bicentennial Medal 1954, Arthur L. Day Medal of Geological Soc. of America 1962, A. L. Day Prize and Lectureship of Nat. Acad. of Sciences 1972, A. G. Werner Medal of German Mineralogical Soc. 1972, Golden Plate Award, American Acad. of Achievement 1976, Wollaston Medal, Geological Soc. of London 1979, Roebling Medal, Mineralogical Soc. of America 1992, Compatriot, Sons of the American Revolution, History of Geology Award, Geological Soc. of America 1998. *Publications:* Generation of Basaltic Magma 1976, The Evolution of the Igneous Rocks: Fiftieth Anniversary Perspectives (editor) 1979, Planned Invasion of Japan 1945: The Siberian Weather Advantage 1997 and numerous papers. *Leisure interests:* camping, trombone, rifle and pistol marksmanship, gardening, philately, genealogy. *Address:* Geophysical Laboratory, 5251 Broad Branch Road, N.W., Washington, DC 20015, U.S.A. *Telephone:* (202) 686-2410. *Fax:* (202) 686-2419.

YON HYONG-MUK; Korean politician; b. 3 Nov. 1931, N. Hamgyong Prov.; ed. university; worked as farm labourer then technician; Deputy to Supreme People's Ass. 1967–; Vice-Dir. then Dir. of Dept., Cen. Cttee. Workers Party of Korea (KWP); mem., KWP Cen. Cttee. Nov. 1970–; Political Bureau 1973–; Vice-Premier, then First Vice-Premier Admin. Council; Sec. to Party Centre; Premier, Admin. Council 1988–92; Kim Il-Sung Medal, Order of the Nat. Flag (First Class), Order of Freedom and Independence (First Class). *Address:* c/o Office of the Premier, Pyongyang, Democratic People's Republic of Korea.

YONGJIAN JIN, Chinese diplomatist; b. 15 Sept. 1934, Jiangsu Prov.; s. of Zhiying Jin and Canzhang Bo; m. Youping Wang 1955; two s.; ed. Beijing Univ.; joined Diplomatic Service 1954, officer People's Inst. of Foreign Affairs 1954–63, Attaché, Embassy of PRC to Kenya 1964–67, officer, African Dept., Ministry of Foreign Affairs 1967–71, Third then Second Sec. Embassy of PRC to Nigeria 1971–76; Rep. of PRC to UN Security Council Cttee. 1977, UN Special Cttee. on Decolonization, and UN Council for Namibia 1977–84; Alt. Rep. of PRC to UN Security Council; Second, First Sec. then Counsellor, Perm. Mission of PRC to UN; Deputy Dir.-Gen. then Dir.-Gen. African Dept., Ministry of Foreign Affairs 1984–88, Dir.-Gen. Dept. of Int. Orgs. and Confs. 1988–90; Deputy Perm. Rep. and Amb. of PRC to UN, Deputy Rep. of PRC to Security Council 1990–92; Amb. and Perm. Rep. of PRC to UN Office, Geneva and other int. orgs. 1992–96; UN Under-Sec.-Gen. for Devt. Support and Man. Services 1996–97, Under-Sec.-Gen. for Gen. Ass. Affairs and Conf. Services June 1997–. *Leisure interests:* walking, playing Chinese chess and bridge. *Address:* United Nations Headquarters, Room S-2963A, New York, NY 10017 (Office); 8 Peter Cooper Road, Apt. 8H, New York, NY 10017, U.S.A. (Home). *Telephone:* (212) 963 8362 (Office). *Fax:* (212) 963 8196 (Office).

YOO CHANG-SOON; Korean politician and businessman; b. 6 Aug. 1918, Anju, Pyongan Namdo; m.; five s. one d.; ed. Hastings Coll., U.S.A.; Branch Dir. Bank of Korea, Tokyo; Head of U.S. Operations, Bank of Korea, New York 1953; Gov. Bank of Korea 1961–62; Minister of Commerce and Industry 1962–63; Chair. Econ. Planning Bd. Feb.–Dec. 1963; Chair. Lotte Confectionery Co. 1967, Counsellor 1985; Chair. Korean Traders' Asscn. 1981–82; Prime Minister, Republic of Korea Jan.–June 1982; Pres. Repub. of Korea Nat. Red Cross 1982–; Chair. UN Korean Asscn. 1981–; mem. Advisory Council on State Affairs; mem. Seoul Olympics Organizing Cttee. 1981. *Leisure interests:* golf, gardening. *Address:* Na-106, Lotte Village, 1494 Sochodong, Socho-gu, Seoul, Republic of Korea.

YOO CHONG HA; Korean politician and diplomatist; b. 28 July 1936; m.; three s.; ed. Seoul Nat. Univ., Bonn Univ.; joined Ministry of Foreign Affairs 1959; Third Sec., Bonn Embassy 1963–68; Consul, Chicago May–Oct. 1968, Islamabad 1968–71; Dir. S.E. Asia Div. Ministry of Foreign Affairs 1971–74; Counsellor, Washington Embassy 1974–77; Deputy Dir.-Gen. American Affairs Bureau, Ministry of Foreign Affairs 1977–78, Dir.-Gen. 1978–80; Minister, Embassy, London 1980–83; Amb. to Sudan 1983–85, to Belgium 1987–89, to EC Feb.–Dec. 1989; Asst. Minister for Econ. Affairs Ministry of Foreign Affairs 1985–87; Vice-Minister of Foreign Affairs 1989–92; Perm. Rep. to UN 1992–94; Sr. Adviser to Pres. for Foreign Policy and Nat. Security 1994–96; Minister of Foreign Affairs 1996–98; Order of Service Merit (Red Stripes). *Address:* c/o Ministry of Foreign Affairs, 77, Sejong-no, Chongno-ku, Seoul, Republic of Korea.

YOON SUNG MIN, Gen.; Korean army officer and politician; b. 15 Oct. 1926, Muan-kun, Cholla-namdo Prov.; m. Chung Hae Woo; two d.; ed. Korea Mil. Acad., Korea Army Coll., Nat. Defence Coll., Grad. School of Public Admin., Seoul Nat. Univ.; Regimental Commdr. 20th Infantry Div. 1964, Asst. Div. Commdr. 8th Infantry Div. 1966, apptd. Brig. Gen. and Asst. Chief of Staff for Personnel, Korea Army 1967; Chief of Staff in Viet Nam 1968; Commanding Gen. First Field Army 1979; Chair. Jt. Chiefs of Staff 1981; Minister of Nat. Defence 1982–86; Standing Advisor Hyundai Precision & Inc. Co. 1991–; awarded Order of Nat. Security Merit, Tongil Medal; Order of Mil. Service Merit, Ulchi Medal, Chung-Mu Medal, etc. *Leisure interests:* reading, golf and tennis.

YORK, H.R.H. the Duke of; Prince Andrew Albert Christian Edward, C.V.O.; Earl of Inverness and Baron Killyleagh; b. 19 Feb. 1960, London; s. of H.M. Queen Elizabeth II (q.v.) and Prince Philip, Duke of Edinburgh (q.v.); m. Sarah Ferguson 1986 (divorced 1996); two d., Beatrice Elizabeth Mary, b. 8 Aug. 1988, Eugenie Victoria Helena, b. 23 March 1990; ed. Heatherdown Preparatory School, Ascot, Gordonstoun School, Scotland, Lakefield Coll. School, Ont., Canada, Britannia Royal Naval Coll., Dartmouth; joined Royal Navy as Seaman Officer, specializing as a pilot 1979, before entering Royal Naval Coll.; flying training with R.A.F. Leeming, Yorks., and helicopter training at Royal Naval Air Station (RNAS) Culdrose, Cornwall; received Wings 1981; joined front-line unit 820 Naval Air Squadron and embarked in Anti-Submarine Warfare Carrier H.M.S. Invincible; participated in Falklands conflict; rank of Lieut. 1984; Personal ADC to H.M. The Queen 1984; served as Flight Pilot in NAS, Type 22 Frigate H.M.S. Brazen 1984–86; returned to 702 NAS as Helicopter Warfare Instructor 1987; joined Type 42 Destroyer H.M.S. Edin. as Officer of the Watch 1988–89; returned to RNAS Portland to form H.M.S. Campbeltown Flight; served as Flight Commdr., 829 NAS 1989–91; Army Command and Staff Course, Staff Coll., Camberley 1992; rank of Lieut. Commdr. 1992; commanded Hunt Class Minehunter H.M.S. Cottesmore 1993–94; Sr. Pilot, 815 NAS, RNAS Portland 1995–96; joined Ministry of Defence, London as a staff officer, Directorate of Naval Operations 1997–99; rank of Commdr., with Diplomacy Section of Naval Staff, London April 1999–; Adm. of the Sea Cadet Corps 1992–; Col.-in-Chief Staffordshire Regt. 1989–, Royal Irish Regt. 1992–, Royal N.Z. Logistic Regt.; Air Commodore R.A.F. Lossiemouth, Morayshire; Patron of over 90 orgs., including Greenwich Hosp., Fight for Sight, Hearing Research Trust, Jubilee Sailing Trust, Royal Aero Club, the Royal Golf Clubs; Trustee Nat. Maritime Museum, Greenwich; Gov. Gordonstoun School; mem. Advisory bd. of Govs., Lakefield Coll. School; Commodore Royal Thames Yacht Club; Elder Brother Trinity House. *Address:* Buckingham Palace, London, SW1A 1AA; Sunninghill Park, Ascot, Berks., SL5 7TH, England.

YORK, Herbert Frank, PH.D.; American physicist; b. 24 Nov. 1921, Rochester, N.Y.; s. of Herbert York and Nellie York; m. Sybil Dunford 1947; one s. two d.; ed. Rochester and California Univs.; joined staff of Calif. Univ. Radiation Lab. 1943; attached to Y-12 Plant, Oak Ridge, Tenn. 1944–45; Univ. of Calif. Graduate School 1945–49; undertook, with Dr. Hugh Bradner, design and execution of major experiment in "Operation Greenhouse" (Eniwetok) 1950; Asst. Prof. of Physics, Univ. of Calif. 1951; headed programme, Livermore weapon devt. lab. 1952–54, Dir. 1954–58; Assoc. Dir. Univ. of Calif. Radiation Lab. 1954–58; Dir. of Research, Advanced Research Projects Div., Inst. for Defense Analyses, Chief Scientist, Dept. of Defense Advanced Research and Devt. Agency 1958; Dir. of Defence Research and Eng. 1958–61; Chancellor, Univ. of Calif. at San Diego 1961–64, 1970–72, Dean of Graduate Studies 1969–70, Dir. Program in Science, Tech. and Public Affairs 1973–88, Prof. of Physics, Univ. of Calif. 1964–; Consultant in Office of Secretary of Defense 1977–81, 1987, in Exec. Office of Pres. 1977–81; mem. Defense Science Bd. 1978–82; Dir. Inst. on Global Conflict and Co-operation 1982–88, Dir. Emer. 1988–; Amb. to Comprehensive Test Ban Negotiations 1979–81; fmr. mem. Army and Air Force Scientific Advisory Bd.; Vice-Chair. President's Science Advisory Cttee. 1965–67, mem. 1957–58,

1964–68; mem. Gen. Advisory Cttee. for Arms Control and Disarmament 1962–69; mem. President's Comm. on Mil. Compensation 1977–78; mem. Bd. of Trustees, Aerospace Corpn. 1961–87, Bd. of Trustees, Inst. for Defense Analyses 1963–95; mem. Bd. of Dirs., Educ. Foundation for Nuclear Science; mem. Exec. Cttee. Fed. of American Scientists 1970–75, Int. Council, Pugwash Movement 1972–76; Personal Rep. of Sec. of Defense at Anti-Satellite Arms Negotiations, Helsinki 1977, Berne 1978; mem. American Acad. of Arts and Sciences. *Publications:* Race to Oblivion 1970, Arms Control Readings 1973, The Advisors 1976, Making Weapons, Talking Peace 1987, A Shield in the Sky (with Sanford Lakoff) 1989, Arms and the Physicist 1995, and various articles on physics and arms control problems. *Address:* University of California, San Diego, 0518, La Jolla, CA 92093 (Office); 6110 Camino de la Costa, La Jolla, CA 92037, U.S.A. (Home). *Telephone:* (619) 459-1776 (Office); (619) 459-1776 (Home). *Fax:* (619) 459-9418.

YORK, Michael (Michael York-Johnson), O.B.E., B.A.; British actor; b. 27 March 1942, Fulmer; s. of Joseph Gwynne and Florence Edith (neé Chown) Johnson; m. Patricia McCallum 1968; ed. Univ. Coll., Oxford; with Dundee Repertory Co. 1964, Nat. Theatre Co. 1965, guest lecturer; Chair. Calif. Youth Theatre; Chevalier Ordre Nat. des. Arts et Lettres. *Stage appearances include:* Any Just Cause 1967, Hamlet 1970, Outcry (Broadway) 1973, Ring Round the Moon 1975, Bent, Cyrano de Bergerac, Whisper in the Mind 1990, The Crucible 1991, Someone to Watch Over Me 1993. *TV appearances include:* The Forsyte Saga, Rebel in the Grave, True Patriot, Much Ado About Nothing, Jesus of Nazareth, A Man Called Intrepid, For Those I Loved, The Weather in The Streets, The Master of Ballantrae, Space, The Far Country, Are You My Mother 1986, Ponce de León 1987, Knot's Landing 1987, The Four Minute Mile 1988, The Lady and the Highwayman 1988, The Heat of the Day 1988, A Duel of Love 1990, The Road to Avonlea 1990, Teklab 1994, September 1995, A Young Connecticut Yankee in King Arthur's Court 1995, Not of This Earth 1995, The Ring 1996, True Women 1996. *Films include:* The Taming of the Shrew 1966, Accident 1966, Red and Blue 1967, Smashing Time 1967, Romeo and Juliet 1967, The Strange Affair 1967, The Guru 1968, Alfred the Great 1968, Justine 1969, Something for Everyone 1969, Zeppelin 1970, La Poudre D'Escampette 1971, Cabaret 1971, England Made Me 1971, Lost Horizon 1972, The Three Musketeers 1973, Murder on the Orient Express 1974, Great Expectations 1974, Conduct Unbecoming 1974, The Four Musketeers 1975, Logan's Run 1976, Seven Nights in Japan, The Last Remake of Beau Geste 1977, The Island of Dr. Moreau 1977, Fedora 1977, The Riddle of the Sands 1978, Final Assignment 1979, Success is The Best Revenge 1984, Dawn 1985, Vengence 1986, The Secret of the Sahara 1987, Imbalances 1987, Lethal Obsession 1987, The Return of the Musketeers 1988, Till We Meet Again 1989, The Heat of the Day 1989, The Night of the Fox 1990, Eline Vere 1990, Duel of Hearts 1990, The Wanderer 1991, The Long Shadow 1991, Wide Sargasso Sea 1991, Rochade 1991, Discretion Assured 1993, The Shadow of a Kiss 1994, Fall from Grace 1994, Gospa 1995, Goodbye America 1996, Austin Powers 1996, Dark Planet 1996, The Ripper 1997, A Knight in Camelot 1998, Perfect Little Angels 1998, Wrongfully Accused 1998, One Hell of a Guy 1998, The Ghostly Rental 1998. *Publications:* The Courage of Conviction (contrib.) 1986, Voices of Survival (contrib.) 1987, Travelling Player (autobiog.) 1991, Accidentally on Purpose (autobiog.) 1992. *Address:* c/o Andrew Manson, 288 Munster Road, London, SW6 6BQ, England. *Telephone:* 0171-386 9158. *Fax:* 0171-381 8874.

YORK, Susannah; British actress; b. 9 Jan. 1942, London; m. Michael Wells 1960 (divorced 1976); one s. one d.; ed. Royal Acad. of Dramatic Art. *Films include:* Tunes of Glory 1960, The Greengage Summer 1961, Freud 1962, Tom Jones 1963, The Seventh Dawn 1964, Act One Scene Nun 1964, Sands of the Kalahari 1965, Scruggs 1966, Kaleidoscope 1966, A Man for All Seasons 1966, Sebastian 1967, The Killing of Sister George 1968, Duffy 1968, Lock up Your Daughters 1969, They Shoot Horses, Don't They? 1969, Country Dance 1970, Jane Eyre 1970, Zee and Co. 1971, Happy Birthday Wanda June 1971, Images 1972 (Best Actress Award, Cannes Film Festival), The Maids, Gold 1974, Conduct Unbecoming 1974, That Lucky Touch 1975, Skyriders 1976, Eliza Fraser 1976, The Shout 1977, The Silent Partner, Superman II 1980, Yellowbeard, Fatal Attraction 1985, A Summer Story 1987, Melancholia 1988, Just Ask for Diamond 1988, Princess 1993. *Plays include:* Wings of a Dove, A Singular Man, Man and Superman, Private Lives, Hedda Gabler (London and New York), Appearances (London and Paris), Peter Pan, Cinderella, The Singular Life of Albert Nobbs, Penthesilea, Fatal Attraction, The Women, The Apple Cart, Agnes of God, The Human Voice, Multiple Choice, A Private Treason, Lyric for a Tango, The Glass Menagerie, A Streetcar Named Desire, Noonbreak, September Tide 1993–94; Dir. Salome (Traverse Theatre, Edin.) 1992, Eagle Has Two Heads (Lilian Bayliss Theatre, London) 1994, The First Years/Beginnings 1995, Camino Real 1997; (with R.S.C.) The Merry Wives of Windsor, Camino Real, Hamlet 1997/98, The Ideal Husband 1998/99. *Television appearances:* The Crucible, Fallen Angels, Second Chance, We'll Meet Again, The Other Side of Me, Macho, Trainer, Devices and Desires; producer: The Big One 1983. *Publications:* children's books: In Search of Unicorns, Lark's Castle. *Leisure interests:* reading, writing, gardening, travelling, riding, theatre and cinema going. *Address:* c/o Peters, Fraser & Dunlop, The Chambers, Chelsea Harbour, London, SW10 0XF, England.

YOSELIANI, Otar Davidovich; Georgian film director; b. 2 Feb. 1934, Tbilisi; s. of David Yoseliani and Maria (Mikaberidze) Yoseliani; m. Rita Semenova 1956; one d.; ed. Moscow Univ., Moscow Cinema Inst.; worked as sailor and miner; Tbilisi film studio 1959–76; teacher of cinema, Tbilisi Acad. of Fine Arts; working in France 1982–. *Films include:* Avril 1962, La Chute des Feuilles 1966 (Fipresci Prize, Cannes), Il était une fois un merle chanteur 1970 (Best Foreign Film of the Year, Italy), Pastorale 1976 (Fipresci Prize, Berlin), Sept pièces pour le cinéma noir et blanc 1982, Euskadi 1983, Les favoris de la lune 1984 (Grand Prix, Venice Festival), Le petit monastère en Toscane 1988, Et la lumière fut 1989 (Grand Prix, Venice Festival), Hunting Butterflies 1992 (Tarkovsky Prize 1993), Georgia Alone (TV documentary) 1994, Les Brigandeurs 1996. *Leisure interest:* speleology. *Address:* Mitskewitch 1 korp., 1 Apt. 38, 380060 Tbilisi, Georgia; 14 rue de Rivoli, 75004 Paris, France. *Telephone:* 385058 (Tbilisi); (1) 40-26-07-18 (Paris).

YOSHIMURA, Yukio, B.A.(ECONS.); Japanese business executive; b. 9 June 1947, Nishinomiya; s. of Kazuo Yoshimura and Itoko Iijima; m. Tomoko Shibazaki 1977; three s.; ed. Tokyo Univ.; Dir. Int. Orgs. Div., Ministry of Finance 1991–92, Int. Banking Div. 1992–95; Counsellor, Minister's Secr., in charge of Int. Public Relations 1995–96, Deputy Dir.-Gen. Int. Finance Bureau 1996–97; Exec. Dir. IMF 1997–; mem. Basle Cttee. on Banking Supervision 1984–85; Alt. Exec. Dir. World Bank 1988–91; Exec. Dir. Inter-American Investment Corpn. 1990–91; mem. Group of Ten Working Party on Electronic Money 1996–97. *Address:* c/o International Monetary Fund, 700 19th Street, N.W., Washington, DC 20431, U.S.A. *Telephone:* (202) 623 7208. *Fax:* (202) 623 4950.

YOSHINAGA, Sayuri; Japanese film actress; b. 1945, m. Tado Okada; ed. Waseda Univ.; film debut in Town with a Cupola 1962; has since appeared in nearly 100 films including The Sound of Waves, The Makioka Sisters, The Diary of Yumechiyo, Ohan, Heaven Station, Killing Time by the Shores of a Mysterious Sea, Joyu; Japan Acad. Award for Best Actress 1985.

YOU XIGUI, Lieut.-Gen.; Chinese army officer; personal bodyguard to Pres. Jiang Zemin 1994–; fmr. acting Dir. Bodyguards Bureau PLA, Dir. 1996–; alt. mem. 15th CCP Cen. Cttee. 1997–. *Address:* People's Liberation Army, c/o Ministry of National Defence, Jingshanqian Jie, Beijing, People's Republic of China.

YOUN, Kong-Hi (Victorinus), S.T.D., D.D.; Korean ecclesiastic; b. 8 Nov. 1924, Jinnampo City, N. Korea; s. of (Peter) Sang Youn and (Victoria) Sang Sook Choi; ed. St. Willibrord's Maj. Seminary, Dok-Won, Urban Coll., Rome, Gregorian Univ., Rome; ordained priest 1950; Asst. Priest, Cathedral of Seoul (Myong-Dong) 1950; Chaplain, Pusan UN P.O.W. Camp 1952, Vice-Pres. Catholic Library, Pusan 1954; teacher, Song-Shin (Holy Ghost) Middle and High School 1956; Sec. Catholic Conf. of Korea 1960; ordained Bishop 1963–; Ordinary of Su-Won Diocese 1963; Admin. Seoul Archdiocese 1967; Archbishop and Ordinary of Kwangju Archdiocese 1973; Rep. Kwangju Catholic Coll. Foundation 1974–; Chair. Episcopal Conf. of Korea 1975; Rep. of Episcopal Cttee. of Bicentennial of Catholic Church in Korea 1980; Episcopal Moderator, Justice and Peace Cttee. 1979–. *Publication:* Radio Message 1963. *Leisure interest:* mountain climbing. *Address:* Archbishop's House, 5-32 Im Dong, Puk-Ku, Kwangju City 500-600, Republic of Korea. *Telephone:* (062) 525-9004. *Fax:* (62) 521-3573.

YOUNES, Mahmoud; Egyptian engineer; b. 3 April 1912, Cairo; m. 1941; two s. one d.; ed. Royal Coll. of Engineers, Cairo Univ. and Staff Officers' Coll.; Engineer with Mechanical and Electrical Dept., Ministry of Public Works, Cairo 1937; army engineer 1937; with Mil. Operations Directorate 1943; lecturer, Staff Officers' Coll. 1944 and 1947; Dir. Technical Affairs Office, G.H.Q. 1952; mem. Permanent Bd. for Development of Nat. Production 1953; Man. Dir. and Chair. Gen. Petroleum Authority 1954; Pres. Engineers' Syndicate 1954–65; Dir. and Chair. Cie. Orientale des Pétroles d'Egypte et Soc. Coopérative des Pétroles 1958–65; Counsellor, Ministry of Commerce and Industry and Mineral Wealth; Man. Dir. and Deputy Chair. Suez Canal Authority 1956, Chair. 1957–65; mem. Nat. Assembly 1964; Deputy Prime Minister for Transport and Communications 1965–67; Minister of Oil and Transport 1967; now in private consulting office in Beirut, Lebanon; Order of Merit (Class I), Order of the Nile (Class III), Military Star, Liberation Medal, Palestine Medal, Grand Cordon of the Order of the Yugoslav Standard, Grand Officer of the Panamanian Nat. Order of Vasco Núñez de Balboa, Republic Medal (Class III), Mil. Service Medal (Class I), Order of The Republic (Class I), and other decorations. *Leisure interests:* swimming, reading. *Address:* 26 July Street 21, Cairo, Egypt. *Telephone:* 750714.

YOUNG, Baroness (Life Peer), cr. 1997, of Old Scone in the County of Perthshire; **Barbara Scott Young,** M.A.; British administrator; b. 8 April 1948, Scone; d. of George Young and Mary Young (née Scott); ed. Perth Acad., Univ. of Edinburgh, Univ. of Strathclyde; Sector Admin. Greater Glasgow Health Bd. 1973–78; Dir. of Planning and Devt., St. Thomas's Health Dist. 1978–79; Dist. Gen. Admin. N.W. Dist. Kensington, Chelsea and Westminster Area Health Authority 1979–82; Dist. Admin. Haringey Health Authority 1982–85; Dist. Gen. Man. Paddington and N. Kensington Health Authority 1985–88, Parkside Health Authority 1988–91; Chief Exec. Royal Soc. for the Protection of Birds 1991–98; Chair. English Nature 1998–; Vice-Chair. of BBC; Pres. Inst. of Health Services Man. 1987–88; Vice-Pres. Flora and Fauna Int. 1998–; patron Inst. of Ecology and Environmental Man. 1993–; mem. BBC Gen. Advisory Council 1985–88, UK Round Table on Sustainable Devt. 1995–, World Council Birdlife Int. 1994–98; Hon. D.Univ. (Stirling) 1995, (Herts.) 1997, Hon. D.Sc. (Cranfield) 1998. *Publica-*

tions: What Women Want (contrib.) 1990, Medical Negligence (contrib.) 1990. *Leisure interests:* cinema, gardening. *Address:* English Nature, Northminster House, Peterborough, PE1 1UA. *Telephone:* (01733) 455000.

YOUNG, Baroness (Life Peer), cr. 1971, of Farnworth in the County Palatine of Lancaster; **Janet Mary Young,** P.C., M.A., D.L.; British politician; b. 23 Oct. 1926, Widnes; d. of John N. L. Baker and Phyllis Hancock; m. Dr. Geoffrey Tyndale Young 1950; three d.; ed. Dragon School, Oxford, Headington School, St. Anne's Coll., Oxford, and New Haven, Conn., U.S.A.; Councillor, Oxford City Council 1957, Alderman and leader of Conservative Group 1967; Baroness in Waiting (Govt. Whip in House of Lords) 1972–73; Parl. Under-Sec. of State, Dept. of Environment 1973–74; Minister of State, Dept. of Educ. and Science 1979–81; Chancellor of Duchy of Lancaster and Leader of House of Lords 1981–82; Minister in charge of Civil Service Dept. 1981; Lord Privy Seal and Leader of House of Lords 1982–83; Minister in charge of Management and Personnel Office 1981–83; Minister of State, FCO 1983–87; a Vice-Chair. Conservative Party Org. 1975–83, Deputy Chair. 1977–79, Co-Chair. Women's Nat. Comm. 1979–83; Dir. Nat. Westminster Bank PLC 1987–96, Marks and Spencer PLC 1987–97; Chair. Ind. Schools Jt. Council June 1989–92, 1994–97; Deputy Lieut. for Oxfordshire Dec. 1989; a Vice-Pres. W. India Cttee. 1987–96, Pres. 1996–; mem. Council of Man., Ditchley Foundation 1990–; Trustee Dorneywood 1992–; a Vice-Pres. Asscn. of Dist. Councils 1990–; Chancellor Univ. of Greenwich 1993–98; Hon. Fellow, Inst. of Civil Engineers, St. Anne's Coll., Oxford; Hon. D.C.L. (Mt. Holyoake Coll.). *Leisure interest:* music. *Address:* House of Lords, London, SW1A 0PW, England.

YOUNG, Andrew; American politician, clergyman and diplomatist; b. 12 March 1932, New Orleans, La.; s. of Andrew J. Young and Daisy Fuller; m. 1st Jean Childs 1954 (died 1994); one s. three d.; m. 2nd Carolyn Watson 1996; ed. Howard Univ. and Hartford Theological Seminary; ordained to ministry, Congregational Church 1955, pastor in Thomasville, Ga. 1955–57; Assoc. Dir. for Youth Work, Nat. Council of Churches 1957–61; Admin. Citizenship Educ. Program, United Church of Christ 1961–64; on staff Southern Christian Leadership Conf. 1961–70, Exec. Dir. 1964–70, Exec. Vice-Pres. 1967–70, Dir.; Chair. U.S. Southern Africa Enterprise Devt. Fund 1994–; mem. House of Reps. 1972, re-elected 1974, 1976; Perm. Rep. to U.N. 1977–79; Mayor of Atlanta 1982–89; Co-Chair. Atlanta Cttee. for the Olympic Games 1996; Vice-Chair. Law Cos. Group Inc. 1990–; Chair. Atlanta Community Relations Comm. 1970–72; Chair. Democratic voter registration drive 1976; organizer of voter registration and community devt. programmes for civil rights movement in 1960s; Medal of Freedom 1980, Légion d'honneur 1982, numerous awards and hon. degrees. *Publication:* An Easy Burden 1996. *Address:* Law International Inc., 1000 Abernathy Road, N.E., Atlanta, GA 30328, U.S.A.

YOUNG, Sir Brian (Walter Mark), Kt.; British administrator; b. 23 Aug. 1922, Ceylon (now Sri Lanka); s. of late Sir Mark Young and Josephine Price; m. Fiona Marjorie Stewart 1947 (died 1997); one s. two d.; ed. Eton Coll., and King's Coll., Cambridge; Asst. Master, Eton Coll., 1947–52; Headmaster of Charterhouse 1952–64; Dir. of Nuffield Foundation 1964–70, Trustee 1978–90; mem. Central Advisory Council for Educ. 1956–59; fmr. mem. U.K. Nat. Comm. for UNESCO; Dir.-Gen. IBA 1970–82; Chair. Christian Aid 1983–90, Associated Bd. Royal Schools of Music 1984–87; mem. Arts Council of Great Britain 1983–88, Exec. Cttee. British Council of Churches 1983–90; Pres. British and Foreign School Soc. 1991–; Trustee Lambeth Palace Library 1984–97, Imperial War Museum 1985–92. *Publications:* Via Vertendi 1952, Intelligent Reading 1964, The Villein's Bible: Stories in Romanesque Carving 1990. *Leisure interests:* watching television, reading, music, travel, Romanesque sculpture. *Address:* Hill End, Woodhill Avenue, Gerrards Cross, Bucks., SL9 8DJ, England. *Telephone:* (01753) 887793.

YOUNG, Sir Colville (Norbert), G.C.M.G., M.B.E., J.P., D.PHIL.; Belizean Governor General and academic; b. 20 Nov. 1932; s. of Henry Oswald Young and Adney Wilhelmina Young (née Waite); m. Norma Eleanor Trapp 1956; three s. one d.; ed. Univ. of West Indies, Univ. of York; Prin. St. Michael's Coll., Belize 1974–76; lecturer in English and Gen. Studies Belize Tech. Coll. 1976–86; Pres. Univ. Coll. of Belize 1986–90, lecturer 1990–93; Gov.-Gen. of Belize 1993–. *Publications:* Creole Proverbs of Belize 1980, Caribbean Corner Calling 1988, Language and Education in Belize 1989, Pataki Full 1990, From One Caribbean Corner (poetry) 1983, contrib. drama and poetry in various anthologies, articles in various publs. *Leisure interests:* creative writing, playing and arranging steelband music. *Address:* Belize House, Belmopan, Belize. *Telephone:* (8) 22521.

YOUNG, Frances Margaret, O.B.E., PH.D.; British professor of theology; b. 25 Nov. 1939, Frome, Somerset; d. of A. Stanley Worrall and Mary Frances (née Marshall) Worrall; m. Robert Charles Young 1964; three s.; ed. Bedford Coll. Univ. of London, Girton Coll. Cambridge and Chicago Divinity School; Research Fellow, Clare Hall, Cambridge 1967–68; temporary lecturer Univ. of Birmingham 1971–73, lecturer 1973–84, sr. lecturer 1984–86, Edward Cadbury Prof. and Head, Dept. of Theology 1986–, Head of School of Philosophy and Theology 1989–93, Dean Faculty of Arts 1995–; ordained Methodist Minister 1984; Hon. D.D. (Univ. of Aberdeen) 1994. *Publications:* Sacrifice and the Death of Christ 1975, Can These Dry Bones Live? 1982, From Nicaea to Chalcedon 1983, Face to Face: A Narrative Essay in the Theology of Suffering 1985, The Art of Performance 1990, The Theology of the Pastoral Letters 1994, Biblical Exegesis and the Formation of Christian Culture 1997. *Leisure interests:* walking, cycling, camping, travel, music, poetry, literature. *Address:* Pro-Vice-Chancellor's Office, University of Birmingham, Birmingham, B15 2TT (Office); 142 Selly Park Road, Birmingham, B29 7LH, England (Home). *Telephone:* (0121) 414 5936 (Office); (0121) 472 4841 (Home).

YOUNG, Rt. Hon. Sir George (Samuel Knatchbull), 6th Bt., M.P., M.A., M.PHIL.; British politician; b. 16 July 1941; s. of Sir George Young, 5th Bt. and Elisabeth Knatchbull-Hugessen; m. Aurelia Nemon-Stuart 1964; two s. two d.; ed. Eton Coll. and Christ Church, Oxford; Economist, Nat. Econ. Devt. Office 1966–67; Kobler Research Fellow, Univ. of Surrey 1967–69; Econ. Adviser, Post Office Corpn. 1969–74; Councillor, London Borough of Lambeth 1968–71; mem. Greater London Council for London Borough of Ealing 1970–73; M.P. for Ealing, Acton 1974–97, for Hampshire N.W. 1997–; Opposition Whip 1976–79; Parl. Under-Sec. of State, Dept. of Health and Social Security 1979–81, Dept. of Environment 1981–86; Dir. Lovell Partnerships 1987–90; Comptroller of H.M. Household 1990; Minister of State, Dept. of Environment 1990–94; Financial Sec. H.M. Treasury 1994–95; Sec. of State for Transport 1995–97; Opposition Front Bench Spokesman for Defence 1997–98; Shadow Leader of the House 1998–; Conservative. *Publications:* Accommodation Services in the U.K. 1970–80, Tourism, Blessing or Blight? 1973. *Leisure interests:* squash, bicycling. *Address:* House of Commons, London, SW1A 0AA, England.

YOUNG, Hugo John Smelter, M.A.; British journalist; b. 13 Oct. 1938, Sheffield; s. of Gerard Young and Diana Young; m. 1st Helen Mason 1966 (died 1989); one s. three d.; m. 2nd Lucy Waring 1990; ed. Ampleforth Coll., Balliol Coll., Oxford; Yorkshire Post 1961; Harkness Fellow 1963; Congressional Fellow, U.S. Congress 1964; Chief Leader Writer, The Sunday Times 1966–77, Political Ed. 1973–84, Jt. Deputy Ed. 1981–84; political columnist, The Guardian 1984–; Dir. The Tablet 1985–; Chair. The Scott Trust 1989–; mem. U.K. Advisory Cttee. Harkness Fellowships 1990–95 (Chair. 1993–95); Hon. D.Litt. (Sheffield Univ.) 1993; British Press Awards, Columnist of the Year 1980, 1983, 1985; Granada TV What the Papers Say Awards Columnist of the Year 1985. *Publications:* (co-author): The Zinoviev Letter 1966, Journey to Tranquillity 1969, No, Minister 1982, But, Chancellor 1984, The Thatcher Phenomenon 1986; The Crossman Affair 1974, One of Us 1989 (revised edn. 1991), This Blessed Plot 1998. *Address:* c/o The Guardian, 119 Farringdon Road, London, EC1 3ER, England.

YOUNG, John Atherton, A.O., D.SC., M.D., F.A.A., F.R.A.C.P.; Australian professor of physiology; b. 18 April 1936, Brisbane, Queensland; s. of William Young and Betty Young (née Atherton); ed. Brisbane Church of England Grammar School, Univ. of Queensland; Jr. Registrar, Royal Brisbane Hosp. 1961; Sr. Research Officer, Kanematsu Inst., Sydney Hosp. 1962–64; C. J. Martin Travelling Fellow of NH and MRC, Physiology Inst., Free Univ. of Berlin 1965–66; Sr. Lecturer, then Assoc. Prof., Univ. of Sydney 1967–76, Prof. of Physiology 1976–, Head of Dept. 1976–89, Dean Faculty of Medicine 1989–97, Pro Vice-Chancellor (Health Sciences) 1994–; Deputy Chair. Cen. Sydney Area Health Service 1993–; Dir. Royal Alexandra Hosp. for Children 1989–; Chair. Bd. of Govs. Menzies School of Health Research, Darwin 1991–96, Deputy Chair. 1997–; Fellow Senate Univ., Sydney 1988–93; Vice-Pres. and Sec. (Biological) Australian Acad. of Science 1998–; Pres. Fed. of Asian and Oceanian Physiological Socs. 1998, Australian Physiological and Pharmacological Soc. 1996–99; Humbold Stiflung Research Prize 1999. *Publications:* Morphology of Salivary Glands 1978, Centenary Book of the University of Sydney Medical School 1983, Across the Years 1987; 8 other scientific books, 200 articles in scientific journals and 4 articles in historical journals. *Leisure interests:* history, music. *Address:* College of Health Sciences, Edward Ford Building (A27), University of Sydney, Sydney, N.S.W. 2006, Australia. *Telephone:* (02) 9351 4600. *Fax:* (02) 9351-9926.

YOUNG, Hon. Sir John (McIntosh), A.C., K.C.M.G., M.A., LL.B.; Australian judge (retd.); b. 17 Dec. 1919, Melbourne; s. of George D. Young and Kathleen M. Young; m. Elisabeth M. Twining 1951; one s. two d.; ed. Geelong Grammar School, Brasenose Coll. Oxford, Inner Temple and Univ. of Melbourne; served Scots Guards 1940–46; admitted Victoria Bar 1948; Assoc. to Mr. Justice Dixon, High Court of Australia 1948; practising barrister 1949–74 (Q.C. 1961); lecturer in Co. Law, Univ. of Melbourne 1957–61; admitted Tasmanian Bar 1964, N.S.W. Bar 1968; consultant, Faculty of Law, Monash Univ. 1968–74; Lieut.-Gov. of Victoria 1974–95; Chief Justice, Supreme Court of Victoria 1974–91; Chair. Police Bd. of Vic. 1992–98; Chancellor, Order of St. John in Australia 1982–91; Chief Scout of Australia 1989–96; Hon. Fellow Brasenose Coll. Oxford 1991, G.C.St.J. 1991; holder of many other public and charitable offices; Hon. LL.D. (Monash) 1986, (Melbourne) 1989. *Publications:* Australian Company Law and Practice (co-author); articles in legal journals. *Leisure interest:* golf. *Address:* 17 Sorrett Avenue, Malvern, Vic. 3144, Australia.

YOUNG, Kirsty; British television presenter; b. 1969, Glasgow; fmrly. with BBC Radio Scotland; fmrly. newsreader Scottish TV, presenter Kirsty (own chatshow); newsreader Channel 5 News 1997–; presenter Talk Radio 1998–. *Address:* c/o Channel 5 Broadcasting Limited, 22 Long Acre, London, W.C.2, England.

YOUNG, Peter Lance, M.I.C.E.; British business executive; b. 26 June 1938, U.K.; m. Susan M. Wilkes 1962; three s. one d.; ed. Chippenham Grammar School; joined RMC Group PLC 1961, mem. Bd. 1977, Deputy Man. Dir.

1992, Man. Dir. 1993, Group Chief Exec. Jan. 1996–. *Leisure interests:* tennis, gardening. *Address:* RMC Group PLC, RMC House, Coldharbour Lane, Thorpe, Egham, Surrey, TW20 8TD, England. *Telephone:* (01932) 568833.

YOUNG, Richard Stuart; British photographer; b. 17 Sept. 1947, Brocket Hall, Herts.; s. of the late David Young and Hilda Ellison; m. 1st Riita Sinikka Harju 1975 (died 1983); two s.; m. 2nd Susan Manije Walker 1985; one d.; career photographer 1974–; solo exhbns. All Hours 1986, Four Stages of Innocence, R.C.A. 1993, Positive View, Saatchi Gallery 1994, The Night is Young, Grosvenor House 1995, Bad Behaviour, Well Hung Gallery, London 1998. *Publications:* By Invitation Only 1981, Paparazzo 1989. *Leisure interests:* films, travel, books, music. *Address:* 110 Highlever Road, London, W10 6PL, England. *Telephone:* 0181-960 4727.

YOUNG, Rosie Margaret, C.B.E., M.D., F.R.C.P., F.R.C.P.(E.), F.R.C.P.(GLAS.), F.R.A.C.P.; British professor of medicine; b. 23 Oct. 1930, Hong Kong; d. of Yeung Shun Hang and Shiu Shui Ying; ed. Univ. of Hong Kong; Prof. of Medicine, Univ. of Hong Kong; Dean, Faculty of Medicine, Univ. of Hong Kong 1983–85, Pro-Vice-Chancellor 1985–93; Chair. Medical Council of Hong Kong 1988–; Overseas Adviser, Royal Coll. of Physicians of Edin. 1987–; mem. Council Royal Australasian Coll. of Physicians 1993–96; J.P. in Hong Kong 1971; Hon. D.Sc. (Hong Kong, Open Learning Inst. of Hong Kong) 1995. *Publications:* over 100 articles in int. medical journals, mostly on diabetes, CHO metabolism and endocrinology. *Address:* Room 413, Professorial Block, Queen Mary Hospital, Hong Kong Special Administrative Region, People's Republic of China. *Telephone:* 2855 4253. *Fax:* 2855 1143.

YOUNG, Wayland (see Kennet, 2nd Baron).

YOUNG OF DARTINGTON, Baron (Life Peer), cr. 1977, of Dartington in the County of Devon; **Michael Young,** PH.D.; British sociologist; b. 9 Aug. 1915, Manchester; m. 1st Joan Lowson 1945; two s. one d.; m. 2nd Sasha Young (died 1993); m. 3rd Dorit Uhlemann 1995; ed. Dartington Hall School, London Univ. and Gray's Inn, London; Dir. of Political and Econ. Planning 1941–45; Sec. Research Dept., Labour Party 1945–51; Dir. Inst. of Community Studies 1953–; Chair. Consumers' Asscn. 1956–65, Pres. 1965–; Chair. Advisory Centre for Educ. 1959–76, Pres. 1976–; Lecturer in Sociology, Cambridge Univ. 1961–63, Trustee, Dartington Hall 1942; Chair. Social Science Research Council 1965–68, Chair. Nat. Extension Coll. 1962; Chair. Int. Extension Coll. 1970–; Dir. Mauritius Coll. of the Air 1972; Visiting Prof. Ahmadu Bello Univ., Nigeria 1974; Chair. Nat. Consumer Council 1975–77, Mutual Aid Centre 1977–, Dartington Inst. of Community Studies 1980–, Tawney Soc. (SDP) 1982–85, College of Health 1983–90, Open Coll. of the Arts 1986–90 (Pres. 1991), Open School 1988–, Education Extra 1990–, Family Covenant Asscn. 1994–, School for Social Entrepreneurs 1997–; Hon. Fellow British Acad. 1995, Churchill Coll. 1995; Prince Albert Medal, R.S.A. 1992. *Publications:* Family and Kinship in East London (with Peter Willmott) 1957, The Rise of the Meritocracy 1959, Family and Class in a London Suburb (with Peter Willmott) 1961, Innovation and Research in Education 1965, Learning Begins at Home 1967, Forecasting and the Social Sciences 1968, The Symmetrical Family (with Peter Willmott) 1973, Poverty Report (Ed.) 1974, Distance Teaching for the Third World 1980 (with others), The Elmhirsts of Dartington 1982, Revolution from Within 1983, The Metronomic Society—Natural Rhythms and Human Timetables 1988, The Rhythms of Society 1988, Life After Work (with Tom Schuller) 1991, Your Head in Mine (poetry) 1994, A Good Death 1996 (with Lesley Cullen). *Address:* 18 Victoria Park Square, London, E2 9PF; House of Lords, London, S.W.1, England.

YOUNG OF GRAFFHAM, Baron (Life Peer), cr. 1984, of Graffham in the County of West Sussex; **David Ivor Young,** P.C., LL.B.; British politician and business executive; b. 27 Feb. 1932, London; s. of Joseph Young and Rebecca Young; m. Lita Marianne Shaw 1956; two d.; ed. Christ Coll., Finchley and Univ. Coll., London; admitted solicitor 1955; solicitor, Malcolm Slowe, London 1955–56; Exec. Great Universal Stores 1956–61; Chair. Eldonwall Ltd. 1961–74, Mfrs. Hanover Property Services Ltd. 1974–80; Chair. Greenwood Homes Ltd. 1976–82; Dir. Centre for Policy Studies 1979–82; Special Adviser Dept. of Industry 1979–82, of Educ. and Science 1981–82; Chair. Manpower Services Comm. 1982–84; mem., Chair. NEDC 1982–89; Minister without Portfolio 1984–85, Sec. of State for Employment 1985–87, for Trade and Industry and Pres. of Bd. of Trade 1987–89; Deputy Chair. Conservative Party 1989–90; Dir. Salomon Inc. 1990–94; Head Supervisory Task Force Salomon Bros. 1991; Chair. Cable and Wireless 1990–95; Chair. Young Associates Ltd. 1996–; Chair. British Org. for Rehabilitation by Training 1975–80 (Pres. 1980–82), Int. Council of Jewish Social and Welfare Services 1981–84, EU–Japan Asscn. 1991–97, UCL Council 1995–, London Philharmonic Trust 1995–98; Pres. Jewish Care 1990–97, Inst. of Dirs. 1993–, Nat. Fed. of Enterprise Agencies 1994–98, W. Sussex Econ. Forum 1996–, Chichester Festival Theatre Productions Co. Ltd. 1997–; Dir. of numerous cos. and orgs. including Young Assocs. Ltd., Powerdesk PLC, UK Lotteries Ltd., Business for Sterling CDT Holdings PLC, Inter Digital Networks Ltd., New Village Properties PLC, Paddington Devt. Corpn. Ltd., Second Opinion Investments Ltd., South Bank Foundation Ltd.; Industrial Adviser, English Industrial Estates Corpn. 1979–80, Special Adviser, mem. 1980–82; Hon. F.R.P.S. 1981; Hon. Fellow Univ. Coll., London 1988. *Publication:* The Enterprise Years: a businessman in the Cabinet 1990. *Leisure interests:* music, book collecting, photography. *Address:* Young Associates Ltd., Harcourt House, 19 Cavendish Square, London, W1M 9AB, England. *Telephone:* 0171-447 8800. Fax: 0171-447 8849.

YOUNGER OF LECKIE, 4th Viscount (cr. 1923); **George (Kenneth Hotson) Younger,** (cr. Baron 1992), K.T., K.C.V.O., P.C., T.D., D.L., F.R.S.E.; British politician, business executive and university chancellor; b. 22 Sept. 1931; s. of late 3rd Viscount Younger of Leckie; m. Diana Rhona Tuck 1954, three s. one d.; ed. Winchester Coll., New Coll., Oxford; commissioned in Argyll and Sutherland Highlanders 1950, served BAOR and Korea 1951, with 7th Bn. Argyll and Sutherland Highlanders, T.A. 1951–65; M.P. for Ayr 1964–92; Scottish Conservative Whip 1965–67; Parl. Under-Sec. of State for Devt., Scottish Office 1970–74; Minister of State for Defence 1974; Sec. of State for Scotland 1979–86, for Defence 1986–89; Dir. Royal Bank of Scotland July 1989– (Chair. June 1990–); Chair. Royal Bank of Scotland Group 1991–; Chancellor, Napier Univ. 1993–; Chair. Siemens Plessey Electronic Systems 1990–98, SPEED PLC 1992–98, Murray Johnston Trusts 1993– (Dir. 1989–, Deputy Chair. 1992–93); Chair. Royal Anniversary Trust 1990–, Romanian Orphanage Trust 1990, Edin. Festival (fmrly. Empire) Theatre Trust 1991–, Royal Armouries 1994–; Deputy Chair. Conservative Party in Scotland 1967–70, Chair. 1974–75; Pres. Nat. Union of Conservative and Unionist Asscns. 1987–88, Royal Highland and Agricultural Soc. 1990; Dir. George Younger & Son Ltd. 1958–68, J. G. Thomson & Co. Ltd., Leith 1962–66, Maclachlans Ltd. 1968–70, Tennant Caledonian Breweries Ltd. 1977–79; Scottish Equitable Life Assurance Soc. 1990–94, PIK Ltd. (fmrly. Ayrshire Community Airport Project) 1991–, Sky Solutions Ltd. 1998–; Brigadier, Queen's Body Guard for Scotland (Royal Company of Archers); Hon. Col. 154 (Lowland) Transport Regt., Royal Corps of Artillery, Territorial & Army Volunteer Reserve 1977–85; Fellow Winchester Coll. 1992– (Warden 1997–); Hon. LL.D. (Glasgow) 1992; Hon. D.Litt. (Napier Univ., Edin.) 1992; Dr. h.c. (Edin.) 1992; Hon. D.Univ. (Paisley Univ.) 1994. *Leisure interests:* music, tennis, sailing, golf. *Address:* Leckie, Gargunnock, Stirlingshire, FK8 3BN, Scotland. *Telephone:* (01786) 860274.

YOUNG-SEEK CHOE, LL.D.; Korean university chancellor; b. 22 Nov. 1921, Woon San; m. Chung-Myung Oh 1943; two s. two d.; ed. Seoul Nat. Univ. and Univ. of Miami; Founder-Pres. Kyung Hee Univ.; Chancellor, Kyung Hee Univ. System; Perpetual Pres. Emer. Int. Asscn. of Univ. Pres. (I.A.U.P.), fmr. Chair.; Chair. High Comm. for Peace; Pres. Inst. of Brighter Soc., Inst. of Int. Peace Studies, Inst. of Asia-Pacific Studies, Center for Reconstruction of Human Soc., Global Co-operation Soc. Club Int.; Chair. Korean Ass. for Reunion of Ten Million Separated Families, Oughtopian Peace Foundation; initiated UN Int. Day and Year of Peace; recipient of 24 hon. degrees and numerous awards and decorations. *Publications include:* Democratic Freedom 1948, Reconstruction of the Human Society 1975, Oughtopia 1979, World Peace Through Pax UN 1984, White Paper on World Peace 1991. *Leisure interests:* golf, tennis, table tennis, travel. *Address:* Office of the Chancellor, Kyung Hee University, 1, Hoiki-Dong, Dondaemoon-Ku, Seoul 130-701 (Office); 7-36, 1-Ka, Myungryun-Dong, Chongro-Ku, Seoul, Republic of Korea (Home). *Telephone:* (82-2) 961-0114 (Office); (82-2) 762-3278 (Home). *Fax:* (82-2) 966-6452 (Office); (82-2) 741-3195 (Home).

YOUSSOUFI, Abderrahmane; Moroccan politician; b. Tangiers; m. Hélène Youssoufi; ed. Univ. de Paris; activist in union and independence movements; mem. Istiqlal –1959; left to help set up Union nat. des forces populaires (UNFP), later Union Socialiste des forces populaires (USFP); Asst. to Medhi Ben Barka; imprisoned 1959 for anti-state activities; given 2-year prison sentence in political trial in 1963; went into exile in France after release in 1964; spokesman for African and Arab nationalist campaigns and human rights; returned to Morocco early 1980s; Sec. Gen. USFP 1992–93 (left party leadership and went into exile again in protest at outcome of 1993 gen. elections); returned to Morocco 1995 to resume Sec. Gen. post; Prime Minister of Morocco Feb. 1998–. *Address:* Office of the Prime Minister, Rabat, Morocco.

YSTAD, Vigdis, D PHIL.; Norwegian professor of Scandinavian literature; b. 13 Jan. 1942, Verdal; d. of Ottar Ystad and Guri Todal; m. 1st Asbjørn Liland 1962, 2nd Daniel Haakonsen 1971; one s. one d.; ed. Univs. of Trondheim and Oslo; lecturer, Univ. of Oslo 1974, Prof. of Scandinavian Literature 1979–, mem. Univ. Bd. 1990–92; Chair. Council for Research in the Humanities 1985; Chair. Bd. Centre for Advanced Study, Norwegian Acad. of Science and Letters 1992–93; Vice-Chair. Nat. Acad. of Dramatic Art 1993–96; mem. Norwegian Research Council 1979–85, Norwegian Govt. Research Cttee. 1982–84; mem. Norwegian Acad. of Science and Letters, Norwegian Acad. for Language and Literature. *Publications:* Kristofer Uppdals Lyrikk 1978, Henrik Ibsens Dikt 1991, Sigrid Undsel: Et kvinneliv-"livets endeløse gåde" 1993, Ibsens dikt og drama 1996, Contemporary Approaches to Ibsen's Drama (Ed.). *Address:* Department of Scandinavian Literature, Box 1013 Blindern, 0315 Oslo (Office); Nils Tollers vei 3, 0851 Oslo, Norway (Home). *Telephone:* 2285 6938 (Office); 2269 1095 (Home).

YU GUANGYUAN; Chinese academic; b. 5 July 1915, Shanghai; ed. Qinghua Univ., Beijing; taught in Physics Dept., Lingnan Univ., Guangzhou 1936–37; engaged in youth movement, land reform, propaganda, culture, journalism, higher educ. and social research 1940s; in CCP Cen. Dept. of Propaganda, in charge of social and natural sciences research 1949–75; mem. Academic Cttee., Acad. of Sciences of China 1955–; Deputy Dir. State Comm. of Science and Tech. 1964–66, 1977–82; Vice-Pres. Acad. of Social Sciences of China 1978–82, Adviser 1982–87; Pres. Soc. for Study of Marxism, Leninism and Mao Zedong Thought 1980, Soc. of Production Power Economics 1980, Soc. of Research in Dialectics of Nature 1980, Soc. of Territorial Econs. 1981; Adviser Environmental Protection Cttee., State Council 1985; Pres. China Environmental Strategy Research Centre 1985; Vice-Pres. China Int. Cultural Centre 1984–; mem. Cen. Advisory Comm. CCP 1982, Pres. Pacific Soc. 1995–. *Publications:* Study of Land Problems in Sui Mi County in China, Exploration of Political Economy of the Socialist Period, Vols. I–V, On the Objective Nature of Law, Thesis, Lectures and Notes on Philosophy, Economy of the Primary Period of Socialist China, On the Reform of the Economic Model of China, Economy-Social Development Strategy, Selected Works on Education, My Educational Ideology 1991, On the Central Place of Socialist Market Economy 1992, and numerous other books on economics and philosophy. *Address:* Chinese Academy of Social Sciences, 5 Jianguomen Nei Da Jie, Beijing 100732, People's Republic of China. *Telephone:* 5137689.

YU GUANGZHONG; Taiwanese university professor, poet, critic and translator; b. 9 Sept. 1928, Nanjing City, Jiangsu Prov.; m. Wo Chun Fan 1956; four d.; ed. Iowa Univ., U.S.A.; Chief Ed. of Blue Stars and Modern Literature; Prof. Taiwan Normal Univ., Chinese Univ. of Hong Kong; Pres. Taipei Chinese Centre, PEN Int. 1990–; Nat. Poetry Prize, Wu San-Lian Prose Prize and six others. *Publications:* Elegy of Boatman, Stalactite, Blue Plume, Sirius, White Jade Bitter Gourd, A Tug of War with Eternity, Dream and Geography. *Leisure interests:* travel, hiking, music, museums. *Address:* Foreign Literature Institute, Sun Yat-sen University, Gaoxiong City, Taiwan. *Telephone:* (07) 5256271. *Fax:* (07) 5253200.

YU KUO-HWA, B.A.; Taiwanese politician and banker; b. 10 Jan. 1914, Chekiang; s. of Choping Yu and Eirying Hu; m. Yu Toong Metsung 1946; two s.; ed. Tsinghua Univ., Harvard Univ. Graduate School, L.S.E.; Sec. to Pres. of Nat. Mil. Council 1936–44; Alt. Exec. Dir. Int. Bank for Reconstruction and Devt. 1947–50, IMF 1951–55; Pres. Cen. Trust of China 1955–61; Chair. Bd. of Dirs. Bank of China 1961–67; Alt. Gov. IBRD 1964–67, Gov. for Repub. of China 1967–69; Minister of Finance 1967–69; Gov. Cen. Bank of China 1969–84; Minister of State 1969–84; Gov. IMF 1969–80, Asian Devt. Bank 1969–84; Prime Minister of Taiwan 1984–89; Sr. Adviser to Pres. of Taiwan 1989–; Vice-Chair. Kuomintang 1997–; mem. Cen. Standing Cttee., Kuomintang 1979–; Chair. Council for Econ. Planning and Devt. 1977–84; Order of Propitious Clouds; Hon. Dr. (St. John's Univ., Jamaica, New York). *Address:* c/o Office of the President, Taipei, Taiwan.

YU MIN; Chinese physicist; b. Aug. 1926, Ninghe Co., Hebei Prov.; ed. Beijing Univ.; mem. Dept. of Math. and Physics, Academia Sinica 1985–; Hon. Special Nat. Prizes of Sciences and Tech. 1987, 1989.

YU WEN; Chinese party official; b. 1918, Shaanxi Prov.; m. Liao Bing; two s. two d.; Deputy Sec.-Gen. Chinese Academy of Sciences 1959; in political disgrace 1967–73; Sec.-Gen. Chinese Acad. of Sciences 1978–83; Perm. Deputy Head, Propaganda Dept. CCP 1983–85; Deputy Sec.-Gen. Presidium 6th NPC 1986–; Deputy to 6th NPC for Qinghai Prov. 1986; mem. Standing Cttee. NPC 1986–; Vice-Chair. Nationalities Cttee. 1986; Head Nat. Examination Cttee. for Higher Posts of Journalists 1983; a Vice-Pres. Chinese Acad. of Social Sciences 1990–; Exec. Vice-Pres. Municipal Party School 1990–; a Vice Pres. Asscn. for Int. Understanding of China 1993–. *Address:* Central Committee of Chinese Communist Party, Beijing, People's Republic of China.

YU YONGBO, Gen.; Chinese army officer and party official; b. 1931, Fuxian Co., Liaoning Prov.; joined CCP 1948; Dir. Political Dept. of PLA Nanjing Mil. Area Command 1985–89; Vice-Dir. PLA Gen. Political Dept. 1989–92, Dir. 1992–; rank of Lieut.-Gen. PLA 1988; mem. Cen. Mil. Comm. 1992–; mem. 14th CCP Cen. Cttee. 1992–97; Deputy Head Work Group for Placement of Demobilized Army Officers 1993–; Deputy Head Leading Group for Cracking Down on Smuggling 1993–; rank of Gen.; mem. 15th CCP Cen. Cttee. 1997–. *Address:* People's Liberation Army Headquarters, c/o Ministry of National Defence, Jingshanqian Jie, Beijing, People's Republic of China.

YU YOUXIAN; Chinese politician; b. 1937, Fenglai Co., Shandong; fmr. Vice-Gov. of Henan; Dir. Bureau of News and Publs., State Council 1993–; mem. CCP Cen. Cttee. for Discipline Inspection 1997. *Address:* Press and Publications Administration, State Council, Beijing, People's Republic of China.

YU ZHEN; Chinese politician; b. 1936, Haiyang, Shandong; Vice-Minister of Light Industry 1985–93, Chair. China Nat. Council of Light Industry 1993–98; Pres. China Nat. Light Industrial Machinery Corpn. 1983–85; Vice-Minister State Econ. and Trade Comm. 1998–. *Address:* State Economics and Trade Commission, Beijing, People's Republic of China. *Telephone:* 8396250.

YU ZHENGSHENG; Chinese politician; b. April 1945, Shaoxin City, Zhejiang Prov.; joined CCP 1964; ed. Harbin Mil. Eng. Inst.; Vice-Chair. Exec. Council of Welfare Fund for the Handicapped 1984; Vice-Sec. CCP Yantai City Cttee. and Vice-Mayor Yantai City 1985, Mayor 1987; Sec. CCP Qingdao City Cttee. and Mayor Qingdao City 1992; alt. mem. 14th CCP Cen. Cttee. 1992; Vice-Minister of Construction 1997–98, Minister 1998–; mem. 15th CCP Cen. Cttee. 1997–. *Address:* Ministry of Construction, Baiwanzhuang, Western Suburb, Beijing 100835, People's Republic of China.

YU ZHENWU, Lieut.-Gen.; Chinese air force officer; b. 1931, Kuangdian Co., Liaoning Prov.; ed. PLA Air Force Aviation School; mem. CCP 1947–; Regt. Chief Navigating Officer, PLA Air Force 1951; served in Korean War 1953; Group Commdr. PLA Air Force 1954–55; Corps Chief Officer in charge of firing training 1957; Regt. Commdr. 1964; Deputy Div. Commdr. 1969–73; Deputy Dir. Mil. Training Dept. PLA Air Force 1973–77, Dir. 1977–79; Corps Commdr. 1979–83; Commdr. Air Force of Guangdong Mil. Dist. 1983–85; Deputy Commdr. PLA Air Force 1985–95, Commdr. 1995–97, now Deputy Sec.; alt. mem. 12th and 13th CCP Cen. Cttee. *Address:* c/o Ministry of National Defence, Jingshanqian Jie, Beijing, People's Republic of China.

YUAN ENFENG; Chinese folk singer; b. 22 Jan. 1940, Shaanxi Prov.; d. of Yuan Zaiming and Li Dexian; m. Sun Shao, composer; three d.; participated in over 3,000 performances, including numerous solo concerts and 1,000 radio and TV programmes; appearances abroad include Romania, Bulgaria, Czechoslovakia, U.S.S.R., Japan, Thailand, Philippines and U.S.A.; Chair. Folk Music Section, Shaanxi Broadcasting Station; Vice-Chair. Shaanxi TV Station; mem. Chinese Musicians' Asscn.; mem. of Bd., Shaanxi Br., Chinese Cultural Exchange Centre; mem. of many other official orgs. *Compositions (with Sun Shao) include:* Millet is Delicious and Caves are Warm, Nowhere is Better than Our North Shaanxi; many recordings and song books. *Address:* Folk Music Section, Provincial Broadcasting and Television Station, Xian, Shaanxi, People's Republic of China. *Telephone:* 24741.

YUAN LONGPING; Chinese agronomist; b. 7 Sept. 1930, Beijing; s. of Yuan Xin-Lie and Hua Jing; m. Deng Ze 1964; three s.; teacher Hunan Prov. 1964–; Deputy, 5th NPC 1978–83; Sr. Rice Breeder Agric. Acad. of Hunan Prov. 1981–; mem. Standing Cttee. 6th CPPCC 1982–; Vice-Chair. CCP 7th Hunan Prov. Cttee.; Dir. Hybrid Rice Research Centre under the Hunan Acad. of Agricultural Sciences 1985–; Gold Medal, UN World Property Org. 1985, Laureate of Science Prize, UNESCO 1987, Rank Prize for Food 1988. *Leisure interests:* violin, swimming. *Address:* Hybrid Rice Research Centre, Changsha, Hunan, People's Republic of China. *Telephone:* 0731-448780. *Fax:* 0731-4448877.

YUAN SHOUFANG, Lieut.-Gen.; Chinese army officer; b. Jan. 1939, Jilin City, Jilin Prov.; joined PLA 1958; joined CCP 1962; ed. PLA Political Acad.; Dir. Army Political Dept. 1983; Vice-Dir. Political Dept. of Ji'nan Mil. Area Command 1985 then Dir.; rank of Maj.-Gen. 1988; Asst. Dir. then Vice-Dir. PLA Gen. Political Dept.; mem. 14th CCP Cen. Comm. for Discipline Inspection 1992; alt. mem. 15th CCP Cen. Cttee. 1997–. *Address:* People's Liberation Army General Political Department, Beijing, People's Republic of China.

YUAN TSEH LEE, M.S., PH.D.; American professor of chemistry; b. 19 Nov. 1936, Hsinchu, Taiwan; s. of Tsefan Lee and Pei Tsai; m. Bernice Wu 1963; two s. one d.; ed. Nat. Taiwan Univ., Nat. Tsinghua Univ. and Univ. of Calif. (Berkeley); postgraduate work in Prof. Bruce Mahan's group, Univ. of Calif. (Berkeley) 1962–67; Post-doctoral Fellow, Harvard Univ. 1967–68; Asst. Prof. Dept. of Chemistry and James Franck Inst. Univ. of Chicago 1968, Assoc. Prof. 1971, Prof. 1973–74; Prof. of Chemistry and Prin. Investigator, Lawrence Berkeley Lab. Univ. of Calif. (Berkeley) 1974; mem. N.A.S., Academia Sinica, Taiwan; Fellow, American Acad. of Arts and Science, American Physical Soc.; Nat. Medal of Science 1986; shared Nobel Prize for Chemistry 1986; Dr. h.c. (Waterloo) 1986; other awards and distinctions. *Address:* Academy Sinica, Nankang, Taipei 11529, Taiwan.

YUAN WEIMIN; Chinese sports administrator and civil servant; b. July 1939, Suzhou, Jiangsu Prov.; joined CCP 1962; joined Chinese Men's Volleyball Team 1962; Chief Coach of Chinese Women's Volleyball Team; Vice-Chair. All-China Sports Fed.; Vice-Chair. Chinese Olympics Cttee.; Chair. Chinese Volleyball Asscn., Chinese Football Asscn.; Exec. Vice-Chair. Asian Volleyball Fed. 1976–84; Vice-Chair. State Comm. for Physical Culture and Sports 1984–98; alt. mem. CCP 12th Cen. Cttee. 1982–87; mem. CCP 13th and 14th Cen. Cttee. 1987–97; alt. mem. CCP 15th Cen. Cttee. 1997–. *Publication:* My Way of Coaching. *Address:* 9 Tiyuguan Road, Chongwen District, Beijing 100763, People's Republic of China.

YUAN ZHONGYI; Chinese archaeologist; b. 1933, Jiangsu Prov.; ed. East China Teachers' Univ.; Vice-Dir. Shaanxi Prov. Archaeological Research Inst. and Curator Qin Shi Huang's Terracotta Army Museum. *Publications:* Studies of the Terracotta Army at Qin Shi Huang's Mausoleum, Pottery Inscriptions of the Qin Dynasty. *Address:* Qin Shi Huang's Terracotta Army Museum, Lintong, Xi'an, People's Republic of China.

YUASA, Joji; Japanese composer and professor of music; b. 12 Aug. 1929, Koriyama City; s. of Daitaro Yuasa and Otoe Yuasa; m. Reiko Suzuki 1958; one s. one d.; ed. Asaka High School, Keio Univ.; orchestral works commissioned by Kousevitzky Music Foundation 1974, Suntory Music Foundation, and by orchestras in Japan, Germany and Finland; Prof. of Music, Univ. of Calif. at San Diego 1981–94, Prof. Emer. 1994–; Prof. of Music, Nihon Univ. 1994–; Visiting Prof., Tokyo Coll. of Music; mem. Experimental Workshop, Tokyo 1952; featured composer, Festival of the Arts of this Century, Hawaii 1970, Pacific Music Festival, Sapporo 1990, Music Today Festival, Tokyo 1992; mem. Int. Jury for World Music Days, Int. Soc. for Contemporary Music (ISCM) 1971, 1983, 1992; Composer-in-Residence, Centre for Music Experiment, Univ. of Calif., San Diego 1976, N.S.W. Conservatorium of Music, Australia 1980, Univ. of Toronto, Canada 1981; a leader for Int. Composers' Workshops, Amsterdam 1984, 1992; 8 awards from ISCM 1971–91, Odaka Prizes for Orchestra 1972, 1988, Kyoto Music Prize Grand Prix 1995. *Compositions include:* Time of Orchestral Time 1976, Scenes from Basho (suite) 1980–89, Revealed Time for viola and orchestra 1986, Cosmos Haptic II for piano 1986, Nine Levels by Ze-Ami for chamber ensemble and quadraphonic tape 1988, Eye on Genesis II for orchestra 1992, Piano Concertino 1994, Symphonic Suite; The Narrow Road into the Deep North: Basho 1995, Libera me, in Requiem of Reconciliation 1995. *Leisure interests:* skiing, reading. *Address:* 1517 Shields Avenue, Encinitas, CA 92024, U.S.A.; 6-8-23-211 Ikegami, Ohta-ku, Tokyo 146, Japan. *Telephone:* (619) 436-3775 (U.S.A.); (03) 3754 -8710 (Japan). *Fax:* (619) 436-0271 (U.S.A.); (03) 3754-7678 (Japan).

YUDASHKIN, Valentin Abramovich; Russian fashion designer; b. 14 Oct. 1963, Bakovka, Moscow Region; m. Marina Vladimirovna Yudashkina; one d.; ed. Moscow Industrial Pedagogical Inst.; fashion designer; f. and artistic dir. Vali-Moda 1987, f. and Dir. Velentin Yudashkin Presents Co. 1989; participated in maj. fashion shows, including Paris 1990–92, Los Angeles (Beverly Hills Hilton), Israel, Egypt, Italy, etc.; costume designer to several Moscow Theatre New Opera productions; opened Valentin Yudashkin House of Fashion 1993; mem. Paris Haute Couture Syndicate 1996. *Address:* Valentin Yudashkin Fashion House, Kutuzovsky pr. 19, Moscow, Russia. *Telephone:* 240 43 01 (Office).

YUE JINGYU; Chinese swimmer; b. March 1975, Shanghai; entered Chinese Women's Swimming Team 1991; broke Olympic record for women's 100m free style and won Gold Medal at 26th Olympics, Atlanta. *Address:* c/o State General Bureau for Physical Culture and Sports, 9 Tiyuguan Road, Chongwen District, Beijing, People's Republic of China.

YUE QIFENG; Chinese government official; b. 1931, Daming Co., Hebei Prov.; joined CCP 1945; Deputy Sec. Hebei Prov. CCP Cttee. 1986–90; Gov. of Liaoning Prov. 1991; Sec. CPC 7th Heilongjiang Prov. Cttee. 1994–; mem. 14th CCP Cen. Cttee. 1992–. *Address:* Heilongjiang Provincial Committee of the CPC, 294 Huayuan Street, Harbin 15011, People's Republic of China. *Telephone:* (451) 3630618. *Fax:* (451) 3635140.

YULDASHEV, Shavkat; Uzbekistan politician; b. 20 Sept. 1943, Namangan; m. Dilbar Yuldasheva; three s. one d.; ed. Moscow Energy Inst.; mem. CPSU 1973–91; engineer, head of the workshop, chief engineer, Inst. of Electronics Uzbek Acad. of Sciences 1968–70; dir. production union Namangantsvet 1970–74, later CPSU functionary; Chair. Cen. Controlling Cttee. of Cen. Cttee. of CP of Uzbekistan 1990–91; Chair. of Supreme Soviet of Uzbekistan 1991–93; U.S.S.R. People's Deputy 1989–91; mem. Cen. Control Comm. CPSU 1990–91. *Address:* House of Government, Tashkent, Uzbekistan.

YUMASHEV, Valentin Borisovich; Russian politician and journalist; b. 15 Dec. 1957, Perm; m; one d.; ed. Moscow State Univ.; errand boy newspaper Komsomolskaya Pravda 1976; corresp., sr. corresp. newspaper Komsomolskaya Pravda 1978–87; Moskovsky Komsomolets 1987–89; took part in election campaign of Boris Yeltsin to Supreme Soviet 1988, 1992, 1996; Head of Div., Ed., Deputy Ed.-in-Chief Ogonyok 1987–96; Adviser to Russian Press on mass media 1996–; Head of Admin. Pres. Yeltsin 1997–98; Adviser to Pres. Yeltsin 1998–; helped Pres. Yeltsin in writing memoirs. *Leisure interest:* tennis. *Address:* Office of the President, Kremlin, korps 1, Moscow, Russia (Office). *Telephone:* (095) 910 1089, 206 6088 (Office).

YUN BULONG; Chinese politician; b. Dec. 1937, Tumed, Inner Mongolia; ed. Taiyuan Eng. Coll. 1962; joined CCP 1958; Vice-Pres. Inner Mongolia Univ. and Sec. CCP Inner Mongolia Univ. Cttee.; Vice-Pres. Higher People's Court of Inner Mongolia; Vice-Chair. Government of Inner Mongolia Autonomous Region 1992–; mem. 15th CCP Cen. Cttee. 1997–. *Address:* Government of Inner Mongolia Autonomous Region, Huhhot, Inner Mongolia, People's Republic of China.

YUNG, Larry; Chinese business executive; s. of Rong Yiren; Man. Dir. Citic Hong Kong (subsidiary of China Int. Trust & Investment, Beijing); Stromme Foundation Prize 1997. *Leisure interest:* golf. *Address:* Citic Hong Kong, c/o China International Trust and Investment Corporation, Capital Mansion, 6 Xianyarunan Lu, Chaoyang Qu, Beijing 100004, People's Republic of China.

YUNUS, Muhammad; Bangladeshi banker and professor; m. Afrizi Yunus; one d.; ed. Vanderbilt Univ.; Prof. of Econs. Chittagong Univ. 1976; f. Grameen Bank Project Dec. 1976, changed to ind. bank, Grameen Bank Sept. 1983, Man. Dir., CEO; Dir. UN Foundation; mem. Int. Advisory Group, Fourth World Conference on Women, Beijing 1993–95, Advisory Council for Sustainable Econ. Devt. 1993–, UN Expert Group on Women and Finance; Hon. LL.D. (Warwick) 1996; Independence Day Award, President's Award and Central Bank Award (all Bangladesh), Ramon Magsaysay Award (Philippines), Aga Khan Award for Architecture, Mohamed Shabdeen Award for Science (Sri Lanka), World Food Prize (U.S.A.). *Address:* Grameen Bank, Mirpur 2, P.O. Box 1216, Dhaka 1216, Bangladesh. *Telephone:* (2) 801542. *Fax:* (2) 803559.

YURSKY, Sergei Yurievich; Russian actor, stage manager, film director and writer; b. 16 March 1935, Leningrad (now St. Petersburg); s. of late Yury Yursky and Eugenia Romanova; m. Natalia Tenyakova 1970, one d.; ed. Leningrad Theatrical Inst.; worked for Gorky Theatre, Leningrad 1957–79, Mossoviet Theatre 1978–87 and other theatres in Moscow, Paris and Brussels; acted in films 1960–; one-man performances in 70 cities in U.S.S.R. 1965–, in Czechoslovakia 1985, Japan 1986, France 1987, 1991, Italy 1987, Switzerland 1989, Israel 1992, Belgium 1993, U.S.A. 1994, Germany 1994. *Stage roles:* over 60, including Chatsky (Woe from Wit) 1963, Tousenbach (Three Sisters) 1965, Victor Frank (Price) 1968, Henry IV (Henry IV) 1969, Molière (Molière; also Dir.) 1973, Groznov (Truth is Good, but Happiness is Better; also Dir.) 1980, Ornifle (Ornifle or Draught; also Dir.) 1986, King Beranger (The King is Dying, Ionescu) 1992, Azriel (Dibouk!) 1992, Glov (after Gamblers XXI, Gogol; also Dir.) 1992, Le Baron Cazou (Les Amants Puérils) 1993, Old Man (after Ionescu, also Dir.) 1994, Foma Opiskin (after Dostoevsky) 1995, Vogler (After The Rehearsal, Bergman) 1996, Malkovic (The Provocation, after Vatsetis; also Dir.) 1997. *Films:* A Man from Nowhere 1969, The Golden Calf 1968, The Little Tragedies 1980, The Fall of Condor 1984, Love and Pigeons 1985, The Abyss 1987, The Picture 1989, Chernov/Chernov (also screenplay and Dir.) 1990 (Prizewinner, Karlovy Vary/Carlsbad Film Festival 1990), The Silencer 1993, Le Bonheur 1993; People's Artist of the R.S.F.S.R. 1987. *Publications:* Who Keeps the Pause 1977, enlarged edn. 1989, During the Timeless Times (short stories) 1989, Recognizing (poetry), The Jest (poetry) 1997. *Address:* Gagarinsky 35-4, 121002 Moscow, Russia. *Telephone:* 241-52-71. *Fax:* 241-52-71.

YUSHCHENKO, Victor; Ukrainian economist and banker; b. 23 Feb. 1954, Khoruzhivka, Sumy Region; m.; one s. one d.; ed. Ternopil Acad., Ukrainian Inst. of Econs. & Agric. Org., Kiev; economist, Br. Dir. U.S.S.R. State Bank, Ulianivskyi Dist., Sumy Region 1976–85, Deputy Dir. of Agric. Credits, Ukrainian HQ 1985–87; Dept. Dir. Ukraina Bank (fmrly. Ukrainian Agro-Industrial Bank) 1987, First Deputy Chair. 1991–93; Gov. Nat. Bank of Ukraine 1993–; Global Finance Award 1997. *Publications:* over 200 articles and research papers in Ukrainian and int. journals. *Leisure interests:* painting, pottery, wood-carving. *Address:* National Bank of Ukraine, 9 Institutska St., 252007 Kiev, Ukraine. *Telephone:* (44) 293-50-73. *Fax:* (44) 293-16-98.

YUSHENKOV, Col. Sergey Nikolayevich, CAND. PHIL.; Russian politician; b. 27 June 1950, Pryamukhino, Tver region; m.; one s. two d.; ed. Novosibirsk Higher Mil. School, Lenin Mil.—Political cadre; teacher of philosophy Mil. Political Acad. 1987–91; active participant of democratic movt.; peoples' deputy of Russia 1990–93, mem. faction Radical Democrats; mem. State Duma 1993–, Chair. Cttee. on Defence 1994–95; mem. Party Democratic Choice of Russia, Deputy Chair. 1995–. *Publications:* books and articles on politics. *Leisure interests:* reading, football, writing humourous short stories. *Address:* State Duma, Okhotny ryad 1, 103009 Moscow, Russia. *Telephone:* (095) 292-92-44.

YUSHKIAVITSHUS, Henrikas Alguirdas; Russian/Lithuanian international civil servant; b. 30 March 1935, Šiauliai, Lithuania; s. of Zigmas Yushkiavitshus and Stefa Biknevitchiute; m. Elena Samuilyte 1961; one d.; ed. Leningrad Electrotechnical Communication Inst.; Dir. Technological Dept. Lithuanian Radio and TV 1960–66; Dir. Tech. Centre, Int. Radio and TV Org. 1966–71; Vice-Chair U.S.S.R. State Cttee. for TV and Radio 1971–90; Chair. Interministerial Cttee. for Radio and TV Devt. and mem. Interministerial Cttee. for Satellite Communications 1971–90; now Asst. Dir.-Gen. for Communication, Information and Informatics, UNESCO; corresp. mem. Russian Eng. Acad., mem. Int. Acad. of Electrotechnical Sciences; Hon. Academician, Russian Acad. of Information; recipient of several Soviet and Russian decorations, etc.; Order of Gediminas, Lithuania 1996, Emmy Directorate Award, U.S. Nat. Acad. of TV Arts and Sciences; Dr. h.c. (Int. Inst. for Advanced Studies in Systems Research and Cybernetics, Canada). *Publications:* contribs. to professional journals. *Leisure interests:* tennis, reading, music. *Address:* UNESCO, 1 rue Miollis, 75732 Paris, Cedex 15 (Office); 23 rue Ginoux, 75015 Paris, France (Home). *Telephone:* 45.68.43.20 (Office); 45.77.20.84 (Home). *Fax:* 45.68.55.81 (Office); 45.77.20.84 (Home).

YUVENALIY, Metropolitan (Vladimir Kyrillovich Poyarkov); Russian Orthodox ecclesiastic; b. 22 Sept. 1935, Yaroslavl; ed. Leningrad Seminary, Moscow Theological Acad.; celibate priest 1960; Sec. Dept. of Foreign Relations Moscow Patriarchy 1960; teacher Moscow Seminary 1961–; Ed. magazine Golos Pravoslavia; Dean Russian Orthodox church in West Berlin 1962–; ordained as archimandrite 1963; Chief Russian Holy Mission in Jerusalem 1963–64; Deputy Chair. Dept. of Foreign Relations of Moscow Patriarchy 1964–72, Chair. 1972–81; ordained as bishop 1963; Bishop of Zaraisk, vicar of Moscow Eparchy 1965–69; Bishop of Tula and Belevsk, Archbishop, Metropolitan 1969–77; perm. mem. Holy Synod 1972–; Metropolitan of Krutitsk and Kolomna 1977–; Chair. Synodal Comm. on Canonization of Saints; Gold Medal For Strengthening of Peace 1968 and other decorations. *Address:* Moscow Patriarchy, Danilovsky val 22, Moscow, Russia. *Telephone:* 235-0454.

Z

ZACHARIUS, Walter, B.A.; American publisher; b. 16 Oct. 1923, New York; s. of Abraham Zacharius and Sara Cohen; m. Alice Riesenberg 1948; one s. one d.; ed. Coll. of City of New York School of Business, New York Univ., New School of Social Research, Empire State Univ.; served U.S. Army 1942–45; circulation depts. McFadden Publishing Inc. 1947, Popular Library Inc. 1948–49, American Mercury Inc. 1949–51; Circulation Dir. Ace News Co., New York 1951–61; Pres. Magnum Royal Publs. Inc., New York 1961–; Pres., Chair. of Bd. Magnum Communications, New York 1961–; Pres. Lancer Books, Inc., New York 1961–75, Walter Zacharius Assoc. 1964–, United Cerebral Palsy of Queens 1986–89; Chair. Bd. Kensington Publishing Corpn., Inc. 1976–; World War II Medal, American Service Medal; European-African-Middle Eastern Service Medal; Public Relations Award-United Cerebral Palsy of Queens 1970, Award of Honor, UJA Fed. Campaign 1987, UJA Fed.'s Distinguished Service Award 1992, Gallatin Div. of New York City Certificate of Distinction 1993. *Leisure interests:* tennis, horseback riding, art collecting, reading, charity work. *Address:* Zebra Books, 850 3rd Avenue, New York, NY 10022 (Office); 1175 York Avenue, 11J, New York, NY 10021, U.S.A. (Home). *Telephone:* (212)-752-0384 (Home).

ZACHAU, Hans G., DR. RER. NAT.; German molecular biologist; b. 16 May 1930, Berlin; s. of Erich Zachau and Gertrud Zachau; m. Elisabeth Vorster 1960; three s.; ed. Univs. of Frankfurt/Main and Tübingen; Postdoctoral Fellow, M.I.T. and Rockefeller Univ. 1956–58; Max-Planck-Inst. für Biochemie, Munich 1958–61; Inst. für Genetik, Cologne 1961–66; Prof. of Physiological Chemistry and Head of Inst., Univ. of Munich 1967–; mem. Deutsche Akad. der Naturforscher Leopoldina, Austrian, Russian and Bavarian Acads., Academia Europaea; Hon. mem. American Soc. of Biological Chemists; Orden pour le merite; Grosses Bundesverdienstkreuz mit Stern; Bayerischer Verdienstorden; Richard Kuhn Medaille, Otto Warburg Medaille, Maximiliansorden. *Publications:* numerous publs. in professional journals. *Address:* Pfingstrosenstr. 5a, 81377 München, Germany. *Telephone:* 5996-429.

ZADEK, Peter; British theatre director; b. 19 May 1926, Berlin, Germany; s. of Paul Zadek and Susi Behr; m. (divorced); one s. one d.; emigrated to U.K. 1933; studied directing at Old Vic, London; Dir. Salome (Oscar Wilde), Sweeney Agonistes (T. S. Eliot) 1945–52; Dir. with BBC-TV, Wales, Dir. The Balcony (Jean Genet), London 1952–57; returned to Fed. Repub. of Germany, Dir. in Cologne, Ulm, Hanover 1958–62, Bremen 1962–67, Wuppertal, Stuttgart, Berlin, Munich, and TV and cinema films 1967–72; worked on Shakespeare cycle 1972–77; directed film Die wilden Fünfziger (The Wild Fifties) 1982; directed Mozart's Marriage of Figaro, Stuttgart 1983; directed plays Berlin, Munich, Hamburg, Vienna, Paris 1983–, including The Merchant of Venice, Vienna 1989, Measure for Measure, Paris; Dir. Berliner Ensemble 1992–95; Dir. Antony and Cleopatra, Vienna and Berlin 1994; subject of books by Volker Canaris 1979, M. Lange 1989 and many articles; Fritz Kortner Prize for Best Dir. 1988, Erwin Piscator Prize, New York 1989, Kainz Medal, Austria 1990; Commdr. des Arts et des Lettres, France 1991. *Publication:* Das wilde Ufer 1990. *Leisure interest:* music. *Address:* Berliner Ensemble, Bertolt-Brecht-Platz 1, 10117 Berlin, Germany; 55060 Vecoli, San Martino in Freddana, Italy. *Telephone:* 0039583-349017.

ZADOK, Haim J.; Israeli politician and lawyer; b. 2 Oct. 1913, Poland; s. of Abraham and Malka Just-Wilkenfeld; m. Esther Berger; two d.; ed. Warsaw Univ. and Jerusalem Law School; joined Labour Zionist Movt. 1930; emigrated to Palestine 1935; with Haganah and Jewish Settlement Police until 1948; with Israel Defence Forces in War of Independence 1948; Deputy Attorney-Gen. 1949–52; pvt. law practice 1952–65, 1967–74, 1978–; Lecturer in Commercial Law, Tel Aviv Law School 1953–61; mem. Knesset (Parl.) 1959–78; Minister of Commerce and Industry 1965–66, concurrently of Devt., of Justice 1974–77, of Religious Affairs June-Nov. 1974, Jan.–June 1977; Chair. Exec. Cttee. Hebrew Univ., Jerusalem 1969–74, Knesset Foreign Affairs and Defence Cttee. 1970–74; mem. Advisory Council, Bank of Israel 1963–74; Lecturer in Govt., Hebrew Univ. 1978–80; Chair. Exec. Cttee. Ben-Gurion Univ. of the Negev 1982–89; Chair. Bd. of Trustees, Int. Centre for Peace in the Middle East 1986–94; Chair. Israel Democracy Inst. 1990–98, Ethics Cttee., Israeli Bar 1992–96; Pres. Press Council 1993–; mem. Leadership Bureau and Political Cttee. Labour Party; Hon. Ph.D. (Ben-Gurion Univ. of the Negev). *Address:* 10 Berkovitch Street, 64238 Tel Aviv, Israel. *Telephone:* (3) 6913718. *Fax:* (3) 6913719.

ZADORNOV, Mikhail Mikhailovich, CAND. ECON.; Russian politician; b. 4 May 1963, Moscow; s. of Mikhail Zadornov and Raisa Zadornova; m. Natalya Zadornova 1982; one d.; ed. G. Plekhanov Inst. of Nat. Econ.; one of authors Programme of Econ. Reforms 500 Days; mem. State Comm. on Econ. Reform, Russian Council of Ministers 1990–91; mem. State Duma (Yabloko faction) 1993–; Chair, Cttee. on Budget, Taxation, Banks and Finances 1994–97; Minister of Finance 1997–. *Leisure interest:* playing football. *Address:* Ministry of Finance, Ilyinka str. 9, 103097 Moscow, Russia. *Telephone:* (095) 298-91-40; (095) 298-93-72.

ZAENTZ, Saul; American film producer; b. Passaic, N.J.; produced: One Flew Over the Cuckoo's Nest 1975 (Acad. Award for Best Picture), Three Warriors 1977, Lord of the Rings 1978, Amadeus 1984, The Unbearable Lightness of Being 1988, A Play in the Fields of the Lord 1991, The English Patient (Acad. Award for Best Picture) 1996; Exec. Producer The Mosquito Coast 1986; Irving G. Thalberg Memorial Award 1996. *Address:* Saul Zaentz & Co., Film Center, 2600 10th Street, Berkeley, CA 94710, U.S.A.

ZAFIROPOULOS, Vassilis S.; Greek diplomatist; b. 24 Jan. 1934; m.; one s.; ed. Univ. of Athens; with Ministry of Finance 1962–67; on secondment in charge of press matters UN Information Centre for Greece, Israel, Turkey and Cyprus, Athens 1967–71; joined Diplomatic Service 1971, Third Sec., Cen. Service of Ministry of Foreign Affairs 1971–73, Second Sec., Greek Consulate, Liege, Belgium 1973–76, First Sec. Embassy, Nicosia and Dir. Greek Press Office in Cyprus 1976–78, Counsellor for Political Affairs, Embassy, London 1980–84, Head of Cyprus Affairs, Ministry of Foreign Affairs 1984–86, Minister Counsellor, Deputy Perm. Rep. to NATO, Brussels 1986–90, Minister Plenipotentiary 1990, Perm. Rep. 1993–96; Amb. to Australia and N.Z. 1991–93, to U.K. 1996–99. *Address:* c/o Ministry of Foreign Affairs, Odos Zalokosta 2, 106 71 Athens, Greece.

ZAGALLO, Mario Jorge Lobo; Brazilian football coach; fmrly. footballer, played in World Cup Final for Brazil 1958, 1962; football coach 1965–, coached Brazilian football team for 1970, 1974 and 1998 World Cups, adviser to nat. coach Brazil 1994; fmrly. nat. coach Kuwait, Saudi Arabia, U.A.E.

ZAGLADIN, Vadim Valentinovich; Russian politician; b. 23 June 1927, Moscow; m. Janetta Rogacheva; one s. three d.; ed. Moscow Inst. of Int. Relations; taught at Moscow Inst. of Int. Relations 1949–54; editorial work on various journals 1954–64; editorial post in Prague 1960–64; mem. CPSU 1955–91; mem. Int. Dept., Cen. Cttee. of CPSU 1964–67, Deputy Head 1967–82, First Deputy Head 1982–88; mem. Cen. Auditing Cttee. 1971–76; cand. mem. Cen. Cttee. of CPSU 1976–81, mem. 1981–90; Deputy, Supreme Soviet of U.S.S.R. and Sec. Foreign Affairs Cttee. 1981–89; Chair. Section of Global Problems of Scientific Council of Pres., U.S.S.R. (now Russian) Acad. of Sciences 1981–; Deputy Chair. Parl. Group of U.S.S.R. 1981–88; Adviser to fmr. Pres. Gorbachev (q.v.) 1988–91; Adviser to Pres., Int. Foundation for Socio-Econ. and Political Studies (Gorbachev Foundation) 1992–; mem. Russian Acad. of Natural Sciences 1992–; Vice-Pres. Asscn. for Euro-Atlantic Co-operation 1991–. *Publications:* over 30 books and numerous articles on political problems. *Address:* Starokonuchenny 26, Apt. 43, 121002 Moscow, Russia. *Telephone:* 241-87-33.

ZAHEDI, Ardeshir, LL.B.; Iranian diplomatist; b. 16 Oct. 1928, Teheran; s. of Gen. Fazlollah and Khadijeh Zahedi; m. Princess Shahnaz Pahlavi 1957 (dissolved 1964); one d.; ed. in Teheran, American Univ. of Beirut and Utah State Univ., U.S.A.; Civil Adjutant to His Imperial Majesty the Shah of Iran 1954–79; Amb. to U.S.A. 1959–61, to U.K. 1962–67; Minister of Foreign Affairs 1967–71; Amb. to U.S.A. 1973–79 to Mexico 1973–76; Hon. LL.D. (Utah State 1960, Chungang Univ. of Seoul 1969, East Texas State 1973, Kent State 1974, St. Louis 1975); sentenced to death (in absentia) by Islamic Revolutionary Court; numerous decorations including Crown with Grand Cordon, Order of Taj (First Class) 1975.

ZAHIR, Abdul; Afghanistan politician; b. 3 May 1910, Lagham; ed. Habibia High School, Kabul and Columbia and Johns Hopkins Univs., U.S.A.; practised medicine in U.S.A. before returning to Kabul 1943; Chief Doctor, Municipal Hosp., Kabul 1943–50; Deputy Minister of Health 1950–55, Minister 1955–58; Amb. to Pakistan 1958–61; Chair. House of the People 1961–64, 1965–69; Deputy Prime Minister and Minister of Health 1964–65; Amb. to Italy 1969–71; Prime Minister 1971–72.

ZAHIR SHAH (see Mohammed Zahir Shah).

ZAHN, Joachim, DR.JUR.; German business executive; b. 24 Jan. 1914, Wuppertal; s. of Hans Zahn; Man. Bd. Deutsche Treuhandgesellschaft 1945–54, Aschaffenburger Zellstoffwerke 1955–58; Dir. Daimler-Benz AG 1958–79, Spokesman, Bd. of Man. 1965–71, Chair. 1971–79; mem. supervisory Bds. of Daimler-Benz AG subsidiary and assoc. cos. Hanomag-Henschel Fahrzeugwerke GmbH, Motoren- und Turbinen-Union, Friedrichshafen and Munich, Mercedes-Benz of N. America, Argentina, Australia, Canada, U.K. and assocs. in Brazil, France, Italy, Spain, South Africa, Switzerland and India; Dir. Fried. Krupp GmbH, Portland Zementwerke, Heidelberg, Frankfurter Versicherung AG, Frankfurter Hypothekenbank, Hannoversche Messe AG, Obermain Schuhfabrik AG; Hon. Vice-Pres. and Treas. Bundesverband der Deutschen Industrie; mem. Bd. Verband der Deutschen Automobilindustrie; Senator Max-Planck-Soc.; Chair. Baden-Württemberg Landeskuratorium des Stifterverbands für die deutsche Wissenschaft; Grosses Bundesverdienstkreuz. *Address:* Gerokstrasse 13B, 70184 Stuttgart, Germany.

ZAHN, Johannes, D.JUR.; German banker; b. 21 Jan. 1907, Aachen; s. of Hans Zahn and Käthe (née Cossel) Zahn; m. Victoria Brandeis 1938 (died 1994); one s. three d.; ed. Tübingen, Bonn and Harvard Univs.; Dept. Man. Reichskreditgesellschaft, Berlin 1937–45; Partner, C. G. Trinkaus, Düsseldorf 1946–71; Exec. Dir. World Bank, Washington 1952–54; Pres. Stock Exchange 1967–77; mem. Bd. Trinkaus and Burkhardt 1972– (Chair

1972–82); Grosses Bundesverdienstkreuz (Germany), Commdr., Ordre Léopold II (Belgium), Ordre de Mérite (Luxembourg), St. Olaf (Norway), Merito Civil (Spain). *Publications:* Der Privatbankier, Zahlung und Zahlungssicherung im Aussenhandel 6 ed. 1985, Banktechnik des Aussenhandels 8 ed. 1987. *Leisure interests:* violin, golf. *Address:* Malkastenstrasse 3, 40211 Düsseldorf, Germany. *Telephone:* (0211) 35 98 37.

ZAHRADNÍK, Rudolf, D.SC., DIPL. ENG.; Czech physical chemist and university professor; b. 20 Oct. 1928, Bratislava; m. Milena Zahradník; one d.; ed. Czech Tech. Univ., Prague; scientific worker Inst. of Labour Hygiene and Diseases, Inst. of Physical Chem. and Electrochem., Prague 1961–83; Prof., Charles Univ., Prague 1967–; Guest Prof. Univs. of Würzburg 1965, Croningen 1967, Osaka 1977, Basel 1981, Vanderbilt Univ. 1990; Dir. Jaroslav Heyrovský Inst. of Physical and Electrochem. Prague 1990–93; Pres. Czech Acad. of Sciences 1993–; Pres. Czech Learned Society 1994–97; mem. many academic and scientific socs. including Int. Acad. of Quantum Molecular Sciences 1982–, World Asscn. of Theoretical Organic Chemists, European Acad. of Arts, Science and Literature, Eds'. Council Special Journals; hon. mem. Swiss-German Chemical Soc.; several hon. degrees including Dr. h.c. (Charles Univ. Prague) 1998, (New York) 1998; Jaroslav Heyrovský Golden Plaque Czech Acad. of Sciences 1990, Medal for Merit, Prague 1998. *Publication:* co-author Basics of Quantum Organic Chemistry 1975, Thinking as Passion (with Lenka Jaklová) 1998. *Leisure interests:* serious music and literature. *Address:* Czech Academy of Sciences, Národni 3, Prague 1 — 11142 (Office); Heřmanova 37, Prague 7 — 170 00, Czech Republic (Home). *Telephone:* 24 22 03 84 (Office); 37 43 67 (Home). *Fax:* 24 22 96 10 (Office).

ZAINUDDIN, Daim, LL.B.; Malaysian politician, lawyer and business executive; b. 1938, Alor Star, Kedah State; ed. London, Univ. of Calif.; called to the Bar Lincoln's Inn; magistrate, then Deputy Public Prosecutor; later set up own law firm; Head Peremba 1979–; mem. Dewan Negara (Senate) 1980–82; mem. Dewan Rakat (House of Reps.) 1982–; Minister of Finance 1984–91; Chair. Fleet Group; Treasurer UMNO; Exec. Dir. Nat. Econ. Action Council 1998–; Econ. Adviser to Prime Minister Mahathir bin Mohammad (q.v.); Minister with Special Functions 1998–; Chair. and Dir. numerous cos. *Address:* Ministry of Special Functions, Kuala Lumpur, Malaysia.

ZAITSEV, Vyacheslav Mikhailovich (Slava); Russian fashion designer; b. 2 March 1938, Ivanovo; one s.; ed. Moscow Textile Inst.; chief designer, All-Union Fashion House 1965–78; chief designer, Moscow Fashion House "Slava Zaitsev" 1982–; Pres. 1991–; took part in Paris fashion show 1988; shows collections worldwide; Prof., Moscow Textile Inst.; Hon. Citizen of Paris 1988; Best designer award (Japan) 1989. *Publications:* The Changing Fasion 1980, This Many-Faced World of Fashion 1980. *Address:* Moscow Fashion House, Prospekt Mira 21, 129110 Moscow, Russia. *Telephone:* (095) 971-11-22. *Fax:* (095) 281-55-75.

ZAITSEV, Yury Vladimirovich, DR. TECH. SC.; Russian engineer and diplomatist; b. 2 Aug. 1933, Moscow; m.; two d.; ed. Kuibyshev Moscow Inst. of Construction Eng., Diplomatic Acad. Ministry of Foreign Affairs; sr. reseacher Centre for Inst. of Scientific Information on construction and architecture U.S.S.R. Acad. of Construction and Architecture 1958–59, Research Inst. of Concrete and Reinforced Concrete 1959–64; Prof., Head of Chair., Pro-rector All-Union Polytechnic Inst. by correspondence 1964–90; Chair. Comm. on Problems of Citizenship at Supreme Soviet, then with Russian Presidency 1990–92; mem. Supreme Soviet of Russian Fed. 1990–93; Perm. Rep. of Russia at int. orgs. in Vienna 1992–97; First Deputy Head, Internal Policy Dept. of Pres. Yeltsin's Admin. 1997–98; mem. Acad. of Tech. Sciences Acad. of Natural Sciences, Acad. of Eng. *Publications include:* 18 monographs, textbooks, over 200 articles in scientific journals. *Address:* President's Administration, Kremlin 1, Moscow, Russia.

ZAJĄC, Stanisław; Polish politician and lawyer; b. 1 May 1949, Święcany, Krosno Prov., m.; two c.; ed. Jagiellonian Univ., Kraków; employee Regional Court, Jasło; advocate in Krosno and Jasło 1980; advocate for the defence during martial law; adviser NSZZ Solidarity, Carpathian Region; Vice-Chair. Christian Nat. Union (ZChN); deputy to Sejm (Parl.) 1991–93, 1997–, Vice-Leader Justice Cttee., mem. Parl. Comm. for Spatial, Bldg. and Housing Policy; mem. Christian Nat. Union Parl. 1991–93; Vice-Marshal of Sejm 1997–; mem. Solidarity Election Action (AWS) Parl. Club. *Address:* Kancelaria Sejmu RP, ul. Wiejska 4/6/8, 00-902 Warsaw, Poland. *Telephone:* (22) 628 87 66.

ZAKHAROV, Aleksander Vladimirovich; Russian business executive; b. 3 Oct. 1955, Moscow; m.; two c.; ed. G. Plekhanov Moscow Inst. of Nat. Econ., All-Union Acad. of Foreign Trade; expert, sr. consultant U.S.S.R. Chamber of Industry and Commerce 1976–89; Deputy rep. U.S.S.R. Chamber of Industry and Commerce in Bulgaria 1989–91; Deputy Dir. Cen. on Interbank Currency Accounts U.S.S.R. State Bank (Gosbank) Sept.–Dec. 1991; Dir. Moscow Interbank Currency Exchange 1992–. *Address:* Moscow Interbank Currency Exchange, Zubovsky blvd., 4, 119021 Moscow, Russia. *Telephone:* (095) 201 2308 (Office).

ZAKHAROV, Mark Anatolievich; Russian stage and film director; b. 13 Oct. 1933, Moscow; m. Nina Lapshinova; one d.; ed. Lunacharsky Theatre Inst.; (now Russian Acad. of Theatre Arts); actor since 1955, stage dir. Theatre of Satire Mayakovsky Theatre 1965–73; Chief Stage Dir. Moscow Theatre of Leninsky Komsomol (now "Lenkom" Theatre) 1973–; teacher, Prof., Russian Acad. of Theatre Arts 1979–; mem. Bd. Theatre Union of Russia 1987–; mem. Pres.'s Council 1996–; Dir. of plays including: Profitable Place by A. Ostrovsky 1967, Yunona and Avos by A. Voznesensky and A. Rybnikov 1981, Three Girls in Blue by L. Petrushevskaya 1985, Dictatorship of Conscience by M. Shatrov 1986, Wise Man by A. Ostrovsky 1989, Pray for the Dead by Sholom-Aleihem 1989, The Marriage of Figaro by Beaumarchais 1993, The Seagull by Chekhov 1994, King's Games by G. Gorin and M. Anderson 1995; TV films: Habitual Miracle 1976, That Very Munchhausen 1979, Formula for Love 1984, To Kill a Dragon 1989; People's Artist of the R.S.F.S.R. 1988. *Publications:* Contacts on Diverse Levels 1988, and numerous publs. on theatre. *Address:* 1st Tverskaya-Yamskaya 7, Apt. 9, Moscow, Russia. *Telephone:* 299-12-61. *Fax:* 299-28-70.

ZAKIS, Juris, DR.SC.; Latvian solid-state physicist; b. 4 Nov. 1936, Ogre, Latvia; s. of Roderickh Zakis and Eugenia Zake; m. Anita Zake 1976; three s. two d.; ed. Univ. of Latvia, Riga; Prof., Rector Univ. of Latvia; U.S.S.R. People's Deputy 1989–91; mem. Parl. of Latvian Ass. 1995–; mem. Latvian Acad. of Sciences; Merited Scientist of Latvia 1986. *Publications:* numerous articles on physics of disordered solids and on higher educ. policy. *Leisure interests:* skiing, linguistics. *Address:* University of Latvia, 19 Rainis Boulevard, Riga, LV-1586, Latvia. *Telephone:* (02) 228928, 229076. *Fax:* (02) 7820113.

ZALYGIN, Sergey Pavlovich; Russian writer; b. 6 Dec. 1913, Durasovka, Bashkir A.S.S.R.; ed. Omsk Agricultural Inst.; worked as engineer-hydrologist with Siberian branch of U.S.S.R. Acad. of Sciences; first works published 1936; (first non-party) Ed.-in-Chief Novy Mir 1986–98; U.S.S.R. People's Deputy 1989–91; Chair. Ecology and Peace (scientific asscn. of ecologists); mem. Russian Acad. of Sciences 1991–, New York Acad. of Sciences; State Prize 1968; Hero of Socialist Labour 1988; Order of Red Banner of Labour, various medals. *Publications include:* Stories 1941, Spring of 1954 1955, Red Clover 1955, Altai Paths 1962, The Salty Ravine 1967–68, My Poet 1969, Traits of the Profession 1970, Commission (novel) 1975, The South American Version (novel) 1978, After the Storm (novel) 1980, Collected Works (6 vols.) 1989–91; Ecological Novel 1993, The Namesakes (novel) 1996, Freedom of Choice: My Democracy (essay) 1996; many works on Chekhov and Tolstoy, and on ecological problems. *Address:* Leninsky Prospekt 28, Apt. 3, 117071 Moscow, Russia. *Telephone:* (095) 423-03-73 (Home).

ZAMACHOWSKI, Zbigniew; Polish actor; b. 17 July 1961, Brzeziny; m.; one s. one d.; ed. State Higher Film, TV and Theatre School, Łódź. *Film roles include:* Zad wielkiego wieloryba 1987, Dotknięci 1988, Bal na dworcu w..., Dekalog X 1989, Ucieczka z kina 'Wolność' 1990, Ferdydurke 1991, Na czarno 1993, Trzy kolory: Biały 1993, Le clandestin (France) 1993, Zawrócony 1994, Pułkownik Kwiatkowski 1995, Sława i chwała 1996, Szczęśliwego Nowego Jorku 1997, "23" 1997, Nie płacz Agnieszko 1997, Ogniem i mienem 1998. *Theatrical roles include:* Płatonow 1992, Amadeus 1993, Wujaszek Wania 1993, Don Juan 1996, Ildefonsjada 1996, Za i przeciw 1997, Ślub 1998; Aleksander Zelwerowicz Award 1993, Gdańsk Film Festival Prize for Best Actor, in Zawrócony 1994. *Address:* c/o Creative Management Concepts, ul. Chełmska 21, 00-724 Warsaw, Poland. *Telephone:* (22) 651 10 50.

ZAMAGNI, Stefano; Italian professor of economics; b. 4 Jan. 1943, Rimini; m. Vera Negri 1968; two d.; ed. Univ. of Milan, Univ. of Oxford, U.K.; Assoc. Dir. and Adjunct Prof., Bologna Center, Johns Hopkins Univ. 1977–; Prof. of Econs., Univ. of Bologna 1985–, Chair. Dept. of Econs. 1985–88, 1991–94, Dean Faculty of Econs. 1994–96, Co-ordinator Ph.D. Programme in Econs. 1989–93; Vice-Pres. Italian Econ. Asscn. 1989–92, State Vic. Bank Visiting Prof., Deakin Univ., Geelong, Australia; McDonnell Visiting Scholar, Wider, Helsinki, Finland; Co-Ed. Economia Politica (quarterly) 1983–, Italian Economic Papers 1990–, Journal of International and Comparative Economics, Ricerche Economiche; mem. Exec. Cttee. Int. Econ. Asscn. 1989–, Pontifical Council on Justice and Peace 1992–, Scientific Cttee., J. Maritain Int. Inst. 1995–, Bd. of Dirs. UNIBANCA 1999–; mem. Acad. of Sciences; Paul Harris Fellow, Rotary Int. 1995; Accademia Lincei Award; St. Vincent Prize in Econs., Capri Prize in Econs. 1995, Golden Sigismondo Prize 1997, Gold Medal, Pio Manzu Int. Centre 1998. *Publications:* Microeconomic Theory 1987, The Economic Theories of Production 1989, History of Economic Thought 1991, Value and Capital—Fifty Years Later (with L. McKenzie) 1991, Firms and Markets 1991, Man—Environment and Development: Toward a Global Approach 1991, Market, State and the Theory of Public Intervention 1992, The Economics of Crime and Illegal Markets 1993, Towards a One World Development Path 1993, The Economics of Altruism 1995, An Evolutionary Dynamic Approach to Altruism 1996, Technological Change: Time-Use Policies and Employment 1996, Globalization as Specificity of Post-Industrial Economy 1997, Civil Economy and Paradoxes of Growth in Post-Fordist Societies 1997, Living in the Global Society 1997, Civil Economy, Cultural Evolution and Participatory Development 1999. *Leisure interests:* sports, theatre, classical music. *Address:* Department of Economics, University of Bologna, Piazza Scaravilli 2, 40126 Bologna, Italy. *Telephone:* (51) 258665. *Fax:* (51) 258040.

ZAMECNIK, Paul Charles, M.D.; American physician; b. 22 Nov. 1912, Cleveland, Ohio; s. of John Zamecnik and Mary McCarthy; m. Mary Connor 1936; one s. two d.; ed. Dartmouth Coll. and Harvard Medical School; Resident, Huntington Memorial Hosp., Boston, Mass. 1936–37; Intern, Univ. Hosps., Cleveland, Ohio 1938–39; Moseley Travelling Fellow of Harvard Univ. at Carlsberg Labs., Copenhagen 1939–40; Fellow Rockefeller Inst., New York 1941–42; Physician, Harvard Univ. and Dir. John Collins Warren

Labs. at Mass. Gen. Hosp. 1956–79, Hon. Physician 1983–, Exec. Sec. of Cttee. on Research 1948–50, Chair. Cttee. on Research 1954–56; Chair. Exec. Cttee. of Depts. of Medicine, Harvard Medical School 1956–61, 1968–71; Collis P. Huntington Prof. of Oncological Medicine, Harvard Medical School 1956–79, Emer. Prof. 1979–; Prin. Scientist Worcester Foundation for Experimental Biology, Shrewsbury, Mass. 1979–97; Chair. SAB Hybridon Inc., Cambridge, Mass. 1991–; Jubilee Lecturer, Biochemical Soc., London 1962; Fogarty Scholar 1975, 1978; Foreign mem. Royal Danish Acad. of Sciences; mem. N.A.S., American Acad. of Arts and Sciences, Asscn. American Physicians, American Asscn. of Biological Chemists, American Asscn. of Cancer Research (Pres. 1964–65); Hon. D.Sc. (Utrecht) 1966, (Columbia) 1971, (Harvard) 1982, (Roger Williams) 1983, (Dartmouth) 1988, (Mass.) 1994; John Collins Warren Triennial Prize 1946, 1950, James Ewing Award 1963, Borden Award in Medical Sciences 1965, American Cancer Soc. Nat. Award 1967, Passano Award 1970, Presidential Medal of Science 1991, Hudson Hoagland Award 1993, City of Medicine Award, Durham, N.C. 1995, City of Worcester Science Award 1996, Lasker Lifetime Science Award 1996, Merck Award, ASBC and MB 1997, Annual Orator, Mass. Medical Soc. 1998. *Publications include:* Historical and Current Aspects of the Problem of Protein Synthesis (Harvey Lectures Series 54) 1960, Unsettled Questions in the Field of Protein Synthesis (Bio-chemical Journal 85) 1962, The Mechanics of Protein Synthesis and its Possible Alterations in the Presence of Oncogenic RNA Viruses (Cancer Research 26) 1966, Antisense Oligonucleotides as Modulators of Genetic Expression 1992, Antisense Therapy of Drug Resistant Malaria and Bacterial Diseases 1995–98. *Leisure interests:* African art, snorkeling. *Address:* Massachusetts General Hospital, 149 13th Street, M.C.: 1494005, Charlestown, MA 02139 (Office); 101 Chestnut Street, Boston, MA 02108, U.S.A. (Home).

ZAMFIR, Gheorghe; Romanian musician; b. 6 April 1941, Găeşti, nr. Bucharest; ed. self-taught and Bucharest Acad. of Music (studied under Fănică Luca); graduated in conducting at Ciprian Porumbescu Conservatory, Bucharest 1968; toured numerous countries in Europe as student and won first prize in many int. competitions; conductor of 'Ciocirlia' Folk Ensemble in Bucharest 1969; Prof. of Pan-Pipes 1970; formed own orchestra 1970; numerous trips to Europe, Australia, S. America, Canada and U.S.A. and recordings. *Address:* 4 rue Tronchet, Paris, France; Dr. Teohari str. 10, Bucharest, Romania.

ZAMMIT, Ninu, B.ARCH.; Maltese politician; b. 1952, Zurrieq; m. Margaret Zahra; one s. two d.; ed. Univ. of Malta; architect and civil engineer 1975; M.P. Nationalist Party 1981–; Party Spokesman for Water and Energy 1985–87; Parl. Sec. for Water and Energy 1987–96; Shadow Minister and Opposition Spokesman for Agric. and Fisheries 1996–98; Minister of Agric. and Fisheries 1998–. *Address:* Ministry of Agriculture and Fisheries, Barriera Wharf, Valletta, CMR 02, Malta. *Telephone:* 225236; 225238. *Fax:* 231294.

ZAMMIT DIMECH, Francis, LL.D.; Maltese politician and lawyer; b. 23 Oct. 1954; s. of George Zammit Dimech; ed. St. Aloysius Coll. and Univ. of Malta; Pres. Students' Rep. Council of Univ. 1978–79; Vice-Pres. Democratic Youth Community of Europe 1981–83; Nationalist Party M.P. 1987–; mem. Maltese Parl. Del. to Parl. Ass. of Council of Europe 1987–92; Parl. Sec. later Minister for Transport and Communications 1990–92, 1992–94; Minister for the Environment 1994–96, 1998–; Shadow Minister and Opposition Spokesman on Public Works and Environment 1996–98; Pres. Exec. Council Nationalist Party 1997. *Publications:* Pull of 76 1980, The Untruth Game 1986. *Address:* Ministry for the Environment, Block B, Floriana CMR 02, Malta. *Telephone:* 222378; 224501. *Fax:* 243306.

ZAMORA RIVAS, Rubén Ignacio; Salvadorean politician; b. 9 Nov. 1942; s. of Ruben Zamora and Lidia Rivas; m. Maria Ester Chamorro 1979; five c.; ed. seminary; abandoned studies for priesthood aged 19 and turned to social activism; joined Christian Democratic Party (f. by José Napoléon Duarte 1960); sometime lecturer, Catholic Univ. San Salvador; arrested for political activities 1977; in exile in U.K. 1977–79; Minister of the Presidency 1979–80; fled to Nicaragua following murder of his brother Mario 1980; founder and leader Social Christian Popular Movt. (MPSC); returned from exile to San Salvador 1987; Vice-Pres. Nat. Ass. 1991–; Presidential Cand. for 1994 elections. *Leisure interests:* reading, playing Nintendo. *Address:* C. Guadalupe, 1313 Final Blvd., Tutunichapa (Office); 204 Ave. Maquilishuat, Col. Vista Hermosa, San Salvador, El Salvador.

ZAMYATIN, Leonid Mitrofanovich; Russian diplomatist and journalist (retd.); b. 9 March 1922, Nizhni Devitsk, Voronezh Region; m. 1946; one d.; ed. Moscow Aviation Inst. and Higher Diplomatic School; mem. CPSU 1944–91; at Ministry of Foreign Affairs 1946–50; First Sec., Secr. of Minister of Foreign Affairs 1950–52; Asst. Head, Third European Dept., Ministry of Foreign Affairs 1952–53; First Sec., Counsellor on Political Questions of U.S.S.R. Mission to UN 1953–57; Soviet Deputy Rep. on Preparatory Cttee., and later on Bd. of Govs., Int. Atomic Energy Agency (IAEA) 1957–59, Soviet Rep. at IAEA 1959–60; Deputy Head, American Countries Dept., Ministry of Foreign Affairs 1960–62, Head of Press Dept. 1962–70, mem. of Collegium of Ministry 1962–70; Dir.-Gen. TASS News Agency 1970–78, Govt. Minister 1972; Deputy to U.S.S.R. Supreme Soviet 1970–89; Chief, Dept. of Int. Information, Cen. Cttee. CPSU 1978–85, mem. Cen. Cttee. 1981; Amb. to U.K. 1986–91; Adviser to Chair. Russian Industrialists' and Entrepreneurs' Union 1992–94, to Pres. Bank of St. Petersburg 1994–; Lenin Prize 1978; orders and medals of U.S.S.R. including Order of Lenin (twice). *Publication:* Gorby and Maggie 1995. *Address:* Leont'yevsky per. 10, 103009 Moscow, Russia. *Telephone:* 229-83-75.

ZANDER, Michael, Q.C., LL.M.; British professor of law; b. 16 Nov. 1932, Berlin, Germany; s. of Walter Zander and Margaret Zander; m. Elizabeth Treeger 1965; one s. one d.; ed. Royal Grammar School, High Wycombe, Jesus Coll. Cambridge and Harvard Law School; Sullivan & Cromwell, New York 1958–59; admitted solicitor of Supreme Court 1962; Asst. Lecturer, London School of Econs. 1963, Lecturer 1965, Sr. Lecturer 1970, Reader 1970, Prof. of Law 1977–98, Emer. Prof. 1998–, Convenor (head) 1984–88, 1997–98; legal corresp. The (Manchester) Guardian 1963–88; mem. Royal Comm. on Criminal Justice 1991–93. *Publications:* Lawyers and the Public Interest 1968, Legal Services for the Community 1978, The Police and Criminal Evidence Act 1984, 1995, A Matter of Justice 1989, Cases and Materials on the English Legal System 1992, The Law-making Process 1996, A Bill of Rights? 1997. *Leisure interests:* swimming (daily), the 'cello (alas, not daily). *Address:* 12 Woodside Avenue, London, N6 4SS, England. *Telephone:* 0181-883 6257. *Fax:* 0181-444 3348.

ZANE, Billy; American actor; b. 24 Feb. 1966, Chicago, Ill.; ed. American School, Switzerland; moved to Hollywood 1984; stage appearances in American Music, New York, The Boys in the Backroom (Actors' Gang, Chicago). *Films:* Back to the Future 1985, Critters 1986, Dead Calm 1989, Back to the Future Part II 1989, Megaville 1990, Memphis Belle 1990, Blood and Concrete: A Love Story 1991, Millions, Femme Fatale 1991, Posse 1993, Orlando 1993, Sniper 1993, Flashfire, Tombstone 1993, The Silence of the Hams 1994, Cyborg Agent, Only You 1994, Tales from the Crypt Presents: Demon Knight 1995, Reflections in the Dark, Danger Zone 1995, The Phantom 1996, This World – Then the Fireworks 1996, Head Above Water 1996, Titanic 1998. *TV:* (series) Twin Peaks; (films) Brotherhood of Justice, The Case of the Hillside Stranglers 1989, Lake Consequence, Running Delilah, The Set Up. *Address:* c/o Creative Artists Agency, 9830 Wilshire Boulevard, Beverly Hills, CA 90212, U.S.A.

ZANG MINGCHANG; Chinese government official; Pres. China Power Investment Corp. *Address:* China Power Investment Corp., c/o Ministry of Power Industry, 137 Fuyou Jie, Xicheng Qu, Beijing 100031, People's Republic of China.

ZANKER, Paul, DR.PHIL.; German professor of archaeology; b. 7 Feb. 1937, Konstanz; ed. Univs. of Munich, Freiburg and Rome; Deutsches Archäologisches Inst. Rome 1963, Dir. 1996–; Asst. Bonn 1964; lecturer, Freiburg 1967; Prof. Göttingen 1972; Prof. of Classical Archaeology, Univ. of Munich 1976; mem. Inst. of Advanced Study, Princeton, N.J.; mem. Bayerische Akad. der Wissenschaften, British Acad., Accademia Europaea (London), Deutsches Archäologisches Inst. *Publications:* Wandel der Hermesgestalt 1965, Forum Augustum 1968, Forum Romanum 1972, Porträts 1973, Klassizistiche Statuen 1974, Provinzielle Kaiserbildnisse 1983, Augustus und die Macht der Bilder 1987, The Mask of Socrates: The Image of the Intellectual in Antiquity 1995. *Address:* Meiserstrasse 10, 80333 Munich, Germany.

ŽANTOVSKÝ, Michael; Czech politician, scientist and translator; b. 3 Jan. 1945, Prague; s. of Jiří Žantovský and Hana Žantovská; m. Kristina Žantovská; one s. one d.; ed. Charles Univ., Prague, McGill Univ., Montreal; scientific worker in a-research inst., Prague 1973–; freelance translator and interpreter 1980–89; activist for ind. creative org. Open Dialogue 1988; founder mem. restored PEN 1989; Press Spokesman for Centre of Civic Forum 1989–90; mem. Advisory Bd. to Pres. Václac Havel (q.v.) 1990–91; Press Spokesman to Pres. 1991–92; with Ministry of Foreign Affairs Aug. 1992; Amb. of Czech Repub. to U.S.A. 1993–97; mem. Senate 1996–; Chair. Senate Comm. for Foreign Affairs, Defence and Security 1996–; mem. Civic Democratic Alliance (ODA) March 1997–, Chair. March–Nov. 1997, Vice-Chair. 1998–. *Publications:* papers in scientific journals on psychological motivation and sexual behaviour, author of plays and translator of numerous papers. *Leisure interest:* tennis. *Address:* Senate, Valdštejnské nám. 4, 118 88, Prague 1, Czech Republic. *Telephone:* 02-570-7-1111.

ZANUCK, Richard Darryl, B.A.; American film company executive; b. 13 Dec. 1934, Beverly Hills, Calif.; s. of Darryl F. Zanuck and Virginia (Fox) Zanuck; m. 1st Lili Gentle; two d.; m. 2nd Linda Harrison 1969; two step-s.; m. 3rd Lili Fini 1978; ed. Harvard Mil. Acad. and Stanford Univ.; Story, Production Asst. Darryl F. Zanuck Productions 1956, Vice-Pres. 1956–62; President's Production Rep. 20th Century-Fox Studios, Beverly Hills 1962–63, Vice-Pres. in charge of Production 1963–69, Pres. 1969–71, Dir. 1966–; Chair. 20th Century-Fox TV Inc.; Sr. Vice-Pres. Warner Bros. Inc. 1971–72; Co-founder, Pres. Zanuck/Brown Co. 1972–88; Founder, Propr. The Zanuck Co. 1989–; mem. Bd. of Govs. Acad. of Motion Picture Arts and Sciences, Screen Producers Guild; Nat. Chair. Fibrosis Asscn. 1966–68; mem. Organizing Cttee. 1984 Olympics; Trustee, Harvard School; shared Irving J. Thalberg Award 1991; Lifetime Achievement Award, Producer's Guild, America 1993. *Producer:* The Sting 1973 (Acad. Award), Jaws 1975, Jaws II 1978, The Island 1980, Neighbors 1982, The Verdict 1983, Cocoon 1985, Target 1985, Cocoon—The Return 1987, Driving Miss Daisy 1989 (Acad. Award), Rush 1991, Rich in Love 1992, Clean State 1993, Wild Bill 1995, Mulholland Falls 1996, Deep Impact 1998. *Address:* Zanuck Co., 9465 Wilshire Boulevard, Beverly Hills, CA 90212, U.S.A.

ZANUSO, Marco; Italian architect; b. 14 May 1916; ed. Politecnico di Milano; architectural practice 1945–; mem. C.I.A.M. 1956–, Istituto Naz. Urbanistica 1956–; Dir. Inst. of Tech. and Faculty of Architecture, Milan Polytechnic 1970; Visiting Prof. of Industrial Design 1976; City Councillor, Milan 1956–60; mem. Building Comm., Milan Corpn. 1961–63, 1967–69; mem. City Devt. Comm., Milan 1969; lecturer, Faculty of Architecture, Milan Polytechnic; Pres. Asscn. for Industrial Design 1966–; numerous gold medals; Int. Plastic Exhbn. Prize, London 1966; Gold Medal, Ministry of Industry and Commerce 1966, etc. *Buildings and projects include:* H.Q. for American Co. 1948; Olivetti buildings, Buenos Aires 1954; Olivetti buildings, São Paulo 1965; Brinnel buildings, Casella d'Asolo 1966; Int. H.Q., S.G.S. Fairchild, Agrate 1967; Olivetti buildings, Scarmagno (Ivrea) 1968; Olivetti factories, Crema and Marcianise 1971; regional H.Q. for Edgars Stores Ltd., Johannesburg 1972; Conference Centre, Grado 1974–75, IBM Bldg. Segrate, Acad. of San Luca 1980, IBM Bldg., San Palomba, Rome 1979–83, restoration Teatro Fossati, Milan 1980–86, Piccolo Theatre project, Milan, 1980–86, water tower, Reggio Emilia 1986, redevt. of fmr. Borletti Bldg. for SIP (telephone co.) 1988–92, bldgs. for SIMA, Puianello, Reggio Emilia 1988–. *Address:* Piazza Castello 20, Milan, Italy (Home). *Telephone:* 866127 (Home).

ZANUSSI, Krzysztof; Polish film director and scriptwriter; b. 17 June 1939, Warsaw; s. of Jerzy and Jadwiga Zanussi; m. Elżbieta Grocholska; ed. Warsaw and Cracow Univs. and Łódź Higher Film School; Dir. TOR State Film Studio 1967–; lecturer, Stage Dept. of Higher State School of Film, TV and Drama, Łódź 1970–72; perm. co-operation with Nat. Film School, U.K. 1977–; has directed numerous short feature films; Vice-Chair., Polish Film Asscn. 1971–81; Pres. European Fed. of Film Dirs. (FERA) 1990–; mem. Pontificia Accademia delle Arti e Lettere; Dr. h.c. (Moscow WGIC) 1998; Special Prize, VII Polish Film Festival 1980, Special Jury Prize, Venice Film Festival 1982, State Prize 1st Class 1984, Vittorio De Sica Int. Film Award, Sorrento 1990; Kt.'s Cross of Order of Polonia Restituta, Gold Cross of Merit 1981, Chevalier de l'Ordre des Sciences et Lettres 1986. *Films include:* Death of Provincial 1966 (awards in Venice, Mannheim, Valladolid and Moscow), Structure of Crystals 1969 (award in Mar del Plata), Family Life 1971 (awards in Chicago, Valladolid and Colombo), Illumination 1973 (Grand prize in Locarno 1973), The Catamount Killing (U.S.A.) 1974, Quarterly Balance 1975 (OCIC Prize, West Berlin Int. Film Festival 1975), Camouflage 1977 (special prize, Teheran Int. Film Festival 1977, Grand Prix, Polish Film Festival 1977), Spiral 1978 (Prize of Journalists, V Polish Film Festival 1978, Cannes 1978, OCIC Prize), Wege in der Nacht 1979 (Fed. Repub. of Germany), Constant Factor (Best Dir. Cannes, OCIC Prize) 1980, Contract (Distribution Prize, Venice Film Festival) 1980, From a Far Country 1980 (Donatello Prize, Florence), Versuchung 1981, Imperative (Special Prize and Passinetti Award, Venice), The Unapproachable 1982, Year of the Quiet Sun 1984 (Grand Prix Golden Lion), The Power of Evil 1985 (OCIC Prize, Montreal), Life for Life (Germany, Poland) 1990. *TV films:* Portrait of the Composer (prizes in Cracow, Leipzig), Face to Face 1967, Credit 1968, Pass Mark 1969, Mountains at Dark 1970, Role (Fed. Repub. of Germany) 1971, Behind the Wall 1971, (Grand Prix, San Remo Int. Film Festival 1972), Hipotese (Fed. Repub. of Germany) 1972, Nachtdienst (Fed. Repub. of Germany) 1975, Penderecki Lutosławski Baird (documentary) 1976, Anatomiestunde (Fed. Repub. of Germany) 1977, Haus der Frauen (Fed. Repub. of Germany) 1978, Mein Krakau (documentary) 1979, Blaubard (Fed. Repub. of Germany, Italy) 1984 (Prize, Venice Film Festival), Mia Varsavia 1987, Erloeschene Zeiten 1987, Stan Posiadania 1989, Wherever You Are (Germany, Poland, U.K.) 1989 (Oecumenical Prize, Moscow, Best Script and Act. European Award, Viareggio 1989), The Silent Touch 1993, At Full Gallop 1995 (Special Jury Prize, Tokyo), Wrong Address (BBC) 1995, Don't Be Afraid (RAI) 1996, Weekend Stories 1995–97, Our God's Brother (Italy, Germany, Poland) 1997. *Stage plays:* One Flew Over the Cuckoo's Nest 1977, Der König stirbt 1980, Mattatoiò 1982, Day and Night, Duo for One 1983, Hiòb, Les Jeux des Femmes (Paris) 1985, Alle Meine Sonne 1986, Giulio Cesare 1986, Alte Zeiten 1988, Koenig Roger 1988, Geburtstag der Infantin 1989, Regina dei Insort 1989, Il Presidente (Rome, Florence) 1994, Death and the Maiden (Poznań and Berlin) 1995, Il Re Pescatore (San Miniatò) 1996, l'uomo che vide (San Miniatò Borgione) 1998, Herodias et Salomé 1998. *Publications:* Nowele Filmowe (short feature films) 1976, Scenariusze Filmowe (film scripts) 1978, Un rigorista nella fortezza assediata 1982, Scenariusze Filmowe (film scripts) II, III 1986, IV 1998, The Time to Die (autobiog.) 1997, Weekend Stories 1997. *Leisure interest:* travel. *Address:* ul. Kaniowska 114, 01-529 Warsaw, Poland; 8 Rue Richepance, Paris 75001, France. *Telephone:* 392556 (Warsaw); 42.97.59.00 (Paris).

ZAPASIEWICZ, Zbigniew; Polish actor; b. 13 Sept. 1934; m.; ed. State Higher Theatre School (PWST), Warsaw; with Współczesny Theatre 1993–; lecturer State Higher Theatre School, Warsaw 1959–, Dean Faculty of Directing 1980–83; over 150 theatre roles. *Film roles include:* Barwy ochronne, Bez znieczulenia, Ziemia obiecana, Matka Królów, Ocalenie. *Address:* Teatr Współczesny, ul. Mokotowska 13, Warsaw, Poland.

ZARB, Frank Gustav, M.B.A.; American government official; b. 17 Feb. 1935, New York; s. of Gustave and Rosemary (née Antinora) Zarb; m. Patricia Koster 1957; one s. one d.; ed. Hofstra Univ.; Graduate trainee, Cities Service Oil Co. 1957–62; Gen. Partner, Goodbody & Co. 1962–69; Exec. Vice-Pres., CBWL-Hayden Stone 1969–71; Asst. Sec., U.S. Dept. of Labor 1971–72; Exec. Vice-Pres. Hayden Stone 1972–73, 1977; Assoc. Dir. Exec. Office of the Pres., Office of Man. and Budget 1973–74; Admin., Fed. Energy Admin. 1974–77; Asst. to the Pres. for Energy Affairs 1976; Gen. Partner Lazard Frères 1977–88; Chair. and C.E.O. Smith Barney, Harris Upham 1988–93, Smith Barney Shearson 1993; Pres., C.E.O. Nat. Asscn. of Securities Dealers 1997–; Dir. Securities Investor Protection Corpn. 1988; Vice-Chair. Group Chief Exec. Travelers Inc. 1993–94; Chair. Pres. CEO Alexander & Alexander Services Inc., New York 1994–97; Bd. Dirs. CS First Boston Inc., Council on Foreign Relations; Chair. Bd. of Trustees, Hofstra Univ.; mem. U.S. Presidential Advisory Cttee. on Fed. Pay, U.S. Investment Policy Advisory Cttee.; mem. Bd. of Trustees Gerald R. Ford Foundation; Distinguished Scholar Award, Hofstra Univ. *Publications:* The Stockmarket Handbook 1969, Handbook of Financial Markets 1981, The Municipal Bond Handbook.

ZARE, Richard Neil, B.A., PH.D.; American professor of chemistry; b. 19 Nov. 1939, Cleveland, Ohio; s. of Milton Zare and Dorothy Sylvia (Amdur) Zare; m. Susan Leigh Shively 1963; three d.; ed. Harvard Univ., Univ. of California, Berkeley; Postdoctoral Research Assoc., Jt. Inst. for Lab. Astrophysics, Univ. of Colo. 1964–65, Asst. Prof., Dept. of Physics and Astrophysics 1966–68, Assoc. Prof. 1968–69; Asst. Prof., Dept. of Chem. M.I.T. 1965–66; Prof. of Chem., Columbia Univ. 1969–77, Higgins Prof. of Natural Science 1975–77; Prof. of Chem., Stanford Univ. 1977– (Marguerite Blake Wilbur Prof. 1987–), Shell Distinguished Prof. of Chem. 1980–85, Fellow 1984–86, Prof. of Physics 1992–; Christensen Fellow, St. Catherine's Coll., Oxford 1982; Chair. Nat. Science Foundation Advisory Panel (Chem. Div.) 1980–82, Div. of Chemical Physics, American Physical Soc. 1985–86, N.A.S. Panel on Science and Tech. Centers 1987; Chair. Nat. Research Council's Comm. on Physical Sciences, Math., and Applications 1992–95, Nat. Science Bd. 1996–; mem. Nat. Research Council's Cttee. on Atomic and Molecular Science 1983–85, Directed Energy Weapons Study Panel of American Physical Soc. 1985–87, Govt.-Univ.-Ind. Roundtable of N.A.S. 1989–, Nat. Science Bd. 1992–; Chair. Bd. of Dirs. Annual Reviews Inc. 1995–; Ed. Chemical Physics Letters 1982–85; mem. Editorial Advisory Bd. Chemical Physics, Journal of Molecular Spectroscopy, Annual Reviews, Molecular Physics, Cambridge Univ. Press; mem. N.A.S. 1976– (mem. Council 1995–), American Chemical Soc., American Acad. of Arts and Sciences, American Philosophical Soc., Chemical Soc. (London); Fellow A.A.A.S., American Physical Soc., Int. Advisory Bd., Optical Soc. of America 1994–; more than 60 distinguished lecturerships; Hon. D.Sc. (Ariz.) 1990; numerous honours and awards, including Nat. Medal of Science 1983, Irving Langmuir Prize of the American Physical Soc. 1985, Kirkwood Award Medal (Yale Univ.) 1986, Willard Gibbs Medal (A.C.S.) 1990, Peter Debye Award (A.C.S.) 1991, N.A.S. Award in Chemical Sciences 1991, Havey Prize 1993, Dannie-Heineman Preis 1993, California Scientist of the Year 1997, Eastern Analytical Symposium Award 1997, NASA Exceptional Scientific Achievement Award 1997, A.C.S. Award in Analytical Chem. 1998. *Publications:* Angular Momentum 1988, Laser Experiments for Beginners 1995; over 550 research articles. *Leisure interests:* chess, cooking, music, theatre. *Address:* Department of Chemistry, Stanford University, Stanford, CA 94305-5080, U.S.A. *Telephone:* (650) 723-3062. *Fax:* (650) 725-0259.

ZASLAVSKAYA, Tatiana Ivanovna, D.ECON.SC.; Russian economist; b. 9 Sept. 1927, Kiev; ed. Moscow Univ.; research at Inst. of Econs. of Acad. of Sciences; mem. CPSU 1954–90; mem. Inst. of Econs. and Org. of Industrial Eng. in Siberian Div. of U.S.S.R. (now Russian) Acad. of Sciences 1963–87; Corresp. mem. U.S.S.R. (now Russian) Acad. of Sciences 1968–, mem. 1981–; Dir. Public Opinion Research Centre, Moscow 1988–91, Head of Dept. 1992–; Pres. of Interdisciplinary Academic Center for Social Sciences (Inter Center), Moscow 1993–; mem. All-Union (now Russian) Agricultural Acad. 1988, Council Int. Fund for Survival and Devt. of Humanity 1988; Pres. Sociological Asscn. of U.S.S.R. (now Russia) 1989–91; U.S.S.R. People's Deputy 1989–91; mem. Pres.'s Consulting Council 1991–; mem. Comm. for Labour, Prices and Social Policy; Hon. mem. Polish Acad. of Sciences; several hon. degrees. *Publications include:* The Principle of Material Interest and Wage-Earning on Soviet Kolkhozes 1958, Contemporary Economics of Kolkhozes 1960, Labour Division on the Kolkhoz 1966, The Migration of the Rural Population in the U.S.S.R. 1970, A Voice of Reform 1989, The Second Socialist Revolution 1991. *Address:* InterCenter C. 282, Vernadskogo prospekt, Moscow, Russia. *Telephone:* 938-21-12.

ZÁTOPEK, Emil; Czech athlete (retd.); b. 19 Sept. 1922, Kopřivnice, Nový Jičín dist.; s. of František Zatopek and Anežka Zátopková; m. Dana Zátopková (Olympic javelin champion, 1952) 1948; ed. Mil. Acad. Hranice; mem. Czechoslovak People's Army 1945–70; stripped of rank of Col. after Soviet-led occupation of Czechoslovakia 1968, rank restored 1990; with Czechoslovak Physical Training Asscn. 1970; 10,000 metres gold medal, 5,000 metres silver medal, Olympic Games, London 1948; 5,000 metres, 10,000 metres and marathon gold medals, Olympic Games, Helsinki 1952; first in 5,000 and 10,000 metres, European Championships 1950; first in 10,000 metres, European Championships 1954; set 18 world records at 5,000 and 10,000 metres, 20, 25 and 30 km., 6, 10 and 15 miles and the one-hour race 1949–55; Meritorious Master of Sports 1948, Order of the Republic 1953, Miroslav Tyrš Medal 1982. *Publications:* My Training and Races 1955, As Told by Dana and Emil 1962. *Leisure interests:* garden, philosophy. *Address:* Nad Kázankou 3, 17100 Prague 7, Czech Republic. *Telephone:* 840 898.

ZATULIN, Konstantin Fedorovich; Russian businessman and economist; b. 7 Sept. 1958, Batumi; m.; one d.; ed. Moscow State Univ.; functionary Cen. Komsomol Cttee. 1988–89; Dir.-Gen. Int. Asscn. of Heads of Enterprises

1989; one of founders Moscow Stock Exchange; Chair. Bd. of Co.-Rostok; Dir.-Gen. Int. Asscn. of leaders of factories 1989–; Pres. Moscow Exchange Union 1992–; mem. Bd. Russian Party of Unity and Consent 1993–94; Chair. Businessman for New Russia Union 1993–; Chair. Cttee. on C.I.S. affairs and connections with compatriots 1994–; mem. State Duma (Parl.) 1993–95; mem. Govt. Comm. on Compatriots Abroad 1994–; Chair. Co-ordination Bd., Employers for New Russia Movt. 1995–; Dir. Inst. for Problems of Diaspora and Integration 1996–; Chair. Fund for Devt. of Econ. Reforms. *Address:* Employers for New Russia, Varvarka 11, 103017 Moscow, Russia. *Telephone:* 206-50-80.

ZAVALA, Silvio, D. EN D.; Mexican historian; b. 7 Feb. 1909, Mérida, Yucatán; s. of Arturo Zavala and Mercedes Vallado; m. Huguette Joris 1951; one s. three d.; ed. Univ. del Sureste, Univ. Nacional Autónoma de México and Univ. Central de Madrid, Spain; Centre of Historical Studies, Madrid 1933–36; Sec. Nat. Museum of Mexico 1937–38; founder and dir. Revista de Historia de América (review of Pan-American Inst. of Geography and History) 1938–65; Pres. Historical Comm. of Pan-American Inst. of Geography and History 1946–65; mem. Colegio de México 1940, Pres. 1963–66, Emer. Prof. 1981–; Dir. Nat. Museum of History, Chapultepec 1946–54; life mem. El Colegio Nacional 1947; Visiting Prof. Univ. de Puerto Rico 1945, Univ. de la Habana 1946; Prof. of History of Social Insts. of America, Univ. Nacional Autónoma de México; Visiting Prof. Mexico City Coll.; Prof. Smith Coll., Mexico; Chief, Section of Educ., Science and Culture of UN 1947; Visiting Lecturer Harvard 1953, Visiting Prof. Washington (Seattle) and Ghent 1956; Perm. del. to UNESCO 1956–62, mem. Exec. Council 1960–66, Vice-Pres. 1962–64; Vice-Pres. Int. Council of Human Sciences and Philosophy 1959–65, Pres. 1965–71; Amb. to France 1966–75; Hon. Pres. Cttee. for 450th Anniversary of Foundation of Mérida de Yucatán; Hon. Pres. 48th Int. Congress of Americanists 1994; mem. Exec. Council, Int. Cttee for Historical Sciences; mem. Nat. Acad. of History and Geography, Mexican Acad. of History 1946, Mexican Acad. of Language 1976; corresp. mem. numerous Acads. of History, etc.; Hon. mem. Historical Asscn. England 1956, Royal Historical Soc., London 1957, American Historical Asscn., Washington, D.C. 1959, Academia Portuguesa da História 1987; Prof. h.c. Colegio de San Nicolás, Morelia, Inst. of Latin American Studies Univ. of Texas; Hon. D.Litt. (Columbia) 1954, (Ghent) 1956, (Toulouse) 1965, (Montpellier) 1967, (Seville) 1990, (Mexico) 1996, (Colima) 1996; Nat. Literary Prize, History Div., Mexico 1969, History Prize, Acad. du Monde Latin, Paris 1974, Arch. C. Gerlach Prize, Panamerican Inst. of Geography and History 1986, Aristotle Medal, UNESCO 1989, Citizen's Merit Medal, Mexico 1991, medals from Universidad Complutense and Panamerican Inst. of Geography and History, El Escorial, Spain 1992, Príncipe de Asturias Prize in Social Sciences 1993, Aguirre Beltrán Medal, Veracruz 1996, Benito Juárez Medal, Sociedad Mexicana de Geografía y Estadística 1997; Grand Officier, Légion d'honneur 1973, Grand-Croix, Ordre nat. du Mérite 1975, Gran Cruz Orden Civil Alfonso X el Sabio 1983, Gran Cruz Orden Isabel la Católica 1997. *Publications:* Columbus' Discovery in Art, XIX and XX Centuries 1991, Bio-Bibliografía de S.Z. 1999, and many works on the Spanish colonization of America, Latin American history, New World history. *Address:* Montes Urales 310, Lomas de Chapultepec, Deleg. M. Hidalgo, México, D.F., 11000 Mexico. *Telephone:* 520 44 18; 520 93 17. *Fax:* 645 04 64.

ZAVALA BAQUERIZO, Jorge Enrique; Ecuadorean lawyer and politician; b. 13 May 1922, Guayaquil; s. of Oswaldo Zavala Arbaiza and Ana C. Baquerizo Germán de Zavala; m. Carolina Egas Núñez de Zavala; four s.; ed. Univ. de Guayaquil; Public Prosecutor, 2nd Criminal Tribunal of Guayas 1947; Prof. of Law, Univ. de Guayaquil; Provincial Counsellor Guayas 1956–58; Vice-Deputy of Guayas 1958–60; Pres. Guayaquil Coll. of Lawyers (twice); Constitutional Vice-Pres. of Republic of Ecuador 1968–72; Minister of Finance and Public Credit 1988–90; Pres. Acad. de Abogados de Guayaquil 1973–74, 1st Nat. Congress of Lawyers 1960, Nat. Comm. of Human Rights, XXV Curso Int. de Criminología; Vice-Pres. various legal confs.; Del. of Sociedad Int. de Criminología; mem. Int. Lawyers' Comm., Int. Lawyers' Asscn., American Bar Asscn., American Judicature Soc., Int. Asscn. of Penal Law, Exec. Cttee. of World Habeas Corpus; Premio Código Civil 1940, Premio Código Penal 1944; Cotenta Prize for university work, Premio al Mérito Científico of Municipality of Guayaquil 1966, 1976; Orden al Mérito en el Grado de Gran Cruz. *Publications:* El Proceso Penal Ecuatoriano, Los Delitos contra la Propiedad, La Pena, Delitos contra la Fe Pública, La Victimiología, El Delito de Cheque sin Provisión de Fondos, and other books on legal topics.

ZAVARZIN, Lieut.-Gen., Victor Mikhailovich; Russian army officer; b. 28 Nov. 1948, Kursk Region; ed. Ordzhonikidze Higher Gen. Army School, Frunze Mil. Acad., Acad. of Gen. Staff; commdg. posts in Middle Asia Command 1970–78; Head of Staff of Div. Far E. Command 1981–85; Head of Staff, Deputy Commd., Commdr. of Div., Commdr. Training Cen. Carpathy Command 1985–90; Commdr. United Russian-Turkmen Armed Force in Turkmenistan 1993–94; Commdr. Forces in Tajikistan 1996–97; Mil. Rep. of Russia to NATO Headquarters, Brussels Nov. 1997–. *Address:* NATO, 1110 Brussels, Belgium.

ZAVGAYEV, Doku Gapurovich, CAND. ECON.; Chechen politician; b. 22 Dec. 1940; ed. Agric. Inst. Acad. of Social Sciences Cen. Cttee. CPSU; mem. CPSU 1966–91; teacher of elementary school, mechanic, engineer of sovkhoz, man. Regional Union Selkhoztechnika, Dir. wine sovkhoz Znamensky, Chair. Nadtechya Regional Exec. Cttee. 1958–72; Chief Repub. Union of sovkhozes 1972–75; Minister of Agric. of Checheno-Ingush S.S.R. 1975–77; head of div., Second Sec. Checheno-Ingush Regional CP Cttee. 1977–89; First Sec. Repub. CP Cttee. 1989–91; Chair. Supreme Soviet of Checheno-Ingush Autonomous S.S.R. 1990–91 (overthrown by D. Dudaev 1991), People's Deputy of R.S.F.S.R. 1990–91; in Admin. of Russian Govt. 1992–95; elected Pres. of Chechen Repub. 1995–96; People's Deputy of Checheno-Ingush Repub. 1990–91; mem. Cen. CPSU Cttee. 1990–91; Russian Amb. to Tanzania 1997–. *Address:* Embassy of Russia, Plot No. 73, Kenyatta Drive, Dar es Salaam, P.O. Box 1905, Tanzania. *Telephone:* 51-361-14.

ZAWADA, Andrzej; Polish mountaineer and geophysicist; b. 16 July 1928, Olsztyn; m.; Anna Milewska; ed.: Univ. of Warsaw, Acad. of Physical Culture, Cracow; mem. staff Inst. of Geophysics, Polish Acad. of Science (PAN) 1955–93. *Expeditions include:* Polish Geophysical Vietnam and Spitsbergen Expedition 1957, 1958, leader Polish Expedition to Pamir 1970, leader Polish Expedition to Kunyang-Chhish, Karakoram 1971, leader Polish Winter Expedition to Noshaq, Hindu Kush 1972/73, leader Polish Winter Expedition to Lhotse, Himalayas 1974, Chief Polish Seismological Spitsbergen Expedition 1976, leader Int. British–Polish Expedition to Hindu Kush 1977, leader Polish Winter Expedition to Mount Everest, Himalayas 1979–80, Chief Polish Seismological Abu Simbel Expedition, Egypt 1981, leader First Winter Reconnaissance to Baltoro Glacier, Karakoram 1983, leader Int. Canadian-Polish Winter Expedition to Cho-Oyu, Himalayas 1984/85, leader Int. Canadian–British–Polish Expedition to K2, Karakoram 1987/88, vice-leader Int. Belgian–Polish Winter Expedition to Everest and Lhotse, Himalayas 1988/89, leader two Polish Winter Expeditions to Nanga Parbat 1996/97, 1997/98. Hon. mem. PZA (Polish Alpine Club), Hon. mem. The Alpine Club (Great Britain), Hon. mem. G.H.M. (Groupe Haut Montagne—France); mem. The Explorers Club; 4 gold medals for mountain-climbing successes. *Publications:* Last Attack on Kunyang-Chhish 1973, History of Polish Alpinism 1985; numerous articles in alpine journals. *Leisure interests:* photography, skiing, water skiing. *Address:* Polski Związek Alpinizmu, ul. E. Ciołka 17, 01-445 Warsaw, Poland. *Telephone:* (22) 36-36-90.

ZAWADZKI, Włodzimierz, PH.D.; Polish scientist; b. 4 Jan. 1939, Warsaw; ed. Warsaw Univ.; Prof. 1985; scientific worker and Prof. Inst. of Physics Polish Acad. of Sciences (PAN) 1961–; with Massachusetts Inst. of Tech., Cambridge, U.S.A. 1965–67, Ecole Normale Supérieure, Paris 1974; Visiting Prof. Linz Univ. 1978, North Texas State Univ. 1980, Tech. Univ., Munich 1981, Innsbruck Univ. 1983, Univ. Sc. et Tech. du Languedoc Montpellier 1984; mem. Polish Physical Soc.; Annual Prize of Polish Science 1973, Maria Sklodowska-Curie Award 1977, State Prize (1st degree, collective) 1978, Mich. Univ. Award 1995, Marian Smoluchowski Medal 1997. *Publications:* over 170 works on theory of semiconductors; also novels and poetry. *Leisure interests:* literature, music, sports, skiing, tennis, basketball. *Address:* al. J. Ch. Szucha 11 m. 26, 00-580 Warsaw, Poland. *Telephone:* (22) 41 02 85.

ZAWINUL, Josef Erich; Austrian jazz musician; b. 7 July 1932, Vienna; s. of Josef and Maria Zawinul; m. Maxine Byars 1964; three s.; ed. Grammar School, Real Gymnasium, Vienna Conservatoire, studied piano under Prof. Valerie Zschörner in Vienna, under Raymond Lewental in New York; studied and played classical, folk and jazz music since early childhood; started as professional musician playing with leading Austrian bands and orchestras throughout Europe 1947–59; moved to U.S.A. 1959; pianist for Dinah Washington (jazz singer) and Joe Williams 1959–61; joined Julian Cannonball Adderley's band, writing songs including Mercy, Mercy, Mercy, and playing in numerous recordings 1961–69; wrote and played on 5 albums of Miles Davis (q.v.) including album in electric jazz In a Silent Way, and Bitches Brew; teamed with Wayne Shorter to form own band Weather Report, working as producer, main composer, and keyboard instrumentalist 1970; Grammy Awards for composition of Mercy, Mercy Mercy 1967, In a Silent Way 1967, Birdland (Best Instrumental Composition) 1977; Weather Report named No. 1 Jazz Band 1972–78, 5 of the 8 Weather Report albums named Jazz Albums of the Year (Downbeat Magazine), No. 1. Synthesizer Player 4 consecutive years, No. 1 Composer, Weather Report No. 1 Group, (Jazz Forum). *Recordings include:* The Rise and Fall of the Third Stream, Zawinul 1969, Weather Report 1971, I Sing the Body Electric 1972, Sweetnighter 1973, Mysterious Traveller 1974, Tale Spinning 1975, Black Market 1976, Heavy Weather 1977, Mr. Gone 1978, Night Passage 1980, Lost Tribes 1992, Amen 1992, Symphony: Stories of the Danube. *Leisure interests:* boxing, soccer, swimming, philosophy. *Address:* International Music Network, 2 Main Street, # F14, Gloucester, MA 01930, U.S.A.

ZEA AGUILAR, Leopoldo, PH.D.; Mexican writer and university professor; b. 30 June 1912, Mexico; s. of Leopoldo Zea and Luz Aguilar; m. 1st Elena Prado Vertiz 1943 (divorced); two s. four d.; m. 2nd María Elena Rodríguez Ozan 1982; Ed. review Tierra Nueva 1940; Prof. Escuela Nacional Preparatoria 1942–47; Prof. Escuela Normal de Maestros 1944–45; Prof. Faculty of Philosophy and Letters, Univ. Nacional Autónoma de México 1944; mem. El Colegio de México 1940; Pres., Cttee. for the History of Ideas, Panamerican Inst. of Geography and History; Chief of Dept. of Univ. Studies, Sec. of Public Educ. 1953–54; research work, 1954–; mem. Soc. Européenne de Culture 1953–; Dir.-Gen. of Cultural Relations Foreign Office; Vice-Pres. Historical Comm. of Pan American Inst. of Geography and History 1961–, Dir. of Faculty of Philosophy and Letters 1966–70, Prof. Emer. 1971; Dir.-Gen. of Cultural Broadcasting 1970–; Co-ordinator, Co-ordination and Diffusion Cen. for Latin American Studies –1994, Univ. Program 1995–; Dr. h.c. (Univ. of Paris X) 1984, (Moscow) 1984, (Univ. de la Repub., Uruguay) 1985, (Univ. Nacional Autónoma, Mexico) 1988, (Univ. Fernando Villareal del

Perú) 1990; Nat. Prize for Sciences and Arts 1980, decorations from Italy, France, Peru, Yugoslavia, Venezuela, Argentina and Spain. *Publications:* El Positivismo en México 1943, Apogeo y Decadencia del Positivismo en México 1944, Ensayos sobre Filosofía en la Historia 1948, Dos Etapas del Pensamiento en Hispanoamérica 1949, La Filosofía como Compromiso 1952, América como Conciencia 1952, Conciencia y posibilidad del Mexicano 1952, El Occidente y la Conciencia de México 1953, La Conciencia del Hombre en la Filosofía 1952, América en la conciencia de Europa 1955, La Filosofía en México 1955, Esquema para una Historia de las ideas en América 1956, Del Liberalismo a la Revolución en la Educación Mexicana 1956, América en la Historia 1957, La Cultura y el Hombre de nuestros Días 1959, Latinoamérica y el Mundo 1960, Ensayos sobre México y Latinoamérica 1960, Democracias y Dictaduras en Latinoamérica 1960, Amerique Latina e la Culture Occidentalie 1961, El Pensamiento Latino-americano 1963, Latinoamérica en la Formación de nuestro tiempo 1965, Antología de la Filosofía Americana Contemporánea 1968, Latin America and the World 1969, Dependencia y Liberación en la Cultura Latinoamericana 1974, Cultura y Filosofía en Latinoamérica 1976, Dialéctica de la Conciencia Americana 1976, Latinoamérica Tercer Mundo 1977, Filosofía de la Historia Americana 1978, Simon Bolivar 1980, Latinoamérica en la Encrucijada de la Historia 1980, Sentido de la Difusion Cultural Latinoamérica 1981, Filosofía de lo Americano 1983, Discurso desde la Marginación y la Barbarie 1988, 500 Años Después. Descubriemento e Identidad Latinoamericana 1990, L'Amérique Latine face à l'histoire 1991. *Leisure interests:* music, art. *Address:* Torre I de Humanidades, 2° piso, Ciudad Universitaria, Mexico, D.F. 03410 (Office); Cerrada de las Margaritas 25, Col. Florida, 01030 México D.F., Mexico (Home). *Telephone:* 622-19-02 (Office); 662-03-77 (Home). *Fax:* 616-25-15.

ZEAYEN, Yusuf; Syrian politician and physician; b. 1931; ed. Univ. of Damascus; Minister of Agrarian Reform 1963; mem. Presidential Council 1964–65; Prime Minister Sept.-Dec. 1965, 1966–68; Baath Party. *Address:* c/o Baath Party, Damascus, Syrian Arab Republic.

ZECCHINI, Salvatore, M.B.A.; Italian lawyer and government official; b. 17 Nov. 1943, Palermo; m. Eliana de Leva 1971; one s. one d.; ed. Columbia Univ. and Univ. of Pennsylvania, U.S.A.; economist, Research Dept. Banca d'Italia, Dir. Research Dept. 1972–81, Dir. 1981–84; Adviser to Govt. of Italy 1978–84; Exec. Dir. IMF 1984–89; Special Counsellor, OECD 1989–90, Asst. Sec.-Gen. 1990–96, Deputy Sec.-Gen. 1996–; Dir. Centre for Co-operation of Economies in Transition 1990–96; Prof. of Int. Econ. Policy, Univ. of Rome 1997–; Econ. Adviser to Minister of Finance 1997–; Dir. Public Investment Evaluation Centre 1997–98. *Publications:* The Transition to a Market Economy (co-ed.) 1991, Lessons from The Economic Transition (ed.) 1996, articles in professional journals and books on econs. and int. finance. *Leisure interests:* history, travel, hiking. *Address:* Ministry of the Treasury and Budget, Via Nerva 1, 00187 Rome, Italy.

ZEDILLO PONCE de LEÓN, Ernesto, D.ECON.; Mexican politician and economist; b. 27 April 1951, Mexico City; m. Nilda Núñez; five c.; ed. Instituto Nacional Politécnico, Bradford, Colorado and Yale Univs.; joined Partido Revolucionario Institucional (PRI) 1971, with Instituto de Estudios Políticos, Económicos y Sociales (Iepes) (affil. to PRI); econ. researcher Dirección Gen. de Programación Económica y Social; Deputy Man. of Finance and Econ. Research, Banco de Mexico (BANXICO), a Dir. in charge of the bank's Ficorca scheme, adviser to Bd. of Dirs.; teacher Colegio de Mexico; Deputy Sec. for Planning and the Budget 1987–88 (f. Programa Nacional de Solidaridad), Sec. 1988–92, Sec. of Public Educ. 1992–93; Pres. of Mexico 1994–; campaign man. for the late Luis Donaldo Colosio (fmr. presidential cand.) 1993. *Address:* Office of the President, Los Pinos, Puerta 1, Col. San Miguel, Chapultepec 11850, México, D.F.; Partido Revolucionario Institucional Insurges Norte 61, 06350 México D.F., Mexico.

ZEFFIRELLI, G. Franco (Corsi); Italian theatrical, opera and film producer and designer; b. 12 Feb. 1923, Florence; ed. Liceo Artistico, Florence and School of Agriculture, Florence; designer Univ. Productions, Florence; actor Morelli Stoppa Co.; collaborated with Salvador Dali on sets for As You Like It 1948; designed sets for A Streetcar Named Desire, Troilus and Cressida, Three Sisters; producer and designer of numerous operas at La Scala, Milan 1952–, and worldwide; cand. Forza Italia 1994–; Prix des Nations 1976. *Operas include:* Lucia di Lammermoor, Cavalleria Rusticana, Pagliacci (Covent Garden) 1959, 1973, Falstaff (Covent Garden) 1961, L'elisir d'amore (Glyndebourne) 1961, Don Giovanni, Alcina (Covent Garden) 1962, Tosca, Rigoletto (Covent Garden) 1964, 1966, 1973, (Metropolitan, New York) 1985, Don Giovanni (Staatsoper-Wien) 1972, (Metropolitan, New York) 1990, Otello (Metropolitan, New York) 1972, Antony and Cleopatra (Metropolitan, New York) 1973, Otello (La Scala) 1976, La Bohème (Metropolitan, New York) 1981, Turandot (La Scala) 1983, 1985, (Metropolitan, New York) 1987, Don Carlos 1992, Carmen 1996. *Theatre:* Romeo and Juliet (Old Vic, London) 1960, Othello (Stratford) 1961, Amleto (Nat. Theatre, London) 1964, After the Fall (Rome) 1964, Who's Afraid of Virginia Woolf (Paris) 1964, (Milan) 1965, La Lupa (Rome) 1965, Much Ado About Nothing (Nat. Theatre, London) 1966, Black Comedy (Rome) 1967, A Delicate Balance (Rome) 1967, Saturday, Sunday, Monday (Nat. Theatre, London) 1973, Filumena (Lyric, London) 1977, Six Characters in Search of an Author (London) 1992. *Films:* The Taming of the Shrew 1966, Florence, Days of Destruction 1966, Romeo and Juliet 1967, Brother Sun and Sister Moon 1973, Jesus of Nazareth 1977, The Champ 1979, Endless Love 1981, La Traviata 1983, Cavalleria Rusticana 1983, Otello 1986, The Young Toscanini 1987, Hamlet 1990, Sparrow 1994, Jane Eyre 1995, Tea With Mussolini 1998. *Ballet:* Swan Lake 1985; produced Beethoven's Missa Solemnis, San Pietro, Rome 1971. *Publication:* Zeffirelli by Zeffirelli (autobiog.) 1986. *Fax:* (39-6) 718.4213.

ZEIDLER, Eberhard Heinrich, O.C., CAND. ARCH., DIPL.ING.; Canadian architect; b. 11 Jan. 1926, Braunsdorf, Germany; s. of Paul Zeidler and Dorothea Dabbert; m. Phyllis Jane Abbott 1957; one s. three d.; ed. Bauhaus Weimar and Univ. Fridericiana, Karlsruhe Technische Hochschule; designer, Prof. Egon Eiermann, Karlsruhe 1949–50; Assoc. with Prof. Emanuel Lindner, Osnabrück 1950–51; Assoc.-in-Charge of Design, W. & W. R. L. Blackwell & Craig, Peterborough 1951–54; partner, Blackwell, Craig & Zeidler Architects, Peterborough and Toronto 1954–57, Craig & Zeidler Architects, Peterborough and Toronto 1957–61, Craig, Zeidler & Strong, Peterborough and Toronto 1961–75, Zeidler Partnership/Architects, Toronto 1975–80, Zeidler Roberts Partnership/Architects, Toronto 1980–; Adjunct Prof. Univ. of Toronto 1983–; Hon. Fellow, American Inst. of Architects; Gold Medal, Royal Architectural Inst. of Canada 1986; more than 100 nat. and int. awards. *Publications:* Healing the Hospital 1974, Multi-use Architecture in the Urban Context 1983. *Leisure interests:* skiing, tennis. *Address:* Zeidler Roberts Partnership/Architects, 315 Queen Street West, Toronto, Ont., M5V 2X2, Canada. *Telephone:* (416) 596-8300. *Fax:* (416) 596-1408.

ZEIGERMAN, Dror, PH.D.; Israeli diplomatist and politician; b. 14 May 1948; s. of Itzchak Zeigerman; m. Asi Sherf; two s. one d.; ed. Hebrew Univ., Jerusalem, George Washington Univ., U.S.A.; mil. service 1966–69; Chair. Students' Union, Hebrew Univ., Jerusalem 1969–70; Sec. Israeli Liberal Party, Jerusalem Br. 1970–73; Gen. Sec. Zionist Council in Israel; Head Students' Dept., Jewish Agency and World Zionist Org. 1977–81; Likud Party mem. Knesset (Parl.), mem. Cttees. on Foreign Relations and Security, Immigration and Absorption, Educ. 1981–84; Head Students' Dept., Zionist Org. in Israel, Special Adviser on Student and Youth Matters to Head of Exec. Cttee. and Zionist Org. 1987–88; Gen. Man. Israel School of Tourism; Consul-Gen. of Israel, Toronto, Canada 1992–95; Amb. to U.K. 1998–. *Leisure interest:* golf. *Address:* Israeli Embassy, 2 Palace Green, London, W8 4QB, England. *Telephone:* 0171-957 9500. *Fax:* 0171-957 9555.

ZELADA DE ANDRES MORENO, Fermín; Spanish banker and lawyer; b. 27 Nov. 1912, La Coruña; m. María del Carmen Jurado y Herrera; six s. three d.; ed. Univs. of Santiago de Compostela, Paris and Milan; Prof. Univ. of Santiago de Compostela, Int. Univ. of Santander; joined Banco Exterior de España as Head of Legal Advisory Office 1948, Gen. Sec. 1958, Chair. Banco Exterior de España 1977–83, Hon. Chair. 1983–; nominated mem. Senate 1977–78. *Address:* c/o Banco de España, Alcalá 50, 28014 Madrid, Spain.

ŻELICHOWSKI, Stanisław; Polish politician; b. 9 April 1944, Księżostany, Zamość Prov.; m.; two c.; ed. Dept. of Forestry, Main School of Farming, Warsaw; began career in Presidium of Dist. People's Council, Ostrołęka; lecturer, Ciechanów Forest Inspectorate 1969; Forest Insp. Dwukoły Forest Inspectorate 1974; mem. Nat. Forestry Council; mem. United Peasants' Party (ZSL) 1970–89; mem. Tribunal of State 1985–89; mem. Main Exec. Cttee. Polish Peasants' Party (PSL) and Pres. Prov. Bd. of PSL, Ciechanów 1990–; Deputy to Sejm (Parl.) 1985–89, 1991–; Minister of Environmental Protection, Natural Resources and Forestry 1993–97. *Address:* Sejm RP, ul. Wiejska 4/6/8, 00-902 Warsaw, Poland. *Telephone:* (22) 694 25 00.

ZELNICK, Strauss, J.D., M.B.A.; American business executive; b. 26 June 1957, Boston; s. of Allan Zelnick and Elsa Lee Strauss; m. Wendy Belzberg 1990; two s.; ed. Wesleyan and Harvard Univs.; called to Bar N.Y. 1984; Dir. Int. TV Columbia Pictures Int. Corpn. 1983–85, Vice-Pres. Int. TV 1985–86; Sr. Vice-Pres. Corp. Devt. Vestron Inc. 1986–87, Exec. Vice-Pres. 1987, Pres., C.O.O. 1988–89; Pres., C.O.O. Twentieth Century Fox 1989–93; Pres., C.E.O. Crystal Dynamics 1993–95; Pres., C.E.O. BMG Entertainment N. America 1995–; Trustee Wesleyan Univ. 1992–. *Leisure interests:* squash, sailing, skiing. *Address:* BMG Entertainment North America, 1540 Broadway, New York, NY 10036, U.S.A.

ZEMAN, Miloš; Czech politician; b. 29 Jan. 1944, Kolín; m. 2nd Ivana Bednarčíková; one s. one d.; ed. School of Econs., Prague; teacher, School of Econs., Prague 1969–70; joined CP of Czechoslovakia 1968; expelled 1970; researcher Prognostic Inst., Prague 1971–89; Chair. Czech Social Democratic Party 1993–; Chair. of Parl. of Czech Repub. 1996–98; mem. Cttee. of Socialist Int. 1997–; Prime Minister of Czech Repub. 1998–; Chair. Cttee. for Protection of Econ. Interests of Czech Repub., Cttee. for Handicapped People 1998–. *Publications:* Confession of a Former Prognosis Maker with J. Bauer 1995, Our Post-Totalitarian Crisis and Its Potential Cure 1992, many articles on econs. in papers and magazines. *Leisure interests:* hiking, cross-country skiing, science fiction, chess. *Address:* Česká strana sociálně demokratická, Hybernská 7, Prague 1, Czech Republic (Office). *Telephone:* 02-2421 9911 (Office).

ZEMAN, Zbyněk Anthony Bohuslav, M.A., D.PHIL.; British historian and writer; b. 18 Oct. 1928, Prague, Czechoslovakia; s. of Jaroslav Zeman and Růžena Zeman; m. Sarah Anthea Collins 1956 (died 1998); two s. one d.; ed. London and Oxford Univs.; Asst. Ed. Foreign Office (Documents on German Foreign Policy) 1957–58; Research Fellow St. Antony's Coll., Oxford 1958–61; mem. ed. staff The Economist 1959–62; Lecturer in Modern History Univ. of St. Andrews 1963–70; Head of Research Amnesty Int. 1970–73; Dir.

European Co-operation Research Group and East-West SPRL 1974–76; Prof. of Cen. and S.E. European Studies Lancaster Univ. 1976–82, Dir. Comenius Centre 1976–82, School of European Studies 1976–82; Research Prof. in European History, Oxford Univ. 1982–96, Emer. Prof. 1996–; Professorial Fellow St. Edmund Hall, Oxford 1983–96; mem. Bd. Inst. of Grad. Studies, Univ. of Prague 1996–; Visiting Prof., Univ. of Prague 1990–91. *Publications:* Germany and the Revolution in Russia 1915–1918 (Ed.) 1958, The Break-up of the Habsburg Empire 1914–1918 1961, Nazi Propaganda 1964, (co-author) The Merchant of Revolution, A Life of Alexander Helphand (Parvus) 1965, Prague Spring 1969, A Diplomatic History of the First World War 1971, (jt. ed.) International Yearbook of East-West Trade 1975, The Masaryks 1976, (co-author) Comecon Oil and Gas 1977, Selling the War: Art and Propaganda in the Second World War 1978, Heckling Hitler: caricatures of the Third Reich 1984, Pursued by a Bear, The Making of Eastern Europe 1989 (revised and enlarged as The Making and Breaking of Communist Europe 1991), The Life of Edvard Beneš 1884–1948 1996, Czechoslovakia in Peace and War 1996. *Address:* Čínská 18, Prague 6, Czech Republic.

ZEMECKIS, Robert; American film director and writer; b. May 1952, Chicago; m. Mary Ellen Trainor; ed. Univ. of Southern Calif.; films include: I Wanna Hold Your Hand (co-screenplay writer) 1978, Romancing the Stone, Back to the Future (co-screenplay writer), II, III, Death Becomes Her (also co-producer), Trespass (co-screenplay writer), Forrest Gump, Who Framed Roger Rabbit?, Contact; several TV films. *Address:* c/o CAA, 9830 Wilshire Boulevard, Beverly Hills, CA 90212, U.S.A.

ZEN, E-An, PH.D.; American geologist; b. 31 May 1928, Beijing, People's Republic of China; s. of Hung-chun Zen and Sophia Heng-chih Chen Zen; ed. Cornell Univ., Harvard Univ.; went to U.S.A. 1946, naturalized U.S. Citizen 1963; Research Assoc. Fellow Woods Hole Oceanographic Inst. 1955–56, Research Assoc. 1956–58; Asst. Prof. Univ. of N.C. 1958–59; Geologist U.S. Geological Survey 1959–80, Research Geologist 1980–89; Adjunct Prof., Univ. of Md. 1990–; Visiting Assoc. Prof. Calif. Inst. of Technology 1962; Crosby Visiting Prof. M.I.T. 1973; Harry H. Hess Sr. Visiting Fellow Princeton Univ. 1981; Fellow Geological Soc. of America (mem. Council 1985–88, Vice-Pres. 1991, Pres. 1992), American Acad. of Arts and Sciences, A.A.A.S., Mineral Soc. of America, Council 1975–77, Pres. 1975–76; mem. Geological Soc. Washington (Pres. 1973); mem. N.A.S.; Arthur L. Day Medal, Geological Soc. of America 1986, Roebling Medal, Mineralogical Soc. of America 1991, Maj. John Coke Medal, Geological Soc. London 1992. *Publications:* about 190 scientific articles and monographs in professional journals. *Address:* Department of Geology, University of Maryland, College Park, MD 20742, U.S.A. *Telephone:* (301) 405-4081.

ZENAWI, Meles; Ethiopian politician and fmr. guerrilla fighter; leader of Ethiopian People's Revolutionary Democratic Front (EPRDF) which overthrew regime of Mengistu Haile Mariam (q.v.) 1991; Acting Head of State of Ethiopia May–June, Pres. 1991–95; Prime Minister 1995–. *Address:* Office of the Prime Minister, P.O. Box 1013, Addis Ababa, Ethiopia. *Telephone:* (1) 552044.

ZENDER, Hans; German composer and conductor; b. 22 Nov. 1936, Wiesbaden; s. of Dr. Franz and Marianne (née Fromm) Zender; m. Gertrud-Maria Achenbach 1962; studied composition and piano; conductor, Freiburg im Breisgau 1959–63; Chief Conductor, Bonn City Theatre 1964–68; Gen. Dir. of Music, Kiel 1969–72; Chief Conductor, Radio Symphony and Chamber Orchestras, Saarbrücken 1972–82; Gen. Dir. of Music (Philharmonia and City Opera), Hamburg 1984–87; Chief Conductor Radio Chamber Orchestra, Netherlands Broadcasting Corpn.; Prin. Guest Conductor Opéra Nat., Brussels 1987–90; Prof. of Composition, Frankfurt Musikhochschule 1988–; mem. Freie Akademie der Künste, Hamburg, Akademie der Künste, Berlin, Bayerische Akademie der Künste; numerous recordings. *Major works include:* Canto I–VIII 1965–96, Zeitströme 1974, Mujinokyo 1975, Litanei 1976, Lo-Shu I–VI 1977–89, Hölderlin Lesen (string quartet) 1979, Dialog mit Haydn 1982, Stephen Climax (opera) 1979–84, Don Quixote (opera) 1989–91, Schubert's Winterreise (for soloists, choir, large orchestra and live electronics) 1993–97. *Publication:* Happy New Ears (essays) 1991, Wir steigen niemals in den selben Fluss (essays) 1996. *Leisure interests:* literature, art. *Address:* Am Rosenheck, 65812 Bad Soden, Germany. *Fax:* 06174/930054.

ZENG PEIYAN; Chinese politician; b. Dec. 1938, Shaoxing City, Zhejiang Prov.; ed. Tsinghua Univ.; joined CCP 1978; Second then First Sec. Commercial Counsellor's Office, Embassy, U.S.A.; Dir. Gen. Office then Dir. Planning Dept. of Ministry of Electronics Industry; Vice-Minister of Electronics Industry 1988; alt. mem. 14th CCP Cen. Cttee. 1992–97; Vice-Minister State Planning Comm. and Vice-Sec.-Gen. Central Finance Leading Group 1993–98; Minister, State Devt. and Planning Comm. 1998–; mem. 15th CCP Cen. Cttee. 1997–. *Address:* State Development and Planning Commission, 38 Yuetan Nan Jie, Beijing, People's Republic of China.

ZENG QINGHONG; Chinese political strategist; s. of Zeng Shan; alt. mem. Cen. Cttee. 1992–, Politburo 1997–; now Chief Strategist to Pres. Jiang Zemin. *Address:* Central Committee of Chinese Communist Party, Beijing, China.

ZENG XIANLIN; Chinese government official; b. 1929, Anyue, Sichuan; Vice-Minister for State Planning Comm. 1986; Vice-Minister for Science and Tech. 1985–87, for State Planning Comm. 1986–87; Minister for Light Industry 1987–93; Vice-Chair. Finance and Econ. Cttee. of 9th NPC 1998–; alt. mem. 13th CCP Cen. Cttee. 1987–92; alt. mem. 14th CCP Cen. Cttee. 1992–97. *Address:* c/o Standing Committee of National People's Congress, Beijing, People's Republic of China.

ZENG YI; Chinese virologist and cancer research specialist; b. 8 March 1929, Guangdong Prov.; s. of Zeng Chin-yao and Chen Chai; m. Li Ze-lin 1953; one s. one d.; ed. Shanghai No. 1 Medical Coll.; Vice-Pres. Chinese Acad. of Preventative Medical Science 1989–; Deputy Dir. AIDS Prevention Dept. 1988–; special interests: tumor viruses, HIV. *Address:* Chinese Academy of Preventative Medicine, 10 Tiantan Xili, Beijing; Institute of Virology, 100 Ying Xin Jie, Beijing, People's Republic of China. *Telephone:* 338621.

ZENTMYER, George Aubrey, Jr., A.B., PH.D.; American professor of plant pathology; b. 9 Aug. 1913, Nebraska; s. of George Aubrey Zentmyer and Mary Strahorn Zentmyer; m. Dorothy Anne Dudley 1941; three d.; ed. Univ. of California; Asst. Forest Pathologist, U.S. Dept. of Agric., San Francisco 1937–40; Asst. Plant Pathologist Conn. Agric. Experimental Station, New Haven 1940–44; Asst. Plant Pathologist Univ. of Calif. 1944–62, Plant Pathologist and Prof. of Plant Pathology 1962–81, Prof. Emer. 1981–, Chair. Dept. of Plant Pathology 1968–73; Pres. American Phytopathological Soc. 1966, Fellow 1968; Pres. Pacific Div. A.A.A.S. 1975; Fellow Explorers Club Bd. of Dirs., American Phytopathology Soc. Foundation 1986– (Vice-Pres. 1991–), UCR Foundation Bd. of Dirs. 1993–94; Pres. Bd. of Dirs., Riverside Hospice 1984; Pres. Bd. of Dirs., UCR Friends of Botanic Gardens 1987–89; Fellow A.A.A.S., mem. Int. Soc. for Plant Pathology, N.A.S., and numerous socs. and cttees.; Assoc. Ed. Annual Review of Phytopathology 1971–; mem. Bd. of Dirs. Calif. Museum of Photography 1987–; Vice-Pres. Bd. of Dirs., Friends of Mission Inn 1990–91, Pres. 1991–93; Guggenheim Fellow, Australia 1964–65, NATO Sr. Science Fellow, England 1971; Award of Honour, Calif. Avocado Soc. 1954, Special Award 1981, Award of Merit, American Phytopathological Soc. 1972, Award of Distinction 1983, Rockefeller Foundation Bellagio Scholar 1985, Emer. Faculty Award, Univ. of Calif., Riverside 1990, Faculty Public Service Award 1991, Lifetime Achievement Award (Pacific Div., American Phytopathological Soc.) 1991. *Publications:* Recent Advances in Pest Control 1957, Plant Disease Development and Control 1968, Plant Pathology: An Advanced Treatise 1977, Soil-Root Interface 1979, Phytophthora: Its Biology, Taxonomy, Ecology, Pathology 1983, Ecology and Management of Soilborne Plant Pathogens 1985, and numerous papers in scientific journals. *Leisure interests:* fishing, sports, stamp collecting, photography. *Address:* Department of Plant Biology, University of California, Riverside, CA 92521 (Office); 708 Via La Paloma, Riverside, CA 92507, U.S.A. (Home). *Fax:* (909) 787-4294.

ZERBO, Col. Saye; Burkinabè politician and army officer; b. Aug. 1932, Tougan; joined French army 1950, Upper Voltan army 1961; fmr. paratrooper; served Indo-China and Algeria; studied Mil. Coll., Fréjus; courses at Artillery School and Staff Coll. 1966; graduated from Ecole supérieure de guerre 1973; Minister of Foreign Affairs 1974–76; Commdr. Combined Regt., Ouagadougou, and Dir. Bureau of Studies, Armed Forces Staff; led coup to depose Pres. Lamizana Nov. 1980; Pres. of Upper Volta (now Burkina Faso) 1980–82 (overthrown in coup Nov. 1982, arrested Sept. 1983, sentenced to 15 years' imprisonment, May 1984).

ZERMATTEN, Maurice; Swiss writer; b. 22 Oct. 1910, Saint Martin; s. of Antoine Zermatten; m. Hélène Kaiser, 1941, two s. four d.; ed. Fribourg Univ.; teacher of French literature; fmr. Pres. Soc. Suisse des écrivains; Dr. h.c. (Univ. of Fribourg); awarded Prix Fondation Schiller 1938, Prix Bodmer 1940, Prix d'honneur Schiller 1946, Grand Prix catholique de littérature, Paris 1959, Grand Prix Gottfried Keller 1960, French Acad. Prize 1961, Prix Monceau 1968, Grand Prix de l'Acad. Française pour le Rayonnement de la langue française, Prix Alpes et Jura, mem. de l'Acad. europeénne des Sciences, des Lettres et des Arts. *Publications:* Le Cœur Inutile, Le Chemin difficile, Contes des Hauts-Pays du Rhône, Les Chapelles Valaisannes, La Colère de Dieu, Le Sang des Morts, Christine, Le Pain Noir, L'Esprit des Tempêtes, Connaissance de Ramuz, Traversée d'un Paradis, Les Mains Pures, Isabelle de Chevron, La Montagne sans Etoiles, Le Lierre et le Figuier, La Fontaine d'Aréthuse, Un Lys de Savoie, Le Bouclier d'Or, Le Cancer des Solitudes, La Rose noire de Marignan, La Louve, Pays sans Chemin, Visages, Les Sèves d'Enfance, Une Soutane aux Orties, La Porte Blanche, Les dernières années de Rainer Maria Rilke, Pour prolonger l'Adieu, Un Amour à Grenchen-Nord, L'Homme aux Herbes, Gonzague de Reynold l'Homme et l'Oeuvre, A l'Est du Grand Couloir, Contes et Légendes de la Montagne valaisanne, L'Epée au Bois dormant, Georges Borgeaud, Théodore Strawinsky, Terre de fer, Ciel d'airain, Vous que je n'ai pas assez aimée, Le Diable à l'Ame, Les Fiancés de la Neige, Vue panoramique sur l'histoire du Valais. *Address:* Rue Gravelone 54, 1950 Sion, Valais, Switzerland. *Telephone:* 027 22 20 84.

ZEROUAL, Gen. Lamine; Algerian head of state and army officer; Minister of Defence July 1993; Supreme Commdr. and C.-in-C. of Armed Forces; Pres. of Algeria 1994–99, also Minister of Defence. *Address:* c/o Office of the President, el-Mouradia, Algiers, Algeria.

ZEVI, Bruno; Italian politician and architect; b. 22 Jan. 1918, Rome; s. of Guido Zevi and Ada Bondí; m. Tullia Calabi 1940; one s. one d.; ed. Graduate School of Design, Harvard Univ. and Faculty of Architecture, Univ. of Rome; left Italy for political reasons 1939–44; Ed. Quaderni Italiani (anti-Fascist magazine smuggled into Italy from U.S.A.) 1941–43; Dir. tech. magazines of U.S. Information Service in Italy 1944–46; co-founder Asscn. for an Organic Architecture in Italy 1945; co-Ed. Metron, an architectural magazine 1945–55; Prof. History of Architecture, Univ. of Venice 1948–63; Prof. History of Architecture, Univ. of Rome 1963–79; Gen. Sec. Italian Town Planning Inst. 1952–68; Hon. Pres. Italian Inst. of Architecture; Ed. L'architettura—cronache e storia 1955–; architectural critic of the weekly L'Espresso 1955–; Hon. Pres. Radical Party 1985–; M.P. 1988–93; Pres. Int. Cttee. of Architectural Critics; Academician Venice Acad. of Art 1953, Accad. di San Luca, Rome 1960–; Hon. mem. Royal Inst. of British Architects; Hon. Fellow American Inst. of Architects. *Publications:* Towards an Organic Architecture 1945, Saper Vedere l'Architettura 1948 (Architecture as Space), Poetica dell'Architettura Neoplastica 1953, Architecture (in International Encyclopaedia of the Arts) 1958, Biagio Rossetti, architetto ferrarese—il primo urbanista moderno europeo 1960, Architettura in nuce 1960, Michelangelo architetto 1964, Erich Mendelsohn: opera completa 1970, Cronache d'architettura 1970–80, Spazi dell'architettura moderna 1973, Il linguaggio moderno dell'architettura (The Modern Language of Architecture) 1973, Architettura e Storiografia 1974, Storia dell'architettura moderna 1975, Editoriali di architettura 1979, Frank Lloyd Wright 1979, Giuseppe Terragni 1980, Pretesti di critica architettonica 1983, Sterzate architettoniche 1992, Languages of Contemporary Architecture 1993, Ebraismo e architettura 1993, Zevi su Zevi: architettura come profezia 1993, Architettura concetti di una Controstoria 1994, Architettura della modernità 1994, Counter-History of Architecture in Italy 1995, Saper vedere la città 1997; Ed. Universale di Architettura (book series). *Leisure interests:* tennis, swimming. *Address:* Via Nomentana 150, 00162-Rome, Italy. *Telephone:* 86320684. *Fax:* 8603662.

ZHAI TAIFENG; Chinese party official; b. May 1933, Tangshan City, Hebei Prov.; joined CCP 1949; ed. Chinese People's Univ. 1955–57; Vice-Chair. Beijing Fed. of Trade Unions 1981; Deputy Sec.-Gen. Propaganda Dept. of CCP Cen. Cttee. 1986, Sec.-Gen. and Vice-Dir. 1991–; Vice-Chair. Chinese Writers' Asscn.; mem. 14th CCP Cen. Comm. for Discipline Inspection 1992–97. *Address:* Propaganda Department, Chinese Communist Party Central Committee, Beijing, People's Republic of China.

ZHANG AIPING, Col.-Gen.; Chinese politician and army officer; b. 1910, Daxian Co., Sichuan Prov.; joined CCP 1928, Red Army 1929; veteran army and party cadre; mil. cadre in East China 1949–54; Deputy Chief of Gen. Staff PLA 1954–67; rank of Col.-Gen. PLA 1955–; alt. mem. 8th Cen. Cttee. CCP 1958; criticized and removed from office during Cultural Revolution 1967; Chair. Science and Tech. Comm. for Nat. Defence 1975–77; Deputy Chief of Gen. Staff PLA 1977; mem. 11th Cen. Cttee. CCP 1977; a Vice-Premier 1980–82; Minister of Defence 1982–88; mem. 12th Cen. CCP Cttee. 1982–85; State Councillor 1982–88; Deputy Sec.-Gen. Mil. Comm. under CCP Cen. Cttee. 1982–88; mem. Cen. Mil. Comm. 1983–88; mem. Standing Cttee. of Cen. Advisory Comm. 1987–92; mem. Presidium 14th CCP Nat. Congress 1992. *Address:* c/o State Council, Beijing, People's Republic of China.

ZHANG BAIFA; Chinese administrator; b. 1934, Xianghe Co., Hebei Prov.; joined CCP 1954; Vice-Minister of State Capital Construction Comm. 1976–82; Vice-Mayor of Beijing Municipality 1982–97; del. 13th Cen. Cttee. CCP 1987–91, del. 14th 1992; Standing Cttee. mem. CPC 7th Beijing Municipal Cttee. 1992–97; Vice-Chair. Capital Planning and Construction Comm. *Address:* c/o Office of Vice-Mayor, Beijing Municipal Government, Beijing City, People's Republic of China.

ZHANG BAOMING; Chinese administrator; b. Nov. 1940, Qiqihar, Heilongjiang Prov.; ed. Fuxin Mining Inst.; joined CCP 1974; Vice-Minister of Coal Industry 1993–98; Dir. State Bureau of Coal Industry 1998–. *Address:* State Bureau of Coal Industry, Beijing, People's Republic of China.

ZHANG BOXING; Chinese party and government official; b. 1930, Baxian Co., Hebei Prov.; joined CCP 1950; Gov. of Shaanxi Prov. 1986; Sec. CCP Shaanxi Prov. Cttee. 1987–94; Chair. Shaanxi Prov. 8th People's Congress, Standing Cttee. 1993; mem. 13th CCP Cen. Cttee. 1987–92, 14th 1992–. *Address:* Shaanxi Provincial Government, Xi'an City, Shaanxi Province, People's Republic of China.

ZHANG CHENGZHI; Chinese writer; b. 1948, Beijing; ed. Beijing Univ.; mem. Inst. of Nationalities, Chinese Acad. of Social Sciences; mem. Chinese Writers' Asscn. *Publications include:* The Black Steed, Rivers of the North, Golden Pastureland.

ZHANG DEJIANG; Chinese politician; b. Nov. 1946, Taian Co., Liaoning Prov.; ed. Yanbian Univ. Kim Il Sung Univ. N. Korea; mem. CCP 1971–; Vice-Pres. Yanbian Univ. 1980–83; Deputy Sec. CCP Yanji City Cttee. 1983–85; Deputy Sec. CCP Yanbian Korean Autonomous Prefectural Cttee. 1985–86; Vice-Minister of Civil Affairs 1986; alt. mem. 14th CCP Cen. Cttee. 1992–97; mem. 15th CCP Cen. Cttee. 1997–; Sec. CCP Jilin Provincial Cttee. 1995–98; Sec. CCP Zhejiang Prov. Cttee. 1998. *Address:* Zhejiang Provincial Committee of Chinese Communist Party, Hangzhou, People's Republic of China.

ZHANG DELIN; Chinese government and party official; b. Aug. 1939, Beijing; ed. Tsinghua Univ., joined CCP 1964; Mayor of Harbin 1990; Vice-Minister of Machine-Bldg. and Electronics 1991; Vice-Minister of Machine-Bldg. 1993; Vice-Sec. CCP Sichuan Provincial Cttee. and Sec. CCP Chongqing City Cttee. 1996; Sec. CCP Chongqing Mun. Cttee. 1997–; mem. 15th CCP Cen. Cttee. 1997–. *Address:* Chinese Communist Party Chongqing Municipal Committee, Chongqing, Sichuan Province, People's Republic of China.

ZHANG DEQIN; Chinese administrator; b. Dec. 1933, Xiaoxian Co., Anhui Prov.; ed. Shanghai Fudan Univ.; Dir. State Bureau for Preservation of Cultural Relics 1988–96, Pres. China Cultural Relics Exchange Asscn. 1996–; mem. 8th Nat. Cttee. CPPCC 1993. *Address:* Administrative Bureau for Museums and Archaeological Data, Beijing, People's Republic of China.

ZHANG DINGHUA; Chinese politician; b. June 1933, Shanxian Co., Henan Prov.; ed. Northwest Univ.; joined CCP 1956; Sec. CCP Dagang Petroleum Admin. Bureau Cttee.; Dir. Propaganda Dept. CCP Tianjin Mun. Cttee., Sec. CCP Tianjin Mun. Comm. for Discipline Inspection; mem. 13th CCP Cen. Comm. for Discipline Inspection 1987; Vice-Sec. CCP Inner Mongolia Autonomous Regional Cttee. 1988; Vice-Chair. and First Sec. Secr. All-China Fed. of Trade Unions 1991–; mem. 14th CCP Cen. Cttee. 1992, 15th CCP Cen. Cttee. 1997–. *Address:* All-China Federation of Trade Unions, 10 Fu Xing Men Wai Jie, Beijing 100865, People's Republic of China.

ZHANG FUSEN; Chinese politician; b. March 1940, Shunyi Co., Beijing Municipality; ed. Tsinghua Univ.; joined CCP 1958; Vice-Sec. then Sec. CCP Haidian Dist. Cttee. of Beijing Municipality 1984; mem. Standing Cttee. of CCP Beijing Mun. Cttee. 1990; Vice-Sec. CCP Xinjiang Uygur Autonomous Regional Cttee. 1990; mem. 14th CCP Cen. Cttee. 1992; Vice-Minister of Justice; Vice-Sec. CCP Beijing Mun. Cttee. 1997–; mem. 15th CCP Cen. Cttee. 1997–. *Address;* Chinese Communist Party Beijing Municipal Committee, Beijing, People's Republic of China.

ZHANG GONG, Gen.; Chinese army officer and party official; b. 1935, Yuanping Co., Shanxi Prov.; joined PLA 1951; CCP 1961; Dir. of Political Dept. Beijing Mil. Area Command 1985; rank of Maj.-Gen. PLA 1988; Political Commissar Chengdu Mil. Region 1992, Political Commisar Acad. of Mil. Sciences 1994–; rank of Gen. 1998; mem. 14th CCP Cen. Cttee. 1992–97, 15th CCP Cen. Cttee. 1997–. *Address:* Academy of Military Science of People's Liberation Army, Xianghongqi, Haidian District, Beijing, People's Republic of China.

ZHANG GUOGUANG; Chinese politician; b. April 1945, Suizhong Co., Liaoning Prov.; joined CCP 1966; ed. Beijing Aeronautics Inst.; Sec. CCP Shenyang City Cttee. 1990; Vice-Sec. CCP Liaoning Provincial Cttee. 1993–; Gov. Liaoning Prov. 1998–; mem. 15th CCP Cen. Cttee. 1997–. *Address:* Liaoning Provincial People's Government, Shenyang, Liaoning Province, People's Republic of China.

ZHANG GUOYING; Chinese party official; b. 1935, Dongguan Co., Guangdong Prov.; Vice-Pres. All-China Women's Fed. Exec. Cttee. 1988–; mem. 12th CCP Cen. Cttee. 1982–87, 13th 1987–92, 14th 1992; a Deputy Sec. CPC 7th Guangdong Prov. Cttee. 1990–; Political Commissar Unit in Tibet 1992–. *Address:* All-China Women's Federation, Beijing, People's Republic of China.

ZHANG HAORUO; Chinese politician and engineer; b. 1932, Gongxian Co., Henan Prov.; ed. Qinghua Univ. and in U.S.S.R.; joined CCP 1950; Gov. of Sichuan Prov. 1988–93; Deputy Sec. CCP Sichuan Prov. 1988–93; Minister of Internal Trade 1993–95; Vice-Chair. and Sec. Party Group, State Comm. for Restructuring the Economy 1995–98; Vice-Chair. Environment and Resources Protection Cttee., 9th NPC 1998–. *Address:* c/o Standing Committee of National People's Congress, Beijing, People's Republic of China.

ZHANG HUSHENG; Chinese journalist; fmr. Dir. Int. Dept., People's Daily, Ed.-in-Chief Overseas Edn. 1991–, Deputy Ed.-in-Chief People's Daily 1995–; Head of Information Bureau of 7th NPC Standing Cttee. *Address:* People's Daily, 2 Jin Tai Xi Lu, Chao Yang Men Wai, Beijing 100733, People's Republic of China. *Telephone:* (10) 65092121. *Fax:* (10) 65091982.

ZHANG JIANMIN; Chinese party official; b. 1931, Beijing; Vice-Mayor of Beijing 1984–93; mem. Standing Cttee., Beijing 1987–; alt. mem. 14th CCP Cen. Cttee. 1992–97; Chair. Beijing Municipal 10th People's Congress, Standing Cttee. 1993–; NPC Deputy, Beijing Municipality. *Address:* Beijing Municipal People's Congress, Beijing, People's Republic of China.

ZHANG JIE, B.A.; Chinese writer; b. 27 April 1937, Beijing; d. of Zhang Shanzhi; m. Sun Youyu 1986; one d.; ed. People's Univ., Beijing; a Deputy Ed.-in-Chief Xinhua News Agency 1986; Visiting Prof., Wesleyan Univ., Middletown, Conn., U.S.A. 1989–90, 1994–95; Council mem. Chinese Asscn. of Writers; mem. Int. PEN (China Br.); mem. Beijing Political Consultative Conf.; Vice-Pres. Beijing Writers' Asscn.; Hon. mem. American Acad. of Arts and Letters; has lectured extensively in Europe and U.S.A.; Nat. Awards for Short Story, Novelette and Novel (only writer to have won all three kinds of awards), Malaparte Prize (Italy) 1989 for As Long as Nothing Happens, Nothing Will, several other awards. *Publications:* Heavy Wings (novel) 1981, As Long as Nothing Happens, Nothing Will (short stories), The Ark (novella) 1983, Smaragd (novella) 1984, Emerald (novella) 1985, Only One Sun (novel) 1988; several other collections of short stories and memoirs. *Leisure interest:* music. *Address:* 501, 97# Qian-Men Xi Da Jie, Beijing 100031, People's Republic of China; c/o Tang Di, 89 Merlin Avenue, North Tarrytown, NY 10591, U.S.A. *Telephone:* (10) 6603 8673 (Beijing).

ZHANG JIN; Chinese scientist and university professor; ed. Qinghua Univ., Beijing, Beijing Univ. of Aeronautics and Astronautics; specializes in computation of structural dynamics and mechanics of new complex materials for aviation industry; Guest Prof. M.I.T., U.S.A.; Prof., Beijing Univ. of Aeronautics and Astronautics; Guest Research Fellow Univ. of Calif., Berkeley, U.S.A. *Publications include:* The Dynamic Mechanism and Application of New Complex Materials (co-author); scientific papers. *Address:* Beijing University of Aeronautics and Astronautics, 37 Xueyuan Road, Beijing 100083, People's Republic of China.

ZHANG JINGFU: Chinese politician; b. 1914, Feidong Co., Anhui Prov.; fmr. Vice-Minister of Local Industry and Vice-Pres. Scientific and Tech. Comm.; alt. mem. 8th Cen. Cttee. of CCP 1956; criticized and removed from office during Cultural Revolution 1967; Minister of Finance 1975–79; Gov. and First Sec. Anhui Prov. Cttee. 1980–81; First Political Comm. Anhui Mil. Div. 1980–82; State Councillor 1982–88; Minister in Charge of State Econ. Comm. 1982–84; mem. State Finance and Econ. Comm.; mem. 12th Cen. CCP Cttee. 1982–87; mem. Standing Comm. of Cen. Advisory Comm. 1987–92; mem. Presidium 14th CCP Nat. Congress 1992; Chair. Guidance Cttee. for State Examinations for Econ. Man. Personnel 1983; Hon. Pres. Soc. for Study of Workers' Educ. 1984; Chair. Nat. Industrial Safety Cttee. 1985; Pres. Chinese Asscn. for Int. Exchange of Personnel 1986–. *Address:* c/o State Economic Commission, Sanlihe, Fuxingmenwai, Beijing, People's Republic of China.

ZHANG JUNJIU; Chinese business executive; Vice-Pres. China North Industries Group 1990–93; Pres. China Ordnance Corpn., China N. Industries Group; Gen. Man. China Armament Industry Gen. Corpn. 1993–; alt. mem. 14th CCP Cen. Cttee. 1992–97; mem. 15th CCP Cen. Cttee. 1997–; Vice-Pres. and First Sec. Secr. of All-China Fed. of Trade Unions 1998–; Vice-Minister, State Comm. of Science, Tech. and Industry for Nat. Defence 1998–. *Address:* China Ordnance Corporation, Beijing, People's Republic of China.

ZHANG KEHUI; Chinese politician; b. Feb. 1928, Zhanghua Co., Taiwan; ed. Taiwan Teachers Coll.; joined CCP 1948; joined Taiwan Democratic Self-Government League 1979; Vice-Dir. Taiwan Affairs Office of State Council 1982–91; Chair. All-China Fed. of Taiwan Compatriots 1991–97; Vice-Chair. Taiwan Democratic Self-Government League 5th Cen. Cttee. 1992, Chair. 6th Cen. Cttee. 1997–; mem. Standing Cttee. 8th NPC 1993–98; Vice-Chair. 9th Nat. Cttee. of CPPCC 1998–. *Address:* National Committee of Chinese People's Political Consultative Conference, 23 Taipingqiao Street, Beijing, People's Republic of China.

ZHANG LIANZHONG, Vice-Adm.; Chinese naval officer; b. 1931, Jiaoxian Co., Shandong Prov.; ed. Navy Submarine Acad., PLA Mil. Acad.; joined PLA 1947, PLA Navy Commdr. 1988–97; joined CCP 1948; rank of Vice-Adm. 1988; alt. mem. 13th CCP Cen. Cttee. 1987–92, 14th 1992–. *Address:* People's Liberation Army Navy Command, Beijing, People's Republic of China.

ZHANG LICHANG; Chinese administrator; b. 1939, Nanpi Co., Hebei Prov.; joined CCP 1966; Vice-Mayor of Tianjin Municipality 1985, Mayor 1993–98; Deputy Sec. CCP 6th Tianjin Municipal Cttee. 1989–92, Sec. CCP 7th Tianjin Municipal Cttee. 1992–98; Chair. Tianjin Municipal People's Congress 1998–; alt. mem. 13th CCP Cen. Cttee. 1987–92, 14th 1992–97; mem. 15th CCP Cen. Cttee. 1997–. *Address:* Tianjin Municipal People's Congress, Tianjin Municipality, People's Republic of China.

ZHANG QUANJING; Chinese politician; b. 1931, Pingyuan Co., Shandong Prov.; mem. CCP 1949–; Deputy Section Chief, CCP Dezhou Pref. Cttee.; Deputy Sec. CCP Dezhou Municipal Cttee. 1950–66; Div. Chief and Deputy Head, Org. Dept. CCP Shandong Provincial Cttee. 1971–86; mem. Standing Cttee. and Head, Org. Dept. CCP Shandong Provincial Cttee. 1986–88; Sec. CCP Shandong Provincial Comm. for Inspecting Discipline 1988; Exec. Deputy Dir. CCP Cen. Cttee. Org. Dept. 1991–94, Head 1994–; mem. 8th CCP Nat. Cttee. 1993–. *Address:* Organization Department, Central Committee of Communist Party of China, Beijing, People's Republic of China.

ZHANG RENWEI; Chinese government official; fmr. Deputy Dir. State Admin. of Bldg. Materials Industry, Dir. Jan. 1994–. *Address:* c/o Ministry of Construction, Baiwanzhuang, Western Suburb, Beijing, People's Republic of China.

ZHANG RENZHI; Chinese landscape artist; b. 7 Dec. 1935, Hebei Prov.; s. of Zhang Pu and Zhang Chen; m. Lang Mei 1966; two s.; ed. Cen. Art Inst.; joined Beijing Art Acad. as professional artist; jt. exhbns. Xinxiang, Henan Prov., Macao, Beijing, Japan 1991, Exhbn. of Buddhism 1991, Nat. Exhbn. 1992, Beseto Arts Festival 1997, etc.; solo exhbns. Tianjin, Shen Zhen City 1992, 'Twenty Nocturnal Pieces', Taiwan 1992, Kuang Tong Prov., also Algeria, Germany, Guyana, U.S.A., Hong Kong, Korea, Japan, Thailand, Malaysia, Singapore; Wintertime Lotus and other works in collection of James Art Museum, Vermont State Univ., U.S.A.; 12 works included in CD-ROM Contemporary Chinese Artists; 2 works in Dictionary of the Achievements of World Chinese Artists; Award of Excellence (for 'Quiet Valley'), Nat. Exhbn. of Fine Arts 1991; prize for 'Lasting Forever' (burnt pine tree). *Publications:* Zhang Renzhi's Album of Paintings, (Vol. 2) 1991. *Leisure interest:* travel. *Address:* Room 501, Building 2, Beijing Arts Institute, Chao Yang District, Beijing, People's Republic of China. *Telephone:* 65013316.

ZHANG RUIFANG; Chinese film producer; b. 1918, Beijing; fmr. Dir. Actors' Section, Shanghai Film Studio; Chair. Shanghai Asscn. of Film Producers 1994–; Hon. mem. Fed. of Chinese Literary and Art Circles 1997–. *Address:* Shanghai Association of Film Producers, Shanghai, People's Republic of China.

ZHANG RUIMIN; Chinese business executive; b. Jan. 1949, Laizhou, Shandong Prov.; Dir. Qingdao Refrigerator Factory 1984–91; Pres. Haier Group 1991–. *Address:* Haier Group, Qingdao, Shandong Province, People's Republic of China.

ZHANG SHENGMAN; Chinese business executive; b. 1957, Shanghai; ed. Fudan Univ., McGill Univ.; Asst. to Exec. Dir. of World Bank 1983–87; section head and then Vice-Dir. Dept of IBRD, Ministry of Finance 1987–92; Deputy Exec. Dir., then Exec. Dir. of IBRD 1992–96; Vice Pres. IBRD 1996–. *Address:* International Bank for Reconstruction and Development, 1818 H Street, N.W., Washington, DC 20433, U.S.A.

ZHANG SHOU; Chinese academic and government official; b. 19 July 1930, Changshu Co., Jiangsu Prov.; ed. Jiaotong Univ.; joined CCP 1949; taught at Jiaotong Univ. 1953–80, Deputy Dir. Dept. of Eng. and Physics 1958–62, Dept. of Naval Architecture 1962–72, Dir. 1972–78; Vice-Pres. Jiaotong Univ. 1979, First Vice-Pres. 1980–82; Visiting Scholar at Univ. of Pennsylvania 1981–82; mem. 12th CCP Cen. Cttee. 1982; mem. 13th CCP Cen. Cttee. 1987–92, 14th CCP Cen. Cttee. 1992–, mem. Finance and Econ. Cttee.; Vice Minister State Planning Comm. 1983–89; Chair. State Econ. Information Centre 1987–89; Pres. China State Shipbldg. Corpn. 1989; Dir. State Information Center 1987; Consultant System Eng. Asscn. of China 1985; Hon. Dir. Computer Asscn. of China 1987; Deputy Head Leading Group for Introducing Foreign Intellectual Resources 1988; Consultant State Natural Science Foundation of China 1987; mem. 8th NPC 1993–, NPC Deputy, Hubei Prov. *Publications:* Hydrostatics of Naval Architecture 1964, A Concise English-Chinese Naval Architecture Dictionary 1973, Econometrics 1984, Scientific Progress and Economic Development 1988, Reform and Development 1988. *Address:* 5 Yuetan Beijie, Beijing, People's Republic of China.

ZHANG SIQING; Chinese judge; b. 1932, Luoyang City, Henan Prov.; joined CCP 1952; Deputy Procurator-Gen. Supreme People's Procuratorate of China 1985–93, Procurator-Gen. 1993–98; alt. mem. 13th CCP Cen. Cttee. 1987–91, 14th 1992–97; mem. 15th CCP Cen. Cttee. 1997–; Vice-Chair. 9th Nat. Cttee. of CPPCC 1998–. *Address:* National Committee of Chinese People's Political Consultative Conference, 23 Taipingqiao Street, Beijing, People's Republic of China.

ZHANG TAIHENG, Gen.; Chinese army officer; b. 1931, Guangrao Co., Shandong; ed. Nanjing Mil. Acad.; joined PLA 1945; platoon leader, 28th Army 1947, Regt. leader 1961; Vice-Commdr. PLA Chengdu Mil. Area Command 1983, Commdr. 1990; Vice-Commdr. Nanjing Mil. Area Command 1992; Commdr. Jinan Mil. Region 1992–96. *Address:* c/o Ministry of National Defence, Jingshanqian Jie, Beijing, People's Republic of China.

ZHANG TANGMIN; Chinese traditional medical practitioner and chemist; b. 19 March 1939, Kai Jai, Sichuan; s. of Zhang He Ming and Tao Kai Yun; m. Sun Ren Ping 1966; two s. one d.; ed. Univ. of Science and Tech. of China; Asst. Researcher Inst. of Chem., Academia Sinica 1962–78, Asst. Prof. 1978–87, Assoc. Prof. 1987; self-taught in traditional Chinese medicine 1964–; assigned to Beijing Xuanwu Hosp. 1981; opened own epilepsy clinic 1981. *Publications:* New Cure for Epilepsy, Can Epilepsy be Cured?, Fringe Science and Epilepsy, Discussions on the Cure for the Abdomen Type of Epilepsy and other works on epilepsy. *Address:* Institute of Chemistry, Academia Sinica, Beijing, 100080, People's Republic of China. *Telephone:* 2553979.

ZHANG WANNIAN, Lieut.-Gen.; Chinese army officer; b. 1 Aug. 1928, Longkou, Shandong; s. of Jin Man Zhang and Li Shi Zhang; m. Pei Zhao Zhong 1954; four d.; alt. mem. 12th CCP Cen. Cttee. 1982, 13th Cen. Cttee. 1987–92; mem. 14th Cen. Cttee. 1992–; mem. Cen. Mil. Comm. 1992–95, Vice-Chair. 1995–98; Deputy Commdr. Wuhan Mil. Region (now Guangzhou Mil. Region) 1982–87, Commdr. 1987–90; Chief of Gen. Staff PLA 1992–95; Commdr. Jinan Mil. Region 1990–92; mem. CCP Politburo; Sec. Secr. CCP Cen. Cttee.; mem. 15th CCP Cen. Cttee. 1997–. *Address:* c/o Chinese Communist Party Central Committee, Zhong Nan Hai, Beijing, People's Republic of China.

ZHANG WANXIN; Chinese petrochemicals executive; b. 5 May 1930, Harbin; s. of Zhang Xinming and Sun Minying; m. Deng Yinin 1958; one s. one d.; Vice-Pres. China Petrochemical Corpn. 1983–88; Chair. and Pres. Int. Multi-Petrochemical Enterprise Ltd. (IMPEL), Hong Kong 1989–94; Chair. and C.E.O. Sino-American Corpn. (SAAX) 1992–; Pres. Creat Group; Vice-Chair. China Taiwan Study Asscn.; Chair. MONTPEL 1992–; Vice-Pres. Devt. Research Centre, State Council; part-time Prof., Tsinghua Univ., Beijing; alt. mem. 12th CCP Cen. Cttee. 1982; alt. mem. 13th CCP Cen. Cttee. 1987; Vice-Chair. China Chemical Eng. and Industry Soc.; Prof. Shenzhen Univ. 1983–88, Tsinghua Univ. 1988–93; mem. CCP Cttee., Beijing Municipality 1981–83; Deputy Chief Exec. Econ., Tech. and Social Devt. Research Center 1988, Vice-Pres. 1991; alt. mem. 12th and 13th CCP Cen. Cttee.; awarded Special Prize of State Cttee. for Science and Tech. 1985. *Leisure interest:* listening to music, liberal arts. *Address:* 225 Chaoyangmen, Nei Dajie, Beijing 100010, People's Republic of China. *Telephone:* (1) 65270800; 68578801. *Fax:* (1) 65236060.

ZHANG WEIQING; Chinese politician; b. 1944, Lintong Co., Shaanxi Prov.; ed. Peking Univ.; joined CCP 1972; Sec. Communist Youth League Shanxi

Provincial Cttee., Vice-Gov. Shanxi Prov.; Vice-Dir. Propaganda Dept. CCP Shanxi Provincial Cttee.; Vice-Minister State Family Planning Comm. 1994–98, Minister 1998–; mem. 15th CCP Cen. Cttee. 1997–. *Address:* State Family Planning Commission, 14 Zhichun Lu, Haidan Qu, Beijing 100088, Beijing, People's Republic of China.

ZHANG WENKANG; Chinese politician; Vice-Minister Ministry of Public Health 1993–98, Minister 1998–; Dir. State Admin. of Traditional Chinese Medicine July 1993–, Drugs Licensing Cttee.; mem. 15th CCP Cen. Cttee. 1997–. *Address:* c/o Ministry of Public Health, 44 Houhaibeiheyan, Xicheng District, Beijing, People's Republic of China.

ZHANG WENYUE; Chinese politician; b. Oct. 1944, Pucheng Co., Fujian Prov.; joined CCP 1965; ed. Beijing Geology Inst.; Dir. Geology and Mineral Resources Bureau of Sichuan Prov.; Dir.-Gen. Office of Ministry of Geology and Mineral Resources 1986; Dir. State Admin. on Mineral Resources 1989; Vice-Minister of Geology and Mineral Resources 1990; mem. CCP Cen. Comm. for Discipline Inspection 1992; Vice-Sec. CCP Xinjiang Uygur Autonomous Regional Cttee. 1995–; mem. 15th CCP Cen. Cttee. 1997–. *Address:* Chinese Communist Party Xinjiang Uygur Autonomous Regional Committee, Urumqi City, Xinjiang Uygur Autonomous Region, People's Republic of China.

ZHANG WULE; Chinese administrator; b. 1937, Anxin Co., Hebei Prov.; ed. Beijing Inst. of Iron and Steel Tech. joined CCP 1982; Vice-Gov. Gansu Prov. 1985–93; a Deputy Sec. CPC 8th Gansu Prov. Cttee. 1993–; alt. mem. 13th Cen. Cttee. CCP 1987–91; mem. 14th 1992; Gov. of Gansu Prov. 1994–96; Vice-Pres. Nat. Cttee. of Economy and Trade 1996–. *Address:* c/o Office of the Governor, Gansu Provincial Government, Shengyang City, People's Republic of China.

ZHANG XIANLIANG; Chinese writer; b. 1936, Jiangsu; fmr. teacher in Beijing and Ningxia; in political disgrace 1957–79; Vice-Pres. Chinese Writers' Asscn. 1985, Best Novel of the Year Awards (China) 1981, 1983, 1984. *Publications include:* Soul and Flesh 1981, Mimosa 1984, Half of Man is Woman 1985, Getting Used to Dying 1989, Grass Soup 1992. *Leisure interest:* Chinese calligraphy. *Address:* Ningxia Writers' Association, Yinchuan City, People's Republic of China.

ZHANG XIAO; Chinese banker; b. 1935; joined CCP 1959; Vice-Pres. of Industrial and Commercial Bank of China 1983; Pres. 1990–97; alt. mem. 14th CPC Cen. Cttee. 1992–. *Address:* c/o Industrial and Commercial Bank of China, Beijing, People's Republic of China.

ZHANG YANNING; Chinese government official; b. 1927, Shenyang, Liaoning; m. Sun Huimin; two s. one d.; Vice-Minister for State Econ. Comm. 1983–88, for Restructuring the Economy 1988, for Production Office of the State Council 1991; mem. State Educ. Comm. 1985; Vice-Pres. and Dir.-Gen. China Enterprise Man. Asscn. 1979, Exec. Vice-Pres. 1990; Vice-Chair. Guidance Cttee. for State Examinations for Econ. Managerial Personnel 1983; Chair. China-Japan Personnel Exchange Cttee. 1985–; Pres. China Enterprise Dirs. Asscn. 1986; mem. 8th NPC 1993–, NPC Deputy Sichuan Prov.; other public appointments. *Address:* 17, Zizhuyuan Nanlu, Haidian District, Beijing 100044, People's Republic of China.

ZHANG YIMOU; Chinese film actor and director; b. 1951, Xi'an, Shanxi Prov.; m. Xiao Hua 1982 (divorced 1990); ed. Xi'an Middle School, Beijing Film Acad.; 8th Golden Rooster Best Actor Award for Old Well 1988. *Films include:* The Old Well, Red Sorghum (Hong Gaoliang), Raise the Red Lantern, The Story of Qiu Ju, Keep Cool 1997; produced Turandot, Beijing 1998. *Address:* Xi'an Film Studio, Xi'an City, Shaanxi Province, People's Republic of China.

ZHANG YOUFU; Chinese ecologist; b. 21 May 1940, Jiangsu Prov.; s. of Zhang Changsheng and Zhong Yinlan; m. Xu Chunlan 1968; two s.; ed. Nanking Univ., Chendu Inst. of Geography, Chinese Acad. of Sciences; has been engaged in research work on biological prevention of mudflow damage, soil and water conservation and forest ecology for 20 years. *Publications:* An Observational Study on Mudflow at Jiangjia Gully, Three Papers 1982, A Brief Introduction of the Programme Against Mudflow By Means of Biology 1983, Mudflow and Forest Vegetation in Jiangjia Gully Basin 1987, Mudflow and its Comprehensive Control 1989, Process of the Erosion, Transportation and Deposition of Debris Flow, Application of Information from Remote Sensing for Preventing Disasters caused by Debris Flow 1990, Application of Information from Remote Sensing for Preventing Disasters caused by Landslides 1990 etc.; papers on measures against debris flow, remote sensing information, etc. *Leisure interest:* photography. *Address:* Chengdu P.O. Box 417, Sichuan 610041, People's Republic of China. *Telephone:* (028) 5581260-375. *Fax:* (0086-028) 5552258.

ZHANG YU; Chinese film actress; b. Oct. 1957, Shanghai City; m. Zhang Jianya; advanced studies, U.S.A. 1985–90; mem. 8th NPC 1993–; Amb. to Guyana 1994–; Hundred Flowers Best Actress Award for Evening Rain 1981; Golden Rooster Best Actress Award for Love at Lushan 1981. *Address:* Embassy of People's Republic of China, 108 Duke Street, Kingston, Georgetown, Guyana; Shanghai Film Studio, 595 Caoxi Beilu Street, Shanghai City, People's Republic of China. *Telephone:* (2) 71651 (Guyana).

ZHANG YUAN; Chinese film director; ed. Beijing Film Acad.; independent film dir. 1989–; Special Jury Prize, Nantes Film Festival for Mama 1991; has directed music videos for leading Chinese rock singer Cui Jian. *Films:* Mama, The Square, Beijing Bastards. *Address:* c/o Beijing Film Academy, Beijing, People's Republic of China.

ZHANG ZHEN, Gen.; Chinese army officer and politician; b. Oct. 1914, Ping Jian Co., Hunan Prov.; joined Red Army 1930, rising to rank of Regimental Chief of Staff; participated in the Long March; Column Chief of Staff Eighth Route Army, Div. Chief of Staff and Brigade Commdr. in New Fourth Army in War against Japan 1937–45; during War of Liberation served as Column Commdr., Political Commissar in Cen. China Field Army, Corps Chief of Staff, Chief of Staff East China Mil. Command and Chief of Staff of Third Field Army 1946–49; Dir. of Operation Dept., HQ of PLA Gen. Staff, Acting Corps Commdr. and Political Commissar, Deputy Commandant and Commandant of the Mil. Coll. of PLA; Deputy Commdr. Wuhan Mil. Command, Deputy Dir. and Dir. of PLA Gen. Logistics Dept., Deputy Chief of PLA Gen. Staff; Lieut.-Gen. 1955; Political Commissar PLA Shanxi Prov. Command 1993, Inner Mongolia Mil. Area Command 1994–; Pres. Nat. Defence Univ., PLA, 1985; a Sr. Advisor China Soc. of Mil. Sciences 1991–; NPC Deputy PLA; alt. mem. 11th Cen. Cttee. CCP; mem. 12th Cen. Cttee. CCP; mem. Cen. Advisory Comm. CCP; mem. 14th Cen. Cttee. CCP 1992–; Vice-Chair. Cen. Mil. Comm. CCP 1992–; rank of Gen. PLA 1988; Amb. to Ukraine 1992–95.

ZHANG ZHIJIAN, Gen.; Chinese army officer; b. 1934, Wenxi Co., Shanxi Prov.; joined PLA 1951; mem. CCP 1956–; teacher, Speeded-Up Educ. School, Chahar Mil. Dist., Hubei (North China) Mil. Region; literacy teacher in div. hosp. of Chinese People's Volunteers, Korea 1953–56; staff officer 1957–69; Chief, Operations and Training Div. PLA Jinan Mil. Region H.Q. 1971–78; Div. Chief of Staff 1978–79; Army Deputy Chief of Staff 1979–80; Div. Commdr. 1980–83; Army Commdr. 1983–85; Deputy Commdr. Jinan Mil. Region 1985; Political Commissar, Chengdu Mil. Region 1994–; rank of Gen. 1998; mem. CCP 15th Cen. Cttee. 1997–. *Address:* Office of the Political Commissar, Chengdu Military Region, People's Republic of China.

ZHANG ZHONGXIAN, Lieut.-Gen.; Chinese army officer; b. Jan. 1926, Weishan Co., Shandong Prov.; s. of Zhixin Zhang and Gaoshi Zhang; m. Yufen Yang 1953; three s. one d.; Political Commissar, Canton Mil. Region, PLA 1985; alt. mem. 12th CCP Cen. Cttee. 1985–87; mem. 13th Cen. Cttee. 1987–92; Standing mem. Party Cttee., Canton Mil. Region 1986–, Political Commissar 1986–; Sec. Party Cttee., Canton Mil. Region 1987; rank of Lieut.-Gen. 1988; mem. Presidium 14th CCP Nat. Congress 1992; mem. 8th NPC 1993–, NPC Deputy, PLA. *Address:* Canton Military Region Headquarters, Guangzhou, Guangdong, People's Republic of China.

ZHANG ZHU; Chinese government official; b. 1929, Dalian, Liaoning; Vice-Minister for Nationatities Affairs Comm. 1986; Pres. Advertising Society, Acad. of Social Sciences 1982; Political Commissar Regional People's Armed Police Corps, Tibet Autonomous Regional People's Govt. 1989–. *Address:* State Nationalities Affairs Commission, Beijing, People's Republic of China.

ZHANG ZONCHU; Chinese scientist; b. 1927; ed. Beijing Univ., Moscow Univ.; mem. Dept. of Earth Sciences, Academia Sinica, 1985–. *Address:* Academia Sinica, 52 San Ji He Road, Beijing 100864, People's Republic of China.

ZHANG ZUOJI; Chinese politician; b. Jan. 1945, Bayan, Heilongjiang Prov.; ed. Heilongjiang Univ.; joined CCP 1972; Vice-Minister of Labour 1993–95; Vice-Chief Sec. of State Council 1995–98; Minister of Labour and Social Security 1998–. *Address:* Ministry of Labour and Social Security, 12 Hepinglizhong Jie, Dongcheng Qu, Beijing 100716, People's Republic of China.

ZHAO DI; Chinese politician; b. 1938, Weinan Co., Shaanxi Prov.; Vice-Mayor Kaifeng City; mem. Standing Cttee. Henan Prov. CCP Cttee. 1983, Deputy Sec. 1984–86; a Vice-Pres. All-China Women's Fed. 1992–, also a Sec. 1991–; alt. mem. CCP Cen. Cttee. 1985–; mem. Standing Cttee. of Cen. Comm. for Discipline Inspection. *Address:* Central Committee of the Chinese Communist Party, Zhongnanhai, Beijing, People's Republic of China.

ZHAO DONGWAN; Chinese politician and mechanical engineer; b. 1926, Henan Prov.; m. Zhang Leiyan 1951; two s. one d.; Vice-Chair. Science and Tech. Comm. 1977; Dir. Cttee. for the Promotion of Int. Measurements 1979; Chinese Chair. PRC-U.S.A. Joint Cttee. on High Energy Physics 1979; Vice-Chair. State Planning Comm. 1982, State Cttee. for the Establishment of Govt. Orgs. 1988–; alt. mem. 12th CCP Cen. Cttee. 1982–87; mem. 13th CCP Cen. Cttee. 1987; mem. Presidium 14th CCP Nat. Congress 1992; Minister of Labour and Personnel 1985–88, Minister of Personnel 1988–93; Vice-Chair. State Cttee. for the Establishment of Govt. Orgs. 1988; Chair. NPC Educ. Science, Culture and Public Health Cttee. 1993–; mem. 8th NPC 1993–, NPC Deputy, Henan Prov. *Leisure interests:* swimming, reading. *Address:* Education, Science, Culture and Public Health Committee, National People's Congress, Beijing, People's Republic of China.

ZHAO FULIN; Chinese politician; b. 1932, Daming Co., Hubei Prov.; mem. CCP 1948–; Asst. Org. Dept. CCP Guanghua Co. Cttee. 1949; mem. Secr. CCP Zaoyang Co. Cttee. 1956–58; Sec. CCP Jiangling Co. Cttee. 1965–66; Deputy Sec. CCP Jingzhou Pref. Cttee. 1966–70, 1972–81, Sec. 1981–85; Deputy Sec. CCP Hubei Provincial Cttee. and Sec. Comm. for Inspecting Discipline 1985; mem. CCP Comm. for Inspecting Discipline 1985; Chair. Guangxi Regional People's Congress Standing Cttee. 1995–, Sec. 7th CCP Guangxi Zhuang Autonomous Regional Cttee.; mem. 13th and 14th CCP

Cen. Cttee. *Address:* Guangxi Regional People's Congress, Guangxi, People's Republic of China.

ZHAO HAIFENG; Chinese party official; b. 1921, Raoyang, Hebei; Vice-Chair. Prov. Revolutionary Cttee., Qinghai 1977–78; Deputy Sec. CCP Cttee., Qinghai 1978–81; Vice-Gov. of Qinghai 1979–81; Perm. Sec. CCP Cttee., Qinghai 1981–83; Chair. Prov. CPPCC Cttee., Qinghai 1981–83; mem. 12th Cen. Cttee. CCP 1982; First Sec. CCP Cttee., Qinghai 1983–85; Chair. Advisory Cttee., CCP Cttee., Qinghai 1985–88; mem. Standing Cttee., 7th CPPCC 1988; mem. 8th CPPCC Nat. Cttee. 1993–. *Address:* Provincial Government, Xining, Qinghai Province, People's Republic of China.

ZHAO JIPING; Chinese composer; b. July 1945, Pingliang, Gansu Prov.; ed. Xi'an Conservatory of Music, Cen. Conservatory of Music; Pres. Shaanxi Prov. Songs and Dance Theatre; wrote music for over 40 films including Yellow Earth, Red Sorghum, Judou, Raise the Red Lantern, To Live, Farewell My Concubine, Five Women and a Rope; maj. works include Qinchuan Lyrics, Silk Road, Elm Flowers (opera); The Soul of the Qin Terracotta Soldier (musical). *Address:* Shaanxi Provincial Songs and Dance Theatre, Wenyi Road, Xi'an, People's Republic of China.

ZHAO NANQI, Gen.; Chinese army officer and party official; b. 1926, Yongji Co., Jilin Prov.; joined CCP 1947; Dir. of PLA Gen. Logistics Dept. 1987–92; mem. PRC Cen. Mil. Comm. 1988–92; rank of Gen. 1988; mem. 14th CCP Cen. Cttee. 1992–97; Commdt. Acad. of Mil. Sciences 1992–95; Vice-Chair. 9th Nat. Cttee. of CPPCC 1998–. *Address:* National Committee of Chinese People's Political Consultative Conference, 23 Taipingqiao Street, Beijing, People's Republic of China.

ZHAO PUCHU; Chinese Buddhist leader, calligrapher, poet and scholar; b. 5 Nov. 1907, Anqin City, Anhui Prov.; organized relief work in Shanghai for refugees from war zones 1937; Chief Leader, Shanghai Union of Charity Orgs. 1948; mem., as Buddhist rep., 1st, 2nd and 3rd CPPCC 1949–59; mem. 1st, 2nd, 3rd, 4th, 5th NPC 1954–78; Standing mem. Nat. Cttee., 4th, 5th CPPCC 1964–78; Vice-Chair. 6th, 7th, 8th, 9th Nat. Cttee., CPPCC 1983–99; Vice-Pres. and Sec.-Gen. Buddhist Asscn. of China 1953–79, Pres. 1980–99; Vice-Chair. Sino-Japanese Friendship Asscn. 1963–66, Adviser 1993–99; mem. Chinese People's Asscn. for Solidarity of Asia and Africa; Vice-Chair. Chinese Calligraphers' Asscn. 1983–85; Pres. Soc. for Study of Sino-Japanese Relations 1985; Hon. Pres. Chinese People's Asscn. for Peace and Disarmament 1985–99; Hon. Chair. China Asscn. for Promoting Democracy 1992; Hon. Vice-Chair. Red Cross Soc. of China 1994; numerous public appts.; Hon. Dr. (Japan Buddhist Univ.) 1982; Hon. D.Litt. (Ryukoko Univ., Japan) 1990; Hon. Ph.D. (Dongguk Univ., Korea) 1992; Buddhist Evangelist Prize 1982, Niwano Peace Prize 1985, Int. Lions Asscn.'s Culture Prize 1997, China, Korea, Japan Culture Prize 1997, Emperor Akihto of Japan Culture Prize 1992. *Publications:* Dishuiji (selected poems) 1964, Pianshiji (collection of poems) 1978, Questions and Answers on Buddhism (Japanese and English edn.) 1980. *Address:* No. 1 Nan Xiao Shuan Hutong, Heping Men, Beijing 100031, People's Republic of China.

ZHAO QI; Chinese artist; b. Aug. 1954, Jinxian, Liaoning Prov.; ed. Lu Xun Acad. of Fine Art; Prof. and Vice-Head Dept. of Chinese Painting, Lu Xun Acad. of Fine Art; numerous paintings of historical subjects. *Address:* Lu Xun Academy of Fine Art, Beijing, People's Republic of China.

ZHAO QING (LUDAN); Chinese dancer and choreographer; b. 16 Nov. 1936, Shanghai City; d. of Zhao Dan and Ye Luxi; m. Chen Mingyuan; ed. Beijing Dancing Coll.; Prin. actress China Opera and Dance Drama Theatre 1959–, First Grade Dancer 1982–; Prin. Dancer Chinese Art Del. to France, England, Italy, U.S.A., U.S.S.R., Poland, Singapore, Japan, Latin America; mem. 8th Nat. Cttee. CPPCC 1993–; mem. China Dancers Asscn.; Gold Medal (World Youth Festival); Excellent Performance Award 1980; First Prize Ministry of Culture for "The Sword" (ballet) 1982. *Performances include:* The Lotus Lantern (ballet), Xiaodao Hui (ballet) 1961, Liang Zhu (ballet) 1962, The Red Silk Dance 1978, The Sword 1980, The Poetry of the Sea 1982, Children of Dragon (TV) 1983–84, Golden Dream (film) 1984–85, Luotuo Xiangzi (ballet) 1986, Luoshen (ballet) 1987, Dance of Calligraphy 1990, The Father and the Daughter (ballet) 1993. *Address:* 2 Nanhuadong Street, Hufang Road, Beijing 100050, People's Republic of China.

ZHAO QIZHENG; Chinese politician; b. Jan. 1940, Beijing; ed. China Science and Tech. Univ. 1963; joined CCP 1979; Vice-Mayor of Shanghai 1991–98; Vice-Dir. then Dir. Information Office of State Council 1998–. *Address:* State Council, Zhongnanhai, Beijing, People's Republic of China.

ZHAO RUICHUN; Chinese artist; b. Nov. 1935, Wenzhou, Zhejiang; s. of Zhao Loshu and Huang Shenghong; m. 1st 1956, one d.; m. 2nd Yun Xiuying, one d.; ed. Chinese Cen. Fine Arts Inst.; lecturer Guangzhou Inst. of Fine Arts 1959–71; teacher Chinese Cen. Fine Arts Inst. 1980–82; painter Guangzhou Art Acad. 1984–; first one-man exhbn. 1962; mem. Chinese Artists' Asscn., Chinese Engraving Asscn.; Sec.-Gen. Chinese Asscn. of Copper-Plate, Lithographic and Silkscreen Engraving; Ed.-in-Chief Modern Engraving; works exhibited in U.S.A., Japan, England, Australia, New Zealand, Ireland, Singapore, Denmark, Switzerland, Korea, Sweden, Thailand, Canada, U.S.S.R., Algeria, Italy and Taiwan. *Publications:* On Engraving Education 1981, Woodcut Techniques 1983, Practice and Theory of Sketching 1986, Silk-screen Plate Techniques 1987. *Leisure interest:* Chinese cooking. *Address:* Guangzhou Academy of Painting, 130 Shuiyin Road, Guangzhou 510075, Guangdong Province; 29 Tian Jin Lane, Wenzhou 325000, Zhejiang, People's Republic of China. *Telephone:* (20) 87724636 (Guangzhou).

ZHAO WEICHEN; Chinese government official; b. 1929, Acheng, Heilongjiang; Vice-Minister of State Econ. Comm. 1983; Vice-Chair. Environmental Protection Cttee., State Council 1984; Deputy Head Leading Group in charge of Sea, Land and Air Ports, State Council 1985; Head Leading Group for Cen. China Power Network, State Council 1984; Head Nat. Leading Group for Packaging Inspection, State Council 1984; Head Leading Group for Import and Export of Grain and Cotton, State Council 1985; Vice-Chair. Guangxi Zhuang Autonomous Regional People's Govt. 1987; mem. CPPCC 8th Nat. Cttee. 1993–; Chair. United Telecommunications Corpn. (UNICOM) 1994–. *Address:* UNICOM, Huibin Building, Yayun Village, Beijing, People's Republic of China. *Telephone:* (10) 64934151. *Fax:* (10) 64934153.

ZHAO YANXIA; Chinese opera singer; b. 1930, Beijing; d. of late Zhao Xiaolou; m. Liu Xinyuan; one d.; Head First Troupe, Beijing Opera Theatre of Beijing. *Address:* c/o Beijing Opera Theatre, Beijing, People's Republic of China. *Telephone:* 660425.

ZHAO ZHIHAO; Chinese government official; b. 1931, Longkou City, Huangxian Co., Shandong Prov.; joined CCP 1947; Sec. CCP Teng and Wenshang Co. Cttee. 1958–82, CCP Qufu Normal Coll. Cttee. 1982–83; Deputy Sec. CCP Shandong Prov. Cttee., Dir. Gen. Office 1983–85; Sec. CCP Zibo Municipal Cttee. 1985–88; Vice-Gov. Shangong Prov. 1988–89, Gov. 1989; mem. 14th CPP Cen. Cttee.; NPC Deputy, Shandong Prov.; Deputy Sec. CCP Shandong Prov. Cttee. 1988–94, Sec. 1994–, now Chair. *Address:* c/o Office of Provincial Governor, Jinan City, Shandong Province, People's Republic of China.

ZHAO ZHONGXIAN, DR.SC.; Chinese physicist; b. 30 Jan. 1941, Liaoning Prov.; s. of Zhao Desheng and Zhang Naibin; m. Zhou Yaqin 1967; two s.; ed. Univ. of Science and Tech. of China; Researcher, Inst. of Physics, Acad. Sinica 1964–, Research Fellow 1986–; Dir. Nat. Lab. for Superconductivity 1991–; mem. CPPCC 1993–; mem. China Asscn. for Science and Tech. 1991; Fellow, Third World Acad. of Sciences 1987, Acad. of Ceramics (Int.) 1989, Chinese Acad. of Sciences 1991; Hon. D.Sc. (Chinese Univ. of Hong Kong) 1988; Physics Award, Third World Acad. of Sciences 1986, Tan Kah-Kee Material Science Prize 1988, Natural Science Prize of China (1st Class) 1990, Wang Dan-ping Science Prize 1992, Science and Tech. Progress Award, Ho Leung Ho Lee Foundation 1997. *Address:* Institute of Physics, Academia Sinica, Zhong Guan Cun, P.O. Box 603, Beijing 100080; Room 1203, Building 811, Zhong Guan Cun, Beijing 100080, People's Republic of China. *Telephone:* (10) 62582190 (Office); (10) 62564951 (Home). *Fax:* (10) 62569220.

ZHARIKOV, Alexander Nikolayevich; Russian trade union official and engineer; b. 2 Jan. 1945, Arsenjevo; s. of Nicolai Philippovich Zharikov and Claudia Egorovna Gorodnicheva; m. Olga Borisovna Suhova 1975; one s.; ed. Leningrad Shipbldg. Inst.; mil. service 1962–66; Sec. of Youth and Student Org. of Leningrad 1971–74; Chair. Student Council of U.S.S.R. 1974–78; Vice-Pres. Int. Union of Students 1978–84; official, Int. Dept. Cen. Cttee. of CPSU 1984–88; Dir. Int. Dept. U.S.S.R. All-Union Council 1988–90; Sec.-Gen. World Fed. of Trade Unions (WFTU) 1990–; Order of Honour (Russia) 1974. *Publications:* book on world student movt. 1979; numerous articles on social issues, labour and trade union relations in newspapers and magazines. *Leisure interests:* swimming, collecting mushrooms, reading, skiing. *Address:* Branicka 112, 14701 Prague 4, Czech Republic (Office). *Telephone:* 02/4446 2140. *Fax:* 02/4446 1378.

ZHARIKOV, Vilen Andreyevich; Russian mineralogist; b. 20 Sept. 1926; m.; two d.; ed. Moscow Inst. of Geological Survey; worked as geologist, jr. then sr. researcher Inst. of Geology of Ore Deposits, Mineralogy and Geochem. 1950–69, Deputy Dir. 1969–79; Dir. Inst. of Experimental Mineralogy 1979–; Corresp. mem. U.S.S.R. (now Russian) Acad. of Sciences 1972, mem. 1987, Academican-Sec. Dept. of Geology, Geophysics, Geochem. and Mining Sciences 1991–96; Counsellor to Pres. 1996–; main research in geophysics and experimental mineralogy, petrology; mem. Petrographic Comm. Russian Acad. of Sciences; Chair. Comm. on Int. Programme of Geologic Correlation; U.S.S.R. State Prize. *Publications:* 6 monographs, dozens of articles and communications in scientific journals. *Address:* Department of Geology, Russian Academy of Sciences, Leninsky prospect 32A, 117334 Moscow, Russia (Office). *Telephone:* 938 0940 (Office, Acad.); 524-50-37 (Inst.).

ZHELEV, Zhelyu, PH.D.; Bulgarian politician; b. 3 March 1935, Veselinovo/Shumen, Varna Region; s. of Mityu Zhelev and Yordanka Nedelcheva; m. Maria Ivanova Marinova 1966; two d.; ed. Univ. of Sofia; fmr. librarian in Veselinovo; joined Bulgarian CP but expelled for criticism of Lenin 1964; unemployed 1966–72; initiator for establishment of Cttee. for Ecological Protection of City of Ruse 1988; Co-Pres. Club for Protection of Glasnost and Restructuring (now Glasnost and Democracy Club) until Nov. 1989; Chair. UDF (opposition party) 1989–90; Pres. of Bulgaria 1990–96. *Publication:* Fascism 1981. *Leisure interests:* hiking, fishing. *Address:* c/o Office of the President, 2 Dondukov Boulevard, Sofia, Bulgaria. *Telephone:* 871767.

ZHEN HAIXIA; Chinese basketball player; b. 1967, Shandong; started playing basketball aged 12; joined nat. team aged 15, now Capt.; also mem. PLA team; Capt. of Chinese basketball team which won Silver Medal at Barcelona Olympic Games 1992, Gold Medal at World Univ. Games 1993,

Silver Medal, Women's World Basketball Championships, Sydney 1994. *Leisure interests:* music, poetry.

ZHENG BIJIAN; Chinese university professor and party official; b. 1932, Fushun Co., Sichuan Prov.; ed. People's Univ. of China; joined CCP 1952; Vice-Pres. Chinese Acad. of Social Sciences and concurrently Dir. of its Research Inst. for Marxism-Leninism and Mao Zedong Thought 1988; mem. 14th CCP Cen. Cttee. 1992–97, 15th CCP Cen. Cttee. 1997–; Exec. Vice-Minister Dept. of Propaganda CCP 1992. *Address:* 5 West Changan Avenue, Beijing 100806, People's Republic of China.

ZHENG SILIN; Chinese administrator; b. May 1940, Wu Co., Jiangsu Prov.; joined CCP 1965; worked at Dandong Automobile Repair Plant, Liaoning Prov. 1965–81; Dir. Dandong TV Parts Factory 1982–83; Vice-Mayor Dandong City 1983–84; Dir. Comm. for Foreign Econ. Relations and Trade, and Asst. Gov., Liaoning Prov. 1984–85; Vice-Gov. Shaanxi Prov. People's Govt. 1989–93; Vice-Minister of Foreign Trade and Econ. Co-operation 1993–94; alt. mem. 13th Cen. Cttee. CCP 1987–92, 14th Cen. Cttee. 1992–97; Deputy Sec. 9th CCP Jiangsu Prov. Cttee.; Acting Gov. of Jiangsu Prov. 1994–95, Gov. 1995–98; Vice-Minister State Econ. and Trade Comm. 1998–; mem. 15th CCP Cen. Cttee. 1997–. *Address:* State Economic and Trade Commission, Beijing, People's Republic of China.

ZHENG TUOBIN; Chinese politician; b. Feb. 1924, Chengcheng Co., Shaanxi Prov.; m. Chen Longzhu; three s.; joined CCP 1938; Commercial Counsellor, Embassy in Moscow 1958–64; disappeared during Cultural Revolution; Deputy Dir. Dept. in Ministry of Foreign Trade 1972; Dir. Third Dept., Ministry of Foreign Trade 1973–77; Leader, trade dels. to Europe, N. America, Asia and Oceania; Vice-Minister of Foreign Trade 1978–81, Minister 1981–82; Vice-Minister of Foreign Econ. Relations and Trade 1982–85, Minister 1985–90; mem. 12th CCP Cen. Cttee. 1982, 13th CCP Cen. Cttee. 1987–92; Sec. Party Group of Ministry of Foreign Econ. Relations and Trade 1985–90; Deputy Dir. Comm. for Commemorating 40th Anniversary of UN 1985. *Leisure interests:* golfing, computers, calligraphy and gardening. *Address:* c/o Ministry of Foreign Trade and Economic Co-operation, 100731 Beijing, People's Republic of China. *Telephone:* 65197542.

ZHENG WANTONG; Chinese politician; b. May 1941, Tianjin; ed. Tianjin Teachers' Coll. 1959; joined CCP 1960; high school teacher, cadre Communist Youth League Hebei Dist. Cttee., Tianjin 1961–70; cadre CCP Hebei Dist. Cttee. 1970–78; cadre then Dir. Gen. Office of CCP Tianjin Municipal Cttee. 1978–83; Chief Sec. CCP Tianjin Municipal Cttee. 1983–88; Vice-Chair. and Sec. Secr. All-China Fed. of Trade Unions 1988–93; Vice-Dir. United Front Work Dept. of CCP Cen. Cttee.; Vice-Chair. All-China Fed. of Industry and Commerce; Vice-Chief Sec. Nat. Cttee. of CPPCC 1993–98; mem. CCP Cen. Cttee. for Discipline Inspection 1997–; Chief Sec. Nat. Cttee. of CPPCC 1998–. *Address:* National Committee of Chinese People's Political Consultative Conference, 23 Taipingqiao Street, Beijing, People's Republic of China.

ZHIRINOVSKY, Vladimir Volfovich, D.PHIL.; Russian politician; b. 25 April 1946, Alma-Ata, Kazakhstan; m. Galina Zhirinovsky; two s.; ed. Inst. of Asian and African Countries, and Faculty of Law, Moscow State Univ.; officer, U.S.S.R. Ministry of Defence, with Gen. Staff of Transcaucasian command 1970–72; with Soviet Soc. of Friendship and Cultural Relations, Cttee. for Peace 1973–83; legal consultant, Mir Publs. 1983–90; f. 1989 and Chair. Liberal-Democratic Party of Soviet Union (now of Russia; LDPR) 1990–; cand. in Russian Presidential Election 1991; mem. State Duma (Parl.) 1993–, Chair. LDPR faction; rank of Lieut.-Col. in Army Reserve 1995. *Publications:* The Last Leap South 1993, Political Landscape of Russia 1995, Economic Ideas of a Politician 1996, Geopolitics and the Russian Question 1997, The Zhirinovsky Phenomenon in Russia 1998, and more than 100 other books and publs. *Leisure interests:* volleyball, swimming. *Address:* State Duma, Okhotny Ryad 1, 103009 Moscow; Liberal-Democratic Party of Russia, 1st Basmanny per. 3, 103045 Moscow, Russia. *Telephone:* (095) 292-80-01, 292-77-11 (Duma); (095) 261-00-33 (Party). *Fax:* (095) 292-37-95 (Duma).

ZHISLIN, Grigory Yefimovich; Russian violinist; b. 14 May 1945, Leningrad (now St. Petersburg); s. of Sarra and Yefim Zhislin; m. Valentina Murashova 1980; one s.; ed. Moscow State Conservatory (pupil of Yuny Yankelevich); winner Int. Competitions of Paganini in Genoa 1967 and Queen Elizabeth in Brussels 1976; concerts in U.S.S.R. and abroad 1966–; participated in maj. music festivals including Maggio Musicale Fiorentino, Warsaw Autumn, Prague Spring, Kuhmi Chamber Music, Berliner Biennale, Pablo Casals in Puerto Rico, Paganini in Genoa and others; teacher Kharkov Inst. of Arts 1971–73, Moscow Gnessin Pedagogical Inst. 1973–, Prof. 1978–90; Royal Coll. of Music London 1990–; Hochschule für Musik Würzburg 1993–; Visiting Prof. Oslo, Cracow, Warsaw Conservatories; master classes U.S.A., Italy, France, Finland, Sweden. *Address:* 25 Whitehall Gardens, London, W3 9RD, England. (Home). *Telephone:* 0181-993 8223. *Fax:* 0181-993 8295.

ZHIVKOV, Zhivko; Bulgarian politician; b. 1915, Toshevtsi, Vidin; ed. Sofia Univ.; Young Communist League 1931–89, CP 1935–89 (expelled Dec. 1989); imprisoned 1942–44; mem. Cen. Cttee., later Sec., Young Communist League; fmr. Deputy to Foreign Minister; Minister of Foreign Trade 1952–57, of Educ. and Culture 1958–59, Deputy Prime Minister 1959–62, First Deputy Chair. Council of Ministers 1962–71, Deputy Chair. 1971–76; Chair. Cttee. for Econ. Co-ordination 1969–89; mem. Cen. Cttee. of Bulgarian Communist Party 1954–89, mem. Political Bureau 1962–76; mem. State Council 1976–89.

ZHONG MING, F.R.S.A.; artist; b. 1949, Beijing, China; elected to Chinese Artists' Asscn. 1980; founder mem. Beijing Oil Painting Research Asscn.; moved to London 1984; exhibited at Open Exhbn. of Royal Soc. of Painters in Watercolour, Bankside Gallery 1984; one-man exhbns. at Camden Arts Centre 1985, Smith's Gallery, Convent Garden 1986, Hong Kong 1988, Taipei 1989; has also exhibited in Japan and Sweden; speaker at int. symposium The Authentic Garden, Leiden, Netherlands 1990. *Publications:* The Craft of Gardens (photographer) 1988; articles on art and cultural subjects in various periodicals. *Address:* 23A Block 2, Ronsdale Garden, 25 Tai Hang Drive, Hong Kong; 51 Sunningwell Road, Oxford, OX1 4SZ, England.

ZHOU DAOJIONG; Chinese banker; b. 1936; ed. Cen. Coll. of Finance; joined CCP 1960; Vice-Pres. of People's Construction Bank of China 1986–90, Pres. 1990–95; fmr. Vice-Pres. State Devt. Bank; Chair. Chinese Securities Regulatory Comm. 1995. *Address:* c/o Chinese Securities Regulatory, Commission, Beijing, People's Republic of China.

ZHOU GANZHI; Chinese architect; b. 1930, Suzhou, Jiangsu Prov.; ed. Tsinghua Univ.; joined CCP 1952; Deputy Office Dir. State Construction Comm.; Vice-Dir. City Planning Research Inst. of State Gen. Admin. of City Construction; Acting Dir. Tianjin City Planning Bureau; Sr. Architect and Pres. China City Planning and Design Research Acad.; Vice-Minister of Urban and Rural Construction and Environment Protection; Vice-Minister of Construction 1952–98; Chair. Standing Cttee. of Civil Eng. and Water Conservancy Eng., Dept. of Chinese Acad. of Eng. 1998–. *Address:* c/o Chinese Academy of Engineering, Beijing, People's Republic of China.

ZHOU GUANGZHAO; Chinese physicist; b. 15 May 1929, Changsha City, Hunan Prov.; m. Zheng Aiqin 1955; one d.; ed. Tsinghua Univ., Peking Univ.; joined CCP 1952; Dir. 9th Research Inst. of Second Ministry of Machine-Bldg. Industry; Research Fellow and Dir. Physics Research Inst. of Chinese Acad. of Sciences; Vice-Pres. Chinese Acad. of Sciences 1960–87, Pres. 1987–; alt. mem. 12th CCP Cen. Cttee. 1982, mem. 1985; mem. 13th CCP Cen. Cttee. 1987–92, 14th Cen. Cttee. 1992–97, 15th CCP Cen. Cttee. 1997–; Vice-Chair. Standing Cttee. of 9th NPC 1998–; took part in making of China's first atomic bomb and hydrogen bomb. *Address:* Chinese Academy of Sciences, 52 San Li He Road, 100864 Beijing, People's Republic of China. *Telephone:* 8597203.

ZHOU JUE; Chinese diplomatist; b. 1927; m. Yu Zhilan; Deputy Dir. West Asia and North Africa Dept., Ministry of Foreign Affairs 1971–73, Acting Dir. 1974–78, Dir. 1979–81; Amb. to Turkey 1981–84, to France 1988–91; Asst. Foreign Minister 1984–87; Vice-Dir. Office of News under State Council 1991; Vice-Chair. Educ., Science, Culture and Public Health Cttee.; mem. 8th NPC 1993–, NPC Deputy, Inner Mongolia. *Address:* c/o Ministry of Foreign Affairs, 225 Chaonei Street, Beijing, People's Republic of China.

ZHOU KEYU, Gen.; Chinese army officer and party official; b. 1929, Funing Co., Jiangsu Prov.; joined CCP 1945, PLA 1947, Deputy Dir. of PLA Gen. Political Dept. 1985, Political Commissar Gen. Logistics Dept. 1990–95; rank of Lieut.-Gen. 1988; mem. 14th CCP Cen. Cttee. 1992–97; Vice-Chair. Legal Affairs Cttee. of 9th NPC 1998–. *Address:* c/o Standing Committee of National People's Congress, Beijing, People's Republic of China.

ZHOU KUNREN, Lieut.-Gen.; Chinese naval officer; b. Sept. 1937, Danyang Co., Jiangsu Prov.; ed. PLA Political Acad. and PLA Univ. of Nat. Defence; joined PLA 1956; mem. CCP 1960–; Vice-Dir. Political Dept. of Navy; rank of Maj.-Gen. 1988; Political Commissar South Sea Fleet; Vice-Political Commissar, PLA Navy 1992, Political Commissar 1992; rank of Lieut.-Gen. 1993; Political Commissar, PLA Gen. Logistics Dept. 1995–; mem. 15th CCP Cen. Cttee. 1997–. *Address:* People's Liberation Army General Logistics Department, Beijing, People's Republic of China.

ZHOU MINGZHEN, PH.D.; Chinese academic; b. 9 Nov. 1918; s. of Henry Zhou and Zhou Chingru; m. Maychen Chay 1940 (deceased); two s. one d.; Prof. Inst. of Vertebrate Palaeontology 1956; Dir. Beijing Natural History Museum; mem. Chinese Acad. of Sciences. *Leisure interests:* photography, music, reading. *Address:* P.O. Box 643, 100044 Beijing, People's Republic of China. *Telephone:* 255 2246.

ZHOU NAN; Chinese government official; b. 1927, Qufu City, Shandong; m. Huang Guo; Counsellor, Chinese Mission to UN and Deputy Rep. of People's Repub. of China (rank of Amb.) 1971–81; Vice-Foreign Minister, Pres. Coll. of Foreign Affairs 1984–90; Dir. Xinhua News Agency, Hong Kong 1990–; mem. CCP Congress 1991; mem. 7th Standing Cttee., NPC 1991, 8th NPC 1993–; mem. 14th CCP Cen. Cttee. 1992–; Dir. Xinhua News Agency, Hong Kong Br. 1990–; Head of del. to Sino-British talks on Hong Kong Question 1984; Head of del. to Sino-Portuguese Talks on Macau Question 1986; Deputy Head Preliminary Working Cttee. of the Preparatory Cttee. of the Hong Kong Special Admin. Region 1993–95, Vice-Chair. Preparatory Cttee. 1995–. *Address:* Hong Kong Bureau of Xinhua News Agency, 387 Queen's Road, East Hong Kong, Hong Kong Special Administrative Region, People's Republic of China. *Telephone:* 28314333.

ZHOU TIENONG; Chinese politician; b. Nov. 1938, Shenyang, Liaoning Prov.; ed. Peking Univ.; teaching asst., lecturer, Assoc. Prof. Northeast Heavy Machinery Coll. 1961–83; Vice-Mayor of Qiqihar, Heilongjiang Prov.

1983–91; Vice-Gov. Heilongjiang Prov. 1991–98; Vice-Chair. Cen. Cttee. of Kuomintang Revolutionary Cttee. 1992–; Vice-Chair. Nat. Cttee. of CPPCC 1998–. *Address:* National Committee of Chinese People's Political Consultative Conference, 23 Taipingqiao Street, Beijing, People's Republic of China.

ZHOU WEIZHI; Chinese politician and musician; b. 1916, Dongtai Co., Jiangsu Prov.; joined CCP 1938; Dir. Central Songs and Dance Troupe; Pres. Cen. Experimental Drama Theatre; Dir. Arts Dept. of Ministry of Culture; Vice-Minister then Acting Minister of Culture; Vice-Chair. Chinese Musicians Asscn.; Chair. China Fed. of Literary and Art Circles 1996. *Address:* Ministry of Culture, Jia 83, Donganmen Bei Jie, Dongcheng Qu, Beijing 100701, Beijing, People's Republic of China.

ZHOU WENYUAN, Maj.-Gen.; Chinese army officer and party official; b. 1940, Tianjin City; ed. Hebei Political Teachers Coll.; joined PLA 1961, Deputy Dir. PLA Gen. Political Dept. 1985; Deputy Political Commissar Shenyang Mil. Region 1993–; joined CCP 1963; alt. mem. 13th CCP Cen. Cttee. 1987–92, 14th 1992–. *Address:* c/o Ministry of National Defence, Jingshanqian Jie, Beijing, People's Republic of China.

ZHOU XIAOYAN; Chinese musician; b. Wuhan City, Hubei Prov.; ed. Shanghai Music School and in France; performed in London, Paris, Geneva, Berlin, Prague and Warsaw; a Vice-Chair. Chinese Musicians' Asscn. 1979–; Dir. of Vocal Dept. Shanghai Conservatory of Music 1987. *Address:* Shanghai Conservatory of Music, Shanghai City, People's Republic of China.

ZHOU XIUJI; Chinese physicist; b. 1936, Zhejiang Prov.; ed. Beijing Univ.; mem. Chinese Acad. of Sciences 1992, Environmental and Resources Protection Cttee. *Address:* State Meteorological Administration, Beijing, People's Republic of China.

ZHOU YONGKANG; Chinese politician; b. Dec. 1942, Wuxi City, Jiangsu Prov.; joined CCP 1964; ed. Beijing Petroleum Inst.; Dir. and Vice.-Sec. CCP Cttee. of Liaohe Petroleum Exploration Bureau; Mayor Panjin City 1983, Vice-Sec. CCP Panjin City Cttee. 1983–85; Vice-Minister of Petroleum Industry 1985; Vice-Gen. Man. Head Office of China Petroleum and Natural Gas Company 1988; alt. mem. 14th CCP Cen. Cttee. 1992; Gen. Man. Head Office of China Petroleum and Natural Gas Company 1997–98; Minister of Land Resources 1998–; mem. 15th CCP Cen. Cttee. 1997–. *Address:* c/o China Petroleum and Natural Gas Company, Beijing, People's Republic of China.

ZHOU YOUGUANG; Chinese economist and linguist; b. 13 Jan. 1906, Changzhou City, Jiangsu Prov.; s. of Zhou Qixian and Xu Wen; m. Zhang Yunhe 1933; one s.; ed. Changzhou High School, St. John's Univ. and Guanghua Univ. 1927; teaching in Guanghua Univ., Shanghai and other univs. 1927–37; Sinhua Bank, Shanghai and Hong Kong 1937–45; Rep. of Sinhua Bank, to New York and London 1946–48; Prof., Fudan Univ. and Shanghai Coll. of Finance and Econs. 1949–55; Research Prof., Cttee. for Written Languages Reform of China 1956–87, Research Prof. State Language Comm. and Chinese Social Sciences Acad., Beijing 1987–; visited U.S.A. 1990. *Publications include:* Language Reform of China 1961, A Free Talk on Chinese Languages 1992, Alphabets of the World (A Chinese View) 1993. *Address:* Chaonei Nanxiaojie 51, 1-301, Beijing, People's Republic of China. *Telephone:* (10) 65254765.

ZHOU ZHENGQING; Chinese business executive and politician; fmr. Deputy Gov. Cen. Bank of China; Deputy Sec. Gen. State Council Sept. 1995–98; mem. Cen. Financial and Econ. Leading Group 1994–; Chair. China Securities Supervisory Comm. 1996–. *Address:* c/o State Council, Beijing, People's Republic of China.

ZHOU ZIYU, Gen.; Chinese army officer; Deputy Dir. PLA Gen. Political Dept.; rank of Gen. 1996; Deputy Sec. Cen. Comm. for Discipline Inspection 1997–; mem. 15th CCP Cen. Cttee. 1997–. *Address:* c/o Central Committee of the Chinese Communist Party, Zhongnanhai, Beijing, People's Republic of China.

ZHU DUNFA, Lieut.-Gen.; Chinese army officer; b. 1927, Peixian Co., Jiangsu Prov.; joined CCP 1945; Deputy Commdr. of PLA Shengyang Mil. Area Command 1985; Commandant PLA Nat. Defence Univ. 1992–95; rank of Lieut.-Gen. 1988; mem. 14th CCP Cen. Cttee. 1992–. *Address:* Shengyang Miltiary Area Command, People's Liberation Army, Shengyang City, Liaoning Province, People's Republic of China.

ZHU GAOFENG; Chinese politician and engineer; b. May 1935, Ningbo, Zhejiang Prov.; ed. Tsinghua Univ., Leningrad Telecommunication Eng. Inst.; joined CCP 1964; technician, engineer, Sr. Engineer and Chief Engineer Ministry of Posts and Telecommunications 1958–82; Vice-Minister of Posts and Telecommunications 1982–98; Vice-Pres. Chinese Acad. of Sciences 1998–. *Address:* Chinese Academy of Sciences, 52 Sanlihe Road, Beijing 100846, People's Republic of China.

ZHU GUANGYA, PH.D.; Chinese physicist and state official; b. 1924, Hubei Prov.; Prof. in Tech. Faculty, Beijing Univ. 1940; mem. Youth League Cen. Cttee. 1953; alt. mem. 9th CCP Cen. Cttee. 1969; mem. 11th CCP Cen. Cttee. 1977; Deputy for PLA to 5th NPC 1978; Vice-Pres. Nuclear Physics Soc. 1980; Vice-Minister, State Scientific and Tech. Comm. 1981–82; Vice-Chair. Science and Tech. Cttee. for Nat. Defence of the PLA 1982–86, Chair. 1986–; mem. 12th CCP Cttee. 1982, 13th Cen. Cttee. 1987–92, 14th Cen. Cttee. 1992–97; Vice-Chair. China Asscn. for Science and Tech. 1986–91, Chair. 1991–95, Hon. Chair. 1996–; mem. Nat. Academic Degrees Cttee. 1988–, Vice-Chair. 1995–; Vice-Chair. 8th Nat. Cttee. of CPPCC 1995–98, 9th Nat. Cttee. 1998–; Pres. Chinese Acad. of Eng. 1994–98; mem. Nat. Leading Group for Science and Tech. 1996–. *Address:* National Committee of Chinese People's Political Consultative Conference, 23 Taipingqiao Street, Beijing, People's Republic of China.

ZHU HOUZE; Chinese party official; b. 16 Jan. 1931, Guiyang Municipality, Guizhou Prov.; s. of Zhu Mei-lu and Xiong Lan-Xian; m. Qiong Zhen-qun 1954; one s. two d.; mem. 12th CCP Cen. Cttee. 1982; Sec. CCP Cttee. Guiyang Municipality 1982; Sec. CCP Cttee., Guizhou Prov. 1983–85; Head, Propaganda Dept. CCP Cen. Cttee. 1985–86; Vice-Pres., Sr. Research Fellow Research Centre for Rural Devt. of the State Council 1987–88; Vice-Chair., First Sec. All-China Fed. of Trade Unions 1989. *Leisure interests:* swimming, music, tennis, photography. *Address:* Jia No. 15, Wan-shou Road, Beijing 100036, People's Republic of China. *Telephone:* (10) 6821.1225. *Fax:* (10) 6821.1225.

ZHU KAIXUAN; Chinese engineer and administrator; b. 1932, Shanghai City; ed. Beijing Aeronautical Inst.; joined CCP 1953; Vice-Minister in charge of State Educ. Comm. 1985–92, Minister 1992–98; Vice-Chair. Acad. Degrees Cttee. under State Council 1988; Head Nat. Co-ordination group for Anti-Illiteracy Work 1994–; alt. mem. 14th CCP Cen. Cttee. 1992–97; Party Group Sec. State Educ. Comm. 1993–98; Chair. Cttee. of Educ., Science, Culture and Public Health, 9th NPC 1998–. *Address:* c/o Standing Committee of National People's Congress, Beijing, People's Republic of China.

ZHU LIANG; Chinese party and government official; b. 1924, Chaoyang Co., Guangdong Prov.; ed. Shanghai Saint John Univ.; joined CCP 1945; Head, Int. Liaison Dept. CCP 1985; a Vice-Pres. Chinese People's Asscn. for Peace and Disarmament 1985–; mem. 13th Cen. Cttee. CCP 1987–91, 14th 1992–; mem. 8th NPC 1993–; Chair. Foreign Affairs Cttee., Repub. of Korea Friendship Group. *Address:* International Liaison Department, Zhonggong Zhongyang, Beijing 100001, People's Republic of China.

ZHU LILAN; Chinese scientist and administrator; b. 18 Aug. 1935, Huzhou Co., Zhejiang Prov.; ed. Odessa Univ. fmr. U.S.S.R.; joined CCP 1956; Vice-Minister in charge of State Science and Tech. Comm. 1986–98, Party Group Sec. 1994–; alt. mem. 14th CCP Cen. Cttee. 1992; mem. Nat. Leading Group for Science and Tech. 1996–98; Minister of Science and Tech. 1998–; mem. 15th CCP Cen. Cttee. 1997–. *Address:* Ministry of Science and Technology, 15B Fuxing Road, Beijing 100862, People's Republic of China. *Telephone:* 6851 2648. *Fax:* 6851 2594.

ZHU LIN; Chinese actress; b. 22 May 1923, Lianyungang City, Jiangsu Prov.; d. of Zhu Xiaofang and Zhao Shouxuan; m. Diao Guangtan 1943; three s. one d.; ed. Huayin Teachers' Coll. and Wuchang Art Training School; actress, Anti-Japanese Performing Group 1938–45, Datong Film Studio 1948–50, China Youth Art Theatre 1950–52, Beijing People's Art Theatre 1953–; Award for Promoting China's Drama 1988, Golden Eagle Prize for Best Supporting Actress, for role of Dowager Empress in film The Last Emperor 1989. *Films:* Weakling, Your Name is Woman 1948, Trials and Hardships 1949, Waiting 1950, The Last Emperor 1989, Su Wu Graze Sheep 1996. *Theatre includes:* Put Down Your Whip 1937, Beautiful Women 1947, Thunderstorm 1953, Three Sisters 1959, Cai Wenji 1959, 1962, 1978, Wu Zetian 1962–64, Death of a Salesman 1983, Win Game 1987, Candied Haws on a Stick 1996, Thunderstorm 1997. *Address:* Room 601, Unit 2, Building 38, Dongzhi Menwai Street, Beijing 100027, People's Republic of China. *Telephone:* 64168165.

ZHU MINGSHAN; Chinese jurist; b. May 1937, Jiutai Co., Jilin Prov.; two s.; ed. People's Univ., Beijing; joined CCP 1961; Judge Criminal Court, Supreme People's Court 1978–82, Vice-Pres. 1982–83, Vice-Pres. Supreme People's Court 1983–. *Address:* Supreme People's Court, 27 Dongjiaomin Xiang, Beijing 100745, People's Republic of China.

ZHU MUZHI; Chinese government official; b. 25 Dec. 1916, Jiangyin City, Jiangsu; s. of Zhu Zushou and He Jiazhen; m. Zhou Luo 1945; one s. two d.; joined CCP 1938; Deputy Ed.-in-Chief Xinhua News Agency 1950, Deputy Dir. 1952; Deputy Dir. New China News Agency (NCNA), State Council 1952–72; Deputy for Jiangsu, 2nd NPC 1958, 3rd NPC 1964; disappeared during Cultural Revolution; Dir. NCNA 1972–77; mem. 10th Cen. Cttee., CCP 1973, 11th Cen. Cttee. 1977; Deputy Dir. Propaganda Dept., CCP Cen. Cttee. 1977; mem. Standing Cttee., Nat. Cttee., 5th CPPCC 1978; mem. Comm. for Inspecting Discipline, CCP Cen. Cttee. 1978; Adviser, Beijing Journalism Studies Soc. 1980; Minister of Culture 1982–86; mem. 12th Cen. Cttee., CCP 1982–85; mem. Advisory Cen. Cttee. CCP 1985, 13th Cen. Cttee. 1987; Dir. Office of News under State Council 1991; mem. Fed. of Literature and Art Circles 1982; Pres. Asscn. for Cultural Exchanges with Foreign Countries 1986–; Pres. China Soc. for the Study of Human Rights 1994–. *Address:* State Council, Beijing, People's Republic of China.

ZHU QIZHEN; Chinese government official; b. 19 Dec. 1927, Jiangsu; m. Wang Yude 1955; one d.; Gen. Office, Ministry of Foreign Affairs 1949–62; Second Sec., First Sec. Chinese Embassy, U.A.R. 1963–68; Div. Chief African Affairs Dept., Ministry of Foreign Affairs 1969–71, Deputy Dir. West Asian and North African Affairs Dept. 1972–73; Counsellor, Chinese Embassy, Australia 1973–76; Deputy Dir. American and Oceanic Dept., Ministry of Foreign Affairs 1977–81, Dir. 1982; Asst. Minister, Ministry of Foreign Affairs 1982–84, Vice-Minister 1984–89; Amb. to U.S.A. 1989–93; mem.

Standing Cttee., Vice-Chair. Foreign Affairs Cttee., 8th NPC 1993–, NPC Deputy, Henan Prov. *Address:* 23 Xi Jiao Min Xiang, Beijing 100805, People's Republic of China. *Telephone:* 6309-9680. *Fax:* 6309-8667.

ZHU RONGJI; Chinese engineer and government official; b. 20 Oct. 1928, Changsha City, Hunan Prov.; ed. Qinghua Univ.; joined CCP 1949; Dir. Tech. Transformation Bureau under State Econ. Comm. 1982–83; Vice-Minister of State Economic Comm. 1983–87; Deputy Sec. Shanghai Municipal Cttee. 1987–89, Sec. 1989–91; Mayor Shanghai Municipal People's Govt. 1988–91; a Vice-Premier, State Council 1991–98, Premier 1998–; Gov. Cen. Bank of PRC 1993–95; alt. mem. 13th CCP Cen. Cttee. 1987–92; mem. 14th CCP Cen. Cttee. 1992–97, mem. 15th CCP Cen. Cttee. 1997–; mem. CCP Politburo 1992–98, 15th NPC 1998–; Pres. Business Man. Inst. 1994–; Prime Minister of PRC 1998–. *Address:* State Council, Xi Changan Jie, Beijing, People's Republic of China.

ZHU SENLIN; Chinese governor; b. 1930, Chuansha Co., Shanghai; ed. Qinghua Univ.; Deputy Sec.-Gen. Guangzhou City Parl. Cttee. and Dir., Gen. Office 1981; later Deputy Sec. Guangzhou City Party Cttee. and Mayor Guangzhou City; mem. Provincial Party Cttee. and mem. and Sec. Guangzhou City Party Cttee.; Deputy Sec., Provincial Vice-Gov. and Acting Provincial Gov. 1991–93; Gov. of Guangdong Prov. 1992–96; alt. mem. 13th CCP Cen. Cttee. and Deputy 7th Nat. People's Congress, Deputy 8th NPC 1993–; Deputy Sec. CPC 7th Guangdong Prov. Cttee. 1991–; mem. 14th CCP Cen. Cttee. 1992–97; Chair. Guangdong People's Congress Standing Cttee. 1996. *Address:* 305 Central Dongpeng Road, Guangzhou, People's Republic of China.

ZHU XU; Chinese actor; b. Feb. 1930, Shenyang, Liaoning Prov.; actor Beijing People's Arts Theatre 1952–; Best Actor Award 9th Tokyo Film Festival (1996) for Face Change. *Address:* Beijing People's Arts Theatre, Beijing, People's Republic of China.

ZHU XUN; Chinese state official; b. 1930, Funing Co., Jiangsu Prov.; ed. China People's Univ. and in U.S.S.R.; Vice-Minister of Geology and Minerals 1982–85, Minister 1985; alt. mem. 12th CCP Cen. Cttee. 1982, mem. 1985–87, mem. 13th CCP Cen. Cttee. 1987–92; mem. 14th CCP Cen. Cttee. 1992–97; Sec.-Gen. 8th Nat. Cttee. CPPCC 1994–98; Chair. Cttee. for Hong Kong, Macao, Taiwan and Overseas Chinese Affairs, 9th Nat. Cttee. of CPPCC 1998–; Hon. mem. Int. Hydrogeologists' Asscn. 1989. *Address:* c/o National Committee of Chinese People's Political Consultative Conference, 23 Taipingqiao Street, Beijing, People's Republic of China.

ZHU YAOHUA; Chinese government official; b. 23 Jan. 1940, Xian Municipality, Shanxi Prov.; m. Li Yazhi 1962; three s.; fmr. Vice-Pres. People's Bank of China; Deputy Dir. Science and Tech. Dept., State Family Planning Comm. April 1992–; Dir. State Admin. of Exchange Control Jan. 1994–. *Leisure interests:* literature, sports. *Address:* State Family Planning Commission, 14 Zhichun Road, Beijing 100088, People's Republic of China. *Telephone:* (10) 62046622. *Fax:* (10) 62051847.

ZHU YINGHUANG; Chinese journalist; b. 28 Dec. 1943, Shanghai; m. Yao Xiang 1972; one d.; Ed.-in-Chief China Daily; Chair. China Daily Newspaper Group. *Address:* China Daily, 15 Huixin Dongjie, Chao Yang Qu, Beijing 100029, People's Republic of China. *Telephone:* (10) 64924488. *Fax:* (10) 64918377.

ZHU YULI; Chinese aviation industry official; Dir. State Bureau of Tech. Supervision 1990–93; Deputy Dir. Econ. and Trade Office State Council 1991, Dir. of Gen. Office of State Council's Leading Group for "Year of Quality, Variety and Economic Results" 1992; Pres. Aviation Industries of China 1993–; mem. 15th CCP Cen. Cttee. 1997–. *Address:* Aviation Industries of China, Beijing, People's Republic of China.

ZHU ZHENDA; Chinese scientist; b. 20 June 1930, Zhejiang Prov.; ed. Nanjing Univ.; Head, Dept. Desert Research, Geography Inst. 1959–65; awarded China Science Congress Prize 1977; Dir., Lanzhou Desert Research Inst. 1981, Chinese Acad. of Sciences 1982. *Address:* Institute of Desert Research, 14 Dong Guan Xilu, Lanzhou, Gansu, People's Republic of China.

ZHUANG XIAOHUI, PH.D.; Chinese embryologist; b. 23 Sept. 1913, Shandong Prov.; m. Zeng Mibai 1948; one s. one d.; ed. Univ. of Munich, Germany; Deputy Dir. Inst. of Experimental Biology 1961–64, Dir. 1964–; Dir. Shanghai Inst. of Cell Biology 1978–84, Hon. Dir. 1985–; mem. Academia Sinica 1980–; mem. 7th CPPCC 1988–. *Address:* Institute of Cell Biology, Academia Sinica, 320 Yueyang Road, Shanghai 200031, People's Republic of China. *Telephone:* (21) 4315030. *Fax:* (21) 4331090.

ZHUMALIYEV, Kubanychbek Myrzabekovich; Kyrgyzstan politician; b. 26 April 1956, Osh Region, Kyrgyzstan; Head, Admin. of Pres. Akayev 1996–98; Prime Minister of Kyrgyzstan 1998–. *Address:* Parliament Buildings, 720003 Bishkek, Kyrgyzstan. *Telephone:* (9961) 22 43 21 (Office).

ZHURKIN, Vitaliy Vladimirovich, DR.PHIL.; Russian political scientist; b. 14 Jan. 1928, Moscow; m. Dina Zhurkina 1961 (died 1997); one s.; ed. Moscow Inst. of Int. Relations; Ed. journal U.S.A.: Economics, Politics, Ideology; Deputy Dir. U.S.A. and Canada Inst. 1971–87; f. and Dir. Inst. of Europe, U.S.S.R. (now Russian) Acad. of Sciences 1987–; Sec. Dept. of World Econ. and Int. Relations, Acad. of Sciences 1991; corresp. mem. U.S.S.R. (now Russian) Acad. of Sciences 1984, mem. 1990; mem. Acad. Europaea 1990, World Acad. of Art and Science 1994; U.S.S.R. State Prize 1980. *Publications:* works on the political and military aspects of contemporary international relations. *Address:* Institute of Europe, 18, Korp. 3, Mokhovaya Str., 103873 Moscow, Russia. *Telephone:* 203-73-43 (Office); 230-00-70 (Home). *Fax:* 200-42-98.

ZHVANETSKY, Mikhail Mikhailovich; Russian writer; b. 6 March 1934, Odessa; s. of Emmanuil Moiseevich Zhvanetsky and Raisa Yakovlevna Zhvanetskaya; two s. one d.; ed. Odessa Inst. of Naval Eng.; worked as technician and engineer, Prodmash factory, Odessa shipbuilding yard 1956–64; literary work 1964–; wrote short stories for Comedy Theatre of A. Raikin; freelance 1970–; performed readings of short stories 1970–; stories banned because of criticism of state; founder and Ed. Magazin journal 1991; Hon. Citizen of Odessa; Triumph Prize 1994. *Publications include:* Meetings in the Streets 1977, A Year For Two (short stories) 1989, My Life, Stay with Me (novel) 1989, Wirbrauchen Helden! (short stories) 1992, My Odessa 1993 (short stories); also stories in newspapers and periodicals. *Address:* Magazin, 1st Tverskaya-Yamskaya 16, 125047 Moscow (Office); Lesnaya Str. 4, Apt. 63, 125047 Moscow, Russia (Home). *Telephone:* (095) 250-37-21 (Office); 187-06-48 (Home).

ZHVANIA, Zurab; Georgian politician; b. 9 Dec. 1963, Tbilisi; m.; two c.; ed. Tbilisi State Univ.; sr. lab. asst., jr. researcher Chair of Physiology of Man and Animals, Tbilisi State Univ. 1985–92; Chair. Cen. Exec. Bd. of Green Party of Georgia 1988–93; Speaker Green Party of Georgia 1990–93; Chair. European Union of Green Parties 1992–93; one of initiators Union of Citizens of Georgia; one of founders, Sec.-Gen. Union of Citizens of Georgia 1993–; mem. Parl. (Green Faction) 1992–95, Chair. 1995–. *Address:* House of Government, Tbilisi, Georgia.

ZI HUAYUN; Chinese dancer and scholar; b. 10 March 1936, Tianjin City; d. of Zi Yaohua and Tong Yijun; m. Wang Shouyin 1960; one s. one d.; ed. Tianjin Nankai High School, Beijing Normal Univ., Beijing Cen. Drama Coll.; dancer, China Cen. Dance Ensemble 1950–; Dir. and Sr. Fellow Dance Research Inst. of Chinese Arts Acad. 1987–; prizes include Gold Medal (for Tibetan Dance), 3rd World Youth Festival, Berlin 1950, Bronze Medal (for Flying Apsara), 5th World Youth Festival, Warsaw 1955, Prize for Excellent Performance, 1st Nat. Dancing Competition 1984. *Publications:* Dance and I 1987, Chinese and Foreign Artists 1989, Introduction to Choreology (Co-author) 1991, Treatises on Choreology (Co-author), The Rise and Development of Chinese Folk Dance during the past 50 years 1992; Chief Ed. of The Art of Dance. *Address:* Dance Research Institute, Chinese Academy of Arts, 17 Qianhai Xijie, Beijing 100009, People's Republic of China.

ZIA, Begum Khaleda; Bangladeshi politician; b. 15 Aug. 1945; d. of late Iskander Majumder and of Begum Taiyaba Majumder; m. Capt. Ziaur Rahman (later Pres. of Bangladesh) 1960 (deceased); two s.; ed. Surendranath Coll., Dinajpur; held captive during Bangladesh's war of independence; Vice-Chair. Nat. Party (BNP) 1982–84, Chair. 1984–; helped to form seven-party alliance leading to ousting Pres. Ershad from power 1990; elected Prime Minister of Bangladesh 1991–96; Chair. SAARC 1993–94. *Leisure interests:* reading, listening to music, gardening. *Address:* BNP, 29 Minto Road, Dhaka, Bangladesh.

ZIEGLER, Jean, D. EN D., D. EN SC.POL.; Swiss university professor, writer and politician; b. 19 April 1934, Berne; s. of Hans Ziegler and Léa Ziegler; m.; one s.; ed. Univs. of Geneva, Berne, Paris-Sorbonne and Columbia Univ. New York; with Swiss American Corpn. New York 1959; jr. lawyer in training with Theodor Haffner, New York; Asst. to Sec.-Gen. of Int. Comm. of Jurists; UN expert, Leopoldville and Elisabethville, Congo 1961–62; Research Assoc. Faculté de Droit, Inst. Africain de Genève 1963; Prof. Inst. d'Etudes Politiques, Univ. of Grenoble 1967; Faculty of Law and Social and Econ. Sciences, Univ. of Berne 1969; Prof. Faculty of Econ. and Social Sciences, Univ. of Geneva and Univ. Inst. of Devt. Studies 1975; Prof. Univ. of Paris I-Sorbonne 1983; numerous research tours in Africa, Latin America and Asia since 1963; City Councillor, Geneva 1963; mem. Swiss Nat. Council 1967–83, 1987–; mem. Fed. Parl. from Geneva; mem. Cen. Cttee. Swiss Socialist Party; mem. Exec. Council, Socialist Int.; Chevalier, Ordre Nat. des Arts et des Lettres. *Publications include:* La Contre-Révolution en Afrique 1963, Vive le pouvoir! ou les délices de la raison d'Etat 1985, Sankara. Un nouveau pouvoir africain (with J. P. Rapp) 1986, Dialogue Est-Ouest (with Y. Popov) 1987, La Suisse lave plus blanc 1990, La victoire des vaincus, oppression et résistance culturelle 1991, Le bonheur d'être Suisse 1993, Il s'agit de ne pas se rendre (with Régis Debray) 1994, L'or du Maniéma (novel) 1996, La Suisse, l'or et les morts 1997; numerous book chapters, articles in reviews, journals, newspapers etc. *Leisure interests:* skiing, tennis, mountaineering. *Address:* University of Geneva, 1211 Geneva 4, Switzerland. *Telephone:* (022) 705 8326. *Fax:* (022) 781 4100.

ZIEGLER, Peter Alfred, PH.D.; Swiss professor of global tectonics; b. 2 Nov. 1928, Winterthur; s. of Eugen Ziegler and Adelheid Riggenbach; m. Yvonne M. Bohrer 1960; two s.; ed. Univ. of Zürich; joined petroleum industry 1955; field geologist in Israel, Madagascar, Algeria; joined Shell Canada 1958; transferred to Shell Int. Petroleum Maatschappij BV, The Hague 1977; tech. adviser, North Sea Exploration 1970–77; exploration consultant Europe, South America; Deputy Head, new ventures and exploration advice with worldwide responsibility 1982; Sr. exploration consultant 1984–88, ind. petroleum exploration consultant 1988–; Hon. Lecturer Univ. of Basel 1990–96, Prof. of Global Geology 1996–; mem. Royal Netherlands Acad., Academia Europaea, Polish Acad. of Arts and Sciences, Russian Acad. of

Natural Sciences; Hon. mem., Geological Soc. London, Polish Geological Soc., European Union of Geosciences; Life mem. Bureau Int. Lithosphere Programme; Dr. h.c. (Moscow State Univ.) 1998; Fourmarier Medal (Geological Soc. Belgium); Van Waterschot van der Gracht Medal (Royal Geological and Mining Soc. of the Netherlands), William Smith Medal (Geological Soc. London), J. Neville George Medal (Geological Soc. Glasgow), Leopold von Buch Medal (Deutsche Geologische Gesellschaft), Robert H. Dott Sr. Memorial Award (American Asscn. of Petroleum Geologists), Special Commendation Award (American Asscn. of Petroleum Geologists), Piotr Leonidovici Kaptsa Medal (Russian Acad. of Natural Sciences), S. Müller Medal, European Geophysical Soc. 1998. *Publications include:* Geological Atlas of Western and Central Europe 1982, Evolution of Arctic-North Atlantic and Western Tethys 1988, Evolution of Laurussia, a study in late Palaeozoic plate tectonics 1989, Geodynamics of Rifting (Ed. and Contrib.) 1992, Structure and Prospects of Alpine Basins and Forelands (Ed. and Contrib.) 1996, Peritethyan Rift and Wrench Basins and Passive Margins (Ed. and Contrib.) 1999. *Leisure interests:* gardening, hiking. *Address:* Kirchweg 41, CH 4102 Binningen, Switzerland. *Telephone:* (061) 4215535. *Fax:* (061) 4215535.

ZIEGLER, Philip Sandeman, C.V.O., M.A., F.R.HIST.S., F.R.S.L.; British writer; b. 24 Dec. 1929, Ringwood, Hants.; s. of Colin Louis Ziegler and Dora Ziegler (née Barnwell); m. 1st Sarah Collins 1960 (deceased), 2nd Mary Clare Charrington 1971; two s. one d.; ed. Eton Coll., New Coll. Oxford; joined Foreign Office 1952, served Vientiane, Paris, Pretoria, Bogotá; Editorial Dir. Collins Publishers 1972, Ed.-in-Chief 1979–80, resgnd. when apptd. to write official biography of the late Earl Mountbatten; Chair. London Library 1979–85, Soc. of Authors 1988–90, Public Lending Right Advisory Cttee. 1993–96; Hon. D.Litt. (Westminster Coll., Mo., U.S.A.) 1987; Chancellor's Essay Prize 1950, Heineman Award 1976. *Publications include:* Duchess of Dino 1962, Addington 1965, The Black Death 1969, William IV 1971, Omdurman 1973, Melbourne 1976, Crown and People 1978, Diana Cooper 1981, Mountbatten 1985, Elizabeth's Britain 1926 to 1986 1986, The Sixth Great Power: Barings 1762–1929 1988, King Edward VIII, The Official Biography 1990; ed.: The Diaries of Lord Louis Mountbatten 1920–1922 1987, Personal Diary of Admiral the Lord Louis Mountbatten 1943–1946 1988, From Shore to Shore: the diaries of Earl Mountbatten of Burma 1953–1979 1989, Brooks's: A Social History (ed. with Desmond Seward) 1991, Wilson: The Authorized Life of Lord Wilson of Rievaulx 1993, London at War: 1939–45 1994, Osbert Sitwell 1998. *Address:* 22 Cottesmore Gardens, London, W8 5PR, England. *Telephone:* 0171-937 1903. *Fax:* 0171-937 5458.

ZIELENKIEWICZ, Wojciech, D.CHEM.; Polish physical chemist; b. 6 June 1933, Warsaw; s. of Edward Zielenkiewicz and Barbara (Szot) Zielenkiewicz; m. Anna Kastrzyńska; one s.; ed. Chemistry Faculty of Warsaw Univ.; researcher, Physical Chemistry Inst. of Polish Acad. of Sciences, Warsaw 1955–, Asst., Lecturer 1955–65, Head, Microcalorimetry Lab. 1965–68, Calorimetry Dept. 1968–, Asst. Prof. 1966–71, Extraordinary Prof. 1971–87, Ordinary Prof. 1987–, Dir. of Inst. 1973–90; Gen.-Dir., Polish Acad. of Sciences (PAN) 1968–69, Deputy Gen. Sec. PAN 1969–72, Deputy Sec. PAN Mathematical, Physical and Chemical Sciences Dept. 1972–80, Sec. of Dept. 1984–89, mem. Presidium 1984–89; Corresp. mem. Real Academia de Ciencias y Artes de Barcelona 1975–, Polish Acad. of Sciences 1977–; titular mem. Thermodynamics Comm. of Int. Union of Pure and Applied Chemistry (IUPAC) 1976–85; Chair. Comm. of Metrology and Scientific Apparatus of Polish Acad. of Sciences; Ed.-in-Chief Bulletin of the Polish Acad. of Sciences, Chemical Sciences Section 1985–94, Int. Journal Scientific Instrumentation 1972–85, Scientific Instrumentation (Warsaw) 1986–; Pres. Polish Asscn. on Calorimetry and Thermal Analysis 1985–91, Hon. mem. 1991–; awards of Science and Tech. Cttee. of PAN, Calvet Medal 1991, W. Świętosławski Medal 1994; Commdr.'s Cross of Order of Polonia Restituta, Gold Cross of Merit, and other decorations. *Publications:* 200 original scientific works in Polish and foreign journals. *Address:* Instytut Chemii Fizycznej PAN, ul. Kasprzaka 44/52, 01-224 Warsaw (Office); ul. L. Schillera 8 m. 30, 00-248 Warsaw, Poland (Home). *Telephone:* (22) 632 43 89 (Office). *Fax:* (22) 632 52 76.

ŽIEMELIS, Vidmantas; Lithuanian lawyer and politician; b. 4 Dec. 1950, Gailiskiai, Moletai Region; ed. Vilnius State Univ.; mem. CPSU –1989, voluntarily withdrew from CP; workman, later legal adviser Amalgamation of Chem. Consumer Products 1977–81; asst. to Prosecutor at Vilnius Prosecutor's Office 1981–84; Prosecutor-Gen. Supervision Dept. Prosecutor's Office Repub. of Lithuania 1984–90; involved in Sajudis movt. from late 1980s; mem. Council of Sajudis, Vilnius City 1989–90; elected Deputy of Supreme Soviet Repub. of Lithuania Feb. 1990; signatory March 11th Act on Re-establishment of Independence; mem. Seimas (Parl.) Repub. of Lithuania 1992–; mem. Cttee. on State Issues and Legal Affairs 1989–96; Minister of Interior 1996–98. *Address:* Ministry of the Interior, Sventaru 2, Vilnius 2600, Lithuania. *Telephone:* (02) 62 67 52 (Office).

ZIENKIEWICZ, Olgierd Cecil, C.B.E., PH.D., D.SC., DIP.ENG., F.I.C.E., F.A.S.C.E., F.R.S., F.ENG.; British professor of engineering; b. 18 May 1921, Caterham; s. of the late Casimir Zienkiewicz and Edith V. Penny; m. Helen J. Fleming 1952; two s. one d.; ed. Katowice, Poland and Imperial Coll., London; consulting eng. 1945–49; Lecturer, Univ. of Edin. 1949–57; Prof. of Structural Mechanics, Northwestern Univ. 1957–61; Prof. and Head Civil Eng. Dept. and Dir. Inst. for Numerical Methods in Eng., Univ. of Wales, Swansea 1961–88, Prof. Emer. 1988–; Naval Sea Systems Command Research Prof. Monterey, Calif. 1979–80; UNESCO Chair. of Numeric Methods in Eng., Univ. of Barcelona 1989–; J. Walter Chair. of Eng., Univ. of Tex., Austin, U.S.A. 1989–97; Hon. founder mem. GAMNI, France; Founder Int. Journal of Numerical Methods in Eng. 1968–; Pres. Int. Asscn. of Computational Mechanics 1986–90; Foreign Assoc. U.S. Nat. Acad. of Eng.; Foreign mem. Polish Acad. of Science 1985; Fellow City and Guilds 1979; Fellow Imperial Coll. 1993; J. A. Ewing Research Medal (Inst. of Civil Engineers) 1980, Newmark Medal (A.S.C.E.) 1980, Worcester W. Reid Medal (A.S.M.E.) 1980, Gauss Medal, Acad. of Science, Braunschweig 1987, The Royal Medal 1990, Gold Medal, Inst. of Structural Eng. 1992, Gold Medal of Inst. of Math. and its Applications 1992, Leonardo da Vinci Medal of European Soc. for Eng. Educ. (SEFI); Chevalier Ordre des Palmes Académiques 1996; recipient of 22 hon. doctorates and other awards and prizes. *Publications:* seven books and numerous articles in professional journals. *Leisure interests:* sailing, skin-diving. *Address:* 29 Somerset Road, Langland, Swansea, SA3 4PG, Wales. *Telephone:* (01792) 368776 (Home).

ZIMAN, John Michael, F.R.S.; British physicist; b. 16 May 1925; s. of the late Solomon Netheim Ziman and of Nellie Francis (née Gaster) Ziman; m. Rosemary Milnes Dixon 1951; two adopted s. two adopted d.; ed. Hamilton High School, New Zealand, Victoria Coll., Wellington, Balliol Coll., Oxford; Junior Lecturer in Mathematics, Oxford Univ. 1951–53, Pressed Steel Ltd. Research Fellow 1953–54; Lecturer in Physics, Cambridge Univ. 1954–64, Fellow of King's Coll. 1957–64, Ed. Cambridge Review 1958–59, Tutor for Advanced Students, King's Coll. 1959–63; Prof. of Theoretical Physics, Univ. of Bristol 1964–69, Melville Wills Prof. 1969–76, Henry Overton Wills Prof. and Dir. H. H. Wills Physics Lab. 1976–81, Prof. Emer. 1989–; Visiting Prof. in Depts. of Social and Econ. Studies and Humanities, Imperial Coll. of Science and Tech. 1982–; Chair. Science Policy Support Group 1986–91; Jt. Ed., Science Progress 1965–; Hon. Ed. Reports on Progress in Physics 1968–76; Gen. Ed. Cambridge Monographs on Physics; Chair. Council for Science and Society; Rutherford Memorial Lecturer in India and Pakistan 1968; Airey Neave Memorial Award 1981. *Publications:* Electrons and Phonons 1960, Electrons in Metals 1963, Camford Observed (with Jasper Rose) 1964, Principles of the Theory of Solids 1965, Public Knowledge 1968, Elements of Advanced Quantum Theory 1969, The Force of Knowledge 1976, Reliable Knowledge 1979, Models of Disorder 1979, Teaching and Learning about Science and Society 1980, Puzzles, Problems and Enigmas 1981, An Introduction to Science Studies 1984, The World of Science and the Rule of Law (with Paul Sieghart and John Humphrey) 1986, Knowing Everything about Nothing 1987, Prometheus Bound 1994, Of One Mind 1995; numerous articles in scientific journals. *Address:* 27 Little London Green, Oakley, Aylesbury, Bucks., HP18 9QL, England. *Telephone:* (01844) 237464. *Fax:* (01844) 237464.

ZIMMER, Hans; film score composer; b. 1958, Frankfurt-am-Main; m. Vicki Carolyn (separated); one d.; ed. in England. *Film scores include:* Driving Miss Daisy, Green Card, Pacific Heights, Backdraft, Rain Man, Regarding Henry, Thelma and Louise, The House of the Spirits, The Lion King (Acad. Award 1994), Crimson Tide, Nine Months, Something to Talk About, Beyond Rangoon, Muppet Treasure Island, Broken Arrow, The Preacher's Wife; in collaboration with Stanley Myers: Eureka, A World Apart, My Beautiful Laundrette.

ZIMMERMAN, Howard Elliot, PH.D.; American professor of chemistry; b. 5 July 1926, New York; m. 1st Jane Kirschenheiter 1950 (deceased); three s.; m. 2nd Martha L. Bailey Kaufman 1975 (divorced 1990); one step-s.; m. 3rd Margaret Jane Vick 1991; ed. Yale and Harvard Univs.; Instructor Northwestern Univ. 1954–55, Asst. Prof. 1955–60; Assoc. Prof. Univ. of Wisconsin 1960–61, Prof. 1961–, Arthur C. Cope Prof. of Chem. 1975– and Hilldale Prof. of Chem. 1990–; mem. several editorial bds. etc.; mem. N.A.S.; Alfred P. Sloan Fellow 1956–60; James Flack Norris Award (American Chem. Soc.) 1976; Halpern Award 1979, Pioneer Award, Nat. Inst. of Chemists 1986, Univ. of Wis. Hilldale Award in Physical Sciences 1990, Arthur C. Cope Scholar Award 1991. *Publications:* Quantum Mechanics for Organic Chemists 1975; 6 book chapters and more than 250 scientific articles. *Address:* Department of Chemistry, University of Wisconsin, 1101 University Avenue, Madison, WI 53706 (Office); 7813 Westchester Drive, Middleton, WI 53562, U.S.A. (Home). *Telephone:* (608) 262-1502 (Office). *Fax:* (608) 265-4534.

ZIMMERMANN, Frank Peter; German violinist; b. 27 Feb. 1965, Duisburg; m. Young Joo Zimmermann; one s.; ed. Folkwang Musikhochschule, Essen, Staatliche Hochschule der Künste, Berlin and with Herman Krebbers in Amsterdam; made debut aged 10 playing Mozart's violin concerto in G major, K 216 in Duisburg; now performs with all maj. orchestras in world and has undertaken extensive tours in Japan and Australia; also gives worldwide recitals, fmrly. with pianist Alexander Lonquich, his regular recital partner until 1994; appeared with English Chamber Orchestra conducted by Sir Colin Davis at Buckingham Palace by special invitation of H.R.H. The Prince of Wales 1991; soloist at Europa Concert given by Berlin Philharmonic under Bernard Haitink at Royal Albert Hall, London and televised live all over world 1993; recordings include concertos of Tchaikovsky, Brahms, Beethoven, Mozart, Prokofiev, Sibelius, Mendelssohn, Dvořák, Glazunov, Berg and Stravinsky; in recital with Alexander Lonquich recorded all Mozart and Prokofiev sonatas and works by Ravel, Debussy, Janáček etc.; Brahms Double Concerto with Heinrich Schiff and London Philharmonic Orchestra 1997; many other recordings; Premio dell'Accademia Musicale Chigiana, Siena 1990, Rheinischer Kulturpreis 1994; numerous awards and prizes for recordings. *Leisure interests:* gastronomy, sports, wine, arts, literature. *Address:* c/o Riaskoff Concert Management, Concertgebouwplein 15, 1071 LL Amsterdam, The Netherlands. *Telephone:* 31 (0)20 664 53 53. *Fax:* 31 (0)20 671 51 06.

ZIMMERMANN, Friedrich, DR.JUR.; German politician; b. 18 July 1925, Munich; s. of Josef and Luise (née Wenger) Zimmermann; m. 1st Erika Mangge 1950 (deceased); one d.; m. 2nd Christel Pratzat 1970 (divorced); one d.; m. 3rd Birgit Kemmler 1988; ed. Univ. of Munich; asst. legal officer, Bavarian State Ministry of Justice 1951–54, legal adviser, Bavarian State Chancellery 1954; called to the Bar, Munich 1963; mem. Supervisory Bd., Adler Feuerversicherung AG, Berlin 1955–82, Versicherung für den öffentlichen Dienst AG im Adler-Iduna-Verbund, Berlin 1978–82, Fernsehstudios München Atelierbetriebsgesellschaft mbH 1974–82, Chair. July–Sept. 1982; Deputy Chair. Advisory Council, Zweites Deutsches Fernsehen 1964–91; mem. CSU 1948–, now mem. Presidium; mem. Bundestag 1957–90; Fed. Minister of the Interior 1982–89, of Transport 1989–91; Bd. Dirs ZDF 1991–; mem. Supervisory Bd. Deutsche Lufthansa, Iduna-Nova-Group, ZDF Enterprises GmbH, Fernsehstudio München GmbH; Grosses Bundesverdienstkreuz mit stern und Schulterband. *Publications:* Anspruch und Leistung: Widmungen für Franz Josef Strauss 1980, Ausgewählte Bundestagsreden. *Leisure interests:* tennis, skiing, hunting. *Address:* Briennerstrasse 28, 80333 München, Germany.

ZIMMERMANN, Reinhard, DR.IUR., LL.D.; German professor of law; b. 10 Oct. 1952, Hamburg; s. of Fritz Zimmermann and Inge Hansen; ed. Univ. of Hamburg and Hamburg Court of Appeal; W. P. Schreiner Chair of Roman and Comparative Law and Head of Dept. Univ. of Cape Town 1981–88, Deputy Dean and Dean, Faculty of Law 1983–88; Vice-Pres. and Pres. Soc. of South African Teachers of Law 1984–86; Prof. of Roman Law, German Pvt. Law and Comparative Legal History, Univ. of Regensburg 1988–, Dean Faculty of Law 1994–96; Visiting Prof. Univ. of Edin., Tulane Univ., Univ. of Stellenbosch, 1990, 1991, 1992, Max Rheinstein Visiting Prof., Univ. of Chicago Law School 1993, Yale Law School 1998; A.L. Goodhart Prof. of Legal Science, Univ. of Cambridge, U.K. 1998/99; Co-Ed. Zeitschrift für Europäisches Privatrecht, Schriftenreihe zur Europäischen Rechtsgeschichte; Foreign mem. Royal Netherlands Acad. of Arts and Sciences; LL.D. h.c. for distinguished published work (Cape Town) 1991; Hon. LL.D (Chicago); Leibniz Prize 1996. *Publications include:* Richterliches Moderationsrecht oder Totalnichtigkeit? 1979, Das römisch-holländische Recht in Südafrika 1983, The Law of Obligations, Roman Foundations of the Civilian Tradition 1993, Southern Cross 1996. *Leisure interests:* field hockey, tennis, running, classical music. *Address:* Universität Regensburg, Juristische Fakultät, Universitätsstr. 31, 93053 Regensburg, Germany. *Telephone:* 0941 943 2632. *Fax:* 0941 943 4965.

ZINDER, Norton David, PH.D.; American geneticist and university professor; b. 7 Nov. 1928, New York, N.Y.; s. of Harry Zinder and Jean Gottesman Zinder; m. Marilyn Esteicher 1949; two s.; ed. Columbia Univ. and Univ. of Wisconsin; Wisconsin Alumni Fund Fellow, Univ. of Wis. 1948–50, Research Asst. 1950–56; Asst., Rockefeller Univ. (then Rockefeller Inst.) 1952–56, Assoc. 1956–58, Assoc. Prof. 1958–64, Prof. 1964–, John D. Rockefeller Jr. Prof. 1977–, Dean Grad. and Postgrad. Studies 1993–95; mem. of following cttees.: Int. Inst. of Cellular and Molecular Pathology (ICP), Brussels 1985, Science and Law sub-cttee. New York City Bar Asscn. 1985, Council on Foreign Relations 1986, NAS/NRC (BAST) Panel on Chemical Weapons Research and Devt. Defense 1986, NAS/NRC Chair. to Review the Army Chemical Weapons Stockpile Disposal Program 1987, Alliance Int. Health Care Trust 1984–; mem. N.A.S., American Acad. of Arts and Sciences, American Soc. of Microbiology, American Soc. of Biological Chemists, Genetics Soc. of America, American Asscn. for the Advancement of Science, American Soc. of Virology; Scholar of American Cancer Soc. 1955–58, Eli Lilly Award in Microbiology 1962, United State Steel Foundation Award of N.A.S. in Molecular Biology 1966, Medal of Excellence from Columbia Univ. 1969, AAAS Award in Scientific Freedom and Responsibility 1982. *Publications:* Infective Heredity in Bacteria, Cold Spring Harbor Symposium on Quantitative Biology XVIII 1953; and scientific articles in learned journals. *Address:* Rockefeller University, 1230 York Avenue, New York, NY 10021 (Office); 450 East 63rd Street, New York City, NY 10021, U.S.A. (Home). *Telephone:* 421-3777.

ZINKERNAGEL, Rolf Martin, PH.D.; Swiss professor of immunology; b. 6 Jan. 1944, Basel; m.; three c.; ed. Mathematisch-Naturwissenschaftliches Gymnasium, Basel, Univ. of Basel, Univ. of Zurich, A.N.U., Canberra; intern Surgical Dept., Clara-Spital Hosp., affiliated to Faculty of Medicine, Univ. of Basel 1969; Postdoctoral Fellow Lab. for Electron Microscopy, Inst. of Anatomy, Univ. of Basel 1969–70; Postdoctoral Fellow Inst. of Biochem., Univ. of Lausanne 1971–73; Visiting Fellow Dept. of Microbiology, John Curtin School of Medical Research, A.N.U., Canberra 1973–75; Assoc. mem. (Asst. Prof.) Dept. of Immunopathology, Research Inst. of Scripps Clinic, La Jolla, Calif. 1976–79, Adjunct Assoc. Prof., Dept. of Pathology 1977–79, Full Prof. Dept. of Immunopathology, Scripps Clinic and Research Foundation 1979; Assoc. Prof. Dept. of Pathology, Univ. Hosp., Univ. of Zurich 1979–88, Full Prof. 1988–92, Head Inst. of Experimental Immunology 1992–; mem. numerous scientific advisory bodies including WHO Group of Experts in Vaccine Devt. 1985–89, advisory council of Cancer Research Inst. 1988–; mem. Ed. Bds. of immunology, pathology, microbiology and virology journals; mem. numerous professional orgs. including Swiss Soc. of Allergy and Immunology 1971–76 (Pres. 1993–94, Hon. mem. 1996–), Acad. Europea 1989–, European Network of Immunological Insts. 1990–, Int. Soc. for Antiviral Research 1990–; Fellow American Acad. of Microbiology 1996, Foreign Fellow Nat. Acad. of Science, U.S.A. 1996, Australian Acad. of Sciences 1996, American Acad. of Arts and Sciences 1998, Royal Soc. 1998, Acad. Royale de Médicine, Belgium 1998, Berlin-Brandenburgische Akad. der Wissenschaften 1998; numerous decorations including Inst. for Cancer Research Award 1987, Nobel Prize for Medicine or Physiology 1996; Dr. h.c. (Liège, A.N.U.) 1996, (Oslo, Quebec, Genoa) 1997, (Latvian Univ., Riga, Agric. Univ. of Warsaw) 1998. *Publications:* numerous articles in learned journals. *Address:* Department of Pathology, University Hospital, Institute of Experimental Immunology, Schmelzbergstrasse 12, CH-8091 Zurich; Rebhusstrasse 47, 8126 Zumikon, Switzerland (Home). *Telephone:* (1) 255 29 89 (Office). *Fax:* (1) 255 44 20 (Office); (1) 918 19 40 (Home).

ZINKEVICIUS, Zigmas, DR. HUM. LIT.; Lithuanian philologist; b. 4 Jan. 1925, Juodausiiai, Ukmerge Region; m. Regina Zinkeviciene; two c.; ed. Vilnius State Univ., lab. asst., Vilnius State Univ. 1946–50; Prof., Chair of Lithuanian Language 1950–56; Deputy Dean, Chair of Philology and History 1956–68, Prof., Head, Dept. of Lithuanian Language 1967–88; Minister of Educ. and Science, Lithuanian Repub. 1996–98; consultant for educ. and science to Lithuanian Pres. 1998–; main research in history of Lithuanian language, dialects and Baltic philology; mem. Swedish Royal Acad. of Letters, History and Antiques, Lithuanian Acad. of Sciences, Norwegian Acad. of Sciences, Lithuanian Catholic Acad. of Sciences 1991, Latvian Acad. of Science; J. G. Herder Award; mem. Editorial Bd. Baltistica Periodical. *Publications:* over 20 books, over 500 articles in Lithuanian and foreign languages. *Leisure interests:* yachting, skiing, motor sports, canoeing and boating. *Address:* L R Vyriasybes kanceliarija, Gedimino pr. 11, LT-2039 Vilnius (Office); Justiniskiu 41-24, LT-2056 Vilnius, Lithuania (Home). *Telephone:* (3702) 41 08 77.

ZINMAN, David Joel; American conductor; b. 9 July 1936, New York; s. of Samuel Zinman and Rachel Ilo (Samuels) Zinman; m. 1st Leslie Heyman (deceased); one s. one d.; m. 2nd Mary Ingham 1974; one s.; ed. Oberlin Conservatory, Ohio and Univ. of Minnesota; studied conducting Berks. Music Center, Tanglewood and with Pierre Monteux; Asst. to Monteux 1961–64; Music Dir. Nederlands Kamerorkest 1964–77; Music Dir. Rochester Philharmonic Orchestra, New York 1974–85, Baltimore Symphony Orchestra 1985–98; Prin. Guest Conductor Rotterdam Philharmonic Orchestra 1977–79, Chief Conductor 1979–82; Music Dir. Tonhalle Orchestra, Zurich 1995–; Music Dir. (desig.) Aspen Music Festival and School 1997, Music Dir. 1998–; numerous recordings; Grand Prix du Disque; Edison Award, Gramophone Best Selling Record (Górecki) 1993, Gramophone Award (Jungle Book) 1994, three Grammy awards, Deutschen Schallplatten Prize. *Address:* Baltimore Symphony Orchestra, 1212 Cathedral Street, Baltimore, MD 21201, U.S.A.

ZINOVIEV, Aleksandr Aleksandrovich, D.PHIL.; Russian philosopher and writer; b. 29 Sept. 1922, Chukhloma, Kostrana Region; ed. Moscow Univ.; mil. service 1944–45; Prof. of Logic & Methodology of Science, Moscow Univ. 1970–78; actively campaigned against party line and discredited in 1970s, expelled 1978, U.S.S.R. Citizenship restored 1990; Research post at Univ. of Munich 1978–; mem. Finnish Acad. of Sciences; Prix Tocqueville 1982. *Publications include:* Philosophical Problems of Polyvalent Logic (Russian 1960, English 1963), Principles of the Logical Theory of Scientific Knowledge 1967 (trans. Eng. 1973), An Essay on Polyvalent Logic 1968 (trans. German 1968); Complex Logic 1970 (trans. German Komplexe Logik 1970), Logical Physics 1972, Logische Sprachregeln (with A. N. Wessel) 1975; non-philosophic works: Ziyayushchiye vysoty (Yawning Heights) 1976 (fiction), The Radiant Future 1978, The Yellow House (2 vols.) 1980, The Reality of Communism 1983, Homo Soveticus 1985, The Way to Calvary 1985, The Madhouse 1986, Para Bellum 1987, Gorbachevism 1988, Perestroika in Partygrad 1992, Russian Experiment 1995.

ZINSOU, Emile Derlin; Benin politician and physician; b. 23 March 1918; ed. Ecole Primaire Supérieure, Ecole Africaine de Médecine, Dakar and Faculté de Médecine, Paris; Represented Dahomey in French Nat. Assembly; fmr. Vice-Pres. Assemblée de l'Union française, Senator, Territorial Council; fmr. Minister of Economy and of The Plan; fmr. Amb. to France; Pres. Supreme Court of Dahomey; Minister of Foreign Affairs 1961–63, 1965–67; Pres. of Dahomey (now Benin) 1968–69; sentenced to death in absentia 1975; pardoned Aug. 1989; Leader Union Nationale pour la Démocratie et le Progrès (UNDP); numerous decorations include Grand Croix Ordre Nat., Dahomey, Grand Officier Légion d'honneur. *Address:* Cotonou, Benin.

ZIV-AV, Itzhak; Israeli administrative official and journalist; b. 4 June 1907, Russia; s. of Abraham and Miriam Ziv-Av; m. Debora Kobrinsky 1934; two s.; ed. Inst. of Pedagogy, Smolensk; farmer and Man. Local Council of Magdiel settlement, Israel 1926–34; Man. Ed. Haboker (daily) 1935–48; Dir. Public Relations Div., Ministry of Defence and GHQ, Israel Defence Forces 1948–52; Dir.-Gen. Israel Farmers' Union 1952–75, Chair. Council 1975–86, Pres. Hon. Court 1986–90; Chair. Exec. Cttee., Co-ordinating Bureau, Israeli Econ. Orgs. 1967–86; Ed. Farmers of Israel monthly 1962–87; mem. Bd. of Dirs. Jewish Nat. Fund; Chair. Bd., Land Devt. Authority 1960–98; mem. Council, State Land Authority 1962–97, Exec. Bd., Int. Fed. Agricultural Producers (IFAP) 1960–80. *Publications:* The Unknown Land, I Seek My Brethren, The Price of Freedom, Forever Ours, From Frontier to Frontier, A World to Live in, Another World, There is a Land, All the Hopes are

Reborn, Beautiful Are the Nights in Canaan, The People of 1948, There is No Other Homeland for Me, and poetry for children. *Leisure interests:* reading, gardening, travel. *Address:* Ramat-Qan 52587, Sh'mueli Street 3, Israel (Home). *Telephone:* 03-7510227 (Home).

ZLENKO, Anatoly Maksimovich; Ukrainian diplomatist; b. 2 June 1938, Kiev Region; s. of Maksim Adamovich Zlenko and Anastasia Efimovna Zlenko; m. Ludmila Ivanovna Zlenko; two d.; ed. Kiev State Univ.; mem. CPSU 1959–91; diplomatic service since 1967, attaché, second sec. Ministry of Foreign Affairs of Ukraine 1967–73; mem. UNESCO Secr., Paris 1973–79; Exec. Sec. Ukrainian Comm. on UNESCO Problems 1979–83; Perm. Rep. of Ukraine in UNESCO 1983–87; Deputy Minister of Foreign Affairs of Ukraine 1987–89, First Deputy Minister 1989–90, Minister 1990–94; Rep. to UN 1994–. *Publications:* articles in Ukrainian and foreign press on int. relations. *Leisure interests:* history, photography, painting, tennis, volleyball. *Address:* Permanent Mission of the Ukraine to the United Nations, 220 East 51st Street, New York, NY 10022, U.S.A.

ŻOCHOWSKI, Ryszard Jacek, DR.MED.; Polish politician and professor of medicine; m.; three s.; Head, Cardiology Dept. Cen. Clinical Hosp. of Ministry of Home Affairs, fmr. Dir. Inst. of Clinical Medicine; Deputy to 1st and 2nd Diets; Minister of Health and Social Welfare 1993; no political affiliation; Pres. Warsaw Medical Soc.; mem. New York Acad. of Sciences. *Publications:* more than 160 scientific papers published in Poland and abroad. *Address:* c/o Ministry of Health and Social Welfare, 00-923 Warsaw, ul. Miodowa 15, Poland.

ZOHAR, Israel; Israeli artist; b. 7 Feb. 1945, Oktubinsk, U.S.S.R.; m. 1st Ruth Bregman 1966 (divorced 1974), 2nd Arna Meyuhas 1974 (divorced 1982), 3rd Wendy Caron 1984; five s. one d.; ed. Bezalel Acad. of Art, Jerusalem and with artists A. Yaskil and Ernst Fuchs; one-man shows: Ahuva Doron Gallery, Tel Aviv 1970, Bergman Gallery, Tel Aviv, Sara Kishon Gallery, Tel Aviv 1977, 1980, 1997, Artist's House, Jerusalem (retrospective) 1982, 13½ Gallery, Tel Aviv 1986, Musée de l'Athenée, Geneva (retrospective) 1987, Roy Miles Gallery, London 1989, 1993, Museum Panorama Mesdag, The Hague (Homage to Vermeer) 1996, Adler Gallery, Gstaad, Switzerland 1996, Catto Gallery, London 1999; group exhbn. Salon des Beaux-Arts, Grand Palais, Paris 1985, Prince Albert Museum, Exeter 1992, Roy Miles Gallery, London 1993; lectured at Hebrew Univ. Jerusalem 1979; maj. works include portraits of H.R.H. The Princess of Wales 1990, Henry Catto (fmr. U.S. Amb. to U.K.) 1990, 24ft x 8ft painting of Jacob's Ladder for Music Festival, Exeter Cathedral, U.K. 1992, portrait of Anne Frank, Music Festival, Bad Kissingen 1992, portrait of Edith Sitwell for Hampstead Festival, London 1995; also writes, adapts and directs plays for theatre including Thomas Mann's Death in Venice (Duke of Cambridge, London), Brecht's The Jewish Wife (Cockpit, London), works by Strindberg, Chekhov, Sartre, Dostoevsky for Café Theatre, London, etc. *Address:* 79 Hornsey Lane, London, N6 5LQ, England. *Telephone:* 0181-341 1754.

ZOLLINGER, Heinrich Fritz, PH.D., D.SC.; Swiss professor and university administrator; b. 29 Nov. 1919, Aarau; s. of Dr. Fritz Zollinger and Helene Prior; m. Heidi Frick 1948; three s.; ed. Fed. Inst. of Tech. (ETH), Univ. of Basel, M.I.T.; Chemist, Dyestuff Research Dept., CIBA Ltd. 1945–60; Lecturer in Dyestuff Chem., Univ. of Basel 1952–60; Prof. of Textile Chem., Fed. Inst. of Tech. 1960–87, Prof. Emer. 1987–, Rector 1973–77; Pres. Organic Chem. Div. of IUPAC 1975–77, Pres. IUPAC 1979–81; Pres. Council Swiss Science Foundation 1979–82; Fellow Swiss Acad. of Eng. 1990; Hon. Fellow, Soc. of Dyers and Colourists (U.K.) 1981, Chem. Soc. of Japan 1985, Swiss Soc. of Dyers and Colourists (SVCC) 1987, Japanese Soc. of Textile Tech. 1989, Textile Inst. (Manchester) 1989, Shenkar Coll., Ramat Gan, Israel 1991, Romanian Soc. of Dyers and Colourists 1992, Swiss Soc. of Friends of the Weizmann Inst. 1993; Foreign Fellow, Royal Swedish Acad. of Eng. 1979, Acad. of Sciences, Göttingen 1984; Hon. Ph.D. (Stuttgart) 1976, (Tokyo Inst. Tech.) 1983; Werner Prize 1959, Ruzicka Award 1960, Lewinstein Award 1964, Conrad Prize 1970, O. N. Witt Gold Medal 1980, M. Kehren Gold Medal 1984; Order of the Rising Sun (Japan) 1989. *Publications:* Chemie der Azofarbstoffe 1958 (Russian 1960), Diazo and Azo Chemistry 1961, Leitfaden der Farbstoffchemie 1970, Chemie und Hochschule 1978, Colour Chemistry 1987, Diazo Chemistry, Part I 1994, Part II 1995, Colour: a multidisciplinary approach 1999; volumes on aromatic chemistry in Int. Review of Science 1973, 1976; 320 scientific papers. *Leisure interests:* clarinet, climbing, skiing, sailing, colour studies. *Address:* Technisch-Chemisches Laboratorium, Eidgenössische Technische Hochschule, Universitätstrasse 6, CH-8092, Zürich (Office); Goldbacherstr. 54, CH-8700 Küsnacht, Switzerland (Home). *Telephone:* 01-632-41-68 (Laboratory); 01-910-53-08 (Home). *Fax:* 01-632-1072.

ZOLOTAS, Xenophon, DR.ECON.; Greek university professor; b. 26 March 1904, Athens; s. of the late Efthymios Zolotas; m. Kallirhoe Ritsos 1958; ed. Univs. of Athens, Leipzig and Paris; Prof. of Econs. Univ. of Thessaloniki 1928, of Athens 1931–68; mem. of Supreme Council of Greece 1932, of Greek del. to the Econ. Council of the Entente Balkanique 1934–39; Chair. Bd. of Dirs., Agricultural Bank of Greece 1936–40; Joint Gov. Bank of Greece (after Liberation) Oct. 1944–45; mem. UNRRA Council 1946; Gov. of IMF for Greece 1946–67, 1974–81, mem. Greek Del. to UN Gen. Ass. 1948–53; Del. to Econ. Comm. for Europe 1949–53; mem. Currency Cttee. 1950, 1974–81; Vice-Chair. ECE 1952; Minister of Co-ordination Oct. 1952; Gov. Bank of Greece 1955–67, 1974–81, Hon. Gov. 1981–; Minister of Econ. Co-ordination July-Nov. 1974; Prime Minister of Greece 1989–90; mem. "Group of Four" for remodelling of OEEC 1960; mem. Acad. of Athens 1952–; Hon. Pres. Int. Econ. Asscn. 1980; Grand Cross of Royal Order of the Phoenix, of the Ordre nat. du Mérite (France), Grand Officier, Légion d'honneur (France) and others. *Publications:* Griechenland auf dem Wege zur Industrialisierung 1926, Wirtschaftsstruktur und Wirtschaftsbeziehungen Griechenlands 1931, L'étalon-or en théorie et en pratique 1933, La question de l'or et le problème monétaire 1938, La théorie économique traverse-t-elle une crise? 1938, La transformation du capitalisme 1953, Monetary Stability and Economic Development 1958, Economic Development and Technical Education 1960, The Problem of the International Monetary Liquidity 1961, Towards a Reinforced Gold Exchange Standard 1961, Economic Development and Private Enterprise 1962, International Monetary Order, Problems and Policies 1962, The Role of the Banks in a Developing Country 1963, The Multicurrency Standard and the International Monetary Fund 1963, Monetary Equilibrium and Economic Development 1965, Remodelling the International Monetary System 1965, Alternative Systems for International Monetary Reform, A Comparative Appraisal 1965, Current Monetary and Economic Developments in Greece 1966, International Labor Migration and Economic Development 1966, Monetary Planning 1967, The Gold Trap and the Dollar 1968, Speculocracy and the International Monetary System 1969, The International Money Mess 1973, From Anarchy to International Monetary Order 1973, The Energy Problem in Greece 1975, Recession and Reflation in the Greek Economy 1975, Developments and Prospects of the Greek Economy 1975, Guidelines for Industrial Development in Greece 1976, Greece in the European Community 1976, International Monetary Vacillations 1976, International Monetary Issues and Development Policies 1977, Inflation and the Monetary Target in Greece 1978, An International Loan Insurance Scheme 1978, The Positive Contribution of Greece to the European Community 1978, The Dollar Crisis and Other Papers 1979, On the Issue of a Stable Monetary Standard 1981, Economic Growth and Declining Social Welfare 1981, The Unruly International Monetary System 1985, The Dollar and the New Form of International Co-operation 1986, The Enigma of the U.S. Trade Deficit 1986, The European Monetary System, the Dollar and the Need for Reform 1987, Co-operation and Disco-ordination in International Monetary Policies, the Need for Rules of Conduct 1988, The European Monetary System and the Challenge of 1992 1988; in Greek: Monetary Stabilization 1929, Economics 1942, Creative Socialism 1944, The Monetary Problem and the Greek Economy 1950, Inflationary Pressures in the Greek Economy 1951, Regional Planning and Economic Development 1961, Human Capital and Economic Development 1968, The Contribution of Exports to Economic Development 1976, Social Welfare and Economic Organization 1976, Consumption, Investment and Monetary Equilibrium 1977, Economic and Monetary Problems in Greece 1979, Progress Towards European Union 1991. *Address:* c/o Bank of Greece, 21 Panepistimou Street, Athens 102 50 (Office); 25 Dionissiou Areopagitou Street, Athens 117 42, Greece (Home). *Telephone:* 3230-317 (Office); 9241-100 (Home).

ZOLOTOV, Yuri Aleksandrovich, DR. CHEM.; Russian chemist; b. 4 Oct. 1932, Vysokovskoye, Moscow Region; m.; two c.; ed. Moscow State Univ.; researcher, Deputy Dir., Head of lab., Inst. of Geochem. and Analytical Chem. 1958–89; Dir. N. Kurnakov Inst. of Gen. and Inorganic Chem. 1990–; corresp. mem., U.S.S.R. (now Russian) Acad. of Sciences 1970, mem. 1987–; main research in analytical chem., extraction of inorganic compounds, ion chromatography; U.S.S.R. State Prize, State Prize of Russia, Prize of U.S.S.R. Council of Ministers. *Leisure interest:* fishing. *Address:* N. Kurnakov Institute of General and Inorganic Chemistry, Leninsky prosp. 31, 117907 Moscow, Russia. *Telephone:* (095) 952 0224 (Office); (095) 132 2010 (Home).

ZOLTÁN, Imre, M.D.; Hungarian obstetrician and gynaecologist; b. 12 Dec. 1909, Budapest; s. of E. Zoltan; m. Edith Rokay 1953; one d.; ed. Pazmany Peter Univ. (now Semmelweis Univ. of Medical Sciences); Asst. in Dept. of Obstetrics and Gynaecology, Univ. Clinic, Pazmany Peter Univ. 1933–46, Assoc. Prof. 1946–50, Prof. and Dir. of Dept. 1950–79; Sec. Gen. Fed. of Hungarian Medical Socs. 1966–70, Pres. 1974–85; Vice-Pres. Int. Fed. of Gynaecology and Obstetrics 1970–73; Dir. Nat. Inst. of Obstetrics and Gynaecology 1973–79, Consulting Prof. 1979–; mem. Presidency of Fed. Hungarian Medical Socs. 1985–. *Publications:* Textbooks of Obstetrics and Gynaecology 1951–70, Caesarian Section in Today's Obstetrics 1961; Co-author: Semmelweis. His Life and Work. *Leisure interests:* sport, tennis, gastronomy. *Address:* Bartók Béla ut. 31, 1114 Budapest, Hungary. *Telephone:* 466-7140.

ZONG PU; Chinese writer; b. (as Feng Zhong Pu) 26 July 1928, Beijing; d. of Feng Youlan and Ren Zaikun; m. Cai Zhongde; one d.; ed. Qinghua Univ.; mem. editorial bds. Literary Gazette and World Literature. *Publications:* The Red Beans 1957, Melody in Dreams (Nat. Prize for Short Stories) 1978, Who Am I? 1979, Lu Lu 1980, The Everlasting Rock (Nat. Prize for novelette) 1980, Fairy Tales from a Windy Cottage 1984, Bear Palm (short stories) 1985, Lilac Knot (essays) (Nat. Prize for essay) 1986, Retreat to the South (Vol. I of Ordeal) 1988, The Story of a Fish (Nat. Prize for Children's Literature), Discourse on an Iron Flute (essays) 1994, Stories of a Windy Cottage (short stories) 1995, Collected Works (4 vols.) 1996, Hiding in the East (Vol. II of Ordeal); numerous essays. *Leisure interests:* music, travel, calligraphy. *Address:* Beijing University, 57 Yan Nan Yuan, Beijing 100871, People's Republic of China.

ZORIN, Leonid Genrikhovich; Russian playwright; b. 3 Nov. 1924, Baku, Azerbaijan; s. of Genzikh Zorin and Polina Zorin; m. 1st 1951 (wife deceased); m. 2nd Tatjana Pospelova 1985; one s.; ed. Azerbaijan State Univ., M. Gorky Inst. of Literature in Moscow; literary ed. Baku Russian Drama Theatre; later freelance, mem. U.S.S.R. Union of Writers 1941–; Grand Prix for the best film script Grandmaster (Festival in Kranje, Yugoslavia), Golden Medal for filmscript Peace to the Newcomer, Venice Film Festival 1961, Prize of All-Union Contest of Playwrights Revival of Russia (for Moscow Nest) 1995, (for Lusgan) 1997. *Plays:* over 40 produced in 15 countries, including Decembrists, Kind Men, The Coronation, The Deck, Warsaw Melody, The Copper Grandmother, The Quotation, The Perished Plot, The Infidelity, The Carnival, The Moscow Nest, Lusgan, The Warsaw Melody 1997, Tsar's Hunt, Roman Comedy. *Film scripts:* 15 including A Man from Nowhere, The Law, Peace to the Newcomer, Granmaster, Transit, The Friends and the Years, Pokrovskye Gates, Tsar's Hunt. *Publications:* (novels and short stories) Old Manuscript 1983, Wanderer 1987, The Topic of the Day 1992, Proscenium 1997; numerous essays; Theatre Fantasy (collection of plays) 1974, Selected Plays (2 vols.) 1986, The Green Notebooks (collection of essays etc.). *Leisure interests:* reading, chess. *Address:* Krasnoarmeyskaya str. 21, Apt. 73, 125319 Moscow, Russia. *Telephone:* (095) 151-43-33 (Home).

ZORRILLA, China; Uruguayan actress, director and producer; b. 1922; d. of Jose Luis Zorrilla de San Martin; unmarried; ed. Royal Acad. of Dramatic Art, London; worked with Ars Pulchra group, Uruguayan Independent Theatre; later worked as journalist and as actress and dir. Nat. Theatre of Uruguay; f. with Antonio Larreta and Enrique Guarnero, Theatre of City of Montevideo 1961; directed show Canciones para mirar, New York 1965 and later in Buenos Aires; staged Jacobo Langsner's El Tobogán and Neil Simon's Plaza Suite, Montevideo 1969; has made several films in Argentina; director, Como en casa (television show); newscaster, Radio Belgrano; noted theatrical appearances including one-woman show Hola, hola, un, dos, tres (toured Argentina, Venezuela and U.S.A.) and as Emily in Spanish-language version of William Luce's The Belle of Amherst throughout Latin America and in U.S.A. 1981.

ZOU CHENGLU (Tsou, C.L.), PH.D.; Chinese biochemist and biophysicist; b. 17 May 1923, Jiangsu; s. of Tsou Dong-hu and Hu Kuei; m. Li Lin (q.v.) 1949; one d.; ed. Cambridge Univ., U.K.; Deputy Dir. Inst. of Biophysics, Academia Sinica 1979–83; Visiting Prof., Harvard Univ., U.S.A. 1981–82; Dir. Nat. Lab. Biomacromolecules 1988–93; Pres. Biochemical Soc. 1993–; mem. Academic Degrees Cttee. under State Council 1986–95; mem. Academia Sinica (Dir. Div. of Biology 1992–); Hon. mem. American Soc. of Biochemistry; mem. Nat. Cttee. CPPCC 1978, 8th Nat. Cttee. 1993–; China Nat. Natural Science Prize, 1st Class (twice). *Publications:* Current Biochemical Research in China (Ed.) 1989; over 180 research papers. *Leisure interest:* music. *Address:* Institute of Biophysics, Academia Sinica, 15 Datum Road, Beijing 100101, People's Republic of China. *Telephone:* 64889870 (Office); 68422342 (Home). *Fax:* 64872026.

ZOU JIAHUA; Chinese engineer and state official; b. Oct. 1926, Shanghai; s. of late Zou Taofen, elder brother of Zou Jingmeng (q.v.); ed. Moscow; joined CCP 1945; fmr. Dir. Shenyang No. 2 Machine Tool Plant; Dir. Machine Tool Inst., First Ministry of Machine Bldg.; Deputy Dir. Communication of Science, Tech. and Industry for Nat. Defence; alt. mem. 12th CCP Cen. Cttee. 1982–87, mem. 1985; Minister of Ordnance Industry 1985–86, of State Machine-Bldg. Industry Comm. 1986–88, of Machine Bldg. and Electronics Industry 1988–93, in charge of State Planning Comm. 1991–93; Vice-Premier 1991–98; State Councillor 1988–91; Chair. State Radio Regulatory Cttee. 1994–; mem. 13th CCP Cen. Cttee. 1987–92, mem. 14th Cen. Cttee. 1992–98; mem. CCP Politburo 1992–98; Vice-Chair. Standing Cttee. of 9th NPC 1998–. *Address:* Standing Committee of National People's Congress, Beijing, People's Republic of China.

ZOU RENJUN, C.CHEM., F.R.S.C.; Chinese scientist; b. 16 Jan. 1927, Suzhou City; s. of late Zou Zhangqin and Deng Aiyun; m. Zhao Yaqin 1951; two d.; ed. Fudan Univ., Shanghai, Tianjin Univ.; Head Teaching Group, Tianjin Inst. of Chemical Tech. 1958; lecturer, Tianjin Inst. of Tech. 1963; Prof., Hebei Inst. of Tech., Tianjin 1979–; Pres. Hebei Acad. of Sciences, Shijiazhuang 1984–88, Hon. Pres. 1988–; Chair. Hebei Asscn. for Science and Tech. 1991–; Fellow Royal Soc. of Chem., London 1982–; numerous awards and prizes, including Gold Medal, State Council of People's Repub. of China 1979, Gay-Lussac Medal, France 1984, Gold Medal, All-China Fed. of Trade Unions 1987, Advanced Worker Award and Gold Medal, State Council 1989. *Publications:* Chemical Reaction Engineering in Basic Organic Chemical Industry 1981, Principles and Techniques of Separation in Petrochemical Industry 1988; more than 50 papers in journals in China, U.S.A., France, Netherlands, Japan etc. *Leisure interest:* music. *Address:* Hebei Academy of Sciences, Friendship Street, Shijiazhuang 050081, People's Republic of China. *Telephone:* 311-336002. *Fax:* 311-332060.

ZOU YONGZHAO, Lieut.-Gen.; Chinese army officer; b. Nov. 1935, Macheng City, Hubei Prov.; ed. Chongqing Artillery School; joined PLA 1950; mem. CCP 1959–; served Korean War 1952; Group Mil. Training Asst. Artillery School, Staff Officer, Deputy Chief and Chief of a Base Mil. Org. Div., Regt. Commdr. PLA Second Artillery 1960–83; Deputy Base Commdr. and Base Commdr. PLA Second Artillery 1983–92; Deputy Commdr. PLA Second Artillery 1992–; rep. to 13th Nat. Congress of CCP 1987. *Address:* c/o Ministry of National Defence, Jingshanqian Jie, Beijing, People's Republic of China.

ZOU YU; Chinese government official; b. 3 Oct. 1922, Guangdong Prov.; m. Xue Xialiang 1953; three s. two d.; ed. Inst. of Shaanbei; Deputy Dir. Public Security Dept. Jilin City 1938–49; Deputy Garrison Commdr. Shanton Dist. 1949–53; Political Commissar Shanton Mil. Sub-Command 1957–75; First Deputy Dir. Guangdong Prov. Public Security Dept., Commr. Shantou Dist., Leader Guangdong Prov. Govt. 1950–77; Dir. State Seismological Bureau, State Council 1978–80; Head China Acad. of Sciences 1978–80; Vice-Minister of Justice 1982–83, Minister 1983–88; Pres. Nat. Lawyers Asscn. 1986–91; Pres. China Univ. of Political Science and Law 1985–88; mem. Standing Cttee., NPC 1983–88; Deputy Dir. Internal and Judicial Affairs Cttee. NPC 1988–93; Pres. China Law Soc. 1991–; mem. Exec. Cttee. LAWASIA 1991, Vice-Pres. 1993; Advisor Internal and Judicial Affairs Cttee. *Publications:* The Strategic Meaning of Spreading Basic Legal Knowledge among the People 1986, The Social Position and Meaning of Civil Conciliation 1987, Dictionary of Jurisprudence 1991. *Leisure interests:* music, painting, calligraphy. *Address:* No. 6 Nam Dajie, Xizhimen, Beijing 100035, People's Republic of China. *Telephone:* (1) 6033363. *Fax:* (1) 6032251.

ZOU YUANXI, PH.D.; Chinese metallurgist; b. Shanghai; ed. Zhejiang Univ. and in U.S.A.; researcher in the field of semiconductor materials; Dir. Shanghai Inst. of Metallurgy, Chinese Acad. of Sciences 1978–83; mem. Chinese Acad. of Sciences 1980–87. *Address:* c/o Institute of Metallurgy, Chinese Academy of Sciences, 865 Changning Road, Shanghai 200050, People's Republic of China.

ZOUBI, Mahmoud al-; Syrian politician; b. 1938, Khirbet Ghazaleh, Dar'a governate; m.; three c.; fmr. Chair. Agric. Centre, al-Ghab; Chair. Agricultural Produce Dept. 1963–64; Dir. of Agric. and Agrarian Reform, al-Ghab Dist. 1964–68, Hama 1969–71; mem. al-Ghab Dist. Baath Party leadership; mem. Admin. Council, Agronomists' Union; mem. People's Ass. 1971; Sec. Bath Party Peasants' Bureau 1972–73; Gen. Dir. Euphrates Basin Investment Establishment 1973–76; reserve mem. Baath Party's Regional Leadership 1975–80, mem. 1980; Speaker, People's Ass. 1981–87; Prime Minister of Syria 1987–. *Address:* Office of the Prime Minister, Damascus, Syria.

ZOUIOUECHE, Nazim Charif Eddine; Algerian engineer and oil company executive; b. 19 Feb. 1940, Algiers; m. Fariel Essid 1971; two s.; ed. Ecole Nat Supérieure des Télécommunications, Ecole Nat. Supérieure du Pétrole, Paris; telecommunications engineer, Ministry of Telecommunications 1965–68; production engineer, Elf/Aquitaine 1968–71; Man. Hassi-Messaoud Dist. 1971–76; Dir. Production Div. Sonatrach 1976–79, Exec. Vice-Pres. and Man. Dir. Sonatrach, in charge of Hydrocarbons Div. 1979–85, C.E.O. Transmediterranean Pipeline Co. 1985–93, Chief of Staff Sonatrach 1994–95, Dir.-Gen. 1995–; Chair. Observatoire Méditerranéen pour l'Energie (OME) 1995–97; mem. Bd. Alfor Drilling Co. (SEDCO/Sonatrach jt. co.) 1977–82. *Leisure interests:* bridge, tennis, horse riding, jogging. *Address:* Sonatrach—Direction Générale, 10 rue du Sahara, Hydra, Algiers, Algeria. *Telephone:* (2) 60.70.00; (2) 60.80.11. *Fax:* (2) 60.24.05.

ZOUMBOULAKIS, Petros I.; Greek artist, stage designer and professor of plastic arts; b. 19 April 1937, Athens; ed. Polytechnic School of Athens; one man shows: Astor Gallery 1970, Zoumboulakis Gallery, Iola 1975, 1977, Rethymnon, Crete 1977, Argo Gallery 1978, Armos Gallery, Thessaloniki 1979, Zalocosta 7 Gallery 1985, New Forms Gallery 1986, 1990, Art Forum Gallery, Thessaloniki 1990, 1992, Agathi Gallery 1991, Citibank, New York 1994; participant in numerous group exhbns. in Greece especially at Nat. Gallery; work also shown in group exhbns. abroad including São Paulo Bienal 1969, Int. Exhbn. of Visual Arts, Moscow 1988, 5th Int. Biennale, Cairo 1994; designer of scenery and costumes for both theatre and cinema; illustrator of textbooks used in Greek schools; teacher in applied arts, drawing, colour and stage design, Doxiadis School of Interior Design 1964–86; works in Nat. Gallery, Ministry of Educ. Collection and many public and pvt. collections at home and abroad. *Address:* Dafnomili 6, 11471 Athens (Studio); Evrou 18-20, 15234 Athens, Greece (Home). *Telephone:* 01-3630028 (Studio); 01-6842088 (Home).

ZOUNGRANA, H.E. Cardinal Paul; Burkinabè ecclesiastic; b. 3 Sept. 1917, Ouagadougou; ed. l'Institut Catholique de Paris, and Univ. Pontificale Grégorienne; ordained priest 1942; mem. Missionary Soc. of Africa; Archbishop of Ouagadougou 1960–95, Archbishop Emer. 1995; cr. Cardinal 1965. *Address:* Archevêché, 01 B.P. 1472, Ouagadougou 01, Burkina Faso.

ZOUNI, Opy; Greek artist; b. 4 Feb. 1941, Cairo; d. of John Sarpakis and Helen Sarpakis; m. Alexander Zounis 1965; two s.; ed. Athens School of Fine Arts; one-woman exhbns. include: Desmos 1973, Athens Gallery 1975, 1978, 1990, 1992, Lausanne Museum of Fine Art 1980, Galerie Jeanneret, Geneva 1982, Contemporary Graphics with Medusa in collaboration with Alexander Iolas 1982, Gallery 3 1984, Peter Noser Gallery, Zurich 1985, Trito Mati 1986, Int. Cultural Centre, Antwerp 1986, Galerie Kara, Geneva 1989, 1991, Vellidio Cultural Centre 1989, Athens French Inst. 1992, Mylos 1993, Galerie Donguy, Paris 1994, Kreonidis Gallery 1996, Art Forum Gallery 1996, Art Athina 4/Amymoni Gallery 1996, Municipal Gallery of Patras; group exhbns. include: Biennials of São Paolo 1979, Alexandria 1970, Ljubljana 1979, 1983, 1985, 1987, Bradford 1984, and numerous int. exhbns. *Publications include:* Symmetry 2 1989, Arte e Tecnologia 1993; bilingual monograph 1997; numerous articles in books and reviews. *Address:* 22 Vrilission Street, 152 36 P. Penteli, Greece. *Telephone:* 8042.950. *Fax:* 8044.264.

ZSÁMBÉKI, Gábor; Hungarian theatrical manager and director; b. 30 Dec. 1943, Pécs; s. of János Zsámbéki and Judit Almásy; two d.; ed. Faculty of

Directing, Budapest Acad. of Dramatic Art and Film Art; Gen. Man. Csiky Gergely Theatre, Kaposvár 1974–78; Prof., Faculty of Acting and Directing, Budapest Acad. of Dramatic Art and Film Art 1978–; Head Dir., Budapest Nat. Theatre 1978–82; Art Dir. Katona József Theatre, Budapest 1982–89, Gen. Man. and Stage Dir. 1989; Stage Dir. Theater tri-bühne, Stuttgart 1988–; mem. Founding Cttee. Union des Théâtres de l'Europe, Paris 1989–. *Productions:* about 150, including classics (Goldoni, Shakespeare, Gogol, Chekhov etc.), modern works (Jarry, Wesker, Gombrowicz) and world premières of contemporary Hungarian plays (Halleluyah by Kornis, Chickenhead by Spiró); productions in more than 50 cities abroad including Cuba, Czechoslovakia, Finland, Germany, Israel, Norway; prizes include: BITEF Prize (for The Government Inspector) 1989, French Critics' Prize for best foreign production (for Ubu Roi, Théâtre de l'Odéon, Paris) 1990, Best Foreign Production (for The Government Inspector), Caracas Int. Festival 1990, Merited Artist of the Hungarian Repub., Kossuth Prize. *Address:* 2011 Budakalász, Duna sétány, Pf. 85, Hungary. *Telephone:* 30-429-309.

ZUBAK, Krešemir; Bosnia and Herzegovina politician; b. 29 Nov. 1947, Doboj; m.; two c.; ed. Sarajevo Univ.; worked in judicial bodies of Bosnia and Herzegovina; Pres. of Higher Court in Doboj; mem. del. of Croatian population to sign the Washington Agreement and Vienna Agreement; elected First Pres. of Fed. of Bosnia and Croatia May 1994–; Croatian Co-Chair. of Bosnia and Herzegovina..

ZUBAKOV, Vice-Adm. Yuri Antonovich; Russian politician; b. 27 Nov. 1944, Chita; ed. KGB Higher School; on staff U.S.S.R. KGB 1966–89; Deputy Head of sector Cen. CPSU Cttee. 1989–90; on staff U.S.S.R. Security Council 1990–91; Deputy Dir. Foreign Intelligence Service U.S.S.R. (later Russia) 1991–96; Deputy Minister of Foreign Affairs 1996–98; Head of Personnel, Pres. Yeltsin's Admin., Minister of Russian Fed. 1998–. *Address:* Administration of the President, Kremlin, korp.14, Moscow, Russia.

ZUBEIDI, Mohammed Hamzah al-; Iraqi politician; Deputy Prime Minister March–Sept. 1991, Prime Minister of Iraq 1991–93. *Address:* c/o Office of the Prime Minister, Baghdad, Iraq.

ZUBERBÜHLER, Daniel; Swiss banking regulator; Dir. Fed. Banking Comm. 1997–. *Address:* Eidgenössische Bankenkommission, Sekretariat, Marktgasse 37, Postfach, 3001 Bern, Switzerland. *Telephone:* (31) 3226911.

ZUCKERMAN, Mortimer Benjamin, B.A., LL.B., LL.M., M.B.A.; American (b. Canadian) real-estate developer, publisher and editor; b. 4 June 1937, Montreal, Quebec; s. of Abraham Zuckerman and Esther Zuckerman; ed. McGill Univ., Pa. Univ., Harvard Univ.; Sr. Vice-Pres. Cabot, Cabot and Forbes 1965–69; lecturer, then Assoc. Prof. Harvard Univ. Grad. School of Design 1966–74; visiting lecturer Yale Univ. 1967–69; Chair. Boston Properties Co. 1970–; Dir. RET Income Foundation 1976–79, Property Capital Trust Co. 1979–80; Pres., Chair. Atlantic Monthly Co., Boston 1980–; Chair., Ed.-in-Chief US News and World Report 1980–; Propr. New York Daily News. *Address:* c/o Boston Properties, 599 Lexington Avenue, New York, NY 10022; US News and World Report, 2400 N. Street, N.W., Washington, DC 20037, U.S.A.

ZUKERMAN, Pinchas; Israeli violinist; b. 16 July 1948, Tel Aviv; s. of Jehuda Zukerman and Miriam Zukerman; m. 1st Eugenia Rich 1968; two d.; m. 2nd Tuesday Weld 1985; ed. Israel Conservatory, Acad. of Music, Tel-Aviv, Juilliard School of Music, New York; studied with Ivan Galamian; début in New York with New York Philharmonic 1969, in U.K. at Brighton Festival 1969; concert and recital performances throughout U.S.A. and Europe; appearances as conductor with orchestras worldwide; has performed at Spoleto, Pablo Casals and Edinburgh Festivals; Dir. S. Bank Summer Music 1978–80; Musical Dir. St. Paul Chamber Orchestra 1980–87; Prin. Conductor Dallas Symphony Orch. 1993–95 (Prin. Conductor Int. Summer Music Festival 1990–95); Music Dir. Nat. Arts Center (desig.) 1998; Hon. D. Mus. (Brown Univ.) 1989; Leventritt Award 1967. *Address:* c/o Shirley Kirshbaum and Associates, 711 West End Avenue, New York, NY 10025, U.S.A. *Telephone:* (212) 222-4843.

ŻUKROWSKI, Wojciech; Polish writer; b. 14 April 1916, Cracow; s. of Zygmunt Żukrowski and Jadwiga Wojtowicz; m. Maria Woltersdorf 1945; one d.; ed. Wrocław Univ. and Jagiellonian Univ., Cracow; War Corresp., North Viet Nam 1954; Counsellor, Polish Embassy, New Delhi 1956–59; Deputy to Sejm (Parl.) 1972–89; Co-Ed. Widnokręgi (monthly) and Nowe Książki; mem. All-Poland Peace Cttee., All-Poland Peace Coalition 1989– (Vice-Chair. Presidium 1989), Chief Council of Union of Fighters for Freedom and Democracy (Z BoWiD); mem. Polish Union of Writers (ZLP), Chair. ZLP Gen. Bd. 1986–90; mem. PEN Club; Chair. Soc. for Polish-Spanish Friendship 1978–85; State Prize 1953, 1978 (1st Class), Ludwik Waryński Prize 1986, Maxim Gorky IBBY Prize 1986, Kt.'s and Officer's Cross, Order Polonia Restituta 1953, 1954, Award of Minister of Nat. Defence 1961, Order of Banner of Labour (1st Class), Prize of Minister of Culture and Art 1963, 1965, 1968, 1969, Pietrzak Prize 1967, Order of Builders of People's Poland 1976, Prize of Prime Minister for literary production for children and youth 1977, Meritorious Activist of Culture 1978, Special Award of Minister of Nat. Defence 1988, and others. *Publications:* Short stories: Z kraju milczenia (From the Land of Silence), Piórkiem flaminga (With a Flamingo's Quill), Córeczka (Little Daughter), Okruchy weselnego tortu (Crumbs from the Wedding Cake), Ręka ojca (Father's Hand); Novels: Dni klęski (Days of Defeat), Skąpani w ogniu, Bathed in Fire (Ministry of Defence Prize 1961), Kamienne Tablice (The Stone Tables) 1966, Szczęściarz (The Lucky Devil), Plaża nad Styksem (Styx Beach) 1976, Zapach psiej sierści 1979; Travel: Dom bez ścian (House without Walls), Wędrówki z moim guru (Wanderings with my Guru: India), W królestwie miliona słoni (In the Kingdom of a Million Elephants: Laos), Nieśmiały narzeczony (Chinese legends); Fairy-tales for children: Porwanie w Tiutiurlistanie 1946, Na tronie w Blabonie 1986; Essays: W głębi zwierciadła (Inside Mirror) 1973, Karambole (Collisions) 1973; Films: Bathed in Fire, Direction Berlin, The Last Days, Lotna, Potop, The Stone Tables. *Leisure interest:* travel. *Address:* 00-324 Warsaw, ul. Karowa 14/16 m. 22, Poland. *Telephone:* 826 16 18.

ZULEEG, Manfred (Friedrich), DR.JUR.; German professor and fmr. international judge; b. 21 March 1935, Creglingen; s. of Ludwig Zuleeg and Thea (née Ohr) Zuleeg; m. Sigrid Feuerhahn 1965; three s. one d.; ed. Univs. of Erlangen and Hamburg, Bologna Center of Johns Hopkins Univ. in Int. Relations; Research Asst., Inst. for Law of the European Communities, Univ. of Cologne 1962–68, Sr. Lecturer 1968–71; Prof. of Public Law and Law of the European Communities, Univ. of Bonn 1971–78; Prof. of Public Law, including European and Public Int. Law, Univ. of Frankfurt 1978–88; Judge, Court of Justice, European Communities 1988–94; Research Fellow Univ. of Calif., Berkeley 1969–70, Visiting Prof. 1996, Jean Monnet Chair. 1998. *Publications:* Die Rechtsform der Subventionen 1965, Das Recht der Europäischen Gemeinschaften im innerstaatlichen Bereich 1969, Subventionskontrolle durch Konkurrentenklage 1974; contrib. to other works. *Leisure interests:* jogging, mountaineering, literature. *Address:* J.W. Goethe-Universität, Senckenberganlage 31, 60054 Frankfurt am Main, Germany. *Telephone:* (069) 798-22382. *Fax:* (069) 798-28750.

ZULFUGAROV, Tofik Nadir ogly; Azerbaijani diplomatist; b. 1 Nov. 1959, Rostov-on-Don; m.; ed. Baku State Univ.; researcher, Inst. of Oriental Studies Azerbaijan Acad. of Sciences 1985–91; researcher, Inst. of History Azerbaijan Acad. of Sciences 1991–92; diplomatic service 1992–; took part in negotiations on regulating Nagorny Karabakh conflict, Head of Azerbaijan del. 1992–; Head, Dept. of Conflict Problems, Azerbaijan Ministry of Foreign Affairs 1993–94, Minister of Foreign Affairs 1998–. *Address:* Ministry of Foreign Affairs, Gendjler Maydani 3, Baku, Azerbaijan. *Telephone:* (8922) 93 82 31 (Office).

ZUMWALT, Admiral Elmo Russell, Jr., B.SC.; American naval officer; b. 29 Nov. 1920, San Francisco, Calif.; s. of Dr. Elmo Russell Zumwalt and Dr. Frances Z. Frank; m. Mouza Coutelais-du-Roche 1945; two s. (one deceased) two d.; ed. U.S. Naval Acad., Naval War Coll., Nat. War Coll.; commissioned Ensign, U.S. Navy 1942, advanced through ranks to Adm. 1970; service on USS Phelps 1942–43, USS Robinson 1943–45, USS Saufley 1945–46, USS Zellars 1946–48; Asst. Prof. Naval Science 1948–50; Commdg. Officer USS Tills 1950–51; Navigator USS Wisconsin 1951–52; Head Shore and Overseas Bases Section, Naval Personnel, Washington 1953–55; Commdg. Officer USS Arnold J. Isbell 1955–57; LT Detailer, Naval Personnel 1957; Special Asst. for Naval Personnel, Officer of Asst. Sec. of the Navy, Washington 1957–58, Exec. Asst., Sr. Aide 1958–59; Commdg. Officer USS Dewey 1959–61; Desk Officer for France, Spain and Portugal, Office of Asst. Sec. of Defense for Int. Security Affairs 1962–63; Dir. Arms Control and Contingency Planning for Cuba 1963; Exec. Asst., Sr. Aide, Sec. of Navy 1963–65; Commdg. Officer Cruiser-Destroyer Flotilla Seven 1965–66; Dir. Chief Naval Operations Systems Analysis Group, Washington 1966–68; Commdr. U.S. Naval Forces, Vietnam, Chief, Naval Advisory Group Vietnam 1968–70; Chief of Naval Operations 1970–74; Pres. Adm. Zumwalt and Assocs. Inc. 1978–85, Pres. Adm. Zumwalt Consultants 1986–; Chair. and C.E.O., American Medical Bldg. 1983–85, Chair. 1985–; Gov. American Stock Exchange 1979–85; Dir. Magellan Aerospace Corpn., Dallas Semiconductor, IDT Corpn., NL Industries; Chair. Phelps-Stokes Fund; Chair. Ethics and Public Policy Center; Distinguished Service Medal with Gold Star, Legion of Merit with Gold Star, Bronze Star Medal with Combat V, Navy Commendation Medal with Combat V, and many other national and foreign decorations; Hon. LL.D. (Villanova, Univ. of N.C., Nat Univ.), Hon. D. Hum. Litt. (U.S. Int. Univ.), Hon. Dr. Public Service (Central Mich. Univ.). *Publications:* On Watch 1976, My Father, My Son 1986, syndicated columns. *Leisure interests:* jogging, tennis. *Address:* Admiral Zumwalt Consultants, 1000 Wilson Boulevard, Suite 3105, Arlington, VA 22209-3901, U.S.A. *Telephone:* (703) 527-5380. *Fax:* (703) 528-5795.

ZUNINO REGGIO, Pio; Italian business executive; b. 8 March 1920, Venice; s. of Mario Zunino Reggio and Isabella Rosso di Cerami; m. Beatrice Zileri Dal Verme 1944; five c.; ed. Univ. of Padua; joined staff of Petrocaltex (later known as Caltex Italiana and from 1967 as Chevron Oil Italiana S.p.A.) 1951; Dir. Bologna Sales Area Office, Caltex 1969, Dir. N. Italy Div. 1964; assigned to Chevron Oil Europe, New York, U.S.A. 1968–69; Sales Man. and mem. Bd. of Dirs. Chevron Oil Italiana S.p.A. 1970, Vice-Pres. and Gen. Man. 1977, Pres. and Man. Dir. 1981–; mem. Bd. of Dirs. of VECAL S.p.A. 1967–70, of CAPO S.p.A. 1969–70; Pres. SERAM S.p.A. 1977–79, 1985–; Vice-Pres. Raffineria di Roma S.p.A. 1981–; Bd. mem. SARPOM S.p.A. 1981–; mem. Exec. Cttee. Italian Petroleum Fed. 1981–; Commendatore dell'Ordine al Merito della Repubblica Italiana 1974. *Leisure interests:* sailing, skiing. *Address:* Chevron Oil Italiana S.p.A., via V. Brancati 60, 00144 Rome (Office); via di Villa Patrizi 4, 00161 Rome, Italy (Home). *Telephone:* (06) 500921 (Office).

ZUNZI (pseudonym of Wong Kee-kwan); Chinese political cartoonist; m. Chan Ya; ed. Chinese Univ. of Hong Kong; worked briefly as print journalist before concentrating on political cartoons; works appear in mass-circulation Chinese-language publications including Ming Pao (daily) and Next (weekly magazine).

ZUO GUANGRUI; Chinese space technologist; b. 1934, Liaoning; ed. Harbin Industrial Univ. 1960; Leader of China's rocket programme; Dir. Beijing Inst. of Control Eng. 1986. *Address:* Beijing Institute of Control Engineering, Beijing, People's Republic of China.

ZURABOV, Aleksander Yuryevich; Russian banker; b. 1956, Leningrad (now St. Petersburg); m.; two c.; ed. Moscow Inst. of Man., Acad. of Int. Trade; with Research Inst. of Marine Transport 1977–89; lecturer Acad. of Int. Trade 1989–91; Head of div., Head of dept., mem. Bd. Dirs. Konversbank 1991–94; Chair. Bd. Dirs., Trust and Investments Bank, also Deputy Chair. Bd. Dirs., MENATEP Bank 1994–95, Pres. MENATEP 1996–. *Address:* MENATEP, Dubininskaya str. 17A, 113054 Moscow, Russia. *Telephone:* (095) 235 9003 (Office).

ZVEREVA, Natalia (Natasha); Belarus tennis player; b. 16 April 1971, Minsk; d. of Marat Zverev and Nina Zvereva; winner doubles French Open (with Larisa Neiland) 1989, (with Gigi Fernandez, q.v.) 1992–95, Wimbledon (with Larisa Neiland) 1991, (with Gigi Fernandez) 1992–94, U.S. Open (with Pam Shriver) 1991, (with Gigi Fernandez) 1992, 1995; winner mixed doubles Australian Open 1990, 1995, doubles (with Gigi Fernandez) 1993–94; Bronze Medallist in doubles (mem. Unified Team), Olympic Games, Barcelona, Spain 1992; winner doubles Pan Pacific (with Gigi Fernandez) 1996. *Leisure interests:* listening to music, watching water polo, table tennis, nightclubs, reading.

ZWANZIG, Robert Walter, M.S., PH.D.; American professor of chemical physics; b. 9 April 1928, Brooklyn, N.Y.; s. of Walter Zwanzig and Bertha Weil Zwanzig; m. Francis Ryder Zwanzig 1953; one s. one d.; ed. Polytechnic Inst. of Brooklyn, Univ. of Southern California and California Inst. of Tech.; Research Fellow, Yale Univ. 1951–54; Asst. Prof. of Chem., Johns Hopkins Univ. 1954–58; Physical Chemist Nat. Bureau of Standards, Washington, D.C. 1958–66; Research Prof., Inst. for Physical Science and Tech., Univ. of Md. 1966–80, Distinguished Prof. of Physical Science 1980–88, (Prof. Emer. 1988–); Research Chemist N.I.H. 1988–; Fellow, American Acad. of Arts and Sciences; mem. N.A.S.; Silver Medal, U.S. Dept. of Commerce; Peter Debye Award in Physical Chem. (A.C.S.) 1976, Irving Langmuir Award in Chemical Physics 1984, Joel Hildebrand Award (A.C.S.) 1994. *Publications:* about 130 articles in scientific periodicals. *Address:* Laboratory of Chemical Physics, National Institutes of Health, Bethesda, MD 20892-0520 (Office); 5314 Sangamore Road, Bethesda, MD 20816, U.S.A. (Home). *Telephone:* (301) 496-8048 (Office). *Fax:* (301) 496-0825.

ZWAVELING, Albert, M.D., PH.D.; Netherlands professor of surgery; b. 21 July 1927, Schoonebeek; s. of Jan H. Zwaveling and Engeline F. (née Hinnen) Zwaveling; m. 1st Susanna M. van Soest 1952 (died 1966); one s.; m. 2nd Anna M. F. Bloem 1969; two s.; ed. State Univ. of Utrecht, University Hosp., Leiden; Mil. doctor (rank of maj.) 1954–57; Gen. Practioner in Indonesia 1957–58; surgical trainee, Leiden 1958–63; Fellow in Oncology, Univ. of Wis., U.S.A. 1963–64; Jr. Consultant 1964–68; Assoc. Prof. of Surgical Oncology, Leiden Univ. 1968–72, Prof. of Surgery 1972; Head, Dept. of Surgery, Univ. Hosp., Leiden 1981–; Chair. Concilium Chirurgicum Utrecht 1985, Medical Staff Univ. Hosp., Leiden 1986; mem. Royal Netherlands Acad. of Sciences 1979; Hon. mem. Dutch Soc. of Oncology, Dutch Asscn. of Surgery 1987, Dutch Asscn. of Surgical Oncology 1991; awarded Rotgans Medal of Nat. Cancer Inst. 1963, Zwanenberg Award 1969. *Publications:* Dutch Textbook of Oncology, Dutch Textbook of Surgery; 6 monographs on oncology, mainly cancer; more than 120 scientific papers. *Leisure interests:* collecting modern plastic art, gardening. *Address:* University Hospital, Leiden (Office); Vlietpark 4, 2355 CT Hoogmade, Netherlands (Home). *Telephone:* 071-264005 (Office); 01712-8622 (Home).

ZWERENZ, Gerhard; German writer; b. 3 June 1925, Gablenz; s. of Rudolf and Liesbeth Zwerenz; m. Ingrid Hoffman 1957; one d.; ed. Univ. of Leipzig; worked as coppersmith 1939–42; army service 1942–44, deserted to join Red Army 1944; P.O.W. in Minsk, U.S.S.R. 1944–48; obliged to serve with G.D.R. police 1948–50; studied at Leipzig Univ. 1952–56; first publication 1956; expelled from CP, fled to W. Berlin 1957; mem. Bundestag 1994–; Ernst Reuter Prize 1975, Carl-von-Ossietzky-preis 1986. *Publications:* 65 books including Aufs Rad geflochten 1959, Die Liebe der toten Männer 1959, Heldengedenktag 1964, Rasputin 1970, Der Widerspruch 1974, Die Westdeutschen 1977, Die Ehe der Maria Braun 1979, Der lange Tod des Rainer-Werner Fassbinder 1982. *Address:* Brunhildensteg 18, 61389 Schmitten, Germany. *Telephone:* (06082) 1078.

ZWICK, Charles John, B.S., PH.D.; American banker and economist; b. 17 July 1926, Plantsville; s. of Louis C. Zwick and Mabel (née Rich) Zwick; m. Joan Cameron 1952; one s. one d.; ed. Univ. of Connecticut and Harvard Univ.; Instructor, Univ. of Conn. 1951; Harvard Univ. 1954–56; Head, Logistics Dept. the RAND Corpn. 1956–63, mem. Research Council 1963–65; Asst. Dir. U.S. Bureau of the Budget 1965–68, Dir. 1968–69; Pres. Southeast Banking Corpn., Miami 1969–; Chair. and C.E.O. 1982–; Chair. Bd. and C.E.O. Southeast Bank 1982–; Dir. Manville Corpn. and numerous other companies; Chair. Pres.'s Comm. on Mil. Compensation; Trustee, Carnegie Endowment for Int. Peace, Chair.; mem. Reserve City Bankers Asscn., The Conference Bd., Council of the Int. Exec. Service Corps, Econ. Soc. of S. Fla., Council of 100. *Address:* 4210 Santa Maria Street, Coral Gables, FL 33146 U.S.A. *Telephone:* 305-666-9208.

ZWICKEL, Klaus; German trades unionist; b. 1935, Heilbronn; apprentice toolmaker, Nordheim; regional admin. Industriegewerkschaft Metall (IG Metall) (Germany's largest trades union); mem. Nat. Cttee. 1986, Deputy Leader 1989–93, Leader Oct. 1993–; Pres. Int. Metallgewerkschaftsbundes (IMB); Deputy Chair. Supervisory Bd. Volkswagen AG 1996–; mem. Supervisory Bds. Mannesmann (Deputy Chair. 1996–), BfG Bank AG. *Address:* Industriegewerkschaft Metall, Lyoner Str. 32, 60519 Frankfurt a.M., Germany. *Telephone:* (69) 6693-0. *Fax:* (69) 6693-2843.

ŻYCIŃSKI, Archbishop Józef, PH.D., D.THEOL.; Polish ecclesiastic; b. 1 Sept. 1948, Stara Wieś; ed. Higher Theological Seminary of the Częstochowa Diocese, Cracow, Pontifical Theology Acad., Cracow, Acad. of Catholic Theology, Warsaw, Catholic Univ. of America, Catholic Univ. of Louvain, ordained priest, Częstochowa 1972; parish curate, Częstochowa Diocese 1972–74; Higher Theological Seminary of the Częstochowa Diocese, Cracow, prefect 1974–78, prefect of studies 1979–83; Pontifical Acad. of Theology, Cracow, deputy dean Philosophy Dept. 1982–85, Prof. 1988, Dean Philosophy Dept. 1988–91; Diocesan Bishop Tarnów Diocese, 1990–97; Metropolitan Archbishop of Lublin 1997–; mem. Catholic Educ. Congregation, Pontifical Council, Main Council of the Polish Episcopate; leader Polish Episcopate Council for Lay Apostolate; leader Programme Council of Catholic Information Agency; mem. European Acad. of Science and Art in Salzburg, Russian Acad. of Natural Sciences, Evolutionary and Theoretical Biology Cttee. of the Polish Acad. of Sciences. *Publications:* The Universe and Philosophy (jtly.) 1980, The Human Person and Philosophy in the Contemporary World (Ed.) 1981, Language and Method 1982, Roads of Those who Think (jtly.) 1981, The Galileo Affair: A Meeting of Faith and Science 1985, The Structure of the Metascientific Revolution 1987, To Philosophise in the Context of Science 1987, The Idea of Unification in Galileo's Epistemology 1987, Three Cultures: Science, the Humanities and Religious Values 1987, Theism and Analytical Philosophy (Vol. 1) 1983, (Vol. 2) 1988, The Universe: Machine or Thought (jtly.) 1988, The Depth of Being 1988, In the Circle of Science and Belief 1989, Documents from UB Country 1989, Three Cultures 1990, Dilemmas of Evolution (jtly.) 1990, Mathematics of Nature, Socratic Meditations (jtly.) 1991, The Debate about Universals and Contemporary Science (jtly.) 1991, The Galileo Affair 1991, The God of Abraham and Whitehead 1991, Reprieving Nature 1992, Unavoidable Questions (jtly.) 1992. Limits of Rationality 1993, Person and Love 1993, Stones and Flowers 1994, Sacrum and Culture 1995, The Seeds of Loneliness 1996, The Elements of Philosophy of Science 1996, Die Zeichen der Hoffnung entdecken 1997, The Invisible Light 1998, The European Community in Spirit 1998. *Leisure interests:* literary dailies, poetry, classical music. *Address:* ul. Prymasa St. Wyszyńskiego 2, skr. poczt. 198, 20-950 Lublin, Poland. *Telephone:* (81) 532 10 58. *Fax:* (81) 532 12 25.

ŻYGULSKI, Kazimierz, H.H.D.; Polish professor and politician; b. 8 Dec. 1919, Wolanka; s. of Zdzisław Zygulski and Maria Zygulska; m. Helena Gutkowa 1955; one s.; ed. Univ. of Lwów (now Lvov, Ukraine); in resistance movt. in Lwów Voivodship during Nazi occupation; imprisoned in U.S.S.R. 1944–56; researcher, Sociology and History of Culture Research Centre of Polish Acad. of Sciences, Łódź 1956–59; scientific worker, Philosophy and Sociology Inst. of Polish Acad. of Sciences, Warsaw 1959–90, Head Culture Research Centre 1961–90, Chair. Scientific Council 1987–90, Extraordinary Prof. 1973–83, Ordinary Prof. 1983–; Pro-Rector, State Film, TV and Theatrical Higher School, Łódź 1970–71; counsellor to Deputy Chair. of Council of Ministers 1971–72; Minister of Culture and Art 1982–86; Pro-Rector, Dir. Scientific Research Centre, Warsaw School of Socioeconomic Sciences 1996–; mem. Polish Cttee. ICOM 1972–90, Presidium State Prizes Cttee. 1975–83, Presidium Nat. Council for Culture 1983–86; Amb. ad personam 1987; Chair. Polish Nat. Comm. for UNESCO 1987–90; mem. UNESCO Exec. Bd. 1987–90, Chair. Int. Cttee. of Extra Govt. Org., UNESCO 1989–90; mem. European Acad. of Arts, Sciences and Humanities 1989–; Officer's Cross Order of Polonia Restituta. *Publications:* Drogi rozwoju kultury masowej (Mass Cultural Ways of Development) 1962, Wstęp do zagadnień kultury (Introduction to the Problems of Culture) 1972, Wartości i wzory kultury (Values and Models of Culture) 1975, Wspólnota śmiechu: Socjologiczne studium komizmu (Community of Laughter: A Sociological Study of the Comical) 1976, Święto i kultura (Holiday and Culture) 1981, Jestem z lwowskiego etapu (I am from Lwów) 1994, Widmo Przyszłości: nowa fala okrueieństwa (Ghost of the future: new wave of atrocities) 1996, Globalne problemy współczesnego świata (The Global Problems of the Contemporary World) 1996, Uwagi o ekstremalnych zjawiskach w kulturze współczesnej (Notes on Extreme Phenomena in Contemporary Culture) 1998; numerous research works and monographs on sociology of culture. *Leisure interests:* history of art, photography. *Address:* ul. Madalińskiego 50/52 m. 23, 02-581 Warsaw, Poland. *Telephone:* (22) 49 81 79.

ŻYLIS-GARA, Teresa; Polish soprano; b. 23 Jan. 1935, Vilnius; m., one c.; ed. State Higher School of Music, Łódź 1954; soloist, Cracow Philharmonic 1954–58 and Cracow Opera 1958–59; foreign contracts in operas: Oberhausen 1961–63, Städtische Bühnen, Dortmund 1963–65, Deutsche Oper am Rhein, Düsseldorf 1965–70; *debuts abroad:* Paris Opera 1966, San Francisco Opera 1968, Metropolitan Opera, New York 1968, Royal Opera House, Covent Garden 1968, Vienna Opera 1970, Nat. Theatre, Prague 1974, Nat. Theatre, Budapest 1976, Great Theatre, Warsaw 1976, La Scala,

Milan 1977, Bolshoi Theatre, Moscow 1978, Teatro Colon, Buenos Aires 1981; *participation in festivals including:* Glyndebourne 1965, Salzburg 1968, Aix-en-Provence 1972, Orange 1975; performances in many countries; regular performances at Metropolitan Opera, New York 1968–; also song recitals; renowned for interpretation of works by Szymanowski; Prime Minister's Prize (1st Class) 1979; Kt.'s Cross Order of Polonia Restituta. *Address:* 16A boulevard de Belgique, Principality of Monaco.

ZYUGANOV, Gennady Adreyevich, D.PHIL.; Russian politician; b. 26 June 1944, Mymrino Village, Orel Region; ed. Orel Pedagogical Inst., Acad. of Social Sciences of Cen. CPSU Cttee.; worked as teacher in a secondary school 1961–65; CP and trade union functionary 1967; First Sec. dist., city, regional Comsomol cttees. of Orel, sec., second sec., head of propaganda div. Orel regional CPSU Cttee. 1974–83; instructor, head of propaganda div. Cen. CPSU Cttee. 1983–89; Deputy Head of Ideology Div. Cen. CPSU Cttee. 1989–90; mem. Politburo, Sec. Cen. Cttee. of CP of Russian Fed.; Chair. Coordination Cttee. of Patriotic Forces of Russia 1992–, Co-Chair. Duma of Russian Nat. Sobor 1992–; Co-Chair. Political Council of the Front of Nat. Salvation 1992–; Chair. Cen. Exec. Cttee. CP of Russian Fed. at the restorative congress of the CP 1993–; mem. State Duma (Parl.) of Russia 1993–, Head of CP faction; CP Presidential Cand. for 1996 Elections. *Publications:* Russia and the Contemporary World 1995, Russia, My Homeland (the Ideology of State Patriotism) 1997. *Address:* Communist Party, Zlatoustinsky per, 8/7, 101000 Moscow; State Duma, Okhotny Ryad 1, 103009 Moscow, Russia. *Telephone:* 206-87-89 (Party); 292-87-44 (Duma). *Fax:* 292-87-42.